PENSION AND EMPLOYEE BENEFITS

CODE · ERISA · REGULATIONS

As of January 1, 2006
Volume 2

ERISA Law and Regulations
Related Laws
Proposed Regulations

CCH Editorial Staff Publication

CCH INCORPORATED
Chicago

A WoltersKluwer Company

Portfolio Managing Editor . . . . Jan Gerstein

Editor . . . . Elizabeth Pope

Production Editor . . . . Lauren Miller

Compiled from

CCH PENSION PLAN GUIDE

As of January 1, 2006

ISBN 0-8080-1448-X

©2006, **CCH** INCORPORATED

4025 W. Peterson Ave.
Chicago, IL 60646-6085
1 800 248-3248
hr.cch.com

ABOUT THIS EDITION

This edition of "Pension and Employee Benefits—Code • ERISA • Regulations" is specially designed to give those involved in the employee benefit plan field instant briefcase and desktop access to selected Internal Revenue Code and ERISA provisions and to corresponding regulatory authority.

Contents—Two-Volume Edition

Volumes 1 and 2 contain the following:

1. The provisions of the Internal Revenue Code (IRC) and regulations dealing with pension plans, profit-sharing and stock bonus plans, deferred compensation, and related employee benefits. Coverage includes all recent law changes, including those made by the Gulf Opportunity Zone Act of 2005 (P.L. 109-135). Also covered are new 2005 final regulations regarding the anti-cutback rules for protected benefits under Code Sec. 411(d)(6), conversions from a traditional to a Roth IRA, and the use of Code Sec. 412(i) plans.

2. The provisions of the Employee Retirement Income Security Act of 1974 (ERISA) and the final or temporary regulations thereunder, including 2005 PBGC regulations relating to the electronic filing of annual financial and actuarial information. Recent law changes have also been reflected.

3. Regulations that have been proposed under the IRC and ERISA, but have not yet been adopted. Some of the proposed IRS regulations may be relied upon by taxpayers until final guidance is issued. Proposed regulation preambles are also included.

4. Relevant non-IRC/non-ERISA provisions of the Bankruptcy Abuse Prevention and Consumer Protection Act of 2005, the Katrina Emergency Tax Relief Act of 2005, the Economic Growth and Tax Relief Reconciliation Act of 2001, the IRS Restructuring and Reform Act of 1998, the Small Business Job Protection Act of 1996, the Health Insurance Portability and Accountability Act of 1996, the GATT (General Agreement on Tariffs and Trade), the Omnibus Budget Reconciliation Act of 1993, the Unemployment Compensation Amendments of 1992, the Revenue Reconciliation Act of 1990, the Omnibus Budget Reconciliation Act of 1989, the Technical and Miscellaneous Revenue Act of 1988, the Omnibus Budget Reconciliation Act of 1987, the Single-Employer Pension Plan Amendments Act of 1986, the Tax Reform Act of 1986, and earlier laws.

Contents—Optional Preambles Volume

In addition to the basic two-volume edition described above, a volume containing official IRS and DOL preambles to final and temporary regulations is also available. The preambles provide introductory material issued with each set of regulations that helps explain their purpose and content.

Contents—Optional Committee Reports Volume

In addition to the basic two-volume edition described above, a volume containing selected committee reports relating to legislation affecting pensions and employee benefits enacted since the passage of ERISA is also available. Readers may search by Code or ERISA section, or by public law number, to find the relevant legislative history.

Finding Devices

Convenient finding lists lead the reader to the materials mentioned above.

Topical Indexes reflect all matters covered in all editions.

This publication is compiled from the CCH PENSION PLAN GUIDE and CCH EMPLOYEE BENEFITS MANAGEMENT, as of January 1, 2006.

January 2006

Table of Contents

VOLUME TWO

FINDING LISTS

TEXT OF ACTS

VOLUME ONE

FINDING LISTS

CODE AND REGULATIONS

Finding List
Employee Retirement Income Security Act of 1974
(ERISA)
P.L. 93-406

Note: Employee Retirement Income Security Act of 1974, Title II (Secs. 1001 to 2008) made amendments to Internal Revenue Code provisions. These amendments are incorporated in place in the Internal Revenue Code provisions in Volume I.

Title I: Protection of Employee Benefit Rights

Title II: Amendments to the Internal Revenue Code Relating to Retirement Plans

[Note: Title II amendments to the Internal Revenue Code, encompassing ERISA Secs. 1011—2008, are incorporated in place in the Internal Revenue Code provisions in Volume I.]

Title III: Jurisdiction, Administration, Enforcement; Joint Pension Task Force, Etc.

Title IV: Plan Termination Insurance

Finding List
Veterans' Employment and Training Service Regulations

Finding List
Employee Benefits Security Administration (formerly Pension and Welfare Benefits Administration) Regulations

Finding List
Joint Board for the Enrollment of Actuaries Regulations

Finding List
Pension Benefit Guaranty Corporation Regulations

Subtitle B—Coverage
Subpart A—General Provisions; Guaranteed Benefits

Subpart B—Limitations on Guaranteed Benefits

Finding List
Age Discrimination in Employment Act of 1967

P.L. 90-202

Finding List
Age Discrimination in Employment Regulations

(Equal Employment Opportunity Commission—DOL)

Finding List
Balanced Budget Act of 1997

P.L. 105-33

Reproduced at the paragraphs noted below are sections of the Balanced Budget Act of 1997 that did not amend any sections of the Internal Revenue Code or any sections of the Employee Retirement Income Security Act of 1974 (ERISA).

Finding List
Bankruptcy Abuse Prevention and Consumer Protection Act of 2005
P.L. 109-08

Reproduced at the paragraphs noted below are excerpts from the Bankruptcy Abuse Prevention and Consumer Protection Act of 2005 that pertain to pensions and employee benefits.

Finding List
Child Support Performance and Incentive Act of 1998
P.L. 105-200

Reproduced at the paragraphs noted below are sections of the Child Support Performance and Incentive Act of 1998 that did not amend any sections of the Internal Revenue Code of 1986 or any sections of the Employee Retirement Income Security Act of 1974 (ERISA).

Finding List
Comprehensive Deposit Insurance Reform and Taxpayer Protection Act of 1991
P.L. 102-242

Reproduced at the paragraphs noted below are sections of the Comprehensive Deposit Insurance Reform and Taxpayer Protection Act of 1991 that did not amend any sections of the Internal Revenue Code or any sections of the Employee Retirement Income Security Act of 1974 (ERISA).

Finding List
Department of Justice Regulations

Procedures Governing Applications for Certificates of Exemption Under the Employee Retirement Income Security of Act of 1974

Finding List
Economic Growth and Tax Relief Reconciliation Act of 2001

P.L. 107-16

Finding List
Health Insurance Portability and Accountability Act of 1996

P.L. 104-191

Reproduced at the paragraphs noted below are sections of the Health Insurance Portability and Accountability Act (HIPAA) that did not amend any sections of the Internal Revenue Code or any sections of the Employee Retirement Income Security Act of 1974 (ERISA).

Finding List
IRS Restructuring and Reform Act of 1998
P.L. 105-206

Reproduced at the paragraphs noted below are sections of the IRS Restructuring and Reform Act of 1998 that did not amend any sections of the Internal Revenue Code of 1986 or any sections of the Employee Retirement Income Security Act of 1974 (ERISA).

Finding List
Katrina Emergency Tax Relief Act
P.L. 109-73

Reproduced at the paragraphs noted below are excerpts from the Katrina Emergency Tax Relief Act that pertain to pensions and employee benefits.

Finding List
Multiemployer Pension Plan Amendments Act of 1980
P.L. 96-364

Reproduced at the paragraphs noted below are sections of the Multiemployer Pension Plan Amendments Act of 1980 (MPPAA) that did not amend any sections of the Internal Revenue Code or any sections of the Employee Retirement Income Security Act of 1974 (ERISA).

Finding List
National Credit Union Administration Regulations

Reproduced at the paragraphs noted below are selected regulations issued by the National Credit Union Administration.

Finding List
Omnibus Budget Reconciliation Act of 1993
P.L. 103-66

Reproduced at the paragraphs noted below are sections of the Omnibus Budget Reconciliation Act of 1993 (OBRA) that did not amend any sections of the Internal Revenue Code or any sections of the Employee Retirement Income Security Act of 1974 (ERISA).

Finding List
Omnibus Budget Reconciliation Act of 1989
P.L. 101-239

Reproduced at the paragraphs noted below are sections of the Omnibus Budget Reconciliation Act of 1989 (OBRA) that did not amend any sections of the Internal Revenue Code or any sections of the Employee Retirement Income Security Act of 1974 (ERISA).

Finding List
Omnibus Budget Reconciliation Act of 1987
P.L. 100-203

Reproduced at the paragraphs noted below are sections of the Omnibus Budget Reconciliation Act of 1987 that did not amend any sections of the Internal Revenue Code of 1986 or any sections of the Employee Retirement Income Security Act of 1974 (ERISA).

Finding List
Retirement Equity Act of 1984
P.L. 98-397

Reproduced at the paragraphs noted below are sections of the Retirement Equity Act of 1984 (REA) that did not amend any sections of the Internal Revenue Code or any sections of the Employee Retirement Income Security Act of 1974 (ERISA).

Finding List
Revenue Reconciliation Act of 1990
P.L. 101-508

Reproduced at the paragraphs noted below are sections of the Revenue Reconciliation Act of 1990 that did not amend any sections of the Internal Revenue Code or any sections of the Employee Retirement Income Security Act of 1974 (ERISA).

Finding List
Omnibus Budget Reconciliation Act of 1985
P.L. 99-272

Reproduced at the paragraphs noted below are sections of the Single-Employer Pension Plan Amendments Act of 1986 (SEPPAA) that did not amend any sections of the Internal Revenue Code or any sections of the Employee Retirement Income Security Act of 1974 (ERISA).

Finding List
Small Business Job Protection Act of 1996
P.L. 104-188

Reproduced at the paragraphs noted below are sections of the Small Business Job Protection Act (SBJPA) that did not amend any sections of the Internal Revenue Code or any sections of the Employee Retirement Income Security Act of 1974 (ERISA).

Finding List
Tax Equity and Fiscal Responsibility Act of 1982
P.L. 97-248

Reproduced at the paragraphs noted below are sections of the Tax Equity and Fiscal Responsibility Act of 1982 (TEFRA) that did not amend any sections of the Internal Revenue Code or any sections of the Employee Retirement Income Security Act of 1974 (ERISA).

Finding List
Tax Reform Act of 1986

P.L. 99-514

Reproduced at the paragraphs noted below are sections of the Tax Reform Act of 1986 (TRA '86) which did not amend any sections of the Internal Revenue Code or any sections of the Employee Retirement Income Security Act of 1974 (ERISA).

Finding List
Tax Reform Act of 1984

P.L. 98-369

Reproduced at the paragraphs noted below are sections of the Tax Reform Act of 1984 (TRA '84) that did not amend any sections of the Internal Revenue Code or any sections of the Employee Retirement Income Security Act of 1974 (ERISA).

Finding List
Taxpayer Relief Act of 1997
P.L. 105-34

Reproduced at the paragraphs noted below are sections of the Taxpayer Relief Act of 1997 (TRA '97) that did not amend any sections of the Internal Revenue Code or any sections of the Employee Retirement Income Security Act of 1974 (ERISA).

Finding List
Technical and Miscellaneous Revenue Act of 1988
P.L. 100-647

Reproduced at the paragraphs noted below are sections of the Technical and Miscellaneous Revenue Act of 1988 which did not amend any sections of the Internal Revenue Code of 1986 or any sections of the Employee Retirement Income Security Act of 1974 (ERISA).

Finding List
Unemployment Compensation Amendments of 1992
P.L. 102-318

Reproduced at the paragraphs noted below are sections of the Unemployment Compensation Amendments of 1992 that did not amend any sections of the Internal Revenue Code or any sections of the Employee Retirement Income Security Act of 1974 (ERISA).

Finding List
Uruguay Round Agreements Act
P.L. 103-465

Reproduced at the paragraphs noted below are sections of the Uruguay Round Agreements Act that did not amend any sections of the Internal Revenue Code or any sections of the Employee Retirement Income Security Act of 1974 (ERISA).

Finding List
ERISA Reorganization Plan

Finding List
Proposed Regulations

Under the Administrative Procedure Act, most new regulations and changes in regulations must be issued in proposed form, and interested parties are then generally given a period of time after the date of publication of the Notice of Proposed Regulations in the *Federal Register* within which to file objections. Sometime thereafter, the regulations are issued in permanent form.

Following is a finding list of proposed regulations in this book relating to employee benefits issued by the Internal Revenue Service, the Labor Department (the Veteran's Employment and Training Service and the Employee Benefits Security Administration), the Pension Benefit Guaranty Corporation, and the Equal Employment Opportunity Commission. The listing is by regulation number. The paragraph and page number give the location of each major regulation section.

Title 26—Internal Revenue Code of 1986—Internal Revenue Service

Title 20—Veterans' Employment and Training Service—Department of Labor

Title 29—Employee Benefits Security Administration (formerly Pension and Welfare Benefits Administration)— Department of Labor

Title 29—Pension Benefit Guaranty Corporation—Department of Labor

Equal Employment Opportunity Commission

U.S. Code-ERISA Locator Table

The Employee Retirement Income Security Act of 1974 (ERISA) is codified at 29 U.S.C. § 1001, *et seq.* Provided below are the Act's section names and the conversion of the U.S. Code sections to ERISA sections.

[The next page is 101.]

Employee Retirement Income Security Act of 1974 (ERISA) (Pension Reform Act of 1974) P.L. 93-406 88 United States Statutes at Large 829 Signed by the President September 2, 1974

>>>→ *Note: ERISA Sec. 1 is reproduced below as it originally appeared in the Employee Retirement Income Security Act of 1974. It is reproduced for historical purposes only. ERISA Sec. 1 is not codified in the United States Code.*

[¶ 14,110] SHORT TITLE AND TABLE OF CONTENTS

Act Sec. 1. This Act may be cited as the "Employee Retirement Income Security Act of 1974".

TABLE OF CONTENTS

TITLE I—PROTECTION OF EMPLOYEE BENEFIT RIGHTS

Subtitle A—General Provisions

[¶ 14,120]
FINDINGS AND DECLARATION OF POLICY

Act Sec. 2. (a) The Congress finds that the growth in size, scope, and numbers of employee benefit plans in recent years has been rapid and substantial; that the operational scope and economic impact of such plans is increasingly interstate; that the continued well-being and security of millions of employees and their dependents are directly affected by these plans; that they are affected with a national public interest; that they have become an important factor affecting the stability of employment and the successful development of industrial relations; that they have become an important factor in commerce because of the interstate character of their activities, and of the activities of their participants, and the employers, employee organizations, and other entities by which they are established or maintained; that a large volume of the activities of such plans is carried on by means of the mails and instrumentalities of interstate commerce; that owing to the lack of employee information and adequate safeguards concerning their operation, it is desirable in the interests of employees and their beneficiaries, and to provide for the general welfare and the free flow of commerce, that disclosure be made and safeguards be provided with respect to the establishment, operation, and administration of such plans; that they substantially affect the revenues of the United States because they are afforded preferential Federal tax treatment; that despite the enormous growth in such plans many employees with long years of employment are losing anticipated retirement benefits owing to the lack of vesting provisions in such plans; that owing to the inadequacy of current minimum standards, the soundness and stability of plans with respect to adequate funds to pay promised benefits may be endangered; that owing to the termination of plans before requisite funds have been accumulated, employees and their beneficiaries have been deprived of anticipated benefits; and that it is therefore desirable in the interests of employees and their beneficiaries, for the protection of the revenue of the United States, and to provide for the free flow of commerce, that minimum standards be provided assuring the equitable character of such plans and their financial soundness.

Act Sec. 2. (b) It is hereby declared to be in the policy of this Act to protect interstate commerce and the interests of participants in employee benefit plans and their beneficiaries, by requiring the disclosure and reporting to participants and beneficiaries of financial and other information with respect thereto, by establishing standards of conduct, responsibility, and obligation for fiduciaries of employee benefit plans, and by providing for appropriate remedies, sanctions, and ready access to the Federal courts.

Act Sec. 2. (c) It is hereby further declared to be the policy of this Act to protect interstate commerce, the Federal taxing power, and the interests of participants in private pension plans and their beneficiaries by improving the equitable character and the soundness of such plans by requiring them to vest the accrued benefits of employees with significant periods of service, to meet minimum standards of funding, and by requiring plan termination insurance.

[¶ 14,130]
DEFINITIONS

Act Sec. 3. For purposes of this title:

(1) The terms "employee welfare benefit plan" and "welfare plan" mean any plan, fund, or program which was heretofore or is hereafter established or maintained by an employer or by an employee organization, or by both, to the extent that such plan, fund, or program was established or is maintained for the purpose of providing for its participants or their beneficiaries, through the purchase of insurance or otherwise, (A) medical, surgical, or hospital care or benefits, or benefits in the event of sickness, accident, disability, death or unemployment, or vacation benefits, apprenticeship or other training programs, or day care centers, scholarship funds, or prepaid legal services, or (B) any benefit described in section 302(c) of the Labor Management Relations Act, 1947 (other than pensions on retirement or death, and insurance to provide such pensions).

(2) (A) Except as provided in subparagraph (B), the terms "employee pension benefit plan" and "pension plan" mean any plan, fund, or program which was heretofore or is hereafter established or maintained by an employer or by an employee organization, or by both, to the extent that by its express terms or as a result of surrounding circumstances such plan, fund, or program—

   (i) provides retirement income to employees, or

   (ii) results in a deferral of income by employees for periods extending to the termination of covered employment or beyond,

regardless of the method of calculating the contributions made to the plan, the method of calculating the benefits under the plan or the method of distributing benefits from the plan.

   (B) The Secretary may by regulation prescribe rules consistent with the standards and purposes of this Act providing one or more exempt categories under which—

   (i) severance pay arrangements, and

   (ii) supplemental retirement income payments, under which the pension benefits of retirees or their beneficiaries are supplemented to take into account some portion or all of the increases in the cost of living (as determined by the Secretary of Labor) since retirement,

shall, for purposes of this title, be treated as welfare plans rather than pension plans. In the case of any arrangement or payment a principal effect of which is the evasion of the standards or purposes of this Act applicable to pension plans, such arrangement or payment shall be treated as a pension plan.

(3) The term "employee benefit plan" or "plan" means an employee welfare benefit plan or an employee pension benefit plan or a plan which is both an employee welfare benefit plan and an employee pension benefit plan.

(4) The term "employee organization" means any labor union or any organization of any kind, or any agency or employee representation committee, association, group, or plan, in which employees participate and which exists for the purpose, in whole or in part, of dealing with employers concerning an employee benefit plan, or other matters incidental to employment relationships; or any employees' beneficiary association organized for the purpose in whole or in part, of establishing such a plan.

(5) The term "employer" means any person acting directly as an employer, or indirectly in the interest of an employer, in relation to an employee benefit plan; and includes a group or association of employers acting for an employer in such capacity.

(6) The term "employee" means any individual employed by an employer.

(7) The term "participant" means any employee or former employee of an employer, or any member or former member of an employee organization, who is or may become eligible to receive a benefit of any type from an employee benefit plan which covers employees of such employer or members of such organization, or whose beneficiaries may be eligible to receive any such benefit.

(8) The term "beneficiary" means a person designated by a participant, or by the terms of an employee benefit plan, who is or may become entitled to a benefit thereunder.

(9) The term "person" means an individual, partnership, joint venture, corporation, mutual company, joint-stock company, trust, estate, unincorporated organization, association, or employee organization.

(10) The term "State" includes any State of the United States, the District of Columbia, Puerto Rico, the Virgin Islands, American Samoa, Guam, Wake Island, and the Canal Zone. The term "United States" when used in the geographic sense means the States and the Outer Continental Shelf lands defined in the Outer Continental Shelf Lands Act (43 U.S.C. 1331-1343).

(11) The term "commerce" means trade, traffic, commerce, transportation, or communication between any State and any place outside thereof.

(12) The term "industry or activity affecting commerce" means any activity, business, or industry in commerce or in which a labor dispute would hinder or obstruct commerce or the free flow of commerce, and includes any activity or industry "affecting commerce" within the meaning of the Labor Management Relations Act, 1947, or the Railway Labor Act.

(13) The term "Secretary" means the Secretary of Labor.

(14) The term "party in interest" means, as to an employee benefit plan—

    (A) any fiduciary (including, but not limited to, any administrator, officer, trustee, or custodian), counsel, or employee of such employee benefit plan;

    (B) a person providing services to such plan;

    (C) an employer any of whose employees are covered by such plan;

    (D) an employee organization any of whose members are covered by such plan;

    (E) an owner, direct or indirect, of 50 percent or more of—

        (i) the combined voting power of all classes of stock entitled to vote or the total value of shares of all classes of stock of a corporation,

        (ii) the capital interest or the profits interest of a partnership, or

        (iii) the beneficial interest of a trust or unincorporated enterprise,

which is an employer or an employee organization described in subparagraph (C) or (D);

    (F) a relative (as defined in paragraph (15)) of any individual described in subparagraph (A), (B), (C), or (E);

    (G) a corporation, partnership, or trust or estate of which (or in which) 50 percent or more of—

        (i) the combined voting power of all classes of stock entitled to vote or the total value of shares of all classes of stock of such corporation,

        (ii) the capital interest or profits interest of such partnership, or

        (iii) the beneficial interest of such trust or estate,

is owned directly or indirectly, or held by persons described in subparagraph (A), (B), (C), (D), or (E);

    (H) an employee, officer, director (or an individual having powers or responsibilities similar to those of officers or directors), or a 10 percent or more shareholder directly or indirectly, of a person described in subparagraph (B), (C), (D), (E), or (G), or of the employee benefit plan; or

    (I) a 10 percent or more (directly or indirectly in capital or profits) partner or joint venturer of a person described in subparagraph (B), (C), (D), (E), or (G).

The Secretary, after consultation and coordination with the Secretary of the Treasury, may by regulation prescribe a percentage lower than 50 percent of subparagraphs (E) and (G) and lower than 10 percent for subparagraph (H) or (I). The Secretary may prescribe regulations for determining the ownership (direct or indirect) of profits and beneficial interests, and the manner in which indirect stockholdings are taken into account. Any person who is a party in interest with respect to a plan to which a trust described in section 501(c)(22) of the Internal Revenue Code of 1986 is permitted to make payments under section 4223 shall be treated as a party in interest with respect to such trust.

(15) The term "relative" means a spouse, ancestor, lineal descendant, or spouse of a lineal descendant.

(16)(A) The term "administrator" means—

    (i) the person specifically so designated by the terms of the instrument under which the plan is operated;

    (ii) if an administrator is not so designated, the plan sponsor; or

    (iii) in the case of a plan for which an administrator is not designated and a plan sponsor cannot be identified, such other person as the Secretary may by regulation prescribe.

    (B) The term "plan sponsor" means (i) the employer in the case of an employee benefit plan established or maintained by a single employer, (ii) the employee organization in the case of a plan established or maintained by an employee organization, or (iii) in the case of a plan established or maintained by two or more employers or jointly by one or more employers and one or more employee organizations, the association, committee, joint board of trustees, or other similar group of representatives of the parties who establish or maintain the plan.

(17) The term "separate account" means an account established or maintained by an insurance company under which income, gains, and losses, whether or not realized, from assets allocated to such account, are, in accordance with the applicable contract, credited to or charged against such account without regard to other income, gains, or losses of the insurance company.

(18) The term "adequate consideration" when used in part 4 of subtitle B means (A) in the case of a security for which there is a generally recognized market, either (i) the price of the security prevailing on a national securities exchange which is registered under section 6 of the Securities Exchange Act of 1934, or (ii) if the security is not traded on such a national securities exchange, a price not less favorable to the plan than the offering price for the security as established by the current bid and asked prices quoted by persons independent of the issuer and of any party in interest; and (B) in the case of an asset other than a security for which there is a generally recognized market, the fair market value of the asset as determined in good faith by the trustee or named fiduciary pursuant to the terms of the plan and in accordance with regulations promulgated by the Secretary.

(19) The term "nonforfeitable" when used with respect to a pension benefit or right means a claim obtained by a participant or his beneficiary to that part of an immediate or deferred benefit under a pension plan which arises from the participant's service, which is unconditional, and which is legally enforceable against the plan. For purposes of this paragraph, a right to an accrued benefit derived from employer contributions shall not be treated as forfeitable merely because the plan contains a provision described in section 203(a)(3).

(20) The term "security" has the same meaning as such term has under section 2(1) of the Securities Act of 1933 (15 U.S.C. 77b(1)).

(21)(A) Except as otherwise provided in subparagraph (B), a person is a fiduciary with respect to a plan to the extent (i) he exercises any discretionary authority or discretionary control respecting management of such plan or exercises any authority or control respecting management or disposition of its assets, (ii) he renders investment advice for a fee or other compensation, direct or indirect, with respect to any moneys or other property of such plan, or has any authority or responsibility to do so, or (iii) he has any discretionary authority or discretionary responsibility in the administration of such plan. Such term includes any person designated under section 405(c)(1)(B).

    (B) If any money or other property of an employee benefit plan is invested in securities issued by an investment company registered under the Investment Company Act of 1940, such investment shall not by itself cause such investment company or such investment company's investment adviser or principal underwriter to be deemed to be a fiduciary or a party in interest as those terms are defined in this title, except insofar as such investment company or its investment adviser or principal underwriter acts in connection with an employee benefit plan covering employees of the investment company, the investment adviser, or its principal underwriter. Nothing contained in this subparagraph shall limit the duties imposed on such investment company, investment adviser, or principal underwriter by any other law.

(22) The term "normal retirement benefit" means the greater of the early retirement benefit under the plan, or the benefit under the plan commencing at normal retirement age. The normal retirement benefit shall be determined without regard to—

    (A) medical benefits, and

    (B) disability benefits not in excess of the qualified disability benefit.

For purposes of this paragraph, a qualified disability benefit is a disability benefit provided by a plan which does not exceed the benefit which would be provided for the participant if he separated from the service at normal retirement age. For purposes of this paragraph, the early retirement benefit under a plan shall be determined without regard to any benefit under the plan which the Secretary of the Treasury finds to be a benefit described in section 204(b)(1)(G).

(23) The term "accrued benefit" means—

(A) in the case of a defined benefit plan, the individual's accrued benefit determined under the plan and, except as provided in section 204(c)(3), expressed in the form of an annual benefit commencing at normal retirement age, or

(B) in the case of a plan which is an individual account plan, the balance of the individual's account.

The accrued benefit of an employee shall not be less than the amount determined under section 204(c)(2)(B) with respect to the employee's accumulated contribution.

(24) The term "normal retirement age" means the earlier of—

(A) the time a plan participant attains normal retirement age under the plan, or

(B) the later of—

(i) the time a plan participant attains age 65, or

(ii) the 5th anniversary of the time a plan participant commenced participation in the plan.

(25) The term "vested liabilities" means the present value of the immediate or deferred benefits available at normal retirement age for participants and their beneficiaries which are nonforfeitable.

(26) The term "current value" means fair market value where available and otherwise the fair value as determined in good faith by a trustee or a named fiduciary (as defined in section 402(a)(2)) pursuant to the terms of the plan and in accordance with regulations of the Secretary, assuming an orderly liquidation at the time of such determination.

(27) The term "present value", with respect to a liability, means the value adjusted to reflect anticipated events. Such adjustments shall conform to such regulations as the Secretary of the Treasury may prescribe.

(28) The term "normal service cost" or "normal cost" means the annual cost of future pension benefits and administrative expenses assigned, under an actuarial cost method, to years subsequent to a particular valuation date of a pension plan. The Secretary of the Treasury may prescribe regulations to carry out this paragraph.

(29) The term "accrued liability" means the excess of the present value, as of a particular valuation date of a pension plan, of the projected future benefit costs and administrative expenses for all plan participants and beneficiaries over the present value of future contributions for the normal cost of all applicable plan participants and beneficiaries. The Secretary of the Treasury may prescribe regulations to carry out this paragraph.

(30) The term "unfunded accrued liability" means the excess of the accrued liability, under an actuarial cost method which so provides, over the present value of the assets of a pension plan. The Secretary of the Treasury may prescribe regulations to carry out this paragraph.

(31) The term "advance funding actuarial cost method" or "actuarial cost method" means a recognized actuarial technique utilized for establishing the amount and incidence of the annual actuarial cost of pension plan benefits and expenses. Acceptable actuarial cost methods shall include the accrued benefit cost method (unit credit method), the entry age normal cost method, the individual level premium cost method, the aggregate cost method, the attained age normal cost method, and the frozen initial liability cost method. The terminal funding cost method and the current funding (pay-as-you-go) cost method are not acceptable actuarial cost methods. The Secretary of the Treasury shall issue regulations to further define acceptable actuarial cost methods.

(32) The term "governmental plan" means a plan established or maintained for its employees by the Government of the United States, by the government of any State or political subdivision thereof, or by any agency or instrumentality of any of the foregoing. The term "governmental plan" also includes any plan to which the Railroad Retirement Act of 1935 or 1937 applies, and which is financed by contributions required under that Act and any plan of an international organization which is exempt from taxation under the provisions of the International Organizations Immunities Act (59 Stat. 669).

(33)(A) The term "church plan" means a plan established and maintained (to the extent required in clause (ii) of subparagraph (B)) for its employees (or their beneficiaries) by a church or by a convention or association of churches which is exempt from tax under section 501 of the Internal Revenue Code of 1986.

(B) The term "church plan" does not include a plan—

(i) which is established and maintained primarily for the benefit of employees (or their beneficiaries) of such church or convention or association of churches who are employed in connection with one or more unrelated trades or businesses (within the meaning of section 513 of the Internal Revenue Code of 1986), or

(ii) if less than substantially all of the individuals included in the plan are individuals described in subparagraph (A) or in clause (ii) of subparagraph (C) (or their beneficiaries).

(C) For purposes of this paragraph—

(i) A plan established and maintained for its employees (or their beneficiaries) by a church or by a convention or association of churches includes a plan maintained by an organization, whether a civil law corporation or otherwise, the principal purpose or function of which is the administration or funding of a plan or program for the provision of retirement benefits or welfare benefits, or both, for the employees of a church or a convention or association of churches, if such organization is controlled by or associated with a church or a convention or association of churches.

(ii) The term employee of a church or a convention or association of churches includes—

(I) a duly ordained, commissioned, or licensed minister of a church in the exercise of his ministry, regardless of the source of his compensation;

(II) an employee of an organization, whether a civil law corporation or otherwise, which is exempt from tax under section 501 of the Internal Revenue Code of 1986 and which is controlled by or associated with a church or a convention or association of churches; and

(III) an individual described in clause (v).

(iii) A church or a convention or association of churches which is exempt from tax under section 501 of the Internal Revenue Code of 1986 shall be deemed the employer of any individual included as an employee under clause (ii).

(iv) An organization, whether a civil law corporation or otherwise, is associated with a church or a convention or association of churches if it shares common religious bonds and convictions with that church or convention or association of churches.

(v) If an employee who is included in a church plan separates from the service of a church or a convention or association of churches or an organization, whether a civil law corporation or otherwise, which is exempt from tax under section 501 of the Internal Revenue Code of 1986 and which is controlled by or associated with a church or a convention or association of churches, the church plan shall not fail to meet the requirements of this paragraph merely because the plan—

(I) retains the employee's accrued benefit or account for the payment of benefits to the employee or his beneficiaries pursuant to the terms of the plan; or

(II) receives contributions on the employee's behalf after the employee's separation from such service, but only for a period of 5 years after such separation, unless the employee is disabled (within the meaning of the disability provisions of the church plan or, if there are no such provisions in the church plan, within the meaning of section 72(m)(7) of the Internal Revenue Code of 1986) at the time of such separation from service.

(D)(i) If a plan established and maintained for its employees (or their beneficiaries) by a church or by a convention or association of churches which is exempt from tax under section 501 of the Internal Revenue Code of 1986 fails to meet one or more of the requirements of this paragraph and corrects its failure to meet such requirements within the correction period, the plan shall be deemed to meet the requirements of this paragraph for the year in which the correction was made and for all prior years.

(ii) If a correction is not made within the correction period, the plan shall be deemed not to meet the requirements of this paragraph beginning with the date on which the earliest failure to meet one or more of such requirements occurred.

(iii) For purposes of this subparagraph, the term "correction period" means—

(I) the period ending 270 days after the date of mailing by the Secretary of the Treasury of a notice of default with respect to the plan's failure to meet one or more of the requirements of this paragraph; or

(II) any period set by a court of competent jurisdiction after a final determination that the plan fails to meet such requirements, or, if the court does not specify such period, any reasonable period determined by the Secretary of the Treasury on the basis of all the facts and circumstances, but in any event not less than 270 days after the determination has become final; or

(III) any additional period which the Secretary of the Treasury determines is reasonable or necessary for the correction of the default, whichever has the latest ending date.

>>>→ *CCH NOTE—: The following public law clarifies the definition of church plans under ERISA Sec. 3(33).*

P.L. 106-244

CHURCH PLAN PARITY AND ENTANGLEMENT PROTECTION ACT

SECTION 1. PURPOSE

The purpose of this Act is only to clarify the application to a church plan that is a welfare plan of State insurance laws that require or solely relate to licensing, solvency, insolvency, or the status of such plan as a single employer plan.

SECTION 2. CLARIFICATION OF CHURCH WELFARE PLAN STATUS UNDER STATE INSURANCE LAW.

(a) In General. For purposes of determining the status of a church plan that is a welfare plan under provisions of a State insurance law described in subsection (b), such church plan (and any trust under such plan) shall be deemed to be a plan sponsored by a single employer that reimburses costs from general church assets, or purchases insurance coverage with general church assets, or both.

(b) State Insurance Law. A State insurance law described in this subsection is a law that—

(1) requires a church plan, or an organization described in section 414(e)(3)(A) of the Internal Revenue Code of 1986 and section 3(33)(C)(i) of the Employee Retirement Income Security Act of 1974 (29 U.S.C. 1002(33)(C)(i)) to the extent that it is administering or funding such a plan, to be licensed; or

(2) relates solely to the solvency or insolvency of a church plan (including participation in State guaranty funds and associations).

(c) Definitions. For purposes of this section:

(1) Church plan. The term "church plan" has the meaning given such term by section 414(e) of the Internal Revenue Code of 1986 and section 3(33) of the Employee Retirement Income Security Act of 1974 (29 U.S.C. 1002(33)).

(2) Reimburses costs from general church assets. The term "reimburses costs from general church assets" means engaging in an activity that is not the spreading of risk solely for the purposes of the provisions of State insurance laws described in subsection (b).

(3) Welfare plan. The term "welfare plan"—

(A) means any church plan to the extent that such plan provides medical, surgical, or hospital care or benefits, or benefits in the event of sickness, accident, disability, death or unemployment, or vacation benefits, apprenticeship or other training programs, or day care centers, scholarship funds, or prepaid legal services; and

(B) does not include any entity, such as a health insurance issuer described in section 9832(b)(2) of the Internal Revenue Code of 1986 or a health maintenance organization described in section 9832(b)(3) of such Code, or any other organization that does business with the church plan or organization sponsoring or maintaining such a plan.

(d) Enforcement Authority. Notwithstanding any other provision of this section, for purposes of enforcing provisions of State insurance laws that apply to a church plan that is a welfare plan, the church plan shall be subject to State enforcement as if the church plan were an insurer licensed by the State.

(e) Application of Section. Except as provided in subsection (d), the application of this section is limited to determining the status of a church plan that is a welfare plan under the provisions of State insurance laws described in subsection (b). This section shall not otherwise be construed to recharacterize the status, or modify or affect the rights, of any plan participant or beneficiary, including participants or beneficiaries who make plan contributions.

---

(34) The term "individual account plan" or "defined contribution plan" means a pension plan which provides for an individual account for each participant and for benefits based solely upon the amount contributed to the participant's account, and any income, expenses, gains and losses, and any forfeitures of accounts of other participants which may be allocated to such participant's account.

(35) The term "defined benefit plan" means a pension plan other than an individual account plan; except that a pension plan which is not an individual account plan and which provides a benefit derived from employer contributions which is based partly on the balance of the separate account of a participant—

(A) for the purposes of section 202, shall be treated as an individual account plan, and

(B) for the purposes of paragraph (23) of this section and section 204, shall be treated as an individual account plan to the extent benefits are based upon the separate account of a participant and as a defined benefit plan with respect to the remaining portion of benefits under the plan.

(36) The term "excess benefit plan" means a plan maintained by an employer solely for the purpose of providing benefits for certain employees in excess of the limitations on contributions and benefits imposed by section 415 of the Internal Revenue Code of 1986 on plans to which that section applies, without regard to whether the plan is funded. To the extent that a separable part of a plan (as determined by the Secretary of Labor) maintained by an employer is maintained for such purpose, that part shall be treated as a separate plan which is an excess benefit plan.

(37)(A) The term "multiemployer plan" means a plan—

(i) to which more than one employer is required to contribute,

(ii) which is maintained pursuant to one or more collective bargaining agreements between one or more employee organizations and more than one employer, and

(iii) which satisfies such other requirements as the Secretary may prescribe by regulation.

(B) For purposes of this paragraph, all trades or businesses (whether or not incorporated) which are under common control within the meaning of section 4001(b)(1) are considered a single employer.

(C) Notwithstanding subparagraph (A), a plan is a multiemployer plan on and after its termination date if the plan was a multiemployer plan under this paragraph for the plan year preceding its termination date.

(D) For purposes of this title, notwithstanding the preceding provisions of this paragraph, for any plan year which began before the date of the enactment of the Multiemployer Pension Plan Amendments Act of 1980, the term "multiemployer plan" means a plan described in section 3(37) of this Act as in effect immediately before such date.

(E) Within one year after the date of the enactment of the Multiemployer Pension Plan Amendments Act of 1980, a multiemployer plan may irrevocably elect, pursuant to procedures established by the corporation and subject to the provisions of sections 4403(b) and (c), that the plan shall not be treated as a multiemployer plan for all puposes under this Act or the Internal Revenue Code of 1954 if for each of the last 3 plan years ending prior to the effective date of the Multiemployer Pension Plan Amendments Act of 1980—

(i) the plan was not a multiemployer plan because the plan was not a plan described in section 3(37)(A)(iii) of this Act and section 414(f)(1)(C) of the Internal Revenue Code of 1954 (as such provisions were in effect on the day before the date of the enactment of the Multiemployer Pension Plan Amendments Act of 1980); and

(ii) the plan had been identified as a plan that was not a multiemployer plan in substantially all its filings with the corporation, the Secretary of Labor and the Secretary of the Treasury.

(F)(i) For purposes of this title a qualified football coaches plan—

(I) shall be treated as a multiemployer plan to the extent not inconsistent with the purposes of this subparagraph; and

(II) notwithstanding section 401(k)(4)(B) of the Internal Revenue Code of 1986, may include a qualified cash and deferred arrangement.

(ii) For purposes of this subparagraph, the term "qualified football coaches plan" means any defined contribution plan which is established and maintained by an organization—

(I) which is described in section 501(c) of such Code;

(II) the membership of which consists entirely of individuals who primarily coach football as full-time employees of 4-year colleges or universities described in section 170(b)(1)(A)(ii) of such Code; and

(III) which was in existence on September 18, 1986.

(38) The term "investment manager" means any fiduciary (other than a trustee or named fiduciary, as defined in section 402(a)(2))—

(A) who has the power to manage, acquire, or dispose of any asset of a plan;

(B) who (i) is registered as an investment adviser under the Investment Advisers Act of 1940; (ii) is not registered as an investment adviser under such Act by reason of paragraph (1) of section 203A(a) of such Act, is registered as an investment adviser under the laws of the State (referred to in such paragraph (1)) in which it maintains its principal office and place of business, and, at the time the fiduciary last filed the registration form most recently filed by the fiduciary with such State in order to maintain the fiduciary's registration under the laws of such State, also filed a copy of such form with the Secretary; (iii) is a bank, as defined in that Act; or (iv) is an insurance company qualified to perform services described in subparagraph (A) under the laws of more than one State; and

(C) has acknowledged in writing that he is a fiduciary with respect to the plan.

(39) The terms "plan year" and "fiscal year of the plan" mean, with respect to a plan, the calendar, policy, or fiscal year on which the records of the plan are kept.

(40)(A) The term "multiple employer welfare arrangement" means an employee welfare benefit plan, or any other arrangement (other than an employee welfare benefit plan), which is established or maintained for the purpose of offering or providing any benefit described in paragraph (1) to the employees of two or more employers (including one or more self-employed individuals), or to their beneficiaries, except that such term does not include any such plan or other arrangement which is established or maintained—

(i) under or pursuant to one or more agreements which the Secretary finds to be collective bargaining agreements,

(ii) by a rural electric cooperative, or

(iii) by a rural telephone cooperative association.

(B) For purposes of this paragraph—

(i) two or more trades or businesses, whether or not incorporated, shall be deemed a single employer if such trades or businesses are within the same control group,

(ii) the term "control group" means a group of trades or businesses under common control,

(iii) the determination of whether a trade or business is under "common control" with another trade or business shall be determined under regulations of the Secretary applying principles similar to the principles applied in determining whether employees of two or more trades or businesses are treated as employed by a single employer under section 4001(b), except that, for purposes of this paragraph, common control shall not be based on an interest of less than 25 percent,

(iv) the term "rural electric cooperative" means—

(I) any organization which is exempt from tax under section 501(a) of the Internal Revenue Code of 1986 and which is engaged primarily in providing electric service on a mutual or cooperative basis, and

(II) any organization described in paragraph (4) or (6) of section 501(c) of the Internal Revenue Code of 1986 which is exempt from tax under section 501(a) of such Code and at least 80 percent of the members of which are organizations described in subclause (I), and

(v) the term "rural telephone cooperative association" means an organization described in paragraph (4) or (6) of section 501(c) of the Internal Revenue Code of 1986 which is exempt from tax under section 501(a) of such Code and at least 80 percent of the members of which are organizations engaged primarily in providing telephone service to rural areas of the United States on a mutual, cooperative, or other basis.

(41) SINGLE-EMPLOYER PLAN. The term "single-employer plan" means an employee benefit plan other than a multiemployer plan.

(41) [*] The term "single-employer plan" means a plan which is not a multiemployer plan.

Amendments

P.L. 105-72, § 1(a):

Amended ERISA Sec. 3(38)(B) by redesignating clauses (ii) and (iii) as clauses (iii) and (iv), respectively; and by striking "who is" and all that followed through clause (i) and inserting clauses (i) and (ii) to read as above, effective July 8, 1997.

Prior to amendment (as effective from 10/11/96 to 10/10/98, as changed by P.L. 104-290, § 308(b)(1)), the section read:

"(B) who is (i) registered as an investment adviser under the Investment Advisers Act of 1940 or under the laws of any State; (ii) is a bank, as defined in that Act; or (iii) is an insurance company qualified to perform services described in subparagraph (A) under the laws of more than one State; and".

Prior to amendment (as effective beginning 10/11/98, following expiration of P.L. 104-290 changes under § 308(b)(2)), the section read:

"(B) who is (i) registered as an investment adviser under the Investment Advisers Act of 1940; (ii) is a bank, as defined in that Act; or (iii) is an insurance company qualified to perform services described in subparagraph (A) under the laws of more than one State; and".

The above amendments are effective July 8, 1997. For a special rule, see Act Sec. 1(c), reproduced below.

Act Sec. 1(c) provides:

(c) Effective Date.—The amendments made by subsection (a) shall take effect on July 8, 1997, except that the requirement of section 3(38)(B)(ii) of the Employee Retirement Income Security Act of 1974 (as amended by this Act) for filing with the Secretary of Labor of a copy of a registration form which has been filed with a State before the date of the enactment of this Act, or is to be filed with a State during the 1-year period beginning with such date, shall be treated as satisfied upon the filing of such a copy with the Secretary at any time during such 1-year period. This section shall supersede section 308(b) of the National Securities Markets Improvement Act of 1996 (and the amendment made thereby).

P.L. 104-290, § 308(b)(1):

Amended ERISA Sec. 3(38) by adding "or under the laws of any State" after "1940".

The above amendment is effective on the date of enactment of this Act. For a special rule, see Act Sec. 308(b)(2), reproduced below.

Act Sec. 308(b)(2) provides:

The amendment made by paragraph (1) shall cease to be effective 2 years after the date of enactment of this Act.

P.L. 102-89, § 2:

Amended ERISA Sec. 3(40) by striking "or" at the end of subparagraph (A)(i); by striking "cooperative." in subparagraph (A)(ii) and adding "cooperative, or"; by adding a new subparagraph (iii) in paragraph (A) to read as above; by striking "and" at the end of subparagraph (B)(iii); by striking "subclause (I)." in subparagraph (B)(iv)(II) and adding "subclause (I), and"; and by adding a new subclause (v) at the end of subparagraph (B) to read as above, effective on the date of enactment.

P.L. 101-508, § 12001(b)(2)(C):

Amended ERISA Sec. 3 by adding a new paragraph (41) to read as above effective for reversions occurring after September 30, 1990 except for the provisions of Act Sec. 12003(b). [* Paragraph (41) was previously enacted in P.L. 101-239—CCH.]

SEC. 12003. EFFECTIVE DATE.

* * *

(b) EXCEPTION.—The amendments made by this subtitle shall not apply to any reversion after September 30, 1990, if—

(1) in the case of plans subject to title IV of the Employee Retirement Income Security Act of 1974, a notice of intent to terminate under such title was provided to participants (or if no participants, to the Pension Benefit Guaranty Corporation) before October 1, 1990,

(2) in the case of plans subject to title I (and not to title IV) of such Act, a notice of intent to reduce future accruals under section 204(h) of such Act was provided to participants in connection with the termination before October 1, 1990,

(3) in the case of plans not subject to title I or IV of such Act, a request for a determination letter with respect to the termination was filed with the Secretary of the Treasury or the Secretary's delegate before October 1, 1990, or

(4) in the case of plans not subject to title I or IV of such Act and having only 1 participant, a resolution terminating the plan was adopted by the employer before October 1, 1990.

P.L. 101-239, §7871(b)(2):

Amended ERISA Sec. 3(24)(B) to read as above, effective for plan years beginning on or after January 1, 1988 and for service performed on or after that date. Prior to amendment, Sec. 3(24)(B) read as follows:

(B) the latest of—

(i) the time a plan participant attains age 65,

(ii) in the case of a plan participant who commences participation in the plan within 5 years before attaining normal retirement age under the plan, the 5th anniversary of the time the plan participant commences participation in the plan, or

(iii) in the case of a plan participant not described in clause (ii), the 10th anniversary of the time the plan participant commences participation in the plan.

P.L. 101-239, §7881(m)(2)(D):

Amended ERISA Sec. 3(23) by adding a new flush sentence to read as above effective December 22, 1987.

P.L. 101-239, §7893(a):

Amended ERISA Sec. 3(37)(B) by striking "section 4001(c)(1)" and inserting "section 4001(b)(1)" effective April 7, 1986.

P.L. 101-239, §7894(a)(1)(A):

Amended ERISA Sec. 3(33)(D)(iii) by inserting "of the Treasury" after "Secretary" each place it appears effective as if included in P.L. 96-364, §407.

P.L. 101-239, §7894(a)(2):

Amended ERISA Sec. 3(37)(F) in clause (i)(II) by striking "such Code" and inserting "the Internal Revenue Code of 1986;" in clause (ii)(I) by inserting "of such Code" after "section 501(c);" and in clause (ii)(II) by inserting "of such Code" after "section 170(b)(1)(A)(ii)" effective as if included in P.L. 100-202, §136.

P.L. 101-239, §7894(a)(3):

Amended ERISA Sec. 3(39) by inserting a comma after "mean" and by inserting "the" before "calendar" effective September 2, 1986.

P.L. 101-239, §7894(a)(4):

Amended ERISA Sec. 3 by adding a new paragraph (41) to read as above effective September 2, 1986.

P.L. 101-239, §7891(a)(1):

Titles I, III, and IV of ERISA (other than sections 3(37)(E), 301(a)(7), and 308, the last sentence of section 408(d), and sections 414(c), 4001(a)(3)(ii), and 4303) are each amended by striking "Internal Revenue Code of 1954" each place it appears and inserting "Internal Revenue Code of 1986" effective April 7, 1986.

P.L. 100-202, §136:

Amended ERISA Sec. 3(37) by adding subparagraph (F) to read as above.

P.L. 99-514, §1897(u)(3):

Repealed section 11016 of P.L. 99-272, effective on April 7, 1986.

P.L. 99-509, §9203(b)(1):

Amended ERISA Sec. 3(24)(B) to read as above, effective with respect to plan years beginning on or after January 1, 1988 and only with respect to service performed on or after such date. See also §9204(c) at ¶ 14,440 (amendment notes). Prior to amendment, Sec. 3(24)(B) read as follows:

(24) The term "normal retirement age" means the earlier of—

* * *

(B) the later of—

(i) the time a plan participant attains age 65, or

(ii) the 10th anniversary of the time a plan participant commenced participation in the plan.

.P.L. 99-272:

Act Sec. 11016(c)(1) amended ERISA Sec. 3(37)(A) by inserting "pension" before "plan" effective on April 7, 1986.

.P.L. 97-473:

Added paragraph (40), effective January 14, 1983.

P.L. 96-364; §§302(a), 305, 407(a), and 409:

Amended Sec. 3(2) by adding "(A) Except as provided in subparagraph (B), the", by renumbering subsections (A) and (B) as (i) and (ii) and by adding new subparagraph (B), effective September 26, 1980.

Amended Sec. 3(14) by adding the last sentence to read as above, effective April 29, 1980.

Amended Sec. 3(33) to read as above, effective January 1, 1974. Prior to amendment, the section read:

"(33)(A) The term 'church plan' means (i) a plan established and maintained for its employees by a church or by a convention or association of churches which is exempt from tax under section 501 of the Internal Revenue Code of 1954, or (ii) a plan described in subparagraph (C).

(B) The term 'church plan' (notwithstanding the provisions of subparagraph (A)) does not include a plan—

(i) which is established and maintained primarily for the benefit of employees (or their beneficiaries) of such church or convention or association of churches who are employed in connection with one or more unrelated trades or businesses (within the meaning of section 513 of the Internal Revenue Code of 1954), or

(ii) which is a plan maintained by more than one employer, if one or more of the employers in the plan is not a church (or a convention or association of churches) which is exempt from tax under section 501 of the Internal Revenue Code of 1954.

(C) Notwithstanding the provisions of subparagraph (B)(ii), a plan in existence on January 1, 1974, shall be treated as a 'church plan' if it is established and maintained by a church or convention or association of churches for its employees and employees of one or more agencies of such church (or convention or association) for the employees of such church (or convention or association) and the employees of one or more agencies of such church (or convention or association), and if such church (or convention or association) and each such agency is exempt from tax under section 501 of the Internal Revenue Code of 1954. The first sentence of this subparagraph shall not apply to any plan maintained for employees of an agency with respect to which the plan was not maintained on January 1, 1974. The first sentence of this subparagraph shall not apply with respect to any plan for any plan year beginning after December 31, 1982."

Amended Sec. 3(37) to read as above generally effective for plan years beginning on or after September 26, 1980. Prior to amendment, the section read:

"(37)(A) The term 'multiemployer plan' means a plan—

(i) to which more than one employer is required to contribute,

(ii) which is maintained pursuant to one or more collective-bargaining agreements between an employee organization and more than one employer,

(iii) under which the amount of contributions made under the plan for a plan year by each employer making such contributions is less than 50 percent of the aggregate amount of contributions made under the plan for that plan year by all employers making such contributions,

(iv) under which benefits are payable with respect to each participant without regard to the cessation of contributions by the employer who had employed that participant except to the extent that such benefits accrued as a result of service with the employer before such employer was required to contribute to such plan, and

(v) which satisfies such other requirements as the Secretary may by regulations prescribe.

(B) For purposes of this paragraph—

(i) if a plan is a multiemployer plan within the meaning of subparagraph (A) for any plan year, clause (iii) of subparagraph (A) shall be applied by substituting '75 percent' for '50 percent' for each subsequent plan year until the first plan year following a plan year in which the plan had one employer who made contributions of 75 percent or more of the aggregate amount of contributions made under the plan for that plan year by all employers making such contributions, and

(ii) all corporations which are members of a controlled group of corporations (within the meaning of section 1563(a) of the Internal Revenue Code of 1954, determined without regard to section 1563(e)(3)(C) of such Code) shall be deemed to be one employer. Effective September 26, 1980, except that the prior law definition will contiinue for plan years beginning before enactment."

Regulations

The following regulations were adopted by FR Doc. 75-21470 under "Title 29—Labor; Chapter XXV—Office of Employee Benefits Security; Part 2510—Definitions of Terms used in Subchapters C, D, E, F, and G of this Chapter." The regulations were published in the Federal Register of August 15, 1975, and are effective August 15, 1975.

[¶ 14,131]

§2510.3-1. **Employee welfare benefit plan.** (a) *General.* (1) The purpose of this section is to clarify the definition of the terms "employee welfare benefit plan" and "welfare plan" for purposes of Title I of the Act and this chapter by identifying certain practices which do not constitute employee welfare benefit plans for those purposes. In addition, the practices listed in this section do not constitute employee pension benefit plans within the meaning of section 3(2) of the Act, and, therefore, do not constitute employee benefit plans within the meaning of section 3(3). Since under section 4(a) of the Act, only employee benefit plans within the meaning of section 3(3) are subject to Title I of the Act, the practices listed in this section are not subject to Title I.

(2) The terms "employee welfare benefit plan" and "welfare plan" are defined in section 3(1) of the Act to include plans providing "(i) medical, surgical, or hospital care or benefits, or benefits in the event of sickness, accident, disability, death or unemployment, or vacation benefits, apprenticeship or other training programs, or day

care centers, scholarship funds, or prepaid legal services, or (ii) any benefit described in section 302(c) of the Labor Management Relations Act, 1947 (other than pensions on retirement or death, and insurance to provide such pensions)." Under this definition only plans which provide benefits described in section 3(1)(A) of the Act or in section 302(c) of the Labor-Management Relations Act 1947 (hereinafter "the LMRA") (other than pensions on retirement or death) constitute welfare plans. For example, a system of payroll deductions by an employer for deposit in savings accounts owned by its employees is not an employee welfare benefit plan within the meaning of section 3(1) of the Act because it does not provide benefits described in section 3(1)(A) of the Act or section 302(c) of the LMRA. (In addition, if each employee has the right to withdraw the balance in his or her account at any time, such a payroll savings plan does not meet the requirements for a pension plan set forth in section 3(2) of the Act and, therefore, is not an employee benefit plan within the meaning of section 3(3) of the Act).

(3) Section 302(c) of the LMRA lists exceptions to the restrictions contained in subsections (a) and (b) of that section on payments and loans made by an employer to individuals and groups representing employees of the employer. Of these exceptions, only those contained in paragraphs (5), (6), (7) and (8) describe benefits provided through employee benefit plans. Moreover, only paragraph (6) describes benefits not described in section 3(1)(A) of the Act. The benefits described in section 302(c)(6) of the LMRA but not in section 3(1)(A) of the Act are "* * * holiday, severance or similar benefits". Thus, the effect of section 3(1)(B) of the Act is to include within the definition of "welfare plan" those plans which provide holiday and severance benefits, and benefits which are similar (for example, benefits which are in substance severance benefits, although not so characterized).

(4) Some of the practices listed in this section as excluded from the definition of "welfare plan" or mentioned as examples of general categories of excluded practices are inserted in response to questions received by the Department of Labor and, in the Department's judgment, do not represent borderline cases under the definition in section 3(1) of the Act. Therefore, this section should not be read as implicitly indicating the Department's views on the possible scope of section 3(1).

(b) *Payroll practices.* For purposes of Title I of the Act and this chapter, the terms "employee welfare benefit plan" and "welfare plan" shall not include—

(1) Payment by an employer of compensation on account of work performed by an employee, including compensation at a rate in excess of the normal rate of compensation on account of performance of duties under other than ordinary circumstances, such as—

(i) Overtime pay,

(ii) Shift premiums,

(iii) Holiday premiums,

(iv) Weekend premiums;

(2) Payment of an employee's normal compensation, out of the employer's general assets, on account of periods of time during which the employee is physically or mentally unable to perform his or her duties, or is otherwise absent for medical reasons (such as pregnancy, a physical examination or psychiatric treatment); and

(3) Payment of compensation, out of the employer's general assets, on account of periods of time during which the employee, although physically and mentally able to perform his or her duties and not absent for medical reasons (such as pregnancy, a physical examination or psychiatric treatment) performs no duties; for example—

(i) Payment of compensation while an employee is on vacation or absent on a holiday, including payment of premiums to induce employees to take vacations at a time favorable to the employer for business reasons,

(ii) Payment of compensation to an employee who is absent while on active military duty,

(iii) Payment of compensation while an employee is absent for the purpose of serving as a juror or testifying in official proceedings,

(iv) Payment of compensation on account of periods of time during which an employee performs little or no productive work while engaged in training (whether or not subsidized in whole or in part by Federal, State or local government funds), and

(v) Payment of compensation to an employee who is relieved of duties while on sabbatical leave or while pursuing further education.

(c) *On-premises facilities.* For purposes of Title I of the Act and this chapter, the terms "employee welfare benefit plan" and "welfare plan" shall not include—

(1) The maintenance on the premises of an employer or of an employee organization of recreation, dining or other facilities (other than day care centers) for use by employees or members; and

(2) The maintenance on the premises of an employer of facilities for the treatment of minor injuries or illness or rendering first aid in case of accidents occurring during working hours.

(d) *Holiday gifts.* For purposes of Title I of the Act and this chapter the terms "employee welfare benefit plan" and "welfare plan" shall not include the distribution of gifts such as turkeys or hams by an employer to employees at Christmas and other holiday seasons.

(e) *Sales to employees.* For purposes of Title I of the Act and this chapter, the terms "employee welfare benefit plan" and "welfare plan" shall not include the sale by an employer to employees of an employer, whether or not at prevailing market prices, of articles or commodities of the kind which the employer offers for sale in the regular course of business.

(f) *Hiring halls.* For purposes of Title I of the Act and this chapter, the terms "employee welfare benefit plan" and "welfare plan" shall not include the maintenance by one or more employers, employee organizations, or both, of a hiring hall facility.

(g) *Remembrance funds.* For purposes of Title I of the Act and this chapter, the terms "employee welfare benefit plan" and "welfare plan" shall not include a program under which contributions are made to provide remembrances such as flowers, an obituary notice in a newspaper or a small gift on occasions such as the sickness, hospitalization, death or termination of employment of employees, or members of an employee organization, or members of their families.

(h) *Strike funds.* For purposes of Title I of the Act and this chapter, the terms "employee welfare benefit plan" and "welfare plan" shall not include a fund maintained by an employee organization to provide payments to its members during strikes and for related purposes.

(i) *Industry advancement programs.* For purposes of Title I of the Act and this chapter, the terms "employee welfare benefit plan" and "welfare plan" shall not include a program maintained by an employer or group or association of employers, which has no employee participants and does not provide benefits to employees or their dependents, regardless of whether the program serves as a conduit through which funds or other assets are channelled to employee benefit plans covered under Title I of the Act.

(j) *Certain group or group-type insurance programs.*

For purposes of Title I of the Act and this chapter, the terms "employee welfare benefit plan" and "welfare plan" shall not include a group or group-type insurance program offered by an insurer to employees or members of an employee organization, under which

(1) no contributions are made by an employer or employee organization;

(2) participation in the program is completely voluntary for employees or members;

(3) the sole functions of the employer or employee organization with respect to the program are, without endorsing the program, to permit the insurer to publicize the program to employees or members, to collect premiums through payroll deductions or dues checkoffs and to remit them to the insurer; and

(4) the employer or employee organization receives no consideration in the form of cash or otherwise in connection with the program, other than reasonable compensation, excluding any profit, for administrative services actually rendered in connection with payroll deductions or dues checkoffs.

(k) *Unfunded scholarship programs.* For purposes of Title I of the Act and this chapter, the terms "employee welfare benefit plan" and "welfare plan" shall not include a scholarship program, including a tuition and education expense refund program, under which payments are made solely from the general assets of an employer or employee organization.

[¶ 14,132]

§ 2510.3-2. **Employee pension benefit plan.** (a) *General.* This section clarifies the limits of the defined terms "employee pension benefit plan" and "pension plan" for purposes of Title I of the Act and this chapter by identifying certain specific plans, funds and programs which do not constitute employee pension benefit plans for those purposes. To the extent that these plans, funds and programs constitute employee welfare benefit plans within the meaning of section 3(1) of the Act and § 2510.3-1 of this part, they will be covered under Title I; however, they will not be subject to parts 2 and 3 of Title I of the Act.

(b) *Severance pay plans.* (1) For purposes of Title I of the Act and this chapter, an arrangement shall not be deemed to constitute an employee pension benefit plan or pension plan solely by reason of the payment of severance benefits on account of the termination of an employee's service, provided that:

(i) Such payments are not contingent, directly or indirectly, upon the employee's retiring;

(ii) The total amount of such payments does not exceed the equivalent of twice the employee's annual compensation during the year immediately preceding the termination of his service; and

(iii) All such payments to any employee are completed,

(A) In the case of an employee whose service is terminated in connection with a limited program of terminations, within the later of 24 months after the termination of the employee's service, or 24 months after the employee reaches normal retirement age; and

(B) In the case of all other employees, within 24 months after the termination of the employee's service.

(2) For purposes of this paragraph (b),

(i) "Annual compensation" means the total of all compensation, including wages, salary, and any other benefit of monetary value, whether paid in the form of cash or otherwise, which was paid as consideration for the employee's service during the year, or which would have been so paid at the employee's usual rate of compensation if the employee had worked a full year.

(ii) "Limited program of terminations" means a program of terminations:

(A) Which, when begun, was scheduled to be completed upon a date certain or upon the occurrence of one or more specified events;

(B) Under which the number, percentage or class or classes of employees whose services are to be terminated is specified in advance; and

(C) Which is described in a written document which is available to the Secretary upon request, and which contains information sufficient to demonstrate that the conditions set forth in subclauses (A) and (B) of this clause (ii) have been met. [Amended February 23, 1979, by FR Doc. 79-5812.]

(c) *Bonus program.* For purposes of Title I of the Act and this chapter, the terms "employee pension benefit plan" and "pension plan" shall not include payments made by an employer to some or all of its employees as bonuses for work performed, unless such payments are systematically deferred to the termination of covered employment or beyond, or so as to provide retirement income to employees.

(d) *Individual Retirement Accounts.* (1) For purposes of Title I of the Act and this chapter, the terms "employee pension benefit plan" and "pension plan" shall not include an individual retirement account described in section 408(a) of the Code, an individual retirement annuity described in section 408(b) of the Internal Revenue Code of 1954 (hereinafter "the Code") and an individual retirement bond described in section 409 of the Code, provided that—

(i) no contributions are made by the employer or employee association;

(ii) participation is completely voluntary for employees or members;

(iii) the sole involvement of the employer or employee organization is without endorsement to permit the sponsor to publicize the program to employees or members, to collect contributions through payroll deductions or dues checkoffs and to remit them to the sponsor; and

(iv) the employer or employee organization receives no consideration in the form of cash or otherwise, other than reasonable compensation for services actually rendered in connection with payroll deductions or dues checkoffs.

(e) *Gratuitous payments to pre-Act retirees.*

For purposes of Title I of the Act and this chapter the terms "employee pension benefit plan" and "pension plan" shall not include voluntary, gratuitous payments by an employer to former employees who separated from the service of the employer if:

(1) payments are made out of the general assets of the employer,

(2) former employees separated from the service of the employer prior to September 2, 1974,

(3) payments made to such employees commenced prior to September 2, 1974, and

(4) each former employee receiving such payments is notified annually that the payments are gratuitous and do not constitute a pension plan.

(f) *Tax sheltered annuities.*

For the purpose of Title I of the Act and this chapter, a program for the purchase of an annuity contract or the establishment of a custodial account described in section 403(b) of the Internal Revenue Code of 1954 (the Code), pursuant to salary reduction agreements or agreements to forego an increase in salary, which meets the requirements of 26 CFR § 1.403(b)-1(b)(3) shall not be "established or maintained by an employer" as that phrase is used in the definition of the terms "employee pension benefit plan" and "pension plan" if

(1) participation is completely voluntary for employees;

(2) all rights under the annuity contract or custodial account are enforceable solely by the employee, by a beneficiary of such employee, or by any authorized representative of such employee or beneficiary;

(3) the sole involvement of the employer, other than pursuant to paragraph (f)(2) above, is limited to any of the following:

(i) permitting annuity contractors (which term shall include any agent or broker who offers annuity contracts or who makes available custodial accounts within the meaning of section 403(b)(7) of the Code) to publicize their products to employees,

(ii) requesting information concerning proposed funding media, products or annuity contractors;

(iii) summarizing or otherwise compiling the information provided with respect to the proposed funding media or products which are made available, or the annuity contractors whose services are provided, in order to facilitate review and analysis by the employees;

(iv) collecting annuity or custodial account considerations as required by salary reduction agreements or by agreements to forego salary increases, remitting such considerations to annuity contractors and maintaining records of such considerations;

(v) holding in the employer's name one or more group annuity contracts covering its employees;

(vi) before February 7, 1978, to have limited the funding media or products available to employees, or the annuity contractors who could approach employees, to those which, in the judgment of the employer, afforded employees appropriate investment opportunities; or

(vii) after February 6, 1978, limiting the funding media or products available to employees, or the annuity contractors who may approach employees, to a number and selection which is designed to afford employees a reasonable choice in light of all relevant circumstances. Relevant circumstances may include, but would not necessarily be limited to, the following types of factors:

(A) the number of employees affected,

(B) the number of contractors who have indicated interest in approaching employees,

(C) the variety of available products,

(D) the terms of the available arrangements,

(E) the administrative burdens and costs to the employer, and

(F) the possible interference with employee performance resulting from direct solicitation by contractors; and

(4) the employer receives no direct or indirect consideration or compensation in cash or otherwise other than reasonable compensation to cover expenses properly and actually incurred by such employer in the performance of the employer's duties pursuant to the salary reduction agreements or agreements to forego salary increases described in this paragraph (f) above.

[Reg. § 2510.3-2(f) was published in the Federal Register of April 20, 1979, effective retroactively from January 1, 1975.]

(g) *Supplemental payment plans.* (1) *General rule.* Generally, an arrangement by which a payment is made by an employer to supplement retirement income is a pension plan. Supplemental payments made on or after September 26, 1980, shall be treated as being made under a welfare plan rather than a pension plan for purposes of Title I of the Act if all of the following conditions are met:

(i) Payment is made for the purpose of supplementing the pension benefits of a participant or his or her beneficiary out of:

(A) the general assets of the employer, or

(B) a separate trust fund established and maintained solely for that purpose.

(ii) The amount payable under the supplemental payment plan to a participant or his or her beneficiary with respect to a month does not exceed the payee's supplemental payment factor ("SPF," as defined in paragraph (g)(3)(i) of this section) for that month, provided however, that unpaid monthly amounts may be cumulated and paid in subsequent months to the participant or his or her beneficiary.

(iii) The payment is not made before the last day of the month with respect to which it is computed.

(2) *Safe harbor for arrangements concerning pre-1977 retirees.* (i) Notwithstanding paragraph (g)(1) of this section, effective January 1, 1975 an arrangement by which a payment is made by an employer to supplement the retirement income of a former employee who separated from the service of the employer prior to January 1, 1977 shall be deemed not to have been made under an employee benefit plan if all of the following conditions are met:

(A) The employer is not obligated to make the payment or similar payments for more than twelve months at a time.

(B) The payment is made out of the general assets of the employer.

(C) The former employee is notified in writing at least once each year in which a payment is made that the payments are not part of an employee benefit plan subject to the protections of the Act.

(D) The former employee is notified in writing at least once each year in which a payment is made of the extent of the employer's obligation, if any, to continue the payments.

(ii) A person who receives a payment on account of his or her relationship to a former employee who retired prior to January 1, 1977 is considered to be a former employee for purposes of this paragraph (g)(2).

(3) *Definitions and special rules.* For purposes of this paragraph (g)—

(i) The term "supplemental payment factor" (SPF) is, for any particular month, the product of: (A) The individual's pension benefit amount (as defined in paragraph (g)(3)(ii) of this section), and (B) the cost of living increase (as defined in paragraph (g)(3)(v) of this section) for that month.

(ii)(A) The term "pension benefit amount" (PBA) means, with regard to a retiree, the amount of pension benefits payable, in the form of the annuity chosen by the retiree, for the first full month that he or she is in pay status under a pension plan (as defined in paragraph (g)(3)(iii) of this section) sponsored by his or her employer or under a multiemployer plan in which his or her employer participates. If the retiree has received a lump-sum distribution from the plan, the PBA for the retiree shall be determined as follows:

(1) If the plan provides an annuity option at the time of the distribution, the PBA shall be computed as if the distribution had been applied on that date to the purchase from the plan of a level straight annuity for the life of the participant if the participant was unmarried at the time of the distribution or a joint and survivor annuity if the participant was married at the time of distribution.

(2) If the plan does not provide an annuity option at the time of the distribution, the PBA shall be computed as if the distribution had been applied on that date to the purchase from an insurance company qualified to do business in a State of a commercially available level straight annuity for the life of the participant if the participant was then single, or a joint and survivor annuity if the participant was then married, based upon the assumption that the participant and beneficiary are standard mortality risks.

(B) If the retiree has received from the plan a series of distributions which do not constitute a lump-sum distribution or an annuity, the PBA for the retiree shall be determined with respect to each distribution according to paragraph (g)(3)(ii)(A) above, or in accordance with a reasonably equivalent method.

(C) The term PBA, with regard to the beneficiary of a plan participant, means: (*1*) The amount of pension benefits, payable in the form of a survivor annuity to the beneficiary, for the first full month that he or she begins to receive the survivor annuity, reduced by: (*2*) Any increases which have been incorporated as part of the survivor annuity under the plan since the participant entered pay status or, if the participant died before the commencement of pension benefits, since the participant's date of death.

(D) Where a plan participant has commenced to receive his or her pension benefits in the form of a straight-life annuity, or another form of an annuity that does not continue after the participant's death in the form of a survivor annuity, no beneficiary of the participant will have a PBA.

(iii) The term "pension plan" means, for purposes of this paragraph (g), a pension plan as defined in section 3(2) of the Act, but not including a plan described in section 4(b), 201(2), or 301(a)(3) of the Act. The term also does not include an arrangement meeting all the conditions of paragraph (g)(1) or (g)(2) of this section or of an arrangement described in § 2510.3-2(e). In the case of a controlled group of corporations within the meaning of section 407(d)(5) of the Act, all pension plans sponsored by members of the group shall be considered to be one pension plan.

(iv) The term "employer" means, for purposes of paragraph (g) of this section, the former employer making the supplemental payment. In the case of a controlled group of corporations within the meaning of section 407(d)(7) of the Act, all members of the controlled group shall be considered to be one employer for purposes of this paragraph (g).

(v) The term "cost of living increase" (CLI) means, as to any month, a percentage equal to the following fraction:

$$\frac{a-b}{b}$$

where a = the CPIU for the month for which a payment is being computed, and b = the CPIU for the first full month the retiree was in pay status. Where the CLI is calculated for the beneficiary of a plan participant, "b" continues to be equal to the CPIU for the first full month the retiree was in pay status. If, however, the participant dies before the commencement of pension benefits, "b" is equal to the CPIU for the first full month the survivor is in pay status.

(vi) The term "CPIU" means the U.S. City Average All Items Consumer Price Index for all Urban Consumers, published by the U.S. Department of Labor, Bureau of Labor Statistics. Data concerning the CPIU for a particular period can be obtained from the U.S. Department of Labor, Bureau of Labor Statistics, Division of Consumer Prices and Price Indexes, Washington, D.C. 20212.

(vii) Where an employer does not pay to a retiree the full amount of the supplemental payments which would be permitted under paragraph (g)(1) of this section, any unpaid amounts may be cumulated and paid in subsequent months to either the retiree or the beneficiary of the retiree. The beneficiary need not be the recipient of a survivor annuity in order to be paid these cumulated supplemental payments.

(4) *Examples.* The following examples illustrate how this paragraph (g) works. As referred to in these examples, the CPIU's for July through November of 1980 are as follows:

July 1980: 247.8

August 1980: 249.4

September 1980: 251.7

October 1980: 253.9

November 1980: 256.2

Example (1)(a). E is an employer. R received monthly benefits of $600 under a straight-life annuity under E's defined benefit pension plan after R retired from E and entered pay status on July 1, 1980. The amount that E may pay to R as supplemental payments under a welfare rather than pension plan with respect to the months of July through September of 1980 is computed as follows:

SPF for July 1980

$$SPF = \frac{a - b}{b} \times PBA$$

$$= \frac{247.8 - 247.8}{247.8} \times \$600 = \$0.00$$

SPF for August 1980

$$SPF = \frac{249.4 - 247.8}{247.8} \times \$600 = \$3.87$$

SPF for September 1980

$$SPF = \frac{251.7 - 247.8}{247.8} \times \$600 = \$9.44$$

Total = $ 0.00
          3.87
          9.44
         $13.31

No supplemental payment may be made to R as a welfare plan payment with respect to July 1980, the month of retirement. The $3.87 that may be paid with respect to August 1980 may be paid at any time after August 31, 1980. The $9.44 that may be paid with respect to September 1980 may be paid at any time after September 30, 1980.

Example (1)(b). S is the beneficiary of R. Because R received pension benefits under a straight-life annuity, S will receive no survivor annuity from E after R's death. S thus will have no PBA after R's death and will not be eligible to receive any supplemental payments from E based on S's PBA. To the extent, however, that R did not receive supplemental payments from E to the maximum limit allowable under paragraph (g)(1), any amounts not paid to R may be cumulated and paid to S after R's death.

Example (2)(a). E is an employer. Q received monthly benefits of $500 in the form of a joint and survivor annuity under E's defined benefit pension plan since retirement from E on July 1, 1980. The amount that E may pay to Q as welfare rather than pension plan payments with respect to the months of July through September of 1980 is computed as follows:

SPF for July 1980

$$SPF = \frac{249.4 - 247.8}{247.8} \times \$500 = \$0.00$$

SPF for August 1980

$$\frac{249.4 - 247.8}{}$$

$$SPF = \frac{}{247.8} \times \$500 = \$3.23$$

SPF for September 1980

$$SPF = \frac{251.7 - 247.8}{247.8} \times \$500 = \$7.87$$

Total = $0.00
         3.23
         7.87
        $11.10

No supplemental payment may be made as a welfare plan payment with respect to July 1980, the month of retirement. The $3.23 that may be paid with respect to August 1980 may be paid at any time after August 31, 1980. The $7.87 that may be paid with respect to September 1980 may be paid at any time after September 30, 1980.

Example (2)(b). Q dies on October 15, 1980 without having received any supplemental payments from E. T is the beneficiary of Q. E pays T a survivor's annuity of $300 beginning in November of 1980. The amount payable to T as a survivor annuity under the plan has not been increased since Q began to receive pension benefits. Thus, T's PBA is $300. The amount that E may pay to T as welfare rather than pension plan payments with respect to the months of July through November 1980 is computed as follows:

SPF for July 1980 = $0.00

SPF for August 1980 = $3.23

SPF for September 1980 = $7.87

SPF for October 1980

$$SPF = \frac{a - b}{b} \times PBA$$

$$= \frac{253.9 - 247.8}{247.8} \times \$500$$

$$= \$12.31$$

(Note that T's "b" is equal to Q's "b".)

SPF for November 1980

$$SPF = \frac{256.2 - 247.8}{247.8} \times \$300 = \$10.17$$

Total that may be paid to T:

The maximum E may pay T with respect to the months of July through November 1980 as welfare rather than pension plan payments is the sum of those months' SPFs, which is $33.58.

Example (3). Assume the same facts as in Example (1)(a), except that R elected to receive a lump-sum distribution rather than a straight-life annuity. If R is unmarried on July 1, 1980, R's PBA is $600 for the remainder of R's life. If R is married to S on July 1, 1980, the PBAs of R and S are based on the annuity that would have been paid under an election to receive a joint and survivor annuity. See paragraph (g)(3)(ii)(A)(1) of this section.

[Added November 4, 1982, by FR Doc. 82-30403 (47 FR 50237).]

[¶ 14,133]

§2510.3-3. **Employee benefit plan.** (a) *General.* This section clarifies the definition in section 3(3) of the term "employee benefit plan" for purposes of Title I of the Act and this chapter. It states a general principle which can be applied to a large class of plans to determine whether they constitute employee benefit plans within the meaning of section 3(3) of the Act. Under section 4(a) of the Act, only employee benefit plans within the meaning of section 3(3) are subject to Title I.

(b) *Plans without employees.* For purposes of Title I of the Act and this chapter, the term "employee benefit plan" shall not include any plan, fund or program, other than an apprenticeship or other training program, under which no employees are participants covered under the plan, as defined in paragraph (d) of this section. For example, a so-called "Keogh" or "H.R. 10" plan under which only partners or only a sole proprietor are participants covered under the plan will not be covered under Title I. However, a Keogh plan under which one or more common law employees in addition to the self-employed individuals are participants covered under the plan, will be covered under Title I. Similarly, partnership buyout agreements described in section 736 of the Internal Revenue Code of 1954 will not be subject to Title I.

(c) *Employees.* For purposes of this section:

(1) An individual and his or her spouse shall not be deemed to be employees with respect to a trade or business, whether incorporated or unincorporated, which is wholly owned by the individual or by the individual and his or her spouse, and

(2) A partner in a partnership and his or her spouse shall not be deemed to be employees with respect to the partnership.

(d) *Participant covered under the plan.* (1)(i) An individual becomes a participant covered under an employee welfare benefit plan on the earlier of—

(A) the date designated by the plan as the date on which the individual begins participation in the plan;

(B) the date on which the individual becomes eligible under the plan for a benefit subject only to occurrence of the contingency for which the benefit is provided; or

(C) the date on which the individual makes a contribution to the plan, whether voluntary or mandatory.

(ii) An individual becomes a participant covered under an employee pension plan—

(A) in the case of a plan which provides for employee contributions or defines participation to include employees who have not yet retired, on the earlier of—

(1) the date on which the individual makes a contribution, whether voluntary or mandatory, or

(2) the date designated by the plan as the date on which the individual has satisfied the plan's age and service requirements for participation, and

(B) in the case of a plan which does not provide for employee contributions and does not define participation to include employees who have not yet retired, the date on which the individual completes the first year of employment which may be taken into account in determining—

(1) whether the individual is entitled to benefits under the plan, or

(2) the amount of benefits to which the individual is entitled,

whichever results in earlier participation.

(2)(i) An individual is not a participant covered under an employee welfare plan on the earliest date on which the individual—

(A) is ineligible to receive any benefit under the plan even if the contingency for which such benefit is provided should occur, and

(B) is not designated by the plan as a participant.

(ii) An individual is not a participant covered under an employee pension plan or a beneficiary receiving benefits under an employee pension plan if—

(A) the entire benefit rights of the individual—

(1) are fully guaranteed by an insurance company, insurance service or insurance organization licensed to do business in a State, and are legally enforceable by the sole choice of the individual against the insurance company, insurance service or insurance organization; and

(2) a contract, policy or certificate describing the benefits to which the individual is entitled under the plan has been issued to the individual; or

(B) the individual has received from the plan a lump-sum distribution or a series of distributions of cash or other property which represents the balance of his or her credit under the plan.

(3)(i) In the case of an employee pension benefit plan, an individual who, under the terms of the plan, has incurred a one-year

break in service after having become a participant covered under the plan, and who has acquired no vested right to a benefit before such break in service is not a participant covered under the plan until the individual has completed a year of service after returning to employment covered by the plan.

(ii) For purposes of paragraph (d)(3)(i) of this section, in the case of an employee pension benefit plan which is subject to section 203 of the Act the term "year of service" shall have the same meaning as in section 203(b)(2)(A) of the Act and any regulations issued under the Act and the term "one-year break in service" shall have the same meaning as in section 203(b)(3)(A) of the Act and any regulations issued under the Act.

[¶ 14,138]

§ 2510.3-21 Definition of "Fiduciary". (a) **[Reserved]**

(b) **[Reserved]**

(c) *Investment advice.* (1) A person shall be deemed to be rendering "investment advice" to an employee benefit plan, within the meaning of section 3(21)(A)(ii) of the Employee Retirement Income Security Act of 1974 (the Act) and this paragraph, only if:

(i) Such person renders advice to the plan as to the value of securities or other property, or makes recommendations as to the advisability of investing in, purchasing, or selling securities or other property; and

(ii) Such person either directly or indirectly (e.g., through or together with any affiliate)—

(A) has discretionary authority or control, whether or not pursuant to agreement, arrangement or understanding, with respect to purchasing or selling securities or other property for the plan; or

(B) renders any advice described in paragraph (c)(1)(i) of this section on a regular basis to the plan pursuant to a mutual agreement, arrangement or understanding, written or otherwise, between such person and the plan or a fiduciary with respect to the plan, that such services will serve as a primary basis for investment decisions with respect to plan assets, and that such person will render individualized investment advice to the plan based on the particular needs of the plan regarding such matters as, among other things, investment policies or strategy, overall portfolio composition, or diversification of plan investments.

(2) A person who is a fiduciary with respect to a plan by reason of rendering investment advice (as defined in paragraph (c)(1) of this section) for a fee or other compensation, direct or indirect, with respect to any moneys or other property of such plan, or having any authority or responsibility to do so, shall not be deemed to be a fiduciary regarding any assets of the plan with respect to which such person does not have any discretionary authority, discretionary control or discretionary responsibility, does not exercise any authority or control, does not render investment advice (as defined in paragraph (c)(1) of this section) for a fee or other compensation, and does not have any authority or responsibility to render such investment advice, provided that nothing in this paragraph shall be deemed to:

(i) Exempt such person from the provisions of section 405(a) of the Act concerning liability for fiduciary breaches by other fiduciaries with respect to any assets of the plan; or

(ii) Exclude such person from the definition of the term "party in interest" (as set forth in section 3(14)(B) of the Act) with respect to any assets of the plan.

(d) *Execution of securities transactions.* (1) A person who is a broker or dealer registered under the Securities Exchange Act of 1934, a reporting dealer who makes primary markets in securities of the United States Government or of an agency of the United States Government and reports daily to the Federal Reserve Bank of New York its positions with respect to such securities and borrowings thereon, or a bank supervised by the United States or a State, shall not be deemed to be a fiduciary, within the meaning of section 3(21)(A) of the Act, with respect to an employee benefit plan solely because such person executes transactions for the purchase or sale of securities on behalf of such plan in the ordinary course of its business as a broker, dealer, or bank, pursuant to instructions of a fiduciary with respect to such plan, if:

(i) Neither the fiduciary nor any affiliate of such fiduciary is such broker, dealer, or bank; and

(ii) The instructions specify (A) the security to be purchased or sold, (B) a price range within which such security is to be purchased or sold, or, if such security is issued by an open-end investment company registered under the Investment Company Act of 1940 (15 U.S.C. 80a-1, et seq.), a price which is determined in accordance with Rule 22c-1 under the Investment Company Act of 1940 (17 CFR 270.22c-1), (C) a time span during which such security may be purchased or sold (not to exceed five business days), and (D) the minimum or maximum quantity of such security which may be purchased or sold within such price range, or, in the case of a security issued by an open-end investment company registered under the Investment Company Act of 1940, the minimum or maximum quantity of such security which may be purchased or sold, or the value of such security in dollar amount which may be purchased or sold, at the price referred to in paragraph (d)(1)(ii)(B) of this section.

(2) A person who is a broker-dealer, reporting dealer, or bank which is a fiduciary with respect to an employee benefit plan solely by reason of the possession or exercise of discretionary authority or discretionary control in the management of the plan or the management or disposition of plan assets in connection with the execution of a transaction or transactions for the purchase or sale of securities on behalf of such plan which fails to comply with the provisions of paragraph (d)(1) of this section, shall not be deemed to be a fiduciary regarding any assets of the plan with respect to which such broker-dealer, reporting dealer or bank does not have any discretionary authority, discretionary control or discretionary responsibility, does not exercise any authority or control, does not render investment advice (as defined in paragraph (c)(1) of this section) for a fee or other compensation, and does not have any authority or responsibility to render such investment advice, provided that nothing in this paragraph shall be deemed to:

(i) Exempt such broker-dealer, reporting dealer, or bank from the provisions of section 405(a) of the Act concerning liability for fiduciary breaches by other fiduciaries with respect to any assets of the plan; or

(ii) Exclude such broker-dealer, reporting dealer, or bank from the definition of the term "party in interest" (as set forth in section 3(14)(B) of the Act) with respect to any assets of the plan.

(e) *Affiliate and control.* (1) For purposes of paragraphs (c) and (d) of this section, an "affiliate" of a person shall include:

(i) Any person directly or indirectly, through one or more intermediaries, controlling, controlled by, or under common control with such person;

(ii) Any officer, director, partner, employee or relative (as defined in section 3(15) of the Act) of such person; and

(iii) Any corporation or partnership of which such person is an officer, director or partner.

(2) For purposes of this paragraph, the term "control" means the power to exercise a controlling influence over the management or policies of a person other than an individual. [§2510.3-21 was filed with the Federal Register on October 28, 1975.]

Regulations

Reg. §2510.3-37 was adopted by FR Doc. 75-30032 under "Title 29—Labor; Chapter XXV—Employee Benefits Security, Office of Department of Labor; Part 2510—Definitions of Terms used in Subchapters C, D, E, F and G of this Chapter." The regulation was published in the *Federal Register* on November 7, 1975, filed November 6, 1975, and effective November 6, 1975 (40 FR 52008). Reg. §2510.3-101 was added by 51 FR 41280, effective March 13, 1987, and amended by 51 FR 47226, December 31, 1986. Reg. §2510.3-102 was adopted by 53 FR 17628, May 17, 1988, and amended by 61 FR 41220 on August 7, 1996, effective February 3, 1997. Reg. §2510.3-102 was further amended by FR Doc. 97-30961, filed with the *Federal Register* on November 24, 1997, published in the *Federal Register* on November 25, 1997, and effective on November 25, 1997 (62 FR 62934). Reg. §2510.3-40 was added on April 9, 2003 (68 FR 17471). Reg. §2510.3-38 was added on August 24, 2004 (69 FR 52119).

[¶ 14,139]

§2510.3-37 **Multiemployer plan.** (a) *General.* Section 3(37) of the Act contains in subparagraph (a)(i)-(iv) a number of criteria which an employee benefit plan must meet in order to be a multiemployer plan under the Act. Section 3(37) also provides that the Secretary may prescribe by regulation other requirements in addition to those contained in subparagraph (a)(i)-(iv). The purpose of this regulation is to establish such requirements.

(b) *Plans in existence before the effective date.* (1) A plan in existence before September 2, 1974, will be considered a multiemployer plan if it satisfies the requirements of section 3(37)(A)(i)-(iv) of the Act.

(2) For purposes of this section, a plan is considered to be in existence if:

(i)(A) The plan was reduced to writing and adopted by the participating employers and the employee organization (including, in the case of a corporate employer, formal approval by an employer's board of directors or shareholders, if required), even though no amounts had been contributed under the plan, and

(B) The plan has not been terminated; or

(ii)(A) There was a legally enforceable agreement to establish such a plan signed by the employers and the employee organization, and

(B) The contributions to be made to the plan were set forth in the agreement.

(iii) If a plan was in existence within the meaning of paragraph (b)(i) or (ii) of this section, any other plan with which such existing plan is merged or consolidated shall also be considered to be in existence.

(c) *Plans not in existence before the effective date.* In addition to the provisions of section 3(37)(A)(i)-(iv) of the Act, a multiemployer plan established on or after September 2, 1974, must meet the requirement that it was established for a substantial business purpose. A substantial business purpose includes the interest of a labor organization in securing an employee benefit plan for its members. The following factors are relevant in determining whether a substantial business purpose existed for the establishment of a plan; any single factor may be sufficient to constitute a substantial business purpose:

(1) The extent to which the plan is maintained by a substantial number of unaffiliated contributing employers and covers a substantial portion of the trade, craft or industry in terms of employees or a substantial number of the employees in the trade, craft or industry in a locality or geographic area;

(2) The extent to which the plan provides benefits more closely related to years of service within the trade, craft or industry rather than with an employer, reflecting the fact that an employee's relationship with an employer maintaining the plan is generally short-term although service in the trade, craft or industry is generally long-term;

(3) The extent to which collective bargaining takes place on matters other than employee benefit plans between the employee organization and the employers maintaining the plan; and

(4) The extent to which the administrative burden and expense of providing benefits through single employer plans would be greater than through a multiemployer plan.

[Adopted by FR Doc. 75-30032, effective November 6, 1975 (40 FR 52008).]

[¶ 14,139A]

§2510.3-38 **Filing requirements for State registered investment advisers to be investment managers.** (a) *General.* Section 3(38) of the Act sets forth the criteria for a fiduciary to be an investment manager for purposes of section 405 of the Act. Subparagraph (B)(ii) of section 3(38) of the Act provides that, in the case of a fiduciary who is not registered under the Investment Advisers Act of 1940 by reason of paragraph (1) of section 203A(a) of such Act, the fiduciary must be registered as an investment adviser under the laws of the State in which it maintains its principal office and place of business, and, at the time the fiduciary files registration forms with such State to maintain the fiduciary's registration under the laws of such State, also files a copy of such forms with the Secretary of Labor. The purpose of this section is to set forth the exclusive means for investment advisers to satisfy the filing obligation with the Secretary described in subparagraph (B)(ii) of section 3(38) of the Act.

(b) *Filing Requirement.* To satisfy the filing requirement with the Secretary in section 3(38)(B)(ii) of the Act, a fiduciary must be registered as an investment adviser with the State in which it maintains its principal office and place of business and file through the Investment Adviser Registration Depository (IARD), in accordance with applicable IARD requirements, the information required to be registered and maintain the fiduciary's registration as an investment adviser in such State. Submitting to the Secretary investment adviser registration forms filed with a State does not constitute compliance with the filing requirement in section 3(38)(B)(ii) of the Act.

(c) *Definitions.* For purposes of this section, the term "Investment Adviser Registration Depository" or "IARD" means the centralized electronic depository described in 17 CFR 275.203-1.

(d) *Cross Reference.* Information for investment advisers on how to file through the IARD is available on the Securities and Exchange Commission website at "http://www.sec.gov/iard."

[¶ 14,139C]

§ 2510.3-40 **Plans Established or Maintained Under or Pursuant to Collective Bargaining Agreements Under Section 4(40)(A) of ERISA.** (a) *Scope and purpose.* Section 3(40)(A) of the Employee Retirement Income Security Act of 1974 (ERISA) provides that the term "multiple employer welfare arrangement" (MEWA) does not include an employee welfare benefit plan that is established or maintained under or pursuant to one or more agreements that the Secretary of Labor (the Secretary) finds to be collective bargaining agreements. This section sets forth criteria that represent a finding by the Secretary whether an arrangement is an employee welfare benefit plan established or maintained under or pursuant to one or more collective bargaining agreements. A plan is established or maintained under or pursuant to collective bargaining if it meets the criteria in this section. However, even if an entity meets the criteria in this section, it will not be an employee welfare benefit plan established or maintained under or pursuant to a collective bargaining agreement if it comes within the exclusions in the section. Nothing in or pursuant to this section shall constitute a finding for any purpose other than the exception for plans established or maintained under or pursuant to one or more collective bargaining agreements under section 3(40) of ERISA. In a particular case where there is an attempt to assert state jurisdiction or the application of state law with respect to a plan or other arrangement that allegedly is covered under Title I of ERISA, the Secretary has set forth a procedure for obtaining individualized findings at 29 CFR part 2570, subpart H.

(b) *General criteria.* The Secretary finds, for purposes of section 3(40) of ERISA, that an employee welfare benefit plan is "established or maintained under or pursuant to one or more agreements which the Secretary finds to be collective bargaining agreements" for any plan year in which the plan meets the criteria set forth in paragraphs (b)(1), (2), (3), and (4) of this section, and is not excluded under paragraph (c) of this section.

(1) The entity is an employee welfare benefit plan within the meaning of section 3(1) of ERISA.

(2) At least 85% of the participants in the plan are:

(i) Individuals employed under one or more agreements meeting the criteria of paragraph (b)(3) of this section, under which contributions are made to the plan, or pursuant to which coverage under the plan is provided;

(ii) Retirees who either participated in the plan at least five of the last 10 years preceding their retirement, or

(A) Are receiving benefits as participants under a multiemployer pension benefit plan that is maintained under the same agreements referred to in paragraph (b)(3) of this section, and

(B) Have at least five years of service or the equivalent under that multiemployer pension benefit plan;

(iii) Participants on extended coverage under the plan pursuant to the requirements of a statute or court or administrative agency decision, including but not limited to the continuation coverage requirements of the Consolidated Omnibus Budget Reconciliation Act of 1985, sections 601-609, 29 U.S.C. 1169, the Family and Medical Leave Act, 29 U.S.C. 2601 et seq., the Uniformed Services Employment and Reemployment Rights Act of 1994, 38 U.S.C. 4301 et seq., or the National Labor Relations Act, 29 U.S.C. 158(a)(5);

(iv) Participants who were active participants and whose coverage is otherwise extended under the terms of the plan, including but not limited to extension by reason of self-payment, hour bank, long or short-term disability, furlough, or temporary unemployment, provided that the charge to the individual for such extended coverage is no more than the applicable premium under section 604 of the Act;

(v) Participants whose coverage under the plan is maintained pursuant to a reciprocal agreement with one or more other employee welfare benefit plans that are established or maintained under or pursuant to one or more collective bargaining agreements and that are multiemployer plans;

(vi) Individuals employed by:

(A) An employee organization that sponsors, jointly sponsors, or is represented on the association, committee, joint board of trustees, or other similar group of representatives of the parties who sponsor the plan;

(B) The plan or associated trust fund;

(C) Other employee benefit plans or trust funds to which contributions are made pursuant to the same agreement described in paragraph (b)(3) of this section; or

(D) An employer association that is the authorized employer representative that actually engaged in the collective bargaining that led to the agreement that references the plan as described in paragraph (b)(3) of this section;

(vii) Individuals who were employed under an agreement described in paragraph (b)(3) of this section, provided that they are employed by one or more employers that are parties to an agreement described in paragraph (b)(3) and are covered under the plan on terms that are generally no more favorable than those that apply to similarly situated individuals described in paragraph (b)(2)(i) of this section;

(viii) Individuals (other than individuals described in paragraph (b)(2)(i) of this section) who are employed by employers that are bound by the terms of an agreement described in paragraph (b)(3) of this section and that employ personnel covered by such agreement, and who are covered under the plan on terms that are generally no more favorable than those that apply to such covered personnel. For this purpose, such individuals in excess of 10% of the total population of participants in the plan are disregarded;

(ix) Individuals who are, or were for a period of at least three years, employed under one or more agreements between or among one or more "carriers" (including "carriers by air") and one or more "representatives" of employees for collective bargaining purposes and as defined by the Railway Labor Act, 45 U.S.C. 151 et seq., providing for such individuals' current or subsequent participation in the plan, or providing for contributions to be made to the plan by such carriers; or

(x) Individuals who are licensed marine pilots operating in United States ports as a state-regulated enterprise and are covered under an employee welfare benefit plan that meets the definition of a qualified merchant marine plan, as defined in section 415(b)(2)(F) of the Internal Revenue Code (26 U.S.C.).

(3) The plan is incorporated or referenced in a written agreement between one or more employers and one or more employee organizations, which agreement, itself or together with other agreements among the same parties:

(i) Is the product of a bona fide collective bargaining relationship between the employers and the employee organization(s);

(ii) Identifies employers and employee organization(s) that are parties to and bound by the agreement;

(iii) Identifies the personnel, job classifications, and/or work jurisdiction covered by the agreement;

(iv) Provides for terms and conditions of employment in addition to coverage under, or contributions to, the plan; and

(v) Is not unilaterally terminable or automatically terminated solely for non-payment of benefits under, or contributions to, the plan.

(4) For purposes of paragraph (b)(3)(i) of this section, the following factors, among others, are to be considered in determining the existence of a bona fide collective bargaining relationship. In any proceeding initiated under 29 CFR part 2570 subpart H, the existence of a bona fide collective bargaining relationship under paragraph (b)(3)(i) shall be presumed where at least four of the factors set out in paragraphs (b)(4)(i) through (viii) of this section are established. In such a proceeding, the Secretary may also consider whether other objective or subjective indicia of actual collective bargaining and representation are present as set out in paragraph (b)(4)(ix) of this section.

(i) The agreement referred to in paragraph (b)(3) of this section provides for contributions to a labor-management trust fund structured according to section 302(c)(5), (6), (7), (8), or (9) of the Taft-Hartley Act, 29 U.S.C. 186(c)(5), (6), (7), (8) or (9), or to a plan lawfully negotiated under the Railway Labor Act;

(ii) The agreement referred to in paragraph (b)(3) of this section requires contributions by substantially all of the participating employers to a multiemployer pension plan that is structured in accordance with section 401 of the Internal Revenue Code (26 U.S.C.) and is either structured in accordance with section 302(c)(5) of the Taft-Hartley Act, 29 U.S.C. 186(c)(5), or is lawfully negotiated under the Railway Labor Act, and substantially all of the active participants covered by the employee welfare benefit plan are also eligible to become participants in that pension plan;

(iii) The predominant employee organization that is a party to the agreement referred to in paragraph (b)(3) of this section has maintained a series of agreements incorporating or referencing the plan since before January 1, 1983;

(iv) The predominant employee organization that is a party to the agreement referred to in paragraph (b)(3) of this section has been a national or international union, or a federation of national and international unions, or has been affiliated with such a union or federation, since before January 1, 1983;

(v) A court, government agency, or other third-party adjudicatory tribunal has determined, in a contested or adversary proceeding, or in a government-supervised election, that the predominant employee organization that is a party to the agreement described in paragraph (b)(3) of this section is the lawfully recognized or designated collective bargaining representative with respect to one or more bargaining units of personnel covered by such agreement;

(vi) Employers who are parties to the agreement described in paragraph (b)(3) of this section pay at least 75% of the premiums or contributions required for the coverage of active participants under the plan or, in the case of a retiree-only plan, the employers pay at least 75% of the premiums or contributions required for the coverage of the retirees. For this purpose, coverage under the plan for dental or vision care, coverage for excepted benefits under 29 CFR 2590.732(b), and amounts paid by participants and beneficiaries as co-payments or deductibles in accordance with the terms of the plan are disregarded;

(vii) The predominant employee organization that is a party to the agreement described in paragraph (b)(3) of this section provides, sponsors, or jointly sponsors a hiring hall(s) and/or a state-certified apprenticeship program(s) that provides services that are available to substantially all active participants covered by the plan;

(viii) The agreement described in paragraph (b)(3) of this section has been determined to be a bona fide collective bargaining agreement for purposes of establishing the prevailing practices with respect to wages and supplements in a locality, pursuant to a prevailing wage statute of any state or the District of Columbia.

(ix) There are other objective or subjective indicia of actual collective bargaining and representation, such as that arm's-length negotiations occurred between the parties to the agreement described in paragraph (b)(3) of this section; that the predominant employee organization that is party to such agreement actively represents employees covered by such agreement with respect to grievances, disputes, or other matters involving employment terms and conditions other than coverage under, or contributions to, the employee welfare benefit plan; that there is a geographic, occupational, trade, organizing, or other rationale for the employers and bargaining units covered by such agreement; that there is a connection between such agreement and the participation, if any, of self-employed individuals in the employee welfare benefit plan established or maintained under or pursuant to such agreement.

(c) *Exclusions.* An employee welfare benefit plan shall not be deemed to be "established or maintained under or pursuant to one or more agreements which the Secretary finds to be collective bargaining agreements" for any plan year in which:

(1) The plan is self-funded or partially self-funded and is marketed to employers or sole proprietors

(i) By one or more insurance producers as defined in paragraph (d) of this section;

(ii) By an individual who is disqualified from, or ineligible for, or has failed to obtain, a license to serve as an insurance producer to the extent that the individual engages in an activity for which such license is required; or

(iii) By individuals (other than individuals described in paragraphs (c)(1)(i) and (ii) of this section) who are paid on a commission-type basis to market the plan.

(iv) For the purposes of this paragraph (c)(1):

(A) "Marketing" does not include administering the plan, consulting with plan sponsors, counseling on benefit design or coverage, or explaining the terms of coverage available under the plan to employees or union members;

(B) "Marketing" does include the marketing of union membership that carries with it plan participation by virtue of such membership, except for membership in unions representing insurance producers themselves;

(2) The agreement under which the plan is established or maintained is a scheme, plan, stratagem, or artifice of evasion, a principal intent of which is to evade compliance with state law and regulations applicable to insurance; or

(3) There is fraud, forgery, or willful misrepresentation as to the factors relied on to demonstrate that the plan satisfies the criteria set forth in paragraph (b) of this section.

(d) *Definitions.* (1) Active participant means a participant who is not retired and who is not on extended coverage under paragraphs (b)(2)(iii) or (b)(2)(iv) of this section.

(2) Agreement means the contract embodying the terms and conditions mutually agreed upon between or among the parties to such agreement. Where the singular is used in this section, the plural is automatically included.

(3) Individual employed means any natural person who furnishes services to another person or entity in the capacity of an employee under common law, without regard to any specialized definitions or interpretations of the terms "employee," "employer," or "employed" under federal or state statutes other than ERISA.

(4) Insurance producer means an agent, broker, consultant, or producer who is an individual, entity, or sole proprietor that is licensed under the laws of the state to sell, solicit, or negotiate insurance.

(5) Predominant employee organization means, where more than one employee organization is a party to an agreement, either the organization representing the plurality of individuals employed under such agreement, or organizations that in combination represent the majority of such individuals.

(e) *Examples.* The operation of the provisions of this section may be illustrated by the following examples.

Example 1. Plan A has 500 participants, in the following 4 categories of participants under paragraph (b)(2) of this section:

Categories of participants	Total number	Nexus group	Non-nexus
1. Individuals working under CBAs	335 (67%)	335 (67%)	0
2. Retirees	50 (10%)	50 (10%)	0
3. "Special Class"—Non-CBA, non-CBA-alumni	100 (20%)	50 (10%)	50 (10%)

Categories of participants	Total number	Nexus group	Non-nexus
4. Non-nexus participants	15 (3%)	0	15 (3%)
Total	500 (100%)	435 (87%)	65 (13%)

In determining whether at least 85% of Plan A's participant population is made up of individuals with the required nexus to the collective bargaining agreement as required by paragraph (b)(2) of this section, the Plan may count as part of the nexus group only 50 (10% of the total plan population) of the 100 individuals described in paragraph (b)(2)(viii) of this section. That is because the number of individuals meeting the category of individuals in paragraph (b)(2)(viii) exceeds 10% of the total participant population by 50 individuals. The paragraph specifies that of those individuals who would otherwise be deemed to be nexus individuals because they are the type of individuals described in paragraph (b)(2)(viii), the number in excess of 10% of the total plan population may not be counted in the nexus group. Here, 50 of the 100 individuals employed by signatory employers, but not covered by the collective bargaining agreement, are counted as nexus individuals and 50 are not counted as nexus individuals. Nonetheless, the Plan satisfies the 85% criterion under paragraph (b)(2) because a total of 435 (335 individuals covered by the collective bargaining agreement, plus 50 retirees, plus 50 individuals employed by signatory employers), or 87%, of the 500 participants in Plan A are individuals who may be counted as nexus participants under paragraph (b)(2). Beneficiaries (e.g., spouses, dependent children, etc.) are not counted to determine whether the 85% test has been met.

Example 2. (i) International Union MG and its Local Unions have represented people working primarily in a particular industry for over 60 years. Since 1950, most of their collective bargaining agreements have called for those workers to be covered by the National MG Health and Welfare Plan. During that time, the number of union-represented workers in the industry, and the number of active participants in the National MG Health and Welfare Plan, first grew and then declined. New Locals were formed and later were shut down. Despite these fluctuations, the National MG Health and Welfare Plan meets the factors described in paragraphs (b)(4)(iii) and (iv) of this section, as the plan has been in existence pursuant to collective bargaining agreements to which the International Union and its affiliates have been parties since before January 1, 1983.

(ii) Assume the same facts, except that on January 1, 1999, International Union MG merged with International Union RE to form International Union MRGE. MRGE and its Locals now represent the active participants in the National MG Health and Welfare Plan and in the National RE Health and Welfare Plan, which, for 45 years, had been maintained under collective bargaining agreements negotiated by International Union RE and its Locals. Since International Union MRGE is the continuation of, and successor to, the MG and RE unions, the two plans continue to meet the factors in paragraphs (b)(4)(iii) and (iv) of this section. This also would be true if the two plans were merged.

(iii) Assume the same facts as in paragraphs (i) and (ii) of this Example. In addition to maintaining the health and welfare plans described in those paragraphs, International Union MG also maintained the National MG Pension Plan and International Union RE maintained the National RE Pension Plan. When the unions merged and the health and welfare plans were merged, National MG Pension Plan and National RE Pension Plan were merged to form National MRGE Pension Plan. When the unions merged, the employees and retirees covered under the pre-merger plans continued to be covered under the post-merger plans pursuant to the collective bargaining agreements and also were given credit in the post-merger plans for their years of service and coverage in the pre-merger plans. Retirees who originally were covered under the pre-merger plans and continue to be covered under the post-merger plans based on their past service and coverage would be considered to be "retirees" for purposes of 2550.3-40(b)(2)(ii). Likewise, bargaining unit alumni who were covered under the pre-merger plans and continued to be covered under the post-merger plans based on their past service and coverage and their continued employment with employers that are parties to an agreement described in paragraph (b)(3) of this section would be considered to be bargaining unit alumni for purposes of 2550.3-40(b)(2)(vii).

Example 3. Assume the same facts as in paragraph (ii) of Example 2 with respect to International Union MG. However, in 1997, one of its Locals and the employers with which it negotiates agree to set up a new multiemployer health and welfare plan that only covers the individuals represented by that Local Union. That plan would not meet the factor in paragraph (b)(4)(iii) of this section, as it has not been incorporated or referenced in collective bargaining agreements since before January 1, 1983.

Example 4. (i) Pursuant to a collective bargaining agreement between various employers and Local 2000, the employers contribute $2 per hour to the Fund for every hour that a covered employee works under the agreement. The covered employees are automatically entitled to health and disability coverage from the Fund for every calendar quarter the employees have 300 hours of additional covered service in the preceding quarter. The employees do not need to make any additional contributions for their own coverage, but must pay $250 per month if they want health coverage for their dependent spouse and children. Because the employer payments cover 100% of the required contributions for the employees' own coverage, the Local 2000 Employers Health and Welfare Fund meets the "75% employer payment" factor under paragraph (b)(4)(vi) of this section.

(ii) Assume, however, that the negotiated employer contribution rate was $1 per hour, and the employees could only obtain health coverage for themselves if they also elected to contribute $1 per hour, paid on a pre-tax basis through salary reduction. The Fund would not meet the 75% employer payment factor, even though the employees' contributions are treated as employer contributions for tax purposes. Under ERISA, and therefore under this section, elective salary reduction contributions are treated as employee contributions. The outcome would be the same if a uniform employee contribution rate applied to all employees, whether they had individual or family coverage, so that the $1 per hour employee contribution qualified an employee for his or her own coverage and, if he or she had dependents, dependent coverage as well.

Example 5. Arthur is a licensed insurance broker, one of whose clients is Multiemployer Fund M, a partially self-funded plan. Arthur takes bids from insurance companies on behalf of Fund M for the insured portion of its coverage, helps the trustees to evaluate the bids, and places the Fund's health insurance coverage with the carrier that is selected. Arthur also assists the trustees of Fund M in preparing material to explain the plan and its benefits to the participants, as well as in monitoring the insurance company's performance under the contract. At the Trustees' request, Arthur meets with a group of employers with which the union is negotiating for their employees' coverage under Fund M, and he explains the cost structure and benefits that Fund M provides. Arthur is not engaged in marketing within the meaning of paragraph (c)(1) of this section, so the fact that he provides these administrative services and sells insurance to the Fund itself does not affect the plan's status as a plan established or maintained under or pursuant to a collective bargaining agreement. This is the case whether or how he is compensated.

Example 6. Assume the same facts as Example 5, except that Arthur has a group of clients who are unrelated to the employers bound by the collective bargaining agreement, whose employees would not be "nexus group" members, and whose insurance carrier has withdrawn from the market in their locality. He persuades the client group to retain him to find them other coverage. The client group has no relationship with the labor union that represents the participants in Fund M. However, Arthur offers them coverage under Fund M and persuades the Fund's Trustees to allow the client group to join Fund M in order to broaden Fund M's contribution base. Arthur's activities in obtaining coverage for the unrelated group under Fund M constitutes marketing through an insurance producer; Fund M is a MEWA under paragraph (c)(1) of this section.

Example 7. Union A represents thousands of construction workers in a three-state geographic region. For many years, Union A has maintained a standard written collective bargaining agreement with several hundred large and small building contractors, covering wages, hours, and other terms and conditions of employment for all work performed in Union A's geographic territory. The terms of those agreements are negotiated every three years between Union A and a multiemployer Association, which signs on behalf of those employers who have delegated their bargaining authority to the Association. Hundreds of other employersincluding both local and traveling contractorshave chosen to become bound to the terms of Union A's standard area agreement for various periods of time and in various ways, such as by signing short-form binders or "me too" agreements, executing a single job or project labor agreement, or entering into a subcontracting arrangement with a signatory employer. All of these employ individuals represented by Union A and contribute to Plan A, a self-insured multiemployer health and welfare plan established and maintained under Union A's standard area agreement. During the past year, the trustees of Plan A have brought lawsuits against several signatory employers seeking contributions allegedly owed, but not paid to the trust. In defending that litigation, a number of employers have sworn that they never intended to operate as union contractors, that their employees want nothing to do with Union A, that Union A procured their assent to the collective bargaining agreement solely by threats and fraudulent misrepresentations, and that Union A has failed to file certain reports required by the Labor Management Reporting and Disclosure Act. In at least one instance, a petition for a decertification election has been filed with the National Labor Relations Board. In this example, Plan A meets the criteria for a regulatory finding under this section that it is a multiemployer plan established and maintained under or pursuant to one or more collective bargaining agreements, assuming that its participant population satisfies the 85% test of paragraph (b)(2) of this section and that none of the disqualifying factors in paragraph (c) of this section is present. Plan A's status for the purpose of this section is not affected by the fact that some of the employers who deal with Union A have challenged Union A's conduct, or have disputed under labor statutes and legal doctrines other than ERISA section 3(40) the validity and enforceability of their putative contract with Union A, regardless of the outcome of those disputes.

Example 8. Assume the same facts as Example 7. Plan A's benefits consultant recently entered into an arrangement with the Medical Consortium, a newly formed organization of health care providers, which allows the Plan to offer a broader range of health services to Plan A's participants while achieving cost savings to the Plan and to participants. Union A, Plan A, and Plan A's consultant each have added a page to their Web sites publicizing the new arrangement with the Medical Consortium. Concurrently, Medical Consortium's Web site prominently publicizes its recent affiliation with Plan A and the innovative services it makes available to the Plan's participants. Union A has mailed out informational packets to its members describing the benefit enhancements and encouraging election of family coverage. Union A has also begun distributing similar material to workers on hundreds of non-union construction job sites within its geographic territory. In this example, Plan A remains a plan established and maintained under or pursuant to one or more collective bargaining agreements under section 3(40) of ERISA. Neither Plan A's relationship with a new organization of health care providers, nor the use of various media to publicize Plan A's attractive benefits throughout the area served by Union A, alters Plan A's status for purpose of this section.

Example 9. Assume the same facts as in Example 7. Union A undertakes an area-wide organizing campaign among the employees of all the health care providers who belong to the Medical Consortium. When soliciting individual employees to sign up as union members, Union A distributes Plan A's information materials and promises to bargain for the same coverage. At the same time, when appealing to the employers in the Medical Consortium for voluntary recognition, Union A promises to publicize the Consortium's status as a group of unionized health care service providers. Union A eventually succeeds in obtaining recognition based on its majority status among the employees working for Medical Consortium employers. The Consortium, acting on behalf of its employer members, negotiates a collective bargaining agreement with Union A that provides terms and conditions of employment, including coverage under Plan A. In this example, Plan A still meets the criteria for a regulatory finding that it is collectively bargained under section 3(40) of ERISA. Union A's recruitment and

representation of a new occupational category of workers unrelated to the construction trade, its promotion of attractive health benefits to achieve organizing success, and the Plan's resultant growth, do not take Plan A outside the regulatory finding.

Example 10. Assume the same facts as in Example 7. The Medical Consortium, a newly formed organization, approaches Plan A with a proposal to make money for Plan A and Union A by enrolling a large group of employers, their employees, and self-employed individuals affiliated with the Medical Consortium. The Medical Consortium obtains employers' signatures on a generic document bearing Union A's name, labeled "collective bargaining agreement," which provides for health coverage under Plan A and compliance with wage and hour statutes, as well as other employment laws. Employees of signatory employers sign enrollment documents for Plan A and are issued membership cards in Union A; their membership dues are regularly checked off along with their monthly payments for health coverage. Self-employed individuals similarly receive union membership cards and make monthly payments, which are divided between Plan A and the Union. Aside from health coverage matters, these new participants have little or no contact with Union A. The new participants enrolled through the Consortium amount to 18% of the population of Plan A during the current Plan Year. In this example, Plan A now fails to meet the criteria in paragraphs (b)(2) and (b)(3) of this section, because more than 15% of its participants are individuals who are not employed under agreements that are the product of a bona fide collective bargaining relationship and who do not fall within any of the other nexus categories set forth in paragraph (b)(2) of this section. Moreover, even if the number of additional participants enrolled through the Medical Consortium, together with any other participants who did not fall within any of the nexus categories, did not exceed 15% of the total participant population under the plan, the circumstances in this example would trigger the disqualification of paragraph (c)(2) of this section, because Plan A now is being maintained under a substantial number of agreements that are a "scheme, plan, stratagem or artifice of evasion" intended primarily to evade compliance with state laws and regulations pertaining to insurance. In either case, the consequence of adding the participants through the Medical Consortium is that Plan A is now a MEWA for purposes of section 3(40) of ERISA and is not exempt from state regulation by virtue of ERISA.

(f) *Cross-reference.* See 29 CFR part 2570, subpart H for procedural rules relating to proceedings seeking an Administrative Law Judge finding by the Secretary under section 3(40) of ERISA.

(g) *Effect of proceeding seeking Administrative Law Judge Section 3(40) Finding.*

(1) An Administrative Law Judge finding issued pursuant to the procedures in 29 CFR part 2570, subpart H will constitute a finding whether the entity in that proceeding is an employee welfare benefit plan established or maintained under or pursuant to an agreement that the Secretary finds to be a collective bargaining agreement for purposes of section 3(40) of ERISA.

(2) Nothing in this section or in 29 CFR part 2570, subpart H is intended to provide the basis for a stay or delay of a state administrative or court proceeding or enforcement of a subpoena.

[¶ 14,139M]

§ 2510.3-101 **Definition of "plan assets"—plan investments.** (a) *In general.* (1) This section describes what constitutes assets of a plan with respect to a plan's investment in another entity for purposes of Subtitle A, and Parts 1 and 4 of Subtitle B, of Title I of the Act and section 4975 of the Internal Revenue Code. Paragraph (a)(2) of this section contains a general rule relating to plan investments. Paragraphs (b) through (f) of this section define certain terms that are used in the application of the general rule. Paragraph (g) of this section describes how the rules in this section are to be applied when a plan owns property jointly with others or where it acquires an equity interest whose value relates solely to identified assets of an issuer. Paragraph (h) of this section contains special rules relating to particular kinds of plan investments. Paragraph (i) describes the assets that a plan acquires when it purchases certain guaranteed mortgage certificates. Paragraph (j) of this section contains examples illustrating the operation of this section. The effective date of this section is set forth in paragraph (k) of this section.

(2) Generally, when a plan invests in another entity, the plan's assets include its investment, but do not, solely by reason of such investment, include any of the underlying assets of the entity. However, in the case of a plan's investment in an equity interest of an entity that is neither a publicly-offered security nor a security issued by an investment company registered under the Investment Company Act of 1940 its assets include both the equity interest and an undivided interest in each of the underlying assets of the entity, unless it is established that—

(i) The entity is an operating company, or

(ii) Equity participation in the entity by benefit plan investors is not significant.

Therefore, any person who exercises authority or control respecting the management or disposition of such underlying assets, and any person who provides investment advice with respect to such assets for a fee (direct or indirect), is a fiduciary of the investing plan.

(b) *"Equity interests" and "publicly-offered securities"*. (1) The term "equity interest" means any interest in an entity other than an instrument that is treated as indebtedness under applicable local law and which has no substantial equity features. A profits interest in a partnership, an undivided ownership interest in property and a beneficial interest in a trust are equity interests.

(2) A "publicly-offered security" is a security that is freely transferrable, part of a class of securities that is widely held and either—

(i) Part of a class of securities registered under section 12(b) or 12(g) of the Securities Exchange Act of 1934, or

(ii) Sold to the plan as part of an offering of securities to the public pursuant to an effective registration statement under the Securities Act of 1933 and the class of securities of which such security is a part is registered under the Securities Exchange Act of 1934 within 120 days (or such later time as may be allowed by the Securities and Exchange Commission) after the end of the fiscal year of the issuer during which the offering of such securities to the public occurred.

(3) For purposes of paragraph (b)(2) of this section, a class of securities is "widely-held" only if it is a class of securities that is owned by 100 or more investors independent of the issuer and of one another. A class of securities will not fail to be widely-held solely because subsequent to the initial offering the number of independent investors falls below 100 as a result of events beyond the control of the issuer.

(4) For purposes of paragraph (b)(2) of this section, whether a security is "freely transferable" is a factual question to be determined on the basis of all relevant facts and circumstances. If a security is part of an offering in which the minimum investment is $10,000 or less, however, the following factors ordinarily will not, alone or in combination, affect a finding that such securities are freely transferable:

(i) Any requirement that not less than a minimum number of shares or units of such security be transferred or assigned by any investor, provided that such requirement does not prevent transfer of all of the then remaining shares or units held by an investor;

(ii) Any prohibition against transfer or assignment of such security or rights in respect thereof to an ineligible or unsuitable investor;

(iii) Any restriction on, or prohibition against, any transfer or assignment which would either result in a termination or reclassification of the entity for federal or state tax purposes or which would violate any state or federal statute, regulation, court order, judicial decree, or rule of law;

(iv) Any requirement that reasonable transfer or administrative fee be paid in connection with a transfer or assignment;

(v) Any requirement that advance notice of a transfer or assignment be given to the entity and any requirement regarding execution of documentation evidencing such transfer or assignment (including documentation setting forth representations from either or both of the transferor or transferee as to compliance with any restriction or requirement described in this paragraph (b)(4) of this section or requiring compliance with the entity's governing instruments);

(vi) Any restriction on substitution of an assignee as a limited partner of a partnership, including a general partner consent requirement, provided that the economic benefits of ownership of the assignee

may be transferred or assigned without regard to such restriction or consent (other than compliance with any other restriction described in this paragraph (b)(4)) of this section;

(vii) Any administrative procedure which establishes an effective date, or an event, such as the completion of the offering, prior to which a transfer or assignment will not be effective; and

(viii) Any limitation or restriction on transfer or assignment which is not created or imposed by the issuer or any person acting for or on behalf of such issuer.

(c) *"Operating company"*. (1) An "operating company" is an entity that is primarily engaged, directly or through a majority owned subsidiary or subsidiaries, in the production or sale of a product or service other than the investment of capital. The term "operating company" includes an entity which is not described in the preceding sentence, but which is a "venture capital operating company" described in paragraph (d) or a "real estate operating company" described in paragraph (e).

(d) *"Venture capital operating company"*. (1) An entity is a "venture capital operating company" for the period beginning on an initial valuation date described in paragraph (d)(5)(i) and ending on the last day of the first "annual valuation period" described in paragraph (d)(5)(ii) (in the case of an entity that is not a venture capital operating company immediately before the determination) or for the 12 month period following the expiration of an "annual valuation period" described in paragraph (d)(5)(ii) (in the case of an entity that is a venture capital operating company immediately before the determination) if—

(i) On such initial valuation date, or at any time within such annual valuation period, at least 50 percent of its assets (other than short-term investments pending long-term commitment or distribution to investors), valued at cost, are invested in venture capital investments described in paragraph (d)(3)(i) or derivative investments described in paragraph (d)(4); and

(ii) During such 12 month period (or during the period beginning on the initial valuation date and ending on the last day of the first annual valuation period), the entity, in the ordinary course of its business, actually exercises management rights of the kind described in paragraph (d)(3)(ii) with respect to one or more of the operating companies in which it invests.

(2)(i) A venture capital operating company described in paragraph (d)(1) shall continue to be treated as a venture capital operating company during the "distribution period" described in paragraph (d)(2)(ii). An entity shall not be treated as a venture capital operating company at any time after the end of the distribution period.

(ii) The "distribution period" referred to in paragraph (d)(2)(i) begins on a date established by a venture capital operating company that occurs after the first date on which the venture capital operating company has distributed to investors the proceeds of at least 50 percent of the highest amount of investments (other than short-term investments made pending long-term commitment or distribution to investors) outstanding at any time from the date it commenced business (determined on the basis of the cost of such investments) and ends on the earlier of—

(A) The date on which the company makes a "new portfolio investment", or

(B) The expiration of 10 years from the beginning of the distribution period.

(iii) For purposes of paragraph (d)(2)(ii)(A), a "new portfolio investment" is an investment other than—

(A) An investment in an entity in which the venture capital operating company had an outstanding venture capital investment at the beginning of the distribution period which has continued to be outstanding at all times during the distribution period, or

(B) A short-term investment pending long-term commitment or distribution to investors.

(3)(i) For purposes of this paragraph (d) a "venture capital investment" is an investment in an operating company (other than a venture capital operating company) as to which the investor has or obtains management rights.

(ii) The term "management rights" means contractual rights directly between the investor and an operating company to substantially participate in, or substantially influence the conduct of, the management of the operating company.

(4)(i) An investment is a "derivative investment" for purposes of this paragraph (d) if it is—

(A) A venture capital investment as to which the investor's management rights have ceased in connection with a public offering of securities of the operating company to which the investment relates, or

(B) An investment that is acquired by a venture capital operating company in the ordinary course of its business in exchange for an existing venture capital investment in connection with:

(1) A public offering of securities of the operating company to which the existing venture capital investment relates, or

(2) A merger or reorganization of the operating company to which the existing venture capital investment relates, provided that such merger or reorganization is made for independent business reasons unrelated to extinguishing management rights.

(ii) An investment ceases to be a derivative investment on the later of:

(A) 10 years from the date of the acquisition of the original venture capital investment to which the derivative investment relates, or

(B) 30 months from the date on which the investment becomes a derivative investment.

(5) For purposes of this paragraph (d) and paragraph (e)—

(i) An "initial valuation date" is the later of—

(A) Any date designated by the company within the 12-month period ending with the effective date of this section, or

(B) The first date on which an entity makes an investment that is not a short-term investment of funds pending long-term commitment.

(ii) An "annual valuation period" is a preestablished annual period, not exceeding 90 days in duration, which begins no later than the anniversary date of an entity's initial valuation date. An annual valuation period, once established, may not be changed except for good cause unrelated to a determination under this paragraph (d) or paragraph (e).

(e) *"Real estate operating company"*. An entity is a "real estate operating company" for the period beginning on an initial valuation date described in paragraph (d)(5)(i) and ending on the last day of the first "annual valuation period" described in paragraph (d)(5)(ii) (in the case of an entity that is not a real estate operating company immediately before the determination) or for the 12-month period following the expiration of an annual valuation period described in paragraph (d)(5)(ii) (in the case of an entity that is a real estate operating company immediately before the determination) if:

(1) On such initial valuation date, or on any date within such annual valuation period, at least 50 percent of its assets, valued at cost (other than short-term investments pending long-term commitment or distribution to investors), are invested in real estate which is managed or developed and with respect to which such entity has the right to substantially participate directly in the management or development activities; and

(2) During such 12-month period (or during the period beginning on the initial valuation date and ending on the last day of the first annual valuation period) such entity in the ordinary course of its business is engaged directly in real estate management or development activities. [Corrected by 51 FR 47226 on December 31, 1986.]

(f) *Participation by benefit plan investors*. (1) Equity participation in an entity by benefit plan investors is "significant" on any date if, immediately after the most recent acquisition of any equity interest in the entity, 25 percent or more of the value of any class of equity interests in the entity is held by benefit plan investors (as defined in paragraph (f)(2)). For purposes of determinations pursuant to this paragraph (f), the value of any equity interests held by a person (other than a benefit plan investor) who has discretionary authority or control with respect to the assets of the entity or any person who provides investment advice for a fee (direct or indirect) with respect to such assets, or any affiliate of such a person, shall be disregarded.

(2) A "benefit plan investor" is any of the following—

(i) Any employee benefit plan (as defined in section 3(3) of the Act), whether or not it is subject to the provisions of Title I of the Act,

(ii) Any plan described in section 4975(e)(1) of the Internal Revenue Code,

(iii) Any entity whose underlying assets include plan assets by reason of a plan's investment in the entity.

(3) An "affiliate" of a person includes any person, directly or indirectly, through one or more intermediaries, controlling, controlled by, or under common control with the person. For purposes of this paragraph (f)(3), "control", with respect to a person other than an individual, means the power to exercise a controlling influence over the management or policies of such person.

(g) *Joint ownership*. For purposes of this section, where a plan jointly owns property with others, or where the value of a plan's equity interest in an entity relates solely to identified property of the entity, such property shall be treated as the sole property of a separate entity.

(h) *Specific rules relating to plan investments*. Notwithstanding any other provision of this section—

(1) Except where the entity is an investment company registered under the Investment Company Act of 1940, when a plan acquires or holds an interest in any of the following entities its assets include its investment and an undivided interest in each of the underlying assets of the entity:

(i) A group trust which is exempt from taxation under section 501(a) of the Internal Revenue Code pursuant to the principles of Rev. Rul. 81-100, 1981-1 C.B. 326,

(ii) A common or collective trust fund of a bank,

(iii) A separate account of an insurance company, other than a separate account that is maintained solely in connection with fixed contractual obligations of the insurance company under which the amounts payable, or credited, to the plan and to any participant or beneficiary of the plan (including an annuitant) are not affected in any manner by the investment performance of the separate account.

(2) When a plan acquires or holds an interest in any entity (other than an insurance company licensed to do business in a State) which is established or maintained for the purpose of offering or providing any benefit described in section 3(1) or section 3(2) of the Act to participants or beneficiaries of the investing plan, its assets will include its investment and an undivided interest in the underlying assets of that entity.

(3) When a plan or a related group of plans owns all of the outstanding equity interests (other than director's qualifying shares) in an entity, its assets include those equity interests and all of the underlying assets of the entity. This paragraph (h)(3) does not apply, however, where all of the outstanding equity interests in an entity are qualifying employer securities described in section 407(d)(5) of the Act, owned by one or more eligible individual account plan(s) (as defined in section 407(d)(3) of the Act) maintained by the same employer, provided that substantially all of the participants in the plan(s) are, or have been, employed by the issuer of such securities or by members of a group of affiliated corporations (as determined under section 407(d)(7) of the Act) of which the issuer is a member.

(4) For purposes of paragraph (h)(3), a "related group" of employee benefit plans consists of every group of two or more employee benefit plans—

(i) Each of which receives 10 percent or more of its aggregate contributions from the same employer or from members of the same controlled group of corporations (as determined under section 1563(a) of the Internal Revenue Code, without regard to section 1563(a)(4) thereof); or

(ii) Each of which is either maintained by, or maintained pursuant to a collective bargaining agreement negotiated by, the same employee organization or affiliated employee organizations. For purposes of this paragraph, an "affiliate" of an employee organization means any person controlling, controlled by, or under common control with such organization, and includes any organization chartered by the same parent body, or governed by the same constitution and bylaws, or having the relation of parent and subordinate.

(i) *Governmental mortgage pools*. (1) Where a plan acquires a guaranteed governmental mortgage pool certificate, as defined in paragraph (i)(2), the plan's assets include the certificate and all of its rights with respect to such certificate under applicable law, but do not, solely by reason of the plan's holding of such certificate, include any of the mortgages underlying such certificate.

(2) A "guaranteed governmental mortgage pool certificate" is a certificate backed by, or evidencing an interest in, specified mortgages or participation interests therein and with respect to which interest and principal payable pursuant to the certificate is guaranteed by the United States or an agency or instrumentality thereof. The term "guaranteed governmental mortgage pool certificate" includes a mortgage pool certificate with respect to which interest and principal payment pursuant to the certificate is guaranteed by:

(i) The Government National Mortgage Association:

(ii) The Federal Home Loan Mortgage Corporation; or

(iii) The Federal National Mortgage Association.

(j) *Examples*. The principles of this section are illustrated by the following examples:

(1) A plan, P, acquires debentures issued by a corporation, T, pursuant to a private offering. T is engaged primarily in investing and reinvesting in precious metals on behalf of its shareholders, all of which are benefit plan investors. By its terms, the debenture is convertible to common stock of T at P's option. At the time of P's acquisition of the debentures, the conversion feature is incidental to T's obligation to pay interest and principal. Although T is not an operating company, P's assets do not include an interest in the underlying assets of T because P has not acquired an *equity* interest in T. However, if P exercises its option to convert the debentures to common stock, it will have acquired an equity interest in T at that time and (assuming that the common stock is not a publicly-offered security and that there has been no change in the composition of the other equity investors in T) P's assets would then include an undivided interest in the underlying assets of T.

(2) A plan, P, acquires a limited partnership interest in a limited partnership, U, which is established and maintained by A, a general partner in U. U has only one class of limited partnership interests. U is engaged in the business of investing and reinvesting in securities. Limited partnership interests in U are offered privately pursuant to an exemption from the registration requirements of the Securities Act of 1933. P acquires 15 percent of the value of all the outstanding limited partnership interests in U, and, at the time of P's investment, a governmental plan owns 15 percent of the value of those interests. U is not an operating company because it is engaged primarily in the investment of capital. In addition, equity participation by benefit plan investors is significant because immediately after P's investment such investors hold more than 25 percent of the limited partnership interests in U. Accordingly, P's assets include an undivided interest in the underlying assets of U, and A is a fiduciary of P with respect to such assets by reason of its discretionary authority and control over U's assets. Although the governmental plan's investment is taken into account for purposes of determining whether equity participation by benefit plan investors is significant, nothing in this section imposes fiduciary obligations on A with respect to that plan.

(3) Assume the same facts as in paragraph (j)(2), except that P acquires only 5 percent of the value of all the outstanding limited partnership interests in U, and that benefit plan investors in the aggregate hold only 10 percent of the value of the limited partnership interests in U. Under these facts, there is no significant equity participation by benefit plan investors in U, and, accordingly, P's assets include its limited partnership interest in U, but do not include any of the underlying assets of U. Thus, A would not be a fiduciary of P by reason of P's investment.

(4) Assume the same facts as in paragraph (j)(3) and that the aggregate value of the outstanding limited partnership interests in U is $10,000 (and that the value of the interests held by benefit plan investors is thus $1000). Also assume that an affiliate of A owns limited partnership interests in U having a value of $6500. The value of the limited partnership interests held by A's affiliate are disregarded for purposes of determining whether there is significant equity participation in U by benefit plan investors. Thus, the percentage of the aggregate value of the limited partnership interests held by benefit plan investors in U for purposes of such a determination is approximately 28.6% ($1000/$3500). Therefore there is significant benefit plan investment in T.

(5) A plan, P, invests in a limited partnership, V, pursuant to a private offering. There is significant equity participation by benefit plan investors in V. V acquires equity positions in the companies in which it invests, and, in connection with these investments, V negotiates terms that give it the right to participate in or influence the management of those companies. Some of these investments are in publicly-offered securities and some are in securities acquired in private offerings. During its most recent valuation period, more than 50 percent of V's assets, valued at cost, consisted of investments with respect to which V obtained management rights of the kind described above. V's managers routinely consult informally with, and advise, the management of only one portfolio company with respect to which it has management rights, although it devotes substantial resources to its consultations with that company. With respect to the other portfolio companies, V relies on the managers of other entities to consult with and advise the companies' management. V is a venture capital operating company and therefore P has acquired its limited partnership investment, but has not acquired an interest in any of the underlying assets of V. Thus, none of the managers of V would be fiduciaries with respect to P solely by reason of its investment. In this situation, the mere fact that V does not participate in or influence the management of all its portfolio companies does not affect its characterization as a venture capital operating company.

(6) Assume the same facts as in paragraph (j)(5) and the following additional facts: V invests in debt securities as well as equity securities of its portfolio companies. In some cases V makes debt investments in companies in which it also has an equity investment; in other cases V only invests in debt instruments of the portfolio company. V's debt investments are acquired pursuant to private offerings and V negotiates covenants that give it the right to substantially participate in or to substantially influence the conduct of the management of the companies issuing the obligations. These covenants give V more significant rights with respect to the portfolio companies' management than the covenants ordinarily found in debt instruments of established, creditworthy companies that are purchased privately by institutional investors. V routinely consults with and advises the management of its portfolio companies. The mere fact that V's investments in portfolio companies are debt, rather than equity, will not cause V to fail to be a venture capital operating company, provided it actually obtains the right to substantially participate in or influence the conduct of the management of its portfolio companies and provided that in the ordinary course of its business it actually exercises those rights.

(7) A plan, P, invests (pursuant to a private offering) in a limited partnership, W, that is engaged primarily in investing and reinvesting assets in equity positions in real property. The properties acquired by W are subject to long-term leases under which substantially all management and maintenance activities with respect to the property are the responsibility of the lessee. W is not engaged in the management or development of real estate merely because it assumes the risks of ownership of income-producing real property, and W is not a real estate operating company. If there is significant equity participation in W by benefit plan investors, P will be considered to have acquired an undivided interest in each of the underlying assets of W.

(8) Assume the same facts as in paragraph (j)(7) except that W owns several shopping centers in which individual stores are leased for relatively short periods to various merchants (rather than owning properties subject to long-term leases under which substantially all management and maintenance activities are the responsibility of the lessee). W retains independent contractors to manage the shopping center properties. These independent contractors negotiate individual leases, maintain the common areas and conduct maintenance activities with respect to the properties. W has the responsibility to supervise and the authority to terminate the independent contractors. During its most recent valuation period more than 50 percent of W's assets, valued at cost, are invested in such properties. W is a real estate operating company. The fact that W does not have its own employees who engage in day-to-day management and development activities is only one factor in determining whether it is actively managing or

developing real estate. Thus, P's assets include its interest in W, but do not include any of the underlying assets of W.

(9) A plan, P, acquires a limited partnership interest in X pursuant to a private offering. There is significant equity participation in X by benefit plan investors. X is engaged in the business of making "convertible loans" which are structured as follows: X lends a specified percentage of the cost of acquiring real property to a borrower who provides the remaining capital needed to make the acquisition. This loan is secured by a mortgage on the property. Under the terms of the loan, X is entitled to receive a fixed rate of interest payable out of the initial cash flow from the property and is also entitled to that portion of any additional cash flow which is equal to the percentage of the acquisition cost that is financed by its loan. Simultaneously with the making of the loan, the borrower also gives X an option to purchase an interest in the property for the original principal amount of the loan at the expiration of its initial term. X's percentage interest in the property, if it exercises this option, would be equal to the percentage of the acquisition cost of the property which is financed by its loan. The parties to the transaction contemplate that the option ordinarily will be exercised at the expiration of the loan term if the property has appreciated in value. X and the borrower also agree that, if the option is exercised, they will form a limited partnership to hold the property. X negotiates loan terms which give it rights to substantially influence, or to substantially participate in, the management of the property which is acquired with the proceeds of the loan. These loan terms give X significantly greater rights to participate in the management of the property than it would obtain under a conventional mortgage loan. In addition, under the terms of the loan, X and the borrower ratably share any capital expenditures relating to the property. During its most recent valuation period, more than 50 percent of the value of X's assets valued at cost consisted of real estate investment of the kind described above. X, in the ordinary course of its business, routinely exercises its management rights and frequently consults with and advises the borrower and the property manager. Under these facts, X is a real estate operating company. Thus, P's assets include its interest in X, but do not include any of the underlying assets of X.

(10) In a private transaction, a plan, P, acquires a 30 percent participation in a debt instrument that is held by a bank. Since the value of the participation certificate relates solely to the debt instrument, that debt instrument is, under paragraph (g), treated as the sole asset of a separate entity. Equity participation in that entity by benefit plan investors is significant since the value of the plan's participation exceeds 25 percent of the value of the instrument. In addition, the hypothetical entity is not an operating company because it is primarily engaged in the investment of capital (*i.e.,* holding the debt instrument). Thus, P's assets include the participation and an undivided interest in the debt instrument, and the bank is a fiduciary of P to the extent it has discretionary authority or control over the debt instrument.

(11) In a private transaction, a plan, P, acquires 30% of the value of class equity securities issued by an operating company, Y. These securities provide that dividends shall be paid solely out of earnings attributable to certain tracts of undeveloped land that are held by Y for investment. Under paragraph (g), the property is treated as the sole asset of a separate entity. Thus, even though Y is an operating company, the hypothetical entity whose sole assets are the undeveloped tracts of land is not an operating company. Accordingly, P is considered to have acquired an undivided interest in the tracts of land held by Y. Thus, Y would be a fiduciary of P to the extent it exercises discretionary authority or control over such property.

(12) A medical benefit plan, P, acquires a beneficial interest in a trust, Z, that is not an insurance company licensed to do business in a State. Under this arrangement, Z will provide the benefits to the participants and beneficiaries of P that are promised under the terms of the plan. Under paragraph (h)(2), P's assets include its beneficial interest in Z and an undivided interest in each of its underlying assets. Thus, persons with discretionary authority or control over the assets of Z would be fiduciaries of P.

(k) *Effective date and transitional rules.* (1) In general, this section is effective for purposes of identifying the assets of a plan on or after March 13, 1987. Except as a defense, this section shall not apply to investments in an entity in existence on March 13, 1987, if no plan

subject to Title I of the Act or plan described in section 4975(e)(1) of the Code (other than a plan described in section 4975(g)(2) or 4975(g)(3)) acquires an interest in the entity from an issuer or underwriter at any time on or after March 13, 1987 except pursuant to a contract binding on the plan in effect on March 13, 1987 with an issuer or underwriter to acquire an interest in the entity.

(2) Notwithstanding paragraph (k)(1), this section shall not, except as a defense, apply to a real estate entity described in section 11018(a) of Pub. L. 99-272.

[Added by 51 FR 41280 on November 13, 1986, effective Mar. 13, 1987.]

[¶ 14,139N]

§ 2510.3-102 **Definition of "plan assets"—participant contributions.** (a) *General rule.* For purposes of subtitle A and parts 1 and 4 of subtitle B of title I of ERISA and section 4975 of the Internal Revenue Code only (but without any implication for and may not be relied upon to bar criminal prosecutions under 18 U.S.C. 664), the assets of the plan include amounts (other than union dues) that a participant or beneficiary pays to an employer, or amounts that a participant has withheld from his wages by an employer, for contribution to the plan as of the earliest date on which such contributions can reasonably be segregated from the employer's general assets.

(b) *Maximum time period for pension benefit plans.*

(1) Except as provided in paragraph (b)(2), of this section, with respect to an employee pension benefit plan as defined in section 3(2) of ERISA, in no event shall the date determined pursuant to paragraph (a) of this section occur later than the 15th business day of the month following the month in which the participant contribution amounts are received by the employer (in the case of amounts that a participant or beneficiary pays to an employer) or the 15th business day of the month following the month in which such amounts would otherwise have been payable to the participant in cash (in the case of amounts withheld by an employer from a participant's wages).

(2) With respect to a SIMPLE plan that involves SIMPLE IRAs (i.e., Simple Retirement Accounts, as described in section 408(p) of the Internal Revenue Code), in no event shall the date determined pursuant to paragraph (a) of this section occur later than the 30th calendar day following the month in which the participant contribution amounts would otherwise have been payable to the participant in cash. [Amended by 62 FR 62934 on November 25, 1997, effective immediately.]

(c) *Maximum time period for welfare benefit plans.* With respect to an employee welfare benefit plan as defined in section 3(1) of ERISA, in no event shall the date determined pursuant to paragraph (a) of this section occur later than 90 days from the date on which the participant contribution amounts are received by the employer (in the case of amounts that a participant or beneficiary pays to an employer) or that date on which such amounts would otherwise have been payable to the participant in cash (in the case of amounts withheld by an employer from a participant's wages).

(d) *Extension of maximum time period for pension plans.* (1) With respect to participant contributions received or withheld by the employer in a single month, the maximum time period provided under paragraph (b) of this section shall be extended for an additional 10 business days for an employer who—

(i) Provides a true and accurate written notice, distributed in a manner reasonably designed to reach all the plan participants within 5 business days after the end of such extension period, stating—

(A) That the employer elected to take such extension for that month;

(B) That the affected contributions have been transmitted to the plan; and

(C) With particularity, the reasons why the employer cannot reasonably segregate the participant contributions within the time period described in paragraph (b) of this section;

(ii) Prior to such extension period, obtains a performance bond or irrevocable letter of credit in favor of the plan and in an amount of not less than the total amount of participant contributions received or withheld by the employer in the previous month; and

(iii) Within 5 business days after the end of such extension period, provides a copy of the notice required under paragraph (d)(1)(i) of this section to the Secretary, along with a certification that such notice was provided to the participants and that the bond or letter of credit required under paragraph (d)(1)(ii) of this section was obtained.

(2) The performance bond or irrevocable letter of credit required in paragraph (d)(1)(ii) of this section shall be guaranteed by a bank or similar institution that is supervised by the Federal government or a State government and shall remain in effect for 3 months after the month in which the extension expires.

(3)(i) An employer may not elect an extension under this paragraph (d) more than twice in any plan year unless the employer pays to the plan an amount representing interest on the participant contributions that were subject to all the extensions within such plan year.

(ii) The amount representing interest in paragraph (d)(3)(i) of this section shall be the greater of—

(A) The amount that otherwise would have been earned on the participant contributions from the date on which such contributions were paid to, or withheld by, the employer until such money is transmitted to the plan had such contributions been invested during such period in the investment alternative available under plan which had the highest rate of return; or

(B) Interest at a rate equal to the underpayment rate defined in section 6621(a)(2) of the Internal Revenue Code from the date on which such contributions were paid to, or withheld by, the employer until such money is fully restored to the plan.

(e) *Definition.* For purposes of this section, the term *business day* means any day other than a Saturday, Sunday or any day designated as a holiday by the Federal Government.

(f) *Examples.* The requirements of this section are illustrated by the following examples:

(1) Employer W is a small company with a small number of employees at a single payroll location. W maintains a plan under section 401(k) of the Code in which all of its employees participate. W's practice is to issue a single check to a trust that maintained under the plan in the amount of the total withheld employee contributions within two business days of the date on which the employees are paid. In view of the relatively small number of employees and the fact that they are paid from a single location, W could reasonably be expected to transmit participant contributions to the trust within two days after the employee's wages are paid. Therefore, the assets of W's 401(k) plan include the participant contributions attributable to such pay periods as of the date two business days from the date the employee's wages are paid.

(2) Employer X is a large national corporation which sponsors a section 401(k) plan. X has several payroll centers and uses an outside payroll processing service to pay employee wages and process deductions. Each payroll center has a different pay period. Each center maintains separate accounts on its books for purposes of accounting for that center's payroll deductions and provides the outside payroll processor the data necessary to prepare employee paychecks and process deductions. The payroll processing service has adopted a procedure under which it issues the employees' paychecks when due and deducts all payroll taxes and elective employee deductions. It deposits withheld income and employment payroll taxes within the time frame specified by 26 CFR 31.6302-1 and forwards a computer data tape representing the total payroll deductions for each employee, for a month's worth of pay periods, to a centralized location in X, within 4 days after the end of the month, where the data tape is checked for accuracy. A single check representing the aggregate participant contributions for the month is then issued to the plan by the employer. X has determined that this procedure, which takes up to 10 business days to complete, permits segregation of participant contributions at the earliest practicable time and avoids mistakes in the allocation of contribution amounts for each participant. Therefore, the assets of X's 401(k) plan would include the participant contributions no later than 10 business days after the end of the month.

(3) Assume the same facts as in paragraph (f)(2) of this section, except that X takes 30 days after receipt of the data tape to issue a check to the plan representing the aggregate participant contributions

for the prior month. X believes that this procedure permits segregation of participant contributions at the earliest practicable time and avoids mistakes in the allocation of contribution amounts for each participant under paragraph (a) and (b) of this section, the assets of the plan include the participant contributions as soon as X could reasonably be expected to segregate the contributions from its general assets, but in no event later than the 15th business day of the month following the month that a participant or beneficiary pays to an employer, or has withheld from his wages by an employer, money for contribution to the plan. The participant contributions become plan assets no later that date.

(4) Employer Y is a medium-sized company which maintains a self-insured contributory group health plan. Several former employees have elected, pursuant to the provisions of ERISA section 602, 29 U.S.C. 1162, to pay Y for continuation of their coverage under the plan. These checks arrive at various times during the month and are deposited in the employer's general account at bank Z. Under paragraphs (a) and (b) of this section, the assets of the plan include the former employees' payments as soon after the checks have cleared the bank as Y could reasonably be expected to segregate the payments from its general assets, but in no event later than the 90 days after a participant or beneficiary, including a former employee, pays to an employer, or has withheld from his wages by an employer, money for contribution to the plan.

(g) *Effective date.* This section is effective February 3, 1997.

(h) *Applicability date for collectively-bargained plans.* (1) Paragraph (b) of this section applies to collectively-bargained plans no sooner that the later of—

(i) February 3, 1997; or

(ii) The first day of the plan year that begins after the expiration of the last to expire of any applicable bargaining agreement in effect on August 7, 1996.

(2) Until paragraph (b) of this section applies to a collectively-bargained plan, paragraph (c) of this section shall apply to such plan as if such plan were an employee welfare benefit plan.

(i) *Optional postponement of applicability.* (1) The application of paragraph (b) of this section (g) shall be postponed for up to an additional 90 days beyond the effective date described in paragraph (g) of this section for an employer who, prior to February 3, 1997—

(i) Provides a true and accurate written notice, distributed in a manner designed to reach all the plan participants before the end of February 3, 1997, stating—

(A) That the employer elected to postpone such applicability;

(B) The date that the postponement will expire; and

(C) With particularity the reasons why the employer cannot reasonably segregate the participant contributions within the time period described in paragraph (b) of this section, by February 3, 1997;

(ii) Obtains a performance bond or irrevocable letter of credit in favor of the plan and in an amount of not less than the total amount of participant contributions received or withheld by the employer in the previous 3 months;

(iii) Provides a copy of the notice required under paragraph (i)(1)(i) of this section to the Secretary, along with a certification that such notice was provided to the participants and that the bond or letter of credit required under paragraph (i)(1)(ii) of this section was obtained; and

(iv) For each month during which such postponement is in effect, provides a true and accurate written notice to the plan participants indicating the date on which the participant contributions received or withheld by the employer during such month were transmitted to the plan.

(2) The notice required in paragraph (i)(1)(iv) of this section shall be distributed in a manner reasonably designed to reach all the plan participants within 10 days after transmission of the affected participant contributions.

(3) The bond or letter of credit required under paragraph (i)(1)(ii) shall be guaranteed by a bank or similar institution that is

supervised by the Federal government or a State government and shall remain in effect for 3 months after the month in which the postponement expires.

    (4) During the period of any postponement of applicability with respect to a plan under this paragraph (i), paragraph (c) of this section shall apply to such plan as if such plan were an employee welfare benefit plan.

[Adopted by 53 FR 17628, May 17, 1988, amended by 61 FR 41220 on August 7, 1996, effective February 3, 1997, and further amended by 62 FR 62934 on November 24, 1997, effective on November 25, 1997.]

[¶ 14,140]
COVERAGE

Act Sec. 4.(a) Except as provided in subsection (b) or (c) and in sections 201, 301, and 401, this title shall apply to any employee benefit plan if it is established or maintained—

    (1) by any employer engaged in commerce or in any industry or activity affecting commerce; or

    (2) by any employee organization or organizations representing employees engaged in commerce or in any industry or activity affecting commerce; or

    (3) by both.

Act Sec. 4. (b) The provisions of this title shall not apply to any employee benefit plan if—

    (1) such plan is a governmental plan (as defined in section 3(32));

    (2) such plan is a church plan (as defined in section 3(33)) with respect to which no election has been made under section 410(d) of the Internal Revenue Code of 1986;

    (3) such plan is maintained solely for the purpose of complying with applicable workmen's compensation laws or unemployment compensation or disability insurance laws;

    (4) such plan is maintained outside of the United States primarily for the benefit of persons substantially all of whom are nonresident aliens; or

    (5) such plan is an excess benefit plan (as defined in section 3(36)) and is unfunded.

The provisions of part 7 of subtitle B shall not apply to a health insurance issuer (as defined in section 706(b)(2)) solely by reason of health insurance coverage (as defined in section 706(b)(1) provided by such issuer in connection with a group health plan (as defined in section 706(a)(1)) if the provisions of this title do not apply to such group health plan.

Act Sec. 4. (c) If a pension plan allows an employee to elect to make voluntary employee contributions to accounts and annuities as provided in section 408(q) of the Internal Revenue Code of 1986, such accounts and annuities (and contributions thereto) shall not be treated as part of such plan (or as a separate pension plan) for purposes of any provision of this title other than section 403(c), 404, or 405 (relating to exclusive benefit, and fiduciary and co-fiduciary responsibilities) and part 5 (relating to administration and enforcement). Such provisions shall apply to such accounts and annuities in a manner similar to their application to a simplified employee pension under section 408(k) of the Internal Revenue Code of 1986.

Amendments

P.L. 107-147, § 411(i)(2):

Amended ERISA Sec. 4(c) by inserting "and part 5 (relating to administration and enforcement" before the period at the end and by adding a new sentence at the end to read as above.

The above amendment is effective for plan years beginning after December 31, 2002, subject to sunset after 2010 under P.L. 107-16, Sec. 901.

P.L. 107-16, § 602(b)(1):

Amended ERISA Sec. 4 by adding at the end a new subsection (c) to read as above.

The above amendment is effective for plan years beginning after December 31, 2002 subject to the sunset after 2010 under P.L. 107-16, Sec. 901.

P.L. 107-16, § 602(b)(2):

Amended ERISA Sec. 4(a) by inserting "or (c)" after "subsection (b)".

The above amendment is effective for plan years beginning after December 31, 2002 subject to the sunset after 2010 under P.L. 107-16, Sec. 901.

P.L. 104-191, § 101(d):

Amended ERISA Sec. 4(b) by adding at the end, after and below paragraph (5), a new sentence to read as above.

The above amendment generally applies with respect to group health plans for plan years beginning after June 30, 1997. For special rules, see Act Sec. 101(g)(2)- (5), reproduced below.

Act Sec. 101(g)(2)-(5) reads as follows:

(g) EFFECTIVE DATES.—

(1) IN GENERAL.—Except as provided in this section, this section (and the amendments made by this section) shall apply with respect to group health plans for plan years beginning after June 30, 1997.

(2) DETERMINATION OF CREDITABLE COVERAGE.—

(A) PERIOD OF COVERAGE.—

(i) IN GENERAL.—Subject to clause (ii), no period before July 1, 1996, shall be taken into account under part 7 of subtitle B of title I of the Employee Retirement Income Security Act of 1974 (as added by this section) in determining creditable coverage.

(ii) SPECIAL RULE FOR CERTAIN PERIODS.—The Secretary of Labor, consistent with section 104, shall provide for a process whereby individuals who need to establish creditable coverage for periods before July 1, 1996, and who would have such coverage credited but for clause (i) may be given credit for creditable coverage for such periods through the presentation of documents or other means.

(B) CERTIFICATIONS, ETC.—

(i) IN GENERAL.—Subject to clauses (ii) and (iii), subsection (e) of section 701 of the Employee Retirement Income Security Act of 1974 (as added by this section) shall apply to events occurring after June 30, 1996.

(ii) NO CERTIFICATION REQUIRED TO BE PROVIDED BEFORE JUNE 1, 1997.—In no case is a certification required to be provided under such subsection before June 1, 1997.

(iii) CERTIFICATION ONLY ON WRITTEN REQUEST FOR EVENTS OCCURRING BEFORE OCTOBER 1, 1996.—In the case of an event occurring after June 30, 1996, and before October 1, 1996, a certification is not required to be provided under such subsection unless an individual (with respect to whom the certification is otherwise required to be made) requests such certification in writing.

(C) TRANSITIONAL RULE.—In the case of an individual who seeks to establish creditable coverage for any period for which certification is not required because it relates to an event occurring before June 30, 1996—

(i) the individual may present other credible evidence of such coverage in order to establish the period of creditable coverage; and

(ii) a group health plan and a health insurance issuer shall not be subject to any penalty or enforcement action with respect to the plan's or issuer's crediting (or not crediting) such coverage if the plan or issuer has sought to comply in good faith with the applicable requirements under the amendments made by this section.

(3) SPECIAL RULE FOR COLLECTIVE BARGAINING AGREEMENTS.—Except as provided in paragraph (2), in the case of a group health plan maintained pursuant to one or more collective bargaining agreements between employee representatives and one or more employers ratified before the date of the enactment of this Act, part 7 of subtitle B of title I of Employee Retirement Income Security Act of 1974 (other than section 701(e) thereof) shall not apply to plan years beginning before the later of—

(A) the date on which the last of the collective bargaining agreements relating to the plan terminates (determined without regard to any extension thereof agreed to after the date of the enactment of this Act), or

(B) July 1, 1997.

For purposes of subparagraph (A), any plan amendment made pursuant to a collective bargaining agreement relating to the plan which amends the plan solely to conform to any requirement of such part shall not be treated as a termination of such collective bargaining agreement.

(4) TIMELY REGULATIONS.—The Secretary of Labor, consistent with section 104, shall first issue by not later than April 1, 1997, such regulations as may be necessary to carry out the amendments made by this section.

(5) LIMITATION ON ACTIONS.—No enforcement action shall be taken, pursuant to the amendments made by this section, against a group health plan or health insurance issuer with respect to a violation of a requirement imposed by such amendments before January 1, 1998, or, if later, the date of issuance of regulations referred to in paragraph (4), if the plan or issuer has sought to comply in good faith with such requirements.

Subtitle B—Regulatory Provisions
Part 1—Reporting and Disclosure

»»→ *Caution: Interpretive Bulletins Relating to Reporting and Disclosure are reproduced beginning at ¶ 14,370.—CCH.*

[¶ 14,210]
DUTY OF DISCLOSURE AND REPORTING

Act Sec. 101. (a) The administrator of each employee benefit plan shall cause to be furnished in accordance with section 104(b) to each participant covered under the plan and to each beneficiary who is receiving benefits under the plan—

(1) a summary plan description described in section 102(a)(1); and

(2) the information described in sections 104(b)(3) and 105(a) and (c).

Act Sec. 101. (b) The administrator shall, in accordance with section 104(a), file with the Secretary—

(1) the annual report containing the information required by section 103; and

(2) terminal and supplementary reports as required by subsection (c) of this section.

Act Sec. 101. (c)(1) Each administrator of an employee pension benefit plan which is winding up its affairs (without regard to the number of participants remaining in the plan) shall, in accordance with regulations prescribed by the Secretary, file such terminal reports as the Secretary may consider necessary. A copy of such report shall also be filed with the Pension Benefit Guaranty Corporation.

(2) The Secretary may require terminal reports to be filed with regard to any employee welfare benefit plan which is winding up its affairs in accordance with regulations promulgated by the Secretary.

(3) The Secretary may require that a plan described in paragraph (1) or (2) file a supplementary or terminal report with the annual report in the year such plan is terminated and that a copy of such supplementary or terminal report in the case of a plan described in paragraph (1) be also filed with the Pension Benefit Guaranty Corporation.

Act Sec. 101. NOTICE OF FAILURE TO MEET MINIMUM FUNDING STANDARDS.—

(d)(1) IN GENERAL. If an employer maintaining a plan other than a multiemployer plan fails to make a required installment or other payment required to meet the minimum funding standard under section 302 to a plan before the 60th day following the due date for such installment or other payment, the employer shall notify each participant and beneficiary (including an alternate payee as defined in section 206(d)(3)(K)) of such plan of such failure. Such notice shall be made at such time and in such manner as the Secretary may prescribe.

(2) SUBSECTION NOT TO APPLY IF WAIVER PENDING. This subsection shall not apply to any failure if the employer has filed a waiver request under section 303 with respect to the plan year to which the required installment relates, except that if the waiver request is denied, notice under paragraph (1) shall be provided within 60 days after the date of such denial.

(3) DEFINITIONS. For purposes of this subsection, the terms "required installment" and "due date" have the same meanings given such terms by section 302(e).

Act Sec. 101. NOTICE OF TRANSFER OF EXCESS PENSION ASSETS TO HEALTH BENEFITS ACCOUNTS.—

(e)(1) NOTICE TO PARTICIPANTS. Not later than 60 days before the date of a qualified transfer by an employee pension benefit plan of excess pension assets to a health benefits account, the administrator of the plan shall notify (in such manner as the Secretary may prescribe) each participant and beneficiary under the plan of such transfer. Such notice shall include information with respect to the amount of excess pension assets, the portion to be transferred, the amount of health benefits liabilities expected to be provided with the assets transferred, and the amount of pension benefits of the participant which will be nonforfeitable immediately after the transfer.

(2) NOTICE TO SECRETARIES, ADMINISTRATOR, AND EMPLOYEE ORGANIZATIONS.—

(A) IN GENERAL. Not later than 60 days before the date of any qualified transfer by an employee pension benefit plan of excess pension assets to a health benefits account, the employer maintaining the plan from which the transfer is made shall provide the Secretary, the Secretary of the Treasury, the administrator, and each employee organization representing participants in the plan a written notice of such transfer. A copy of any such notice shall be available for inspection in the principal office of the administrator.

(B) INFORMATION RELATING TO TRANSFER. Such notice shall identify the plan from which the transfer is made, the amount of the transfer, a detailed accounting of assets projected to be held by the plan immediately before and immediately after the transfer, and the current liabilities under the plan at the time of the transfer.

(C) AUTHORITY FOR ADDITIONAL REPORTING REQUIREMENTS. The Secretary may prescribe such additional reporting requirements as may be necessary to carry out the purposes of this section.

(3) DEFINITIONS. For purposes of paragraph (1), any term used in such paragraph which is also used in section 420 of the Internal Revenue Code of 1986 (as in effect on the date of the enactment of the American Jobs Creation Act of 2004) shall have the same meaning as when used in such section.

»»→ *Caution: ERISA Sec. 101(f), as added by P.L. 108-218, generally applies to plan years beginning after December 31, 2004.*

Act Sec. 101. MULTIEMPLOYER DEFINED BENEFIT PLAN FUNDING NOTICES.—

(f)(1) IN GENERAL. The administrator of a defined benefit plan which is a multiemployer plan shall for each plan year provide a plan funding notice to each plan participant and beneficiary, to each labor organization representing such participants or beneficiaries, to each employer that has an obligation to contribute under the plan, and to the Pension Benefit Guaranty Corporation.

(2) Information contained in notices.—

(A) Identifying information. Each notice required under paragraph (1) shall contain identifying information, including the name of the plan, the address and phone number of the plan administrator and the plan's principal administrative officer, each plan sponsor's employer identification number, and the plan number of the plan.

(B) Specific information. A plan funding notice under paragraph (1) shall include—

(i) a statement as to whether the plan's funded current liability percentage (as defined in section 302(d)(8)(B)) for the plan year to which the notice relates is at least 100 percent (and, if not, the actual percentage);

(ii) a statement of the value of the plan's assets, the amount of benefit payments, and the ratio of the assets to the payments for the plan year to which the notice relates;

(iii) a summary of the rules governing insolvent multiemployer plans, including the limitations on benefit payments and any potential benefit reductions and suspensions (and the potential effects of such limitations, reductions, and suspensions on the plan); and

(iv) a general description of the benefits under the plan which are eligible to be guaranteed by the Pension Benefit Guaranty Corporation, along with an explanation of the limitations on the guarantee and the circumstances under which such limitations apply.

(C) Other information. Each notice under paragraph (1) shall include any additional information which the plan administrator elects to include to the extent not inconsistent with regulations prescribed by the Secretary.

(3) Time for providing notice. Any notice under paragraph (1) shall be provided no later than two months after the deadline (including extensions) for filing the annual report for the plan year to which the notice relates.

(4) Form and manner. Any notice under paragraph (1)—

(A) shall be provided in a form and manner prescribed in regulations of the Secretary,

(B) shall be written in a manner so as to be understood by the average plan participant, and

(C) may be provided in written, electronic, or other appropriate form to the extent such form is reasonably accessible to persons to whom the notice is required to be provided..

Act Sec. 101. REPORTING BY CERTAIN ARRANGEMENTS. (g) The Secretary may, by regulation, require multiple employer welfare arrangements providing benefits consisting of medical care (within the meaning of section 706(a)(2)) which are not group health plans to report, not more frequently than annually, in such form and such manner as the Secretary may require for the purpose of determining the extent to which the requirements of part 7 are being carried out in connection with such benefits.

Act Sec. 101. SIMPLE RETIREMENT ACCOUNTS.—

(h)(1) NO EMPLOYER REPORTS. Except as provided in this subsection, no report shall be required under this section by an employer maintaining a qualified salary reduction arrangement under section 408(p) of the Internal Revenue Code of 1986.

(2) SUMMARY DESCRIPTION. The trustee of any simple retirement account established pursuant to a qualified salary reduction arrangement under section 408(p) of such Code shall provide to the employer maintaining the arrangement each year a description containing the following information:

(A) The name and address of the employer and the trustee.

(B) The requirements for eligibility for participation.

(C) The benefits provided with respect to the arrangement.

(D) The time and method of making elections with respect to the arrangement.

(E) The procedures for, and effects of, withdrawals (including rollovers) from the arrangement.

(3) EMPLOYEE NOTIFICATION. The employer shall notify each employee immediately before the period for which an election described in section 408(p)(5)(C) of such Code may be made of the employee's opportunity to make such election. Such notice shall include a copy of the description described in paragraph (2).

Act Sec. 101. NOTICE OF BLACKOUT PERIODS TO PARTICIPANT OR BENEFICIARY UNDER INDIVIDUAL ACCOUNT PLAN—

(i)(1) DUTIES OF PLAN ADMINISTRATOR-. In advance of the commencement of any blackout period with respect to an individual account plan, the plan administrator shall notify the plan participants and beneficiaries who are affected by such action in accordance with this subsection.

(2) NOTICE REQUIREMENTS—

(A) IN GENERAL. The notices described in paragraph (1) shall be written in a manner calculated to be understood by the average plan participant and shall include—

(i) the reasons for the blackout period,

(ii) an identification of the investments and other rights affected,

(iii) the expected beginning date and length of the blackout period,

(iv) in the case of investments affected, a statement that the participant or beneficiary should evaluate the appropriateness of their current investment decisions in light of their inability to direct or diversify assets credited to their accounts during the blackout period, and

(v) such other matters as the Secretary may require by regulation.

(B) NOTICE TO PARTICIPANTS AND BENEFICIARIES-. Except as otherwise provided in this subsection, notices described in paragraph (1) shall be furnished to all participants and beneficiaries under the plan to whom the blackout period applies at least 30 days in advance of the blackout period.

(C) EXCEPTION TO 30-DAY NOTICE REQUIREMENT- In any case in which—

(i) a deferral of the blackout period would violate the requirements of subparagraph (A) or (B) of section 404(a)(1), and a fiduciary of the plan reasonably so determines in writing, or

(ii) the inability to provide the 30-day advance notice is due to events that were unforeseeable or circumstances beyond the reasonable control of the plan administrator, and a fiduciary of the plan reasonably so determines in writing, subparagraph (B) shall not apply, and the notice shall be furnished to all participants and beneficiaries under the plan to whom the blackout period applies as soon as reasonably possible under the circumstances unless such a notice in advance of the termination of the blackout period is impracticable.

(D) WRITTEN NOTICE. The notice required to be provided under this subsection shall be in writing, except that such notice may be in electronic or other form to the extent that such form is reasonably accessible to the recipient.

(E) NOTICE TO ISSUERS OF EMPLOYER SECURITIES SUBJECT TO BLACKOUT PERIOD. In the case of any blackout period in connection with an individual account plan, the plan administrator shall provide timely notice of such blackout period to the issuer of any employer securities subject to such blackout period.

(3) EXCEPTION FOR BLACKOUT PERIODS WITH LIMITED APPLICABILITY-. In any case in which the blackout period applies only to 1 or more participants or beneficiaries in connection with a merger, acquisition, divestiture, or similar transaction involving the plan or plan sponsor and occurs solely in connection with becoming or ceasing to be a participant or beneficiary under the plan by reason of such merger, acquisition, divestiture, or transaction, the requirement of this subsection that the notice be provided to all participants and beneficiaries shall be treated as met if the notice required under paragraph (1) is provided to such participants or beneficiaries to whom the blackout period applies as soon as reasonably practicable.

(4) CHANGES IN LENGTH OF BLACKOUT PERIOD-. If, following the furnishing of the notice pursuant to this subsection, there is a change in the beginning date or length of the blackout period (specified in such notice pursuant to paragraph (2)(A)(iii)), the administrator shall provide affected participants and beneficiaries notice of the change as soon as reasonably practicable. In relation to the extended blackout period, such notice shall meet the requirements of paragraph (2)(D) and shall specify any material change in the matters referred to in clauses (i) through (v) of paragraph (2)(A).

(5) REGULATORY EXCEPTIONS-. The Secretary may provide by regulation for additional exceptions to the requirements of this subsection which the Secretary determines are in the interests of participants and beneficiaries.

(6) GUIDANCE AND MODEL NOTICES-. The Secretary shall issue guidance and model notices which meet the requirements of this subsection.

(7) BLACKOUT PERIOD-. For purposes of this subsection—

(A) IN GENERAL-. The term 'blackout period' means, in connection with an individual account plan, any period for which any ability of participants or beneficiaries under the plan, which is otherwise available under the terms of such plan, to direct or diversify assets credited to their accounts, to obtain loans from the plan, or to obtain distributions from the plan is temporarily suspended, limited, or restricted, if such suspension, limitation, or restriction is for any period of more than 3 consecutive business days.

(B) EXCLUSIONS. The term 'blackout period' does not include a suspension, limitation, or restriction—

(i) which occurs by reason of the application of the securities laws (as defined in section 3(a)(47) of the Securities Exchange Act of 1934),

(ii) which is a change to the plan which provides for a regularly scheduled suspension, limitation, or restriction which is disclosed to participants or beneficiaries through any summary of material modifications, any materials describing specific investment alternatives under the plan, or any changes thereto, or

(iii) which applies only to 1 or more individuals, each of whom is the participant, an alternate payee (as defined in section 206(d)(3)(K)), or any other beneficiary pursuant to a qualified domestic relations order (as defined in section 206(d)(3)(B)(i)).

(8) INDIVIDUAL ACCOUNT PLAN—

(A) IN GENERAL. For purposes of this subsection, the term 'individual account plan' shall have the meaning provided such term in section 3(34), except that such term shall not include a one-participant retirement plan.

(B) ONE-PARTICIPANT RETIREMENT PLAN-. For purposes of subparagraph (A), the term 'one-participant retirement plan' means a retirement plan that—

(i) on the first day of the plan year—

(I) covered only the employer (and the employer's spouse) and the employer owned the entire business (whether or not incorporated), or

(II) covered only one or more partners (and their spouses) in a business partnership (including partners in an S or C corporation (as defined in section 1361(a) of the Internal Revenue Code of 1986)),

(ii) meets the minimum coverage requirements of section 410(b) of the Internal Revenue Code of 1986 (as in effect on the date of the enactment of this paragraph) without being combined with any other plan of the business that covers the employees of the business,

(iii) does not provide benefits to anyone except the employer (and the employer's spouse) or the partners (and their spouses),

(iv) does not cover a business that is a member of an affiliated service group, a controlled group of corporations, or a group of businesses under common control, and

(v) does not cover a business that leases employees.

Act Sec. 101. CROSS REFERENCE.—

(j) For regulations relating to coordination of reports to the Secretaries of Labor and the Treasury, see section 3004.

Amendments

P.L. 108-357, § 709(a)(1):

Act. Sec. 709(a)(1) amended ERISA Sec. 101(e)(3) by striking "Pension Funding Equity Act of 2004" and inserting "American Jobs Creation Act of 2004."

P.L. 108-218, § 204(b):

Act. Sec. 204(b) amended ERISA Sec. 101(e)(3) by replacing "Tax Relief Extension Act of 1999" with "Pension Funding Equity Act of 2004."

P.L. 108-218, § 103(a):

Act Sec. 103(a) amended ERISA Sec. 101 by inserting after subsection (e), subsection (f) to read as above. The amendment applies to plan years beginning after December 31, 2004.

Act Sec. 103 provides:

(c) Regulations and Model Notice.—The Secretary of Labor shall, not later than 1 year after the date of the enactment of this Act, issue regulations (including a model notice) necessary to implement the amendments made by this section.

P.L. 107-204, § 306(b)(1):

Act. Sec. 306(b)(1) amended ERISA Sec. 101 by redesignating the second subsection (h) as subsection (j) and inserting after the first subsection (h), subsection (i) to read as above.

P.L. 107-204, § 306(c):

Act. Sec. 306(c) EFFECTIVE DATE-T he provisions of this section (including the amendments made thereby) shall take effect 180 days after the date of the enactment of this Act. Good faith compliance with the requirements of such provisions in advance of the issuance of applicable regulations thereunder shall be treated as compliance with such provisions.

P.L. 106-170, § 535(a)(2)(A):

Act. Sec. 535(a)(2)(A) amended ERISA Sec. 101(e)(3) by striking "January 1, 1995" and inserting "the date of the enactment of the Tax Relief Extension Act of 1999".

The above amendment applies to qualified transfers occurring after December 17, 1999.

P.L. 105-200, § 402(h)(1):

Repealed ERISA Sec. 101(f). Prior to repeal, ERISA Sec. 101(f) read as follows:

Act. Sec. 101. (f) INFORMATION NECESSARY TO COMPLY WITH MEDICARE AND MEDICAID COVERAGE DATA BANK REQUIREMENTS.—

(1) PROVISION OF INFORMATION BY GROUP HEALTH PLAN UPON REQUEST OF EMPLOYER.—

(A) IN GENERAL.—An employer shall comply with the applicable requirements of section 1144 of the Social Security Act (as added by section 13581 of the Omnibus Budget Reconciliation Act of 1993). Upon the request of an employer maintaining a group health plan, any plan sponsor, plan administrator, insurer, third-party administra-

tor, or other person who maintains under the plan the information necessary to enable the employer to comply with the applicable requirements of section 1144 of the Social Security Act shall, in such form and manner as may be prescribed in regulations of the Secretary (in consultation with the Secretary of Health and Human Services), provide such information (not inconsistent with paragraph (2))—

(i) in the case of a request by an employer described in subparagraph (B) and a plan that is not a multiemployer plan or a component of an arrangement described in subparagraph (C), to the Medicare and Medicaid Coverage Data Bank;

(ii) in the case of a plan that is a multiemployer plan or is a component of an arrangement described in subparagraph (C), to the employer or to such Data Bank, at the option of the plan; and

(iii) in any other case, to the employer or to such Data Bank, at the option of the employer.

(B) EMPLOYER DESCRIBED.—An employer is described in this subparagraph for any calendar year if such employer normally employed fewer than 50 employees on a typical business day during such calendar year.

(C) ARRANGEMENT DESCRIBED.—An arrangement described in this subparagraph is any arrangement in which two or more employers contribute for the purpose of providing group health plan coverage for employees.

(2) INFORMATION NOT REQUIRED TO BE PROVIDED.—Any plan sponsor, plan administrator, insurer, third-party administrator, or other person described in paragraph (1)(A) (other than the employer) that maintains the information under the plan shall not provide to an employer in order to satisfy the requirements of section 1144 of the Social Security Act, and shall not provide to the Data Bank under such section, information that pertains in any way to—

(A) the health status of a participant, or of the participant's spouse, dependent child, or other beneficiary,

(B) the cost of coverage provided to any participant or beneficiary, or

(C) any limitations on such coverage specific to any participant or beneficiary.

(3) REGULATIONS.—The Secretary may, in consultation with the Secretary of Health and Human Service, prescribe such regulations as are necessary to carry out this subsection.

The above repeal is effective as if included in P.L. 104-226 (October 2, 1996).

P.L. 105-34, § 1503(a):

Amended ERISA Sec. 101(b) by striking paragraphs (1), (2), and three and redesignating paragraphs (4) and (5) as (1) and (2), respectively. Prior to amendment, the three paragraphs read as follows:

(1) the summary plan description described in section 102(a)(1);

(2) a plan description containing the matter required in section 102(b);

(3) modifications and changes referred to in section 102(a)(2).

The above amendment is effective August 5, 1997.

P.L. 104-188, § 1421(d)(1):

Amended ERISA Sec. 101 by redesignating subsection (g) as subsection (h) and by inserting after subsection (f) the new subsection (g) to read as above.

The above amendments apply to tax years beginning after December 31, 1996.

P.L. 104-191, § 101(e)(1):

Amended ERISA Sec. 101 by redesignating subsection (g) as subsection (h) and by inserting after subsection (f) the new subsection (g) to read as above.

The above amendments generally apply with respect to group health plans for plan years beginning after June 30, 1997. For special rules, see Act Sec. 101(g)(2)- (5), reproduced below.

Act Sec. 101(g)(2)-(5) reads as follows:

(g) EFFECTIVE DATES.—

(1) IN GENERAL.—Except as provided in this section, this section (and the amendments made by this section) shall apply with respect to group health plans for plan years beginning after June 30, 1997.

(2) DETERMINATION OF CREDITABLE COVERAGE.—

(A) PERIOD OF COVERAGE.—

(i) IN GENERAL.—Subject to clause (ii), no period before July 1, 1996, shall be taken into account under part 7 of subtitle B of title I of the Employee Retirement Income Security Act of 1974 (as added by this section) in determining creditable coverage.

(ii) SPECIAL RULE FOR CERTAIN PERIODS.—The Secretary of Labor, consistent with section 104, shall provide for a process whereby individuals who need to establish creditable coverage for periods before July 1, 1996, and who would have such coverage credited but for clause (i) may be given credit for creditable coverage for such periods through the presentation of documents or other means.

(B) CERTIFICATIONS, ETC.—

(i) IN GENERAL.—Subject to clauses (ii) and (iii), subsection (e) of section 701 of the Employee Retirement Income Security Act of 1974 (as added by this section) shall apply to events occurring after June 30, 1996.

(ii) NO CERTIFICATION REQUIRED TO BE PROVIDED BEFORE JUNE 1, 1997.—In no case is a certification required to be provided under such subsection before June 1, 1997.

(iii) CERTIFICATION ONLY ON WRITTEN REQUEST FOR EVENTS OCCURRING BEFORE OCTOBER 1, 1996.—In the case of an event occurring after June 30, 1996, and before October 1, 1996, a certification is not required to be provided under such subsection unless an individual (with respect to whom the certification is otherwise required to be made) requests such certification in writing.

(C) TRANSITIONAL RULE.—In the case of an individual who seeks to establish creditable coverage for any period for which certification is not required because it relates to an event occurring before June 30, 1996—

(i) the individual may present other credible evidence of such coverage in order to establish the period of creditable coverage; and

(ii) a group health plan and a health insurance issuer shall not be subject to any penalty or enforcement action with respect to the plan's or issuer's crediting (or not crediting) such coverage if the plan or issuer has sought to comply in good faith with the applicable requirements under the amendments made by this section.

(3) SPECIAL RULE FOR COLLECTIVE BARGAINING AGREEMENTS.—Except as provided in paragraph (2), in the case of a group health plan maintained pursuant to one or more collective bargaining agreements between employee representatives and one or more employers ratified before the date of the enactment of this Act, part 7 of subtitle B of title I of Employee Retirement Income Security Act of 1974 (other than section 701(e) thereof) shall not apply to plan years beginning before the later of—

(A) the date on which the last of the collective bargaining agreements relating to the plan terminates (determined without regard to any extension thereof agreed to after the date of the enactment of this Act), or

(B) July 1, 1997.

For purposes of subparagraph (A), any plan amendment made pursuant to a collective bargaining agreement relating to the plan which amends the plan solely to conform to any requirement of such part shall not be treated as a termination of such collective bargaining agreement.

(4) TIMELY REGULATIONS.—The Secretary of Labor, consistent with section 104, shall first issue by not later than April 1, 1997, such regulations as may be necessary to carry out the amendments made by this section.

(5) LIMITATION ON ACTIONS.—No enforcement action shall be taken, pursuant to the amendments made by this section, against a group health plan or health insurance issuer with respect to a violation of a requirement imposed by such amendments before January 1, 1998, or, if later, the date of issuance of regulations referred to in paragraph (4), if the plan or issuer has sought to comply in good faith with such requirements.

P.L. 103-66, § 4301(b)(1):

Amended ERISA Sec. 101 by redesignating subsection (f) as subsection (g) and by inserting after subsection (e) the new subsection (f) to read as above.

The above amendments are effective on August 10, 1993. Any plan amendment required to be made by Act Sec. 4301 need not be made before the first plan year beginning on or after January 1, 1994 if: (1) the plan is operated in accordance with Act Sec. 4301 during the period after August 9, 1993 and before such first plan year; and (2) the amendment applies retroactively to this period. A plan will not be treated as failing to be operated in accordance with plan provisions merely because it operates in accordance with the effective date requirements.

P.L. 101-508, Sec. 12012(d)(1):

Amended ERISA Sec. 101 by redesignating subsection (e) as subsection (f) and adding new subsection (e) to read as above effective for qualified transfers under Code Sec. 420 made after November 5, 1990.

P.L. 101-239, § 7881(b)(5)(A):

Amended ERISA Sec. 101(d)(1) by striking "an employer of a plan" and inserting "an employer maintaining a plan" effective for plan years beginning after December 31, 1987.

P.L. 101-239, § 7881(b)(5)(C):

Amended P.L. 100-203, § 9304(d) by striking "Section" and inserting "Effective with respect to plan years beginning after December 31, 1987, section" effective for plan years beginning after December 31, 1987.

P.L. 101-239, § 7894(b)(1):

Amended the heading for part 1 of subtitle B of title I of ERISA by striking "Part I" and inserting "Part 1" effective September 2, 1974.

P.L. 101-239, § 7894(b)(2):

Amended ERISA Sec. 101(a)(2) by striking "section" and inserting "sections" effective September 2, 1974.

P.L. 100-203, § 9304(d):

Amended ERISA Sec. 101 by redesignating subsection (d) as (e) and adding new subsection (d) to read as above, effective for plan years beginning after December 31, 1987.

Regulations

Reg. § 2520.101-1 (¶ 14,211) was published in the *Federal Register* on April 23, 1976 (41 FR 16957). Interim Reg. § 2520.101-2 (¶ 14,212) was published in the *Federal Register* on February 11, 2000 (65 FR 7152), and was effective April 11, 2000. Final Reg. § 2520.101-2 (¶ 14,212A) was published in the *Federal Register* on April 9, 2003 (68 FR 17493), and is effective January 1, 2004. Interim Reg. § 2520.101-3 was published in the *Federal Register* on October 21, 2002 (67 FR 64765) and was effective January 26, 2003. Reg. § 2520.101-3 was revised and finalized on January 24, 2003 (68 FR 3715).

Subpart A—General Reporting and Disclosure Requirements

[¶ 14,211]

§ 2520.101-1 **Duty of reporting and disclosure**. The procedures for implementing the plan administrator's duty of reporting to the Secretary of Labor and disclosing information to participants and beneficiaries are located in Subparts D, E, and F of this part [see Finding Lists in Volume 1—CCH].

[¶ 14,212]

§ 2520.101-2 **Annual reporting by multiple employer welfare arrangements and certain other entities offering or providing coverage for medical care to the employees of two or more employers.**

(a) *Basis and scope.* Section 101(g){h}[1] of the Act permits the Secretary of Labor to require, by regulation, multiple employer welfare arrangements (MEWAs) providing benefits that consist of medical care

(within the meaning of section 733(a)(2) of the Act), and that are not group health plans, to report, not more frequently than annually, in such form and manner as the Secretary may require, for the purpose of determining the extent to which the requirements of part 7 of the Act are being carried out in connection with such benefits. Section 734 of the Act provides that the Secretary may promulgate such regulations as may be necessary or appropriate to carry out the provisions of part 7 of the Act. This section sets out requirements for annual reporting by MEWAs that provide benefits that consist of medical care and by certain entities that claim not to be a MEWA solely due to the exception in section 3(40)(A)(i) of the Act (Entities Claiming Exception or ECEs). These requirements apply regardless of whether the MEWA or ECE is a group health plan.

(b) *Definitions.* As used in this section, the following definitions apply:

Administrator means—

---

[1] Section 1421(d)(1) of the Small Business Job Protection Act of 1996 (Pub. L. 104-188) created a new section 101(g) of ERISA relating to Simple Retirement Accounts. Subsequently, section 101(e)(1) of HIPAA also created a new section 101(g) of ERISA relating to MEWA reporting. Accordingly, when referring to section 101(g) of ERISA relating to MEWA reporting, this document cites section 101(g){h} of ERISA.

(1) The person specifically so designated by the terms of the instrument under which the MEWA or ECE is operated;

(2) If the MEWA or ECE is a group health plan and the administrator is not so designated, the plan sponsor (as defined in section 3(16)(B) of the Act); or

(3) In the case of a MEWA or ECE for which an administrator is not designated and a plan sponsor cannot be identified, the person or persons actually responsible (whether or not so designated under the terms of the instrument under which the MEWA or ECE is operated) for the control, disposition, or management of the cash or property received by or contributed to the MEWA or ECE, irrespective of whether such control, disposition, or management is exercised directly by such person or persons or indirectly through an agent, custodian, or trustee designated by such person or persons.

Entity Claiming Exception (ECE) means an entity that claims it is not a MEWA due to the exception in section 3(40)(A)(i) of the Act. (In general, this exception is for entities that are established and maintained under or pursuant to one or more agreements that the Secretary finds to be collective bargaining agreements).

Group health plan means a *group health plan* within the meaning of section 733(a) of the Act and § 2590.701-2.

Health insurance issuer means a *health insurance issuer* within the meaning of section 733(b)(2) of the Act and § 2590.701-2.

Medical care means *medical care* within the meaning of section 733(a)(2) of the Act and § 2590.701-2.

Multiple employer welfare arrangement (MEWA) means a multiple employer welfare arrangement within the meaning of section 3(40) of the Act.

Origination means the occurrence of any of the following three events (and a MEWA or ECE is considered to have been *originated* when any of the following three events occurs)—

(1) The MEWA or ECE first begins offering or providing coverage for medical care to the employees of two or more employers (including one or more self-employed individuals);

(2) The MEWA or ECE begins offering or providing coverage for medical care to the employees of two or more employers (including one or more self-employed individuals) after a merger with another MEWA or ECE (unless all of the MEWAs or ECEs that participate in the merger previously were last originated at least three years prior to the merger); or

(3) The number of employees receiving coverage for medical care under the MEWA or ECE is at least 50 percent greater than the number of such employees on the last day of the previous calendar year (unless the increase is due to a merger with another MEWA or ECE under which all MEWAs and ECEs that participate in the merger were last originated at least three years prior to the merger).

(c) *Persons required to report.* (1) *General rule.* Except as provided in paragraph (c)(2) of this section, the following persons are required to report under this section—

(i) The administrator of a MEWA that offers or provides benefits consisting of medical care, regardless of whether the entity is a group health plan; and

(ii) The administrator of an ECE that offers or provides benefits consisting of medical care during the first three years after the ECE is originated.

(2) *Exception.* Nothing in this paragraph (c) shall be construed to require reporting under this section by the administrator of a MEWA or ECE if the MEWA or ECE is licensed or authorized to operate as a health insurance issuer in every State in which it offers or provides coverage for medical care to employees.

(3) *Construction.* For purposes of this section, the following rules of construction apply—

(i) Whether or not an entity is a MEWA or ECE is determined by the administrator acting in good faith. Therefore, if an administrator makes a good faith determination at the time when a filing under this section would otherwise be required that the entity is maintained pursuant to one or more collective bargaining agreements, the entity is an ECE, and the administrator of the ECE is not required

to file if its most recent origination was more than three years. Even if the entity is later determined to be a MEWA, filings are not required prior to the determination that the entity is a MEWA if at the time the filings were otherwise due, the administrator made a good faith determination that the entity was an ECE. However, filings are required for years after the determination that the entity is a MEWA.

(ii) In contrast, while an administrator's good faith determination that an entity is an ECE may eliminate the requirement that the administrator of the entity file under this section for more than three years after the entity's origination date, the administrator's determination, nonetheless, does not affect the applicability of State law to the entity. Accordingly, incorrectly claiming the exception may eliminate the need to file under this section, if the claiming of the exception is done in good faith. However, the claiming of the exception for ECEs under this filing requirement does not prevent the application of State law to an entity that is later determined to be a MEWA. This is because the filing, or the failure to file, under this section does not in any way affect the application of State law to a MEWA.

(d) *Information to be reported.* (1) The annual report required by this section shall consist of a completed copy of the Form M-1 "Annual Report for Multiple Employer Welfare Arrangements (MEWAs) and Certain Entities Claiming Exception (ECEs)" (Form M-1) and any additional statements required in the instructions to the Form M-1. This report is available by calling 1-800-998-7542 and on the Internet at http://www.dol.gov/dol/pwba.

(2) The Secretary may reject any filing under this section if the Secretary determines that the filing is incomplete, in accordance with § 2560.502c-5.

(3) If the Secretary rejects a filing under paragraph (d)(2) of this section, and if a revised filing satisfactory to the Secretary is not submitted within 45 days after the notice of rejection, the Secretary may bring a civil action for such relief as may be appropriate (including penalties under section 502(c)(5) of the Act and § 2560.502c-5).

(e) *Timing.* (1) *Period to be Reported.* A completed copy of the Form M-1 is required to be filed for each calendar year during all or part of which the MEWA or ECE offers or provides coverage for medical care to the employees of two or more employers (including one or more self-employed individuals).

(2) *Filing deadline.* (i) *General March 1 filing due date.* Subject to the transition rule described in paragraph (e)(2)(ii) of this section, a completed copy of the Form M-1 is required to be filed on or before each March 1 that follows a period to be reported (as described in paragraph (e)(1) of this section). However, if March 1 is a Saturday, Sunday, or federal holiday, the form must be filed no later than the next business day.

(ii) *Transition rule for Year 2000 filings.* For the year 1999 period to be reported, a completed copy of the Form M-1 is required to be filed no later than May 1, 2000.

(iii) *Special rule requiring a 90-Day Origination Report when a MEWA or ECE is originated.* (A) *In general.* Subject to paragraph (e)(2)(ii)(B) of this section, when a MEWA or ECE is originated, the administrator of the MEWA or ECE is also required to file a completed copy of the Form M-1 within 90 days of the origination date (unless 90 days after the origination date is a Saturday, Sunday, or federal holiday, in which case the form must be filed no later than the next business day).

(B) *Exceptions.* (1) Paragraph (d)(2)(ii)(A) of this section does not apply if the origination occurred between October 1 and December 31.

(2) Paragraph (d)(2)(ii)(A) of this section does not apply before May 1, 2000. Therefore, for an entity that is originated, for example, on January 1, 2000, no 90-day origination report is required. Nonetheless, for an entity originated, for example, on April 1, 2000, a 90-day origination report is required to be completed and filed no later than June 30, 2000.

(iv) *Extensions.* An extension may be granted for filing a report if the administrator complies with the extension procedure prescribed in the Instructions to the Form M-1.

(f) *Filing address.* A completed copy of the Form M-1 is filed with the Secretary by sending it to the address prescribed in the Instructions to the Form M-1.

(g) *Civil penalties and procedures.* For information on civil penalties under section 502(c)(5) of the Act for persons who fail to file the information required under this section (including a transition rule applicable to filings due in the year 2000), see § 2560.502c-5. For information relating to administrative hearings and appeals in connection with the assessment of civil penalties under section 502(c)(5) of the Act, see § 2570.90 *et seq.*

(h) *Examples.* The rules of this section are illustrated by the following examples:

Example 1. (i) MEWA *A* began offering coverage for medical care to the employees of two or more employers July 1, 1989 (and continuous to offer such coverage). MEWA *A* does not claim the exception under section 3(40)(A)(i) of ERISA.

(ii) In this *Example 1,* the administrator of MEWA *A* must file a completed copy of the Form M-1 by May 1, 2000. Furthermore, the administrator of MEWA *A* must file the Form M-1 annually by every March 1 thereafter.

Example 2. (i) ECE *B* began offering coverage for medical care to the employees of two or more employers on January 1, 1992. ECE *B* has not been involved in any mergers and in 1999 the number of employees to which ECE *B* provides coverage for medical care is not at least 50 percent greater than the number of such employees on December 31, 1998.

(ii) In this *Example 2,* ECE *B* was originated was on January 1, 1992 has not been originated since then. Therefore, the administrator of ECE *B* is not required to file a Form M-1 on May 1, 2000 because the last time the ECE *B* was originated was January 1, 1992 which more than 3 years prior to May 1, 2000.

Example 3. (i) ECE *C* began offering coverage for medical care to the employees of two or more employers on July 1, 1998.

(ii) In this *Example 3,* the administrator of ECE *C* must file a completed copy of the Form M-1 by May 1, 2000 because the last date *A* was originated was July 1, 1998, which is less than 3 years prior to the May 1, 2000 due date. Furthermore, the administrator of ECE *C* must file a year 2000 annual report by March 1, 2001 (because July 1, 1998 is less than three years prior to March 1, 2001). However, if ECE *C* is not involved in any mergers that would result in a new origination date and if ECE *C* does not experience a growth of 50 percent or more in the number of employees to which ECE *C* provides coverage from the last day of the previous calendar year to any day in the current calendar year, then no Form M-1 report is required to be filed after March 1, 2001.

Example 4. (i) MEWA *D* begins offering coverage to the employees of two or more employers on January 1, 2000. MEWA *D* is licensed or authorized to operate as a health insurance issuer in every State in which it offers coverage for medical care to employees.

(ii) In this *Example 4,* the administrator of MEWA *D* is not required to file Form M-1 on May 1, 2000 because it is licensed or authorized to operate as a health insurance issuer in every State in which it offers coverage for medical care to employees.

Example 5. (i) MEWA *E* is originated on September 1, 2000.

(ii) In this *Example 5,* because MEWA *E* was originated on September 1, 2000, the administrator of MEWA *E* must file a completed copy of the Form M-1 on or before November 30, 2000 (which is 90 days after the origination date). In addition, the administrator of MEWA *E* must file a completed copy of the Form M-1 annually by every March 1 thereafter.

(i) *Compliance dates.* (1) Subject to paragraph (i)(2) of this section, reports filed pursuant to this reporting requirement are first due by May 1, 2000. (Therefore, on May 1, 2000, filings are due with respect to MEWAs or ECEs that provided coverage in calendar year 1999.)

(2) 90-Day Origination Reports (described in paragraph (e)(2)(ii) of this section) are first due by May 1, 2000. Therefore, for an entity that is originated, for example, on January 1, 2000, no 90-day origination report is required. Nonetheless, for an entity originated, for

example, on April 1, 2000, a 90-day origination report is required to be completed and filed no later than June 30, 2000. [Added February 11, 2000, by 65 FR 7152.]

⨠⨠⨠→ **Caution: Final Reg. § 2520.101-2 effective date: January 1, 2004.**

[¶ 14,212A]

§ 2520.101-2 **Annual Reporting by Multiple Employer Welfare Arrangements and Certain Other Entities Offering or Providing Coverage for Medical Care to the Employees of Two or More Employers.**

(a) *Basis and scope.* Section 101(g) of the Employee Retirement Income Security Act (ERISA) permits the Secretary of Labor to require, by regulation, multiple employer welfare arrangements (MEWAs) providing benefits that consist of medical care (within the meaning of section 733(a)(2) of ERISA), and that are not group health plans, to report, not more frequently than annually, in such form and manner as the Secretary may require, for the purpose of determining the extent to which the requirements of part 7 of subtitle B of title I of ERISA (part 7) are being carried out in connection with such benefits. Section 734 of ERISA provides that the Secretary may promulgate such regulations as may be necessary or appropriate to carry out the provisions of part 7. This section sets out requirements for annual reporting by MEWAs that provide benefits that consist of medical care and by certain entities that claim not to be a MEWA solely due to the exception in section 3(40)(A)(i) of ERISA (referred to in this section as Entities Claiming Exception or ECEs). These requirements apply regardless of whether the MEWA or ECE is a group health plan.

(b) *Definitions.* As used in this section, the following definitions apply:

Administrator means—

(1) The person specifically so designated by the terms of the instrument under which the MEWA or ECE is operated;

(2) If the MEWA or ECE is a group health plan and the administrator is not so designated, the plan sponsor (as defined in section 3(16)(B) of ERISA); or

(3) In the case of a MEWA or ECE for which an administrator is not designated and a plan sponsor cannot be identified, jointly and severally the person or persons actually responsible (whether or not so designated under the terms of the instrument under which the MEWA or ECE is operated) for the control, disposition, or management of the cash or property received by or contributed to the MEWA or ECE, irrespective of whether such control, disposition, or management is exercised directly by such person or persons or indirectly through an agent, custodian, or trustee designated by such person or persons.

Entity Claiming Exception (ECE) means an entity that claims it is not a MEWA on the basis that the entity is established or maintained pursuant to one or more agreements that the Secretary finds to be collective bargaining agreements within the meaning of section 3(40)(A)(i) of ERISA and 29 CFR 2510.3-40.

Excepted benefits means excepted benefits within the meaning of section 733(c) of ERISA and 29 CFR 2590.732(b).

Group health plan means a group health plan within the meaning of section 733(a) of ERISA and 29 CFR 2590.701-2.

Health insurance issuer means a health insurance issuer within the meaning of section 733(b)(2) of ERISA and 29 CFR 2590.701-2.

Medical care means medical care within the meaning of section 733(a)(2) of ERISA and 29 CFR 2590.701-2.

Multiple employer welfare arrangement (MEWA) means a multiple employer welfare arrangement within the meaning of section 3(40) of ERISA and 29 CFR 2510.3-40.

Origination means the occurrence of any of the following three events (and a MEWA or ECE is considered to have been originated when any of the following three events occurs)—

(1) The MEWA or ECE first begins offering or providing coverage for medical care to the employees of two or more employers (including one or more self-employed individuals);

(2) The MEWA or ECE begins offering or providing coverage for medical care to the employees of two or more employers (including

one or more self-employed individuals) after a merger with another MEWA or ECE (unless all of the MEWAs or ECEs that participate in the merger previously were last originated at least three years prior to the merger); or

(3) The number of employees receiving coverage for medical care under the MEWA or ECE is at least 50 percent greater than the number of such employees on the last day of the previous calendar year (unless the increase is due to a merger with another MEWA or ECE under which all MEWAs and ECEs that participate in the merger were last originated at least three years prior to the merger).

(c) *Persons required to report.* (1) *General rule.* Except as provided in paragraph (c)(2) of this section, the following persons are required to report under this section—

(i) The administrator of a MEWA that offers or provides benefits consisting of medical care, regardless of whether the entity is a group health plan; and

(ii) The administrator of an ECE that offers or provides benefits consisting of medical care during the first three years after the ECE is originated.

(2) *Exceptions.* (i) Nothing in this paragraph (c) shall be construed to require reporting under this section by the administrator of a MEWA or ECE if the MEWA or ECE—

(A) Is licensed or authorized to operate as a health insurance issuer in every state in which it offers or provides coverage for medical care to employees;

(B) Provides coverage that consists solely of excepted benefits, which are not subject to Part 7. If the MEWA or ECE provides coverage that consists of both excepted benefits and other benefits for medical care that are not excepted benefits, the administrator of the MEWA or ECE is required to report under this section;

(C) Is a group health plan that is not subject to ERISA, including a governmental plan, church plan, or a plan maintained solely for the purpose of complying with workmen's compensation laws, within the meaning of sections (4)(b)(1), 4(b)(2), or 4(b)(3) of ERISA, respectively; or

(D) Provides coverage only through group health plans that are not covered by ERISA, including governmental plans, church plans, or plans maintained solely for the purpose of complying with workmen's compensation laws within the meaning of sections 4(b)(1), 4(b)(2), or 4(b)(3) of ERISA, respectively (or other arrangements not covered by ERISA, such as health insurance coverage offered to individuals other than in connection with a group health plan, known as individual market coverage);

(ii) Nothing in this paragraph (c) shall be construed to require reporting under this section by the administrator of an entity that would not constitute a MEWA or ECE but for the following circumstances:

(A) The entity provides coverage to the employees of two or more trades or businesses that share a common control interest of at least 25 percent at any time during the plan year, applying the principles of section 414(b) or (c) of the Internal Revenue Code (26 U.S.C.);

(B) The entity provides coverage to the employees of two or more employers due to a change in control of businesses (such as a merger or acquisition) that occurs for a purpose other than avoiding Form M-1 filing and is temporary in nature. For purposes of this paragraph, "temporary" means the MEWA or ECE does not extend beyond the end of the plan year following the plan year in which the change in control occurs; or

(C) The entity provides coverage to persons (excluding spouses and dependents) who are not employees or former employees of the plan sponsor, such as non-employee members of the board of directors or independent contractors, and the number of such persons who are not employees or former employees does not exceed one percent of the total number of employees or former employees covered under the arrangement, determined as of the last day of the year to be reported or, in the case of a 90-day origination report, determined as of the 60th day following the origination date.

(d) *Information to be reported.* (1) The annual report required by this section shall consist of a completed copy of the Form M-1 Annual Report for Multiple Employer Welfare Arrangements (MEWAs) and Certain Entities Claiming Exception (ECEs) and any additional statements required in the Instructions to the Form M-1.

(2) The Secretary may reject any filing under this section if the Secretary determines that the filing is incomplete, in accordance with 29 CFR 2560.502c-5.

(3) If the Secretary rejects a filing under paragraph (d)(2) of this section, and if a revised filing satisfactory to the Secretary is not submitted within 45 days after the notice of rejection, the Secretary may bring a civil action for such relief as may be appropriate (including penalties under section 502(c)(5) of ERISA and 29 CFR 2560.502c-5).

(e) *Reporting requirement and timing.* (1) Period for which report is required. A completed copy of the Form M-1 is required to be filed for each calendar year during all or part of which the MEWA or ECE offers or provides coverage for medical care to the employees of two or more employers (including one or more self-employed individuals).

(2) *Filing deadline.* (i) *General.* March 1 filing due date for annual filings. A completed copy of the Form M-1 is required to be filed on or before each March 1 that follows a period to be reported (as described in paragraph (e)(1) of this section). However, if March 1 is a Saturday, Sunday, or federal holiday, the form must be filed no later than the next business day.

(ii) Special rule requiring a 90-Day Origination Report when a MEWA or ECE is originated. (A) In general. Subject to paragraph (e)(2)(ii)(B) of this section, when a MEWA or ECE is originated, the administrator of the MEWA or ECE is also required to file a completed copy of the Form M-1 within 90 days of the origination date (unless 90 days after the origination date is a Saturday, Sunday, or federal holiday, in which case the form must be filed no later than the next business day).

(B) *Exception.* Paragraph (e)(2)(ii)(A) of this section does not apply if the origination occurred between October 1 and December 31. (Thus, no 90-day origination report is due when an entity is originated between October 1 and December 31. However, the March 1 filing deadline of paragraph (e)(2)(i) of this section continues to apply.)

(iii) *Extensions.* An extension may be granted for filing a report if the administrator complies with the extension procedure prescribed in the Instructions to the Form M-1.

(f) *Filing address.* A completed copy of the Form M-1 is filed with the Secretary by sending it to the address prescribed in the Instructions to the Form M-1.

(g) *Civil penalties and procedures.* For information on civil penalties under section 502(c)(5) of ERISA for persons who fail to file the information required under this section, see 29 CFR 2560.502c-5. For information relating to administrative hearings and appeals in connection with the assessment of civil penalties under section 502(c)(5) of ERISA, see 29 CFR 2570.90 through 2570.101.

(h) *Examples.* The rules of this section are illustrated by the following examples:

Example 1. (i) *Facts.* MEWA A began offering coverage for medical care to the employees of two or more employers July 1, 1989 (and continues to offer such coverage). MEWA A does not claim the exception under section 3(40)(A)(i) of ERISA.

(ii) *Conclusion.* In this Example 1, the administrator of MEWA A must file a completed copy of the Form M-1 each year by March 1.

Example 2. (i) *Facts.* ECE B began offering coverage for medical care to the employees of two or more employers on January 1, 1992. ECE B has not been involved in any mergers and the number of employees to which ECE B provides coverage for medical care has not grown by more than 50 percent in any given year.

(ii) *Conclusion.* In this Example 2, ECE B was originated on January 1, 1992 and has not been originated since then. Therefore, the administrator of ECE B is not required to file a 2003 Form M-1 on March 1, 2004 because the last time the ECE B was originated was January 1, 1992 which is more than 3 years prior to March 1, 2004.

Example 3. (i) *Facts.* ECE C began offering coverage for medical care to the employees of two or more employers on July 1, 2004.

(ii) *Conclusion.* In this Example 3, the administrator of ECE C must file a completed copy of the 2004 Form M-1 on or before September 29, 2004 (which is 90 days after the origination date). In addition, the administrator of ECE C must file an updated copy of the 2004 Form M-1 by March 1, 2005 because the last date C was originated was July 1, 2004, which is less than 3 years prior to the March 1, 2005 due date. Furthermore, the administrator of ECE C must file a 2005 Form M-1 by March 1, 2006 and a 2006 Form M-1 by March 1, 2007 (because July 1, 2004 is less than three years prior to March 1, 2006 and March 1, 2007, respectively). However, if ECE C is not involved in any mergers that would result in a new origination date and if ECE C does not experience a growth of 50 percent or more in the number of employees to which ECE C provides coverage from the last day of the previous calendar year to any day in the current calendar year, then no Form M-1 report is required to be filed after March 1, 2007.

Example 4. (i) *Facts.* MEWA D begins offering coverage to the employees of two or more employers on January 1, 2000. MEWA D is licensed or authorized to operate as a health insurance issuer in every state in which it offers coverage for medical care to employees.

(ii) *Conclusion.* In this Example 4, the administrator of MEWA D is not required to file Form M-1 because it is licensed or authorized to operate as a health insurance issuer in every state in which it offers coverage for medical care to employees.

Example 5. (i) *Facts.* MEWA E is originated on September 1, 2004.

(ii) *Conclusion.* In this Example 5, because MEWA E was originated on September 1, 2004, the administrator of MEWA E must file a completed copy of the Form M-1 on or before November 30, 2004 (which is 90 days after the origination date). In addition, the administrator of MEWA E must file a completed copy of the Form M-1 annually by every March 1 thereafter.

Example 6. (i) *Facts.* Company F maintains a group health plan that provides benefits for medical care for its employees (and their dependents). Company F establishes a joint venture in which it has a 25 percent stock ownership interest, determined by applying the principles under section 414(b) of the Internal Revenue Code, and transfers some of its employees to the joint venture. Company F continues to cover these transferred employees under its group health plan.

(ii) *Conclusion.* In this Example 6, the administrator is not required to file the Form M-1 because Company F's group health plan meets the exception to the filing requirement in paragraph (c)(2)(ii)(A) of this section. This is because Company F's group health plan would not constitute a MEWA but for the fact that it provides coverage to two or more trades or businesses that share a common control interest of at least 25 percent.

Example 7. (i) *Facts.* Company G maintains a group health plan that provides benefits for medical care for its employees. The plan year of Company G's group health plan is the fiscal year for Company G, which is October 1st—September 30th. Therefore, October 1, 2004— September 30, 2005 is the 2005 plan year. Company G decides to sell a portion of its business, Division X, to Company H. Company G signs an agreement with Company H under which Division X will be transferred to Company H, effective September 30, 2005. The change in control of Division X therefore occurs on September 30, 2005. Under the terms of the agreement, Company G agrees to continue covering all of the employees that formerly worked for Division X under its group health plan until Company H has established a new group health plan to cover these employees. Under the terms of the agreement, it is anticipated that Company G will not be required to cover the employees of Division X under its group health plan beyond the end of the 2006 plan year, which is the plan year following the plan year in which the change in control of Division X occurs.

(ii) *Conclusion.* In this Example 7, the administrator of Company G's group health plan is not required to file the Form M-1 on March 1, 2006 for fiscal year 2005 because it is subject to the exception to the filing requirement in paragraph (c)(2)(ii)(B) of this section for an entity that would not constitute a MEWA but for the fact that it is created by a change in control of businesses that occurs for a purpose other than to avoid filing the Form M-1 and is temporary in nature. Under the exception, "temporary" means the MEWA does not extend

beyond the end of the plan year following the plan year in which the change in control occurs. The administrator is not required to file the 2005 Form M-1 because it is anticipated that Company G will not be required to cover the employees of Division X under its group health plan beyond the end of the 2006 plan year, which is the plan year following the plan year in which the change in control of businesses occurred.

Example 8. (i) *Facts.* Company I maintains a group health plan that provides benefits for medical care for its employees (and their dependents) as well as certain independent contractors who are self-employed individuals. The plan is therefore a MEWA. The administrator of Company I's group health plan uses calendar year data to report for purposes of the Form M-1. The administrator of Company I's group health plan determines that the number of independent contractors covered under the group health plan as of the last day of calendar year 2004 is less than one percent of the total number of employees and former employees covered under the plan determined as of the last day of calendar year 2004.

(ii) *Conclusion.* In this Example 8, the administrator of Company I's group health plan is not required to file a Form M-1 for calendar year 2004 (which is otherwise due by March 1, 2005) because it is subject to the exception to the filing requirement provided in paragraph (c)(2)(ii)(C) of this section for entities that cover a very small number of persons who are not employees or former employees of the plan sponsor.

[Added by EBSA on April 9, 2003 by 68 FR 17493.]

[¶ 14,213]

§2520.101-3 **Notice of blackout periods under individual account plans.**

(a) *In general.* In accordance with section 101(i) of the Act, the administrator of an individual account plan, within the meaning of paragraph (d)(2) of this section, shall provide notice of any blackout period, within the meaning of paragraph (d)(1) of this section, to all participants and beneficiaries whose rights under the plan will be temporarily suspended, limited, or restricted by the blackout period (the "affected participants and beneficiaries") and to issuers of employer securities subject to such blackout period in accordance with this section.

(b) *Notice to participants and beneficiaries.* (1) *Content.* The notice required by paragraph (a) of this section shall be written in a manner calculated to be understood by the average plan participant and shall include—

(i) The reasons for the blackout period;

(ii) A description of the rights otherwise available to participants and beneficiaries under the plan that will be temporarily suspended, limited or restricted by the blackout period (e.g., right to direct or diversify assets in individual accounts, right to obtain loans from the plan, right to obtain distributions from the plan), including identification of any investments subject to the blackout period;

(iii) The length of the blackout period by reference to:

(A) The expected beginning date and ending date of the blackout period; or

(B) The calendar week during which the blackout period is expected to begin and end, provided that during such weeks information as to whether the blackout period has begun or ended is readily available, without charge, to affected participants and beneficiaries, such as via a toll-free number or access to a specific web site, and the notice describes how to access the information;

(iv) In the case of investments affected, a statement that the participant or beneficiary should evaluate the appropriateness of their current investment decisions in light of their inability to direct or diversify assets in their accounts during the blackout period (a notice that includes the advisory statement contained in paragraph 4. of the model notice in paragraph (e)(2) of this section will satisfy this requirement);

(v) In any case in which the notice required by paragraph (a) of this section is not furnished at least 30 days in advance of the last date on which affected participants and beneficiaries could exercise affected rights immediately before the commencement of the blackout period, except for a notice furnished pursuant to paragraph (b)(2)(ii)(C) of this section:

(A) A statement that Federal law generally requires that notice be furnished to affected participants and beneficiaries at least 30 days in advance of the last date on which participants and beneficiaries could exercise the affected rights immediately before the commencement of a blackout period (a notice that includes the statement contained in paragraph 5. of the model notice in paragraph (e)(2) of this section will satisfy this requirement), and

(B) An explanation of the reasons why at least 30 days advance notice could not be furnished; and

(vi) The name, address and telephone number of the plan administrator or other contact responsible for answering questions about the blackout period.

(2) *Timing.* (i) The notice described in paragraph (a) of this section shall be furnished to all affected participants and beneficiaries at least 30 days, but not more than 60 days, in advance of the last date on which such participants and beneficiaries could exercise the affected rights immediately before the commencement of any blackout period.

(ii) The requirement to give at least 30 days advance notice contained in paragraph (b)(2)(i) of this section shall not apply in any case in which—

(A) A deferral of the blackout period in order to comply with paragraph (b)(2)(i) of this section would result in a violation of the requirements of section 404(a)(1)(A) or (B) of the Act, and a fiduciary of the plan reasonably so determines in writing;

(B) The inability to provide the advance notice of a blackout period is due to events that were unforeseeable or circumstances beyond the reasonable control of the plan administrator, and a fiduciary of the plan reasonably so determines in writing; or

(C) The blackout period applies only to one or more participants or beneficiaries solely in connection with their becoming, or ceasing to be, participants or beneficiaries of the plan as a result of a merger, acquisition, divestiture, or similar transaction involving the plan or plan sponsor.

(iii) In any case in which paragraph (b)(2)(ii) of this section applies, the administrator shall furnish the notice described in paragraph (a) of this section to all affected participants and beneficiaries as soon as reasonably possible under the circumstances, unless such notice in advance of the termination of the blackout period is impracticable.

(iv) Determinations under paragraph (b)(2)(ii)(A) and (B) of this section must be dated and signed by the fiduciary.

(3) *Form and manner of furnishing notice.* The notice required by paragraph (a) of this section shall be in writing and furnished to affected participants and beneficiaries in any manner consistent with the requirements of Sec. 2520.104b-1 of this chapter, including paragraph (c) of that section relating to the use of electronic media.

(4) *Changes in length of blackout period.* If, following the furnishing of a notice pursuant to this section, there is a change in the length of the blackout period (specified in such notice pursuant to paragraph (b)(1)(iii) of this section), the administrator shall furnish all affected participants and beneficiaries an updated notice explaining the reasons for the change and identifying all material changes in the information contained in the prior notice. Such notice shall be furnished to all affected participants and beneficiaries as soon as reasonably possible, unless such notice in advance of the termination of the blackout period is impracticable.

(c) *Notice to issuer of employer securities.* (1) The notice required by paragraph (a) of this section shall be furnished to the issuer of any employer securities held by the plan and subject to the blackout period. Such notice shall contain the information described in paragraph (b)(1)(i), (ii), (iii) and (vi) of this section and shall be furnished in accordance with the time frames prescribed in paragraph (b)(2) of this section. In the event of a change in the length of the blackout period specified in such notice, the plan administrator shall furnish an updated notice to the issuer in accordance with the requirements of paragraph (b)(4) of this section.

(2) For purposes of this section, notice to the agent for service of legal process for the issuer shall constitute notice to the issuer, unless the issuer has provided the plan administrator with the name of another person for service of notice, in which case the plan administrator shall furnish notice to such person. Such notice shall be in writing, except that the notice may be in electronic or other form to the extent the person to whom notice must be furnished consents to receive the notice in such form.

(3) If the issuer designates the plan administrator as the person for service of notice pursuant to paragraph (c)(2) of this section, the issuer shall be deemed to have been furnished notice on the same date as notice is furnished to affected participants and beneficiaries pursuant to paragraph (b) of this section.

(d) *Definitions.* For purposes of this section—

(1) *Blackout period*—

(i) *General.* The term "blackout period" means, in connection with an individual account plan, any period for which any ability of participants or beneficiaries under the plan, which is otherwise available under the terms of such plan, to direct or diversify assets credited to their accounts, to obtain loans from the plan, or to obtain distributions from the plan is temporarily suspended, limited, or restricted, if such suspension, limitation, or restriction is for any period of more than three consecutive business days.

(ii) *Exclusions.* The term "blackout period" does not include a suspension, limitation, or restriction—

(A) Which occurs by reason of the application of the securities laws (as defined in section 3(a)(47) of the Securities Exchange Act of 1934);

(B) Which is a regularly scheduled suspension, limitation, or restriction under the plan (or change thereto), provided that such suspension, limitation or restriction (or change) has been disclosed to affected plan participants and beneficiaries through the summary plan description, a summary of material modifications, materials describing specific investment alternatives under the plan and limits thereon or any changes thereto, participation or enrollment forms, or any other documents and instruments pursuant to which the plan is established or operated that have been furnished to such participants and beneficiaries;

(C) Which occurs by reason of a qualified domestic relations order or by reason of a pending determination (by the plan administrator, by a court of competent jurisdiction or otherwise) whether a domestic relations order filed (or reasonably anticipated to be filed) with the plan is a qualified order within the meaning of section 206(d)(3)(B)(i) of the Act; or

(D) Which occurs by reason of an act or a failure to act on the part of an individual participant or by reason of an action or claim by a party unrelated to the plan involving the account of an individual participant.

(2) *Individual account plan.* The term "individual account plan" shall have the meaning provided such term in section 3(34) of the Act, except that such term shall not include a "one-participant retirement plan" within the meaning of paragraph (d)(3) of this section.

(3) *One-participant retirement plan.* The term "one-participant retirement plan" means a one-participant retirement plan as defined in section 101(i)(8)(B) of the Act.

(4) *Issuer.* The term "issuer" means an issuer as defined in section 3 of the Securities Exchange Act of 1934 (15 U.S.C. 78c), the securities of which are registered under section 12 of the Securities Exchange Act of 1934, or that is required to file reports under section 15(d) of the Securities Exchange Act of 1934, or files or has filed a registration statement that has not yet become effective under the Securities Act of 1933 (15 U.S.C. 77a et seq.), and that it has not withdrawn.

(5) *Calendar week.* For purposes of paragraph (b)(1)(iii)(B), the term "calendar week" means a seven day period beginning on Sunday and ending on Saturday.

(e) *Model notice.* (1) *General.* The model notice set forth in paragraph (e)(2) of this section is intended to assist plan administrators in discharging their notice obligations under this section. Use of the model notice is not mandatory. However, a notice that uses the statements provided in paragraphs 4. and 5.(A) of the model notice will be deemed to satisfy the notice content requirements of paragraph (b)(1)(iv) and (b)(1)(v)(A), respectively, of this section. With regard to all other information required by paragraph (b)(1) of this section, compliance with the notice content requirements will depend on the facts and circumstances pertaining to the particular blackout period and plan.

(2) *Form and content of model notice.*

Important Notice Concerning Your Rights

Under The [Enter Name of Individual Account Plan]

[Enter date of notice]

1. This notice is to inform you that the [enter name of plan] will be [enter reasons for blackout period, as appropriate: changing investment options, changing recordkeepers, etc.].

2. As a result of these changes, you temporarily will be unable to [enter as appropriate: direct or diversify investments in your individual accounts (if only specific investments are subject to the blackout, those investments should be specifically identified), obtain a loan from the plan, or obtain a distribution from the plan]. This period, during which you will be unable to exercise these rights otherwise available under the plan, is called a "blackout period." Whether or not you are planning retirement in the near future, we encourage you to carefully consider how this blackout period may affect your retirement planning, as well as your overall financial plan.

3. The blackout period for the plan [enter the following as appropriate: is expected to begin on [enter date] and end [enter date]/ is expected to begin during the week of [enter date] and end during the week of [enter date]. During these weeks, you can determine whether the blackout period has started or ended by [enter instructions for use toll-free number or accessing web site].

4. [In the case of investments affected by the blackout period, add the following: During blackout period you will be unable to direct

or diversify the assets held in your plan account. For this reason, it is very important that you review and consider the appropriateness of your current investments in light of your inability to direct or diversify those investments during the blackout period. For your long-term retirement security, you should give careful consideration to the importance of a well-balanced and diversified investment portfolio, taking into account all your assets, income and investments.] [If the plan permits investments in individual securities, add the following: You should be aware that there is a risk to holding substantial portions of your assets in the securities of any one company, as individual securities tend to have wider price swings, up and down, in short periods of time, than investments in diversified funds. Stocks that have wide price swings might have a large loss during the blackout period, and you would not be able to direct the sale of such stocks from your account during the blackout period.]

5. [If timely notice cannot be provided (see paragraph (b)(1)(v) of this section) enter: (A) Federal law generally requires that you be furnished notice of a blackout period at least 30 days in advance of the last date on which you could exercise your affected rights immediately before the commencement of any blackout period in order to provide you with sufficient time to consider the effect of the blackout period on your retirement and financial plans. (B) [Enter explanation of reasons for inability to furnish 30 days advance notice.]]

6. If you have any questions concerning this notice, you should contact [enter name, address and telephone number of the plan administrator or other contact responsible for answering questions about the blackout period].

(f) *Effective date.* This section shall be effective and shall apply to any blackout period commencing on or after January 26, 2003. For the period January 26, 2003 to February 25, 2003, plan administrators shall furnish notice as soon as reasonably possible.

[Reg. § 2520.101-3 was added by FR Doc. 02-26522, interim regulations, published in the *Federal Register* October 21, 2002, effective January 26, 2003 (67 FR 64765). Reg. § 2520.101-3 was revised and finalized on January 24, 2003 (68 FR 3715).]

[¶ 14,220]
SUMMARY PLAN DESCRIPTION

Act Sec. 102. (a) A summary plan description of any employee benefit plan shall be furnished to participants and beneficiaries as provided in section 104(b). The summary plan description shall include the information described in subsection (b), shall be written in a manner calculated to be understood by the average plan participant, and shall be sufficiently accurate and comprehensive to reasonably apprise such participants and beneficiaries of their rights and obligations under the plan. A summary of any material modification in the terms of the plan and any change in the information required under subsection (b) shall be written in a manner calculated to be understood by the average plan participant and shall be furnished in accordance with section 104(b)(1).

Act Sec. 102. The summary plan description shall contain the following information: The name and type of administration of the plan; in the case of a group health plan (as defined in section 706(a)(1)), whether a health insurance issuer (as defined in section 706(b)(2)) is responsible for the financing or administration (including payment of claims) of the plan and (if so) the name and address of such issuer; the name and address of the person designated as agent for the service of legal process, if such person is not the administrator; the name and address of the administrator; names, titles, and addresses of any trustee or trustees (if they are persons different from the administrator); a description of the relevant provisions of any applicable collective bargaining agreement; the plan's requirements respecting eligibility for participation and benefits; a description of the provisions providing for nonforfeitable pension benefits; circumstances which may result in disqualification, ineligibility, or denial or loss of benefits; the source of financing of the plan and the identity of any organization through which benefits are provided; the date of the end of the plan year and whether the records of the plan are kept on a calendar, policy, or fiscal year basis; the procedures to be followed in presenting claims for benefits under the plan including the office at the Department of Labor through which participants and beneficiaries may seek assistance or information regarding their rights under this Act and the Health Insurance Portability and Accountability Act of 1996 with respect to health benefits that are offered through a group health plan (as defined in section 706(a)(1) and the remedies available under the plan for the redress of claims which are denied in whole or in part (including procedures required under section 503 of this Act).

Amendments

P.L. 105-34, § 1503(b)(1):

Amended ERISA Sec. 102(a) by striking paragraph (2) and by striking (a)(1) and inserting (a). Prior to amendment, ERISA Sec. 102(a)(2) read as follows:

(2) A plan description (containing the information required by subsection (b)) of any employee benefit plan shall be prepared on forms prescribed by the Secretary, and shall be filed with the Secretary as required by section 104(a)(1). Any material modification in the terms of the plan and any change in the information described in subsection (b) shall be filed in accordance with section 104(a)(1)(D).

P.L. 105-34, § 1503(b)(2):

Amended ERISA Sec. 102 by striking "PLAN DESCRIPTION AND" in the heading and ERISA Sec. 102(b) by striking "The plan description and summary plan description shall contain" and inserting "The summary plan description shall contain."

The above amendments are effective August 5, 1997.

P.L. 104-191, § 101(c)(2):

Amended ERISA Sec. 102(b) by inserting "in the case of a group health plan (as defined in section 706(a)(1)), whether a health insurance issuer (as defined in section 706(b)(2)) is responsible for the financing or administration (including payment of

claims) of the plan and (if so) the name and address of such issuer;" after "type of administration of the plan" and by inserting "including the office at the Department of Labor through which participants and beneficiaries may seek assistance or information regarding their rights under this Act and the Health Insurance Portability and Accountability Act of 1996 with respect to health benefits that are offered through a group health plan (as defined in section 706(a)(1)" after "benefits under the plan".

The above amendments generally apply with respect to group health plans for plan years beginning after June 30, 1997. For special rules, see Act Sec. 101(g)(2)-(5), reproduced below.

Act Sec. 101(g)(2)-(5) reads as follows:

(g) Effective Dates.—

(1) In General.—Except as provided in this section, this section (and the amendments made by this section) shall apply with respect to group health plans for plan years beginning after June 30, 1997.

(2) Determination of creditable coverage.—

(A) Period of coverage.—

(i) In general.—Subject to clause (ii), no period before July 1, 1996, shall be taken into account under part 7 of subtitle B of title I of the Employee Retirement Income Security Act of 1974 (as added by this section) in determining creditable coverage.

(ii) SPECIAL RULE FOR CERTAIN PERIODS.—The Secretary of Labor, consistent with section 104, shall provide for a process whereby individuals who need to establish creditable coverage for periods before July 1, 1996, and who would have such coverage credited but for clause (i) may be given credit for creditable coverage for such periods through the presentation of documents or other means.

(B) CERTIFICATIONS, ETC.—

(i) IN GENERAL.—Subject to clauses (ii) and (iii), subsection (e) of section 701 of the Employee Retirement Income Security Act of 1974 (as added by this section) shall apply to events occurring after June 30, 1996.

(ii) NO CERTIFICATION REQUIRED TO BE PROVIDED BEFORE JUNE 1, 1997.—In no case is a certification required to be provided under such subsection before June 1, 1997.

(iii) CERTIFICATION ONLY ON WRITTEN REQUEST FOR EVENTS OCCURRING BEFORE OCTOBER 1, 1996.—In the case of an event occurring after June 30, 1996, and before October 1, 1996, a certification is not required to be provided under such subsection unless an individual (with respect to whom the certification is otherwise required to be made) requests such certification in writing.

(C) TRANSITIONAL RULE.—In the case of an individual who seeks to establish creditable coverage for any period for which certification is not required because it relates to an event occurring before June 30, 1996—

(i) the individual may present other credible evidence of such coverage in order to establish the period of creditable coverage; and

(ii) a group health plan and a health insurance issuer shall not be subject to any penalty or enforcement action with respect to the plan's or issuer's crediting (or not crediting) such coverage if the plan or issuer has sought to comply in good faith with the applicable requirements under the amendments made by this section.

(3) SPECIAL RULE FOR COLLECTIVE BARGAINING AGREEMENTS.—Except as provided in paragraph (2), in the case of a group health plan maintained pursuant to one or more collective bargaining agreements between employee representatives and one or more employers ratified before the date of the enactment of this Act, part 7 of subtitle B of title I of Employee Retirement Income Security Act of 1974 (other than section 701(e) thereof) shall not apply to plan years beginning before the later of—

(A) the date on which the last of the collective bargaining agreements relating to the plan terminates (determined without regard to any extension thereof agreed to after the date of the enactment of this Act), or

(B) July 1, 1997.

For purposes of subparagraph (A), any plan amendment made pursuant to a collective bargaining agreement relating to the plan which amends the plan solely to conform to any requirement of such part shall not be treated as a termination of such collective bargaining agreement.

(4) TIMELY REGULATIONS.—The Secretary of Labor, consistent with section 104, shall first issue by not later than April 1, 1997, such regulations as may be necessary to carry out the amendments made by this section.

(5) LIMITATION ON ACTIONS.—No enforcement action shall be taken, pursuant to the amendments made by this section, against a group health plan or health insurance issuer with respect to a violation of a requirement imposed by such amendments before January 1, 1998, or, if later, the date of issuance of regulations referred to in paragraph (4), if the plan or issuer has sought to comply in good faith with such requirements.

Regulations

Reg. § 2520.102-1 was adopted by FR Doc. 76-11859 (41 FR 16957) under "Title 29—Labor; Chapter XXV—Office of Employee Benefits Security; Subchapter C—Reporting and Disclosure Under the Employee Retirement Income Security Act of 1974; Part 2520—Rules and Regulations for Reporting and Disclosure." The regulation was filed with the *Federal Register* on April 22, 1976, and published in the *Federal Register* on April 23, 1976. Reg. §§ 2520.102-2 through 2520.102-4 were adopted by FR Doc. 77-7637, filed with the *Federal Register* on March 11, 1977, and published in the *Federal Register* on March 15, 1977 (42 FR 14266). Reg. § 2520.102-3(m) and 2520.102-3(t) are interim as well as proposed regulations. The regulations are effective March 15, 1977. Reg. § 2520.102-3 was amended by FR Doc. 20810, filed with the *Federal Register* on July 18, 1977, published in the *Federal Register* on July 19, 1977, effective July 19, 1977 (42 FR 37178). Reg. § 2520.102-5 was added by FR Doc. 81-2105, filed with the *Federal Register* on January 19, 1981, published in the *Federal Register* on January 21, 1981, effective February 20, 1981 (46 FR 5882). Reg. § 2520.102-3(q) was amended, § 2520.102-3(u) and (v) were added, § 2520.104b-1(c) was added, § 2520.104b-3(a) was amended, § 2520.104b-3(d) and § 2520.104b-3(e) were added by FR Doc. 97-8173, interim regulations, filed with the *Federal Register* on April 1, 1997, published in the *Federal Register* on April 8, 1997, effective June 1, 1997 (62 FR 16979). Reg. § 2520.102-3 was officially corrected on June 10, 1997 (62 FR 31690). Reg. § 2520.102-3 was amended, effective June 1, 1997 (62 FR 36205). Reg. § 2520.102-3(u) was amended, effective September 9, 1998 (63 FR 48371). Reg. §§ 2520.102-3 (d), (j), (l), (m)(3), (o), (q), (s), (t)(2) and (u) were amended effective January 20, 2001 and published in the *Federal Register* on November 21, 2000 (65 FR 70225). Reg. § 2520.102-3(m)(4) was added effective January 20, 2001 and published in the *Federal Register* on November 21, 2000 (65 FR 70225). Reg. § 2520.102-5 was removed effective January 20, 2001 and published in the *Federal Register* on November 21, 2000 (65 FR 70225). Reg. §§ 2520.104b-3 (a), (d) and (e) were amended effective January 20, 2001 and published in the *Federal Register* on November 21, 2000 (65 FR 70225).ERISA Reg. Sec. 2520.102-1 was removed and reserved by 67 FR 771 and published in the *Federal Register* on January 7, 2002. ERISA Reg. Sec. 2520.102-4 was revised by 67 FR 771 and published in the *Federal Register* on January 7, 2002.

Subpart B—Contents of Plan Description and Summary Plan Description

[¶ 14,221]

§ 2520.102-1 **Plan description**. Reserved. [67 FR 771, 1/7/02].

[¶ 14,222]

§ 2520.102-2 **Style and format of summary plan description**. (a) *Method of presentation*. The summary plan description shall be written in a manner calculated to be understood by the average plan participant and shall be sufficiently comprehensive to apprise the plan's participants and beneficiaries of their rights and obligations under the plan. In fulfilling these requirements, the plan administrator shall exercise considered judgment and discretion by taking into account such factors as the level of comprehension and education of typical participants in the plan and the complexity of the terms of the plan. Consideration of these factors will usually require the limitation or elimination of technical jargon and of long, complex sentences, the use of clarifying examples and illustrations, the use of clear cross-references and a table of contents.

(b) *General format*. The format of the summary plan description must not have the effect of misleading, misinforming or failing to inform participants and beneficiaries. Any description of exceptions, limitations, reductions, and other restrictions of plan benefits shall not be minimized, rendered obscure, or otherwise made to appear unimportant. Such exceptions, limitations, reductions, or restrictions of plan benefits shall be described or summarized in a manner not less prominent than the style, captions, printing type, and prominence used to describe or summarize plan benefits. The advantages and disadvantages of the plan shall be presented without either exaggerating the benefits or minimizing the limitations. The description or summary of restrictive plan provisions need not be disclosed in the summary plan description in close conjunction with the description or summary of benefits, provided that adjacent to the benefit description the page on which the restrictions are described is noted.

(c) *Foreign languages*. In the case of either—

(1) A plan that covers fewer than 100 participants at the beginning of a plan year, and in which 25 percent or more of all plan participants are literate only in the same non-English language, or

(2) A plan which covers 100 or more participants at the beginning of the plan year, and in which the lesser of: (i) 500 or more participants, or (ii) 10% or more of all plan participants are literate only in the same non-English language, so that a summary plan description in English would fail to inform these participants adequately of their rights and obligations under the plan, the plan administrator for such plan shall provide these participants with an English-language summary plan description which prominently displays a notice, in the non-English language common to these participants, offering them assistance. The assistance provided need not involve written materials, but shall be given in the non-English language common to these participants and shall be calculated to provide them with a reasonable opportunity to become informed as to their rights and obligations under the plan. The notice offering assistance contained in the summary plan description shall clearly set forth in the non-English language common to such participants the procedures they must follow in order to obtain such assistance.

Example. Employer A maintains a pension plan which covers 1000 participants. At the beginning of a plan year five hundred of Employer A's covered employees are literate only in Spanish, 101 are literate only in Vietnamese, and the remaining 399 are literate in English. Each of the 1000 employees receives a summary plan description in English, containing an assistance notice in both Spanish and Vietnamese stating the following:

This booklet contains a summary in English of your plan rights and benefits under Employer A Pension Plan. If you have difficulty understanding any part of this booklet, contact Mr. John Doe, the plan administrator, at his office in Room 123, 456 Main St., Anywhere City, State 20001. Office hours are from 8:30 A.M. to 5:00 P.M. Monday through Friday. You may also call the plan administrator's office at 202 555-2345 for assistance. [Added by 42 FR 14266, effective March 15, 1977.]

[¶ 14,223]

§ 2520.102-3 **Contents of summary plan description**. Section 102 of the Act specifies information that must be included in the summary plan description. The summary plan description must accurately reflect the contents of the plans as of a date not earlier than 120 days prior to the date such summary plan description is disclosed. The following information shall be included in the summary plan description of both employee welfare benefit plans and employee pension benefit plans, except as stated otherwise in subsection (j) through (n):

(a) The name of the plan, and, if different, the name by which the plan is commonly known by its participants and beneficiaries;

(b) The name and address of—

(1) In the case of a single employer plan, the employer whose employees are covered by the plan,

(2) In the case of a plan maintained by an employee organization for its members, the employee organization that maintains the plan,

(3) In the case of a collectively-bargained plan established or maintained by one or more employers and one or more employee organizations, the association, committee, joint board of trustees, parent, or most significant employer of a group of employers all of which contribute to the same plan, or other similar representative of the parties who established or maintain the plan, as well as:

(i) A statement that a complete list of the employers and employee organizations sponsoring the plan may be obtained by participants and beneficiaries upon written request to the plan administrator, and is available for examination by participants and beneficiaries, as required by § § 2520.104b-1 and 2520.104b-30, or,

(ii) A statement that participants and beneficiaries may receive from the plan administrator, upon written request, information as to whether a particular employer or employee organization is a sponsor of the plan and, if the employer or employee organization is a plan sponsor, the sponsor's address.

(4) In the case of a plan established or maintained by two or more employers, the association, committee, joint board of trustees, parent, or most significant employer of a group of employers all of which contribute to the same plan, or other similar representative of the parties who established or maintain the plan, as well as:

(i) A statement that a complete list of the employers sponsoring the plan may be obtained by participants and beneficiaries upon written request to the plan administrator, and is available for examination by participants and beneficiaries, as required by § § 2520.104b-1 and 2520.104b-30, or,

(ii) A statement that participants and beneficiaries may receive from the plan administrator, upon written request, information as to whether a particular employer is a sponsor of the plan and, if the employer is a plan sponsor, the sponsor's address. [Amended by 42 FR 37178, effective July 19, 1977.]

(c) The employer identification number (EIN) assigned by the Internal Revenue Service to the plan sponsor and the plan number assigned by the plan sponsor. (For further detailed explanation, see the instructions to the plan description Form EBS-1 and "Identification Numbers Under ERISA" (Publ. 1004), published jointly by DOL, IRS, and PBGC);

(d) The type of pension or welfare plan, e.g. pension plans—defined benefit, defined contribution, 401(k), cash balance, money purchase, profit sharing, ERISA section 404(c) plan, etc., and for welfare plans—group health plans, disability, pre-paid legal services, etc. [Amended 11/21/00 by 65 FR 70225. Corrected by PWBA on 7/2/01, 66 FR 34994. Corrected by PWBA on 7/11/01, 66 FR 36368.]

(e) The type of administration of the plan, *e.g.*, contract administration, insurer administration, etc.;

(f) The name, business address, and business telephone number of the plan administrator as that term is defined by section 3(16) of the Act;

(g) The name of the person designated as agent for service of legal process, and the address at which process may be served on such person, and in addition, a statement that service of legal process may be made upon a plan trustee or the plan administrator;

(h) The name, title, and address of the principal place of business of each trustee of the plan;

(i) If a plan is maintained pursuant to one or more collective bargaining agreements, a statement that the plan is so maintained, and that a copy of any such agreement may be obtained by participants and beneficiaries upon written request to the plan administrator, and is available for examination by participants and beneficiaries, as required by § § 2520.104b-1 and 2520.104b-30. For the purpose of this paragraph, a plan is maintained pursuant to a collective bargaining agreement if such agreement controls any duties, rights or benefits under the plan, even though such agreement has been superseded in part for other purposes;

(j) The plan's requirements respecting eligibility for participation and for benefits. The summary plan description shall describe the plan's provisions relating to eligibility to participate in the plan and the information identified in paragraphs (j)(1), (2) and (3) of this section, as appropriate. [Amended 11/21/00 by 65 FR 70225.]

(1) For employee pension benefit plans, it shall also include a statement describing the plan's normal retirement age, as that term is defined in section 3(24) of the Act, and a statement describing any other conditions which must be met before a participant will be eligible to receive benefits. Such plan benefits shall be described or summarized. In addition, the summary plan description shall include a description of the procedures governing qualified domestic relations order (QDRO) determinations or a statement indicating that participants and beneficiaries can obtain, without charge, a copy of such procedures from the plan administrator. [Amended 11/21/00 by 65 FR 70225.]

(2) For employee welfare benefit plans, it shall also include a statement of the conditions pertaining to eligibility to receive benefits, and a description or summary of the benefits. In the case of a welfare plan providing extensive schedules of benefits (a group health plan, for example), only a general description of such benefits is required if reference is made to detailed schedules of benefits which are available without cost to any participant or beneficiary who so requests. In addition, the summary plan description shall include a description of the procedures governing qualified medical child support order (QMCSO) determinations or a statement indicating that participants and beneficiaries can obtain, without charge, a copy of such procedures from the plan administrator. [Amended 11/21/00 by 65 FR 70225.]

(3) For employee welfare benefit plans that are group health plans, as defined in section 733(a)(1) of the Act, the summary plan description shall include a description of: any cost-sharing provisions, including premiums, deductibles, coinsurance, and copayment amounts for which the participant or beneficiary will be responsible; any annual or lifetime caps or other limits on benefits under the plan; the extent to which preventive services are covered under the plan; whether, and under what circumstances, existing and new drugs are covered under the plan; whether, and under what circumstances, coverage is provided for medical tests, devices and procedures; provisions governing the use of network providers, the composition of the provider network, and whether, and under what circumstances, coverage is provided for out-of-network services; any conditions or limits on the selection of primary care providers or providers of speciality medical care; any conditions or limits applicable to obtaining emergency medical care; and any provisions requiring preauthorizations or utilization review as a condition to obtaining a benefit or service under the plan. In the case of plans with provider networks, the listing of providers may be furnished as a separate document that accompanies the plan's SPD, provided that the summary plan description contains a general description of the provider network and provided further that the SPD contains a statement that provider lists are furnished automatically, without charge, as a separate document. [Added 11/21/00 by 65 FR 70225. Corrected by PWBA on 7/2/01, 66 FR 34994. Corrected by PWBA on 7/11/01, 66 FR 36368.]

(k) In the case of an employee pension benefit plan, a statement describing any joint and survivor benefits provided under the plan, including any requirement that an election be made as a condition to select or reject the joint and survivor annuity;

(l) For both pension and welfare benefit plans, a statement clearly identifying circumstances which may result in disqualification, ineligibility, or denial, loss, forfeiture, suspension, offset, reduction, or recovery (e.g., by exercise of subrogation or reimbursement rights) of any benefits that a participant or beneficiary might otherwise reasonably expect the plan to provide on the basis of the description of benefits required by paragraphs (j) and (k) of this section. In addition to other required information, plans must include a summary of any plan provisions governing the authority of the plan sponsors or others to terminate the plan or amend or eliminate benefits under the plan and the circumstances, if any, under which the plan may be terminated or benefits may be amended or eliminated; a summary of any plan provisions governing the benefits, rights and obligations of participants and beneficiaries under the plan on termination of the plan or amendment or elimination of benefits under the plan, including, in the case of an employee pension benefit plan, a summary of any provisions relating to the accrual and the vesting of pension benefits under the plan upon termination; and a summary of any plan provisions governing the allocation and disposition of assets of the plan upon termination. Plans also shall include a summary of any provisions that may result in the imposition of a fee or charge on a participant or beneficiary, or on an individual account thereof, the payment of which is a condition to the receipt of benefits under the plan. The foregoing summaries shall be disclosed in accordance with the requirements under 29 CFR 2520.102-2(b). [Amended 11/21/00 by 65 FR 70225.]

(m) For an employee pension benefit plan the following information:

(1) if the benefits of the plan are not insured under Title IV of the Act, a statement of this fact, and the reason for the lack of insurance; and

(2) if the benefits of the plan are insured under Title IV of the Act, a statement of this fact, a summary of the pension benefit guaranty provisions of Title IV, and a statement indicating that further information on the provisions of Title IV can be obtained from the plan administrator or the Pension Benefit Guaranty Corporation. The address of the PBGC shall be provided.

(3) A summary plan description for a single-employer plan will be deemed to comply with paragraph (m)(2) of this section if it includes the following statement:

Your pension benefits under this plan are insured by the Pension Benefit Guaranty Corporation (PBGC), a federal insurance agency. If the plan terminates (ends) without enough money to pay all benefits, the PBGC will step in to pay pension benefits. Most people receive all of the pension benefits they would have received under their plan, but some people may lose certain benefits.

The PBGC guarantee generally covers: (1) Normal and early retirement benefits; (2) disability benefits if you become disabled before the plan terminates; and (3) certain benefits for your survivors.

The PBGC guarantee generally does not cover: (1) Benefits greater than the maximum guaranteed amount set by law for the year in which the plan terminates; (2) some or all of benefit increases and new benefits based on plan provisions that have been in place for fewer than 5 years at the time the plan terminates; (3) benefits that are not vested because you have not worked long enough for the company; (4) benefits for which you have not met all of the requirements at the time the plan terminates; (5) certain early retirement payments (such as supplemental benefits that stop when you become eligible for Social Security) that result in an early retirement monthly benefit greater than your monthly benefit at the plan's normal retirement age; and (6) nonpension benefits, such as health insurance, life insurance, certain death benefits, vacation pay, and severance pay.

Even if certain of your benefits are not guaranteed, you still may receive some of those benefits from the PBGC depending on how much money your plan has and on how much the PBGC collects from employers.

For more information about the PBGC and the benefits it guarantees, ask your plan administrator or contact the PBGC's Technical

Assistance Division, 1200 K Street N.W., Suite 930, Washington, D.C. 20005-4026 or call 202-326-4000 (not a toll-free number). TTY/TDD users may call the federal relay service toll-free at 1-800-877-8339 and ask to be connected to 202-326-4000. Additional information about the PBGC's pension insurance program is available through the PBGC's website on the Internet at http://www.pbgc.gov. [Added by 42 FR 37178, effective July 19, 1977. Amended 11/21/00 by 65 FR 70225.]

(4) A summary plan description for a multiemployer plan will be deemed to comply with paragraph (m)(2) of this section if it includes the following statement:

Your pension benefits under this multiemployer plan are insured by the Pension Benefit Guaranty Corporation (PBGC), a federal insurance agency. A multiemployer plan is a collectively bargained pension arrangement involving two or more unrelated employers, usually in a common industry.

Under the multiemployer plan program, the PBGC provides financial assistance through loans to plans that are insolvent. A multiemployer plan is considered insolvent if the plan is unable to pay benefits (at least equal to the PBGC's guaranteed benefit limit) when due.

The maximum benefit that the PBGC guarantees is set by law. Under the multiemployer program, the PBGC guarantee equals a participant's years of service multiplied by (1) 100% of the first $5 of the monthly benefit accrual rate and (2) 75% of the next $15. The PBGC's maximum guarantee limit is $16.25 per month times a participant's years of service. For example, the maximum annual guarantee for a retiree with 30 years of service would be $5,850.

The PBGC guarantee generally covers: (1) Normal and early retirement benefits; (2) disability benefits if you become disabled before the plan becomes insolvent; and (3) certain benefits for your survivors.

The PBGC guarantee generally does not cover: (1) Benefits greater than the maximum guaranteed amount set by law; (2) benefit increases and new benefits based on plan provisions that have been in place for fewer than 5 years at the earlier of: (i) The date the plan terminates or (ii) the time the plan becomes insolvent; (3) benefits that are not vested because you have not worked long enough; (4) benefits for which you have not met all of the requirements at the time the plan becomes insolvent; and (5) nonpension benefits, such as health insurance, life insurance, certain death benefits, vacation pay, and severance pay.

For more information about the PBGC and the benefits it guarantees, ask your plan administrator or contact the PBGC's Technical Assistance Division, 1200 K Street, N.W., Suite 930, Washington, D.C. 20005-4026 or call 202-326-4000 (not a toll-free number). TTY/TDD users may call the federal relay service toll-free at 1-800-877-8339 and ask to be connected to 202-326-4000. Additional information about the PBGC's pension insurance program is available through the PBGC's website on the Internet at http://www.pbgc.gov. [Added 11/21/00 by 65 FR 70225.]

(n) In the case of an employee pension benefit plan, a description and explanation of the plan provisions for determining years of service for eligibility to participate, vesting, and breaks in service, and years of participation for benefit accrual. The description shall state the service required to accrue full benefits and the manner in which accrual of benefits is prorated for employees failing to complete full service for a year.

(o) In the case of a group health plan, within the meaning of section 607(1) of the Act, subject to the continuation coverage provisions of Part 6 of Title I of ERISA, a description of the rights and obligations of participants and beneficiaries with respect to continuation coverage, including, among other things, information concerning qualifying events and qualified beneficiaries, premiums, notice and election requirements and procedures, and duration of coverage. [Amended 11/21/00 by 65 FR 70225.]

(p) The sources of contributions to the plan—for example, employer, employee organization, employees—and the method by which the amount of contribution is calculated. Defined benefit pension plans may state without further explanation that the contribution is actuarially determined.

(q) The identity of any funding medium used for the accumulation of assets through which benefits are provided. The summary plan description shall identify any insurance company, trust fund, or any other institution, organization, or entity which maintains a fund on behalf of the plan or through which the plan is funded or benefits are provided. If a health insurance issuer, within the meaning of section 733(b)(2) of the Act, is responsible, in whole or in part, for the financing or administration of a group health plan, the summary plan description shall indicate the name and address of the issuer, whether and to what extent benefits under the plan are guaranteed under a contract or policy of insurance issued by the issuer, and the nature of any administrative services (e.g., payment of claims) provided by the issuer. [Amended by 62 FR 16979, effective June 1, 1997. Amended 11/21/00 by 65 FR 70225.]

(r) The date of the end of the year for purposes of maintaining the plan's fiscal records;

(s) The procedures governing claims for benefits (including procedures for obtaining preauthorizations, approvals, or utilization review decisions in the case of group health plan services or benefits, and procedures for filing claim forms, providing notifications of benefit determinations, and reviewing denied claims in the case of any plan), applicable time limits, and remedies available under the plan for the redress of claims which are denied in whole or in part (including procedures required under section 503 of Title I of the Act). The plan's claims procedures may be furnished as a separate document that accompanies the plan's SPD, provided that the document satisfies the style and format requirements of 29 CFR 2520.102-2 and, provided further that the SPD contains a statement that the plan's claims procedures are furnished automatically, without charge, as a separate document. [Amended 11/21/00 by 65 FR 70225.]

(t)(1) The statement of ERISA rights authorized by section 104(c) of the Act, containing the items of information applicable to the plan included in the model statement of subparagraph (2) of this paragraph. Items which are not applicable to the plan are not required to be included. The statement may contain explanatory and descriptive provisions in addition to those prescribed in paragraph (t)(2) of this section. However, the style and format of the statement must not have the effect of misleading, misinforming or failing to inform participants and beneficiaries of a plan. All such information shall be written in a manner calculated to be understood by the average plan participant, taking into account factors such as the level of comprehension and education of typical participants in the plan and the complexity of the items required under this subparagraph to be included in the statement. Inaccurate, incomprehensible or misleading explanatory material will fail to meet the requirements of this section. The statement of ERISA rights (the model statement or a statement prepared by the plan), must appear as one consolidated statement. If a plan finds it desirable to make additional mention of certain rights elsewhere in the summary plan description, it may do so. The summary plan description may state that the statement of ERISA rights is required by federal law and regulation.

(2) A summary plan description will be deemed to comply with the requirements of paragraph (t)(1) of this section if it includes the following statement; items of information which are not applicable to a particular plan should be deleted:

As a participant in (name of plan) you are entitled to certain rights and protections under the Employee Retirement Income Security Act of 1974 (ERISA). ERISA provides that all plan participants shall be entitled to:

Receive Information About Your Plan and Benefits

Examine, without charge, at the plan administrator's office and at other specified locations, such as worksites and union halls, all documents governing the plan, including insurance contracts and collective bargaining agreements, and a copy of the latest annual report (Form 5500 Series) filed by the plan with the U.S. Department of Labor and available at the Public Disclosure Room of the Employee Benefits Security Administration. [EBSA technical correction, 68 FR 16399 (April 3, 2003).]

Obtain, upon written request to the plan administrator, copies of documents governing the operation of the plan, including insurance contracts and collective bargaining agreements, and copies of the latest annual report (Form 5500 Series) and updated summary plan description. The administrator may make a reasonable charge for the copies.

Receive a summary of the plan's annual financial report. The plan administrator is required by law to furnish each participant with a copy of this summary annual report.

Obtain a statement telling you whether you have a right to receive a pension at normal retirement age (age * * *) and if so, what your benefits would be at normal retirement age if you stop working under the plan now. If you do not have a right to a pension, the statement will tell you how many more years you have to work to get a right to a pension. This statement must be requested in writing and is not required to be given more than once every twelve (12) months. The plan must provide the statement free of charge.

Continue Group Health Plan Coverage

Continue health care coverage for yourself, spouse or dependents if there is a loss of coverage under the plan as a result of a qualifying event. You or your dependents may have to pay for such coverage. Review this summary plan description and the documents governing the plan on the rules governing your COBRA continuation coverage rights.

Reduction or elimination of exclusionary periods of coverage for preexisting conditions under your group health plan, if you have creditable coverage from another plan. You should be provided a certificate of creditable coverage, free of charge, from your group health plan or health insurance issuer when you lose coverage under the plan, when you become entitled to elect COBRA continuation coverage, when your COBRA continuation coverage ceases, if you request it before losing coverage, or if you request it up to 24 months after losing coverage. Without evidence of creditable coverage, you may be subject to a preexisting condition exclusion for 12 months (18 months for late enrollees) after your enrollment date in your coverage.

Prudent Actions by Plan Fiduciaries

In addition to creating rights for plan participants ERISA imposes duties upon the people who are responsible for the operation of the employee benefit plan. The people who operate your plan, called "fiduciaries" of the plan, have a duty to do so prudently and in the interest of you and other plan participants and beneficiaries. No one, including your employer, your union, or any other person, may fire you or otherwise discriminate against you in any way to prevent you from obtaining a (pension, welfare) benefit or exercising your rights under ERISA.

Enforce Your Rights

If your claim for a (pension, welfare) benefit is denied or ignored, in whole or in part, you have a right to know why this was done, to obtain copies of documents relating to the decision without charge, and to appeal any denial, all within certain time schedules.

Under ERISA, there are steps you can take to enforce the above rights. For instance, if you request a copy of plan documents or the latest annual report from the plan and do not receive them within 30 days, you may file suit in a Federal court. In such a case, the court may require the plan administrator to provide the materials and pay you up to $110 a day until you receive the materials, unless the materials were not sent because of reasons beyond the control of the administrator. If you have a claim for benefits which is denied or ignored, in whole or in part, you may file suit in a state or Federal court. In addition, if you disagree with the plan's decision or lack thereof concerning the qualified status of a domestic relations order or a medical child support order, you may file suit in Federal court. If it should happen that plan fiduciaries misuse the plan's money, or if you are discriminated against for asserting your rights, you may seek assistance from the U.S. Department of Labor, or you may file suit in a Federal court. The court will decide who should pay court costs and legal fees. If you are successful the court may order the person you have sued to pay these costs and fees. If you lose, the court may order you to pay these costs and fees, for example, if it finds your claim is frivolous.

Assistance with Your Questions

If you have any questions about your plan, you should contact the plan administrator. If you have any questions about this statement or about your rights under ERISA, or if you need assistance in obtaining documents from the plan administrator, you should contact the nearest office of the Employee Benefits Security Administration, U.S. Department of Labor, listed in your telephone directory or the Division of Technical Assistance and Inquiries, Employee Benefits Security

Administration, U.S. Department of Labor, 200 Constitution Avenue N.W., Washington, D.C. 20210. You may also obtain certain publications about your rights and responsibilities under ERISA by calling the publications hotline of the Employee Benefits Security Administration. [Amended by 62 FR 16979, effective June 1, 1997. Amended 11/21/00 by 65 FR 70225. EBSA technical correction, 68 FR 16399 (April 3, 2003).]

(u)(1) For a group health plan, as defined in section 733(a)(1) of the Act, that provides maternity or newborn infant coverage, a statement describing any requirements under federal or state law applicable to the plan, and any health insurance coverage offered under the plan, relating to hospital length of stay in connection with childbirth for the mother or newborn child. If federal law applies in some areas in which the plan operates and state law applies in other areas, the statement should describe the different areas and the federal or state law requirements applicable in each.

(2) In the case of a group health plan subject to section 720 of the Act, the summary plan description will be deemed to have complied with paragraph (u)(1) of this section relating to the required description of federal law requirements if it includes the following statement in the summary plan description:

Group health plans and health insurance issuers generally may not, under Federal law, restrict benefits for any hospital length of stay in connection with childbirth for the mother or newborn child to less than 48 hours following a vaginal delivery, or less than 96 hours following a cesarean section. However, Federal law generally does not prohibit the mother's or newborn's attending provider, after consulting with the mother, from discharging the mother or her newborn earlier than 48 hours (or 96 hours as applicable). In any case, plans and issuers may not, under Federal law, require that a provider obtain authorization from the plan or the insurance issuer for prescribing a length of stay not in excess of 48 hours (or 96 hours). [Added by 63 FR 48371 effective September 9, 1998. Amended 11/21/00 by 65 FR 70225.]

(v) *Applicability dates.* [Added by 42 FR 37178, effective July 19, 1977. Amended by 62 FR 16979, effective June 1, 1997. Corrected June 10, 1997, by 62 FR 31690. Amended by 62 FR 36205, effective June 1, 1997. Removed 11/21/00 by 65 FR 70225.]

[¶ 14,224]

§ 2520.102-4 **Option for different summary plan descriptions**. In some cases an employee benefit plan may provide different benefits for various classes of participants and beneficiaries. For example, a plan amendment altering benefits may apply to only those participants who are employees of an employer when the amendment is adopted and to employees who later become participants, but not to participants who no longer are employees when the amendment is adopted. (See § 2520.104b-4.) Similarly, a plan may provide for different benefits for participants employed at different plants of the employer, or for different classes of participants in the same plant. In such cases the plan administrator may fulfill the requirement to furnish a summary plan description to participants covered under the plan and beneficiaries receiving benefits under the plan by furnishing to each member of each class of participants and beneficiaries a copy of a summary plan description appropriate to that class. Each summary plan description so prepared shall follow the style and format prescribed in § 2520.102-2, and shall contain all information which is required to be contained in the summary plan description under § 2520.102-3. It may omit information which is not applicable to the class of participants or beneficiaries to which it is furnished. It should also clearly identify on the first page of the text the class of participants and beneficiaries for which it has been prepared and the plan's coverage of other classes. Revised by 67 FR 771, effective March 8, 2002. [Added by 42 FR 14266, effective March 15, 1977.]

[¶ 14,225]

§ 2520.102-5 **Limited exemption with respect to summary plan descriptions of welfare plans providing benefits through a qualified health maintenance organization**. [Added by 46 FR 5882, originally scheduled to be effective February 20, 1981. However, the effective date was delayed under the President's regulation freeze until March 30, 1981 (46 FR 11253). Removed 11/21/00 by 65 FR 70225.]

[¶ 14,230]
ANNUAL REPORTS

Act Sec. 103.(a)(1)(A) An annual report shall be published with respect to every employee benefit plan to which this part applies. Such report shall be filed with the Secretary in accordance with section 104(a), and shall be made available and furnished to participants in accordance with section 104(b).

(B) The annual report shall include the information described in subsections (b) and (c) and where applicable subsections (d) and (e) and shall also include—

(i) a financial statement and opinion, as required by paragraph (3) of this subsection, and

(ii) an actuarial statement and opinion, as required by paragraph (4) of this subsection.

(2) If some or all of the information necessary to enable the administrator to comply with the requirements of this title is maintained by—

(A) an insurance carrier or other organization which provides some or all of the benefits under the plan, or holds assets of the plan in a separate account,

(B) a bank or similar institution which holds some or all of the assets of the plan in a common or collective trust or a separate trust, or custodial account, or

(C) a plan sponsor as defined in section 3(16)(B),

such carrier, organization, bank, institution, or plan sponsor shall transmit and certify the accuracy of such information to the administrator within 120 days after the end of the plan year (or such other date as may be prescribed under regulations of the Secretary).

(3)(A) Except as provided in subparagraph (C), the administrator of an employee benefit plan shall engage, on behalf of all plan participants, an independent qualified public accountant, who shall conduct such an examination of any financial statements of the plan, and of other books and records of the plan, as the accountant may deem necessary to enable the accountant to form an opinion as to whether the financial statements and schedules required to be included in the annual report by subsection (b) of this section are presented fairly in conformity with generally accepted accounting principles applied on a basis consistent with that of the preceding year. Such examination shall be conducted in accordance with generally accepted auditing standards, and shall involve such tests of the books and records of the plan as are considered necessary by the independent qualified public accountant. The independent qualified public accountant shall also offer his opinion as to whether the separate schedules specified in subsection (b)(3) of this section and the summary material required under section 104(b)(3) present fairly, and in all material respects the information contained therein when considered in conjunction with the financial statements taken as a whole. The opinion by the independent qualified public accountant shall be made a part of the annual report. In a case where a plan is not required to file an annual report, the requirements of this paragraph shall not apply. In a case where by reason of section 104(a)(2) a plan is required only to file a simplified annual report, the Secretary may waive the requirements of this paragraph.

(B) In offering his opinion under this section the accountant may rely on the correctness of any actuarial matter certified to by an enrolled actuary, if he so states his reliance.

(C) The opinion required by subparagraph (A) need not be expressed as to any statements required by subsection (b)(3)(G) prepared by a bank or similar institution or insurance carrier regulated and supervised and subject to periodic examination by a State or Federal agency if such statements are certified by the bank, similar institution, or insurance carrier as accurate and are made a part of the annual report.

(D) For purposes of this title, the term "qualified public accountant" means—

(i) a person who is a certified public accountant, certified by a regulatory authority of a State;

(ii) a person who is a licensed public accountant, licensed by a regulatory authority of a State; or

(iii) a person certified by the Secretary as a qualified public accountant in accordance with regulations published by him for a person who practices in States where there is no certification or licensing procedure for accountants.

(4)(A) The administrator of an employee pension benefit plan subject to the reporting requirement of subsection (d) of this section shall engage, on behalf of all plan participants, an enrolled actuary who shall be responsible for the preparation of the materials comprising the actuarial statement required under subsection (d) of this section. In a case where a plan is not required to file an annual report, the requirement of this paragraph shall not apply, and, in a case where by reason of section 104(a)(2), a plan is required only to file a simplified report, the Secretary may waive the requirement of this paragraph.

(B) The enrolled actuary shall utilize such assumptions and techniques as are necessary to enable him to form an opinion as to whether the contents of the matters reported under subsection (d) of this section—

(i) are in the aggregate reasonably related to the experience of the plan and to reasonable expectations; and

(ii) represent his best estimate of anticipated experience under the plan. The opinion by the enrolled actuary shall be made with respect to, and shall be made a part of, each annual report.

(C) For purposes of this title, the term "enrolled actuary" means an actuary enrolled under subtitle C of title III of this Act.

(D) In making a certification under this section the enrolled actuary may rely on the correctness of any accounting matter under section 103(b) as to which any qualified public accountant has expressed an opinion, if he so states his reliance.

Act Sec. 103. (b) An annual report under this section shall include a financial statement containing the following information:

(1) With respect to an employee welfare benefit plan: a statement of assets and liabilities; a statement of changes in fund balance; and a statement of changes in financial position. In the notes to financial statements, disclosures concerning the following items shall be considered by the accountant: a description of the plan including any significant changes in the plan made during the period and the impact of such changes on benefits; a description of material lease commitments, other commitments, and contingent liabilities; a description of agreements and transactions with persons known to be parties in interest; a general description of priorities upon termination of the plan; information concerning whether or not a tax ruling or determination letter has been obtained; and any other matters necessary to fully and fairly present the financial statements of the plan.

(2) With respect to an employee pension benefit plan: a statement of assets and liabilities, and a statement of changes in net assets available for plan benefits which shall include details of revenues and expenses and other changes aggregated by general source and application. In the notes to financial statements, disclosures concerning the following items shall be considered by the accountant: a description of the plan including any significant changes in the plan made during the period and the impact of such changes on benefits; the funding policy (including policy with respect to prior service cost), and any changes in such policies during the year; a description of any significant changes in plan benefits made during the period; a description of material lease commitments, other commitments, and contingent liabilities; a description of agreements and transactions with persons known to be parties in interest; a general description of priorities upon termination of the plan; information concerning whether or not a tax ruling or determination letter has been obtained; and any other matters necessary to fully and fairly present the financial statements of such pension plan.

(3) With respect to all employee benefit plans, the statement required under paragraph (1) or (2) shall have attached the following information in separate schedules:

(A) a statement of the assets and liabilities of the plan aggregated by categories and valued at their current value, and the same data displayed in comparative form for the end of the previous fiscal year of the plan;

(B) a statement of receipts and disbursements during the preceding twelve-month period aggregated by general sources and applications;

(C) a schedule of all assets held for investment purposes aggregated and identified by issuer, borrower, or lessor, or similar party to the transaction (including a notation as to whether such party is known to be a party in interest), maturity date, rate of interest, collateral, par or maturity value, cost, and current value;

(D) a schedule of each transaction involving a person known to be party in interest, the identity of such party in interest and his relationship or that of any other party in interest to the plan, a description of each asset to which the transaction relates; the purchase or selling price in case of a sale or purchase, the rental in case of a lease, or the interest rate and maturity date in case of a loan; expenses incurred in connection with the transaction; the cost of the asset, the current value of the asset, and the net gain (or loss) on each transaction;

(E) a schedule of all loans or fixed income obligations which were in default as of the close of the plan's fiscal year or were classified during the year as uncollectable and the following information with respect to each loan on such schedule (including a notation as to whether parties involved are known to be parties in interest): the original principal amount of the loan, the amount of principal and interest received during the reporting year, the unpaid balance, the identity and address of the obligor, a detailed description of the loan (including date of making and maturity, interest rate, the type and value of collateral, and other material terms), the amount of principal and interest overdue (if any) and an explanation thereof;

(F) a list of all leases which were in default or were classified during the year as uncollectable; and the following information with respect to each lease on such schedule (including a notation as to whether parties involved are known to be parties in interest): the type of property leased (and, in the case of fixed assets such as land, buildings, leasehold, and so forth, the location of the property), the identity of the lessor or lessee from or to whom the plan is leasing, the relationship of such lessors and lessees, if any, to the plan, the employer, employee organization, or any other party in interest, the terms of the lease regarding rent, taxes, insurance, repairs, expenses, and renewal options; the date the leased property was purchased and its cost, the date the property was leased and its approximate value at such date, the gross rental receipts during the reporting period, expenses paid for the leased property during the reporting period, the net receipts from the lease, the amounts in arrears, and a statement as to what steps have been taken to collect amounts due or otherwise remedy the default;

(G) if some or all of the assets of a plan or plans are held in a common or collective trust maintained by a bank or similar institution or in a separate account maintained by an insurance carrier or a separate trust maintained by a bank as trustee, the report shall include the most recent annual statement of assets and liabilities of such common or collective trust, and in the case of a separate account or a separate trust, such other information as is required by the administrator in order to comply with this subsection; and

(H) a schedule of each reportable transaction, the name of each party to the transaction (except that, in the case of an acquisition or sale of a security on the market, the report need not identify the person from whom the security was acquired or to whom it was sold) and a description of each asset to which the transaction applies; the purchase or selling price in case of a sale or purchase, the rental in case of a lease, or the interest rate and maturity date in case of a loan; expenses incurred in connection with the transaction; the cost of the asset, the current value of the asset, and the net gain (or loss) on each transaction. For purposes of the preceding sentence, the term "reportable transaction" means a transaction to which the plan is a party if such transaction is—

(i) a transaction involving an amount in excess of 3 percent of the current value of the assets of the plan;

(ii) any transaction (other than a transaction respecting a security) which is part of a series of transactions with or in conjunction with a person in a plan year, if the aggregate amount of such transaction exceeds 3 percent of the current value of the assets of the plan;

(iii) a transaction which is part of a series of transactions respecting one or more securities of the same issuer, if the aggregate amount of such transactions in the plan year exceeds 3 percent of the current value of the assets of the plan; or

(iv) a transaction with or in conjunction with a person respecting a security, if any other transaction with or in conjunction with such person in the plan year respecting a security is required to be reported by reason of clause (i).

(4) The Secretary may, by regulation, relieve any plan from filing a copy of a statement of assets and liabilities (or other information) described in paragraph (3)(G) if such statement and other information is filed with the Secretary by the bank or insurance carrier which maintains the common or collective trust or separate account.

Act Sec. 103. (c) The administrator shall furnish as a part of a report under this section the following information:

(1) The number of employees covered by the plan.

(2) The name and address of each fiduciary.

(3) Except in the case of a person whose compensation is minimal (determined under regulations of the Secretary) and who performs solely ministerial duties (determined under such regulations), the name of each person (including but not limited to, any consultant, broker, trustee, accountant, insurance carrier, actuary, administrator, investment manager, or custodian who rendered services to the plan or who had transactions with the plan) who received directly or indirectly compensation from the plan during the preceding year for services rendered to the plan or its participants, the amount of such compensation, the nature of his services to the plan or its participants, his relationship to the employer of the employees covered by the plan, or the employee organization, and any other office, position, or employment he holds with any party in interest.

(4) An explanation of the reason for any change in appointment of trustee, accountant, insurance carrier, enrolled actuary, administrator, investment manager, or custodian.

(5) Such financial and actuarial information including but not limited to the material described in subsections (b) and (d) of this section as the Secretary may find necessary or appropriate.

Act Sec. 103. (d) With respect to an employee pension benefit plan (other than (A) a profit sharing, savings, or other plan, which is an individual account plan, (B) a plan described in section 301(b), or (C) a plan described both in section 4021(b) and in paragraph (1), (2), (3), (4), (5), (6), or (7) of section 301(a)) an annual report under this section for a plan year shall include a complete actuarial statement applicable to the plan year which shall include the following:

(1) The date of the plan year, and the date of the actuarial valuation applicable to the plan year for which the report is filed.

(2) The date and amount of the contribution (or contributions) received by the plan for the plan year for which the report is filed and contributions for prior plan years not previously reported.

(3) The following information applicable to the plan year for which the report is filed: the normal costs, the accrued liabilities, an identification of benefits not included in the calculation; a statement of the other facts and actuarial assumptions and methods used to determine costs, and a justification for any change in actuarial assumptions or cost methods; and the minimum contribution required under section 302.

(4) The number of participants and beneficiaries, both retired and nonretired, covered by the plan.

(5) The current value of the assets accumulated in the plan, and the present value of the assets of the plan used by the actuary in any computation of the amount of contributions to the plan required under section 302 and a statement explaining the basis of such valuation of present value of assets.

(6) Information required in regulations of the Pension Benefit Guaranty Corporation with respect to:

(A) the current value of the assets of the plan,

(B) the present value of all nonforfeitable benefits for participants and beneficiaries receiving payments under the plan,

(C) the present value of all nonforfeitable benefits for all other participants and beneficiaries,

(D) the present value of all accrued benefits which are not nonforfeitable (including a separate accounting of such benefits which are benefit commitments, as defined in section 4001(a)(16)), and

(E) the actuarial assumptions and techniques used in determining the values described in subparagraphs (A) through (D).

(7) A certification of the contribution necessary to reduce the accumulated funding deficiency to zero.

(8) A statement by the enrolled actuary—

(A) that to the best of his knowledge the report is complete and accurate, and

(B) the requirements of section 302(c)(3) (relating to reasonable actuarial assumptions and methods) have been complied with.

(9) A copy of the opinion required by subsection (a)(4).

(10) A statement by the actuary which discloses—

(A) any event which the actuary has not taken into account, and

(B) any trend which, for purposes of the actuarial assumptions used, was not assumed to continue in the future,

but only if, to the best of the actuary's knowledge, such event or trend may require a material increase in plan costs or required contribution rates.

(11) If the current value of the assets of the plan is less than 70 percent of the current liability under the plan (within the meaning of section 302(d)(7)), the percentage which such value is of such liability.

(12) Such other information regarding the plan as the Secretary may by regulation require.

(13) Such other information as may be necessary to fully and fairly disclose the actuarial position of the plan.

Such actuary shall make an actuarial valuation of the plan for every third plan year, unless he determines that a more frequent valuation is necessary to support his opinion under subsection (a)(4) of this section.

Act Sec. 103. (e) If some or all of the benefits under the plan are purchased from and guaranteed by an insurance company, insurance service, or other similar organization, a report under this section shall include a statement from such insurance company, service, or other similar organization covering the plan year and enumerating—

(1) the premium rate for subscription charge and the total premium or subscription charges paid to each such carrier, insurance service, or other similar organization and the approximate number of persons covered by each class of such benefits; and

(2) the total amount of premiums received, the approximate number of persons covered by each class of benefits, and the total claims paid by such company, service, or other organization; dividends or retroactive rate adjustments, commissions, and administrative service or other fees or other specific acquisition costs paid by such company, service, or other organization; any amounts held to provide benefits after retirement; the remainder of such premiums; and the names and addresses of the brokers, agents, or other persons to whom commissions or fees were paid, the amount paid to each, and for what purpose. If any such company, service, or other organization does not maintain separate experience records covering the specific groups it serves, the report shall include in lieu of the information required by the foregoing provisions of this paragraph (A) a statement as to the basis of its premium rate or subscription charge, the total amount of premiums or subscription charges received from the plan, and a copy of the financial report of the company, service or other organization and (B) if such company, service, or organization incurs specific costs in connection with the acquisition or retention of any particular plan or plans, a detailed statement of such costs.

Amendments

P.L. 101-239, §7881(j)(1):

Amended ERISA Sec. 103(d)(11) by striking "60 percent" and inserting "70 percent" and by striking "such percentage" and inserting "the percentage which such value is of such liability" effective with respect to reports required to be filed after December 31, 1987.

P.L. 100-203, §9342(a)(1):

Amended ERISA Sec. 103(d) by redesignating paragraphs (11) and (12) as paragraphs (12) and (13), respectively, and by inserting paragraph (11) to read as above, effective with respect to reports required to be filed after December 31, 1987.

P.L. 99-272, §11016(b)(1):

Amended ERISA Sec. 103(d)(6) to read as above, effective on April 7, 1986.

Prior to the amendment, ERISA Sec. 103(d)(6) read as follows:

(6) The present value of all of the plan's liabilities for nonforfeitable pension benefits allocated by the termination priority categories as set forth in section 4044 of this Act, and the actuarial assumptions used in these computations. The Secretary shall establish regulations defining (for purposes of this section) "termination priority categories" and acceptable methods, including approximate methods, for allocating the plan's liabilities to such termination priority categories.

P.L. 96-364, §307:

Added new subsection 103(d)(10) to read as above and renumbered old subsections 103(d)(10) and (11) to be 103(11) and (12), respectively, effective September 26, 1980.

Regulations

The following regulations on annual reporting requirements were adopted, effective generally for plan years beginning in 1977, by FR Doc. 78-6073 under "Title 29—Labor," "Chapter XXV—Pension and Welfare Benefit Programs, Department of Labor," "Part 2520—Rules and Regulations for Reporting and Disclosure." The regulations were filed with the Federal Register on March 9, 1978, and published in the Federal Register on March 10, 1978 (41 FR 10130). Reg. §§ 2520.103-1—2520.103-6 and §§ 2520.103-9—2520.103-12 were amended by 65 FR 21067 and published in the *Federal Register* on April 19, 2000 (65 FR 21067).

Subpart C—Annual Report Requirements

[¶ 14,231A]

§ 2520.103-1 **Contents of the annual report.** (a) *General.* The administrator of a plan required to file an annual report in accordance with section 104(a)(1) of the Act shall include with the annual report the information prescribed in paragraph (a)(1) of this section or in the limited exemption or alternative method of compliance described in paragraph (a)(2) of this section.

(1) The annual report shall contain the information prescribed in section 103 of the Act.

(2) Under the authority of sections 104(a)(3) and 110 of the Act, a limited exemption or alternative method of compliance is prescribed for employee welfare and pension benefit plans, respectively, which cover 100 or more participants at the beginning of the plan year. A plan electing the limited exemption or alternative method of compliance shall file an annual report containing the information prescribed in paragraph (b) of this section and shall furnish a summary annual report as prescribed in § 2520.104b-10. [Amended on March 1, 1989 by 54 FR 8624.]

(b) *Contents of the annual report for plans with 100 or more participants electing the limited exemption or alternative method of compliance.* Except as provided in paragraph (d) of this section and in §§ 2520.103-2 and 2520.104-44, the annual report of an employee benefit plan covering 100 or more participants at the beginning of the plan year which elects the limited exemption or alternative method of compliance described in paragraph (a)(2) of this section shall include:

(1) A Form 5500 "Annual Return/Report of Employee Benefit Plan" and any statements or schedules required to be attached to the form, completed in accordance with the instructions for the form, including Schedule A (Insurance Information), Schedule B (Actuarial Information), Schedule C (Service Provider Information), Schedule D (DFE/Participating Plan Information), Schedule G (Financial Transaction Schedules), Schedule H (Financial Information), Schedule R (Retirement Plan Information), and the other financial schedules described in § 2520.103-10. See the instructions for this form. [Amended on March 1, 1989 by 54 FR 8624; amended April 19 by 65 FR 21080.]

(2) Separate financial statements (in addition to the information required by paragraph (b)(1) of this section), if such financial statements are prepared in order for the independent qualified public accountant to form the opinion required by section 103(a)(3)(A) of the Act and § 2520.103-1(b)(5). These statements shall include the following:

(i) A statement of assets and liabilities at current value presented in comparative form for the beginning and end of the year. The statement of plan assets and liabilities shall include the assets and liabilities required to be reported on Form 5500; however, the assets and liabilities may be aggregated into categories in a manner other than that used on Form 5500. [Amended on March 1, 1989 by 54 FR 8624; amended on April 19, 2000 by 65 FR 21080.]

(ii) Separate or combined statements of plan income and expenses and of changes in net assets which include the categories of income, expense, and changes in assets required to be reported on the Form 5500; however, the income, expense, and changes in net assets may be aggregated into categories in a manner other than that used on Form 5500. [Amended on March 1, 1989 by 54 FR 8624.]

(3) Notes to the financial statements described in paragraphs (b)(1) or (2) of this section which contain a description of the accounting principles and practices reflected in the financial statements and, if applicable, variances from generally accepted accounting principles; a description of the plan, including any significant changes in the plan made during the period and the impact of such changes on benefits; the funding policy (including policy with respect to prior service cost) and any changes in such policy from the prior year, a description of material lease commitments, other commitments, and contingent liabil-

ities; a description of agreements and transactions with persons known to be parties in interest; a general description of priorities upon termination of the plan; information concerning whether or not a tax ruling or determination letter has been obtained; an explanation of the differences, if any, between the information contained in the separate financial statements and the assets, liabilities, income, expenses and changes in net assets as required to be reported on the Form 5500, and any other matters necessary to fully and fairly present the financial condition of the plan. [Amended on March 1, 1989 by 54 FR 8624.]

(4) In the case of a plan, some or all of the assets of which are held in a pooled separate account maintained by an insurance company, or a common or collective trust maintained by a bank or similar institution, a copy of the annual statement of assets and liabilities of such account or trust for the fiscal year of the account or trust which ends with or within the plan year for which the annual report is made as required to be furnished to the administrator by such account or trust under § 2520.103-5(c). Although the statement of assets and liabilities referred to in § 2520.103-5(c) shall be considered part of the plan's annual report, such statement of assets and liabilities need not be filed with the plan's annual report. See §§ 2520.103-3 and 2520.103-4 for reporting requirements for plans some or all of the assets of which are held in a pooled separate account maintained by an insurance company, or a common or collective trust maintained by a bank or similar institution. [Amended April 19, 2000 by 65 FR 21080.]

(5) A report of an independent qualified public accountant.

(i) *Technical requirements.* The accountant's report—

(A) Shall be dated;

(B) Shall be signed manually;

(C) Shall indicate the city and state where issued; and

(D) Shall identify without detailed enumeration the financial statements and schedules covered by the report.

(ii) *Representations as to the audit.* The accountant's report—

(A) Shall state whether the audit was made in accordance with generally accepted auditing standards; and

(B) Shall designate any auditing procedures deemed necessary by the accountant under the circumstances of the particular case which have been omitted, and the reasons for their omission. Authority for the omission of certain procedures which independent accountants might ordinarily employ in the course of an audit made for the purpose of expressing the opinions required by paragraph (b)(5)(iii) of this section is contained in §§ 2520.103-8 and 2520.103-12. [Amended by 51 FR 41285 on Nov. 13, 1986; amended on March 1, 1989 by 54 FR 8624.]

(iii) *Opinion to be expressed.* The accountant's report shall state clearly:

(A) The opinion of the accountant in respect of the financial statements and schedules covered by the report and the accounting principles and practices reflected therein; and

(B) The opinion of the accountant as to the consistency of the application of the accounting principles with the application of such principles in the preceding year or as to any changes in such principles which have a material effect on the financial statements.

(iv) *Exceptions.* Any matters to which the accountant takes exception shall be clearly identified, the exception thereto specifically and clearly stated, and, to the extent practicable, the effect of the matters to which the accountant takes exception on the related financial statements given. The matters to which the accountant takes exception shall be further identified as (A) those that are the result of DOL regulations, and (B) all others.

(c) *Contents of the annual report for plans with fewer than 100 participants.* Except as provided in paragraph (d) of this section and in

§§ 2520.104-43 and 2520.104a-6, the annual report of an employee benefit plan which covers fewer than 100 participants at the beginning of the plan year shall include a Form 5500 "Annual Return/Report of Employee Benefit Plan" and any statements or schedules required to be attached to the form, completed in accordance with the instructions for the form, including Schedule A (Insurance Information), Schedule B (Actuarial Information), Schedule D (DFE/Participating Plan Information), Schedule I (Financial Information—Small Plan), and Schedule R (Retirement Plan Information). See the instructions for this form. [Amended on July 29, 1980 by 45 FR 51446; amended on March 1, 1989 by 54 FR 8624; amended on April 19, 2000 by 65 FR 21080.]

(d) *Special rule.* If a plan has between 80 and 120 participants (inclusive) as of the beginning of the plan year, the plan administrator may elect to file the same category of annual report (i.e., the annual report for plans with 100 or more participants under paragraph (b) of this section or the annual report for plans with fewer than 100 participants under paragraph (c) of this section) that was filed for the previous plan year. [Added on July 29, 1980 by 45 FR 51446; amended on March 1, 1989 by 54 FR 8624; amended April 19, 2000 by FR 65 21080.]

(e) *Plans which participate in a master trust.* The plan administrator of a plan which participates in a master trust shall file an annual report on Form 5500 in accordance with the instructions for the form relating to master trusts and master trust investment accounts. For purposes of annual reporting, a master trust is a trust for which a regulated financial institution serves as trustee or custodian (regardless of whether such institution exercises discretionary authority or control respecting the management of assets held in the trust) and in which assets of more than one plan sponsored by a single employer or by a group of employers under common control are held. For purpose of this paragraph, a regulated financial institution is a bank, trust company, or similar financial institution regulated, supervised, and subject to periodic examination by a State or Federal agency. Common control is determined on the basis of all relevant facts and circumstances (whether or not such employers are incorporated). [Added on December 10, 1981, by 46 FR 61074; amended on March 1, 1989 by 54 FR 8624; amended April 19, 2000 by FR 65 21080.]

(f) *Electronic filing.* The Form 5500 "Annual Return/Report of Employee Benefit Plan" may be filed electronically or through other media in accordance with the instructions accompanying the form, provided the plan administrator maintains an original copy, with all required signatures, as part of the plan's records. [Added April 19, 2000 by FR 65 21080.]

[¶ 14,231B]
§ 2520.103-2 **Contents of the annual report for a group insurance arrangement.** (a) *General.* (1) A trust or other entity described in § 2520.104-43(b) that files an annual report for purposes of § 2520.104-43 shall include in such report the items set forth in paragraph (b) of this section.

(b) *Contents.* (1) A Form 5500 "Annual Return/Report of Employee Benefit Plan" and any statements or schedules required to be attached to the form, completed in accordance with the instructions for the form, including Schedule A (Insurance Information), Schedule C (Service Provider Information), Schedule D (DFE/Participating Plan Information), Schedule G (Financial Transaction Schedules), Schedule H (Financial Information), and the other financial schedules described in § 2520.103-10. See the instructions for this form. [Amended on March 1, 1989 by 54 FR 8624; amended April 19, 2000 by 65 FR 21080.]

(2) Separate financial statements (in addition to the information required by paragraph (b)(1) of this section), if such financial statements are prepared in order for the independent qualified public accountant to form the opinion required by section 103(a)(3)(A) of the Act and § 2520.103-2(b)(5). These financial statements shall include the following:

(i) A statement of all trust assets and liabilities at current value presented in comparative form for the beginning and end of the year. The statement of trust assets and liabilities shall include the assets and liabilities required to be reported on the Form 5500; however, the assets and liabilities may be aggregated into categories in a

manner other than that used on Form 5500. [Amended on March 1, 1989 by 54 FR 8624; amended April 19, 2000 by 65 FR 21080.]

(ii) Separate or combined statements of all trust income and expenses and changes in net assets which includes the categories of income, expense, and changes in assets required to be reported on the Form 5500; however, the income, expense, and changes in assets may be aggregated into categories in a manner other than that used on Form 5500. [Amended on March 1, 1989 by 54 FR 8624.]

(3) Notes to the financial statements described in paragraphs (b)(1) or (2) of this section which contain a description of the accounting principles and practices reflected in the financial statements and, if applicable, variances from generally accepted accounting principles; a description of the group insurance arrangement including any significant changes in the group insurance arrangement made during the period and the impact of such changes on benefits; a description of material lease commitments, other commitments, and contingent liabilities; a description of agreements and transactions with persons known to be parties in interest; a general description of priorities upon termination of the plan; an explanation of the differences, if any, between the information contained in the separate financial statements and the assets, liabilities, income, expenses and changes in net assets as required to be reported on the Form 5500; and any other matters necessary to fully and fairly present the financial condition of the plan. [Amended on March 1, 1989 by 54 FR 8624.]

(4) In the case of a group insurance arrangement some or all of the assets of which are held in a pooled separate account maintained by an insurance carrier, or in a common or collective trust maintained by a bank, trust company or similar institution, a copy of the annual statement of assets and liabilities of such account or trust for the fiscal year of the account or trust which ends with or within the plan year for which the annual report is made as required to be furnished by such account or trust under § 2520.103-5(c). Although the statement of assets and liabilities referred to in § 2520.103-5(c) shall be considered part of the group insurance arrangement's annual report, such statement of assets and liabilities need not be filed with its annual report. See §§ 2520.103-3 and 2520.103-4 for reporting requirements for plans some or all of the assets of which are held in a pooled separate account maintained by an insurance company, or a common or collective trust maintained by a bank or similar institution, and see § 2520.104-43(b)(2) for when the terms "group insurance arrangement" or "trust or other entity" shall be, respectively, used in place of the terms "plan" and "plan administrator." [Amended April 19, 2000 by 65 FR 21080.]

(5) A report of an independent qualified public accountant.

(i) *Technical requirements.* The accountant's report—

(A) Shall be dated;

(B) Shall be signed manually;

(C) Shall indicate the city and State where issued; and

(D) Shall identify without detailed enumeration the financial statements and schedules covered by the report.

(ii) *Representations as to the audit.* The accountant's report—

(A) Shall state whether the audit was made in accordance with generally accepted auditing standards; and

(B) Shall designate any auditing procedures deemed necessary by the accountant under the circumstances of the particular case, which have been omitted, and the reasons for their omission. Authority for the omission of certain procedures which independent accountants might ordinarily employ in the course of an audit made for the purpose of expressing the opinions required by paragraph (b)(5)(iii) of this section is contained in § 2520.103-8.

(iii) *Opinion to be expressed.* The accountant's report shall state clearly:

(A) The opinion of the accountant in respect of the financial statements and schedules covered by the report and the accounting principles and practices reflected therein; and

(B) The opinion of the accountant as to the consistency of the application of the accounting principles with the application of such principles in the preceding year, or as to any changes in such principles which have a material effect on the financial statements.

(iv) *Exceptions.* Any matters to which the accountant takes exception shall be clearly identified, the exception thereto specifically and clearly stated, and, to the extent practicable, the effect of the matters to which the accountant takes exception on the related financial statements given. The matters to which the accountant takes exception shall be further identified as to (a) those that are the result of DOL regulations and (b) all others. [Added March 9, 1978, by 43 F.R. 10130.]

(c) *Electronic filing.* The Form 5500 "Annual Return/Report of Employee Benefit Plan" may be filed electronically or through other media in accordance with the instructions accompanying the form, provided the trust or other entity described in § 2520.104-43(b) maintains an original copy, with all required signatures, as part of the trust's or entity's records. [Added April 19, 2000 by 65 FR 21081.]

[¶ 14,231C]

§ 2520.103-3 **Exemption from certain annual reporting requirements for assets held in a common or collective trust.** (a) *General.* Under the authority of sections 103(b)(3)(G), 103(b)(4), 104(a)(2)(B), 104(a)(3), 110 and 505 of the Act, a plan whose assets are held in whole or in part in a common or collective trust maintained by a bank, trust company, or similar institution which meets the requirements of paragraph (b) of this section shall include as part of the annual report required to be filed under §§ 2520.104a-5 or 2520.104a-6 the information described in paragraph (c) of this section. Such plan is not required to include in its annual report information concerning the individual transactions of the common or collective trust. This exemption has no application to assets not held in such trusts. [Amended April 19, 2000 by 65 FR 21081.]

(b) *Application.* This provision applies only to a plan some or all of the assets of which are held in a common or collective trust maintained by a bank, trust company, or similar institution regulated and supervised and subject to periodic examination by a State or Federal agency. For purposes of this section, (1) a common or collective trust is a trust which consists of the assets of two or more participating entities and is maintained for the collective investment and reinvestment of assets contributed thereto, and (2) plans maintained by a single employer or by the members of a controlled group of corporations, as defined in section 1563(a) of the Internal Revenue Code of 1954, shall be deemed to be a single participating entity.

(c) *Contents.* (1) A plan which meets the requirements of paragraph (b) of this section, and which invests in a common or collective trust that files a Form 5500 report in accordance with § 2520.103-9, shall include in its annual report: information required by the instructions to Schedule H (Financial Information) or Schedule I (Financial Information—Small Plan) about the current value of and net investment gain or loss relating to the units of participation in the common or collective trust held by the plan; identifying information about the common or collective trust including its name, employer identification number, and any other information required by the instructions to the Schedule D (DFE/Participating Plan Information); and such other information as is required in the separate statements and schedules of the annual report about the value of the plan's units of participation in the common or collective trust and transactions involving the acquisition and disposition by the plan of units of participation in the common or collective trust. [Amended April 18, 2000 by 65 FR 21081.]

(2) A plan which meets the requirements of paragraph (b) of this section, and which invests in a common or collective trust that does not file a Form 5500 report in accordance with § 2520.103-9, shall include in its annual report: information required by the instructions to Schedule H (Financial Information) or Schedule I (Financial Information—Small Plan) about the current value of the plan's allocable portion of the underlying assets and liabilities of the common or collective trust and the net investment gain or loss relating to the units of participation in the common or collective trust held by the plan; identifying information about the common or collective trust including its name, employer identification number, and any other information required by the instructions to the Schedule D (DFE/Participating Plan Information); and such other information as is required in the separate statements and schedules of the annual report about the value of the plan's units of participation in the common or collective trust and transactions involving the acquisition and disposition by the plan of units of participation

in the common or collective trust. [Added March 9, 1978, by 43 FR 10130; amended April 19, 2000 by 65 FR 21081.]

[¶ 14,231D]

§ 2520.103-4 **Exemption from certain annual reporting requirements for assets held in an insurance company pooled separate account.** (a) *General.* Under the authority of sections 103(b)(3)(G), 103(b)(4), 104(a)(2)(B), 104(a)(3), 110 and 505 of the Act, a plan whose assets are held in whole or in part in a pooled separate account of an insurance carrier which meets the requirements of paragraph (b) of this section shall include as part of the annual report required to be filed under § 2520.104a-5 or § 2520.104a-6 the information described in paragraph (c) of this section. Such plan is not required to include in its annual report information concerning the individual transactions of the pooled separate account. This exemption has no application to assets not held in such a pooled separate account. [Amended April 19, 2000 by 65 FR 21081.]

(b) *Application.* This provision applies only to a plan some or all of the assets of which are held in a pooled separate account of an insurance carrier regulated and supervised and subject to periodic examination by a State agency. For purposes of this section, (1) a pooled separate account is an account which consists of the assets of two or more participating entities and is maintained for the collective investment and reinvestment of assets contributed thereto, and (2) plans maintained by a single employer or by members of a controlled group of corporations, as defined in section 1563(a) of the Internal Revenue Code of 1954, shall be deemed to be a single participating entity.

(c) *Contents.* (1) A plan which meets the requirements of paragraph (b) of this section, and which invests in a pooled separate account that files a Form 5500 report in accordance with § 2520.103-9, shall include in its annual report: information required by the instructions to Schedule H (Financial Information) or Schedule I (Financial Information—Small Plan) about the current value of, and net investment gain or loss relating to, the units of participation in the pooled separate account held by the plan; identifying information about the pooled separate account including its name, employer identification number, and any other information required by the instructions to the Schedule D (DFE/Participating Plan Information); and such other information as is required in the separate statements and schedules of the annual report about the value of the plan's units of participation in the pooled separate accounts and transactions involving the acquisition and disposition by the plan of units of participation in the pooled separate account. [Amended on April 19, 2000 by 65 FR 21081.]

(2) A plan which meets the requirements of paragraph (b) of this section, and which invests in a pooled separate account that does not file a Form 5500 report in accordance with § 2520.103-9, shall include in its annual report: information required by the instructions to Schedule H (Financial Information) or Schedule I (Financial Information—Small Plan) about the current value of the plan's allocable portion of the underlying assets and liabilities of the pooled separate account and the net investment gain or loss relating to the units of participation in the pooled separate account held by the plan; identifying information about the pooled separate account including its name, employer identification number, and any other information required by the instructions to the Schedule D (DFE/Participating Plan Information); and such other information as is required in the separate statements and schedules of the annual report about the value of the plan's units of participation in the pooled separate account and transactions involving the acquisition and disposition by the plan of units of participation in the pooled separate account. [Added March 9, 1978, by 43 FR 10130; amended April 19, 2000 by 65 FR 21081].

[¶ 14,231E]

§ 2520.103-5 **Transmittal and certification of information to plan administrator for annual reporting purposes.** (a) *General.* In accordance with section 103(a)(2) of the Act, an insurance carrier or other organization which provides benefits under the plan or holds plan assets, a bank or similar institution which holds plan assets, or a plan sponsor shall transmit and certify such information as needed by the administrator to file the annual report under section 104(a)(1) of the Act and § 2520.104a-5 or § 2520.104a-6:

(1) Within 9 months after the close of the plan year which begins in 1975 or September 30, 1976, whichever is later, and

(2) Within 120 days after the close of any plan year which begins after December 31, 1975.

(b) *Application.* This requirement applies with respect to—

(1) An insurance carrier or other organization which:

(i) Provides from its general asset account funds for the payment of benefits under a plan, or

(ii) Holds assets of a plan in a separate account;

(2) A bank, trust company, or similar institution which holds assets of a plan in a common or collective trust, separate trust, or custodial account; and

(3) A plan sponsor as defined in section 3(16)(B) of the Act.

(c) *Contents.* The information required to be provided to the administrator shall include—

(1) In the case of an insurance carrier or other organization which:

(i) Provides funds from its general asset account for the payment of benefits under a plan, upon request of the plan administrator, such information as is contained within the ordinary business records of the insurance carrier or other organization and is needed by the plan administrator to comply with the requirements of section 104(a)(1) of the Act and § 2520.104a-5 or § 2520.104a-6;

(ii) Holds assets of a plan in a pooled separate account and files a Form 5500 report pursuant to § 2520.103-9 for the participating plan's plan year—

(A) A copy of the annual statement of assets and liabilities of the separate account for the fiscal year of such account ending with or within the plan year for which the participating plan's annual report is made,

(B) A statement of the value of the plan's units of participation in the separate account,

(C) The Employer Identification Number (EIN) of the separate account, entity number required for purposes of completing the Form 5500 and any other identifying number assigned by the insurance carrier to the separate account,

(D) A statement that a filing pursuant to § 2520.103-9(c) will be made for the separate account (for its fiscal year ending with or within the participating plan's plan year) on or before the filing due date for such account in accordance with the Form 5500 instructions, and

(E) Upon request of the plan administrator, any other information that can be obtained from the ordinary business records of the insurance carrier and that is needed by the plan administrator to comply with the requirements of section 104(a)(1) of the Act and § 2520.104a-5 or § 2520.104a-6; [Amended April 19, 2000 by 65 FR 21081.]

(iii) Holds assets of a plan in a pooled separate account and does not file a Form 5500 report pursuant to § 2520.103-9 for the participating plan's plan year—

(A) A copy of the annual statement of assets and liabilities of the separate account for the fiscal year of such account that ends with or within the plan year for which the participating plan's annual report is made,

(B) A statement of the value of the plan's units of participation in the separate account,

(C) The EIN of the separate account and any other identifying number assigned by the insurance carrier to the separate account,

(D) A statement that a filing pursuant to § 2520.103-9(c) will not be made for the separate account for its fiscal year ending with or within the participating plan's plan year, and

(E) Upon request of the plan administrator, any other information that can be obtained from the ordinary business records of the insurance carrier and that is needed by the plan administrator to comply with the requirements of section 104(a)(1) of the Act and § 2520.104a-5 or § 2520.104a-6. [Added April 19, 2000 by 65 FR 21081.]

(iv) Holds assets of a plan in a separate account which is not exempted from certain reporting requirements under § 2520.103-4, a listing of all transactions of the separate account and, upon request of the plan administrator, such information as is contained within the ordinary business records of the insurance carrier and is needed by the plan administrator to comply with the requirements of section 104(a)(1) of the Act and § 2520.104a-5 or § 2520.104a-6. [Amended April 19, 2000 by 65 FR 21081.]

(2) In the case of a bank, trust company, or similar institution holding assets of a plan—

(i) In a common or collective trust that files a Form 5500 report pursuant to § 2520.103-9 for the participating plan's plan year—

(A) A copy of the annual statement of assets and liabilities of the common or collective trust for the fiscal year of such trust ending with or within the plan year for which the participating plan's annual report is made,

(B) A statement of the value of the plan's units of participation in the common or collective trust,

(C) The EIN of the common or collective trust, entity number assigned for purposes of completing the Form 5500 and any other identifying number assigned by the bank, trust company, or similar institution,

(D) A statement that a filing pursuant to § 2520.103-9(c) will be made for the common or collective trust (for its fiscal year ending with or within the participating plan's plan year) on or before the filing due date for such trust in accordance with the Form 5500 instructions, and

(E) Upon request of the plan administrator, any other information that can be obtained from the ordinary business records of the bank, trust company or similar institution and that is needed by the plan administrator to comply with the requirements of section 104(a)(1) of the Act and § § 2520.104a-5 or 2520.104a-6. [Amended April 19, 2000 by 65 FR 21082.]

(ii) In a common or collective trust that does not file a Form 5500 report pursuant to § 2520.103-9 for the participating plan's plan year—

(A) A copy of the annual statement of assets and liabilities of the common or collective trust for the fiscal year of such account that ends with or within the plan year for which the participating plan's annual report is made,

(B) A statement of the value of the plan's units of participation in the common or collective trust,

(C) The EIN of the common or collective trust and any other identifying number assigned by the bank, trust company or similar institution,

(D) A statement that a filing pursuant to § 2520.103-9(c) will not be made for the common or collective trust for its fiscal year ending with or within the participating plan's plan year, and

(E) Upon request of the plan administrator, any other information that can be obtained from the ordinary business records of the bank, trust company or similar institution and that is needed by the plan administrator to comply with the requirements of section 104(a)(1) of the Act and § § 2520.104a-5 or 2520.104a-6. [Added April 19, 2000 by 65 FR 21082.]

(iii) In a trust which is not exempted from certain reporting requirements under § 2520.103-3, a listing of all transactions of the separate trust and, upon request of the the plan administrator, such information as is contained within the ordinary business records of the bank, trust company, or similar institution and is needed by the plan administrator to comply with the requirements of section 104(a)(1) of the Act and § 2520.104a-5. [Amended April 19, 2000 by 65 FR 21082.]

(iv) In a custodial account, upon request of the plan administrator, such information as is contained within the ordinary business records of the bank, trust company, or similar institution and is needed by the plan administrator to comply with the requirements of section 104(a)(1) of the Act and § 2520.104a-5 or § 2520.104a-6. [Amended April 19, 2000 by 65 FR 21082.]

(3) In the case of a plan sponsor, a listing of all transactions directly or indirectly involving plan assets engaged in by the plan sponsor and such information as is needed by the plan administrator to

comply with the requirements of section 104(a)(1) of the Act and § 2520.104a-5 or § 2520.104a-6.

(d) *Certification.* (1) An insurance carrier or other organization, a bank, trust company, or similar institution, or plan sponsor, as described in paragraph (b) of this section, shall certify to the accuracy and completeness of the information described in paragraph (c) of this section by a written declaration which is signed by a person authorized to represent the insurance carrier, bank, or plan sponsor. Such certification will serve as a written assurance of the truth of the facts stated therein.

(2) *Example of Certification.* The XYZ Bank (Insurance Carrier) hereby certifies that the foregoing statement furnished pursuant to 29 CFR 2520.103-5(c) is complete and accurate. [Added March 9, 1978, by 43 FR 10130.]

[¶ 14,231F]

§ 2520.103-6 **Definition of reportable transaction for Annual Return/Report.** (a) *General.* General. For purposes of preparing the schedule of reportable transactions described in § 2520.103-10(b)(6), and subject to the exceptions provided in § § 2520.103-3, 2520.103-4 and 2520.103-12, with respect to individual transactions by a common or collective trust, pooled separate account, or a 103-12 investment entity, a reportable transaction includes any transaction or series of transactions described in paragraph (c) of this section. [Corrected April 4, 1978, by 43 FR 14009; amended April 19, 2000 by 65 FR 21082.]

(b) *Definitions.* (1)(i) Except as provided in paragraphs (c)(2) and (d)(1)(vi) of this section (relating to assets acquired or disposed of during the plan year), "current value" shall mean the current value, as defined in section 3(26) of the Act, of plan assets as of the beginning of the plan year, or the end of the previous plan year. [Amended July 1, 1996 by 61 FR 33847.]

(ii) Except as provided in paragraphs (c)(2) and (d)(1)(vi) of this section (relating to assets acquired or disposed of during the plan year), with respect to schedules of reportable transactions for the initial plan year of a plan, "current value" shall mean the current value, as defined in section 3(26) of the Act, of plan assets at the end of a plan's initial plan year. [Amended April 19, 2000 by 65 FR 21082.]

(2)(i) A "transaction with respect to securities" is any purchase, sale, or exchange of securities. A transaction with respect to securities for purposes of this section occurs on either the trade date or settlement date of a purchase, sale, or exchange of securities; either the trade date or settlement date must be used consistently during the plan year for the purposes of this section. For the purposes of this section, except as provided in paragraph (b)(2)(ii) of this section, "securities" includes a unit of participation in a common or collective trust or a pooled separate account.

(ii) Solely for purposes of paragraph (c)(1)(iv) of this section, the term "securities", as it applies to any transaction involving a bank or insurance company regulated by a Federal or State agency, an investment company registered under the Investment Company Act of 1940, or a broker-dealer registered under the Securities Exchange Act of 1934, shall not include:

(A) Debt obligations of the United States or any United States agency with a maturity of not more than one year;

(B) Debt obligations of the United States or any United States agency with a maturity of more than one year if purchased or sold, under a repurchase agreement having a term of less than 91 days;

(C) Interests issued by a company registered under the Investment Company Act of 1940;

(D) Bank certificates of deposit with a maturity of not more than one year;

(E) Commercial paper with a maturity of not more than nine months if it is ranked in the highest rating category for commercial paper by at least two nationally recognized statistical rating services and is issued by a company required to file reports under section 13 of the Securities Exchange Act of 1934;

(F) Participations in a bank common or collective trust;

(G) Participations in an insurance company pooled separate account;

(3)(i) Except as provided by paragraph (b)(3)(ii) of this section, a transaction is "with or in conjunction with a person" for purposes of this section if that person benefits from, executes, facilitates, participates, promotes, or solicits a transaction or part of a transaction involving plan assets.

(ii) Solely for the purposes of paragraph (c)(1)(iv) of this section, a transaction shall not be considered "with or in conjunction with a person" if:

(A) That person is a broker-dealer registered under the Securities Exchange Act of 1934;

(B) The transaction involves the purchase or sale of securities listed on a national securities exchange registered under section 6 of the Securities Exchange Act of 1934 or quoted on NASDAQ; and

(C) The broker-dealer does not purchase or sell securities involved in the transaction for its own account or the account of an affiliated person.

(c) *Application.* (1) Except as provided in paragraph (c)(4) of this section, this provision applies to—

(i) A transaction within the plan year, with respect to any plan asset, involving an amount in excess of 3 percent of the current value of plan assets;

(ii) Any series of transactions (other than transactions with respect to securities) within the plan year with or in conjunction with the same person which, when aggregated, regardless of the category of asset and the gain or loss on any transation, involves an amount in excess of 3 percent of the current value of plan assets;

(iii) Any transaction within the plan year involving securities of the same issue if within the plan year any series of transactions with respect to such securities, when aggregated, involves an amount in excess of 3 percent of the current value of plan assets; and

(iv) Any transaction within the plan year with respect to securities with or in conjunction with a person if any prior or subsequent single transaction within the plan year with such person with respect to securities exceeds 3 percent of the current value of plan assets.

(2) For purposes of determining whether any 3 percent transactions occur, the "current value" of an asset acquired or disposed of during the plan year is the current value, as defined in section 3(26) of the Act, at the time of acquisition or disposition of such asset.

(3) Plans whose assets are held in whole or in part in a common or collective trust or a pooled separate account, as provided in § § 2520.103-3 and 2520.103-4, and which satisfy the requirements of those sections, are not required to prepare schedules of reportable transactions with respect to the individual transactions of the common or collective trust or pooled separate account.

(4) For plan years beginning on or after January 1, 1988, 5 percent shall be substituted for 3 percent in paragraphs (c)(1) and (2) of this section for purposes of determining whether a transaction or series of transactions constitutes a reportable transaction under this section. [Amended on March 1, 1989 by 54 FR 8624.]

(d) *Contents.* (1) The schedule of transactions shall include the following information as to each transaction or series of transactions:

(i) The name of each party, except that in the case of a transaction or series of transactions involving a purchase or sale of a security on the market, the schedule need not include the person from whom it was purchased or to whom it was sold. A purchase or sale on the market is a purchase or sale of a security through a registered broker-dealer acting as a broker under the Securities Exchange Act of 1934;

(ii) A brief description of each asset;

(iii) The purchase or selling price in the case of a purchase or sale, the rental in the case of a lease, and the amount of principal, interest rate, payment schedule (e.g., fully amortized, partly amortized with balloon) and maturity date in the case of a loan;

(iv) Expenses incurred, including, but not limited to, any fees or commissions;

(v) The cost of any asset;

(vi) The current value of any asset acquired or disposed of at the time of acquisition or disposition; and

(vii) The net gain or loss.

(2) The schedule of transactions with respect to a series of transactions described in subparagraph (c)(1)(iii) may include the following information for each issue in lieu of the information prescribed in paragraphs (d)(1)(i)—(vii):

(i) The total number of purchases of such securities made by the plan within the plan year;

(ii) The total number of sales of such securities made by the plan within the plan year;

(iii) The total dollar value of such purchases;

(iv) The total dollar value of such sales;

(v) The net gain or loss as a result of these transactions.

(e) *Examples*. These examples are effective for reporting for plan years beginning on or after January 1, 1988.

(1) At the beginning of the plan year, XYZ plan has 10 percent of the current value of its plan assets invested in ABC common stock. Halfway through the plan year, XYZ purchases ABC common stock in a single transaction in an amount equal to 6 percent of the current value of plan assets. At about this time, XYZ plan also purchases a commercial development property in an amount equal to 8 percent of the current value of plan assets. Under paragraph (c)(1)(i) of this section, the 6 percent stock transaction is a reportable transaction for the plan year because it exceeds 5 percent of the current value of plan assets. The 8 percent land transaction is also reportable under paragraph (c)(1)(i) of this section because it exceeds 5 percent of the current value of plan assets.

(2) During the plan year, AAA plan purchases a commercial lot from ZZZ corporation at a cost equal to 2 percent of the current value of the plan assets. Two months later, AAA plan loans ZZZ corporation an amount of money equal to 3.5 percent of the current value of plan assets. Under the provisions of paragraph (c)(1)(ii) of this section, the plan has engaged in a reportable series of transactions with or in conjunction with the same person, ZZZ corporation, which when aggregated involves 5.5 percent of plan assets.

(3) During the plan year NMN plan sells to OPO corporation a commercial property that represents 3.5 percent of the current value of plan assets. OPO simultaneously executes a note and mortgage on the purchased property to NMN which represents 3 percent of the current value of plan assets. Under the provisions of paragraph (c)(1)(ii) of this section, NMN has engaged in a reportable series of transactions with or in conjunction with the same person, OPO corporation, consisting of a simultaneous sale of property and a loan, which, when aggregated, involves 6.5 percent of the current value of plan assets.

(4) At the beginning of the plan year, ABC plan has 10 percent of the current value of plan assets invested equally in a combination of XYZ Corporation common stock and XYZ preferred stock. One month into the plan year, ABC sells some of its XYZ common stock in an amount equal to 2 percent of the current value of plan assets.

(i) Six weeks later the plan sells XYZ preferred stock in an amount equal to 4 percent of the current value of plan assets. A reportable series of transactions has not occurred because only transactions involving securities of the same issue are to be aggregated under paragraph (c)(1)(iii) of this section.

(ii) Two weeks later when the ABC plan purchases XYZ common stock in an amount equal to 3.5 percent of the current value of plan assets, a reportable series of transactions under paragraph (c)(1)(iii) of this section has occurred. The sale of XYZ common stock worth 2 percent of plan assets and the purchase of XYZ common stock worth 3.5 percent of plan assets aggregate to exceed 5 percent of the total value of plan assets.

(5) At the beginning of the plan year, Plan X purchases through broker-dealer Y common stock of Able Industries in an amount equal to 6 percent of plan assets. The common stock of Able Industries is not listed on any national securities exchange or quoted on NASDAQ. This purchase is a reportable transaction under paragraph (c)(1)(i) of this section. Three months later, Plan X purchases short term debt obligations of Charley Company through broker-dealer Y in the amount of 0.2 percent of plan assets. This purchase is also a reportable transaction under the provisions of paragraph (c)(1)(iv) of this section.

(6) At the beginning of the plan year, Plan X purchases from Bank B certificates of deposit having a 180 day maturity in an amount equal to 6 percent of plan assets. Bank B is a national bank regulated by the Comptroller of the Currency. This purchase is a reportable transaction under paragraph (c)(1)(i) of this section. Three months later, Plan X purchases through Bank B 91-day Treasury bills in the amount of 0.2 percent of plan assets. This purchase is not a reportable transaction under paragraph (c)(1)(iv) of this section because the purchase of the Treasury bills as well as the purchase of the certificates of deposit are not considered to involve a security under the definition of "securities" in paragraph (b)(2)(ii) of this section. [Corrected April 4, 1978, by 43 FR 14009; amended on March 1, 1989 by 54 FR 8624.]

(7) At the beginning of the plan year, Plan X purchases through broker-dealer Y common stock of Able Industries, a New York Stock Exchange listed security, in an amount equal to 6 percent of plan assets. This purchase is a reportable transaction under paragraph (c)(1)(i) of this section. Three months later, Plan X purchases through broker-dealer Y, acting as agent, common stock of Baker Corporation, also a New York Stock Exchange listed security, in an amount equal to 0.2 percent of plan assets. This latter purchase is not a reportable transaction under paragraph (c)(1)(iv) of this section because it is not a transaction "with or in conjunction with a person" pursuant to paragraph (b)(3)(ii) of this section. [Added March 9, 1978, by 43 FR 10130; amended on March 1, 1989 by 54 FR 8624.]

(f) *Special rule for certain participant-directed transactions*. Participant or beneficiary directed transactions under an individual account plan shall not be taken into account under paragraph (c)(1) of this section for purposes of preparing the schedule of reportable transactions described in this section. For purposes of this section only, a transaction will be considered directed by a participant or beneficiary if it has been authorized by such participant or beneficiary. [Added April 19, 2000 by 65 FR 21082.]

⫸ *Caution: Regulation §2520.103-7 was officially removed by 61 FR 33847 on July 1, 1996.*

[¶ 14,231G]

§2520.103-7 **Special accounting rules for plans filing the initial (1975) annual report**. (a) *General*. (1) The administrator of an employee benefit plan which meets the requirements described in paragraph (b)(1) and elects to file an annual report containing the items prescribed in §2520.103-1(b) or §2520.103-2(b) is not required to comply with the accounting requirements described in paragraph (c)(1) of this section.

(2) Under the authority of sections 110 and 104(a)(3) of the Act, the administrator of any employee benefit plan which meets the requirements described in paragraph (b)(2) is not required to comply with the accounting requirements described in paragraph (c)(2) of this section.

(b) *Application*. With respect to the annual report described in §2520.103-1 or §2520.103-2, filed in accordance with §2520.104a-5 or §2520.104a-6 for the plan year beginning in 1975,

(1) The administrator of a plan which covers 100 or more participants as of the beginning of the plan year or the trust or other entity which files an annual report in accordance with §2520.104-43 is not required to comply with the accounting requirements described in paragraph (c)(1) of this section; and

(2) The administrator of a plan which covers fewer than 100 participants as of the beginning of the plan year is not required to comply with the accounting requirements described in paragraph (c)(2) of this section.

(c) *Excepted requirements*. (1) In the case of a plan which covers 100 or more participants as of the beginning of the plan year,

(i) To display at current value the statement of the assets and liabilities of the plan, as of the end of the previous plan year;

(ii) To engage an independent qualified public accountant to conduct an examination of the plan's financial statements for the plan year immediately preceding the plan year or trust year covered by the initial annual report; and

(iii) To include within the initial annual report the opinion of an independent qualified public accountant as to whether the financial statements for the close of the initial plan year are presented on a basis consistent with that of the preceding year.

(2) In the case of a plan which covers fewer than 100 participants at the beginning of the plan year, to display at current value the statement of the assets and liabilities of the plan displayed in Item 13 of the 1975 Form 5500-C or Item 12 of the 1975 Form 5500-K as of the end of the previous plan year or as of the beginning of the plan year subject to the initial annual report. [Added March 9, 1978, by 43 F.R. 10130.]

[¶ 14,231H]

§ 2520.103-8 **Limitation on scope of accountant's examination.** (a) *General.* Under the authority of section 103(a)(3)(C) of the Act, the examination and report of an independent qualified public accountant need not extend to any statement or information prepared and certified by a bank or similar institution or insurance carrier. A plan, trust or other entity which meets the requirements of paragraph (b) of this section is not required to have covered by the accountant's examination or report any of the information described in paragraph (c) of this section.

(b) *Application.* This section applies to any plan, trust or other entity some or all of the assets of which are held by a bank or similar institution or insurance carrier which is regulated and supervised and subject to periodic examination by a State or Federal agency.

(c) *Excluded information.* Any statements or information certified to by a bank or similar institution or insurance carrier described in paragraph (b) of this section, provided that the statements or information regarding assets so held are prepared and certified to by the bank or insurance carrier in accordance with § 2520.103-5. [Added March 9, 1978 by 43 FR 10130.]

[¶ 14,231I]

§ 2520.103-9 **Direct filing for bank or insurance carrier trusts and accounts.** (a) *General.* Under the authority of sections 103(b)(4), 104(a)(3), 110 and 505 of the Act, an employee benefit plan, some or all of the assets of which are held in a common or collective trust or a pooled separate account described in section 103(b)(3)(G) of the Act and §§ 2520.103-3 and 2520.103-4, is relieved from including in its annual report information about the current value of the plan's allocable portion of assets and liabilities of the common or collective trust or pooled separate account and information concerning the individual transactions of the common or collective trust or pooled separate account, provided that the plan meets the requirements of paragraph (b) of this section, and, provided further, that the bank or insurance carrier which holds the plan's assets meets the requirements of paragraph (c) of this section. [Amended April 19, 2000 by 65 FR 21802.]

(b) *Application.* A plan whose assets are held in a common or collective trust or a pooled separate account described in section 103(b)(3)(G) of the Act and §§ 2520.103-3 and 2520.103-4, provided the plan administrator, on or before the end of the plan year, provides the bank or insurance carrier which maintains the common or collective trust or pooled separate account with the plan number, and name and Employer Identification Number of the plan sponsor as will be reported on the plan's annual report. [Amended April 19, 2000 by 65 FR 21802.]

(c) *Separate filing by common or collective trusts and pooled separate accounts.* The bank or insurance carrier which maintains the common or collective trust or pooled separate account in which assets of the plan are held shall file, in accordance with the instructions for the form, a completed Form 5500 "Annual Return/Report of Employee Benefit Plan" and any statements or schedules required to be attached to the form for the common or collective trust or pooled separate account, including Schedule D (DFE/Participating Plan Information) and Schedule H (Financial Information). See the instructions for this form. The information reported shall be for the fiscal year of such trust or account ending with or within the plan year for which the annual report of the plan is made. [Added March 9, 1978, by 43 FR 10130; corrected April 4, 1978, by 43 FR 14009; amended July 29, 1980 by 45 FR 51446; amended April 19, 2000 by 65 FR 21083.]

(d) *Method of filing.* The Form 5500 "Annual Return/Report of Employee Benefit Plan" may be filed electronically or through other media in accordance with the instructions accompanying the form, provided the bank or insurance company which maintains the common or collective trust or pooled separate account maintains an original copy, with all required signatures, as part of its records. [Added April 19, 2000 by 65 FR 21803].

[¶ 14,231J]

§ 2520.103-10 **Annual Report Financial Schedules.** (a) *General.* The administrator of a plan filing an annual report pursuant to § 2520.103-1(a)(2) or the report for a group insurance arrangement pursuant to § 2520.103-2 shall, as provided in the instructions to the Form 5500 "Annual Return/Report of Employee Benefit Plan," include as part of the annual report the separate financial schedules described in paragraph (b) of this section. [Amended April 19, 2000 by 65 FR 21803].

(b) *Schedules.* (1) Assets held for investment.

(i) A schedule of all assets held for investment purposes at the end of the plan year (see § 2520.103-11) with assets aggregated and identified by:

(A) Identity of issue, borrower, lessor or similar party to the transaction (including a notation as to whether such party is known to be a party in interest);

(B) Description of investment including maturity date, rate of interest, collateral, par, or maturity value;

(C) Cost; and

(D) Current value, and, in the case of a loan, the payment schedule.

(ii) Except as provided in the Form 5500 and the instructions thereto, in the case of assets or investment interests of two or more plans maintained in one trust, all entries on the schedule of assets held for investment purposes that relate to the trust shall be completed by including the plan's allocable portion of the trust. [Amended April 19, 2000 by 65 FR 21803].

(2) *Assets acquired and disposed within the plan year.* (i) A schedule of all assets acquired and disposed of within the plan year (see § 2520.103-11) with assets aggregated and identified by:

(A) Identity of issue, borrower, issuer or similar party;

(B) Descriptions of investment including maturity date, rate of interest, collateral, par, or maturity value;

(C) Cost of acquisitions; and

(D) Proceeds of dispositions.

(ii) Except as provided in the Form 5500 and the instructions thereto, in the case of assets or investment interests of two or more plans maintained in one trust, all entries on the schedule of assets held for investment purposes that relate to the trust shall be completed by including the plan's allocable portion of the trust. [Amended April 19, 2000 by 65 FR 21803].

(3) *Party in interest transactions.* A schedule of each transaction involving a person known to be a party in interest except do not include:

(i) A transaction to which a statutory exemption under part 4 of title I applies;

(ii) A transaction to which an administrative exemption under section 408(a) of the Act applies; or

(iii) A transaction to which the exemptions of section 4975(c) or 4975(d) of the Internal Revenue Code (Title 26 of the United States Code) applies. [Amended April 19, 2000 by 65 FR 21803].

(4) *Obligations in default.* A schedule of all loans or fixed income obligations which were in default as of the end of the plan year or were classified during the year as uncollectible. [Amended April 19, 2000 by 65 FR 21803].

(5) *Leases in default.* A schedule of all leases which were in default or were classified during the year as uncollectible. [Amended April 19, 2000 by 65 FR 21803].

(6) *Reportable transactions.* A schedule of all reportable transactions as defined in § 2520.103-6. [Amended on March 1, 1989 by 54 FR 8624; amended Apri 19, 2000 by 65 FR 21083.]

(c) *Format requirements for certain schedules.* See the instructions to the Form 5500 "Annual Return/Report of Employee Benefit Plan" as to the format requirement for the schedules referred to in paragraphs (b)(1), (b)(2) or (b)(6) of this section. [Added April 19, 2000 by 65 FR 21803].

[¶ 14,231K]

§ 2520.103-11 **Assets held for investment purposes.** (a) *General.* For purposes of preparing the schedule of assets held for investment purposes described in § 2520.103-10(b)(1) and (2), assets held for investment purposes include those assets described in paragraph (b) of this section. [Amended April 19, 2000 by 65 FR 21083.]

(b) *Definitions.* (1) Assets held for investment purposes shall include:

(i) Any investment asset held by the plan on the last day of the plan year; and

(ii) Any investment asset which was purchased at any time during the plan year and was sold at any time before the last day of the plan year, except as provided by paragraphs (b)(2) and (b)(3) of this section.

(2) Assets held for investment purposes shall not include any investment which was not held by the plan on the last day of the plan year for which the annual report is filed if that investment falls within any of the following categories:

(i) Debt obligations of the United States or any agency of the United States;

(ii) Interests issued by a company registered under the Investment Company Act of 1940;

(iii) Bank certificates of deposit with a maturity of not more than one year;

(iv) Commercial paper with a maturity of not more than nine months if it is ranked in the highest rating category by at least two nationally recognized statistical rating services and is issued by a company required to file reports with the Securities and Exchange Commission under section 13 of the Securities Exchange Act of 1934;

(v) Participations in a bank common or collective trust;

(vi) Participations in an insurance company pooled separate account;

(vii) Securities purchased from a person registered as a broker-dealer under the Securities Exchange Act of 1934 and listed on a national securities exchange registered under section 6 of the Securities Exchange Act of 1934 or quoted on NASDAQ;

(3) Assets held for investment purposes shall not include any investment which was not held by the plan on the last day of the plan year for which the annual report is filed if that investment is reported on the annual report of that same plan in any of the following:

(i) The schedule of each transaction involving a person known to be a party in interest required by section 103(b)(3)(D) of the Act and § 2520.103-10(b)(3);

(ii) The schedule of loans or fixed income obligations in default required by section 103(b)(3)(E) of the Act and § 2520.103-10(b)(4);

(iii) The schedule of leases in default or classified as uncollectible required by section 103(b)(3)(F) of the Act and § 2520.103-10(b)(5); or

(iv) The schedule of reportable transactions required by section 103(b)(3)(H) of the Act and § 2520.103-10(b)(6).

(c) *Examples.* (1) On February 1, 1977, plan N purchases an interest in registered investment company F (fund F). Fund F is not a party in interest with respect to plan N. On November 1, 1977, plan N sells this interest in fund F and purchases 1,000 shares of stock S, which the plan holds for the rest of the plan year. Plan N mustinclude in its schedule of assets held for investment purposes the 1,000 shares of stock S under paragraph (b)(1) of this section, but need not include the interest in fund F because of Paragraph (b)(2)(ii) of this section.

(2) On February 1, 1977, plan N purchases a parcel of real estate from Mr. M, who is not a party in interest with respect to plan N. On November 1, 1977, plan N sells the parcel of real estate for cash to Mr. X, who is not a party in interest with respect to plan N. Plan N uses

the cash from this transaction to purchase a 1-year certificate of deposit in bank B, which it holds until maturity in 1978. Plan N must include in its schedule of assets held for investment purposes the 1-year certificate of deposit in bank B under paragraph (b)(1)(i) of this section, and must also include the parcel of real estate under paragraph (b)(1)(ii) of this section.

(d) *Special rule for certain participant-directed transactions.* Cost information may be omitted from the schedule of assets held for investment purposes for assets described in paragraphs (b)(1)(i) and (b)(1)(ii) of this section only with respect to participant or beneficiary directed transactions under an individual account plan. For purposes of this section only, a transaction will be considered directed by a participant or beneficiary if it has been authorized by such participant or beneficiary. [Added April 19, 2000 by 65 FR 21083.]

[¶ 14,231L]

§ 2520.103-12 **Limited exemption and alternative method of compliance for annual reporting of investments in certain entities.** (a) This section prescribes an exemption from and alternative method of compliance with the annual reporting requirements of Part 1 of Title I of ERISA for employee benefit plans whose assets are invested in certain entities described in paragraph (c). A plan utilizing this method of reporting shall include as part of its annual report the current value of its investment or units of participation in the entity in the manner prescribed by the Return/Report Form and the instructions thereto. The plan is not required to include in its annual report any information regarding the underlying assets or individual transactions of the entity, provided the information described in paragraph (b) regarding the entity is reported directly to the Department on behalf of the plan administrator on or before the filing due date for the entity in accordance with the instructions to the Form 5500 Annual Return/ Report. The information described in paragraph (b), however, shall be considered as part of the annual report for purposes of the requirements of section 104(a)(1) of the Act and §§ 2520.104a-5 and 2520.104a-6. [Amended April 19, 2000 by 65 FR 21083.]

(b) The following information must be filed regarding the entity described in paragraph (c) of this section:

(1) A Form 5500 "Annual Return/Report of Employee Benefit Plan" and any statements or schedules required to be attached to the form for such entity, completed in accordance with the instructions for the form, including Schedule A (Insurance Information), Schedule C (Service Provider Information), Schedule D (DFE/Participating Plan Information), Schedule G (Financial Transaction Schedules), Schedule H (Financial Information), and the schedules described in § 2520.103-10(b)(1) and (b)(2). See the instructions for this form. The information reported shall be for the fiscal year of such entity ending with or within the plan year for which the annual report of the plan is made.

(2) A report of an independent qualified public accountant regarding the financial statements and schedules described in paragraph (b)(1) of this section which meets the requirements of § 2520.103-1(b)(5). [Amended April 19, 2000 by 65 FR 21084.]

(c) This method of reporting is available to any employee benefit plan which has invested in an entity the assets of which are deemed to include plan assets under § 2510.3-101, provided the entity holds the assets of two or more plans which are not members of a "related group" of employee benefit plans as that term is defined in paragraph (e) of this section. The method of reporting is not available for investments in an insurance company pooled separate account or a common or collective trust maintained by a bank, trust company, or similar institution.

(d) The examination and report of an independent qualified public accountant required by § 2520.103-1 for a plan utilizing the method of reporting described in this section need not extend to any information concerning an entity which is reported directly to the Department under paragraph (b) of this section.

(e) A "related group" of employee benefit plans consists of every group of two or more employee benefit plans—

(1) Each of which receives 10 percent or more of its aggregate contributions from the same employer or from members of the same controlled group of corporations (as determined under section 1563(a)

of the Internal Revenue Code, without regard to section 1563(a)(4) thereof); or

(2) Each of which is either maintained by, or maintained pursuant to a collective bargaining agreement negotiated by, the same employee organization or affiliated employee organizations. For purposes of this paragraph, an "affiliate" of an employee organization means any person controlling, controlled by, or under common control with such organization, and includes any organization chartered by the same parent body, or governed by the same constitution and bylaws, or having the relation of parent and subordinate. [Added by 51 FR 41285 on November 13, 1986]

(f) *Method of filing.* The Form 5500 "Annual Return/Report of Employee Benefit Plan" may be filed electronically or through other media in accordance with the instructions accompanying the form provided the entity described in paragraph (c) of this section maintains an original copy, with all required signatures, as part of its records. [Added April 19, 2000 by 65 FR 21084.]

[**¶ 14,232—14,234b Reserved.** Temporary and proposed Reg. §§ 2520.104-41—2520.104-46, 2520.104a-5, 2520.104a-6, 2520.104b-10—2520.104b-12 formerly appeared at the above paragraphs. Sections 2520.104b-10—2520.104b-12 are at ¶ 14,249I—14,249K. Final regulations for the other sections have been adopted and are at ¶ 14,247U—14,247Z, 14,248D, and 14,248E.]

[¶ 14,240]
FILING WITH SECRETARY AND FURNISHING INFORMATION TO PARTICIPANTS

Sec. 104. (a)(1) The administrator of any employee benefit plan subject to this part shall file with the Secretary the annual report for a plan year within 210 days after the close of such year (or within such time as may be required by regulations promulgated by the Secretary in order to reduce duplicative filing). The Secretary shall make copies of such annual reports available for inspection in the public document room of the Department of Labor.

(2)(A) With respect to annual reports required to be filed with the Secretary under this part, he may by regulation prescribe simplified annual reports for any pension plan which covers less than 100 participants.

(B) Nothing contained in this paragraph shall preclude the Secretary from requiring any information or data from any such plan to which this part applies where he finds such data or information is necessary to carry out the purposes of this title nor shall the Secretary be precluded from revoking provisions for simplified reports for any such plan if he finds it necessary to do so in order to carry out the objectives of this title.

(3) The Secretary may by regulation exempt any welfare benefit plan from all or part of the reporting and disclosure requirements of this title, or may provide for simplified reporting and disclosure if he finds that such requirements are inappropriate as applied to welfare benefit plans.

(4) The Secretary may reject any filing under this section—

(A) if he determines that such filing is incomplete for purposes of this part; or

(B) if he determines that there is any material qualification by an accountant or actuary contained in an opinion submitted pursuant to section 103(a)(3)(A) or section 103(a)(4)(B).

(5) If the Secretary rejects a filing of a report under paragraph (4) and if a revised filing satisfactory to the Secretary is not submitted within 45 days after the Secretary makes his determination under paragraph (4) to reject the filing, and if the Secretary deems it in the best interest of the participants, he may take any one or more of the following actions—

(A) retain an independent qualified public accountant (as defined in section 103(a)(3)(D)) on behalf of the participants to perform an audit,

(B) retain an enrolled acutary (as defined in section 103(a)(4)(C) of this Act) on behalf of the plan participants, to prepare an actuarial statement,

(C) bring a civil action for such legal or equitable relief as may be appropriate to enforce the provisions of this part, or

(D) take any other action authorized by this title.

The administrator shall permit such accountant or actuary to inspect whatever books and records of the plan are necessary for such audit. The plan shall be liable to the Secretary for the expenses for such audit or report, and the Secretary may bring an action against the plan in any court of competent jurisdiction to recover such expenses.

(6) The administrator of any employee benefit plan subject to this part shall furnish to the Secretary, upon request, any documents relating to the employee benefit plan, including but not limited to, the latest summary plan description (including any summaries of plan changes not contained in the summary plan description), and the bargaining agreement, trust agreement, contract, or other instrument under which the plan is established or operated.

Act Sec. 104. (b) Publication of the summary plan descriptions and annual reports shall be made to participants and beneficiaries of the particular plan as follows:

(1) The administrator shall furnish to each participant, and each beneficiary receiving benefits under the plan, a copy of the summary, plan description, and all modifications and changes referred to in section 102(a)—

(A) within 90 days after he becomes a participant, or (in the case of a beneficiary) within 90 days after he first receives benefits, or

(B) if later, within 120 days after the plan becomes subject to this part.

The administrator shall furnish to each participant, and each beneficiary receiving benefits under the plan, every fifth year after the plan becomes subject to this part an updated summary plan description described in section 102 which integrates all plan amendments made within such five-year period, except that in a case where no amendments have been made to a plan during such five-year period this sentence shall not apply. Notwithstanding the foregoing, the administrator shall furnish to each participant, and to each beneficiary receiving benefits under the plan, the summary plan description described in section 102 every tenth year after the plan becomes subject to this part. If there is a modification or change described in section 102(a) (other than a material reduction in covered services or benefits provided in the case of a group health plan (as defined in section 706(a)(1)), a summary description of such modification or change shall be furnished not later than 210 days after the end of the plan year in which the change is adopted to each participant, and to each beneficiary who is receiving benefits under the plan. If there is a modification or change described in section 102(a) that is a material reduction in covered services or benefits provided under a group health plan (as defined in section 706(a)(1)), a summary description of such modification or change shall be furnished to participants and beneficiaries not later than 60 days after the date of the adoption of the modification or change. In the alternative, the plan sponsors may provide such description at regular intervals of not more than 90 days. The Secretary shall issue regulation within 180 days after the date of enactment of the Health Insurance Portability and Accountability Act of 1996, providing alternative mechanisms to delivery by mail through which group health plans (as so defined) may notify participants and beneficiaries of material reductions in covered services or benefits.

(2) The administrator shall make copies of the latest updated summary plan description and the latest annual report and the bargaining agreement, trust agreement, contract, or other instruments under which the plan was established or is operated available for examination by any plan participant or beneficiary in the principal office of the administrator and in such other places as may be necessary to make available all pertinent information to all participants (including such places as the Secretary may prescribe by regulations).

(3) Within 210 days after the close of the fiscal year of the plan, the administrator shall furnish to each participant, and to each beneficiary receiving benefits under the plan, a copy of the statements and schedules, for such fiscal year, described in subparagraphs (A) and (B) of section 103(b)(3) and such other material (including the percentage determined under section 103(d)(11)) as is necessary to fairly summarize the latest annual report.

(4) The administrator shall, upon written request of any participant or beneficiary, furnish a copy of the latest updated summary plan description, and the latest annual report, any terminal report, the bargaining agreement, trust agreement, contract, or other instruments under which the plan is established or operated. The administrator may make a reasonable charge to cover the cost of furnishing such complete copies. The Secretary may by regulation prescribe the maximum amount which will constitute a reasonable charge under the preceding sentence.

Act Sec. 104. (c) The Secretary may by regulation require that the administrator of any employee benefit plan furnish to each participant and to each beneficiary receiving benefits under the plan a statement of the rights of participants and beneficiaries under this title.

Act Sec. 104. CROSS REFERENCE.

(d) **For regulations respecting coordination of reports to the Secretaries of Labor and the Treasury, see section 3004.**

Amendments

P.L. 105-34, § 1503(c)(1):

Amended ERISA Sec. 104(a)(1) to read as above. Previously, the paragraph read as follows:

Act Sec. 104. (a)(1) The administrator of any employee benefit plan subject to this part shall file with the Secretary—

(A) the annual report for a plan year within 210 days after the close of such year (or within such time as may be required by regulations promulgated by the Secretary in order to reduce duplicative filing);

(B) the plan description within 120 days after such plan becomes subject to this part and an updated plan description, no more frequently than once every 5 years, as the Secretary may require;

(C) a copy of the summary plan description at the time such summary plan description is required to be furnished to participants and beneficiaries pursuant to subsection (b)(1)(B) of this section; and

(D) modifications and changes referred to in section 102(a)(2) within 60 days after such modification or change is adopted or occurs, as the case may be.

The Secretary shall make copies of such plan descriptions, summary plan descriptions, and annual reports available for inspection in the public document room of the Department of Labor. The administrator shall also furnish to the Secretary, upon request, any documents relating to the employee benefit plan, including but not limited to the bargaining agreement, trust agreement, contract, or other instrument under which the plan is established or operated.

P.L. 105-34, § 1503(c)(2):

Added ERISA Sec. 104(a)(6) to read as above.

The above amendment is effective August 5, 1997.

P.L. 105-34, § 1503(d)(1):

Amended ERISA Sec. 104(b)(1) by striking "section 102(a)(1)" each place it appears and inserting "section 102(a)."

The above amendment is effective August 5, 1997.

P.L. 105-34, § 1503(d)(2):

Amended ERISA Sec. 104(b)(2) by striking "the plan description and" and inserting "the latest updated summary plan description and."

The above amendment is effective August 5, 1997.

P.L. 105-34, § 1503(d)(3):

Amended ERISA Sec. 104(b)(4) by striking "the plan description."

The above amendment is effective August 5, 1997.

P.L. 101-191, § 101(c)(1):

Amended ERISA Sec. 104(b)(1) by striking "102(a)(1)," and inserting "102(a)(1) (other than a material reduction in covered services or benefits provided in the case of a group health plan (as defined in section 706(a)(1))),"; and adding at the end three new sentences to read as above.

The above amendments generally apply with respect to group health plans for plan years beginning after June 30, 1997. For special rules, see Act Sec. 101(g)(2)-(5), reproduced below.

Act Sec. 101(g)(2)-(5) reads as follows:

(g) EFFECTIVE DATES.—

(1) IN GENERAL.—Except as provided in this section, this section (and the amendments made by this section) shall apply with respect to group health plans for plan years beginning after June 30, 1997.

(2) DETERMINATION OF CREDITABLE COVERAGE.—

(A) PERIOD OF COVERAGE.—

(i) IN GENERAL.—Subject to clause (ii), no period before July 1, 1996, shall be taken into account under part 7 of subtitle B of title I of the Employee Retirement Income Security Act of 1974 (as added by this section) in determining creditable coverage.

(ii) SPECIAL RULE FOR CERTAIN PERIODS.—The Secretary of Labor, consistent with section 104, shall provide for a process whereby individuals who need to establish creditable coverage for periods before July 1, 1996, and who would have such coverage credited but for clause (i) may be given credit for creditable coverage for such periods through the presentation of documents or other means.

(B) CERTIFICATIONS, ETC.—

(i) IN GENERAL.—Subject to clauses (ii) and (iii), subsection (e) of section 701 of the Employee Retirement Income Security Act of 1974 (as added by this section) shall apply to events occurring after June 30, 1996.

(ii) NO CERTIFICATION REQUIRED TO BE PROVIDED BEFORE JUNE 1, 1997.—In no case is a certification required to be provided under such subsection before June 1, 1997.

(iii) CERTIFICATION ONLY ON WRITTEN REQUEST FOR EVENTS OCCURRING BEFORE OCTOBER 1, 1996.—In the case of an event occurring after June 30, 1996, and before October 1, 1996, a certification is not required to be provided under such subsection unless an individual (with respect to whom the certification is otherwise required to be made) requests such certification in writing.

(C) TRANSITIONAL RULE.—In the case of an individual who seeks to establish creditable coverage for any period for which certification is not required because it relates to an event occurring before June 30, 1996—

(i) the individual may present other credible evidence of such coverage in order to establish the period of creditable coverage; and

(ii) a group health plan and a health insurance issuer shall not be subject to any penalty or enforcement action with respect to the plan's or issuer's crediting (or not crediting) such coverage if the plan or issuer has sought to comply in good faith with the applicable requirements under the amendments made by this section.

(3) SPECIAL RULE FOR COLLECTIVE BARGAINING AGREEMENTS.—Except as provided in paragraph (2), in the case of a group health plan maintained pursuant to one or more collective bargaining agreements between employee representatives and one or more employers ratified before the date of the enactment of this Act, part 7 of subtitle B of title I of Employee Retirement Income Security Act of 1974 (other than section 701(e) thereof) shall not apply to plan years beginning before the later of—

(A) the date on which the last of the collective bargaining agreements relating to the plan terminates (determined without regard to any extension thereof agreed to after the date of the enactment of this Act), or

(B) July 1, 1997.

For purposes of subparagraph (A), any plan amendment made pursuant to a collective bargaining agreement relating to the plan which amends the plan solely to conform to any requirement of such part shall not be treated as a termination of such collective bargaining agreement.

(4) TIMELY REGULATIONS.—The Secretary of Labor, consistent with section 104, shall first issue by not later than April 1, 1997, such regulations as may be necessary to carry out the amendments made by this section.

(5) LIMITATION ON ACTIONS.—No enforcement action shall be taken, pursuant to the amendments made by this section, against a group health plan or health insurance issuer with respect to a violation of a requirement imposed by such amendments before January 1, 1998, or, if later, the date of issuance of regulations referred to in paragraph (4), if the plan or issuer has sought to comply in good faith with such requirements.

P.L. 101-239, § 7894(b)(3):

Amended ERISA Sec. 104(a)(5)(B) by striking the period and inserting a comma, effective September 2, 1974.

P.L. 101-239, § 7894(b)(4):

Amended ERISA Sec. 104(b)(1) by striking the comma after "summary" effective September 2, 1974.

P.L. 100-203, § 9342(a)(2):

Amended ERISA Sec. 104(b)(3) by striking out "such other material" and inserting "such other material (including the precentage determined under section 103(d)(11)" instead, effective December 17, 1987 for reports required to be filed after December 31, 1987.

P.L. 99-272, § 11016(b)(2):

Amended ERISA Sec. 104(a)(2)(A) by striking out the second sentence, effective on April 7, 1986.

Prior to amendment, the second sentence read:

In addition, and without limiting the foregoing sentence, the Secretary may waive or modify the requirements of section 103(d)(6) in such cases or categories of cases as to which he finds that (i) the interests of the plan participants are not harmed thereby and (ii) the expense of compliance with the specific requirements of section 103(d)(6) is not justified by the needs of the participants, the Pension Benefit Guaranty Corporation, and the Department of Labor for some portion or all of the information otherwise required under section 103(d)(6).

Regulations

Reg. § 2520.104-3 was adopted by FR Doc. 75-11656 under "Title 29—Labor; Chapter XXV—Office of Employee Benefits Security; Part 2520—Rules and Regulations for Reporting and Disclosure." The regulation was filed with the Federal Register on April 30, 1975, and published in the Federal Register on May 5, 1975. Reg. § 2520.104-3 was amended and Reg. § § 2520.104-2, and 2520.104-20—2520.104-25 were adopted by FR Doc. 75-21470, effective August 15, 1975, and published in the Federal Register on August 15, 1975. Reg. § § 2520.104-1, 2520.104-5, 2520.104-6, 2520.104a-1, 2520.104a-2, 2520.104a-4, 2520.104b-1, 2520.104b-5 and 2520.104b-30 were adopted by FR Doc. 76-11859 (41 FR 16957) filed with the Federal Register on April 22, 1976, published in the Federal Register of April 23, 1976, and effective April 23, 1976. Reg. § § 2520.104-4, 2520.104-26, 2520.104-27, 2520.104a-3, 2520.104b-2, 2520.104b-3, and 2520.104b-4 were adopted by FR Doc. 77-7637, filed with the Federal Register on March 11, 1977, and published in the Federal Register and effective on March 15, 1977 (42 FR 14266). Reg. § § 2520.104-26, 2520.104-27, 2520.104b-(2)(d)(2), 2520.104b-2(e)(2), and 2520.104b-2(f) are interim as well as proposed regulations. Reg. § § 2520.104-5 and 2520.104-6 were amended by FR Doc. 77-7464 (42 FR 14280), published in the Federal Register of March 15, 1977, and effective March 15, 1977. The following sections or portions of sections, previously published as interim rules on March 15, 1977, were made final by FR Doc. 20810 (42 FR 37178), effective July 19, 1977: § § 2520.104-26, 2520.104-27, and

2520.104b-2. At the same time, the following sections were adopted as interim rules: §§ 2520.104-5, 2520.104-6, 2520.104-28, 2520.104a-5, 2520.104b-2(a)(3), and 2520.104b-4. Reg. §§ 2520.104-41—2520.104-46, 2520.104a-5, and 2520.104a-6, were adopted by 41 FR 10130, effective generally for plan years beginning 1977 and thereafter. Reg. §§ 2520.104-20, 2520.104-21, and 2520.104a-4 were amended at the same time. Reg. § 2520.104b-10 was adopted by 44 FR 19400, published on April 3, 1979. The following interim rules were made final by FR Doc. 80-6528 (45 FR 14029), effective April 3, 1980; Reg. § 2520.104-5, 2520.104-6, 2520.104-28, 2520.104a-7, 2520.104b-2(a)(3), and 2520.104b-4. Reg. § 2520.104-48 was adopted by 45 FR 24866 and published on April 11, 1980. Reg. § 2520.104-49 was adopted by 46 FR 1261 and published in the Federal Register on January 6, 1981. Reg. § 2520.104-50 was adopted by 46 FR 1265 and published in the Federal Register on January 6, 1981. Reg. §§ 2520.104-23(b)(2)(ii) and 2520.104-44(b)(1)(ii) were amended by 46 FR 5882 and published in the *Federal Register* on January 21, 1981. Reg. §§ 2520.104b-1 and 2520.104b-3 were amended by 62 FR 36205, effective June 1, 1997, and published in the *Federal Register* on July 7, 1997. Reg. §§ 2520.104-21, 2520.104-41, 2520.104-43, 2520.104-44, 2520.104-46 and 2520.104(b)-10 were amended by 65 FR 21067 and published in the *Federal Register* on April 19, 2000. Reg §§ 2520.104-41 and 2520.104-46 were amended by 65 FR 62957 and published in the *Federal Register* on October 19, 2000.ERISA Reg. Secs. 2520.104-4, 2520.104-20, 2520.104-21,2520.104-26, 2520.104-27, and 2520.104b-2 were revised effective March 8, 2002 and published in the *Federal Register* on January 7, 2002 (67 FR 771). ERISA Reg. Secs. 2520.104-23, 2520.104-24, 2520.104-25, 2520.104-43, 2520.104-44, 2520.104a-5, 2520.104b-1, and 2520.104b-3 were amended effective March 8, 2002 and published in the *Federal Register* on January 7, 2992 (67 FR 771). ERISA Reg. Secs. 2520.104a-2, 2520.104a-3, 2520.104a-4, and 2520.104a-7 were removed and reserved effective March 8, 2002 (67 FR 771, 1/7/02). Reg. § 2520.104b-1 was amended by the PWBA on April 9, 2003 by 67 FR 17264. Reg. §§ 2520.104-22, 2520.104-23, and 2530.104b-10 were amended by EBSA on April 3, 2003 by 68 FR 16399.

Subpart D—Provisions Applicable to Both Reporting and Disclosure Requirements

[¶ 14,243]

§ 2520.104-1 **General**. The administrator of an employee benefit plan covered by Part 1 of Title I of the Act must file reports and additional information with the Secretary of Labor, and disclose reports, statements, and documents to plan participants and to beneficiaries receiving benefits from the plan. The regulations contained in this Subpart are applicable to both the reporting and disclosure requirements of Part 1 of Title I of the Act. Regulations concerning only a plan administrator's duty of reporting to the Secretary of Labor are set forth in Subpart E of this part, and those applicable only to the duty of disclosure to participants and beneficiaries are set forth in Subpart F of this part. [Added by 41 FR 16957, effective April 23, 1976.]

➤➤➤ *Caution: Regulation § 2520.104-2 officially removed and reserved by 61 FR 33847 on July 1, 1996*

[¶ 14,244]

§ 2520.104-2 **Postponing effective date of annual reporting requirements and extending WPPDA reporting requirements.** (a) *Postponing reports under the Act.* The January 1, 1975, effective date for the annual financial reporting and related disclosure requirements of section 103 of the Act is postponed for any employee benefit plan having a plan year other than a calendar year. These requirements shall become effective as to such plans on the first day of the first plan year beginning after January 1, 1975. Specifically, the administrator of a non-calendar year plan (1) is not required to file an annual financial report with the Secretary under sections 103(a)(1)(A) and 104(a)(1)(A) of the Act until the required time (210 days or such other time as the Secretary of Labor sets by regulation) after the end of the first plan year which begins after January 1, 1975, and (2) is not required to furnish participants covered under the plan and beneficiaries receiving benefits under the plan with statements of the plan's assets, liabilities, receipts, disbursements, and a summary of the latest annual report, as required by sections 103(a)(1)(A) and 104(b)(3) of the Act, until the required time after the end of the first year which begins after January 1, 1975. The requirement of section 104(b)(2) of the Act to make copies of the latest annual report available for inspection, and the requirement of section 104(b)(4) of the Act to furnish, upon written request of a participant or beneficiary, a copy of the latest annual report, do not take effect until the required time after the end of the first plan year which begins after January 1, 1975.

Example. A plan with a plan year beginning on April 1, 1975, files an annual report with the Secretary within the required time after March 31, 1976. The plan also furnishes participants covered under the plan and beneficiaries receiving benefits under the plan with statements of the plan's assets and liabilities and receipts and disbursements, and a summary of the latest annual report, by the same date. The following disclosure requirements are also complied with by the same date: A copy of the annual report is made available for inspection by any plan participant or beneficiary in the principal office of the administrator and in such other places as may be necessary to make available all pertinent information to all participants; and the plan administrator supplies a copy of the annual report to any participant or beneficiary who requests it in writing.

(b) *Extending WPPDA reporting.* The repeal of the annual reporting requirements of section 7 and the requirements for disclosure to participants and beneficiaries relating to annual reports of section 8(a)(2) of the Welfare and Pension Plans Disclosure Act (29 U.S.C. 306) are postponed from January 1, 1975 for any employee benefit plan having a plan year other than a calendar year. For non-calendar year plans subject to the WPPDA, the reporting and disclosure provisions of the WPPDA shall remain in force and effect through the last day of any plan year beginning before January 1, 1975, and ending after December 31, 1974.

(c) *Effect on other provisions.* This postponement does not delay the effective date of any other provisions of Part 1 of Title I of the Act.

➤➤➤ *Caution: Regulation § 2520.104-3 officially removed and reserved by 61 FR 33847 on July 1, 1996*

[¶ 14,245]

§ 2520.104-3 **Deferral of certain initial reporting and disclosure requirements.** (a) Under the authority of section 104(a)(3) of the Act, certain reporting and disclosure requirements of employee welfare benefit plans are deferred. This deferral is set forth in paragraph (c) of this section and applies to welfare plans subject to Part 1 of Title I of the Act on or before January 31, 1976. Welfare plans which become subject to Part 1 on or after February 1, 1976 shall meet the general reporting and disclosure provisions set forth in that part and regulations issued thereunder.

(b) Under the authority of section 110 of the Act, an alternative method of compliance is provided for employee pension benefit plans subject to Part 1 of Title I of the Act on or before January 31, 1976. This alternative, set forth in paragraph (c) of this section, permits an administrator of a pension plan to defer compliance with certain reporting and disclosure requirements. Pension plans which become subject to Part 1 of Title I of the Act on or after February 1, 1976 shall meet the general reporting and disclosure provisions set forth in that part and regulations issued thereunder.

(c) The administrator of a welfare plan described in paragraph (a) of this section or of a pension plan using the alternative specified in paragraph (b) of this section:

(1) Shall file a short form plan description consisting of the first two pages of Department of Labor Form EBS-1 (not including schedules A, B and C) and the signature page (item 38 only), on or before the later of—

(i) August 31, 1975, or

(ii) The 120th day after the plan becomes subject to Part I;

(2) May defer compliance with the following provisions of Part 1 of Title I of the Act until May 30, 1976—

(i) Subsection (a)(1)(C) and (b)(1) of section 104 of the Act, to the extent that they require plan administrators to file with the Secretary, and furnish to plan participants and beneficiaries, copies of a summary plan description,

(ii) Section 104(a)(1)(B) of the Act, which requires plan administrators to file a plan description with the Secretary.

(iii) Section 104(b)(2) of the Act to the extent that it requires plan administrators to make copies of the plan description available for examination by any plan participant and beneficiary of certain places, and

(iv) Section 104(b)(4) of the Act to the extent that it requires plan administrators to furnish a copy of the latest summary plan description and plan description to any participants or beneficiary upon written request; and

(3) Shall not be required to comply with the provisions of sections 104(a)(1)(D) and 104(b)(1) of the Act, to the extent that they require plan administrators to file with the Secretary of Labor, and to furnish to plan participants and beneficiaries summaries of, material modifications to the plan and changes in information required to be included in the plan description or summary plan description, as the case may be, which—

(i) Are adopted or occurred prior to May 30, 1976,

(ii) Are effective on May 30, 1976, and

(iii) Are incorporated in the initial plan description and summary plan description. [Amended August 15, 1975, by F.R.Doc. 75-21470.]

[¶ 14,245A]

§ 2520.104-4 **Alternative method of compliance for certain successor pension plans.** (a) *General.* Under the authority of section 110 of the Act, this section sets forth an alternative method of compliance for certain successor pension plans in which some participants and beneficiaries not only have their rights set out in the plan, but also retain eligibility for certain benefits under the terms of a former plan which has been merged into the successor. This section is applicable only to plan mergers which occur after the issuance by the successor plan of the initial summary plan description under the Act. Under the alternative method, the plan administrator of the successor plan is not required to describe relevant provisions of merged plans in summary plan descriptions of the successor plan furnished after the merger to that class of participants and beneficiaries still affected by the terms of the merged plans. Revised by 67 FR 771, effective March 8, 2002. [Amended by 42 F.R. 37178, effective July 19, 1977.]

(b) *Scope and application.* This alternative method of compliance is available only if:

(1) The plan administrator of the successor plan furnishes to the participants covered under the merged plan and beneficiaries receiving pension benefits under the merged plan within 90 days after the effective date of the merger—

(i) A copy of the most recent summary plan description of the successor plan;

(ii) A copy of any summaries of material modifications to the successor plan not incorporated in the most recent summary plan description; and

(iii) A separate statement containing a brief description of the merger; a description of the provisions of, and benefits provided by, the merged and successor plans which are applicable to the participants and beneficiaries of the merged plan; and a notice that copies of the merged and successor plan documents, as well as the plan merger documents (including the portions of any corporate merger documents which describe or control the plan merger), are available for inspection and that copies may be obtained upon written request for a duplication charge (pursuant to § 2520.104b-30); and

(2) After the merger, the plan administrator, in all subsequent summary plan descriptions furnished pursuant to § 2520.104b-2(a)—

(i) Clearly and conspicuously identifies the class of participants and beneficiaries affected by the provisions of the merged plan, and

(ii) States that the documents described in paragraph (b)(1) of this section are available for inspection and that copies may be obtained upon written request for a duplication charge (pursuant to § 2520.104(b)-30). [Added by 42 F.R. 14266, effective March 15, 1977, and amended by 42 FR 37178, effective July 19, 1977.]

⟩⟩⟩➔ *Caution: Regulation § 2520.104-5 officially removed and reserved by 61 FR 33847 on July 1, 1996*

[¶ 14,246]

§ 2520.104-5 **Deferral of certain reporting and disclosure requirements relating to the summary plan description for welfare plans.** (a) *General Rule.* Under the authority of section 104(a)(3) of the Act, employee welfare benefit plans described in and meeting the conditions of paragraph (b) may defer certain reporting and disclosure requirements that apply on and after July 15, 1977. These requirements may be deferred until dates that are no earlier than November 16, 1977, as provided in paragraph (c). The requirements that may be deferred include filing a copy of a summary plan description with the Secretary, furnishing a copy of a summary plan description to participants of a plan, filing material modifications to the plan and changes in the information required to be included in the summary plan description with the Secretary, furnishing a summary description of such modifications or changes to participants of a plan, and furnishing a copy of the latest summary plan description to participants and beneficiaries upon written request.

(b) *Application.* (1) in the case of a welfare plan which became subject to the provisions of Part 1, Title I of the Act on or before March 2, 1976, the plan administrator may defer until the time specified in paragraph (c) compliance with the requirements set forth in paragraph (a), if the administrator:

(i) Furnished an ERISA Notice which met the requirements of § 2520.104b-5 on or before May 30, 1976 to each participant covered under the plan as of March 2, 1976,

(ii) Furnished an ERISA Notice which met the requirements of § 2520.104b-5 to each person who became a participant covered under the plan after March 2, 1976 and before December 2, 1976, within 90 days after that person became a participant covered under the plan and

(iii) Furnished a copy of the ERISA Notice, without charge, upon request to any participant covered under the plan or beneficiary to whom no copy of the Notice had been previously furnished.

(2) In the case of a welfare plan which became subject to the provisions of Part 1, Title I of the Act after March 2, 1976 but before December 2, 1976, the plan administrator may defer until the time specified in paragraph (c) compliance with the requirements set forth in paragraph (a) if the administrator:

(i) Furnished an ERISA Notice which met the requirements of § 2520.104b-5 within 90 days after the date the plan became subject to the provision of Part 1, Title I, to each person who was a participant covered under the plan on the date the plan became subject to the provisions of Part 1, Title I;

(ii) Furnished an ERISA Notice which met the requirements of § 2520.104b-5 to each person who became a participant covered under the plan after the date on which the plan became subject to the provisions of Part 1, Title I and before December 2, 1976, within 90 days after that person became a participant covered under the plan; and

(iii) Furnished a copy of the ERISA Notice, without charge, upon request to any participant covered under the plan or beneficiary to whom no copy of the Notice had been previously furnished.

(3) In the case of a welfare plan which became subject to the provisions of Part 1, Title I of the Act on or after December 2, 1976, but before the date of publication of these regulations, the administrator may defer compliance with the requirements set forth in paragraph (a) until the time set in paragraph (c).

(c) The administrator of a welfare plan described in paragraph (b) who elected to defer compliance with the requirements described in paragraph (a) shall comply with such requirements by November 16, 1977. [Added by 41 FR 16957, effective April 23, 1976; amended by 41 FR 55510, filed with the Federal Register on December 20, 1977, by 42 FR 14280, effective March 15, 1977, and by 42 FR 37178, effective July 19, 1977; finalized by 45 FR 14029, effective April 3, 1980.]

⫸→ Caution: Regulation § 2520.104-6 officially removed and reserved by 61 FR 33847 on July 1, 1996

[¶ 14,246A]

§ 2520.104-6 **Deferral of certain reporting and disclosure requirements relating to the summary plan description for pension plans.** (a) *General Rule.* Under the authority of section 110 of the Act, an alternative method of compliance which defers certain reporting and disclosure requirements that apply on and after May 30, 1976 is provided for employee pension benefit plans described in and meeting the conditions of paragraph (b). The alternative method of compliance permits pension plans to defer these requirements until the times set forth in paragraphs (c) or (d). The requirements which may be deferred include filing a copy of the summary plan description with the Secretary, furnishing a copy of the summary plan description to participants and beneficiaries of a plan, filing material modifications and changes in the information required to be included in the summary plan description with the Secretary, furnishing a summary description of such modifications or changes to participants and beneficiaries of a plan, and furnishing a copy of the latest summary plan description upon written request.

(b) *Application.* (1) In the case of a pension plan which became subject to the provisions of Part 1, Title I of the Act on or before March 2, 1976, the plan administrator may defer until the times specified in paragraph (c)(1) compliance with the requirements set forth in paragraph (a), if the administrator:

(i) Furnished an ERISA Notice which met the requirements of § 2520.104b-5 on or before May 30, 1976 to each participant covered under the plan and beneficiary receiving benefits as of March 2, 1976.

(ii) Furnished an ERISA Notice to each person who became a participant covered under the plan or a beneficiary receiving benefits after March 2, 1976 but more than 120 days before the date prescribed in paragraph (c)(1), within 90 days after that person became a participant covered under the plan or beneficiary receiving benefits, and

(iii) Furnished a copy of the ERISA Notice, without charge, upon request to any participant covered under the plan or beneficiary receiving benefits to whom no copy of the Notice had been previously furnished.

(2) In the case of a pension plan which became subject to the provisions of Part 1, Title I of the Act after March 2, 1976 but before December 2, 1976, the plan administrator may defer until the times specified by paragraph (c)(1) compliance with the requirements set forth in paragraph (a) if the administrator:

(i) Furnished an ERISA Notice which met the requirements of § 2520.104b-5 within 90 days after the date the plan became subject to the provisions of Part 1, Title I to each person who was a participant covered under the plan or beneficiary receiving benefits on the date the plan became subject to the provisions of Part 1, Title I;

(ii) Furnished an ERISA Notice which met the requirements of § 2520.104b-5 to each person who became a participant covered under the plan or a beneficiary receiving benefits after the date on which the plan became subject to the provisions of Part 1 Title I but more than 120 days before the date prescribed in paragraph (c)(1), within 90 days after that person became a participant covered under the plan or a beneficiary receiving benefits; and

(iii) Furnished a copy of the ERISA Notice, without charge, upon request to any participant covered under the plan or beneficiary receiving benefits to whom no copy of the Notice had been previously furnished.

(3) In the case of a pension plan which became subject to the provisions of Part 1, Title I of the Act on or after December 2, 1976 but before March 17, 1977, the administrator may defer compliance with the requirements set forth in paragraph (a) until the times specified in paragraph (c)(1).

(4) In the case of a pension plan, other than a pension plan described in subparagraph (5), which became subject to the provisions of Part 1, Title I of the Act on or after March 17, 1977 and before July 19, 1977, the administrator may defer compliance with the requirements set forth in paragraph (a) until the time specified in paragraph (c)(2).

(5) In the case of a master, prototype, or practitioner pattern plan which became subject to the provisions of Part I, Title 1 of the Act on or after March 17, 1977, the administrator may defer compliance with the requirements set forth in paragraphs (a) until the times specified in paragraph (d).

(c)(1) The administrator of a pension plan described in paragraph (b)(1), (b)(2), or (b)(3) who elected to defer compliance with the requirements described in paragraph (a)—

(i)(A) And who files a request for a determination letter within the period prescribed in section 401(b) of the Internal Revenue Code of 1954 and the regulations issued pursuant thereto, shall have complied with the requirements described in paragraph (a) by the later of November 16, 1977 or 90 days after the date on which notice of the final determination with respect to the request for a determination letter is issued by the Internal Revenue Service, the request is withdrawn or the request is otherwise finally disposed of.

(B) For the purpose of computing the periods of time described in subparagraph (A) above, a notice of determination, opinion letter or notification letter from the Internal Revenue Service will be deemed to be issued on the later of the date of such document or the date of postmark thereon. The date of withdrawal of a request for a determination letter, opinion letter or notification letter will be deemed to be the later of the date on the document withdrawing the request or the postmark thereon. The date of "other disposition" will be the later of the date on the docuement notifying of such other disposition or the postmark on such document.

(ii) And who does not file a request for a determination letter within the period prescribed in section 401(b) of the Internal Revenue Code and the regulations issued pursuant thereto, shall have complied with the requirements described in paragraph (a) by the later of November 16, 1977 or the close of the period prescribed in section 401(b) of the Internal Revenue Code of 1054 and the regulations issued pursuant thereto.

(2) The administrator of a pension plan described in paragraph (b)(4) who defers compliance with the requirements described in paragraph (a) shall have complied with such requirements by November 16, 1977.

(d) *Special rule for plans adopting master, prototype or practitioner pattern plans after March 17, 1977.* The administrator of a pension plan which adopts a master, prototype, or practitioner pattern plan on or after March 17, 1977 may defer compliance with the statutory requirements described in paragraph (a) until the later of—

(1) The end of the applicable remedial amemdment period described in 26 CFR § 1.401b-1(d)(1) or (2) of regulations issued by the Internal Revenue Service under section 401(b) of the Internal Revenue Code of 1954, or

(2) November 16, 1977. [Added by 41 FR 16957, effective April 23, 1976; amended by 42 FR 14280, effective March 15, 1977, and by 42 FR 3178, effective July 19, 1977; amended and finalized by 45 FR 14029, effective April 3, 1980.]

[¶ 14,247]

§ 2520.104-20 **Limited exemption for certain small welfare plans.** (a) *Scope.* Under the authority of section 104(a)(3) of the Act, the administrator of any employee welfare benefit plan which covers fewer than 100 participants at the beginning of the plan year and which meets the requirements of paragraph (b) of this section is exempted from certain reporting and disclosure provisions of the Act. Specifically, the administrator of such plan is not required to file with the Secretary an annual or terminal report. In addition, the administrator of a plan exempted under this section—

(1) Is not required to furnish participants covered under the plan and beneficiaries receiving benefits under the plan with statements of the plan's assets and liabilities and receipts and disbursements and a summary of the annual report required by section 104(b)(3) of the Act;

(2) Is not required to furnish upon written request of any participant or beneficiary a copy of the annual report and any terminal report, as required by section 104(b)(4) of the Act; and

(3) Is not required to make copies of the annual report available for examination by any participant or beneficiary in the principal office

of the administrator and such other places as may be necessary, as required by section 104(b)(2) of the Act. [Revised by 67 FR 771, effective March 8, 2002.]

(b) *Application*. This exemption applies only to welfare benefit plans—

(1) Which have fewer than 100 participants at the beginning of the plan year;

(2)(i) For which benefits are paid as needed solely from the general assets of the employer or employee organization maintaining the plan, or

(ii) The benefits of which are provided exclusively through insurance contracts or policies issued by an insurance company or similar organization which is qualified to do business in any State or through a qualified health maintenance organization as defined in section 1310(d) of the Public Health Service Act, as amended, 42 U.S.C. § 300e-9(d), the premiums for which are paid directly by the employer or employee organization from its general assets or partly from its general assets and partly from contributions by its employees or members, *Provided,* that contributions by participants are forwarded by the employer or employee organization within three months of receipt, or [Amended by 46 FR 5882, originally scheduled to be effective February 20, 1981. However, the effective date was delayed under the President's regulation freeze until March 30, 1981 (46 FR 11253).]

(iii) Both; and

(3) for which, in the case of an insured plan—

(i) Refunds, to which contributing participants are entitled, are returned to them within three months of receipt by the employer or employee organization, and

(ii) Contributing participants are informed upon entry into the plan of the provisions of the plan concerning the allocation of refunds.

(c) *Limitations*. This exemption does not exempt the administrator of an employee benefit plan from any other requirement of title I of the Act, including the provisions which require that plan administrators furnish copies of the summary plan description to participants and beneficiaries (section 104(b)(1)) and furnish certain documents to the Secretary of Labor upon request (section 104(a)(6)), and which authorize the Secretary of Labor to collect information and data from employee benefit plans for research and analysis (section 513). [Revised by 67 FR 771, effective March 8, 2002.]

(d) *Examples*. (1) A welfare plan has 75 participants at the beginning of the plan year and 105 participants at the end of the plan year. Plan benefits are fully insured and premiums are paid directly to the insurance company by the employer pursuant to an insurance contract purchased with premium payments derived half from the general assets of the employer and half from employee contributions (which the employer forwards within three months of receipt). Refunds to the plan are paid to participating employees within three months of receipt as provided in the plan and as described to each participant upon entering the plan. The plan appoints the employer as its plan administrator. The employer, as plan administrator, provides summary plan descriptions to participants and beneficiaries. He also makes copies of certain plan documents available at the plan's principal office and such other places as necessary to give participants reasonable access to them. The exemption provided by § 2520.104-20 applies even though the plan has more than 100 participants by the end of the plan year, because it had fewer than 100 participants at the beginning of the plan year and otherwise satisfied the conditions of the exemption.

(2) A welfare plan is established and maintained in the same way as the plan described in example (1), except that a trade association which sponsors the plan is the holder of the insurance contract. Since the plan still sends the premium payments directly to the insurance company, the exemption applies, as in example (1). [Amended March 9, 1978, by 43 F.R. 10130.]

[¶ 14,247A]

§ 2520.104-21 **Limited exemption for certain group insurance arrangements**. (a) *Scope*. Under the authority of section 104(a)(3) of the Act, the administrator of any employee welfare benefit plan which covers fewer than 100 participants at the beginning of the plan year and which meets the requirements of paragraph (b) of this section is exempted from certain reporting and disclosure provisions of the Act. Specifically, the administrator of such plan is not required to file with the Secretary a terminal report or furnish upon written request of any participant or beneficiary a copy of any terminal report as required by section 104 (b) (4) of the Act. [Revised by 67 FR 771, effective March 8, 2002.]

(b) *Application*. This exemption applies only to welfare plans, each of which has fewer than 100 participants at the beginning of the plan year and which are part of a group insurance arrangement if such arrangement:

(1) Provides benefits to the employees of two or more unaffiliated employers, but not in connection with a multiemployer plan as defined in section 3(37) of the Act and any regulations prescribed under the Act concerning section 3(37);

(2) Fully insures one or more welfare plans of each participating employer through insurance contracts purchased solely by the employers or purchased partly by the employers and partly by their participating employees, with all benefit payments made by the insurance company: *Provided,* That—

(i) Contributions by participating employees are forwarded by the employers within three months of receipt,

(ii) Refunds, to which contributing participants are entitled, are returned to them within three months of receipt, and

(iii) Contributing participants are informed upon entry into the plan of the provisions of the plan concerning the allocation of refunds; and

(3) Uses a trust (or other entity such as a trade association) as the holder of the insurance contracts and uses a trust as the conduit for payment of premiums to the insurance company. [Amended April 19, 2000 by 65 FR 21084.]

(c) *Limitations*. This exemption does not exempt the administrator of an employee benefit plan from any other requirement of title I of the Act, including the provisions which require that plan administrators furnish copies of the summary plan description to participants and beneficiaries (section 104(b)(1)), file an annual report with the Secretary of Labor (section 104(a)(1)(A)) and furnish certain documents to the Secretary of Labor upon request (section 104(a)(6)), and authorize the Secretary of Labor to collect information and data from employee benefit plans for research and analysis (section 513). [Revised by 67 FR 771, effective March 8, 2002.]

(d) *Examples*. (1) A welfare plan has 25 participants at the beginning of the plan year. It is part of a group insurance arrangement of a trade association which provides benefits to employees of two or more unaffiliated employers, but not in connection with a multiemployer plan as defined in the Act. Plan benefits are fully insured pursuant to insurance contracts purchased with premium payments derived half from employee contributions (which the employer forwards within three months of receipt) and half from the general assets of each participating employer. Refunds to the plan are paid to participating employees within three months of receipt as provided in the plan and as described to each participant upon entering the plan. The trade association holds the insurance contracts. A trust acts as a conduit for payments, receiving premium payments from participating employers and paying the insurance company. The plan appoints the trade association as its plan administrator. The association, as plan administrator, provides summary plan descriptions to participants and beneficiaries, enlisting the help of participating employers in carrying out this distribution. The plan administrator also makes copies of certain plan documents available to the plan's principal office and such other places as necessary to give participants reasonable access to them. The plan administrator files with the Secretary an annual report covering activities of the plan, as required by the Act and such regulations as the Secretary may issue. The exemption provided by this section applies because the conditions of paragraph (b) have been satisfied. [Amended April 19, 2000 by 65 FR 21084.]

(2) Assume the same facts as paragraph (d)(1) of this section except that the premium payments for the insurance company are paid from the trust to an independent insurance brokerage firm acting as the agent of the insurance company. The trade association is the holder

of the insurance contract. The plan appoints an officer of the participating employer as the plan administrator. The officer, as plan administrator, performs the same reporting and disclosure functions as the administrator in paragraph (d)(1) of this section, enlisting the help of the association in providing summary plan descriptions and necessary information. The exemption provided by this section applies. [Amended April 19, 2000 by 65 FR 21084.]

(3) The facts are the same as paragraph (d)(1) of this section except the welfare plan has 125 participants at the beginning of the plan year. The exemption provided by this section does not apply because the plan had 100 or more participants at the beginning of the plan year. See, however, § 2520.104-43. [Amended April 19, 2000 by 65 FR 21084.]

(4) The facts are the same as paragraph (d)(2) of this section except the welfare plan has 125 participants. The exemption provided by this section does not apply because the plan had 100 or more participants at the beginning of the plan year. See, however, § 2520.104-43. [Amended March 9, 1978, by 41 F.R. 10130; amended April 19, 2000 by 65 FR 21084.]

(e) *Applicability date.* For purposes of paragraph (b)(3) of this section, the arrangement may continue to use an entity (such as a trade association) as the conduit for the payment of insurance premiums to the insurance company for reporting years of the arrangement beginning before January 1, 2001. [Added April 19, 2000 by 65 FR 21084.]

[¶ 14,247B]

§ 2520.104-22 **Exemption from reporting and disclosure requirements for apprenticeship and training plans**. (a) An employee welfare benefit plan that provides exclusively apprenticeship training benefits or other training benefits or that provides exclusively apprenticeship and training benefits shall not be required to meet any requirement of Part 1 of the Act, provided that the administrator of such plan: (1) has filed with the Secretary the notice described in paragraph (b) of this section; (2) takes steps reasonably designed to ensure that the information required to be contained in such notice is disclosed to employees of employers contributing to the plan who may be eligible to enroll in any course of study sponsored or established by the plan; and (3) makes such notice available to such employees upon request.

(b) The notice referred to in paragraph (a) of this section shall contain accurate information concerning: (1) the name of the plan; (2) the Employer Identification Number (EIN) of the plan sponsor; (3) the name of the plan administrator; (4) the name and location of an office or person from whom an interested individual can obtain: [i] a description of any existing or anticipated future course of study sponsored or established by the plan, including any prerequisites for enrolling in such course; and [ii] a description of the procedure by which to enroll in such course. [Amended March 10, 1980, by 45 FR 15527.]

⫸→ Caution: *The filing address below applies to any disclosures required to be furnished on or after January 1, 2004.*

(c) *Filing Address.* The notice referred to in paragraph (a) of this section shall be filed with the Secretary of Labor by mailing it to: Apprenticeship and Training Plan Exemption, Employee Benefits Security Administration, Room N-1513, U.S. Department of Labor, 200 Constitution Avenue NW., Washington, DC 20210, or by delivering it during normal working hours to the Employee Benefits Security Administration, Room N-1513, U.S. Department of Labor, 200 Constitution Avenue NW., Washington, DC. [Amended on March 1, 1989 by 54 FR 8624. Amended by EBSA on April 3, 2003 by 68 FR 16399.]

[¶ 14,247C]

§ 2520.104-23 **Alternative method of compliance for pension plans for certain selected employees**. (a) *Purpose and scope.* (1) This section contains an alternative method of compliance with the reporting and disclosure requirements of Part 1 of Title I of the Employee Retirement Income Security Act of 1974 for unfunded or insured pension plans maintained by an employer for a select group of management or highly compensated employees, pursuant to the authority of the Secretary of Labor under section 110 of the Act (88 Stat. 851).

(2) Under section 110 of the Act, the Secretary is authorized to prescribe an alternative method for satisfying any requirement of Part 1

of Title I of the Act with respect to any pension plans, or class of pension plans, subject to such requirement.

(b) *Filing obligation.* Under the authority of section 110 of the Act, an alternative form of compliance with the reporting and disclosure requirements of Part 1 of the Act is provided for certain pension plans for a select group of management or highly compensated employees. The administrator of a pension plan described in paragraph (d) shall be deemed to satisfy the reporting and disclosure provisions of Part 1 of Title I of the Act by—

(1) Filing a statement with the Secretary of Labor that includes the name and address of the employer, the employer identification number (EIN) assigned by the Internal Revenue Service, a declaration that the employer maintains a plan or plans primarily for the purpose of providing deferred compensation for a select group of management or highly compensated employees, and a statement of the number of such plans and the number of employees in each, and

(2) Providing plan documents, if any, to the Secretary upon request as required by section 104(a)(6) of the Act. Only one statement need be filed for each employer maintaining one or more of the plans described in paragraph (d) of this section. For plans in existence on May 4, 1975, the statement shall be filed on or before August 31, 1975. For a plan to which Part 1 of Title I of the Act becomes applicable after May 4, 1975, the statement shall be filed within 120 days after the plan becomes subject to Part 1. [Revised by 67 FR 771, effective March 8, 2002.]

⫸→ Caution: *The filing address below applies to any disclosures required to be furnished on or after January 1, 2004.*

(c) *Filing Address.* Statements may be filed with the Secretary of Labor by mailing them addressed to: Top Hat Plan Exemption, Employee Benefits Security Administration, Room N-1513, U.S. Department of Labor, 200 Constitution Avenue NW., Washington, DC 20210, or by delivering it during normal working hours to the Employee Benefits Security Administration, Room N-1513, U.S. Department of Labor, 200 Constitution Avenue NW., Washington, D.C. [Amended on March 1, 1989 by 54 FR 8624. Amended by EBSA on April 3, 2003 by 68 FR 16399.]

(d) *Application.* The alternative form of compliance described in paragraph (b) of this section is available only to employee pension benefit plans—

(1) Which are maintained by an employer primarily for the purpose of providing deferred compensation for a select group of management or highly compensated employees, and

(2) For which benefits (i) are paid as needed solely from the general assets of the employer, (ii) are provided exclusively through insurance contracts or policies, the premiums for which are paid directly by the employer from its general assets, issued by an insurance company or similar organization which is qualified to do business in any State, or (iii) both. [Amended by EBSA on April 3, 2003 by 68 FR 16399.]

[¶ 14,247D]

§ 2520.104-24 **Exemption for welfare plans for certain selected employees**. (a) *Purpose and scope.* (1) This section, under the authority of section 104(a)(3) of the Employee Retirement Income Security Act of 1974, exempts unfunded or insured welfare plans maintained by an employer for the purpose of providing benefits for a select group of management or highly compensated employees from the reporting and disclosure provisions of Part 1 of Title I of the Act, except for the requirement to provide plan documents to the Secretary of Labor upon request under section 104(a)(1) of the Act.

(2) Under section 104(a)(3) of the Act, the Secretary is authorized to exempt by regulation any welfare benefit plan from all or part of the reporting and disclosure requirements of Title I of the Act.

(b) *Exemption.* Under the authority of section 104(a)(3) of the Act, each employee welfare benefit plan described in paragraph (c) of this section is exempted from the reporting and disclosure provisions of Part 1 of Title I of the Act, except for providing plan documents to the Secretary of Labor upon request as required by section 104(a)(6). [Revised by 67 FR 771, effective March 8, 2002.]

(c) *Application.* This exemption is available only to employee welfare benefit plans:

(1) Which are maintained by an employer primarily for the purpose of providing benefits for a select group of management or highly compensated employees, and

(2) For which benefits (i) are paid as needed solely from the general assets of the employer, (ii) are provided exclusively through insurance contracts or policies, the premiums for which are paid directly by the employer from its general assets, issued by an insurance company or similar organization which is qualified to do business in any State, or (iii) both.

[¶ 14,247E]

§ 2520.104-25 **Exemption from reporting and disclosure for day care centers**. Under the authority of section 104(a)(3) of the Act, day care centers are exempted from the reporting and disclosure provisions of Part 1 of Title I of the Act, except for providing plan documents to the Secretary upon request as required under section 104(a)(6) of the Act. [Revised by 67 FR 771, effective March 8, 2002.]

[¶ 14,247F]

§ 2520.104-26 **Limited exemption for certain dues financed welfare plans maintained by employee organizations**. (a) *Scope.* Under the authority of section 104(a)(3) of the Act, a welfare benefit plan that meets the requirements of paragraph (b) of this section is exempted from the provisions of the Act that require filing with the Secretary an annual report and furnishing a summary annual report to participants and beneficiaries. Such plans may use a simplified method of reporting and disclosure to comply with the requirement to furnish a summary plan description to participants and beneficiaries, as follows:

(1) In lieu of filing an annual report with the Secretary or distibuting a summary annual report, a filing is made of Report Form LM-2 or LM-3, pursuant to the Labor-Management Reporting and Disclosure Act (LMRDA) and regulations thereunder, and

(2) In lieu of a summary plan description, the employee organization constitution or by-laws may be furnished in accordance with Sec. 2520.104b-2 to participants and beneficiaries together with any supplement to such document necessary to meet the requirements of Secs. 2520.102-2 and 2520.102-3.

(3)(i) The plan meets the requirements for furnishing a summary plan description of § 2520.104b-2(f), except the requirement of subparagraph (1) of that paragraph to have furnished the summary plan description before the date of publication of these regulations. The employee organization constitution or by-laws may be used as the summary plan description, if they meet the requirements of that paragraph.

(ii) Notwithstanding subparagraph (i), if any provisions of such documents indicate that a certain portion of members' dues or a certain portion of the employee organization's assets will be used only for the payment of benefits, although such portion of dues or assets may legally be used for general employee organization purposes, or may be subject to the claims of general creditors of the employee organization, such documents may nevertheless be used as the summary plan description provided that:

(A) The supplement required by § 2520.104b-2(f) contains a clear statement that such portion of dues or assets may legally be used for general employee organization purposes or may be subject to the claims of general creditors of the employee organization, and

(B) The employee organization constitution or by-laws are amended as soon as possible following normal procedures (e.g., at the next regularly scheduled employee organization convention, in the case of a constitution or by-laws which provide for amendment in regularly scheduled conventions) to reflect accurately the status of the plan. [Revised by 67 FR 771, effective March 8, 2002.]

(b) *Application.* This exemption is available only to welfare benefit plans maintained by an employee organization, as that term is defined in section 3(4) of the Act, paid for out of the employee organization's assets, which are derived wholly or partly from membership dues, and which cover employee organization members and their beneficiaries.

(c) *Limitations.* This exemption does not exempt the administrator from any other requirement of Part 1 of Title I of the Act. [Added by 42 FR 37178, effective July 19, 1977.]

[¶ 14,247G]

§ 2520.104-27 **Alternative method of compliance for certain dues financed pension plans maintained by employee organizations**. (a) *Scope.* Under the authority of section 110 of the Act, a pension benefit plan that meets the requirements of paragraph (b) of this section is exempted from the provisions of the Act that require an annual report and furnishing a summary annual report to participants and beneficiaries receiving benefits. Such plans may use a simplified method of reporting and disclosure to comply with the requirement to furnish a summary plan description to participants and beneficiaries receiving benefits, as follows:

(1) In lieu of filing an annual report with the Secretary or distributing a summary annual report, a filing is made of Report Form LM-2 or LM-3, pursuant to the Labor-Management Reporting and Disclosure Act (LMRDA) and regulations thereunder, and

(2) In lieu of a summary plan description, the employee organization constitution or bylaws may be furnished in accordance with Sec. 2520.104b-2 to participants and beneficiaries together with any supplement to such document necessary to meet the requirements of Secs. 2520.102-2 and 2520.102-3.

(3)(i) The plan meets the requirements for furnishing the summary plan description of § 2520.104b-2(f) except the requirement of subparagraph (1) of that paragraph to have furnished the summary plan description before the date of publication of these regulations. The employee organization constitution or by-laws may be used as the summary plan description, if they meet the requirements of that paragraph.

(ii) Notwithstanding subparagraph (i), if any provisions of such documents indicate that a certain portion of members' dues or a certain portion of the employee organization's assets will be used only for the payment of benefits, although such portion of dues or assets may legally be used for general employee organization purposes, or may be subject to the claims of general creditors of the employee organization, such documents may nevertheless be used as the summary plan description provided that:

(A) The supplement required by § 2520.104b-2(f) contains a clear statement that such portion of dues or assets may legally be used for general employee organization purposes or may be subject to the claims of general creditors of the employee organization, and

(B) The employee organization constitution or by-laws are amended as soon as possible following normal procedures (e.g., at the next regularly scheduled employee organization convention, in the case of a constitution or by-laws which provide for amendment in regularly scheduled conventions) to reflect accurately the status of the plan.

(b) *Application.* This exemption is available only to pension benefit plans maintained by an employee organization, as that term is defined in section 3(4) of the Act, paid for out of the employee organization's general assets, which are derived wholly or partly from membership dues, and which cover employee organization members and their beneficiaries.

(c) *Limitations.* This exemption does not exempt the administrator from any other requirement of Part 1 of Title I of the Act. [Added by 42 FR 37178, effective July 19, 1977.]

⫸ Caution: Regulation § 2520.104-28 was officially removed and reserved by 61 FR 33847 on July 1, 1996

[¶ 14,247H]

§ 2520.104-28 **Extension of time for filing and disclosure of the initial summary plan description**. (a) *General.* An employee benefit plan may, for good cause as determined by the plan administrator, extend the date to file and disclose the initial summary plan description or supplement for a period of 60 days from the date provided in § 2520.104a-3 and § 2520.104b-2. This extension is available to all employee benefit plans except for those plans described in paragraph (c), which may use the extension procedure provided under that paragraph.

(b) *Requirements.* In order for an employee benefit plan to extend the date for filing and disclosure of the initial summary plan description or supplement, the plan administrator of a plan must—

(1) Determine that there is good cause for the extension. The following are examples of situations for which good cause could be found. This list is not exclusive and other situations may also constitute good cause for extending the date for filing and disclosure:

(i) A plan whose summary plan description or supplement is being prepared by a consulting company, insurance carrier or service, or other person that engages in the preparation of summary plan descriptions or supplements, where the volume of work of such persons exceeds the capacity to finish preparation of these documents before the time to file and disclose them under §2520.104a-3 and §2520.104b-2.

(ii) A plan of a plan sponsor which has 20 or more classes of participants for which separate summary plan descriptions or supplements will be filed and disclosed.

(2) Furnish with the initial summary plan description or supplement a statement describing the good cause for which the date for filing and disclosure was extended.

(c) *Plans involved in collective bargaining negotiations.* The plan administrator of a plan which by the terms of a collective bargaining agreement may be the subject of collective bargaining negotiations within a period of 120 days prior to, or after, the date for filing and disclosure of the summary plan description or supplement under §2520.104a-3 and §2520.104b-2, may extend the requirement to file and disclose the summary plan description or supplement for a period not to exceed 90 days from the date of conclusion of the new collective bargaining agreement. A statement explaining the basis upon which the date was extended must be furnished with the summary plan description or supplement.

(d) *Limitation.* This extension procedure is available only for an employee benefit plan which is subject to Part 1 of Title I on or before July 19, 1977. [Added by 42 FR 37178, published July 19, 1977; amended and finalized by 45 FR 14029, effective April 3, 1980.]

[¶ 14,247U]

§2520.104-41 **Simplified annual reporting requirements for plans with fewer than 100 participants.** (a) *General.* (1) Under the authority of section 104(a)(2)(A), the Secretary of Labor may prescribe simplified annual reporting for employee pension benefit plans with fewer than 100 participants.

(2) Under the authority of section 104(a)(3), the Secretary of Labor may provide a limited exemption for any employee welfare benefit plan with respect to certain annual reporting requirements.

(b) *Application.* The administrator of an employee pension or welfare benefit plan which covers fewer than 100 participants at the beginning of the plan year and the administrator of an employee pension or welfare benefit plan described in §2520.103-1(d) may file the simplified annual report described in paragraph (c) of this section in lieu of the annual report described in §2520.103-1(b). [Corrected April 4, 1978, by 43 FR 14010. Amended July 29, 1980 by 45 FR 51446; amended April 19, 2000 by 65 FR 21084.]

(c) *Contents.* The administrator of an employee pension or welfare benefit plan described in paragraph (b) of this section shall file, in the manner described in §2520.104a-5, a completed Form 5500 "Annual Return/Report of Employee Benefit Plan," including any required schedules or statements prescribed by the instructions to the form, and, unless waived by Sec. 2520.104-46, a report of an independent qualified public accountant meeting the requirements of Sec. 2520.103-1(b). [Amended March 1, 1989 by 54 FR 8624; amended July 29, 1980 by 45 FR 51446; amended April 19, 2000 by 65 FR 21084; amended October 19, 2000 by 65 FR 62957.]

[¶ 14,247V]

§2520.104-42 **Waiver of certain actuarial information in the annual report.** Under the authority of §104(a)(2)(A) of ERISA, the requirement of section 103(d)(6) of ERISA that the annual report include as part of the actuarial statement (Schedule B) the present value of all of the plan's liabilities for nonforfeitable pension benefits allocated by termination priority categories, as set forth in section 4044 of Title IV of ERISA, and the actuarial assumptions used in these computations, is waived. [Amended January 23, 1979, by 44 FR 5440.]

[¶ 14,247W]

§2520.104-43 **Exemption from annual reporting requirement for certain group insurance arrangements.** (a) *General.* Under the authority of section 104(a)(3) of the Act, the administrator of an employee welfare benefit plan which meets the requirements of paragraph (b) of this section is not required to file an annual report with the Secretary of Labor as required by section 104(a)(1) of the Act. [Revised by 67 FR 771, effective March 8, 2002.]

(b) *Application.* (1) This exemption applies only to a welfare plan for a plan year in which (i) such plan meets the requirements of §2520.104-21, except the requirement that the plan cover fewer than 100 participants at the beginning of the plan year, and (ii) an annual report containing the items set forth in §2520.103-2 has been filed with the Secretary of Labor in accordance with §§2520.104a-6 by the trust or other entity which is the holder of the group insurance contracts by which plan benefits are provided. [Amended April 19, 2000 by 65 FR 21084.]

(2) For purposes of this section, the terms "group insurance arrangement" or "trust or other entity" shall be used in place of the terms "plan" and "plan administrator," as applicable, in §§2520.103-3, 2520.103-4, 2520.103-6, 2520.103-8, 2520.103-9 and 2520.103-10. [Amended April 19, 2000 by 65 FR 21084.]

(c) *Limitation.* This provision does not exempt the administrator of an employee benefit plan which meets the requirements of paragraph (b) from furnishing a copy of a summary annual report to participants and beneficiaries of the plan, as required by section 104(b)(3) of the Act. [Added March 9, 1978, by 43 F.R. 10130.]

[¶ 14,247X]

§2520.104-44 **Limited exemption and alternative method of compliance for annual reporting by unfunded plans and by certain insured plans.** (a) *General.* (1) Under the authority of section 104(a)(3) of the Act, the Secretary of Labor may exempt an employee welfare benefit plan from any or all of the reporting and disclosure requirements of Title I. An employee welfare benefit plan which meets the requirements of paragraph (b)(1) of this section is not required to comply with the annual reporting requirements described in paragraph (c) of this section. [Amended July 29, 1980 by 45 FR 51446.]

(2) Under the authority of section 110 of the Act, an alternative method of compliance is prescribed for certain employee pension benefit plans subject to Part 1, Title I of the Act. An employee pension benefit plan which meets the requirements of paragraph (b)(2) and (b)(3) of this section is not required to comply with the annual reporting requirements described in paragraph (c) of this section. [Amended April 19, 2000 by 65 FR 21085.]

(b) *Application.* This section applies only to:

(1) An employee welfare benefit plan under the terms of which benefits are to be paid—

(i) Solely from the general assets of the employer or employee organization maintaining the plan;

(ii) The benefits of which are provided exclusively through insurance contracts or policies issued by an insurance company or similar organization which is qualified to do business in any State or through a qualified health maintenance organization as defined in section 1310(d) of the Public Health Service Act, as amended, 42 U.S.C. §300e-9(d), the premiums for which are paid directly by the employer or employee organization from its general assets or partly from its general assets and partly from contributions by its employees or members, provided that any plan assets held by such an insurance company are held solely in the general account of such company or organization, contributions by participants are forwarded by the employer or employee organization within three months of receipt and, in the case of a plan that provides for the return of refunds to contributing participants, such refunds are returned to them within three months of receipt by the employer or employee organization, or [Amended by 46 FR 5882, originally scheduled to be effective February 20, 1981. However, the effective date was delayed under the President's regulation freeze until March 30, 1981 (46 FR 11253).]

(iii) Partly in the manner specified in paragraph (b)(1)(i) of this section and partly in the manner specified in paragraph (b)(1)(ii) of this section;

(2) A pension benefit plan the benefits of which are provided exclusively through allocated insurance contracts or policies which are issued by, and pursuant to the specific terms of such contracts or policies benefit payments are fully guaranteed by an insurance company or similar organization which is qualified to do business in any State, and the premiums for which are paid directly by the employer or employee organization from its general assets or partly from its general assets and partly from contributions by its employees or members: *Provided,* That contributions by participants are forwarded by the employer or employee organization to the insurance company or organization within three months of receipt and, in the case of a plan that provides for the return of refunds to contributing participants, such refunds are returned to them within three months of receipt by the employer or employee organization; and [Amended April 19, 2000 by 65 FR 21805.]

(3) A pension plan using a tax deferred annuity arrangement under section 403(b)(1) of the Internal Revenue Code (Title 26 of the United States Code) and/or a custodial account for regulated investment company stock under Code section 403(b)(7) as the sole funding vehicle for providing pension benefits. [Added April 19, 2000 by 65 FR 21085.]

(c) *Contents.* An employee benefit plan described in paragraph (b) of this section is exempt from complying with the following annual reporting requirements:

(1) Completing certain items of the annual report relating to financial information and transactions entered into by the plan as described in the instructions to the Form 5500 "Annual Return/Report of Employee Benefit Plan" and accompanying schedules; [Amended July 29, 1980 by 45 FR 51446; amended April 19, 2000 by 65 FR 21085.]

(2) Engaging an independent qualified public accountant pursuant to section 103(a)(3)(A) of the Act and § 2520.103-1(b) to conduct an examination of the financial statements and schedules of the plan; and

(3) Including in the annual report a report of an independent qualified public accountant concerning the financial statements and schedules required to be a part of the annual report pursuant to section 103(b) of the Act and § 2520.103-1(b).

(d) *Limitation.* This section does not exempt any plan from filing an annual report form with the Secretary in accordance with section 104(a)(1) of the Act and § 2520.104a-5. [Revised by 67 FR 771, effective Match 8, 2002.]

(e) *Example.* A welfare plan which is funded entirely with insurance contracts and which meets all the requirements of exemption under § 2520.104-20 except that it covers 100 or more participants at the beginning of the plan year is not exempt from the annual reporting requirements under § 2520.104-20, but is exempt from certain reporting requirements under § 2520.104-44. Under the latter section, such a welfare plan should file Form 5500, including Schedule A "Insurance Information." However, the plan is not required to engage an independent qualified public accountant and need not complete certain items on Form 5500. [Added March 9, 1978, by 43 FR 10130 and amended by 45 FR 51446 on July 29, 1980.]

»»→ *Caution: Regulation § 2520.104-45 was officially removed and reserved by 61 FR 33847 on July 1, 1996.*

[¶ 14,247Y]

§ 2520.104-45 **Temporary exemption from reporting insurance fees and commissions for insured plans with fewer than 100 participants**. (a) *General.* (1) Under the authority of section 104(a)(3) of the Act, the Secretary of Labor may exempt an employee welfare benefit plan from any or all of the reporting and disclosure requirements of Title I. The administrator of an employee welfare benefit plan which meets the requirements of paragraph (b) of this section is exempt from complying with the annual reporting requirements described in paragraph (c) of this section.

(2) Under the authority of section 110 of the Act, the Secretary of Labor may prescribe an alternative method of compliance for employee pension benefit plans subject to Part 1, Title I, of the Act. The administrator of an employee pension benefit plan which meets the requirements of paragraph (b) of this section is not required to comply with the annual reporting requirements described in paragraph (c) of this section.

(b) *Application.* (1) The provisions of this section apply only to welfare and pension plans which cover fewer than 100 participants at the beginning of the plan year and which provide benefits in whole or in part through insurance contracts or policies issued by an insurance company or similar organization which is qualified to do business in any State.

(c) *Contents.* A plan which meets the requirements of paragraph (b) is not required to include in the annual report filed in accordance with section 104(a)(1)(A) of the Act and § 2520.104a-5 or § 2520.104a-6 the following information described under sections 103(c) and (e) of the Act:

(1) The name and address of any insurance agent, broker or other person to whom insurance commissions, salaries or fees are paid;

(2) the amount paid to each; and

(3) The purpose for which such payment is made.

(d) *Limitation.* The provisions of this section apply only to the annual report required to be filed for the plan years beginning in 1975 and 1976. [Added March 9, 1978, by 43 FR 10130.]

[¶ 14,247Z]

§ 2520.104-46 **Waiver of examination and report of an independent qualified public accountant for employee benefit plans with fewer than 100 participants**. (a) *General.* (1) Under the authority of section 103(a)(3)(A) of the Act, the Secretary may waive the requirements of section 103(a)(3)(A) in the case of a plan for which simplified annual reporting has been prescribed in accordance with section 104(a)(2) of the Act.

(2) Under the authority of section 104(a)(3) of the Act the Secretary may exempt any employee welfare benefit plan from certain annual reporting requirements.

(b) *Application.* (1)(i) The administrator of an employee pension benefit plan for which simplified annual reporting has been prescribed in accordance with section 104(a)(2)(A) of the Act and Sec. 2520.104-41 is not required to comply with the annual reporting requirements described in paragraph (c) of this section, provided that with respect to each plan year for which the waiver is claimed—

(A)(1) At least 95 percent of the assets of the plan constitute qualifying plan assets within the meaning of paragraph (b)(1)(ii) of this section, or

(2) Any person who handles assets of the plan that do not constitute qualifying plan assets is bonded in accordance with the requirements of section 412 of the Act and the regulations issued thereunder, except that the amount of the bond shall not be less than the value of such assets;

(B) The summary annual report, described in Sec. 2520.104b-10, includes, in addition to any other required information:

(1) Except for qualifying plan assets described in paragraph (b)(1)(ii)(A), (B) and (F) of this section, the name of each regulated financial institution holding (or issuing) qualifying plan assets and the amount of such assets reported by the institution as of the end of the plan year;

(2) The name of the surety company issuing the bond, if the plan has more than 5% of its assets in non-qualifying plan assets;

(3) A notice indicating that participants and beneficiaries may, upon request and without charge, examine, or receive copies of, evidence of the required bond and statements received from the regulated financial institutions describing the qualifying plan assets; and

(4) A notice stating that participants and beneficiaries should contact the Regional Office of the U.S. Department of Labor's Employee Benefits Security Administration if they are unable to examine or obtain copies of the regulated financial institution statements

or evidence of the required bond, if applicable; and [EBSA technical correction, 68 FR 16399 (April 3, 2003).]

(C) in response to a request from any participant or beneficiary, the administrator, without charge to the participant or beneficiary, makes available for examination, or upon request furnishes copies of, each regulated financial institution statement and evidence of any bond required by paragraph (b)(1)(i)(A)(2).

(ii) For purposes of paragraph (b)(1), the term "qualifying plan assets" means:

(A) Qualifying employer securities, as defined in section 407(d)(5) of the Act and the regulations issued thereunder;

(B) Any loan meeting the requirements of section 408(b)(1) of the Act and the regulations issued thereunder;

(C) Any assets held by any of the following institutions:

(1) A bank or similar financial institution as defined in Sec. 2550.408b-4(c);

(2) An insurance company qualified to do business under the laws of a state;

(3) An organization registered as a broker-dealer under the Securities Exchange Act of 1934; or

(4) Any other organization authorized to act as a trustee for individual retirement accounts under section 408 of the Internal Revenue Code.

(D) Shares issued by an investment company registered under the Investment Company Act of 1940;

(E) Investment and annuity contracts issued by any insurance company qualified to do business under the laws of a state; and,

(F) In the case of an individual account plan, any assets in the individual account of a participant or beneficiary over which the participant or beneficiary has the opportunity to exercise control and with respect to which the participant or beneficiary is furnished, at least annually, a statement from a regulated financial institution referred to in paragraphs (b)(1)(ii)(C), (D) or (E) of this section describing the assets held (or issued) by such institution and the amount of such assets.

(iii)(A) For purposes of this paragraph (b)(1), the determination of the percentage of all plan assets consisting of qualifying plan assets with respect to a given plan year shall be made in the same manner as the amount of the bond is determined pursuant to Secs. 2580.412-11, 2580.412-14, and 2580.412-15.

(B) *Examples.* Plan A, which reports on a calendar year basis, has total assets of $600,000 as of the end of the 1999 plan year. Plan A's assets, as of the end of year, include: investments in various bank, insurance company and mutual fund products of $520,000; investments in qualifying employer securities of $40,000; participant loans, meeting the requirements of ERISA section 408(b)(1), totaling $20,000; and a $20,000 investment in a real estate limited partnership. Because the only asset of the plan that does not constitute a "qualifying plan asset" is the $20,000 real estate investment and that investment represents less than 5% of the plan's total assets, no bond would be required under the proposal as a condition for the waiver for the 2000 plan year. By contrast, Plan B also has total assets of $600,000 as of the end of the 1999 plan year, of which $558,000 constitutes "qualifying plan assets" and $42,000 constitutes non-qualifying plan assets. Because 7%—more than 5%—of Plan B's assets do not constitute "qualifying plan assets," Plan B, as a condition to electing the waiver for the 2000 plan year, must ensure that it has a fidelity bond in an amount equal to at least $42,000 covering persons handling non-qualifying plan assets. Inasmuch as compliance with section 412 requires the amount of bonds to be not less than 10% of the amount of all the plan's funds or other property handled, the bond acquired for section 412 purposes may be adequate to cover the non-qualifying plan assets without an increase (i.e., if the amount of the bond determined to be needed for the relevant persons for section 412 purposes is at least $42,000). As demonstrated by the foregoing example, where a plan has more than 5% of its assets in non-qualifying plan assets, the bond required by the proposal is for the total amount of the non-qualifying plan assets, not just the amount in excess of 5%. [Added March 9, 1978, by 43 FR 10130. Amended October 19, 2000 by 65 FR 62957.]

(2) The administrator of an employee welfare benefit plan that covers fewer than 100 participants at the beginning of the plan year is not required to comply with annual reporting requirements described in paragraph (c) of this section.

(c) *Waiver.* The administrator of a plan described in paragraph (b)(1) or (2) of this section is not required to:

(1) Engage an independent qualified public accountant to conduct an examination of the financial statements of the plan;

(2) Include within the annual report the financial statements and schedules prescribed in section 103(b) of the Act and §§ 2520.103-1, 2520.103-2, and 2520.103-10; and

(3) Include within the annual report a report of an independent qualified public accountant as prescribed in section 103(a)(3)(A) of the Act and § 2520.103-1.

(d) *Limitations.* (1) The waiver described in this section does not affect the obligation of a plan described in paragraph (b)(1) or (2) of this section to file a Form 5500 "Annual Return/Report of Employee Benefit Plan," including any required schedules or statements prescribed by the instructions to the form. See Sec. 2520.104-41. [Amended April 19, 2000 by 65 FR 21085 and October 19, 2000 by 65 FR 62957.]

(2) For purposes of this section, an employee pension benefit plan for which simplified annual reporting has been prescribed includes an employee pension benefit plan which elects to file a Form 5500 as a small plan pursuant to Sec. 2520.103-1(d) with respect to the plan year for which the waiver is claimed. See Sec. 2520.104-41. [Corrected April 4, 1978 by 43 FR 14010; amended July 29, 1980 by 45 FR 51446; amended March 1, 1989 by 54 FR 8624; amended October 19, 2000 by 65 FR 62957.]

(3) For purposes of this section, an employee welfare benefit plan that covers fewer than 100 participants at the beginning of the plan year includes an employee welfare benefit plan which elects to file a Form 5500 as a small plan pursuant to Sec. 2520.103-1(d) with respect to the plan year for which the waiver is claimed. See Sec. 2520.104-41.

(4) A plan that elects to file a Form 5500 as a large plan pursuant to Sec. 2520.103-1(d) may not claim a waiver under this section. [Amended October 19, 2000 by 65 FR 62957.]

[¶ 14,247ZA]

§ 2520.104-47 **Limited exemption and alternative method of compliance for filing of insurance company financial reports**. An administrator of an employee benefit plan to which section 103(e)(2) of the Act applies shall be deemed in compliance with the requirement to include with its annual report a copy of the financial report of the insurance company, insurance service or similar organization, provided that the administrator files a copy of such report within 45 days of receipt of a written request for such report by the Secretary of Labor. [Added by 45 FR 14034, effective March 4, 1980.]

[¶ 14,247ZB]

§ 2520.104-48 **Alternative Method of Compliance for Model Simplified Employee Pensions—IRS Form 5305-SEP**. Under the authority of section 110 of the Act the provisions of this section are prescribed as an alternative method of compliance with the reporting and disclosure requirements set forth in Part 1 of Title I of the Employee Retirement Income Security Act of 1974 in the case of a simplified employee pension (SEP) described in section 408(k) of the Internal Revenue Code of 1954 as amended (the Code) that is created by use without modification of Internal Revenue Service (IRS) Form *5305-SEP.*

(a) At the time an employee becomes eligible to participate in the SEP (whether at the creation of the SEP or thereafter), the administrator of the SEP (generally the employer establishing and maintaining the SEP) shall furnish the employee with a copy of the completed and unmodified IRS Form *5305-SEP* used to create the SEP, including (1) the completed Contribution Agreement, (2) the General Information and Guidelines, and (3) the Questions and Answers.

(b) Following the end of each calendar year the administrator of the SEP shall notify each participant in the SEP in writing of any employer contributions made under the Contribution Agreement to the participant's individual retirement account or individual retirement annuity (IRA) for that year.

(c) If the employer establishing and maintaining the SEP selects, recommends, or in any other way influences employees to choose a particular IRA or type of IRA into which contributions under the SEP will be made, and if that IRA is subject to restrictions on a participant's ability to withdraw funds (other than restrictions imposed by the Code that apply to all IRAs), the administrator of the SEP shall give to each employee, in writing, within 90 days of the adoption of this regulation or at the time such employee becomes eligible to participate in the SEP, whichever is later, a clear explanation of those restrictions and a statement to the effect that other IRAs, into which rollovers or employee contributions may be made, may not be subject to such restrictions. [Added by 45 FR 24866, adopted and effective April 8, 1980.]

[¶ 14,247ZC]

§ 2520.104-49 **Alternative method of compliance for certain simplified employee pensions**. Under the authority of section 110 of the Act, the provisions of this section are prescribed as an alternative method of compliance with the reporting and disclosure requirements set forth in Part 1 of Title I of the Act for a simplified employee pension (SEP) described in section 408(k) of the Internal Revenue Code of 1954 as amended, except for (1) a SEP that is created by proper use of Internal Revenue Service Form *5305-SEP,* or (2) a SEP in connection with which the employer who establishes or maintains the SEP selects, recommends or influences its employees to choose the IRAs into which employer contributions will be made and those IRAs are subjectto provisions that prohibit withdrawal of funds by participants for any period of time.

(a) At the time an employee becomes eligible to participate in the SEP (whether at the creation of the SEP or thereafter) or up to 90 days after the effective date of this regulation, whichever is later, the administrator of the SEP (generally the employer establishing or maintaining the SEP) shall furnish the employee in writing with:

(1) Specific information concerning the SEP, including:

(i) The requirements for employee participation in the SEP,

(ii) The formula to be used to allocate employer contributions made under the SEP to each participant's individual retirement account or annuity (IRA).

(iii) The name or title of the individual who is designated by the employer to provide additional information to participants concerning the SEP, and

(iv) If the employer who establishes or maintains the SEP selects, recommends or substantially influences its employees to choose the IRAs into which employer contributions under the SEP will be made, a clear explanation of the terms of those IRAs, such as the rate(s) of return and any restrictions on a participant's ability to roll over or withdraw funds from the IRAs, including restrictions that allow rollovers or withdrawals but reduce earnings of the IRAs or impose other penalties.

(2) General information concerning SEPs and IRAs, including a clear explanation of:

(i) What a SEP is and how it operates,

(ii) The statutory provisions prohibiting discrimination in favor of highly compensated employees.

(iii) A participant's right to receive contributions under a SEP-and the allowable sources of contributions to a SEP-related IRA (SEP-IRA),

(iv) The statutory limits on contributions to SEP-IRAs,

(v) The consequences of excess contributions to a SEP-IRA and how to avoid excess contributions,

(vi) A participant's rights with respect to contributions made under a SEP to his or her IRA(s),

(vii) How a participant must treat contributions to a SEP-IRA for tax purposes,

(viii) The statutory provisions concerning withdrawal of funds from a SEP-IRA and the consequences of a premature withdrawal, and

(ix) A participant's ability to roll over or transfer funds from a SEP-IRA to another IRA, SEP-IRA, or retirement bond, and how such a

rollover or transfer may be effected without causing adverse tax consequences.

(3) A statement to the effect that:

(i) IRAs other than the IRA(s) into which employer contributions will be made under the SEP may provide different rates of return and may have different terms concerning, among other things, transfers and withdrawals of funds from the IRA(s),

(ii) In the event a participant is entitled to make a contribution or rollover to an IRA, such contribution or rollover can be made to an IRA other than the one into which employer contributions under the SEP are to be made, and

(iii) Depending on the terms of the IRA into which employer contributions are made, a participant may be able to make rollovers or transfers of funds from that IRA to another IRA.

(4) A description of the disclosure required by the Internal Revenue Service to be made to individuals for whose benefit an IRA is established by the financial institution or other person who sponsors the IRA(s) into which contributions will be made under the SEP.

(5) A statement that, in addition to the information provided to an employee at the time he or she becomes eligible to participate in a SEP, the administrator of the SEP must furnish each participant:

(i) Within 30 days of the effective date of any amendment to the terms of the SEP, a copy of the amendment and a clear written explanation of its effects, and

(ii) No later than the later of:

(A) January 31 of the year following the year for which a contribution is made,

(B) 30 days after a contribution is made, or

(C) 30 days after the effective date of this regulation written notification of any employer contributions made under the SEP to that participant's IRA(s).

(6) In the case of a SEP that provides for integration with Social Security.

(i) A statement that Social Security taxes paid by the employer on account of a participant will be considered as an employer contribution under the SEP to a participant's SEP-IRA for purposes of determining the amount contributed to the SEP-IRA(s) of a participant by the employer pursuant to the allocation formula,

(ii) A description of the effect that integration with Social Security would have on employer contributions under a SEP, and

(iii) The integration formula, which may constitute part of the allocation formula required by paragraph (a)(1)(ii) of this section.

(b)(1) The requirements of paragraphs (a)(1)(i), (a)(1)(ii), (a)(1)(iii) and (a)(6)(i) of this regulation may be met by furnishing the SEP agreement to participants, provided that the SEP agreement is written in a manner reasonably calculated to be understood by the average plan participant.

(2) The requirements of paragraph (a)(1)(iv) of this regulation may be met through disclosure materials furnished by the financial institution in which the participant's IRA is maintained, provided the materials contain the information specified in such paragraph.

(c) No later than the later of:

(1) January 31 of the year following the year for which a contribution is made,

(2) 30 days after a contribution is made, or

(3) 30 days after the effective date of this regulation the administrator of the SEP shall notify a participant in the SEP in writing of any employer contributions made under the SEP to the participant's IRA(s).

(d) Within 30 days of the effective date of any amendment to the terms of the SEP, the administrator shall furnish each participant a copy of the amendment and a clear explanation in writing of its effect. [Adopted by 46 FR 1261, originally scheduled to be effective February 6, 1981. However, the effective date was delayed under the President's regulation freeze at least until March 30, 1981 (46 FR 10465).]

[¶ 14,247ZD]

§ 2520.104-50 **Short plan years, deferral of accountant's examination and report**. (a) *Definition of "short plan year".* For purposes of this section, a short plan year is a plan year, as defined in section 3(39) of the Act, of seven or fewer months' duration, which occurs in the event that—(1) a plan is established or commences operations; (2) a plan is merged or consolidated with another plan or plans; (3) a plan is terminated; or (4) the annual date on which the plan year begins is changed.

(b) *Deferral of accountant's report.* A plan administrator is not required to include the report of an independent qualified public accountant in the annual report for the first of two consecutive plan years, one of which is a short plan year, provided that the following conditions are satisfied:

(1) The annual report for the first of the two consecutive plan years shall include:

(i) Financial statements and accompanying schedules prepared in conformity with the requirements of section 103(b) of the Act and regulations promulgated thereunder;

(ii) An explanation why one of the two plan years is of seven or fewer months' duration; and

(iii) A statement that the annual report for the immediately following plan year will include a report of an independent qualified public accountant with respect to the financial statements and accompanying schedules for both of the two plan years.

(2) The annual report for the second of the two consecutive plan years shall include:

(i) Financial statements and accompanying schedules prepared in conformity with section 103(b) of the Act and regulations promulgated thereunder with respect to both plan years;

(ii) A report of an independent qualified public accountant with respect to the financial statements and accompanying schedules for both plan years; and

(iii) A statement identifying any material differences between the unaudited financial information relating to, and contained in the annual report for, the first of the two consecutive plan years and the audited financial information relating to that plan year contained in the annual report for the immediately following plan year.

(c) *Accountant's examination and report.* The examination by the accountant which serves as the basis for the portion of his report relating to the first of the two consecutive plan years may be conducted at the same time as the examination which serves as the basis for the portion of his report relating to the immediately following plan year. The report of the accountant shall be prepared in conformity with section 103(a)(3)(A) of the Act and regulations thereunder. [Adopted December 30, 1980 by 46 FR 1265, effective December 29, 1980.]

Subpart E—Reporting Requirements

[¶ 14,248]

§ 2520.104a-1 **Filing with the Secretary of Labor.** (a) *General reporting requirements.* Part 1 of Title I of the Act requires that the administrator of an employee benefit plan subject to the provisions of Part 1 file with the Secretary of Labor certain reports and additional documents. Each report filed shall accurately and comprehensively detail the information required. Where a form is prescribed, the reports shall be filed on that form. The Secretary may reject any incomplete filing. Reports and documents shall be filed as specified in this part.

(b) *Exemption for certain welfare plans.* See §§ 2520.104-20, 2520.104-21, 2520.104-22, 2520.104-24, and 2520.104-25.

(c) *Alternative method of compliance for pension plans for certain selected employees.* See § 2520.104-23. [Added by 41 FR 16957, effective April 23, 1976.]

[¶ 14,248A]

§ 2520.104a-2 **Plan description reporting requirements.** [Reserved.] [67 FR 771, 1/7/02.]

[¶ 14,248B]

§ 2520.104a-3 **Summary plan description.** [Reserved.] [67 FR 771, 1/7/02.]

[¶ 14,248C]

§ 2520.104a-4 **Material modifications to the plan and changes in plan description information.** [Reserved.] [67 FR 771, 1/7/02.]

[¶ 14,248D]

§ 2520.104a-5 **Annual reporting filing requirements.** (a) *Filing obligation.* Except as provided in § 2520.104a-6, the administrator of an employee benefit plan required to file an annual report pursuant to section 104(a)(1) of the Act shall file an annual report containing the items prescribed in § 2520.103-1 within:

(1) Eleven and one half months after the close of the plan year which begins in 1975, or December 15, 1977, whichever is later; and

(2) Seven months after the close of any plan year which begins after December 31, 1975, unless extended. See "When to file" instructions of the appropriate annual Return/Report Form. [Corrected April 4, 1978, by 43 FR 14010.]

(b) *Where to file.* The annual report described in § 2520.103-1 shall be filed in accordance with and at the address provided in the instructions to the Annual Return/Report Form. [Added March 9, 1978, by 43 FR 10130. Revised by 67 FR 771, effective March 8, 2002.]

[¶ 14,248E]

§ 2520.104a-6 **Annual reporting for plans which are part of a group insurance arrangement.** (a) *General.* A trust or other entity described in § 2520.104-43(b) that files an annual report in accordance with the terms of subsections (b) and (c) shall be deemed to have filed such report in accordance with § 2520.104a-6 for purposes of § 2520.104-43.

(b) *Date of filing.* The annual report shall be filed within:

(1) Eleven and one-half months after the close of the fiscal year of the trust or other entity described in § 2520.104-43 which begins in 1975 or December 15, 1977, whichever is later; and

(2) Seven months after the close of the fiscal year of the trust or other entity which begins after December 31, 1975, unless extended. See "When to file" instructions of the appropriate Annual Return/ Report Form. [Corrected April 4, 1978, by 43 FR 14010.]

(c) *Where to file.* The annual report prescribed in § 2520.103-2 shall be filed in accordance with and at the address provided in the instructions to the Annual Return/Report Form. [Added March 9, 1978, by 43 FR 10130.]

[¶ 14,248F]

§ 2520.104a-7 **Summary of material modifications.** [Reserved.] [67 FR 771, 1/7/02.]

[¶ 14,248G]

§ 2520.104a-8 **Requirement to furnish documents to the Secretary of Labor on request.** (a) *In general.*

(1) Under section 104(a)(6) of the Act, the administrator of an employee benefit plan subject to the provisions of part 1 of title I of the Act is required to furnish to the Secretary, upon request, any documents relating to the employee benefit plan. For purposes of section 104(a)(6) of the Act, the administrator of an employee benefit plan shall furnish to the Secretary, upon service of a written request, a copy of:

(i) The latest updated summary plan description (including any summaries of material modifications to the plan or changes in the information required to be included in the summary plan description); and

(ii) Any other document described in section 104(b)(4) of the Act with respect to which a participant or beneficiary has requested, in writing, a copy from the plan administrator and which the administrator has failed or refused to furnish to the participant or beneficiary.

(2) Multiple requests for document(s). Multiple requests under this section for the same or similar document or documents shall be considered separate requests for purposes of § 2560.502c-6(a).

(b) For purposes of this section, a participant or beneficiary will include any individual who is:

(1) A participant or beneficiary within the meaning of ERISA sections 3(7) and 3(8), respectively;

(2) An alternate payee under a qualified domestic relations order (see ERISA section 206(d)(3)(K)) or prospective alternate payee (spouses, former spouses, children or other dependents);

(3) A qualified beneficiary under COBRA (see ERISA section 607(3)) or prospective qualified beneficiary (spouse or dependent child);

(4) An alternate recipient under a qualified medical child support order (see ERISA section 609(a)(2)(C)) or a prospective alternate recipient; or

(5) A representative of any of the foregoing.

(c) *Service of request.* Requests under this section shall be served in accordance with § 2560.502c-6(i).

(d) *Furnishing documents.* A document shall be deemed to be furnished to the Secretary on the date the document is received by the Department of Labor at the address specified in the request; or, if a document is delivered by certified mail, the date on which the document is mailed to the Department of Labor at the address specified in the request.

Subpart F—Disclosure Requirements

[¶ 14,249]

§ 2520.104b-1 **Disclosure.** (a) *General disclosure requirements.* The administrator of an employee benefit plan covered by Title I of the Act must disclose certain material, including reports, statements, notices, and other documents, to participants, beneficiaries and other specified individuals. Disclosure under Title I of the Act generally takes three forms. First, the plan administrator must, by direct operation of law, furnish certain material to all participants covered under the plan and beneficiaries receiving benefits under the plan (other than beneficiaries under a welfare plan) at stated times or if certain events occur. Second, the plan administrator must furnish certain material to individual participants and beneficiaries upon their request. Third, the plan administrator must make certain material available to participants and beneficiaries for inspection at reasonable times and places.

(b) *Fulfilling the disclosure obligation.* (1) Except as provided in paragraph (e) of this section, where certain material, including reports, statements, notices and other documents, is required under Title I of the Act, or regulations issued thereunder, to be furnished either by direct operation of law or on individual request, the plan administrator shall use measures reasonably calculated to ensure actual receipt of the material by plan participants, beneficiaries and other specified individuals. Material which is required to be furnished to all participants covered under the plan and beneficiaries receiving benefits under the plan (other than beneficiaries under a welfare plan) must be sent by a method or methods of delivery likely to result in full distribution. For example in-hand delivery to an employee at his or her worksite is acceptable. However, in no case is it acceptable merely to place copies of the material in a location frequented by participants. It is also acceptable to furnish such material as a special insert in a periodical distributed to employees such as a union newspaper or a company publication if the distribution list for the periodical is comprehensive and up-to-date and a prominent notice on the front page of the periodical advises readers that the issue contains an insert with important information about rights under the plan and the Act which should be read and retained for future reference. If some participants and beneficiaries are not on the mailing list, a periodical must be used in conjunction with other methods of distribution such that the methods taken together are reasonably calculated to ensure actual receipt.

Material distributed through the mail may be sent by first, second, or third-class mail. However, distribution by second or third-class mail is acceptable only if return and forwarding postage is guaranteed and address correction is requested. Any material sent by second or third-class mail which is returned with an address correction shall be sent again by first-class mail or personally delivered to the participant at his or her worksite.

(2) For purposes of section 104(b)(4) of the Act, materials furnished upon written request shall be mailed to an address provided by the requesting participant or beneficiary or personally delivered to the participant or beneficiary.

(3) For purposes of section 104(b)(2) of the Act, where certain documents are required to be made available for examination by participants and beneficiaries in the principal office of the plan administrator and in such other places as may be necessary to make available all pertinent information to all participants and beneficiaries, disclosure shall be made pursuant to the provisions of this paragraph.

Such documents must be current, readily accessible, and clearly identified, and copies must be available in sufficient number to accommodate the expected volume of inquiries. Plan administrators shall make copies of the latest annual report, and the bargaining agreement, trust agreement, contract, or other instruments under which the plan is established or operated available at all times in their principal offices. They are not required to maintain these plan documents at all times at each employer establishment or union hall or office as described in paragraphs (b)(3)(i), (ii), and (iii) of this section, but the documents must be made available at any such location within ten calendar days following the day on which a request for disclosure at that location is made.

Plan administrators shall make plan documents available at the appropriate employer establishment or union meeting hall or office within the required ten day period when a request is made directly to the plan administrator or through a procedure establishing reasonable rules governing the making of requests for examination of plan documents. If a plan administrator prescribes such a procedure and communicates it to plan participants and beneficiaries, a plan administrator will not be required to comply with a request made in a manner which does not conform to the established procedure. In order to comply with the requirements of this section, a procedure for making requests to examine plan documents must permit requests to be made in a reasonably convenient manner both directly to the plan administrator and at each employer establishment, or union meeting hall or office where documents must be made available in accordance with this paragraph. If no such reasonable procedure is established, a good faith effort by a participant or beneficiary to request examination of plan documents will be deemed a request to the plan administrator for purposes of this paragraph.

(i) In the case of a plan not maintained according to a collective bargaining agreement, including a plan maintained by a single employer with more than one establishment, a multiple employer plan, and a plan maintained by a controlled group of corporations (within the meaning of § 1563(a) of the Internal Revenue Code of 1954 (the Code), determined without regard to § 1563(a)(4) and (e)(3)(C) of the Code), documents shall be made available for examination in the principal office of the employer and at each employer establishment in which at least 50 participants covered under a plan are customarily working. "Establishment" means a single physical location where business is conducted or where services or industrial operations are performed. Where employees are engaged in activities which are physically dispersed, such as agriculture, construction, transportation, and communications, the "establishment" shall be the place to which employees report each day. When employees do not usually work at, or report to, a single establishment—for example, traveling salesmen, technicians, and engineers—the establishment shall be the location from which the employees customarily carry out their activities—for example the field office of an engineering firm servicing at least 50 participants covered under the plan.

(ii) In the case of a plan maintained solely by an employee organization, the plan administrator shall take measures to ensure that documents are available for examination at the meeting hall or office of each union local in which there are at least 50 participants covered under the plan. Such measures shall include distributing copies of the documents to each union local in which there are at least 50 participants covered under the plan.

(iii) In the case of a plan maintained according to a collective bargaining agreement, including a collectively bargained single employer plan with more than one establishment, a collectively bargained multiple employer plan, and a multiemployer plan which meets the definition of section 3(37) of the Act, § 2510.3-37 of this chapter, and section 414(b) of the Internal Revenue Code of 1954 and 26 CFR § 1.414(f) (40 CFR 43034), documents shall be made available for examination in the principal office of the employee organization and at each employer establishment in which at least 50 participants covered under the plan are customarily working. In employment situations where employees do not usually work at, or report to, a single establishment, the plan administrator shall take measures to ensure that plan documents are available for examination at the meeting hall or office of each union local in which there are at least 50 participants covered under the plan. [Revised by 67 FR 771, effective March 8, 2002. Revised by 67 FR 17263, April 9, 2002]

(c) *Disclosure through electronic media.* (1) Except as otherwise provided by applicable law, rule or regulation, the administrator of an employee benefit plan furnishing documents through electronic media is deemed to satisfy the requirements of paragraph (b)(1) of this section with respect to an individual described in paragraph (c)(2) if:

(i) The administrator takes appropriate and necessary measures reasonably calculated to ensure that the system for furnishing documents—

(A) Results in actual receipt of transmitted information (e.g., using return-receipt or notice of undelivered electronic mail features, conducting periodic reviews or surveys to confirm receipt of the transmitted information); and

(B) Protects the confidentiality of personal information relating to the individual's accounts and benefits (e.g., incorporating into the system measures designed to preclude unauthorized receipt of or access to such information by individuals other than the individual for whom the information is intended);

(ii) The electronically delivered documents are prepared and furnished in a manner that is consistent with the style, format and content requirements applicable to the particular document;

(iii) Notice is provided to each participant, beneficiary or other individual, in electronic or non-electronic form, at the time a document is furnished electronically, that apprises the individual of the significance of the document when it is not otherwise reasonably evident as transmitted (e.g., the attached document describes changes in the benefits provided by your plan) and of the right to request and obtain a paper version of such document; and

(iv) Upon request, the participant, beneficiary or other individual is furnished a paper version of the electronically furnished documents.

(2) Paragraph (c)(1) shall only apply with respect to the following individuals:

(i) A participant who—

(A) Has the ability to effectively access documents furnished in electronic form at any location where the participant is reasonably expected to perform his or her duties as an employee; and

(B) With respect to whom access to the employer's or plan sponsor's electronic information system is an integral part of those duties; or

(ii) A participant, beneficiary or any other person entitled to documents under Title I of the Act or regulations issued thereunder (including, but not limited to, an "alternate payee" within the meaning of section 206(d)(3) of the Act and a "qualified beneficiary" within the meaning of section 607(3) of the Act) who—

(A) Except as provided in paragraph (c)(2)(ii) (B) of this section, has affirmatively consented, in electronic or non-electronic form, to receiving documents through electronic media and has not withdrawn such consent;

(B) In the case of documents to be furnished through the Internet or other electronic communication network, has affirmatively consented or confirmed consent electronically, in a manner that reasonably demonstrates the individual's ability to access information in the electronic form that will be used to provide the information that is the subject of the consent, and has provided an address for the receipt of electronically furnished documents;

(C) Prior to consenting, is provided, in electronic or non-electronic form, a clear and conspicuous statement indicating:

(1) The types of documents to which the consent would apply;

(2) That consent can be withdrawn at any time without charge;

(3) The procedures for withdrawing consent and for updating the participant's, beneficiary's or other individual's address for receipt of electronically furnished documents or other information;

(4) The right to request and obtain a paper version of an electronically furnished document, including whether the paper version will be provided free of charge; and

(5) Any hardware and software requirements for accessing and retaining the documents; and

(D) Following consent, if a change in hardware or software requirements needed to access or retain electronic documents creates a material risk that the individual will be unable to access or retain electronically furnished documents:

(1) Is provided with a statement of the revised hardware or software requirements for access to and retention of electronically furnished documents;

(2) Is given the right to withdraw consent without charge and without the imposition of any condition or consequence that was not disclosed at the time of the initial consent; and

(3) Again consents, in accordance with the requirements of paragraph (c)(2)(ii)(A) or paragraph (c)(2)(ii)(B) of this section, as applicable, to the receipt of documents through electronic media.

This paragraph (c) applies on or after June 1, 1997. [Added by 62 FR 16979, April 8, 1997.] [Revised by 67 FR 17263, April 9, 2002.]

(d) *Participant and beneficiary status for purposes of sections 101(a) and 104(b)(1) of the Act and Subpart F of this part.*—See §§ 2510.3-3(d)(1), 2510.3-3(d)(2), and 2520.3-3(d)(3) of this chapter. (Approved by the Office of Management and Budget under control number 1210-0039.) [Added by 41 FR 16957, effective April 23, 1976. Amended by 62 FR 36205, effective June 1, 1997.]

(e) *Limitations.* This section does not apply to disclosures required under provisions of part 2 and part 3 of the Act over which the Secretary of the Treasury has interpretative and regulatory authority pursuant to Reorganization Plan No. 4 of 1978.

[Added by 67 FR 17263, April 9, 2002.]

[¶ 14,249A]

§ 2520.104b-2 **Summary plan description.** (a) *Obligation to furnish.* Under the authority of sections 104(b)(1) and 104(c) of the Act, the plan administrator of an employee benefit plan subject to the provisions of Part 1 of Title I shall furnish a copy of the summary plan description and a statement of ERISA rights as provided in § 2520.102-3(t), to each participant covered under the plan (as defined in § 2510.3-(d)), and each beneficiary receiving benefits under a pension plan on or before the later of:

(1) The date which is 90 days after the employee becomes a participant, or (in the case of a beneficiary receiving benefits under a pension plan) within 90 days after he or she first receives benefits, except as provided in § 2520.104b-4(a), or,

(2) Within 120 days after the plan becomes subject to Part 1 of Title I.

(3)(i) A plan becomes subject to Part 1 of Title I on the first day on which an employee is credited with an hour of service under § 2530.200b-2 or § 2530.200b-3. Where a plan is made prospectively effective to take effect after a certain date or after a condition is satisfied, the day upon which the plan becomes subject to Part 1 of Title I is the day after such date or condition is satisfied. Where a plan is adopted with a retroactive effective date, the 120 day period begins on the day after the plan is adopted. Where a plan is made retroactively effective dependent on a condition, the day on which the plan becomes subject to Part 1 of Title I is the day after the day on which the condition is satisfied. Where a plan is made retroactively effective subject to a contingency which may or may not occur in the future, the day on which the plan becomes subject to Part 1, Title I is the day after the day on which the contingency occurs.

(ii) *Examples*: Company A is negotiating the purchase of Company B. On September 1, 1978, as part of the negotiations, Company A adopts a pension plan covering the employees of Company B, contingent on the successful conclusion of its negotiations to purchase Company B. The plan provides that it shall take effect on the first day of the calendar year in which the purchase is concluded. On February 1, 1979, the negotiations conclude with Company A's purchase of Company B. The plan therefore becomes effective on February 1, 1979, retroactive to January 1, 1979. The summary plan description must be filed and disclosed no later than 120 days after February 1, 1979. [Amended by 42 FR 37178, effective July 19, 1977; amended and finalized by 45 FR 14029, effective April 3, 1980.]

(b) *Periods for furnishing updated summary plan description.* (1) For purposes of the requirement to furnish the updated summary plan description to each participant and each beneficiary receiving benefits under the plan (other than beneficiaries receiving benefits under a welfare plan) required by section 104(b)(1) of the Act, the administrator of an employee benefit plan shall furnish such updated summary plan description no later than 210 days following the end of the plan year within which occurs the later of—

(i) November 16, 1983, or

(ii) Five years after the last date a change in the information required to be disclosed by section 102 or 29 CFR 2520.102-3 would have been reflected in the most recently distributed summary plan description (or updated summary plan description), as described in section 102 of the Act.

(2) In the case of a plan to which no amendments have been made between the end of the time period covered by the last distributed summary plan description (or updated summary plan description), described in section 102 of the Act, and the next occurring applicable date described in paragraph (b)(1)(i) or (ii) of this section, for purposes of the requirement to furnish the updated summary plan description to each participant, and to each beneficiary receiving benefits under the plan (other than beneficiaries receiving benefits under a welfare plan), required by section 104(b)(1) of the Act, the administrator of an employee benefit plan shall furnish such updated summary plan description no later than 210 days following the end of the plan year within which occurs ten years after the last date a change in the information required to be disclosed by section 102 or 29 CFR 2520.102-3 would have beend reflected in the most recently distributed summary plan description (or updated summary plan description), as described in action 102 of the Act. [Paragraph (b) was amended on July 1, 1996 by 61 FR 33847.]

>>>→ Caution: Regulation § 2520.104(b)-2(c) removed and reserved officially by 61 FR 33847 on July 1, 1996.

(c) *Alternative ERISA Notice requirements.* A plan which elected to comply with the alternative ERISA Notice procedure provided in § 2520.104-5 or § 2520.104-6 is not required to furnish a copy of the summary plan description to participants and beneficiaries until the time described in the applicable section, and will be deemed to have satisfied the requirements of section 104(b)(1)(B) of the Act until such time. Thereafter, the requirements of section 104(b)(1)(B) of the Act and this section must be met in full.

>>>→ Caution: Regulation § 2520.104(b)-2(d) removed and reserved officially by 61 FR 33847 on July 1, 1996.

(d) *Use of form EBS-1 as summary plan description.* (1) The plan administrator of an employee benefit plan shall be deemed to have satisfied the requirements of section 104(b)(1)(B) of the Act and this section for the initial disclosure of the summary plan description if the plan administrator filed a summary plan description pursuant to proposed § 2520.104a-3(d) of the June 9, 1975, proposed regulations (40 FR 24642); § 2520.104-3 as issued on April 30, 1975 (40 FR 19469; see also 40 FR 20628, May 12, 1975); proposed §§ 2522.40 and 2523.30 as published on December 4, 1974, (39 FR 42241); and the instructions on old form EBS-1 (bearing print date 4-75), and if the plan administrator furnished copies of a complete Form EBS-1 bearing print date 4-75 to participants covered under the plan and beneficiaries receiving benefits under the plan.

(2) Under the authority of section 104(c) of the Act, a plan described in subparagraph (1) shall furnish to participants covered under the plan and beneficiaries receiving benefits under the plan a statement of ERISA rights which complies with § 2520.102-3(t) by November 16, 1977.

>>>→ Caution: Regulation § 2520.104(b)-2(e) removed and reserved officially by 61 FR 33847 on July 1, 1996.

(e) *Disclosure obligation for plans which filed and disclosed by May 30, 1976 in reliance upon regulations of the Department.* (1) The plan administrator of an employee benefit plan shall be deemed to have satisfied the requirements of section 104(b)(1)(B) of the Act and this section for the initial disclosure of the summary plan description if the plan administrator filed a summary plan description based upon the final regulations published in the FEDERAL REGISTER on August 15, 1975 (40 FR 34526) and on specific sections of the proposed regulations published in the FEDERAL REGISTER on June 9, 1975 (40 FR 24642) in reliance upon the preamble to the final regulations published in the FEDERAL REGISTER on April 23, 1976 (41 FR 16957) and announced in Departmental press release USDL 76-706, published April 21, 1976, and if the plan administrator furnished to participants covered under the plan and pension plan beneficiaries receiving benefits under the plan copies of such summary plan description.

(2) Under the authority of section 104(c) of the Act, a plan described in subparagraph (1) shall furnish to participants covered under the plan and beneficiaries receiving benefits under the plan a statement of ERISA rights which complies with § 2520.102-3(t) by November 16, 1977.

>>>→ Caution: Regulation § 2520.104(b)-2(f) removed and reserved officially by 61 FR 33847 on July 1, 1996.

(f) *Disclosure obligation for all other plans which previously disclosed the summary plan description.* (1) This section applies to those employee benefit plans which have disclosed to participants covered under the plan and beneficiaries receiving benefits under a pension plan, a summary plan description on or after September 2, 1974, and before March 15, 1977, and which are not described in paragraph (4) or (e) of this section.

(2) The plan administrator of an employee benefit plan described in subparagraph (1) shall be deemed to have satisfied the requirements of section 104(b)(1)(B) of the Act of this section for the initial disclosure of the summary plan description and the disclosure of the first updated summary plan description if the plan administrator:

(i) Furnishes to participants covered under the plan and pension plan beneficiaries receiving benefits under the plan by November 16, 1977, a copy of a supplement to the summary plan description which includes any items of information required by § 2520.102-3 which were not included in the earlier document and which, taken together with the earlier document, meets the style and format requirements of § 2520.102-2. The requirement of § 2520.102-2(b) that benefit restrictions be described or cross-referenced adjacent to the description of benefits will be deemed satisfied if the supplement contains a statement which references participants to the descriptions of benefits and benefit restrictions in the summary plan description and describes their relationship;

(ii) Files with the Secretary, by November 16, 1977, a copy of the summary plan description described in paragraph (f)(1) and a copy of the supplement described in paragraph (f)(2)(i); and

(iii) Furnishes to participants and beneficiaries a summary plan description which meets the requirements of §§ 2520.102-2 and 2520.102-3 within five years (or ten years) of the date of disclosure described in subparagraph (i).

(g) *Terminated plans.* (1) If, on or before the date by which a plan is required to furnish a summary plan description or updated summary plan description to participants and pension plan beneficiaries under this section, the plan has terminated within the meaning of paragraph (g)(2) of this section, the administrator of such plan is not required to furnish to participants covered under the plan or to beneficiaries receiving benefits under the plan a summary plan description.

(2) For purposes of this section, a plan shall be considered terminated if:

(i) in the case of an employee pension benefit plan, all distributions to participants and beneficiaries have been completed; and

(ii) in the case of an employee welfare benefit plan, no claims can be incurred which will result in a liability of the plan to pay benefits. A claim is incurred upon the occurrence of the event or condition from which the claim arises (whether or not discovered). [Revised by 67 FR 771, effective March 8, 2002.]

Reg. § 2520.104b-2(g)(2)(ii)   ¶14,249A

>>> *Caution: Regulation § 2520.104(b)-2(h) removed and reserved officially by 61 FR 33847 on July 1, 1996.*

(h) *Alternative requirements for plans subject to the alternative ERISA Notice requirements.* See § 2520.104-5 or § 2520.104-6. See § 2510.3-3(d).

(i) *Style and format of the summary plan description.* See § 2520.102-2.

(j) *Contents of the summary plan description.* See § 2520.102-3.

(k) *Option for different summary plan descriptions.* See § 2520.102-4, § 2520.104-26, and § 2520.104-27.

(l) *Employee benefit plan—participant covered under a plan.* See § 2510.3-3(d). [Added by 42 FR 14266, effective March 15, 1977; and amended by 42 FR 37178, effective July 19, 1977.]

[¶ 14,249B]

§ 2520.104b-3 **Summary of material modifications to the plan and changes in the information required to be included in the summary plan description.** (a) The administrator of an employee benefit plan subject to the provisions of Part 1 of Title I of the Act shall, in accordance with § 2520.104b-1(b), furnish a summary description of any material modification to the plan and any change in the information required by section 102(b) of the Act and § 2520.102-3 of these regulations to be included in the summary plan description to each participant covered under the plan and each beneficiary receiving benefits under the plan. Except as provided in paragraph (d) of this section, the plan administrator shall furnish this summary, written in a manner calculated to be understood by the average plan participant, not later than 210 days after the close of the plan year in which the modification or change was adopted. This disclosure date is not affected by retroactive application to a prior plan year of an amendment which makes a material modification to the plan; a modification does not occur before it is adopted. For example, a calendar year plan adopts a modification in April 1978. The modification, by its terms, applies retroactively to the 1977 plan year. A summary description of the material modification is furnished on or before July 29, 1979. A plan which adopts an amendment which makes a material modification to the plan which takes effect on a date in the future must disclose a summary of that modification within 210 days after the close of the plan year in which the modification or change is adopted. Under the authority of sections 104(a)(3) and 110 of the Act, a summary description of a material modification or change is not required to be disclosed if it is rescinded or otherwise does not take effect. For example, a calendar year plan adopts a modification in June 1978. The modification, by its terms, becomes effective beginning in plan year 1979. Before the beginning of plan year 1979, the prospective modification is withdrawn. No summary of the material modification is required to be disclosed. [Amended 11/21/00 by 65 FR 70225.]

(b) The summary of material modifications to the plan or changes in information required to be included in the summary plan description need not be furnished separately if the changes or modifications are described in a timely summary plan description. For example, a calendar year plan adopts a material modification on June 3, 1976. The modification is incorporated in a summary plan description furnished on July 15, 1977. No separate summary of the material modification is furnished. The plan adopts another material modification September 15, 1977. A separate summary of the modification is furnished on or before July 29, 1978.

(c) The copy of the summary plan description furnished in accordance with §§ 2520.104b-2(a)(1)(i) and 2520.104b-4 shall be accompanied by all summaries of material modifications or changes in information required to be included in the summary plan description which have not been incorporated into that summary plan description.

(d) *Special rule for group health plans.* (1) *General.* Except as provided in paragraph (d)(2) of this section, the administrator of a group health plan, as defined in section 733(a)(1) of the Act, shall furnish to each participant covered under the plan a summary, written in a manner calculated to be understood by the average plan participant, of any modification to the plan or change in the information required to be included in the summary plan description, within the meaning of paragraph (a) of this section, that is a material reduction in covered services or benefits not later than 60 days after the date of adoption of the modification or change.

(2) *90-day alternative rule.* The administrator of a group health plan shall not be required to furnish a summary of any material reduction in covered services or benefits within the 60-day period described in paragraph (d)(1) of this section to any participant covered under the plan who would reasonably be expected to be furnished such summary in connection with a system of communication maintained by the plan sponsor or administrator, with respect to which plan participants are provided information concerning their plan, including modifications and changes thereto, at regular intervals of not more than 90 days and such communication otherwise meets the disclosure requirements of 29 CFR 2520.104b-1.

(3) *"Material reduction".* (i) For purposes of this paragraph (d), a "material reduction in covered services or benefits" means any modification to the plan or change in the information required to be included in the summary plan description that, independently or in conjunction with other contemporaneous modifications or changes, would be considered by the average plan participant to be an important reduction in covered services or benefits under the plan.

(ii) A "reduction in covered services or benefits" generally would include any plan modification or change that: eliminates benefits payable under the plan; reduces benefits payable under the plan, including a reduction that occurs as a result of a change in formulas, methodologies or schedules that serve as the basis for making benefit determinations; increases premiums, deductibles, coinsurance, copayments, or other amounts to be paid by a participant or beneficiary; reduces the service area covered by a health maintenance organization; establishes new conditions or requirements (e.g., preauthorization requirements) to obtaining services or benefits under the plan. [Added by 62 FR 16979, April 8, 1997. Amended 11/21/00 by 65 FR 70225. Corrected by PWBA on 7/2/01, 66 FR 34994.]

(e) *Applicability date.* Paragraph (d) of this section is applicable as of the first day of the first plan year beginning after June 30, 1997. [Added by 62 FR 16979, April 8, 1997. Amended 11/21/00 by 65 FR 70225.]

(f) *Alternative requirements for plans subject to alternative ERISA Notice requirements.* Reserved. [67 FR 771, 1/7/02.]

(g) *Filing obligation for all other plans which previously filed and disclosed the summary plan description.* Reserved. [67 FR 771, 1/7/02.]

[¶ 14,249C]

§ 2520.104b-4 **Alternative methods of compliance for furnishing the summary plan description and summaries of material modifications of a pension plan to a retired participant, a separated participant with vested benefits, and a beneficiary receiving benefits.** Under the authority of section 110 of the Act, in the case of an employee pension benefit plan—

(a) *Summary plan descriptions.* A plan administrator will be deemed to satisfy the requirements of section 104(b)(1) of the Act and § 2520.104b-2(a) to furnish a copy of the initial summary plan description to a retired participant, a beneficiary receiving benefits, or a separated participant with vested benefits ("vested separated participant") if, no earlier than the date stated in subparagraph (4) of this paragraph.

(1) In the case of a retired participant or a beneficiary receiving benefits, a document is furnished which—

(i) Meets the requirements of §§ 2520.102-2 and 2520.102-3 except paragraphs (b)(3), (b)(4), (j), (k), (l), (n), (o), and (p);

(ii) Contains a statement that the benefit payment presently being received by the retired participant or beneficiary receiving benefits will continue in the same amount and for the period provided in the mode of settlement selected at retirement, and will not be changed except as described in subparagraph (iii); and

(iii) Contains a statement describing any plan provision under which the present benefit payment may be reduced, changed, terminated, forfeited, or suspended;

(2) In the case of a vested separated participant, a document is furnished which—

(i) Meets the requirements of §§ 2520.102-2 and 2520.102-3 except paragraphs (b)(3), (b)(4), (j), (l), (n), (o), (p), and (r);

(ii)(A) If at or after separation, a separated vested participant was furnished a statement of the dollar amount of the vested benefit or the method of computation of the benefit, includes a statement that the dollar amount of the vested benefit was previously furnished and that a copy of the previously furnished statement of the dollar amount of such vested benefit or method of computation of the benefit may be obtained from the plan upon request;

(B) If the vested separate participant was not furnished a statement of the dollar amount of the vested benefit or the method of computation of the benefit, the plan furnishes either a statement of the dollar amount of the vested benefit, or a statement of the formula used to determine the dollar amount of the vested benefit;

(iii) Includes a statement of the form in which the benefits will be paid and duration of the payment period or a description of the optional modes of payment available under the plan; and

(iv) Includes a statement describing any plan provision under which a benefit may be reduced, changed, terminated, forfeited, or suspended; or

(3)(i) Such retired participant, vested separated participant, or beneficiary receiving benefits was furnished with a copy of a document which—

(A) Satisfies the requirements of section 102(a)(1) of the Act and § 2520.102-2 (relating to the style and format of the summary plan description) and § 2520.102-3 (relating to the content of the summary plan description);

(B) Describes the rights and obligations under the plan of such retired participant, vested separated participant, or beneficiary receiving benefits as of the date stated in subparagraph (4);

(ii) In the case of a person who retired, became a beneficiary, or separated with vested benefits before November 16, 1977, a document will be deemed to comply with the requirements of subparagraph (i) if the document omitted only information described in one or more of the provisions of § 2520.102-3 listed below, provided that a supplement containing such information, which meets the requirements of § 2520.102-2, is furnished to the retired participant, vested separated participant, or beneficiary receiving benefits by November 16, 1977.

(A) Employer identification number (EIN), as required by § 2520.102-3(c);

(B) Type of administration, as required by § 2520.102-3(e);

(C) Name of agent for service of legal process, as required by § 2520.102-3(g);

(D) Names and addresses of trustees, as required by § 2520.102-3(h);

(E) Statement regarding plan termination insurance as required by § 2520.102-3(m);

(F) Date of the end of the fiscal year, as required by § 2520.102-3(r); or

(G) Statement of ERISA rights, as required by § 2520.102-3(t).

(4) For purposes of this paragraph the dates are: for a vested separated participant, the date of separation; for a beneficiary, the date on which payment of benefits commences; and for a retired participant, the date of retirement.

(b) *Updated summary plan descriptions.* A copy of an updated summary plan description need not be furnished as prescribed in section 104(b)(1) of the Act and § 2520.104b-2(b) to a retired participant, vested separated participant, or a beneficiary receiving benefits if—

(1)(i) On or after the date stated in subparagraph (ii), the retired participant, vested separated participant, or beneficiary is furnished with a copy of the most recent summary plan description and a copy of any summaries of material modifications not incorporated in such summary plan description;

(ii) For purposes of subparagraph (i) the dates are: for a retired participant, the date of retirement; for a vested separated partici-

pant, the date of separation; and for a beneficiary, the date on which payment of benefits commences;

(2) No later than the date on which an updated summary plan description is furnished to participants and beneficiaries as prescribed by section 104(b)(1) of the Act and § 2520.104b-2(b), a retired participant, vested separated participant, or beneficiary receiving benefits is furnished a notice containing the following:

(i) A statement that the benefit rights of such retired participant, vested separated participant, or beneficiary receiving benefits are set forth in the earlier summary plan description and any subsequently furnished summaries of material modifications (see paragraph (c)), and

(ii) A statement that such retired participant, vested separated participant, or beneficiary receiving benefits may obtain a copy of the earlier summary plan description and summaries of material modifications described in subparagraph (i), and the updated summary plan description, without charge, upon request, from the plan administrator; and

(3) The plan administrator furnishes a copy of the documents described in subparagraph (2)(ii) to such retired participant, vested separated participant or beneficiary, without charge, upon request.

(c) *Summary of material modifications or changes.* A summary description of a material modification to the plan or a change in the information required to be included in the summary plan description need not be furnished to a retired participant, a vested separated participant or a beneficiary receiving benefits under the plan, within the time prescribed in section 104(b)(1) of the Act and § 2520.104b-3 for furnishing summary descriptions of such modifications and changes, if the material modification or change in no way affects such retired participant's, vested separated participant's, or beneficiary's rights under the plan. For example, a change in trustees is information which such a person may need to know in order to make inquiries about his or her rights expeditiously, and hence must be furnished. On the other hand, a modification in benefits under the plan to which such retired participant, vested separated participant, or beneficiary had not at any time been entitled (and would not in the future be entitled) would not affect his or her rights and hence need not be furnished. If such retired participant, vested separated participant, or beneficiay requests a copy of a summary description of a material modification or a change which was not furnished, the plan administrator shall furnish the copy, without charge.

»»→ *Caution: Regulation § 2520.104b-4(d) removed and reserved officially by 61 FR 33847 on July 1, 1996.*

(d) *Special rule for a plan which has previously furnished a summary plan description.* A plan described in § 2520.104b-2(e) or (f) which did not specify and identify those items of information in the summary plan description pertinent to a class of participants or beneficiaries as required by § 2520.102-2 must furnish, by November 16, 1977, a supplement to the class which—

(1) Identifies the information not relevant to the class, and

(2) Provides the information required to be furnished to the class under § 2520.102-3, or under an alternative provided by this section. [Added by 42 FR 14266, effective March 15, 1977; amended by 42 FR 37178, effective July 19, 1977; amended and finalized by 45 FR 14029, effective April 3, 1980.]

»»→ *Caution: Regulation § 2520.104b-5 removed and reserved officially by 61 FR 33847 on July 1, 1996.*

[¶ 14,249D]

§ 2520.104b-5 **ERISA Notice.** (a) *Obligation to furnish.* The administrator of an employee benefit plan who elects the deferral provided by § 2520.104-5 or 104-6 must furnish a copy of an ERISA Notice to participants and beneficiaries as described in those sections.

(b) *Content, style and format.*

The ERISA Notice shall include:

(1) the name of the plan,

(2) the name, business address, business telephone number and Employer Identification Number of the plan administrator,

(3) a statement describing certain reporting and disclosure provisions of the Act, including the requirements to:

(i) file with the Secretary of Labor a plan description, in accordance with sections 104(a)(1)(B) of the Act,

(ii) file with the Secretary an annual financial statement, in accordance with section 104(a)(1)(A) of the Act,

(iii) furnish to participants and beneficiaries a summary of the annual financial report, in accordance with section 104(b)(3) of the Act,

(iv) furnish plan documents and information at a reasonable charge upon written request of a participant or beneficiary, in accordance with section 104(b)(4) of the Act, and

(v) make plan documents available for examination at the plan administrator's office and certain other locations, in accordance with section 104(b)(2) of the Act,

(4) a statement that fiduciaries have obligations imposed by the Act to act prudently and solely in the interest of participants and beneficiaries of the plan,

(5) in the case of pension plans,

(i) a statement that the plan must meet certain new standards for participation, vesting and accrual of benefits and a brief statement of them, and

(ii) a general explanation of the plan amendment process that the plan has followed or will follow to comply with ERISA, including the dates of the first plan year to which amendments must apply, and the impact of any retroactive amendment.

The ERISA Notice may contain explanatory and descriptive provisions in addition to those prescribed herein. However, the style and format of the ERISA notice shall not have the effect of misleading, misinforming or failing to inform participants and beneficiaries of a plan. Any additional explanatory information shall be written in a manner calculated to be understood by the average plan participant, taking into account factors such as the level of comprehension and education of typical participants in the plan and the complexity of the items required under this section to be included in the ERISA Notice. Inaccurate or misleading explanatory material will fail to meet the requirements of this section.

(c) *Model ERISA Notice.*

A plan administrator who uses the sample language of paragraph (1) or (2) will be deemed to meet the requirements of this section unless he has reason to know that the use of such language would be seriously misleading or incomplete as applied to the plan.

(1) *Model ERISA Notice for pension plans.*

On Labor Day of 1974 a new law was enacted to protect the interests of workers in pension and welfare benefits connected with their jobs. Its title is "Employee Retirement Income Security Act of 1974", but it is often referred to by its initials—ERISA.

ERISA requires plan administrators—the people who run plans—to tell you the most important facts you need to know, in writing and free of charge. They must also let you look at plan documents, and buy copies of them at reasonable cost if you ask. ERISA says that pension plans must give you certain minimum rights. For example, ERISA controls when you can join the plan. Also, a great many people have control over employee benefit plans. ERISA says that these people—called "fiduciaries"—must act solely in your interest and must be prudent in carrying out their plan duties. ERISA also has other special rules that limit what a fiduciary is allowed to do. Fiduciaries who violate ERISA may be removed, and may have to make good losses they cause to the plan.

Because ERISA contains many provisions which may affect your retirement benefits, you should contact (name of plan administrator, business address, business telephone and Employer Identification Number) before making decisions about your future or retirement plans.

ERISA requires (name of administrator), the administrator of (name of plan), to file certain information about the plan with the U.S. Department of Labor. A description of the plan's provisions must be filed with the Department of Labor by May 30, 1976. (Name of Administrator) must also file an annual report with the Department of Labor by (date). The annual report gives detailed financial information about the

plan. (Name of plan administrator) is also required to send a summary of the annual financial report to you, at no charge.

In addition, plan documents and other plan information must be provided to you by (name of plan administrator) if you request this information in writing. (Name of Plan Administrator) may make a reasonable charge for these documents. You may wish to find out how much the charge will be before making a written request. However, all plan documents must be made available for your examination at (office address of plan administrator) and certain other locations, such as worksites and union halls, at no charge.

ERISA also requires the (name of plan) to meet certain new standards for pension plans. These minimum standards determine when an employee must become eligible to participate in a plan, when he or she has a vested right (one which cannot be taken away, except in limited circumstances) to certain benefits, and the rate at which benefits must accrue in the participant's behalf.

(Choose the appropriate one of the following two paragraphs.)

Optional Paragraph 1.

The (name of plan) has NOT been amended to meet these standards yet. ERISA requires that (name of plan) apply the new standards to the plan year starting on (start of 1976 plan year). But ERISA does not require the plan to make amendments by (start of 1976 plan year). The amendments may come later. When they are made, they must be applied back to (start of 1976 plan year). For example, if you were not eligible to join the plan under the rule in force (start of 1976 plan year), but the amendment would make you eligible, the plan must count you as a member starting with (start of 1976 plan year).

Optional Paragraph 2.

The (name of plan) already has been amended. However, further plan amendments may have to be made to comply with ERISA standards. (Name of plan administrator) will provide information regarding these amendments.

As a result of the modifications which will be made, your right to a pension and the form and amount of your pension may be affected. Regardless of your age, if you are thinking about changing jobs or retiring you should contact (administrator, personnel office) about your pension situation before making any decisions.

If you have any questions about this Notice or your rights, contact (name of plan administrator). Also, the nearest Area Office of the Labor Department has people who will be able to assist you or provide you with additional information.

(2) *Model ERISA Notice for welfare plans.*

On Labor Day of 1974 a new law was enacted to protect the interests of workers in pension and welfare benefits connected with their jobs. Its title is "Employee Retirement Income Security Act of 1974" but it is often referred to by its initials—ERISA.

ERISA requires plan administrators—the people who run plans—to tell you the most important facts you need to know, in writing and free of charge. They must also let you look at plan documents, and buy copies of them at reasonable cost if you ask.

Also, a great many people have control over employee benefit plans. ERISA says that these people—called "fiduciaries"—must act solely in your interest and be prudent in carrying out their plan duties. ERISA also has other special rules that limit what a fiduciary is allowed to do. Fiduciaries who violate ERISA may be removed, and have to make good losses they cause to the plan.

ERISA requires (name of administrator), the administrator of (name of plan), to file certain information about the plan with the U.S. Department of Labor. A description of the plan's provisions must be filed with the Department of Labor by May 30, 1976. (Name of Administrator) must also file an annual report with the Department of Labor by (date). The annual report gives detailed financial information about the plan. (Name of plan administrator) is also required to send a summary of the annual financial report to you, at no charge.

In addition, plan documents and other plan information must be provided to you by (name of plan administrator) if you request this information in writing. (Name of Plan Administrator) may make a reasonable charge for these documents. You may wish to find out how much the charge will be before making a written request. However, all plan documents must be made available for your examination at (office

¶14,249D Reg. §2520.104b-5(b)(3)

address of plan administrator) and certain other locations, such as worksite and union halls, at no charge.

Certain amendments in the (name of plan) may have been made or may be made to meet the requirements of ERISA. (Name of plan administrator) will provide information regarding these amendments.

If you have any questions about this Notice of your rights, contact (name of plan administrator). Also, the nearest Area Office of the Labor Department has people who will be able to assist you or provide you with additional information.

(d) *Obligation to furnish for certain multiemployer plans.* In the case of a multiemployer plan which was in existence on January 1, 1974, and which does not, as of May 30, 1976, maintain complete records of participants covered under the plan, the Secretary will consider that the plan administrator has used methods reasonably calculated to ensure timely receipt of the ERISA Notice by participants covered under the plan and beneficiaries receiving benefits under a pension plan if the plan administrator takes the following measures for compliance:

(1) No later than May 30, 1976, the plan administrator shall furnish a copy of the ERISA Notice to all participants and beneficiaries of a pension plan who, as of March 2, 1976, are receiving benefits under the plan.

(2) No later than May 30, 1976, the plan administrator shall take measures to distribute copies of the ERISA Notice to substantially all individuals who, as of March 2, 1976, are participants covered under the plan and who can be identified. These measures may include the following:

(i) The plan administrator may deliver copies of the ERISA Notice to employers whose employees are participants covered under the plan, or employee organizations whose members are participants covered under the plan, or to both, in sufficient quantity and sufficiently in advance of May 30, 1976, to enable such employers or employee organizations to furnish them to employees or members who are participants covered under the plan by that date.

(ii) The administrator may publish the ERISA Notice before May 30, 1976, in a periodical or periodicals, the circulation of which includes participants covered under the plan.

(3) The plan administrator shall take measures to ensure that all individuals who become participants covered under the plan after March 2, 1976 (see § 2520.104-5 and .104-6) receive copies of the ERISA Notice within 90 days after becoming such participants. These measures may include the following:

(i) The plan administrator may deliver copies of the ERISA Notice to employers whose employees are participants covered under the plan, to employee organizations whose members are participants covered under the plan, or to both, in sufficient quantity and with sufficient frequency to enable such employers or employee organizations to furnish them to participants within 90 days after they become participants covered under the plan.

(ii) The plan administrator may publish the ERISA Notice or a statement that the Notice may be secured on request free of charge and how it may be secured, in a periodical or periodicals, the circulation of which includes participants covered under the plan, at regular intervals after May 30, 1976.

(4) In instances where the plan administrator relies on employers or employee organizations to perform duties relating to the distribution of the ERISA Notice to participants covered under the plan, the plan administrator should take whatever steps are necessary and feasible under the circumstances to ensure that employers or employee organizations actually perform those duties. For example, after a prompt meeting of the Board of Trustees of a multiemployer plan, a plan administrator secures written commitments from appropriate employers and employee organizations that they will distribute copies of the ERISA Notice to identifiable participants covered under the plan who are in their workforce or membership. [Added by 41 FR 16957, effective April 23, 1976].

[¶ 14,249H]

§ 2520.104b-10 **Summary Annual Report**. (a) *Obligation to furnish.* Except as otherwise provided in paragraphs (g) of this section, the administrator of any employee benefit plan shall furnish annually to

each participant of such plan and to each beneficiary receiving benefits under such plan (other than beneficiaries under a welfare plan) a summary annual report conforming to the requirements of this section. Such furnishing of the summary annual report shall take place in accordance with the requirements of § 2520.104b-1 of this part.

[Amended on July 20, 1982, by 47 FR 31871.]

(b) [Amended on July 20, 1982, by 47 FR 31871; reserved April 19, 2000 by 65 FR 21085.] [REMOVED and RESERVED on April 19, 2000 by 65 FR 21805.]

(c) *When to furnish.* Except as otherwise provided in this paragraph (c), the summary annual report required by paragraph (a) of this section shall be furnished within nine months after the close of the plan year. [Amended on April 19, 2000 by 65 FR 21805.]

(1) In the case of a welfare plan described in § 2520.104-43 of this part, such furnishing shall take place within 9 months after the close of the fiscal year of the trust or other entity which files the annual report under § 2520.104a-6 of this part.

(2) When an extension of time in which to file an annual report has been granted by the Internal Revenue Service, such furnishing shall take place within 2 months after the close of the period for which the extension was granted.

[Amended on July 20, 1982, by 47 FR 31871.]

(d) *Contents, style and format.* Except as otherwise provided in this paragraph (d), the summary annual report furnished to participants and beneficiaries of an employee pension benefit plan pursuant to this section shall consist of a completed copy of the form prescribed in subparagraph (3) of this paragraph (d), and the summary annual report furnished to participants and beneficiaries of an employee welfare benefit plan pursuant to this section shall consist of a completed copy of the form prescribed in subparagraph (4) of this paragraph (d). The information used to complete the form shall be based upon information contained in the most recent annual report of the plan which is required to be filed in accordance with section 104(a)(1) of the Act.

(1) Any portion of the forms set forth in this paragraph (d) which is not applicable to the plan to which the summary annual report relates, or which would require information which is not required to be reported on the annual report of that plan, may be omitted.

(2) Where the plan administrator determines that additional explanation of any information furnished pursuant to this paragraph (d) is necessary to fairly summarize the annual report, such explanation shall be set forth following the completed form required by this paragraph (d) and shall be headed, "Additional Explanation."

(3) *Form for Summary Annual Report Relating to Pension Plans.*

Summary Annual Report for (name of plan)

This is a summary of the annual report for (name of plan and EIN) for (period covered by this report). The annual report has been filed with the Employee Benefits Security Administration, as required under the Employee Retirement Income Security Act of 1974 (ERISA). [Corrected by DOL, 65 FR 35568, June 5, 2000. Amended by EBSA, 68 FR 16399, April 3, 2003.]

Basic Financial Statement

Benefits under the plan are provided by (indicate funding arrangements). Plan expenses were ($). These expenses included ($) in administrative expenses and ($) in benefits paid to participants and beneficiaries, and ($) in other expenses. A total of (   ) persons were participants in or beneficiaries of the plan at the end of the plan year, although not all of these persons had yet earned the right to receive benefits. [Amended on April 19, 2000 by 65 FR 21805.]

[If the plan is funded other than solely by allocated insurance contracts:]

The value of plan assets, after subtracting liabilities of the plan, was ($) as of (the end of the plan year), compared to ($) as of (the beginning of the plan year). During the plan year the plan experienced an (increase) (decrease) in its net assets of ($). This (increase) (decrease) includes unrealized appreciation or depreciation in the value of plan assets; that is, the difference between the value of the plan's assets at the end of the year and the value of the assets at the beginning of the year or the cost of assets acquired during the year. The plan had total income of ($　　), including employer contributions of ($　　), employee contributions of ($　　), (gains) (losses) of ($　　), from the sale of assets, and earnings from investments of ($　　).

[If any funds are used to purchase allocated insurance contracts:]

The plan has (a) contract(s) with (name of insurance carrier(s)) which allocate(s) funds toward (state whether individual policies, group deferred annuities or other). The total premiums paid for the plan year ending (date) were ($　　).

[Officially corrected May 31, 1979, and published in the *Federal Register* of June 1, 1979 (44 FR 31640).]

Minimum Funding Standards

[If the plan is a defined benefit plan:]

An actuary's statement shows that (enough money was contributed to the plan to keep it funded in accordance with the minimum funding standards of ERISA) (not enough money was contributed to the plan to keep it funded in accordance with the minimum funding standards of ERISA. The amount of the deficit was $　　).

[If the plan is a defined contribution plan covered by funding requirements:]

(Enough money was contributed to the plan to keep it funded in accordance with the minimum funding standards of ERISA) (Not enough money was contributed to the plan to keep it funded in accordance with the minimum funding standards of ERISA. The amount of the deficit was $　　).

Your Rights to Additional Information

You have the right to receive a copy of the full annual report, or any part thereof, on request. The items listed below are included in that report: [*Note*—list only those items which are actually included in the latest annual report]

1. an accountant's report; [Amended on April 19, 2000 by 65 FR 21805.]

2. financial information and information on payments to service providers; [Amended on April 19, 2000 by 65 FR 21805.]

3. assets held for investment; [Amended on April 19, 2000 by 65 FR 21805.]

4. fiduciary information, including non-exempt transactions between the plan and parties-in-interest (that is, persons who have certain relationships with the plan); [Amended on April 19, 2000 by 65 FR 21805.]

5. loans or other obligations in default or classified as uncollectible; [Amended on April 19, 2000 by 65 FR 21805.]

6. leases in default or classified as uncollectible; [Amended on April 19, 2000 by 65 FR 21805.]

7. transactions in excess of 5 percent of the plan assets; [Amended on April 19, 2000 by 65 FR 21805.]

8. insurance information including sales commissions paid by insurance carriers; [Amended on April 19, 2000 by 65 FR 21805.]

9. information regarding any common or collective trusts, pooled separate accounts; master trusts or 103-12 investment entities in which the plan participates, and [Added on April 19, 2000 by 65 FR 21805.]

10. actuarial information regarding the funding of the plan.

To obtain a copy of the full annual report, or any part thereof, write or call the office of (name), who is (state title: e.g., the plan administrator), (business address and telephone number). The charge to cover copying costs will be ($　　) for the full annual report, or ($　　) per page for any part thereof. [Added on April 19, 2000 by 65 FR 21805.]

You also have the right to receive from the plan administrator, on request and at no charge, a statement of the assets and liabilities of the plan and accompanying notes, or a statement of income and expenses of the plan and accompanying notes, or both. If you request a copy of the full annual report from the plan administrator, these two statements and accompanying notes will be included as part of that report. The charge to cover copying costs given above does not include a charge for the copying of these portions of the report because these portions are furnished without charge.

You also have the legally protected right to examine the annual report at the main office of the plan (　　address　　), (at any other location where the report is available for examination), and at the U.S. Department of Labor in Washington, D.C., or to obtain a copy from the U.S. Department of Labor upon payment of copying costs. Requests to the Department should be addressed to: Public Disclosure Room, Room N-1513, Employee Benefits Security Administration, U.S. Department of Labor, 200 Constitution Avenue, N.W., Washington, D.C. 20210. [Corrected by DOL, 65 FR 35568, June 5, 2000. Amended by EBSA, 68 FR 16399, April 3, 2003.]

(4) *Form for Summary Annual Report Relating to Welfare Plans*

Summary Annual Report for (name of plan)

This is a summary of the annual report of the (name of plan, EIN and type of welfare plan) for (period covered by this report). The annual report has been filed with the Employee Benefits Security Administration as required under the Employee Retirement Income Security Act of 1974 (ERISA).[Corrected by DOL, 65 FR 35568, June 5, 2000. Amended by EBSA, 68 FR 16399, April 3, 2003.]

[If any benefits under the plan are provided on an uninsured basis:]

(Name of sponsor) has committed itself to pay (all, certain) (state type of) claims incurred under the terms of the plan.

[If any of the funds are used to purchase insurance contracts:]

Insurance Information

The plan has (a) contract(s) with (name of insurance carrier(s) to pay (all, certain) (state type of) claims incurred under the terms of the plan. The total premiums paid for the plan year ending (　　date　　) were ($　　).

[If applicable add:]

Because (it is a) (they are) so called "experience-rated" contract(s), the premium costs are affected by, among other things, the number and size of claims. Of the total insurance premiums paid for the plan year ending (date), the premiums paid under such "experience-rated" contract(s) were ($　　) and the total of all benefit claims paid under the(se) experience-rated contract(s) during the plan year was ($　　).

[If any funds of the plan are held in trust or in a separately maintained fund:]

Basic Financial Statement

The value of plan assets, after subtracting liabilities of the plan, was ($　　) as of (the end of plan year), compared to ($　　) as of (the beginning of the plan year). During the plan year the plan experienced an (increase) (decrease) in its net assets of ($　　). This (increase) (decrease) includes unrealized appreciation or depreciation in the value of plan assets; that is, the difference between the value of the plan's assets at the end of the year and the value of the assets at the beginning of the year or the cost of assets acquired during the year. During the plan year, the plan had total income of ($　　) including employer contributions of ($　　), employee contributions of ($　　), realized (gains) (losses) of ($　　) from the sale of assets, and earnings from investments of ($　　).

Plan expenses were ($　　). These expenses included ($　　) in administrative expenses, ($　　) in benefits paid to participants and beneficiaries, and ($　　) in other expenses.

[Officially corrected on May 31, 1979, and published in the *Federal Register* of June 1, 1979 (44 FR 31640).]

Your Rights to Additional Information

You have the right to receive a copy of the full annual report, or any part thereof, on request. The items listed below are included in that report: [Note—list only those items which are actually included in the latest annual report]

1. an accountant's report; [Amended on April 19, 2000 by 65 FR 21805.]

2. financial information and information on payments to service providers; [Amended on April 19, 2000 by 65 FR 21805.]

3. assets held for investment; [Amended on April 19, 2000 by 65 FR 21805.]

4. fiduciary information, including non-exempt transactions between the plan and parties-in-interest (that is, persons who have certain relationships with the plan); [Amended on April 19, 2000 by 65 FR 21805.]

5. loans or other obligations in default or classified as uncollectible; [Amended on April 19, 2000 by 65 FR 21805.]

6. leases in default or classified as uncollectible; [Amended on April 19, 2000 by 65 FR 21805.]

7. transactions in excess of 5 percent of the plan assets; [Amended on April 19, 2000 by 65 FR 21805.]

8. insurance information including sales commissions paid by insurance carriers; and [Added on April 19, 2000 by 65 FR 21805.]

9. information regarding any common or collective trusts, pooled separate accounts, master trusts or 103-12 investment entities in which the plan participates. [Added on April 19, 2000 by 65 FR 21805.]

To obtain a copy of the full annual report, or any part thereof, write or call the office of (name), who is (state title: e.g., the plan administrator), (business address and telephone number). The charge to cover copying costs will be ($) for the full annual report, or ($) per page for any part thereof.

You also have the right to receive from the plan administrator, on request and at no charge, a statement of the assets and liabilities of the plan and accompanying notes, or a statement of income and expenses of the plan and accompanying notes, or both. If you request a copy of the full annual report from the plan administrator, these two statements and accompanying notes will be included as part of that report. The charge to cover copying costs given above does not include a charge for the copying of these portions of the report because these portions are furnished without charge.

You also have the legally protected right to examine the annual report at the main office of the plan (address), (at any other location where the report is available for examination), and at the U.S. Depart-ment of Labor in Washington, D.C. or to obtain a copy from the U.S. Department of Labor upon payment of copying costs. Requests to the Department should be addressed to: Public Disclosure Room, Room N1513, Employee Benefits Security Administration, U.S. Department of Labor, 200 Constitution Avenue, N.W., Washington, D.C. 20210. [Amended April 19, 2000 by 65 FR 21085. Amended by EBSA, 68 FR 16399, April 3, 2003.]

(e) *Foreign languages.* In the case of either—

(1) A plan which covers fewer than 100 participants at the beginning of a plan year in which 25 percent or more of all plan participants are literate only in the same non-English language; or

(2) A plan which covers 100 or more participants in which 500 or more participants or 10 percent or more of all plan participants, whichever is less, are literate only in the same non-English language—

The plan administrator for such plan shall provide these participants with an English-language summary annual report which prominently displays a notice, in the non-English language common to these participants, offering them assistance. The assistance provided need not involve written materials, but shall be given in the non-English language common to these participants. The notice offering assistance shall clearly set forth any procedures participants must follow to obtain such assistance.

[Amended on July 20, 1982, by 47 FR 31871; amended April 19, 2000 by 65 FR 21085.]

(f) *Furnishing of additional documents to participants and beneficiaries.* A plan administrator shall promptly comply with any request by a participant or beneficiary for additional documents made in accordance with the procedures or rights described in paragraph (d) of this section.

[Amended on July 20, 1982, by 47 FR 31871; amended April 19, 2000 by 65 FR 21085.]

(g) *Exemptions.* Notwithstanding the provisions of this section, a summary annual report is not required to be furnished with respect to the following:

(1) A totally unfunded welfare plan described in 29 CFR 2520.104-44(b)(1)(i); (2) a welfare plan which meets the requirements of 29 CFR 2520.104-20(b); (3) an apprenticeship or other training plan which meets the requirements of 29 CFR 2520.104-22; (4) a pension plan for selected employees which meets the requirements of 29 CFR 2520.104-23; (5) a welfare plan for selected employees which meets the requirements of 29 CFR 2520.104-24; (6) a day care center referred to in 29 CFR 2520.104-25; (7) a dues financed welfare plan which meets the requirements of 29 CFR 2520.104-26; and (8) a dues financed pension plan which meets the requirements of 29 CFR 2520.104-27. [Added by 44 FR 19400, effective June 5, 1979.]

[Appendix to Summary Annual Report Regulation (§2520.104b-10) appears on page 18,197.—CCH.]

APPENDIX TO §2520.104b-10—THE SUMMARY ANNUAL REPORT (SAR) UNDER ERISA: A CROSS-REFERENCE TO THE ANNUAL REPORT

SAR Item	Form 5500 Large Plan Filer Line Items	Form 5500 Small Plan Filer Line Items
A. PENSION PLAN		
1. Funding arrangement	Form 5500 — 9a	Same.
2. Total plan expenses	Sch. H — 2j	Sch. I — 2i.
3. Administrative expenses	Sch. H — 2i(5)	Not applicable.
4. Benefits paid	Sch. H — 2e(4)	Sch. I — 2e.
5. Other expenses	Sch. H — Subtract the sum of 2e(4) & 2i(5) from 2j	Sch. I — 2h.
6. Total participants	Form 5500 — 7f	Same.
7. Value of plan assets (net):		
a. End of plan year	Sch. H — 1l [Col. (b)]	Sch. I — 1c [Col. (b)].
b. Beginning of plan year	Sch. H — 1l [Col. (a)]	Sch. I — 1c [Col. (a)].
8. Change in net assets	Sch. H — Subtract 1l [Col. (a) from 1l[Col. (b)]	Sch. I — Subtract 1c [Col. (a) from 1c [Col. (b)].
9. Total income	Sch. H — 2d	Sch. I — 2d.
a. Employer contributions	Sch. H — 2a(1)(A) & 2a(2) if applicable	Sch. I — 2a(1) & 2b if applicable.

SAR Item	Form 5500 Large Plan Filer Line Items	Form 5500 Small Plan Filer Line Items
b. Employee contributions	Sch. H — 2a(1)(B) & 2a(2) if applicable	Sch. I — 2a(2) & 2b if applicable.
c. Gains (losses) from sale of assets .	Sch. H — 2b(4)(C)	Not applicable.
d. Earnings from investments	Sch. H — Subtract the sum of 2a(3), 2b(4)(C) and 2C from 2d.	Sch. I — 2c.
10. Total insurance premiums	Total of all Schs. A — 5b	Total of all Schs. A — 5b.
11. Funding deficiency:		
a. Defined benefit plans	Sch. B — 10	Same.
b. Defined contribution plans	Sch. R — 6c, if more than zero	Same.
B. WELFARE PLAN		
1. Name of insurance carrier	All Schs. A — 1(a)	Same.
2. Total (experience rated and non-experienced rated) insurance premiums.	All Schs. A — Sum of 8a(4) and 9(a)	Same.
3. Experience rated premiums	All Schs. A — 8a(4)	Same.
4. Experience rated claims	All Schs. A — 8b(4)	Same.
5. Value of plan assets (net):		
a. End of plan year	Sch H. — 1l [Col. (b)]	Sch. I — 1c [Col. (b)].
b. Beginning of plan year	Sch H. — 1l [Col. (a)]	Sch. I — 1c [Col. (a)].
6. Change in net assets	Sch. H — Subtract 1l [Col. (a)] from 1l [Col. (b)]	Sch. I — Subtract 1c [Col. (a)] from 1c [Col. (b)].
7. Total income	Sch. H — 2d	Sch. I — 2d.
a. Employer contributions	Sch. H — 2a(1)(A) & 2a(2) if applicable	Sch. I — 2a(1) & 2b if applicable.
b. Employee contributions	Sch. H — 2a(1)(B) & 2a(2) if applicable	Sch. I — 2a(2) & 2b if applicable.
c. Gains (losses) from sale of assets .	Sch. H — 2b(4)(C)	Not applicable.
d. Earnings from investments	Sch. H — Subtract the sum of 2a(3), 2b(4)(C) and 2c from 2d.	Sch. I — 2c.
8. Total plan expenses	Sch. H — 2j	Sch. I — 2i.
9. Administrative expenses	Sch. H — 2i(5)	Not applicable.
10. Benefits paid	Sch. H — 2e(4)	Sch. I — 2e.
11. Other expenses	Sch. H — Subtract the sum of 2e(4) & 2i(5) from 2j	Sch. I — 2h.

[44 FR 19403, April 3, 1979, as amended by 44 FR 31640, June 1, 1979, by 47 FR 31871 on July 20, 1982, and by 54 FR 8624 on March 1, 1989; amended April 19, 2000 by 65 FR 21085; amended April 3, 2003 by 68 FR 16399.]

Temporary and Proposed Regulations

The temporary and proposed Reg. § 2520.104b-12 was filed with the *Federal Register* on February 9, 1977, and published in the *Federal Register* on February 11, 1977. It is effective upon publication in the *Federal Register*.

[¶ 14,249K]

§ 2520.104b-12. **Summary Annual Report for 1975 Plan Year— Optional Method of Distribution for Certain Multiemployer Plans.**

»»→ Caution: Regulation § 2520.104b-12 was officially removed by 61 FR 33847 on July 1, 1996.

§ 2520.104b-12. Summary Annual Report for 1975 Plan Year— Optional Method of Distribution for Certain Multiemployer Plans. (a) In the case of a multiemployer plan which

(1) is required to disclose a summary annual report to its participants and beneficiaries under section 104(b)(3) of the Act and § 2520.104b-10 or § 2520.104b-11, and

(2) does not, as of the date for disclosure of the summary annual report described in those sections, maintain complete records of participants covered under the plan, the administrator of such plan will be deemed to have used methods reasonably calculated to ensure timely receipt of the summary annual report by participants covered under the plan, as required by § 2520.104b-1 (relating to methods of disclosure), if the administrator meets the requirements of paragraph (b).

(b) No later than the dates set forth in § 2520.104b-10(b) or § 2520.104b-11(a), as appropriate, the administrator shall take measures to furnish copies of the summary annual report to substantially all individuals who, as of the date of such disclosure, are participants covered under the plan who can be identified. These measures may include the following.

(1) The administrator may deliver copies of the summary annual report to employers whose employees are participants covered under the plan, or employee organizations whose members are participants covered under the plan, or to both, in sufficient quantity and sufficiently in advance of the date by which disclosure must be made to enable such employers or employee organizations to furnish them by that date to employees or members who are participants covered under the plan. The administrator shall take whatever steps are necessary and feasible under the circumstances to ensure that employers or employee organizations actually perform those duties. For example, an administrator secures written commitments from appropriate employers and employee organizations that they will furnish copies of the summary annual report to identifiable participants covered under the plan who are in their workforce or membership; or

(2) The administrator may publish the summary annual report, on or before the date by which disclosure must be made, in a periodical or periodicals, the circulation of which includes participants covered under the plan.

(c) *Limitations.* (1) This section applies to only the summary annual report required to be disclosed for the plan year which began in 1975.

(2) This section does not exempt an administrator from the requirement of § 2520.104b-1 to furnish copies of the summary annual report to participants and beneficiaries receiving benefits under a pension plan.

This regulation shall take effect upon publication in the Federal Register.

[¶ 14,249Z]

§ 2520.104b-30 **Charges for documents.** (a) *Application.* The plan administrator of an employee benefit plan may impose a reasonable charge to cover the cost of furnishing to participants and beneficiaries upon their written request as required under section 104(b)(4) of the Act, copies of the following information, statements or documents: the latest updated summary plan description, plan description, and the latest annual report, any terminal report, the bargaining agreement, trust agreement, contract, or other instruments under which the plan is established or operated. No charge may be assessed for furnishing information, statements or documents as required by other provisions of the Act, which include, in Part 1 of Title I, sections 104(b)(1), (2), (3) and (c) and 105(a) and (c). [Corrected by 41 FR 37575.]

(b) *Reasonableness.* The charge assessed by the plan administrator to cover the costs of furnishing documents is reasonable if it is equal to the actual cost per page to the plan for the least expensive means of acceptable reproduction, but in no event may such charge exceed 25 cents per page. For example, if a plan printed a large number of pamphlets at $1.00 per 50-page pamphlet, the actual cost of reproduction for the entire pamphlet ($1.00) would be equal to 2 cents per page. If only one page of such a pamphlet were requested, the actual cost of providing that page from the printed copy would be $1.00, since the copy would no longer be complete. In such a case, the least expensive means of acceptable reproduction would be individually reproducing the page requested at a charge of no more than 25 cents. On the other hand, if six pages of the same plan document were requested and each page cost 20 cents to be reproduced, the actual cost of providing those pages would be $1.20. In such a case, if a printed copy is available, the least expensive means of acceptable reproduction would be to use pages from the printed copy at a charge of no more than $1.00. No other charge for furnishing documents, such as handling or postage charges, will be deemed reasonable. The plan administrator shall provide information to a plan participant or beneficiary, upon request, about the charge that would be made to provide a copy of material described in this paragraph. [Added by 41 FR 16957, effective April 23, 1976.]

[¶ 14,250]
REPORTING OF PARTICIPANT'S BENEFIT RIGHTS

Act Sec. 105. (a) Each administrator of an employee pension benefit plan shall furnish to any plan participant or beneficiary who so requests in writing, a statement indicating, on the basis of the latest available information—

(1) the total benefits accrued, and

(2) the nonforfeitable pension benefits, if any, which have accrued, or the earliest date on which benefits will become nonforfeitable.

Act Sec. 105. (b) In no case shall a participant or beneficiary be entitled under this section to receive more than one report described in subsection (a) during any one 12-month period.

Act Sec. 105. (c) Each administrator required to register under section 6057 of the Internal Revenue Code of 1986 shall, before the expiration of the time prescribed for such registration, furnish to each participant described in subsection (a)(2)(C) of such section, an individual statement setting forth the information with respect to such participant required to be contained in the registration statement required by section 6057(a)(2) of such Code. Such statement shall also include a notice to the participant of any benefits which are forfeitable if the participant dies before a certain date.

Act Sec. 105. (d) Subsection (a) of this section shall apply to a plan to which more than one unaffiliated employer is required to contribute only to the extent provided in regulations prescribed by the Secretary in coordination with the Secretary of the Treasury.

Amendments

P.L. 101-239, § 7891(a)(1):

Titles I, III, and IV of ERISA (other than sections 3(37)(E), 301(a)(7), and 308, the last sentence of section 408(d), and sections 414(c), 4001(a)(3)(ii), and 4303) are each amended by striking "Internal Revenue Code of 1954" each place it appears and inserting "Internal Revenue Code of 1986," effective October 22, 1986.

P.L. 101-239, § 7894(b)(5):

Amended ERISA Sec. 105(b) by striking "12 month" and inserting "12-month," effective September 2, 1974.

P.L. 98-397, § 106

Act Sec. 106 amended ERISA Sec. 105(c) by adding the last sentence at the end thereof.

The above amendment applies to plan years beginning after December 31, 1984.

However, Act Sec. 302(b) provides:

(b) Special Rule for Collective Bargaining Agreements.—In the case of a plan maintained pursuant to 1 or more collective bargaining agreements between employee representatives and 1 or more employers ratified before the date of enactment of this Act, except as provided in subsection (d) or section 303, the amendments made by this Act shall not apply to plan years beginning before the earlier of—(1) the date on which the last of the collective bargaining agreements relating to the plan terminates (determined without regard to any extension thereof agreed to after the date of the enactment of this Act), or

(2) January 1, 1987.

For purposes of paragraph (1), any plan amendment made pursuant to a collective bargaining agreement relating to the plan which amends the plan solely to conform to any requirement added by title I or II shall not be treated as a termination of such collective bargaining agreement.

[¶ 14,260]
REPORTS MADE PUBLIC INFORMATION

Act Sec. 106. (a) Except as provided in subsection (b), the contents of the annual reports, statements, and other documents filed with the Secretary pursuant to this part shall be public information and the Secretary shall make any such information and data available for inspection in the public document room of the Department of Labor. The Secretary may use the information and data for statistical and research purposes, and compile and publish such studies, analyses, reports, and surveys based thereon as he may deem appropriate.

Act Sec. 106. (b) Information described in sections 105(a) and 105(c) with respect to a participant may be disclosed only to the extent that information respecting that participant's benefits under title II of the Social Security Act may be disclosed under such Act.

Amendment

P.L. 105-34, § 1503(d)(4):

Amended ERISA Sec. 106(a) by striking "descriptions," effective August 5, 1997.

P.L. 101-239, § 7894(b)(6):

Amended ERISA Sec. 106(b) by striking "section" and inserting "sections" effective September 2, 1974.

[¶ 14,270]
RETENTION OF RECORDS

Act Sec. 107. Every person subject to a requirement to file any report or to certify any information therefor under this title or who would be subject to such a requirement but for an exemption or simplified reporting requirement under section 104(a)(2) or (3) of this title shall maintain records on the matters of which disclosure is required which will provide in sufficient detail the necessary basic information and data from which the documents thus required may be verified, explained, or clarified, and checked for accuracy and completeness, and shall include vouchers, worksheets, receipts, and applicable resolutions, and shall keep such records available for examination for a period of not less than six years after the filing date of the documents based on the information which they contain, or six years after the date on which such documents would have been filed but for an exemption or simplified reporting requirement under section 104(a)(2) or (3).

Amendment

P.L. 105-34, § 1503(d)(5):

Amended ERISA Sec. 107 by striking "description or" effective August 5, 1997.

Regulations

The following regulations under Code Section 107 were adopted under document number RIN 1210-AA71 under the title "Final Rules Relating to Use of Electronic Communication and Recordkeeping Technologies by Employee Pension and Welfare Benefit Plans". The regulation was filed with the Federal Register on April 8, 2002 and published on April 9, 2002 (67 FR 17264).

[¶ 14,270B]

Subpart G - Recordkeeping Requirements

Sec. 2520.107-1 Use of electronic media for maintenance and retention of records.—(a) *Scope and purpose.* Sections 107 and 209 of the Employee Retirement Income Security Act of 1974, as amended (ERISA), contain certain requirements relating to the maintenance of records for reporting and disclosure purposes and for determining the pension benefits to which participants and beneficiaries are or may become entitled. This section provides standards applicable to both pension and welfare plans concerning the use of electronic media for the maintenance and retention of records required to be kept under sections 107 and 209 of ERISA.

(b) *General requirements.* The record maintenance and retention requirements of sections 107 and 209 of ERISA are satisfied when using electronic media if: (1) The electronic recordkeeping system has reasonable controls to ensure the integrity, accuracy, authenticity and reliability of the records kept in electronic form;

(2) The electronic records are maintained in reasonable order and in a safe and accessible place, and in such manner as they may be readily inspected or examined (for example, the recordkeeping system should be capable of indexing, retaining, preserving, retrieving and reproducing the electronic records);

(3) The electronic records are readily convertible into legible and readable paper copy as may be needed to satisfy reporting and disclosure requirements or any other obligation under Title I of ERISA;

(4) The electronic recordkeeping system is not subject, in whole or in part, to any agreement or restriction that would, directly or indi-

rectly, compromise or limit a person's ability to comply with any reporting and disclosure requirement or any other obligation under Title I of ERISA; and

(5) Adequate records management practices are established and implemented (for example, following procedures for labeling of electronically maintained or retained records, providing a secure storage environment, creating back-up electronic copies and selecting an off-site storage location, observing a quality assurance program evidenced by regular evaluations of the electronic recordkeeping system including periodic checks of electronically maintained or retained records, and retaining paper copies of records that cannot be clearly, accurately or completely transferred to an electronic recordkeeping system).

(c) *Legibility and readability.* All electronic records must exhibit a high degree of legibility and readability when displayed on a video display terminal or other method of electronic transmission and when reproduced in paper form. The term "legibility" means the observer must be able to identify all letters and numerals positively and quickly to the exclusion of all other letters or numerals. The term "readability" means that the observer must be able to recognize a group of letters or numerals as words or complete numbers.

(d) *Disposal of original paper records.* Original paper records may be disposed of any time after they are transferred to an electronic recordkeeping system that complies with the requirements of this section, except such original records may not be discarded if the electronic record would not constitute a duplicate or substitute record under the terms of the plan and applicable federal or state law. [Added by 67 FR 17264, effective October 9, 2002.]

[¶ 14,280]

RELIANCE ON ADMINISTRATIVE INTERPRETATIONS

Act Sec. 108. In any criminal proceeding under section 501 based on any act or omission in alleged violation of this part or section 412, no person shall be subject to any liability or punishment for or on account of the failure of such person to

(1) comply with this part or section 412, if he pleads and proves that the act or omission complained of was in good faith, in conformity with, and in reliance on any regulation or written ruling of the Secretary, or

(2) publish and file any information required by any provision of this part if he pleads and proves that he published and filed such information in good faith, and in conformity with any regulation or written ruling of the Secretary issued under this part regarding the filing of such reports. Such a defense, if established, shall be a bar to the action or proceeding, notwithstanding that

(A) after such act or omission, such interpretation or opinion is modified or rescinded or is determined by judicial authority to be invalid or of no legal effect, or

(B) after publishing or filing the annual reports and other reports required by this title, such publication or filing is determined by judicial authority not to be in conformity with the requirements of this part.

Amendment

P.L. 105-34, § 1503(d)(6):

Amended ERISA Sec. 108(2)(B) by striking "plan description, annual reports," and inserting "annual reports" effective August 5, 1997.

P.L. 101-239, § 7894(b)(7):

Amended ERISA Sec. 108 by striking "act of omission" and inserting "act or omission" effective September 2, 1974.

[¶ 14,290]

FORMS

Act Sec. 109.(a) Except as provided in subsection (b) of this section, the Secretary may require that any information required under this title to be submitted to him, including but not limited to the information required to be filed by the administrator pursuant to section 103(b)(3) and (c), must be submitted on such forms as he may prescribe.

Act Sec. 109. (b) The financial statement and opinion required to be prepared by an independent qualified public accountant pursuant to section 103(a)(3)(A), the actuarial statement required to be prepared by an enrolled actuary pursuant to section 103(a)(4)(A) and the summary plan description required by section 102(a) shall not be required to be submitted on forms.

Act Sec. 109. (c) The Secretary may prescribe the format and content of the summary plan description, the summary of the annual report described in section 104(b)(3) and any other report, statements or documents (other than the bargaining agreement, trust agreement, contract, or other instrument under which the plan is established or operated), which are required to be furnished or made available to plan participants and beneficiaries receiving benefits under the plan.

[¶ 14,300]

ALTERNATIVE METHODS OF COMPLIANCE

Act Sec. 110.(a) The Secretary on his own motion or after having received the petition of an administrator may prescribe an alternative method for satisfying any requirement of this part with respect to any pension plan, or class of pension plans, subject to such requirement if he determines—

(1) that the use of such alternative method is consistent with the purposes of this title and that it provides adequate disclosure to the participants and beneficiaries in the plan, and adequate reporting to the Secretary.

(2) that the application of such requirement of this part would—

(A) increase the costs to the plan, or

(B) impose unreasonable administrative burdens with respect to the operation of the plan, having regard to the particular characteristics of the plan or the type of plan involved; and

(3) that the application of this part would be adverse to the interests of plan participants in the aggregate.

Act Sec. 110. (b) An alternative method may be prescribed under subsection (a) by regulation or otherwise. If an alternative method is prescribed other than by regulation, the Secretary shall provide notice and an opportunity for interested persons to present their views, and shall publish in the Federal Register the provisions of such alternative method.

[¶ 14,310]
REPEAL AND EFFECTIVE DATE

Act Sec. 111. (a)(1) The Welfare and Pension Plans Disclosure Act is repealed except that such Act shall continue to apply to any conduct and events which occurred before the effective date of this part.

(2)(A) Section 664 of title 18, United States Code, is amended by striking out "any such plan subject to the provisions of the Welfare and Pension Plans Disclosure Act" and inserting in lieu thereof "any employee benefit plan subject to any provision of title I of the Employee Retirement Income Security Act of 1974".

(B)(i) Section 1027 of such title 18 is amended by striking out "Welfare and Pension Plans Disclosure Act" and inserting in lieu thereof "title I of the Employee Retirement Income Security Act of 1974", and by striking out "Act" each place it appears and inserting in lieu thereof "title".

(ii) The heading for such section is amended by striking out "WELFARE AND PENSION PLANS DISCLOSURE ACT" and inserting in lieu thereof "EMPLOYEE RETIREMENT INCOME SECURITY ACT OF 1974".

(iii) The table of sections of chapter 47 of such title 18 is amended by striking out "Welfare and Pension Plans Disclosure Act" in the item relating to section 1027 and inserting in lieu thereof "Employee Retirement Income Security Act of 1974".

(C) Section 1954 of such title 18 is amended by striking out "any plan subject to the provisions of the Welfare and Pension Plans Disclosure Act as amended" and inserting in lieu thereof "any employee welfare benefit plan or employee pension benefit plan, respectively, subject to any provision of title I of the Employee Retirement Income Security Act of 1974"; and by striking out "sections 3(3) and 5(b)(1) and (2) of the Welfare and Pension Plans Disclosure Act, as amended" and inserting in lieu thereof "sections 3(4) and (3)(16) of the Employee Retirement Income Security Act of 1974".

(D) Section 211 of the Labor-Management Reporting and Disclosure Act of 1959 (29 U.S.C. 441) is amended by striking out "Welfare and Pension Plans Disclosure Act" and inserting in lieu thereof "Employee Retirement Income Security Act of 1974".

Act Sec. 111. (b)(1) Except as provided in paragraph (2), this part (including the amendments and repeals made by subsection (a)) shall take effect on January 1, 1975.

(2) In the case of a plan which has a plan year which begins before January 1, 1975, and ends after December 31, 1974, the Secretary may postpone by regulation the effective date of the repeal of any provision of the Welfare and Pension Plans Disclosure Act (and of any amendment made by subsection (a)(2)) and the effective date of any provision of this part, until the beginning of the first plan year of such plan which begins after January 1, 1975.

Act Sec. 111. (c) The provisions of this title authorizing the Secretary to promulgate regulations shall take effect on the date of enactment of this Act.

Act Sec. 111. (d) Subsections (b) and (c) shall not apply with respect to amendments made to this part in provisions enacted after the date of the enactment of this Act.

Amendment

P.L. 101-239, §7894(h)(1):

Amended ERISA Sec. 111 by adding new subsection (d) to read as above effective September 2, 1974.

Interpretive Bulletins

Interpretive Bulletin ERISA IB RD 75-1 was adopted by FR Doc. 75-31318 under "Title 29—Labor; Chapter XXV—Office of Employee Benefits Security; Part 2556—Interpretive Bulletins Relating to Reporting and Disclosure." The bulletin was published in the Rules and Regulations section of the Federal Register on November 20, 1975 (40 FR 53998). The bulletin was filed with the Federal Register on November 19, 1975. The notice on the addition of a new Part 2556, "Interpretive Bulletins Relating to Reporting and Disclosure" to Title 29 of the Code of Federal Regulations was published in the Federal Register of November 20, 1975 (40 FR 53998). ERISA IB RD 75-1 was redesignated as Reg. §2509.75-9 under "Part 2509—Interpretive Bulletins Relating to the Employee Retirement Income Security Act of 1974" by FR Doc. 76-966 (41 FR 1906), filed with the Federal Register on January 12, 1976, and published in the Federal Register of January 13, 1976.

Regulations

[¶ 14,370]

§2509.75-9 **Independence of Accountant Retained by Employee Benefit Plan**. The Department of Labor today announced guidelines for determining when a qualified public accountant is independent for purposes of auditing and rendering an opinion on the financial information required to be included in the annual report filed with the Department.

Section 103(a)(3)(A) requires that the accountant retained by an employee benefit plan be "independent" for purposes of examining plan financial information and rendering an opinion on the financial statements and schedules required to be contained in the annual report.

Under the authority of section 103(a)(3)(A) the Department of Labor will not recognize any person as an independent qualified public accountant who is in fact not independent with respect to the employee benefit plan upon which that account renders an opinion in the annual report filed with the Department of Labor. For example, an accountant will not be considered independent with respect to a plan if:

(1) During the period of professional engagement to examine the financial statements being reported, at the date of the opinion, or during the period covered by the financial statements, the accountant or his or her firm or a member thereof had, or was committed to acquire, any direct financial interest or any material indirect financial

interest in such plan, or the plan sponsor, as that term is defined in section 3(16)(B) of the Act.

(2) During the period of professional engagement to examine the financial statements being reported, at the date of the opinion, or during the period covered by the financial statements, the accountant, his or her firm or a member thereof was connected as a promoter, underwriter, investment advisor, voting trustee, director, officer, or employee of the plan or plan sponsor except that a firm will not be deemed not independent in regard to a particular plan if a former officer or employee of such plan or plan sponsor is employed by the firm and such individual has completely diassociated himself from the plan or plan sponsor and does not participate in auditing financial statements of the plan covering any period of his or her employment by the plan or plan sponsor. For the purpose of this bulletin the term "member" means all partners or shareholder employees in the firm and all professional employees participating in the audit or located in an office of the firm participating in a significant portion of the audit;

(3) An accountant or a member of an accounting firm maintains financial records for the employee benefit plan.

However, an independent qualified public accountant may permissably engage in or have members of his or her firm engage in certain activities which will not have the effect of removing recognition of his or her independence. For example, (1) an accountant will not fail to be recognized as independent if at or during the period of his or her professional engagement with the employee benefit plan the accountant or his or her firm is retained or engaged on a professional basis by the plan sponsor, as that term is defined in section 3(16)(B) of the Act. However, to retain recognition of independence under such circumstances the accountant must not violate the prohibitions against recognition of independence established under paragraphs (1), (2) or (3) of this interpretive bulletin: (2) the rendering of services by an actuary associated with an accountant or accounting firm shall not impair the accountant's or accounting firm's independence. However, it should be noted that the rendering of services to a plan by an actuary and accountant employed by the same firm may constitute a prohibited transaction under section 406(a)(1)(C) of the Act. The rendering of

such multiple services to a plan by a firm will be the subject of a later interpretive bulletin that will be issued by the Department of Labor.

In determining whether an accountant or accounting firm is not, in fact, independent with respect to a particular plan, the Department of Labor will give appropriate consideration to all relevant circumstances, including evidence bearing on all relationships between the accountant or accounting firm and that of the plan sponsor or any affiliate thereof, and will not confine itself to the relationships existing in connection with the filing of annual reports with the Department of Labor.

Further interpretive bulletins may be issued by the Department of Labor concerning the question of independence of an accountant retained by an employee benefit plan. [Amended by 40 FR 59728, filed with the Federal Register December 29, 1975, and published in the Federal Register December 30, 1975.]

Part 2—Participation and Vesting

[¶ 14,410]
COVERAGE

Act Sec. 201. This part shall apply to any employee benefit plan described in section 4(a) (and not exempted under section 4(b)) other than—

(1) an employee welfare benefit plan;

(2) a plan which is unfunded and is maintained by an employer primarily for the purpose of providing deferred compensation for a select group of management or highly compensated employees;

(3)(A) a plan established and maintained by a society, order, or association described in section 501(c)(8) or (9) of the Internal Revenue Code of 1986, if no part of the contributions to or under such plan are made by employers of participants in such plan, or

(B) a trust described in section 501(c)(18) of such Code;

(4) a plan which is established and maintained by a labor organization described in section 501(c)(5) of the Internal Revenue Code of 1986 and which does not at any time after the date of enactment of this Act provide for employer contributions;

(5) any agreement providing payments to a retired partner or a deceased partner's successor in interest, as described in section 736 of the Internal Revenue Code of 1986;

(6) an individual retirement account or annuity described in section 408 of the Internal Revenue Code of 1954, or a retirement bond described in section 409 of the Internal Revenue Code of 1954 (as effective for obligations issued before January 1, 1984);

(7) an excess benefit plan; or

(8) any plan, fund or program under which an employer, all of whose stock is directly or indirectly owned by employees, former employees or their beneficiaries proposes through an unfunded arrangement to compensate retired employees for benefits which were forfeited by such employees under a pension plan maintained by a former employer prior to the date such pension plan became subject to this Act.

Amendments

P.L. 101-239, § 7894(c)(1):

Amended ERISA Sec. 201, in pargraph 6, by striking "or" at the end; in paragraph (7) by striking "plan." and inserting "plan; or;" and in paragraph (8), by striking "Any" and inserting "any" effective as if included in P.L. 96-364, § 411.

P.L. 101-239, § 7894(c)(11):

Amended ERISA Sec. 201(6) by striking "section 409 of such Code" and inserting "section 409 of the Internal Revenue Code of 1954 (as effective for obligations issued before January 1, 1984)" effective as if included in P.L. 98-369, § 491(b).

P.L. 101-239, § 7891(a)(1):

Titles I, III, and IV of ERISA (other than sections 3(37)(E), 301(a)(7), and 308, the last sentence of section 408(d), and sections 414(c), 4001(a)(3)(ii), and 4303) are each amended by striking "Internal Revenue Code of 1954" each place it appears and inserting "Internal Revenue Code of 1986" effective October 22, 1986.

P.L. 96-364, § 411(a):

Added new section 201(8), effective September 26, 1980.

Regulations

The following regulations were adopted under "Title 29—Labor," "Chapter XXV—Pension and Welfare Benefit Programs, Department of Labor," "Subchapter C—Minimum Standards for Employee Pension Benefit Plans Under the Employee Retirement Income Security Act of 1974," "Part 2530—Rules and Regulations for Minimum Standards for Employee Pension Benefit Plans." The regulations were filed with the Federal Register on December 23, 1976, and published in the Federal Register of December 28, 1976 (41 FR 56462).

Subpart A—Scope and General Provisions

§ 2530.200a **Scope.**

[¶ 14,411]

§ 2530.200a-1 **Relationship of the Act and Internal Revenue Code of 1954.**

(a) Part 2 of Title I of the Employee Retirement Income Security Act of 1974 (hereinafter referred to as "the Act") contains minimum standards that a plan which is an employee pension benefit plan within the meaning of section 3(2) of the Act and which is covered under Part 2 must satisfy. (For a general explanation of the coverage of Part 2, see § 2530.201-1.) Substantially identical requirements are imposed by Subchapter D of Chapter 1 of Subtitle A of the Internal Revenue Code of 1954 (hereinafter referred to as "the Code") for plans seeking qualification for certain tax benefits under the Code. In general, the Code provisions apply to "qualified" pension, profitsharing, and stock bonus plans described in section 401(a) of the Code, annuity plans described in section 403(a) of the Code and bond purchase plans described in section 405(a) of the Code. The standards contained in Title I of the Act generally apply to both "non-qualified" and "qualified" employee pen-

sion benefit plans. The standards contained in the Act, and the related Code provisions, are "minimum" standards. In general, more liberal plan provisions (in terms of the benefit to be derived by the employee) are not prohibited.

(b) For a definition of the term "employee pension benefit plan", see section 3(2) of the Act and § 2510.3-2.

(c) For a statement of the coverage of Part 2 of Title I of the Act, see sections 4 and 201 of the Act and §§ 2510.3-2, 2510.3-3, 2530.201-1 and 2530.201-2.

[¶ 14,411A]

§ 2530.200a-2 **Treasury regulations for purposes of the Act.**

Regulations prescibed by the Secretary of the Treasury or his delegate under sections 410 and 411 of the Code (relating to minimum standards for participation and vesting) shall apply for purposes of sections 202 through 204 of the Act. Thus, except for those provisions (such as the definition of an hour of service or a year of service) for which authority to prescribe regulations is specifically delegated to the Secretary of Labor, regulations prescribed by the Secretary of the Treasury shall also be used to implement the related provisions contained in the Act. Those regulations specify the credit that must be given to an employee for years of service and years of participation completed by the employee. The allocation of regulatory jurisdiction between the Secretary of the Treasury or his delegate and the Secretary of Labor is governed by Titles I through III of the Act. *See* section 3002 of the Act (88 Stat. 996).

[¶ 14,411B]

§ 2530.200a-3 **Labor regulations for purposes of the Internal Revenue Code of 1954.**

The Secretary of Labor is specifically authorized to prescribe certain regulations (generally relating to hour of service, year of service, break in service, year of participation and special rules for seasonal and maritime industries) applicable to both Title I of the Act and sections 410 and 411 of the Code. These regulations are contained in this Subpart (A) and Subpart (B) of this part (2530) and must be integrated with regulations prescribed by the Secretary of the Treasury or his delegate under section 410 of the Code (relating to minimum participation standards), 411(a) of the Code (relating to minimum vesting standards) and 411(b) of the Code (relating to benefit accrual requirements). The allocation of regulatory jurisdiction between the Secretary of Labor and the Secretary of the Treasury or his delegate is governed by Titles I through III of the Act. *See* section 3002 of the Act (88 Stat. 996).

[¶ 14,412]

§ 2530.200b-1 **Computation periods.**

(a) *General.* Under sections 202, 203 and 204 of the Act and sections 410 and 411 of the Code, an employee's statutory entitlements with regard to participation, vesting and benefit accrual are generally determined by reference to years of service and years of participation completed by the employee and one-year breaks in service incurred by the employee. The units used for determining an employee's credit towards statutory participation, vesting and benefit accrual entitlements are in turn defined in terms of the number of hours of service credited to the employee during a specified period—in general, a twelve-consecutive-month period—referred to herein as a "computation period". A plan must designate eligibility computation periods pursuant to § 2530.202-2 and vesting computation periods pursuant to § 2530.203-2, and, under certain circumstances, a defined benefit plan must designate accrual computation periods pursuant to § 2530.204-2. An employee who is credited with 1000 hours of service during an eligibility computation period must generally be credited with a year of service for purposes of section 202 of the Act and section 410 of the Code (relating to minimum participation standards). An employee who is credited with 1000 hours of service during a vesting computation period must generally be credited with a year of service for purposes of section 203 of the Act and 411(a) of the Code (relating to minimum vesting standards). An employee who completes 1000 hours of service during an accrual computation period must, under certain circumstances, be credited with at least a partial year of participation for purposes of section 204 of the Act and section 411(b) of the Code (relating to benefit accrual requirements). With respect to benefit accrual, however, the plan may not be required to credit an employee with a full year of participation and, therefore, full accrual for such year of participation unless the employee is credited with the number of hours of service or other permissible units of credit prescribed under the plan for crediting of a full year of participation (*see* § 2530.204-2 (c) and (d)). It should be noted that under some of the equivalencies which a plan may use under § 2530.200b-3 to determine the number of units of service to be credited to an employee in a computation period, an employee must be credited with a year of service or partial year of participation if the employee is credited with a number of units of service which is less than 1000 in a computation period. *See also* § 2530.200b-9, relating to elapsed time.

(b) *Rules generally applicable to computation periods.* In general, employment at the beginning or the end of an applicable computation period or on any particular date during the computation period is not determinative of whether the employee is credited with a year of service or a partial year of participation, or incurs a break in service, for the computation period. Rather, these determinations generally must be made solely with reference to the number of hours (or other units of

service) which are credited to the employee during the applicable computation period. For example, an employee who is credited with 1000 hours of service during any portion of a vesting computation period must be credited with a year of service for that computation period regardless of whether the employee is employed by the employer on the first or the last day of the computation period. It should be noted, however, that in certain circumstances, a plan may provide that certain consequences follow from an employee's failure to be employed on a particular date. For example, under section 202(a)(4) of the Act and section 410(a)(4) of the Code, a plan may provide that an individual otherwise entitled to commence participation in the plan on a specified date does not commence participation on that date if he or she was separated from the service before that date. Similarly, under section 204(b)(1) of the Act and section 411(b)(1) of the Code, a plan which is not a defined benefit plan is not subject to section 204 (b)(1) and (b)(3) of the Act and section 411 (b)(1) and (b)(3) of the Code. Such a plan, therefore, may provide that an individual who has been a participant in the plan, but who has separated from service before the date on which the employer's contributions to the plan or forfeitures are allocated among participant's accounts or before the last day of the vesting computation period, does not share in the allocation of such contributions or forfeitures even though the individual is credited with 1000 or more hours of service for the applicable vesting computation period. Under certain circumstances, however, such a plan provision may result in discrimination prohibited under section 401(a)(4) of the Code. *See* Revenue Ruling 76-250, I.R.B 1976-27.

[¶ 14,412A]

§ 2530.200b-2 **Hour of service.**

(a) *General rule.* An hour of service which must, as a minimum, be counted for the purposes of determining a year of service, a year of participation for benefit accrual, a break in service and employment commencement date (or reemployment commencement date) under sections 202, 203 and 204 of the Act and sections 410 and 411 of the Code, is an hour of service as defined in paragraphs (a) (1), (2) and (3) of this section. The employer may round up hours at the end of a computation period or more frequently.

(1) An hour of service is each hour for which an employee is paid, or entitled to payment, for the performance of duties for the employer during the applicable computation period.

(2) An hour of service is each hour for which an employee is paid, or entitled to payment, by the employer on account of a period of time during which no duties are performed (irrespective of whether the employment relationship has terminated) due to vacation, holiday, illness, incapacity (including disability), layoff, jury duty, military duty or leave of absence. Notwithstanding the preceding sentence,

(i) No more than 501 hours of service are required to be credited under this paragraph (a)(2) to an employee on account of any single continuous period during which the employee performs no duties (whether or not such period occurs in a single computation period);

(ii) An hour for which an employee is directly or indirectly paid, or entitled to payment, on account of a period during which no duties are performed is not required to be credited to the employee if such payment is made or due under a plan maintained solely for the purpose of complying with applicable workmen's compensation, or unemployment compensation or disability insurance laws; and

(iii) Hours of service are not required to be credited for a payment which solely reimburses an employee for medical or medically related expenses incurred by the employee.

For purposes of this paragraph (a)(2), a payment shall be deemed to be made by or due from an employer regardless of whether such payment is made by or due from the employer directly, or indirectly through, among others, a trust fund, or insurer, to which the employer contributes or pays premiums and regardless of whether contributions made or due to the trust fund, insurer or other entity are for the benefit of particular employees or are on behalf of a group of employees in the aggregate.

(3) An hour of service is each hour for which back pay, irrespective of mitigation of damages, is either awarded or agreed to by the employer. The same hours of service shall not be credited both under paragraph (a)(1) or paragraph (a)(2), as the case may be, and under

this paragraph (a)(3). Thus, for example, an employee who receives a back pay award following a determination that he or she was paid at an unlawful rate for hours of service previously credited will not be entitled to additional credit for the same hours of service. Crediting of hours of service for back pay awarded or agreed to with respect to periods described in paragraph (a)(2) shall be subject to the limitations set forth in that paragraph. For example, no more than 501 hours of service are required to be credited for payments of back pay, to the extent that such back pay is agreed to or awarded for a period of time during which an employee did not or would not have performed duties.

(b) *Special rule for determining hours of service for reasons other than the performance of duties.* In the case of a payment which is made or due on account of a period during which an employee peforms no duties, and which results in the crediting of hours of service under paragraph (a)(2) of this section, or in the case of an award or agreement for back pay, to the extent that such award or agreement is made with respect to a period described in paragraph (a)(2) of this section, the number of hours of service to be credited shall be determined as follows:

(1) *Payments calculated on the basis of units of time.* (i) Except as provided in paragraph (b)(3) of this section, in the case of a payment made or due which is calculated on the basis of units of time, such as hours, days, weeks or months, the number of hours of service to be credited shall be the number of regularly scheduled working hours included in the units of time on the basis of which the payment is calculated. For purposes of the preceding sentence, in the case of an employee without a regular work schedule, a plan may provide for the calculation of the number of hours to be credited on the basis of a 40-hour workweek or an 8-hour workday, or may provide for such calculation on any reasonable basis which reflects the average hours worked by the employee, or by other employees in the same job classification, over a representative period of time, provided that the basis so used is consistently applied with respect to all employees within the same job classifications, reasonably defined. Thus, for example, a plan may not use a 40-hour workweek as a basis for calculating the number of hours of service to be credited for periods of paid absences for one employee while using an average based on hours worked over a representative period of time as a basis for such calculation for another, similarly situated employee.

(ii) *Examples.* The following examples illustrate the rules in paragraph (b)(1) of this section without regard to paragraphs (b) (2) and (3).

(A) Employee A was paid for 6 hours of sick leave at his normal hourly rate. The payment was therefore calculated on the basis of units of time (hours). A must, therefore, be credited with 6 hours of service for the 6 hours of sick leave.

(B) Employee B was paid his normal weekly salary for 2 weeks of vacation. The payment was therefore calculated on the basis of units of time (weeks). B is scheduled to work 37 ½ hours per week (although from time to time working overtime). B must, therefore, be credited with 75 hours of service for the vacation (37 ½ hours per week multiplied by 2 weeks).

(C) Employee C spent 3 weeks on a paid vacation. C's salary is established at an annual rate but is paid on a bi-weekly basis. The amount of salary payments attributable to be paid vacation was calculated on the basis of units of time (weeks). C has no regular work schedule but works at least 50 hours per week. The plan provides for the calculation of hours of service to be credited to employees in C's situation for periods of paid absences on the basis of a 40-hour workweek. C must, therefore, be credited with 120 hours of service for the vacation (3 weeks multiplied by 40 hours per week).

(D) Employee D spent 2 weeks on vacation, for which he was paid $150. Although D has no regular work schedule, the $150 payment was established on the assumption that an employee in D's position works an average of 30 hours per week at a rate of $2.50 per hour. The payment of $150 was therefore calculated on the basis of units of time (weeks). The plan provides for the calculation of hours of service to be credited to employees in D's situation for periods of paid absences on the basis of the average number of hours worked by an employee over a period of 6 months. D's employer's records show that D worked an average of 28 hours per week for a 6-month period. D

must, therefore, be credited with 56 hours of service for the vacation (28 hours per week multiplied by 2 weeks).

(E) Employee E is regularly scheduled to work a 40-hour week. During a computation period E is incapacitated as a result of injury for a period of 11 weeks. Under the sick leave policy of E's employer E is paid his normal weekly salary for the first 8 weeks of his incapacity. After 8 weeks the employer ceases to pay E's normal salary but, under a disability insurance program maintained by the employer, E receives payments equal to 65% of his normal weekly salary for the remaining 3 weeks during which E is incapacitated. For the period during which he is incapacitated, therefore, E receives credit for 440 hours of service (11 weeks multiplied by 40 hours per week) regardless of the fact that payments to E for the last 3 weeks of the period during which he was incapacitated were made in amounts less than E's normal compensation.

(2) *Payments not calculated on the basis of units of time.* (i) Except as provided in paragraph (b)(3) of this section, in the case of a payment made or due, which is not calculated on the basis of units of time, the number of hours of service to be credited shall be equal to the amount of the payment divided by the employee's most recent hourly rate of compensation (as determined under paragraph (b)(2)(ii) of this section) before the period during which no duties are performed.

(ii) For purposes of paragraph (b)(2)(i) of this section an employee's hourly rate of compensation shall be determined as follows:

(A) In the case of an employee whose compensation is determined on the basis of an hourly rate, such hourly rate shall be the employee's most recent hourly rate of compensation.

(B) In the case of an employee whose compensation is determined on the basis of a fixed rate for specified periods of time (other than hours) such as days, weeks or months, the employee's hourly rate of compensation shall be the employee's most recent rate of compensation for a specified period of time (other than an hour), divided by the number of hours regularly scheduled for the performance of duties during such period of time. For purposes of the preceding sentence, in the case of an employee without a regular work schedule, the plan may provide for the calculation of the employee's hourly rate of compensation on the basis of a 40-hour workweek, an 8-hour workday, or may provide for such calculation on any reasonable basis which reflects the average hours worked by the employee over a representative period of time, provided that the basis so used is consistently applied with respect to all employees within the same job classifications, reasonably defined.

(C) In the case of an employee whose compensation is not determined on the basis of a fixed rate for specified periods of time, the employee's hourly rate of compensation shall be the lowest hourly rate of compensation paid to employees in the same job classification as that of the employee or, if no employees in the same job classification have an hourly rate, the minimum wage as established from time to time under section 6(a)(1) of the Fair Labor Standards Act of 1938, as amended.

(iii) *Examples.* The following examples illustrate the rules in paragraph (b)(2) of this section without regard to paragraphs (b) (1) and (3).

(A) As a result of an injury, an employee is incapacitated for 5 weeks. A lump sum payment of $500 is made to the employee with respect to the injury under a disability insurance plan maintained by the employee's employer. At the time of the injury, the employee's rate of pay was $3.00 per hour. The employee must, therefore, be credited with 167 hours of service ($500 divided by $3.00 per hour).

(B) Same facts as in Example (A), above, except that at the time of the injury, the employee's rate of pay was $160 per week and the employee has a regular work schedule of 40 hours per week. The employee's hourly rate of compensation is, therefore, $4.00 per hour ($160 per week divided by 40 hours per week) and the employee must be credited with 125 hours of service for the period of absence ($500 divided by $4.00 per hour).

(C) An employee is paid at an hourly rate of $3.00 per hour and works a regular schedule of 40 hours per week. The employee is disabled for 26 weeks during a computation period. For the first 12 weeks of disability, the employee is paid his normal weekly earnings of

$120 per week by the employer. Thereupon, a lump-sum disability payment of $1000 is made to the employee under a disability insurance plan maintained by the employer. Under paragraph (a)(3)(i) of this section, the employee is credited with 501 hours of service for the period of disability (lesser of 501 hours—the maximum number of hours required to be credited for a period of absence—or the sum of 12 weeks multiplied by 40 hours per week plus $1000 divided by $3.00 per hour).

(3) *Rule against double credit.* (i) Notwithstanding paragraphs (b) (1) and (2) of this section, an employee is not required to be credited on account of a period during which no duties are performed with a number of hours of service which is greater than the number of hours regularly scheduled for the performance of duties during such period. For purposes of applying the preceding sentence in the case of an employee without a regular work schedule, a plan may provide for the calculation of the number of hours of service to be credited to the employee for a period during which no duties are performed on the basis of a 40-hour workweek or an 8-hour workday, or may provide for such calculation on any reasonable basis which reflects the average hours worked by the employee, or by other employees in the same job classification, over a representative period of time, provided that the basis so used is consistently applied with respect to all employees within the same job classifications, reasonably defined.

(ii) *Examples.* (A) Employee A has a regular 40-hour work-week. Each year Employee A is entitled to pay for a two-week vacation, in addition to receiving normal wages for all hours worked, regardless of whether A actually takes a vacation and regardless of the duration of his vacation. The vacation payments are, therefore, calculated on the basis of units of time (weeks). In computation period I, A takes no vacation but receives vacation pay. A is entitled to no credit for hours of service for the vacation payment made in computation period I because the payment was not made on account of a period during which no duties were performed. In computation period II, A takes a vacation of one week in duration, although receiving pay for a two-week vacation. A is entitled to be credited with 40 hours of service for his one-week vacation in computation period II even though paid for two weeks of vacation. In computation period III, A takes a vacation for a period lasting more than 2 weeks. A is entitled to be credited with 80 hours of service for his vacation in computation period III (40 hours per week multiplied by 2 weeks) even though the vacation lasted more than 2 weeks.

(B) Employee B has no regular work schedule. As a result of an injury, B is incapacitated for 1 day. A lump-sum payment of $500 is made to A with respect to the injury under an insurance program maintained by the employer. A pension plan maintained by the employer provides for the calculation of the number of hours of service to be credited to an employee without a regular work schedule on the basis of an 8-hour day. A is therefore required to be credited with no more than 8 hours for the day during which he was incapacitated, even though A's rate of pay immediately before the injury was $3.00 per hour.

(c) *Crediting of hours of service to computation periods.* (1) Except as provided in paragraph (c)(4) of this section, hours of service described in paragraph (a)(1) of this section shall be credited to the computation period in which the duties are performed.

(2) Except as provided in paragraph (c)(4) of this section, hours of service described in paragraph (a)(2) of this section shall be credited as follows:

(i) Hours of service credited to an employee on account of a payment which is calculated on the basis of units of time, such as hours, days, weeks or months, shall be credited to the computation period or computation periods in which the period during which no duties are performed occurs, beginning with the first unit of time to which the payment relates.

(ii) Hours of service credited to an employee by reason of a payment which is not calculated on the basis of units of time shall be credited to the computation period in which the period during which no duties are performed occurs, or if the period during which no duties are performed extends beyond one computation period, such hours of service shall be allocated between not more than the first two computation periods on any reasonable basis which is consistently applied with

respect to all employees within the same job classifications, reasonably defined.

(3) Except as provided in paragraph (c)(4) of this section, hours of service described in paragraph (a)(3) of this section shall be credited to the computation period or periods to which the award or agreement for back pay pertains, rather than to the computation period in which the award, agreement or payment is made.

(4) In the case of hours of service to be credited to an employee in connection with a period of no more than 31 days which extends beyond one computation period, all such hours of service may be credited to the first computation period or the second computation period. Crediting of hours of service under this subparagraph must be done consistently with respect to all employees within the same job classifications, reasonably defined.

(5) *Examples.* The following examples are intended to illustrate paragraph (c)(4) of this section.

(i) An employer maintaining a plan pays employees on a bi-weekly basis. The plan designates the calendar year as the vesting computation period. The employer adopts the practice of crediting hours of service for the performance of duties during a bi-weekly payroll period to the vesting computation period in which the payroll period ends. Thus, when a payroll period ends on January 7, 1978, all hours of service to be credited to employees for the performance of duties during that payroll period are credited to the vesting computation period beginning on January 1, 1978. This practice is consistent with paragraph (c)(4) of this section, even though some hours of service credited to the computation period beginning on January 1, 1978, are attributable to duties performed during the previous vesting computation period.

(ii) An employer maintains a sick leave policy under which an employee is entitled to a certain number of hours of sick leave each year, on account of which the employee is paid his or her normal rate of compensation. An employee with a work schedule of 8 hours per day, 5 days per week, is sick from December 26, 1977 through January 4, 1978. Under the employer's sick leave policy, the employee is entitled to compensation for the entire period. A plan maintained by the employer establishes a calendar-year vesting computation period. The period from December 26, 1977 through December 31, 1977 includes 5 working days; the period from January 1, 1978 through January 4, 1978 includes 3 working days. Unless the plan adopts the alternative method for crediting service under paragraph (c)(4) of this section (illustrated in Example (iii), below) for the period of paid sick leave, the plan, pursuant to paragraph (c)(2)(i) of this section, must credit the employee with 40 hours of service in the 1977 vesting computation period (5 days multiplied by 8 hours per day) and 24 hours of service in the 1978 vesting computation period (3 days multiplied by 8 hours per day).

(iii) Same facts as in Example (ii), above, except that the plan adopts the practice of crediting hours of service for sick leave and other periods of compensated absences to the vesting computation period in which the employer's bi-weekly payroll period ends. The employee returns to work on January 5, 1978 and works for 2 days. For the 2-week payroll period ending on January 8, 1978, the employee may be credited with 80 hours of service in the 1978 vesting computation period (64 hours of service for the paid sick leave and 16 hours of service for the 2 days during which duties were performed).

(d) *Other Federal law.* Nothing in this section shall be construed to alter, amend, modify, invalidate, impair or supersede any law of the United States or any rule or regulation issued under any such law. Thus, for example, nothing in this section shall be construed as denying an employee credit for an "hour of service" if credit is required by separate federal law. Furthermore, the nature and extent of such credit shall be determined under such law.

(e) *Additional examples.* (1) During a computation period, an employee was paid for working 38 ¼ hours a week for 45 weeks. During the remaining 7 weeks of the computation period the employee was not employed by this employer. The employee completed 1,721 ¼ hours of service (45 weeks worked multiplied by 38 ¼ hours per week). The employer may also round up hours at the end of the computation period or more frequently. Thus, this employee could be credited with 1,722 hours of service (or, if the employer rounded up at the end of each week, 39 hours of service per week, resulting in credit for 1,755 hours of service).

(2) During a computation period, an employee was paid for a workweek of 40 hours per week for 40 weeks and, including overtime, for working 50 hours per week for 8 weeks. The employee completed 2,000 hours of service (40 weeks multiplied by 40 hours per week, plus 8 weeks worked multiplied by 50 hours per week).

(3) During a computation period, an employee was paid for working 2 regularly scheduled 40-hour weeks and then became disabled. The employee was disabled through the remainder of the computation period and the following computation period. Throughout the period of disability, payments were made to the employee as follows: for the first month of a period of disability, the employer continued to pay the employee's normal compensation at the same rate as before the disability occurred; thereupon, under the employer's disability insurance policy, payments were made to the employee in amounts equal to 80 percent of the employee's compensation before the disability. For the first computation period the employee is credited with 80 hours of service for the performance of duties (2 weeks multiplied by 40 hours per week) and 501 hours of service for the period of disability (the lesser of 501 hours of service or 50 weeks multiplied by 40 hours per week), or a total of 581 hours of service; for the second computation period the employee is credited with no hours of service because, under paragraph (a)(2)(i) of this section, the maximum of 501 hours of service has been credited for the period of disability in the first computation period.

(4) An employee has a regularly scheduled 5-day, 40-hour week. During a computation period the employee works for the first week, spends the second week on a paid vacation, returns to work for an hour and is then disabled for the remainder of the computation period. Payments under a disability plan maintained by the employer are made to the employee on account of the period of disability. The employee is credited with 582 hours of service for the computation period (40 hours for the period of paid vacation; 41 hours for the performance of duties; 501 hours for the period of disability).

(5) Same facts as in Example (4), above, except that the employee's period of disability begins before the employee returns from vacation to the performance of duties. The employee is credited with only 541 hours of service, because the paid vacation and the disability together constitute a single, continuous period during which no duties were performed and, therefore, under paragraph (a)(2)(i) of this section, no more than 501 hours of service are required to be credited for such period.

(6) During a computation period, an employee worked 40 hours a week for the first 2 weeks. The employee then began serving on active duty in the Armed Forces of the United States, which service occupied the remaining 50 weeks of the computation period. The employee would be credited with 80 hours (2 weeks worked multiplied by 40 hours) plus such credit as may be prescribed by separate Federal laws relating to military service. The nature and extent of the credit that the employee receives upon his return and the purpose for which such credit is given, e.g., the percentage of his or her accrued benefits derived from employer contributions which are nonforfeitable (or vested), will depend upon the interpretation of the federal law governing veterans' reemployment rights.

(f) *Plan document.* A plan which credits service on the basis of hours of service must state in the plan document the definition of hours of service set forth in paragraph (a) of this section, but is not required to state the rules set forth in paragraphs (b) and (c) of this section if they are incorporated by reference.

[¶ 14,412B]

§ 2530.200b-3 **Determination of service to be credited to employees.**

(a) *General rule.* For the purpose of determining the hours of service which must be credited to an employee for a computation period, a plan shall determine hours of service from records of hours worked and hours for which payment is made or due or shall use an equivalency permitted under paragraphs (d), (e) or (f) of this section to determine hours of service. Any records may be used to determine hours of service to be credited to employees under a plan, even though

such records are maintained for other purposes, provided that they accurately reflect the actual number of hours of service with which an employee is required to be credited under § 2530.200b-2(a). Payroll records, for example, may provide sufficiently accurate data to serve as a basis for determining hours of service. If, however, existing records do not accurately reflect the actual number of hours of service with which an employee is entitled to be credited, a plan must either develop and maintain adequate records or use one of the permitted equivalencies. A plan may in any case credit hours of service under any method which results in the crediting of no less than the actual number of hours of service required to be credited under § 2530.200b-2(a) to each employee in a computation period, even though such method may result in the crediting of hours of service in excess of the number of hours required to be credited under § 2530.200b-2. A plan is not required to prescribe in its documents which records are to be used to determine hours of service.

(b) *Determination of pre-effective date hours of service.* To the extent that a plan is required to determine hours of service completed before the effective date of Part 2 of Title I of the Act (see section 211 of the Act), the plan may use whatever records may be reasonably accessible to it and may make whatever calculations are necessary to determine the approximate number of hours of service completed before such effective date. For example, if a plan or an employer maintaining a plan has, or has access to, only the records of compensation of employees for the period before the effective date, it may derive the pre-effective date hours of service by using the hourly rate for the period or the hours customarily worked. If accessible records are insufficient to make an approximation of the number of pre-effective date hours of service for a particular employee or group of employees, the plan may make a reasonable estimate of the hours of service completed by such employee or employees during the particular period. For example, if records are available with respect to some employees, the plan may estimate the hours of other employees in the same job classification based on these records. A plan may use any of the equivalencies permitted under this section, or the elapsed time method of crediting service permitted under this section, or the elapsed time method of crediting service permitted under § 2530.200b-9, to determine hours of service completed before the effective date of Part 2 of Title I of the Act.

(c) *Use of equivalencies for determining service to be credited to employees.* (1) The equivalencies permitted under paragraphs (d), (e) and (f) of this section are methods of determining service to be credited to employees during computation periods which are alternatives to the general rule for determining hours of service set forth in paragraph (a) of this section. The equivalencies are designed to enable a plan to determine the amount of service to be credited to an employee in a computation period on the basis of records which do not accurately reflect the actual number of hours of service required to be credited to the employee under § 2530.200b-2(a). However, the equivalencies may be used even if such records are maintained. Any equivalency used by a plan must be set forth in the document under which the plan is maintained.

(2) A plan may use different methods of crediting service, including equivalencies permitted under paragraphs (d), (e) and (f) of this section and the method of crediting service under the general rule set forth in § 2530.200b-2(a), for different classifications of employees covered under the plan or for different purposes, provided that such classifications are reasonable and are consistently applied. Thus, for example, a plan may provide that part-time employees are credited under the general method of crediting service set forth in § 2530.200b-2 and full-time employees are credited under a permissible equivalency. A classification, however, will not be deemed to be reasonable or consistently applied if such classification is designed with an intent to preclude an employee or employees from attaining statutory entitlement with respect to eligibility to participate, vesting or benefit accrual. For example, a classification applied so that any employee credited with less than 1,000 hours of service during a given 12-consecutive-month period would be considered part-time and subject to the general method of crediting service rather than an equivalency would not be reasonable.

(3) Notwithstanding paragraphs (c) (1) and (2) of this section, the use of a permissible equivalency for some, but not all, purposes or

the use of a permissible equivalency for some, but not all, employees may, under certain circumstances, result in discrimination prohibited under section 401(a) of the Code, even though it is permitted under this section.

(d) *Equivalencies based on working time.* (1) *Hours worked.* A plan may determine service to be credited to an employee on the basis of hours worked, as defined in paragraph (d)(3)(i) of this section, if 870 hours worked are treated as equivalent to 1,000 hours of service and 435 hours worked are treated as equivalent to 500 hours of service.

(2) *Regular time hours.* A plan may determine service to be credited to an employee on the basis of regular time hours, as defined in paragraph (d)(3)(ii) of this section, if 750 regular time hours are treated as equivalent to 1,000 hours of service and 375 regular time hours are treated as equivalent to 500 hours of service.

(3) For purposes of this section:

(i) The term "hours worked" shall mean hours of service described in § 2530.200b-2(a)(1), hours for which back pay, irrespective of mitigation of damages, is awarded or agreed to by an employer, to the extent that such award or agreement is intended to compensate an employee for periods during which the employee would have been engaged in the performance of duties for the employer.

(ii) The term "regular time hours" shall mean hours worked, except hours for which a premium rate is paid because such hours are in excees of the maximum workweek applicable to an employee under section 7(a) of the Fair Labor Standards Act of 1938, as amended, or because such hours are in excess of a bona fide standard workweek or workday.

(4) A plan determining service to be credited to an employee on the basis of hours worked or regular time hours shall credit hours worked or regular time hours, as the case may be, to computation periods in accordance with the rules for crediting hours of service to computation periods set forth in § 2520.200b-2(c).

(5) *Examples.* (i) A defined benefit plan uses the equivalency based on hours worked permitted under paragarph (d)(1) of this section. The plan uses the same 12-consecutive-month period for the vesting and accrual computation periods. The plan credits a participant with each hour for which the participant is paid, or entitled to payment, for the performance of duties for the employer during a computation period (as well as each hour for which back pay is awarded or agreed to). During a vesting/accrual computation period Participant A is credited with 870 hours worked. A is credited with a year of service for purposes of vesting for the computation period and with at least a partial year of participation for purposes of accrual, as if A had been credited with 1000 hours of service during the computation period. During the same computation period Participant B is credited with 436 hours of service. B is not credited with a year of service for purposes of vesting or a partial year of participation for purposes of accrual for the computation period, but does not incur a one-year break in service for the computation period, as if B had been credited with 501 hours of service during the computation period.

(ii) A plan uses the equivalency based on regular time hours permitted under paragraph (d)(2) of this section. During a computation period a participant works 370 regular time hours and 20 overtime hours. The participant incurs a one-year break in service for the computation period because he has not been credited with 375 regular hours in the computation period.

(e) *Equivalencies based on periods of employment.* (1) Except as provided in paragraphs (e)(4) and (6) of this section, a plan may determine the number of hours of service to be credited to employees in a computation period on the following bases:

(i) On the basis of days of employment, if an employee is credited with 10 hours of service for each day for which the employee would be required to be credited with at least one hour of service under § 2530.200b-2;

(ii) On the basis of weeks of employment, if an employee is credited with 45 hours of service for each week for which the employee would be required to be credited with at least one hour of service under § 2530.200b-2;

(iii) On the basis of semi-monthly payroll periods, if an employee is credited with 95 hours of service for each semi-monthly payroll period for which the employee would be required to be credited with at least one hour of service under § 2530.200b-2; or

(iv) On the basis of months of employment, if an employee is credited with 190 hours of service for each month for which the employee would be required to be credited with at least one hour of service under § 2530.200b-2.

(2) Except as provided in paragraphs (e)(4) and (6) of this section, a plan may determine the number of hours of service to be credited to employees in a computation period on the basis of shifts if an employee is credited with the number of hours included in a shift for each shift for which the employee would be required to be credited with at least one hour of service under § 2530.200b-2. If a plan uses the equivalency based on shifts permitted under this paragraph, the times of the beginning and end of each shift used as a basis for the determination of service shall be set forth in a document referred to in the plan.

(3) *Examples.* The following examples illustrate the application of paragraphs (e)(1) and (2) of this section:

(i) A plan uses the equivalency based on weeks of employment permitted under paragraph (e)(1)(ii) of this section. An employee works for one hour on the first workday of a week and then takes leave without pay for the entire remainder of the week. The plan must credit the employee with 45 hours of service for the week.

(ii) A plan uses the equivalency based on weeks of employment permitted under paragraph (e)(1)(ii) of this section. An employee spends a week on vacation with pay. The plan must credit the employee with 45 hours of service for the week.

(iii) A plan uses the equivalency based on weeks of employment permitted under paragraph (e)(1)(ii) of this section. An employee spends two days of a week on vacation with pay and the remainder of the week on leave without pay. The plan must credit the employee with 45 hours of service for the week.

(iv) A plan uses the equivalency based on weeks of employment permitted under paragraph (e)(1)(ii) of this section. An employee spends the entire week on leave without pay. The plan is not required to credit the employee with any hours of service for the week because no payment was made to the employee for the week of leave and, therefore, under § 2530.200b-2 no hours of service would be credited to the employee for the week of leave.

(v) The workday of an employer maintaining a plan is scheduled in shifts. Ordinarily, each shift is 6 hours in duration. At certain times, however, the employer schedules 8-hour shifts in order to meet increased demand. Such shifts are described in a collective bargaining agreement referred to in the plan documents. The plan must credit an employee with 6 hours of service for each 6-hour shift for which the employee would be credited with one hour of service under § 2530.200b-2, and with 8 hours of service for each such 8-hour shift.

(vi) An employer's workday is divided into three 8-hour shifts, each employee generally working 5 shifts per week. A plan maintained by the employer uses the equivalency based on shifts permitted under paragraph (e)(2) of this section. An employee is on vacation with pay for 2 weeks, during which, in the ordinary course of his work schedule, he would have worked 10 shifts. The employee must be credited with 80 hours of service for the vacation (10 shifts multiplied by 8 hours per shift).

(vii) An employer's workday is divided into 3 8-hour shifts, each employee generally working 1 shift per workday. A plan maintained by the employer uses the equivalency based on shifts permitted under paragraph (e)(2) of this section. On a certain day, an employee works his normal 8-hour shift and an hour during the following shift. In addition to 8 hours service for the first shift, the employee must be credited with 8 hours of service for the following shift, since he would be entitled to be credited with at least one hour of service for the second shift under § 2530.200b-2.

(viii) A plan uses the equivalency based on days permitted under paragraph (e)(1)(i) of this section. During a computation period an employee spends 2 weeks on vacation with pay. In the ordinary course of the employee's regular work schedule, the employee would be engaged in the performance of duties for 10 days during the 2-week vacation period. Under § 2530.200b-2, the employee would be credited

184 Labor Laws & Regulations

with at least one hour of service for each of the 10 days during the 2-week vacation for which the employee would ordinarily be engaged in the performance of duties. Under paragraph (e)(4) of this section, the employee is credited with 100 hours of service for the 2-week vacation (10 days multiplied by 10 hours of service per day).

(4) For purposes of this paragraph, in the case of a payment described in § 2530.20b-2(b)(2) (relating to payments not calculated on the basis of units of time), a plan using an equivalency based on units of time permitted under this paragraph shall credit the employee with the number or hours of service determined under subparagraph (2) of § 2530.200b-2(b), and, to the extent applicable, paragraph (e)(3), containing the rule against double crediting, of § 2530.200b-2(b). For example, if an employee with a regular work schedule of 40 hours per week paid at a rate of $3.00 per hour is incapacitated for a period of 4 weeks and receives a lump sum payment of $500 for his incapacity, the employee must be credited with 160 hours of service for the period of incapacity, regardless of whether the plan uses an equivalency permitted under this paragraph (see example at § 2530.200b-2(b)(2)(iii)(A)). If, however, the employee is incapacitated for only 3 weeks, under § 2530.200b-2(b)(3) the employee is not required to be credited with more than 120 hours of service (lesser of 167 hours of service determined under the preceding sentence or 3 weeks multiplied by 40 hours per week).

(5) For purposes of this paragraph, in the case of a payment to an employee calculated on the basis of units of time which are greater than the periods of employment used by a plan as a basis for determining service to be credited to the employee under this paragraph, the plan shall credit the employee with the number of periods of employment which, in the course of the employees' regular work schedule, would be included in the unit or units of time on the basis of which the payment is calculated. For example, a plan uses the equivalency based on days permitted under paragraph (e)(1)(i) of this section. During a computation period an employee spends 2 weeks on vacation with pay. In the ordinary course of the employee's regular work schedule, the employee would be engaged in the performance of duties for 10 days during the 2-week vacation period. Under § 2530.200b-2, the employee would be credited with at least one hour of service for each of the 10 days off during the 2-week vacation for which the employee would ordinarily be engaged in the performance of duties. Under this subparagraph the employee is credited with 100 hours of service for the 2-week vacation (10 days multiplied by 10 hours of service per day). If, however, the employee, although paid for a 2-week vacation, spends only one week on vacation, under § 2530.200b-2(b)(3) the employee is not required to be credited with more than 50 hours of service (5 days multiplied by 10 hours per day).

(6) For purposes of this paragraph, in the case of periods of time used as a basis for determining service to be credited to an employee which extend into two computation periods, the plan may credit all hours of service (or other units of service) credited for such a period to the first computation period or the second computation period, or may allocate such hours of service (or other units of service) between the two computation periods on a pro rata basis. Crediting of service under this subparagraph must be done consistently with respect to all employees within the same job classifications, reasonably defined.

(7) A plan may combine an equivalency based on working time permitted under paragraph (d) of this section (i.e., hours worked or regular time hours) with an equivalency based on periods of employment permitted under this paragraph if the following conditions are met:

(i) The plan credits an employee with the number of hours worked or regular time hours, as the case may be, equal to the number of hours of service which would be credited to the employee under paragraphs (e)(1) and (2) of this section, for each period of employment for which the employee would be credited with one hour worked or one regular time hour; and

(ii) The plan treats hours worked and regular time hours in the manner prescribed under paragraphs (d)(1) and (d)(2) of this section.

(8) *Example.* The following example illustrates the application of paragraph (e)(7) of this section. A plan uses the equivalency based

on weeks of employment permitted under paragraph (e)(1)(ii) of this section in conjunction with the equivalency based on hours worked permitted under paragraph (d)(1) of this section, as provided in paragraph (e)(7) of this section. During a vesting computation period an employee is paid for the performance of duties for at least 1 hour in each of the first 20 weeks of the computation period and spends the next 2 weeks on a paid vacation. The employee thereupon terminates employment performing no further duties for the employer, and receiving no further compensation in the computation period. The employee is therefore credited with 900 hours worked for the vesting computation period (20 weeks multiplied by 45 hours per week), receiving no credit for the two weeks of paid vacation. The employee is credited with a year of service for the vesting computation period because he has been credited with more than 870 hours for the computation period.

(f) *Equivalencies based on earnings.* (1) In the case of an employee whose compensation is determined on the basis of an hourly rate, a plan may determine the number of hours to be credited the employee in a computation period on the basis of earnings, if:

(i) The employee is credited with the number of hours equal to the total of the employee's earnings from time to time during the computation period divided by the employee's hourly rate as in effect at such times during the computation period, or equal to the employee's total earnings for the performance of duties during the computation period divided by the employee's lowest hourly rate of compensation during the computation period, or by the lowest hourly rate of compensation payable to an employee in the same, or a similar, job classification, reasonably defined; and

(ii) 870 hours credited under paragraph (f)(1)(i) of this section are treated as equivalent to 1,000 hours of service, and 435 hours credited under paragraph (f)(1)(i) of this section are treated as equivalent to 500 hours of service.

For purposes of this paragraph (f)(1), a plan may divide earnings at premium rates for overtime by the employee's hourly rate for overtime, rather than the regular time hourly rate.

(2) In the case of an employee whose compensation is determined on a basis other than an hourly rate, a plan may determine the number of hours to be credited to the employee in a computation period on the basis of earnings if:

(i) The employee is credited with the number of hours equal to the employee's total earnings for the performance of duties during the computation period divided by the employee's lowest hourly rate of compensation during the computation period, determined under paragraph (f)(3) of this section; and

(ii) 750 hours credited under paragraph (f)(2)(i) of this section are treated as equivalent to 1,000 hours of service, and 375 hours credited under paragraph (f)(2)(i) of this section are treated as equivalent to 500 hours of service.

(3) For purposes of paragraph (f)(2) of this section, an employee's hourly rate of compensation shall be determined as follows:

(i) In the case of an employee whose compensation is determined on the basis of a fixed rate for a specified period of time (other than an hour) such as a day, week or month, the employee's hourly rate of compensation shall be the employee's lowest rate of compensation during a computation period for such specified period of time divided by the number of hours regularly scheduled for the performance of duties during such period of time. For purposes of the preceding sentence, in the case of an employee without a regular work schedule, the plan may provide for the calculation of the employee's hourly rate of compensation on the basis of a 40-hour workweek or an 8-hour workday, or may provide for such calculation on any reasonable basis which reflects the average hours worked by the employee over a representative period of time, provided that the basis so used is consistently applied to all employees within the same job classifications, reasonably defined.

(ii) In the case of an employee whose compensation is not determined on the basis of a fixed rate for a specified period of time, the employee's hourly rate of compensation shall be the lowest hourly rate of compensation payable to employees in the same job classification as the employee, or, if no employees in the same job classification have an hourly rate, the minimum wage as established from time to

¶14,412B   Reg. §2530.200b-3(e)(4)

time under section 6(a)(1) of the Fair Labor Standards Act of 1938, as amended.

(4) *Examples.* (i) In a particular job classification employees' wages range from $3.00 per hour to $4.00 per hour. To determine the number of hours to be credited to an employee in that job classification who is compensated at a rate of $4.00 per hour, a plan may divide the employee's total earnings during the computation period for the performance of duties either by $3.00 per hour (the lowest hourly rate of compensation in the job classification) or by $4.00 per hour (the employee's own hourly rate of compensation).

(ii) An hourly employee's total earnings for the performance of duties during a vesting computation period amount to $4,350. During that calendar year, the employee's lowest hourly rate of compensation was $5.00 per hour. The plan may determine the number of hours to be credited to the employee for that vesting computation period by dividing $4,350 by $5.00 per hour. The employee is credited with 870 hours for the vesting computation period and is, therefore, credited with a year of service for purposes of vesting.

(iii) During the first 3 months of a vesting computation period an hourly employee is paid at a rate of $3.00 per hour and earns $675 for the performance of duties; during the next 6 months, the employee is paid at a rate of $3.50 per hour and earns $1,575 for the performance of duties; during the final 3 months the employee is paid at a rate of $3.60 per hour and earns $810 for the performance of duties. The plan may determine the number of hours to be credited to the employee in the computation period under the equivalency set forth in paragraph (f)(1) of this section either (A) by dividing the employee's earnings for each period during which the employee was paid at a separate rate ($675 divided by $3.00 per hour equals 225 hours; $1,575 divided by $3.50 per hour equals 450 hours; $810 divided by $3.60 per hour equals 225 hours) and adding the hours so obtained (900 hours), or (B) by dividing the employee's total compensation for the vesting computation period by the employee's lowest hourly rate during the computation period ($3,020 divided by $3.00 per hour equals 1,009 ⅔ hours). The plan may also divide the employee's total compensation during the computation period by the lowest hourly rate payable to an employee in the same, or a similar, job classification.

(iv) During a plan's computation period an hourly employee's total earnings for the performance of duties consist of $7,500 at a basic rate of $5.00 per hour and $750 at an overtime rate of $7.50 per hour for hours worked in excess of 40 in a week. If the plan uses the equivalency permitted under paragraph (f)(1) of this section, the plan may adjust for the overtime rate in calculating the number of hours to be credited to the employee. Thus, the plan may calculate the number of hours to be credited to the employee by adding the employee's earnings at the basic rate divided by the basic rate and the employee's earnings at the overtime rate divided by the overtime rate ($7,500 divided by $5.00 per hour, plus $750 divided by $7.50 per hour, or 1,500 hours plus 100 hours), resulting in credit for 1,600 hours for the computation period.

(v) During a plan's vesting computation period an employee's lowest weekly rate of compensation is $400 per week. The employee has a regular work schedule of 40 hours per week. The employee's lowest hourly rate during the vesting computation period is, therefore, $10 per hour ($400 per week divided by 40 hours per week). During the vesting computation period, the employee receives a total of $7,500 for the performance of duties. The plan determines the number of regular time hours to be credited to the employee for the computation period by dividing $7,500 by $10 per hour. The employee is credited with 750 hours for the computation period and is, therefore, credited with a year of service for purposes of vesting.

[¶ 14,412C]
§ 2530.200b-4 One-year break in service.

(a) *Computation period.* (1) Under sections 202(b) and 203(b)(3) of the Act and sections 410(a)(5) and 411(a)(6) of the Code, a plan may provide that an employee incurs a one-year break in service for a computation period or periods if the employee fails to complete more than 500 hours of service or, in the case of any maritime industry, 62 days of service in such period or periods.

(2) For purposes of section 202(b) of the Act and section 410(a)(5) of the Code, relating to one-year breaks in service for eligibility to participate, in determining whether an employee incurs a one-year break in service, a plan shall use the eligibility computation period designated under § 2530.202-2(b) for measuring years of service after the initial eligibility computation period.

(3) For purposes of section 203(b)(3) of the Act and section 411(a)(6) of the Code, relating to breaks in service for purposes of vesting, in determining whether an employee incurs a one-year break in service, a plan shall use the vesting computation period designated under § 2530.203-2(a).

(4) For rules regarding service which is not required to be taken into account for purposes of benefit accrual, *see* § 2530.204-1(b)(1).

(b) *Service following a break in service.* (1) For purposes of section 202(b)(3) of the Act and section 410(a)(5)(C) of the Code (relating to completion of a year of service for eligibility to participate after a one-year break in service), the following rules shall be applied in measuring completion of a year of service upon an employee's return after a one-year break in service:

(i) In the case of a plan which, after the initial eligibility computation period, measures years of service for purposes of eligibility to participate on the basis of eligibility computation periods beginning on anniversaries of an employee's employment commencement date, as permitted under § 2530.202-2(b)(1), the plan shall use the 12-consecutive-month period beginning on an employee's reemployment commencement date (as defined in paragraph (b)(1)(iii) and (iv) of this section) and, where necessary, subsequent 12-consecutive-month periods beginning on anniversaries of the reemployment commencement date.

(ii) In the case of a plan which, after the initial eligibility computation period, measures years of service for eligibility to participate on the basis of plan years beginning with the plan year which includes the first anniversary of the initial eligibility computation period, as permitted under § 2530.202-2(b)(2), the plan shall use the 12-consecutive-month period beginning on an employee's reemployment commencement date (as defined in paragraph (b)(1)(iii) and (iv) of this section) and, where necessary, plan years beginning with the plan year which includes the first anniversary of the employee's reemployment commencement date.

(iii) Except as provided in paragraph (b)(1)(iv) of this section, an employee's reemployment commencement date shall be the first day on which the employee is entitled to be credited with an hour of service described in § 2530.200b-2(a)(1) after the first eligibility computation period in which the employee incurs a one-year break in service following an eligibility computation period in which the employee is credited with more than 500 hours of service.

(iv) In the case of an employee who is credited with no hours of service in an eligibility computation period beginning after the employee's reemployment commencement date established under subparagraph (b)(1)(iii) of this section, the employee shall be treated as having a new reemployment commencement date as of the first day on which the employee is entitled to be credited with an hour of service described in § 2530.200b-2(a)(1) after such eligibility computation period.

(2) For purposes of section 203(b)(3)(B) of the Act and section 411(a)(6)(B) of the Code (relating to the completion of a year of service for vesting following a one-year break in service), in measuring completion of a year of service upon an employee's return after a one-year break in service, a plan shall use the vesting computation period designated under § 2530.203-2. In the case of a plan which designates a separate vesting computation period for each employee (rather than one vesting computation period for all employees), when an employee who has incurred a one-year break in service later completes an initial hour of service, the plan may change the employee's vesting computation period to a 12-consecutive-month period beginning on the day on which such initial hour of service is completed, provided that the plan follows the rules for changing the vesting computation period set forth in § 2530.203-2(c)(1). Specifically, such a plan must ensure that as a result of the change of the vesting computation period of an employee who has incurred a one-year break in service to the 12-month period

beginning on the first day on which the employee later completes an initial hour of service, the employee's vested percentage of the accrued benefit derived from employer contributions will not be less on any date after the change than such nonforfeitable percentage would be in the absence of the change. As under §2530.203-2(c)(i), the plan will be deemed to satisfy the requirement of that paragraph if, in the case of an employee who has incurred a one-year break in service, the vesting computation period beginning on the day on which the employee completes an hour of service after the one-year break in service begins before the end of the last vesting computation period established before the change of vesting computation periods and, if the employee is credited with 1000 hours of service in both such vesting computation periods, the employee is credited with 2 years of service for purposes of vesting.

(3) For purposes of section 203(b)(3)(B) of the Act and section 411(a)(6)(B) of the Code (relating to the completion of a year of service for vesting following a one-year break in service), in measuring completion of a year of service upon an employee's return after a one-year break in service, a plan shall use the vesting computation period designated under §2530.203-2. In the case of a plan which designates a separate vesting computation period for each employee (rather than one vesting computation period for all employees), when an employee who has incurred a one-year break in service later completes an initial hour of service, the plan may change the employee's vesting computation period to a 12-consecutive-month period beginning on the day on which such initial hour of service is completed, provided that the plan follows the rules for changing the vesting computation period set forth in §2530.203-2(c)(1).

(4) *Examples.* (i) Employer X maintains a pension plan. The plan uses a calendar year vesting computation period and plan year. As conditions for participation, the plan requires that an employee of X complete one year of service and attain age 25, and, in accordance with §2530.202-2(b)(2), provides that after the initial eligibility computation period, plan years will be used as eligibility computation periods, beginning with the plan year which includes the first anniversary of an employee's employment commencement date. Thus, under paragraph (a)(2) of this section, the plan must use plan years in measuring one-year breaks in service for eligibility to participate. The plan provides that an employee acquires a nonforfeitable right to 100 percent of the accrued benefit derived from employer contributions upon completion of 10 years of service. Under the plan, for purposes of vesting, years of service completed before an employee attains age 22 are not taken into account. The plan also provides that if an employee has incurred a one-year break in service, in computing the employee's period of service for eligibility to participate, years of service before such break will not be taken into account until the employee has completed a year of service with X after the employee's return. The plan further provides that in the case of an employee who has no vested right to an accrued benefit derived from employer contributions, years of service for purposes of eligibility to participate or vesting before a one-year break in service for eligibility or vesting (as the case may be) shall not be required to be taken into account if the number of consecutive one-year breaks in service equals or exceeds the aggregate number of such years of service before such consecutive one-year breaks in service.

(A) Employee A commences employment with X on January 1, 1976 at age 30 and completes a year of service for eligibility to participate and vesting in both the 1976 and 1977 computation periods. A becomes a participant in the plan on January 1, 1977. A terminates employment with X on November 3, 1977, after completing 1000 hours of service; completes no hours of service in 1978, incurring a one-year break in service; and is reemployed by X on June 1, 1979. A completes 800 hours of service during the remainder of 1979 and 600 hours of service from January 1, 1980 through May 31, 1980. Under paragraph (b)(1)(iii) of this section, A's reemployment commencement date is June 1, 1979. By June 1, 1980, A has completed a year of service during the eligibility computation period following his return, and receives credit for his pre-break service to the extent required under section 202 of the Act and section 410 of the Code and the regulations thereunder. The plan is not, however, required to credit A with a year of service for vesting during 1979 because he failed to complete 1,000 hours of service during that vesting computation period. If A completes 400 or more hours of service from June 1, 1980 to December 31, 1980, then A

will be credited with one year of service for vesting purposes for the 1980 vesting computation period.

(B) Employee B was born on February 22, 1955 and commenced employment with Employer X on July 1, 1975. B is credited with a year of service for eligibility to participate in the plan for the eligibility computation period beginning on his employment commencement date (July 1, 1975) and a year of service for eligibility and vesting for the 1976 and 1977 plan years. As of the end of the 1977 plan year, B is credited with 3 years of service for purposes of eligibility to participate, but only one year of service for purposes of vesting. Not having attained age 25, however, B is not admitted to participation in the plan upon completion of his first year of service with X. In the 1978 plan year, B fails to be credited with 500 hours of service, thereby incurring a one-year break in service. As a result of B's one-year break in service in the 1978 plan year, the year of service for vesting which was earlier credited to B for the 1977 plan year is disregarded because the one-year break in service equals the one year of service credited to B before the one-year break in service. After the end of the 1978 plan year, B does not perform an hour of service with X until February 3, 1979. February 3, 1979, therefore, is B's reemployment commencement date under paragraph (b)(1)(i) of this section. B fails to be credited with 1000 hours of service in the first eligibility computation period beginning on February 3, 1979, and also for the vesting computation period beginning January 1, 1979. Because, in accordance with §2530.202-2(b)(2), the plan provides that after the initial eligibility computation period, plan years will be used as eligibility computation periods, under paragraph (b)(1)(ii) of this section the plan must provide that, in measuring completion of a year of service for eligibility to participate after a one-year break in service, plan years beginning with the plan year which includes an employee's reemployment commencement date will be used. B is credited with 1000 hours of service for the plan year beginning on January 1, 1980 and is therefore credited with a year of service for the 1980 plan year. Under section 202(b)(3) of the Act and section 410(a)(5)(C) of the Code, as a consequence of B's completion of a year of service in the 1980 plan year, B's service before his one-year break in service in the 1978 plan year must be taken into account for eligibility purposes. As conditions of participation, the plan requires that an employee attain age 25 and complete one year of service. Upon his completion of a year of service for the 1980 plan year, B is deemed to have met the plan's participation requirements as of February 22, 1980, his twenty-fifth birthday, because the year of service completed by B in B's eligibility computation period beginning on January 1, 1976 is taken into account for eligibility purposes.

(ii) Employer Y maintains a defined benefit pension plan. The plan provides that an employee acquires a nonforfeitable right to 100 percent of the employee's accrued benefit derived from employer contributions upon completion of 10 years of service. As conditions for participation, the plan requires that an employee of Y complete one year of service and provides that if an employee has incurred a one-year break in service, in computing the employee's period of service for eligibility to participate, years of service before such break will not be taken into account until the employee has completed a year of service with Y after the employee's return. In accordance with §2530.202-2(b)(1), the plan provides that after the initial eligibility computation period, eligibility computation periods beginning on anniversaries of an employee's employment commencement date will be used. Thus, under paragraph (a)(1) of this section, the plan must use computation periods beginning on anniversaries of the employee's employment commencement date in measuring one-year breaks in service. Employee C's employment commencement date with Y is February 1, 1975. C is credited with a year of service for eligibility to participate in the eligibility computation period beginning on C's employment commencement date and meets the plan's eligibility requirements as of February 1, 1976. In accordance with the provisions of the plan, C commences participation in the plan as of July 1, 1976. C is thereafter credited with a year of service for eligibility to participate in each of the eligibility computation periods beginning on anniversaries of C's employment commencement date (February 1) in 1976, 1977, 1978 and 1979. Thus, as of February 1, 1980, C is credited with 5 years of service for eligibility to participate. In the eligibility computation period beginning on February 1, 1980, C fails to be credited with more than 500 hours of service and therefore incurs a one-year break in service. In the eligibility computation period beginning on February 1,

1981, C is not credited with an hour of service for the performance of duties until March 1, 1981. Under paragraph (b)(1)(iii) of this section, March 1, 1981 is C's reemployment commencement date. C terminates employment with Y on May 1, 1981 and fails to be credited with 1000 hours of service in the 12-consecutive-month period beginning on March 1, 1981, or with more than 500 hours of service in the eligibility computation period beginning on February 1, 1981, thereby incurring a second one-year break in service for eligibility to participate. C is credited with no hours of service in the eligibility computation period beginning on February 1, 1982, thereby incurring a third one-year break in service for eligibility to participate, and is likewise credited with no hours of service in the 12-consecutive-month period beginning on March 1, 1982, the anniversary of B's reemployment commencement date. Under paragraph (b)(1)(iv) of this section, C must therefore be treated as having a new reemployment commencement date as of the first day following the close of the eligibility computation period beginning on February 1, 1982. On January 1, 1984 (before the end of the eligibility computation period beginning February 1, 1983) C is rehired by Y and is credited with an hour of service for the performance of duties. C is therefore treated as having a new reemployment commencement date of January 1, 1984. C fails to be credited with more than 500 hours of service in the eligibility computation period beginning on February 1, 1983, thereby incurring a fourth one-year break in service, and fails to be credited with 1000 hours of service in the 12-consecutive-month period beginning on March 1, 1983, the anniversary of C's original reemployment commencement date. However, in the 12-consecutive-month period beginning on January 1, 1984, C is credited with 1000 hours of service, thus meeting the plan's requirement that an employee who has incurred a one-year break in service for eligibility to participate must complete a year of service upon the employee's return in order for years of service before the one-year break in service to be taken into account for purposes of eligibility. Because C's years of service completed before C's first one-year break in service must be taken into account under section 202(b) of the Act and section 410(b)(5) of the Code for purposes of eligibility to participate, under § 2530.204-2(a)(2) the period beginning on July 1, 1976 (the earliest date on which C was a participant) and extending until January 31, 1980 (the last day before C's first one-year break in service) must be taken into account for purposes of benefit accrual.

(c) *Prior service for eligibility to participate.* For rules relating to computing service preceding a break in service for the purpose of eligibility to participate in the plan, *see* § 2530.202-2(c).

(d) *Prior service for vesting.* For rules relating to computing service preceding a break in service for the purpose of credit toward vesting, see § 2530.203-2(d).

[¶ 14,412D]

§ 2530.200b-5 **Seasonal industries.** [Reserved.]

[¶ 14,412E]

§ 2530.200b-6 **Maritime industry.**

(a) *General.* Sections 202(a)(3)(D), 203(b)(2)(D) and 204(b)(3)(E) of the Act and sections 410(a)(3)(D) and 411(a)(5)(D) and (b)(3)(E) of the Code contain special provisions applicable to the maritime industry. In general, those provisions permit statutory standards otherwise expressed in terms of 1,000 hours of service to be applied to employees in the maritime industry as if such standards were expressed in terms of 125 days of service. A plan covering employees in the maritime industry may nevertheless credit service to such employees on the basis of hours of service, as prescribed in § 2530.200b-2, including the use of any equivalency permitted under § 2530.200b-3, or may credit service to such employees on the basis of elapsed time, as permitted under § 2530.200b-9.

(b) *Definition.* For purposes of sections 202, 203, and 204 of the Act and sections 410 and 411 of the Code, the maritime industry is that industry in which employees perform duties on board commercial, exploratory, service or other vessels moving on the high seas, inland waterways, Great Lakes, coastal zones, harbors and noncontiguous areas, or on offshore ports, platforms or other similar sites.

(c) *Computation periods.* For employees in the maritime industry, computation periods shall be established as for employees in any other industry.

(d) *Year of service.* To the extent that a plan covers employees engaged in the maritime industry, and credits service for such employees on the basis of days of service, such employees who are credited with 125 days of service in the applicable computation period must be credited with a year of service. In the case of a plan covering both employees engaged in the maritime industry and employees not engaged in the maritime industry, service of employees not engaged in the maritime industry shall not be determined on the basis of days of service.

(e) *Year of paticipation for benefit accrual.* A plan covering employees engaged in the maritime industry may determine such an employee's period of service for purposes of benefit accrual on any basis permitted under § 2530.204-2 and § 2530.204-3. For purposes of § 2530.204-2(c) (relating to partial years of participation), in the case of an employee engaged in the maritime industry who is credited by the plan on the basis of days of service and whose service is not less than 125 days of service during an accrual computation period, the calculation of such employee's period of service for purposes of benefit accrual shall be treated as not made on a reasonable and consistent basis if service during such computation period is not taken into account. Thus, the employee must be credited with at least a partial year of participation (but not necessarily a full year of participation) for that accrual computation period, in accordance with § 2530.204-2(c).

(f) *Employment commencement date.* For purposes of § 2530.200b-4 (relating to breaks in service) and § 2530.202-2 (relating to eligibility computation periods):

(1) The employment commencement date of an employee engaged in the maritime industry who is credited by the plan on the basis of days of service shall be the first day for which the employee is entitled to be credited with a day of service described in § 2530.200b-7(a)(1).

(2)(i) Except as provided in paragraph (f)(2)(ii) of this section, the reemployment commencement date of an employee engaged in the maritime industry shall be the first day for which the employee is entitled to be credited with a day of service described in § 2530.200b-7(a)(1) after the first eligibility computation period in which the employee incurs a one-year break in service following an eligibility computation period in which the employee is credited with more than 62 days of service.

(ii) In the case of an employee engaged in the maritime industry who is credited with no hours of service in an eligibility computation period beginning after the employee's reemployment commencement date established under paragraph (f)(2)(i) of this section, the employee shall be treated as having a new reemployment commencement date as of the first day for which the employee is entitled to be credited with a day of service described in § 2530.200b-7(a)(1) after such eligibility computation period.

[¶ 14,412F]

§ 2530.200b-7 **Day of service for employees in the maritime industry.**

(a) *General rule.* A day of service in the maritime industry which must, as a minimum, be counted for the purposes of determining a year of service, a year of participation for benefit accrual, a break in service and an employment commencement date (or reemployment commencement date) under sections 202, 203 and 204 of the Act and sections 410 and 411 of the Code by a plan that credits service by days of service rather than hours of service (as prescribed in § 2530.200b-2, or under equivalencies permitted under § 2530.200b-3) or elapsed time (as permitted under § 2530.200b-9), is a day of service as defined in paragraphs (a)(1), (2) and (3) of this section.

(1) A day of service is each day for which an employee is paid, or entitled to payment for the performance of duties for the employer during the applicable computation period.

(2) A day of service is each day for which an employee is paid, or entitled to payment, by the employer on account of a period of time during which no duties are performed (irrespective of whether the

employment relationship has terminated) due to vacation, holiday, illness, incapacity (including disability), layoff, jury duty, military duty or leave of absence. Notwithstanding the preceding sentence;

      (i) No more than 63 days of service are required to be credited under this paragraph (a)(2) to an employee on account of any single continuous period during which the employee performs no duties (whether or not such period occurs in a single computation period);

      (ii) A day for which an employee is directly or indirectly paid, or entitled to payment, on account of a period during which no duties are performed is not required to be credited to the employee if such payment is made or due under a plan maintained solely for the purpose of complying with applicable workmen's compensation (including maintenance and care), or unemployment compensation or disability insurance laws; and

      (iii) Days of service are not required to be credited for a payment which solely reimburses an employee for medical or medically related expenses incurred by the employee.

For purposes of this paragraph (a)(2), a payment shall be deemed to be made by or due from an employer regardless of whether such payment is made by or due from the employer directly, or indirectly through, among others, a trust, fund, or insurer, to which the employer contributes or pays premiums, and regardless of whether contributions made or due to the trust, fund, insurer or other entity are for the benefit of particular employees or are made on behalf of a group of employees in the aggregate.

      (3) A day of service is each day for which back pay, irrespective of mitigation of damages, has been either awarded or agreed to by the employer. Days of service shall not be credited both under paragraph (a)(1) or paragraph (a)(2), as the case may be, and under this subparagraph. Thus, for example, an employee who receives a back pay award following a determination that he or she was paid at an unlawful rate for days of service previously credited will not be entitled to additional credit for the same days of service. Crediting of days of service for back pay awarded or agreed to with respect to periods described in paragraph (a)(2) shall be subject to the limitations set forth in that paragraph. For example, no more than 63 days of service are required to be credited for payments of back pay, to the extent that such back pay is agreed to or awarded for a period of time during which an employee did not or would not have performed duties.

      (b) *Special rule for determining days of service for reasons other than the performance of duties.* In the case of a payment which is made or due on account of a period during which an employee performs no duties, and which results in the crediting of days of service under paragraph (a)(3) of this section, or, in the case of an award or agreement for back pay, to the extent that such award or agreement is made with respect to a period described in paragraph (a)(2) of this section, the number of days of service to be credited shall be determined as follows:

      (1) *Payments calculated on the basis of units of time.* In the case of a payment made or due which is calculated on the basis of units of time, such as days, weeks or months, the number of days of service to be credited shall be the number of regularly scheduled working days included in the units of time on the basis of which the payment is calculated. For purposes of the preceding sentence, in the case of an employee without a regular work schedule, a plan may provide for the calculation of the number of days of service to be credited on the basis of a 5-day workweek, or may provide for such calculation on any reasonable basis which reflects the average days worked by the employee, or by other employees in the same job classification, over a representative period of time, provided that the basis so used is consistently applied with respect to all employees within the same job classifications, reasonably defined.

      (2) *Payments not calculated on the basis of units of time.* Except as provided in paragraph (b)(3) of this section, in the case of a payment made or due, which is not calculated on the basis of units of time, the number of days of service to be credited shall be equal to the amount of the payment divided by the employee's most recent daily rate of compensation before the period during which no duties are performed.

      (3) *Rule against double credit.* Notwithstanding paragraphs (b)(1) and (2) of this section, an employee is not required to be credited on account of a period during which no duties are performed with a number of days of service which is greater than the number of days regularly scheduled for the performance of duties during such period. For purposes of the preceding sentence, in the case of an employee without a regular work schedule, a plan may provide for the calculation of the number of days of service to be credited to the employee for a period during which no duties are performed on the basis of a 5-day workweek, or may provide for such calculation on any reasonable basis which reflects the average hours worked by the employee, or by other employees in the same job classification, over a representative period of time, provided that the basis so used is consistently applied with respect to all employees in the same job classifications, reasonably defined.

      (c) *Crediting of days of service to computation periods.* (1) Except as provided in paragraph (c)(4) of this section, days of service described in paragraph (a)(1) of this section shall be credited to the computation period in which the duties are performed.

      (2) Except as provided in paragraph (c)(4) of this section, days of service described in paragraph (a)(2) of this section shall be credited as follows:

      (i) Days of service credited to an employee on account of a payment which is calculated on the basis of units of time, such as days, weeks or months, shall be credited to the computation period or computation periods in which the period during which no duties are performed occurs, beginning with the first unit of time to which the payment relates.

      (ii) Days of service credited to an employee by reason of a payment which is not calculated on the basis of units of time shall be credited to the computation period in which the period during which no duties are performed occurs, or if the period during which no duties are performed extends beyond one computation period, such hours of service shall be allocated between not more than the first two computation periods on any reasonable basis which is consistently applied with respect to all employees within the same job classifications, reasonably defined.

      (3) Except as provided in paragraph (c)(4) of this section, days of service described in paragraph (a)(3) of this section shall be credited to the computation period or periods to which the award or agreement for back pay pertains, rather than to the computation period in which the award, agreement or payment is made.

      (4) In the case of days of service to be credited to an employee in connection with a period of no more than 31 days which extends beyond one computation period, all such days of service may be credited to the first computation period or the second computation period. Crediting of days of service under this subparagraph must be done consistently with respect to all employees with the same job classifications, reasonably defined.

      (d) *Other federal law.* Nothing in this section shall be construed to alter, amend, modify, invalidate, impair or supersede any law of the United States or any rule or regulation issued under any such law. Thus, for example, nothing in this section shall be construed as denying an employee credit for a day of service if credit is required by separate federal law. Furthermore, the nature and extent of such credit shall be determined under such law.

      (e) *Nondaily employees.* For maritime employees whose compensation is not determined on the basis of certain amounts for each day worked during a given period, service shall be credited on the basis of hours of service as determined in accordance with §2530.200b-2(a) (including use of any equivalency permitted under §2530.200b-3) or on the basis of elapsed time, as permitted under §2530.200b-9.

      (f) *Plan document.* A plan which credits service on the basis of days of service must state in the plan document the definition of days of service set forth in paragraph (a) of this section, but is not required to state the rules set forth in paragraph (b) and (c) if they are incorporated by reference.

[¶ 14,412G]

§ 2530.200b-8 **Determination of days of service to be credited to maritime employees**.

(a) *General rule*. For the purpose of determining the days of service which must be credited to an employee for a computation period, a plan shall determine days of service from records of days worked and days for which payment is made or due. Any records may be used to determine days of service to be credited to employees under a plan, even though such records are maintained for other purposes, provided that they accurately reflect the actual number of days of service with which an employee is required to be credited under § 2530.200b-7(a). Payroll records, for example, may provide sufficiently accurate data to serve as a basis for determining days of service. If, however, existing records do not accurately reflect the actual number of days of service with which an employee is entitled to be credited, a plan must develop and maintain adequate records. A plan may in any case credit days of service under any method which results in the crediting of no less than the actual number of days of service required to be credited under § 2530.200b-7(a) to each employee in a computation period, even though such method may result in the crediting of days of service in excess of the number of days required to be credited under § 2530.200b-7(a). A plan is not required to prescribe in its documents which records are to be used to determine days of service.

(b) *Determination of pre-effective date days of service*. To the extent that a plan is required to determine days of service completed before the effective date of Part 2 of Title I of the Act (*see* section 211 of the Act), the plan may use whatever records may be reasonably accessible to it and may make whatever calculations are necessary to determine the approximate number of hours of service completed before such effective date. For example, if a plan or an employer maintaining the plan has, or has access to, only the records of compensation of employees for the period before the effective date, it may derive the pre-effective date days of service by using the daily rate for the period or the days customarily worked. If accessible records are insufficient to make an approximation of the number of pre-effective date days of service for a particular employee or group of employees, the plan may make a reasonable estimate of the days of service completed by such employee or employees during the particular period. For example, if records are available with respect to some employees, the plan may estimate the days of service of other employees in the same job classification based on these records. A plan may use the elapsed time method prescribed under § 2530.200b-9 to determine days of service completed before the effective date of Part 2 of Title I of the Act.

⋙→ *Caution: The following regulation was formerly temporary and proposed. It has since been amended, finalized and redesignated as IRS Reg. § 1.410(a)-7 at ¶ 12,162 because of the ERISA Reorganization Plan which transferred jurisdiction of this subject matter to the IRS. The regulation below was subsequently deleted by the DOL from its regulations (45 FR 40987). It is retained here in its temporary and proposed form for historical purposes.*

[¶ 14,413]

§ 2530.200b-9 **Elapsed time**.

(a) *General*. (1) *Introduction to elapsed time method of crediting service*. (i) § 2530.200b-2 sets forth the general method of crediting service for an employee. The general method is based upon the actual counting of hours of service during the applicable 12-consecutive-month computation period. The equivalencies set forth in § 2530.200b-3 are also methods for crediting hours of service during computation periods. Under the general method and the equivalencies, an employee receives a year's credit (in units of years of service or years of participation) for a computation period during which the employee is credited with a specified number of hours of service. In general, an employee's statutory entitlement with respect to eligibility to participate, vesting and benefit accrual is determined by totalling the number of years' credit to which an employee is entitled.

(ii) Under the alternative method set forth in this section, by contrast, an employee's statutory entitlement with respect to eligibility to participate, vesting and benefit accrual is not based upon the actual completion of a specified number of hours of service during a 12-con-

secutive-month period. Instead, such entitlement is determined generally with reference to the total period of time which elapses while the employee is employed (i.e., while the employment relationship exists) with the employer or employers maintaining the plan. The alternative method set forth in this section is designed to enable a plan to lessen the administrative burdens associated with the maintenance of records of an employee's hours of service by permitting each employee to be credited with his or her total period of service with the employer or employers maintaining the plan, irrespective of the actual hours of service completed in any 12-consecutive-month period.

(2) *Overview of the operation of the elapsed time method*. (i) Under the elapsed time method of crediting service, a plan is generally required to take into account the period of time which elapses while the employee is employed (i.e., while the employment relationship exists) with the employer or employers maintaining the plan, regardless of the actual number of hours he or she completes during such period. Under this alternative method of crediting service, an employee's service is required to be taken into account for purposes of eligibility to participate and vesting as of the date he or she first performs an hour of service within the meaning of § 2530.200b-2(a)(1) for the employer or employers maintaining the plan. Service is required to be taken into account for the period of time from the date the employee first performs such an hour of service until the date he or she severs from service with the employer or employers maintaining the plan.

(ii) The date the employee severs from service is the earlier of the date the employee quits, is discharged, retires or dies, or the first anniversary of the date the employee is absent from service for any other reason (e.g., disability, vacation, leave of absence, layoff, etc.). Thus, for example, if an employee quits, the severance from service date is the date the employee quits. On the other hand, if an employee is granted a leave of absence (and if no intervening event occurs), the severance from service date will occur one year after the date the employee was first absent on leave, and this one year of absence is required to be taken into account as service for the employer or employers maintaining the plan. Because the severance from service date occurs on the earlier of two possible dates (i.e., quit, discharge, retirement or death *or* the first anniversary of an absence from service for any other reason), a quit, discharge, retirement or death within the year after the beginning of an absence for any other reason results in an immediate severance from service. Thus, for example, if an employee dies at the end of a four-week absence resulting from illness, the severance from service date is the date of death, rather than the first anniversary date of the first day of absence for illness.

(iii) In addition, for purposes of eligibility to participate and vesting under the elapsed time method of crediting service, an employee who has severed from service by reason of a quit, discharge or retirement may be entitled to have a period of time of 12 months or less taken into account by the employer or employers maintaining the plan if the employee returns to service within a certain period of time and performs an hour of service within the meaning of § 2530.200b-2(a)(1). In general, the period of time during which the employee must return to service begins on the date the employee severs from service as a result of a quit, discharge or retirement and ends on the first anniversary of such date. However, if the employee is absent for any other reason (e.g., layoff) and then quits, is discharged or retires, the period of time during which the employee may return and receive credit begins on the severance from service date and ends one year after the first day of absence (e.g., first day of layoff). As a result of the operation of these rules, a severance from service (e.g., a quit), or an absence (e.g., layoff) followed by a severance from service, never results in a period of time of more than one year being required to be taken into account after an employee severs from service or is absent from service.

(iv) For purposes of benefit accrual under the elapsed time method of crediting service, an employee is entitled to have his or her service taken into account from the date he or she begins to participate in the plan until the severance from service date. Periods of severance under any circumstances are not required to be taken into account. For example, a participant who is discharged on December 14, 1980 and rehired on October 14, 1981 is not required to be credited with the 10 month period of severance for benefit accrual purposes.

(3) *Overview of certain concepts relating to the elapsed time method.* (i) *General.* The rules with respect to the elapsed time method of crediting service are based on certain concepts which are defined in paragraph (b) of this section. These concepts are applied in the substantive rules contained in paragraphs (c), (d), (e), (f) and (g) of this section. The purpose of this subparagraph is to summarize these concepts.

(ii) *Employment commencement date.* (A) A concept which is necessary in order to credit service accurately under any service crediting method is the establishment of a starting point for crediting service. The employment commencement date, which is the date on which an employee first performs an hour of service within the meaning of § 2530.200b-2(a)(1) for the employer or employers maintaining the plan, is used throughout Part 2530 to establish the date upon which an employee must begin to receive credit for certain purposes (e.g. eligibility to participate and vesting).

(B) In order to credit accurately an employee's total service with an employer or employers maintaining the plan, a plan also may provide for an "adjusted" employment commencement date (i.e., a recalculation of the employment commencement date to reflect non-creditable periods of severance) or a reemployment commencement date as defined in paragraph (b)(3) of this section. Fundamentally, all three concepts rely upon the performance of an hour of service to provide a starting point for crediting service. One purpose of these three concepts is to enable plans to satisfy the requirements of this section in a variety of ways.

(C) The fundamental rule with respect to these concepts is that any plan provision is permissible so long as it satisfies the minimum standards. Thus, for example, although the rules of this section provide that credit must begin on the employment commencement date, a plan is permitted to "adjust" the employment commencement date to reflect periods of time for which service is not required to be credited. Similarly, a plan may wish to credit service under the elapsed time method as discrete periods of service and provide for a reemployment commencement date. Certain plans may wish to provide for both concepts, although it is not a requirement of this section that plans so provide.

(iii) *Severance from service date.* Another fundamental concept of the elapsed time method of crediting service is the severance from service date, which is defined as the earlier of the date on which an employee quits, retires, is discharged or dies, or the first anniversary of the first date of absence for any other reason. One purpose of the severance from service date is to provide the endpoint for crediting service under the elapsed time method. As a general proposition, service is credited from the employment commencement date (i.e., the starting point) until the severance from service date (i.e., the endpoint). A complementary purpose of the severance from service date is to establish the starting point for measuring a period of severance from service in order to determine a "break in service" (see paragraph (a)(3)(v) of this section). A third purpose of such date is to establish the starting point for measuring the period of time which may be required to be taken into account under the service spanning rules (see paragraph (a)(3)(vi) of this section).

(iv) *Period of service.* A third elapsed time concept is the use of the "period of service" rather than the "year of service" in determining service to be taken into account for purposes of eligibility to participate, vesting and benefit accrual. For purposes of eligibility to participate and vesting, the period of service runs from the employment commencement date or reemployment commencement date until the severance from service date. For purposes of benefit accrual, a period of service runs from the date that a participant commences participation under the plan until the severance from service date. Because the endpoint of the period of service is marked by the severance from service date, an employee is credited with the period of time which runs during any absence from service (other than for reasons of a quit, retirement, discharge or death) which is 12 months or less. Thus, for example, a three week absence for vacation is taken into account as part of a period of service and does not trigger a severance from service date.

(v) *Period of severance.* A period of severance begins on the severance from service date and ends when an employee returns to

service with the employer or employers maintaining the plan. The purpose of the period of severance is to apply the statutory "break in service" rules to an elapsed time method of crediting service.

(vi) *Service spanning.* Under the elapsed time method of crediting service, a plan is required to credit periods of service and, under the service spanning rules, certain periods of severance of 12 months or less for purposes of eligibility to participate and vesting. Under the first service spanning rule, if an employee severs from service as a result of quit, discharge or retirement and then returns to service within 12 months, the period of severance is required to be taken into account. However, a situation may arise in which an employee is absent from service for any reason other than quit, discharge, retirement or death and during the absence a quit, discharge or retirement occurs. The second service spanning rule provides in that set of circumstances that a plan is required to take into account the period of time between the severance from service date (i.e., the date of quit, discharge or retirement) and the first anniversary of the date on which the employee was first absent, if the employee returns to service on or before such first anniversary date.

(4) *Scope.* (i) Except for certain provisions for which the Secretary of Labor has been specifically authorized to prescribe regulations, regulations prescribed by the Secretary of the Treasury under sections 410 and 411 of the Code shall, pursuant to section 3002(c) of the Act, implement the counterpart provisions of sections 202, 203 and 204 of the Act. Certain provisions for which the Secretary of Labor has been authorized to prescribe regulations relate to the methods for computing service to be credited to an employee, such as the calculation of an hour of service, year of service, year of participation and breaks in service, and such concepts are implemented in Part 2530. Accordingly, because elapsed time represents an alternative method of crediting service, this alternative method is set forth in Part 2530.

(ii) In order to clarify and illustrate the elapsed time method of crediting service, this section restates certain statutory provisions for which the Secretary of the Treasury has been authorized to prescribe regulations. In certain instances, as a result of the nature of the elapsed time method of crediting service, it has been necessary in this section to recast these concepts in a mode consistent with and solely for the purpose of using the elapsed time method. Thus, for example, due to the lack of computation periods under the elapsed time method of crediting service, a plan using elapsed time may disregard service for vesting purposes prior to the date an employee attains the age of 22, while under the general rule under section 203(b)(1)(A) of the Act, 411(a)(4)(A) of the Code and Treasury Department regulations under section 411(a) of the Code, contained in 26 CFR, a plan may disregard service for vesting computation periods prior to the vesting computation period during which an employee attains the age of 22. Except as otherwise expressly provided in this section, the rules applicable to the general methods of crediting service are also applicable to the elapsed time method of crediting service.

(5) *Application of elapsed time method to sections 202, 203 or 204 of the Act and sections 410 and 411 of the Code.* (i) The substantive rules for crediting service under the elapsed time method with respect to eligibility to participate are contained in paragraph (c), the rules with respect to vesting are contained in paragraph (d), and the rules with respect to benefit accrual are contained in paragraph (e). The format of the rules is designed to enable a plan to use the elapsed time method of crediting service either for all purposes or for any one or combination of purposes under Part 2 of Title I of the Act and the counterpart provisions of the Code. Thus, for example, a plan may credit service for eligibility to participate purposes by the use of the general method of crediting service set forth in § 2530.200b-2 or by the use of any of the equivalencies set forth in § 2530.200b-3, while the plan may credit service for vesting and benefit accrual purposes by the use of the elapsed time method of crediting service.

(ii) A plan using the elapsed time method of crediting service for one or more classifications of employees covered under the plan may use the general method of crediting service set forth in § 2530.200b-2 or any of the equivalencies set forth in § 2530.200b-3 for other classifications of employees, provided that such classifications are reasonable and are consistently applied. Thus, for example, a plan may provide that part-time employees are credited under the general method of crediting service set forth in §2530.200b-2 and full-time employees are credited under the elapsed time method. A classification, however, will not be deemed to be reasonable or consistently applied if such classification is designed with an intent to preclude an employee or employees from attaining his or her statutory entitlement with respect to eligibility to participate, vesting or benefit accrual. For example, a classification applied so that any employee credited with less than 1,000 hours of service during a given 12-consecutive-month period would be considered part-time and subject to the general method of crediting service rather than the elapsed time method would not be reasonable.

(iii) Notwithstanding paragraph (a) (5) i and (ii) of this section, the use of the elapsed time method for some purposes or the use of the elapsed time method for some employees may, under certain circumstances result in discrimination prohibited under section 401(a)(4) of the Code, even though the use of the elapsed time method for such purposes and for such employees is permitted under this section.

(b) *Definitions.* (1) *Employment commencement date.* For purposes of this section, the term "employment commencement date" shall mean the date on which the employee first performs an hour of service within the meaning of §2530.200b-2(a)(1) for the employer or employers maintaining the plan.

(2) *Severance from service date.* For purposes of this section, a "severance from service" shall occur on the earlier of—

(i) The date on which an employee quits, retires, is discharged or dies; or

(ii) The first anniversary of the first date of a period in which an employee remains absent from service (with or without pay) with the employer or employers maintaining the plan for any reason other than quit, retirement, discharge or death, such as vacation, holiday, sickness, disability, leave of absence or layoff.

(3) *Reemployment commencement date.* For purposes of this section, the term "reemployment commencement date" shall mean the first date, following a period of severance from service which is not required to take into account under the service spanning rules in paragraphs (c)(2)(iii) and (d)(1)(iii) of this section, on which the employee performs an hour of service within the meaning of paragraph §2530.200b-2(a)(1) for the employer or employers maintaining the plan.

(4) *Participation commencement date.* For purposes of this section, the term "participation commencement date" shall mean the date a participant first commences participation under the plan.

(5) *Period of severance.* For purposes of this section, the term "period of severance" shall mean the period of time commencing on the severance from service date and ending on the date on which the employee again performs an hour of service within the meaning of §2530.200b-2(a)(1) for an employer or employers maintaining the plan.

(6) *Period of service.* (i) *General rule.* For purposes of this section, the term "period of service" shall mean a period of service commencing on the employee's employment commencement date or reemployment commencement date, whichever is applicable, and ending on the severance from service date.

(ii) *Aggregation rule.* Unless a plan provides in some manner for an "adjusted" employment commencement date or similar method of consolidating periods of service, periods of service shall be aggregated unless such periods may be disregarded under section 202(b) or 203(b) of the Act and section 410(a)(5) or 411(a)(4) of the Code.

(iii) *Other federal law.* Nothing in this section shall be construed to alter, amend, modify, invalidate, impair or supersede any law of the United States or any rule or regulation issued under any such law. Thus, for example, nothing in this section shall be construed as denying an employee credit for a "period of service" if credit is required by separate federal law. Furthermore, the nature and extent of such credit shall be determined under such law.

(c) *Eligibility to participate.* (1) *General rule.* For purposes of section 202(a)(1)(A) of the Act and section 410(a)(1)(A) of the Code, a plan generally may not require as a condition of participation in the plan that an employee complete a period of service with the employer or employers maintaining the plan extending beyond the later of—

(i) The date on which the employee attains the age of 25; or

(ii) The date on which the employee completes a one-year period of service.

See regulations, relating to eligibility to participate rules (section 410(a) of the Code), prescribed by the Secretary of the Treasury in 26 CFR.

(2) *Determination of one-year period of service.* (i) For purposes of determining the date on which an employee satisfies the service requirement for initial eligibility to participate under the plan, a plan, using the elapsed time method of crediting service, shall provide that an employee who completes the 1-year period of service requirement on the first anniversary of his employment commencement date satisfies the minimum service requirement as of such date. In the case of an employee who fails to complete a one-year period of service on the first anniversary of his employment commencement date, a plan which does not contain a provision permitted by section 202(b)(4) of the Act and section 410(a)(5)(D) of the Code (rule of parity) shall provide for the aggregation of periods of service so that a one-year period of service shall be completed as of the date the employee completes 12 months of service (30 days are deemed to be a month in the case of the aggregation of fractional months) or 365 days of service.

(ii) For purposes of section 202(a)(1)(B)(i) of the Act and section 410(a)(1)(B)(i) of the Code, a "3-year period of service" shall be deemed to be "3 years of service."

(iii) *Service spanning rules.* In determining a 1-year period of service for purposes of initial eligibility to participate and a period of service for purposes of retention of eligibility to participate, in addition to taking into account an employee's period of service, a plan shall take into account the following periods of severance—

(A) If an employee severs from service by reason of a quit, discharge or retirement and the employee then performs an hour of service within the meaning of §2530.200b-2(a)(1) within 12 months of the severance from service date, the plan is required to take into account the period of severance; and

(B) Notwithstanding paragraph (c)(2)((iii)(A) of this section, if an employee severs from service by reason of a quit, discharge or retirement during an absence from service of 12 months or less for any reason other than a quit, discharge, retirement or death, and then performs an hour of service within the meaning of §2530.200b-2(a)(1) within 12 months of the date on which the employee was first absent from service, the plan is required to take into account the period of severance.

(iv) For purposes of determining an employee's retention of eligibility to participate in the plan, a plan shall take into account an employee's entire period of service unless certain periods of service may be disregarded under section 202(b) of the Act and section 410(a)(5) of the Code.

(v) *Example.* Employee W, age 31, completed 6 months of service and was laid off. After 2 months of layoff, W quit. Five months later, W returned to service. For purposes of eligibility to participate, W was required to be credited with 13 months of service (8 months of service and 5 months of severance). If, on the other hand, W had not returned to service within the first 10 months of severance (i.e., within 12 months after the first day of layoff), W would be required to be credited with eight months of service.

(3) *Entry date requirements.* (i) *General rule.* For purposes of section 202(a)(4) of the Act and section 410(a)(4) of the Code, it is necessary for a plan to provide that any employee who has satisfied the minimum age and service requirements, and who is otherwise entitled to participate in the plan, commences participation in the plan no later than the earlier of—

(A) The first day of the first plan year beginning after the date on which such employee satisfied such requirements, or

(B) The date six months after the date on which he satisfied such requirements, unless such employee was separated from service before the date referred to in subparagraph (A) or (B), whichever is applicable.

(ii) *Separation from service.* (A) *Definition.* For purposes of this section, the term "separated from service" includes a severance from service or an absence from service for any reason other than a quit, discharge, retirement or death, regardless of the duration of such absence. Accordingly, if an employee is laid off for a period of six weeks, the employee shall be deemed to be "separated from service" during such period for purposes of the entry date requirements.

(B) *Application.* A period of severance which is taken into account under the service spanning rules in paragraph (c)(2)(iii) of this section or an absence of 12 months or less may result in an employee satisfying the plan's minimum service requirement during such period of time. In addition, once an employee satisfies the plan's minimum service requirement, either before or during such period of time, such period of time may contain an entry date applicable to such employee. In the case of an employee whose period of severance is taken into account and such period contains an entry date applicable to the employee, he or she shall be made a participant in the plan (if otherwise eligible) no later than the date on which he or she ended the period of severance. In the case of an employee whose period of absence contains an entry date applicable to such employee, he or she, no later than the date such absence ended, shall be made a participant in the plan (if otherwise eligible) as of the first applicable entry date which occurred during such absence from service.

(iii) *Examples.* For purposes of the following examples, assume that the plan provides for a minimum age requirement of 25 and a minimum service requirement of one year, and provides for semiannual entry dates.

(A) Employee A, age 35, worked for 10 months in a job classification covered under the plan, became disabled for nine consecutive months and then returned to service. During the period of absence, A completed a 1-year period of service and passed a semiannual entry date after satisfying the minimum service requirement. Accordingly, the plan is required to make A a participant no later than his return to service effective as of the applicable entry date.

(B) Employee B, after satisfying the minimum age and service requirements, quit work before the next semi-annual entry date, and then returned to service before incurring a 1-year period of severance, but after such semi-annual entry date. Employee B is entitled to become a participant immediately upon his return to service effective as of the date of his return.

See regulations, relating to eligibility to participate rules (Section 410(a) of the Code), prescribed by the Secretary of the Treasury in 26 CFR.

(4) *Break in service.* For purposes of applying the break in service rules under sections 202(b)(2) and (3) of the Act and sections 410(a)(5)(B) and (C) of the Code, the term "1-year period of severance" shall be substituted for the term "1-year break in service." A 1-year period of severance shall be determined on the basis of a 12-consecutive-month period beginning on the severance from service date and ending on the first anniversary of such date provided that the employee during such 12-consecutive-month period does not perform an hour of service within the meaning of §2530.200b-2(a)(1) for the employer or employers maintaining the plan.

(5) *One-year hold-out.* (i) *General rule.* (A) For purposes of section 202(b)(3) of the Act and section 410(a)(5)(C) of the Code, in determining the period of service of an employee who has incurred a 1-year period of severance, a plan may disregard the employee's period of service before such period of severance until the employee completes a 1-year period of service after such period of severance.

(B) *Example.* Assume that a plan provides for a minimum service requirement of 1 year and provides for semi-annual entry dates, but does not contain the provisions permitted by section 202(b)(4) of the Act and section 410(a)(5)(D) of the Code (relating to the rule of parity). Employee G, age 40, completed a seven-month period of service, quit and then returned to service 15 months later, thereby incurring a 1-year period of severance. After working four months, G was laid off for nine months and then returned to work again. Although the

plan may hold employee G out from participation in the plan until the completion of a 1-year period of service after the 1-year (or greater) period of severance, once the 1-year hold-out is completed the plan is required to provide the employee with such statutory entitlement as arose during the 1-year hold-out. Accordingly, employee G satisfied the 1-year of service requirement as of the first month of layoff, and G is entitled to become a participant in the plan immediately upon his return to service after the nine month layoff effective as of the first applicable entry date occurring after the date on which he satisfied the 1-year of service requirement (i.e., the first applicable entry date after the first month of layoff).

See regulations, relating to eligibility to participate rules (Section 410(a) of the Code), prescribed by the Secretary of the Treasury in 26 CFR.

(6) *Rule of parity.* (i) *General rule.* For purposes of section 202(b)(4) of the Act and section 410(a)(5)(D) of the Code, in the case of a participant who does not have any nonforfeitable right under the plan to his accrued benefit derived from employer contributions and who incurs a 1-year period of severance, a plan, in determining an employee's period of service for purposes of section 202(a)(1) of the Act and section 410(a)(1) of the Code, may disregard his period of service if his latest period of severance equals or exceeds his prior period of service, whether or not consecutive, completed before such period of severance.

(ii) In determining whether a completely nonvested employee's service may be disregarded under the rule of parity, a plan is not permitted to apply the rule until the employee incurs a 1-year period of severance. Accordingly, a plan may not disregard a period of service of less than one year until an employee has incurred a period of severance of at least one year.

(iii) *Example.* Assume that a plan provides for a minimum service requirement of one year and provides for the rule of parity. An employee works for three months, quits and then is rehired 10 months later. Such employee is entitled to receive 13 months of credit for purposes of eligibility to participate and vesting (see service spanning rules). Although the period of severance exceeded the period of service, the three months of service may not be disregarded because no 1-year period of severance occurred.

See regulations, relating to eligibility to participate rules (Section 410(a) of the Code), prescribed by the Secretary of the Treasury in 26 CFR.

(d) *Vesting.* (1) *General rule.* (i) For purposes of section 203(a)(2) of the Act and section 411(a)(2) of the Code, relating to vesting in accrued benefits derived from employer contributions, a plan, which determines service to be taken in account on the basis of elapsed time, shall provide that an employee is credited with a number of years of service equal to at least the number of whole years of the employee's period of service, whether or not such periods of service were completed consecutively.

(ii) In order to determine the number of whole years of an employee's period of service, a plan shall provide that nonsuccessive periods of service must be aggregated and that less than whole year periods of service (whether or not consecutive) must be aggregated on the basis that 12 months of service (30 days are deemed to be a month in the case of the aggregation of fractional months) or 365 days of service equal a whole year of service.

(iii) *Service spanning rules.* In determining a participant's period of service for vesting purposes, a plan shall take into account the following periods of severance—

(A) If an employee severs from service by reason of a quit, discharge or retirement and the employee then performs an hour of service within the meaning of §2530.200b-2(a)(1) within 12 months of the severance from service date, the plan is required to take into account the period of severance; and

(B) Notwithstanding subparagraph (d)(1)((iii)(A) of this section, if an employee severs from service by reason of a quit, discharge or retirement during an absence from service of 12 months or less for any reason other than a quit, discharge, retirement or death, and then performs an hour of service within the meaning of §2530.200b-2(a)(1) within 12 months of the date on which the employee was first absent from service, the plan is required to take into account the period of severance.

(iv) For purposes of determining an employee's nonforfeitable percentage of accrued benefits derived from employer contributions, a plan, after calculating an employee's period of service in the manner prescribed in this paragraph, may disregard any remaining less than whole year, 12-month or 365-day period of service. Thus, for example, if a plan provides for the statutory five to fifteen year graded vesting, an employee with a period (or periods) of service which yield 5 whole year periods of service and an additional 321-day period of service is twenty-five percent vested in his or her employer-derived accrued benefits (based solely on the 5 whole year periods of service).

(2) *Service which may be disregarded.* (i) For purposes of section 203(b)(1) of the Act and section 411(a)(4) of the Code, in determining the nonforfeitable percentage of an employee's right to his or her accrued benefits derived from employer contributions, all of an employee's period or periods of service with an employer or employers maintaining the plan shall be taken into account unless such service may be disregarded under paragraph (d)(2)(ii) of this section.

(ii) For purposes of paragraph (d)(2)(i) of this section, the following periods of service may be disregarded—

(A) The period of service completed by an employee before the date on which he attains age 22;

(B) In the case of a plan which requires mandatory employee contributions, the period of service which falls within the period of time to which a particular employee contribution relates if the employee had the opportunity to make a contribution for such period of time and failed to do so;

(C) The period of service during any period for which the employer did not maintain the plan or a predecessor plan;

(D) The period of service which is not required to be taken into account by reason of a period of severance which constitutes a break in service within the meaning of paragraph (d)(4) of this section;

(E) The period of service completed by an employee prior to January 1, 1971, unless the employee completes a period of service of at least 3 years at any time after December 31, 1970; and

(F) The period of service completed before the first plan year for which this section applies to the plan, if such service would have been disregarded under the plan rules relating to breaks in service.

See regulations, relating to service which may be disregarded (Section 411(a) of the Code), prescribed by the Secretary of the Treasury in 26 CFR.

(3) *Seasonal industry.* (Reserved.)

(4) *Break in service.* For purposes of applying the break in service rules, the term "1-year period of severance" shall be substituted for the term "1-year break in service." A 1-year period of serverance shall be a 12-consecutive-month period beginning on the severance from service date and ending on the first anniversary of such date, provided that the employee during such 12-consecutive-month period fails to perform an hour of service within the meaning of § 2530.200b-2(a)(1) for an employer or employers maintaining the plan.

(5) *One-year hold-out.* For purposes of section 203(b)(3)(B) of the Act and section 411(a)(6)(B) of the Code, in determining the nonforfeitable percentage of the right to accrued benefits derived from employer contributions of an employee who has incurred a 1-year period of severance, the period of service completed before such period of severance is not required to be taken into account until the employee has completed a 1-year period of service after his return to service.

See regulations, relating to vesting rules (Section 411(a) of the Code), prescribed by the Secretary of the Treasury under 26 CFR.

(6) *Vesting in pre-break accruals.* For purposes of section 203(b)(3)(C) of the Act and section 411(a)(6)(C) of the Code, a "1-year period of severance" shall be deemed to constitute a "1-year break in service."

See regulations, relating to vesting rules (Section 411(a) of the Code), prescribed by the Secretary of the Treasury under 26 CFR.

(7) *Rule of parity.* (i) *General rule.* For purposes of section 203(b)(3)(D) of the Act and section 411(a)(6)(D) of the Code, in the case of an employee who is a nonvested participant in employer-derived benefits at the time he incurs a 1-year period of severance, the period of service completed by such participant before such period of severance is not required to be taken into account for purposes of determining the vested percentage of his or her right to employer-derived benefits if at such time the consecutive period of severance equals or exceeds his prior period of service, whether or not consecutive, completed before such period of severance.

See regulations, relating to vesting rules (Section 411(a) of the Code), prescribed by the Secretary of Treasury under 26 CFR.

(e) *Benefit accrual.* (1) For purposes of section 204 of the Act and section 411(b) of the Code, a plan may provide that a participant's service with an employer or employers maintaining the plan be determined on the basis of the participant's total period of service beginning on the participation commencement date and ending on the severance from service date.

(2) Under section 204(b)(3)(A) of the Act and section 411(b)(3)(A) of the Code, a defined benefit pension plan may determine an employee's service for purposes of benefit accrual on any basis which is reasonable and consistent and which takes into account all service during the employee's participation in the plan which is included in a period of service required to be taken into account under section 202(b) of the Act and section 410(a) of the Code (relating to service which must be taken into account for purposes of determining an employee's eligibility to participate). A plan which provides for the determination of an employee's service with an employer or employers maintaining the plan on the basis permitted under paragraph (e)(1) of this section will be deemed to meet the requirements of section 204(b)(3)(A) of the Act and section 411(b)(3)(A) of the Code, provided that the plan meets the requirements of § 2530.204-3, relating to plans which determine an employee's service for purposes of benefit accrual on a basis other than computation periods. Specifically, under § 2530.204-3, it must be possible to provide that, despite the fact that benefit accrual under such a plan is not based on computation periods, the plan's provisions meet at least one of the three benefit accrual rules of section 204(b)(1) of the Act and section 411(b)(1) of the Code under all circumstances. Further, § 2530.204-3 prohibits such a plan from disregarding service under section 204(b)(3)(C) of the Act and section 411(b)(3)(C) of the Code (which would otherwise permit a plan to disregard service performed by an employee during a computation period in which the employee is credited with less than 1,000 hours).

See regulations, relating to benefit accrual rules (Section 411(b) of the Code), prescribed by the Secretary of the Treasury under 26 CFR.

(f) *Transfers between methods of crediting service*

(1) *Single plan.* A plan may provide that an employee's service for purposes of eligibility to participate, vesting or benefit accrual shall be determined on the basis of computation periods under the general method set forth in § 2530.200b-1 for certain classes of employees but under the alternative method permitted under this section for other classes of employees if the plan provides as follows—

(i) In the case of an employee who transfers from a class of employees whose service is determined on the basis of computation periods to a class of employees whose service is determined on the alternative basis permitted under this section, the employee shall receive credit, as of the date of the transfer, for a period of service consisting of—

(A) A number of years equal to the number of years of service credited to the employee before the computation period during which the transfer occurs; and

(B) The greater of (1) the period of time beginning on the first day of the computation period during which the transfer occurs and ending on the date of such transfer or (2) the service taken into account under the computation periods method as of the date of the transfer.

If the period of service for which an employee receives credit under this paragraph (f)(1)(i) consists of the total of the periods of service determined under paragraph (f)(1)(i)(A) plus paragraph (f)(1)(i)(B)(1) of this section, the employee shall receive credit for service subsequent to the transfer commencing on the date the transfer occurs. If such period of service consists of the total of the amounts of service determined under paragraph (f)(1)(i)(A) plus paragraph (f)(1)(i)(B)(2) of this section, the employee shall receive credit for service subsequent to the transfer commencing on the day after the last day of the computation during which the transfer occurred.

(ii) In the case of an employee who transfers from a class of employees whose service is determined on the alternative basis permitted under this section to a class of employees whose service is determined on the basis of computation periods—

(A) The employee shall receive credit, as of the date of the transfer, for a number of years of service equal to the number of 1-year periods of service credited to the employee as of the date of the transfer, and

(B) The employee shall receive credit in the computation period which includes the date of the transfer, for a number of hours of service determined by applying one of the equivalencies set forth in § 2530.200b-4(e)(1) to any fractional part of a year credited to the employee under this section as of the date of the transfer. Such equivalency shall be set forth in the plan and shall apply to all similarly situated employees.

(2) *More than one plan*. In the case of an employee who transfers from a plan using either the general method of determining service on the basis of computation periods set forth in § 2530.200b-1 or the method of determining service permitted under this section to a plan using the other method of determining service, all service required to be credited under the plan to which the employee transfers shall be determined under the method of determining service used by such plan. Accordingly, to the extent that service credited to the employee under the plan from which he or she transfers must also be credited to the employee under the plan to which he or she transfers, such service must be redetermined under the latter plan.

(g) *Amendments to change method of crediting service*. A plan may be amended to change the method of crediting service for any purpose or for any class of employees between the general method set forth in § 2530.200b-1 and the method permitted under this section, if such amendment contains provisions under which each employee with respect to whom the method of crediting service is changed is treated in the same manner as an employee who transfers from one class of employees to another under paragraph (f)(1) of this section.

[¶ 14,414]

§ 2530.201-1　**Coverage; general**.

Coverage of the provisions of Part 2 of Title I of the Act is determined under a multiple step process. First, the plan must be an employee benefit plan as defined under section 3(3) of the Act and § 2510.3-3. (See also the definitions of employee welfare benefit plan, section 3(1) of the Act and § 2510.3-1 and employee pension benefit plan, section 3(2) of the Act and § 2510.3-2.) Second, the employee benefit plan must be subject to Title I of the Act. Coverage for Title I is specified in section 4 of the Act. Third, section 201 of the Act specifies the employee benefit plans subject to Title I which are not subject to the minimum standards of Part 2 of Title I of the Act. Section 2530.201-2 specifies the employee benefit plans subject to Title I of the Act which are exempted from coverage under Part 2 of Title I of the Act and this Part (2530).

[¶ 14,415]

§ 2530.201-2　**Plans covered by part 2530**.

This part (2530) shall apply to any employee benefit plan described in section 4(a) of the Act (and not exempted under section 4(b)) other than—

(a) An employee welfare benefit plan as defined in section 3(1) of the Act and § 2510.3-1;

(b) A plan which is unfunded and is maintained by an employer primarily for the purpose of providing deferred compensation for a select group of management or highly compensated employees;

(1) (Reserved.)

(2) (Reserved.)

(c) A plan established and maintained by a society, order, or association described in section 501(c)(8) or (9) of the Code, if no part of the contributions to or under such plan are made by employers of participants in such plan;

(d) A trust described in section 501(c)(18) of the Code:

(e) A plan which is established and maintained by a labor organization described in section 501(c)(5) of the Code and which does not at any time after the date of enactment of the Act provide for employer contributions;

(f) An agreement providing payments to a retired partner or a deceased partner's successor in interest, as described in section 736 of the Code;

(g) An individual retirement account or annuity described in section 408 of the Code, or a retirement bond described in section 409 of the Code;

(h) An excess benefit plan as described in section 3(36) of the Act.

[¶ 14,420]
MINIMUM PARTICIPATION STANDARDS

Act Sec. 202. (a)(1)(A) No pension plan may require, as a condition of participation in the plan, that an employee complete a period of service with the employer or employers maintaining the plan extending beyond the later of the following dates—

(i) the date on which the employee attains the age of 21; or

(ii) the date on which he completes 1 year of service.

(B)(i) In the case of any plan which provides that after not more than 2 years of service each participant has a right to 100 percent of his accrued benefit under the plan which is nonforfeitable at the time such benefit accrues, clause (ii) of subparagraph (A) shall be applied by substituting "2 years of service" for "1 year of service".

(ii) In the case of any plan maintained exclusively for employees of an educational organization (as defined in section 170(b)(1)(A)(ii) of the Internal Revenue Code of 1986) by an employer which is exempt from tax under section 501(a) of such Code, which provides that each participant having at least 1 year of service has a right to 100 percent of his accrued benefit under the plan which is nonforfeitable at the time such benefit accrues, clause (i) of subparagraph (A) shall be applied by substituting "26" for "21". This clause shall not apply to any plan to which clause (i) applies.

(2) No pension plan may exclude from participation (on the basis of age) employees who have attained a specified age.

(3)(A) For purposes of this section, the term "year of service" means a 12-month period during which the employee has not less than 1,000 hours of service. For purposes of this paragraph, computation of any 12-month period shall be made with reference to the date on which the employee's employment commenced, except that, in accordance with regulations prescribed by the Secretary, such computation may be made by reference to the first day of a plan year in the case of an employee who does not complete 1,000 hours of service during the 12-month period beginning on the date his employment commenced.

(B) In the case of any seasonal industry where the customary period of employment is less than 1,000 hours during a calendar year, the term "year of service" shall be such period as may be determined under regulations prescribed by the Secretary.

(C) For purposes of this section, the term "hour of service" means a time of service determined under regulations prescribed by the Secretary.

(D) For purposes of this section, in the case of any maritime industry, 125 days of service shall be treated as 1,000 hours of service. The Secretary may prescribe regulations to carry out the purposes of this subparagraph.

(4) A plan shall be treated as not meeting the requirements of paragraph (1) unless it provides that any employee who has satisfied the minimum age and service requirements specified in such paragraph, and who is otherwise entitled to participate in the plan, commences participation in the plan no later than the earlier of—

(A) the first day of the first plan year beginning after the date on which such employee satisfied such requirements, or

(B) the date 6 months after the date on which he satisfied such requirements, unless such employee was separated from the service before the date referred to in subparagraph (A) or (B), whichever is applicable.

Act Sec. 202. (b)(1) Except as otherwise provided in paragraphs (2), (3), and (4), all years of service with the employer or employers maintaining the plan shall be taken into account in computing the period of service for purposes of subsection (a)(1).

(2) In the case of any employee who has any 1-year break in service (as defined in section 203(b)(3)(A)) under a plan to which the service requirements of clause (i) of subsection (a)(1)(B) apply, if such employee has not satisfied such requirements, service before such break shall not be required to be taken into account.

(3) In computing an employee's period of service for purposes of subsection (a)(1) in the case of any participant who has any 1-year break in service (as defined in section 203(b)(3)(A)), service before such break shall not be required to be taken into account under the plan until he has completed a year of service (as defined in subsection (a)(3)) after his return.

(4)(A) For purposes of paragraph (1), in the case of a nonvested participant, years of service with the employer or employers maintaining the plan before any period of consecutive 1-year breaks in service shall not be required to be taken into account in computing the period of service if the number of consecutive 1-year breaks in service within such period equals or exceeds the greater of—

(i) 5, or

(ii) the aggregated number of years of service before such period.

(B) If any years of service are not required to be taken into account by reason of a period of breaks in service to which subparagraph (A) applies, such years of service shall not be taken into account in applying subparagraph (A) to a subsequent period of breaks in service.

(C) For purposes of subparagraph (A), the term "nonvested participant" means a participant who does not have any nonforfeitable right under the plan to an accrued benefit derived from employer contributions.

(5)(A) In the case of each individual who is absent from work for any period—

(i) by reason of the pregnancy of the individual,

(ii) by reason of the birth of a child of the individual,

(iii) by reason of the placement of a child with the individual in connection with the adoption of such child by such individual, or

(iv) for purposes of caring for such child for a period beginning immediately following such birth or placement,

the plan shall treat as hours of service, solely for purposes of determining under this subsection whether a 1-year break in service (as defined in section 203(b)(3)(A)) has occurred, the hours described in subparagraph (B).

(B) The hours described in this subparagraph are—

(i) the hours of service which otherwise would normally have been credited to such individual but for such absence, or

(ii) in any case in which the plan is unable to determine the hours described in clause (i), 8 hours of service per day of such absence,

except that the total number of hours treated as hours of service under this subparagraph by reason of any such pregnancy or placement shall not exceed 501 hours.

(C) The hours described in subparagraph (B) shall be treated as hours of service as provided in this paragraph—

(i) only in the year in which the absence from work begins, if a participant would be prevented from incurring a 1-year break in service in such year solely because the period of absence is treated as hours of service as provided in subparagraph (A); or

(ii) in any other case, in the immediately following year.

(D) For purposes of this paragraph, the term "year" means the period used in computations pursuant to section 202(a)(3)(A).

(E) A plan may provide that no credit will be given pursuant to this paragraph unless the individual furnishes to the plan administrator such timely information as the plan may reasonably require to establish—

(i) that the absence from work is for reasons referred to in subparagraph (A), and

(ii) the number of days for which there was such an absence.

Amendments

P.L. 101-239, §7891(a)(1):

Titles I, III, and IV of ERISA (other than sections 3(37)(E), 301(a)(7), and 308, the last sentence of section 408(d), and sections 414(c), 4001(a)(3)(ii), and 4303) are each amended by striking "Internal Revenue Code of 1954" each place it appears and inserting "Internal Revenue Code of 1986" effective October 22, 1986.

P.L. 101-239, §7892(a):

Amended ERISA Sec. 202(a)(2) by striking out the comma.

P.L. 101-239, §7894(c)(2)(A):

Amended ERISA Sec. 202(a)(1)(B)(ii) by striking "institution" and inserting "organization" effective September 2, 1974.

P.L. 101-239, §7894(c)(2)(B):

Amended ERISA Sec. 202(b)(2) by striking "the plan" and inserting "a plan" effective September 2, 1974.

P.L. 99-514, §1113(d)(3):

Amended ERISA Sec. 202(a)(1)(B)(i) by striking out "3 years" and substituting "2 years" instead, effective for plan years beginning after 1988, but subject to the special rules of Act Sec. 1113(e)[(f)](2) and (3), which provide:

(2) SPECIAL RULE FOR COLLECTIVE BARGAINING AGREEMENTS.—In the case of a plan maintained pursuant to 1 or more collective bargaining agreements between employee representatives and 1 or more employers ratified before March 1, 1986, the amendments made by this section shall not apply to employees covered by any such agreement in plan years beginning before the earlier of—

(A) the later of—

(i) January 1, 1989, or

(ii) the date on which the last of such collective bargaining agreements terminates (determined without regard to any extension thereof after February 28, 1986), or

(B) January 1, 1991.

(3) PARTICIPATION REQUIRED.—The amendments made by this section shall not apply to any employee who does not have 1 hour of service in any plan year to which the amendments made by this section apply.

P.L. 99-509; §9203(a)(1):

Amended ERISA Sec. 202(a)(2) by striking out "unless" and all that followed and inserting a period. This amendment is effective with respect to plan years beginning on or after January 1, 1988 and only with respect to service performed on or after such date. See also §9204(c) at ¶14,440 (amendment notes). Prior to amendment, Sec. (a)(2) read as follows:

(2) No pension plan may exclude from participation (on the basis of age) employees who have attained a specified age, unless—

(A) the plan is a—

(i) defined benefit plan, or

(ii) target benefit plan (as defined under regulations prescribed by the Secretary of the Treasury), and

(B) such employees begin employment with the employer after they have attained a specified age which is not more than 5 years before the normal retirement age under the plan.

P.L. 98-397, §102:

Act Sec. 102(a)(1) amended ERISA Sec. 202(a)(1)(A)(i) by striking out "25" and inserting in lieu thereof "21."

Act. Sec. 102(a)(2) amended ERISA Sec. 202(a)(1)(B)(ii) by striking out "'30' for '25'" and inserting in lieu thereof "'26' for '21'."

Act. Sec. 102(d)(1) amended ERISA Sec. 202(b)(4) by striking out the prior law and replacing it with new paragraph (4). Prior to amendment, ERISA Sec. 202(b)(4) read as follows:

(4) In the case of an employee who does not have any nonforfeitable right to an accrued benefit derived from employer contributions, years of service with the employer or employers maintaining the plan before a break in service shall not be required to be taken into account in computing the period of service for purposes of subsection (a)(1) if the number of consecutive 1-year breaks in service equals or exceeds the aggregate number of such years of service before such break. Such aggregate number

of years of service before such break shall be deemed not to include any years of service not required to be taken into account under this paragraph by reason of any prior break in service.

Act Sec. 102(e) amended ERISA Sec. 202(b) by adding at the end thereof a new paragraph (5) to read as above.

The above amendments are generally effective for plan years beginning after December 31, 1984. However, Act Sec. 303(a)(1) and (2) provide the following:

SEC. 303. TRANSITIONAL RULES.

(a) Amendments Relating to Vesting Rules; Breaks in Service; Maternity or Paternity Leave.—

(1) Minimum Age for Vesting.—The amendments made by sections 102(b) and 202(b) shall apply in the case of participants who have at least 1 hour of service under

the plan on or after the first day of the first plan year of which the amendments made by this Act apply.

(2) Break in Service Rules.—If, as of the day before the first day of the first plan year to which the amendments made by this Act apply, section 202(a) or (b) or 203(b) of the Employee Retirement Income Security Act of 1974 or section 410(a) or 411(a) of the Internal Revenue Code of 1954 (as in effect on the day before the date of the enactment of this Act) would not require any service to be taken into account, nothing in the amendments made by subsections (c) and (d) of section 102 of this Act and subsections (c) and (d) of section 202 of this Act shall be construed as requiring such service to be taken into account under such section 202(a) or (b), 203(b), 410(a), or 411(a); as the case may be.

Also, see Act Sec. 302(b) for a special rule for collective bargaining agreements at ¶ 14,250.09.

Regulations

The following regulations were adopted under "Title 29—Labor," "Chapter XXV—Pension and Welfare Benefit Programs, Department of Labor," "Subchapter C—Minimum Standards for Employee Pension Benefit Plans Under the Employee Retirement Income Security Act of 1974," "Part 2530—Rules and Regulations for Minimum Standards for Employee Pension Benefit Plans." The regulations were filed with the Federal Register on December 23, 1976, and published in the Federal Register of December 28, 1976 (41 FR 56462).

Subpart B—Participation, Vesting and Benefit Accrual

[¶ 14,421]

§ 2530.202-1 **Eligibility to participate; general.**

(a) Section 202 of the Act and section 410 of the Code contain minimum participation standards relating to certain employee pension benefit plans. In general, an employee pension benefit plan may not require, as a condition of participation in the plan, that an employee complete a period of service with the employer or employers maintaining the plan in excess of limits established by section 202 of the Act and section 410 of the Code and the regulations issued thereunder. Service for this purpose is measured in units of years of service. Section 2530.202-2 sets forth rules relating to the computation periods which a plan must use to determine whether an employee has completed a year of service for purposes of eligibility to participate ("eligibility computation periods").

(b) For rules relating to service with the employer or employers maintaining the plan, see § 2530.210.

[¶ 14,422]

§ 2530.202-2 **Eligibility computation period.**

(a) *Initial eligibility computation period*. For purposes of section 202(a)(1)(A)(ii) of the Act and section 410(a)(1)(A)(ii) of the Code, the initial eligibility computation period the plan must use is the 12-consecutive-month-period beginning on the employment commencement date. An employee's employment commencement date is the first day for which the employee is entitled to be credited with an hour of service described in § 2530.200b-2(a)(1) for an employer maintaining the plan. (For establishment of a reemployment commencement date following a break in service, see § 2530.200b-4(b)(1)(iii) and (iv)).

(b) *Eligibility computation periods after the initial eligibility computation period*. In measuring years of service for purposes of eligibility to participate after the initial eligibility computation period, a plan may adopt either of the following alternatives:

(1) A plan may designate 12-consecutive-month periods beginning on the first anniversary of an employee's employment commencement date and succeeding anniversaries thereof as the eligibility computation period after the initial eligibility computation period; or

(2) A plan may designate plan years beginning with the plan year which includes the first anniversary of an employee's employment commencement date as the eligibility computation period after the initial eligibility computation period (without regard to whether the employee is entitled to be credited with 1000 hours of service during such period), provided that an employee who is credited with 1000 hours of service in both the initial eligibility computation period and the plan year which includes the first anniversary of the employee's employment commencement date is credited with two years of service for purposes of eligibility to participate.

(c) *Service prior to a break in service*. For purposes of applying section 202(b)(4) of the Act and section 410(a)(5)(D) of the Code (relating to years of service completed prior to a break in service for purposes of eligibility to participate), the computation periods used by a plan in determining years of service before such break shall be the

eligibility computation periods established in accordance with paragraphs (a) and (b) of this section.

(d) *Plans with three-year 100 percent vesting*. A plan which, under 202(a)(1)(B)(i) of the Act and section 410a(1)(B)(i) of the Code, requires more than one year of service for eligibility to participate in the plan shall use an initial eligibility computation period established under paragraph (a) of this section and eligibility computation periods designated in accordance with paragraph (b) of this section. Thus, for the eligibility computation period after the initial eligibility computation period, such a plan may designate either eligibility computation periods beginning on anniversaries of an employee's employment commencement date or plan years beginning with the plan year which includes the anniversary of the first day of the initial eligibility computation period.

(e) *Alternative eligibility computation period*. The following rule is designed primarily for a plan using a recordkeeping system which does not permit the plan to identify an employee's employment commencement date (or, in the case of an employee who has incurred a one-year break in service, the employee's reemployment computation date), but which does permit the plan to identify a period of no more than 31 days during which the employee's employment commencement date (or reemployment commencement date) occurred.

(1) A plan may be an initial eligibility computation period (or initial computation period for measuring completion of a year of service upon an employee's return after a one-year break in service) beginning on the first day of a period of no more than 31 days during which an employee's employment commencement date (or reemployment commencement date) occurs and ending on the anniversary of the last day of such period.

(2) If a plan uses an initial eligibility computation period (or initial computation period for measuring completion of a year of service upon an employee's return after a one-year break in service) permitted under paragraph (e)(1) of this section, the plan shall use the following computation periods after the initial computation period:

(i) If the plan does not use plan years for computation periods after the initial computation period, the plan shall use computation periods beginning on anniversaries of the first day of the initial computation period and ending on anniversaries of the last day of the initial computation period, and including a period of at least 12 consecutive months.

(ii) If the plan uses plan years for computation periods after the initial computation period, the plan shall use plan years beginning with the plan year which includes the anniversary of the first day of the initial computation period.

(3) For purposes of determining an employee's commencement of participation under section 202(a)(4) of the Act and section 410(a)(4) of the Code, regardless of whether an eligibility computation period permitted under this paragraph includes a period longer than 12 consecutive months, an employee who completes 1000 hours of service in such eligibility computation period shall be treated as having satisfied the plan's service requirement for eligibility to participate as of the last day of the 12-consecutive-month period beginning on the first day of such eligibility computation period. In the case of a plan described in section 202(a)(1)(B)(i) of the Act and section 410(a)(1)(B)(i) of the

Code, the requirement of the preceding sentence shall apply only with respect to the last year of service required under the plan for eligibility to participate.

(4) *Example.* A plan maintained by Employer X obtains records from X which indicate the number of hours worked by an employee during a monthly payroll period. The records do not, however, break down the number of hours worked by an employee by days. Thus, after a new employee has begun employment with X it is impossible for the plan to ascertain the employee's employment commencement date from the records furnished by X (although it is possible for the plan to determine the month during which an employee's employment commencement date occurred). For administrative convenience, in conjunction with the equivalency based on hours worked permitted under §2530.200b-3(d)(1), and with the method of crediting hours of service to computation periods set forth in §2530.200b-2(c)(4), the plan uses the alternative initial eligibility computation period permitted under this paragraph. The plan provides that an employee's initial eligibility computation period shall be the period beginning on the first day of the first monthly payroll period for which the employee is entitled to credit for the performance of duties and ending on the last day of the monthly payroll period which includes the anniversary of the last day of the initial monthly payroll period. This condition ensures that the initial eligibility computation period will include the 12-consecutive-month

period beginning on the employee's employment commencement date and ending on the day before the anniversary of the employee's employment commencement date. If, however, an employee completes the plan's requirement of one year of service for eligibility to participate (i.e., completion of 870 hours worked in an eligibility computation period) in the initial eligibility computation period, the plan provides that the employee is deemed to have satisfied the plan's service requirements for eligibility to participate as of the day before the anniversary of the first day of the initial eligibility computation period. This provision ensures that no employee who has in fact completed 1000 hours of service in the 12-consecutive-month period beginning on the employee's employment commencement date will be admitted to participation later than the date specified under section 202(a)(4) of the Act and section 410(a)(4) of the Code. For example, in the case of an employee who begins employment in January, 1977, the employee's initial eligibility computation period begins on January 1, 1977 and ends on January 31, 1978. If the employee completes 879 hours worked in the initial eligibility computation period, the employee is treated as having met the plan's service requirements for eligibility to participate as of December 31, 1977. If the plan provides for semi-annual entry dates of January 1 and July 1, and the employee has met any eligibility requirements of the plan other than the minimum service requirements as of December 31, 1977, the plan must provide that the employee commences participation as of January 1, 1978.

[¶14,430]
MINIMUM VESTING STANDARDS

Act Sec. 203. (a) Each pension plan shall provide that an employee's right to his normal retirement benefit is nonforfeitable upon the attainment of normal retirement age and in addition shall satisfy the requirements of paragraphs (1) and (2) of this subsection.

(1) A plan satisfies the requirements of this paragraph if an employee's rights in his accrued benefit derived from his own contributions are nonforfeitable.

(2) Except as provided in paragraph (4), a plan satisfies the requirements of this paragraph if it satisfies the requirements of subparagraph (A) or (B).

(A) A plan satisfies the requirements of this subparagraph if an employee who has completed at least 5 years of service has a nonforfeitable right to 100 percent of the employee's accrued benefit derived from employer contributions.

(B) A plan satisfies the requirements of this subparagraph if an employee has a nonforfeitable right to a percentage of the employee's accrued benefit derived from employer contributions determined under the following table:

Years of service:	The nonforfeitable percentage is:
3	20
4	40
5	60
6	80
7 or more	100

(3)(A) A right to an accrued benefit derived from employer contributions shall not be treated as forfeitable solely because the plan provides that it is not payable if the participant dies (except in the case of a survivor annuity which is payable as provided in section 205).

(B) A right to an accrued benefit derived from employer contributions shall not be treated as forfeitable solely because the plan provides that the payment of benefits is suspended for such period as the employee is employed, subsequent to the commencement of payment of such benefits—

(i) in the case of a plan other than a multiemployer plan, by an employer who maintains the plan under which such benefits were being paid; and

(ii) in the case of a multiemployer plan, in the same industry, in the same trade or craft, and the same geographic area covered by the plan, as when such benefits commenced.

The Secretary shall prescribe such regulations as may be necessary to carry out the purposes of this subparagraph, including regulations with respect to the meaning of the term "employed".

(C) A right to an accrued benefit derived from employer contributions shall not be treated as forfeitable solely because plan amendments may be given retroactive application as provided in section 302(c)(8).

(D)(i) A right to an accrued benefit derived from employer contributions shall not be treated as forfeitable solely because the plan provides that, in the case of a participant who does not have a nonforfeitable right to at least 50 percent of his accrued benefit derived from employer contributions, such accrued benefit may be forfeited on account of the withdrawal by the participant of any amount attributable to the benefit derived from mandatory contributions (as defined in the last sentence of section 204(c)(2)(C)) made by such participant.

(ii) Clause (i) shall not apply to a plan unless the plan provides that any accrued benefit forfeited under a plan provision described in such clause shall be restored upon repayment by the participant of the full amount of the withdrawal described in such clause plus, in the case of a defined benefit plan, interest. Such interest shall be computed on such amount at the rate determined for purposes of section 204(c)(2)(C) (if such subsection applies) on the date of such repayment (computed annually from the date of such withdrawal). The plan provision required under this clause may provide that such repayment must be made (I) in the case of a withdrawal on account of separation from service, before the earlier of 5 years after the first date on which the participant is subsequently re-employed by the employer, or the close of the first period of 5 consecutive 1-year breaks in service commencing after the withdrawal; or (II) in the case of any other withdrawal, 5 years after the date of the withdrawal.

(iii) In the case of accrued benefits derived from employer contributions which accrued before the date of the enactment of this Act, a right to such accrued benefit derived from employer contributions shall not be treated as forfeitable solely because the plan provides that an amount of such accrued benefit may be forfeited on account of the withdrawal by the participant of an amount attributable to the benefit derived from mandatory contributions, made by such participant before the date of the enactment of this Act if such amount forfeited is proportional to such amount withdrawn. This clause shall not apply to any plan to which any mandatory contribution is made after the date of the enactment of this Act. The Secretary of the Treasury shall prescribe such regulations as may be necessary to carry out the purposes of this clause.

(iv) For purposes of this subparagraph, in the case of any class-year plan, a withdrawal of employee contributions shall be treated as a withdrawal of such contributions on a plan year by plan year basis in succeeding order of time.

(v) CROSS REFERENCE.. **For nonforfeitability where the employee has a nonforfeitable right to at least 50 percent of his accrued benefit, see section 206(c).**

(E)(i) A right to an accrued benefit derived from employer contributions under a multiemployer plan shall not be treated as forfeitable solely because the plan provides that benefits accrued as a result of service with the participant's employer before the employer had an obligation to contribute under the plan may not be payable if the employer ceases contributions to the multiemployer plan.

(ii) A participant's right to an accrued benefit derived from employer contributions under a multiemployer plan shall not be treated as forfeitable solely because—

(I) the plan is amended to reduce benefits under section 4244A or 4281, or

(II) benefit payments under the plan may be suspended under section 4245 or 4281.

(F) A matching contribution (within the meaning of section 401(m) of the Internal Revenue Code of 1986) shall not be treated as forfeitable merely because such contribution is forfeitable if the contribution to which the matching contribution relates is treated as an excess contribution under section 401(k)(8)(B) of such Code, an excess deferral under section 402(g)(2)(A) of such Code, or an excess aggregate contribution under section 401(m)(6)(B) of such Code.

(4) In the case of matching contributions (as defined in section 401(m)(4)(A) of the Internal Revenue Code of 1986), paragraph (2) shall be applied—

(A) by substituting "3 years" for "5 years" in subparagraph (A), and

(B) by substituting the following table for the table contained in subparagraph (B):

Years of service:	The nonforfeitable percentage is:
2	20
3	40
4	60
5	80
6 or more	100.

Act Sec. 203.(b)(1) In computing the period of service under the plan for purposes of determining the nonforfeitable percentage under subsection (a)(2), all of an employee's years of service with the employer or employers maintaining the plan shall be taken into account, except that the following may be disregarded:

(A) years of service before age 18,

(B) years of service during a period for which the employee declined to contribute to a plan requiring employee contributions;

(C) years of service with an employer during any period for which the employer did not maintain the plan or a predecessor plan, defined by the Secretary of the Treasury;

(D) service not required to be taken into account under paragraph (3);

(E) years of service before January 1, 1971, unless the employee has had at least 3 years of service after December 31, 1970;

(F) years of service before this part first applies to the plan if such service would have been disregarded under the rules of the plan with regard to breaks in service, as in effect on the applicable date; and

(G) in the case of a multiemployer plan, years of service—

(i) with an employer after—

(I) a complete withdrawal of such employer from the plan (within the meaning of section 4203); or

(II) to the extent permitted by regulations prescribed by the Secretary of the Treasury, a partial withdrawal described in section 4205(b)(2)(A)(i) in connection with the decertification of the collective bargaining representative; and

(ii) with any employer under the plan after the termination date of the plan under section 4048.

(2)(A) For purposes of this section, except as provided in subparagraph (C), the term "year of service" means a calendar year, plan year, or other 12-consecutive-month period designated by the plan (and not prohibited under regulations prescribed by the Secretary) during which the participant has completed 1,000 hours of service.

(B) For purposes of this section, the term "hour of service" has the meaning provided by section 202(a)(3)(C).

(C) In the case of any seasonal industry where the customary period of employment is less than 1,000 hours during a calendar year, the term "year of service" shall be such period as determined under regulations of the Secretary.

(D) For purposes of this section, in the case of any maritime industry, 125 days of service shall be treated as 1,000 hours of service. The Secretary may prescribe regulations to carry out the purposes of this subparagraph.

(3)(A) For purposes of this paragraph, the term "1-year break in service" means a calendar year, plan year, or other 12-consecutive-month period designated by the plan (and not prohibited under regulations prescribed by the Secretary) during which the participant has not completed more than 500 hours of service.

(B) For purposes of paragraph (1), in the case of any employee who has any 1-year break in service, years of service before such break shall not be required to be taken into account until he has completed a year of service after his return.

(C) For purposes of paragraph (1), in the case of any participant in an individual account plan or an insured defined benefit plan which satisfies the requirements of subsection 204(b)(1)(F) who has 5 consecutive 1-year breaks in service, years of service after such 5-year period shall not be required to be taken into account for purposes of determining the nonforfeitable percentage of his accrued benefit derived from employer contributions which accrued before such 5-year period.

(D)(i) For purposes of paragraph (1), in the case of a nonvested participant, years of service with the employer or employers maintaining the plan before any period of consecutive 1-year breaks in service shall not be required to be taken into account if the number of consecutive 1-year breaks in service within such period equals or exceeds the greater of—

(I) 5, or

(II) the aggregate number of years of service before such period.

(ii) If any years of service are not required to be taken into account by reason of a period of breaks in service to which clause (i) applies, such years of service shall not be taken into account in applying clause (i) to a subsequent period of breaks in service.

(iii) For purposes of clause (i), the term "nonvested participant" means a participant who does not have any nonforfeitable right under the plan to an accrued benefit derived from employer contributions.

(E)(i) In the case of each individual who is absent from work for any period—

(I) by reason of the pregnancy of the individual,

(II) by reason of the birth of a child of the individual,

(III) by reason of the placement of a child with the individual in connection with the adoption of such child by such individual, or

(IV) for purposes of caring for such child for a period beginning immediately following such birth or placement,

the plan shall treat as hours of service, solely for purposes of determining under this paragraph whether a 1-year break in service has occurred, the hours described in clause (ii).

(ii) The hours described in this clause are—

(I) the hours of service which otherwise would normally have been credited to such individual but for such absence, or

(II) in any case in which the plan is unable to determine the hours described in subclause (I), 8 hours of service per day of absence,

except that the total number of hours treated as hours of service under this clause by reason of pregnancy or placement shall not exceed 501 hours.

(iii) The hours described in clause (ii) shall be treated as hours of service as provided in this subparagraph—

(I) only in the year in which the absence from work begins, if a participant would be prevented from incurring a 1-year break in service in such year solely because the period of absence is treated as hours of service as provided in clause (i); or

(II) in any other case, in the immediately following year.

(iv) For purposes of this subparagraph, the term "year" means the period used in computations pursuant to paragraph (2).

(v) A plan may provide that no credit will be given pursuant to this subparagraph unless the individual furnishes to the plan administrator such timely information as the plan may reasonably require to establish—

(I) that the absence from work is for reasons referred to in clause (i), and

(II) the number of days for which there was such an absence.

(4) Cross references.—

(A) For definitions of "accrued benefit" and "normal retirement age", see sections 3 (23) and (24).

(B) For effect of certain cash out distributions, see section 204(d)(1).

Act Sec. 203.(c)(1)(A) A plan amendment changing any vesting schedule under the plan shall be treated as not satisfying the requirements of subsection (a)(2) if the nonforfeitable percentage of the accrued benefit derived from employer contributions (determined as of the later of the date such amendment is adopted, or the date such amendment becomes effective) of any employee who is a participant in the plan is less than such nonforfeitable percentage computed under the plan without regard to such amendment.

(B) A plan amendment changing any vesting schedule under the plan shall be treated as not satisfying the requirements of subsection (a)(2) unless each participant having not less than 3 years of service is permitted to elect, within a reasonable period after adoption of such amendment, to have his nonforfeitable percentage computed under the plan without regard to such amendment.

(2) Subsection (a) shall not apply to benefits which may not be provided for designated employees in the event of early termination of the plan under provisions of the plan adopted pursuant to regulations prescribed by the Secretary of the Treasury to preclude the discrimination prohibited by section 401(a)(4) of the Internal Revenue Code of 1986.

(3)(A) The requirements of subsection (a)(2) shall be treated as satisfied in the case of a class-year plan if such plan provides that 100 percent of each employee's right to or derived from the contributions of the employer on the employee's behalf with respect to any plan year is nonforfeitable not later than when such participant was performing services for the employer as of the close of each of 5 plan years (whether or not consecutive) after the plan year for which the contributions were made.

(B) For purposes of subparagraph (A) if—

(i) any contributions are made on behalf of a participant with respect to any plan year, and

(ii) before such participant meets the requirements of subparagraph (A), such participant was not performing services for the employer as of the close of any of 5 consecutive plan years after such plan year,

then the plan may provide that the participant forfeits any right to or derived from the contributions made with respect to such plan year.

(C) For purposes of this part, the term "class year plan" means a profit-sharing, stock bonus, or money purchase plan which provides for the separate nonforfeitability of employees' rights to or derived from the contributions for each plan year.

Act Sec. 203. (d) A pension plan may allow for nonforfeitable benefits after a lesser period and in greater amounts than are required by this part.

Act Sec. 203.(e)(1) If the present value of any nonforfeitable benefit with respect to a participant in a plan exceeds $5,000, the plan shall provide that such benefit may not be immediately distributed without the consent of the participant.

(2) For purposes of paragraph (1), the present value shall be calculated in accordance with section 205(g)(3).

(3) This subsection shall not apply to any distribution of dividends to which section 404(k) of the Internal Revenue Code of 1986 applies.

(4) A plan shall not fail to meet the requirements of this subsection if, under the terms of the plan, the present value of the nonforfeitable accrued benefit is determined without regard to that portion of such benefit which is attributable to rollover contributions (and earnings allocable thereto). For purposes of this subparagraph, the term "rollover contributions" means any rollover contribution under sections 402(c), 403(a)(4), 403(b)(8), 408(d)(3)(A)(ii), and 457(e)(16) of the Internal Revenue Code of 1986.

Amendments

P.L. 108-311, §408(b)(8):

Amended ERISA §203(b)(4) by adding "or more" after "6" in the last line of the table.

P.L. 107-16, §633(b)(1):

Act Sec. 633(b)(1) amended ERISA Sec. 203(a)(2) by striking "A plan" and inserting "Except as provided in paragraph (4), a plan".

P.L. 107-16, §633(b)(2):

Act Sec. 633(b)(2) amended ERISA Sec. 203(a) by adding subsection (4) at the end to read as above.

P.L. 107-16, §633(c):

Act Sec. 633(c) governs the effective date of the above amendments:

"(c) Effective Dates.—

(1) In general.—Except as provided in paragraph (2), the amendments made by this section shall apply to contributions for plan years beginning after December 31, 2001.

(2) Collective bargaining agreements.—In the case of a plan maintained pursuant to one or more collective bargaining agreements between employee representatives and one or more employers ratified by the date of the enactment of this Act, the amendments made by this section shall not apply to contributions on behalf of employees covered by any such agreement for plan years beginning before the earlier of—

(A) the later of—

(i) the date on which the last of such collective bargaining agreements terminates (determined without regard to any extension thereof on or after such date of the enactment); or

(ii) January 1, 2002; or

(B) January 1, 2006.

(3) Service required.—With respect to any plan, the amendments made by this section shall not apply to any employee before the date that such employee has 1 hour of service under such plan in any plan year to which the amendments made by this section apply."

P.L. 107-16, §648(a)(2):

Act Sec. 648(a)(2) amended ERISA Sec. 203(e) by adding subsection (4) at the end to read as above.

The above amendment applies to distributions after December 31, 2001.

P.L. 105-34, §1071(b)(1):

Act Sec. 1071(b)(1) amended ERISA Sec. 203(e)(1) by striking "$3,500" and inserting "$5,000".

The above amendment is effective for plan years beginning after August 5, 1997.

P.L. 104-188, §1442(b):

Act Sec. 1442(b) amended ERISA Sec. 203(a)(2) by striking "subparagraph (A), (B), or (C)" and inserting "subparagraph (A) or (B)"; and by striking subparagraph (C). Prior to amendment, ERISA Sec. 203(a)(2)(C) read as follows:

(C) A plan satisfies the requirements of this subparagraph if—

(i) the plan is a multiemployer plan (within the meaning of section 3(37)), and

(ii) under the plan—

(I) an employee who is covered pursuant to a collective bargaining agreement described in section 3(37)(A)(ii) and who has completed at least 10 years of service has a nonforfeitable right to 100 percent of the employee's accrued benefit derived from employer contributions, and

(II) the requirements of subparagraph (A) or (B) are met with respect to employees not described in subclause (I).

The above amendments apply to plan years beginning on or after the earlier of:

(1) the later of—

(A) January 1, 1997, or

(B) the date on which the last of the collective bargaining agreements pursuant to which the plan is maintained terminates (determined without regard to any extension thereof after the date of the enactment of this Act), or

(2) January 1, 1999.

Such amendments shall not apply to any individual who does not have more than 1 hour of service under the plan on or after the 1st day of the 1st plan year to which such amendments apply.

P.L. 103-465, §767(c)(1):

Act Sec. 767(c)(1) amended ERISA Sec. 203(e)(2) to read as above. Prior to amendment, ERISA Sec. 203(e)(2) read as follows:

(2)(A) For purposes of paragraph (1), the present value shall be calculated—

(i) by using an interest rate no greater than the applicable interest rate if the vested accrued benefit (using such rate) is not in excess of $25,000, and

(ii) by using an interest rate no greater than 120 percent of the applicable interest rate if the vested accrued benefit exceeds $25,000 (as determined under clause (i)).

In no event shall the present value determined under subclause (II) be less than $25,000.

(B) For purposes of subparagraph (A), the term "applicable interest rate" means the interest rate which would be used (as of the date of the distribution) by the Pension Benefit Guaranty Corporation for purposes of determining the present value of a lump-sum distribution on plan termination.

The above amendment applies to plan years and limitation years beginning after December 31, 1994, except that an employer may elect to treat the amendments made by this section as being effective on or after December 8, 1994. For special rules, see Act Sec. 767(e)(2)-(3), below.

Act Sec. 767(e)(2)-(3) provides:

(2) NO REDUCTION IN ACCRUED BENEFITS.—A participant's accrued benefit shall not be considered to be reduced in violation of section 411(d)(6) of the Internal Revenue Code of 1986 or section 204(g) of the Employee Retirement Income Security Act of 1974 merely because (A) the benefit is determined in accordance with section 417(e)(3)(A) of such Code, as amended by this Act, or section 205(g)(3) of the Employee Retirement Income Security Act of 1974, as amended by this Act or (B) the plan applies section 415(b)(2)(E) of such Code, as amended by this Act.

(3) SECTION 415.

(A) NO REDUCTION REQUIRED.—An accrued benefit shall not be required to be reduced below the accrued benefit as of the last day of the last plan year beginning before January 1, 1995, merely because of the amendments made by subsection (b).

(B) TIMING OF PLAN AMENDMENT.—A plan that operates in accordance with the amendments made by subsection (b) shall not be treated as failing to satisfy section 401(a) of the Internal Revenue Code of 1986 or as not being operated in accordance with the provisions of the plan until such date as the Secretary of the Treasury provides merely because the plan has not been amended to include the amendments made by subsection (b).

P.L. 101-239, §7861(a)(1):

Amended ERISA Sec. 203(a)(2) by striking "following" the first place it appears and by striking "414(f)(1)(B)" in subparagraph (C)(ii)(I) and inserting "3(37)(A)(ii)".

P.L. 101-239, §7861(a)(2):

Amended P.L. 99-514, §1113(e)(3) by striking "Section 202(B)(i)" and inserting "Section 202(a)(1)(B)(i)".

P.L. 101-239, §7861(a)(3):

Redesignated the second subsection (e) of P.L. 99-514, §1113 as subsection (f).

P.L. 101-239, §7861(a)(4):

Added a new paragraph (4) to P.L. 99-514, §1113(f).

If years of service equal or exceed—

5	....
6	....
7	....
8	....
9	....
10	....

(ii) Notwithstanding clause (i), a plan shall not be treated as satisfying the requirements of this subparagraph unless any participant who has completed at least 10 years of service has a nonforfeitable right to not less than 50 percent of his accrued benefit derived from employer contributions and to not less than an additional 10 percent for each additional year of service thereafter.

P.L. 101-239, §7861(a)(5)(B):

Amended ERISA Sec. 203(a)(3) by adding a new subparagraph (F) to read as above.

P.L. 101-239, §7861(a)(6)(B):

Amended ERISA Sec. 203(b)(1)(A) to read as above. Prior to amendment, ERISA Sec. 203(b)(1)(A) read as follows:

(A) years of service before age 18, except that in the case of a plan which does not satisfy subparagraph (A) or (B) of subsection (a)(2), the plan may not disregard any such year of service during which the employee was a participant;

P.L. 101-239, §7862(d)(5) and (10):

Amended ERISA Sec. 203(e)(1) to read as above. Previously the subsection read as follows:

(e)(1) If the present value of any vested accrued benefit exceeds $3,500, a pension plan shall provide that such benefit may not be immediately distributed without the consent of the participant.

The above amendments are effective October 22, 1986.

P.L. 101-239, §7891(a)(1):

Titles I, III, and IV of ERISA (other than sections 3(37)(E), 301(a)(7), and 308, the last sentence of section 408(d), and sections 414(c), 4001(a)(3)(ii), and 4303) are each amended by striking "Internal Revenue Code of 1954" each place it appears and inserting "Internal Revenue Code of 1986" effective October 22, 1986.

P.L. 101-239, §7891(b)(2):

Amended ERISA Sec. 203(e)(2)(B) by striking "APPLICABLE INTEREST RATE.—" effective October 22, 1986.

P.L. 101-239, §7894(c)(3):

Amended ERISA Sec. 203(a)(3)(D)(v) by striking "**nonforfeitably**" and inserting "**nonforfeitability**" effective September 2, 1974.

P.L. 99-514, §1113(d)(4)(A):

Amended ERISA Sec. 203(c)(1)(B) by striking out "5 years" and inserting "3 years" instead.

P.L. 99-514, §1113(e)(1):

Amended paragraph 2 to read as above in section 203(a). Prior to amendment, paragraph (2) read as follows:

(2) A plan satisfies the requirement of this paragraph if it satisfies the requirements of subparagraph (A), (B), or (C).

(A) A plan satisfies the requirements of this subparagraph if an employee who has at least 10 years of service has a nonforfeitable right to 100 percent of his accrued benefit derived from employer contributions.

(B) A plan satisfies the requirements of this subparagraph if an employee who has completed at least 5 years of service has a nonforfeitable right to a percentage of his accrued benefit derived from employer contributions which percentage is not less than the percentage determined under the following table:

Years of service:	Nonforfeitable percentage
5	25
6	30
7	35
8	40
9	45
10	50
11	60
12	70
13	80
14	90
15 or more	100

(C)(1) A plan satisfies the requirements of this subparagraph if a participant who is not separated from the service, who has completed at least 5 years of service, and with respect to whom the sum of his age and years of service equals or exceeds 45, has a nonforfeitable right to a percentage of his accrued benefit derived from employer contributions determined under the following table:

and sum of age and service equals or exceeds—	then the nonforfeitable percentage is—
45	50
47	60
49	70
51	80
53	90
55	100

P.L. 99-514, §1113(e)(2):

Struck out paragraph (3), section 203(c). Prior to its repeal, paragraph (3) read as follows:

Act Sec. 203. (c) * * *

(3) The requirements of subsection (a)(2) shall be deemed to be satisfied in the case of a class year plan if such plan provides that 100 percent of each employee's right to or

derived from the contributions of the employer on his behalf with respect to any plan year are nonforfeitable not later than the end of the 5th plan year following the plan year for which such contributions were made. For purposes of this part, the term "class year plan" means a profit sharing, stock bonus, or money purchase plan which provides for the separate nonforfeitability of employees' rights to or derived from the contributions for each plan year.

P.L. 99-514, § 1113(f):

Section (f) provides as follows:

(f) EFFECTIVE DATES.—

(1) IN GENERAL.—Except as provided in paragraph (2), the amendments made by this section shall apply to plan years beginning after December 31, 1988.

(2) SPECIAL RULE FOR COLLECTIVE BARGAINING AGREEMENTS.—In the case of a plan maintained pursuant to 1 or more collective bargaining agreements between employee representatives and 1 or more employers ratified before March 1, 1986, the amendments made by this section shall not apply to employees covered by any such agreement in plan years beginning before the earlier of—

(A) the later of—

(i) January 1, 1989, or

(ii) the date on which the last of such collective bargaining agreements terminates (determined without regard to any extension thereof after February 28, 1986), or

(B) January 1, 1991.

(3) PARTICIPATION REQUIRED.—The amendments made by this section shall not apply to any employee who does not have 1 hour of service in any plan year to which the amendments made by this section apply.

(4) REPEAL OF CLASS YEAR VESTING.—If a plan amendment repealing class year vesting is adopted after October 22, 1986, such amendment shall not apply to any employee for the 1st plan year to which the amendments made by subsections (b) and (e)(2) apply (and any subsequent plan year) of—

(A) such plan amendment would reduce the nonforfeitable right of such employee for such year, and

(B) such employee has at least 1 hour of service before the adoption of such plan amendment and after the beginning of such 1st plan year.

This paragraph shall not apply to an employee who has 5 consecutive 1-year breaks in service (as defined in section 411(a)(6)(A) of the Internal Revenue Code of 1986) which include the 1st day of the 1st plan year to which the amendments made by subsection (b) and (e)(2) apply. A plan shall not be treated as failing to meet the requirements of section 401(a)(26) of such Code by reason of complying with the provisions of this paragraph.

P.L. 99-514, § 1139(c)(1):

Amended ERISA Sec. 203(e)(2) to read as above. Prior to amendment, ERISA Sec. 203(e)(2) read as follows:

(2) For purposes of paragraph (1), the present value shall be calculated by using an interest rate not greater than the interest rate which would be used (as of the date of the distribution) by the Pension Benefit Guaranty Corporation for purposes of determining the present value of a lump-sum distribution on plan termination.

The above amendment applies to distributions in plan years beginning after December 31, 1984, except that such amendments shall not apply to any distributions in plan years beginning after December 31, 1984, and before January 1, 1987, if such distributions were made in accordance with the requirements of the regulations issued under the Retirement Equity Act of 1984. However, for a special rule, see Act Sec. 1139(d)(2) below.

Act Sec. 1139(d)(2) provides:

(2) Reduction in Accrued Benefits.—

(A) In General.—If a plan—

(i) adopts a plan amendment before the close of the first plan year beginning on or before January 1, 1989, which provides for the calculation of the present value of the accrued benefit in the manner provided by the amendments made by this section, and

(ii) the plan reduces the accrued benefits for any plan year to which such plan amendment applies in accordance with such plan amendment,

such reduction shall not be treated as a violation of section 411(d)(6) of the Internal Revenue Code of 1986 or section 204(g) of the Employee Retirement Income Security Act of 1974 (29 U.S.C. 1054(g)).

(B) Special Rule.—In the case of a plan maintained by a corporation incorporated on April 11, 1934, which is headquartered in Tarrant County, Texas—

(i) such a plan may be amended to remove the option of an employee to receive a lump sum distribution (within the meaning of section 402(e)(5) of such Code) if such amendment—

(I) is adopted within 1 year of the date of the enactment of this Act, and

(II) is not effective until 2 years after the employees are notified of such amendment, and

(ii) the present value of any vested accrued benefit of such plan determined during the 3-year period beginning on the date of the enactment of this Act shall be determined under the applicable interest rate (within the meaning of section 411(a)(11)(B)(ii) of such Code), except that if such value (as so determined) exceeds $50,000, then the value of any excess over $50,000 shall be determined by using the interest rate specified in the plan as of August 16, 1986.

P.L. 99-514, § 1898(a)(1)(B):

Amended ERISA Sec. 203(c)(3) to read as above. The amendment is to take effect according to the provision of Act Sec. 1898(a)(1)(C) which provides:

(C) EFFECTIVE DATE.—The amendments made by this paragraph shall apply to contributions made for plan years beginning after the date of the enactment of this Act; except that, in the case of a plan described in section 302(b) of the Retirement Equity Act of 1984, such amendments shall not apply to any plan year to which the amendments made by such Act do not apply by reason of such section 302(b).

P.L. 99-514, § 1898(a)(4)(B)(i):

Amended ERISA Sec. 203(a)(3)(D)(ii), last sentence, to read as above. This amendment is effective for plan years beginning after 1984. Prior to amendment, the last sentence read as follows:

In the case of a defined contribution plan the plan provision required under this clause may provide that such repayment must be made before the participant has any 1-year break in service commencing after the withdrawal.

P.L. 99-514, § 1898(d)(1)(B):

Amended ERISA Sec. 203(e)(1) to read as above. This amendment is effective for plan years beginning after 1984. Prior to amendment, paragraph (1) read as follows:

Act Sec. 203. (e)(1) If the present value of any accrued benefit exceeds $3,500, such benefit shall not be treated as nonforfeitable if the plan provides that the present value of such benefit could be immediately distributed without the consent of the participant.

P.L. 99-514, § 1898(d)(2)(B):

Amended ERISA Sec. 203(e)(3) to read as above, effective for distributions made after 1984.

P.L. 98-397, §§ 102 and 105:

Act Sec. 102(b) amended ERISA Sec. 203(b)(1)(A) by striking out "22" and inserting "18" in its place.

For the effective date of the above amendment, see Act Sec. 303(a)(1) which is reproduced in the amendment notes to ERISA Sec. 202 at ¶ 102.

Act Sec. 102(c) amended ERISA Sec. 203(b)(3)(C): (1) by striking out "any 1-year break in service" and inserting in lieu thereof "5 consecutive 1-year breaks in service", and (2) by striking out "such break" each place it appeared and inserting in lieu thereof "such 5-year period".

Act Sec. 102(d)(2) amended ERISA Sec. 203(b)(3)(D) by striking out the prior law and replacing it with new subparagraph (D). Prior to amendment, ERISA Sec. 203(b)(3)(D) read as follows:

(D) For purposes of paragraph (1), in the case of a participant who, under the plan, does not have any nonforfeitable right to an accrued benefit derived from employer contributions, years of service before any 1-year break in service shall not be required to be taken into account if the number of consecutive 1-year breaks in service equals or exceeds the aggregate number of such years of service prior to such break. Such aggregate number of years of service before such break shall be deemed not to include any years of service not required to be taken into account under this subparagraph by reason of any prior break in service.

Act Sec. 102(e)(2) amended ERISA Sec. 203(b)(3) by adding at the end thereof new subparagraph (E) to read as above.

Act Sec. 105(a) added new ERISA Sec. 203(e) to read as above.

The above amendments generally are effective for plan years beginning after December 31, 1984.

However, Act Secs. 303(a)(3) and (b) provide:

(a)(3) Maternity or Paternity Leave.—The amendments made by sections 102(e) and 202(e) shall apply in the case of absences from work which begin on or after the first day of the first plan year to which the amendments made by this Act apply.

(b) Special Rule for Amendments Relating to Maternity or Paternity Absences.—If a plan is administered in a manner which would meet the amendments made by sections 102(e) and 202(e) (relating to certain maternity or paternity absences not treated as breaks in service), such plan need not be amended to meet such requirements until the earlier of—

(1) the date on which such plan is first otherwise amended after the date of the enactment of this Act, or

(2) the beginning of the first plan year beginning after December 31, 1986.

Also, see Act Sec. 302(b) for a special rule for collecting bargaining agreements at ¶ 14,250.09.

P.L. 96-364, § 303:

Added new subsections 203(a)(3)(E) and 203(b)(1)(G), effective September 26, 1980.

Regulations

The following regulations were adopted on December 23, 1976, and were published in the Federal Register of December 28, 1976 (41 FR 56462). Reg. § 2530.203-3 was adopted on January 26, 1981, and was published in the Federal Register of January 27, 1981 (46 FR 8894). The regulation was due to take effect on May 27, 1981, but the effective date was delayed until final amendments to the regulation were adopted. The amendments were adopted on December 1, 1981 (46 FR 59243), and, accordingly, the regulation is effective January 1, 1982.

§ 2530.203-1 **Vesting; general.**

(a) Section 203 of the Act and section 411(a) of the Code contain minimum vesting standards relating to certain employee pension benefit plans. In general, a pension plan subject to section 203 of the Act or section 411(a) of the Code must meet certain requirements relating to an employee's nonforfeitable ("vested") right to his or her normal retirement benefit. One of these requirements specifies that an employee's accrued benefit derived from employer contributions must be vested in accordance with certain schedules. The schedules (or alternative minimum vesting standards) are generally based on the employee's number of years of service with the employer or employers maintaining the plan. Section 2530.203-2 sets forth rules relating to the computation periods used to determine whether an employee has completed a year of service for vesting purposes ("vesting computation periods").

(b) For rules relating to service with the employer or employers maintaining the plan, *see* § 2530.210.

§ 2530.203-2 **Vesting computation period.** (a) *Designation of vesting computation periods.* Except as provided in paragraph (b) of this section, a plan may designate any 12-consecutive-month period as the vesting computation period. The period so designated must apply equally to all participants. This requirement may be satisfied even though the actual 12-consecutive-month periods are not the same for all employees (e.g., if the designated vesting computation period is the 12-consecutive-month period beginning on an employee's employment commencement date and anniversaries of that date). The plan is prohibited, however, from using any period that would result in artificial postponement of vesting credit, such as a period measured by anniversaries of the date four months following the employment commencement date.

(b) *Plans with 3-year 100 percent vesting.* For rules regarding when a participant has a nonforfeitable right to his accrued benefit, see section 202(a)(1)(B)(i) of the Act and 410(a)(1)(B)(i) of the Code and regulations issued thereunder.

(c) *Amendments to change the vesting computation period.* (1) A plan may be amended to change the vesting computation period to a different 12-consecutive-month period provided that as a result of such change no employee's vested percentage of the accrued benefit derived from employer contributions is less on any date after such change than such vested percentage would be in the absence of such change. A plan amendment changing the vesting computation period shall be deemed to comply with the requirements of this subparagraph if the first vesting computation period established under such amendment begins before the last day of the preceding vesting computation period and an employee who is credited with 1,000 hours of service in both the vesting computation period under the plan before the amendment and the first vesting computation period under the plan as amended is credited with 2 years of service for those vesting computation periods. For example, a plan which has been using a calendar year vesting computation period is amended to provide for a July 1—June 30 vesting computation period starting in 1977. Employees who complete more than 1,000 hours of service in both of the 12-month periods extending from January 1, 1977 to December 31, 1977 and from July 1, 1977 to June 30, 1978 are advanced two years on the plan's vesting schedule. The plan is deemed to meet the requirements of this subparagraph.

(2) For additional requirements pertaining to changes in the vesting schedule, see section 203(c)(1) of the Act and section 411(a)(10) of the Code and the regulations issued thereunder.

(d) *Service preceding a break in service.* For purposes of applying section 203(b)(3)(D) of the Act and section 411(a)(6)(D) of the Code (relating to counting years of service before a break in service for vesting purposes), the computation periods used by the plan in computing years of service before such break must be the vesting computation periods. (For application of the break in service rules, see section 203(b)(3)(D) and section 411 (a)(6)(D) of the Code and regulations issued thereunder.)

§ 2530.203-3 **Suspension of pension benefits upon reemployment of retirees.** (a) *General.* Section 203(a)(3)(B) of the Act provides that the right to the employer-derived portion of an accrued pension benefit shall not be treated as forfeitable solely because an employee pension benefit plan provides that the payment of benefits is suspended during certain periods of reemployment which occur subsequent to the commencement of payment of such benefits. This section sets forth the circumstances and conditions under which such benefit payments may be suspended. A plan may provide for the suspension of pension benefits which commence prior to the attainment of normal retirement age, or for the suspension of that portion of pension benefits which exceeds the normal retirement benefit, or both, for any reemployment and without regard to the provisions of section 203(a)(3)(B) and this regulation to the extent (but only to the extent) that suspension of such benefits does not affect a retiree's entitlement to normal retirement benefits payable after attainment of normal retirement age, or the actuarial equivalent thereof.

(b) *Suspension rules.* (1) *General rule.* A plan may provide for the permanent withholding of an amount which does not exceed the suspendible amount of an employee's accrued benefit for each calendar month, or for each four or five week payroll period ending in a calendar month, during which an employee is employed in "section 203(a)(3)(B) service" as described in § 2530.203-3(c).

[Amended by F.R. Doc. 81-34837 on December 1, 1981 (46 FR 59243)]

(2) *Resumption of payments.* If benefit payments have been suspended pursuant to paragraph (b)(1) of this section, payments shall resume no later than the first day of the third calendar month after the calendar month in which the employee ceases to be employed in section 203(a)(3)(B) service: *Provided,* That the employee has complied with any reasonable procedure adopted by the plan for notifying the plan that he has ceased such employment. The initial payment upon resumption shall include the payment scheduled to occur in the calendar month when payments resume and any amounts withheld during the period between the cessation of employment and the resumption of payments, less any amounts which are subject to offset.

(3) *Offset rules.* A plan which provides for the permanent withholding of benefits may deduct from benefit payments to be made by the plan payments previously made by the plan during those calendar months or pay periods in which the employee was employed in section 203(a)(3)(B) service, *Provided,* That such deduction or offset does not exceed in any one month 25 percent of that month's total benefit payment which would have been due but for the offset (excluding the initial payment described in paragraph (b)(2) of this section, which may be subject to offset without limitation).

[Amended by F.R. Doc. 81-34837 on December 1, 1981 (46 FR 59243)]

(4) *Notification.* No payment shall be withheld by a plan pursuant to this section unless the plan notifies the employee by personal delivery or first class mail during the first calendar month or payroll period in which the plan withholds payments that his benefits are suspended. Such notification shall contain a description of the specific reasons why benefit payments are being suspended, a general description of the plan provisions relating to the suspension of payments, a copy of such provisions, and a statement to the effect that applicable Department of Labor regulations may be found in § 2530.203-3 of the Code of Federal Regulations. In addition, the suspension notification shall inform the employee of the plan's procedure for affording a review of the suspension of benefits. Requests for such reviews may be considered in accordance with the claims procedure adopted by the plan pursuant to section 503 of the Act and applicable regulations. In the case of a plan which requires the filing of a benefit resumption notice as a condition precedent to the resumption of benefits, the suspension notification shall also describe the procedure for filing such notice and include the forms (if any) which must be filed. Furthermore, if a plan intends to offset any suspendible amounts actually paid during the periods of employment in section 203(a)(3)(B) service, the notification shall identify specifically the periods of employment, the suspendible amounts which are subject to offset, and the manner in which

the plan intends to offset such suspendible amounts. Where the plan's summary plan description (SPD) contains information which is substantially the same as information required by this subparagraph (4), the suspension notification may refer the employee to relevant pages of the SPD for information as to a particular item, provided the employee is informed how to obtain a copy of the SPD, or relevant pages thereof, and provided requests for referenced information are honored within a reasonable period of time, not to exceed 30 days.

[Amended by F.R. Doc. 81-34837 on December 1, 1981 (46 FR 59243)]

(5) *Verification.* A plan may provide that an employee must notify the plan of any employment. A plan may request from an employee access to reasonable information for the purpose of verifying such employment. Furthermore, a plan may provide that an employee must, at such time and with such frequency as may be reasonable, as a condition to receiving future benefit payments, either certify that he is unemployed or provide factual information sufficient to establish that any employment does not constitute section 203(a)(3)(B) service if specifically requested by the plan administrator. Once an employee has furnished the required certification or information, the plan must forward, at the next regularly scheduled time for payment of benefits, all payments which had been withheld pursuant to this subparagraph (5) except to the extent that payments may be withheld and offset pursuant to other provisions of this regulation.

(6) *Status determination.* If a plan provides for benefits suspension, the plan shall adopt a procedure, and so inform employees, whereunder an employee may request, and the plan administrator in a reasonable amount of time will render, a determination of whether specific contemplated employment will be section 203(a)(3)(B) service for purposes of plan provisions concerning suspension of benefits. Requests for status determinations may be considered in accordance with the claims procedure adopted by the plan pursuant to section 503 of the Act and applicable regulations.

(7) *Presumptions.* (i) A plan which has adopted verification requirements described in paragraph (b)(5) of this section, and which complies with the notice requirements set forth in paragraph (b)(7)(ii) of this section may provide that whenever the plan fiduciaries become aware that a retiree is employed in section 203(a)(3)(B) service and the retiree has not complied with the plan's reporting requirements with regard to that employment, the plan fiduciaries may, unless it is unreasonable under the circumstances to do so, act on the basis of a rebuttable presumption that the retiree had worked a period exceeding the plan's minimum number of hours for that month. In addition, a plan covering persons employed in the building trades which has adopted verification requirements described in paragraph (b)(5) of this section and which complies with the notice requirements set forth in paragraph (b)(7)(ii) of this section may provide that whenever the plan fiduciaries become aware that a retiree is employed in section 203(a)(3)(B) service at a construction site and the retiree has not complied with the plan's reporting requirements with regard to that employment, then the plan fiduciaries may, unless it is unreasonable under the circumstances to do so, act on the basis of a rebuttable presumption that the retiree engaged in such employment for the same employer in work at that site for so long before the work in question as that same employer performed that work at that construction site.

(ii) A plan which provides for a presumption described in paragraph (b)(7)(i) of this section may employ such presumption only if the following requirements are met. The plan must describe its employment verification requirements and the nature and effect of such presumption in the plan's summary plan description and in any communication to plan participants which relates to such verification requirements (for example, employment reporting reminders or forms), and retirees must be furnished such disclosure, whether through receipt of the above communications or by special distribution, at least once every 12 months.

(c) *Section 202(a)(3)(B) Service.* (1) *Plans other than multiemployer plans.* In the case of a plan other than a multiemployer plan, as defined in section 3(37) of the Act, the employment of an employee, subsequent to the time the payment of benefits commenced or would have commenced if the employee had not remained in or returned to employment, results in section 203(a)(3)(B) service during a calendar month, or during a four or five week payroll period ending in a calendar month, if the employee, in such month or payroll period,

Completes 40 or more hours of service (as defined in 29 CFR 2530.200b-2(a)(1) and (2)) for an employer which maintains the plan, including employers described in §2530.210(d) and (e), as of the time that the payment of benefits commenced or would have commenced if the employee had not remained in or returned to employment; or

Receives from such employer payment for any such hours of service performed on each of 8 or more days (or separate work shifts) in such month or payroll period, *Provided,* That the plan has not for any purpose determined or used the actual number of hours of service which would be required to be credited to the employee under §2530.200b-(2)(a).

[Amended by F.R. Doc. 81-34837 on December 1, 1981 (46 FR 59243)]

(2) *Multiemployer plans.* In the case of a multiemployer plan, as defined in section 3(37) of the Act, the employment of an employee subsequent to the time the payment of benefits commenced or would have commenced if the employee had not remained in or returned to employment results in section 203(a)(3)(B) service during a calendar month, or during a four or five week payroll period ending in a calendar month, if the employee, in such month or payroll period:

—Completes 40 or more hours of service (as defined in §2530.200b-2(a)(1) and 2)); or

—Receives payment for any such hours of service performed on each of 8 or more days (or separate work shifts) in such month or payroll period, *Provided,* That the plan has not for any purpose determined or used the actual number of hours of service which would be required to be credited to the employee under §2530.200b-2(a); in

—An industry in which employees covered by the plan were employed and accrued benefits under the plan as a result of such employment at the time that the payment of benefits commenced or would have commenced if the employee had not remained in or returned to employment, and

—A trade or craft in which the employee was employed at any time under the plan, and

—The geographic area covered by the plan at the time that the payment of benefits commenced or would have commenced if the employee had not remained in or returned to employment.

[Amended by F.R. Doc. 81-34837 on December 1, 1981 (46 FR 59243)]

(i) *Industry.* The term "industry" means the business activities of the types engaged in by any employers maintaining the plan.

• *Example.* One of the employers contributing to a multiemployer plan engages in heavy construction, another in textile manufacturing, and another in communications. Employee E began his career as an employee of an employer engaged in heavy construction. Later E was employed by an employer in communications. With both employers, E accrued benefits under the plan. If E retires and then becomes reemployed in the same trade or craft and in the same geographic area, employment by E in either heavy construction, communications or textile manufacturing, whether or not with an employer who contributes to the plan or in a self-employed capacity, may be considered by the plan to be employment in the same industry, assuming that employees covered by the plan were accruing benefits as a result of employment in these industries at the time E commenced receiving benefits. This is true even though E did not previously accrue benefits as a result of employment with an employer engaged in textile manufacturing because other employees covered by the plan were employed in that industry and were accruing benefits under the plan as a result of such employment at the time when benefit payments to E commenced or would have commenced if E had not returned to employment.

(ii) *Trade or craft.* A trade or craft is (A) a skill or skills, learned during a significant period of training or practice, which is applicable in occupations in some industry, (B) a skill or skills relating to selling, retailing, managerial, clerical or professional occupations, or (C) supervisory activities relating to a skill or skills described in (A) or (B) of this paragraph (c)(2)(ii). For purposes of this paragraph (c)(2)(ii), the determination whether a particular job classification, job description or industrial occupation constitutes or is included in a trade or craft shall be based upon the facts and circumstances of each case. Factors which may be examined include whether there is a customary and substantial period of practical, on-the-job training or a period of related supplementary instruction. Notwithstanding any other factor, the registration of an apprenticeship program with the Bureau of Apprenticeship and Training of the Employment Training Administration of the U.S. Department of Labor is sufficient for the conclusion that a skill or skills which is the subject of the apprenticeship program constitutes a trade or craft.

• *Example.* Participation in a multiemployer plan is limited solely to electricians. Electrician E retired and then became reemployed as a foreman of electricians. Because a "trade or craft" includes related supervisory activities, E remains within his trade or craft for purposes of this section.

(iii) *Geographic area covered by the plan.* (A) With the exception of a plan covering employees in a maritime industry, the "geographic area covered by the plan" consists of any state or any province of Canada in which contributions were made or were required to be made by or on behalf of an employer and the remainder of any Standard Metropolitan Statistical Area (SMSA) which falls in part within such state, determined as of the time that the payment of benefits commenced or would have commenced if the employee had not returned to employment.

• *Example.* A multiemployer plan covers plumbers in Pennsylvania. All contributing employers have always been located within Pennsylvania. Accordingly, the "geographic area covered by the plan" consists of Pennsylvania and any SMSAs which fall in part within Pennsylvania. Thus, for example, in the case of the Philadelphia SMSA, Burlington, Camden and Gloucester Counties in New Jersey are within the "geographic area covered by the plan".

(B) [Reserved—for definition of the geographic area covered by a plan that covers employees in a maritime industry.]

For purposes of this paragraph (c)(2)(iii), contributions shall not include amounts contributed: after December 31, 1978 by or on behalf of an employer where no contributions were made by or on behalf of that employer before that date, if the primary purpose of such contribution

is to allow for the suspension of plan benefits in a geographic area not otherwise covered by the plan; or with respect to isolated projects performed in states where plan participants were not otherwise employed.

(3) *Employment in a maritime industry.* For plans covering employees employed in a maritime industry, as defined in § 2530.200b-6, the standard of "five or more days of service, as defined in § 2530.200b-7(a)(1)" shall be used in lieu of the standard "40 or more hours of sservice", for purposes of determining whether an employee is employed in section 203(a)(3)(B) service.

(d) *Suspendable amount.* (1) *Life annuity.* In the case of benefits payable periodically on a monthly basis for as long as a life (or lives) continues, such as a straight life annuity or a qualified joint and survivor annuity, a plan may provide that an amount not greater than the portion of a monthly benefit payment derived from employer contributions may be withheld permanently for a calendar month, or for a four or five week payroll period ending in a calendar month, in which the employee is employed in section 203(a)(3)(B) service.

(2) *Other benefit forms.* In the case of benefits payable in a form other than the form described in paragraph (d)(1) of this section, a plan may provide for the permanent withholding of an amount of the employer-derived portion of benefit payments for a calendar month, or for a four or five week payroll period ending in a calendar month, in which the employee is employed in section 203(a)(3)(B) service, not exceeding the lesser of—

(i) The amount of benefits which would have been payable to the employee if he had been receiving monthly benefits under the plan since actual retirement based on a single life annuity commencing at actual retirement age; or

(ii) The actual amount paid or scheduled to be paid to the employee for such month. Payments which are scheduled to be paid less frequently than monthly may be converted to monthly payments for purposes of this paragraph (d)(2)(ii).

[Amended by F.R. Doc. 81-34847 on December 1, 1981 (46 FR 59243)]

[¶ 14,440]
BENEFIT ACCRUAL REQUIREMENTS

Act Sec. 204.(a) Each pension plan shall satisfy the requirements of subsection (b)(3), and—

(1) in the case of a defined benefit plan, shall satisfy the requirements of subsection (b)(1); and

(2) in the case of a defined contribution plan, shall satisfy the requirements of subsection (b)(2).

Act Sec. 204.(b)(1)(A) A defined benefit plan satisfies the requirements of this paragraph if the accrued benefit to which each participant is entitled upon his separation from the service is not less than—

(i) 3 percent of the normal retirement benefit to which he would be entitled at the normal retirement age if he commenced participation at the earliest possible entry age under the plan and served continuously until the earlier of age 65 or the normal retirement age specified under the plan, multiplied by

(ii) the number of years (not in excess of 33 1/3) of his participation in the plan.

In the case of a plan providing retirement benefits based on compensation during any period, the normal retirement benefit to which a participant would be entitled shall be determined as if he continued to earn annually the average rate of compensation which he earned during consecutive years of service, not in excess of 10, for which his compensation was the highest. For purposes of this subparagraph, social security benefits and all other relevant factors used to compute benefits shall be treated as remaining constant as of the current year for all years after such current year.

(B) A defined benefit plan satisfies the requirements of this paragraph for a particular plan year if under the plan the accrued benefit payable at the normal retirement age is equal to the normal retirement benefit and the annual rate at which any individual who is or could be a participant can accrue the retirement benefits payable at normal retirement age under the plan for any later plan year is not more than 133 1/3 percent of the annual rate at which he can accrue benefits for any plan year beginning on or after such particular plan year and before such later plan year. For purposes of this subparagraph—

(i) any amendment to the plan which is in effect for the current year shall be treated as in effect for all other plan years;

(ii) any change in an accrual rate which does not apply to any individual who is or could be a participant in the current year shall be disregarded;

(iii) the fact that benefits under the plan may be payable to certain employees before normal retirement age shall be disregarded; and

(iv) social security benefits and all other relevant factors used to compute benefits shall be treated as remaining constant as of the current year for all years after the current year.

(C) A defined benefit plan satisfies the requirements of this paragraph if the accrued benefit to which any participant is entitled upon his separation from the service is not less than a fraction of the annual benefit commencing at normal retirement age to which he would be entitled under the plan as in effect on the date of his separation if he continued to earn annually until normal retirement age the same rate of compensation upon which his normal retirement benefit would be computed under the plan, determined as if he had attained normal retirement age on the date any such determination is made (but taking into account no more than the 10 years of service immediately preceding his separation from service). Such fraction shall be a fraction, not exceeding 1, the numerator of which is the total number of his years of participation in the plan (as of the date of his separation from the service) and the denominator of which is the total number of years he would have participated in the plan if he separated from the service at the normal retirement age. For purposes of this subparagraph, social security benefits and all other relevant factors used to compute benefits shall be treated as remaining constant as of the current year for all years after such current year.

(D) Subparagraphs (A), (B), and (C) shall not apply with respect to years of participation before the first plan year to which this section applies but a defined benefit plan satisfies the requirement of this subparagraph with respect to such years of participation only if the accrued benefit of any participant with respect to such years of participation is not less than the greater of—

(i) his accrued benefit determined under the plan, as in effect from time to time prior to the date of the enactment of this Act, or

(ii) an accrued benefit which is not less than one-half of the accrued benefit to which such participant would have been entitled if subparagraph (A), (B), or (C) applied with respect to such years of participation.

(E) Notwithstanding subparagraphs (A), (B), and (C) of this paragraph, a plan shall not be treated as not satisfying the requirements of this paragraph solely because the accrual of benefits under the plan does not become effective until the employee has two continuous years of service. For purposes of this subparagraph, the term "years of service" has the meaning provided by section 202(a)(3)(A).

(F) Notwithstanding subparagraphs (A), (B), and (C), a defined benefit plan satisfies the requirements of this paragraph if such plan—

(i) is funded exclusively by the purchase of insurance contracts, and

(ii) satisfies the requirements of paragraphs (2) and (3) of section 301(b) (relating to certain insurance contract plans),

but only if an employee's accrued benefit as of any applicable date is not less than the cash surrender value his insurance contracts would have on such applicable date if the requirements of paragraphs (4), (5), and (6) of section 301(b) were satisfied.

(G) Notwithstanding the preceding subparagraphs, a defined benefit plan shall be treated as not satisfying the requirements of this paragraph if the participant's accrued benefit is reduced on account of any increase in his age or service. The preceding sentence shall not apply to benefits under the plan commencing before benefits payable under title II of the Social Security Act which benefits under the plan—

(i) do not exceed such social security benefits, and

(ii) terminate when such social security benefits commence.

(H)(i) Notwithstanding the preceding subparagraphs, a defined benefit plan shall be treated as not satisfying the requirements of this paragraph if, under the plan, an employee's benefit accrual is ceased, or the rate of an employee's benefit accrual is reduced, because of the attainment of any age.

(ii) A plan shall not be treated as failing to meet the requirements of this subparagraph solely because the plan imposes (without regard to age) a limitation on the amount of benefits that the plan provides or a limitation on the number of years of service or years of participation which are taken into account for purposes of determining benefit accrual under the plan.

(iii) In the case of any employee who, as of the end of any plan year under a defined benefit plan, has attained normal retirement age under such plan—

(I) if distribution of benefits under such plan with respect to such employee has commenced as of the end of such plan year, then any requirement of this subparagraph for continued accrual of benefits under such plan with respect to such employee during such plan year shall be treated as satisfied to the extent of the actuarial equivalent of in-service distribution of benefits, and

(II) if distribution of benefits under such plan with respect to such employee has not commenced as of the end of such year in accordance with section 206(a)(3), and the payment of benefits under such plan with respect to such employee is not suspended during such plan year pursuant to section 203(a)(3)(B), then any requirement of this subparagraph for continued accrual of benefits under such plan with respect to such employee during such plan year shall be treated as satisfied to the extent of any adjustment in the benefit payable under the plan during such plan year attributable to the delay in the distribution of benefits after the attainment of normal retirement age.

The preceding provisions of this clause shall apply in accordance with regulations of the Secretary of the Treasury. Such regulations may provide for the application of the preceding provisions of this clause, in the case of any such employee, with respect to any period of time within a plan year.

(iv) Clause (i) shall not apply with respect to any employee who is a highly compensated employee (within the meaning of section 414(q) of the Internal Revenue Code of 1986) to the extent provided in regulations prescribed by the Secretary of the Treasury for purposes of precluding discrimination in favor of highly compensated employees within the meaning of subchapter D of chapter 1 of the Internal Revenue Code of 1986.

(v) A plan shall not be treated as failing to meet the requirements of clause (i) solely because the subsidized portion of any early retirement benefit is disregarded in determining benefit accruals.

(vi) Any regulations prescribed by the Secretary of the Treasury pursuant to clause (v) of section 411(b)(1)(H) of the Internal Revenue Code of 1986 shall apply with respect to the requirements of this subparagraph in the same manner and to the same extent as such regulations apply with respect to the requirement of such section 411(b)(1)(H).

(2)(A) A defined contribution plan satisfies the requirements of this paragraph if, under the plan, allocations to the employee's account are not ceased, and the rate at which amounts are allocated to the employee's account is not reduced, because of the attainment of any age.

(B) A plan shall not be treated as failing to meet the requirements of subparagraph (A) solely because the subsidized portion of any early retirement benefit is disregarded in determining benefit accruals.

(C) Any regulations prescribed by the Secretary of the Treasury pursuant to subparagraphs (B) and (C) of section 411(b)(2) of the Internal Revenue Code of 1986 shall apply with respect to the requirements of this paragraph in the same manner and to the same extent as such regulations apply with respect to the requirements of such section 411(b)(2).

(3) A plan satisfies the requirements of this paragraph if—

(A) in the case of a defined benefit plan, the plan requires separate accounting for the portion of each employee's accrued benefit derived from any voluntary employee contributions permitted under the plan; and

(B) in the case of any plan which is not a defined benefit plan, the plan requires separate accounting for each employee's accrued benefit.

(4)(A) For purposes of determining an employee's accrued benefit, the term "year of participation" means a period of service (beginning at the earliest date on which the employee is a participant in the plan and which is included in a period of service required to be taken into account under section 202(b), determined without regard to section 202(b)(5)) as determined under regulations prescribed by the Secretary which provide for the calculation of such period on any reasonable and consistent basis.

(B) For purposes of this paragraph, except as provided in subparagraph (C), in the case of any employee whose customary employment is less than full time, the calculation of such employee's service on any basis which provides less than a ratable portion of the accrued benefit to which he would be entitled under the plan if his customary employment were full time shall not be treated as made on a reasonable and consistent basis.

(C) For purposes of this paragraph, in the case of an employee whose service is less than 1,000 hours during any calendar year, plan year or other 12-consecutive-month period designated by the plan (and not prohibited under regulations prescribed by the Secretary), the calculation of his period of service shall not be treated as not made on a reasonable and consistent basis merely because such service is not taken into account.

(D) In the case of any seasonal industry where the customary period of employment is less than 1,000 hours during a calendar year, the term "year of participation" shall be such period as determined under regulations prescribed by the Secretary.

(E) For purposes of this subsection in the case of any maritime industry, 125 days of service shall be treated as a year of participation. The Secretary may prescribe regulations to carry out the purposes of this subparagraph.

Act. Sec. 204.(c)(1) For purposes of this section and section 203 an employee's accrued benefit derived from employer contributions as of any applicable date is the excess (if any) of the accrued benefit for such employee as of such applicable date over the accrued benefit derived from contributions made by such employee as of such date.

(2)(A) In the case of a plan other than a defined benefit plan, the accrued benefit derived from contributions made by an employee as of any applicable date is—

(i) except as provided in clause (ii), the balance of the employee's separate account consisting only of his contributions and the income, expenses, gains, and losses attributable thereto, or

(ii) if a separate account is not maintained with respect to an employee's contributions under such a plan, the amount which bears the same ratio to his total accrued benefit as the total amount of the employee's contributions (less withdrawals) bears to the sum of such contributions and the contributions made on his behalf by the employer (less withdrawals).

(B) DEFINED BENEFIT PLANS. In the case of a defined benefit plan, the accrued benefit derived from contributions made by an employee as of any applicable date is the amount equal to the employee's accumulated contributions expressed as an annual benefit commencing at normal retirement age, using an interest rate which would be used under the plan under section 205(g)(3) (as of the determination date).

(C) For purposes of this subsection, the term "accumulted contributions" means the total of—

(i) all mandatory contributions made by the employee,

(ii) interest (if any) under the plan to the end of the last plan year to which section 203(a)(2) does not apply (by reason of the applicable effective date) and

(iii) interest on the sum of the amounts determined under clauses (i) and (ii) compounded annually—

(I) at the rate of 120 percent of the Federal midterm rate (as in effect under section 1274 of the Internal Revenue Code of 1986 for the 1st month of a plan year for the period beginning with the 1st plan year to which subsection (a)(2) applies by reason of the applicable effective date) and ending with the date on which the determination is being made, and

(II) at the interest rate which would be used under the plan under section 205(g)(3) (as of the determination date) for the period beginning with the determination date and ending on the date on which the employee attains normal retirement age.

For purposes of this subparagraph, the term "mandatory contributions" means amounts contributed to the plan by the employee which are required as a condition of employment, as a condition of participation in such plan, or as a condition of obtaining benefits under the plan attributable to employer contributions.

(D) The Secretary of the Treasury is authorized to adjust by regulation the conversion factor described in subparagraph (B) from time to time as he may deem necessary. No such adjustment shall be effective for a plan year beginning before the expiration of 1 year after such adjustment is determined and published.

(3) For purposes of this section, in the case of any defined benefit plan, if an employee's accrued benefit is to be determined as an amount other than an annual benefit commencing at normal retirement age, or if the accrued benefit derived from contributions made by an employee is to be determined with respect to a benefit other than an annual benefit in the form of a single life annuity (without ancillary benefits) commencing at normal retirement age, the employee's accrued benefit, or the accrued benefits derived from contributions made by an employee, as the case may be, shall be the actuarial equivalent of such benefit or amount determined under paragraph (1) or (2).

(4) In the case of a defined benefit plan which permits voluntary employee contributions, the portion of an employee's accrued benefit derived from such contributions shall be treated as an accrued benefit derived from employee contributions under a plan other than a defined benefit plan.

Act Sec. 204. (d) Notwithstanding section 203(b)(1), for purposes of determining the employee's accrued benefit under the plan, the plan may disregard service performed by the employee with respect to which he has received—

(1) a distribution of the present value of his entire nonforfeitable benefit if such distribution was in an amount (not more than $5,000) perrmitted under regulations prescribed by the Secretary of the Treasury, or

(2) a distribution of the present value of his nonforfeitable benefit attributable to such service which he elected to receive.

Paragraph (1) shall apply only if such distribution was made on termination of the employee's participation in the plan. Paragraph (2) shall apply only if such distribution was made on termination of the employee's participation in the plan or under such other circumstances as may be provided under regulations prescribed by the Secretary of the Treasury.

Act Sec. 204. (e) For purposes of determining the employee's accrued benefit, the plan shall not disregard service as provided in subsection (d) unless the plan provides an opportunity for the participant to repay the full amount of a distribution described in subsection (d) with, in the case of a defined benefit plan, interest at the rate determined for purposes of subsection (c)(2)(C) and provides that upon such repayment the employee's accrued benefit shall be recomputed by taking into account service so disregarded. This subsection shall apply only in the case of a participant who—

(1) received such a distribution in any plan year to which this section applies, which distribution was less than the present value of his accrued benefit,

(2) resumes employment covered under the plan, and

(3) repays the full amount of such distribution with, in the case of a defined benefit plan, interest at the rate determined for purposes of subsection (c)(2)(C).

The plan provision required under this subsection may provide that such repayment must be made (A) in the case of a withdrawal on account of separation from service, before the earlier of 5 years after the first date on which the participant is subsequently re-employed by the employer, or the close of the first period of 5 consecutive 1-year breaks in service commencing after the withdrawal; or (B) in the case of any other withdrawal, 5 years after the date of the withdrawal.

Act Sec. 204. (f) For the purposes of this part, an employer shall be treated as maintaining a plan if any employee of such employer accrues benefits under such plan by reason of service with such employer.

Act Sec. 204. (g)(1) The accrued benefit of a participant under a plan may not be decreased by an amendment of the plan, other than an amendment described in section 302(c)(8) or section 4281.

(2) For purposes of paragraph (1), a plan amendment which has the effect of—

(A) eliminating or reducing an early retirement benefit or a retirement-type subsidy (as defined in regulations), or

(B) eliminating an optional form of benefit,

with respect to benefits attributable to service before the amendment shall be treated as reducing accrued benefits. In the case of a retirement-type subsidy, the preceding sentence shall apply only with respect to a participant who satisfies (either before or after the amendment) the preamendment conditions for the subsidy. The Secretary of the Treasury shall by regulations provide that this paragraph shall not apply to any plan amendment which reduces or eliminates benefits or subsidies which create significant burdens or complexities for the plan and plan participants, unless such amendment adversely affects the rights of any participant in a more than de minimis manner. The Secretary of the Treasury may by regulations provide that this subparagraph shall not apply to a plan amendment described in subparagraph (B) (other than a plan amendment having an effect described in subparagraph (A)).

(3) For purposes of this subsection, any—

(A) tax credit employee stock ownership plan (as defined in section 409(a) of the Internal Revenue Code of 1986), or

(B) employee stock ownership plan (as defined in section 4975(e)(7) of such Code),

shall not be treated as failing to meet the requirements of this subsection merely because it modifies distribution options in a nondiscriminatory manner.

(4)(A) A defined contribution plan (in this subparagraph referred to as the 'transferee plan') shall not be treated as failing to meet the requirements of this subsection merely because the transferee plan does not provide some or all of the forms of distribution previously available under another defined contribution plan (in this subparagraph referred to as the "transferor plan") to the extent that—

(i) the forms of distribution previously available under the transferor plan applied to the account of a participant or beneficiary under the transferor plan that was transferred from the transferor plan to the transferee plan pursuant to a direct transfer rather than pursuant to a distribution from the transferor plan;

(ii) the terms of both the transferor plan and the transferee plan authorize the transfer described in clause (i);

(iii) the transfer described in clause (i) was made pursuant to a voluntary election by the participant or beneficiary whose account was transferred to the transferee plan;

(iv) the election described in clause (iii) was made after the participant or beneficiary received a notice describing the consequences of making the election; and

(v) the transferee plan allows the participant or beneficiary described in clause (iii) to receive any distribution to which the participant or beneficiary is entitled under the transferee plan in the form of a single sum distribution.

(B) Subparagraph (A) shall apply to plan mergers and other transactions having the effect of a direct transfer, including consolidations of benefits attributable to different employers within a multiple employer plan.

(5) Except to the extent provided in regulations promulgated by the Secretary of the Treasury, a defined contribution plan shall not be treated as failing to meet the requirements of this subsection merely because of the elimination of a form of distribution previously available thereunder. This paragraph shall not apply to the elimination of a form of distribution with respect to any participant unless—

(A) a single sum payment is available to such participant at the same time or times as the form of distribution being eliminated; and

(B) such single sum payment is based on the same or greater portion of the participant's account as the form of distribution being eliminated.

Act Sec. 204.(h)(1) An applicable pension plan may not be amended so as to provide for a significant reduction in the rate of future benefit accrual unless the plan administrator provides the notice described in paragraph (2) to each applicable individual (and to each employee organization representing applicable individuals).

(2) The notice required by paragraph (1) shall be written in a manner calculated to be understood by the average plan participant and shall provide sufficient information (as determined in accordance with regulations prescribed by the Secretary of the Treasury) to allow applicable individuals to understand the effect of the plan amendment. The Secretary of the Treasury may provide a simplified form of notice for, or exempt from any notice requirement, a plan—

(A) which has fewer than 100 participants who have accrued a benefit under the plan, or

(B) which offers participants the option to choose between the new benefit formula and the old benefit formula.

(3) Except as provided in regulations prescribed by the Secretary of the Treasury, the notice required by paragraph (1) shall be provided within a reasonable time before the effective date of the plan amendment.

(4) Any notice under paragraph (1) may be provided to a person designated, in writing, by the person to which it would otherwise be provided.

(5) A plan shall not be treated as failing to meet the requirements of paragraph (1) merely because notice is provided before the adoption of the plan amendment if no material modification of the amendment occurs before the amendment is adopted.

(6)(A) In the case of any egregious failure to meet any requirement of this subsection with respect to any plan amendment, the provisions of the applicable pension plan shall be applied as if such plan amendment entitled all applicable individuals to the greater of—

(i) the benefits to which they would have been entitled without regard to such amendment, or

(ii) the benefits under the plan with regard to such amendment.

(B) For purposes of subparagraph (A), there is an egregious failure to meet the requirements of this subsection if such failure is within the control of the plan sponsor and is—

(i) an intentional failure (including any failure to promptly provide the required notice or information after the plan administrator discovers an unintentional failure to meet the requirements of this subsection),

(ii) a failure to provide most of the individuals with most of the information they are entitled to receive under this subsection, or

(iii) a failure which is determined to be egregious under regulations prescribed by the Secretary of the Treasury.

(7) The Secretary of the Treasury may by regulations allow any notice under this subsection to be provided by using new technologies.

(8) For purposes of this subsection—

(A) The term "applicable individual" means, with respect to any plan amendment—

(i) each participant in the plan; and

(ii) any beneficiary who is an alternate payee (within the meaning of section 206(d)(3)(K)) under an applicable qualified domestic relations order (within the meaning of section 206(d)(3)(B)(i)),

whose rate of future benefit accrual under the plan may reasonably be expected to be significantly reduced by such plan amendment.

(B) The term "applicable pension plan" means—

(i) any defined benefit plan; or

(ii) an individual account plan which is subject to the funding standards of section 412 of the Internal Revenue Code of 1986.

(9) For purposes of this subsection, a plan amendment which eliminates or reduces any early retirement benefit or retirement-type subsidy (within the meaning of subsection (g)(2)(A)) shall be treated as having the effect of reducing the rate of future benefit accrual.

Act Sec. 204.(i)(1) In the case of a plan described in paragraph (3) which is maintained by an employer that is a debtor in a case under title 11, United States Code, or similar Federal or State law, no amendment of the plan which increases the liabilities of the plan by reason of—

(A) any increase in benefits,

(B) any change in the accrual of benefits, or

(C) any change in the rate at which benefits become nonforfeitable under the plan,

with respect to employees of the debtor, shall be effective prior to the effective date of such employers' plan of reorganization.

(2) Paragraph (1) shall not apply to any plan amendment that—

(A) the Secretary of the Treasury determines to be reasonable and that provides for only de minimis increases in the liabilities of the plan with respect to employees of the debtor,

(B) only repeals an amendment described in section 302(e)(8),

(C) is required as a condition of qualification under part I of subchapter D of chapter 1 of the Internal Revenue Code of 1986, or

(D) was adopted prior to, or pursuant to a collective bargaining agreement entered into prior to, the date on which the employer became a debtor in a case under title 11, United States Code, or similar Federal or State law.

(3) This subsection shall apply only to plans (other than multiemployer plans) covered under section 4021 of this Act for which the funded current liability percentage (within the meaning of section 302(d)(8) of this Act) is less than 100 percent after taking into account the effect of the amendment.

(4) For purposes of this subsection, the term "employer" has the meaning set forth in section 302(c)(11)(A), without regard to section 302(c)(11)(B).

Act Sec. 204. CROSS REFERENCE.—

(j) For special rules relating to plan provisions adopted to preclude discrimination see section 203(c)(2).

Amendments

P.L. 107-147, §411(u)(2):

Act Sec. 411(u)(2) amended ERISA Sec. 204(h)(9) by striking the word "significantly" each time it appears.

The above amendment is effective for years beginning after December 31, 2001, subject to sunset after 2010 under P.L. 107-16, Sec. 901.

P.L. 107-16, § 645(a)(2):

Act Sec. 645(a)(2) amended ERISA Sec. 204(g) by adding subsections (4) and (5) to read as above.

The above amendment is effective for years beginning after December 31, 2001; subject to sunset after 2010 under P.L. 107-16, Sec. 901.

P.L. 107-16, § 645(b)(2):

Act Sec. 645(b)(2) amended ERISA Sec. 204(g)(2) by inserting after the second sentence the following: "The Secretary of the Treasury shall by regulations provide that this paragraph shall not apply to any plan amendment which reduces or eliminates benefits or subsidies which create significant burdens or complexities for the plan and plan participants, unless such amendment adversely affects the rights of any participant in a more than de minimis manner.".

P.L. 107-16, § 659(b):

Act Sec. 659(b) amended ERISA Sec. 204(h) to read as above. Previously, paragraph 204(h) read as follows:

"(h)(1) A plan described in paragraph (2) may not be amended so as to provide for a significant reduction in the rate of future benefit accrual, unless, after adoption of the plan amendment and not less than 15 days before the effective date of the plan amendment, the plan administrator provides a written notice, setting forth the plan amendment and its effective date, to—

(A) each participant in the plan,

(B) each beneficiary who is an alternate payee (within the meaning of section 206(d)(3)(K)) under an applicable qualified domestic relations order (within the meaning of section 206(d)(3)(B)(i)), and

(C) each employee organization representing participants in the plan, except that such notice shall instead be provided to a person designated, in writing, to receive such notice on behalf of any person referred to in paragraph (A), (B), or (C).

(2) A plan is described in this paragraph if such plan is—

(A) a defined benefit plan, or

(B) an individual account plan which is subject to the funding standards of section 302."

P.L. 107-16, § 659(c):

Act Sec. 659(c) provides the following effective dates:

"(c) EFFECTIVE DATES.—

(1) IN GENERAL.—The amendments made by this section shall apply to plan amendments taking effect on or after the date of the enactment of this Act.

(2) TRANSITION.—Until such time as the Secretary of the Treasury issues regulations under sections 4980F(e)(2) and (3) of the Internal Revenue Code of 1986, and section 204(h) of the Employee Retirement Income Security Act of 1974, as added by the amendments made by this section, a plan shall be treated as meeting the requirements of such sections if it makes a good faith effort to comply with such requirements.

(3) SPECIAL NOTICE RULE.—

(A) IN GENERAL.—The period for providing any notice required by the amendments made by this section shall not end before the date which is 3 months after the date of the enactment of this Act.

(B) REASONABLE NOTICE.—The amendments made by this section shall not apply to any plan amendment taking effect on or after the date of the enactment of this Act if, before April 25, 2001, notice was provided to participants and beneficiaries adversely affected by the plan amendment (or their representatives) which was reasonably expected to notify them of the nature and effective date of the plan amendment."

P.L. 105-34, § 1071(b)(2):

Act Sec. 1071(b)(2) amended ERISA Sec. 204(d)(1) by striking "$3,500" and inserting "$5,000".

The above amendment is effective for plan years beginning after August 5, 1997.

P.L. 103-465, § 766(a):

Act Sec. 766(a) amended ERISA Sec. 204 by redesignating subsection (i) as (j) and inserting after subsection (h) subsection (i), to read as above.

The above amendments apply to plan amendments adopted on or after December 8, 1994.

P.L. 101-239, § 7862(b)(2):

Amended ERISA Sec. 204(h)(2) by adjusting the left-hand margin of the material preceding subparagraph (A) effective October 22, 1986.

P.L. 101-239, § 7871(a)(1):

Amended ERISA Sec. 204(b)(2) by striking subparagraph (B) and by redesignating subparagraphs (C) and (D) as subparagraphs (B) and (C), respectively. Previously, subparagraph (B) read as follows:

(B) Subparagraph (A) shall not apply with respect to any employee who is a highly compensated employee (within the meaning of section 414(q) of the Internal Revenue Code of 1986) to the extent provided in regulations prescribed by the Secretary of the Treasury for purposes of precluding discrimination in favor of highly compensated employees within the meaning of subchapter D of chapter 1 of the Internal Revenue Code of 1986.

P.L. 101-239, § 7871(a)(3):

Amended ERISA Sec. 204(b)(2)(C), as redesignated by § 7863(a)(1) above, by striking "(C) and (D)" and inserting "(B) and (C)."

P.L. 101-239, § 7881(m)(2)(A):

Amended ERISA Sec. 204(c)(2)(C)(iii) to read as above. Previously, subparagraph (iii) read as follows:

(iii) interest on the sum of the amounts determined under clauses (i) and (ii) compounded annually at the rate of 120 percent of the Federal mid-term rate (as in

effect under section 1274 of the Internal Revenue Code of 1986 for the 1st month of a plan year) from the beginning of the first plan year to which section 203(a)(2) applies (by reason of the applicable effective date) to the date upon which the employee would attain normal retirement age.

P.L. 101-239, § 7881(m)(2)(B):

Amended ERISA Sec. 204(c)(2)(B) to read as above. Previously, paragraph (B) read as follows:

(B)(i) In the case of a defined benefit plan providing an annual benefit in the form of a single life annuity (without ancillary benefits) commencing at normal retirement age, the accrued benefit derived from contributions made by an employee as of any applicable date is the annual benefit equal to the employee's accumulated contributions multiplied by the appropriate conversion factor.

(ii) For purposes of clause (i), the term "appropriate conversion factor" means the factor necessary to convert an amount equal to the accumulated contributions to a single annuity (without ancillary benefits) commencing at normal retirement age and shall be 10 percent for a normal retirement age of 65 years. For other normal retirement ages the conversion factor shall be determined in accordance with regulations prescribed by the Secretary of the Treasury or his delegate.

P.L. 101-239, § 7881(m)(2)(C):

Amended ERISA Sec. 204(c)(2) by striking subparagraph (E). Previously subparagraph (E) read as follows:

(E) The accrued benefit derived from employee contributions shall not exceed the greater of—

(i) the employee's accrued benefit under the plan, or

(ii) the accrued benefit derived from employee contributions determined as though the amounts calculated under clauses (ii) and (iii) of subparagraph (C) were zero.

The above amendments are effective October 21, 1986.

P.L. 101-239, § 7891(a)(1):

Titles I, III, and IV of ERISA (other than sections 3(37)(E), 301(a)(7), and 308, the last sentence of section 408(d), and sections 414(c), 4001(a)(3)(ii), and 4303) are each amended by striking "Internal Revenue Code of 1954" each place it appears and inserting "Internal Revenue Code of 1986."

P.L. 101-239, § 7894(c)(4):

Amended ERISA Sec. 204(b)(1)(A) in the last sentence by striking "suparagraph" and inserting "subparagraph."

P.L. 101-239, § 7894(c)(5):

Amended ERISA Sec. 204(b)(1)(E) in the last sentence by striking "years" and inserting "year."

P.L. 101-239, § 7894(c)(6):

Amended ERISA Sec. 204(d) to remove the indentation of the term "paragraph" the first place it appeared in the matter following paragraph (2).

The above amendments are effective October 22, 1986.

P.L. 100-203, § 9346(a)(1):

Amended ERISA Sec. 204(c)(2)(C)(iii) by striking "5 percent per annum" and inserting "120 percent of the Federal mid-term rate (as in effect under section 1274 of the Internal Revenue Code of 1986 for the 1st month of a plan year)" instead.

P.L. 100-203, § 9346(a)(2):

Amended ERISA Sec. 204(c)(2)(D) by striking ", the rate of interest described in clause (iii) of subparagraph (C), or both,"; and by striking the second sentence.

P.L. 99-514, § 1113(e)(4)(B):

Amended ERISA Sec. 204(i) to read as above. Prior to amendment, section (i) read as follows:

(i) Cross Reference.

For special rules relating to class year plans and plan provisions adopted to preclude discrimination, see sections 203(c)(2) and (3).

For effective dates, see Act Sec. 1113(e) in amendment notes under ERISA Sec. 203.

P.L. 99-514, § 1879(u)(1):

Amended ERISA Sec. 204(h) by striking out "single-employer plan" and inserting in lieu thereof "plan described in paragraphs (2)"; by redesignating paragraphs (1), (2), and (3) as subparagraphs (A), (B), and (C), respectively; by striking out "paragraph (1), (2), or (3)" and inserting in lieu thereof "subparagraph (A), (B), or (C)"; by inserting "(1)" after "(h)"; and by adding paragraph (2) to read as above.

P.L. 99-514, § 1879(u)(4):

Act Sec. 1879(u)(4) provides as follows:

(4) EFFECTIVE DATE.—

(A) GENERAL RULE.—Except as provided in subparagraph (B), the preceding provisions of this subsection shall be effective as if such provisions were included in the enactment of the Single-Employer Pension Plan Amendments Act of 1986.

(B) SPECIAL RULE.—Subparagraph (B) of section 204(h)(2) of the Employee Retirement Income Security Act of 1974 (as amended by paragraph (1)) shall apply only with respect to plan amendments adopted on or after the date of the enactment of this Act.

P.L. 99-514, § 1898(a)(4)(B)(ii):

Amended ERISA Sec. 204(e), last sentence to read as above, effective for plan years beginning after 1984. Prior to amendment, the last sentence read as follows:

In the case of a defined contribution plan, the plan provision required under this subsection may provide that such repayment must be made before the participant has 5 consecutive 1-year breaks in service commencing after such withdrawal.

P.L. 99-514, § 1898(f)(1):

Added ERISA Sec. 204(g)(3) to read as above, effective for years beginning after 1984.

P.L. 99-514, § 1898(f)(2):

Amended ERISA Sec. 204(g)(1) by striking out "section 302(c)(8)" and inserting "section 302(c)(8) or 4281" instead, effective for plan years beginning after 1984.

P.L. 99-509, § 9202(a)(1):

Amended ERISA Sec. 204(a) to read as above. Prior to amendment, Sec. 204(a) read as follows:

Act Sec. 204. (a) Each pension plan shall satisfy the requirements of subsection (b)(2), and in the case of a defined benefit plan shall also satisfy the requirements of subsection (b)(1).

This amendment is effective with respect to plan years beginning on or after January 1, 1988 and only with respect to employees who have 1 hour of service in any plan year to which the amendment applies.

P.L. 99-509, § 9204(a)(3) and (c):

Secs. 9204(a)(3) and (c) provide as follows:

(b)(2) SPECIAL RULES FOR COLLECTIVELY BARGAINED PLANS.—In the case of a plan maintained pursuant to 1 or more collective bargaining agreements between employee representatives and 1 or more employers ratified before March 1, 1986, paragraph (1) shall be applied to benefits pursuant to, and individuals covered by, any such agreement by substituting for "January 1, 1988" the date of the commencement of the first plan year beginning on or after the earlier of—

(A) the later of—

(i) January 1, 1988, or

(ii) the date on which the last of such collective bargaining agreements terminate (determined without regard to any extension thereof after February 28, 1986), or

(B) January 1, 1990.

* * *

(c) PLAN AMENDMENTS.—If any amendment made by this subtitle requires an amendment to any plan, such plan amendment shall not be required to be made before the first plan year beginning on or after January 1, 1989, if—

(1) during the period after such amendment takes effect and before such first plan year, the plan is operated in accordance with the requirements of such amendment, and

(2) such plan amendment applies retroactively to the period after such amendment takes effect and such first plan year.

A pension plan shall not be treated as failing to provide definitely determinable benefits or contributions, or to be operated in accordance with the provisions of the plan, merely because it operates in accordance with this subsection.

P.L. 99-509, § 9202(a)(2):

Amended ERISA Sec. 204(b)(1) by adding a new subparagraph (H) to read as above.

This amendment is effective with respect to plan years beginning on or after January 1, 1988 and only with respect to, employees who have 1 hour of service in any plan year to which the amendment applies.

P.L. 99-509, § 9202(a)(3):

Amended ERISA Sec. 204(b) by redesignating paragraphs (2) and (3) as paragraphs (3) and (4), respectively, and adding a new paragraph (2) to read as above.

This amendment is effective with respect to plan years beginning on or after January 1, 1988 and only with respect to employees who have 1 hour of service in any plan year to which the amendment applies.

P.L. 99-272:

Act Sec. 11006(a) amended ERISA Sec. 204 by redesignating section (h) as section (i) and by adding a new section (h) to read as above, effective for plan amendments adopted on or after January 1, 1986. Act Sec. 11006(b) also contains the following provisions:

"... except that, in the case of plan amendments adopted on or after January 1, 1986, and on or before the date of the enactment of this Act, the requirements of section 204(h) of the Employee Retirement Income Security Act of 1974 (as added by this section) shall be treated as met if the written notice required under such section 204(h) is provided before 60 days after the date of the enactment of this Act."

P.L. 98-397, §§ 102, 105 and 301:

Act Sec. 102(e)(3) amended ERISA Sec. 204(b)(3)(A) by inserting ", determined without regard to section 202(b)(5)" after "section 202(b)."

For the effective date of the above amendment, see Act Sec. 303(b), which appears in the amendment notes for ERISA Sec. 203 at ¶ 103.

Act Sec. 102(f) amended ERISA Sec. 204(e) by striking out "any 1-year break in service" and inserting in lieu thereof "5 consecutive 1-year breaks in service."

Act. Sec. 105(b) amended ERISA Sec. 204(d)(1) by striking out "$1,750" and inserting in lieu thereof "$3,500."

The above amendments apply to plan years beginning after December 31, 1984.

Act Sec. 301(a)(2) amended ERISA Sec. 204(g) by striking out the prior law and replacing it with new subsection (g) to read as above. Prior to amendment, ERISA Sec. 204(g) read as follows:

(g) The accrued benefit of a participant under a plan may not be decreased by an amendment of the plan, other than an amendment described in section 302(c)(8).

The above amendment applies to plan amendments made after July 30, 1984 but a special rule under Act Sec. 302(d)(2) also provides:

(2) Special Rule for Collective Bargaining Agreements.—In the case of a plan maintained pursuant to 1 or more collective bargaining agreements entered into before January 1, 1985, which are—

(A) between employee representatives and 1 or more employers, and

(B) successor agreements to 1 or more collective bargaining agreements which terminate after July 30, 1984, and before January 1, 1985, the amendments made by section 301 shall not apply to plan amendments adopted before April 1, 1985, pursuant to such successor agreements (without regard to any modification or reopening after December 31, 1984).

Regulations

The following regulations were adopted under "Title 29—Labor," "Chapter XXV—Pension and Welfare Benefit Programs, Department of Labor," "Subchapter C—Minimum Standards for Employee Pension Benefit Plans Under the Employee Retirement Income Security Act of 1974," "Part 2530—Rules and Regulations for Minimum Standards for Employee Pension Benefit Plans." The regulations were filed with the Federal Register on December 23, 1976, and published in the Federal Register of December 28, 1976 (41 FR 56462).

[¶ 14,441]
§ 2530.204-1 Year of participation for benefit accrual.

(a) *General.* Section 204(b)(1) of the Act and section 411(b)(1) of the Code contain certain requirements relating to benefit accrual under a defined benefit pension plan. Some of these requirements are based on the number of years of participation included in an employee's period of service. Paragraph (b) of this section relates to service which must be taken into account in determining an employee's period of service for purposes of benefit accrual. Section 2530.204-2 sets forth rules relating to the computation periods to be used in measuring years of participation for benefit accrual ("accrual computation periods").

(b) *Service which may be disregarded for purposes of benefit accrual.* (1) In calculating an employee's period of service for purposes of benefit accrual under a defined benefit pension plan, section 204(b)(3) of the Act and section 411(b)(3) of the Code permit the following service to be disregarded: service before an employee first becomes a participant in the plan; service which is not required to be taken into account under section 202(b) of the Act and section 410(b)(5) of the Code (relating to one-year breaks in service for purposes of eligibility to participate); and service which is not required to be taken into account under section 204(b)(3)(C) of the Act and section 411(b)(3)(C) of the Code (relating to 12-consecutive-month periods during which an employee's service is less than 1000 hours). In addition, in calculating an employee's period of service for purposes of benefit accrual, a defined benefit plan shall not be required to take into

account service before the conclusion of a series of consecutive 1-year breaks in service occurs which permits a plan to disregard prior service under section 203(b)(3)(D) of the Act and section 411(a)(6)(D) of the Code.

(2) *Example.* The following example illustrates paragraph (b)(1) of this section. A plan has a calendar year vesting and accrual computation period and, under § 2530.202-2(a) and (b)(1), uses eligibility computation periods beginning on an employee's employment commencement date and anniversaries thereof. The plan provides that an employee who has at least 10 years of service has a vested right to 100 percent of his accrued benefit derived from employer contributions. The plan provides that an employee who is credited with at least 1,000 hours of service in a calendar year accrual computation period is credited with at least partial year of participation for purposes of benefit accrual. An employee whose birthday is October 16, 1956, begins employment with an employer maintaining the plan on January 1, 1977. Under § 2530.202-2(a)(1), January 1, 1977 is the employee's employment commencement date and the calendar year 1977 is the employee's initial eligibility computation period. The employee completes at least 1,000 hours of service in each of the calendar years from 1977 through 1981. On January 1, 1982 the employee is admitted to participation in the plan, having met the plan's age requirement (25 years) and service requirement (one year of service) for eligibility to participate. In 1982, the employee is credited with the number of hours of service required for a full year of participation (i.e., more than 1,000 hours of service). Under § 2530.202-2(c), for purposes of applying section

202(b)(4) of the Act and section 410(a)(5)(D) of the Code (relating to years of service completed before a break in service for purposes of eligibility to participate), eligibility computation periods beginning on the employee's employment commencement date and anniversaries thereof are used under the plan to measure service prior to a break in service (in addition, under § 2530.200b-4(a)(2), the same eligibility computation periods are used in measuring one-year breaks in service for purposes of eligibility to participate). Thus, as of January 1, 1983, the employee is credited with six years of service for purposes of eligibility to participate and is credited with one year of participation. In accordance with section 203(b)(1)(A) of the Act and section 411(a)(4)(A) of the Code, the plan provides that years of service completed before age 22 are disregarded for purposes of vesting. As of January 1, 1983, therefore, the employee is credited with four years of service for purposes of vesting. In 1983 the employee terminates employment with the employer, incurrinng one-year breaks in service in each of the calendar years from 1983 through 1986. As of December 31, 1986, the employee's consecutive one-year breaks in service equal the employee's four years of service for vesting before such breaks. Under section 203(b)(3)(D) of the Act and section 410(a)(5)(D) of the Code and the terms of the plan, the four years of service for vesting completed by the employee before his four consecutive one-year breaks in service are not taken into account for purposes of vesting. Under paragraph (b)(1) of this section, therefore, in calculating the employee's period of service for purposes of benefit accrual, the plan may disregard the year of participation completed by the employee before his four consecutive one-year breaks in service for vesting, because the four consecutive one-year breaks in service equal the four years of service credited to the employee for vesting. The employee is re-employed by the employer on January 1, 1987 completing an hour of service on that date. Under § 2530.-200b-4(b)(1), therefore, January 1, 1987 is the employee's reemployment commencement date. In 1987, the employee completes the number of hours of service required for a full year of participation (i.e., more than 1,000 hours of service). For 1987, therefore, the employee is credited with a year of service for purposes of eligibility to participate and vesting, and with a year of participation. As of December 31, 1987, the employee is credited with one year of service for purposes of vesting, since service before the employee's four consecutive one-year breaks in service—including the year of service completed in 1982—is not taken into account. Because under paragraph (b)(1) of this section, the year of participation credited to the employee for 1982 is not required to be taken into account for purposes of benefit accrual, the employee is credited with one year of participation as of December 31, 1987.

[¶ 14,442]

§ 2530.204-2 **Accrual computation period.**

(a) *Designation of accrual computation periods.* A plan may designate any 12-consecutive-month period as the accrual computation period except that the period so designated must apply equally to all participants. This requirement may be satisfied even though the actual time periods are not the same for all participants. For example, the accrual computation period may be designated as the vesting computation period, the plan year, or the 12-consecutive-month period beginning on either of two semi-annual dates designated for entry to participation under a plan.

(b) *Participation prior to effective date.* For purposes of applying the accrual rules of section 204(b)(1)(D) of the Act and section 411(b)(1)(D) of the Code (relating to accrual requirements for defined benefit plans for periods prior to the effective date of those sections), all service from the date of participation in the plan, as determined in accordance with applicable plan provisions, shall be taken into account in determining an employee's period of service. When the plan documents do not provide a definite means for determining the date of commencement of participation, the date of commencement of employment covered under the plan during the period that the employer maintained the plan shall be presumed to be the date of commencement of participation in the plan. The plan may rebut this presumption by demonstrating from circumstances surrounding the operation of the plan, such as the date of commencement of mandatory employee contributions, that participation actually began on a later date.

(c) *Partial year of participation.* (1) Under section 204(b)(3)(C) of the Act and section 411(b)(3)(C) of the Code, in calculating an employee's period of service for purposes of benefit accrual, a plan is not required to take into account a 12-consecutive-month period during which the employee's service is less than 1000 hours of service. In measuring an employee's service for purposes of section 204(b)(3)(C) of the Act and section 411(b)(3)(C) of the Code, a plan shall use the accrual computation period designated under paragraph (a) of this section. Under section 204(b)(3)(B) of the Act and section 411(b)(3)(B) of the Code, in the case of an employee whose service is not less than 1,000 hours of service during an accrual computation period, the calculation of such employee's period of service will not be treated as made on a reasonable and consistent basis unless service during such computation period is taken into account. To the extent that the employee's service during the accrual computation period is less than the service required under the plan for a full year of participation, the employee must be credited with a partial year of participation equivalent to no less than a ratable portion of a full year of participation.

(2) For purposes of calculating the portion of a full year of participation to be credited to an employee whose service during a computation period is not less than 1,000 hours of service but is less than service required for a full year of participation in the plan, the plan may credit the employee with a greater portion of a full year of participation than a ratable portion, or may credit an employee with a full year of participation even though the employee's service is less than the service required for a full year of participation, provided that such crediting is reasonable and is consistent for all employees within the same job classifications, reasonably established.

(3) In the case of an employee who commences participation in a plan (or recommences participation in the plan upon the employee's return after one or more 1-year breaks in service) on a date other than the first day of an applicable accrual computation period, all hours of service required to be credited to the employee during the entire accrual computation period, including hours of service credited to the employee for the portion of the computation period before the date on which the employee commences (or recommences) participation, shall be taken into account in determining whether the employee has 1,000 or more hours of service for purposes of section 204(b)(3)(C) of the Act and section 411(b)(3)(C) of the Code. If such employee's service is not less than 1,000 hours in such accrual computation period, the employee must be credited with a partial year of participation which is equivalent to no less than a ratable portion of a full year of participation for service credited to the employee for the portion of the computation period after the date of commencement (or recommencement) of participation.

(4) *Examples.* The following are examples of reasonable and consistent methods for crediting partial years of participation:

(i) A plan requires 2,000 hours of service for a full year of participation. An employee who is credited during a computation period with no less than 1,000 hours of service but less than 2,000 hours of service is credited with a partial year of participation equal to a portion of a full year of participation determined by dividing the number of hours of service credited to the employee by 2,000.

(ii) A plan requires 2,000 hours of service for a full year of participation. The plan credits service in an accrual computation period in accordance with the following table:

Hours of service credited:	Percentage of full year of participation credited
1000	50
1001 to 1200	60
1201 to 1400	70
1401 to 1600	80
1601 to 1800	90
1801 and above	100

Under this method of crediting partial years of participation, each employee who is credited with not less than 1,000 hours of service is credited with at least a ratable portion of a full year of participation.

(iii) A plan provides that each employee who is credited with at least 1,000 hours of service in an accrual computation period must receive credit for at least a partial year of participation for that computation period. For full accrual, however, the plan requires that an employee must be credited with a specified number of hours worked; employees who meet the 1,000 hours of service requirement but who are not credited with the specified number of hours worked required for a full year of participation are credited with a partial year of participation on a pro rata basis. For example, if the plan requires 1,500 hours worked for full accrual, an employee with 1,500 hours worked would be credited with full accrual, but an employee with 1,000 hours worked and 500 other hours of service would be credited with ⅔ of full accrual. The plan's method of crediting service for accrual purposes is consistent with the requirements of this paragraph. It should be noted, however, that use of hours worked as a basis for prorating benefit accrual may result in discrimination prohibited under section 401(a)(4) of the Code.

(iv) Employee A is employed on June 1, 1980 in service covered by a plan with a calendar year accrual computation period, and which requires 1,800 hours of service for a full accrual. Employee A completes 500 hours from June 1, 1980 to December 31, 1980, and completes 100 hours per month in each month during 1981. A is admitted to participation on July 1, 1981. A is credited with 1,200 hours of service for the accrual computation period beginning January 1, 1981. Under the rules set forth in paragraph (c)(3) of this section, A is required to be credited with not less than one-third of a full accrual (600 hours divided by 1,800 hours).

(d) *Prohibited double proration.* (1) In the case of a defined benefit plan that (i) defines benefits on a basis which has the effect of prorating benefits to reflect less than full-time employment or less than maximum compensation and (ii) does not adjust less-than-full-time service to reflect the equivalent of full-time hours or compensation (as the case may be), the plan may not further prorate benefit accrual under section 204(b)(3)(B) of the Act and section 411(b)(3)(B) of the Code by crediting less than full years of participation, as would otherwise be permitted under paragraph (c) of this section. These plans must credit, except when service may be disregarded under section 204(b)(3)(C) of the Act and section 411(b)(3)(C) of the Code (relating to less than 1000 hours of service), less-than-full-time employees with a full year of participation for the purpose of accrual of benefits.

(2) *Examples.* (i) A plan's defined benefit formula provides that the annual retirement benefit shall be 2 percent of the average compensation in all years of participation multiplied by the number of years of participation. Employee A is a full-time employee who has completed 2,000 hours during each of 20 accrual computation periods. A's average hourly rate was $5 an hour. Thus, A's average compensation for each year during participation in the plan is $10,000 ($5 per hour multiplied by 2,000 hours). If the plan states that a full year of participation is 2,000 hours, then A's annual retirement benefits, if he retired at that time, would be $4,000 ($10,000 per year of compensation × .02 × 20 years of participation). Employee B, however, is a part-time employee who completes 1,000 hours of service during each of 20 accrual computation periods. Like A, B's average hourly rate is $5 per hour. B's average compensation is $5,000 ($5 per hour multiplied by 1,000 hours). Thus, the plan's benefit formula, by basing benefits on an employee's average compensation in all years of participation, in effect prorates benefits to reflect the fact that during B's participation in the plan, he has earned less than the maximum compensation that a full-time employee paid at the same rate could earn during the same period of participation in the plan. Under the rule of subparagraph (1), therefore, the plan is not permitted to prorate B's years of participation to reflect B's less than full-time employment throughout his participation in the plan. Therefore, B's annual retirement benefit would be $2,000 ($5,000 average compensation × .02 × 20 years of participation). (If double proration were permitted, then B's total years of participation would be only 10 since he would be credited with only one-half of a year of participation during each of the accrual computation periods (1,000/2,000). Thus, B's annual retirement benefit would be $1,000— i.e., $5,000 average compensation × .02 × 10 years of participation.)

(ii) If the plan adjusts the average compensation during plan participation to reflect full compensation, then the plan may prorate years of participation. Thus, the average full annual compensation for B

would be $10,000 rather than the $5,000 actually paid. Employee B's annual retirement benefit would then be $2,000 ($10,000 average full compensation × .02 × 10 years of participation).

(e) *Amendments to change accrual computation periods.* (1) A plan may be amended to change the accrual computation period to a different 12-consecutive-month period, provided that the period between the end of the last accrual computation period under the plan as in effect before such amendment and the beginning of the first accrual computation period under the plan as amended is treated as a partial accrual computation period in accordance with the rules set forth in subparagraph (2) of this paragraph.

(2) In the case of a partial accrual computation period, the following rules shall apply:

(i) A plan having a minimum service requirement expressed in hours of service (or other units of service) for benefit accrual in a full accrual computation period (as permitted under section 204(b)(3)(B) of the Act and section 411(b)(3)(B) of the Code) may apply a minimum service requirement for benefit accrual in a full accrual computation period, multiplied by the ratio of the length of the partial accrual computation period to a full year.

(ii) In the case of a participant who meets a plan's minimum service requirement for benefit accrual in a partial accrual computation period (as permitted under subparagraph (2)(i) of this paragraph), the plan shall credit the participant with at least a partial year of participation for purposes of benefit accrual. Credit for a partial accrual computation period shall be determined in accordance with paragraphs (c) and (d) of this section.

(3) *Example.* Effective October 1, 1977, a plan is amended to change the accrual computation period from the 12-consecutive-month period beginning on January 1 to the 12-consecutive-month period beginning on October 1. The period from January 1, 1977 to September 30, 1977 must be treated as a partial accrual computation period. The plan has a requirement that a participant must be credited with 1,000 hours of service in an accrual computation period in order to be credited with a year of participation for purposes of benefit accrual. For the partial accrual computation period the plan may require a participant to be credited with 750 hours of service in the partial accrual computation period in order to receive credit for purposes of benefit accrual (1,000 hours of service multiplied by the ratio of 9 months to 12 months). To the extent permitted under paragraph (d) of this section, the plan may prorate accrual credit on whatever basis the plan uses to prorate accrual credit for employees whose service is 1,000 hours of service or more but less than service required for full accrual in a full accrual computation period.

[¶ 14,443]

§ 2530.204-3 Alternative computation methods for benefit accrual.

(a) *General.* Under section 204(b)(3)(A) of the Act and section 411(b)(3)(A) of the Code, a defined benefit pension plan may determine an employee's service for purposes of benefit accrual on the basis of accrual computation periods, as specified in § 2530.204-2, or on any other basis which is reasonable and consistent and which takes into account all covered service during the employee's participation in the plan which is included in a period of service required to be taken into account under section 202(b) of the Act and section 410(a)(5) of the Code. If, however, a plan determines an employee's service for purposes of benefit accrual on a basis other than computation periods, it must be possible to prove that, despite the fact that benefit accrual under the plan is not based on computation periods, the plan's provisions meet at least one of the three benefit accrual rules of section 204(b)(1) of the Act and section 411(b)(1) of the Code under all circumstances. Further, a plan which does not provide for benefit accrual on the basis of computation periods may not disregard service under section 204(b)(3)(C) of the Act and section 411(b)(3)(C) of the Code.

(b) *Examples.* The following are examples of methods of determining an employee's period of service for purposes of benefit accrual under which an employee's period of service is not determined on the basis of computation periods but which may be used by a plan provided that the requirements of paragraph (a) of this section are met:

(1) *Career Compensation.* A defined benefit formula based on a percentage of compensation earned in a participant's career or during participation, with no variance depending on hours completed in given periods.

(2) *Credited Hours.* A defined benefit formula pursuant to which an employee is credited with a specified amount of accrual for each hour of service (or hour worked or regular time hour) completed by the employee during his or her career.

(3) *Elapsed Time.* See § 2530.200b-9 (e).

[¶ 14,444]

§ 2530.204-4 **Deferral of Benefit Accrual.** For purposes of section 204(b)(1)(E) of the Act and section 411(b)(1)(E) of the Code (which permit deferral of benefit accrual until an employee has two continuous years of service), an employee shall be credited with a year of service for each computation period in which he or she completes 1,000 hours of service. The computation period shall be the eligibility computation period designated in accordance with § 2530.202-2.

[¶ 14,450]
REQUIREMENT OF JOINT AND SURVIVOR ANNUITY AND PRERETIREMENT SURVIVOR ANNUITY

Act Sec. 205. (a) Each pension plan to which this section applies shall provide that

(1) in the case of a vested participant who does not die before the annuity starting date, the accrued benefit payable to such participant shall be provided in the form of a qualified joint and survivor annuity, and

(2) in the case of a vested participant who dies before the annuity starting date and who has a surviving spouse, a qualified preretirement survivor annuity shall be provided to the surviving spouse of such participant.

Act Sec. 205. (b)(1) This section shall apply to—

(A) any defined benefit plan,

(B) any individual account plan which is subject to the funding standards of section 302, and

(C) any participant under any other individual account plan unless—

(i) such plan provides that the participant's nonforfeitable accrued benefit (reduced by any security interest held by the plan by reason of a loan outstanding to such participant) is payable in full, on the death of the participant, to the participant's surviving spouse (or, if there is no surviving spouse or the surviving spouse consents in the manner required under subsection (c)(2), to a designated beneficiary),

(ii) such participant does not elect the payment of benefits in the form of a life annuity, and

(iii) with respect to such participant, such plan is not a direct or indirect transferee (in a transfer after December 31, 1984) of a plan which is described in subparagraph (A) or (B) or to which this clause applied with respect to the participant.

Clause (iii) of subparagraph (C) shall apply only with respect to the transferred assets (and income therefrom) if the plan separately accounts for such assets and any income therefrom.

(2)(A) In the case of—

(i) a tax credit employee stock ownership plan (as defined in section 409(a) of the Internal Revenue Code of 1986), or

(ii) an employee stock ownership plan (as defined in section 4975(e)(7) of such Code),

subsection (a) shall not apply to that portion of the employee's accrued benefit to which the requirements of section 409(h) of such Code apply.

(B) Subparagraph (A) shall not apply with respect to any participant unless the requirements of clause (i), (ii), and (iii) of paragraph (1)(C) are met with respect to such participant.

(3) A plan shall not be treated as failing to meet the requirements of paragraph (1)(C) or (2) merely because the plan provides that benefits will not be payable to the surviving spouse of the participant unless the participant and such spouse had been married throughout the 1-year period ending on the earlier of the participant's annuity starting date or the date of the participant's death.

(4) This section shall not apply to a plan which the Secretary of the Treasury or his delegate has determined is a plan described in section 404(c) of the Internal Revenue Code of 1986 (or a continuation thereof) in which participation is substantially limited to individuals who, before January 1, 1976, ceased employment covered by the plan.

Act Sec. 205. (c)(1) A plan meets the requirements of this section only if—

(A) under the plan, each participant—

(i) may elect at any time during the applicable election period to waive the qualified joint and survivor annuity form of benefit or the qualified preretirement survivor annuity form of benefit (or both), and

(ii) may revoke any such election at any time during the applicable election period, and

(B) the plan meets the requirements of paragraphs (2), (3), and (4).

(2) Each plan shall provide that an election under paragraph (1)(A)(i) shall not take effect unless—

(A)(i) the spouse of the participant consents in writing to such election, (ii) such election designates a beneficiary (or a form of benefits) which may not be changed without spousal consent (or the consent of the spouse expressly permits designations by the participant without any requirement of further consent by the spouse), and (iii) the spouse's consent acknowledges the effect of such election and is witnessed by a plan representative or a notary public, or

(B) it is established to the satisfaction of a plan representative that the consent required under subparagraph (A) may not be obtained because there is no spouse, because the spouse cannot be located, or because of such other circumstances as the Secretary of the Treasury may by regulations prescribe.

Any consent by a spouse (or establishment that the consent of a spouse may not be obtained) under the preceding sentence shall be effective only with respect to such spouse.

(3)(A) Each plan shall provide to each participant, within a reasonable period of time before the annuity starting date (and consistent with such regulations as the Secretary of the Treasury may prescribe) a written explanation of—

(i) the terms and conditions of the qualified joint and survivor annuity,

(ii) the participant's right to make, and the effect of, an election under paragraph (1) to waive the joint and survivor annuity form of benefit,

(iii) the rights of the participant's spouse under paragraph (2), and

(iv) the right to make, and the effect of, a revocation of an election under paragraph (1).

(B)(i) Each plan shall provide to each participant, within the applicable period with respect to such participant (and consistent with such regulations as the Secretary may prescribe), a written explanation with respect to the qualified preretirement survivor annuity comparable to that required under subparagraph (A).

(ii) For purposes of clause (i), the term "applicable period" means, with respect to a participant, whichever of the following periods ends last:

(I) The period beginning with the first day of the plan year in which the participant attains age 32 and ending with the close of the plan year preceding the plan year in which the participant attains age 35.

(II) A reasonable period after the individual becomes a participant.

(III) A reasonable period ending after paragraph (5) ceases to apply to the participant.

(IV) A reasonable period ending after section 205 applies to the participant.

In the case of a participant who separates from service before attaining age 35, the applicable period shall be a reasonable period after separation.

(4) Each plan shall provide that, if this section applies to a participant when part or all of the participant's accrued benefit is to be used as security for a loan, no portion of the participant's accrued benefit may be used as security for such loan unless—

(A) the spouse of the participant (if any) consents in writing to such use during the 90-day period ending on the date on which the loan is to be so secured, and

(B) requirements comparable to the requirements of paragraph (2) are met with respect to such consent.

(5) (A) The requirements of this subsection shall not apply with respect to the qualified joint and survivor annuity form of benefit or the qualified preretirement survivor annuity form of benefit, as the case may be, if such benefit may not be waived or another beneficiary selected and if the plan fully subsidizes the costs of such benefit.

(B) For purposes of subparagraph (A), a plan fully subsidizes the costs of a benefit if under the plan the failure to waive such benefit by a participant would not result in a decrease in any plan benefits with respect to such participant and would not result in increased contributions from such participant.

(6) If a plan fiduciary acts in accordance with part 4 of this subtitle in—

(A) relying on a consent or revocation referred to in paragraph (1) (A), or

(B) making a determination under paragraph (2),

then such consent, revocation, or determination shall be treated as valid for purposes of discharging the plan from liability to the extent of payments made pursuant to such Act.

(7) For purposes of this subsection, the term "applicable election period" means—

(A) in the case of an election to waive the qualified joint and survivor annuity form of benefit, the 90-day period ending on the annuity starting date, or

(B) in the case of an election to waive the qualified preretirement survivor annuity, the period which begins on the first day of the plan year in which the participant attains age 35 and ends on the date of the participant's death.

In the case of a participant who is separated from service, the applicable election period under subparagraph (B) with respect to benefits accrued before the date of such separation from service shall not begin later than such date.

(8) Notwithstanding any other provision of this subsection—

(A) (i) A plan may provide the written explanation described in paragraph (3) (A) after the annuity starting date. In any case to which this subparagraph applies, the applicable election period under paragraph (7) shall not end before the 30th day after the date on which such explanation is provided.

(ii) The Secretary of the Treasury may by regulations limit the application of clause (i), except that such regulations may not limit the period of time by which the annuity starting date precedes the provision of the written explanation other than by providing that the annuity starting date may not be earlier than termination of employment.

(B) A plan may permit a participant to elect (with any applicable spousal consent) to waive any requirement that the written explanation be provided at least 30 days before the annuity starting date (or to waive the 30-day requirement under subparagraph (A)) if the distribution commences more than 7 days after such explanation is provided.

Act Sec. 205. (d) For purposes of this section, the term "qualified joint and survivor annuity" means an annuity—

(1) for the life of the participant with a survivor annuity for the life of the spouse which is not less than 50 percent of (and is not greater than 100 percent of) the amount of the annuity which is payable during the joint lives of the participant and the spouse, and

(2) which is the actuarial equivalent of a single annuity for the life of the participant.

Such term also includes any annuity in a form having the effect of an annuity described in the preceding sentence.

Act Sec. 205. (e) For purposes of this section—

(1) Except as provided in paragraph (2), the term "qualified preretirement survivor annuity" means a survivor annuity for the life of the surviving spouse of the participant if—

(A) the payments to the surviving spouse under such annuity are not less than the amounts which would be payable as a survivor annuity under the qualified joint and survivor annuity under the plan (or the actuarial equivalent thereof) if—

(i) in the case of a participant who dies after the date on which the participant attained the earliest retirement age, such participant had retired with an immediate qualified joint and survivor annuity on the day before the participant's date of death, or

(ii) in the case of a participant who dies on or before the date on which the participant would have attained the earliest retirement age, such participant had—

(I) separated from service on the date of death,

(II) survived to the earliest retirement age,

(III) retired with an immediate qualified joint and survivor annuity at the earliest retirement age, and

(IV) died on the day after the day on which such participant would have attained the earliest retirement age, and

(B) under the plan, the earliest period for which the surviving spouse may receive a payment under such annuity is not later than the month in which the participant would have attained the earliest retirement age under the plan.

In the case of an individual who separated from service before the date of such individual's death, subparagraph (a) (ii) (I) shall not apply.

(2) In the case of any individual account plan or participant described in subparagraph (B) or (C) of subsection (b) (1), the term "qualified preretirement survivor annuity" means an annuity for the life of the surviving spouse the actuarial equivalent of which is not less than 50 percent of the portion of the account balance of the participant (as of the date of death) to which the participant had a nonforfeitable right (within the meaning of section 203).

(3) For purposes of paragraphs (1) and (2), any security interest held by the plan by reason of a loan outstanding to the participant shall be taken into account in determining the amount of the qualified preretirement survivor annuity.

Act Sec. 205. (f) (1) Except as provided in paragraph (2), a plan may provide that a qualified joint and survivor annuity (or a qualified preretirement survivor annuity) will not be provided unless the participant and spouse had been married throughout the 1-year period ending on the earlier of—

(A) the participant's annuity starting date, or

(B) the date of the participant's death.

(2) For purposes of paragraph (1), if—

(A) a participant marries within 1 year before the annuity starting date, and

(B) the participant and the participant's spouse in such marriage have been married for at least a 1-year period ending on or before the date of the participant's death,

such participant and such spouse shall be treated as having been married throughout the 1-year period ending on the participant's annuity starting date.

Act Sec. 205. (g) (1) A plan may provide that the present value of a qualified joint and survivor annuity or a qualified preretirement survivor annuity will be immediately distributed if such value does not exceed the amount that can be distributed without the participant's consent under section 203 (e). No distribution may be made under the preceding sentence after the annuity starting date unless the participant and the spouse of the participant (or where the participant has died, the surviving spouse) consent in writing to such distribution.

(2) If—

(A) the present value of the qualified joint and survivor annuity or the qualified preretirement survivor annuity exceeds the amount that can be distributed without the participant's consent under section 203(e), and

(B) the participant and the spouse of the participant (or where the participant has died, the surviving spouse) consent in writing to the distribution, the plan may immediately distribute the present value of such annuity.

(3) DETERMINATION OF PRESENT VALUE.—

(A) IN GENERAL.—

(i) PRESENT VALUE. Except as provided in subparagraph (B), for purposes of paragraphs (1) and (2), the present value shall not be less than the present value calculated by using the applicable mortality table and the applicable interest rate.

(ii) DEFINITIONS. For purposes of clause (i)—

(I) APPLICABLE MORTALITY TABLE. The term "applicable mortality table" means the table prescribed by the Secretary of the Treasury. Such table shall be based on the prevailing commissioners' standard table (described in section 807(d)(5)(A) of the Internal Revenue Code of 1986) used to determine reserves for group annuity contracts issued on the date as of which present value is being determined (without regard to any other subparagraph of section 807(d)(5) of such Code).

(II) APPLICABLE INTEREST RATE. The term "applicable interest rate" means the annual rate of interest on 30-year Treasury securities for the month before the date of distribution or such other time as the Secretary of the Treasury may by regulations prescribe.

(B) EXCEPTION. In the case of a distribution from a plan that was adopted and in effect prior to the date of the enactment of the Retirement Protection Act of 1994, the present value of any distribution made before the earlier of—

(i) the later of when a plan amendment applying subparagraph (A) is adopted or made effective, or

(ii) the first day of the first plan year beginning after December 31, 1999,

shall be calculated, for purposes of paragraphs (1) and (2), using the interest rate determined under the regulations of the Pension Benefit Guaranty Corporation for determining the present value of a lump sum distribution on plan termination that were in effect on September 1, 1993, and using the provision of the plan as in effect on the day before such date of enactment; but only if such provisions of the plan met the requirements of section 205(g)(3) as in effect on the date before such date of enactment.

Act Sec. 205. (h) For purposes of this section—

(1) The term "vested participant" means any participant who has a nonforfeitable right (within the meaning of section 3(19)) to any portion of such participant's accrued benefit.

(2)(A) The term "annuity starting date" means—

(i) the first day of the first period for which an amount is paid as an annuity, or

(ii) in the case of a benefit not payable in the form of an annuity, the first day on which all events have occurred which entitle the participant to such benefit.

(B) For purposes of subparagraph (A), the first day of the first period for which a benefit is to be received by reason of disability shall be treated as the annuity starting date only if such benefit is not an auxiliary benefit.

(3) The term "earliest retirement age" means the earliest date on which, under the plan, the participant could elect to receive retirement benefits.

Act Sec. 205. (i) A plan may take into account in any equitable manner (as determined by the Secretary of the Treasury) any increased costs resulting from providing a qualified joint or survivor annuity or a qualified preretirement survivor annuity.

Act Sec. 205. (j) If the use of any participant's accrued benefit (or any portion thereof) as security for a loan meets the requirements of subsection (c)(4), nothing in this section shall prevent any distribution required by reason of a failure to comply with the terms of such loan.

Act Sec. 205. (k) No consent of a spouse shall be effective for purposes of subsection (g)(1) or (g)(2) (as the case may be) unless requirements comparable to the requirements for spousal consent to an election under subsection (c)(1)(A) are met.

Act Sec. 205. (l) In prescribing regulations under this section, the Secretary of the Treasury shall consult with the Secretary of Labor.

Amendments

P.L. 107-147, §411(r)(2):

Act Sec. 411(r)(2)(A) amended ERISA Sec. 205(g)(1) by striking "exceed the dollar limit under section 203(e)(1)" and inserting "exceed the amount that can be distributed without the participant's consent under section 203(e)."

Act Sec. 411(r)(2)(B) amended ERISA Sec. 205(g)(2)(A) by striking "exceeds the dollar limit under section 203(e)(1)" and inserting "exceeds the amount that can be distributed without the participant's consent under section 203(e)."

P.L. 105-34, §1601(d)(5):

Act Sec. 1601(d)(5) amended ERISA Sec. 205(c)(8)(A)(ii) by striking "Secretary" and inserting "Secretary of the Treasury".

The above amendment is effective with respect to plan years beginning after December 31, 1996.

P.L. 105-34, §1071(g)(1):

Act Sec. 1071(g)(1) amended ERISA Sec. 205(g)(1) by striking "$3,500" and inserting "$5,000".

P.L. 105-34, §1071(g)(2):

Act Sec. 1071(g)(2) amended ERISA Sec. 205(g)(2) by striking "$3,500" and inserting "$5,000".

The above amendments are effective for plan years beginning after August 5, 1997.

P.L. 104-188, §1451(b):

Act Sec. 1451(b) amended ERISA Sec. 205(c) by adding at the end the new paragraph (8) to read as above.

The above amendment applies to plan years beginning after December 31, 1996.

P.L. 103-465, §767(c)(2):

Act Sec. 767(c)(2) amended ERISA Sec. 205(g)(3) to read as above. Prior to amendment, ERISA Sec. 205(g)(3) read as follows:

(3)(A) For purposes of paragraphs (1) and (2), the present value shall be calculated—

(i) by using an interest rate no greater than the applicable interest rate if the vested accrued benefit (using such rate) is not in excess of $25,000, and

(ii) by using an interest rate no greater than 120 percent of the applicable interest rate if the vested accrued benefit exceeds $25,000 (as determined under clause (i)).

In no event shall the present value determined under subclause (II) be less than $25,000.

(B) For purposes of subparagraph (A), the term "applicable interest rate" means the interest rate which would be used (as of the date of the distribution) by the Pension Benefit Guaranty Corporation for purposes of determining the present value of a lump sum distribution on plan termination.

The above amendment applies to plan years and limitation years beginning after December 31, 1994, except that an employer may elect to treat the amendments made by this section as being effective on or after December 8, 1994. For special rules, see Act Sec. 767(e)(2)-(3), following ERISA Sec. 203(e).

P.L. 101-239, §7862(d)(1)(B):

Amended ERISA Sec. 205(c)(3)(B)(ii) by striking clause (V) and inserting a new flush sentence to read as above effective for plan years beginning after 1984. Previously, clause (V) read as follows:

(V) A reasonable period after separation from service in case of a participant who separates before attaining age 35.

P.L. 101-239, §7862(d)(3):

Amended ERISA Sec. 205(h) in paragraph (1), by striking "the term" and inserting "The term", and by striking "benefit," and inserting "benefit."; and in paragraph (3), by striking "the term" and inserting "The term", effective for plan years beginning after 1984.

P.L. 101-239, §7862(d)(6):

Amended ERISA Sec. 205(c)(3)(B)(ii) by striking "401(a)(11)" and inserting "205" effective for plan years beginning after 1984.

P.L. 101-239, §7862(d)(8):

Amended ERISA Sec. 205(e)(2) by striking "nonforfeitable accrued benefit" and inserting "nonforfeitable right (within the meaning of section 203)" effective for plan years beginning after 1984.

P.L. 101-239, §7862(d)(9)(B):

Redesignated paragraph (3) of ERISA Sec. 205(b) (as added by P.L. 99-514, §1898(b)(14)(B)) as paragraph (4) effective for plan years beginning after 1984.

P.L. 101-239, §7891(e):

Amended ERISA Sec. 205(h) by striking "the term" and inserting "The term" and by striking "benefit," and inserting "benefit." in paragraph (1) and by striking "the term" and inserting "The term" in paragraph (3) effective October 22, 1986.

P.L. 101-239, §7894(c)(7):

Amended ERISA Sec. 205(c)(6) by striking "act" and inserting "Act" effective September 2, 1974.

P.L. 99-514, §1139(c)(2):

Amended paragraph (3) of Sec. 205(g) to read as above. Prior to amendment, paragraph (3) read as follows:

Act Sec. 205(g).

* * *

(3) For purposes of paragraphs (1) and (2), the present value of a qualified joint and survivor annuity or a qualified preretirement survivor annuity shall be determined as of the date of the distribution and by using an interest rate not greater than the interest rate which would be used (as of the date of the distribution) by the Pension Benefit Guaranty Corporation for purposes of determining the present value of a lump-sum distribution on plan termination.

P.L. 99-514, §1139(d):

Act Sec. 1139(d) provides as follows:

(d) EFFECTIVE DATE.—

(1) IN GENERAL.—The amendments made by this section shall apply to distributions in plan years beginning after December 31, 1984, except that such amendments shall not apply to any distributions in plan years beginning after December 31, 1984, and before January 1, 1987, if such distributions were made in accordance with the requirements of the regulations issued under the Retirement Equity Act of 1984.

(2) Reduction in Accrued Benefits.—

(A) IN GENERAL.—If a plan—

(i) adopts a plan amendment before the close of the first plan year beginning on or before January 1, 1989, which provides for the calculation of the present value of the accrued benefits in the manner provided by the amendments made by this section, and

(ii) the plan reduces the accrued benefits for any plan year to which such plan amendment applies in accordance with such plan amendment,

such reduction shall not be treated as a violation of section 411(d)(6) of the Internal Revenue Code of 1986 or section 204(g) of the Employee Retirement Income Security Act of 1974 (29 U.S.C. 1054(g)).

(B) SPECIAL RULE.—In the case of a plan maintained by a corporation incorporated on April 11, 1934, which is headquartered in Tarrant County, Texas—

(i) such plan may be amended to remove the option of an employee to receive a lump-sum distribution (within the meaning of section 402(e)(5) of such Code) if such amendment—

(I) is adopted within 1 year of the date of the enactment of this Act, and

(II) is not effective until 2 years after the employees are notified of such amendment, and

(ii) the present value of any vested accrued benefit of such plan determined during the 3-year period beginning on the date of the enactment of this Act shall be determined under the applicable interest rate (within the meaning of section 411(a)(11)(B)(ii) of such Code), except that if such value (as so determined) exceeds $50,000, then the value of any excess over $50,000 shall be determined by using the interest rate specified in the plan as of August 16, 1986.

P.L. 99-514, §1145(b):

Amended ERISA Sec. 205(b) by adding a new paragraph (3) to read as above, effective for taxable years beginning after 1984.

P.L. 99-514, §1898(b)(1)(B):

Amended ERISA Sec. 205(e)(1) by adding a new sentence at the end to read as above, effective for plan years beginning after 1984.

P.L. 99-514, §1898(b)(2)(B)(i):

Amended ERISA Sec. 205(b)(1)(C)(iii) by striking out "a transferee" and inserting "a direct or indirect transferee (in a transfer after December 31, 1984)" instead, effective for plan years beginning after 1984.

P.L. 99-514, §1898(b)(2)(B)(ii):

Amended ERISA Sec. 205(b)(1) by adding a new sentence at the end to read as above, effective for plan years beginning after 1984.

P.L. 99-514, §1898(b)(3)(B):

Amended ERISA Sec. 205(a)(1) by striking out "who retires under the plan" and inserting "who does not die before the annuity starting date" instead, effective for plan years beginning after 1984.

P.L. 99-514, §1898(b)(4)(B)(i):

Amended ERISA Sec. 205(c)(1)(B) by striking "paragraphs (2) and (3)" and inserting "paragraphs (2), (3), and (4)" instead.

P.L. 99-514, §1898(b)(4)(B)(ii):

Amended ERISA Sec. 205(c) by redesignating paragraphs (4), (5), and (6) as (5), (6), and (7), respectively and by adding a new paragraph (4) to read as above.

P.L. 99-514, §1898(b)(4)(C):

Subsection (C) provides as follows:

(C) Effective dates.—

(i) The amendments made by this paragraph shall apply with respect to loans made after August 18, 1985.

(ii) In the case of any loan which was made on or before August 18, 1985, and which is secured by a portion of the participant's accrued benefit, nothing in the amendments made by sections 103 and 203 of the Retirement Equity Act of 1984 shall prevent any distribution required by reason of a failure to comply with the terms of such loan.

(iii) For purposes of this subparagraph, any loan which is revised, extended, renewed, or renegotiated after August 18, 1985, shall be treated as made after August 18, 1985.

P.L. 99-514, §1898(b)(5)(B):

Amended ERISA Sec. 205(c)(3)(B) to read as above, effective for plan years beginning after 1984. Prior to amendment, subparagraph (B) read as follows:

(B) Each plan shall provide to each participant, within the period beginning with the first day of the plan year in which the participant attains age 32 and ending with the close of the plan year preceding the plan year in which the participant attains age 35 (and consistent with such regulations as the Secretary of the Treasury may prescribe), a written explanation with respect to the qualified preretirement survivor annuity comparable to that required under subparagraph (A).

P.L. 99-514, §1898(b)(6)(B):

Amended ERISA Sec. 205(c)(2)(A) to read as above, effective for plan years beginning after 1984. Prior to amendment, subparagraph (A) read as follows:

(A) the spouse of the participant consents in writing to such election, and the spouse's consent acknowledges the effect of such election and is witnessed by a plan representative or a notary public, or

P.L. 99-514, §1898(b)(7)(B):

Amended ERISA Sec. 205(b)(1)(C) by striking out "the participant's nonforfeitable accrued benefit" and inserting "the participant's nonforfeitable accrued benefit (reduced by any security interest held by the plan by reason of a loan outstanding to such participant)" instead, effective for plan years beginning after 1984.

P.L. 99-514, §1898(b)(8)(B):

Amended ERISA Sec. 205(h)(1) by striking out "the accrued benefit derived from employer contributions" and inserting "such participant's accrued benefit" instead, effective for plan years beginning after 1984.

P.L. 99-514, §1898(b)(9)(B)(i):

Amended ERISA Sec. 205(e)(2) by striking "the account balance of the participant as of the date of death" and inserting "the portion of the account balance of the participant (as of the date of death) to which the participant had a nonforfeitable accrued benefit" instead, effective for plan years beginning after 1984.

P.L. 99-514, §1898(b)(9)(B)(ii):

Added ERISA Sec. 205(e)(3) to read as above, effective for plan years beginning after 1984.

P.L. 99-514, §1898(b)(10)(B):

Redesignated ERISA Sec. 205(k) as (l) and added new subsection (k) to read as above, effective for plan years beginning after 1984.

P.L. 99-514, §1898(b)(11)(B):

Amended ERISA Sec. 205(c)(5)(A) by striking "if the plan" and inserting "if such benefit may not be waived or another beneficiary selected and if the plan" instead, effective for plan years beginning after 1984.

P.L. 99-514, §1898(b)(12)(B):

Amended ERISA Sec. 205(h)(2) to read as above, effective for plan years beginning after 1984. Prior to amendment, paragraph (2) read as follows:

Act Sec. 205. (h) For purposes of this section—

* * *

(2) the term "annuity starting date" means the first day of the first period for which an amount is received as an annuity (whether by reason of retirement or disability), and

P.L. 99-514, §1898(b)(13)(B):

Amended ERISA Sec. 205(b)(1)(C)(i) by striking out "subsection (c)(2)(A)" and inserting "subsection (c)(2)" instead, effective for plan years beginning after 1984.

P.L. 99-514, §1898(b)(14)(B):

Added ERISA Sec. 205(b)(3) to read as above, effective for plan years beginning after 1984.

P.L. 98-397, §103:

Act Sec. 103 amended ERISA Sec. 205 by striking out the prior law and replacing it with new section 205. Prior to amendment, ERISA Sec. 205 read as follows:

(a) If a pension plan provides for the payment of benefits in the form of an annuity, such plan shall provide for the payment of annuity benefits in a form having the effect of a qualified joint and survivor annuity.

(b) In the case of a plan which provides for the payment of benefits before the normal retirement age as defined in section 3(24), the plan is not required to provide for the payment of annuity benefits in a form having the effect of a qualfied joint and survivor annuity during the period beginning on the date on which the employee enters into the plan as a participant and ending on the later of—

(1) the date the employee reaches the earliest retirement age, or

(2) the first day of the 120th month beginning before the date on which the employee reaches normal retirement age.

(c)(1) A plan described in subsection (b) does not meet the requirements of subsection (a) unless, under the plan, a participant has a reasonable period in which he may elect the qualified joint and survivor annuity form with respect to the period beginning on the date on which the period described in subsection (b) ends and ending on the date on which he reaches normal retirement age if he continues his employment during that period.

(2) A plan does not meet the requirements of this subsection unless, in the case of such election, the payments under the survivor annuity are not less than the payments which would have been made under the joint annuity to which the participant would have been entitled if he had made an election under this subsection immediately prior to his retirement and if his retirement had occurred on the date immediately preceding the date of his death and within the period within which an election can be made.

(d) A plan shall not be treated as not satisfying the requirements of this section solely because the spouse of the participant is not entitled to receive a survivor annuity (whether or not an election has been made under subsection (c)) unless the participant and his spouse have been married throughout the 1-year period ending on the date of such participant's death.

(e) A plan shall not be treated as satisfying the requirements of this section unless, under the plan, each participant has a reasonable period (as prescribed by the Secretary of the Treasury by regulations) before the annuity starting date during which he may elect in writing (after having received a written explanation of the terms and conditions of the joint and survivor annuity and the effect of an election under this subsection) not to take such joint and survivor annuity.

(f) A plan shall not be treated as not satisfying the requirements of this section solely because, under the plan there is a provision that any election under subsection (c) or (e), and any revocation of any such election, does not become effective (or ceases to be effective) if the participant dies within a period (not in excess of 2 years) beginning on the date of such election or revocation, as the case may be. The preceding sentence does not apply unless the plan provision described in the preceding sentence also provides that such an election or revocation will be given effect in any case in which—

(1) the participant dies from accidental causes,

(2) a failure to give effect to the election or revocation would deprive the participant's survivor of a survivor annuity, and

(3) such election or revocation is made before such accident occurred.

(g) For purposes of this section:

(1) The term "annuity starting date" means the first day of the first period for which an amount is received as an annuity (whether by reason of retirement or by reason or disability).

(2) The term "earliest retirement age" means the earliest date on which, under the plan, the participant could elect to receive retirement benefits.

(3) The term "qualified joint and survivor annuity" means an annuity for the life of the participant with a survivor annuity for the life of his spouse which is not less than one-half or, or greater than, the amount of the annuity payable during the joint lives of the participant and his spouse and which is the actuarial equivalent of a single annuity for the life of the participant.

(h) For the purposes of this section, a plan may take into account in any equitable fashion (as determined by the Secretary of the Treasury) any increased costs resulting from providing joint and survivor annuity benefits under an election made under subsection (c).

(i) This section shall apply only if—

(1) the annuity starting date did not occur before the effective date of this section, and

(2) the participant was an active participant in the plan on or after such effective date.

Generally, the above amendment is effective for plan years beginning after December 31, 1984. However, Act Secs. 303(c) and (e) provide:

(c) Requirement of Joint and Survivor Annuity and Preretirement Survivor Annuity.—

(1) Requirement That Participant Have at Least 1 Hour of Service or Paid Leave on or After Date of Enactment.—The amendments made by sections 103 and 203 shall apply only in the case of participants who have at least 1 hour of service under the plan on or after the date of the enactment of this Act or have at least 1 hour of paid leave on or after such date of enactment.

(2) Requirement That Preretirement Survivor Annuity Be Provided in Case of Certain Participants Dying on or After Date of Enactment.—In the case of any participant—

(A) who has at least 1 hour of service under the plan on or after the date of the enactment of this Act or has at least 1 hour of paid leave on or after such date of enactment.

(B) who dies before the annuity starting date, and

(C) who dies on or after the date of the enactment of this Act and before the first day of the first plan year to which the amendments made by this Act apply.

the amendments made by sections 103 and 203 shall be treated as in effect as of the time of such participant's death.

(3) Spousal Consent Required for Certain Elections After Date of Enactment.—Any election after December 31, 1984, and before the first day of the first plan year to which the amendments made by this Act apply not to take a joint and survivor annuity shall not be effective unless the requirements of section 205(c)(2) of the Employee Retirement Income Security Act of 1974 (as amended by section 103 of this Act) and section 417(a)(2) of the Internal Revenue Code of 1954 (as added by section 203 of this Act) are met with respect to such election.

(e) Treatment of Certain Participants Who Separate From Service Before Date of Enactment.—

(1) Joint and Survivor Annuity Provisions of Employee Retirement Income Security Act of 1974 Apply to Certain Participants.—If—

(A) a participant had at least 1 hour of service under the plan on or after September 2, 1974.

(B) section 205 of the Employee Retirement Income Security Act of 1974 and section 401(a)(11) of the Internal Revenue Code of 1954 (as in effect on the day before the date of the enactment of this Act) would not (but for this paragraph) apply to such participant,

(C) the amendments made by section 103 and 203 of this Act do not apply to such participant, and

(D) as of the date of the enactment of this Act, the participant's annuity starting date has not occurred and the participant is alive,

then such participant may elect to have section 205 of the Employee Retirement Income Security Act of 1974 and section 401(a)(11) of the Internal Revenue Code of 1954 (as in effect on the day before the date of the enactment of this Act) apply.

(2) Treatment of Certain Participants Who Perform Service on or After January 1, 1976.—If—

(A) a participant had at least 1 hour of service in the first plan year beginning on or after January 1, 1976,

(B) the amendments made by sections 103 and 203 would not (but for this paragraph) apply to such participant,

(C) when such participant separated from service, such participant had at least 10 years of service under the plan and had a nonforfeitable right to all (or any portion) of such participant's accrued benefit derived from employer contributions, and

(D) as of the date of the enactment of this Act, such participant's annuity starting date has not occurred and such participant is alive, then such participant may elect to have the qualified preretirement survivor annuity requirements of the amendments made by sections 103 and 203 apply.

Also, see Act Sec. 303(b) for a special rule for collective bargaining agreements at ¶ 14,250.09.

[¶ 14,460]
OTHER PROVISIONS RELATING TO FORM AND PAYMENT OF BENEFITS

Act Sec. 206. (a) Each pension plan shall provide that unless the participant otherwise elects, the payment of benefits under the plan to the participant shall begin not later than the 60th day after the latest of the close of the plan year in which—

(1) occurs the date on which the participant attains the earlier of age 65 or the normal retirement age specified under the plan,

(2) occurs the 10th anniversary of the year in which the participant commenced participation in the plan, or

(3) the participant terminates his service with the employer.

In the case of a plan which provides for the payment of an early retirement benefit, such plan shall provide that a participant who satisfied the service requirements for such early retirement benefit, but separated from the service (with any nonforfeitable right to an accrued benefit) before satisfying the age requirement for such early retirement benefit, is entitled upon satisfaction of such age requirement to receive a benefit not less than the benefit to which he would be entitled at the normal retirement age, actuarially reduced under regulations prescribed by the Secretary of the Treasury.

Act Sec. 206. (b) If—

(1) a participant or beneficiary is receiving benefits under a pension plan, or

(2) a participant is separated from the service and has nonforfeitable rights to benefits,

a plan may not decrease benefits of such a participant by reason of any increase in the benefit levels payable under title II of the Social Security Act or the Railroad Retirement Act of 1937, or any increase in the wage base under such title II, if such increase takes place after the date of the enactment of this Act or (if later) the earlier of the date of first entitlement of such benefits or the date of such separation.

Act Sec. 206. (c) No pension plan may provide that any part of a participant's accrued benefit derived from employer contributions (whether or not otherwise nonforfeitable) is forfeitable solely because of withdrawal by such participant of any amount attributable to the benefit derived from contributions made by such participant. The preceding sentence shall not apply (1) to the accrued benefit of any participant unless, at the time of such withdrawal, such participant has a nonforfeitable right to at least 50 percent of such accrued benefit, or (2) to the extent that an accrued benefit is permitted to be forefeited in accordance with section 203(a)(3)(D)(iii).

Act Sec. 206. (d) (1) Each pension plan shall provide that benefits provided under the plan may not be assigned or alienated.

(2) For the purposes of paragraph (1) of this subsection, there shall not be taken into account any voluntary and revocable assignment of not to exceed 10 percent of any benefit payment, or of any irrevocable assignment or alienation of benefits executed before the date of enactment of this Act. The preceding sentence shall not apply to any assignment or alienation made for the purposes of defraying plan administration costs. For purposes of this paragraph a loan made to a participant or beneficiary shall not be treated as an assignment or alienation if such loan is secured by the participant's accrued nonforfeitable benefit and is exempt from the tax imposed by section 4975 of the Internal Revenue Code of 1986 (relating to tax on prohibited transactions) by reason of section 4975(d) (1) of such Code.

(3) (A) Paragraph (1) shall apply to the creation, assignment, or recognition of a right to any benefit payable with respect to a participant pursuant to a domestic relations order, except that paragraph (1) shall not apply if the order is determined to be a qualified domestic relations order. Each pension plan shall provide for the payment of benefits in accordance with the applicable requirements of any qualified domestic relations order.

(B) For purposes of this paragraph—

(i) the term "qualified domestic relations order" means a domestic relations order—

(I) which creates or recognizes the existence of an alternate payee's right to, or assigns to an alternative payee the right to, receive all or a portion of the benefits payable with respect to a participant under a plan, and

(II) with respect to which the requirements of subparagraphs (C) and (D) are met, and

(ii) the term "domestic relations order" means any judgment, decree, or order (including approval of a property settlement agreement) which—

(I) relates to the provisions of child support, alimony payments, or marital property rights to a spouse, former spouse, child, or other dependent of a participant, and

(II) is made pursuant to a State domestic relations law (including a community property law).

(C) A domestic relations order meets the requirements of this subparagraph only if such order clearly specifies—

(i) the name and the last known mailing address (if any) of the participant and the name and mailing address of each alternate payee covered by the order,

(ii) the amount or percentage of the participant's benefits to be paid by the plan to each such alternate payee, or the manner in which such amount or percentage is to be determined,

(iii) the number of payments or period to which such order applies, and

(iv) each plan to which such order applies.

(D) A domestic relations order meets the requirements of this subparagraph only if such order—

(i) does not require a plan to provide any type or form of benefits, or any option, not otherwise provided under the plan,

(ii) does not require the plan to provide increased benefits (determined on the basis of actuarial value), and

(iii) does not require the payment of benefits to an alternate payee which are required to be paid to another alternate payee under another order previously determined to be a qualified domestic relations order.

(E) (i) A domestic relations order shall not be treated as failing to meet the requirements of clause (i) of subparagraph (D) solely because such order requires that payment of benefits be made to an alternate payee—

(I) in the case of any payment before a participant has separated from service, on or after the date on which the participant attains (or would have attained) the earliest retirement age,

(II) as if the participant had retired on the date on which such payment is to begin under such order (but taking into account only the present value of benefits actually accrued and not taking into account the value of any employer subsidy for early retirement), and

(III) in any form in which such benefits may be paid under the plan to the participant (other than in the form of a joint and survivor annuity with respect to the alternate payee and his or her subsequent spouse).

For purposes of subclause (II), the interest rate assumption used in determining the present value shall be the interest rate specified in the plan or, if no rate is specified, 5 percent.

(ii) For purposes of this subparagraph, the term 'earliest retirement age' means the earlier of—

(I) the date on which the participant is entitled to a distribution under the plan, or

(II) the later of the date of the participant attains age 50 or the earliest date on which the participant could begin receiving under the plan if the participant separated from service.

(F) To the extent provided in any qualified domestic relations order—

(i) the surviving former spouse of a participant shall be treated as a surviving spouse of such participant for purposes of section 205 (and any spouse of the participant shall not be treated as a spouse of the participant for such purposes), and

(ii) if married for at least 1 year, the surviving former spouse shall be treated as meeting the requirements of section 205(f).

(G) (i) In the case of any domestic relations order received by a plan—

(I) the plan administrator shall promptly notify the participant and each alternate payee of the receipt of such order and the plan's procedures for determining the qualified status of domestic relations orders, and

(II) within a reasonable period after receipt of such order, the plan administrator shall determine whether such order is a qualified domestic relations order and notify the participant and each alternate payee of such determination.

(ii) Each plan shall establish reasonable procedures to determine the qualified status of domestic relations orders and to administer distributions under such qualified orders.

Such procedures—

(I) shall be in writing,

(II) shall provide for the notification of each person specified in a domestic relations order as entitled to payment of benefits under the plan (at the address included in the domestic relations order) of such procedures promptly upon receipt by the plan of the domestic relations order, and

(III) shall permit an alternate payee to designate a representative for receipt of copies of notices that are sent to the alternate payee with respect to a domestic relations order.

(H) (i) During any period in which the issue of whether a domestic relations order is a qualified domestic relations order is being determined (by the plan administrator, by a court of competent jurisdiction, or otherwise), the plan administrator shall separately account for the amounts (hereinafter in this subparagraph referred to as the "segregated amounts") which would have been payable to the alternate payee during such period if the order had been determined to be a qualified domestic relations order.

(ii) If within the 18-month period described in clause (c) the order (or modification thereof) is determined to be a qualified domestic relations order, the plan administrator shall pay the segregated amounts (including any interest thereon) to the person or persons entitled thereto.

(iii) If within the 18-month period described in clause (v)—

(I) it is determined that the order is not a qualified domestic relations order, or

(II) the issue as to whether such order is a qualified domestic relations order is not resolved,

then the plan administrator shall pay the segregated amounts (including any interest thereon) to the person or persons who would have been entitled to such amounts if there had been no order.

(iv) Any determination that an order is a qualified domestic relations order which is made after the close of the 18-month period described in clause (v) shall be applied prospectively only.

(v) For purposes of this subparagraph, the 18-month period described in this clause is the 18-month period beginning with the date on which the first payment would be required to be made under the domestic relations order.

(I) If a plan fiduciary acts in accordance with part 4 of this subtitle in—

(i) treating a domestic relations order as being (or not being) a qualified domestic relations order, or

(ii) taking action under subparagraph (H),

then the plan's obligation to the participant and each alternate payee shall be discharged to the extent of any payment made pursuant to such Act.

(J) A person who is an alternate payee under a qualified domestic relations order shall be considered for purposes of any provision of this Act a beneficiary under the plan. Nothing in the preceding sentence shall permit a requirement under section 4001 of the payment of more than 1 premium with respect to a participant for any period.

(K) The term "alternate payee" means any spouse, former spouse, child, or other dependent of a participant who is recognized by a domestic relations order as having a right to receive all, or a portion of, the benefits payable under a plan with respect to such participant.

(L) This paragraph shall not apply to any plan to which paragraph (1) does not apply.

(M) Payment of benefits by a pension plan in accordance with the applicable requirements of a qualified domestic relations order shall not be treated as garnishment for purposes of section 303(a) of the Consumer Credit Protection Act.

(N) In prescribing regulations under this paragraph, the Secretary shall consult with the Secretary of the Treasury.

(4) Paragraph (1) shall not apply to any offset of a participant's benefits provided under an employee pension benefit plan against an amount that the participant is ordered or required to pay to the plan if—

(A) the order or requirement to pay arises—

(i) under a judgment of conviction for a crime involving such plan,

(ii) under a civil judgment (including a consent order or decree) entered by a court in an action brought in connection with a violation (or alleged violation) of part 4 of this subtitle, or

(iii) pursuant to a settlement agreement between the Secretary and the participant, or a settlement agreement between the Pension Benefit Guaranty Corporation and the participant, in connection with a violation (or alleged violation) of part 4 of this subtitle by a fiduciary or any other person,

(B) the judgment, order, decree, or settlement agreement expressly provides for the offset of all or part of the amount ordered or required to be paid to the plan against the participant's benefits provided under the plan, and

(C) in a case in which the survivor annuity requirements of section 205 apply with respect to distributions from the plan to the participant, if the participant has a spouse at the time at which the offset is to be made—

(i) either—

(I) such spouse has consented in writing to such offset and such consent is witnessed by a notary public or representative of the plan (or it is established to the satisfaction of a plan representative that such consent may not be obtained by reason of circumstances described in section 205(c)(2)(B)), or

(II) an election to waive the right of the spouse to a qualified joint and survivor annuity or a qualified preretirement survivor annuity is in effect in accordance with the requirements of section 205(c),

(ii) such spouse is ordered or required in such judgment, order, decree, or settlement to pay an amount to the plan in connection with a violation of part 4 of this subtitle, or

(iii) in such judgment, order, decree, or settlement, such spouse retains the right to receive the survivor annuity under a qualified joint and survivor annuity provided pursuant to section 205(a)(1) and under a qualified preretirement survivor annuity provided pursuant to section 205(a)(2), determined in accordance with paragraph (5).

A plan shall not be treated as failing to meet the requirements of section 205 solely by reason of an offset under this paragraph.

(5)(A) The survivor annuity described in paragraph (4)(C)(iii) shall be determined as if—

(i) the participant terminated employment on the date of the offset,

(ii) there was no offset,

(iii) the plan permitted commencement of benefits only on or after normal retirement age,

(iv) the plan provided only the minimum-required qualified joint and survivor annuity, and

(v) the amount of the qualified preretirement survivor annuity under the plan is equal to the amount of the survivor annuity payable under the minimum-required qualified joint and survivor annuity.

(B) For purposes of this paragraph, the term "minimum-required qualified joint and survivor annuity" means the qualified joint and survivor annuity which is the actuarial equivalent of the participant's accrued benefit (within the meaning of section 3(23)) and under which the survivor annuity is 50 percent of the amount of the annuity which is payable during the joint lives of the participant and the spouse.

(e) LIMITATION ON DISTRIBUTIONS OTHER THAN LIFE ANNUITIES PAID BY THE PLAN.—

(1) IN GENERAL. Notwithstanding any other provision of this part, the fiduciary of a pension plan that is subject to the additional funding requirements of section 302(d) shall not permit a prohibited payment to be made from a plan during a period in which such plan has a liquidity shortfall (as defined in section 302(e)(5)).

(2) PROHIBITED PAYMENT. For purposes of paragraph (1), the term "prohibited payment" means—

(A) any payment, in excess of the monthly amount paid under a single life annuity (plus any social security supplements described in the last sentence of section 204(b)(1)(G)), to a participant or beneficiary whose annuity starting date (as defined in section 205(h)(2)), that occurs during the period referred to in paragraph (1),

(B) any payment for the purchase of an irrevocable commitment from an insurer to pay benefits, and

(C) any other payment specified by the Secretary of the Treasury by regulations.

(3) PERIOD OF SHORTFALL. For purposes of this subsection, a plan has a liquidity shortfall during the period that there is an underpayment of an installment under section 302(e) by reason of paragraph (5)(A) thereof.

(4) COORDINATION WIHT OTHER PROVISIONS. Compliance with this subsection shall not constitute a violation of any other provision of this Act.

(f) MISSING PARTICIPANTS IN TERMINATED PLANS. In the case of a plan covered by title IV, the plan shall provide that, upon termination of the plan, benefits of missing participants shall be treated in accordance with section 4050.

P.L. 105-34, §1502(a):

Act Sec. 1502(a) amended ERISA Sec. 206(d) by adding paragraphs (4) and (5) to read as above.

The above amendment applies to judgments, orders, and decrees issued, and settlement agreements entered into, on or after August 5, 1997.

P.L. 103-465, §761(a)(9)(B)(i):

Act Sec. 761(a)(9)(B)(i) amended ERISA Sec. 206 by adding subsection (e) to read as above.

The above amendment applies to plan years beginning after December 31, 1994.

P.L. 103-465, §776(c)(2):

Act Sec. 776(c)(2) amended ERISA Sec. 206 by adding subsection (f) to read as above.

The above amendment is effective with respect to distributions that occur in plan years commencing after final regulations implementing these provisions are prescribed by the Pension Benefit Guaranty Corporation.

P.L. 101-239, §7894(c)(8):

Amended ERISA Sec. 206(a)(1) by inserting "occurs" after "(1)," effective September 2, 1974.

P.L. 101-239, §7894(c)(9):

Amended ERISA Sec. 206(d)(3)(I) by striking "act" and inserting "Act," effective as if included in P.L. 98-397, §104.

P.L. 99-514, §1898(c)(2)(B)(i):

Amended ERISA Sec. 206(d)(3)(H)(i) by striking out "shall segregate in a separate account in the plan or in an escrow account the amounts" and inserted "shall separately account for the amounts (hereinafter in this subparagraph referred to as the 'segregated amounts')" instead, effective January 1, 1985.

P.L. 99-514, §1898(c)(2)(B)(ii):

Amended ERISA Sec. 206(d)(3)(h)(ii) by striking out "18-months" and inserting "the 18-month period described in clause (c)" and by striking out "plus any interest" and inserting "including any interest" instead, effective January 1, 1985.

P.L. 99-514, §1898(c)(2)(B)(iii):

Amended ERISA Sec. 206(d)(3)(H)(iii) by striking out "18-months" and inserting "the 18-month period described in clause (v)" and by striking out "plus any interest" and inserting "including any interest" instead, effective January 1, 1985.

P.L. 99-514, §1898(c)(2)(B)(iv):

Amended ERISA Sec. 206(d)(3)(H)(iv) by striking out "the 18-month period" and inserting "the 18-month period described in clause (v)" instead, effective January 1, 1985.

P.L. 99-514, §1898(c)(2)(B)(v):

Added ERISA Sec. 206(d)(3)(H)(v) to read as above, effective January 1, 1985.

P.L. 99-514, §1898(c)(4)(B):

Amended ERISA Sec. 206(d)(3) by redesignating subparagraph (L) as (N) and by inserting a new subparagraph (L) to read as above, effective January 1, 1985.

P.L. 99-514, §1898(c)(5):

Added new ERISA Sec. 206(d)(3)(M) to read as above, effective January 1, 1985.

P.L. 99-514, §1898(c)(6)(B):

Amended ERISA Sec. 206(d)(3)(F)(i) by striking out "section 205" and inserting "section 205 (and any spouse of the participant shall not be treated as a spouse of the participant for such purposes)" instead, effective January 1, 1985.

P.L. 99-514, §1898(c)(7)(B):

Amended ERISA Sec. 206(d)(3)(F)(ii) by striking out "the former spouse" and inserting "the surviving former spouse" instead, effective January 1, 1985.

Amended ERISA Sec. 206(d)(3)(G)(i)(I) by striking out "any other alternate payee" and inserting "each alternate payee" instead, effective January 1, 1985.

Amended ERISA Sec. 206(d)(3)(E) by striking out "In the case of any payment before a participant has separated from service, a" in clause (i) and inserting "A" and by inserting "in the case of any payment before a participant has separated from service," before "on or" in subclause (I), effective January 1, 1985.

Amended ERISA Sec. 206(d)(3)(E)(ii) to read as above, effective January 1, 1985. Prior to amendment, clause (ii) read as follows:

(ii) For purposes of this subparagraph, the term "earliest retirement age" has the meaning given such term by section 205(h)(3), except that in the case of any individual account plan, the earliest retirement age shall be the date which is 10 years before the normal retirement age.

P.L. 98-397, §104:

Act Sec. 104(a) amended ERISA Sec. 206(d) by adding a new paragraph (3) to read as above.

The above amendment is to take effect as provided by Act Sec. 303(d) which follows:

(d) Amendments Relating to Assignments in Divorce, Etc., Proceedings.—The amendments made by sections 104 and 204 shall take effect on January 1, 1985, except that in the case of a domestic relations order entered before such date, the plan administrator—

(1) shall treat such order as a qualified domestic relations order if such administrator is paying benefits pursuant to such order on such date, and

(2) may treat any other such order entered before such date as a qualified domestic relations order even if such order does not meet the requirements of such amendments.

[¶ 14,470]
TEMPORARY VARIANCES FROM CERTAIN VESTING REQUIREMENTS

Act Sec. 207. In the case of any plan maintained on January 1, 1974, if, not later than 2 years after the date of enactment of this Act, the administrator petitions the Secretary, the Secretary may prescribe an alternate method which shall be treated as satisfying the requirements of section 203(a)(2) or 204(b)(1) (other than subparagraph (D) thereof) or both for a period of not more than 4 years. The Secretary may prescribe such alternate method only when he finds that—

(1) the application of such requirements would increase the costs of the plan to such an extent that there would result a substantial risk to the voluntary continuation of the plan or a substantial curtailment of benefit levels or the levels of employees' compensation,

(2) the application of such requirement or discontinuance of the plan would be adverse to the interests of plan participants in the aggregate, and

(3) a waiver or extension of time granted under section 303 or 304 of this Act would be inadequate.

In the case of any plan with respect to which an alternate method has been prescribed under the preceding provisions of this subsection for a period of not more than 4 years, if, not later than 1 year before the expiration of such period, the administrator petitions the Secretary for an extension of such alternate method, and the Secretary makes the findings required by the preceding sentence, such alternate method may be extended for not more than 3 years.

[¶ 14,480]
MERGERS AND CONSOLIDATIONS OF PLANS OR TRANSFERS OF PLAN ASSETS

Act Sec. 208. A pension plan may not merge or consolidate with, or transfer its assets or liabilities to, any other plan after the date of the enactment of this Act, unless each participant in the plan would (if the plan then terminated) receive a benefit immediately after the merger, consolidation, or transfer which is equal to or greater than the benefit he would have been entitled to receive immediately before the merger, consolidation, or transfer (if the plan had then terminated). The preceding sentence shall not apply to any transaction to the extent that participants either before or after the transaction are covered under a multiemployer plan to which title IV of this Act applies.

Amendment

P.L. 96-364, §402(b)(1):

Amended Sec. 208, effective September 26, 1980, by striking out the last sentence which read "This paragraph shall apply in the case of a multiemployer plan only to the extent determined by the Pension Benefit Guaranty Corporation" and inserting the new last sentence to read as above.

[¶ 14,490]
RECORDKEEPING AND REPORTING REQUIREMENTS

Act Sec. 209.(a)(1) Except as provided by paragraph (2) every employer shall, in accordance with regulations prescribed by the Secretary, maintain records with respect to each of his employees sufficient to determine the benefits due or which may become due to such employees. The plan administrator shall make a report, in such manner and at such time as may be provided in regulations prescribed by the Secretary, to each employee who is a participant under the plan and who—

(A) requests such report, in such manner and at such time as may be provided in such regulations,

(B) terminates his service with the employer, or

(C) has a 1-year break in service (as defined in section 203(b)(3)(A)).

The employer shall furnish to the plan administrator the information necessary for the administrator to make the reports required by the preceding sentence. Not more than one report shall be required under subparagraph (A) in any 12-month period. Not more than one report shall be required under subparagraph (C) with respect to consecutive 1-year breaks in service. The report required under this paragraph shall be sufficient to inform the employee of his accrued benefits under the plan and the percentage of such benefits which are nonforfeitable under the plan.

(2) If more than one employer adopts a plan, each such employer shall, in accordance with regulations prescribed by the Secretary, furnish to the plan administrator the information necessary for the administrator to maintain the records and make the reports required by paragraph (1). Such administrator shall maintain the records and, to the extent provided under regulations prescribed by the Secretary, make the reports, required by paragraph (1).

Act Sec. 209. (b) If any person who is required, under subsection (a), to furnish information or maintain records for any plan year fails to comply with such requirement, he shall pay to the Secretary a civil penalty of $10 for each employee with respect to whom such failure occurs, unless it is shown that such failure is due to reasonable cause.

[¶ 14,500]
PLANS MAINTAINED BY MORE THAN ONE EMPLOYER, PREDECESSOR PLANS, AND EMPLOYER GROUPS

Act Sec. 210.(a) Notwithstanding any other provision of this part or part 3, the following provisions of this subsection shall apply to a plan maintained by more than one employer:

(1) Section 202 shall be applied as if all employees of each of the employers were employed by a single employer.

(2) Sections 203 and 204 shall be applied as if all such employers constituted a single employer, except that the application of any rules with respect to breaks in service shall be made under regulations prescribed by the Secretary.

(3) The minimum funding standard provided by section 302 shall be determined as if all participants in the plan were employed by a single employer.

Act Sec. 210. (b) For purposes of this part and part 3—

(1) in any case in which the employer maintains a plan of a predecessor employer, service for such predecessor shall be treated as service for the employer, and

(2) in any case in which the employer maintains a plan which is not the plan maintained by a predecessor employer, service for such predecessor shall, to the extent provided in regulations prescribed by the Secretary of the Treasury, be treated as service for the employer.

Act Sec. 210. (c) For purposes of sections 202, 203, and 204, all employees of all corporations which are members of a controlled group of corporations (within the meaning of section 1563(a) of the Internal Revenue Code of 1986, determined without regard to section 1563(a)(4) and (e)(3)(C) of such Code) shall be treated as employed by a single employer. With respect to a plan adopted by more than one such corporation, the minimum funding standard of section 302 shall be determined as if all such employers were a single employer, and allocated to each employer in accordance with regulations prescribed by the Secretary of the Treasury.

Act Sec. 210. (d) For purposes of sections 202, 203, and 204, under regulations prescribed by the Secretary of the Treasury, all employees of trades or businesses (whether or not incorporated) which are under common control shall be treated as employed by a single employer. The regulations prescribed under this subsection shall be based on principles similar to the principles which apply in the case of subsection (c).

Amendments

P.L. 101-239, § 7894(c)(10):

Amended ERISA Sec. 210(c) by striking "such code" and inserting "such Code" effective September 2, 1974.

P.L. 101-239, § 7891(a)(1):

Titles I, III, and IV of ERISA (other than sections 3(37)(E), 301(a)(7), and 308, the last sentence of section 408(d), and sections 414(c), 4001(a)(3)(ii), and 4303) are each amended by striking "Internal Revenue Code of 1954" each place it appears and inserting "Internal Revenue Code of 1986" effective October 22, 1986.

Regulations

The following regulations were adopted under "Title 29—Labor," "Chapter XXV—Pension and Welfare Benefit Programs, Department of Labor," "Subchapter C—Minimum Standards for Employee Pension Benefit Plans Under the Employee Retirement Income Security Act of 1974," "Part 2530—Rules and Regulations for Minimum Standards for Employee Pension Benefit Plans." The regulations were filed with the Federal Register on December 23, 1976, and published in the Federal Register of December 28, 1976 (41 FR 56462).

Subpart D—Plan Administration as Related to Benefits

[¶ 14,501]
§ 2530.210 **Employer or employers maintaining the plan.**

(a) *General statutory provisions.* (1) *Eligibility to participate and vesting.* Except as otherwise provided in sections 202(b) or 203(b)(1) of the Act and sections 410(a)(5), 411(a)(5) and 411(a)(6) of the Code, all years of service with the employer or employers maintaining the plan shall be taken into account for purposes of section 202 of the Act and section 410 of the Code (relating to minimum eligibility standards) and section 203 of the Act and section 411(a) of the Code (relating to minimum vesting standards).

(2) *Accrual of benefits.* Except as otherwise provided in section 202(b) of the Act and section 410(a)(5) of the Code, all years of participation under the plan must be taken into account for purposes of section 204 of the Act and section 411(b) of the Code (relating to benefit accrual). Section 204(b) of the Act and 411(b) of the Code require only that periods of actual participation in the plan (e.g., covered service) be taken into account for purposes of benefit accrual.

(b) *General rules concerning service to be credited under this section.* Section 210 of the Act and sections 413(c), 414(b) and 414(c) of the Code provide rules applicable to sections 202, 203, and 204 of the Act and sections 410, 411(a) and 411(b) of the Code for purposes of determining who is an "employer or employers maintaining the plan" and, accordingly, what service is required to be taken into account in the case of a plan maintained by more than one employer. Paragraphs (c) through (e) of this section set forth the rules for determining

service required to be taken into account in the case of a plan or plans maintained by multiple employers, controlled groups of corporations and trades or businesses under common control. Note throughout that every mention of multiple employer plans includes multiemployer plans. *See* § 2530.210(c)(3). Paragraph (f) of this section sets forth special break-in-service rules for such plans. Paragraph (g) of this section applies the break-in-service rules of sections 202(b)(4) and 203(b)(3)(D) of the Act and sections 410(a)(5)(D) and 411(a)(6)(D) of the Code (rule of parity) to such plans.

(c) *Multiple employer plans.* (1) *Eligibility to participate and vesting.* A multiple employer plan shall be treated as if all maintaining employers constitute a single employer so long as an employee is employed in either covered service or contiguous noncovered service. Accordingly, except as referred to in paragraph (a)(1) and provided in paragraph (f) of this section, in determining an employee's service for eligibility to participate and vesting purposes, all covered service with an employer or employers maintaining the plan and all contiguous noncovered service with an employer or employers maintaining the plan shall be taken into account. Thus, for example, if an employee in service covered under a multiple employer plan leaves covered service with one employer maintaining the plan and is employed immediately thereafter in covered service with another employer maintaining the plan, the plan is required to credit all hours of service with both employers for purposes of participation and vesting. If an employee moves from contiguous noncovered to covered service, or from covered service to contiguous noncovered service, with the same employer, the plan is required to credit all hours of service with such employer for purposes of eligibility to participate and vesting.

(2) *Benefit accrual.* A multiple employer plan shall be treated as if all maintaining employers constitute a single employer so long as an employee is employed in covered service. Accordingly, except as referred to in paragraph (a)(2) and provided in paragraph (f) of this section, in determining a participant's service for benefit accrual purposes, all covered service with an employer or employers maintaining the plan shall be taken into account.

(3) *Definitions.* (i) For purposes of this section, the term "multiple employer plan" shall mean a multiemployer plan as defined in section 3(37) of the Act and section 414(f) of the Code or a multiple employer plan within the meaning of sections 413 (b) and (c) of the Code and the regulations issued thereunder. Notwithstanding the preceding sentence, a plan maintained solely by members of the same controlled group of corporations within the meaning of paragraph (d) of this section or by trades or businesses which are under the common control of one person or group of persons within the meaning of paragraph (e) of this section shall not be deemed to be a multiple employer plan for purposes of this section, and such plan is required to apply the rules under this section which are applicable to controlled groups of corporations or commonly controlled trades or businesses respectively.

(ii) For purposes of this section, the term "covered service" shall mean service with an employer or employers maintaining the plan within a job classification or class of employees covered under the plan.

(iii) For purposes of this section the term "noncovered service" shall mean service with an employer or employers maintaining the plan which is not covered service.

(iv)(A) *General.* For purposes of this section noncovered service shall be deemed "contiguous" if (1) the noncovered service precedes or follows covered service and (2) no quit, discharge or retirement occurs between such covered service and noncovered service.

(B) *Exception.* Notwithstanding the preceding paragraph, in the case of a controlled group of corporations within the meaning of paragraph (d) of this section or trades or businesses which are under the common control of one person or group of persons within the meaning of paragraph (e) of this section, any transfer of an employee from one member of the controlled group to another member or from one trade or business under common control to another trade or business under the common control of the same person or group of persons shall result in the period of noncovered service which immediately precedes or follows such transfer being deemed "noncontiguous" for purposes of paragraph (c) of this section.

Diagram No. 1. **(Multiple Employer Plan.)**

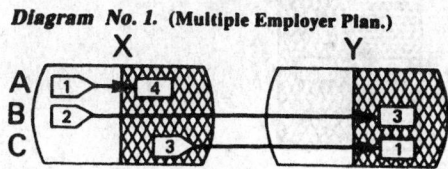

Assume for purposes of diagram No. 1 that X and Y are both employers who are required to contribute to a multiple employer plan and that neither employer maintains any other plan. Covered service is represented by the shaded segments of the diagram. After completing 1 year of noncovered service, employee A immediately enters covered service with X and completes 4 years of covered service. For purposes of eligibility to participate and vesting, the plan is required to credit employee A with 5 years of service with employer X because his period of service with X includes a period of covered service and a period of contiguous noncovered service. On the other hand, employee B, immediately after completing 2 years of noncovered service with X, enters covered service with Y. Because B quit employment with X, his period of noncovered service with X is not contiguous and, therefore, is not required to be taken into account. In the case of employee C, the plan is required to take into account all service with employers X and Y because employee C is employed in covered service with both employers.

Diagram No. 2. **(Multiple Employer Plan— Noncovered Service.)**

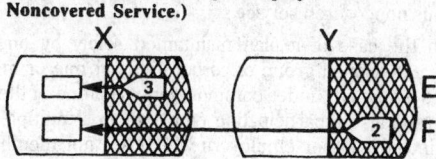

The multiple employer plan rules with respect to noncovered service are illustrated in diagram No. 2. Assume that X and Y are both employers who are required to contribute to a multiple employer plan and that neither employer maintains any other plan. Covered service is represented by the shaded segments of the diagram. Employee E completed 3 years of service with employer X in covered service and then immediately entered noncovered service with X. Because E's noncovered service is contiguous, the plan is required to take into account all service with X for purposes of eligibility to participate and vesting under the multiple employer plan. Employee F does not continue to receive credit; F quit the employment of Y and entered noncovered service with X.

(d) *Controlled groups of corporations.* (1) With respect to a plan maintained by one or more members of a controlled group of corporations (within the meaning of section 1563(a) of the Code, determined without regard to section 1563 (a)(4) and (e)(3)(C)), all employees of such corporations shall be treated as employed by a single employer.

(2) Accordingly, except as referred to in paragraph (a)(1) and provided in paragraph (f) of this section, in determining an employee's service for eligibility to participate and vesting purposes, all service with any employer which is a member of the controlled group of corporations shall be taken into account. Except as referred to in paragraph (a)(2) and provided in paragraph (f) of this section, in determining a participant's service for benefit accrual purposes, all service during periods of participation covered under the plan with any employer which is a member of the controlled group of corporations shall be taken into account.

(e) *Commonly controlled trades or businesses.* With respect to a plan maintained only by one or more trades or businesses (whether or not incorporated) which are under common control within the meaning of section 414(c) of the Code and the regulations issued thereunder, all employees of such trades or businesses shall be treated as employed by a single employer. Accordingly, except as referred to in paragraph (a)(1) and provided in paragraph (f) of this section, in determining an employee's service for eligibility to participate and vesting purposes, all service with any employer which is under common control shall be taken into account. Except as referred to in paragraph (a)(2) and provided in paragraph (f) of this section, in determining a participant's service for benefit accrual purposes, all service during periods of participation covered under the plan with any employer which is under common control shall be taken into account.

Diagram No. 3. **(Controlled Group or Commonly Controlled Trade or Business.)**

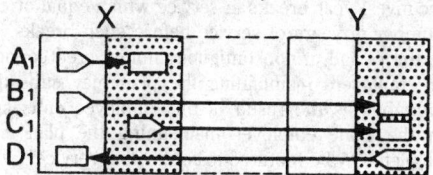

Assume for purposes of diagram No. 3 that X and Y are either members of the same controlled group of corporations or trades or businesses which are under the same common control. The dotted segments of the diagram represent plan coverage under plans separately maintained by X and Y. Neither employer maintains any other plans. Because A1, B1, C1, and D1 have their service with X and Y treated as if X and Y were a single employer, the plans are required to take into account all service with X and Y for eligibility to participate and vesting purposes.

(f) *Special break in service rules.* (1) In addition to service which may be disregarded under the statutory provisions referred to in paragraph (a) of this section, a multiple employer plan may disregard noncontiguous noncovered service.

(2) In the case of a plan maintained solely by one or more members of a controlled group of corporations or one or more trades or businesses which are under common control, if one of the maintaining employers is also a participating employer in a multiple employer plan which includes other employers which are not members of the controlled group or commonly controlled trades or businesses, service with such other employer maintaining the multiple employer plan may be disregarded by the controlled group or commonly controlled plan.

Diagram No. 4. (Break in Service Rules.)

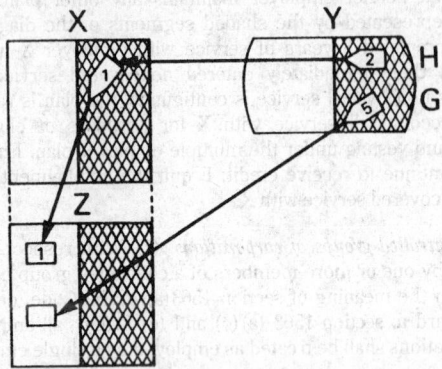

Diagram No. 4 illustrates the break in service rules of paragraph (f) of this section. Assume for purposes of diagram no. 4 that employer Z is controlled by employer X but employer Y's only relation to X and Z is that X, Y and Z are required to contribute to a multiple employer plan. The multiple employer plan, represented by the shaded segments of the diagram, provides for 100% vesting after 10 years. X, Y and Z maintain no other plans.

Employee G completed 5 years of covered service with employer Y, and then moved to noncovered service with employer Z. G's noncovered service is noncontiguous (see employee F in diagram No. 2 above), and such service may be disregarded for purposes of the multiple employer plan under the rule in paragraph (f)(1).

Employee H completed 2 years of covered service with employer Y and then entered covered service with employer X for 1 year. The multiple employer plan is required to credit H with 3 years of service. H then entered noncovered service with employer Z. H's noncovered service is noncontiguous (see employee F in diagram No. 2 above), and such service may be disregarded for purposes of the multiple employer plan under the rule in paragraph (f)(1).

(g) *Rule of parity.* For purposes of sections 202(b)(4) and 203(b)(3)(D) of the Act and sections 410(a)(5)(D) and 411(a)(6)(D) of the Code, in the case of an employee who is a nonvested participant in employer-derived accrued benefits at the time he incurs a 1-year break in service, years of service completed by such employee before such break are not required to be taken into account if at such time he incurs consecutive 1-year breaks in service which equal or exceed the aggregate number of years of service before such breaks. This is so even though the period of noncontiguous noncovered service with an employer or employers maintaining the plan may subsequently be deemed contiguous as the result of the employee entering covered service with the same employer maintaining the plan and, consequently, such plan may be required to credit such service.

Diagram No. 5. (Rule of Parity.)

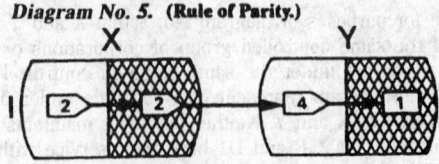

Assume for purposes of diagram No. 5 that X and Y are both employers who are required to contribute to a multiple employer plan which contains a provision applying the rule of parity. Covered service is represented by the shaded segments of the diagram. The plan has 100% vesting after ten years. X and Y maintain no other plan.

The multiple employer plan credited employee I with 4 years of service with X when he quit employment with X and entered noncovered service with Y. As a result of 4 years of noncontiguous noncovered service with Y, employee I incurred 4 consecutive 1-year breaks in service, so that the multiple employer plan may disregard his prior service (i.e., the 4 years of service with X).

When employee I entered covered service with Y (as a "new employee"), his 4 years of noncontiguous service with Y became contiguous for purposes of the multiple employer plan. Consequently, after 1 year of covered service with Y, the plan is required to credit employee I with 5 years of service.

(h) *Example.* Under section 203(b)(1)(C) of the Act and section 411(a)(4)(C) of the Code, service with an employer prior to such employer's adoption of the plan need not be taken into account. The following example demonstrates that this rule applies even if an employee is employed in contiguous noncovered service. The example is applicable to any plan subject to the rules of this section. However, for purposes of clarity, the example assumes that X and Y are required to contribute to a multiple employer plan.

Assume that employee D completed 3 years of covered service with employer Y as of the date X adopts the plan. Immediately after X's adoption of the plan D left covered service with Y and D entered covered service with X. His prior covered service with Y is required to be counted, and D remains a participant.

On the other hand, if D had entered service with X anytime prior to X's adoption of the plan and subsequently was covered by the plan when X adopted it, his prior service with Y must also be counted, unless such service may be disregarded under the break in service rules because the period of service with X before X's adoption of the plan was equal to or greater than his prior service with Y. For example, if X adopted the plan three years after D began employment with X, and consequently after D had incurred 3 consecutive 1-year breaks in service, his prior service with Y could be disregarded.

(i) *Comprehensive diagram.* (No. 6)

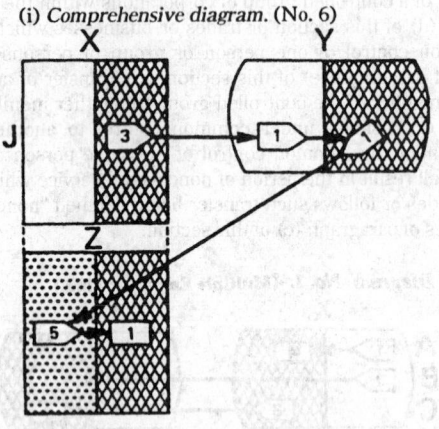

Assume for purposes of diagram No. 6 that employer Z is controlled by employer X within the meaning of paragraph (d) but employer Y's only relation to X and Z is that X, Y and Z are required to contribute to a multiple employer plan. The shaded segments represent coverage under the multiple employer plan which contains a provision applying the rule of parity. The dotted segment represents a separate plan maintained by Z. Both plans have 100% vesting after 10 years.

Employee J completed 3 years of service with employer X in covered service with the multiple employer plan. J then entered noncovered service with Y and remained with Y for 1 year, and thereby incurred a 1-year break in service under the multiple employer plan. J then entered covered service with employer Y, thereby causing the noncovered service with Y to become contiguous. Covered service with X and contiguous noncovered and covered service with Y must be taken into account for purposes of the multiple employer plan; accordingly, that plan is required to credit J with a total of 5 years of service.

J then left service with Y and entered noncovered service (with respect to the multiple employer plan) with Z. J remained in noncovered service with Z (with respect to the multiple employer plan) for 5 years and thereby incurred 5 consecutive 1-year breaks in service for purposes of the multiple employer plan. Consequently, the prior service with X and Y may be disregarded for purposes of the multiple employer plan.

J then entered covered service under the multiple employer plan with Z and completed 1 year of service. Because the 5 years of noncovered service with Z is contiguous with the 1 year of covered service, the multiple employer plan is now required to credit J with 6 years of service for purposes of eligibility to participate and vesting.

For purposes of Z's controlled group plan (i.e., dotted segment), employee J is entitled to receive credit for 9 years of service. The 3 years of service with X, a member of the controlled group, may not be disregarded under the rule of parity because J incurred only 2 consecutive 1-year breaks in service while employed with Y. When J entered service with Z covered under Z's controlled group plan, the 3 years of service with X were still required to be credited by the controlled group plan. In addition, J must receive credit for the 5 years of service with Z covered under the controlled group plan. Finally, when J moved to service with Z covered under the multiple employer plan the controlled group plan was required to credit J with an additional year of service.

[¶ 14,510]
EFFECTIVE DATES

Act Sec. 211.(a) Except as otherwise provided in this section, this part shall apply in the case of plan years beginning after the date of the enactment of this Act.

Act Sec. 211.(b)(1) Except as otherwise provided in subsection (d), sections 205, 206(d), and 208 shall apply with respect to plan years beginning after December 31, 1975.

(2) Except as otherwise provided in subsections (c) and (d) in the case of a plan in existence on January 1, 1974, this part shall apply in the case of plan years beginning after December 31, 1975.

Act Sec. 211.(c)(1) In the case of a plan maintained on January 1, 1974, pursuant to one or more agreements which the Secretary finds to be collective bargaining agreements between employee organizations and one or more employers, no plan shall be treated as not meeting the requirements of sections 204 and 205 solely by reason of a supplementary or special plan provision (within the meaning of paragraph (2)) for any plan year before the year which begins after the earlier of—

(A) the date on which the last of such agreements relating to the plan terminates (determined without regard to any extension thereof agreed to after the date of the enactment of this Act), or

(B) December 31, 1980.

For purposes of subparagraph (A) and section 307(c), any plan amendment made pursuant to a collective bargaining agreement relating to the plan which amends the plan solely to conform to any requirement contained in this Act or the Internal Revenue Code of 1986 shall not be treated as a termination of such collective bargaining agreement. This paragraph shall not apply unless the Secretary determines that the participation and vesting rules in effect on the date of enactment of this Act are not less favorable to participants, in the aggregate, than the rules provided under sections 202, 203, and 204.

(2) For purposes of paragraph (1), the term "supplementary or special plan provision" means any plan provision which—

(A) provides supplementary benefits, not in excess of one-third of the basic benefit, in the form of an annuity for the life of the participant, or

(B) provides that, under a contractual agreement based on medical evidence as to the effects of working in an adverse environment for an extended period of time, a participant having 25 years of service is to be treated as having 30 years of service.

(3) This subsection shall apply with respect to a plan if (and only if) the application of this subsection results in a later effective date for this part than the effective date required by subsection (b).

Act Sec. 211. (d) If the administrator of a plan elects under section 1017(d) of this Act to make applicable to a plan year and to all subsequent plan years the provisions of the Internal Revenue Code of 1986 relating to participation, vesting, funding, and form of benefit, this part shall apply to the first plan year to which such election applies and to all subsequent plan years.

Act Sec. 211.(e)(1) No pension plan to which section 202 applies may make effective any plan amendment with respect to breaks in service (which amendment is made or becomes effective after January 1, 1974, and before the date on which section 202 first becomes effective with respect to such plan) which provides that any employee's participation in the plan would commence at any date later than the later of—

(A) the date on which his participation would commence under the break in service rules of section 202(b), or

(B) the date on which his participation would commence under the plan as in effect on January 1, 1974.

(2) No pension plan to which section 203 applies may make effective any plan amendment with respect to breaks in service (which amendment is made or becomes effective after January 1, 1974, and before the date on which section 203 first becomes effective with respect to such plan) if such amendment provides that the nonforfeitable benefit derived from employer contributions to which any employee would be entitled is less than the lesser of the nonforfeitable benefit derived from employer contributions to which he would be entitled under—

(A) the break in service rules of section 202(b)(3), or

(B) the plan as in effect on January 1, 1974.

Subparagraph (B) shall not apply if the break in service rules under the plan would have been in violation of any law or rule of law in effect on January 1, 1974.

Act Sec. 211. (f) The preceding provisions of this section shall not apply with respect to amendments made to this part in provisions enacted after the date of the enactment of this Act.

Amendments

P.L. 99-272:

P.L. 101-239, §7891(a)(1):

Titles I, III, and IV of ERISA (other than sections 3(37)(E), 301(a)(7), and 308, the last sentence of section 408(d), and sections 414(c), 4001(a)(3)(ii), and 4303) are each amended by striking "Internal Revenue Code of 1954" each place it appears and inserting "Internal Revenue Code of 1986" effective October 22, 1986.

P.L. 101-239, §7894(h)(2):

Amended ERISA Sec. 211 by adding new subsection (f) to read as above effective September 2, 1974.

Act Sec. 11015(a)(1)(B) amended ERISA Sec. 211(c)(1) by striking out "306(c)" and inserting "307(c)" in its place, effective with respect to applications for waivers, extensions and modifications filed on or after April 7, 1986.

[¶ 14,515 Reserved. Temporary regulations on Minimum Standards for Employee Pension Benefit Plans Under the Employee Retirement Income Security Act of 1974, effective under the Special Reliance Procedure, were formerly reproduced at this point. Final Minimum Standard Regulations have been adopted. They appear at ¶ 14,411-14,415, 14,421, 14,422, 14,431, 14,432, 14,441-14,444, and 14,501.]

Regulations

Interpretive Bulletin ERISA IB 76-1 was adopted under "Title 29—Labor; Chapter XXV—Office of Employee Benefits Security; Part 2509—Interpretive Bulletins Relating to the Employee Retirement Income Security Act of 1974—§2509.76-1" [Interpretive Bulletin Relating to Guidelines on Seasonal Industries]. The Bulletin was filed with the Federal Register on January 21, 1976 41 (FR 3289). [ERISA IB 76-1 was rescinded by ERISA IB 76-2, Reg. §2509.76-2, at ¶ 14,521.]

[¶ 14,520]

§ 2509.76-1 Interpretive bulletin relating to guidelines on seasonal industries. [*] On January 16, 1976, the Department of Labor issued an interpretive bulletin, designated ERISA IB 76-1, establishing guidelines on seasonal industries under the Employee Retirement Income Security Act of 1974 (the Act). The guidelines enable employee pension benefit plans to comply with the Act until regulations can be issued under sections 202(a)(3)(B), 203(b)(2)(C) and 204(b)(3)(D) of the Act. Plans may rely on these guidelines, as provided in ERISA IB 75-10 and TIR-1415 (November 5, 1975), for computing service to be credited to employees in seasonal industries.

The Act makes special provision for a "seasonal" industry where the "customary period of employment" is less than 1,000 hours of service during a year. The provisions of the Act concerning participation, vesting and benefit accrual are applicable to plans, rather than to industries. It is therefore necessary to provide guidance for plans in an industry with customary annual employment of less than 1,000 hours for purposes of applying the special provision.

The guidelines establish two tests to determine whether a plan covers employees in a seasonal industry. First, a seasonality percentage test is used to measure peaking of hours of service, in order to limit seasonality to those business activities with at least one concentrated period of employment during a year. This is a primary characteristic of seasonality. Under this test, the seasonality percentage is met where the total hours completed by all employees who are covered by a plan, or would be covered but for the plan's minimum service requirements, in any three-month period is 150% or more of the total hours in any other three-month period during the fifteen months immediately preceding the plan year to which the test is applied. Under the second test, the customary period of employment is less than 1,000 hours if 50% or more of the employees described in the previous sentence have completed less than 1,000 hours of service during the twelve calendar months immediately preceding the plan year under consideration. If the plan meets these two tests for seasonality, the plan covers employees in a seasonal industry, and all employees who are covered or would be covered by the plan must be credited for participation, vesting and benefit accrual for the plan year on the basis of a 500 hour standard rather than the normal 1,000 hour standard.

Paragraph (b) sets forth in detail the first test for determining whether a plan covers employees in a seasonal industry and provides that a plan must meet the seasonality percentage test measured in units of thirteen overlapping three-month periods during the fifteen calendar months immediately preceding the plan year. By spanning a fifteen-month period, the seasonality percentage test insures measurement of all annual peaks. If only a twelve-month period were used, a plan year might begin in the midst of an annual peak period, and the highest three-month period actually occurring each year would not be measured under the test. The fifteen-month period covers all three-consecutive-month combinations during a year.

Paragraph (c) allows the exclusion of certain periods from the seasonality percentage test in the situation where a catastrophic event, unrelated to the business activities of the employer maintaining the plan, restricts operations for a significant period of time.

The guidelines follow:

Guidelines on seasonal industries.

(a) *General rule.* A plan covers employees in a seasonal industry for a plan year if—

(1) the hours of service of all employees covered by the plan (or who would be covered by the plan if they satisfied the minimum service requirements set by the plan as a condition for eligibility to participate) meet the seasonality percentage test set forth in paragraph (b) and

(2) Fifty percent or more of the employees described in paragraph (1) have less than 1,000 hours of service in the twelve calendar months immediately preceding the plan year to which this rule is being applied.

(b) *Seasonality percentage test* is a test by which hours of service are measured in each of thirteen different three-month periods that occur during the fifteen calendar months immediately preceding the

plan year to which this rule is being applied. If the total hours of service completed by all employees described in paragraph (a)(1) within any one such three-month period is 150% or more of the total hours completed by all such employees in any other such three-month period, then the plan meets the seasonality percentage test. For example, assume that the total hours of service for all employees described in paragraph (a)(1) are as shown below for each of the three-month periods in the 15-month period. The plan is on a calendar year basis.

(1)	Oct.-Dec.	1974	7,500
(2)	Nov.-Jan.	1975	8,000
(3)	Dec.-Feb.	1975	8,000
(4)	Jan.-Mar.	1975	7,000
(5)	Feb.-Apr.	1975	6,500
(6)	Mar.-May	1975	6,500
(7)	Apr.-June	1975	8,000
(8)	May-July	1975	9,500
(9)	June-Aug.	1975	9,000
(10)	July-Sept.	1975	7,500
(11)	Aug.-Oct.	1975	6,000
(12)	Sept.-Nov.	1975	6,500
(13)	Oct.-Dec.	1975	7,500

The plan meets the seasonality percentage test in the 15-month period because the total hours in either period 8 or period 9 are equal to or more than 150% of the total hours in period 11. Therefore the plan meets the test of paragraph (a)(1) for the 1976 plan year.

(c) *Limitation on the use of the seasonality percentage test.* A plan is not required to include in the seasonality percentage test any period which contains a calendar month during which 50% or more of the employees described in paragraph (a)(1) were unable to complete an hour of service for 15 or more days as a result of a rare, atypical and nonrecurring event rather than the seasonal nature of employment. For the purposes of this paragraph, any fire, flood, explosion, earthquake or other event which is not a normal occurrence in the operations of a seasonal industry shall be deemed a rare, atypical and nonrecurring event.

If a plan—

(1) Excludes a three-month period or periods from the seasonality percentage test for the reasons set forth in this paragraph; and

(2) Fails to meet the seasonality percentage test for the plan year to which the test (measured now by less than thirteen three-month periods) is applied, seasonality shall be determined by applying the tests of seasonality set forth in paragraph (a) to the prior plan year.

(d) *Year of service.* An employee in a seasonal industry completes a year of service for the purposes of vesting and eligibility to participate if the employee completes 500 or more hours of service (or, in the case of a seasonal maritime industry, 62 or more days of service) in the respective computation periods beginning with or within the plan year for which the industry is determined to be seasonal.

(e) *Year of participation.* (1) An employee in a seasonal industry completes at least a partial year of participation for the purposes of benefit accrual if the employee completes 500 or more hours of service (or, in the case of a seasonal maritime industry, 62 or more days of service) in an accrual computation period beginning with or within the plan year for which the industry is determined to be seasonal.

(2) When partial years of participation are computed under § 2530.204-2(c), the number 500 will be substituted for the number 1,000 in determining the largest number of hours that a plan may require during the period for an employee to obtain credit for a partial year of participation for the purposes of benefit accrual. All other calculations shall remain the same.

(f) *Breaks in service.* For purposes of sections 202(b), 203(b)(3) and 204(b)(3)(A) of the Act and sections 410(a)(5), 411(a)(6) and 411(b)(3)(A) of the Code, a plan may charge an employee in a seasonal

---

[*] § 2509.76-1 was rescinded by § 2509.76-2.

industry with a break in service for a computation period beginning with or within the plan year for which the industry is determined to be seasonal if the employee fails to complete more than 250 hours of service or, in the case of any seasonal maritime industry, 31 days of service in such period. All other rules relating to breaks in service, such as use of certain computation periods, are the same for employees in seasonal industries as for employees in other industries.

>>> *Caution: Regulation § 2509.76-2 was officially removed by 61 FR 33847 on July 1, 1996.*

[¶ 14,521]

§ 2509.76-2 **Interpretive bulletin rescinding guidelines on seasonal industries.** The Department of Labor has determined that the guidelines on seasonal industries, ERISA IB 76-1 published at 41 F.R. 3290 on January 22, 1976, should be rescinded. The Department will issue guidelines or a regulation on seasonal industries in the future.

In consideration of the foregoing, the guidelines on seasonal industries published in the *Federal Register* at 41 FR 3290 on January 22, 1976, and issued as ERISA IB 76-1 are hereby rescinded. (Added February 19, 1976, by 41 F.R. 7749.)

>>> *Caution: Regulation § 2509.76-3 was officially removed by 61 FR 33847 on July 1, 1996.*

[¶ 14,522]

§ 2509.76-3 **Interpretive bulletin withdrawing definition of seasonal industries from ERISA guidelines.** (a) The Department of Labor, with the concurrence of the Internal Revenue Service, has determined that the definition of seasonal industries should be withdrawn from the ERISA Guidelines. See TIR No. 1415 (November 5, 1975) and ERISA IB 75-10 (published November 5, 1975, originally numbered IB MS-75-1).

(b) On January 22, 1976, the Department of Labor issued guidelines on seasonal industries in ERISA IB 76-1, published at 41 FR 3290. In consideration of comments relating to the adverse impact of the guidelines on seasonal industries upon plans in industries which are

generally recognized as nonseasonal, the Department, on February 20, 1976, issued an interpretive bulletin rescinding such guidelines. See ERISA IB 76-2 published at 41 FR 7749.

(c) The definition of seasonal industries is currently part of the ERISA Guidelines. For employers who wish to adopt new plans or amend existing plans to take advantage of the Special Reliance Procedure contained in TIR No. 1416 released on November 5, 1975, the ERISA Guidelines provide a fixed body of law for such purposes. In consideration of the need for employers who wish to take advantage of the Special Reliance Procedure to act promptly, and in view of the time delays which may be involved in formulating a revised definition of seasonal industries, the Department intends to withdraw the definition of seasonal industries from the schedule of documents comprising the ERISA Guidelines.

(d) The Employee Retirement Income Security Act of 1974 (ERISA) and relevant portions of the Internal Revenue Code of 1954 (the Code) provide that in the case of any seasonal industry where the customary period of employment is less than 1,000 hours during a calendar year, the term "year of service", for eligibility purposes, shall be such period as may be determined under regulations prescribed by the Secretary of Labor. ERISA § 202(a)(3)(B) and § 410(a)(3)(B) of the Code. Similar provisions apply to a year of service for vesting purposes and a year of participation for benefit accrual purposes. ERISA §§ 203(b)(2)(C) and 204(b)(3)(D) and Code §§ 411(a)(5)(C) and 411(b)(3)(D). Presently, there is no published guidance concerning the definition of a seasonal industry with a customary period of employment of less than 1,000 hours during a calendar year nor any special rules concerning the definition of a year of service or a year of participation in such industry. In the absence of regulations issued by the Secretary defining seasonal industries, the general standards for determining a year of service for eligibility to participate and vesting purposes, and a year of participation for benefit accrual purposes, apply to all plans.

(e) In consideration of the foregoing, the definition of seasonal industries is hereby withdrawn from the ERISA Guidelines. (Added June 21, 1976, by 41 F.R. 24999.)

Part 3—Funding

[¶ 14,610]
COVERAGE

Act Sec. 301. (a) This part shall apply to any employee pension benefit plan described in section 4(a), (and not exempted under section 4(b)), other than—

(1) an employee welfare benefit plan;

(2) an insurance contract plan described in subsection (b);

(3) a plan which is unfunded and is maintained by an employer primarily for the purpose of providing deferred compensation for a select group of management or highly compensated employees;

(4)(A) a plan which is established and maintained by a society, order, or association described in section 501(c)(8) or (9) of the Internal Revenue Code of 1986, if no part of the contributions to or under such plan are made by employers of participants in such plan; or

(B) a trust described in section 501(c)(18) of such Code;

(5) a plan which has not at any time after the date of enactment of this Act provided for employer contributions;

(6) an agreement providing payments to a retired partner or deceased partner or a deceased partner's successor in interest as described in section 736 of the Internal Revenue Code of 1986;

(7) an individual retirement account or annuity as described in section 408 of the Internal Revenue Code of 1954 or a retirement bond described in section 409 of the Internal Revenue Code of 1954 (as effective for obligations issued before January 1, 1984);

(8) an individual account plan (other than a money purchase plan) and a defined benefit plan to the extent it is treated as an individual account plan (other than a money purchase plan) under section 3(35)(B) of this title;

(9) an excess benefit plan; or

(10) any plan, fund or program under which an employer, all of whose stock is directly or indirectly owned by employees, former employees or their beneficiaries, proposes through an unfunded arrangement to compensate retired employees for benefits which were forfeited by such employees under a pension plan maintained by a former employer prior to the date such pension plan became subject to this Act.

Act Sec. 301. (b) For the purposes of paragraph (2) of subsection (a) a plan is an "insurance contract plan" if—

(1) the plan is funded exclusively by the purchase of individual insurance contracts,

(2) such contracts provide for level annual premium payments to be paid extending not later than the retirement age for each individual participating in the plan, and commencing with the date the individual became a participant in the plan (or, in the case of an increase in benefits, commencing at the time such increase becomes effective),

(3) benefits provided by the plan are equal to the benefits provided under each contract at normal retirement age under the plan and are guaranteed by an insurance carrier (licensed under the laws of a State to do business with the plan) to the extent premiums have been paid,

(4) premiums payable for the plan year, and all prior plan years under such contracts have been paid before lapse or there is reinstatement of the policy,

(5) no rights under such contracts have been subject to a security interest at any time during the plan year, and

(6) no policy loans are outstanding at any time during the plan year.

A plan funded exclusively by the purchase of group insurance contracts which is determined under regulations prescribed by the Secretary of the Treasury to have the same characteristics as contracts described in the preceding sentence shall be treated as a plan described in this subsection.

Act Sec. 301. (c) This part applies, with respect to a terminated multiemployer plan to which section 4021 applies, until the last day of the plan year in which the plan terminates, within the meaning of section 4041A(a)(2).

Act Sec. 301. (d) Any amount of any financial assistance from the Pension Benefit Guaranty Corporation to any plan, and any repayment of such amount, shall be taken into account under this section in such manner as determined by the Secretary of the Treasury.

Amendments

P.L. 101-239, §7891(a)(1):

Titles I, III, and IV of ERISA (other than sections 3(37)(E), 301(a)(7), and 308, the last sentence of section 408(d), and sections 414(c), 4001(a)(3)(ii), and 4303) are each amended by striking "Internal Revenue Code of 1954" each place it appears and inserting "Internal Revenue Code of 1986" effective October 22, 1986.

P.L. 101-239, §7894(d)(1):

Amended ERISA Sec. 301, in paragraph (8), by striking "or" at the end; in paragraph (9), by striking "plan." and inserting "plan; or;" and, in paragraph (10), by striking "Any" and inserting "any" effective as if included in P.L. 96-364, §411.

P.L. 101-239, §7894(d)(4):

Amended ERISA Sec. 301(a)(7) by striking "section 409 of such Code" and inserting "section 409 of the Internal Revenue Code of 1954 (as effective for obligations issued before January 1, 1984)" effective as if included in P.L. 98-369, §491(b).

P.L. 96-364, §§304(a) and 411(b):

Added new section 301(a)(10) and new sections 301(c) and (d), effective September 26, 1980.

[¶ 14,620]
MINIMUM FUNDING STANDARDS

Act Sec. 302.(a)(1) Every employee pension benefit plan subject to this part shall satisfy the minimum funding standard (or the alternative minimum funding standard under section 305) for any plan year to which this part applies. A plan to which this part applies shall have satisfied the minimum funding standard for such plan for a plan year if as of the end of such plan year the plan does not have an accumulated funding deficiency.

(2) For the purposes of this part, the term "accumulated funding deficiency" means for any plan the excess of the total charges to the funding standard account for all plan years (beginning with the first plan year to which this part applies) over the total credits to such account for such years or, if less, the excess of the total charges to the alternative minimum funding standard account for such plan years over the total credits to such account for such years.

(3) In any plan year in which a multiemployer plan is in reorganization, the accumulated funding deficiency of the plan shall be determined under section 4243.

Act Sec. 302.(b)(1) Each plan to which this part applies shall establish and maintain a funding standard account. Such account shall be credited and charged solely as provided in this section.

(2) For a plan year, the funding standard account shall be charged with the sum of—

(A) the normal cost of the plan for the plan year,

(B) the amounts necessary to amortize in equal annual installments (until fully amortized)—

(i) in the case of a plan in existence on January 1, 1974, the unfunded past service liability under the plan on the first day of the first plan year to which this part applies, over a period of 40 plan years,

(ii) in the case of a plan which comes into existence after January 1, 1974, the unfunded past service liability under the plan on the first day of the first plan year to which this part applies, over a period of 30 plan years,

(iii) separately, with respect to each plan year, the net increase (if any) in unfunded past service liability under the plan arising from plan amendments adopted in such year, over a period of 30 plan years,

(iv) separately, with respect to each plan year, the net experience loss (if any) under the plan, over a period of 5 plan years (15 plan years in the case of a multiemployer plan), and

(v) separately, with respect to each plan year, the net loss (if any) resulting from changes in actuarial assumptions used under the plan, over a period of 10 plan years (30 plan years in the case of a multiemployer plan),

(C) the amount necessary to amortize each waived funding deficiency (within the meaning of section 303(c)) for each prior plan year in equal annual installments (until fully amortized) over a period of 5 plan years in the case of a multiemployer plan),

(D) the amount necessary to amortize in equal annual installments (until fully amortized) over a period of 5 plan years any amount credited to the funding standard account under paragraph (3)(D), and

(E) the amount necessary to amortize in equal annual installments (until fully amortized) over a period of 20 years the contributions which would be required to be made under the plan but for the provisions of subsection (c)(7)(A)(i)(I).

(3) For a plan year, the funding standard account shall be credited with the sum of—

(A) the amount considered contributed by the employer to or under the plan for the plan year,

(B) the amount necessary to amortize in equal annual installments (until fully amortized)—

(i) separately, with respect to each plan year, the net decrease (if any) in unfunded past service liability under the plan arising from plan amendments adopted in such year, over a period of 30 plan years,

(ii) separately, with respect to each plan year, the net experience (if any) under the plan, over a period of 5 plan years (15 plan years in the case of a multiemployer plan), and

(iii) separately, with respect to each plan year, the net gain (if any) resulting from changes in actuarial assumptions used under the plan, over a period of 10 plan years (30 plan years in the case of a multiemployer plan),

(C) the amount of the waived funding deficiency (within the meaning of section 303(c)) for the plan year, and

(D) in the case of a plan year for which the accumulated funding deficiency is determined under the funding standard account if such plan year follows a plan year for which such deficiency was determined under the alternative minimum funding standard, the excess (if any) of any debit balance in the funding standard account (determined without regard to this subparagraph) over any debit balance in the alternative minimum funding standard account.

(4) Under regulations prescribed by the Secretary of the Treasury, amounts required to be amortized under paragraph (2) or paragraph (3), as the case may be—

(A) may be combined into one amount under such paragraph to be amortized over a period determined on the basis of the remaining amortization period for all items entering into such combined amount, and

(B) may be offset against amounts required to be amortized under the other such paragraph, with the resulting amount to be amortized over a period determined on the basis of the remaining amortization periods for all items entering into whichever of the two amounts being offset is the greater.

(5) Interest.—

(A) In General. The funding standard account (and items therein) shall be charged or credited (as determined under regulations prescribed by the Secretary of the Treasury) with interest at the appropriate rate consistent with the rate or rates of interest used under the plan to determine costs.

(B) Required Change of Interest Rate. For purposes of determining a plan's current liability and for purposes of determining a plan's required contribution under section 302(d) for any plan year—

(i) In General. If any rate of interest used under the plan to determine cost is not within the permissible range, the plan shall establish a new rate of interest within the permissible range.

(ii) Permissible Range. For purposes of this subparagraph—

(I) In General. Except as provided in subclause (II) or (III), the term "permissible range" means a rate of interest which is not more than 10 percent above, and not more than 10 percent below, the weighted average of the rates of interest on 30-year Treasury securities during the 4-year period ending on the last day before the beginning of the plan year.

(II) Special rule for years 2004 and 2005. In the case of plan years beginning after December 31, 2003, and before January 1, 2006, the term 'permissible range' means a rate of interest which is not above, and not more than 10 percent below, the weighted average of the rates of interest on amounts invested conservatively in long-term investment grade corporate bonds during the 4-year period ending on the last day before the beginning of the plan year. Such rates shall be determined by the Secretary of the Treasury on the basis of 2 or more indices that are selected periodically by the Secretary of the Treasury and that are in the top 3 quality levels available. The Secretary of the Treasury shall make the permissible range, and the indices and methodology used to determine the average rate, publicly available.

(III) Secretarial Authority. If the Secretary finds that the lowest rate of interest permissible under subclause (I) or (II) is unreasonably high, the Secretary may prescribe a lower rate of interest, except that such rate may not be less than 80 percent of the average rate determined under such subclause.

(iii) Assumptions. Notwithstanding subsection (c)(3)(A)(i), the interest rate used under the plan shall be—

(I) determined without taking into account the experience of the plan and reasonable expectations, but

(II) consistent with the assumptions which reflect the purchase rates which would be used by insurance companies to satisfy the liabilities under the plan.

(6) In the case of a plan which, immediately before the date of the enactment of the Multiemployer Pension Plan Amendments Act of 1980, was a multiemployer plan (within the meaning of section 3(37) as in effect immediately before such date)—

(A) any amount described in paragraph (2)(B)(ii), (2)(B)(iii), or (3)(B)(i) of this subsection which arose in a plan year beginning before such date shall be amortized in equal annual installments (until fully amortized) over 40 plan years beginning with the plan year in which the amount arose;

(B) any amount described in paragraph (2)(B)(iv) or (3)(B)(ii) of this subsection which arose in a plan year beginning before such date shall be amortized in equal annual installments (until fully amortized) over 20 plan years, beginning with the plan year in which the amount arose;

(C) any change in past service liability which arises during the period of 3 plan years beginning on or after such date, and results from a plan amendment adopted before such date, shall be amortized in equal annual installments (until fully amortized) over 40 plan years, beginning with the plan year in which the change arises; and

(D) any change in past service liability which arises during the period of 2 plan years beginning on or after such date, and results from the changing of a group of participants from one benefit level to another benefit level under a schedule of plan benefits which—

(i) was adopted before such date, and

(ii) was effective for any plan participant before the beginning of the first plan year beginning on or after such date,

shall be amortized in equal annual installments (until fully amortized) over 40 plan years, beginning with the plan year in which the increase arises.

(7) For purposes of this part—

(A) Any amount received by a multiemployer plan in payment of all or part of an employer's withdrawal liability under part 1 of subtitle E of title IV shall be considered an amount contributed by the employer to or under the plan. The Secretary of the Treasury may prescribe by regulation additional charges and credits to a multiemployer plan's funding standard account to the extent necessary to prevent withdrawal liability payments from being unduly reflected as advance funding for plan liabilities.

(B) If a plan is not in reorganization in the plan year but was in reorganization in the immediately preceding plan year, any balance in the funding standard account at the close of such immediately preceding plan year—

(i) shall be eliminated by an offsetting credit or charge (as the case may be), but

(ii) shall be taken into account in subsequent plan years by being amortized in equal annual installments (until fully amortized) over 30 plan years.

The preceding sentence shall not apply to the extent of any accumulated funding deficiency under section 418B(a) of the Internal Revenue Code of 1986 as of the end of the last plan year that the plan was in reorganization.

(C) Any amount paid by a plan during a plan year to the Pension Benefit Guaranty Corporation pursuant to section 4222 or to a fund exempt under section 501(c)(22) of such Code pursuant to section 4223 shall reduce the amount of contributions considered received by the plan for the plan year.

(D) Any amount paid by an employer pending a final determination of the employer's withdrawal liability under part 1 of subtitle E of title IV and subsequently refunded to the employer by the plan shall be charged to the funding standard account in accordance with regulations prescribed by the Secretary.

(E) For purposes of the full funding limitation under subsection (c)(7), unless otherwise provided by the plan, the accrued liability under a multiemployer plan shall not include benefits which are not nonforfeitable under the plan after the termination of the plan (taking into consideration section 411(d)(3) of the Internal Revenue Code of 1986).

(F) Election for deferral of charge for portion of net experience loss.—

(i) In general. With respect to the net experience loss of an eligible multiemployer plan for the first plan year beginning after December 31, 2001, the plan sponsor may elect to defer up to 80 percent of the amount otherwise required to be charged under paragraph (2)(B)(iv) for any plan year beginning after June 30, 2003, and before July 1, 2005, to any plan year selected by the plan from either of the 2 immediately succeeding plan years.

(ii) Interest. For the plan year to which a charge is deferred pursuant to an election under clause (i), the funding standard account shall be charged with interest on the deferred charge for the period of deferral at the rate determined under section 304(a) for multiemployer plans.

(iii) Restrictions on benefit increases. No amendment which increases the liabilities of the plan by reason of any increase in benefits, any change in the accrual of benefits, or any change in the rate at which benefits become nonforfeitable under the plan shall be adopted during any period for which a charge is deferred pursuant to an election under clause (i), unless—

(I) the plan's enrolled actuary certifies (in such form and manner prescribed by the Secretary of the Treasury) that the amendment provides for an increase in annual contributions which will exceed the increase in annual charges to the funding standard account attributable to such amendment, or

(II) the amendment is required by a collective bargaining agreement which is in effect on the date of enactment of this subparagraph.

If a plan is amended during any such plan year in violation of the preceding sentence, any election under this paragraph shall not apply to any such plan year ending on or after the date on which such amendment is adopted.

(iv) Eligible multiemployer plan. For purposes of this subparagraph, the term 'eligible multiemployer plan' means a multiemployer plan—

(I) which had a net investment loss for the first plan year beginning after December 31, 2001, of at least 10 percent of the average fair market value of the plan assets during the plan year, and

(II) with respect to which the plan's enrolled actuary certifies (not taking into account the application of this subparagraph), on the basis of the acutarial assumptions used for the last plan year ending before the date of the enactment of this subparagraph, that the plan is projected to have an accumulated funding deficiency (within the meaning of subsection (a)(2)) for any plan year beginning after June 30, 2003, and before July 1, 2006.

For purposes of subclause (I), a plan's net investment loss shall be determined on the basis of the actual loss and not under any actuarial method used under subsection (c)(2).

(v) Exception to treatment of eligible multiemployer plan. In no event shall a plan be treated as an eligible multiemployer plan under clause (iv) if—

(I) for any taxable year beginning during the 10- year period preceding the first plan year for which an election is made under clause (i), any employer required to contribute to the plan failed to timely pay any excise tax imposed under section 4971 of the Internal Revenue Code of 1986 with respect to the plan,

(II) for any plan year beginning after June 30, 1993, and before the first plan year for which an election is made under clause (i), the average contribution required to be made by all employers to the plan does not exceed 10 cents per hour or no employer is required to make contributions to the plan, or

(III) with respect to any of the plan years beginning after June 30, 1993, and before the first plan year for which an election is made under clause (i), a waiver was granted under section 303 of this Act or section 412(d) of the Internal Revenue Code of 1986 with respect to the plan or an extension of an amortization period was granted under section 304 of this Act or section 412(e) of such Code with respect to the plan.

(vi) Notice. If a plan sponsor makes an election under this subparagraph or section 412(b)(7)(F) of the Internal Revenue Code of 1986 for any plan year, the plan administrator shall provide, within 30 days of filing the election for such year, written notice of the election to participants and beneficiaries, to each labor organization representing such participants or beneficiaries, to each employer that has an obligation to contribute under the plan, and to the Pension Benefit Guaranty Corporation. Such notice shall include with respect to any election the amount of any charge to be deferred and the period of the deferral. Such notice shall also include the maximum guaranteed monthly benefits which the Pension Benefit Guaranty Corporation would pay if the plan terminated while underfunded.

(vii) Election. An election under this subparagraph shall be made at such time and in such manner as the Secretary of the Treasury may prescribe..

Act Sec. 302.(c)(1) For purposes of this part, normal costs, accrued liability, past service liabilities, and experience gains and losses shall be determined under the funding method used to determine costs under the plan.

(2)(A) For purposes of this part, the value of the plan's assets shall be determined on the basis of any reasonable actuarial method of valuation which takes into account fair market value and which is permitted under regulations prescribed by the Secretary of the Treasury.

(B) For purposes of this part, the value of a bond or other evidence of indebtedness which is not in default as to principal or interest may, at the election of the plan administrator, be determined on an amortized basis running from initial cost at purchase to par value at maturity or earliest call date. Any election under this subparagraph shall be made at such time and in such manner as the Secretary of the Treasury shall by regulations provide, shall apply to all such evidences of indebtedness, and may be revoked only with the consent of the Secretary of the Treasury. In the case of a plan other than a multiemployer plan, this subparagraph shall not apply, but the Secretary of the Treasury may by regulations provide that the value of any dedicated bond portfolio of such plan shall be determined by using the interest rate under subsection (b)(5).

(3) For purposes of this section, all costs, liabilities, rates of interest, and other factors under the plan shall be determined on the basis of actuarial assumptions and methods—

(A) in the case of—

(i) a plan other than a multiemployer plan, each of which is reasonable (taking into account the experience of the plan and reasonable expectations) or which, in the aggregate, result in a total contribution equivalent to that which would be determined if each such assumption and method were reasonable, or

(ii) a multiemployer plan, which, in the aggregate, are reasonable (taking into account the experiences of the plan and reasonable expectations), and

(B) which, in combination, offer the actuary's best estimate of anticipated experience under the plan.

(4) For purposes of this section, if—

(A) a change in benefits under the Social Security Act or in other retirement benefits created under Federal or State law, or

(B) a change in the definition of the term "wages" under section 3121 of the Internal Revenue Code of 1954, or a change in the amount of such wages taken into account under regulations prescribed for purposes of section 401(a)(5) of the Internal Revenue Code of 1986,

results in an increase or decrease in accrued liability under a plan, such increase or decrease shall be treated as an experience loss or gain.

(5)(A) IN GENERAL. If the funding method for a plan is changed, the new funding method shall become the funding method used to determine costs and liabilities under the plan only if the change is approved by the Secretary of the Treasury. If the plan year for a plan is changed, the new plan year shall become the plan year for the plan only if the change is approved by the Secretary of the Treasury.

(B) APPROVAL REQUIRED FOR CERTAIN CHANGES IN ASSUMPTIONS BY CERTAIN SINGLE-EMPLOYER PLANS SUBJECT TO ADDITIONAL FUNDING REQUIREMENT.—

(i) IN GENERAL. No actuarial assumption (other than the assumptions described in subsection (d)(7)(C)) used to determine the current liability for a plan to which this subparagraph applies may be changed without the approval of the Secretary of the Treasury.

(ii) PLANS TO WHICH SUBPARAGRAPH APPLIES. This subparagraph shall apply to a plan only if—

(I) the plan is a defined benefit plan (other than a multiemployer plan) to which title IV applies;

(II) the aggregate unfunded vested benefits as of the close of the preceding plan year (as determined under section 4006(a)(3)(E)(iii)) of such plan and all other plans maintained by the contributing sponsors (as defined in section 4001(a)(13)) and members of such sponsors' controlled groups (as defined in section 4001(a)(14)) which are covered by title IV (disregarding plans with no unfunded vested benefits) exceed $50,000,000; and

(III) the change in assumptions (determined after taking into account any changes in interest rate and mortality table) results in a decrease in the unfunded current liability of the plan for the current plan year that exceeds $50,000,000, or that exceeds $5,000,000 and that is 5 percent or more of the current liability of the plan before such change.

(6) If, as of the close of a plan year, a plan would (without regard to this paragraph) have an accumulated funding deficiency (determined without regard to the alternative minimum funding standard account permitted under section 305) in excess of the full funding limitation—

(A) the funding standard account shall be credited with the amount of such excess, and

(B) all amounts described in paragraphs (2)(B), (C), and (D) and (3)(B) of subsection (b) which are required to be amortized shall be considered fully amortized for purposes of such paragraphs.

(7) FULL-FUNDING LIMITATION.—

(A) IN GENERAL. For purposes of paragraph (6), the term "full-funding limitation" means the excess (if any) of—

(i) the lesser of (I) in the case of plan years beginning before January 1, 2004, the applicable percentage of current liability (including the expected increase in current liability due to benefits accruing during the plan year), or (II) the accrued liability (including normal cost) under the plan (determined under the entry age normal funding method if such accrued liability cannot be directly calculated under the funding method used for the plan), over

(ii) the lesser of—

(I) the fair market value of the plan's assets, or

(II) the value of such assets determined under paragraph (2).

(B) CURRENT LIABILITY. For purposes of subparagraph (D) and subclause (I) of subparagraph (A)(i), the term "current liability" has the meaning given such term by subsection (d)(7) (without regard to subparagraphs (C) and (D) thereof) and using the rate of interest used under subsection (b)(5)(B).

(C) SPECIAL RULE FOR PARAGRAPH (6)(B). For purposes of paragraph (6)(B), subparagraph (A)(i) shall be applied without regard to subclause (I) thereof.

(D) REGULATORY AUTHORITY. The Secretary of the Treasury may by regulations provide—

(i) for adjustments to the percentage contained in subparagraph (A)(i) to take into account the respective ages or lengths of service of the participants and

(ii) alternative methods based on factors other than current liability for the determination of the amount taken into account under subparagraph (A)(i).

(E) MINIMUM AMOUNT.—

(i) IN GENERAL. In no event shall the full-funding limitation determined under subparagraph (A) be less than the excess (if any) of—

(I) 90 percent of the current liability of the plan (including the expected increase in current liability due to benefits accruing during the plan year), over

(II) the value of the plan's assets determined under paragraph (2).

(ii) CURRENT LIABILITY; ASSETS. For purposes of clause (i)—

(I) the term "current liability" has the meaning given such term by subsection (d)(7) (without regard to subparagraph (D) thereof), and

(II) assets shall not be reduced by any credit balance in the funding standard account.

(F) APPLICABLE PERCENTAGE. For purposes of subparagraph (A)(i)(I), the applicable percentage shall be determined in accordance with the following table:

"In the case of any plan year beginning in—	The applicable percentage is—
2002	165
2003	170.

(8) For purposes of this part, any amendment applying to a plan year which—

(A) is adopted after the close of such plan year but no later than 2 ½ months after the close of the plan year (or, in the case of a multiemployer plan, no later than 2 years after the close of such plan year),

(B) does not reduce the accrued benefit of any participant determined as of the beginning of the first plan year to which the amendment applies, and

(C) does not reduce the accrued benefit of any participant determined as of the time of adoption except to the extent required by the circumstances,

shall, at the election of the plan administrator, be deemed to have been made on the first day of such plan year. No amendment described in this paragraph which reduces the accrued benefits of any participant shall take effect unless the plan administrator files a notice with the Secretary notifying him of such amendment and the Secretary has approved such amendment or, within 90 days after the date on which such notice was filed, failed to disapprove such amendment. No amendment described in this subsection shall be approved by the Secretary unless he determines that such amendment is necessary because of a substantial business hardship (as determined under section 303(b)) and that waiver under section 303(a) is unavailable or inadequate.

(9)(A) For purposes of this part, a determination of experience gains and losses and a valuation of the plan's liability shall be made not less frequently than once every year, except that such determination shall be made more frequently to the extent required in particular cases under regulations prescribed by the Secretary of the Treasury.

(B)(i) Except as provided in clause (ii), the valuation referred to in subparagraph (A) shall be made as of a date within the plan year to which the valuation refers or within one month prior to the beginning of such year.

(ii) The valuation referred to in subparagraph (A) may be made as of a date within the plan year prior to the year to which the valuation refers if, as of such date, the value of the assets of the plan are not less than 100 percent of the plan's current liability (as defined in paragraph (7)(B)).

(iii) Information under clause (ii) shall, in accordance with regulations, be actuarially adjusted to reflect significant differences in participants.

(iv) A change in funding method to use a prior year valuation, as provided in clause (ii), may not be made unless as of the valuation date within the prior plan year, the value of the assets of the plan are not less than 125 percent of the plan's current liability (as defined in paragraph (7)(B)).

(10) For purposes of this section—

(A) In the case of a defined benefit plan other than a multiemployer plan, any contributions for a plan year made by an employer during the period—

(i) beginning on the day after the last day of such plan year, and

(ii) ending on the date which is 8 ½ months after the close of the plan year, shall be deemed to have been made on such last day.

(B) In the case of a plan not described in subparagraph (A), any contributions for a plan year made by an employer after the last day of such plan year, but not later than two and one-half months after such day, shall be deemed to have been made on such last day. For purposes of this subparagraph, such two and one-half month period may be extended for not more than six months under regulations prescribed by the Secretary of the Treasury.

(11) LIABILITY FOR CONTRIBUTIONS.—

(A) IN GENERAL. Except as provided in subparagraph (B), the amount of any contribution required by this section and any required installments under subsection (e) shall be paid by the employer responsible for contributing to or under the plan the amount described in subsection (b)(3)(A).

(B) JOINT AND SEVERAL LIABILITY WHERE EMPLOYER MEMBER OF CONTROLLED GROUP.—

(i) IN GENERAL. In the case of a plan other than a multiemployer plan, if the employer referred to in subparagraph (A) is a member of a controlled group, each member of such group shall be jointly and severally liable for payment of such contribution or required installment.

(ii) CONTROLLED GROUP. For purposes of clause (i), the term "controlled group" means any group treated as a single employer under subsection (b), (c), (m), or (o) of section 414 of the Internal Revenue Code of 1986.

(12) ANTICIPATION OF BENEFIT INCREASES EFFECTIVE IN THE FUTURE. In determining projected benefits, the funding method of a collectively bargained plan described in section 413(a) of the Internal Revenue Code of 1986 (other than a multiemployer plan) shall anticipate benefit increases scheduled to take effect during the term of the collective bargaining agreement applicable to the plan.

Act Sec. 302. ADDITIONAL FUNDING REQUIREMENTS FOR PLANS WHICH ARE NOT MULTIEMPLOYER PLANS.—

(d)(1) IN GENERAL. In the case of a defined benefit plan (other than a multiemployer plan) to which this subsection applies under paragraph (9) for any plan year, the amount charged to the funding standard account for such plan year shall be increased by the sum of—

(A) the excess (if any) of—

(i) the deficit reduction contribution determined under paragraph (2) for such plan year, over

(ii) the sum of the charges for such plan year under subsection (b)(2), reduced by the sum of the credits for such plan year under subparagraph (B) of subsection (b)(3), plus

(B) the unpredictable contingent event amount (if any) for such plan year.

Such increase shall not exceed the amount which, after taking into account charges (other than the additional charge under this subsection) and credits under subsection (b), is necessary to increase the funded current liability percentage (taking into account the expected increase in current liability due to benefits accruing during the plan year) to 100 percent.

(2) DEFICIT REDUCTION CONTRIBUTION. For purposes of paragraph (1), the deficit reduction contribution determined under this paragraph for any plan year is the sum of—

(A) the unfunded old liability amount,

(B) the unfunded new liability amount,

(C) the expected increase in current liability due to benefits accruing during the plan year, and

(D) the aggregate of the unfunded mortality increase amounts.

(3) UNFUNDED OLD LIABILITY AMOUNT. For purposes of this subsection—

(A) IN GENERAL. The unfunded old liability amount with respect to any plan year for any plan year is the amount necessary to amortize the unfunded old liability under the plan in equal annual installments over a period of 18 plan years (beginning with the 1st plan year beginning after December 31, 1988).

(B) UNFUNDED OLD LIABILITY. The term "unfunded old liability" means the unfunded current liability of the plan as of the beginning of the 1st plan year beginning after December 31, 1987 (determined without regard to any plan amendment increasing liabilities adopted after October 16, 1987).

(C) SPECIAL RULES FOR BENEFIT INCREASES UNDER EXISTING COLLECTIVE BARGAINING AGREEMENTS.—

(i) IN GENERAL. In the case of a plan maintained pursuant to 1 or more collective bargaining agreements between employee representatives and the employer ratified before October 17, 1987, the unfunded old liability amount with respect to such plan for any plan year shall be increased by the amount necessary to amortize the unfunded existing benefit increase liability in equal annual installments over a period of 18 plan years beginning with—

(I) the plan year in which the benefit increase with respect to such liability occurs, or

(II) if the taxpayer elects, the 1st plan year beginning after December 31, 1988.

(ii) UNFUNDED EXISTING BENEFIT INCREASE LIABILITIES. For purposes of clause (i), the unfunded existing benefit increase liability means, with respect to any benefit increase under the agreements described in clause (i) which takes effect during or after the 1st plan year beginning after December 31, 1987, the unfunded current liability determined—

(I) by taking into account only liabilities attributable to such benefit increase, and

(II) by reducing (but not below zero) the amount determined under paragraph (8)(A)(ii) by the current liability determined without regard to such benefit increase.

(iii) EXTENSIONS, MODIFICATIONS, ETC. NOT TAKEN INTO ACCOUNT. For purposes of this subparagraph, any extension, amendment, or other modification of an agreement after October 16, 1987, shall not be taken into account.

(D) SPECIAL RULE FOR REQUIRED CHANGES IN ACTUARIAL ASSUMPTIONS.—

(i) IN GENERAL. The unfunded old liability amount with respect to any plan for any plan year shall be increased by the amount necessary to amortize the amount of additional unfunded old liability under the plan in equal annual installments over a period of 12 plan years (beginning with the first plan year beginning after December 31, 1994).

(ii) ADDITIONAL UNFUNDED OLD LIABILITY. For purposes of clause (i), the term "additional unfunded old liability" means the amount (if any) by which—

(I) the current liability of the plan as of the beginning of the first plan year beginning after December 31, 1994, valued using the assumptions required by paragraph (7)(C) as in effect for plan years beginning after December 31, 1994, exceeds

(II) the current liability of the plan as of the beginning of such first plan year, valued using the same assumptions used under subclause (I) (other than the assumptions required by paragraph (7)(C)), using the prior interest rate, and using such mortality assumptions as were used to determine current liability for the first plan year beginning after December 31, 1992.

(iii) PRIOR INTEREST RATE. For purposes of clause (ii), the term 'prior interest rate' means the rate of interest that is the same percentage of the weighted average under subsection (b)(5)(B)(ii)(I) for the first plan year beginning after December 31, 1994, as the rate of interest used by the plan to determine current liability for the first plan year beginning after December 31, 1992, is of the weighted average under subsection (b)(5)(B)(ii)(I) for such first plan year beginning after December 31, 1992.

(E) OPTIONAL RULE FOR ADDITIONAL UNFUNDED OLD LIABILITY.—

(i) IN GENERAL. If an employer makes an election under clause (ii), the additional unfunded old liability for purposes of subparagraph (D) shall be the amount (if any) by which—

(I) the unfunded current liability of the plan as of the beginning of the first plan year beginning after December 31, 1994, valued using the assumptions required by paragraph (7)(C) as in effect for plan years beginning after December 31, 1994, exceeds

(II) the unamortized portion of the unfunded old liability under the plan as of the beginning of the first plan year beginning after December 31, 1994.

(ii) ELECTION.—

(I) An employer may irrevocably elect to apply the provisions of this subparagraph as of the beginning of the first plan year beginning after December 31, 1994.

(II) If an election is made under this clause, the increase under paragraph (1) for any plan year beginning after December 31, 1994, and before January 1, 2002, to which this subsection applies (without regard to this subclause) shall not be less than the increase that would be required under paragraph (1) if the provisions of this title as in effect for the last plan year beginning before January 1, 1995, had remained in effect.

(4) UNFUNDED NEW LIABILITY AMOUNT. For purposes of this subsection—

(A) IN GENERAL. The unfunded new liability amount with respect to any plan for any plan year is the applicable percentage of the unfunded new liability.

(B) UNFUNDED NEW LIABILITY. The term "unfunded new liability" means the unfunded current liability of the plan for the plan year determined without regard to—

(i) the unamortized portion of the unfunded old liability, the unamortized portion of the additional unfunded old liability, the unamortized portion of each unfunded mortality increase, and the unamortized portion of the unfunded existing benefit increase liability, and

(ii) the liability with respect to any unpredictable contingent event benefits (without regard to whether the event has occurred).

(C) APPLICABLE PERCENTAGE. The term "applicable percentage" means, with respect to any plan year, 30 percent, reduced by the products of—

(i) .40 multiplied by

(ii) the number of percentage points (if any) by which the funded current liability percentage exceeds 60 percent.

(5) UNPREDICTABLE CONTINGENT EVENT AMOUNT.—

(A) IN GENERAL. The unpredictable contingent event amount with respect to a plan for any plan year is an amount equal to the greatest of—

(i) the applicable percentage of the product of—

(I) 100 percent, reduced (but not below zero) by the funded current liability percentage for the plan year, multiplied by

(II) the amount of unpredictable contingent event benefits paid during the plan year, including (except as provided by the Secretary of the Treasury) any payment for the purchase of an annuity contract for a participant or beneficiary with respect to such benefits, or

(ii) the amount which would be determined for the plan year if the unpredictable contingent event benefit liabilities were amortized in equal annual installments over 7 plan years (beginning with the plan year in which such event occurs), or

(iii) the additional amount that would be determined under paragraph (4)(A) if the unpredictable contingent event benefit liabilities were included in unfunded new liability notwithstanding paragraph (4)(B)(ii).

(B) APPLICABLE PERCENTAGE.—

In the case of plan years beginning in:	The applicable percentage is:
1989 and 1990	5
1991	10
1992	15
1993	20
1994	30
1995	40
1996	50
1997	60
1998	70
1999	80
2000	90
2001 and thereafter	100

(C) PARAGRAPH NOT TO APPLY TO EXISTING BENEFITS. This paragraph shall not apply to unpredictable contingent event benefits (and liabilities attributable thereto) for which the event occurred before the first plan year beginning after December 31, 1988.

(D) SPECIAL RULE FOR FIRST YEAR OF AMORTIZATION. Unless the employer elects otherwise, the amount determined under subparagraph (A) for the plan year in which the event occurs shall be equal to 150 percent of the amount determined under subparagraph (A)(i). The amount under subparagraph (A)(ii) for subsequent plan years in the amortization period shall be adjusted in the manner provided by the Secretary of the Treasury to reflect the application of this subparagraph.

(E) LIMITATION. The present value of the amounts described in subparagraph (A) with respect to any one event shall not exceed the unpredictable contingent event benefit liabilities attributable to that event.

(6) SPECIAL RULES FOR SMALL PLANS.—

(A) PLANS WITH 100 OR FEWER PARTICIPANTS. This subsection shall not apply to any plan for any plan year if on each day during the preceding plan year such plan had no more than 100 participants.

(B) PLANS WITH MORE THAN 100 BUT NOT MORE THAN 150 PARTICIPANTS. In the case of a plan to which subparagraph (A) does not apply and which on each day during the preceding plan year had no more than 150 participants, the amount of the increase under paragraph (1) for such plan year shall be equal to the product of—

(i) such increase determined without regard to this subparagraph, multiplied by

(ii) 2 percent for the highest number of participants in excess of 100 on any such day.

(C) AGGREGATION OF PLANS. For purposes of this paragraph, all defined benefit plans maintained by the same employer (or any member of such employer's controlled group) shall be treated as 1 plan, but only employees of such employer or member shall be taken into account.

(7) CURRENT LIABILITY. For purposes of this subsection—

(A) IN GENERAL. The term "current liability" means all liabilities to participants and their beneficiaries under the plan.

(B) TREATMENT OF UNPREDICTABLE CONTINGENT EVENT BENEFITS.—

(i) IN GENERAL. For purposes of subparagraph (A), any unpredictable contingent event benefit shall not be taken into account until the event on which the benefit is contingent occurs.

(ii) UNPREDICTABLE CONTINGENT EVENT BENEFIT. The term "unpredictable contingent event benefit" means any benefit contingent on an event other than—

(I) age, service compensation, death or disability, or

(II) an event which is reasonably and reliably predictable (as determined by the Secretary of the Treasury).

(C) INTEREST RATE AND MORTALITY ASSUMPTIONS USED. Effective for plan year beginning after December 31, 1994—

(i) INTEREST RATE.—

(I) IN GENERAL. The rate of interest used to determine current liability under this subsection shall be the rate of interest used under subsection (b)(5), except that the highest rate in the permissible range under subparagraph (B)(ii) thereof shall not exceed the specified percentage under subclause (II) of the weighted average referred to in such subparagraph.

(II) SPECIFIED PERCENTAGE. For purposes of subclause (I), the specified percentage shall be determined as follows:

In the case of plan years beginning in calendar year:	The specified percentage is:
1995	109
1996	108
1997	107
1998	106
1999 and thereafter	105 .

(III) SPECIAL RULE FOR 2002 AND 2003. For a plan year beginning in 2002 or 2003, notwithstanding subclause (I), in the case that the rate of interest used under subsection (b)(5) exceeds the highest rate permitted under subclause (I), the rate of interest used to determine current liability under this subsection may exceed the rate of interest otherwise permitted under subclause (I); except that such rate of interest shall not exceed 120 percent of the weighted average referred to in subsection (b)(5)(B)(ii).

(ii) MORTALITY TABLES.—

(I) COMMISSIONERS' STANDARD TABLE. In the case of plan years beginning before the first plan year to which the first tables prescribed under subclause (II) apply, the mortality table used in determining current liability under this subsection shall be the table prescribed by the Secretary of the Treasury which is based on the prevailing commissioners' standard table (described in section 807(d)(5)(A) of the Internal Revenue Code of 1986) used to determine reserves for group annuity contracts issued on January 1, 1993.

(II) SECRETARIAL AUTHORITY. The Secretary of the Treasury may by regulation prescribe for plan years beginning after December 31, 1999, mortality tables to be used in determining current liability under this subsection. Such tables shall be based upon the actual experience of pension plans and projected trends in such experience. In prescribing such tables, the Secretary of the Treasury shall take into account results of available independent studies of mortality of individuals covered by pension plans.

(III) PERIODIC REVIEW. The Secretary of the Treasury shall periodically (at least every 5 years) review any tables in effect under this subsection and shall, to the extent the Secretary determines necessary, by regulation update the tables to reflect the actual experience of pension plans and projected trends in such experience.

(iii) SEPARATE MORTALITY TABLES FOR THE DISABLED. Notwithstanding clause (ii)—

(I) IN GENERAL. In the case of plan years beginning after December 31, 1995, the Secretary of the Treasury shall establish mortality tables which may be used (in lieu of the tables under clause (ii)) to determine current liability under this subsection for individuals who are entitled to benefits under the plan on account of disability. Such Secretary shall establish separate tables for individuals whose disabilities occur in plan years beginning before January 1, 1995, and for individuals whose disabilities occur in plan years beginning on or after such date.

(II) SPECIAL RULE FOR DISABILITIES OCCURRING AFTER 1994. In the case of disabilities occurring in plan years beginning after December 31, 1994, the tables under subclause (I) shall apply only with respect to individuals described in such subclause who are disabled within the meaning of title II of the Social Security Act and the regulations thereunder.

(III) PLAN YEARS BEGINNING IN 1995. In the case of any plan year beginning in 1995, a plan may use its own mortality assumptions for individuals who are entitled to benefits under the plan on account of disability.

(IV) SPECIAL RULE FOR 2004 AND 2005. For plan years beginning in 2004 or 2005, notwithstanding subclause (I), the rate of interest used to determine current liability under this subsection shall be the rate of interest under subsection (b)(5).

(D) CERTAIN SERVICE DISREGARDED.—

(i) IN GENERAL. In the case of a participant to whom this subparagraph applies, only the applicable percentage of the years of service before such individual became a participant shall be taken into account in computing the current liability of the plan.

(ii) APPLICABLE PERCENTAGE. For purposes of this subparagraph, the applicable percentage shall be determined as follows:

If the years of participation are:	The applicable percentage is:
1	20
2	40

If the years of participation are:	The applicable percentage is:
3	60
4	80
5 or more	100.

(iii) PARTICIPANTS TO WHOM SUBPRARGRAPH APPLIES. This subparagraph shall apply to any participant who, at the time of becoming a participant—

(I) has not accrued any other benefit under any defined benefit plan (whether or not terminated) maintained by the employer or a member of the same controlled group of which the employer is *a* member,

(II) who first becomes a participant under the plan in a plan year beginning after December 31, 1987, and

(III) has years of service greater than the minimum years of service necessary for eligibility to participate in the plan.

(iv) ELECTION. An employer may elect not to have this subparagraph apply. Such an election, once made, may be revoked only with the consent of the Secretary of the Treasury.

(8) OTHER DEFINITIONS. For purposes of this subsection—

(A) UNFUNDED CURRENT LIABILITY. The term "unfunded current liability" means, with respect to any plan year, the excess (if any) of—

(i) the current liability under the plan, over

(ii) value of the plan's assets determined under subsection (c)(2).

(B) FUNDED CURRENT LIABILITY PERCENTAGE. The term "funded current liability percentage" means, with respect to any plan year, the percentage which—

(i) the amount determined under subparagraph (A)(ii), is of

(ii) the current liability under the plan.

(C) CONTROLLED GROUP. The term "controlled group" means any group treated as a single employer under subsection (b), (c), (m), and (o) of section 414 of the Internal Revenue Code of 1986.

(D) ADJUSTMENTS TO PREVENT OMISSIONS AND DUPLICATIONS. The Secretary of the Treasury shall provide such adjustments in the unfunded old liability amount, the unfunded new liability amount, the unpredictable contingent event amount, the current payment amount, and any other charges or credits under this section as are necessary to avoid duplication or omission of any factors in the determination of such amounts, charges, or credits.

(E) DEDUCTION FOR CREDIT BALANCES. For purposes of this subsection, the amount determined under subparagraph (A)(ii) shall be reduced by any credit balance in the funding standard account. The Secretary of the Treasury may provide for such reduction for purposes of any other provision which references this subsection.

(9) APPLICABILITY OF SUBSECTION.—

(A) IN GENERAL. Except as provided in paragraph (6)(A), this subsection shall apply to a plan for any plan year if its funded current liability percentage for such year is less than 90 percent.

(B) EXCEPTION FOR CERTAIN PLANS AT LEAST 80 PERCENT FUNDED. Subparagraph (A) shall not apply to a plan for a plan year if—

(i) the funded current liability percentage for the plan year is at least 80 percent, and

(ii) such percentage for each of the 2 immediately preceding plan years (or each of the 2d and 3d immediately preceding plan years) is at least 90 percent.

(C) FUNDED CURRENT LIABILITY PERCENTAGE. For purposes of subparagraphs (A) and (B), the term "funded current liability percentage" has the meaning given such term by paragraph (8)(B), except that such percentage shall be determined for any plan year—

(i) without regard to paragraph (8)(E), and

(ii) by using the rate of interest which is the highest rate allowable for the plan year under paragraph (7)(C).

(D) TRANSITION RULES. For purposes of this paragraph:

(i) FUNDED PERCENTAGE FOR YEARS BEFORE 1995. The funded current liability percentage for any plan year beginning before January 1, 1995, shall be treated as not less than 90 percent only if for such plan year the plan met one of the following requirements (as in effect for such year):

(I) The full-funding limitation under subsection (c)(7) for the plan was zero.

(II) The plan had no additional funding requirement under this subsection (or would have had no such requirement if its funded current liability percentage had been determined under subparagraph (C)).

(III) The plan's additional funding requirement under this subsection did not exceed the lesser of 0.5 percent of current liability or $5,000,000.

(ii) SPECIAL RULE FOR 1995 AND 1996. For purposes of determining whether subparagraph (B) applies to any plan year beginning in 1995 or 1996, a plan shall be treated as meeting the requirements of subparagraph (B)(ii) if the plan met the requirements of clause (i) of this subparagraph for any two of the plan years beginning in 1992, 1993, and 1994 (whether or not consecutive).

(10) UNFUNDED MORTALITY INCREASE AMOUNT.—

(A) IN GENERAL. The unfunded mortality increase amount with respect to each unfunded mortality increase is the amount necessary to amortize such increase in equal annual installments over a period of 10 plan years (beginning with the first plan year for which a plan uses any new mortality table issued under paragraph (7)(C)(ii)(II) or (III)).

(B) UNFUNDED MORTALITY INCREASE. For purposes of subparagraph (A), the term "unfunded mortality increase" means an amount equal to the excess of—

(i) the current liability of the plan for the first plan year for which a plan uses any new mortality table issued under paragraph (7)(C)(ii)(II) or (III), over

(ii) the current liability of the plan for such plan year which would have been determined if the mortality table in effect for the preceding plan year had been used.

(11) PHASE-IN OF INCREASES IN FUNDING REQUIRED BY RETIREMENT PROTECTION ACT OF 1994.—

(A) IN GENERAL. For any applicable plan year, at the election of the employer, the increase under paragraph (1) shall not exceed the greater of—

(i) the increase that would be required under paragraph (1) if the provisions of this title as in effect for plan years beginning before January 1, 1995, had remained in effect, or

(ii) the amount which, after taking into account charges (other than the additional charge under this subsection) and credits under subsection (b), is necessary to increase the funded current liability percentage (taking into account the expected increase in current liability due to benefits accruing during the plan year) for the applicable plan year to a percentage equal to the sum of the initial funded current liability percentage of the plan plus the applicable number of percentage points for such applicable plan year.

(B) APPLICABLE NUMBER OF PERCENTAGE POINTS.—

(i) INITIAL FUNDED CURRENT LIABILITY PERCENTAGE OF 75 PERCENT OR LESS. Except as provided in clause (ii), for plans with an initial funded current liability percentage of 75 percent or less, the applicable number of percentage points for the applicable plan year is:

In the case of applicable plan years beginning in:	*The applicable number of percentage points is:*
1995	3
1996	6
1997	9
1998	12
1999	15
2000	19
2001	24

(ii) OTHER CASES. In the case of a plan to which this clause applies, the applicable number of percentage points for any such applicable plan year is the sum of—

(I) 2 percentage points;

(II) the applicable number of percentage points (if any) under this clause for the preceding applicable plan year;

(III) the product of .10 multiplied by the excess (if any) of (a) 85 percentage points over (b) the sum of the initial funded current liability percentage and the number determined under subclause (II);

(IV) for applicable plan years beginning in 2000, 1 percentage point; and

(V) for applicable plan years beginning in 2001, 2 percentage points.

(iii) PLANS TO WHICH CLAUSE (ii) APPLIES.—

(I) IN GENERAL. Clause (ii) shall apply to a plan for an applicable plan year if the initial funded current liability percentage of such plan is more than 75 percent.

(II) PLANS INITIALLY UNDER CLAUSE (i). In the case of a plan which (but for this subclause) has an initial funded current liability percentage of 75 percent or less, clause (ii) (and not clause (i)) shall apply to such plan with respect to applicable plan years beginning after the first applicable plan year for which the sum of the initial funded current liability percentage and the applicable number of percentage points (determined under clause (i)) exceeds 75 percent. For purposes of applying clause (ii) to such a plan, the initial funded current liability percentage of such plan shall be treated as being the sum referred to in the preceding sentence.

(C) DEFINITIONS. For purposes of this paragraph—

(i) The term "applicable plan year" means a plan year beginning after December 31, 1994, and before January 1, 2002.

(ii) The term "initial funded current liability percentage" means the funded current liability percentage as of the first day of the first plan year beginning after December 31, 1994.

(12) ELECTION FOR CERTAIN PLANS.—

(a) Amendment of ERISA. Section 302(d) of the Employee Retirement Income Security Act of 1974 (29 U.S.C. 1082(d)) is amended by adding at the end the following new paragraph:

(12) Election for certain plans.—

(A) In general. In the case of a defined benefit plan established and maintained by an applicable employer, if this subsection did not apply to the plan for the plan year beginning in 2000 (determined without regard to paragraph (6)), then, at the election of the employer, the increased amount under paragraph (1) for any applicable plan year shall be the greater of—

(i) 20 percent of the increased amount under paragraph (1) determined without regard to this paragraph, or

(ii) the increased amount which would be determined under paragraph (1) if the deficit reduction contribution under paragraph (2) for the applicable plan year were determined without regard to subparagraphs (A), (B), and (D) of paragraph (2).

(B) Restrictions on benefit increases. No amendment which increases the liabilities of the plan by reason of any increase in benefits, any change in the accrual of benefits, or any change in the rate at which benefits become nonforfeitable under the plan shall be adopted during any applicable plan year, unless—

(i) the plan's enrolled actuary certifies (in such form and manner prescribed by the Secretary of the Treasury) that the amendment provides for an increase in annual contributions which will exceed the increase in annual charges to the funding standard account attributable to such amendment, or

(ii) the amendment is required by a collective bargaining agreement which is in effect on the date of enactment of this subparagraph.

If a plan is amended during any applicable plan year in violation of the preceding sentence, any election under this paragraph shall not apply to any applicable plan year ending on or after the date on which such amendment is adopted.

(C) Applicable employer. For purposes of this paragraph, the term 'applicable employer' means an employer which is—

(i) a commercial passenger airline,

(ii) primarily engaged in the production or manufacture of a steel mill product or the processing of iron ore pellets, or

(iii) an organization described in section 501(c)(5) of the Internal Revenue Code of 1986 and which established the plan to which this paragraph applies on June 30, 1955.

(D) Applicable plan year. For purposes of this paragraph—

(i) In general. The term 'applicable plan year' means any plan year beginning after December 27, 2003, and before December 28, 2005, for which the employer elects the application of this paragraph.

(ii) Limitation on number of years which may be elected. An election may not be made under this paragraph with respect to more than 2 plan years.

(E) Notice requirements for plans electing alternative deficit reduction contributions.—

(i) In general. If an employer elects an alternative deficit reduction contribution under this paragraph and section 412(l)(12) of the Internal Revenue Code of 1986 for any year, the employer shall provide, within 30 days of filing the election for such year, written notice of the election to participants and beneficiaries and to the Pension Benefit Guaranty Corporation.

(ii) Notice to participants and beneficiaries. The notice under clause (i) to participants and beneficiaries shall include with respect to any election—

(I) the due date of the alternative deficit reduction contribution and the amount by which such contribution was reduced from the amount which would have been owed if the election were not made, and

(II) a description of the benefits under the plan which are eligible to be guaranteed by the Pension Benefit Guaranty Corporation and an explanation of the limitations on the guarantee and the circumstances under which such limitations apply, including the maximum guaranteed monthly benefits which the Pension Benefit Guaranty Corporation would pay if the plan terminated while underfunded.

(iii) Notice to pbgc. The notice under clause (i) to the Pension Benefit Guaranty Corporation shall include—

(I) the information described in clause (ii)(I),

(II) the number of years it will take to restore the plan to full funding if the employer only makes the required contributions, and

(III) information as to how the amount by which the plan is underfunded compares with the capitalization of the employer making the election.

(F) Election. An election under this paragraph shall be made at such time and in such manner as the Secretary of the Treasury may prescribe..

Act Sec. 302. QUARTERLY CONTRIBUTIONS REQUIRED.—

(e)(1) IN GENERAL. If a defined benefit plan (other than a multiemployer plan) which has a funded current liability percentage (as defined in subsection (d)(8)) for the preceding plan year of less than 100 percent fails to pay the full amount of a required installment for *the plan year,* then the rate of interest charged to the funding standard account under subsection (b)(5) with respect to the amount of the underpayment for the period of the underpayment shall be equal to the greater of—

(A) 175 percent of the Federal mid-term rate (as in effect under section 1274 of the Internal Revenue Code of 1986 for the 1st month of such plan year), or

(B) the rate of interest used under the plan in determining costs (including adjustments under subsection (b)(5)(B)).

(2) AMOUNT OF UNDERPAYMENT, PERIOD OF UNDERPAYMENT. For purposes of paragraph (1)—

(A) AMOUNT. The amount of the underpayment shall be the excess of—

(i) the required installment, over

(ii) the amount (if any) of the installment contributed to or under the plan on or before the due date for the installment.

(B) PERIOD OF UNDERPAYMENT. The period for which any interest is charged under this subsection with respect to any portion of the underpayment shall run from the due date for the installment to the date on which such portion is contributed to or under the plan (determined without regard to subsection (c)(10)).

(C) ORDER OF CREDITING CONTRIBUTIONS. For purposes of subparagraph (A)(ii), contributions shall be credited against unpaid required installments in the order in which such installments are required to be paid.

(3) NUMBER OF REQUIRED INSTALLMENTS: DUE DATES. For purposes of this subsection—

(A) PAYABLE IN 4 INSTALLMENTS. There shall be 4 required installments for each plan year.

(B) TIME FOR PAYMENT OF INSTALLMENTS.—

In the case of the following required installments:	The due date is:
1st	April 15
2nd	July 15
3rd	October 15
4th	January 15 of the following year

(4) AMOUNT OF REQUIRED INSTALLMENT. For purposes of this subsection—

(A) IN GENERAL. The amount of any required installment shall be the applicable percentage of the required annual payment.

(B) REQUIRED ANNUAL PAYMENT. For purposes of subparagraph (A), the term "required annual payment" means the lesser of—

(i) 90 percent of the amount required to be contributed to or under the plan by the employer for the plan year under section 412 of the Internal Revenue Code of 1986 (without regard to any waiver under subsection (d) thereof), or

(ii) 100 percent of the amount so required for the preceding plan year. Clause (ii) shall not apply if the preceding plan year was not a year of 12 months.

(C) APPLICABLE PERCENTAGE. For purposes of subparagraph (A), the applicable percentage shall be determined in accordance with the following table:

For plan years beginning in:	The applicable percentage is:
1989	6.25
1990	12.50

For plan years beginning in:	The applicable percentage is:
1991	18.75
1992 and thereafter	25.00

(D) Special rules for unpredictable contingent event benefits. In the case of a plan to which subsection (d) applies for any calendar year and which has any unpredictable contingent event benefit liabilities—

(i) Liabilities not taken into account. Such liabilities shall not be taken into account in computing the required annual payment under subparagraph (B).

(ii) Increase in installments. Each required installment shall be increased by the greatest of—

(I) the unfunded percentage of the amount of benefits described in subsection (d)(5)(A)(i) paid during the 3-month period preceding the month in which the due date for such installment occurs,

(II) 25 percent of the amount determined under subsection (d)(5)(A)(ii) for the plan year, or

(III) 25 percent of the amount determined under subsection (d)(5)(A)(iii) for the plan year.

(iii) Unfunded percentage. For purposes of clause (ii)(I), the term "unfunded percentage" means the percentage determined under subsection (d)(5)(A)(i)(I) for the plan year.

(iv) Limitation on increase. In no event shall the increases under clause (ii) exceed the amount necessary to increase the funded current liability percentage (within the meaning of subsection (d)(8)(B)) for the plan year to 100 percent.

(5) Liquidity requirement.—

(A) In general. A plan to which this paragraph applies shall be treated as failing to pay the full amount of any required installment to the extent that the value of the liquid assets paid in such installment is less than the liquidity shortfall (whether or not such liquidity shortfall exceeds the amount of such installment required to be paid but for this paragraph).

(B) Plans to which paragraph applies. This paragraph shall apply to a defined benefit plan (other than a multiemployer plan or a plan described in subsection (d)(6)(A)) which—

(i) is required to pay installments under this subsection for a plan year, and

(ii) has a liquidity shortfall for any quarter during such plan year.

(C) Period of underpayment. For purposes of paragraph (1), any portion of an installment that is treated as not paid under subparagraph (A) shall continue to be treated as unpaid until the close of the quarter in which the due date for such installment occurs.

(D) Limitation on increase. If the amount of any required installment is increased by reason of subparagraph (A), in no event shall such increase exceed the amount which, when added to prior installments for the plan year, is necessary to increase the funded current liability percentage (taking into account the expected increase in current liability due to benefits accruing during the plan year) to 100 percent.

(E) Definitions. For purposes of this paragraph—

(i) Liquidity shortfall. The term "liquidity shortfall" means, with respect to any required installment, an amount equal to the excess (as of the last day of the quarter for which such installment is made) of the base amount with respect to such quarter over the value (as of such last day) of the plan's liquid assets.

(ii) Base amount.—

(I) In general. The term "base amount" means, with respect to any quarter, an amount equal to 3 times the sum of the adjusted disbursements from the plan for the 12 months ending on the last day of such quarter.

(II) Special rule. If the amount determined under subclause (I) exceeds an amount equal to 2 times the sum of the adjusted disbursements from the plan for the 36 months ending on the last day of the quarter and an enrolled actuary certifies to the satisfaction of the Secretary of the Treasury that such excess is the result of nonrecurring circumstances, the base amount with respect to such quarter shall be determined without regard to amounts related to those nonrecurring circumstances.

(iii) Disbursements from the plan. The term "disbursements from the plan" means all disbursements from the trust, including purchases of annuities, payments of single sums and other benefits, and administrative expenses.

(iv) Adjusted disbursements. The term "adjusted disbursements" means disbursements from the plan reduced by the product of—

(I) the plan's funded current liability percentage (as defined in subsection (d)(8)) for the plan year, and

(II) the sum of the purchases of annuities, payments of single sums, and such other disbursements as the Secretary of the Treasury shall provide in regulations.

(v) Liquid assets. The term "liquid assets" means cash, marketable securities and such other assets as specified by the Secretary of the Treasury in regulations.

(vi) Quarter. The term "quarter" means, with respect to any required installment, the 3-month period preceding the month in which the due date for such installment occurs.

(F) Regulations. The Secretary of the Treasury may prescribe such regulations as are necessary to carry out this paragraph.

(6) Fiscal years and short years.—

(A) Fiscal years. In applying this subsection to a plan year beginning on any date other than January 1, there shall be substituted for the months specified in this subsection, the months which correspond thereto.

(B) Short plan year. This section shall be applied to plan years of less than 12 months in accordance with regulations prescribed by the Secretary of the Treasury.

(7) SPECIAL RULE FOR 2002—. In any case in which the interest rate used to determine current liability is determined under subsection (d)(7)(C)(i)(III), for purposes of applying paragraphs (1) and (4)(B)(ii) for plan years beginning in 2002, the current liability for the preceding plan year shall be redetermined using 120 percent as the specified percentage determined under subsection (d)(7)(C)(i)(II).

Act Sec. 302. IMPOSITION OF LIEN WHERE FAILURE TO MAKE REQUIRED CONTRIBUTIONS.—

(f)(1) IN GENERAL. In the case of a plan *covered under section 4021 of this Act* if—

(A) any person fails to make a required installment under subsection (e) or any other payment required under this section before the due date for such installment or other payment, and

(B) the unpaid balance of such installment or other payment (including interest), when added to the aggregate unpaid balance of all preceding such installments or other payments for which payment was not made before the due date (including interest), exceeds $1,000,000,

then there shall be a lien in favor of the plan in the amount determined under paragraph (3) upon all property and rights to property, whether real or personal, belonging to such person and any other person who is a member of the same controlled group of which such person is a member.

(2) PLANS TO WHICH SUBSECTION APPLIES. This subsection shall apply to a defined benefit plan (other than a multiemployer plan) for any plan year for which the funded current liability percentage (within the meaning of subsection (d)(8)(B)) of such plan is less than 100 percent.

(3) AMOUNT OF LIEN. For purposes of paragraph (1), the amount of the lien shall be equal to the aggregate unpaid balance of required installments and other payments required under this section (including interest)—

(A) for plan years beginning after 1987, and

(B) for which payment has not been made before the due date.

(4) NOTICE OF FAILURE; LIEN.—

(A) NOTICE OF FAILURE. A person committing a failure described in paragraph (1) shall notify the Pension Benefit Guaranty Corporation of such failure within 10 days of the due date for the required installment or other payment.

(B) PERIOD OF LIEN. The lien imposed by paragraph (1) shall arise on the due date for the required installment or other payment and shall continue until the last day of the first plan year in which the plan ceases to be described in paragraph (1)(B). Such lien shall continue to run without regard to whether such plan continues to be described in paragraph (2) during the period referred to in the preceding sentence.

(C) CERTAIN RULES TO APPLY. Any amount with respect to which a lien is imposed under paragraph (1) shall be treated as taxes due and owing the United States and rules similar to the rules of subsections (c), (d), and (e) of section 4068 shall apply with respect to a lien imposed by subsection (a) and the amount with respect to such lien.

(5) ENFORCEMENT. Any lien created under paragraph (1) may be perfected and enforced only by the Pension Benefit Guaranty Corporation, or at the direction of the Pension Benefit Guaranty Corporation, by the contributing sponsor (or any member of the controlled group of the contributing sponsor).

(6) DEFINITIONS. For purposes of this subsection—

(A) DUE DATE; REQUIRED INSTALLMENT. The term "due date" and "required installment" have the meanings given such terms by subsection (e), except that in the case of a payment other than a required installment, the due date shall be the date such payment is required to be made under this section.

(B) CONTROLLED GROUP. The term "controlled group" means any group treated under subsections (b), (c), (m), and (o) of section 414 of the Internal Revenue Code of 1986.

Act Sec. 302. QUALIFIED TRANSFERS TO HEALTH BENEFIT ACCOUNTS. (g) For purposes of this section, in the case of a qualified transfer (as defined in section 420 of the Internal Revenue Code of 1986)—

(1) any assets transferred in a plan year on or before the valuation date for such year (and any income allocable thereto) shall, for purposes of subsection (c)(7), be treated as assets in the plan as of the valuation date for such year, and

(2) the plan shall be treated as having a net experience loss under subsection (b)(2)(B)(iv) in an amount equal to the amount of such transfer (reduced by any amounts transferred back to the plan under section 420(c)(1)(B) of such Code) and for which amortization charges begin for the first plan year after the plan year in which such transfer occurs, except that such subsection shall be applied to such amount by substituting "10 plan years" for "5 plan years".

Act Sec. 302. CROSS REFERENCE.—

(h) For alternative amortization method for certain multiemployer plans see section 1013(d) of this Act.

Amendments

P.L. 109-135, §412:

Amended ERISA Sec. 302(e)(4)(B)(i) by striking "subsection (c)" and inserting "subsection (d)".

P.L. 108-218, §104(a):

Amended ERISA Sec. 302(b)(7) by adding sub paragraph F.

P.L. 108-218, §102(a):

Amended ERISA Sec. 302(d) by adding paragraph 12.

Act Sec. 102 provides:

(c) Effect of Election.—

An election under section 302(d)(12) of the Employee Retirement Income Security Act of 1974 or section 412(l)(12) of the Internal Revenue Code of 1986 (as added by this section) with respect to a plan shall not invalidate any obligation (pursuant to a collective bargaining agreement in effect on the date of the election) to provide benefits, to change the accrual of benefits, or to change the rate at which benefits become nonforfeitable under the plan.

(d) Penalty for Failing To Provide Notice.

Section 502(c)(3) of the Employee Retirement Income Security Act of 1974 (29 U.S.C. 1132(c)(3)) is amended by inserting "or who fails to meet the requirements of section 302(d)(12)(E) with respect to any person" after "101(e)(2) with respect to any person".

P.L. 108-218, §101(a):

Amended ERISA Sec. 302(b)(5)(B) by redesignating and amending subclause II as subclause III and by adding new subclause II to read as above.

Amended ERISA Sec. 302(e) to read as above.

Act Sec. 101 provides:

(c) Provisions Relating to Plan Amendments.

(1) In general.—

If this subsection applies to any plan or annuity contract amendment—

(A) such plan or contract shall be treated as being operated in accordance with the terms of the plan or contract during the period described in paragraph (2)(B)(i), and

(B) except as provided by the Secretary of the Treasury, such plan shall not fail to meet the requirements of section 411(d)(6) of the Internal Revenue Code of 1986 and section 204(g) of the Employee Retirement Income Security Act of 1974 by reason of such amendment.

(2) Amendments to which section applies.—

(A) In general. This subsection shall apply to any amendment to any plan or annuity contract which is made—

(i) pursuant to any amendment made by this section, and

(ii) on or before the last day of the first plan year beginning on or after January 1, 2006.

(B) Conditions.—

This subsection shall not apply to any plan or annuity contract amendment unless—

(i) during the period beginning on the date the amendment described in subparagraph (A)(ii) takes effect and ending on the date described in subparagraph (A)(ii) (or, if earlier, the date the plan or contract amendment is adopted), the plan or contract is operated as if such plan or contract amendment were in effect; and

(ii) such plan or contract amendment applies retroactively for such period.

(d) Effective Dates.—

(1) In general.

Except as provided in paragraphs (2) and (3), the amendments made by this section shall apply to plan years beginning after December 31, 2003.

(2) Lookback rules.

For purposes of applying subsections (d)(9)(B)(ii) and (e)(1) of section 302 of the Employee Retirement Income Security Act of 1974 and subsections (l)(9)(B)(ii) and (m)(1) of section 412 of the Internal Revenue Code of 1986 to plan years beginning after December 31, 2003, the amendments made by this section may be applied as if such amendments had been in effect for all prior plan years. The Secretary of the Treasury may prescribe simplified assumptions which may be used in applying the amendments made by this section to such prior plan years.

(3) Transition rule for Section 415 limitation.

In the case of any participant or beneficiary receiving a distribution after December 31, 2003 and before January 1, 2005, the amount payable under any form of benefit subject to section 417(e)(3) of the Internal Revenue Code of 1986 and subject to adjustment under section 415(b)(2)(B) of such Code shall not, solely by reason of the amendment made by subsection (b)(4), be less than the amount that would have been so payable had the amount payable been determined using the applicable interest rate in effect as of the last day of the last plan year beginning before January 1, 2004.

P.L. 107-147, § 405(b):

Act Sec. 405(b)(1) amended ERISA Sec. 302(d)(7)(C)(i) by adding subclause III to read as above.

Act Sec. 405(b)(2) amended ERISA Sec. 302(e) by adding paragraph (7) to read as above.

P.L. 107-147, § 411(v)(2):

Act Sec. 411(v)(2) amended ERISA Sec. 302(c)(9)(B)(ii) by striking "125 percent" and inserting "100 percent" and by adding clause iv to read as above.

The above amendment applies to plan years beginning after December 31, 2001, subject to sunset after 2010 under P.L. 107-16, Sec. 901.

P.L. 107-16, § 651(b)(1):

Act Sec. 651(b)(1) amended ERISA Sec. 302(c)(7) by striking "the applicable percentage" in subparagraph (A)(i)(I) and inserting "in the case of plan years beginning before January 1, 2004, the applicable percentage".

P.L. 107-16, § 651(b)(2):

Act Sec. 651(b)(2) amended ERISA Sec. 302(c)(7) by amending subparagraph (F) to read as follows:

"(F) APPLICABLE PERCENTAGE.—For purposes of subparagraph (A)(i)(I), the applicable percentage shall be determined in accordance with the following table:

"In the case of any plan year beginning in—	The applicable percentage is—
2002	165
2003	170 ."

Prior to amendment, ERISA Sec. 302(c)(7)(F) read as follows:

"(F) APPLICABLE PERCENTAGE.—For purposes of subparagraph (A)(i)(I), the applicable percentage shall be determined in accordance with the following table:

In the case of any plan year beginning in—	The applicable percentage is—
1999 or 2000	155
2001 or 2002	160
2003 or 2004	165
2005 and succeeding years	170 ."

P.L. 107-16, § 661(b):

Act Sec. 661(b) amended ERISA Sec. 302(c)(9) by inserting "(A)" after "(9)", and by adding at the end the following:

"(B)(i) Except as provided in clause (ii), the valuation referred to in subparagraph (A) shall be made as of a date within the plan year to which the valuation refers or within one month prior to the beginning of such year.

"(ii) The valuation referred to in subparagraph (A) may be made as of a date within the plan year prior to the year to which the valuation refers if, as of such date, the value of the assets of the plan are not less than 125 percent of the plan's current liability (as defined in paragraph (7)(B)).

"(iii) Information under clause (ii) shall, in accordance with regulations, be actuarially adjusted to reflect significant differences in participants.".

The above amendments apply to plan years beginning after December 31, 2001 subject to sunset after 2010 under P.L. 107-16, Sec. 901.

P.L. 105-34, § 1521(b)(A):

Act Sec. 1521(b)(A) amended ERISA Sec. 302(c)(7) by striking "150 percent" in subparagraph (A)(i)(I) and inserting "the applicable percentage;" and by adding subparagraph (F) to read as above.

P.L. 105-34, § 1521(c)(2):

Act Sec. 1521(c)(2) amended ERISA Sec. 302(b)(2) by striking "and" at the end of subparagraph (b)(2)(C) and deleting the period at the end of (b)(2)(D) and inserting ", and" at the end of (b)(2)(D) and by adding subparagraph (b)(2)(E) to read as above.

P.L. 105-34, § 1521(c)(3):

Act Sec. 1521(c)(3)(B) amended ERISA Sec. 302(c)(7)(D) by adding "and" at the end of clause (i), by striking ", and" at the end of clause (ii) and inserting a period, and by striking clause (iii). Prior to amendment, clause (iii) to read as follows:

(iii) for the treatment under this section of contributions which would be required to be made under the plan but for the provisions of subparagraph (A)(i)(I).

The above amendments apply to plan years beginning after December 31, 1998. But see Act Sec. 1521(d)(2) below for a special rule.

P.L. 105-34, § 1521(d)(2):

(2) SPECIAL RULE FOR UNAMORTIZED BALANCES UNDER EXISTING LAW.—The unamortized balance (as of the close of the plan year preceding the plan's first year beginning in 1999) of any amortization base established under section 412(c)(7)(D)(iii) of such Code and section 302(c)(7)(D)(iii) of such Act (as repealed by subsection (c)(3)) for any plan year beginning before 1999 shall be amortized in equal annual installments (until fully amortized) over a period of years equal to the excess of—

(A) 20 years, over

(B) the number of years since the amortization base was established.

P.L. 105-34, § 1604(b)(2):

Act Sec. 1604(b)(2) amended ERISA Sec. 302(e)(5)(E)(ii) by striking "clause (i)" and inserting "subclause (I)."

The above amendment applies to plan years beginning after December 31, 1994.

P.L. 103-465, § 761(a)(1)(A):

Act Sec. 761(a)(1)(A) amended ERISA Sec. 302(d)(1) by striking "which has an unfunded current liability" and inserting "to which this subsection applies under paragraph (9)".

P.L. 103-465, § 761(a)(1)(B):

Act Sec. 761(a)(1)(B) amended ERISA Sec. 302(d) by adding paragraph (9) to read as above.

P.L. 103-465, § 761(a)(2)(A):

Act Sec. 761(a)(2)(A) amended ERISA Sec. 302(d)(1)(A)(ii) to read as above. Prior to amendment, ERISA Sec. 302(d)(1)(A)(ii) read as follows:

(ii) the sum of the charges for such plan year under subparagraph (B) (other than clauses (iv) and (v) thereof), (C), and (D) of subsection (b)(2), reduced by the sum of the credits for such plan year under subparagraph (B)(i) of subsection (b)(3), plus

P.L. 103-465, § 761(a)(2)(B):

Act Sec. 761(a)(2)(B) amended the last sentence of ERISA Sec. 302(d)(1) to read as above. Prior to amendment, the last sentence of ERISA Sec. 302(d)(1) read as follows:

Such increase shall not exceed the amount necessary to increase the funded current liability percentage to 100 percent.

P.L. 103-465, § 761(a)(3):

Act Sec. 761(a)(3) amended ERISA Sec. 302(d)(2) by striking "plus" at the end of subparagraph (A); by striking the period at the end of subparagraph (B) and inserting ", plus"; and by adding at the end subparagraph (C) to read as above.

P.L. 103-465, § 761(a)(4)(A):

Act Sec. 761(a)(4)(A) amended ERISA Sec. 302(d)(3) by adding subparagraphs (D) and (E) to read as above.

P.L. 103-465, § 761(a)(4)(B):

Act Sec. 761(a)(4)(B) amended ERISA Sec. 302(d)(4)(B)(i) by inserting ", the unamortized portion of the additional unfunded old liability," after "old liability".

P.L. 103-465, § 761(a)(5):

Act Sec. 761(a)(5) amended ERISA Sec. 302(d)(4)(C) by striking ".25" and inserting ".40", and by striking "35" and inserting "60".

P.L. 103-465, § 761(a)(6)(A):

Act Sec. 761(a)(6)(A) amended ERISA Sec. 302(d)(5)(A) by striking "greater of" and inserting "greatest of" before clause (i); by striking "or" at the end of clause (i); by striking the period at the end of clause (ii) and inserting ", or"; and by adding after clause (ii) a new clause (iii) to read as above.

P.L. 103-465, § 761(a)(6)(B):

Act Sec. 761(a)(6)(B) amended ERISA Sec. 302(d)(5) by adding subparagraph (E) to read as above.

P.L. 103-465, § 761(a)(6)(C):

Act Sec. 761(a)(6)(C) amended ERISA Sec. 302(e)(4)(D)(ii) by striking "greater of" and inserting "greatest of" before subclause (I); by striking "or" at the end of subclause (I); by striking the period at the end of subclause (II) and inserting ", or"; and by adding subclause (III) to read as above.

P.L. 103-465, § 761(a)(7)(A):

Act Sec. 761(a)(7)(A) amended ERISA Sec. 302(d)(7)(C) to read as above. Prior to amendment, ERISA Sec. 302(d)(7)(C) read as follows:

(C) Interest Rates Used.—The rate of interest used to determine current liability shall be the rate of interest used under subsection (b)(5).

P.L. 103-465, § 761(a)(7)(B)(i):

Act Sec. 761(a)(7)(B)(i) amended ERISA Sec. 302(d)(2), as amended by Act Sec. 761(a)(3), by striking "plus" at the end of subparagraph (B); by striking the period at the end of subparagraph (C), and inserting ", and"; and by adding subparagraph (D) to read as above.

P.L. 103-465, § 761(a)(7)(B)(ii):

Act Sec. 761(a)(7)(B)(ii) amended ERISA Sec. 302(d), as amended by Act Sec. 761(a)(1), by adding paragraph (10) to read as above.

P.L. 103-465, § 761(a)(7)(B)(iii):

Act Sec. 761(a)(7)(B)(iii) amended ERISA Sec. 302(d)(4)(B)(i), as amended by Act. Sec. 761(a)(4)(B), by inserting "the unamortized portion of each unfunded mortality increase," after "additional unfunded old liability".

P.L. 103-465, § 761(a)(8):

Act Sec. 761(a)(8) amended ERISA Sec. 302(d), as amended by Act Sec. 761(a)(7), by adding paragraph (11) to read as above.

The above amendments apply to plan years beginning after December 31, 1994.

P.L. 103-465, § 761(a)(9)(A):

Act Sec. 761(a)(9)(A) amended ERISA Sec. 302(e) by redesignating paragraph (5) as paragraph (6) and by inserting new paragraph (5) to read as above.

The above amendments apply to plan years beginning after December 31, 1994.

P.L. 103-465, §764(a):

Act Sec. 764(a) amended ERISA Sec. 302(e)(1) by inserting "which has a funded current liability percentage (as defined in subsection (d)(8)) for the preceding plan year of less than 100 percent" before "fails", and by striking "any plan year" and inserting "the plan year".

The above amendment applies to plan years beginning after December 8, 1994.

P.L. 103-465, §768(b)(1):

Act Sec. 768(b)(1) amended ERISA Sec. 302(f)(1) by striking "to which this section applies" and inserting "covered under section 4021 of this Act".

P.L. 103-465, §768(b)(2):

Act Sec. 768(b)(2) amended ERISA Sec. 302(f)(3) to read as above. Prior to amendment, ERISA Sec. 302(f)(3) read as follows:

(3) AMOUNT OF LIEN.—For purposes of paragraph (1), the amount of the lien shall be equal to the lesser of—

(A) the amount by which the unpaid balances described in paragraph (1)(B) (including interest) exceed $1,000,000, or

(B) the aggregate unpaid balance of required installments and other payments required under this section (including interest)—

(i) for plan years beginning after 1987, and

(ii) for which payment has not been made before the due date.

P.L. 103-465, §768(b)(3):

Act Sec. 768(b)(3) amended ERISA Sec. 302(f)(4)(B) by striking "60th day following the" preceding "due date for the required installment".

The above amendments are effective for installments and other payments required under section 412 of the Internal Revenue Code of 1986 or under part 3 of subtitle B of the Employee Retirement Income Security Act of 1974 that become due on or after December 8, 1994.

P.L. 103-465, §769(a) & (b):

Act Sec. 769(a) & (b) provide:

ACT SEC. 769. SPECIAL FUNDING RULES FOR CERTAIN PLANS.

(a) FUNDING RULES NOT TO APPLY TO CERTAIN PLANS.—Any changes made by this Act to section 412 of the Internal Revenue Code of 1986 or to part 3 of subtitle B of title I of the Employee Retirement Income Security Act of 1974 shall not apply to—

(1) a plan which is, on the date of enactment of this Act, subject to a restoration payment schedule order issued by the Pension Benefit Guaranty Corporation that meets the requirements of section 1.412(c)(1)-3 of the Treasury Regulations, or

(2) a plan established by an affected air carrier (as defined under section 4001(a)(14)(C)(ii)(I) of such Act) and assumed by a new plan Sponsor pursuant to the terms of a written agreement with the Pension Benefit Guaranty Corporation dated January 5, 1993, and approved by the United States Bankruptcy Court for the District of Delaware on December 30, 1992.

(b) CHANGE IN ACTUARIAL METHOD.—Any amortization installments for bases established under section 412(b) of the Internal Revenue Code of 1986 and section 302(b) of the Employee Retirement Income Security Act of 1974 for plan years beginning after December 31, 1987, and before January 1, 1993, by reason of nonelective changes under the frozen entry age actuarial cost method shall not be included in the calculation of offsets under section 412(l)(1)(A)(ii) of such Code and section 302(d)(1)(A)(ii) of such Act for the 1st 5 plan years beginning after December 31, 1994.

The above provisions are effective December 8, 1994.

P.L. 103-465, §761(a)(10):

Act Sec. 761(a)(10) amended ERISA Sec. 302(c)(7) by inserting "(including the expected increase in current liability due to benefits accruing during the plan year)" after "current liability" in clause (i), and adding subparagraph (E) to read as above.

Act Sec. 761(a)(10)(C) amended ERISA Sec. 302(c)(7)(B) to read as above. Prior to amendment, it read as follows: "CURRENT LIABILITY.—For purposes of paragraphs (A) and (D), the term 'current liability' has the meaning given such term by subsection (d)(7) (without regard to subparagraph (D) thereof.)"

The above amendments apply to plan years beginning after December 31, 1994.

P.L. 103-465, §762(a):

Act Sec. 762(a) amended ERISA Sec. 302(c)(5) by striking "If the funding method" and inserting the following: "(A) IN GENERAL.—If the funding method", and by adding subparagraph (B) to read as above.

The above amendments apply to changes in assumptions for plan years beginning after October 28, 1993. For special rules, see Act Sec. 762(b)(2), below.

Act Sec. 762(b)(2) provides:

(2) CERTAIN CHANGES CEASE TO BE EFFECTIVE.—In the case of changes in assumptions for plan years beginning after December 31, 1992, and on or before October 28, 1993, such changes shall cease to be effective for plan years beginning after December 31, 1994, if—

(A) such change would have required the approval of the Secretary of the Treasury had such amendment applied to such change, and

(B) such change is not so approved.

P.L. 103-465, §763(a):

Act Sec. 763(a) amended ERISA Sec. 302(c) by adding subparagraph (12) to read as above.

The above amendment shall apply to plan years beginning after December 31, 1994, with respect to collective bargaining agreements in effect on or after January 1, 1995.

P.L. 101-508, Sec. 12012(c):

Amended ERISA Sec. 302 by redesignating subsection (g) as subsection (h) and adding new subsection (g) to read as above effective for qualified transfers under Code Sec. 420 made after November 5, 1990.

P.L. 101-508, Sec. 12012(c):

Amended ERISA Sec. 302 by redesignating subsection (g) as subsection (h) effective for qualified transfers under Code Sec. 420 made after November 5, 1990.

P.L. 101-239, §7881(a)(1)(B):

Amended ERISA Sec. 302(d)(3)(C)(ii)(II) by inserting "(but not below zero)" after "reducing."

P.L. 101-239, §7881(a)(2)(B):

Amended ERISA Sec. 302(d)(4)(B)(i) by inserting "and the unamortized portion of the unfunded existing benefit increase liability" after "liability."

P.L. 101-239, §7881(a)(3)(B):

Amended ERISA Sec. 302(d)(5)(C) by striking "October 17, 1987" and inserting "the first plan year beginning after December 31, 1988."

P.L. 101-239, §7881(a)(4)(B):

Amended ERISA Sec. 302(d)(7)(D) by striking "and" at the end of clause (iii)(I) and by striking the period at the end of clause (iii)(II) and inserting, "and" and by adding new subclause (IV) at the end of clause (iii) and also by adding a new clause (iv) to read as above.

P.L. 101-239, §7881(a)(5)(B):

Amended ERISA Sec. 302(d)(8) by striking "reduced by any credit balance in the funding standard account" in subparagraph (A)(ii) and by adding a new subparagraph (E).

The above amendments are effective for plan years beginning after December 31, 1988.

P.L. 101-239, §7881(a)(6)(B):

Amended ERISA Sec. 302(c)(9) by striking "three years" and inserting "year."

P.L. 101-239, §7881(b)(1)(B):

Amended ERISA Sec. 302(c)(10)(A) by inserting "defined benefit" before "plan other."

P.L. 101-239, §7881(b)(2)(B):

Amended ERISA Sec. 302(c)(10)(B) by striking "multiemployer plan" and inserting "plan not described in subparagraph (A)."

P.L. 101-239, §7881(b)(3)(B):

Amended ERISA Sec. 302(e)(1) by inserting "defined benefit" before "plan (other."

P.L. 101-239, §7881(b)(4)(B):

Amended ERISA Sec. 302(e)(4)(D) to read as above. Prior to amendment, subparagraph (D) read as follows:

(D) Special Rules for Unpredictable Contingent Event Benefits.—In the case of a plan with any unpredictable contingent event benefit liabilities—

(i) such liabilities shall not be taken into account in computing the required annual payment under subparagraph (B), and

(ii) each required installment shall be increased by the greater of—

(I) the amount of benefits described in subsection (d)(5)(A)(i) paid during the 3-month period preceding the month in which the due date for such installment occurs, or

(II) 25 percent of the amount determined under subsection (d)(5)(A)(ii) for the plan year.

P.L. 101-239, §7881(b)(6)(B)(i):

Amended ERISA Sec. 302(e)(1)(B) to read as above. Prior to amendment, subparagraph (B) read as follows:

(B) the rate under subsection (b)(5).

The above amendments are effective for plan years beginning after December 31, 1988.

P.L. 101-239, §7881(d)(1)(B):

Amended ERISA Sec. 302(b)(5)(B)(iii) by striking "for purposes of this section and for purposes of determining current liability."

P.L. 101-239, §7881(d)(2)(A):

Amended ERISA Sec. 302(b)(5)(B) by adding new material after the heading and before clause (i) to read as above.

P.L. 101-239, §7881(d)(2)(B):

Amended ERISA Sec. 302(b)(5) by striking material following the heading and preceding subparagraph (A). Prior to being stricken, the material read as follows:

For purposes of determining a plan's current liability and for purposes of determining a plan's required contribution under section 412(l) for any plan year—

P.L. 101-239, § 7881(d)(2)(C):

Amended ERISA Sec. 302(b)(5)(B)(ii)(I) by striking "average weight" and inserting "the weighted average of the rates."

P.L. 101-239, § 7881(d)(3):

Amended P.L. 100-203, § 9307(f) to read as below.

The above amendments are effective for years beginning after December 31, 1987.

P.L. 101-239, § 7891(a)(1):

Titles I, III, and IV of ERISA (other than sections 3(37)(E), 301(a)(7), and 308, the last sentence of section 408(d), and sections 414(c), 4001(a)(3)(ii), and 4303) are each amended by striking "Internal Revenue Code of 1954" each place it appears and inserting "Internal Revenue Code of 1986" effective October 22, 1986.

P.L. 101-239, § 7894(d)(2):

Amended ERISA Sec. 302(b)(3)(B)(ii), by striking the period and inserting a comma, effective September 2, 1974.

P.L. 101-239, § 7894(d)(5):

Amended ERISA Sec. 302(c)(6) by striking "subsection (g)" and inserting "section 305."

The above amendments are effective for plan years beginning after December 31, 1987.

P.L. 100-203, § 9301(b):

Amended ERISA Sec. 302(c)(7) to read as above, effective for years beginning after December 31, 1987. Prior to amendment, ERISA Sec. 302(c)(7) read as follows:

(7) For purposes of paragraph (6), the term "full funding limitation" means the excess (if any) of—

(A) the accrued liability (including normal cost) under the plan (determined under the entry age normal funding method if such accrued liability cannot be directly calculated under the funding method used for the plan), over

(B) the lesser of the fair market value of the plan's assets or the value of such assets determined under paragraph (2).

P.L. 100-203, § 9303(d)(2):

Amended ERISA Sec. 302(c)(2)(B) by adding a new sentence at the end to read as above, effective for years beginning after December 31, 1987.

P.L. 100-203, § 9304(a)(2):

Amended ERISA Sec. 302(c)(10) to read as above, effective for plan years beginning after December 31, 1987. Prior to amendment, ERISA Sec. 302(c)(10) read as follows:

(10) For purposes of this part, any contributions for a plan year made by an employer after the last day of such plan year, but not later than 2 ½ months after such day, shall be deemed to have been made on such last day. For purposes of this paragraph, such 2 ½ month period may be extended for not more than 6 months under regulations prescribed by the Secretary of the Treasury.

P.L. 100-203, § 9303(b)(1):

Amended ERISA Sec. 302 by adding subsection (d) to read as above, effective for plan years beginning after December 31, 1988.

P.L. 100-203, § 9304(b)(2):

Amended ERISA Sec. 302 by adding subsection (e) to read as above, effective for plan years beginning after 1988.

P.L. 100-203, § 9304:

ERISA Sec. 302(d) was redesignated as subsection (e), which was redesignated as subsection (f), which was redesignated as subsection (g).

P.L. 100-203, § 9307(a)(2)(A):

Amended ERISA Sec. 302(b)(2)(B)(iv), (2)(C) and (3)(B)(ii) by striking out "15 plan years" and inserting in lieu thereof "5 plan years (15 plan years in the case of a multiemployer plan)", effective for years beginning after December 31, 1987.

P.L. 100-203, § 9307(a)(2)(B):

Amended ERISA Sec. 302(b)(2)(B)(iv) and (3)(B)(iii) by striking out "30 plan years" and inserting in lieu thereof "10 plan years (30 plan years in the case of a multiemployer plan)", effective for years beginning after December 31, 1987.

P.L. 100-203, § 9307(b)(2):

Amended ERISA Sec. 302(c)(3) to read as above, effective for years beginning after December 31, 1987. Prior to amendment, ERISA Sec. 302(c)(3) read as follows:

(3) For purposes of this part, all costs, liabilities, rates of interest, and other factors under the plan shall be determined on the basis of actuarial assumptions and methods which, in the aggregate, are reasonable (taking into account the experience of the plan

and reasonable expectations) and which, in combination, offer the actuary's best estimate of anticipated experience under the plan.

P.L. 100-203, § 9307(e)(2):

Amended ERISA Sec. 302(b)(5) to read as above, effective for years beginning after December 31, 1987. Prior to amendment, ERISA Sec. 302(b)(5) read as follows:

(5) The funding standard account (and items therein) shall be charged or credited (as determined under regulations prescribed by the Secretary of the Treasury) with interest at the appropriate rate consistent with the rate or rates of interest used under the plan to determine costs.

P.L. 100-203, § 9307(f):

(f) EFFECTIVE DATE.—

(1) IN GENERAL.—Except as provided in paragraph (2), the amendments made by this section shall apply to years beginning after December 31, 1987.

(2) AMORTIZATION OF GAINS AND LOSSES.—Sections 412(b)(2)(B)(iv) and 412(b)(3)(B)(ii) of the Internal Revenue Code of 1986 and sections 302(b)(2)(B)(iv) and 302(b)(3)(B)(ii) of the Employee Retirement Income Security Act of 1974 (as amended by paragraphs (1)(A) and (2)(A) of subsection a)) shall apply to gains and losses established in years beginning after December 31, 1987. For purposes of the preceding sentence, any gain or loss determined by a valuation occurring as of January 1, 1988, shall be treated as established in years beginning before 1988, or at the election of the employer, shall be amortized in accordance with Internal Revenue Service Notice 89-52.

P.L. 100-203, § 9405(b)(2):

Amended ERISA Sec. 302(c) by adding paragraph (11) to read as above, effective for plan years beginning after December 31, 1987.

P.L. 100-203, § 9304(e)(2):

Amended ERISA Sec. 302 by adding subsection (f) to read as above, effective for plan years beginning after December 31, 1987.

P.L. 96-364, § 304:

Amended subsections 302(b)(2) and (3) to read as above and added new subsections 302(a)(3) and 302(b)(6) and (7), effective September 26, 1980.

Prior to being amended, subsections 302(b)(2) and (3) read:

"(2) For a plan year, the funding standard account shall be charged with the sum of—

(A) the normal cost of the plan for the plan year,

(B) the amounts necessary to amortize in equal annual installments (until fully amortized)—

(i) in the case of a plan in existence on January 1, 1974, the unfunded past service liability under the plan on the first day of the first plan year to which this part applies, over a period of 40 plan years,

(ii) in the case of a plan which comes into existence after January 1, 1974, the unfunded past service liability under the plan on the first day of the first plan year to which this part applies, over a period of 30 plan years (40 plan years in the case of a multiemployer plan),

(iii) separately, with respect to each plan year, the net increase (if any) in unfunded past service liability under the plan arising from plan amendments adopted in such year, over a period of 30 plan years (40 plan years in the case of a multiemployer plan),

(iv) separately, with respect to each plan year, the net experience loss (if any) under the plan, over a period of 15 plan years (20 plan years in the case of a multiemployer plan), and

(v) separately, with respect to each plan year, the net loss (if any) resulting from changes in actuarial assumptions used under the plan, over a period of 30 plan years,

(C) the amount necessary to amortize each waived funding deficiency (within the meaning of section 303(c)) for each prior plan year in equal annual installments (until fully amortized) over a period of 15 plan years, and

(D) the amount necessary to amortize in equal annual installments (until fully amortized) over a period of 5 plan years any amount credited to the funding standard account under paragraph (3)(D).

(3) For a plan year, the funding standard account shall be credited with the sum of—

(A) the amount considered contributed by the employer to or under the plan for the plan year,

(B) the amount necessary to amortize in equal annual installments (until fully amortized)—

(i) separately, with respect to each plan year, the net decrease (if any) in unfunded past service liability under the plan arising from plan amendments adopted in such year, over a period of 30 plan years (40 plan years in the case of a multiemployer plan),

(ii) separately, with respect to each plan year, the net experience gain (if any) under the plan, over a period of 15 plan years (20 plan years in the case of a multiemployer plan), and * * *"

[¶ 14,630]
VARIANCE FROM MINIMUM FUNDING STANDARD

Act Sec. 303. (a) If an employer, or in the case of a multiemployer plan, 10 percent or more of the number of employers contributing to or under the plan are unable to satisfy the minimum funding standard for a plan year without temporary substantial business hardship (substantial business hardship in the case of a multiemployer plan) and if application of the standard would be adverse to the interests of plan participants in the aggregate, the Secretary of the Treasury may waive the requirements of section 302(a) for such year with respect to all or any portion of the minimum funding standard other than the portion thereof determined under section 302(b)(2)(C). The Secretary of the Treasury shall not waive the minimum funding standard with respect to a plan for more than 3 of any 15 (5 of any 15 in the case of a multiemployer plan) consecutive plan years. The interest rate used for purposes of computing the amortization charge described in subsection (b)(2)(C) for any plan year shall be—

(1) in the case of a plan other than a multiemployer plan, the greater of (A) 150 percent of the Federal mid-term rate (as in effect under section 1274 of the Internal Revenue Code of 1986 for the 1st month of such plan year), or (B) the rate of interest used under the plan in determining costs (including adjustments under section 302(b)(5)(B)), and

(2) in the case of a multiemployer plan, the rate determined under section 6621(b) of such Code.

Act Sec. 303. (b) For purposes of this part, the factors taken into account in determining temporary substantial business hardship (substantial business hardship in the case of a multiemployer plan) shall include (but shall not be limited to) whether—

(1) the employer is operating at an economic loss,

(2) there is substantial unemployment or underemployment in the trade or business and in the industry concerned,

(3) the sales and profits of the industry concerned are depressed or declining, and

(4) it is reasonable to expect that the plan will be continued only if the waiver is granted.

Act Sec. 303. (c) For purposes of this part, the term "waived funding deficiency" means the portion of the minimum funding standard (determined without regard to subsection (b)(3)(C) of section 302) for a plan year waived by the Secretary of the Treasury and not satisfied by employer contributions.

Act Sec. 303. SPECIAL RULES.—

(d)(1) APPLICATION MUST BE SUBMITTED BEFORE DATE 2 ½ MONTHS AFTER CLOSE OF YEAR. In the case of a plan other than a multiemployer plan, no waiver may be granted under this section with respect to any plan for any plan year unless an application therefor is submitted to the Secretary of the Treasury not later than the 15th day of the 3rd month beginning after the close of such plan year.

(2) SPECIAL RULE IF EMPLOYER IS MEMBER OF CONTROLLED GROUP.—

(A) IN GENERAL. In the case of a plan other than a multiemployer plan, if an employer is a member of a controlled group, the temporary substantial business hardship requirements of subsection (a) shall be treated as met only if such requirements are met—

(i) with respect to such employer, and

(ii) with respect to the controlled group of which such employer is a member (determined by treating all members of such group as a single employer).

The Secretary of the Treasury may provide that an analysis of trade or business or industry of a member need not be conducted if the Secretary of the Treasury determines such analysis is not necessary because the taking into account of such member would not significantly affect the determination under this subsection.

(B) CONTROLLED GROUP. For purposes of subparagraph (A), the term "controlled group" means any group treated as a single employer under subsection (b), (c), (m), or (o) of section 414 of the Internal Revenue Code of 1986.

Act Sec. 303. (e)(1) The Secretary of the Treasury shall, before granting a waiver under this section, require each applicant to provide evidence satisfactory to such Secretary that the applicant has provided notice of the filing of the application for such waiver to each employee organization representing employees covered by the affected plan, and each affected party (as defined in section 4001(a)(21)) other than the Pension Benefit Guaranty Corporation. Such notice shall include a description of the extent to which the plan is funded for benefits which are guaranteed under title IV and for benefit liabilities.

(2) The Secretary of the Treasury shall consider any relevant information provided by a person to whom notice was given under paragraph (1).

Act Sec. 303. CROSS REFERENCE. (f) For corresponding duties of the Secretary of the Treasury with regard to implementation of the Internal Revenue Code of 1986, see section 412(d) of such Code.

Amendments

P.L. 101-239, §7881(b)(6)(B)(ii):

Amended ERISA Sec. 303(a)(1)(B) by inserting "(including adjustments under section 302(b)(5)(B))" after "costs."

P.L. 101-239, §7881(b)(7):

Amended ERISA Sec. 303(a) by redesignating subparagraphs (A) and (B) as paragraphs (1) and (2), respectively, and by adjusting the left-hand margination thereof 4 ems to the left; in paragraph (1) (as redesignated), by redesignating clauses (i) and (ii) as subparagraphs (A) and (B), respectively; and in paragraph (2) (as redesignated), by inserting "of such Code" after "section 6621(b)" effective for applications submitted after December 17, 1987 and waivers granted pursuant to such applications.

P.L. 101-239, §7881(b)(8):

Amended ERISA Sec. 303(f) as redesignated by P.L. 100-203, §9306(a)(2) by transferring it to immediately after subsection (e), effective for plan years beginning after December 31, 1987.

P.L. 101-239, §7881(c)(2):

Amended ERISA Sec. 303(e)(1) by striking "the benefit liabilities" and inserting "for benefit liabilities" effective for applications submitted after March 21, 1987.

P.L. 101-239, §7881(c)(3):

Amended P.L. 100-203, §9306(f)(3) to read as below, effective December 22, 1987.

P.L. 100-203, §9306(a)(2)(A):

Amended ERISA Sec. 303 by redesignating subsection (d) as (f) and inserting a new subsection (d)(1) to read as above, effective for plan years beginning after December 31, 1987.

P.L. 100-203, §9306(a)(2)(B):

Amended ERISA Secs. 303(a) and (b) by striking out "substantial business hardship" and inserting in lieu thereof "temporary substantial business hardship (substantial business hardship in the case of a multiemployer plan)," effective for applications submitted after December 17, 1987 and waivers granted pursuant to such applications.

P.L. 100-203, §9306(a)(2)(C):

Amended ERISA Sec. 303(d) by adding a new paragraph (2) to read as above, effective for applications submitted after December 17, 1987 and for waivers granted pursuant to such applications.

P.L. 100-203, §9306(b)(2):

Amended ERISA Sec. 303(a) by striking out "more than 5 of any 15" and inserting "more than 3 of any 15 (5 of any 15 in the case of a multiemployer plan)," effective for applications submitted after December 17, 1987 and waivers granted pursuant to such applications.

P.L. 100-203, §9306(c)(2)(A):

Amended ERISA Sec. 303(a) by striking out the last sentence and inserting the new last sentence to read as above, effective for applications submitted after December 17, 1987 and waivers granted pursuant to such applications. Prior to amendment, the last sentence read: "The interest rate used for purposes of computing the amortization charge described in section 302(b)(2)(C) for a variance granted under this subsection shall be the rate determined under section 6621(b) of the Internal Revenue Code of 1954."

P.L. 100-203, §9306(d)(2):

Amended ERISA Sec. 303(e)(1) by striking out "plan," and adding the new material at the end of the sentence, effective for applications submitted after March 21, 1987.

P.L. 101-239, §7891(a)(1):

Titles I, III, and IV of ERISA (other than sections 3(37)(E), 301(a)(7), and 308, the last sentence of section 408(d), and sections 414(c), 4001(a)(3)(ii), and 4303) are each amended by striking "Internal Revenue Code of 1954" each place it appears and inserting "Internal Revenue Code of 1986" effective October 22, 1986.

P.L. 100-203, §9306(f)(3):

(3) SUBSECTION (b).—The amendments made by subsection (b) shall apply to waivers for plan years beginning after December 31, 1987. For purposes of applying such amendments, the number of waivers which may be granted for plan years after December 31, 1987, shall be determined without regard to any waivers granted for plan years beginning before January 1, 1988.

P.L. 99-272:

Act Sec. 11015(b)(1)(A) amended ERISA Sec. 303(a) by adding a new sentence at the end of the subsection, to read as above, effective with respect to terminations pursuant to notices of intent filed with the PBGC on or after January 1, 1986 or proceeding begun on or after that date.

Act Sec. 11016(c)(2) amended ERISA Sec. 303 by adding a new subsection (e) to read as above, effective on April 7, 1986.

[¶ 14,640]
EXTENSION OF AMORTIZATION PERIODS

Act Sec. 304.(a) The period of years required to amortize any unfunded liability (described in any clause of subsection (b)(2)(B) of section 302) of any plan may be extended by the Secretary for a period of time (not in excess of 10 years) if he determines that such extension would carry out the purpose of this Act and would provide adequate protection for participants under the plan and their beneficiaries and if he determines that the failure to permit such extension would—

(1) result in—

(A) a substantial risk to the voluntary continuation of the plan, or

(B) a substantial curtailment of pension benefit levels or employee compensation, and

(2) be adverse to the interests of plan participants in the aggregate.

In the case of a plan other than a multiemployer plan, the interest rate applicable for any plan year under any arrangement entered into by the Secretary in connection with an extension granted under this subsection shall be the greater of (A) 150 percent of the Federal mid-term rate (as in effect under section 1274 of the Internal Revenue Code of 1986 for the 1st month of such plan year), or (B) the rate of interest used under the plan in determining costs. In the case of a multiemployer plan, such rate shall be the rate determined under section 6621(b) of such Code.

Act Sec. 304.(b)(1) (1) No amendment of the plan which increases the liabilities of the plan by reason of any increase in benefits, any change in the accrual of benefits, or any change in the rate at which benefits become nonforfeitable under the plan shall be adopted if a waiver under section 303(a) or an extension of time under subsection (a) of this section is in effect with respect to the plan, or if a plan amendment described in section 302(c)(8) has been made at any time in the preceding 12 months (24 months in the case of a multiemployer plan). If a plan is amended in violation of the preceding sentence, any such waiver, or extension of time, shall not apply to any plan year ending on or after the date on which such amendment is adopted.

(2) Paragraph (1) shall not apply to any plan amendment which—

(A) the Secretary determines to be reasonable and which provides for only de minimis increases in the liabilities of the plan,

(B) only repeals an amendment described in section 302(c)(8), or

(C) is required as a condition of qualification under part I of subchapter D, of chapter 1, of the Internal Revenue Code of 1986.

Act Sec. 304.(c)(1) (1) The Secretary of the Treasury shall, before granting an extension under this section, require each applicant to provide evidence satisfactory to such Secretary that the applicant has provided notice of the filing of the application for such extension to each employee organization representing employees covered by the affected plan.

(2) The Secretary of the Treasury shall consider any relevant information provided by a person to whom notice was given under paragraph (1).

Amendments

P.L. 101-239, §7894(d)(3):

Amended ERISA Sec. 304(b)(2)(A), by striking the period and inserting a comma, effective September 2, 1974.

P.L. 101-239, §7891(a)(1):

Titles I, III, and IV of ERISA (other than sections 3(37)(E), 301(a)(7), and 308, the last sentence of section 408(d), and sections 414(c), 4001(a)(3)(ii), and 4303) are each amended by striking "Internal Revenue Code of 1954" each place it appears and inserting "Internal Revenue Code of 1986" effective October 22, 1986.

P.L. 100-203, §9306(c)(2)(B):

Amended ERISA Sec. 304(a) by striking out the last sentence and inserting a new last sentence to read as above, effective for applications for waivers submitted after Decem-

ber 17, 1987 and waivers granted pursuant to such waivers. Prior to amendment, the last sentence read as follows:

The interest rate applicable under any arrangement entered into by the Secretary in connection with an extension granted under this subsection shall be the rate determined under section 6621(b) of the Internal Revenue Code of 1954.

P.L. 99-272:

Act Sec. 11015(b)(1)(B) amended ERISA Sec. 304 by adding the new sentence following paragraph (2) to read as above, effective with respect to terminations pursuant to notices of intent filed with the PBGC on or after January 1, 1986 and proceedings begun on or after that date.

Act Sec. 11016(c)(3) amended ERISA Sec. 304 by adding a new subsection (c) to read as above, effective on April 7, 1986.

[¶ 14,650]
ALTERNATIVE MINIMUM FUNDING STANDARD

Act Sec. 305.(a) A plan which uses a funding method that requires contributions in all years not less than those required under the entry age normal funding method may maintain an alternative minimum funding standard account for any plan year. Such account shall be credited and charged solely as provided in this section.

Act Sec. 305. (b) For a plan year the alternative minimum funding standard accounts shall be—

(1) charged with the sum of—

(A) the lesser of normal cost under the funding method used under the plan or normal cost determined under the unit credit method.

(B) the excess, if any, of the present value of accrued benefits under the plan over the fair market value of the assets, and

(C) an amount equal to the excess, if any, of credits to the alternative minimum funding standard account for all prior plan years over charges to such account for all such years, and

(2) credited with the amount considered contributed by the employer to or under the plan (within the meaning of section 302(c)(10)) for the plan year.

Act Sec. 305. (c) The alternative minimum funding standard account (and items therein) shall be charged or credited with interest in the manner provided under section 302(b)(5) with respect to the funding standard account.

[¶ 14,655]
SECURITY FOR WAIVERS OF MINIMUM FUNDING STANDARD AND EXTENSIONS OF AMORTIZATION PERIOD

Act Sec. 306.(a) SECURITY MAY BE REQUIRED.—

(1) IN GENERAL. Except as provided in subsection (c), the Secretary of the Treasury may require an employer maintaining a defined benefit plan which is a single-employer plan (within the meaning of section 4001(a)(15)) to provide security to such plan as a condition for granting or modifying a waiver under section 303 or an extension under section 304.

(2) SPECIAL RULES. Any security provided under paragraph (1) may be perfected and enforced only by the Pension Benefit Guaranty Corporation or, at the direction of the Corporation, by a contributing sponsor (within the meaning of section 4001(a)(13)) or a member of such sponsor's controlled group (within the meaning of section 4001(a)(14)).

Act Sec. 306. CONSULTATION WITH THE PENSION BENEFIT GUARANTY CORPORATION. (b) Except as provided in subsection (c), the Secretary of the Treasury shall, before granting or modifying a waiver under section 303 or an extension under section 304 with respect to a plan described in subsection (a)(1)—

(1) provide the Pension Benefit Guaranty Corporation with—

(A) notice of the compelled application for any waiver, extension, or modification, and

(B) an opportunity to comment on such application within 30 days after receipt of such notice, and

(2) consider—

(A) any comments of the Corporation under paragraph (1)(B), and

(B) any views of any employee organization representing participants in the plan which are submitted in writing to the Secretary of the Treasury in connection with such application.

Information provided to the corporation under this subsection shall be considered tax return information and subject to the safeguarding and reporting requirements of section 6103(p) of the Internal Revenue Code of 1986.

Act Sec. 306. EXCEPTION FOR CERTAIN WAIVERS AND EXTENSIONS.—

(c)(1) IN GENERAL. The preceding provisions of this section shall not apply to any plan with respect to which the sum of—

(A) the outstanding balance of the accumulated funding deficiencies (within the meaning of section 302(a)(2) of this Act and section 412(a) of the Internal Revenue Code of 1986) of the plan,

(B) the outstanding balance of the amount of waived funding deficiencies of the plan waived under section 303 of this Act or section 412(d) of such Code, and

(C) the outstanding balance of the amount of decreases in the minimum funding standard allowed under section 304 of this Act or section 412(e) of such Code,

is less than $1,000,000.

(2) ACCUMULATED FUNDING DEFICIENCIES. For purposes of paragraph (1)(A), accumulated funding deficiencies shall include any increase in such amount which would result if all applications for waivers of the minimum funding standard under section 303 of this Act or section 412(d) of the Internal Revenue Code of 1986 and for extensions of amortization period under section 304 of this Act or section 412(e) of such Code which are pending with respect to such plan were denied.

Amendments

P.L. 101-239, §7891(a)(1):

Titles I, III, and IV of ERISA (other than sections 3(37)(E), 301(a)(7), and 308, the last sentence of section 408(d), and sections 414(c), 4001(a)(3)(ii), and 4303) are each amended by striking "Internal Revenue Code of 1954" each place it appears and inserting "Internal Revenue Code of 1986" effective October 22, 1986.

P.L. 100-203, §9306(e)(2):

Amended ERISA Sec. 306(c)(1) by striking out "$2,000,000" and inserting in lieu thereof "$1,000,000", effective for waiver applications submitted after December 17, 1987 and waivers granted pursuant to such applications.

P.L. §99-272:

Act Sec. 11015(a)(1)(A) added new ERISA Sec. 306 to read as above, effective with respect to applications for waivers, extensions and modifications filed on or after April 7, 1986.

[¶ 14,657]
SECURITY REQUIRED UPON ADOPTION OF PLAN AMENDMENT RESULTING IN SIGNIFICANT UNDERFUNDING

Act Sec. 307.(a) IN GENERAL. If—

(1) a defined benefit plan (other than a multiemployer plan) to which the requirements of section 302 apply adopts an amendment an effect of which is to increase current liability under the plan for a plan year, and

(2) the funded current liability percentage of the plan for the plan year in which the amendment takes effect is less than 60 percent, including the amount of the unfunded current liability under the plan attributable to the plan amendment.

the contributing sponsor (or any member of the controlled group of the contributing sponsor) shall provide security to the plan.

Act Sec. 307. FORM OF SECURITY. (b) The security required under subsection (a) shall consist of—

(1) a bond issued by a corporate surety company that is an acceptable surety for purposes of section 412,

(2) cash, or United States obligations which mature in 3 years or less, held in escrow by a bank or similar financial institution, or

(3) such other form of security as is satisfactory to the Secretary of the Treasury and the parties involved.

Act Sec. 307. AMOUNT OF SECURITY. (c) The security shall be in an amount equal to the excess of—

(1) the lesser of—

(A) the amount of additional plan assets which would be necessary to increase the funded current liability percentage under the plan to 60 percent, including the amount of the unfunded current liability under the plan attributable to the plan amendment, or

(B) the amount of the increase in current liability under the plan attributable to the plan amendment and any other plan amendments adopted after December 22, 1987, and before such plan amendment, over

(2) $10,000,000.

Act Sec. 307. RELEASE OF SECURITY. (d) The security shall be released (and any amounts thereunder shall be refunded together with any interest accrued thereon) at the end of the first plan year which ends after the provision of the security and for which the funded current liability percentage under the plan is not less than 60 percent. The Secretary of the Treasury may prescribe regulations for partial releases of the security by reason of increases in the funded current liability percentage.

Act Sec. 307. NOTICE. (e) A contributing sponsor which is required to provide security under subsection (a) shall notify the Pension Benefit Guaranty Corporation within 30 days after the amendment requiring such security takes effect. Such notice shall contain such information as the Corporation may require.

Act Sec. 307. DEFINITIONS. (f) For purposes of this section, the terms "current liability", "funded current liability percentage", and "unfunded current liability" shall have the meanings given such terms by section 302(d), except that in computing unfunded current liability there shall not be taken into account any unamortized portion of the unfunded old liability amount as of the close of the plan year.

Amendments

P.L. 101-239, §7881(i)(1)(B):

Amended ERISA Sec. 307(c)(1)(B) by inserting "and any other plan amendments adopted after December 22, 1987, and before such plan amendment" after "amendment."

P.L. 101-239, §7881(i)(2):

Amended ERISA Sec. 307(d) by inserting "of the Treasury" after "Secretary."

P.L. 101-239, §7881(i)(3)(A):

Amended ERISA Sec. 307 by redesignating subsection (e) as subsection (f) and adding new subsection (e) to read as above.

P.L. 101-239, §7881(i)(4)(B):

Amended ERISA Sec. 307(a)(1) by inserting "to which the requirements of section 302 apply" after "multiemployer plan)."

The above amendments are effective as if included in P.L. 100-203, §9341(b).

P.L. 101-239, §7881(i)(5):

Amended P.L. 100-203, §9341(c) to read as below, effective December 22, 1987.

P.L. 100-203, §9341(b)(2):

Added ERISA Sec. 307, to read as above, effective for plan amendments made after December 22, 1987 except for plan amendments adopted by collective bargaining agreements ratified before December 22, 1987.

P.L. 101-203, § 9341(c):

(c) EFFECTIVE DATE.—

(1) IN GENERAL.—Except as provided in this subsection, the amendments made by this section shall apply to plan amendments adopted after the date of the enactment of this Act.

(2) COLLECTIVE BARGAINING AGREEMENTS.—In the case of a plan maintained pursuant to 1 or more collective bargaining agreements between employee representatives and 1 or more employers ratified before the date of the enactment of this Act, the amendments made by this section shall not apply to plan amendments adopted pursuant to collective bargaining agreements ratified before the date of enactment (without regard to any extension, amendment, or modification of such agreements on or after such date of enactment).

[¶ 14,660]
EFFECTIVE DATES

Act Sec. 308. (a) Except as otherwise provided in this section, this part shall apply in the case of plan years beginning after the date of the enactment of this Act.

Act Sec. 308. (b) Except as otherwise provided in subsections (c) and (d), in the case of a plan in existence on January 1, 1974, this part shall apply in the case of plan years beginning after December 31, 1975.

Act Sec. 308. (c) (1) In the case of a plan maintained on January 1, 1974, pursuant to one or more agreements which the Secretary finds to be collective bargaining agreements between employee organizations and one or more employers, this part shall apply only with respect to plan years beginning after the earlier of the date specified in subparagraph (A) or (B) of section 211(c)(1).

(2) This subsection shall apply with respect to a plan if (and only if) the application of this subsection results in a later effective date for this part than the effective date required by subsection (b).

Act Sec. 308. (d) In the case of a plan the administrator of which elects under section 1017(d) of this Act to have the provisions of the Internal Revenue Code of 1954 relating to participation, vesting, funding, and form of benefit to apply to a plan year and to all subsequent plan years, this part shall apply to plan years beginning on the earlier of the first plan year to which such election applies or the first plan year determined under subsections (a), (b), and (c) of this section.

Act Sec. 308. (e) In the case of a plan maintained by a labor organization which is exempt from tax under section 501(c)(5) of the Internal Revenue Code of 1954 exclusively for the benefit of its employees and their beneficiaries, this part shall be applied by substituting for the term "December 31, 1975" in subsection (b), the earlier of—

(1) the date on which the second convention of such labor organization held after the date of the enactment of this Act ends, or

(2) December 31, 1980,

but in no event shall a date earlier than the later of December 31, 1975, or the date determined under subsection (c) be substituted.

Act Sec. 308. (f) The preceding provisions of this section shall not apply with respect to amendments made to this part in provisions enacted after the date of the enactment of this Act.

Amendments

P.L. 101-239, § 7984(h)(3):

Amended ERISA by adding subsection (f).

P.L. 100-203, § 9341(b):

Redesignated ERISA Sec. 307 as ERISA Sec. 308, to read as above, effective for plan amendments made after December 22, 1987 except for plan amendments adopted by collective bargaining agreements ratified before December 22, 1987.

P.L. 99-272, § 11015(a)(1)(A):

Redesignated ERISA Sec. 306 as ERISA Sec. 307, effective with respect to applications for waivers, extensions and modifications filed on or after April 7, 1986.

Regulations

Interpretive Bulletin ERISA IB MS 75-1 has been redesignated as Reg. § 2509.75-10 as section of "Part 2509—Interpretive Bulletins Relating to the Employee Retirement Income Security Act of 1974; Chapter XXV—Office of Employee Benefits Security—Title 29—Labor," filed with the Federal Register on January 21, 1976 (41 FR 3289).

»»→ *Caution: The Reliance Period and the deadline dates have expired.*

[¶ 14,671]

§ 2509.75-10 **Interpretive bulletin relating to the ERISA Guidelines and the Special Reliance Procedure.** On November 5, 1975, the Department of Labor (the "Department") and the Internal Revenue Service (the "Service") announced the publication of a compendium of authoritative rules (hereinafter referred to as the "ERISA Guidelines") relating to ERISA requirements. *See* T.I.R. No. 1415 (November 5, 1975) issued by the Service. These rules were published in recognition of the need to provide an immediate and complete set of interim guidelines to facilitate (1) adoption of new employee pension benefit plans (hereinafter referred to as "plans"), and (2) prompt amendment of existing plans, in conformance with the applicable requirements of the Employee Retirement Income Security Act of 1974 ("ERISA") pending the issuance of final regulations or other rules. These rules govern the application of (1) the qualification requirements of the Internal Revenue Code of 1954 (the "Code") added or amended by ERISA, and (2) the requirements of the provisions of parts 2 and 3 of Title I of ERISA paralleling such qualification requirements (both such sets of requirements hereinafter referred to collectively as the "new qualification requirements").

The ERISA Guidelines incorporate by reference the documents relating to the new qualification requirements heretofore published by the Department and by the Service as temporary or proposed regulations, revenue rulings, revenue procedures, questions and answers, technical information releases, and other issuances. The ERISA Guidelines also incorporate additional documents published on November 5, 1975, or to be published forthwith, which are necessary to complete the interim guidelines relating to the new qualification requirements. See the schedule set forth below for a complete list and brief description of the documents comprising the ERISA Guidelines.

The Department and the Service emphasized that the ERISA Guidelines constitute the entire set of interim rules of the Department and the Service for satisfying the new qualification requirements, and thus provide authoritative guidance in respect of the new statutory requirements bearing on qualification. These rules are applicable to individually designed plans and to multiemployer (or other multiple employer) plans, and may be relied upon until amended or supplemented by final regulations or other rules. Moreover, the Department and the Service announced that any provisions of final regulations or other rules which amend or supplement the rules contained in the ERISA Guidelines will generally be prospective only from the date of publication. Further, in the case of employee plan provisions adopted or amended before the date of such publication which satisfy the ERISA Guidelines, such final regulations or other rules will generally be made effective for plan years commencing after such date, except in unusual circumstances.

The Service further announced that the ERISA Guidelines incorporate the procedures that will enable employers to obtain determination letters as to the qualification of pension, annuity, profit sharing, stock bonus and bond purchase plans which satisfy the requirements of sections 401(a), 403(a) and 405(a) of the Code, as amended by ERISA. The Service also pointed out that the ERISA Guidelines will enable sponsors of master and prototype plans (whether newly established or amended) to obtain opinion letters as to the acceptability of the form of such plans, and further, that employers who establish plans designed to meet the requirements of section 301(d) of the Tax Reduction Act of 1975 (relating to employee stock ownership plans) will be able to obtain determination letters as to the acceptability of such plans (whether or not such plans are intended to be qualified).

To facilitate further the adoption of new plans and the prompt amendment of existing plans in conformance with the new qualification requirements, the Service announced on November 5, 1975, the adoption of a special procedure (hereinafter referred to as the "Special Reliance Procedure") pursuant to which the adoption, on or before May 30, 1976, of new plans and amendments of existing plans may be effectuated with full reliance upon the rules which comprise the ERISA Guidelines and without regard to any amendment or supplementation of such rules before such date. Therefore, except in unusual circumstances (described in Technical Information Release No. 1416 (November 5, 1975)), plans which comply with the Special Reliance Procedure shall generally be considered by the Service as satisfying the qualification requirements of the Code added or amended by ERISA for plan years commencing on or before December 31, 1976, to which such requirements are applicable, notwithstanding the date when final regulations or other rules hereafter published which amend or supplement the rules comprising the ERISA Guidelines may otherwise be made effective. Reference is hereby made to Technical Information Release No. 1416 (November 5, 1975) for a description of the Special Reliance Procedure.

The Department announced that plans which comply with the Special Reliance Procedure will be considered by the Department as satisfying the requirements of the provisions of parts 2 and 3 of Title I of ERISA which parallel the qualification requirements of the Code added or amended by ERISA to the same extent as such plans are considered by the Service as satisfying, in accordance with the terms of the Special Reliance Procedure, such qualification requirements.

The availability of the Special Reliance Procedure will substantially diminish the occasions for plans to avail themselves of the right to satisfy, for tax purposes, the qualification requirements of the Code (added or amended by ERISA) by retroactive amendments adopted during or after the close of a plan year, in accordance with section 401(b) of the Code and the temporary regulations thereunder. The Department pointed out that no explicit parallel provision to section 401(b) of the Code is contained in Title I of ERISA. Nevertheless, to the extent retroactive amendments to a plan are made to satisfy the requirements of parts 2 and 3 of Title I of ERISA which parallel the qualification requirements of the Code added or amended by ERISA, the Department noted that such plan will be in compliance with such requirements if such an amendment designed to satisfy such requirements (1) is adopted by the end of the plan year to which such requirements are applicable, and (2) is made effective for all purposes for such entire plan year.

The schedule of documents comprising the ERISA Guidelines follows.

ERISA GUIDELINES
SCHEDULE OF DOCUMENTS

Publication Date[1]	Document [1]	Subject [1]	Code and ERISA Sections [1]
1/ 8/75	TIR 1334 [¶ 17,248]	Questions and answers relating to defined contribution plans subject to ERISA	410,411, *et al.*
4/21/75	40 F.R. 17576 [¶ 20,120]	Notice of Proposed Rule Making: Qualification (& other aspects) of HR-10 plans	401(c), 401(d), 401(e), 46, 50A, 72,404(e), 901 and 1379
6/ 4/75	T.D. 7358 [¶ 13,913—13,914]	Temporary Regulations: Notification of Interested Parties	7476
7/14/75	T.D. 7367 [¶ 13,915]	Temporary Regulations: Notice of determination of qualification	7476
9/ 8/75	40 F.R. 41654 [¶ 14,515]	Department of Labor — Minimum Standards for hours of service, years of service, and breaks in service relating to participation, vesting, and accrual of benefits[2]	401(a)(3)(B), 411(a)(5)(C), and ERISA sections 202, 203, and 204
9/17/75	TIR 1403 [¶ 17,443]	Questions and answers relating mainly to defined benefit plans subject to ERISA (addition to TIR 1334)	410, 411, *et al.*
9/18/75	40 F.R. 43034 [¶ 20,129]	Notice of Proposed Rule Making: Definitions of multiemployer plan and plan administrator	414(f) and (g)
9/29/75	T.D. 7377 [¶ 11,721]	Temporary Regulations: Certain retroactive amendments of employee plans[3]	401(b)
10/ 3/75	T.D. 7379 [¶ 11,719]	Temporary Regulations: Qualified joint and survivor annuities[4]	401(a)(11)
10/ 3/75	T.D. 7380 [¶ 12,155—12,171]	Temporary Regulations: Minimum Participation Standards[4a]	410
10/ 8/75	T.D. 7381 [¶ 11,720]	Temporary Regulations: Commencement of Benefits[5]	401(a)(14)

[1] [Bracketed material relates to additions made by CCH after ERISA IB-MS-75-1 was originally issued. Bracketed paragraph numbers refer to the paragraphs where the Documents are reported in the CCH PENSION PLAN GUIDE.—CCH.]

[2] [Final regulations on minimum standards for hours of service, years of service, and breaks in service relating to participation, vesting, and accrual of benefits have been adopted by the Department of Labor. They were published in the *Federal Register* (41 FR 56462) on December 28, 1976. The final regulations appear at ¶ 14,411—14,415, 14,421—14,422, 14,431—14,432, 14,441—14,444, and 14,501.—CCH.]

[3] [Final regulations on retroactive plan changes were adopted by T.D. 7437. The final regulations appear at ¶ 11,721.—CCH.]

[4] [Final regulations on joint and survivor annuities were adopted by T.D. 7458. The final regulations appear at ¶ 11,719.—CCH.]

[4a] [Final regulations on minimum participation standards were adopted by T.D. 7508. The final regulations appear at ¶ 12,156—12,163, 12,171, 12,311, and 12,312.—CCH.]

[5] [Final regulations on the commencement of benefits under qualified trusts were adopted by T.D. 7436. The final regulations appear at ¶ 11,720.—CCH.]

Publication Date[1]	Document[1]	Subject[1]	Code and ERISA Sections[1]
10/15/75	T.D. 7382 [¶ 11,720A]	Temporary Regulations: Requirement that benefits under a qualified plan are not decreased on account of certain Social Security increases[6]	401(a)(15)
10/16/75	T.D. 7383 [¶ 11,731]	Temporary Regulations: Nonbank trustees of pension and profit sharing trusts benefiting owner-employees	401(d)(1)
10/16/75	40 F.R. 48517 [¶ 20,136]	Notice of Proposed Rule Making: Certain Custodial Accounts	401(f)
10/30/75	TIR 1408 [¶ 17,445]	Questions & Answers relating to mergers, consolidations, etc.	401(a)(12) and 414(l)
11/3/75	Rev. Rul. 75-480, 1975-44 IRB [¶ 19,394]	Updating of Rev. Rul. 71-446 to reflect changes mandated by ERISA	401(a)(5)
11/3/75	Rev. Rul. 75-481, 1975-44 IRB [¶ 19,395]	Guidelines for determining whether contributions or benefits under plan satisfy the limitations of section 415 of the Code[7]	401(a)(16) and 415
11/3/75	TIR 1411, Rev. Proc. 75-49, 1975-48 IRB [¶ 17,250]	Vesting and discrimination	401(a)(4) and 411(d)(1)
2/2/76	TIR 1441, Rev. Proc. 76-11, 1976-9 IRB [¶ 17,456]	[Vesting and discrimination]	[401(a)(4) and 411(d)(1)]
11/4/75	TIR 1413 [¶ 17,446]	Questions & Answers relating to Employee Stock Ownership Plans[8]	401, 4975, and section 301(d) of the Tax Reduction Act of 1975
11/5/75	T.D. 7387 [¶ 11,720D, 12,211—12,231]	Temporary Regulations on Minimum Vesting Standards[8a]	411
11/5/75	T.D. 7388 [¶ 12,365]	Controlled groups, businesses under common control, etc.	414(b) and (c)
4/6/76	IR-1589 [¶ 17,052]	Nonforfeiture of employee-derived accrued benefit upon death	411(a)(1)
1/21/76[9]	41 F.R. 3290	Department of Labor — Interpretive Bulletin; Definition of Seasonal Industries	410(a)(3)(B), 411(a)(5)(C), and ERISA sections 202(a)(3)(C), 203(b)(2)(C)
11/7/75	40 F.R. 52008 [¶ 14,139]	Department of Labor—additional requirements applicable to definition of multiemployer plan	404(f) and ERISA section 3(37)
		Department of Labor—suspension of benefits upon reemployment of retiree	411(a)(3)(B) and ERISA section 201(a)(3)(A)
12/3/75	TIR's 1422 and 1430 [¶ 17,450, 17,454]	Assignment or alienation of plan benefits[10]	401(a)(13)
12/3/75	TIR's 1422 and 1430 [¶ 17,450, 17,454]	Assignment or alienation of plan benefits[10]	401(a)(13)
1/28/76	TIR 1439; Rev. Rul. 76-47 [¶ 19,403]	Appropriate conversion factor	411(c)(2)(B)(ii)

Part 4—Fiduciary Responsibility

[¶ 14,710]
ERISA Sec. 401, COVERAGE

Act Sec. 401. (a) This part shall apply to any employee benefit plan described in section 4(a) (and not exempted under section 4(b)), other than—

(1) a plan which is unfunded and is maintained by an employer primarily for the purpose of providing deferred compensation for a select group of management or highly compensated employees; or

(2) any agreement described in section 736 of the Internal Revenue Code of 1986, which provides payments to a retired partner or deceased partner or a deceased partner's successor in interest.

Act Sec. 401. (b) For purposes of this part:

---

[6] [Final regulations under Code Sec. 401 on benefits under qualified plans not being decreased on account of certain social security increases were adopted by T.D. 7434. The final regulations appear at ¶ 11,720A.—CCH.]

[7] [Rev. Rul. 75-481: 1975-2 CB 188 has been modified by Rev. Rul. 76-318 at ¶ 19,415 and Rev. Rul. 77-24 at ¶ 19,424.—CCH.]

[8] [Final regulations on excise taxes for employee stock ownership plans were adopted by T.D. 7506. The final regulations appear at ¶ 13,644, 13,647B, and 13,647C.]

[8a] [Final regulations on minimum vesting standards were adopted by T.D. 7501. The final regulations appear at ¶ 11,700A, 11,720D, 11,859, 12,211—12,231, 12,311, 12,312, and 13,302.]

[9] [The Interpretive Bulletin on Seasonal Industries, § 2509.76-1, ¶ 14,520, was rescinded by ERISA IB 76-2 (§ 2509.76-2), reproduced at ¶ 14,521. It was officially withdrawn from the ERISA Guidelines by § 2509.76-3 at ¶ 14,522.]

[10] [Final regulations on assignment or alienation of benefits were adopted by T.D. 7534 on February 5, 1978. The final regulations appear at ¶ 11,719B.]

[10] [Final regulations on assignment or alienation of benefits were adopted by T.D. 7534 on February 5, 1978. The final regulations appear at ¶ 11,719B.]

(1) In the case of a plan which invests in any security issued by an investment company registered under the Investment Company Act of 1940, the assets of such plan shall be deemed to include such security but shall not, solely by reason of such investment, be deemed to include any assets of such investment company.

(2) In the case of a plan to which a guaranteed benefit policy is issued by an insurer, the assets of such plan shall be deemed to include such policy, but shall not, solely by reason of the issuance of such policy, be deemed to include any assets of such insurer. For purposes of this paragraph:

(A) The term "insurer" means an insurance company, insurance service, or insurance organization, qualified to do business in a State.

(B) The term "guaranteed benefit policy" means an insurance policy or contract to the extent that such policy or contract provides for benefits the amount of which is guaranteed by the insurer. Such term includes any surplus in a separate account, but excludes any other portion of a separate account.

Act Sec. 401.(c)(1)(A) (A) Not later than June 30, 1997, the Secretary shall issue proposed regulations to provide guidance for the purpose of determining, in cases where an insurer issues 1 or more policies to or for the benefit of an employee benefit plan (and such policies are supported by assets of such insurer's general account), which assets held by the insurer (other than plan assets held in its separate accounts) constitute assets of the plan for purposes of this part and section 4975 of the Internal Revenue Code of 1986 and to provide guidance with respect to the application of this title to the general account assets of insurers.

(B) The proposed regulations under subparagraph (A) shall be subject to public notice and comment until September 30, 1997.

(C) The Secretary shall issue final regulations providing the guidance described in subparagraph (A) not later than December 31, 1997.

(D) Such regulations shall only apply with respect to policies which are issued by an insurer on or before December 31, 1998, to or for the benefit of an employee benefit plan which is supported by assets of such insurer's general account. With respect to policies issued on or before December 31, 1998, such regulations shall take effect at the end of the 18-month period following the date on which such regulations become final.

(2) The Secretary shall ensure that the regulations issued under paragraph (1)—

(A) are administratively feasible, and

(B) protect the interests and rights of the plan and of its participants and beneficiaries (including meeting the requirements of paragraph (3)).

(3) The regulations prescribed by the Secretary pursuant to paragraph (1) shall require, in connection with any policy issued by an insurer to or for the benefit of an employee benefit plan to the extent that the policy is not a guaranteed benefit policy (as defined in subsection (b)(2)(B))—

(A) that a plan fiduciary totally independent of the insurer authorize the purchase of such policy (unless such purchase is a transaction exempt under section 408(b)(5)),

(B) that the insurer describe (in such form and manner as shall be prescribed in such regulations), in annual reports and in policies issued to the policyholder after the date on which such regulations are issued in final form pursuant to paragraph (1)(C)—

(i) a description of the method by which any income and expenses of the insurer's general account are allocated to the policy during the term of the policy and upon the termination of the policy, and

(ii) for each report, the actual return to the plan under the policy and such other financial information as the Secretary may deem appropriate for the period covered by each such annual report,

(C) that the insurer disclose to the plan fiduciary the extent to which alternative arrangements supported by assets of separate accounts of the insurer (which generally hold plan assets) are available, whether there is a right under the policy to transfer funds to a separate account and the terms governing any such right, and the extent to which support by assets of the insurer's general account and support by assets of separate accounts of the insurer might pose differing risks to the plan, and

(D) that the insurer manage those assets of the insurer which are assets of such insurer's general account (irrespective of whether any such assets are plan assets) with the care, skill, prudence, and diligence under the circumstances then prevailing that a prudent man acting in a like capacity and familiar with such matters would use in the conduct of an enterprise of a like character and with like aims, taking into account all obligations supported by such enterprise.

(4) Compliance by the insurer with all requirements of the regulations issued by the Secretary pursuant to paragraph (1) shall be deemed compliance by such insurer with sections 404, 406, and 407 with respect to those assets of the insurer's general account which support a policy described in paragraph (3).

(5)(A) Subject to subparagraph (B), any regulations issued under paragraph (1) shall not take effect before the date on which such regulations become final.

(B) No person shall be subject to liability under this part or section 4975 of the Internal Revenue Code of 1986 for conduct which occurred before the date which is 18 months following the date described in subparagraph (A) on the basis of a claim that the assets of an insurer (other than plan assets held in a separate account) constitute assets of the plan, except—

(i) as otherwise provided by the Secretary in regulations intended to prevent avoidance of the regulations issued under paragraph (1), or

(ii) as provided in an action brought by the Secretary pursuant to paragraph (2) or (5) of section 502(a) for a breach of fiduciary responsibilities which would also constitute a violation of Federal or State criminal law.

The Secretary shall bring a cause of action described in clause (ii) if a participant, beneficiary, or fiduciary demonstrates to the satisfaction of the Secretary that a breach described in clause (ii) has occurred.

(6) Nothing in this subsection shall preclude the application of any Federal criminal law.

(7) For purposes of this subsection, the term "policy" includes a contract.

Amendment

P.L. 104-188, §1460(a):

Amended ERISA Act Sec. 401 by adding at the end a new subsection (c) to read as above.

The above amendment is effective January 1, 1975, except that it shall not apply to any civil action commenced before November 7, 1995.

P.L. 101-239, §7891(a)(1):

Titles I, III, and IV of ERISA (other than sections 3(37)(E), 301(a)(7), and 308, the last sentence of section 408(d), and sections 414(c), 4001(a)(3)(ii), and 4303) are each amended by striking "Internal Revenue Code of 1954" each place it appears and inserting "Internal Revenue Code of 1986" effective October 22, 1986.

Regulations

Reg. §2550.401b-1 was adopted by FR Doc. 82-13400 and was filed with the Federal Register on May 13, 1982 (47 FR 21241). The regulation is effective June 17, 1982. **Note:** This regulation was removed from Part 2550 by 51 FR 41262 on Nov. 13, 1986, effective as of Mar. 13, 1987. Reg. §2550.401c-1 was filed with the Federal Register January 5, 2000 (65 FR 613).

[¶ 14,713]

§2550.401b-1 Definition of "plan assets"—Governmental mortgage pools. (a) *In General.* (1) Where an employee benefit plan acquires a guaranteed governmental mortgage pool certificate, as defined in paragraph (b), then, for purposes of part 4 of Title I of the Act and section 4975 of the Internal Revenue Code, the plan's assets include the certificate and all of its rights with respect to such certifi-

cate under applicable law, but do not, solely by reason of the plan's holding of such certificate, include any of the mortgages underlying such certificate.

(b) A "guaranteed governmental mortgage pool certificate" is a certificate backed by, or evidencing an interest in, specified mortgages or participation interests therein and with respect to which interest and principal payable pursuant to the certificate is guaranteed by the United

States or an agency or instrumentality thereof. The term "guaranteed governmental mortgage pool certificate" includes a mortgage pool certificate with respect to which interest and principal payable pursuant to the certificate is guaranteed by:

(1) The Government National Mortgage Association;

(2) The Federal Home Loan Mortgage Corporation; or

(3) The Federal National Mortgage Association.

[¶ 14,714]

§ 2550.401c-1 **Definition of "plan assets"—insurance company general accounts.** (a) *In General.* (1) This section describes, in the case where an insurer issues one or more policies to or for the benefit of an employee benefit plan (and such policies are supported by assets of an insurance company's general account), which assets held by the insurer (other than plan assets held in its separate accounts) constitute plan assets for purposes of Subtitle A, and Parts 1 and 4 of Subtitle B, of Title I of the Employee Retirement Income Security Act of 1974 (ERISA or the Act) and section 4975 of the Internal Revenue Code (the Code), and provides guidance with respect to the application of Title I of the Act and section 4975 of the Code to the general account assets of insurers.

(2) Generally, when a plan has acquired a Transition Policy (as defined in paragraph (h)(6) of this section), the plan's assets include the Transition Policy, but do not include any of the underlying assets of the insurer's general account if the insurer satisfies the requirements of paragraphs (c) through (f) of this section or, if the requirements of paragraphs (c) through (f) were not satisfied, the insurer cures the non-compliance through satisfaction of the requirements in paragraph (i)(5) of this section.

(3) For purposes of paragraph (a)(2) of this section, a plan's assets will not include any of the underlying assets of the insurer's general account if the insurer fails to satisfy the requirements of paragraphs (c) through (f) of this section solely because of the takeover of the insurer's operations from management as a result of the granting of a petition filed in delinquency proceedings in the State court where the insurer is domiciled.

(b) *Approval by fiduciary independent of the issuer.*

(1) *In general.* An independent plan fiduciary who has the authority to manage and control the assets of the plan must expressly authorize the acquisition or purchase of the Transition Policy. For purposes of this paragraph, a fiduciary is not independent if the fiduciary is an affiliate of the insurer issuing the policy.

(2) Notwithstanding paragraph (b)(1) of this section, the authorization by an independent plan fiduciary is not required if:

(i) The insurer is the employer maintaining the plan, or a party in interest which is wholly owned by the employer maintaining the plan; and

(ii) The requirements of section 408(b)(5) of the Act are met.[1]

(c) *Duty of disclosure.*

(1) *In general.* An insurer shall furnish the information described in paragraphs (c)(3) and (c)(4) of this section to a plan fiduciary acting on behalf of a plan to which a Transition Policy has been issued. Paragraph (c)(2) of this section describes the style and format of such disclosure. Paragraph (c)(3) of this section describes the content of the initial disclosure. Paragraph (c)(4) of this section describes the information that must be disclosed by the insurer at least once per year for as long as the Transition Policy remains outstanding.

(2) *Style and format.* The disclosure required by this paragraph should be clear and concise and written in a manner calculated to be understood by a plan fiduciary, without relinquishing any of the substantive detail required by paragraphs (c)(3) and (c)(4) of this section. The information does not have to be organized in any particular order but should be presented in a manner which makes it easy to understand the operation of the Transition Policy.

(3) *Initial disclosure.* The insurer must provide to the plan, either as part of an amended policy, or as a separate written document, the disclosure information set forth in paragraphs (c)(3)(i) through (iv)

of this section. The disclosure must include all of the following information which is applicable to the Transition Policy:

(i) A description of the method by which any income and any expense of the insurer's general account are allocated to the policy during the term of the policy and upon its termination, including:

(A) A description of the method used by the insurer to determine the fees, charges, expenses or other amounts that are, or may be, assessed against the policyholder or deducted by the insurer from any accumulation fund under the policy, including the extent and frequency with which such fees, charges, expenses or other amounts may be modified by the insurance company;

(B) A description of the method by which the insurer determines the return to be credited to any accumulation fund under the policy, including a description of the method used to allocate income and expenses to lines of business, business segments, and policies within such lines of business and business segments, and a description of how any withdrawals, transfers, or payments will affect the amount of the return credited;

(C) A description of the rights which the policyholder or plan participants have to withdraw or transfer all or a portion of any accumulation fund under the policy, or to apply the amount of a withdrawal to the purchase of guaranteed benefits or to the payment of benefits, and the terms on which such withdrawals or other applications of funds may be made, including a description of any charges, fees, credits, market value adjustments, or any other charges or adjustments, both positive and negative;

(D) A statement of the method used to calculate any charges, fees, credits or market value adjustments described in paragraph (c)(3)(i)(C) of this section, and, upon the request of a plan fiduciary, the insurer must provide within 30 days of the request:

(1) The formula actually used to calculate the market value adjustment, if any, to be applied to the unallocated amount in the accumulation fund upon distribution of a lump sum payment to the policyholder, and

(2) The actual calculation, as of a specified date that is no earlier than the last contract anniversary preceding the date of the request, of the applicable market value adjustment, including a description of the specific variables used in the calculation, the value of each of the variables, and a general description of how the value of each of those variables was determined.

(3) If the formula is based on interest rate guarantees applicable to new contracts of the same class or classes, and the duration of the assets underlying the accumulation fund, the contract must describe the process by which those components are ascertained or obtained. If the formula is based on an interest rate implicit in an index of publicly traded obligations, the identity of the index, the manner in which it is used, and identification of the source or publication where any data used in the formula can be found, must be disclosed;

(ii) A statement describing the expense, income and benefit guarantees under the policy, including a description of the length of such guarantees, and of the insurer's right, if any, to modify or eliminate such guarantees;

(iii) A description of the rights of the parties to make or discontinue contributions under the policy, and of any restrictions (such as timing, minimum or maximum amounts, and penalties and grace periods for late payments) on the making of contributions under the policy, and the consequences of the discontinuance of contributions under the policy; and

(iv) A statement of how any policyholder or participant-initiated withdrawals are to be made: first-in, first-out (FIFO) basis, last-in, first-out (LIFO) basis, pro rata or another basis.

(4) *Annual disclosure.* At least annually and not later than 90 days following the period to which it relates, an insurer shall provide the following information to each plan to which a Transition Policy has been issued:

(i) The balance of any accumulation fund on the first day and last day of the period covered by the annual report;

---

[1] The Department notes that, because section 401(c)(1)(D) of the Act and the definition of Transition Policy preclude the issuance of any additional Transition Policies after December 31, 1998, the requirement for independent fiduciary authorization of the acquisition or purchase of the Transition Policy in paragraph (b) no longer has any application.

(ii) Any deposits made to the accumulation fund during such annual period;

(iii) An itemized statement of all income attributed to the policy or added to the accumulation fund during the period, and a description of the method used by the insurer to determine the precise amount of income;

(iv) The actual rate of return credited to the accumulation fund under the policy during such period, stating whether the rate of return was calculated before or after deduction of expenses charged to the accumulation fund;

(v) Any other additions to the accumulation fund during such period;

(vi) An itemized statement of all fees, charges, expenses or other amounts assessed against the policy or deducted from the accumulation fund during the reporting year, and a description of the method used by the insurer to determine the precise amount of the fees, charges and other expenses;

(vii) An itemized statement of all benefits paid, including annuity purchases, to participants and beneficiaries from the accumulation fund;

(viii) The dates on which the additions or subtractions were credited to, or deducted from, the accumulation fund during such period;

(ix) A description, if applicable, of all transactions with affiliates which exceed 1 percent of group annuity reserves of the general account for the prior reporting year;

(x) A statement describing any expense, income and benefit guarantees under the policy, including a description of the length of such guarantees, and of the insurer's right, if any, to modify or eliminate such guarantees. However, the information on guarantees does not have to be provided annually if it was previously disclosed in the insurance policy and has not been modified since that time;

(xi) A good faith estimate of the amount that would be payable in a lump sum at the end of such period pursuant to the request of a policyholder for payment or transfer of amounts in the accumulation fund under the policy after the insurer deducts any applicable charges and makes any appropriate market value adjustments, upward or downward, under the terms of the policy. However, upon the request of a plan fiduciary, the insurer must provide within 30 days of the request the information contained in paragraph (c) (3) (i) (D) as of a specified date that is no earlier than the last contract anniversary preceding the date of the request; and

(xii) An explanation that the insurer will make available promptly upon request of a plan, copies of the following publicly available financial data or other publicly available reports relating to the financial condition of the insurer:

(A) National Association of Insurance Commissioners Statutory Annual Statement, with Exhibits, General Interrogatories, and Schedule D, Part 1A, Sections 1 and 2 and Schedule S—Part 3E;

(B) Rating agency reports on the financial strength and claims-paying ability of the insurer;

(C) Risk adjusted capital ratio, with a brief description of its derivation and significance, referring to the risk characteristics of both the assets and the liabilities of the insurer;

(D) Actuarial opinion of the insurer's Appointed Actuary certifying the adequacy of the insurer's reserves as required by New York State Insurance Department Regulation 126 and comparable regulations of other States; and

(E) The insurer's most recent SEC Form 10K and Form 10Q (stock companies only).

(d) *Alternative separate account arrangements.*

(1) In general. An insurer must provide the plan fiduciary with the following additional information at the same time as the initial disclosure required under paragraph (c)(3) of this section:

(i) A statement explaining the extent to which alternative contract arrangements supported by assets of separate accounts of insurers are available to plans;

(ii) A statement as to whether there is a right under the policy to transfer funds to a separate account and the terms governing any such right; and

(iii) A statement explaining the extent to which general account contracts and separate account contracts of the insurer may pose differing risks to the plan.

(2) An insurer will be deemed to comply with the requirements of paragraph (d)(1)(iii) of this section if the disclosure provided to the plan includes the following statement:

a. Contractual arrangements supported by assets of separate accounts may pose differing risks to plans from contractual arrangements supported by assets of general accounts. Under a general account contract, the plan's contributions or premiums are placed in the insurer's general account and commingled with the insurer's corporate funds and assets (excluding separate accounts and special deposit funds). The insurance company combines in its general account premiums received from all of its lines of business. These premiums are pooled and invested by the insurer. General account assets in the aggregate support the insurer's obligations under all of its insurance contracts, including (but not limited to) its individual and group life, health, disability, and annuity contracts. Experience rated general account policies may share in the experience of the general account through interest credits, dividends, or rate adjustments, but assets in the general account are not segregated for the exclusive benefit of any particular policy or obligation. General account assets are also available to the insurer for the conduct of its routine business activities, such as the payment of salaries, rent, other ordinary business expenses and dividends.

b. An insurance company separate account is a segregated fund which is not commingled with the insurer's general assets. Depending on the particular terms of the separate account contract, income, expenses, gains and losses associated with the assets allocated to a separate account may be credited to or charged against the separate account without regard to other income, expenses, gains, or losses of the insurance company, and the investment results passed through directly to the policyholders. While most, if not all, general account investments are maintained at book value, separate account investments are normally maintained at market value, which can fluctuate according to market conditions. In large measure, the risks associated with a separate account contract depend on the particular assets in the separate account.

c. The plan's legal rights vary under general and separate account contracts. In general, an insurer is subject to ERISA's fiduciary responsibility provisions with respect to the assets of a separate account (other than a separate account registered under the Investment Company Act of 1940) to the extent that the investment performance of such assets is passed directly through to the plan policyholders. ERISA requires insurers, in administering separate account assets, to act solely in the interest of the plan's participants and beneficiaries; prohibits self-dealing and conflicts of interest; and requires insurers to adhere to a prudent standard of care. In contrast, ERISA generally imposes less stringent standards in the administration of general account contracts which were issued on or before December 31, 1998.

d. On the other hand, State insurance regulation is typically more restrictive with respect to general accounts than separate accounts. However, State insurance regulation may not provide the same level of protection to plan policyholders as ERISA regulation. In addition, insurance company general account policies often include various guarantees under which the insurer assumes risks relating to the funding and distribution of benefits. Insurers do not usually provide any guarantees with respect to the investment returns on assets held in separate accounts. Of course, the extent of any guarantees from any general account or separate account contract will depend upon the specific policy terms.

e. Finally, separate accounts and general accounts pose differing risks in the event of the insurer's insolvency. In the event of insolvency, funds in the general account are available to meet the claims of the insurer's general creditors, after payment of amounts due under certain priority claims, including amounts owed to its policyholders. Funds held in a separate account as reserves for its policy obligations, however, may be protected from the claims of creditors other than the policyholders participating in the separate account. Whether separate account funds will be granted this protection will depend upon the terms of the applicable policies and the provisions of any applicable laws in effect at the time of insolvency.

(e) *Termination procedures.* Within 90 days of written notice by a policyholder to an insurer, the insurer must permit the policyholder to exercise the right to terminate or discontinue the policy and to elect to receive without penalty either:

(1) A lump sum payment representing all unallocated amounts in the accumulation fund. For purposes of this paragraph (e)(1), the term penalty does not include a market value adjustment (as defined in paragraph (h)(7)of this section) or the recovery of costs actually incurred which would have been recovered by the insurer but for the termination or discontinuance of the policy, including any unliquidated acquisition expenses, to the extent not previously recovered by the insurer; or

(2) A book value payment of all unallocated amounts in the accumulation fund under the policy in approximately equal annual installments, over a period of no longer than 10 years, together with interest computed at an annual rate which is no less than the annual rate which was credited to the accumulation fund under the policy as of the date of the contract termination or discontinuance, minus 1 percentage point. Notwithstanding paragraphs (e)(1) and (e)(2) of this section, the insurer may defer, for a period not to exceed 180 days, amounts required to be paid to a policyholder under this paragraph for any period of time during which regular banking activities are suspended by State or federal authorities, a national securities exchange is closed for trading (except for normal holiday closings), or the Securities and Exchange Commission has determined that a state of emergency exists which may make such determination and payment impractical.

(f) *Insurer-initiated amendments.* In the event the insurer makes an insurer-initiated amendment (as defined in paragraph (h)(8) of this section), the insurer must provide written notice to the plan at least 60 days prior to the effective date of the insurer-initiated amendment. The notice must contain a complete description of the amendment and must inform the plan of its right to terminate or discontinue the policy and withdraw all unallocated funds without penalty by sending a written request within such 60 day period to the name and address contained in the notice. The plan must be offered the election to receive either a lump sum or an installment payment as described in paragraph (e)(1) and (e)(2) of this section. An insurer-initiated amendment shall not apply to a contract if the plan fiduciary exercises its right to terminate or discontinue the contract within such 60 day period and to receive a lump sum or installment payment.

(g) *Prudence.* An insurer shall manage those assets of the insurer which are assets of such insurer's general account (irrespective of whether any such assets are plan assets) with the care, skill, prudence and diligence under the circumstances then prevailing that a prudent man acting in a like capacity and familiar with such matters would use in the conduct of an enterprise of a like character and with like aims, taking into account all obligations supported by such enterprise. This prudence standard applies to the conduct of all insurers with respect to policies issued to plans on or before December 31, 1998, and differs from the prudence standard set forth in section 404(a)(1)(B) of the Act. Under the prudence standard provided in this paragraph, prudence must be determined by reference to all of the obligations supported by the general account, not just the obligations owed to plan policyholders. The more stringent standard of prudence set forth in section 404(a)(1)(B) of the Act continues to apply to any obligations which insurers may have as fiduciaries which do not arise from the management of general account assets, as well as to insurers' management of plan assets maintained in separate accounts. The terms of this section do not modify or reduce the fiduciary obligations applicable to insurers in connection with policies issued after December 31, 1998, which are supported by general account assets, including the standard of prudence under section 404(a)(1)(B) of the Act.

(h) *Definitions.* For purposes of this section:

(1) An affiliate of an insurer means:

(i) Any person, directly or indirectly, through one or more intermediaries, controlling, controlled by, or under common control with the insurer,

(ii) Any officer of, director of, 5 percent or more partner in, or highly compensated employee (earning 5 percent or more of the yearly wages of the insurer) of, such insurer or of any person described in paragraph (h)(1)(i) of this section including in the case of an insurer,

an insurance agent or broker thereof (whether or not such person is a common law employee) if such agent or broker is an employee described in this paragraph or if the gross income received by such agent or broker from such insurer exceeds 5 percent of such agent's gross income from all sources for the year, and

(iii) Any corporation, partnership, or unincorporated enterprise of which a person described in paragraph (h)(1)(ii) of this section is an officer, director, or a 5 percent or more partner.

(2) The term control means the power to exercise a controlling influence over the management or policies of a person other than an individual.

(3) The term guaranteed benefit policy means a policy described in section 401(b)(2)(B) of the Act and any regulations promulgated thereunder.

(4) The term insurer means an insurer as described in section 401(b)(2)(A) of the Act.

(5) The term accumulation fund means the aggregate net considerations (i.e., gross considerations less all deductions from such considerations) credited to the Transition Policy plus all additional amounts, including interest and dividends, credited to such Transition Policy less partial withdrawals, benefit payments and less all charges and fees imposed against this accumulated amount under the Transition Policy other than surrender charges and market value adjustments.

(6) The term Transition Policy means:

(i) A policy or contract of insurance (other than a guaranteed benefit policy) that is issued by an insurer to, or on behalf of, an employee benefit plan on or before December 31, 1998, and which is supported by the assets of the insurer's general account.

(ii) A policy will not fail to be a Transition Policy merely because the policy is amended or modified:

(A) To comply with the requirements of section 401(c) of the Act and this section; or

(B) Pursuant to a merger, acquisition, demutualization, conversion, or reorganization authorized by applicable State law, provided that the premiums, policy guarantees, and the other terms and conditions of the policy remain the same, except that a membership interest in a mutual insurance company may be eliminated from the policy in exchange for separate consideration (e.g., shares of stock or policy credits).

(7) For purposes of this section, the term market value adjustment means an adjustment to the book value of the accumulation fund to accurately reflect the effect on the value of the accumulation fund of its liquidation in the prevailing market for fixed income obligations, taking into account the future cash flows that were anticipated under the policy. An adjustment is a market value adjustment within the meaning of this definition only if the insurer has determined the amount of the adjustment pursuant to a method which was previously disclosed to the policyholder in accordance with paragraph (c)(3)(i)(D) of this section, and the method permits both upward and downward adjustments to the book value of the accumulation fund.

(8) The term insurer-initiated amendment is defined in paragraphs (h)(8)(i), (ii) and (iii) of this section as:

(i) An amendment to a Transition Policy made by an insurer pursuant to a unilateral right to amend the policy terms that would have a material adverse effect on the policyholder; or

(ii) Any of the following unilateral changes in the insurer's conduct or practices with respect to the policyholder or the accumulation fund under the policy that result in a material reduction of existing or future benefits under the policy, a material reduction in the value of the policy or a material increase in the cost of financing the plan or plan benefits:

(A) A change in the methodology for assessing fees, expenses, or other charges against the accumulation fund or the policyholder;

(B) A change in the methodology used for allocating income between lines of business, or product classes within a line of business;

(C) A change in the methodology used for determining the rate of return to be credited to the accumulation fund under the policy;

(D) A change in the methodology used for determining the amount of any fees, charges, expenses, or market value adjustments applicable to the accumulation fund under the policy in connection with the termination of the contract or withdrawal from the accumulation fund;

(E) A change in the dividend class to which the policy or contract is assigned;

(F) A change in the policyholder's rights in connection with the termination of the policy, withdrawal of funds or the purchase of annuities for plan participants; and

(G) A change in the annuity purchase rates guaranteed under the terms of the contract or policy, unless the new rates are more favorable for the policyholder.

(iii) For purposes of this definition, an insurer-initiated amendment is material if a prudent fiduciary could reasonably conclude that the amendment should be considered in determining how or whether to exercise any rights with respect to the policy, including termination rights.

(iv) For purposes of this definition, the following amendments or changes are not insurer-initiated amendments:

(A) Any amendment or change which is made with the affirmative consent of the policyholder;

(B) Any amendment or change which is made in order to comply with the requirements of section 401(c) of the Act and this section; or

(C) Any amendment or change which is made pursuant to a merger, acquisition, demutualization, conversion, or reorganization authorized by applicable State law, provided that the premiums, policy guarantees, and the other terms and conditions of the policy remain the same, except that a membership interest in a mutual insurance company may be eliminated from the policy in exchange for separate consideration (e.g., shares of stock or policy credits).

(i) *Limitation on liability.*

(1) No person shall be subject to liability under Parts 1 and 4 of Title I of the Act or section 4975 of the Internal Revenue Code of 1986 for conduct which occurred prior to the applicability dates of the regulation on the basis of a claim that the assets of an insurer (other than plan assets held in a separate account) constitute plan assets. Notwithstanding the provisions of this paragraph (i)(1), this section shall not:

(i) Apply to an action brought by the Secretary of Labor pursuant to paragraphs (2) or (5) of section 502(a) of ERISA for a breach of fiduciary responsibility which would also constitute a violation of Federal or State criminal law;

(ii) Preclude the application of any Federal criminal law; or

(iii) Apply to any civil action commenced before November 7, 1995.

(2) Nothing in this section relieves any person from any State law regulating insurance which imposes additional obligations or duties upon insurers to the extent not inconsistent with the provisions of this section. Therefore, nothing in this section should be construed to preclude a State from requiring insurers to make additional disclosures to policyholders, including plans. Nor does this section prohibit a State from imposing additional substantive requirements with respect to the management of general accounts or from otherwise regulating the relationship between the policyholder and the insurer to the extent not inconsistent with the provisions of this section.

(3) Nothing in this section precludes any claim against an insurer or other person for violations of the Act which do not require a finding that the underlying assets of a general account constitute plan assets, regardless of whether the violation relates to a Transition Policy.

(4) If the requirements in paragraphs (c) through (f) of this section are not met with respect to a plan that has purchased or acquired a Transition Policy, and the insurer has not cured the non-compliance through satisfaction of the requirements in paragraph (i)(5) of this section, the plan's assets include an undivided interest in the underlying assets of the insurer's general account for that period of time for which the requirements are not met. However, an insurer's failure to comply with the requirements of this section with respect to any particular Transition Policy will not result in the underlying assets of the general account constituting plan assets with respect to other Transition Policies if the insurer is otherwise in compliance with the requirements contained in this section.

(5) Notwithstanding paragraphs (a)(2) and (i)(4) of this section, a plan's assets will not include an undivided interest in the underlying assets of the insurer's general account if the insurer made reasonable and good faith attempts at compliance with each of the requirements of paragraphs (c) through (f) of this section, and meets each of the following conditions:

(i) The insurer has in place written procedures that are reasonably designed to assure compliance with the requirements of paragraphs (c) through (f) of this section, including procedures reasonably designed to detect any instances of non-compliance.

(ii) No later than 60 days following the earlier of the insurer's detection of an instance of non-compliance or the receipt of written notice of non-compliance from the plan, the insurer complies with the requirements of paragraphs (c) through (f) of this section. If the insurer has failed to pay a plan the amounts required under paragraphs (e) or (f) of this section within 90 days of receiving written notice of termination or discontinuance of the policy, the insurer must make all corrections and adjustments necessary to restore to the plan the full amounts that the plan would have received but for the insurer's non-compliance within the applicable 60 day period; and

(iii) The insurer makes the plan whole for any losses resulting from the non-compliance as follows:

(A) If the insurer has failed to comply with the disclosure or notice requirements set forth in paragraphs (c), (d) and (f) of this section, then the insurer must make the plan whole for any losses resulting from its non-compliance within the earlier of 60 days of detection by the insurer or sixty days following the receipt of written notice from the plan; and

(B) If the insurer has failed to pay a plan any amounts required under paragraphs (e) or (f) of this section within 90 days of receiving written notice of termination or discontinuance of the policy, the insurer must pay to the plan interest on any amounts restored pursuant to paragraph (i)(5)(ii) of this section at the "underpayment rate" as set forth in 26 U.S.C. sections 6621 and 6622. Such interest must be paid within the earlier of 60 days of detection by the insurer or sixty days following receipt of written notice of non-compliance from the plan.

(j) *Applicability dates.*

(1) In general. Except as provided in paragraphs (j)(2) through (4) of this section, this section is applicable on July 5, 2001.

(2) Paragraph (c) relating to initial disclosures and paragraph (d) relating to separate account disclosures are applicable on July 5, 2000.

(3) The first annual disclosure required under paragraph (c)(4) of this section shall be provided to each plan not later than 18 months following January 5, 2000.

(4) Paragraph (f), relating to insurer-initiated amendments, is applicable on January 5, 2000.

(k) *Effective date.* This section is effective January 5, 2000.

[¶ 14,720]
ESTABLISHMENT OF PLAN

Act Sec. 402. (a)(1) Every employee benefit plan shall be established and maintained pursuant to a written instrument. Such instrument shall provide for one or more named fiduciaries who jointly or severally shall have authority to control and manage the operation and administration of the plan.

(2) For purposes of this title, the term "named fiduciary" means a fiduciary who is named in the plan instrument, or who, pursuant to a procedure specified in the plan, is identified as a fiduciary (A) by a person who is an employer or employee organization with respect to the plan or (B) by such an employer and such an employee organization acting jointly.

Act Sec. 402. (b) Every employee benefit plan shall—

(1) provide a procedure for establishing and carrying out a funding policy and method consistent with the objectives of the plan and the requirements of this title,

(2) describe any procedure under the plan for the allocation of responsibilities for the operation and administration of the plan (including any procedure described in section 405(c)(1)),

(3) provide a procedure for amending such plan, and for identifying the persons who have authority to amend the plan, and

(4) specify the basis on which payments are made to and from the plan.

Act Sec. 402. (c) Any employee benefit plan may provide—

(1) that any person or group of persons may serve in more than one fiduciary capacity with respect to the plan (including service both as trustee and administrator);

(2) that a named fiduciary, or a fiduciary designated by a named fiduciary pursuant to a plan procedure described in section 405(c)(1), may employ one or more persons to render advice with regard to any responsibility such fiduciary has under the plan; or

(3) that a person who is a named fiduciary with respect to control or management of the assets of the plan may appoint an investment manager or managers to manage (including the power to acquire and dispose of) any assets of a plan.

[¶ 14,730]
ESTABLISHMENT OF TRUST

Act Sec. 403.(a) Except as provided in subsection (b), all assets of an employee benefit plan shall be held in trust by one or more trustees. Such trustee or trustees shall be either named in the trust instrument or in the plan instrument described in section 402(a) or appointed by a person who is a named fiduciary, and upon acceptance of being named or appointed, the trustee or trustees shall have exclusive authority and discretion to manage and control the assets of the plan, except to the extent that—

(1) the plan expressly provides that the trustee or trustees are subject to the direction of a named fiduciary who is not a trustee, in which case the trustees shall be subject to proper directions of such fiduciary which are made in accordance with the terms of the plan and which are not contrary to this Act, or

(2) authority to manage, acquire, or dispose of assets of the plan is delegated to one or more investment managers pursuant to section 402(c)(3).

Act Sec. 403. (b) The requirements of subsection (a) of this section shall not apply—

(1) to any assets of a plan which consist of insurance contracts or policies issued by an insurance company qualified to do business in a State;

(2) to any assets of such an insurance company or any assets of a plan which are held by such an insurance company;

(3) to a plan—

(A) some or all of the participants of which are employees described in section 401(c)(1) of the Internal Revenue Code of 1986; or

(B) which consists of one or more individual retirement accounts described in section 408 of the Internal Revenue Code of 1986;

to the extent that such plan's assets are held in one or more custodial accounts which qualify under section 401(f) and 408(h) of such Code, whichever is applicable.

(4) to a plan which the Secretary exempts from the requirement of subsection (a) and which is not subject to any of the following provisions of this Act—

(A) part 2 of this subtitle,

(B) part 3 of this subtitle, or

(C) title IV of this Act;

(5) to a contract established and maintained under section 403(b) of the Internal Revenue Code of 1986 to the extent that the assets of the contract are held in one or more custodial accounts pursuant to section 403(b)(7) of such Code; or

(6) any plan, fund or program under which an employer, all of whose stock is directly or indirectly owned by employees, former employees or their beneficiaries, proposes through an unfunded arrangement to compensate retired employees for benefits which were forfeited by such employees under a pension plan maintained by a former employer prior to the date such pension plan became subject to this Act.

Act Sec. 403.(c)(1) (1) Except as provided in paragraph (2), (3) or (4) or subsection (d), or under section 4042 and 4044 (relating to termination of insured plans), or under section 420 of the Internal Revenue Code of 1986 (as in effect on the date of the enactment of the American Jobs Creation Act of 2004), the assets of a plan shall never inure to the benefit of any employer and shall be held for the exclusive purposes of providing benefits to participants in the plan and their beneficiaries and defraying reasonable expenses of administering the plan.

(2)(A) In the case of a contribution, or a payment of withdrawal liability under part 1 of subtitle E of title IV—

(i) if such contribution or payment is made by an employer to a plan (other than a multiemployer plan) by a mistake of fact, paragraph (1) shall not prohibit the return of such contribution to the employer within one year after the payment of the contribution, and

(ii) if such contribution or payment is made by an employer to a multiemployer plan by a mistake of act or law (other than a mistake relating to whether the plan is described in section 401(a) of the Internal Revenue Code of 1986 or the trust which is part of such plan is exempt from taxation under section 501(a) of such Code), paragraph (1) shall not prohibit the return of such contribution or payment to the employer within 6 months after the plan administrator determines that the contribution was made by such a mistake.

(B) If a contribution is conditioned on initial qualification of the plan under section 401 or 403(a) of the Internal Revenue Code of 1986, and if the plan receives an adverse determination with respect to its initial qualification, then paragraph (1) shall not prohibit the return of such contribution to the employer within one year after such determination, but only if the application for the determination is made by the time prescribed by law for filing the employer's return for the taxable year in which such plan was adopted, or such later date as the Secretary of the Treasury may prescribe.

(C) If a contribution is conditioned upon the deductibility of the contribution under section 404 of the Internal Revenue Code of 1986, then, to the extent the deduction is disallowed, paragraph (1) shall not prohibit the return to the employer of such contribution (to the extent disallowed) within one year after the disallowance of the deduction.

(3) In the case of a withdrawal liability payment which has been determined to be an overpayment, paragraph (1) shall not prohibit the return of such payment to the employer within 6 months after the date of such determination.

Act Sec. 403.(d)(1) Upon termination of a pension plan to which section 4021 does not apply at the time of termination and to which this part applies (other than a plan to which no employer contributions have been made) the assets of the plan shall be allocated in accordance with the provisions of section 4044 of this Act, except as otherwise provided in regulations of the Secretary.

(2) (2) The assets of a welfare plan which terminates shall be distributed in accordance with the terms of the plan, except as otherwise provided in regulations of the Secretary.

Amendments

P.L. 108-357, § 709(a)(2):

Act Sec. 709(a)(2) amended ERISA Sec. 403(c)(1) by striking "Pension Funding Equity Act of 2004" and inserting "American Jobs Creation Act of 2004."

P.L. 108-218, § 204(b):

Act Sec. 204(b)(2) amended ERISA Sec. 403(c)(1) by striking "Tax Relief Extension Act of 1999" and inserting "Pension Funding Equity Act of 2004."

P.L. 106-170, §535(a)(2)(B):

Act Sec. 535(a)(2)(B) amended ERISA Sec. 403(c)(1) by striking "January 1, 1995" and inserting "the date of the enactment of the Tax Relief Extension Act of 1999".

The above amendment applies to qualified transfers occurring after December 17, 1999.

P.L. 101-508, Sec. 12012(a):

Amended ERISA Sec. 403(c)(1) by inserting ", or under section 420 of the Internal Revenue Code of 1986 (as in effect on January 1, 1991)" after "insured plans)" effective for qualified transfers under Code Sec. 420 made after November 5, 1990.

P.L. 101-239, §7881(k):

Amended ERISA Sec. 403(c) by striking paragraph (3) and redesignating paragraph (4) as paragraph (3) effective December 22, 1987. Prior to being stricken, paragraph (3) read as follows:

(3) In the case of a contribution which would otherwise be an excess contribution (as defined in section 4979(c) of the Internal Revenue Code of 1986) paragraph (1) shall not prohibit a correcting distribution with respect to such contribution from the plan to the employer to the extent permitted in such section to avoid payment of an excise tax on excess contributions under such section.

P.L. 101-239, §7891(a)(1):

Titles I, III, and IV of ERISA (other than sections 3(37)(E), 301(a)(7), and 308, the last sentence of section 408(d), and sections 414(c), 4001(a)(3)(ii), and 4303) are each amended by striking "Internal Revenue Code of 1954" each place it appears and inserting "Internal Revenue Code of 1986" effective October 22, 1986.

P.L. 101-239, §7894(e)(3):

Amended ERISA Sec. 403(b)(3) by redesignating clauses (i) and (ii) as subparagraphs (A) and (B), respectively; by striking "to the extent" and all that followed through "applicable" in subparagraph (B) (as redesignated); and by adding the new material that follows subparagraph (B) effective September 2, 1974. Prior to amendment, ERISA Sec. 403(b)(3) read as follows:

(3) to a plan—

(i) some or all of the participants of which are employees described in section 401(c)(1) of the Internal Revenue Code of 1954; or

(ii) which consists of one or more individual retirement accounts described in section 408 of the Internal Revenue Code of 1954, to the extent that such plan's assets are held in one or more custodial accounts which qualify under section 401(f) or 408(h) of such Code, whichever is applicable;

P.L. 100-203, §9343(c)(1):

Amended ERISA Sec. 403(c)(2)(B) to read as above, effective December 22, 1987. Prior to amendment, subparagraph (B) read as follows:

(B) If a contribution is conditioned on qualification of the plan under section 401, 403(a), or 405(a) of the Internal Revenue Code of 1954, and if the plan does not qualify, then paragraph (1) shall not prohibit the return of such contribution to the employer within one year after the date of denial of qualification of the plan.

P.L. 100-203, §9343(c)(2):

Amended ERISA Sec. 403(c)(3) by striking out "4972(b) of the Internal Revenue Code of 1954" and inserting "4979(c) of the Internal Revenue Code of 1986" instead.

P.L. 96-364, §§310, 402(b)(2), 410(a) and 411(c):

Added new subsection 403(b)(6), amended section 403(c)(1) by substituting "(3) or (4)" for (3) and added new section 403(c)(4), effective September 26, 1980.

Sec. 403(c)(2)(A) was amended to read as above. Prior to its amendment, section 403(c)(2)(A) read:

"(2)(A) In the case of a contribution which is made by an employer by a mistake of fact, paragraph (1) shall not prohibit the return of such contribution to the employer within one year after the payment of the contribution."

Act Sec. 410(c) provides:

"(c) The amendment made by this section shall take effect on January 1, 1975, except that in the case of contributions received by a collectively bargained plan maintained by more than one employer before the date of enactment of this Act, any determination by the plan administrator that any such contribution was made by mistake of fact or law before such date shall be deemed to have been made on such date of enactment."

Regulations

Reg. §§2550.403a-1 and 2550.403b-1 were adopted by FR Doc. 82-13400 and were filed with the Federal Register on May 13, 1982 (47 FR 21241). The regulations are effective June 17, 1982.

Subchapter F—Fiduciary Responsibility Under the Employee Retirement Income Security Act of 1974

Part 2550—Rules and Regulations for Fiduciary Responsibility

[¶ 14,733]

§2550.403a-1 **Establishment of trust.** (a) *In General.* Except as otherwise provided in §403b-1, all assets of an employee benefit plan shall be held in trust by one or more trustees pursuant to a written trust instrument.

(b) *Specific applications.* (1) The requirements of paragraph (a) of this section will not fail to be satisfied merely because securities of a plan are held in the name of a nominee or in street name, provided such securities are held on behalf of the plan by:

(i) A bank or trust company that is subject to supervision by the United States or a State, or a nominee of such bank or trust company;

(ii) A broker or dealer registered under the Securities Exchange Act of 1934, or a nominee of such broker or dealer; or

(iii) A "clearing agency," as defined in section 3(a)(23) of the Securities Exchange Act of 1934, or its nominee.

(2) Where a corporation described in section 501(c)(2) of the Internal Revenue Code holds property on behalf of a plan, the requirements of paragraph (a) of this section are satisfied with respect to such property if all the stock of such corporation is held in trust on behalf of the plan by one or more trustees.

(3) If the assets of an entity in which a plan invests include plan assets by reason of the plan's investment in the entity, the requirements of paragraph (a) of this section are satisfied with respect to such investment if the indicia of ownership of the plan's interest in the entity are held in trust on behalf of the plan by one or more trustees.

(c) *Requirements concerning trustees.* The trustee or trustees referred to in paragraphs (a) and (b) shall be either named in the trust instrument or in the plan instrument described in section 402(a) of the Act, or appointed by a person who is a named fiduciary (within the meaning of section 402(a)(2) of the Act). Upon acceptance of being named or appointed, the trustee or trustees shall have exclusive authority and discretion to manage and control the assets of the plan, except to the extent that:

(1) The plan instrument or the trust instrument expressly provides that the trustee or trustees are subject to the direction of a named fiduciary who is not a trustee, in which case the trustees shall be subject to the proper directions of such fiduciary which are made in accordance with the terms of the plan and which are not contrary to the provisions of Title I of the Act of Chapter XXV of this Title, or

(2) Authority to manage, acquire or dispose of assets of the plan is delegated to one or more investment managers (within the meaning of section 3(38) of the Act) pursuant to section 402(c)(3) of the Act.

[¶ 14,734]

§2550.403b-1 **Exemptions from trust requirement.** (a) *Statutory exemptions.* The requirements of section 403(a) of the Act and section 403a-1 shall not apply—

(1) To any assets of a plan which consist of insurance contracts or policies issued by an insurance company qualified to do business in a State;

(2) To any assets of such an insurance company or any assets of a plan which are held by such an insurance company.

(3) To plan—

(i) Some or all of the participants of which are employees described in section 401(c)(1) of the Internal Revenue Code of 1954; or

(ii) Which consists of one or more individual retirement accounts described in section 408 of the Internal Revenue Code of 1954 to the extent that such plan's assets are held in one or more custodial accounts which qualify under section 401(f) or 408(h) of such Code, whichever is applicable;

(4) To a contract established and maintained under section 403(b) of the Internal Revenue Code of 1954 to the extent that the assets of the contract are held in one or more custodial accounts pursuant to section 403(b)(7) of such Code.

(5) To any plan, fund or program under which as employer, all of whose stock is directly or indirectly owned by employees, former employees or their beneficiaries, proposes through an unfunded arrangement to compensate retired employees for benefits which were forfeited by such employees under a pension plan maintained by a former employer prior to the date such pension plan became subject to the Act.

(b) [Reserved]

[¶ 14,740]
FIDUCIARY DUTIES

Act Sec. 404 (a)(1) Subject to sections 403(c) and (d), 4042, and 4044, a fiduciary shall discharge his duties with respect to a plan solely in the interest of the participants and beneficiaries and—

(A) for the exclusive purpose of:

(i) providing benefits to participants and their beneficiaries; and

(ii) defraying reasonable expenses of administering the plan;

(B) with the care, skill, prudence, and diligence under the circumstances then prevailing that a prudent man acting in a like capacity and familiar with such matters would use in the conduct of an enterprise of a like character and with like aims;

(C) by diversifying the investments of the plan so as to minimize the risk of large losses, unless under the circumstances it is clearly prudent not to do so; and

(D) in accordance with the documents and instruments governing the plan insofar as such documents and instruments are consistent with the provisions of this title and Title IV.

(2) In the case of an eligible individual account plan (as defined in section 407(d)(3)), the diversification requirement of paragraph (1)(C) and the prudence requirement (only to the extent that it requires diversification) of paragraph (1)(B) is not violated by acquisition or holding of qualifying employer real property or qualifying employer securities (as defined in section 407(d)(4) and (5)).

Act Sec. 404. (b) Except as authorized by the Secretary by regulation, no fiduciary may maintain the indicia of ownership of any assets of a plan outside the jurisdiction of the district courts of the United States.

Act Sec. 404. (c)(1) In the case of a pension plan which provides for individual accounts and permits a participant or beneficiary to exercise control over assets in his account, if a participant or beneficiary exercises control over the assets in his account (as determined under regulations of the Secretary)—

(A) such participant or beneficiary shall not be deemed to be a fiduciary by reason of such exercise, and

(B) no person who is otherwise a fiduciary shall be liable under this part for any loss, or by reason of any breach, which results from such participant's or beneficiary's exercise of control.

(2) In the case of a simple retirement account established pursuant to a qualified salary reduction arrangement under section 408(p) of the Internal Revenue Code of 1986, a participant or beneficiary shall, for purposes of paragraph (1), be treated as exercising control over the assets in the account upon the earliest of—

(A) an affirmative election among investment options with respect to the initial investment of any contribution,

(B) a rollover to any other simple retirement account or individual retirement plan, or

(C) one year after the simple retirement account is established.

No reports, other than those required under section 101(g), shall be required with respect to a simple retirement account established pursuant to such a qualified salary reduction arrangement.

(3) In the case of a pension plan which makes a transfer to an individual retirement account or annuity of a designated trustee or issuer under section 401(a)(31)(B) of the Internal Revenue Code of 1986, the participant or beneficiary shall, for purposes of paragraph (1), be treated as exercising control over the assets in the account or annuity upon—

(A) the earlier of—

(i) a rollover of all or a portion of the amount to another individual retirement account or annuity; or

(ii) one year after the transfer is made; or

(B) a transfer that is made in a manner consistent with guidance provided by the Secretary.

Act Sec. 404. (d)(1) If, in connection with the termination of a pension plan which is a single-employer plan, there is an election to establish or maintain a qualified replacement plan, or to increase benefits, as provided under section 4980(d) of the Internal Revenue Code of 1986, a fiduciary shall discharge the fiduciary's duties under this title and title IV in accordance with the following requirements:

(A) In the case of a fiduciary of the terminated plan, any requirement—

(i) under section 4980(d)(2)(B) of such Code with respect to the transfer of assets from the terminated plan to a qualified replacement plan, and

(ii) under section 4980(d)(2)(B)(ii) or 4980(d)(3) of such Code with respect to any increase in benefits under the terminated plan.

(B) In the case of a fiduciary of a qualified replacement plan, any requirement—

(i) under section 4980(d)(2)(A) of such Code with respect to participation in the qualified replacement plan of active participants in the terminated plan,

(ii) under section 4980(d)(2)(B) of such Code with respect to the receipt of assets from the terminated plan, and

(iii) under section 4980(d)(2)(C) of such Code with respect to the allocation of assets to participants of the qualified replacement plan.

(2) For purposes of this subsection—

(A) any term used in this subsection which is also used in section 4980(d) of the Internal Revenue Code of 1986 shall have the same meaning as when used in such section, and

(B) any reference in this subsection to the Internal Revenue Code of 1986 shall be a reference to such Code as in effect immediately after the enactment of the Omnibus Budget Reconciliation Act of 1990.

Amendments

P.L. 107-147, §411(t):

Amended ERISA Sec. 404(c)(3) by striking "the earlier of" the second place it appears in subparagraph (A) and by striking "if the transfer" and inserting "a transfer that."

The above amendments shall apply to distributions made ater final regulations implementing Act Sec. 657(c)(2)(A) are amended, subject to sunset after 2010 under P.L. 107-16, Sec. 901.

P.L. 107-16, §657(c)(1):

Amended ERISA Sec. 404(c) by adding at the end a new paragraph (3) to read as above.

The above amendments shall apply to distributions made after final regulations implementing Act Sec. 657(c)(2)(A) are amended, subject to sunset after 2010 under P.L. 107-16, Sec. 901.

P.L. 104-188, Sec. 1421(d)(2):

Amended ERISA Sec. 404(c) by inserting (1) after "(c)", by redesignating paragraphs (1) and (2) as subparagraphs (A) and (B), respectively, and by adding at the end a new paragraph (2) to read as above.

The above amendments apply to tax years beginning after December 31, 1996.

P.L. 101-508, Sec. 12001(b)(1):

Amended ERISA Sec. 404 by adding a new subsection (d) to read as above effective for reversions occurring after September 30, 1990 except for the provisions of Act Sec. 12003(b). See P.L. 101-508, Sec. 12001(b)(2)(A) below for exceptions to effective date.

P.L. 101-508, Sec. 12001(b)(2)(A):

Amended ERISA Sec. 404(a)(1)(D) by striking "or title IV" and inserting "and title IV" effective for reversions occurring after September 30, 1990 except for the provisions of Act Sec. 12003(b).

SEC. 12003. EFFECTIVE DATE.

* * *

(b) EXCEPTION.—The amendments made by this subtitle shall not apply to any reversion after September 30, 1990, if—

(1) in the case of plans subject to title IV of the Employee Retirement Income Security Act of 1974, a notice of intent to terminate under such title was provided to participants (or if no participants, to the Pension Benefit Guaranty Corporation) before October 1, 1990,

(2) in the case of plans subject to title I (and not to title IV) of such Act, a notice of intent to reduce future accruals under section 204(h) of such Act was provided to participants in connection with the termination before October 1, 1990,

(3) in the case of plans not subject to title I or IV of such Act, a request for a determination letter with respect to the termination was filed with the Secretary of the Treasury or the Secretary's delegate before October 1, 1990, or

(4) in the case of plans not subject to title I or IV of such Act and having only 1 participant, a resolution terminating the plan was adopted by the employer before October 1, 1990.

P.L. 96-364, § 309:

Amended subsection 404(a)(1)(D) by adding "or Title IV" at the end of the subsection, effective September 26, 1980.

Regulations

Reg. § 2550.404a-1 was filed with the Federal Register on June 25, 1979. Reg. § 2550.404b-1 was adopted by FR Doc. 77-29187, filed with the Federal Register on September 30, 1977, and published in the Federal Register of October 4, 1977 (42 FR 54122). Reg. § 2550.404c-1 was adopted by FR Doc. 92-24357, filed with the Federal Register on October 9, 1992 and published in the Federal Register of October 13, 1992 (57 FR 46906). Reg. § 2550.404a-2 was adopted by FR Doc. 04-21591, filed with the Federal Register on September 27, 2004 and published in the Federal Register on September 28, 2004 (69 FR 58017).

[¶ 14,742]

§ 2550.404a-1 **Investment duties.** (a) *In general.* Section 404(a)(1)(B) of the Employee Retirement Income Security Act of 1974 (the Act) provides, in part, that a fiduciary shall discharge his duties with respect to a plan with the care, skill, prudence, and diligence under the circumstances then prevailing that a prudent man acting in a like capacity and familiar with such matters would use in the conduct of an enterprise of a like character and with like aims.

(b) *Investment Duties.* (1) With regard to an investment or investment course of action taken by a fiduciary of an employee benefit plan pursuant to his investment duties, the requirements of section 404(a)(1)(B) of the Act set forth in subsection (a) of this section are satisfied if the fiduciary (A) has given appropriate consideration to those facts and circumstances that, given the scope of such fiduciary's investment duties, the fiduciary knows or should know are relevant to the particular investment or investment course of action involved, including the role the investment or investment course of action plays in that portion of the plan's investment portfolio with respect to which the fiduciary has investment duties; and (B) has acted accordingly.

(2) For purposes of paragraph (1) of this subsection, "appropriate consideration" shall include, but is not necessarily limited to, (A) a determination by the fiduciary that the particular investment or investment course of action is reasonably designed, as part of the portfolio (or, where applicable, that portion of the plan portfolio with respect to which the fiduciary has investment duties), to further the purposes of the plan, taking into consideration the risk of loss and the opportunity for gain (or other return) associated with the investment or investment course of action, and (B) consideration of the following factors as they relate to such portion of the portfolio:

(i) the composition of the portfolio with regard to diversification;

(ii) the liquidity and current return of the portfolio relative to the anticipated cash flow requirement of the plan, and

(iii) the projected return of the portfolio relative to the funding objectives of the plan.

(3) An investment manager appointed, pursuant to the provisions of section 402(c)(3) of the Act, to manage all or part of the assets of a plan, may, for purposes of compliance with the provisions of paragraphs (1) and (2) of this subsection, rely on, and act upon the basis of, information pertaining to the plan provided by or at the direction of the appointing fiduciary, if—

(A) such information is provided for the stated purpose of assisting the manager in the performance of his investment duties, and

(B) the manager does not know and has no reason to know that the information is incorrect.

(c) *Definitions.* For purposes of this section:

(1) The term "investment duties" means any duties imposed upon, or assumed or undertaken by, a person in connection with the investment of plan assets which make or will make such person a fiduciary of an employee benefit plan or which are performed by such person as a fiduciary of an employee benefit plan as defined in section 3(21)(A)(i) or (ii) of the Act.

(2) The term "investment course of action" means any series or program of investments or actions related to a fiduciary's performance of his investment duties.

(3) The term "plan" means an employee benefit plan to which Title I of the Act applies.

[¶ 14,742A]

§ 2550.404a-2 **Safe harbor for automatic rollovers to individual retirement plans.** (a) *In general.* (1) Pursuant to section 657(c) of the Economic Growth and Tax Relief Reconciliation Act of 2001, Public Law 107-16, June 7, 2001, 115 Stat. 38, this section provides a safe harbor under which a fiduciary of an employee pension benefit plan subject to Title I of the Employee Retirement Income Security Act of 1974, as amended (the Act), 29 USC 1001 et seq., will be deemed to have satisfied his or her fiduciary duties under section 404(a) of the Act in connection with an automatic rollover of a mandatory distribution described in section 401(a)(31)(B) of the Internal Revenue Code of 1986, as amended (the Code). This section also provides a safe harbor for certain other mandatory distributions not described in section 401(a)(31)(B) of the Code.

(2) The standards set forth in this section apply solely for purposes of determining whether a fiduciary meets the requirements of this safe harbor. Such standards are not intended to be the exclusive means by which a fiduciary might satisfy his or her responsibilities under the Act with respect to rollovers of mandatory distributions described in paragraphs (c) and (d) of this section.

(b) *Safe harbor.* A fiduciary that meets the conditions of paragraph (c) or paragraph (d) of this section is deemed to have satisfied his or her duties under section 404(a) of the Act with respect to both the selection of an individual retirement plan provider and the investment of funds in connection with the rollover of mandatory distributions described in those paragraphs to an individual retirement plan, within the meaning of section 7701(a)(37) of the Code.

(c) *Conditions.* With respect to an automatic rollover of a mandatory distribution described in section 401(a)(31)(B) of the Code, a fiduciary shall qualify for the safe harbor described in paragraph (b) of this section if:

(1) The present value of the nonforfeitable accrued benefit, as determined under section 411(a)(11) of the Code, does not exceed the maximum amount under section 401(a)(31)(B) of the Code;

(2) The mandatory distribution is to an individual retirement plan within the meaning of section 7701(a)(37) of the Code;

(3) In connection with the distribution of rolled-over funds to an individual retirement plan, the fiduciary enters into a written agreement with an individual retirement plan provider that provides:

(i) the rolled-over funds shall be invested in an investment product designed to preserve principal and provide a reasonable rate of return, whether or not such return is guaranteed, consistent with liquidity;

(ii) for purposes of paragraph (c)(3)(i) of this section, the investment product selected for the rolled-over funds shall seek to maintain, over the term of the investment, the dollar value that is equal to the amount invested in the product by the individual retirement plan;

(iii) the investment product selected for the rolled-over funds shall be offered by a state or federally regulated financial institution, which shall be: a bank or savings association, the deposits of which are insured by the Federal Deposit Insurance Corporation; a credit union, the member accounts of which are insured within the meaning of section 101(7) of the Federal Credit Union Act; an insurance company, the products of which are protected by state guaranty associations; or an investment company registered under the Investment Company Act of 1940;

(iv) all fees and expenses attendant to an individual retirement plan, including investments of such plan, (e.g., establishment charges, maintenance fees, investment expenses, termination costs and surrender charges) shall not exceed the fees and expenses charged by the individual retirement plan provider for comparable individual retirement plans established for reasons other than the receipt of a rollover distribution subject to the provisions of section 401(a)(31)(B) of the Code; and

(v) the participant on whose behalf the fiduciary makes an automatic rollover shall have the right to enforce the terms of the contractual agreement establishing the individual retirement plan, with regard to his or her rolled-over funds, against the individual retirement plan provider.

(4) Participants have been furnished a summary plan description, or a summary of material modifications, that describes the plan's automatic rollover provisions effectuating the requirements of section 401(a)(31)(B) of the Code, including an explanation that the mandatory distribution will be invested in an investment product designed to preserve principal and provide a reasonable rate of return and liquidity, a statement indicating how fees and expenses attendant to the individual retirement plan will be allocated (i.e., the extent to which expenses will be borne by the account holder alone or shared with the distributing plan or plan sponsor), and the name, address and phone number of a plan contact (to the extent not otherwise provided in the summary plan description or summary of material modifications) for further information concerning the plan's automatic rollover provisions, the individual retirement plan provider and the fees and expenses attendant to the individual retirement plan; and

(5) Both the fiduciary's selection of an individual retirement plan and the investment of funds would not result in a prohibited transaction under section 406 of the Act, unless such actions are exempted from the prohibited transaction provisions by a prohibited transaction exemption issued pursuant to section 408(a) of the Act.

(d) *Mandatory distributions of $1,000 or less.* A fiduciary shall qualify for the protection afforded by the safe harbor described in paragraph (b) of this section with respect to a mandatory distribution of one thousand dollars ($1,000) or less described in section 411(a)(11) of the Code, provided there is no affirmative distribution election by the participant and the fiduciary makes a rollover distribution of such amount into an individual retirement plan on behalf of such participant in accordance with the conditions described in paragraph (c) of this section, without regard to the fact that such rollover is not described in section 401(a)(31)(B) of the Code.

(e) *Effective date.* This section shall be effective and shall apply to any rollover of a mandatory distribution made on or after March 28, 2005.

[¶ 14,743]

§ 2550.404b-1 **Maintenance of the indicia of ownership of plan assets outside the jurisdiction of the district courts of the United States.** (a) No fiduciary may maintain the indicia of ownership of any assets of a plan outside the jurisdiction of the district courts of the United States, unless: [Amended by 64 FR 1266, originally scheduled to be effective February 6, 1981. However, the effective date was delayed under the President's regulation freeze until March 30, 1981 (46 FR 10465).]

(1) Such assets are (i) Securities issued by a person, as defined in section 3(9) of the Employee Retirement Income Security Act of 1974 (Act) (other than an individual), which is not organized under the laws of the United States or a State and does not have its principal place of business within the United States, (ii) securities issued by a government other than the government of the United States or of a State, or any political subdivision, agency or instrumentality of such a government, (iii) securities issued by a person, as defined in section 3(9) of the Act (other than an individual), the principal trading market for which securities is outside the jurisdiction of the district courts of the United States, or (iv) currency issued by a government other than the government of the United States if such currency is maintained outside the jurisdiction of the district courts of the United States solely as an incident to the purchase, sale or maintenance of securities described in paragraph (a)(1) of this section; and

(2)(i) Such assets are under the management and control of a fiduciary which is a corporation or partnership organized under the laws of the United States or a State, which fiduciary has its principal place of business within the United States and which is—

(A) A bank as defined in section 202(a)(2) of the Investment Advisers Act of 1940 that has, as of the last day of its most recent fiscal year, equity capital in excess of $1,000,000;

(B) An insurance company which is qualified under the laws of more than one State to manage, acquire, or dispose of any asset of a plan, which company has, as of the last day of its most recent fiscal year, net worth in excess of $1,000,000 and which is subject to supervision and examination by the State authority having supervision over insurance companies; or

(C) An investment adviser registered under the Investment Advisers Act of 1940 that has, as of the last day of its most recent fiscal year, total client assets under its management and control in excess [of] $50,000,000 and either *(1)* Shareholders' or partners' equity in excess of $750,000 or *(2)* all of its obligations and liabilities assumed or guaranteed by a person described in paragraph (a)(2)(i)(A), (B), or (C) *(1)* or (a)(2)(ii)(A) *(2)* of this section; or

(ii) Such indicia of ownership are either

(A) In the physical possession of, or, as a result of normal business operations, are in transit to the physical possession of, a person which is organized under the laws of the United States or a State, which person has its principal place of business in the United States and which is—

(1) A bank as defined in section 202(a)(2) of the Investment Advisers Act of 1940 that has, as of the last day of its most recent fiscal year, equity capital in excess of $1,000,000;

(2) A broker or dealer registered under the Securities Exchange Act of 1934 that has, as of the last day of its most recent fiscal year, net worth in excess of $750,000; or

(3) A broker or dealer registered under the Securities Exchange Act of 1934 that has all of its obligations and liabilities assumed or guaranteed by a person described in paragraph (a)(2)(i)(A), (B), or (C) *(1)* or (a)(2)(ii)(A) *(2)* of this section; or

(B) Maintained by a broker or dealer, described in paragraph (a)(2)(ii)(A) *(2)* or *(3)* of this section, in the custody of an entity designated by the Securities and Exchange Commission as a "satisfactory control location" with respect to such broker or dealer pursuant to Rule 15c3-3 under the Securities Exchange Act of 1934, provided that:

(1) Such entity holds the indicia of ownership as agent for the broker or dealer, and

(2) Such broker or dealer is liable to the plan to the same extent it would be if it retained the physical possession of the indicia of ownership pursuant to paragraph (a)(2)(ii)(A) of this section. [Amended by 46 FR 1266, originally scheduled to be effective February 6, 1981. However, the effective date was delayed under the President's regulation freeze until March 30, 1981 (46 FR 10465).]

(C) Maintained by a bank described in paragraph (a)(2)(ii)(A) *(1)*, in the custody of an entity that is a foreign securities depository, foreign clearing agency which acts as a securities depository, or foreign bank, which entity is supervised or regulated by a government agency or regulatory authority in the foreign jurisdiction having authority over such depositories, clearing agencies or banks, provided that:

(1) the foreign entity holds the indicia of ownership as agent for the bank;

(2) the bank is liable to the plan to the same extent it would be if it retained the physical possession of the indicia of ownership within the United States;

(3) the indicia of ownership are not subject to any right, charge, security interest, lien or claim of any kind in favor of the foreign entity except for their safe custody or administration;

(4) beneficial ownership of the assets represented by the indicia of ownership is freely transferable without the payment of money or value other than for safe custody or administration; and

(5) upon request by the plan fiduciary who is responsible for the selection and retention of the bank, the bank identifies to such fiduciary the name, address and principal place of business of the

foreign entity which acts as custodian for the plan pursuant to this paragraph (a)(2)(ii)(C), and the name and address of the governmental agency or other regulatory authority that supervises or regulates that foreign entity. [Added by 46 FR 1266, originally scheduled to be effective February 6, 1981. However, the effective date was delayed under the President's regulation freeze until March 30, 1981 (46 FR 10465).]

(b) Notwithstanding any requirement of paragraph (a) of this section, a fiduciary with respect to a plan may maintain in Canada the indicia of ownership of plan assets which are attributable to a contribution made on behalf of a plan participant who is a citizen or resident of Canada, if such indicia of ownership must remain in Canada in order for the plan to qualify for and maintain tax exempt status under the laws of Canada or to comply with other applicable laws of Canada or any Province of Canada.

(c) For purposes of this regulation:

(1) the term "management and control" means the power to direct the acquisition or disposition through purchase, sale, pledging, or other means; and

(2) the term "depository" means any company, or agency or instrumentality of government, that acts as a custodian of securities in connection with a system for the central handling of securities whereby all securities of a particular class or series of any issuer deposited within the system are treated as fungible and may be transferred, loaned, or pledged by bookkeeping entry without physical delivery of securities certificates. [Amended by 46 FR 1266, originally scheduled to be effective February 6, 1981. However, the effective date was delayed under the President's regulation freeze until March 30, 1981 (46 FR 10465).]

[¶ 14,744]

§ 2550.404c-1 **ERISA section 404(c) plans.** (a) *In general.* (1) Section 404(c) of the Employee Retirement Income Security Act of 1974 (ERISA or the Act) provides that if a pension plan that provides for individual accounts permits a participant or beneficiary to exercise control over assets in his account and that participant or beneficiary in fact exercises control over assets in his account, then the participant or beneficiary shall not be deemed to be a fiduciary by reason of his exercise of control and no person who is otherwise a fiduciary shall be liable for any loss, or by reason of any breach, which results from such exercise of control. This section describes the kinds of plans that are "ERISA section 404(c) plans," the circumstances in which a participant or beneficiary is considered to have exercised independent control over the assets in his account as contemplated by section 404(c), and the consequences of a participant's or beneficiary's exercise of control.

(2) The standards set forth in this section are applicable solely for the purpose of determining whether a plan is an ERISA section 404(c) plan and whether a particular transaction engaged in by a participant or beneficiary of such plan is afforded relief by section 404(c). Such standards, therefore, are not intended to be applied in determining whether, or to what extent, a plan which does not meet the requirements for an ERISA section 404(c) plan or a fiduciary with respect to such a plan satisfies the fiduciary responsibility or other provisions of Title I of the Act.

(b) *ERISA section 404(c) plans.*

(1) *In general.* An "ERISA section 404(c) plan" is an individual account plan described in section 3(34) of the Act that:

(i) Provides an opportunity for a participant or beneficiary to exercise control over assets in his individual account (see paragraph (b)(2) of this section); and

(ii) Provides a participant or beneficiary an opportunity to choose, from a broad range of investment alternatives, the manner in which some or all of the assets in his account are invested (see paragraph (b)(3) of this section).

(2) *Opportunity to exercise control.* (i) A plan provides a participant or beneficiary an opportunity to exercise control over assets in his account only if:

(A) Under the terms of the plan, the participant or beneficiary has a reasonable opportunity to give investment instructions (in writing or otherwise, with an opportunity to obtain written confirmation

of such instructions) to an identified plan fiduciary who is obligated to comply with such instructions except as otherwise provided in paragraphs (b)(2)(ii)(B) and (d)(2)(ii) of this section; and

(B) The participant or beneficiary is provided or has the opportunity to obtain sufficient information to make informed decisions with regard to investment alternatives available under the plan, and incidents of ownership appurtenant to such investments. For purposes of this subparagraph, a participant or beneficiary will not be considered to have sufficient investment information unless—

(1) the participant or beneficiary is provided by an identified plan fiduciary (or a person or persons designated by the plan fiduciary to act on his behalf):

(i) an explanation that the plan is intended to constitute a plan described in section 404(c) of the Employee Retirement Income Security Act, and Title 29 of the *Code of Federal Regulations* Section 2550.404c-1, and that the fiduciaries of the plan may be relieved of liability for any losses which are the direct and necessary result of investment instructions given by such participant or beneficiary;

(ii) a description of the investment alternatives available under the plan and, with respect to each designated investment alternative, a general description of the investment objectives and risk and return characteristics of each such alternative, including information relating to the type and diversification of assets comprising the portfolio of the designated investment alternative;

(iii) identification of any designated investment managers;

(iv) an explanation of the circumstances under which participants and beneficiaries may give investment instructions and an explanation of any specified limitations on such instructions under the terms of the plan, including any restrictions on transfers to or from a designated investment alternative, and any restrictions on the exercise of voting, tender and similar rights appurtenant to a participant's or beneficiary's investment in an investment alternative;

(v) a description of any transaction fees and expenses which affect the participant's or beneficiary's account balance in connection with purchases or sales of interests in investment alternatives (e.g., commissions, sales loads, deferred sales charges, redemption or exchange fees);

(vi) the name, address, and phone number of the plan fiduciary (and, if applicable, the person or persons designated by the plan fiduciary to act on his behalf) responsible for providing the information described in paragraph (b)(2)(i)(B)(2) upon request of a participant or beneficiary and a description of the information described in paragraph (b)(2)(i)(B)(2) which may be obtained on request;

(vii) in the case of plans which offer an investment alternative which is designed to permit a participant or beneficiary to directly or indirectly acquire or sell any employer security (employer security alternative), a description of the procedures established to provide for the confidentiality of information relating to the purchase, holding and sale of employer securities, and the exercise of voting, tender and similar rights, by participants and beneficiaries, and the name, address and phone number of the plan fiduciary responsible for monitoring compliance with the procedures (see subparagraphs (d)(2)(ii)(E)(4)(vii), (viii) and (ix) of this section); and

(viii) in the case of an investment alternative which is subject to the Securities Act of 1933, and in which the participant or beneficiary has no assets invested, immediately following the participant's or beneficiary's initial investment, a copy of the most recent prospectus provided to the plan. This condition will be deemed satisfied if the participant or beneficiary has been provided with a copy of such most recent prospectus immediately prior to the participant's or beneficiary's initial investment in such alternative;

(ix) subsequent to an investment in an investment alternative, any materials provided to the plan relating to the exercise of voting, tender or similar rights which are incidental to the holding in the account of the participant or beneficiary of an ownership interest in such alternative to the extent that such rights are passed through to participants and beneficiaries under the terms of the plan, as well as a description of or reference to plan provisions relating to the exercise of voting, tender or similar rights.

(2) the participant or beneficiary is provided by the identified plan fiduciary (or a person or persons designated by the plan fiduciary to act on his behalf), either directly or upon request, the following information, which shall be based on the latest information available to the plan:

(i) a description of the annual operating expenses of each designated investment alternative (e.g., investment management fees, administrative fees, transaction costs) which reduce the rate of return to participants and beneficiaries, and the aggregate amount of such expenses expressed as a percentage of average net assets of the designated investment alternative;

(ii) copies of any prospectuses, financial statements and reports, and of any other materials relating to the investment alternatives available under the plan, to the extent such information is provided to the plan;

(iii) a list of the assets comprising the portfolio of each designated investment alternative which constitutes plans assets within the meaning of 29 CFR 2510.3-101, the value of each such asset (or the proportion of the investment alternative which it comprises), and, with respect to each such asset which is a fixed rate investment contract issued by a bank, savings and loan association or insurance company, the name of the issuer of the contract, the term of the contract and the rate of return on the contract;

(iv) information concerning the value of shares or units in designated investment alternatives available to participants and beneficiaries under the plan, as well as the past and current investment performance of such alternatives, determined, net of expenses, on a reasonable and consistent basis; and

(v) information concerning the value of shares or units in designated investment alternatives held in the account of the participant or beneficiary.

(ii) A plan does not fail to provide an opportunity for a participant or beneficiary to exercise control over his individual account merely because it—

(A) *Imposes charges for reasonable expenses.* A plan may charge participants' and beneficiaries' accounts for the reasonable expenses of carrying out investment instructions, provided that procedures are established under the plan to periodically inform such participants and beneficiaries of actual expenses incurred with respect to their respective individual accounts;

(B) *Permits a fiduciary to decline to implement investment instructions by participants and beneficiaries.* A fiduciary may decline to implement participant and beneficiary instructions which are described at paragraph (d)(2)(ii) of this section, as well as instructions specified in the plan, including instructions—

(1) which would result in a prohibited transaction described in ERISA section 406 or section 4975 of the Internal Revenue Code, and

(2) which would generate income that would be taxable to the plan;

(C) *Imposes reasonable restrictions on frequency of investment instructions.* A plan may impose reasonable restrictions on the frequency with which participants and beneficiaries may give investment instructions. In no event, however, is such a restriction reasonable unless, with respect to each investment alternative made available by the plan, it permits participants and beneficiaries to give investment instructions with a frequency which is appropriate in light of the market volatility to which the investment alternative may reasonably be expected to be subject, provided that—

(1) At least three of the investment alternatives made available pursuant to the requirements of paragraph (b)(3)(i)(B) of this section, which constitute a broad range of investment alternatives, permit participants and beneficiaries to give investment instructions no less frequently than once within any three month period; and

(2)(i) At least one of the investment alternatives meeting the requirements of paragraph (b)(2)(ii) (C)(*1*) of this section permits participants and beneficiaries to give investment instructions with regard to transfers into the investment alternative as frequently as participants and beneficiaries are permitted to give investment instruc-

tions with respect to any investment alternative made available by the plan which permits participants and beneficiaries to give investment instructions more frequently than once within any three month period; or

(ii) With respect to each investment alternative which permits participants and beneficiaries to give investment instructions more frequently than once within any three month period, participants and beneficiaries are permitted to direct their investments from such alternative into an income producing, low risk, liquid fund, subfund, or account as frequently as they are permitted to give investment instructions with respect to each such alternative and, with respect to such fund, subfund or account, participants and beneficiaries are permitted to direct investments from the fund, subfund or account to an investment alternative meeting the requirements of paragraph (b)(2)(ii)(C)(*1*) as frequently as they are permitted to give investment instructions with respect to that investment alternative; and

(3) With respect to transfers from an investment alternative which is designed to permit a participant or beneficiary to directly or indirectly acquire or sell any employer security (employer security alternative) either:

(i) All of the investment alternatives meeting the requirements of paragraph (b)(2)(ii)(C)(*1*) of this section must permit participants and beneficiaries to give investment instructions with regard to transfers into each of the investment alternatives as frequently as participants and beneficiaries are permitted to give investment instructions with respect to the employer security alternative; or

(ii) Participants and beneficiaries are permitted to direct their investments from each employer security alternative into an income producing, low risk, liquid fund, subfund, or account as frequently as they are permitted to give investment instructions with respect to such employer security alternative and, with respect to such fund, subfund, or account, participants and beneficiaries are permitted to direct investments from the fund, subfund or account to each investment alternative meeting the requirements of paragraph (b)(2)(ii)(C)(*1*) as frequently as they are permitted to give investment instructions with respect to each such investment alternative.

(iii) Paragraph (c) of this section describes the circumstances under which a participant or beneficiary will be considered to have exercised independent control with respect to a particular transaction.

(3) Broad range of investment alternatives. (i) A plan offers a broad range of investment alternatives only if the available investment alternatives are sufficient to provide the participant or beneficiary with a reasonable opportunity to:

(A) Materially affect the potential return on amounts in his individual account with respect to which he is permitted to exercise control and the degree of risk to which such amounts are subject;

(B) Choose from at least three investment alternatives:

(1) each of which is diversified;

(2) each of which has materially different risk and return characteristics;

(3) which in the aggregate enable the participant or beneficiary by choosing among them to achieve a portfolio with aggregate risk and return characteristics at any point within the range normally appropriate for the participant or beneficiary; and

(4) each of which when combined with investments in the other alternatives tends to minimize through diversification the overall risk of a participant's or beneficiary's portfolio;

(C) Diversify the investment of that portion of his individual account with respect to which he is permitted to exercise control so as to minimize the risk of large losses, taking into account the nature of the plan and the size of participants' or beneficiaries' accounts. In determining whether a plan provides the participant or beneficiary with a reasonable opportunity to diversify his investments, the nature of the investment alternatives offered by the plan and the size of the portion of the individual's account over which he is permitted to exercise control must be considered. Where such portion of the account of any participant or beneficiary is so limited in size that the opportunity to invest in look-through investment vehicles is the only prudent means to assure an opportunity to achieve appropriate diversification, a plan may satisfy the requirements of this paragraph only by offering look-through investment vehicles.

(ii) *Diversification and look-through investment vehicles.* Where look-through investment vehicles are available as investment alternatives to participants and beneficiaries, the underlying investments of the look-through investment vehicles shall be considered in determining whether the plan satisfies the requirements of subparagraphs (b)(3)(i)(B) and (b)(3)(i)(C).

(c) *Exercise of control.* (1) *In general.* (i) Sections 404(c)(1) and 404(c)(2) of the Act and paragraphs (a) and (d) of this section apply only with respect to a transaction where a participant or beneficiary has exercised independent control in fact with respect to the investment of assets in his individual account under an ERISA section 404(c) plan.

(ii) For purposes of sections 404(c)(1) and 404(c)(2) of the Act and paragraphs (a) and (d) of this section, a participant or beneficiary will be deemed to have exercised control with respect to the exercise of voting, tender and similar rights appurtenant to the participant's or beneficiary's ownership interest in an investment alternative, provided that the participant's or beneficiary's investment in the investment alternative was itself the result of an exercise of control, the participant or beneficiary was provided a reasonable opportunity to give instruction with respect to such incidents of ownership, including the provision of the information described in paragraph (b)(2)(i)(B)(*1*)(*ix*) of this section, and the participant or beneficiary has not failed to exercise control by reason of the circumstances described in paragraph (c)(2) with respect to such incidents of ownership.

(2) *Independent control.* Whether a participant or beneficiary has exercised independent control in fact with respect to a transaction depends on the facts and circumstances of the particular case. However, a participant's or beneficiary's exercise of control is not independent in fact if:

(i) The participant or beneficiary is subjected to improper influence by a plan fiduciary or the plan sponsor with respect to the transaction;

(ii) A plan fiduciary has concealed material non-public facts regarding the investment from the participant or beneficiary, unless the disclosure of such information by the plan fiduciary to the participant or beneficiary would violate any provision of federal law or any provision of state law which is not preempted by the Act; or

(iii) The participant or beneficiary is legally incompetent and the responsible plan fiduciary accepts the instructions of the participant or beneficiary knowing him to be legally incompetent.

(3) *Transactions involving a fiduciary.* In the case of a sale, exchange or leasing of property (other than a transaction described in paragraph (d)(2)(ii)(E) of this section) between an ERISA section 404(c) plan and a plan fiduciary or an affiliate of such a fiduciary, or a loan to a plan fiduciary or an affiliate of such a fiduciary, the participant or beneficiary will not be deemed to have exercised independent control unless the transaction is fair and reasonable to him. For purposes of this paragraph (c)(3), a transaction will be deemed to be fair and reasonable to a participant or beneficiary if he pays no more than, or receives no less than, adequate consideration (as defined in section 3(18) of the Act) in connection with the transaction.

(4) *No obligation to advise.* A fiduciary has no obligation under part 4 of Title I of the Act to provide investment advice to a participant or beneficiary under an ERISA section 404(c) plan.

(d) *Effect of independent exercise of control.* (1) *Participant or beneficiary not a fiduciary.* If a participant or beneficiary of an ERISA section 404(c) plan exercises independent control over assets in his individual account in the manner described in paragraph (c), then such participant or beneficiary is not a fiduciary of the plan by reason of such exercise of control.

(2) *Limitation on liability of plan fiduciaries.* (i) If a participant or beneficiary of an ERISA section 404(c) plan exercises independent control over assets in his individual account in the manner described in paragraph (c), then no other person who is a fiduciary with respect to such plan shall be liable for any loss, or with respect to any breach of

part 4 of Title I of the Act, that is the direct and necessary result of that participant's or beneficiary's exercise of control.

(ii) Paragraph (d)(2)(i) does not apply with respect to any instruction which, if implemented—

(A) Would not be in accordance with the documents and instruments governing the plan insofar as such documents and instruments are consistent with the provisions of Title I of ERISA;

(B) Would cause a fiduciary to maintain the indicia of ownership of any assets of the plan outside the jurisdiction of the district courts of the United States other than as permitted by section 404(b) of the Act and 29 C.F.R. § 2550.404b-1;

(C) Would jeopardize the plan's tax qualified status under the Internal Revenue Code;

(D) Could result in a loss in excess of a participant's or beneficiary's account balance; or

(E) Would result in a direct or indirect:

(*1*) Sale, exchange, or lease of property between a plan sponsor or any affiliate of the sponsor and the plan except for the acquisition or disposition of any interest in a fund, subfund or portfolio managed by a plan sponsor or an affiliate of the sponsor, or the purchase or sale of any qualifying employer security (as defined in section 407(d)(5) of the Act) which meets the conditions of section 408(e) of ERISA and section (d)(2)(ii)(E)(*4*) below;

(*2*) Loan to a plan sponsor or any affiliate of the sponsor;

(*3*) Acquisition or sale of any employer real property (as defined in section 407(d)(2) of the Act); or

(*4*) Acquisition or sale of any employer security except to the extent that:

(*i*) such securities are qualifying employer securities (as defined in section 407(d)(5) of the Act);

(*ii*) such securities are stock or an equity interest in a publicly traded partnership (as defined in section 7704(b) of the Internal Revenue Code of 1986), but only if such partnership is an existing partnership as defined in section 10211(c)(2)(A) of the Revenue Act of 1987 (Public Law 100-203);

(*iii*) such securities are publicly traded on a national exchange or other generally recognized market;

(*iv*) such securities are traded with sufficient frequency and in sufficient volume to assure that participant and beneficiary directions to buy or sell the security may be acted upon promptly and efficiently;

(*v*) information provided to shareholders of such securities is provided to participants and beneficiaries with accounts holding such securities;

(*vi*) voting, tender and similar rights with respect to such securities are passed through to participants and beneficiaries with accounts holding such securities;

(*vii*) information relating to the purchase, holding, and sale of securities, and the exercise of voting, tender and similar rights with respect to such securities by participants and beneficiaries, is maintained in accordance with procedures which are designed to safeguard the confidentiality of such information, except to the extent necessary to comply with Federal laws or state laws not preempted by the Act;

(*viii*) the plan designates a fiduciary who is responsible for ensuring that: the procedures required under subparagraph (d)(2)(ii)(E)(*4*)(*vii*) are sufficient to safeguard the confidentiality of the information described in that subparagraph, such procedures are being followed, and the independent fiduciary required by subparagraph (d)(2)(ii)(E)(*4*)(*ix*) is appointed; and

(*ix*) an independent fiduciary is appointed to carry out activities relating to any situations which the fiduciary designated by the plan for purposes of subparagraph (d)(2)(ii)(E)(*4*)(*viii*) determines involve a potential for undue employer influence upon participants and beneficiaries with regard to the direct or indirect exercise of shareholder rights. For purposes of this subparagraph, a fiduciary is not independent if the fiduciary is affiliated with any sponsor of the plan.

(iii) The individual investment decisions of an investment manager who is designated directly by a participant or beneficiary or who manages a look-through investment vehicle in which a participant or beneficiary has invested are not direct and necessary results of the designation of the investment manager or of investment in the look-through investment vehicle. However, this paragraph (d)(2)(iii) shall not be construed to result in liability under section 405 of ERISA with respect to a fiduciary (other than the investment manager) who would otherwise be relieved of liability by reason of section 404(c)(2) of the Act and paragraph (d) of this section.

(3) *Prohibited transactions.* The relief provided by section 404(c) of the Act and this section applies only to the provisions of part 4 of title I of the Act. Therefore, nothing in this section relieves a disqualified person from the taxes imposed by sections 4975(a) and (b) of the Internal Revenue Code with respect to the transactions prohibited by section 4975(c)(1) of the Code.

(e) *Definitions.* For purposes of this section:

(1) "Look-through investment vehicle" means:

(i) An investment company described in section 3(a) of the Investment Company Act of 1940, or a series investment company described in section 18(f) of the 1940 Act or any of the segregated portfolios of such company;

(ii) A common or collective trust fund or a pooled investment fund maintained by a bank or similar institution, a deposit in a bank or similar institution, or a fixed rate investment contract of a bank or similar institution;

(iii) A pooled separate account or a fixed rate investment contract of an insurance company qualified to do business in a State; or

(iv) Any entity whose assets include plan assets by reason of a plan's investment in the entity;

(2) "Adequate consideration" has the meaning given it in section 3(18) of the Act and in any regulations under this title;

(3) An "affiliate" of a person includes the following:

(i) Any person directly or indirectly controlling, controlled by, or under common control with the person;

(ii) Any officer, director, partner, employee, an employee of an affiliated employer, relative (as defined in section 3(15) of ERISA), brother, sister, or spouse of a brother or sister, of the person; and

(iii) Any corporation or partnership of which the person is an officer, director or partner.

For purposes of this paragraph (e)(3), the term "control" means, with respect to a person other than an individual, the power to exercise a controlling influence over the management or policies of such person.

(4) A "designated investment alternative" is a specific investment identified by a plan fiduciary as an available investment alternative under the plan.

(f) *Examples.* The provisions of this section are illustrated by the following examples. Examples (5) through (11) assume that the participant has exercised independent control with respect to his individual account under an ERISA section 404(c) plan described in paragraph (b) and has not directed a transaction described in paragraph (d)(2)(ii).

(1) Plan A is an individual account plan described in section 3(34) of the Act. The plan states that a plan participant or beneficiary may direct the plan administrator to invest any portion of his individual account in a particular diversified equity fund managed by an entity which is not affiliated with the plan sponsor, or any other asset administratively feasible for the plan to hold. However, the plan provides that the plan administrator will not implement certain listed instructions for which plan fiduciaries would not be relieved of liability under section 404(c) (see paragraph (d)(2)(ii)). Plan participants and beneficiaries are permitted to give investment instructions during the first week of each month with respect to the equity fund and at any time with respect to other investments. The plan provides for the pass-through of voting, tender and similar rights incidental to the holding in the account of a participant or beneficiary of an ownership interest in the equity fund or any other investment alternative available under the plan. The plan administrator of plan A provides each participant and beneficiary with the information described in subparagraphs (*i*), (*ii*), (*iv*), (*v*), (*vi*) and (*vii*) of paragraph (b)(2)(i)(B)(*1*) upon their entry

into the plan, and provides updated information in the event of any material change in the information provided. Immediately following an investment by a participant or beneficiary in the equity fund, the plan administrator provides a copy of the most recent prospectus received from the fund to the investing participant or beneficiary. Immediately following any investment by a participant or beneficiary in any other investment alternative which is subject to the Securities Act of 1933, the plan administrator provides the participant or beneficiary with the most recent prospectus received from that investment alternative (see paragraph (b)(2)(i)(B)(*1*)(*viii*)). Finally, subsequent to any investment by a participant or beneficiary, the plan administrator forwards to the investing participant or beneficiary any materials provided to the plan relating to the exercise of voting, tender or similar rights attendant to ownership of an interest in such investment (see paragraph (b)(2)(i)(B)(*1*)(*ix*)). Upon request, the plan administrator provides each participant or beneficiary with copies of any prospectuses, financial statements and reports, and any other materials relating to the investment alternatives available under the plan which are received by the plan (see paragraph (b)(2)(i)(B)(*2*)(*ii*)). Also upon request, the plan administrator provides each participant and beneficiary with the other information required by paragraph (b)(2)(i)(B)(*2*) with respect to the equity fund, which is a designated investment alternative, including information concerning the latest available value of the participant's or beneficiary's interest in the equity fund (*see* paragraph (b)(2)(i)(B)(*2*)(*v*)). Plan A meets the requirements of paragraphs (b)(2)(i)(B)(*1*) and (*2*) of this section regarding the provision of investment information. Note: The regulation imposes no additional obligation on the administrator to furnish or make available materials relating to the companies in which the equity fund invests (e.g., prospectuses, proxies, etc.).

(2) Plan C is an individual account plan described in section 3(34) of the Act under which participants and beneficiaries may choose among three investment alternatives which otherwise meet the requirements of paragraph (b) of this section. The plan permits investment instruction with respect to each investment alternative only on the first 10 days of each calendar quarter, i.e. January 1-10, April 1-10, July 1-10 and October 1-10. Plan C satisfies the condition of paragraph (b)(2)(ii)(C)(*1*) that instruction be permitted not less frequently than once within any three month period, since there is not any three month period during which control could not be exercised.

(3) Assume the same facts as in paragraph (f)(2), except that investment instruction may only be given on January 1, April 4, July 1 and October 1. Plan C is not an ERISA section 404(c) plan because it does not satisfy the condition of paragraph (b)(2)(ii)(C)(*1*) that instruction be permitted not less frequently than once within any three month period. Under these facts, there is a three month period, e.g., January 2 through April 1, during which control could not be exercised by participants and beneficiaries.

(4) Plan D is an individual account plan described in section 3(34) of the Act under which participants and beneficiaries may choose among three diversified investment alternatives which constitute a broad range of investment alternatives. The plan also permits investment instruction with respect to an employer securities alternative but provides that a participant or beneficiary can invest no more than 25% of his account balance in this alternative. This restriction does not affect the availability of relief under section 404(c) inasmuch as it does not relate to the three diversified investment alternatives and, therefore, does not cause the plan to fail to provide an opportunity to choose from a broad range of investment alternatives.

(5) A participant, P, independently exercises control over assets in his individual account plan by directing a plan fiduciary, F, to invest 100% of his account balance in a single stock. P is not a fiduciary with respect to the plan by reason of his exercise of control and F will not be liable for any losses that necessarily result from P's investment instruction.

(6) Assume the same facts as in paragraph (f)(5), except that P directs F to purchase the stock from B, who is a party in interest with respect to the plan. Neither P nor F has engaged in a transaction prohibited under section 406 of the Act: P because he is not a fiduciary with respect to the plan by reason of his exercise of control and F because he is not liable for any breach of part 4 of Title I that is the direct and necessary consequence of P's exercise of control. However,

a prohibited transaction under section 4975(c) of the Internal Revenue Code may have occurred, and, in the absence of an exemption, tax liability may be imposed pursuant to sections 4975(a) and (b) of the Code.

(7) Assume the same facts as in paragraph (f)(5), except that P does not specify that the stock be purchased from B, and F chooses to purchase the stock from B. In the absence of an exemption, F has engaged in a prohibited transaction described in 406(a) of ERISA because the decision to purchase the stock from B is not a direct or necessary result of P's exercise of control.

(8) Pursuant to the terms of the plan, plan fiduciary F designates three reputable investment managers whom participants may appoint to manage assets in their individual accounts. Participant P selects M, one of the designated managers, to manage the assets in his account. M prudently manages P's account for 6 months after which he incurs losses in managing the account through his imprudence. M has engaged in a breach of fiduciary duty because M's imprudent management of P's account is not a direct or necessary result of P's exercise of control (the choice of M as manager). F has no fiduciary liability for M's imprudence because he has no affirmative duty to advise P (see paragraph (c)(4)) and because F is relieved of co-fiduciary liability by reason of section 404(c)(2) (see paragraph (d)(2)(iii)). F does have a duty to monitor M's performance to determine the suitability of continuing M as an investment manager, however, and M's imprudence would be a factor which F must consider in periodically reevaluating its decision to designate M.

(9) Participant P instructs plan fiduciary F to appoint G as his investment manager pursuant to the terms of the plan which provide P total discretion in choosing an investment manager. Through G's imprudence, G incurs losses in managing P's account. G has engaged in a breach of fiduciary duty because G's imprudent management of P's account is not a direct or necessary result of P's exercise of control (the choice of G as manager). Plan fiduciary F has no fiduciary liability for G's imprudence because F has no obligation to advise P (see paragraph (c)(4)) and because F is relieved of co-fiduciary liability for G's actions by reason of section 404(c)(2) (see paragraph (d)(2)(iii)). In addition, F also has no duty to determine the suitability of G as an investment manager because the plan does not designate G as an investment manager.

(10) Participant P directs a plan fiduciary, F, a bank, to invest all of the assets in his individual account in a collective trust fund managed by F that is designed to be invested solely in a diversified portfolio of common stocks. Due to economic conditions, the value of the common stocks in the bank collective trust fund declines while the value of publicly-offered fixed income obligations remains relatively stable. F is not liable for any losses incurred by P solely because his individual account was not diversified to include fixed income obligations. Such losses are the direct result of P's exercise of control; moreover, under paragraph (c)(4) of this section F has no obligation to advise P regarding his investment decisions.

(11) Assume the same facts as in paragraph (f)(10) except that F, in managing the collective trust fund, invests the assets of the fund solely in a few highly speculative stocks. F is liable for losses resulting from its imprudent investment in the speculative stocks and for its failure to diversify the assets of the account. This conduct involves a separate breach of F's fiduciary duty that is not a direct or necessary result of P's exercise of control (see paragraph (d)(2)(iii)).

(g) *Effective date.* (1) *In general.* Except as provided in paragraph (g)(2), this section is effective with respect to transactions occurring on or after the first day of the second plan year beginning on or after October 13, 1992.

(2) This section is effective with respect to transactions occurring under a plan maintained pursuant to one or more collective bargaining agreements between employee representatives and one or more employers ratified before October 13, 1992 after the later of the date determined under paragraph (g)(1) or the date on which the last collective bargaining agreement terminates. For purposes of this paragraph (g)(2), any extension or renegotiation of a collective bargaining agreement which is ratified on or after October 13, 1992 is to be disregarded in determining the date on which the agreement terminates.

(3) Transactions occurring before the date determined under paragraph (g)(1) or (2) of this section, as applicable, are governed by section 404(c) of the Act without regard to the regulation.

[¶ 14,746]

§ 2509.94-1 **Interpretive Bulletin relating to the fiduciary standard under ERISA in considering economically targeted investments.** This Interpretive Bulletin sets forth the Department of Labor's interpretation of section 403 and 404 of the Employee Retirement Income Security Act of 1974 (ERISA), as applied to employee benefit plan investments in "economically targeted investments" (ETIs). Sections 403 and 404, in part, require that a fiduciary of a plan act prudently, and to diversify plan investments so as to minimize the risk of large losses, unless under the circumstances it is clearly prudent not to do so. In addition, these sections require that a fiduciary act solely in the interest of the plan's participants and beneficiaries and for the exclusive purpose of providing benefits to their participants and beneficiaries. The Department has construed the requirements that a fiduciary act solely in the interest of, and for the exclusive purpose of providing benefits to, participants and beneficiaries as prohibiting a fiduciary from subordinating the interests of participants and beneficiaries in their retirement income to unrelated objectives.

With regard to investing plan assets, the Department has issued a regulation, at 29 C.F.R. 2550.404a-1, interpreting the prudence requirements of ERISA as they apply to the investment duties of fiduciaries of employee benefit plans. The regulation provides that the prudence requirements of section 404(a)(1)(B) are satisfied if (1) the fiduciary making an investment or engaging in an investment course of action has given appropriate consideration to those facts and circumstances that, given the scope of the fiduciary's investment duties, the fiduciary knows or should know are relevant, and (2) the fiduciary acts accordingly. This includes giving appropriate consideration to the role that the investment or investment course of action plays (in terms of such factors as diversification, liquidity and risk/return characteristics) with respect to that portion of the plan's investment portfolio within the scope of the fiduciary's responsibility.

Other facts and circumstances relevant to an investment or investment course of action would, in the view of the Department, include consideration of the expected return on alternative investments with similar risks available to the plan. It follows that, because every investment necessarily causes a plan to forgo other investment opportunities, an investment will not be prudent if it would be expected to provide a plan with a lower rate of return than available alternative investments with commensurate degrees of risk or is riskier than alternative available investments with commensurate rates of return.

The fiduciary standards applicable to ETIs—that is, investments selected for the economic benefits they confer on others apart from their investment return to the employee benefit plan—are no different than the standards applicable to plan investments generally. Therefore, if the above requirements are met, the selection of an ETI, or the engaging in an investment course of action intended to result in the selection of ETIs, will not violate section 404(a)(1)(A) and (B) and the exclusive purpose requirements of section 403.

Signed at Washington, DC, this 17th day of June 1994.

[Added by FR Doc. 94-15162, filed with the Federal Register on June 22, 1994, and published in the Federal Register of June 23, 1994 (59 FR 32606).]

[¶ 14,746A]

§ 2509.94-2 **Interpretive Bulletin relating to written statements of investment policy, including proxy voting policy or guidelines.** This interpretive bulletin sets forth the Department of Labor's (the Department) interpretation of sections 402, 403 and 404 of the Employee Retirement Income Security Act of 1974 (ERISA) as those sections apply to voting of proxies on securities held in employee benefit plan investment portfolios and the maintenance of and compliance with statements of investment policy, including proxy voting policy. In addition, this interpretive bulletin provides guidance on the appropriateness under ERISA of active monitoring of corporate management by plan fiduciaries.

(1) Proxy Voting

The fiduciary act of managing plan assets that are shares of corporate stock includes the voting of proxies appurtenant to those shares of stock. As a result, the responsibility for voting proxies lies exclusively with the plan trustee except to the extent that either (1) the trustee is subject to the directions of a named fiduciary pursuant to ERISA § 403(a)(1); or (2) the power to manage, acquire or dispose of the relevant assets has been delegated by a named fiduciary to one or more investment managers pursuant to ERISA § 403(a)(2). Where the authority to manage plan assets has been delegated to an investment manager pursuant to § 403(a)(2), no person other than the investment manager has authority to vote proxies appurtenant to such plan assets except to the extent that the named fiduciary has reserved to itself (or to another named fiduciary so authorized by the plan document) the right to direct a plan trustee regarding the voting of proxies. In this regard, a named fiduciary, in delegating investment management authority to an investment manager, could reserve to itself the right to direct a trustee with respect to the voting of all proxies or reserve to itself the right to direct a trustee as to the voting of only those proxies relating to specified assets or issues.

If the plan document or investment management agreement provides that the investment manager is not required to vote proxies, but does not expressly preclude the investment manager from voting proxies, the investment manager would have exclusive responsibility for voting proxies. Moreover, an investment manager would not be relieved of its own fiduciary responsibilities by following directions of some other person regarding the voting of proxies, or by delegating such responsibility to another person. If, however, the plan document or the investment management contract expressly precludes the investment manager from voting proxies, the responsibility for voting proxies would lie exclusively with the trustee. The trustee, however, consistent with the requirements of ERISA § 403(a)(1), may be subject to the directions of a named fiduciary if the plan so provides.

The fiduciary duties described at ERISA § 404(a)(1)(A) and (B), require that, in voting proxies, the responsible fiduciary consider those factors that may affect the value of the plan's investment and not subordinate the interests of the participants and beneficiaries in their retirement income to unrelated objectives. These duties also require that the named fiduciary appointing an investment manager periodically monitor the activities of the investment manager with respect to the management of plan assets, including decisions made and actions taken by the investment manager with regard to proxy voting decisions. The named fiduciary must carry out this responsibility solely in the interest of the participants and beneficiaries and without regard to its relationship to the plan sponsor.

It is the view of the Department that compliance with the duty to monitor necessitates proper documentation of the activities that are subject to monitoring. Thus, the investment manager or other responsible fiduciary would be required to maintain accurate records as to proxy voting. Moreover, if the named fiduciary is to be able to carry out its responsibilities under ERISA § 404(a) in determining whether the investment manager is fulfilling its fiduciary obligations in investing plans assets in a manner that justifies the continuation of the management appointment, the proxy voting records must enable the named fiduciary to review not only the investment manager's voting procedure with respect to plan-owned stock, but also to review the actions taken in individual proxy voting situations.

The fiduciary obligations of prudence and loyalty to plan participants and beneficiaries require the responsible fiduciary to vote proxies on issues that may affect the value of the plan's investment. Although the same principles apply for proxies appurtenant to shares of foreign corporations, the Department recognizes that in voting such proxies, plans may, in some cases, incur additional costs. Thus, a fiduciary should consider whether the plan's vote, either by itself or together with the votes of other shareholders, is expected to have an effect on the value of the plan's investment that will outweigh the cost of voting. Moreover, a fiduciary, in deciding whether to purchase shares of a foreign corporation, should consider whether the difficulty and expense in voting the shares is reflected in their market price.

(2) Statements of Investment Policy

The maintenance by an employee benefit plan of a statement of investment policy designed to further the purposes of the plan and its funding policy is consistent with the fiduciary obligations set forth in

ERISA § 404(a)(1)(A) and (B). Since the fiduciary act of managing plan assets that are shares of corporate stock includes the voting of proxies appurtenant to those shares of stock, a statement of proxy voting policy would be an important part of any comprehensive statement of investment policy. For purposes of this document, the term "statement of investment policy" means a written statement that provides the fiduciaries who are responsible for plan investments with guidelines or general instructions concerning various types or categories of investment management decisions, which may include proxy voting decisions. A statement of investment policy is distinguished from directions as to the purchase or sale of a specific investment at a specific time or as to voting specific plan proxies.

In plans where investment management responsibility is delegated to one or more investment managers appointed by the named fiduciary pursuant to ERISA § 402(c)(3), inherent in the authority to appoint an investment manager, the named fiduciary responsible for appointment of investment managers has the authority to condition the appointment on acceptance of a statement of investment policy. Thus, such a named fiduciary may expressly require, as a condition of the investment management agreement, that an investment manager comply with the terms of a statement of investment policy which sets forth guidelines concerning investments and investment courses of action which the investment manager is authorized or is not authorized to make. Such investment policy may include a policy or guidelines on the voting of proxies on shares of stock for which the investment manager is responsible. In the absence of such an express requirement to comply with an investment policy, the authority to manage the plan assets placed under the control of the investment manager would lie exclusively with the investment manager. Although a trustee may be subject to the directions of a named fiduciary pursuant to ERISA § 403(a)(1), an investment manager who has authority to make investment decisions, including proxy voting decisions, would never be relieved of its fiduciary responsibility if it followed directions as to specific investment decisions from the named fiduciary or any other person.

Statements of investment policy issued by a named fiduciary authorized to appoint investment managers would be part of the "documents and instruments governing the plan" within the meaning of ERISA § 404(a)(1)(D). An investment manager to whom such investment policy applies would be required to comply with such policy, pursuant to ERISA § 404(a)(1)(D) insofar as the policy directives or guidelines are consistent with titles I and IV of ERISA. Therefore, if, for example, compliance with the guidelines in a given instance would be imprudent, then the investment manager's failure to follow the guidelines would not violate ERISA § 404(a)(1)(D). Moreover, ERISA § 404(a)(1)(D) does not shield the investment manager from liability for imprudent actions taken in compliance with a statement of investment policy.

The plan document or trust agreement may expressly provide a statement of investment policy to guide the trustee or may authorize a named fiduciary to issue a statement of investment policy applicable to a trustee. Where a plan trustee is subject to an investment policy, the trustee's duty to comply with such investment policy would also be analyzed under ERISA § 404(a)(1)(D). Thus, the trustee would be required to comply with the statement of investment policy unless, for example, it would be imprudent to do so in a given instance.

Maintenance of a statement of investment policy by a named fiduciary does not relieve the named fiduciary of its obligations under ERISA § 404(a) with respect to the appointment and monitoring of an investment manager or trustee. In this regard, the named fiduciary appointing an investment manager must periodically monitor the investment manager's activities with respect to management of the plan assets. Moreover, compliance with ERISA § 404(a)(1)(B) would require maintenance of proper documentation of the activities of the investment manager and of the named fiduciary of the plan in monitoring the activities of the investment manager. In addition, in the view of the Department, a named fiduciary's determination of the terms of a statement of investment policy is an exercise of fiduciary responsibility and, as such, statements may need to take into account factors such as the plan's funding policy and its liquidity needs as well as issues of prudence, diversification and other fiduciary requirements of ERISA.

An investment manager of a pooled investment vehicle that holds assets of more than one employee benefit plan may be subject to a proxy voting policy of one plan that conflicts with the proxy voting policy of another plan. Compliance with ERISA § 404(a)(1)(D) would require such investment manager to reconcile, insofar as possible, the conflicting policies (assuming compliance with each policy would be consistent with ERISA § 404(a)(1)(D)) and, if necessary and to the extent permitted by applicable law, vote the relevant proxies to reflect such policies in proportion to each plan's interest in the pooled investment vehicle. If, however, the investment manager determines that compliance with conflicting voting policies would violate ERISA § 404(a)(1)(D) in a particular instance, for example, by being imprudent or not solely in the interest of plan participants, the investment manager would be required to ignore the voting policy that would violate ERISA § 404(a)(1)(D) in that instance. Such an investment manager may, however, require participating investors to accept the investment manager's own investment policy statement, including any statement of proxy voting policy, before they are allowed to invest. As with investment policies originating from named fiduciaries, a policy initiated by an investment manager and adopted by the participating plans would be regarded as an instrument governing the participating plans, and the investment manager's compliance with such a policy would be governed by ERISA § 404(a)(1)(D).

(3) Shareholder Activism

An investment policy that contemplates activities intended to monitor or influence the management of corporations in which the plan owns stock is consistent with a fiduciary's obligations under ERISA where the responsible fiduciary concludes that there is a reasonable expectation that such monitoring or communication with management, by the plan alone or together with other shareholders, is likely to enhance the value of the plan's investment in the corporation, after taking into account the costs involved. Such a reasonable expectation may exist in various circumstances, for example, where plan investments in corporate stock are held as long-term investments or where a plan may not be able to easily dispose such an investment. Active monitoring and communication activities would generally concern such issues as the independence and expertise of candidates for the corporation's board of directors and assuring that the board has sufficient information to carry out its responsibility to monitor management. Other issues may include such matters as consideration of the appropriateness of executive compensation, the corporation's policy regarding mergers and acquisitions, the extent of debt financing and capitalization, the nature of long-term business plans, the corporation's investment in training to develop its work force, other workplace practices and financial and non-financial measures of corporate performance. Active monitoring and communication may be carried out through a variety of methods including by means of correspondence and meetings with corporate management as well as by exercising the legal rights of a shareholder.

[Added by FR Doc. 94-18198, filed with the Federal Register on July 28, 1994, and published in the Federal Register on July 29, 1994 (59 FR 38860).]

[¶ 14,746AA]
§ 2509.94-3 **Interpretive Bulletin relating to in-kind contributions to employee benefit plans.**

(a) *General.* This bulletin sets forth the views of the Department of Labor (the Department) concerning in-kind contributions (*i.e.,* contributions of property other than cash) in satisfaction of an obligation to contribute to an employee benefit plan to which part 4 of Title I of the Employee Retirement Income Security Act of 1974 (ERISA) or a plan to which section 4975 of the Internal Revenue Code (the Code) applies. (For purposes of this document the term "plan" shall refer to either or both types of such entities as appropriate). Section 406(a)(1)(A) of ERISA provides that a fiduciary with respect to a plan shall not cause the plan to engage in a transaction if the fiduciary knows or should know that the transaction constitutes a direct or indirect sale or exchange of any property between a plan and a "party in interest" as defined in section 3(14) of ERISA. The Code imposes a two-tier excise tax under section 4975(c)(1)(A) an any direct or indirect sale or exchange of any property between a plan and a "disqualified person" as defined in section 4975(e)(2) of the Code. An employer or

employee organization that maintains a plan is included within the definitions of "party in interest" and "disqualified person."[1]

In *Commissioner of Internal Revenue v. Keystone Consolidated Industries, Inc.,*—U.S.—, 113 S. Ct. 2006 (1993), the Supreme Court held that an employer's contribution of unencumbered real property to a tax-qualified defined benefit pension plan was a sale or exchange prohibited under section 4975 of the Code where the stated fair market value of the property was credited against the employer's obligation to the defined benefit pension plan. The parties stipulated that the property was contributed to the plan free of encumbrances and the stated fair market value of the property was not challenged. 113 S. Ct. at 2009. In reaching its holding the Court construed section 4975(f)(3) of the Code (and therefore section 406(c) of ERISA), regarding transfers of encumbered property, not as a limitation but rather as extending the reach of section 4975(c)(1)(A) of the Code (and thus section 406(a)(1)(A) of ERISA) to include contributions of encumbered property that do not satisfy funding obligations. *Id.* at 2013. Accordingly, the Court concluded that the contribution of unencumbered property was prohibited under section 4975(c)(1)(A) of the Code (and thus section 406(a)(1)(A) of ERISA) as "at least both an indirect type of sale and a form of exchange, since the property is exchanged for diminution of the employer's funding obligation." 113 S. Ct. at 2012.

(b) *Defined benefit plans.* Consistent with the reasoning of the Supreme Court in *Keystone,* because an employer's or plan sponsor's in-kind contribution to a defined benefit pension plan is credited to the plan's funding standard account it would constitute a transfer to reduce an obligation of the sponsor or employer to the plan. Therefore, in the absence of an applicable exemption, such a contribution would be prohibited under section 406(a)(1)(A) of ERISA and section 4975(c)(1)(A) of the Code. Such an in-kind contribution would constitute a prohibited transaction even if the value of the contribution is in excess of the sponsor's or employer's funding obligation for the plan year in which the contribution is made and thus is not used to reduce the plan's accumulated funding deficiency for that plan year because the contribution would result in a credit against funding obligations which might arise in the future.

(c) *Defined contribution and welfare plans.* In the context of defined contribution pension plans and welfare plans, it is the view of the Department that an in-kind contribution to a plan that reduces an obligation of a plan sponsor or employer to make a contribution measured in terms of cash amounts would constitute a prohibited transaction under section 406(a)(1)(A) of ERISA (and section 4975(c)(1)(A) of the Code) unless a statutory or administrative exemption under section 408 of ERISA (or sections 4975(c)(2) or (d) of the Code) applies. For example, if a profit sharing plan required the employer to make annual contributions "in cash or in kind" equal to a given percentage of the employer's net profits for the year, an in-kind contribution used to reduce this obligation would constitute a prohibited transaction in the absence of an exemption because the amount of the contribution obligation is measured in terms of cash amounts (a percentage of profits) even though the terms of the plan purport to permit in-kind contributions.

Conversely, a transfer of unencumbered property to a welfare benefit plan that does not relieve the sponsor or employer of any present or future obligation to make a contribution that is measured in terms of cash amounts would not constitute a prohibited transaction under section 406(a)(1)(A) of ERISA or section 4975(c)(1)(A) of the Code. The same principles apply to defined contribution plans that are not subject to the minimum funding requirements of section 302 of ERISA or section 412 of the Code. For example, where a profit sharing or stock bonus plan, by its terms, is funded solely at the discretion of the sponsoring employer, and the employer is not otherwise obligated to make a contribution measured in terms of cash amounts, a contribution of unencumbered real property would not be a prohibited sale or exchange between the plan and the employer. If, however, the same employer had made an enforceable promise to make a contribution measured in terms of cash amounts to the plan, a subsequent contribu-

---

[1] Under Reorganization Plan No. 4 of 1978 (43 FR 47713, October 17, 1978), the authority of the Secretary of the Treasury to issue rulings under the prohibited transactions provisions of section 4975 of the Code has been transferred, with certain exceptions

not here relevant, to the Secretary of Labor. Except with respect to the types of plans covered, the prohibited transaction provisions of section 406 of ERISA generally parallel the prohibited transaction of provisions of section 4975 of the Code.

tion of unencumbered real property made to offset such an obligation would be a prohibited sale or exchange.

(d) *Fiduciary standards.* Independent of the application of the prohibited transaction provisions, fiduciaries of plans covered by part 4 of Title I of ERISA must determine that acceptance of an in-kind contribution is consistent with ERISA's general standards of fiduciary conduct. It is the view of the Department that acceptance of an in-kind contribution is a fiduciary act subject to section 404 of ERISA. In this regard, sections 406(a)(1)(A) and (B) of ERISA require that fiduciaries discharge their duties to a plan solely in the interests of the participants and beneficiaries, for the exclusive purpose of providing benefits and defraying reasonable administrative expenses, and with the care, skill, prudence, and diligence under the circumstances then prevailing that a prudent person acting in a like capacity and familiar with such matters would use in the conduct of an enterprise of a like character and with like aims. In addition, section 406(a)(1)(C) requires generally that fiduciaries diversify plan assets so as to minimize the risk of large losses. Accordingly, the fiduciaries of a plan must act "prudently," "solely in the interest" of the plan's participants and beneficiaries and with a view to the need to diversify plan assets when deciding whether to accept in-kind contributions. If accepting an in-kind contribution is not "prudent," not "solely in the interest" of the participants and beneficiaries of the plan, or would result in an improper lack of diversification of plan assets, the responsible fiduciaries of the plan would be liable for any losses resulting from such a breach of fiduciary responsibility, even if a contribution in kind does not constitute a prohibited transaction under section 406 of ERISA. In this regard, a fiduciary should consider any liabilities appurtenant to the in-kind contribution to which the plan would be exposed as a result of acceptance of the contribution.

[¶ 14,746B]

§ 2509.95-1 Interpretive Bulletin relating to the fiduciary standard under ERISA when selecting an annuity provider.

(a) *Scope.* This Interpretive Bulletin provides guidance concerning certain fiduciary standards under part 4 of title I of the Employee Retirement Income Security Act of 1974 (ERISA), 29 U.S.C. 1104-1114, applicable to the selection of annuity providers for the purpose of pension plan benefit distributions where the plan intends to transfer liability for benefits to the annuity provider.

(b) *In General.* Generally, when a pension plan purchases an annuity from an insurer as a distribution of benefits, it is intended that the plan's liability for such benefits is transferred to the annuity provider. The Department's regulation defining the term "participant covered under the plan" for certain purposes under title I of ERISA recognizes that such a transfer occurs [[Page 12330]] when the annuity is issued by an insurance company licensed to do business in a State. 29 CFR 2510.3-3(d)(2)(ii). Although the regulation does not define the term "participant" or "beneficiary" for purposes of standing to bring an action under ERISA Sec. 502(a), 29 U.S.C. 1132(a), it makes clear that the purpose of a benefit distribution annuity is to transfer the plan's liability with respect to the individual's benefits to the annuity provider.

Pursuant to ERISA section 404(a)(1), 29 U.S.C. 1104(a)(1), fiduciaries must discharge their duties with respect to the plan solely in the interest of the participants and beneficiaries. Section 404(a)(1)(A), 29 U.S.C. 1104(a)(1)(A), states that the fiduciary must act for the exclusive purpose of providing benefits to the participants and beneficiaries and defraying reasonable plan administration expenses. In addition, section 404(a)(1)(B), 29 U.S.C. 1104(a)(1)(B), requires a fiduciary to act with the care, skill, prudence and diligence under the prevailing circumstances that a prudent person acting in a like capacity and familiar with such matters would use.

(c) *Selection of Annuity Providers.* The selection of an annuity provider for purposes of a pension benefit distribution, whether upon separation or retirement of a participant or upon the termination of a plan, is a fiduciary decision governed by the provisions of part 4 of title I of ERISA. In discharging their obligations under section 404(a)(1), 29 U.S.C. 1104(a)(1), to act solely in the interest of participants and beneficiaries and for the exclusive purpose of providing benefits to the participants and beneficiaries as well as defraying reasonable expenses of administering the plan, fiduciaries choosing an annuity provider for

the purpose of making a benefit distribution must take steps calculated to obtain the safest annuity available, unless under the circumstances it would be in the interests of participants and beneficiaries to do otherwise. In addition, the fiduciary obligation of prudence, described at section 404(a)(1)(B), 29 U.S.C. 1104(a)(1)(B), requires, at a minimum, that plan fiduciaries conduct an objective, thorough and analytical search for the purpose of identifying and selecting providers from which to purchase annuities. In conducting such a search, a fiduciary must evaluate a number of factors relating to a potential annuity provider's claims paying ability and creditworthiness. Reliance solely on ratings provided by insurance rating services would not be sufficient to meet this requirement. In this regard, the types of factors a fiduciary should consider would include, among other things:

(1) the quality and diversification of the annuity provider's investment portfolio;

(2) the size of the insurer relative to the proposed contract;

(3) the level of the insurer's capital and surplus;

(4) the lines of business of the annuity provider and other indications of an insurer's exposure to liability;

(5) the structure of the annuity contract and guarantees supporting the annuities, such as the use of separate accounts;

(6) the availability of additional protection through state guaranty associations and the extent of their guarantees. Unless they possess the necessary expertise to evaluate such factors, fiduciaries would need to obtain the advice of a qualified, independent expert. A fiduciary may conclude, after conducting an appropriate search, that more than one annuity provider is able to offer the safest annuity available.

(d) *Costs and Other Considerations.* The Department recognizes that there are situations where it may be in the interest of the participants and beneficiaries to purchase other than the safest available annuity. Such situations may occur where the safest available annuity is only marginally safer, but disproportionately more expensive than competing annuities, and the participants and beneficiaries are likely to bear a significant portion of that increased cost. For example, where the participants in a terminating pension plan are likely to receive, in the form of increased benefits, a substantial share of the cost savings that would result from choosing a competing annuity, it may be in the interest of the participants to choose the competing annuity. It may also be in the interest of the participants and beneficiaries to choose a competing annuity of the annuity provider offering the safest available annuity is unable to demonstrate the ability to administer the payment of benefits to the participants and beneficiaries. The Department notes, however, that increased cost or other considerations could never justify putting the benefits of annuitized participants and beneficiaries at risk by purchasing an unsafe annuity.

In contrast to the above, a fiduciary's decision to purchase more risky, lower-priced annuities in order to ensure or maximize a reversion of excess assets that will be paid solely to the employer-sponsor in connection with the termination of an over-funded pension plan would violate the fiduciary's duties under ERISA to act solely in the interest of the plan participants and beneficiaries. In such circumstances, the interests of those participants and beneficiaries who will receive annuities lies in receiving the safest annuity available and other participants and beneficiaries have no countervailing interests. The fiduciary in such circumstances must make diligent efforts to assure that the safest available annuity is purchased.

Similarly, a fiduciary may not purchase a riskier annuity solely because there are insufficient assets in a defined benefit plan to purchase a safer annuity. The fiduciary may have to condition the purchase of annuities on additional employer contributions sufficient to purchase the safest available annuity.

(e) *Conflicts of Interest.* Special care should be taken in reversion situations where fiduciaries selecting the annuity provider have an interest in the sponsoring employer which might affect their judgment and therefore create the potential for a violation of ERISA Sec. 406(b)(1). As a practical matter, many fiduciaries have this conflict of interest and therefore will need to obtain and follow independent expert advice calculated to identify those insurers with the highest claims-paying ability willing to write the business.

[Added by FR Doc. 95-5321, filed with the Federal Register on March 3, 1995, and published in the Federal Register on March 6, 1995 (60 FR 12328).]

[¶ 14,746C]
§2509.96-1 Interpretive Bulletin relating to participant investment education.

(a) *Scope.* This interpretive bulletin sets forth the Department of Labor's interpretation of section 3(21)(A)(ii) of the Employee Retirement Income Security Act of 1974, as amended (ERISA), and 29 CFR 2510.3-21(c) as applied to the provision of investment-related educational information to participants and beneficiaries in participant-directed individual account pension plans (*i.e.*, pension plans that permit participants and beneficiaries to direct the investment of assets in their individual accounts, including plans that meet the requirements of the Department's regulations at 29 CFR 2550.404c-1).

(b) *General.* Fiduciaries of an employee benefit plan are charged with carrying out their duties prudently and solely in the interest of participants and beneficiaries of the plan, and are subject to personal liability to, among other things, make good any losses to the plan resulting from a breach of their fiduciary duties. ERISA sections 403, 404 and 409, 29 U.S.C. 1103, 1104, and 1109. Section 404(c) of ERISA provides a limited exception to these rules for a pension plan that permits a participant or beneficiary to exercise control over the assets in his or her individual account. The Department of Labor's regulation, at 29 CFR 2550.404c-1, describes the kinds of plans to which section 404(c) applies, the circumstances under which a participant or beneficiary will be considered to have exercised independent control over the assets in his or her account, and the consequences of a participant's or beneficiary's exercise of such control.[1]

With both an increase in the number of participant-directed individual account plans and the number of investment options available to participants and beneficiaries under such plans, there has been an increasing recognition of the importance of providing participants and beneficiaries, whose investment decisions will directly affect their income at retirement, with information designed to assist them in making investment and retirement-related decisions appropriate to their particular situations. Concerns have been raised, however, that the provision of such information may in some situations be Viewed as rendering "investment advice for a fee or other compensation," within the meaning of ERISA section 3(21)(A)(ii), thereby giving rise to fiduciary status and potential liability under ERISA for investment decisions of plan participants and beneficiaries.

In response to these concerns, the Department of Labor is clarifying herein the applicability of ERISA section 3(21)(A)(ii) and 29 CFR 2510.3-21(c) to the provision of investment-related educational information to participants and beneficiaries in participant directed individual account plans.[2] In providing this clarification, the Department does not address the "fee or other compensation, direct or indirect," which is a necessary element of fiduciary status under ERISA section 3(21)(A)(ii).[3]

(c) *Investment Advice.* Under ERISA section 3(21)(A)(ii), a person is considered a fiduciary with respect to an employee benefit plan to the extent that person "renders investment advice for a fee or other compensation, direct or indirect, with respect to any moneys or other property of such plan, or has any authority to do so. . . ." The Department issued a regulation, at 29 CFR 2510.3-21(c), describing the circumstances under which a person will be considered to be render-

ing "investment advice" within the meaning of section 3(21)(A)(ii). Because section 3(21)(A)(ii) applies to advice with respect to "any moneys or other property" of a plan and 29 CFR 2510.3-21(c) is intended to clarify the application of that section, it is the view of the Department of Labor that the criteria set forth in the regulation apply to determine whether a person renders "investment advice" to a pension plan participant or beneficiary who is permitted to direct the investment of assets in his or her individual account.

Applying 29 CFR 2510.3-21(c) in the context of providing investment-related information to participants and beneficiaries of participant-directed individual account pension plans, a person will be considered to be rendering "investment advice," within the meaning of ERISA section 3(21)(A)(ii), to a participant or beneficiary only if: (i) the person renders advice to the participant or beneficiary as to the value of securities or other property, or makes recommendations as to the advisability of investing in, purchasing, or selling securities or other property (2510.3-21(c)(1)(i)); and (ii) the person, either directly or indirectly, (A) has discretionary authority or control with respect to purchasing or selling securities or other property for the participant or beneficiary (2510.3-21(c)(1)(ii)(A)), or (B) renders the advice on a regular basis to the participant or beneficiary, pursuant to a mutual agreement, arrangement or understanding (written or otherwise) with the participant or beneficiary that the advice will serve as a primary basis for the participant's or beneficiary's investment decisions with respect to plan assets and that such person will render individualized advice based on the particular needs of the participant or beneficiary (2510.3-21(c)(1)(ii)(B)).[4]

Whether the provision of particular investment-related information or materials to a participant or beneficiary constitutes the rendering of "investment advice," within the meaning of 29 CFR 2510.3-21(c)(1), generally can be determined only by reference to the facts and circumstances of the particular case with respect to the individual plan participant or beneficiary. To facilitate such determinations, however, the Department of Labor has identified, in paragraph (d), below, examples of investment-related information and materials which if provided to plan participants and beneficiaries would not, in the view of the Department, result in the rendering of "investment advice" under ERISA section 3(21)(A)(ii) and 29 CFR 2510.3-21(c).

(d) *Investment Education.* For purposes of ERISA section 3(21)(A)(ii) and 29 CFR 2510.3-21(c), the Department of Labor has determined that the furnishing of the following categories of information and materials to a participant or beneficiary in a participant-directed individual account pension plan will not constitute the rendering of "investment advice," irrespective of who provides the information (*e.g.*, plan sponsor, fiduciary or service provider), the frequency with which the information is shared, the form in which the information and materials are provided (*e.g.*, on an individual or group basis, in writing or orally, or via video or computer software), or whether an identified category of information and materials is furnished alone or in combination with other identified categories of information and materials:

(1) *Plan Information.* (i) Information and materials that inform a participant or beneficiary about the benefits of plan participation, the benefits of increasing plan contributions, the impact of preretirement withdrawals on retirement income, the terms of the plan, or the operation of the plan; or

(ii) information such as that described in 29 CFR 2550.404c-1(b)(2)(i) on investment alternatives under the plan (*e.g.*, descriptions of investment objectives and philosophies, risk and return characteristics, historical return information, or related prospectuses).[5]

---

[1] The section 404(c) regulation conditions relief from fiduciary liability on, among other things, the participant or beneficiary being provided or having the opportunity to obtain sufficient investment information regarding the investment alternatives available under the plan in order to make informed investment decisions. Compliance with this condition, however, does not require that participants and beneficiaries be offered or provided either investment advice or investment education, *e.g.* regarding general investment principles and strategies, to assist them in making investment decisions. 29 CFR 2550.404c-1(c)(4).

[2] Issues relating to the circumstances under which information provided to participants and beneficiaries may affect a participant's or beneficiary's ability to exercise independent control over the assets in his or her account for purposes of relief from fiduciary liability under ERISA section 404(c) are beyond the scope of this interpretive bulletin. Accordingly, no inferences should be drawn regarding such issues. See 29 CFR 2550.404c-1(c)(2). It is the view of the Department, however, that the provision of investment-related information

and material to participants and beneficiaries in accordance with paragraph (d) of this interpretive bulletin will not, in and of itself, affect the availability of relief under section 404(c).

[3] The Department has expressed the view that, for purposes of section 3(21)(A)(ii), such fees or other compensation need not come from the plan and should be deemed to include all fees or other compensation incident to the transaction in which the investment advice has been or will be rendered. See A.O. 83-60A (Nov. 21, 1983); *Reich* v. *McManus*, 883 F. Supp. 1144 (N.D. *Ill.* 1995).

[4] This IB does not address the application of 29 CFR 2510.3-21(c) to communications with fiduciaries of participant-directed individual account pension plans.

[5] Descriptions of investment alternatives under the plan may include information relating to the generic asset class (*e.g.*, equities, bonds, or cash) of the investment alternatives. 29 CFR 2550.404c-1(b)(2)(i)(B)(*1*)(*ii*).

The information and materials described above relate to the plan and plan participation, without reference to the appropriateness of any individual investment option for a particular participant or beneficiary under the plan. The information, therefore, does not contain either "advice" or "recommendations" within the meaning of 29 CFR 2510.3-21(c)(1)(i). Accordingly, the furnishing of such information would not constitute the rendering of "investment advice" for purposes of section 3(21)(A)(ii) of ERISA.

(2) *General Financial and Investment Information.* Information and materials that inform a participant or beneficiary about: (i) general financial and investment concepts, such as risk and return, diversification, dollar cost averaging, compounded return, and tax deferred investment; (ii) historic differences in rates of return between different asset classes (*e.g.*, equities, bonds, or cash) based on standard market indices; (iii) effects of inflation; (iv) estimating future retirement income needs; (v) determining investment time horizons; and (vi) assessing risk tolerance.

The information and materials described above are general financial and investment information that have no direct relationship to investment alternatives available to participants and beneficiaries under a plan or to individual participants or beneficiaries. The furnishing of such information, therefore, would not constitute rendering "advice" or making "recommendations" to a participant or beneficiary within the meaning of 29 CFR 2510.3-21(c)(1)(i). Accordingly, the furnishing of such information would not constitute the rendering of "investment advice" for purposes of section 3(21)(A)(ii) of ERISA.

(3) *Asset Allocation Models.* Information and materials (*e.g.*, pie charts, graphs, or case studies) that provide a participant or beneficiary with models, available to all plan participants and beneficiaries, of asset allocation portfolios of hypothetical individuals with different time horizons and risk profiles, where: (i) such models are based on generally accepted investment theories that take into account the historic returns of different asset classes (*e.g.*, equities, bonds, or cash) over defined periods of time; (ii) all material facts and assumptions on which such models are based (*e.g.*, retirement ages, life expectancies, income levels, financial resources, replacement income ratios, inflation rates, and rates of return) accompany the models; (iii) to the extent that an asset allocation model identifies any specific investment alternative available under the plan, the model is accompanied by a statement indicating that other investment alternatives having similar risk and return characteristics may be available under the plan and identifying where information on those investment alternatives may be obtained; and (iv) the asset allocation models are accompanied by a statement indicating that, in applying particular asset allocation models to their individual situations, participants or beneficiaries should consider their other assets, income, and investments (*e.g.*, equity in a home, IRA investments, savings accounts, and interests in other qualified and non-qualified plans) in addition to their interests in the plan.

Because the information and materials described above would enable a participant or beneficiary to assess the relevance of an asset allocation model to his or her individual situation, the furnishing of such information would not constitute a "recommendation" within the meaning of 29 CFR 2510.3-21(c)(1)(i) and, accordingly, would not constitute "investment advice" for purposes of section 3(21)(A)(ii) of ERISA. This result would not, in the view of the Department, be affected by the fact that a plan offers only one investment alternative in a particular asset class identified in an asset allocation model.

(4) *Interactive Investment Materials.* Questionnaires, worksheets, software, and similar materials which provide a participant or beneficiary the means to estimate future retirement income needs and assess the impact of different asset allocations on retirement income, where: (i) such materials are based on generally accepted investment theories that take into account the historic returns of different asset classes (*e.g.*, equities, bonds, or cash) over defined periods of time; (ii) there is an objective correlation between the asset allocations generated by the materials and the information and data supplied by the participant or beneficiary; (iii) all material facts and assumptions (*e.g.*, retirement ages, life expectancies, income levels, financial resources,

replacement income ratios, inflation rates, and rates of return) which may affect a participant's or beneficiary's assessment of the different asset allocations accompany the materials or are specified by the participant or beneficiary; (iv) to the extent that an asset allocation generated by the materials identifies any specific investment alternative available under the plan, the asset allocation is accompanied by a statement indicating that other investment alternatives having similar risk and return characteristics may be available under the plan and identifying where information on those investment alternatives may be obtained; and (v) the materials either take into account or are accompanied by a statement indicating that, in applying particular asset allocations to their individual situations, participants or beneficiaries should consider their other assets, income, and investments (*e.g.*, equity in a home, IRA investments, savings accounts, and interests in other qualified and non-qualified plans) in addition to their interests in the plan.

The information provided through the use of the above-described materials enables participants and beneficiaries independently to design and assess multiple asset allocation models, but otherwise these materials do not differ from asset allocation models based on hypothetical assumptions. Such information would not constitute a "recommendation" within the meaning of 29 CFR 2510.3-21(c)(1)(i) and, accordingly, would not constitute "investment advice" for purposes of section 3(21)(A)(ii) of ERISA.

The Department notes that the information and materials described in subparagraphs (1)-(4) above merely represent examples of the type of information and materials which may be furnished to participants and beneficiaries without such information and materials constituting "investment advice." In this regard, the Department recognizes that there may be many other examples of information, materials, and educational services which, if furnished to participants and beneficiaries, would not constitute "investment advice." Accordingly, no inferences should be drawn from subparagraphs (1)-(4), above, with respect to whether the furnishing of any information, materials or educational services not described therein may constitute "investment advice." Determinations as to whether the provision of any information, materials or educational services not described herein constitutes the rendering of "investment advice" must be made by reference to the criteria set forth in 29 CFR 2510.3-21(c)(1).

(e) *Selection and Monitoring of Educators and Advisors.* As with any designation of a service provider to a plan, the designation of a person(s) to provide investment educational services or investment advice to plan participants and beneficiaries is an exercise of discretionary authority or control with respect to management of the plan; therefore, persons making the designation must act prudently and solely in the interest of the plan participants and beneficiaries, both in making the designation(s) and in continuing such designation(s). See ERISA sections 3(21)(A)(i) and 404(a), 29 U.S.C. 1002(21)(A)(i) and 1104(a). In addition, the designation of an investment advisor to serve as a fiduciary may give rise to co-fiduciary liability if the person making and continuing such designation in doing so fails to act prudently and solely in the interest of plan participants and beneficiaries; or knowingly participates in, conceals or fails to make reasonable efforts to correct a known breach by the investment advisor. See ERISA section 405(a), 29 U.S.C. 1105(a). The Department notes, however, that, in the context of an ERISA section 404(c) plan, neither the designation of a person to provide education nor the designation of a fiduciary to provide investment advice to participants and beneficiaries would, in itself, give rise to fiduciary liability for loss, or with respect to any breach of part 4 of title I of ERISA, that is the direct and necessary result of a participant's or beneficiary's exercise of independent control. 29 CFR 2550.404c-1(d). The Department also notes that a plan sponsor or fiduciary would have no fiduciary responsibility or liability with respect to the actions of a third party selected by a participant or beneficiary to provide education or investment advice where the plan sponsor or fiduciary neither selects nor endorses the educator or advisor, nor otherwise makes arrangements with the educator or advisor to provide such services.

[Added by FR Doc. 96-14093, filed with the Federal Register on June 10, 1996, and published in the Federal Register on June 11, 1996 (61 FR 29586).]

[¶ 14,750]
LIABILITY FOR BREACH BY CO-FIDUCIARY

Act Sec. 405. (a) In addition to any liability which he may have under any other provision of this part, a fiduciary with respect to a plan shall be liable for a breach of fiduciary responsibility of another fiduciary with respect to the same plan in the following circumstances:

(1) if he participates knowingly in, or knowingly undertakes to conceal, an act or omission of such other fiduciary, knowing such act or omission is a breach;

(2) if, by his failure to comply with section 404(a)(1) in the administration of his specific responsibilities which give rise to his status as a fiduciary, he has enabled such other fiduciary to commit a breach; or

(3) if he has knowledge of a breach by such other fiduciary, unless he makes reasonable efforts under the circumstances to remedy the breach.

Act Sec. 405. (b)(1) Except as otherwise provided in subsection (d) and in section 403(a)(1) and (2), if the assets of a plan are held by two or more trustees—

(A) each shall use reasonable care to prevent a co-trustee from committing a breach; and

(B) they shall jointly manage and control the assets of the plan, except that nothing in this subparagraph (B) shall preclude any agreement, authorized by the trust instrument, allocating specific responsibilities, obligations, or duties among trustees, in which event a trustee to whom certain responsibilities, obligations, or duties have not been allocated shall not be liable by reason of this subparagraph (B) either individually or as a trustee for any loss resulting to the plan arising from the acts or omissions on the part of another trustee to whom such responsibilities, obligations, or duties have been allocated.

(2) Nothing in this subsection shall limit any liability that a fiduciary may have under subsection (a) or any other provision of this part.

(3)(A) In the case of a plan the assets of which are held in more than one trust, a trustee shall not be liable under paragraph (1) except with respect to an act or omission of a trustee of a trust of which he is a trustee.

(B) No trustee shall be liable under this subsection for following instructions referred to in section 403(a)(1).

Act Sec. 405. (c)(1) The instrument under which a plan is maintained may expressly provide for procedures (A) for allocating fiduciary responsibilities (other than trustee responsibilities) among named fiduciaries, and (B) for named fiduciaries to designate persons other than named fiduciaries to carry out fiduciary responsibilities (other than trustee responsibilities) under the plan.

(2) If a plan expressly provides for a procedure described in paragraph (1), and pursuant to such procedure any fiduciary responsibility of a named fiduciary is allocated to any person, or a person is designated to carry out any such responsibility, then such named fiduciary shall not be liable for an act or omission of such person in carrying out such responsibility except to the extent that—

(A) the named fiduciary violated section 404(a)(1)—

(i) with respect to such allocation or designation,

(ii) with respect to the establishment or implementation of the procedure under paragraph (1), or

(iii) in continuing the allocation or designation; or

(B) the named fiduciary would otherwise be liable in accordance with subsection (a).

(3) For purposes of this subsection, the term "trustee responsibility" means any responsibility provided in the plan's trust instrument (if any) to manage or control the assets of the plan, other than a power under the trust instrument of a named fiduciary to appoint an investment manager in accordance with section 402(c)(3).

Act Sec. 405. (d)(1) If an investment manager or managers have been appointed under section 402(c)(3), then, notwithstanding subsections (a)(2) and (3) and subsection (b), no trustee shall be liable for the acts or omissions of such investment manager or managers, or be under an obligation to invest or otherwise manage any asset of the plan which is subject to the management of such investment manager.

(2) Nothing in this subsection shall relieve any trustee of any liability under this part for any act of such trustee.

[¶ 14,760]
PROHIBITED TRANSACTIONS

Act Sec. 406. (a) Except as provided in section 408:

(1) A fiduciary with respect to a plan shall not cause the plan to engage in a transaction, if he knows or should know that such transaction constitutes a direct or indirect—

(A) sale or exchange, or leasing, of any property between the plan and a party in interest;

(B) lending of money or other extension of credit between the plan and a party in interest;

(C) furnishing of goods, services, or facilities between the plan and a party in interest;

(D) transfer to, or use by or for the benefit of, a party in interest, of any assets of the plan; or

(E) acquisition, on behalf of the plan, of any employer security or employer real property in violation of section 407(a).

(2) No fiduciary who has authority or discretion to control or manage the assets of a plan shall permit the plan to hold any employer security or employer real property if he knows or should know that holding such security or real property violates section 407(a).

Act Sec. 406. (b) A fiduciary with respect to a plan shall not—

(1) deal with the assets of the plan in his own interest or for his own account,

(2) in his individual or in any other capacity act in any transaction involving the plan on behalf of a party (or represent a party) whose interests are adverse to the interests of the plan or the interests of its participants or beneficiaries, or

(3) receive any consideration for his own personal account from any party dealing with such plan in connection with a transaction involving the assets of the plan.

Act Sec. 406. (c) A transfer of real or personal property by a party in interest to a plan shall be treated as a sale or exchange if the property is subject to a mortgage or similar lien which the plan assumes or if it is subject to a mortgage or similar lien which a party-in-interest placed on the property within the 10-year period ending on the date of the transfer.

[¶ 14,770]
10 PERCENT LIMITATION WITH RESPECT TO ACQUISITION AND HOLDING OF EMPLOYER SECURITIES AND EMPLOYER REAL PROPERTY BY CERTAIN PLANS

Act Sec. 407. (a) Except as otherwise provided in this section and section 414:

(1) A plan may not acquire or hold—

(A) any employer security which is not a qualifying employer security, or

(B) any employer real property which is not qualifying employer real property.

(2) A plan may not acquire any qualifying employer security or qualifying employer real property, if immediately after such acquisition the aggregate fair market value of employer securities and employer real property held by the plan exceeds 10 percent of the fair market value of the assets of the plan.

(3)(A) After December 31, 1984, a plan may not hold any qualifying employer securities or qualifying employer real property (or both) to the extent that the aggregate fair market value of such securities and property determined on December 31, 1984, exceeds 10 percent of the greater of—

    (i) the fair market value of the assets of the plan, determined on December 31, 1984, or

    (ii) the fair market value of the assets of the plan determined on January 1, 1975.

(B) Subparagraph (A) of this paragraph shall not apply to any plan which on any date after December 31, 1974, and before January 1, 1985, did not hold employer securities or employer real property (or both) the aggregate fair market value of which determined on such date exceeded 10 percent of the greater of—

    (i) the fair market value of the assets of the plan, determined on such date, or

    (ii) the fair market value of the assets of the plan determined on January 1, 1975.

(4)(A) After December 31, 1979, a plan may not hold any employer securities or employer real property in excess of the amount specified in regulations under subparagraph (B). This subparagraph shall not apply to a plan after the earliest date after December 31, 1974, on which it complies with such regulations.

(B) Not later than December 31, 1976, the Secretary shall prescribe regulations which shall have the effect of requiring that a plan divest itself of 50 percent of the holdings of employer securities and employer real property which the plan would be required to divest before January 1, 1985, under paragraph (2) or subsection (c) (whichever is applicable).

Act Sec. 407. (b)(1) Subsection (a) of this section shall not apply to any acquisition or holding of qualifying employer securities or qualifying employer real property by an eligible individual account plan.

(2)(A) If this paragraph applies to an eligible individual account plan, the portion of such plan which consists of applicable elective deferrals (and earnings allocable thereto) shall be treated as a separate plan—

    (i) which is not an eligible individual account plan, and

    (ii) to which the requirements of this section apply.

(B)(i) This paragraph shall apply to any eligible individual account plan if any portion of the plan's applicable elective deferrals (or earnings allocable thereto) are required to be invested in qualifying employer securities or qualifying employer real property or both—

    (I) pursuant to the terms of the plan, or

    (II) at the direction of a person other than the participant on whose behalf such elective deferrals are made to the plan (or a beneficiary).

    (ii) This paragraph shall not apply to an individual account plan for a plan year if, on the last day of the preceding plan year, the fair market value of the assets of all individual account plans maintained by the employer equals not more than 10 percent of the fair market value of the assets of all pension plans (other than multiemployer plans) maintained by the employer.

    (iii) This paragraph shall not apply to an individual account plan that is an employee stock ownership plan as defined in section 4975(e)(7) of the Internal Revenue Code of 1986.

    (iv) This paragraph shall not apply to an individual account plan if, pursuant to the terms of the plan, the portion of any employee's applicable elective deferrals which is required to be invested in qualifying employer securities and qualifying employer real property for any year may not exceed 1 percent of the employee's compensation which is taken into account under the plan in determining the maximum amount of the employee's applicable elective deferrals for such year.

(C) For purposes of this paragraph, the term "applicable elective deferral" means any elective deferral (as defined in section 402(g)(3)(A) of the Internal Revenue Code of 1986) which is made pursuant to a qualified cash or deferred arrangement as defined in section 401(k) of the Internal Revenue Code of 1986.

(3) CROSS REFERENCES.—

(A) For exemption from diversification requirements for holding of qualifying employer securities and qualifying employer real property by eligible individual account plans, see section 404(a)(2).

(B) For exemption from prohibited transactions for certain acquisitions of qualifying employer securities and qualifying employer real property which are not in violation of 10 percent limitation, see section 408(e).

(C) For transitional rules respecting securities or real property subject to binding contracts in effect on June 30, 1974, see section 414(c).

Act Sec. 407. (c)(1) A plan which makes the election under paragraph (3) shall be treated as satisfying the requirement of subsection (a)(3) if and only if employer securities held on any date after December 31, 1974 and before January 1, 1985 have a fair market value, determined as of December 31, 1974, not in excess of 10 percent of the lesser of—

(A) the fair market value of the assets of the plan determined on such date (disregarding any portion of the fair market value of employer securities which is attributable to appreciation of such securities after December 31, 1974) but not less than the fair market value of plan assets on January 1, 1975, or

(B) an amount equal to the sum of (i) the total amount of the contributions to the plan received after December 31, 1974, and prior to such date, plus (ii) the fair market value of the assets of the plan, determined on January 1, 1975.

(2) For purposes of this subsection, in the case of an employer security held by a plan after January 1, 1975, the ownership of which is derived from ownership of employer securities held by the plan on January 1, 1975, or from the exercise of rights derived from such ownership, the value of such security held after January 1, 1975, shall be based on the value as of January 1, 1975, of the security from which ownership was derived. The Secretary shall prescribe regulations to carry out this paragraph.

(3) An election under this paragraph may not be made after December 31, 1975. Such an election shall be made in accordance with regulations prescribed by the Secretary, and shall be irrevocable. A plan may make an election under this paragraph only if on January 1, 1975, the plan holds no employer real property. After such election and before January 1, 1985 the plan may not acquire any employer real property.

Act Sec. 407. (d) For purposes of this section—

(1) The term "employer security" means a security issued by an employer of employees covered by the plan, or by an affiliate of such employer. A contract to which section 408(b)(5) applies shall not be treated as a security for purposes of this section.

(2) The term "employer real property" means real property (and related personal property) which is leased to an employer of employees covered by the plan, or to an affiliate of such employer. For purposes of determining the time at which a plan acquires employer real property for purposes of this section, such property shall be deemed to be acquired by the plan on the date on which the plan acquires the property or on the date on which the lease to the employer (or affiliate) is entered into, whichever is later.

(3)(A) The term "eligible individual account plan" means an individual account plan which is (i) a profit-sharing, stock bonus, thrift, or savings plan; (ii) an employee stock ownership plan; or (iii) a money purchase plan which was in existence on the date of enactment of this Act and which on such date invested primarily in qualifying employer securities. Such term excludes an individual retirement account or annuity described in section 408 of the Internal Revenue Code of 1986.

(B) Notwithstanding subparagraph (A), a plan shall be treated as an eligible individual account plan with respect to the acquisition or holding of qualifying employer real property or qualifying employer securities only if such plan explicitly provides for acquisition and holding of qualifying employer securities or qualifying employer real property (as the case may be). In the case of a plan in existence on the date of enactment of this Act, this subparagraph shall not take effect until January 1, 1976.

(C) The term "eligible individual account plan" does not include any individual account plan the benefits of which are taken into account in determining the benefits payable to a participant under any defined benefit plan.

(4) The term "qualifying employer real property" means parcels of employer real property—

(A) if a substantial number of the parcels are dispersed geographically;

(B) if each parcel of real property and the improvements thereon are suitable (or adaptable without excessive cost) for more than one use;

(C) even if all of such real property is leased to one lessee (which may be an employer, or an affiliate of an employer); and

(D) if the acquisition and retention of such property comply with the provisions of this part (other than section 404(a)(1)(B) to the extent it requires diversification, and sections 404(a)(1)(C), 406, and subsection (a) of this section).

(5) The term "qualifying employer security" means an employer security which is—

(A) stock,

(B) a marketable obligation (as defined in subsection (e)), or

(C) an interest in a publicly traded partnership (as defined in section 7704(b) of the Internal Revenue Code of 1986), but only if such partnership is an existing partnership as defined in section 10211(c)(2)(A) of the Revenue Act of 1987 (Public Law 100-203).

After December 17, 1987, in the case of a plan other than an eligible individual account plan, an employer security described in subparagraph (A) or (C) shall be considered a qualifying employer security only if such employer security satisfies the requirements of subsection (f)(1).

(6) The term "employee stock ownership plan" means an individual account plan—

(A) which is a stock bonus plan which is qualified, or a stock bonus plan and money purchase plan both of which are qualified, under section 401 of the Internal Revenue Code of 1954, and which is designed to invest primarily in qualifying employer securities, and

(B) which meets such other requirements as the Secretary of the Treasury may prescribe by regulation.

(7) A corporation is an affiliate of an employer if it is a member of any controlled group of corporations (as defined in section 1563(a) of the Internal Revenue Code of 1986, except that "applicable percentage" shall be substituted for "80 percent" wherever the latter percentage appears in such section) of which the employer who maintains the plan is a member. For purposes of the preceding sentence, the term "applicable percentage" means 50 percent, or such lower percentage as the Secretary may prescribe by regulation. A person other than a corporation shall be treated as an affiliate of an employer to the extent provided in regulations of the Secretary. An employer which is a person other than a corporation shall be treated as affiliated with another person to the extent provided by regulations of the Secretary. Regulations under this paragraph shall be prescribed only after consultation and coordination with the Secretary of the Treasury.

(8) The Secretary may prescribe regulations specifying the extent to which conversion, splits, the exercise of rights, and similar transactions are not treated as acquisitions.

(9) For purposes of this section, an arrangement which consists of a defined benefit plan and an individual account plan shall be treated as 1 plan if the benefits of such individual account plan are taken into account in determining the benefits payable under such defined benefit plan.

Act Sec. 407. (e) For purposes of subsection (d)(5), the term "marketable obligation" means a bond, debenture, note, or certificate, or other evidence of indebtedness (hereinafter in this subsection referred to as "obligation") if—

(1) such obligation is acquired—

(A) on the market, either (i) at the price of the obligation prevailing on a national securities exchange which is registered with the Securities and Exchange Commission, or (ii) if the obligation is not traded on such a national securities exchange, at a price not less favorable to the plan than the offering price for the obligation as established by current bid and asked prices quoted by persons independent of the issuer;

(B) from an underwriter, at a price (i) not in excess of the public offering price for the obligation as set forth in a prospectus or offering circular filed with the Securities and Exchange Commission, and (ii) at which a substantial portion of the same issue is acquired by persons independent of the issuer; or

(C) directly from the issuer, at a price not less favorable to the plan than the price paid currently for a substantial portion of the same issue by persons independent of the issuer;

(2) immediately following acquisition of such obligation—

(A) not more than 25 percent of the aggregate amount of obligations issued in such issue and outstanding at the time of acquisition is held by the plan, and

(B) at least 50 percent of the aggregate amount referred to in subparagraph (A) is held by persons independent of the issuer; and

(3) immediately following acquisition of the obligation, not more than 25 percent of the assets of the plan is invested in obligations of the employer or an affiliate of the employer.

Act Sec. 407. (f)(1) Stock satisfies the requirements of this paragraph if, immediately following the acquisition of such stock—

(A) no more than 25 percent of the aggregate amount of stock of the same class issued and outstanding at the time of acquisition is held by the plan, and

(B) at least 50 percent of the aggregate amount referred to in subparagraph (A) is held by persons independent of the issuer.

(2) Until January 1, 1993, a plan shall not be treated as violating subsection (a) solely by holding stock which fails to satisfy the requirements of paragraph (1) if such stock—

(A) has been so held since December 17, 1987, or

(B) was acquired after December 17, 1987, pursuant to a legally binding contract in effect on December 17, 1987, and has been so held at all times after the acquisition.

Amendments

P.L. 105-34, §1524(a):

Amended ERISA Sec. 407(b) by redesignating paragraph (2) as paragraph (3) and by inserting after paragraph (1) new paragraph (2) to read as above.

The amendments made above apply to elective deferrals for plan years beginning after December 31, 1998.

P.L. 101-540, §1:

Amended ERISA Sec. 407(d)(5) to read as above. Previously, Sec. 407(d)(5) read as follows:

(5) The term "qualifying employer security" means an employer security which is stock or a marketable obligation (as defined in subsection (e)). After December 17, 1987, in the case of a plan, other than an eligible individual account plan, stock shall be considered a qualifying employer security only if such stock satisfies the requirements of subsection (f)(1).

The above amendment is effective for interests in publicly traded partnerships acquired before, on, or after January 1, 1987.

P.L. 101-239, §7881(1)(2):

Amended ERISA Sec. 407(d)(9) by striking "such arrangement" and inserting "such individual account plan."

The above amendment is effective for arrangements established after December 22, 1987.

P.L. 101-239, §7881(1)(3):

Amended ERISA Sec. 407(f) in paragraph (1) by striking "this subsection" and inserting "this paragraph" and by striking paragraph (3). Prior to being stricken, paragraph (3) read as follows:

(3) After December 17, 1987, no plan may acquire stock which does not satisfy the requirements of paragraph (1) unless the acquisition is made pursuant to a legally binding contract in effect on such date.

The above changes are effective December 22, 1987.

P.L. 101-239, §7881(1)(4):

Amended ERISA Sec. 407(f) in paragraph (1) by inserting ", immediately following the acquisition of such stock" after "if."

The above changes are effective December 22, 1987.

P.L. 101-239, §7891(a)(1):

Titles I, III, and IV of ERISA (other than sections 3(37)(E), 301(a)(7), and 308, the last sentence of section 408(d), and sections 414(c), 4001(a)(3)(ii), and 4303) are each amended by striking "Internal Revenue Code of 1954" each place it appears and inserting "Internal Revenue Code of 1986."

The above changes are effective October 22, 1986.

P.L. 101-239, §7894(e)(2):

Amended ERISA Sec. 407(d)(6)(A) by inserting "plan" after "money purchase" and by striking "employee securities" and inserting "employer securities." effective for arrangements established after December 17, 1987.

The above amendment is effective for arrangements established after December 22, 1987.

P.L. 100-203, §9345(a)(1):

Amended ERISA Sec. 407(d)(3) by adding subparagraph (c) to read as above.

The above amendment is effective for arrangements established after December 22, 1987.

P.L. 100-203, §9345(a)(2):

Amended ERISA Sec. 407(d) by adding paragraph (9) to read as above.

The above amendment is effective for arrangements established after December 22, 1987.

P.L. 100-203, §9345(b)(1):

Amended ERISA Sec. 407(d)(5) by adding the second sentence to read as above.

The above amendment is effective December 22, 1987.

P.L. 100-203, §9345(b)(2):

Amended ERISA Sec. 407 by adding subsection (f) to read as above.

The above amendment is effective December 22, 1987.

Regulations

The following regulations were adopted by FR Doc. 77-27315, filed with the Federal Register on September 19, 1977, and published in the Federal Register of September 20, 1977 (42 FR 47198).

[¶ 14,771]

§2550.407a-1 **General rule for the acquisition and holding of employer securities and employer real property.** (a) *In General.* Section 407(a)(1) of the Employee Retirement Income Security Act of 1974 (the Act) states that except as otherwise provided in section 407 and section 414 of the Act, a plan may not acquire or hold any employer security which is not a qualifying employer security or any employer real property which is not qualifying employer real property. Section 406(a)(1)(E) prohibits a fiduciary from knowingly causing a plan to engage in a transaction which constitutes a direct or indirect acquisition, on behalf of a plan, of any employer security or employer real property in violation of section 407(a), and section 406(a)(2) prohibits a fiduciary who has authority or discretion to control or manage assets of a plan to permit the plan to hold any employer security or employer real property if he knows or should know that holding such security or real property violates section 407(a).

(b) *Requirements applicable to all plans.* A plan may hold or acquire only employer securities which are qualifying employer securities and employer real property which is qualifying employer real property. A plan may not hold employer securities and employer real property which are not qualifying employer securities and qualifying employer real property, except to the extent that:

(1) The employer security is held by a plan which has made an election under section 407(c)(3) of the Act; or

(2) The employer security is a loan or other extension of credit which satisfies the requirements of section 414(c)(1) of the Act or the employer real property is leased to the employer pursuant to a lease which satisfies the requirements of section 414(c)(2) of the Act.

[¶ 14,771A]

§2550.407a-2 **Limitation with respect to the acquisition of qualifying employer securities and qualifying employer real property.** (a) *In general.* Section 407(a)(2) of the Employee Retirement Income Security Act of 1974 (the Act) provides that a plan may not acquire any qualifying employer security or qualifying employer real property, if immediately after such acquisition the aggregate fair market value of qualifying employer securities and qualifying employer real property held by the plan exceeds 10 percent of the fair market value of the assets of the plan.

(b) *Acquisition.* For purposes of section 407(a) of the Act, an acquisition by a plan of qualifying employer securities or qualifying employer real property shall include, but not be limited to, an acquisition by purchase, by the exchange of plan assets, by the exercise of warrants or rights, by the conversion of a security (except any acquisition pursuant to a conversion exempt under section 408(b)(7) of the Act), by default of a loan where the qualifying employer security or qualifying employer real property was security for the loan, or by the contribution of such securities or real property to the plan. However, an acquisition of a security shall not be deemed to have occurred if a plan acquires the security as a result of a stock dividend or stock split.

(c) *Fair market value—Indebtedness incurred in connection with the acquisition of a plan asset.* In determining whether a plan is in compliance with the limitation on the acquisition of qualifying employer securities and qualifying employer real property in section 407(a)(2), the limitation on the holding of qualifying employer securities and qualifying employer real property in section 407(a)(3) and §2550.407a-3 thereunder, and the requirement regarding the disposition of employer securities and employer real property in section 407(a)(4) and §2550.407a-4 thereunder, the fair market value of total plan assets shall be the fair market value of such assets less the unpaid amount of:

(1) Any indebtedness incurred by the plan in acquiring such assets;

(2) Any indebtedness incurred before the acquisition of such assets if such indebtedness would not have been incurred but for such acquisition; and

(3) Any indebtedness incurred after the acquisition of such assets if such indebtedness would not have been incurred but for such acquisition and the incurrence of such indebtedness was reasonably foreseeable at the time of such acquisition. However, the fair market value of qualifying employer securities and qualifying employer real property shall be the fair market value of such assets without any reduction for the unpaid amount of any indebtedness incurred by the plan in connection with the acquisition of such employer securities and employer real property.

(d) *Examples.* (1) Plan assets have a fair market value of $100,000. The plan has no liabilities other than liabilities for vested benefits of participants and does not own any employer securities or employer real property. The plan proposes to acquire qualifying employer securities with a fair market value of $10,000 by paying $1,000 in cash and borrowing $9,000. The fair market value of plan assets would be $100,000 ($100,000 of plan assets less $1,000 cash payment plus $10,000 of employer securities less $9,000 indebtedness), the fair market value of the qualifying employer securities would be $10,000, which is 10 percent of the fair market value of plan assets. Accordingly, the acquisition would not contravene section 407(a).

(2) Plan assets have a fair market value of $100,000. The plan has liabilities of $20,000 which were incurred in connection with the acquisition of those assets, and does not own any employer securities or employer real property. The plan proposes to pay cash for qualifying employer securities with a fair market value of $10,000. The fair market value of plan assets would be $80,000 ($100,000 of plan assets less $10,000 cash payment plus $10,000 of employer securities less $20,000 indebtedness), the fair market value of the qualifying employer securities would be $10,000, which is 12.5 percent of the fair market value of plan assets. Accordingly, the acquisition would contravene section 407(a).

⋙→ *Caution: Regulation §2550.407a-3 was officially removed by 61 FR 33847 on July 1, 1996.*

[¶ 14,771B]

§2550.407a-3 **Limitation with respect to the holding of qualifying employer securities and qualifying employer real property.** (a) *In general.* (1) Section 407(a)(3) of the Employee Retirement Income Security Act of 1974 (the Act) provides that a plan (other than an eligible individual account plan) may not hold, after December 31, 1984, any qualifying employer securities or qualifying employer real property (or both) to the extent that the aggregate fair market value of such securities and property, determined on December 31, 1984, exceeds 10 percent of the greater of:

(i) The fair market value of the assets of the plan, determined on December 31, 1984, or

(ii) The fair market value of the assets of the plan determined on January 1, 1975.

(2) Section 407(a)(3)(B) makes section 407(a)(3)(A) inapplicable to a plan which on any date after December 31, 1974, and before January 1, 1985, did not hold qualifying employer securities or qualifying employer real property (or both) the aggregate fair market value of which determined on such date exceeded 10 percent of the greater of:

(i) The fair market value of the assets of the plan, determined on such date, or

(ii) The fair market value of the assets determined on January 1, 1975.

(b) *Ten percent limitation.* (1) The requirement of section 407(a)(3) that a plan hold no more than 10 percent of the fair market value of its assets in qualifying employer securities or qualifying employer real property (or both) can be met at any time between December 31, 1974, and January 1, 1985. In accordance with section 407(a)(3)(B) of the Act, if at any time between December 31, 1974 and January 1, 1985, the fair market value of qualifying employer securities and qualifying employer real property does not exceed 10 percent of the fair market value of total plan assets, the plan will be in compliance with the holding requirements of section 407(a)(3), notwithstanding any subsequent increase in such percentage above 10 percent which occurs as the result of changes in the fair market value of either the qualifying employer securities or qualifying employer real property, or the other assets of the plan. Moreover, if such percentage falls below 10 percent, the plan may acquire additional qualifying employer securities or qualifying employer real property not to exceed the limitation on such acquisitions contained in section 407(a)(2).

(2) *Example.* On January 1, 1975 a plan holds qualifying employer real property with a fair market value of $200,000 and has total assets with a fair market value of $1,000,000. The plan would have to divest qualifying employer securities or qualifying employer real property with a value of $100,000 to comply with section 407(a)(3). If, however, there is a substantial rise in the market value of the plan's other assets in 1976 and the first quarter of 1977 so that the fair market value of total plan assets on March 31, 1977, is $2,000,000, but the aggregate fair market value of the qualifying employer securities and qualifying employer real property is still $200,000, the 10 percent holding requirement of section 407(a)(3) would have been met on March 31, 1977. Henceforth, the plan would not be subject to the holding limitations of section 407(a)(3), but only the limitations regarding the acquisition of qualifying employer securities and qualifying employer real property set forth in section 407(a)(2) of the Act. If the plan does not acquire any additional employer securities or employer real property, and if, in 1978, the fair market value of other plan assets decreases to $1,500,000 while the fair market value of qualifying employer securities and qualifying employer real property held by the plan remains at $200,000, or even increases to $300,000, the plan will not contravene the holding requirement of section 407(a)(3), inasmuch as the plan was in compliance with that requirement on March 31, 1977. If, on February 1, 1980, the fair market value of total plan assets is $2,500,000 and the fair market value of qualifying employer securities and qualifying employer real property is $200,000, the plan may acquire additional qualifying employer securities and qualifying employer real property in the amount of $50,000.

(c) *Fair market value—Indebtedness incurred in connection with the acquisition of a plan asset.* In determining whether a plan is in compliance with the limitation on the holding of qualifying employer securities and qualifying employer real property in section 407(a)(3), the fair market value of total plan assets, qualifying employer securities and qualifying employer real property for purposes of section 407(a)(3) and this section shall be determined in accordance with the provisions of §2550.407(a)-2(c).

»→ *Caution: Regulation §2550.407a-4 was officially removed by 61 FR 33847 on July 1, 1996.*

[¶ 14,771C]

§2550.407a-4 **Divestiture of employer securities and real property by December 31, 1979.** (a) *In general.* Section 407(a)(4)(A) of the Employee Retirement Income Security Act of 1974 (the Act) provides that a plan may not hold, after December 31, 1979, any employer securities or employer real property in excess of the amount specified in regulations promulgated by the Secretary of Labor under section 407(a)(4)(B) of the Act. That section directs the Secretary to prescribe regulations which shall have the effect of requiring a plan to divest 50 percent of the holdings of employer securities and employer real property which the plan would be required to divest before January 1, 1985, under sections 407(a)(3) or 407(c) of the Act.

(b) *Fair market value—Indebtedness incurred in connection with the acquisition of a plan asset.* In determining whether a plan is in compliance with the requirement regarding the disposition of employer securities and employer real property set forth in section 407(a)(4), the fair market value of total plan assets, employer securities and employer real property for purposes of section 407(a)(4) and this section shall be determined in accordance with the provisions of §2550.407a-2(c).

(c) *Fifty percent divestiture.* (1) *Divestiture which would be required under section 407(a)(3).* (i) A plan which would be required to divest qualifying employer securities or qualifying employer real property before January 1, 1985, pursuant to section 407(a)(3), and which has not met the requirements of that section by December 31, 1979, will be in compliance with the requirements of section 407(a)(4) of the Act and this section if the plan divests by December 31, 1979, qualifying employer securities and qualifying employer real property which have, on any date between December 31, 1974, and January 1, 1980 (hereafter referred to as the "valuation date"), a fair market value equal to 50 percent of the amount by which such qualifying employer securities and qualifying employer real property exceed 10 percent of the fair market value of plan assets as of the valuation date. For purposes of this section, the fair market value of plan assets on the valuation date shall be deemed to be an amount equal to:

(A) The fair market value of the assets of the plan on the valuation date, or

(B) An actuarial estimate of the fair market value of the assets of the plan on any date between December 31, 1979 and January 1, 1985. The actuarial estimate under paragraph (c)(1)(i)(B) of this section must be made in good faith and its basis must be set forth in writing.

(ii) The fair market value of qualifying employer securities and qualifying employer real property which must be divested pursuant to paragraph (c)(1)(i) of this section shall be reduced by an amount equal to the fair market value of any qualifying employer security which is a loan or other extension of credit that satisfies the requirements of section 414(c)(1) of the Act or any qualifying employer real property leased to the employer pursuant to a lease that satisfies the requirements of section 414(c)(2) of the Act.

(iii) *Examples.* (A) On January 1, 1975, the assets of a plan have a fair market value of $800,000. On December 31, 1977, plan assets have a fair market value of $900,000 and the actuarial estimate of the fair market value of plan assets as of December 31, 1984, is $1,000,000. The plan has chosen December 31, 1977, as the valuation date, and has decided that for purposes of section 407(a)(4) and §2550.407a-4 the fair market value of plan assets on the valuation date shall be the actuarial estimate of the fair market value of plan assets as of December 31, 1984, which is $1,000,000. The qualifying employer securities and qualifying employer real property held by the plan on December 31, 1977 have a fair market value of $200,000. A qualifying employer security, which has a fair market value of $25,000, is a loan by the plan which meets the conditions of section 414(c)(1) of the Act. The fair market value of qualifying employer securities and qualifying employer real property held by the plan exceed by $100,000 10 percent of the greater of the fair market value of plan assets on January 1, 1975, or the valuation date. In order to comply with section 407(a)(4) of the Act and this section, the plan ordinarily would have to divest, by December 31, 1979, $50,000 of qualifying employer securities or qualifying employer real property, which would be 50 percent of the amount which exceeds 10 percent of plan assets. However, because qualifying employer securities which have a fair market value of $25,000 are held by the plan pursuant to the transitional rules of section 414(c)(1) of the Act, the plan will have to divest by December 31, 1979, only $25,000 of qualifying employer securities and qualifying employer real property because it may subtract the fair market value of any qualifying employer securities or qualifying employer real property held by the plan which satisfies the requirements of the transitional rules of section 414(c)(1) or (2) of the Act from any amounts which it is required to divest.

        (B) Same facts as example (A) except that the plan has $100,000 in indebtedness outstanding, which was incurred in connection with the acquisition of a plan asset (other than qualifying employer securities or qualifying employer real property). For purposes of determining the percentage of plan assets represented by the investment in qualifying employer securities and qualifying employer real property, the fair market value of plan assets on the valuation date is $900,000 ($1,000,000 less $100,000 in indebtedness). The fair market value of qualifying employer securities and qualifying employer real property (i.e., $200,000) held by the plan exceeds 10 percent (i.e., $90,000) of the fair market value of plan assets by $110,000. In order to comply with section 407(a)(4) of the Act and this section, the plan would be required to divest $30,000 of qualifying employer securities or qualifying employer real property by December 31, 1979, which would be 50 percent of $110,000, less the fair market value of qualifying employer securities or qualifying employer real property held pursuant to section 414(c)(1) or (2) of the Act.

        (2) *Divestiture which would be required under section 407(c).* (i) Notwithstanding the prohibition of section 407(a)(1)(A) of the Act regarding the holding of employer securities, and subject to the limitations of section 407(c)(1) of the Act, section 407(c) permits a plan which has made a valid election under section 407(c)(3) to hold an employer security which is neither a qualifying employer security nor a loan or other extension of credit covered by the transitional provisions of section 414(c)(1) of the Act. An election under section 407(c) must have been made before January 1, 1976, and in accordance with § 2550.407c-3 (41 FR 43726, September 23, 1975). A plan which has made a valid election under section 407(c)(3) will be in compliance with the requirements of section 407(a)(4) of the Act and this section if, by December 31, 1979, the plant divests employer securities which have on any date between December 31, 1974 and January 1, 1980 (hereafter referred to as the "valuation date"), a fair market value determined as of December 31, 1974 equal to 50 percent of the amount in excess of 10 percent of the lesser of:

        (A) The fair market value of the assets of the plan determined on the valuation date (disregarding any portion of the fair market value of employer securities which is attributable to appreciation of such securities after December 31, 1974) but not less than the fair market value of the plan assets on January 1, 1975, or

        (B) An amount equal to the sum of (1) The total amount of the contributions to the plan received after December 31, 1974 and prior to the valuation date, plus (2) The fair market value of the assets of the plan, determined as of January 1, 1975.

For purposes of this paragraph (c)(2), the fair market value of plan assets on the valuation date shall be deemed to be an amount equal to (1) the fair market value of the assets of the plan on the valuation date, or (2) an actuarial estimate of the fair market value of the assets of the plan on any date between December 31, 1979 and January 1, 1985. The actuarial estimate must be made in good faith and its basis must be set forth in writing.

        (ii) The fair market value of employer securities which must be divested pursuant to this section shall be reduced by an amount equal to the fair market value of any employer security which is a loan or other extension of credit that satisfies the requirements of section 414(c)(1) of the Act.

        (iii) *Examples.* (A) A plan has made a valid election under section 407(c) of the Act and has been in compliance with the requirements of section 407(c)(3). On January 1, 1975, total plan assets have a fair market value of $105,000 and employer securities have a fair market value of $15,000. On June 30, 1975, the fair market value of plan assets is $105,000, and the actuarial estimate of the fair market value of plan assets as of December 31, 1984 is $145,000. The plan has chosen June 30, 1975 as the valuation date and has decided that for purposes of section 407(a)(4) and § 2550.407a-4 the fair market value of plan assets on the valuation date shall be the actuarial estimate of the fair market value of assets as of December 31, 1984, which is $145,000. No contributions have been made to the plan from December 31, 1974, to June 30, 1975, and the employer securities held by the plan on June 30, 1975, are the same employer securities held on January 1, 1975. Five thousand dollars of employer securities held by the plan is a loan which meets the conditions of section 414(c)(1) of the Act. One thousand dollars of employer securities is neither qualifying employer securities nor a loan or other extension of credit covered by the provisions of section 414(c)(1). Ten percent of the fair market value of plan assets on the valuation date is $14,500; and 10 percent of the sum of the amount of contributions received after December 31, 1974, and prior to July 1, 1975 (nothing, because no contributions were received) plus the fair market value of plan assets on January 1, 1975 ($105,000) is $10,500. Ordinarily, as of December 31, 1979, the plan would have to divest employer securities in excess of 50 percent of the fair market value of the lesser of these amounts. The fair market value of employer securities held by the plan exceeds the lesser of these amounts by $4,500 and 50 percent of $4,500 is $2,250. However, because $5,000 of employer securities is a loan covered by the provisions of section 414(c)(1), the amount of employer securities which would have to be divested is reduced by $5,000. Accordingly, the plan is not required to divest any employer securities by December 31, 1979.

        (B) A plan has made a valid election under section 407(c) and has been in compliance with the requirements of section 407(c)(3). On January 1, 1975, total plan assets have a fair market value of $100,000 and employer securities have a fair market value of $30,000. On April 30, 1977, the fair market value of total plan assets is $110,000, none of which is attributable to appreciation of employer securities after December 31, 1974. The actuarial estimate of the fair market value of plan assets as of December 31, 1984 is $160,000. Contributions to the plan from December 31, 1974, through April 30, 1977, total $12,000. The plan has chosen April 30, 1977 as the valuation date and has decided that the fair market value of plan assets on the valuation date shall be the actuarial estimate of the fair market value of plan assets as of December 31, 1984, which is $160,000. The employer securities held on April 30, 1977, are the same employer securities held on January 1, 1975. Ten percent of the fair market value of plan assets on the valuation date is $16,000; and 10 percent of the sum of the amount of contributions received after December 31, 1974, and prior to May 1, 1977, plus the fair market value of plan assets on January 1, 1975, is $11,200. The fair market value of employer securities held by the plan exceeds the lesser of these two amounts by $13,800. In order to comply with section 407(a)(4) of the Act and this section, the plan would be required to divest, by December 31, 1979, $9,400 of employer securities.

Temporary Regulations

        The following temporary regulations were adopted effective September 18, 1975, under "Title 29—Labor; Chapter XXV—Office of Employee Benefits Security; Subchapter F—Fiduciary Responsibility under the Employee Retirement Security Act of 1974; § 2550.407c-3 of Part 2550—Rules and Regulations for Fiduciary Responsibility." The temporary regulations were published in the Federal Register of September 23, 1975.

»» → *Caution: Regulation § 2550.407c-3 was officially removed by 61 FR 33847 on July 1, 1996.*

[¶ 14,775]

§ 2550.407c-3. **Election by plan to utilize the alternate method of calculation of value of employer securities.** (a) *In general.* If an employee benefit plan holds no employer real property (as defined in section 407(d)(2) of the Employee Retirement Income Security Act of 1974 (the "Act")) on January 1, 1975, it may elect under section 407(c)(3) of the Act to utilize the alternate method of calculation of value of employer securities set forth in section 407(c) of the Act for the purpose of satisfying the requirement of section 407(a)(3) of the Act relating to the limitation on holding by certain employee benefit plans of qualifying employer securities and qualifying employer real property.

(b) *Election is irrevocable.* An election by a plan under section 407(c)(3) of the Act shall be binding with respect to such plan and, once made, shall be irrevocable.

(c) *Procedure for making election.* (1) *Time of election.* An election under this section must be made before January 1, 1976. An election will be deemed to be timely filed only if received at the Office of Employee Benefits Security, Labor-Management Services Administration, U.S. Department of Labor, Washington, D.C. 20216 on or before 5 p.m., December 31, 1975, or, if mailed by certified or registered mail, postmarked prior to January 1, 1976.

(2) *By whom election is to be made.* The election provided by this section may be made only by the plan administrator of the plan.

(3) *Manner of making election.* The plan administrator shall file a statement containing the following information: (i) the name and address of the plan; (ii) the EIN number of the plan; (iii) the WP number of the plan (if any); (iv) the name and address of the plan administrator; (v) a statement that on January 1, 1975, the plan held no employer real property; and (vi) a statement that the plan elects to use the alternate method of valuation of employer securities provided under section 407(c)(3) of the Act.

(d) *Limitation on acquisition of employer real property.* After making an election under this section, and before January 1, 1985, the plan may not acquire any employer real property.

Regulations

The following regulations under Act Secs. 407 and 408 were adopted by FR Doc. 77-25695, filed with the Federal Register on August 30, 1977, and published in the Federal Register of September 2, 1977 (42 FR 44384).

[¶ 14,776E]

§ 2550.407d-5. **Definition of the term "qualifying employer security".** (a) *In general.* For purposes of this section and section 407(d)(5) of the Employee Retirement Income Security Act of 1974 (the Act), the term "qualifying employer security" means an employer security which is:

(1) Stock; or

(2) A marketable obligation, as defined in paragraph (b) of this section and section 407(e) of the Act.

(b) For purposes of paragraph (a)(2) of this section and section 407(d)(5) of the Act, the term "marketable obligation" means a bond, debenture, note, or certificate, or other evidence of indebtedness (hereinafter in this paragraph referred to as "obligation") if:

(1) Such obligation is acquired—

(i) On the market, either

(A) At the price of the obligation prevailing on a national securities exchange which is registered with the Securities and Exchange Commission, or

(B) If the obligation is not traded on such a national securities exchange, at a price not less favorable to the plan than the offering price for the obligation as established by current bid and asked prices quoted by persons independent of the issuer;

(ii) From an underwriter, at a price—

(A) Not in excess of the public offering price for the obligation as set forth in a prospectus or offering circular filed with the Securities and Exchange Commission, and

(B) At which a substantial portion of the same issue is acquired by persons independent of the issuer; or

(iii) Directly from the issuer at a price not less favorable to the plan than the price paid currently for a substantial portion of the same issue by persons independent of the issuer;

(2) Immediately following acquisition of such obligation,

(i) Not more than 25 percent of the aggregate amount of obligations issued in such issue and outstanding at the time of acquisition is held by the plan, and

(ii) At least 50 percent of the aggregate amount referred to in paragraph (A) is held by persons independent of the issuer; and

(3) Immediately following acquisition of the obligation, not more than 25 percent of the assets of the plan is invested in obligations of the employer or an affiliate of the employer.

[¶ 14,776F]

§ 2550.407d-6. **Definition of the term "employee stock ownership plan".** (a) *In general.* (1) *Type of plan.* To be an "ESOP" (employee stock ownership plan), a plan described in section 407(d)(6)(A) of the Employee Retirement Income Security Act of 1974 (the Act) must meet the requirements of this section. See section 407(d)(6)(B).

(2) *Designation as ESOP.* To be an ESOP, a plan must be formally designated as such in the plan document.

(3) *Retroactive amendment.* A plan meets the requirements of this section as of the date that it is designated as an ESOP if it is amended retroactively to meet, and in fact does meet, such requirements at any of the following times:

(i) 12 months after the date on which the plan is designated as an ESOP;

(ii) 90 days after a determination letter is issued with respect to the qualification of the plan as an ESOP under this section, but only if the determination is requested by the date in paragraph (a)(3)(i) of this section; or

(iii) A later date approved by the Internal Revenue Service district director.

(4) *Addition to other plan.* An ESOP may form a portion of a plan the balance of which includes a qualified pension, profit-sharing, or stock bonus plan which is not an ESOP. A reference to an ESOP includes an ESOP that forms a portion of another plan.

(5) *Conversion of existing plan to an ESOP.* If an existing pension, profit-sharing, or stock bonus plan is converted into an ESOP, the requirements of section 404 of the Act, relating to fiduciary duties, and section 401(a) of the Internal Revenue Code (the Code), relating to requirements for plans established for the exclusive benefit of employees, apply to such conversion. A conversion may constitute a termination of an existing plan. For definition of a termination, see the regulations under section 411(d)(3) of the Code and section 4041(f) of the Act.

(6) *Certain arrangements barred.* (i) *Buy-sell agreements.* An arrangement involving an ESOP that creates a put option must not provide for the issuance of put options other than as provided under § 2550.408b-3(j), (k) and (l). Also, an ESOP must not otherwise obligate itself to acquire securities from a particular security holder at an indefinite time determined upon the happening of an event such as the death of the holder.

(b) *Plan designed to invest primarily in qualifying employer securities.* A plan constitutes an ESOP only if the plan specifically states that it is designed to invest primarily in qualifying employer securities. Thus, a stock bonus plan or a money purchase pension plan constituting an ESOP may invest part of its assets in other than qualifying employer securities. Such plan will be treated the same as other stock bonus plans or money purchase pension plans qualified under section 401(a) of the Code with respect to those investments.

(c) Regulations of the Secretary of the Treasury. A plan constitutes an ESOP for a plan year only if it meets such other requirements as the Secretary of the Treasury may prescribe by regulation under section 4975(e)(7) of the Code. (See 26 CFR 54.4975-11).

⟫→ *Caution: Note: Various Prohibited Transaction Exemptions that have been granted are enumerated in the Finding Lists and the Current Finding Lists.—CCH.*

[¶ 14,780]
EXEMPTIONS FROM PROHIBITED TRANSACTIONS

Act Sec. 408.(a) The Secretary shall establish an exemption procedure for purposes of this subsection. Pursuant to such procedure, he may grant a conditional or unconditional exemption of any fiduciary or transaction, or class of fiduciaries or transactions, from all or part of the restrictions imposed by sections 406 and 407(a). Action under this subsection may be taken only after consultation and coordination with the Secretary of the Treasury. An exemption granted under this section shall not relieve a fiduciary from any other applicable provision of this Act. The Secretary may not grant an exemption under this subsection unless he finds that such exemption is—

(1) administratively feasible,

(2) in the interests of the plan and of its participants and beneficiaries, and

(3) protective of the rights of participants and beneficiaries of such plan.

Before granting an exemption under this subsection from section 406(a) or 407(a), the Secretary shall publish notice in the Federal Register of the pendency of the exemption, shall require that adequate notice be given to interested persons, and shall afford interested persons opportunity to present views. The Secretary may not grant an exemption under this subsection from section 406(b) unless he affords an opportunity for a hearing and makes a determination on the record with respect to the findings required by paragraphs (1), (2), and (3) of this subsection.

Act Sec. 408. (b) The prohibitions provided in section 406 shall not apply to any of the following transactions:

(1) Any loans made by the plan to parties in interest who are participants or beneficiaries of the plan if such loans (A) are available to all such participants and beneficiaries on a reasonably equivalent basis, (B) are not made available to highly compensated employees (within the meaning of section 414(g) of the Internal Revenue Code of 1986) in an amount greater than the amount made available to other employees, (C) are made in accordance with specific provisions regarding such loans set forth in the plan, (D) bear a reasonable rate of interest, and (E) are adequately secured. A loan made by a plan shall not fail to meet the requirements of the preceding sentence by reason of a loan repayment suspension described under section 414(u)(4) of the Internal Revenue Code of 1986.

(2) Contracting or making reasonable arrangements with a party in interest for office space, or legal, accounting, or other services necessary for the establishment or operation of the plan, if no more than reasonable compensation is paid therefor.

(3) A loan to an employee stock ownership plan (as defined in section 407(d)(6)), if—

(A) such loan is primarily for the benefit of participants and beneficiaries of the plan, and

(B) such loan is at an interest rate which is not in excess of a reasonable rate.

If the plan gives collateral to a party in interest for such loan, such collateral may consist only of qualifying employer securities (as defined in section 407(d)(5)).

(4) The investment of all or part of a plan's assets in deposits which bear a reasonable interest rate in a bank or similar financial institution supervised by the United States or a State, if such bank or other institution is a fiduciary of such plan and if—

(A) the plan covers only employees of such bank or other institution and employees of affiliates of such bank or other institution, or

(B) such investment is expressly authorized by a provision of the plan or by a fiduciary (other than such bank or institution or affiliate thereof) who is expressly empowered by the plan to so instruct the trustee with respect to such investment.

(5) Any contract for life insurance, health insurance, or annuities with one or more insurers which are qualified to do business in a State, if the plan pays no more than adequate consideration, and if each such insurer or insurers is—

(A) the employer maintaining the plan, or

(B) a party in interest which is wholly owned (directly or indirectly) by the employer maintaining the plan, or by any person which is a party in interest with respect to the plan, but only if the total premiums and annuity considerations written by such insurers for life insurance, health insurance, or annuities for all plans (and their employers) with respect to which such insurers are parties in interest (not including premiums or annuity considerations written by the employer maintaining the plan) do not exceed 5 percent of the total premiums and annuity considerations written for all lines of insurance in that year by such insurers (not including premiums or annuity considerations written by the employer maintaining the plan).

(6) The providing of any ancillary service by a bank or similar financial institution supervised by the United States or a State, if such bank or other institution is a fiduciary of such plan, and if—

(A) such bank or similar financial institution has adopted adequate internal safeguards which assure that the providing of such ancillary service is consistent with sound banking and financial practice, as determined by Federal or State supervisory authority, and

(B) the extent to which such ancillary service is provided is subject to specific guidelines issued by such bank or similar financial institution (as determined by the Secretary after consultation with Federal and State supervisory authority), and adherence to such guidelines would reasonably preclude such bank or similar financial institution from providing such ancillary service (i) in an excessive or unreasonable manner, and (ii) in a manner that would be inconsistent with the best interests of participants and beneficiaries of employee benefit plans.

Such ancillary services shall not be provided at more than reasonable compensation.

(7) The exercise of a privilege to convert securities, to the extent provided in regulations of the Secretary, but only if the plan receives no less than adequate consideration pursuant to such conversion.

(8) Any transaction between a plan and (i) a common or collective trust fund or pooled investment fund maintained by a party in interest which is a bank or trust company supervised by a State or Federal agency or (ii) a pooled investment fund of an insurance company qualified to do business in a State, if—

(A) the transaction is a sale or purchase of an interest in the fund,

(B) the bank, trust company, or insurance company receives not more than reasonable compensation, and

(C) such transaction is expressly permitted by the instrument under which the plan is maintained, or by a fiduciary (other than the bank, trust company, or insurance company, or an affiliate thereof) who has authority to manage and control the assets of the plan.

(9) The making by a fiduciary of a distribution of the assets of the plan in accordance with the terms of the plan if such assets are distributed in the same manner as provided under section 4044 of this Act (relating to allocation of assets).

(10) Any transaction required or permitted under part 1 of subtitle E of title IV.

(11) A merger of multiemployer plans, or the transfer of assets or liabilities between multiemployer plans, determined by the Pension Benefit Guaranty Corporation to meet the requirements of section 4231.

(12) The sale by a plan to a party in interest on or after December 18, 1987, of any stock, if—

(A) the requirements of paragraphs (1) and (2) of subsection (e) are met with respect to such stock,

(B) on the later of the date on which the stock was acquired by the plan, or January 1, 1975, such stock constituted a qualifying employer security (as defined in section 407(d)(5) as then in effect), and

(C) such stock does not constitute a qualifying employer security (as defined in section 407(d)(5) as in effect at the time of the sale).

(13) Any transfer made before January 1, 2014, of excess pension assets from a defined benefit plan to a retiree health account in a qualified transfer permitted under section 420 of the Internal Revenue Code of 1986 (as in effect on the date of the enactment of the American Jobs Creation Act of 2004).

Act Sec. 408. (c) Nothing in section 406 shall be construed to prohibit any fiduciary from—

(1) receiving any benefit to which he may be entitled as a participant or beneficiary in the plan, so long as the benefit is computed and paid on a basis which is consistent with the terms of the plan as applied to all other participants and beneficiaries;

(2) receiving any reasonable compensation for services rendered, or for the reimbursement of expenses properly and actually incurred, in the performance of his duties with the plan; except that no person so serving who already receives full-time pay from an employer or an association of employers, whose employees are participants in the plan, or from an employee organization whose members are participants in such plan shall receive compensation from such plan, except for reimbursement of expenses properly and actually incurred; or

(3) serving as a fiduciary in addition to being an officer, employee, agent, or other representative of a party in interest.

(d)(1) Section 407(b) and subsections (b), (c), and (e) of this section shall not apply to a transaction in which a plan directly or indirectly—

(A) lends any part of the corpus or income of the plan to,

(B) pays any compensation for personal services rendered to the plan to, or

(C) acquires for the plan any property from, or sells any property to,

any person who is with respect to the plan an owner-employee (as defined in section 401(c)(3) of the Internal Revenue Code of 1986), a member of the family (as defined in section 267(c)(4) of such Code) of any such owner-employee, or any corporation in which any such owner-employee owns, directly or indirectly, 50 percent or more of the total combined voting power of all classes of stock entitled to vote or 50 percent or more of the total value of shares of all classes of stock of the corporation.

(2)(A) For purposes of paragraph (1), the following shall be treated as owner-employees:

(i) A shareholder-employee.

(ii) A participant or beneficiary of an individual retirement plan (as defined in section 7701(a)(37) of the Internal Revenue Code of 1986).

(iii) An employer or association of employees which establishes such an individual retirement plan under section 408(c) of such Code.

(B) Paragraph (1)(C) shall not apply to a transaction which consists of a sale of employer securities to an employee stock ownership plan (as defined in section 407(d)(6)) by a shareholder-employee, a member of the family (as defined in section 267(c)(4) of such Code) of any such owner-employee, or a corporation in which such a shareholder-employee owns stock representing a 50 percent or greater interest described in paragraph (1).

(C) For purposes of paragraph (1)(A), the term "owner-employee" shall only include a person described in clause (ii) or (iii) of subparagraph (A).

(3) For purposes of paragraph (2), the term "shareholder-employee" means an employee or officer of an S corporation (as defined in section 1361(a)(1) of such Code) who owns (or is considered as owning within the meaning of section 318(a)(1) of such Code) more than 5 percent of the outstanding stock of the corporation on any day during the taxable year of such corporation.

Act Sec. 408. (e) Sections 406 and 407 shall not apply to the acquisition or sale by a plan of qualifying employer securities (as defined in section 407(d)(5)) or acquisition, sale or lease by a plan of qualifying employer real property (as defined in section 407(d)(4))—

(1) if such acquisition, sale, or lease is for adequate consideration (or in the case of a marketable obligation, at a price not less favorable to the plan than the price determined under section 407(e)(1)),

(2) if no commission is charged with respect thereto, and

(3) if—

(A) the plan is an eligible individual account plan (as defined in section 407(d)(3)), or

(B) in the case of an acquisition or lease of qualifying employer real property by a plan which is not an eligible individual account plan, or of an acquisition of qualifying employer securities by such a plan, the lease or acquisition is not prohibited by section 407(a).

Act Sec. 408. (f) Section 406(b)(2) shall not apply to any merger or transfer described in subsection (b)(11).

Amendments

P.L. 108-357, §709(a)(3):

Act Sec. 709(a)(3) amended ERISA Sec. 408(b)(13) by striking "Pension Funding Equity Act of 2004" and inserting "American Jobs Creation Act of 2004."

P.L. 108-218, §204(b):

Act Sec. 535(b)(3) amended ERISA Sec. 408(b)(13) by striking "January 1, 2006" and inserting "January 1, 2014" and by striking "Tax Relief Extension Act of 1999" and inserting "Pension Funding Equity Act of 2004".

P.L. 107-16, §612(b):

Act Sec. 612(b) amended ERISA Sec. 408(d)(2) by adding at the end new subparagraph (C) to read as above.

The above amendment applies to years beginning after December 31, 2001.

P.L. 106-170, §535(b)(2)(C):

Act Sec. 535(b)(2)(C) amended ERISA Sec. 408(b)(13) by striking "in a taxable year beginning before January 1, 2001" and inserting "made before January 1, 2006" and by striking "January 1, 1995" and inserting "the date of the enactment of the Tax Relief Extension Act of 1999".

The above amendment applies to qualified transfers occurring after December 17, 1999.

P.L. 105-34, Sec. 1506(b)(2):

Amended ERISA Sec. 408(d) to read as above. Prior to amendment, the subsection read as follows:

Act Sec. 408. (d) Section 407(b) and subsections (b), (c), and (e) of this section shall not apply to any transaction in which a plan, directly or indirectly—

(1) lends any part of the corpus or income of the plan to;

(2) pays any compensation for personal services rendered to the plan to; or

(3) acquires for the plan any property from or sells any property to;

any person who is with respect to the plan an owner-employee (as defined in section 401(c)(3) of the Internal Revenue Code of 1986), a member of the family (as defined in section 267(c)(4) of such Code) of any such owner-employee, or a corporation controlled by any such owner-employee through the ownership, directly or indirectly, of 50 percent or more of the total combined voting power of all classes of stock entitled to vote or 50 percent or more of the total value of shares of all classes of stock of the

corporation. For purposes of this subsection a shareholder employee (as defined in section 1379 of the Internal Revenue Code of 1954 as in effect on the day before the date of the enactment of the Subchapter S Revision Act of 1982) and a participant or beneficiary of an individual retirement account or individual retirement annuity described in section 408 of the Internal Revenue Code of 1954 or a retirement bond described in section 409 of the Internal Revenue Code of 1954 (as effective for obligations issued before January 1, 1984) and an employer or association of employers which establishes such an account or annuity under section 408(c) of such Code shall be deemed to be an owner-employee.

The above amendment applies to taxable years beginning after December 31, 1997.

P.L. 104-188, Sec. 1704(n)(2):

Amended ERISA Sec. 408(b)(1) by adding a new sentence at the end to read as above.

The above amendment is effective as of December 12, 1994.

P.L. 101-508, Sec. 12012(b):

Amended ERISA Sec. 408(b) by adding new paragraph (13) effective for qualified transfers under Code Sec. 420 made after November 5, 1990.

P.L. 101-239, §7881(l)(5):

Amended ERISA Sec. 408(b) by adding a new paragraph (12) to read as above effective December 22, 1987.

P.L. 101-239, §7891(a)(2):

Amended ERISA Sec. 408(d), last sentence (as amended by section 7894(e)(4)(A)(i)), by striking "section 408 of the Internal Revenue Code of 1954" and inserting "section 408 of the Internal Revenue Code of 1986" and by striking "section 408(c) of such Code" and inserting "section 408(c) of the Internal Revenue Code of 1986" effective December 22, 1987.

P.L. 101-239, §7894(e)(4):

Amended ERISA Sec. 408(d), the last sentence, by striking "individual retirement account, individual retirement annuity, or an individual retirement bond (as defined in section 408 or 409 of the Internal Revenue Code of 1954)" and inserting "individual retirement account or individual retirement annuity described in section 408 of the Internal Revenue Code of 1954 or a retirement bond described in section 409 of the Internal Revenue Code of 1954 (as effective for obligations issued before January 1,

1984)"; and by striking "section 408(c) of such code" and inserting "section 408(c) of such Code" effective as if included in P.L. 98-369, § 491(b).

P.L. 99-514, § 1114(b)(15)(B):

Struck out "highly compensated employees, officers, or shareholders" and inserted "highly compensated employees (within the meaning of section 414(g) of the Internal Revenue Code of 1986)" in ERISA Sec. 408(b), effective for years beginning after December 31, 1988.

P.L. 99-514, § 1898(i):

Amended ERISA Sec. 408(d) by striking out "(a)", effective for transactions after the date of enactment.

P.L. 97-354, § 5(a)(43):

Added the words, "as in effect on the day before the date of the enactment of the Subchapter S Revision Act of 1982," after the words "section 1379 of the Internal Revenue Code of 1954" in subsection 408(d).

P.L. 96-364, § 308:

Added new subsections 408(b)(10) and (11) and new section 408(f), effective September 26, 1980.

Regulations

The following regulations were adopted under "Title 29—Labor," "Chapter XXV—Pension and Welfare Benefit Programs," "Subchapter F—Employee Retirement Income Security Act of 1974," "Part 2550—Rules and Regulations for Fiduciary Responsibility." The regulations were filed with the Federal Register on June 21, 1977, and published in the Federal Register on June 24, 1977 (42 FR 32389). Reg. § 2550.408b-1 was filed with the Federal Register on July 19, 1989, and published in the Federal Register on July 20, 1989 (54 FR 30520). Reg. § 2550.408e was adopted on July 29, 1980, and published in the Federal Register on August 1, 1980 (45 FR 51194).

[¶ 14,781]

§ 2550.408b-1 General statutory exemption for loans to plan participants and beneficiaries who are parties in interest with respect to the plan.

(a)(1) *In general.* Section 408(b)(1) of the Employee Retirement Income Security Act of 1974 (the Act or ERISA) exempts from the prohibitions of section 406(a), 406(b)(1) and 406(b)(2) loans by a plan to parties in interest who are participants or beneficiaries of the plan, provided that such loans:

(i) Are available to all such participants and beneficiaries on a reasonably equivalent basis;

(ii) Are not made available to highly compensated employees, officers or shareholders in an amount greater than the amount made available to other employees;

(iii) Are made in accordance with specific provisions regarding such loans set forth in the plan;

(iv) Bear a reasonable rate of interest; and

(v) Are adequately secured.

The Internal Revenue Code (the Code) contains parallel provisions to section 408(b)(1) of the Act. Effective, December 31, 1978, section 102 of Reorganization Plan No. 4 of 1987 (43 FR 47713, October 17, 1978) transferred the authority of the Secretary of the Treasury to promulgate regulations of the type published herein to the Secretary of Labor. Therefore, all references herein to section 408(b)(1) of the Act should be read to include reference to the parallel provisions of section 4975(d)(1) of the Code.

Section 1114(b)(15)(B) of the Tax Reform Act of 1986 amended section 408(b)(1)(B) of ERISA by deleting the phrase "highly compensated employees, officers or shareholders" and substituting the phrase "highly compensated employees (within the meaning of section 414(q) of the Internal Revenue Code of 1986)." Thus, for plans with participant loan programs which are subject to the amended section 408(b)(1)(B), the requirements of this regulation should be read to conform with the amendment.

(2) *Scope.* Section 408(b)(1) of the Act does not contain an exemption from acts described in section 406(b)(3) of the Act (prohibiting fiduciaries from receiving consideration for their own personal account from any party dealing with a plan in connection with a transaction involving plan assets). If a loan from a plan to a participant who is a party in interest with respect to that plan involves an act described in section 406(b)(3), such an act constitutes a separate transaction which is not exempt under section 408(b)(1) of the Act. The provisions of section 408(b)(1) are further limited by section 408(d) of the Act (relating to transactions with owner-employees and related persons).

(3) *Loans.* (i) Section 408(b)(1) of the Act provides relief from the prohibitions of section 406(a), 406(b)(1) and 406(b)(2) for the making of a participant loan. The term "participant loan" refers to a loan which is arranged and approved by the fiduciary administering the loan program primarily in the interest of the participant and which otherwise satisfies the criteria set forth in section 408(b)(1) of the Act. The existence of a participant loan or participant loan program will be determined upon consideration of all relevant facts and circumstances.

Thus, for example, the mere presence of a loan document appearing to satisfy the requirements of section 408(b)(1) will not be dispositive of whether a participant loan exists where the subsequent administration of the loan indicates that the parties to the loan agreement did not intend the loan to be repaid. Moreover, a loan program containing a precondition designed to benefit a party in interest (other than the participant) is not afforded relief by section 408(b)(1) or this regulation. In this regard, section 408(b)(1) recognizes that a program of participant loans, like other plan investments, must be prudently established and administered for the exclusive purpose of providing benefits to participants and beneficiaries of the plan.

(ii) For the purpose of this regulation, the term "loan" will include any renewal or modification of an existing loan agreement, provided that, at the time of each such renewal or modification, the requirements of section 408(b)(1) and this regulation are met.

(4) *Examples.* The following examples illustrate the provisions of § 2550.408b-1(a).

Example (1): T, a trustee of plan P, has exclusive discretion over the management and disposition of plan assets. As a result, T is a fiduciary with respect to P under section 3(21)(A) of the Act and a party in interest with respect to P pursuant to section 3(14)(A) of the Act. T is also a participant in P. Among T's duties as fiduciary is the administration of a participant loan program which meets the requirements of section 408(b)(1) of the Act. Pursuant to strict objective criteria stated under the program, T, who participates in all loan decisions, receives a loan on the same terms as other participants. Although the exercise of T's discretion on behalf of himself may constitute an act of self-dealing described in section 406(b)(1), section 408(b)(1) provides an exemption from section 406(b)(1). As a result, the loan from P to T would be exempt under section 408(b)(1), provided the conditions of that section are otherwise satisfied.

Example (2): P is a plan covering all the employees of E, the employer who established and maintained P. F is a fiduciary with respect to P and an officer of E. The plan documents governing P give F the authority to establish a participant loan program in accordance with section 408(b)(1) of the Act. Pursuant to an arrangement with E, F establishes such a program but limits the use of loan funds to investments in a limited partnership which is established and maintained by E as general partner. Under these facts, the loan program and any loans made pursuant to this program are outside the scope of relief provided by section 408(b)(1) because the loan program is designed to operate for the benefit of E. Under the circumstances described, the diversion of plan assets for E's benefit would also violate sections 403(c)(1) and 404(a) of the Act.

Example (3): Assume the same facts as in Example 2, above, except that F does not limit the use of loan funds. However, E pressures his employees to borrow funds under P's participant loan program and then reloans the loan proceeds to E. F, unaware of E's activities, arranges and approves the loans. If the loans meet all the conditions of section 408(b)(1), such loans will be exempt under that section. However, E's activities would cause the entire transaction to be viewed as an indirect transfer of plan assets between P and E, who is a party in interest with respect to P, but not the participant borrowing from P. By coercing the employee to engage in loan transactions for its benefit, E has engaged in separate transactions that are not exempt under section 408(b)(1). Accordingly, E would be liable for the payment of excise taxes under section 4975 of the Code.

Example (4): Assume the same facts as in Example 2, above, except that, in return for structuring and administering the loan program as indicated, E agrees to pay F an amount equal to 10 percent of the funds loaned under the program. Such a payment would result in a separate transaction not covered by section 408(b)(1). This transaction would be prohibited under section 406(b)(3) since F would be receiving consideration from a party in connection with a transaction involving plan assets.

Example (5): F is a fiduciary with respect to plan P. D is a party in interest with respect to plan P. Section 406(a)(1)(B) of the Act would prohibit F from causing P to lend money to D. However, F enters into an agreement with Z, a plan participant, whereby F will cause P to make a participant loan to Z with the express understanding that Z will subsequently lend the loan proceeds to D. An examination of Z's credit standing indicates that he is not creditworthy and would not, under normal circumstances, receive a loan under the conditions established by the participant loan program. F's decision to approve the participant loan to Z on the basis of Z's prior agreement to lend the money to D violates the exclusive purpose requirements of sections 403(c) and 404(a). In effect, the entire transaction is viewed as an indirect transfer of plan assets between P and D, and not a loan to a participant exempt under section 408(b)(1). Z's lack of credit standing would also cause the transaction to fail under section 408(b)(1)(A) of the Act.

Example (6): F is a fiduciary with respect to Plan P. Z is a plan participant. Z and D are both parties in interest with respect to P. F approves a participant loan to Z in accordance with the conditions established under the participant loan program. Upon receipt of the loan, Z intends to lend the money to D. If F has approved this loan solely upon consideration of those factors which would be considered in a normal commercial setting by an entity in the business of making comparable loans, Z's subsequent use of the loan proceeds will not affect the determination of whether loans under P's program satisfy the conditions of section 408(b)(1).

Example (7): A is the trustee of a small individual account plan. D, the president of the plan sponsor, is also a participant in the plan. Pursuant to a participant loan program meeting the requirements of section 408(b)(1), D applies for a loan to be secured by a parcel of real property. D does not intend to repay the loan; rather, upon eventual default, he will permit the property to be foreclosed upon and transferred to the plan in discharge of his legal obligation to repay the loan. A, aware of D's intention, approves the loan. D fails to make two consecutive quarterly payments of principal and interest under the note evidencing the loan thereby placing the loan in default. The plan then acquires the real property upon foreclosure. Such facts and circumstances indicate that the payment of money from the plan to D was not a participant loan eligible for the relief afforded by section 408(b)(1). In effect, this transaction is a prohibited sale or exchange of property between a plan and a party in interest from the time D receives the money.

Example (8): Plan P establishes a participant loan program. All loans are subject to the condition that the borrowed funds must be used to finance home purchases. Interest rates on the loans are the same as those charged by a local savings and loan association under similar circumstances. A loan by P to a participant to finance a home purchase would be subject to the relief provided by section 408(b)(1) provided that the conditions of 408(b)(1) are met. A participant loan program which is established to make loans for certain stated purposes (e.g., hardship, college tuition, home purchases, etc.) but which is not otherwise designed to benefit parties in interest (other than plan participants) would not, in itself, cause such program to be ineligible for the relief provided by section 408(b)(1). However, fiduciaries are cautioned that operation of a loan program with limitations may result in loans not being made available to all participants and beneficiaries on a reasonably equivalent basis.

(b) *Reasonably Equivalent Basis.* (1) Loans will not be considered to have been made available to participants and beneficiaries on a reasonably equivalent basis unless:

    (i) Such loans are available to all plan participants and beneficiaries without regard to any individual's race, color, religion, sex, age or national origin;

    (ii) In making such loans, consideration has been given only to those factors which would be considered in a normal commercial setting by an entity in the business of making similar types of loans. Such factors may include the applicant's creditworthiness and financial need; and

    (iii) An evaluation of all relevant facts and circumstances indicates that, in actual practice, loans are not unreasonably withheld from any applicant.

    (2) A participant loan program will not fail the requirement of paragraph (b)(1) of this section or §2550.408b-1(c) if the program establishes a minimum loan amount of up to $1,000, provided that the loans granted meet the requirements of §2550.408b-1(f).

    (3) *Examples.* The following examples illustrate the provisions of §2550.408b-1(b)(1):

Example (1): T, a trustee of plan P, has exclusive discretion over the management and disposition of plan assets. T's duties include the administration of a participant loan program which meets the requirements of section 408(b)(1) of the Act. T receives a participant loan at a lower interest rate than the rate made available to other plan participants of similar financial condition or creditworthiness with similar security. The loan by P to T would not be covered by the relief provided by section 408(b)(1) because loans under P's program are not available to all plan participants on a reasonably equivalent basis.

Example (2): Same facts as in Example 1, except that T is a member of a committee of trustees responsible for approving participant loans. T pressures the committee to refuse loans to other qualified participants in order to assure that the assets allocated to the participant loan program would be available for a loan by P to T. The loan by P to T would not be covered by the relief provided by section 408(b)(1) since participant loans have not been made available to all participants and beneficiaries on a reasonably equivalent basis.

Example (3): T is the trustee of plan P, which covers the employees of E. A, B and C are employees of E, participants in P, and friends of T. The documents governing P provide that T, in his discretion, may establish a participant loan program meeting certain specified criteria. T institutes such a program and tells A, B and C of his decision. Before T is able to notify P's other participants and beneficiaries of the loan program, A, B, and C file loan applications which, if approved, will use up substantially all of the funds set aside for the loan program. Approval of these applications by T would represent facts and circumstances showing that loans under P's program are not available to all participants and beneficiaries on a reasonably equivalent basis.

(c) *Highly Compensated Employees.* (1) Loans will not be considered to be made available to highly compensated employees, officers or shareholders in an amount greater than the amount made available to other employees if, upon consideration of all relevant facts and circumstances, the program does not operate to exclude large numbers of plan participants from receiving loans under the program.

    (2) A participant loan program will not fail to meet the requirement in paragraph (c)(1), of this section, merely because the plan documents specifically governing such loans set forth either (i) a maximum dollar limitation, or (ii) a maximum percentage of vested accrued benefit which no loan may exceed.

    (3) If the second alternative in paragraph (c)(2) of this section (maximum percentage of vested accrued benefit) is chosen, a loan program will not fail to meet this requirement solely because maximum loan amounts will vary directly with the size of the participant's accrued benefit.

    (4) *Examples.* The following examples illustrate the provisions of §2550.408b-1(c).

Example (1): The documents governing plan P provide for the establishment of a participant loan program in which the amount of any loan under the program (when added to the outstanding balances of any other loans under the program to the same participant) does not exceed the lesser of (i) $50,000, or (ii) one-half of the present value of that participant's vested accrued benefit under the plan (but not less than $10,000). P's participant loan program does not fail to meet the requirement in section 408(b)(1)(B) of the Act, and would be covered by the relief provided by section 408(b)(1) if the other conditions of that section are met.

Example (2): The documents governing plan T provide for the establishment of a participant loan program in which the minimum loan amount would be $25,000. The documents also require that the only security acceptable under the program would be the participant's vested accrued benefit. A, the plan fiduciary administering the loan program, finds that because of the restrictions in the plan documents only 20 percent of the plan participants, all of whom earn in excess of $75,000 a year, would meet the threshold qualifications for a loan. Most of these participants are high-level supervisors or corporate officers. Based on these facts, it appears that loans under the program would be made available to highly compensated employees in an amount greater than the amount made available to other employees. As a result, the loan program would fail to meet the requirement in section 408(b)(1)(B) of the Act and would not be covered by the relief provided in section 408(b)(1).

(d) *Specific Plan Provisions*. For the purpose of section 408(b)(1) and this regulation, the Department will consider that participant loans granted or renewed at any time prior to the last day of the first plan year beginning on or after January 1, 1989, are made in accordance with specific provisions regarding such loans set forth in the plan if:

(1) The plan provisions regarding such loans contain (at a minimum) an explicit authorization for the plan fiduciary responsible for investing plan assets to establish a participant loan program; and

(2) For participant loans granted or renewed on or after the last day of the first plan year beginning on or after January 1, 1989, the participant loan program which is contained in the plan or in a written document forming part of the plan includes, but need not be limited to, the following:

(i) The identity of the person or positions authorized to administer the participant loan program;

(ii) A procedure for applying for loans;

(iii) The basis on which loans will be approved or denied;

(iv) Limitations (if any) on the types and amount of loans offered;

(v) The procedure under the program for determining a reasonable rate of interest;

(vi) The types of collateral which may secure a participant loan; and

(vii) The events constituting default and the steps that will be taken to preserve plan assets in the event of such default.

Example (1): Plan P authorizes the trustee to establish a participant loan program in accordance with section 408(b)(1) of the Act. Pursuant to this explicit authority, the trustee establishes a written program which contains all of the information required by § 2550.408b-1(d)(2). Loans made pursuant to this authorization and the written loan program will not fail under section 408(b)(1)(C) of the Act merely because the specific provisions regarding such loans are contained in a separate document forming part of the plan. The specific provisions describing the loan program, whether contained in the plan or in a written document forming part of a plan, do affect the rights and obligations of the participants and beneficiaries under the plan and, therefore, must in accordance with section 102(a)(1) of the Act, be disclosed in the plan's summary plan description.

(e) *Reasonable Rate of Interest*. A loan will be considered to bear a reasonable rate of interest if such loan provides the plan with a return commensurate with the interest rates charged by persons in the business of lending money for loans which would be made under similar circumstances.

Example (1): Plan P makes a participant loan to A at the fixed interest rate of 8% for 5 years. The trustees, prior to making the loan, contacted two local banks to determine under what terms the banks would make a similar loan taking into account A's creditworthiness and the collateral offered. One bank would charge a variable rate of 10% adjusted monthly for a similar loan. The other bank would charge a fixed rate of 12% under similar circumstances. Under these facts, the loan to A would not bear a reasonable rate of interest because the loan did not provide P with a return commensurate with interest rates

charged by persons in the business of lending money for loans which would be made under similar circumstances. As a result, the loan would fail to meet the requirements of section 408(b)(1)(D) and would not be covered by the relief provided by section 408(b)(1) of the Act.

Example (2): Pursuant to the provisions of plan P's participant loan program, T, the trustee of P, approves a loan to M, a participant and party in interest with respect to P. At the time of execution, the loan meets all of the requirements of section 408(b)(1) of the Act. The loan agreement provides that at the end of two years M must pay the remaining balance in full or the parties may renew for an additional two-year period. At the end of the initial two-year period, the parties agree to renew the loan for an additional two years. At the time of renewal, however, A fails to adjust the interest rate charged on the loan in order to reflect current economic conditions. As a result, the interest rate on the renewal fails to provide a "reasonable rate of interest" as required by section 408(b)(1)(D) of the Act. Under such circumstances, the loan would not be exempt under section 408(b)(1) of the Act from the time of renewal.

Example (3): The documents governing plan P's participant loan program provide that loans must bear an interest rate no higher than the maximum interest rate permitted under State X's usury law. Pursuant to the loan program, P makes a participant loan to A, a plan participant, at a time when the interest rates charged by financial institutions in the community (not subject to the usury limit) for similar loans are higher than the usury limit. Under these circumstances, the loan would not bear a reasonable rate of interest because the loan does not provide P with a return commensurate with the interest rates charged by persons in the business of lending money under similar circumstances. In addition, participant loans that are artificially limited to the maximum usury ceiling then prevailing call into question the status of such loans under sections 403(c) and 404(a) where higher yielding comparable investment opportunities are available to the plan.

(f) *Adequate Security*. (1) A loan will be considered to be adequately secured if the security posted for such loan is something in addition to and supporting a promise to pay, which is so pledged to the plan that it may be sold, foreclosed upon, or otherwise disposed of upon default of repayment of the loan, the value and liquidity of which security is such that it may reasonably be anticipated that loss of principal or interest will not result from the loan. The adequacy of such security will be determined in light of the type and amount of security which would be required in the case of an otherwise identical transaction in a normal commercial setting between unrelated parties on arm's-length terms. A participant's vested accrued benefit under a plan may be used as security for a participant loan to the extent of the plan's ability to satisfy the participant's outstanding obligation in the event of default.

(2) For purposes of this paragraph, (i) no more than 50% of the present value of a participant's vested accrued benefit may be considered by a plan as security for the outstanding balance of all plan loans made to that participant; (ii) a plan will be in compliance with paragraph (f)(2)(i) of this section if, with respect to any participant, it meets the provisions of paragraph (f)(2)(i) of this section immediately after the origination of each participant loan secured in whole or in part by that participant's vested accrued benefit; and (iii) any loan secured in whole or in part by a portion of a participant's vested accrued benefit must also meet the requirements of paragraph (f)(1) of this section.

(g) *Effective Date*. This section is effective for all participant loans granted or renewed after October 18, 1989, except with respect to paragraph (d)(2) of this section relating to specific plan provisions. Paragraph (d)(2) of this section is effective for participant loans granted or renewed on or after the last day of the first plan year beginning on or after January 1, 1989.

(Approved by the Office of Management and Budget under control number 1210-0076)

Signed this 14th day of July, 1989.

Ann L. Combs,

Deputy Assistant Secretary for Policy Pension and Welfare Benefits Administration, U.S. Department of Labor.

[¶ 14,782]

§ 2550.408b-2 General statutory exemption for services of office space.

(a) *In general.* Section 408(b)(2) of the Employee Retirement Income Security Act of 1974 (the Act) exempts from the prohibitions of section 406(a) of the Act payment by a plan to a party in interest, including a fiduciary, for office space or any service (or a combination of services) if (1) such office space or service is necessary for the establishment or operation of the plan; (2) such office space or service is furnished under a contract or arrangement which is reasonable; and (3) no more than reasonable compensation is paid for such office space or service. However, section 408(b)((2) does not contain an exemption from acts described in section 406(b)(1) of the Act (relating to fiduciaries dealing with the assets of plans in their own interest or for their own account), section 406(b)(2) of the Act (relating to fiduciaries in their individual or in any other capacity acting in any transaction involving the plan on behalf of a party (or representing a party) whose interests are adverse to the interests of the plan or the interests of its participants or beneficiaries) or section 406(b)(3) of the Act (relating to fiduciaries receiving consideration for their own personal account from any party dealing with a plan in connection with a transaction involving the assets of the plan). Such acts are separate transactions not described in section 408(b)(2). See §§ 2550.408b-2(e) and (f) for guidance as to whether transactions relating to the furnishing of office space or services by fiduciaries to plans involve acts described in section 406(b)(1) of the Act. Section 408(b)(2) of the Act does not contain an exemption from other provisions of the Act, such as section 404, or other provisions of law which may impose requirements or restrictions relating to the transactions which are exempt under section 408(b)(2). See, for example, section 401 of the Internal Revenue Code of 1954. The provisions of section 408(b)(2) of the Act are further limited by section 408(d) of the Act (relating to transactions with owner-employees and related persons).

(b) *Necessary service.* A service is necessary for the establishment or operation of a plan within the meaning of section 408(b)(2) of the Act and § 2550.408b-2(a)(1) if the service is appropriate and helpful to the plan obtaining the service in carrying out the purposes for which the plan is established or maintained. A person providing such a service to a plan (or a person who is a party in interest solely by reason of a relationship to such a service provider described in section 3 (14) (F), (G), (H), or (I) of the Act) may furnish goods which are necessary for the establishment or operation of the plan in the course of, and incidental to, the furnishing of such service to the plan.

(c) *Reasonable contract or arrangement.* No contract or arrangement is reasonable within the meaning of section 408(b)(2) of the Act and § 2550.408b-2(a)(2) if it does not permit termination by the plan without penalty to the plan on reasonably short notice under the circumstances to prevent the plan from becoming locked into an arrangement that has become disadvantageous. A long-term lease which may be terminated prior to its expiration (without penalty to the plan) on reasonably short notice under the circumstances is not generally an unreasonable arrangement merely because of its long term. A provision in a contract or other arrangement which reasonably compensates the service provider or lessor for loss upon early termination of the contract, arrangement or lease is not a penalty. For example, a minimal fee in a service contract which is charged to allow recoupment of reasonable startup costs is not a penalty. Similarly, a provision in a lease for a termination fee that covers reasonably foreseeable expenses related to the vacancy and reletting of the office space upon early termination of the lease is not a penalty. Such a provision does not reasonably compensate for loss if it provides for payment in excess of actual loss or if it fails to require mitigation of damages.

(d) *Reasonable compensation.* Section 408(b)(2) of the Act and § 2550.408b-2(a)(3) permit a plan to pay a party in interest reasonable compensation for the provision of office space or services described in section 408(b)(2). Section 2550.408c-2 of these regulations contains provisions relating to what constitutes reasonable compensation for the provision of services.

(e) *Transactions with fiduciaries.* (1) *In general.* If the furnishing of office space or a service involves an act described in section 406(b)

of the Act (relating to acts involving conflicts of interest by fiduciaries), such an act constitutes a separate transaction which is not exempt under section 408(b)(2) of the Act. The prohibitions of section 406(b) supplement the other prohibitions of section 406(a) of the Act by imposing on parties in interest who are fiduciaries a duty of undivided loyalty to the plans for which they act. These prohibitions are imposed upon fiduciaries to deter them from exercising the authority, control, or responsibility which makes such persons fiduciaries when they have interests which may conflict with the interests of the plans for which they act. In such cases, the fiduciaries have interests in the transactions which may affect the exercise of their best judgment as fiduciaries. Thus, a fiduciary may not use the authority, control, or responsibility which makes such a person a fiduciary to cause a plan to pay an additional fee to such fiduciary (or to a person in which such fiduciary has an interest which may affect the exercise of such fiduciary's best judgment as a fiduciary) to provide a service. Nor may a fiduciary use such authority, control, or responsibility to cause a plan to enter into a transaction involving plan assets whereby such fiduciary (or a person in which such fiduciary has an interest which may affect the exercise of such fiduciary's best judgment as a fiduciary) will receive consideration from a third party in connection with such transaction. A person in which a fiduciary has an interest which may affect the exercise of such fiduciary's best judgment as a fiduciary includes, for example, a person who is a party in interest by reason of a relationship to such fiduciary described in section 3(14) (E), (F), (G), (H), or (I).

(2) *Transactions not described in section 406(b)(1).* A fiduciary does not engage in an act described in section 406(b)(1) of the Act if the fiduciary does not use any of the authority, control or responsibility which makes such person a fiduciary to cause a plan to pay additional fees for a service furnished by such fiduciary or to pay a fee for a service furnished by a person in which such fiduciary has an interest which may affect the exercise of such fiduciary's best judgment as a fiduciary. This may occur, for example, when one fiduciary is retained on behalf of a plan by a second fiduciary to provide a service for an additional fee. However, because the authority, control or responsibility which makes a person a fiduciary may be exercised "in effect" as well as in form, mere approval of the transaction by a second fiduciary does not mean that the first fiduciary has not used any of the authority, control or responsibility which makes such person a fiduciary to cause the plan to pay the first fiduciary an additional fee for a service. See paragraph (f) below.

(3) *Services without compensation.* If a fiduciary provides services to a plan without the receipt of compensation or other consideration (other than reimbursement of direct expenses properly and actually incurred in the performance of such services within the meaning of § 2550.408c-2(b)(3)), the provision of such services does not, in and of itself, constitute an act described in section 406(b) of the Act. The allowance of a deduction to an employer under section 162 or 212 of the Code for the expense incurred in furnishing office space or services to a plan established or maintained by such employer does not constitute compensation or other consideration.

(f) *Examples.* The provisions of § 2550.408b-2(e) may be illustrated by the following examples.

Example (1). E, an employer whose employees are covered by plan P, is a fiduciary of P. I is a professional investment adviser in which E has no interest which may affect the exercise of E's best judgment as a fiduciary. E causes P to retain I to provide certain kinds of investment advisory services of a type which causes I to be a fiduciary of P under section 3(21)(A)(ii) of the Act. Thereafter, I proposes to perform for additional fees portfolio evaluation services in addition to the services currently provided. The provision of such services is arranged by I and approved on behalf of the plan by E. I has not engaged in an act described in section 406(b)(1) of the Act, because I did not use any of the authority, control or responsibility which makes I a fiduciary (the provision of investment advisory services) to cause the plan to pay I additional fees for the provision of the portfolio evaluation services. E has not engaged in an act which is described in section 406(b)(1). E, as the fiduciary who has the responsibility to be prudent in his selection and retention of I and the other investment advisers of the plan, has an interest in the purchase by the plan of portfolio evaluation services. However, such an interest is not an interest which may affect the exercise of E's best judgment as a fiduciary.

Example (2). D, a trustee of plan P with discretion over the management and disposition of plan assets, relies on the advice of C, a consultant to P, as to the investment of plan assets, thereby making C a fiduciary of the plan. On January 1, 1978, C recommends to D that the plan purchase an insurance policy from U, an insurance company which is not a party in interest with respect to P. C thoroughly explains the reasons for the recommendation and makes a full disclosure concerning the fact that C will receive a commission from U upon the purchase of the policy by P. D considers the recommendation and approves the purchase of the policy by P. C receives a commission. Under such circumstances, C has engaged in an act described in section 406(b)(1) of the Act (as well as sections 406(b)(2) and (3) of the Act) because C is in fact exercising the authority, control or responsibility which makes C a fiduciary to cause the plan to purchase the policy. However, the transaction is exempt from the prohibited transaction provisions of section 406 of the Act, if the requirements of Prohibited Transaction Exemption 77-9 are met.

Example (3). Assume the same facts as in Example (2) except that the nature of C's relationship with the plan is not such that C is a fiduciary of P. The purchase of the insurance policy does not involve an act described in section 406(b)(1) of the Act (or sections 406(b) (2) or (3) of the Act) because such sections only apply to acts by fiduciaries.

Example (4). E, an employer whose employees are covered by plan P, is a fiduciary with respect to P. A, who is not a party in interest with respect to P, persuades E that the plan needs the services of a professional investment adviser and that A should be hired to provide the investment advice. Accordingly, E causes P to hire A to provide investment advice of the type which makes A a fiduciary under §2510.3-21(c)(1)(ii)(B). Prior to the expiration of A's first contract with P, A persuades E to cause P to renew A's contract with P to provide the same services for additional fees in view of the increased costs in providing such services. During the period of A's second contract, A provides additional investment advice services for which no additional charge is made. Prior to the expiration of A's second contract, A persuades E to cause P to renew his contract for additional fees in view of the additional services A is providing. A has not engaged in an act described in section 406(b)(1) of the Act, because A has not used any of the authority, control or responsibility which makes A a fiduciary (the provision of investment advice) to cause the plan to pay additional fees for A's services.

Example (5). F, a trustee of plan P with discretion over the management and disposition of plan assets, retains C to provide administrative services to P of the type which makes C a fiduciary under section 3(21)(A)(iii). Thereafter, C retains F to provide for additional fees actuarial and various kinds of administrative services in addition to the services F is currently providing to P. Both F and C have engaged in an act described in section 406(b)(1) of the Act. F, regardless of any intent which he may have had at the time he retained C, has engaged in such an act because F has, in effect, exercised the authority, control or responsibility which makes F a fiduciary to cause the plan to pay F additional fees for the services. C, whose continued employment by P depends on F, has also engaged in such an act, because C has an interest in the transaction which might affect the exercise of C's best judgment as a fiduciary. As a result, C has dealt with plan assets in his own interest under section 406(b)(1).

Example (6). F, a fiduciary of plan P with discretionary authority respecting the management of P, retains S, the son of F, to provide for a fee various kinds of administrative services necessary for the operation of the plan. F has engaged in an act described in section 406(b)(1) of the Act because S is a person in whom F has an interest which may affect the exercise of F's best judgment as a fiduciary. Such act is not exempt under section 408(b)(2) of the Act irrespective of whether the provision of the services by S is exempt.

Example (7). T, one of the trustees of plan P, is president of bank B. The bank proposes to provide administrative services to P for a fee. T physically absents himself from all consideration of B's proposal and does not otherwise exercise any of the authority, control or responsibility which makes T a fiduciary to cause the plan to retain B. The other trustees decide to retain B. T has not engaged in an act described in section 406(b)(1) of the Act. Further, the other trustees have not

engaged in an act described in section 406(b)(1) merely because T is on the board of trustees of P. This fact alone would not make them have an interest in the transaction which might affect the exercise of their best judgment as fiduciaries.

[¶ 14,783]
§2550.408b-3 **Loans to Employee Stock Ownership Plans.**

(a) *Definitions.* When used in this section, the terms listed below have the following meanings:

(1) *ESOP.* The term "ESOP" refers to an employee stock ownership plan that meets the requirements of section 407(d)(6) of the Employee Retirement Income Security Act of 1974 (the Act) and 29 CFR 2550.407d-6. It is not synonymous with "stock bonus plan." A stock bonus plan must, however, be an ESOP to engage in an exempt loan. The qualification of an ESOP under section 401(a) of the Internal Revenue Code (the Code) and 26 CFR 54.4975-11 will not be adversely affected merely because it engages in a non-exempt loan.

(2) *Loan.* The term "loan" refers to a loan made to an ESOP by a party in interest or a loan to an ESOP which is guaranteed by a party in interest. It includes a direct loan of cash, a purchase-money transaction, and an assumption of the obligation of an ESOP. "Guarantee" includes an unsecured guarantee and the use of assets of a party in interest as collateral for a loan, even though the use of assets may not be a guarantee under applicable state law. An amendment of a loan in order to qualify as an exempt loan is not a refinancing of the loan or the making of another loan.

(3) *Exempt loan.* The term "exempt loan" refers to a loan that satisfies the provisions of this section. A "non-exempt loan" is one that fails to satisfy such provisions.

(4) *Publicly traded.* The term "publicly traded" refers to a security that is listed on a national securities exchange registered under section 6 of the Securities Exchange Act of 1934 (15 U.S.C. 78f) or that is quoted on a system sponsored by a national securities association registered under section 15 A(b) of the Securities Exchange Act (15 U.S.C. 78o).

(5) *Qualifying employer security.* The term "qualifying employer security" refers to a security described in 29 CFR 2550.407d-5.

(b) *Statutory exemption.* (1) *Scope.* Section 408(b)(3) of the Act provides an exemption from the prohibited transaction provisions of sections 406(a) and 406(b)(1) of the Act (relating to fiduciaries dealing with the assets of plans in their own interest or for their own account) and 406(b)(2) of the Act (relating to fiduciaries in their individual or in any other capacity acting in any transaction involving the plan on behalf of a party (or representing a party) whose interests are adverse to the interests of the plan or the interests of its participants or beneficiaries). Section 408(b)(3) does not provide an exemption from the prohibitions of section 406(b)(3) of the Act (relating to fiduciaries receiving consideration for their own personal account from any party dealing with a plan in connection with a transaction involving the income or assets of the plan).

(2) *Special scrutiny of transaction.* The exemption under section 408(b)(3) includes within its scope certain transactions in which the potential for self-dealing by fiduciaries exists and in which the interests of fiduciaries may conflict with the interests of participants. To guard against these potential abuses, the Department of Labor will subject these transactions to special scrutiny to ensure that they are primarily for the benefit of participants and their beneficiaries. Although the transactions need not be arranged and approved by an independent fiduciary, fiduciaries are cautioned to scrupulously exercise their discretion in approving them. For example, fiduciaries should be prepared to demonstrate compliance with the net effect test and the arm's-length standard under paragraphs (c)(2) and (3) of this section. Also, fiduciaries should determine that the transaction is truly arranged primarily in the interest of participants and their beneficiaries rather than, for example, in the interest of certain selling shareholders.

(c) *Primary benefit requirement.* (1) *In general.* An exempt loan must be primarily for the benefit of the ESOP participants and their beneficiaries. All the surrounding facts and circumstances, including those described in paragraphs (c) (2) and (3) of this section, will be considered in determining whether such loan satisfies this requirement. However, no loan will satisfy such requirement unless it satisfies the requirements of paragraphs (d), (e) and (f) of this section.

(2) *Net effect on plan assets.* At the time that a loan is made, the interest rate for the loan and the price of securities to be acquired with the loan proceeds should not be such that plan assets might be drained off.

(3) *Arm's-length standard.* The terms of a loan, whether or not between independent parties, must, at the time the loan is made, be at least as favorable to the ESOP as the terms of a comparable loan resulting from arm's-length negotiations between independent parties.

(d) *Use of loan proceeds.* The proceeds of an exempt loan must be used, within a reasonable time after their receipt, by the borrowing ESOP only for any or all of the following purposes:

(1) To acquire qualifying employer securities.

(2) To repay such loan.

(3) To repay a prior exempt loan. A new loan, the proceeds of which are so used, must satisfy the provisions of this section.

Except as provided in paragraphs (i) and (j) of this section or as otherwise required by applicable law, no security acquired with the proceeds of an exempt loan may be subject to a put, call, or other option, or buy-sell or similar arrangement while held by and when distributed from a plan, whether or not the plan is then an ESOP.

(e) *Liability and collateral of ESOP for loan.* An exempt loan must be without recourse against the ESOP. Furthermore, the only assets of the ESOP that may be given as collateral on an exempt loan are qualifying employer securities of two classes: those acquired with the proceeds of the exempt loan and those that were used as collateral on a prior exempt loan repaid with the proceeds of the current exempt loan. No person entitled to payment under the exempt loan shall have any right to assets of the ESOP other than:

(1) Collateral given for the loan,

(2) Contributions (other than contributions of employer securities) that are made under an ESOP to meet its obligations under the loan, and

(3) Earnings attributable to such collateral and the investment of such contributions.

The payments made with respect to an exempt loan by the ESOP during a plan year must not exceed an amount equal to the sum of such contributions and earnings received during or prior to the year less such payments in prior years. Such contributions and earnings must be accounted for separately in the books of account of the ESOP until the loan is repaid.

(f) *Default.* In the event of default upon an exempt loan, the value of plan assets transferred in satisfaction of the loan must not exceed the amount of default. If the lender is a party in interest, a loan must provide for a transfer of plan assets upon default only upon and to the extent of the failure of the plan to meet the payment schedule of the loan. For purposes of this paragraph, the making of a guarantee does not make a person a lender.

(g) *Reasonable rate of interest.* The interest rate of a loan must not be in excess of a reasonable rate of interest. All relevant factors will be considered in determining a reasonable rate of interest, including the amount and duration of the loan, the security and guarantee (if any) involved, the credit standing of the ESOP and the guarantor (if any), and the interest rate prevailing for comparable loans. When these factors are considered, a variable interest rate may be reasonable.

(h) *Release from encumbrance.* (1) *General rule.* In general, an exempt loan must provide for the release from encumbrance of plan assets used as collateral for the loan under this paragraph. For each plan year during the duration of the loan, the number of securities released must equal the number of encumbered securities held immediately before release for the current plan year multiplied by a fraction. The numerator of the fraction is the amount of principal and interest paid for the year. The denominator of the fraction is the sum of the numerator plus the principal and interest to be paid for all future years.

See § 2550.408b-3(h)(4). The number of future years under the loan must be definitely ascertainable and must be determined without taking into account any possible extensions or renewal periods. If the interest rate under the loan is variable, the interest to be paid in future years must be computed by using the interest rate applicable as of the end of the plan year. If collateral includes more than one class of securities, the number of securities of each class to be released for a plan year must be determined by applying the same fraction to each class.

(2) *Special rule.* A loan will not fail to be exempt merely because the number of securities to be released from encumbrance is determined solely with reference to principal payments. However, if release is determined with reference to principal payments only, the following three additional rules apply. The first rule is that the loan must provide for annual payments of principal and interest at a cumulative rate that is not less rapid at any time than level annual payments of such amounts for 10 years. The second rule is that interest included in any payment is disregarded only to the extent that it would be determined to be interest under standard loan amortization tables. The third rule is that subdivision (2) is not applicable from the time that, by reason of a renewal, extension, or refinancing, the sum of the expired duration of the exempt loan, the renewal period, the extension period, and the duration of a new exempt loan exceeds 10 years.

(3) *Caution against plan disqualification.* Under an exempt loan, the number of securities released from encumbrance may vary from year to year. The release of securities depends upon certain employer contributions and earnings under the ESOP. Under 26 CFR 54.4975-11(d)(2) actual allocations to participants' accounts are based upon assets withdrawn from the suspense account. Nevertheless, for purposes of applying the limitations under section 415 of the Code to these allocations, under 26 CFR 54.4975-11(a)(8)(ii) contributions used by the ESOP to pay the loan are treated as annual additions to participants' accounts. Therefore, particular caution must be exercised to avoid exceeding the maximum annual additions under section 415 of the Code. At the same time, release from encumbrance in annually varying numbers may reflect a failure on the part of the employer to make substantial and recurring contributions to the ESOP which will lead to loss of qualification under section 401(a) of the Code. The Internal Revenue Service will observe closely the operation of ESOPs that release encumbered securities in varying annual amounts, particularly those that provide for the deferral of loan payments or for balloon payments. See 26 CFR 54.4975-7(b)(8)(iii).

(4) *Illustration.* The general rule under paragraph (h)(1) of this section operates as illustrated in the following example:

Example. Corporation X establishes an ESOP that borrows $750,000 from a bank. X guarantees the loan which is for 15 years at 5% interest and is payable in level annual amounts of $72,256.72. Total payments on the loan are $1,083,850.80. The ESOP uses the entire proceeds of the loan to acquire 15,000 shares of X stock which is used as collateral for the loan. The number of securities to be released for the first year is 1,000 shares, i.e., 15,000 shares × $72,256.72/$1,083,850.80 = 15,000 shares × $\frac{1}{15}$. The number of securities to be released for the second year is 1,000 shares, i.e., 14,000 shares × $72,256.72/$1,011,594.08 = 14,000 shares × $\frac{1}{14}$. If all loan payments are made as originally scheduled, the number of securities released in each succeeding year of the loan will also be 1,000.

[Officially corrected by 42 FR 45907.]

(i) *Right of first refusal.* Qualifying employer securities acquired with proceeds of an exempt loan may, but need not, be subject to a right of first refusal. However, any such right must meet the requirements of this paragraph. Securities subject to such right must be stock or an equity security, or a debt security convertible into stock or an equity security. Also, they must not be publicly traded at the time the right may be exercised. The right of first refusal must be in favor of the employer, the ESOP, or both in any order of priority. The selling price and other terms under the right must not be less favorable to the seller than the greater of the value of the security determined under 26 CFR 54.4975-11(d)(5), or the purchase price and other terms offered by a buyer, other than the employer or the ESOP, making a good faith offer to purchase the security. The right of first refusal must lapse no later than 14 days after the security holder gives written notice to the holder of the right that an offer by a third party to purchase the security has been received.

(j) *Put option.* A qualifying employer security acquired with the proceeds of an exempt loan by an ESOP after September 30, 1976, must be subject to a put option if it is not publicly traded when distributed or if it is subject to a trading limitation when distributed. For purposes of this paragraph, a "trading limitation" on a security is a restriction under any Federal or State securities law or any regulation thereunder, or an agreement (not prohibited by this section) affecting the security which would make the security not as freely tradable as one not subject to such restriction. The put option must be exercisable only by a participant, by the participant's donees, or by a person (including an estate or its distributee) to whom the security passes by reason of a participant's death. (Under this paragraph "participant" means a participant and the beneficiaries of the participant under the ESOP.) The put option must permit a participant to put the security to the employer. Under no circumstances may the put option bind the ESOP. However, it may grant the ESOP an option to assume the rights and obligations of the employer at the time that the put option is exercised. If it is known at the time a loan is made that Federal or state law will be violated by the employer's honoring such put option, the put option must permit the security to be put, in a manner consistent with such law, to a third party (e.g., an affiliate of the employer or a shareholder other than the ESOP) that has substantial net worth at the time the loan is made and whose net worth is reasonably expected to remain substantial.

[Officially corrected by 42 FR 45907.]

(k) *Duration of put option.* (1) *General rule.* A put option must be exercisable at least during a 15-month period which begins the date the security subject to the put option is distributed by the ESOP.

(2) *Special rule.* In the case of a security that is publicly traded without restriction when distributed but ceases to be so traded within 15 months after distribution, the employer must notify each security holder in writing on or before the tenth day after the date the security ceases to be so traded that for the remainder of the 15-month period the security is subject to a put option. The number of days between the tenth day and the date on which notice is actually given, if later than the tenth day, must be added to the duration of the put option. The notice must inform distributees of the terms of the put options that they are to hold. The terms must satisfy the requirements of paragraphs (j) through (l) of this section.

(l) *Other put option provisions.* (1) *Manner of exercise.* A put option is exercised by the holder notifying the employer in writing that the put option is being exercised.

(2) *Time excluded from duration of put option.* The period during which a put option is exercisable does not include any time when a distributee is unable to exercise it because the party bound by the put option is prohibited from honoring it by applicable Federal or state law.

(3) *Price.* The price at which a put option must be exercisable is the value of the security, determined in accordance with paragraph (d)(5) of 26 CFR 54.4975-11.

(4) *Payment terms.* The provisions for payment under a put option must be reasonable. The deferral of payment is reasonable if adequate security and a reasonable interest rate are provided for any credit extended and if the cumulative payments at any time are no less than the aggregate of reasonable periodic payments as of such time. Periodic payments are reasonable if annual installments, beginning with 30 days after the date the put option is exercised, are substantially equal. Generally, the payment period may not end more than 5 years after the date the put option is exercised. However, it may be extended to a date no later than the earlier of 10 years from the date the put option is exercised or the date the proceeds of the loan used by the ESOP to acquire the security subject to such put option are entirely repaid.

(5) *Payment restrictions.* Payment under a put option may be restricted by the terms of a loan, including one used to acquire a security subject to a put option, made before November 1, 1977. Otherwise, payment under a put option must not be restricted by the provisions of a loan or any other arrangement, including the terms of

the employer's articles of incorporation, unless so required by applicable state law.

(m) *Other terms of loan.* An exempt loan must be for a specific term. Such loan may not be payable at the demand of any person, except in the case of default.

(n) *Status of plan as ESOP.* To be exempt, a loan must be made to a plan that is an ESOP at the time of such loan. However, a loan to a plan formally designated as an ESOP at the time of the loan that fails to be an ESOP because it does not comply with section 401(a) of the Code or 26 CFR 54.4975-11 will be exempt as of the time of such loan if the plan is amended retroactively under section 401(b) of the Code or 26 CFR 54.4975-11(a)(4).

(o) *Special rules for certain loans.* (1) *Loans made before January 1, 1976.* A loan made before January 1, 1976, or made afterwards under a binding agreement in effect on January 1, 1976 (or under renewals permitted by the terms of such an agreement on that date) is exempt for the entire period of such loan if it otherwise satisfies the provisions of this section for such period, even though it does not satisfy the following provisions of this section:

(i) The last sentence of paragraph (d);

(ii) Paragraphs (e), (f), and (h) (1) and (2); and

(iii) Paragraphs (i) through (m), inclusive.

(2) *Loans made after December 31, 1975, but before (November 1, 1977).* A loan made after December 31, 1975, but before November 1, 1977, or made afterwards under a binding agreement in effect on November 1, 1977 (or under renewals permitted by the terms of such an agreement on that date) is exempt for the entire period of such loan if it otherwise satisfies the provisions of this section for such period even though it does not satisfy the following provisions of this section:

(i) Paragraph (f);

(ii) The three provisions of paragraph (h)(2); and (iii) paragraph (i).

(3) *Release rule.* Notwithstanding paragraphs (o) (1) and (2) of this section, if the proceeds of a loan are used to acquire securities after November 1, 1977, the loan must comply by such date with the provisions of paragraph (h) of this section.

(4) *Default rule.* Notwithstanding paragraphs (o) (1) and (2) of this section, a loan by a party in interest other than a guarantor must satisfy the requirements of paragraph (f) of this section. A loan will satisfy these requirements if it is retroactively amended before November 1, 1977, to satisfy these requirements.

(5) *Put option rule.* With respect to a security distributed before November 1, 1977, the put option provisions of paragraphs (j), (k), and (l) of this section will be deemed satisfied as of the date the security is distributed if by December 31, 1977, the security is subject to a put option satisfying such provisions. For purposes of satisfying such provisions, the security will be deemed distributed on the date the put option is issued. However, the put option provisions need not be satisfied with respect to a security that is not owned on November 1, 1977, by a person in whose hands a put option must be exercisable.

[Added August 30, 1977, by 42 FR 44384; officially corrected by 42 FR 45907.]

[¶ 14,784]

§ 2550.408b-4 Statutory exemption for investments in deposits of banks or similar financial institutions.

(a) *In general.* Section 408(b)(4) of the Employee Retirement Income Security Act of 1974 (the Act) exempts from the prohibitions of section 406 of the Act the investment of all or a part of a plan's assets in deposits bearing a reasonable rate of interest in a bank or similar financial institution supervised by the United States or a State, even though such bank or similar financial institution is a fiduciary or other party in interest with respect to the plan, if the conditions of either § 2550.408b-4(b)(1) or § 2550.408b-4(b)(2) are met. Section 408(b)(4) provides an exemption from sections 406(b)(1) of the Act (relating to fiduciaries dealing with the assets of plans in their own interest or for their own account) and 406(b)(2) of the Act (relating to fiduciaries in their individual or in any other capacity acting in any transaction involving the plan on behalf of a party (or representing a party) whose interests are adverse to the interests of the plan or the interests of its participants or beneficiaries), as well as section 406(a)(1), because section 408(b)(4) contemplates a bank or similar financial institution causing a plan for which it acts as a fiduciary to invest plan assets in its own deposits if the requirements of section 408(b)(4) are met. However, it does not provide an exemption from section 406(b)(3) of the Act (relating to fiduciaries receiving consideration for their own personal account from any party dealing with a plan in connection with a transaction involving the assets of the plan). The receipt of such consideration is a separate transaction not described in the statutory exemption. Section 408(b)(4) does not contain an exemption from other provisions of the Act, such as section 404, or other provisions of law which may impose requirements or restrictions relating to the transactions which are exempt under section 408(b)(4) of the Act. See, for example, section 401 of the Internal Revenue Code of 1954 (Code). The provisions of section 408(b)(4) of the Act are further limited by section 408(d) of the Act (relating to transactions with owner-employees and related persons).

[Officially corrected by 42 FR 36823.]

(b)(1) *Plan covering own employees.* Such investment may be made if the plan is one which covers only the employees of the bank or similar financial institution, the employees of any of its affiliates, or the employees of both.

(2) *Other plans.* Such investment may be made if the investment is expressly authorized by a provision of the plan or trust instrument or if the investment is expressly authorized (or made) by a fiduciary of the plan (other than the bank or similar financial institution or any of its affiliates) who has authority to make such investments, or to instruct the trustee or other fiduciary with respect to investments, and who has no interest in the transaction which may affect the exercise of such authorizing fiduciary's best judgment as a fiduciary so as to cause such authorization to constitute an act described in section 406(b) of the Act. Any authorization to make investments contained in a plan or trust instrument will satisfy the requirement of express authorization for investments made prior to November 1, 1977. Effective November 1, 1977, in the case of a bank or similar financial institution that invests plan assets in deposits in itself or its affiliates under an authorization contained in a plan or trust instrument, such authorization must name such bank or similar financial institution and must state that such bank or similar financial institution may make investments in deposits which bear a reasonable rate of interest in itself (or in an affiliate).

(3) *Example.* B, a bank, is the trustee of plan P's assets. The trust instruments give the trustees the right to invest plan assets in its discretion. B invests in the certificates of deposit of bank C, which is a fiduciary of the plan by virtue of performing certain custodial and administrative services. The authorization is sufficient for the plan to make such investment under section 408(b)(4). Further, such authorization would suffice to allow B to make investments in deposits in itself prior to November 1, 1977. However, subsequent to October 31, 1977, B may not invest in deposits in itself, unless the plan or trust instrument specifically authorizes it to invest in deposits of B.

(c) *Definitions.* (1) The term "bank or similar financial institution" includes a bank (as defined in section 581 of the Code), a domestic building and loan association (as defined in section 7701(a)(19) of the Code), and a credit union (as defined in section 101(6) of the Federal Credit Union Act).

(2) A person is an affiliate of a bank or similar financial institution if such person and such bank or similar financial institution would be treated as members of the same controlled group of corporations or as members of two or more trades or businesses under common control within the meaning of section 414(b) or (c) of the Code and the regulations thereunder.

(3) The term "deposits" includes any account, temporary or otherwise, upon which a reasonable rate of interest is paid, including a certificate of deposit issued by a bank or similar financial institution.

[¶ 14,786]
§ 2550.408b-6 Statutory exemption for ancillary services by a bank or similar financial institution.

(a) *In general.* Section 408(b)(6) of the Employee Retirement Income Security Act of 1974 (the Act) exempts from the prohibitions of section 406 of the Act the provision of certain ancillary services by a bank or similar financial institution (as defined in § 2550.408b-4(c)(1)) supervised by the United States or a State to a plan for which it acts as a fiduciary if the conditions of § 2550.408b-6(b) are met. Such ancillary services include services which do not meet the requirements of section 408(b)(2) of the Act because the provision of such services involves an act described in section 406(b)(1) of the Act (relating to fiduciaries dealing with the assets of plans in their own interest or for their own account) by the fiduciary bank or similar financial institution or an act described in section 406(b)(2) of the Act (relating to fiduciaries in their individual or in any other capacity acting in any transaction involving the plan on behalf of a party (or representing a party) whose interests are adverse to the interests of the plan or the interests of its participants or beneficiaries). Section 408(b)(6) provides an exemption from sections 406(b)(1) and (2) because section 408(b)(6) contemplates the provision of such ancillary services without the approval of a second fiduciary (as described in § 2550.408b-2(e)(2)) if the conditions of § 2550.408b-6(b) are met. Thus, for example, plan assets held by a fiduciary bank which are reasonably expected to be needed to satisfy current plan expenses may be placed by the bank in a non-interest-bearing checking account if the conditions of § 2550.408b-6(b) are met, notwithstanding the provisions of section 408(b)(4) of the Act (relating to investments in bank deposits). However, section 408(b)(6) does not provide an exemption for an act described in section 406(b)(3) of the Act (relating to fiduciaries receiving consideration for their own personal account from any party dealing with a plan in connection with a transaction involving the assets of the plan). The receipt of such consideration is a separate transaction not described in section 408(b)(6). Section 408(b)(6) does not contain an exemption from other provisions of the Act, such as section 404, or other provisions of law which may impose requirements or restrictions relating to the transactions which are exempt under section 408(b)(6) of the Act. See, for example, section 401 of the Internal Revenue Code of 1954. The provisions of section 408(b)(6) of the Act are further limited by section 408(d) of the Act (relating to transactions with owner-employees and related persons).

[Officially corrected by 42 FR 36823.]

(b) *Conditions.* Such service must be provided—

(1) At not more than reasonable compensation;

(2) Under adequate internal safeguards which assure that the provision of such service is consistent with sound banking and financial practice, as determined by Federal or State supervisory authority; and

(3) Only to the extent that such service is subject to specific guidelines issued by the bank or similar financial institution which meet the requirements of § 2550.408b-6(c).

(c) *Specific guidelines.* [Reserved]

[¶ 14,788]
§ 2550.408c-2 Compensation for services.

(a) *In general.* Section 408(b)(2) of the Employee Retirement Income Security Act of 1974 (the Act) refers to the payment of reasonable compensation by a plan to a party in interest for services rendered to the plan. Section 408(c)(2) of the Act and §§ 2550.408c-2(b)(1) through 2550.408c-2(b)(4) clarify what constitutes reasonable compensation for such services.

(b)(1) *General rule.* Generally, whether compensation is "reasonable" under sections 408(b)(2) and 408(c)(2) of the Act depends on the particular facts and circumstances of each case.

(2) *Payments to certain fiduciaries.* Under sections 408(b)(2) and 408(c)(2) of the Act, the term "reasonable compensation" does not include any compensation to a fiduciary who is already receiving full-time pay from an employer or association of employers (any of whose employees are participants in the plan) or from an employee organization (any of whose members are participants in the plan), except for the

reimbursement of direct expenses properly and actually incurred and not otherwise reimbursed. The restrictions of this paragraph (b)(2) do not apply to a party in interest who is not a fiduciary.

(3) *Certain expenses not direct expenses.* An expense is not a direct expense to the extent it would have been sustained had the service not been provided or if it represents an allocable portion of overhead costs.

(4) *Expense advances.* Under sections 408(b)(2) and 408(c)(2) of the Act, the term "reasonable compensation", as applied to a fiduciary or an employee of a plan, includes an advance to such a fiduciary or employee by the plan to cover direct expenses to be properly and actually incurred by such person in the performance of such person's duties with the plan if:

(i) The amount of such advance is reasonable with respect to the amount of the direct expense which is likely to be properly and actually incurred in the immediate future (such as during the next month); and

(ii) The fiduciary or employee accounts to the plan at the end of the period covered by the advance for the expenses properly and actually incurred.

(5) *Excessive compensation.* Under sections 408(b)(2) and 408(c)(2) of the Act, any compensation which would be considered excessive under 26 CFR 1.162-7 (Income Tax Regulations relating to compensation for personal services which constitutes an ordinary and necessary trade or business expense) will not be "reasonable compensation". Depending upon the facts and circumstances of the particular situation, compensation which is not excessive under 26 CFR 1.162-7 may, nevertheless, not be "reasonable compensation" within the meaning of sections 408(b)(2) and 408(c)(2) of the Act.

[¶ 14,789]

§ 2550.408e Statutory exemption for acquisition or sale of qualifying employer securities and for acquisition, sale or lease of qualifying employer real property.

(a) *General.* Section 408(e) of the Employee Retirement Income Security Act of 1974 (the Act) exempts from the prohibitions of section 406(a) and 406(b)(1) and (2) of the Act any acquisition or sale by a plan of qualifying employer securities (as defined in section 407(d)(5) of the Act), or any acquisition, sale or lease by a plan of qualifying employer

real property (as defined in section 407(d)(4) of the Act) if certain conditions are met. The conditions are that

(1) The acquisition, sale or lease must be for adequate consideration (which is defined in paragraph (d) of this section);

(2) No commission may be charged directly or indirectly to the plan with respect to the transaction; and

(3) In the case of an acquisition or lease of qualifying employer real property, or an acquisition of qualifying employer securities, by a plan other than an eligible individual account plan (as defined in section 407(d)(3) of the Act), the acquisition or lease must comply with the requirements of section 407(a) of the Act.

(b) *Acquisition.* For purposes of section 408(e) and this section, an acquisition by a plan of qualifying employer securities or qualifying employer real property shall include, but not be limited to, an acquisition by purchase, by the exchange of plan assets, by the exercise of warrants or rights, by the conversion of a security, by default of a loan where the qualifying employer security or qualifying employer real property was security for the loan, or in connection with the contribution of such securities or real property to the plan. However, an acquisition of a security shall not be deemed to have occurred if a plan acquires the security as a result of a stock dividend or stock split.

(c) *Sale.* For purposes of section 408(e) and this section, a sale of qualifying employer real property or qualifying employer securities shall include any disposition for value.

(d) *Adequate Consideration.* For purposes of section 408(e) and this section, adequate consideration means:

(1) In the case of a marketable obligation, a price not less favorable to the plan than the price determined under section 407(e)(1) of the Act; and

(2) In all other cases, a price not less favorable to the plan than the price determined under section 3(18) of the Act.

(e) *Commission.* For purposes of section 408(e) and this section, the term "commission" includes any fee, commission or similar charge paid in connection with a transaction, except that the term "commission" does not include a charge incurred for the purpose of enabling the appropriate plan fiduciaries to evaluate the desirability of entering into a transaction to which this section would apply, such as an appraisal or investment advisory fee.

Regulations

The following regulations were adopted under "Title 29—Labor," "Chapter XXV—Pension and Welfare Benefit Programs," "Subchapter F—Employee Retirement Income Security Act of 1974," "Part 2570 Subpart B—Procedures for Filing and Processing Prohibited Transaction Exemption Applications." The regulations were filed with the Federal Register on August 9, 1990 and published in the Federal Register on August 10, 1990 (55 FR 32836).

Subpart B—Procedures for Filing and Processing Prohibited Transaction Exemption Applications

[¶ 14,789C]

§ 2570.30 Scope of rules.

(a)(1) The rules of procedure set forth in this subpart apply to all applications for exemption which the Department has authority to issue under:

(i) Section 408(a) of the Employee Retirement Income Security Act of 1974 (ERISA);

(ii) Section 4975(c)(2) of the Internal Revenue Code of 1986 (the Code) (see Reorganization Plan No. 4 of 1978); or

(iii) The Federal Employees' Retirement System Act of 1986 (FERSA) (5 U.S.C. 8477(c)(3)).

(b) The Department will generally treat any exemption application which is filed solely under section 408(a) of ERISA or solely under section 4975(c)(2) of the Code as an exemption filed under both section 408(a) and section 4975(c)(2) if it relates to a transaction that would be prohibited both by ERISA and by the corresponding provisions of the Code.

(c) The procedures set forth in this subpart represent the exclusive means by which the Department will issue administrative exemptions. The Department will not issue exemptions upon oral request

alone. Likewise, the Department will not grant exemptions orally. An applicant for an administrative exemption may request and receive oral advice from Department employees in preparing an exemption application. However, such advice does not constitute part of the administrative record and is not binding on the Department in its processing of an exemption application or in its examination or audit of a plan.

[¶ 14,789D]

§ 2570.31 Definitions.

For purposes of these procedures, the following definitions apply:

(a) An *affiliate* of a person means—

(1) Any person directly or indirectly through one or more intermediaries, controlling, controlled by, or under common control with the person;

(2) Any director of, relative of, or partner in, any such person;

(3) Any corporation, partnership, trust, or unincorporated enterprise of which such person is an officer, director, or a 5 percent or more partner or owner; and

(4) Any employee or officer of the person who—

(i) Is highly compensated (as defined in section 4975(e)(2)(H) of the Code), or

(ii) Has direct or indirect authority, responsibility, or control regarding the custody, management, or disposition of plan assets.

(b) A *class exemption* is an administrative exemption, granted under section 408(a) of ERISA, section 4975(c)(2) of the Code, and/or 5 U.S.C. 8477(c)(3), which applies to any parties in interest within the class of parties in interest specified in the exemption who meet the conditions of the exemption.

(c) *Department* means the U.S. Department of Labor and includes the Secretary of Labor or his delegate exercising authority with respect to prohibited transaction exemptions to which this subpart applies.

(d) *Exemption transaction* means the transaction or transactions for which an exemption is requested.

(e) An *individual exemption* is an administrative exemption, granted under section 408(a) of ERISA, section 4975(c)(2) of the Code, and/or 5 U.S.C. 8477(c)(3), which applies only to the specific parties in interest named or otherwise defined in the exemption.

(f) A *party in interest* means a person described in section 3(14) of ERISA or 5 U.S.C. 8477(a)(4) and includes a *disqualified person,* as defined in section 4975(e)(2) of the Code.

(g) *Pooled fund* means an account or fund for the collective investment of the assets of two or more unrelated plans, including (but not limited to) a pooled separate account maintained by an insurance company and a common or collective trust fund maintained by a bank or similar financial institution.

[¶ 14,789E]
§ 2570.32 Persons who may apply for exemptions.

(a) The Department may initiate exemption proceedings on its own motion. In addition, the Department will initiate exemption proceedings upon the application of:

(1) Any party in interest to a plan who is or may be a party to the exemption transaction;

(2) Any plan which is a party to the exemption transaction; or

(3) In the case of an application for an exemption covering a class of parties in interest or a class of transactions, in addition to any person described in paragraphs (a)(1) and (a)(2) of this section, an association or organization representing parties in interest who may be parties to the exemption transaction.

(b) An application by or for a person described in paragraph (a) of this section, may be submitted by the applicant or by his authorized representatives. If the application is submitted by a representative of the applicant, the representative must submit proof of his authority in the form of:

(1) A power of attorney; or

(2) A written certification from the applicant that the representation is authorized.

(c) If the authorized representative of an applicant submits an application for an exemption to the Department together with proof of his authority to file the application as required by paragraph (b) of this section, the Department will direct all correspondence and inquiries concerning the application to the representative unless requested to do otherwise by the applicant.

[¶ 14,789F]
§ 2570.33 Applications the Department will not ordinarily consider.

(a) The Department will not ordinarily consider:

(1) An application that fails to include all the information required by §§ 2570.34 and 2570.35 or otherwise fails to conform to the requirements of these procedures; or

(2) An application for exemption involving a transaction or transactions which are the subject of an investigation for possible violations of part 1 or 4 of subtitle B of title I of ERISA or section 8477 or 8478 of FERSA or an application for an exemption involving a party in interest who is the subject of such an investigation or who is a defendant in an action by the Department or the Internal Revenue Service to enforce the above-mentioned provisions of ERISA or FERSA.

(b) If for any reason the Department decides not to consider an exemption application, it will inform the applicant of that decision in writing and of the reasons therefor.

(c) An application for an individual exemption relating to a specific transaction or transactions will ordinarily not be considered separately if the Department is considering a class exemption relating to the same type of transaction or transactions.

[¶ 14,789G]
§ 2570.34 Information to be included in every exemption application.

(a) All applications for exemptions must contain the following information:

(1) The name(s) of the applicant(s);

(2) A detailed description of the exemption transaction and the parties in interest for whom an exemption is requested, including a description of any larger integrated transaction of which the exemption transaction is a part;

(3) Whether the affected plan(s) and any parties in interest will be represented by the same person with regard to the exemption application;

(4) Reasons a plan would have for entering into the exemption transaction;

(5) The prohibited transaction provisions from which exemptive relief is requested and the reason why the transaction would violate each such provision;

(6) Whether the exemption transaction is customary for the industry or class involved;

(7) Whether the exemption transaction is or has been the subject of an investigation or enforcement action by the Department or by the Internal Revenue Service; and

(8) The hardship or economic loss, if any, which would result to the person or persons on behalf of whom the exemption is sought, to affected plans, and to their participants and beneficiaries from denial of the exemption.

(b) All applications for exemption must also contain the following:

(1) A statement explaining why the requested exemption would be—

(i) Administratively feasible;

(ii) In the interests of affected plans and their participants and beneficiaries, and

(iii) Protective of the rights of participants and beneficiaries of affected plans.

(2) With respect to the notification of interested persons required by § 2570.43:

(i) A description of the interested persons to whom the applicant intends to provide notice;

(ii) The manner in which the applicant will provide such notice; and

(iii) An estimate of the time the applicant will need to furnish notice to all interested persons following publication of a notice of the proposed exemption in the **Federal Register.**

(3) If an advisory opinion has been requested with respect to any issue relating to the exemption transaction—

(i) A copy of the letter concluding the Department's action on the advisory opinion request; or

(ii) If the Department has not yet concluded its action on the request:

(A) A copy of the request or the date on which it was submitted together with the Department's correspondence control number as indicated in the acknowledgement letter; and

(B) An explanation of the effect of a favorable advisory opinion upon the exemption transaction.

(4) If the application is to be signed by anyone other than an individual party in interest seeking exemptive relief on his own behalf, a statement which—

(i) Identifies the individual who will be signing the application and his position with the applicant; and

(ii) Explains briefly the basis of his familiarity with the matters discussed in the application.

(5)(i) A declaration in the following form: Under penalty of perjury, I declare that I am familiar with the matters discussed in this application and, to the best of my knowledge and belief, the representations made in this application are true and correct.

(ii) This declaration must be dated and signed by:

(A) The applicant himself in the case of an individual party in interest seeking exemptive relief on his own behalf;

(B) A corporate officer or partner where the applicant is a corporation or partnership;

(C) A designated officer or official where the applicant is an association, organization or other unincorporated enterprise;

(D) The plan fiduciary who has the authority, responsibility, and control with respect to the exemption transaction where the applicant is a plan.

(iii) Specialized statements from third-party experts, such as appraisals or analyses of market conditions, submitted to support an application for exemption must also be accompanied by a statement of consent from such expert acknowledging that he or she knows that his or her statement is being submitted to the Department as part of an application for exemption.

(iv) For those applications requiring an independent fiduciary to represent the plan in the exemption transaction, each statement submitted by said independent fiduciary must contain a signed and dated declaration under penalty of perjury that, to the best of said fiduciary's knowledge and belief, the representations made in such statement are true and correct.

(c) An application for exemption may also include a draft of the requested exemption which defines the transaction and parties in interest for which exemptive relief is sought and the specific conditions under which the exemption would apply.

[¶ 14,789H]

§ 2570.35 Information to be included in applications for individual exemptions only.

(a) Except as provided in paragraph (c) of this section, every application for an individual exemption must include, in addition to the information specified in § 2570.34, the following information:

(1) The name, address, telephone number, and type of plan or plans to which the requested exemption applies;

(2) The Employer Identification Number (EIN) and the plan number (PN) used by such plan or plans in all reporting and disclosure required by the Department;

(3) Whether any plan or trust affected by the requested exemption has ever been found by the Department, the Internal Revenue Service, or by a court to have violated the exclusive benefit rule of section 401(a) of the Code, or to have engaged in a prohibited transaction under section 503(b) of the Code or corresponding provisions of prior law, section 4975(c)(1) of the Code, section 406 or 407(a) of ERISA, or 5 U.S.C. 8477(c)(3);

(4) Whether any relief under section 408(a) of ERISA, section 4975(c)(2) of the Code, or 5 U.S.C. 8477(c)(3) has been requested by, or provided to, the applicant or any of the parties on behalf of whom the exemption is sought and, if so, the exemption application number or the prohibited transaction exemption number;

(5) Whether the applicant or any of the parties in interest involved in the exemption transaction is currently, or has been within the last five years, a defendant in any lawsuit or criminal action concerning such person's conduct as a fiduciary or party in interest with respect to any plan;

(6) Whether the applicant or any of the parties in interest involved in the exemption transaction has, within the last 13 years, been convicted of any crime described in section 411 of ERISA;

(7) Whether, within the last five years, any plan affected by the exemption transaction or any party in interest involved in the exemption transaction has been under investigation or examination by, or has been engaged in litigation or a continuing controversy with, the Department, the Internal Revenue Service, the Justice Department, the Pension Benefit Guaranty Corporation, or the Federal Retirement Thrift Investment Board involving compliance with provisions of ERISA, provisions of the Code relating to employee benefit plans, or provisions of FERSA relating to the Federal Thrift Savings Fund. If so, the applicant must submit copies of all correspondence with the Department, the

Internal Revenue Service, the Justice Department, the Pension Benefit Guaranty Corporation, or the Federal Retirement Thrift Investment Board regarding the substantive issues involved in the investigation, examination, litigation, or controversy which relate to compliance with the provisions of part 1 or 4 of subtitle B of title I of ERISA, section 4975 of the Code, or section 8477 or 8478 of FERSA. For this purpose, the term "examination" does not include routine audits conducted by the Department pursuant to section 8477(g) of FERSA;

(8) Whether any plan affected by the requested exemption has experienced a reportable event under section 4043 of ERISA;

(9) Whether a notice of intent to terminate has been filed under section 4041 of ERISA respecting any plan affected by the requested exemption;

(10) Names, addresses, and taxpayer identifying numbers of all parties in interest involved in the subject transaction;

(11) The estimated number of participants and beneficiaries in each plan affected by the requested exemption as of the date of the application;

(12) The percentage of the fair market value of the total assets of each affected plan that is involved in the exemption transaction;

(13) Whether the exemption transaction has been consummated or will be consummated only if the exemption is granted;

(14) If the exemption transaction has already been consummated:

(i) The circumstances which resulted in plan fiduciaries causing the plan(s) to engage in the subject transaction before obtaining an exemption from the Department;

(ii) Whether the transaction has been terminated;

(iii) Whether the transaction has been corrected as defined in Code section 4975(f)(5);

(iv) Whether Form 5330, Return of Excise Taxes Related to Employee Benefit Plans, has been filed with the Internal Revenue Service with respect to the transaction; and

(v) Whether any excise taxes due under section 4975(a) and (b) of the Code by reason of the transaction have been paid.

(15) The name of every person who has investment discretion over any assets involved in the exemption transaction and the relationship of each such person to the parties in interest involved in the exemption transaction and the affiliates of such parties in interest;

(16) Whether or not the assets of the affected plan(s) are invested in loans to any party in interest involved in the exemption transaction, in property leased to any such party in interest, or in securities issued by any such party in interest, and, if such investments exist, a statement for each of these three types of investments which indicates:

(i) The type of investment to which the statement pertains;

(ii) The aggregate fair market value of all investments of this type as reflected in the plan's most recent annual report;

(iii) The approximate percentage of the fair market value of the plan's total assets as shown in such annual report that is represented by all investments of this type; and

(iv) The statutory or administrative exemption covering these investments, if any.

(17) The approximate aggregate fair market value of the total assets of each affected plan;

(18) The person(s) who will bear the costs of the exemption application and of notifying interested persons; and

(19) Whether an independent fiduciary is or will be involved in the exemption transaction and, if so, the names of the persons who will bear the cost of the fee payable to such fiduciary.

(b) Each application for an individual exemption must also include:

(1) True copies of all contracts, deeds, agreements, and instruments, as well as relevant portions of plan documents, trust agreements, and any other documents bearing on the exemption transaction;

(2) A discussion of the facts relevant to the exemption transaction that are reflected in these documents and an analysis of their bearing on the requested exemption; and

(3) A copy of the most recent financial statements of each plan affected by the requested exemption.

(c) *Special rule for applications for individual exemption involving pooled funds:*

(1) The information required by paragraphs (a)(8) through (12) of this section is not required to be furnished in an application for individual exemption involving one or more pooled funds;

(2) The information required by paragraphs (a)(1) through (7) and (a)(13) through (19) of this section and by paragraphs (b)(1) through (3) of this section must be furnished by reference to the pooled fund, rather than to the plans participating therein. (For purposes of this paragraph, the information required by paragraph (a)(16) of this section relates solely to other pooled fund transactions with, and investments in, parties in interest involved in the exemption transaction which are also sponsors of plans which invest in the pooled fund.);

(3) The following information must also be furnished—

(i) The estimated number of plans that are participating (or will participate) in the pooled fund; and

(ii) The minimum and maximum limits imposed by the pooled fund (if any) on the portion of the total assets of each plan that may be invested in the pooled fund.

(4) Additional requirements for applications for individual exemption involving pooled funds in which certain plans participate.

(i) This paragraph applies to any application for individual exemption involving one or more pooled funds in which any plan participating therein—

(A) Invests an amount which exceeds 20% of the total assets of the pooled fund, or

(B) Covers employees of:

(I) The party sponsoring or maintaining the pooled fund, or any affiliate of such party, or

(II) Any fiduciary with investment discretion over the pooled fund's assets, or any affiliate of such fiduciary.

(ii) The exemption application must include, with respect to each plan described in paragraph (c)(4)(i) of this section, the information required by paragraphs (a)(1) through (3), (a)(5) through (7), (a)(10), (a)(12) through (16) and, (a)(18) and (19), of this section. The information required by this paragraph must be furnished by reference to the plan's investment in the pooled fund (e.g., the names, addresses and taxpayer identifying numbers of all fiduciaries responsible for the plan's investment in the pooled fund [§ 2570.35(a)(10)], the percentage of the assets of the plan invested in the pooled fund [§ 2570.35(a)(12)], whether the plan's investment in the pooled fund has been consummated or will be consummated only if the exemption is granted [§ 2570.35(a)(13)], etc.).

(iii) The information required by paragraph (c)(4) of this section is in addition to the information required by paragraphs (c)(2) and (3) of this section relating to information furnished by reference to the pooled fund.

(5) The special rule and the additional requirements described in paragraphs (c)(1) through (4) of this section do not apply to an individual exemption request solely for the investment by a plan in a pooled fund. Such an application must provide the information required by paragraphs (a) and (b) of this section.

[¶ 14,789I]

§ 2570.36 **Where to file an application.**

The Department's prohibited transaction exemption program is administered by the Employee Benefits Security Administration (EBSA). Any exemption application governed by these procedures should be mailed or otherwise delivered to: Exemption Application, EBSA, Office of Exemption Determinations, Division of Exemptions, U.S. Department of Labor, 200 Constitution Avenue NW., Washington, DC 20210. [EBSA technical correction, 68 FR 16399 (April 3, 2003).]

[¶ 14,789J]

§ 2570.37 **Duty to amend and supplement exemption applications.**

(a) During the pendency of his exemption application, an applicant must promptly notify the Division of Exemptions in writing if he discovers that any material fact or representation contained in his application or in any documents or testimony provided in support of the application is inaccurate, if any such fact or representation changes during this period, or if, during the pendency of the application, anything occurs that may affect the continuing accuracy of any such fact or representation.

(b) If, at any time during the pendency of his exemption application, an applicant or any other party in interest who would participate in the exemption transaction becomes the subject of an investigation or enforcement action by the Department, the Internal Revenue Service, the Justice Department, the Pension Benefit Guaranty Corporation, or the Federal Retirement Thrift Investment Board involving compliance with provisions of ERISA, provisions of the Code relating to employee benefit plans, or provisions of FERSA relating to the Federal Thrift Savings Fund, the applicant must promptly notify the Division of Exemptions.

(c) The Department may require an applicant to provide documentation it considers necessary to verify any statements contained in the application or in supporting materials or documents.

[¶ 14,789K]

§ 2570.38 **Tentative denial letters.**

(a) If, after reviewing an exemption file, the Department concludes that it will not grant the exemption, it will notify the applicant in writing of its tentative denial of the exemption application. At the same time, the Department will provide a short statement of the reasons for its tentative denial.

(b) An applicant will have 20 days from the date of a tentative denial letter to request a conference under § 2570.40 of these procedures and/or to notify the Department of its intent to submit additional information in writing under § 2570.39 of these procedures. If the Department does not receive a request for a conference or a notification of intent to submit additional information within that time, it will issue a final denial letter pursuant to § 2570.41.

(c) The Department need not issue a tentative denial letter to an applicant before issuing a final denial letter where the Department has conducted a hearing on the exemption pursuant to either § 2570.46 or § 2570.47 of these procedures.

[¶ 14,789L]

§ 2570.39 **Opportunities to submit additional information.**

(a) An applicant may notify the Department of its intent to submit additional information supporting an exemption application either by telephone or by letter sent to the address furnished in the applicant's tentative denial letter. At the same time, the applicant should indicate generally the type of information that he will submit.

(b) An applicant will have 30 days from the date of the notification discussed in paragraph (a) of this section to submit in writing all of the additional information he intends to provide in support of his application. All such information must be accompanied by a declaration under penalty of perjury attesting to the truth and correctness of the information provided, which is dated and signed by a person qualified under § 2570.34(b)(5) of these procedures to sign such a declaration.

(c) If, for reasons beyond his control, an applicant is unable to submit in writing all the additional information he intends to provide in support of his application within the 30-day period described in paragraph (b) of this section, he may request an extension of time to furnish the information. Such requests must be made before the expiration of the 30-day period and will be granted only in unusual circumstances and for limited periods of time.

(d) If an applicant is unable to submit all of the additional information he intends to provide in support of his exemption application within the 30-day period specified in paragraph (b) of this section, or within any additional period of time granted to him pursuant to paragraph (c) of this section, the applicant may withdraw the exemption application before expiration of the applicable time period and reinstate it later pursuant to § 2570.44 of these procedures.

(e) The Department will issue, without further notice, a final denial letter denying the requested exemption pursuant to § 2570.41 of these procedures where—

(1) The Department has not received the additional information that the applicant indicated he would submit within the 30-day period

described in paragraph (b) of this section, or within any additional period of time granted pursuant to paragraph (c) of this section;

(2) The applicant did not request a conference pursuant to §2570.38(b) of these procedures; and

(3) The applicant has not withdrawn his application as permitted by paragraph (d) of this section.

[¶ 14,789M]
§ 2570.40 **Conferences.**

(a) Any conference between the Department and an applicant pertaining to a requested exemption will be held in Washington, DC, except that a telephone conference will be held at the applicant's request.

(b) An applicant is entitled to only one conference with respect to any exemption application. An applicant will not be entitled to a conference, however, where the Department has held a hearing on the exemption under either §2570.46 or §2570.47 of these procedures.

(c) Insofar as possible, conferences will be scheduled as joint conferences with all applicants present where:

(1) More than one applicant has requested an exemption with respect to the same or similar types of transactions;

(2) The Department is considering the applications together as a request for a class exemption;

(3) The Department contemplates not granting the exemption; and

(4) More than one applicant has requested a conference.

(d) The Department will attempt to schedule a conference under this section for a mutually convenient time during the 45-day period following the later of—

(1) The date the Department receives the applicant's request for a conference, or

(2) The date the Department notifies the applicant, after reviewing additional information submitted pursuant to §2570.39, that it is still not prepared to propose the requested exemption.

If the applicant is unable to attend a conference at any of the times proposed by the Department during this 45-day period or if the applicant fails to appear for a scheduled conference, he will be deemed to have waived his right to a conference unless circumstances beyond his control prevent him from scheduling a conference or attending a scheduled conference within this period.

(e) Within 20 days after the date of any conference held under this section, the applicant may submit to the Department a written record of any additional data, arguments, or precedents discussed at the conference but not previously or adequately presented in writing.

[¶ 14,789N]
§ 2570.41 **Final denial letters.**

(a) The Department will issue a final denial letter denying a requested exemption where:

(1) The conditions for issuing a final denial letter specified in §2570.38(b) or §2570.39(e) of these procedures are satisfied;

(2) After issuing a tentative denial letter under §2570.38 of this part and considering the entire record in the case, including all written information submitted pursuant to §2570.39 and §2570.40(e) of these procedures, the Department decides not to propose an exemption or to withdraw an exemption already proposed; or

(3) After proposing an exemption and conducting a hearing on the exemption under either §2570.46 or §2570.47 of this part and after considering the entire record in the case, including the record of the hearing, the Department decides to withdraw the proposed exemption.

[¶ 14,789O]
§ 2570.42 **Notice of proposed exemption.**

If the Department tentatively decides, based on all the information submitted by an applicant, that the exemption should be granted, it will publish a notice of proposed exemption in the **Federal Register.** The notice will:

(a) Explain the exemption transaction and summarize the information received by the Department in support of the exemption;

(b) Specify any conditions under which the exemption is proposed;

(c) Inform interested persons of their right to submit comments in writing to the Department relating to the proposed exemption and establish a deadline for receipt of such comments;

(d) If the proposed exemption includes relief from the prohibitions of section 406(b) of ERISA, section 4975(c)(1)(E) or (F) of the Code, or section 8477(c)(2) of FERSA, inform interested persons of their right to request a hearing under §2570.46 of this part and establish a deadline for receipt of requests for such hearings.

[¶ 14,789P]
§ 2570.43 **Notification of interested persons by applicant.**

(a) If, as set forth in the exemption application, the notification that an applicant intends to provide to interested persons upon publication of a notice of proposed exemption in the **Federal Register** is inadequate, the Department will so inform the applicant and will secure the applicant's written agreement to provide what it considers to be adequate notice under the circumstances.

(b) If a notice of proposed exemption is published in the **Federal Register** in accordance with §2570.42 of this part, the applicant must notify interested persons of the pendency of the exemption in the manner and time period specified in the application or in any superseding agreement with the Department. Any such notification must include:

(1) A copy of the notice of proposed exemption; and

(2) A supplemental statement in the following form:

You are hereby notified that the United States Department of Labor is considering granting an exemption from the prohibited transaction restrictions of the Employee Retirement Income Security Act of 1974, the Internal Revenue Code of 1986, or the Federal Employees' Retirement System Act of 1986. The exemption under consideration is explained in the enclosed Notice of Proposed Exemption. As a person who may be affected by this exemption, you have the right to comment on the proposed exemption by [date].[1] [If you may be adversely affected by the grant of the exemption, you also have the right to request a hearing on the exemption by [date].][2]

Comments or requests for a hearing should be addressed to: Office of Exemption Determinations, Employee Benefits Security Administration, Room ___[3] U.S. Department of Labor, 200 Constitution Avenue NW., Washington, DC 20210, ATTENTION: Application No. ___.[4] [EBSA technical correction, 68 FR 16399 (April 3, 2003).]

The Department will make no final decision on the proposed exemption until it reviews all comments received in response to the enclosed notice. If the Department decides to hold a hearing on the exemption before making its final decision, you will be notified of the time and place of the hearing.

(c) The method used to furnish notice to interested persons must be reasonably calculated to ensure that interested persons actually receive the notice. In all cases, personal delivery and delivery by first-class mail will be considered reasonable methods of furnishing notice.

(d) After furnishing the notice required by this section, an applicant must provide the Department with a statement confirming that notice was furnished to the persons and in the manner and time designated in its exemption application or in any superseding agreement with the Department. This statement must be accompanied by a declaration under penalty of perjury attesting to the truth of the infor-

---

[1] The applicant will write in this space the date of the last day of the time period specified in the notice of proposed exemption.

[2] To be added in the case of an exemption that provides relief from section 406(b) of ERISA or corresponding sections of the Code or FERSA.

[3] The applicant will fill in the room number of the Division of Exemptions. As of the date of this final regulation, the room number of the Division of Exemption was N-5671.

[4] The applicant will fill in the exemption application number, which is stated in the notice of proposed exemption, as well as in all correspondence from the Department to the applicant regarding the application.

mation provided in the statement and signed by a person qualified under § 2570.34(b)(5) of these procedures to sign such a declaration. No exemption will be granted until such a statement and its accompanying declaration have been furnished to the Department.

[¶ 14,789Q]

§ 2570.44 Withdrawal of exemption applications.

(a) An applicant may withdraw his application for an exemption at any time by informing the Department, either orally or in writing, of his intent to withdraw.

(b) Upon receiving an applicant's notice of intent to withdraw an application for an individual exemption, the Department will confirm by letter the applicant's withdrawal of the application and will terminate all proceedings relating to the application. If a notice of proposed exemption has been published in the Federal Register, the Department will publish a notice withdrawing the proposed exemption.

(c) Upon receiving an applicant's notice of intent to withdraw an application for a class exemption or for an individual exemption that is being considered with other applications as a request for a class exemption, the Department will inform any other applicants for the exemption of the withdrawal. The Department will continue to process other applications for the same exemption. If all applicants for a particular class exemption withdraw their applications, the Department may either terminate all proceedings relating to the exemption or propose the exemption on its own motion.

(d) If, following the withdrawal of an exemption application, an applicant decides to reapply for the same exemption, he may submit a letter to the Department requesting that the application be reinstated and referring to the application number assigned to the original application. If, at the time the original application was withdrawn, any additional information to be submitted to the Department under § 2570.39 of these procedures was outstanding, that information must accompany the letter requesting reinstatement of the application. However, the applicant need not resubmit information previously furnished to the Department in connection with a withdrawn application unless reinstatement of the application is requested more than two years after the date of its withdrawal.

(e) Any request for reinstatement of a withdrawn application submitted in accordance with paragraph (d) of this section, will be granted by the Department, and the Department will take whatever steps remained at the time the application was withdrawn to process the application.

[¶ 14,789R]

§ 2570.45 Requests for reconsideration.

(a) The Department will entertain one request for reconsideration of an exemption application that has been finally denied pursuant to § 2570.41(a)(2) or (a)(3) of this part if the applicant presents in support of the application significant new facts or arguments, which, for good reason, could not have been submitted for the Department's consideration during its initial review of the exemption application.

(b) A request for reconsideration of a previously denied application must be made within 180 days after the issuance of the final denial letter and must be accompanied by a copy of the Department's final letter denying the exemption and a statement setting forth the new information and/or arguments that provide the basis for reconsideration.

(c) A request for reconsideration must also be accompanied by a declaration under penalty of perjury attesting to the truth of the new information provided, which is signed by a person qualified under § 2570.34(b)(5) of these procedures to sign such a declaration.

(d) If, after reviewing a request for reconsideration, the Department decides that the facts and arguments presented do not warrant reversal of its original decision to deny the exemption, it will send a letter to the applicant reaffirming that decision.

(e) If, after reviewing a request for reconsideration, the Department decides, based on the new facts and arguments submitted, to reconsider its denial letter, it will notify the applicant of its intent to reconsider the application in light of the new information presented. The Department will then take whatever steps remained at the time it issued its final denial letter to process the exemption application.

(f) If, at any point during its subsequent processing of the application, the Department decides again that the exemption is unwarranted, it will issue a letter affirming its final denial.

[¶ 14,789S]

§ 2570.46 Hearings in opposition to exemptions from restrictions on fiduciary self-dealing.

(a) Any interested person who may be adversely affected by an exemption which the Department proposes to grant from the restrictions of section 406(b) of ERISA, section 4975(c)(1)(E) or (F) of the Code, or section 8477(c)(2) of FERSA may request a hearing before the Department within the period of time specified in the Federal Register notice of the proposed exemption. Any such request must state:

(1) The name, address, and telephone number of the person making the request;

(2) The nature of the person's interest in the exemption and the manner in which the person would be adversely affected by the exemption; and

(3) A statement of the issues to be addressed and a general description of the evidence to be presented at the hearing.

(b) The Department will grant a request for a hearing made in accordance with paragraph (a) of this section where a hearing is necessary to fully explore material factual issues identified by the person requesting the hearing. However, the Department may decline to hold a hearing where:

(1) The request for the hearing does not meet the requirements of paragraph (a);

(2) The only issues identified for exploration at the hearing are matters of law; or

(3) The factual issues identified can be fully explored through the submission of evidence in written form.

(c) An applicant for an exemption must notify interested persons in the event that the Department schedules a hearing on the exemption. Such notification must be given in the form, time, and manner prescribed by the Department. Ordinarily, however, adequate notification can be given by providing to interested persons a copy of the notice of hearing published by the Department in the Federal Register within 10 days of its publication, using any of the methods approved in § 2570.43(c) of this part.

(d) After furnishing the notice required by paragraph (c) of this section, an applicant must submit a statement confirming that notice was given in the form, manner, and time prescribed. This statement must be accompanied by a declaration under penalty of perjury attesting to the truth of the information provided in the statement, which is signed by a person qualified under § 2570.34(b)(5) of these procedures to sign such a declaration.

[¶ 14,789T]

§ 2570.47 Other hearings.

(a) In its discretion, the Department may schedule a hearing on its own motion where it determines that issues relevant to the exemption can be most fully or expeditiously explored at a hearing.

(b) An applicant for an exemption must notify interested persons of any hearing on an exemption scheduled by the Department in the manner described in § 2570.46(c). In addition, the applicant must submit a statement subscribed as true under penalty of perjury like that required in § 2570.46(d).

[¶ 14,789U]

§ 2570.48 Decision to grant exemptions.

(a) If, after considering all the facts and representations submitted by an applicant in support of an exemption application, all the comments received in response to a notice of proposed exemption, and the record of any hearing held in connection with the proposed exemption, the Department determines that the exemption should be granted, it will publish a notice in the Federal Register granting the exemption.

(b) A Federal Register notice granting an exemption will summarize the transaction or transactions for which exemptive relief has been granted and will specify the conditions under which such exemptive relief is available.

[¶ 14,789V]

§ 2570.49 **Limits on the effect of exemptions.**

(a) An exemption does not take effect or protect parties in interest from liability with respect to the exemption transaction unless the material facts and representations contained in the application and in any materials and documents submitted in support of the application were true and complete.

(b) An exemption is effective only for the period of time specified and only under the conditions set forth in the exemption.

(c) Only the specific parties to whom an exemption grants relief may rely on the exemption. If the notice granting an exemption does not limit exemptive relief to specific parties, all parties to the exemption transaction may rely on the exemption.

[¶ 14,789W]

§ 2570.50 **Revocation or modification of exemptions.**

(a) If, after an exemption takes effect, changes in circumstances, including changes in law or policy, occur which call into question the continuing validity of the Department's original conclusions concerning the exemption, the Department may take steps to revoke or modify the exemption.

(b) Before revoking or modifying an exemption, the Department will publish a notice of its proposed action in the Federal Register and provide interested persons with an opportunity to comment on the proposed revocation or modification. In addition, the Department will give the applicant at least 30 days notice in writing of the proposed revocation or modification and the reasons therefor and will provide the applicant with the opportunity to comment on the revocation or modification.

(c) Ordinarily the revocation or modification of an exemption will have prospective effect only.

[¶ 14,789X]

§ 2570.51 **Public inspection and copies.**

(a) The administrative record of each exemption application will be open to public inspection and copying at the Public Disclosure Branch, EBSA, U.S. Department of Labor, 200 Constitution Avenue, N.W., Washington, DC 20210. [EBSA technical correction, 68 FR 16399 (April 3, 2003).]

(b) Upon request, the staff of the Public Disclosure Branch will furnish photocopies of an administrative record, or any specified portion of that record, for a specified charge per page.

[¶ 14,789Y]

§ 2570.52 **Effective date.**

This regulation is effective with respect to all applications for exemptions filed with the Department under section 408(a) of ERISA, section 4975(c)(2) of the Code, or 5 U.S.C. 8477(c)(3) at any time on or after September 10, 1990. Applications for exemptions under section 408(a) of ERISA and/or section 4975 of the Code filed before September 10, 1990, are governed by ERISA Procedure 75-1. Applications for exemption under 5 U.S.C. 8477(c)(3) filed before September 10, 1990, but after December 29, 1988 are governed by part 2585 of chapter XXV of title 29 of the *Code of Federal Regulations* (section 29 CFR part 2585 as revised July 1, 1990). Applications under 5 U.S.C. 8477(c)(3) filed before December 29, 1988 are governed by ERISA Procedure 75-1.

Regulations

The following final regulations, published in the *Federal Register* on April 9, 2003 (68 FR 17484) set forth an administrative procedure for obtaining a determination by the Secretary of Labor as to whether a particular employee benefit plan is established or maintained under or pursuant to one or more agreements that are collective bargaining agreements for purposes of ERISA Sec. 3(40). They replace proposed regulations (CCH PENSION PLAN GUIDE ¶ 20,534F), published in the *Federal Register* on October 27, 2000 (65 FR 64498).

⫸→ *Caution: These regulations are effective on June 9, 2003.*

Subpart H—Procedures for Issuance of Findings Under ERISA Sec. 3(40)

[¶ 14,789Z-1]

§ 2570.150 **Scope of rules.**

The rules of practice set forth in this subpart H apply to "section 3(40) Finding Proceedings" (as defined in § 2570.152(g)), under section 3(40) of the Employee Retirement Income Security Act of 1974 (ERISA or the Act). Refer to 29 CFR 2510.3-40 for the definition of relevant terms of section 3(40) of ERISA, 29 U.S.C. 1002(40). To the extent that the regulations in this subpart differ from the regulations in subpart A of 29 CFR part 18, the regulations in this subpart apply to matters arising under section 3(40) of ERISA rather than the rules of procedure for administrative hearings published by the Department's Office of Administrative Law Judges in subpart A of 29 CFR part 18. These proceedings shall be conducted as expeditiously as possible, and the parties shall make every effort to avoid delay at each stage of the proceedings.

[¶ 14,789Z-2]

§ 2570.151 **In general.**

If there is an attempt to assert state jurisdiction or the application of state law, either by the issuance of a state administrative or court subpoena to, or the initiation of administrative or judicial proceedings against, a plan or other arrangement that alleges it is covered by title I of ERISA, 29 U.S.C. 1003, the plan or other arrangement may petition the Secretary to make a finding under section 3(40)(A)(i) of ERISA that it is a plan established or maintained under or pursuant to an agreement or agreements that the Secretary finds to be collective bargaining agreements for purposes of section 3(40) of ERISA.

[¶ 14,789Z-3]

§ 2570.152 **Definitions.**

For section 3(40) Finding Proceedings, this section shall apply instead of the definitions in 29 CFR 18.2.

(a) ERISA means the Employee Retirement Income Security Act of 1974, et seq., 29 U.S.C. 1001, et seq., as amended.

(b) Order means the whole or part of a final procedural or substantive disposition by the administrative law judge of a matter under section 3(40) of ERISA. No order will be appealable to the Secretary except as provided in this subpart.

(c) Petition means a written request under the procedures in this subpart for a finding by the Secretary under section 3(40) of ERISA that a plan is established or maintained under or pursuant to one or more collective bargaining agreements.

(d) Petitioner means the plan or arrangement filing a petition.

(e) Respondent means:

(1) A state government instrumentality charged with enforcing the law that is alleged to apply or which has been identified as asserting jurisdiction over a plan or other arrangement, including any agency, commission, board, or committee charged with investigating and enforcing state insurance laws, including parties joined under § 2570.153;

(2) The person or entity asserting that state law or state jurisdiction applies to the petitioner;

(3) The Secretary of Labor; and

(4) A state not named in the petition that has intervened under § 2570.153(b).

(f) *Secretary* means the Secretary of Labor, and includes, pursuant to any delegation or sub-delegation of authority, the Assistant Secretary for Employee Benefits Security or other employee of the Employee Benefits Security Administration.

(g) *Section 3(40) Finding Proceeding* means a proceeding before the Office of Administrative Law Judges (OALJ) relating to whether the Secretary finds an entity to be a plan to be established or maintained under or pursuant to one or more collective bargaining agreements within the meaning of section 3(40) of ERISA.

[¶ 14,789Z-4]
§ 2570.153 **Parties.**

For section 3(40) Finding Proceedings, this section shall apply instead of 29 CFR 18.10.

(a) The term "party" with respect to a Section 3(40) Finding Proceeding means the petitioner and the respondents.

(b) States not named in the petition may participate as parties in a Section 3(40) Finding Proceeding by notifying the OALJ and the other parties in writing prior to the date for filing a response to the petition. After the date for service of responses to the petition, a state not named in the petition may intervene as a party only with the consent of all parties or as otherwise ordered by the ALJ.

(c) The Secretary of Labor shall be named as a "respondent" to all actions.

(d) The failure of any party to comply with any order of the ALJ may, at the discretion of the ALJ, result in the denial of the opportunity to present evidence in the proceeding.

[¶ 14,789Z-5]
§ 2570.154 **Filing and contents of petition.**

(a) A person seeking a finding under section 3(40) of ERISA must file a written petition by delivering or mailing it to the Chief Docket Clerk, Office of Administrative Law Judges (OALJ), 800 K Street, NW., Suite 400, Washington, DC 20001-8002, or by making a filing by any electronic means permitted under procedures established by the OALJ.

(b) The petition shall—

(1) Provide the name and address of the entity for which the petition is filed;

(2) Provide the names and addresses of the plan administrator and plan sponsor(s) of the plan or other arrangement for which the finding is sought;

(3) Identify the state or states whose law or jurisdiction the petitioner claims has been asserted over the petitioner, and provide the addresses and names of responsible officials;

(4) Include affidavits or other written evidence showing that:

(i) State jurisdiction has been asserted over or legal process commenced against the petitioner pursuant to state law;

(ii) The petitioner is an employee welfare benefit plan as defined at section 3(1) of ERISA (29 U.S.C. 1002(1)) and 29 CFR 2510.3-1 and is covered by title I of ERISA (see 29 U.S.C. 1003);

(iii) The petitioner is established or maintained for the purpose of offering or providing benefits described in section 3(1) of ERISA (29 U.S.C. 1002(1)) to employees of two or more employers (including one or more self-employed individuals) or their beneficiaries;

(iv) The petitioner satisfies the criteria in 29 CFR 2510.3-40(b); and

(v) Service has been made as provided in § 2570.155.

(5) The affidavits shall set forth such facts as would be admissible in evidence in a proceeding under 29 CFR part 18 and shall show affirmatively that the affiant is competent to testify to the matters stated therein. The affidavit or other written evidence must set forth specific facts showing the factors required under paragraph (b)(4) of this section.

[¶ 14,789Z-6]
§ 2570.155 **Service.**

For section 3(40) proceedings, this section shall apply instead of 29 CFR 18.3.

(a) *In general.* Copies of all documents shall be served on all parties of record. All documents should clearly designate the docket number, if any, and short title of all matters. All documents to be filed shall be delivered or mailed to the Chief Docket Clerk, Office of Administrative Law Judges (OALJ), 800 K Street, NW., Suite 400, Washington, DC 20001-8002, or to the OALJ Regional Office to which the proceeding may have been transferred for hearing. Each document filed shall be clear and legible.

(b) *By parties.* All motions, petitions, pleadings, briefs, or other documents shall be filed with the Office of Administrative Law Judges with a copy, including any attachments, to all other parties of record. When a party is represented by an attorney, service shall be made upon the attorney. Service of any document upon any party may be made by personal delivery or by mailing by first class, prepaid U.S. mail, a copy to the last known address. The Secretary shall be served by delivery to the Associate Solicitor, Plan Benefits Security Division, ERISA Section 3(40) Proceeding, PO Box 1914, Washington, DC 20013. The person serving the document shall certify to the manner and date of service.

(c) *By the Office of Administrative Law Judges.* Service of orders, decisions and all other documents shall be made to all parties of record by regular mail to their last known address.

(d) *Form of pleadings.*

(1) Every pleading shall contain information indicating the name of the Employee Benefits Security Administration (EBSA) as the agency under which the proceeding is instituted, the title of the proceeding, the docket number (if any) assigned by the OALJ and a designation of the type of pleading or paper (e.g., notice, motion to dismiss, etc.). The pleading or paper shall be signed and shall contain the address and telephone number of the party or person representing the party. Although there are no formal specifications for documents, they should be typewritten when possible on standard size 8 1/2 × 11 inch paper.

(2) Illegible documents, whether handwritten, typewritten, photocopies, or otherwise, will not be accepted. Papers may be reproduced by any duplicating process provided all copies are clear and legible.

[¶ 14,789Z-7]
§ 2570.156 **Expedited proceedings.**

For section 3(40) Finding Proceedings, this section shall apply instead of 29 CFR 18.42.

(a) At any time after commencement of a proceeding, any party may move to advance the scheduling of a proceeding, including the time for conducting discovery.

(b) Except when such proceedings are directed by the Chief Administrative Law Judge or the administrative law judge assigned, any party filing a motion under this section shall:

(1) Make the motion in writing;

(2) Describe the circumstances justifying advancement;

(3) Describe the irreparable harm that would result if the motion is not granted; and

(4) Incorporate in the motion affidavits to support any representations of fact.

(c) Service of a motion under this section shall be accomplished by personal delivery, or by facsimile, followed by first class, prepaid, U.S. mail. Service is complete upon personal delivery or mailing.

(d) Except when such proceedings are required, or unless otherwise directed by the Chief Administrative Law Judge or the administrative law judge assigned, all parties to the proceeding in which the motion is filed shall have ten (10) days from the date of service of the motion to file an opposition in response to the motion.

(e) Following the timely receipt by the administrative law judge of statements in response to the motion, the administrative law judge may advance pleading schedules, discovery schedules, prehearing conferences, and the hearing, as deemed appropriate; provided, however, that a hearing on the merits shall not be scheduled with less than five (5) working days notice to the parties, unless all parties consent to an earlier hearing.

(f) When an expedited hearing is held, the decision of the administrative law judge shall be issued within twenty (20) days after receipt of the transcript of any oral hearing or within twenty (20) days after the filing of all documentary evidence if no oral hearing is conducted.

[¶ 14,789Z-8]

§ 2570.157 **Allocation of burden of proof.**

For purposes of a final decision under § 2570.158 (Decision of the Administrative Law Judge) or § 2570.159 (Review by the Secretary), the petitioner shall have the burden of proof as to whether it meets 29 CFR 2510.3-40.

[¶ 14,789Z-9]

§ 2570.158 **Decision of the Administrative Law Judge.**

For section 3(40) finding proceedings, this section shall apply instead of 29 CFR 18.57.

(a) *Proposed findings of fact, conclusions of law, and order.* Within twenty (20) days of filing the transcript of the testimony, or such additional time as the administrative law judge may allow, each party may file with the administrative law judge, subject to the judge's discretion under 29 CFR 18.55, proposed findings of fact, conclusions of law, and order together with the supporting brief expressing the reasons for such proposals. Such proposals and brief shall be served on all parties, and shall refer to all portions of the record and to all authorities relied upon in support of each proposal.

(b) *Decision based on oral argument in lieu of briefs.* In any case in which the administrative law judge believes that written briefs or proposed findings of fact and conclusions of law may not be necessary, the administrative law judge shall notify the parties at the opening of the hearing or as soon thereafter as is practicable that he or she may wish to hear oral argument in lieu of briefs. The administrative law judge shall issue his or her decision at the close of oral argument, or within 30 days thereafter.

(c) *Decision of the administrative law judge.* Within 30 days, or as soon as possible thereafter, after the time allowed for the filing of the proposed findings of fact, conclusions of law, and order, or within thirty (30) days after receipt of an agreement containing consent findings and order disposing of the disputed matter in whole, the administrative law judge shall make his or her decision. The decision of the administrative law judge shall include findings of fact and conclusions of law, with reasons therefore, upon each material issue of fact or law presented on the record. The decision of the administrative law judge shall be based upon the whole record. It shall be supported by reliable and probative evidence. Such decision shall be in accordance with the regulations found at 29 CFR 2510.3-40 and shall be limited to whether the petitioner, based on the facts presented at the time of the proceeding, is a plan established or maintained under or pursuant to collective bargaining for the purposes of section 3(40) of ERISA.

[¶ 14,789Z-10]

§ 2570.159 **Review by the Secretary.**

(a) A request for review by the Secretary of an appealable decision of the administrative law judge may be made by any party. Such a request must be filed within 20 days of the issuance of the final decision or the final decision of the administrative law judge will become the final agency order for purposes of 5 U.S.C. 701 et seq.

(b) A request for review by the Secretary shall state with specificity the issue(s) in the administrative law judge's final decision upon which review is sought. The request shall be served on all parties to the proceeding.

(c) The review by the Secretary shall not be a de novo proceeding but rather a review of the record established by the administrative law judge.

(d) The Secretary may, in his or her discretion, allow the submission of supplemental briefs by the parties to the proceeding.

(e) The Secretary shall issue a decision as promptly as possible, affirming, modifying, or setting aside, in whole or in part, the decision under review, and shall set forth a brief statement of reasons therefor. Such decision by the Secretary shall be the final agency action within the meaning of 5 U.S.C. 704.

[¶ 14,790]

LIABILITY FOR BREACH OF FIDUCIARY DUTY

Act Sec. 409. (a) Any person who is a fiduciary with respect to a plan who breaches any of the responsibilities, obligations, or duties imposed upon fiduciaries by this title shall be personally liable to make good to such plan any losses to the plan resulting from each such breach, and to restore to such plan any profits of such fiduciary which have been made through use of assets of the plan by the fiduciary, and shall be subject to such other equitable or remedial relief as the court may deem appropriate, including removal of such fiduciary. A fiduciary may also be removed for a violation of section 411 of this Act.

Act Sec. 409. (b) No fiduciary shall be liable with respect to a breach of fiduciary duty under this title if such breach was committed before he became a fiduciary or after he ceased to be a fiduciary.

[¶ 14,800]

EXCULPATORY PROVISIONS; INSURANCE

Act Sec. 410. (a) Except as provided in section 405(b)(1) and 405(d), any provision in an agreement or instrument which purports to relieve a fiduciary from responsibility or liability for any responsibility, obligation, or duty under this part shall be void as against public policy.

Act Sec. 410. (b) Nothing in this subpart shall preclude—

(1) a plan from purchasing insurance for its fiduciaries or for itself to cover liability or losses occurring by reason of the act or omission of a fiduciary, if such insurance permits recourse by the insurer against the fiduciary in the case of a breach of a fiduciary obligation by such fiduciary;

(2) a fiduciary from purchasing insurance to cover liability under this part from and for his own account; or

(3) an employer or an employee organization from purchasing insurance to cover potential liability of one or more persons who serve in a fiduciary capacity with regard to an employee benefit plan.

[¶ 14,810]

PROHIBITION AGAINST CERTAIN PERSONS HOLDING CERTAIN POSITIONS

Act Sec. 411. (a) No person who has been convicted of, or has been imprisoned as a result of his conviction of, robbery, bribery, extortion, embezzlement, fraud, grand larceny, burglary, arson, a felony violation of Federal or State law involving substances defined in section 102(6) of the Comprehensive Drug Abuse Prevention and Control Act of 1970, murder, rape, kidnaping, perjury, assault with intent to kill, any crime described in section 9(a)(1) of the Investment Company Act of 1940 (15 U.S.C. 80a-9(a)(1)), a violation of any provision of this Act, a violation of section 302 of the Labor-Management Relations Act, 1947 (29 U.S.C. 186), a violation of chapter 63 of title 18, United States Code, a violation of section 874, 1027, 1503, 1505, 1506, 1510, 1951, or 1954 of title 18, United States Code, a violation of the Labor-Management Reporting and Disclosure Act of 1959 (29 U.S.C. 401), any felony involving abuse or misuse of such person's position or employment in a labor organization or employee benefit plan to seek or obtain an illegal gain at the expense of the members of the labor organization or the beneficiaries of the employee benefit plan, or conspiracy to commit any such crimes or attempt to commit any such crimes, or a crime in which any of the foregoing crimes is an element, shall serve or be permitted to serve—

(1) as an administrator, fiduciary, officer, trustee, custodian, counsel, agent, employee, or representative in any capacity of any employee benefit plan,

(2) as a consultant or adviser to an employee benefit plan, including but not limited to any entity whose activities are in whole or substantial part devoted to providing goods or services to any employee benefit plan, or

(3) in any capacity that involves decisionmaking authority or custody or control of the moneys, funds, assets, or property of any employee benefit plan,

during or for the period of thirteen years after such conviction or after the end of such imprisonment, whichever is later, unless the sentencing court on the motion of the person convicted sets a lesser period of at least three years after such conviction or after the end of such imprisonment, whichever is later, or unless prior to the end of such period, in the case of a person so convicted or imprisoned (A) his citizenship rights, having been revoked as a result of such conviction, have been fully restored, or (B) if the offense is a Federal offense, the sentencing judge or, if the offense is a State or local offense, the United States district court for the district in which the offense was committed, pursuant to sentencing guidelines and policy statements under section 994(a) of title 28, United States Code, determines that such person's service in any capacity referred to in paragraphs (1) through (3) would not be contrary to the purposes of this title. Prior to making any such determination the court shall hold a hearing and shall give notice to such proceeding by certified mail to the Secretary of Labor and to State, county, and Federal prosecuting officials in the jurisdiction or jurisdictions in which such person was convicted. The court's determination in any such proceeding shall be final. No person shall knowingly hire, retain, employ, or otherwise place any other person to serve in any capacity in violation of this subsection. Notwithstanding the preceding provisions of this subsection, no corporation or partnership will be precluded from acting as an administrator, fiduciary, officer, trustee, custodian, counsel, agent, or employee of any employee benefit plan or as a consultant to any employee benefit plan without a notice, hearing, and determination by such court that such service would be inconsistent with the intention of this section.

Act Sec. 411. (b) Any person who intentionally violates this section shall be fined not more than $10,000 or imprisoned for not more than five years, or both.

Act Sec. 411. (c) For the purposes of this section:

(1) A person shall be deemed to have been "convicted" and under the disability of "conviction" from the date of the judgment of the trial court, regardless of whether that judgment remains under appeal.

(2) The term "consultant" means any person who, for compensation, advises or represents an employee benefit plan or who provides other assistance to such plan, concerning the establishment or operation of such plan.

(3) A period of parole shall not be considered as part of a period of imprisonment.

Act Sec. 411. (d) Whenever any person—

(1) by operation of this section, has been barred from office or other position in an employee benefit plan as a result of a conviction, and

(2) has filed an appeal of that conviction,

any salary which would be otherwise due such person by virtue of such office or position, shall be placed in escrow by the individual or organization responsible for payment of such salary. Payment of such salary into escrow shall continue for the duration of the appeal or for the period of time during which such salary would be otherwise due, whichever period is shorter. Upon the final reversal of such person's conviction on appeal, the amounts in escrow shall be paid to such person. Upon the final sustaining of that person's conviction on appeal, the amounts in escrow shall be returned to the individual or organization responsible for payments of those amounts. Upon final reversal of such person's conviction, such person shall no longer be barred by this statute from assuming any position from which such person was previously barred.

Amendments:

P.L. 100-182, § 15:

Amended Sec. 411(a), (1) by striking out "the United States Parole Commission" and inserting in lieu thereof "if the offense is a Federal offense, the sentencing judge or, if the offense is a State or local offense, the United States district court for the district in which the offense was committed, pursuant to sentencing guidelines and policy statements under section 994(a) of title 28, United States Code,";

(2) by striking out "Commission shall" and inserting in lieu thereof "court shall";

(3) by striking out "Commission's" and inserting in lieu thereof "court's";

(4) by striking out "such Parole Commission" and inserting in lieu thereof "such court"; and

(5) by striking out "and administrative hearing" and inserting in lieu thereof "a hearing".

P.L. 100-182, Sec. 26, provides that the amendments apply with respect to offenses committed after enactment (December 7, 1987).

P.L. 98-473, § 802:

Amended Sec. 411 to read as reflected above. Prior to the amendment, Sec. 411 read as follows:

" **Act Sec. 411.** (a) No person who has been convicted of, or has been imprisoned as a result of his conviction of, robbery, bribery, extortion, embezzlement, fraud, grand larceny, burglary, arson, a felony violation of Federal or State law involving substances defined in section 102(6) of the Comprehensive Drug Abuse Prevention and Control Act of 1970, murder, rape, kidnaping, perjury, assault with intent to kill, any crime described in section 9(a)(1) of the Investment Company Act of 1940 (15 U.S.C. 80a-9(a)(1)), a violation of any provision of this Act, a violation of section 302 of the Labor-Management Relations Act, 1947 (29 U.S.C. 186), a violation of chapter 63 of title 18, United States Code, a violation of section 874, 1027, 1503, 1505, 1506, 1510, 1951, or 1954 of title 18, United States Code, a violation of the Labor-Management Reporting and Disclosure Act of 1959 (29 U.S.C. 401), or conspiracy to commit any such crimes or attempt to commit any such crimes, or a crime in which any of the foregoing crimes is an element, shall serve or be permitted to serve—

"(1) as an administrator, fiduciary, officer, trustee, custodian, counsel, agent, or employee of any employee benefit plan, or

"(2) as a consultant to any employee benefit plan,

during or for five years after such conviction or after the end of such imprisonment, whichever is the later, unless prior to the end of such five-year period, in the case of a person so convicted or imprisoned, (A) his citizenship rights, having been revoked as a result of such conviction, have been fully restored, or (B) if the offense is a Federal offense, the sentencing judge or, if the offense is a State or local offense, on motion of the United States Department of Justice, the district court of the United States for the district in which the offense was committed, pursuant to sentencing guidelines and policy statements issued pursuant to 28 U.S.C. 994(a), determines that such person's service in any capacity referred to in paragraph (1) or (2) would not be contrary to the purposes of this title. Prior to making any such determination the court shall hold a hearing and shall give notice of such proceeding by certified mail to the State, county, and Federal prosecuting officials in the jurisdiction or jurisdictions in which such

person was convicted. The court's determination in any such proceeding shall be final. No person shall knowingly permit any other person to serve in any capacity referred to in paragraph (1) or (2) in violation of this subsection. Notwithstanding the preceding provisions of this subsection, no corporation or partnership will be precluded from acting as an administrator, fiduciary, officer, trustee, custodian, counsel, agent, or employee, of any employee benefit plan or as a consultant to any employee benefit plan without a notice, hearing, and determination by such court of parole that such service would be inconsistent with the intention of this section.

" **Act Sec. 411.** (b) Any person who intentionally violates this section shall be fined not more than $10,000 or imprisoned for not more than one year, or both.

" **Act Sec. 411.** (c) For the purposes of this section:

"(1) A person shall be deemed to have been 'convicted' and under the disability of 'conviction' from the date of the judgment of the trial court or the date of the final sustaining of such judgment on appeal, whichever is the later event.

"(2) The term 'consultant' means any person who, for compensation, advises or represents an employee benefit plan or who provides other assistance to such plan, concerning the establishment or operation of such plan.

"(3) A period of parole or supervised release shall not be considered as part of a period of imprisonment."

P.L. 98-473, Sec. 804, provides: "(a) The amendments made by section 802 and section 803 of this title shall take effect with respect to any judgment of conviction entered by the trial court after the date of enactment of this title (October 12, 1984), except that that portion of such amendments relating to the commencement of the period of disability shall apply to any judgment of conviction entered prior to the date of enactment of this title (October 12, 1984), if a right of appeal or an appeal from such judgment is pending on the date of enactment of this title.

"(b) Subject to subsection (a) the amendments made by sections 803 and 804 shall not affect any disability under section 411 of the Employee Retirement Income Security Act of 1974 or under section 504 of the Labor-Management Reporting and Disclosure Act of 1959 in effect on the date of enactment of this title (October 12, 1984)."

P.L. 98-473, § § 229 and 230:

Amended Sec. 411(a) and 411(a)(3) to read as reflected in the amendment note immediately above as follows:

(1) in Sec. 411(a), by deleting "the Board of Parole of the United States Department of Justice" and substituting "if the offense is a Federal offense, the sentencing judge, or, if the offense is a State or local offense, on motion of the United States Department of Justice, the district court of the United States for the district in which the offense was committed, pursuant to sentencing guidelines and policy statements issued pursuant to 28 U.S.C. 994(a),"

(2) by deleting "Board" and "Board's" and substituting "court" and "court's" respectively, and

(3) by deleting "an administrative" and substituting "a."

In Sec. 411(c)(3) "or supervised release" was added after "parole."

Under Sec. 235 of P.L. 98-473, the above described amendments take effect on November 1, 1986.

Regulations

The following regulations were adopted effective March 5, 1979, under "Title 28—Judicial Administration; Chapter 1—Department of Justice; Part 4—Procedure Governing Applications for Certificates of Exemption under the Labor-Management Reporting and Disclosure Act of 1959, and the Employee Retirement Income Security Act of 1974." The regulations were published in the Federal Register of February 2, 1979 (44 FR 6890).

[¶ 14,811]

§ 4.1 **Definitions.** As used in this part:

(a) "Labor Act" means the Labor-Management Reporting and Disclosure Act of 1959 (73 Stat. 519).

(b) "Pension Act" means the Employee Retirement Income Security Act of 1974 (Pub. L. 93-406) (88 Stat. 829).

(c) "Acts" means both of the above statutes.

(d) "Commission" means the United States Parole Commission.

(e) "Secretary" means the Secretary of Labor or his designee.

(f) For proceedings under the "Labor Act"

(1) "Employer" means the labor organization, or person engaged in an industry or activity affecting commerce, or group or association of employers dealing with any labor organization, which an applicant under § 4.2 desires to serve in a capacity for which he is ineligible under section 504(a) of the "Labor Act".

(2) All other terms used in this part shall have the same meaning as identical or comparable terms when those terms are used in the "Labor Act".

(g) For proceedings under the "Pension Act"

(1) "Employer" means the employee benefit plan with which an applicant under § 4.2 desires to serve in a capacity for which he is ineligible under section 411(a) of the "Pension Act" (29 U.S.C. section 1111).

(2) All other terms used in this part shall have the same meaning as identical or comparable terms when those terms are used in the "Pension Act".

[¶ 14,811A]

§ 4.2 **Who may apply for Certificate of Exemption.** Any person who has been convicted of any of the crimes enumerated in section 504(a) of the "Labor Act" whose service, present or prospective, as described in that section is or would be prohibited by that section because of such a conviction or a prison term resulting therefrom; or any person who has been convicted of any of the crimes enumerated in section 411(a) of the "Pension Act" (29 U.S.C. section 1111) whose service, present or prospective, as described in that section is or would be prohibited by that section because of such a conviction or a prison term resulting therefrom, may apply to the Commission for a Certificate of Exemption from such a prohibition under the applicable Act.

[¶ 14,811B]

§ 4.3 **Contents of application.** A person applying for a Certificate of Exemption shall file with the Office of General Counsel, U.S. Parole Commission, 320 First St., NW., Washington, D.C. 20537, a signed application under oath, in seven copies, which shall set forth clearly and completely the following information:

(a) The name and address of the applicant and any other names used by the applicant and dates of such use.

(b) A statement of all convictions and imprisonments which prohibit the applicant's service under the provisions of the applicable Act.

(c) Whether any citizenship rights were revoked as a result of conviction or imprisonment and if so the name of the court and date of judgment thereof and the extent to which such rights have been restored.

(d) The name and location of the employer and a description of the office or paid position, including the duties thereof, for which a Certificate of Exemption is sought.

(e) A full explanation of the reasons or grounds relied upon to establish that the applicant's service in the office or employment for which a Certificate of Exemption is sought would not be contrary to the purposes of the applicable Act.

(f) A statement that the applicant does not, for the purpose of the proceeding, contest the validity of any conviction.

[¶ 14,811C]

§ 4.4 **Supporting affidavit; additional information.** (a) Each application filed with the Commission must be accompanied by a signed affidavit, in 7 copies, setting forth the following concerning the personal history of the applicant:

(1) Place and date of birth. If the applicant was not born in the United States, the time of first entry and port of entry, whether he is a citizen of the United States, and if naturalized, when, where and how he became naturalized and the number of his Certificate of Naturalization.

(2) Extent of education, including names of schools attended.

(3) History of marital and family status, including a statement as to whether any relatives by blood or marriage are currently serving in any capacity with any employee benefit plan, or labor organization, group or association of employers dealing with labor organizations or industrial labor relations group, or currently advising or representing any employer with respect to employee organizing, concerted activities, or collective bargaining activities.

(4) Present employment, including office or offices held, with a description of the duties thereof.

(5) History of employment, including military service, in chronological order.

(6) Licenses held, at the present time or at any time in the past five years, to possess or carry firearms.

(7) Veterans Administration claim number and regional office handling claim, if any.

(8) A listing (not including traffic offenses for which a fine of not more than $25 was imposed or collateral of not more than $25 was forfeited) by date and place of all arrests, convictions for felonies, misdemeanors, or offenses and all imprisonment or jail terms resulting therefrom, together with a statement of the circumstances of each violation which led to arrest or conviction.

(9) Whether applicant was ever on probation or parole, and if so the names of the courts by which convicted and the dates of conviction.

(10) Names and locations of all employee benefit plans, labor organizations or employer groups with which the applicant has ever been associated or employed, and all employers or employee benefit plans which he has advised or represented concerning employee organizing, concerted activities, or collective bargaining activities together with a description of the duties performed in each such employment or association.

(11) A statement of applicant's net worth, including all assets held by him or in the names of others for him, the amount of each liability owed by him or by him together with any other person and the amount and sources of all income during the immediately preceding five calendar years plus income to date of application.

(12) Any other information which the applicant feels will assist the Commission in making its determination.

(b) The Commission may require of the applicant such additional information as it deems appropriate for the proper consideration and disposition of his application.

[¶ 14,812]

§ 4.5 **Character endorsements.** Each application filed with the Commission must be accompanied by letters or other forms of statement (in three copies) from six persons addressed to the Chairman, U.S. Parole Commission, attesting to the character and reputation of the applicant. The statement as to character shall indicate the length of time the writer has known the applicant, and shall describe applicant's character traits as they relate to the position for which the exemption is sought and the duties and responsibilities thereof. The statement as to reputation shall attest to applicant's reputation in his community or in his circle of business or social acquaintances. Each letter or other form of statement shall indicate that it has been submitted in compliance with procedures under the respective Act and that applicant has informed the writer of the factual basis of his application. The persons submitting letters or other forms of statement shall not include relatives by blood or marriage, prospective employers, or persons serving in any official capacity with an employee benefit plan, labor organization, group or association of employers dealing with labor organizations or industrial labor relations group.

[¶ 14,812A]

§ 4.6 **Institution of proceedings.** All applications and supporting documents received by the Commission shall be reviewed for completeness by the Office of General Counsel of the Parole Commission and if complete and fully in compliance with the regulations of this part the Office of General Counsel shall accept them for filing. Applicant and/or his representative will be notified by the Office of General Counsel of any deficiency in the application and supporting documents. The amount of time allowed for deficiencies to be remedied will be specified in said notice. In the event such deficiencies are not remedied within the specified period or any extension thereof, granted after application to the Commission in writing within the specified period, the application shall be deemed to have been withdrawn and notice thereof shall be given to applicant.

[¶ 14,812B]

§ 4.7 **Notice of hearing; postponements.** Upon the filing of an application, the Commission shall: (a) set the application for a hearing on a date within a reasonable time after its filing and notify the applicant of such date by certified mail; (b) give notice, as required by the respective Act, to the appropriate State, County, or Federal prosecuting officials in the jurisdiction or jurisdictions in which the applicant was convicted that an application for a Certificate of Exemption has been filed and the date for hearing thereon; and (c) notify the Secretary that an application has been filed and the date for hearing thereon and furnish him copies of the application and all supporting documents. Any party may request a postponement of a hearing date in writing from the Office of General Counsel at any time prior to ten (10) days before the scheduled hearing. No request for postponement other than the first for any party will be considered unless a showing is made of cause entirely beyond the control of the requester. The granting of such requests will be within the discretion of the Commission. In the event of a failure to appear on the hearing date as originally scheduled or extended, the absent party will be deemed to have waived his right to a hearing. The hearing will be conducted with the parties present participating and documentation, if any, of the absent party entered into the record.

[¶ 14,812C]

§ 4.8 **Hearing.** The hearing on the appplication shall be held at the offices of the Commission in Washington, D.C., or elsewhere as the Commission may direct. The hearing shall be held before the Commission, before one or more Commissioners or before one or more administrative law judges appointed as provided by section 11 of the Administrative Procedure Act (5 U.S.C. 3105) as the Commission by order shall determine. Hearings shall be conducted in accordance with sections 7 and 8 of the Administrative Procedure Act (5 U.S.C. 556, 557).

[¶ 14,813]

§ 4.9 **Representation.** The applicant may be represented before the Commission by any person who is a member in good standing of the bar of the Supreme Court of the United States or of the highest court of any State or territory of the United States, or the District of Columbia, and who is not under any order of any court suspending, enjoining, restraining, or disbarring him from, or otherwise restricting him in, the practice of law. Whenever a person acting in a representative capacity appears in person or signs a paper in practice before the Commission, his personal appearance or signature shall constitute a representation to the Commission that under the provisions of this part and applicable law he is authorized and qualified to represent the particular person in whose behalf he acts. Further proof of a person's authority to act in a representative capacity may be required. When any applicant is represented by an attorney at law, any notice or other written communication required or permitted to be given to or by such applicant shall be given to or by such attorney. If an applicant is represented by more than one attorney, service by or upon any one of such attorneys shall be sufficient.

[¶ 14,813A]

§ 4.10 **Waiver of oral hearing.** The Commission upon receipt of a statement from the Secretary that he does not object, and in the absence of any request for oral hearing from the others to whom notice has been sent pursuant to § 4.7 may grant an application without receiving oral testimony with respect to it.

[¶ 14,813B]

§ 4.11 **Appearance; testimony; cross-examination.** (a) The applicant shall appear and, except as otherwise provided in § 4.10, shall testify at the hearing and may cross-examine witnesses.

(b) The Secretary and others to whom notice has been sent pursuant to § 4.7 shall be afforded an opportunity to appear and present evidence and cross-examine witnesses, at any hearing.

(c) In the discretion of the Commission or presiding officer, other witnesses may testify at the hearing.

[¶ 14,813C]

§ 4.12 **Evidence which may be excluded.** The Commission or officer presiding at the hearing may exclude irrelevant, untimely, immaterial, or unduly repetitious evidence.

[¶ 14,814]

§ 4.13 **Record for decision; receipt of documents comprising record; timing and extension.** (a) The application and all supporting documents, the transcript of the testimony and oral argument at the hearing, together with any exhibits received and other documents filed pursuant to these procedures and/or the Administrative Procedures Act shall be made parts of the record for decision.

(b) At the conclusion of the hearing the presiding officer shall specify the time for submission of proposed findings of fact and conclusions of law (unless waived by the parties); transcript of the hearing, and supplemental exhibits, if any. He shall set a tentative date for the recommended decision based upon the timing of these preliminary steps. Extensions of time may be requested by any party, in writing, from the Parole Commission. Failure of any party to comply with the time frame as established or extended will be deemed to be a waiver on his part of his right to submit the document in question. The adjudication will proceed and the absence of said document and reasons therefor will be noted in the record.

[¶ 14,814A]

§ 4.14 **Administrative law judge's recommended decision; exceptions thereto; oral argument before Commission.** Whenever the hearing is conducted by an administrative law judge, at the conclusion of the hearing he shall submit a recommended decision to the Commission, which shall include a statement of findings and conclusions, as well as the reasons therefor. The applicant, the Secretary and others to whom notice has been sent pursuant to § 4.7 may file with the Commission, within 10 days after having been furnished a copy of the recommended decision, exceptions thereto and reasons in support thereof. The Commission may order the taking of additional evidence and may request the applicant and others to appear before it. The Commission may invite oral argument before it on such questions as it desires.

[¶ 14,814B]

§ 4.15 **Certificate of Exemption.** The applicant, the Secretary and others to whom notice has been sent pursuant to § 4.7 shall be served a copy of the Commission's decision and order with respect to each application. Whenever the Commission decision is that the application be granted, the Commission shall issue a Certificate of Exemption to the applicant. The Certificate of Exemption shall extend only to the stated employment with the prospective employer named in the application.

[¶ 14,814C]

§ 4.16 **Rejection of application.** No application for a Certificate of Exemption shall be accepted from any person whose application for a Certificate of Exemption has been withdrawn, deemed withdrawn due to failure to remedy deficiencies in a timely manner, or denied by the Commission within the preceding 12 months.

[¶ 14,815]

§ 4.17 **Availability of decisions.** The Commission's Decisions under both Acts are available for examination in the Office of the U.S. Parole Commission, 320 First Street, NW., Washington, D.C. 20537. Copies will be mailed upon written request to the Office of General Counsel, U.S. Parole Commission at the above address at a cost of ten cents per page.

Dated: January 26, 1979.

CECIL C. McCALL,

Chairman,

United States Parole Commission.

[FR Doc. 79-3641, filed 2-1-79; 8:45 a.m.]

[¶ 14,820]
BONDING

Act Sec. 412. (a) Every fiduciary of an employee benefit plan and every person who handles funds or other property of such a plan (hereafter in this section referred to as "plan official") shall be bonded as provided in this section; except that—

    (1) where such plan is one under which the only assets from which benefits are paid are the general assets of a union or of an employer, the administrator, officers, and employees of such plan shall be exempt from the bonding requirements of this section, and

    (2) no bond shall be required of a fiduciary (or of any director, officer, or employee of such fiduciary) if such fiduciary—

        (A) is a corporation organized and doing business under the laws of the United States or of any State;

        (B) is authorized under such laws to exercise trust powers or to conduct an insurance business;

        (C) is subject to supervision or examination by Federal or State authority; and

        (D) has at all times a combined capital and surplus in excess of such a minimum amount as may be established by regulations issued by the Secretary, which amount shall be at least $1,000,000.

Paragraph (2) shall apply to a bank or other financial institution which is authorized to exercise trust powers and the deposits of which are not insured by the Federal Deposit Insurance Corporation, only if such bank or institution meets bonding or similar requirements under State law which the Secretary determines are at least equivalent to those imposed on banks by Federal law.

The amount of such bond shall be fixed at the beginning of each fiscal year of the plan. Such amount shall be not less than 10 per centum of the amount of funds handled. In no case shall such bond be less than $1,000 nor more than $500,000, except that the Secretary, after due notice and opportunity for hearing to all interested parties, and after consideration of the record, may prescribe an amount in excess of $500,000, subject to the 10 per centum limitation of the preceding sentence. For purposes of fixing the amount of such bond, the amount of funds handled shall be determined by the funds handled by the person, group, or class to be covered by such bond and by their predecessor or predecessors, if any, during the preceding reporting year, or if the plan has no preceding reporting year, the amount of funds to be handled during the current reporting year by such person, group, or class, estimated as provided in regulations of the Secretary. Such bond shall provide protection to the plan against loss by reason of acts of fraud or dishonesty on the part of the plan official, directly or through connivance with others. Any bond shall have as surety thereon a corporate surety company which is an acceptable surety on Federal bonds under authority granted by the Secretary of the Treasury pursuant to sections 9304-9308 of title 31. Any bond shall be in a form or of a type approved by the Secretary, including individual bonds or schedule or blanket forms of bonds which cover a group or class.

Act Sec. 412. (b) It shall be unlawful for any plan official to whom subsection (a) applies, to receive, handle, disburse, or otherwise exercise custody or control of any of the funds or other property of any employee benefit plan, without being bonded as required by subsection (a) and it shall be unlawful for any plan official of such plan, or any other person having authority to direct the performance of such functions, to permit such functions, or any of them, to be performed by any plan official, with respect to whom the requirements of subsection (a) have not been met.

Act Sec. 412. (c) It shall be unlawful for any person to procure any bond required by subsection (a) from any surety or other company or through any agent or broker in whose business operations such plan or any party in interest in such plan has any control or significant financial interest, direct or indirect.

Act Sec. 412. (d) Nothing in any other provision of law shall require any person, required to be bonded as provided in subsection (a) because he handles funds or other property of an employee benefit plan, to be bonded insofar as the handling by such person of the funds or other property of such plan is concerned.

Act Sec. 412. (e) The Secretary shall prescribe such regulations as may be necessary to carry out the provisions of this section including exempting a plan from the requirements of this section where he finds that (1) other bonding arrangements or (2) the overall financial condition of the plan would be adequate to protect the interests of the beneficiaries and participants. When, in the opinion of the Secretary, the administrator of a plan offers adequate evidence of the financial responsibility of the plan, or that other bonding arrangements would provide adequate protection of the beneficiaries and participants, he may exempt such plan from the requirements of this section.

Amendment:

P.L. 97-258, § 4(b):

In subsection (a), "sections 9304-9308 of Title 31" was substituted for "sections 6 through 13 of Title 6, United States Code" on authority of Pub. L. 97-258, § 4(B), Sept. 13, 1982, 96 Stat. 1067, effective January 1, 1975.

ERISA Section 412, BONDING

The following temporary regulations were adopted effective January 10, 1975, under "Title 29—Labor; Chapter XXV—Office of Employee Benefits Security; Subchapter F—Fiduciary Responsibility; § 2550.412-1 of Part 2550—Bonding Requirements." The temporary regulations were published in the Federal Register of January 10, 1975[1] and were amended on June 28, 1985 (50 FR 26705).

[¶ 14,821]

§ 2550.412-1 of Part 2550 **Temporary bonding requirements.**
(a) Pending the issuance of permanent regulations with respect to the bonding provisions under section 412 of the Employee Retirement Income Security Act of 1974 (the Act), any plan official, as defined in section 412(a) of the Act, shall be deemed to be in compliance with the bonding requirements of the Act if he or she is bonded under a bond which would have been in compliance with section 13 of the Welfare and Pension Plans Disclosure Act, as amended (the WPPDA), and with the basic bonding requirements of Subparts A through E of Part 2580, Title 29, Code of Federal Regulations and with the prohibition against bonding by parties interested in the plan contained in Subpart G of Part 2580 of such Title, or would be exempt from such bonding requirements because bonding would not be required under the exemption provisions contained in Subpart F of Part 2580 of such Title. "Part 2580 of Title 29 of the *Code of Federal Regulations* incorporates material previously designated as Subparts A through E of Part 464, Subpart B of Part 465 and Part 485 of Title 29 of the *Code of Federal Regulations*." The requirements which are set forth in the temporary regulations hereby adopted shall be applicable to all employee benefit plans covered by the Act, including those plans which were not covered by the WPPDA. Thus, for example, the regulations so adopted are applicable to plans containing fewer than 26 participants, although such plans were not covered by the WPPDA.

(b) For the purpose of this temporary regulation, any bond or rider thereto obtained by a plan official which contains a reference to the WPPDA will be construed by the Secretary to refer to the Act, provided that the surety company so agrees.

---

[1] This was Part 2555 before redesignation by the Department of Labor. Part 2555 is reserved.

(c) For the purpose of this regulation, (1) any reference to section 13 of th WPPDA or any subsection thereof in the regulations issued under the WPPDA and which are incorporated by reference by this temporary regulation shall be deemed to refer to section 412 of the Act, or the corresponding subsection thereof, (2) where the particular phrases set forth in the Act are not identical to the phrases in the WPPDA and the regulations issued pursuant thereto, the phrases appearing in the Act shall be substituted by operation of law, and (3) where the phrases are identical but the meaning is different, the meaning given such phrases by the Act shall govern. For example, the phrase "administrators, officers, and employees of any employee wel-

fare benefit plan or of any employee pension benefit plan subject to this Act who handle funds or other property of such plan" which appears in section 13 of the WPPDA and the regulations issued thereunder shall be construed to mean, for purposes of this regulation, "plan officials"', which is the term appearing in section 412 of the Act, and the terms "employee welfare benefit plan" and "employee pension benefit plan" shall be given the meaning assigned to them by the Act, and not the meaning set forth in the WPPDA.

(d) The requirements of this temporary regulation, as set forth in paragraphs (a) through (c), shall remain in effect pending the issuance of permanent regulations by the Secretary.

Temporary Regulations

The following temporary regulations were originally adopted on January 10, 1985 under Subchapter B of Chapter IV of Title 29 of the Code of Federal Regulations and were issued under the authority of the Office of Pension and Welfare Programs. As the result of a Department of Labor reorganization, the temporary regulations were transferred, effective June 28, 1985, to Chapter XXV (Office of Pension and Welfare Benefit Programs) of Title 29 (50 FR 26705).

Subchapter I—Temporary Bonding Rules Under the Employee Retirement Income Security Act of 1974

Part 2580—Temporary Bonding Rules

Subpart A—Criteria for Determining Who Must Be Bonded

[¶ 14,822]

§2580.412-1. **Statutory Provisions**. Section 13(a) of the Welfare and Pension Plans Disclosure Act of 1958, as amended, states, in part, that—

Every administrator, officer and employee of any employee welfare benefit plan or of any employee pension benefit plan subject to this Act who handles funds or other property of such plan shall be bonded as herein provided; except that, where such plan is one under which the only assets from which benefits are paid are the general assets of a union or of an employer, the administrator, officers and employees of such plan shall be exempt from the bonding requirements of this section.

. . . Such bond shall provide protection to the plan against loss by reason of acts of fraud or dishonesty on the part of such administrator, officer, or employee, directly or through connivance with others.

[¶ 14,822A]

§2580.412-2. **Plans exempt from the coverage of section 13**. Only completely unfunded plans in which the plan benefits derive solely from the general assets of a union[1] or employer, and in which plan assets are not segregated in any way from the general assets of a union or employer and remain solely within the general assets until the time of distribution of benefits, shall be exempt from the bonding provisions. As such, the language "where such plan is one under which the only assets from which benefits are paid are the general assets of a union or of an employer" shall not be deemed to exempt a plan from the coverage of section 13 if the plan is one in which:

(a) Any benefits thereunder are provided or underwritten by an insurance carrier or service or other organization, or

(b) There is a trust or other separate entity to which contributions are made or out of which benefits are paid, or

(c) Contributions to the plan are made by the employees, either through withholding or otherwise, or from any source other than the employer or union involved, or

(d) There is a separately maintained bank account or separately maintained books and records for the plan or other evidence of the existence of a segregated or separately maintained or administered fund out of which plan benefits are to be provided.

As a general rule, the presence of special ledger accounts or accounting entries for plan funds as an integral part of the general books and records of an employer or union shall not, in and of itself, be deemed sufficient evidence of segregation of plan funds to take a plan out of the exempt category, but shall be considered along with the other factors

and criteria discussed above in determining whether the exemption applies. Again, it should be noted, however, that the fact that a plan is not exempt from the coverage of section 13 does not necessarily mean that its administrators, officers or employees are required to be bonded. As stated previously, this will depend in each case on whether or not they "handle" funds or other property of the plan within the meaning of section 13 and under the standards set forth in section 2580.412-6.

[¶ 14,822B]

§2580.412-3. **Plan administrators, officers and employees for purposes of section 13.**—

(a) *Administrator*. (1) For purposes of the bonding provisions, the term "administrator" is defined in the same manner as under section 5 of the Act and refers to—

(i) The person or persons designated by the terms of the plan or the collective bargaining agreement with responsibility for the ultimate control, disposition, or management of the money received or contributed; or

(ii) In the absence of such designation, the person or persons actually responsible for the control, disposition, or management of the money received or contributed, irrespective of whether such control, disposition, or management is exercised directly or through an agent or trustee designated by such person or persons.

(2) Where by virtue of this definition, or regulations, interpretations or opinions issued with respect thereto, the term embodies natural persons such as members of the board of trustees of a trust, the bonding requirements shall apply to such persons.

(3) However, when by virtue of this definition or regulations, interpretations, or opinions issued with respect thereto, the administrator in a given case is an entity such as a partnership, corporation, mutual company, joint stock company, trust, unincorporated organization, union or employees' beneficiary association, the term shall be deemed to apply, in meeting the bonding requirements, only to those natural persons who—

(i) Are vested under the authority of the entity-administrator with the responsibility for carrying out functions constituting control, disposition or management of the money received or contributed within the definition of administrator, or who, acting on behalf of or under the actual or apparent authority of the entity-administrator, actually perform such functions, and who

(ii) "Handle" funds or other property of the plan within the meaning of these regulations.

(b) *Officers*. For purposes of the bonding provisions, the term "officer" shall include any person designated by the terms of a plan or collective bargaining agreement as an officer, any person performing or authorized to perform executive functions of the plan or any member of a board of trustees or similar governing body of a plan. The term shall include such persons regardless of whether they are representatives of

---

[1] For purposes of the exemption discussed in §2580.412-2, the term "union" shall include " * * * any organization of any kind or any agency or employee representation committee, association, group, or plan, in which employees participate and which elects for

the purpose in whole or in part, of dealing with employers concerning an employee welfare or pension benefit plan, or other matters incidental to employment relationships * * *" (29 U.S.C. 302(a)(3)).

or selected by an employer, employees or an employee organization. In its most frequent application the term will encompass those natural persons appointed or elected as officers of the plan or as members of boards or committees performing executive or supervisory functions for the plan, but who do not fall within the definition of administrator.

(c) *Employees.* For purposes of the bonding provisions the term "employee" shall, to the extent a person performs functions not falling within the definition of officer or administrator, include any employee who performs work for or directly related to a covered plan, regardless of whether technically he is employed, directly or indirectly, by or for a plan, a plan administrator, a trust, or by an employee organization or employer within the meaning of section 3(3) or 3(4) of the Act.

(d) *Other persons covered.* For purposes of the bonding provisions, the terms "administrator, officer, or employee" shall include any persons performing functions for the plan normally performed by administrators, officers, or employees of a plan. As such, the terms shall include persons indirectly employed, or otherwise delegated, to perform such work for the plan, such as pension consultants and planners, and attorneys who perform "handling" functions within the meaning of § 2580.412-6. On the other hand, the terms would not include those brokers or independent contractors who have contracted for the performance of functions which are not ordinarily carried out by the administrators, officers, or employees of a plan, such as securities brokers who purchase and sell securities or armored motor vehicle companies. (Amended by F.R. Doc. 69-3030, published in Federal Register March 13, 1969.)

(e) [Deleted by F.R. Doc. 69-3030, published in Federal Register March 13, 1969.]

[¶ 14,822C]

§ 2580.412-4. **"Funds or other property" of a plan.** The affirmative requirement for bonding persons falling within the definition of administrator, officer or employee is applicable only if they handle "funds or other property" of the plan concerned. The term "funds or other property" is intended to encompass all property which is used or may be used as a source for the payment of benefits to plan participants. It does not include permanent assets used in the operation of the plan such as land and buildings, furniture and fixtures or office and delivery equipment used in the operation of the plan. It does include all items in the nature of quick assets, such as cash, checks and other negotiable instruments, government obligations and marketable securities. It also includes all other property or items convertible into cash or having a cash value and held or acquired for the ultimate purpose of distribution to plan participants or beneficiaries. In the case of a plan which has investments, this would include all the investments of the plan even though not in the nature of quick assets, such as land and buildings, mortgages, and securities in closely held corporations. However, in a given case, the question of whether a person was "handling" such "funds or other property" so as to require bonding would depend on whether his relationship to this property was such that there was a risk that he, alone or in connivance with others, could cause a loss of such "funds or other property" through fraud or dishonesty.

[¶ 14,822D]

§ 2580.412-5. **Determining when "funds or other property" belong to a plan.** With respect to any contribution to a plan from any source, including employers, employees or employee organizations, the point at which any given item or amount becomes "funds or other property" of a plan for purposes of the bonding provisions shall be determined as described in this section.

(a) Where the plan administrator is a board of trustees, person or body other than the employer or employee organization establishing the plan, a contribution to the plan from any source shall become "funds or other property" of the plan at the time it is received by the plan administrator. Employee contributions collected by an employer and later turned over to the plan administrator would not become "funds or other property" of the plan until receipt by the plan administrator.

(b) Where the employer or employee organization establishing the plan is itself the plan administrator:

(1) Contributions from employees or other persons who are plan participants would normally become "funds or other property" of the plan at the time they are received by the employer or employee organization, except however that contributions made by withholding from employees' salaries shall not be considered "funds or other property" of the plan for purposes of the bonding provisions so long as they are retained in and not segregated in any way from the general assets of the withholding employer or employee organization.

(2) Contributions made to a plan by such employer or employee organization and contributions made by withholdings from employees' salaries would normally become "funds or other property" of the plan if and when they are taken out of the general assets of the employer or employee organization and placed in a special bank account or investment account; or identified on a separate set of books and records; or paid over to a corporate trustee or used to purchase benefits from an insurance carrier or service or other organization; or otherwise segregated, paid out or used for plan purposes, whichever shall occur first. Thus, if a plan is operated by a corporate trustee and no segregation from general assets is made of monies to be turned over to the corporate trustee prior to the actual transmittal of such monies, the contribution represented in the transmission becomes "funds or other property" of the plan at the time of receipt by the corporate trustee. On the other hand, if a special fund is first established from which monies are paid over to the corporate trustee, a given item would become "funds or other property" of the plan at the time it is placed in the special fund. Similarly, if plan benefits are provided through the medium of an insurance carrier or service or other organization and no segregation from general assets of monies used to purchase such benefits is made prior to turning such monies over to the organization contracting to provide benefits, plan funds or other property come into being at the time of receipt of payment for such benefits by the insurance carrier or service or other organization. In such a case, the "funds or other property" of the plan would be represented by the insurance contract or other obligations to pay benefits and would not be normally subject to "handling". Bonding would not be required for any person with respect to the purchase of such benefits directly from general assets nor with respect to the bare existence of the contract obligation to pay benefits. However, if the particular arrangement were such that monies derived from, or by virtue of, the contract did subsequently flow back to the plan, bonding may be required if such monies returned to the plan are handled by plan administrators, officers or employees. (Further discussion on bonding of insured plans is contained in § 2580.412-6(b)(7).)

[¶ 14,822E]

§ 2580.412-6. **Determining when "funds or other property" are "handled" so as to require bonding.**—

(a) *General scope of term.* (1) A plan administrator, officer, or employee shall be deemed to be "handling" funds or other property of a plan, so as to require bonding under section 13, whenever his duties or activities with respect to given funds or other property are such that there is a risk that such funds or other property could be lost in the event of fraud or dishonesty on the part of such person, acting either alone or in collusion with others. While ordinarily, those plan administrators, officers and employees who "handle" within the meaning of section 13 will be those persons with duties related to the receipt, safekeeping and disbursement of funds, the scope of the term "handles" and the prohibitions of paragraph (b) of section 13 shall be deemed to encompass any relationship of an administrator, officer or employee with respect to funds or other property which can give rise to a risk of loss through fraud or dishonesty. This shall include relationships such as those which involve access to funds or other property or decision making powers with respect to funds or property which can give rise to such risk of loss.

(2) Section 13 contains no exemptions based on the amount or value of funds or other property "handled," nor is the determination of the existence of risk of loss based on the amount involved. However, regardless of the amount involved, a given duty or relationship to funds or other property shall not be considered "handling," and bonding is not required, where it occurs under conditions and circumstances in which the risk that a loss will occur through fraud or dishonesty is negligible. This may be the case where the risk of mishandling is precluded by the nature of the funds or other property (e.g., checks, securities or title papers which can not be negotiated by the persons performing duties with respect to them). It may also be the case where

significant risk of mishandling in the performance of duties of an essentially clerical character is precluded by fiscal controls.

(b) *General criteria for determining "handling."*

Subject to the application of the basic standard of risk of loss to each situation, general criteria for determining whether there is "handling" so as to require bonding are:

(1) *Physial contact.* Physical contact with cash, checks or similar property generally constitutes "handling." However, persons who from time to time perform counting, packaging, tabulating, messenger or similar duties of an essentially clerical character involving physical contact with funds or other property would not be "handling" when they perform these duties under conditions and circumstances where risk of loss is negligible because of factors such as close supervision and control or the nature of the property.

(2) *Power to exercise physical contact or control.* Whether or not physical contact actually takes place, the power to secure physical possession of cash, checks or similar property through factors such as access to a safe deposit box or similar depository, access to cash or negotiable assets, powers of custody or safekeeping, power to withdraw funds from a bank or other account generally constitutes "handling," regardless of whether the person in question has specific duties in these matters regardless of whether the power or access is authorized.

(3) *Power to transfer to oneself or a third party or to negotiate for value.* With respect to property such as mortgages, title to land and buildings, or securities, while physical contact or the possibility of physical contact may not, of itself, give rise to risk of loss so as to constitute "handling," a person shall be regarded as "handling" such items where he, through actual or apparent authority, can cause those items to be transferred to himself or to a third party or to be negotiated for value.

(4) *Disbursement.* Persons who actually disburse funds or other property, such as officers or trustees authorized to sign checks or other negotiable instruments, or persons who make cash disbursements, shall be considered to be "handling" such funds or property. Whether other persons who may influence, authorize or direct disbursements or the signing or endorsing of checks or similar instruments will be considered to be "handling" funds or other property shall be determined by reference to the particular duties or responsibilities of such persons as applied to the basic criteria of risk of loss.

(5) *Signing or endorsing checks or other negotiable instruments.* In connection with disbursements or otherwise, any persons with the power to sign or endorse checks or similar instruments or otherwise render them transferable, whether individually or as co-signers with one or more persons, shall each be considered to be "handling" such funds or other property.

(6) *Supervisory or decision making responsibility.* To the extent a person's supervisory or decision making responsibility involves factors in relationship to funds discussed in subparagraphs (1), (2), (3), (4), or (5) of this paragraph, such persons shall be considered to be "handling" in the same manner as any person to whom the criteria of those paragraphs apply. To the extent that only general responsibility for the conduct of the business affairs of the plan is involved, including such functions as approval of contracts, authorization of disbursements, auditing of accounts, investment decisions, determination of benefit claims and similar responsibilities, such persons shall be considered to be "handling" whenever the facts of the particular case raise the possibility that funds or other property of the plan are likely to be lost in the event of their fraud or dishonesty. The mere fact of general supervision would not necessarily, in and of itself, mean that such persons are "handling." Factors to be accorded weight are the system of fiscal controls, the closeness and continuity of supervision, who is in fact charged with, or actually exercising final responsibility for determining whether specific disbursements, investments, contracts, or benefit claims are bona fide, regular and made in accordance with the applicable trust instrument or other plan documents.

(i) For example, persons having supervisory or decision making responsibility would be "handling" to the extent they:

(a) Act in the capacity of plan "administrator" and have ultimate responsibility for the plan within the meaning of the definition of "administrator" (except to the extent that it can be shown that such persons could not, in fact, cause a loss to the plan to occur through fraud or dishonesty);

(b) Exercise close supervision over corporate trustees or other parties charged with dealing with plan funds or other property; exercise such close control over investment policy that they, in effect, determine all specific investments;

(c) Conduct, in effect, a continuing daily audit of the persons who "handle" funds;

(d) Regularly review and have veto power over the actions of a disbursing officer whose duties are essentially ministerial.

(ii) On the other hand, persons having supervisory or decision making responsibility would not be "handling" to the extent:

(a) They merely conduct a periodic or sporadic audit of the persons who "handle" funds;

(b) Their duties with repect to investment policy are essentially advisory;

(c) They make a broad general allocation of funds or general authorization of disbursements intended to permit expenditures by a disbursing officer who has final responsibility for determining the propriety of any specific expenditure and making the actual disbursement;

(d) A bank or corporate trustee has all the day to day functions of administering the plan;

(e) They are in the nature of a Board of Directors of a corporation or similar authority acting for the corporation rather than for the plan and do not perform specific functions with respect to the operations of the plan.

(7) *Insured plan arrangements.* In many cases, plan contributions made by employers or employee organizations or by withholding from employees' salaries are not segregated from the general assets of the employer or employee organization until payment for purchase of benefits from an insurance carrier or service or other organization. No bonding is required with respect to the payment of premiums or other payments made to purchase such benefits directly from general assets, nor with respect to the bare existence of the contract obligation to pay benefits. Such arrangements would not normally be subject to bonding except to the extent that monies returned by way of benefit payments, cash surrender, dividends, credits or otherwise, and which by the terms of the plan belonged to the plan (rather than to the employer, employee organization, insurance carrier or service or other organization) were subject to "handling" by plan administrators, officers or employees.

Subpart B—Scope and Form of the Bond

[¶ 14,822F]

§ 2580.412-7. **Statutory provision—Scope of the bond**. The statute requires that the bond shall provide protection to the plan against loss by reason of acts of fraud or dishonesty on the part of a plan administrator, officer, or employee, directly or through connivance with others.

[¶ 14,822G]

§ 2580.412-8. **The nature of the duties or activities to which the bonding requirement relates**. The bond required under section 13 is limited to protection for those duties and activities from which loss can arise through fraud or dishonesty. It is not required to provide the same scope of coverage that is required in faithful discharge of duties bonds under the Labor-Management Reporting and Disclosure Act of 1959 or in the faithful performance bonds of public officials.

[¶ 14,822H]

§ 2580.412-9. **Meaning of fraud or dishonesty**. The term "fraud or dishonesty" shall be deemed to encompass all those risks of loss that might arise through dishonest or fraudulent acts in handling of funds as delineated in section 2580.412-6. As such, the bond must provide recovery for loss occasioned by such acts even though no personal gain accrues to the person committing the act and the act is not subject to punishment as a crime or misdemeanor, provided that within the law of the state in which the act is committed, a court would afford recovery under a bond providing protection against fraud or dishonesty. As usually applied under state laws, the term "fraud or dishonesty" encompasses such matters as larceny, theft, embezzlement, forgery, misappropriation, wrongful abstraction, wrongful conversion, willful misapplication or any other fraudulent or dishonest acts. For the purposes of section 13, other fraudulent or dishonest acts shall also be deemed to include acts where losses result through any act or arrangement prohibited by Title 18, Section 1954 of the United States Code.

[¶ 14,822I]

§ 2580.412-10. **Individual or schedule or blanket form of bonds**. Section 13 provides that "any bond shall be in a form or of a type approved by the Secretary, including individual bonds or schedule or blanket forms of bonds which cover a group or class". Any form of bond which may be described as individual, schedule or blanket in form or any combination of such forms of bonds shall be acceptable to meet the requirements of section 13, provided that in each case, the form of the bond, in its particular clauses and application, is not inconsistent with meeting the substantive requirements of the statute for the persons and plan involved and with meeting the specific requirements of the regulations in this part. Basic types of bonds in general usage are:

(a) *Individual Bond* covers a named individual in a stated penalty.

(b) *Name Schedule Bond* covers a number of named individuals in the respective amounts set opposite their names.

(c) *Position Schedule Bond* covers each of the occupants of positions listed in the schedule in the respective amounts set opposite such positions.

(d) *Blanket Bonds* cover all the insured's officers and employees with no schedule or list of those covered being necessary and with all new officers and employees bonded automatically, in a blanket penalty which takes two forms—an aggregate penalty bond and a multiple penalty bond—which are described below:

(1) The aggregate penalty blanket bond such as the Commercial Blanket Bond; the amount of the bond is available for dishonesty losses caused by persons covered thereunder or losses in which such person is concerned or implicated. Payment of loss on account of any such person does not reduce the amount of coverage available for losses other than those caused by such person or in which he was concerned or implicated.

(2) The multiple penalty bond such as the Blanket Position Bond giving separate coverage on each person for a uniform amount—the net effect being the same as though a separate bond were issued on each person covered thereunder and all of such bonds being for a uniform amount.

> NOTE: For the purpose of section 13 blanket bonds which are either aggregate penalty or multiple penalty in form shall be permissible if they otherwise meet the requirements of the Act and the regulations in this part.

Bonding, to the extent required, of persons indirectly employed, or otherwise delegated, to perform functions for the plan which are normally performed by "administrators, officers, or employees" as described in section 2580.412-3 may be accomplished either by including them under individual or schedule bonds or other forms of bonds meeting the requirements of the Act, or naming them in what is known under general trade usage as an "Agents Rider" attached to a Blanket Bond.

Subpart C—Amount of the Bond

[¶ 14,822J]

§ 2580.412-11. **Statutory provision**. Section 13 requires that the amount of the bond be fixed at the beginning of each calendar, policy or other fiscal year, as the case may be, which constitutes the reporting year of the plan for purposes of the reporting provisions of the Act. The amount of the bond shall be not less than 10 per centum of the amount of funds handled, except that any such bond shall be in at least the amount of $1,000 and no such bond shall be required in an amount in excess of $500,000: *Provided,* That the Secretary, after due notice and opportunity for hearing to all interested parties, and after consideration of the record, may prescribe an amount in excess of $500,000, which in no event shall exceed 10 per centum of the funds handled. For purposes of fixing the amount of such bond, the amount of funds handled

shall be determined by the funds handled by the person, group, or class to be covered by such bond and by their predecessor or predecessors, if any, during the preceding reporting year, or if the plan has no preceding reporting year, the amount of funds to be handled during the current reporting year by such person, group, or class, estimated as provided in the regulations in this part. With respect to persons required to be bonded, section 13 shall be deemed to require the bond to insure from the first dollar of loss up to the requisite bond amount and not to permit the use of deductible or similar features whereby a portion of the risk within such requisite bond amount is assumed by the insured. Any request for variance from these requirements shall be made pursuant to the provisions of section 13(e) of the Act.

[¶ 14,822K]

§ 2580.412-12. **Relationship of determining the amount of the bond to "handling"**. A determination of whether persons falling within the definition of administrator, officer or employee are required to be bonded depends on whether they "handle" funds or other property. Determining the amount of the bond is an aspect of the same process in that it requires a determination of what funds or other property are being handled or what amounts of funds of other property are subject to risk of loss with respect to the duties or powers of an administrator, officer or employee of a covered plan. Once this calculation is made, the required amount for which that person must be covered by a bond, either by himself or as a part of a group or class being bonded under a blanket or schedule bond, is not less than 10 percent of the amount "handled" or $1,000, whichever is the greater amount, except that no such bond shall be required in an amount greater than $500,000 by virtue of these regulations. (See § 2580.412-17).

[¶ 14,822L]

§ 2580.412-13. **The meaning of "funds" in determining the amount of the bond**. The amount of the bond depends on the amount of "funds" "handled," and shall be sufficient to provide bonding protection against risk of loss through fraud or dishonesty for all plan funds, including other property similar to funds or in the nature of funds. As such, the term "funds" shall be deemed to include and be equivalent to "funds and other property" of the plan as described in ¶ 2580.412-4. With respect to any item of "funds or other property" which does not have a cash or readily ascertainable market value, the value of such property may be estimated on such basis as will reasonably reflect the loss the plan might suffer if it were mishandled.

[¶ 14,822M]

§ 2580.412-14. **Determining the amount of funds "handled" during the preceding reporting year**. (a) The amount of funds "handled" by each person falling within the definition of administrator, officer, or employee (or his predecessors) during the preceding reporting year shall be the total of funds subject to risk of loss, within the meaning of the definition of "handling" (see § 2580.412-6), through acts of fraud or dishonesty, directly or in connivance with others, by such person or his predecessors during the preceding reporting year. The relationship of the determination of the amount of funds "handled" to the determination of who is "handling" can best be illustrated by a situation that commonly arises with respect to executive personnel of a plan, where a bank or corporate trustee has the responsibility for the receipt, safekeeping, physical handling and investment of a plan's assets and the basic function of the executive personnel is to authorize payments to beneficiaries and payments for services to the corporate trustee, the actuary and the employees of the plan itself. Normally, in any given year, only a small portion of the plan's total assets is disbursed, and the question arises as to whether an administrator or executive personnel are "handling" only the amounts actually disbursed each year or whether they are "handling" the total amounts of the assets. The answer to this question depends on the same basic criterion that governs all questions of "handling", namely, the possibility of loss. If the authorized duties of the persons in question are strictly limited to disbursements of benefits and payments for services, and the fiscal controls and practical realities of the situation are such that these persons cannot gain access to funds which they are not legitimately allowed to disburse, the amount on which the bond is based may be limited to the amount actually disbursed in the reporting year. This would depend, in part, on the extent to which the bank or corporate trustee which has physical possession of the funds also has final responsibility for questioning and limiting disbursements from the plan, and on whether this responsibility is embodied in the original plan instruments. On the other hand, where insufficient fiscal controls exist so that the persons involved have free access to, or can obtain control of, the total amount of the fund, the bond shall reflect this fact and the amount "handled" shall be based on the total amount of the fund. This would generally occur with respect to persons such as the "administrator," regardless of what functions are performed by a bank or corporate trustee, since the "administrator" by definition retains ultimate power to revoke any arrangement with a bank or corporate trustee. In such case, the "administrator" would have the power to commit the total amount of funds involved to his control, unless the plan itself or other specific agreement (1) prevents the "administrator" from so doing or (2) requires that revocation cannot be had unless a new agreement providing for similar controls and limitations on the "handling" of funds is simultaneously entered into.

(b) Where the circumstances of "handling" are such that the total amount of a given account or fund is subject to "handling," the amount "handled" shall include the total of all such funds on hand at the beginning of the reporting year, plus any items received during the year for any reason, such as contributions or income, or items received as a result of sales, investments, reinvestments, interest or otherwise. It would not, however, be necessary to count the same item twice in arriving at the total funds "handled" by a given person during a reporting year. For example, a given person may have various duties or powers involving receipt, safekeeping or disbursement of funds which would place him in contact with the same funds at several times during the same year. Different duties, however, would not make it necessary to count the same item twice in arriving at the total "handled" by him. Similarly, where a person has several different positions with respect to a plan, it would not be necessary to count the same funds each time that they are "handled" by him in these different positions, so long as the amount of the bond is sufficient to meet the 10 percent requirement with respect to the total funds "handled" by him subject to risk of loss through fraud or dishonesty, whether acting alone or in a collusion with others. In general, once an item properly within the catergory of "funds" has been counted as "handled" by a given person, it need not be counted again even though it should subsequently be "handled" by the same person during the same year.

[¶ 14,822N]

§ 2580.412-15. **Procedures to be used for estimating the amount of funds to be "handled" during the current reporting year in those cases where there is no preceding reporting year**. If for any reason a plan does not have a complete preceding reporting year, the amount "handled" by persons required to be covered by a bond shall be estimated at the beginning of the calendar, policy or other fiscal year, as the case may be, which would constitute either the operating year or the reporting year of the plan, whichever shall occur first, as follows:

(a) In the case of a plan having a previous experience year, even though it has no preceding reporting year, the estimate of the amount to be "handled" for any person required to be covered shall be based on the experience in the previous year by applying the same standards and criteria as in a plan which has a preceding reporting year. Similarly, where a plan is recently established, but has had, at the time a bond is obtained, sufficient experience to reasonably estimate a complete year's experience for persons required to be bonded, the amount of funds to be "handled" shall be projected to the complete year on the basis of the period in which the plan has had experience, unless, to the knowledge of the plan administrator, the given period of experience is so seasonal or unrepresentative of the complete year's experience as not to provide a reasonable basis for projecting the estimate for the complete year.

(b) Where a plan does not have any prior experience sufficient to allow it to estimate the amount "handled" in the manner outlined in paragraph (a) of this section, the amount to be "handled" by the administrators, officers and employees of the plan during the current reporting year shall be that amount initially required to fund or set up the plan, plus the amount of contributions required to be made under the plan formula from any source during the current reporting year. In most cases, the amount of contributions will be calculated by multiply-

ing the total yearly contribution per participant required by the plan formula from either employers, employees, employer organizations or any other source) by the number of participants in the plan at the beginning of such reporting year. In cases where the per capita contribution cannot readily be determined, such as in the case of certain insured plans covered by the Act, the amount of contributions shall be estimated on the amount of insurance premiums which are actuarially estimated as necessary to support the plan, or on such other actuarially estimated basis as may be applicable. In the case of a newly formed profit-sharing plan covered by the Act, if the employer establishing the plan has a previous year of experience, the amount of contributions required by the plan formula shall be estimated on the basis of the profits of the previous year. The amount of the bond shall then be fixed at 10 percent of this calculation, but not more than $500,000. A bond for such amount shall be obtained in any form the plan desires on all persons who are administrators, officers or employees of the plan and who "handle" funds or other property of the plan.

[¶ 14,822O]

§ 2580.412-16. **Amount of bond required in given types of bonds or where more than one plan is insured in the same bond**. (a) As indicated in § 464.11, the Act permits the use of blanket, schedule and individual forms of bonds so long as the amount of the bond penalty is sufficient to meet the requirements of the Act for any person who is an administrator, officer or employee of a plan handling funds or other property of the plan. Such person must be bonded for 10 percent of the amount he handles, and the amount of the bond must be sufficient to indemnify the plan for any losses in which such person is involved up to that amount.

(b) When individual or schedule bonds are written, the bond amount for each person must represent not less than 10 percent of the funds "handled" by the named individual or by the person in the position. When a blanket bond is written, the amount of the bond shall be at least 10% of the highest amount handled by any administrator, officer or employee to be covered under the bond. It should also be noted that if an individual or group or class covered under a blanket bond "handle" a large amount of funds or other property, while the remaining bondable persons "handle" only a smaller amount, it is permissible to obtain a blanket bond in an amount sufficient to meet the 10 percent requirements for all except the individual, group or class "handling" the larger amounts, with respect to whom excess indemnity shall be secured in an amount sufficient to meet the 10 percent requirement.

(c) The Act does not prohibit more than one plan from being named as insured under the same bond. However, any such bond must allow for recovery by each plan in an amount at least equal to that which would be required if bonded separately. This requirement has application where a person or persons sought to be bonded pursuant to the requirements of section 13 have "handling" functions in more than one plan covered under the bond. Where such is the case, the amount of the bond must be sufficient to cover any such persons having functions in more than one plan for at least 10 percent of the total amount "handled" by them in all the plans covered under the bond. For example, X is the administrator of two welfare plans run by the same employer and he "handled" $100,000 in the preceding reporting year for Plan A and $500,000 in the preceding reporting year for Plan B. If both plans are covered under the same bond, the amount of the bond with respect to X shall be at least $60,000 or ten percent of the total "handled" by X for both plans covered under the bond in which X has powers and duties of "handling" since Plan B is required to carry bond in at least the amount of $50,000 and Plan A, $10,000.

(d) Additionally, in order to meet the requirement that each plan be protected, it shall be necessary that arrangement be made either by the terms of the bond or rider to the bond or by separate agreement among the parties concerned, that payment of a loss sustained by one of such insureds shall not work to the detriment of any other plan covered under the bond with respect to the amount for which that plan is required to be covered. For example, if Plan A suffered a loss of $30,000 as described above and such loss was recompensed in its entirety by the surety company, it would receive $20,000 more than the $10,000 protection required under Section 13, and only $30,000 would be available for recovery with respect to further losses caused by X. In a subsequently discovered defalcation of $40,000 by X from Plan B, it would be necessary that the bond, rider, or separate agreement provide that such amount of recovery paid to Plan A, in excess of the $10,000 for which it is required to be covered, be made available by such insured to, or held for the use of, Plan B in such amount as Plan B would receive if bonded separately. Thus, in the instant case, Plan B would be able to recover the full $40,000 of its loss. Where the funds or other property of several plans are commingled (if permitted by law) with each other or with other funds, such arrangement shall allow recovery to be attributed proportionately to the amount for which each plan is required to be protectd. Thus, in the instant case, if funds or other property were commingled, and X caused a loss of these funds through fraud or dishonesty, one-sixth of the loss would be attributable to Plan A and five-sixths of the loss attributable to Plan B.

(e) The maximum amount of any bond with respect to any person in any one plan is $500,000, but bonds covering more than one plan may be required to be over $500,000 in order to meet the requirements of the Act, since persons covered by such a bond may have "handling" functions in more than one plan. The $500,000 limitations for such persons applies only with respect to each separate plan in which they have such functions. The minimum bond coverage for any administrator, officer, or employee "handling" funds or other property of a plan is $1,000 as respects each plan in which he has "handling" functions.

[¶ 14,822P]

§ 2580.412-17. **Bonds over $500,000.** The Labor-Management Services Administrator, after due notice and opportunity for hearing to all interested parties, and after consideration of the record, may prescribe an amount in excess of $500,000, which in no event shall exceed 10 per centum of the funds "handled." Any requirement for bonding in excess of $500,000 shall be according to such other regulations as the Secretary may prescribe.

Subpart D—General Bond Rules

[¶ 14,822Q]

§ 2580.412-18. **Naming of insureds.** Since section 13 is intended to protect funds or other property of all plans involved, bonds under this section shall allow for enforcement or recovery by those persons usually authorized to act for such plans in such matters. In most cases, the naming of the plan or plans as insured will provide for such recovery. Where it is not clear that such recovery will be provided, however, a rider shall be attached to the bond or separate agreement made among the parties concerned to make certain that any reimbursement collected under the bond will be for the benefit and use of the plan suffering a loss. Such rider or agreement shall always be required as respects any bond (a) where the employer or employee organization is first named joint insured with one or more plans, or (b) two or more plans are named joint insureds under a single bond with the first named acting for all insureds for the purpose of orderly servicing of the bond.

[¶ 14,822R]

§ 2580.412-19. **Term of the bond, discovery period, other bond clauses.**—

(a) *Term of the bond.* The amount of any required bond must in each instance be based on the amount of funds "handled" and must be fixed or estimated at the beginning of the plan's reporting year, that is, as soon after the date when such year begins as the necessary information from the preceding reporting year can practically be ascertained. This does not mean, however, that a new bond must be obtained each year. There is nothing in the Act that prohibits a bond for a term longer than one year, with whatever advantages such a bond might offer by way of a lower premium. However, at the beginning of each reporting year the bond shall be in at least the requisite amount. If, for any reason, the bond is below the required level at that time, the existing bond shall either be increased to the proper amount, or a supplemental bond shall be obtained.

(b) *Discovery period.* A discovery period of no less than one year after the termination or cancellation of the bond is required. Any standard form written on a "discovery" basis, i.e., providing that a loss must be discovered within the bond period as a prerequisite to recovery of such loss, however, will not be required to have a discovery

period if it contains a provision giving the insured the right to purchase a discovery period of one year in the event of termination or cancellation and the insured has already given the surety notice that it desires such discovery period.

(c) *Other bond clauses.* A bond shall not be adequate to meet the requirements of section 13, if, with respect to bonding coverage required under section 13, it contains a clause, or is otherwise, in contravention of the law of the State in which it is executed.

[¶ 14,822S]

§ 2580.412-20. **Use of existing bonds, separate bonds and additional bonding.**—

(a) *Additional bonding.* Section 13 neither prevents additional bonding beyond that required by its terms, nor prescribes the form in which additional coverage may be taken. Thus, so long as a particular bond meets the requirements of the regulations in this part as to the persons required to be bonded and provides coverage for such persons in at least the minimum required amount, additional coverage as to persons or amount may be taken in any form, either on the same or separate bond.

(b) *Use of existing bonds.* Insofar as a bond currently in use is adequate to meet the requirements of the Act and the regulations in this part or may be made adequate to meet these requirements through rider, modification or separate agreement between the parties, no further bonding is required.

(c) *Use of separate bonds.* The choice of whether persons required to be bonded should be bonded separately or under the same bond, whether given plans should be bonded separately or under the same bond, whether existing bonds should be used or separate bonds for Welfare and Pension Plans Disclosure Act bonding should be obtained, or whether the bond is underwritten by a single surety company or more than one surety company, either separately or on a cosurety basis, is left to the judgment of the parties concerned, so long as the bonding program adopted meets the requirements of the Act and the regulations in this part.

Subpart E—Qualified Agents, Brokers and Surety Companies for the Placing of Bonds

[¶ 14,822T]

§ 2580.412-21. **Corporate sureties holding, grants of authority from the Secretary of the Treasury.** (a) The provisions of section 13 require that any surety company with which a bond is placed pursuant to that section must be a corporate surety which holds a grant of authority from the Secretary of the Treasury under the Act of July 30, 1947 (6 U.S.C. 6-13), as an acceptable surety on Federal bonds. The Act provides, among other things, that in order for a surety company to be eligible for such grant of authority, it must be incorporated under the laws of the United States or of any State and the Secretary of the Treasury shall be satisfied of certain facts relating to its authority and capitalization. Such grants of authority are evidenced by Certificates of Authority which are issued by the Secretary of the Treasury and which expire on the April 30 following the date of their issuance. A list of the companies holding such Certificates of Authority is published annually in the Federal Register, usually in May or June. Changes in the list, occurring between May 1 and April 30, either by addition to or removal from the list of companies, are also published in the Federal Register following each such change.

(b) Where a surety becomes insolvent and is placed in receivership, or if for any other reason the Secretary of the Treasury determines that its financial condition is not satisfactory to him and he revokes the authority of such company to act as an acceptable surety under the Act of July 30, 1947, the "administrator" of the insured plan shall, upon knowledge of such facts, be responsible for securing a new bond with an acceptable surety.

(c) In obtaining or renewing a bond, the plan administrator shall assure that the surety is one which satisfies the requirements of this section. If the bond is for a term of more than one year, the plan administrator, at the beginning of each reporting year, shall assure that the surety continues to satisfy the requirements of this subpart.

[¶ 14,822U]

§ 2580.412-22. **Interests held in agents, brokers and surety companies**. Section 13(c) prohibits the placing of bonds, required to be obtained pursuant to section 13, with any surety or other company, or through any agent or broker in whose business operations a plan or any party in interest in a plan has significant control or financial interest, direct or indirect. An interpretation of this section has been issued (Part 485 of this chapter).

Subpart F—Exemptions

BONDS PLACED WITH CERTAIN REINSURING COMPANIES

[¶ 14,822V]

§ 2580.412-23. **Exemption**. An exemption from the bonding requirements of the Welfare and Pension Plans Disclosure Act is granted by this section whereby bonding arrangements (which otherwise comply with the requirements of section 13 of the Act and the regulations issued thereunder) with companies authorized by the Secretary of the Treasury as acceptable reinsurers on Federal bonds will satisfy the bonding requirements of the Act. (Amended by F.R. Doc. 63-11370, published in Federal Register October 29, 1963.)

[¶ 14,822W]

§ 2580.412-24. **Conditions of exemption**. (a) This exemption obtains only with respect to the requirement of section 13(a) of the Act that all bonds required thereunder shall have as surety thereon, a corporate surety company, which is an acceptable surety on Federal bonds under authority granted by the Secretary of the Treasury pursuant to the Act of July 30, 1947 (6 U.S.C. 6-13).

(b) The exemption is granted upon the condition that if for any reason the authority of any such company to act as an acceptable reinsuring company is terminated, the administrator of a plan insured with such company, shall, upon knowledge of such fact, be responsible for securing a new bond with a company acceptable under the Act and the exemptions issued thereunder.

(c) In obtaining or renewing a bond, the plan administrator shall ascertain that the surety is one which satisfies the requirements of the Act and the exemptions thereunder. If the bond is for a term of more than one year, the plan administrator, at the beginning of each reporting year, shall ascertain that the surety continues to do so. (Amended by F.R. Doc. 63-11370, published in Federal Register October 29, 1963.)

BONDS PLACED WITH UNDERWRITERS AT LLOYDS, LONDON

[¶ 14,822X]

§ 2580.412-25. **Exemption**. An exemption from the bonding requirements of subsection 13(a) of the Welfare and Pension Plans Disclosure Act is granted by this section whereby arrangements (which otherwise comply with the requirements of section 13 of the Act and the regulations issued thereunder), with the Underwriters at Lloyds, London will satisfy the bonding requirements of the Act.

[¶ 14,822Y]

§ 2580.412-26. **Conditions of exemption**. (a) This exemption obtains only with respect to the requirements of section 13(a) of the Act that all bonds required thereunder shall have assurety thereon, a corporate surety company, which is an acceptable surety on Federal bonds under authority granted by the Secretary of the Treasury, pursuant to the Act of July 30, 1947 (6 U.S.C. 6-13).

(b) This exemption is granted on the following conditions:

(1) Underwriters at Lloyds, London shall continue to be licensed in a state of the United States to enter into bonding arrangements of the type required by the Act.

(2) Underwriters at Lloyds, London shall file with the Office of Pension and Welfare Benefit Programs two (2) copies of each annual statement required to be made to the Commissioner of Insurance of those states in which Underwriters at Lloyds, London are licensed. Copies of annual statements shall be filed with the Office of Pension and Welfare Benefit Programs within the same period required by the respective states.

(3) All bonding arrangements entered into by Underwriters at Lloyds, London under section 13 of the Act shall contain a "Service of

Suit Clause" in substantial conformity with that set forth in the petition for exemption.

BANKING INSTITUTIONS SUBJECT TO FEDERAL REGULATION

[¶ 14,822Z]

§ 2580.412-27. **Exemption**. An exemption from the bonding requirements of subsections 13(a) and (b) of the Welfare and Pension Plans Disclosure Act is granted whereby banking institutions and trust companies specified in § 2580.412-28 are not required to comply with subsections 13(a) and (b) of the Act, with respect to welfare and pension benefit plans covered by the Act. (Amended by F.R. Doc. 69-3030, published in Federal Register March 13, 1969.)

[¶ 14,823]

§ 2580.412-28. **Conditions of exemption**. This exemption applies only to those banking institutions and trust companies subject to regulation and examination by the Comptroller of the Currency or the Board of Governors of the Federal Reserve System, or the Federal Deposit Insurance Corporation.

[¶ 14,823A]

§ 2580.412-29. **Exemption**. An exemption from the bonding requirements of subsections 13(a) and (b) of the Welfare and Pension Plans Disclosure Act is granted whereby savings and loan associations (including building and loan associations, cooperative banks and homestead associations) specified in § 2580.412-30 are not required to comply with subsections 13(a) and (b) of the Act, with respect to welfare and pension benefit plans covered by the Act for the benefit of their own employees, where such a savings and loan association is the administrator of such plans. (Added by F.R. Doc. 67-4967, published in Federal Register May 4, 1967.)

[¶ 14,823B]

§ 2580.412-30. **Conditions of exemption**. This exemption applies only to those savings and loan associations (including building and loan associations, cooperative banks and homestead associations) subject to regulation and examination by the Federal Home Loan Bank Board. (Added by F.R. Doc. 67-4967, published in Federal Register May 4, 1967.)

INSURANCE CARRIERS, SERVICE AND OTHER SIMILAR ORGANIZATIONS

[¶ 14,823C]

§ 2580.412-31. **Exemption**. An exemption from the bonding requirements of subsections 13(a) and (b) of the Welfare and Pension Plans Disclosure Act is granted whereby any insurance carrier or service or other similar organization specified in § 2580.412-32 is not required to comply with subsections 13(a) and (b) of the Act with respect to any welfare or pension benefit plan covered by the Act which is established or maintained for the benefit of persons other than the employees of such insurance carrier or service or other similar organization. (Added by F.R. Doc. 69-3030, published in Federal Register March 13, 1969.)

[¶ 14,823D]

§ 2580.412-32. **Conditions of exemption**. This exemption applies only to those insurance carriers, service or other similar organizations providing or underwriting welfare or pension plan benefits in accordance with State law. (Added by F.R. Doc. 69-3030, published in Federal Register March 13, 1969.)

Subpart G—Prohibition Against Bonding by Parties Interested in the Plan

[¶ 14,823E]

§ 2580.412-33. **Introductory statement**. (a) This part discusses the meaning and scope of Section 13(c) of the Welfare and Pension Plans Disclosure Act of 1958 (76 Stat. 39, 29 U.S.C. 308d (c)) (hereinafter referred to as the Act). This provision makes it unlawful "for any person to procure any bond [required by the Act] from any surety or other company or through any agent or broker in whose business operations such plan or any party in interest in such plan has any significant control or financial interest, direct or indirect." Because the prohibition contained in this provision is broadly stated, it becomes a matter of importance to determine more specifically the types of arrangements intended to be prohibited.

(b) The provisions of Section 13 of the Act, including 13(c) are subject to the general investigatory authority of the Director, Office of Labor-Management and Welfare-Pension Reports, embodied in Section 9 of the Act. The correctness of an interpretation of these provisions can be determined finally and authoritatively only by the courts. It is necessary, however, for the Labor-Management Services Administrator (hereafter referred to as "the administrator") to reach informed conclusions as to the meaning of the law to enable him to carry out his statutory duties of administration and enforcement. The interpretations of the Administrator contained in this part, which are issued upon the advice of the Solicitor of Labor, indicate the construction of the law which will guide the Administrator in performing his duties unless and until he is directed otherwise by authoritative rulings of the courts or unless and until he subsequently decides that his prior interpretation is incorrect. Under Section 12 of the Act, the interpretations contained in this part, if relied upon in good faith, will constitute a defense in any action or proceeding based on any act or omission in alleged violation of Section 13(c) of the Act. The omission, however, to discuss a particular problem in this part, or in interpretations supplementing it, should not be taken to indicate the adoption of any position by the Administrator with respect to such problem or to constitute an administrative interpretation or practice. Interpretations of the Administrator with respect to 13(c) are set forth in this part to provide those affected by the provisions of the Act with "a practical guide * * * as to how the office representing the public interest in its enforcement will seek to apply it" (*Skidmore v. Swift & Co.,* 323 U.S. 134, 138).

(c) To the extent that prior opinions and interpretations relating to 13(c) are inconsistent with the principles stated in this part, they are hereby rescinded and withdrawn.

[¶ 14,823F]

§ 2580.412-34. **General**. The purpose of Section 13(c), as shown by its legislative history, is similar to a closely related provision contained in Section 502(a) of the Labor-Management Reporting and Disclosure Act of 1959 (73 Stat. 536; 29 U.S.C. 502(a)). The fundamental purpose of Congress under 13(c) is to insure against potential abuses arising from significant financial or other influential interests affecting the objectivity of the plan or parties in interest in the plan and agents, brokers, or surety or other companies, in securing and providing the bond specified in Section 13(a). As will be explained more fully below, this prohibition, however, was not intended to preclude the placing of bonds through or with certain parties in interest in plans which provide a variety of services to the plan, one of which is a bonding service.

[¶ 14,823G]

§ 2580.412-35. **Disqualification of agents, brokers and sureties**. Since 13(c) is to be construed as disqualifying any agent, broker, surety or other company from having a bond placed through or with it, if the plan or any party in interest in the plan has a significant financial interest or control in such agent, broker, surety or other company, a question of fact will necessarily arise in many cases as to whether the financial interest or control held is sufficiently significant to disqualify the agent, broker, or surety. Although no rule of guidance can be established to govern each and every case in which this question arises, in general, the essential test is whether the existing financial interest or control held is incompatible with an unbiased exercise of judgment in regard to procuring the bond or bonding the plan's personnel. In regard to the foregoing, it is also to be pointed out that lack of knowledge or consent on the part of persons responsible for procuring bonds with respect to the existence of a significant financial interest or control rendering the bonding arrangement unlawful will not be deemed a mitigating factor where such persons have failed to make a reasonable examination into the pertinent circumstances affecting the procuring of the bond.

[¶ 14,823H]

§ 2580.412-36. **Application of 13(c) to "party in interest"**. (a) Under 13(c), an agent, broker or surety or other company is disqualified from having a bond placed through or with it if a "party in interest" in the plan has any significant control or financial interest in such agent, broker, surety or other company. Section 3(13) of the Act defines the term "party in interest" to mean "any administrator, officer, trustee, custodian, counsel, or employee of any employee welfare benefit plan or employee pension benefit plan, or a person providing benefit plan services to any such plan, or an employer any of whose employees are covered by such a plan or officer or employee or agent of such employer, or an officer or agent or employee of an employee organization having members covered by such plan."

(b) A basic question presented is whether the effect of 13(c) is to prohibit persons from placing a bond through or with any "party in interest" in the plan. The language used in 13(c) appears to indicate that in this connection the intent of Congress was to eliminate those instances where the existing financial interest or control held by the "party in interest" in the agent, broker, surety or other company is incompatible with an unbiased exercise of judgment in regard to procuring the bond or bonding the plan's personnel. Accordingly, not all parties in interest are disqualified from procuring or providing bonds for the plan. Thus where a "party in interest" or its affiliate provides multiple benefit plan services to plans, persons are not prohibited from availing themselves of the bonding services provided by the "party in interest" or its affiliate merely because the plan has already availed itself, or will avail itself, of other services provided by the "party in interest." In this case, it is inherent in the nature of the "party in interest" or its affiliate as an individual or organization providing multiple benefit plan services, one of which is a bonding service, that the existing financial interest or control held is not, in and of itself, incompatible with an unbiased exercise of judgment in regard to procuring the bond or bonding the plan's personnel. In short, there is no distinction between this type of relationship and the ordinary arm's length business relationship which may be established between a plan-customer and an agent, broker or surety company, a relationship which Congress could not have intended to disturb. On the other hand, where a "party in interest" in the plan or an affiliate does not provide a bonding service as part of its general business operations, 13(c) would prohibit any person from procuring the bond through or with any agent, broker, surety or other company, with respect to which the "party in interest" has any significant control or financial interest, direct or indirect. In this case, the failure of the "party in interest" or its affiliate to provide a bonding service as part of its general business operations misses the possibility of less than an arm's length business relationship between the plan and the agent, broker, surety or other company since the objectivity of either the plan or the agent, broker or surety may be influenced by the "party in interest".

(c) The application of the principles discussed in this section is illustrated by the following examples:

Example (1). B, a broker, renders actuarial and consultant services to plan P. B has also procured a group life insurance policy for plan P. B may also place a bond for P with surety company S, provided that neither B nor P has any significant control or financial interest, direct or indirect, in S and provided that neither P nor any other "party in interest" in P, e.g., an officer of the plan, has any significant control or financial interest, direct or indirect, in B or S.

Example (2). I, a life insurance company, has provided a group life insurance policy for plan P. I is affiliated with S, a surety company, and has a significant financial interest or control in S. P is not prohibited from obtaining a bond from S since I's affiliation with S does not ordinarily, in and of itself, affect the objectivity of P in procuring the bond or the objectivity of S in bonding P's personnel. However, if any other "party in interest" as defined in Section 3(13) of the Act, such as the employer whose employees are covered by P, should have a significant financial interest or control in S, S could not write the bond for P, since the employer's interest affects the objectivity of P and S.

[¶ 14,830]
LIMITATION ON ACTIONS

Act Sec. 413. No action may be commenced under this title with respect to a fiduciary's breach of any responsibility, duty, or obligation under this part, or with respect to a violation of this part, after the earlier of—

(1) six years after (A) the date of the last action which constituted a part of the breach or violation, or (B) in the case of an omission, the latest date on which the fiduciary could have cured the breach or violation, or

(2) three years after the earliest date on which the plaintiff had actual knowledge of the breach or violation

except that in the case of fraud or concealment, such action may be commenced not later than six years after the date of discovery of such breach or violation.

Amendments

P.L. 101-239, § 7881(j)(4):

Amended ERISA Sec. 413(2) by striking the comma effective December 17, for reports required to be filed after December 31, 1987.

P.L. 101-239, § 7894(e)(5):

Amended ERISA Sec. 413 by striking "(a)" effective September 2, 1974.

P.L. 100-203, § 9342(b):

Amended ERISA Sec. 413(a)(2) by striking "A" and "or B" and all that followed through "title", to read as above, effective December 17, 1987 for reports required to be filed after December 31, 1987. Prior to amendment, 413(a)(2) reads as follows:

(2) three years after the earliest date (A) on which the plaintiff had actual knowledge of the breach or violation, or (B) on which a report from which he could reasonably be expected to have obtained knowledge of such breach or violation was filed with the Secretary under this title;

[¶ 14,840]
EFFECTIVE DATE

Act Sec. 414.(a) Except as provided in subsections (b), (c), and (d), this part shall take effect on January 1, 1975.

Act Sec. 414.(b)(1) The provisions of this part authorizing the Secretary to promulgate regulations shall take effect on the date of enactment of this Act.

(2) Upon application of a plan, the Secretary may postpone until not later than January 1, 1976, the applicability of any provision of sections 402, 403 (other than 403(c)), 405 (other than 405(a) and (d)), and 410(a), as it applies to any plan in existence on the date of enactment of this Act if he determines such postponement is (A) necessary to amend the instrument establishing the plan under which the plan is maintained and (B) not adverse to the interest of participants and beneficiaries.

(3) This part shall take effect on the date of enactment of this Act with respect to a plan which terminates after June 30, 1974, and before January 1, 1975, and to which at the time of termination section 4021 applies.

Act Sec. 414. (c) Sections 406 and 407(a) (relating to prohibited transactions) shall not apply—

(1) until June 30, 1984, to a loan of money or other extension of credit between a plan and a party in interest under a binding contract in effect on July 1, 1974 (or pursuant to renewals of such a contract), if such loan or other extension of credit remains at least as favorable to the plan as an arm's-length transaction with an unrelated party would be, and if the execution of the contract, the making of the loan, or the extension of credit was not, at the time of such execution, making, or extension, a prohibited transaction (within the meaning of section 503(b) of the Internal Revenue Code of 1986 or the corresponding provisions of prior law);

(2) until June 30, 1984, to a lease or joint use of property involving the plan and a party in interest pursuant to a binding contract in effect on July 1, 1974 (or pursuant to renewals of such a contract), if such lease or joint use remains at least as favorable to the plan as an arm's-length transaction with an unrelated party would be and if the execution of the contract was not, at the time of such execution, a prohibited transaction (within the meaning of section 503(b) of the Internal Revenue Code of 1986 or the corresponding provisions of prior law);

(3) until June 30, 1984, to the sale, exchange, or other disposition of property described in paragraph (2) between a plan and a party in interest if—

(A) in the case of a sale, exchange, or other disposition of the property by the plan to the party in interest, the plan receives an amount which is not less than the fair market value of the property at the time of such disposition; and

(B) in the case of the acquisition of the property by the plan, the plan pays an amount which is not in excess of the fair market value of the property at the time of such acquisition;

(4) until June 30, 1977, to the provision of services, to which paragraphs (1), (2), and (3) do not apply between a plan and a party in interest—

(A) under a binding contract in effect on July 1, 1974 (or pursuant to renewals of such contract), or

(B) if the party in interest ordinarily and customarily furnished such services on June 30, 1974, if such provision of services remains at least as favorable to the plan as an arm's-length transaction with an unrelated party would be and if such provision of services was not, at the time of such provision, a prohibited transaction (within the meaning of section 503(b) of the Internal Revenue Code of 1954) or the corresponding provisions of prior law; or

(5) the sale, exchange, or other disposition of property which is owned by a plan on June 30, 1974, and all times thereafter, to a party in interest, if such plan is required to dispose of such property in order to comply with the provisions of section 407(a) (relating to the prohibition against holding excess employer securities and employer real property), and if the plan receives not less than adequate consideration.

Act Sec. 414. (d) Any election, or failure to elect, by a disqualified person under section 2003(c)(1)(B) of this Act shall be treated for purposes of this part (but not for purposes of section 514) as an act or omission occurring before the effective date of this part.

Act Sec. 414. (e) The preceding provisions of this section shall not apply with respect to amendments made to this part in provisions enacted after the date of the enactment of this Act.

Amendments

P.L. 101-239, § 7891(a)(1):

Titles I, III, and IV of ERISA (other than sections 3(37)(E), 301(a)(7), and 308, the last sentence of section 408(d), and sections 414(c), 4001(a)(3)(ii), and 4303) are each amended by striking "Internal Revenue Code of 1954" each place it appears and inserting "Internal Revenue Code of 1986" effective October 22, 1986.

P.L. 101-239, § 7894(e)(6):

Amended ERISA Sec. 414(c)(2) by striking "1954)" and inserting "1986" and by striking "prior law" and inserting "prior law)" effective September 2, 1974.

P.L. 101-239, § 7894(h)(4):

Amended ERISA Sec. 414 by adding new subsection (e) to read as above.

Regulations

The following regulations were adopted effective November 21, 1974, under "Title 29—Labor; Chapter XXV—Office of Employee Benefits Security; Subchapter F—Fiduciary Responsibility; § 2550.414b-1 of Part 2550—Guidelines for Submission of Applicaton for Postponement of the Effective Date of Certain Fiduciary Responsibility Provisions." The regulations were published in the Federal Register of November 21, 1974.[1] Amendments were made by FR Doc. 75-15215 and published in the Federal Register on June 11, 1975, effective on publication. The regulations at ¶ 14,845 were added by FR Doc. 77-17895, effective June 21, 1977.

---

[1] § 2550.414b-1 of Part 2550 was Part 2550. See ¶ 23,887.

»»→ *Caution: Regulation § 2550.414b-1 was officially removed by 61 FR 33847 on July 1, 1996.*

[¶ 14,841]

§ 2550.414b-1 **Guidelines.**

(a) *Purpose.* The purpose of this regulation is to issue guidelines to assist applicants seeking postponement of the effective date of certain fiduciary responsibility provisions of the Employee Retirement Income Security Act of 1974 (the Act). In general, the fiduciary responsibility provisions of Part 4 of Title I of the Act are effective on January 1, 1975. However, section 414(b)(2) of the Act provides that for plans in existence on September 2, 1974, the Secretary of Labor (the Secretary) may, upon application, postpone until not later than January 1, 1976, the effective date of certain provisions respecting establishment of plans (section 402), establishment of trusts (section 403, other than subsection (c)), liability for breach by co-fiduciaries (section 405, other than subsections (a) and (d)) and exculpatory clauses (section 410(a)). Such a postponement shall be allowed where the Secretary determines that the delay is (1) necessary to amend the instrument or instruments under which the plan is established or maintained and (2) not adverse to the interest of plan participants and beneficiaries. It should be noted that under the terms of section 414(b)(2), no postponement may be given for the applicability of the provisions of section 403(c), which precludes plan assets from inuring to the benefit of any employer; section 405(a), which sets forth general rules regarding co-fiduciary liability; and section 405(d), dealing with trustee liability where an investment manager has been appointed in accordance with section 402(c)(3) of the Act.

Since the provisions as to which the effective date may be postponed were not required by previously existing Federal law and will necessitate amendment of many existing plans to comply with or take these provisions into account, the Secretary has prepared these guidelines setting forth the application procedure and the kind of information the Secretary will require to make a determination.

(b) *Who may submit an application for postponement.* Any plan administrator, trustee, named fiduciary, or other individual duly authorized to act on behalf of a plan may apply for a postponement.

(c) *Procedure for submitting application.* Applications for postponement subject to this regulation shall be sent in duplicate by first-class mail, postage prepaid, to the Office of Employee Benefits Security, Labor-Management Services Administration, U.S. Department of Labor, P.O. Box 176, Washington, D.C. 20044, or shall be delivered by hand to Room 3311, U.S. Department of Labor, 14th Street and Constitution Avenue, N.W., Washington, D.C. An application submitted by mail shall be deemed to be submitted as of the date of the postmark. See § 2550.414b-1(h) for submittal deadlines.

(d) *Format and content of application.* In order to enable the Secretary to expeditiously process applications under this regulation, those applications which are submitted in duplicate and which include the following information in the following order will be processed first, and applications which do not contain such information will be disapproved, subject to § 2550.414b-1(h):

(1) The name of the plan and the name and address of the individual making the application on behalf of the plan (applicant) and the basis for his or her authority to make the application on behalf of the plan;

(2) The WP number assigned to the plan, if it has previously filed under the Welfare and Pension Plans Disclosure Act with the Office of Labor-Management and Welfare Pension Reports of the Department of Labor;

(3) The employer identification number (EIN) assigned by the Internal Revenue Service to the plan sponsor (as defined in section 3(16)(b) of the Act) and, if the plan sponsor has assigned a plan identification number to the plan pursuant to instructions of Internal Revenue Service Form 4848, the Plan Identification Number;

(4) A statement that the plan was in existence on September 2, 1974;

(5) A statement that the method of notification used or to be used will afford reasonable notice to plan participants in accordance with the provisions of § 2550.414b-1(f) of the application for postponement and of their right to file comments under § 2550.414b-1(e);

(6) An enumeration of the specific fiduciary responsibility sessions (or provisions of such sections) listed in section 414(b)(2) of the Act for which a postponement of the effective date is requested. If a postponement for all such provisions is sought, the applicant may merely state that a postponement is requested for all provisions listed in section 414(b)(2);

(7) A statement disclosing the reason why a postponement is necessary, the date until which such postponement is requested (see § 2550.414b-1(g)), and why such postponement will not be adverse to the interest of plan participants and beneficiaries. If the applicant is requesting a postponement of the applicability of section 410(a) of the Act, a separate explanation should be given of the reasons therefor;

(8) If the plan is an employee pension benefit plan (as defined in section 3(2) of the Act) and is requesting a postponement of the applicability of the provisions of section 403(a) of the Act, a statement that, to the extent that plan assets would otherwise be required to be held in trust under the provisions of section 403 of the Act, such assets that are held by a party in interest are held in a manner that would reasonably be expected to protect the plan against loss resulting from the satisfaction of a creditor's claim against the party in interest;

(9) A statement by the applicant that if any of the material facts contained in or underlying the statements made in the application is discovered by the applicant to be inaccurate, the applicant will promptly notify the Secretary in writing of such inaccuracy specifying the reasons for the inaccuracy; and

(10) A duly notarized certification by the person signing the application for postponement on behalf of the plan that he or she is duly authorized to execute the application on behalf of the plan, and that, under applicable penalties of law, the information in the application is, to the best of his or her knowledge and belief, true, correct and complete.

(e) *Comments by participants and beneficiaries.* Plan participants and beneficiaries and their authorized representatives may submit written comments respecting any application for postponement made under § 2550.414b-1(d) at any time after such application is filed, specifying any objections which they may have. A collective bargaining representative for a plan participant or beneficiary shall be deemed to be an authorized representative for purposes of this Part.

Such comments shall be submitted at any time before the expiration of the period of the postponement of the Office of Employee Benefits Security, Labor-Management Services Administration, U.S. Department of Labor, P.O. Box 176, Washington, D.C. 20044.

(f) *Notification to participants.* (1) The applicant shall employ methods reasonably calculated to provide plan participants with notification that an application for postponement has been filed with the Secretary of Labor, describing in language calculated to be understood by the average plan participant the sections (or provisions of sections) of the act for which the delay has been requested, the date until which such postponement has been requested, the reasons for requesting the postponement, why the postponement will not adversely affect the interest of plan participants and beneficiaries, and stating that plan participants and beneficiaries may comment on the requested postponement by writing to the Office of Employee Benefits Security, Labor-Management Services Administration, U.S. Department of Labor, P.O. Box 176, Washington, D.C. 20044.

(2) Notice must be in writing and must be reasonably calculated to reach a substantial number of plan participants. While there is no prescribed form or method of delivery for adequate notice, and while other forms or methods of delivery may be deemed acceptable under the particular circumstances involved, any of the following shall be deemed adequate notice to plan participants:

(A) The prominent posting, not later than 30 days after the date of application for postponement, of the notification required by paragraph (a) above at those locations customarily used by the employer for notices to employees with regard to labor-management relations matters at worksites of plan participants or, if the plan is maintained pursuant to a collective bargaining agreement and notices to employees with regard to labor-management relations matters are ordinarily posted at locations such as local union meeting places, at such locations;

(B) The mailing by first-class mail, not later than 30 days after the date of the application for postponement, of the notification required by paragraph (a) above to the last known address of substantially all plan participants;

(C) The publishing, not later than 60 days after the date of the application for postponement, of the notification required by paragraph (a) above in a publication which is directed to a substantial number of plan participants; or

(D) The utilization of any combination of the above methods reasonably calculated to so notify a substantial number of plan participants.

If the plan is the subject of one or more collective bargaining agreements, the applicant shall also mail the notification required by paragraph (a) above by first-class mail, not later than 15 days after the date of application for postponement, to each collective bargaining agent representing participants covered by the plan.

(3) In the case of a plan which applied for a postponement of the applicability of sections 402, 403 (other than 403(c)) and 405 (other than 405(a) and (d)), the application of which has been approved under paragraph (h), and which has not been amended so as to comply with such sections before July 1, 1975, the applicant or any other person authorized to file an application for a plan under paragraph (b) shall employ methods reasonably calculated to provide plan participants and, if the plan is the subject of one or more collective bargaining agreements, each collective bargaining agent representing participants covered by the plan, with notification that the Secretary of Labor has extended postponements of the applicability of those sections to the plan until not later than January 1, 1976. This notification shall comply with the requirements of subparagraph (2) of this paragraph. [Amended on June 11, 1975, by F.R. Doc. 75-15215.]

(g) *Length of postponement.* (1) All postponements of the applicability of section 410(a) of the Act approved by the Secretary shall be effective for a period of time not extending beyond June 30, 1975.

(2) All postponements of sections 402, 403 (other than 403(c)) and 405 (other than 405(a) and (d)) of the Act approved by the

Secretary shall be effective for a period of time extending through December 31, 1975. [Amended on June 11, 1975, by F.R. Doc. 75-15215.]

(h) *Notification of Secretary's decision with respect to postponement; effect of non-notification.* (1) It is contemplated that notification to applicants of approval or disapproval will be made before January 1, 1975, respecting those applications submitted on or before December 10, 1974;

(2) In the case of applications submitted after December 10, 1974, and before January 1, 1975, notification of approval or disapproval will be made as expeditiously as possible, and in the case of any application submitted on or before December 31, 1974, as to which notification of approval or disapproval has not been made before January 1, 1975, the application shall be deemed to be approved, subject to the provisions of § 2550.414b-1(i).

(3) In any case in which notification of approval is made before January 1, 1975, and the disapproval is based on receipt of an incomplete application, the applicant shall have a period of 30 days from the date of such notification to submit an amended application, and the application shall be deemed approved during such period.

(4) Applications will not be accepted after December 31, 1974, except for good cause shown for the failure to submit a timely application.

(i) *Revocation of modification of postponement.* The Secretary may revoke or modify any postponements approved (or deemed approved) under § 2550.414b-1(h) if, upon receipt of comments or upon investigation (or, in the case of an application received too late for review and notification before January 1, 1975, upon review of the application) he determines that such postponement is not necessary to amend the instrument establishing the plan or is adverse to the interest of participants and beneficiaries. Before issuing any proposed decision of revocation or modification, the Secretary shall give the applicant and any persons who filed comments 45 days written notice of the proposed revocation or modification and the reasons therefor and an opportunity to file comments with respect to the proposed action, in accordance with procedures designated in the notice.

Regulations

The following regulations under Act Sec. 414 were adopted by FR Doc. 81-2445, filed with the Federal Register on January 22, 1981, and published in the Federal Register of January 23, 1981 (46 FR 7320). § § 2550.414c-1 and 2550.414c-2 are effective January 1, 1975.

⫸ Caution: *Regulation § 2550.414c-1 was officially removed by 61 FR 33847 on July 1, 1996.*

[¶ 14,844A]

§ 2550.414c-1 **Transitional rule relating to certain loans or other extensions of credit prior to June 30, 1984.** (a) Before June 30, 1984, sections 406 and 407(a) of the Employee Retirement Income Security Act of 1974 shall not apply with respect to a loan of money or other extension of credit between a plan and a party in interest under a binding contract in effect on July 1, 1974, or pursuant to renewals of such a contract, if such loan or other extension of credit remains at least as favorable to the plan as an arm's-length transaction with an unrelated party would be, and if the execution of the contract, the making of the loan, or the extension of credit was not, at the time of such execution, making, or extension, a prohibited transaction within the meaning of section 503(b) of the Internal Revenue Code of 1954 or the corresponding provisions of prior law.

(b) For purposes of this section,

(1) "Binding contract" means a contract which is binding under applicable state law;

(2) A loan or other extension of credit will not be considered to "remain at least as favorable to the plan as an arm's-length transaction with an unrelated party would be" unless:

(i) Such loan or extension of credit, at the time of the execution of the contract and any renewal, is on terms at least as favorable to the plan as those which reasonably would be expected to exist in the case of an otherwise identical transaction in a normal commercial setting between the plan and the party in interest if they were unrelated parties, and

(ii) The plan requires termination or modification of the contract at such time as, and in such manner and to such extent that, it reasonably would be expected to require such termination or modification in the case of an otherwise identical transaction in a normal commercial setting with the party in interest if they were unrelated parties; and

(3) "Renewal" of a contract means only a renewal which:

(i) The plan reasonably would be expected to agree to in the case of an otherwise identical transaction in a normal commercial setting with the party in interest if they were unrelated parties, and

(ii) Except to the extent required by paragraph (b)(2)(ii) of this section, does not result in any substantial change or modification of the terms of the existing contract.

⫸ Caution: *Regulation § 2550.414c-2 was officially removed by 61 FR 33847 on July 1, 1996.*

[¶ 14,844B]

§ 2550.414c-2 **Transitional rule relating to certain leases or joint uses of property prior to June 30, 1984.** (a) Before June 30, 1984, sections 406 and 407(a) of the Employee Retirement Income Security Act of 1974 shall not apply with respect to a lease or joint use of property involving the plan and a party in interest pursuant to a binding contract in effect on July 1, 1974, or pursuant to renewals of such a contract, if such lease or joint use remains at least as favorable to the plan as an arm's length transaction with an unrelated party would be and if the execution of the contract was not, at the time of such execution, a prohibited transaction within the meaning of section 503(b) of the Internal Revenue Code of 1954 or the corresponding provisions of prior law.

(b) For purposes of this section,

(1) "Binding contract" means a contract which is binding under applicable state law;

(2) A lease or joint use of property will not be considered to "remain at least as favorable to the plan as an arm's-length transaction with an unrelated party would be" unless:

(i) The contract for such lease or joint use of property, at the time of the execution and any renewal thereof, is on terms at least as favorable to the plan as those which reasonably would be expected to exist in the case of an otherwise identical transaction in a normal commercial setting between the plan and the party in interest if they were unrelated parties, and

(ii) The plan requires termination or modification of the contract at such time as, and in such manner and to such extent that, it reasonably would be expected to require such termination or modification in the case of an otherwise identical transaction in a normal commercial setting with the party in interest if they were unrelated parties; and

(3) "Renewal" of a contract means only a renewal which:

(i) The plan reasonably would be expected to agree to in the case of an otherwise identical transaction in a normal commercial setting with the party in interest if they were unrelated parties, and

(ii) Except to the extent required by paragraph (b)(2)(ii) of this section, does not result in any substantial change or modification of the terms of the existing contract.

⋙→ Caution: *Regulations § 2550.414c-3 was officially removed by 61 FR 33847 on July 1, 1996.*

[¶ 14,844C]

§ 2550.414c-3 **Transitional rule relating to certain sales, exchanges, or other dispositions of property prior to June 30, 1984.** (a) Before June 30, 1984, sections 406 and 407(a) of the Employee Retirement Income Security Act of 1974 shall not apply with respect to a sale, exchange, or other disposition of leased or jointly used property described in 29 CFR 2550.414c-2 between a plan and a party in interest: *Provided,* That:

(1) In the case of a sale, exchange, or other disposition of such property by the plan to the party in interest, the plan receives an amount which is not less than the fair market value of the property at the time of such disposition; and

(2) In the case of the acquisition of such property by the plan, the plan pays an amount which is not in excess of the fair market value of the property at the time of such acquisition.

(b) For purposes of this section:

(1) The term "property described in 29 CFR 2550.414c-2" means any property subject to a lease or joint use involving a plan and a party in interest under a binding contract in effect on July 1, 1974, or pursuant to renewals of such contracts;

(2) A property will not be regarded as the subject of a lease or joint use between a plan and a party in interest if one or more unrelated persons leases or jointly uses any portion or portions of such property representing a total value equal to or greater than the value of the portion of the property leased to or jointly used by one or more parties in interest. Property leased or jointly used by a party in interest which is subleased to or jointly used with an unrelated party shall not, solely because of such sublease or use, be considered property leased to or jointly used by an unrelated party.

(3)(A) Subject to the provisions of subparagraph (B) of this paragraph, "fair market value" shall be determined by the plan trustee or named fiduciary in light of the facts and circumstances of the particular case.

(B) In determining the fair market value of leased or jointly used property pursuant to subparagraph (A) of this paragraph, the plan trustee or named fiduciary shall not take into account any diminution in value resulting from

(i) Any encumbrance arising out of a lease or joint use which violates any provision of the Act, and

(ii) Any encumbrance, arising out of a lease or joint use, to the extent such encumbrance extends beyond June 30, 1984.

(4) The term "property" means any property or part thereof. [Reg. § 2550.414c-3 was originally scheduled to be effective February 23, 1981. However, the effective date was delayed under the President's regulation freeze until March 30, 1981 (46 FR 11253).]

⋙→ Caution: *Regulation § 2550.414c-4 was officially removed by 61 FR 33847 on July 1, 1996.*

[¶ 14,845]

§ 2550.414c-4 **Transitional rule for the provision of certain services until June 30, 1977.**

(a) *In general.* Section 414(c)(4) of the Employee Retirement Income Security Act of 1974 (the Act) provides that sections 406 and 407(a) shall not apply to the provision of services before June 30, 1977, between a plan and a party in interest if the three requirements contained in section 414(c)(4) are met. The first requirement is that such services must be provided either (1) under a binding contract in effect on July 1, 1974 (or pursuant to a renewal or modification of such contract), or (2) by a party in interest who ordinarily and customarily furnished such services on June 30, 1974. The second requirement is that the services be provided on terms that remain at least as favorable to the plan as an arm's-length transaction with an unrelated party would be. For this purpose, such services are provided on terms that remain at least as favorable to the plan as an arm's-length transaction with an unrelated party would be, if at the time of execution (or renewal) of such binding contract, the contract (or renewal) is on terms at least as favorable to the plan as an arm's-length transaction with an unrelated party would be. However, if in a normal commercial setting an unrelated party in the position of the plan could be expected to insist upon a renegotiation or termination of a binding contract, the plan must so act. Thus, for example, if a party in interest provides services to a plan on a month-to-month basis, and a party in the position of the plan could be expected to renegotiate the price paid under such contract because of a decline in the fair market value of such services, the plan must so act in order to avoid participation in a prohibited transaction. The third requirement is that the provision of services must not be, or have been, at the time of such provision a prohibited transaction within the meaning of section 503(b) of the Internal Revenue Code of 1954 or the corresponding provisions of prior law. If these three requirements are met, section 406 of the Act will apply neither to services provided before June 30, 1977 (both to customers to whom such services were being provided on June 30, 1974, and to new customers) nor to the receipt of compensation therefor. Thus, if these three requirements are met, section 406 of the Act will not apply until June 30, 1977, to the provision of services to a plan by a party in interest (including a fiduciary) even if such services could not be furnished pursuant to the exemption provisions of sections 408(b)(2) or (6) of the Act and §§ 2550.408b-2 and 2550.408b-6. For example, if the three requirements of section 414(c)(4) of the Act are met, a person serving as a fiduciary to a plan who already receives full-time pay from an employer or an association of employers, whose employees are participants in such plan, or from an employee organization whose members are participants in such plan, may continue to receive reasonable compensation from the plan for services rendered to the plan before June 30, 1977. Similarly, until June 30, 1977, a plan consultant who may be a fiduciary because of the nature of the consultative and administrative services being provided may, if these three requirements are met, continue to cause the sale of insurance to the plan and continue to receive commissions for such sales from the insurance company writing the policy. Further, if the three requirements of section 414(c)(4) of the Act are met, a securities broker-dealer who renders investment advice to a plan for a fee, thereby becoming a fiduciary, may furnish other services to the plan, such as brokerage services, and receive compensation therefor. Also, if a registered representative of such a broker-dealer were a fiduciary, the registered representative may receive compensation, including commissions, for brokerage services performed before June 30, 1977.

[Officially corrected by 42 FR 36823.]

(b) *Persons deemed to be June 30, 1974, service providers.* A party in interest with respect to a plan which did not, on June 30, 1974, ordinarily and customarily furnish a particular service, will nevertheless be considered to have ordinarily and customarily furnished such service on June 30, 1974, for purposes of this section and section 414(c)(4) of the Act, if either of the following conditions are met:

(1) At least 50 percent of the outstanding beneficial interests of such party in interest are owned directly or through one or more intermediaries by the same person or persons who owned, directly or through one or more intermediaries, at least 50 percent of the outstanding beneficial interests of a person who ordinarily and customarily furnished such service on June 30, 1974; or

(2) Control or the power to exercise a controlling influence over the management and policies of such party in interest is possessed, directly or through one or more intermediaries, by the same person or persons who possessed, directly or through one or more intermediaries, control or the power to exercise a controlling influence over the management and policies of a person who ordinarily and customarily furnished such service on June 30, 1974.

For purposes of paragraph (b) of this section, a person shall be deemed to be an "intermediary" of another person if at least 50 percent of the outstanding beneficial interest of such person are owned by such other person, directly or indirectly, or if such other person controls or has the power to exercise a controlling influence over the management and policies of such person.

(c) *Examples.* The following examples apply the principles enunciated in paragraph (b) of this section.

Example (1). A owns 50 percent of the outstanding beneficial interests of ABC Partnership which ordinarily and customarily furnished certain services on June 30, 1974. On July 2, 1974, ABC Partnership was incorporated into ABC Corporation with one class of stock outstanding. A owns 50 percent of the shares of such stock. ABC Corporation furnishes the same services that were furnished by ABC Partnership on June 30, 1974. ABC Corporation will be deemed to have ordinarily and customarily furnished such services on June 30, 1974, for purposes of section 414(c)(4) of the Act.

Example (2). A and B together own 100 percent of the beneficial interests of AB Partnership, which ordinarily and customarily furnished certain services on June 30, 1974. On September 1, 1974, AB Partnership was incorporated into AB Corporation with one class of stock outstanding. A and B each own 20 percent of such outstanding class of stock and together have control over the management and policies of AB Corporation. AB Corporation furnishes the same services that were furnished by AB Partnership on June 30, 1974. AB Corporation will be deemed to have ordinarily and customarily furnished such services on June 30, 1974, for purposes of section 414(c)(4) of the Act.

Example (3). On June 30, 1974, M Corporation was ordinarily and customarily furnishing certain services. On that date, X, Y, and Z together owned 50 percent of all classes of the outstanding shares of M Corporation. On January 28, 1975, all of the shareholders of M Corporation exchanged their shares in M Corporation for shares of a new N Corporation. As a result of that exchange, X, Y, and Z together own 50 percent of the common stock of N Corporation, the only class of N Corporation stock outstanding after the exchange. N Corporation furnishes the services formerly furnished by M Corporation. N Corporation will be deemed to have ordinarily and customarily furnished such services on June 30, 1974, for purposes of section 414(c)(4) of the Act.

Example (4). I Corporation ordinarily and customarily furnished certain services on June 30, 1974. On November 3, 1975, I Corporation organizes a wholly-owned subsidiary, S Corporation, which furnishes the same services ordinarily and customarily furnished by I Corporation on June 30, 1974. S Corporation will be deemed to have ordinarily and customarily furnished such services on June 30, 1974, for purposes of section 414(c)(4) of the Act.

Example (5). X Corporation, wholly owned and controlled by A, ordinarily and customarily furnished certain services on June 30, 1974. Y Corporation did not perform such services on that date. On January 2, 1976, X Corporation is merged into Y Corporaton and, although A received less than 50 percent of the total outstanding shares of Y Corporation, after such merger A has control over the management and policies of Y Corporation. Y Corporation furnishes the same services that were formerly furnished by X Corporation. Y Corporation will be deemed to have ordinarily and customarily furnished such services on June 30, 1974, for purposes of section 414(c)(4) of the Act. [Officially corrected by 42 FR 36823.]

Regulations

The following regulations were adopted under "Title 29—Labor; Chapter XXV—Office of Employee Benefits Security; Part 2555—Interpretive Bulletins Relating to Fiduciary Responsibility." The regulations were filed with the Federal Register on July 25, 1975, and published in the Federal Register of July 28, 1975. The regulations were renumbered under a new "Part 2509—Interpretive Bulletins Relating to the Employee Retirement Income Security Act of 1974" by FR Doc. 76-966, 41 FR 1906, filed with the Federal Register on January 12, 1976, and published in the Federal Register of January 13, 1976. Reg Sec. 2509.75-5 was amended on August 24, 2004 by 69 FR 52119.

⟫⟫→ *Caution: Regulation 2509.75-1 was officially removed by 61 FR 33847 on July 1, 1996.*

[¶ 14,875]

§ 2509.75-1 **Interpretive bulletin relating to section 414(c)(4) of the Employee Retirement Income Security Act of 1974.** This regulation, formerly reproduced at this point, was replaced by § 2550.414c-4 at ¶ 14,845 [FR Doc. 77-17895, filed with the Federal Register on June 21, 1977, and published in the Federal Register on June 24, 1977].

[¶ 14,876]

§ 2509.75-2 **Interpretive bulletin relating to prohibited transactions.** On February 6, 1975, the Department of Labor issued an an interpretive bulletin, ERISA IB 75-2, with respect to whether a party in interest has engaged in a prohibited transaction with an employee benefit plan where the party in interest has engaged in a transaction with a corporation or partnership (within the meaning of section 7701 of the Internal Revenue Code of 1954) in which the plan has invested.

On November 13, 1986 the Department published a final regulation dealing with the definition of "plan assets". See § 2510.3-101 of this title. Under that regulation, the assets of certain entities in which plans invest would include "plan assets" for purposes of the fiduciary responsibility provisions of the Act. Section 2510.3-101 applies only for purposes of identifying plan assets on or after the effective date of that section, however, and § 2510.3-101 does not apply to plan investments in certain entities that qualify for the transitional relief provided for in paragraph (k) of that section. The principles discussed in paragraph (a)

of this Interpretive Bulletin continue to be applicable for purposes of identifying assets of a plan for periods prior to the effective date of § 2510.3-101 and for investments that are subject to the transitional rule in § 2510.3-101(k). Paragraphs (b) and (c) of this Interpretive Bulletin, however, relate to matters outside the scope of § 2510.3-101, and nothing in that section affects the continuing application of the principles discussed in those parts.

(a) *Principles applicable to plan investments to which § 2510.3-101 does not apply.* Generally, investment by a plan in securities (within the meaning of section 3(20) of the Employee Retirement Income Security Act of 1974) of a corporation or partnership will not, solely by reason of such investment, be considered to be an investment in the underlying assets of such corporation or partnership so as to make such assets of the entity "plan assets" and thereby make a subsequent transaction between the party in interest and the corporation or partnership a prohibited transaction under section 406 of the Act.

For example, where a plan acquires a security of a corporation or a limited partnership interest in a partnership, a subsequent lease or sale of property between such corporation or partnership and a party in interest will not be a prohibited transaction solely by reason of the plan's investment in the corporation or partnership.

This general proposition, as applied to corporations and partnerships, is consistent with section 401(b)(1) of the Act, relating to plan investments in investment companies registered under the Investment Company Act of 1940. Under section 401(b)(1), an investment by a plan in securities of such an investment company may be made without causing, solely by reason of such investment, any of the assets of the investment company to be considered to be assets of the plan.

»»→ *Caution: Regulation § 2509.75-2 was officially amended by removing and reserving paragraph (b) by 61 FR 33847 on July 1, 1996.*

(b) *Contracts of policies of insurance.* If an insurance company issues a contract or policy of insurance to a plan and places the consideration for such contract or policy in its general asset account, the assets in such account shall not be considered to be plan assets. Therefore, a subsequent transaction involving the general asset account between a party in interest and the insurance company will not, solely because the plan has been issued such a contract or policy of insurance, be a prohibited transaction.

(c) *Applications of the fiduciary responsibility rules.* The preceding paragraphs do not mean that an investment of plan assets in a security of a corporation or partnership may not be a prohibited transaction. For example, section 406(a)(1)(D) prohibits the direct or indirect transfer to, or use by or for the benefit of, a party in interest of any assets of the plan and section 406(b)(1) prohibits a fiduciary from dealing with the assets of the plan in his own interest or for his own account.

Thus, for example, if there is an arrangement under which a plan invests in, or retains its investment in, an investment company and as part of the arrangement it is expected that the investment company will purchase securities from a party in interest, such arrangement is a prohibited transaction.

Similarly, the purchase by a plan of an insurance policy pursuant to an arrangement under which it is expected that the insurance company will make a loan to a party in interest is a prohibited transaction.

Moreover, notwithstanding the foregoing, if a transaction between a party in interest and a plan would be a prohibited transaction, then such a transaction between a party in interest and such corporation or partnership will ordinarily be a prohibited transaction if the plan may, by itself, require the corporation or partnership to engage in such transaction.

Similarly, if a transaction between a party in interest and a plan would be a prohibited transaction, then such a transaction between a party in interest and such corporation or partnership will ordinarily be a prohibited transaction if such party in interest, together with one or more persons who are parties in interest by reason of such persons' relationship (within the meaning of section 3(14)(E) through (I)) to such party in interest may, with the aid of the plan but without the aid of any other persons, require the corporation or partnership to engage in such a transaction. However, the preceding sentence does not apply if the parties in interest engaging in the transaction, together with one or more persons who are parties in interest by reason of such persons' relationship (within the meaning of section 3(14)(E) through (I)) to such party in interest, may, by themselves, require the corporation or partnership to engage in the transaction.

Further, the Department of Labor emphasizes that it would consider a fiduciary who makes or retains an investment in a corporation or partnership for the purpose of avoiding the application of the fiduciary responsibility provisions of the Act to be in contravention of the provisions of section 404(a) of the Act. [Amended by 51 FR 41262 on November 13, 1986, effective Mar. 13, 1987].

[¶ 14,877]

§ 2509.75-3 **Interpretive bulletin relating to investments by employee benefit plans in securities of registered investment companies.** On March 12, 1975, the Department of Labor issued an interpretive bulletin, ERISA IB 75-3, with regard to its interpretation of section 3(21)(B) of the Employee Retirement Income Security Act of 1974. That section provides that an investment by an employee benefit plan in securities issued by an investment company registered under the Investment Company Act of 1940 shall not by itself cause the investment company, its investment adviser or principal underwriter to be deemed to be a fiduciary or party in interest "except insofar as such investment company or its investment adviser or principal underwriter acts in connection with an employee benefit plan covering employees of the investment company, the investment adviser, or its principal underwriter."

The Department of Labor interprets this section as an elaboration of the principle set forth in section 401(b)(1) of the Act and ERISA IB 75-2

(issued February 6, 1975) that the assets of an investment company shall not be deemed to be assets of a plan solely by reason of an investment by such plan in the shares of such investment company. Consistent with this principle, the Department of Labor interprets this section to mean that a person who is connected with an investment company, such as the investment company itself, its investment adviser or its principal underwriter, is not to be deemed to be a fiduciary of or party in interest with respect to a plan solely because the plan has invested in the investment company's shares.

This principle applies, for example, to a plan covering employees of an investment adviser to an investment company where the plan invests in the securities of the investment company. In such a case the investment company or its principal underwriter is not be be deemed to be a fiduciary of or party in interest with respect to the plan solely because of such investment.

On the other hand, the exception clause in section 3(21) emphasizes that if an investment company, its investment adviser or its principal underwriter is a fiduciary or party in interest for a reason other than the investment in the securities of the investment company, such a person remains a party in interest or fiduciary. Thus, in the preceding example, since an employer is a party in interest, the investment adviser remains a party in interest with respect to a plan covering its employees.

The Department of Labor emphasized that an investment adviser, principal underwriter or investment company which is a fiduciary by virtue of section 3(21)(A) of the Act is subject to the fiduciary responsibility provisions of Part 4 of Title I of the Act, including those relating to fiduciary duties under section 404.

[¶ 14,878]

§ 2509.75-4 **Interpretive bulletin relating to indemnification of fiduciaries.** On June 4, 1975, the Department of Labor issued an interpretive bulletin, ERISA IB 75-4, announcing the Department's interpretation of section 410(a) of the Employee Retirement Income Security Act of 1974, insofar as that section relates to indemnification of fiduciaries. Section 410(a) states, in relevant part, that "any provision in an agreement or instrument which purports to relieve a fiduciary from responsibility or liability for any responsibilty, obligation, or duty under this part shall be void as against public policy."

The Department of Labor interprets this section to permit indemnification agreements which do not relieve a fiduciary of responsibility or liability under Part 4 of Title I. Indemnification provisions which leave the fiduciary fully responsible and liable, but merely permit another party to satisfy any liability incurred by the fiduciary in the same manner as insurance purchased under section 410(b)(3), are therefore not void under section 410(a).

Examples of such indemnification provisions are:

(1) Indemnification of a plan fiduciary by (a) an employer, any of whose employees are covered by the plan, or an affiliate (as defined in section 407(d)(7) of the Act) of such employer, or (b) an employee organization, any of whose members are covered by the plan; and

(2) Indemnification by a plan fiduciary of the fiduciary's employees who actually perform the fiduciary services.

The Department of Labor interprets section 410(a) as rendering void any arrangement for indemnification of a fiduciary of an employee benefit plan by the plan. Such an arrangement would have the same result as an exculpatory clause, in that it would, in effect, relieve the fiduciary of responsibility and liability to the plan by abrogating the plan's right to recovery from the fiduciary for breaches of fiduciary obligations.

While indemnification arrangements do not contravene the provisions of section 410(a), parties entering into an indemnification agreement should consider whether the agreement complies with the other provisions of Part 4 of Title I of the Act and with other applicable laws.

[¶ 14,879]

§ 2509.75-5 **Questions and answers relating to fiduciary responsibility.** On June 25, 1975, the Department of Labor issued an interpretive bulletin, ERISA IB 75-5, containing questions and answers relating to certain aspects of the recently enacted Employee Retirement Income Security Act of 1974 (the "Act").

Pending the issuance of regulations or other guidelines, persons may rely on the answers to these questions in order to resolve the issues that are specifically considered. No inferences should be drawn regarding issues not raised which may be suggested by a particular question and answer or as to why certain questions, and not others, are included. Furthermore, in applying the questions and answers, the effect of subsequent legislation, regulations, court decisions, and interpretive bulletins must be considered. To the extent that plans utilize or rely on these answers and the requirements of regulations subsequently adopted vary from the answers relied on, such plans may have to be amended.

An index of the questions and answers, relating them to the appropriate sections of the Act, is also provided.

INDEX KEY TO QUESTION PREFIXES

D—Refers to Definitions.
FR—Refers to Fiduciary Responsibility.

D-1 Q: Is an attorney, accountant, actuary or consultant who renders legal, accounting, actuarial or consulting services to an employee benefit plan (other than an investment adviser to the plan) a fiduciary to the plan solely by virtue of the rendering of such services, absent a showing that such consultant (a) exercises discretionary authority or discretionary control respecting the management of the plan, (b) exercises authority or control respecting management or disposition of the plan's assets, (c) renders investment advice for a fee, direct or indirect, with respect to the assets of the plan, or has any authority or responsibility to do so, or (d) has any discretionary authority or discretionary responsibility in the administration of the plan?

A: No. However, while attorneys, accountants, actuaries and consultants performing their usual professional functions will ordinarily not be considered fiduciaries, if the factual situation in a particular case falls within one of the categories described in clauses (a) through (d) of this question, such persons would be considered to be fiduciaries within the meaning of section 3(21) of the Act. The Internal Revenue Service notes that such persons would also be considered to be fiduciaries within the meaning of section 4975(e)(3) of the Internal Revenue Code of 1954.

FR-1 Q: If an instrument establishing an employee benefit plan provides that the plan committee shall control and manage the operation and administration of the plan and specifies who shall constitute the plan committee (either by position or by naming individuals to the committee), does such provision adequately satisfy the requirement in section 402(a) that a "named fiduciary" be provided for in a plan instrument?

A: Yes. While the better practice would be to state explicitly that the plan committee is the "named fiduciary" for purposes of the Act, clear identification of one or more persons, by name or title, combined with a statement that such person or persons have authority to control and manage the operation and administration of the plan, satisfies the "named fiduciary" requirement of section 402(a). The purpose of this requirement is to enable employees and other interested persons to ascertain who is responsible for operating the plan. The instrument in the above example, which provides that "the plan committee shall control and manage the operation and administration of the plan," and specifies, by name or position, who shall constitute the committee, fulfills this requirement.

FR-2 Q: In a union negotiated employee benefit plan, the instrument establishing the plan provides that a joint board on which employees and employers are equally represented shall control and manage the operation and administration of the plan. Does this provision adequately satisfy the requirement in section 402(a) that a "named fiduciary" be provided for in a plan instrument?

A: Yes, for the reasons stated in response to question FR-1. The joint board is clearly identified as the entity which has authority to control and manage the operation and administration of the plan, and the persons designated to be members of such joint board would be named fiduciaries under section 402(a).

FR-3 Q: May an employee benefit plan covering employees of a corporation designate the corporation as the "named fiduciary" for purposes of section 402(a)(1) of the Act?

A: Yes, it may. Section 402(a)(2) of the Act states that a "named fiduciary" is a fiduciary either named in the plan instrument or designated according to a procedure set forth in the plan instrument. A fiduciary is a "person" falling within the definition of fiduciary set forth in section 3(21)(A) of the Act. A "person" may be a corporation under the definition of person contained in section 3(9) of the Act. While such designation satisfies the requirement of enabling employees and other interested persons to ascertain the person or persons responsible for operating the plan, a plan instrument which designates a corporation as "named fiduciary" should provide for designation by the corporation of specified individuals or other persons to carry out specified fiduciary responsibilities under the plan, in accordance with section 405(c)(1)(B) of the Act.

FR-4 Q: A defined benefit pension plan's procedure for establishing and carrying out a funding policy provides that the plan's trustees shall, at a meeting duly called for the purpose, establish a funding policy and method which satisfies the requirements of Part 3 of Title I of the Act, and shall meet annually at a stated time of the year to review such funding policy and method. It further provides that all actions taken with respect to such funding policy and method and the reasons therefor shall be recorded in the minutes of the trustees' meetings. Does this procedure comply with section 402(b)(1) of the Act?

A: Yes. The above procedure specifies who is to establish the funding policy and method for the plan, and provides for a written record of the actions taken with respect to such funding policy and method, including the reasons for such actions. The purpose of the funding policy requirement set forth in section 402(b)(1) is to enable plan participants and beneficiaries to ascertain that the plan has a funding policy that meets the requirements of Part 3 of Title I of the Act. The procedure set forth above meets that requirement.

FR-5 Q: Must a welfare plan in which the benefits are paid out of the general assets of the employer have a procedure for establishing and carrying out a funding policy set forth in the plan instrument?

A: No. Section 402(b)(1) requires that the plan provide for such a procedure "consistent with the objectives of the plan" and requirements of Title I of the Act. In stituations in which a plan is unfunded and Title I of the Act does not require the plan to be funded, there is no need to provide for such a procedure. If the welfare plan were funded, a procedure consistent with the objectives of the plan would have to be established.

FR-6 Q: May an investment adviser which is neither a bank nor an insurance company, and which is neither registered under the Investment Advisers Act of 1940 nor registered as an investment adviser in the State where it maintains its principal office and place of business, be appointed an investment manager under section 402(c)(3) of the Act?

A: No. The only persons who may be appointed an investment manager under section 402(c)(3) of the Act are persons who meet the requirements of section 3(38) of the Act—namely, banks (as defined in the Investment Advisers Act of 1940), insurance companies qualified under the laws of more than one state to manage, acquire and dispose of plan assets, persons registered as investment advisers under the Investment Advisers Act of 1940, or persons not registered under the Investment Advisers Act by reason of paragraph 1 of section 203A(a) of that Act who are registered as investment advisers in the State where they maintain their principal office and place of business in accordance with ERISA section 3(38) and who have met the filing requirements of 29 CFR 2510.3-38.

FR-7 Q: May an investment adviser that has a registration application pending for federal registration under the Investment Advisers Act of 1940, or pending with the appropriate state regulatory body under State investment adviser registration laws if relying on the provisions of 29 CFR 2510.3-38 to qualify as a state-registered investment manager, function as an investment manager under the Act prior to the effective date of their federal or state registration?

A: No, for the reasons stated in the answer to FR-6 above.

FR-8 Q: Under the temporary bonding regulation set forth in 29 CFR § 2550.412-1, must a person who renders investment advice to a plan for a fee or other compensation, direct or indirect, but who does not exercise or have the right to exercise discretionary authority with respect to the assets of the plan, be bonded solely by reason of the provision of such investment advice?

A: No. A person who renders investment advice, but who does not exercise or have the right to exercise discretionary authority with respect to plan assets, is not required to be bonded solely by reason of the provision of such investment advice. Such a person is not considered to be "handling" funds within the meaning of the temporary bonding regulation set forth in 29 CFR § 2550.412-1, which incorporates by reference 29 CFR § 464.7. For purposes of the temporary bonding regulation, only those fiduciaries who handle funds must be bonded. If, in addition to the rendering of investment advice, such person performs any additional function which constitutes the handling of plan funds under 29 CFR § 464.7, the person would have to be bonded.

FR-9 Q: May an employee benefit plan purchase a bond covering plan officials?

A: Yes. The bonding requirement, which applies, with certain exceptions, to every plan official under section 412(a) of the Act, is for the protection of the plan and does not benefit any plan official or relieve any plan official of any obligation to the plan. The purchase of such bond by a plan will not, therefore, be considered to be in contravention of sections 406(a) or (b) of the Act.

FR-10 Q: An employee benefit plan is considering the construction of a building to house the administration of the plan. One trustee has proposed that the building be constructed on a cost plus basis by a particular contractor without competitive bidding. When the trustee was questioned by another trustee as to the basis of choice of the contractor, the impact of the building on the plan's administrative costs, whether a cost plus contract would yield a better price to the plan than a fixed price basis, and why a negotiated contract would be better than letting the contract for competitive bidding, no satisfactory answers were provided. Several of the trustees have argued that letting such a contract would be a violation of their general fiduciary responsibilities. Despite their arguments, a majority of the trustees appear to be ready to vote to construct the building as proposed. What should the minority trustees do to protect themselves from liability under section 409(a) of the Act and section 405(b)(1)(A) of the Act?

A: Here, where a majority of trustees appear ready to take action which would clearly be contrary to the prudence requirement of section 404(a)(1)(B) of the Act, it is incumbent on the minority trustees to take all reasonable and legal steps to prevent the action. Such steps might include preparations to obtain an injunction from a Federal District court under section 502(a)(3) of the Act, to notify the Labor Department, or to publicize the vote if the decision is to proceed as proposed. If, having taken all reasonable and legal steps to prevent the imprudent action, the minority trustees have not succeeded, they will not incur liability for the action of the majority. Mere resignation, however, without taking steps to prevent the imprudent action, will not suffice to avoid liability for the minority trustees once they have knowledge that the imprudent action is under consideration.

More generally, trustees should take great care to document adequately all meetings where actions are taken with respect to management and control of plan assets. Written minutes of all actions taken should be kept describing the action taken, and stating how each trustee voted on each matter. If, as in the case above, trustees object to a proposed action on the grounds of possible violation of the fiduciary responsibility provisions of the Act, the trustees so objecting should insist that their objections and the responses to such objections be included in the record of the meeting. It should be noted that, where a trustee believes that a cotrustee has already committed a breach, resignation by the trustee as a protest against such breach will not

generally be considered sufficient to discharge the trustee's positive duty under section 405(a)(3) to make reasonable efforts under the circumstances to remedy the breach. [Amended by 69 FR 52119 on August 24, 2004, effective October 25, 2004.]

[¶ 14,880]

§ 2509.75-6 **Interpretive bulletin relating to section 408(c)(2) of the Employee Retirement Income Security Act of 1974.** This regulation, formerly reproduced at this point, was replaced by § 2550.408c-2 at ¶ 14,788 [FR Doc. 77-17895, filed with the Federal Register on June 21, 1977, and published in the Federal Register on June 24, 1977].

»»→ *Caution: Regulation § 2509.75-7 was officially removed by 61 FR 33847 on July 1, 1996.*

[¶ 14,881]

§ 2509.75-7 **Interpretive bulletin supplementing ERISA IB 75-1, relating to section 414(c)(4) of the Employee Retirement Income Security Act of 1974.** This regulation, formerly reproduced at this point, was replaced by § 2550.414c-4 at ¶ 14,845 [FR Doc. 77-17895, filed with the Federal Register on June 21, 1977, and published in the Federal Register on June 24, 1977].

[¶ 14,882]

§ 2509.75-8 **Questions and answers relating to fiduciary responsibility under the Employee Retirement Income Security Act of 1974.** On October 3, 1975, the Department of Labor issued questions and answers relating to certain aspects of fiduciary responsibility under the Act, thereby supplementing ERISA IB 75-5 (29 CFR 2555.75-5) which was issued on June 24, 1975, and published in the FEDERAL REGISTER on July 28, 1975 (40 FR 31598).

Pending the issuance of regulations or other guidelines, persons may rely on the answers to these questions in order to resolve the issues that are specifically considered. No inferences should be drawn regarding issues not raised which may be suggested by a particular question and answer or as to why certain questions, and not others, are included. Furthermore, in applying the questions and answers, the effect of subsequent legislation, regulations, court decisions, and interpretive bulletins must be considered. To the extent that plans utilize or rely on these answers and the requirements of regulations subsequently adopted vary from the answers relied on, such plans may have to be amended.

An index of the questions and answers, relating them to the appropriate sections of the Act, is also provided.

INDEX KEY TO QUESTION PREFIXES

D—Refers to Definitions.
FR—Refers to Fiduciary Responsibility.

Sec. No.:	Question No.
3(21)(A)	D-2, D-3, D-4, D-5.
3(38)	FR-15.
402(c)(1)	FR-12.
402(c)(2)	FR-15.
402(c)(3)	FR-15.
403(a)(2)	FR-15.
404(a)(1)(B)	FR-11, FR-17.
405(a)	FR-13, FR-14, FR-16.
405(c)(1)	FR-12, FR-15.
405(c)(2)	D-4, FR-13, FR-14, FR-16.
412	D-2.

NOTE: Questions D-2, D-3, D-4, and D-5 relate to not only section 3(21)(A) of Title I of the Act, but also section 4975(c)(3) of the Internal Revenue Code (section 2003 of the Act). The Internal Revenue Service has indicated its concurrence with the answers to these questions.

D-2 Q: Are persons who have no power to make any decisions as to plan policy, interpretations, practices or procedures, but who perform the following administrative functions for an employee benefit plan, within a framework of policies, interpretations, rules, practices and procedures made by other persons, fiduciaries with respect to the plan:

(1) Application of rules determining eligibility for participation or benefits;

(2) Calculation of services and compensation credits for benefits;

(3) Preparation of employee communications material;

(4) Maintenance of participants' service and employment records;

(5) Preparation of reports required by government agencies;

(6) Calculation of benefits;

(7) Orientation of new participants and advising participants of their rights and options under the plan;

(8) Collection of contributions and application of contributions as provided in the plan;

(9) Preparation of reports concerning participants' benefits;

(10) Processing of claims; and

(11) Making recommendations to others for decisions with respect to plan administration?

A: No. Only persons who perform one or more of the functions described in section 3(21)(A) of the Act with respect to an employee benefit plan are fiduciaries. Therefore, a person who performs purely ministerial functions such as the types described above for an employee benefit plan within a framework of policies, interpretations, rules, practices and procedures made by other persons is not a fiduciary because such person does not have discretionary authority or discretionary control respecting management of the plan, does not exercise any authority or control respecting management or disposition of the assets of the plan, and does not render investment advice with respect to any money or other property of the plan and has no authority or responsibility to do so.

However, although such a person may not be a plan fiduciary, he may be subject to the bonding requirements contained in section 412 of the Act if he handles funds or other property of the plan within the meaning of applicable regulations.

The Internal Revenue Service notes that such persons would not be considered plan fiduciaries within the meaning of section 4975(e)(3) of the Internal Revenue Code of 1954.

D-3 Q: Does a person automatically become a fiduciary with respect to a plan by reason of holding certain positions in the administration of such plan?

A: Some offices or positions of an employee benefit plan by their very nature require persons who hold them to perform one or more of the functions described in section 3(21)(A) of the Act. For example, a plan administrator or a trustee of a plan must, by the very nature of his position, have "discretionary authority or discretionary responsibility in the administration" of the plan within the meaning of section 3(21)(A)(iii) of the Act. Persons who hold such positions will therefore be fiduciaries.

Other offices and positions should be examined to determine whether they involve the performance of any of the functions described in section 3(21)(A) of the Act. For example, a plan might designate as a "benefit supervisor" a plan employee whose sole function is to calculate the amount of benefits to which each plan participant is entitled in accordance with a mathematical formula contained in the written instrument pursuant to which the plan is maintained. The benefit supervisor, after calculating the benefits, would then inform the plan administrator of the results of his calculations, and the plan administrator would authorize the payment of benefits to a particular plan participant. The benefit supervisor does not perform any of the functions described in section 3(21)(A) of the Act and is not, therefore, a plan fiduciary. However, the plan might designate as a "benefit supervisor" a plan employee who has the final authority to authorize or disallow benefit payments in cases where a dispute exists as to the interpretation of plan provisions relating to eligibility for benefits. Under these circumstances, the benefit supervisor would be a fiduciary within the meaning of section 3(21)(A) of the Act.

The Internal Revenue Service notes that it would reach the same answer to this question under section 4975(e)(3) of the Internal Revenue Code of 1954.

D-4 Q: In the case of a plan established and maintained by an employer, are members of the board of directors of the employer fiduciaries with respect to the plan?

A: Members of the board of directors of an employer which maintains an employee benefit plan will be fiduciaries only to the extent that they have responsibility for the functions described in section 3(21)(A) of the Act. For example, the board of directors may be responsible for the selection and retention of plan fiduciaries. In such a case, members of the board of directors exercise "discretionary authority or discretionary control respecting management of such plan" and are, therefore, fiduciaries with respect to the plan. However, their responsibility, and, consequently, their liability, is limited to the selection and retention of fiduciaries (apart from co-fiduciary liability arising under circumstances described in section 405(a) of the Act). In addition, if the directors are made named fiduciaries of the plan, their liability may be limited pursuant to a procedure provided for in the plan instrument for the allocation of fiduciary responsibilities among named fiduciaries or for the designation of persons other than named fiduciaries to carry out fiduciary responsibilities, as provided in section 405(c)(2).

The Internal Revenue Service notes that it would reach the same answer to this question under section 4975(e)(3) of the Internal Revenue Code of 1954.

D-5 Q: Is an officer or employee of an employer or employee organization which sponsors an employee benefit plan a fiduciary with respect to the plan solely by reason of holding such office or employment if he or she performs none of the functions described in section 3(21)(A) of the Act?

A: No, for the reasons stated in response to question D-2.

The Internal Revenue Service notes that it would reach the same answer to this question under section 4975(e)(3) of the Internal Revenue Code of 1954.

FR-11 Q: In discharging fiduciary responsibilities, may a fiduciary with respect to a plan rely on information, data, statistics or analyses provided by other persons who perform purely ministerial functions for such plan, such as those persons described in D-2 above?

A: A plan fiduciary may rely on information, data, statistics or analyses furnished by persons performing ministerial functions for the plan, provided that he has exercised prudence in the selection and retention of such persons. The plan fiduciary will be deemed to have acted prudently in such selection and retention if, in the exercise of ordinary care in such situation, he has no reason to doubt the competence, integrity or responsibility of such persons.

FR-12 Q: How many fiduciaries must an employee benefit plan have?

A: There is no required number of fiduciaries that a plan must have. Each plan must, of course, have at least one named fiduciary who serves as plan administrator and, if plan assets are held in trust, the plan must have at least one trustee. If these requirements are met, there is no limit on the number of fiduciaries a plan may have. A plan may have as few or as many fiduciaries as are necessary for its operation and administration. Under section 402(c)(1) of the Act, if the plan so provides, any person or group of persons may serve in more than one fiduciary capacity, including serving both as trustee and administrator. Conversely, fiduciary responsibilities not involving management and control of plan assets may, under section 405(c)(1) of the Act, be allocated among named fiduciaries and named fiduciaries may designate persons other than named fiduciaries to carry out such fiduciary responsibilities, if the plan instrument expressly provides procedures for such allocation or designation.

FR-13 Q: If the named fiduciaries of an employee benefit plan allocate their fiduciary responsibilities among themselves in accordance with a procedure set forth in the plan for the allocation of responsibilities for operation and administration of the plan, to what extent will a named fiduciary be relieved of liability for acts and omissions of other named fiduciaries in carrying out fiduciary responsibilities allocated to them?

A: If named fiduciaries of a plan allocate responsibilities in accordance with a procedure for such allocation set forth in the plan, a named fiduciary will not be liable for acts and omissions of other named fiduciaries in carrying out fiduciary responsibilities which have been allocated to them, except as provided in section 405(a) of the Act, relating to the general rules of co-fiduciary responsibility, and section 405(c)(2)(A) of the Act, relating in relevant part to standards for establishment and implementation of allocation procedures.

However, if the instrument under which the plan is maintained does not provide for a procedure for the allocation of fiduciary responsibilities among named fiduciaries, any allocation which the named fiduciaries may make among themselves will be ineffective to relieve a named fiduciary from responsibility or liability for the performance of fiduciary responsibilities allocated to other named fiduciaries.

FR-14 Q: If the named fiduciaries of an employee benefit plan designate a person who is not a named fiduciary to carry out fiduciary responsibilities, to what extent will the named fiduciaries be relieved of liability for the acts and omissions of such person in the performance of his duties?

A: If the instrument under which the plan is maintained provides for a procedure under which a named fiduciary may designate persons who are not named fiduciaries to carry out fiduciary responsibilities, named fiduciaries of the plan will not be liable for acts and omissions of a person who is not a named fiduciary in carrying out the fiduciary responsibilities which such person has been designated to carry out, except as provided in section 405(a) of the Act, relating to the general rules of co-fiduciary liability, and section 405(c)(2)(A) of the Act, relating in relevant part to the designation of persons to carry out fiduciary responsibilities.

However, if the instrument under which the plan is maintained does not provide for a procedure for the designation of persons who are not named fiduciaries to carry out fiduciary responsibilities, then any such designation which the named fiduciaries may make will not relieve the named fiduciaries from responsibility or liability for the acts and omissions of the persons so designated.

FR-15 Q: May a named fiduciary delegate responsibility for management and control of plan assets to anyone other than a person who is an investment manager as defined in section 3(38) of the Act so as to be relieved of liability for the acts and omissions of the person to whom such responsibility is delegated?

A: No. Section 405(c)(1) does not allow named fiduciaries to delegate to others authority or discretion to manage or control plan assets. However, under the terms of sections 403(a)(2) and 402(c)(3) of the Act, such authority and discretion may be delegated to persons who are investment managers as defined in section 3(38) of the Act. Further, under section 402(c)(2) of the Act, if the plan so provides, a named fiduciary may employ other persons to render advice to the named fiduciary to assist the named fiduciary in carrying out his investment responsibilities under the plan.

FR-16 Q: Is a fiduciary who is not a named fiduciary with respect to an employee benefit plan personally liable for all phases of the management and administration of the plan?

A: A fiduciary with respect to the plan who is not a named fiduciary is a fiduciary only to the extent that he or she performs one or more of the functions described in section 3(21)(A) of the Act. The personal liability of a fiduciary who is not a named fiduciary is generally limited to the fiduciary functions, which he or she performs with respect to the plan. With respect to the extent of liability of a named fiduciary of a plan where duties are properly allocated among named fiduciaries or where named fiduciaries properly designate other persons to carry out certain fiduciary duties, see question FR-13 and FR-14.

In addition, any fiduciary may become liable for breaches of fiduciary responsibility committed by another fiduciary of the same plan under circumstances giving rise to cofiduciary liability, as provided in section 405(a) of the Act.

FR-17 Q: What are the ongoing responsibilities of a fiduciary who has appointed trustees or other fiduciaries with respect to these appointments?

A: At reasonable intervals the performance of trustees and other fiduciaries should be reviewed by the appointing fiduciary in such manner as may be reasonably expected to ensure that their performance has been in compliance with the terms of the plan and statutory standards, and satisfies the needs of the plan. No single procedure will be appropriate in all cases; the procedure adopted may vary in accordance with the nature of the plan and other facts and circumstances relevant to the choice of the procedure.

Signed at Washington, D.C. this 3rd day of October 1975.

[§ 2555.75-8 filed with the Federal Register as FR Doc. 75-27156 on October 6, 1975, and published in the Federal Register of October 9, 1975 (40 FR 47491).]

[¶ 14,883]

§ 2509.78-1 **Interpretive Bulletin relating to payments by certain employee welfare benefit plans.** The Department of Labor today announced its interpretation of certain provisions of Part 4 of Title I of the Employee Retirement Income Security Act of 1974 (ERISA), as those sections apply to a payment by multiple employer vacation plans of a sum of money to which a participant or beneficiary of the plan is entitled to a party other than the participant or beneficiary.[1]

Section 402(b)(4) of ERISA requires every employee benefit plan to specify the basis on which payments are made to and from the plan.

Section 403(c)(1) of ERISA generally requires the assets of an employee benefit plan to be held for the exclusive purpose of providing benefits to participants in the plan and their beneficiaries[2] and defraying reasonable expenses of administering the plan. Similarly, section 404(a)(1)(A) requires a plan fiduciary to discharge his duties with respect to a plan solely in the interest of the participants and beneficiaries of the plan and for the exclusive purpose of providing benefits to participants and their beneficiaries and defraying reasonable expenses of administering the plan. Section 404(a)(1)(D) further requires the fiduciary to act in accordance with the documents and instruments governing the plan insofar as such documents and instruments are consistent with the provisions of Title I of ERISA.

In addition, section 406(a) of ERISA specifically prohibits a fiduciary with respect to a plan from causing the plan to engage in a transaction if he knows or should know that such transaction constitutes, *inter alia*, a direct or indirect: furnishing of goods, services or facilities between the plan and a party in interest (section 406(a)(1)(C)); or transfer to, or use by or for the benefit of, a party in interest of any assets of the plan (section 406(a)(1)(D)). Section 406(b)(2) of ERISA prohibits a plan fiduciary from acting in any transaction involving the plan on behalf of a party, or representing a party, whose interests are adverse to the interests of the plan or of its participants or beneficiaries.

In this regard, however, Prohibited Transaction Exemptions 76-1, Part C, (41 FR 12740, March 26, 1976) and 77-10 (42 FR 33918, July 1, 1977) exempt from the prohibitions of section 406(a) and 406(b)(2), respectively, the provision of administrative services by a multiple employer plan if specified conditions are met. These conditions are: (a) the plan receives reasonable compensation for the provision of the services (for purposes of the exemption, "reasonable compensation" need not include a profit which would ordinarily have been received in an arm's length transaction, but must be sufficient to reimburse the plan for its costs); (b) the arrangement allows any multiple employer plan which is a party to the transaction to terminate the relationship on a reasonably short notice under the circumstances; and (c) the plan complies with certain recordkeeping requirements. It should be noted that plans not subject to Prohibited Transaction Exemptions 76-1 and 77-10—i.e., plans that are not multiple employer plans—cannot rely upon these exemptions.

A payment by a vacation plan of all or any portion of benefits to which a plan participant or beneficiary is entitled to a party other than the participant or beneficiary will comply with the above-mentioned sections of ERISA if the arrangement pursuant to which payments are made does not constitute a prohibited transaction under ERISA and:

(1) The plan documents expressly state that benefits payable under the plan to a participant or beneficiary may, at the direction of the participant or beneficiary, be paid to a third party rather than to the participant or beneficiary;

(2) The participant or beneficiary directs in writing that the plan trustee(s) shall pay a named third party all or a specified portion of the sum of money which would otherwise be paid under the plan to him or her; and

(3) A payment is made to a third party only when or after the money would otherwise be payable to the plan participant or beneficiary.

---

[1] Multiple employer vacation plans generally consist of trust funds to which employers are obligated to make contributions pursuant to collective bargaining agreements. Benefits are generally paid at specified intervals (usually annually or semi-annually) and such benefits are neither contingent upon the occurrence of a specified event nor restricted to use for a specified purpose when paid to the participant.

[2] Section 403(c) and (d) provide certain exceptions to this requirement, not here relevant.

In the case of a multiple employer plan (as defined in Prohibited Transaction Exemption 76-1, Part C, Section III), if the arrangement to make payments to a third party is a prohibited transaction under ERISA, the arrangement will comply with the above-mentioned sections of ERISA if the conditions of Prohibited Transaction Exemptions 76-1, Part C, and 77-10 and the above three paragraphs are met. In this regard, it is the view of the Department that the mere payment of money to which a participant or beneficiary is entitled, at the direction of the participant or beneficiary, to a third party who is a party in interest would not constitute a transfer of plan assets prohibited under section 406(a)(1)(D). It is also the view of the Department that if a trustee or other fiduciary of a plan, in addition to his duties with respect to the plan, serves in a decision making capacity with another party, the mere fact that the fiduciary effects payments to such party of money to which a participant is entitled at the direction of the participant and in accordance with specific provisions of governing plan documents and instruments, does not amount to a prohibited transaction under section 406(b)(2).

It should be noted that the interpretation set forth herein deals solely with the application of the provisions of Title I of ERISA to the arrangements described herein. It does not deal with the application of any other statute to such arrangements. Specifically, no opinion is expressed herein as to the application of section 302 of the Labor Management Relations Act, 1947 or the Internal Revenue Code of 1954 (particularly the provisions of section 501(c)(9) of the Code). [Added by FR Doc. 78-34599, filed with the Federal Register on December 14, 1978, and published in the Federal Register of December 15, 1978 (43 FR 58565. The regulation is effective December 15, 1978.]

Part 5—Administration and Enforcement

[¶ 14,910]
CRIMINAL PENALTIES

Act Sec. 501. Any person who willfully violates any provision of part 1 of this subtitle, or any regulation or order issued under any such provision, shall upon conviction be fined not more than $100,000 or imprisoned not more than 10 years, or both; except that in the case of such violation by a person not an individual, the fine imposed upon such person shall be a fine not exceeding $500,000.

Amendments

P.L. 107-204, §904

Act Sec. 904 amended ERISA Sec. 501 by striking "$5,000" and inserting "$100,000," by striking "one year" and inserting "10 years" and by striking "$100,000" and inserting "$500,000."

[¶ 14,920]
CIVIL ENFORCEMENT

Act Sec. 502. (a) A civil action may be brought—

(1) by a participant or beneficiary—

(A) for the relief provided for in subsection (c) of this section, or

(B) to recover benefits due to him under the terms of his plan, to enforce his rights under the terms of the plan, or to clarify his rights to future benefits under the terms of the plan;

(2) by the Secretary, or by a participant, beneficiary or fiduciary for appropriate relief under section 409;

(3) by a participant, beneficiary, or fiduciary (A) to enjoin any act or practice which violates any provision of this title or the terms of the plan, or (B) to obtain other appropriate equitable relief (i) to redress such violations or (ii) to enforce any provisions of this title or the terms of the plan;

(4) by the Secretary, or by a participant, or beneficiary for appropriate relief in the case of a violation of [section] 105(c);

(5) except as otherwise provided in subsection (b), by the Secretary (A) to enjoin any act or practice which violates any provision of this title, or (B) to obtain other appropriate equitable relief (i) to redress such violation or (ii) to enforce any provision of this title;

(6) by the Secretary to collect any civil penalty under paragraph (2), (4), (5), (6), or (7) of subsection (c) or under subsection (i) or (l);

(7) by a State to enforce compliance with a qualified medical child support order (as defined in section 609(a)(2)(A));

(8) by the Secretary, or by an employer or other person referred to in section 101(f)(1), (A) to enjoin any act or practice which violates subsection (f) of section 101, or (B) to obtain appropriate equitable relief (i) to redress such violation or (ii) to enforce such subsection; or

(9) in the event that the purchase of an insurance contract or insurance annuity in connection with termination of an individual's status as a participant covered under a pension plan with respect to all or any portion of the participant's pension benefit under such plan constitutes a violation of part 4 of this title or the terms of the plan, by the Secretary, by any individual who was a participant or beneficiary at the time of the alleged violation, or by a fiduciary, to obtain appropriate relief, including the posting of security if necessary, to assure receipt by the participant or beneficiary of the amounts provided or to be provided by such insurance contract or annuity, plus reasonable prejudgment interest on such amounts.

Act Sec. 502. (b)(1) In the case of a plan which is qualified under section 401(a), 403(a), or 405(a) of the Internal Revenue Code of 1986 (or with respect to which an application to so qualify has been filed and has not been finally determined) the Secretary may exercise his authority under subsection (a)(5) with respect to a violation of or the enforcement of, parts 2 and 3 of this subtitle (relating to participation, vesting, and funding), only if—

(A) requested by the Secretary of the Treasury, or

(B) one or more participants, beneficiaries, or fiduciaries, of such plan request in writing (in such manner as the Secretary shall prescribe by regulation) that he exercise such authority on their behalf. In the case of such a request under this paragraph he may exercise such authority only if he determines that such violation affects, or such enforcement is necessary to protect, claims of participants or beneficiaries to benefits under the plan.

(2) The Secretary shall not initiate an action to enforce section 515.

(3) The Secretary is not authorized to enforce under this part any requirement of part 7 against a health insurance issuer offering health insurance coverage in connection with a group health plan (as defined in section 706(a)(1)). Nothing in this paragraph shall affect the authority of the Secretary to issue regulations to carry out such part.

Act Sec. 502. (c)(1) Any administrator (A) who fails to meet the requirements of paragraph (1) or (4) of section 606, section 101(e)(1), or section 101(f) with respect to a participant or beneficiary, or (B) who fails or refuses to comply with a request for any information which such administrator is required by this title to furnish to a participant or beneficiary (unless such failure or refusal results from matters reasonably beyond the control of the administrator) by mailing the material requested to the last known address of the requesting participant or beneficiary within 30 days after such request may in the court's discretion be personally liable to such participant or beneficiary in the amount of up to $100 a day from the date of such failure or refusal, and the court may in its discretion order such other relief as it deems proper. For purposes of this paragraph, each violation described in subparagraph (A) with respect to any single participant, and each violation described in subparagraph (B) with respect to any single participant or beneficiary, shall be treated as a separate violation.

(2) The Secretary may assess a civil penalty against any plan administrator of up to $1,000 a day from the date of such plan administrator's failure or refusal to file the annual report required to be filed with the Secretary under section 101(b)(4). For purposes of this paragraph, an annual report, that has been rejected under section 104(a)(4) for failure to provide material information shall not be treated as having been filed with the Secretary.

(3) Any employer maintaining a plan who fails to meet the notice requirement of section 101(d) with respect to any participant or beneficiary or who fails to meet the requirements of section 101(e)(2) with respect to any person may in the court's discretion be liable to such participant or beneficiary or to such person in the amount of up to $100 a day from the date of such failure, and the court may in its discretion order such other relief as it deems proper.

(4) The Secretary may assess a civil penalty of not more than $1,000 a day for each violation by any person of section 302(b)(7)(F)(vi).

(5) The Secretary may asses a civil penalty against any person of up to $1,000 a day from the date of the persons' failure or refusal to file the information required to be filed by such person with the Secretary under regulations prescribed pursuant to section 101(g).

(6) If, within 30 days of a request by the Secretary to a plan administrator for documents under section 104(a)(6), the plan administrator fails to furnish the material requested to the Secretary, the Secretary may assess a civil penalty against the plan administrator of up to $100 a day from the date of such failure (but in no event in excess of $1,000 per request). No penalty shall be imposed under this paragraph for any failure resulting from matters reasonably beyond the control of the plan administrator.

(7) The Secretary may assess a civil penalty against a plan administrator of up to $100 a day from the date of the plan administrator's failure or refusal to provide notice to participants and beneficiaries in accordance with section 101(i). For purposes of this paragraph, each violation with respect to any single participant or beneficiary shall be treated as a separate violation.

(8) The Secretary and the Secretary of Health and Human Services shall maintain such ongoing consultation as may be necessary and appropriate to coordinate enforcement under this subsection with enforcement under section 1144(c)(8) of the Social Security Act.

Act Sec. 502. (d)(1) An employee benefit plan may sue or be sued under this title as an entity. Service of summons, subpoena, or other legal process of a court upon a trustee or an administrator of an employee benefit plan in his capacity as such shall constitute service upon the employee benefit plan. In a case where a plan has not designated in the summary plan description of the plan an individual as agent for the service of legal process, service upon the Secretary shall constitute such service. The Secretary, not later than 15 days after receipt of service under the preceding sentence, shall notify the administrator or any trustee of the plan of receipt of such service.

(2) Any money judgment under this title against an employee benefit plan shall be enforceable only against the plan as an entity and shall not be enforceable against any other person unless liability against such person is established in his individual capacity under this title.

Act Sec. 502. (e)(1) Except for actions under subsection (a)(1)(B) of this section, the district courts of the United States shall have exclusive jurisdiction of civil actions under this title brought by the Secretary or by a participant, beneficiary, fiduciary, or any person referred to in section 101(f)(1). State courts of competent jurisdiction and district courts of the United States shall have concurrent jurisdiction of actions under paragraphs (1)(B) and (7) of subsection (a) of this section.

(2) Where an action under this title is brought in a district court of the United States, it may be brought in the district where the plan is administered, where the breach took place, or where a defendant resides or may be found, and process may be served in any other district where a defendant resides or may be found.

Act Sec. 502. (f) The district courts of the United States shall have jurisdiction, without respect to the amount in controversy or the citizenship of the parties, to grant the relief provided for in subsection (a) of this section in any action.

Act Sec. 502. (g)(1) In any action under this title (other than an action described in paragraph (2)) by a participant, beneficiary, or fiduciary, the court in its discretion may allow a reasonable attorney's fee and costs of action to either party.

(2) In any action under this title by a fiduciary for or on behalf of a plan to enforce section 515 in which a judgment in favor of the plan is awarded, the court shall award the plan—

(A) the unpaid contributions,

(B) interest on the unpaid contributions,

(C) an amount equal to the greater of—

(i) interest on the unpaid contributions, or

(ii) liquidated damages provided for under the plan in an amount not in excess of 20 percent (or such higher percentage as may be permitted under Federal or State law) of the amount determined by the court under subparagraph (A),

(D) reasonable attorney's fees and costs of the action, to be paid by the defendant, and

(E) such other legal or equitable relief as the court deems appropriate.

For purposes of this paragraph, interest on unpaid contributions shall be determined by using the rate provided under the plan, or, if none, the rate prescribed under section 6621 of the Internal Revenue Code of 1986.

Act Sec. 502. (h) A copy of the complaint in any action under this title by a participant, beneficiary, or fiduciary (other than an action brought by one or more participants or beneficiaries under subsection (a)(1)(B) which is solely for the purpose of recovering benefits due such participants under the terms of the plan) shall be served upon the Secretary and the Secretary of the Treasury by certified mail. Either Secretary shall have the right in his discretion to intervene in any action, except that the Secretary of the Treasury may not intervene in any action under part 4 of this subtitle. If the Secretary brings an action under subsection (a) on behalf of a participant or beneficiary, he shall notify the Secretary of the Treasury.

Act Sec. 502. (i) In the case of a transaction prohibited by section 406 by a party in interest with respect to a plan to which this part applies, the Secretary may assess a civil penalty against such party in interest. The amount of such penalty may not exceed 5 percent of the amount involved in each such transaction (as defined in section 4975(f)(4) of the Internal Revenue Code of 1986) for each year or part thereof during which the prohibited transaction continues, except that, if the transaction is not corrected (in such manner as the Secretary shall prescribe in regulations which shall be consistent with section 4975(f)(5) of such Code) within 90 days after notice from the Secretary (or such longer period as the Secretary may permit), such penalty may be in an amount not more than 100 percent of the amount involved. This subsection shall not apply to a transaction with respect to a plan described in section 4975(e)(1) of such Code.

Act Sec. 502. (j) In all civil actions under this title, attorneys appointed by the Secretary may represent the Secretary (except as provided in section 518(a) of title 28, United States Code), but all such litigation shall be subject to the direction and control of the Attorney General.

(k) Suits by an administrator, fiduciary, participant, or beneficiary of an employee benefit plan to review a final order of the Secretary, to restrain the Secretary from taking any action contrary to the provisions of this Act, or to compel him to take action required under this title, may be brought in the district court of the United States for the district where the plan has its principal office, or in the United States District Court for the District of Columbia.

Act Sec. 502. (l)(1) In the case of—

(A) any breach of fiduciary responsibility under (or other violation of) part 4 by a fiduciary, or

(B) any knowing participation in such a breach or violation by any other person,

the Secretary shall assess a civil penalty against such fiduciary or other person in an amount equal to 20 percent of the applicable recovery amount.

(2) For purposes of paragraph (1), the term "applicable recovery amount" means any amount which is recovered from a fiduciary or other person with respect to a breach or violation described in paragraph (1)—

(A) pursuant to any settlement agreement with the Secretary, or

(B) ordered by a court to be paid by such fiduciary or other person to a plan or its participants and beneficiaries in a judicial proceeding instituted by the Secretary under subsection (a)(2) or (a)(5).

(3) The Secretary may, in the Secretary's sole discretion, waive or reduce the penalty under paragraph (1) if the Secretary determines in writing that—

(A) the fiduciary or other person acted reasonably and in good faith, or

(B) it is reasonable to expect that the fiduciary or other person will not be able to restore all losses to the plan (or to provide the relief ordered pursuant to subsection (a)(9)) without severe financial hardship unless such waiver or reduction is granted.

(4) The penalty imposed on a fiduciary or other person under this subsection with respect to any transaction shall be reduced by the amount of any penalty or tax imposed on such fiduciary or other person with respect to such transaction under subsection (i) of this section and section 4975 of the Internal Revenue Code of 1986.

Act Sec. 502. (m) In the case of a distribution to a pension plan participant or beneficiary in violation of section 206(e) by a plan fiduciary, the Secretary shall assess a penalty against such fiduciary in an amount equal to the value of the distribution. Such penalty shall not exceed $10,000 for each such distribution.

Amendments

P.L. 108-218, §104(a):

Act Sec. 103(a)(2) amended ERISA Sec. 502(c)(4) to read as above.

P.L. 108-218, §103(b):

Act Sec. 103(b) amended ERISA Sec. 502(c)(1) by striking "or section 101(e)(1)" and inserting ", section 101(e)(1), or section 101(f)" The amendment shall apply to plan years beginning after December 31, 2004.

Act Sec. 103 provides:

(c) Regulations and Model Notice.—The Secretary of Labor shall, not later than 1 year after the date of the enactment of this Act, issue regulations (including a model notice) necessary to implement the amendments made by this section.

P.L. 107-204, §306(b)(3)(A):

Act Sec. 306(b)(3)(A) amended ERISA Sec. 502(a)(6) by striking "(5), or (6)" and inserting "(5), (6), or (7)." See P.L. 107-204, §306(c) below for effective date.

P.L. 107-204, §306(b)(3)(B) and (C):

Act Sec. 306(b)(3)(B) amended ERISA Sec. 502(c) by redesignating paragraph (7) as paragraph (8) and inserting new paragraph (7) to read as above. See P.L. 107-204, §306(c) for effective date.

P.L. 107-204, §306(c):

(c) Effective Date—The provisions of this section (including the amendments made thereby) shall take effect 180 days after the date of the enactment of this Act. Good faith compliance with the requirements of such provisions in advance of the issuance of applicable regulations thereunder shall be treated as compliance with such provisions.

P.L. 105-34, §1503(c)(2)(B):

Act Sec. 1503(c)(2)(B) amended ERISA Sec. 502(c) by redesignating paragraph (6) as paragraph (7) and by inserting after paragraph (5) a new paragraph (6) to read as above.

The above amendments are effective August 5, 1997.

P.L. 105-34, §1503(d)(7):

Act Sec. 1503(d)(7) amended ERISA Sec. 502(a)(6) by striking "or (5)" and inserting "(5), or (6)"

The above amendment is effective August 5, 1997.

P.L. 104-191, §101(b):

Act Sec. 101(b) amended ERISA Sec. 502(b) by adding at the end a new paragraph (3) to read as above.

P.L. 104-191, §101(e)(2)(A):

Act Sec. 101(e)(2)(A) amended ERISA Sec. 502(a)(6) by striking "under subsection (c)(2) or (i) or (l)" and inserting "under paragraph (2), (4), or (5) of subsection (c) or under subsection (i) or (l)"; and ERISA Sec. 502(c), the last two sentences, by striking "For purposes of this paragraph" and all that follows through "The Secretary and" and inserting:

"(5) The Secretary may assess a civil penalty against any person of up to $1,000 a day from the date of the person's failure or refusal to file the information required to be filed by such person with the Secretary under regulations prescribed pursuant to section 101(g).

(6) The Secretary and"

P.L. 104-191, §101(e)(2)(B):

Act Sec. 101(e)(2)(B) amended ERISA Sec. 502(c)(1) by adding at the end a new sentence to read as above.

The above amendments generally apply with respect to group health plans for plan years beginning after June 30, 1997. For special rules, see Act Sec. 101(g)(2)-(5), reproduced below.

Act Sec. 101(g)(2)-(5) reads as follows:

(g) Effective Dates.—

(1) In general.—Except as provided in this section, this section (and the amendments made by this section) shall apply with respect to group health plans for plan years beginning after June 30, 1997.

(2) Determination of creditable coverage.—

(A) Period of coverage.—

(i) In general.—Subject to clause (ii), no period before July 1, 1996, shall be taken into account under part 7 of subtitle B of title I of the Employee Retirement Income Security Act of 1974 (as added by this section) in determining creditable coverage.

(ii) Special rule for certain periods.—The Secretary of Labor, consistent with section 104, shall provide for a process whereby individuals who need to establish creditable coverage for periods before July 1, 1996, and who would have such coverage credited but for clause (i) may be given credit for creditable coverage for such periods through the presentation of documents or other means.

(B) Certifications, etc.—

(i) In general.—Subject to clauses (ii) and (iii), subsection (e) of section 701 of the Employee Retirement Income Security Act of 1974 (as added by this section) shall apply to events occurring after June 30, 1996.

(ii) No certification required to be provided before June 1, 1997.—In no case is a certification required to be provided under such subsection before June 1, 1997.

(iii) Certification only on written request for events occurring before October 1, 1996.—In the case of an event occurring after June 30, 1996, and before October 1, 1996, a certification is not required to be provided under such subsection unless an individual (with respect to whom the certification is otherwise required to be made) requests such certification in writing.

(C) Transitional rule.—In the case of an individual who seeks to establish creditable coverage for any period for which certification is not required because it relates to an event occurring before June 30, 1996—

(i) the individual may present other credible evidence of such coverage in order to establish the period of creditable coverage; and

(ii) a group health plan and a health insurance issuer shall not be subject to any penalty or enforcement action with respect to the plan's or issuer's crediting (or not crediting) such coverage if the plan or issuer has sought to comply in good faith with the applicable requirements under the amendments made by this section.

(3) Special rule for collective bargaining agreements.—Except as provided in paragraph (2), in the case of a group health plan maintained pursuant to one or more collective bargaining agreements between employee representatives and one or more employers ratified before the date of the enactment of this Act, part 7 of subtitle B of title I of Employee Retirement Income Security Act of 1974 (other than section 701(e) thereof) shall not apply to plan years beginning before the later of—

(A) the date on which the last of the collective bargaining agreements relating to the plan terminates (determined without regard to any extension thereof agreed to after the date of the enactment of this Act), or

(B) July 1, 1997.

For purposes of subparagraph (A), any plan amendment made pursuant to a collective bargaining agreement relating to the plan which amends the plan solely to conform to any requirement of such part shall not be treated as a termination of such collective bargaining agreement.

(4) Timely regulations.—The Secretary of Labor, consistent with section 104, shall first issue by not later than April 1, 1997, such regulations as may be necessary to carry out the amendments made by this section.

(5) Limitation on actions.—No enforcement action shall be taken, pursuant to the amendments made by this section, against a group health plan or health insurance issuer with respect to a violation of a requirement imposed by such amendments before January 1, 1998, or, if later, the date of issuance of regulations referred to in paragraph (4), if the plan or issuer has sought to comply in good faith with such requirements.

P.L. 103-465, §761(a)(9)(B)(ii):

Act Sec. 761(a)(9)(B)(ii) amended ERISA Sec. 502 by adding subsection (m) to read as above.

The above amendment applies to plan years beginning after December 31, 1994.

P.L. 103-401:

Amended ERISA Sec. 502(a) by adding subparagraph (9). In addition, in ERISA Sec. 502(l)(3)(B), the words "(or to provide the relief ordered pursuant to subsection (a)(9))" were added after "to restore all losses to the plan".

Under Sec. 5 of P.L. 103-401, the above amendments apply to any legal proceeding pending, or brought, on or after May 31, 1993.

Sec. 4 of P.L. 103-401, entitled, "Effect on Other Provisions," provides, "Nothing in this Act shall be construed to limit the legal standing of individuals to bring a civil action as participants or beneficiaries under section 502(a) of the Employee Retirement Income Security Act of 1974 (29 U.S.C. §1132(a)), and nothing in this Act shall affect the responsibilities, obligations, or duties imposed upon fiduciaries by title I of the Employee Retirement Income Security Act of 1974."

P.L. 103-66, §4301(c)(1):

Amended ERISA Sec. 502(a) by striking "or" at the end of paragraph (5), by striking the period and inserting a semicolon in paragraph (6), and by adding new paragraphs (7) and (8) to read as above.

The above amendments are effective on August 10, 1993. Any plan amendment required to be made by Act Sec. 4301 need not be made before the first plan year beginning on or after January 1, 1994 if: (1) the plan is operated in accordance with Act Sec. 4301 during the period after August 9, 1993 and before such first plan year; and (2) the amendment applies retroactively to this period. A plan will not be treated as failing to be operated in accordance with plan provisions merely because it operates in accordance with the effective date requirements.

P.L. 103-66, §4301(c)(2):

Amended ERISA Sec. 502(c) by adding at the end new paragraph (4) to read as above.

The above amendments are effective on August 10, 1993. Any plan amendment required to be made by Act Sec. 4301 need not be made before the first plan year beginning on or after January 1, 1994 if: (1) the plan is operated in accordance with Act Sec. 4301 during the period after August 9, 1993 and before such first plan year; and (2) the amendment applies retroactively to this period. A plan will not be treated as failing to be operated in accordance with plan provisions merely because it operates in accordance with the effective date requirements.

P.L. 103-66, §4301(c)(3):

Amended ERISA Sec. 502(e)(1) by striking "or fiduciary" in the first sentence and inserting "fiduciary, or any person referred to in section 101(f)(1)"; and by striking "subsection (a)(1)(B)" in the second sentence and inserting "paragraphs (1)(B) and (7) of subsection (a)."

The above amendments are effective on August 10, 1993. Any plan amendment required to be made by Act. Sec. 4301 need not be made before the first plan year beginning on or after January 1, 1994 if: (1) the plan is operated in accordance with Act Sec. 4301 during the period after August 9, 1993 and before such first plan year; and (2) the amendment applies retroactively to this period. A plan will not be treated as failing to be operated in accordance with plan provisions merely because it operates in accordance with the effective date requirements.

P.L. 101-508, Sec. 12012(d)(2)(A):

Amended ERISA Sec. 502(c)(1) by inserting "or section 101(e)(1)" after "section 606" effective for qualified transfers under Code Sec. 420 made after November 5, 1990.

P.L. 101-508, Sec. 12012(d)(2)(B):

Amended ERISA Sec. 502(c)(3) by inserting "or who fails to meet the requirements of section 101(e)(2) with respect to any person" after "beneficiary" the first place it appears and by inserting "or to such person" after "beneficiary" the second place it appears effective for qualified transfers under Code Sec. 420 made after November 5, 1990.

P.L. 101-239, § 2101(a):

Amended ERISA Sec. 502 by adding new subsection (l) to read as above, effective for any breach of fiduciary responsibility or other violation occurring on or after December 19, 1989.

P.L. 101-239, § 2101(b):

Amended ERISA Sec. 502(a)(6) by inserting "or (l)" after "subsection (i)" effective for any breach of fiduciary responsibility or other violation occurring on or after December 19, 1989.

P.L. 101-239, § 7881(b)(5)(B):

Amended ERISA Sec. 502(c) by adding a new paragraph (3) to read as above, effective for reports required to be filed after December 31, 1987.

P.L. 101-239, § 7881(j)(2):

Amended ERISA Sec. 502(a)(6) by striking "subsection (i)" and inserting "subsection (c)(2) or (i)" effective December 22, 1987.

P.L. 101-239, § 7881(j)(3):

Amended ERISA Sec. 502(c)(2) by inserting "against any plan administrator" after "civil penalty" and by striking "a plan administrator's" and inserting "such plan administrator's" effective for reports to be filed after December 31, 1987.

P.L. 101-239, § 7894(f)(1):

Amended ERISA Sec. 502(b)(1) by striking "respct" and inserting "respect" effective September 2, 1974.

P.L. 101-239, § 7891(a)(1):

Titles I, III, and IV of ERISA (other than sections 3(37)(E), 301(a)(7), and 308, the last sentence of section 408(d), and sections 414(c), 4001(a)(3)(ii), and 4303) are each amended by striking "Internal Revenue Code of 1954" each place it appears and inserting "Internal Revenue Code of 1986" effective October 22, 1986.

P.L. 100-203, § 9342(c)(1):

Amended ERISA Sec. 502 by inserting (1) after (c) and by striking "(1) who" and "(2) who" and inserting "(A) who" and "(B) who", respectively, to read as above, effective for reports required to be filed after December 31, 1987.

P.L. 100-203, § 9342(c)(2):

Amended ERISA Sec. 502(c) by adding paragraph (2) to read as above, effective for reports required to be filed after December 31, 1987.

P.L. 100-203, § 9344:

Amended ERISA Sec. 502(i) by striking the second sentence and inserting a new sentence, to read as above, effective December 22, 1987. Prior to amendment, subsection (i) read as follows:

(i) In the case of a transaction prohibited by section 406 by a party in interest with respect to a plan to which this part applies, the Secretary may assess a civil penalty against such party in interest. The amount of such penalty may not exceed 5 percent of the amount involved (as defined in section 4975(f)(4) of the Internal Revenue Code of 1954); except that if the transaction is not corrected (in such manner as the Secretary shall prescribe by regulation, which regulations shall be consistent with section 4975(f)(5) of such Code) within 90 days after notice from the Secretary (or such longer period as the Secretary may permit), such penalty may be in an amount not more than 100 percent of the amount involved. This subsection shall not apply to a transaction with respect to a plan described in section 4975(e)(1) of such Code.

P.L. 99-272:

Act Sec. 10002(b) amended ERISA Sec. 502(c) by inserting after "any administrator (1) who fails to meet the requirements of paragraph (1) or (4) of section 606 with respect to a participant or beneficiary, or (2)," effective for plan years beginning on or after July 1, 1986, subject to the rules at ¶ 15,045.

P.L. 96-364, § 306(b):

Act Sec. 306(b) renumbered subsections 502(b)(1)(A) and (B) and added new subsection 502(b)(2); renumbered section 502(g)(1) and inserted "(other than an action described in paragraph (2))" between "title" and "by" therein; and added new subsection 502(g)(2) effective September 26, 1980.

Regulations

The following regulations were adopted under "Title 29—Labor", "Chapter XXV—Pension and Welfare Benefit Programs, Department of Labor", "Subchapter G—Administration and Enforcement Under the Employee Retirement Income Security Act of 1974", "Part 2560—Rules and Regulations for Administration and Enforcement". The regulations were published in the *Federal Register* on October 27, 1978 (43 F.R. 50174), and filed October 20, 1978. The regulations are effective retroactively from January 1, 1975. ERISA Reg. Sec. 2560.502c-2 was amended effective March 8, 2002 and published in the *Federal Register* on January 7, 2002 (67 FR 771) and revised by the PWBA on January 24, 2003 (68 FR 3729).

Subchapter G—Administration and Enforcement Under the Employee Retirement Income Security Act of 1974

Part 2560—Rules and Regulations for Administration and Enforcement

[¶ 14,925]

§ 2560.502-1 **Requests for enforcement pursuant to section 502(b)(2).** (a) *Form, content, and filing.* All requests by participants, beneficiaries, and fiduciaries for the Secretary of Labor to exercise his enforcement authority pursuant to section 502(a)(5), 29 U.S.C. 1132(a)(5), with respect to a violation of, or the enforcement of, Parts 2 and 3 of Title I of the Employee Retirement Income Security Act of 1974 (Act) shall be in writing and shall contain information sufficient to

form a basis for identifying the participant, beneficiary or fiduciary and the plan involved. All such requests shall be considered filed if they are directed to and received by any office or official of the Department of Labor or referred to and received by any such office or official by any party to whom such writing is directed.

(b) *Consideration.* The Secretary of Labor retains discretion to determine whether any enforcement proceeding should be commenced in the case of any request received pursuant to paragraph (a) of this section, and he may, but shall not be required to, exercise his authority pursuant to section 502(a)(5) of the Act only if he determines that such violation affects, or such enforcement is necessary to protect, claims of participants or beneficiaries to benefits under the plan.

Regulations

The following regulation was published in the *Federal Register* on June 23, 1989 (54 FR 26890). The regulation is effective with respect to annual reports required to be filed for plan years beginning on or after January 1, 1988. Regulation § 2560.502c-5 was added by 65 FR 7181 on February 11, 2000. Regulations § 2560.502c-2, § 2560.502c-5, § 2560.502c-6, and § 2560.502c-7 were revised by PWBA in 67 FR 64774 on October 21, 2002 and in 68 FR 3729 on January 24, 2003. Regulation § 2560.502c-5 was amended and revised by 68 FR 17503 on April 9, 2003.

[¶ 14,925A]

§ 2560.502c-2 **Civil penalties under section 502(c)(2).**

(a) *In general.* (1) Pursuant to the authority granted the Secretary under section 502(c)(2) of the Employee Retirement Income Security Act of 1974, as amended (the Act), the administrator (within the meaning of section 3(16)(A)) of an employee benefit plan (within the meaning of section 3(3) and § 2510.3-1, *et seq.*) for which an annual report is required to be filed under section 101(b)(1) shall be liable for civil penalties assessed by the Secretary under section 502(c)(2) of the

Act in each case in which there is a failure or refusal to file the annual report required to be filed under section 101(b)(1).

(2) For purposes of this section, a failure or refusal to file the annual report required to be filed under section 101(b)(1) shall mean a failure or refusal to file, in whole or in part, that information described in section 103 and § 2520.103-1, et seq., on behalf of the plan at the time and in the manner prescribed therefor. [Revised by 67 FR 771, effective March 8, 2002.]

(b) *Amount assessed.* (1) The amount assessed under section 502(c)(2) shall be determined by the Department of Labor, taking into consideration the degree and/or willfulness of the failure or refusal to file the annual report. However, the amount assessed under section 502(c)(2) of the Act shall not exceed $1,000 a day (or such other maximum amount as may be established by regulation pursuant to the Federal Civil Penalties Inflation Adjustment Act of 1990, as amended), computed from the date of the administrator's failure or refusal to file the annual report and, except as provided in paragraph (b)(2) of this section, continuing up to the date on which an annual report satisfactory to the Secretary is filed. (Revised by PWBA in 68 FR 3729 on 1-24-03).

(2) If upon receipt of a notice of intent to assess a penalty (as described in paragraph (c) of this section) the administrator files a statement of reasonable cause for the failure to file, in accordance with paragraph (e) of this section, a penalty shall not be assessed for any day from the date the Department serves the administrator with a copy of such notice until the day after the Department serves notice on the administrator of its determination on reasonable cause and its intention to assess a penalty (as described in paragraph (g) of this section).

(3) For purposes of this paragraph, the date on which the administrator failed or refused to file the annual report shall be the date on which the annual report was due (determined without regard to any extension for filing). An annual report which is rejected under section 104(a)(4) for a failure to provide material information shall be treated as a failure to file an annual report when a revised report satisfactory to the Department is not filed within 45 days of the date of the Department's notice of rejection.

A penalty shall not be assessed under section 502(c)(2) for any day earlier than the day after the date of an administrator's failure or refusal to file the annual report if a revised filing satisfactory to the Department is not submitted within 45 days of the date of the notice of rejection by the Department.

(c) *Notice of intent to assess a penalty.* Prior to the assessment of any penalty under section 502(c)(2), the Department shall provide to the administrator of the plan a written notice indicating the Department's intent to assess a penalty under section 502(c)(2), the amount of such penalty, the period to which the penalty applies, and the reason(s) for the penalty.

(d) *Reconsideration or waiver of penalty to be assessed.* The Department may determine that all or part of the penalty amount in the notice of intent to assess a penalty shall not be assessed on a showing that the administrator complied with the requirements of section 101(b)(1) of the Act or on a showing by the administrator of mitigating circumstances regarding the degree or willfulness of the noncompliance. [Revised by PWBA in 67 FR 64774 on 10-21-02 and in 68 FR 3729 on 1-24-03.]

(e) *Showing of reasonable cause.* Upon issuance by the Department of a notice of intent to assess a penalty, the administrator shall have thirty (30) days from the date of service of the notice, as described in paragraph (i) of this section, to file a statement of reasonable cause explaining why the penalty, as calculated, should be reduced, or not be assessed, for the reasons set forth in paragraph (d) of this section. Such statement must be made in writing and set forth all the facts alleged as reasonable cause for the reduction or nonassessment of the penalty. The statement must contain a declaration by the administrator that the statement is made under the penalties of perjury. [Revised by PWBA in 67 FR 64774 on 10-21-02 and in 68 FR 3729 on 1-24-03.]

(f) *Failure to file a statement of reasonable cause.* Failure of an administrator to file a statement of reasonable cause within the thirty (30) day period described in paragraph (e) of this section shall be deemed to constitute a waiver of the right to appear and contest the facts alleged in the notice of intent, and such failure shall be deemed an admission of the facts alleged in the notice for purposes of any proceeding involving the assessment of a civil penalty under section 502(c)(2) of the Act. Such notice shall then become a final order of the Secretary, within the meaning of section 2570.61(g) of this chapter, forty-five (45) days from the date of service of the notice. [Revised by PWBA in 67 FR 64774 on 10-21-02 and in 68 FR 3729 on 1-24-03.]

(g) *Notice of the determination on statement of reasonable cause.* (1) The Department, following a review of all the facts alleged in support of no assessment or a complete or partial waiver of the penalty,

shall notify the administrator, in writing, of its determination to waive the penalty, in whole or in part, and/or assess a penalty. If it is the determination of the Department to assess a penalty, the notice shall indicate the amount of the penalty, not to exceed the amount described in paragraph (c) of this section. This notice is a "pleading" for purposes of Sec. 2570.61(m) of this chapter. [Revised by PWBA in 67 FR 64774 on 10-21-02 and in 58 FR 3729 on 1-24-03.]

(2) Except as provided in paragraph (h) of this section, a notice issued pursuant to paragraph (g)(1) of this section, indicating the Department's intention to assess a penalty shall become a final order, within the meaning of Sec. 2570.61(g), forty-five (45) days from the date of service of the notice. [Revised by PWBA in 67 FR 64774 on 10-21-02 and in 68 FR 3729 on 1-24-03.]

(h) *Administrative hearing.* A notice issued pursuant to paragraph (g) of this section will not become a final order, within the meaning of Sec. 2570.61(g) of this chapter, if, within 30 days from the date of the service of the notice, the administrator or a representative thereof files a request for a hearing under Sec. Sec. 2570.60 through 2570.71 of this chapter, and files an answer to the notice. The request for hearing and answer must be filed in accordance with Sec. 2570.62 of this chapter and Sec. 18.4 of this title. The answer opposing the proposed sanction shall be in writing, and supported by reference to specific circumstances or facts surrounding the notice of determination issued pursuant to paragraph (g) of this section. [Revised by PWBA in 67 FR 64774 on 10-21-02 and in 68 FR 3729 on 1-24-03.]

(i) *Service of notices and filing of statements.* (1) Service of a notice for purposes of paragraphs (c) and (g) of this section shall be made:[Revised by PWBA in 67 FR 64774 on 10-21-02 and in 68 FR 3729 on 1-24-03.]

(i) By delivering a copy to the administrator or representative thereof;

(ii) By leaving a copy at the principal office, place of business, or residence of the administrator or representative thereof; or

(iii) By mailing a copy to the last known address of the administrator or representative thereof.

(2) If service is accomplished by certified mail, service is complete upon mailing. If service is by regular mail, service is complete upon receipt by the addressee. When service of a notice under paragraph (c) or (g) of this section is by certified mail, five (5) days shall be added to the time allowed by these rules for the filing of a statement, or a request for hearing and answer, as applicable. [Revised by PWBA in 67 FR 64774 on 10-21-02 and in 68 FR 3729 on 1-24-03.]

(3) For purposes of this section, a statement of reasonable cause shall be considered filed: [Added by PWBA in 67 FR 64774 on 10-21-02 and revised in 68 FR 3729 on 1-24-03.]

(i) Upon mailing, if accomplished using United States Postal Service certified mail or Express Mail; [Added by PWBA in 67 FR 64774 on 10-21-02 and revised in 68 FR 3729 on 1-24-03.]

(ii) Upon receipt by the delivery service, if accomplished using a "designated private delivery service" within the meaning of 26 U.S.C. 7502(f); [Added by PWBA in 67 FR 64774 on 10-21-02 and revised in 68 FR 3729 on 1-24-03.]

(iii) Upon transmittal, if transmitted in a manner specified in the notice of intent to assess a penalty as a method of transmittal to be accorded such special treatment; or [Added by PWBA in 67 FR 64774 on 10-21-02 and revised in 68 FR 3729 on 1-24-03.]

(iv) In the case of any other method of filing, upon receipt by the Department at the address provided in the notice of intent to assess a penalty. [Added by PWBA in 67 FR 64774 on 10-21-02 and revised in 68 FR 3729 on 1-24-03.]

(j) *Liability.* (1) If more than one person is responsible as administrator for the failure to file the annual report, all such persons shall be jointly and severally liable with respect to such failure.

(2) Any person against whom a civil penalty has been assessed under section 502(c)(2) pursuant to a final order, within the meaning of § 2570.61(g), shall be personally liable for the payment of such penalty.

(k) *Cross-reference.* See §§ 2570.60 through 71 of this chapter for procedural rules relating to administrative hearings under section 502(c)(2) of the Act.

[¶ 14,925D]

§ 2560.502c-5 Civil penalties under section 502(c)(5).

(a) *In general.* (1) Pursuant to the authority granted the Secretary under section 502(c)(5) of the Employee Retirement Income Security Act of 1974, as amended (the Act), the administrator of a multiple employer welfare arrangement (MEWA) (within the meaning of section 3(40)(A) of the Act) that is not a group health plan, and that provides benefits consisting of medical care (within the meaning of section 733(a)(2)), for which a report is required to be filed under section 101(g) of the Act and 29 CFR 2520.101-2, shall be liable for civil penalties assessed by the Secretary under section 502(c)(5) of the Act for each failure or refusal to file a completed report required to be filed under section 101(g) and 29 CFR 2520.101-2. The term "administrator" is defined in 29 CFR 2520.101-2(b).

(2) For purposes of this section, a failure or refusal to file the report required to be filed under section 101(g) shall mean a failure or refusal to file, in whole or in part, that information described in section 101(g) and 29 CFR 2520.101-2, on behalf of the MEWA, at the time and in the manner prescribed therefor.

(b) *Amount assessed.* (1) The amount assessed under section 502(c)(5) shall be determined by the Department of Labor, taking into consideration the degree and/or willfulness of the failure to file the report. However, the amount assessed under section 502(c)(5) of the Act shall not exceed $1,000 a day, computed from the date of the administrator's failure or refusal to file the report and, except as provided in paragraph (b)(2) of this section, continuing up to the date on which a report meeting the requirements of section 101(g) and 29 CFR 2520.101-2, as determined by the Secretary, is filed.

(2) If, upon receipt of a notice of intent to assess a penalty (as described in paragraph (c) of this section), the administrator files a statement of reasonable cause for the failure to file, in accordance with paragraph (e) of this section, a penalty shall not be assessed for any day from the date the Department serves the administrator with a copy of such notice until the day after the Department serves notice on the administrator of its determination on reasonable cause and its intention to assess a penalty (as described in paragraph (g) of this section).

(3) For purposes of this paragraph, the date on which the administrator failed or refused to file the report shall be the date on which the report was due (determined without regard to any extension of time for filing). A report which is rejected under 29 CFR 2520.101-2 shall be treated as a failure to file a report when a revised report meeting the requirements of this section is not filed within 45 days of the date of the Department's notice of rejection. If a revised report meeting the requirements of this section, as determined by the Secretary, is not submitted within 45 days of the date of the notice of rejection by the Department, a penalty shall be assessed under section 502(c)(5) beginning on the day after the date of the administrator's failure or refusal to file the report.

(c) *Notice of intent to assess a penalty.* Prior to the assessment of any penalty under section 502(c)(5), the Department shall provide to the administrator of the MEWA a written notice indicating the Department's intent to assess a penalty under section 502(c)(5), the amount of such penalty, the period to which the penalty applies, and a statement of the facts and the reason(s) for the penalty.

(d) *Reconsideration or waiver of penalty to be assessed.* The Department may determine that all or part of the penalty amount in the notice of intent to assess a penalty shall not be assessed on a showing that the administrator complied with the requirements of section 101(g) of the Act or on a showing by the administrator of mitigating circumstances regarding the degree or willfulness of the noncompliance.

(e) *Showing of reasonable cause.* Upon issuance by the Department of a notice of intent to assess a penalty, the administrator shall have thirty (30) days from the date of service of the notice, as described in paragraph (i) of this section, to file a statement of reasonable cause explaining why the penalty, as calculated, should be reduced, or not be assessed, for the reasons set forth in paragraph (d) of this section. Such statement must be made in writing and set forth all the facts alleged as reasonable cause for the reduction or nonassessment of the penalty. The statement must contain a declaration by the administrator that the statement is made under the penalties of perjury.

(f) *Failure to file a statement of reasonable cause.* Failure of an administrator to file a statement of reasonable cause within the thirty (30) day period described in paragraph (e) of this section shall be deemed to constitute a waiver of the right to appear and contest the facts alleged in the notice of intent, and such failure shall be deemed an admission of the facts alleged in the notice for purposes of any proceeding involving the assessment of a civil penalty under section 502(c)(5) of the Act. Such notice shall then become a final order of the Secretary, within the meaning of 29 CFR 2570.91(g), forty-five (45) days from the date of service of the notice.

(g) *Notice of the determination on statement of reasonable cause.* (1) The Department, following a review of all the facts alleged in support of no assessment or a complete or partial waiver of the penalty, shall notify the administrator, in writing, of its determination to waive the penalty, in whole or in part, and/or assess a penalty. If it is the determination of the Department to assess a penalty, the notice shall indicate the amount of the penalty, not to exceed the amount described in paragraph (c) of this section, and a brief statement of the reasons for assessing the penalty. This notice is a "pleading" for purposes of 29 CFR 2570.91(m).

(2) Except as provided in paragraph (h) of this section, a notice issued pursuant to paragraph (g)(1) of this section, indicating the Department's intention to assess a penalty, shall become a final order, within the meaning of 29 CFR 2570.91(g), forty-five (45) days from the date of service of the notice.

(h) *Administrative hearing.* A notice issued pursuant to paragraph (g) of this section will not become a final order, within the meaning of 29 CFR 2570.91(g), if, within thirty (30) days from the date of the service of the notice, the administrator or a representative thereof files a request for a hearing under 29 CFR 2570.90 through 2570.101, and files an answer to the notice. The request for hearing and answer must be filed in accordance with 29 CFR 2570.92 and 18.4. The answer opposing the proposed sanction shall be in writing, and supported by reference to specific circumstances or facts surrounding the notice of determination issued pursuant to paragraph (g) of this section.

(i) *Service of notices and filing of statements.* (1) Service of a notice for purposes of paragraphs (c) and (g) of this section shall be made:

(i) By delivering a copy to the administrator or representative thereof;

(ii) By leaving a copy at the principal office, place of business, or residence of the administrator or representative thereof; or

(iii) By mailing a copy to the last known address of the administrator or representative thereof.

(2) If service is accomplished by certified mail, service is complete upon mailing. If service is by regular mail, service is complete upon receipt by the addressee. When service of a notice under paragraph (c) or (g) of this section is by certified mail, five (5) days shall be added to the time allowed by these rules for the filing of a statement, or a request for hearing and answer, as applicable.

(3) For purposes of this section, a statement of reasonable cause shall be considered filed:

(i) Upon mailing, if accomplished using United States Postal Service certified mail or Express Mail;

(ii) Upon receipt by the delivery service, if accomplished using a "designated private delivery service" within the meaning of 26 U.S.C. 7502(f);

(iii) Upon transmittal, if transmitted in a manner specified in the notice of intent to assess a penalty as a method of transmittal to be accorded such special treatment; or

(iv) In the case of any other method of filing, upon receipt by the Department at the address provided in the notice of intent to assess a penalty.

(j) *Liability.* (1) If more than one person is responsible as administrator for the failure to file the report, all such persons shall be jointly and severally liable with respect to such failure.

(2) Any person against whom a civil penalty has been assessed under section 502(c)(5) pursuant to a final order, within the meaning of 29 CFR 2570.91(g), shall be personally liable for the payment of such penalty.

(k) *Cross-reference*. See 29 CFR 2570.90 through 2570.101 for procedural rules relating to administrative hearings under section 502(c)(5) of the Act.

[¶ 14,925E]
§ 2560.502c-6 Civil penalties under section 502(c)(6).

(a) *In general*. (1) Pursuant to the authority granted the Secretary under section 502(c)(6) of the Employee Retirement Income Security Act of 1974, as amended (the Act), the administrator (within the meaning of section 3(16)(A) of the Act) of an employee benefit plan (within the meaning of section 3(3) of the Act and § 2510.3-1 of this chapter) shall be liable for civil penalties assessed by the Secretary under section 502(c)(6) of the Act in each case in which there is a failure or refusal to furnish to the Secretary documents requested under section 104(a)(6) of the Act and § 2520.104a-8 of this chapter.

(2) For purposes of this section, a failure or refusal to furnish documents shall mean a failure or refusal to furnish, in whole or in part, the documents requested under section 104(a)(6) of the Act and § 2520.104a-8 of this chapter at the time and in the manner prescribed in the request.

(b) *Amount assessed*. (1) The amount assessed under section 502(c)(6) of the Act shall be determined by the Department of Labor, taking into consideration the degree and/or willfulness of the failure or refusal to furnish any document or documents requested by the Department under section 104(a)(6) of the Act. However, the amount assessed under section 502(c)(6) of the Act shall not exceed $100 a day or $1,000 per request (or such other maximum amounts as may be established by regulation pursuant to the Federal Civil Penalties Inflation Adjustment Act of 1990, as amended), computed from the date of the administrator's failure or refusal to furnish any document or documents requested by the Department. [Revised by PWBA in 68 FR 3729 on 1-24-03].

(2) For purposes of calculating the amount to be assessed under this section, the date of a failure or refusal to furnish documents shall not be earlier than the thirtieth day after service of the request under section 104(a)(6) of ERISA and § 2520.104a-8 of this chapter.

(c) *Notice of intent to assess a penalty*. Prior to the assessment of any penalty under section 502(c)(6) of the Act, the Department shall provide to the administrator of the plan a written notice that indicates the Department's intent to assess a penalty under section 502(c)(6) of the Act, the amount of the penalty, the period to which the penalty applies, and the reason(s) for the penalty.

(d) *Reconsideration of waiver of penalty to be assessed*. The Department may determine that all or part of the penalty amount in the notice of intent to assess a penalty shall not be assessed on a showing that the administrator complied with the requirements of section 104(a)(6) of the Act or on a showing by the administrator of mitigating circumstances regarding the degree or willfulness of the noncompliance. [Revised by PWBA in 67 FR 64774 on 10-21-02 and in 68 FR 3729 on 1-24-03.]

(e) *Showing of reasonable cause*. Upon issuance by the Department of a notice of intent to assess a penalty, the administrator shall have thirty (30) days from the date of service of the notice, as described in paragraph (i) of this section, to file a statement of reasonable cause explaining why the penalty, as calculated, should be reduced, or not be assessed, for the reasons set forth in paragraph (d) of this section. Such statement must be in writing and set forth all the facts alleged as reasonable cause for the reduction or nonassessment of the penalty. The statement must contain a declaration by the administrator that the statement is made under the penalties of perjury. [Revised by PWBA in 67 FR 64774 on 10-21-02 and in 68 FR 3729 on 1-24-03.]

(f) *Failure to file a statement of reasonable cause*. Failure to file a statement of reasonable cause within the 30-day period described in paragraph (e) of this section shall be deemed to constitute a waiver of the right to appear and contest the facts alleged in the notice of intent, and such failure shall be deemed an admission of the facts alleged in the notice for purposes of any proceeding involving the assessment of a civil penalty under section 502(c)(6) of the Act. Such notice shall then become a final order of the Secretary, within the meaning of § 2570.111(g) of this chapter, forty-five (45) days from the date of service of the notice. [Revised by PWBA in 67 FR 64774 on 10-21-02 and in 68 FR 3729 on 1-24-03.]

(g) *Notice of determination on statement of reasonable cause*. (1) The Department, following a review of all of the facts alleged in support of no assessment or a complete or partial waiver of the penalty, shall notify the administrator, in writing, of its determination not to assess or to waive the penalty, in whole or in part, and/or assess a penalty. If it is the determination of the Department to assess a penalty, the notice shall indicate the amount of the penalty, not to exceed the amount described in paragraph (c) of this section. This notice is a "pleading" for purposes of Sec. 2570.111(m) of this chapter. [Revised by PWBA in 67 FR 64774 on 10-21-02 and in 68 FR 3729 on 1-24-03.]

(2) Except as provided in paragraph (h) of this section, a notice issued pursuant to paragraph (g)(1) of this section, indicating the Department's intention to assess a penalty, shall become a final order, within the meaning of Sec. 2570.111(g) of this chapter, forty-five (45) days from the date of service of the notice. [Revised by PWBA in 67 FR 64774 on 10-21-02 and in 68 FR 3729 on 1-24-03.]

(h) *Administrative hearing*. A notice issued pursuant to paragraph (g) of this section will not become a final order, within the meaning of Sec. 2570.91(g) of this chapter, if, within thirty (30) days from the date of the service of the notice, the administrator or a representative thereof files a request for a hearing under Sec. Sec. 2570.110 through 2570.121 of this chapter, and files an answer to the notice. The request for hearing and answer must be filed in accordance with Sec. 2570.112 of this chapter and Sec. 18.4 of this title. The answer opposing the proposed sanction shall be in writing, and supported by reference to specific circumstances or facts surrounding the notice of determination issued pursuant to paragraph (g) of this section. [Revised by PWBA in 67 FR 64774 on 10-21-02 and in 68 FR 3729 on 1-24-03.]

(i) *Service of notices and filing of statements*. (1) Service of a notice for purposes of paragraphs (c) and (g) of this section shall be made:

(i) By delivering a copy to the administrator or representative thereof; [Revised by PWBA in 67 FR 64774 on 10-21-02 and in 68 FR 3729 on 1-24-03.]

(ii) By leaving a copy at the principal office, place of business, or residence of the administrator or representative thereof; or

(iii) By mailing a copy to the last known address of the administrator or representative thereof.

(2) If service is accomplished by certified mail, service is complete upon mailing. If service is by regular mail, service is complete upon receipt by the addressee. When service of a notice under paragraph (c) or (g) of this section is by certified mail, five (5) days shall be added to the time allowed by these rules for the filing of a statement, or a request for hearing and answer, as applicable. [Revised by PWBA in 67 FR 64774 on 10-21-02 and 68 FR 3729 on 1-24-03.]

(3) For purposes of this section, a statement of reasonable cause shall be considered filed: [Added by PWBA in 67 FR 64774 on 10-21-02.]

(i) Upon mailing, if accomplished using United States Postal Service certified mail or Express Mail; [Added by PWBA in 67 FR 64774 on 10-21-02.]

(ii) Upon receipt by delivery service, if accomplished using a "designated private delivery service" within the meaning of 26 U.S.C. 7502(f); [Added by PWBA in 67 FR 64774 on 10-21-02.]

(iii) Upon transmittal, if transmitted in a manner specified in the notice of intent to assess a penalty as a method of transmittal to be accorded such special treatment; or [Added by PWBA in 67 FR 64774 on 10-21-02.]

(iv) In the case of any other method of filing, upon receipt by the Department at the address provided in the notice of intent to assess a penalty. [Added by PWBA in 67 FR 64774 on 10-21-02.]

(j) *Liability*. (1) If more than one person is responsible as administrator for the failure to furnish the document or documents requested under section 104(a)(6) of the Act and its implementing regulations (§ 2520.104a-8 of this chapter), all such persons shall be jointly and severally liable with respect to such failure.

(2) Any person, or persons under paragraph (j)(1) of this section, against whom a civil penalty has been assessed under section 502(c)(6) of the Act pursuant to a final order, within the meaning of §2570.111(g) of this chapter, shall be personally liable for the payment of such penalty.

(k) *Cross-reference.* See §§2570.110 through 2570.121 of this chapter for procedural rules relating to administrative hearings under section 502(c)(6) of the Act.

Regulations

The following regulations regarding inflationary adjustments to ERISA civil monetary penalties were published in the *Federal Register* on October 21, 2002 (67 FR 64774) and revised by the PWBA on January 24, 2003 (68 FR 3729).

[¶ 14,925F]
§2560.502c-7 Civil penalties under section 502(c)(7).

(a) *In general.* Pursuant to the authority granted the Secretary under section 502(c)(7) of the Employee Retirement Income Security Act of 1974, as amended (the Act), the administrator (within the meaning of section 3(16)(A) of the Act) of an individual account plan (within the meaning of section 101(i)(8) of the Act and Sec. 2520.101-3(d)(2) of this chapter), shall be liable for civil penalties assessed by the Secretary under section 502(c)(7) of the Act for failure or refusal to provide notice of a blackout period to affected participants and beneficiaries in accordance with section 101(i) of the Act and Sec. 2520.101-3 of this chapter.

(2) For purposes of this section, a failure or refusal to provide a notice of blackout period shall mean a failure or refusal, in whole or in part, to provide notice of a blackout period to an affected plan participant or beneficiary at the time and in the manner prescribed by section 101(i) of the Act and Sec. 2520.101-3 of this chapter. [Revised by PWBA in 68 FR 3729 on 1-24-03.]

(b) *Amount assessed.* (1) The amount assessed under section 502(c)(7) of the Act for each separate violation shall be determined by the Department of Labor, taking into consideration the degree and/or willfulness of the failure or refusal to provide a notice of blackout period. However, the amount assessed for each violation under section 502(c)(7) of the Act shall not exceed $100 a day (or such other maximum amount as may be established by regulation pursuant to the Federal Civil Penalties Inflation Adjustment Act of 1990, as amended), computed from the date of the administrator's failure or refusal to provide a notice of blackout period up to an including the date that is the final day of the blackout period for which the notice was required. [Revised by PWBA in 68 FR 3729 on 1-24-03.]

(2) For purposes of calculating the amount to be assessed under this section, a failure or refusal to provide a notice of blackout period with respect to any single participant or beneficiary shall be treated as a separate violation under section 101(i) of the Act and Sec. 2520.101-3 of this chapter.

(c) *Notice of intent to assess a penalty.* Prior to the assessment of any penalty under section 502(c)(7) of the Act, the Department shall provide to the administrator of the plan a written notice indicating the Department's intent to assess a penalty under section 502(c)(7) of the Act, the amount of such penalty, the number of participants and beneficiaries on which the penalty is based, the period to which the penalty applies, and the reason(s) for the penalty. [Revised by PWBA in 68 FR 3729 on 1-24-03.]

(d) *Reconsideration or waiver of penalty to be assessed.* The Department may determine that all or part of the penalty amount in the notice of intent to assess a penalty shall not be assessed on a showing that the administrator complied with the requirements of section 101(i) of the Act or on a showing by the administrator of mitigating circumstances regarding the degree or wilfulness of the noncompliance. [Revised by PWBA in 68 FR 3729 on 1-24-03.]

(e) *Showing of reasonable cause.* Upon issuance by the Department of a notice of intent to assess a penalty, the administrator shall have thirty (30) days from the date of service of the notice, as described in paragraph (i) of this section, to file a statement of reasonable cause explaining why the penalty, as calculated, should be reduced, or not be assessed, for the reasons set forth in paragraph (d) of this section. Such statement must be in writing and set forth all the facts alleged as reasonable cause for the reduction or nonassessment of the penalty. The statement must contain a declaration by the administrator that the statement is made under the penalties of perjury. [Revised by PWBA in 68 FR 3729 on 1-24-03.]

(f) *Failure to file a statement of reasonable cause.* Failure to file a statement of reasonable cause within the 30 day period described in paragraph (e) of this section shall be deemed to constitute a waiver of the right to appear and contest the facts alleged in the notice of intent, and such failure shall be deemed an admission of the facts alleged in the notice for purposes of any proceeding involving the assessment of a civil penalty under section 502(c)(7) of the Act. Such notice shall then become a final order of the Secretary, within the meaning of §2570.131(g) of this chapter, forty-five (45) days from the date of service of the notice. [Revised by PWBA in 68 FR 3729 on 1-24-03.]

(g) *Notice of determination on statement of reasonable cause.* (1) The Department, following a review of all of the facts in a statement of reasonable cause alleged in support of no assessment or a complete or partial waiver of the penalty, shall notify the administrator, in writing, of its determination on the statement of reasonable cause and its determination whether to waive the penalty, in whole or in part, and/or assess a penalty. If it is the determination of the Department to assess a penalty, the notice shall indicate the amount of the penalty assessment, not to exceed the amount described in paragraph (c) of this section. This notice is a "pleading" for purposes of Sec. 2570.131(m) of this chapter.

(2) Except as provided in paragraph (h) of this section, a notice issued pursuant to paragraph (g)(1) of this section, indicating the Department's determination to assess a penalty, shall become a final order, within the meaning of Sec. 2570.131(g) of this chapter, forty-five (45) days from the date of service of the notice. [Revised by PWBA in 68 FR 3729 on 1-24-03.]

(h) *Administrative hearing.* A notice issued pursuant to paragraph (g) of this section will not become a final order, within the meaning of Sec. 2570.131(g) of this chapter, if, within thirty (30) days from the date of the service of the notice, the administrator or a representative thereof files a request for a hearing under Sec. Sec. 2570.130 through 2570.141 of this chapter, and files an answer to the notice. The request for hearing and answer must be filed in accordance with Sec. 2570.132 of this chapter and Sec. 18.4 of this title. The answer opposing the proposed sanction shall be in writing, and supported by reference to specific circumstances or facts surrounding the notice of determination issued pursuant to paragraph (g) of this section. [Revised by PWBA in 68 FR 3729 on 1-24-03.]

(i) *Service of notices and filing of statements.* (1) Service of a notice for purposes of paragraphs (c) and (g) of this section shall be made:

(i) By delivering a copy to the administrator or representative thereof;

(ii) By leaving a copy at the principal office, place of business, or residence of the administrator or representative thereof; or

(iii) By mailing a copy to the last known address of the administrator or representative thereof.

(2) If service is accomplished by certified mail, service is complete upon mailing. If service is by regular mail, service is complete upon receipt by the addressee. When service of a notice under paragraph (c) or (g) of this section is by certified mail, five (5) days shall be added to the time allowed by these rules for the filing of a statement, or a request for hearing and answer, as applicable.

(3) For purposes of this section, a statement of reasonable cause shall be considered filed:

(i) Upon mailing, if accomplished using United States Postal Service certified mail or Express Mail;

(ii) Upon receipt by delivery service, if accomplished using a "designated private delivery service" within the meaning of 26 U.S.C. 7502(f);

(iii) Upon transmittal, if transmitted in a manner specified in the notice of intent to assess a penalty as a method of transmittal to be accorded such special treatment; or

(iv) In the case of any other method of filing, upon receipt by the Department at the address provided in the notice of intent to assess a penalty. [Revised by PWBA in 68 FR 3729 on 1-24-03.]

(j) *Liability.* (1) If more than one person is responsible as administrator for the failure to provide a notice of blackout period under section 101(i) of the Act and its implementing regulations (Sec. 2520.101-3 of this chapter), all such persons shall be jointly and severally liable for such failure.

(2) Any person, or persons under paragraph (j)(1) of this section, against whom a civil penalty has been assessed under section 502(c)(7) of the Act pursuant to a final order, within the meaning of §2570.131(g) of this chapter, shall be personally liable for the payment of such penalty. [Revised by PWBA in 68 FR 3729 on 1-24-03.]

(k) *Cross-reference.* See Sec. Sec. 2570.130 through 2570.141 of this chapter for procedural rules relating to administrative hearings under section 502(c)(7) of the Act. [Revised by PWBA in 68 FR 3729 on 1-24-03.]

Regulations

The following regulation was adopted under "Title 29—Labor, Chapter XXV—Pension and Welfare Benefit Administration, Department of Labor, Subchapter G—Administration and Enforcement under the Employee Retirement Income Security Act of 1974, Part 2560—Rules and Regulations for Administration and Enforcement." The regulation was filed with the Federal Register on September 23, 1988 and published in the Federal Register of September 26, 1988 (53 FR 37474). The regulation is effective October 26, 1988.

[¶ 14,926]
§ 2560.502i-1 Civil Penalties Under Section 502(i).

(a) *In general.* Section 502(i) of the Employee Retirement Income Security Act of 1974 (ERISA or the Act) permits the Secretary of Labor to assess a civil penalty against a party in interest who engages in a prohibited transaction with respect to an employee benefit plan other than a plan described in section 4975(e)(1) of the Internal Revenue Code (the Code). The initial penalty under section 502(i) is five percent of the total "amount involved" in the prohibited transaction (unless a lesser amount is otherwise agreed to by the parties). However, if the prohibited transaction is not corrected during the "correction period," the civil penalty shall be 100 percent of the "amount involved" (unless a lesser amount is otherwise agreed to by the parties). Paragraph (b) of this section defines the term "amount involved," paragraph (c) defines the term "correction," and paragraph (d) defines the term "correction period." Paragraph (e) illustrates the computation of the civil penalty under section 502(i). Paragraph (f) is a cross reference to the Department's procedural rules for section 502(i) proceedings.

(b) *Amount involved.* Section 502(i) of ERISA states that the term "amount involved" in that section shall be defined as it is defined under section 4975(f)(4) of the Code. As provided in 26 CFR 141.4975.13, 26 CFR 53.4941(e)-1(b) is controlling with respect to the interpretation of the term "amount involved" under section 4975 of the Code. Accordingly, the Department of Labor will apply the principles set out at 26 CFR 53.4941(e)-1(b) in determining the "amount involved" in a transaction subject to the civil penalty provided by section 502(i) of the Act and this section.

(c) *Correction.* Section 502(i) of ERISA states that the term "correction" shall be defined in a manner that is consistent with the definition of that term under section 4975(f)(5) of the Code. As provided in 26 CFR 141.4975-13, 26 CFR 53.4941(e)-1(c) is controlling with respect to the interpretation of the term "correction" for purposes of section 4975 of the Code. Accordingly, the Department of Labor will apply the principles set out in 26 CFR 53.4941(e)-(1)(c) in interpreting the term "correction" under section 502(i) of the Act and this section.

(d) *Correction Period.* (1) In general, the "correction period" begins on the date the prohibited transaction occurs and ends 90 days after a final agency order with respect to such transaction.

(2) When a party in interest seeks judicial review within 90 days of a final agency order in an ERISA section 502(i) proceeding, the correction period will end 90 days after the entry of a final order in the judicial action.

(3) The following examples illustrate the operation of this paragraph:

(i) A party in interest receives notice of the Department's intent to impose the section 502(i) penalty and does not invoke the ERISA section 502(i) prohibited transaction penalty proceedings described in §2570.1 of this chapter within 30 days of such notice. As provided in §2570.5 of this chapter, the notice of the intent to impose a penalty becomes a final order after 30 days. Thus, the "correction period" ends 90 days after the expiration of the 30-day period.

(ii) A party in interest contests a proposed section 502(i) penalty, but does not appeal an adverse decision of the administrative law judge in the proceeding. As provided in §2570.10(a) of this chapter, the decision of the administrative law judge becomes a final order of the Department unless the decision is appealed within 20 days after the date of such order. Thus, the correction period ends 90 days after the expiration of such 20-day period.

(iii) The Secretary of Labor issues to a party in interest a decision upholding an administrative law judge's adverse decision. As provided in §2570.12(b) of this chapter, the decision of the Secretary becomes a final order of the Department immediately. Thus, the correction period will end 90 days after the issuance of the Secretary's order unless the party in interest judicially contests the order within that 90-day period. If the party in interest so contests the order, the correction period will end 90 days after the entry of a final order in the judicial action.

(e) *Computation of the Section 502(i) penalty.* (1) In general, the civil penalty under section 502(i) is determined by applying the applicable percentage (five percent or one hundred percent) to the aggregate amount involved in the transaction. However, a continuing prohibited transaction, such as a lease or a loan, is treated as giving rise to a separate event subject to the sanction for each year (as measured from the anniversary date of the transaction) in which the transaction occurs.

(2) The following examples illustrate the computation of the section 502(i) penalty:

(i) An employee benefit plan purchases property from a party in interest at a price of $10,000. The fair market value of the property is $5,000. The "amount involved" in that transaction, as determined under 26 CFR 53.4941(e)-1(b), is $10,000 (the greater of the amount paid by the plan or the fair market value of the property). The initial five percent penalty under section 502(i) is $500 (five percent of $10,000).

(ii) An employee benefit plan executes a four-year lease with a party in interest at an annual rental of $10,000 (which is the fair rental value of the property). The amount involved in each year of that transaction, as determined under 26 CFR 53.4941(e)-1(b), is $10,000. The amount of the initial sanction under ERISA section 502(i) would be a total of $5,000: $2,000 ($10,000 × 5% × 4 with respect to the rentals paid in the first year of the lease); $1,500 ($10,000 × 5% × 3 with respect to the second year); $1,000 ($10,000 × 5% × 2 with respect to the third year); $500 ($10,000 × 5% × 1 with respect to the fourth year).

(f) *Cross Reference.* See §§2570.1-2570.12 of this chapter for procedural rules relating to section 502(i) penalty proceedings.

Regulations

The following regulations were adopted under "Title 29—Labor," "Chapter XXV—Pension and Welfare Benefits Administration, Department of Labor," "Subchapter G—Administration and Enforcement Under the Employee Retirement Income Security Act of 1974," "Part 2570—Procedural

Regulations Under the Employee Retirement Income Security Act." The regulations were filed with the *Federal Register* on September 23, 1988 and published in the *Federal Register* of September 26, 1988 (53 FR 37474). The regulations are effective October 26, 1988. Subpart C (Reg. §§2570.60-2570.71) was published in the *Federal Register* on June 26, 1989 (54 FR 26895). It is effective on July 26, 1989. Regulations §2570.61 and §2570.64 were revised by PWBA in 67 FR 64774 on October 21, 2002 and in 68 FR 3729 on January 24, 2003. Regulation §2570.3 was amended on April 9, 2003 (68 FR 17506).

Subpart A—Procedures for the Assessment of Civil Sanctions Under ERISA Section 502(i)

[¶ 14,928]

§2570.1 **Scope of rules**.

The rules of practice set forth in this part are applicable to "prohibited transaction penalty proceedings" (as defined in §2570.2(o) of this part) under section 502(i) of the Employee Retirement Income Security Act of 1974. The rules of procedure for administrative hearings published by the department's Office of Administrative Law Judges at Part 18 of this Title will apply to matters arising under ERISA section 502(i) except as modified by this section. These proceedings shall be conducted as expeditiously as possible, and the parties shall make every effort to avoid delay at each stage of the proceedings.

[¶ 14,928A]

§2570.2 **Definitions**.

For prohibited transaction penalty proceedings, this section shall apply in lieu of the definitions in §18.2 of this title:

(a) "Adjudicatory proceeding" means a judicial-type proceeding leading to the formulation of a final order;

(b) "Administrative law judge" means an administrative law judge appointed pursuant to the provisions of 5 U.S.C. 3105;

(c) "Answer" is defined for these proceedings as set forth in §18.5(d)(2) of this title;

(d) "Commencement of proceeding" is the filing of an answer by the respondent;

(e) "Consent agreement" means any written document containing a specified proposed remedy or other relief acceptable to the Department and consenting parties;

(f) "ERISA" means the Employee Retirement Income Security Act of 1974, as amended;

(g) "Final order" means the final decision or action of the Department of Labor concerning the assessment of a civil sanction under ERISA section 502(i) against a particular party. Such final order may result from a decision of an administrative law judge or the Secretary, or the failure of a party to invoke the procedures for hearings or appeals under this title. Such a final order shall constitute final agency action within the meaning of 5 U.S.C. 704;

(h) "Hearing" means that part of a proceeding which involves the submission of evidence, either by oral presentation or written submission, to the administrative law judge;

(i) "Notice" means any document, however designated, issued by the Department of Labor which initiates an adjudicatory proceeding under ERISA section 502(i);

(j) "Order" means the whole or any part of a final procedural or substantive disposition of a matter under ERISA section 502(i);

(k) "Party" includes a person or agency named or admitted as a party to a proceeding;

(l) "Person" includes an individual, partnership, corporation, employee benefit plan, association, exchange or other entity or organization;

(m) "Petition" means a written request, made by a person or party, for some affirmative action;

(n) "Pleading" means the notice, the answer to the notice, any supplement or amendment thereto, and any reply that may be permitted to any answer, supplement or amendment;

(o) "Prohibited transaction penalty proceeding" means a proceeding relating to the assessment of the civil penalty provided for in section 502(i) of ERISA;

(p) "Respondent" means the party against whom the Department is seeking to assess a civil sanction under ERISA section 502(i);

(q) "Secretary" means the Secretary of Labor and includes, pursuant to any delegation of authority by the Secretary, any assistant secretary (including the Assistant Secretary for Employee Benefits Security), administrator, commissioner, appellate body, board, or other official; [EBSA technical correction, 68 FR 16399 (April 3, 2003).]

(r) "Solicitor" means the Solicitor of Labor or his or her delegate.

[¶ 14,928A-1]

§2570.3 **Service: copies of documents and pleadings**.

For prohibited transaction penalty proceedings, this section shall apply in lieu of §18.3 of this title.

(a) *General*. Copies of all documents shall be served on all parties of record. All documents should clearly designate the docket number, if any, and short title of all matters. All documents shall be delivered or mailed to the Chief Docket Clerk, Office of Administrative Law Judges, 800 K Street, NW., Suite 400, Washington, DC 20001-8002, or to the OALJ Regional Office to which the proceeding may have been transferred for hearing. Each document filed shall be clear and legible.

(b) *By parties*. All motions, petitions, pleadings, briefs or other documents shall be filed with the Office of Administrative Law Judges with a copy including any attachments to all other parties of record. When a party is represented by an attorney, service shall be made upon the attorney. Service of any document upon any party may be made by personal delivery or by mailing a copy to the last known address. The Department shall be served by delivery to the Associate Solicitor, Plan Benefits Security Division, ERISA Section 502(i) Proceeding, P.O. Box 1914, Washington, DC 20013. The person serving the document shall certify to the manner and date of service.

(c) *By the Office of Administrative Law Judges*. Service of orders, decisions and all other documents, except notices, shall be made by regular mail to the last known address.

(d) *Service of notices*. (1) Service of notices shall be made either:

(i) By delivering a copy to the individual, any partner, any officer of a corporation, or any attorney of record;

(ii) By leaving a copy at the principal office, place of business, or residence of such individual, partner, officer or attorney; or

(iii) By mailing a copy to the last known address of such individual, partner, officer or attorney.

(2) If service is accomplished by certified mail, service is complete upon mailing. If done by regular mail, service is complete upon receipt by the addressee.

(e) *Form of pleadings*. (1) Every pleading shall contain information indicating the name of the Employee Benefits Security Administration (EBSA) as the agency under which the proceeding is instituted, the title of the proceeding, the docket number (if any) assigned by the Office of Administrative Law Judges and a designation of the type of pleading or paper (e.g., notice, motion to dismiss, etc.). The pleading or paper shall be signed and shall contain the address and telephone number of the party or person representing the party. Although there are no formal specifications for documents, they should be typewritten when possible on standard size 8 ½ × 11 inch paper. [EBSA technical correction, 68 FR 16399 (April 3, 2003).]

(2) Illegible documents, whether handwritten, typewritten, photocopied, or otherwise, will not be accepted. Papers may be reproduced by any duplicating process provided all copies are clear and legible.

[¶ 14,928A-2]

§2570.4 **Parties**.

For prohibited transaction penalty proceedings, this section shall apply in lieu of §18.10 of this title.

(a) The term "party" wherever used in these rules shall include any natural person, corporation, employee benefit plan, association, firm, partnership, trustee, receiver, agency, public or private organization, or government agency. A party against whom a civil sanction is sought shall be designated as "respondent." The Department shall be designated as "complainant."

(b) Other persons organizations shall be permitted to participate as parties only if the administrative law judge finds that the final decision could directly and adversely affect them or the class they represent, that they may contribute materially to the disposition of the proceedings and their interest is not adequately represented by existing parties, and that in the discretion of the administrative law judge the participation of such persons or organizations would be appropriate.

(c) A person or organization not named as a respondent wishing to participate as a party under this section shall submit a petition to the administrative law judge within fifteen (15) days after the person or organization has knowledge of or should have known about the proceeding. The petition shall be filed with the administrative law judge and served on each person or organization who has been made a party at the time of filing. Such petition shall concisely state:

(1) Petitioner's interest in the proceeding;

(2) How his or her participation as a party will contribute materially to the disposition of the proceeding;

(3) Who will appear for petitioner;

(4) The issues on which petitioner wishes to participate; and

(5) Whether petitioner intends to present witnesses.

(d) Objections to the petition may be filed by a party within fifteen (15) days of the filing of the petition. If objections to the petition are filed, the administrative law judge shall then determine whether petitioners have the requisite interest to be a party in the proceedings, as defined in paragraph (b) of this section, and shall permit or deny participation accordingly. Where petitions to participate as parties are made by individuals or groups with common interests, the administrative law judge may request all such petitioners to designate a single representative, or he or she may recognize one or more of such petitioners. The administrative law judge shall give each such petitioner as well as the parties, written notice of the decision on his or her petition. For each petition granted, the administrative law judge shall provide a brief statement of the basis of the decision. If the petition is denied, he or she shall briefly state the grounds for denial and shall then treat the petition as a request for participation as amicus curiae.

[¶ 14,928A-3]
§ 2570.5 Consequences of default.

For prohibited transaction penalty proceedings, this section shall apply in lieu of § 18.5(b) of this title. Failure of the respondent to file an answer within the 30 day time period provided in § 18.5 of this title shall be deemed to constitute a waiver of his right to appear and contest the allegations of the notice, and such failure shall be deemed to be an admission of the facts as alleged in the notice for purposes of the prohibited transaction penalty proceeding. Such notice shall then become the final order of the Secretary, except that the administrative law judge may set aside a default entered under this provision where there is proof of defective notice.

[¶ 14,928A-4]
§ 2570.6 Consent order or settlement.

For prohibited transaction penalty proceedings, the following shall apply in lieu of § 18.9 of this title.

(a) *General*. At any time after the commencement of a proceeding, but at least five (5) days prior to the date set for hearing, the parties jointly may move to defer the hearing for a reasonable time to permit negotiation of a settlement or an agreement containing findings and an order disposing of the whole or any part of the proceeding. The allowance of such deferment and the duration thereof shall be in the discretion of the administrative law judge, after consideration of such factors as the nature of the proceeding, the requirements of the public interest, the representations of the parties and the probability of reaching an agreement which will result in a just disposition of the issues involved.

(b) *Content*. Any agreement containing consent findings and an order disposing of a proceeding or any part thereof shall also provide:

(1) That the order shall have the same force and effect as an order made after full hearing;

(2) That the entire record on which any order may be based shall consist solely of the notice and the agreement;

(3) A waiver of any further procedural steps before the administrative law judge;

(4) A waiver of any right to challenge or contest the validity of the order and decision entered into in accordance with the agreement; and

(5) That the order and decision of the administrative law judge shall be final agency action.

(c) *Submission*. On or before the expiration of the time granted for negotiations, but, in any case, at least five (5) days prior to the date set for hearing, the parties or their authorized representative or their counsel may:

(1) Submit the proposed agreement containing consent findings and an order to the administrative law judge; or

(2) Notify the administrative law judge that the parties have reached a full settlement and have agreed to dismissal of the action subject to compliance with the terms of the settlement; or

(3) Inform the administrative law judge that agreement cannot be reached.

(d) *Disposition*. In the event a settlement containing consent findings and an order is submitted within the time allowed therefor, the administrative law judge shall issue a decision incorporating such findings and agreement within thirty (30) days of his receipt of such document. The decision of the administrative law judge shall incorporate all of the findings, terms, and conditions of the settlement agreement and consent order of the parties. Such decision shall become final agency action within the meaning of 5 U.S.C. 704.

(e) *Settlement without consent of all parties*. In cases in which some, but not all, of the parties to a proceeding submit a consent agreement to the administrative law judge, the following procedure shall apply:

(1) If all of the parties have not consented to the proposed settlement submitted to the administrative law judge, then such non-consenting parties must receive notice, and a copy, of the proposed settlement at the time it is submitted to the administrative law judge;

(2) Any non-consenting party shall have fifteen (15) days to file any objections to the proposed settlement with the administrative law judge and all other parties;

(3) If any party submits an objection to the proposed settlement, the administrative law judge shall decide within thirty (30) days after receipt of such objections whether he shall sign or reject the proposed settlement. Where the record lacks substantial evidence upon which to base a decision or there is a genuine issue of material fact, then the administrative law judge may establish procedures for the purpose of receiving additional evidence upon which a decision on the contested issues may reasonably be based;

(4) If there are no objections to the proposed settlement, or if the administrative law judge decides to sign the proposed settlement after reviewing any such objections, the administrative law judge shall incorporate the consent agreement into a decision meeting the requirements of paragraph (d) of this section.

[¶ 14,928A-5]
§ 2570.7 Scope of discovery.

For prohibited transaction penalty proceedings, this section shall apply in lieu of § 18.14 of this title.

(a) A party may file a motion to conduct discovery with the administrative law judge. The motion for discovery shall be granted by the administrative law judge only upon a showing of good cause. In order to establish "good cause" for the purposes this section, a party must show that the discovery requested relates to a genuine issue as to a material fact that is relevant to the proceeding. The order of the administrative law judge shall expressly limit the scope and terms of discovery to that for which "good cause" has been shown, as provided in this paragraph.

(b) A party may obtain discovery of documents and tangible things otherwise discoverable under paragraph (a) of this section and prepared in anticipation of or for the hearing by or for another party's representative (including his or her attorney, consultant, surety, indemnitor, insurer, or agent) only upon a showing that the party seeking discovery has substantial need of the materials or information in the preparation of his or her case and that he or she is unable without undue hardship to obtain the substantial equivalent of the materials or information by other means. In ordering discovery of such materials when the required showing has been made, the administrative law judge shall protect against disclosure of the mental impressions, conclusions, opinions, or legal theories of an attorney or other representative of a party concerning the proceeding.

[¶ 14,928A-6]

§ 2570.8 **Summary decision**.

For prohibited transaction penalty proceedings, this section shall apply in lieu of § 18.41 of this title.

(a) *No genuine issue of material fact*. (1) Where no genuine issue of a material fact is found to have been raised, the administrative law judge may issue a decision which, in the absence of an appeal pursuant to §§ 2570.10-2570.12 of this part, shall become a final order.

(2) A decision made under this paragraph shall include a statement of:

(i) Findings of fact and conclusions of law, and the reasons therefor, on all issues presented; and

(ii) Any terms and conditions of the rule or order.

(3) A copy of any decision under this paragraph shall be served on each party.

(b) *Hearings on issue of fact*. Where a genuine question of material fact is raised, the administrative law judge shall, and in any other case may, set the case for an evidentiary hearing.

[¶ 14,928A-7]

§ 2570.9 **Decision of the administrative law judge**.

For prohibited transaction penalty proceedings, this section shall apply in lieu of § 18.57 of this title

(a) *Proposed findings of fact, conclusions, and order*. Within twenty (20) days of the filing of the transcript of the testimony or such additional time as the administrative law judge may allow, each party may file with the administrative law judge, subject to the judge's discretion, proposed findings of fact, conclusions of law, and order together with a supporting brief expressing the reasons for such proposals. Such proposals and brief shall be served on all parties, and shall refer to all portions of the record and to all authorities relied upon in support of each proposal.

(b) *Decision of the administrative law judge*. Within a reasonable time after the time allowed for the filing of the proposed findings of fact, conclusions of law, and order, or within thirty (30) days after receipt of an agreement containing consent findings and order disposing of the disputed matter in whole, the administrative law judge shall make his or her decision. The decision of the administrative law judge shall include findings of fact and conclusions of law with reasons therefor upon each material issue of fact of law presented on the record. The decision of the administrative law judge shall be based upon the whole record. In a contested case in which the Department and the Respondent have presented their positions to the administrative law judge pursuant to the procedures for prohibited transaction penalty proceedings as set forth in this part, the penalty (if any) which may be included in the decision of the administrative law judge shall be limited to the sanction expressly provided for in section 502(i) of ERISA. It shall be supported by reliable and probative evidence. The decision of the administrative law judge shall become final agency action within the meaning of 5 U.S.C. 704 unless an appeal is made pursuant to the procedures set forth in §§ 2570.10-2570.12.

[¶ 14,928A-8]

§ 2570.10 **Review by the Secretary**.

(a) The Secretary may review a decision of an administrative law judge. Such a review may occur only when a party files a notice of appeal from a decision of an administrative law judge within twenty (20) days of the issuance of such decision. In all other cases, the decision of the administrative law judge shall become final agency action within the meaning of 5 U.S.C. 704.

(b) A notice of appeal to the Secretary shall state with specificity the issue(s) in the decision of the administrative law judge on which the party is seeking review. Such notice of appeal must be served on all parties of record.

(c) Upon receipt of a notice of appeal, the Secretary shall request the Chief Administrative Law Judge to submit to him a copy of the entire record before the administrative law judge.

[¶ 14,928A-9]

§ 2570.11 **Scope of review**.

The review of the Secretary shall not be a *de novo* proceeding but rather a review of the record established before the administrative law judge. There shall be no opportunity for oral argument.

[¶ 14,928A-10]

§ 2570.12 **Procedures for review by the Secretary**.

(a) Upon receipt of a notice of appeal, the Secretary shall establish a briefing schedule which shall be served on all parties of record. Upon motion of one or more of the parties, the Secretary may, in his discretion, permit the submission of reply briefs.

(b) The Secretary shall issue a decision as promptly as possible after receipt of the briefs of the parties. The Secretary may affirm, modify, or set aside, in whole or in part, the decision on appeal and shall issue a statement of reasons and bases for the action(s) taken. Such decision by the Secretary shall be final agency action within the meaning of 5 U.S.C. 704.

Subpart C—Procedures for the Assessment of Civil Penalties Under ERISA Section 502(c)(2)

[¶ 14,928B]

§ 2570.60 **Scope of rules**.

The rules of practice set forth in this subpart are applicable to "502(c)(2) civil penalty proceedings" (as defined in § 2570.61(n) of this subpart) under section 502(c)(2) of the Employee Retirement Income Security Act of 1974. The rules of procedure for administrative hearings published by the Department's Office of Law Judges at Part 18 of this Title will apply to matters arising under ERISA section 502(c)(2) except as modified by this section. These proceedings shall be conducted as expeditiously as possible, and the parties shall make every effort to avoid delay at each stage of the proceedings.

[¶ 14,928B-1]

§ 2570.61 **Definitions**.

For 502(c)(2) civil penalty proceedings, this section shall apply in lieu of the definitions in § 18.2 of this title:

(a) "Adjudicatory proceeding" means a judicial-type proceeding before an administrative law judge leading to the formulation of a final order;

(b) "Administrative law judge" means an administrative law judge appointed pursuant to the provisions of 5 U.S.C. 3105;

(c) Answer means a written statement that is supported by reference to specific circumstances or facts surrounding the notice of determination issued pursuant to Sec. 2560.502c-2(g) of this chapter. [Revised by PWBA in 67 FR 64774 on 10-21-02 and in 68 FR 3729 on 1-24-03.]

(d) "Commencement of proceeding" is the filing of an answer by the respondent;

(e) "Consent agreement" means any written document containing a specified proposed remedy or other relief acceptable to the Department and consenting parties;

(f) "ERISA" means the Employee Retirement Income Security Act of 1974, as amended;

(g) "Final Order" means the final decision or action of the Department of Labor concerning the assessment of a civil penalty under ERISA section 502(c)(2) against a particular party. Such final order may result from a decision of an administrative law judge or the Secretary, the failure of a party to file a statement of reasonable cause described in § 2560.502c-2(e) within the prescribed time limits, or the failure of a party to invoke the procedures for hearings or appeals under this title within the prescribed time limits. Such a final order shall constitute final agency action within the meaning of 5 U.S.C. 704;

(h) "Hearing" means that part of a proceeding which involves the submission of evidence, either by oral presentation or written submission, to the administrative law judge;

(i) "Order" means the whole or any part of a final procedural or substantive disposition of a matter under ERISA section 502(c)(2);

(j) "Party" includes a person or agency named or admitted as a party to a proceeding;

(k) "Person" includes an individual, partnership, corporation, employee benefit plan, association, exchange or other entity or organization;

(l) "Petition" means a written request, made by a person or party, for some affirmative action;

(m) "Pleading" means the notice as defined in § 2560.502c-2(g), the answer to the notice, any supplement or amendment thereto, and any reply that may be permitted to any answer, supplement or amendment;

(n) "502(c)(2) civil penalty proceeding" means an adjudicatory proceeding relating to the assessment of a civil penalty provided for in section 502(c)(2) of ERISA;

(o) "Respondent" means the party against whom the Department is seeking to assess a civil sanction under ERISA section 502(c)(2);

(p) "Secretary" means the Secretary of Labor and includes, pursuant to any delegation of authority by the Secretary, any assistant secretary (including the Assistant Secretary for Employee Benefits Security), administrator, commissioner, appellate body, board, or other official; and [EBSA technical correction, 68 FR 16399 (April 3, 2003).]

(q) "Solicitor" means the Solicitor of Labor or his or her delegate.

[¶ 14,928B-2]
§ 2570.62 **Service: Copies of documents and pleadings**.

For 502(c)(2) penalty proceedings, this section shall apply in lieu of § 18.3 of this title.

(a) *General*. Copies of all documents shall be served on all parties of record. All documents should clearly designate the docket number, if any, and short title of all matters. All documents to be filed shall be delivered or mailed to the Chief Docket Clerk, Office of Administrative Law Judges, 800 K Street, N.W., Suite 400, Washington, DC 20001-8002, or to the OALJ Regional Office to which the proceeding may have been transferred for hearing. Each document filed shall be clear and legible. [Address changed by 56 FR 54708 on October 22, 1991.]

(b) *By parties*. All motions, petitions, pleadings, briefs, or other documents shall be filed with the Office of Administrative Law Judges with a copy, including any attachments, to all other parties of record. When a party is represented by an attorney, service shall be made upon the attorney. Service of any document upon any party may be made by personal delivery or by mailing a copy to the last known address. The Department shall be served by delivery to the Associate Solicitor, Plan Benefits Security Division, ERISA section 502(c)(2) Proceeding, P.O. Box 1914, Washington, DC 20013. The person serving the document shall certify to the manner and date of service.

(c) *By the Office of Administrative Law Judges*. Service of orders, decisions and all other documents shall be made by regular mail to the last known address.

(d) *Form of pleadings*. (1) Every pleading shall contain information indicating the name of the Employee Benefits Security Administration (EBSA) as the agency under which the proceeding is instituted, the title of the proceeding, the docket number (if any) assigned by the Office of Administrative Law Judges and a designation of the type of pleading or paper (e.g., notice, motion to dismiss, etc.). The pleading or paper shall be signed and shall contain the address and telephone number of the party or person representing the party. Although there are no formal specifications for documents, they should be typewritten when possible on standard size 8 ½ × 11 inch paper. [EBSA technical correction, 68 FR 16399 (April 3, 2003).]

(2) Illegible documents, whether handwritten, typewritten, photocopies, or otherwise, will not be accepted. Papers may be reproduced by any duplicating process provided all copies are clear and legible.

[¶ 14,928B-3]
§ 2570.63 **Parties, how designated**.

For 502(c)(2) civil penalty proceedings, this section shall apply in lieu of § 18.10 of this title.

(a) The term "party" wherever used in these rules shall include any natural person, corporation, employee benefit plan, association, firm, partnership, trustee, receiver, agency, public or private organization, or government agency. A party against whom a civil penalty is sought shall be designated as "respondent." The Department shall be designated as the "complainant."

(b) Other persons or organizations shall be permitted to participate as parties only if the administrative law judge finds that the final decision could directly and adversely affect them or the class they represent, that they may contribute materially to the disposition of the proceedings and their interest is not adequately represented by existing parties, and that in the discretion of the administrative law judge the participation of such persons or organizations would be appropriate.

(c) A person or organization not named as a respondent wishing to participate as a party under this section shall submit a petition to the administrative law judge within fifteen (15) days after the person or organization has knowledge of or should have known about the proceeding. The petition shall be filed with the administrative law judge and served on each person or organization who has been made a party at the time of filing. Such petition shall concisely state:

(1) Petitioner's interest in the proceeding;

(2) How his or her participation as a party will contribute materially to the disposition of the proceeding;

(3) Who will appear for petitioner;

(4) The issues on which petitioner wishes to participate; and

(5) Whether petitioner intends to present witnesses.

(d) Objections to the petition may be filed by a party within fifteen (15) days of the filing of the petition. If objections to the petition are filed, the administrative law judge shall then determine whether petitioners have the requisite interest to be a party in the proceedings, as defined in paragraph (b) of this section, and shall permit or deny participation accordingly. Where petitions to participate as parties are made by individuals or groups with common interests, the administrative law judge may request all such petitioners to designate a single representative, or he or she may recognize one or more of such petitioners. The administrative law judge shall give each such petitioner as well as the parties, written notice of the decision on his or her petition. For each petition granted, the administrative law judge shall provide a brief statement of the basis of the decision. If the petition is denied, he or she shall briefly state the grounds for denial and shall then treat the petition as a request for participation as amicus curiae.

[¶ 14,928B-4]
§ 2570.64 **Consequences of default**.

For 502(c)(2) civil penalty proceedings, this section shall apply in lieu of Sec. 18.5(a) and (b) of this title. Failure of the respondent to file an answer to the notice of determination described in Sec. 2560.502c-2(g) of this chapter within the 30-day period provided by Sec. 2560.502c-2(h) of this chapter shall be deemed to constitute a waiver of his or her right to appear and contest the allegations of the notice of determination, and such failure shall be deemed to be an admission of the facts as alleged in the notice for purposes of any proceeding involving the assessment of a civil penalty under section 502(c)(2) of the Act. Such notice shall then become the final order of the Secretary, within the meaning of Sec. 2570.61(g) of this subpart, forty-five (45) days from the date of service of the notice. [Revised by PWBA in 67 FR 64774 on 10-21-02 and in 68 FR 3729 on 1-24-03.]

[¶ 14,928B-5]
§ 2570.65 **Consent order or settlement**.

For 502(c)(2) civil penalty proceedings, the following shall apply in lieu of § 18.9 of this title.

(a) *General*. At any time after the commencement of a proceeding, but at least five (5) days prior to the date set for hearing, the parties jointly may move to defer the hearing for a reasonable time to permit negotiation of a settlement or an agreement containing findings and an order disposing of the whole or any part of the proceeding. The allowance of such and the duration thereof shall be in the discretion of the administrative law judge, after consideration of such factors as the nature of the proceeding, the requirements of the public interest, the representations of the parties and the probability of reaching an agreement which will result in a just disposition of the issues involved.

(b) *Content*. Any agreement containing consent findings and an order disposing of a proceeding or any part thereof shall also provide:

(1) That the order shall have the same force and effect as an order made after full hearing;

(2) That the entire record on which any order may be based shall consist solely of the notice and the agreement;

(3) A waiver of any further procedural steps before the administrative law judge;

(4) A waiver of any right to challenge or contest the validity of the order and decision entered into in accordance with the agreement; and

(5) That the order and decision of the administrative law judge shall be final agency action.

(c) *Submission*. On or before the expiration of the time granted for negotiations, but, in any case, at least five (5) days prior to the date set for hearing, the parties or their authorized representative or their counsel may:

(1) Submit the proposed agreement containing consent findings and an order to the administrative law judge; or

(2) Notify the administrative law judge that the parties have reached a full settlement and have agreed to dismissal of the action subject to compliance with the terms of the settlement; or

(3) Inform the administrative law judge that agreement cannot be reached.

(d) *Disposition*. In the event a settlement agreement containing consent findings and an order is submitted within the time allowed therefore, the administrative law judge shall issue a decision incorporating such findings and agreement within thirty (30) days of his receipt of such document. The decision of the administrative law judge shall incorporate all of the findings, terms, and conditions of the settlement agreement and consent order of the parties. Such decision shall become final agency action within the meaning of 5 U.S.C. 704.

(e) *Settlement without consent of all parties*. In cases in which some, but not all, of the parties to a proceeding submit a consent agreement to the administrative law judge, the following procedure shall apply:

(1) If all of the parties have not consented to the proposed settlement submitted to the administrative law judge, then such non-consenting parties must receive notice, and a copy, of the proposed settlement at the time it is submitted to the administrative law judge;

(2) Any non-consenting party shall have fifteen (15) days to file any objections to the proposed settlement with the administrative law judge and all other parties;

(3) If any party submits an objection to the proposed settlement, the administrative law judge shall decide within thirty (30) days after receipt of such objections whether he shall sign or reject the proposed settlement. Where the record lacks substantial evidence upon which to base a decision or there is a genuine issue of material fact, then the administrative law judge may establish procedures for the purpose of receiving additional evidence upon which a decision on the contested issues may reasonably be based;

(4) If there are no objections to the proposed settlement, or if the administrative law judge decides to sign the proposed settlement after reviewing any such objections, the administrative law judge shall incorporate the consent agreement into a decision meeting the requirements of paragraph (d) of this section.

¶14,928B-6   Reg. §2570.65(a)

§ 2570.66 **Scope of discovery**.

For 502(c)(2) civil penalty proceedings, this section shall apply in lieu of § 18.14 of this title.

(a) A party may file a motion to conduct discovery with the administrative law judge. The motion for discovery shall be granted by the administrative law judge only upon a showing of good cause. In order to establish "good cause" for the purposes of this section, a party must show that the discovery requested relates to a genuine issue as to a material fact that is relevant to the proceeding. The order of the administrative law judge shall expressly limit the scope and terms of discovery to that for which "good cause" has been shown, as provided in this paragraph.

(b) A party may obtain discovery of documents and tangible things otherwise discoverable under paragraph (a) of this section and prepared in anticipation of or for the hearing by or for another party's representative (including his or her attorney, consultant, surety, indemnitor, insurer, or agent) only upon showing that the party seeking discovery has substantial need of the materials or information in the preparation of his or her case and that he or she is unable without undue hardship to obtain the substantial equivalent of the materials or information by other means. In ordering discovery of such materials when the required showing has been made, the administrative law judge shall protect against disclosure of the mental impressions, conclusions, opinions, or legal theories of an attorney or other representatives of a party concerning the proceeding.

§ 2570.67 **Summary decision**.

For 502(c)(2) civil penalty proceedings, this section shall apply in lieu of § 18.41 of this title.

(a) *No genuine issue of material of fact*. (1) Where no issue of a material of fact is found to have been raised, the administrative law judge may issue a decision which, in the absence of an appeal pursuant to § § 2570.69 through 71 of this subpart, shall become a final order.

(2) A decision made under this paragraph shall include a statement of:

(i) Findings of fact and conclusions of law, and the reasons therefor, on all issues presented; and

(ii) Any terms and conditions of the rule or order.

(3) A copy of any decision under this paragraph shall be served on each party.

(b) *Hearings on issues of fact*. Where a genuine question of material of fact is raised, the administrative law judge shall, and in any other case may, set the case for an evidentiary hearing.

§ 2570.68 **Decision of the administrative law judge**.

For 502(c)(2) civil penalty proceedings, this section shall apply in lieu of § 18.57 of this title.

(a) *Proposed findings of fact, conclusions, and order*. Within twenty (20) days of the filing of the transcript of the testimony of such additional time as the administrative law judge may allow, each party may file with the administrative law judge, subject to the judge's discretion, proposed findings of fact, conclusions of law, and order together with a supporting brief expressing the reasons for such proposals. Such proposals and briefs shall be served on all parties, and shall refer to all portions of the record and to all authorities relied upon in support of each proposal.

(b) *Decision of the administrative law judge*. Within a reasonable time after the time allowed for the filing of the proposed findings of fact, conclusions of law, and order, or within thirty (30) days after receipt of an agreement containing consent findings and order disposing of the disputed matter in whole, the administrative law judge shall make his or her decision. The decision of the administrative law judge shall include findings of fact and conclusions of law with reasons therefor upon each material issue of fact or law presented on the record. The decision of the administrative law judge shall be based upon the whole record. In a contested case in which the Department and the Respondent have presented their positions to the administrative law judge pursuant to the procedures for 502(c)(2) civil penalty proceedings as set forth in this subpart, the penalty (if any) which may be included in the decision of the administrative law judge shall be limited to the penalty expressly provided for in section 502(c)(2) of ERISA. It shall be supported by reliable and probative evidence. The decision of the administrative law judge shall become final agency action within the meaning of 5 U.S.C. 704 unless an appeal is made pursuant to the procedures set forth in §§2570.69 through 2570.71.

[¶ 14,928B-9]
§2570.69 **Review by the Secretary**.

(a) The Secretary may review a decision of an administrative law judge. Such a review may occur only when a party files a notice of appeal from a decision of an administrative law judge within twenty (20) days of the issuance of such decision. In all other cases, the decision of the administrative law judge shall become final agency action within the meaning of 5 U.S.C. 704.

(b) A notice of appeal to the Secretary shall state with specificity the issue(s) in the decision of the administrative law judge on which the party is seeking review. Such notice of appeal must be served on all parties of record.

(c) Upon receipt of a notice of appeal, the Secretary shall request the Chief Administrative Law Judge to submit to him or her a copy of the entire record before the administrative law judge.

[¶ 14,928B-10]
§2570.70 **Scope of review**.

The review of the Secretary shall not be *de novo* proceeding but rather a review of the record established before the administrative law judge. There shall be no opportunity for oral argument.

[¶ 14,928B-11]
§2570.71 **Procedures for review by the Secretary**.

(a) Upon receipt of the notice of appeal, the Secretary shall establish a briefing schedule which shall be served on all parties of record. Upon motion of one or more of the parties, the Secretary may, in his or her discretion, permit the submission of reply briefs.

(b) The Secretary shall issue a decision as promptly as possible after receipt of the briefs of the parties. The Secretary may affirm, modify, or set aside, in whole or in part, the decision on appeal and shall issue a statement of reasons and bases for the action(s) taken. Such decision by the Secretary shall be final agency action within the meaning of 5 U.S.C. 704.

[Subpart C was added on June 26, 1989 (54 FR 26895).]

Interim Regulations

The following interim regulations were adopted under "Title 29—Labor," "Chapter XXV—Pension and Welfare Benefits Administration, Department of Labor," "Subchapter G—Administration and Enforcement Under the Employee Retirement Income Security Act of 1974," and "Part 2570—Procedural Regulations Under the Employee Retirement Income Security Act." The regulations were published in the *Federal Register* on June 20, 1990 (55 FR 25284). The regulations were effective June 20, 1990. Regulations §2570.94 and §2570.114 were revised by PWBA in 67 FR 64774 on October 21, 2002. Regulation 2570.82 was amended by EBSA in 68 FR 16399 on April 3, 2003.

Subpart D—Procedure for the Assessment of Civil Penalties Under ERISA Section 502(l)

[¶ 14,928C]
§2570.80 **Scope of rules**.

The rules of practice set forth in this subpart are applicable to "502(l) civil penalty proceedings" (as defined in §2570.82 of this subpart) under section 502(l) of the Employee Retirement Income Security Act of 1974 (ERISA or the Act). Refer to 29 CFR 2560.5021 for the definition of the relevant terms of ERISA section 502(l).

[¶ 14,928D]
§2570.81 **In general**.

Section 502(l) of the Employee Retirement Income Security Act of 1974 (ERISA or the Act) requires the Secretary of Labor to assess a civil penalty against a fiduciary who breaches a fiduciary responsibility under, or commits any other violation of part 4 of Title I of ERISA or any other person who knowingly participates in such breach or violation. The penalty under section 502(l) is equal to 20 percent of the "applicable recovery amount" paid pursuant to any settlement agreement with the Secretary or ordered by a court to be paid in a judicial proceeding instituted by the Secretary under section 502(a)(2) or (a)(5). The Secretary may, in the Secretary's sole discretion, waive or reduce the penalty if the Secretary determines in writing that:

(a) The fiduciary or other person acted reasonably and in good faith, or

(b) It is reasonable to expect that the fiduciary or other person will not be able to restore all losses to the plan or any participant or beneficiary of such plan without severe financial hardship unless such waiver or reduction is granted.

The penalty imposed on a fiduciary or other person with respect to any transaction shall be reduced by the amount of any penalty or tax imposed on such fiduciary or other person with respect to such transaction under section 502(i) or section 4975 of the Internal Revenue Code of 1986 (the Code).

[¶ 14,928E]
§2570.82 **Definitions**.

For purposes of this section:

(a) *502(l) civil penalty proceedings* means an adjudicatory proceeding relating to the assessment of a civil penalty provided in section 502(l) of ERISA;

(b) *Notice of assessment* means any document, however designated, issued by the Secretary which contains a specified assessment, in monetary terms, of a civil penalty under ERISA section 502(l). A "notice of assessment" will contain a brief factual description of the violation for which the assessment is being made, the identity of the person being assessed, and the amount of the assessment and the basis for assessing that particular person that particular penalty amount;

(c) *Person* includes an individual, partnership, corporation, employee benefit plan, association, exchange or other entity or organization;

(d) *Petition* means a written request, made by a person, for a waiver or reduction of the civil penalty described herein; and

(e) *Secretary* means the Secretary of Labor and includes, pursuant to any delegation of authority by the Secretary, the Assistant Secretary for Pension and Welfare Benefits, Regional Directors for Employee Benefits Security, or Deputy Area Directors for Pension and Welfare Benefits. [Amended by EBSA, 68 FR 16399, April 3, 2003.]

[¶ 14,928F]
§2570.83 **Assessment of civil penalty**.

(a) Except as described in §§2570.85 and 2570.86 below, subsequent to the payment of the applicable recovery amount pursuant to either a settlement agreement or a court order, the Secretary shall serve on the person liable for making such payment a notice of assessment of civil penalty equal to 20 percent of the applicable recovery amount.

(b) Service of such notice shall be made either:

(1) By delivering a copy to the person being assessed; if the person is an individual, to the individual; if the person is a partnership, to any partner; if the person is a corporation, association, exchange, or other entity or organization, to any officer of such entity; of the person is an employee benefit plan, to a trustee of such plan; or to any attorney representing any such person;

(2) By leaving a copy at the principal office, place of business, or residence of such individual, partner, officer, trustee, or attorney; or

(3) By mailing a copy to the last known address of such individual, partner, officer, trustee, or attorney.

If service is accomplished by certified mail, service is complete upon mailing. If done by regular mail, service is complete upon receipt by the addressee.

[¶ 14,928G]

§ 2570.84 **Payment of civil penalty.**

(a) The civil penalty must be paid within 60 days of service of the notice of assessment.

(b) At any time prior to the expiration of the payment period for the assessed penalty, any person who has committed, or knowingly participated in, a breach or violation, or has been alleged by the Secretary to have so committed or participated, may submit a written request for a conference with the Secretary to discuss the calculation of the assessed penalty. A person will be entitled under this section to one such conference per assessment. If such written request is submitted during the 60 day payment period described in subparagraph (a), such a request will not toll the running of that payment period.

(c) The notice of assessment will become a final order (within the meaning of 5 U.S.C. 704) on the first day following the 60 day payment period, subject to any tolling caused by a petition to waive or reduce described in paragraph 2570.85.

[¶ 14,928H]

§ 2570.85 **Waiver or reduction of civil penalty.**

(a) At any time prior to the expiration of the payment period for the assessed penalty, any person who has committed, or knowingly participated in, a breach or violation, or has been alleged by the Secretary to have so committed or participated, may petition the Secretary to waive or reduce the penalty under this section on the basis that:

(1) The person acted reasonably and in good faith in engaging in the breach or violation; or

(2) The person will not be able to restore all losses to the plan or participant or beneficiary of such plan without severe financial hardship unless such waiver or reduction is granted.

(b) All petitions for waiver or reduction shall be in writing and contain the following information:

(1) The name of the petitioner(s);

(2) A detailed description of the breach or violation which is the subject of the penalty;

(3) A detailed recitation of the facts which support one, or both, of the bases for waiver or reduction described in § 2570.85(a) of this part, accompanied by underlying documentation supporting such factual allegations;

(4) A declaration, signed and dated by the petitioner(s), in the following form: Under penalty of perjury, I declare that, to the best of my knowledge and belief, the representations made in this petition are true and correct.

(c) If a petition for waiver or reduction is submitted during the 60 day payment period described in § 2570.84(a) above, the payment

period for the penalty in question will be tolled pending Departmental consideration of the petition. During such consideration, the applicant is entitled to one conference with the Secretary, but the Secretary, in his or her sole discretion, may schedule or hold additional conferences with the petitioner concerning the factual allegations contained in the petition.

(d) Based solely on his or her discretion, the Secretary will determine whether to grant such a waiver or reduction. Pursuant to the procedure described in § 2570.83(b), the petitioner will be served with a written determination informing him or her of the Secretary's decision. Such written determination shall briefly state the grounds for the Secretary's decision, and shall be final and non-reviewable. In the case of a determination not to waive, the payment period for the penalty in question, if previously initiated, will resume as of the date of service of the Secretary's written determination.

[¶ 14,928I]

§ 2570.86 **Reduction of Penalty by Other Penalty Assessments.**

The penalty assessed on a person pursuant to this section with respect to any transaction shall be reduced by the amount of any penalty or tax imposed on such person with respect to such transaction under ERISA section 502(i) and section 4975 of the Code. Prior to a reduction of penalty under this paragraph, the person being assessed must provide proof to the Department of the payment of the penalty or tax and the amount of that payment.

Submissions of proof of other penalty or tax assessments will not toll the 60 day payment period, if previously initiated.

[¶ 14,928J]

§ 2570.87 **Revision of assessment.**

If, based on the procedures described in §§ 2570.84, 2570.85, or 2570.86, the assessed penalty amount is revised, the person being assessed will receive a revised notice of assessment and will be obligated to pay the revised assessed penalty within the relevant 60 day payment period (as determined by the applicable procedure in §§ 2570.84, 2570.85, or 2570.86), and, if necessary, any excess penalty payment will be refunded as soon as administratively feasible. The revised notice of assessment will revoke any previously issued notice of assessment with regard to the transaction in question and will become a final order (within the meaning of 5 U.S.C. 704) the later of the first day following the 60 day payment period or the date of its service on the person being assessed, pursuant to the service procedures described in § 2570.83(b).

[¶ 14,928K]

§ 2570.88 **Effective Date.**

This section is effective June 20, 1990 and shall apply to assessments under section 502(l) made by the Secretary after June 20, 1990 based on any breach or violation occurring on or after December 19, 1989.

Regulations

The following regulations were adopted under "Title 29—Labor," "Chapter XXV—Pension and Welfare Benefits Administration, Department of Labor," "Subchapter G—Administration and Enforcement Under the Employee Retirement Income Security Act of 1974," "Part 2570—Procedural Regulations Under the Employee Retirement Income Security Act." The interim regulations were filed with the *Federal Register* on February 11, 2000 (65 FR 7185). The regulations are effective April 11, 2000. Regulation § 2570.94 was revised by the PWBA on January 24, 2003 (68 FR 3729). They were amended and revised on April 9, 2003 (68 FR 17506).

Subpart E—Procedures for the Assessment of Civil Penalties Under ERISA Section 502(c)(5)

[¶ 14,928M]

§ 2570.90 **Scope of rules.**

The rules of practice set forth in this subpart are applicable to "502(c)(5) civil penalty proceedings" (as defined in 2570.91(n)) under section 502(c)(5) of the Employee Retirement Income Security Act of 1974. The rules of procedure for administrative hearings published by the Department's Office of Administrative Law Judges in subpart A of 29 CFR part 18 will apply to matters arising under ERISA section 502(c)(5) except as described by this section. These proceedings shall be conducted as expeditiously as possible, and the parties shall make every effort to avoid delay at each stage of the proceedings.

[¶ 14,928M-1]

§ 2570.91 **Definitions.**

For 502(c)(5) civil penalty proceedings, this section shall apply in lieu of the definitions in § 18.2 of this title.

(a) *Adjudicatory proceeding* means a judicial-type proceeding before an administrative law judge leading to the formulation of a final order;

(b) *Administrative law judge* means an administrative law judge appointed pursuant to the provisions of 5 U.S.C. 3105;

(c) *Answer* means a written statement that is supported by reference to specific circumstances or facts surrounding the notice of determination issued pursuant to 29 CFR 2560.502c-5(g);

(d) *Commencement of proceeding* is the filing of an answer by the respondent;

(e) *Consent agreement* means any written document containing a specified proposed remedy or other relief acceptable to the Department and consenting parties;

(f) *ERISA* means the Employee Retirement Income Security Act of 1974, as amended;

(g) *Final order* means the final decision or action of the Department of Labor concerning the assessment of a civil penalty under ERISA section 502(c)(5) against a particular party. Such final order may result from a decision of an administrative law judge or the Secretary, the failure of a party to file a statement of reasonable cause described in 29 CFR 2560.502c-5(e) within the prescribed time limits, or the failure of a party to invoke the procedures for hearings or appeals under this title within the prescribed time limits. Such a final order shall constitute final agency action within the meaning of 5 U.S.C. 704;

(h) *Hearing* means that part of a proceeding which involves the submission of evidence, either by oral presentation or written submission, to the administrative law judge;

(i) *Order* means the whole or any part of a final procedural or substantive disposition of a matter under ERISA section 502(c)(5);

(j) *Party* includes a person or agency named or admitted as a party to a proceeding;

(k) *Person* includes an individual, partnership, corporation, employee benefit plan, association, exchange, or other entity or organization;

(l) *Petition* means a written request, made by a person or party, for some affirmative action;

(m) *Pleading* means the notice as defined in 29 CFR 2560.502c-5(g), the answer to the notice, any supplement or amendment thereto, and any reply that may be permitted to any answer, supplement or amendment;

(n) *502(c)(5) civil penalty proceeding* means an adjudicatory proceeding relating to the assessment of a civil penalty provided for in section 502(c)(5) of ERISA;

(o) *Respondent* means the party against whom the Department is seeking to assess a civil sanction under ERISA section 502(c)(5);

(p) *Secretary* means the Secretary of Labor and includes, pursuant to any delegation of authority by the Secretary, any assistant secretary (including the Assistant Secretary for Employee Benefits Security), administrator, commissioner, appellate body, board, or other official of the Department of Labor; and

(q) *Solicitor* means the Solicitor of Labor or his or her delegate.

[¶ 14,928M-2]
§ 2570.92 **Service: Copies of documents and pleadings**.

For 502(c)(5) penalty proceedings, this section shall apply in lieu of 29 CFR 18.3.

(a) *In general*. Copies of all documents shall be served on all parties of record. All documents should clearly designate the docket number, if any, and short title of all matters. All documents to be filed shall be delivered or mailed to the Chief Docket Clerk, Office of Administrative Law Judges (OALJ), 800 K Street, NW., Suite 400, Washington, DC 20001-8002, or to the OALJ Regional Office to which the proceeding may have been transferred for hearing. Each document filed shall be clear and legible.

(b) *By parties*. All motions, petitions, pleadings, briefs, or other documents shall be filed with the Office of Administrative Law Judges with a copy, including any attachments, to all other parties of record. When a party is represented by an attorney, service shall be made upon the attorney. Service of any document upon any party may be made by personal delivery or by mailing a copy to the last known address. The Department shall be served by delivery to the Associate Solicitor, Plan Benefits Security Division, ERISA Section 502(c)(5) Proceeding, P.O. Box 1914, Washington, DC 20013. The person serving the document shall certify to the manner and date of service.

(c) *By the Office of Administrative Law Judges*. Service of orders, decisions and all other documents shall be made by regular mail to the last known address.

(d) *Form of pleadings—*

(1) Every pleading shall contain information indicating the name of the Employee Benefits Security Administration (EBSA) as the agency under which the proceeding is instituted, the title of the proceeding, the docket number (if any) assigned by the Office of Administrative Law Judges and a designation of the type of pleading or paper (e.g., notice, motion to dismiss, etc.). The pleading or paper shall be signed and shall contain the address and telephone number of the party or person representing the party. Although there are no formal specifications for documents, they should be typewritten when possible on standard size 8 1/2 × 11 inch paper.

(2) Illegible documents, whether handwritten, typewritten, photocopies, or otherwise, will not be accepted. Papers may be reproduced by any duplicating process provided all copies are clear and legible.

[¶ 14,928M-3]
§ 2570.93 **Parties, how designated**.

For 502(c)(5) civil penalty proceedings, this section shall apply in lieu of 29 CFR 18.10.

(a) The term party wherever used in this subpart shall include any natural person, corporation, employee benefit plan, association, firm, partnership, trustee, receiver, agency, public or private organization, or government agency. A party against whom a civil penalty is sought shall be designated as "respondent." The Department shall be designated as the "complainant."

(b) Other persons or organizations shall be permitted to participate as parties only if the administrative law judge finds that the final decision could directly and adversely affect them or the class they represent, that they may contribute materially to the disposition of the proceedings and their interest is not adequately represented by existing parties, and that in the discretion of the administrative law judge the participation of such persons or organizations would be appropriate.

(c) A person or organization not named as a respondent wishing to participate as a party under this section shall submit a petition to the administrative law judge within fifteen (15) days after the person or organization has knowledge of or should have known about the proceeding. The petition shall be filed with the administrative law judge and served on each person or organization who has been made a party at the time of filing. Such petition shall concisely state:

(1) Petitioner's interest in the proceeding;

(2) How his or her participation as a party will contribute materially to the disposition of the proceeding;

(3) Who will appear for petitioner;

(4) The issues on which petitioner wishes to participate; and

(5) Whether petitioner intends to present witnesses.

(d) Objections to the petition may be filed by a party within fifteen (15) days of the filing of the petition. If objections to the petition are filed, the administrative law judge shall then determine whether petitioners have the requisite interest to be a party in the proceedings, as defined in paragraph (b) of this section, and shall permit or deny participation accordingly. Where petitions to participate as parties are made by individuals or groups with common interests, the administrative law judge may request all such petitioners to designate a single representative, or he or she may recognize one or more of such petitioners. The administrative law judge shall give each such petitioner as well as the parties, written notice of the decision on his or her petition. For each petition granted, the administrative law judge shall provide a brief statement of the basis of the decision. If the petition is denied, he or she shall briefly state the grounds for denial and shall then treat the petition as a request for participation as amicus curiae.

[¶ 14,928M-4]
§ 2570.94 **Consequences of default**.

For 502(c)(5) civil penalty proceedings, this section shall apply in lieu of 29 CFR 18.5(a) and (b). Failure of the respondent to file an answer to the notice of determination described in 29 CFR 2560.502c-5(g) within the 30 day period provided by 29 CFR 2560.502c-5(h) shall be deemed to constitute a waiver of his or her right to appear and contest the allegations of the notice of determination, and such failure shall be deemed to be an admission of the facts as alleged in the notice for purposes of any proceeding involving the assessment of a civil penalty under section 502(c)(5) of the Act. Such notice shall then become a final order of the Secretary, within the meaning of §2570.91(g), forty-five (45) days from the date of the service of the notice.

[¶ 14,928M-5]
§2570.95 Consent order or settlement.

For 502(c)(5) civil penalty proceedings, the following shall apply in lieu of 29 CFR 18.9.

(a) *In general.* At any time after the commencement of a proceeding, but at least five (5) days prior to the date set for hearing, the parties jointly may move to defer the hearing for a reasonable time to permit negotiation of a settlement or an agreement containing findings and an order disposing of the whole or any part of the proceeding. The allowance of such deferment and the duration thereof shall be in the discretion of the administrative law judge, after consideration of such factors as the nature of the proceeding, the requirements of the public interest, the representations of the parties and the probability of reaching an agreement which will result in a just disposition of the issues involved.

(b) *Content.* Any agreement containing consent findings and an order disposing of a proceeding or any part thereof shall also provide:

(1) That the order shall have the same force and effect as an order made after full hearing;

(2) That the entire record on which any order may be based shall consist solely of the notice and the agreement;

(3) A waiver of any further procedural steps before the administrative law judge;

(4) A waiver of any right to challenge or contest the validity of the order and decision entered into in accordance with the agreement; and

(5) That the order and decision of the administrative law judge shall be final agency action.

(c) *Submission.* On or before the expiration of the time granted for negotiations, but, in any case, at least five (5) days prior to the date set for hearing, the parties or their authorized representative or their counsel may:

(1) Submit the proposed agreement containing consent findings and an order to the administrative law judge;

(2) Notify the administrative law judge that the parties have reached a full settlement and have agreed to dismissal of the action subject to compliance with the terms of the settlement; or

(3) Inform the administrative law judge that agreement cannot be reached.

(d) *Disposition.* In the event that a settlement agreement containing consent findings and an order is submitted within the time allowed therefor, the administrative law judge shall issue a decision incorporating such findings and agreement within thirty (30) days of receipt of such document. The decision of the administrative law judge shall incorporate all of the findings, terms, and conditions of the settlement agreement and consent order of the parties. Such decision shall become a final agency action within the meaning of 5 U.S.C. 704.

(e) *Settlement without consent of all parties.* In cases in which some, but not all, of the parties to a proceeding submit a consent agreement to the administrative law judge, the following procedure shall apply:

(1) If all of the parties have not consented to the proposed settlement submitted to the administrative law judge, then such non-consenting parties must receive notice, and a copy, of the proposed settlement at the time it is submitted to the administrative law judge;

(2) Any non-consenting party shall have fifteen (15) days to file any objections to the proposed settlement with the administrative law judge and all other parties;

(3) If any party submits an objection to the proposed settlement, the administrative law judge shall decide within thirty (30) days after receipt of such objections whether to sign or reject the proposed settlement. Where the record lacks substantial evidence upon which to base a decision or there is a genuine issue of material fact, then the administrative law judge may establish procedures for the purpose of

receiving additional evidence upon which a decision on the contested issues may reasonably be based;

(4) If there are no objections to the proposed settlement, or if the administrative law judge decides to sign the proposed settlement after reviewing any such objections, the administrative law judge shall incorporate the consent agreement into a decision meeting the requirements of paragraph (d) of this section.

[¶ 14,928M-6]
§2570.96 Scope of discovery.

For 502(c)(5) civil penalty proceedings, this section shall apply in lieu of 29 CFR 18.14.

(a) A party may file a motion to conduct discovery with the administrative law judge. The motion for discovery shall be granted by the administrative law judge only upon a showing of good cause. In order to establish "good cause" for the purposes of this section, a party must show that the discovery requested relates to a genuine issue as to a material fact that is relevant to the proceeding. The order of the administrative law judge shall expressly limit the scope and terms of discovery to that for which "good cause" has been shown, as provided in this paragraph.

(b) A party may obtain discovery of documents and tangible things otherwise discoverable under paragraph (a) of this section and prepared in anticipation of or for the hearing by or for another party's representative (including his or her attorney, consultant, surety, indemnitor, insurer, or agent) only upon showing that the party seeking discovery has substantial need of the materials or information in the preparation of his or her case and that he or she is unable without undue hardship to obtain the substantial equivalent of the materials or information by other means. In ordering discovery of such materials when the required showing has been made, the administrative law judge shall protect against disclosure of the mental impressions, conclusions, opinions, or legal theories of an attorney or other representative of a party concerning the proceeding.

[¶ 14,928M-7]
§2570.97 Summary decision.

For 502(c)(5) civil penalty proceedings, this section shall apply in lieu of 29 CFR 18.41.

(a) *No genuine issue of material fact.*

(1) Where no issue of material fact is found to have been raised, the administrative law judge may issue a decision which, in the absence of an appeal pursuant to §§2570.99 through 2570.101, shall become a final order.

(2) A decision made under this paragraph shall include a statement of:

(i) Findings of fact and conclusions of law, and the reasons therefore, on all issues presented; and

(ii) Any terms and conditions of the rule or order.

(3) A copy of any decision under this paragraph shall be served on each party.

(b) *Hearings on issues of fact.* Where a genuine question of material fact is raised, the administrative law judge shall, and in any other case may, set the case for an evidentiary hearing.

[¶ 14,928M-8]
§2570.98 Decision of the administrative law judge.

For 502(c)(5) civil penalty proceedings, this section shall apply in lieu of 29 CFR 18.57.

(a) *Proposed findings of fact, conclusions, and order.* Within twenty (20) days of the filing of the transcript of the testimony or such additional time as the administrative law judge may allow, each party may file with the administrative law judge, subject to the judge's discretion, proposed findings of fact, conclusions of law, and an order together with a supporting brief expressing the reasons for such proposals. Such proposals and briefs shall be served on all parties, and shall refer to all portions of the record and to all authorities relied upon in support of each proposal.

(b) *Decision of the administrative law judge.* Within a reasonable time after the time allowed for the filing of the proposed findings of fact, conclusions of law, and order, or within thirty (30) days after receipt of an agreement containing consent findings and an order disposing of the disputed matter in whole, the administrative law judge shall make his or her decision. The decision of the administrative law judge shall include findings of fact and conclusions of law with reasons therefor upon each material issue of fact or law presented on the record. The decision of the administrative law judge shall be based upon the whole record. In a contested case in which the Department and the Respondent have presented their positions to the administrative law judge pursuant to the procedures for 502(c)(5) civil penalty proceedings as set forth in this subpart, the penalty (if any) which may be included in the decision of the administrative law judge shall be limited to the penalty expressly provided for in section 502(c)(5) of ERISA. It shall be supported by reliable and probative evidence. The decision of the administrative law judge shall become a final agency action within the meaning of 5 U.S.C. 704 unless an appeal is made pursuant to the procedures set forth in §§ 2570.99 through 2570.101.

[¶ 14,928M-9]
§ 2570.99 **Review by the Secretary**.

(a) The Secretary may review a decision of an administrative law judge. Such a review may occur only when a party files a notice of appeal from a decision of an administrative law judge within twenty (20) days of the issuance of such decision. In all other cases, the decision of the administrative law judge shall become final agency action within the meaning of 5 U.S.C. 704.

(b) A notice of appeal to the Secretary shall state with specificity the issue(s) in the decision of the administrative law judge on which the party is seeking review. Such notice of appeal must be served on all parties of record.

(c) Upon receipt of a notice of appeal, the Secretary shall request the Chief Administrative Law Judge to submit to him or her a copy of the entire record before the administrative law judge.

[¶ 14,928M-10]
§ 2570.100 **Scope of review**.

The review of the Secretary shall not be a de novo proceeding but rather a review of the record established before the administrative law judge. There shall be no opportunity for oral argument.

[¶ 14,928M-11]
§ 2570.101 **Procedures for review by the Secretary**.

(a) Upon receipt of the notice of appeal, the Secretary shall establish a briefing schedule which shall be served on all parties of record. Upon motion of one or more of the parties, the Secretary may, in his or her discretion, permit the submission of reply briefs.

(b) The Secretary shall issue a decision as promptly as possible after receipt of the briefs of the parties. The Secretary may affirm, modify, or set aside, in whole or in part, the decision on appeal and shall issue a statement of reasons and bases for the action(s) taken. Such decision by the Secretary shall be final agency action within the meaning of 5 U.S.C. 704.

Regulations

The following regulations were adopted under "Title 29—Labor," "Chapter XXV—Pension and Welfare Benefits Administration, Department of Labor," "Subchapter—Administration and Enforcement Under the Employee Retirement Income Security Act of 1974," Part 2570—Procedural Regulations Under the Employee Retirement Income Security Act." The regulation was filed with the *Federal Register* on January 4, 2002 and published in the *Federal Register* on January 7, 2002 (67 FR 777). The regulation is effective March 8, 2002. Reg. § 2570.114 was revised by EBSA on January 24, 2003 (68 FR 3729).

Subpart F—Procedures for the Assessment of Civil Penalties Under ERISA Section 502(c)(6)

[¶ 14,928Q]
§ 2570.110 **Scope of rules**.

The rules of practice set forth in this subpart are applicable to "502(c)(6) civil penalty proceedings" (as defined in § 2570.111(n) of this subpart) under section 502(c)(6) of the Employee Retirement Income Security Act of 1974. The rules of procedure for administrative hearings published by the Department's Office of Law Judges at Part 18 of this title will apply to matters arising under ERISA section 502(c)(6) except as modified by this section. These proceedings shall be conducted as expeditiously as possible, and the parties shall make every effort to avoid delay at each stage of the proceedings.

[¶ 14,928R]
§ 2570.111 **Definitions**.

For section 502(c)(6) civil penalty proceedings, this section shall apply in lieu of the definitions in § 18.2 of this title:

(a) *Adjudicatory proceeding* means a judicial-type proceeding before an administrative law judge leading to the formulation of a final order;

(b) *Administrative law judge* means an administrative law judge appointed pursuant to the provisions of 5 U.S.C. 3105;

(c) *Answer* means a written statement that is supported by reference to specific circumstances or facts surrounding the notice of determination issued pursuant to § 2560.502c-6(g) of this chapter;

(d) *Commencement of proceeding* is the filing of an answer by the respondent;

(e) *Consent agreement* means any written document containing a specified proposed remedy or other relief acceptable to the Department and consenting parties;

(f) *ERISA* means the Employee Retirement Income Security Act of 1974, as amended;

(g) *Final order* means the final decision or action of the Department of Labor concerning the assessment of a civil penalty under

ERISA section 502(c)(6) against a particular party. Such final order may result from a decision of an administrative law judge or the Secretary, the failure of a party to file a statement of matters reasonably beyond the control of the plan administrator described in § 2560.502c-6(e) of this chapter within the prescribed time limits, or the failure of a party to invoke the procedures for hearings or appeals under this title within the prescribed time limits. Such a final order shall constitute final agency action within the meaning of 5 U.S.C. 704;

(h) *Hearing* means that part of a proceeding which involves the submission of evidence, either by oral presentation or written submission, to the administrative law judge;

(i) *Order* means the whole or any part of a final procedural or substantive disposition of a matter under ERISA section 502(c)(6);

(j) *Party* includes a person or agency named or admitted as a party to a proceeding;

(k) *Person* includes an individual, partnership, corporation, employee benefit plan, association, exchange or other entity or organization;

(l) *Petition* means a written request, made by a person or party, for some affirmative action;

(m) *Pleading* means the notice as defined in § 2560.502c-6(g) of this chapter, the answer to the notice, any supplement or amendment thereto, and any reply that may be permitted to any answer, supplement or amendment;

(n) *502(c)(6) civil penalty proceeding* means an adjudicatory proceeding relating to the assessment of a civil penalty provided for in section 502(c)(6) of ERISA;

(o) *Respondent* means the party against whom the Department is seeking to assess a civil sanction under ERISA section 502(c)(6);

(p) *Secretary* means the Secretary of Labor and includes, pursuant to any delegation of authority by the Secretary, any assistant secretary (including the Assistant Secretary for Employee Benefits Security), administrator, commissioner, appellate body, board, or other official; and [EBSA technical correction, 68 FR 16399 (April 3, 2003).]

(q) *Solicitor* means the Solicitor of Labor or his or her delegate.

[¶ 14,928S]

§ 2570.112 Service: Copies of documents and pleadings.

For 502(c)(6) penalty proceedings, this section shall apply in lieu of § 18.3 of this title.

(a) *General.* Copies of all documents shall be served on all parties of record. All documents should clearly designate the docket number, if any, and short title of all matters. All documents to be filed shall be delivered or mailed to the Chief Docket Clerk, Office of Administrative Law Judges, 800 K Street, NW., Suite 400, Washington, DC 20001-8002, or to the OALJ Regional Office to which the proceeding may have been transferred for hearing. Each document filed shall be clear and legible.

(b) *By parties.* All motions, petitions, pleadings, briefs, or other documents shall be filed with the Office of Administrative Law Judges with a copy, including any attachments, to all other parties of record. When a party is represented by an attorney, service shall be made upon the attorney. Service of any document upon any party may be made by personal delivery or by mailing a copy to the last known address. The Department shall be served by delivery to the Associate Solicitor, Plan Benefits Security Division, ERISA section 502(c)(6) Proceeding, P.O. Box 1914, Washington, DC 20013. The person serving the document shall certify to the manner and date of service.

(c) *By the Office of Administrative Law Judges.* Service of orders, decisions and all other documents shall be made by regular mail to the last known address.

(d) *Form of pleadings.*

(1) Every pleading shall contain information indicating the name of the Employee Benefits Security Administration (EBSA) as the agency under which the proceeding is instituted, the title of the proceeding, the docket number (if any) assigned by the Office of Administrative Law Judges and a designation of the type of pleading or paper (e.g., notice, motion to dismiss, etc.). The pleading or paper shall be signed and shall contain the address and telephone number of the party or person representing the party. Although there are no formal specifications for documents, they should be typewritten when possible on standard size 8 1/2 x 11 inch paper. [EBSA technical correction, 68 FR 16399 (April 3, 2003).]

(2) Illegible documents, whether handwritten, typewritten, photocopied, or otherwise, will not be accepted. Papers may be reproduced by any duplicating process provided all copies are clear and legible.

[¶ 14,928T]

§ 2570.113 Parties, how designated.

For 502(c)(6) civil penalty proceedings, this section shall apply in lieu of § 18.10 of this title.

(a) The term "party" wherever used in this subpart shall include any natural person, corporation, employee benefit plan, association, firm, partnership, trustee, receiver, agency, public or private organization, or government agency. A party against whom a civil penalty is sought shall be designated as "respondent". The Department shall be designated as the "complainant".

(b) Other persons or organizations shall be permitted to participate as parties only if the administrative law judge finds that the final decision could directly and adversely affect them or the class they represent, that they may contribute materially to the disposition of the proceedings and their interest is not adequately represented by existing parties, and that in the discretion of the administrative law judge the participation of such persons or organizations would be appropriate.

(c) A person or organization not named as a respondent wishing to participate as a party under this section shall submit a petition to the administrative law judge within fifteen (15) days after the person or organization has knowledge of or should have known about the proceeding. The petition shall be filed with the administrative law judge and served on each person or organization who has been made a party at the time of filing. Such petition shall concisely state:

(1) Petitioner's interest in the proceeding;

(2) How his or her participation as a party will contribute materially to the disposition of the proceeding;

(3) Who will appear for petitioner;

(4) The issues on which petitioner wishes to participate; and

(5) Whether petitioner intends to present witnesses.

(d) Objections to the petition may be filed by a party within fifteen (15) days of the filing of the petition. If objections to the petition are filed, the administrative law judge shall then determine whether petitioner has the requisite interest to be a party in the proceedings, as defined in paragraph (b) of this section, and shall permit or deny participation accordingly. Where petitions to participate as parties are made by individuals or groups with common interests, the administrative law judge may request all such petitioners to designate a single representative, or he or she may recognize one or more of such petitioners. The administrative law judge shall give each such petitioner, as well as the parties, written notice of the decision on his or her petition. For each petition granted, the administrative law judge shall provide a brief statement of the basis of the decision. If the petition is denied, he or she shall briefly state the grounds for denial and shall then treat the petition as a request for participation as amicus curiae.

[¶ 14,928U]

§ 2570.114 Consequences of default.

For 502(c)(6) civil penalty proceedings, this section shall apply in lieu of § 18.5 (a) and (b) of this title. Failure of the respondent to file an answer to the notice of determination described in § 2560.502c-6(g) of this chapter within the 30-day period provided by § 2560.502c-6(h) of this chapter shall be deemed to constitute a waiver of his or her right to appear and contest the allegations of the notice of determination, and such failure shall be deemed to be an admission of the facts as alleged in the notice for purposes of any proceeding involving the assessment of a civil penalty under section 502(c)(6) of the Act. Such notice shall then become the final order of the Secretary, within the meaning of Sec. 2570.111(g) of this subpart, forty-five (45) days from the date of service of the notice. [Revised by PWBA in 67 FR 64774 on 10-21-02 and in 68 FR 3729 on 1-24-03.]

[¶ 14,928V]

§ 2570.115 Consent order or settlement.

For 502(c)(6) civil penalty proceedings, the following shall apply in lieu of § 18.9 of this title.

(a) *General.* At any time after the commencement of a proceeding, but at least five (5) days prior to the date set for hearing, the parties jointly may move to defer the hearing for a reasonable time to permit negotiation of a settlement or an agreement containing findings and an order disposing of the whole or any part of the proceeding. The allowance of such a deferral and the duration thereof shall be in the discretion of the administrative law judge, after consideration of such factors as the nature of the proceeding, the requirements of the public interest, the representations of the parties, and the probability of reaching an agreement which will result in a just disposition of the issues involved.

(b) *Content.* Any agreement containing consent findings and an order disposing of a proceeding or any part thereof shall also provide:

(1) That the order shall have the same force and effect as an order made after full hearing;

(2) That the entire record on which any order may be based shall consist solely of the notice and the agreement;

(3) A waiver of any further procedural steps before the administrative law judge;

(4) A waiver of any right to challenge or contest the validity of the order and decision entered into in accordance with the agreement; and

(5) That the order and decision of the administrative law judge shall be final agency action.

(c) *Submission.* On or before the expiration of the time granted for negotiations, but, in any case, at least five (5) days prior to the date set for hearing, the parties or their authorized representative or their counsel may:

(1) Submit the proposed agreement containing consent findings and an order to the administrative law judge; or

(2) Notify the administrative law judge that the parties have reached a full settlement and have agreed to dismissal of the action subject to compliance with the terms of the settlement; or

(3) Inform the administrative law judge that agreement cannot be reached.

(d) *Disposition*. In the event a settlement agreement containing consent findings and an order is submitted within the time allowed therefor, the administrative law judge shall issue a decision incorporating such findings and agreement within 30 days of his receipt of such document. The decision of the administrative law judge shall incorporate all of the findings, terms, and conditions of the settlement agreement and consent order of the parties. Such decision shall become final agency action within the meaning of 5 U.S.C. 704.

(e) *Settlement without consent of all parties*. In cases in which some, but not all, of the parties to a proceeding submit a consent agreement to the administrative law judge, the following procedure shall apply:

(1) If all of the parties have not consented to the proposed settlement submitted to the administrative law judge, then such non-consenting parties must receive notice, and a copy, of the proposed settlement at the time it is submitted to the administrative law judge;

(2) Any non-consenting party shall have fifteen (15) days to file any objections to the proposed settlement with the administrative law judge and all other parties;

(3) If any party submits an objection to the proposed settlement, the administrative law judge shall decide within 30 days after receipt of such objections whether he shall sign or reject the proposed settlement. Where the record lacks substantial evidence upon which to base a decision or there is a genuine issue of material fact, then the administrative law judge may establish procedures for the purpose of receiving additional evidence upon which a decision on the contested issues may reasonably be based;

(4) If there are no objections to the proposed settlement, or if the administrative law judge decides to sign the proposed settlement after reviewing any such objections, the administrative law judge shall incorporate the consent agreement into a decision meeting the requirements of paragraph (d) of this section.

[¶ 14,928W]

§ 2570.116 **Scope of discovery**.

For 502(c)(6) civil penalty proceedings, this section shall apply in lieu of § 18.14 of this title.

(a) A party may file a motion to conduct discovery with the administrative law judge. The motion for discovery shall be granted by the administrative law judge only upon a showing of good cause. In order to establish "good cause" for the purposes of this section, a party must show that the discovery requested relates to a genuine issue as to a material fact that is relevant to the proceeding. The order of the administrative law judge shall expressly limit the scope and terms of discovery to that for which "good cause" has been shown, as provided in this paragraph.

(b) A party may obtain discovery of documents and tangible things otherwise discoverable under paragraph (a) of this section and prepared in anticipation of or for the hearing by or for another party's representative (including his or her attorney, consultant, surety, indemnitor, insurer, or agent) only upon showing that the party seeking discovery has substantial need of the materials or information in the preparation of his or her case and that he or she is unable without undue hardship to obtain the substantial equivalent of the materials or information by other means. In ordering discovery of such materials when the required showing has been made, the administrative law judge shall protect against disclosure of the mental impressions, conclusions, opinions, or legal theories of an attorney or other representatives of a party concerning the proceeding.

[¶ 14,928X]

§ 2570.117 **Summary decision**.

For 502(c)(6) civil penalty proceedings, this section shall apply in lieu of § 18.41 of this title.

(a) *No genuine issue of material fact*.

(1) Where no issue of a material fact is found to have been raised, the administrative law judge may issue a decision which, in the absence of an appeal pursuant to §§ 2570.119 through 2570.121 of this subpart, shall become a final order.

(2) A decision made under this paragraph (a) shall include a statement of:

(i) Findings of fact and conclusions of law, and the reasons therefor, on all issues presented; and

(ii) Any terms and conditions of the rule or order.

(3) A copy of any decision under this paragraph shall be served on each party.

(b) *Hearings on issues of fact*. Where a genuine question of a material fact is raised, the administrative law judge shall, and in any other case may, set the case for an evidentiary hearing.

[¶ 14,928Y]

§ 2570.118 **Decision of the administrative law judge**.

For 502(c)(6) civil penalty proceedings, this section shall apply in lieu of § 18.57 of this title.

(a) *Proposed findings of fact, conclusions, and order*. Within twenty (20) days of the filing of the transcript of the testimony, or such additional time as the administrative law judge may allow, each party may file with the administrative law judge, subject to the judge's discretion, proposed findings of fact, conclusions of law, and order together with a supporting brief expressing the reasons for such proposals. Such proposals and briefs shall be served on all parties, and shall refer to all portions of the record and to all authorities relied upon in support of each proposal.

(b) *Decision of the administrative law judge*. Within a reasonable time after the time allowed for the filing of the proposed findings of fact, conclusions of law, and order, or within 30 days after receipt of an agreement containing consent findings and order disposing of the disputed matter in whole, the administrative law judge shall make his or her decision. The decision of the administrative law judge shall include findings of fact and conclusions of law with reasons therefor upon each material issue of fact or law presented on the record. The decision of the administrative law judge shall be based upon the whole record. In a contested case in which the Department and the Respondent have presented their positions to the administrative law judge pursuant to the procedures for 502(c)(6) civil penalty proceedings as set forth in this subpart, the penalty (if any) which may be included in the decision of the administrative law judge shall be limited to the penalty expressly provided for in section 502(c)(6) of ERISA. It shall be supported by reliable and probative evidence. The decision of the administrative law judge shall become final agency action within the meaning of 5 U.S.C. 704 unless an appeal is made pursuant to the procedures set forth in §§ 2570.119 through 2570.121.

[¶ 14,928Z]

§ 2570.119 **Review by the Secretary**.

(a) The Secretary may review a decision of an administrative law judge. Such a review may occur only when a party files a notice of appeal from a decision of an administrative law judge within twenty (20) days of the issuance of such decision. In all other cases, the decision of the administrative law judge shall become final agency action within the meaning of 5 U.S.C. 704.

(b) A notice of appeal to the Secretary shall state with specificity the issue(s) in the decision of the administrative law judge on which the party is seeking review. Such notice of appeal must be served on all parties of record.

(c) Upon receipt of a notice of appeal, the Secretary shall request the Chief Administrative Law Judge to submit to him or her a copy of the entire record before the administrative law judge.

[¶ 14,928Z-1]

§ 2570.120 **Scope of review**.

The review of the Secretary shall not be a de novo proceeding but rather a review of the record established before the administrative law judge. There shall be no opportunity for oral argument.

[¶ 14,928Z-2]

§ 2570.121 **Procedures for review by the Secretary.**

(a) Upon receipt of the notice of appeal, the Secretary shall establish a briefing schedule which shall be served on all parties of record. Upon motion of one or more of the parties, the Secretary may, in his or her discretion, permit the submission of reply briefs.

(b) The Secretary shall issue a decision as promptly as possible after receipt of the briefs of the parties. The Secretary may affirm, modify, or set aside, in whole or in part, the decision on appeal and shall issue a statement of reasons and bases for the action(s) taken. Such decision by the Secretary shall be final agency action within the meaning of 5 U.S.C. 704.

Regulations

The following regulations regarding inflationary adjustments to ERISA civil monetary penalties were published in the *Federal Register* on October 21, 2002 (67 FR 64774) and revised by the PWBA on January 24, 2003 (68 FR 3729).

Subpart G—Procedures for the Assessment of Civil Penalties Under ERISA Section 502(c)(7)

[¶ 14,928MM]

§ 2570.130 **Scope of rules**. The rules of practice set forth in this subpart are applicable to "502(c)(7) civil penalty proceedings" (as defined in Sec. 2570.131(n) of this subpart) under section 502(c)(7) of the Employee Retirement Income Security Act of 1974, as amended (the Act). The rules of procedure for administrative hearings published by the Department's Office of Administrative Law Judges at Part 18 of this title will apply to matters arising under ERISA section 502(c)(7) except as modified by this subpart. These proceedings shall be conducted as expeditiously as possible, and the parties shall make every effort to avoid delay at each stage of the proceedings. [Revised by PWBA in 67 FR 64774 on 10-21-02 and in 68 FR 3729 on 1-24-03.]

[¶ 14,928NN]

§ 2570.131 **Definitions**. For 502(c)(7) civil penalty proceedings, this section shall apply in lieu of the definitions in Sec. 18.2 of this title:

(a) *Adjudicatory proceeding* means a judicial-type proceeding before an administrative law judge leading to the formulation of a final order;

(b) *Administrative law judge* means an administrative law judge appointed pursuant to the provisions of 5 U.S.C. 3105;

(c) *Answer* means a written statement that is supported by reference to specific circumstances or facts surrounding the notice of determination issued pursuant to Sec. 2560.502c-7(g) of this chapter;

(d) *Commencement of proceeding* is the filing of an answer by the respondent;

(e) *Consent agreement* means any written document containing a specified proposed remedy or other relief acceptable to the Department and consenting parties;

(f) *ERISA* means the Employee Retirement Income Security Act of 1974, as amended;

(g) *Final order* means the final decision or action of the Department of Labor concerning the assessment of a civil penalty under ERISA section 502(c)(7) against a particular party. Such final order may result from a decision of an administrative law judge or the Secretary, the failure of a party to file a statement of reasonable cause described in Sec. 2560.502c-7(e) of this chapter within the prescribed time limits, or the failure of a party to invoke the procedures for hearings or appeals under this title within the prescribed time limits. Such a final order shall constitute final agency action within the meaning of 5 U.S.C. 704;

(h) *Hearing* means that part of a proceeding which involves the submission of evidence, by either oral presentation or written submission, to the administrative law judge;

(i) *Order* means the whole or any part of a final procedural or substantive disposition of a matter under ERISA section 502(c)(7);

(j) *Party* includes a person or agency named or admitted as a party to a proceeding;

(k) *Person* includes an individual, partnership, corporation, employee benefit plan, association, exchange or other entity or organization;

(l) *Petition* means a written request, made by a person or party, for some affirmative action;

(m) *Pleading* means the notice as defined in Sec. 2560.502c-7(g) of this chapter, the answer to the notice, any supplement or amendment thereto, and any reply that may be permitted to any answer, supplement or amendment;

(n) *502(c)(7) civil penalty proceeding* means an adjudicatory proceeding relating to the assessment of a civil penalty provided for in section 502(c)(7) of ERISA;

(o) *Respondent* means the party against whom the Department is seeking to assess a civil sanction under ERISA section 502(c)(7);

(p) *Secretary* means the Secretary of Labor and includes, pursuant to any delegation of authority by the Secretary, any assistant secretary (including the Assistant Secretary for Employee Benefits Security), administrator, commissioner, appellate body, board, or other official; and [EBSA technical correction, 68 FR 16399 (April 3, 2003).]

(q) *Solicitor* means the Solicitor of Labor or his or her delegate. [Revised by PWBA in 67 FR 64774 on 10-21-02 and in 68 FR 3729 on 1-24-03.]

[¶ 14,928OO]

§ 2570.132 **Service: Copies of documents and pleadings**. For 502(c)(7) penalty proceedings, this section shall apply in lieu of Sec. 18.3 of this title.

(a) General. Copies of all documents shall be served on all parties of record. All documents should clearly designate the docket number, if any, and short title of all matters. All documents to be filed shall be delivered or mailed to the Chief Docket Clerk, Office of Administrative Law Judges, 800 K Street, NW, Suite 400, Washington, DC 20001-8002, or to the OALJ Regional Office to which the proceeding may have been transferred for hearing. Each document filed shall be clear and legible.

(b) By parties. All motions, petitions, pleadings, briefs, or other documents shall be filed with the Office of Administrative Law Judges with a copy, including any attachments, to all other parties of record. When a party is represented by an attorney, service shall be made upon the attorney. Service of any document upon any party may be made by personal delivery or by mailing a copy to the last known address. The Department shall be served by delivery to the Associate Solicitor, Plan Benefits Security Division, ERISA section 502(c)(7) Proceeding, P.O. Box 1914, Washington, DC 20013. The person serving the document shall certify to the manner and date of service.

(c) By the Office of Administrative Law Judges. Service of orders, decisions and all other documents shall be made by regular mail to the last known address.

(d) Form of pleadings. (1) Every pleading shall contain information indicating the name of the Employee Benefits Security Administration (EBSA) as the agency under which the proceeding is instituted, the title of the proceeding, the docket number (if any) assigned by the Office of Administrative Law Judges and a designation of the type of pleading or paper (e.g., notice, motion to dismiss, etc.). The pleading or paper shall be signed and shall contain the address and telephone number of the party or person representing the party. Although there are no formal specifications for documents, they should be typewritten when possible on standard size 8 1/2 x 11 inch paper. [EBSA technical correction, 68 FR 16399 (April 3, 2003).]

(2) Illegible documents, whether handwritten, typewritten, photocopied, or otherwise, will not be accepted. Papers may be reproduced by any duplicating process provided all copies are clear and legible. [Revised by PWBA in 67 FR 64774 on 10-21-02 and in 68 FR 3729 on 1-24-03.]

[¶ 14,928PP]

§ 2570.133 **Parties, how designated**. For 502(c)(7) civil penalty proceedings, this section shall apply in lieu of Sec. 18.10 of this title.

(a) The term "party" wherever used in this subpart shall include any natural person, corporation, employee benefit plan, association, firm, partnership, trustee, receiver, agency, public or private organization, or government agency. A party against whom a civil penalty is sought shall be designated as "respondent." The Department shall be designated as the "complainant."

(b) Other persons or organizations shall be permitted to participate as parties only if the administrative law judge finds that the final decision could directly and adversely affect them or the class they represent, that they may contribute materially to the disposition of the proceedings and their interest is not adequately represented by existing parties, and that in the discretion of the administrative law judge the participation of such persons or organizations would be appropriate.

(c) A person or organization not named as a respondent wishing to participate as a party under this section shall submit a petition to the administrative law judge within fifteen (15) days after the person or organization has knowledge of or should have known about the proceeding. The petition shall be filed with the administrative law judge and served on each person who or organization that has been made a party at the time of filing. Such petition shall concisely state:

(1) Petitioner's interest in the proceeding;

(2) How his or her participation as a party will contribute materially to the disposition of the proceeding;

(3) Who will appear for petitioner;

(4) The issues on which petitioner wishes to participate; and

(5) Whether petitioner intends to present witnesses.

(d) Objections to the petition may be filed by a party within fifteen (15) days of the filing of the petition. If objections to the petition are filed, the administrative law judge shall then determine whether petitioner has the requisite interest to be a party in the proceedings, as defined in paragraph (b) of this section, and shall permit or deny participation accordingly. Where petitions to participate as parties are made by individuals or groups with common interests, the administrative law judge may request all such petitioners to designate a single representative, or he or she may recognize one or more of such petitioners. The administrative law judge shall give each such petitioner, as well as the parties, written notice of the decision on his or her petition. For each petition granted, the administrative law judge shall provide a brief statement of the basis of the decision. If the petition is denied, he or she shall briefly state the grounds for denial and shall then treat the petition as a request for participation as amicus curiae. [Revised by PWBA in 67 FR 64774 on 10-21-02 and in 68 FR 3729 on 1-24-03.]

[¶ 14,928QQ]

§ 2570.134 **Consequences of default.** For 502(c)(7) civil penalty proceedings, this section shall apply in lieu of Sec. 18.5 (a) and (b) of this title. Failure of the respondent to file an answer to the notice of determination described in Sec. 2560.502c-7(g) of this chapter within the 30 day period provided by Sec. 2560.502c-7(h) of this chapter shall be deemed to constitute a waiver of his or her right to appear and contest the allegations of the notice of determination, and such failure shall be deemed to be an admission of the facts as alleged in the notice for purposes of any proceeding involving the assessment of a civil penalty under section 502(c)(7) of the Act. Such notice shall then become the final order of the Secretary, within the meaning of Sec. 2570.131(g) of this subpart, forty-five (45) days from the date of service of the notice. [Revised by PWBA in 67 FR 64774 on 10-21-02 and in 68 FR 3729 on 1-24-03.]

[¶ 14,928RR]

§ 2570.135 **Consent order or settlement**. For 502(c)(7) civil penalty proceedings, the following shall apply in lieu of Sec. 18.9 of this title.

(a) *General.* At any time after the commencement of a proceeding, but at least five (5) days prior to the date set for hearing, the parties jointly may move to defer the hearing for a reasonable time to permit negotiation of a settlement or an agreement containing findings and an order disposing of the whole or any part of the proceeding. The allowance of such a deferral and the duration thereof shall be in the discretion of the administrative law judge, after consideration of such factors as the nature of the proceeding, the requirements of the public interest, the representations of the parties, and the probability of reaching an agreement which will result in a just disposition of the issues involved.

(b) *Content.* Any agreement containing consent findings and an order disposing of a proceeding or any part thereof shall also provide:

(1) That the order shall have the same force and effect as an order made after full hearing;

(2) That the entire record on which any order may be based shall consist solely of the notice and the agreement;

(3) A waiver of any further procedural steps before the administrative law judge;

(4) A waiver of any right to challenge or contest the validity of the order and decision entered into in accordance with the agreement; and

(5) That the order and decision of the administrative law judge shall be final agency action.

(c) *Submission.* On or before the expiration of the time granted for negotiations, but, in any case, at least five (5) days prior to the date set for hearing, the parties or their authorized representative or their counsel may:

(1) Submit the proposed agreement containing consent findings and an order to the administrative law judge; or

(2) Notify the administrative law judge that the parties have reached a full settlement and have agreed to dismissal of the action subject to compliance with the terms of the settlement; or

(3) Inform the administrative law judge that agreement cannot be reached.

(d) *Disposition.* In the event a settlement agreement containing consent findings and an order is submitted within the time allowed therefor, the administrative law judge shall issue a decision incorporating such findings and agreement within 30 days of his receipt of such document. The decision of the administrative law judge shall incorporate all of the findings, terms, and conditions of the settlement agreement and consent order of the parties. Such decision shall become final agency action within the meaning of 5 U.S.C. 704.

(e) *Settlement without consent of all parties.* In cases in which some, but not all, of the parties to a proceeding submit a consent agreement to the administrative law judge, the following procedure shall apply:

(1) If all of the parties have not consented to the proposed settlement submitted to the administrative law judge, then such nonconsenting parties must receive notice, and a copy, of the proposed settlement at the time it is submitted to the administrative law judge;

(2) Any non-consenting party shall have fifteen (15) days to file any objections to the proposed settlement with the administrative law judge and all other parties;

(3) If any party submits an objection to the proposed settlement, the administrative law judge shall decide within 30 days after receipt of such objections whether he shall sign or reject the proposed settlement. Where the record lacks substantial evidence upon which to base a decision or there is a genuine issue of material fact, then the administrative law judge may establish procedures for the purpose of receiving additional evidence upon which a decision on the contested issues may reasonably be based;

(4) If there are no objections to the proposed settlement, or if the administrative law judge decides to sign the proposed settlement after reviewing any such objections, the administrative law judge shall incorporate the consent agreement into a decision meeting the requirements of paragraph (d) of this section. [Revised by PWBA in 67 FR 64774 on 10-21-02 and in 68 FR 3729 on 1-24-03.]

[¶ 14,928SS]

§ 2570.136 **Scope of discovery**. For 502(c)(7) civil penalty proceedings, this section shall apply in lieu of Sec. 18.14 of this title.

(a) A party may file a motion to conduct discovery with the administrative law judge. The motion for discovery shall be granted by the administrative law judge only upon a showing of good cause. In order to establish "good cause" for the purposes of this section, a party must show that the discovery requested relates to a genuine issue as to a material fact that is relevant to the proceeding. The order of the administrative law judge shall expressly limit the scope and terms of discovery to that for which "good cause" has been shown, as provided in this paragraph.

(b) A party may obtain discovery of documents and tangible things otherwise discoverable under paragraph (a) of this section and prepared in anticipation of or for the hearing by or for another party's representative (including his or her attorney, consultant, surety, indemnitor, insurer, or agent) only upon showing that the party seeking discovery has substantial need of the materials or information in the preparation of his or her case and that he or she is unable without undue hardship to obtain the substantial equivalent of the materials or information by other means. In ordering discovery of such materials when the required showing has been made, the administrative law judge shall protect against disclosure of the mental impressions, conclusions, opinions, or legal theories of an attorney or other representatives of a party concerning the proceeding. [Revised by PWBA in 67 FR 64774 on 10-21-02 and in 68 FR 3729 on 1-24-03.]

[¶ 14,928TT]

§ 2570.137 **Summary decision**. For 502(c)(7) civil penalty proceedings, this section shall apply in lieu of Sec. 18.41 of this title.

(a) *No genuine issue of material fact.* (1) Where no issue of a material fact is found to have been raised, the administrative law judge may issue a decision which, in the absence of an appeal pursuant to Sec. Sec. 2570.139 through 2570.141 of this subpart, shall become a final order.

(2) A decision made under paragraph (a) of this section shall include a statement of:

(i) Findings of fact and conclusions of law, and the reasons therefor, on all issues presented; and

(ii) Any terms and conditions of the rule or order.

(3) A copy of any decision under this paragraph shall be served on each party.

(b) *Hearings on issues of fact.* Where a genuine question of a material fact is raised, the administrative law judge shall, and in any other case may, set the case for an evidentiary hearing. [Revised by PWBA in 67 FR 64774 on 10-21-02 and in 68 FR 3729 on 1-24-03.]

[¶ 14,928UU]

§ 2570.138 **Decision of the administrative law judge**. For 502(c)(7) civil penalty proceedings, this section shall apply in lieu of Sec. 18.57 of this title.

(a) *Proposed findings of fact, conclusions, and order.* Within twenty (20) days of the filing of the transcript of the testimony, or such additional time as the administrative law judge may allow, each party may file with the administrative law judge, subject to the judge's discretion, proposed findings of fact, conclusions of law, and order together with a supporting brief expressing the reasons for such proposals. Such proposals and briefs shall be served on all parties, and shall refer to all portions of the record and to all authorities relied upon in support of each proposal.

(b) *Decision of the administrative law judge.* Within a reasonable time after the time allowed for the filing of the proposed findings of fact, conclusions of law, and order, or within thirty (30) days after receipt of an agreement containing consent findings and order disposing of the disputed matter in whole, the administrative law judge shall make his or her decision. The decision of the administrative law judge shall include findings of fact and conclusions of law with reasons therefor upon each material issue of fact or law presented on the record. The decision of the administrative law judge shall be based upon the whole record. In a contested case in which the Department and the Respondent have presented their positions to the administrative law judge pursuant to the procedures for 502(c)(7) civil penalty proceedings as set forth in this subpart, the penalty (if any) which may be included in the decision of the administrative law judge shall be limited to the penalty expressly provided for in section 502(c)(7) of ERISA. It shall be supported by reliable and probative evidence. The decision of the administrative law judge shall become final agency action within the meaning of 5 U.S.C. 704 unless an appeal is made pursuant to the procedures set forth in Sec. Sec. 2570.139 through 2570.141 of this subpart. [Revised by PWBA in 67 FR 64774 on 10-21-02 and in 68 FR 3729 on 1-24-03.]

[¶ 14,928VV]

§ 2570.139 **Review by the Secretary**.

(a) The Secretary may review a decision of an administrative law judge. Such a review may occur only when a party files a notice of appeal from a decision of an administrative law judge within twenty (20) days of the issuance of such decision. In all other cases, the decision of the administrative law judge shall become final agency action within the meaning of 5 U.S.C. 704.

(b) A notice of appeal to the Secretary shall state with specificity the issue(s) in the decision of the administrative law judge on which the party is seeking review. Such notice of appeal must be served on all parties of record.

(c) Upon receipt of a notice of appeal, the Secretary shall request the Chief Administrative Law Judge to submit to him or her a copy of the entire record before the administrative law judge. [Revised by PWBA in 67 FR 64774 on 10-21-02 and in 68 FR 3729 on 1-24-03.]

[¶ 14,928WW]

§ 2570.140 **Scope of review**. The review of the Secretary shall not be a de novo proceeding but rather a review of the record established before the administrative law judge. There shall be no opportunity for oral argument. [Revised by PWBA in 67 FR 64774 on 10-21-02 and in 68 FR 3729 on 1-24-03.]

[¶ 14,928XX]

§ 2570.141 **Procedures for review by the Secretary**.

(a) Upon receipt of the notice of appeal, the Secretary shall establish a briefing schedule which shall be served on all parties of record. Upon motion of one or more of the parties, the Secretary may, in his or her discretion, permit the submission of reply briefs.

(b) The Secretary shall issue a decision as promptly as possible after receipt of the briefs of the parties. The Secretary may affirm, modify, or set aside, in whole or in part, the decision on appeal and shall issue a statement of reasons and bases for the action(s) taken. Such decision by the Secretary shall be final agency action within the meaning of 5 U.S.C. 704. [Revised by PWBA in 67 FR 64774 on 10-21-02 and in 68 FR 3729 on 1-24-03.]

Regulations

The following regulations regarding inflationary adjustments to ERISA civil monetary penalties were published in the *Federal Register* on July 29, 1997 (62 FR 40696). The regulations are to be applied to violations occurring after the effective date. On August 3, 1999 (64 FR 42246), the regulations contained herein were transferred from Subpart E of part 2570 to Subpart A of a new part 2575 of Chapter XXV of title 29 of the Code of Federal Regulation (CFR) and were redesignated accordingly. The transfer was performed to simplify the organization and numbering of procedure regulations in part 2570 of the CFR. The contents of the regulations was not altered during the redesign. The regulations were amended and revised at § 2575.100, § 2575.502c-5, and § 2575.502c-6 by PWBA final regulations published in the *Federal Register* on January 22, 2003 (68 FR 2875).

Part 2575, Subpart A—Adjustment of Civil Penalties Under ERISA Title I

[¶ 14,929A]

§ 2575.100 **In general.**

Section 31001(s) of the Debt Collection Improvement Act of 1996 (the Act, Public Law 104-134, 110 Stat. 1321-373) amended the Federal Civil Penalties Inflation Adjustment Act of 1990 (the 1990 Act, Public Law 101-410, 104 Stat. 890) to require generally that the head of each Federal agency adjust the civil monetary penalties subject to its jurisdiction for inflation within 180 days after enactment of the Act and at least once every four years thereafter. [Redesignated as ERISA Reg. Sec. 2575.100, 64 FR 42245, August 3, 1999. Amended and revised by PWBA on January 22, 2003 (68 FR 1875)].

[¶ 14,929B]

§ 2575.209b-1 **Adjusted civil penalty under section 209(b).**

In accordance with the requirements of the 1990 Act, as amended, the amount of the civil monetary penalty established by section 209(b) of the Employee Retirement Income Security Act of 1974, as amended (ERISA), is hereby increased from $10 for each employee to $11 for each employee. This adjusted penalty applies only to violations occurring after July 29, 1997 [Redesignated as ERISA Reg. Sec. 2575.209b-1, 64 FR 42245, August 3, 1999].

[¶ 14,929C]

§ 2575.502c-1 **Adjusted civil penalty under section 502(c)(1).**

In accordance with the requirements of the 1990 Act, as amended, the maximum amount of the civil monetary penalty established by section 502(c)(1) of the Employee Retirement Income Security Act of 1974, as amended (ERISA), is hereby increased from $100 a day to $110 a day. This adjusted penalty applies only to violations occurring after July 29, 1997 [Redesignated as ERISA Reg. Sec. 2575.502c-1, 64 FR 42245, August 3, 1999].

[¶ 14,929D]

§ 2575.502c-2 **Adjusted civil penalty under section 502(c)(2).**

In accordance with the requirements of the 1990 Act, as amended, the maximum amount of the civil monetary penalty established by section 502(c)(2) of the Employee Retirement Income Security Act of 1974, as amended (ERISA), is hereby increased from $1000 a day to $1100 a day. This adjusted penalty applies only to violations occurring after July 29, 1997 [Redesignated as ERISA Reg. Sec. 2575.502c-2, 64 FR 42245, August 3, 1999].

[¶ 14,929E]

§ 2575.502c-3 **Adjusted civil penalty under section 502(c)(3).**

In accordance with the requirements of the 1990 Act, as amended, the maximum amount of the civil monetary penalty established by section 502(c)(3) of the Employee Retirement Income Security Act of 1974, as amended (ERISA), is hereby increased from $100 a day to $110 a day. This adjusted penalty applies only to violations occurring

after July 29, 1997 [Redesignated as ERISA Reg. Sec. 2575.502c-3, 64 FR 42245, August 3, 1999].

[¶ 14,929G]

§ 2575.502c-5 **Adjusted civil penalty under section 502(c)(5).**

In accordance with the requirements of the 1990 Act, as amended, the maximum amount of the civil monetary penalty established by section 502(c)(5) of the Employee Retirement Income Security Act of 1974, as amended (ERISA), is hereby increased from $1,000 a day to $1,100 a day. This adjusted penalty applies only to violations occurring after March 24, 2003. [Redesignated as ERISA Reg. Sec. 2575.502c-3, 64 FR 42245, August 3, 1999. Amended and revised by PWBA on January 22, 2003 (68 FR 2875)].

[¶ 14,929H]

§ 2575.502c-6 **Adjusted civil penalty under section 502(c)(6).**

In accordance with the requirements of the 1990 Act, as amended, the maximum amount of the civil monetary penalty established by section 502(c)(6) of the Employee Retirement Income Security Act of 1974, as amended (ERISA), is hereby increased from $100 a day but in no event in excess of $1,000 per request to $110 a day but in no event in excess of $1,100 per request. This adjusted penalty applies only to violations occurring after March 24, 2003. [Redesignated as ERISA Reg. Sec. 2575.502c-3, 64 FR 42245, August 3, 1999. Amended and revised by PWBA on January 22, 2003 (68 FR 2875)].

[¶ 14,929L]

Part 2575, Subpart B. Reserved [Added and Reserved, 64 FR 42245, August 3, 1999].

[¶ 14,929M]

Part 2575, Subpart C. Reserved [Added and Reserved, 64 FR 42245, August 3, 1999].

[¶ 14,929N]

Part 2575, Subpart D. Reserved [Added and Reserved, 64 FR 42245, August 3, 1999].

[¶ 14,930]
CLAIMS PROCEDURE

Act Sec. 503. In accordance with regulations of the Secretary, every employee benefit plan shall—

(1) provide adequate notice in writing to any participant or beneficiary whose claim for benefits under the plan has been denied, setting forth the specific reasons for such denial, written in a manner calculated to be understood by the participant, and

(2) afford a reasonable opportunity to any participant whose claim for benefits has been denied for a full and fair review by the appropriate named fiduciary of the decision denying the claim.

Regulations

The following regulations were adopted under "Title 29—Labor," "Chapter XXV—Pension and Welfare Benefit Programs," "Subchapter G—Administration and Enforcement Under the Employee Retirement Income Security Act of 1974," "Part 2560—Rules and Regulations for Administration and Enforcement." The regulations were filed with the Federal Register on May 25, 1977, and published in the *Federal Register* of May 27, 1977 (42 FR 27426). The regulations are effective for claims filed on or after October 1, 1977. Regulation § 2560.503-1 was amended by revising paragraph (b)(1)(i) and adding a new paragraph (j) by 46 FR 5882 and published in the *Federal Register* on January 21, 1981. The regulations were amended by 65 FR 70264 and published in the *Federal Register* on November 21, 2000. Regulation Sec. 2560.503-1 was amended by revising paragraph (o) by 66 FR 35885 and published in the *Federal Register* on July 9, 2001.

[¶ 14,931]

§ 2560.503-1 **Claims procedure.**

(a) *Scope and purpose.* In accordance with the authority of sections 503 and 505 of the Employee Retirement Income Security Act of 1974 (ERISA or the Act), 29 U.S.C. 1133, 1135, this section sets forth minimum requirements for employee benefit plan procedures pertaining to claims for benefits by participants and beneficiaries (hereinafter referred to as claimants). Except as otherwise specifically provided in this section, these requirements apply to every employee benefit plan described in section 4(a) and not exempted under section 4(b) of the Act.

(b) *Obligation to establish and maintain reasonable claims procedures.* Every employee benefit plan shall establish and maintain reasonable procedures governing the filing of benefit claims, notification of benefit determinations, and appeal of adverse benefit determinations

(hereinafter collectively referred to as claims procedures). The claims procedures for a plan will be deemed to be reasonable only if—

(1) The claims procedures comply with the requirements of paragraphs (c), (d), (e), (f), (g), (h), (i), and (j) of this section, as appropriate, except to the extent that the claims procedures are deemed to comply with some or all of such provisions pursuant to paragraph (b)(6) of this section;

(2) A description of all claims procedures (including, in the case of a group health plan within the meaning of paragraph (m)(6) of this section, any procedures for obtaining prior approval as a prerequisite for obtaining a benefit, such as preauthorization procedures or utilization review procedures) and the applicable time frames is included as part of a summary plan description meeting the requirements of 29 CFR 2520.102-3;

(3) The claims procedures do not contain any provision, and are not administered in a way, that unduly inhibits or hampers the initiation or processing of claims for benefits. For example, a provision or

practice that requires payment of a fee or costs as a condition to making a claim or to appealing an adverse benefit determination would be considered to unduly inhibit the initiation and processing of claims for benefits. Also, the denial of a claim for failure to obtain a prior approval under circumstances that would make obtaining such prior approval impossible or where application of the prior approval process could seriously jeopardize the life or health of the claimant (e.g., in the case of a group health plan, the claimant is unconscious and in need of immediate care at the time medical treatment is required) would constitute a practice that unduly inhibits the initiation and processing of a claim;

(4) The claims procedures do not preclude an authorized representative of a claimant from acting on behalf of such claimant in pursuing a benefit claim or appeal of an adverse benefit determination. Nevertheless, a plan may establish reasonable procedures for determining whether an individual has been authorized to act on behalf of a claimant, provided that, in the case of a claim involving urgent care, within the meaning of paragraph (m)(1) of this section, a health care professional, within the meaning of paragraph (m)(7) of this section, with knowledge of a claimant's medical condition shall be permitted to act as the authorized representative of the claimant; and

(5) The claims procedures contain administrative processes and safeguards designed to ensure and to verify that benefit claim determinations are made in accordance with governing plan documents and that, where appropriate, the plan provisions have been applied consistently with respect to similarly situated claimants.

(6) In the case of a plan established and maintained pursuant to a collective bargaining agreement (other than a plan subject to the provisions of section 302(c)(5) of the Labor Management Relations Act, 1947 concerning joint representation on the board of trustees)—

(i) Such plan will be deemed to comply with the provisions of paragraphs (c) through (j) of this section if the collective bargaining agreement pursuant to which the plan is established or maintained sets forth or incorporates by specific reference—

(A) Provisions concerning the filing of benefit claims and the initial disposition of benefit claims, and

(B) A grievance and arbitration procedure to which adverse benefit determinations are subject.

(ii) Such plan will be deemed to comply with the provisions of paragraphs (h), (i), and (j) of this section (but will not be deemed to comply with paragraphs (c) through (g) of this section) if the collective bargaining agreement pursuant to which the plan is established or maintained sets forth or incorporates by specific reference a grievance and arbitration procedure to which adverse benefit determinations are subject (but not provisions concerning the filing and initial disposition of benefit claims).

(c) *Group health plans.* The claims procedures of a group health plan will be deemed to be reasonable only if, in addition to complying with the requirements of paragraph (b) of this section—

(1)(i) The claims procedures provide that, in the case of a failure by a claimant or an authorized representative of a claimant to follow the plan's procedures for filing a pre-service claim, within the meaning of paragraph (m)(2) of this section, the claimant or representative shall be notified of the failure and the proper procedures to be followed in filing a claim for benefits. This notification shall be provided to the claimant or authorized representative, as appropriate, as soon as possible, but not later than 5 days (24 hours in the case of a failure to file a claim involving urgent care) following the failure. Notification may be oral, unless written notification is requested by the claimant or authorized representative.

(ii) Paragraph (c)(1)(i) of this section shall apply only in the case of a failure that—

(A) Is a communication by a claimant or an authorized representative of a claimant that is received by a person or organizational unit customarily responsible for handling benefit matters; and

(B) Is a communication that names a specific claimant; a specific medical condition or symptom; and a specific treatment, service, or product for which approval is requested.

(2) The claims procedures do not contain any provision, and are not administered in a way, that requires a claimant to file more than two appeals of an adverse benefit determination prior to bringing a civil action under section 502(a) of the Act;

(3) To the extent that a plan offers voluntary levels of appeal (except to the extent that the plan is required to do so by State law), including voluntary arbitration or any other form of dispute resolution, in addition to those permitted by paragraph (c)(2) of this section, the claims procedures provide that:

(i) The plan waives any right to assert that a claimant has failed to exhaust administrative remedies because the claimant did not elect to submit a benefit dispute to any such voluntary level of appeal provided by the plan;

(ii) The plan agrees that any statute of limitations or other defense based on timeliness is tolled during the time that any such voluntary appeal is pending;

(iii) The claims procedures provide that a claimant may elect to submit a benefit dispute to such voluntary level of appeal only after exhaustion of the appeals permitted by paragraph (c)(2) of this section;

(iv) The plan provides to any claimant, upon request, sufficient information relating to the voluntary level of appeal to enable the claimant to make an informed judgment about whether to submit a benefit dispute to the voluntary level of appeal, including a statement that the decision of a claimant as to whether or not to submit a benefit dispute to the voluntary level of appeal will have no effect on the claimant's rights to any other benefits under the plan and information about the applicable rules, the claimant's right to representation, the process for selecting the decisionmaker, and the circumstances, if any, that may affect the impartiality of the decisionmaker, such as any financial or personal interests in the result or any past or present relationship with any party to the review process; and

(v) No fees or costs are imposed on the claimant as part of the voluntary level of appeal.

(4) The claims procedures do not contain any provision for the mandatory arbitration of adverse benefit determinations, except to the extent that the plan or procedures provide that:

(i) The arbitration is conducted as one of the two appeals described in paragraph (c)(2) of this section and in accordance with the requirements applicable to such appeals; and

(ii) The claimant is not precluded from challenging the decision under section 502(a) of the Act or other applicable law.

(d) *Plans providing disability benefits.* The claims procedures of a plan that provides disability benefits will be deemed to be reasonable only if the claims procedures comply, with respect to claims for disability benefits, with the requirements of paragraphs (b), (c)(2), (c)(3), and (c)(4) of this section.

(e) *Claim for benefits.* For purposes of this section, a claim for benefits is a request for a plan benefit or benefits made by a claimant in accordance with a plan's reasonable procedure for filing benefit claims. In the case of a group health plan, a claim for benefits includes any pre-service claims within the meaning of paragraph (m)(2) of this section and any post-service claims within the meaning of paragraph (m)(3) of this section.

(f) *Timing of notification of benefit determination.* (1) *In general.* Except as provided in paragraphs (f)(2) and (f)(3) of this section, if a claim is wholly or partially denied, the plan administrator shall notify the claimant, in accordance with paragraph (g) of this section, of the plan's adverse benefit determination within a reasonable period of time, but not later than 90 days after receipt of the claim by the plan, unless the plan administrator determines that special circumstances require an extension of time for processing the claim. If the plan administrator determines that an extension of time for processing is required, written notice of the extension shall be furnished to the claimant prior to the termination of the initial 90day period. In no event shall such extension exceed a period of 90 days from the end of such initial period. The extension notice shall indicate the special circumstances requiring an extension of time and the date by which the plan expects to render the benefit determination.

(2) *Group health plans.* In the case of a group health plan, the plan administrator shall notify a claimant of the plan's benefit determi-

nation in accordance with paragraph (f)(2)(i), (f)(2)(ii), or (f)(2)(iii) of this section, as appropriate.

(i) *Urgent care claims.* In the case of a claim involving urgent care, the plan administrator shall notify the claimant of the plan's benefit determination (whether adverse or not) as soon as possible, taking into account the medical exigencies, but not later than 72 hours after receipt of the claim by the plan, unless the claimant fails to provide sufficient information to determine whether, or to what extent, benefits are covered or payable under the plan. In the case of such a failure, the plan administrator shall notify the claimant as soon as possible, but not later than 24 hours after receipt of the claim by the plan, of the specific information necessary to complete the claim. The claimant shall be afforded a reasonable amount of time, taking into account the circumstances, but not less than 48 hours, to provide the specified information. Notification of any adverse benefit determination pursuant to this paragraph (f)(2)(i) shall be made in accordance with paragraph (g) of this section. The plan administrator shall notify the claimant of the plan's benefit determination as soon as possible, but in no case later than 48 hours after the earlier of—

(A) The plan's receipt of the specified information, or

(B) The end of the period afforded the claimant to provide the specified additional information.

(ii) *Concurrent care decisions.* If a group health plan has approved an ongoing course of treatment to be provided over a period of time or number of treatments—

(A) Any reduction or termination by the plan of such course of treatment (other than by plan amendment or termination) before the end of such period of time or number of treatments shall constitute an adverse benefit determination. The plan administrator shall notify the claimant, in accordance with paragraph (g) of this section, of the adverse benefit determination at a time sufficiently in advance of the reduction or termination to allow the claimant to appeal and obtain a determination on review of that adverse benefit determination before the benefit is reduced or terminated.

(B) Any request by a claimant to extend the course of treatment beyond the period of time or number of treatments that is a claim involving urgent care shall be decided as soon as possible, taking into account the medical exigencies, and the plan administrator shall notify the claimant of the benefit determination, whether adverse or not, within 24 hours after receipt of the claim by the plan, provided that any such claim is made to the plan at least 24 hours prior to the expiration of the prescribed period of time or number of treatments. Notification of any adverse benefit determination concerning a request to extend the course of treatment, whether involving urgent care or not, shall be made in accordance with paragraph (g) of this section, and appeal shall be governed by paragraph (i)(2)(i), (i)(2)(ii), or (i)(2)(iii), as appropriate.

(iii) *Other claims.* In the case of a claim not described in paragraphs (f)(2)(i) or (f)(2)(ii) of this section, the plan administrator shall notify the claimant of the plan's benefit determination in accordance with either paragraph (f)(2)(iii)(A) or (f)(2)(iii)(B) of this section, as appropriate.

(A) *Pre-service claims.* In the case of a pre-service claim, the plan administrator shall notify the claimant of the plan's benefit determination (whether adverse or not) within a reasonable period of time appropriate to the medical circumstances, but not later than 15 days after receipt of the claim by the plan. This period may be extended one time by the plan for up to 15 days, provided that the plan administrator both determines that such an extension is necessary due to matters beyond the control of the plan and notifies the claimant, prior to the expiration of the initial 15-day period, of the circumstances requiring the extension of time and the date by which the plan expects to render a decision. If such an extension is necessary due to a failure of the claimant to submit the information necessary to decide the claim, the notice of extension shall specifically describe the required information, and the claimant shall be afforded at least 45 days from receipt of the notice within which to provide the specified information. Notification of any adverse benefit determination pursuant to this paragraph (f)(2)(iii)(A) shall be made in accordance with paragraph (g) of this section.

(B) *Post-service claims.* In the case of a post-service claim, the plan administrator shall notify the claimant, in accordance with paragraph (g) of this section, of the plan's adverse benefit determination within a reasonable period of time, but not later than 30 days after receipt of the claim. This period may be extended one time by the plan for up to 15 days, provided that the plan administrator both determines that such an extension is necessary due to matters beyond the control of the plan and notifies the claimant, prior to the expiration of the initial 30-day period, of the circumstances requiring the extension of time and the date by which the plan expects to render a decision. If such an extension is necessary due to a failure of the claimant to submit the information necessary to decide the claim, the notice of extension shall specifically describe the required information, and the claimant shall be afforded at least 45 days from receipt of the notice within which to provide the specified information.

(3) *Disability claims.* In the case of a claim for disability benefits, the plan administrator shall notify the claimant, in accordance with paragraph (g) of this section, of the plan's adverse benefit determination within a reasonable period of time, but not later than 45 days after receipt of the claim by the plan. This period may be extended by the plan for up to 30 days, provided that the plan administrator both determines that such an extension is necessary due to matters beyond the control of the plan and notifies the claimant, prior to the expiration of the initial 45-day period, of the circumstances requiring the extension of time and the date by which the plan expects to render a decision. If, prior to the end of the first 30-day extension period, the administrator determines that, due to matters beyond the control of the plan, a decision cannot be rendered within that extension period, the period for making the determination may be extended for up to an additional 30 days, provided that the plan administrator notifies the claimant, prior to the expiration of the first 30-day extension period, of the circumstances requiring the extension and the date as of which the plan expects to render a decision. In the case of any extension under this paragraph (f)(3), the notice of extension shall specifically explain the standards on which entitlement to a benefit is based, the unresolved issues that prevent a decision on the claim, and the additional information needed to resolve those issues, and the claimant shall be afforded at least 45 days within which to provide the specified information.

(4) *Calculating time periods.* For purposes of paragraph (f) of this section, the period of time within which a benefit determination is required to be made shall begin at the time a claim is filed in accordance with the reasonable procedures of a plan, without regard to whether all the information necessary to make a benefit determination accompanies the filing. In the event that a period of time is extended as permitted pursuant to paragraph (f)(2)(iii) or (f)(3) of this section due to a claimant's failure to submit information necessary to decide a claim, the period for making the benefit determination shall be tolled from the date on which the notification of the extension is sent to the claimant until the date on which the claimant responds to the request for additional information.

(g) *Manner and content of notification of benefit determination.* (1) Except as provided in paragraph (g)(2) of this section, the plan administrator shall provide a claimant with written or electronic notification of any adverse benefit determination. Any electronic notification shall comply with the standards imposed by 29 CFR 2520.104b-1(c)(1)(i), (iii), and (iv). The notification shall set forth, in a manner calculated to be understood by the claimant—

(i) The specific reason or reasons for the adverse determination;

(ii) Reference to the specific plan provisions on which the determination is based;

(iii) A description of any additional material or information necessary for the claimant to perfect the claim and an explanation of why such material or information is necessary;

(iv) A description of the plan's review procedures and the time limits applicable to such procedures, including a statement of the claimant's right to bring a civil action under section 502(a) of the Act following an adverse benefit determination on review;

(v) In the case of an adverse benefit determination by a group health plan or a plan providing disability benefits,

(A) If an internal rule, guideline, protocol, or other similar criterion was relied upon in making the adverse determination, either the specific rule, guideline, protocol, or other similar criterion; or a statement that such a rule, guideline, protocol, or other similar criterion was relied upon in making the adverse determination and that a copy of such rule, guideline, protocol, or other criterion will be provided free of charge to the claimant upon request; or

(B) If the adverse benefit determination is based on a medical necessity or experimental treatment or similar exclusion or limit, either an explanation of the scientific or clinical judgment for the determination, applying the terms of the plan to the claimant's medical circumstances, or a statement that such explanation will be provided free of charge upon request.

(vi) In the case of an adverse benefit determination by a group health plan concerning a claim involving urgent care, a description of the expedited review process applicable to such claims.

(2) In the case of an adverse benefit determination by a group health plan concerning a claim involving urgent care, the information described in paragraph (g)(1) of this section may be provided to the claimant orally within the time frame prescribed in paragraph (f)(2)(i) of this section, provided that a written or electronic notification in accordance with paragraph (g)(1) of this section is furnished to the claimant not later than 3 days after the oral notification.

(h) *Appeal of adverse benefit determinations.* (1) In general. Every employee benefit plan shall establish and maintain a procedure by which a claimant shall have a reasonable opportunity to appeal an adverse benefit determination to an appropriate named fiduciary of the plan, and under which there will be a full and fair review of the claim and the adverse benefit determination.

(2) *Full and fair review.* Except as provided in paragraphs (h)(3) and (h)(4) of this section, the claims procedures of a plan will not be deemed to provide a claimant with a reasonable opportunity for a full and fair review of a claim and adverse benefit determination unless the claims procedures—

(i) Provide claimants at least 60 days following receipt of a notification of an adverse benefit determination within which to appeal the determination;

(ii) Provide claimants the opportunity to submit written comments, documents, records, and other information relating to the claim for benefits;

(iii) Provide that a claimant shall be provided, upon request and free of charge, reasonable access to, and copies of, all documents, records, and other information relevant to the claimant's claim for benefits. Whether a document, record, or other information is relevant to a claim for benefits shall be determined by reference to paragraph (m)(8) of this section;

(iv) Provide for a review that takes into account all comments, documents, records, and other information submitted by the claimant relating to the claim, without regard to whether such information was submitted or considered in the initial benefit determination.

(3) *Group health plans.* The claims procedures of a group health plan will not be deemed to provide a claimant with a reasonable opportunity for a full and fair review of a claim and adverse benefit determination unless, in addition to complying with the requirements of paragraphs (h)(2)(ii) through (iv) of this section, the claims procedures—

(i) Provide claimants at least 180 days following receipt of a notification of an adverse benefit determination within which to appeal the determination;

(ii) Provide for a review that does not afford deference to the initial adverse benefit determination and that is conducted by an appropriate named fiduciary of the plan who is neither the individual who made the adverse benefit determination that is the subject of the appeal, nor the subordinate of such individual;

(iii) Provide that, in deciding an appeal of any adverse benefit determination that is based in whole or in part on a medical judgment, including determinations with regard to whether a particular treatment, drug, or other item is experimental, investigational, or not medically necessary or appropriate, the appropriate named fiduciary shall consult

with a health care professional who has appropriate training and experience in the field of medicine involved in the medical judgment;

(iv) Provide for the identification of medical or vocational experts whose advice was obtained on behalf of the plan in connection with a claimant's adverse benefit determination, without regard to whether the advice was relied upon in making the benefit determination;

(v) Provide that the health care professional engaged for purposes of a consultation under paragraph (h)(3)(iii) of this section shall be an individual who is neither an individual who was consulted in connection with the adverse benefit determination that is the subject of the appeal, nor the subordinate of any such individual; and

(vi) Provide, in the case of a claim involving urgent care, for an expedited review process pursuant to which—

(A) A request for an expedited appeal of an adverse benefit determination may be submitted orally or in writing by the claimant; and

(B) All necessary information, including the plan's benefit determination on review, shall be transmitted between the plan and the claimant by telephone, facsimile, or other available similarly expeditious method.

(4) *Plans providing disability benefits.* The claims procedures of a plan providing disability benefits will not, with respect to claims for such benefits, be deemed to provide a claimant with a reasonable opportunity for a full and fair review of a claim and adverse benefit determination unless the claims procedures comply with the requirements of paragraphs (h)(2)(ii) through (iv) and (h)(3)(i) through (v) of this section.

(i) *Timing of notification of benefit determination on review.* (1) *In general.* (i) Except as provided in paragraphs (i)(1)(ii), (i)(2), and (i)(3) of this section, the plan administrator shall notify a claimant in accordance with paragraph (j) of this section of the plan's benefit determination on review within a reasonable period of time, but not later than 60 days after receipt of the claimant's request for review by the plan, unless the plan administrator determines that special circumstances (such as the need to hold a hearing, if the plan's procedures provide for a hearing) require an extension of time for processing the claim. If the plan administrator determines that an extension of time for processing is required, written notice of the extension shall be furnished to the claimant prior to the termination of the initial 60-day period. In no event shall such extension exceed a period of 60 days from the end of the initial period. The extension notice shall indicate the special circumstances requiring an extension of time and the date by which the plan expects to render the determination on review.

(ii) In the case of a plan with a committee or board of trustees designated as the appropriate named fiduciary that holds regularly scheduled meetings at least quarterly, paragraph (i)(1)(i) of this section shall not apply, and, except as provided in paragraphs (i)(2) and (i)(3) of this section, the appropriate named fiduciary shall instead make a benefit determination no later than the date of the meeting of the committee or board that immediately follows the plan's receipt of a request for review, unless the request for review is filed within 30 days preceding the date of such meeting. In such case, a benefit determination may be made by no later than the date of the second meeting following the plan's receipt of the request for review. If special circumstances (such as the need to hold a hearing, if the plan's procedures provide for a hearing) require a further extension of time for processing, a benefit determination shall be rendered not later than the third meeting of the committee or board following the plan's receipt of the request for review. If such an extension of time for review is required because of special circumstances, the plan administrator shall provide the claimant with written notice of the extension, describing the special circumstances and the date as of which the benefit determination will be made, prior to the commencement of the extension. The plan administrator shall notify the claimant, in accordance with paragraph (j) of this section, of the benefit determination as soon as possible, but not later than 5 days after the benefit determination is made.

(2) *Group health plans.* In the case of a group health plan, the plan administrator shall notify a claimant of the plan's benefit determi-

nation on review in accordance with paragraphs (i)(2)(i) through (iii), as appropriate.

(i) *Urgent care claims.* In the case of a claim involving urgent care, the plan administrator shall notify the claimant, in accordance with paragraph (j) of this section, of the plan's benefit determination on review as soon as possible, taking into account the medical exigencies, but not later than 72 hours after receipt of the claimant's request for review of an adverse benefit determination by the plan.

(ii) *Pre-service claims.* In the case of a pre-service claim, the plan administrator shall notify the claimant, in accordance with paragraph (j) of this section, of the plan's benefit determination on review within a reasonable period of time appropriate to the medical circumstances. In the case of a group health plan that provides for one appeal of an adverse benefit determination, such notification shall be provided not later than 30 days after receipt by the plan of the claimant's request for review of an adverse benefit determination. In the case of a group health plan that provides for two appeals of an adverse determination, such notification shall be provided, with respect to any one of such two appeals, not later than 15 days after receipt by the plan of the claimant's request for review of the adverse determination.

(iii) *Post-service claims.* (A) In the case of a post-service claim, except as provided in paragraph (i)(2)(iii)(B) of this section, the plan administrator shall notify the claimant, in accordance with paragraph (j) of this section, of the plan's benefit determination on review within a reasonable period of time. In the case of a group health plan that provides for one appeal of an adverse benefit determination, such notification shall be provided not later than 60 days after receipt by the plan of the claimant's request for review of an adverse benefit determination. In the case of a group health plan that provides for two appeals of an adverse determination, such notification shall be provided, with respect to any one of such two appeals, not later than 30 days after receipt by the plan of the claimant's request for review of the adverse determination.

(B) In the case of a multiemployer plan with a committee or board of trustees designated as the appropriate named fiduciary that holds regularly scheduled meetings at least quarterly, paragraph (i)(2)(iii)(A) of this section shall not apply, and the appropriate named fiduciary shall instead make a benefit determination no later than the date of the meeting of the committee or board that immediately follows the plan's receipt of a request for review, unless the request for review is filed within 30 days preceding the date of such meeting. In such case, a benefit determination may be made by no later than the date of the second meeting following the plan's receipt of the request for review. If special circumstances (such as the need to hold a hearing, if the plan's procedures provide for a hearing) require a further extension of time for processing, a benefit determination shall be rendered not later than the third meeting of the committee or board following the plan's receipt of the request for review. If such an extension of time for review is required because of special circumstances, the plan administrator shall notify the claimant in writing of the extension, describing the special circumstances and the date as of which the benefit determination will be made, prior to the commencement of the extension. The plan administrator shall notify the claimant, in accordance with paragraph (j) of this section, of the benefit determination as soon as possible, but not later than 5 days after the benefit determination is made.

(3) *Disability claims.* (i) Except as provided in paragraph (i)(3)(ii) of this section, claims involving disability benefits (whether the plan provides for one or two appeals) shall be governed by paragraph (i)(1) of this section, except that a period of 45 days shall apply instead of 60 days for purposes of that paragraph.

(ii) In the case of a multiemployer plan with a committee or board of trustees designated as the appropriate named fiduciary that holds regularly scheduled meetings at least quarterly, paragraph (i)(3)(i) of this section shall not apply, and the appropriate named fiduciary shall instead make a benefit determination no later than the date of the meeting of the committee or board that immediately follows the plan's receipt of a request for review, unless the request for review is filed within 30 days preceding the date of such meeting. In such case, a benefit determination may be made by no later than the date of the second meeting following the plan's receipt of the request for

review. If special circumstances (such as the need to hold a hearing, if the plan's procedures provide for a hearing) require a further extension of time for processing, a benefit determination shall be rendered not later than the third meeting of the committee or board following the plan's receipt of the request for review. If such an extension of time for review is required because of special circumstances, the plan administrator shall notify the claimant in writing of the extension, describing the special circumstances and the date as of which the benefit determination will be made, prior to the commencement of the extension. The plan administrator shall notify the claimant, in accordance with paragraph (j) of this section, of the benefit determination as soon as possible, but not later than 5 days after the benefit determination is made.

(4) *Calculating time periods.* For purposes of paragraph (i) of this section, the period of time within which a benefit determination on review is required to be made shall begin at the time an appeal is filed in accordance with the reasonable procedures of a plan, without regard to whether all the information necessary to make a benefit determination on review accompanies the filing. In the event that a period of time is extended as permitted pursuant to paragraph (i)(1), (i)(2)(iii)(B), or (i)(3) of this section due to a claimant's failure to submit information necessary to decide a claim, the period for making the benefit determination on review shall be tolled from the date on which the notification of the extension is sent to the claimant until the date on which the claimant responds to the request for additional information.

(5) *Furnishing documents.* In the case of an adverse benefit determination on review, the plan administrator shall provide such access to, and copies of, documents, records, and other information described in paragraphs (j)(3), (j)(4), and (j)(5) of this section as is appropriate.

(j) *Manner and content of notification of benefit determination on review.* The plan administrator shall provide a claimant with written or electronic notification of a plan's benefit determination on review. Any electronic notification shall comply with the standards imposed by 29 CFR 2520.104b-1(c)(1)(i), (iii), and (iv). In the case of an adverse benefit determination, the notification shall set forth, in a manner calculated to be understood by the claimant—

(1) The specific reason or reasons for the adverse determination;

(2) Reference to the specific plan provisions on which the benefit determination is based;

(3) A statement that the claimant is entitled to receive, upon request and free of charge, reasonable access to, and copies of, all documents, records, and other information relevant to the claimant's claim for benefits. Whether a document, record, or other information is relevant to a claim for benefits shall be determined by reference to paragraph (m)(8) of this section;

(4) A statement describing any voluntary appeal procedures offered by the plan and the claimant's right to obtain the information about such procedures described in paragraph (c)(3)(iv) of this section, and a statement of the claimant's right to bring an action under section 502(a) of the Act; and

(5) In the case of a group health plan or a plan providing disability benefits—

(i) If an internal rule, guideline, protocol, or other similar criterion was relied upon in making the adverse determination, either the specific rule, guideline, protocol, or other similar criterion; or a statement that such rule, guideline, protocol, or other similar criterion was relied upon in making the adverse determination and that a copy of the rule, guideline, protocol, or other similar criterion will be provided free of charge to the claimant upon request;

(ii) If the adverse benefit determination is based on a medical necessity or experimental treatment or similar exclusion or limit, either an explanation of the scientific or clinical judgment for the determination, applying the terms of the plan to the claimant's medical circumstances, or a statement that such explanation will be provided free of charge upon request; and

(iii) The following statement: "You and your plan may have other voluntary alternative dispute resolution options, such as mediation. One way to find out what may be available is to contact your local

U.S. Department of Labor Office and your State insurance regulatory agency."

(k) *Preemption of State law.* (1) Nothing in this section shall be construed to supersede any provision of State law that regulates insurance, except to the extent that such law prevents the application of a requirement of this section.

(2)(i) For purposes of paragraph (k)(1) of this section, a State law regulating insurance shall not be considered to prevent the application of a requirement of this section merely because such State law establishes a review procedure to evaluate and resolve disputes involving adverse benefit determinations under group health plans so long as the review procedure is conducted by a person or entity other than the insurer, the plan, plan fiduciaries, the employer, or any employee or agent of any of the foregoing.

(ii) The State law procedures described in paragraph (k)(2)(i) of this section are not part of the full and fair review required by section 503 of the Act. Claimants therefore need not exhaust such State law procedures prior to bringing suit under section 502(a) of the Act.

(l) *Failure to establish and follow reasonable claims procedures.* In the case of the failure of a plan to establish or follow claims procedures consistent with the requirements of this section, a claimant shall be deemed to have exhausted the administrative remedies available under the plan and shall be entitled to pursue any available remedies under section 502(a) of the Act on the basis that the plan has failed to provide a reasonable claims procedure that would yield a decision on the merits of the claim.

(m) *Definitions.* The following terms shall have the meaning ascribed to such terms in this paragraph (m) whenever such term is used in this section:

(1)(i) A "claim involving urgent care" is any claim for medical care or treatment with respect to which the application of the time periods for making non-urgent care determinations—

(A) Could seriously jeopardize the life or health of the claimant or the ability of the claimant to regain maximum function, or,

(B) In the opinion of a physician with knowledge of the claimant's medical condition, would subject the claimant to severe pain that cannot be adequately managed without the care or treatment that is the subject of the claim.

(ii) Except as provided in paragraph (m)(1)(iii) of this section, whether a claim is a "claim involving urgent care" within the meaning of paragraph (m)(1)(i)(A) of this section is to be determined by an individual acting on behalf of the plan applying the judgment of a prudent layperson who possesses an average knowledge of health and medicine.

(iii) Any claim that a physician with knowledge of the claimant's medical condition determines is a "claim involving urgent care" within the meaning of paragraph (m)(1)(i) of this section shall be treated as a "claim involving urgent care" for purposes of this section.

(2) The term "pre-service claim" means any claim for a benefit under a group health plan with respect to which the terms of the plan condition receipt of the benefit, in whole or in part, on approval of the benefit in advance of obtaining medical care.

(3) The term "post-service claim" means any claim for a benefit under a group health plan that is not a pre-service claim within the meaning of paragraph (m)(2) of this section.

(4) The term "adverse benefit determination" means any of the following: a denial, reduction, or termination of, or a failure to provide or make payment (in whole or in part) for, a benefit, including any such denial, reduction, termination, or failure to provide or make payment that is based on a determination of a participant's or beneficiary's eligibility to participate in a plan, and including, with respect to group health plans, a denial, reduction, or termination of, or a failure to provide or make payment (in whole or in part) for, a benefit resulting from the application of any utilization review, as well as a failure to cover an item or service for which benefits are otherwise provided because it is determined to be experimental or investigational or not medically necessary or appropriate.

(5) The term "notice" or "notification" means the delivery or furnishing of information to an individual in a manner that satisfies the standards of 29 CFR 2520.104b-1(b) as appropriate with respect to material required to be furnished or made available to an individual.

(6) The term "group health plan" means an employee welfare benefit plan within the meaning of section 3(1) of the Act to the extent that such plan provides "medical care" within the meaning of section 733(a) of the Act.

(7) The term "health care professional" means a physician or other health care professional licensed, accredited, or certified to perform specified health services consistent with State law.

(8) A document, record, or other information shall be considered "relevant" to a claimant's claim if such document, record, or other information

(i) Was relied upon in making the benefit determination;

(ii) Was submitted, considered, or generated in the course of making the benefit determination, without regard to whether such document, record, or other information was relied upon in making the benefit determination;

(iii) Demonstrates compliance with the administrative processes and safeguards required pursuant to paragraph (b)(5) of this section in making the benefit determination; or

(iv) In the case of a group health plan or a plan providing disability benefits, constitutes a statement of policy or guidance with respect to the plan concerning the denied treatment option or benefit for the claimant's diagnosis, without regard to whether such advice or statement was relied upon in making the benefit determination.

(n) *Apprenticeship plans.* This section does not apply to employee benefit plans that solely provide apprenticeship training benefits.

(o) *Applicability dates*

(1) Except as provided in paragraph (o)(2) of this section, this section shall apply to claims filed under a plan on or after January 1, 2002.

(2) This section shall apply to claims filed under a group health plan on or after the first day of the first plan year beginning on or after July 1, 2002, but in no event later than January 1, 2003. [Revised July 9, 2001, 66 FR 35885.]

[¶ 14,940]
INVESTIGATIVE AUTHORITY

Act Sec. 504. (a) The Secretary shall have the power, in order to determine whether any person has violated or is about to violate any provision of this title or any regulation or order thereunder—

(1) to make an investigation, and in connection therewith to require the submission of reports, books, and records, and the filing of data in support of any information required to be filed with the Secretary under this title, and

(2) to enter such places, inspect such books and records and question such persons as he may deem necessary to enable him to determine the facts relative to such investigation, if he has reasonable cause to believe there may exist a violation of this title or any rule or regulation issued thereunder or if the entry is pursuant to an agreement with the plan.

The Secretary may make available to any person actually affected by any matter which is the subject of an investigation under this section, and to any department or agency of the United States, information concerning any matter which may be the subject of such investigation; except that any information obtained by the Secretary pursuant to section 6103(g) of the Internal Revenue Code of 1954 shall be made available only in accordance with regulations prescribed by the Secretary of the Treasury.

Act Sec. 504. (b) The Secretary may not under the authority of this section require any plan to submit to the Secretary any books or records of the plan more than once in any 12 month period, unless the Secretary has reasonable cause to believe there may exist a violation of this title or any regulation or order thereunder.

Act Sec. 504. (c) For the purposes of any investigation provided for in this title, the provisions of section 9 and 10 (relating to the attendance of witnesses and the production of books, records, and documents) of the Federal Trade Commission Act (15 U.S.C. 49, 50) are hereby made applicable (without regard to any limitation in such sections respecting persons, partnerships, banks, or common carriers) to the jurisdiction, powers, and duties of the Secretary or any officers designated by him. To the extent he considers appropriate, the Secretary may delegate his investigative functions under this section with respect to insured banks acting as fiduciaries of employee benefit plans to the appropriate Federal banking agency (as defined in section 3(q) of the Federal Deposit Insurance Act (12 U.S.C. 1813(q))).

[¶ 14,950]
REGULATIONS

Act Sec. 505. Subject to title III and section 109, the Secretary may prescribe such regulations as he finds necessary or appropriate to carry out the provisions of this title. Among other things, such regulations may define accounting, technical and trade terms used in such provisions; may prescribe forms; and may provide for the keeping of books and records, and for the inspection of such books and records (subject to section 504(a) and (b)).

[¶ 14,960]
COORDINATION AND RESPONSIBILITY OF AGENCIES ENFORCING EMPLOYEE RETIREMENT INCOME SECURITY ACT AND RELATED FEDERAL LAWS

Act Sec. 506.(a) COORDINATION WITH OTHER AGENCIES AND DEPARTMENTS. In order to avoid unnecessary expense and duplication of functions among Government agencies, the Secretary may make such arrangements or agreements for cooperation or mutual assistance in the performance of his functions under this title and the functions of any such agency as he may find to be practicable and consistent with law. The Secretary may utilize, on a reimbursable or other basis, the facilities or services of any department, agency, or establishment of the United States or of any State or political subdivision of a State, including the services of any of its employees, with the lawful consent of such department, agency, or establishment; and each department, agency, or establishment of the United States is authorized and directed to cooperate with the Secretary and, to the extent permitted by law, to provide such information and facilities as he may request for his assistance in the performance of his functions under this title. The Attorney General or his representative shall receive from the Secretary for appropriate action such evidence developed in the performance of his functions under this title as may be found to warrant consideration for criminal prosecution under the provisions of this title or other Federal law.

Act Sec. 506. RESPONSIBILITY FOR DETECTING AND INVESTIGATING CIVIL AND CRIMINAL VIOLATIONS OF EMPLOYEE RETIREMENT INCOME SECURITY ACT AND RELATED FEDERAL LAWS. (b) The Secretary shall have the responsibility and authority to detect and investigate and refer, where appropriate, civil and criminal violations related to the provisions of this title and other related Federal laws, including the detection, investigation, and appropriate referrals of related violations of title 18 of the United States Code. Nothing in this subsection shall be construed to preclude other appropriate Federal agencies from detecting and investigating civil and criminal violations of this title and other related Federal laws.

Act Sec. 506. COORDINATION OF ENFORCEMENT WITH STATES WITH RESPECT TO CERTAIN ARRANGEMENTS. (c) A State may enter into an agreement with the Secretary for delegation to the State of some or all of the Secretary's authority under sections 502 and 504 to enforce the requirements under part 7 in connection with multiple employer welfare arrangements, providing medical care (within the meaning of section 706(a)(2)), which are not group health plans.

Amendment

P.L. 104-191, § 101(e)(3):

Added Sec. 506(c) to read as above.

The above amendment generally applies with respect to group health plans for plan years beginning after June 30, 1997. For special rules, see Act Sec. 101(g)(2)-(5), reproduced after ERISA Act Sec. 502.

P.L. 98-473, § 805:

Added Sec. 506(b) and the section heading to Sec. 506(a) and amended the title of the section. Prior to amendment, the section heading was as follows: "OTHER AGENCIES AND DEPARTMENTS."

[¶ 14,970]
ADMINISTRATION

Act Sec. 507.(a) Subchapter II of chapter 5, and chapter 7, of title 5, United States Code (relating to administrative procedure), shall be applicable to this title.

Act Sec. 507. (b) Section 5108 of title 5, United States Code, is amended by adding at the end thereof the following new subsection:

"(f) In addition to the number of positions authorized by subsection (a), the Secretary of Labor is authorized, without regard to any other provision of this section, to place 1 position in the Department of Labor in grade GS-18, and a total of 20 positions in the Department of Labor in grades GS-16 and 17."

Act Sec. 507. (c) No employee of the Department of Labor or the Department of the Treasury shall administer or enforce this title or the Internal Revenue Code of 1954 with respect to any employee benefit plan under which he is a participant or beneficiary, any employee organization of which he is a member, or any employer organization in which he has an interest. This subsection does not apply to an employee benefit plan which covers only employees of the United States.

[¶ 14,980]
APPROPRIATIONS

Act Sec. 508. There are hereby authorized to be appropriated such sums as may be necessary to enable the Secretary to carry out his functions and duties under this Act.

[¶ 14,990]
SEPARABILITY PROVISIONS

Act Sec. 509. If any provision of this Act, or the application of such provision to any person or circumstances, shall be held invalid, the remainder of this Act, or the application of such provision to persons or circumstances other than those as to which it is held invalid, shall not be affected thereby.

[¶ 15,000]
INTERFERENCE WITH RIGHTS PROTECTED UNDER ACT

Act Sec. 510. It shall be unlawful for any person to discharge, fine, suspend, expel, discipline, or discriminate against a participant or beneficiary for exercising any right to which he is entitled under the provisions of an employee benefit plan, this title, section 3001, or the Welfare and Pension Plans Disclosure Act, or for the purpose of interfering with the attainment of any right to which such participant may become entitled under the plan, this title, or the Welfare and Pension Plans Disclosure Act. It shall be unlawful for any person to discharge, fine, suspend, expel, or discriminate against any person because he has given information or has testified or is about to testify in any inquiry or proceeding relating to this Act or the Welfare and Pension Plans Disclosure Act. The provisions of section 502 shall be applicable in the enforcement of this section.

[¶ 15,010]
COERCIVE INTERFERENCE

Act Sec. 511. It shall be unlawful for any person through the use of fraud, force, violence, or threat of the use of force or violence, to restrain, coerce, intimidate, or attempt to restrain, coerce, or intimidate any participant or beneficiary for the purpose of interfering with or preventing the exercise of any right to which he is or may become entitled under the plan, this title, section 3001, or the Welfare and Pension Plans Disclosure Act. Any person who willfully violates this section shall be fined $10,000 or imprisoned for not more than one year, or both.

[¶ 15,020]
ADVISORY COUNCIL

Act Sec. 512. (a) (1) There is hereby established an Advisory Council on Employee Welfare and Pension Benefit Plans (hereinafter in this section referred to as the "Council") consisting of fifteen members appointed by the Secretary. Not more than eight members of the Council shall be members of the same political party.

(2) Members shall be persons qualified to appraise the programs instituted under this Act.

(3) Of the members appointed, three shall be representatives of employee organizations (at least one of whom shall be representative of any organization members of which are participants in a multiemployer plan); three shall be representatives of employers (at least one of whom shall be representative of employers maintaining or contributing to multiemployer plans); three representatives shall be appointed from the general public, one of whom shall be a person representing those receiving benefits from a pension plan; and there shall be one representative each from the fields of insurance, corporate trust, actuarial counseling, investment counseling, investment management, and the accounting field.

(4) Members shall serve for terms of three years except that of those first appointed, five shall be appointed for terms of one year, five shall be appointed for terms of two years, and five shall be appointed for terms of three years. A member may be reappointed. A member appointed to fill a vacancy shall be appointed only for the remainder of such term. A majority of members shall constitute a quorum and action shall be taken only by a majority vote of those present and voting.

Act Sec. 512. (b) It shall be the duty of the Council to advise the Secretary with respect to the carrying out of his functions under this Act and to submit to the Secretary recommendations with respect thereto. The Council shall meet at least four times each year and at such other times as the Secretary requests. In his annual report submitted pursuant to section 513(b), the Secretary shall include each recommendation which he has received from the Council during the preceding calendar year.

Act Sec. 512. (c) The Secretary shall furnish to the Council an executive secretary and such secretarial, clerical, and other services as are deemed necessary to conduct its business. The Secretary may call upon other agencies of the Government for statistical data, reports, and other information which will assist the Council in the performance of its duties.

Act Sec. 512. (d) (1) Members of the Council shall each be entitled to receive the daily equivalent of the annual rate of basic pay in effect for grade GS-18 of the General Schedule for each day (including travel time) during which they are engaged in the actual performance of duties vested in the Council.

(2) While away from their homes or regular places of business in the performance of services for Council, members of the Council shall be allowed travel expenses, including per diem in lieu of subsistence, in the same manner as persons employed intermittently in the Government service are allowed expenses under section 5703(b) of title 5 of the United States Code.

Act Sec. 512. (e) Section 14(a) of the Federal Advisory Committee Act (relating to termination) shall not apply to the Council.

[¶ 15,030]
RESEARCH, STUDIES, AND ANNUAL REPORT

Act Sec. 513. (a) (1) The Secretary is authorized to undertake research and surveys and in connection therewith to collect, compile, analyze and publish data, information, and statistics relating to employee benefit plans, including retirement, deferred compensation, and welfare plans, and types of plans not subject to this Act.

(2) The Secretary is authorized and directed to undertake research studies relating to pension plans, including but not limited to (A) the effects of this title upon the provisions and costs of pension plans, (B) the role of private pensions in meeting the economic security needs of the Nation, and (C) the operation of private pension plans including types and levels of benefits, degree of reciprocity of portability, and financial and actuarial characteristics and practice, and methods of encouraging the growth of the private pension system.

(3) The Secretary may, as he deems appropriate or necessary, undertake other studies relating to employee benefit plans, the matters regulated by this title, and the enforcement procedures provided for under this title.

(4) The research, surveys, studies, and publications referred to in this subsection may be conducted directly, or indirectly through grant or contract agreements.

Act Sec. 513. (b) The Secretary shall submit annually a report to the Congress covering his administration of this title for the preceding year, and including (1) an explanation of any variances or extensions granted under section 110, 207, 303, or 304 and the projected date for terminating the variance; (2) the status of cases in enforcement status; (3) recommendations received from the Advisory Council during the preceding year; and (4) such information, data, research findings, studies, and recommendations for further legislation in connection with the matters covered by this title as he may find advisable.

Act Sec. 513. (c) The Secretary is authorized and directed to cooperate with the Congress and its appropriate committees, subcommittees, and staff in supplying data and any other information, and personnel and services, required by the Congress in any study, examination, or report by the Congress relating to pension benefit plans established or maintained by States or their political subdivisions.

[¶ 15,040]
EFFECT ON OTHER LAWS

Act Sec. 514. (a) Except as provided in subsection (b) of this section, the provisions of this title and title IV shall supersede any and all State laws insofar as they may now or hereafter relate to any employee benefit plan described in section 4(a) and not exempt under section 4(b). This section shall take effect on January 1, 1975.

Act Sec. 514. (b) (1) This section shall not apply with respect to any cause of action which arose, or any act or omission which occurred, before January 1, 1975.

(2) (A) Except as provided in subparagraph (B), nothing in this title shall be construed to exempt or relieve any person from any law of any State which regulates insurance, banking, or securities.

(B) Neither an employee benefit plan described in section 4(a), which is not exempt under section 4(b) (other than a plan established primarily for the purpose of providing death benefits), nor any trust established under such a plan, shall be deemed to be an insurance company or other insurer, bank, trust company, or investment company or to be engaged in the business of insurance or banking for purposes of any law of any State purporting to regulate insurance companies, insurance contracts, banks, trust companies, or investment companies.

(3) Nothing in this section shall be construed to prohibit use by the Secretary of services or facilities of a State agency as permitted under section 506 of this Act.

(4) Subsection (a) shall not apply to any generally applicable criminal law of a state.

(5)(A) Except as provided in subparagraph (B), subsection (a) shall not apply to tthe Hawaii Prepaid Health Care Act (Haw.Rev.Stat. §§ 393-1 through 393-51).

(B) Nothing in subparagraph (A) shall be construed to exempt from subsection (a)—

(i) any State tax law relating to employee benefit plans, or

(ii) any amendment of the Hawaii Prepaid Health Care Act enacted after September 2, 1974, to the extent it provides for more than the effective administration of such Act as in effect on such date.

(C) Notwithstanding subparagraph (A), parts 1 and 4 of this subtitle, and the preceding sections of this part to the extent they govern matters which are governed by the provisions of such parts 1 and 4 and the preceding sections of this part, shall supersede the Hawaii Prepaid Health Care Act (as in effect on or after the date of the enactment of this paragraph), but the Secretary may enter into cooperative arrangements under paragraph and section 506 with officials of the State of Hawaii to assist them in effectuating the policies of provisions of such Act which are superseded by such parts.

(6)(A) Notwithstanding any other provision of this section—

(i) in the case of an employee welfare benefit plan which is a multiple employer welfare arrangement and is fully insured (or which is a multiple employer welfare arrangement subject to an exemption under subparagraph (B)), any law of any State which regulates insurance may apply to such arrangement to the extent that such law provides—

(I) standards, requiring the maintenance of specified levels of reserves and specified levels of contributions, which any such plan, or any trust established under such a plan, must meet in order to be considered under such law able to pay benefits in full when due, and

(II) provisions to enforce such standards, and

(ii) in the case of any other employee welfare benefit plan which is a multiple employer welfare arrangement, in addition to this title, any law of any State which regulates insurance may apply to the extent not inconsistent with the preceding sections of this title.

(B) The Secretary may, under regulations which may be prescribed by the Secretary, exempt from subparagraph (A)(ii), individually or by class, multiple employer welfare arrangements which are not fully insured. Any such exemption may be granted with respect to any arrangement or class of arrangements only if such arrangement or each arrangement which is a member of such class meets the requirements of section 3(1) and section 4 necessary to be considered an employee welfare benefit plan to which this title applies.

(C) Nothing in subparagraph (A) shall affect the manner or extent to which the provisions of this title apply to an employee welfare benefit plan which is not a multiple employer welfare arrangement and which is a plan, fund, or program participating in, subscribing to, or otherwise using a multiple employer welfare arrangement to fund or administer benefits to such plan's participants and beneficiaries.

(D) For purposes of this paragraph, a multiple employer welfare arrangement shall be considered fully insured only if the terms of the arrangement provide for benefits the amount of all of which the Secretary determines are guaranteed under a contract, or policy of insurance, issued by an insurance company, insurance service, or insurance organization, qualified to conduct business in a State.

(7) Subsection (a) shall not apply to qualified domestic relations orders (within the meaning of section 206(d)(3)(B)(i)), qualified medical child support orders (within the meaning of section 609(a)(2)(A)), and the provisions of law referred to in section 609(a)(2)(B)(ii) to the extent they apply to qualified medical child support orders.

(8) Subsection (a) of this section shall not be construed to preclude any State cause of action—

(A) with respect to which the State exercises its acquired rights under section 609(b)(3) with respect to a group health plan (as defined in section 607(1)), or

(B) for recoupment of payment with respect to items or services pursuant to a State plan for medical assistance approved under title XIX of the Social Security Act which would not have been payable if such acquired rights had been executed before payment with respect to such items or services by the group health plan.

(9) For additional provisions relating to group health plans, see section 704.

Act Sec. 514. (c) For purposes of this section:

(1) The term "State law" includes all laws, decisions, rules, regulations, or other State action having the effect of law, of any State. A law of the United States applicable only to the District of Columbia shall be treated as a State law rather than a law of the United States.

(2) The term "State" includes a State, any political subdivisions thereof, or any agency or intrumentality of either, which purports to regulate, directly or indirectly, the terms and conditions of employee benefit plans covered by this title.

Act Sec. 514. (d) Nothing in this title shall be construed to alter, amend, modify, invalidate, impair, or supersede any law of the United States (except as provided in sections 111 and 507(b)) or any rule or regulation issued under any such law.

Amendments

P.L. 105-200, § 402(h)(2)(A)(ii):

Amended ERISA Sec. 514(b)(7) by striking "enforced by" and inserting "they apply to" to read as above.

The above amendment is effective August 10, 1993, as if included in ther enactment of P.L. 103-66, Sec. 4301(c)(4)(A).

P.L. 104-191, § 101(f)(1):

Amended ERISA Sec. 514(b) by adding at the end a new paragraph (9) to read as above.

The above amendment generally applies with respect to group health plans for plan years beginning after June 30, 1997. For special rules, see Act Sec. 101(g)(2)-(5), reproduced after ERISA Act Sec. 701.

P.L. 103-66, § 4301(c)(4)(A):

Amended ERISA Sec. 514 by inserting in subsection (b)(7) ", qualified medical child support orders (within the meaning of section 609(a)(2)(A)), and the provisions of law referred to in section 609(a)(2)(B)(ii) to the extent enforced by qualified medical child support orders" before the period.

The above amendment is effective on August 10, 1993. Any plan amendment required to be made by Act Sec. 4301 need not be made before the first plan year beginning on or after January 1, 1994 if: (1) the plan is operated in accordance with Act Sec. 4301 during the period after August 9, 1993 and before such first plan year; and (2) the amendment applies retroactively to this period. A plan will not be treated as failing to be operated in accordance with plan provisions merely because it operates in accordance with the effective date requirements.

P.L. 103-66, Sec. 4301(c)(4)(A) was amended by Sec. 402(h)(1)(i) of P.L. 105-200 by striking "subsection (b)(7)(D)" and inserting "subsection (b)(7)" effective August 10, 1993.

P.L. 103-66, § 4301(c)(4)(B):

Amended ERISA Sec. 514 by striking subsection (b)(8) and inserting new subsection (b)(8) to read as above.

The above amendment is effective on August 10, 1993. Any plan amendment required to be made by Act Sec. 4301 need not be made before the first plan year beginning on or after January 1, 1994 if: (1) the plan is operated in accordance with Act Sec. 4301 during the period after August 9, 1993 and before such first plan year; and (2) the amendment applies retroactively to this period. A plan will not be treated as failing to be operated in accordance with plan provisions merely because it operates in accordance with the effective date requirements.

P.L. 101-239, § 7894(f)(2):

Amended ERISA Sec. 514(b)(5)(C) by striking "such parts" the second place it appeared and inserting "such parts 1 and 4 and the preceding sections of this part" effective as if included in P.L. 97-473, § 301.

P.L. 101-239, § 7894(f)(3):

Amended ERISA Sec. 514(b)(6)(B) by striking section 3(l) and inserting "section 3(1)" effective as if included in P.L. 97-473, § 302.

P.L. 99-272, § 9503(d)(1):

Amended ERISA Sec. 514 by adding new paragraph (8), to take effect pursuant to § 9503(d)(2), which provided:

(2)(A) Except as provided in subparagraph (B), the amendment made by paragraph (1) shall become effective on October 1, 1986.

(B) In the case of a plan maintained pursuant to one or more collective bargaining agreements between employee representatives and one or more employers ratified on or before the date of the enactment of this Act, the amendment made by paragraph (1) shall become effective on the later of—

(i) October 1, 1986; or

(ii) the earlier of—

(I) the date on which the last of the collective bargaining agreements under which the plan is maintained, which were in effect on the date of the enactment of this Act, terminates (determined without regard to any extension thereof agreed to after the date of the enactment of this Act); or

(II) three years after the date of the enactment of this Act.

P.L. 98-397, §104:

Act Sec. 104(b) amended ERISA Sec. 514(b) by adding new paragraph (7).

For the effective date of the above amendment, see Act Sec. 303(d), which appears in the amendment note for ERISA Sec. 206 at ¶ 14,460.

P.L. 97-473, §301:

Amended Sec. 514(b) by adding new paragraph (5), effective January 14, 1983. Sec. 301(b) of the Act provided: "The amendment made by this section shall not be considered a precedent with respect to extending such amendment to any other State law."

P.L. 97-473, §302:

Amended Sec. 514(b) by adding new paragraph (6), effective January 14, 1983.

[¶ 15,043]
DELINQUENT CONTRIBUTIONS

Act Sec. 515. Every employer who is obligated to make contributions to a multi-employer plan under the terms of the plan or under the terms of a collectively bargained agreement shall to the extent not inconsistent with law, make such contributions in accordance with the terms and conditions of such plan or such agreement.

Amendment

P.L. 96-364, §306:

Added new section 515, effective September 26, 1980.

[¶ 15,043C]
OUTREACH TO PROMOTE RETIREMENT INCOME SAVINGS

Act Sec. 516.(a) IN GENERAL. The Secretary shall maintain an ongoing program of outreach to the public designed to effectively promote retirement income savings by the public.

(b) METHODS. The Secretary shall carry out the requirements of subsection (a) by means which shall ensure effective communication to the public, including publication of public service announcements, public meetings, creation of educational materials, and establishment of a site on the Internet.

(c) INFORMATION TO BE MADE AVAILABLE. The information to be made available by the Secretary as part of the program of outreach required under subsection (a) shall include the following:

(1) a description of the vehicles currently available to individuals and employers for creating and maintaining retirement income savings, specifically including information explaining to employers, in simple terms, the characteristics and operation of the different retirement savings vehicles, including the steps to establish each such vehicle; and

(2) information regarding matters relevant to establishing retirement income savings, such as—

(A) the forms of retirement income savings;

(B) the concept of compound interest;

(C) the importance of commencing savings early in life;

(D) savings principles;

(E) the importance of prudence and diversification in investing;

(F) the importance of the timing of investments; and

(G) the impact on retirement savings of life's uncertainties, such as living beyond one's life expectancy.

(d) ESTABLISHMENT OF SITE ON THE INTERNET. The Secretary shall establish a permanent site on the Internet concerning retirement income savings. The site shall contain at least the following information:

(1) a means for individuals to calculate their estimated retirement savings needs, based on their retirement income goal as a percentage of their preretirement income;

(2) a description in simple terms of the common types of retirement income savings arrangements available to both individuals and employers (specifically including small employers), including information on the amount of money that can be placed into a given vehicle, the tax treatment of the money, the amount of accumulation possible through different typical investment options and interest rate projections, and a directory of resources of more descriptive information;

(3) materials explaining to employers in simple terms, the characteristics and operation of the different retirement savings arrangements for their workers and what the basic legal requirements are under this Act and the Internal Revenue Code of 1986, including the steps to establish each such arrangement;

(4) copies of all educational materials developed by the Department of Labor, and by other Federal agencies in consultation with such Department, to promote retirement income savings by workers and employers; and

(5) links to other sites maintained on the Internet by governmental agencies and nonprofit organizations that provide additional detail on retirement income savings arrangements and related topics on savings or investing.

(e) COORDINATION. The Secretary shall coordinate the outreach program under this section with similar efforts undertaken by other public and private entities.

Amendment

P.L. 105-92, §3(a):

Added new section 516, to read as above.

[¶ 15,043F]
NATIONAL SUMMIT ON RETIREMENT SAVINGS

Act Sec. 517.(a) AUTHORITY TO CALL SUMMIT. Not later than July 15, 1998, the President shall convene a National Summit on Retirement Income Savings at the White House, to be co-hosted by the President and the Speaker and the Minority Leader of the House of Representatives and the Majority Leader and Minority Leader of the Senate. Such a National Summit shall be convened thereafter in 2001 and 2005 on or after September 1 of each year involved. Such a National Summit shall—

(1) advance the public's knowledge and understanding of retirement savings and its critical importance to the future well-being of American workers and their families;

(2) facilitate the development of a broad-based, public education program to encourage and enhance individual commitment to a personal retirement savings strategy;

(3) develop recommendations for additional research, reforms, and actions in the field of private pensions and individual retirement savings; and

(4) disseminate the report of, and information obtained by, the National Summit and exhibit materials and works of the National Summit.

(b) PLANNING AND DIRECTION. The National Summit shall be planned and conducted under the direction of the Secretary, in consultation with, and with the assistance of, the heads of such other Federal departments and agencies as the President may designate. Such assistance may include the assignment of personnel. The Secretary shall, in planning and conducting the National Summit, consult with the congressional leaders specified in subsection (e)(2). The Secretary shall also, in carrying out the Secretary's duties under this subsection, consult and coordinate with at least one organization made up of private sector businesses and associations partnered with Government entities to promote long-term financial security in retirement through savings.

(c) PURPOSE OF NATIONAL SUMMIT. The purpose of the National Summit shall be—

(1) to increase the public awareness of the value of personal savings for retirement;

(2) to advance the public's knowledge and understanding of retirement savings and its critical importance to the future well-being of American workers and their families;

(3) to facilitate the development of a broad-based, public education program to encourage and enhance individual commitment to a personal retirement savings strategy;

(4) to identify the problems workers have in setting aside adequate savings for retirement;

(5) to identify the barriers which employers, especially small employers, face in assisting their workers in accumulating retirement savings;

(6) to examine the impact and effectiveness of individual employers to promote personal savings for retirement among their workers and to promote participation in company savings options;

(7) to examine the impact and effectiveness of government programs at the Federal, State, and local levels to educate the public about, and to encourage, retirement income savings;

(8) to develop such specific and comprehensive recommendations for the legislative and executive branches of the Government and for private sector action as may be appropriate for promoting private pensions and individual retirement savings; and

(9) to develop recommendations for the coordination of Federal, State, and local retirement income savings initiatives among the Federal, State, and local levels of government and for the coordination of such initiatives.

(d) SCOPE OF NATIONAL SUMMIT. The scope of the National Summit shall consist of issues relating to individual and employer-based retirement savings and shall not include issues relating to the old-age, survivors, and disability insurance program under title II of the Social Security Act.

(e) NATIONAL SUMMIT PARTICIPANTS.—

(1) IN GENERAL. To carry out the purposes of the National Summit, the National Summit shall bring together—

(A) professionals and other individuals working in the fields of employee benefits and retirement savings;

(B) Members of Congress and officials in the executive branch;

(C) representatives of State and local governments;

(D) representatives of private sector institutions, including individual employers, concerned about promoting the issue of retirement savings and facilitating savings among American workers; and

(E) representatives of the general public.

(2) STATUTORILY REQUIRED PARTICIPATION. The participants in the National Summit shall include the following individuals or their designees:

(A) the Speaker and the Minority Leader of the House of representatives;

(B) the Majority Leader and the Minority Leader of the Senate;

(C) the Chairman and ranking Member of the Committee on Education and the Workforce of the House of Representatives;

(D) the Chairman and ranking Member of the Committee on Labor and Human Resources of the Senate;

(E) the Chairman and ranking Member of the Special Committee on Aging of the Senate;

(F) the Chairman and ranking Member of the Subcommittees on Labor, Health and Human Services, and Education of the Senate and House of Representatives; and

(G) the parties referred to in subsection (b).

(3) ADDITIONAL PARTICIPANTS.—

(A) IN GENERAL. There shall be not more than 200 additional participants. Of such additional participants—

(i) one-half shall be appointed by the President, in consultation with the elected leaders of the President's party in Congress (either the Speaker of the House of Representatives or the Minority Leader of the House of Representatives, and either the Majority Leader or the Minority Leader of the Senate; and

(ii) one-half shall be appointed by the elected leaders of Congress of the party to which the President does not belong (one-half of that allotment to be appointed by either the Speaker of the House of Representatives or the Minority Leader of the House of Representatives, and one-half of that allotment to be appointed by either the Majority Leader or the Minority Leader of the Senate).

(B) APPOINTMENT REQUIREMENTS. The additional participants described in subparagraph (A) shall be—

(i) appointed not later than January 31, 1998;

(ii) selected without regard to political affiliation or past partisan activity; and

(iii) representative of the diversity of thought in the fields of employee benefits and retirement income savings.

(4) PRESIDING OFFICERS. The National Summit shall be presided over equally by representatives of the executive and legislative branches.

(f) NATIONAL SUMMIT ADMINISTRATION—

(1) ADMINISTRATION. In administering this section, the Secretary shall—

(A) request the cooperation and assistance of such other Federal departments and agencies and other parties referred to in subsection (b) as may be appropriate in the carrying out of this section;

(B) furnish all reasonable assistance to State agencies, area agencies, and other appropriate organizations to enable them to organize and conduct conferences in conjunction with the National Summit;

(C) make available for public comment a proposed agenda for the National Summit that reflects to the greatest extent possible the purposes for the National Summit set out in this section;

(D) prepare and make available background materials for the use of participants in the National Summit that the Secretary considers necessary; and

(E) appoint and fix the pay of such additional personnel as may be necessary to carry out the provisions of this section without regard to provisions of title 5, United States Code, governing appointments in the competitive service, and without regard to chapter 51 and subchapter III of chapter 53 of such title relating to classification and General Schedule pay rates.

(2) DUTIES. The Secretary shall, in carrying out the responsibilities and functions of the Secretary under this section, and as part of the National Summit, ensure that—

(A) the National Summit shall be conducted in a manner that ensures broad participation of Federal, State, and local agencies and private organizations, professionals, and others involved in retirement income savings and provides a strong basis for assistance to be provided under paragraph (1)(B);

(B) the agenda prepared under paragraph (1)(C) for the National Summit is published in the Federal Register; and

(C) the personnel appointed under paragraph (1)(E) shall be fairly balanced in terms of points of views represented and shall be appointed without regard to political affiliation or previous partisan activities.

(3) NONAPPLICATION OF FACA. The provisions of the Federal Advisory Committee Act (5 U.S.C. App.) shall not apply to the National Summit.

(g) REPORT. The Secretary shall prepare a report describing the activities of the National Summit and shall submit the report to the President, the Speaker and Minority Leader of the House of Representatives, the Majority and Minority Leaders of the Senate, and the chief executive officers of the States not later than 90 days after the date on which the National Summit is adjourned.

(h) DEFINITION. For purposes of this section, the term 'State' means a State, the District of Columbia, the Commonwealth of Puerto Rico, the Commonwealth of the Northern Mariana Islands, Guam, the Virgin Islands, American Samoa, and any other territory or possession of the United States.

(i) AUTHORIZATION OF APPROPRIATIONS.—

(1) IN GENERAL. There is authorized to be appropriated for fiscal years beginning on or after October 1, 1997, such sums as are necessary to carry out this section.

(2) AUTHORIZATION TO ACCEPT PRIVATE CONTRIBUTIONS. In order to facilitate the National Summit as a public-private partnership, the Secretary may accept private contributions, in the form of money, supplies, or services, to defray the costs of the National Summit.

(j) FINANCIAL OBLIGATION FOR FISCAL YEAR 1998. The financial obligation for the Department of Labor for fiscal year 1998 shall not exceed the lesser of—

(1) one-half of the costs of the National Summit; or

(2) $250,000.

The private sector organization described in subsection (b) and contracted with by the Secretary shall be obligated for the balance of the cost of the National Summit.

(k) CONTRACTS. The Secretary may enter into contracts to carry out the Secretary's responsibilities under this section. The Secretary shall enter into a contract on a sole-source basis to ensure the timely completion of the National Summit in fiscal year 1998.

Amendment

P.L. 105-92, §4(a):

Added new section 517, to read as above.

[¶ 15,043H]

AUTHORITY TO POSTPONE CERTAIN DEADLINES BY REASON OF A PRESIDENTIALLY DECLARED DISASTER OR TERRORISTIC OR MILITARY ACTIONS

Act Sec. 518. In the case of a pension or other employee benefit plan, or any sponsor, administrator, participant, beneficiary, or other person with respect to such plan, affected by a Presidentially declared disaster (as defined in section 1033 (h) (3) of the Internal Revenue Code of 1986) or a terroristic or military action (as defined in section 692 (c) (2) of such Code), the Secretary may, notwithstanding any other provision of law prescribe, by notice or otherwise, a period of up to 1 year which may be disregarded in determining the date by which any action is required or permitted to be completed underthis Act. No plan shall be treated as failing to be operated in accordance with the terms of the plan solely as the result of disregarding any period by reason of the preceding sentence.

Amendment

P.L. 107-134, §112(c)(1):

Added new section 518, to read as above. This section applies to disasters and terroristic or military actions occurring on or after September 11, 2001, with respect to

any action of the Secretary of the Treasury, Secretary of Labor, or the PBGC occurring on or after January 23, 2002.

Part 6—Group Health Plans

[¶ 15,045]

PLANS MUST PROVIDE CONTINUATION COVERAGE TO CERTAIN INDIVIDUALS

Act Sec. 601.(a) IN GENERAL. The plan sponsor of each group health plan shall provide, in accordance with this part, that each qualified beneficiary who would lose coverage under the plan as a result of a qualifying event is entitled, under the plan, to elect, within the election period, continuation coverage under the plan.

Act Sec. 601. (b) EXCEPTION FOR CERTAIN PLANS. Subsection (a) shall not apply to any group health plan for any calendar year if all employers maintaining such plan normally employed fewer than 20 employees on a typical business day during the preceding calendar year.

Amendments

P.L. 101-239, §7862(c)(1)(B):

Amended ERISA Sec. 601(b) by striking the last sentence, effective for years beginning after December 31, 1986. Prior to being striken, the last sentence read:

Under regulations, rules similar to the rules of subsections (a) and (b) of section 52 of the Internal Revenue Code of 1954 (relating to employers under common control) shall apply for purposes of this subsection.

P.L. 99-272:

Act Sec. 10002(a) added new ERISA Sec. 601 to read as above, effective for plan years beginning after July 1, 1986 except for the special rule which applies to collective bargaining agreements. When the amendments become effective the plan is subject to certain notification requirements. Act Secs. 10002(d) and (e) provide as follows:

(d) Effective Dates.—

(1) General rule.—The amendments made by this section shall apply to plan years beginning on or after July 1, 1986.

(2) Special rule for collective bargaining agreements.—In the case of a group health plan maintained pursuant to one or more collective bargaining agreements.—In the case of a group health plan maintained pursuant to one or more collective bargaining agreements between employee representatives and one or more employers ratified before the date of the enactment of this Act, the amendments made by this section shall not apply to plan years beginning before the later of—

(A) the date on which the last of the collective bargaining agreements relating to the plan terminates (determined without regard to any extension thereof agreed to after the date of the enactment of this Act), or

(B) January 1, 1987.

For purposes of subparagraph (A), any plan amendment made pursuant to a collective bargaining agreement relating to the plan which amends the plan solely to conform to any requirement added by this section shall not be treated as a termination of such collective bargaining agreement.

(e) Notification to Covered Employees.—At the time that the amendments made by this section apply to a group health plan (within the meaning of section 607(1) of the Employee Retirement Income Security Act of 1974), the plan shall notify each covered employee, and spouse of the employee (if any), who is covered under the plan at that time of the continuation coverage required under part 6 of subtitle B of title I of such Act. The notice furnished under this subsection is in lieu of notice that may otherwise be required under section 601(1) of such Act with respect to such individuals.

[¶ 15,045F]
CONTINUATION COVERAGE

Act Sec. 602. For purposes of section 601, the term "continuation coverage" means coverage under the plan which meets the following requirements:

(1) TYPE OF BENEFIT COVERAGE. The coverage must consist of coverage which, as of the time the coverage is being provided, is identical to the coverage provided under the plan to similarly situated beneficiaries under the plan with respect to whom a qualifying event has not occurred. If coverage is modified under the plan for any group of similarly situated beneficiaries, such coverage shall also be modified in the same manner for all individuals who are qualified beneficiaries under the plan pursuant to this part in connection with such group.

(2) PERIOD OF COVERAGE. The coverage must extend for at least the period beginning on the date of the qualifying event and ending not earlier than the earliest of the following:

(A) MAXIMUM REQUIRED PERIOD.—

(i) GENERAL RULE FOR TERMINATIONS AND REDUCED HOURS. In the case of a qualifying event described in section 603(2), except as provided in clause (ii), the date which is 18 months after the date of the qualifying event.

(ii) SPECIAL RULE FOR MULTIPLE QUALIFYING EVENTS. If a qualifying event (other than a qualifying event described in section 603(6)) occurs during the 18 months after the date of a qualifying event described in section 603(2), the date which is 36 months after the date of the qualifying event described in section 603(2).

(iii) SPECIAL RULE FOR CERTAIN BANKRUPTCY PROCEEDINGS. In the case of a qualifying event described in section 603(6) (relating to bankruptcy proceedings), the date of the death of the covered employee or qualified beneficiary (described in section 607(3)(C)(iii)), or in the case of the surviving spouse or dependent children of the covered employee, 36 months after the date of the death of the covered employee.

(iv) GENERAL RULE FOR OTHER QUALIFYING EVENTS. In the case of a qualifying event not described in section 603(2) or 603(6), the date which is 36 months after the date of the qualifying event.

(v) MEDICARE ENTITLEMENT FOLLOWED BY QUALIFYING EVENT. In the case of a qualifying event described in section 603(2) that occurs less than 18 months after the date the covered employee became entitled to benefits under title XVIII of the Social Security Act, the period of coverage for qualified beneficiaries other than the covered employee shall not terminate under this subparagraph before the close of the 36-month period beginning on the date the covered employee became so entitled.

In the case of a qualified beneficiary who is determined, under title II or XVI of the Social Security Act, to have been disabled at any time during the first 60 days of continuation coverage under this part, any reference in clause (i) or (ii) to 18 months is deemed a reference to 29 months (with respect to all qualified beneficiaries), but only if the qualified beneficiary has provided notice of such determination under section 606(3) before the end of such 18 months.

(B) END OF PLAN. The date on which the employer ceases to provide any group health plan to any employee.

(C) FAILURE TO PAY PREMIUM. The date on which coverage ceases under the plan by reason of a failure to make timely payment of any premium required under the plan with respect to the qualified beneficiary. The payment of any premium (other than any payment referred to in the last sentence of paragraph (3)) shall be considered to be timely if made within 30 days after the date due or within such longer period as applies to or under the plan.

(D) GROUP HEALTH PLAN COVERAGE OR MEDICARE ENTITLEMENT. The date on which the qualified beneficiary first becomes, after the date of the election—

(i) covered under any other group health plan (as an employee or otherwise which does not contain any exclusion or limitation with respect to any preexisting condition of such beneficiary) (other than such an exclusion or limitation which does not apply to (or is satisfied by) such beneficiary by reason of chapter 100 of the Internal Revenue Code of 1986, part 7 of this subtitle, or title XXVII of the Public Health Service Act), or

(ii) in the case of a qualified beneficiary other than a qualified beneficiary described in section 607(3)(C) entitled to benefits under title XVIII of the Social Security Act.

(E) TERMINATION OF EXTENDED COVERAGE FOR DISABILITY. In the case of a qualified beneficiary who is disabled at any time during the first 60 days of continuation coverage under this part, the month that begins more than 30 days after the date of the final determination under title II or XVI of the Social Security Act that the qualified beneficiary is no longer disabled.

(3) PREMIUM REQUIREMENTS. The plan may require payment of a premium for any period of continuation coverage, except that such premium—

(A) shall not exceed 102 percent of the applicable premium for such period, and

(B) may, at the election of the payor, be made in monthly installments.

In no event may the plan require the payment of any premium before the day which is 45 days after the day on which the qualified beneficiary made the initial election for continuation coverage. In the case of an individual described in the last sentence of paragraph (2)(A), any reference in subparagraph (A) of this paragraph to "102 percent" is deemed a reference to "150 percent" for any month after the 18th month of continuation coverage described in clause (i) or (ii) of paragraph (2)(A).

(4) NO REQUIREMENT OF INSURABILITY. The coverage may not be conditioned upon, or discriminate on the basis of lack of, evidence of insurability.

(5) CONVERSION OPTION. In the case of a qualified beneficiary whose period of continuation coverage expires under paragraph (2)(A), the plan must, during the 180-day period ending on such expiration date, provide to the qualified beneficiary the option of enrollment under a conversion health plan otherwise generally available under the plan.

Amendments

P.L. 104-191, §421(b)(1)(A):

Act Sec. 421(b)(1)(A) amended ERISA Sec. 602(2)(A), the last sentence thereof, by striking "an individual" and inserting "a qualified beneficiary"; by striking "at the time of a qualifying event described in section 603(2)" and inserting "at any time during the first 60 days of continuation coverage under this part"; by striking "with respect to such event"; and by inserting "(with respect to all qualified beneficiaries)" after "29 months". Prior to amendment, the last sentence of ERISA Sec. 602(2)(A) read as follows:

In the case of an individual who is determined, under title II or XVI of the Social Security Act, to have been disabled at the time of a qualifying event described in section 603(2), any reference in clause (i) or (ii) to 18 months with respect to such event is deemed a reference to 29 months, but only if the qualified beneficiary has provided notice of such determination under section 606(3) before the end of such 18 months.

P.L. 104-191, §421(b)(2):

Act Sec. 421(b)(2) amended ERISA Sec. 602(2)(D)(i) by inserting before ", or" the following: "(other than such an exclusion or limitation which does not apply to (or is satisfied by) such beneficiary by reason of chapter 100 of the Internal Revenue Code of 1986, part 7 of this subtitle, or title XXVII of the Public Health Service Act)".

P.L. 104-191, §421(b)(3):

Act Sec. 421(b)(3) amended ERISA Sec. 602(2)(E) by striking "at the time of a qualifying event described in section 603(2)" and inserting "at any time during the first 60 days of continuation coverage under this part".

The above amendments are effective on January 1, 1997, regardless of whether the qualifying event occurred before, on, or after such date. For a special rule, see Act Sec. 421(e), reproduced below.

Act Sec. 421(e) provides:

(e) NOTIFICATION OF CHANGES.—Not later than November 1, 1996, each group health plan (covered under title XXII of the Public Health Service Act, part 6 of subtitle B of title I of the Employee Retirement Income Security Act of 1974, and section 4980B(f) of the Internal Revenue Code of 1986) shall notify each qualified beneficiary who has elected continuation coverage under such title, part or section of the amendments made by this section.

P.L. 104-188, §1704(g)(1)(B):

Act Sec. 1704(g)(1)(B) amended ERISA Sec. 602(2)(A) by striking clause (v) and adding a new clause (v) to read as above. Prior to amendment, clause (v) read as follows:

(v) QUALIFYING EVENT INVOLVING MEDICARE ENTITLEMENT.—In the case of an event described in section 603(4) (without regard to whether such event is a qualifying event), the period of coverage for qualified beneficiaries other than the covered employee for such event or any subsequent qualifying event shall not terminate before the close of the 36-month period beginning on the date the covered employee becomes entitled to benefits under title XVIII of the Social Security Act.

The above amendment is effective as of December 12, 1994.

P.L. 101-239, §6703(a):

Act Sec. 6703(a)(1) amended ERISA Sec. 602(2)(A) by adding a new sentence after and below clause (iv) to read as above.

Act Sec. 6703(a)(2) amended ERISA Sec. 602(2) by adding a new subparagraph (E) to read as above.

P.L. 101-239, §6703(b):

Act Sec. 6703(b) amended ERISA Sec. 602(3) by adding in the matter after and below subparagraph (B) a new sentence to read as above.

The above amendments apply to plan years beginning on or after December 19, 1989, regardless of whether the qualifying event occurred before, on, or after that date.

P.L. 101-239, §7862(c)(2)(A):

Amended ERISA Sec. 602(2)(D) by striking "ELIGIBILITY" in the heading and inserting "ENTITLEMENT" and by inserting "which does not contain any exclusion or limitation with respect to any preexisting condition of such beneficiary" after "or otherwise)" in subclause (i), applicable to qualifying events occurring after December 31, 1989.

P.L. 101-239, §7862(c)(4)(A):

Amended the last sentence of ERISA Sec. 602(3) to read as above effective October 22, 1986.

P.L. 101-239, §7862(c)(5)(B):

Amended ERISA Sec. 602(2)(A) by adding a new clause at the end effective October 22, 1986.

P.L. 101-239, §7871(c):

Amended ERISA Sec. 602(2)(A)(iii) by inserting "section" before "603(6)" effective as if included in P.L. 99-509, §9501(b)(1)(B).

P.L. 99-514, §1895(d)(1)(B), (d)(2)(B), (d)(3)(B), and (d)(4)(B):

Amended Sec. 602(1) by adding the sentence at the end to read as above.

Amended Sec. 602(2)(A) to read as above. Prior to amendment, the section read as follows:

(A) MAXIMUM PERIOD.—In the case of—

(i) a qualifying event described in section 603(2) (relating to terminations and reduced hours), the date which is 18 months after the date of the qualifying event, and

(ii) any qualifying event not described in clause (i), the date which is 36 months after the date of the qualifying event.

Amended Sec. 602(2)(C) by adding the last sentence to read as above.

Amended Sec. 602(2) by striking out subparagraph (E), by amending clause (i) of subparagraph (D) to read as above and by amending the heading to read as above. Prior to amendment, the heading and Secs. 602(2)(D)(i) and (E) read as follows:

(2) PERIOD OF COVERAGE.—

(D) REEMPLOYMENT OR MEDICARE ELIGIBILITY.—The date on which the qualified beneficiary first becomes, after the date of the election—

(i) a covered employee under any other group health plan, or

(ii) entitled to benefits under title XVIII of the Social Security Act.

(E) REMARRIAGE OF SPOUSE.—In the case of an individual who is a qualified beneficiary by reason of being the spouse of a covered employee, the date on which the beneficiary remarries and becomes covered under a group health plan.

The above amendments are effective for plan years beginning after July 1, 1986 except for plans maintained under collective bargaining agreements in which case the amendments do not apply to plan years beginning before the later of (1) the date the last of the collective bargaining agreements terminate, or (2) January 1, 1987.

P.L. 99-509, §9501(b)(1)(B):

Amended ERISA Sec. 602(2)(A)

(i) in clause (ii), by inserting "(other than a qualifying event described in section 603(6))" after "qualifying event" the first place it appears,

(ii) in clause (iii), by inserting "or 603(6)" after "603(2)",

(iii) by redesignating clause (iii) as clause (iv),

and by adding a new subclause (iii) to read as above, effective for plan years beginning after July 1, 1986 except for plans maintained under collective bargaining agreements in which case the amendments do not apply to plan years beginning before the later of (1) the date the last of the collective bargaining agreements terminate, or (2) January 1, 1987.

P.L. 99-509, §9501(b)(2)(B):

Amended ERISA Sec. 602(2)(D) by inserting "in the case of a qualified beneficiary other than a qualified beneficiary described in section 607(3)(C)" before "entitled", effective for plan years beginning after July 1, 1986 except for plans maintained under collective bargaining agreements in which case the amendments do not apply to plan years beginning before the later of (1) the date the last of the collective bargaining agreements terminate, or (2) January 1, 1987.

P.L. 99-272:

Act Sec. 10002(a) added ERISA Sec. 602 to read as above, effective for plan years beginning after July 1, 1986, subject to the special rules discussed at ¶ 15,045.

[¶ 15,045L]
QUALIFYING EVENT

Act Sec. 603. For purposes of this part, the term "qualifying event" means, with respect to any covered employee, any of the following events which, but for the continuation coverage required under this part, would result in the loss of coverage of a qualified beneficiary:

(1) The death of the covered employee.

(2) The termination (other than by reason of such employee's gross misconduct), reduction of hours, of the covered employee's employment.

(3) The divorce or legal separation of the covered employee from the employee's spouse.

(4) The covered employee becoming entitled to benefits under title XVIII of the Social Security Act.

(5) A dependent child ceasing to be a dependent child under the generally applicable requirements of the plan.

(6) A proceeding in a case under title 11, United States Code, commencing on or after July 1, 1986, with respect to the employer from whose employment the covered employee retired at any time.

In the case of an event described in paragraph (6), a loss of coverage includes a substantial elimination of coverage with respect to a qualified beneficiary described in section 607(3)(C) within one year before or after the date of commencement of the proceeding.

Amendment

P.L. 99-509, §9501(a)(2):

Amended ERISA Sec. 603 by adding a new subsection (6) to read as above, effective for plan years beginning after July 1, 1986 except for plans maintained under collective bargaining agreements in which case the amendments do not apply to plan years

beginning before the later of (1) the date the last of the collective bargaining agreements terminate, or (2) January 1, 1987.

P.L. 99-272:

Act Sec. 10002(a) added ERISA Sec. 603 to read as above, effective for plan years beginning after July 1, 1986, subject to the special rules discussed at ¶ 15,045.

[¶ 15,045P]
APPLICABLE PREMIUM

Act Sec. 604. For purposes of this part—

(1) IN GENERAL. The term "applicable premium" means, with respect to any period of continuation coverage of qualified beneficiaries, the cost to the plan for such period of the coverage for similarly situated beneficiaries with respect to whom a qualifying event has not occurred (without regard to whether such cost is paid by the employer or employee).

(2) SPECIAL RULE FOR SELF-INSURED PLANS. To the extent that a plan is a self-insured plan—

(A) IN GENERAL. Except as provided in subparagraph (B), the applicable premium for any period of continuation coverage of qualified beneficiaries shall be equal to a reasonable estimate of the cost of providing coverage for such period for similarly situated beneficiaries which—

(i) is determined on an actuarial basis, and

(ii) takes into account such factors as the Secretary may prescribe in regulations.

(B) DETERMINATION ON BASIS OF PAST COST. If an administrator elects to have this subparagraph apply, the applicable premium for any period of continuation coverage of qualified beneficiaries shall be equal to—

(i) the cost to the plan for similarly situated beneficiaries for same period occurring during the preceding determination period under paragraph (3), adjusted by

(ii) the percentage increase or decrease in the implicit price deflator of the gross national product (calculated by the Department of Commerce and published in the Survey of Current Business) for the 12-month period ending on the last day of the sixth month of such preceding determination period.

(C) SUBPARAGRAPH (B) NOT TO APPLY WHERE SIGNIFICANT CHANGE. An administrator may not elect to have subparagraph (B) apply in any case in which there is any significant difference, between the determination period and the preceding determination period, in coverage under, or in employees covered by, the plan. The determination under the preceding sentence for any determination period shall be made at the same time as the determination under paragraph (3).

(3) DETERMINATION PERIOD. The determination of any applicable premium shall be made for a period of 12 months and shall be made before the beginning of such period.

Amendment:

P.L. 99-272:

Act Sec. 10002(a) added ERISA Sec. 604 to read as above, effective for plan years beginning after July 1, 1986, subject to the special rules discussed at ¶ 15,045.

[¶ 15,045T]
ELECTION

Act Sec. 605.(a) IN GENERAL. For purposes of this part—

(1) ELECTION PERIOD. The term "election period" means the period which—

(A) begins not later than the date on which coverage terminates under the plan by reason of a qualifying event,

(B) is of at least 60 days' duration, and

(C) ends not earlier than 60 days after the later of—

(i) the date described in subparagraph (A), or

(ii) in the case of any qualified beneficiary who receives notice under section 606(4), the date of such notice.

(2) EFFECT OF ELECTION ON OTHER BENEFICIARIES. Except as otherwise specified in an election, any election of continuation coverage by a qualified beneficiary described in subparagraph (A)(i) or (B) of section 607(3) shall be deemed to include an election of continuation coverage on behalf of any other qualified beneficiary who would lose coverage under the plan by reason of the qualifying event. If there is a choice among types of coverage under the plan, each qualified beneficiary is entitled to make a separate election among such types of coverage.

Act Sec. 605. TEMPORARY EXTENSION OF **COBRA** ELECTION PERIOD FOR CERTAIN INDIVIDUALS—

(b)(1) IN GENERAL. In the case of a nonelecting TAA-eligible individual and notwithstanding subsection (a), such individual may elect continuation coverage under this part during the 60-day period that begins on the first day of the month in which the individual becomes a TAA-eligible individual, but only if such election is made not later than 6 months after the date of the TAA-related loss of coverage.

(2) COMMENCEMENT OF COVERAGE; NO REACH-BACK. Any continuation coverage elected by a TAA-eligible individual under paragraph (1) shall commence at the beginning of the 60-day election period described in such paragraph and shall not include any period prior to such 60-day election period.

(3) PREEXISTING CONDITIONS. With respect to an individual who elects continuation coverage pursuant to paragraph (1), the period—

(A) beginning on the date of the TAA-related loss of coverage, and

(B) ending on the first day of the 60-day election period described in paragraph (1), shall be disregarded for purposes of determining the 63-day periods referred to in section 701(c)(2), section 2701(c)(2) of the Public Health Service Act, and section 9801(c)(2) of the Internal Revenue Code of 1986.

(4) DEFINITIONS. For purposes of this subsection:

(A) NONELECTING TAA-ELIGIBLE INDIVIDUAL. The term 'nonelecting TAA-eligible individual' means a TAA-eligible individual who—

(i) has a TAA-related loss of coverage; and

(ii) did not elect continuation coverage under this part during the TAA-related election period.

(B) TAA- ELIGIBLE INDIVIDUAL. The term 'TAA-eligible individual' means—

(i) an eligible TAA recipient (as defined in paragraph (2) of section 35(c) of the Internal Revenue Code of 1986), and

(ii) an eligible alternative TAA recipient (as defined in paragraph (3) of such section).

(C) TAA- RELATED ELECTION PERIOD. The term 'TAA-related election period' means, with respect to a TAA-related loss of coverage, the 60-day election period under this part which is a direct consequence of such loss.

(D) TAA- RELATED LOSS OF COVERAGE. The term 'TAA-related loss of coverage' means, with respect to an individual whose separation from employment gives rise to being an TAA-eligible individual, the loss of health benefits coverage associated with such separation.

Amendment

P.L. 107-210, §203(e)(1):

Act Sec. 203(e)(1) amended ERISA Sec. 605 by inserting "(a) IN GENERAL—" before "For purposes of this part"; and by adding paragraph (b) to read as above.

P.L. 99-514, §1895(d)(5)(B):

Amended Sec. 605(2) by inserting "of continuation coverage" after "any election" and by adding the sentence at the end of the section, effective for plan years beginning after July 1, 1986, subject to the special rules at ¶ 15,045.

P.L. 99-272:

Act Sec. 10002(a) added ERISA Sec. 605 to read as above, effective for plan years beginning after July 1, 1986, subject to the special rules discussed at ¶ 15,045.

[¶ 15,046]
NOTICE REQUIREMENTS

Act Sec. 606.(a) IN GENERAL. In accordance with regulations prescribed by the Secretary—

(1) the group health plan shall provide, at the time of commencement of coverage under the plan, written notice to each covered employee and spouse of the employee (if any) of the rights provided under this subsection,

(2) the employer of an employee under a plan must notify the administrator of a qualifying event described in paragraph (1), (2), (4), or (6) of section 603 within 30 days (or, in the case of a group health plan which is a multiemployer plan, such longer period of time as may be provided in the terms of the plan) of the date of the qualifying event,

(3) each covered employee or qualified beneficiary is responsible for notifying the administrator of the occurrence of any qualifying event described in paragraph (3) or (5) of section 603 within 60 days after the date of the qualifying event and each qualified beneficiary who is determined, under title II or XVI of the Social Security Act, to have been disabled at any time during the first 60 days of continuation coverage under this part is responsible for notifying the plan administrator of such determination within 60 days after the date of the determination and for notifying the plan administrator within 30 days after the date of any final determination under such title or titles that the qualified beneficiary is no longer disabled, and

(4) the administrator shall notify—

(A) in the case of a qualifying event described in paragraph (1), (2), (4) or (6) of section 603, any qualified beneficiary with respect to such event, and

(B) in the case of a qualifying event described in paragraph (3) or (5) of section 603 where the covered employee notifies the administrator under paragraph (3), any qualified beneficiary with respect to such event, of such beneficiary's rights under this subsection.

Act Sec. 606. ALTERNATIVE MEANS OF COMPLIANCE WITH REQUIREMENT FOR NOTIFICATION OF MULTIEMPLOYER PLANS BY EMPLOYERS. (b) The requirements of subsection (a)(2) shall be considered satisfied in the case of a multiemployer plan in connection with a qualifying event described in paragraph (2) of section 603 if the plan provides that the determination of the occurrence of such qualifying event will be made by the plan administrator.

Act Sec. 606. RULES RELATING TO NOTIFICATION OF QUALIFIED BENEFICIARIES BY PLAN ADMINISTRATOR. (c) For purposes of subsection (a)(4), any notification shall be made within 14 days (or, in the case of a group health plan which is a multiemployer plan, such longer period of time as may be provided in the terms of the plan) of the date on which the administrator is notified under paragraph (2) or (3), whichever is applicable, and any such notification to an individual who is a qualified beneficiary as the spouse of the covered employee shall be treated as notification to all other qualified beneficiaries residing with such spouse at the time such notification is made.

Amendments

P.L. 104-191, § 421(b)(2):

Act Sec. 421(b)(2) amended ERISA Sec. 606(a)(3) by striking "at the time of a qualifying event described in section 603(2)" and inserting "at any time during the first 60 days of continuation coverage under this part".

The above amendment is effective on January 1, 1997, regardless of whether the qualifying event occurred before, on, or after such date. For a special rule, see Act Sec. 421(e), reproduced below.

Act Sec. 421(e) provides:

(e) NOTIFICATION OF CHANGES.—Not later than November 1, 1996, each group health plan (covered under title XXII of the Public Health Service Act, part 6 of subtitle B of title I of the Employee Retirement Income Security Act of 1974, and section 4980B(f) of the Internal Revenue Code of 1986) shall notify each qualified beneficiary who has elected continuation coverage under such title, part or section of the amendments made by this section.

P.L. 101-239, § 6703(c):

Act Sec. 6703(c) amended ERISA Sec. 606(a)(3) by inserting before the comma the following:

"and each qualified beneficiary who is determined, under title II or XVI of the Social Security Act, to have been disabled at the time of a qualifying event described in section 603(2) is responsible for notifying the plan administrator of such determination within 60 days after the date of the determination and for notifying the plan administrator within 30 days after the date of any final determination under such title or titles that the qualified beneficiary is no longer disabled".

The above amendment applies to plan years beginning on or after December 19, 1989, regardless of whether the qualifying event occurred before, on, or after that date.

P.L. 101-239, § 7891(d)(1)(A)(i)(I):

Amended ERISA Sec. 606(2) by inserting after "30 days" new material to read as above, effective for plan years beginning on or after January 1, 1990.

P.L. 101-239, § 7891(d)(1)(A)(i)(II):

Amended ERISA Sec. 606(c) (as redesignated) by inserting after "14 days" new material to read as above, effective for plan years beginning on or after January 1, 1990.

P.L. 101-239, § 7891(d)(1)(A)(ii):

Amended ERISA Sec. 606 by inserting "(a) IN GENERAL.—" before "In accordance", by striking "for purposes of paragraph (4)," and inserting "(c) RULES RELATING TO NOTIFICATION OF QUALIFIED BENEFICIARIES BY PLAN ADMINISTRATOR.—For purposes of subsection (a)(4)," and by inserting after subsection (a)(4) (as designated by this amendment) new subsection (b) to read as above, effective for plan years beginning on or after January 1, 1990.

P.L. 99-514, § 1895(d)(6)(B):

Amended Sec. 606(3) by inserting "within 60 days after the date of the qualifying event" after "section 603" effective with respect to qualifying events occurring after the date of enactment.

P.L. 99-272:

Act Sec. 10002(a) added ERISA Sec. 606 to read as above, effective for plan years beginning after July 1, 1986, subject to the special rules discussed at ¶ 15,045.

Regulations

The following regulations were adopted and published in the *Federal Register* on May 26, 2004 (69 FR 30084), amending Part 2590, Subpart A under "Chapter XXV of Title 29 of the Code of Federal Regulations; Subchapter L—Group Health Plans; Part 2590—Rules and Regulations for Group Health Plans."

Subchapter L—Group Health Plans

Part 2590—Rules and Regulations for Group Health Plans

Subpart A—Requirements Relating to Access and Renewability of Coverage, and Limitations on Preexisting Condition Exclusion Periods

[¶ 15,046B-1]

§ 2590.606-1. **General Notice of Continuation Coverage.**

(a) *General.* Pursuant to section 606(a)(1) of the Employee Retirement Income Security Act of 1974, as amended (the Act), the administrator of a group health plan subject to the continuation coverage requirements of Part 6 of title I of the Act shall provide, in accordance with this section, written notice to each covered employee and spouse of the covered employee (if any) of the right to continuation coverage provided under the plan.

(b) *Timing of notice.* (1) The notice required by paragraph (a) of this section shall be furnished to each employee and each employee's spouse, not later than the earlier of:

(i) The date that is 90 days after the date on which such individual's coverage under the plan commences, or, if later, the date

that is 90 days after the date on which the plan first becomes subject to the continuation coverage requirements; or

(ii) The first date on which the administrator is required, pursuant to § 2590.606-4(b), to furnish the covered employee, spouse, or dependent child of such employee notice of a qualified beneficiary's right to elect continuation coverage.

(2) A notice that is furnished in accordance with paragraph (b)(1) of this section shall, for purposes of section 606(a)(1) of the Act, be deemed to be provided at the time of commencement of coverage under the plan.

(3) In any case in which an administrator is required to furnish a notice to a covered employee or spouse pursuant to paragraph (b)(1)(ii) of this section, the furnishing of a notice to such individual in accordance with § 2590.606-4(b) shall be deemed to satisfy the requirements of this section.

(c) *Content of notice.* The notice required by paragraph (a) of this section shall be written in a manner calculated to be understood by the average plan participant and shall contain the following information:

(1) The name of the plan under which continuation coverage is available, and the name, address and telephone number of a party or parties from whom additional information about the plan and continuation coverage can be obtained;

(2) A general description of the continuation coverage under the plan, including identification of the classes of individuals who may become qualified beneficiaries, the types of qualifying events that may give rise to the right to continuation coverage, the obligation of the employer to notify the plan administrator of the occurrence of certain qualifying events, the maximum period for which continuation coverage may be available, when and under what circumstances continuation coverage may be extended beyond the applicable maximum period, and the plan's requirements applicable to the payment of premiums for continuation coverage;

(3) An explanation of the plan's requirements regarding the responsibility of a qualified beneficiary to notify the administrator of a qualifying event that is a divorce, legal separation, or a child's ceasing to be a dependent under the terms of the plan, and a description of the plan's procedures for providing such notice;

(4) An explanation of the plan's requirements regarding the responsibility of qualified beneficiaries who are receiving continuation coverage to provide notice to the administrator of a determination by the Social Security Administration, under title II or XVI of the Social Security Act (42 U.S.C. 401 *et seq.* or 1381 *et seq.*), that a qualified beneficiary is disabled, and a description of the plan's procedures for providing such notice;

(5) An explanation of the importance of keeping the administrator informed of the current addresses of all participants or beneficiaries under the plan who are or may become qualified beneficiaries; and

(6) A statement that the notice does not fully describe continuation coverage or other rights under the plan and that more complete information regarding such rights is available from the plan administrator and in the plan's SPD.

(d) *Single notice rule.* A plan administrator may satisfy the requirement to provide notice in accordance with this section to a covered employee and the covered employee's spouse by furnishing a single notice addressed to both the covered employee and the covered employee's spouse, if, on the basis of the most recent information available to the plan, the covered employee's spouse resides at the same location as the covered employee, and the spouse's coverage under the plan commences on or after the date on which the covered employee's coverage commences, but not later than the date on which the notice required by this section is required to be provided to the covered employee. Nothing in this section shall be construed to create a requirement to provide a separate notice to dependent children who share a residence with a covered employee or a covered employee's spouse to whom notice is provided in accordance with this section. [Technical correction made June 23, 2004 (69 FR 34920)]

(e) *Notice in summary plan description.* A plan administrator may satisfy the requirement to provide notice in accordance with this section by including the information described in paragraphs (c)(1), (2), (3), (4), and (5) of this section in a summary plan description meeting the requirements of § 2520.102-3 of this Chapter furnished in accordance with paragraph (b) of this section.

(f) *Delivery of notice.* The notice required by this section shall be furnished in a manner consistent with the requirements of § 2520.104b-1 of this Chapter, including paragraph (c) of that section relating to the use of electronic media.

(g) *Model notice.* The appendix to this section contains a model notice that is intended to assist administrators in discharging the notice obligations of this section. Use of the model notice is not mandatory. The model notice reflects the requirements of this section as they would apply to single-employer group health plans and must be modified if used to provide notice with respect to other types of group health plans, such as multiemployer plans or plans established and maintained by employee organizations for their members. In order to use the model notice, administrators must appropriately add relevant information where indicated in the model notice, select among alternative language, and supplement the model notice to reflect applicable plan provisions. Items of information that are not applicable to a particular plan may be deleted. Use of the model notice, appropriately modified and supplemented, will be deemed to satisfy the notice content requirements of paragraph (c) of this section.

(h) *Applicability.* This section shall apply to any notice obligation described in this section that arises on or after the first day of the first plan year beginning on or after November 26, 2004.

[¶ 15,046B-2]
§ 2590.606-1. **Appendix to § 2590.606-1.**
MODEL GENERAL NOTICE OF COBRA CONTINUATION COVERAGE RIGHTS
(For use by single-employer group health plans)
** CONTINUATION COVERAGE RIGHTS UNDER COBRA**
Introduction

You are receiving this notice because you have recently become covered under a group health plan (the Plan). This notice contains important information about your right to COBRA continuation coverage, which is a temporary extension of coverage under the Plan. **This notice generally explains COBRA continuation coverage, when it may become available to you and your family, and what you need to do to protect the right to receive it.**

The right to COBRA continuation coverage was created by a federal law, the Consolidated Omnibus Budget Reconciliation Act of 1985 (COBRA). COBRA continuation coverage can become available to you when you would otherwise lose your group health coverage. It can also become available to other members of your family who are covered under the Plan when they would otherwise lose their group health coverage. For additional information about your rights and obligations under the Plan and under federal law, you should review the Plan's Summary Plan Description or contact the Plan Administrator.

What is COBRA Continuation Coverage?

COBRA continuation coverage is a continuation of Plan coverage when coverage would otherwise end because of a life event known as a "qualifying event." Specific qualifying events are listed later in this notice. After a qualifying event, COBRA continuation coverage must be offered to each person who is a "qualified beneficiary." You, your spouse, and your dependent children could become qualified beneficiaries if coverage under the Plan is lost because of the qualifying event. Under the Plan, qualified beneficiaries who elect COBRA continuation coverage [*choose and enter appropriate information:* must pay *or* are not required to pay] for COBRA continuation coverage.

If you are an employee, you will become a qualified beneficiary if you lose your coverage under the Plan because either one of the following qualifying events happens:

• Your hours of employment are reduced, or

• Your employment ends for any reason other than your gross misconduct.

If you are the spouse of an employee, you will become a qualified beneficiary if you lose your coverage under the Plan because any of the following qualifying events happens:

• Your spouse dies;

• Your spouse's hours of employment are reduced;

• Your spouse's employment ends for any reason other than his or her gross misconduct;

• Your spouse becomes entitled to Medicare benefits (under Part A, Part B, or both); or

• You become divorced or legally separated from your spouse.

Your dependent children will become qualified beneficiaries if they lose coverage under the Plan because any of the following qualifying events happens:

• The parent-employee dies;

• The parent-employee's hours of employment are reduced;

• The parent-employee's employment ends for any reason other than his or her gross misconduct;

• The parent-employee becomes entitled to Medicare benefits (Part A, Part B, or both);

• The parents become divorced or legally separated; or

• The child stops being eligible for coverage under the plan as a "dependent child."

[*If the Plan provides retiree health coverage, add the following paragraph:*]

Sometimes, filing a proceeding in bankruptcy under title 11 of the United States Code can be a qualifying event. If a proceeding in bankruptcy is filed with respect to [*enter name of employer sponsoring the plan*], and that bankruptcy results in the loss of coverage of any retired employee covered under the Plan, the retired employee will become a qualified beneficiary with respect to the bankruptcy. The retired employee's spouse, surviving spouse, and dependent children will also become qualified beneficiaries if bankruptcy results in the loss of their coverage under the Plan.

When is COBRA Coverage Available?

The Plan will offer COBRA continuation coverage to qualified beneficiaries only after the Plan Administrator has been notified that a qualifying event has occurred. When the qualifying event is the end of employment or reduction of hours of employment, death of the employee, [*add if Plan provides retiree health coverage:* commencement of a proceeding in bankruptcy with respect to the employer,] or the employee's becoming entitled to Medicare benefits (under Part A, Part B, or both), the employer must notify the Plan Administrator of the qualifying event.

You Must Give Notice of Some Qualifying Events

For the other qualifying events (*divorce* or *legal separation* of the employee and spouse or a *dependent child's losing eligibility for coverage* as a dependent child), you must notify the Plan Administrator within 60 days [*or enter longer period permitted under the terms of the Plan*] after the qualifying event occurs. You must provide this notice to: [*Enter name of appropriate party*]. [*Add description of any additional Plan procedures for this notice, including a description of any required information or documentation.*]

How is COBRA Coverage Provided?

Once the Plan Administrator receives notice that a qualifying event has occurred, COBRA continuation coverage will be offered to each of the qualified beneficiaries. Each qualified beneficiary will have an independent right to elect COBRA continuation coverage. Covered employees may elect COBRA continuation coverage on behalf of their spouses, and parents may elect COBRA continuation coverage on behalf of their children.

COBRA continuation coverage is a temporary continuation of coverage. When the qualifying event is the death of the employee, the employee's becoming entitled to Medicare benefits (under Part A, Part B, or both), your divorce or legal separation, or a dependent child's losing eligibility as a dependent child, COBRA continuation coverage lasts for up to a total of 36 months. When the qualifying event is the end of employment or reduction of the employee's hours of employment, and the employee became entitled to Medicare benefits less than 18 months before the qualifying event, COBRA continuation coverage for qualified beneficiaries other than the employee lasts until 36 months after the date of Medicare entitlement. For example, if a covered employee becomes entitled to Medicare 8 months before the date on which his employment terminates, COBRA continuation coverage for his spouse and children can last up to 36 months after the date of Medicare entitlement, which is equal to 28 months after the date of the qualifying event (36 months minus 8 months). Otherwise, when the qualifying event is the end of employment or reduction of the employee's hours of employment, COBRA continuation coverage generally lasts for only up to a total of 18 months. There are two ways in which this 18-month period of COBRA continuation coverage can be extended.

Disability extension of 18-month period of continuation coverage

If you or anyone in your family covered under the Plan is determined by the Social Security Administration to be disabled and you notify the Plan Administrator in a timely fashion, you and your entire family may be entitled to receive up to an additional 11 months of COBRA continuation coverage, for a total maximum of 29 months. The disability would have to have started at some time before the 60th day of COBRA continuation coverage and must last at least until the end of the 18-month period of continuation coverage. [*Add description of any additional Plan procedures for this notice, including a description of any*

required information or documentation, the name of the appropriate party to whom notice must be sent, and the time period for giving notice].

Second qualifying event extension of 18-month period of continuation coverage

If your family experiences another qualifying event while receiving 18 months of COBRA continuation coverage, the spouse and dependent children in your family can get up to 18 additional months of COBRA continuation coverage, for a maximum of 36 months, if notice of the second qualifying event is properly given to the Plan. This extension may be available to the spouse and any dependent children receiving continuation coverage if the employee or former employee dies, becomes entitled to Medicare benefits (under Part A, Part B, or both), or gets divorced or legally separated, or if the dependent child stops being eligible under the Plan as a dependent child, but only if the event would have caused the spouse or dependent child to lose coverage under the Plan had the first qualifying event not occurred.

If You Have Questions

Questions concerning your Plan or your COBRA continuation coverage rights should be addressed to the contact or contacts identified below. For more information about your rights under ERISA, including COBRA, the Health Insurance Portability and Accountability Act (HIPAA), and other laws affecting group health plans, contact the nearest Regional or District Office of the U.S. Department of Labor's Employee Benefits Security Administration (EBSA) in your area or visit the EBSA website at www.dol.gov/ebsa. (Addresses and phone numbers of Regional and District EBSA Offices are available through EBSA's website.)

Keep Your Plan Informed of Address Changes

In order to protect your family's rights, you should keep the Plan Administrator informed of any changes in the addresses of family members. You should also keep a copy, for your records, of any notices you send to the Plan Administrator.

Plan Contact Information

[*Enter name of group health plan and name (or position), address and phone number of party or parties from whom information about the plan and COBRA continuation coverage can be obtained on request.*]

[¶ 15,046B-3]
§ 2590.606-2. Notice Requirement for Employers.

(a) *General.* Pursuant to section 606(a)(2) of the Employee Retirement Income Security Act of 1974, as amended (the Act), except as otherwise provided herein, the employer of a covered employee under a group health plan subject to the continuation coverage requirements of Part 6 of title I of the Act shall provide, in accordance with this section, notice to the administrator of the plan of the occurrence of a qualifying event that is the covered employee's death, termination of employment (other than by reason of gross misconduct), reduction in hours of employment, Medicare entitlement, or a proceeding in a case under title 11, United States Code, with respect to the employer from whose employment the covered employee retired at any time.

(b) *Timing of notice.* The notice required by this section shall be furnished to the administrator of the plan —

(1) In the case of a plan that provides, with respect to a qualifying event, pursuant to section 607(5) of the Act, that continuation coverage and the applicable period for providing notice under section 606(a)(2) of the Act shall commence on the date of loss of coverage, not later than 30 days after the date on which a qualified beneficiary loses coverage under the plan due to the qualifying event;

(2) In the case of a multiemployer plan that provides, pursuant to section 606(a)(2) of the Act, for a longer period of time within which employers may provide notice of a qualifying event, not later than the end of the period provided pursuant to the plan's terms for such notice; and

(3) In all other cases, not later than 30 days after the date on which the qualifying event occurred.

(c) *Content of notice.* The notice required by this section shall include sufficient information to enable the administrator to determine the plan, the covered employee, the qualifying event, and the date of the qualifying event.

(d) *Multiemployer plan special rules.* This section shall not apply to any employer that maintains a multiemployer plan, with respect to qualifying events affecting coverage under such plan, if the plan provides, pursuant to section 606(b) of the Act, that the administrator shall determine whether such a qualifying event has occurred.

(e) *Applicability.* This section shall apply to any notice obligation described in this section that arises on or after the first day of the first plan year beginning on or after November 26, 2004.

[¶ 15,046B-4]

§ 2590.606-3. **Notice Requirements for Covered Employees and Qualified Beneficiaries.**

(a) *General.* In accordance with the authority of sections 505 and 606(a)(3) of the Employee Retirement Income Security Act of 1974, as amended (the Act), this section sets forth requirements for group health plans subject to the continuation coverage requirements of Part 6 of title I of the Act with respect to the responsibility of covered employees and qualified beneficiaries to provide the following notices to administrators:

(1) Notice of the occurrence of a qualifying event that is a divorce or legal separation of a covered employee from his or her spouse;

(2) Notice of the occurrence of a qualifying event that is a beneficiary's ceasing to be covered under a plan as a dependent child of a participant;

(3) Notice of the occurrence of a second qualifying event after a qualified beneficiary has become entitled to continuation coverage with a maximum duration of 18 (or 29) months;

(4) Notice that a qualified beneficiary entitled to receive continuation coverage with a maximum duration of 18 months has been determined by the Social Security Administration, under title II or XVI of the Social Security Act (42 U.S.C. 401 *et seq.* or 1381 *et seq.*) (SSA), to be disabled at any time during the first 60 days of continuation coverage; and

(5) Notice that a qualified beneficiary, with respect to whom a notice described in paragraph (a)(4) of this section has been provided, has subsequently been determined by the Social Security Administration, under title II or XVI of the SSA to no longer be disabled.

(b) *Reasonable procedures.* (1) A plan subject to the continuation coverage requirements shall establish reasonable procedures for the furnishing of the notices described in paragraph (a) of this section.

(2) For purposes of this section, a plan's notice procedures shall be deemed reasonable only if such procedures:

(i) Are described in the plan's summary plan description required by § 2520.102-3 of this Chapter;

(ii) Specify the individual or entity designated to receive such notices;

(iii) Specify the means by which notice may be given;

(iv) Describe the information concerning the qualifying event or determination of disability that the plan deems necessary in order to provide continuation coverage rights consistent with the requirements of the Act; and

(v) Comply with the requirements of paragraphs (c), (d), and (e) of this section.

(3) A plan's procedures will not fail to be reasonable, pursuant to this section, solely because the procedures require a covered employee or qualified beneficiary to utilize a specific form to provide notice to the administrator, provided that any such form is easily available, without cost, to covered employees and qualified beneficiaries.

(4) If a plan has not established reasonable procedures for providing a notice required by this section, such notice shall be deemed to have been provided when a written or oral communication identifying a specific event is made in a manner reasonably calculated to bring the information to the attention of any of the following:

(i) In the case of a single-employer plan, the person or organizational unit that customarily handles employee benefits matters of the employer;

(ii) In the case of a plan to which more than one unaffiliated employer contributes, or which is established or maintained by an employee organization, either the joint board, association, committee, or other similar group (or any member of any such group) administering the plan, or the person or organizational unit to which claims for benefits under the plan customarily are referred; or

(iii) In the case of a plan the benefits of which are provided or administered by an insurance company, insurance service, or other similar organization subject to regulation under the insurance laws of one or more States, the person or organizational unit that customarily handles claims for benefits under the plan or any officer of the insurance company, insurance service, or other similar organization.

(c) *Periods of time for providing notice.* A plan may establish a reasonable period of time for furnishing any of the notices described in paragraph (a) of this section, provided that any time limit imposed by the plan with respect to a particular notice may not be shorter than the time limit described in this paragraph (c) with respect to that notice.

(1) *Time limits for notices of qualifying events.* The period of time for furnishing a notice described in paragraph (a)(1), (2), or (3) of this section may not end before the date that is 60 days after the latest of:

(i) The date on which the relevant qualifying event occurs;

(ii) The date on which the qualified beneficiary loses (or would lose) coverage under the plan as a result of the qualifying event; or

(iii) The date on which the qualified beneficiary is informed, through the furnishing of the plan's summary plan description or the notice described in § 2590.606-1, of both the responsibility to provide the notice and the plan's procedures for providing such notice to the administrator.

(2) *Time limits for notice of disability determination.* (i) Subject to paragraph (c)(2)(ii) of this section, the period of time for furnishing the notice described in paragraph (a)(4) of this section may not end before the date that is 60 days after the latest of:

(A) The date of the disability determination by the Social Security Administration;

(B) The date on which a qualifying event occurs;

(C) The date on which the qualified beneficiary loses (or would lose) coverage under the plan as a result of the qualifying event; or

(D) The date on which the qualified beneficiary is informed, through the furnishing of the summary plan description or the notice described in § 2590.606-1, of both the responsibility to provide the notice and the plan's procedures for providing such notice to the administrator.

(ii) Notwithstanding paragraph (c)(2)(i) of this section, a plan may require the notice described in paragraph (a)(4) of this section to be furnished before the end of the first 18 months of continuation coverage.

(3) *Time limits for notice of change in disability status.* The period of time for furnishing the notice described in paragraph (a)(5) of this section may not end before the date that is 30 days after the later of:

(i) The date of the final determination by the Social Security Administration, under title II or XVI of the SSA, that the qualified beneficiary is no longer disabled; or

(ii) The date on which the qualified beneficiary is informed, through the furnishing of the plan's summary plan description or the notice described in § 2590.606-1, of both the responsibility to provide the notice and the plan's procedures for providing such notice to the administrator.

(d) *Required contents of notice.* (1) A plan may establish reasonable requirements for the content of any notice described in this section, provided that a plan may not deem a notice to have been provided untimely if such notice, although not containing all of the information required by the plan, is provided within the time limit established under the plan in conformity with paragraph (c) of this section, and the administrator is able to determine from such notice the plan, the covered employee and qualified beneficiary(ies), the qualifying event or disability, and the date on which the qualifying event (if any) occurred.

(2) An administrator may require a notice that does not contain all of the information required by the plan to be supplemented with the additional information necessary to meet the plan's reasonable content requirements for such notice in order for the notice to be deemed to have been provided in accordance with this section.

(e) *Who may provide notice.* With respect to each of the notice requirements of this section, any individual who is either the covered employee, a qualified beneficiary with respect to the qualifying event, or any representative acting on behalf of the covered employee or qualified beneficiary may provide the notice, and the provision of notice by one individual shall satisfy any responsibility to provide notice on behalf of all related qualified beneficiaries with respect to the qualifying event.

(f) *Plan provisions.* To the extent that a plan provides a covered employee or qualified beneficiary a period of time longer than that specified in this section to provide notice to the administrator, the terms of the plan shall govern the time frame for such notice.

(g) *Additional rights to continuation coverage.* Nothing in this section shall be construed to preclude a plan from providing, in accordance with its terms, continuation coverage to a qualified beneficiary although a notice requirement of this section was not satisfied.

(h) *Applicability.* This section shall apply to any notice obligation described in this section that arises on or after the first day of the first plan year beginning on or after November 26, 2004.

[¶ 15,046B-5]
§ 2590.606-4. Notice Requirements for Plan Administrators.

(a) *General.* Pursuant to section 606(a)(4) of the Employee Retirement Income Security Act of 1974, as amended (the Act), the administrator of a group health plan subject to the continuation coverage requirements of Part 6 of title I of the Act shall provide, in accordance with this section, notice to each qualified beneficiary of the qualified beneficiary's rights to continuation coverage under the plan.

(b) *Notice of right to elect continuation coverage.* (1) Except as provided in paragraph (b)(2) or (3) of this section, upon receipt of a notice of qualifying event furnished in accordance with § 2590.606-2 or § 2590.606-3, the administrator shall furnish to each qualified beneficiary, not later than 14 days after receipt of the notice of qualifying event, a notice meeting the requirements of paragraph (b)(4) of this section.

(2) In the case of a plan with respect to which an employer of a covered employee is also the administrator of the plan, except as provided in paragraph (b)(3) of this section, if the employer is otherwise required to furnish a notice of a qualifying event to an administrator pursuant to § 2590.606-2, the administrator shall furnish to each qualified beneficiary a notice meeting the requirements of paragraph (b)(4) of this section not later than 44 days after:

(i) In the case of a plan that provides, with respect to the qualifying event, that continuation coverage and the applicable period for providing notice under section 606(a)(2) of the Act shall commence with the date of loss of coverage, the date on which a qualified beneficiary loses coverage under the plan due to the qualifying event; or

(ii) In all other cases, the date on which the qualifying event occurred.

(3) In the case of a plan that is a multiemployer plan, a notice meeting the requirements of paragraph (b)(4) of this section shall be furnished not later than the later of:

(i) The end of the time period provided in paragraph (b)(1) of this section; or

(ii) The end of the time period provided in the terms of the plan for such purpose.

(4) The notice required by this paragraph (b) shall be written in a manner calculated to be understood by the average plan participant and shall contain the following information:

(i) The name of the plan under which continuation coverage is available; and the name, address and telephone number of the party

responsible under the plan for the administration of continuation coverage benefits;

(ii) Identification of the qualifying event;

(iii) Identification, by status or name, of the qualified beneficiaries who are recognized by the plan as being entitled to elect continuation coverage with respect to the qualifying event, and the date on which coverage under the plan will terminate (or has terminated) unless continuation coverage is elected;

(iv) A statement that each individual who is a qualified beneficiary with respect to the qualifying event has an independent right to elect continuation coverage, that a covered employee or a qualified beneficiary who is the spouse of the covered employee (or was the spouse of the covered employee on the day before the qualifying event occurred) may elect continuation coverage on behalf of all other qualified beneficiaries with respect to the qualifying event, and that a parent or legal guardian may elect continuation coverage on behalf of a minor child;

(v) An explanation of the plan's procedures for electing continuation coverage, including an explanation of the time period during which the election must be made, and the date by which the election must be made;

(vi) An explanation of the consequences of failing to elect or waiving continuation coverage, including an explanation that a qualified beneficiary's decision whether to elect continuation coverage will affect the future rights of qualified beneficiaries to portability of group health coverage, guaranteed access to individual health coverage, and special enrollment under Part 7 of title I of the Act, with a reference to where a qualified beneficiary may obtain additional information about such rights; and a description of the plan's procedures for revoking a waiver of the right to continuation coverage before the date by which the election must be made;

(vii) A description of the continuation coverage that will be made available under the plan, if elected, including the date on which such coverage will commence, either by providing a description of the coverage or by reference to the plan's summary plan description;

(viii) An explanation of the maximum period for which continuation coverage will be available under the plan, if elected; an explanation of the continuation coverage termination date; and an explanation of any events that might cause continuation coverage to be terminated earlier than the end of the maximum period;

(ix) A description of the circumstances (if any) under which the maximum period of continuation coverage may be extended due either to the occurrence of a second qualifying event or a determination by the Social Security Administration, under title II or XVI of the Social Security Act (42 U.S.C. 401 *et seq.* or 1381 *et seq.*) (SSA), that the qualified beneficiary is disabled, and the length of any such extension;

(x) In the case of a notice that offers continuation coverage with a maximum duration of less than 36 months, a description of the plan's requirements regarding the responsibility of qualified beneficiaries to provide notice of a second qualifying event and notice of a disability determination under the SSA, along with a description of the plan's procedures for providing such notices, including the times within which such notices must be provided and the consequences of failing to provide such notices. The notice shall also explain the responsibility of qualified beneficiaries to provide notice that a disabled qualified beneficiary has subsequently been determined to no longer be disabled;

(xi) A description of the amount, if any, that each qualified beneficiary will be required to pay for continuation coverage;

(xii) A description of the due dates for payments, the qualified beneficiaries' right to pay on a monthly basis, the grace periods for payment, the address to which payments should be sent, and the consequences of delayed payment and non-payment;

(xiii) An explanation of the importance of keeping the administrator informed of the current addresses of all participants or beneficiaries under the plan who are or may become qualified beneficiaries; and

(xiv) A statement that the notice does not fully describe continuation coverage or other rights under the plan, and that more complete information regarding such rights is available in the plan's summary plan description or from the plan administrator.

(c) *Notice of unavailability of continuation coverage.* (1) In the event that an administrator receives a notice furnished in accordance with § 2590.606-3 relating to a qualifying event, second qualifying event, or determination of disability by the Social Security Administration regarding a covered employee, qualified beneficiary, or other individual and determines that the individual is not entitled to continuation coverage under Part 6 of title I of the Act, the administrator shall provide to such individual an explanation as to why the individual is not entitled to continuation coverage.

(2) The notice required by this paragraph (c) shall be written in a manner calculated to be understood by the average plan participant and shall be furnished by the administrator in accordance with the time frame set out in paragraph (b) of this section that would apply if the administrator received a notice of qualifying event and determined that the individual was entitled to continuation coverage.

(d) *Notice of termination of continuation coverage.* (1) The administrator of a plan that is providing continuation coverage to one or more qualified beneficiaries with respect to a qualifying event shall provide, in accordance with this paragraph (d), notice to each such qualified beneficiary of any termination of continuation coverage that takes effect earlier than the end of the maximum period of continuation coverage applicable to such qualifying event.

(2) The notice required by this paragraph (d) shall be written in a manner calculated to be understood by the average plan participant and shall contain the following information:

(i) The reason that continuation coverage has terminated earlier than the end of the maximum period of continuation coverage applicable to such qualifying event;

(ii) The date of termination of continuation coverage; and

(iii) Any rights the qualified beneficiary may have under the plan or under applicable law to elect an alternative group or individual coverage, such as a conversion right.

(3) The notice required by this paragraph (d) shall be furnished by the administrator as soon as practicable following the administrator's determination that continuation coverage shall terminate.

(e) *Special notice rules.* The notices required by paragraphs (b), (c), and (d) of this section shall be furnished to each qualified beneficiary or individual, except that:

(1) An administrator may provide notice to a covered employee and the covered employee's spouse by furnishing a single notice addressed to both the covered employee and the covered employee's spouse, if, on the basis of the most recent information available to the plan, the covered employee's spouse resides at the same location as the covered employee; and

☐ End of employment
☐ Death of employee
☐ Entitlement to Medicare

Each person ("qualified beneficiary") in the category(ies) checked below is entitled to elect COBRA continuation coverage, which will continue group health care coverage under the Plan for up to ___ months [*enter 18 or 36, as appropriate and check appropriate box or boxes; names may be added*]:

☐ Employee or former employee
☐ Spouse or former spouse
☐ Dependent child(ren) covered under the Plan on the day before the event that caused the loss of coverage
☐ Child who is losing coverage under the Plan because he or she is no longer a dependent under the Plan

If elected, COBRA continuation coverage will begin on [*enter date*] and can last until [*enter date*]. [*Add, if appropriate:* You may elect any of the following options for COBRA continuation coverage: [*list available coverage options*].

COBRA continuation coverage will cost: [*enter amount each qualified beneficiary will be required to pay for each option per month of coverage and any other permitted coverage periods.*] You do not have to send any payment with the Election Form. Important additional information

(2) An administrator may provide notice to each qualified beneficiary who is the dependent child of a covered employee by furnishing a single notice to the covered employee or the covered employee's spouse, if, on the basis of the most recent information available to the plan, the dependent child resides at the same location as the individual to whom such notice is provided.

(f) *Delivery of notice.* The notices required by this section shall be furnished in any manner consistent with the requirements of § 2520.104b-1 of this Chapter, including paragraph (c) of that section relating to the use of electronic media.

(g) *Model notice.* The appendix to this section contains a model notice that is intended to assist administrators in discharging the notice obligations of paragraph (b) of this section. Use of the model notice is not mandatory. The model notice reflects the requirements of this section as they would apply to single-employer group health plans and must be modified if used to provide notice with respect to other types of group health plans, such as multiemployer plans or plans established and maintained by employee organizations for their members. In order to use the model notice, administrators must appropriately add relevant information where indicated in the model notice, select among alternative language and supplement the model notice to reflect applicable plan provisions. Items of information that are not applicable to a particular plan may be deleted. Use of the model notice, appropriately modified and supplemented, will be deemed to satisfy the notice content requirements of paragraph (b)(4) of this section.

(h) *Applicability.* This section shall apply to any notice obligation described in this section that arises on or after the first day of the first plan year beginning on or after November 26, 2004.

[¶ 15,046B-6]
§ 2590.606-4. **Appendix to § 2590.606-4.**
MODEL COBRA CONTINUATION COVERAGE ELECTION NOTICE
(For use by single-employer group health plans)
[*Enter date of notice*]
Dear: [*Identify the qualified beneficiary(ies), by name or status*]

This notice contains important information about your right to continue your health care coverage in the [*enter name of group health plan*] (the Plan). Please read the information contained in this notice very carefully.

To elect COBRA continuation coverage, follow the instructions on the next page to complete the enclosed Election Form and submit it to us.

If you do not elect COBRA continuation coverage, your coverage under the Plan will end on [*enter date*] due to [*check appropriate box*]:

☐ Reduction in hours of employment
☐ Divorce or legal separation
☐ Loss of dependent child status

about payment for COBRA continuation coverage is included in the pages following the Election Form.

If you have any questions about this notice or your rights to COBRA continuation coverage, you should contact [*enter name of party responsible for COBRA administration for the Plan, with telephone number and address*].

COBRA CONTINUATION COVERAGE ELECTION FORM

INSTRUCTIONS: To elect COBRA continuation coverage, complete this Election Form and return it to us. Under federal law, you must have 60 days after the date of this notice to decide whether you want to elect COBRA continuation coverage under the Plan.

Send completed Election Form to: [*Enter Name and Address*]

This Election Form must be completed and returned by mail [*or describe other means of submission and due date*]. If mailed, it must be post-marked no later than [*enter date*].

If you do not submit a completed Election Form by the due date shown above, you will lose your right to elect COBRA continuation coverage. If you reject COBRA continuation coverage before the due date, you may change your mind as long as you furnish a

completed Election Form before the due date. However, if you change your mind after first rejecting COBRA continuation coverage, your COBRA continuation coverage will begin on the date you furnish the completed Election Form.

Name	Date of Birth	Relationship to Employee	SSN (or other identifier)

a. _____

[*Add if appropriate:* Coverage option elected:]

_____

c. _____

[*Add if appropriate:* Coverage option elected:]

_____

Signature _____

Print Name _____

_____

Print Address

IMPORTANT INFORMATION ABOUT YOUR COBRA CONTINUATION COVERAGE RIGHTS

What is continuation coverage?

Federal law requires that most group health plans (including this Plan) give employees and their families the opportunity to continue their health care coverage when there is a "qualifying event" that would result in a loss of coverage under an employer's plan. Depending on the type of qualifying event, "qualified beneficiaries" can include the employee (or retired employee) covered under the group health plan, the covered employee's spouse, and the dependent children of the covered employee.

Continuation coverage is the same coverage that the Plan gives to other participants or beneficiaries under the Plan who are not receiving continuation coverage. Each qualified beneficiary who elects continuation coverage will have the same rights under the Plan as other participants or beneficiaries covered under the Plan, including [*add if applicable:* open enrollment and] special enrollment rights.

How long will continuation coverage last?

In the case of a loss of coverage due to end of employment or reduction in hours of employment, coverage generally may be continued only for up to a total of 18 months. In the case of losses of coverage due to an employee's death, divorce or legal separation, the employee's becoming entitled to Medicare benefits or a dependent child ceasing to be a dependent under the terms of the plan, coverage may be continued for up to a total of 36 months. When the qualifying event is the end of employment or reduction of the employee's hours of employment, and the employee became entitled to Medicare benefits less than 18 months before the qualifying event, COBRA continuation coverage for qualified beneficiaries other than the employee lasts until 36 months after the date of Medicare entitlement. This notice shows the maximum period of continuation coverage available to the qualified beneficiaries.

Continuation coverage will be terminated before the end of the maximum period if:

• any required premium is not paid in full on time,

• a qualified beneficiary becomes covered, after electing continuation coverage, under another group health plan that does not impose any pre-existing condition exclusion for a pre-existing condition of the qualified beneficiary,

Read the important information about your rights included in the pages after the Election Form.

I (We) elect COBRA continuation coverage in the [*enter name of plan*] (the Plan) as indicated below:

b. _____

[*Add if appropriate:* Coverage option elected:]

_____

Date _____

Relationship to individual(s) listed above

_____

Telephone number

• a qualified beneficiary becomes entitled to Medicare benefits (under Part A, Part B, or both) after electing continuation coverage, [Technical correction made June 23, 2004 (69 FR 34920)] or

• the employer ceases to provide any group health plan for its employees.

Continuation coverage may also be terminated for any reason the Plan would terminate coverage of a participant or beneficiary not receiving continuation coverage (such as fraud).

[*If the maximum period shown on page 1 of this notice is less than 36 months, add the following three paragraphs:*]

How can you extend the length of COBRA continuation coverage?

If you elect continuation coverage, an extension of the maximum period of coverage may be available if a qualified beneficiary is disabled or a second qualifying event occurs. You must notify [*enter name of party responsible for COBRA administration*] of a disability or a second qualifying event in order to extend the period of continuation coverage. Failure to provide notice of a disability or second qualifying event may affect the right to extend the period of continuation coverage.

Disability

An 11-month extension of coverage may be available if any of the qualified beneficiaries is determined by the Social Security Administration (SSA) to be disabled. The disability has to have started at some time before the 60th day of COBRA continuation coverage and must last at least until the end of the 18-month period of continuation coverage. [*Describe Plan provisions for requiring notice of disability determination, including time frames and procedures.*] Each qualified beneficiary who has elected continuation coverage will be entitled to the 11-month disability extension if one of them qualifies. If the qualified beneficiary is determined by SSA to no longer be disabled, you must notify the Plan of that fact within 30 days after SSA's determination.

Second Qualifying Event

An 18-month extension of coverage will be available to spouses and dependent children who elect continuation coverage if a second qualifying event occurs during the first 18 months of continuation coverage. The maximum amount of continuation coverage available when a second qualifying event occurs is 36 months. Such second qualifying events may include the death of a covered employee, divorce or separation from the covered employee, the covered employee's becoming entitled to Medicare benefits (under Part A, Part B, or both), or a dependent child's ceasing to be eligible for coverage as a dependent under the Plan. These events can be a second qualifying event only if they would have caused the qualified beneficiary to lose coverage under the Plan if the first qualifying event had not occurred. You must notify the Plan within 60 days after a second qualifying event occurs if you want to extend your continuation coverage.

How can you elect COBRA continuation coverage?

To elect continuation coverage, you must complete the Election Form and furnish it according to the directions on the form. Each qualified beneficiary has a separate right to elect continuation coverage. For example, the employee's spouse may elect continuation coverage even if the employee does not. Continuation coverage may be elected for only one, several, or for all dependent children who are qualified beneficiaries. A parent may elect to continue coverage on behalf of any dependent children. The employee or the employee's spouse can elect continuation coverage on behalf of all of the qualified beneficiaries.

In considering whether to elect continuation coverage, you should take into account that a failure to continue your group health coverage will affect your future rights under federal law. First, you can lose the right to avoid having pre-existing condition exclusions applied to you by other group health plans if you have more than a 63-day gap in health coverage, and election of continuation coverage may help you not have such a gap. Second, you will lose the guaranteed right to purchase individual health insurance policies that do not impose such pre-existing condition exclusions if you do not get continuation coverage for the maximum time available to you. Finally, you should take into account that you have special enrollment rights under federal law. You have the right to request special enrollment in another group health plan for which you are otherwise eligible (such as a plan sponsored by your spouse's employer) within 30 days after your group health coverage ends because of the qualifying event listed above. You will also have the same special enrollment right at the end of continuation coverage if you get continuation coverage for the maximum time available to you.

How much does COBRA continuation coverage cost?

Generally, each qualified beneficiary may be required to pay the entire cost of continuation coverage. The amount a qualified beneficiary may be required to pay may not exceed 102 percent (or, in the case of an extension of continuation coverage due to a disability, 150 percent) of the cost to the group health plan (including both employer and employee contributions) for coverage of a similarly situated plan participant or beneficiary who is not receiving continuation coverage. The required payment for each continuation coverage period for each option is described in this notice.

[*If employees might be eligible for trade adjustment assistance, the following information may be added*: The Trade Act of 2002 created a new tax credit for certain individuals who become eligible for trade adjustment assistance and for certain retired employees who are receiving pension payments from the Pension Benefit Guaranty Corporation (PBGC) (eligible individuals). Under the new tax provisions, eligible individuals can either take a tax credit or get advance payment of 65% of premiums paid for qualified health insurance, including continuation coverage. If you have questions about these new tax provisions, you may call the Health Coverage Tax Credit Customer Contact Center toll-free at 1-866-628-4282. TTD/TTY callers may call toll-free at 1-866-626-4282. More information about the Trade Act is also available at *www.doleta.gov/tradeact/2002act_index.asp.*

When and how must payment for COBRA continuation coverage be made?

First payment for continuation coverage

If you elect continuation coverage, you do not have to send any payment with the Election Form. However, you must make your first payment for continuation coverage not later than 45 days after the date of your election. (This is the date the Election Notice is post-marked, if mailed.) If you do not make your first payment for continuation coverage in full not later than 45 days after the date of your election, you will

lose all continuation coverage rights under the Plan. You are responsible for making sure that the amount of your first payment is correct. You may contact [*enter appropriate contact information, e.g., the Plan Administrator or other party responsible for COBRA administration under the Plan*] to confirm the correct amount of your first payment.

Periodic payments for continuation coverage

After you make your first payment for continuation coverage, you will be required to make periodic payments for each subsequent coverage period. The amount due for each coverage period for each qualified beneficiary is shown in this notice. The periodic payments can be made on a monthly basis. Under the Plan, each of these periodic payments for continuation coverage is due on the [*enter due day for each monthly payment*] for that coverage period. [*If Plan offers other payment schedules, enter with appropriate dates:* You may instead make payments for continuation coverage for the following coverage periods, due on the following dates:]. If you make a periodic payment on or before the first day of the coverage period to which it applies, your coverage under the Plan will continue for that coverage period without any break. The Plan [*select one:* will *or* will not] send periodic notices of payments due for these coverage periods.

Grace periods for periodic payments

Although periodic payments are due on the dates shown above, you will be given a grace period of 30 days after the first day of the coverage period [*or enter longer period permitted by Plan*] to make each periodic payment. Your continuation coverage will be provided for each coverage period as long as payment for that coverage period is made before the end of the grace period for that payment. [*If Plan suspends coverage during grace period for nonpayment, enter and modify as necessary:* However, if you pay a periodic payment later than the first day of the coverage period to which it applies, but before the end of the grace period for the coverage period, your coverage under the Plan will be suspended as of the first day of the coverage period and then retroactively reinstated (going back to the first day of the coverage period) when the periodic payment is received. This means that any claim you submit for benefits while your coverage is suspended may be denied and may have to be resubmitted once your coverage is reinstated.]

If you fail to make a periodic payment before the end of the grace period for that coverage period, you will lose all rights to continuation coverage under the Plan.

Your first payment and all periodic payments for continuation coverage should be sent to:

[*enter appropriate payment address*]

For more information

This notice does not fully describe continuation coverage or other rights under the Plan. More information about continuation coverage and your rights under the Plan is available in your summary plan description or from the Plan Administrator.

If you have any questions concerning the information in this notice, your rights to coverage, or if you want a copy of your summary plan description, you should contact [*enter name of party responsible for COBRA administration for the Plan, with telephone number and address*].

For more information about your rights under ERISA, including COBRA, the Health Insurance Portability and Accountability Act (HIPAA), and other laws affecting group health plans, contact the U.S. Department of Labor's Employee Benefits Security Administration (EBSA) in your area or visit the EBSA website at *www.dol.gov/ebsa.* (Addresses and phone numbers of Regional and District EBSA Offices are available through EBSA's website.)

Keep Your Plan Informed of Address Changes

In order to protect your and your family's rights, you should keep the Plan Administrator informed of any changes in your address and the addresses of family members. You should also keep a copy, for your records, of any notices you send to the Plan Administrator.

[¶ 15,046F]
DEFINITIONS AND SPECIAL RULES

Act Sec. 607. For purposes of this part—

(1) GROUP HEALTH PLAN. The term "group health plan" means an employee welfare benefit plan providing medical care (as defined in section 213(d) of the Internal Revenue Code of 1986) to participants or beneficiaries directly or through insurance, reimbursement, or otherwise. Such term shall not include any plan substantially all of the coverage under which is for qualified long-term care services (as defined in section 7702B(c) of such Code).

(2) COVERED EMPLOYEE. The term "covered employee" means an individual who is (or was) provided coverage under a group health plan by virtue of the performance of services by the individual for 1 or more persons maintaining the plan (including as an employee defined in section 401(c)(1) of the Internal Revenue Code of 1986).

(3) QUALIFIED BENEFICIARY—

(A) IN GENERAL. The term "qualified beneficiary" means, with respect to a covered employee under a group health plan, any other individual who, on the day before the qualifying event for that employee, is a beneficiary under the plan—

(i) as the spouse of the covered employee, or

(ii) as the dependent child of the employee.

Such term shall also include a child who is born to or placed for adoption with the covered employee during the period of continuation coverage under this part.

(B) SPECIAL RULE FOR TERMINATIONS AND REDUCED EMPLOYMENT. In the case of a qualifying event described in section 603(2), the term "qualified beneficiary" includes the covered employee.

(C) SPECIAL RULE FOR RETIREES AND WIDOWS. In the case of a qualifying event described in section 603(6), the term qualified beneficiary includes a covered employee who had retired on or before the date of substantial elimination of coverage and any other individual who, on the day before such qualifying event, is a beneficiary under the plan—

(i) as the spouse of the covered employee,

(ii) as the dependent child of the employee, or

(iii) as the surviving spouse of the covered employee.

(4) EMPLOYER. Subsection (n) (relating to leased employees) and subsection (t) (relating to application of controlled group rules to certain employee benefits) of section 414 of the Internal Revenue Code of 1986 shall apply for purposes of this part in the same manner and to the same extent as such subsections apply for purposes of section 106 of such Code. Any regulations prescribed by the Secretary pursuant to the preceding sentence shall be consistent and coextensive with any regulations prescribed for similar purposes by the Secretary of the Treasury (or such Secretary's delegate) under such subsections.

(5) OPTIONAL EXTENSION OF REQUIRED PERIODS. A group health plan shall not be treated as failing to meet the requirements of this part solely because the plan provides both—

(A) that the period of extended coverage referred to in section 602(2) commences with the date of the loss of coverage, and

(B) that the applicable notice period provided under section 606(a)(2) commences with the date of the loss of coverage.

Amendments

P.L. 104-191, §321(d)(2):

Amended ERISA Sec. 607(1) by adding a new sentence at the end to read as above.

The above amendment applies to contracts issued after December 31, 1996. For special rules, see Act Sec. 321(f)(2)-(5), reproduced below:

(2) CONTINUATION OF EXISTING POLICIES.—In the case of any contract issued before January 1, 1997, which met the long-term care insurance requirements of the State in which the contract was situated at the time the contract was issued—

(A) such contract shall be treated for purposes of the Internal Revenue Code of 1986 as a qualified long-term care insurance contract (as defined in section 7702B(b) of such Code), and

(B) services provided under, or reimbursed by, such contract shall be treated for such purposes as qualified long-term care services (as defined in section 7702B(c) of such Code).

In the case of an individual who is covered on December 31, 1996, under a State long-term care plan (as defined in section 7702B(f)(2) of such Code), the terms of such plan on such date shall be treated for purposes of the preceding sentence as a contract issued on such date which met the long-term care insurance requirements of such State.

(3) EXCHANGES OF EXISTING POLICIES.—If, after the date of enactment of this Act and before January 1, 1998, a contract providing for long-term care insurance coverage is exchanged solely for a qualified long-term care insurance contract (as defined in section 7702B(b) of such Code), no gain or loss shall be recognized on the exchange. If, in addition to a qualified long-term care insurance contract, money or other property is received in the exchange, then any gain shall be recognized to the extent of the sum of the money and the fair market value of the other property received. For purposes of this paragraph, the cancellation of a contract providing for long-term care insurance coverage and reinvestment of the cancellation proceeds in a qualified long-term care insurance contract within 60 days thereafter shall be treated as an exchange.

(4) ISSUANCE OF CERTAIN RIDERS PERMITTED.—For purposes of applying sections 101(f), 7702, and 7702A of the Internal Revenue Code of 1986 to any contract—

(A) the issuance of a rider which is treated as a qualified long-term care insurance contract under section 7702B, and

(B) the addition of any provision required to conform any other long-term care rider to be so treated,

shall not be treated as a modification or material change of such contract.

(5) APPLICATION OF PER DIEM LIMITATION TO EXISTING CONTRACTS.—The amount of per diem payments made under a contract issued on or before July 31, 1996, with respect to an insured which are excludable from gross income by reason of section 7702B of the Internal Revenue Code of 1986 (as added by this section) shall not be reduced under subsection (d)(2)(B) thereof by reason of reimbursements received under a contract issued on or before such date. The preceding sentence shall cease to apply as of the date (after July 31, 1996) such contract is exchanged or there is any contract modifica-

tion which results in an increase of such per diem payments or the amount of such reimbursements.

P.L. 104-191, §421(b)(3):

Amended ERISA Sec. 607(3)(A) by adding a new flush sentence at the end to read as above.

The above amendment is effective on January 1, 1997, regardless of whether the qualifying event occurred before, on, or after such date. For a special rule, see Act Sec. 421(e), reproduced below.

Act Sec. 421(e) provides:

(e) NOTIFICATION OF CHANGES.—Not later than November 1, 1996, each group health plan (covered under title XXII of the Public Health Service Act, part 6 of subtitle B of title I of the Employee Retirement Income Security Act of 1974, and section 4980B(f) of the Internal Revenue Code of 1986) shall notify each qualified beneficiary who has elected continuation coverage under such title, part or section of the amendments made by this section.

P.L. 101-239, §7862(c)(2)(A):

Amended ERISA Sec. 607(2) by striking "the individual's employment or previous employment with an employer" and inserting "the performance of services by the individual for 1 or more persons maintaining the plan (including as an employee defined in section 401(c)(1) of the Internal Revenue Code of 1986)," effective for plan years beginning after December 31, 1989.

P.L. 101-239, §7891(a)(1):

Titles I, III, and IV of ERISA (other than sections 3(37)(E), 301(a)(7), and 308, the last sentence of section 408(d), and sections 414(c), 4001(a)(3)(ii), and 4303) are each amended by striking "Internal Revenue Code of 1954" each place it appears and inserting "Internal Revenue Code of 1986" effective October 22, 1986.

P.L. 101-239, §7891(d)(2)(B)(i):

Amended ERISA Sec. 607 by inserting "AND SPECIAL RULES" after "DEFINITIONS" in the heading and by adding new paragraph (5) to read as above, effective for plan years beginning on or after January 1, 1990.

P.L. 101-239, §7862(c)(6):

Repealed Sec. 3011(b)(6) of the Technical and Miscellaneous Revenue Act of 1988 (P.L. 100-647), effective as if included in Sec. 3011(b).

P.L. 100-647, §3011(b)(6):

Amended ERISA Sec. 607(1) by striking out "section 162(i)(3) of the Internal Revenue Code of 1954" and inserting in lieu thereof "section 162(i)(2) of the Internal Revenue Code of 1986".

The above amendment shall apply to tax years beginning after December 31, 1988, but shall not apply to any plan for any plan year to which section 162(k) of the Internal Revenue Code of 1986 (as in effect on the date before the date of

enactment of this Act) did not apply by reason of section 10001(e)(2) of the Consolidated Budget Reconciliation Act of 1985.

P.L. 99-514, §1895(d)(8):

Added Sec. 607(1) to read as above, effective for plan years beginning after July 1, 1986, subject to the special rules discussed at ¶ 15,045. Prior to amendment, Sec. 607(1) read as follows:

(1) GROUP HEALTH PLAN.—The term "group health plan" means an employee welfare benefit plan that is a group health plan (within the meaning of section 162(i)(3) of the Internal Revenue Code of 1954).

P.L. 99-514 §1895(d)(9):

Added Sec. 607(4) to read as above, effective subject to the rules under Act Sec. 1151(k), which provides as follows:

(k) EFFECTIVE DATES.—

(l) IN GENERAL.—The amendments made by this section shall apply to years beginning after the later of—

(A) December 31, 1987, or

(B) the earlier of—

(i) the date which is 3 months after the date on which the Secretary of the Treasury or his delegate issues such regulations as are necessary to carry out the provisions of section 89 of the Internal Revenue Code of 1986 (as added by this section), or

(ii) December 31, 1988.

(2) SPECIAL RULE FOR COLLECTIVE BARGAINING PLAN.—In the case of a plan maintained pursuant to 1 or more collective bargaining agreements between employee representatives and 1 or more employers ratified before March 1, 1986, the amendments made by this section shall not apply to employees covered by such an agreement in years beginning before the earlier of—

(A) the date on which the last of such collective bargaining agreements terminates (determined without regard to any extension thereof after February 28, 1986), or

(B) January 1, 1991.

A plan shall not be required to take into account employees to which the preceding sentence applies for purposes of applying section 89 of the Internal Revenue Code of 1986 (as added by this section) to employees to which the preceding sentence does not apply for any year preceding the year described in the preceding sentence.

* * *

P.L. 99-509, §9501(c)(2):

Amended ERISA Sec. 607(3) by adding a new paragraph (C) to read as above effective for plan years beginning after July 1, 1986 except for plans maintained under collective bargaining agreements in which case the amendments do not apply to plan years beginning before the later of (1) the date the last of the collective bargaining agreements terminates, or (2) January 1, 1987.

P.L. 99-272:

Act Sec. 10002(a) added ERISA Sec. 607 to read as above, effective for plan years beginning after July 1, 1986, subject to the special rules discussed at ¶ 15,045.

[¶ 15,046L]
REGULATIONS

Act Sec. 608. The Secretary may prescribe regulations to carry out the provisions of this part.
Amendment

P.L. 99-272:

Act Sec. 10002(a) added ERISA Sec. 608 to read as above, effective for plan years beginning after July 1, 1986, subject to the special rules discussed at ¶ 15,045.

[¶ 15,046M]
ADDITIONAL STANDARDS FOR GROUP HEALTH PLANS

Act Sec. 609.(a) GROUP HEALTH PLAN COVERAGE PURSUANT TO MEDICAL CHILD SUPPORT ORDERS.—

(1) In General. Each group health plan shall provide benefits in accordance with the applicable requirements of any qualified medical child support order. A qualified medical child support order with respect to any participant or beneficiary shall be deemed to apply to each group health plan which has received such order, from which the participant or beneficiary is eligible to receive benefits, and with respect to which the requirements of paragraph (4) are met.

(2) Definitions. For purposes of this subsection—

(A) Qualified Medical Child Support Order. The term "qualified medical child support order" means a medical child support order—

(i) which creates or recognizes the existence of an alternate recipient's right to, or assigns to an alternate recipient the right to, receive benefits for which a participant or beneficiary is eligible under a group health plan, and

(ii) with respect to which the requirements of paragraphs (3) and (4) are met.

(B) Medical Child Support Order. The term "medical child support order" means any judgment, decree, or order (including approval of a settlement agreement) which—

(i) provides for child support with respect to a child of a participant under a group health plan or provides for health benefit coverage to such a child, is made pursuant to a State domestic relations law (including a community property law), and relates to benefits under such plan, or

(ii) is made pursuant to a law relating to medical child support described in section 1908 of the Social Security Act (as added by section 13822 of the Omnibus Budget Reconciliation Act of 1993) with respect to a group health plan,

if such judgment, decree, or order (I) is issued by a court of competent jurisdiction or (II) is issued through an administrative process established under State law and has the force and effect of law under applicable State law.

For purposes of this subparagraph, an administrative notice which is issued pursuant to an administrative process referred to in subclause (II) of the preceding sentence and which has the effect of an order described in clause (i) or (ii) of the preceding sentence shall be treated as such an order.

(C) Alternate Recipient. The term "alternate recipient" means any child of a participant who is recognized under a medical child support order as having a right to enrollment under a group health plan with respect to such participant.

(D) Child. The term "child" includes any child adopted by, or placed for adoption with, a participant of a group health plan.

(3) Information to be Included in Qualified Order. A medical child support order meets the requirements of this paragraph only if such order clearly specifies—

(A) the name and the last known mailing address (if any) of the participant and the name and address of each alternate recipient covered by the order, except that, to the extent provided in the order, the name and mailing address of an official of a State or a political subdivision thereof may be substituted for the mailing address of any such alternate recipient,

(B) a reasonable description of the type of coverage to be provided to each such alternate recipient, or the manner in which such type of coverage is to be determined, and

(C) the period to which such order applies.

(4) Restrictions on New Types or Forms of Benefits. A medical child support order meets the requirements of this paragraph only if such order does not require a plan to provide any type or form of benefit, or any option, not otherwise provided under the plan, except to the extent necessary to meet the requirements of a law relating to medical child support described in section 1908 of the Social Security Act (as added by section 13822 of the Omnibus Budget Reconciliation Act of 1993).

(5) Procedural Requirements.—

(A) Timely Notifications and Determinations. In the case of any medical child support order received by a group health plan—

(i) the plan administrator shall promptly notify the participant and each alternate recipient of the receipt of such order and the plan's procedures for determining whether medical child support orders are qualified medical child support orders, and

(ii) within a reasonable period after receipt of such order, the plan administrator shall determine whether such order is a qualified medical child support order and notify the participant and each alternate recipient of such determination.

(B) Establishment of Procedures for Determining Qualified Status of Orders. Each group health plan shall establish reasonable procedures to determine whether medical child support orders are qualified medical child support orders and to administer the provision of benefits under such qualified orders. Such procedures—

(i) shall be in writing,

(ii) shall provide for the notification of each person specified in a medical child support order as eligible to receive benefits under the plan (at the address included in the medical child support order) of such procedures promptly upon receipt by the plan of the medical child support order, and

(iii) shall permit an alternate recipient to designate a representative for receipt of copies of notices that are sent to the alternate recipient with respect to a medical child support order.

(C) National medical support notice deemed to be a qualified medical child support order.—

(i) In general. If the plan administrator of a group health plan which is maintained by the employer of a noncustodial parent of a child or to which such an employer contributes receives an appropriately completed National Medical Support Notice promulgated pursuant to section 401(b) of the Child Support Performance and Incentive Act of 1998 in the case of such child, and the Notice meets the requirements of paragraphs (3) and (4), the Notice shall be deemed to be a qualified medical child support order in the case of such child.

(ii) Enrollment of child in plan. In any case in which an appropriately completed National Medical Support Notice is issued in the case of a child of a participant under a group health plan who is a noncustodial parent of the child, and the Notice is deemed under clause (i) to be a qualified medical child support order, the plan administrator, within 40 business days after the date of the Notice, shall—

(I) notify the State agency issuing the Notice with respect to such child whether coverage of the child is available under the terms of the plan and, if so, whether such child is covered under the plan and either the effective date of the coverage or, if necessary, any steps to be taken by the custodial parent (or by the official of a State or political subdivision thereof substituted for the name of such child pursuant to paragraph (3)(A)) to effectuate the coverage; and

(II) provide to the custodial parent (or such substituted official) a description of the coverage available and any forms or documents necessary to effectuate such coverage.

(iii) Rule of construction. Nothing in this subparagraph shall be construed as requiring a group health plan, upon receipt of a National Medical Support Notice, to provide benefits under the plan (or eligibility for such benefits) in addition to benefits (or eligibility for benefits) provided under the terms of the plan as of immediately before receipt of such Notice.

(6) Actions Taken by Fiduciaries. If a plan fiduciary acts in accordance with part 4 of this subtitle in treating a medical child support order as being (or not being) a qualified medical child support order, then the plan's obligation to the participant and each alternate recipient shall be discharged to the extent of any payment made pursuant to such act of the fiduciary.

(7) Treatment of Alternate Recipients.—

(A) Treatment as Beneficiary Generally. A person who is an alternate recipient under a qualified medical child support order shall be considered a beneficiary under the plan for purposes of any provision of this Act.

(B) Treatment as Participant for Purposes of Reporting and Disclosure Requirements. A person who is an alternate recipient under any medical child support order shall be considered a participant under the plan for purposes of the reporting and disclosure requirements of part 1.

(8) Direct Provision of Benefits Provided to Alternate Recipients. Any payment for benefits made by a group health plan pursuant to a medical child support order in reimbursement for expenses paid by an alternate recipient or an alternate recipient's custodial parent or legal guardian shall be made to the alternate recipient or the alternate recipient's custodial parent or legal guardian.

(9) Payment to state official treated as satisfaction of plan's obligation to make payment to alternate recipient. Payment of benefits by a group health plan to an official of a State or a political subdivision thereof whose name and address have been substituted for the address of an alternate recipient in a qualified medical child support order, pursuant to paragraph (3)(A), shall be treated, for purposes of this title, as payment of benefits to the alternate recipient.

Act Sec. 609. RIGHTS OF STATES WITH RESPECT TO GROUP HEALTH PLANS WHERE PARTICIPANTS OR BENEFICIARIES THEREUNDER ARE ELIGIBLE FOR MEDICAID BENEFITS.—

(b)(1) Compliance by Plans with Assignment of Rights. A group health plan shall provide that payment for benefits with respect to a participant under the plan will be made in accordance with any assignment of rights made by or on behalf of such participant or a beneficiary of the participant as required by a State plan for medical assistance approved under title XIX of the Social Security Act pursuant to section 1912(a)(1)(A) of such Act (as in effect on the date of the enactment of the Omnibus Budget Reconciliation Act of 1993).

(2) Enrollment and Provision of Benefits Without Regard to Medicaid Eligibility. A group health plan shall provide that, in enrolling an individual as a participant or beneficiary or in determining or making any payments for benefits of an individual as a participant or beneficiary, the fact that the individual is eligible for or is provided medical assistance under a State plan for medical assistance approved under title XIX of the Social Security Act will not be taken into account.

(3) Acquisition by States of Rights of Third Parties. A group health plan shall provide that, to the extent that payment has been made under a State plan for medical assistance approved under title XIX of the Social Security Act in any case in which a group health plan has a legal liability to make payment for items or services constituting such assistance, payment for benefits under the plan will be made in accordance with any State law which provides that the State has acquired the rights with respect to a participant to such payment for such items or services.

Act Sec. 609. GROUP HEALTH PLAN COVERAGE OF DEPENDENT CHILDREN IN CASES OF ADOPTION.—

(c)(1) Coverage Effective upon Placement for Adoption. In any case in which a group health plan provides coverage for dependent children of participants or beneficiaries, such plan shall provide benefits to dependent children placed with participants or beneficiaries for adoption under the same terms and conditions as apply in the case of dependent children who are natural children of participants or beneficiaries under the plan, irrespective of whether the adoption has become final.

(2) Restrictions Based on Preexisting Conditions at Time of Placement for Adoption Prohibited. A group health plan may not restrict coverage under the plan of any dependent child adopted by a participant or beneficiary, or placed with a participant or beneficiary for adoption, solely on the basis of a preexisting condition of such child at the time that such child would otherwise become eligible for coverage under the plan, if the adoption or placement for adoption occurs while the participant or beneficiary is eligible for coverage under the plan.

(3) Definitions. For purposes of this subsection—

(A) Child. The term "child" means, in connection with any adoption, or placement for adoption, of the child, an individual who has not attained age 18 as of the date of such adoption or placement for adoption.

(B) Placement for Adoption. The term "placement," or being "placed," for adoption, in connection with any placement for adoption of a child with any person, means the assumption and retention by such person of a legal obligation for total or partial support of such child in anticipation of adoption of such child. The child's placement with such person terminates upon the termination of such legal obligation.

Act Sec. 609. CONTINUED COVERAGE OF COSTS OF A PEDIATRIC VACCINE UNDER GROUP HEALTH PLANS. (d) A group health plan may not reduce its coverage of the costs of pediatric vaccines (as defined under section 1928(h)(6) of the Social Security Act as amended by section 13830 of the Omnibus Budget Reconciliation Act of 1993) below the coverage it provided as of May 1, 1993.

Act Sec. 609. REGULATIONS. (e) Any regulations prescribed under this section shall be prescribed by the Secretary of Labor, in consultation with the Secretary of Health and Human Services.

Amendments

P.L. 105-200, §401(d):

Amended ERISA Sec. 609(a)(5) by adding subparagraph (C) to read as above.

The above amendment is effective July 16, 1998.

P.L. 105-200, §402(h)(2)(A)(iii):

Amended ERISA Sec. 609(a)(2)(B)(ii) by striking "enforced by" and inserting "is made pursuant to" to read as above.

The above amendment is effective August 10, 1993.

P.L. 105-200, §402(h)(2)(B):

Amended ERISA Sec. 609(a)(2) by adding subparagraph (D) to read as above.

The above amendment is effective July 16, 1998.

P.L. 105-200, §402(h)(3)(A):

Amended ERISA Sec. 609(a)(9) by striking "the name and address" and inserting "the address" to read as above.

The above amendment is effective with respect to medical child support orders issued on or after August 5, 1997.

P.L. 105-33, §5611(a):

Amended ERISA Sec. 609(a)(3)(A) by adding at the end new material to read as above.

The above amendment is effective with respect to medical child support orders issued on or after August 5, 1997.

P.L. 105-33, §5611(b):

Amended ERISA Sec. 609(a) by adding a new paragraph (9) to read as above.

The above amendment is effective with respect to medical child support orders issued on or after August 5, 1997.

P.L. 105-33, §5612(a):

Amended ERISA Sec. 609(a)(2)(B) by adding at the end a new sentence to read as above.

The above amendment is effective on August 22, 1996. For a special rule, see Act Sec. 381(b)(2), reproduced below.

P.L. 105-33, §5613(a):

Amended ERISA Sec. 609(a)(3) in subparagraph (B), by striking "by the plan;" by adding "and" at the end of subparagraph (B); in subparagraph (C), by striking ", and"

and inserting a period; and by striking subparagraph (D). Prior to being striken, subparagraph (D) read as follows:

(D) each plan to which such order applies.

The above amendments are effective with respect to medical child support orders issued on or after August 5, 1997.

P.L. 104-193, §381(a):

Amended ERISA Sec. 609(a)(2)(B) by striking "issued by a court of competent jurisdiction"; by striking the period at the end of clause (ii) and inserting a comma; and by adding, after and below clause (ii), the following: "if such judgment, decree, or order (I) is issued by a court of competent jurisdiction or (II) is issued through an administrative process established under State law and has the force and effect of law under applicable State law."

The above amendments are effective on August 22, 1996. For a special rule, see Act Sec. 381(b)(2), reproduced below.

Act Sec. 381(b)(2) provides:

(2) PLAN AMENDMENTS NOT REQUIRED UNTIL JANUARY 1, 1997.—Any amendment to a plan required to be made by an amendment made by this section shall not be required to be made before the 1st plan year beginning on or after January 1, 1997,if—

(A) during the period after the date before the date of the enactment of this Act and before such 1st plan year, the paln is operated in accordance with the requirements of the amendments made by this section; and

(B) such plan amendment applies retroactively to the period after the date before the date of the enactment of this Act and before such 1st plan year.

A plan shall not be treated as failing to be operated in accordance with the provisions of the plan merely because it operates in accordance with this paragraph.

P.L. 103-66, §4301(a):

Added ERISA Sec. 609 to read as above.

The above amendments are effective on August 10, 1993. Any plan amendment required to be made by Act Sec. 4301 need not be made before the first plan year beginning on or after January 1, 1994 if: (1) the plan is operated in accordance with Act Sec. 4301 during the period after August 9, 1993 and before such first plan year; and (2) the amendment applies retroactively to this period. A plan will not be treated as failing to be operated in accordance with plan provisions merely because it operates in accordance with the effective date requirements.

Regulations

The following regulations regarding a National Medical Support Notice were adopted by the Pension and Welfare Benefits Administration. The regulations were published in the *Federal Register* on December 27, 2000 (65 FR 82127) and became effective January 26, 2001. Reg. §2590.609-1 was reserved and §2590.609-2 was added on December 27, 2000 (65 FR 82127).

[¶ 15,047H]

§2590.609-1 **[Reserved on 12/27/00 by 65 FR 82129].**

[¶ 15,047I]

§2590.609-2 **National Medical Support Notice.** (a) This section promulgates the National Medical Support Notice (the Notice), as mandated by section 401(b) of the Child Support Performance and Incentive Act of 1998 (Pub. L. 105-200). If the Notice is appropriately completed and satisfies paragraphs (3) and (4) of section 609(a) of the Employee Retirement Income Security Act (ERISA), the Notice is deemed to be a qualified medical child support order (QMCSO) pursuant to ERISA section 609(a)(5)(C). Section 609(a) of ERISA delineates the rights and obligations of the alternate recipient (child), the participant, and the group health plan under a QMCSO. A copy of the Notice is available on the Internet at http://www.dol.gov/dol/ebsa. [EBSA technical correction, 68 FR 16399 (April 3, 2003).]

(b) For purposes of this section, a plan administrator shall find that a Notice is appropriately completed if it contains the name of an Issuing Agency, the name and mailing address (if any) of an employee who is a participant under the plan, the name and mailing address of one or more alternate recipient(s) (child(ren)) of the participant) (or the name and address of a substituted official or agency which has been

substituted for the mailing address of the alternate recipient(s)), and identifies an underlying child support order.

(c)(1) Under section 609(a)(3)(A) of ERISA, in order to be qualified, a medical child support order must clearly specify the name and the last known mailing address (if any) of the participant and the name and mailing address of each alternate recipient covered by the order, except that, to the extent provided in the order, the name and mailing address of an official of a State or a political subdivision thereof may be substituted for the mailing address of any such alternate recipient. Section 609(a)(3)(B) of ERISA requires a reasonable description of the type of coverage to be provided to each such alternate recipient, or the manner in which such type of coverage is to be determined. Section 609(a)(3)(C) of ERISA requires that the order specify the period to which such order applies.

(2) The Notice satisfies ERISA section 609(a)(3)(A) by including the necessary identifying information described in §2590.609-2(b).

(3) The Notice satisfies ERISA section 609(a)(3)(B) by having the Issuing Agency identify either the specific type of coverage or all available group health coverage. If an employer receives a Notice that does not designate either specific type(s) of coverage or all available coverage, the employer and plan administrator should assume that all are designated. The Notice further satisfies ERISA section

609(a)(3)(B) by instructing the plan administrator that if a group health plan has multiple options and the participant is not enrolled, the Issuing Agency will make a selection after the Notice is qualified, and, if the Issuing Agency does not respond within 20 days, the child will be enrolled under the plan's default option (if any).

(4) Section 609(a)(3)(C) of ERISA is satisfied because the Notice specifies that the period of coverage may only end for the alternate recipient(s) when similarly situated dependents are no longer eligible for coverage under the terms of the plan, or upon the occurrence of certain specified events.

(d)(1) Under ERISA section 609(a)(4), a qualified medical child support order may not require a plan to provide any type or form of benefit, or any option, not otherwise provided under the plan, except to the extent necessary to meet the requirements of a law relating to medical child support described in section 1908 of the Social Security Act, 42 U.S.C. 1396g-1.

(2) The Notice satisfies the conditions of ERISA section 609(a)(4) because it requires the plan to provide to an alternate recipient only those benefits that the plan provides to any dependent of a participant who is enrolled in the plan, and any other benefits that are necessary to meet the requirements of a State law described in such section 1908.

(e) For the purposes of this section, an "Issuing Agency" is a State agency that administers the child support enforcement program under Part D of Title IV of the Social Security Act. [Added on 12/27/00 by 65 FR 82127.]

Appendix: National Medical Support Notice.

CCH Note: The following Appendix, which follows Reg. §2590.609-2 in the Federal Register dated December 27, 2000, does not appear in the Code of Federal Regulations.

APPENDIX
NATIONAL MEDICAL SUPPORT NOTICE
PART A
NOTICE TO WITHHOLD FOR HEALTH CARE COVERAGE

This Notice is issued under section 466(a)(19) of the Social Security Act, section 609(a)(5)(C) of the Employee Retirement Income Security Act of 1974 (ERISA), and for State and local government and church plans, sections 401(e) and (f) of the Child Support Performance and Incentive Act of 1998.

Issuing Agency: _____
Issuing Agency Address: _____
_____
Date of Notice: _____
Case Number: _____
Telephone Number: _____
FAX Number: _____

Court or Administrative Authority: _____
Date of Support Order: _____
Support Order Number: _____

RE* _____

_____)
Employer/Withholder's Federal EIN Number

Employee's Name (Last, First, MI)

_____)
Employer/Withholder's Name

Employee's Social Security Number

_____)
Employer/Withholder's Address

Employee's Mailing Address

_____)
Custodial Parent's Name (Last, First, MI)

_____)
Custodial Parent's Mailing Address

Substituted Official/Agency Name and Address

_____)
Child(ren)'s Mailing Address (if different from Custodial Parent's)

_____)
_____)
_____)
Name, Mailing Address, and Telephone
Number of a Representative of the Child(ren)

Child(ren)'s Name(s)	DOB	SSN	Child(ren)'s Name(s)	DOB	SSN
_____	_____	_____	_____	_____	_____
_____	_____	_____	_____	_____	_____
_____	_____	_____	_____	_____	_____

The order requires the child(ren) to be enrolled in [ ] any health coverages available; or [] only the following coverage(s): __Medical; __Dental; __Vision; __Prescription drug; __Mental health; __Other (specify):_____

THE PAPERWORK REDUCTION ACT OF 1995 (P.L. 104-13) Public reporting burden for this collection of information is estimated to average 10 minutes per response, including the time reviewing instructions, gathering and maintaining the data needed, and reviewing the collection of information. An agency may not conduct or sponsor, and a person is not required to respond to, a collection of information unless it displays a currently valid OMB control number. OMB control number: 0970-0222 Expiration Date: 12/31/2003.

EMPLOYER RESPONSE

If either 1, 2, or 3 below applies, check the appropriate box and return this Part A to the Issuing Agency within 20 business days after the date of the Notice, or sooner if reasonable. NO OTHER ACTION IS NECESSARY. If neither 1, 2, nor 3 applies, forward Part B to the appropriate plan administrator(s) within 20 business days after the date of the Notice, or sooner if reasonable. Check number 4 and return this Part A to the Issuing Agency if the Plan Administrator informs you that the child(ren) is/are enrolled in an option under the plan for which you have determined that the employee contribution exceeds the amount that may be withheld from the employee's income due to State or Federal withholding limitations and/or prioritization.

□ 1. Employer does not maintain or contribute to plans providing dependent or family health care coverage.

□ 2. The employee is among a class of employees (for example, part-time or non-union) that are not eligible for family health coverage under any group health plan maintained by the employer or to which the employer contributes.

□ 3. Health care coverage is not available because employee is no longer employed by the employer:

Date of termination: _____

Last known address: _____

Last known telephone number: _____

New employer (if known): _____

New employer address: _____

New employer telephone number: _____

□ 4. State or Federal withholding limitations and/or prioritization prevent the withholding from the employee's income of the amount required to obtain coverage under the terms of the plan.

Employer Representative:

Name: _____ Telephone Number: _____

Title: _____ Date: _____

EIN (if not provided by Issuing Agency on Notice to Withhold for Health Care Coverage): _____

INSTRUCTIONS TO EMPLOYER

This document serves as notice that the employee identified on this National Medical Support Notice is obligated by a court or administrative child support order to provide health care coverage for the child(ren) identified on this Notice. This National Medical Support Notice replaces any Medical Support Notice that the Issuing Agency has previously served on you with respect to the employee and the children listed on this Notice.

The document consists of **Part A - Notice to Withhold for Health Care Coverage** for the employer to withhold any employee contributions required by the group health plan(s) in which the child(ren) is/are enrolled; and **Part B - Medical Support Notice to the Plan Administrator**, which must be forwarded to the administrator of each group health plan identified by the employer to enroll the eligible child(ren).

EMPLOYER RESPONSIBILITIES

1.   If the individual named above is not your employee, or if family health care coverage is not available, please complete item 1, 2, or 3 of the Employer Response as appropriate, and return it to the Issuing Agency. NO FURTHER ACTION IS NECESSARY.

2.   If family health care coverage is available for which the child(ren) identified above may be eligible, you are required to:

        a.   Transfer, not later than 20 business days after the date of this Notice, a copy of **Part B - Medical Support Notice to the Plan Administrator** to the administrator of each appropriate group health plan for which the child(ren) may be eligible, and

        b.   Upon notification from the plan administrator(s) that the child(ren) is/are enrolled, either

                1) withhold from the employee's income any employee contributions required under each group health plan, in accordance with the applicable law of the employee's principal place of employment and transfer employee contributions to the appropriate plan(s), or

                2) complete item 4 of the Employer Response to notify the Issuing Agency that enrollment cannot be completed because of prioritization or limitations on withholding.

        c.   If the plan administrator notifies you that the employee is subject to a waiting period that expires more than 90 days from the date of its receipt of **Part B of** this Notice, or whose duration is determined by a measure other than the passage of time (for example, the completion of a certain number of hours worked), notify the plan administrator when the employee is eligible to enroll in the plan and that this Notice requires the enrollment of the child(ren) named in the Notice in the plan.

LIMITATIONS ON WITHHOLDING

The total amount withheld for both cash and medical support cannot exceed ___% of the employee's aggregate disposable weekly earnings. The employer may not withhold more under this National Medical Support Notice than the lesser of:

      1.   The amounts allowed by the Federal Consumer Credit Protection Act (15 U.S.C., section 1673(b));

      2.   The amounts allowed by the State of the employee's principal place of employment; or

      3.   The amounts allowed for health insurance premiums by the child support order, as indicated here:_____.

The Federal limit applies to the aggregate disposable weekly earnings (ADWE). ADWE is the net income left after making mandatory deductions such as State, Federal, local taxes; Social Security taxes; and Medicare taxes.

PRIORITY OF WITHHOLDING

If withholding is required for employee contributions to one or more plans under this notice and for a support obligation under a separate notice and available funds are insufficient for withholding for both cash and medical support contributions, the employer must withhold amounts for purposes of cash support and medical support contributions in accordance with the law, if any, of the State of the employee's principal place of employment requiring prioritization between cash and medical support, as described here:_____
_____.

DURATION OF WITHHOLDING

The child(ren) shall be treated as dependents under the terms of the plan. Coverage of a child as a dependent will end when similarly situated dependents are no longer eligible for coverage under the terms of the plan. However, the continuation coverage provisions of ERISA may entitle the child to continuation coverage under the plan. The employer must continue to withhold employee contributions and may not disenroll (or eliminate coverage for) the child(ren) unless:

      1.   The employer is provided satisfactory written evidence that:

    a.   The court or administrative child support order referred to above is no longer in effect; or

    b.   The child(ren) is or will be enrolled in comparable coverage which will take effect no later than the effective date of disenrollment from the plan; or

2.   The employer eliminates family health coverage for all of its employees.

POSSIBLE SANCTIONS

An employer may be subject to sanctions or penalties imposed under State law and/or ERISA for discharging an employee from employment, refusing to employ, or taking disciplinary action against any employee because of medical child support withholding, or for failing to withhold income, or transmit such withheld amounts to the applicable plan(s) as the Notice directs.

NOTICE OF TERMINATION OF EMPLOYMENT

In any case in which the above employee's employment terminates, the employer must promptly notify the Issuing Agency listed above of such termination. This requirement may be satisfied by sending to the Issuing Agency a copy of any notice the employer is required to provide under the continuation coverage provisions of ERISA or the Health Insurance Portability and Accountability Act.

EMPLOYEE LIABILITY FOR CONTRIBUTION TO PLAN

The employee is liable for any employee contributions that are required under the plan(s) for enrollment of the child(ren) and is subject to appropriate enforcement. The employee may contest the withholding under this Notice based on a mistake of fact (such as the identity of the obligor). Should an employee contest the withholding under this Notice, the employer must proceed to comply with the employer responsibilities in this Notice until notified by the Issuing Agency to discontinue withholding. To contest the withholding under this Notice, the employee should contact the Issuing Agency at the address and telephone number listed on the Notice. With respect to plans subject to ERISA, it is the view of the Department of Labor that Federal Courts have jurisdiction if the employee challenges a determination that the Notice constitutes a Qualified Medical Child Support Order.

CONTACT FOR QUESTIONS

If you have any questions regarding this Notice, you may contact the Issuing Agency at the address and telephone number listed above.

NATIONAL MEDICAL SUPPORT NOTICE OMB NO. 1210-0113
PART B
MEDICAL SUPPORT NOTICE TO PLAN ADMINISTRATOR

This Notice is issued under section 466(a)(19) of the Social Security Act, section 609(a)(5)(C) of the Employee Retirement Income Security Act of 1974, and for State and local government and church plans, sections 401(e) and (f) of the Child Support Performance and Incentive Act of 1998. Receipt of this Notice from the Issuing Agency constitutes receipt of a Medical Child Support Order under applicable law. The rights of the parties and the duties of the plan administrator under this Notice are in addition to the existing rights and duties established under such law.

Issuing Agency: _____

Issuing Agency Address: _____
_____

Date of Notice: _____
Case Number: _____
Telephone Number: _____
FAX Number: _____

Court or Administrative Authority: _____
Date of Support Order: _____
Support Order Number: _____

RE* _____

Employer/Withholder's Federal EIN Number

Employee's Name (Last, First, MI)

Employer/Withholder's Name

Employee's Social Security Number

Employer/Withholder's Address

Employee's Address

Custodial Parent's Name (Last, First, MI)

Custodial Parent's Mailing Address

Substituted Official/Agency Name and Address

Child(ren)'s Mailing Address (if Different from Custodial Parent's)

Name(s), Mailing Address, and Telephone Number of a Representative of the Child(ren)

Child(ren)'s Name(s)   DOB   SSN   Child(ren)'s Name(s)   DOB   SSN

The order requires the child(ren) to be enrolled in [] any health coverages available; or [] only the following coverage(s): __medical; __dental; __vision; __prescription drug; __mental health; __other (specify):_____

PLAN ADMINISTRATOR RESPONSE

(To be completed and returned to the Issuing Agency within 40 business days after the date of the Notice, or sooner if reasonable)

This Notice was received by the plan administrator on _____.

☐ 1. This Notice was determined to be a "qualified medical child support order," on _____. Complete **Response 2 or 3, and 4**, if applicable.

2. The participant (employee) and alternate recipient(s) (child(ren)) are to be enrolled in the following family coverage.
    ☐ a. The child(ren) is/are currently enrolled in the plan as a dependent of the participant.
    ☐ b. There is only one type of coverage provided under the plan. The child(ren) is/are included as dependents of the participant under the plan.
    ☐ c. The participant is enrolled in an option that is providing dependent coverage and the child(ren) will be enrolled in the same option.
    ☐ d. The participant is enrolled in an option that permits dependent coverage that has not been elected; dependent coverage will be provided.

Coverage is effective as of __/__/____ (includes waiting period of less than 90 days from date of receipt of this Notice).   The child(ren) has/have been enrolled in the following option: _____. Any necessary withholding should commence if the employer determines that it is permitted under State and Federal withholding and/or prioritization limitations.

☐ 3. There is more than one option available under the plan and the participant is not enrolled. The Issuing Agency must select from the available options. Each child is to be included as a dependent under one of the available options that provide family coverage. If the Issuing Agency does not reply within 20 business days of the date this Response is returned, the child(ren), and the participant if necessary, will be enrolled in the plan's default option, if any: _____.

☐ 4. The participant is subject to a waiting period that expires __/__/____ (more than 90 days from the date of receipt of this Notice), or has not completed a waiting period which is determined by some measure other than the passage of time, such as the completion of a certain number of hours worked (describe here: _____). At the completion of the waiting period, the plan administrator will process the enrollment.

☐ 5. This Notice does not constitute a "qualified medical child support order" because:
    ☐ The name of the ☐ child(ren) or ☐ participant is unavailable.
    ☐ The mailing address of the ☐ child(ren) (or a substituted official) or ☐ participant is unavailable.
    ☐ The following child(ren) is/are at or above the age at which dependents are no longer eligible for coverage under the plan _____ (insert name(s) of child(ren)).

Plan Administrator or Representative:

Name: _____ Telephone Number: _____

Title: _____ Date: _____

Address: _____

INSTRUCTIONS TO PLAN ADMINISTRATOR

This Notice has been forwarded from the employer identified above to you as the plan administrator of a group health plan maintained by the employer (or a group health plan to which the employer contributes) and in which the noncustodial parent/participant identified above is enrolled or is eligible for enrollment.

This Notice serves to inform you that the noncustodial parent/participant is obligated by an order issued by the court or agency identified above to provide health care coverage for the child(ren) under the group health plan(s) as described on **Part B**.

(A) If the participant and child(ren) and their mailing addresses (or that of a Substituted Official or Agency) are identified above, and if coverage for the child(ren) is or will become available, this Notice constitutes a "qualified medical child support order"(QMCSO) under ERISA or CSPIA, as applicable. (If any mailing address is not present, but it is reasonably accessible, this Notice will not fail to be a QMCSO on that basis.) You must, within 40 business days of the date of this Notice, or sooner if reasonable:

    (1) Complete Part B - Plan Administrator Response - and send it to the Issuing Agency:

    (a) if you checked Response 2:

        (i) notify the noncustodial parent/participant named above, each named child, and the custodial parent that coverage of the child(ren) is or will become available (notification of the custodial parent will be deemed notification of the child(ren) if they reside at the same address);

        (ii) furnish the custodial parent a description of the coverage available and the effective date of the coverage, including, if not already provided, a summary plan description and any forms, documents, or information necessary to effectuate such coverage, as well as information necessary to submit claims for benefits;

    (b) if you checked Response 3:

        (i) if you have not already done so, provide to the Issuing Agency copies of applicable summary plan descriptions or other documents that describe available coverage including the additional participant contribution necessary to obtain coverage for the child(ren) under each option and whether there is a limited service area for any option;

        (ii) if the plan has a default option, you are to enroll the child(ren) in the default option if you have not received an election from the Issuing Agency within 20 business days of the date you returned the Response. If the plan does not have a default option, you are to enroll the child(ren) in the option selected by the Issuing Agency.

(c) if the participant is subject to a waiting period that expires more than 90 days from the date of receipt of this Notice, or has not completed a waiting period whose duration is determined by a measure other than the passage of time (for example, the completion of a certain number of hours worked), complete Response 4 on the Plan Administrator Response and return to the employer and the Issuing Agency, and notify the participant and the custodial parent; and upon satisfaction of the period or requirement, complete enrollment under Response 2 or 3, and

(d) upon completion of the enrollment, transfer the applicable information on Part B - Plan Administrator Response to the employer for a determination that the necessary employee contributions are available. Inform the employer that the enrollment is pursuant to a National Medical Support Notice.

(B) If within 40 business days of the date of this Notice, or sooner if reasonable, you determine that this Notice does not constitute a QMCSO, you must complete Response 5 of Part B - Plan Administrator Response and send it to the Issuing Agency, and inform the noncustodial parent/participant, custodial parent, and child(ren) of the specific reasons for your determination.

(C) Any required notification of the custodial parent, child(ren) and/or participant that is required may be satisfied by sending the party a copy of the Plan Administrator Response, if appropriate.

UNLAWFUL REFUSAL TO ENROLL

Enrollment of a child may not be denied on the ground that: (1) the child was born out of wedlock; (2) the child is not claimed as a dependent on the participant's Federal income tax return; (3) the child does not reside with the participant or in the plan's service area; or (4) because the child is receiving benefits or is eligible to receive benefits under the State Medicaid plan. If the plan requires that the participant be enrolled in order for the child(ren) to be enrolled, and the participant is not currently enrolled, you must enroll both the participant and the child(ren). All enrollments are to be made without regard to open season restrictions.

PAYMENT OF CLAIMS

A child covered by a QMCSO, or the child's custodial parent, legal guardian, or the provider of services to the child, or a State agency to the extent assigned the child's rights, may file claims and the plan shall make payment for covered benefits or reimbursement directly to such party.

PERIOD OF COVERAGE

The alternate recipient(s) shall be treated as dependents under the terms of the plan. Coverage of an alternate recipient as a dependent will end when similarly situated dependents are no longer eligible for coverage under the terms of the plan. However, the continuation coverage provisions of ERISA or other applicable law may entitle the alternate recipient to continue coverage under the plan. Once a child is enrolled in the plan as directed above, the alternate recipient may not be disenrolled unless:

(1) The plan administrator is provided satisfactory written evidence that either:
(a) the court or administrative child support order referred to above is no longer in effect, or
(b) the alternate recipient is or will be enrolled in comparable coverage which will take effect no later than the effective date of disenrollment from the plan;

(2) The employer eliminates family health coverage for all of its employees; or

(3) Any available continuation coverage is not elected, or the period of such coverage expires.

CONTACT FOR QUESTIONS

If you have any questions regarding this Notice, you may contact the Issuing Agency at the address and telephone number listed above.

Paperwork Reduction Act Notice

The Issuing Agency asks for the information on this form to carry out the law as specified in the Employee Retirement Income Security Act or the Child Support Performance and Incentive Act, as applicable. You are required to give the Issuing Agency the information. You are not required to respond to this collection of information unless it displays a currently valid OMB control number. The Issuing Agency needs the information to determine whether health care coverage is provided in accordance with the underlying child support order. The Average time needed to complete and file the form is estimated below. These times will vary depending on the individual circumstances.

Learning about the law or the form	....	**Preparing the form**
First Notice 1 hr.__		1 hr., 45 min.
Subsequent ----- Notices		35 min.

Part 7—Group Health Plan Portability, Access, and Renewability Requirements

[¶ 15,049H]
INCREASED PORTABILITY THROUGH LIMITATION ON PREEXISTING CONDITION EXCLUSIONS

Act Sec. 701.(a) LIMITATIONS ON PREEXISTING CONDITION EXCLUSION PERIOD; CREDITING FOR PERIODS OF PREVIOUS COVERAGE. Subject to subsection (d), a group health plan, and a health insurance issuer offering group health insurance coverage, may, with respect to a participant or beneficiary, impose a preexisting condition exclusion only if—

(1) such exclusion relates to a condition (whether physical or mental), regardless of the cause of the condition, for which medical advice, diagnosis, care, or treatment was recommended or received within the 6-month period ending on the enrollment date;

(2) such exclusion extends for a period of not more than 12 months (or 18 months in the case of a late enrollee) after the enrollment date; and

(3) the period of any such preexisting condition exclusion is reduced by the aggregate of the periods of creditable coverage (if any, as defined in subsection (c)(1)) applicable to the participant or beneficiary as of the enrollment date.

Act Sec. 701. DEFINITIONS. (b) For purposes of this part—

(1) PREEXISTING CONDITION EXCLUSION.—

(A) IN GENERAL. The term "preexisting condition exclusion" means, with respect to coverage, a limitation or exclusion of benefits relating to a condition based on the fact that the condition was present before the date of enrollment for such coverage, whether or not any medical advice, diagnosis, care, or treatment was recommended or received before such date.

(B) TREATMENT OF GENETIC INFORMATION. Genetic information shall not be treated as a condition described in subsection (a)(1) in the absence of a diagnosis of the condition related to such information.

(2) ENROLLMENT DATE. The term "enrollment date" means, with respect to an individual covered under a group health plan or health insurance coverage, the date of enrollment of the individual in the plan or coverage or, if earlier, the first day of the waiting period for such enrollment.

(3) LATE ENROLLEE. The term "late enrollee" means, with respect to coverage under a group health plan, a participant or beneficiary who enrolls under the plan other than during—

(A) the first period in which the individual is eligible to enroll under the plan, or

(B) a special enrollment period under subsection (f).

(4) WAITING PERIOD. The term "waiting period" means, with respect to a group health plan and an individual who is a potential participant or beneficiary in the plan, the period that must pass with respect to the individual before the individual is eligible to be covered for benefits under the terms of the plan.

Act Sec. 701. RULES RELATING TO CREDITING PREVIOUS COVERAGE.—

(c)(1) CREDITABLE COVERAGE DEFINED. For purposes of this part, the term "creditable coverage" means, with respect to an individual, coverage of the individual under any of the following:

(A) A group health plan.

(B) Health insurance coverage.

(C) Part A or part B of title XVIII of the Social Security Act.

(D) Title XIX of the Social Security Act, other than coverage consisting solely of benefits under section 1928.

(E) Chapter 55 of title 10, United States Code.

(F) A medical care program of the Indian Health Service or of a tribal organization.

(G) A State health benefits risk pool.

(H) A health plan offered under chapter 89 of title 5, United States Code.

(I) A public health plan (as defined in regulations).

(J) A health benefit plan under section 5(e) of the Peace Corps Act (22 U.S.C. 2504(e)).

Such term does not include coverage consisting solely of coverage of excepted benefits (as defined in section 706(c)).

(2) Not counting periods before significant breaks in coverage.—

(A) IN GENERAL. A period of creditable coverage shall not be counted, with respect to enrollment of an individual under a group health plan, if, after such period and before the enrollment date, there was a 63-day period during all of which the individual was not covered under any creditable coverage.

(B) WAITING PERIOD NOT TREATED AS A BREAK IN COVERAGE. For purposes of subparagraph (A) and subsection (d)(4), any period that an individual is in a waiting period for any coverage under a group health plan (or for group health insurance coverage) or is in an affiliation period (as defined in subsection (g)(2)) shall not be taken into account in determining the continuous period under subparagraph (A).

(3) METHOD OF CREDITING COVERAGE.—

(A) STANDARD METHOD. Except as otherwise provided under subparagraph (B), for purposes of applying subsection (a)(3), a group health plan, and a health insurance issuer offering group health insurance coverage, shall count a period of creditable coverage without regard to the specific benefits covered during the period.

(B) ELECTION OF ALTERNATIVE METHOD. A group health plan, or a health insurance issuer offering group health insurance coverage, may elect to apply subsection (a)(3) based on coverage of benefits within each of several classes or categories of benefits specified in regulations rather than as provided under subparagraph (A). Such election shall be made on a uniform basis for all participants and beneficiaries. Under such election a group health plan or issuer shall count a period of creditable coverage with respect to any class or category of benefits if any level of benefits is covered within such class or category.

(C) PLAN NOTICE. In the case of an election with respect to a group health plan under subparagraph (B) (whether or not health insurance coverage is provided in connection with such plan), the plan shall—

(i) prominently state in any disclosure statements concerning the plan, and state to each enrollee at the time of enrollment under the plan, that the plan has made such election, and

(ii) include in such statements a description of the effect of this election.

(4) ESTABLISHMENT OF PERIOD. Periods of creditable coverage with respect to an individual shall be established through presentation of certifications described in subsection (e) or in such other manner as may be specified in regulations.

Act Sec. 701. EXEMPTIONS.—

(d)(1) EXCLUSION NOT APPLICABLE TO CERTAIN NEWBORNS. Subject to paragraph (4), a group health plan, and a health insurance issuer offering group health insurance coverage, may not impose any preexisting condition exclusion in the case of an individual who, as of the last day of the 30-day period beginning with the date of birth, is covered under creditable coverage.

(2) EXCLUSION NOT APPLICABLE TO CERTAIN ADOPTED CHILDREN. Subject to paragraph (4), a group health plan, and a health insurance issuer offering group health insurance coverage, may not impose any preexisting condition exclusion in the case of a child who is adopted or placed for adoption before attaining 18 years of age and who, as of the last day of the 30-day period beginning on the date of the adoption or placement for adoption, is covered under creditable coverage. The previous sentence shall not apply to coverage before the date of such adoption or placement for adoption.

(3) EXCLUSION NOT APPLICABLE TO PREGNANCY. A group health plan, and health insurance issuer offering group health insurance coverage, may not impose any preexisting condition exclusion relating to pregnancy as a preexisting condition.

(4) LOSS IF BREAK IN COVERAGE. Paragraphs (1) and (2) shall no longer apply to an individual after the end of the first 63-day period during all of which the individual was not covered under any creditable coverage.

Act Sec. 701. CERTIFICATIONS AND DISCLOSURE OF COVERAGE.—

(e)(1) REQUIREMENT FOR CERTIFICATION OF PERIOD OF CREDITABLE COVERAGE.—

(A) IN GENERAL. A group health plan, and a health insurance issuer offering group health insurance coverage, shall provide the certification described in subparagraph (B)—

(i) at the time an individual ceases to be covered under the plan or otherwise becomes covered under a COBRA continuation provision,

(ii) in the case of an individual becoming covered under such a provision, at the time the individual ceases to be covered under such provision, and

(iii) on the request on behalf of an individual made not later than 24 months after the date of cessation of the coverage described in clause (i) or (ii), whichever is later.

The certification under clause (i) may be provided, to the extent practicable, at a time consistent with notices required under any applicable COBRA continuation provision.

(B) CERTIFICATION. The certification described in this subparagraph is a written certification of—

(i) the period of creditable coverage of the individual under such plan and the coverage (if any) under such COBRA continuation provision, and

(ii) the waiting period (if any) (and affiliation period, if applicable) imposed with respect to the individual for any coverage under such plan.

(C) ISSUER COMPLIANCE. To the extent that medical care under a group health plan consists of group health insurance coverage, the plan is deemed to have satisfied the certification requirement under this paragraph if the health insurance issuer offering the coverage provides for such certification in accordance with this paragraph.

(2) DISCLOSURE OF INFORMATION ON PREVIOUS BENEFITS. In the case of an election described in subsection (c)(3)(B) by a group health plan or health insurance issuer, if the plan or issuer enrolls an individual for coverage under the plan and the individual provides a certification of coverage of the individual under paragraph (1)—

(A) upon request of such plan or issuer, the entity which issued the certification provided by the individual shall promptly disclose to such requesting plan or issuer information on coverage of classes and categories of health benefits available under such entity's plan or coverage, and

(B) such entity may charge the requesting plan or issuer for the reasonable cost of disclosing such information.

(3) REGULATIONS. The Secretary shall establish rules to prevent an entity's failure to provide information under paragraph (1) or (2) with respect to previous coverage of an individual from adversely affecting any subsequent coverage of the individual under another group health plan or health insurance coverage.

Act Sec. 701. SPECIAL ENROLLMENT PERIODS.—

(f)(1) INDIVIDUALS LOSING OTHER COVERAGE. A group health plan, and a health insurance issuer offering group health insurance coverage in connection with a group health plan, shall permit an employee who is eligible, but not enrolled, for coverage under the terms of the plan (or a dependent of such an employee if the dependent is eligible, but not enrolled, for coverage under such terms) to enroll for coverage under the terms of the plan if each of the following conditions is met:

(A) The employee or dependent was covered under a group health plan or had health insurance coverage at the time coverage was previously offered to the employee or dependent.

(B) The employee stated in writing at such time that coverage under a group health plan or health insurance coverage was the reason for declining enrollment, but only if the plan sponsor or issuer (if applicable) required such a statement at such time and provided the employee with notice of such requirement (and the consequences of such requirement) at such time.

(C) The employee's or dependent's coverage described in subparagraph (A)—

(i) was under a COBRA continuation provision and the coverage under such provision was exhausted; or

(ii) was not under such a provision and either the coverage was terminated as a result of loss of eligibility for the coverage (including as a result of legal separation, divorce, death, termination of employment, or reduction in the number of hours of employment) or employer contributions toward such coverage were terminated.

(D) Under the terms of the plan, the employee requests such enrollment not later than 30 days after the date of exhaustion of coverage described in subparagraph (C)(i) or termination of coverage or employer contribution described in subparagraph (C)(ii).

(2) FOR DEPENDENT BENEFICIARIES—

(A) IN GENERAL. If—

(i) a group health plan makes coverage available with respect to a dependent of an individual,

(ii) the individual is a participant under the plan (or has met any waiting period applicable to becoming a participant under the plan and is eligible to be enrolled under the plan but for a failure to enroll during a previous enrollment period), and

(iii) a person becomes such a dependent of the individual through marriage, birth, or adoption or placement for adoption,

the group health plan shall provide for a dependent special enrollment period described in subparagraph (B) during which the person (or, if not otherwise enrolled, the individual) may be enrolled under the plan as a dependent of the individual, and in the case of the birth or adoption of a child, the spouse of the individual may be enrolled as a dependent of the individual if such spouse is otherwise eligible for coverage.

(B) Dependent special enrollment period. A dependent special enrollment period under this subparagraph shall be a period of not less than 30 days and shall begin on the later of—

(i) the date dependent coverage is made available, or

(ii) the date of the marriage, birth, or adoption or placement for adoption (as the case may be) described in subparagraph (A)(iii).

(C) No waiting period. If an individual seeks to enroll a dependent during the first 30 days of such a dependent special enrollment period, the coverage of the dependent shall become effective—

(i) in the case of marriage, not later than the first day of the first month beginning after the date the completed request for enrollment is received;

(ii) in the case of a dependent's birth, as of the date of such birth; or

(iii) in the case of a dependent's adoption or placement for adoption, the date of such adoption or placement for adoption.

Act Sec. 701. Use of Affiliation Period by HMOs as Alternative to Preexisting Condition Exclusion.—

(g)(1) In general. In the case of a group health plan that offers medical care through health insurance coverage offered by a health maintenance organization, the plan may provide for an affiliation period with respect to coverage through the organization only if—

(A) no preexisting condition exclusion is imposed with respect to coverage through the organization,

(B) the period is applied uniformly without regard to any health status-related factors, and

(C) such period does not exceed 2 months (or 3 months in the case of a late enrollee).

(2) Affiliation period.—

(A) Defined. For purposes of this part, the term "affiliation period" means a period which, under the terms of the health insurance coverage offered by the health maintenance organization, must expire before the health insurance coverage becomes effective. The organization is not required to provide health care services or benefits during such period and no premium shall be charged to the participant or beneficiary for any coverage during the period.

(B) Beginning. Such period shall begin on the enrollment date.

(C) Runs concurrently with waiting periods. An affiliation period under a plan shall run concurrently with any waiting period under the plan.

(3) Alternative methods. A health maintenance organization described in paragraph (1) may use alternative methods, from those described in such paragraph, to address adverse selection as approved by the State insurance commissioner or official or officials designated by the State to enforce the requirements of part A of title XXVII of the Public Health Service Act for the State involved with respect to such issuer.

Amendments

P.L. 104-191, §101(a):

Added ERISA Act Sec. 701 to read as above.

The above amendments generally apply with respect to group health plans for plan years beginning after June 30, 1997. For special rules, see Act Sec. 101(g)(2)-(5), reproduced below.

Act Sec. 101(g)(2)-(5) reads as follows:

(g) Effective Dates.—

(1) In general.—Except as provided in this section, this section (and the amendments made by this section) shall apply with respect to group health plans for plan years beginning after June 30, 1997.

(2) Determination of creditable coverage.—

(A) Period of coverage.—

(i) In general.—Subject to clause (ii), no period before July 1, 1996, shall be taken into account under part 7 of subtitle B of title I of the Employee Retirement Income Security Act of 1974 (as added by this section) in determining creditable coverage.

(ii) Special rule for certain periods.—The Secretary of Labor, consistent with section 104, shall provide for a process whereby individuals who need to establish creditable coverage for periods before July 1, 1996, and who would have such coverage credited but for clause (i) may be given credit for creditable coverage for such periods through the presentation of documents or other means.

(B) Certifications, etc.—

(i) In general.—Subject to clauses (ii) and (iii), subsection (e) of section 701 of the Employee Retirement Income Security Act of 1974 (as added by this section) shall apply to events occurring after June 30, 1996.

(ii) No certification required to be provided before June 1, 1997.—In no case is a certification required to be provided under such subsection before June 1, 1997.

(iii) Certification only on written request for events occurring before October 1, 1996.—In the case of an event occurring after June 30, 1996, and before October 1, 1996, a certification is not required to be provided under such subsection unless an individual (with respect to whom the certification is otherwise required to be made) requests such certification in writing.

(C) Transitional rule.—In the case of an individual who seeks to establish creditable coverage for any period for which certification is not required because it relates to an event occurring before June 30, 1996—

(i) the individual may present other credible evidence of such coverage in order to establish the period of creditable coverage; and

(ii) a group health plan and a health insurance issuer shall not be subject to any penalty or enforcement action with respect to the plan's or issuer's crediting (or not crediting) such coverage if the plan or issuer has sought to comply in good faith with the applicable requirements under the amendments made by this section.

(3) Special rule for collective bargaining agreements.—Except as provided in paragraph (2), in the case of a group health plan maintained pursuant to one or more collective bargaining agreements between employee representatives and one or more employers ratified before the date of the enactment of this Act, part 7 of subtitle B of title I of Employee Retirement Income Security Act of 1974 (other than section 701(e) thereof) shall not apply to plan years beginning before the later of—

(A) the date on which the last of the collective bargaining agreements relating to the plan terminates (determined without regard to any extension thereof agreed to after the date of the enactment of this Act), or

(B) July 1, 1997.

For purposes of subparagraph (A), any plan amendment made pursuant to a collective bargaining agreement relating to the plan which amends the plan solely to conform to any requirement of such part shall not be treated as a termination of such collective bargaining agreement.

(4) Timely regulations.—The Secretary of Labor, consistent with section 104, shall first issue by not later than April 1, 1997, such regulations as may be necessary to carry out the amendments made by this section.

(5) Limitation on actions.—No enforcement action shall be taken, pursuant to the amendments made by this section, against a group health plan or health insurance issuer with respect to a violation of a requirement imposed by such amendments before January 1, 1998, or, if later, the date of issuance of regulations referred to in paragraph (4), if the plan or issuer has sought to comply in good faith with such requirements.

Regulations

The following regulations were adopted by 62 FR 16894 and published in the Federal Register on April 8, 1997, under "Chapter XXV of Title 29 of the Code of Federal Regulations; Subchapter L—Health Insurance Portability and Renewability for Group Health Plans; Part 2590—Rules and Regulations for Health Insurance Portability and Renewability for Group Health Plans." Reg. §§ 2590.701-2—2590.701-6 were officially corrected on June 10, 1997, by 62 FR 31690. Reg. §§ 2590.701-3—2590.701-6 were amended by 62 FR 35904 and published in the *Federal Register* on July 2, 1997. Reg. §§ 2590.701-1, 2590.701-2, 2590.701-3, 2590.701-4, 2590.701-5, 2590.701-6, and 2590.701-7 were revised by T.D. 9166 on December 30, 2004 (69 FR 78720).

[¶ 15,049I]

§ 2590.701-1 **Basis and scope.** (a) *Statutory basis.* This Subpart B implements Part 7 of Subtitle B of Title I of the Employee Retirement Income Security Act of 1974, as amended (hereinafter ERISA or the Act).

(b) *Scope.* A group health plan or health insurance issuer offering group health insurance coverage may provide greater rights to participants and beneficiaries than those set forth in this Subpart B. This Subpart B sets forth minimum requirements for group health plans and health insurance issuers offering group health insurance coverage concerning:

(1) Limitations on a preexisting condition exclusion period.

(2) Certificates and disclosure of previous coverage.

(3) Rules relating to counting creditable coverage.

(4) Special enrollment periods.

(5) Prohibition against discrimination on the basis of health factors.

(6) Use of an affiliation period by an HMO as an alternative to a preexisting condition exclusion.

[¶ 15,049J]

§ 2590.701-2 **Definitions.** Unless otherwise provided, the definitions in this section govern in applying the provisions of §§ 2590.701 through 2590.734.

Affiliation period means a period of time that must expire before health insurance coverage provided by an HMO becomes effective, and during which the HMO is not required to provide benefits.

COBRA definitions:

(1) *COBRA* means Title X of the Consolidated Omnibus Budget Reconciliation Act of 1985, as amended.

(2) *COBRA continuation coverage* means coverage, under a group health plan, that satisfies an applicable COBRA continuation provision.

(3) *COBRA continuation provision* means sections 601-608 of the Act, section 4980B of the Internal Revenue Code (other than paragraph (f)(1) of such section 4980B insofar as it relates to pediatric vaccines), or Title XXII of the PHS Act.

(4) *Exhaustion of COBRA continuation coverage* means that an individual's COBRA continuation coverage ceases for any reason other than either failure of the individual to pay premiums on a timely basis, or for cause (such as making a fraudulent claim or an intentional misrepresentation of a material fact in connection with the plan). An individual is considered to have exhausted COBRA continuation coverage if such coverage ceases—

(i) Due to the failure of the employer or other responsible entity to remit premiums on a timely basis;

(ii) When the individual no longer resides, lives, or works in the service area of an HMO or similar program (whether or not within the choice of the individual) and there is no other COBRA continuation coverage available to the individual; or

(iii) When the individual incurs a claim that would meet or exceed a lifetime limit on all benefits and there is no other COBRA continuation coverage available to the individual.

Condition means a *medical condition.*

Creditable coverage means *creditable coverage* within the meaning of § 2590.701-4(a).

Dependent means any individual who is or may become eligible for coverage under the terms of a group health plan because of a relationship to a participant.

Enroll means to become covered for benefits under a group health plan (that is, when coverage becomes effective), without regard to when the individual may have completed or filed any forms that are required in order to become covered under the plan. For this purpose, an individual who has health coverage under a group health plan is enrolled in the plan regardless of whether the individual elects coverage, the individual is a dependent who becomes covered as a result of an election by a participant, or the individual becomes covered without an election.

Enrollment date definitions (*enrollment date, first day of coverage,* and *waiting period*) are set forth in § 2590.701-3(a)(3)(i), (ii), and (iii).

Excepted benefits means the benefits described as excepted in § 2590.732(c).

Genetic information means information about genes, gene products, and inherited characteristics that may derive from the individual or a family member. This includes information regarding carrier status and information derived from laboratory tests that identify mutations in specific genes or chromosomes, physical medical examinations, family histories, and direct analysis of genes or chromosomes.

Group health insurance coverage means health insurance coverage offered in connection with a group health plan.

Group health plan or *plan* means a *group health plan* within the meaning of § 2590.732(a).

Group market means the market for health insurance coverage offered in connection with a group health plan. (However, certain very small plans may be treated as being in the individual market, rather than the group market; see the definition of *individual market* in this section.)

Health insurance coverage means benefits consisting of medical care (provided directly, through insurance or reimbursement, or otherwise) under any hospital or medical service policy or certificate, hospital or medical service plan contract, or HMO contract offered by a health insurance issuer. Health insurance coverage includes group health insurance coverage, individual health insurance coverage, and short-term, limited-duration insurance.

Health insurance issuer or *issuer* means an insurance company, insurance service, or insurance organization (including an HMO) that is required to be licensed to engage in the business of insurance in a State and that is subject to State law that regulates insurance (within the meaning of section 514(b)(2) of the Act). Such term does not include a group health plan.

Health maintenance organization or *HMO* means—

(1) A federally qualified health maintenance organization (as defined in section 1301(a) of the PHS Act);

(2) An organization recognized under State law as a health maintenance organization; or

(3) A similar organization regulated under State law for solvency in the same manner and to the same extent as such a health maintenance organization.

Individual health insurance coverage means health insurance coverage offered to individuals in the individual market, but does not include short-term, limited-duration insurance. Individual health insurance coverage can include dependent coverage.

Individual market means the market for health insurance coverage offered to individuals other than in connection with a group health plan. Unless a State elects otherwise in accordance with section 2791(e)(1)(B)(ii) of the PHS Act, such term also includes coverage offered in connection with a group health plan that has fewer than two participants who are current employees on the first day of the plan year.

Internal Revenue Code means the Internal Revenue Code of 1986, as amended (Title 26, United States Code).

Issuer means a *health insurance issuer.*

Late enrollment definitions (*late enrollee* and *late enrollment*) are set forth in § 2590.701-3(a)(3)(v) and (vi).

Medical care means amounts paid for—

(1) The diagnosis, cure, mitigation, treatment, or prevention of disease, or amounts paid for the purpose of affecting any structure or function of the body;

(2) Transportation primarily for and essential to medical care referred to in paragraph (1) of this definition; and

(3) Insurance covering medical care referred to in paragraphs (1) and (2) of this definition.

Medical condition or *condition* means any condition, whether physical or mental, including, but not limited to, any condition resulting from illness, injury (whether or not the injury is accidental), pregnancy, or congenital malformation. However, genetic information is not a condition.

Participant means *participant* within the meaning of section 3(7) of the Act.

Placement, or being placed, for adoption means the assumption and retention of a legal obligation for total or partial support of a child by a person with whom the child has been placed in anticipation of the child's adoption. The child's placement for adoption with such person ends upon the termination of such legal obligation.

Plan year means the year that is designated as the plan year in the plan document of a group health plan, except that if the plan document does not designate a plan year or if there is no plan document, the plan year is—

(1) The deductible or limit year used under the plan;

(2) If the plan does not impose deductibles or limits on a yearly basis, then the plan year is the policy year;

(3) If the plan does not impose deductibles or limits on a yearly basis, and either the plan is not insured or the insurance policy is not renewed on an annual basis, then the plan year is the employer's taxable year; or

(4) In any other case, the plan year is the calendar year.

Preexisting condition exclusion means *preexisting condition exclusion* within the meaning of § 2590.701-3(a)(1).

Public health plan means *public health plan* within the meaning of § 2590.701-4(a)(1)(ix).

Public Health Service Act (PHS Act) means the Public Health Service Act (42 U.S.C. 201, *et seq.*).

Short-term, limited-duration insurance means health insurance coverage provided pursuant to a contract with an issuer that has an expiration date specified in the contract (taking into account any extensions that may be elected by the policyholder without the issuer's consent) that is less than 12 months after the original effective date of the contract.

Significant break in coverage means a *significant break in coverage* within the meaning of § 2590.701-4(b)(2)(iii).

Special enrollment means enrollment in a group health plan or group health insurance coverage under the rights described in § 2590.701-6.

State means each of the several States, the District of Columbia, Puerto Rico, the Virgin Islands, Guam, American Samoa, and the Northern Mariana Islands.

State health benefits risk pool means a *State health benefits risk pool* within the meaning of § 2590.701-4(a)(1)(vii).

Waiting period means *waiting period* within the meaning of § 2590.701-3(a)(3)(iii).

[¶ 15,049K]

§ 2590.701-3 **Limitations on preexisting condition exclusion period.** (a) *Preexisting condition exclusion.* (1) *Defined.* (i) A *preexisting condition exclusion* means a limitation or exclusion of benefits relating to a condition based on the fact that the condition was present before the effective date of coverage under a group health plan or group health insurance coverage, whether or not any medical advice, diagnosis, care, or treatment was recommended or received before that day. A preexisting condition exclusion includes any exclusion applicable to an individual as a result of information relating to an individual's health status before the individual's effective date of coverage under a group health plan or group health insurance coverage, such as a condition identified as a result of a pre-enrollment questionnaire or physical examination given to the individual, or review of medical records relating to the pre-enrollment period.

(ii) *Examples.* The rules of this paragraph (a)(1) are illustrated by the following examples:

Example 1. (i) *Facts.* A group health plan provides benefits solely through an insurance policy offered by Issuer *S*. At the expiration of the policy, the plan switches coverage to a policy offered by Issuer *T*. Issuer *T*'s policy excludes benefits for any prosthesis if the body part was lost before the effective date of coverage under the policy.

(ii) *Conclusion.* In this *Example 1*, the exclusion of benefits for any prosthesis if the body part was lost before the effective date of coverage is a preexisting condition exclusion because it operates to exclude benefits for a condition based on the fact that the condition was present before the effective date of coverage under the policy. (Therefore, the exclusion of benefits is required to comply with the limitations on preexisting condition exclusions in this section. For an example illustrating the application of these limitations to a succeeding insurance policy, see *Example 3* of paragraph (a)(3)(iv) of this section.)

Example 2. (i) *Facts.* A group health plan provides coverage for cosmetic surgery in cases of accidental injury, but only if the injury occurred while the individual was covered under the plan.

(ii) *Conclusion.* In this *Example 2*, the plan provision excluding cosmetic surgery benefits for individuals injured before enrolling in the plan is a preexisting condition exclusion because it operates to exclude benefits relating to a condition based on the fact that the

condition was present before the effective date of coverage. The plan provision, therefore, is subject to the limitations on preexisting condition exclusions in this section.

Example 3. (i) *Facts.* A group health plan provides coverage for the treatment of diabetes, generally not subject to any lifetime dollar limit. However, if an individual was diagnosed with diabetes before the effective date of coverage under the plan, diabetes coverage is subject to a lifetime limit of $10,000.

(ii) *Conclusion.* In this *Example 3*, the $10,000 lifetime limit is a preexisting condition exclusion because it limits benefits for a condition based on the fact that the condition was present before the effective date of coverage. The plan provision, therefore, is subject to the limitations on preexisting condition exclusions in this section.

Example 4. (i) *Facts.* A group health plan provides coverage for the treatment of acne, subject to a lifetime limit of $2,000. The plan counts against this $2,000 lifetime limit acne treatment benefits provided under prior health coverage.

(ii) *Conclusion.* In this *Example 4*, counting benefits for a specific condition provided under prior health coverage against a lifetime limit for that condition is a preexisting condition exclusion because it operates to limit benefits for a condition based on the fact that the condition was present before the effective date of coverage. The plan provision, therefore, is subject to the limitations on preexisting condition exclusions in this section.

Example 5. (i) *Facts.* When an individual's coverage begins under a group health plan, the individual generally becomes eligible for all benefits. However, benefits for pregnancy are not available until the individual has been covered under the plan for 12 months.

(ii) *Conclusion.* In this *Example 5*, the requirement to be covered under the plan for 12 months to be eligible for pregnancy benefits is a subterfuge for a preexisting condition exclusion because it is designed to exclude benefits for a condition (pregnancy) that arose before the effective date of coverage. Because a plan is prohibited under paragraph (b)(5) of this section from imposing any preexisting condition exclusion on pregnancy, the plan provision is prohibited. However, if the plan provision included an exception for women who were pregnant before the effective date of coverage under the plan (so that the provision applied only to women who became pregnant on or after the effective date of coverage) the plan provision would not be a preexisting condition exclusion (and would not be prohibited by paragraph (b)(5) of this section).

Example 6. (i) *Facts.* A group health plan provides coverage for medically necessary items and services, generally including treatment of heart conditions. However, the plan does not cover those same items and services when used for treatment of congenital heart conditions.

(ii) *Conclusion.* In this *Example 6*, the exclusion of coverage for treatment of congenital heart conditions is a preexisting condition exclusion because it operates to exclude benefits relating to a condition based on the fact that the condition was present before the effective date of coverage. The plan provision, therefore, is subject to the limitations on preexisting condition exclusions in this section.

Example 7. (i) *Facts.* A group health plan generally provides coverage for medically necessary items and services. However, the plan excludes coverage for the treatment of cleft palate.

(ii) *Conclusion.* In this *Example 7*, the exclusion of coverage for treatment of cleft palate is not a preexisting condition exclusion because the exclusion applies regardless of when the condition arose relative to the effective date of coverage. The plan provision, therefore, is not subject to the limitations on preexisting condition exclusions in this section.

Example 8. (i) *Facts.* A group health plan provides coverage for treatment of cleft palate, but only if the individual being treated has been continuously covered under the plan from the date of birth.

(ii) *Conclusion.* In this *Example 8*, the exclusion of coverage for treatment of cleft palate for individuals who have not been covered under the plan from the date of birth operates to exclude benefits in relation to a condition based on the fact that the condition was present before the effective date of coverage. The plan provision, therefore, is subject to the limitations on preexisting condition exclusions in this section.

(2) *General rules.* Subject to paragraph (b) of this section (prohibiting the imposition of a preexisting condition exclusion with respect to certain individuals and conditions), a group health plan, and a health insurance issuer offering group health insurance coverage, may impose, with respect to a participant or beneficiary, a preexisting condition exclusion only if the requirements of this paragraph (a)(2) are satisfied.

(i) *6-month look-back rule.* A preexisting condition exclusion must relate to a condition (whether physical or mental), regardless of the cause of the condition, for which medical advice, diagnosis, care, or treatment was recommended or received within the 6-month period (or such shorter period as applies under the plan) ending on the enrollment date.

(A) For purposes of this paragraph (a)(2)(i), medical advice, diagnosis, care, or treatment is taken into account only if it is recommended by, or received from, an individual licensed or similarly authorized to provide such services under State law and operating within the scope of practice authorized by State law.

(B) For purposes of this paragraph (a)(2)(i), the 6-month period ending on the enrollment date begins on the 6-month anniversary date preceding the enrollment date. For example, for an enrollment date of August 1, 1998, the 6-month period preceding the enrollment date is the period commencing on February 1, 1998 and continuing through July 31, 1998. As another example, for an enrollment date of August 30, 1998, the 6-month period preceding the enrollment date is the period commencing on February 28, 1998 and continuing through August 29, 1998.

(C) The rules of this paragraph (a)(2)(i) are illustrated by the following examples:

Example 1. (i) *Facts.* Individual A is diagnosed with a medical condition 8 months before A's enrollment date in Employer R's group health plan. A's doctor recommends that A take a prescription drug for 3 months, and A follows the recommendation.

(ii) *Conclusion.* In this *Example 1,* Employer R's plan may impose a preexisting condition exclusion with respect to A's condition because A received treatment during the 6-month period ending on A's enrollment date in Employer R's plan by taking the prescription medication during that period. However, if A did not take the prescription drug during the 6-month period, Employer R's plan would not be able to impose a preexisting condition exclusion with respect to that condition.

Example 2. (i) *Facts.* Individual B is treated for a medical condition 7 months before the enrollment date in Employer S's group health plan. As part of such treatment, B's physician recommends that a follow-up examination be given 2 months later. Despite this recommendation, B does not receive a follow-up examination, and no other medical advice, diagnosis, care, or treatment for that condition is recommended to B or received by B during the 6-month period ending on B's enrollment date in Employer S's plan.

(ii) *Conclusion.* In this *Example 2,* Employer S's plan may not impose a preexisting condition exclusion with respect to the condition for which B received treatment 7 months prior to the enrollment date.

Example 3. (i) *Facts.* Same facts as Example 2, except that Employer S's plan learns of the condition and attaches a rider to B's certificate of coverage excluding coverage for the condition. Three months after enrollment, B's condition recurs, and Employer S's plan denies payment under the rider.

(ii) *Conclusion.* In this *Example 3,* the rider is a preexisting condition exclusion and Employer S's plan may not impose a preexisting condition exclusion with respect to the condition for which B received treatment 7 months prior to the enrollment date. (In addition, such a rider would violate the provisions of § 2590.702, even if B had received treatment for the condition within the 6-month period ending on the enrollment date.)

Example 4. (i) *Facts.* Individual C has asthma and is treated for that condition several times during the 6-month period before C's enrollment date in Employer T's plan. Three months after the enrollment date, C begins coverage under Employer T's plan. Two months later, C is hospitalized for asthma.

(ii) *Conclusion.* In this *Example 4,* Employer T's plan may impose a preexisting condition exclusion with respect to C's asthma because care relating to C's asthma was received during the 6-month period ending on C's enrollment date (which, under the rules of paragraph (a)(3)(i) of this section, is the first day of the waiting period).

Example 5. (i) *Facts.* Individual D, who is subject to a preexisting condition exclusion imposed by Employer U's plan, has diabetes, as well as retinal degeneration, a foot condition, and poor circulation (all of which are conditions that may be directly attributed to diabetes). D receives treatment for these conditions during the 6-month period ending on D's enrollment date in Employer U's plan. After enrolling in the plan, D stumbles and breaks a leg.

(ii) *Conclusion.* In this *Example 5,* the leg fracture is not a condition related to D's diabetes, retinal degeneration, foot condition, or poor circulation, even though they may have contributed to the accident. Therefore, benefits to treat the leg fracture cannot be subject to a preexisting condition exclusion. However, any additional medical services that may be needed because of D's preexisting diabetes, poor circulation, or retinal degeneration that would not be needed by another patient with a broken leg who does not have these conditions may be subject to the preexisting condition exclusion imposed under Employer U's plan.

(ii) *Maximum length of preexisting condition exclusion.* A preexisting condition exclusion is not permitted to extend for more than 12 months (18 months in the case of a late enrollee) after the enrollment date. For example, for an enrollment date of August 1, 1998, the 12-month period after the enrollment date is the period commencing on August 1, 1998 and continuing through July 31, 1999; the 18-month period after the enrollment date is the period commencing on August 1, 1998 and continuing through January 31, 2000.

(iii) *Reducing a preexisting condition exclusion period by creditable coverage.* (A) The period of any preexisting condition exclusion that would otherwise apply to an individual under a group health plan is reduced by the number of days of creditable coverage the individual has as of the enrollment date, as counted under § 2590.701-4. Creditable coverage may be evidenced through a certificate of creditable coverage (required under § 2590.701-5(a)), or through other means in accordance with the rules of § 2590.701-5(c).

(B) The rules of this paragraph (a)(2)(iii) are illustrated by the following example:

Example. (i) *Facts.* Individual D works for Employer X and has been covered continuously under X's group health plan. D's spouse works for Employer Y. Y maintains a group health plan that imposes a 12-month preexisting condition exclusion (reduced by creditable coverage) on all new enrollees. D enrolls in Y's plan, but also stays covered under X's plan. D presents Y's plan with evidence of creditable coverage under X's plan.

(ii) *Conclusion.* In this *Example,* Y's plan must reduce the preexisting condition exclusion period that applies to D by the number of days of coverage that D had under X's plan as of D's enrollment date in Y's plan (even though D's coverage under X's plan was continuing as of that date).

(iv) *Other standards.* See § 2590.702 for other standards in this Subpart B that may apply with respect to certain benefit limitations or restrictions under a group health plan. Other laws may also apply, such as the Uniformed Services Employment and Reemployment Rights Act (USERRA), which can affect the application of a preexisting condition exclusion to certain individuals who are reinstated in a group health plan following active military service.

(3) *Enrollment definitions.* (i) *Enrollment date* means the first day of coverage (as described in paragraph (a)(3)(ii) of this section) or, if there is a waiting period, the first day of the waiting period. If an individual receiving benefits under a group health plan changes benefit packages, or if the plan changes group health insurance issuers, the individual's enrollment date does not change.

(ii) *First day of coverage* means, in the case of an individual covered for benefits under a group health plan, the first day of coverage under the plan and, in the case of an individual covered by health insurance coverage in the individual market, the first day of coverage under the policy or contract.

(iii) *Waiting period* means the period that must pass before coverage for an employee or dependent who is otherwise eligible to enroll under the terms of a group health plan can become effective. If an employee or dependent enrolls as a late enrollee or special enrollee, any period before such late or special enrollment is not a waiting period. If an individual seeks coverage in the individual market, a waiting period begins on the date the individual submits a substantially complete application for coverage and ends on—

(A) If the application results in coverage, the date coverage begins;

(B) If the application does not result in coverage, the date on which the application is denied by the issuer or the date on which the offer of coverage lapses.

(iv) The rules of paragraphs (a)(3)(i), (ii), and (iii) of this section are illustrated by the following examples:

Example 1. (i) *Facts.* Employer *V*'s group health plan provides for coverage to begin on the first day of the first payroll period following the date an employee is hired and completes the applicable enrollment forms, or on any subsequent January 1 after completion of the applicable enrollment forms. Employer *V*'s plan imposes a preexisting condition exclusion for 12 months (reduced by the individual's creditable coverage) following an individual's enrollment date. Employee *E* is hired by Employer *V* on October 13, 1998 and on October 14, 1998 *E* completes and files all the forms necessary to enroll in the plan. *E*'s coverage under the plan becomes effective on October 25, 1998 (which is the beginning of the first payroll period after *E*'s date of hire).

(ii) *Conclusion.* In this *Example 1, E*'s enrollment date is October 13, 1998 (which is the first day of the waiting period for *E*'s enrollment and is also *E*'s date of hire). Accordingly, with respect to *E*, the permissible 6-month period in paragraph (a)(2)(i) is the period from April 13, 1998 through October 12, 1998, the maximum permissible period during which Employer *V*'s plan can apply a preexisting condition exclusion under paragraph (a)(2)(ii) is the period from October 13, 1998 through October 12, 1999, and this period must be reduced under paragraph (a)(2)(iii) by *E*'s days of creditable coverage as of October 13, 1998.

Example 2. (i) *Facts.* A group health plan has two benefit package options, Option 1 and Option 2. Under each option a 12-month preexisting condition exclusion is imposed. Individual *B* is enrolled in Option 1 on the first day of employment with the employer maintaining the plan, remains enrolled in Option 1 for more than one year, and then decides to switch to Option 2 at open season.

(ii) *Conclusion.* In this *Example 2, B* cannot be subject to any preexisting condition exclusion under Option 2 because any preexisting condition exclusion period would have to begin on *B*'s enrollment date, which is *B*'s first day of coverage, rather than the date that *B* enrolled in Option 2. Therefore, the preexisting condition exclusion period expired before *B* switched to Option 2.

Example 3. (i) *Facts.* On May 13, 1997, Individual *E* is hired by an employer and enrolls in the employer's group health plan. The plan provides benefits solely through an insurance policy offered by Issuer *S*. On December 27, 1998, *E*'s leg is injured in an accident and the leg is amputated. On January 1, 1999, the plan switches coverage to a policy offered by Issuer *T*. Issuer *T*'s policy excludes benefits for any prosthesis if the body part was lost before the effective date of coverage under the policy.

(ii) *Conclusion.* In this *Example 3, E*'s enrollment date is May 13, 1997, *E*'s first day of coverage. Therefore, the permissible 6-month look-back period for the preexisting condition exclusion imposed under Issuer *T*'s policy begins on November 13, 1996 and ends on May 12, 1997. In addition, the 12- month maximum permissible preexisting condition exclusion period begins on May 13, 1997 and ends on May 12, 1998. Accordingly, because no medical advice, diagnosis, care, or treatment was recommended to or received by *E* for the leg during the 6-month look-back period (even though medical care was provided within the 6-month period preceding the effective date of *E*'s coverage under Issuer *T*'s policy), Issuer *T* may not impose any preexisting condition exclusion with respect to *E*. Moreover, even if *E* had received

treatment during the 6-month look-back period, Issuer *T* still would not be permitted to impose a preexisting condition exclusion because the 12-month maximum permissible preexisting condition exclusion period expired on May 12, 1998 (before the effective date of *E*'s coverage under Issuer *T*'s policy).

Example 4. (i) *Facts.* A group health plan limits eligibility for coverage to full-time employees of Employer *Y*. Coverage becomes effective on the first day of the month following the date the employee becomes eligible. Employee *C* begins working full-time for Employer *Y* on April 11. Prior to this date, *C* worked part-time for *Y*. *C* enrolls in the plan and coverage is effective May 1.

(ii) *Conclusion.* In this *Example 4, C*'s enrollment date is April 11 and the period from April 11 through April 30 is a waiting period. The period while *C* was working parttime, and therefore not in an eligible class of employees, is not part of the waiting period.

Example 5. (i) *Facts.* To be eligible for coverage under a multiemployer group health plan in the current calendar quarter, the plan requires an individual to have worked 250 hours in covered employment during the previous quarter. If the hours requirement is satisfied, coverage becomes effective on the first day of the current calendar quarter. Employee *D* begins work on January 28 and does not work 250 hours in covered employment during the first quarter (ending March 31). *D* works at least 250 hours in the second quarter (ending June 30) and is enrolled in the plan with coverage effective July 1 (the first day of the third quarter).

(ii) *Conclusion.* In this *Example 5, D*'s enrollment date is the first day of the quarter during which *D* satisfies the hours requirement, which is April 1. The period from April 1 through June 30 is a waiting period.

(v) *Late enrollee* means an individual whose enrollment in a plan is a late enrollment.

(vi) (A) *Late enrollment* means enrollment of an individual under a group health plan other than—

(1) On the earliest date on which coverage can become effective for the individual under the terms of the plan; or

(2) Through special enrollment. (For rules relating to special enrollment, see § 2590.701-6.)

(B) If an individual ceases to be eligible for coverage under the plan, and then subsequently becomes eligible for coverage under the plan, only the individual's most recent period of eligibility is taken into account in determining whether the individual is a late enrollee under the plan with respect to the most recent period of coverage. Similar rules apply if an individual again becomes eligible for coverage following a suspension of coverage that applied generally under the plan.

(vii) *Examples.* The rules of paragraphs (a)(3)(v) and (vi) of this section are illustrated by the following examples:

Example 1. (i) *Facts.* Employee *F* first becomes eligible to be covered by Employer *W*'s group health plan on January 1, 1999 but elects not to enroll in the plan until a later annual open enrollment period, with coverage effective January 1, 2001. *F* has no special enrollment right at that time.

(ii) *Conclusion.* In this *Example 1, F* is a late enrollee with respect to *F*'s coverage that became effective under the plan on January 1, 2001.

Example 2. (i) *Facts.* Same facts as *Example 1,* except that *F* terminates employment with Employer *W* on July 1, 1999 without having had any health insurance coverage under the plan. *F* is rehired by Employer *W* on January 1, 2000 and is eligible for and elects coverage under Employer *W*'s plan effective on January 1, 2000.

(ii) *Conclusion.* In this *Example 2, F* would not be a late enrollee with respect to *F*'s coverage that became effective on January 1, 2000.

(b) *Exceptions pertaining to preexisting condition exclusions.* (1) *Newborns.* (i) *In general.* Subject to paragraph (b)(3) of this section, a group health plan, and a health insurance issuer offering group health insurance coverage, may not impose any preexisting condition exclusion on a child who, within 30 days after birth, is covered under any creditable coverage. Accordingly, if a child is enrolled in a group health plan (or other creditable coverage) within 30 days after birth and subsequently enrolls in another group health plan without a significant break in coverage (as described in § 2590.701-4(b)(2)(iii)), the other plan may not impose any preexisting condition exclusion on the child.

(ii) *Examples.* The rules of this paragraph (b)(1) are illustrated by the following examples:

Example 1. (i) *Facts.* Individual *E*, who has no prior creditable coverage, begins working for Employer *W* and has accumulated 210 days of creditable coverage under Employer *W*'s group health plan on the date *E* gives birth to a child. Within 30 days after the birth, the child is enrolled in the plan. Ninety days after the birth, both *E* and the child terminate coverage under the plan. Both *E* and the child then experience a break in coverage of 45 days before *E* is hired by Employer *X* and the two are enrolled in Employer *X*'s group health plan.

(ii) *Conclusion.* In this *Example 1,* because *E*'s child is enrolled in Employer *W*'s plan within 30 days after birth, no preexisting condition exclusion may be imposed with respect to the child under Employer *W*'s plan. Likewise, Employer *X*'s plan may not impose any preexisting condition exclusion on *E*'s child because the child was covered under creditable coverage within 30 days after birth and had no significant break in coverage before enrolling in Employer *X*'s plan. On the other hand, because *E* had only 300 days of creditable coverage prior to *E*'s enrollment date in Employer *X*'s plan, Employer *X*'s plan may impose a preexisting condition exclusion on *E* for up to 65 days (66 days if the 12-month period after *E*'s enrollment date in *X*'s plan includes February 29).

Example 2. (i) *Facts.* Individual *F* is enrolled in a group health plan in which coverage is provided through a health insurance issuer. *F* gives birth. Under State law applicable to the health insurance issuer, health care expenses incurred for the child during the 30 days following birth are covered as part of *F*'s coverage. Although *F* may obtain coverage for the child beyond 30 days by timely requesting special enrollment and paying an additional premium, the issuer is prohibited under State law from recouping the cost of any expenses incurred for the child within the 30-day period if the child is not later enrolled.

(ii) *Conclusion.* In this *Example 2,* the child is covered under creditable coverage within 30 days after birth, regardless of whether the child enrolls as a special enrollee under the plan. Therefore, no preexisting condition exclusion may be imposed on the child unless the child has a significant break in coverage.

(2) *Adopted children.* Subject to paragraph (b)(3) of this section, a group health plan, and a health insurance issuer offering group health insurance coverage, may not impose any preexisting condition exclusion on a child who is adopted or placed for adoption before attaining 18 years of age and who, within 30 days after the adoption or placement for adoption, is covered under any creditable coverage. Accordingly, if a child is enrolled in a group health plan (or other creditable coverage) within 30 days after adoption or placement for adoption and subsequently enrolls in another group health plan without a significant break in coverage (as described in § 2590.701-4(b)(2)(iii)), the other plan may not impose any preexisting condition exclusion on the child. This rule does not apply to coverage before the date of such adoption or placement for adoption.

(3) *Significant break in coverage.* Paragraphs (b)(1) and (2) of this section no longer apply to a child after a significant break in coverage. (*See* § 2590.701-4(b)(2)(iii) for rules relating to the determination of a significant break in coverage.)

(4) *Special enrollment.* For special enrollment rules relating to new dependents, see § 2590.701-6(b).

(5) *Pregnancy.* A group health plan, and a health insurance issuer offering group health insurance coverage, may not impose a preexisting condition exclusion relating to pregnancy.

(6) *Genetic information.* (i) A group health plan, and a health insurance issuer offering group health insurance coverage, may not impose a preexisting condition exclusion relating to a condition based solely on genetic information. However, if an individual is diagnosed with a condition, even if the condition relates to genetic information,

the plan may impose a preexisting condition exclusion with respect to the condition, subject to the other limitations of this section.

(ii) The rules of this paragraph (b)(6) are illustrated by the following example:

Example. (i) *Facts.* Individual *A* enrolls in a group health plan that imposes a 12-month maximum preexisting condition exclusion. Three months before *A*'s enrollment, *A*'s doctor told *A* that, based on genetic information, *A* has a predisposition towards breast cancer. *A* was not diagnosed with breast cancer at any time prior to *A*'s enrollment date in the plan. Nine months after *A*'s enrollment date in the plan, *A* is diagnosed with breast cancer.

(ii) *Conclusion.* In this *Example,* the plan may not impose a preexisting condition exclusion with respect to *A*'s breast cancer because, prior to *A*'s enrollment date, *A* was not diagnosed with breast cancer.

(c) *General notice of preexisting condition exclusion.* A group health plan imposing a preexisting condition exclusion, and a health insurance issuer offering group health insurance coverage subject to a preexisting condition exclusion, must provide a written general notice of preexisting condition exclusion to participants under the plan and cannot impose a preexisting condition exclusion with respect to a participant or a dependent of the participant until such a notice is provided.

(1) *Manner and timing.* A plan or issuer must provide the general notice of preexisting condition exclusion as part of any written application materials distributed by the plan or issuer for enrollment. If the plan or issuer does not distribute such materials, the notice must be provided by the earliest date following a request for enrollment that the plan or issuer, acting in a reasonable and prompt fashion, can provide the notice.

(2) *Content.* The general notice of preexisting condition exclusion must notify participants of the following:

(i) The existence and terms of any preexisting condition exclusion under the plan. This description includes the length of the plan's look-back period (which is not to exceed 6 months under paragraph (a)(2)(i) of this section); the maximum preexisting condition exclusion period under the plan (which cannot exceed 12 months (or 18-months for late enrollees) under paragraph (a)(2)(ii) of this section); and how the plan will reduce the maximum preexisting condition exclusion period by creditable coverage (described in paragraph (a)(2)(iii) of this section).

(ii) A description of the rights of individuals to demonstrate creditable coverage, and any applicable waiting periods, through a certificate of creditable coverage (as required by § 2590.701-5(a)) or through other means (as described in § 2590.701-5(c)). This must include a description of the right of the individual to request a certificate from a prior plan or issuer, if necessary, and a statement that the current plan or issuer will assist in obtaining a certificate from any prior plan or issuer, if necessary.

(iii) A person to contact (including an address or telephone number) for obtaining additional information or assistance regarding the preexisting condition exclusion.

(3) *Duplicate notices not required.* If a notice satisfying the requirements of this paragraph (c) is provided to an individual, the obligation to provide a general notice of preexisting condition exclusion with respect to that individual is satisfied for both the plan and the issuer.

(4) *Example with sample language.* The rules of this paragraph (c) are illustrated by the following example, which includes sample language that plans and issuers can use as a basis for preparing their own notices to satisfy the requirements of this paragraph (c):

Example. (i) *Facts.* A group health plan makes coverage effective on the first day of the first calendar month after hire and on each January 1 following an open season. The plan imposes a 12-month maximum preexisting condition exclusion (18 months for late enrollees) and uses a 6-month lookback period. As part of the enrollment application materials, the plan provides the following statement:

This plan imposes a preexisting condition exclusion. This means that if you have a medical condition before coming to our plan, you might have to wait a certain period of time before the plan will provide coverage for that condition. This exclusion applies only to conditions for which medical advice, diagnosis, care, or treatment was recommended or received within a six-month period. Generally, this six-month period ends the day before your coverage becomes effective. However, if you were in a waiting period for coverage, the six-month period ends on the day before the waiting period begins. The preexisting condition exclusion does not apply to pregnancy nor to a child who is enrolled in the plan within 30 days after birth, adoption, or placement for adoption.

This exclusion may last up to 12 months (18 months if you are a late enrollee) from your first day of coverage, or, if you were in a waiting period, from the first day of your waiting period. However, you can reduce the length of this exclusion period by the number of days of your prior "creditable coverage." Most prior health coverage is creditable coverage and can be used to reduce the preexisting condition exclusion if you have not experienced a break in coverage of at least 63 days. To reduce the 12-month (or 18-month) exclusion period by your creditable coverage, you should give us a copy of any certificates of creditable coverage you have. If you do not have a certificate, but you do have prior health coverage, we will help you obtain one from your prior plan or issuer. There are also other ways that you can show you have creditable coverage. Please contact us if you need help demonstrating creditable coverage.

All questions about the preexisting condition exclusion and creditable coverage should be directed to Individual *B* at Address *M* or Telephone Number *N*.

(ii) *Conclusion.* In this Example, the plan satisfies the general notice requirement of this paragraph (c), and thus also satisfies this requirement for any issuer providing the coverage.

(d) *Determination of creditable coverage.* (1) *Determination within reasonable time.* If a group health plan or health insurance issuer offering group health insurance coverage receives creditable coverage information under § 2590.701-5, the plan or issuer is required, within a reasonable time following receipt of the information, to make a determination regarding the amount of the individual's creditable coverage and the length of any exclusion that remains. Whether this determination is made within a reasonable time depends on the relevant facts and circumstances. Relevant facts and circumstances include whether a plan's application of a preexisting condition exclusion would prevent an individual from having access to urgent medical care.

(2) *No time limit on presenting evidence of creditable coverage.* A plan or issuer may not impose any limit on the amount of time that an individual has to present a certificate or other evidence of creditable coverage.

(3) *Example.* The rules of this paragraph (d) are illustrated by the following example:

Example. (i) *Facts.* A group health plan imposes a preexisting condition exclusion period of 12 months. After receiving the general notice of preexisting condition exclusion, Individual *H* develops an urgent health condition before receiving a certificate of creditable coverage from *H*'s prior group health plan. *H* attests to the period of prior coverage, presents corroborating documentation of the coverage period, and authorizes the plan to request a certificate on *H*'s behalf in accordance with the rules of § 2590.701-5.

(ii) *Conclusion.* In this *Example,* the plan must review the evidence presented by *H* and make a determination of creditable coverage within a reasonable time that is consistent with the urgency of *H*'s health condition. (This determination may be modified as permitted under paragraph (f) of this section.)

(e) *Individual notice of period of preexisting condition exclusion.* After an individual has presented evidence of creditable coverage and after the plan or issuer has made a determination of creditable coverage under paragraph (d) of this section, the plan or issuer must provide the individual a written notice of the length of preexisting condition exclusion that remains after offsetting for prior creditable coverage. This individual notice is not required to identify any medical conditions specific to the individual that could be subject to the exclusion. A plan or issuer is not required to provide this notice if the plan or issuer does not impose any preexisting condition exclusion on the individual or if

the plan's preexisting condition exclusion is completely offset by the individual's prior creditable coverage.

(1) *Manner and timing.* The individual notice must be provided by the earliest date following a determination that the plan or issuer, acting in a reasonable and prompt fashion, can provide the notice.

(2) *Content.* A plan or issuer must disclose—

(i) Its determination of any preexisting condition exclusion period that applies to the individual (including the last day on which the preexisting condition exclusion applies);

(ii) The basis for such determination, including the source and substance of any information on which the plan or issuer relied;

(iii) An explanation of the individual's right to submit additional evidence of creditable coverage; and

(iv) A description of any applicable appeal procedures established by the plan or issuer.

(3) *Duplicate notices not required.* If a notice satisfying the requirements of this paragraph (e) is provided to an individual, the obligation to provide this individual notice of preexisting condition exclusion with respect to that individual is satisfied for both the plan and the issuer.

(4) *Examples.* The rules of this paragraph (e) are illustrated by the following examples:

Example 1. (i) *Facts.* A group health plan imposes a preexisting condition exclusion period of 12 months. After receiving the general notice of preexisting condition exclusion, Individual *G* presents a certificate of creditable coverage indicating 240 days of creditable coverage. Within seven days of receipt of the certificate, the plan determines that *G* is subject to a preexisting condition exclusion of 125 days, the last day of which is March 5. Five days later, the plan notifies *G* that, based on the certificate *G* submitted, *G* is subject to a preexisting condition exclusion period of 125 days, ending on March 5. The notice also explains the opportunity to submit additional evidence of creditable coverage and the plan's appeal procedures. The notice does not identify any of *G*'s medical conditions that could be subject to the exclusion.

(ii) *Conclusion.* In this *Example 1,* the plan satisfies the requirements of this paragraph (e).

Example 2. (i) *Facts.* Same facts as in *Example 1,* except that the plan determines that *G* has 430 days of creditable coverage based on *G*'s certificate indicating 430 days of creditable coverage under *G*'s prior plan.

(ii) *Conclusion.* In this *Example 2,* the plan is not required to notify *G* that *G* will not be subject to a preexisting condition exclusion.

(f) *Reconsideration.* Nothing in this section prevents a plan or issuer from modifying an initial determination of creditable coverage if it determines that the individual did not have the claimed creditable coverage, provided that—

(1) A notice of the new determination (consistent with the requirements of paragraph (e) of this section) is provided to the individual; and

(2) Until the notice of the new determination is provided, the plan or issuer, for purposes of approving access to medical services (such as a presurgery authorization), acts in a manner consistent with the initial determination.

[¶ 15,049L]

§ 2590.701-4 **Rules relating to creditable coverage.** (a) *General rules.* (1) *Creditable coverage.* For purposes of this section, except as provided in paragraph (a)(2) of this section, the term *creditable coverage* means coverage of an individual under any of the following:

(i) A group health plan as defined in § 2590.732(a).

(ii) Health insurance coverage as defined in § 2590.701-2 (whether or not the entity offering the coverage is subject to Part 7 of Subtitle B of Title I of the Act, and without regard to whether the coverage is offered in the group market, the individual market, or otherwise).

(iii) Part A or B of Title XVIII of the Social Security Act (Medicare).

(iv) Title XIX of the Social Security Act (Medicaid), other than coverage consisting solely of benefits under section 1928 of the Social Security Act (the program for distribution of pediatric vaccines).

(v) Title 10 U.S.C. Chapter 55 (medical and dental care for members and certain former members of the uniformed services, and for their dependents; for purposes of Title 10 U.S.C. Chapter 55, *uniformed services* means the armed forces and the Commissioned Corps of the National Oceanic and Atmospheric Administration and of the Public Health Service).

(vi) A medical care program of the Indian Health Service or of a tribal organization.

(vii) A State health benefits risk pool. For purposes of this section, a *State health benefits risk pool* means—

(A) An organization qualifying under section 501(c)(26) of the Internal Revenue Code;

(B) A qualified high risk pool described in section 2744(c)(2) of the PHS Act; or

(C) Any other arrangement sponsored by a State, the membership composition of which is specified by the State and which is established and maintained primarily to provide health coverage for individuals who are residents of such State and who, by reason of the existence or history of a medical condition—

(1) Are unable to acquire medical care coverage for such condition through insurance or from an HMO, or

(2) Are able to acquire such coverage only at a rate which is substantially in excess of the rate for such coverage through the membership organization.

(viii) A health plan offered under Title 5 U.S.C. Chapter 89 (the Federal Employees Health Benefits Program).

(ix) A public health plan. For purposes of this section, a *public health plan* means any plan established or maintained by a State, the U.S. government, a foreign country, or any political subdivision of a State, the U.S. government, or a foreign country that provides health coverage to individuals who are enrolled in the plan.

(x) A health benefit plan under section 5(e) of the Peace Corps Act (22 U.S.C. 2504(e)).

(xi) Title XXI of the Social Security Act (State Children's Health Insurance Program).

(2) *Excluded coverage.* Creditable coverage does not include coverage of solely excepted benefits (described in § 2590.732).

(3) *Methods of counting creditable coverage.* For purposes of reducing any preexisting condition exclusion period, as provided under § 2590.701-3(a)(2)(iii), the amount of an individual's creditable coverage generally is determined by using the standard method described in paragraph (b) of this section. A plan or issuer may use the alternative method under paragraph (c) of this section with respect to any or all of the categories of benefits described under paragraph (c)(3) of this section.

(b) *Standard method.* (1) *Specific benefits not considered.* Under the standard method, the amount of creditable coverage is determined without regard to the specific benefits included in the coverage.

(2) *Counting creditable coverage.* (i) *Based on days.* For purposes of reducing the preexisting condition exclusion period that applies to an individual, the amount of creditable coverage is determined by counting all the days on which the individual has one or more types of creditable coverage. Accordingly, if on a particular day an individual has creditable coverage from more than one source, all the creditable coverage on that day is counted as one day. Any days in a waiting period for coverage are not creditable coverage.

(ii) *Days not counted before significant break in coverage.* Days of creditable coverage that occur before a significant break in coverage are not required to be counted.

(iii) *Significant break in coverage defined.* A significant break in coverage means a period of 63 consecutive days during each of which an individual does not have any creditable coverage. (*See also* § 2590.731(c)(2)(iii) regarding the applicability to issuers of State insurance laws that require a break of more than 63 days before an individ-

ual has a significant break in coverage for purposes of State insurance law.)

(iv) *Periods that toll a significant break.* Days in a waiting period and days in an affiliation period are not taken into account in determining whether a significant break in coverage has occurred. In addition, for an individual who elects COBRA continuation coverage during the second election period provided under the Trade Act of 2002, the days between the date the individual lost group health plan coverage and the first day of the second COBRA election period are not taken into account in determining whether a significant break in coverage has occurred.

(v) *Examples.* The rules of this paragraph (b)(2) are illustrated by the following examples:

Example 1. (i) *Facts.* Individual *A* has creditable coverage under Employer *P*'s plan for 18 months before coverage ceases. *A* is provided a certificate of creditable coverage on *A*'s last day of coverage. Sixty-four days after the last date of coverage under *P*'s plan, *A* is hired by Employer *Q* and enrolls in *Q*'s group health plan. *Q*'s plan has a 12-month preexisting condition exclusion.

(ii) *Conclusion.* In this *Example 1, A* has a break in coverage of 63 days. Because *A*'s break in coverage is a significant break in coverage, *Q*'s plan may disregard *A*'s prior coverage and *A* may be subject to a 12-month preexisting condition exclusion.

Example 2. (i) *Facts.* Same facts as *Example 1,* except that *A* is hired by *Q* and enrolls in *Q*'s plan on the 63rd day after the last date of coverage under *P*'s plan.

(ii) *Conclusion.* In this *Example 2, A* has a break in coverage of 62 days. Because *A*'s break in coverage is not a significant break in coverage, *Q*'s plan must count *A*'s prior creditable coverage for purposes of reducing the plan's preexisting condition exclusion period that applies to *A.*

Example 3. (i) *Facts.* Same facts as *Example 1,* except that *Q*'s plan provides benefits through an insurance policy that, as required by applicable State insurance laws, defines a significant break in coverage as 90 days.

(ii) *Conclusion.* In this *Example 3,* under State law, the issuer that provides group health insurance coverage to *Q*'s plan must count *A*'s period of creditable coverage prior to the 63-day break. (However, if *Q*'s plan was a self-insured plan, the coverage would not be subject to State law. Therefore, the health coverage would not be governed by the longer break rules and *A*'s previous health coverage could be disregarded.)

Example 4. —[Reserved]

Example 5. (i) *Facts.* Individual *C* has creditable coverage under Employer *S*'s plan for 200 days before coverage ceases. *C* is provided a certificate of creditable coverage on *C*'s last day of coverage. *C* then does not have any creditable coverage for 51 days before being hired by Employer *T. T*'s plan has a 3-month waiting period. *C* works for *T* for 2 months and then terminates employment. Eleven days after terminating employment with *T, C* begins working for Employer *U. U*'s plan has no waiting period, but has a 6-month preexisting condition exclusion.

(ii) *Conclusion.* In this *Example 5, C* does not have a significant break in coverage because, after disregarding the waiting period under *T*'s plan, *C* had only a 62-day break in coverage (51 days plus 11 days). Accordingly, *C* has 200 days of creditable coverage, and *U*'s plan may not apply its 6-month preexisting condition exclusion with respect to *C.*

Example 6. —[Reserved]

Example 7. (i) *Facts.* Individual *E* has creditable coverage under Employer *X*'s plan. *E* is provided a certificate of creditable coverage on *E*'s last day of coverage. On the 63rd day without coverage, *E* submits a substantially complete application for a health insurance policy in the individual market. *E*'s application is accepted and coverage is made effective 10 days later.

(ii) *Conclusion.* In this *Example 7,* because *E* applied for the policy before the end of the 63rd day, the period between the date of application and the first day of coverage is a waiting period and no significant break in coverage occurred even though the actual period without coverage was 73 days.

Example 8. (i) *Facts.* Same facts as *Example 7,* except that *E*'s application for a policy in the individual market is denied.

(ii) *Conclusion.* In this *Example 8,* even though *E* did not obtain coverage following application, the period between the date of application and the date the coverage was denied is a waiting period. However, to avoid a significant break in coverage, no later than the day after the application for the policy is denied *E* would need to do one of the following: submit a substantially complete application for a different individual market policy; obtain coverage in the group market; or be in a waiting period for coverage in the group market.

(vi) *Other permissible counting methods.* (A) *Rule.* Notwithstanding any other provisions of this paragraph (b)(2), for purposes of reducing a preexisting condition exclusion period (but not for purposes of issuing a certificate under § 2590.701-5), a group health plan, and a health insurance issuer offering group health insurance coverage, may determine the amount of creditable coverage in any other manner that is at least as favorable to the individual as the method set forth in this paragraph (b)(2), subject to the requirements of other applicable law.

(B) *Example.* The rule of this paragraph (b)(2)(vi) is illustrated by the following example:

Example. (i) *Facts.* Individual *F* has coverage under Group Health Plan *Y* from January 3, 1997 through March 25, 1997. *F* then becomes covered by Group Health Plan *Z*. *F*'s enrollment date in Plan *Z* is May 1, 1997. Plan *Z* has a 12-month preexisting condition exclusion.

(ii) *Conclusion.* In this *Example,* Plan *Z* may determine, in accordance with the rules prescribed in paragraphs (b)(2)(i), (ii), and (iii) of this section, that *F* has 82 days of creditable coverage (29 days in January, 28 days in February, and 25 days in March). Thus, the preexisting condition exclusion will no longer apply to *F* on February 8, 1998 (82 days before the 12-month anniversary of *F*'s enrollment (May 1)). For administrative convenience, however, Plan *Z* may consider that the preexisting condition exclusion will no longer apply to *F* on the first day of the month (February 1).

(c) *Alternative method.* (1) *Specific benefits considered.* Under the alternative method, a group health plan, or a health insurance issuer offering group health insurance coverage, determines the amount of creditable coverage based on coverage within any category of benefits described in paragraph (c)(3) of this section and not based on coverage for any other benefits. The plan or issuer may use the alternative method for any or all of the categories. The plan or issuer may apply a different preexisting condition exclusion period with respect to each category (and may apply a different preexisting condition exclusion period for benefits that are not within any category). The creditable coverage determined for a category of benefits applies only for purposes of reducing the preexisting condition exclusion period with respect to that category. An individual's creditable coverage for benefits that are not within any category for which the alternative method is being used is determined under the standard method of paragraph (b) of this section.

(2) *Uniform application.* A plan or issuer using the alternative method is required to apply it uniformly to all participants and beneficiaries under the plan or health insurance coverage. The use of the alternative method is required to be set forth in the plan.

(3) *Categories of benefits.* The alternative method for counting creditable coverage may be used for coverage for the following categories of benefits—

(i) Mental health;

(ii) Substance abuse treatment;

(iii) Prescription drugs;

(iv) Dental care; or

(v) Vision care.

(4) *Plan notice.* If the alternative method is used, the plan is required to—

(i) State prominently that the plan is using the alternative method of counting creditable coverage in disclosure statements concerning the plan, and State this to each enrollee at the time of enrollment under the plan; and

(ii) Include in these statements a description of the effect of using the alternative method, including an identification of the categories used.

(5) *Disclosure of information on previous benefits.* See § 2590.701-5(b) for special rules concerning disclosure of coverage to a plan, or issuer, using the alternative method of counting creditable coverage under this paragraph (c).

(6) *Counting creditable coverage.* (i) *In general.* Under the alternative method, the group health plan or issuer counts creditable coverage within a category if any level of benefits is provided within the category. Coverage under a reimbursement account or arrangement, such as a flexible spending arrangement (as defined in section 106(c)(2) of the Internal Revenue Code), does not constitute coverage within any category.

(ii) *Special rules.* In counting an individual's creditable coverage under the alternative method, the group health plan, or issuer, first determines the amount of the individual's creditable coverage that may be counted under paragraph (b) of this section, up to a total of 365 days of the most recent creditable coverage (546 days for a late enrollee). The period over which this creditable coverage is determined is referred to as the determination period. Then, for the category specified under the alternative method, the plan or issuer counts within the category all days of coverage that occurred during the determination period (whether or not a significant break in coverage for that category occurs), and reduces the individual's preexisting condition exclusion period for that category by that number of days. The plan or issuer may determine the amount of creditable coverage in any other reasonable manner, uniformly applied, that is at least as favorable to the individual.

(iii) *Example.* The rules of this paragraph (c)(6) are illustrated by the following example:

Example. (i) *Facts.* Individual *D* enrolls in Employer *V*'s plan on January 1, 2001. Coverage under the plan includes prescription drug benefits. On April 1, 2001, the plan ceases providing prescription drug benefits. *D*'s employment with Employer *V* ends on January 1, 2002, after *D* was covered under Employer *V*'s group health plan for 365 days. *D* enrolls in Employer *Y*'s plan on February 1, 2002 (*D*'s enrollment date). Employer *Y*'s plan uses the alternative method of counting creditable coverage and imposes a 12-month preexisting condition exclusion on prescription drug benefits.

(ii) *Conclusion.* In this *Example,* Employer *Y*'s plan may impose a 275-day preexisting condition exclusion with respect to *D* for prescription drug benefits because *D* had 90 days of creditable coverage relating to prescription drug benefits within *D*'s determination period.

[¶ 15,049M]

§ 2590.701-5 **Certification and disclosure of previous coverage.** (a) *Certificate of creditable coverage.* (1) *Entities required to provide certificate.* (i) *In general.* A group health plan, and each health insurance issuer offering group health insurance coverage under a group health plan, is required to furnish certificates of creditable coverage in accordance with this paragraph (a).

(ii) *Duplicate certificates not required.* An entity required to provide a certificate under this paragraph (a) with respect to an individual satisfies that requirement if another party provides the certificate, but only to the extent that the certificate contains the information required in paragraph (a)(3) of this section. For example, in the case of a group health plan funded through an insurance policy, the issuer satisfies the certification requirement with respect to an individual if the plan actually provides a certificate that includes all the information required under paragraph (a)(3) of this section with respect to the individual.

(iii) *Special rule for group health plans.* To the extent coverage under a plan consists of group health insurance coverage, the plan satisfies the certification requirements under this paragraph (a) if any issuer offering the coverage is required to provide the certificates pursuant to an agreement between the plan and the issuer. For example, if there is an agreement between an issuer and a plan sponsor under which the issuer agrees to provide certificates for individuals covered under the plan, and the issuer fails to provide a certificate to an individual when the plan would have been required to provide one under this paragraph (a), then the issuer, but not the plan, violates the certification requirements of this paragraph (a).

    (iv) *Special rules for issuers.* (A) *(1) Responsibility of issuer for coverage period.* An issuer is not required to provide information regarding coverage provided to an individual by another party.

    (2) Example. The rule of this paragraph (a)(1)(iv)(A) is illustrated by the following example:

    Example. (i) *Facts.* A plan offers coverage with an HMO option from one issuer and an indemnity option from a different issuer. The HMO has not entered into an agreement with the plan to provide certificates as permitted under paragraph (a)(1)(iii) of this section.

    (ii) *Conclusion.* In this *Example,* if an employee switches from the indemnity option to the HMO option and later ceases to be covered under the plan, any certificate provided by the HMO is not required to provide information regarding the employee's coverage under the indemnity option.

    (B) *(1) Cessation of issuer coverage prior to cessation of coverage under a plan.* If an individual's coverage under an issuer's policy or contract ceases before the individual's coverage under the plan ceases, the issuer is required to provide sufficient information to the plan (or to another party designated by the plan) to enable the plan (or other party), after cessation of the individual's coverage under the plan, to provide a certificate that reflects the period of coverage under the policy or contract. By providing that information to the plan, the issuer satisfies its obligation to provide an automatic certificate for that period of creditable coverage with respect to the individual under paragraph (a)(2)(ii) of this section. The issuer, however, must still provide a certificate upon request as required under paragraph (a)(2)(iii) of this section. In addition, the issuer is required to cooperate with the plan in responding to any request made under paragraph (b)(2) of this section (relating to the alternative method of counting creditable coverage). Moreover, if the individual's coverage under the plan ceases at the time the individual's coverage under the issuer's policy or contract ceases, the issuer must still provide an automatic certificate under paragraph (a)(2)(ii) of this section. If an individual's coverage under an issuer's policy or contract ceases on the effective date for changing enrollment options under the plan, the issuer may presume (absent information to the contrary) that the individual's coverage under the plan continues. Therefore, the issuer is required to provide information to the plan in accordance with this paragraph (a)(1)(iv)(B)(*1*) (and is not required to provide an automatic certificate under paragraph (a)(2)(ii) of this section).

    (2) Example. The rule of this paragraph (a)(1)(iv)(B) is illustrated by the following example:

    Example. (i) *Facts.* A group health plan provides coverage under an HMO option and an indemnity option through different issuers, and only allows employees to switch on each January 1. Neither the HMO nor the indemnity issuer has entered into an agreement with the plan to provide certificates as permitted under paragraph (a)(1)(iii) of this section.

    (ii) *Conclusion.* In this *Example,* if an employee switches from the indemnity option to the HMO option on January 1, the indemnity issuer must provide the plan (or a person designated by the plan) with appropriate information with respect to the individual's coverage with the indemnity issuer. However, if the individual's coverage with the indemnity issuer ceases at a date other than January 1, the issuer is instead required to provide the individual with an automatic certificate.

    (2) *Individuals for whom certificate must be provided; timing of issuance.* (i) *Individuals.* A certificate must be provided, without charge, for participants or dependents who are or were covered under a group health plan upon the occurrence of any of the events described in paragraph (a)(2)(ii) or (iii) of this section.

    (ii) *Issuance of automatic certificates.* The certificates described in this paragraph (a)(2)(ii) are referred to as automatic certificates.

    (A) *Qualified beneficiaries upon a qualifying event.* In the case of an individual who is a qualified beneficiary (as defined in section 607(3) of the Act) entitled to elect COBRA continuation coverage, an automatic certificate is required to be provided at the time the individual would lose coverage under the plan in the absence of COBRA continuation coverage or alternative coverage elected instead of COBRA continuation coverage. A plan or issuer satisfies this requirement if it provides the automatic certificate no later than the time a notice is required to be furnished for a qualifying event under section 606 of the Act (relating to notices required under COBRA).

    (B) *Other individuals when coverage ceases.* In the case of an individual who is not a qualified beneficiary entitled to elect COBRA continuation coverage, an automatic certificate must be provided at the time the individual ceases to be covered under the plan. A plan or issuer satisfies the requirement to provide an automatic certificate at the time the individual ceases to be covered if it provides the automatic certificate within a reasonable time after coverage ceases (or after the expiration of any grace period for nonpayment of premiums).

    (1) The cessation of temporary continuation coverage (TCC) under Title 5 U.S.C. Chapter 89 (the Federal Employees Health Benefit Program) is a cessation of coverage upon which an automatic certificate must be provided.

    (2) In the case of an individual who is entitled to elect to continue coverage under a State program similar to COBRA and who receives the automatic certificate not later than the time a notice is required to be furnished under the State program, the certificate is deemed to be provided within a reasonable time after coverage ceases under the plan.

    (3) If an individual's coverage ceases due to the operation of a lifetime limit on all benefits, coverage is considered to cease for purposes of this paragraph (a)(2)(ii)(B) on the earliest date that a claim is denied due to the operation of the lifetime limit.

    (C) *Qualified beneficiaries when COBRA ceases.* In the case of an individual who is a qualified beneficiary and has elected COBRA continuation coverage (or whose coverage has continued after the individual became entitled to elect COBRA continuation coverage), an automatic certificate is to be provided at the time the individual's coverage under the plan ceases. A plan, or issuer, satisfies this requirement if it provides the automatic certificate within a reasonable time after coverage ceases (or after the expiration of any grace period for nonpayment of premiums). An automatic certificate is required to be provided to such an individual regardless of whether the individual has previously received an automatic certificate under paragraph (a)(2)(ii)(A) of this section.

    (iii) *Any individual upon request.* A certificate must be provided in response to a request made by, or on behalf of, an individual at any time while the individual is covered under a plan and up to 24 months after coverage ceases. Thus, for example, a plan in which an individual enrolls may, if authorized by the individual, request a certificate of the individual's creditable coverage on behalf of the individual from a plan in which the individual was formerly enrolled. After the request is received, a plan or issuer is required to provide the certificate by the earliest date that the plan or issuer, acting in a reasonable and prompt fashion, can provide the certificate. A certificate is required to be provided under this paragraph (a)(2)(iii) even if the individual has previously received a certificate under this paragraph (a)(2)(iii) or an automatic certificate under paragraph (a)(2)(ii) of this section.

    (iv) *Examples.* The rules of this paragraph (a)(2) are illustrated by the following examples:

    Example 1. (i) *Facts.* Individual *A* terminates employment with Employer Q. *A* is a qualified beneficiary entitled to elect COBRA continuation coverage under Employer *Q*'s group health plan. A notice of the rights provided under COBRA is typically furnished to qualified beneficiaries under the plan within 10 days after a covered employee terminates employment.

    (ii) *Conclusion.* In this *Example 1,* the automatic certificate may be provided at the same time that *A* is provided the COBRA notice.

Example 2. (i) *Facts.* Same facts as *Example 1*, except that the automatic certificate for *A* is not completed by the time the COBRA notice is furnished to *A*.

(ii) *Conclusion.* In this *Example 2*, the automatic certificate may be provided after the COBRA notice but must be provided within the period permitted by law for the delivery of notices under COBRA.

Example 3. (i) *Facts.* Employer *R* maintains an insured group health plan. *R* has never had 20 employees and thus *R*'s plan is not subject to the COBRA continuation provisions. However, *R* is in a State that has a State program similar to COBRA. *B* terminates employment with *R* and loses coverage under *R*'s plan.

(ii) *Conclusion.* In this *Example 3*, the automatic certificate must be provided not later than the time a notice is required to be furnished under the State program.

Example 4. (i) *Facts.* Individual *C* terminates employment with Employer *S* and receives both a notice of *C*'s rights under COBRA and an automatic certificate. *C* elects COBRA continuation coverage under Employer *S*'s group health plan. After four months of COBRA continuation coverage and the expiration of a 30-day grace period, *S*'s group health plan determines that *C*'s COBRA continuation coverage has ceased due to a failure to make a timely payment for continuation coverage.

(ii) *Conclusion.* In this *Example 4*, the plan must provide an updated automatic certificate to *C* within a reasonable time after the end of the grace period.

Example 5. (i) *Facts.* Individual *D* is currently covered under the group health plan of Employer *T*. *D* requests a certificate, as permitted under paragraph (a)(2)(iii) of this section. Under the procedure for *T*'s plan, certificates are mailed (by first class mail) 7 business days following receipt of the request. This date reflects the earliest date that the plan, acting in a reasonable and prompt fashion, can provide certificates.

(ii) *Conclusion.* In this *Example 5*, the plan's procedure satisfies paragraph (a)(2)(iii) of this section.

(3) *Form and content of certificate.* (i) *Written certificate.* (A) *In general.* Except as provided in paragraph (a)(3)(i)(B) of this section, the certificate must be provided in writing (or any other medium approved by the Secretary).

(B) *Other permissible forms.* No written certificate is required to be provided under this paragraph (a) with respect to a particular event described in paragraph (a)(2)(ii) or (iii) of this section, if—

(*1*) An individual who is entitled to receive the certificate requests that the certificate be sent to another plan or issuer instead of to the individual;

(*2*) The plan or issuer that would otherwise receive the certificate agrees to accept the information in this paragraph (a)(3) through means other than a written certificate (such as by telephone); and

(*3*) The receiving plan or issuer receives the information from the sending plan or issuer through such means within the time required under paragraph (a)(2) of this section.

(ii) *Required information.* The certificate must include the following—

(A) The date the certificate is issued;

(B) The name of the group health plan that provided the coverage described in the certificate;

(C) The name of the participant or dependent with respect to whom the certificate applies, and any other information necessary for the plan providing the coverage specified in the certificate to identify the individual, such as the individual's identification number under the plan and the name of the participant if the certificate is for (or includes) a dependent;

(D) The name, address, and telephone number of the plan administrator or issuer required to provide the certificate;

(E) The telephone number to call for further information regarding the certificate (if different from paragraph (a)(3)(ii)(D) of this section);

(F) Either—

(*1*) A statement that an individual has at least 18 months (for this purpose, 546 days is deemed to be 18 months) of creditable coverage, disregarding days of creditable coverage before a significant break in coverage, or

(*2*) The date any waiting period (and affiliation period, if applicable) began and the date creditable coverage began;

(G) The date creditable coverage ended, unless the certificate indicates that creditable coverage is continuing as of the date of the certificate; and

(H) An educational statement regarding HIPAA, which explains:

(*1*) The restrictions on the ability of a plan or issuer to impose a preexisting condition exclusion (including an individual's ability to reduce a preexisting condition exclusion by creditable coverage);

(*2*) Special enrollment rights;

(*3*) The prohibitions against discrimination based on any health factor;

(*4*) The right to individual health coverage;

(*5*) The fact that state law may require issuers to provide additional protections to individuals in that State; and

(*6*) Where to get more information.

(iii) *Periods of coverage under the certificate.* If an automatic certificate is provided pursuant to paragraph (a)(2)(ii) of this section, the period that must be included on the certificate is the last period of continuous coverage ending on the date coverage ceased. If an individual requests a certificate pursuant to paragraph (a)(2)(iii) of this section, the certificate provided must include each period of continuous coverage ending within the 24-month period ending on the date of the request (or continuing on the date of the request). A separate certificate may be provided for each such period of continuous coverage.

(iv) *Combining information for families.* A certificate may provide information with respect to both a participant and the participant's dependents if the information is identical for each individual. If the information is not identical, certificates may be provided on one form if the form provides all the required information for each individual and separately States the information that is not identical.

(v) *Model certificate.* The requirements of paragraph (a)(3)(ii) of this section are satisfied if the plan or issuer provides a certificate in accordance with a model certificate authorized by the Secretary.

(vi) *Excepted benefits; categories of benefits.* No certificate is required to be furnished with respect to excepted benefits described in § 2590.732(c). In addition, the information in the certificate regarding coverage is not required to specify categories of benefits described in § 2590.701-4(c) (relating to the alternative method of counting creditable coverage). However, if excepted benefits are provided concurrently with other creditable coverage (so that the coverage does not consist solely of excepted benefits), information concerning the benefits may be required to be disclosed under paragraph (b) of this section.

(4) *Procedures.* (i) *Method of delivery.* The certificate is required to be provided to each individual described in paragraph (a)(2) of this section or an entity requesting the certificate on behalf of the individual. The certificate may be provided by first-class mail. (*See also* § 2520.104b-1, which permits plans to make disclosures under the Act—including the furnishing of certificates—through electronic means if certain standards are met.) If the certificate or certificates are provided to the participant and the participant's spouse at the participant's last known address, then the requirements of this paragraph (a)(4) are satisfied with respect to all individuals residing at that address. If a dependent's last known address is different than the participant's last known address, a separate certificate is required to be provided to the dependent at the dependent's last known address. If separate certificates are being provided by mail to individuals who reside at the same address, separate mailings of each certificate are not required.

(ii) *Procedure for requesting certificates.* A plan or issuer must establish a written procedure for individuals to request and receive

Reg. §2590.701-5(a)(4)(ii)   ¶15,049M

certificates pursuant to paragraph (a)(2)(iii) of this section. The written procedure must include all contact information necessary to request a certificate (such as name and phone number or address).

(iii) *Designated recipients.* If an automatic certificate is required to be provided under paragraph (a)(2)(ii) of this section, and the individual entitled to receive the certificate designates another individual or entity to receive the certificate, the plan or issuer responsible for providing the certificate is permitted to provide the certificate to the designated individual or entity. If a certificate is required to be provided upon request under paragraph (a)(2)(iii) of this section and the individual entitled to receive the certificate designates another individual or entity to receive the certificate, the plan or issuer responsible for providing the certificate is required to provide the certificate to the designated individual or entity.

(5) *Special rules concerning dependent coverage.* (i)(A) *Reasonable efforts.* A plan or issuer is required to use reasonable efforts to determine any information needed for a certificate relating to dependent coverage. In any case in which an automatic certificate is required to be furnished with respect to a dependent under paragraph (a)(2)(ii) of this section, no individual certificate is required to be furnished until the plan or issuer knows (or making reasonable efforts should know) of the dependent's cessation of coverage under the plan.

(B) *Example.* The rules of this paragraph (a)(5)(i) are illustrated by the following example:

Example. (i) *Facts.* A group health plan covers employees and their dependents. The plan annually requests all employees to provide updated information regarding dependents, including the specific date on which an employee has a new dependent or on which a person ceases to be a dependent of the employee.

(ii) *Conclusion.* In this *Example*, the plan has satisfied the standard in this paragraph (a)(5)(i) of this section that it make reasonable efforts to determine the cessation of dependents' coverage and the related dependent coverage information.

(ii) *Special rules for demonstrating coverage.* If a certificate furnished by a plan or issuer does not provide the name of any dependent covered by the certificate, the procedures described in paragraph (c)(5) of this section may be used to demonstrate dependent status. In addition, these procedures may be used to demonstrate that a child was covered under any creditable coverage within 30 days after birth, adoption, or placement for adoption. *See also* § 2590.701-3(b), under which such a child cannot be subject to a preexisting condition exclusion.

(6) *Special certification rules for entities not subject to Part 7 of Subtitle B of Title I of the Act.* (i) *Issuers.* For special rules requiring that issuers not subject to Part 7 of Subtitle B of Title I of the Act provide certificates consistent with the rules in this section, including issuers offering coverage with respect to creditable coverage described in sections 701(c)(1)(G), (I), and (J) of the Act (coverage under a State health benefits risk pool, a public health plan, and a health benefit plan under section 5(e) of the Peace Corps Act), see sections 2743 and 2721(b)(1)(B) of the PHS Act (requiring certificates by issuers in the individual market, and issuers offering health insurance coverage in connection with a group health plan, including a church plan or a governmental plan (such as the Federal Employees Health Benefits Program (FEHBP)). (However, this section does not require a certificate to be provided with respect to shortterm, limited-duration insurance, as described in the definition of *individual health insurance coverage* in § 2590.701-2, that is not provided by a group health plan or issuer offering health insurance coverage in connection with a group health plan.)

(ii) *Other entities.* For special rules requiring that certain other entities not subject to Part 7 of Subtitle B of Title I of the Act provide certificates consistent with the rules in this section, see section 2791(a)(3) of the PHS Act applicable to entities described in sections 2701(c)(1)(C), (D), (E), and (F) of the PHS Act (relating to Medicare, Medicaid, TRICARE, and Indian Health Service), section 2721(b)(1)(A) of the PHS Act applicable to nonfederal governmental plans generally, section 2721(b)(2)(C)(ii) of the PHS Act applicable to nonfederal governmental plans that elect to be excluded from the requirements of

Subparts 1 through 3 of Part A of Title XXVII of the PHS Act, and section 9832(a) of the Internal Revenue Code applicable to group health plans, which includes church plans (as defined in section 414(e) of the Internal Revenue Code).

(b) *Disclosure of coverage to a plan or issuer using the alternative method of counting creditable coverage.* (1) *In general.* After an individual provides a certificate of creditable coverage to a plan or issuer using the alternative method under § 2590.701-4(c), that plan or issuer (requesting entity) must request that the entity that issued the certificate (prior entity) disclose the information set forth in paragraph (b)(2) of this section. The prior entity is required to disclose this information promptly.

(2) *Information to be disclosed.* The prior entity is required to identify to the requesting entity the categories of benefits with respect to which the requesting entity is using the alternative method of counting creditable coverage, and the requesting entity may identify specific information that the requesting entity reasonably needs in order to determine the individual's creditable coverage with respect to any such category.

(3) *Charge for providing information.* The prior entity may charge the requesting entity for the reasonable cost of disclosing such information.

(c) *Ability of an individual to demonstrate creditable coverage and waiting period information.* (1) *Purpose.* The rules in this paragraph (c) implement section 701(c)(4) of the Act, which permits individuals to demonstrate the duration of creditable coverage through means other than certificates, and section 701(e)(3) of the Act, which requires the Secretary to establish rules designed to prevent an individual's subsequent coverage under a group health plan or health insurance coverage from being adversely affected by an entity's failure to provide a certificate with respect to that individual.

(2) *In general.* If the accuracy of a certificate is contested or a certificate is unavailable when needed by an individual, the individual has the right to demonstrate creditable coverage (and waiting or affiliation periods) through the presentation of documents or other means. For example, the individual may make such a demonstration when—

(i) An entity has failed to provide a certificate within the required time;

(ii) The individual has creditable coverage provided by an entity that is not required to provide a certificate of the coverage pursuant to paragraph (a) of this section;

(iii) The individual has an urgent medical condition that necessitates a determination before the individual can deliver a certificate to the plan; or

(iv) The individual lost a certificate that the individual had previously received and is unable to obtain another certificate.

(3) *Evidence of creditable coverage.* (i) *Consideration of evidence.* (A) A plan or issuer is required to take into account all information that it obtains or that is presented on behalf of an individual to make a determination, based on the relevant facts and circumstances, whether an individual has creditable coverage. A plan or issuer shall treat the individual as having furnished a certificate under paragraph (a) of this section if—

(1) The individual attests to the period of creditable coverage;

(2) The individual also presents relevant corroborating evidence of some creditable coverage during the period; and

(3) The individual cooperates with the plan's or issuer's efforts to verify the individual's coverage.

(B) For purposes of this paragraph (c)(3)(i), cooperation includes providing (upon the plan's or issuer's request) a written authorization for the plan or issuer to request a certificate on behalf of the individual, and cooperating in efforts to determine the validity of the corroborating evidence and the dates of creditable coverage. While a plan or issuer may refuse to credit coverage where the individual fails to cooperate with the plan's or issuer's efforts to verify coverage, the plan or issuer may not consider an individual's inability to obtain a certificate to be evidence of the absence of creditable coverage.

(ii) *Documents.* Documents that corroborate creditable coverage (and waiting or affiliation periods) include explanations of benefits (EOBs) or other correspondence from a plan or issuer indicating coverage, pay stubs showing a payroll deduction for health coverage, a health insurance identification card, a certificate of coverage under a group health policy, records from medical care providers indicating health coverage, third party statements verifying periods of coverage, and any other relevant documents that evidence periods of health coverage.

(iii) *Other evidence.* Creditable coverage (and waiting or affiliation periods) may also be corroborated through means other than documentation, such as by a telephone call from the plan or provider to a third party verifying creditable coverage.

(iv) *Example.* The rules of this paragraph (c)(3) are illustrated by the following example:

Example. (i) *Facts.* Individual *F* terminates employment with Employer *W* and, a month later, is hired by Employer *X*. *X*'s group health plan imposes a preexisting condition exclusion of 12 months on new enrollees under the plan and uses the standard method of determining creditable coverage. *F* fails to receive a certificate of prior coverage from the self-insured group health plan maintained by *F*'s prior employer, *W*, and requests a certificate. However, *F* (and *X*'s plan, on *F*'s behalf and with *F*'s cooperation) is unable to obtain a certificate from *W*'s plan. *F* attests that, to the best of *F*'s knowledge, *F* had at least 12 months of continuous coverage under *W*'s plan, and that the coverage ended no earlier than *F*'s termination of employment from *W*. In addition, *F* presents evidence of coverage, such as an explanation of benefits for a claim that was made during the relevant period.

(ii) *Conclusion.* In this *Example*, based solely on these facts, *F* has demonstrated creditable coverage for the 12 months of coverage under *W*'s plan in the same manner as if *F* had presented a written certificate of creditable coverage.

(4) *Demonstrating categories of creditable coverage.* Procedures similar to those described in this paragraph (c) apply in order to determine the duration of an individual's creditable coverage with respect to any category under paragraph (b) of this section (relating to determining creditable coverage under the alternative method).

(5) *Demonstrating dependent status.* If, in the course of providing evidence (including a certificate) of creditable coverage, an individual is required to demonstrate dependent status, the group health plan or issuer is required to treat the individual as having furnished a certificate showing the dependent status if the individual attests to such dependency and the period of such status and the individual cooperates with the plan's or issuer's efforts to verify the dependent status.

[¶ 15,049N]

§ 2590.701-6 **Special enrollment periods.** (a) *Special enrollment for certain individuals who lose coverage.* (1) *In general.* A group health plan, and a health insurance issuer offering health insurance coverage in connection with a group health plan, is required to permit current employees and dependents (as defined in § 2590.701-2) who are described in paragraph (a)(2) of this section to enroll for coverage under the terms of the plan if the conditions in paragraph (a)(3) of this section are satisfied. The special enrollment rights under this paragraph (a) apply without regard to the dates on which an individual would otherwise be able to enroll under the plan.

(2) *Individuals eligible for special enrollment.* (i) *When employee loses coverage.* A current employee and any dependents (including the employee's spouse) each are eligible for special enrollment in any benefit package under the plan (subject to plan eligibility rules conditioning dependent enrollment on enrollment of the employee) if—

(A) The employee and the dependents are otherwise eligible to enroll in the benefit package;

(B) When coverage under the plan was previously offered, the employee had coverage under any group health plan or health insurance coverage; and

(C) The employee satisfies the conditions of paragraph (a)(3)(i), (ii), or (iii) of this section and, if applicable, paragraph (a)(3)(iv) of this section.

(ii) *When dependent loses coverage.* (A) A dependent of a current employee (including the employee's spouse) and the employee each are eligible for special enrollment in any benefit package under the plan (subject to plan eligibility rules conditioning dependent enrollment on enrollment of the employee) if—

(1) The dependent and the employee are otherwise eligible to enroll in the benefit package;

(2) When coverage under the plan was previously offered, the dependent had coverage under any group health plan or health insurance coverage; and

(3) The dependent satisfies the conditions of paragraph (a)(3)(i), (ii), or (iii) of this section and, if applicable, paragraph (a)(3)(iv) of this section.

(B) However, the plan or issuer is not required to enroll any other dependent unless that dependent satisfies the criteria of this paragraph (a)(2)(ii), or the employee satisfies the criteria of paragraph (a)(2)(i) of this section.

(iii) *Examples.* The rules of this paragraph (a)(2) are illustrated by the following examples:

Example 1. (i) *Facts.* Individual *A* works for Employer *X*. *A*, *A*'s spouse, and *A*'s dependent children are eligible but not enrolled for coverage under *X*'s group health plan. *A*'s spouse works for Employer *Y* and at the time coverage was offered under *X*'s plan, *A* was enrolled in coverage under *Y*'s plan. Then, *A* loses eligibility for coverage under *Y*'s plan.

(ii) *Conclusion.* In this *Example 1*, because *A* satisfies the conditions for special enrollment under paragraph (a)(2)(i) of this section, *A*, *A*'s spouse, and *A*'s dependent children are eligible for special enrollment under *X*'s plan.

Example 2. (i) *Facts.* Individual *A* and *A*'s spouse are eligible but not enrolled for coverage under Group Health Plan *P* maintained by *A*'s employer. When *A* was first presented with an opportunity to enroll *A* and *A*'s spouse, they did not have other coverage. Later, *A* and *A*'s spouse enroll in Group Health Plan *Q* maintained by the employer of *A*'s spouse. During a subsequent open enrollment period in *P*, *A* and *A*'s spouse did not enroll because of their coverage under *Q*. They then lose eligibility for coverage under *Q*.

(ii) *Conclusion.* In this *Example 2*, because *A* and *A*'s spouse were covered under *Q* when they did not enroll in *P* during open enrollment, they satisfy the conditions for special enrollment under paragraphs (a)(2)(i) and (ii) of this section. Consequently, *A* and *A*'s spouse are eligible for special enrollment under *P*.

Example 3. (i) *Facts.* Individual *B* works for Employer *X*. *B* and *B*'s spouse are eligible but not enrolled for coverage under *X*'s group health plan. *B*'s spouse works for Employer *Y* and at the time coverage was offered under *X*'s plan, *B*'s spouse was enrolled in self-only coverage under *Y*'s group health plan. Then, *B*'s spouse loses eligibility for coverage under *Y*'s plan.

(ii) *Conclusion.* In this *Example 3*, because *B*'s spouse satisfies the conditions for special enrollment under paragraph (a)(2)(ii) of this section, both *B* and *B*'s spouse are eligible for special enrollment under *X*'s plan.

Example 4. (i) *Facts.* Individual *A* works for Employer *X*. *X* maintains a group health plan with two benefit packages—an HMO option and an indemnity option. Self-only and family coverage are available under both options. *A* enrolls for self-only coverage in the HMO option. *A*'s spouse works for Employer *Y* and was enrolled for self-only coverage under *Y*'s plan at the time coverage was offered under *X*'s plan. Then, *A*'s spouse loses coverage under *Y*'s plan. *A* requests special enrollment for *A* and *A*'s spouse under the plan's indemnity option.

(ii) *Conclusion.* In this *Example 4*, because *A*'s spouse satisfies the conditions for special enrollment under paragraph (a)(2)(ii) of this section, both *A* and *A*'s spouse can enroll in either benefit package under *X*'s plan. Therefore, if *A* requests enrollment in accordance with the requirements of this section, the plan must allow *A* and *A*'s spouse to enroll in the indemnity option.

(3) *Conditions for special enrollment.* (i) *Loss of eligibility for coverage.* In the case of an employee or dependent who has coverage that is not COBRA continuation coverage, the conditions of this paragraph (a)(3)(i) are satisfied at the time the coverage is terminated as a result of loss of eligibility (regardless of whether the individual is eligible for or elects COBRA continuation coverage). Loss of eligibility under this paragraph (a)(3)(i) does not include a loss due to the failure of the employee or dependent to pay premiums on a timely basis or termination of coverage for cause (such as making a fraudulent claim or an intentional misrepresentation of a material fact in connection with the plan). Loss of eligibility for coverage under this paragraph (a)(3)(i) includes (but is not limited to)—

(A) Loss of eligibility for coverage as a result of legal separation, divorce, cessation of dependent status (such as attaining the maximum age to be eligible as a dependent child under the plan), death of an employee, termination of employment, reduction in the number of hours of employment, and any loss of eligibility for coverage after a period that is measured by reference to any of the foregoing;

(B) In the case of coverage offered through an HMO, or other arrangement, in the individual market that does not provide benefits to individuals who no longer reside, live, or work in a service area, loss of coverage because an individual no longer resides, lives, or works in the service area (whether or not within the choice of the individual);

(C) In the case of coverage offered through an HMO, or other arrangement, in the group market that does not provide benefits to individuals who no longer reside, live, or work in a service area, loss of coverage because an individual no longer resides, lives, or works in the service area (whether or not within the choice of the individual), and no other benefit package is available to the individual;

(D) A situation in which an individual incurs a claim that would meet or exceed a lifetime limit on all benefits; and

(E) A situation in which a plan no longer offers any benefits to the class of similarly situated individuals (as described in § 2590.702(d)) that includes the individual.

(ii) *Termination of employer contributions.* In the case of an employee or dependent who has coverage that is not COBRA continuation coverage, the conditions of this paragraph (a)(3)(ii) are satisfied at the time employer contributions towards the employee's or dependent's coverage terminate. Employer contributions include contributions by any current or former employer that was contributing to coverage for the employee or dependent.

(iii) *Exhaustion of COBRA continuation coverage.* In the case of an employee or dependent who has coverage that is COBRA continuation coverage, the conditions of this paragraph (a)(3)(iii) are satisfied at the time the COBRA continuation coverage is exhausted. For purposes of this paragraph (a)(3)(iii), an individual who satisfies the conditions for special enrollment of paragraph (a)(3)(i) of this section, does not enroll, and instead elects and exhausts COBRA continuation coverage satisfies the conditions of this paragraph (a)(3)(iii). (*Exhaustion of COBRA continuation coverage* is defined in § 2590.701-2.)

(iv) *Written statement.* A plan may require an employee declining coverage (for the employee or any dependent of the employee) to State in writing whether the coverage is being declined due to other health coverage only if, at or before the time the employee declines coverage, the employee is provided with notice of the requirement to provide the statement (and the consequences of the employee's failure to provide the statement). If a plan requires such a statement, and an employee does not provide it, the plan is not required to provide special enrollment to the employee or any dependent of the employee under this paragraph (a)(3). A plan must treat an employee as having satisfied the plan requirement permitted under this paragraph (a)(3)(iv) if the employee provides a written statement that coverage was being declined because the employee or dependent had other coverage; a plan cannot require anything more for the employee to satisfy the plan's requirement to provide a written statement. (For example, the plan cannot require that the statement be notarized.)

(v) The rules of this paragraph (a)(3) are illustrated by the following examples:

Example 1. (i) *Facts.* Individual *D* enrolls in a group health plan maintained by Employer *Y*. At the time *D* enrolls, *Y* pays 70 percent of the cost of employee coverage and *D* pays the rest. *Y* announces that beginning January 1, *Y* will no longer make employer contributions towards the coverage. Employees may maintain coverage, however, if they pay the total cost of the coverage.

(ii) *Conclusion.* In this *Example 1,* employer contributions towards *D*'s coverage ceased on January 1 and the conditions of paragraph (a)(3)(ii) of this section are satisfied on this date (regardless of whether *D* elects to pay the total cost and continue coverage under *Y*'s plan).

Example 2. (i) *Facts.* A group health plan provides coverage through two options—Option 1 and Option 2. Employees can enroll in either option only within 30 days of hire or on January 1 of each year. Employee *A* is eligible for both options and enrolls in Option 1. Effective July 1 the plan terminates coverage under Option 1 and the plan does not create an immediate open enrollment opportunity into Option 2.

(ii) *Conclusion.* In this *Example 2, A* has experienced a loss of eligibility for coverage that satisfies paragraph (a)(3)(i) of this section, and has satisfied the other conditions for special enrollment under paragraph (a)(2)(i) of this section. Therefore, if *A* satisfies the other conditions of this paragraph (a), the plan must permit *A* to enroll in Option 2 as a special enrollee. (*A* may also be eligible to enroll in another group health plan, such as a plan maintained by the employer of *A*'s spouse, as a special enrollee.) The outcome would be the same if Option 1 was terminated by an issuer and the plan made no other coverage available to *A*.

Example 3. (i) *Facts.* Individual *C* is covered under a group health plan maintained by Employer *X*. While covered under *X*'s plan, *C* was eligible for but did not enroll in a plan maintained by Employer *Z*, the employer of *C*'s spouse. *C* terminates employment with *X* and loses eligibility for coverage under *X*'s plan. *C* has a special enrollment right to enroll in *Z*'s plan, but *C* instead elects COBRA continuation coverage under *X*'s plan. *C* exhausts COBRA continuation coverage under *X*'s plan and requests special enrollment in *Z*'s plan.

(ii) *Conclusion.* In this *Example 3, C* has satisfied the conditions for special enrollment under paragraph (a)(3)(iii) of this section, and has satisfied the other conditions for special enrollment under paragraph (a)(2)(i) of this section. The special enrollment right that *C* had into *Z*'s plan immediately after the loss of eligibility for coverage under *X*'s plan was an offer of coverage under *Z*'s plan. When *C* later exhausts COBRA coverage under *X*'s plan, *C* has a second special enrollment right in *Z*'s plan.

(4) *Applying for special enrollment and effective date of coverage.* (i) A plan or issuer must allow an employee a period of at least 30 days after an event described in paragraph (a)(3) of this section (other than an event described in paragraph (a)(3)(i)(D)) to request enrollment (for the employee or the employee's dependent). In the case of an event described in paragraph (a)(3)(i)(D) of this section (relating to loss of eligibility for coverage due to the operation of a lifetime limit on all benefits), a plan or issuer must allow an employee a period of at least 30 days after a claim is denied due to the operation of a lifetime limit on all benefits.

(ii) Coverage must begin no later than the first day of the first calendar month beginning after the date the plan or issuer receives the request for special enrollment.

(b) *Special enrollment with respect to certain dependent beneficiaries.* (1) *In general.* A group health plan, and a health insurance issuer offering health insurance coverage in connection with a group health plan, that makes coverage available with respect to dependents is required to permit individuals described in paragraph (b)(2) of this section to be enrolled for coverage in a benefit package under the terms of the plan. Paragraph (b)(3) of this section describes the required special enrollment period and the date by which coverage must begin. The special enrollment rights under this paragraph (b) apply without regard to the dates on which an individual would otherwise be able to enroll under the plan.

(2) *Individuals eligible for special enrollment.* An individual is described in this paragraph (b)(2) if the individual is otherwise eligible

for coverage in a benefit package under the plan and if the individual is described in paragraph (b)(2)(i), (ii), (iii), (iv), (v), or (vi) of this section.

(i) *Current employee only.* A current employee is described in this paragraph (b)(2)(i) if a person becomes a dependent of the individual through marriage, birth, adoption, or placement for adoption.

(ii) *Spouse of a participant only.* An individual is described in this paragraph (b)(2)(ii) if either —

(A) The individual becomes the spouse of a participant; or

(B) The individual is a spouse of a participant and a child becomes a dependent of the participant through birth, adoption, or placement for adoption.

(iii) *Current employee and spouse.* A current employee and an individual who is or becomes a spouse of such an employee, are described in this paragraph (b)(2)(iii) if either—

(A) The employee and the spouse become married; or

(B) The employee and the spouse are married and a child becomes a dependent of the employee through birth, adoption, or placement for adoption.

(iv) *Dependent of a participant only.* An individual is described in this paragraph (b)(2)(iv) if the individual is a dependent (as defined in § 2590.701- 2) of a participant and the individual has become a dependent of the participant through marriage, birth, adoption, or placement for adoption.

(v) *Current employee and a new dependent.* A current employee and an individual who is a dependent of the employee, are described in this paragraph (b)(2)(v) if the individual becomes a dependent of the employee through marriage, birth, adoption, or placement for adoption.

(vi) *Current employee, spouse, and a new dependent.* A current employee, the employee's spouse, and the employee's dependent are described in this paragraph (b)(2)(vi) if the dependent becomes a dependent of the employee through marriage, birth, adoption, or placement for adoption.

(3) *Applying for special enrollment and effective date of coverage.* (i) *Request.* A plan or issuer must allow an individual a period of at least 30 days after the date of the marriage, birth, adoption, or placement for adoption (or, if dependent coverage is not generally made available at the time of the marriage, birth, adoption, or placement for adoption, a period of at least 30 days after the date the plan makes dependent coverage generally available) to request enrollment (for the individual or the individual's dependent).

(ii) *Reasonable procedures for special enrollment.* [Reserved]

(iii) *Date coverage must begin.* (A) *Marriage.* In the case of marriage, coverage must begin no later than the first day of the first calendar month beginning after the date the plan or issuer receives the request for special enrollment.

(B) *Birth, adoption, or placement for adoption.* Coverage must begin in the case of a dependent's birth on the date of birth and in the case of a dependent's adoption or placement for adoption no later than the date of such adoption or placement for adoption (or, if dependent coverage is not made generally available at the time of the birth, adoption, or placement for adoption, the date the plan makes dependent coverage available).

(4) *Examples.* The rules of this paragraph (b) are illustrated by the following examples:

Example 1. (i) *Facts.* An employer maintains a group health plan that offers all employees employee-only coverage, employee-plus-spouse coverage, or family coverage. Under the terms of the plan, any employee may elect to enroll when first hired (with coverage beginning on the date of hire) or during an annual open enrollment period held each December (with coverage beginning the following January 1). Employee *A* is hired on September 3. *A* is married to *B*, and they have no children. On March 15 in the following year a child *C* is born to *A* and *B*. Before that date, *A* and *B* have not been enrolled in the plan.

(ii) *Conclusion.* In this *Example 1,* the conditions for special enrollment of an employee with a spouse and new dependent under paragraph (b)(2)(vi) of this section are satisfied. If *A* satisfies the conditions of paragraph (b)(3) of this section for requesting enrollment timely, the plan will satisfy this paragraph (b) if it allows *A* to enroll either with employee-only coverage, with employee-plus-spouse coverage (for *A* and *B*), or with family coverage (for *A, B,* and *C*). The plan must allow whatever coverage is chosen to begin on March 15, the date of *C*'s birth.

Example 2. (i) *Facts.* Individual *D* works for Employer X. *X* maintains a group health plan with two benefit packages—an HMO option and an indemnity option. Self-only and family coverage are available under both options. *D* enrolls for self-only coverage in the HMO option. Then, a child, E, is placed for adoption with *D*. Within 30 days of the placement of *E* for adoption, *D* requests enrollment for *D* and *E* under the plan's indemnity option.

(ii) *Conclusion.* In this *Example 2,* D and E satisfy the conditions for special enrollment under paragraphs (b)(2)(v) and (b)(3) of this section. Therefore, the plan must allow *D* and *E* to enroll in the indemnity coverage, effective as of the date of the placement for adoption.

(c) *Notice of special enrollment.* At or before the time an employee is initially offered the opportunity to enroll in a group health plan, the plan must furnish the employee with a notice of special enrollment that complies with the requirements of this paragraph (c).

(1) *Description of special enrollment rights.* The notice of special enrollment must include a description of special enrollment rights. The following model language may be used to satisfy this requirement:

If you are declining enrollment for yourself or your dependents (including your spouse) because of other health insurance or group health plan coverage, you may be able to enroll yourself and your dependents in this plan if you or your dependents lose eligibility for that other coverage (or if the employer stops contributing towards your or your dependents' other coverage). However, you must request enrollment within [insert "30 days" or any longer period that applies under the plan] after your or your dependents' other coverage ends (or after the employer stops contributing toward the other coverage).

In addition, if you have a new dependent as a result of marriage, birth, adoption, or placement for adoption, you may be able to enroll yourself and your dependents. However, you must request enrollment within [insert "30 days" or any longer period that applies under the plan] after the marriage, birth, adoption, or placement for adoption.

To request special enrollment or obtain more information, contact [insert the name, title, telephone number, and any additional contact information of the appropriate plan representative].

(2) *Additional information that may be required.* The notice of special enrollment must also include, if applicable, the notice described in paragraph (a)(3)(iv) of this section (the notice required to be furnished to an individual declining coverage if the plan requires the reason for declining coverage to be in writing).

(d) *Treatment of special enrollees.* (1) If an individual requests enrollment while the individual is entitled to special enrollment under either paragraph (a) or (b) of this section, the individual is a special enrollee, even if the request for enrollment coincides with a late enrollment opportunity under the plan. Therefore, the individual cannot be treated as a late enrollee.

(2) Special enrollees must be offered all the benefit packages available to similarly situated individuals who enroll when first eligible. For this purpose, any difference in benefits or cost-sharing requirements for different individuals constitutes a different benefit package. In addition, a special enrollee cannot be required to pay more for coverage than a similarly situated individual who enrolls in the same coverage when first eligible. The length of any preexisting condition exclusion that may be applied to a special enrollee cannot exceed the length of any preexisting condition exclusion that is applied to similarly situated individuals who enroll when first eligible. For rules prohibiting the application of a preexisting condition exclusion to certain newborns, adopted children, and children placed for adoption, see § 2590.701-3(b).

(3) The rules of this section are illustrated by the following example:

Example. (i) *Facts.* Employer *Y* maintains a group health plan that has an enrollment period for late enrollees every November 1 through November 30 with coverage effective the following January 1. On October 18, Individual *B* loses coverage under another group health plan and satisfies the requirements of paragraphs (a)(2), (3), and (4) of this section. *B* submits a completed application for coverage on November 2.

(ii) *Conclusion.* In this *Example, B* is a special enrollee. Therefore, even though *B*'s request for enrollment coincides with an open enrollment period, *B*'s coverage is required to be made effective no later than December 1 (rather than the plan's January 1 effective date for late enrollees).

[¶ 15,049O]

§ 2590.701-7 **HMO affiliation period as an alternative to a preexisting condition exclusion.** (a) *In general.* A group health plan offering health insurance coverage through an HMO, or an HMO that offers health insurance coverage in connection with a group health plan, may impose an affiliation period only if each of the following requirements is satisfied—

(1) No preexisting condition exclusion is imposed with respect to any coverage offered by the HMO in connection with the particular group health plan.

(2) No premium is charged to a participant or beneficiary for the affiliation period.

(3) The affiliation period for the HMO coverage is imposed consistent with the requirements of § 2590.702 (prohibiting discrimination based on a health factor).

(4) The affiliation period does not exceed 2 months (or 3 months in the case of a late enrollee).

(5) The affiliation period begins on the enrollment date, or in the case of a late enrollee, the affiliation period begins on the day that would be the first day of coverage but for the affiliation period.

(6) The affiliation period for enrollment in the HMO under a plan runs concurrently with any waiting period.

(b) *Examples.* The rules of paragraph (a) of this section are illustrated by the following examples:

Example 1. (i) *Facts.* An employer sponsors a group health plan. Benefits under the plan are provided through an HMO, which imposes a two-month affiliation period. In order to be eligible under the plan, employees must have worked for the employer for six months. Individual *A* begins working for the employer on February 1.

(ii) *Conclusion.* In this *Example 1,* Individual *A*'s enrollment date is February 1 (see § 2590.701-3(a)(2)), and both the waiting period and the affiliation period begin on this date and run concurrently. Therefore, the affiliation period ends on March 31, the waiting period ends on July 31, and *A* is eligible to have coverage begin on August 1.

Example 2. (i) *Facts.* A group health plan has two benefit package options, a fee-forservice option and an HMO option. The HMO imposes a 1-month affiliation period. Individual *B* is enrolled in the fee-for-service option for more than one month and then decides to switch to the HMO option at open season.

(ii) *Conclusion.* In this *Example 2,* the HMO may not impose the affiliation period with respect to *B* because any affiliation period would have to begin on *B*'s enrollment date in the plan rather than the date that *B* enrolled in the HMO option. Therefore, the affiliation period would have expired before *B* switched to the HMO option.

Example 3. (i) *Facts.* An employer sponsors a group health plan that provides benefits through an HMO. The plan imposes a two-month affiliation period with respect to salaried employees, but it does not impose an affiliation period with respect to hourly employees.

(ii) *Conclusion.* In this *Example 3,* the plan may impose the affiliation period with respect to salaried employees without imposing any affiliation period with respect to hourly employees (unless, under the circumstances, treating salaried and hourly employees differently does not comply with the requirements of § 2590.702).

(c) *Alternatives to affiliation period.* An HMO may use alternative methods in lieu of an affiliation period to address adverse selection, as approved by the State insurance commissioner or other official designated to regulate HMOs. However, an arrangement that is in the nature of a preexisting condition exclusion cannot be an alternative to an affiliation period. Nothing in this part requires a State to receive proposals for or approve alternatives to affiliation periods.

[¶ 15,049P]

§ 2590.701-8 **Interaction with the Family and Medical Leave Act.** [Reserved].

[¶ 15,050A]
PROHIBITING DISCRIMINATION AGAINST INDIVIDUAL PARTICIPANTS AND BENEFICIARIES BASED ON HEALTH STATUS

Act Sec. 702.(a) IN ELIGIBILITY TO ENROLL.—

(1) IN GENERAL. Subject to paragraph (2), a group health plan, and a health insurance issuer offering group health insurance coverage in connection with a group health plan, may not establish rules for eligibility (including continued eligibility) of any individual to enroll under the terms of the plan based on any of the following health status-related factors in relation to the individual or a dependent of the individual:

    (A) Health status.

    (B) Medical condition (including both physical and mental illnesses).

    (C) Claims experience.

    (D) Receipt of health care.

    (E) Medical history.

    (F) Genetic information.

    (G) Evidence of insurability (including conditions arising out of acts of domestic violence).

    (H) Disability.

(2) NO APPLICATION TO BENEFITS OR EXCLUSIONS. To the extent consistent with section 701, paragraph (1) shall not be construed—

    (A) to require a group health plan, or group health insurance coverage, to provide particular benefits other than those provided under the terms of such plan or coverage, or

    (B) to prevent such a plan or coverage from establishing limitations or restrictions on the amount, level, extent, or nature of the benefits or coverage for similarly situated individuals enrolled in the plan or coverage.

(3) CONSTRUCTION. For purposes of paragraph (1), rules for eligibility to enroll under a plan include rules defining any applicable waiting periods for such enrollment.

Act Sec. 702. IN PREMIUM CONTRIBUTIONS.—

(b)(1) IN GENERAL. A group health plan, and a health insurance issuer offering health insurance coverage in connection with a group health plan, may not require any individual (as a condition of enrollment or continued enrollment under the plan) to pay a premium or contribution which is greater than such premium or contribution for a similarly situated individual enrolled in the plan on the basis of any health status-related factor in relation to the individual or to an individual enrolled under the plan as a dependent of the individual.

(2) CONSTRUCTION. Nothing in paragraph (1) shall be construed—

(A) to restrict the amount that an employer may be charged for coverage under a group health plan; or

(B) to prevent a group health plan, and a health insurance issuer offering group health insurance coverage, from establishing premium discounts or rebates or modifying otherwise applicable copayments or deductibles in return for adherence to programs of health promotion and disease prevention.

Amendments

P.L. 104-191, § 101(a):

Added ERISA Act Sec. 702 to read as above.

The above amendments generally apply with respect to group health plans for plan years beginning after June 30, 1997. For special rules, see Act Sec. 101(g)(2)-(5), reproduced after ERISA Act Sec. 701 above.

Regulations

The following regulations were adopted by 62 FR 16894 and published in the Federal Register on April 8, 1997, under "Chapter XXV of Title 29 of the Code of Federal Regulations; Subchapter L—Health Insurance Portability and Renewability for Group Health Plans; Part 2590—Rules and Regulations for Health Insurance Portability and Renewability for Group Health Plans." They were revised January 8, 2001 by 66 FR 1377 and amended March 9, 2001 by 66 FR 14,076.

[¶ 15,050A-1]

§ 2590.702 Prohibiting discrimination against participants and beneficiaries based on a health factor.

(a) *Health factors.* (1) The term *health factor* means, in relation to an individual, any of the following health status-related factors:

(i) Health status;

(ii) Medical condition (including both physical and mental illnesses), as defined in § 2590.701-2;

(iii) Claims experience;

(iv) Receipt of health care;

(v) Medical history;

(vi) Genetic information, as defined in § 2590.701-2;

(vii) Evidence of insurability; or

(viii) Disability.

(2) Evidence of insurability includes—

(i) Conditions arising out of acts of domestic violence; and

(ii) Participation in activities such as motorcycling, snowmobiling, all-terrain vehicle riding, horseback riding, skiing, and other similar activities.

(3) The decision whether health coverage is elected for an individual (including the time chosen to enroll, such as under special enrollment or late enrollment) is not, itself, within the scope of any health factor. (However, under § 2590.701-6, a plan or issuer must treat special enrollees the same as similarly situated individuals who are enrolled when first eligible.)

(b) *Prohibited discrimination in rules for eligibility.* (1) *In general.* (i) A group health plan, and a health insurance issuer offering health insurance coverage in connection with a group health plan, may not establish any rule for eligibility (including continued eligibility) of any individual to enroll for benefits under the terms of the plan or group health insurance coverage that discriminates based on any health factor that relates to that individual or a dependent of that individual. This rule is subject to the provisions of paragraph (b)(2) of this section (explaining how this rule applies to benefits), paragraph (b)(3) of this section (allowing plans to impose certain preexisting condition exclusions), paragraph (d) of this section (containing rules for establishing groups of similarly situated individuals), paragraph (e) of this section (relating to nonconfinement, actively-at-work, and other service requirements), paragraph (f) of this section (relating to bona fide wellness programs), and paragraph (g) of this section (permitting favorable treatment of individuals with adverse health factors).

(ii) For purposes of this section, rules for eligibility include, but are not limited to, rules relating to—

(A) Enrollment;

(B) The effective date of coverage;

(C) Waiting (or affiliation) periods;

(D) Late and special enrollment;

(E) Eligibility for benefit packages (including rules for individuals to change their selection among benefit packages);

(F) Benefits (including rules relating to covered benefits, benefit restrictions, and cost-sharing mechanisms such as coinsurance, copayments, and deductibles), as described in paragraphs (b)(2) and (3) of this section;

(G) Continued eligibility; and

(H) Terminating coverage (including disenrollment) of any individual under the plan.

(iii) The rules of this paragraph (b)(1) are illustrated by the following examples:

Example 1. (i) *Facts.* An employer sponsors a group health plan that is available to all employees who enroll within the first 30 days of their employment. However, employees who do not enroll within the first 30 days cannot enroll later unless they pass a physical examination.

(ii) *Conclusion.* In this *Example 1*, the requirement to pass a physical examination in order to enroll in the plan is a rule for eligibility that discriminates based on one or more health factors and thus violates this paragraph (b)(1).

Example 2. (i) *Facts.* Under an employer's group health plan, employees who enroll during the first 30 days of employment (and during special enrollment periods) may choose between two benefit packages: an indemnity option and an HMO option. However, employees who enroll during late enrollment are permitted to enroll only in the HMO option and only if they provide evidence of good health.

(ii) *Conclusion.* In this *Example 2*, the requirement to provide evidence of good health in order to be eligible for late enrollment in the HMO option is a rule for eligibility that discriminates based on one or more health factors and thus violates this paragraph (b)(1). However, if the plan did not require evidence of good health but limited late enrollees to the HMO option, the plan's rules for eligibility would not discriminate based on any health factor, and thus would not violate this paragraph (b)(1), because the time an individual chooses to enroll is not, itself, within the scope of any health factor.

Example 3. (i) *Facts.* Under an employer's group health plan, all employees generally may enroll within the first 30 days of employment. However, individuals who participate in certain recreational activities, including motorcycling, are excluded from coverage.

(ii) *Conclusion.* In this *Example 3*, excluding from the plan individuals who participate in recreational activities, such as motorcycling, is a rule for eligibility that discriminates based on one or more health factors and thus violates this paragraph (b)(1).

Example 4. (i) *Facts.* A group health plan applies for a group health policy offered by an issuer. As part of the application, the issuer receives health information about individuals to be covered under the plan. Individual A is an employee of the employer maintaining the plan. A and A's dependents have a history of high health claims. Based on the information about A and A's dependents, the issuer excludes A and A's dependents from the group policy it offers to the employer.

(ii) *Conclusion.* In this *Example 4*, the issuer's exclusion of A and A's dependents from coverage is a rule for eligibility that discriminates based on one or more health factors, and thus violates this paragraph (b)(1). (If the employer is a small employer under 45 CFR 144.103 (generally, an employer with 50 or fewer employees), the issuer also may violate 45 CFR 146.150, which requires issuers to offer all the policies they sell in the small group market on a guaranteed available basis to all small employers and to accept every eligible individual in every small employer group.) If the plan provides coverage through this policy and does not provide equivalent coverage for A and A's dependents through other means, the plan will also violate this paragraph (b)(1).

(2) *Application to benefits.* (i) *General rule.* (A) Under this section, a group health plan or group health insurance issuer is not required to provide coverage for any particular benefit to any group of similarly situated individuals.

(B) However, benefits provided under a plan or through group health insurance coverage must be uniformly available to all similarly situated individuals (as described in paragraph (d) of this section). Likewise, any restriction on a benefit or benefits must apply uniformly to all similarly situated individuals and must not be directed at individual participants or beneficiaries based on any health factor of the participants or beneficiaries (determined based on all the relevant facts and circumstances). Thus, for example, a plan or issuer may limit or exclude benefits in relation to a specific disease or condition, limit or exclude benefits for certain types of treatments or drugs, or limit or exclude benefits based on a determination of whether the benefits are experimental or not medically necessary, but only if the benefit limitation or exclusion applies uniformly to all similarly situated individuals and is not directed at individual participants or beneficiaries based on any health factor of the participants or beneficiaries. In addition, a plan or issuer may impose annual, lifetime, or other limits on benefits and may require the satisfaction of a deductible, copayment, coinsurance, or other cost-sharing requirement in order to obtain a benefit if the limit or cost-sharing requirement applies uniformly to all similarly situated individuals and is not directed at individual participants or beneficiaries based on any health factor of the participants or beneficiaries. In the case of a cost-sharing requirement, see also paragraph (b)(2)(ii) of this section, which permits variances in the application of a cost-sharing mechanism made available under a bona fide wellness program. (Whether any plan provision or practice with respect to benefits complies with this paragraph (b)(2)(i) does not affect whether the provision or practice is permitted under any other provision of the Act, the Americans with Disabilities Act, or any other law, whether State or federal.)

(C) For purposes of this paragraph (b)(2)(i), a plan amendment applicable to all individuals in one or more groups of similarly situated individuals under the plan and made effective no earlier than the first day of the first plan year after the amendment is adopted is not considered to be directed at any individual participants or beneficiaries.

(D) The rules of this paragraph (b)(2)(i) are illustrated by the following examples:

Example 1. (i) *Facts.* A group health plan applies a $500,000 lifetime limit on all benefits to each participant or beneficiary covered under the plan. The limit is not directed at individual participants or beneficiaries.

(ii) *Conclusion.* In this *Example 1*, the limit does not violate this paragraph (b)(2)(i) because $500,000 of benefits are available uniformly to each participant and beneficiary under the plan and because the limit is applied uniformly to all participants and beneficiaries and is not directed at individual participants or beneficiaries.

Example 2. (i) *Facts.* A group health plan has a $2 million lifetime limit on all benefits (and no other lifetime limits) for participants covered under the plan. Participant *B* files a claim for the treatment of AIDS. At the next corporate board meeting of the plan sponsor, the claim is discussed. Shortly thereafter, the plan is modified to impose a $10,000 lifetime limit on benefits for the treatment of AIDS, effective before the beginning of the next plan year.

(ii) *Conclusion.* Under the facts of this *Example 2*, the plan violates this paragraph (b)(2)(i) because the plan modification is directed at *B* based on *B*'s claim.

Example 3. (i) A group health plan applies for a group health policy offered by an issuer. Individual *C* is covered under the plan and has an adverse health condition. As part of the application, the issuer receives health information about the individuals to be covered, including information about *C*'s adverse health condition. The policy form offered by the issuer generally provides benefits for the adverse health condition that *C* has, but in this case the issuer offers the plan a policy modified by a rider that excludes benefits for *C* for that condition. The exclusionary rider is made effective the first day of the next plan year.

(ii) *Conclusion.* In this *Example 3*, the issuer violates this paragraph (b)(2)(i) because benefits for *C*'s condition are available to other individuals in the group of similarly situated individuals that includes *C* but are not available to *C*. Thus, the benefits are not uniformly available to all similarly situated individuals. Even though the exclusionary rider is made effective the first day of the next plan year, because the rider does not apply to all similarly situated individuals, the issuer violates this paragraph (b)(2)(i).

Example 4. (i) *Facts.* A group health plan has a $2,000 lifetime limit for the treatment of temporomandibular joint syndrome (TMJ). The limit is applied uniformly to all similarly situated individuals and is not directed at individual participants or beneficiaries.

(ii) *Conclusion.* In this *Example 4*, the limit does not violate this paragraph (b)(2)(i) because $2000 of benefits for the treatment of TMJ are available uniformly to all similarly situated individuals and a plan may limit benefits covered in relation to a specific disease or condition if the limit applies uniformly to all similarly situated individuals and is not directed at individual participants or beneficiaries.

Example 5. (i) *Facts.* A group health plan applies a $2 million lifetime limit on all benefits. However, the $2 million lifetime limit is reduced to $10,000 for any participant or beneficiary covered under the plan who has a congenital heart defect.

(ii) *Conclusion.* In this *Example 5*, the lower lifetime limit for participants and beneficiaries with a congenital heart defect violates this paragraph (b)(2)(i) because benefits under the plan are not uniformly available to all similarly situated individuals and the plan's lifetime limit on benefits does not apply uniformly to all similarly situated individuals.

Example 6. (i) *Facts.* A group health plan limits benefits for prescription drugs to those listed on a drug formulary. The limit is applied uniformly to all similarly situated individuals and is not directed at individual participants or beneficiaries.

(ii) *Conclusion.* In this *Example 6*, the exclusion from coverage of drugs not listed on the drug formulary does not violate this paragraph (b)(2)(i) because benefits for prescription drugs listed on the formulary are uniformly available to all similarly situated individuals and because the exclusion of drugs not listed on the formulary applies uniformly to all similarly situated individuals and is not directed at individual participants or beneficiaries.

Example 7. (i) *Facts.* Under a group health plan, doctor visits are generally subject to a $250 annual deductible and 20 percent coinsurance requirement. However, prenatal doctor visits are not subject to any deductible or coinsurance requirement. These rules are applied uniformly to all similarly situated individuals and are not directed at individual participants or beneficiaries.

(ii) *Conclusion.* In this *Example 7*, imposing different deductible and coinsurance requirements for prenatal doctor visits and other visits does not violate this paragraph (b)(2)(i) because a plan may establish different deductibles or coinsurance requirements for different services if the deductible or coinsurance requirement is applied uniformly to all similarly situated individuals and is not directed at individual participants or beneficiaries.

(ii) *Cost-sharing mechanisms and wellness programs.* A group health plan or group health insurance coverage with a cost-sharing mechanism (such as a deductible, copayment, or coinsurance) that requires a higher payment from an individual, based on a health factor of that individual or a dependent of that individual, than for a similarly situated individual under the plan (and thus does not apply uniformly to all similarly situated individuals) does not violate the requirements of this paragraph (b)(2) if the payment differential is based on whether an individual has complied with the requirements of a bona fide wellness program.

(iii) *Specific rule relating to source-of-injury exclusions.* (A) If a group health plan or group health insurance coverage generally provides benefits for a type of injury, the plan or issuer may not deny benefits otherwise provided for treatment of the injury if the injury results from an act of domestic violence or a medical condition (including both physical and mental health conditions).

(B) The rules of this paragraph (b)(2)(iii) are illustrated by the following examples:

Example 1. (i) *Facts.* A group health plan generally provides medical/surgical benefits, including benefits for hospital stays, that are medically necessary. However, the plan excludes benefits for self-inflicted injuries or injuries sustained in connection with attempted suicide. Individual *D* suffers from depression and attempts suicide. As a result, *D* sustains injuries and is hospitalized for treatment of the injuries. Pursuant to the exclusion, the plan denies *D* benefits for treatment of the injuries.

(ii) *Conclusion.* In this *Example 1*, the suicide attempt is the result of a medical condition (depression). Accordingly, the denial of benefits for the treatments of D's injuries violates the requirements of this paragraph (b)(2)(iii) because the plan provision excludes benefits for treatment of an injury resulting from a medical condition.

Example 2. (i) *Facts.* A group health plan provides benefits for head injuries generally. The plan also has a general exclusion for any injury sustained while participating in any of a number of recreational activities, including bungee jumping. However, this exclusion does not apply to any injury that results from a medical condition (nor from domestic violence). Participant *E* sustains a head injury while bungee jumping. The injury did not result from a medical condition (nor from domestic violence). Accordingly, the plan denies benefits for *E*'s head injury.

(ii) *Conclusion.* In this *Example 2*, the plan provision that denies benefits based on the source of an injury does not restrict benefits based on an act of domestic violence or any medical condition. Therefore, the provision is permissible under this paragraph (b)(2)(iii) and does not violate this section. (However, if the plan did not allow *E* to enroll in the plan (or applied different rules for eligibility to *E*) because *E* frequently participates in bungee jumping, the plan would violate paragraph (b)(1) of this section.)

(3) *Relationship to § 2590.701-3.* (i) A preexisting condition exclusion is permitted under this section if it—

(A) Complies with § 2590.701-3;

(B) Applies uniformly to all similarly situated individuals (as described in paragraph (d) of this section); and

(C) Is not directed at individual participants or beneficiaries based on any health factor of the participants or beneficiaries. For purposes of this paragraph (b)(3)(i)(C), a plan amendment relating to a preexisting condition exclusion applicable to all individuals in one or more groups of similarly situated individuals under the plan and made effective no earlier than the first day of the first plan year after the amendment is adopted is not considered to be directed at any individual participants or beneficiaries.

(ii) The rules of this paragraph (b)(3) are illustrated by the following examples:

Example 1. (i) *Facts.* A group health plan imposes a preexisting condition exclusion on all individuals enrolled in the plan. The exclusion applies to conditions for which medical advice, diagnosis, care, or treatment was recommended or received within the six-month period ending on an individual's enrollment date. In addition, the exclusion generally extends for 12 months after an individual's enrollment date, but this 12-month period is offset by the number of days of an individual's creditable coverage in accordance with § 2590.701-3. There is nothing to indicate that the exclusion is directed at individual participants or beneficiaries.

(ii) *Conclusion.* In this *Example 1*, even though the plan's preexisting condition exclusion discriminates against individuals based on one or more health factors, the preexisting condition exclusion does not violate this section because it applies uniformly to all similarly situated individuals, is not directed at individual participants or beneficiaries, and complies with § 2590.701-3 (that is, the requirements relating to the six-month look-back period, the 12-month (or 18-month) maximum exclusion period, and the creditable coverage offset).

Example 2. (i) *Facts.* A group health plan excludes coverage for conditions with respect to which medical advice, diagnosis, care, or treatment was recommended or received within the six-month period ending on an individual's enrollment date. Under the plan, the preexisting condition exclusion generally extends for 12 months, offset by creditable coverage. However, if an individual has no claims in the first six months following enrollment, the remainder of the exclusion period is waived.

(ii) *Conclusion.* In this *Example 2*, the plan's preexisting condition exclusions violate this section because they do not meet the requirements of this paragraph (b)(3); specifically, they do not apply

uniformly to all similarly situated individuals. The plan provisions do not apply uniformly to all similarly situated individuals because individuals who have medical claims during the first six months following enrollment are not treated the same as similarly situated individuals with no claims during that period. (Under paragraph (d) of this section, the groups cannot be treated as two separate groups of similarly situated individuals because the distinction is based on a health factor.)

(c) *Prohibited discrimination in premiums or contributions.* (1) *In general.* (i) A group health plan, and a health insurance issuer offering health insurance coverage in connection with a group health plan, may not require an individual, as a condition of enrollment or continued enrollment under the plan or group health insurance coverage, to pay a premium or contribution that is greater than the premium or contribution for a similarly situated individual (described in paragraph (d) of this section) enrolled in the plan or group health insurance coverage based on any health factor that relates to the individual or a dependent of the individual.

(ii) Discounts, rebates, payments in kind, and any other premium differential mechanisms are taken into account in determining an individual's premium or contribution rate. (For rules relating to cost-sharing mechanisms, see paragraph (b)(2) of this section (addressing benefits).)

(2) *Rules relating to premium rates.* (i) *Group rating based on health factors not restricted under this section.* Nothing in this section restricts the aggregate amount that an employer may be charged for coverage under a group health plan.

(ii) *List billing based on a health factor prohibited.* However, a group health insurance issuer, or a group health plan, may not quote or charge an employer (or an individual) a different premium for an individual in a group of similarly situated individuals based on a health factor. (But see paragraph (g) of this section permitting favorable treatment of individuals with adverse health factors.)

(iii) *Examples.* The rules of this paragraph (c)(2) are illustrated by the following examples:

Example 1. (i) *Facts.* An employer sponsors a group health plan and purchases coverage from a health insurance issuer. In order to determine the premium rate for the upcoming plan year, the issuer reviews the claims experience of individuals covered under the plan. The issuer finds that Individual *F* had significantly higher claims experience than similarly situated individuals in the plan. The issuer quotes the plan a higher per-participant rate because of *F*'s claims experience.

(ii) *Conclusion.* In this *Example 1*, the issuer does not violate the provisions of this paragraph (c)(2) because the issuer blends the rate so that the employer is not quoted a higher rate for *F* than for a similarly situated individual based on *F*'s claims experience.

Example 2. (i) *Facts.* Same facts as *Example 1*, except that the issuer quotes the employer a higher premium rate for *F*, because of *F*'s claims experience, than for a similarly situated individual.

(ii) *Conclusion.* In this *Example 2*, the issuer violates this paragraph (c)(2). Moreover, even if the plan purchased the policy based on the quote but did not require a higher participant contribution for *F* than for a similarly situated individual, the issuer would still violate this paragraph (c)(2) (but in such a case the plan would not violate this paragraph (c)(2)).

(3) *Exception for bona fide wellness programs.* Notwithstanding paragraphs (c)(1) and (2) of this section, a plan may establish a premium or contribution differential based on whether an individual has complied with the requirements of a bona fide wellness program.

(d) *Similarly situated individuals.* The requirements of this section apply only within a group of individuals who are treated as similarly situated individuals. A plan or issuer may treat participants as a group of similarly situated individuals separate from beneficiaries. In addition, participants may be treated as two or more distinct groups of similarly situated individuals and beneficiaries may be treated as two or more distinct groups of similarly situated individuals in accordance with the rules of this paragraph (d). Moreover, if individuals have a choice of two or more benefit packages, individuals choosing one benefit package may be treated as one or more groups of similarly situated individuals distinct from individuals choosing another benefit package.

(1) *Participants.* Subject to paragraph (d)(3) of this section, a plan or issuer may treat participants as two or more distinct groups of similarly situated individuals if the distinction between or among the groups of participants is based on a bona fide employment-based classification consistent with the employer's usual business practice. Whether an employment-based classification is bona fide is determined on the basis of all the relevant facts and circumstances. Relevant facts and circumstances include whether the employer uses the classification for purposes independent of qualification for health coverage (for example, determining eligibility for other employee benefits or determining other terms of employment). Subject to paragraph (d)(3) of this section, examples of classifications that, based on all the relevant facts and circumstances, may be bona fide include full-time versus part-time status, different geographic location, membership in a collective bargaining unit, date of hire, length of service, current employee versus former employee status, and different occupations. However, a classification based on any health factor is not a bona fide employment-based classification, unless the requirements of paragraph (g) of this section are satisfied (permitting favorable treatment of individuals with adverse health factors).

(2) *Beneficiaries.* (i) Subject to paragraph (d)(3) of this section, a plan or issuer may treat beneficiaries as two or more distinct groups of similarly situated individuals if the distinction between or among the groups of beneficiaries is based on any of the following factors:

(A) A bona fide employment-based classification of the participant through whom the beneficiary is receiving coverage;

(B) Relationship to the participant (e.g., as a spouse or as a dependent child);

(C) Marital status;

(D) With respect to children of a participant, age or student status; or

(E) Any other factor if the factor is not a health factor.

(ii) Paragraph (d)(2)(i) of this section does not prevent more favorable treatment of individuals with adverse health factors in accordance with paragraph (g) of this section.

(3) *Discrimination directed at individuals.* Notwithstanding paragraphs (d)(1) and (2) of this section, if the creation or modification of an employment or coverage classification is directed at individual participants or beneficiaries based on any health factor of the participants or beneficiaries, the classification is not permitted under this paragraph (d), unless it is permitted under paragraph (g) of this section (permitting favorable treatment of individuals with adverse health factors). Thus, if an employer modified an employment-based classification to single out, based on a health factor, individual participants and beneficiaries and deny them health coverage, the new classification would not be permitted under this section.

(4) *Examples.* The rules of this paragraph (d) are illustrated by the following examples:

Example 1. (i) *Facts.* An employer sponsors a group health plan for full-time employees only. Under the plan (consistent with the employer's usual business practice), employees who normally work at least 30 hours per week are considered to be working full-time. Other employees are considered to be working part-time. There is no evidence to suggest that the classification is directed at individual participants or beneficiaries.

(ii) *Conclusion.* In this *Example 1,* treating the full-time and part-time employees as two separate groups of similarly situated individuals is permitted under this paragraph (d) because the classification is bona fide and is not directed at individual participants or beneficiaries.

Example 2. (i) *Facts.* Under a group health plan, coverage is made available to employees, their spouses, and their dependent children. However, coverage is made available to a dependent child only if the dependent child is under age 19 (or under age 25 if the child is continuously enrolled full-time in an institution of higher learning (full-time students)). There is no evidence to suggest that these classifications are directed at individual participants or beneficiaries.

(ii) *Conclusion.* In this *Example 2,* treating spouses and dependent children differently by imposing an age limitation on dependent children, but not on spouses, is permitted under this paragraph (d). Specifically, the distinction between spouses and dependent children is permitted under paragraph (d)(2) of this section and is not prohibited under paragraph (d)(3) of this section because it is not directed at individual participants or beneficiaries. It is also permissible to treat dependent children who are under age 19 (or full-time students under age 25) as a group of similarly situated individuals separate from those who are age 25 or older (or age 19 or older if they are not full-time students) because the classification is permitted under paragraph (d)(2) of this section and is not directed at individual participants or beneficiaries.

Example 3. (i) *Facts.* A university sponsors a group health plan that provides one health benefit package to faculty and another health benefit package to other staff. Faculty and staff are treated differently with respect to other employee benefits such as retirement benefits and leaves of absence. There is no evidence to suggest that the distinction is directed at individual participants or beneficiaries.

(ii) *Conclusion.* In this *Example 3,* the classification is permitted under this paragraph (d) because there is a distinction based on a bona fide employment-based classification consistent with the employer's usual business practice and the distinction is not directed at individual participants and beneficiaries.

Example 4. (i) *Facts.* An employer sponsors a group health plan that is available to all current employees. Former employees may also be eligible, but only if they complete a specified number of years of service, are enrolled under the plan at the time of termination of employment, and are continuously enrolled from that date. There is no evidence to suggest that these distinctions are directed at individual participants or beneficiaries.

(ii) *Conclusion.* In this *Example 4,* imposing additional eligibility requirements on former employees is permitted because a classification that distinguishes between current and former employees is a bona fide employment-based classification that is permitted under this paragraph (d), provided that it is not directed at individual participants or beneficiaries. In addition, it is permissible to distinguish between former employees who satisfy the service requirement and those who do not, provided that the distinction is not directed at individual participants or beneficiaries. (However, former employees who do not satisfy the eligibility criteria may, nonetheless, be eligible for continued coverage pursuant to a COBRA continuation provision or similar State law.)

Example 5. (i) *Facts.* An employer sponsors a group health plan that provides the same benefit package to all seven employees of the employer. Six of the seven employees have the same job title and responsibilities, but Employee *G* has a different job title and different responsibilities. After *G* files an expensive claim for benefits under the plan, coverage under the plan is modified so that employees with *G*'s job title receive a different benefit package that includes a lower lifetime dollar limit than in the benefit package made available to the other six employees.

(ii) *Conclusion.* Under the facts of this *Example 5,* changing the coverage classification for *G* based on the existing employment classification for *G* is not permitted under this paragraph (d) because the creation of the new coverage classification for *G* is directed at *G* based on one or more health factors.

(e) *Nonconfinement and actively-at-work provisions.* (1) *Nonconfinement provisions.* (i) *General rule.* Under the rules of paragraphs (b) and (c) of this section, a plan or issuer may not establish a rule for eligibility (as described in paragraph (b)(1)(ii) of this section) or set any individual's premium or contribution rate based on whether an individual is confined to a hospital or other health care institution. In addition, under the rules of paragraphs (b) and (c) of this section, a plan or issuer may not establish a rule for eligibility or set any individual's premium or contribution rate based on an individual's ability to engage in normal life activities, except to the extent permitted under paragraphs (e)(2)(ii) and (3) of this section (permitting plans and issuers, under certain circumstances, to distinguish among employees based on the performance of services).

(ii) *Examples.* The rules of this paragraph (e)(1) are illustrated by the following examples:

Example 1. (i) *Facts.* Under a group health plan, coverage for employees and their dependents generally becomes effective on the first day of employment. However, coverage for a dependent who is confined to a hospital or other health care institution does not become effective until the confinement ends.

(ii) *Conclusion.* In this *Example 1*, the plan violates this paragraph (e)(1) because the plan delays the effective date of coverage for dependents based on confinement to a hospital or other health care institution.

Example 2. (i) *Facts.* In previous years, a group health plan has provided coverage through a group health insurance policy offered by Issuer *M.* However, for the current year, the plan provides coverage through a group health insurance policy offered by Issuer *N.* Under Issuer *N*'s policy, items and services provided in connection with the confinement of a dependent to a hospital or other health care institution are not covered if the confinement is covered under an extension of benefits clause from a previous health insurance issuer.

(ii) *Conclusion.* In this *Example 2*, Issuer *N* violates this paragraph (e)(1) because the group health insurance coverage restricts benefits (a rule for eligibility under paragraph (b)(1)) based on whether a dependent is confined to a hospital or other health care institution that is covered under an extension of benefits clause from a previous issuer. This section does not affect any obligation Issuer *M* may have under applicable State law to provide any extension of benefits and does not affect any State law governing coordination of benefits.

(2) *Actively-at-work and continuous service provisions.* (i) *General rule.* (A) Under the rules of paragraphs (b) and (c) of this section and subject to the exception for the first day of work described in paragraph (e)(2)(ii) of this section, a plan or issuer may not establish a rule for eligibility (as described in paragraph (b)(1)(ii) of this section) or set any individual's premium or contribution rate based on whether an individual is actively at work (including whether an individual is continuously employed), unless absence from work due to any health factor (such as being absent from work on sick leave) is treated, for purposes of the plan or health insurance coverage, as being actively at work.

(B) The rules of this paragraph (e)(2)(i) are illustrated by the following examples:

Example 1. (i) *Facts.* Under a group health plan, an employee generally becomes eligible to enroll 30 days after the first day of employment. However, if the employee is not actively at work on the first day after the end of the 30-day period, then eligibility for enrollment is delayed until the first day the employee is actively at work.

(ii) *Conclusion.* In this *Example 1*, the plan violates this paragraph (e)(2) (and thus also violates paragraph (b) of this section). However, the plan would not violate paragraph (e)(2) or (b) of this section if, under the plan, an absence due to any health factor is considered being actively at work.

Example 2. (i) *Facts.* Under a group health plan, coverage for an employee becomes effective after 90 days of continuous service; that is, if an employee is absent from work (for any reason) before completing 90 days of service, the beginning of the 90-day period is measured from the day the employee returns to work (without any credit for service before the absence).

(ii) *Conclusion.* In this *Example 2*, the plan violates this paragraph (e)(2) (and thus also paragraph (b) of this section) because the 90-day continuous service requirement is a rule for eligibility based on whether an individual is actively at work. However, the plan would not violate this paragraph (e)(2) or paragraph (b) of this section if, under the plan, an absence due to any health factor is not considered an absence for purposes of measuring 90 days of continuous service.

(ii) *Exception for the first day of work.* (A) Notwithstanding the general rule in paragraph (e)(2)(i) of this section, a plan or issuer may establish a rule for eligibility that requires an individual to begin work for the employer sponsoring the plan (or, in the case of a multiemployer plan, to begin a job in covered employment) before coverage becomes effective, provided that such a rule for eligibility applies regardless of the reason for the absence.

(B) The rules of this paragraph (e)(2)(ii) are illustrated by the following examples:

Example 1. (i) *Facts.* Under the eligibility provision of a group health plan, coverage for new employees becomes effective on the first day that the employee reports to work. Individual *H* is scheduled to begin work on August 3. However, *H* is unable to begin work on that day because of illness. *H* begins working on August 4, and *H*'s coverage is effective on August 4.

(ii) *Conclusion.* In this *Example 1*, the plan provision does not violate this section. However, if coverage for individuals who do not report to work on the first day they were scheduled to work for a reason unrelated to a health factor (such as vacation or bereavement) becomes effective on the first day they were scheduled to work, then the plan would violate this section.

Example 2. (i) *Facts.* Under a group health plan, coverage for new employees becomes effective on the first day of the month following the employee's first day of work, regardless of whether the employee is actively at work on the first day of the month. Individual *J* is scheduled to begin work on March 24. However, *J* is unable to begin work on March 24 because of illness. *J* begins working on April 7 and *J*'s coverage is effective May 1.

(ii) *Conclusion.* In this *Example 2*, the plan provision does not violate this section. However, as in *Example 1*, if coverage for individuals absent from work for reasons unrelated to a health factor became effective despite their absence, then the plan would violate this section.

(3) *Relationship to plan provisions defining similarly situated individuals.* (i) Notwithstanding the rules of paragraphs (e)(1) and (2) of this section, a plan or issuer may establish rules for eligibility or set any individual's premium or contribution rate in accordance with the rules relating to similarly situated individuals in paragraph (d) of this section. Accordingly, a plan or issuer may distinguish in rules for eligibility under the plan between full-time and part-time employees, between permanent and temporary or seasonal employees, between current and former employees, and between employees currently performing services and employees no longer performing services for the employer, subject to paragraph (d) of this section. However, other federal or State laws (including the COBRA continuation provisions and the Family and Medical Leave Act of 1993) may require an employee or the employee's dependents to be offered coverage and set limits on the premium or contribution rate even though the employee is not performing services.

(ii) The rules of this paragraph (e)(3) are illustrated by the following examples:

Example 1. (i) *Facts.* Under a group health plan, employees are eligible for coverage if they perform services for the employer for 30 or more hours per week or if they are on paid leave (such as vacation, sick, or bereavement leave). Employees on unpaid leave are treated as a separate group of similarly situated individuals in accordance with the rules of paragraph (d) of this section.

(ii) *Conclusion.* In this *Example 1*, the plan provisions do not violate this section. However, if the plan treated individuals performing services for the employer for 30 or more hours per week, individuals on vacation leave, and individuals on bereavement leave as a group of similarly situated individuals separate from individuals on sick leave, the plan would violate this paragraph (e) (and thus also would violate paragraph (b) of this section) because groups of similarly situated individuals cannot be established based on a health factor (including the taking of sick leave) under paragraph (d) of this section.

Example 2. (i) *Facts.* To be eligible for coverage under a bona fide collectively bargained group health plan in the current calendar quarter, the plan requires an individual to have worked 250 hours in covered employment during the three-month period that ends one month before the beginning of the current calendar quarter. The distinction between employees working at least 250 hours and those working less than 250 hours in the earlier three-month period is not directed at individual participants or beneficiaries based on any health factor of the participants or beneficiaries.

(ii) *Conclusion.* In this *Example 2*, the plan provision does not violate this section because, under the rules for similarly situated individuals allowing full-time employees to be treated differently than part-time employees, employees who work at least 250 hours in a three-month period can be treated differently than employees who fail to work 250 hours in that period. The result would be the same if the plan permitted individuals to apply excess hours from previous periods to satisfy the requirement for the current quarter.

Example 3. (i) *Facts.* Under a group health plan, coverage of an employee is terminated when the individual's employment is terminated, in accordance with the rules of paragraph (d) of this section. Employee *B* has been covered under the plan. *B* experiences a disabling illness that prevents *B* from working. *B* takes a leave of absence under the Family and Medical Leave Act of 1993. At the end of such leave, *B* terminates employment and consequently loses coverage under the plan. (This termination of coverage is without regard to whatever rights the employee (or members of the employee's family) may have for COBRA continuation coverage.)

(ii) *Conclusion.* In this *Example 3*, the plan provision terminating *B*'s coverage upon *B*'s termination of employment does not violate this section.

Example 4. (i) *Facts.* Under a group health plan, coverage of an employee is terminated when the employee ceases to perform services for the employer sponsoring the plan, in accordance with the rules of paragraph (d) of this section. Employee *C* is laid off for three months. When the layoff begins, *C*'s coverage under the plan is terminated. (This termination of coverage is without regard to whatever rights the employee (or members of the employee's family) may have for COBRA continuation coverage.)

(ii) *Conclusion.* In this *Example 4*, the plan provision terminating *C*'s coverage upon the cessation of *C*'s performance of services does not violate this section.

(f) *Bona fide wellness programs.* [Reserved.]

(g) *More favorable treatment of individuals with adverse health factors permitted.* (1) *In rules for eligibility.* (i) Nothing in this section prevents a group health plan or group health insurance issuer from establishing more favorable rules for eligibility (described in paragraph (b)(1) of this section) for individuals with an adverse health factor, such as disability, than for individuals without the adverse health factor. Moreover, nothing in this section prevents a plan or issuer from charging a higher premium or contribution with respect to individuals with an adverse health factor if they would not be eligible for the coverage were it not for the adverse health factor. (However, other laws, including State insurance laws, may set or limit premium rates; these laws are not affected by this section.)

(ii) The rules of this paragraph (g)(1) are illustrated by the following examples:

Example 1. (i) *Facts.* An employer sponsors a group health plan that generally is available to employees, spouses of employees, and dependent children until age 23. However, dependent children who are disabled are eligible for coverage beyond age 23.

(ii) *Conclusion.* In this *Example 1*, the plan provision allowing coverage for disabled dependent children beyond age 23 satisfies this paragraph (g)(1) (and thus does not violate this section).

Example 2. (i) *Facts.* An employer sponsors a group health plan, which is generally available to employees (and members of the employee's family) until the last day of the month in which the employee ceases to perform services for the employer. The plan generally charges employees $50 per month for employee-only coverage and $125 per month for family coverage. However, an employee who ceases to perform services for the employer by reason of disability may remain covered under the plan until the last day of the month that is 12 months after the month in which the employee ceased to perform services for the employer. During this extended period of coverage, the plan charges the employee $100 per month for employee-only coverage and $250 per month for family coverage. (This extended period of coverage is without regard to whatever rights the employee (or members of the employee's family) may have for COBRA continuation coverage.)

(ii) *Conclusion.* In this *Example 2*, the plan provision allowing extended coverage for disabled employees and their families satisfies this paragraph (g)(1) (and thus does not violate this section). In addition, the plan is permitted, under this paragraph (g)(1), to charge

the disabled employees a higher premium during the extended period of coverage.

Example 3. (i) *Facts.* To comply with the requirements of a COBRA continuation provision, a group health plan generally makes COBRA continuation coverage available for a maximum period of 18 months in connection with a termination of employment but makes the coverage available for a maximum period of 29 months to certain disabled individuals and certain members of the disabled individual's family. Although the plan generally requires payment of 102 percent of the applicable premium for the first 18 months of COBRA continuation coverage, the plan requires payment of 150 percent of the applicable premium for the disabled individual's COBRA continuation coverage during the disability extension if the disabled individual would not be entitled to COBRA continuation coverage but for the disability.

(ii) *Conclusion.* In this *Example 3*, the plan provision allowing extended COBRA continuation coverage for disabled individuals satisfies this paragraph (g)(1) (and thus does not violate this section). In addition, the plan is permitted, under this paragraph (g)(1), to charge the disabled individuals a higher premium for the extended coverage if the individuals would not be eligible for COBRA continuation coverage were it not for the disability. (Similarly, if the plan provided an extended period of coverage for disabled individuals pursuant to State law or plan provision rather than pursuant to a COBRA continuation coverage provision, the plan could likewise charge the disabled individuals a higher premium for the extended coverage.)

(2) *In premiums or contributions.* (i) Nothing in this section prevents a group health plan or group health insurance issuer from charging individuals a premium or contribution that is less than the premium (or contribution) for similarly situated individuals if the lower charge is based on an adverse health factor, such as disability.

(ii) The rules of this paragraph (g)(2) are illustrated by the following example:

Example. (i) *Facts.* Under a group health plan, employees are generally required to pay $50 per month for employee-only coverage and $125 per month for family coverage under the plan. However, employees who are disabled receive coverage (whether employee-only or family coverage) under the plan free of charge.

(ii) *Conclusion.* In this *Example*, the plan provision waiving premium payment for disabled employees is permitted under this paragraph (g)(2) (and thus does not violate this section).

(h) *No effect on other laws.* Compliance with this section is not determinative of compliance with any other provision of the Act (including the COBRA continuation provisions) or any other State or federal law, such as the Americans with Disabilities Act. Therefore, although the rules of this section would not prohibit a plan or issuer from treating one group of similarly situated individuals differently from another (such as providing different benefit packages to current and former employees), other federal or State laws may require that two separate groups of similarly situated individuals be treated the same for certain purposes (such as making the same benefit package available to COBRA qualified beneficiaries as is made available to active employees). In addition, although this section generally does not impose new disclosure obligations on plans and issuers, this section does not affect any other laws, including those that require accurate disclosures and prohibit intentional misrepresentation.

(i) *Applicability dates.* (1) *Paragraphs applicable May 8, 2001.* Paragraphs (a)(1), (a)(2)(i), (b)(1)(i), (b)(1)(iii) *Example 1*, (b)(2)(i)(A), (b)(2)(ii), (c)(1)(i), (c)(2)(i), and (c)(3) of this section and this paragraph (*i*)(1) apply to group health plans and health insurance issuers offering group health insurance coverage May 8, 2001. [Amended 3/9/01 by 66 FR 14,076.]

(2) *Paragraphs applicable for plan years beginning on or after July 1, 2001.* Except as provided in paragraph (*i*)(3) of this section, the provisions of this section not listed in paragraph (*i*)(1) of this section apply to group health plans and health insurance issuers offering group health insurance coverage for plan years beginning on or after July 1, 2001. Except as provided in paragraph (*i*)(3) of this section, with respect to efforts to comply with section 702 of the Act before the first plan year beginning on or after July 1, 2001, the Secretary will not take

any enforcement action against a plan that has sought to comply in good faith with section 702 of the Act.

(3) *Transitional rules for individuals previously denied coverage based on a health factor.* This paragraph (*i*) (3) provides rules relating to individuals previously denied coverage under a group health plan or group health insurance coverage based on a health factor of the individual. Paragraph (*i*) (3) (i) clarifies what constitutes a denial of coverage under this paragraph (*i*) (3). Paragraph (*i*) (3) (ii) of this section applies with respect to any individual who was denied coverage if the denial was not based on a good faith interpretation of section 702 of the Act or the Secretary's published guidance. Under that paragraph, such an individual must be allowed to enroll retroactively to the effective date of section 702 of the Act, or, if later, the date the individual meets eligibility criteria under the plan that do not discriminate based on any health factor. Paragraph (*i*) (3) (iii) of this section applies with respect to any individual who was denied coverage based on a good faith interpretation of section 702 of the Act or the Secretary's published guidance. Under that paragraph, such an individual must be given an opportunity to enroll effective July 1, 2001. In either event, whether under paragraph (*i*) (3) (ii) or (iii) of this section, the Secretary will not take any enforcement action with respect to denials of coverage addressed in this paragraph (*i*) (3) if the plan has complied with the transitional rules of this paragraph (*i*) (3).

(i) *Denial of coverage clarified.* For purposes of this paragraph (*i*) (3), an individual is considered to have been denied coverage if the individual—

(A) Failed to apply for coverage because it was reasonable to believe that an application for coverage would have been futile due to a plan provision that discriminated based on a health factor; or

(B) Was not offered an opportunity to enroll in the plan and the failure to give such an opportunity violates this section.

(ii) *Individuals denied coverage without a good faith interpretation of the law.* (A) *Opportunity to enroll required.* If a plan or issuer has denied coverage to any individual based on a health factor and that denial was not based on a good faith interpretation of section 702 of the Act or any guidance published by the Secretary, the plan or issuer is required to give the individual an opportunity to enroll (including notice of an opportunity to enroll) that continues for at least 30 days. This opportunity must be presented not later than May 8, 2001. [Amended 3/9/01 by 66 FR 14,076.]

(1) If this enrollment opportunity was presented before or within the first plan year beginning on or after July 1, 1997 (or in the case of a collectively bargained plan, before or within the first plan year beginning on the effective date for the plan described in section 101(g)(3) of the Health Insurance Portability and Accountability Act of 1996), the coverage must be effective within that first plan year.

(2) If this enrollment opportunity is presented after such plan year, the individual must be given the choice of having the coverage effective on either of the following two dates—

(i) The date the plan receives a request for enrollment in connection with the enrollment opportunity; or

(ii) Retroactively to the first day of the first plan year beginning on the effective date for the plan described in sections 101(g)(1) and (3) of the Health Insurance Portability and Accountability Act of 1996 (or, if the individual otherwise first became eligible to enroll for coverage after that date, on the date the individual was otherwise eligible to enroll in the plan). If an individual elects retroactive coverage, the plan or issuer is required to provide the benefits it would have provided if the individual had been enrolled for coverage during that period (irrespective of any otherwise applicable plan provisions governing timing for the submission of claims). The plan or issuer may require the individual to pay whatever additional amount the individual would have been required to pay for the coverage (but the plan or issuer cannot charge interest on that amount).

(B) *Relation to preexisting condition rules.* For purposes of Part 7 of Subtitle B of Title I of the Act, the individual may not be treated as a late enrollee or as a special enrollee. Moreover, the individual's enrollment date is the effective date for the plan described in sections 101(g)(1) and (3) of the Health Insurance Portability and Accountability Act (or, if the individual otherwise first became eligible

to enroll for coverage after that date, on the date the individual was otherwise eligible to enroll in the plan), even if the individual chooses under paragraph (*i*) (3) (ii) (A) of this section to have coverage effective only prospectively. In addition, any period between the individual's enrollment date and the effective date of coverage is treated as a waiting period.

(C) *Examples.* The rules of this paragraph (*i*) (3) (ii) are illustrated by the following examples:

Example 1. (i) *Facts.* Employer *X* maintains a group health plan with a plan year beginning October 1 and ending September 30. Individual *F* was hired by Employer *X* before the effective date of section 702 of the Act. Before the effective date of section 702 of the Act for this plan (October 1, 1997), the terms of the plan allowed employees and their dependents to enroll when the employee was first hired, and on each January 1 thereafter, but in either case, only if the individual could pass a physical examination. *F*'s application to enroll when first hired was denied because *F* had diabetes and could not pass a physical examination. Upon the effective date of section 702 of the Act for this plan (October 1, 1997), the plan is amended to delete the requirement to pass a physical examination. In November of 1997, the plan gives *F* an opportunity to enroll in the plan (including notice of the opportunity to enroll) without passing a physical examination, with coverage effective January 1, 1998.

(ii) *Conclusion.* In this *Example 1*, the plan complies with the requirements of this paragraph (*i*) (3) (ii).

Example 2. (i) *Facts.* The plan year of a group health plan begins January 1 and ends December 31. Under the plan, a dependent who is unable to engage in normal life activities on the date coverage would otherwise become effective is not enrolled until the dependent is able to engage in normal life activities. Individual *G* is a dependent who is otherwise eligible for coverage, but is unable to engage in normal life activities. The plan has not allowed *G* to enroll for coverage.

(ii) *Conclusion.* In this *Example 2*, beginning on the effective date of section 702 of the Act for the plan (January 1, 1998), the plan provision is not permitted under any good faith interpretation of section 702 of the Act or any guidance published by the Secretary. Therefore, the plan is required, not later than May 8, 2001 to give *G* an opportunity to enroll (including notice of the opportunity to enroll), with coverage effective, at *G*'s option, either retroactively from January 1, 1998 or prospectively from the date *G*'s request for enrollment is received by the plan. If *G* elects coverage to be effective beginning January 1, 1998, the plan can require *G* to pay any required employee premiums for the retroactive coverage. [Amended 3/9/01 by 66 FR 14,076.]

(iii) *Individuals denied coverage based on a good faith interpretation of the law.* (A) *Opportunity to enroll required.* If a plan or issuer has denied coverage to any individual before the first day of the first plan year beginning on or after July 1, 2001 based in part on a health factor and that denial was based on a good faith interpretation of section 702 of the Act or guidance published by the Secretary, the plan or issuer is required to give the individual an opportunity to enroll (including notice of an opportunity to enroll) that continues for at least 30 days, with coverage effective no later than July 1, 2001. Individuals required to be offered an opportunity to enroll include individuals previously offered enrollment without regard to a health factor but subsequently denied enrollment due to a health factor.

(B) *Relation to preexisting condition rules.* For purposes of Part 7 of Subtitle B of Title I of the Act, the individual may not be treated as a late enrollee or as a special enrollee. Moreover, the individual's enrollment date is the effective date for the plan described in sections 101(g)(1) and (3) of the Health Insurance Portability and Accountability Act (or, if the individual otherwise first became eligible to enroll for coverage after that date, on the date the individual was otherwise eligible to enroll in the plan). In addition, any period between the individual's enrollment date and the effective date of coverage is treated as a waiting period.

(C) *Example.* The rules of this paragraph (*i*) (3) (iii) are illustrated by the following example:

Example. (i) *Facts.* Individual *H* was hired by Employer *Y* on May 3, 1995. *Y* maintains a group health plan with a plan year beginning on February 1. Under the terms of the plan, employees and their dependents are allowed to enroll when the employee is first hired (without a requirement to pass a physical examination), and on each February 1 thereafter if the individual can pass a physical examination. *H* chose not to enroll for coverage when hired in May of 1995. On February 1, 1997, *H* tried to enroll for coverage under the plan. However, *H* was denied coverage for failure to pass a physical examination. Shortly thereafter, *Y*'s plan eliminated late enrollment, and *H* was not given another opportunity to enroll in the plan. There is no evidence to suggest that *Y*'s plan was acting in bad faith in denying coverage under the plan beginning on the effective date of section 702 of the Act (February 1, 1998).

(ii) *Conclusion.* In this *Example*, because coverage previously had been made available with respect to *H* without regard to any

health factor of *H* and because *Y*'s plan was acting in accordance with a good faith interpretation of section 702 (and guidance published by the Secretary), the failure of *Y*'s plan to allow *H* to enroll effective February 1, 1998 was permissible on that date. However, under the transitional rules of this paragraph (*i*)(3)(iii), *Y*'s plan must give *H* an opportunity to enroll that continues for at least 30 days, with coverage effective no later than July 1, 2001. (In addition, February 1, 1998 is *H*'s enrollment date under the plan and the period between February 1, 1998 and July 1, 2001 is treated as a waiting period. Accordingly, any preexisting condition exclusion period permitted under § 2590.701-3 will have expired before July 1, 2001.)

Historical Comment: Amended 3/9/01 by 66 FR 14,076.

[¶ 15,050B]
GUARANTEED RENEWABILITY IN MULTIEMPLOYER PLANS AND MULTIPLE EMPLOYER WELFARE ARRANGEMENTS

Act Sec. 703. A group health plan which is a multiemployer plan or which is a multiple employer welfare arrangement may not deny an employer whose employees are covered under such a plan continued access to the same or different coverage under the terms of such a plan, other than—

(1) for nonpayment of contributions;

(2) for fraud or other intentional misrepresentation of material fact by the employer;

(3) for noncompliance with material plan provisions;

(4) because the plan is ceasing to offer any coverage in a geographic area;

(5) in the case of a plan that offers benefits through a network plan, there is no longer any individual enrolled through the employer who lives, resides, or works in the service area of the network plan and the plan applies this paragraph uniformly without regard to the claims experience of employers or any health status-related factor in relation to such individuals or their dependents; and

(6) for failure to meet the terms of an applicable collective bargaining agreement, to renew a collective bargaining or other agreement requiring or authorizing contributions to the plan, or to employ employees covered by such an agreement.

Amendments

P.L. 104-191, § 101(a):

Added ERISA Act Sec. 703 to read as above.

The above amendments generally apply with respect to group health plans for plan years beginning after June 30, 1997. For special rules, see Act Sec. 101(g)(2)- (5), reproduced after ERISA Act Sec. 701 above.

Regulations

The following regulations were adopted by 62 FR 16894 and published in the Federal Register on April 8, 1997, under "Chapter XXV of Title 29 of the Code of Federal Regulations; Subchapter L—Health Insurance Portability and Renewability for Group Health Plans; Part 2590—Rules and Regulations for Health Insurance Portability and Renewability for Group Health Plans."

[¶ 15,050B-1]
§ 2590.703 **Guaranteed renewability in multiemployer plans and multiple employer welfare arrangements. [Reserved]**

⋙→ *Caution: Effective for plan years beginning on or after January 1, 1998, Act Sec. 704, below, is redesignated as Act Sec. 731. See ¶ 15,051A.—CCH.*

[¶ 15,050C]
PREEMPTION; STATE FLEXIBILITY; CONSTRUCTION

Act Sec. 704.(a) CONTINUED APPLICABILITY OF STATE LAW WITH RESPECT TO HEALTH INSURANCE ISSUERS.—

(1) IN GENERAL. Subject to paragraph (2) and except as provided in subsection (b), this part shall not be construed to supersede any provision of State law which establishes, implements, or continues in effect any standard or requirement solely relating to health insurance issuers in connection with group health insurance coverage except to the extent that such standard or requirement prevents the application of a requirement of this part.

(2) CONTINUED PREEMPTION WITH RESPECT TO GROUP HEALTH PLANS. Nothing in this part shall be construed to affect or modify the provisions of section 514 with respect to group health plans.

Act Sec. 704. SPECIAL RULES IN CASE OF PORTABILITY REQUIREMENTS.—

(b)(1) IN GENERAL. Subject to paragraph (2), the provisions of this part relating to health insurance coverage offered by a health insurance issuer supersede any provision of State law which establishes, implements, or continues in effect a standard or requirement applicable to imposition of a preexisting condition exclusion specifically governed by section 701 which differs from the standards or requirements specified in such section.

(2) EXCEPTIONS. Only in relation to health insurance coverage offered by a health insurance issuer, the provisions of this part do not supersede any provision of State law to the extent that such provision—

(A) substitutes for the reference to "6-month period" in section 701(a)(1) a reference to any shorter period of time;

(B) substitutes for the reference to "12 months" and "18 months" in section 701(a)(2) a reference to any shorter period of time;

(C) substitutes for the references to "63 days" in sections 701(c)(2)(A) and (d)(4)(A) a reference to any greater number of days;

(D) substitutes for the reference to "30-day period" in sections 701(b)(2) and (d)(1) a reference to any greater period;

(E) prohibits the imposition of any preexisting condition exclusion in cases not described in section 701(d) or expands the exceptions described in such section;

(F) requires special enrollment periods in addition to those required under section 701(f); or

(G) reduces the maximum period permitted in an affiliation period under section 701(g)(1)(B).

Act Sec. 704. Rules of Construction. (c) Nothing in this part shall be construed as requiring a group health plan or health insurance coverage to provide specific benefits under the terms of such plan or coverage.

Act Sec. 704. Definitions. (d) For purposes of this section—

(1) State law. The term "State law" includes all laws, decisions, rules, regulations, or other State action having the effect of law, of any State. A law of the United States applicable only to the District of Columbia shall be treated as a State law rather than a law of the United States.

(2) State. The term "State" includes a State, the Northern Mariana Islands, any political subdivisions of a State or such Islands, or any agency or instrumentality of either.

Amendments

P.L. 104-204, § 603(a)(3):

Redesignated ERISA Act Sec. 704 as ERISA Act Sec. 731.

The above amendment shall apply with respect to group health plans for plan years beginning on or after January 1, 1998.

P.L. 104-191, § 101(a):

Added ERISA Act Sec. 704 to read as above.

The above amendments generally apply with respect to group health plans for plan years beginning after June 30, 1997. For special rules, see Act Sec. 101(g)(2)- (5), reproduced after ERISA Act Sec. 701 above.

≫→ *Caution: Effective for plan years beginning on or after January 1, 1998, Act Sec. 705, below, is redesignated as Act Sec. 732. See ¶ 15,051B.—CCH.*

[¶ 15,050D]
SPECIAL RULES RELATING TO GROUP HEALTH PLANS

Act Sec. 705.(a) General Exception for Certain Small Group Health Plans. The requirements of this part shall not apply to any group health plan (and group health insurance coverage offered in connection with a group health plan) for any plan year if, on the first day of such plan year, such plan has less than 2 participants who are current employees.

Act Sec. 705. Exception for Certain Benefits. (b) The requirements of this part shall not apply to any group health plan (and group health insurance coverage) in relation to its provision of excepted benefits described in section 706(c)(1).

Act Sec. 705. Exception for Certain Benefits of Certain Conditions Met.—

(c)(1) Limited, excepted benefits. The requirements of this part shall not apply to any group health plan (and group health insurance coverage offered in connection with a group health plan) in relation to its provision of excepted benefits described in section 706(c)(2) if the benefits—

(A) are provided under a separate policy, certificate, or contract of insurance; or

(B) are otherwise not an integral part of the plan.

(2) Noncoordinated, excepted benefits. The requirements of this part shall not apply to any group health plan (and group health insurance coverage offered in connection with a group health plan) in relation to its provision of excepted benefits described in section 706(c)(3) if all of the following conditions are met:

(A) The benefits are provided under a separate policy, certificate, or contract of insurance.

(B) There is no coordination between the provision of such benefits and any exclusion of benefits under any group health plan maintained by the same plan sponsor.

(C) Such benefits are paid with respect to an event without regard to whether benefits are provided with respect to such an event under any group health plan maintained by the same plan sponsor.

(3) Supplemental excepted benefits. The requirements of this part shall not apply to any group health plan (and group health insurance coverage) in relation to its provision of excepted benefits described in section 706(c)(4) if the benefits are provided under a separate policy, certificate, or contract of insurance.

Act Sec. 705. Treatment of Partnerships. (d) For purposes of this part—

(1) Treatment as a group health plan. Any plan, fund, or program which would not be (but for this subsection) an employee welfare benefit plan and which is established or maintained by a partnership, to the extent that such plan, fund, or program provides medical care (including items and services paid for as medical care) to present or former partners in the partnership or to their dependents (as defined under the terms of the plan, fund, or program), directly or through insurance, reimbursement, or otherwise, shall be treated (subject to paragraph (2)) as an employee welfare benefit plan which is a group health plan.

(2) Employer. In the case of a group health plan, the term "employer" also includes the partnership in relation to any partner.

(3) Participants of group health plans. In the case of a group health plan, the term "participant" also includes—

(A) in connection with a group health plan maintained by a partnership, an individual who is a partner in relation to the partnership, or

(B) in connection with a group health plan maintained by a self-employed individual (under which one or more employees are participants), the self-employed individual,

if such individual is, or may become, eligible to receive a benefit under the plan or such individual's beneficiaries may be eligible to receive any such benefit.

Amendments

P.L. 104-204, § 603(a)(3):

Redesignated ERISA Act Sec. 705 as ERISA Act Sec. 732.

The above amendment shall apply with respect to group health plans for plan years beginning on or after January 1, 1998.

P.L. 104-191, § 101(a):

Added ERISA Act Sec. 705 to read as above.

The above amendments generally apply with respect to group health plans for plan years beginning after June 30, 1997. For special rules, see Act Sec. 101(g)(2)- (5), reproduced after ERISA Act Sec. 701 above.

≫→ *Caution: Effective for plan years beginning on or after January 1, 1998, Act Sec. 706, below, is redesignated as Act Sec. 733. See ¶ 15,051C.—CCH.*

[¶ 15,050E]
DEFINITIONS

Act Sec. 706.(a) Group Health Plan. For purposes of this part—

(1) In general. The term "group health plan" means an employee welfare benefit plan to the extent that the plan provides medical care (as defined in paragraph (2) and including items and services paid for as medical care) to employees or their dependents (as defined under the terms of the plan) directly or through insurance, reimbursement, or otherwise.

(2) MEDICAL CARE. The term "medical care" means amounts paid for—

(A) the diagnosis, cure, mitigation, treatment, or prevention of disease, or amounts paid for the purpose of affecting any structure or function of the body,

(B) amounts paid for transportation primarily for and essential to medical care referred to in subparagraph (A), and

(C) amounts paid for insurance covering medical care referred to in subparagraphs (A) and (B).

Act Sec. 706. DEFINITIONS RELATING TO HEALTH INSURANCE. (b) For purposes of this part—

(1) HEALTH INSURANCE COVERAGE. The term "health insurance coverage" means benefits consisting of medical care (provided directly, through insurance or reimbursement, or otherwise and including items and services paid for as medical care) under any hospital or medical service policy or certificate, hospital or medical service plan contract, or health maintenance organization contract offered by a health insurance issuer.

(2) HEALTH INSURANCE ISSUER. The term "health insurance issuer" means an insurance company, insurance service, or insurance organization (including a health maintenance organization, as defined in paragraph (3)) which is licensed to engage in the business of insurance in a State and which is subject to State law which regulates insurance (within the meaning of section 514(b)(2)). Such term does not include a group health plan.

(3) HEALTH MAINTENANCE ORGANIZATION. The term "health maintenance organization" means—

(A) a federally qualified health maintenance organization (as defined in section 1301(a) of the Public Health Service Act (42 U.S.C. 300e(a))),

(B) an organization recognized under State law as a health maintenance organization, or

(C) a similar organization regulated under State law for solvency in the same manner and to the same extent as such a health maintenance organization.

(4) GROUP HEALTH INSURANCE COVERAGE. The term "group health insurance coverage" means, in connection with a group health plan, health insurance coverage offered in connection with such plan.

Act Sec. 706. EXCEPTED BENEFITS. (c) For purposes of this part, the term "excepted benefits" means benefits under one or more (or any combination thereof) of the following:

(1) BENEFITS NOT SUBJECT TO REQUIREMENTS.—

(A) Coverage only for accident, or disability income insurance, or any combination thereof.

(B) Coverage issued as a supplement to liability insurance.

(C) Liability insurance, including general liability insurance and automobile liability insurance.

(D) Workers' compensation or similar insurance.

(E) Automobile medical payment insurance.

(F) Credit-only insurance.

(G) Coverage for on-site medical clinics.

(H) Other similar insurance coverage, specified in regulations, under which benefits for medical care are secondary or incidental to other insurance benefits.

(2) BENEFITS NOT SUBJECT TO REQUIREMENTS IF OFFERED SEPARATELY.—

(A) Limited scope dental or vision benefits.

(B) Benefits for long-term care, nursing home care, home health care, community-based care, or any combination thereof.

(C) Such other similar, limited benefits as are specified in regulations.

(3) BENEFITS NOT SUBJECT TO REQUIREMENTS IF OFFERED AS INDEPENDENT, NONCOORDINATED BENEFITS.—

(A) Coverage only for a specified disease or illness.

(B) Hospital indemnity or other fixed indemnity insurance.

(4) BENEFITS NOT SUBJECT TO REQUIREMENTS IF OFFERED AS SEPARATE INSURANCE POLICY. Medicare supplemental health insurance (as defined under section 1882(g)(1) of the Social Security Act), coverage supplemental to the coverage provided under chapter 55 of title 10, United States Code, and similar supplemental coverage provided to coverage under a group health plan.

Act Sec. 706. OTHER DEFINITIONS. (d) For purposes of this part—

(1) COBRA CONTINUATION PROVISION. The term "COBRA continuation provision" means any of the following:

(A) Part 6 of this subtitle.

(B) Section 4980B of the Internal Revenue Code of 1986, other than subsection (f)(1) of such section insofar as it relates to pediatric vaccines.

(C) Title XXII of the Public Health Service Act.

(2) HEALTH STATUS-RELATED FACTOR. The term "health status-related factor" means any of the factors described in section 702(a)(1).

(3) NETWORK PLAN. The term "network plan" means health insurance coverage offered by a health insurance issuer under which the financing and delivery of medical care (including items and services paid for as medical care) are provided, in whole or in part, through a defined set of providers under contract with the issuer.

(4) PLACED FOR ADOPTION. The term "placement", or being "placed", for adoption, has the meaning given such term in section 609(c)(3)(B).

Amendments

P.L. 104-204, §603(a)(3):

Redesignated ERISA Act Sec. 706 as ERISA Act Sec. 733.

The above amendment shall apply with respect to group health plans for plan years beginning on or after January 1, 1998.

P.L. 104-191, §101(a):

Added ERISA Act Sec. 706 to read as above.

The above amendments generally apply with respect to group health plans for plan years beginning after June 30, 1997. For special rules, see Act Sec. 101(g)(2)- (5), reproduced after ERISA Act Sec. 701 above.

Regulations

»»→ *Caution: Effective for plan years beginning on or after January 1, 1998, Act Sec. 707, below, is redesignated as Act Sec. 734. See ¶ 15,051D.—CCH.*

[¶ 15,050F] **Act Sec. 707.** The Secretary, consistent with section 104 of the Health Care Portability and Accountability Act of 1996, may promulgate such regulations as may be necessary or appropriate to carry out the provisions of this part. The Secretary may promulgate any interim final rules as the Secretary determines are appropriate to carry out this part.

Amendments

P.L. 104-204, §603(a)(3):

Redesignated ERISA Act Sec. 707 as ERISA Act Sec. 734.

The above amendment shall apply with respect to group health plans for plan years beginning on or after January 1, 1998.

P.L. 104-191, § 101(a):

Added ERISA Act Sec. 707 to read as above.

The above amendments generally apply with respect to group health plans for plan years beginning after June 30, 1997. For special rules, see Act Sec. 101(g)(2)-(5), reproduced after ERISA Act Sec. 701 above.

[¶ 15,050J]
STANDARDS RELATING TO BENEFITS FOR MOTHERS AND NEWBORNS

Act Sec. 711.(a) REQUIREMENTS FOR MINIMUM HOSPITAL STAY FOLLOWING BIRTH. (1) IN GENERAL. A group health plan, and a health insurance issuer offering group health insurance coverage, may not—

(A) except as provided in paragraph (2)—

(i) restrict benefits for any hospital length of stay in connection with childbirth for the mother or newborn child, following a normal vaginal delivery, to less than 48 hours, or

(ii) restrict benefits for any hospital length of stay in connection with childbirth for the mother or newborn child, following a cesarean section, to less than 96 hours; or

(B) require that a provider obtain authorization from the plan or the issuer for prescribing any length of stay required under subparagraph (A) (without regard to paragraph (2)).

(2) EXCEPTION. Paragraph (1)(A) shall not apply in connection with any group health plan or health insurance issuer in any case in which the decision to discharge the mother or her newborn child prior to the expiration of the minimum length of stay otherwise required under paragraph (1)(A) is made by an attending provider in consultation with the mother.

Act Sec. 711. PROHIBITIONS. (b) A group health plan, and a health insurance issuer offering group health insurance coverage in connection with a group health plan, may not—

(1) deny to the mother or her newborn child eligibility, or continued eligibility, to enroll or to renew coverage under the terms of the plan, solely for the purpose of avoiding the requirements of this section;

(2) provide monetary payments or rebates to mothers to encourage such mothers to accept less than the minimum protections available under this section;

(3) penalize or otherwise reduce or limit the reimbursement of an attending provider because such provider provided care to an individual participant or beneficiary in accordance with this section;

(4) provide incentives (monetary or otherwise) to an attending provider to induce such provider to provide care to an individual participant or beneficiary in a manner inconsistent with this section; or

(5) subject to subsection (c)(3), restrict benefits for any portion of a period within a hospital length of stay required under subsection (a) in a manner which is less favorable than the benefits provided for any preceding portion of such stay.

Act Sec. 711. RULES OF CONSTRUCTION.—

(c)(1) Nothing in this section shall be construed to require a mother who is a participant or beneficiary—

(A) to give birth in a hospital; or

(B) to stay in the hospital for a fixed period of time following the birth of her child.

(2) This section shall not apply with respect to any group health plan, or any group health insurance coverage offered by a health insurance issuer, which does not provide benefits for hospital lengths of stay in connection with childbirth for a mother or her newborn child.

(3) Nothing in this section shall be construed as preventing a group health plan or issuer from imposing deductibles, coinsurance, or other cost-sharing in relation to benefits for hospital lengths of stay in connection with childbirth for a mother or newborn child under the plan (or under health insurance coverage offered in connection with a group health plan), except that such coinsurance or other cost-sharing for any portion of a period within a hospital length of stay required under subsection (a) may not be greater than such coinsurance or cost-sharing for any preceding portion of such stay.

Act Sec. 711. NOTICE UNDER GROUP HEALTH PLAN. (d) The imposition of the requirements of this section shall be treated as a material modification in the terms of the plan described in section 102(a)(1), for purposes of assuring notice of such requirements under the plan; except that the summary description required to be provided under the last sentence of section 104(b)(1) with respect to such modification shall be provided by not later than 60 days after the first day of the first plan year in which such requirements apply.

Act Sec. 711. LEVEL AND TYPE OF REIMBURSEMENTS. (e) Nothing in this section shall be construed to prevent a group health plan or a health insurance issuer offering group health insurance coverage from negotiating the level and type of reimbursement with a provider for care provided in accordance with this section.

Act Sec. 711. PREEMPTION; EXCEPTION FOR HEALTH INSURANCE COVERAGE IN CERTAIN STATES.—

(f)(1) IN GENERAL. The requirements of this section shall not apply with respect to health insurance coverage if there is a State law (as defined in section 731(d)(1)) for a State that regulates such coverage that is described in any of the following subparagraphs:

(A) Such State law requires such coverage to provide for at least a 48-hour hospital length of stay following a normal vaginal delivery and at least a 96-hour hospital length of stay following a cesarean section.

(B) Such State law requires such coverage to provide for maternity and pediatric care in accordance with guidelines established by the American College of Obstetricians and Gynecologists, the American Academy of Pediatrics, or other established professional medical associations.

(C) Such State law requires, in connection with such coverage for maternity care, that the hospital length of stay for such care is left to the decision of (or required to be made by) the attending provider in consultation with the mother.

(2) CONSTRUCTION. Section 731(a)(1) shall not be construed as superseding a State law described in paragraph (1).

Amendments

P.L. 104-204, § 603(a)(5):

Added ERISA Sec. 711 to read as above.

The above amendment shall apply with respect to group health plans for plan years beginning on or after January 1, 1998.

Regulations

The following regulations were adopted by 62 FR 16894 and published in the Federal Register on April 8, 1997, under "Chapter XXV of Title 29 of the Code of Federal Regulations; Subchapter L—Health Insurance Portability and Renewability for Group Health Plans; Part 2590—Rules and Regulations for Health Insurance Portability and Renewability for Group Health Plans." The regulations were amended by 63 FR 5745 and published in the Federal Register on October 27, 1998. The heading was revised by T.D. 9166 (69 FR 78720) on December 30, 2004.

Subpart B—Health Coverage Portability, Nondiscrimination, and Renewability

[¶ 15,050J-1]

§ 2590.711 **Standards relating to benefits for mothers and newborns**.

(a) *Hospital length of stay.* (1) *General rule.* Except as provided in paragraph (a)(5) of this section, a group health plan, or a health insurance issuer offering group health insurance coverage, that provides benefits for a hospital length of stay in connection with childbirth for a mother or her newborn may not restrict benefits for the stay to less than—

    (i) 48 hours following a vaginal delivery; or

    (ii) 96 hours following a delivery by cesarean section.

(2) *When stay begins.* (i) *Delivery in a hospital.* If delivery occurs in a hospital, the hospital length of stay for the mother or newborn child begins at the time of delivery (or in the case of multiple births, at the time of the last delivery).

    (ii) *Delivery outside a hospital.* If delivery occurs outside a hospital, the hospital length of stay begins at the time the mother or newborn is admitted as a hospital inpatient in connection with childbirth. The determination of whether an admission is in connection with childbirth is a medical decision to be made by the attending provider.

(3) *Examples.* The rules of paragraphs (a)(1) and (2) of this section are illustrated by the following examples. In each example, the group health plan provides benefits for hospital lengths of stay in connection with childbirth and is subject to the requirements of this section, as follows:

    Example 1. (i) A pregnant woman covered under a group health plan goes into labor and is admitted to the hospital at 10 p.m. on June 11. She gives birth by vaginal delivery at 6 a.m. on June 12.

    (ii) In this *Example 1*, the 48-hour period described in paragraph (a)(1)(i) of this section ends at 6 a.m. on June 14.

    Example 2. (i) A woman covered under a group health plan gives birth at home by vaginal delivery. After the delivery, the woman begins bleeding excessively in connection with the childbirth and is admitted to the hospital for treatment of the excessive bleeding at 7 p.m. on October 1.

    (ii) In this *Example 2*, the 48-hour period described in paragraph (a)(1)(i) of this section ends at 7 p.m. on October 3.

    Example 3. (i) A woman covered under a group health plan gives birth by vaginal delivery at home. The child later develops pneumonia and is admitted to the hospital. The attending provider determines that the admission is not in connection with childbirth.

    (ii) In this *Example 3*, the hospital length-of-stay requirements of this section do not apply to the child's admission to the hospital because the admission is not in connection with childbirth.

(4) *Authorization not required.* (i) *In general.* A plan or issuer may not require that a physician or other health care provider obtain authorization from the plan or issuer for prescribing the hospital length of stay required under paragraph (a)(1) of this section. (*See also* paragraphs (b)(2) and (c)(3) of this section for rules and examples regarding other authorization and certain notice requirements.)

    (ii) *Example.* The rule of this paragraph (a)(4) is illustrated by the following example:

    Example. (i) In the case of a delivery by cesarean section, a group health plan subject to the requirements of this section automatically provides benefits for any hospital length of stay of up to 72 hours. For any longer stay, the plan requires an attending provider to complete a certificate of medical necessity. The plan then makes a determination, based on the certificate of medical necessity, whether a longer stay is medically necessary.

    (ii) In this *Example*, the requirement that an attending provider complete a certificate of medical necessity to obtain authorization for the period between 72 hours and 96 hours following a delivery by cesarean section is prohibited by this paragraph (a)(4).

(5) *Exceptions.* (i) *Discharge of mother.* If a decision to discharge a mother earlier than the period specified in paragraph (a)(1) of this section is made by an attending provider, in consultation with the mother, the requirements of paragraph (a)(1) of this section do not apply for any period after the discharge.

    (ii) *Discharge of newborn.* If a decision to discharge a newborn child earlier than the period specified in paragraph (a)(1) of this section is made by an attending provider, in consultation with the mother (or the newborn's authorized representative), the requirements of paragraph (a)(1) of this section do not apply for any period after the discharge.

    (iii) *Attending provider defined.* For purposes of this section, *attending provider* means an individual who is licensed under applicable State law to provide maternity or pediatric care and who is directly responsible for providing maternity or pediatric care to a mother or newborn child.

    (iv) *Example.* The rules of this paragraph (a)(5) are illustrated by the following example:

    Example. (i) A pregnant woman covered under a group health plan subject to the requirements of this section goes into labor and is admitted to a hospital. She gives birth by cesarean section. On the third day after the delivery, the attending provider for the mother consults with the mother, and the attending provider for the newborn consults with the mother regarding the newborn. The attending providers authorize the early discharge of both the mother and the newborn. Both are discharged approximately 72 hours after the delivery. The plan pays for the 72-hour hospital stays.

    (ii) In this *Example*, the requirements of this paragraph (a) have been satisfied with respect to the mother and the newborn. If either is readmitted, the hospital stay for the readmission is not subject to this section.

(b) *Prohibitions.* (1) *With respect to mothers.* (i) *In general.* A group health plan, and a health insurance issuer offering group health insurance coverage, may not—

    (A) Deny a mother or her newborn child eligibility or continued eligibility to enroll or renew coverage under the terms of the plan solely to avoid the requirements of this section; or

    (B) Provide payments (including payments-in-kind) or rebates to a mother to encourage her to accept less than the minimum protections available under this section.

    (ii) *Examples.* The rules of this paragraph (b)(1) are illustrated by the following examples. In each example, the group health plan is subject to the requirements of this section, as follows:

    Example 1. (i) A group health plan provides benefits for at least a 48-hour hospital length of stay following a vaginal delivery. If a mother and newborn covered under the plan are discharged within 24 hours after the delivery, the plan will waive the copayment and deductible.

    (ii) In this *Example 1*, because waiver of the copayment and deductible is in the nature of a rebate that the mother would not receive if she and her newborn remained in the hospital, it is prohibited by this paragraph (b)(1). (In addition, the plan violates paragraph (b)(2) of this section because, in effect, no copayment or deductible is required for the first portion of the stay and a double copayment and a deductible are required for the second portion of the stay.)

    Example 2. (i) A group health plan provides benefits for at least a 48-hour hospital length of stay following a vaginal delivery. In the event that a mother and her newborn are discharged earlier than 48 hours and the discharges occur after consultation with the mother in accordance with the requirements of paragraph (a)(5) of this section, the plan provides for a follow-up visit by a nurse within 48 hours after the discharges to provide certain services that the mother and her newborn would otherwise receive in the hospital.

    (ii) In this *Example 2*, because the follow-up visit does not provide any services beyond what the mother and her newborn would receive in the hospital, coverage for the follow-up visit is not prohibited by this paragraph (b)(1).

(2) *With respect to benefit restrictions.* (i) *In general.* Subject to paragraph (c)(3) of this section, a group health plan, and a health insurance issuer offering group health insurance coverage, may not restrict the benefits for any portion of a hospital length of stay required under paragraph (a) of this section in a manner that is less favorable than the benefits provided for any preceding portion of the stay.

(ii) *Example.* The rules of this paragraph (b)(2) are illustrated by the following example:

Example. (i) A group health plan subject to the requirements of this section provides benefits for hospital lengths of stay in connection with childbirth. In the case of a delivery by cesarean section, the plan automatically pays for the first 48 hours. With respect to each succeeding 24-hour period, the participant or beneficiary must call the plan to obtain precertification from a utilization reviewer, who determines if an additional 24-hour period is medically necessary. If this approval is not obtained, the plan will not provide benefits for any succeeding 24-hour period.

(ii) In this *Example*, the requirement to obtain precertification for the two 24-hour periods immediately following the initial 48-hour stay is prohibited by this paragraph (b)(2) because benefits for the latter part of the stay are restricted in a manner that is less favorable than benefits for a preceding portion of the stay. (However, this section does not prohibit a plan from requiring precertification for any period after the first 96 hours.) In addition, if the plan's utilization reviewer denied any mother or her newborn benefits within the 96-hour stay, the plan would also violate paragraph (a) of this section.

(3) *With respect to attending providers.* A group health plan, and a health insurance issuer offering group health insurance coverage, may not directly or indirectly—

(i) Penalize (for example, take disciplinary action against or retaliate against), or otherwise reduce or limit the compensation of, an attending provider because the provider furnished care to a participant or beneficiary in accordance with this section; or

(ii) Provide monetary or other incentives to an attending provider to induce the provider to furnish care to a participant or beneficiary in a manner inconsistent with this section, including providing any incentive that could induce an attending provider to discharge a mother or newborn earlier than 48 hours (or 96 hours) after delivery.

(c) *Construction.* With respect to this section, the following rules of construction apply:

(1) *Hospital stays not mandatory.* This section does not require a mother to—

(i) Give birth in a hospital; or

(ii) Stay in the hospital for a fixed period of time following the birth of her child.

(2) *Hospital stay benefits not mandated.* This section does not apply to any group health plan, or any group health insurance coverage, that does not provide benefits for hospital lengths of stay in connection with childbirth for a mother or her newborn child.

(3) *Cost-sharing rules.* (i) *In general.* This section does not prevent a group health plan or a health insurance issuer offering group health insurance coverage from imposing deductibles, coinsurance, or other cost-sharing in relation to benefits for hospital lengths of stay in connection with childbirth for a mother or a newborn under the plan or coverage, except that the coinsurance or other cost-sharing for any portion of the hospital length of stay required under paragraph (a) of this section may not be greater than that for any preceding portion of the stay.

(ii) *Examples.* The rules of this paragraph (c)(3) are illustrated by the following examples. In each example, the group health plan is subject to the requirements of this section, as follows:

Example 1. (i) A group health plan provides benefits for at least a 48-hour hospital length of stay in connection with vaginal deliveries. The plan covers 80 percent of the cost of the stay for the first 24-hour period and 50 percent of the cost of the stay for the second 24-hour period. Thus, the coinsurance paid by the patient increases from 20 percent to 50 percent after 24 hours.

(ii) In this *Example 1*, the plan violates the rules of this paragraph (c)(3) because coinsurance for the second 24-hour period of the 48-hour stay is greater than that for the preceding portion of the stay. (In addition, the plan also violates the similar rule in paragraph (b)(2) of this section.)

Example 2. (i) A group health plan generally covers 70 percent of the cost of a hospital length of stay in connection with childbirth. However, the plan will cover 80 percent of the cost of the stay if the participant or beneficiary notifies the plan of the pregnancy in advance of admission and uses whatever hospital the plan may designate.

(ii) In this *Example 2*, the plan does not violate the rules of this paragraph (c)(3) because the level of benefits provided (70 percent or 80 percent) is consistent throughout the 48-hour (or 96-hour) hospital length of stay required under paragraph (a) of this section. (In addition, the plan does not violate the rules in paragraph (a)(4) or (b)(2) of this section.)

(4) *Compensation of attending provider.* This section does not prevent a group health plan or a health insurance issuer offering group health insurance coverage from negotiating with an attending provider the level and type of compensation for care furnished in accordance with this section (including paragraph (b) of this section).

(d) *Notice requirement.* See 29 CFR 2520.102-3(u) and (v)(2) (relating to the disclosure requirement under section 711(d) of the Act).

(e) *Applicability in certain States.* (1) *Health insurance coverage.* The requirements of section 711 of the Act and this section do not apply with respect to health insurance coverage offered in connection with a group health plan if there is a State law regulating the coverage that meets any of the following criteria:

(i) The State law requires the coverage to provide for at least a 48-hour hospital length of stay following a vaginal delivery and at least a 96-hour hospital length of stay following a delivery by cesarean section.

(ii) The State law requires the coverage to provide for maternity and pediatric care in accordance with guidelines established by the American College of Obstetricians and Gynecologists, the American Academy of Pediatrics, or any other established professional medical association.

(iii) The State law requires, in connection with the coverage for maternity care, that the hospital length of stay for such care is left to the decision of (or is required to be made by) the attending provider in consultation with the mother. State laws that require the decision to be made by the attending provider with the consent of the mother satisfy the criterion of this paragraph (e)(1)(iii).

(2) *Group health plans.* (i) *Fully-insured plans.* For a group health plan that provides benefits solely through health insurance coverage, if the State law regulating the health insurance coverage meets any of the criteria in paragraph (e)(1) of this section, then the requirements of section 711 of the Act and this section do not apply.

(ii) *Self-insured plans.* For a group health plan that provides all benefits for hospital lengths of stay in connection with childbirth other than through health insurance coverage, the requirements of section 711 of the Act and this section apply.

(iii) *Partially-insured plans.* For a group health plan that provides some benefits through health insurance coverage, if the State law regulating the health insurance coverage meets any of the criteria in paragraph (e)(1) of this section, then the requirements of section 711 of the Act and this section apply only to the extent the plan provides benefits for hospital lengths of stay in connection with childbirth other than through health insurance coverage.

(3) *Relation to section 731(a) of the Act.* The preemption provisions contained in section 731(a)(1) of the Act and § 2590.731(a) do not supersede a State law described in paragraph (e)(1) of this section.

(4) *Examples.* The rules of this paragraph (e) are illustrated by the following examples:

Example 1. (i) A group health plan buys group health insurance coverage in a State that requires that the coverage provide for at least a

48-hour hospital length of stay following a vaginal delivery and at least a 96-hour hospital length of stay following a delivery by cesarean section.

(ii) In this *Example 1*, the coverage is subject to State law, and the requirements of section 711 of the Act and this section do not apply.

Example 2. (i) A self-insured group health plan covers hospital lengths of stay in connection with childbirth in a State that requires health insurance coverage to provide for maternity care in accordance with guidelines established by the American College of Obstetricians and Gynecologists and to provide for pediatric care in accordance with guidelines established by the American Academy of Pediatrics.

(ii) In this *Example 2*, even though the State law satisfies the criterion of paragraph (e)(1)(ii) of this section, because the plan provides benefits for hospital lengths of stay in connection with childbirth other than through health insurance coverage, the plan is subject to the requirements of section 711 of the Act and this section.

(f) *Effective date.* Section 711 of the Act applies to group health plans, and health insurance issuers offering group health insurance coverage, for plan years beginning on or after January 1, 1998. This section applies to group health plans, and health insurance issuers offering group health insurance coverage, for plan years beginning on or after January 1, 1999.

[¶ 15,050K]
PARITY IN THE APPLICATION OF CERTAIN LIMITS TO MENTAL HEALTH BENEFITS

Act Sec. 712.(a) IN GENERAL. (1) Aggregate lifetime limits. In the case of a group health plan (or health insurance coverage offered in connection with such a plan) that provides both medical and surgical benefits and mental health benefits—

(A) NO LIFETIME LIMIT. If the plan or coverage does not include an aggregate lifetime limit on substantially all medical and surgical benefits, the plan or coverage may not impose any aggregate lifetime limit on mental health benefits.

(B) LIFETIME LIMIT. If the plan or coverage includes an aggregate lifetime limit on substantially all medical and surgical benefits (in this paragraph referred to as the "applicable lifetime limit"), the plan or coverage shall either—

(i) apply the applicable lifetime limit both to the medical and surgical benefits to which it otherwise would apply and to mental health benefits and not distinguish in the application of such limit between such medical and surgical benefits and mental health benefits; or

(ii) not include any aggregate lifetime limit on mental health benefits that is less than the applicable lifetime limit.

(C) RULE IN CASE OF DIFFERENT LIMITS. In the case of a plan or coverage that is not described in subparagraph (A) or (B) and that includes no or different aggregate lifetime limits on different categories of medical and surgical benefits, the Secretary shall establish rules under which subparagraph (B) is applied to such plan or coverage with respect to mental health benefits by substituting for the applicable lifetime limit an average aggregate lifetime limit that is computed taking into account the weighted average of the aggregate lifetime limits applicable to such categories.

(2) ANNUAL LIMITS. In the case of a group health plan (or health insurance coverage offered in connection with such a plan) that provides both medical and surgical benefits and mental health benefits—

(A) NO ANNUAL LIMIT. If the plan or coverage does not include an annual limit on substantially all medical and surgical benefits, the plan or coverage may not impose any annual limit on mental health benefits.

(B) ANNUAL LIMIT. If the plan or coverage includes an annual limit on substantially all medical and surgical benefits (in this paragraph referred to as the "applicable annual limit"), the plan or coverage shall either—

(i) apply the applicable annual limit both to medical and surgical benefits to which it otherwise would apply and to mental health benefits and not distinguish in the application of such limit between such medical and surgical benefits and mental health benefits; or

(ii) not include any annual limit on mental health benefits that is less than the applicable annual limit.

(C) RULE IN CASE OF DIFFERENT LIMITS. In the case of a plan or coverage that is not described in subparagraph (A) or (B) and that includes no or different annual limits on different categories of medical and surgical benefits, the Secretary shall establish rules under which subparagraph (B) is applied to such plan or coverage with respect to mental health benefits by substituting for the applicable annual limit an average annual limit that is computed taking into account the weighted average of the annual limits applicable to such categories.

Act Sec. 712. CONSTRUCTION. (b) Nothing in this section shall be construed—

(1) as requiring a group health plan (or health insurance coverage offered in connection with such a plan) to provide any mental health benefits; or

(2) in the case of a group health plan (or health insurance coverage offered in connection with such a plan) that provides mental health benefits, as affecting the terms and conditions (including cost sharing, limits on numbers of visits or days of coverage, and requirements relating to medical necessity) relating to the amount, duration, or scope of mental health benefits under the plan or coverage, except as specifically provided in subsection (a) (in regard to parity in the imposition of aggregate lifetime limits and annual limits for mental health benefits).

Act Sec. 712. EXEMPTIONS.—

(c)(1) SMALL EMPLOYER EXEMPTION.—

(A) IN GENERAL. This section shall not apply to any group health plan (and group health insurance coverage offered in connection with a group health plan) for any plan year of a small employer.

(B) SMALL EMPLOYER. For purposes of subparagraph (A), the term "small employer" means, in connection with a group health plan with respect to a calendar year and a plan year, an employer who employed an average of at least 2 but not more than 50 employees on business days during the preceding calendar year and who employs at least 2 employees on the first day of the plan year.

(C) APPLICATION OF CERTAIN RULES IN DETERMINATION OF EMPLOYER SIZE. For purposes of this paragraph—

(i) APPLICATION OF AGGREGATION RULE FOR EMPOYERS. Rules similar to the rules under subsections (b), (c), (m), and (o) of section 414 of the Internal Revenue Code of 1986 shall apply for purposes of treating persons as a single employer.

(ii) EMPLOYERS NOT IN EXISTENCE IN PRECEDING YEAR. In the case of an employer which was not in existence throughout the preceding calendar year, the determination of whether such employer is a small employer shall be based on the average number of employees that it is reasonably expected such employer will employ on business days in the current calendar year.

(iii) PREDECESSORS. Any reference in this paragraph to an employer shall include a reference to any predecessor of such employer.

(2) INCREASED COST EXEMPTION. This section shall not apply with respect to a group health plan (or health insurance coverage offered in connection with a group health plan) if the application of this section to such plan (or to such coverage) results in an increase in the cost under the plan (or for such coverage) of at least 1 percent.

Act Sec. 712. SEPARATE APPLICATION TO EACH OPTION OFFERED. (d) In the case of a group health plan that offers a participant or beneficiary two or more benefit package options under the plan, the requirements of this section shall be applied separately with respect to each such option.

Act Sec. 712. DEFINITIONS. (e) For purposes of this section—

(1) AGGREGATE LIFETIME LIMIT. The term "aggregate lifetime limit" means, with respect to benefits under a group health plan or health insurance coverage, a dollar limitation on the total amount that may be paid with respect to such benefits under the plan or health insurance coverage with respect to an individual or other coverage unit.

(2) ANNUAL LIMIT. The term "annual limit" means, with respect to benefits under a group health plan or health insurance coverage, a dollar limitation on the total amount of benefits that may be paid with respect to such benefits in a 12-month period under the plan or health insurance coverage with respect to an individual or other coverage unit.

(3) MEDICAL OR SURGICAL BENEFITS. The term "medical or surgical benefits" means benefits with respect to medical or surgical services, as defined under the terms of the plan or coverage (as the case may be), but does not include mental health benefits.

(4) MENTAL HEALTH BENEFITS. The term "mental health benefits" means benefits with respect to mental health services, as defined under the terms of the plan or coverage (as the case may be), but does not include benefits with respect to treatment of substance abuse or chemical dependency.

Act Sec. 712. SUNSET. (f) This section shall not apply to benefits for services furnished after December 31, 2006.

Amendments

P.L. 109-151, § 1(a)

Act Sec. 1(a) amended ERISA § 712(f) by striking "December 31, 2005" and inserting "December 31, 2006."

The above amendment is effective on the date of enactment of this Act (December 30, 2005).

P.L. 108-311, § 302(b):

Amended ERISA § 712 by striking "on or after December 31, 2004" and inserting "after December 31, 2005".

The above amendment is effective on October 4, 2004 (the date of enactment of P.L. 108-311).

P.L. 108-197, § 2:

Amended ERISA Sec. 712 (f) by striking "December 31, 2003," and inserting "December 31, 2004."

P.L. 107-313, § 2:

Amended ERISA Sec. 712 (f) by striking "December 31, 2002," and inserting "December 31, 2003."

P.L. 107-116, § 701(a):

Amended ERISA Sec. 712(f) by striking "September 30, 2001," and inserting "December 31, 2002."

P.L. 104-204, § 702(a):

Added ERISA Sec. 712 to read as above.

The above amendment shall apply with respect to group health plans for plan years beginning on or after January 1, 1998.

Regulations

The following regulations were adopted by 62 FR 16894 and published in the *Federal Register* on April 8, 1997, under "Chapter XXV of Title 29 of the Code of Federal Regulations; Subchapter L—Health Insurance Portability and Renewability for Group Health Plans; Part 2590—Rules and Regulations for Health Insurance Portability and Renewability for Group Health Plans." Reg. § 2590.712 was amended by T.D. 8741, which was published in the *Federal Register* on Dec. 22, 1997 (62 FR 66932) and was amended on Sept. 27, 2002 (67 FR 60859), on April 14, 2003 (68 FR 18048), on January 26, 2004 (69 FR 3815), and on December 17, 2004 (69 FR 75797).

[¶ 15,050K-1]

§ 2590.712 **Parity in the application of certain limits to mental health benefits.**

(a) *Definitions.* For purposes of this section, except where the context clearly indicates otherwise, the following definitions apply:

Aggregate lifetime limit means a dollar limitation on the total amount of specified benefits that may be paid under a group health plan (or group health insurance coverage offered in connection with such a plan) for an individual (or for a group of individuals considered a single unit in applying this dollar limitation, such as a family or an employee plus spouse).

Annual limit means a dollar limitation on the total amount of specified benefits that may be paid in a 12-month period under a plan (or group health insurance coverage offered in connection with such a plan) for an individual (or for a group of individuals considered a single unit in applying this dollar limitation, such as a family or an employee plus spouse).

Medical/surgical benefits means benefits for medical or surgical services, as defined under the terms of the plan or group health insurance coverage, but does not include mental health benefits.

Mental health benefits means benefits for mental health services, as defined under the terms of the plan or group health insurance coverage, but does not include benefits for treatment of substance abuse or chemical dependency.

(b) *Requirements regarding limits on benefits.* (1) *In general.* (i) *General parity requirement.* A group health plan (or health insurance coverage offered by an issuer in connection with a group health plan) that provides both medical/surgical benefits and mental health benefits must comply with paragraph (b)(2), (3), or (6) of this section.

(ii) *Exception.* The rule in paragraph (b)(1)(i) of this section does not apply if a plan, or coverage, satisfies the requirements of paragraph (e) or (f) of this section.

(2) *Plan with no limit or limits on less than one-third of all medical/surgical benefits.* If a plan (or group health insurance coverage) does not include an aggregate lifetime or annual limit on any medical/surgical benefits or includes aggregate lifetime or annual limits that apply to less than one-third of all medical/surgical benefits, it may not impose an aggregate lifetime or annual limit, respectively, on mental health benefits.

(3) *Plan with a limit on at least two-thirds of all medical/surgical benefits.* If a plan (or group health insurance coverage) includes an aggregate lifetime or annual limit on at least two-thirds of all medical/surgical benefits, it must either—

(i) Apply the aggregate lifetime or annual limit both to the medical/surgical benefits to which the limit would otherwise apply and to mental health benefits in a manner that does not distinguish between the medical/surgical and mental health benefits; or

(ii) Not include an aggregate lifetime or annual limit on mental health benefits that is less than the aggregate lifetime or annual limit, respectively, on the medical/surgical benefits.

(4) *Examples.* The rules of paragraphs (b)(2) and (3) of this section are illustrated by the following examples:

Example 1. (i) Prior to the effective date of the mental health parity provisions, a group health plan had no annual limit on medical/surgical benefits and had a $10,000 annual limit on mental health benefits. To comply with the parity requirements of this paragraph (b), the plan sponsor is considering each of the following options:

(A) Eliminating the plan's annual limit on mental health benefits;

(B) Replacing the plan's previous annual limit on mental health benefits with a $500,000 annual limit on all benefits (including medical/surgical and mental health benefits); and

(C) Replacing the plan's previous annual limit on mental health benefits with a $250,000 annual limit on medical/surgical benefits and a $250,000 annual limit on mental health benefits.

(ii) In this *Example 1*, each of the three options being considered by the plan sponsor would comply with the requirements of this section because they offer parity in the dollar limits placed on medical/surgical and mental health benefits.

Example 2. (i) Prior to the effective date of the mental health parity provisions, a group health plan had a $100,000 annual limit on medical/surgical inpatient benefits, a $50,000 annual limit on medical/surgical outpatient benefits, and a $100,000 annual limit on all mental health benefits. To comply with the parity requirements of this paragraph (b), the plan sponsor is considering each of the following options:

(A) Replacing the plan's previous annual limit on mental health benefits with a $150,000 annual limit on mental health benefits; and

(B) Replacing the plan's previous annual limit on mental health benefits with a $100,000 annual limit on mental health inpatient benefits and a $50,000 annual limit on mental health outpatient benefits.

(ii) In this *Example 2*, each option under consideration by the plan sponsor would comply with the requirements of this section because they offer parity in the dollar limits placed on medical/surgical and mental health benefits.

Example 3. (i) A group health plan that is subject to the requirements of this section has no aggregate lifetime or annual limit for either medical/surgical benefits or mental health benefits. While the plan provides medical/surgical benefits with respect to both network and out-of-network providers, it does not provide mental health benefits with respect to out-of-network providers.

(ii) In this *Example 3*, the plan complies with the requirements of this section because they offer parity in the dollar limits placed on medical/surgical and mental health benefits.

Example 4. (i) Prior to the effective date of the mental health parity provisions, a group health plan had an annual limit on medical/surgical benefits and a separate but identical annual limit on mental health benefits. The plan included benefits for treatment of substance abuse and chemical dependency in its definition of mental health benefits. Accordingly, claims paid for treatment of substance abuse and chemical dependency were counted in applying the annual limit on mental health benefits. To comply with the parity requirements of this paragraph (b), the plan sponsor is considering each of the following options:

(A) Making no change in the plan so that claims paid for treatment of substance abuse and chemical dependency continue to count in applying the annual limit on mental health benefits;

(B) amending the plan to count claims paid for treatment of substance abuse and chemical dependency in applying the annual limit on medical/surgical benefits (rather than counting those claims in applying the annual limit on mental health benefits);

(C) amending the plan to provide a new category of benefits for treatment of chemical dependency and substance abuse that is subject to a separate, lower limit and under which claims paid for treatment of substance abuse and chemical dependency are counted only in applying the annual limit on this separate category; and

(D) amending the plan to eliminate distinctions between medical/surgical benefits and mental health benefits and establishing an overall limit on benefits offered under the plan under which claims paid for treatment of substance abuse and chemical dependency are counted with medical/surgical benefits and mental health benefits in applying the overall limit.

(ii) In this *Example 4*, the group health plan is described in paragraph (b)(3) of this section. Because mental health benefits are defined in paragraph (a) of this section as excluding benefits for treatment of substance abuse and chemical dependency, the inclusion of benefits for treatment of substance abuse and chemical dependency in applying an aggregate lifetime limit or annual limit on mental health benefits under option (A) of this *Example 4* would not comply with the requirements of paragraph (b)(3) of this section. However, options (B), (C), and (D) of this *Example 4* would comply with the requirements of paragraph (b)(3) of this section because they offer parity in the dollar limits placed on medical/surgical and mental health benefits.

(5) *Determining one-third and two-thirds of all medical/surgical benefits.* For purposes of this paragraph (b), the determination of whether the portion of medical/surgical benefits subject to a limit represents one-third or two-thirds of all medical/surgical benefits is based on the dollar amount of all plan payments for medical/surgical benefits expected to be paid under the plan for the plan year (or for the portion of the plan year after a change in plan benefits that affects the applicability of the aggregate lifetime or annual limits). Any reasonable method may be used to determine whether the dollar amounts expected to be paid under the plan will constitute one-third or two-thirds of the dollar amount of all plan payments for medical/surgical benefits.

(6) *Plan not described in paragraph (b)(2) or (3) of this section.* (i) *In general.* A group health plan (or group health insurance coverage) that is not described in paragraph (b)(2) or (3) of this section, must either—

(A) Impose no aggregate lifetime or annual limit, as appropriate, on mental health benefits; or

(B) Impose an aggregate lifetime or annual limit on mental health benefits that is no less than an average limit calculated for medical/surgical benefits in the following manner. The average limit is calculated by taking into account the weighted average of the aggregate lifetime or annual limits, as appropriate, that are applicable to the categories of medical/surgical benefits. Limits based on delivery systems, such as inpatient/outpatient treatment or normal treatment of common, low-cost conditions (such as treatment of normal births), do not constitute categories for purposes of this paragraph (b)(6)(i)(B). In addition, for purposes of determining weighted averages, any benefits that are not within a category that is subject to a separately-designated limit under the plan are taken into account as a single separate category by using an estimate of the upper limit on the dollar amount that a plan may reasonably be expected to incur with respect to such benefits, taking into account any other applicable restrictions under the plan.

(ii) *Weighting.* For purposes of this paragraph (b)(6), the weighting applicable to any category of medical/surgical benefits is determined in the manner set forth in paragraph (b)(5) of this section for determining one-third or two-thirds of all medical/surgical benefits.

(iii) *Example.* The rules of this paragraph (b)(6) are illustrated by the following example:

Example. (i) A group health plan that is subject to the requirements of this section includes a $100,000 annual limit on medical/surgical benefits related to cardio-pulmonary diseases. The plan does not include an annual limit on any other category of medical/surgical benefits. The plan determines that 40% of the dollar amount of plan payments for medical/surgical benefits are related to cardio-pulmonary diseases. The plan determines that $1,000,000 is a reasonable estimate of the upper limit on the dollar amount that the plan may incur with respect to the other 60% of payments for medical/surgical benefits.

(ii) In this *Example*, the plan is not described in paragraph (b)(3) of this section because there is not one annual limit that applies to at least two-thirds of all medical/surgical benefits. Further, the plan is not described in paragraph (b)(2) of this section because more than one-third of all medical/surgical benefits are subject to an annual limit. Under this paragraph (b)(6), the plan sponsor can choose either to include no annual limit on mental health benefits, or to include an annual limit on mental health benefits that is not less than the weighted average of the annual limits applicable to each category of medical/surgical benefits. In this example, the minimum weighted average annual limit that can be applied to mental health benefits is $640,000 (40% × $100,000 + 60% × $1,000,000 = $640,000).

(c) *Rule in the case of separate benefit packages.* If a group health plan offers two or more benefit packages, the requirements of this section, including the exemption provisions in paragraph (f) of this section, apply separately to each benefit package. Examples of a group health plan that offers two or more benefit packages include a group health plan that offers employees a choice between indemnity coverage or HMO coverage, and a group health plan that provides one benefit package for retirees and a different benefit package for current employees.

(d) *Applicability.* (1) *Group health plans.* The requirements of this section apply to a group health plan offering both medical/surgical benefits and mental health benefits regardless of whether the mental health benefits are administered separately under the plan.

(2) *Health insurance issuers.* The requirements of this section apply to a health insurance issuer offering health insurance coverage for both medical/surgical benefits and mental health benefits in connection with a group health plan.

(3) *Scope.* This section does not—

(i) Require a group health plan (or health insurance issuer offering coverage in connection with a group health plan) to provide any mental health benefits; or

(ii) Affect the terms and conditions (including cost sharing, limits on the number of visits or days of coverage, requirements relating to medical necessity, requiring prior authorization for treatment, or requiring primary care physicians' referrals for treatment) relating to the amount, duration, or scope of the mental health benefits under the plan (or coverage) except as specifically provided in paragraph (b) of this section.

(e) *Small employer exemption.* (1) *In general.* The requirements of this section do not apply to a group health plan (or health insurance issuer offering coverage in connection with a group health plan) for a plan year of a small employer. For purposes of this paragraph (e), the term *small employer* means, in connection with a group health plan with respect to a calendar year and a plan year, an employer who employed an average of at least two but not more than 50 employees on business days during the preceding calendar year and who employs at least two employees on the first day of the plan year. See section 732(a) of the Act and § 2590.732(a), which provide that this section (and certain other sections) does not apply to any group health plan (and health insurance issuer offering coverage in connection with a group health plan) for any plan year if, on the first day of the plan year, the plan has fewer than two participants who are current employees.

(2) *Rules in determining employer size.* For purposes of paragraph (e)(1) of this section—

(i) All persons treated as a single employer under subsections (b), (c), (m), and (o) of section 414 of the Internal Revenue Code of 1986 (26 U.S.C. 414) are treated as one employer;

(ii) If an employer was not in existence throughout the preceding calendar year, whether it is a small employer is determined based on the average number of employees the employer reasonably expects to employ on business days during the current calendar year; and

(iii) Any reference to an employer for purposes of the small employer exemption includes a reference to a predecessor of the employer.

(f) *Increased cost exemption.* (1) *In general.* A group health plan (or health insurance coverage offered in connection with a group health plan) is not subject to the requirements of this section if the requirements of this paragraph (f) are satisfied. If a plan offers more than one benefit package, this paragraph (f) applies separately to each benefit package. Except as provided in paragraph (h) of this section, a plan must comply with the requirements of paragraph (b)(1)(i) of this section for the first plan year beginning on or after January 1, 1998, and must continue to comply with the requirements of paragraph (b)(1)(i) of this section until the plan satisfies the requirements in this paragraph (f). In no event is the exemption of this paragraph (f) effective until 30 days after the notice requirements in paragraph (f)(3) of this section are satisfied. If the requirements of this paragraph (f) are satisfied with respect to a plan, the exemption continues in effect (at the plan's discretion) until December 31, 2005, even if the plan subsequently purchases a different policy from the same or a different issuer and regardless of any other changes to the plan's benefit structure. [Amended by EBSA on 9/27/02 (67 FR 60859), on 4/14/03 (68 FR 18048), on 1/26/2004 (69 FR 3815), and on 12/17/2004 (69 FR 75797.]

(2) *Calculation of the one-percent increase.* (i) *Ratio.* A group health plan (or group health insurance coverage) satisfies the requirements of this paragraph (f)(2) if the application of paragraph (b)(1)(i) of this section to the plan (or to such coverage) results in an increase in the cost under the plan (or for such coverage) of at least one percent. The application of paragraph (b)(1)(i) of this section results in an increased cost of at least one percent under a group health plan (or for

such coverage) only if the ratio below equals or exceeds 1.01000. The ratio is determined as follows:

(A) The incurred expenditures during the base period, divided by,

(B) The incurred expenditures during the base period, reduced by—

(1) The claims incurred during the base period that would have been denied under the terms of the plan absent plan amendments required to comply with this section; and

(2) Administrative expenses attributable to complying with the requirements of this section.

(ii) *Formula.* The ratio of paragraph (f)(2)(i) of this section is expressed mathematically as follows:

$$\frac{IE}{IE - (CE + AE)} \geq 1.01000$$

(A) *IE* means the incurred expenditures during the base period.

(B) *CE* means the claims incurred during the base period that would have been denied under the terms of the plan absent plan amendments required to comply with this section

(C) *AE* means administrative costs related to claims in *CE* and other administrative costs attributable to complying with the requirements of this section.

(iii) *Incurred expenditures. Incurred expenditures* means actual claims incurred during the base period and reported within two months following the base period, and administrative costs for all benefits under the group health plan, including mental health benefits and medical/surgical benefits, during the base period. Incurred expenditures do not include premiums.

(iv) *Base period. Base period* means the period used to calculate whether the plan may claim the one-percent increased cost exemption in this paragraph (f). The base period must begin on the first day in any plan year that the plan complies with the requirements of paragraph (b)(1)(i) of this section and must extend for a period of at least six consecutive calendar months. However, in no event may the base period begin prior to September 26, 1996 (the date of enactment of the Mental Health Parity Act (Pub. L. 104-204, 110 Stat. 2944)).

(v) *Rating pools.* For plans that are combined in a pool for rating purposes, the calculation under this paragraph (f)(2) for each plan in the pool for the base period is based on the incurred expenditures of the pool, whether or not all the plans in the pool have participated in the pool for the entire base period. (However, only the plans that have complied with paragraph (b)(1)(i) of this section for at least six months as a member of the pool satisfy the requirements of this paragraph (f)(2).) Otherwise, the calculation under this paragraph (f)(2) for each plan is calculated by the plan administrator (or issuer) based on the incurred expenditures of the plan.

(vi) *Examples.* The rules of this paragraph (f)(2) are illustrated by the following examples:

Example 1. (i) A group health plan has a plan year that is the calendar year. The plan satisfies the requirements of paragraph (b)(1)(i) of this section as of January 1, 1998. On September 15, 1998, the plan determines that $1,000,000 in claims have been incurred during the period between January 1, 1998 and June 30, 1998 and reported by August 30, 1998. The plan also determines that $100,000 in administrative costs have been incurred for all benefits under the group health plan, including mental health benefits. Thus, the plan determines that its incurred expenditures for the base period are $1,100,000. The plan also determines that the claims incurred during the base period that would have been denied under the terms of the plan absent plan amendments required to comply with this section are $40,000 and that administrative expenses attributable to complying with the requirements of this section are $10,000. Thus, the total amount of expenditures for the base period had the plan not been amended to comply with the requirements of paragraph (b)(1)(i) of this section are $1,050,000 ($1,100,000 - ($40,000 + $10,000) = $1,050,000).

(ii) In this *Example 1*, the plan satisfies the requirements of this paragraph (f)(2) because the application of this section results in an increased cost of at least one percent under the terms of the plan ($1,100,000/$1,050,000 = 1.04762).

Example 2. (i) A health insurance issuer sells a group health insurance policy that is rated on a pooled basis and is sold to 30 group health plans. One of the group health plans inquires whether it qualifies for the one-percent increased cost exemption. The issuer performs the calculation for the pool as a whole and determines that the application of this section results in an increased cost of 0.500 percent (for a ratio under this paragraph (f)(2) of 1.00500) for the pool. The issuer informs the requesting plan and the other plans in the pool of the calculation.

(ii) In this *Example 2*, none of the plans satisfy the requirements of this paragraph (f)(2) and a plan that purchases a policy not complying with the requirements of paragraph (b)(1)(i) of this section violates the requirements of this section. In addition, an issuer that issues to any of the plans in the pool a policy not complying with the requirements of paragraph (b)(1)(i) of this section violates the requirements of this section.

Example 3. (i) A partially insured plan is collecting the information to determine whether it qualifies for the exemption. The plan administrator determines the incurred expenses for the base period for the self-funded portion of the plan to be $2,000,000 and the administrative expenses for the base period for the self-funded portion to be $200,000. For the insured portion of the plan, the plan administrator requests data from the insurer. For the insured portion of the plan, the plan's own incurred expenses for the base period are $1,000,000 and the administrative expenses for the base period are $100,000. The plan administrator determines that under the self-funded portion of the plan, the claims incurred for the base period that would have been denied under the terms of the plan absent the amendment are $0 because the self-funded portion does not cover mental health benefits and the plan's administrative costs attributable to complying with the requirements of this section are $1,000. The issuer determines that under the insured portion of the plan, the claims incurred for the base period that would have been denied under the terms of the plan absent the amendment are $25,000 and the administrative costs attributable to complying with the requirements of this section are $1,000. Thus, the total incurred expenditures for the plan for the base period are $3,300,000 ($2,000,000 + $200,000 + $1,000,000 + $100,000 = $3,300,000) and the total amount of expenditures for the base period had the plan not been amended to comply with the requirements of paragraph (b)(1)(i) of this section are $3,273,000 ($3,300,000 - ($0 + $1,000 + $25,000 + $1,000) = $3,273,000).

(ii) In this *Example 3*, the plan does not satisfy the requirements of this paragraph (f)(2) because the application of this section does not result in an increased cost of at least one percent under the terms of the plan ($3,300,000/$3,273,000 = 1.00825).

(3) *Notice of exemption.* (i) *Participants and beneficiaries.* (A) *In general.* A group health plan must notify participants and beneficiaries of the plan's decision to claim the onepercent increased cost exemption. The notice must include the following information:

(1) A statement that the plan is exempt from the requirements of this section and a description of the basis for the exemption;

(2) The name and telephone number of the individual to contact for further information;

(3) The plan name and plan number (PN);

(4) The plan administrator's name, address, and telephone number;

(5) For single-employer plans, the plan sponsor's name, address, and telephone number (if different from paragraph (f)(3)(i)(A)(*3*) of this section) and the plan sponsor's employer identification number (EIN);

(6) The effective date of the exemption;

(7) The ability of participants and beneficiaries to contact the plan administrator to see how benefits may be affected as a result of the plan's claim of the exemption; and

(8) The availability, upon request and free of charge, of a summary of the information required under paragraph (f)(4) of this section.

(B) *Use of summary of material reductions in covered services or benefits.* A plan may satisfy the requirements of paragraph (f)(3)(i)(A) of this section by providing participants and beneficiaries (in accordance with paragraph (f)(3)(i)(C) of this section) with a summary of material reductions in covered services or benefits required under § 2520.104b-3(d) that also includes the information of this paragraph (f)(3)(i). However, in all cases, the exemption is not effective until 30 days after notice has been sent.

(C) *Delivery.* The notice described in this paragraph (f)(3)(i) is required to be provided to all participants and beneficiaries. The notice may be furnished by any method of delivery that satisfies the requirements of section 104(b)(1) of ERISA (e.g., first-class mail). If the notice is provided to the participant at the participant's last known address, then the requirements of this paragraph (f)(3)(i) are satisfied with respect to the participant and all beneficiaries residing at that address. If a beneficiary's last known address is different from the participant's last known address, a separate notice is required to be provided to the beneficiary at the beneficiary's last known address.

(D) *Example.* The rules of this paragraph (f)(3)(i) are illustrated by the following example:

Example. (i) A group health plan has a plan year that is the calendar year and has an open enrollment period every November 1 through November 30. The plan determines on September 15 that it satisfies the requirements of paragraph (f)(2) of this section. As part of its open enrollment materials, the plan mails, on October 15, to all participants and beneficiaries a notice satisfying the requirements of this paragraph (f)(3)(i).

(ii) In this *Example*, the plan has sent the notice in a manner that complies with this paragraph (f)(3)(i).

(ii) *Federal agencies.* (A) *Church plans.* A church plan (as defined in section 414(e) of the Internal Revenue Code) claiming the exemption of this paragraph (f) for any benefit package must provide notice to the Department of the Treasury. This requirement is satisfied if the plan sends a copy, to the address designated by the Secretary in generally applicable guidance, of the notice described in paragraph (f)(3)(i) of this section identifying the benefit package to which the exemption applies.

(B) *Group health plans subject to Part 7 of Subtitle B of Title I of ERISA.* A group health plan subject to Part 7 of Subtitle B of Title I of ERISA, and claiming the exemption of this paragraph (f) for any benefit package, must provide notice to the Department of Labor. This requirement is satisfied if the plan sends a copy, to the address designated by the Secretary in generally applicable guidance, of the notice described in paragraph (f)(3)(i) of this section identifying the benefit package to which the exemption applies.

(C) *Nonfederal governmental plans.* A group health plan that is a nonfederal governmental plan claiming the exemption of this paragraph (f) for any benefit package must provide notice to the Department of Health and Human Services (HHS). This requirement is satisfied if the plan sends a copy, to the address designated by the Secretary in generally applicable guidance, of the notice described in paragraph (f)(3)(i) of this section identifying the benefit package to which the exemption applies.

(4) *Availability of documentation.* The plan (or issuer) must make available to participants and beneficiaries (or their representatives), on request and at no charge, a summary of the information on which the exemption was based. An individual who is not a participant or beneficiary and who presents a notice described in paragraph (f)(3)(i) of this section is considered to be a representative. A representative may request the summary of information by providing the plan a copy of the notice provided to the participant under paragraph (f)(3)(i) of this section with any individually identifiable information redacted. The summary of information must include the incurred expenditures, the base period, the dollar amount of claims incurred during the base period that would have been denied under the terms of the plan absent amendments required to comply with paragraph (b)(1)(i) of this section, the administrative costs related to those claims, and other administrative costs attributable to complying with the requirements of this

section. In no event should the summary of information include any individually identifiable information.

(g) *Special rules for group health insurance coverage.* (1) *Sale of nonparity policies.* An issuer may sell a policy without parity (as described in paragraph (b) of this section) only to a plan that meets the requirements of paragraphs (e) or (f) of this section.

(2) *Duration of exemption.* After a plan meets the requirements of paragraph (f) of this section, the plan may change issuers without having to meet the requirements of paragraph (f) of this section again before December 31, 2005. [Amended by EBSA on 9/27/02 (67 FR 60859), on 4/14/03 (68 FR 18048), on 1/26/2004 (69 FR 3815), and on 12/17/2004 (69 FR 75797).]

(h) *Effective dates.* (1) *In general.* The requirements of this section are applicable for plan years beginning on or after January 1, 1998.

(2) *Limitation on actions.* (i) Except as provided in paragraph (h)(3) of this section, no enforcement action is to be taken by the Secretary against a group health plan that has sought to comply in good faith with the requirements section 712 of the Act, with respect to a violation that occurs before the earlier of—

(A) The first day of the first plan year beginning on or after April 1, 1998; or

(B) January 1, 1999.

(ii) Compliance with the requirements of this section is deemed to be good faith compliance with the requirements of section 712 of Part 7 of Subtitle B of Title I of ERISA.

(iii) The rules of this paragraph (h)(2) are illustrated by the following examples:

Example 1. (i) A group health plan has a plan year that is the calendar year. The plan complies with section 712 of Part 7 of Subtitle B of Title I of ERISA in good faith using assumptions inconsistent with paragraph (b)(6) of this section relating to weighted averages for categories of benefits.

(ii) In this *Example 1*, no enforcement action may be taken against the plan with respect to a violation resulting solely from those assumptions and occurring before January 1, 1999.

Example 2. (i) A group health plan has a plan year that is the calendar year. For the entire 1998 plan year, the plan applies a $1,000,000 annual limit on medical/surgical benefits and a $100,000 annual limit on mental health benefits.

(ii) In this *Example 2*, the plan has not sought to comply with the requirements of section 712 of the Act in good faith and this paragraph (h)(2) does not apply.

(3) *Transition period for increased cost exemption.* (i) *In general.* No enforcement action will be taken against a group health plan that is subject to the requirements of this section based on a violation of this section that occurs before April 1, 1998 solely because the plan claims the increased cost exemption under section 712(c)(2) of Part 7 of Subtitle B of Title I of ERISA based on assumptions inconsistent with the rules under paragraph (f) of this section, provided that a plan amendment that complies with the requirements of paragraph (b)(1)(i) of this section is adopted and effective no later than March 31, 1998 and the plan complies with the notice requirements in paragraph (h)(3)(ii) of this section.

(ii) *Notice of plan's use of transition period.* (A) A group health plan satisfies the requirements of this paragraph (h)(3)(ii) only if the plan provides notice to the applicable federal agency and posts such notice at the location(s) where documents must be made available for examination by participants and beneficiaries under section 104(b)(2) of ERISA and the regulations thereunder (29 CFR 2520.104b-1(b)(3)). The notice must indicate the plan's decision to use the transition period in paragraph (h)(3)(i) of this section by 30 days after the first day of the plan year beginning on or after January 1, 1998, but in no event later than March 31, 1998. For a group health plan that is a church plan, the applicable federal agency is the Department of the Treasury. For a group health plan that is subject to Part 7 of Subtitle B of Title I of ERISA, the applicable federal agency is the Department of Labor. For a group health plan that is a nonfederal governmental plan, the applicable federal agency is the Department of Health and Human Services. The notice must include—

(1) The name of the plan and the plan number (PN);

(2) The name, address, and telephone number of the plan administrator;

(3) For single-employer plans, the name, address, and telephone number of the plan sponsor (if different from the plan administrator) and the plan sponsor's employer identification number (EIN);

(4) The name and telephone number of the individual to contact for further information; and

(5) The signature of the plan administrator and the date of the signature.

(B) The notice must be provided at no charge to participants or their representative within 15 days after receipt of a written or oral request for such notification, but in no event before the notice has been sent to the applicable federal agency.

(i) *Sunset.* This section does not apply to benefits for services furnished on or after December 31, 2005.

[Amended December 19, 1997 by T.D. 8741 and by EBSA on 9/27/02 (67 FR 60859), on 4/14/03 (68 FR 18048), on 1/26/2004 (69 FR 3815), and on 12/17/2004 (69 FR 75797).]

[¶ 15,050P]
MANDATED COVERAGE OF POST-MASTECTOMY RECONSTRUCTIVE SURGERY

Act Sec. 713. REQUIRED COVERAGE FOR RECONSTRUCTIVE SURGERY FOLLOWING MASTECTOMIES.

Act. Sec. 713 IN GENERAL. (a) A group health plan, and a health insurance issuer providing health insurance coverage in connection with a group health plan, that provides medical and surgical benefits with respect to a mastectomy shall provide, in a case of a participant or beneficiary who is receiving benefits in connection with a mastectomy and who elects breast reconstruction in connection with such mastectomy, coverage for—

"(1) reconstruction of the breast on which the mastectomy has been performed;

"(2) surgery and reconstruction of the other breast to produce a symmetrical appearance; and

"(3) prostheses and physical complications all stages of mastectomy, including lymphedemas; in a manner determined in consultation with the attending physician and the patient. Such coverage may be subject to annual deductibles and coinsurance provisions as may be deemed appropriate and as are consistent with those established for other benefits under the plan or coverage. Written notice of the availability of such coverage shall be delivered to the participant upon enrollment and annually thereafter.

Act Sec. 713. NOTICE. (b) A group health plan, and a health insurance issuer providing health insurance coverage in connection with a group health plan, shall provide notice to each participant and beneficiary under such plan regarding the coverage required by this section in accordance with regulations promulgated by the Secretary. Such notice shall be in writing and prominently positioned in any literature or correspondence made available or distributed by the plan or issuer and shall be transmitted—

"(1) in the next mailing made by the plan or issuer to the participant or beneficiary;

"(2) as part of any yearly informational packet sent to the participant or beneficiary; or

"(3) not later than January 1, 1999; whichever is earlier.

Act Sec. 713. PROHIBITIONS. (c) A group health plan, and a health insurance issuer offering group health insurance coverage in connection with a group health plan, may not—

"(1) deny to a patient eligibility, or continued eligibility, to enroll or to renew coverage under the terms of the plan, solely for the purpose of avoiding the requirements of this section; and

"(2) penalize or otherwise reduce or limit the reimbursement of an attending provider, or provide incentives (monetary or otherwise) to an attending provider, to induce such provider to provide care to an individual participant or beneficiary in a manner inconsistent with this section.

Act Sec. 713. Rule of Construction. (d) Nothing in this section shall be construed to prevent a group health plan or a health insurance issuer offering group health insurance coverage from negotiating the level and type of reimbursement with a provider for care provided in accordance with this section.

Act Sec. 713. Preemption, Relation to State Laws.—

(e)

"(1) In General. Nothing in this section shall be construed to preempt any State law in effect on the date of enactment of this section with respect to health insurance coverage that requires coverage of at least the coverage of reconstructive breast surgery otherwise required under this section.

"(2) ERISA. Nothing in this section shall be construed to affect or modify the provisions of section 514 with respect to group health plans."

Amendments

P.L. 105-277, § 902(a):

Subpart B of part 7 of subtitle B of title I of the Employee Retirement Income Security Act of 1974 (29 U.S.C. 1185 et seq.) is amended by adding at the end the above new section:

(b) Clerical Amendment. The table of contents in section 1 of the Employee Retirement Income Security Act of 1974 (29 U.S.C. 1001 note) is amended by inserting after the item relating to section 712 the following new item:

Sec. 713. Required coverage reconstructive surgery following mastectomies.".

(c) Effective Dates.

(1) In General. The amendments made by this section shall apply with respect to plan years beginning on or after the date of enactment of this Act.

(2) Special Rule for Collective Bargaining Agreements. In the case of a group health plan maintained pursuant to 1 or more collective bargaining agreements between employee representatives and 1 or more employers, any plan amendment made pursuant to a collective bargaining agreement relating to the plan which amends the plan solely to conform to any requirement added by this section shall not be treated as a termination of such collective bargaining agreement.

>>> *Caution: Act Sec. 731, below, formerly Act Sec. 704, was redesignated as Act Sec. 731 by P.L. 104-204, to apply with respect to group health plans for plan years beginning on or after January 1, 1998.—CCH.*

[¶ 15,051A]
PREEMPTION; STATE FLEXIBILITY; CONSTRUCTION

Act Sec. 731.(a) Continued Applicability of State Law with Respect to Health Insurance Issuers.—

(1) In General. Subject to paragraph (2) and except as provided in subsection (b), this part shall not be construed to supersede any provision of State law which establishes, implements, or continues in effect any standard or requirement solely relating to health insurance issuers in connection with group health insurance coverage except to the extent that such standard or requirement prevents the application of a requirement of this part.

(2) Continued Preemption with Respect to Group Health Plans. Nothing in this part shall be construed to affect or modify the provisions of section 514 with respect to group health plans.

Act Sec. 731. Special Rules in Case of Portability Requirements.—

(b)(1) In General. Subject to paragraph (2), the provisions of this part relating to health insurance coverage offered by a health insurance issuer supersede any provision of State law which establishes, implements, or continues in effect a standard or requirement applicable to imposition of a preexisting condition exclusion specifically governed by section 701 which differs from the standards or requirements specified in such section.

(2) Exceptions. Only in relation to health insurance coverage offered by a health insurance issuer, the provisions of this part do not supersede any provision of State law to the extent that such provision—

(A) substitutes for the reference to "6-month period" in section 701(a)(1) a reference to any shorter period of time;

(B) substitutes for the reference to "12 months" and "18 months" in section 701(a)(2) a reference to any shorter period of time;

(C) substitutes for the references to "63 days" in sections 701(c)(2)(A) and (d)(4)(A) a reference to any greater number of days;

(D) substitutes for the reference to "30-day period" in sections 701(b)(2) and (d)(1) a reference to any greater period;

(E) prohibits the imposition of any preexisting condition exclusion in cases not described in section 701(d) or expands the exceptions described in such section;

(F) requires special enrollment periods in addition to those required under section 701(f); or

(G) reduces the maximum period permitted in an affiliation period under section 701(g)(1)(B).

Act Sec. 731. Rules of Construction. (c) Except as provided in section 711, nothing in this part shall be construed as requiring a group health plan or health insurance coverage to provide specific benefits under the terms of such plan or coverage.

Act Sec. 731. Definitions. (d) For purposes of this section—

(1) State Law. The term "State law" includes all laws, decisions, rules, regulations, or other State action having the effect of law, of any State. A law of the United States applicable only to the District of Columbia shall be treated as a State law rather than a law of the United States.

(2) State. The term "State" includes a State, the Northern Mariana Islands, any political subdivisions of a State or such Islands, or any agency or instrumentality of either.

Amendments

P.L. 104-204, § 603(a)(3):

Redesignated ERISA Act Sec. 704 as ERISA Act Sec. 731.

P.L. 104-204, § 603(b)(1):

Amended ERISA Act Sec. 731 by striking "Nothing" and inserting "Except as provided in section 711, nothing".

The above amendments shall apply with respect to group health plans for plan years beginning on or after January 1, 1998.

P.L. 104-191, § 101(a):

Added ERISA Act Sec. 704 to read as above.

The above amendments generally apply with respect to group health plans for plan years beginning after June 30, 1997. For special rules, see Act Sec. 101(g)(2)- (5), reproduced after ERISA Act Sec. 701 above.

Regulations

The following regulations were adopted by 62 FR 16894 and published in the Federal Register on April 8, 1997, under "Chapter XXV of Title 29 of the Code of Federal Regulations; Subchapter L—Health Insurance Portability and Renewability for Group Health Plans; Part 2590—Rules and Regulations for Health Insurance Portability and Renewability for Group Health Plans." They were officially corrected on June 10, 1997, by 62 FR 31690. Reg. § 2590.731 was revised by T.D. 9166 on December 30, 2004 (69 FR 78720) and corrected on April 25, 2005 (70 FR 21146).

Subpart C—General Provisions

[¶ 15,051A-1]

§ 2590.731. **Preemption; State flexibility; construction.** (a) *Continued applicability of State law with respect to health insurance issuers.* Subject to paragraph (b) of this section and except as provided in paragraph (c) of this section, part 7 of subtitle B of Title I of the Act is not to be construed to supersede any provision of State law which establishes, implements, or continues in effect any standard or requirement solely relating to health insurance issuers in connection with group health insurance coverage except to the extent that such standard or requirement prevents the application of a requirement of this part.

(b) *Continued preemption with respect to group health plans.* Nothing in part 7 of subtitle B of Title I of the Act affects or modifies the provisions of section 514 of the Act with respect to group health plans.

(c) *Special rules.* (1) *In general.* Subject to paragraph (c)(2) of this section, the provisions of part 7 of subtitle B of Title I of the Act relating to health insurance coverage offered by a health insurance issuer supersede any provision of State law which establishes, implements, or continues in effect a standard or requirement applicable to imposition of a preexisting condition exclusion specifically governed by section 701 which differs from the standards or requirements specified in such section.

(2) *Exceptions.* Only in relation to health insurance coverage offered by a health insurance issuer, the provisions of this part do not supersede any provision of State law to the extent that such provision—

(i) Shortens the period of time from the "6-month period" described in section 701(a)(1) of the Act and § 2590.701-3(a)(2)(i) (for

purposes of identifying a preexisting condition); [Corrected 4/25/05 by 70 FR 21146.]

(ii) Shortens the period of time from the "12 months" and "18 months" described in section 701(a)(2) of the Act and § 2590.701-3(a)(2)(ii) (for purposes of applying a preexisting condition exclusion period); [Corrected 4/25/05 by 70 FR 21146.]

(iii) Provides for a greater number of days than the "63-day period" described in sections 701(c)(2)(A) and (d)(4)(A) of the Act and §§ 2590.701-3(a)(2)(iii) and 2590.701-4 (for purposes of applying the break in coverage rules); [Corrected 4/25/05 by 70 FR 21146.]

(iv) Provides for a greater number of days than the "30-day period" described in sections 701(b)(2) and (d)(1) of the Act and § 2590.701-3(b) (for purposes of the enrollment period and preexisting condition exclusion periods for certain newborns and children that are adopted or placed for adoption);

(v) Prohibits the imposition of any preexisting condition exclusion in cases not described in section 701(d) of the Act or expands the exceptions described therein;

(vi) Requires special enrollment periods in addition to those required under section 701(f) of the Act; or

(vii) Reduces the maximum period permitted in an affiliation period under section 701(g)(1)(B) of the Act.

(d) *Definitions.* (1) *State law.* For purposes of this section the term *State law* includes all laws, decisions, rules, regulations, or other State action having the effect of law, of any State. *A* law of the United States applicable only to the District of Columbia is treated as a State law rather than a law of the United States.

(2) *State.* For purposes of this section the term *State* includes a State (as defined in § 2590.701-2), any political subdivisions of a State, or any agency or instrumentality of either.

»»→ *Caution: Act Sec. 732, below, formerly Act Sec. 705, was redesignated as Act Sec. 732 by P.L. 104-204, to apply with respect to group health plans for plan years beginning on or after January 1, 1998.—CCH.*

[¶ 15,051B]
SPECIAL RULES RELATING TO GROUP HEALTH PLANS

Act Sec. 732.(a) GENERAL EXCEPTION FOR CERTAIN SMALL GROUP HEALTH PLANS. The requirements of this part (other than section 711) shall not apply to any group health plan (and group health insurance coverage offered in connection with a group health plan) for any plan year if, on the first day of such plan year, such plan has less than 2 participants who are current employees.

Act Sec. 732. EXCEPTION FOR CERTAIN BENEFITS. (b) The requirements of this part shall not apply to any group health plan (and group health insurance coverage) in relation to its provision of excepted benefits described in section 733(c)(1).

Act Sec. 732. EXCEPTION FOR CERTAIN BENEFITS OF CERTAIN CONDITIONS MET.—

(c)(1) LIMITED, EXCEPTED BENEFITS. The requirements of this part shall not apply to any group health plan (and group health insurance coverage offered in connection with a group health plan) in relation to its provision of excepted benefits described in section 733(c)(2) if the benefits—

(A) are provided under a separate policy, certificate, or contract of insurance; or

(B) are otherwise not an integral part of the plan.

(2) NONCOORDINATED, EXCEPTED BENEFITS. The requirements of this part shall not apply to any group health plan (and group health insurance coverage offered in connection with a group health plan) in relation to its provision of excepted benefits described in section 733(c)(3) if all of the following conditions are met:

(A) The benefits are provided under a separate policy, certificate, or contract of insurance.

(B) There is no coordination between the provision of such benefits and any exclusion of benefits under any group health plan maintained by the same plan sponsor.

(C) Such benefits are paid with respect to an event without regard to whether benefits are provided with respect to such an event under any group health plan maintained by the same plan sponsor.

(3) SUPPLEMENTAL EXCEPTED BENEFITS. The requirements of this part shall not apply to any group health plan (and group health insurance coverage) in relation to its provision of excepted benefits described in section 733(c)(4) if the benefits are provided under a separate policy, certificate, or contract of insurance.

Act Sec. 732. TREATMENT OF PARTNERSHIPS. (d) For purposes of this part—

(1) TREATMENT AS A GROUP HEALTH PLAN. Any plan, fund, or program which would not be (but for this subsection) an employee welfare benefit plan and which is established or maintained by a partnership, to the extent that such plan, fund, or program provides medical care (including items and services paid for as medical care) to present or former partners in the partnership or to their dependents (as defined under the terms of the plan, fund, or program), directly or through insurance, reimbursement, or otherwise, shall be treated (subject to paragraph (2)) as an employee welfare benefit plan which is a group health plan.

(2) EMPLOYER. In the case of a group health plan, the term "employer" also includes the partnership in relation to any partner.

(3) PARTICIPANTS OF GROUP HEALTH PLANS. In the case of a group health plan, the term "participant" also includes—

(A) in connection with a group health plan maintained by a partnership, an individual who is a partner in relation to the partnership, or

(B) in connection with a group health plan maintained by a self-employed individual (under which one or more employees are participants), the self-employed individual,

if such individual is, or may become, eligible to receive a benefit under the plan or such individual's beneficiaries may be eligible to receive any such benefit.

Amendments

P.L. 104-204, §603(a)(3):

Redesignated ERISA Act Sec. 705 as ERISA Act Sec. 732.

P.L. 104-204, §603(b)(2):

Amended ERISA Act Sec. 732(a) by inserting "(other than section 711)" after "part".

P.L. 104-204, §603(b)(3)(I):

Amended ERISA Act Sec. 732(b) by striking "section 706(c)(1)" and inserting "section 733(c)(1)".

P.L. 104-204, §603(b)(3)(J):

Amended ERISA Act Sec. 732(c)(1) by striking "section 706(c)(2)" and inserting "section 733(c)(2)".

P.L. 104-204, §603(a)(3)(K):

Amended ERISA Act Sec. 732(c)(2) by striking "section 706(c)(3)" and inserting "section 733(c)(3)".

P.L. 104-204, §603(a)(3)(L):

Amended ERISA Act Sec. 732(c)(3) by striking "section 706(c)(4)" and inserting "section 733(c)(4)".

The above amendments shall apply with respect to group health plans for plan years beginning on or after January 1, 1998.

P.L. 104-191, §101(a):

Added ERISA Act Sec. 705 to read as above.

The above amendments generally apply with respect to group health plans for plan years beginning after June 30, 1997. For special rules, see Act Sec. 101(g)(2)- (5), reproduced after ERISA Act Sec. 701 above.

Regulations

The following regulations were adopted by 62 FR 16894 and published in the Federal Register on April 8, 1997, under "Chapter XXV of Title 29 of the Code of Federal Regulations; Subchapter L—Health Insurance Portability and Renewability for Group Health Plans; Part 2590—Rules and Regulations for Health Insurance Portability and Renewability for Group Health Plans." Reg. § 2590.732 was revised by T.D. 9166 on December 30, 2004 (69 FR 78720).

[¶ 15,051B-1]

§ 2590.732. **Special rules relating to group health plans.** (a) *Group health plan.* (1) *Defined.* A group health plan means an employee welfare benefit plan to the extent that the plan provides medical care (including items and services paid for as medical care) to employees (including both current and former employees) or their dependents (as defined under the terms of the plan) directly or through insurance, reimbursement, or otherwise.

(2) *Determination of number of plans.* [Reserved]

(b) *General exception for certain small group health plans.* The requirements of this part, other than § 2590.711, do not apply to any group health plan (and group health insurance coverage) for any plan year if, on the first day of the plan year, the plan has fewer than two participants who are current employees.

(c) *Excepted benefits.* (1) *In general.* The requirements of this Part do not apply to any group health plan (or any group health insurance coverage) in relation to its provision of the benefits described in paragraph (c)(2), (3), (4), or (5) of this section (or any combination of these benefits).

(2) *Benefits excepted in all circumstances.* The following benefits are excepted in all circumstances—

(i) Coverage only for accident (including accidental death and dismemberment);

(ii) Disability income coverage;

(iii) Liability insurance, including general liability insurance and automobile liability insurance;

(iv) Coverage issued as a supplement to liability insurance;

(v) Workers' compensation or similar coverage;

(vi) Automobile medical payment insurance;

(vii) Credit-only insurance (for example, mortgage insurance); and

(viii) Coverage for on-site medical clinics.

(3) *Limited excepted benefits.* (i) *In general.* Limited-scope dental benefits, limited-scope vision benefits, or longterm care benefits are excepted if they are provided under a separate policy, certificate, or contract of insurance, or are otherwise not an integral part of a group health plan as described in paragraph (c)(3)(ii) of this section. In addition, benefits provided under a health flexible spending arrangement are excepted benefits if they satisfy the requirements of paragraph (c)(3)(v) of this section.

(ii) *Not an integral part of a group health plan.* For purposes of this paragraph (c)(3), benefits are not an integral part of a group health plan (whether the benefits are provided through the same plan or a separate plan) only if the following two requirements are satisfied—

(A) Participants must have the right to elect not to receive coverage for the benefits; and

(B) If a participant elects to receive coverage for the benefits, the participant must pay an additional premium or contribution for that coverage.

(iii) *Limited scope.* (A) *Dental benefits.* Limited scope dental benefits are benefits substantially all of which are for treatment of the mouth (including any organ or structure within the mouth).

(B) *Vision benefits.* Limited scope vision benefits are benefits substantially all of which are for treatment of the eye.

(iv) *Long-term care.* Long-term care benefits are benefits that are either—

(A) Subject to State long-term care insurance laws;

(B) For qualified long-term care services, as defined in section 7702B(c)(1) of the Internal Revenue Code, or provided under a qualified long-term care insurance contract, as defined in section 7702B(b) of the Internal Revenue Code; or

(C) Based on cognitive impairment or a loss of functional capacity that is expected to be chronic.

(v) *Health flexible spending arrangements.* Benefits provided under a health flexible spending arrangement (as defined in section 106(c)(2) of the Internal Revenue Code) are excepted for a class of participants only if they satisfy the following two requirements—

(A) Other group health plan coverage, not limited to excepted benefits, is made available for the year to the class of participants by reason of their employment; and

(B) The arrangement is structured so that the maximum benefit payable to any participant in the class for a year cannot exceed two times the participant's salary reduction election under the arrangement for the year (or, if greater, cannot exceed $500 plus the amount of the participant's salary reduction election). For this purpose, any amount that an employee can elect to receive as taxable income but elects to apply to the health flexible spending arrangement is considered a salary reduction election (regardless of whether the amount is characterized as salary or as a credit under the arrangement).

(4) *Noncoordinated benefits.* (i) *Excepted benefits that are not coordinated.* Coverage for only a specified disease or illness (for example, cancer-only policies) or hospital indemnity or other fixed indemnity insurance is excepted only if it meets each of the conditions specified in paragraph (c)(4)(ii) of this section. To be hospital indemnity or other fixed indemnity insurance, the insurance must pay a fixed dollar amount per day (or per other period) of hospitalization or illness (for example, $100/day) regardless of the amount of expenses incurred.

(ii) *Conditions.* Benefits are described in paragraph (c)(4)(i) of this section only if—

(A) The benefits are provided under a separate policy, certificate, or contract of insurance;

(B) There is no coordination between the provision of the benefits and an exclusion of benefits under any group health plan maintained by the same plan sponsor; and

(C) The benefits are paid with respect to an event without regard to whether benefits are provided with respect to the event under any group health plan maintained by the same plan sponsor.

(iii) *Example.* The rules of this paragraph (c)(4) are illustrated by the following example:

Example. (i) *Facts.* An employer sponsors a group health plan that provides coverage through an insurance policy. The policy provides benefits only for hospital stays at a fixed percentage of hospital expenses up to a maximum of $100 a day.

(ii) *Conclusion.* In this *Example,* even though the benefits under the policy satisfy the conditions in paragraph (c)(4)(ii) of this section, because the policy pays a percentage of expenses incurred rather than a fixed dollar amount, the benefits under the policy are not excepted benefits under this paragraph (c)(4). This is the result even if, in practice, the policy pays the maximum of $100 for every day of hospitalization.

(5) *Supplemental benefits.* (i) The following benefits are excepted only if they are provided under a separate policy, certificate, or contract of insurance—

(A) Medicare supplemental health insurance (as defined under section 1882(g)(1) of the Social Security Act; also known as Medigap or MedSupp insurance);

(B) Coverage supplemental to the coverage provided under Chapter 55, Title 10 of the United States Code (also known as TRICARE supplemental programs); and

(C) Similar supplemental coverage provided to coverage under a group health plan. To be similar supplemental coverage, the coverage must be specifically designed to fill gaps in primary coverage, such as coinsurance or deductibles. Similar supplemental coverage does not include coverage that becomes secondary or supplemental only under a coordination-of-benefits provision.

(ii) The rules of this paragraph (c)(5) are illustrated by the following example:

Example. (i) *Facts.* An employer sponsors a group health plan that provides coverage for both active employees and retirees. The coverage for retirees supplements benefits provided by Medicare, but does not meet the requirements for a supplemental policy under section 1882(g)(1) of the Social Security Act.

(ii) *Conclusion.* In this *Example,* the coverage provided to retirees does not meet the definition of supplemental excepted benefits under this paragraph (c)(5) because the coverage is not Medicare supplemental insurance as defined under section 1882(g)(1) of the Social Security Act, is not a TRICARE supplemental program, and is not supplemental to coverage provided under a group health plan.

(d) *Treatment of partnerships.* For purposes of this part:

(1) *Treatment as a group health plan.* Any plan, fund, or program that would not be (but for this paragraph (d)) an employee welfare benefit plan and that is established or maintained by a partnership, to the extent that the plan, fund, or program provides medical care (including items and services paid for as medical care) to present or former partners in the partnership or to their dependents (as defined under the terms of the plan, fund, or program), directly or through insurance, reimbursement, or otherwise, is treated (subject to paragraph (d)(2)) as an employee welfare benefit plan that is a group health plan.

(2) *Employment relationship.* In the case of a group health plan, the term *employer* also includes the partnership in relation to any bona fide partner. In addition, the term *employee* also includes any bona fide partner. Whether or not an individual is a bona fide partner is determined based on all the relevant facts and circumstances, including whether the individual performs services on behalf of the partnership.

(3) *Participants of group health plans.* In the case of a group health plan, the term participant also includes any individual described in paragraph (d)(3)(i) or (ii) of this section if the individual is, or may become, eligible to receive a benefit under the plan or the individual's beneficiaries may be eligible to receive any such benefit.

(i) In connection with a group health plan maintained by a partnership, the individual is a partner in relation to the partnership.

(ii) In connection with a group health plan maintained by a self-employed individual (under which one or more employees are participants), the individual is the self-employed individual.

(e) *Determining the average number of employees.* [Reserved]

⋙→ *Caution: Act Sec. 733, below, formerly Act Sec. 706, was redesignated as Act Sec. 733 by P.L. 104-204, to apply with respect to group health plans for plan years beginning on or after January 1, 1998.—CCH.*

[¶ 15,051C]
DEFINITIONS

Act Sec. 733.(a) GROUP HEALTH PLAN. For purposes of this part—

(a)(1) IN GENERAL. The term "group health plan" means an employee welfare benefit plan to the extent that the plan provides medical care (as defined in paragraph (2) and including items and services paid for as medical care) to employees or their dependents (as defined under the terms of the plan) directly or through insurance, reimbursement, or otherwise.

(2) MEDICAL CARE. The term "medical care" means amounts paid for—

(A) the diagnosis, cure, mitigation, treatment, or prevention of disease, or amounts paid for the purpose of affecting any structure or function of the body,

(B) amounts paid for transportation primarily for and essential to medical care referred to in subparagraph (A), and

(C) amounts paid for insurance covering medical care referred to in subparagraphs (A) and (B).

Act Sec. 733. DEFINITIONS RELATING TO HEALTH INSURANCE. (b) For purposes of this part—

(b)(1) HEALTH INSURANCE COVERAGE. The term "health insurance coverage" means benefits consisting of medical care (provided directly, through insurance or reimbursement, or otherwise and including items and services paid for as medical care) under any hospital or medical service policy or certificate, hospital or medical service plan contract, or health maintenance organization contract offered by a health insurance issuer.

(2) HEALTH INSURANCE ISSUER. The term "health insurance issuer" means an insurance company, insurance service, or insurance organization (including a health maintenance organization, as defined in paragraph (3)) which is licensed to engage in the business of insurance in a State and which is subject to State law which regulates insurance (within the meaning of section 514(b)(2)). Such term does not include a group health plan.

(3) HEALTH MAINTENANCE ORGANIZATION. The term "health maintenance organization" means—

(A) a federally qualified health maintenance organization (as defined in section 1301(a) of the Public Health Service Act (42 U.S.C. 300e(a))),

(B) an organization recognized under State law as a health maintenance organization, or

(C) a similar organization regulated under State law for solvency in the same manner and to the same extent as such a health maintenance organization.

(4) GROUP HEALTH INSURANCE COVERAGE. The term "group health insurance coverage" means, in connection with a group health plan, health insurance coverage offered in connection with such plan.

Act Sec. 733. EXCEPTED BENEFITS. (c) For purposes of this part, the term "excepted benefits" means benefits under one or more (or any combination thereof) of the following:

(1) BENEFITS NOT SUBJECT TO REQUIREMENTS.—

(A) Coverage only for accident, or disability income insurance, or any combination thereof.

(B) Coverage issued as a supplement to liability insurance.

(C) Liability insurance, including general liability insurance and automobile liability insurance.

(D) Workers' compensation or similar insurance.

(E) Automobile medical payment insurance.

(F) Credit-only insurance.

(G) Coverage for on-site medical clinics.

(H) Other similar insurance coverage, specified in regulations, under which benefits for medical care are secondary or incidental to other insurance benefits.

(2) BENEFITS NOT SUBJECT TO REQUIREMENTS IF OFFERED SEPARATELY.—

(A) Limited scope dental or vision benefits.

(B) Benefits for long-term care, nursing home care, home health care, community-based care, or any combination thereof.

(C) Such other similar, limited benefits as are specified in regulations.

(3) BENEFITS NOT SUBJECT TO REQUIREMENTS IF OFFERED AS INDEPENDENT, NONCOORDINATED BENEFITS.—

(A) Coverage only for a specified disease or illness.

(B) Hospital indemnity or other fixed indemnity insurance.

(4) BENEFITS NOT SUBJECT TO REQUIREMENTS IF OFFERED AS SEPARATE INSURANCE POLICY. Medicare supplemental health insurance (as defined under section 1882(g)(1) of the Social Security Act), coverage supplemental to the coverage provided under chapter 55 of title 10, United States Code, and similar supplemental coverage provided to coverage under a group health plan.

Act Sec. 733. OTHER DEFINITIONS. (d) For purposes of this part—

(1) COBRA CONTINUATION PROVISION. The term "COBRA continuation provision" means any of the following:

(A) Part 6 of this subtitle.

(B) Section 4980B of the Internal Revenue Code of 1986, other than subsection (f)(1) of such section insofar as it relates to pediatric vaccines.

(C) Title XXII of the Public Health Service Act.

(2) HEALTH STATUS-RELATED FACTOR. The term "health status-related factor" means any of the factors described in section 702(a)(1).

(3) NETWORK PLAN. The term "network plan" means health insurance coverage offered by a health insurance issuer under which the financing and delivery of medical care (including items and services paid for as medical care) are provided, in whole or in part, through a defined set of providers under contract with the issuer.

(4) PLACED FOR ADOPTION. The term "placement", or being "placed", for adoption, has the meaning given such term in section 609(c)(3)(B).

Amendments

P.L. 104-204, § 603(a)(3):

Redesignated ERISA Act Sec. 706 as ERISA Act Sec. 733.

The above amendment shall apply with respect to group health plans for plan years beginning on or after January 1, 1998.

P.L. 104-191, § 101(a):

Added ERISA Act Sec. 706 to read as above.

The above amendments generally apply with respect to group health plans for plan years beginning after June 30, 1997. For special rules, see Act Sec. 101(g)(2)- (5), reproduced after ERISA Act Sec. 701 above.

>>>→ *Caution: Act Sec. 734, below, formerly Act Sec. 707, was redesignated as Act Sec. 734 by P.L. 104-204, to apply with respect to group health plans for plan years beginning on or after January 1, 1998.—CCH.*

[¶ 15,051D]
REGULATIONS

Act Sec. 734. The Secretary, consistent with section 104 of the Health Care Portability and Accountability Act of 1996, may promulgate such regulations as may be necessary or appropriate to carry out the provisions of this part. The Secretary may promulgate any interim final rules as the Secretary determines are appropriate to carry out this part.

Amendments

P.L. 104-204, § 603(a)(3):

Redesignated ERISA Act Sec. 707 as ERISA Act Sec. 734.

The above amendment shall apply with respect to group health plans for plan years beginning on or after January 1, 1998.

P.L. 104-191, § 101(a):

Added ERISA Act Sec. 707 to read as above.

The above amendments generally apply with respect to group health plans for plan years beginning after June 30, 1997. For special rules, see Act Sec. 101(g)(2)- (5), reproduced after ERISA Act Sec. 701 above.

Regulations

The following regulations were adopted by 62 FR 16894 and published in the Federal Register on April 8, 1997, under "Chapter XXV of Title 29 of the Code of Federal Regulations; Subchapter L—Health Insurance Portability and Renewability for Group Health Plans; Part 2590—Rules and Regulations for Health Insurance Portability and Renewability for Group Health Plans."

[¶ 15,051D-1]

§ 2590.734. **Enforcement.** [Reserved.]

Regulations

The following regulations were adopted by 62 FR 16894 and published in the Federal Register on April 8, 1997, under "Chapter XXV of Title 29 of the Code of Federal Regulations; Subchapter L—Health Insurance Portability and Renewability for Group Health Plans; Part 2590—Rules and Regulations for Health Insurance Portability and Renewability for Group Health Plans." They were officially corrected on June 10, 1997, by 62 FR 31690. Revised January 8, 2001 by 66 FR 1377. Reg. § 2590.736 was revised by T.D. 9166 on December 30, 2004 (69 FR 78720).

[¶ 15,051E-1]
§ 2590.736. **Applicability dates.** Sections 2590.701-1 through 2590.701-8 and 2590.731 through 2590.736 are applicable for plan years beginning on or after July 1, 2005. Until the applicability date for this regulation, plans and issuers are required to continue to comply with the corresponding sections of 29 CFR part 2590, contained in the 29 CFR, parts 1927 to end, edition revised as of July 1, 2004.

TITLE II—AMENDMENTS TO THE INTERNAL REVENUE CODE RELATING TO RETIREMENT PLANS

Subtitle A—Participation, Vesting, Funding Administration, Etc.

Part 1—Participation, Vesting, and Funding

[¶ 15,052]
AMENDMENT OF INTERNAL REVENUE CODE OF 1954

Act Sec. 1001. Except as otherwise expressly provided, whenever in this title an amendment or repeal is expressed in terms of an amendment to, or repeal of, a section or other provision, the reference shall be considered to be made to a section or other provision of the Internal Revenue Code of 1954.

CCH Note: New and Amended Code Provisions

Title II amendments to the Internal Revenue Code of 1954, encompassing Act Secs. 1011-2008, are incorporated in place in the "Internal Revenue Code—Regulations.". The division contains the new and amended code provisions with controlling committee reports and applicable regulations.

Excerpts from Title II that do not amend the Internal Revenue Code are reproduced below.

[¶ 15,060]
MINIMUM VESTING STANDARDS

Act Sec. 1012.

* * *

(c) VARIATIONS FROM CERTAIN VESTING AND ACCRUED BENEFITS REQUIREMENTS. Inthe case of any plan maintained on January 1, 1974, if, not later than 2 years after the date of the enactment of this Act, the plan administrator petitions the Secretary of Labor, the Secretary of Labor may prescribe an alternate method which shall be treated as satisfying the requirements of subsection (a)(2) of section 411 of the Internal Revenue Code of 1954, or of subsection (b)(1) (other than subparagraph (D) thereof) of such section 411, or of both such provisions for a period of not more than 4 years. The Secretary may prescribe such alternate method only when he finds that—

(1) the application of such requirements would increase the costs of the plan to such an extent that there would result a substantial risk to the voluntary continuation of the plan or a substantial curtailment of benefit levels or the levels of employees' compensation,

(2) the application of such requirements or discontinuance of the plan would be adverse to the interests of plan participants in the aggregate, and

(3) a waiver or extension of time granted under section 412(d) or (e) would be inadequate.

In the case of any plan withh respect to which an alternate method has been prescribed under the preceding provisions of this subsection for a period of not more than 4 years, if, not later than 1 year before the expiration of such period, the plan administrator petitions the Secretary of Labor for an extension of such alternate method, and the Secretary makes the findings required by the preceding sentence, such alternate method may be extended for not more than 3 years.

[¶ 15,062]
CERTAIN PUERTO RICAN PENSION PLANS

Act Sec. 1022.

* * *

(i) CERTAIN PUERTO RICAN PENSION, ETC., PLANS TO BE EXEMPT FROM TAX UNDER SECTION 501(A).—

(1) GENERAL RULE. Effective for taxable years beginning after December 31, 1973, for purposes of section 501(a) of the Internal Revenue Code of 1954 (relating to exemption from tax), any trust forming part of a pension, profitsharing, or stock bonus plan all of the participants of which are residents of the Commonwealth of Puerto Rico shall be treated as an organization described in section 401(a) of such Code if such trust—

(A) forms part of a pension, profitsharing, or stock bonus plan, and

(B) is exempt from income tax under the laws of the Commonwealth of Puerto Rico.

(2) Election to have provisions of, and amendments made by, title II of this act apply.—

(A) If the administrator of a pension, profitsharing, or stock bonus plan which is created or organized in Puerto Rico elects, at such time and in such manner as the Secretary of the Treasury may require, to have the provisions of this paragraph apply, for plan years beginning after the date of election, any trust forming a part of such plan shall be treated as a trust created or organized in the United States for purposes of section 401(a) of the Internal Revenue Code of 1954.

(B) An election under subparagraph (A), once made, is irrevocable.

(C) This paragraph applies to plan years beginning after the date of enactment of this Act.

(D) The source of any distributions made under a plan which makes an election under this paragraph to participants and beneficiaries residing outside of the United States shall be determined, for purposes of subchapter N of chapter 1 of the Internal Revenue Code of 1954, by the Secretary of the Treasury in accordance with regulations prescribed by him. For purposes of this subparagraph the United States means the United States as defined in section 7701(a)(9) of the Internal Revenue Code of 1954.

[¶ 15,065]
EFFECTIVE DATES

Act Sec. 1024. Except as otherwise provided in section 1021, the amendments made by section 1021 shall apply to plan years to which part I applies. Except as otherwise provided in section 1022, the amendments made by section 1022 shall apply to plan years in which part I applies. Section 1023 shall take effect on the date of the enactment of this Act.

[¶ 15,070]
DUTIES OF SECRETARY OF HEALTH, EDUCATION, AND WELFARE

Act Sec. 1032. Title XI of the Social Security Act (relating to general provisions) is amended by adding at the end of part A thereof the following new section:

"NOTIFICATION OF SOCIAL SECURITY CLAIMANT WITH RESPECT TO DEFERRED VESTED BENEFITS

"Sec. 1131. (a) Whenever—

"(1) the Secretary makes a finding of fact and a decision as to—

"(A) the entitlement of any individual to monthly benefits under section 202, 223, or 228,

"(B) the entitlement of any individual to a lump-sum death payment payable under section 202(i) on account of the death of any person to whom such individual is related by blood, marriage, or adoption, or

"(C) the entitlement under section 226 of any individual to hospital insurance benefits under part A of title XVIII, or

"(2) the Secretary is requested to do so—

"(A) by any individual with respect to whom the Secretary holds information obtained under section 6057 of the Internal Revenue Code of 1954, or

"(B) in the case of the death of the individual referred to in subparagraph (A), by the individual who would be entitled to payment under section 204(d) of this Act,

he shall transmit to the individual referred to in paragraph (1) or the individual making the request under paragraph (2) any information, as reported by the employer, regarding any deferred vested benefit transmitted to the Secretary pursuant to such section 6057 with respect to the individual referred to in paragraph (1) or (2)(A) or the person on whose wages and self-employment income entitlement (or claim of entitlement) is based.

"(b)(1) For purposes of section 201(g)(1), expenses incurred in the administration of subsection (a) shall be deemed to be expenses incurred for the administration of title II.

"(2) There are hereby authorized to be appropriated to the Federal Old-Age and Survivors Insurance Trust Fund for each fiscal year (commencing with the fiscal year ending June 30, 1974) such sums as the Secretary deems necessary on account of additional administrative expenses resulting from the enactment of the provisions of subsection (a)."

[¶ 15,075]
EFFECTIVE DATES

Act Sec. 1034. This part shall take effect upon the date of the enactment of this Act; except that—

(1) the requirements of section 6059 of the Internal Revenue Code of 1954 shall apply only with respect to plan years to which part I of this title applies,

(2) the requirements of section 6057 of such Code shall apply only with respect to plan years beginning after December 31, 1975,

(3) the requirements of section 6058(a) of such Code shall apply only with respect to plan years beginning after the date of the enactment of this Act, and

(4) the amendments made by section 1032 shall take effect on January 1, 1978.

[¶ 15,080]
TAX COURT PROCEDURE

Act Sec. 1041.

* * *

(d) EFFECTIVE DATE. The amendments made by this section shall apply to pleadings filed more than 1 year after the date of the enactment of this Act.

Part 5—Internal Revenue Service

[¶ 15,081]
ESTABLISHMENT OF OFFICE

Act Sec. 1051.

* * *

(b) SALARIES.—

(1) ASSISTANT COMMISSIONER. Section 5109 of title 5, United States Code, is amended by adding at the end thereof the following new subsection:

"(c) The position held by the employee appointed under section 7802(b) of the Internal Revenue Code of 1954 is classified at GS-18, and is in addition to the number of positions authorized by section 5108(a) of this title."

(2) CLASSIFICATION OF POSITIONS AT GS-16 AND 17. Section 5108 of title 5, United States Code, is amended by adding at the end thereof the following new subsection:

"(e) In addition to the number of positions authorized by subsection (a), the Commissioner of Internal Revenue is authorized, without regard to any other provision of this section, to place a total of 20 positions in the Internal Revenue Service in GS-16 and 17."

* * *

Act Sec. 1051. EFFECTIVE DATE. (d) The amendments made by this section shall take effect on the 90th day after the date of the enactment of this Act.

[¶ 15,082]
AUTHORIZATION OF APPROPRIATIONS

Act Sec. 1052. There is authorized to be appropriated to the Department of the Treasury for the purpose of carrying out all functions of the Office of Employee Plans and Exempt Organizations for each fiscal year beginning after June 30, 1974, an amount equal to the sum of—

(1) so much of the collections from the taxes imposed under section 4940 of such Code (relating to excise tax based on investment income) as would have been collected if the rate of tax under such section was 2 percent during the second preceding fiscal year, and

(2) the greater of—

(A) an amount equal to the amount described in paragraph (1), or

(B) $30,000,000.

Subtitle B—Other Amendments to the Internal Revenue Code Relating to Retirement Plans

[¶ 15,090]
CONTRIBUTIONS ON BEHALF OF SELF-EMPLOYED INDIVIDUALS AND SHAREHOLDER-EMPLOYEES

Act Sec. 2001.(i) EFFECTIVE DATES.—

(1) The amendments made by subsections (a) and (b) apply to taxable years beginning after December 31, 1973.

(2) The amendments made by subsection (c) apply to—

(A) taxable years beginning after December 31, 1975, and

(B) any other taxable years beginning after December 31, 1973, for which contributions were made under the plan in excess of the amounts permitted to be made under sections 404(e) and 1379(b) as in effect on the day before the date of the enactment of this Act.

(3) The amendments made by subsection (d) apply to taxable years beginning after December 31, 1975.

(4) The amendments made by subsections (e) and (f) apply to contributions made in taxable years beginning after December 31, 1975.

(5) The amendments made by subsection (g) apply to distributions made in taxable years beginning after December 31, 1975.

(6) The amendments made by subsection (h) apply to taxable years ending after the date of enactment of this Act.

[¶ 15,091]
LIMITATIONS ON BENEFITS AND CONTRIBUTIONS

Act Sec. 2004.(a) PLAN REQUIREMENTS.—

* * *

(3) SPECIAL RULE FOR CERTAIN PLANS IN EFFECT ON DATE OF ENACTMENT [September 2, 1974]. In any case in which, on the date of enactment [September 2, 1974] of this Act, an individual is a participant in both a defined benefit plan and a definedcontribution plan maintained by the same employer, and the sum of the defined benefit plan fraction and the defined contribution plan fraction for the year during which such date occurs exceeds 1.4, the sum of such fractions may continue to exceed 1.4 if—

(A) the defined benefit plan fraction is not increased, by amendment of the plan or otherwise, after the date of enactment [September 2, 1974] of this Act, and

(B) no contributions are made under the defined contribution plan after such date.

A trust which is part of a pension, profit-sharing, or stock bonus plan described in the preceding sentence shall not be treated as not constituting a qualified trust under section 401(a) of the Internal Revenue Code of 1954 on account of the provisions of section 415(e) of such Code, as long as it is described in the preceding sentence of this subsection.

* * *

Act Sec. 2004. EFFECTIVE DATE.—

(d)(1) GENERAL RULE. The amendments made by this section shall apply to years beginning after December 31, 1975. The Secretary of the Treasury shall prescribe such regulations as may be necessary to carry out the provisions of this paragraph.

(2) TRANSITION RULE FOR DEFINED BENEFIT PLANS. In the case of an individual who was an active participant in a defined benefit plan before October 3, 1973, if—

(A) the annual benefit (within the meaning of section 415(b)(2) of the Internal Revenue Code of 1954) payable to such participant on retirement does not exceed 100 percent of his annual rate of compensation on the earlier of (i) October 2, 1973, or (ii) the date on which he separated from the service of the employer,

(B) such annual benefit is no greater than the annual benefit which would have been payable to such participant on retirement if (i) all the terms and conditions of such plan in existence on such date had remained in existence until such retirement, and (ii) his compensation taken into account for any period after October 2, 1973, had not exceeded his annual rate of compensation on such date, and

(C) in the case of a participant who separated from the service of the employer prior to October 2, 1973, such annual benefit is no greater than his vested accrued benefit as of the date he separated from the service,

then such annual benefit shall be treated as not exceeding the limitation of subsection (b) of section 415 of the Internal Revenue Code of 1954.

[¶ 15,093]
TAXATION OF CERTAIN LUMP SUM DISTRIBUTIONS

Act Sec. 2005.

* * *

(d) EFFECTIVE DATE. The amendments made by this section shall apply only with respect to distributions or payments made after December 31, 1973, in taxable years beginning after such date.

[¶ 15,095]
RULES FOR CERTAIN NEGOTIATED PLANS

Act Sec. 2007.

* * *

(c) EFFECTIVE DATE. The amendments made by this section shall apply to taxable years ending on or after June 30, 1972.

[¶ 15,096]
CERTAIN ARMED FORCES SURVIVOR ANNUITIES

Act Sec. 2008.

* * *

(c) EFFECTIVE DATES. The amendments made by this section apply to taxable years ending on or after September 21, 1972. The amendments made by paragraphs (3) and (4) of subsection (b) apply with respect to individuals dying on or after such date.

TITLE III—JURISDICTION, ADMINISTRATION, ENFORCEMENT; JOINT PENSION TASK FORCE, ETC.

Subtitle A—Jurisdiction, Administration, and Enforcement

[¶ 15,110]

PROCEDURES IN CONNECTION WITH THE ISSUANCE OF CERTAIN DETERMINATION LETTERS BY THE SECRETARY OF THE TREASURY

Act Sec. 3001.(a) Before issuing an advance determination of whether a pension, profit-sharing, or stock bonus plan, a trust which is a part of such a plan, or an annuity or bond purchase plan meets the requirements of part I of subchapter D of chapter 1 of the Internal Revenue Code of 1986, the Secretary of the Treasury shall require the person applying for the determination to provide, in addition to any material and information necessary for such determination, such other material and information as may reasonably be made available at the time such application is made as the Secretary of Labor may require under title I of this Act for the administration of that title. The Secretary of the Treasury shall also require that the applicant provide evidence satisfactory to the Secretary that the applicant has notified each employee who qualifies as an interested party (within the meaning of regulations prescribed under section 7476(b)(1) of such Code (relating to declaratory judgments in connection with the qualification of certain retirement plans)) of the application for a determination.

Act Sec. 3001.(b)(1) Whenever an application is made to the Secretary of the Treasury for a determination of whether a pension, profit-sharing, or stock bonus plan, a trust which is a part of such a plan, or an annuity or bond purchase plan meets the requirements of part I of subchapter D of chapter 1 of the Internal Revenue Code of 1986, the Secretary shall upon request afford an opportunity to comment on the application at any time within 45 days after receipt thereof to—

    (A) any employee or class of employee qualifying as an interested party within the meaning of the regulations referred to in subsection (a),

    (B) the Secretary of Labor, and

    (C) the Pension Benefit Guaranty Corporation.

    (2) The Secretary of Labor may not request an opportunity to comment upon such an application unless he has been requested in writing to do so by the Pension Benefit Guaranty Corporation or by the lesser of—

    (A) 10 employees, or

    (B) 10 percent of the employees

who qualify as interested parties within the meaning of the regulations referred to in subsection (a). Upon receiving such a request, the Secretary of Labor shall furnish a copy of the request to the Secretary of the Treasury within 5 days (excluding Saturdays, Sundays, and legal public holidays (as set forth in section 6103 of title 5, United States Code)).

    (3) Upon receiving such a request from the Secretary of Labor, the Secretary of the Treasury shall furnish to the Secretary of Labor such information held by the Secretary of the Treasury relating to the application as the Secretary of Labor may request.

    (4) The Secretary of Labor shall, within 30 days after receiving a request from the Pension Benefit Guaranty Corporation or from the necessary number of employees who qualify as interested parties, notify the Secretary of the Treasury, the Pension Benefit Guaranty Corporation, and such employees with respect to whether he is going to comment on the application to which the request relates and with respect to any matters raised in such request on which he is not going to comment. If the Secretary of Labor indicates in the notice required under the preceding sentence that he is not going to comment on all or part of the matters raised in such request, the Secretary of the Treasury shall afford the corporation, and such employees, an opportunity to comment on the application with respect to any matter on which the Secretary of Labor has declined to comment.

Act Sec. 3001. (c) The Pension Benefit Guaranty Corporation and, upon petition of a group of employees referred to in subsection (b)(2), the Secretary of Labor, may intervene in any action brought for declaratory judgment under section 7476 of the Internal Revenue Code of 1986 in accordance with the provisions of such section. The Pension Benefit Guaranty Corporation is permitted to bring an action under such section 7476 under such rules as may be prescribed by the United States Tax Court.

Act Sec. 3001. (d) If the Secretary of the Treasury determines that a plan or trust to which this section applies meets the applicable requirements of part I of subchapter D of chapter 1 of the Internal Revenue Code of 1986 and issues a determination letter to the applicant, the Secretary shall notify the Secretary of Labor of his determination and furnish such information and material relating to the application and determination held by the Secretary of the Treasury as the Secretary of Labor may request for the proper administration of title I of this Act. The Secretary of Labor shall accept the determination of the Secretary of the Treasury as prima facie evidence of initial compliance by the plan with the standards of parts 2, 3, and 4 of subtitle B of title I of this Act. The determination of the Secretary of the Treasury shall not be prima facie evidence on issues relating solely to part 4 of subtitle B of title I. If an application for such a determination is withdrawn, or if the Secretary of the Treasury issues a determination that the plan or trust does not meet the requirements of such part I, the Secretary shall notify the Secretary of Labor of the withdrawal or determination.

Act Sec. 3001. (e) This section does not apply with respect to an application for any plan received by the Secretary of the Treasury before the date on which section 410 of the Internal Revenue Code of 1986 applies to the plan, or on which such section will apply if the plan is determined by the Secretary to be a qualified plan.

Amendments

P.L. 101-239, §7891(a)(1):

    Titles I, III, and IV of ERISA (other than sections 3(37)(E), 301(a)(7), and 308, the last sentence of section 408(d), and sections 414(c), 4001(a)(3)(ii), and 4303) are each

amended by striking "Internal Revenue Code of 1954" each place it appears and inserting "Internal Revenue Code of 1986" effective October 22, 1986.

P.L. 100-203, §9343(b):

    Amended ERISA Sec. 3001(d) by adding a new sentence after the second sentence, to read as above, effective December 22, 1987.

[¶ 15,120]

PROCEDURES WITH RESPECT TO CONTINUED COMPLIANCE WITH REQUIREMENTS RELATING TO PARTICIPATION, VESTING, AND FUNDING STANDARDS

Act Sec. 3002.(a) In carrying out the provisions of part I of subchapter D of chapter 1 of the Internal Revenue Code of 1986 with respect to whether a plan or a trust meets the requirements of section 410(a) or 411 of such Code (relating to minimum participation standards and minimum vesting standards, respectively), the Secretary of the Treasury shall notify the Secretary of Labor when the Secretary of the Treasury issues a preliminary notice of intent to disqualify related to the plan or trust or, if earlier, at the time of commencing any proceeding to determine whether the plan or trust satisfies such requirements. Unless the Secretary of the Treasury finds that the collection of a tax imposed under the Internal Revenue Code of 1986 is in jeopardy, the Secretary of the Treasury shall not issue a determination that the plan or trust does not satisfy the requirements of such section until the expiration of a period of 60 days after the date on which he notifies the Secretary of Labor of such review. The Secretary of the Treasury, in his discretion, may extend the 60-day period referred to in the preceding sentence if he determines that such an extension would enable the Secretary of Labor to obtain compliance with such requirements by the plan within the extension period. Except as otherwise provided in this Act, the Secretary of Labor shall not generally apply part 2 of title I of this Act to any plan or trust subject to sections 410(a) and 411 of such Code, but shall refer alleged general violations of the vesting or participation standards to the Secretary of the Treasury. (The preceding sentence shall not apply to matters relating to individual benefits.)

Act Sec. 3002. (b) Unless the Secretary of the Treasury finds that the collection of a tax is in jeopardy, in carrying out the provisions of section 4971 of the Internal Revenue Code of 1986 (relating to taxes on the failure to meet minimum funding standards), the Secretary of the Treasury shall notify the Secretary of

Labor before sending a notice of deficiency with respect to any tax imposed under that section on an employer, and, in accordance with the provisions of subsection (d) of that section, afford the Secretary of Labor an opportunity to comment on the imposition of the tax imposed under section 4971(b) of such Code in appropriate cases. Upon receiving a written request from the Secretary of Labor or from the Pension Benefit Guaranty Corporation, the Secretary of the Treasury shall cause an investigation to be commenced expeditiously with respect to whether the tax imposed under section 4971 of such Code should be applied with respect to any employer to which the request relates. The Secretary of the Treasury and the Secretary of Labor shall consult with each other from time to time with respect to the provisions of section 412 of the Internal Revenue Code of 1986 (relating to minimum funding standards) and with respect to the funding standards applicable under title I of this Act in order to coordinate the rules applicable under such standards.

Act Sec. 3002. (c) Regulations prescribed by the Secretary of the Treasury under sections 410(a), 411, and 412 of the Internal Revenue Code of 1986 (relating to minimum participation standards, minimum vesting standards, and minimum funding standards, respectively) shall also apply to the minimum participation, vesting, and funding standards set forth in parts 2 and 3 of subtitle B of title I of this Act. Except as otherwise expressly provided in this Act, the Secretary of Labor shall not prescribe other regulations under such parts, or apply the regulations prescribed by the Secretary of the Treasury under sections 410(a), 411, 412 of the Internal Revenue Code of 1986 and applicable to the minimum participation, vesting, and funding standards under such parts in a manner inconsistent with the way such regulations apply under sections 410(a), 411, and 412 of such Code.

Act Sec. 3002. (d) The Secretary of Labor and the Pension Benefit Guaranty Corporation, before filing briefs in any case involving the construction or application of minimum participation standards, minimum vesting standards, or minimum funding standards under title I of this Act, shall afford the Secretary of the Treasury a reasonable opportunity to review any such brief. The Secretary of the Treasury shall have the right to intervene in any such case.

Act Sec. 3002. (e) The Secretary of the Treasury shall consult with the Pension Benefit Guaranty Corporation with respect to any proposed or final regulation authorized by subpart C of part I of subchapter D of chapter 1 of the Internal Revenue Code of 1986, or by sections 4241 through 4245 of this Act, before publishing any such proposed or final regulation.

Amendments

P.L. 101-239, §7891(a)(1):

Titles I, III, and IV of ERISA (other than sections 3(37)(E), 301(a)(7), and 308, the last sentence of section 408(d), and sections 414(c), 4001(a)(3)(ii), and 4303) are each amended by striking "Internal Revenue Code of 1954" each place it appears and inserting "Internal Revenue Code of 1986".

P.L. 96-364, §402(b)(3):

Amended Sec. 3002 effective September 26, 1980 by adding at the end thereof the new subsection (e).

[¶ 15,130]
PROCEDURES IN CONNECTION WITH PROHIBITED TRANSACTIONS

Act Sec. 3003. (a) Unless the Secretary of the Treasury finds that the collection of a tax is in jeopardy, in carrying out the provisions of section 4975 of the Internal Revenue Code of 1986 (relating to tax on prohibited transactions) the Secretary of the Treasury shall, in accordance with the provisions of subsection (h) of such section, notify the Secretary of Labor before sending a notice of deficiency with respect to the tax imposed by subsection (a) or (b) of such section, and, in accordance with the provisions of subsection (h) of such section, afford the Secretary an opportunity to comment on the imposition of the tax in any case. The Secretary of the Treasury shall have authority to waive the imposition of the tax imposed under section 4975(b) in appropriate cases. Upon receiving a written request from the Secretary of Labor or from the Pension Benefit Guaranty Corporation, the Secretary of the Treasury shall cause an investigation to be carried out with respect to whether the tax imposed by section 4975 of such Code should be applied to any person referred to in the request.

Act Sec. 3003. (b) The Secretary of the Treasury and the Secretary of Labor shall consult with each other from time to time with respect to the provisions of section 4975 of the Internal Revenue Code of 1986 (relating to tax on prohibited transactions) and with respect to the provisions of title I of this Act relating to prohibited transactions and exemptions therefrom in order to coordinate the rules applicable under such standards.

Act Sec. 3003. (c) Whenever the Secretary of Labor obtains information indicating that a party-in-interest or disqualified person is violating section 406 of this Act, he shall transmit such information to the Secretary of the Treasury.

Amendment

P.L. 101-239, §7891(a)(1):

Titles I, III, and IV of ERISA (other than sections 3(37)(E), 301(a)(7), and 308, the last sentence of section 408(d), and sections 414(c), 4001(a)(3)(ii), and 4303) are each amended by striking "Internal Revenue Code of 1954" each place it appears and inserting "Internal Revenue Code of 1986".

[¶ 15,140]
COORDINATION BETWEEN THE DEPARTMENT OF THE TREASURY AND THE DEPARTMENT OF LABOR

Act Sec. 3004. (a) Whenever in this Act or in any provision of law amended by this Act the Secretary of the Treasury and the Secretary of Labor are required to carry out provisions relating to the same subject matter (as determined by them) they shall consult with each other and shall develop rules, regulations, practices, and forms which, to the extent appropriate for the efficient administration of such provisions are designed to reduce duplication of effort, duplication of reporting, conflicting or overlapping requirements, and the burden of compliance with such provisions by plan administrators, employers, and participants and beneficiaries.

Act Sec. 3004. (b) In order to avoid unnecessary expense and duplication of functions among Government agencies, the Secretary of the Treasury and the Secretary of Labor may make such arrangements or agreements for cooperation or mutual assistance in the performance of their functions under this Act, and the functions of any such agency as they find to be practicable and consistent with law. The Secretary of the Treasury and the Secretary of Labor may utilize, on a reimbursable or other basis, the facilities or services, of any department, agency, or establishment of the United States or of any State or political subdivision of a State, including the services of any of its employees, with the lawful consent of such department, agency, or establishment; and each department, agency, or establishment of the United States is authorized and directed to cooperate with the Secretary of the Treasury and the Secretary of Labor and, to the extent permitted by law, to provide such information and facilities as they may request for their assistance in the performance of their functions under this Act. The Attorney General or his representative shall receive from the Secretary of the Treasury and the Secretary of Labor for appropriate action such evidence developed in the performance of their functions under this Act as may be found to warrant consideration for criminal prosecution under the provisions of this title or other Federal law.

Subtitle B—Joint Pension, Profit-Sharing, and Employee Stock Ownership Plan Task Force; Studies

Part 1—Joint Pension, Profit-Sharing, and Employee Stock Ownership Plan Task Force

[¶ 15,150]
ESTABLISHMENT

Act Sec. 3021. The staffs of the Committee on Ways and Means and the Committee on Education and Labor of the House of Representatives, the Joint Committee on Internal Revenue Taxation, and the Committee on Finance and the Committee on Labor and Public Welfare of the Senate shall carry out the duties assigned under this title to the Joint Pension, Profit-Sharing, and Employee Stock Ownership Plan Task Force. By agreement among the chairmen of such Committees, the Joint Pension, Profit-Sharing, and Employee Stock Ownership Plan Task Force shall be furnished with office space, clerical personnel, and such supplies and equipment as may be necessary for the Joint Pension, Profit-Sharing, and Employee Stock Ownership Plan Task Force to carry out its duties under this title.

P.L. 94-455, §803(i):

Amended Sec. 3021 by striking out "Joint Pension" each place it appeared and substituting in its place "Joint Pension, Profit-Sharing, and Employee Stock Ownership

Plan." The amendment is applicable to taxable years beginning after December 31, 1974.

[¶ 15,160]
DUTIES

Act Sec. 3022.(a) The Joint Pension, Profit-Sharing, and Employee Stock Ownership Plan Task Force shall, within 24 months after the date of enactment of this Act, make a full study and review of—

(1) the effect of the requirements of section 411 of the Internal Revenue Code of 1986 and of section 203 of this Act to determine the extent of discrimination, if any, among employees in various age groups resulting from the application of such requirements;

(2) means of providing for the portability of pension rights among different pension plans;

(3) the appropriate treatment under title IV of this Act (relating to termination insurance) of plans established and maintained by small employers;

(4) the broadening of stock ownership, particularly with regard to employee stock ownership plans (as defined in section 4975(e)(7) of the Internal Revenue Code of 1986 and section 407(d)(6) of this Act) and all other alternative methods for broadening stock ownership to the American labor force and others;

(5) the effects and desirability of the Federal preemption of State and local law with respect to matters relating to pension and similar plans; and

(6) such other matter as any of the committees referred to in section 3021 may refer to it.

Act Sec. 3022. (b) The Joint Pension, Profit-Sharing, and Employee Stock Ownership Plan Task Force shall report the results of its study and review to each of the committees referred to in section 3021.

P.L. 101-239, §7891(a)(1):

Title I, III, and IV of ERISA (other than sections 3(37)(E), 301(a)(7), and 308, the last sentence of section 408(d), and sections 414(c), 4001(a)(3)(ii), and 4303) are each amended by striking "Internal Revenue Code of 1954" each place it appears and inserting "Internal Revenue Code of 1986".

P.L. 94-455, §803(i):

Amended Sec. 3022 by striking out "Joint Pension" each place it appeared and substituting in its place "Joint Pension, Profit-Sharing, and Employee Stock Ownership Plan." In addition, subsection (a)(4) was added. The amendments are applicable to taxable years beginning after December 31, 1974.

Part 2—Other Studies

[¶ 15,170]
CONGRESSIONAL STUDY

Act Sec. 3031.(a) The Committee on Education and Labor and the Committee on Ways and Means of the House of Representatives and the Committee on Finance and the Committee on Labor and Public Welfare of the Senate shall study retirement plans established and maintained or financed (directly or indirectly) by the Government of the United States, by any State (including the District of Columbia) or political subdivision thereof, or by any agency or instrumentality of any of the foregoing. Such study shall include analysis of—

(1) the adequacy of existing levels of participation, vesting, and financing arrangements,

(2) existing fiduciary standards, and

(3) the necessity for Federal legislation and standards with respect to such plans.

In determining whether any such plan is adequately financed, each committee shall consider the necessity for minimum funding standards, as well as the taxing power of the government maintaining the plan.

Act Sec. 3031. (b) Not later than December 31, 1976, the Committee on Education and Labor and the Committee on Ways and Means shall each submit to the House of Representatives the results of the studies conducted under this section, together with such recommendations as they deem appropriate. The Committee on Finance and the Committee on Labor and Public Welfare shall each submit to the Senate the results of the studies conducted under this section together with such recommendations as they deem appropriate not later than such date.

[¶ 15,180]
PROTECTION FOR EMPLOYEES UNDER FEDERAL PROCUREMENT, CONSTRUCTION, AND RESEARCH CONTRACTS AND GRANTS

Act Sec. 3032.(a) The Secretary of Labor shall, during the 2-year period beginning on the date of the enactment of this Act, conduct a full and complete study and investigation of the steps necessary to be taken to insure that professional, scientific, and technical personnel and others working in associated occupations employed under Federal procurement, construction, or research contracts or grants will, to the extent feasible, be protected against forfeitures of pension or retirement rights or benefits, otherwise provided, as a consequence of job transfers or loss of employment resulting from terminations or modifications of Federal contracts, grants, or procurement policies. The Secretary of Labor shall report the results of his study and investigation to the Congress within 2 years after the date of the enactment of this Act. The Secretary of Labor is authorized, to the extent provided by law, to obtain the services of private research institutions and such other persons by contract or other arrangement as he determines necessary in carrying out the provisions of this section.

Act Sec. 3032. (b) In the course of conducting the study and investigation described in subsection (a), and in developing the regulations referred to in subsection (c), the Secretary of Labor shall consult—

(1) with appropriate professional societies, business organizations, and labor organizations, and

(2) with the heads of interested Federal departments and agencies.

Act Sec. 3032. (c) Within 1 year after the date on which he submits his report to the Congress under subsection (a), the Secretary of Labor shall, if he determines it to be feasible, develop regulations which will provide the protection of pension and retirement rights and benefits referred to in subsection (a).

Act Sec. 3032.(d)(1) Any regulations developed pursuant to subsection (c) shall take effect if, and only if—

(A) the Secretary of Labor, not later than the day which is 3 years after the date of the enactment of this Act, delivers a copy of such regulations to the House of Representatives and a copy to the Senate, and

(B) before the close of the 120-day period which begins on the day on which the copies of such regulations are delivered to the House of Representatives and to the Senate, neither the House of Representatives nor the Senate adopts, by an affirmative vote of a majority of those present and voting in that House, a resolution of disapproval.

(2) For purposes of this subsection, the term "resolution of disapproval" means only a resolution of either House of Congress, the matter after the resolving clause of which is as follows: "That the . . . does not favor the taking effect of the regulations transmitted to the Congress by the Secretary of Labor on . . . ", the first blank space therein being filled with the name of the resolving House and the second blank space therein being filled with the day and year.

(3) A resolution of disapproval in the House of Representatives shall be referred to the Committee on Education and Labor. A resolution of disapproval in the Senate shall be referred to the Committee on Labor and Public Welfare.

(4)(A) If the committee to which a resolution of disapproval has been referred has not reported it at the end of 7 calendar days after its introduction, it is in order to move either to discharge the committee from further consideration of the resolution or to discharge the committee from further consideration of any other resolution of disapproval which has been referred to the committee.

(B) A motion to discharge may be made only by an individual favoring the resolution, is highly privileged (except that it may not be made after the committee has reported a resolution of disapproval), and debate thereon shall be limited to not more than 1 hour, to be divided equally between those favoring and those opposing the resolution. An amendment to the motion is not in order, and it is not in order to move to reconsider the vote by which the motion is agreed to or disagreed to.

(C) If the motion to discharge is agreed to or disagreed to, the motion may not be renewed, nor may another motion to discharge the committee be made with respect to any other resolution of disapproval.

(5)(A) When the committee has reported, or has been discharged from further consideration of, a resolution of disapproval, it is at any time thereafter in order (even though a previous motion to the same effect has been disagreed to) to move to proceed to the consideration of the resolution. The motion is highly privileged and is not debatable. An amendment to the motion is not in order, and it is not in order to move to reconsider the vote by which the motion is agreed to or disagreed to.

(B) Debate on the resolution of disapproval shall be limited to not more than 10 hours, which shall be divided equally between those favoring and those opposing the resolution. A motion further to limit debate is not debatable. An amendment to, or motion to recommit, the resolution is not in order, and it is not in order to move to reconsider the vote by which the resolution is agreed to or disagreed to.

(6)(A) Motions to postpone, made with respect to the discharge from committee or the consideration of a resolution of disapproval, and motions to proceed to the consideration of other business, shall be decided without debate.

(B) Appeals from the decisions of the Chair relating to the application of the rules of the House of Representatives or the Senate, as the case may be, to the procedure relating to any resolution of disapproval shall be decided without debate.

(7) Whenever the Secretary of Labor transmits copies of the regulations to the Congress, a copy of such regulations shall be delivered to each House of Congress on the same day and shall be delivered to the Clerk of the House of Representatives if the House is not in session and to the Secretary of the Senate if the Senate is not in session.

(8) The 120 day period referred to in paragraph (1) shall be computed by excluding—

(A) the days on which either House is not in session because of an adjournment of more than 3 days to a day certain or an adjournment of the Congress sine die, and

(B) any Saturday and Sunday, not excluded under subparagraph (A), when either House is not in session.

(9) This subsection is enacted by the Congress—

(A) as an exercise of the rulemaking power of the House of Representatives and the Senate, respectively, and as such they are deemed a part of the rules of each House, respectively, but applicable only with respect to the procedure to be followed in that House in the case of resolutions of disapproval described in paragraph (2); and they supersede other rules only to the extent that they are inconsistent therewith; and

(B) with full recognition of the constitutional right of either House to change the rules (so far as relating to the procedures of that House) at any time, in the same manner and to the same extent as in the case of any other rule of that House.

Subtitle C—Enrollment of Actuaries

[¶ 15,210]
ESTABLISHMENT OF JOINT BOARD FOR THE ENROLLMENT OF ACTUARIES

Act Sec. 3041. The Secretary of Labor and the Secretary of the Treasury shall, not later than the last day of the first calendar month beginning after the date of the enactment of this Act, establish a Joint Board for the Enrollment of Actuaries (hereinafter in this part referred to as the "Joint Board").

Regulations

The following regulations were adopted by 40 FR 18776, filed with the Federal Register on April 25, 1975, and published in the Federal Register on April 30, 1975, under "Title 20—Employees' Benefits;" "Chapter VIII—Joint Board for the Enrollment of Actuaries;" "Part 900—Statement of Organization." The Bylaws of the Joint Board for the Enrollment of Actuaries are reproduced following the regulations.

[¶ 15,211]
§ 900.1 **Basis.** This Statement is issued by the Joint Board for the Enrollment of Actuaries (the Joint Board) pursuant to the requirement of section 552 of Title 5 of the United States Code that every agency shall publish in the FEDERAL REGISTER a description of its central and field organization.

[¶ 15,212]
§ 900.2 **Establishment.** The Joint Board has been established by the Secretary of Labor and the Secretary of the Treasury pursuant to section 3041 of the Employee Retirement Income Security Act of 1974 (29 U.S.C. 1241). Bylaws of the Board have been issued by the two Secretaries.[1]

BYLAWS OF THE JOINT BOARD FOR THE ENROLLMENT OF ACTUARIES

>>> *CCH Note:: The Bylaws signed on April 27, 1981, appear below*

Pursuant to the Provisions of the Employee Retirement Income Security Act of 1974

(Public Law No. 93-406)

SECTION 1. *Name.*

The name of the organization is the Joint Board for the Enrollment of Actuaries, hereinafter referred to as the Joint Board.

SECTION 2. *Offices.*

The principal office of the Joint Board shall be in the City of Washington, District of Columbia. The Joint Board may have additional offices at such other places as it may deem necessary or desirable for the conduct of its business.

[1] Copy filed with the Office of the Federal Register. Copies may also be obtained from the Executive Director of the Board.

SECTION 3. *Membership.*

(a) (i) The Joint Board shall be composed of five members, three to be appointed by and to serve at the pleasure of the Secretary of the Treasury for three-year terms and two to be appointed by and to serve at the pleasure of the Secretary of Labor for three-year terms. Members of the Joint Board may be appointed for successive three-year terms. To the extent feasible, two of the members appointed by the Secretary of the Treasury and one of the members appointed by the Secretary of Labor shall be actuaries.

(ii) Any Joint Board member who has served three years or more on the date the Bylaws are adopted shall be considered to have served a three-year term and will be subject to reappointment within 30 days from the date of such adoption. The terms of all Joint Board members shall run from the dates of appointment.

(b) A Chairman shall be elected for a one-year term by the Board from among its members. No Chairman shall serve in that capacity for two consecutive terms. The Chairman may designate an Acting Chairman from among the Joint Board members.

(c) A Secretary of the Joint Board shall be elected for a one-year term by the Board from among its members. No Secretary shall serve in that capacity for two consecutive terms. The Secretary of the Joint Board may designate an Acting Secretary from among the Joint Board members.

(d) The Pension Benefit Guaranty Corporation may designate a representative to sit with, and participate in, the discussions of the Joint Board.

(e) The Secretary of the Treasury may appoint one alternate member of the Joint Board. The alternate member shall serve at the pleasure of the Secretary of the Treasury for a three-year term. An alternate member may be appointed for successive three-year terms. The alternate member shall serve on the Joint Board only at such time that one of the Joint Board members appointed by the Secretary of the Treasury (i) has left service on the Joint Board, (ii) is incapacitated for health reasons, or (iii) is unable to participate at meetings of the Joint Board because of a detail or assignment away from his/her regular employment. An alternate member serving on the Joint Board pursuant to this subsection shall be considered a Joint Board member for quorum and voting purposes.

(f) The Secretary of Labor may appoint one alternate member of the Joint Board. The alternate member shall serve at the pleasure of the Secretary of Labor for a three-year term. An alternate member may be appointed for successive three-year terms. The alternate member shall serve on the Joint Board only at such time that one of the Joint Board members appointed by the Secretary of Labor (i) has left service on the Joint Board, (ii) is incapacitated for health reasons, or (iii) is unable to participate at meetings of the Joint Board because of a detail or assignment away from his/her regular employment. An alternate member serving on the Joint Board pursuant to this subsection shall be considered a Joint Board member for quorum and voting purposes.

(g) Members of the Joint Board, who shall be Federal employees, shall serve without compensation from the Board.

SECTION 4. *Powers of the Joint Board.*

(a) The Joint Board shall issue, after approval by the Secretaries of Labor and Treasury, or their delegates, regulations establishing standards and qualifications for the enrollment of persons performing actuarial services with respect to certain employee-benefit plans covered by the Employee Retirement Income Security Act of 1974.

(b) If the Joint Board finds that any person applying for enrollment satisfies the standards and qualifications referred to in Section 4(a) above, the Joint Board shall enroll such individual.

(c) The Joint Board may after an opportunity for a hearing suspend or terminate the enrollment of an individual if the Board finds that such individual has failed to discharge his duties under the Act or does not satisfy the requirement for enrollment in effect at the time of his enrollment.

(d) The Joint Board shall have all such powers, and shall establish and administer necessary policies and procedures, for the performance of the functions assigned to it under Title III, Subtitle C, of the Employee Retirement Income Security Act of 1974.

SECTION 5. *Administration.*

(a) There is established in the Joint Board, an Executive Director. The Executive Director shall be appointed by the Secretary of the Treasury. Authority for administration of the Joint Board, including the hiring of appropriate staff, supervision of personnel, organization, and budget practices, shall be delegated to the Executive Director. In addition, the Executive Director shall provide for the conduct of disciplinary proceedings relating to enrolled actuaries; shall make inquiries with respect to matters under his/her jurisdiction; and shall perform such other duties as are necessary or appropriate to carry out his/her functions under these Bylaws or as are prescribed by the Joint Board.

(b) The Departments of Treasury and Labor shall provide the Joint Board with sufficient support services to perform its functions.

(c) Administrative expenses incurred by the Joint Board in the performance of its duties shall be paid by the Departments of Treasury and Labor.

SECTION 6. *Meetings.*

Regular meetings of the Joint Board shall be held at such times as the Chairman shall select. Special meetings of the Joint Board shall be called by the Chairman on the request of any other member. Reasonable notice of any meetings shall be given to each member. The Secretary of the Joint Board shall keep its minutes, and as soon as practicable after each meeting a draft of the minutes of such meeting shall be distributed to each member of the Board for correction or approval.

SECTION 7. *Quorum.*

(a) A majority of the members, including at least one member appointed by each Department, shall constitute a quorum for the transaction of business. Any act of a majority of the members present at any meeting at which there is a quorum shall be the act of the Board.

(b) A resolution of the Joint Board signed by all of its members shall have the same force and effect as if agreed to at a duly called meeting and shall be recorded in the minutes of the Joint Board.

SECTION 8. *Place of Meetings: Use of Conference Call Communications Equipment.*

Meetings of the Joint Board shall be held in the offices of the Department of the Treasury unless otherwise determined by the Joint Board or the Chairman. Any member may participate in a meeting of the Board through the use of conference call telephone or similar communications equipment, by means of which all persons participating in the meeting can simultaneously speak to and hear each other. Any member so participating in a meeting shall be deemed present for all purposes. Actions taken by the Joint Board at meetings conducted through the use of such equipment, including the votes of each member, shall be recorded in the usual manner in the minutes of the meetings of the Joint Board.

SECTION 9. *Amendments.*

These bylaws may be amended or new bylaws adopted by the Secretaries of Treasury and Labor acting jointly. The Joint Board may recommend such amendment or revision, provided a copy of any proposed amendments has been delivered to each member at least seven days prior to the adoption of such recommendation.

Pursuant to Paragraph 4 of the Order dated October 31, 1974, establishing the Joint Board for the Enrollment of Actuaries, we hereby approve these Bylaws as the Bylaws of the Joint Board, thereby revoking all other Bylaws previously approved.

Raymond J. Donovan

Secretary of Labor

Date: April 10, 1981

Donald T. Regan

Secretary of the Treasury

Date: April 27, 1981

[¶ 15,213]

§ 900.3 **Composition.** Pursuant to the Bylaws, the Joint Board consists of three members appointed by the Secretary of the Treasury and two appointed by the Secretary of Labor. The Board elects a Chairman from among the Treasury Representatives and a Secretary from among the Department of Labor Representatives. The Pension Benefit Guaranty Corporation may designate a non-voting representative to sit with, and participate in, the discussions of the Board. All decisions of the Board are made by simple majority vote.

[¶ 15,214]

§ 900.4 **Meetings.** The Joint Board meets on the call of the Chairman at such times as are necessary in order to consider matters requiring action. Minutes are kept of each meeting by the Secretary.

[¶ 15,215]

§ 900.5 **Staff.** (a) The Executive Director advises and assists the Joint Board directly in carrying out its responsibilities under the Act and performs such other functions as the Board may delegate to him.

(b) Members of the staffs of the Departments of the Treasury and of Labor, by arrangement with the Joint Board, perform such services as may be appropriate in assisting the Board in the discharge of its responsibilities.

[¶ 15,216]

§ 900.6 **Offices.** The Joint Board does not maintain offices separate from those of the Departments of the Treasury and Labor. Its post office address is Joint Board for the Enrollment of Actuaries, c/o Department of the Treasury, Washington, D.C. 20220.

[¶ 15,217]

§ 900.7 **Delegations of authority.** As occasion warrants, the Joint Board may delegate functions to the Chairman or the Executive Director, including the authority to receive applications and to give notice of actions. Any such delegation of authority is conferred by resolution of the Board.

[¶ 15,220]
ENROLLMENT BY JOINT BOARD

Act Sec. 3042. (a) The Joint Board shall, by regulations, establish reasonable standards and qualifications for persons performing actuarial services with respect to plans to which this Act applies and, upon application by any individual, shall enroll such individual if the Joint Board finds that such individual satisfies such standards and qualifications. With respect to individuals applying for enrollment before January 1, 1976, such standards and qualifications shall include a requirement for an appropriate period of responsible actuarial experience relating to pension plans. With respect to individuals applying for enrollment on or after January 1, 1976, such standards and qualifications shall include—

(1) education and training in actuarial mathematics and methodology, as evidenced by—

(A) a degree in actuarial mathematics or its equivalent from an accredited college or university,

(B) successful completion of an examination in actuarial mathematics and methodology to be given by the Joint Board, or

(C) successful completion of other actuarial examinations deemed adequate by the Joint Board, and

(2) an appropriate period of responsible actuarial experience.

Notwithstanding the preceding provisions of this subsection, the Joint Board may provide for the temporary enrollment for the period ending on January 1, 1976, of actuaries under such interim standards as it deems adequate.

Act Sec. 3042. (b) The Joint Board may, after notice and an opportunity for a hearing, suspend or terminate the enrollment of an individual under this section if the Joint Board finds that such individual—

(1) has failed to discharge his duties under this Act, or

(2) does not satisfy the requirements for enrollment as in effect at the time of his enrollment.

The Joint Board may also, after notice and opportunity for hearing, suspend or terminate the temporary enrollment of an individual who fails to discharge his duties under this Act or who does not satisfy the interim enrollment standards.

Regulations

The following regulations were adopted by FR Doc. 76-1156 (41 FR 2080) under "Title 20—Employees' Benefits"; "Chapter VIII—Joint Board for the Enrollment of Actuaries"; "Part 901—Regulations Governing the Performance of Actuarial Services Under the Employee Retirement Income Security Act of 1974" and "Part 902—Rules Regarding Availability of Information." The temporary regulations which were filed with the Federal Register on August 26, 1975, published in the Federal Register of August 27, 1975, have been superseded. Identical proposed regulations that were also published in the Federal Register of August 27, 1975, have been adopted with certain changes (41 FR 2080). In the case of *Sol Tabor v. Joint Board for the Enrollment of Actuaries* the regulations were vacated for failure to comply with the Administrative Procedure Act. The regulations have been reissued (42 FR 39200). They were filed with the Federal Register on July 29, 1977, and published in the Federal Register on August 3, 1977.

Regulations under Title 20—"Employee Benefits," Chapter VIII, Part 901, "Regulations Governing the Performance of Actuarial Services Under the Employee Retirement Income Security Act of 1974" were amended in Subpart B, § 901.11 and Subpart C, § 901.20 and Subparts D and E were adopted by FR Doc. 78-25172 (43 FR 39756) which was filed with the Federal Register on September 6, 1978 and published in the Register on September 7, 1978.

[¶ 15,221]
§ 901.0 Performance of Actuarial Services Under ERISA

Scope. This part contains rules governing the performance of actuarial services under the Employee Retirement Income Security Act of 1974, hereinafter also referred to as ERISA. Subpart A of this part sets forth definitions and eligibility to perform actuarial services; Subpart B of this part sets forth rules governing the enrollment of actuaries; Subpart C of this part sets forth standards of performance to which enrolled actuaries must adhere; Subpart D of this part is reserved and will set forth rules applicable to suspension and termination of enrollment; and Subpart E of this part sets forth general provisions.

Subpart A—Definitions and Eligibility to Perform Actuarial Services

[¶ 15,222]
§ 901.1 Definitions. As used in this part, the term:

(a) *"Actuarial experience"* means the performance of or the direct supervision of, services involving the application of principles of probability and compound interest to determine the present value of payments to be made upon the fulfillment of certain specified conditions or the occurrence of certain specified events.

(b) *"Responsible actuarial experience"* means actuarial experience:

(1) involving participation in making determinations that the methods and assumptions adopted in the procedures followed in actuarial services are appropriate in the light of all pertinent circumstances, and

(2) Demonstrating a thorough understanding of the principles and alternatives involved in such actuarial services.

(c) *"Month of responsible actuarial experience"* means a month during which the actuary spent a substantial amount of time in responsible actuarial experience.

(d) *"Responsible pension actuarial experience"* means responsible actuarial experience involving valuations of the liabilities of pension plans, wherein the performance of such valuations requires the application of principles of life contingencies and compound interest in the determination, under one or more standard actuarial cost methods, of such of the following as may be appropriate in the particular case:

(1) Normal cost.

(2) Accrued liability.

(3) Payment required to amortize a liability or other amount over a period of time.

(4) Actuarial gain or loss.

(e) "*Month of responsible pension actuarial experience*" means a month during which the actuary spent a substantial amount of time in responsible pension actuarial experience.

(f) "*Applicant*" means an individual who has filed an application to become an enrolled actuary.

(g) "*Enrolled actuary*" means an individual who has satisfied the standards and qualifications as set forth in this part and who has been approved by the Joint Board (or its designee) to perform actuarial services required under ERISA or regulations thereunder.

(h) "*Actuarial services*" means performance of actuarial valuations and preparation of any actuarial reports.

[¶ 15,222A]

§ 901.2 **Eligibility to perform actuarial services**. (a) *Enrolled actuary*. Subject to the standards of performance set forth in Subpart C of this part, any individual who is an enrolled actuary as defined in § 901.1(g) may perform actuarial services required under ERISA or regulations thereunder. Where a corporation, partnership, or other entity is engaged to provide actuarial services, such services may be provided on its behalf only by an enrolled actuary who is an employee, partner or consultant.

(b) *Government officers and employees*. No officer or employee of the United States in the executive, legislative, or judicial branch of the Government, or in any agency of the United States, including the District of Columbia, may perform actuarial services required under ERISA or regulations thereunder if such services would be in violation of 18 U.S.C. 205. No Member of Congress or Resident Commissioner (elect or serving) may perform such actuarial services if such services would be in violation of 18 U.S.C. 203 or 205.

(c) *Former government officers and employees*. (1) *Personal and substantial participation in the performance of actuarial services*. No former officer or employee of the executive branch of the United States Government, of any independent agency of the United States, or of the District of Columbia, shall perform actuarial services required under ERISA or regulations thereunder or aid or assist in the performance of such actuarial services, in regard to particular matters, involving a specific party or parties, in which the individual participated personally and substantially as such officer or employee.

(2) *Official responsibility*. No former officer or employee of the executive branch of the United States Government, of any independent agency of the United States, or of the District of Columbia, shall, within 1 year after his employment has ceased, perform actuarial services required under ERISA or regulations thereunder in regard to any particular matter involving a specific party or parties which was under the individual's official responsibility as an officer or employee of the Government at any time within a period of 1 year prior to the termination of such responsibility.

Subpart B—Enrollment of Actuaries

[¶ 15,223]

§ 901.10 **Application for enrollment**. (a) *Form*. As a requirement for enrollment, an applicant shall file with the Executive Director of the Joint Board a properly executed application on a form or forms specified by the Joint Board, and shall agree to comply with the regulations of the Joint Board.

(b) *Additional information*. The Joint Board or Executive Director, as a condition to consideration of an application for enrollment, may require the applicant to file additional information and to submit to written or oral examination under oath or otherwise.

(c) *Denial of application*. If the Joint Board proposes to deny an application for enrollment, the Executive Director shall notify the applicant in writing of the proposed denial and the reasons therefor, of his rights to request reconsideration, of the address to which such request should be made and the date by which such request must be made. The applicant may, within 30 days from the date of the written proposed denial, file a written request for reconsideration therefrom, together with his reasons in support thereof, to the Joint Board. The Joint Board may afford an applicant the opportunity to make a personal appearance before the Joint Board. A decision on the request for reconsideration shall be rendered by the Joint Board as soon as practicable. In the absence of a request for reconsideration within the aforesaid 30 days, the proposed denial shall, without further proceeding, constitute a final decision of denial by the Joint Board.

[¶ 15,223A]

§ 901.11 **Enrollment procedures**. (a) *Enrollment*. The Joint Board shall enroll each applicant it determines has met the requirements of these regulations, and shall so notify the applicant. Subject to the provisions of Subpart D of this part, an individual must renew his or her enrollment in the manner described in paragraph (d) of this section. [Amended by 53 FR 34484, 9-7-88.]

(b) *Enrollment certificate*. The Joint Board (or its designee) shall issue a certificate of enrollment to each actuary who is duly enrolled under this part.

(c) *Rosters*. The Executive Director shall maintain rosters of all actuaries who are duly enrolled under this part and of all individuals whose enrollment has been suspended or terminated.

(d) *Renewal of enrollment*. To maintain active enrollment to perform actuarial services under the Employee Retirement Income Security Act of 1974, each enrolled actuary is required to have his/her enrollment renewed as set forth herein. Failure by an individual to receive notification of the renewal requirement from the Joint Board will not be justification for circumvention of such requirement.

(1) All individuals enrolled before January 1, 1990 shall apply for renewal of enrollment on the prescribed form before March 1, 1990. The effective date of renewal for such individuals is April 1, 1990.

(2) Thereafter, applications for renewal will be required of all enrolled actuaries between October 1, 1992 and March 1, 1993, and between October 1 and March 1 of every third year period subsequent thereto.

(3) The Executive Director of the Joint Board will notify each enrolled actuary of the renewal of enrollment requirement at his/her address of record with the Joint Board.

(4) A reasonable non-refundable fee may be charged for each application for renewal of enrollment filed.

(5) Forms required for renewal may be obtained form the Executive Director, Joint Board for the Enrollment of Actuaries, c/o Department of the Treasury, Washington, D.C. 20220.

(e) *Condition for renewal: continuing professional education*. To qualify for renewal of enrollment, an enrolled actuary must certify, on the form prescribed by the Executive Director, that he/she has satisfied the following continuing professional education requirements.

(1) *For renewed enrollment effective April 1, 1990*.

(i) A minimum of 10 hours of continuing education credit must be completed between (the effective date of these regulations) and December 31, 1989. Of the 10 hours, at least 6 hours must be comprised of core subject matter; the remainder may be comprised of non-core subject matter.

(ii) An individual who receives initial enrollment between October 1, 1988 and December 31, 1989 is exempt from the continuing education requirement for the enrollment cycle ending December 31, 1989, but is required to file a timely application for renewal of enrollment effective April 1, 1990.

(2) *For renewed enrollment effective April 1, 1993 and every third year thereafter*.

(i) A minimum of 36 hours of continuing education credit must be completed between January 1, 1990 and December 31, 1992, and between January 1 and December 31 for each three-year period subsequent thereto. Each such three-year period is known as an enrollment cycle. Of the 36 hours, at least 18 must be comprised of core subject matter; the remainder may be of a non-core nature.

(ii) An individual who receives initial enrollment during the first or second year of an enrollment cycle must satisfy the following requirements by the end of the enrollment cycle: Those enrolled during the first year of an enrollment cycle must complete 24 hours of continuing education; those enrolled during the second year of an enrollment cycle must complete 12 hours of continuing education. At least one half of the applicable hours must be comprised of core subject matter; the remainder may be comprised of non-core subject matter. For purposes of this paragraph, credit will be awarded for continuing education completed after January 1 of the year in which initial enrollment was received.

(iii) An individual who receives initial enrollment during the third year of an enrollment cycle is exempt from the continuing education requirements until the next enrollment cycle, but must file a timely application for renewal.

(3) Enrolled actuaries whose enrollment status would have expired under previous regulations during the five-year period from October 1, 1988 are not subject to compliance with such previous regulations addressing renewal of enrollment. Their enrollment status will not be adversely affected provided they comply with requirements of this part.

(f) *Qualifying continuing education.* (1) *In general.* To qualify for continuing education credit consistent with the requirements of the above subsections, a course of learning must be a qualifying program comprised of core and/or non-core subject matter conducted by a qualifying sponsor.

(i) Core subject matter is program content designed to enhance the knowledge of an enrolled actuary with respect to matters directly related to the performance of pension actuarial services under ERISA or the Internal Revenue Code. Such core subject matter includes the characteristics of actuarial cost methods under ERISA, actuarial assumptions, minimum funding standards, Title IV of ERISA, requirements with respect to the valuation of plan assets, requirements for qualification of pension plans, maximum deductible contributions, tax treatments of distributions from qualified pension plans, excise taxes related to the funding of qualified pension plans and standards of performance for actuarial services.

(ii) Non-core subject matter is program content designed to enhance the knowledge of an enrolled actuary in matters related to the performance of pension actuarial services. Examples include economics, computer programs, pension accounting, investment and finance, risk theory, communication skills and business and general tax law.

(iii) The Joint Board may publish other topics or approve other topics which may be included in a qualifying program as core or non-core subject matter.

(iv) Repeated taking of the same course of study cannot be used to satisfy the continuing education requirements of the regulations. If the major content of a program or session differs substantively from a previous one bearing the same or similar title, it may be used to satisfy such requirements.

(2) *Qualifying Programs.* (i) *Formal programs.* Formal programs qualify as continuing education programs if they:

A. Require attendance by at least three individuals engaged in substantive pension service in addition to the instructor, discussion leader or speaker;

B. Require that the program be conducted by a qualified instructor, discussion leader or speaker, i.e. a person whose background, training, education and/or experience is appropriate for instructing or leading a discussion on the subject matter of the particular program; and

C. Require a written outline and/or textbook and cerfificate of attendance provided by the sponsor, all of which must be retained by the enrolled actuary for a three year period following the end of the enrollment cycle.

(ii) *Correspondence or individual study programs (including audio and/or video taped programs).* Qualifying continuing education programs include correspondence or individual study programs completed on an individual basis by the enrolled actuary and conducted by qualifying sponsors. The allowable credit hours for such programs will be measured on a basis comparable to the measurement of a seminar or course for credit in an accredited educational institution. Such programs qualify as continuing education programs if they:

(A) Require registration of the participants by the sponsor;

(B) Provide a means for measuring completion by the participants (e.g., written examination); and

(C) Require a written outline and/or textbook and certificate of completion provided by the sponsor. Such certificate must be retained by the participant for a three year period following the end of an enrollment cycle.

(iii) *Teleconferencing:.* Programs utilizing teleconferencing or other communications technologies qualify for continuing education purposes if they either:

(A) Meet all the requirements of formal programs, execpt that they may include a sign-on/sign-off capacity or similar technique in lieu of the physical attendance of participants; or

(B) Meet all the requirements of correspondence or individual study programs.

(iv) *Serving as an instructor, discussion leader or speaker.*

(A) Four hours of continuing education credit will be awarded for each contact hour completed as an instructor, discussion leader or speaker at an educational program which meets the continuing education requirements of this section, in recognition of both presentation and preparation time.

(B) The credit for instruction and preparation may not exceed 50% of the continuing education requirement for an enrollment cycle.

(C) Presentation of the same material as an instructor, discussion leader or speaker more than one time in any 36 month period will not qualify for continuing education credit. A program will not be considered to consist of the same material if a substantial portion of the content has been revised to reflect changes in the law or in the state of the art relative to the performance of pension actuarial service.

(D) Credit as an instructor, discussion leader or speaker will not be awarded to panelists, moderators or others whose contribution does not constitute a substantial portion of the program. However, such individuals may be awarded credit for attendance, provided the other provisions of this section are met.

(E) The nature of the subject matter will determine if credit will be of a core or non-core nature.

(v) *Credit for published articles, books, films, audio and video tapes, etc.*

(A) Continuing education credit will be awarded for the creation of materials for publication or distribution with respect to matters directly related to the continuing professional education requirements of this section.

(B) The credit allowed will be on the basis of one hour credit for each hour of preparation time of the material. It will be the responsibility of the person claiming the credit to maintain records to verify preparation time.

(C) Publication or distribution may utilize any available technology for the dissemination of written, visual or auditory materials.

(D) The materials must be available on reasonable terms for acquisition and used by all enrolled actuaries.

(E) The credit for the creation of materials may not exceed 25% of the continuing education requirement of any enrollment cycle.

(F) The nature of the subject matter will determine if credit will be of a core or non-core nature.

(G) Publication of the same material more than one time will not qualify for continuing education credit. A publication will not be considered to consist of the same material if a substantial portion has been revised to reflect changes in the law or in the state of the art relating to the performance of pension actuarial service.

(vi) *Service on Joint Board advisory committee(s)*. Continuing education credit may be awarded by the Joint Board for service on (any of) its advisory committee(s), to the extent that the Board considers warranted by the service rendered.

(vii) *Preparation of Joint Board examination*. Continuing educational credit may be awarded by the Joint Board for participation in drafting questions for use on Joint Board examinations or in pretesting its examinations, to the extent the Board determines suitable. Such credit may be not exceed 50% of the continuing professional education requirement for the applicable enrollment cycle.

(viii) *Society examinations*. Individuals may earn continuing professional education credit for achieving a passing grade on proctored examinations sponsored by a professional organization or society recognized by the Joint Board. Such credit is limited to the number of hours scheduled for each examination and may be applied only as non-core credit provided the content of the examination is non-core.

(ix) *Pension law examination*. Individuals may establish eligibility for renewal of enrollment for any enrollment cycle by:

(A) Achieving a passing score on the pension law actuarial examination offered by the Joint Board and administered under this part during the applicable enrollment cycle; and

(B) Completing a minimum of 12 hours of qualifying continuing education in core subject matter during the same applicable enrollment cycle.

(C) This option of satisfying the continuing professional education requirements is not available to those who receive initial enrollment during the enrollment cycle.

(g) *Sponsors*. (1) Sponsors are those responsible for presenting programs.

(2) To qualify as a sponsor, a program presenter must:

(i) Be an accredited educational institution;

(ii) Be recognized for continuing education purposes by the lincensing body of any State, possession, territory, Commonwealth, or the District of Columbia responsible for the issuance of a license in the field of actuarial science, insurance, accounting or law;

(iii) Be recognized by the Executive Director of the Joint Board as a professional organization or society whose programs include offering continuing professional education opportunities in subject matter within the scope of this section; or

(iv) File a sponsor agreement with the Executive Director of the Joint Board to obtain approval of the program as a qualifying continuing education program.

(3) Professional organizations or societies and others wishing to be considering as qualifying sponsors shall request such status of the Executive Director of the Joint Board and furnish information in support of the request together with any further information deemed necessary by the Executive Director.

(4) A qualifying sponsor must ensure the program complies with the following requirements:

(i) Programs must be developed by individual(s) qualified in the subject matter.

(ii) Program subject matter must be current.

(iii) Instructors, discussion leaders, and speakers must be qualified with respect to program content.

(iv) Programs must include some means for evaluation of technical content and presentation.

(v) Certificates of completion must be provided those who have successfully completed the program.

(vi) Records must be maintained by the sponsor to verify satisfaction of the requirements of this section. Such records must be retained for a period of three years following the end of the enrollment cycle in which the program is held. In the case of programs of more than one session, records must be maintained to verify completion of the program and attendance by each participant at each session of the program.

(5) Sponsor agreements and qualified professional organization or society sponsors approved by the Executive Director wil remain in effect for one enrollment cycle. The names of such sponsors will be published on a periodic basis.

(h) *Measurement of continuing education course work*. (1) All continuing education programs will be measured in terms of credit hours. The shortest recognized program will be one credit hour.

(2) A credit hour is 50 minutes of continuous participation in a program. Each session in a program must be at least one full credit hour, i.e., 50 minutes. For example, a single-session program lasting 100 minutes will count as two credit hours, and a program comprised of three 75 minute sessions (225 minutes) constitutes four credit hours. However, at the end of an enrollment cycle, an individual may total the number of minutes of sessions of at least one credit hour in duration attended during the cycle and divided by fifty. For example, attending three 75 minutes segments at two separate programs will accord an individual nine credit hours (450 minutes divided by 50) toward fulfilling the minimum number of continuing professional education hours. It will not be permissible to merge non-core hours with core hours.

For university or college courses, each "semester" hour credit will equal 15 credit hours and each "quarter" hour credit will equal 10 credit hours. Measurements of other formats of university or college courses will be handled on a comparable basis.

(i) *Record keeping requirements*. (1) Each individual applying for renewal shall retain for a period of three years following the end of an enrollment cycle the information required with regard to qualifying continuing professional education credit hours. Such information shall include:

(i) The name of the sponsoring organization;

(ii) The location of the program;

(iii) The title of the program and description of its content, e.g., course syllabus and/or textbooks;

(iv) The dates attended;

(v) The credit hours claimed and whether core or non-core subject matter;

(vi) The name(s) of the instructor(s), discussion leader(s), or speaker(s), if appropriate;

(vii) The certificate of completion and/or signed statement of the hours of attendance obtained from the sponsor; and

(viii) The total core and non-core credit.

(2) To receive continuing education credit for service completed as an instructor, discussion leader, or speaker, the following information must be maintained for a period of three years following the end of the applicable enrollment cycle.

(i) The name of the sponsoring organization;

(ii) The location of the program;

(iii) The title of the program and description of its content;

(iv) The dates of the program; and

(v) The credit hours claimed and whether core or non-core subject matter;

(3) To receive continuing education credit for a publication, the following information must be maintained for a period of three years following the end of the applicable enrollment cycle.

(i) The publisher;

(ii) The title of the publication;

(iii) A copy of the publication;

(iv) The date of publication;

(v) The credit hours claimed;

(vi) Whether core or non-core subject matter; and

(vii) The availability and distribution of the publications to enrolled actuaries.

(j) *Waivers*. (1) Waiver from the continuing education requirements for a given period may be granted by the Executive Director of the Joint Board for the following reasons:

(i) Physical incapacity, which prevented compliance with the continuing education requirements;

(ii) Extended active military duty;

(iii) Absence from the individual's country of residence for an extended period of time due to employment or other reasons, provided the individual does not perform services as an enrolled actuary during such absence; and

(iv) Other compelling reasons, which will be considered on a case-by-case basis.

(2) A request for waiver must be accompanied by appropriate documentation. The individual will be required to furnish any additional documentation or explanation deemed necessary by the Executive Director of the Joint Board. Examples of appropriate documentation could be a medical certificate, military orders, etc.

(3) A request for waiver must be filed no later than the last day of the renewal application period.

(4) If a request for waiver is not approved, the individual will be so notified by the Executive Director of the Joint Board and placed on a roster of inactive enrolled individuals.

(5) If a request for waiver is approved, the individual will be so notified.

(6) Those who are granted waivers are required to file timely applications for renewal of enrollment.

(k) *Failure to comply.* (1) Compliance by an individual with the requirements of this part shall be determined by the Executive Director of the Joint Board. An individual who applies for renewal of enrollment but who fails to meet the requirements of eligibility for renewal will be notified by the Executive Director at his/her last known address by first class mail. The notice will state the basis for the non-compliance and will provide the individual an opportunity to furnish in writing, within 60 days of the date of the notice, information relating to the matter. Such information will be considered by the Executive Director in making a final determination as to eligibility for renewal of enrollment.

(2) The Executive Director of the Joint Board may require any individual, by first class mail sent to his/her mailing address of record within the Joint Board, to provide copies of any records required to be maintained under this section. The Executive Director may disallow any continuing professional education hours claimed if the individual concerned fails to comply with such requirements.

(3) An individual whose application for renewal is not approved may seek review of the matter by the Joint Board. A request for review and the reasons in support of the request must be filed with the Joint Board within 30 days of the date of the non-approved notice.

(4) An individual who has not filed a timely application for renewal of enrollment, who has not made a timely response to the notice of non-compliance with the renewal requirements, or who has not satisfied the requirements of eligibility for renewal will be placed on a roster of inactive enrolled actuaries for a period of three years from the date renewal would have been effective. During this time, the individual will be ineligible to perform services as an enrolled actuary and to practice before the Internal Revenue Service.

(5) During inactive enrollment status or at any other time an individual is ineligible to perform services as an enrolled actuary and to practice before the Internal Revenue Service, the individual shall not in any manner, directly or indirectly, indicate he or she is so enrolled, or use the term "enrolled actuary," the designation "E. A.," or other form of reference to eligibility to perform services as an enrolled actuary.

(6) An individual placed in an inactive status must file an application for renewal of enrollment and satisfy the requirements for renewal as set forth in this section within three years from the date renewal would have been effective. The name of such individual otherwise will be removed from the inactive enrollment roster and his/her enrollment will terminate. Eligibility for enrollment must then be reestablished by the individual as provided in this part.

(7) An individual placed in an inactive status may satisfy the requirements for renewal of enrollment at any time during his/her period of inactive enrollment. If such satisfaction includes completing the continuing education requirement, the application for renewal may be filed immediately upon such completion. Continuing education credit under this subsection may not be used to satisfy the requirements of the enrollment cycle in which the individual has been placed back on the active roster.

(8) An individual in inactive status remains subject to the jurisdiction of the Joint Board and/or the Department of the Treasury with respect to disciplinary matters.

(9) An individual who is in good faith has certified that he/she has satisfied the continuing professional education requirements of this section will not be considered to be in non-compliance with such requirements on the basis of a program he/she has attended being found inadequate or not in compliance with the requirements for renewal. Such individual will be granted renewal, but the Executive Director may require such individual to remedy the resulting shortfall by earning replacement credit during the cycle in which renewal was granted or within a reasonable time period as determined by the Executive Director. For example, if six of the credit hours claimed were disallowed, the individual may be required to present 42 credit hours instead of the minimum 36 credit hours to qualify for renewal related to the next cycle.

(l) *Inactive retirement status.* An individual who no longer performs services as an enrolled actuary may request placement in an inactive retirement status at any time and such individual will be placed in such status. The individual will be ineligible to perform services as an enrolled actuary. Such individual must file a timely application for renewal of enrollment at each applicable renewal cycle provided in this part. An individual who is placed in an inactive retirement status may be reinstated to active enrollment status upon filing an application for renewal of enrollment and providing evidence of the completion of the required continuing professional education hours for the applicable enrollment cycle. An individual in inactive retirement status remains subject to the jurisdiction of the Joint Board and/or the Department of the Treasury with respect to disciplinary matters.

(m) *Renewal while under suspension or disbarment.* An individual who is ineligible to perform actuarial services and/or to practice before the Internal Revenue Service by virtue of disciplinary action is required to meet the requirements for renewal of enrollment during the period of such ineligibility.

(n) *Verification.* The Executive Director of the Joint Board or his/her designee may review the continuing education records of an enrolled actuary and/or qualified sponsor, including attending programs, in a manner deemed appropriate to determine compliance with the requirements and standards for the renewal of enrollment as provided in this section.

[¶ 15,223B]

§ 901.12 **Eligibility for enrollment of individuals applying for enrollment before January 1, 1976**. (a) *In general*. An individual applying before January 1, 1976, to be an enrolled actuary must fulfill the experience requirements of paragraph (b) of this section and either the examination requirements of paragraph (c) of this section or the educational requirements of paragraph (d) of this section.

(b) *Qualifying experience*. Within a 15 year period immediately preceding the date of application, the applicant shall have completed either:

(1) A minimum of 36 months of responsible pension actuarial experience, or

(2) A minimum of 60 months of responsible actuarial experience, including at least 18 months of responsible pension actuarial experience.

(c) *Examination requirement*. The applicant shall satisfactorily complete the Joint Board examination requirement of paragraph (c)(1) of this section or the organization examination requirement of paragraph (c)(2) of this section.

(1) *Joint Board examination*. To satisfy the Joint Board examination requirement, the applicant shall have completed, to the satisfaction of the Joint Board, an examination prescribed by the Joint Board in actuarial mathematics and methodology related to pension plans, including the funding requirements of ERISA.

(2) *Organization examination.* (i) To satisfy the organization examination requirement, the applicant shall, before March 1, 1975, have attained by proctored examination one of the following classes of qualification in one of the following organizations:

    (A) Member of the American Academy of Actuaries,

    (B) Fellow or Member of the American Society of Pension Actuaries,

    (C) Fellow or Associate of the Casualty Actuarial Society,

    (D) Fellow or Member of the Conference of Actuaries in Public Practice,

    (E) Fellow or Associate of the Society of Actuaries, or

    (F) A class attained by proctored examination in any other actuarial organization in the United States or elsewhere if the Joint Board determines that the subject matter included in such examination, complexity of questions, and the minimum acceptable qualifying score are at least comparable to proctored examinations administered by any of the above organizations before March 1, 1975; or

    (ii) On or after March 1, 1975, the applicant shall have attained one of the classes of qualification specified in paragraph (c)(2)(i) of this section, the attainment of such qualification having been by proctored examination under requirements determined by the Joint Board to be of not lower standards than the requirements for qualification during the 12 months immediately preceding March 1, 1975.

(d) *Qualifying formal education.* Prior to filing an application, the applicant shall have satisfied one of the following educational requirements:

    (1) Received a bachelor's or higher degree from an accredited college or university, such degree having been granted after the satisfactory completion of a course of study in which the major area of concentration was actuarial science, or

    (2) Received a bachelor's or higher degree from an accredited college or university, such degree having been granted after the satisfactory completion of a course of study in which the major area of concentration was mathematics, statistics, or computer science, and shall have successfully completed at least 6 semester hours or 9 quarter hours of courses in life contingencies at an accredited college or university.

(e) *Disreputable conduct.* The applicant may be denied enrollment if it is found that he/she, after his/her eighteenth birthday, has:

    (1) Engaged in any conduct evidencing fraud, dishonesty or breach of trust, or

    (2) Been convicted of any of the offenses referred to in section 411 of ERISA, or

    (3) Submitted false or misleading information on an application for enrollment to perform actuarial services or in any oral or written information submitted in connection therewith or in any report presenting actuarial information to any person, knowing the same to be false or misleading.

[¶ 15,223C]

§901.13 **Eligibility for enrollment of individuals applying for enrollment on or after January 1, 1976.** (a) *In general.* An individual applying on or after January 1, 1976, to be an enrolled actuary, must fulfill the experience requirement of paragraph (b) of this section, the basic actuarial knowledge requirement of paragraph (c) of this section, and the pension actuarial knowledge requirement of paragraph (d) of this section.

(b) *Qualifying experience.* Within a 10 year period immediately preceding the date of application, the applicant shall have completed either:

    (1) A minimum of 36 months of responsible pension actuarial experience, or

    (2) A minimum of 60 months of responsibile actuarial experience, including at least 18 months of responsible pension actuarial experience.

(c) *Basic actuarial knowledge.* The applicant shall demonstrate knowledge of basic actuarial mathematics and methodology by one of the following:

    (1) *Joint Board basic examination.* Successful completion, to a score satisfactory to the Joint Board, of an examination, prescribed by the Joint Board, in basic actuarial mathematics and methodology including compound interest, principles of life contingencies, commutation functions, multiple-decrement functions, and joint life annuities.

    (2) *Organization basic examinations.* Successful completion, to a score satisfactory to the Joint Board, of one or more proctored examinations which are given by an actuarial organization and which the Joint Board has determined cover substantially the same subject areas, have at least a comparable level of difficulty, and require at least the same competence as the Joint Board basic examination referred to in paragraph (c)(1) of this section.

    (3) *Qualifying formal education.* Receipt of a bachelor's or higher degree from an accredited college or university after the satisfactory completion of a course of study:

      (i) In which the major area of concentration was actuarial mathematics, or

      (ii) Which included at least as many semester hours or quarter hours each in mathematics, statistics, actuarial mathematics and other subjects as the Board determines represent equivalence to paragraph (c)(3)(i) of this section.

(d) *Pension actuarial knowledge.* The applicant shall demonstrate pension actuarial knowledge by one of the following:

    (1) *Joint Board pension examination.* Successful completion, to a score satisfactory to the Joint Board, of an examination, prescribed by the Joint Board, in actuarial mathematics and methodology relating to pension plans, including the provisions of ERISA relating to the minimum funding requirements and allocation of assets on plan termination.

    (2) *Organization pension examinations.* Successful completion, to a score satisfactory to the Joint Board, of one or more proctored examinations which are given by an actuarial organization and which the Joint Board has determined cover substantially the same subject areas, have at least a comparable level of difficulty, and require at least the same competence as the Joint Board pension examination referred to in paragraph (d)(1) of this section.

(e) *Form; fee.* An applicant who wishes to take an examination administered by the Joint Board under paragraph (c)(1) or (d)(1) of this section shall file an application on a form prescribed by the Joint Board. Such application shall be accompanied by a check or money order in the amount set forth on the application form, payable to the Treasury of the United States. The amount represents a fee charged to each applicant for examination and is designed to cover the costs assessed the Joint Board for the administration of the examination. The fee shall be retained by the United States whether or not the applicant successfully completes the examination or is enrolled. [Added by 44 FR 68457, effective November 13, 1979.]

(f) *Denial of enrollment.* An applicant may be denied enrollment if:

    (1) The Joint Board finds that the applicant, during the 15-year period immediately preceding the date of application and on or after the applicant's eighteenth birthday has engaged in disreputable conduct. The term disreputable conduct includes, but is not limited to:

      (i) An adjudication, decision, or determination by a court of law, a duly constituted licensing or accreditation authority (other than the Joint Board), or by any federal or state agency, board, commission, hearing examiner, administrative law judge, or other official administrative authority, that the applicant has engaged in conduct evidencing fraud, dishonesty or breach of trust.

      (ii) Giving false or misleading information, or participating in any way in the giving of false or misleading information, to the Department of the Treasury or the Department of Labor or the Pension Benefit Guaranty Corporation or any officer or employee thereof in connection with any matter pending or likely to be pending before them, knowing such information to be false or misleading.

      (iii) Willfully failing to make a federal tax return in violation of the revenue laws of the United States, or evading, attempting to evade, or participating in any way in evading or attempting to evade any federal tax or payment thereof, knowingly counseling or suggesting to a client or prospective client an illegal plan to evade federal taxes or payment thereof, or concealing assets of himself or another to evade federal taxes or payment thereof.

(iv) Directly or indirectly attempting to influence, or offering or agreeing to attempt to influence, the official action of any officer or employee of the Department of the Treasury or the Department of Labor or the Pension Benefit Guaranty Corporation by the use of threats, false accusations, duress or coercion, by the offer of any special inducement or promise of advantage or by the bestowing of any gift, favor, or thing of value.

(v) Disbarment or suspension from practice as an actuary, attorney, certified public accountant, public accountant, or an enrolled agent by any duly constituted authority of any state, possession, territory, commonwealth, the District of Columbia, by any Federal Court of record, or by the Department of the Treasury.

(vi) Contemptuous conduct in connection with matters before the Department of Labor or the Pension Benefit Guaranty Corporation, including the use of abusive language, making false accusations and statements knowing them to be false, or circulating or publishing malicious or libelous matter.

(2) The applicant has been convicted of any of the offenses referred to in section 411 of ERISA.

(3) The applicant has submitted false or misleading information on an application for enrollment to perform actuarial services or in any oral or written information submitted in connection therewith or in any report presenting actuarial information to any person, knowing the same to be false or misleading. [Added November 12, 1976, by 41 FR 49970. Amended by 43 FR 39756, filed with the Federal Register September 6, 1978, and published in the Federal Register on September 6, 1978.]

Subpart C—Standards of Performance for Enrolled Actuaries

[¶ 15,224]

§ 901.20 **Standards of performance of actuarial services**. In the discharge of duties required by ERISA of enrolled actuaries with respect to any plan to which the Act applies:

(a) *In general.* An enrolled actuary shall undertake an actuarial assignment only when qualified to do so.

(b) *Professional duty.* An enrolled actuary shall not perform actuarial services for any person or organization which he/she believes or has reasonable grounds for believing may utilize his/her services in a fraudulent manner or in a manner inconsistent with law.

(c) *Advice or explanations.* An enrolled actuary shall provide to the plan administrator upon appropriate request, supplemental advice or explanation relative to any report signed or certified by such enrolled actuary.

(d) *Conflicts of interest.* In any situation in which the enrolled actuary has a conflict of interest with respect to the performance of actuarial services, of which the enrolled actuary has knowledge, he/she shall not perform such actuarial services except after full disclosure has been made to plan trustees, any named fiduciary of the plan, the plan administrator, and, if the plan is subject to a collective bargaining agreement, the collective bargaining representative.

(e) *Assumptions, calculations and recommendations.* The enrolled actuary shall exercise due care, skill, prudence and diligence to ensure that:

(1) The actuarial assumptions are reasonable in the aggregate and the actuarial cost method and the actuarial method of valuation of assets are appropriate.

(2) The calculations are accurately carried out, and

(3) The report, any recommendations to the plan administrator and any supplemental advice or explanation relative to the report reflect the results of the calculations.

(f) *Report or certificate.* An enrolled actuary shall include in any report or certificate stating actuarial costs or liabilities, a statement or reference describing or clearly identifying the data, any material inadequacies therein and the implications thereof, and the actuarial methods and assumptions employed.

(g) *Utilization of enrolled actuary designation.* An enrolled actuary shall not advertise his/her status as an enrolled actuary in any solicitation related to the performance of actuarial services, and shall not employ, accept employment in partnership, corporate, or any other form, or share fees with, any individual or entity who so solicits. However, the use of the term "enrolled actuary" to identify an individual who is named on the stationery, letterhead or business card of an enrolled actuary, or of a partnership, association, or corporation shall not be considered in violation of this section. In addition, the term "enrolled actuary" may appear after the general listing of an enrolled actuary's name in a telephone directory provided such listing is not of a distinctive nature.

(h) *Notification.* An enrolled actuary shall provide written notification of the nonfiling of any actuarial document he/she has signed upon discovery of the non-filing. Such notification shall be made to the office of the Internal Revenue Service, the Department of Labor, or the Pension Benefit Guaranty Corporation where such document should have been filed. [Amended by 43 FR 39756, filed with the Federal Register September 6, 1978, and published in the Federal Register on September 6, 1978.]

Subpart D—Suspension and Termination of Enrollment

[¶ 15,224A]

§ 901.30 **Authority to suspend or terminate enrollment**. Under Section 3042(b) of ERISA the Joint Board may, after notice and opportunity for a hearing, suspend or terminate the enrollment of an enrolled actuary if the Joint Board finds that such enrolled actuary

(a) has failed to discharge his/her duties under ERISA, or

(b) does not satisfy the requirements for enrollment in effect at the time of his/her enrollment.

[¶ 15,224B]

§ 901.31 **Grounds for suspension or termination of enrollment**. (a) *Failure to satisfy requirements for enrollment.* The enrollment of an actuary may be terminated if it is found that the actuary did not satisfy the eligibility requirements set forth in §§ 901.12 or 901.13, whichever is applicable.

(b) *Failure to discharge duties.* The enrollment of an actuary may be suspended or terminated if it is found that the actuary, following enrollment, failed to discharge his/her duties under ERISA. Such duties include those set forth in § 901.20.

(c) *Disreputable conduct.* The enrollment of an actuary may be suspended or terminated if it is found that the actuary has, at any time after he/she applied for enrollment, engaged in any conduct set forth in § 901.13(e)(1)(i)(vi) or other conduct evidencing fraud, dishonesty, or breach of trust. Such other conduct includes, but is not limited to, the following:

(1) Conviction of any criminal offense under the laws of the United States (including Section 411 of ERISA, 29 U.S.C. 1111), any State thereof, the District of Columbia, or any territory or possession of the United States, which evidences fraud, dishonesty, or breach of trust.

(2) Knowingly filing false or altered documents, affidavits, financial statements or other papers on matters relating to employee benefit plans or actuarial services.

(3) Knowingly making false or misleading representations, either orally or in writing, on matters relating to employee benefit plans or actuarial services, or knowingly failing to disclose information relative to such matters.

(4) The use of false or misleading representations with intent to deceive a client or prospective client, or of intimations that the actuary is able to obtain special consideration or action from an officer or employee of any agency or court authorized to determine the validity of pension plans under ERISA.

(5) Willful violation of any of the regulations contained in this part.

[¶ 15,224C]

§ 901.32 **Receipt of information concerning enrolled actuaries**. If an officer or employee of the Department of the Treasury, the Department of Labor, the Pension Benefit Guaranty Corporation, or a member of the Joint Board has reason to believe that an enrolled actuary has violated any provision of this part, or if any such officer, employee or member receives information to that effect, he/she may make a written report thereof, which report or a copy thereof shall be forwarded to the Executive Director. If any other person has information of any such violation, he/she may make a report thereof to the Executive Director or to any officer or employee of the Department of the Treasury, the Department of Labor, or to the Pension Benefit Guaranty Corporation.

[¶ 15,224D]

§ 901.33 **Initiation of proceeding.** Whenever the Executive Director has reason to believe that an enrolled actuary has violated any provision of the laws or regulations governing enrollment, such individual may be reprimanded or a proceeding may be initiated for the suspension or termination of such individual's enrollment. A reprimand as used in this paragraph is a statement informing the enrolled actuary that, in the opinion of the Executive Director, his/her conduct is in violation of the regulations and admonishing the enrolled actuary that repetition of the conduct occasioning the reprimand may result in the institution of a proceeding for the suspension or termination of the actuary's enrollment. A proceeding for suspension or termination of enrollment shall be initiated by a complaint naming the respondent actuary, signed by the Executive Director and filed in the Executive Director's office. Except in cases where the nature of the proceeding or the public interest does not permit, a proceeding will not be initiated under this section until the facts which may warrant such a proceeding have been called to the attention of the actuary in writing and he/she has been given an opportunity to respond to the allegations of misconduct.

[¶ 15,224E]

§ 901.34 **Conferences.** (a) *In general.* The Executive Director may confer with an enrolled actuary concerning allegations of his/her misconduct whether or not a proceeding for suspension or termination has been initiated against him/her. If the conference results in agreement as to certain facts or other matters in connection with such a proceeding, such agreement may be entered in the record at the request of the actuary or the Executive Director.

(b) *Voluntary suspension or termination of enrollment.* An enrolled actuary, in order to avoid the initiation or conclusion of a suspension or termination proceeding, may offer his/her consent to suspension or termination of enrollment or may offer his/her resignation. The Executive Director may accept the offered resignation or may suspend or terminate enrollment in accordance with the consent offered.

[¶ 15,224F]

§ 901.35 **Contents of complaint.** (a) *Charges.* A complaint initiating a suspension or termination proceeding shall describe the allegations which are the basis for the proceeding, and fairly inform the respondent of the charges against him/her.

(b) *Answer.* In the complaint, or in a separate paper attached to the complaint, notice shall be given of the place at, and time within which the respondent shall file an answer, which time shall not be less than 15 days from the date of service of the complaint. Notice shall be given that a decision by default may be rendered against the respondent if an answer is not filed as required.

[¶ 15,224G]

§ 901.36 **Service of complaint and other papers.** (a) *Complaint.* The complaint or a copy thereof may be served upon the respondent by certified mail, or first-class mail as hereinafter provided, by delivering it to the respondent, or the respondent's attorney or agent of record either in person or by leaving it at the office or place of business of the respondent, the attorney or agent, or in any other manner which may have been agreed to in writing by the respondent. Where the service is by certified mail, the return post office receipt signed by or on behalf of the respondent shall be proof of service. If the certified matter is not claimed or accepted by the respondent and is returned undelivered, complete service may be made upon the respondent by mailing the complaint to him/her by first-class mail, addressed to the respondent at the last address known to the Executive Director. If service is made upon the respondent or his/her attorney or agent in person or by

leaving the complaint at the office or place of business of the respondent, attorney, or agent, the verified return by the person making service, setting forth the manner of service, shall be proof of such service.

(b) *Service of papers other than complaint.* Any paper other than the complaint may be served upon the respondent as provided in paragraph (a) of this section or by mailing the paper by first-class mail to the respondent at the last address known to the Executive Director or by mailing the paper by first-class mail to the respondent's attorney or agent. Such mailing shall constitute complete service. Notices may also be served upon the respondent or his/her attorney or agent by telegraph.

(c) *Filing of papers.* Whenever the filing of a paper is required or permitted in connection with a suspension or termination proceeding, and the place of filing is not specified by this subpart or by rule or order of the Administrative Law Judge, the paper shall be filed with the Executive Director of the Joint Board for the Enrollment of Actuaries, Treasury Department, Washington, D.C. 20220. All papers shall be filed in duplicate.

[¶ 15,224H]

§ 901.37 **Answer.** (a) *Filing.* The respondent's answer shall be filed in writing within the time specified in the complaint or notice of initiation of the proceeding, unless, on application, the time is extended by the Executive Director or the Administrative Law Judge. The answer shall be filed in duplicate with the Executive Director.

(b) *Contents.* The answer shall contain a statement of facts which constitute the grounds of defense and it shall specifically admit or deny each allegation set forth in the complaint, except that the respondent shall not deny a material allegation in the complaint which he/she knows to be true, or state that he/she is without sufficient information to form a belief when in fact the respondent possesses such information. The respondent may also state affirmatively special matters of defense.

(c) *Failure to deny or answer allegations in the complaint.* Every allegation in the complaint which is not denied in the answer shall be deemed to be admitted and may be considered as proven, and no further evidence in respect of such allegation need be adduced at a hearing. Failure to file an answer within the time prescribed in the notice to the respondent, except as the time for answer is extended by the Executive Director or the Administrative Law Judge, shall constitute an admission of the allegations of the complaint and a waiver of hearing, and the Administrative Law Judge may make a decision by default, without a hearing or further procedure.

[¶ 15,224I]

§ 901.38 **Supplemental charges.** If it appears to the Executive Director that the respondent in his/her answer falsely and in bad faith denies a material allegation of fact in the complaint or states that the respondent has no knowledge sufficient to form a belief when he/she in fact possesses such knowledge, or if it appears that the respondent has knowingly introduced false testimony during proceedings for suspension or termination of his/her enrollment, the Executive Director may file supplemental charges against the respondent. Such supplemental charges may be tried with other charges in the case, provided the respondent is given due notice thereof and is afforded an opportunity to prepare a defense thereto.

[¶ 15,224J]

§ 901.39 **Reply to answer.** No reply to the respondent's answer shall be required, but the Executive Director may file a reply at his/her discretion or at the request of the Administrative Law Judge.

[¶ 15,224K]

§ 901.40 **Proof; variance; amendment of pleadings.** In the case of a variance between the allegations in a pleading and the evidence adduced in support of the pleading, the Administrative Law Judge may order or authorize amendment of the pleading to conform to the evidence, provided that the party who would otherwise be prejudiced by the amendment is given reasonable opportunity to meet the allegations of the pleading as amended. The Administrative Law Judge shall make findings on any issue presented by the pleadings as so amended.

[¶ 15,224L]

§ 901.41 **Motions and requests**. Motions and requests may be filed with the Executive Director or with the Administrative Law Judge.

[¶ 15,224M]

§ 901.42 **Representation**. A respondent or proposed respondent may appear at conference or hearing in person or may be represented by counsel or other representative. The Executive Director may be represented by an attorney or other employee of the Treasury Department.

[¶ 15,224N]

§ 901.43 **Administrative Law Judge**. (a) *Appointment*. An Administrative Law Judge, appointed as provided by section 11 of the Administrative Procedure Act, 60 Stat. 244 (5 U.S.C. 3105), shall conduct proceedings upon complaints for the suspension or termination of enrolled actuaries.

(b) *Power of Administrative Law Judge*. Among other powers, the Administrative Law Judge shall have authority, in connection with any suspension or termination proceeding of an enrolled actuary, to do the following:

(1) Administer oaths and affirmations;

(2) Make rulings upon motions and requests, which may not be appealed before the close of a hearing except at the discretion of the Administrative Law Judge;

(3) Determine the time and place of hearing and regulate its course of conduct;

(4) Adopt rules of procedure and modify the same as required for the orderly disposition of proceedings;

(5) Rule upon offers of proof, receive relevant evidence, and examine witnesses;

(6) Take or authorize the taking of depositions;

(7) Receive and consider oral or written argument on facts or law;

(8) Hold or provide for the holding of conferences for the settlement or simplification of the issues by consent of the parties;

(9) Perform such acts and take such measures as are necessary or appropriate to the efficient conduct of any proceeding; and

(10) Make initial decisions.

[¶ 15,224O]

§ 901.44 **Hearings**. (a) *In general*. The Administrative Law Judge shall preside at the hearing on a complaint for the suspension or termination of an enrolled actuary. Hearing shall be stenographically recorded and transcribed and the testimony of witnesses shall be taken under oath or affirmation. Hearings will be conducted pursuant to Section 7 of the Administrative Procedure Act, 60 Stat. 241 (5 U.S.C. 556).

(b) *Failure to appear*. If either party to the proceeding fails to appear at the hearing, after due notice thereof has been sent to the parties, the Administrative Law Judge may make a decision against the absent party by default.

[¶ 15,224P]

§ 901.45 **Evidence**. (a) *In general*. The rules of evidence prevailing in courts of law and equity are not controlling in hearings on complaints for the suspension or the termination of the enrollment of enrolled actuaries. However, the Administrative Law Judge shall exclude evidence which is irrelevant, immaterial, or unduly repetitious.

(b) *Depositions*. The deposition of any witness taken pursuant to § 901.46 may be admitted.

(c) *Proof of documents*. Official documents, records, and papers of the Department of the Treasury, the Department of Labor, the Pension Benefit Guaranty Corporation, the Joint Board for the Enrollment of Actuaries or the Office of the Executive Director of the Joint Board for the Enrollment of Actuaries shall be admissible into evidence without the production of an officer or employee to authenticate them. Any such documents, records, and papers may be evidenced by a copy attested to or identified by an officer or employee of the Department of

the Treasury, the Department of Labor, the Pension Benefit Guaranty Corporation, the Joint Board for the Enrollment of Actuaries, or the Office of the Executive Director of the Joint Board for the Enrollment of Actuaries, as the case may be.

(d) *Exhibits*. If any document, record, or other paper is introduced into evidence as an exhibit, the Administrative Law Judge may authorize the withdrawal of the exhibit subject to any conditions which he/she deems proper.

(e) *Objections*. Objections to evidence shall state the grounds relied upon, and the record shall not include argument thereon, except as ordered by the Administrative Law Judge. Rulings on such objections shall be part of the record. No exception to the ruling is necessary to preserve the rights of the parties.

[¶ 15,224Q]

§ 901.46 **Depositions**. Depositions for use at a hearing may, with the written approval of the Administrative Law Judge, be taken by either the Executive Director or the respondent or their duly authorized representatives. Depositions may be taken upon oral or written interrogatories, upon not less than 10 days written notice to the other party, before any officer duly authorized to administer an oath for general purposes or before an officer or employee of the Department of the Treasury, the Department of Labor, the Pension Benefit Guaranty Corporation, or the Joint Board who is authorized to administer an oath. Such notice shall state the names of the witnesses and the time and place where the depositions are to be taken. The requirement of 10 days notice may be waived by the parties in writing, and depositions may then be taken from the persons and at the times and places mutually agreed upon by the parties. When a deposition is taken upon written interrogatories, any cross-examination shall be upon written interrogatories. Copies of such written interrogatories shall be served upon the other party with the notice, and the copies of any written cross-interrogatories shall be mailed or delivered to the opposing party at least five days before the date of taking the depositions, unless the parties mutually agree otherwise. A party upon whose behalf a deposition is taken must file it with the Administrative Law Judge and serve one copy upon the opposing party. Expenses in the reporting of depositions shall be borne by the party at whose instance the deposition is taken.

[¶ 15,224R]

§ 901.47 **Transcript**. In cases where the hearing is stenographically reported by a Government contract reporter, copies of the transcript may be obtained from the reporter at rates not to exceed the minimum rates fixed by contract between the Government and the reporter. Where the hearing is stenographically reported by a regular employee of the Department of the Treasury, the Department of Labor, the Pension Benefit Guaranty Corporation, or the Joint Board, a copy thereof will be supplied to the respondent either without charge or upon the payment of a reasonable fee. Copies of exhibits introduced at the hearing or at the taking of depositions will be supplied to parties upon the payment of a reasonable fee (31 U.S.C. 483a).

[¶ 15,224S]

§ 901.48 **Proposed findings and conclusions**. Except in cases where the respondent has failed to answer the complaint or where a party has failed to appear at the hearing, the Administrative Law Judge, before making his/her decision, shall give the parties a reasonable opportunity to submit proposed findings and conclusions and supporting reasons therefor.

[¶ 15,224T]

§ 901.49 **Decision of the Administrative Law Judge**. As soon as practicable after the conclusion of a hearing and the receipt of any proposed findings and conclusions timely submitted by the parties, the Administrative Law Judge shall make the initial decision in the case. The decision should be based solely upon the pleading, the testimony and exhibits received in evidence at the hearing or specifically authorized to be subsequently submitted under the applicable laws and regulations. The decision shall include (a) a statement of findings and conclusions, as well as the reasons or basis therefor, upon all the material issues of fact or law presented on the record, and (b) an order of suspension, termination or reprimand or an order of dismissal of the complaint. The Administrative Law Judge shall file the decision with the Executive Director and shall transmit a copy thereof to the respondent or his/her attorney or agent of record. In the absence of an appeal to the Joint Board or review of the decision upon motion of the Joint Board, the decision of the Administrative Law Judge shall without further proceedings become the decision of the Joint Board 30 days from the date of the Administrative Law Judge's decision.

[¶ 15,224U]

§ 901.50 **Appeal to the Joint Board**. Within 30 days from the date of the Administrative Law Judge's decision, either party may appeal to the Joint Board for the Enrollment of Actuaries. The appeal shall be filed with the Executive Director in duplicate and shall include exceptions to the decision of the Administrative Law Judge and supporting reasons for such exceptions. If an appeal is filed by the Executive Director, a copy of it shall be transmitted to the respondent. Within 30 days after receipt of an appeal or copy thereof, the other party may file a reply brief in duplicate with the Executive Director. If the reply brief is filed by the Executive Director, a copy thereof shall be transmitted to the respondent. Upon the filing of an appeal and a reply brief, if any, the Executive Director shall transmit the entire record to the joint board.

[¶ 15,224V]

§ 901.51 **Decision of the Joint Board**. On appeal from or review of the initial decision of the Administrative Law Judge, the Joint Board for the Enrollment of Actuaries will make the final decision. In making its decision the Joint Board will review the record of such portions thereof as may be cited by the parties to permit limiting of the issues. A copy of the Joint Board's decision shall be transmitted to the respondent by the Executive Director.

[¶ 15,224W]

§ 901.52 **Effect of suspension, termination or resignation of enrollment; surrender of enrollment certificate**. If the respondent's enrollment is suspended, the respondent shall not thereafter be permitted to perform actuarial services under ERISA during the period of suspension. If the respondent's enrollment is terminated, the respondent shall not thereafter be permitted to perform actuarial services under ERISA unless and until authorized to do so by the Executive Director pursuant to § 901.54. The respondent shall surrender his/her enrollment certificate to the Executive Director for cancellation in the case of a termination or resignation of enrollment or for retention during a period of suspension.

[¶ 15,224X]

§ 901.53 **Notice of suspension, termination or resignation of enrollment**. Upon the resignation or the issuance of a final order suspending or terminating the enrollment of an actuary, the Executive Director shall give notice thereof to appropriate officers and employees of the Department of the Treasury, the Department of Labor, the Pension Benefit Guaranty Corporation, and to other interested departments and agencies of the Federal Government.

[¶ 15,224Y]

§ 901.54 **Petition for reinstatement**. Any individual whose enrollment has been terminated may petition the Executive Director for reinstatement after the expiration of five years following such termination. Reinstatement may not be granted unless the Executive Director, with the approval of the Joint Board, is satisfied that the petitioner is not likely to conduct himself/herself thereafter contrary to the regulations in this part, and that granting such reinstatement would not be contrary to the public interest.

Subpart E—General Provisions

[¶ 15,225]

§ 901.70 **Records**. (a) *Availability*. There are made available for public inspection at the Office of the Executive Director of the Joint Board for the Enrollment of Actuaries a roster of all persons enrolled to perform actuarial services under ERISA and a roster of all persons whose enrollments to perform such services have been suspended or terminated. Other records may be disclosed upon specific request, in accordance with the applicable disclosure and privacy statutes.

(b) *Disciplinary procedures*. A request by an enrolled actuary that a hearing in a disciplinary proceeding concerning him/her be public, and that the record thereof be made available for inspection by interested persons may be granted if written agreement is reached in advance to protect from disclosure tax information which is confidential, in accordance with applicable statutes and regulations.

[¶ 15,225A]

§ 901.71 **Special orders**. The Joint Board reserves the power to issue such special orders as it may deem proper in any case within the purview of this part.

[¶ 15,226]
Availability of Information

§ 902.1 **Scope**. This part is issued by the Joint Board for the Enrollment of Actuaries (the "Joint Board") pursuant to the requirements of section 552 of Title 5 of the United States Code, including the requirements that every Federal agency shall publish in the FEDERAL REGISTER, for the guidance of the public, descriptions of the established places at which, the officers from whom, and the methods whereby, the public may obtain information, make submittals or requests, or obtain decisions.

[¶ 15,226A]

§ 902.2 **Definitions**. (a) *"Records of the Joint Board"*. For purposes of this Part, the term "records of the Joint Board" means rules, statements, opinions, orders, memoranda, letters, reports, accounts and other papers containing information in the possession of the Joint Board that constitute part of the Joint Board's official files.

(b) *"Unusual Circumstances"*. For purposes of this part, "unusual circumstances" means, but only to the extent reasonably necessary for the proper processing of the particular request:

(1) The need to search for and collect the requested records from other establishments that are separate from the Joint Board's office processing the request;

(2) The need to search for, collect, and appropriately examine a voluminous amount of separate and distinct records which are demanded in a single request; or

(3) The need for consultation, which shall be conducted with all practicable speed, with another agency having a substantial interest in the determination of the request.

[¶ 15,226B]

§ 902.3 **Published information**. (a) *Federal Register*. Pursuant to sections 552 and 553 of Title 5 of the United States Code, and subject to the provisions of § 902.5, the Joint Board publishes in the FEDERAL REGISTER for the guidance of the public, in addition to this part, descriptions of its organization and procedures, substantive rules of general applicability, and, as may from time to time be appropriate, statements of general policy, and interpretations of general applicability.

(b) *Other published information*. From time to time, the Joint Board issues statements to the press relating to its operations.

(c) *Obtaining printed information*. If not available through the Government Printing Office, printed information released by the Joint Board may be obtained without cost from the Executive Director of the Joint Board ("Executive Director").

[¶ 15,226C]

§ 902.4 **Access to records**. (a) *General rule*. All records of the Joint Board, including information set forth in section 552(a)(2) of Title 5 of the United States Code, are made available to any person, upon request, for inspection and copying in accordance with the provisions of this section and subject to the limitations stated in section 552(b) of Title 5 of the United States Code. Records falling within such limitations may nevertheless be made available in accordance with this section to the extent consistent, in the judgment of the Chairman of the Joint Board ("Chairman"), with the effective performance of the Joint Board's statutory responsibilities and with the avoidance of injury to a public or private interest intended to be protected by such limitations.

(b) *Obtaining access to records*. Records of the Joint Board subject to this section are available by appointment for public inspection or copying during regular business hours on regular business days at the office of the Executive Director. Every request for access to such records, other than published records described in §902.3, shall be signed and submitted in writing to the Executive Director, Joint Board for the Enrollment of Actuaries, c/o Department of the Treasury, Washington, D.C. 20220, shall state the name and address of the person requesting such access, and shall describe such records in a manner reasonably sufficient to permit their identification without undue difficulty.

(c) *Fees.* A fee at the rate of $5.00 per hour or fraction thereof or the time required to locate such records, plus ten cents per standard page for any copying thereof, shall be paid by any person requesting records other than published records described in §902.3. In addition, the cost of postage and any packaging and special handling shall be paid by the requester. Documents shall be provided without charge or at a reduced charge where the Chairman determines that waiver or reduction of the fee is in the public interest because furnishing the information can be considered as primarily benefitting the general public.

(d) *Actions on request.* The Executive Director shall within ten days (excepting Saturdays, Sundays and legal public holidays) from receipt of request, determine whether to comply with such requests for records and shall immediately notify in writing the person making such request of such determination and the reason therefor, and of the right of such person to appeal any adverse determination, as provided in §902.5. In unusual circumstances, the time limit for the determination may be extended by written notice to the person making such request, setting forth the reasons for such extension and the date on which the

determination is expected to be dispatched. No such notice shall specify a date that will result in an extension of more than ten working days.

§902.5 **Appeal.** (a) Any person denied access to records requested under §902.4, may within thirty days after notification of such denial, file a signed written appeal to the Joint Board. The appeal shall provide the name and address of the appellant, the identification of the records denied, and the dates of the original request and its denial.

(b) The Joint Board shall act upon any such appeal within twenty days (excepting Saturdays, Sundays and legal public holidays) of its receipt unless for unusual circumstances the time for such action is deferred, subject to §902.4(b), for not more than ten days. If action upon any such appeal is so deferred, the Joint Board shall notify the requester of the reasons for such deferral and the date on which the final reply is expected to be dispatched. If it is determined that the appeal from the initial denial shall be denied (in whole or in part), the requester shall be notified in writing of the denial, of the reasons therefor, of the fact the Joint Board is responsible for the denial, and of the provisions of section 552(a)(4) of Title 5 of the United States Code for judicial review of the determination.

(c) Any extension or extensions of time under §§902.4(d) and 902.5(b) shall not cumulatively total more than ten days (excepting Saturdays, Sundays and legal public holidays). If an extension is invoked in connection with an initial determination under §902.4(d), any unused days of such extension may be invoked in connection with the determination on appeal under §902.5(a), by written notice from the Joint Board.

AMENDMENT OF INTERNAL REVENUE CODE

Act Sec. 3043. Section 7701(a) of the Internal Revenue Code of 1986 (relating to definitions) is amended by adding at the end thereof the following new paragraph:

[Code Sec. 7701(a)(35)]

(35) **ENROLLED ACTUARY.** The term 'enrolled actuary' means a person who is enrolled by the Joint Board for the Enrollment of Actuaries established under subtitle C of the title III of the Employee Retirement Income Security Act of 1974."

[The above amendment to the Internal Revenue Code of 1954 is incorporated in place in the "Internal Revenue Code—Regulations."]

Amendment

P.L. 101-239, §7891(a)(1):

Titles I, III, and IV of ERISA (other than sections 3(37)(E), 301(a)(7), and 308, the last sentence of section 408(d), and sections 414(c), 4001(a)(3)(ii) and 4303) are each

amended by striking "Internal Revenue Code of 1954" each place it appears and inserting "Internal Revenue Code of 1986" effective October 22, 1986.

TITLE IV—PLAN TERMINATION INSURANCE
Subtitle A—Pension Benefit Guaranty Corporation (Part 4000)

Part 4000—Filing, Issuance, Computation of Time, and Record Retention

Regulations

The following regulations were adopted by the Pension Benefit Guaranty Corporation on July 1, 1996 (61 FR 34002), and officially corrected on December 26, 1996 (61 FR 67942). Prior to July 1, 1996, PBGC regulations were under Chapter XXVI of Title 29 of the Code of Federal Regulations. Effective July 1, 1996, PBGC regulations were moved to Chapter XL, and were renumbered and reorganized. Reg. §4000.2 was amended effective August 11, 1997 (62 FR 36993). Reg. §4000.1—4000.54 were revised on October 28, 2003 (68 FR 61344). Reg. Secs. 4000.3, 4000.4, 4000.23, and 4000.29 were revised on March 9, 2005 (70 FR 11540).

Subpart A—Filing Rules

§4000.1 **What are these filing rules about?**

Where a particular regulation calls for their application, the rules in this subpart A of part 4000 tell you what filing methods you may use for any submission (including a payment) to us. They do not cover an issuance from you to anyone other than the PBGC, such as a notice to participants. Also, they do not cover filings with us that are not made under our regulations, such as procurement filings, litigation filings, and applications for employment with us. (Subpart B tells you what methods you may use to issue a notice or otherwise provide information to any person other than us. Subpart C tells you how we determine your filing or issuance date. Subpart D tells you how to compute

various periods of time. Subpart E tells you how to maintain required records in electronic form.)

§4000.2 **What definitions do I need to know for these rules?**

You need to know two definitions from Sec. 4001.2 of this chapter: PBGC and person. You also need to know the following definitions:

Filing means any notice, information, or payment that you submit to us under our regulations.

Issuance means any notice or other information you provide to any person other than us under our regulations.

We means the PBGC.

You means the person filing with us.

[¶ 15,302A]

§4000.3 What methods of filing may I use?

(a) *Paper filings.* Except for the filings listed in paragraph (b) of this section, you may file any submission with us by hand, mail, or commercial delivery service.

(b) *Electronic filings.* You must submit the information required under 29 CFR part 4010 electronically in accordance with the instructions on the PBGC's Web site, except as otherwise provided by the PBGC.

(c) *Information on electronic filings.* Current information on electronic filings, including permitted methods, fax numbers, and e-mail addresses, is—

(1) On our Web site, *http://www.pbgc.gov;*

(2) In our various printed forms and instructions packages; and

(3) Available by contacting our Customer Service Center at 1200 K Street, NW., Washington, DC, 20005- 4026; telephone 1-800-400-7242 (for participants), or 1-800-736-2444 (for practitioners). (TTY/TDD users may call the Federal relay service toll-free at 1-800-877-8339 and ask to be connected to the appropriate number.)

[¶ 15,302B]

§4000.4 Where do I file my submission?

To find out where to send your submission, visit our Web site at http://www.pbgc.gov, see the instructions to our forms, or call our Customer Service Center (1-800-400-7242 for participants, or 1-800-736-2444 for practitioners; TTY/TDD users may call the Federal relay service toll-free at 1-800-877-8339 and ask to be connected to the appropriate number.) Because we have different addresses for different types of filings, you should make sure to use the appropriate address for your type of filing. For example, some filings (such as premium payments) must be sent to a specified bank, while other filings (such as the Standard Termination Notice (Form 500)) must be sent to the appropriate department at our offices in Washington, DC. You do not have to address electronic submissions made through our Web site. We are responsible for ensuring that such submissions go to the proper place.

[¶ 15,302C]

§4000.5 Does the PBGC have discretion to waive these filing requirements?

We retain the discretion to waive any requirement under this part, at any time, if warranted by the facts and circumstances.

Subpart B—Issuance Rules

[¶ 15,302I]

§4000.11 What are these issuance rules about?

Where a particular regulation calls for their application, the rules in this subpart B of part 4000 tell you what methods you may use to issue a notice or otherwise provide information to any person other than us (e.g., a participant or beneficiary). They do not cover payments to third parties. In some cases, the PBGC regulations tell you to comply with requirements that are found somewhere other than in the PBGC's own regulations (e.g., requirements under the Internal Revenue Code). If so, you must comply with any applicable issuance rules under those other requirements. (Subpart A tells you what filing methods you may use for filings with us. Subpart C tells you how we determine your filing or issuance date. Subpart D tells you how to compute various periods of time. Subpart E tells you how to maintain required records in electronic form.)

[¶ 15,302J]

§4000.12 What definitions do I need to know for these rules?

You need to know two definitions from Sec. 4001.2 of this chapter: PBGC and person. You also need to know the following definitions:

Filing means any notice, information, or payment that you submit to us under our regulations.

Issuance means any notice or other information you provide to any person other than us under our regulations.

We means the PBGC.

You means the person providing the issuance to a third party.

[¶ 15,302K]

§4000.13 What methods of issuance may I use?

(a) *In general.* You may use any method of issuance, provided you use measures reasonably calculated to ensure actual receipt of the material by the intended recipient. Posting is not a permissible method of issuance under the rules of this part.

(b) *Electronic safe-harbor metho* d. Section 4000.14 provides a safe-harbor method for meeting the requirements of paragraph (a) of this section when providing an issuance using electronic media.

[¶ 15,302L]

§4000.14 What is the safe-harbor method for providing an issuance by electronic media?

(a) *In general.* Except as otherwise provided by applicable law, rule or regulation, you satisfy the requirements of Sec. 4000.13 if you follow the methods described at paragraph (b) of this section when providing an issuance by electronic media to any person described in paragraph (c) or (d) of this section.

(b) *Issuance requirements.* (1) You must take appropriate and necessary measures reasonably calculated to ensure that the system for furnishing documents—

(i) Results in actual receipt of transmitted information (e.g., using return-receipt or notice of undelivered electronic mail features, conducting periodic reviews or surveys to confirm receipt of the transmitted information); and

(ii) Protects confidential information relating to the intended recipient (e.g., incorporating into the system measures designed to preclude unauthorized receipt of or access to such information by anyone other than the intended recipient);

(2) You prepare and furnish electronically delivered documents in a manner that is consistent with the style, format and content requirements applicable to the particular document;

(3) You provide each intended recipient with a notice, in electronic or non-electronic form, at the time a document is furnished electronically, that apprises the intended recipient of—

(i) The significance of the document when it is not otherwise reasonably evident as transmitted (e.g., "The attached participant notice contains information on the funding level of your defined benefit pension plan and the benefits guaranteed by the Pension Benefit Guaranty Corporation."); and

(ii) The intended recipient's right to request and obtain a paper version of such document; and

(4) You give the intended recipient, upon request, a paper version of the electronically furnished documents.

(c) *Employees with electronic access.* This section applies to a participant who—

(1) Has the ability to effectively access the document furnished in electronic form at any location where the participant is reasonably expected to perform duties as an employee; and

(2) With respect to whom access to the employer's electronic information system is an integral part of those duties.

(d) *Any person.* This section applies to any person who—

(1) Except as provided in paragraph (d)(2) of this section, has affirmatively consented, in electronic or non-electronic form, to receiving documents through electronic media and has not withdrawn such consent;

(2) In the case of documents to be furnished through the Internet or other electronic communication network, has affirmatively consented or confirmed consent electronically, in a manner that reasonably demonstrates the person's ability to access information in the electronic form that will be used to provide the information that is the subject of the consent, and has provided an address for the receipt of electronically furnished documents;

(3) Prior to consenting, is provided, in electronic or non-electronic form, a clear and conspicuous statement indicating:

(i) The types of documents to which the consent would apply;

(ii) That consent can be withdrawn at any time without charge;

(iii) The procedures for withdrawing consent and for updating the participant's, beneficiary's or other person's address for receipt of electronically furnished documents or other information;

(iv) The right to request and obtain a paper version of an electronically furnished document, including whether the paper version will be provided free of charge;

(v) Any hardware and software requirements for accessing and retaining the documents; and

(4) Following consent, if a change in hardware or software requirements needed to access or retain electronic documents creates a material risk that the person will be unable to access or retain electronically furnished documents,

(i) Is provided with a statement of the revised hardware or software requirements for access to and retention of electronically furnished documents;

(ii) Is given the right to withdraw consent without charge and without the imposition of any condition or consequence that was not disclosed at the time of the initial consent; and

(iii) Again consents, in accordance with the requirements of paragraph (d)(1) or paragraph (d)(2) of this section, as applicable, to the receipt of documents through electronic media.

[¶ 15,302M]

§ 4000.15 **Does the PBGC have discretion to waive these issuance requirements?**

We retain the discretion to waive any requirement under this part, at any time, if warranted by the facts and circumstances.

Subpart C—Determining Filing and Issuance Dates

[¶ 15,302S]

§ 4000.21 **What are these rules for determining the filing or issuance date about?**

Where the particular regulation calls for their application, the rules in this subpart C of part 4000 tell you how we will determine the date you send us a filing and the date you provide an issuance to someone other than us (such as a participant). These rules do not cover payments to third parties. In addition, they do not cover filings with us that are not made under our regulations, such as procurement filings, litigation filings, and applications for employment with us. In some cases, the PBGC regulations tell you to comply with requirements that are found somewhere other than in the PBGC's own regulations (e.g., requirements under the Internal Revenue Code (Title 26, USC)). In meeting those requirements, you should follow any applicable rules under those requirements for determining the filing and issuance date. (Subpart A tells you what filing methods you may use for filings with us. Subpart B tells you what methods you may use to issue a notice or otherwise provide information to any person other than us. Subpart D tells you how to compute various periods of time. Subpart E tells you how to maintain required records in electronic form.)

[¶ 15,302T]

§ 4000.22 **What definitions do I need to know for these rules?**

You need to know two definitions from Sec. 4001.2 of this chapter: PBGC and person. You also need to know the following definitions:

Business day means a day other than a Saturday, Sunday, or Federal holiday. We means the PBGC.

You means the person filing with us or the person providing the issuance to a third party.

[¶ 15,302U]

§ 4000.23 **When is my submission or issuance treated as filed or issued?**

(a) *Filed or issued when sent.* Generally, we treat your submission as filed, or your issuance as provided, on the date you send it, if you meet certain requirements. The requirements depend upon the method you use to send your submission or issuance (see Sec. Sec. 4000.24 through 4000.29). (Certain filings are always treated as filed when

received, as explained in paragraph (b)(2) of this section.) A submission made through our Web site is considered to have been sent when you perform the last act necessary to indicate that your submission is filed and cannot be further edited or withdrawn.

(b) *Filed or issued when received.* (1) *In genera* l. If you do not meet the requirements for your submission or issuance to be treated as filed or issued when sent (see Sec. Sec. 4000.24 through 4000.32), we treat it as filed or issued on the date received in a permitted format at the proper address.

(2) *Certain filings always treated as filed when received.* We treat the following submissions as filed on the date we receive your submission, no matter what method you use:

(i) *Applications for benefits.* An application for benefits or related submission (unless the instructions for the applicable forms provide for an earlier date);

(ii) *Advance notice of reportable events.* Information required under subpart C of part 4043 of this chapter, dealing with advance notice of reportable events;

(iii) *Form 200 filings.* Information required under subpart D of part 4043 of this chapter, dealing with notice of certain missed minimum funding contributions; and

(iv) *Requests for approval of multiemployer plan amendments.* A request for approval of an amendment filed with the PBGC pursuant to part 4220 of this chapter.

(3) *Determining our receipt date for your filing.* If we receive your submission at the correct address by 5 p.m. (our time) on a business day, we treat it as received on that date. If we receive your submission at the correct address after 5 p.m. on a business day, or anytime on a weekend or Federal holiday, we treat it as received on the next business day. For example, if you send your fax or e-mail of a Form 200 filing to us in Washington, DC, on Friday, March 15, from California at 3 p.m. (Pacific standard time), and we receive it immediately at 6 p.m. (our time), we treat it as received on Monday, March 18. A submission made through our Web site is considered to have been received when we receive an electronic signal that you have performed the last act necessary to indicate that your submission is filed and cannot be further edited or withdrawn.

[¶ 15,302V]

§ 4000.24 **What if I mail my submission or issuance using the U.S. Postal Service?**

(a) *In general.* Your filing or issuance date is the date you mail your submission or issuance using the U.S. Postal Service if you meet the requirements of paragraph (b) of this section, and you mail it by the last scheduled collection of the day. If you mail it later than that, or if there is no scheduled collection that day, your filing or issuance date is the date of the next scheduled collection. If you do not meet the requirements of paragraph (b), your filing or issuance date is the date of receipt at the proper address.

(b) *Requirements for "send date".* Your submission or issuance must meet the applicable postal requirements, be properly addressed, and you must use First-Class Mail (or a U.S. Postal Service mail class that is at least the equivalent of First-Class Mail, such as Priority Mail or Express Mail). However, if you are filing an advance notice of reportable event or a Form 200 (notice of certain missed contributions), see Sec. 4000.23(b); these filings are always treated as filed when received.

(c) *Presumptions.* We make the following presumptions—

(1) *U.S. Postal Service postmark.* If you meet the requirements of paragraph (b) of this section and your submission or issuance has a legible U.S. Postal Service postmark, we presume that the postmark date is the filing or issuance date. However, you may prove an earlier date under paragraph (a) of this section.

(2) *Private meter postmark.* If you meet the requirements of paragraph (b) of this section and your submission or issuance has a legible postmark made by a private postage meter (but no legible U.S.

Postal Service postmark) and arrives at the proper address by the time reasonably expected, we presume that the metered postmark date is your filing or issuance date. However, you may prove an earlier date under paragraph (a) of this section.

(d) *Examples*. (1) You mail your issuance using the U.S. Postal Service and meet the requirements of paragraph (b) of this section. You deposit your issuance in a mailbox at 4 p.m. on Friday, March 15 and the next scheduled collection at that mailbox is 5 p.m. that day. Your issuance date is March 15. If on the other hand you deposit it at 6 p.m. and the next collection at that mailbox is not until Monday, March 18, your issuance date is March 18.

(2) You mail your submission using the U.S. Postal Service and meet the requirements of paragraph (b) of this section. You deposit your submission in the mailbox at 4 p.m. on Friday, March 15, and the next scheduled collection at that mailbox is 5 p.m. that day. If your submission does not show a March 15 postmark, then you may prove to us that you mailed your submission by the last scheduled collection on March 15.

[¶ 15,302W]
§ 4000.25 What if I use the postal service of a foreign country?

If you send your submission or issuance using the postal service of a foreign country, your filing or issuance date is the date of receipt at the proper address.

[¶ 15,302X]
§ 4000.26 What if I use a commercial delivery service?

(a) *In general*. Your filing or issuance date is the date you deposit your submission or issuance with the commercial delivery service if you meet the requirements of paragraph (b) of this section, and you deposit it by the last scheduled collection of the day for the type of delivery you use (such as two-day delivery or overnight delivery). If you deposit it later than that, or if there is no scheduled collection that day, your filing or issuance date is the date of the next scheduled collection. If you do not meet the requirements of paragraph (b), your filing or issuance date is the date of receipt at the proper address. However, if you are filing an advance notice of reportable event or a Form 200 (notice of certain missed contributions), see Sec. 4000.23(b); these filings are always treated as filed when received.

(b) *Requirements for "send date"*. Your submission or issuance must meet the applicable requirements of the commercial delivery service, be properly addressed, and—

(1) *Delivery within two days*. It must be reasonable to expect your submission or issuance will arrive at the proper address by 5 p.m. on the second business day after the next scheduled collection; or

(2) *Designated delivery service*. You must use a "designated delivery service" under section 7502(f) of the Internal Revenue Code (Title 26, USC). Our Web site, http://www.pbgc.gov, lists those designated delivery services. You should make sure that both the provider and the particular type of delivery (such as two-day delivery) are designated.

(c) *Example*. You send your submission by commercial delivery service using two-day delivery. In addition, you meet the requirements of paragraph (b) of this section. Suppose that the deadline for two-day delivery at the place you make your deposit is 8 p.m. on Friday, March 15. If you deposit your submission by that deadline, your filing date is March 15. If, instead, you deposit it after the 8 p.m. deadline and the next collection at that site for two-day delivery is on Monday, March 18, your filing date is March 18.

[¶ 15,302Y]
§ 4000.27 What if I hand deliver my submission or issuance?

Your filing or issuance date is the date of receipt of your hand-delivered submission or issuance at the proper address. A hand-delivered issuance need not be delivered while the intended recipient is physically present. For example, unless you have reason to believe that the intended recipient will not receive the notice within a reasonable amount of time, a notice is deemed to be received when you place it in the intended recipient's office mailbox. Our Web site, http://

www.pbgc.gov, and the instructions to our forms, identify the proper addresses for filings with us.

[¶ 15,302Z]
§ 4000.28 What if I send a computer disk?

(a) *In general*. We determine your filing or issuance date for a computer disk as if you had sent a paper version of your submission or issuances if you meet the requirements of paragraph (b) of this section.

(1) *Filings*. For computer-disk filings, we may treat your submission as invalid if you fail to meet the requirements of paragraph (b)(1) or (b)(3) of this section.

(2) *Issuances*. For computer-disk issuances, we may treat your issuance as invalid if—

(i) You fail to meet the requirements ("using measures reasonably calculated to ensure actual receipt") of Sec. 4000.13(a), or

(ii) You fail to meet the contact information requirements of paragraph (b)(3) of this section.

(b) *Requirements*. To get the filing date under paragraph (a) of this section, you must meet the requirements of paragraphs (b)(1) and (b)(3). To get the issuance date under paragraph (a), you must meet the requirements of paragraphs (b)(2) and (b)(3).

(1) *Technical requirements for filings*. For filings, your electronic disk must comply with any technical requirements for that type of submission (our Web site, http://www.pbgc.gov, identifies the technical requirements for each type of filing).

(2) *Technical requirements for issuances*. For issuances, you must comply with the safe-harbor method under Sec. 4000.14.

(3) *Identify contact person*. For filings and issuances, you must include, in a paper cover letter or on the disk's label, the name and telephone number of the person to contact if we or the intended recipient is unable to read the disk.

[¶ 15,302AA]
§ 4000.29 What if I use electronic delivery?

(a) *In general*. Your filing or issuance date is the date you electronically transmit your submission or issuance to the proper address if you meet the requirements of paragraph (b) of this section. Note that we always treat an advance notice of reportable event and a Form 200 (notice of certain missed contributions) as filed when received. A submission made through our Web site is considered to have been transmitted when you perform the last act necessary to indicate that your submission is filed and cannot be further edited or withdrawn. You do not have to address electronic submissions made through our Web site. We are responsible for ensuring that such submissions go to the proper place.

(1) *Filings*. For electronic filings, if you fail to meet the requirements of paragraph (b)(1) or (b)(3) of this section, we may treat your submission as invalid.

(2) *Issuances*. For electronic issuances, we may treat your issuance as invalid if—

(i) You fail to meet the requirements ("using measures reasonably calculated to ensure actual receipt") of Sec. 4000.13(a), or

(ii) You fail to meet the contact information requirements of paragraph (b)(3) of this section.

(b) *Requirements*. To get the filing date under paragraph (a) of this section, you must meet the requirements of paragraphs (b)(1) and (b)(3). To get the issuance date under paragraph (a), you must meet the requirement of paragraphs (b)(2) and (b)(3).

(1) *Technical requirements for filings*. For filings, your electronic submission must comply with any technical requirements for that type of submission (our Web site, http://www.pbgc.gov, identifies the technical requirements for each type of filing).

(2) T *echnical requirements for issuances*. For issuances, you must comply with the safe-harbor method under Sec. 4000.14.

(3) *Identify contact person.* For an e-mail submission or issuance with an attachment, you must include, in the body of your e-mail, the name and telephone number of the person to contact if we or the intended recipient needs you to resubmit your filing or issuance.

(c) *Failure to meet address requirement.* If you send your electronic submission or issuance to the wrong address (but you meet the requirements of paragraph (b) of this section), your filing or issuance date is the date of receipt at the proper address.

[¶ 15,302BB]
§4000.30 What if I need to resend my filing or issuance for technical reasons?

(a) *Request to resubmit.* (1) *Filing.* We may ask you to resubmit all or a portion of your filing for technical reasons (for example, because we are unable to open an attachment to your e-mail). In that case, your submission (or portion) is invalid. However, if you comply with the request or otherwise resolve the problem (e.g., by providing advice that allows us to open the attachment to your e-mail) by the date we specify, your filing date for the submission (or portion) that we asked you to resubmit is the date you filed your original submission. If you comply with our request late, your submission (or portion) will be treated as filed on the date of your resubmission.

(2) *Issuance.* The intended recipient may, for good reason (of a technical nature), ask you to resend all or a portion of your issuance (for example, because of a technical problem in opening an attachment to your e-mail). In that case, your issuance (or portion) is invalid. However, if you comply with the request or otherwise resolve the problem (e.g., by providing advice that the recipient uses to open the attachment to your e-mail), within a reasonable time, your issuance date for the issuance (or portion) that the intended recipient asked you to resend is the date you provided your original issuance. If you comply with the request late, your issuance (or portion) will be treated as provided on the date of your reissuance.

(b) *Reason to believe submission or issuance not received or defective.* If you have reason to believe that we have not received your submission (or have received it in a form that is not useable), or that the intended recipient has not received your issuance (or has received it in a form that is not useable), you must promptly resend your submission or issuance to get your original filing or issuance date. However, we may require evidence to support your original filing or issuance date. If you are not prompt, or you do not provide us with any evidence we may require to support your original filing or issuance date, your filing or issuance date is the filing or issuance date of your resubmission or reissuance.

[¶ 15,302CC]
§4000.31 Is my issuance untimely if I miss a few participants or beneficiaries?

The PBGC will not treat your issuance as untimely based on your failure to provide the issuance to a participant or beneficiary in a timely manner if—

(a) The failure resulted from administrative error;

(b) The failure involved only a de minimis percentage of intended recipients; and

(c) You resend the issuance to the intended recipient promptly after discovering the error.

[¶ 15,302DD]
§4000.32 Does the PBGC have discretion to waive any requirements under this part?

We retain the discretion to waive any requirement under this part, at any time, if warranted by the facts and circumstances.

Subpart D—Computation of Time
[¶ 15,302MM]
§4000.41 What are these computation-of-time rules about?

The rules in this subpart D of part 4000 tell you how to compute time periods under our regulations (e.g., for filings with us and issuances to third parties) where the particular regulation calls for their application. (There are specific exceptions or modifications to these rules in Sec.

4007.6 of this chapter (premium payments), Sec. 4050.6(d)(3) of this chapter (payment of designated benefits for missing participants), and Sec. 4062.10 of this chapter (employer liability payments). In some cases, the PBGC regulations tell you to comply with requirements that are found somewhere other than in the PBGC's own regulations (e.g., requirements under the Internal Revenue Code (Title 26, USC)). In meeting those requirements, you should follow any applicable computation-of-time rules under those other requirements. (Subpart A tells you what filing methods you may use for filings with us. Subpart B tells you what methods you may use to issue a notice or otherwise provide information to any person other than us. Subpart C tells you how we determine your filing or issuance date. Subpart E tells you how to maintain required records in electronic form.)

[¶ 15,302NN]
§4000.42 What definitions do I need to know for these rules?

You need to know two definitions from Sec. 4001.2 of this chapter: PBGC and person. You also need to know the following definitions:

Business day means a day other than a Saturday, Sunday, or Federal holiday.

We means the PBGC.

You means the person responsible, under our regulations, for the filing or issuance to which these rules apply.

[¶ 15,302OO]
§4000.43 How do I compute a time period?

(a) *In general.* If you are computing a time period to which this part applies, whether you are counting forwards or backwards, the day after (or before) the act, event, or default that begins the period is day one, the next day is day two, and so on. Count all days, including weekends and Federal holidays. However, if the last day you count is a weekend or Federal holiday, extend or shorten the period (whichever benefits you in complying with the time requirement) to the next regular business day. The examples in paragraph (d) of this section illustrate these rules.

(b) *When date is designated.* In some cases, our regulations designate a specific day as the end of a time period, such as "the last day" of a plan year or "the fifteenth day" of a calendar month. In these cases, you simply use the designated day, together with the weekend and holiday rule of paragraph (a) of this section.

(c) *When counting months.* If a time period is measured in months, first identify the date (day, month, and year) of the act, event, or default that begins the period. The corresponding day of the following (or preceding) month is one month later (or earlier), and so on. For example, two months after July 15 is September 15. If the period ends on a weekend or Federal holiday, follow the weekend and holiday rule of paragraph (a) of this section. There are two special rules for determining what the corresponding day is when you start counting on a day that is at or near the end of a calendar month:

(1) *Special "last-day" rule.* If you start counting on the last day of a calendar month, the corresponding day of any calendar month is the last day of that calendar month. For example, a three-month period measured from November 30 ends (if counting forward) on the last day of February (the 28th or 29th) or (if counting backward) on the last day of August (the 31st).

(2) *Special February rule.* If you start counting on the 29th or 30th of a calendar month, the corresponding day of February is the last day of February. For example, a one-month period measured from January 29 ends on the last day of February (the 28th or 29th).

(d) *Examples.* (1) *Counting backwards.* Suppose you are required to file an advance notice of reportable event for a transaction that is effective December 31. Under our regulations, the notice is due at least 30 days before the effective date of the event. To determine your deadline, count December 30 as day 1, December 29 as day 2, December 28 as day 3, and so on. Therefore, December 1 is day 30. Assuming that day is not a weekend or holiday, your notice is timely if you file it on or before December 1.

(2) *Weekend or holiday rule.* Suppose you are filing a notice of intent to terminate. The notice must be issued at least 60 days and no

more than 90 days before the proposed termination date. Suppose the 60th day before the proposed termination date is a Saturday. Your notice is timely if you issue it on the following Monday even though that is only 58 days before the proposed termination date. Similarly, if the 90th day before the proposed termination date is Wednesday, July 4 (a Federal holiday), your notice is timely if you issue it on Tuesday, July 3, even though that is 91 days before the proposed termination date.

(3) *Counting months.* Suppose you are required to issue a Participant Notice two months after December 31. The deadline for the Participant Notice is the last day of February (the 28th or 29th). If the last day of February is a weekend or Federal holiday, your deadline is extended until the next day that is not a weekend or Federal holiday.

Subpart E—Electronic Means of Record Retention

[¶ 15,302WW]

§ 4000.51 **What are these record retention rules about?**

The rules in this subpart E of part 4000 tell you what methods you may use to meet any record retention requirement under our regulations if you choose to use electronic means. The rules for who must retain the records, how long the records must be maintained, and how records must be made available to us are contained in the specific part where the record retention requirement is found. (Subpart A tells you what filing methods you may use for filings with us and how we determine your filing date. Subpart B tells you what methods you may use to issue a notice or otherwise provide information to any person other than us. Subpart C tells you how we determine your filing or issuance date. Subpart D tells you how to compute various periods of time.)

[¶ 15,302XX]

§ 4000.52 **What definitions do I need to know for these rules?**

You need to know two definitions from Sec. 4001.2 of this chapter: PBGC and person. You also need to know the following definitions:

We means the PBGC.

You means the person subject to the record retention requirement.

[¶ 15,302YY]

§ 4000.53 **May I use electronic media to satisfy PBGC's record retention requirements?**

General requirements. You may use electronic media to satisfy the record maintenance and retention requirements of this chapter if:

(a) The electronic recordkeeping system has reasonable controls to ensure the integrity, accuracy, authenticity and reliability of the records kept in electronic form;

(b) The electronic records are maintained in reasonable order and in a safe and accessible place, and in such manner as they may be readily inspected or examined (for example, the recordkeeping system should be capable of indexing, retaining, preserving, retrieving and reproducing the electronic records);

(c) The electronic records are readily convertible into legible and readable paper copy as may be needed to satisfy reporting and disclosure requirements or any other obligation under section 302(f)(4), section 307(e), or Title IV of ERISA;

(d) The electronic recordkeeping system is not subject, in whole or in part, to any agreement or restriction that would, directly or indirectly, compromise or limit a person's ability to comply with any reporting and disclosure requirement or any other obligation under section 302(f)(4), section 307(e), or Title IV of ERISA;

(e) Adequate records management practices are established and implemented (for example, following procedures for labeling of electronically maintained or retained records, providing a secure storage environment, creating back-up electronic copies and selecting an off-site storage location, observing a quality assurance program evidenced by regular evaluations of the electronic recordkeeping system including periodic checks of electronically maintained or retained records; and retaining paper copies of records that cannot be clearly, accurately or completely transferred to an electronic recordkeeping system); and

(f) All electronic records exhibit a high degree of legibility and readability when displayed on a video display terminal or other method of electronic transmission and when reproduced in paper form. The term "legibility" means the observer must be able to identify all letters and numerals positively and quickly to the exclusion of all other letters or numerals. The term "readability" means that the observer must be able to recognize a group of letters or numerals as words or complete numbers.

[¶ 15,302ZZ]

§ 4000.54 **May I dispose of original paper records if I keep electronic copies?**

You may dispose of original paper records any time after they are transferred to an electronic recordkeeping system that complies with the requirements of this subpart, except such original records may not be discarded if the electronic record would not constitute a duplicate or substitute record under the terms of the plan and applicable federal or state law.

[¶ 15,310]
DEFINITIONS

Act Sec. 4001.(a) For purposes of this title, the term—

(1) "administrator" means the person or persons described in paragraph (16) of section 3 of this Act;

(2) "substantial employer", for any plan year of a single-employer plan, means one or more persons—

    (A) who are contributing sponsors of the plan in such plan year,

    (B) who, at any time during such plan year, are members of the same control group, and

    (C) whose required contributions to the plan for each plan year constituting one of—

        (i) the two immediately preceding plan years, or

        (ii) the first two of the three immediately preceding plan years,

total an amount greater than or equal to 10 percent of all contributions required to be paid to or under the plan for such plan year;

(3) "multiemployer plan" means a plan—

    (A) to which more than one employer is required to contribute,

    (B) which is maintained pursuant to one or more collective bargaining agreements between one or more employee organizations and more than one employer, and

    (C) which satisfies such other requirements as the Secretary of Labor may prescribe by regulation,

    except that, in applying this paragraph—

        (i) a plan shall be considered a multiemployer plan on and after its termination date if the plan was a multiemployer plan under this paragraph for the plan year preceding such termination, and

        (ii) for any plan year which began before the date of the enactment of the Multiemployer Pension Plan Amendments Act of 1980, the term "multiemployer plan" means a plan described in section 414(f) of the Internal Revenue Code of 1954 as in effect immediately before such date;

(4) "corporation", except where the context clearly requires otherwise, means the Pension Benefit Guaranty Corporation established under section 4002;

(5) "fund" means the appropriate fund established under section 4005;

(6) "basic benefits" means benefits guaranteed under section 4022 (other than under section 4022(c)), or under section 4022A (other than under section 4022A(g));

(7) "non-basic benefits" means benefits guaranteed under section 4022(c) or 4022A(g);

(8) "nonforfeitable benefit" means, with respect to a plan, a benefit for which a participant has satisfied the conditions for entitlement under the plan or the requirements of this Act (other than submission of a formal application, retirement, completion of a required waiting period, or death in the case of a benefit which returns all or a portion of a participant's accumulated mandatory employee contributions upon the participant's death), whether or not the benefit may subsequently be reduced or suspended by a plan amendment, an occurrence of any condition, or operation of this Act or the Internal Revenue Code of 1986;

(9) "reorganization index" means the amount determined under section 4241(b);

(10) "plan sponsor" means, with respect to a multiemployer plan—

(A) the plan's joint board of trustees, or

(B) if the plan has no joint board of trustees, the plan administrator;

(11) "contribution base unit" means a unit with respect to which an employer has an obligation to contribute under a multiemployer plan, as defined in regulations prescribed by the Secretary of the Treasury;

(12) "outstanding claim for withdrawal liability" means a plan's claim for the unpaid balance of the liability determined under part 1 of subtitle E for which demand has been made, valued in accordance with regulations prescribed by the corporation;

(13) "contributing sponsor", of a single-employer plan, means a person described in section 302(c)(11)(A) of this Act (without regard to section 302(c)(11)(B) of this Act) or section 412(c)(11)(A) of the Internal Revenue Code of 1986 (without regard to section 412(c)(11)(B) of such Code).

(14) in the case of a single-employer plan—

(A) "controlled group" means, in connection with any person, a group consisting of such person and all other persons under common control with such person;

(B) the determination of whether two or more persons are under "common control" shall be made under regulations of the corporation which are consistent and coextensive with regulations prescribed for similar purposes by the Secretary of the Treasury under subsections (b) and (c) of section 414 of the Internal Revenue Code of 1986; and

(C)(i) notwithstanding any other provision of this title, during any period in which an individual possesses, directly or indirectly, the power to direct or cause the direction of the management and policies of an affected air carrier of which he was an accountable owner, whether through the ownership of voting securities, by contract, or otherwise, the affected air carrier shall be considered to be under common control not only with those persons described in subparagraph (B), but also with all related persons; and

(ii) for purposes of this subparagraph, the term—

(I) "affected air carrier" means an air carrier, as defined in section 101(3) of the Federal Aviation Act of 1958, that holds a certificate of public convenience and necessity under section 401 of such Act for route number 147, as of November 12, 1991;

(II) "related person" means any person which was under common control (as determined under subparagraph (B)) with an affected air carrier on October 10, 1991, or any successor to such related person;

(III) "accountable owner" means any individual who on October 10, 1991, owned directly or indirectly through the application of section 318 of the Internal Revenue Code of 1986 more than 50 percent of the total voting power of the stock of an affected air carrier;

(IV) "successor" means any person that acquires, directly or indirectly through the application of section 318 of the Internal Revenue Code of 1986, more than 50 percent of the total voting power of the stock of a related person, more than 50 percent of the total value of the securities (as defined in section 3(20) of this Act) of the related person, more than 50 percent of the total value of the assets of the related person, or any person into which such related person shall be merged or consolidated; and

(V) "individual" means a living human being;

(15) "single-employer plan" means any defined benefit plan (as defined in section 3(35)) which is not a multiemployer plan;

(16) "benefit liabilities" means the benefits of their employees and their beneficiaries under the plan (within the meaning of section 401(a)(2) of the Internal Revenue Code of 1986);

(17) "amount of unfunded guaranteed benefits", of a participant or beneficiary as of any date under a single-employer plan, means an amount equal to the excess of—

(A) the actuarial present value (determined as of such date on the basis of assumptions prescribed by the corporation for purposes of section 4044) of the benefits of the participant or beneficiary under the plan which are guaranteed under section 4022, over

(B) the current value (as of such date) of the assets of the plan which are required to be allocated to those benefits under section 4044;

(18) "amount of unfunded benefit liabilities" means, as of any date, the excess (if any) of—

(A) the value of the benefit liabilities under the plan (determined as of such date on the basis of assumptions prescribed by the corporation for purposes of section 4044), over

(B) the current value (as of such date) of the assets of the plan;

(19) "outstanding amount of benefit liabilities" means, with respect to any plan, the excess (if any) of—

(A) the value of the benefit liabilities under the plan (determined as of the termination date on the basis of assumptions prescribed by the corporation for purposes of section 4044), over

(B) the value of the benefit liabilities which would be so determined by only taking into account benefits which are guaranteed under section 4022 or to which assets of the plan are allocated under section 4044;

(20) "person" has the meaning set forth in section 3(9);

(21) "affected party" means, with respect to a plan—

(A) each participant in the plan,

(B) each beneficiary under the plan who is a beneficiary of a deceased participant or who is an alternate payee (within the meaning of section 206(d)(3)(K)) under an applicable qualified domestic relations order (within the meaning of section 206(d)(3)(B)(i)),

(C) each employee organization representing participants in the plan, and

(D) the corporation,

except that, in connection with any notice required to be provided to the affected party, if an affected party has designated, in writing, a person to receive such notice on behalf of the affected party, any reference to the affected party shall be construed to refer to such person.

Act Sec. 4001. (b)(1) An individual who owns the entire interest in an unincorporated trade or business is treated as his own employer, and a partnership is treated as the employer of each partner who is an employee within the meaning of section 401(c)(1) of the Internal Revenue Code of 1986. For purposes of this title, under regulations prescribed by the corporation, all employees of trades or businesses (whether or not incorporated) which are under common control shall be treated as employed by a single employer and all such trades and businesses as a single employer. The regulations prescribed under the preceding sentence shall be consistent and coextensive with regulations prescribed for similar purposes by the Secretary of the Treasury under section 414(c) of the Internal Revenue Code of 1986.

(2) For purposes of subtitle E—

(A) except as otherwise provided in subtitle E, contributions or other payments shall be considered under a plan for a plan year if they are made within the period prescribed under section 412(c)(10) of the Internal Revenue Code of 1986 (determined, in the case of a terminated plan, as if the plan had continued beyond the termination date), and

(B) the term "Secretary of the Treasury" means the Secretary of the Treasury or such Secretary's delegate.

Amendments

P.L. 103-465, §761(a)(11):

Act Sec. 761(a)(11) amended ERISA Sec. 4001(a)(13) by striking "means a person—"and all that follows and inserting "means a person described in section 302(c)(11)(A) of this Act (without regard to section 302(c)(11)(B) of this Act) or section 412(c)(11)(A) of the Internal Revenue Code of 1986 (without regard to section 412(c)(11)(B) of such Code)." Prior to amendment, ERISA Sec. 4001(a)(13) read as follows:

(13) "contributing sponsor", of a single-employer plan, means a person—

(A) who is responsible, in connection with such plan, for meeting the funding requirements under section 302 of this Act or section 412 of the Internal Revenue Code of 1986, or

(B) who is a member of the controlled group of a person described in subparagraph (A), has been responsible for meeting such funding requirements, and has employed a significant number (as may be defined in regulations of the corporation) of participants under such plan while such person was so responsible;

The above amendment is effective as if included in the Pension Protection Act.

P.L. 102-229, §214:

Amended ERISA Sec. 4001(a)(14) by striking "and" at the end of subparagraph (A), adding "and" at the end of subparagraph (B) and by adding a new subparagraph (C) to read as above, effective December 13, 1991.

P.L. 101-239, §7891(a)(1):

Titles I, III, and IV of ERISA (other than sections 3(37)(E), 301(a)(7), and 308, the last sentence of section 408(d), and sections 414(c), 4001(a)(3)(ii), and 4303) are each amended by striking "Internal Revenue Code of 1954" each place it appears and inserting "Internal Revenue Code of 1986" effective October 22, 1986.

P.L. 100-203, §9312(b)(4):

Amended ERISA Sec. 4001(a)(16) to read as above, effective for (A) plan terminations under section 4041(c) of ERISA with respect to which notices of intent to terminate are provided under section 4041(a)(2) of ERISA after December 17, 1987, and (B) plan terminations with respect to which proceedings are instituted by the Pension Benefit Guaranty Corporation under section 4042 of ERISA after December 17, 1987.

Prior to amendment ERISA Sec. 4001(a)(16) read as follows:

(16) "benefit commitments", to a participant or beneficiary as of any date under a single-employer plan, means all benefits provided by the plan with respect to the participant or beneficiary which—

(A) are guaranteed under section 4022,

(B) would be guaranteed under section 4022, but for the operation of subsection 4022(b), or

(C) constitute—

(i) early retirement supplements or subsidies, or

(ii) plant closing benefits,

irrespective of whether any such supplements, subsidies, or benefits are benefits guaranteed under section 4022, if the participant or beneficiary has satisfied, as of such date, all of the conditions required of him or her under the provisions of the plan to establish entitlement to the benefits, except for the submission of a formal application, retirement, completion of a required waiting period subsequent to application for benefits, or designation of a beneficiary;

P.L. 100-203, §9312(b)(5):

Amended ERISA Sec. 4001(a)(19) to read as above. For the effective date, see Act Sec. 9312(b)(4), above.

Prior to amendment, ERISA Sec. 4001(a)(19) read as follows:

(19) "outstanding amount of benefit commitments", of a participant or beneficiary under a terminated single-employer plan, means the excess of—

(A) the actuarial present value (determined as of the termination date on the basis of assumptions prescribed by the corporation for purposes of section 4044) of the benefit commitments to such participant or beneficiary under the plan, over

(B) the actuarial present value (determined as of such date on the basis of assumptions prescribed by the corporation for purposes of section 4044) of the benefits of such

participants or beneficiary which are guaranteed under section 4022 or to which assets of the plan are required to be allocated under section 4044;

P.L. 100-203, §9313(a)(3)(F):

Amended ERISA Sec. 4001(a)(18) to read as above, effective for plan termination under section 4041 of ERISA for which notices of intent to terminate are provided under section 4041(a)(2) of ERISA after December 17, 1987.

Prior to amendment, ERISA Sec. 4001(a)(18) read as follows:

(18) "amounts of unfunded benefit commitments", of a participant or beneficiary as of any date under a single-employer plan, means an amount equal to the excess of—

(A) the actuarial present value (determined as of such date on the basis of assumptions prescribed by the corporation for purposes of section 4044) of the benefit commitments to the participant or beneficiary under the plan, over

(B) the current value (as of such date) of the assets of the plan which are required to be allocated to those benefit commitments under section 4044;

P.L. 99-272:

Act Sec. 11004(a) amended ERISA Sec. 4001(a) by striking paragraph (2) and inserting a new paragraph (2) to read as above.

Prior to amendment, ERISA Sec. 4001(a)(2) read as follows:

(2) "substantial employer" means for any plan year an employer (treating employers who are members of the same affiliated group, within the meaning of section 1563(a) of the Internal Revenue Code of 1954, determined without regard to section 1563(a)(4) and (e)(3)(C) of such Code, as one employer) who has made contributions to or under a plan under which more than one employer (other than a multiemployer plan) makes contributions for each of—

(A) the two immediately preceding plan years, or

(B) the second and third preceding plan years,

equaling or exceeding 10 percent of all employer contributions paid to or under that plan for each such year;

Act Sec. 11004(a) also amended ERISA Sec. 4001(a) by striking "and" which followed paragraph (11), struck the period following "corporation" at the end of paragraph (12) and inserted a semicolon and added new paragraphs (13)—(21) to read as above.

Act Sec. 11004(b) amended ERISA Sec. 4001(b) by inserting (1) and (b) and by adding new paragraph (2) to read as above.

Act Sec. 11004(b) also struck out amendments made by section 402(a)(1)(F) of the Multiemployer Pension Plan Amendments Act of 1980 which added new paragraphs to ERISA Sec. 4001(c)(1) which read:

(2) For purposes of this title, "single-employer plan" means, except as otherwise specifically provided in this title, any plan which is not a multiemployer plan.

(3) For purposes of this title, except as otherwise provided in this title, contributions or other payments shall be considered made under a plan for a plan year if they are made within the period prescribed under section 412(c)(10) of the Internal Revenue Code of 1954.

(4) For purposes of subtitle E, "Secretary of the Treasury" means the Secretary of the Treasury or such Secretary's delegate.

These amendments apply with respect to terminations pursuant to notices of intent filed with the PBGC on or after January 1, 1986 and proceedings begun after that date.

P.L. 96-364, §402(a)(1):

Amended Sec. 4001, effective September 26, 1980 by: inserting in subsection (a)(2) "(other than a multiemployer plan)"; inserting subsection (a)(3), prior to the amendment subsection (a)(3) read "'multiemployer plan' means a multi-employer plan as defined in section 414(f) of the Internal Revenue Code of 1954 (as added by this Act but without regard to whether such section is in effect on the date of enactment of this Act)"; inserting subsection (a)(6), prior to the amendment subsection (A)(6) read "'basic benefits' means benefits guaranteed under section 4022 other than under section 4022(c)"; inserting "or 4022(A)g;" at the end of subsection (a)(7); inserting new subsections (a)(8) through (a)(12). Act Sec. 402(a)(1) added new paragraphs (2), (3), (4) to subsection (c)(1) (as redesignated); however, no redesignation was made in the law. Therefore, the provisions of subsection (b) have been designated as paragraph (b)(1) to which paragraphs (2) through (4) have been added.

Regulations

The following regulations were adopted by the Pension Benefit Guaranty Corporation on July 1, 1996 (61 FR 34002). Prior to July 1, 1996, PBGC regulations were under Chapter XXVI of Title 29 of the Code of Federal Regulations. Effective July 1, 1996, PBGC regulations were moved to Chapter XL, and were renumbered and reorganized. Reg. §4001.2 was amended December 2, 1996 (61 FR 63988), effective January 1, 1997 and was corrected July 1, 1997 (62 FR 35342), effective July 1, 1996. Reg. §4001.2 was amended November 7, 1997 (62 FR 60424), effective January 1, 1998. Reg. §4001.2 was officially corrected on December 30, 1997 (62 FR 67728).

[¶ 15,315]

§4001.1 **Purpose and scope.** This part contains definitions of certain terms used in this chapter and the regulations under which the PBGC makes various controlled group determinations.

[¶ 15,315A]

§4001.2 **Definitions.** For purposes of this chapter (unless otherwise indicated or required by the context):

Affected party means, with respect to a plan—

(1) Each participant in the plan;

(2) Each beneficiary of a deceased participant;

(3) Each alternate payee under an applicable qualified domestic relations order, as defined in section 206(d)(3) of ERISA;

(4) Each employee organization that currently represents any group of participants;

(5) For any group of participants not currently represented by an employee organization, the employee organization, if any, that last

represented such group of participants within the 5-year period preceding issuance of the notice of intent to terminate; and

(6) the PBGC. If an affected party has designated, in writing, a person to receive a notice on behalf of the affected party, any reference to the affected party (in connection with the notice) shall be construed to refer to such person.

Annuity means a series of periodic payments to a participant or surviving beneficiary for a fixed or contingent period.

Basic-type benefit means a benefit that is guaranteed under the provisions of part 4022 of this chapter or would be guaranteed if the guarantee limits in §§ 4022.22 through 4022.27 of this chapter did not apply. [Corrected 12/30/97, by 62 FR 67728.]

Benefit liabilities means the benefits of participants and their beneficiaries under the plan (within the meaning of section 401(a)(2) of the Code).

Code means the Internal Revenue Code of 1986, as amended.

Complete withdrawal means a complete withdrawal as described in section 4203 of ERISA.

Contributing sponsor means a person who is a contributing sponsor as defined in section 4001(a)(13) of ERISA.

Controlled group means, in connection with any person, a group consisting of such person and all other persons under common control with such person, determined under section 4001.3 of this part. For purposes of determining the persons liable for contributions under section 412(c)(11)(B) of the Code or section 302(c)(11)(B) of ERISA, or for premiums under section 4007(e)(2) of ERISA, a controlled group also includes any group treated as a single employer under section 414(m) or (o) of the Code. Any reference to a plan's controlled group means all contributing sponsors of the plan and all members of each contributing sponsor's controlled group. [Amended 12/2/96 by 61 FR 63989.]

Corporation means the Pension Benefit Guaranty Corporation, except where the context demonstrates that a different meaning is intended.

Defined benefit plan means a plan described in section 3(35) of ERISA.

Distress termination means the voluntary termination of a single-employer plan in accordance with section 4041(c) of ERISA and part 4041, subpart C, of this chapter.

Distribution date means:

(1) Except as provided in paragraph (2)—

(i) For benefits provided through the purchase of irrevocable commitments, the date on which the obligation to provide the benefits passes from the plan to the insurer; and

(ii) For benefits provided other than through the purchase of irrevocable commitments, the date on which the benefits are delivered to the participant or beneficiary (or to another plan or benefit arrangement or other recipient authorized by the participant or beneficiary in accordance with applicable law and regulations) personally or by deposit with a mail or courier service (as evidenced by a postmark or written receipt); or

(2) The deemed distribution date (as defined in § 4050.2) in the case of a designated benefit paid to the PBGC in accordance with part 4050 of this chapter (dealing with missing participants). [Amended 11/7/97 by 62 FR 60424. Generally, for fully-funded, single-employer pension plans which issued their first notice of intent to terminate before January 1, 1998, an unamended definition applies. Paragraph (2) previously read: (2) Other than for purposes of determining the interest rate to be used in calculating the value of a benefit to be paid as a lump sum to a late-discovered participant, the deemed distribution date (as defined in § 4050.2) in the case of a designated benefit paid to the PBGC, a benefit provided after the deemed distribution date to a late-discovered participant, or an irrevocable commitment purchased from an insurer after the deemed distribution date for a recently-missing participant in accordance with part 4050 of this chapter (dealing with missing participants).]

EIN means the nine-digit employer identification number assigned by the Internal Revenue Service to a person. [Amended 12/2/96 by 61 FR 63988.]

Employer means all trades or businesses (whether or not incorporated) that are under common control, within the meaning of § 4001.3 of this chapter.

ERISA means the Employee Retirement Income Security Act of 1974, as amended.

Fair market value means the price at which property would change hands between a willing buyer and a willing seller, neither being under any compulsion to buy or sell and both having reasonable knowledge of relevant facts.

FOIA means the Freedom of Information Act, as amended (5 U.S.C. 552).

Funding standard account means an account established and maintained under section 302(b) of ERISA or section 412(b) of the Code.

Guaranteed benefit means a benefit under a single-employer plan that is guaranteed by the PBGC under section 4022(a) of ERISA and part 4022 of this chapter, or a benefit under a multiemployer plan that is guaranteed by the PBGC under section 4022A of ERISA.

Insurer means a company authorized to do business as an insurance carrier under the laws of a State or the District of Columbia.

Irrevocable commitment means an obligation by an insurer to pay benefits to a named participant or surviving beneficiary, if the obligation cannot be cancelled under the terms of the insurance contract (except for fraud or mistake) without the consent of the participant or beneficiary and is legally enforceable by the participant or beneficiary.

IRS means the Internal Revenue Service.

Mandatory employee contributions means amounts contributed to the plan by a participant that are required as a condition of employment, as a condition of participation in such plan, or as a condition of obtaining benefits under the plan attributable to employer contributions.

Mass withdrawal means:

(1) The withdrawal of every employer from the plan (2) The cessation of the obligation of all employers to contribute under the plan, or (3) The withdrawal of substantially all employers pursuant to an agreement or arrangement to withdraw. [Corrected 7/1/97 by 62 FR 35342.]

Multiemployer Act means the Multiemployer Pension Plan Amendments Act of 1980.

Multiemployer plan means a plan that is described in section 4001(a)(3) of ERISA and that is covered by title IV of ERISA.

Multiple employer plan means a single-employer plan maintained by two or more contributing sponsors that are not members of the same controlled group, under which all plan assets are available to pay benefits to all plan participants and beneficiaries.

Nonbasic-type benefit means any benefit provided by a plan other than a basic-type benefit.

Nonforfeitable benefit means a benefit described in section 4001(a)(8) of ERISA. Benefits that become nonforfeitable solely as a result of the termination of a plan will be considered forfeitable.

Normal retirement age means the age specified in the plan as the normal retirement age. This age shall not exceed the later of age 65 or the age attained after 5 years of participation in the plan. If no normal retirement age is specified in the plan, it is age 65.

Notice of intent to terminate means the notice of a proposed termination of a single-employer plan, as required by section 4041(a)(2) of ERISA and § 4041.21 (in a standard termination) or § 4041.41 (in a distress termination) of this chapter.

PBGC means the Pension Benefit Guaranty Corporation.

Person means a person defined in section 3(9) of ERISA.

Plan means a defined benefit plan within the meaning of section 3(35) of ERISA that is covered by title IV of ERISA.

Plan administrator means an administrator, as defined in section 3(16)(A) of ERISA.

Plan sponsor means, with respect to a multiemployer plan, the person described in section 4001(a)(10) of ERISA.

Plan year means the calendar, policy, or fiscal year on which the records of the plan are kept.

PN means the three-digit plan number assigned to a plan. [Amended 12/2/96 by 61 FR 63988.]

Proposed termination date means the date specified as such by the plan administrator of a single-employer plan in a notice of intent to terminate or, if later, in the standard or distress termination notice, in accordance with section 4041 of ERISA and part 4041 of this chapter.

Single-employer plan means any defined benefit plan (as defined in section 3(35) of ERISA) that is not a multiemployer plan (as defined in section 4001(a)(3) of ERISA) and that is covered by title IV of ERISA.

Standard termination means the voluntary termination, in accordance with section 4041(b) of ERISA and part 4041, subpart B, of this chapter, of a single-employer plan that is able to provide for all of its benefit liabilities when plan assets are distributed.

Substantial owner means a substantial owner as defined in section 4022(b)(5)(A) of ERISA.

Sufficient for benefit liabilities means that there is no amount of unfunded benefit liabilities, as defined in section 4001(a)(18) of ERISA.

Sufficient for guaranteed benefits means that there is no amount of unfunded guaranteed benefits, as defined in section 4001(a)(17) of ERISA.

Termination date means the date established pursuant to section 4048(a) of ERISA.

Title IV benefit means the guaranteed benefit plus any additional benefits to which plan assets are allocated pursuant to section 4044 of ERISA and part 4044 of this chapter.

Voluntary employee contributions means amounts contributed by an employee to a plan, pursuant to the provisions of the plan, that are not mandatory employee contributions. [Amended 12/2/96 by 61 FR 63988; corrected 7/1/97 by 62 FR 35342.]

[¶ 15,315B]

§4001.3 **Trades or businesses under common control; controlled groups.** For purposes of title IV of ERISA:

(a)(1) The PBGC will determine that trades and businesses (whether or not incorporated) are under common control if they are "two or more trades or businesses under common control", as defined in regulations prescribed under section 414(c) of the Code.

(2) The PBGC will determine that all employees of trades or businesses (whether or not incorporated) which are under common control shall be treated as employed by a single employer, and all such trades and businesses shall be treated as a single employer.

(3) An individual who owns the entire interest in an unincorporated trade or business is treated as his own employer, and a partnership is treated as the employer of each partner who is an employee within the meaning of section 401(c)(1) of the Code.

(b) In the case of a single-employer plan:

(1) In connection with any person, a controlled group consists of that person and all other persons under common control with such person.

(2) Persons are under common control if they are members of a "controlled group of corporations", as defined in regulations prescribed under section 414(b) of the Code, or if they are "two or more trades or businesses under common control", as defined in regulations prescribed under section 414(c) of the Code.

[¶ 15,320]
PENSION BENEFIT GUARANTY CORPORATION

Act Sec. 4002.(a) There is established within the Department of Labor a body corporate to be known as the Pension Benefit Guaranty Corporation. In carrying out its functions under this title, the corporation shall be administered by the chairman of the board of directors in accordance with policies established by the board. The purposes of this title, which are to be carried out by the corporation, are—

(1) to encourage the continuation and maintenance of voluntary private pension plans for the benefit of their participants,

(2) to provide for the timely and uninterrupted payment of pension benefits to participants and beneficiaries under plans to which this title applies, and

(3) to maintain premiums established by the corporation under section 4006 at the lowest level consistent with carrying out its obligations under this title.

Act Sec. 4002. (b) To carry out the purposes of this title, the corporation has the powers conferred on a nonprofit corporation under the District of Columbia Nonprofit Corporation Act and, in addition to any specific power granted to the corporation elsewhere in this title or under that Act, the corporation has the power—

(1) to sue and be sued, complain and defend, in its corporate name and through its own counsel, in any court, State or Federal;

(2) to adopt, alter, and use a corporate seal, which shall be judicially noticed;

(3) to adopt, amend, and repeal, by the board of directors, bylaws, rules, and regulations relating to the conduct of its business and the exercise of all other rights and powers granted to it by this Act and such other bylaws, rules, and regulations as may be necessary to carry out the purposes of this title;

(4) to conduct its business (including the carrying on of operations and the maintenance of offices) and to exercise all other rights and powers granted to it by this Act in any State or other jurisdiction without regard to qualification, licensing, or other requirements imposed by law in such State or other jurisdiction;

(5) to lease, purchase, accept gifts or donations of, or otherwise to acquire, to own, hold, improve, use, or otherwise deal in or with, and to sell, convey, mortgage, pledge, lease, exchange, or otherwise dispose of, any property, real, personal or mixed, or any interest therein wherever situated;

(6) to appoint and fix the compensation of such officers, attorneys, employees, and agents as may be required, to determine their qualifications, to define their duties and, to the extent desired by the corporation, require bonds for them and fix the penalty thereof, and to appoint and fix the compensation of experts and consultants in accordance with the provisions of section 3109 of title 5, United States Code;

(7) to utilize the personnel and facilities of any other agency or department of the United States Government, with or without reimbursement, with the consent of the head of such agency or department; and

(8) to enter into contracts, to execute instruments, to incur liabilities, and to do any and all other acts and things as may be necessary or incidental to the conduct of its business and the exercise of all other rights and powers granted to the corporation by this Act.

Act Sec. 4002. (c) Section 5108 of title 5, United States Code, is amended by adding at the end thereof the following new subsection:

"(g) In addition to the number of positions authorized by subsection (a), the Pension Benefit Guaranty Corporation is authorized, without regard to any other provision of this section, to place one position in the corporation at GS-18 and a total of 10 positions in the corporation at GS-16 and 17.".

Act Sec. 4002. (d) The board of directors of the corporation consists of the Secretary of the Treasury, the Secretary of Labor, and the Secretary of Commerce. Members of the board shall serve without compensation, but shall be reimbursed for travel, subsistence, and other necessary expenses incurred in the performance of their duties as members of the board. The Secretary of Labor is the chairman of the board of directors.

Act Sec. 4002. (e) The board of directors shall meet at the call of its chairman, or as otherwise provided by the bylaws of the corporation.

Act Sec. 4002. (f) As soon as practicable, but not later than 180 days after the date of enactment of this Act, the board of directors shall adopt initial bylaws and rules relating to the conduct of the business of the corporation. Thereafter, the board of directors may alter, supplement, or repeal any existing bylaw or rule, and may adopt additional bylaws and rules from time to time as may be necessary. The chairman of the board shall cause a copy of the bylaws of the corporation to be published in the Federal Register not less often than once each year.

Act Sec. 4002. (g)(1) The corporation, its property, its franchise, capital, reserves, surplus, and its income (including, but not limited to, any income of any fund established under section 4005), shall be exempt from all taxation now or hereafter imposed by the United States (other than taxes imposed under chapter 21 of the Internal Revenue Code of 1954, relating to Federal Insurance Contributions Act, and chapter 23 of such Code, relating to Federal Unemployment Tax Act), or by any State or local taxing authority, except that any real property and any tangible personal property (other than cash and securities) of the corporation shall be subject to State and local taxation to the same extent according to its value as other real and tangible personal property is taxed.

(2) The receipts and disbursements of the corporation in the discharge of its functions shall be included in the totals of the budget of the United States Government. The United States is not liable for any obligation or liability incurred by the corporation.

(3) Section 101 of the Government Corporation Control Act (31 U.S.C. 846) is amended by inserting before the period a semicolon and the following: "and Pension Benefit Guaranty Corporation".

Act Sec. 4002. (h)(1) There is established an advisory committee to the corporation, for the purpose of advising the corporation as to its policies and procedures relating to (A) the appointment of trustees in termination proceedings, (B) investment of moneys, (C) whether plans being terminated should be liquidated immediately or continued in operation under a trustee, and (D) such other issues as the corporation may request from time to time. The advisory committee may also recommend persons for appointment as trustees in termination proceedings, make recommendations with respect to the investment of moneys in the funds, and advise the corporation as to whether a plan subject to being terminated should be liquidated immediately or continued in operation under a trustee.

(2) The advisory committee consists of seven members appointed, from among individuals recommended by the board of directors, by the President. Of the seven members, two shall represent the interests of employee organizations, two shall represent the interests of employers who maintain pension plans, and three shall represent the interests of the general public. The President shall designate one member as chairman at the time of the appointment of that member.

(3) Members shall serve for terms of 3 years each, except that, of the members first appointed, one of the members representing the interests of employee organizations, one of the members representing the interests of employers, and one of the members representing the interests of the general public shall be appointed for terms of 2 years each, one of the members representing the interests of the general public shall be appointed for a term of 1 year, and the other members shall be appointed to full 3-year terms. The advisory committee shall meet at least six times each year and at such other times as may be determined by the chairman or requested by any three members of the advisory committee.

(4) Members shall be chosen on the basis of their experience with employee organizations, with employers who maintain pension plans, with the administration of pension plans, or otherwise on account of outstanding demonstrated ability in related fields. Of the members serving on the advisory committee at any time, no more than four shall be affiliated with the same political party.

(5) An individual appointed to fill a vacancy occurring other than by the expiration of a term of office shall be appointed only for the unexpired term of the member he succeeds. Any vacancy occurring in the office of a member of the advisory committee shall be filled in the manner in which that office was originally filled.

(6) The advisory committee shall appoint and fix the compensation of such employees as it determines necessary to discharge its duties, including experts and consultants in accordance with the provisions of section 3109 of title 5, United States Code. The corporation shall furnish to the advisory committee such professional, secretarial, and other services as the committee may request.

(7) Members of the advisory committee shall, for each day (including travel time) during which they are attending meetings or conferences of the committee or otherwise engaged in the business of the committee, be compensated at a rate fixed by the corporation which is not in excess of the daily equivalent of the annual rate of basic pay in effect for grade GS-18 of the General Schedule, and while away from their homes or regular places of business they may be allowed travel expenses, including per diem in lieu of subsistence, as authorized by section 5703 of title 5, United States Code.

(8) The Federal Advisory Committee Act does not apply to the advisory committee established by this subsection.

Act Sec. 4002. SPECIAL RULES REGARDING DISASTERS, ETC. (i) In the case of a pension or other employee benefit plan, or any sponsor, administrator, participant, beneficiary, or other person with respect to such plan, affected by a Presidentially declared disaster (as defined in section 1033 (h)(3) of the Internal Revenue Code of 1986) or a terroristic or military action (as defined in section 692 (c)(2) of such Code), the corporation may, notwithstanding any other provision of law, prescribe, by notice or otherwise, a period of up to 1 year which may be disregarded in determining the date by which any action is required or permitted to be completed under this Act. No plan shall be treated as failing to be operated in accordance with the terms of the plan solely as the result of disregarding any period by reason of the preceding sentence.

Amendments:

P.L. 107-134, §112(c)(2):

Amended Sec. 4002 by adding subsection (i). The amendment applies to disasters and terroristic or military actions occurring on or after September 11, 2001, with respect to any action of the Secretary of the Treasury, Secretary of Labor, or the PBGC occurring on or after January 23, 2002.

P.L. 96-364, §§403(1) and 406:

Amended Sec. 4002(b)(3) to read as above, effective September 26, 1980 by inserting "and such other bylaws, rules, and regulations as may be necessary to carry out the purposes of this title" after "Act" and amended Sec. 4002(g)(2) to read as above. Prior to amendment, Sec. 4002(g)(2) read as follows: "The receipts and disbursements of the

corporation in the discharge of its functions shall not be included in the totals of the budget of the United States Government and shall be exempt from any general limitations imposed by statute on budget outlays of the United States. Except as explicitly provided in this title, the United States is not liable for any obligation or liability incurred by the corporation." The amendment applies to fiscal years beginning after September 30, 1980.

P.L. 94-455, §1510:

Amended Sec. 4002(g)(1) by inserting "by the United States (other than taxes imposed under chapter 21 of the Internal Revenue Code of 1954, relating to Federal Insurance Contributions Act, and chapter 23 of such Code, relating to Federal Unemployment Tax Act, or" immediately after the word "imposed." The amendment is effective September 2, 1974.

Regulations

The following regulations were adopted by the Pension Benefit Guaranty Corporation on July 1, 1996 (61 FR 34002). Prior to July 1, 1996, PBGC regulations were under Chapter XXVI of Title 29 of the Code of Federal Regulations. Effective July 1, 1996, PBGC regulations were moved to Chapter XL, and were renumbered and reorganized.

[¶ 15,321]

§4002.1 **Name.** The name of the Corporation is the Pension Benefit Guaranty Corporation.

[¶ 15,321A]

§4002.2 **Offices.** The principal office of the Corporation shall be in the Metropolitan area of the City of Washington, District of Columbia. The Corporation may have additional offices at such other places as the Board of Directors may deem necessary or desirable to the conduct of its business.

[¶ 15,321B]

§4002.3 **Board of Directors.** (a) The Board of Directors shall establish the policies of the Corporation and shall perform the other functions assigned to the Board of Directors in title IV of the Employee Retirement Income Security Act of 1974. The Board of Directors of the Corporation shall be composed of the Secretary of Labor, the Secretary of the Treasury, and the Secretary of Commerce. Members of the Board shall serve without compensation, but shall be reimbursed by

the Corporation for travel, subsistence, and other necessary expenses incurred in the performance of their duties as members of the Board. A person at the time of a meeting of the Board of Directors who is serving as Secretary of Labor, Secretary of the Treasury or Secretary of Commerce in an acting capacity, shall serve as a member of the Board of Directors with the same authority and effect as the designated Secretary.

(b) The following powers are expressly reserved to the Board of Directors and shall not be delegated:

(1) Approval of all final substantive regulations prior to publication in the Federal Register, except for amendments to the regulations on Allocation of Assets in Single-employer Plans and Duties of Plan Sponsor Following Mass Withdrawal (parts 4044 and 4281 of this chapter) establishing new interest rates and factors, which may be approved by the Executive Director of the PBGC.

(2) Approval of all reports or recommendations to the Congress that are required by statute;

(3) Establishment from time to time of the Corporation's budget and debt ceiling up to the statutory limit;

(4) Determination from time to time of limits on advances to the revolving funds administered by the Corporation pursuant to section 4005(a) of ERISA;

(5) Final decision on any policy matter that would materially affect the rights of a substantial number of employers or covered participants and beneficiaries.

(c) Final non-substantive regulations and all proposed regulations shall be approved by the Executive Director prior to publication in the Federal Register; provided that all proposed substantive regulations shall first be circulated for review to the Board of Directors or their designees, and may thereafter be issued by the Executive Director after responding to any comments made within 21 days after circulation of the proposed regulation, or, if no comments are received, after expiration of the 21-day period.

[¶ 15,321C]

§4002.4 **Chairman.** The Secretary of Labor shall be the Chairman of the Board of Directors and he shall be the administrator of the Corporation with responsibility for its management, including overall supervision of the Corporation's personnel, organization, and budget practices, and shall exercise such incidental powers as may be necessary to carry out his administrative responsibilities. The Chairman may delegate his administrative responsibilities.

[¶ 15,321D]

§4002.5 **Quorum.** A majority of the Directors shall constitute a quorum for the transaction of business. Any act of a majority of the Directors present at any meeting at which there is a quorum shall be the act of the Board, except as may otherwise be provided in these bylaws.

[¶ 15,321E]

§4002.6 **Meetings.** Regular meetings of the Board of Directors shall be held at such times as the Chairman shall select. Special meetings of the Board of Directors shall be called by the Chairman on the request of any other Director. Reasonable notice of any meetings shall be given to each Director. The General Counsel of the Corporation shall serve as Secretary to the Board of Directors and keep its minutes. As soon as practicable after each meeting, a draft of the minutes of such meeting shall be distributed to each member of the Board for correction or approval.

[¶ 15,321F]

§4002.7 **Place of meetings; use of conference call communications equipment.** Meetings of the Board of Directors shall be held at the principal office of the Corporation unless otherwise determined by the Board of Directors or the Chairman. Any Director may participate in a meeting of the Board of Directors through the use of conference call telephone or similar communications equipment, by means of which all persons participating in the meeting can simultaneously speak to and hear each other. Any Director so participating in a meeting shall be deemed present for all purposes. Actions taken by the Board of Directors at meetings conducted through the use of such equipment, including the votes of each member, shall be recorded in the usual manner in the minutes of the meetings of the Board of Directors. A resolution of the Board of Directors signed by each of its three members shall have the same force and effect as if agreed at a duly called meeting and shall be recorded in the minutes of the Board of Directors.

[¶ 15,321G]

§4002.8 **Alternate voting procedure.** (a) A Director shall be deemed to have participated in a meeting of the Board of Directors for all purposes if,

(1) That Director was represented at that meeting by an individual who was designated to act on his behalf, and

(2) That Director ratified in writing the actions taken by his designee at that meeting within a reasonable period of time after such meeting.

(b) For purposes of this section, a Director, including an individual serving as Acting Secretary, shall designate a representative at a level not below that of Assistant Secretary within his Department. Such designation shall be in writing and shall be effective until withdrawn or until a date specified therein.

(c) For purposes of this section, a Director's approval of the minutes of a meeting of the Board of Directors shall constitute ratification of the actions of his designee at such meeting.

[¶ 15,321H]

§4002.9 **Amendments.** These bylaws may be amended or new bylaws adopted by unanimous vote of the Board.

[¶ 15,330]
INVESTIGATORY AUTHORITY; COOPERATION WITH OTHER AGENCIES; CIVIL ACTIONS

Act Sec. 4003. (a) The corporation may make such investigations as it deems necessary to enforce any provision of this title or any rule or regulation thereunder, and may require or permit any person to file with it a statement in writing, under oath or otherwise as the corporation shall determine, as to all the facts and circumstances concerning the matter to be investigated. The corporation shall annually audit a statistically significant number of plans terminating under section 4041(b) to determine whether participants and beneficiaries have received their benefit commitments and whether section 4050(a) has been satisfied. Each audit shall include a statistically significant number of participants and beneficiaries.

Act Sec. 4003. (b) For the purpose of any such investigation, or any other proceeding under this title, any member of the board of directors of the corporation, or any officer designated by the chairman, may administer oaths and affirmations, subpena witnesses, compel their attendance, take evidence, and require the production of any books, papers, correspondence, memoranda, or other records which the corporation deems relevant or material to the inquiry.

Act Sec. 4003. (c) In case of contumacy by, or refusal to obey a subpena issued to, any person, the corporation may invoke the aid of any court of the United States within the jurisdiction of which such investigation or proceeding is carried on, or where such person resides or carries on business, in requiring the attendance and testimony of witnesses and the production of books, papers, correspondence, memoranda, and other records. The court may issue an order requiring such person to appear before the corporation, or member or officer designated by the corporation, and to produce records or to give testimony related to the matter under investigation or in question. Any failure to obey such order of the court may be punished by the court as a contempt thereof. All process in any such case may be served in the judicial district in which such person is an inhabitant or may be found.

Act Sec. 4003. (d) In order to avoid unnecessary expense and duplication of functions among government agencies, the corporation may make such arrangements or agreements for cooperation or mutual assistance in the performance of its functions under this title as is practicable and consistent with law. The corporation may utilize the facilities or services of any department, agency, or establishment of the United States or of any State or political subdivision of a State, including the services of any of its employees, with the lawful consent of such department, agency, or establishment. The head of each department, agency, or establishment of the United States shall cooperate with the corporation and, to the extent permitted by law, provide such information and facilities as it may request for its assistance in the performance of its functions under this title. The Attorney General or his representative shall receive from the corporation for appropriate action such evidence developed in the performance of its functions under this title as may be found to warrant consideration for criminal prosecution under the provisions of this or any other Federal law.

Act Sec. 4003. (e)(1) Civil actions may be brought by the corporation for appropriate relief, legal or equitable or both, to enforce

     (A) the provisions of this title, and

     (B) in the case of a plan which is covered under this title (other than a multiemployer plan) and for which the conditions for imposition of a lien described in section 302(f)(1)(A) and (B) of this Act or section 412(n)(1)(A) and (B) of this Act or section 412(n)(1)(A) and (B) of the Internal Revenue Code of 1986 have been met, section 302 of this Act and section 412 of such Code.

     (2) Except as otherwise provided in this title, where such an action is brought in a district court of the United States, it may be brought in the district where the plan is administered, where the violation took place, or where a defendant resides or may be found, and process may be served in any other district where a defendant resides or may be found.

(3) The district courts of the United States shall have jurisdiction of actions brought by the corporation under this title without regard to the amount in controversy in any such action.

(4) [Repealed]

(5) In any action brought under this title, whether to collect premiums, penalties, and interest under section 4007 or for any other purpose, the court may award to the corporation all or a portion of the costs of litigation incurred by the corporation in connection with such action.

(6)(A) Except as provided in subparagraph (C), an action under this subsection may not be brought after the later of—

(i) 6 years after the date on which the cause of action arose, or

(ii) 3 years after the applicable date specified in subparagraph (B).

(B)(B)(i) Except as provided in clause (ii), the applicable date specified in this subparagraph is the earliest date on which the corporation acquired or should have acquired actual knowledge of the existence of such cause of action.

(ii) If the corporation brings the action as a trustee, the applicable date specified in this subparagraph is the date on which the corporation became a trustee with respect to the plan if such date is later than the date described in clause (i).

(C) In the case of fraud or concealment, the period described in subparagraph (A)(ii) shall be extended to 6 years after the applicable date specified in subparagraph (B).

Act Sec. 4003.(f)(1) Except with respect to withdrawal liability disputes under part 1 of subtitle E, any person who is a fiduciary, employer, contributing sponsor, member of a contributing sponsor's controlled group, participant, or beneficiary, and is adversely affected by any action of the corporation with respect to a plan in which such person has an interest, or who is an employee organization representing such a participant or beneficiary so adversely affected for purposes of collective bargaining with respect to such plan, may bring an action against the corporation for appropriate equitable relief in the appropriate court.

(2) For purposes of this subsection, the term "appropriate court" means—

(A) the United States district court before which proceedings under section 4041 or 4042 are being conducted,

(B) if no such proceedings are being conducted, the United States district court for the judicial district in which the plan has its principal office, or

(C) the United States District Court for the District of Columbia.

(3) In any action brought under this subsection, the court may award all or a portion of the costs and expenses incurred in connection with such action to any party who prevails or substantially prevails in such action.

(4) This subsection shall be the exclusive means for bringing actions against the corporation under this title, including actions against the corporation in its capacity as a trustee under section 4042 or 4049.

(5)(A) Except as provided in subparagraph (C), an action under this subsection may not be brought after the later of—

(i) 6 years after the date on which the cause of action arose, or

(ii) 3 years after the applicable date specified in subparagraph (B).

(B)(i) Except as provided in clause (ii), the applicable date specified in this subparagraph is the earliest date on which the plaintiff acquired or should have acquired actual knowledge of the existence of such cause of action.

(ii) In the case of a plaintiff who is a fiduciary bringing the action in the exercise of fiduciary duties, the applicable date specified in this subparagraph is the date on which the plaintiff became a fiduciary with respect to the plan if such date is later than the date specified in clause (i).

(C) In the case of fraud or concealment, the period described in subparagraph (A)(ii) shall be extended to 6 years after the applicable date specified in subparagraph (B).

(6) The district courts of the United States have jurisdiction of actions brought under this subsection without regard to the amount in controversy.

(7) In any suit, action, or proceeding in which the corporation is a party, or intervenes under section 4301, in any State court, the corporation may, without bond or security, remove such suit, action, or proceeding from the state court to the United States district court for the district or division in which such suit, action, or proceeding is pending by following any procedure for removal now or hereafter in effect.

Amendments:

P.L. 103-465, §773(a):

Act Sec. 773(a) amended ERISA Sec. 4003(e)(1) to read as above. Prior to amendment, ERISA Sec. 4003(e)(1) read as follows:

(e)(1) Civil actions may be brought by the corporation for appropriate relief, legal or equitable or both, to enforce the provisions of this title.

The above amendment is effective for installments and other payments required under ERISA Sec. 302 or Code Sec. 412 that become due on or after December 8, 1994.

P.L. 103-465, §776(b)(1):

Act Sec. 776(b)(1) amended ERISA Sec. 4003(a) in the second sentence by inserting before the period the following: "and whether section 4050(a) has been satisfied".

The above amendment is effective with respect to distributions that occur in plan years commencing after final regulations implementing the amendment are prescribed by the Pension Benefit Guaranty Corporation.

P.L. 99-272:

Act Sec. 11014(b)(2) amended ERISA Sec. 4003(e) by adding a new paragraph (6) to read as above, effective with respect to actions filed after April 7, 1986.

Act Sec. 11014(b)(1) amended ERISA Sec. 4003(f) to read as above, effective with respect to actions filed after April 7, 1986. Prior to amendment, Sec. 4003(f) read as follows:

Act Sec. 4003. (f) Except as provided in section 4301(a)(2), any participant beneficiary plan administrator, or employer adversely affected by any action of the corporation, or by a receiver or trustee appointed by the corporation, with respect to a plan in which such participant, beneficiary, plan administrator or employer has an interest, may bring

an action against the corporation, receiver or trustee in the appropriate court. For purposes of this subsection the term "appropriate court" means the United States district court before which proceedings under section 4041 or 4042 of this title are being conducted, or if no such proceedings are being conducted the United States district court for the district in which the plan has its principal office, or the United States district court for the District of Columbia. The district courts of the United States have jurisdiction of actions brought under this subsection without regard to the amount in controversy. In any suit, action, or proceeding in which the corporation is a party, or intervenes under section 4301, an [sic] any State court, the corporation may, without bond or security, remove such suit, action, or proceeding from the State court to the United States District Court for the district or division embracing the place where the same is pending by following any procedure for removal now or hereafter in effect.

Act Sec. 11016(c)(5) amended ERISA Sec. 4003(a) by adding a new sentence at the end of the subsection, effective on April 7, 1986.

P.L. 98-620, §402(33):

Repealed ERISA Sec. 4003(e)(4) effective November 8, 1984, but the repeal does not apply to cases pending on that date. Prior to repeal, ERISA Sec. 4003(e)(4) read:

"(4) Upon application by the corporation to a court of the United States for expedited handling of any case in which the corporation is a party, it is the duty of that court to assign such case for hearing at the earliest practical date and to cause such case to be in every way expedited."

P.L. 96-364, §§402(a)(2) and 403(k):

Amended Sec. 4003 effective September 26, 1980 by: striking out in subsection (a) "determine whether any person has violated or is about to violate" and inserting "enforce"; striking out in subsection (e)(1) "redress violations of" and inserting "enforce"; and inserting at the end of subsection (f) the new sentence.

Regulations

The following regulations were adopted by the Pension Benefit Guaranty Corporation on July 1, 1996 (61 FR 34002). Prior to July 1, 1996, PBGC regulations were under Chapter XXVI of Title 29 of the Code of Federal Regulations. Effective July 1, 1996, PBGC regulations were moved to Chapter XL, and were renumbered and reorganized. On October 28, 2003, § 4003.9 and § 4003.10 were revised and § 4003.33 and § 4003.53 were amended (68 FR 61344).

Subpart A—General Provisions

[¶ 15,331]

§ 4003.1 **Purpose and scope.** (a) *Purpose.* This part sets forth the rules governing the issuance of all initial determinations by the PBGC on cases pending before it involving the matters set forth in paragraph (b) of this section and the procedures for requesting and obtaining administrative review by the PBGC of those determinations. Subpart A contains general provisions. Subpart B sets forth rules governing the issuance of all initial determinations of the PBGC on matters covered by this part. Subpart C establishes procedures governing the reconsideration by the PBGC of initial determinations relating to the matters set forth in paragraphs (b)(1) through (b)(4). Subpart D establishes procedures governing administrative appeals from initial determinations relating to the matters set forth in paragraphs (b)(5) through (b)(10).

(b) *Scope.* This part applies to the following determinations made by the PBGC in cases pending before it and to the review of those determinations:

(1) Determinations that a plan is covered under section 4021 of ERISA;

(2) Determinations with respect to premiums, interest and late payment penalties pursuant to section 4007 of ERISA;

(3) Determinations with respect to voluntary terminations under section 4041 of ERISA, including—

(i) A determination that a notice requirement or a certification requirement under section 4041 of ERISA has not been met,

(ii) A determination that the requirements for demonstrating distress under section 4041(c)(2)(B) of ERISA have not been met, and

(iii) A determination with respect to the sufficiency of plan assets for benefit liabilities or for guaranteed benefits;

(4) Determinations with respect to allocation of assets under section 4044 of ERISA, including distribution of excess assets under section 4044(d);

(5) Determinations that a plan is not covered under section 4021 of ERISA;

(6) Determinations under section 4022(a) or (c) or section 4022A(a) of ERISA with respect to benefit entitlement of participants and beneficiaries under covered plans and determinations that a domestic relations order is or is not a qualified domestic relations order under section 206(d)(3) of ERISA and section 414(p) of the Code;

(7) Determinations under section 4022(b) or (c), section 4022A (b) through (e), or section 4022B of ERISA of the amount of benefits payable to participants and beneficiaries under covered plans;

(8) Determinations of the amount of money subject to recapture pursuant to section 4045 of ERISA;

(9) Determinations of the amount of liability under section 4062(b)(1), section 4063, or section 4064 of ERISA;

(10) Determinations—

(i) That the amount of a participant's or beneficiary's benefit under section 4050(a)(3) of ERISA has been correctly computed based on the designated benefit paid to the PBGC under section 4050(b)(2) of ERISA, or

(ii) That the designated benefit is correct, but only to the extent that the benefit to be paid does not exceed the participant's or beneficiary's guaranteed benefit.

(c) *Matters not covered by this part.* Nothing in this part limits—

(1) The authority of the PBGC to review, either upon request or on its own initiative, a determination to which this part does not apply when, in its discretion, the PBGC determines that it would be appropriate to do so, or

(2) The procedure that the PBGC may utilize in reviewing any determination to which this part does not apply.

[¶ 15,331A]

§ 4003.2 **Definitions.** The following terms are defined in § 4001.2 of this chapter: Code, contributing sponsor, controlled group, ERISA, multiemployer plan, PBGC, person, plan administrator, and single-employer plan.

In addition, for purposes of this part:

Aggrieved person means any participant, beneficiary, plan administrator, contributing sponsor of a single-employer plan or member of such a contributing sponsor's controlled group, plan sponsor of a multiemployer plan, or employer that is adversely affected by an initial determination of the PBGC with respect to a pension plan in which such person has an interest. The term "beneficiary" includes an alternate payee (within the meaning of section 206(d)(3)(K) of ERISA) under a qualified domestic relations order (within the meaning of section 206(d)(3)(B) of ERISA).

Appeals Board means a board consisting of three PBGC officials. The Executive Director shall appoint a senior PBGC official to serve as Chairperson and three or more other PBGC officials to serve as regular Appeals Board members. The Chairperson shall designate the three officials who will constitute the Appeals Board with respect to a case, provided that a person may not serve on the Appeals Board with respect to a case in which he or she made a decision regarding the merits of the determination being appealed. The Chairperson need not serve on the Appeals Board with respect to all cases.

Appellant means any person filing an appeal under subpart D of this part.

Director means the Director of any department of the PBGC and includes the Executive Director of the PBGC, Deputy Executive Directors, and the General Counsel.

[¶ 15,331B]

§ 4003.3 **PBGC assistance in obtaining information.** A person who lacks information or documents necessary to file a request for review pursuant to subpart C or D of this part, or necessary to a decision whether to seek review, or necessary to participate in an appeal pursuant to § 4003.57 of this part or necessary to a decision whether to participate, may request the PBGC's assistance in obtaining information or documents in the possession of a party other than the PBGC. The request shall state or describe the missing information or documents, the reason why the person needs the information or documents, and the reason why the person needs the assistance of the PBGC in obtaining the information or documents. The request may also include a request for an extension of time to file pursuant to § 4003.4 of this part.

[¶ 15,331C]

§ 4003.4 **Extension of tim** e. (a) *General rule.* When a document is required under this part to be filed within a prescribed period of time, an extension of time to file will be granted only upon good cause shown and only when the request for an extension is made before the expiration of the time prescribed. The request for an extension shall be in writing and state why additional time is needed and the amount of additional time requested. The filing of a request for an extension shall stop the running of the prescribed period of time. When a request for an extension is granted, the PBGC shall notify the person requesting the extension, in writing, of the amount of additional time granted. When a request for an extension is denied, the PBGC shall so notify the requestor in writing, and the prescribed period of time shall resume running from the date of denial.

(b) *Disaster relief.* When the President of the United States declares that, under the Disaster Relief Act of 1974, as amended (42 U.S.C. 5121, 5122(2), 5141(b)), a major disaster exists, the Executive Director of the PBGC (or his or her designee) may, by issuing one or more notices of disaster relief, extend the due date for filing a request for reconsideration under § 4003.32 or an appeal under § 4003.52 by up to 180 days.

(1) The due date extension or extensions shall be available only to an aggrieved person who is residing in, or whose principal place of business is within, a designated disaster area, or with respect to whom the office of the service provider, bank, insurance company, or other person maintaining the information necessary to file the request for reconsideration or appeal is within a designated disaster area; and

(2) The request for reconsideration or appeal shall identify the filing as one for which the due date extension is available.

[¶ 15,331D]

§ 4003.5 **Non-timely request for review.** The PBGC will process a request for review of an initial determination that was not filed within the prescribed period of time for requesting review (see §§4003.32 and 4003.52) if—

(a) The person requesting review demonstrates in his or her request that he or she did not file a timely request for review because he or she neither knew nor, with due diligence, could have known of the initial determination; and

(b) The request for review is filed within 30 days after the date the aggrieved person, exercising due diligence at all relevant times, first learned of the initial determination where the requested review is reconsideration, or within 45 days after the date the aggrieved person, exercising due diligence at all relevant times, first learned of the initial determination where the request for review is an appeal.

[¶ 15,331E]

§4003.6 **Representation**. A person may file any document or make any appearance that is required or permitted by this part on his or her own behalf or he or she may designate a representative. When the representative is not an attorney-at-law, a notarized power of attorney, signed by the person making the designation, which authorizes the representation and specifies the scope of representation shall be filed with the PBGC in accordance with §4003.9(b) of this part.

[¶ 15,331F]

§4003.7 **Exhaustion of administrative remedies**. Except as provided in §4003.22(b), a person aggrieved by an initial determination of the PBGC covered by this part, other than a determination subject to reconsideration that is issued by a Department Director, has not exhausted his or her administrative remedies until he or she has filed a request for reconsideration under subpart C of this part or an appeal under subpart D of this part, whichever is applicable, and a decision granting or denying the relief requested has been issued.

[¶ 15,331G]

§4003.8 **Request for confidential treatment**. If any person filing a document with the PBGC believes that some or all of the information contained in the document is exempt from the mandatory public disclosure requirements of the Freedom of Information Act, 5 U.S.C. 552, he or she shall specify the information with respect to which confidentiality is claimed and the grounds therefor.

[¶ 15,331H]

§4003.9 **Method and date of filing**. (a) *Method of filing*. The PBGC applies the rules in subpart A of part 4000 of this chapter to determine permissible methods of filing with the PBGC under this part.

(b) *Date of filing*. The PBGC applies the rules in subpart C of part 4000 of this chapter to determine the date that a submission under this part was filed with the PBGC.

[¶ 15,331I]

§4003.10 **Computation of time**. The PBGC applies the rules in subpart D of part 4000 of this chapter to compute any time period under this part.

Subpart B—Initial Determinations

[¶ 15,332]

§4003.21 **Form and contents of initial determinations**. All determinations to which this subpart applies shall be in writing, shall state the reason for the determination, and, except when effective on the date of issuance as provided in §4003.22(b), shall contain notice of the right to request review of the determination pursuant to subpart C or subpart D of this part, as applicable, and a brief description of the procedures for requesting review.

[¶ 15,332A]

§4003.22 **Effective date of determinations**. (a) *General Rule*. Except as provided in paragraph (b) of this section, an initial determination covered by this subpart will not become effective until the prescribed period of time for filing a request for reconsideration under subpart C of this part or an appeal under subpart D of this part, whichever is applicable, has elapsed. The filing of a request for review under subpart C or D of this part shall automatically stay the effectiveness of a determination until a decision on the request for review has been issued by the PBGC.

(b) *Exception*. The PBGC may, in its discretion, order that the initial determination in a case is effective on the date it is issued. When the PBGC makes such an order, the initial determination shall state that the determination is effective on the date of issuance and that there is no obligation to exhaust administrative remedies with respect to that determination by seeking review of it by the PBGC.

Subpart C—Reconsideration of Initial Determinations

[¶ 15,333]

§4003.31 **Who may request reconsideration**. Any person aggrieved by an initial determination of the PBGC to which this subpart applies may request reconsideration of the determination.

[¶ 15,333A]

§4003.32 **When to request reconsideration**. Except as provided in §§4003.4 and 4003.5, a request for reconsideration must be filed within 30 days after the date of the initial determination of which reconsideration is sought or, when administrative review includes a procedure in §4903.33 of this chapter, by a date 60 days (or more) thereafter that is specified in the PBGC's notice of the right to request review.

[¶ 15,333B]

§4003.33 **[Amended]**. A request for reconsideration shall be submitted to the Director of the department within the PBGC that issued the initial determination, except that a request for reconsideration of a determination described in §4003.1(b)(3)(ii) shall be submitted to the Executive Director. See Sec. 4000.4 of this chapter for information on where to file.

[¶ 15,333C]

§4003.34 **Form and contents of request for reconsideration**. A request for reconsideration shall—

(a) Be in writing;

(b) Be clearly designated as a request for reconsideration;

(c) Contain a statement of the grounds for reconsideration and the relief sought; and

(d) Reference all pertinent information already in the possession of the PBGC and include any additional information believed to be relevant.

[¶ 15,333D]

§4003.35 **Final decision on request for reconsideration**. (a) Except as provided in paragraphs (a)(1) or (a)(2), final decisions on requests for reconsideration will be issued by the same department of the PBGC that issued the initial determination, by an official whose level of authority in that department is higher than that of the person who issued the initial determination.

(1) When an initial determination is issued by a Department Director, the Department Director (or an official designated by the Department Director) will issue the final decision on request for reconsideration of a determination other than one described in §4003.1(b)(3)(ii).

(2) The Executive Director (or an official designated by the Executive Director) will issue the final decision on a request for reconsideration of a determination described in §4003.1(b)(3)(ii).

(b) The final decision on a request for reconsideration shall be in writing, specify the relief granted, if any, state the reason(s) for the decision, and state that the person has exhausted his or her administrative remedies.

Subpart D—Administrative Appeals

[¶ 15,334]

§4003.51 **Who may appeal or participate in appeals**. Any person aggrieved by an initial determination to which this subpart applies may file an appeal. Any person who may be aggrieved by a decision under this subpart granting the relief requested in whole or in part may participate in the appeal in the manner provided in §4003.57.

[¶ 15,334A]

§4003.52 **When to file**. Except as provided in §§4003.4 and 4003.5, an appeal under this subpart must be filed within 45 days after the date of the initial determination being appealed or, when administrative review includes a procedure in §4903.33 of this chapter, by a date 60 days (or more) thereafter that is specified in the PBGC's notice of the right to request review.

[¶ 15,334B]

§4003.53 **[Amended]**. An appeal or a request for an extension of time to appeal shall be submitted to the Appeals Board, Pension Benefit Guaranty Corporation, 1200 K Street NW., Washington, DC 20005-4026. See Sec. 4000.4 of this chapter for additional information on where to file.

[¶ 15,334C]

§4003.54 **Contents of appeal**. (a) An appeal shall—

(1) Be in writing;

(2) Be clearly designated as an appeal;

(3) Contain a statement of the grounds upon which it is brought and the relief sought;

(4) Reference all pertinent information already in the possession of the PBGC and include any additional information believed to be relevant;

(5) State whether the appellant desires to appear in person or through a representative before the Appeals Board; and

(6) State whether the appellant desires to present witnesses to testify before the Appeals Board, and if so, state why the presence of witnesses will further the decision-making process.

(b) In any case where the appellant believes that another person may be aggrieved if the PBGC grants the relief sought, the appeal shall also include the name(s) and address(es) (if known) of such other person(s).

[¶ 15,334D]

§4003.55 **Opportunity to appear and to present witnesses**. (a) At the discretion of the Appeals Board, any appearance permitted under this subpart may be before a hearing officer designated by the Appeals Board.

(b) An opportunity to appear before the Appeals Board (or a hearing officer) and an opportunity to present witnesses will be permitted at the discretion of the Appeals Board. In general, an opportunity to appear will be permitted if the Appeals Board determines that there is a dispute as to a material fact; an opportunity to present witnesses will be permitted when the Appeals Board determines that witnesses will contribute to the resolution of a factual dispute.

(c) Appearances permitted under this section will take place at the main offices of the PBGC, 1200 K Street NW., Washington, DC 20005-4026, unless the Appeals Board, in its discretion, designates a different location, either on its own initiative or at the request of the appellant or a third party participating in the appeal.

[¶ 15,334E]

§4003.56 **Consolidation of appeals**. (a) *When consolidation may be required*. Whenever multiple appeals are filed that arise out of the same or similar facts and seek the same or similar relief, the Appeals Board may, in its discretion, order the consolidation of all or some of the appeals.

(b) *Representation of parties*. Whenever the Appeals Board orders the consolidation of appeals, the appellants may designate one (or more) of their number to represent all of them for all purposes relating to their appeals.

(c) *Decision by Appeals Board*. The decision of the Appeals Board in a consolidated appeal shall be binding on all appellants whose appeals were subject to the consolidation.

[¶ 15,334F]

§4003.57 **Appeals affecting third parties**. (a) Before the Appeals Board issues a decision granting, in whole or in part, the relief requested in an appeal, it shall make a reasonable effort to notify third persons who will be aggrieved by the decision of the following:

(1) The pendency of the appeal;

(2) The grounds upon which the appeal is based;

(3) The grounds upon which the Appeals Board is considering reversing the initial determination;

(4) The right to submit written comments on the appeal;

(5) The right to request an opportunity to appear in person or through a representative before the Appeals Board and to present witnesses; and

(6) That no further opportunity to present information to the PBGC with respect to the determination under appeal will be provided.

(b) Written comments and a request to appear before the Appeals Board must be filed within 45 days after the date of the notice from the Appeals Board.

(c) If more than one third party is involved, their participation in the appeal may be consolidated pursuant to the provisions of §4003.56.

[¶ 15,334G]

§4003.58 **Powers of the Appeals Board**. In addition to the powers specifically described in this part, the Appeals Board may request the submission of any information or the appearance of any person it considers necessary to resolve a matter before it and to enter any order it considers necessary for or appropriate to the disposition of any matter before it.

[¶ 15,334H]

§4003.59 **Decision by the Appeals Board**. (a) In reaching its decision, the Appeals Board shall consider those portions of the file relating to the initial determination, all material submitted by the appellant and any third parties in connection with the appeal, and any additional information submitted by PBGC staff.

(b) The decision of the Appeals Board constitutes the final agency action by the PBGC with respect to the determination which was the subject of the appeal and is binding on all parties who participated in the appeal and who were notified pursuant to §4003.57 of their right to participate in the appeal.

(c) The decision of the Appeals Board shall be in writing, specify the relief granted, if any, state the bases for the decision, including a brief statement of the facts or legal conclusions supporting the decision, and state that the appellant has exhausted his or her administrative remedies.

[¶ 15,334I]

§4003.60 **Referral of appeal to the Executive Director**. The Appeals Board may, in its discretion, refer any appeal to the Executive Director of the PBGC for decision. In such a case, the Executive Director shall have all the powers vested in the Appeals Board by this subpart and the decision of the Executive Director shall meet the requirements of and have the effect of a decision issued under §4003.59 of this part.

[¶ 15,334J]

§4003.61 **Action by a single Appeals Board member**. (a) *Authority to act*. Notwithstanding any other provision of this part, any member of the Appeals Board has the authority to take any action that the Appeals Board could take with respect to a routine appeal as defined in paragraph (b) of this section.

(b) *Routine appeal defined*. For purposes of this section, a routine appeal is any appeal that does not raise a significant issue of law or a precedent-setting issue. This would generally include any appeal that—

(1) Is outside the jurisdiction of the Appeals Board (for example, an appeal challenging the plan's termination date);

(2) Is filed by a person other than an aggrieved person or an aggrieved person's authorized representative;

(3) Is untimely and presents no grounds for waiver or extension of the time limit for filing the appeal, or only grounds that are clearly without merit;

(4) Presents grounds that clearly warrant or clearly do not warrant the relief requested;

(5) Presents only factual issues that are not reasonably expected to affect other appeals (for example, the participant's date of birth or date of hire); or

(6) Presents only issues that are controlled by settled principles of existing law, including Appeals Board precedent (for example, an issue of plan interpretation that has been resolved by the Appeals

Board in a decision on an appeal by another participant in the same plan).

[¶ 15,340]
[SEC. 4004 REPEALED]

Act Sec. 4004 Repealed.
Amendment:

P.L. 99-272:

Act Sec. 11016(c)(6) repealed ERISA Sec. 4004, effective on April 7, 1986.

Prior to repeal, ERISA Sec. 4004 read as follows:

TEMPORARY AUTHORITY FOR INITIAL PERIOD

Act Sec. 4004. (a) Notwithstanding anything to the contrary in this title, the corporation may, upon receipt of notice that a plan is to be terminated or upon making a determination described in section 4042, appoint a receiver whose powers shall take effect immediately. The receiver shall assume control of such plan and its assets, protecting the interests of all interested persons during subsequent proceedings.

(b) (1) Within a reasonable time, not exceeding 20 days, after the appointment of a receiver under subsection (a), the corporation shall apply to an appropriate United States district court for a decree approving such appointment. The court to which application is made shall issue a decree approving such appointment unless it determines that such approval would not be in the best interests of the participants and beneficiaries of the plan.

(2) If the court to which application is made under paragraph (1) dismisses the application with prejudice, or if the corporation fails to apply for a degree under paragraph (1) within 20 days after the appointment of the receiver, the receiver shall transfer all assets and records of the plan held by him to the plan administrator within 3 business days after such dismissal or the expiration of the 20 day period. The receiver shall not be liable to the plan or to any other person for his acts as receiver other than for willful misconduct, or for conduct in violation of the provisions of part 4 of subpart B of title I of this Act (except to the extent that the provisions of section 4042(d)(1)(A) provide otherwise).

(c) The corporation is authorized, as an alternative to appointing a receiver under subsection (a), to direct a plan administrator to apply to a district court of the United States for the appointment of a receiver to assume control of the plan and its assets for the purpose of protecting the interests of all interested persons until the plan can be terminated under the provisions of this title.

(d) A receiver appointed under this section has the powers of a trustee under section 4042(d)(1)(A) and (B), and shall report to the corporation and the court on the plan from time to time as required by either the corporation or the court. As soon as practicable after his appointment, a receiver appointed under this section shall determine whether the assets of the plan are sufficient to discharge when due all obligations of the plan with respect to benefits guaranteed under this title in accordance with the requirements of section 4044. If the determination of the receiver is approved by the corporation and the court, the receiver shall proceed as if he were a trustee appointed under section 4042.

(e) A receiver may not be appointed under this section more than 270 days after the date of enactment of this Act.

(f) In addition to its other powers under this title, for only the first 270 days after the date of enactment of this Act the corporation may—

(1) contract for printing without regard to the provisions of chapter 5 of this title 44, United States Code,

(2) waive any notice required under this title if corporation finds that a waiver is necessary or appropriate.

(3) extend the 90-day period referred to in section 4041(a) for an additional 90 days without the agreement of the plan administrator and without application to a court as required under section 4041(d), and

(4) Waive the application of the provisions of sections 4062, 4063, and 4064 to, or reduce the liability imposed under such sections on, any employer with respect to a plan terminating during that 270 day period if the corporation determines that such waiver or reduction is necessary to avoid unreasonable hardship in any case in which the employer was not able, as a practical matter, to continue the plan.

[¶ 15,350]
ESTABLISHMENT OF PENSION BENEFIT GUARANTY FUNDS

Act Sec. 4005. (a) There are established on the books of the Treasury of the United States four revolving funds to be used by the corporation in carrying out its duties under this title. One of the funds shall be used with respect to basic benefits guaranteed under section 4022, one of the funds shall be used with respect to basic benefits guaranteed under section 4022A, one of the funds shall be used with respect to nonbasic benefits guaranteed under section 4022 (if any), and the remaining fund shall be used with respect to nonbasic benefits guaranteed under section 4022A (if any), other than subsection (g)(2) thereof (if any). Whenever in this title reference is made to the term "fund" the reference shall be considered to refer to the appropriate fund established under this subsection.

Act Sec. 4005. (b)(1) Each fund established under this section shall be credited with the appropriate portion of—

(A) funds borrowed under subsection (c),

(B) premiums, penalties, interest, and charges collected under this title,

(C) the value of the assets of a plan administered under section 4042 by a trustee to the extent that they exceed the liabilities of such plan,

(D) the amount of any employer liability payments under subtitle D, to the extent that such payments exceed liabilities of the plan (taking into account all other plan assets),

(E) earnings on investments of the fund or on assets credited to the fund under this subsection,

(F) attorney's fees awarded to the corporation, and

(G) receipts from any other operations under this title.

(2) Subject to the provisions of subsection (a), each fund shall be available—

(A) for making such payments as the corporation determines are necessary to pay benefits guaranteed under section 4022 or 4022A or benefits payable under section 4050,

(B) to purchase assets from a plan being terminated by the corporation when the corporation determines such purchase will best protect the interests of the corporation, participants in the plan being terminated, and other insured plans,

(C) to repay to the Secretary of the Treasury such sums as may be borrowed (together with interest thereon) under subsection (c), and

(D) to pay the operational and administrative expenses of the corporation, including reimbursement of the expenses incurred by the Department of the Treasury in maintaining the funds, and the Comptroller General in auditing the corporation.

(E) to pay to participants and beneficiaries the estimated amount of benefits which are guaranteed by the corporation under this title and the estimated amount of other benefits to which plan assets are allocated under section 4044, under single-employer plans which are unable to pay benefits when due or which are abandoned.

(3) Whenever the corporation determines that the moneys of any fund are in excess of current needs, it may request the investment of such amounts as it determines advisable by the Secretary of the Treasury in obligations issued or guaranteed by the United States but, until all borrowings under subsection (c) have been repaid, the obligations in which such excess moneys are invested may not yield a rate of return in excess of the rate of interest payable on such borrowings.

Act Sec. 4005. (c) The corporation is authorized to issue to the Secretary of the Treasury notes or other obligations in an aggregate amount of not to exceed $100,000,000, in such forms and denominations, bearing such maturities, and subject to such terms and conditions as may be prescribed by the Secretary of the Treasury. Such notes or other obligations shall bear interest at a rate determined by the Secretary of the Treasury, taking into consideration the current average market yield on outstanding marketable obligations of the United States of comparable maturities during the month preceding the issuance of such notes or other obligations of the corporation. The Secretary of the Treasury is authorized and directed to purchase any notes or other obligations issued by the corporation under this subsection, and for that purpose he is authorized to use as a public debt transaction the proceeds from the sale of any securities issued under the Second Liberty Bond Act, as amended, and the purposes for which securities may be issued under that Act, as amended, are extended to include any purchase of such notes and obligations. The Secretary of the Treasury may at any time sell any of the notes or other obligations acquired by him under this subsection. All redemptions, purchases, and sales by the Secretary of the Treasury of such notes or other obligations shall be treated as public debt transactions of the United States.

Act Sec. 4005. (d) (1) A fifth fund shall be established for the reimbursement of uncollectible withdrawal liability under section 4222, and shall be credited with the appropriate—

    (A) premiums, penalties, and interest charges collected under this title, and

    (B) earnings on investments of the fund or on assets credited to the fund.

The fund shall be available to make payments pursuant to the supplemental program established under section 4222, including those expenses and other charges determined to be appropriate by the corporation.

    (2) The corporation may invest amounts of the fund in such obligations as the corporation considers appropriate.

Act Sec. 4005. (e) (1) A sixth fund shall be established for the supplemental benefit guarantee program provided under section 4022A(g)(2).

    (2) Such fund shall be credited with the appropriate—

    (A) premiums, penalties, and interest charges collected under section 4022A(g)(2), and

    (B) earnings on investments of the fund or on assets credited to the fund.

The fund shall be available for making payments pursuant to the supplemental benefit guarantee program established under section 4022A(g)(2), including those expenses and other charges determined to be appropriate by the corporation.

    (3) The corporation may invest amounts of the fund in such obligations as the corporation considers appropriate.

Act Sec. 4005. (f) (1) A seventh fund shall be established and credited with—

    (A) premiums, penalties, and interest charges collected under section 4006(a)(3)(A)(i) (not described in subparagraph (B)) to the extent attributable to the amount of the premium in excess of $8.50,

    (B) premiums, penalties, and interest charges collected under section 4006(a)(3)(E), and

    (C) earnings on investments of the fund or on assets credited to the fund.

    (2) Amounts in the fund shall be available for transfer to other funds established under this section with respect to a single-employer plan but shall not be available to pay—

    (A) administrative costs of the corporation, or

    (B) benefits under any plan which was terminated before October 1, 1988, unless no other amounts are available for such payment.

The corporation may invest amounts of the fund in such obligations as the corporation considers appropriate.

Act Sec. 4005. (g) (1) Amounts in any fund established under this section may be used only for the purposes for which such fund was established and may not be used to make loans to (or on behalf of) any other fund or to finance any other activity of the corporation.

    (2) None of the funds borrowed under subsection (c) may be used to make loans to (or on behalf of) any fund other than a fund described in the second sentence of subsection (a).

    (3) Any repayment to the corporation of any amount paid out of any fund in connection with a multiemployer plan shall be deposited in such fund.

Act Sec. 4005. (h) Any stock in a person liable to the corporation under this title which is paid to the corporation by such person or a member of such person's controlled group in satisfaction of such person's liability under this title may be voted only by the custodial trustees or outside money managers of the corporation.

Amendment:

P.L. 103-465, § 776(b)(2):

Act Sec. 776(b)(2) amended ERISA Sec. 4005(b)(2)(A) by inserting "or benefits payable under section 4050" after "section 4022A".

The above amendment is effective with respect to distributions that occur in plan years commencing after final regulations implementing the amendment are prescribed by the Pension Benefit Guaranty Corporation.

P.L. 100-203, § 9312(c)(4):

Amended ERISA Sec. 4005(g) by striking out "or fiduciaries with respect to trusts to which the requirements of section 4049 apply", effective for (A) plan terminations under section 4041(c) of ERISA with respect to which notices of intent to terminate are provided under section 4041(a)(2) of ERISA after December 17, 1987, and (B) plan terminations with respect to which proceedings are instituted by the Pension Benefit Guaranty Corporation under section 4042 of ERISA after December 17, 1987.

P.L. 100-203, § 9331(d):

Amending ERISA Sec. 4005 by redesignating subsections (f) and (g) as subsections (g) and (h) and by adding subsection (f), to read as above, effective for fiscal years beginning after September 30, 1988.

P.L. 99-272:

Act Sec. 11016(a)(1) amended ERISA Sec. 4005(b)(2) by striking out "and" at the end of subparagraph (C), striking out the period at the end of subparagraph (D) and by adding a new subparagraph (E) to read as above.

Act Sec. 11016(a)(2) amended ERISA Sec. 4005(b)(1) by striking out "and" at the end of subparagraph (E), by redesignating subparagraph (F) as (G) and by adding a new subparagraph (F) to read as above.

Act Sec. 11016(c)(7) amended ERISA Sec. 4005 by adding a new subsection (g) to read as above.

These amendments take effect on the date of enactment.

P.L. 96-364, § 403(a):

Amended Sec. 4005(a) to read as above and added new subsections (d), (e), and (f), effective September 26, 1980. Prior to amendment, Sec. 4005(a) read as follows:

"(a) There are established on the books of the Treasury of the United States four revolving funds to be used by the corporation in carrying out its duties under this title. One of the funds shall be used in connection with benefits guaranteed under sections 4022 and 4023 (but not non-basic benefits) with respect to plans other than multiemployer plans, one of the funds shall be used with respect to such benefits guaranteed under such sections (other than non-basic benefits) for multiemployer plans, one of the funds shall be used with respect to non-basic benefits, if any are guaranteed by the corporation under section 4022, for plans which are not multiemployer plans, and the remaining fund shall be used with respect to non-basic benefits, if any are guaranteed by the corporation under section 4022, for multiemployer plans. Whenever in this title reference is made to the term 'fund' the reference shall be considered to refer to the appropriate fund established under this subsection."

[¶ 15,360]
PREMIUM RATES

Act Sec. 4006. (a) (a) (1) The corporation shall prescribe such schedules of premium rates and bases for the application of those rates as may be necessary to provide sufficient revenue to the fund for the corporation to carry out its functions under this title. The premium rates charged by the corporation for any period shall be uniform for all plans, other than multiemployer plans, insured by the corporation with respect to basic benefits guaranteed by it under section 4022, and shall be uniform for all multiemployer plans with respect to basic benefits guaranteed by it under section 4022A.

    (2) The corporation shall maintain separate schedules of premium rates, and bases for the application of those rates, for—

    (A) basic benefits guaranteed by it under section 4022 for single-employer plans,

    (B) basic benefits guaranteed by it under section 4022A for multiemployer plans,

    (C) nonbasic benefits guaranteed by it under section 4022 for single-employer plans,

    (D) nonbasic benefits guaranteed by it under section 4022A for multiemployer plans, and

    (E) reimbursements of uncollectible withdrawal liability under section 4222.

The corporation may revise such schedules whenever it determines that revised schedules are necessary. Except as provided in section 4022A(f), in order to place a revised schedule described in subparagraph (A) and (B) in effect, the corporation shall proceed in accordance with subsection (b)(1), and such schedule shall apply only to plan years beginning more than 30 days after the date on which a joint resolution approving such revised schedule is enacted.

    (3)(A) Except as provided in subparagraph (C), the annual premium rate payable to the corporation by all plans for basic benefits guaranteed under this title is—

(i) in the case of a single-employer plan, for plan years beginning after December 31, 1990, an amount equal to the sum of $19 plus the additional premium (if any) determined under subparagraph (E) for each individual who is a participant in such plan during the plan year;

(ii) in the case of a multiemployer plan, for the plan year within which the date of enactment of the Multiemployer Pension Plan Amendments Act of 1980 falls, an amount for each individual who is a participant in such plan for such plan year equal to the sum of—

(I) 50 cents, multiplied by a fraction the numerator of which is the number of months in such year ending on or before such date and the denominator of which is 12, and

(II) $1.00, multiplied by a fraction equal to 1 minus the fraction determined under clause (i),

(iii) in the case of a multiemployer plan, for plan years beginning after the date of enactment of the Multiemployer Pension Plan Amendments Act of 1980, an amount equal to—

(I) $1.40 for each participant, for the first, second, third, and fourth plan years,

(II) $1.80 for each participant, for the fifth and sixth plan years,

(III) $2.20 for each participant, for the seventh and eighth plan years, and

(IV) $2.60 for each participant, for the ninth plan year, and for each succeeding plan year.

(B) the Corporation may prescribe by regulation the extent to which the rate described in subparagraph (A)(i) applies more than once for any plan year to an individual participating in more than one plan maintained by the same employer and the corporation may prescribe regulations under which the rate described in subparagraph (A)(iii) will not apply to the same participant in any multiemployer plan more than once for any plan year.

(C)(i) If the sum of—

(I) the amounts in any fund for basic benefits guaranteed for multiemployer plans, and

(II) the value of any assets held by the corporation for payment of basic benefits guaranteed for multiemployer plans,

is for any calendar year less than 2 times the amount of basic benefits guaranteed by the corporation under this title for multiemployer plans which were paid out of any such fund or assets during the preceding calendar year, the annual premium rates under subparagraph (A) shall be increased to the next highest premium level necessary to insure that such sum will be at least 2 times greater than such amount during the following calendar year.

(ii) If the board of directors of the corporation determines that an increase in the premium rates under subparagraph (A) is necessary to provide assistance to plans which are receiving assistance under section 4261 and to plans the board finds are reasonably likely to require such assistance, the board may order such increase in the premium rates.

(iii) The maximum annual premium rate which may be established under this subparagraph is $2.60 for each participant.

(iv) The provisions of this subparagraph shall not apply if the annual premium rate is increased to a level in excess of $2.60 per participant under any other provisions of this title.

(D)(i) Not later than 120 days before the date on which an increase under subparagraph (C)(ii) is to become effective, the corporation shall publish in the Federal Register a notice of the determination described in subparagraph (C)(ii), the basis for the determination, the amount of the increase in the premium, and the anticipated increase in premium income that would result from the increase in the premium rate. The notice shall invite public comment, and shall provide for a public hearing if one is requested. Any such hearing shall be commenced not later than 60 days before the date on which the increase is to become effective.

(ii) The board of directors shall review the hearing record established under clause (i) and shall, not later than 30 days before the date on which the increase is to become effective, determine (after the consideration of the comments received) whether the amount of the increase should be changed and shall publish its determination in the Federal Register.

(E)(i) The additional premium determined under this subparagraph with respect to any plan for any plan year shall be an amount equal to the amount determined under clause (ii) divided by the number of participants in such plan as of the close of the preceding plan year.

(ii) The amount determined under this clause for any plan year shall be an amount equal to $9.00 for each $1,000 (or fraction thereof) of unfunded vested benefits under the plan as of the close of the preceding plan year.

(iii) For purposes of clause (ii)—

(I) Except as provided in subclause (II) or (III) the term "unfunded vested benefits" means the amount which would be the unfunded current liability (within the meaning of section 302(d)(8)(A)) if only vested benefits were taken in account.

(II) The interest rate used in valuing vested benefits for purposes of subclause (I) shall be equal to the applicable percentage of the annual yield on 30-year Treasury securities for the month preceding the month in which the plan year begins. For purposes of this subclause, the applicable percentage is 80 percent for plan years beginning before July 1, 1997, 85 percent for plan years beginning after June 30, 1997, and before the 1st plan year to which the first tables prescribed under section 302(d)(7)(C)(ii)(II) apply, and 100 percent for such 1st plan year and subsequent plan years.

(III) In the case of any plan year for which the applicable percentage under subclause (II) is 100 percent, the value of the plan's assets used in determining unfunded current liability under subclause (I) shall be their fair market value.

(IV) In the case of plan years beginning after December 31, 2001, and before January 1, 2004, subclause (II) shall be applied to substituting '100 percent' for '85 percent'. Subclause (III) shall be applied for such years without regard to the preceding sentence. Any reference to this clause or this subparagraph by any other sections or subsections (other than sections 4005, 4010, 4011, and 4043) shall be treated as a reference to this clause or this subparagraph without regard to this subclause.

(V) In the case of plan years beginning after December 31, 2003, and before January 1, 2006, the annual yield taken into account under subclause (II) shall be the annual rate of interest determined by the Secretary of the Treasury on amounts invested conservatively in long-term investment grade corporate bonds for the month preceding the month in which the plan year begins. For purposes of the preceding sentence, the Secretary of the Treasury shall determine such rate of interest on the basis of 2 or more indices that are selected periodically by the Secretary of the Treasury and that are in the top 3 quality levels available. The Secretary of the Treasury shall make the permissible range, and the indices and methodology used to determine the rate, publicly available..

(iv) No premium shall be determined under this subparagraph for any plan year if, as of the close of the preceding plan year, contributions to the plan for the preceding plan year were not less than the full funding limitation for the preceding year under section 412(c)(7) of the Internal Revenue Code of 1986.

(v) No premium shall be determined under this subparagraph for any plan year if, as of the close of the preceding plan year, contributions to the plan for the preceding plan year were not less than the full funding limitation for the preceding plan year under section 412(c)(7) of the Internal Revenue Code of 1986.

(4) The corporation may prescribe, subject to the enactment of a joint resolution in accordance with this section or section 4022A(f), alternative schedules of premium rates, and bases for the application of those rates, for basic benefits guaranteed by it under sections 4022 and 4022A based, in whole or in part, on the risks insured by the corporation in each plan.

(5)(A) In carrying out its authority under paragraph (1) to establish schedules of premium rates, and bases for the application of those rates, for nonbasic benefits guaranteed under sections 4022 and 4022A, the premium rates charged by the corporation for any period for nonbasic benefits guaranteed shall—

(i) be uniform by category of nonbasic benefits guaranteed,

(ii) be based on the risks insured in each category, and

(iii) reflect the experience of the corporation (including experience which may be reasonably anticipated) in guaranteeing such benefits.

(B) Notwithstanding subparagraph (A), premium rates charged to any multiemployer plan by the corporation for any period for supplemental guarantees under section 4022A(g)(2) may reflect any reasonable considerations which the corporation determines to be appropriate.

(6)(A) In carrying out its authority under paragraph (1) to establish premium rates and bases for basic benefits guaranteed under section 4022 with respect to single-employer plans, the corporation shall establish such rates and bases in coverage schedules is accordance with the provisions of this paragraph.

(B) The corporation may establish annual premiums for single-employer plans composed of the sum of—

(i) a charge based on a rate applicable to the excess, if any, of the present value of the basic benefits of the plan which are guaranteed over the value of the assets of the plan, not in excess of 0.1 percent, and

(ii) an additional charge based on a rate applicable to the present value of the basic benefits of the plan which are guaranteed.

The rate for the additional charge referred to in clause (ii) shall be set by the corporation for every year at a level which the corporation estimates will yield total revenue approximately equal to the total revenue to be derived by the corporation from the charges referred to in clause (i) of this subparagraph.

(C) The corporation may establish annual premiums for single-employer plans based on—

(i) the number of participants in a plan, but such premium rates shall not exceed the rates described in paragraph (3),

(ii) unfunded basic benefits guaranteed under this title, but such premium rates shall not exceed the limitations applicable to charges referred to in subparagraph (B)(i), or

(iii) total guaranteed basic benefits, but such premium rates shall not exceed the rates for additional charges referred to in subparagraph (B)(ii).

If the corporation uses two or more of the rate bases described in this subparagraph, the premium rates shall be designed to produce approximately equal amounts of aggregate premium revenue from each of the rate bases used.

(D) For purposes of this paragraph, the corporation shall by regulation define the terms "value of assets" and "present value of the benefits of the plan which are guaranteed" in a manner consistent with the purposes of this title and the provisions of this section.

Act Sec. 4006.(b)(1) In order to place a revised schedule (other than a schedule described in subsection (a)(2)(C), (D), or (E)) in effect, the corporation shall transmit the proposed schedule, its proposed effective date, and the reasons for its proposal to the Committee on Ways and Means and the Committee on Education and Labor of the House of Representatives, and to the Committee on Finance and the Committee on Labor and Human Resources of the Senate.

(2) The succeeding paragraphs of this subsection are enacted by Congress as an exercise of the rulemaking power of the Senate and the House of Representatives, respectively, and as such they shall be deemed a part of the rules of each House, respectively, but applicable only with respect to the procedure to be followed in that House in the case of resolutions described in paragraph (3). They shall supersede other rules only to the extent that they are inconsistent therewith. They are enacted with full recognition of the constitutional right of either House to change the rules (so far as relating to the procedure of that House) at any time, in the same manner and to the same extent as in the case of any rule of that House.

(3) For the purpose of the succeeding paragraphs of this subsection, "resolution" means only a joint resolution, the matter after the resolving clause of which is as follows: "The proposed revised schedule transmitted to Congress by the Pension Benefit Guaranty Corporation on . . . is hereby approved.", the blank space therein being filled with the date on which the corporation's message proposing the rate was delivered.

(4) A resolution shall be referred to the Committee on Ways and Means and the Committee on Education and Labor of the House of Representatives and to the Committee on Finance and the Committee on Labor and Human Resources of the Senate.

(5) If a committee to which has been referred a resolution has not reported it before the expiration of 10 calendar days after its introduction, it shall then (but not before) be in order to move to discharge the committee from further consideration of that resolution, or to discharge the committee from further consideration of any other resolution with respect to the proposed adjustment which has been referred to the committee. The motion to discharge may be made only by a person favoring the resolution, shall be highly privileged (except that it may not be made after the committee has reported a resolution with respect to the same proposed rate), and debate thereon shall be limited to not more than 1 hour, to be divided equally between those favoring and those opposing the resolution. An amendment to the motion is not in order, and it is not in order to move to reconsider the vote by which the motion is agreed to or disagreed to. If the motion to discharge is agreed to or disagreed to, the motion may not be renewed, nor may another motion to discharge the committee be made with respect to any other resolution with respect to the same proposed rate.

(6) When a committee has reported, or has been discharged from further consideration of a resolution, it is at any time thereafter in order (even though a previous motion to the same effect has been disagreed to) to move to proceed to the consideration of the resolution. The motion is highly privileged and is not debatable. An amendment to the motion is not in order, and it is not in order to move to reconsider the vote by which the motion is agreed to or disagreed to. Debate on the resolution shall be limited to not more than 10 hours, which shall be divided equally between those favoring and those opposing the resolution. A motion further to limit debate is not debatable. An amendment to, or motion to recommit, the resolution is not in order, and it is not in order to move to reconsider the vote by which the resolution is agreed to or disagreed to.

(7) Motions to postpone, made with respect to the discharge from committee, or the consideration of, a resolution and motions to proceed to the consideration of other business shall be decided without debate. Appeals from the decisions of the Chair relating to the application of the rules of the Senate or the House of Representatives, as the case may be, to the procedure relating to a resolution shall be decided without debate.

Act Sec. 4006.(c)(1) Except as provided in subsection (a)(3), and subject to paragraph (2), the rate for all plans for basic benefits guaranteed under this title with respect to plan years ending after September 2, 1974, is—

(A) in the case of each plan which was not a multiemployer plan in a plan year—

(i) with respect to each plan year beginning before January 1, 1978, an amount equal to $1 for each individual who was a participant in such plan during the plan year, and

(ii) with respect to each plan year beginning after December 31, 1977, and before January 1, 1986, an amount equal to $2.60 for each individual who was a participant in such plan during the plan year, and

(iii) with respect to each plan year beginning after December 31, 1985, and before January 1, 1988, an amount equal to $8.50 for each individual who was a participant in such plan during the plan year, and

(iv) with respect to each plan year beginning after December 31, 1987, and before January 1, 1991, an amount equal to $16 for each individual who was a participant in such plan during the plan year, and

(B) in the case of each plan which was a multiemployer plan in a plan year, an amount equal to 50 cents for each individual who was a participant in such plan during the plan year.

(2) The rate applicable under this subsection for the plan year preceding September 1, 1975, is the product of—

(A) the rate described in the preceding sentence; and

(B) a fraction—

(i) the numerator of which is the number of calendar months in the plan year which ends after September 2, 1974, and before the date on which the new plan year commences, and

(ii) the denominator of which is 12.

Amendments

P.L. 108-311, §403(d):

Amended ERISA §4006(a)(3)(E)(iii)(IV) by inserting "or this subparagraph" after "this clause" both places it appears and by inserting "(other than sections 4005, 4010, 4011, and 4043" after "subsections".

The above amendment is effective as if included in the provisions of the Job Creation and Worker Assistance Act of 2002 to which they relate.

P.L. 108-218, §101(a):

Act Sec. 101(a) amended ERISA Sec. 4006(a)(3)(E) by adding subclause V to read as above.

Act Sec. 101 provides:

(c) Provisions Relating to Plan Amendments.—

(1) In general.

If this subsection applies to any plan or annuity contract amendment—

(A) such plan or contract shall be treated as being operated in accordance with the terms of the plan or contract during the period described in paragraph (2)(B)(i), and

(B) except as provided by the Secretary of the Treasury, such plan shall not fail to meet the requirements of section 411(d)(6) of the Internal Revenue Code of 1986 and section 204(g) of the Employee Retirement Income Security Act of 1974 by reason of such amendment.

(2) Amendments to which section applies.—

(A) In general.—

This subsection shall apply to any amendment to any plan or annuity contract which is made—

(i) pursuant to any amendment made by this section, and

(ii) on or before the last day of the first plan year beginning on or after January 1, 2006.

(B) Conditions.—

This subsection shall not apply to any plan or annuity contract amendment unless—

(i) during the period beginning on the date the amendment described in subparagraph (A)(i) takes effect and ending on the date described in subparagraph (A)(ii) (or, if earlier, the date the plan or contract amendment is adopted), the plan or contract is operated as if such plan or contract amendment were in effect; and

(ii) such plan or contract amendment applies retroactively for such period.

(d) Effective Dates.—

(1) In general.—Except as provided in paragraphs (2) and (3), the amendments made by this section shall apply to plan years beginning after December 31, 2003.

(2) Lookback rules.—For purposes of applying subsections (d)(9)(B)(ii) and (e)(1) of section 302 of the Employee Retirement Income Security Act of 1974 and subsections (l)(9)(B)(ii) and (m)(1) of section 412 of the Internal Revenue Code of 1986 to plan years beginning after December 31, 2003, the amendments made by this section may be applied as if such amendments had been in effect for all prior plan years. The Secretary of the Treasury may prescribe simplified assumptions which may be used in applying the amendments made by this section to such prior plan years.

(3) Transition rule for section 415 limitation.—In the case of any participant or beneficiary receiving a distribution after December 31, 2003 and before January 1, 2005, the amount payable under any form of benefit subject to section 417(e)(3) of the Internal Revenue Code of 1986 and subject to adjustment under section 415(b)(2)(B) of such Code shall not, solely by reason of the amendment made by subsection (b)(4), be less than the amount that would have been so payable had the amount payable been determined using the applicable interest rate in effect as of the last day of the last plan year beginning before January 1, 2004.

P.L. 107-147, §405(c):

Act Sec. 405(c) amended ERISA Sec. 4006(a)(3)(E)(iii) to add subclause III to read as above.

P.L. 103-465, §774(b)(1):

Act Sec. 774(b)(1) amended ERISA Sec. 4006(a)(3)(E)(iii)(II) by striking "80 percent" and inserting "the applicable percentage", and by adding at the end a new sentence to read as above.

P.L. 103-465, §774(b)(2):

Act Sec. 774(b)(2) amended ERISA Sec. 4006(a)(3)(E)(iii) by inserting "or (III)" after "subclause (II)" in subclause (I), and by adding new subclause (III) to read as above.

The above amendments apply to plan years beginning after December 8, 1994. For special rules, see Act Sec. 774(c) below.

P.L. 103-465, §774(a)(1):

Act Sec. 774(a)(1) amended ERISA Sec. 4006(a)(3)(E) by striking clause (iv), and by redesignating clause (v) as clause (iv) to read as above. Prior to amendment, ERISA Sec. 4006(a)(3)(E)(iv) read as follows:

(iv)(I) Except as provided in this clause, the aggregate increase in the premium payable with respect to any participant by reason of this subparagraph shall not exceed $53.

(II) If an employer made contributions to a plan during 1 or more of the 5 plan years preceding the 1st plan year to which this subparagraph applies in an amount not less than the maximum amount allowable as a deduction with respect to such contributions under section 404 of such Code, the dollar amount in effect under subclause (I) for the 1st 5 plan years to which this subparagraph applies shall be reduced by $3 for each plan year for which such contributions were made in such amount.

The above amendment is effective for plan years beginning on or after July 1, 1994. For special rules, see Act Secs. 774(a)(2)(B) and 774(c), below.

Act Sec. 774(a)(2)(B) provides:

(B) TRANSITION RULE.—In the case of plan years beginning on or after July 1, 1994, and before July 1, 1996, the additional premium payable with respect to any participant by reason of the amendments made by this section shall not exceed the sum of—

(i) $53, and

(ii) the product derived by multiplying—

(I) the excess (if any) of the amount determined under clause (i) of section 4006(a)(3)(E) of the Employee Retirement Income Security Act of 1974, over $53, by

(II) the applicable percentage.

For purposes of this subparagraph, the applicable percentage shall be the percentage specified in the following table:

For the plan year beginning:		The applicable percentage
on or after	but before	is:
July 1, 1994	July 1, 1995	20 percent
July 1, 1995	July 1, 1996	60 percent

Act Sec. 774(c) provides:

(e) TRANSITION RULE FOR CERTAIN REGULATED PUBLIC UTILITIES.—In the case of a regulated public utility described in section 7701(a)(33)(A)(i) of the Internal Revenue Code of 1986, the amendments made by this section shall not apply to plan years beginning before the earlier of—

(1) January 1, 1998, or

(2) the date the regulated public utility begins to collect from utility customers rates that reflect the costs incurred or projected to be incurred for additional premiums under section 4006(a)(3)(E) of the Employee Retirement Income Security Act of 1974 pursuant to final and nonappealable determinations by all public utility commissions (or other authorities having jurisdiction over the rates and terms of service by the regulated public utility) that the costs are just and reasonable and recoverable from customers of the regulated public utility.

P.L. 101-508, Sec. 12021(a)(1):

Amended ERISA Sec. 4006(a)(3)(A)(i) by striking "for plan years beginning after December 31, 1987, an amount equal to the sum of $16" and inserting "for plan years beginning after December 31, 1990, an amount equal to the sum of $19" effective for plan years beginning after December 31, 1990.

P.L. 101-508, Sec. 12021(a)(2):

Amended ERISA Sec. 4006(c)(1)(A) by adding a new clause (iv) to read as above effective for plan years beginning after December 31, 1990.

P.L. 101-508, Sec. 12021(b):

Amended ERISA Sec. 4006(a)(3)(E) by striking "$6.00" in clause (ii) and inserting "$9.00" and by striking "$34" in clause (iv)(I) and inserting "$53" effective for plan years beginning after December 31, 1990.

P.L. 101-239, §7881(h)(1):

Amended ERISA Sec. 4006(a)(3)(E) by adding a new clause (v) at the end.

P.L. 100-203, §9331(a):

Amended ERISA Sec. 4006(a)(3)(A)(i) by striking out "for plan years beginning after December 31, 1985, an amount equal to $8.50" and inserting "for plan years beginning after December 31, 1987, an amount equal to the sum of $16 plus the additional premium (if any) determined under subparagraph (E), to read as above, effective December 22, 1987.

P.L. 100-203, §9331(b):

Amended ERISA Sec. 4006(a)(3) by adding subparagraph (E), to read as above, effective December 22, 1987.

P.L. 100-203, §9331(e):

Amended ERISA Sec. 4006(c)(1)(A) by striking out "and" at the end of clause (i), by inserting "and before January 1, 1986," after "after December 31, 1977," and by adding subparagraph (iii), to read as above, effective for plan years beginning after December 31, 1987.

P.L. 99-272:

Act Sec. 11005(a)(1) amended ERISA Sec. 4006(a)(3)(A)(i) by striking out "for plan years beginning after December 31, 1977, an amount equal to $2.60" and inserting "for plan years beginning after December 31, 1985, an amount equal to $8.50."

Act Sec. 11005(a)(2) amended ERISA Sec. 4006(c)(1) by striking out subparagraph (A) and inserting a new subparagraph (A) to read as above. Prior to the amendment, ERISA Sec. 4006(c)(1)(A) read as follows:

(A) in the case of each plan which was not a multiemployer plan in a plan year, an amount equal to $1 for each individual who was a participant in such plan during the plan year, and

Act Sec. 11005(b) amended ERISA Sec. 4006(a) by striking out the last sentence in paragraph (1) and by adding a new paragraph (6) to read as above. Prior to amendment, the last sentence of ERISA Sec. 4006(a)(1) read as follows:

In establishing annual premiums with respect to plans, other than multiemployer plans, paragraphs (5) and (6) of this subsection (as in effect before the enactment of the Multiemployer Pension Plan Amendments Act of 1980) shall continue to apply.

Act Sec. 11005(c)(1) amended ERISA Sec. 4006(a)(2) by striking out "the Congress approves such revised schedule by a concurrent resolution" and inserting "a joint resolution approving such revised schedule is enacted."

Act Sec. 11005(c)(2) amended ERISA Sec. 4006(a)(4) by striking out "approval by the Congress" and inserting "the enactment of a joint resolution."

Act Sec. 11005(c)(3) amended ERISA Sec. 4006(b)(3) by striking out "concurrent" and inserting "joint," by striking out "That the Congress favors the" and inserting "The," and by inserting "is hereby approved." before the period preceding the quotation marks,

The above amendments are effective for plan years beginning after December 31, 1985 except for the amendment made by Act Sec. 11005(b) which is effective as of September 26, 1980.

P.L. 96-364, § 105:

Amended section 4006(a) to read as above; amended section 4006(b) by substituting "Committee on Labor and Human Resources" for "Committee on Labor and Public Welfare," striking out "coverage" and by substituting "(C), (D), or (E)" for "(B) or (C)"; and by adding new section 4006(c), effective September 26, 1980.

Section 4006(a) prior to amendment read:

"(a)(1) The corporation shall prescribe such insurance premium rates and such coverage schedules for the application of those rates as may be necessary to provide sufficient revenue to the fund for the corporation to carry out its functions under this title. The premium rates charged by the corporation for any period shall be uniform for all plans, other than miltiemployer plans insured by the corporation, with respect to basic benefits guaranteed by it under section 4022, and shall be uniform for all multiemployer plans with respect to basic benefits guaranteed by it under such section. The premium rates charged by the corporation for any period for non-basic benefits guaranteed by it shall be uniform by category of non-basic benefit guaranteed, shall be based on the risk insured in each category, and shall reflect the experience of the corporation (including reasonably anticipated experience) in guaranteeing such benefits.

(2) The corporation shall maintain separate coverage schedules for—

(A) basic benefits guaranteed by it under section 4022 for—

(i) plans which are multiemployer plans, and

(ii) plans which are not multiemployer plans,

(B) employers insured under section 4023 against liability under subtitle D of this title, and

(C) non-basic benefits.

Except as provided in paragraph (3), the corporation may revise such schedules whenever it determines that revised rates are necessary, but a revised schedule described in subparagraph (A) shall apply only to plan years beginning more than 30 days after the date on which the Congress approves such revised schedule by a concurrent resolution.

(3) Except as provided in paragraph (4), the rate for all plans for benefits guaranteed under section 4022 (other than non-basic benefits) with respect to plan years ending no more than 35 months after the effective date of this title is—

(A) in the case of each plan which is not a multiemployer plan, an amount equal to one dollar for each individual who is a participant in such plan at any time during the plan year; and

(B) in the case of a multiemployer plan, an amount equal to fifty cents for each individual who is a participant in such plan at any time during such plan year.

The rate applicable under this paragraph to any plan the plan year of which does not begin on the date of enactment of this Act is a fraction of the rate described in the preceding sentence, the numerator of which is the number of months which end before the date on which the new plan year commences and the denominator of which is 12.

The corporation is authorized to prescribe regulations under which the rate described in subparagraph (B) will not apply to the same participant in any multiemployer plan more than once for any plan year.

(4) Upon notification filed with the corporation not less than 60 days after the date on which the corporation publishes the rates applicable under paragraph (5), at the election of a plan the rate applicable to that plan with respect to the second full plan year to which this section applies beginning after the date of enactment of this Act shall be the greater of—

(A) an alternative rate determined under paragraph (5), or

(B) one-half of the rate applicable to the plan under paragraph (3).

In the case of a multiemployer plan, the rate prescribed by this paragraph (at the election of a plan) for the second full plan year is also the applicable rate for plan years succeeding the second full plan year and ending before the full plan year first commencing after December 31, 1977.

(5) In carrying out its authority under paragraph (1) to establish premium rates and bases for basic benefits guaranteed under section 4022 the corporation shall establish such rates and bases in coverage schedules for plan years beginning 24 months or more after the date of enactment of this Act in accordance with the provisions of the paragraph. The corporation shall publish the rate schedules first applicable under this paragraph in the Federal Register not later than 270 days after the date of enactment of this Act.

(A) The corporation may establish annual premiums composed of—

(i) a rate applicable to the excess, if any, of the present value of the basic benefits of the plan which are guaranteed over the value of the assets of the plan, not in excess of 0.1 percent for plans which are not multiemployer plans and not in excess of 0.025 percent for multiemployer plans, and

(ii) an additional charge base on the rate applicable to the present value of the basic benefits of the plan which are guaranteed, determined separately for multiemployer plans and for plans which are not multiemployer plans.

The rate for the additional charge referred to in clause (ii) shall be set by the corporation for every year at a level (determined separately for multiemployer plans and for plans which are not multiemployer plans) which the corporation estimates will yield total revenue approximately equal to the total revenue to be derived by the corporation from the premiums referred to in clause (i) of this subparagraph.

(B) The corporation may establish annual premiums based on—

(i) the number of participants in a plan, but such premium rates shall not exceed the rates described in paragraph (3),

(ii) unfunded basic benefits guaranteed under this title, but such premium rates shall not exceed the limitations applicable under subparagraph (A)(i), or

(iii) total guaranteed basic benefits, but such premium rates may not exceed the rates determined under subparagraph (A)(ii).

If the corporation uses 2 or more of the rate bases described in this subparagraph, the premium rates shall be designed to produce approximately equal amounts of aggregate premium revenue from each of the rate bases used.

(6) The corporation shall by regulation define the terms 'value or the assets' and 'present value of the benefits of the plan which are guaranteed' in a manner consistent with the purposes of this title and the provisions of this section."

Regulations

The following regulations were adopted by the Pension Benefit Guaranty Corporation on July 1, 1996 (61 FR 34002). Prior to July 1, 1996, PBGC regulations were under Chapter XXVI of Title 29 of the Code of Federal Regulations. Effective July 1, 1996, PBGC regulations were moved to Chapter XL, and were renumbered and reorganized. Reg. § 4006.5 was amended November 7, 1997 (62 FR 60424), effective January 1, 1998. Regs. § 4006.2, § 4006.5, and § 4006.6 were amended December 1, 2000 (65 FR 75160), effective January 1, 2001.

[¶ 15,361]

§ 4006.1 **Purpose and scope.** This part, which applies to all plans covered by title IV of ERISA, provides rules for computing the premiums imposed by sections 4006 and 4007 of ERISA. (See part 4007 of this chapter for rules for the payment of premiums, including due dates and late payment charges.)

[¶ 15,361A]

§ 4006.2 **Definitions.** The following terms are defined in § 4001.2 of this chapter: Code, contributing sponsor, ERISA, fair market value, insurer, irrevocable commitment, multiemployer plan, notice of intent to terminate, PBGC, plan administrator, plan, plan year, and single-employer plan.

In addition, for purposes of this part:

New plan means a plan that became effective within the premium payment year and includes a plan resulting from a consolidation or spinoff. A plan that meets this definition is considered to be a new plan even if the plan constitutes a successor plan within the meaning of section 4021(a) of ERISA.

Newly-covered plan means a plan that is not a new plan and that was not covered by title IV of ERISA immediately prior to the premium payment year.

Participant has the meaning described in Sec. 4006.6. [Amended 12/1/00 by 65 FR 75160.]

Premium payment year means the plan year for which the premium is being paid.

Short plan year means a plan year that is less than twelve full months.

[¶ 15,361B]

§ 4006.3 **Premium rate.** Subject to the provisions of § 4006.5 (dealing with exemptions and special rules), the premium paid for basic benefits guaranteed under section 4022(a) of ERISA shall equal the flat-rate premium under paragraph (a) of this section plus, in the case of a single-employer plan, the variable-rate premium under paragraph (b) of this section.

(a) *Flat-rate premium.* The flat-rate premium is equal to the number of participants in the plan on the last day of the plan year preceding the premium payment year, multiplied by—

(1) $19 for a single-employer plan, or

(2) $2.60 for a multiemployer plan.

(b) *Variable-rate premium.* The variable-rate premium is $9 for each $1,000 of a single-employer plan's unfunded vested benefits, as determined under § 4006.4.

[¶ 15,361C]

§ 4006.4 **Determination of unfunded vested benefits.** (a) *General rule.* Except as permitted by paragraph (c) of this section or as provided in the exemptions and special rules under § 4006.5, the amount of a plan's unfunded vested benefits (as defined in paragraph (b) of this section) shall be determined as of the last day of the plan year preceding the premium payment year, based on the plan provisions and the plan's population as of that date. The determination shall be made in accordance with paragraph (a)(1) or (a)(2), and shall be certified to in accordance with paragraph (a)(4).

(1) unfunded vested benefits shall be determined using the actuarial assumptions and methods described in paragraph (a)(3) for the plan year preceding the premium payment year (or, in the case of a new or newly-covered plan, for the premium payment year), except to the extent that other actuarial assumptions or methods are specifically prescribed by this section or are necessary to reflect the occurrence of a significant event described in paragraph (d) of this section between the date of the funding valuation and the last day of the plan year preceding the premium payment year. (If the plan does a valuation as of the last day of the plan year preceding the premium payment year, no separate adjustment for significant events is needed.)

(2) Under this rule, the determination of the unfunded vested benefits may be based on a plan valuation done as of the first day of the premium payment year, provided that—

(i) The actuarial assumptions and methods used are those described in paragraph (a)(3) for the premium payment year, except to the extent that other actuarial assumptions or methods are specifically prescribed by this section or are required to make the adjustment described in paragraph (a)(2)(ii) of this section; and

(ii) If an enrolled actuary determines that there is a material difference between the values determined under the valuation and the values that would have been determined as of the last day of the preceding plan year, the valuation results are adjusted to reflect appropriately the values as of the last day of the preceding plan year. (This adjustment need not be made if the unadjusted valuation would result in greater unfunded vested benefits.)

(3) For purposes of paragraphs (a)(1) and (a)(2), the actuarial assumptions and methods for a plan year are those used by the plan for purposes of determining the additional funding requirement under section 302(d) of ERISA and section 412(1) of the Code (or, in the case of a plan that is not required to determine such additional funding requirement, any assumptions and methods that would be permitted for such purpose if the plan were so required).

(4) In the case of any plan that determines the amount of its unfunded vested benefits under the general rule described in this paragraph, an enrolled actuary must certify, in accordance with the PBGC annual Premium Payment Package provided for in §4007.3 of this part, that the determination was made in a manner consistent with generally accepted actuarial principles and practices.

(b) *Unfunded vested benefits.* The amount of a plan's unfunded vested benefits under this section shall be the excess of the plan's vested benefits amount (determined under paragraph (b)(1) of this section) over the value of the plan's assets (determined under paragraph (b)(2) of this section).

(1) *Vested benefits amount.* A plan's vested benefits amount under this section shall be the plan's current liability (within the meaning of section 302(d)(7) of ERISA and section 412(1)(7) of the Code) determined by taking into account only vested benefits and by using an interest rate equal to the applicable percentage of the annual yield for 30-year Treasury constant maturities, as reported in Federal Reserve Statistical Release G.13 and H.15, for the calendar month preceding the calendar month in which the premium payment year begins. If the interest rate (or rates) used by the plan to determine current liability was (or were all) not greater than the required interest rate, the vested benefits need not be revalued if an enrolled actuary certifies that the interest rate (or interest rates) used was (or were all) not greater than the required interest rate. For purposes of this paragraph (b)(1) (subject to the provisions of §4006.5(g), dealing with plans of regulated public utilities), the applicable percentage is—

(i) For a premium payment year that begins before July 1997, 80 percent;

(ii) For a premium payment year that begins after June 1997 and before the first premium payment year to which the first tables prescribed under section 302(d)(7)(C)(ii)(II) of ERISA and section 412(1)(7)(C)(ii)(II) of the Code apply, 85 percent; and

(iii) For the first premium payment year to which the first tables prescribed under section 302(d)(7)(C)(ii)(II) of ERISA and section 412(1)(7)(C)(ii)(II) of the Code apply and any subsequent plan year, 100 percent.

(2) *Value of assets.*

(i) *Actuarial value.* For a premium payment year that is described in paragraph (b)(1)(i) or (b)(1)(ii) of this section, the value of the plan's assets shall be their actuarial value determined in accordance with section 302(c)(2) of ERISA and section 412(c)(2) of the Code.

(ii) *Fair market value.* For a premium payment year that is described in paragraph (b)(1)(iii) of this section, the value of the plan's assets shall be their fair market value.

(iii) *Use of credit balance.* The value of the plan's assets shall not be reduced by a credit balance in the funding standard account.

(iv) *Contributions.* Contributions owed for any plan year preceding the premium payment year shall be included for plans with 500 or more participants and may be included for any other plan. Contributions may be included only to the extent such contributions have been paid into the plan on or before the earlier of the due date for payment of the variable-rate portion of the premium under §4007.11 or the date that portion is paid. Contributions included that are paid after the last day of the plan year preceding the premium payment year shall be discounted at the plan asset valuation rate (on a simple or compound basis in accordance with the plan's discounting rules) to such last day to reflect the date(s) of payment. Contributions for the premium payment year may not be included for any plan.

(c) *Alternative method for calculating unfunded vested benefits.* In lieu of determining the amount of the plan's unfunded vested benefits pursuant to paragraph (a) of this section, a plan administrator may calculate the amount of a plan's unfunded vested benefits under this paragraph (c) using the plan's Form 5500, Schedule B, for the plan year preceding the premium payment year. Pursuant to this paragraph (c), unfunded vested benefits shall be determined, in accordance with the Premium Payment Package, from values for the plan's vested benefits and assets that are required to be reported on the plan's Schedule B. The value of the vested benefits shall be adjusted in accordance with paragraph (c)(1) of this section to reflect accruals during the plan year preceding the premium payment year and with paragraph (c)(2) of this section to reflect the interest rate prescribed in paragraph (b)(1) of this section, and the value of the assets shall be adjusted in accordance with paragraph (c)(4) of this section. (If the plan administrator certifies that the interest rate (or rates) used to determine the vested benefit values taken from the Schedule B was (or were all) not greater than the interest rate prescribed in paragraph (b)(1) of this section, the interest rate adjustment prescribed in paragraph (c)(2) of this section is not required.) The resulting unfunded vested benefits amount shall be adjusted in accordance with paragraph (c)(5) of this section to reflect the passage of time from the date of the Schedule B data to the last day of the plan year preceding the premium payment year.

(1) *Vested benefits adjustment for accruals.* The total value of the plan's current liability as of the first day of the plan year preceding the premium payment year for vested benefits of active and terminated vested participants not in pay status, computed in accordance with section 302(d)(7) of ERISA and section 412(l)(7) of the Code, shall be adjusted to reflect the increase in vested benefits attributable to accruals during the plan year preceding the premium payment year by multiplying that value by 1.07.

(2) *Vested benefits interest rate adjustment.* The value of vested benefits as entered on the Schedule B shall be adjusted in accordance with the following formula (except as provided in paragraph (c)(3) of this section) to reflect the interest rate prescribed in paragraph (b)(1) of this section:

$$VB_{adj} = VB_{pay} \times .94^{(RIR-BIR)} + VB_{non\text{-}pay} \times .94^{(RIB-BIR)} \times ((100 + BIA)/(100 + (RIR))^{(ARA-50)}; \text{where—}$$

(i) VB_{adj} is the adjusted vested benefits amount (as of the first day of the plan year preceding the premium payment year) under the alternative calculation method;

(ii) VB_{PAY} is the plan's current liability as of the first day of the plan year preceding the premium payment year for vested benefits of participants and beneficiaries in pay status, computed in accordance with section 302(d)(7) of ERISA and section 412(l)(7) of the Code;

(iii) VB $_{NON-PAY}$ is the total of the plan's current liability as of the first day of the plan year preceding the premium payment year for vested benefits of active and terminated vested participants not in pay status, computed in accordance with section 302(d)(7) of ERISA and section 412(l)(7) of the Code, multiplied by 1.07 in accordance with paragraph (c)(1) of this section;

(iv) RIR is the required interest rate prescribed in paragraph (b)(1) of this section;

(v) BIR is the post-retirement current liability interest rate used to determine the pay-status current liability figure referred to in paragraph (c)(2)(ii) of this section;

(vi) BIA is the pre-retirement current liability interest rate used to determine the pre-pay-status current liability figures referred to in paragraph (c)(2)(iii) of this section; and

(vii) ARA is the plan's assumed weighted average retirement age.

(3) *Optional use of substitution factors in interest rate adjustment formula.* In lieu of the term, .94 $^{(RIR-BIR)}$, in the formula prescribed by paragraph (c)(2) of this section, a plan administrator may use the optional substitution factor provided in the Premium Payment Package.

(4) *Adjusted value of plan assets.* The value of plan assets shall be the actuarial value of plan assets as of the first day of the plan year preceding the premium payment year, determined in accordance with section 302(c)(2) of ERISA and section 412(c)(2) of the Code without reduction for any credit balance in the plan's funding standard account, unless that amount was determined as of a date other than the first day of the plan year preceding the premium payment year or the premium payment year is described in §4006.4(b)(1)(iii). In either of those events, the value of plan assets shall be the current value of assets (as reported on Form 5500) as of that first day or (if Form 5500-EZ is filed) as of the last day of the plan year preceding the Schedule B year. The value of assets from the Schedule B shall be adjusted in accordance with paragraph (b)(2) of this section, except that the amount of all contributions that are included in the value of assets and that were made after the first day of the plan year preceding the premium payment year shall be discounted to such first day at the interest rate prescribed in paragraph (b)(1) of this section for the premium payment year, compounded annually except that simple interest may be used for any partial years.

(5) *Adjustment for passage of time.* The amount of the plan's unfunded vested benefits shall be adjusted to reflect the passage of time between the date of the Schedule B data (the first day of the plan year preceding the premium payment year) and the last day of the plan year preceding the premium payment year in accordance with the following formula:

$$UVB_{adj} = (VB_{adj} - A_{adj}) \times (1 + RIR/100)^Y; \text{ where—}$$

(i) UVB $_{adj}$ is the amount of the plan's adjusted unfunded vested benefits;

(ii) VB $_{adj}$ is the value of the adjusted vested benefits calculated in accordance with paragraphs (c)(1) and (c)(2) of this section;

(iii) A $_{adj}$ is the adjusted asset amount calculated in accordance with paragraph (c)(3) of this section; (iv) RIR is the required interest rate prescribed in paragraph (b)(1) of this section; and

(v) Y is deemed to be equal to 1 (unless the plan year preceding the premium payment year is a short plan year, in which case Y is the number of years between the first day and the last day of the short plan year, expressed as a decimal fraction of 1.0 with two digits to the right of the decimal point).

(d) *Restrictions on alternative calculation method for large plans.*

(1) The alternative calculation method described in paragraph (c) of this section may be used for a plan with 500 or more participants as of the last day of the plan year preceding the premium payment year only if—

(i) No significant event, as described in paragraph (d)(2) of this section, has occurred between the first day and the last day of the plan year preceding the premium payment year, and an enrolled actuary so certifies in accordance with the Premium Payment Package; or

(ii) An enrolled actuary makes an appropriate adjustment to the value of unfunded vested benefits to reflect the occurrence of significant events that have occurred between those dates and certifies to that fact in accordance with the Premium Payment Package.

(2) The significant events described in this paragraph are—

(i) An increase in the plan's actuarial costs (consisting of the plan's normal cost under section 302(b)(2)(A) of ERISA and section 412(b)(2)(A) of the Code, amortization charges under section 302(b)(2)(B) of ERISA and section 412(b)(2)(B) of the Code, and amortization credits under section 302(b)(3)(B) of ERISA and section 412(b)(3)(B) of the Code) attributable to a plan amendment, unless the cost increase attributable to the amendment is less than 5 percent of the actuarial costs determined without regard to the amendment;

(ii) The extension of coverage under the plan to a new group of employees resulting in an increase of 5 percent or more in the plan's liability for accrued benefits;

(iii) A plan merger, consolidation or spinoff that is not de minimis pursuant to the regulations under section 414(l) of the Code;

(iv) The shutdown of any facility, plant, store, etc., that creates immediate eligibility for benefits that would not otherwise be immediately payable for participants separating from service;

(v) The offer by the plan for a temporary period to permit participants to retire at benefit levels greater than that to which they would otherwise be entitled;

(vi) A cost-of-living increase for retirees resulting in an increase of 5 percent or more in the plan's liability for accrued benefits; and

(vii) Any other event or trend that results in a material increase in the value of unfunded vested benefits.

[¶ 15,361D]

§4006.5 **Exemptions and special rules.** (a) *Variable-rate premium exemptions.* A plan described in any of paragraphs (a)(1)-(a)(5) of this section is not required to determine its unfunded vested benefits under §4006.4 and does not owe a variable-rate premium under §4006.3(b).

(1) *Certain fully funded plans.* A plan is described in this paragraph if the plan had fewer than 500 participants on the last day of the plan year preceding the premium payment year, and an enrolled actuary certifies in accordance with the Premium Payment Package that, as of that date, the plan had no unfunded vested benefits (valued at the interest rate prescribed in §4006.4(b)(1)).

(2) *Plans without vested benefit liabilities.* A plan is described in this paragraph if it did not have any participants with vested benefits as of the last day of the plan year preceding the premium payment year, and the plan administrator so certifies in accordance with the Premium Payment Package.

(3) *Section 412(i) plans.* A plan is described in this paragraph if the plan was a plan described in section 412(i) of the Code and the regulations thereunder on the last day of the plan year preceding the premium payment year and the plan administrator so certifies, in accordance with the Premium Payment Package. [Amended 12/1/00 by 65 FR 75160.]

(4) *Plans terminating in standard terminations.* The exemption for a plan described in this paragraph is conditioned upon the plan's making a final distribution of assets in a standard termination. If a plan is ultimately unable to do so, the exemption is revoked and all variable-rate amounts not paid pursuant to this exemption are due retroactive to the applicable due date(s). A plan is described in this paragraph if—

(i) The plan administrator has issued notices of intent to terminate the plan in a standard termination in accordance with section 4041(a)(2) of ERISA; and

(ii) The proposed termination date set forth in the notice of intent to terminate is on or before the last day of the plan year preceding the premium payment year.

(5) *Plans at full funding limit.* A plan is described in this paragraph if, on or before the earlier of the due date for payment of the variable-rate portion of the premium under §4007.11 or the date that portion is paid, the plan's contributing sponsor or contributing spon-

sors made contributions to the plan for the plan year preceding the premium payment year in an amount not less than the full funding limitation for such preceding plan year under section 302(c)(7) of ERISA and section 412(c)(7) of the Code (determined in accordance with paragraphs (a)(5)(i) and (a)(5)(ii) of this section). In order for a plan to qualify for this exemption, an enrolled actuary must certify that the plan has met the requirements of this paragraph.

(i) *Determination of full funding limitation.* The determination of whether contributions for the preceding plan year were in an amount not less than the full funding limitation under section 302(c)(7) of ERISA and section 412(c)(7) of the Code for such preceding plan year shall be based on the methods of computing the full funding limitation, including actuarial assumptions and funding methods, used by the plan (provided such assumptions and methods met all requirements, including the requirements for reasonableness, under section 302 of ERISA and section 412 of the Code) with respect to such preceding plan year. Plan assets shall not be reduced by the amount of any credit balance in the plan's funding standard account.

(ii) *Rounding of de minimis amounts.* Any contribution that is rounded down to no less than the next lower multiple of one hundred dollars (in the case of full funding limitations up to one hundred thousand dollars) or to no less than the next lower multiple of one thousand dollars (in the case of full funding limitations above one hundred thousand dollars) shall be deemed for purposes of this paragraph to be in an amount equal to the full funding limitation.

(b) *Special rule for determining vested benefits for certain large plans.* With respect to a plan that had 500 or more participants on the last day of the plan year preceding the premium payment year, if an enrolled actuary determines pursuant to §4006.4(a) that the actuarial value of plan assets equals or exceeds the value of all benefits accrued under the plan (valued at the interest rate prescribed in §4006.4(b)(1)), the enrolled actuary need not determine the value of the plan's vested benefits, and may instead report in the Premium Payment Package the value of the accrued benefits.

(c) *Special rule for determining unfunded vested benefits for plans terminating in distress or involuntary terminations.* A plan described in this paragraph may determine its unfunded vested benefits by using the special alternative calculation method set forth in this paragraph. A plan is described in this paragraph if it has issued notices of intent to terminate in a distress termination in accordance with section 4041(a)(2) of ERISA with a proposed termination date on or before the last day of the plan year preceding the premium payment year, or if the PBGC has instituted proceedings to terminate the plan in accordance with section 4042 of ERISA and has sought a termination date on or before the last day of the plan year preceding the premium payment year. Pursuant to this paragraph, a plan shall determine its unfunded vested benefits in accordance with the alternative calculation method in §4006.4(c), except that—

(1) The calculation shall be based on the Form 5500, Schedule B, for the plan year which includes (in the case of a distress termination) the proposed termination date or (in the case of an involuntary termination) the termination date sought by the PBGC, or, if no Schedule B is filed for that plan year, on the Schedule B for the immediately preceding plan year;

(2) All references in §4006.4(c) and §4006.4(d) to the first day of the plan year preceding the premium payment year shall be deemed to refer to the first day of the plan year for which the Schedule B was filed;

(3) The value of the sum of the plan's current liability as of the first day of the plan year preceding the premium payment year for vested benefits of active and terminated vested participants not in pay status, computed in accordance with section 302(d)(7) of ERISA and section 412(l)(7) of the Code, shall be adjusted (in lieu of the adjustment required by §4006.4(c)(1)) by multiplying that value by the sum of 1 plus the product of .07 and the number of years (rounded to the nearest hundredth of a year) between the date of the Schedule B data and (in the case of a distress termination) the proposed termination date or (in the case of an involuntary termination) the termination date sought by the PBGC; and

(4) The exponent, "Y," in the time adjustment formula of §4006.4(c)(5) shall be deemed to equal the number of years (rounded

to the nearest hundredth of a year) between the date of the Schedule B data and the last day of the plan year preceding the premium payment year.

(d) *Special determination date rule for new and newly-covered plans.* In the case of a new plan or a newly-covered plan, all references in §§4006.3, 4006.4, and paragraphs (a) and (b) of this section to the last day of the plan year preceding the premium payment year shall be deemed to refer to the first day of the premium payment year or, if later, the date on which the plan became effective for benefit accruals for future service, and for purposes of determining the plan's premium, the number of plan participants, and (for a single-employer plan) the amount of the plan's unfunded vested benefits and the applicability of any exemption or special rule under paragraph (a) or (b) of this section, shall be determined as of such first day or later date.

(e) *Special determination date rule for certain mergers and spinoffs.*

(1) With respect to a plan described in paragraph (e)(2) of this section, all references in §§4006.3, 4006.4, and this section, as applicable, to the last day of the plan year preceding the premium payment year shall be deemed to refer to the first day of the premium payment year.

(2) A plan is described in this paragraph (e)(2) if—

(i) The plan engages in a merger or spinoff that is not de minimis pursuant to the regulations under section 414(l) of the Code (in the case of single-employer plans) or pursuant to part 4231 of this chapter (in the case of multiemployer plans), as applicable;

(ii) The merger or spinoff is effective on the first day of the plan's premium payment year; and

(iii) The plan is the transferee plan in the case of a merger or the transferor plan in the case of a spinoff.

(f) *Proration for certain short plan years.* The premium for a plan that has a short plan year as described in this paragraph (f) is prorated by the number of months in the short plan year (treating a part of a month as a month). The proration applies whether or not the short plan year ends by the premium due date for the short plan year. For purposes of this paragraph (f), there is a short plan year in the following circumstances:

(1) *New plan.* A new or newly-covered plan becomes effective for premium purposes on a date other than the first day of its first plan year.

(2) *Change in plan year.* A plan amendment changes the plan year, but only if the plan does not merge into or consolidate with another plan or otherwise cease its independent existence either during the short plan year or at the beginning of the full plan year following the short plan year.

(3) *Distribution of assets.* The plan's assets (other than any excess assets) are distributed pursuant to the plan's termination.

(4) *Appointment of trustee.* The plan is a single-employer plan, and a plan trustee is appointed pursuant to section 4042 of ERISA. [Amended 12/1/00 by 65 FR 75160.]

[¶ 15,361E]

§4006.6 **Definition of "participant".** (a) *General rule.* For purposes of this part and part 4007 of this chapter, an individual is considered to be a participant in a plan on any date if the plan has benefit liabilities with respect to the individual on that date.

(b) *Loss or distribution of benefit.* For purposes of this section, an individual is treated as no longer being a participant—

(1) In the case of an individual with no vested accrued benefit, after—

(i) The individual incurs a one-year break in service under the terms of the plan,

(ii) The individual's entire "zero-dollar" vested accrued benefit is deemed distributed under the terms of the plan, or

(iii) The individual dies; and

(2) In the case of a living individual whose accrued benefit is fully or partially vested, or a deceased individual whose accrued benefit was fully or partially vested at the time of death, after—

(i) An insurer makes an irrevocable commitment to pay all benefit liabilities with respect to the individual, or

(ii) All benefit liabilities with respect to the individual are otherwise distributed.

(c) *Examples.* The operation of this section is illustrated by the following examples:

Example 1. Participation under a calendar-year plan begins upon commencement of employment, and the only benefit provided by the plan is an accrued benefit (expressed as a life annuity beginning at age 65) of $30 per month times full years of service. The plan credits a ratable portion of a full year of service for service of at least 1,000 hours but less than 2,000 hours in a service computation period that begins on the date when the participant commences employment and each anniversary of that date. John and Mary both commence employment on July 1, 2000. On December 31, 2000 (the snapshot date for the plan's 2001 premium), John has credit for 988 hours of service and Mary has credit for 1,006 hours of service. For purposes of this section, Mary is considered to have an accrued benefit, and John is considered not to have an accrued benefit. Thus, the plan is considered to have benefit liabilities with respect to Mary, but not John, on December 31, 2000; and Mary, but not John, must be counted as a participant for purposes of computing the plan's 2001 premium.

Example 2. The plan also provides that a participant becomes vested five years after commencing employment and defines a one-year break in service as a service computation period in which less than 500 hours of service is performed. On February 1, 2002, John has an accrued benefit of $18 per month beginning at age 65 based on credit for 1,200 hours of service in the service computation period that began July 1, 2000. However, John has credit for only 492 hours of service in the service computation period that began July 1, 2001. On February 1, 2002, John terminates his employment. On December 31, 2002 (the snapshot date for the 2003 premium), John has incurred a one-year break in service, and thus is not counted as a participant for purposes of computing the plan's 2003 premium.

Example 3. On January 1, 2004, the plan is amended to provide that if a vested participant whose accrued benefit has a present value of $5,000 or less leaves employment, the benefit will be immediately cashed out. On December 30, 2005, Jane, who has a vested benefit with a present value of less than $5,000, leaves employment. Because of reasonable administrative delay in determining the amount of the benefit to be paid, the plan does not pay Jane the value of her benefit until January 9, 2006. Under the provisions of this section, Jane is treated as not having an accrued benefit on December 31, 2005 (the snapshot date for the 2006 premium), because Jane's benefit is treated as having been paid on December 30, 2005. Thus, Jane is not counted as a participant for purposes of computing the plan's 2006 premium.

Example 4. If the plan amendment had instead provided for cashouts as of the first of the month following termination of employment, and the plan paid Jane the value of her benefit on January 1, 2006, Jane would be treated under the provisions of this section as having an accrued benefit on December 31, 2005, and would thus be counted as a participant for purposes of computing the plan's 2006 premium. [Added 12/1/00 by 65 FR 75160.]

[¶ 15,370]
PAYMENT OF PREMIUMS

Act Sec. 4007. (a) The designated payor of each plan shall pay the premiums imposed by the corporation under this title with respect to that plan when they are due. Any employer obtaining contingent liability coverage under section 4023 shall pay the premiums imposed by the corporation under that section when due. Premiums imposed by this title on the date of enactment (applicable to that portion of any plan year during which such date occurs) are due within 30 days after such date. Premiums imposed by this title on the first plan year commencing after the date of enactment of this Act are due within 30 days after such plan year commences. Premiums shall continue to accrue until a plan's assets are distributed pursuant to a termination procedure, or until a trustee is appointed pursuant to section 4042, whichever is earlier. The corporation may waive or reduce premiums for a multiemployer plan for any plan year during which such plan receives financial assistance from the corporation under section 4261, except that any amount so waived or reduced shall be treated as financial assistance under such section.

Act Sec. 4007. (b) If any basic benefit premium is not paid when it is due the corporation is authorized to assess a late payment charge of not more than 100 percent of the premium payment which was not timely paid. The preceding sentence shall not apply to any payment of premium made within 60 days after the date on which payment is due, if before such date, the designated payor obtains a waiver from the corporation based upon a showing of substantial hardship arising from the timely payment of the premium. The corporation is authorized to grant a waiver under this subsection upon application made by the designated payor, but the corporation may not grant a waiver if it appears that the designated payor will be unable to pay the premium within 60 days after the date on which it is due. If any premium is not paid by the last date prescribed for a payment, interest on the amount of such premium at the rate imposed under section 6601(a) of the Internal Revenue Code of 1986 (relating to interest on underpayment, nonpayment, or extensions of time for payment of tax) shall be paid for the period from such last date to the date paid.

Act Sec. 4007. (c) If any designated payor fails to pay a premium when due, the corporation is authorized to bring a civil action in any district court of the United States within the jurisdiction of which the plan assets are located, the plan is administered, or in which a defendant resides or is found for the recovery of the amount of the premium, penalty, and interest, and process may be served in any other district. The district courts of the United States shall have jurisdiction over actions brought under this subsection by the corporation without regard to the amount in controversy.

Act. Sec. 4007. (d) The corporation shall not cease to guarantee basic benefits on account of the failure of a designated payor to pay any premium when due.

Act Sec. 4007. (e)(1) For purposes of this section, the term "designated payor" means—

(A) the contributing sponsor or plan administrator in the case of a single-employer plan, and

(B) the plan administrator in the case of a multiemployer plan.

(2) If the contributing sponsor of any single-employer plan is a member of a controlled group, each member of such group shall be jointly and severally liable for any premiums required to be paid by such contributing sponsor. For purposes of the preceding sentence, the term "controlled group" means any group treated as a single employer under subsection (b), (c), (m), or (o) of section 414 of the Internal Revenue Code of 1986.

Amendments

P.L. 101-239, §7891(a)(1):

Titles I, III, and IV of ERISA (other than sections 3(37)(E), 301(a)(7), and 308, the last sentence of section 408(d), and sections 414(c), 4001(a)(3)(ii), and 4303) are each amended by striking "Internal Revenue Code of 1954" each place it appears and inserting "Internal Revenue Code of 1986" effective October 22, 1986.

P.L. 100-203, §9331(c)(1):

Amended ERISA Sec. 4007 by striking out "plan administrator" and replacing it with "designated payor", to read as above, effective for plan years beginning after December 31, 1987.

P.L. 100-203, §9331(c)(2):

Amended ERISA Sec. 4007 by adding subsection (e), to read as above, effective from plan years beginning after December 31, 1987.

P.L. 96-364, §§402(a)(3) and 403(b):

Amended Sec. 4007(a), effective September 26, 1980 by striking out the second sentence and by inserting a new sentence at the end thereof.

Regulations

The following regulations were adopted by the Pension Benefit Guaranty Corporation on July 1, 1996 (61 FR 34002). Prior to July 1, 1996, PBGC regulations were under Chapter XXVI of Title 29 of the Code of Federal Regulations. Effective July 1, 1996, PBGC regulations were moved to Chapter XL, and were renumbered and reorganized. Reg. §4007.10 was amended July 9, 1997 (62 FR 36663), effective August 8, 1997. Reg. §4007.8 was revised November 26, 1999 (64 FR 66383), effective December 27, 1999. Reg §4007.8 was amended December 1, 2000 (65 FR 75160), effective January 1, 2001. Reg. §4007.3, Reg. §4007.5, Reg. §4007.6, and Reg. §4007.10 were amended October 28, 2003 (68 FR 61344).

[¶ 15,371]

§ 4007.1 **Purpose and scope.** This part, which applies to all plans that are covered by title IV of ERISA, provides procedures for paying the premiums imposed by sections 4006 and 4007 of ERISA. (See part 4006 of this chapter for premium rates and computational rules.)

[¶ 15,371A]

§ 4007.2 **Definitions.** (a) The following terms are defined in § 4001.2 of this chapter: Code, contributing sponsor, ERISA, insurer, IRS, multiemployer plan, notice of intent to terminate, PBGC, plan, plan administrator, plan year, and single-employer plan.

(b) For purposes of this part, the following terms are defined in § 4006.2 of this chapter: new plan, newly covered plan, participant, premium payment year, and short plan year.

[¶ 15,371B]

§ 4007.3 **Filing requirements; method of filing.** (a) *Filing require-ments.* The estimation, declaration, reconciliation and payment of pre-miums shall be made using the forms prescribed by and in accordance with the instructions in the PBGC annual Premium Payment Package. The plan administrator of each covered plan shall file the prescribed form or forms, and any premium payments due, no later than the applicable due date specified in Sec. 4007.11.

(b) *Method of filing.* The PBGC applies the rules in subpart A of part 4000 of this chapter to determine permissible methods of filing with the PBGC under this part.

[Amended 10/28/2003 by 68 FR 61344]

[¶ 15,371C]

§ 4007.4 **Filing address.** Plan administrators shall file all forms required to be filed under this part and all payments for premiums, interest, and penalties required to be made under this part at the address specified in the Premium Payment Package.

[¶ 15,371D]

§ 4007.5 **Date of filing.** The PBGC applies the rules in subpart C of part 4000 of this chapter to determine the date that a submission under this part was filed with the PBGC.

[Amended 10/28/2003 by 68 FR 61344]

[¶ 15,371E]

§ 4007.6 **Computation of time.** The PBGC applies the rules in subpart D of part 4000 of this chapter to compute any time period under this part. However, for purposes of determining the amount of a late payment interest charge under Sec. 4007.7 or of a late payment penalty charge under Sec. 4007.8, the rule in Sec. 4000.43(a) of this chapter governing periods ending on weekends or Federal holidays does not apply.

[Amended 10/28/2003 by 68 FR 61344]

[¶ 15,371F]

§ 4007.7 **Late payment interest charges.** (a) If any premium pay-ment due under this part is not paid by the due date prescribed for such payment by § 4007.11, an interest charge will accrue on the unpaid amount at the rate imposed under section 6601(a) of the Code for the period from the date payment is due to the date payment is made. Late payment interest charges are compounded daily.

(b) When PBGC issues a bill for premium payments necessary to reconcile the premiums paid with the actual premium due, interest will be accrued on the unpaid premium until the date of the bill if paid no later than 30 days after the date of such bill. If the bill is not paid within the 30-day period following the date of such bill, interest will continue to accrue throughout such 30-day period and thereafter, until the date paid.

(c) PBGC bills for interest assessed under this section will be deemed paid when due if paid no later than 30 days after the date of such bills. Otherwise, interest will accrue in accordance with paragraph (a) of this section on the amount of the bill from the date of the bill until the date of payment.

[¶ 15,371G]

§ 4007.8 **Late payment penalty charges.** (a) *Penalty charge.* If any premium payment due under this part is not paid by the due date under

Sec. 4007.11, the PBGC will assess a late payment penalty charge as determined under this paragraph (a), except to the extent the charge is waived under paragraphs (b) through (g) of this section. The charge will be no more than 100% of the unpaid premium. The charge will be based on the number of months (counting any portion of a month as a whole month) from the due date to the date of payment and is subject to a floor of $25 (or, if less, the amount of the unpaid premium).

(1) *Penalty rate for post-1995 premium payment years.* This para-graph (a)(1) applies to the premium for any premium payment year beginning after 1995. The penalty rate is—

(i) 1% per month (for all months) on any amount of unpaid premium that is paid on or before the date the PBGC issues a written notice to any person liable for the plan's premium that there is or may be a premium delinquency (e.g., a premium bill, a letter initiating a premium compliance review, or a letter questioning a failure to make a premium filing); or

(ii) 5% per month (for all months) on any amount of unpaid premium that is paid after that date.

(2) *Penalty rate for pre-1996 premium payment years.* This para-graph (a)(2) applies to the premium for any premium payment year beginning before 1996. The penalty rate is 5% per month (for all months) on any amount of unpaid premium.

(b) *Hardship waiver.* The PBGC may grant a waiver based upon a showing of substantial hardship as provided in section 4007(b) of ERISA.

(c) *Reasonable cause waiver.* The PBGC may, upon any demon-stration of reasonable cause, waive all or part of a late payment penalty charge.

(d) *Waiver on PBGC's own initiative.* The PBGC may, on its own initiative, waive all or part of a late payment penalty charge.

(e) *Grace period.* With respect to any PBGC bill for a premium underpayment, the PBGC will waive any late payment penalty charge accruing after the date of the bill, provided the premium underpayment is paid within 30 days after the date of the bill.

(f) *Safe-harbor relief for certain large plans.* This waiver applies in the case of a plan for which a reconciliation filing is required under Sec. 4007.11(a)(2)(iii). The PBGC will waive the penalty on any underpay-ment of the flat-rate premium for the period that ends on the date the reconciliation filing is due if fewer than 500 participants are reported for the plan year preceding the premium payment year (determined in accordance with paragraph (h) of this section).

(g) *Safe-harbor relief for plans that make minimum estimated pay-ment.* This waiver applies in the case of a plan for which a reconciliation filing is required under Sec. 4007.11(a)(2)(iii). The PBGC will waive the penalty on any underpayment of the flat-rate premium for the period that ends on the date the reconciliation filing is due if, by the date the flat-rate premium for the premium payment year is due under Sec. 4007.11(a)(2)(i), the plan administrator pays at least the lesser of—

(1) 90% of the flat-rate premium due for the premium payment year; or

(2) 100% of the flat-rate premium that would be due for the premium payment year if the number of participants for that year were the lesser of—

(i) The number of participants for whom premiums were required to be paid for the plan year preceding the premium payment year; or

(ii) The number of participants reported for the plan year preceding the premium payment year (determined in accordance with paragraph (h) of this section).

(h) *Reported participant count.* For purposes of paragraphs (f) and (g)(2) of this section, the number of participants reported for the plan year preceding the premium payment year is the number of participants last reported under this part to the PBGC (for the plan year preceding the premium payment year) by the date the flat-rate pre-mium for the premium payment year is due under Sec. 4007.11(a)(2)(i).[Revised 11/16/99 by 64 FR 66383.]

(i) *Safe harbor relief for certain plan amendments prospectively changing plan year.* This waiver applies in the case of a plan for which a reconciliation filing is required under Sec. 4007.11(a)(2)(iii). The PBGC will waive the penalty on any underpayment of the flat-rate premium for the period that ends on the date the reconciliation filing is due if, by the date the flat-rate premium for the premium payment year is due under Sec. 4007.11(a)(2)(i),—

(1) The plan has been amended to change its plan year and the amendment as in effect on that date makes the premium payment year a short year that will end after that date; and

(2) The plan administrator pays at least the lesser of—

(i) The amount determined under Sec. 4007.8(g) based on the actual length of the premium payment year, or

(ii) The amount determined under Sec. 4007.8(g) based on the length that the premium payment year would have if the new plan year cycle began as anticipated by the amendment. [Added 12/1/00 by 65 FR 75160.]

[¶ 15,371H]

§4007.9 Coverage for guaranteed basic benefits. (a) The failure by a plan administrator to pay the premiums due under this part will not result in that plan's loss of coverage for basic benefits guaranteed under sections 4022(a) or 4022A(a) of ERISA.

(b) The payment of the premiums imposed by this part will not result in coverage for basic benefits guaranteed under sections 4022(a) or 4022A(a) of ERISA for plans not covered under title IV of ERISA.

[¶ 15,371I]

§4007.10 Recordkeeping; audits; disclosure of information. (a) *Retention of records to support premium payments.* (1) *In general.* All plan records, including calculations and other data prepared by an enrolled actuary or, for a plan described in section 412(i) of the Code, by the insurer from which the insurance contracts are purchased, that are necessary to support or to validate premium payments under this part shall be retained by the plan administrator for a period of six years after the premium due date. Records that must be retained pursuant to this paragraph include, but are not limited to, records that establish the number of plan participants and that reconcile the calculation of the plan's unfunded vested benefits with the actuarial valuation upon which the calculation was based.

(2) *Electronic recordkeeping.* The plan administrator may use electronic media for maintenance and retention of records required by this part in accordance with the requirements of subpart E of part 4000 of this chapter.

[Amended 10/28/2003 by 68 FR 61344]

(b) *PBGC audit.* Premium payments under this part are subject to audit by the PBGC. If, upon audit, the PBGC determines that a premium due under this part was underpaid, the late payment interest charges under §4007.7 and the late payment penalty charges under §4007.8 shall apply to the unpaid balance from the premium due date to the date of payment. In determining the premium due, if, in the judgment of the PBGC, the plan's records fail to establish the number of plan participants with respect to whom premiums were required for any premium payment year, the PBGC may rely on data it obtains from other sources (including the IRS and the Department of Labor) for presumptively establishing the number of plan participants for premium computation purposes.

(c) *Providing record information.* (1) *In general.* The plan administrator shall make the records retained pursuant to paragraph (a) of this section available to the PBGC upon request for inspection and photocopying (or, for electronic records, inspection, electronic copying, and printout) at the location where they are kept (or another, mutually agreeable, location) and shall submit information in such records to the PBGC within 45 days of the date of the PBGC's written request therefor, or by a different time specified therein.

[Amended 10/28/2003 by 68 FR 61344]

(2) *Extension.* Except as provided in paragraph (c)(3) of this section, the plan administrator may automatically extend the period described in paragraph (c)(1) by submitting a certification to the PBGC prior to the expiration of that time period. The certification shall—

(i) Specify a date to which the time period described in paragraph (c)(1) is extended that is no more than 90 days from the date of the PBGC's written request for information; and

(ii) Contain a statement, certified to by the plan administrator under penalty of perjury (18 U.S.C. § 1001), that, despite reasonable efforts, the additional time is necessary to comply with the PBGC's request.

(3) *Shortening of time period.* The PBGC may in its discretion shorten the time period described in paragraph (c)(1) or (c)(2) of this section where it determines that collection of unpaid premiums (or any associated interest or penalties) would otherwise be jeopardized. If the PBGC shortens the time period described in paragraph (c)(1), no extension is available under paragraph (c)(2).

(d) *Address and timeliness.* Information required to be submitted under paragraph (c) of this section shall be submitted to the address specified in the PBGC's request. The timeliness of a submission shall be determined in accordance with §§4007.5 and 4007.6. [Amended 7/9/97 by 62 FR 36663.]

[¶ 15,371J]

§4007.11 Due dates. (a) *In general.* The premium filing due date for small plans is prescribed in paragraph (a)(1) of this section and the premium filing due dates for large plans are prescribed in paragraph (a)(2) of this section.

(1) *Plans with fewer than 500 participants.* If the plan has fewer than 500 participants, as determined under paragraph (b) of this section, the due date is the fifteenth day of the tenth full calendar month following the end of the plan year preceding the premium payment year.

(2) *Plans with 500 or more participants.* If the plan has 500 or more participants, as determined under paragraph (b) of this section—

(i) The due date for the flat-rate premium required by §4006.3(a) is the last day of the second full calendar month following the close of the plan year preceding the premium payment year; and

(ii) The due date for the variable-rate premium required by §4006.3(b) for single-employer plans is the fifteenth day of the tenth full calendar month following the end of the plan year preceding the premium payment year.

(iii) If the number of plan participants on the last day of the plan year preceding the premium payment year is not known by the date specified in paragraph (a)(2)(i) of this section, a reconciliation filing (on the form prescribed by this part) and any required premium payment or request for refund shall be made by the date specified in paragraph (a)(2)(ii) of this section.

(3) Plans that change plan years. For any plan that changes its plan year, the premium form or forms and payment or payments for the short plan year shall be filed by the applicable due date or dates specified in paragraphs (a)(1), (a)(2), or (c) of this section. For the plan year that follows a short plan year, the due date or dates for the premium forms and payments shall be, with respect to each such due date, the later of—

(i) The applicable due date or dates specified in paragraph (a)(1) or (a)(2) of this section; or

(ii) 30 days after the date on which the amendment changing the plan year was adopted.

(b) *Participant count rule for purposes of determining filing due dates.* For purposes of determining under paragraph (a) of this section whether a plan has fewer than 500 participants, or 500 or more participants, the plan administrator shall use—

(1) For a single-employer plan, the number of participants for whom premiums were payable for the plan year preceding the premium payment year, or

(2) For a multiemployer plan,—

(i) If the premium payment year is the plan's second plan year, the first day of the first plan year; or

(ii) If the premium payment year is the plan's third or a subsequent plan year, the last day of the second preceding plan year.

(c) *Due dates for new and newly covered plans.* Notwithstanding paragraph (a) of this section, the premium form and all premium payments due for the first plan year of coverage of any new plan or newly covered plan shall be filed on or before the latest of—

    (1) The fifteenth day of the tenth full calendar month that began on or after the later of—

        (i) The first day of the premium payment year; or

        (ii) The day on which the plan became effective for benefit accruals for future service;

    (2) 90 days after the date of the plan's adoption; or

    (3) 90 days after the date on which the plan became covered by title IV of ERISA.

(d) *Continuing obligation to file.* The obligation to file the form or forms prescribed by this part and to pay any premiums due continues through the plan year in which all plan assets are distributed pursuant to a plan's termination or in which a trustee is appointed under section 4042 of ERISA, whichever occurs earlier. The entire premium computed under this part is due, irrespective of whether the plan is entitled to a refund for a short plan year pursuant to § 4006.5(f).

(e) *Improper filings.* Any form not filed in accordance with this part, not filed in accordance with the instructions in the Premium Payment Package, not accompanied by the required premium payment, or otherwise incomplete, may, in the discretion of the PBGC, be returned with any payment accompanying the form to the plan administrator, and such payment shall be treated as not having been made.

[Amended 12/14/98 by 63 FR 68684.]

[¶ 15,371K]

§ 4007.12 **Liability for single-employer premiums.** (a) The designation under this part of the plan administrator as the person required to file the applicable forms and to submit the premium payment for a single-employer plan is a procedural requirement only and does not alter the liability for premium payments imposed by section 4007 of ERISA. Pursuant to section 4007(e) of ERISA, both the plan administrator and the contributing sponsor of a single-employer plan are liable for premium payments, and, if the contributing sponsor is a member of a controlled group, each member of the controlled group is jointly and severally liable for the required premiums. Any entity that is liable for required premiums is also liable for any interest and penalties assessed with respect to such premiums.

(b) For any plan year in which a plan administrator issues (pursuant to section 4041(a)(2) of ERISA) notices of intent to terminate in a distress termination under section 4041(c) of ERISA or the PBGC initiates a termination proceeding under section 4042 of ERISA, and for each plan year thereafter, the obligation to pay the premiums (and any interest or penalties thereon) imposed by ERISA and this part for a single-employer plan shall be an obligation solely of the contributing sponsor and the members of its controlled group, if any.

(Approved by the Office of Management and Budget under control number 1212-0009)

[Amended 7/9/97 by 62 FR 36663.]

[¶ 15,380]
REPORT BY THE CORPORATION

Act Sec. 4008. As soon as practicable after the close of each fiscal year the corporation shall transmit to the President and the Congress a report relative to the conduct of its business under this title for that fiscal year. The report shall include financial statements setting forth the finances of the corporation at the end of such fiscal year and the result of its operations (including the source and application of its funds) for the fiscal year and shall include an actuarial evaluation of the expected operations and status of the funds established under section 4005 for the next five years (including a detailed statement of the actuarial assumptions and methods used in making such evaluation).

[¶ 15,390]
PORTABILITY ASSISTANCE

Act Sec. 4009. The corporation shall provide advice and assistance to individuals with respect to evaluating the economic desirability of establishing individual retirement accounts or other forms of individual retirement savings for which a deduction is allowable under section 219 of the Internal Revenue Code of 1986 and with respect to evaluating the desirability, in particular cases, of transferring amounts representing an employee's interest in a qualified plan to such an account upon the employee's separation from service with an employer.

Amendment

P.L. 101-239, § 7891(a)(1):

Titles I, III, and IV of ERISA (other than sections 3(37)(E), 301(a)(7), and 308, the last sentence of section 408(d), and sections 414(c), 4001(a)(3)(ii), and 4303) are each

amended by striking "Internal Revenue Code of 1954" each place it appears and inserting "Internal Revenue Code of 1986" effective October 22, 1986.

[¶ 15,395]
AUTHORITY TO REQUIRE CERTAIN INFORMATION

Act Sec. 4010.(a) INFORMATION REQUIRED. Each person described in subsection (b) shall provide the corporation annually, on or before a date specified by the corporation in regulations, with—

    (1) such records, documents, or other information that the corporation specifies in regulations as necessary to determine the liabilities and assets of plans covered by this title; and

    (2) copies of such person's audited (or, if unavailable, unaudited) financial statements, and such other financial information as the corporation may prescribe in regulations.

(b) PERSONS REQUIRED TO PROVIDE INFORMATION. The persons covered by subsection (a) are each contributing sponsor, and each member of a contributing sponsor's controlled group, of a single-employer plan covered by this title, if—

    (1) the aggregate unfunded vested benefits at the end of the preceding plan year (as determined under section 4006(a)(3)(E)(iii)) of plans maintained by the contributing sponsor and the members of its controlled group exceed $50,000,000 (disregarding plans with no unfunded vested benefits);

    (2) the conditions for imposition of a lien described in section 302(f)(1)(A) and (B) of this Act or section 412(n)(1)(A) and (B) of the Internal Revenue Code of 1986 have been met with respect to any plan maintained by the contributing sponsor or any member of its controlled group; or

    (3) minimum funding waivers in excess of $1,000,000 have been granted with respect to any plan maintained by the contributing sponsor or any member of its controlled group, and any portion thereof is still outstanding.

(c) INFORMATION EXEMPT FROM DISCLOSURE REQUIREMENTS. —Any information or documentary material submitted to the corporation pursuant to this section shall be exempt from disclosure under section 552 of title 5, United States Code, and no such information or documentary material may be made public, except as may be relevant to any administrative or judicial action or proceeding. Nothing in this section is intended to prevent disclosure to either body of Congress or to any duly authorized committee or subcommittee of the Congress.

Amendment

P.L. 103-465, § 772(a):

Act Sec. 772(a) amended subtitle A of title IV of ERISA by adding new section 4010 to read as above.

The above amendment is effective on December 8, 1994.

Regulations

The following regulations were adopted by the Pension Benefit Guaranty Corporation on July 1, 1996 (61 FR 34002). Prior to July 1, 1996, PBGC regulations were under Chapter XXVI of Title 29 of the Code of Federal Regulations. Effective July 1, 1996, PBGC regulations were moved to Chapter XL, and were renumbered and reorganized. Reg. 4010.13 was amended effective August 11, 1997 (62 FR 36993). Reg. § 4010.10 was amended on October 28, 2003 (68 FR 61344). Reg. Secs. 4010.3—4010.9 were revised on March 9, 2005 (70 FR 11540).

[¶ 15,396]

§ 4010.1 **Purpose and scope.** This part prescribes the requirements for annual filings with the PBGC under section 4010 of ERISA. This part applies to filers for any information year ending on or after December 31, 1995.

[¶ 15,396A]

§ 4010.2 **Definitions.** The following terms are defined in § 4001.2 of this chapter: benefit liabilities, Code, contributing sponsor, controlled group, ERISA, fair market value, IRS, PBGC, person, plan, and plan year.

In addition, for purposes of this part:

Exempt entity means a person who does not have to file information and about whom information does not have to be filed, as described in § 4010.4(d) of this part.

Exempt plan means a plan about which actuarial information does not have to be filed, as described in § 4010.8(c) of this part.

Fair market value of the plan's assets means the fair market value of the plan's assets at the end of the plan year ending within the filer's information year (determined without regard to any contributions receivable).

Filer means a person who is required to file reports, as described in § 4010.4 of this part.

Fiscal year means, with respect to a person, the person's annual accounting period or, if the person has not adopted a closing date, the calendar year.

Information year means the year determined under § 4010.5 of this part.

[¶ 15,396B]

§ 4010.3 **Filing requirement.** (a) *In general.* Except as provided in § 4010.8(c) (relating to exempt plans) and except where waivers have been granted under § 4010.11, each filer shall submit to the PBGC annually, on or before the due date specified in § 4010.10, all information specified in § 4010.6(a) with respect to all members of a controlled group and all plans maintained by members of a controlled group. Under § 4000.3(b) of this chapter, except as otherwise provided by the PBGC, the information shall be submitted electronically in accordance with the instructions on the PBGC's Web site.

(b) *Single controlled group submission.* Any filer or other person may submit the information specified in § 4010.6(a) on behalf of one or more members of a filer's controlled group.

[¶ 15,396C]

§ 4010.4 **Filers.** (a) *General.* A contributing sponsor of a plan and each member of the contributing sponsor's controlled group is a filer with respect to an information year (unless exempted under paragraph (d) of this section) if—

(1) the aggregate unfunded vested benefits of all plans (including any exempt plans) maintained by the members of the contributing sponsor's controlled group exceed $50 million (disregarding those plans with no unfunded vested benefits);

(2) any member of a controlled group fails to make a required installment or other required payment to a plan and, as a result, the conditions for imposition of a lien described in section 302(f)(1)(A) and (B) of ERISA or section 412(n)(1)(A) and (B) of the Code have been met during the information year, and the required installment or other required payment is not made within ten days after its due date; or

(3) Any plan maintained by a member of a controlled group has been granted one or more minimum funding waivers under section 303 of ERISA or section 412(d) of the Code, totaling in excess of $1 million and, as of the end of the plan year ending within the information year, any portion thereof is still outstanding (determined in accordance with paragraph (c) of this section).

(b) *Unfunded vested benefits.* (1) *General.* For purposes of the $50 million test in paragraph (a)(1) of this section, the value of a plan's unfunded vested benefits is determined at the end of the plan year ending within the filer's information year in accordance with section 4006(a)(3)(E)(iii) of ERISA and § 4006.4 of this chapter (without reference to the exemptions and special rules under § 4006.5 of this chapter).

(2) *Contributions.* For purposes of determining the value of a plan's unfunded vested benefits under paragraph (b)(1) of this section, contributions made after the end of the plan year ending within the filer's information year are taken into account for that plan year only to the extent that they are—

(i) Paid on or before the filing due date under § 4010.10(a) (without regard to the alternative due date under § 4010.10(b));

(ii) Attributable to that plan year for funding purposes under ERISA section 302(c)(1) and section 412(c)(10) of the Code; and

(iii) Discounted in accordance with § 4006.4(b)(2)(iv) if unfunded vested benefits are determined under § 4006.4(b) or in accordance with § 4006.4(c)(4) if unfunded vested benefits are determined under § 4006.4(c).

(c) *Outstanding waiver.* Before the end of the statutory amortization period, a portion of a minimum funding waiver for a plan is considered outstanding unless—

(1) a credit balance exists in the funding standard account (described in section 302(b) of ERISA and section 412(b) of the Code) that is no less than the outstanding balance of all waivers for the plan;

(2) a waiver condition or contractual obligation requires that a credit balance as described in paragraph (c)(1) continue to be maintained as of the end of each plan year during the remainder of the statutory amortization period for the waiver; and

(3) no portion of any credit balance described in paragraph (c)(1) is used to make any required installment under section 302(e) of ERISA or section 412(m) of the Code for any plan year during the remainder of the statutory amortization period.

(d) *Exempt entities.* A person is an exempt entity if the person—

(1) is not a contributing sponsor of a plan (other than an exempt plan);

(2) has revenue for its fiscal year ending within the controlled group's nformation year that is five percent or less of the controlled group's revenue for the fiscal year(s) ending within the information year;

(3) has annual operating income for the fiscal year ending within the controlled group's information year that is no more than the greater of—

(i) five percent of the controlled group's annual operating income for the fiscal year(s) ending within the information year, or

(ii) $5 million; and

(4) has net assets at the end of the fiscal year ending within the controlled group's information year that is no more than the greater of—

(i) five percent of the controlled group's net assets at the end of the fiscal year(s) ending within the information year, or

(ii) $5 million.

[¶ 15,396D]

§ 4010.5 **Information year.** (a) *Determinations based on information year.* An information year is used under this part to determine which persons are filers (§ 4010.4), what information a filer must submit (§§ 4010.6-4010.9), whether a plan is an exempt plan (§ 4010.8(c)), and the due date for submitting the information (§ 4010.10(a)).

(b) *General.* Except as provided in paragraph (c) of this section, a person's information year shall be the fiscal year of the person. A filer is not required to change its fiscal year or the plan year of a plan, to report financial information for any accounting period other than an existing fiscal year, or to report actuarial information for any plan year other than an existing plan year.

(c) *Controlled group members with different fiscal years.* (1) *Use of calendar year.* If members of a controlled group (disregarding any exempt entity) report financial information on the basis of different fiscal years, the information year shall be the calendar year.

(2) *Example.* Filers A and B are members of the same controlled group. Filer A has a July 1 fiscal year, and filer B has an October 1 fiscal year. The information year is the calendar year. Filer A's financial information with respect to its fiscal year ending June 30, 2004, and filer B's financial information with respect to its fiscal year ending September 30, 2004, must be submitted to the PBGC following the end of the 2004 calendar year (the calendar year in which those fiscal years end). If filer B were an exempt entity, the information year would be filer A's July 1 fiscal year.

[¶ 15,396E]

§ 4010.6 **Information to be filed.** (a) *General.* (1) *Current filers.* A filer must submit the information specified in § 4010.7 (identifying information), § 4010.8 (plan actuarial information) and § 4010.9 (financial information) with respect to each member of the filer's controlled group and each plan maintained by any member of the controlled group, and any other information relating to the information specified in §§ 4010.7 through 4010.9, as specified in the instructions on the PBGC's website.

(2) *Previous filers.* If a filer for the immediately preceding information year is not required to file for the current information year, the filer must submit information, in accordance with the instructions on the PBGC's website, demonstrating why a filing is not required for the current information year.

(b) *Additional information.* By written notification, the PBGC may require any filer to submit additional actuarial or financial information that is necessary to determine plan assets and liabilities for any period through the end of the filer's information year, or the financial status of a filer for any period through the end of the filer's information year (including information on exempt entities and exempt plans). The information must be submitted within ten days after the date of the written notification or by a different time specified therein.

(c) *Previous submissions.* If any required information has been previously submitted to the PBGC, a filer may incorporate this information into the required submission by referring to the previous submission.

[¶ 15,396F]

§ 4010.7 **Identifying information.** (a) *Filers.* Each filer is required to provide, in accordance with the instructions on the PBGC's website, the following identifying information with respect to each member of the controlled group (excluding exempt entities)—

(1) *Current members.* For an entity that is a member of the controlled group as of the end of the filer's information year—

(i) The name, address, and telephone number of the entity and the legal relationships with other members of the controlled group (for example, parent, subsidiary);

(ii) The nine-digit Employer Identification Number (EIN) assigned by the IRS to the entity (or if there is no EIN for the entity, an explanation);

(iii) If the entity became a member of the controlled group during the information year, the date the entity became a member of the controlled group; and

(2) *Former members.* For any entity that ceased to be a member of the controlled group during the filer's information year, the date the entity ceased to be a member of the controlled group and the identifying information required by paragraph (a)(1) of this section as of the date immediately preceding the date the entity left the controlled group.

(b) *Plans.* Each filer is required to provide, in accordance with the instructions on the PBGC's website, the following identifying informa-

tion with respect to each plan (including exempt plans) maintained by any member of the controlled group (including exempt entities)—

(1) *Current plans.* For a plan that is maintained by the controlled group as of the last day of the filer's information year—

(i) The name of the plan;

(ii) The EIN and the three-digit Plan Number (PN) assigned by the contributing sponsor to the plan (or if there is no EIN or PN for the plan, an explanation);

(iii) If the EIN or PN of the plan has changed since the beginning of the filer's information year, the previous EIN or PN and an explanation;

(iv) If the plan had not been maintained by the controlled group immediately before the filer's information year, the date the plan was first maintained by the controlled group during the information year; and

(v) If, as of any day during the information year, the plan was frozen (for eligibility or benefit accrual purposes), a description of the date and the nature of the freeze (*e.g.*, service is frozen but pay is not).

(2) *Former plans.* For a plan that ceased to be maintained by the controlled group during the filer's information year, the date the plan ceased to be so maintained, identification of the controlled group currently maintaining the plan, and the identifying information required by paragraph (b)(1) as of the date immediately preceding that date.

[¶ 15,396G]

§ 4010.8 **Plan actuarial information.** (a) *Required information.* For each plan (other than an exempt plan) maintained by any member of the filer's controlled group, each filer is required to provide, in accordance with the instructions on the PBGC's website, the following actuarial information—

(1) The number of—

(i) Retired participants and beneficiaries receiving payments;

(ii) Terminated vested participants, and

(iii) Active participants;

(2) The fair market value of the plan's assets;

(3) The value of the plan's benefit liabilities, setting forth separately the value of the liabilities attributable to retired participants and beneficiaries receiving payments, terminated vested participants, and active participants, determined (in accordance with paragraph (d) of this section) at the end of the plan year ending within the filer's information year;

(4) A description of the actuarial assumptions for interest (*i.e.*, the specific interest rate(s), such as 5%), mortality, retirement age, and loading for administrative expenses, as used to determine the benefit liabilities in paragraph (a)(3) of this section; and

(5) A copy of the actuarial valuation report for the plan year ending within the filer's information year that contains or is supplemented by the following information—

(i) Each amortization base and related amortization charge or credit to the funding standard account (as defined in section 302(b) of ERISA or section 412(b) of the Code) for that plan year (excluding the amount considered contributed to the plan as described in section 302(b)(3)(A) of ERISA or section 412(b)(3)(A) of the Code),

(ii) The itemized development of the additional funding charge payable for that plan year pursuant to section 412(l) of the Code,

(iii) The minimum funding contribution and the maximum deductible contribution for that plan year,

(iv) The actuarial assumptions and methods used for that plan year for purposes of section 302(b) and (d) of ERISA or section 412(b) and (l) of the Code (and any change in those assumptions and methods since the previous valuation and justifications for any change),

(v) A summary of the principal eligibility and benefit provisions on which the valuation of the plan was based (and any changes to those provisions since the previous valuation), along with descriptions of any benefits not included in the valuation, any significant events that occurred during that plan year, and the plan's early retirement factors,

(vi) The current liability, vested and nonvested, calculated pursuant to section 412 of the Code, setting forth separately the value of the liabilities attributable to retired participants and beneficiaries receiving payments, terminated vested participants, and active participants,

(vii) The expected increase in current liability due to benefits accruing during the plan year, and

(viii) The expected plan disbursements for the plan year; and

(6) A written certification by an enrolled actuary that, to the best of his or her knowledge and belief, the actuarial information submitted is true, correct, and complete and conforms to all applicable laws and regulations, provided that this certification may be qualified in writing, but only to the extent the qualification(s) are permitted under 26 CFR 301.6059-1(d).

(b) *Alternative compliance for plan actuarial information.* If any of the information specified in paragraph (a)(5) of this section is not available by the date specified in § 4010.10(a), a filer may satisfy the requirement to provide such information by—

(1) Including a statement, with the material that is submitted to the PBGC, that the filer will file the unavailable information by the alternative due date specified in § 4010.10(b), and

(2) Filing such information (along with a certification by an enrolled actuary under paragraph (a)(6) of this section) with the PBGC by that alternative due date.

(c) *Exempt plan.* The actuarial information specified in this section is not required with respect to a plan that, as of the end of the plan year ending within the filer's information year, has fewer than 500 participants or has benefit liabilities (determined in accordance with paragraph (d) of this section) equal to or less than the fair market value of the plan's assets, provided that the plan—

(1) has received, on or within ten days after their due dates, all required installments or other payments required to be made during the information year under section 302 of ERISA or section 412 of the Code; and

(2) has no minimum funding waivers outstanding (as described in § 4010.4(c) of this part) as of the end of the plan year ending within the information year.

(d) *Value of benefit liabilities.* The value of a plan's benefit liabilities at the end of a plan year shall be determined using the plan census data described in paragraph (d)(1) of this section and the actuarial assumptions and methods described in paragraph (d)(2) or, where applicable, (d)(3) of this section.

(1) *Census data.* (i) *Census data period.* Plan census data shall be determined (for all plans for any information year) either as of the end of the plan year or as of the beginning of the next plan year.

(ii) *Projected census data.* If actual plan census data is not available, a plan may use a projection of plan census data from a date within the plan year. The projection must be consistent with projections used to measure pension obligations of the plan for financial statement purposes and must give a result appropriate for the end of the plan year for these obligations. For example, adjustments to the projection process will be required where there has been a significant event (such as a plan amendment or a plant shutdown) that has not been reflected in the projection data.

(2) *Actuarial assumptions and methods.* The value of benefit liabilities shall be determined using the assumptions and methods applicable to the valuation of benefits to be paid as annuities in trusteed plans terminating at the end of the plan year (as prescribed in §§ 4044.51 through 4044.57 of this chapter).

(3) *Special actuarial assumptions for exempt plan determination.* Solely for purposes of determining whether a plan is an exempt plan, the value of benefit liabilities may be determined by substituting for the retirement age assumptions in paragraph (d)(2) the retirement age assumptions used by the plan for that plan year for purposes of section 302(d) of ERISA or section 412(l) of the Code.

§ 4010.9 **Financial information.** (a) *General.* Except as provided in this section, each filer is required to provide, in accordance with the instructions on the PBGC's Web site, the following financial information for each controlled group member (other than an exempt entity)—

(1) audited financial statements for the fiscal year ending within the information year (including balance sheets, income statements, cash flow statements, and notes to the financial statements);

(2) if audited financial statements are not available by the date specified in § 4010.10(a), unaudited financial statements for the fiscal year ending within the information year; or

(3) if neither audited nor unaudited financial statements are available by the date specified in § 4010.10(a), copies of federal tax returns for the tax year ending within the information year.

(b) *Consolidated financial statements.* If the financial information of a controlled group member is combined with the information of other group members in consolidated financial statements, a filer may provide the following financial information in lieu of the information required in paragraph (a) of this section—

(1) the audited consolidated financial statements for the filer's information year or, if the audited consolidated financial statements are not available by the date specified in § 4010.10(a), unaudited consolidated financial statements for the fiscal year ending within the information year; and

(2) for each controlled group member included in the consolidated financial statements (other than an exempt entity), the member's revenues and operating income for the information year, and net assets at the end of the information year.

(c) *Subsequent submissions.* If unaudited financial statements are submitted as provided in paragraph (a)(2) or (b)(1) of this section, audited financial statements must thereafter be filed within 15 days after they are prepared. If federal tax returns are submitted as provided in paragraph (a)(3) of this section, audited and unaudited financial statements must thereafter be filed within 15 days after they are prepared.

(d) *Submission of public information.* If any of the financial information required by paragraphs (a) through (c) of this section is publicly available, the filer, in lieu of submitting such information to the PBGC, may include a statement with the other information that is submitted to the PBGC indicating when such financial information was made available to the public and where the PBGC may obtain it. For example, if the controlled group member has filed audited financial statements with the Securities and Exchange Commission, it need not file the financial statements with PBGC but instead can identify the SEC filing as part of its submission under this part.

(e) *Inclusion of information about non-filers and exempt entities.* Consolidated financial statements provided pursuant to paragraph (b)(1) of this section may include financial information of persons who are not controlled group members (e.g., joint ventures) or are exempt entities.

§ 4010.10 **Due date and filing with the PBGC.** (a) *Due date.* Except as permitted under paragraph (b) of this section, a filer shall file the information required under this part with the PBGC on or before the 105th day after the close of the filer's information year.

(b) *Alternative due date.* A filer that includes the statement specified in § 4010.8(b)(1) with its submission to the PBGC by the date specified in paragraph (a) of this section must submit the actuarial information specified in § 4010.8(b)(2) within 15 days after the deadline for filing the plan's annual report (Form 5500 series) for the plan year ending within the filer's information year (see § 2520.104a-5(a)(2) of this title).

(c) *How and where to file.* The PBGC applies the rules in subpart A of part 4000 of this chapter to determine permissible methods of filing with the PBGC under this part. See Sec. 4000.4 of this chapter for information on where to file [Amended 10/28/2003 by 68 FR 61344].

(d) *Date of filing.* The PBGC applies the rules in subpart C of part 4000 of this chapter to determine the date that a submission under this part was filed with the PBGC [Amended 10/28/2003 by 68 FR 61344].

(e) *Computation of time.* The PBGC applies the rules in subpart D of part 4000 of this chapter to compute any time period under this part [Amended 10/28/2003 by 68 FR 61344].

[¶ 15,396J]

§ 4010.11 **Waivers and extensions.** The PBGC may waive the requirement to submit information with respect to one or more filers or plans or may extend the applicable due date or dates specified in § 4010.10 of this part. The PBGC will exercise this discretion in appropriate cases where it finds convincing evidence supporting a waiver or extension; any waiver or extension may be subject to conditions. A request for a waiver or extension must be filed in writing with the PBGC at the address provided in § 4010.10(c) no later than 15 days before the applicable date specified in § 4010.10 of this part, and must state the facts and circumstances on which the request is based.

[¶ 15,396K]

§ 4010.12 **Confidentiality of information submitted.** In accordance with § 4901.21(a)(3) of this chapter and section 4010(c) of ERISA, any information or documentary material that is not publicly available and is submitted to the PBGC pursuant to this part shall not be made public, except as may be relevant to any administrative or judicial action or proceeding or for disclosures to either body of Congress or to any duly authorized committee or subcommittee of the Congress.

[¶ 15,396L]

§ 4010.13 **Penalties.** If all of the information required under this part is not provided within the specified time limit, the PBGC may assess a separate penalty under section 4071 of ERISA against the filer and each member of the filer's controlled group (other than an exempt entity) of up to $1,100 a day for each day that the failure continues. The PBGC may also pursue other equitable or legal remedies available to it under the law. [Amended by 62 FR 36993, effective August 11, 1997.]

[¶ 15,396M]

§ 4010.14 **OMB control number.** The collection of information requirements contained in this part have been approved by the Office of Management and Budget under OMB Control Number 1212-0049.

[¶ 15,400]
NOTICE TO PARTICIPANTS

Act Sec. 4011.(a) IN GENERAL. The plan administrator of a plan subject to the additional premium under section 4006(a)(3)(E) shall provide, in a form and manner and at such time as prescribed in regulations of the corporation, notice to plan participants and beneficiaries of the plan's funding status and the limits on the corporation's guaranty should the plan terminate while underfunded.

Such notice shall be written in a manner as to be understood by the average plan participant.

(b) EXCEPTION. Subsection (a) shall not apply to any plan to which section 302(d) does not apply for the plan year by reason of paragraph (9) thereof.

Amendment

P.L. 103-465, § 775(a):

Act Sec. 775(a) amended subtitle A of title IV of ERISA by adding new section 4011 to read as above.

The above amendment is effective for plan years beginning after December 8, 1994.

Regulations

The following regulations were adopted by the Pension Benefit Guaranty Corporation on July 1, 1996 (61 FR 34002). Prior to July 1, 1996, PBGC regulations were under Chapter XXVI of Title 29 of the Code of Federal Regulations. Effective July 1, 1996, PBGC regulations were moved to Chapter XL, and were renumbered and reorganized. Reg. § 4011.1 was amended effective August 11, 1997 (62 FR 36993). Appendix A of Reg. § 4011 was amended effective August 17, 1998 (63 FR 38305). Reg. § 4011.9 was amended October 28, 2003 (68 FR 61344).

[¶ 15,401]

§ 4011.1 **Purpose and scope.** This part prescribes rules and procedures for complying with the requirements of section 4011 of ERISA. This part applies for any plan year beginning on or after January 1, 1995, with respect to any single-employer plan that is covered by section 4021 of ERISA.

[¶ 15,401A]

§ 4011.2 **Definitions.** The following terms are defined in § 4001.2 of this chapter: contributing sponsor, employer, ERISA, normal retirement age, PBGC, person, plan, plan administrator, plan year, and single-employer plan.

In addition, for purposes of this part:

Participant has the meaning in § 4041.2 of this chapter.

Participant Notice means the notice required pursuant to section 4011 of ERISA and this part.

[¶ 15,401B]

§ 4011.3 **Notice requirement.** (a) *General.* Except as otherwise provided in this part, the plan administrator of a plan must provide a Participant Notice for a plan year if a variable rate premium is payable for the plan under section 4006(a)(3)(E) of ERISA and part 4006 of this chapter for that plan year, unless, for that plan year or for the prior plan year, the plan meets the Deficit Reduction Contribution ("DRC") Exception Test in paragraph (b) of this section. The DRC Exception Test may be applied using the Small Plan DRC Exception Test rules in § 4011.4(b), where applicable.

(b) *DRC Exception Test.* (1) *Basic rule.* A plan meets the DRC Exception Test for a plan year if it is exempt from the requirements of section 302(d) of ERISA for that plan year by reason of section

302(d)(9), without regard to the small plan exemption in section 302(d)(6)(A).

(2) *1994 plan year.* A plan satisfies the DRC Exception Test for the 1994 plan year if, for any two of the plan years beginning in 1992, 1993, and 1994 (whether or not consecutive), the plan satisfies any requirement of section 302(d)(9)(D)(i) of ERISA.

(c) *Penalties for non-compliance.* If a plan administrator fails to provide a Participant Notice within the specified time limit or omits material information from a Participant Notice, the PBGC may assess a penalty under section 4071 of ERISA of up to $1,100 a day for each day that the failure continues. [Amended by 62 FR 36993, effective August 11, 1997.]

[¶ 15,401C]

§ 4011.4 **Small plan rules.** (a) *1995 plan year exemption.* A plan that is exempt from the requirements of section 302(d) of ERISA for the 1994 or 1995 plan year by reason of section 302(d)(6)(A) is exempt from the Participant Notice requirement for the 1995 plan year.

(b) *Small Plan DRC Exception Test.* In determining whether the Participant Notice requirement applies for a plan year beginning after 1995, the plan administrator of a plan that is exempt from the requirements of section 302(d) of ERISA by reason of section 302(d)(6)(A) for the plan year being tested may use any one or more of the following rules in determining whether the plan meets the DRC Exception Test for that plan year:

(1) *Use of Schedule B data.* For any plan year for which the plan is exempt from the requirements of section 302(d) of ERISA by reason of section 302(d)(6)(A), provided both of the following adjustments are made—

(i) The market value of the plan's assets as of the beginning of the plan year (as required to be reported on Form 5500, Schedule B) may be substituted for the actuarial value of the plan's assets as of the valuation date; and

(ii) The plan's current liability for all participants' total benefits as of the beginning of the plan year (as required to be reported on Form 5500, Schedule B) may be substituted for the plan's current liability as of the valuation date.

(2) *Pre-1995 plan year 90 percent test.* A plan that is exempt from the requirements of section 302(d) of ERISA for a pre-1995 plan year by reason of section 302(d)(6)(A) satisfies the requirements of section 302(d)(9)(D)(i) for that pre-1995 plan year if the ratio of its assets to its current liability for that plan year is at least 90 percent. For this purpose, the plan's assets are valued without subtracting any credit balance under section 302(b) of ERISA, and its current liability is determined using the highest interest rate allowable for the plan year under section 302(d)(7)(C).

(3) *Interest rate adjustment.* If the interest rate used to calculate current liability for a plan year is less than the highest rate allowable for the plan year under section 302(d)(7)(C) of ERISA, the current liability may be reduced by one percent for each tenth of a percentage point by which the highest rate exceeds the rate so used.

[¶ 15,401D]

§4011.5 **Exemption for new and newly-covered plans.** A plan (other than a plan resulting from a consolidation or spinoff) is exempt from the Participant Notice requirement for the first plan year for which the plan must pay premiums under parts 4006 and 4007 of this chapter.

[¶ 15,401E]

§4011.6 **Mergers, consolidations, and spinoffs.** In the case of a plan involved in a merger, consolidation, or spinoff transaction that becomes effective during a plan year, the plan administrator shall apply the requirements of section 4011 of ERISA and of this part for that plan year in a reasonable manner to ensure that the Participant Notice serves its statutory purpose.

[¶ 15,401F]

§4011.7 **Persons entitled to receive notice.** The plan administrator must provide the Participant Notice to each person who is a participant, a beneficiary of a deceased participant, an alternate payee under an applicable qualified domestic relations order (as defined in section 206(d)(3) of ERISA), or an employee organization that represents any group of participants for purposes of collective bargaining. To determine who is a person that must receive the Participant Notice for a plan year, the plan administrator may select any date during the period beginning with the last day of the previous plan year and ending with the day on which the Participant Notice for the plan year is due, provided that a change in the date from one plan year to the next does not exclude a substantial number of participants and beneficiaries.

[¶ 15,401G]

§4011.8 **Time of notice.** The plan administrator must issue the Participant Notice for a plan year no later than two months after the deadline (including extensions) for filing the annual report for the previous plan year (see §2520.104a-5(a)(2) of this title). The plan administrator may change the date of issuance from one plan year to the next, provided that the effect of any change is not to avoid disclosing a minimum funding waiver under §4011.10(b)(5) or a missed contribution under §4011.10(b)(6). When the President of the United States declares that, under the Disaster Relief Act of 1974, as amended (42 U.S.C. 5121, 5122(2), 5141(b)), a major disaster exists, the PBGC may extend the due date for providing the Participant Notice by up to 180 days.

[¶ 15,401H]

§4011.9 **Method and date of issuance of notice; computation of time.** (a) *Method of issuance.* The PBGC applies the rules in subpart B of part 4000 of this chapter to determine permissible methods of issuance of the Participant Notice. The Participant Notice may be issued together with another document, such as the summary annual report required under section 104(b)(3) of ERISA for the prior plan year, but must be in a separate document.

(b) *Issuance date.* The PBGC applies the rules in subpart C of part 4000 of this chapter to determine the date the Participant Notice was issued

(c) *Computation of time.* The PBGC applies the rules in subpart D of part 4000 of this chapter to compute any time period for issuances under this part. [Amended 10/28/2003 by 68 FR 61344]

[¶ 15,401I]

§4011.10 **Form of notice.** (a) *General.* The Participant Notice (and any additional information under paragraph (d) of this section) shall be readable and written in a manner calculated to be understood by the average plan participant and not to mislead recipients. The Model Participant Notice in Appendix A to this part (when properly completed) is an example of a Participant Notice meeting the requirements of this section.

(b) *Content.* The Participant Notice for a plan year shall include—

(1) Identifying information (the name of the plan and the contributing sponsor, the employer identification number of the contributing sponsor, the plan number, the date (at least the month and year) on which the Participant Notice is issued, and the name, title, address and telephone number of the person(s) who can provide information about the plan's funding);

(2) A statement to the effect that the Participant Notice is required by law;

(3) The Notice Funding Percentage for the plan year, determined in accordance with paragraph (c) of this section, and the date as of which the Notice Funding Percentage is determined;

(4) A statement to the effect that—

(i) To pay pension benefits, the employer is required to contribute money to the plan over a period of years;

(ii) A plan's funding percentage does not take into consideration the financial strength of the employer; and

(iii) The employer, by law, must pay for all pension benefits, but benefits may be at risk if the employer faces a severe financial crisis or is in bankruptcy;

(5) If, for any of the five plan years immediately preceding the plan year, the plan has been granted a minimum funding waiver under section 303 of ERISA that has not (as of the end of the prior plan year) been fully repaid, a statement identifying each such plan year and an explanation of a minimum funding waiver;

(6) For any payment subject to the requirements of this paragraph, a statement identifying the due date for the payment and noting that the payment has or has not been made and (if made) the date of the payment. Once participants have been notified (under this part or Title I of ERISA) of a missed contribution that is subject to the requirements of this paragraph, the delinquency need not be reported in a Participant Notice for a subsequent plan year if the missed contribution has been paid in full by the time the subsequent Participant Notice is issued. The payments subject to the requirements of this paragraph are—

(i) Any minimum funding payment necessary to satisfy the minimum funding standard under section 302(a) of ERISA for any plan year beginning on or after January 1, 1994, if not paid by the earlier of the due date for that payment (the latest date allowed under section 302(c)(10)) or the date of issuance of the Participant Notice; and

(ii) An installment or other payment required by section 302 of ERISA for a plan year beginning on or after January 1, 1995, that was not paid by the 60th day after the due date for that payment;

(7) A statement to the effect that if a plan terminates before all pension benefits are fully funded, the PBGC pays most persons all pension benefits, but some persons may lose certain benefits that are not guaranteed;

(8) A summary of plan benefits guaranteed by the PBGC, with an explanation of the limitations on such guarantee; and

(9) A statement that further information about the PBGC's guarantee may be obtained by requesting a free copy of the booklet "Your Guaranteed Pension" from Consumer Information Center, Dept.

YGP, Pueblo, Colorado 81009. The Participant Notice may include a statement that the booklet may be obtained through electronic access via the World Wide Web from the PBGC Homepage at http://www.pbgc.gov/ygp.htm.

(c) *Notice Funding Percentage—*

(1) *General Rule.* The Notice Funding Percentage that must be included in the Participant Notice for a plan year is the "funded current liability percentage" (as that term is defined in section 302(d)(9)(C) of ERISA) for that plan year or the prior plan year.

(2) *Small plans.* A plan that is exempt from the requirements of section 302(d) of ERISA for a plan year by reason of section 302(d)(6)(A) may determine its funded current liability percentage for that plan year using the Small Plan DRC Exception Test rules in §4011.4(b).

(d) *Additional information.* The plan administrator may include with the Participant Notice any information not described in paragraph (b) of this section only if it is in a separate document.

(e) *Foreign languages.* In the case of a plan that (as of the date selected under §4011.7) covers the numbers or percentages specified in §2520.104b-10(e) of this title of participants literate only in the same non-English language, the plan administrator shall provide those participants either—

(1) An English-language Participant Notice that prominently displays a legend, in their common non-English language, offering them assistance in that language, and clearly setting forth any procedures participants must follow to obtain such assistance, or

(2) A Participant Notice in that language.

[¶ 15,401J]

§4011.11 **OMB control number.** The collections of information contained in this part have been approved by the Office of Management and Budget under OMB control number 1212-0050.

[¶ 15,401K]

§4011.11 **Appendix A to Part 4011: Model Participant Notice.**

The following is an example of a Participant Notice that satisfies the requirements of §4011.10 when the required information is filled in (subject to §§4011.10(d)-(e), where applicable).

Notice to Participants of [Plan Name]

The law requires that you receive information on the funding level of your defined benefit pension plan and the benefits guaranteed by the Pension Benefit Guaranty Corporation (PBGC), a federal insurance agency. YOUR PLAN'S FUNDING

As of [DATE], your plan had [INSERT NOTICE FUNDING PERCENTAGE (DETERMINED IN ACCORDANCE WITH §4011.10(c))] percent of the money needed to pay benefits promised to employees and retirees.

To pay pension benefits, your employer is required to contribute money to the pension plan over a period of years. A plan's funding percentage does not take into consideration the financial strength of the employer. Your employer, by law, must pay for all pension benefits, but your benefits may be at risk if your employer faces a severe financial crisis or is in bankruptcy.

[INCLUDE THE FOLLOWING PARAGRAPH ONLY IF, FOR ANY OF THE PREVIOUS FIVE PLAN YEARS, THE PLAN HAS BEEN GRANTED AND HAS NOT FULLY REPAID A FUNDING WAIVER.]

Your plan received a funding waiver for [LIST ANY OF THE FIVE PREVIOUS PLAN YEARS FOR WHICH A FUNDING WAIVER WAS GRANTED AND HAS NOT BEEN FULLY REPAID]. If a company is experiencing temporary financial hardship, the Internal Revenue Service may grant a funding waiver that permits the company to delay contributions that fund the pension plan.

[INCLUDE THE FOLLOWING WITH RESPECT TO ANY UNPAID OR LATE PAYMENT THAT MUST BE DISCLOSED UNDER §4011.10(b)(6):]

Your plan was required to receive a payment from the employer on [LIST APPLICABLE DUE DATE(S)]. That payment [has not been made] [was made on [LIST APPLICABLE PAYMENT DATE(S)]].

PBGC GUARANTEES

When a pension plan ends without enough money to pay all benefits, the PBGC steps in to pay pension benefits. The PBGC pays most people all pension benefits, but some people may lose certain benefits that are not guaranteed.

The PBGC pays pension benefits up to certain maximum limits.

• The maximum guaranteed benefit is [INSERT FROM TABLE IN APPENDIX B] per month or [INSERT FROM TABLE IN APPENDIX B] per year for a 65-year-old person in a plan that terminates in [INSERT APPLICABLE YEAR].

• The maximum benefit may be reduced for an individual who is younger than age 65. For example, it is [INSERT FROM TABLE IN APPENDIX B] per month or [INSERT FROM TABLE IN APPENDIX B] per year for an individual who starts receiving benefits at age 55. [IN LIEU OF AGE 55, YOU MAY ADD OR SUBSTITUTE ANY AGE(S) RELEVANT UNDER THE PLAN. FOR EXAMPLE, YOU MAY ADD OR SUBSTITUTE THE MAXIMUM BENEFIT FOR AGES 62 OR 60 FROM THE TABLE IN APPENDIX B. IF THE PLAN PROVIDES FOR NORMAL RETIREMENT BEFORE AGE 65, YOU MUST INCLUDE THE NORMAL RETIREMENT AGE.]

[IF THE PLAN DOES NOT PROVIDE FOR COMMENCEMENT OF BENEFITS BEFORE AGE 65, YOU MAY OMIT THIS PARAGRAPH.]

• The maximum benefit will also be reduced when a benefit is provided for a survivor.

The PBGC does not guarantee certain types of benefits.

[INCLUDE THE FOLLOWING GUARANTEE LIMITS THAT APPLY TO THE BENEFITS AVAILABLE UNDER YOUR PLAN.]

• The PBGC does not guarantee benefits for which you do not have a vested right when a plan ends, usually because you have not worked enough years for the company.

• The PBGC does not guarantee benefits for which you have not met all age, service, or other requirements at the time the plan ends.

• Benefit increases and new benefits that have been in place for less than a year are not guaranteed. Those that have been in place for less than 5 years are only partly guaranteed.

• Early retirement payments that are greater than payments at normal retirement age may not be guaranteed. For example, a supplemental benefit that stops when you become eligible for Social Security may not be guaranteed.

• Benefits other than pension benefits, such as health insurance, life insurance, death benefits, vacation pay, or severance pay, are not guaranteed.

• The PBGC generally does not pay lump sums exceeding $5,000.

WHERE TO GET MORE INFORMATION

Your plan, [EIN-PN], is sponsored by [CONTRIBUTING SPONSOR(S)]. If you would like more information about the funding of your plan, contact [INSERT NAME, TITLE, BUSINESS ADDRESS AND PHONE NUMBER OF INDIVIDUAL OR ENTITY].

For more information about the PBGC and the benefits it guarantees, you may request a free copy of "Your Guaranteed Pension" by writing to Consumer Information Center, Dept. YGP, Pueblo, Colorado 81009.

[THE FOLLOWING SENTENCE MAY BE INCLUDED:] "Your Guaranteed Pension" is also available from the PBGC Homepage on the World Wide Web at http://www.pbgc.gov/ygp.htm.

Issued: [INSERT AT LEAST MONTH AND YEAR]

§ 4011.11 **Appendix B to Part 4011: Table of Maximum Guaranteed Benefits.**

The maximum guaranteed benefit for an individual starting to receive benefits at the age listed below is the amount (monthly or annual) listed below:

If a plan terminates in–	Age 65		Age 62		Age 60		Age 55	
	Monthly	Annual	Monthly	Annual	Monthly	Annual	Monthly	Annual
1995	$2,573.86	$30,886.32	$2,033.35	$24,400.20	$1,673.01	$20,076.12	$1,158.24	$13,898.88
1996	$2,642.05	$31,704.60	$2,087.22	$25,046.64	$1,717.33	$20,607.96	$1,188.92	$14,267.04
1997	$2,761.36	$33,136.32	$2,181.47	$26,177.64	$1,794.88	$21,538.56	$1,242.61	$14,911.32
1998	$2,880.68	$34,568.16	$2,275.74	$27,308.88	$1,872.44	$22,469.28	$1,296.31	$15,555.72
1999	$3,051.14	$36,613.68	$2,410.40	$28,924.80	$1,983.24	$23,798.88	$1,373.01	$16,476.12
2000	$3,221.59	$38,659.08	$2,545.06	$30,540.72	$2,094.03	$25,128.36	$1,449.72	$17,396.64
2001	$3,392.05	$40,704.60	$2,679.72	$32,156.64	$2,204.83	$26,457.96	$1,526.42	$18,317.04
2002	$3,579.55	$42,954.60	$2,827.84	$33,934.08	$2,326.71	$27,920.52	$1,610.80	$19,329.60
2003	$3,664.77	$43,977.24	$2,895.17	$34,742.04	$2,382.10	$28,585.20	$1,649.15	$19,789.80
2004	$3,698.86	$44,386.32	$2,922.10	$35,065.20	$2,404.26	$28,851.12	$1,664.49	$19,973.88
2005	$3,801.14	$45,613.68	$3,002.90	$36,034.80	$2,470.74	$29,648.88	$1,710.51	$20,526.12
2006	$3,971.59	$47,659.08	$3,137.56	$37,650.72	$2,581.53	$30,978.36	$1,787.22	$21,446.64

The maximum guaranteed benefit for an individual starting to receive benefits at ages other than those listed above can be determined by applying the PBGC's regulation on computation of maximum guaranteeable benefits (29 CFR 4022.22).

Subtitle B—Coverage

[¶ 15,410]
PLANS COVERED

Act Sec. 4021. (a) Except as provided in subsection (b), this title applies to any plan (including a successor plan) which, for a plan year—

(1) is an employee pension benefit plan (as defined in paragraph (2) of section 3 of this Act) established or maintained—

(A) by an employer engaged in commerce or in any industry or activity affecting commerce, or

(B) by any employee organization, or organization representing employees, engaged in commerce or in any industry or activity affecting commerce, or

(C) by both, which has, in practice, met the requirements of part I of subchapter D of chapter 1 of the Internal Revenue Code of 1986 (as in effect for the preceding 5 plan years of the plan) applicable to plans described in paragraph (2) for the preceding 5 plan years; or

(2) is, or has been determined by the Secretary of the Treasury to be, a plan described in section 401(a) of the Internal Revenue Code of 1986, or which meets, or has been determined by the Secretary of the Treasury to meet, the requirements of section 404(a)(2) of such Code.

For purposes of this title, a successor plan is considered to be a continuation of a predecessor plan. For this purpose, unless otherwise specifically indicated in this title, a successor plan is a plan which covers a group of employees which includes substantially the same employees as a previously established plan, and provides substantially the same benefits as that plan provided.

(b) This section does not apply to any plan—

(1) which is an individual account plan, as defined in paragraph (34) of section 3 of this Act,

(2) established and maintained for its employees by the Government of the United States, by the government of any State or political subdivision thereof, or by any agency or instrumentality of any of the foregoing, or to which the Railroad Retirement Act of 1935 or 1937 applies and which is financed by contributions required under that Act,

(3) which is a church plan as defined in section 414(e) of the Internal Revenue Code of 1986, unless that plan has made an election under section 410(d) of such Code, and has notified the corporation in accordance with procedures prescribed by the corporation, that it wishes to have the provisions of this part apply to it,

(4)(A) established and maintained by a society, order, or association described in section 501(c)(8) or (9) of the Internal Revenue Code of 1986, if no part of the contributions to or under the plan is made by employers of participants in the plan, or

(B) of which a trust described in section 501(c)(18) of such Code is a part;

(5) which has not at any time after the date of enactment of this Act provided for employer contributions;

(6) which is unfunded and which is maintained by an employer primarily for the purpose of providing deferred compensation for a select group of management or highly compensated employees;

(7) which is established and maintained outside of the United States primarily for the benefit of individuals substantially all of whom are nonresident aliens;

(8) which is maintained by an employer solely for the purpose of providing benefits for certain employees in excess of the limitations on contributions and benefits imposed by section 415 of the Internal Revenue Code of 1986 on plans to which that section applies, without regard to whether the plan is funded, and, to the extent that a separable part of a plan (as determined by the corporation) maintained by an employer is maintained for such purpose, that part shall be treated for purposes of this title, as a separate plan which is an excess benefit plan;

(9) which is established and maintained exclusively for substantial owners as defined in section 4022(b)(6);

(10) of an international organization which is exempt from taxation under the International Organizations Immunities Act;

(11) maintained solely for the purpose of complying with applicable workmen's compensation laws or unemployment compensation or disability insurance laws;

(12) which is a defined benefit plan, to the extent that it is treated as an individual account plan under paragraph (35)(B) of section 3 of this Act; or

(13) established and maintained by a professional service employer which does not at any time after the date of enactment of this Act have more than 25 active participants in the plan.

Act Sec. 4021.(c)(1) For purposes of subsection (b)(1), the term "individual account plan" does not include a plan under which a fixed benefit is promised if the employer or his representative participated in the determination of that benefit.

(2) For purposes of this paragraph and for purposes of subsection (b)(13)—

(A) the term "professional service employer" means any proprietorship, partnership, corporation, or other association or organization (i) owned or controlled by professional individuals or by executors or administrators of professional individuals, (ii) the principal business of which is the performance of professional services, and

(B) the term "professional individuals" includes[,] but is not limited to, physicians, dentists, chiropractors, osteopaths, optometrists, other licensed practitioners of the healing arts, attorneys at law, public accountants, public engineers, architects, draftsmen, actuaries, psychologists, social or physical scientists, and performing artists.

(3) In the case of a plan established and maintained by more than one professional service employer, the plan shall not be treated as a plan described in subsection (b)(13) if, at any time after the date of enactment of this Act the plan has more than 25 active participants.

Amendments

P.L. 101-239, §7891(a)(1):

Titles I, III, and IV of ERISA (other than sections 3(37)(E), 301(a)(7), and 308, the last sentence of section 408(d), and sections 414(c), 4001(a)(3)(ii), and 4303) are each amended by striking "Internal Revenue Code of 1954" each place it appears and inserting "Internal Revenue Code of 1986" effective October 22, 1986.

P.L. 101-239, §7894(g)(3)(A):

Amended ERISA Sec. 4021(a) by striking "this section" and inserting "this title" effective September 2, 1974.

P.L. 96-364, §402(a)(4):

Amended Sec. 4021(a) effective September 26, 1980 by inserting in the last sentence "unless otherwise specifically indicated in this title," before "a successor plan".

[¶ 15,420]
SINGLE-EMPLOYER PLAN BENEFITS GUARANTEED

Act Sec. 4022.(a) Subject to the limitations contained in subsection (b), the corporation shall guarantee, in accordance with this section, the payment of all nonforfeitable benefits (other than benefits becoming nonforfeitable solely on account of the termination of a plan) under a single-employer plan which terminates at a time when this title applies to it.

Act Sec. 4022.(b)(1) Except to the extent provided in paragraph (7)—

(A) no benefits provided by a plan which has been in effect for less than 60 months at the time the plan terminates shall be guaranteed under this section, and

(B) any increase in the amount of benefits under a plan resulting from a plan amendment which was made, or became effective, whichever is later, within 60 months before the date on which the plan terminates shall be disregarded.

(2) For purposes of this subsection, the time a successor plan (within the meaning of section 4021(a)) has been in effect includes the time a previously established plan (within the meaning of section 4021(a)) was in effect. For purposes of determining what benefits are guaranteed under this section in the case of a plan to which section 4021 does not apply on the day after the date of enactment of this Act, the 60-month period referred to in paragraph (1) shall be computed beginning on the first date on which such section does apply to the plan.

(3) The amount of monthly benefits described in subsection (a) provided by a plan, which are guaranteed under this section with respect to a participant, shall not have an actuarial value which exceeds the actuarial value of a monthly benefit in the form of a life annuity commencing at age 65 equal to the lesser of—

(A) his average monthly gross income from his employer during the 5 consecutive calendar year period (or, if less, during the number of calendar years in such period in which he actively participates in the plan) during which his gross income from that employer was greater than during any other such period with that employer determined by dividing $1/12$ of the sum of all such gross income by the number of such calendar years in which he had such gross income, or

(B) $750 multiplied by a fraction, the numerator of which is the contribution and benefit base (determined under section 230 of the Social Security Act) in effect at the time the plan terminates and the denominator of which is such contribution and benefit base in effect in calendar year 1974.

The provisions of this paragraph do not apply to non-basic benefits.

The maximum guaranteed monthly benefit shall not be reduced solely on account of the age of a participant in the case of a benefit payable by reason of disability that occurred on or before the termination date, if the participant demonstrates to the satisfaction of the corporation that the Social Security Administration has determined that the participant satisfies the definition of disability under title II or XVI of the Social Security Act, and the regulations thereunder. If a benefit payable by reason of disability is converted to an early or normal retirement benefit for reasons other than a change in the health of the participant, such early or normal retirement benefit shall be treated as a continuation of the benefit payable by reason of disability and this subparagraph shall continue to apply.

(4)(A) The actuarial value of a benefit, for purposes of this subsection, shall be determined in accordance with regulations prescribed by the corporation.

(B) For purposes of paragraph (3)—

(i) the term "gross income" means "earned income" within the meaning of section 911(b) of the Internal Revenue Code of 1986 (determined without regard to any community property laws),

(ii) in the case of a participant in a plan under which contributions are made by more than one employer, amounts received as gross income from any employer under that plan shall be aggregated with amounts received from any other employer under that plan during the same period, and

(iii) any non-basic benefit shall be disregarded.

(5)(A) For purposes of this title, the term "substantial owner" means an individual who—

(i) owns the entire interest in an unincorporated trade or business,

(ii) in the case of a partnership, is a partner who owns, directly or indirectly, more than 10 percent of either the capital interest or the profits interest in such partnership, or

(iii) in the case of a corporation, owns, directly or indirectly, more than 10 percent in value of either the voting stock of that corporation or all the stock of that corporation.

For purposes of clause (iii) the constructive ownership rules of section 1563(e) of the Internal Revenue Code of 1986 shall apply (determined without regard to section 1563(e)(3)(C)). For purposes of this title an individual is also treated as a substantial owner with respect to a plan if, at any time within the 60 months preceding the date on which the determination is made, he was a substantial owner under the plan.

(B) In the case of a participant in a plan under which benefits have not been increased by reason of any plan amendments and who is covered by the plan as a substantial owner, the amount of benefits guaranteed under this section shall not exceed the product of—

(i) a fraction (not to exceed 1) the numerator of which is the number of years the substantial owner was an active participant in the plan, and the denominator of which is 30, and

(ii) the amount of the substantial owner's monthly benefits guaranteed under subsection (a) (as limited under paragraph (3) of this subsection).

(C) In the case of a participant in a plan, other than a plan described in subparagraph (B), who is covered by the plan as a substantial owner, the amount of the benefit guaranteed under this section shall, under regulations prescribed by the corporation, treat each benefit increase attributable to a plan amendment as if it were provided under a new plan. The benefits guaranteed under this section with respect to all such amendments shall not exceed the amount which would be determined under subparagraph (B) if subparagraph (B) applied.

(6)(A) No benefits accrued under a plan after the date on which the Secretary of the Treasury issues notice that he has determined that any trust which is a part of a plan does not meet the requirements of section 401(a) of the Internal Revenue Code of 1986, or that the plan does not meet the requirements of section 404(a)(2) of such Code, are guaranteed under this section unless such determination is erroneous. This subparagraph does not apply if the Secretary subsequently issues a notice that such trust meets the requirements of section 401(a) of such Code or that the plan meets the requirements of section 404(a)(2) of such Code and if the Secretary determines that the trust or plan has taken action necessary to meet such requirements during the period between the issuance of the notice referred to in the preceding sentence and the issuance of the notice referred to in this sentence.

(B) No benefits accrued under a plan after the date on which an amendment of the plan is adopted which causes the Secretary of the Treasury to determine that any trust under the plan has ceased to meet the requirements of section 401(a) of the Internal Revenue Code of 1986 or that the plan has ceased to meet the requirements of section 404(a)(2) of such Code, are guaranteed under this section unless such determination is erroneous. This subparagraph shall not apply if the amendment is revoked as of the date it was first effective or amended to comply with such requirements.

(7) Benefits described in paragraph (1) are guaranteed only to the extent of the greater of—

(A) 20 percent of the amount which, but for the fact that the plan or amendment has not been in effect for 60 months or more, would be guaranteed under this section, or

(B) $20 per month,

multiplied by the number of years (but not more than 5) the plan or amendment, as the case may be, has been in effect. In determining how many years a plan or amendment has been in effect for purposes of this paragraph, the first 12 months beginning with the date on which the plan or amendment is made or first becomes effective (whichever is later) constitutes one year, and each consecutive period of 12 months thereafter constitutes an additional year. This paragraph does not apply to benefits payable under a plan unless the corporation finds substantial evidence that the plan was terminated for a reasonable business purpose and not for the purpose of obtaining the payment of benefits by the corporation under this title.

Act Sec. 4022. (c)(1) In addition to benefits paid under the preceding provision of this section with respect to a terminated plan, the corporation shall pay the portion of the amount determined under paragraph (2) which is allocated with respect to each participant under section 4044(a). Such payment shall be made to such participant or to such participant's beneficiaries (including alternate payees, within the meaning of section 206(d)(3)(K)).

(2) The amount determined under this paragraph is an amount equal to the product derived by multiplying—

(A) the outstanding amount of benefit liabilities under the plan (including interest calculated from the termination date), by

(B) the applicable recovery ratio.

(3)(A) Except as provided in subparagraph (C), for purposes of this subsection, the term "recovery ratio" means the average ratio, with respect to prior plan terminations described in subparagraph (B), of—

(i) the value of the recovery of the corporation under section 4062, 4063, or 4064 in connection with such prior terminations, to

(ii) the amount of unfunded benefit liabilities under such plans as of the termination date in connection with such prior terminations.

(B) A plan termination described in this subparagraph is a termination with respect to which—

(i) the corporation has determined the value of recoveries under section 4062, 4063, or 4064, and

(ii) notices of intent to terminate were provided after December 17, 1987, and during the 5-Federal fiscal year period ending with the fiscal year preceding the fiscal year in which occurs the date of the notice of intent to terminate with respect to the plan termination for which the recovery ratio is being determined.

(C) In the case of a terminated plan with respect to which the outstanding amount of benefit liabilities exceeds $20,000,000, for purposes of this section, the term "recovery ratio" means, with respect to the termination of such plan, the ratio of—

(i) the value of the recoveries of the corporation under section 4062, 4063, or 4064 in connection with such plan, to

(ii) the amount of unfunded benefit liabilities under such plan as of the termination date.

(4) Determinations under this subsection shall be made by the corporation. Such determinations shall be binding unless shown by clear and convincing evidence to be unreasonable.

Act Sec. 4022. (d) The corporation is authorized to guarantee the payment of such other classes of benefits and to establish the terms and conditions under which such other classes of benefits are guaranteed as it determines to be appropriate.

Act Sec. 4022. (e) For purposes of subsection (a), a qualified preretirement survivor annuity (as defined in section 205(e)(1)) with respect to a participant under a terminated single-employer plan shall not be treated as forfeitable solely because the participant has not died as of the termination date.

(f) For purposes of this section, the effective date of a plan amendment described in section 204(i)(1) shall be the effective date of the plan of reorganization of the employer described in section 204(i)(1) or, if later, the effective date stated in such amendment.

Amendments

P.L. 103-465, §777(a):

Act Sec. 777(a) amended ERISA Sec. 4022(b)(3) by adding at the end new sentences to read as above.

The above amendment is effective for plan terminations under ERISA Sec. 4041(c) with respect to which notices of intent to terminate are provided under ERISA Sec. 4041(a)(2), or under ERISA Sec. 4042 with respect to which proceedings are instituted by the corporation, on or after December 8, 1994.

P.L. 103-465, §766(c):

Act Sec. 766(c) amended ERISA Sec. 4022 by inserting new subsection (f) to read as above.

The above amendment applies to plan amendments adopted on or after December 8, 1994.

P.L. 101-239, §7881(f)(1):

Amended P.L. 100-203, §9312(b)(3)(B)(i) by striking "section 4022(c)(1)" in subclause (I) and inserting "section 4022(c)(3)", and by striking "subparagraph (B) of section 4022(c)(1)" and inserting "subparagraph (C) of section 4022(c)(3)."

P.L. 101-239, §7881(f)(4):

Amended ERISA Sec. 4022(c)(1) by striking "(in the case of a deceased participant)."

P.L. 101-239, §7881(f)(5):

Amended ERISA Sec. 4022(c)(3)(B)(ii) by inserting new material after "1987."

P.L. 101-239, §7881(f)(6):

Amended P.L. 100-203, §9312(b)(3)(B) by striking clause (ii).

P.L. 101-239, §7881(f)(11):

Amended ERISA Sec. 4022(c)(1) by striking "section 4044(a), to such participant" and inserting "section 4044(a). Such payment shall be made to such participant".

The above amendments are effective as if included in P.L. 100-203, §9312(b)(3)(A).

P.L. 101-239, §7891(a)(1):

Titles I, III, and IV of ERISA (other than sections 3(37)(E), 301(a)(7), and 308, the last sentence of section 408(d), and sections 414(c), 4001(a)(3)(ii), and 4303) are each amended by striking "Internal Revenue Code of 1954" each place it appears and inserting "Internal Revenue Code of 1986" effective October 22, 1986.

P.L. 101-239, §7894(g)(1):

Amended ERISA Sec. 4022(b)(2) by striking "60 month" and inserting "60-month."

P.L. 101-239, §7894(g)(3)(B):

Amended ERISA Sec. 4022(a) by striking "section 4021" and inserting "this title."

The above amendments are effective September 2, 1974.

P.L. 100-203, §9312(b)(3)(A):

Amended ERISA Sec. 4022 by redesignating subsections (c) and (d) as (d) and (e) and adding new subsection (c) to read as above, effective for (A) plan terminations under section 4041(c) of ERISA with respect to which notices of intent to terminate are provided under section 4041(a)(2) of ERISA after December 17, 1987, and (B) plan terminations with respect to which proceedings are instituted by the Pension Benefit Guaranty Corporation under section 4042 of ERISA after December 17, 1987.

P.L. 100-203, §9312(b)(3)(B):

(B) TRANSITIONAL RULE.—

(i) IN GENERAL.—In the case of any plan termination to which the amendments made by this section apply and with respect to which notices of intent to terminate were provided on or before December 17, 1990—

(I) subparagraph (A) of section 4022(c)(3) of ERISA (as amended by this paragraph) shall not apply, and

(II) subparagraph (C) of section 4022(c)(3) of ERISA (as so amended) shall apply irrespective of the outstanding amount of benefit liabilities under the plan.

P.L. 99-272:

Act Sec. 11016(c)(8) amended ERISA Sec. 4022(b)(7) by striking "following" and inserting "beginning with" in its place. Act Sec. 11016(c)(9) added a new subsection (d) to read as above. These amendments apply on April 7, 1986.

P.L. 99-364, §403(c):

Amended Sec. 4022, effective September 26, 1980 by changing the title to read as above (previously it read "Benefits Guaranteed"), amended subsection (a) to read as above, substituted "(7)" for "(8)" in subparagrah (b)(1), and struck subparagraph (b)(5) and renumbered subparagraphs (b)(6)-(8) as (b)(5), (b)(6) and (b)(7). Prior to amendment, subsection (a) read:

"Subject to the limitations contained in subsection (b), the corporation shall guarantee the payment of all nonforfeitable benefits (other than benefits becoming nonforfeitable solely on account of the termination of a plan) under the terms of a plan which terminates at a time when section 4021 applies to it."

Prior to amendment, subparagraph (b)(5) read:

"Notwithstanding paragraph (3), no person shall receive from the corporation for basic benefits with respect to a participant an amount, or amounts, with an actuarial value which exceeds a monthly benefit in the form of a life annuity commencing at age 65 equal to the amount determined under paragraph (3)(B) at the time of the last plan termination."

Regulations

The following regulations were adopted by the Pension Benefit Guaranty Corporation on July 1, 1996 (61 FR 34002). Prior to July 1, 1996, PBGC regulations were under Chapter XXVI of Title 29 of the Code of Federal Regulations. Effective July 1, 1996, PBGC regulations were moved to Chapter XL, and were renumbered and reorganized. Reg. §4022.61 was amended November 7, 1997 (62 FR 60424), effective January 1, 1998. Reg. §§4022.1, 4022.24 and 4022.26 were officially corrected December 30, 1997 (62 FR 67728). Reg. §§4022.81, 4022.82, and 4022.83 were amended May 28, 1998 (63 FR 29353), effective May 29, 1998. Reg. §4022.7 was amended July 15, 1998 (63 FR 38305), effective July 16, 1998 and on March 17, 2000 (65 FR 14751), effective May 1, 2000. The Appendix to Part 4022 was amended and added to on March 17, 2000 (65 FR 14751 and 14753), effective May 1, 2000. Reg. §§4022.4, 4022.6, 4022.7, 4022.21, 4022.25, 4022.81 were amended April 8, 2002 (67 FR 16949), effective June 1, 2002. Reg §§4022.8, 4022.9, 4022.10, 4022.91, 4022.92, 4022.93, 4022.94, 4022.95, 4022.101, 4022.102, 4022.103, and 4022.104 were added April 8, 2002 (67 FR 16949), effective June 1, 2002. Reg. §4022.9 was amended on October 28, 2003 (68 FR 61344).

Subpart A—General Provisions; Guaranteed Benefits

[¶ 15,421]

§4022.1 **Purpose and scope.** The purpose of this part is to prescribe rules governing the calculation and payment of benefits payable in terminated single-employer plans under section 4022 of ERISA. Subpart A, which applies to each plan providing benefits guaranteed under title IV of ERISA, contains definitions applicable to all subparts, and describes benefits that are guaranteed by the PBGC subject to the limitations set forth in Subpart B. Subpart C is reserved for rules relating to the calculation and payment of unfunded nonguaranteed benefits under section 4022(c) of ERISA. Subpart D prescribes procedures that minimize the overpayment of benefits by plan administrators after initiating distress terminations of single-employer plans that are not expected to be sufficient for guaranteed benefits. Subpart E sets forth the method of recoupment of benefit payments in excess of the amounts permitted under sections 4022, 4022B, and 4044 of ERISA from participants and beneficiaries in PBGC-trusteed plans, and provides for reimbursement of benefit underpayments. (The provisions of this part have not been amended to take account of changes made in section 4022 of ERISA by sections 766 and 777 of the Retirement Protection Act of 1994.) [Corrected 12/30/97 by 62 FR 67728.]

[¶ 15,421A]

§4022.2 **Definitions.** The following terms are defined in §4001.2 of this chapter: annuity, Code, employer, ERISA, guaranteed benefit, mandatory employee contributions, nonforfeitable benefit, normal retirement age, notice of intent to terminate, PBGC, person, plan, plan administrator, plan year, proposed termination date, substantial owner, and title IV benefit.

In addition, for purposes of this part (unless otherwise required by the context):

Accumulated mandatory employee contributions means mandatory employee contributions plus interest credited on those contributions under the plan, or, if greater, interest required by section 204(c) of ERISA.

Benefit in pay status means that one or more benefit payments have been made or would have been made except for administrative delay.

Benefit increase means any benefit arising from the adoption of a new plan or an increase in the value of benefits payable arising from an amendment to an existing plan. Such increases include, but are not limited to, a scheduled increase in benefits under a plan or plan amendment, such as a cost-of-living increase, and any change in plan provisions which advances a participant's or beneficiary's entitlement to a benefit, such as liberalized participation requirements or vesting schedules, reductions in the normal or early retirement age under a

plan, and changes in the form of benefit payments. In the case of a plan under which the amount of benefits depends on the participant's salary and the participant receives a salary increase the resulting increase in benefits to which the participant becomes entitled will not, for the purpose of this part, be treated as a benefit increase. Similarly, in the case of a plan under which the amount of benefits depends on the participant's age or service, and the participant becomes entitled to increased benefits solely because of advancement in age or service, the increased benefits to which the participant becomes entitled will not, for the purpose of this part, be treated as a benefit increase.

Covered employment means employment with respect to which benefits accrue under a plan.

Pension benefit means a benefit payable as an annuity, or one or more payments related thereto, to a participant who permanently leaves or has permanently left covered employment, or to a surviving beneficiary, which payments by themselves or in combination with Social Security, Railroad Retirement, or workmen's compensation benefits provide a substantially level income to the recipient.

Straight life annuity means a series of level periodic payments payable for the life of the recipient, but does not include any combined annuity form, including an annuity payable for a term certain and life.

[¶ 15,421B]

§4022.3 **Guaranteed benefits.** Except as otherwise provided in this part, the PBGC will guarantee the amount, as of the termination date, of a benefit provided under a plan to the extent that the benefit does not exceed the limitations in ERISA and in subpart B, if—

(a) The benefit is a nonforfeitable benefit;

(b) The benefit qualifies as a pension benefit as defined in §4022.2; and

(c) The participant is entitled to the benefit under §4022.4.

[¶ 15,421C]

§4022.4 **Entitlement to a benefit.** (a) A participant or his surviving beneficiary is entitled to a benefit if under the provisions of a plan:

(1) The benefit was in pay status on the date of the termination of the plan.

(2) A benefit payable at normal retirement age is an optional form of payment to the benefit otherwise payable at such age and the participant elected the benefit before the termination date of the plan.

(3) Except for a benefit described in paragraph (a)(2) of this section, before the termination date or on or before the termination date, in the case of a requirement that a participant attain a particular age, earn a particular amount of service, become disabled, or die the participant had satisfied the conditions of the plan necessary to estab-

lish the right to receive the benefit prior to such date prior to or on such date, in the case of a requirement that a participant attain a particular age, earn a particular amount of service, become disabled, or die other than application for the benefit, satisfaction of a waiting period described in the plan, or retirement; or [Amended by 67 FR 16949, April 8, 2002.]

(4) Absent an election by the participant, the benefit would be payable upon retirement.

(5) In the case of a benefit that returns all or a portion of a participant's accumulated mandatory employee contributions upon death, the participant (or beneficiary) had satisfied the conditions of the plan necessary to establish the right to the benefit other than death or designation of a beneficiary.

(b) If none of the conditions set forth in paragraph (a) of this section is met, the PBGC will determine whether the participant is entitled to a benefit on the basis of the provisions of the plan and the circumstances of the case.

[¶ 15,421D]

§ 4022.5 **Determination of nonforfeitable benefits**. (a) A guaranteed benefit payable to a surviving beneficiary is not considered to be forfeitable solely because the plan provides that the benefit will cease upon the remarriage of such beneficiary or his attaining a specified age. However, the PBGC will observe the provisions of the plan relating to the effect of such remarriage or attainment of such specified age on the surviving beneficiary's eligibility to continue to receive benefit payments.

(b) Any other provision in a plan that the right to a benefit in pay status will cease or be suspended upon the occurrence of any specified condition does not automatically make that benefit forfeitable. In each such case the PBGC will determine whether the benefit is forfeitable.

(c) A benefit guaranteed under § 4022.6 shall not be considered forfeitable solely because the plan provides that upon recovery of the participant the benefit will cease.

[¶ 15,421E]

§ 4022.6 **Annuity payable for total disability**. (a) Except as provided in paragraph (b) of this section, an annuity which is payable (or would be payable after a waiting period described in the plan, whether or not the participant is in receipt of other benefits during such waiting period), under the terms of a plan on account of the total and permanent disability of a participant which is expected to last for the life of the participant and which began on or before the termination date is considered to be a pension benefit. [Amended by 67 FR 16949, April 8, 2002.]

(b) In any case in which the PBGC determines that the standards for determining such total and permanent disability under a plan were unreasonable, or were modified in anticipation of termination of the plan, the disability benefits payable to a participant under such standard shall not be guaranteed unless the participant meets the standards of the Social Security Act and the regulations promulgated thereunder for determining total disability.

(c) For the purpose of this section, a participant may be required, upon the request of the PBGC, to submit to an examination or to submit proof of continued total and permanent disability. If the PBGC finds that a participant is no longer so disabled, it may suspend, modify, or discontinue the payment of the disability benefit.

[¶ 15,421F]

§ 4022.7 **Benefits payable in a single installment**. (a) *Alternative benefit*. If a benefit that is guaranteed under this part is payable in a single installment or substantially so under the terms of the plan, or an option elected under the plan by the participant, the benefit will not be guaranteed or paid as such, but the PBGC will guarantee the alternative benefit, if any, in the plan which provides for the payment of equal periodic installments for the life of the recipient. If the plan provides more than one such annuity, the recipient may within 30 days after notification of the proposed termination of the plan elect to receive one of those annuities. If the plan does not provide such an annuity, the PBGC will guarantee an actuarially equivalent life annuity.

(b)(1) *Payment in lump sum*. Notwithstanding paragraph (a) of this section:

(i) *In general*. If the lump sum value of a benefit (or of an estimated benefit) payable by the PBGC is $5,000 or less and the benefit is not yet in pay status, the benefit (or estimated benefit) may be paid in a lump sum.

(ii) *Annuity option*. If the PBGC would otherwise make a lump sum payment in accordance with paragraph (b)(1)(i) of this section and the monthly benefit (or the estimated monthly benefit) is equal to or greater than $25 (at normal retirement age and in the normal form for an unmarried participant), the PBGC will provide the option to receive the benefit in the form of an annuity.

(iii) *Election of QPSA lump sum*. If the lump sum value of annuity payments under a qualified preretirement survivor annuity (or under an estimated qualified preretirement survivor annuity) is $5,000 or less, the benefit is not yet in pay status, and the participant dies after the termination date, the benefit (or estimated benefit) may be paid in a lump sum if so elected by the surviving spouse.

(iv) *Payments to estates*. The PBGC may pay any annuity payments payable to an estate in a single installment without regard to the threshold in paragraph (b)(1)(i) of this section if so elected by the estate. The PBGC will discount the annuity payments using the federal mid-term rate (as determined by the Secretary of the Treasury pursuant to section 1274(d)(1)(C)(ii) of the Code) applicable for the month the participant died based on monthly compounding. [Amended by 67 FR 16949, April 8, 2002.]

(2) *Return of employee contributions—*

(i) *General*. Notwithstanding any other provision of this part, the PBGC may pay in a single installment (or a series of installments) instead of as an annuity, the value of the portion of an individual's basic-type benefit derived from mandatory employee contributions, if:

(A) The individual elects payment in a single installment (or a series of installments) before the sixty-first (61st) day after the date he or she receives notice that such an election is available; and

(B) Payment in a single installment (or a series of installments) is consistent with the plan's provisions. For purposes of this part, the portion of an individual's basic-type benefit derived from mandatory employee contributions is determined under § 4044.12 (priority category 2 benefits) of this chapter, and the value of that portion is computed under the applicable rules contained in part 4044, subpart B, of this chapter.

(ii) *Set-off for distributions after termination*. The amount to be returned under paragraph (b)(2)(i) of this section is reduced by the set-off amount. The set-off amount is the amount by which distributions made to the individual after the termination date exceed the amount that would have been distributed, exclusive of mandatory employee contributions, if the individual had withdrawn the mandatory employee contributions on the termination date.

Example: Participant A is receiving a benefit of $600 per month when the plan terminates, $200 of which is derived from mandatory employee contributions. If the participant had withdrawn his contributions on the termination date, his benefit would have been reduced to $400 per month. The participant receives two monthly payments after the termination date. The set-off amount is $400. (The $600 actual payment minus the $400 the participant would have received if he had withdrawn his contributions multiplied by the two months for which he received the extra payment.)

(c) *Death benefits—*

(1) *General*. Notwithstanding paragraph (a) of this section, a benefit that would otherwise be guaranteed under the provisions of this subpart, except for the fact that it is payable solely in a single installment (or substantially so) upon the death of a participant, shall be paid by the PBGC as an annuity that has the same value as the single installment. The PBGC will in each case determine the amount and duration of the annuity based on all the facts and circumstances.

(2) *Exception*. Upon the death of a participant the PBGC may pay in a single installment (or a series of installments) that portion of the participant's accumulated mandatory employee contributions that is

payable under the plan in a single installment (or a series of installments) upon the participant's death.

(d) *Determination of lump sum amount.* For purposes of paragraph (b)(1) of this section—

(1) *Benefits disregarded.* In determining whether the lump-sum value of a benefit is $5,000 or less, the PBGC may disregard the value of any benefits the plan or the PBGC previously paid in lump-sum form or the plan paid by purchasing an annuity contract, the value of any benefits returned under paragraph (b)(2) of this section, and the value of any benefits the PBGC has not yet determined under section 4022(c) of ERISA.

(2) *Actuarial assumptions.* The PBGC will calculate the lump sum value of a benefit by valuing the monthly annuity benefits payable in the form determined under §4044.51(a) of this chapter and commencing at the time determined under §4044.51(b) of this chapter. The actuarial assumptions used will be those described in §4044.52, except that—

(i) *Loading for expenses.* There will be no adjustment to reflect the loading for expenses;

(ii) *Mortality rates and interest assumptions.* The mortality rates in appendix A to this part and the interest assumptions in appendix B to this part will apply; and

(iii) *Date for determining lump sum value.* The date as of which a lump sum value is calculated is the termination date, except that in the case of a subsequent insufficiency it is the date described in section 4062(b)(1)(B) of ERISA. [Amended by 67 FR 16949, April 8, 2002.]

(3) *Date for determining lump sum value.* The date as of which a lump sum value is calculated is the termination date, except that in the case of a subsequent insufficiency it is the date described in section 4062(b)(1)(B) of ERISA. [Amended on 3/17/00 by 65 FR 14751.]

(e) *Publication of lump sum rates.* The PBGC will provide two sets of lump sum interest rates as follows—

(1) In appendix B to this part, the lump sum interest rates for PBGC payments, as provided under paragraph (d)(2) of this section; and

(2) In appendix C to this part, the lump sum interest rates for private-sector payments. [Added on 3/17/00 by 65 FR 14753.]

[¶ 15,421G]

§4022.8 Form of payment.

(a) *In general.* This section applies where benefits are not already in pay status. Except as provided in §4022.7 (relating to the payment of lump sums), the PBGC will pay benefits—

(1) In the automatic PBGC form described in paragraph (b) of this section; or

(2) If an optional PBGC form described in paragraph (c) of this section is elected, in that optional form.

(b) *Automatic PBGC form.*

(1) *Participants.*

(i) *Married participants.* The automatic PBGC form with respect to a participant who is married at the time the benefit enters pay status is the form a married participant would be entitled to receive from the plan in the absence of an election.

(ii) *Unmarried participants.* The automatic PBGC form with respect to a participant who is unmarried at the time the benefit enters pay status is the form an unmarried person would be entitled to receive from the plan in the absence of an election.

(2) *Beneficiaries.*

(i) *QPSA beneficiaries.* The automatic PBGC form with respect to the spouse of a married participant in a plan with a termination date on or after August 23, 1984, who dies before his or her benefit enters pay status is the qualified preretirement survivor annuity such a

spouse would be entitled to receive from the plan in the absence of an election. The PBGC will not charge the participant or beneficiary for this survivor benefit coverage for the time period beginning on the plan's termination date (regardless of whether the plan would have charged).

(ii) *Alternate payees.* The automatic PBGC form with respect to an alternate payee with a separate interest under a qualified domestic relations order is the form an unmarried participant would be entitled to receive from the plan in the absence of an election.

(c) *Optional PBGC forms.*

(1) *Participant and beneficiary elections.* A participant may elect any optional form described in paragraphs (c)(4) or (c)(5) of this section. A beneficiary described in paragraph (b)(2) of this section (a QPSA beneficiary or an alternate payee) may elect any optional form described in paragraphs (c)(4)(i) through (c)(4)(iv) of this section.

(2) *Permitted designees.* A participant or beneficiary, whether married or unmarried, who elects an optional form with a survivor feature (e.g., a 5-year certain-and-continuous annuity or, in the case of a participant, a joint-and-50%-survivor annuity) may designate either a spouse or a non-spouse beneficiary to receive survivor benefits. An optional joint-life form must be payable to a natural person or (with the consent of the PBGC) to a trust for the benefit of one or more natural persons.

(3) *Spousal consent.* In the case of a participant who is married at the time the benefit enters pay status, the election of an optional form or the designation of a non-spouse beneficiary is valid only if the participant's spouse consents.

(4) *Permitted optional single-life forms.* The PBGC may offer benefits in the following single-life forms:

(i) A straight-life annuity;

(ii) A 5-year certain-and-continuous annuity;

(iii) A 10-year certain-and-continuous annuity;

(iv) A 15-year certain-and-continuous annuity; and

(v) The form an unmarried person would be entitled to receive from the plan in the absence of an election.

(5) *Permitted optional joint-life forms.* The PBGC may offer benefits in the following joint-life forms:

(i) A joint-and-50%-survivor annuity;

(ii) A joint-and-50%-survivor- "pop-up" annuity (i.e., where the participant's benefit "pops up" to the unreduced level if the beneficiary dies first);

(iii) A joint-and-75%-survivor annuity; and

(iv) A joint-and-100%-survivor annuity.

(6) *Determination of benefit amount; starting benefit.* To determine the amount of the benefit in an optional PBGC form—

(i) *Single-life forms.* In the case of an optional PBGC form under paragraph (c)(4) of this section, the PBGC will first determine the amount of the benefit in the form the plan would pay to an unmarried participant in the absence of an election.

(ii) *Joint-life forms.* In the case of an optional PBGC form under paragraph (c)(5) of this section, the PBGC will first determine the amount of the benefit in the form the plan would pay to a married participant in the absence of an election. For this purpose, the PBGC will treat a participant who designates a non-spouse beneficiary as being married to a person who is the same age as that non-spouse beneficiary.

(7) *Determination of benefit amount; conversion factors.* The PBGC will convert the benefit amount determined under paragraph (c)(6) of this section to the optional form elected, using PBGC factors based on—

(i) *Mortality.* Unisex mortality rates that are a fixed blend of 50 percent of the male mortality rates and 50 percent of the female mortality rates from the 1983 Group Annuity Mortality Table as prescribed in Rev. Rul. 95-6, 1995-1 C.B. 80 (Internal Revenue Service

Cumulative Bulletins are available from the Superintendent of Documents, Government Printing Office, Washington, DC 20402); and

(ii) *Interest*. An interest rate of six percent.

(8) *Determination of benefit amount; limitation*. The PBGC will limit the benefit amount determined under paragraph (c)(7) of this section to the amount of the benefit it would pay in the form of a straight life annuity under paragraph (c)(4)(i) of this section.

(9) *Incidental benefits*. The PBGC will not pay an optional PBGC form with a death benefit (e.g., a joint-and-50%-survivor annuity) unless the death benefit would be an "incidental death benefit" under 26 CFR 1.401-1(b)(1)(i). If the death benefit would not be an "incidental death benefit," the PBGC may instead offer a modified version of the optional form under which the death benefit would be an "incidental death benefit."

(d) *Change in benefit form*. Once payment of a benefit starts, the benefit form cannot be changed.

(e) *PBGC discretion*. The PBGC may make other optional annuity forms available subject to the rules in paragraph (c) of this section.

[¶ 15,421H]
§ 4022.9 **Time of payment; benefit applications**.

(a) *Time of payment*. A participant may start receiving an annuity benefit from —the PBGC (subject to the PBGC's rules for starting benefit payments) on his or her Earliest PBGC Retirement Date as determined under § 4022.10 of this subchapter or, if later, the plan's termination date.

(b) *Elections and consents*. The PBGC may prescribe the time and manner for benefit elections to be made and spousal consents to be provided.

(c) *Benefit applications*. The PBGC is not required to accept any application for benefits not made in accordance with its forms and instructions.

(d) *Filing with the PBGC*—. (1) *Method and date of filing*. The PBGC applies the rules in subpart A of part 4000 of this chapter to determine permissible methods of filing with the PBGC under this part. Benefit applications and related submissions are treated as filed on the date received by the PBGC unless the instructions for the applicable form provide for an earlier date. Subpart C of part 4000 of this chapter provides rules for determining when the PBGC receives a submission.

(2) *Where to file*. See Sec. 4000.4 of this chapter for information on where to file.

(3) *Computation of time*. The PBGC applies the rules in subpart D of part 4000 of this chapter to compute any time period for filing under this part.

[Amended 10/28/2003 by 68 FR 61344]

[¶ 15,421I]
§ 4022.10 **Earliest PBGC Retirement Date.**

The Earliest PBGC Retirement Date for a participant is the earliest date on which the participant could retire under plan provisions for purposes of section 4044(a)(3)(B) of ERISA. The Earliest PBGC Retirement Date is determined in accordance with this § 4022.10. For purposes of this § 4022.10, "age" means the participant's age as of his or her last birthday (unless otherwise required by the context).

(a) *Immediate annuity at or after age 55*. If the earliest date on which a participant could separate from service with the right to receive an immediate annuity is on or after the date the participant reaches age 55, the Earliest PBGC Retirement Date for the participant is the earliest date on which the participant could separate from service with the right to receive an immediate annuity.

(b) *Immediate annuity before age 55*. If the earliest date on which a participant could separate from service with the right to receive an immediate annuity is before the date the participant reaches age 55, the Earliest PBGC Retirement Date for the participant is the date the participant reaches age 55 (except as provided in paragraph (c) of this section).

(c) *Facts and circumstances*. If a participant could separate from service with the right to receive an immediate annuity before the date the participant reaches age 55, the PBGC will make a determination, under the facts and circumstances, as to whether the participant could retire under plan provisions for purposes of section 4044(a)(3)(B) of ERISA on an earlier date. If the PBGC determines, under the facts and circumstances, that the participant could retire under plan provisions for those purposes on an earlier date, that earlier date is the Earliest PBGC Retirement Date for the participant. In making this determination, the PBGC will take into account plan provisions (e.g., the general structure of the provisions, the extent to which the benefit is subsidized, and whether eligibility for the benefit is based on a substantial service or age-and-service requirement), the age at which employees customarily retire (under the particular plan or in the particular company or industry, as appropriate), and all other relevant considerations. Neither a plan's reference to a separation from service at a particular age as a "retirement" nor the ability of a participant to receive an immediate annuity at a particular age necessarily makes the date the participant reaches that age the Earliest PBGC Retirement Date for the participant. The Earliest PBGC Retirement Date determined by the PBGC under this paragraph (c) will never be earlier than the earliest date the participant could separate from service with the right to receive an immediate annuity.

(d) *Examples*. The following examples illustrate the operation of the rules in paragraphs (a) through (c) of this section.

(1) *Normal retirement age*. A plan's normal retirement age is age 65. The plan does not offer a consensual lump sum or an immediate annuity upon separation before normal retirement age. The Earliest PBGC Retirement Date for a participant who, as of the plan's termination date, is age 50 is the date the participant reaches age 65.

(2) *Early retirement age*. A plan's normal retirement age is age 65. The plan specifies an early retirement age of 60 with 10 years of service. The plan does not offer a consensual lump sum or an immediate annuity upon separation before early retirement age. The Earliest PBGC Retirement Date for a participant who, as of the plan's termination date, is age 55 and has completed 10 years of service is the date the participant reaches age 60.

(3) *Separation at any age*. A plan's normal retirement age is age 65. The plan specifies an early retirement age of 60 but offers an immediate annuity upon separation regardless of age. The Earliest PBGC Retirement Date for a participant who, as of the plan's termination date, is age 35 is the date the participant reaches age 55, unless the PBGC determines under the facts and circumstances that the participant could "retire" for purposes of ERISA section 4044(a)(3)(B) on an earlier date, in which case the participant's Earliest PBGC Retirement Date would be that earlier date.

(4) *Age 50 retirement common*. A plan's normal retirement age is age 60. The plan specifies an early retirement age of 50 but offers an immediate annuity upon separation regardless of age. The Earliest PBGC Retirement Date for a participant who, as of the plan's termination date, is age 35 is the date the participant reaches age 55, unless the PBGC determines under the facts and circumstances that the participant could retire for purposes of ERISA section 4044(a)(3)(B) on an earlier date, in which case the Earliest PBGC Retirement Date would be that earlier date. For example, if it were common for participants to retire at age 50, the PBGC could determine that the participant's Earliest PBGC Retirement Date would be the date the participant reached age 50.

(5) *"30-and-out" benefit*. A plan's normal retirement age is age 65. The plan offers an immediate annuity upon separation regardless of age and a fully-subsidized annuity upon separation with 30 years of service. The Earliest PBGC Retirement Date for a participant who, as of the plan's termination date, is age 48 and has completed 30 years of service is the date the participant reaches age 55, unless the PBGC determines under the facts and circumstances that the participant could retire for purposes of ERISA section 4044(a)(3)(B) on an earlier date, in which case the participant's Earliest PBGC Retirement Date

would be that earlier date. In this example, the PBGC generally would determine under the facts and circumstances that the participant's Earliest PBGC Retirement Date is the date the participant completed 30 years of service.

(6) *Typical airline pilots' plan.* An airline pilots' plan has a normal retirement age of 60. The plan specifies an early retirement age of 50 (with 5 years of service). The Earliest PBGC Retirement Date for a participant who, as of the plan's termination date, is age 48 and has completed five years of service would be the date the participant reaches age 55, unless the PBGC determines under the facts and circumstances that the participant could retire for purposes of ERISA section 4044(a)(3)(B) on an earlier date, in which case the participant's Earliest PBGC Retirement Date would be that earlier date. In this example, the PBGC generally would determine under the facts and circumstances that the participant's Earliest PBGC Retirement Date is the date the participant reaches age 50. If the plan instead had provided for early retirement before age 50, the PBGC would consider all the facts and circumstances (including the plan's normal retirement age and the age at which employees customarily retire in the airline industry) in determining whether to treat the date the participant reaches the plan's early retirement age as the participant's Earliest PBGC Retirement Date.

(e) *Special rule for "window" provisions.* For purposes of paragraphs (a), (b), and (c) of this section, the PBGC will treat a participant as being able, under plan provisions, to separate from service with the right to receive an immediate annuity on a date before the plan's termination date only if—

(1) Eligibility for that immediate annuity continues through the earlier of—

(i) The plan's termination date; or

(ii) The date the participant actually separates from service with the right to receive an immediate annuity; and

(2) The participant satisfies the conditions for eligibility for that immediate annuity on or before the plan's termination date.

Subpart B—Limitations on Guaranteed Benefits

[¶ 15,422]

§ 4022.21 **Limitations; in general**. (a)(1) Subject to paragraphs (b), (c) and (d) of this section, the PBGC will not guarantee that part of an installment payment that exceeds the dollar amount payable as a straight life annuity commencing at normal retirement age, or thereafter, to which a participant would have been entitled under the provisions of the plan in effect on the termination date, on the basis of his credited service to such date. If the plan does not provide a straight life annuity either as its normal form of retirement benefit or as an option to the normal form, the PBGC will for purposes of this paragraph convert the plan's normal form benefit to a straight life annuity of equal actuarial value as determined by the PBGC.

(2) The limitation of paragraph (a)(1) of this section shall not apply to:

(i) A survivor's benefit payable as an annuity on account of the death of a participant that occurred on or before the plan's termination date and before the participant retired; [Amended by 67 FR 16949, April 8, 2002.]

(ii) A disability pension described in section 4022.6 of this part; or

(iii) A benefit payable in non-level installments that in combination with Social Security, Railroad Retirement, or workman's compensation benefits yields a substantially level income if the projected income from the plan benefit over the expected life of the recipient does not exceed the value of the straight life annuity described in paragraph (a)(1) of this section.

(b) The PBGC will not guarantee the payment of that part of any benefit that exceeds the limitations in section 4022(b) of ERISA and this subpart B.

(c)(1) Except as provided in paragraph (c)(2) of this section, the PBGC does not guarantee a benefit payable in a single installment (or substantially so) upon the death of a participant or his surviving beneficiary unless that benefit is substantially derived from a reduction in the pension benefit payable to the participant or surviving beneficiary.

(2) Paragraphs (a) and (c)(1) of this section do not apply to that portion of accumulated mandatory employee contributions payable under a plan upon the death of a participant, and such a benefit is a pension benefit for purposes of this part.

(d) The PBGC will not guarantee a joint-life annuity benefit payable to other than—

(1) Natural persons; or

(2) A trust or estate for the benefit of one or more natural persons. [Amended by 67 FR 16949, April 8, 2002.]

[¶ 15,422A]

§ 4022.22 **Maximum guaranteeable benefit**. Subject to section 4022B of ERISA and part 4022B of this chapter, benefits payable with respect to a participant under a plan shall be guaranteed only to the extent that such benefits do not exceed the actuarial value of a benefit in the form of a life annuity payable in monthly installments, commencing at age 65 equal to the lesser of the amounts computed in paragraphs (a) and (b) of this section.

(a) One-twelfth of the participant's average annual gross income from his employer during either his highest-paid five consecutive calendar years in which he was an active participant under the plan, or if he was not an active participant throughout the entire such period, the lesser number of calendar years within that period in which he was an active participant under the plan.

(1) As used in this paragraph, "gross income" means "earned income" as defined in section 911(b) of the Code, determined without regard to any community property laws.

(2) For the purposes of this paragraph, if the plan is one to which more than one employer contributes, and during any calendar year the participant received gross income from more than one such contributing employer, then the amounts so received shall be aggregated in determining the participant's gross income for the calendar year.

(b) $750 multiplied by the fraction x/$13,200 where "x" is the Social Security contribution and benefit base determined under section 230 of the Social Security Act in effect at the termination date of the plan.

[¶ 15,422B]

§ 4022.23 **Computation of maximum guaranteeable benefits**. (a) *General.* Where a benefit is payable in any manner other than as a monthly benefit payable for life commencing at age 65, the maximum guaranteeable monthly amount of such benefit shall be computed by applying the applicable factor or factors set forth in paragraphs (c)-(e) of this section to the monthly amount computed under § 4022.22. In the case of a step-down life annuity, the maximum guaranteeable monthly amount of such benefit shall be computed in accordance with paragraph (f) of this section.

(b) *Application of adjustment factors to monthly amount computed under § 4022.22.* (1) Each percentage increase or decrease computed under paragraphs (c), (d), and (e) of this section shall be added to or subtracted from a base of 1.00, and the resulting amounts shall be multiplied.

(2) The monthly amount computed under § 4022.22 shall be multiplied by the product computed pursuant to paragraph (b)(1) of this section in order to determine the participant's and/or beneficiary's maximum benefit guaranteeable.

(c) *Annuitant's age factor.* If a participant or the beneficiary of a deceased participant is entitled to and chooses to receive his benefit at an age younger than 65, the monthly amount computed under § 4022.22 shall be reduced by the following amounts for each month up to the number of whole months below age 65 that corresponds to the later of the participant's age at the termination date or his age at the time he begins to receive the benefit: For each of the 60 months immediately preceding the 65th birthday, the reduction shall be 7/12 of 1%; For each of the 60 months immediately preceding the 60th birthday, the reduction shall be 4/12 of 1%; For each of the 120 months immediately preceding the 55th birthday, the reduction shall be 2/12 of 1%; and For each succeeding 120 months period, the monthly percentage reduction shall be 1/2 of that used for the preceding 120 month period.

(d) *Factor for benefit payable in a form other than as a life annuity.* When a benefit is in a form other than a life annuity payable in monthly installments, the monthly amount computed under §4022.22 shall be adjusted by the appropriate factors on a case-by-case basis by PBGC. This paragraph sets forth the adjustment factors to be used for several common benefit forms payable in monthly installments.

(1) *Period certain and continuous annuity.* A period certain and continuous annuity means an annuity which is payable in periodic installments for the participant's life, but for not less than a specified period of time whether or not the participant dies during that period. The monthly amount of a period certain and continuous annuity computed under §4022.22 shall be reduced by the following amounts for each month of the period certain subsequent to the termination date:

For each month up to 60 months deduct 1/24 of 1%;

For each month beyond 60 months deduct 1/12 of 1%.

(i) A cash refund annuity means an annuity under which if the participant dies prior to the time when he has received pension payments equal to a fixed sum specified in the plan, then the balance is paid as a lump-sum death benefit. A cash refund annuity shall be treated as a benefit payable for a period certain and continuous. The period of certainty shall be computed by dividing the amount of the lump-sum refund by the monthly amount to which the participant is entitled under the terms of the plan.

(ii) An installment refund annuity means an annuity under which if the participant dies prior to the time he has received pension payments equal to a fixed sum specified in the plan, then the balance is paid as a death benefit in periodic installments equal in amount to the participant's periodic benefit. An installment refund annuity shall be treated as a benefit payable for a period certain and continuous. The period of certainty shall be computed by dividing the amount of the remaining refund by the monthly amount to which the participant is entitled under the terms of the plan.

(2) *Joint and survivor annuity (contingent basis).* A joint and survivor annuity (contingent basis) means an annuity which is payable in periodic installments to a participant for his life and upon his death is payable to his beneficiary for the beneficiary's life in the same or in a reduced amount. The monthly amount of a joint and survivor annuity

(contingent basis) computed under §4022.22 shall be reduced by an amount equal to 10% plus 2/10 of 1% for each percentage point in excess of 50% of the participant's benefit that will continue to be paid to the beneficiary. If the benefit payable to the beneficiary is less than 50 percent of the participant's benefit, PBGC shall provide the adjustment factors to be used.

(3) *Joint and survivor annuity (joint basis).* A joint and survivor annuity (joint basis) means an annuity which is payable in periodic installments to a participant and upon his death or the death of his beneficiary is payable to the survivor for the survivor's life in the same or in a reduced amount. The monthly amount of a joint and survivor annuity (joint basis) computed under §4022.22 shall be reduced by an amount equal to 4/10 of 1% for each percentage point in excess of 50% of the participant's original benefit that will continue to be paid to the survivor. If the benefit payable to the survivor is less than 50 percent of the participant's original benefit, PBGC shall provide the adjustment factors to be used.

(e) When a benefit is payable in a form described in paragraph (d) (2) or (3) of this section, and the beneficiary's age is different from the participant's age, by 15 years or less, the monthly amount computed under §4022.22 shall be adjusted by the following amounts: If the beneficiary is younger than the participant, deduct 1% for each year of the age difference; If the beneficiary is older than the participant, add 1/2 of 1% for each year of the age difference. In computing the difference in ages, years over 65 years of age shall not be counted. If the difference in age between the beneficiary and the participant is greater than 15 years, PBGC shall provide the adjustment factors to be used.

(f) *Step-down life annuity.* A step-down life annuity means an annuity payable in a certain amount for the life of the participant plus a temporary additional amount payable until the participant attains an age specified in the plan.

(1) The temporary additional amount payable under a step-down life annuity shall be converted to a life annuity payable in monthly installments by multiplying the appropriate factor based on the participant's age and the number of remaining years of the temporary additional benefit by the amount of the temporary additional benefit. The factors to be used are set forth in the table below. The amount of the monthly benefit so calculated shall be added to the level amount of the monthly benefit payable for life to determine the level-life annuity that is equivalent to the step-down life annuity.

Factors for Converting Temporary Additional Benefit Under Step-Down Life Annuity

Age of participant[1] at the later of the date the temporary additional benefit commences or the date of plan termination	Number of years temporary additional benefit is payable under the plan as of the date of plan termination[2]									
	1	2	3	4	5	6	7	8	9	10
45	0.060	0.117	0.170	0.220	0.268	0.315	0.355	0.395	0.435	0.475
46	.061	.119	.173	.224	.273	.321	.362	.403	.444	.485
47	.062	.121	.176	.228	.278	.327	.369	.411	.453	.495
48	.063	.123	.179	.232	.283	.333	.376	.419	.462	.505
49	.064	.125	.182	.236	.288	.339	.383	.427	.471	.515
50	.065	.127	.185	.240	.293	.345	.390	.435	.480	.525
51	.066	.129	.188	.244	.298	.351	.397	.443	.489	.535
52	.067	.131	.191	.248	.303	.357	.404	.451	.498	.545
53	.068	.133	.194	.252	.308	.363	.411	.459	.507	.555
54	.069	.135	.197	.256	.313	.369	.418	.467	.516	.565
55	.070	.137	.200	.260	.318	.375	.425	.475	.525	.575
56	.072	.141	.206	.268	.328	.387	.439	.491	.543	...
57	.074	.145	.212	.276	.338	.399	.453	.507	...	...
58	.076	.149	.218	.284	.348	.411	.467	...	...	...
59	.078	153	.224	.292	.358	.423	...	...	...	...
60	.080	.157	.230	.300	.368	...	...	...	...	...
61	.082	.161	.236	.308	...	...	...	...	...	...
62	.084	.165	.242	...						

Age of participant[1] at the later of the date the temporary additional benefit commences or the date of plan termination	Number of years temporary additional benefit is payable under the plan as of the date of plan termination[2]									
	1	2	3	4	5	6	7	8	9	10
63	.086	.169	...	...	...	...	...	...	...	...
64	.088	...	...	...	...	...	...	...	...	...

[1] Age of participant is his age at his last birthday.

[2] If the benefit is payable for less than 1 yr, the appropriate factor is obtained by multiplying the factor for 1 yr by a fraction, the numerator of which is the number of months the benefit is payable, and the denominator of which is 12. If the benefit is payable for 1 or more whole years, plus an additional number of months less than 12, the appropriate factor is obtained by linear interpolation between the factor for the number of whole years the benefit is payable and the factor for the next year.

(2) If a participant is entitled to and chooses to receive a step-down life annuity at an age younger than 65, the monthly amount computed under §4022.22 shall be adjusted by applying the factors set forth in paragraph (c) of this section in the manner described in paragraph (b) of this section.

(3) If the level-life monthly benefit calculated pursuant to paragraph (f)(1) of this section exceeds the monthly amount calculated pursuant to paragraph (f)(2) of this section, then the monthly maximum benefit guaranteeable shall be a step-down life annuity under which the monthly amount of the temporary additional benefit and the amount of the monthly benefit payable for life, respectively, shall bear the same ratio to the monthly amount of the temporary additional benefit and the monthly benefit payable for life provided under the plan, respectively, as the monthly benefit calculated pursuant to paragraph (f)(2) of this section bears to the monthly benefit calculated pursuant to paragraph (f)(1) of this section.

[¶ 15,422C]

§4022.24 **Benefit increases**. (a) *Scope*. This section applies:

(1) To all benefit increases, as defined in §4022.2, payable with respect to a participant other than a substantial owner, which have been in effect for less than five years preceding the termination date; and

(2) To all benefit increases payable with respect to a substantial owner, which have been in effect for less than 30 years preceding the termination date.

(b) *General rule*. Benefit increases described in paragraph (a) of this section shall be guaranteed only to the extent provided in §4022.25 with respect to a participant other than a substantial owner and in §4022.26 with respect to a participant who is a substantial owner.

(c) *Computation of guaranteeable benefit increases*. Except as provided in paragraph (d) of this section pertaining to multiple benefit increases, the amount of a guaranteeable benefit increase shall be the amount, if any, by which the monthly benefit calculated pursuant to paragraph (c)(1) of this section (the monthly benefit provided under the terms of the plan as of the termination date, as limited by §4022.22) exceeds the monthly benefit calculated pursuant to paragraph (c)(4) of this section (the monthly benefit which would have been payable on the termination date if the benefit provided subsequent to the increase were equivalent, as of the date of the increase, to the benefit provided prior to the increase).

(1) Determine the amount of the monthly benefit payable on the termination date (or, in the case of a deferred benefit, the monthly benefit which will become payable thereafter) under the terms of the plan subsequent to the increase, using service credited to the participant as of the termination date, that is guaranteeable pursuant to §4022.22;

(2) Determine, as of the date of the benefit increase, in accordance with the provisions of §4022.23, the factors which would be used to calculate the monthly maximum benefit guaranteeable (i) under the terms of the plan prior to the increase and (ii) under the terms of the plan subsequent to the increase. However, when the benefit referred to in paragraph (c)(2)(ii) of this section is a joint and survivor benefit deferred as of the termination date and there is no beneficiary on that date, the factors computed in paragraph (c)(2)(ii) of this section shall be determined as if the benefit were payable only to the participant.

Each set of factors determined under this paragraph shall be stated in the manner set forth in §4022.23(b)(1);

(3) Multiply the monthly benefit which would have been payable (or, in the case of a deferred benefit, would have become payable) under the terms of the plan prior to the increase based on service credited to the participant as of the termination date by a fraction, the numerator of which is the product of the factors computed pursuant to paragraph (c)(2)(ii) of this section and the denominator of which is the product of the factors computed pursuant to paragraph (c)(2)(i) of this section.

(4) Calculate the amount of the monthly benefit which would be payable on the termination date if the monthly benefit computed in paragraph (c)(3) of this section had been payable commencing on the date of the benefit increase (or, in the case of a deferred benefit, would have become payable thereafter.) In the case of a benefit which does not become payable until subsequent to the termination date, the amount of the monthly benefit determined pursuant to this paragraph is the same as the amount of the monthly benefit calculated pursuant to paragraph (c)(3) of this section.

(d) *Multiple benefit increases.* (1) Where there has been more than one benefit increase described in paragraph (a) of this section, the amounts of guaranteeable benefit increases shall be calculated beginning with the earliest increase, and each such amount (except for the amount resulting from the final benefit increase) shall be multiplied by a fraction, the numerator of which is the product of the factors, stated in the manner set forth in §4022.23(b)(1), used to calculate the monthly maximum guaranteeable benefit under §4022.22 and the denominator of which is the product of the factors used in the calculation under paragraph (c)(2)(i) of this section.

(2) Each benefit increase shall be treated separately for the purposes of §4022.25, except as otherwise provided in paragraph (d) of that section, and for the purposes of §4022.26, as appropriate.

(e) For the purposes of §§4022.22 through 4022.27, a benefit increase is deemed to be in effect commencing on the later of its adoption date or its effective date. [Corrected 12/30/97 by 62 FR 67728.]

[¶ 15,422D]

§4022.25 **Five-year phase-in of benefit guarantee for participants other than substantial owners**. (a) *Scope.* This section applies to the guarantee of benefit increases which have been in effect for less than five years with respect to participants other than substantial owners.

(b) *Phase-in formula.* The amount of a benefit increase computed pursuant to §4022.24 shall be guaranteed to the extent provided in the following formula: the number of years the benefit increase has been in effect, not to exceed five, multiplied by the greater of (1) 20 percent of the amount computed pursuant to §4022.24; or (2) $20 per month.

(c) *Computation of years.* In computing the number of years a benefit increase has been in effect, each complete 12-month period ending on or before the termination date during which such benefit increase was in effect constitutes one year. [Amended by 67 FR 16949, April 8, 2002.]

(d) *Multiple benefit increases.* In applying the formula contained in paragraph (b) of this section, multiple benefit increases within any 12-month period ending on or before the termination date and calculated from that date are aggregated and treated as one benefit increase. [Amended by 67 FR 16949, April 8, 2002.]

(e) Notwithstanding the provisions of paragraph (b) of this section, a benefit increase described in paragraph (a) of this section shall be guaranteed only if PBGC determines that the plan was terminated for a reasonable business purpose and not for the purpose of obtaining the payment of benefits by PBGC.

[¶ 15,422E]

§ 4022.26 **Phase-in of benefit guarantee for participants who are substantial owners.** (a) *Scope.* This section shall apply to the guarantee of all benefits described in subpart A (subject to the limitations in § 4022.21) with respect to participants who are substantial owners at the termination date or who were substantial owners at any time within the 5-year period preceding that date. [Corrected 12/30/97 by 62 FR 67728.]

(b) *Phase-in formula when there have been no benefit increases.* Benefits provided by a plan under which there has been no benefit increase, other than the adoption of the plan, shall be guaranteed to the extent provided in the following formula: The monthly amount computed under § 4022.22 multiplied by a fraction not to exceed 1, the numerator of which is the number of full years prior to the termination date that the substantial owner was an active participant under the plan, and the denominator of which is 30. Active participation under a plan commences at the later of the date on which the plan is adopted or becomes effective.

(c) *Phase-in formula when there have been benefit increases.* If there has been a benefit increase under the plan, other than the adoption of the plan, benefits provided by each such increase shall be guaranteed to the extent provided in the following formula: The amount of the guaranteeable benefit increase computed under § 4022.24 multiplied by a fraction not to exceed 1, the numerator of which is the number of full years prior to the termination date that the benefit increase was in effect and during which the substantial owner was an active participant under the plan, and the denominator of which is 30. However, in no event shall the total benefits guaranteed under all such benefit increases exceed the benefits which are guaranteed under paragraph (b) of this section with respect to a plan described therein.

(d) For the purpose of computing the benefits guaranteed under this section, in the case of a substantial owner who becomes an active participant under a plan after a benefit increase (other than the adoption of the plan) has been put into effect, the plan as it exists at the time he commences his participation shall be deemed to be the original plan with respect to him.

[¶ 15,422F]

§ 4022.27 **Effect of tax disqualification.** (a) *General rule.* Except as provided in paragraph (b) of this section, benefits accrued under a plan after the date on which the Secretary of the Treasury or his delegate issues a notice that any trust which is part of the plan no longer meets the requirements of section 401(a) of the Code or that the plan no longer meets the requirements of section 404(a) of the Code or after the date of adoption of a plan amendment that causes the issuance of such a notice shall not be guaranteed under this part.

(b) *Exceptions.* The restriction on the guarantee of benefits set forth in paragraph (a) of this section shall not apply if:

(1) The Secretary of the Treasury or his delegate issues a notice stating that the original notice referred to in paragraph (a) of this section was erroneous;

(2) The Secretary of the Treasury or his delegate finds that, subsequent to the issuance of the notice referred to in paragraph (a) of this section, appropriate action has been taken with respect to the trust or plan to cause it to meet the requirements of sections 401(a) or 404(a)(2) of the Code, respectively, and issues a subsequent notice stating that the trust or plan meets such requirements; or

(3) The plan amendment is revoked retroactively to its original effective date.

Subpart C—Calculation and Payment of Unfunded Nonguaranteed Benefits [Reserved].

[¶ 15,422G]
Subpart D—Benefit Reductions in Terminating Plans

[¶ 15,423]

§ 4022.61 **Limitations on benefit payments by plan administrator.** (a) *General.* When section 4041.42 of this chapter requires a plan administrator to reduce benefits, the plan administrator shall limit benefit payments in accordance with this section. [Amended 11/7/97 by 62 FR 60424. Generally, for fully-funded, single-employer pension plans which issued their first notice of intent to terminate before January 1, 1998, an unamended regulation applies. The paragraph previously read: (a) General. When section 4041.4 of this chapter requires a plan administrator to reduce benefits, the plan administrator shall limit benefit payments in accordance with this section.]

(b) *Accrued benefit at normal retirement.* Except to the extent permitted by paragraph (d) of this section, a plan administrator may not pay that portion of a monthly benefit payable with respect to any participant that exceeds the participant's accrued benefit payable at normal retirement age under the plan. For the purpose of applying this limitation, post-retirement benefit increases, such as cost-of-living adjustments, are not considered to increase a participant's benefit beyond his or her accrued benefit payable at normal retirement age.

(c) *Maximum guaranteeable benefit.* Except to the extent permitted by paragraph (d) of this section, a plan administrator may not pay that portion of a monthly benefit payable with respect to any participant, as limited by paragraph (b) of this section, that exceeds the maximum guaranteeable benefit under section 4022(b)(3)(B) of ERISA and § 4022.22(b) of this part, adjusted for age and benefit form, for the year of the proposed termination date.

(d) *Estimated benefit payments.* A plan administrator shall pay the monthly benefit payable with respect to each participant as determined under § 4022.62 or § 4022.63, whichever produces the higher benefit.

(e) *PBGC authority to modify procedures.* In order to avoid abuse of the plan termination insurance system, inequitable treatment of participants and beneficiaries, or the imposition of unreasonable burdens on terminating plans, the PBGC may authorize or direct the use of alternative procedures for determining benefit reductions.

(f) *Examples.* This section is illustrated by the following examples:

Example 1— Facts. On October 10, 1992, a plan administrator files with the PBGC a notice of intent to terminate in a distress termination that includes December 31, 1992, as the proposed termination date. A participant who is in pay status on December 31, 1992, has been receiving his accrued benefit of $2,500 per month under the plan. The benefit is in the form of a joint and survivor annuity (contingent basis) that will pay 50 percent of the participant's benefit amount (i.e., $1,250 per month) to his surviving spouse following the death of the participant. On December 31, 1992, the participant is age 66, and his wife is age 56.

Benefit reductions. Paragraph (b) of this section requires the plan administrator to cease paying benefits in excess of the accrued benefit payable at normal retirement age. Because the participant is receiving only his accrued benefit, no reduction is required under paragraph (b).

Paragraph (c) of this section requires the plan administrator to cease paying benefits in excess of the maximum guaranteeable benefit, adjusted for age and benefit form in accordance with the provisions of subpart B. The maximum guaranteeable benefit for plans terminating in 1992, the year of the proposed termination date, is $2,352.27 per month, payable in the form of a single life annuity at age 65. Because the participant is older than age 65, no adjustment is required under § 4022.23(c) based on the annuitant's age factor. The benefit form is a joint and survivor annuity (contingent basis), as defined in § 4022.23(d)(2). The required benefit reduction for this benefit form under § 4022.23(d) is 10 percent. The corresponding adjustment factor is 0.90 (1.00 – 0.10). The benefit reduction factor to adjust for the age difference between the participant and the beneficiary is computed under § 4022.23(e). In computing the difference in ages, years over 65 years of age are not taken into account. Therefore, the age difference is

9 years (65 – 56). The required percentage reduction when the beneficiary is 9 years younger than the participant is 9 percent. The corresponding adjustment factor is 0.91 (1.00 – 0.09).

The maximum guaranteeable benefit adjusted for age and benefit form is $1,926.51 ($2,352.27 × 0.90 × 0.91) per month. Therefore, the plan administrator must reduce the participant's benefit payment from $2,500 to $1,926.51. If the participant dies after December 31, 1992, the plan administrator will pay his spouse $963.26 (0.50 × $1,926.51) per month.

Example 2— Facts. The benefit of a participant who retired under a plan at age 60 is a reduced single life annuity of $400 per month plus a temporary supplement of $400 per month payable until age 62 (i.e., a step-down benefit). The participant's accrued benefit under the plan is $450 per month, payable from the plan's normal retirement age. On the proposed termination date, June 30, 1992, the participant is 61 years old.

The maximum guaranteeable benefit adjusted for age under § 4022.23(c) of this chapter is $1,693.63 ($2,352.27 × 0.72) per month. Since the benefit is payable as a single life annuity, no adjustment is required under § 4022.23(d) for benefit form.

Benefit reductions. The plan benefit of $800 per month payable until age 62 exceeds the participant's accrued benefit at normal requirement age of $450 per month. Paragraph (b) of this section requires that, except to the extent permitted by paragraph (d), the plan benefit must be reduced to $450 per month. Since the levelized benefit of $404.10 ((0.082 × 50) + $400) per month, determined under § 4022.23(f), is less than the adjusted maximum guaranteeable benefit of $1,693.63 per month, no further reduction in the $450 per month benefit payment is required under paragraph (c) of this section. The plan administrator next would determine the amount of the participant's estimated benefit under paragraph (d).

Example 3— Facts. A retired participant is receiving a reduced early retirement benefit of $1,100 per month plus a temporary supplement of $700 per month payable until age 62. The benefit is in the form of a single life annuity. On the proposed termination date, November 30, 1992, the participant is 56 years old.

The participant's accrued benefit at normal retirement age under the plan is $1,200 per month. The maximum guaranteeable benefit adjusted for age is $1,152.61 ($2,352.27 × 0.49) per month. A form adjustment is not required.

Benefit reductions. The plan benefit of $1,800 per month payable from age 56 to age 62 exceeds the participant's accrued benefit at normal retirement age of $1,200 per month. Therefore, under paragraph (b) of this section, the plan administrator must reduce the temporary supplement to $100 per month.

For the purpose of determining whether the reduced benefit, i.e., a level-life annuity of $1,100 per month and a temporary annuity supplement of $100 per month to age 62, exceeds the maximum guaranteeable benefit adjusted for age, the temporary annuity supplement of $100 per month is converted to a level-life annuity equivalent in accordance with § 4022.23(f) of this chapter. The level-life annuity equivalent is $38.70 ($100 × 0.387). This, added to the life annuity of $1,100 per month, equals $1,138.70. Since the maximum guaranteeable benefit of $1,152.61 per month exceeds $1,138.70 per month, no further reduction is required under paragraph (c) of this section.

The plan administrator next would determine the participant's estimated benefit under paragraph (d). Assume that the estimated benefit under paragraph (d) is $780 per month until age 62 and $715 per month thereafter. The plan administrator would pay the participant $780 per month, reduced to $715 per month at age 62, subject to the final benefit determination made under title IV.

Example 4— Facts. A retired participant is receiving a reduced early retirement benefit of $2,650 per month plus a temporary supplement of $800 per month payable until age 62. The benefit is in the form of a joint and survivor annuity (contingent basis) that will pay 50 percent of the participant's benefit amount to his surviving spouse following the death of the participant. On the proposed termination date, December 20, 1992, the participant and his spouse are each 56 years old.

The participant's accrued benefit at normal retirement age under the plan is $3,000 per month. The maximum guaranteeable benefit adjusted for age and the joint and survivor annuity (contingent basis) annuity form is $1,037.35 per month. An adjustment for age difference is not required because the participant and his spouse are the same age.

Benefit reductions. The plan benefit of $3,450 per month payable from age 56 to age 62 exceeds the participant's accrued benefit at normal retirement age, which is $3,000 per month. Therefore, under paragraph (b) of this section, the plan administrator must reduce the participant's benefit so that it does not exceed $3,000 per month.

The level-life equivalent of the participant's reduced benefit, determined using the § 4022.23(f) adjustment factor, is $2,785.45 (($350 × 0.387) + $2,650) per month. Since this benefit exceeds the participant's maximum guaranteeable benefit of $1,037.35 per month, the plan administrator must reduce the participant's benefit payment so that it does not exceed the maximum guaranteeable benefit.

The ratio of (i) the participant's maximum guaranteeable benefit to (ii) the level-life equivalent of the participant's reduced benefit (computed under the "accrued for normal retirement age" limitation) is used in converting the level-life maximum guaranteeable benefit to the step-down benefit form. The level-life equivalent of the reduced benefit computed under the "accrued for normal retirement age" limitation is 37.24 percent ($1,037.35/$2,785.45). Thus, the plan administrator must reduce the participant's level-life benefit of $2,650 per month to $986.86 ($2,650 x 0.3724) and must further reduce the reduced temporary benefit of $350 per month to $130.34 ($350 × 0.3724). Under paragraph (c) of this section, therefore, the participant's maximum guaranteeable benefit is $1,117.20 ($986.86 + $130.34) per month to age 62 and $986.86 per month thereafter, subject to any adjustment under paragraph (d) of this section.

Assume that the estimated benefit under paragraph (d) is $1,005.48 per month to age 62 and $888.17 per month thereafter. The plan administrator would reduce the participant's benefit from $3,450 per month to $1,005.48 per month and pay this amount until age 62, at which time the benefit payment would be reduced to $888.17 per month, subject to the final benefit determination made under title IV.

[¶ 15,423A]

§ 4022.62 **Estimated guaranteed benefit**. (a) *General.* The estimated guaranteed benefit payable with respect to each participant who is not a substantial owner is computed under paragraph (c) of this section. The estimated guaranteed benefit payable with respect to each participant who is a substantial owner is computed under paragraph (d) of this section.

(b) *Rules for determining benefits.* For the purposes of determining entitlement to a benefit and the amount of the estimated benefit under this section, the following rules apply:

(1) *Participants in pay status on the proposed termination date.* For benefits payable with respect to a participant who is in pay status on or before the proposed termination date, the plan administrator shall use the participant's age and benefit payable under the plan as of the proposed termination date.

(2) *Participants who enter pay status after the proposed termination date.* For benefits payable with respect to a participant who enters pay status after the proposed termination date, the plan administrator shall use the participant's age as of the benefit commencement date and his or her service and compensation as of the proposed termination date.

(3) *Participants with new benefits or benefit improvements.* For the purpose of determining the estimated guaranteed benefit under paragraph (c) of this section, only new benefits and benefit improvements that affect the benefit of the participant or beneficiary for whom the determination is made are taken into account.

(4) *Limitations on estimated guaranteed benefits.* For the purpose of determining the estimated guaranteed benefit under paragraph (c) or (d) of this section, the benefit determined under paragraph (b)(1) or (b)(2) of this section is subject to the limitations set forth in § 4022.61(b) and (c).

(c) *Estimated guaranteed benefit payable with respect to a participant who is not a substantial owner.* For benefits payable with respect to a participant who is not a substantial owner, the estimated guaranteed benefit is determined under paragraph (c)(1) of this section, if no portion of the benefit is subject to the phase-in of plan termination insurance guarantees set forth in section 4022(b)(1) of ERISA. In any other case, the estimated guaranteed benefit is determined under paragraph (c)(2). "Benefit subject to phase-in" means a benefit that is subject to the phase-in of plan termination insurance guarantees set forth in section 4022(b)(1) of ERISA, determined without regard to section 4022(b)(7) of ERISA.

(1) *Participants with no benefits subject to phase-in.* In the case of a participant or beneficiary with no benefit improvement (as defined in paragraph (c)(2)(ii)) or new benefit (as defined in paragraph (c)(2)(i)) in the five years preceding the proposed termination date, the estimated guaranteed benefit is the benefit to which he or she is entitled under the rules in paragraph (b) of this section.

(2) *Participants with benefits subject to phase-in.* In the case of a participant or beneficiary with a benefit improvement or new benefit in the five years preceding the proposed termination date, the estimated guaranteed benefit is the benefit to which he or she is entitled under the rules in paragraph (b) of this section, multiplied by the multiplier determined according to paragraphs (i), (ii), and (iii), but not less than the benefit to which he or she would have been entitled if the benefit improvement or new benefit had not been adopted.

(i) From column (a) of Table I, select the line that applies according to the number of full years before the proposed termination date since the plan was last amended to provide for a new benefit (or the number of full years since the plan was established, if it has never been amended to provide for a new benefit). "New benefit" means a change in the terms of the plan that results in (a) a participant's or a beneficiary's eligibility for a benefit that was not previously available or to which he or she was not entitled (excluding a benefit that is actuarially equivalent to the normal retirement benefit to which the participant was previously entitled) or (b) an increase of more than twenty percent in the benefit to which a participant is entitled upon entering pay status before his or her normal retirement age under the plan. "New benefits" result from liberalized participation or vesting requirements, reductions in the age or service requirements for receiving unreduced benefits, additions of actuarially subsidized benefits, and increases in actuarial subsidies. The establishment of a plan creates a new benefit as of the effective date of the plan. A change in the amount of a benefit is not deemed to be a "new benefit" if it results solely from a benefit improvement. "New benefit" and "benefit improvement" are mutually exclusive terms.

(ii) If there was no benefit improvement under the plan during the one-year period ending on the proposed termination date, use the multiplier set forth in column (b) of Table I on the line selected from column (a). "Benefit improvement" means a change in the terms of the plan that results in (a) an increase in the benefit to which a participant is entitled at his or her normal retirement age under the plan or (b) an increase in the benefit to which a participant or beneficiary in pay status is entitled.

(iii) If there was any benefit improvement during the one-year period ending on the proposed termination date, use the multiplier set forth in column (c) of Table I on the line selected from column (a).

TABLE I.—APPLICABLE MULTIPLIER IF—

Full years since last new benefit (a)	No benefit improvement during last year (b)	Benefit improvement during last year (c)
Five or more	.90	.80
Four	.80	.70
Three	.65	.55
Two	.50	.45

Full years since last new benefit (a)	No benefit improvement during last year (b)	Benefit improvement during last year (c)
Fewer than two	.35	.30

Note: The foregoing method of estimating guaranteed benefits is based upon the PBGC's experience with a wide range of plans and may not provide accurate estimates in certain circumstances. In accordance with §4022.61(e), a plan administrator may use a different method of estimation if he or she demonstrates to the PBGC that his proposed method will be more equitable to participants and beneficiaries. The PBGC may require the use of a different method in certain cases.

(d) *Estimated guaranteed benefit payable with respect to a substantial owner.* For benefits payable with respect to each participant who is a substantial owner and who commenced participation under the plan fewer than five full years before the proposed termination date, the estimated guaranteed benefit is determined under paragraph (d)(1). With respect to any other substantial owner, the estimated guaranteed benefit is determined under paragraph (d)(2).

(1) *Fewer than five years of participation.* The estimated guaranteed benefit under this paragraph is the benefit to which the substantial owner is entitled, as determined under paragraph (b) of this section, multiplied by a fraction, not to exceed one, the numerator of which is the number of full years prior to the proposed termination date that the substantial owner was an active participant under the plan and the denominator of which is thirty.

(2) *Five or more years of participation.* The estimated guaranteed benefit under this paragraph is the lesser of—

(i) the estimated guaranteed benefit calculated under paragraph (d)(1) of this section; or

(ii) the benefit to which the substantial owner would have been entitled as of the proposed termination date (or benefit commencement date in the case of a substantial owner whose benefit commences after the proposed termination date) under the terms of the plan in effect when he or she first began participation, as limited by §4022.61 (b) and (c), multiplied by a fraction, not to exceed one, the numerator of which is two times the number of full years of his or her active participation under the plan prior to the proposed termination date and the denominator of which is thirty.

(e) *Examples.* This section is illustrated by the following examples:

Example 1— Facts. A participant who is not a substantial owner retired on December 31, 1991, at age 60 and began receiving a benefit of $600 per month. On January 1, 1989, the plan had been amended to allow participants to retire with unreduced benefits at age 60. Previously, a participant who retired before age 65 was subject to a reduction of 1/15 for each year by which his or her actual retirement age preceded age 65. On January 1, 1992, the plan's benefit formula was amended to increase benefits for participants who retired before January 1, 1992. As a result, the participant's benefit was increased to $750 per month. There have been no other pertinent amendments. The proposed termination date is December 15, 1992.

Estimated guaranteed benefit. No reduction is required under §4022.61(b) or (c) because the participant's benefit does not exceed either the participant's accrued benefit at normal retirement age or the maximum guaranteeable benefit. (Post-retirement benefit increases are not considered as increasing accrued benefits payable at normal retirement age.)

The amendment as of January 1, 1989, resulted in a "new benefit" because the reduction in the age at which the participant could receive unreduced benefits increased the participant's benefit entitlement at actual retirement age by 5/15, which is more than a 20 percent increase. The amendment of January 1, 1992, which increased the participant's benefit to $750 per month, is a "benefit improvement" because it is an increase in the amount of benefit for persons in pay status. (No percentage test applies in determining whether such an increase is a benefit improvement.)

The multiplier for computing the amount of the estimated guaranteed benefit is taken from the third row of Table I (because the last new benefit had been in effect for 3 full years as of the proposed termination date) and column (c) (because there was a benefit improvement within the 1-year period preceding the proposed termination date). This multiplier is 0.55. Therefore, the amount of the participant's estimated guaranteed benefit is $412.50 (0.55 × $750) per month.

Example 2— Facts. A participant who is not a substantial owner terminated employment on December 31, 1990. On January 1, 1992, she reached age 65 and began receiving a benefit or $250 per month. She had completed 3 years of service at her termination of employment and was fully vested in her accrued benefit. The plan's vesting schedule had been amended on July 1, 1988. Under the schedule in effect before the amendment, a participant with 5 years of service was 100 percent vested. There have been no other pertinent amendments. The proposed termination date is December 31, 1992.

Estimated guaranteed benefit. No reduction is required under §4022.61(b) or (c) because the participant's benefit does not exceed either her accrued benefit at normal retirement age or the maximum guaranteeable benefit. The plan's change of vesting schedule created a new benefit for the participant. Because the amendment was in effect for 4 full years before the proposed termination date, the second row of Table I is used to determine the applicable multiplier for estimating the amount of the participant's guaranteed benefit. Because the participant did not receive any benefit improvement during the 12-month period ending on the proposed termination date, column (b) of the table is used. Therefore, the multiplier is 0.80, and the amount of the participant's estimated guaranteed benefit is $200 (0.80 × $250) per month.

Example 3— Facts. A participant who is a substantial owner retired prior to the proposed termination date after 5 1/2 years of active participation in the plan. The benefit under the terms of the plan when he first began active participation was $800 per month. On the proposed termination date of April 30, 1992, he was entitled to receive a benefit of $2000 per month. No reduction of this benefit is required under §4022.61(b) or (c).

Estimated guaranteed benefit. Paragraph (d)(2) of this section is used to compute the amount of the estimated guaranteed benefit of substantial owners with 5 or more years of active participation prior to the proposed termination date. Consequently, the amount of this participant's estimated guaranteed benefit is the lesser of—

(i) the amount calculated as if he had been an active participant in the plan for fewer than 5 full years on the proposed termination date, or $333.33 ($2000 × 5/30) per month, or

(ii) the amount to which he would have been entitled as of the proposed termination date under the terms of the plan when he first began participation, as limited by §4022.61(b) and (c), multiplied by 2 times the number of years of active participation and divided by 30, or $266.67 ($800 × 2 × 5/30) per month. Therefore, the amount of the participant's estimated guaranteed benefit is $266.67 per month.

[¶ 15,423B]

§4022.63 **Estimated title IV benefit**. (a) *General*. If the conditions specified in paragraph (b) exist, the plan administrator shall determine each participant's estimated title IV benefit. The estimated title IV benefit payable with respect to each participant who is not a substantial owner is computed under paragraph (c) of this section. The estimated title IV benefit payable with respect to each participant who is a substantial owner is computed under paragraph (d) of this section.

(b) *Conditions for use of this section.* The conditions set forth in this paragraph must be satisfied in order to make use of the procedures set forth in this section. If the specified conditions exist, estimated title IV benefits must be determined in accordance with these procedures (or in accordance with alternative procedures authorized by the PBGC under §4022.61(f)) for each participant and beneficiary whose benefit under the plan exceeds the limitations contained in §4022.61(b) or (c) or who is a substantial owner or the beneficiary of a substantial owner. If the specified conditions do not exist, title IV benefits may be estimated by the plan administrator in accordance with procedures authorized by the PBGC, but no such estimate is required. The conditions are as follows:

(1) An actuarial valuation of the plan has been performed for a plan year beginning not more than eighteen months before the proposed termination date. If the interest rate used to value plan liabilities in this valuation exceeded the applicable valuation interest rates and

factors under appendix B to part 4044 of this chapter in effect on the proposed termination date, the value of benefits in pay status and the value of vested benefits not in pay status on the valuation date must be converted to the PBGC's valuation rates and factors.

(2) The plan has been in effect for at least five full years before the proposed termination date, and the most recent actuarial valuation demonstrates that the value of plan assets, reduced by employee contributions remaining in the plan and interest credited thereon under the terms of the plan, exceeds the present value, adjusted as required under paragraph (b)(1), of all plan benefits in pay status on the valuation date.

(c) *Estimated title IV benefit payable with respect to a participant who is not a substantial owner.* For benefits payable with respect to a participant who is not a substantial owner, the estimated title IV benefit is the estimated priority category 3 benefit computed under this paragraph. Priority category 3 benefits are payable with respect to participants who were, or could have been, in pay status three full years prior to the proposed termination date. The estimated priority category 3 benefit is computed by multiplying the benefit payable with respect to the participant under §4022.62(b)(1) and (b)(2) by a fraction, not to exceed one—

(1) The numerator of which is the benefit that would be payable with respect to the participant at normal retirement age under the provisions of the plan in effect on the date five full years before the proposed termination date, based on the participant's age, service, and compensation as of the earlier of the participant's benefit commencement date or the proposed termination date, and

(2) The denominator of which is the benefit that would be payable with respect to the participant at normal retirement age under the provisions of the plan in effect on the proposed termination date, based on the participant's age, service, and compensation as of the earlier of the participant's benefit commencement date or the proposed termination date.

(d) *Estimated title IV benefit payable with respect to a substantial owner.* For benefits payable with respect to a participant who is a substantial owner, the estimated title IV benefit is the higher of the benefit computed under paragraph (c) of this section or the benefit computed under this paragraph.

(1) The plan administrator shall first calculate the estimated guaranteed benefit payable with respect to the substantial owner as if he or she were not a substantial owner, using the method set forth in §4022.62(c).

(2) The benefit computed under paragraph (d)(1) shall be multiplied by the priority category 4 funding ratio. The category 4 funding ratio is the ratio of x to y, not to exceed one, where—

(i) in a plan with priority category 3 benefits, x equals plan assets minus employee contributions remaining in the plan on the valuation date, with interest credited thereon under the terms of the plan, and the present value of benefits in pay status, and y equals the present value of all vested benefits not in pay status minus such employee contributions and interest; or

(ii) in a plan with no priority category 3 benefits, x equals plan assets minus employee contributions remaining in the plan on the valuation date, with interest credited thereon under the terms of the plan, and y equals the present value of all vested benefits minus such employee contributions and interest.

(e) *Examples.* This section is illustrated by the following examples:

Example 1— Facts. A participant who is not a substantial owner was eligible to retire 3 1/2 years before the proposed termination date. The participant retired 2 years before the proposed termination date with 20 years of service. Her final 5 years' average salary was $45,000, and she was entitled to an unreduced early retirement benefit of $1,500 per month payable as a single life annuity. This retirement benefit does not exceed the limitation in §4022.61(b) or (c).

On the participant's benefit commencement date, the plan provided for a normal retirement benefit of 2 percent of the final 5 years' salary times the number of years of service. Five years before the proposed termination date, the percentage was 1 1/2 percent. The amendments improving benefits were put into effect 3 1/2 years prior to the proposed termination date. There were no other amendments during the 5-year period.

The participant's estimated guaranteed benefit computed under § 4022.62(c) is $1,500 per month times 0.90 (the factor from column (b) of Table I in § 4022.62(c)(2)), or $1,350 per month. It is assumed that the plan meets the conditions set forth in paragraph (b) of this section, and the plan administrator is therefore required to estimate the title IV benefit.

Estimated title IV benefit. For a participant who is not a substantial owner, the amount of the estimated title IV benefit is the estimated priority category 3 benefit computed under paragraph (c) of this section. This amount is computed by multiplying the participant's benefit under the plan as of the later of the proposed termination date or the benefit commencement date by the ratio of (i) the normal retirement benefit under the provisions of the plan in effect 5 years before the proposed termination date and (ii) the normal retirement benefit under the plan provisions in effect on the proposed termination date.

Thus, the numerator of the ratio is the benefit that would be payable to the participant under the normal retirement provisions of the plan 5 years before the proposed termination date, based on her age, service, and compensation on her benefit commencement date. The denominator of the ratio is the benefit that would be payable to the participant under the normal retirement provisions of the plan in effect on the proposed termination date, based on her age, service, and compensation as of the earlier of her benefit commencement date or the proposed termination date. Since the only different factor in the numerator and denominator is the salary percentage, the amount of the estimated title IV benefit is $1,125 (0.015/0.020 × $1,500) per month. This amount is less than the estimated guaranteed benefit of $1,350 per month. Therefore, in accordance with § 4022.61(d), the benefit payable to the participant is $1,350 per month.

Example 2— Facts. A participant who is a substantial owner retires at the plan's normal retirement age, having completed 5 years of active participation in the plan, on October 31, 1992, which is the proposed termination date. Under provisions of the plan in effect 5 years prior to the proposed termination date, the participant is entitled to a single life annuity of $500 per month. Under the most recent plan amendments, which were put into effect 1 1/2 years prior to the proposed termination date, the participant is entitled to a single life annuity of $1,000 per month. The participant's estimated guaranteed benefit computed under § 4022.62(d)(2) is $166.67 per month.

It is assumed that all of the conditions in paragraph (b) of this section have been met. Plan assets equal $2 million. The present value of all benefits in pay status is $1.5 million based on applicable PBGC interest rates. There are no employee contributions and the present value of all vested benefits that are not in pay status is $0.75 million based on applicable PBGC interest rates.

Estimated title IV benefit. Paragraph (d) of this section provides that the amount of the estimated title IV benefit payable with respect to a participant who is a substantial owner is the higher of the estimated priority category 3 benefit computed under paragraph (c) of this section or the estimated priority category 4 benefit computed under paragraph (d) of this section.

Under paragraph (c), the participant's estimated priority category 3 benefit is $500 ($1,000 × $500/$1000) per month.

Under paragraph (d), the participant's estimated priority category 4 benefit is the estimated guaranteed benefit computed under § 4022.62(c) (i.e., as if the participant were not a substantial owner) multiplied by the priority category 4 funding ratio. Since the plan has priority category 3 benefits, the ratio is determined under paragraph (d)(2)(i). The numerator of the ratio is plan assets minus the present value of benefits in pay status. The denominator of the ratio is the present value of all vested benefits that are not in pay status. The participant's estimated guaranteed benefit under § 4022.62(c) is $1,000 per month times 0.90 (the factor from column (b) of Table I in § 4022.62(c)(2)), or $900 per month. Multiplying $900 by the category 4 funding ratio of 2/3 (($2 million—$1.5 million)/$0.75 million) produces an estimated category 4 benefit of $600 per month.

Because the estimated category 4 benefit so computed is greater than the estimated category 3 benefit so computed, the estimated category 4 benefit is the estimated title IV benefit. Because the estimated category 4 benefit so computed is greater than the estimated

guaranteed benefit of $166.67 per month, in accordance with § 4022.61(d), the benefit payable to the participant is the estimated category 4 benefit of $600 per month.

Subpart E—PBGC Recoupment and Reimbursement of Benefit Overpayments and Underpayments

[¶ 15,424]

§ 4022.81 **General rules.** (a) *Recoupment of benefit overpayments.* If at any time the PBGC determines that net benefits paid with respect to any participant in a PBGC-trusteed plan exceed the total amount to which the participant (and any beneficiary) is entitled up to that time under title IV of ERISA, and the participant (or beneficiary) is, as of the termination date, entitled to receive future benefit payments, the PBGC will recoup the net overpayment in accordance with paragraph (c) of this section and § 4022.82. Notwithstanding the previous sentence, the PBGC may, in its discretion, recover overpayments by methods other than recouping in accordance with the rules in this subpart. The PBGC will not normally do so unless net benefits paid after the termination date exceed those to which a participant (and any beneficiary) is entitled under the terms of the plan before any reductions under subpart D.

(b) *Reimbursement of benefit underpayments.* If at any time the PBGC determines that net benefits paid with respect to a participant in a PBGC-trusteed plan are less than the amount to which the participant (and any beneficiary) is entitled up to that time under title IV of ERISA, the PBGC will reimburse the participant or beneficiary for the net underpayment in accordance with paragraphs (c) and (d) of this section and § 4022.83.

(c) *Amount to be recouped or reimbursed.* In order to determine the amount to be recouped from, or reimbursed to, a participant (or beneficiary), the PBGC will calculate a monthly account balance for each month ending after the termination date. The PBGC will start with a balance of zero as of the end of the calendar month ending immediately prior to the termination date and determine the account balance as of the end of each month thereafter as follows:

(1) *Debit for overpayments.* the PBGC will subtract from the account balance the amount of overpayments made in that month. Only overpayments made on or after the latest of the proposed termination date, the termination date, or, if no notice of intent to terminate was issued, the date on which proceedings to terminate the plan are instituted pursuant to section 4042 of ERISA will be included.

(2) *Credit for underpayments.* The PBGC will add to the account balance the amount of underpayments made in that month. Only underpayments made on or after the termination date will be included.

(3) *Credit for interest on net underpayments.* If at the end of a month there is a positive account balance (a net underpayment), the PBGC will add to the account balance interest thereon for that month using—

(i) For months after May 1998, the applicable federal mid-term rate (as determined by the Secretary of the Treasury pursuant to section 1274(d)(1)(c)(ii) of the Code) for that month (or, where the rate for a month is not available at the time the PBGC calculates the amount to be recouped or reimbursed, the most recent month for which the rate is available) based on monthly compounding; and

(ii) For May 1998 and earlier months, the immediate annuity rate established for lump sum valuations as set forth in Table II of Appendix B of part 4044 of this chapter.

(4) *No interest on net overpayments.* If at the end of the month, there is a negative account balance (a net overpayment), there will be no interest adjustment for that month.

(d) *Death of participant.* (1) *Benefit overpayments.* If the PBGC determines that, at the time of a participant's death, there was a net overpayment to the participant—

(i) *Future annuity payments.* If the participant was entitled to future annuity payments as of the plan's termination date, the PBGC will (except as provided in paragraph (a) of this section) recoup the overpayment from the person (if any) who is receiving survivor benefits under the annuity.

(ii) *No future annuity payments.* If the participant was not entitled to future annuity benefits as of the plan's termination date, the PBGC may seek repayment of the overpayment from the participant's estate.

(2) *Benefit underpayments.* If the PBGC determines that, at the time of a participant's death, there was a net underpayment to the participant—

(i) *Future annuity payments.* If the benefit is in the form of a joint-and-survivor or other annuity under which payments may continue after the participant's death, the PBGC will pay the underpayment to the person who is receiving survivor benefits; for this purpose, if the person receiving survivor benefits is an alternate payee under a qualified domestic relations order, the PBGC will treat the benefit as if payments do not continue after the participant's death (see paragraph (d)(2)(ii) of this section).

(ii) *No future annuity payments.* If the benefit is not in the form of a joint-and-survivor or other annuity (e.g., a certain-and-continuous annuity) under which payments may continue after the participant's death or although the benefit is in such a form payments do not continue after the participant's death (i.e., in the case of a joint-and-survivor annuity, the person designated to receive survivor benefits predeceased the participant or, in the case of another annuity under which payments may continue after the participant's death the participant died with no payments owed for future periods), the PBGC will pay the underpayment to the person determined under the rules in §§ 4022.91 through 4022.95. [Added by 67 FR 16949, April 8, 2002.]

[¶ 15,424A]

§ 4022.82 **Method of recoupment.** (a) *Future benefit reductions.* The PBGC will recoup net overpayments of benefits by reducing the amount of each future benefit payment to which the participant or any beneficiary is entitled by the fraction determined under paragraphs (a)(1) and (a)(2) of this section, except that benefit reduction will cease when the amount (without interest) of the net overpayment is recouped. Notwithstanding the preceding sentence, the PBGC may accept repayment ahead of the recoupment schedule.

(1) *Computation.* The PBGC will determine the fractional multiplier by dividing the amount of the net overpayment by the present value of the benefit payable with respect to the participant under title IV of ERISA. The PBGC will determine the present value of the benefit to which a participant or beneficiary is entitled under title IV of ERISA as of the termination date, using the PBGC interest rates and factors in effect on that date. The PBGC may, however, utilize a different date of determination if warranted by the facts and circumstances of a particular case.

(2) *Limitation on benefit reduction.* Except as provided in paragraph (a)(1) of this section, the PBGC will reduce benefits with respect to a participant or beneficiary by no more than the greater of—

(i) ten percent per month; or

(ii) the amount of benefit per month in excess of the maximum guaranteeable benefit payable under section 4022(b)(3)(B) of ERISA, determined without adjustment for age and benefit form.

(3) *PBGC notice to participant or beneficiary.* Before effecting a benefit reduction pursuant to this paragraph, the PBGC will notify the participant or beneficiary in writing of the amount of the net overpayment and of the amount of the reduced benefit computed under this section.

(4) *Waiver of de minimis amounts.* The PBGC may, in its discretion, decide not to recoup net overpayments that it determines to be de minimis.

(5) *Final installment.* The PBGC will cease recoupment one month early if the amount remaining to be recouped in the final month is less than the amount of the monthly reduction.

(b) *Full repayment through repayment.* Recoupment under this section constitutes full repayment of the net overpayment.

[¶ 15,424B]

§ 4022.83 **PBGC reimbursement of benefit underpayments.** When the PBGC determines that there has been a net benefit underpayment made with respect to a participant, it shall pay the participant or beneficiary the amount of the net underpayment, determined in accordance with § 4022.81(c), in a single payment.

[¶ 15,424C]

§ 4022.83 **Appendix A to Part 4022: Lump Sum Mortality Rates.**

Age x	q_x	Age x	q_x	Age x	q_x	Age x	q_x
12	0.000000	36	0.001513	60	0.014162	84	0.112816
13	0.000000	37	0.001643	61	0.015509	85	0.122079
14	0.000000	38	0.001792	62	0.017010	86	0.132174
15	0.000000	39	0.001948	63	0.018685	87	0.143179
16	0.001437	40	0.002125	64	0.020517	88	0.155147
17	0.001414	41	0.002327	65	0.022562	89	0.168208
18	0.001385	42	0.002556	66	0.024847	90	0.182461
19	0.001351	43	0.002818	67	0.027232	91	0.198030
20	0.001311	44	0.003095	68	0.029634	92	0.215035
21	0.001267	45	0.003410	69	0.032073	93	0.232983
22	0.001219	46	0.003769	70	0.034743	94	0.252545
23	0.001167	47	0.004180	71	0.037667	95	0.273878
24	0.001149	48	0.004635	72	0.040871	96	0.297152
25	0.001129	49	0.005103	73	0.044504	97	0.322553
26	0.001107	50	0.005616	74	0.048504	98	0.349505
27	0.001083	51	0.006196	75	0.052913	99	0.378865
28	0.001058	52	0.006853	76	0.057775	100	0.410875
29	0.001083	53	0.007543	77	0.063142	101	0.445768
30	0.001111	54	0.008278	78	0.068628	102	0.483830
31	0.001141	55	0.009033	79	0.074648	103	0.524301
32	0.001173	56	0.009875	80	0.081256	104	0.568365
33	0.001208	57	0.010814	81	0.088518	105	0.616382
34	0.001297	58	0.011863	82	0.096218	106	0.668696
35	0.001398	59	0.012952	83	0.104310	107	0.725745

Age x	q_x	Age x	q_x	Age x	q_x
108	0.786495	109	0.852659	110	0.924666
				111	1.000000

[Amended 3/17/2000 by 65 FR 14753.]

[¶ 15,424D]

§ 4022.83 **Appendix B to Part 4022: Lump Sum Interest Rates for PBGC Payments.**

[In using this table: (1) For benefits for which the participant or beneficiary is entitled to be in pay status on the valuation date, the immediate annuity rate shall apply; (2) For benefits for which the deferral period is y years (where y is an integer and $0 < y$ [is less than or equal to] n_1), interest rate i_1 shall apply from the valuation date for a period of y years; thereafter the immediate annuity rate shall apply; (3) For benefits for which the deferral period is y years (where y is an integer and $n_1 < y$ [is less than or equal to] $n_1 + n_2$); interest rate i_2 shall apply from the valuation date for a period of $y - n_1$ years, interest rate i_1 shall apply for the following n_1 years; thereafter the immediate annuity rate shall apply; (4) For benefits for which the deferral period is y years (where y is an integer and $y < n_1 + n_2$), interest rate i_3 shall apply from the valuation date for a period of $y - n_1 - n_2$ years; interest rate i_2 shall apply for the following n_2 years; interest rate i_1 shall apply for the following n_1 years; thereafter the immediate annuity rate shall apply.] [Amended 3/17/00 by 65 FR 14751, 14753.]

Rate set	For plans with a valuation date		Immediate annuity rate (percent)	Deferred annuities (percent)				
	On or After	Before		i_1	i_2	i_3	n_1	n_2
1	11-1-93	12-1-93	4.25	4.00	4.00	4.00	7	8
2	12-1-93	1-1-94	4.25	4.00	4.00	4.00	7	8
3	1-1-94	2-1-94	4.50	4.00	4.00	4.00	7	8
4	2-1-94	3-1-94	4.50	4.00	4.00	4.00	7	8
5	3-1-94	4-1-94	4.50	4.00	4.00	4.00	7	8
6	4-1-94	5-1-94	4.75	4.00	4.00	4.00	7	8
7	5-1-94	6-1-94	5.25	4.50	4.00	4.00	7	8
8	6-1-94	7-1-94	5.25	4.50	4.00	4.00	7	8
9	7-1-94	8-1-94	5.50	4.75	4.00	4.00	7	8
10	8-1-94	9-1-94	5.75	5.00	4.00	4.00	7	8

Rate set	For plans with a valuation date		Immediate annuity rate (percent)	Deferred annuities (percent)				
	On or After	Before		i_1	i_2	i_3	n_1	n_2
11	9-1-94	10-1-94	5.50	4.75	4.00	4.00	7	8
12	10-1-94	11-1-94	5.50	4.75	4.00	4.00	7	8
13	11-1-94	12-1-94	6.00	5.25	4.00	4.00	7	8
14	12-1-94	1-1-95	6.25	5.50	4.25	4.00	7	8
15	1-1-95	2-1-95	6.00	5.25	4.00	4.00	7	8
16	2-1-95	3-1-95	6.00	5.25	4.00	4.00	7	8
17	3-1-95	4-1-95	6.00	5.25	4.00	4.00	7	8
18	4-1-95	5-1-95	5.75	5.00	4.00	4.00	7	8
19	5-1-95	6-1-95	5.50	4.75	4.00	4.00	7	8
20	6-1-95	7-1-95	5.50	4.75	4.00	4.00	7	8

Rate set	For plans with a valuation date		Immediate annuity rate (percent)	Deferred annuities (percent)				
	On or After	Before		i_1	i_2	i_3	n_1	n_2
21	7-1-95	8-1-95	4.75	4.00	4.00	4.00	7	8
22	8-1-95	9-1-95	4.75	4.00	4.00	4.00	7	8
23	9-1-95	10-1-95	5.00	4.25	4.00	4.00	7	8
24	10-1-95	11-1-95	4.75	4.00	4.00	4.00	7	8
25	11-1-95	12-1-95	4.75	4.00	4.00	4.00	7	8
26	12-1-95	1-1-96	4.50	4.00	4.00	4.00	7	8
27	1-1-96	2-1-96	4.50	4.00	4.00	4.00	7	8
28	2-1-96	3-1-96	4.25	4.00	4.00	4.00	7	8
29	3-1-96	4-1-96	4.25	4.00	4.00	4.00	7	8
30	4-1-96	5-1-96	4.75	4.00	4.00	4.00	7	8

Rate set	For plans with a valuation date		Immediate annuity rate (percent)	Deferred annuities (percent)				
	On or After	Before		i_1	i_2	i_3	n_1	n_2
31	5-1-96	6-1-96	5.00	4.25	4.00	4.00	7	8
32	6-1-96	7-1-96	5.00	4.25	4.00	4.00	7	8
33	7-1-96	8-1-96	5.00	4.25	4.00	4.00	7	8
34	8-1-96	9-1-96	5.25	4.50	4.00	4.00	7	8
35	9-1-96	10-1-96	5.25	4.50	4.00	4.00	7	8
36	10-1-96	11-1-96	5.25	4.50	4.00	4.00	7	8
37	11-1-96	12-1-96	5.00	4.25	4.00	4.00	7	8
38	12-1-96	1-1-97	4.75	4.00	4.00	4.00	7	8
39	1-1-97	2-1-97	4.50	4.00	4.00	4.00	7	8
40	2-1-97	3-1-97	4.75	4.00	4.00	4.00	7	8

Rate set	For plans with a valuation date		Immediate annuity rate (percent)	Deferred annuities (percent)				
	On or After	Before		i_1	i_2	i_3	n_1	n_2
41	3-1-97	4-1-97	5.00	4.25	4.00	4.00	7	8
42	4-1-97	5-1-97	4.75	4.00	4.00	4.00	7	8
43	5-1-97	6-1-97	5.00	4.25	4.00	4.00	7	8
44	6-1-97	7-1-97	5.25	4.50	4.00	4.00	7	8
45	7-1-97	8-1-97	5.25	4.50	4.00	4.00	7	8
46	8-1-97	9-1-97	4.75	4.00	4.00	4.00	7	8
47	9-1-97	10-1-97	4.50	4.00	4.00	4.00	7	8
48	10-1-97	11-1-97	4.75	4.00	4.00	4.00	7	8
49	11-1-97	12-1-97	4.50	4.00	4.00	4.00	7	8
50	12-1-97	1-1-98	4.50	4.00	4.00	4.00	7	8

Rate set	For plans with a valuation date		Immediate annuity rate (percent)	Deferred annuities (percent)				
	On or After	Before		i_1	i_2	i_3	n_1	n_2
51	1-1-98	2-1-98	4.25	4.00	4.00	4.00	7	8
52	2-1-98	3-1-98	4.25	4.00	4.00	4.00	7	8
53	3-1-98	4-1-98	4.25	4.00	4.00	4.00	7	8
54	4-1-98	5-1-98	4.25	4.00	4.00	4.00	7	8
55	5-1-98	6-1-98	4.25	4.00	4.00	4.00	7	8
56	6-1-98	7-1-98	4.25	4.00	4.00	4.00	7	8
57	7-1-98	8-1-98	4.00	4.00	4.00	4.00	7	8
58	8-1-98	9-1-98	4.00	4.00	4.00	4.00	7	8
59	9-1-98	10-1-98	4.00	4.00	4.00	4.00	7	8
60	10-1-98	11-1-98	4.00	4.00	4.00	4.00	7	8

Rate set	For plans with a valuation date		Immediate annuity rate (percent)	Deferred annuities (percent)				
	On or After	Before		i_1	i_2	i_3	n_1	n_2
61	11-1-98	12-1-98	3.75	4.00	4.00	4.00	7	8
62	12-1-98	1-1-99	4.00	4.00	4.00	4.00	7	8
63	1-1-99	2-1-99	4.00	4.00	4.00	4.00	7	8
64	2-1-99	3-1-99	4.00	4.00	4.00	4.00	7	8
65	3-1-99	4-1-99	4.00	4.00	4.00	4.00	7	8
66	4-1-99	5-1-99	4.25	4.00	4.00	4.00	7	8
67	5-1-99	6-1-99	4.25	4.00	4.00	4.00	7	8
68	6-1-99	7-1-99	4.25	4.00	4.00	4.00	7	8
69	7-1-99	8-1-99	4.50	4.00	4.00	4.00	7	8
70	8-1-99	9-1-99	5.00	4.25	4.00	4.00	7	8

Rate set	For plans with a valuation date		Immediate annuity rate (percent)	Deferred annuities (percent)				
	On or After	Before		i_1	i_2	i_3	n_1	n_2
71	9-1-99	10-1-99	5.00	4.25	4.00	4.00	7	8
72	10-1-99	11-1-99	5.00	4.25	4.00	4.00	7	8
73	11-1-99	12-1-99	5.00	4.25	4.00	4.00	7	8
74	12-1-99	1-1-00	5.25	4.50	4.00	4.00	7	8
75	1-1-00	2-1-00	5.00	4.25	4.00	4.00	7	8
76	2-1-00	3-1-00	5.25	4.50	4.00	4.00	7	8
77	3-1-00	4-1-00	5.25	4.50	4.00	4.00	7	8
78	4-1-00	5-1-00	5.25	4.50	4.00	4.00	7	8
79	5-1-00	6-1-00	5.25	4.50	4.00	4.00	7	8
80	6-1-00	7-1-00	5.25	4.50	4.00	4.00	7	8

Rate set	For plans with a valuation date		Immediate annuity rate (percent)	Deferred annuities (percent)				
	On or After	Before		i_1	i_2	i_3	n_1	n_2
81	7-1-00	8-1-00	5.50	4.75	4.00	4.00	7	8
82[1]	8-1-00	9-1-00	5.25	4.50	4.00	4.00	7	8
83[2]	9-1-00	10-1-00	5.25	4.50	4.00	4.00	7	8
84[3]	10-1-00	11-1-00	5.00	4.25	4.00	4.00	7	8
85[4]	11-1-00	12-1-00	5.25	4.50	4.00	4.00	7	8
86[5]	12-1-00	1-1-01	5.25	4.50	4.00	4.00	7	8
87[6]	1-1-01	2-1-01	5.00	4.25	4.00	4.00	7	8
88[7]	2-1-01	3-1-01	4.75	4.00	4.00	4.00	7	8
89[8]	3-1-01	4-1-01	4.75	4.00	4.00	4.00	7	8
90[9]	4-1-01	5-1-01	4.75	4.00	4.00	4.00	7	8

Rate set	For plans with a valuation date		Immediate annuity rate (percent)	Deferred annuities (percent)				
	On or After	Before		i_1	i_2	i_3	n_1	n_2
91[10]	5-1-01	6-1-01	4.75	4.00	4.00	4.00	7	8
92[11]	6-1-01	7-1-01	5.00	4.25	4.00	4.00	7	8
93[12]	7-1-01	8-1-01	5.00	4.25	4.00	4.00	7	8
94[13]	8-1-01	9-1-01	4.75	4.00	4.00	4.00	7	8
95[14]	9-1-01	10-1-01	4.50	4.00	4.00	4.00	7	8
96[15]	10-1-01	11-1-01	4.50	4.00	4.00	4.00	7	8
97[16]	11-1-01	12-1-01	4.75	4.00	4.00	4.00	7	8
98[17]	12-1-01	1-1-02	4.50	4.00	4.00	4.00	7	8
100[19]	2-1-02	3-1-02	4.75	4.00	4.00	4.00	7	8

Rate set	For plans with a valuation date		Immediate annuity rate (percent)	Deferred annuities (percent)				
	On or After	Before		i_1	i_2	i_3	n_1	n_2
101[20]	3-1-02	4-1-02	4.50	4.00	4.00	4.00	7	8
102[21]	4-1-02	5-1-02	4.25	4.00	4.00	4.00	7	8
103[22]	5-1-02	6-1-02	4.75	4.00	4.00	4.00	7	8
104[23]	6-1-02	7-1-02	4.50	4.00	4.00	4.00	7	8
105[24]	7-1-02	8-1-02	4.50	4.00	4.00	4.00	7	8
106[25]	8-1-02	9-1-02	4.25	4.00	4.00	4.00	7	8
107[26]	9-1-02	10-1-02	4.25	4.00	4.00	4.00	7	8
108[27]	10-1-02	11-1-02	4.00	4.00	4.00	4.00	7	8
109[28]	11-1-02	12-1-02	3.75	4.00	4.00	4.00	7	8
110[29]	12-1-02	1-1-03	4.00	4.00	4.00	4.00	7	8

Rate set	For plans with a valuation date		Immediate annuity rate (percent)	Deferred annuities (percent)				
	On or After	Before		i_1	i_2	i_3	n_1	n_2
111[30]	1-1-03	2-1-03	4.00	4.00	4.00	4.00	7	8
112[31]	2-1-03	3-1-03	3.75	4.00	4.00	4.00	7	8
113[32]	3-1-03	4-1-03	3.75	4.00	4.00	4.00	7	8

Rate set	For plans with a valuation date		Immediate annuity rate (percent)	Deferred annuities (percent)				
	On or After	Before		i_1	i_2	i_3	n_1	n_2
114[33]	4-1-03	5-1-03	3.50	4.00	4.00	4.00	7	8
115[34]	5-1-03	6-1-03	3.50	4.00	4.00	4.00	7	8
116[35]	6-1-03	7-1-03	3.50	4.00	4.00	4.00	7	8
117[36]	7-1-03	8-1-03	3.00	4.00	4.00	4.00	7	8
118[37]	8-1-03	9-1-03	3.00	4.00	4.00	4.00	7	8
119[38]	9-1-03	10-1-03	3.50	4.00	4.00	4.00	7	8
120[39]	10-1-03	11-1-03	3.50	4.00	4.00	4.00	7	8
121[40]	11-1-03	12-1-03	3.25	4.00	4.00	4.00	7	8
122[41]	12-1-03	1-1-04	3.25	4.00	4.00	4.00	7	8

Rate set	For plans with a valuation date		Immediate annuity rate (percent)	Deferred annuities (percent)				
	On or After	Before		i_1	i_2	i_3	n_1	n_2
123[42]	1-1-04	2-1-04	3.25	4.00	4.00	4.00	7	8
124[43]	2-1-04	3-1-04	3.25	4.00	4.00	4.00	7	8
125[44]	3-1-04	4-1-04	3.00	4.00	4.00	4.00	7	8
126[45]	4-1-04	5-1-04	3.00	4.00	4.00	4.00	7	8
127[46]	5-1-04	6-1-04	3.00	4.00	4.00	4.00	7	8
128[47]	6-1-04	7-1-04	3.50	4.00	4.00	4.00	7	8
129[48]	7-1-04	8-1-04	3.50	4.00	4.00	4.00	7	8
130[49]	8-1-04	9-1-04	3.50	4.00	4.00	4.00	7	8
131[50]	9-1-04	10-1-04	3.25	4.00	4.00	4.00	7	8
132[51]	10-1-04	11-1-04	3.00	4.00	4.00	4.00	7	8
133[52]	11-1-04	12-1-04	2.75	4.00	4.00	4.00	7	8
134[53]	12-1-04	1-1-05	2.75	4.00	4.00	4.00	7	8

Rate set	For plans with a valuation date		Immediate annuity rate (percent)	Deferred annuities (percent)				
	On or After	Before		i_1	i_2	i_3	n_1	n_2
135[54]	1-1-05	2-1-05	3.00	4.00	4.00	4.00	7	8
136[55]	2-1-05	3-1-05	3.00	4.00	4.00	4.00	7	8
137[56]	3-1-05	4-1-05	2.75	4.00	4.00	4.00	7	8
138[57]	4-1-05	5-1-05	2.75	4.00	4.00	4.00	7	8
139[58]	5-1-05	6-1-05	2.75	4.00	4.00	4.00	7	8
140[59]	6-1-05	7-1-05	2.50	4.00	4.00	4.00	7	8
141[60]	7-1-05	8-1-05	2.50	4.00	4.00	4.00	7	8
142[61]	8-1-05	9-1-05	2.25	4.00	4.00	4.00	7	8
143[62]	9-1-05	10-1-05	2.50	4.00	4.00	4.00	7	8
144[63]	10-1-05	11-1-05	2.25	4.00	4.00	4.00	7	8
145[64]	11-1-05	12-1-05	2.50	4.00	4.00	4.00	7	8
146[65]	12-1-05	1-1-06	2.75	4.00	4.00	4.00	7	8

Rate set	For plans with a valuation date		Immediate annuity rate (percent)	Deferred annuities (percent)				
	On or After	Before		i_1	i_2	i_3	n_1	n_2
147[66]	1-1-06	2-1-06	2.75	4.00	4.00	4.00	7	8

[1] 65 FR 43694—7/14/00.
[2] 65 FR 49737—8/15/00.
[3] 65 FR 55986—9/15/00.
[4] 65 FR 60859—10/13/00.
[5] 65 FR 68892—11/15/00.
[6] 65 FR 78414—12/15/00.
[7] 66 FR 2822—1/12/01.
[8] 66 FR 10365—2/15/01.
[9] 66 FR 15031—3/15/01.
[10] 66 FR 19089—4/13/01.
[11] 66 FR 26791—5/15/01.
[12] 66 FR 32543—6/15/01.
[13] 66 FR 36702—7/13/01.
[14] 66 FR 42737—8/15/01.

Reg. §4022.83 ¶15,424D

[15] 66 FR 47885—9/14/01.
[16] 66 FR 52315—10/15/01.
[17] 66 FR 57369—11/15/01.
[18] 66 FR 64744—12/14/01.
[19] 67 FR 1861—1/15/02.
[20] 67 FR 7076—2/15/02.
[21] 67 FR 11572—3/15/02.
[22] 67 FR 18112—4/15/02.
[23] 67 FR 34610—5/15/02.
[24] 67 FR 40850—6/14/02.
[25] 67 FR 46376—7/15/02.
[26] 67 FR 53307—8/15/02.
[27] 67 FR 57949—9/13/02.
[28] 67 FR 63544—10/15/02.
[29] 67 FR 69121—11/15/02.
[30] 67 FR 76682—12/13/02.
[31] 68 FR 1965—1/15/03.
[32] 68 FR 7419—2/14/03.
[33] 68 FR 12303—3/14/03.
[34] 68 FR 18122—4/15/03.
[35] 68 FR 26206—5/15/03.
[36] 68 FR 35294—6/13/03.
[37] 68 FR 41714—7/15/03.
[38] 68 FR 48787—8/15/03.
[39] 68 FR 53880—9/15/03.
[40] 68 FR 59315—10/15/03.
[41] 68 FR 64525—11/14/03.
[42] 68 FR 69606—12/15/03.
[43] 69 FR 2299—1/15/04.
[44] 69 FR 7119—2/13/04.
[45] 69 FR 12072—3/15/04.
[46] 69 FR 19925—4/15/04.
[47] 69 FR 26769—5/14/04.
[48] 69 FR 33302—6/15/04.
[49] 69 FR 42333—7/15/04.
[50] 69 FR 50070—8/13/04.
[51] 69 FR 55500—9/15/04.
[52] 69 FR 61150—10/15/04.
[53] 69 FR 65543—11/15/04.
[54] 69 FR 74973—12/15/04.
[55] 70 FR 2568—1/14/05.
[56] 70 FR 7651—2/15/05.
[57] 70 FR 12585—3/15/05.
[58] 70 FR 19890—4/15/05.
[59] 70 FR 25470—5/13/05.
[60] 70 FR 34655—6/15/05.
[61] 70 FR 40882—7/15/05.
[62] 70 FR 47725—8/15/05.
[63] 70 FR 54477—9/15/05.
[64] 70 FR 60002—10/14/05.
[65] 70 FR 69277—11/15/05.
[66] 70 FR 74200—12/15/05.

[¶ 15,424E]

§ 4022.83 **Appendix C to Part 4022: Lump Sum Interest Rates for Private-Sector payments.**

[In using this table: (1) For benefits for which the participant or beneficiary is entitled to be in pay status on the valuation date, the immediate annuity rate shall apply; (2) For benefits for which the deferral period is y years (where y is an integer and $0 \le y \le n_1$), interest rate i_1 shall apply from the valuation date for a period of y years, and thereafter the immediate annuity rate shall apply; (3) For benefits for which the deferral period is y years (where y is an integer and $n_1 \le y \le n_1 + n_2$), interest rate i_2 shall apply from the valuation date for a period of $y - n_1$ years, interest rate i_1 shall apply for the following n_1 years, and thereafter the immediate annuity rate shall apply; (4) For benefits for which the deferral period is y years (where y is an integer and $y > n_1 + n_2$), interest rate i_3 shall apply from the valuation date for a period of $y-n_1-n_2$ years, interest rate i_2 shall apply for the following n_2 years, interest rate i_1 shall apply for the following n_1 years, and thereafter the immediate annuity rate shall apply.][Amended 3/17/00 by 65 FR 14751, 14753.]

Rate set	For plans with a valuation date		Immediate annuity rate (percent)	Deferred annuities (percent)				
	On or After	Before		i_1	i_2	i_3	n_1	n_2
1	11-1-93	12-1-93	4.25	4.00	4.00	4.00	7	8
2	12-1-93	1-1-94	4.25	4.00	4.00	4.00	7	8
3	1-1-94	2-1-94	4.50	4.00	4.00	4.00	7	8
4	2-1-94	3-1-94	4.50	4.00	4.00	4.00	7	8

Rate set	For plans with a valuation date On or After	For plans with a valuation date Before	Immediate annuity rate (percent)	Deferred annuities (percent) i_1	i_2	i_3	n_1	n_2
5	3-1-94	4-1-94	4.50	4.00	4.00	4.00	7	8
6	4-1-94	5-1-94	4.75	4.00	4.00	4.00	7	8
7	5-1-94	6-1-94	5.25	4.50	4.00	4.00	7	8
8	6-1-94	7-1-94	5.25	4.50	4.00	4.00	7	8
9	7-1-94	8-1-94	5.50	4.75	4.00	4.00	7	8
10	8-1-94	9-1-94	5.75	5.00	4.00	4.00	7	8

Rate set	For plans with a valuation date On or After	For plans with a valuation date Before	Immediate annuity rate (percent)	Deferred annuities (percent) i_1	i_2	i_3	n_1	n_2
11	9-1-94	10-1-94	5.50	4.75	4.00	4.00	7	8
12	10-1-94	11-1-94	5.50	4.75	4.00	4.00	7	8
13	11-1-94	12-1-94	6.00	5.25	4.00	4.00	7	8
14	12-1-94	1-1-95	6.25	5.50	4.25	4.00	7	8
15	1-1-95	2-1-95	6.00	5.25	4.00	4.00	7	8
16	2-1-95	3-1-95	6.00	5.25	4.00	4.00	7	8
17	3-1-95	4-1-95	6.00	5.25	4.00	4.00	7	8
18	4-1-95	5-1-95	5.75	5.00	4.00	4.00	7	8
19	5-1-95	6-1-95	5.50	4.75	4.00	4.00	7	8
20	6-1-95	7-1-95	5.50	4.75	4.00	4.00	7	8

Rate set	For plans with a valuation date On or After	For plans with a valuation date Before	Immediate annuity rate (percent)	Deferred annuities (percent) i_1	i_2	i_3	n_1	n_2
21	7-1-95	8-1-95	4.75	4.00	4.00	4.00	7	8
22	8-1-95	9-1-95	4.75	4.00	4.00	4.00	7	8
23	9-1-95	10-1-95	5.00	4.25	4.00	4.00	7	8
24	10-1-95	11-1-95	4.75	4.00	4.00	4.00	7	8
25	11-1-95	12-1-95	4.75	4.00	4.00	4.00	7	8
26	12-1-95	1-1-96	4.50	4.00	4.00	4.00	7	8
27	1-1-96	2-1-96	4.50	4.00	4.00	4.00	7	8
28	2-1-96	3-1-96	4.25	4.00	4.00	4.00	7	8
29	3-1-96	4-1-96	4.25	4.00	4.00	4.00	7	8
30	4-1-96	5-1-96	4.75	4.00	4.00	4.00	7	8

Rate set	For plans with a valuation date On or After	For plans with a valuation date Before	Immediate annuity rate (percent)	Deferred annuities (percent) i_1	i_2	i_3	n_1	n_2
31	5-1-96	6-1-96	5.00	4.25	4.00	4.00	7	8
32	6-1-96	7-1-96	5.00	4.25	4.00	4.00	7	8
33	7-1-96	8-1-96	5.00	4.25	4.00	4.00	7	8
34	8-1-96	9-1-96	5.25	4.50	4.00	4.00	7	8
35	9-1-96	10-1-96	5.25	4.50	4.00	4.00	7	8
36	10-1-96	11-1-96	5.25	4.50	4.00	4.00	7	8
37	11-1-96	12-1-96	5.00	4.25	4.00	4.00	7	8
38	12-1-96	1-1-97	4.75	4.00	4.00	4.00	7	8
39	1-1-97	2-1-97	4.50	4.00	4.00	4.00	7	8

Rate set	For plans with a valuation date On or After	For plans with a valuation date Before	Immediate annuity rate (percent)	Deferred annuities (percent) i_1	i_2	i_3	n_1	n_2
40	2-1-97	3-1-97	4.75	4.00	4.00	4.00	7	8
41	3-1-97	4-1-97	5.00	4.25	4.00	4.00	7	8
42	4-1-97	5-1-97	4.75	4.00	4.00	4.00	7	8
43	5-1-97	6-1-97	5.00	4.25	4.00	4.00	7	8
44	6-1-97	7-1-97	5.25	4.50	4.00	4.00	7	8
45	7-1-97	8-1-97	5.25	4.50	4.00	4.00	7	8
46	8-1-97	9-1-97	4.75	4.00	4.00	4.00	7	8

Rate set	For plans with a valuation date		Immediate annuity rate (percent)	Deferred annuities (percent)				
	On or After	Before		i_1	i_2	i_3	n_1	n_2
47	9-1-97	10-1-97	4.50	4.00	4.00	4.00	7	8
48	10-1-97	11-1-97	4.75	4.00	4.00	4.00	7	8
49	11-1-97	12-1-97	4.50	4.00	4.00	4.00	7	8

Rate set	For plans with a valuation date		Immediate annuity rate (percent)	Deferred annuities (percent)				
	On or After	Before		i_1	i_2	i_3	n_1	n_2
50	12-1-97	1-1-98	4.50	4.00	4.00	4.00	7	8
51	1-1-98	2-1-98	4.25	4.00	4.00	4.00	7	8
52	2-1-98	3-1-98	4.25	4.00	4.00	4.00	7	8
53	3-1-98	4-1-98	4.25	4.00	4.00	4.00	7	8
54	4-1-98	5-1-98	4.25	4.00	4.00	4.00	7	8
55	5-1-98	6-1-98	4.25	4.00	4.00	4.00	7	8
56	6-1-98	7-1-98	4.25	4.00	4.00	4.00	7	8
57	7-1-98	8-1-98	4.00	4.00	4.00	4.00	7	8
58	8-1-98	9-1-98	4.00	4.00	4.00	4.00	7	8
59	9-1-98	10-1-98	4.00	4.00	4.00	4.00	7	8

Rate set	For plans with a valuation date		Immediate annuity rate (percent)	Deferred annuities (percent)				
	On or After	Before		i_1	i_2	i_3	n_1	n_2
60	10-1-98	11-1-98	4.00	4.00	4.00	4.00	7	8
61	11-1-98	12-1-98	3.75	4.00	4.00	4.00	7	8
62	12-1-98	1-1-99	4.00	4.00	4.00	4.00	7	8
63	1-1-99	2-1-99	4.00	4.00	4.00	4.00	7	8
64	2-1-99	3-1-99	4.00	4.00	4.00	4.00	7	8
65	3-1-99	4-1-99	4.00	4.00	4.00	4.00	7	8
66	4-1-99	5-1-99	4.25	4.00	4.00	4.00	7	8
67	5-1-99	6-1-99	4.25	4.00	4.00	4.00	7	8
68	6-1-99	7-1-99	4.25	4.00	4.00	4.00	7	8
69	7-1-99	8-1-99	4.50	4.00	4.00	4.00	7	8

Rate set	For plans with a valuation date		Immediate annuity rate (percent)	Deferred annuities (percent)				
	On or After	Before		i_1	i_2	i_3	n_1	n_2
70	8-1-99	9-1-99	5.00	4.25	4.00	4.00	7	8
71	9-1-99	10-1-99	5.00	4.25	4.00	4.00	7	8
72	10-1-99	11-1-99	5.00	4.25	4.00	4.00	7	8
73	11-1-99	12-1-99	5.00	4.25	4.00	4.00	7	8
74	12-1-99	1-1-00	5.25	4.50	4.00	4.00	7	8
75	1-1-00	2-1-00	5.00	4.25	4.00	4.00	7	8
76	2-1-00	3-1-00	5.25	4.50	4.00	4.00	7	8
77	3-1-00	4-1-00	5.25	4.50	4.00	4.00	7	8
78	4-1-00	5-1-00	5.25	4.50	4.00	4.00	7	8
79	5-1-00	6-1-00	5.25	4.50	4.00	4.00	7	8

Rate set	For plans with a valuation date		Immediate annuity rate (percent)	Deferred annuities (percent)				
	On or After	Before		i_1	i_2	i_3	n_1	n_2
80	6-1-00	7-1-00	5.25	4.50	4.00	4.00	7	8
81	7-1-00	8-1-00	5.50	4.75	4.00	4.00	7	8
82 [1]	8-1-00	9-1-00	5.25	4.50	4.00	4.00	7	8
83 [2]	9-1-00	10-1-00	5.25	4.50	4.00	4.00	7	8
84 [3]	10-1-00	11-1-00	5.00	4.25	4.00	4.00	7	8
85 [4]	11-1-00	12-1-00	5.25	4.50	4.00	4.00	7	8
86 [5]	12-1-00	1-1-01	5.25	4.50	4.00	4.00	7	8
87 [6]	1-1-01	2-1-01	5.00	4.25	4.00	4.00	7	8
88 [7]	2-1-01	3-1-01	4.75	4.00	4.00	4.00	7	8

¶15,424E   Reg. §4022.83

Rate set	For plans with a valuation date		Immediate annuity rate (percent)	Deferred annuities (percent)				
	On or After	Before		i_1	i_2	i_3	n_1	n_2
89[8]	3-1-01	4-1-01	4.75	4.00	4.00	4.00	7	8
90[9]	4-1-01	5-1-01	4.75	4.00	4.00	4.00	7	8

Rate set	For plans with a valuation date		Immediate annuity rate (percent)	Deferred annuities (percent)				
	On or After	Before		i_1	i_2	i_3	n_1	n_2
91[10]	5-1-01	6-1-01	4.75	4.00	4.00	4.00	7	8
92[11]	6-1-01	7-1-01	5.00	4.25	4.00	4.00	7	8
93[12]	7-1-01	8-1-01	5.00	4.25	4.00	4.00	7	8
94[13]	8-1-01	9-1-01	4.75	4.00	4.00	4.00	7	8
95[14]	9-1-01	10-1-01	4.50	4.00	4.00	4.00	7	8
96[15]	10-1-01	11-1-01	4.50	4.00	4.00	4.00	7	8
97[16]	11-1-01	12-1-01	4.75	4.00	4.00	4.00	7	8
98[17]	12-1-01	1-1-02	4.50	4.00	4.00	4.00	7	8
99[18]	1-1-02	2-1-02	4.50	4.00	4.00	4.00	7	8
100[19]	2-1-02	3-1-02	4.75	4.00	4.00	4.00	7	8

Rate set	For plans with a valuation date		Immediate annuity rate (percent)	Deferred annuities (percent)				
	On or After	Before		i_1	i_2	i_3	n_1	n_2
101[20]	3-1-02	4-1-02	4.50	4.00	4.00	4.00	7	8
102[21]	4-1-02	5-1-02	4.25	4.00	4.00	4.00	7	8
103[22]	5-1-02	6-1-02	4.75	4.00	4.00	4.00	7	8
104[23]	6-1-02	7-1-02	4.50	4.00	4.00	4.00	7	8
105[24]	7-1-02	8-1-02	4.50	4.00	4.00	4.00	7	8
106[25]	8-1-02	9-1-02	4.25	4.00	4.00	4.00	7	8
107[26]	9-1-02	10-1-02	4.25	4.00	4.00	4.00	7	8
108[27]	10-1-02	11-1-02	4.00	4.00	4.00	4.00	7	8
109[28]	11-1-02	12-1-02	3.75	4.00	4.00	4.00	7	8
110[29]	12-1-02	1-1-03	4.00	4.00	4.00	4.00	7	8

Rate set	For plans with a valuation date		Immediate annuity rate (percent)	Deferred annuities (percent)				
	On or After	Before		i_1	i_2	i_3	n_1	n_2
111[30]	1-1-03	2-1-03	4.00	4.00	4.00	4.00	7	8
112[31]	2-1-03	3-1-03	3.75	4.00	4.00	4.00	7	8
113[32]	3-1-03	4-1-03	3.75	4.00	4.00	4.00	7	8
114[33]	4-1-03	5-1-03	3.50	4.00	4.00	4.00	7	8
115[34]	5-1-03	6-1-03	3.50	4.00	4.00	4.00	7	8
116[35]	6-1-03	7-1-03	3.50	4.00	4.00	4.00	7	8
117[36]	7-1-03	8-1-03	3.00	4.00	4.00	4.00	7	8
118[37]	8-1-03	9-1-03	3.00	4.00	4.00	4.00	7	8
119[38]	9-1-03	10-1-03	3.50	4.00	4.00	4.00	7	8
120[39]	10-1-03	11-1-03	3.50	4.00	4.00	4.00	7	8
121[40]	11-1-03	12-1-03	3.25	4.00	4.00	4.00	7	8
122[41]	12-1-03	1-1-04	3.25	4.00	4.00	4.00	7	8

Rate set	For plans with a valuation date		Immediate annuity rate (percent)	Deferred annuities (percent)				
	On or After	Before		i_1	i_2	i_3	n_1	n_2
123[42]	1-1-04	2-1-04	3.25	4.00	4.00	4.00	7	8
124[43]	2-1-04	3-1-04	3.25	4.00	4.00	4.00	7	8
125[44]	3-1-04	4-1-04	3.00	4.00	4.00	4.00	7	8
126[45]	4-1-04	5-1-04	3.00	4.00	4.00	4.00	7	8
127[46]	5-1-04	6-1-04	3.00	4.00	4.00	4.00	7	8
128[47]	6-1-04	7-1-04	3.50	4.00	4.00	4.00	7	8
129[48]	7-1-04	8-1-04	3.50	4.00	4.00	4.00	7	8
130[49]	8-1-04	9-1-04	3.50	4.00	4.00	4.00	7	8

Rate set	For plans with a valuation date		Immediate annuity rate (percent)	Deferred annuities (percent)				
	On or After	Before		i_1	i_2	i_3	n_1	n_2
131[50]	9-1-04	10-1-04	3.25	4.00	4.00	4.00	7	8
132[51]	10-1-04	11-1-04	3.00	4.00	4.00	4.00	7	8
133[52]	11-1-04	12-1-04	2.75	4.00	4.00	4.00	7	8
134[53]	12-1-04	1-1-05	2.75	4.00	4.00	4.00	7	8

Rate set	For plans with a valuation date		Immediate annuity rate (percent)	Deferred annuities (percent)				
	On or After	Before		i_1	i_2	i_3	n_1	n_2
135[54]	1-1-05	2-1-05	3.00	4.00	4.00	4.00	7	8
136[55]	2-1-05	3-1-05	3.00	4.00	4.00	4.00	7	8
137[56]	3-1-05	4-1-05	2.75	4.00	4.00	4.00	7	8
138[57]	4-1-05	5-1-05	2.75	4.00	4.00	4.00	7	8
139[58]	5-1-05	6-1-05	2.75	4.00	4.00	4.00	7	8
140[59]	6-1-05	7-1-05	2.50	4.00	4.00	4.00	7	8
141[60]	7-1-05	8-1-05	2.50	4.00	4.00	4.00	7	8
142[61]	8-1-05	9-1-05	2.25	4.00	4.00	4.00	7	8
143[62]	9-1-05	10-1-05	2.50	4.00	4.00	4.00	7	8
144[63]	10-1-05	11-1-05	2.25	4.00	4.00	4.00	7	8
145[64]	11-1-05	12-1-05	2.50	4.00	4.00	4.00	7	8
146[65]	12-1-05	1-1-06	2.75	4.00	4.00	4.00	7	8

Rate set	For plans with a valuation date		Immediate annuity rate (percent)	Deferred annuities (percent)				
	On or After	Before		i_1	i_2	i_3	n_1	n_2
147[66]	1-1-06	2-1-06	2.75	4.00	4.00	4.00	7	8

[1] 65 FR 43694—7/14/00.
[2] 65 FR 49737—8/15/00.
[3] 65 FR 55896—9/15/00.
[4] 65 FR 60859—10/13/00.
[5] 65 FR 68892—11/15/00.
[6] 65 FR 78414—12/15/00.
[7] 66 FR 2822—1/12/01.
[8] 66 FR 10365—2/15/01.
[9] 66 FR 15031—3/15/01.
[10] 66 FR 19089—4/13/01.
[11] 66 FR 26791—5/15/01.
[12] 66 FR 32543—6/15/01.
[13] 66 FR 36702—7/13/01.
[14] 66 FR 42737—8/15/01.
[15] 66 FR 47885—9/14/01.
[16] 66 FR 52315—10/15/01.
[17] 66 FR 57369—11/15/01.
[18] 66 FR 64744—12/14/01.
[19] 67 FR 1861—1/15/02.
[20] 67 FR 7076—2/15/02.
[21] 67 FR 11572—3/15/02.
[22] 67 FR 18112—4/15/02.
[23] 67 FR 34610—5/15/02.
[24] 67 FR 40850—6/14/02.
[25] 67 FR 46376—7/15/02.
[26] 67 FR 53307—8/15/02.
[27] 67 FR 57949—9/13/02.
[28] 67 FR 63544—10/15/02.
[29] 67 FR 69121—11/15/02.
[30] 67 FR 76682—12/13/02.
[31] 68 FR 1965—1/15/03.
[32] 68 FR 7419—2/14/03.
[33] 68 FR 12303—3/14/03.
[34] 68 FR 18122—4/15/03.
[35] 68 FR 26206—5/15/03.
[36] 68 FR 35294—6/13/03.
[37] 68 FR 41714—7/15/03.
[38] 68 FR 48787—8/15/03.

[39] 68 FR 53880—9/15/03.
[40] 68 FR 59315—10/15/03.
[41] 68 FR 64525—11/14/03.
[42] 68 FR 69606—12/15/03.
[43] 69 FR 2299—1/15/04.
[44] 69 FR 7119—2/13/04.
[45] 69 FR 12072—3/15/04.
[46] 69 FR 19925—4/15/04.
[47] 69 FR 26769—5/14/04.
[48] 69 FR 33302—6/15/04.
[49] 69 FR 42333—7/15/04.
[50] 69 FR 50070—8/13/04.
[51] 69 FR 55500—9/15/04.
[52] 69 FR 61150—10/15/04.
[53] 69 FR 65543—11/15/04.
[54] 69 FR 74973—12/15/04.
[55] 70 FR 2568—1/14/05.
[56] 70 FR 7651—2/15/05.
[57] 70 FR 12585—3/15/05.
[58] 70 FR 19890—4/15/05.
[59] 70 FR 25470—5/13/05.
[60] 70 FR 34655—6/15/05.
[61] 70 FR 40882—7/15/05.
[62] 70 FR 47725—8/15/05.
[63] 70 FR 54477—9/15/05.
[64] 70 FR 60002—10/14/05.
[65] 70 FR 69277—11/15/05.
[66] 70 FR 74200—12/15/05.

[¶ 15,424F]

§ 4022.83 Appendix D to Part 4022: Maximum Guaranteeable Monthly Benefit.

The following table lists by year the maximum guaranteeable monthly benefit payable in the form of a life annuity commencing at age 65 as described by § 4022.22(b) to a participant in a plan that terminated in that year:

Year	Maximum guaranteeable monthly benefit
1974	$750.00
1975	801.14
1976	869.32
1977	937.50
1978	1,005.68
1979	1,073.86
1980	1,159.09
1981	1,261.36
1982	1,380.68
1983	1,517.05
1984	1,602.27
1985	1,687.50
1986	1,789.77
1987	1,857.95
1988	1,909.09
1989	2,028.41
1990	2,164.77
1991	2,250.00
1992	2,352.27
1993	2,437.50
1994	2,556.82
1995	2,573.86
1996	2,642.05
1997	2,761.36
1998	2,880.68

Year	Maximum guaranteeable monthly benefit
1999	3,051.14
2000[1]	3,221.59
2001[2]	3,392.05
2002[3]	3,579.55
2003[4]	3,664.77
2004[5]	3,698.86
2005[6]	3,801.14
2006[7]	3,971.59

[1] [Amended 3/17/00 by 65 FR 14751, 14753.]
[2] [Amended 12/1/00 by 66 FR 75165.]
[3] [Amended 11/30/01 by 66 FR 59695.]
[4] [Amended 12/2/02 by 67 FR 71470.]
[5] [Amended 12/1/03 by 68 FR 67032.]
[6] [Amended 12/1/04 by 69 FR 69820.]
[7] [Amended 12/1/05 by 70 FR 72074.]

Subpart F—Certain Payments Owed Upon Death

[¶ 15,425]

§ 4022.91 When do these rules apply?

(a) *Types of benefits.* Provided the conditions in paragraphs (b) and (c) of this section are satisfied, these rules (§§ 4022.91 through 4022.95) apply to any benefits we may owe you (including benefits we owe you because your plan owed them) at the time of your death, such as a payment of a lump-sum benefit that we calculated as of your plan's termination date but have not yet paid you or a back payment to reimburse you for monthly underpayments. We may owe you benefits at the time of your death if—

(1) You are a participant in a terminated plan;

(2) You are a beneficiary (including an alternate payee) of a participant; or

(3) You are a designee or other payee (e.g., a participant's next of kin) under these rules, as explained in § 4022.93.

(b) *Payments do not continue after death.* These rules apply only if payments do not continue after your death. (If payments continue after your death, we will make up any underpayment to you at the time of your death under the rule in § 4022.81(d)(2)(i) by paying it to the person who is entitled to receive those continuing payments.) Payments do not continue after your death if—

(1) Your benefit is not in the form of a joint-and-survivor or other annuity under which payments may continue after your death (e.g., a certain-and-continuous annuity);

(2) Your benefit is in the form of a joint-and-survivor annuity and the person designated to receive survivor benefits died before you; or

(3) Your benefit is in the form of another type of annuity under which payments may continue after your death (e.g., a certain-and-continuous annuity) but you die with no payments owed for future periods.

(c) *Time of death.* These rules apply only if you die—

(1) On or after the date we take over your plan (as trustee); or

(2) Before the date we take over your plan, to the extent that, by that date, the plan administrator has not paid all benefits owed to you at the time of your death.

(d) *Effect of plan or will.* These rules apply even if there is a contrary provision in a plan or will.

[¶ 15,425A]

§ 4022.92 **What definitions do I need to know for these rules?**

You need to know three definitions from § 4001.2 of this chapter (PBGC, person, and plan) and the following definitions:

"We" means the PBGC.

"You" means the person to whom we may owe benefits at the time of death.

[¶ 15,425B]

§ 4022.93 **Who will get benefits the PBGC may owe me at the time of my death?**

(a) *In general.* Except as provided in paragraphs (b) and (c) of this section (which explain what happens if you die before the date we take over your plan or within 180 days after the date we take over your plan), we will pay any benefits we owe you at the time of your death to the person(s) surviving you in the following order—

(1) *Designee with the PBGC.* The person(s) you designated with us to get any benefits we may owe you at the time of your death. See § 4022.94 for information on designating with us.

(2) *Spouse. Your spouse.* We will consider a person to whom you are married to be your spouse even if you and that person are separated, unless a decree of divorce or annulment has been entered in a court.

(3) *Children.* Your children and descendants of your deceased children.

(i) *Adopted children.* In determining who is a child or descendant, an adopted child is treated the same way as a natural child.

(ii) *Child dies before parent.* If one of your children dies before you, any of your grandchildren through that deceased child will equally divide that deceased child's share; if one of your grandchildren through that deceased child dies before that deceased child, any of your great-grandchildren through that deceased grandchild will equally divide that deceased grandchild's share; and so on.

(4) *Parents. Your parents.* A parent includes an adoptive parent.

(5) *Estate.* Your estate, provided your estate is open.

(6) *Next of kin.* Your next of kin in accordance with applicable state law.

(b) *Pre-trusteeship deaths.* If you die before the date we take over your plan and, by that date, the plan administrator has not paid all benefits owed to you at the time of your death, we will pay any benefits we owe you at the time of your death to the person(s) designated by or under the plan to get those benefits (provided the designation clearly applies to those benefits). If there is no such designation, we will pay those benefits to your spouse, children, parents, estate, or next of kin under the rules in paragraphs (a) (2) through (a) (6) of this section.

(c) *Deaths shortly after trusteeship.* If you die within 180 days after the date we take over your plan and you have not designated anyone with the PBGC under paragraph (a) (1) of this section, we will pay any benefits we owe you at the time of your death to the person(s) designated by or under the plan to get those benefits (provided the designation clearly applies to those benefits) before paying those benefits to your spouse, children, parents, estate, or next of kin under the rules in paragraphs (a) (2) through (a) (6) of this section.

[¶ 15,425C]

§ 4022.94 **What are the PBGC's rules on designating a person to get benefits the PBGC may owe me at the time of my death?**

(a) *When you may designate.* At any time on or after the date we take over your plan, you may designate with us who will get any benefits we owe you at the time of your death.

(b) *Change of designee.* If you want to change the person(s) you designate with us, you must submit another designation to us.

(c) *If your designee dies before you.*

(1) *In general.* If the person(s) you designate with us dies before you or at the same time as you, we will treat you as not having designated anyone with us (unless you named an alternate designee who survives you). Therefore, you should keep your designation with us current.

(2) *Simultaneous deaths.* If you and a person you designated die as a result of the same event, we will treat you and that person as having died at the same time, provided you and that person die within 30 days of each other.

[¶ 15,425D]

§ 4022.95 **Examples.**

The following examples show how the rules in §§ 4022.91 through 4022.94 apply. For examples on how these rules apply in the case of a certain-and-continuous annuity, see § 4022.104.

At the time of his death, Charlie was receiving payments under a joint-and-survivor annuity. Charlie designated Ellen to receive survivor benefits under his joint-and-survivor annuity. We underpaid Charlie for periods before his death. At the time of his death, we owed Charlie a back payment to reimburse him for those underpayments.

(a) *Example 1:* where surviving beneficiary is alive at participant's death. Ellen survived Charlie. As explained in § 4022.91(b), because Ellen is entitled to survivor benefits under the joint-and-survivor annuity, we would pay Ellen the back payment.

(b) *Example 2:* where surviving beneficiary predeceases participant. Ellen died before Charlie. As explained in §§ 4022.91(b) and 4022.93, because benefits do not continue after Charlie's death under the joint-and-survivor annuity, we would pay the back payment to the person(s) Charlie designated to receive any payments we might owe him at the time of his death. If Charlie did not designate anyone to receive those payments or his designee died before him, we would pay the back payment to the person(s) surviving Charlie in the following order: spouse, children, parents, estate and next of kin.

Subpart G—Certain-and-Continuous and Similar Annuity Payments Owed for Future Periods After Death

[¶ 15,426]

§ 4022.101 **When do these rules apply?**

(a) *In general.* These rules (§§ 4022.101 through 4022.104) apply only if you die—

(1) *Required payments for future periods.* Without having received all required payments for future periods under a form of annuity promising that, regardless of a participant's death, there will be annuity payments for a certain period of time (e.g., a certain-and-continuous annuity) or until a certain amount is paid (e.g., a cash-refund annuity or installment-refund annuity);

(2) *No surviving beneficiary.* Without a surviving beneficiary designated to receive the payments described in paragraph (a)(1) of this section; and

(3) *Time of death.*

(i) On or after the date we take over your plan (as trustee); or

(ii) Before the date we take over your plan, to the extent that, by that date, the plan administrator has not paid any required payments for future periods.

(b) *Effect of plan or will.* These rules apply even if there is a contrary provision in a plan or will.

(c) *Payments owed at time of death.* See §§4022.91 through 4022.95 for rules that apply to benefits we may owe you at the time of your death, such as a correction for monthly underpayments.

[¶ 15,426A]

§4022.102 **What definitions do I need to know for these rules?**

You need to know three definitions from §4001.2 of this chapter (PBGC, person, and plan) and the following definitions:

"We" means the PBGC.

"You" means the person who might die—

(1) Without having received all required payments for future periods under a form of annuity promising that, regardless of a participant's death, there will be annuity payments for a certain period of time (e.g., a certain-and-continuous annuity) or until a certain amount is paid (e.g., a cash-refund annuity or installment-refund annuity); and

(2) Without a surviving beneficiary designated to receive the payments described in paragraph (1) of this definition.

[¶ 15,426B]

§4022.103 **Who will get benefits if I die when payments for future periods under a certain-and-continuous or similar annuity are owed upon my death?**

If you die at a time when payments are owed for future periods under a form of annuity promising that, regardless of a participant's death, there will be annuity payments for a certain period of time (e.g., a certain-and-continuous annuity) or until a certain amount is paid (e.g., a cash-refund annuity or installment-refund annuity), and there is no surviving beneficiary designated to receive such payments, we will pay the remaining payments to the person determined under the rules in §4022.93.

[¶ 15,426C]

§4022.104 **Examples.**

The following examples show how the rules in §§4022.101 through 4022.103 and 4022.91 through 4022.94 apply in the case of a certain-and-continuous annuity.

(a) *C&C annuity with no underpayment.* At the time of his death, Charlie was receiving payments (in the correct amount) under a 5-year certain-and-continuous annuity. Charlie designated Ellen to receive any payments we might owe for periods after his death (but did not designate an alternate beneficiary to receive those payments in case Ellen died before him). Charlie died with three years of payments remaining.

(1) *Example 1:* where surviving beneficiary predeceases participant. Ellen died before Charlie. As explained in §§4022.103 and

4022.93, we would pay the remaining three years of payments to the person(s) surviving Charlie in the following order: spouse, children, parents, estate and next of kin.

(2) *Example 2:* where surviving beneficiary dies during certain period. Ellen survived Charlie and lived another year. We pay Ellen one year of payments. As explained in §§4022.103 and 4022.93, we would pay the remaining two years of payments to the person Ellen designated to receive any payments we might owe for periods after Ellen's death. If Ellen did not designate anyone to receive those payments or her designee died before her, we would pay the remaining year of payments to the person(s) surviving Ellen in the following order: spouse, children, parents, estate, next of kin.

(b) *C&C annuity with underpayment.* At the time of his death, Charlie was receiving payments under a 5-year certain-and-continuous annuity. Charlie designated Ellen to receive any payments we might owe for periods after his death. We underpaid Charlie for periods before his death. At the time of his death, we owed Charlie a back payment to reimburse him for those underpayments.

(1) *Example 3:* where participant dies during certain period. Charlie died with three years of payments remaining. Ellen survived Charlie and lived at least another three years. We pay Ellen the remaining three years of payments. As explained in §4022.91(b), because Ellen is entitled to survivor benefits under the certain-and-continuous annuity, we would pay Ellen the back payment for the underpayments to Charlie (and for any underpayments to Ellen).

(2) *Example 4:* where participant and surviving beneficiary die during certain period. Charlie died with three years of payments remaining. Ellen survived Charlie and lived another year. We paid Ellen one year of payments. Ellen designated Jean to receive any payments we might owe for periods after Ellen's death. Jean survived Ellen and lives at least another two years. We pay Jean the remaining two years of payments. As explained in §4022.91(b), because Jean is entitled to survivor benefits under the certain-and-continuous annuity, we would pay Jean the back payment for the underpayments to Charlie (and for any underpayments to Ellen).

(3) *Example 5:* where participant dies after certain period. Charlie died after receiving seven years of payments. As explained in §§4022.91(b) and 4022.93, because benefits do not continue after Charlie's death under the certain-and-continuous annuity, we would pay the back payment to the person(s) Charlie designated to receive any payments we might owe him at the time of his death in case he died after the end of certain period. If Charlie did not designate anyone to receive those payments or his designee died before him, we would pay the back payment to the person(s) surviving Charlie in the following order: spouse, children, parents, estate and next of kin.

[¶ 15,429H]
MULTIEMPLOYER PLAN BENEFITS GUARANTEED

Act Sec. 4022A.(a) The corporation shall guarantee, in accordance with this section, the payment of all nonforfeitable benefits (other than benefits becoming nonforfeitable solely on account of the termination of a plan) under a multiemployer plan—

(1) to which this title applies, and

(2) which is insolvent under section 4245(b) or 4281(d)(2).

Act Sec. 4022A.(b)(1)(A) For purposes of this section, a benefit or benefit increase which has been in effect under a plan for less than 60 months is not eligible for the corporation's guarantee. For purposes of this paragraph, any month of any plan year during which the plan was insolvent or terminated (within the meaning of section 4041A(a)(2)) shall not be taken into account.

(B) For purposes of this section, a benefit or benefit increase which has been in effect under a plan for less than 60 months before the first day of the plan year for which an amendment reducing the benefit or the benefit increase is taken into account under section 4244A(a)(2) in determining the minimum contribution requirement for the plan year under section 4243(b) is not eligible for the corporation's guarantee.

(2) For purposes of this section—

(A) the date on which a benefit or a benefit increase under a plan is first in effect is the later of—

(i) the date on which the documents establishing or increasing the benefit were executed, or

(ii) the effective date of the benefit or benefit increase;

(B) the period of time for which a benefit or a benefit increase has been in effect under a successor plan includes the period of time for which the benefit or benefit increase was in effect under a previous established plan; and

(C) in the case of a plan to which section 4021 did not apply on September 3, 1974, the time periods referred to in this section are computed beginning on the date on which section 4021 first applies to the plan.

Act Sec. 4022A.(c)(1) Except as provided in subsection (g), the monthly benefit of a participant or a beneficiary which is guaranteed under this section by the corporation with respect to a plan is the product of—

(A) 100 percent of the accrual rate up to $11, plus 75 percent of the lesser of—

(i) $33, or

(ii) the accrual rate, if any, in excess of $11, and

(B) the number of the participant's years of credited service.

(2) For purposes of this section, the accrual rate is—

(A) the monthly benefit of the participant or beneficiary which is described in subsection (a) and which is eligible for the corporation's guarantee under subsection (b), except that such benefit shall be—

(i) no greater than the monthly benefit which would be payable under the plan at normal retirement age in the form of a single life annuity, and

(ii) determined without regard to any reduction under section 411(a)(3)(E) of the Internal Revenue Code of 1986; divided by

(B) the participant's years of credited service.

(3) For purposes of this subsection—

(A) a year of credited service is a year in which the participant completed—

(i) a full year of participation in the plan, or

(ii) any period of service before participation which is credited for purposes of benefit accrual as the equivalent of a full year of participation;

(B) any year for which the participant is credited for purposes of benefit accrual with a fraction of the equivalent of a full year of participation shall be counted as such a fraction of a year of credited service; and

(C) years of credited service shall be determined by including service which may otherwise be disregarded by the plan under section 411(a)(3)(E) of the Internal Revenue Code of 1986.

Act Sec. 4022A. (d) In the case of a benefit which has been reduced under section 411(a)(3)(E) of the Internal Revenue Code of 1954, the corporation shall guarantee the lesser of—

(1) the reduced benefit, or

(2) the amount determined under subsection (c).

Act Sec. 4022A. (e) The corporation shall not guarantee benefits under a multiemployer plan which, under section 4022(b)(6), would not be guaranteed under a single-employer plan.

Act Sec. 4022A. (f)(1) No later than 5 years after the date of the enactment of the Multiemployer Pension Plan Amendments Act of 1980, and at least every fifth year thereafter, the corporation shall—

(A) conduct a study to determine—

(i) the premiums needed to maintain the basic-benefit guarantee levels for multiemployer plans described in subsection (c), and

(ii) whether the basic-benefit guarantee levels for multiemployer plans may be increased without increasing the basic-benefit premiums for multiemployer plans under this title; and

(B) report such determinations to the Committee on Ways and Means and the Committee on Education and Labor of the House of Representatives and to the Committee on Finance and the Committee on Labor and Human Resources of the Senate.

(2)(A) If the last report described in paragraph (1) indicates that a premium increase is necessary to support the existing basic-benefit guarantee levels for multiemployer plans, the corporation shall transmit to the Committee on Ways and Means and the Committee on Education and Labor of the House of Representatives and to the Committee on Finance and the Committee on Labor and Human Resources of the Senate by March 31 of any calendar year in which congressional action under this subsection is requested—

(i) a revised schedule of basic-benefit guarantees for multiemployer plans which would be necessary in the absence of an increase in premiums approved in accordance with section 4006(b),

(ii) a revised schedule of basic-benefit premiums for multiemployer plans which is necessary to support the existing basic-benefit guarantees for such plans, and

(iii) a revised schedule of basic-benefit guarantees for multiemployer plans for which the schedule of premiums necessary is higher than the existing premium schedule for such plans but lower than the revised schedule of premiums for such plans specified in clause (ii), together with such schedule of premiums.

(B) The revised schedule of increased premiums referred to in subparagraph (A)(ii) or (A)(iii) shall go into effect as approved by the enactment of a joint resolution.

(C) If an increase in premiums is not so enacted, the revised guarantee schedule described in subparagraph (A)(i) shall go into effect on the first day of the second calendar year following the year in which such revised guarantee schedule was submitted to the Congress.

(3)(A) If the last report described in paragraph (1) indicates that basic-benefit guarantees for multiemployer plans can be increased without increasing the basic-benefit premiums for multiemployer plans under this title, the corporation shall submit to the Committee on Ways and Means and the Committee on Education and Labor of the House of Representatives and to the Committee on Finance and the Committee on Labor and Human Resources of the Senate by March 31 of the calendar year in which congressional action under this paragraph is requested—

(i) a revised schedule of increases in the basic-benefit guarantees which can be supported by the existing schedule of basic-benefit premiums for multiemployer plans, and

(ii) a revised schedule of basic-benefit premiums sufficient to support the existing basic-benefit guarantees.

(B) The revised schedules referred to in subparagraph (A)(i) or subparagraph (A)(ii) shall go into effect as approved by the enactment of a joint resolution.

(4)(A) The succeeding subparagraphs of this paragraph are enacted by the Congress as an exercise of the rulemaking power of the Senate and the House of Representatives, respectively, and as such they shall be deemed a part of the rules of each House, respectively, but applicable only with respect to the procedure to be followed in that House in the case of joint resolutions (as defined in subparagraph (B)). Such subparagraphs shall supersede other rules only to the extent that they are inconsistent therewith. They are enacted with full recognition of the constitutional right of either House to change the rules (so far as relating to the procedure of that House) at any time, in the same manner, and to the same extent as in the case of any rule of that House.

(B) For purposes of this subsection, "joint resolution" means only a concurrent resolution, the matter after the resolving clause of which is as follows: "The proposed schedule described in   transmitted to the Congress by the Pension Benefit Guaranty Corporation on   is hereby approved.", the first blank space therein being filled with "section 4022A(f)(2)(A)(ii) of the Employee Retirement Income Security Act of 1974", "section 4022A(f)(2)(A)(iii) of the Employee Retirement Income Security Act of 1974", "section 4022A(f)(3)(A)(i) of the Employee Retirement Income Security Act of 1974", or "section 4022A(f)(3)(A)(ii) of the Employee Retirement Income Security Act of 1974" (whichever is applicable), and the second blank space therein being filled with the date on which the corporation's message proposing the revision was submitted.

(C) The procedure for disposition of a concurrent resolution shall be the procedure described in section 4006(b)(4) through (7).

Act Sec. 4022A. (g)(1) The corporation may guarantee the payment of such other classes of benefits under multiemployer plans, and establish the terms and conditions under which those other classes of benefits are guaranteed, as it determines to be appropriate.

(2)(A) The corporation shall prescribe regulations to establish a supplemental program to guarantee benefits under multiemployer plans which would be guaranteed under this section but for the limitations in subsection (c). Such regulations shall be proposed by the corporation no later than the end of the 18th calendar month following the date of the enactment of the Multiemployer Pension Plan Amendment Act of 1980. The regulations shall make coverage under the supplemental program available no later than January 1, 1983. Any election to participate in the supplemental program shall be on a voluntary basis and a plan electing such coverage shall continue to pay the premiums required under section 4006(a)(2)(B) to the revolving fund used pursuant to section 4005 in connection with benefits otherwise guaranteed under this section. Any such election shall be irrevocable, except to the extent otherwise provided by regulations prescribed by the corporation.

(B) The regulations prescribed under this paragraph shall provide—

(i) that a plan must elect coverage under the supplemental program within the time permitted by the regulations;

(ii) unless the corporation determines otherwise, that a plan may not elect supplemental coverage unless the value of the assets of the plan as of the end of the plan year preceding the plan year in which the election must be made is an amount equal to 15 times the total amount of the benefit payments made under the plan for that year; and

(iii) such other reasonable terms and conditions for supplemental coverage, including funding standards and any other reasonable limitations with respect to plans or benefits covered or to means of program financing, as the corporation determines are necessary and appropriate for a feasible supplemental program consistent with the purposes of this title.

(3) Any benefits guaranteed under this subsection shall be considered nonbasic benefits for purposes of this title.

(4)(A) No revised schedule of premiums under this subsection, after the initial schedule, shall go into effect unless—

(i) the revised schedule is submitted to the Congress, and

(ii) a joint resolution described in subparagraph (B) is not enacted before the close of the 60th legislative day after such schedule is submitted to the Congress.

(B) For purposes of subparagraph (A), a joint resolution described in this subparagraph is a joint resolution the matter after the resolving clause of which is as follows: "The revised premium schedule transmitted to the Congress by the Pension Benefit Guaranty Corporation under section 4022A(g)(4) of the Employee Retirement Income Security Act of 1974 on   is hereby disapproved.", the blank space therein being filed with the date on which the revised schedule was submitted.

(C) For purposes of subparagraph (A), the term "legislative day" means any calendar day other than a day on which either House is not in session because of a sine die adjournment or an adjournment of more than 3 days to a day certain.

(D) The procedure for disposition of a joint resolution described in subparagraph (B) shall be the procedure described in paragraphs (4) through (7) of section 4006(b).

(5) Regulations prescribed by the corporation to carry out the provisions of this subsection, may, to the extent provided therein, supersede the requirements of sections 4245, 4261, and 4281, and the requirements of section 418E of the Internal Revenue Code of 1986, but only with respect to benefits guaranteed under this subsection.

Act Sec. 4022A.(h)(1) Except as provided in paragraph (3), subsections (b) and (c) shall not apply with respect to the nonforfeitable benefits accrued as of July 29, 1980, with respect to a participant or beneficiary under a multiemployer plan—

(1) who is in pay status on July 29, 1980, or

(2) who is within 36 months of the normal retirement age and has a nonforfeitable right to a pension as of that date.

(2) The benefits described in paragraph (1) shall be guaranteed by the corporation in the same manner and to the same extent as benefits are guaranteed by the corporation under section 4022 (without regard to this section).

(3) This subsection does not apply with respect to a plan for plan years following a plan year—

(A) in which the plan has terminated within the meaning of section 4041A(a)(2), or

(B) in which it is determined by the corporation that substantially all the employers have withdrawn from the plan pursuant to an agreement or arrangement to withdraw.

Amendments

P.L. 106-554, §951:

Act Sec. 951(a)(1) amended ERISA Sec. 4022A(c)(1) by striking "$5" each place it appears and inserting "$11".

Act Sec. 951(a)(2) amended ERISA Sec. 4022A(c)(1)(A)(i) by striking "$15" and inserting "$33".

Act Sec. 951(a)(3) amended ERISA Sec. 4022A(c) by striking paragraphs (2), (5), and (6) and by redesignating paragraphs (3) and (4) as paragraphs (2) and (3).

Prior to amendment, ERISA Sec. 4022A(c)(2) read as follows:

"(2) Except as provided in paragraph (6) of this subsection and in subsection (g), in applying paragraph (1) with respect to a plan described in paragraph (5)(A), the term '65 percent' shall be substituted in paragraph (1)(A) for the term '75 percent'."

Prior to amendment, ERISA Sec. 4022A(c)(5) read as follows:

"(5)(A) A plan is described in this subparagraph if—

(i) the first plan year—

(I) in which the plan is insolvent under section 4245(b) or 4281(d)(2), and

(II) for which benefits are required to be suspended under section 4245, or reduced or suspended under section 4281, until they do not exceed the levels provided in this subsection,

begins before the year 2000; and

(ii) the plan sponsor has not established to the satisfaction of the corporation that, during the period of 10 consecutive plan years (or of such lesser number of plan years for which the plan was maintained) immediately preceding the first plan year to which the minimum funding standards of section 412 of the Internal Revenue Code of 1986 apply, the total amount of the contributions required under the plan for each plan year was at least equal to the sum of—

(I) the normal cost for that plan year, and

(II) the interest for the plan year (determined under the plan) on the unfunded past service liability for that plan year, determined as of the beginning of that plan year.

(B) A plan shall not be considered to be described in subparagraph (A) if—

(i) it is established to the satisfaction of the corporation that—

(I) the total amount of the contributions received under the plan for the plan years for which the actuarial valuations (performed during the period described in subparagraph (A)(ii)) were performed was at least equal to the sum described in subparagraph (A)(ii); or

(II) the rates of contribution to the plan under the collective bargaining agreements negotiated when the findings of such valuations were available were reasonably expected to provide such contributions;

(ii) the number of actuarial valuations performed during the period described in subparagraph (A)(ii) is—

(I) at least 2, in any case in which such period consists of more than 6 plan years, and

(II) at least 1, in any case in which such period consists of 6 or fewer plan years; and

(iii) if the proposition described in clause (i)(I) is to be established, the plan sponsor certifies that to the best of the plan sponsor's knowledge there is no information available which establishes that the total amount of the contributions received under the plan for any plan year during the period described in subparagraph (A)(ii) for which no valuation was performed is less than the sum described in subparagraph (A)(ii)."

Prior to amendment, ERISA Sec. 4022A(c)(6) read as follows:

"(6) Notwithstanding paragraph (2), in the case of a plan described in paragraph (5)(A), if for any period of 3 consecutive plan years beginning with the first plan year to which the minimum funding standards of section 412 of the Internal Revenue Code of 1986 apply, the value of the assets of the plan for each such plan year is an amount equal to at least 8 times the benefit payments for such plan year—

(A) paragraph (2) shall not apply to such plan; and

(B) the benefit of a participant or beneficiary guaranteed by the corporation with respect to the plan shall be an amount determined under paragraph (1)."

The above amendements shall apply to any multiemployer plan that has not received financial assistance (within the meaning of section 4261 of the Employee Retirement Income Security Act of 1974) within the 1-year period ending on the date of the enactment of this Act.

Amendments

P.L. 101-239, §7891(a)(1):

Titles I, III, and IV of ERISA (other than sections 3(37)(E), 301(a)(7), and 308, the last sentence of section 408(d), and sections 414(c), 4001(a)(3)(ii), and 4303) are each amended by striking "Internal Revenue Code of 1954" each place it appears and inserting "Internal Revenue Code of 1986" effective October 22, 1986.

P.L. 101-239, §7893(b):

Amended ERISA Sec. 4022A(f)(2)(B) by striking "the the enactment" and inserting "the enactment" effective for plan years beginning after December 31, 1985.

P.L. 101-239, §7894(g)(3)(C):

Amended ERISA Sec. 4022A(a)(1) by striking "section 4021" and inserting "this title" effective as if included in P.L. 96-364, §102.

P.L. 99-272:

Act Sec. 11005(c)(4) amended ERISA Sec. 4022A(f)(2)(B) by striking out "Congress by concurrrent resolution" and inserting "the enactment of a joint resolution."

Act Sec. 11005(c)(5) amended ERISA Sec. 4022A(f)(2)(C) by striking out "approved" and inserting "so enacted."

Act Sec. 11005(c)(6) amended ERISA Sec. 4022A(f)(3)(B) by striking out "Congress by a concurrent resolution" and inserting "enactment of a joint resolution."

Act Sec. 11005(c)(7) amended ERISA Sec. 4022A(f)(4)(A) by striking out "concurrent" and inserting "joint."

Act Sec. 11005(c)(8) amended ERISA Sec. 4022A(f)(4)(B) by striking out "concurrent" each place it appeared and inserting "joint" instead; by striking out "That the Congress favors the" and inserting "The;" and, by inserting "is hereby approved" immediately before the period preceding the quotation marks.

Act Sec. 11005(c)(9) amended ERISA Sec. 4022A(f)(4)(C) by striking out "concurrent" and inserting "joint."

Act Sec. 11005(c)(10) amended ERISA Sec. 4022A(g)(4)(A)(ii) by striking out "concurrent" and inserting "joint" and by striking out "adopted" and inserting "enacted."

Act Sec. 11005(c)(11) amended ERISA Sec. 4022A(g)(4)(B) by striking out "concurrent" each place it appeared and inserting "joint" instead; by striking out "That the

Congress disapproves the" and inserting "The;" and by inserting "is hereby disapproved" immediately before the period preceding the quotation marks.

Act Sec. 11005(c)(12) amended ERISA Sec. 4022A(g)(4)(D) by striking out "concurrent" and inserting "joint."

These amendments are effective for plan years beginning after December 31, 1985.

P.L. 96-364, §102:

Added new section 4022A, effective September 26, 1980.

[¶ 15,429L]
AGGREGATE LIMIT ON BENEFITS GUARANTEED

Act Sec. 4022B. (a) Notwithstanding sections 4022 and 4022A, no person shall receive from the corporation pursuant to a guarantee by the corporation of basic benefits with respect to a participant under all multiemployer and single employer plans an amount, or amounts, with an actuarial value which exceeds the actuarial value of a monthly benefit in the form of a life annuity commencing at age 65 equal to the amount determined under section 4022(b)(3)(B) as of the date of the last plan termination.

Act Sec. 4022B. (b) For purposes of this section—

(1) the receipt of benefits under a multiemployer plan receiving financial assistance from the corporation shall be considered the receipt of amounts from the corporation pursuant to a guarantee by the corporation of basic benefits except to the extent provided in regulations prescribed by the corporation, and

(2) the date on which a multiemployer plan, whether or not terminated, begins receiving financial assistance from the corporation shall be considered a date of plan termination.

Amendment:

P.L. 96-364, §102:

Added new ERISA section 4022B, effective September 26, 1980.

Regulations

The following regulations were adopted by the Pension Benefit Guaranty Corporation on July 1, 1996 (61 FR 34002). Prior to July 1, 1996, PBGC regulations were under Chapter XXVI of Title 29 of the Code of Federal Regulations. Effective July 1, 1996, PBGC regulations were moved to Chapter XL, and were renumbered and reorganized. Reg. §4022B.1 was revised April 8, 2002 (67 FR 16949), effective June 1, 2002.

[¶ 15,429M]

§4022B.1 **Aggregate payments limitation.** (a) *Benefits with respect to two or more plans.* If a person (or persons) is entitled to benefits payable with respect to one participant in two or more plans, the aggregate benefits payable by PBGC from its funds is limited by §4022.22 of this chapter (without regard to §4022.22(a)). The PBGC will determine the limitation as of the date of the last plan termination.

(b) *Benefits with respect to two or more participants.* The PBGC will not aggregate the benefits payable with respect to one participant with the benefits payable with respect to any other participant (e.g., if an individual is entitled to benefits both as a participant and as the spouse of a deceased participant). [Revised by 67 FR 16949, April 8, 2002.]

[¶ 15,430]
PLAN FIDUCIARIES

Act Sec. 4023. Notwithstanding any other provision of this Act, a fiduciary of a plan to which section 4021 applies is not in violation of the fiduciary's duties as a result of any act or of any withholding of action required by this title.

Amendments:

P.L. 96-364, §402(a)(5):

Added new ERISA section 4023 to read as above, effective September 26, 1980.

P.L. 96-364, §107:

Repealed ERISA section 4023 (as in effect immediately before the date of enactment of this Act [September 26, 1980]). Prior to its repeal, section 4023 read:

" CONTINGENT LIABILITY COVERAGE

"(a) The corporation shall insure any employer who maintains or contributes to or under a plan to which section 4021 applies against the payment of any liability imposed on him under subtitle D of this title in the event of a termination of that plan. The corporation may develop arrangements with persons engaged in the business of providing insurance under which the insurance coverage described in the preceding sentence could be provided in whole or in part by such private insurers. In developing such arrangements the corporation shall devise a system under which risks are equitably distributed between the corporation and private insurers with respect to the classes of employers insured by each.

"(b) The corporation is authorized to prescribe and collect in such manner as it determines to be appropriate premiums for insurance offered under subsection (a). If the corporation requires all employers to which this title applies to purchase coverage under this section, the provisions of section 4007(b) and (c) apply to the collection of premiums under this section. The premiums shall be determined by the corporation and revised by it from time to time as may be necessary, and shall be chargeable at a

rate sufficient to fund any payment by the corporation becoming necessary under such coverage.

"(c) If the corporation is, in its determination, able to develop a satisfactory arrangement with private insurers, within 36 months after the date of enactment of this Act, to carry out the program of insurance authorized by this section in whole or in part, the corporation is authorized to require employers to elect coverage by such private insurance or by the corporation at such times and in such manner as the corporation determines necessary.

"(d) No payment may be made by the corporation under any insurance provided by it under this section unless the premiums on such insurance have been paid by the employer and the insurance has been in effect (with respect to any benefit) for more than 60 months. The corporation is authorized to prescribe conditions under which no payment will be made by it under any insurance offered under this section without regard to whether premiums for such insurance have been paid.

"(e) Nothing in this section precludes the purchase by the employer of insurance from any other person, or limits the circumstances under which that insurance is payable, or in any way limits the terms and conditions of such insurance, except that the corporation may prescribe as a condition precedent to the purchase of such insurance the payment of a reinsurance premium or other reasonable fee under this section determined by the corporation to be necessary to assure the liquidity and adequacy of any fund or funds established to carry out the provisions of this section.

"(f) In carrying out its duties under subsection (a) to develop arrangements with private insurers the corporation shall consider as an alternative or as a supplement to private insurance the feasibility of using private industry guarantees, indemnities, or letters of credit."

Subtitle C—Terminations

[¶ 15,440]
TERMINATION OF SINGLE-EMPLOYER PLANS

Act Sec. 4041.(a) GENERAL RULES GOVERNING SINGLE-EMPLOYER PLAN TERMINATIONS.—

(1) EXCLUSIVE MEANS OF PLAN TERMINATION. Except in the case of a termination for which proceedings are otherwise instituted by the corporation as provided in section 4042, a single-employer plan may be terminated only in a standard termination under subsection (b) or a distress termination under subsection (c).

(2) 60- DAY NOTICE OF INTENT TO TERMINATE. Not less than 60 days before the proposed termination date of a standard termination under subsection (b) or a distress termination under subsection (c), the plan administrator shall provide to each affected party (other than the corporation in the case of a standard termination) a written notice of intent to terminate stating that such termination is intended and the proposed termination date. The written notice shall include any related additional information required in regulations of the corporation.

(3) ADHERENCE TO COLLECTIVE BARGAINING AGREEMENTS. The corporation shall not proceed with a termination of a plan under this section if the termination would violate the terms and conditions of an existing collective bargaining agreement. Nothing in the preceding sentence shall be construed as limiting the authority of the corporation to institute proceedings to involuntarily terminate a plan under section 4042.

Act Sec. 4041. STANDARD TERMINATION OF SINGLE-EMPLOYER PLANS.—

(b) (1) GENERAL REQUIREMENTS. A single-employer plan may terminate under a standard termination only if—

    (A) the plan administrator provides the 60-day advance notice of intent to terminate to affected parties required under subsection (a) (2),

    (B) the requirements of subparagraphs (A) and (B) of paragraph (2) are met,

    (C) the corporation does not issue a notice of noncompliance under subparagraph (C) of paragraph (2), and

    (D) when the final distribution of assets occurs, the plan is sufficient for benefit liabilities (determined as of the termination date).

(2) TERMINATION PROCEDURE.—

    (A) NOTICE TO THE CORPORATION. As soon as practicable after the date on which the notice of intent to terminate is provided pursuant to subsection (a) (2), the plan administrator shall send a notice to the corporation setting forth—

        (i) certification by an enrolled actuary—

            (I) of the projected amount of the assets of the plan (as of a proposed date of final distribution of assets),

            (II) of the actuarial present value (as of such date) of the benefit liabilities (determined as of the proposed termination date) under the plan, and

            (III) that the plan is projected to be sufficient (as of such proposed date of final distribution) for such benefit liabilities,

        (ii) such information as the corporation may prescribe in regulations as necessary to enable the corporation to make determinations under subparagraph (C), and

        (iii) certification by the plan administrator that—

            (I) the information on which the enrolled actuary based the certification under clause (i) is accurate and complete, and

            (II) the information provided to the corporation under clause (ii) is accurate and complete.

Clause (i) and clause (iii) (I) shall not apply to a plan described in section 412 (i) of the Internal Revenue Code of 1986.

    (B) NOTICE TO PARTICIPANTS AND BENEFICIARIES OF BENEFIT COMMITMENTS [LIABILITIES]. No later than the date on which a notice is sent by the plan administrator under subparagraph (A), the plan administrator shall send a notice to each person who is a participant or beneficiary under the plan—

        (i) specifying the amount of the benefit liabilities (if any) attributable to such person as of the proposed termination date and the benefit form on the basis of which such amount is determined and

        (ii) including the following information used in determining such benefit liabilities:

            (I) the length of service,

            (II) the age of the participant or beneficiary,

            (III) wages,

            (IV) the assumptions, including the interest rate, and

            (V) such other information as the corporation may require.

Such notice shall be written in such manner as is likely to be understood by the participant or beneficiary and as may be prescribed in regulations of the corporation.

    (C) NOTICE FROM THE CORPORATION OF NONCOMPLIANCE.—

        (i) IN GENERAL. Within 60 days after receipt of the notice under subparagraph (A), the corporation shall issue a notice of noncompliance to the plan administrator if—

            (I) it determines, based on the notice sent under paragraph (2) (A) of subsection (b), that there is reason to believe that the plan is not sufficient for benefit liabilities,

            (II) it otherwise determines, on the basis of information provided by affected parties or otherwise obtained by the corporation, that there is reason to believe that the plan is not sufficient for benefit liabilities, or

            (III) it determines that any other requirement of subparagraph (A) or (B) of this paragraph or of subsection (a) (2) has not been met, unless it further determines that the issuance of such notice would be inconsistent with the interests of participants and beneficiaries.

        (ii) EXTENSION. The corporation and the plan administrator may agree to extend the 60-day period referred to in clause (i) by a written agreement signed by the corporation and the plan administrator before the expiration of the 60-day period. The 60-day period shall be extended as provided in the agreement and may be further extended by subsequent written agreements signed by the corporation and the plan administrator made before the expiration of a previously agreed upon extension of the 60-day period. Any extension may be made upon such terms and conditions (including the payment of benefits) as are agreed upon by the corporation and the plan administrator.

    (D) FINAL DISTRIBUTION OF ASSETS IN ABSENCE OF NOTICE OF NONCOMPLIANCE. The plan administrator shall commence the final distribution of assets pursuant to the standard termination of the plan as soon as practicable after the expiration of the 60-day (or extended) period referred to in subparagraph (C), but such final distribution may occur only if—

        (i) the plan administrator has not received during such period a notice of noncompliance from the corporation under subparagraph (C), and

        (ii) when such final distribution occurs, the plan is sufficient for benefit liabilities (determined as of the termination date).

(3) METHODS OF FINAL DISTRIBUTION OF ASSETS.—

    (A) IN GENERAL. In connection with any final distribution of assets pursuant to the standard termination of the plan under this subsection, the plan administrator shall distribute the assets in accordance with section 4044. In distributing such assets, the plan administrator shall—

        (i) purchase irrevocable commitments from an insurer to provide all benefit liabilities under the plan, or

        (ii) in accordance with the provisions of the plan and any applicable regulations, otherwise fully provide all benefit liabilities under the plan. A transfer of assets to the corporation in accordance with section 4050 on behalf of a missing participant shall satisfy this subparagraph with respect to such participant.

(B) CERTIFICATION TO THE CORPORATION OF FINAL DISTRIBUTION OF ASSETS. Within 30 days after the final distribution of assets is completed pursuant to the standard termination of the plan under this subsection, the plan administrator shall send a notice to the corporation certifying that the assets of the plan have been distributed in accordance with the provisions of subparagraph (A) so as to pay all benefit liablities under the plan.

(4) CONTINUING AUTHORITY. Nothing in this section shall be construed to preclude the continued exercise by the corporation, after the termination date of a plan terminated in a standard termination under this subsection, of its authority under section 4003 with respect to matters relating to the termination. A certification under paragraph (3)(B) shall not affect the corporation's obligations under section 4022.

Act Sec. 4041. DISTRESS TERMINATION OF SINGLE-EMPLOYER PLANS.—

(c)(1) IN GENERAL. A single-employer plan may terminate under a distress termination only if—

(A) the plan administrator provides the 60-day advance notice of intent to terminate to affected parties required under subsection (a)(2),

(B) the requirements of subparagraph (A) of paragraph (2) are met, and

(C) the corporation determines that the requirements of subparagraph (B) of paragraph (2) are met.

(2) TERMINATION REQUIREMENTS.—

(A) INFORMATION SUBMITTED TO THE CORPORATION. As soon as practicable after the date on which the notice of intent to terminate is provided pursuant to subsection (a)(2), the plan administrator shall provide the corporation, in such form as may be prescribed by the corporation in regulations, the following information:

(i) such information as the corporation may prescribe by regulation as necessary to make determinations under subparagraph (B) and paragraph (3);

(ii) unless the corporation determines the information is not necessary for purposes of paragraph (3)(A) or section 4062, certification by an enrolled actuary of—

(I) the amount (as of the proposed termination date and, if applicable, the proposed distribution date) of the current value of the assets of the plan,

(II) the actuarial present value (as of such dates) of the benefit liabilities under the plan,

(III) whether the plan is sufficient for benefit liabilities as of such dates,

(IV) the actuarial present value (as of such dates) of benefits under the plan guaranteed under section 4022, and

(V) whether the plan is sufficient for guaranteed benefits as of such dates;

(iii) in any case in which the plan is not sufficient for benefit liabilities as of such date—

(I) the name and address of each participant and beneficiary under the plan as of such date, and

(II) such other information as shall be prescribed by the corporation by regulation as necessary to enable the corporation to be able to make payments to participants and beneficiaries as required under section 4022(c); and

(iv) certification by the plan administrator that—

(I) the information on which the enrolled actuary based the certifications under clause (ii) as accurate and complete, and

(II) the information provided to the corporation under clauses (i) and (iii) is accurate and complete.

Clause (ii) and clause (iv)(I) shall not apply to a plan described in section 412(i) of the Internal Revenue Code of 1986.

(B) DETERMINATION BY THE CORPORATION OF NECESSARY DISTRESS CRITERIA. Upon receipt of the notice of intent to terminate required under subsection (a)(2) and the information required under subparagraph (A), the corporation shall determine whether the requirements of this subparagraph are met as provided in clause (i), (ii), or (iii). The requirements of this subparagraph are met if each person who is (as of the proposed termination date) a contributing sponsor of such plan or a member of such sponsor's controlled group meets the requirements of any of the following clauses:

(i) LIQUIDATION IN BANKRUPTCY OR INSOLVENCY PROCEEDINGS. The requirements of this clause are met by a person if—

(I) such person has filed or has had filed against such person, as of the proposed termination date, a petition seeking liquidation in a case under title 11, United States Code, or under any similar Federal law or law of a State or political subdivision of a State (or a case described in clause (ii) filed by or against such person has been converted, as of such date, to a case in which liquidation is sought), and

(II) such case has not, as of the proposed termination date, been dismissed.

(ii) REORGANIZATION IN BANKRUPTCY OR INSOLVENCY PROCEEDINGS. The requirements of this clause are met by a person if—

(I) such person has filed, or has had filed against such person, as of the proposed termination date, a petition seeking reorganization in a case under title 11, United States Code, or under any similar law of a State or political subdivision of a State (or a case described in clause (i) filed by or against such person has been converted, as of such date, to such a case in which reorganization is sought),

(II) such case has not, as of the proposed termination date, been dismissed,

(III) such person timely submits to the corporation any request for the approval of the bankruptcy court (or other appropriate court in a case under such similar law of a State or political subdivision) of the plan termination, and

(IV) the bankruptcy court (or such other appropriate court) determines that, unless the plan is terminated, such person will be unable to pay all its debts pursuant to a plan of reorganization and wil be unable to continue in business outside a Chapter 11 reorganization process and approves the termination.

(iii) TERMINATION REQUIRED TO ENABLE PAYMENT OF DEBTS WHILE STAYING IN BUSINESS OR TO AVOID UNREASONABLY BURDENSOME PENSION COSTS CAUSED BY DECLINING WORKFORCE. The requirements of this clause are met by a person if such person demonstrates to the satisfaction of the corporation that—

(I) unless a distress termination occurs, such person will be unable to pay such person's debts when due and will be unable to continue in business, or

(II) the costs of providing pension coverage have become unreasonably burdensome to such person, solely as a result of a decline of such person's workforce covered by participants under all single-employer plans of which such person is a contributing sponsor.

(C) NOTIFICATION OF DETERMINATIONS BY THE CORPORATION. The corporation shall notify the plan administrator as soon as practicable of its determinations made pursuant to subparagraph (B).

(3) TERMINATION PROCEDURE.—

(A) DETERMINATIONS BY THE CORPORATION RELATING TO PLAN SUFFICIENCY FOR GUARANTEED BENEFITS AND FOR BENEFIT LIABILITIES. If the corporation determines that the requirements for a distress termination set forth in paragraphs (1) and (2) are met, the corporation shall—

(i) determine that the plan is sufficient for guaranteed benefits (as of the termination date) or that the corporation is unable to make such determination on the basis of information made available to the corporation,

(ii) determine that the plan is sufficient for benefit liabilities (as of the termination date) or that the corporation is unable to make such determination on the basis of information made available to the corporation, and

(iii) notify the plan administrator of the determinations made pursuant to this subparagraph as soon as practicable.

(B) IMPLEMENTATION OF TERMINATION. After the corporation notifies the plan administrator of its determinations under subparagraph (A), the termination of the plan shall be carried out as soon as practicable, as provided in clause (i), (ii), or (iii).

(i) CASES OF SUFFICIENCY FOR BENEFIT LIABILITIES. In any case in which the corporation determines that the plan is sufficient for benefit liabilities, the plan administrator shall proceed to distribute the plan's assets, and make certification to the corporation with respect to such distribution, in the manner described in subsection (b)(3), and shall take such other actions as may be appropriate to carry out the termination of the plan.

(ii) CASES OF SUFFICIENCY FOR GUARANTEED BENEFITS WITHOUT A FINDING OF SUFFICIENCY FOR BENEFIT LIABILITIES. In any case in which the corporation determines that the plan is sufficient for guaranteed benefits, but further determines that it is unable to determine that the plan is sufficient for benefit liabilities on the basis of the information made available to it, the plan administrator shall proceed to distribute the plan's assets in the manner described in subsection (b)(3), make certification to the corporation that the distribution has occurred, and take such actions as may be appropriate to carry out the termination of the plan.

(iii) CASES WITHOUT ANY FINDING OF SUFFICIENCY. In any case in which the corporation determines that it is unable to determine that the plan is sufficient for guaranteed benefits on the basis of the information made available to it, the corporation shall commence proceedings in accordance with section 4042.

(C) FINDINGS AFTER AUTHORIZED COMMENCEMENT OF TERMINATION THAT PLAN IS UNABLE TO PAY BENEFITS. (i) FINDING WITH RESPECT TO BENEFIT LIABILITIES WHICH ARE NOT GUARANTEED BENEFITS. If, after the plan administrator has begun to terminate the plan as authorized under subparagraph (B)(i), the plan administrator finds that the plan is unable, or will be unable, to pay benefit liabilities which are not benefits guaranteed by the corporation under section 4022, the plan administrator shall notify the corporation of such findings as soon as practicable thereafter.

(ii) FINDING WITH RESPECT TO GUARANTEED BENEFITS. If, after the plan administrator has begun to terminate the plan as authorized by subparagraph (B)(i) or (ii), the plan administrator finds that the plan is unable, or will be unable, to pay all benefits under the plan which are guaranteed by the corporation under section 4022, the plan administrator shall notify the corporation of such finding as soon as practicable thereafter. If the corporation concurs in the finding of the plan administrator (or the corporation itself makes such a finding), the corporation shall institute appropriate proceedings under section 4042.

(D) ADMINISTRATION OF THE PLAN DURING INTERIM PERIOD.—. (i) IN GENERAL. The plan administrator shall—

(I) meet the requirements of clause (ii) for the period commencing on the date on which the plan administrator provides a notice of distress termination to the corporation under subsection (a)(2) and ending on the date on which the plan administrator receives notification from the corporation of its determinations under subparagraph (A), and

(II) meet the requirements of clause (ii) commencing on the date on which the plan administrator or the corporation makes a finding under subparagraph (C)(ii).

(ii) REQUIREMENTS. The requirements of this clause are met by the plan administrator if the plan administrator—

(I) refrains from distributing assets or taking any other actions to carry out the proposed termination under this subsection,

(II) pays benefits attributable to employer contributions, other than death benefits, only in the form of an annuity,

(III) does not use plan assets to purchase irrevocable commitments to provide benefits from an insurer, and

(IV) continues to pay all benefit liabilities under the plan, but, commencing on the proposed termination date, limits the payment of benefits under the plan to those benefits which are guaranteed by the corporation under section 4022 or to which assets are required to be allocated under section 4044.

In the event the plan administrator is later determined not to have met the requirements for distress termination, any benefits which are not paid solely by reason of compliance with subclause (IV) shall be due and payable immediately (together with interest, at a reasonable rate, in accordance with regulations of the corporation).

Act Sec. 4041. SUFFICIENCY. (d) For purposes of this section—

(1) SUFFICIENCY FOR BENEFIT LIABILITIES. A single-employer plan is sufficient for benefit liabilities if there is no amount of unfunded benefit liabilities under the plan.

(2) SUFFICIENCY FOR GUARANTEED BENEFITS. A single-employer plan is sufficient for guaranteed benefits if there is no amount of unfunded guaranteed benefits under the plan.

Act Sec. 4041. LIMITATION ON THE CONVERSION OF A DEFINED BENEFIT PLAN TO A DEFINED CONTRIBUTION PLAN. (e) The adoption of an amendment to a plan which causes the plan to become a plan described in section 4021(b)(1) constitutes a termination of the plan. Such an amendment may take effect only after the plan satisfies the requirements for standard termination under subsection (b) or distress termination under subsection (c).

Amendments

P.L. 103-465, § 776(b)(3):

Act Sec. 776(b)(3) amended ERISA Sec. 4041(b)(3)(A)(ii) by adding at the end a new sentence to read as above.

The above amendment is effective with respect to distributions that occur in plan years commencing after final regulations implementing the amendment are prescribed by the Pension Benefit Guaranty Corporation.

P.L. 103-465, § 778(a):

Act Sec. 778(a) amended ERISA Sec. 4041(b)(2)(C)(i) by striking subclause (I) and inserting new subclause (I) to read as above. Prior to amendment, ERISA Sec. 4041(b)(2)(C)(i)(I) read as follows:

(I) it has reason to believe that any requirement of subsection (a)(2) and subparagraph (A) or (B) has not been met, or

Act Sec. 778(a) also amended ERISA Sec. 4041(b)(2)(C)(i) by striking the period at the end of subclause (II) and inserting ", or"; and by adding a new subclause (III) to read as above.

The above amendments apply to any plan termination under ERISA Sec. 4041(b) with respect to which the Pension Benefit Guaranty Corporation has not, as of the date of enactment, issued a notice of noncompliance that has become final, or otherwise issued a final determination that the plan termination is nullified.

P.L. 103-465, § 778(b):

Act Sec. 778(b) amended ERISA Sec. 4041(c)(2)(B)(i)(I) by inserting after "under any similar" the following: "Federal law or".

The above amendment is effective as if included in the Single-Employer Pension Plan Amendments Act of 1986.

P.L. 101-239, § 7881(f)(7):

Amended ERISA Sec. 4041(c) by striking "(or its designee under section 4049(b))" in paragraph (2)(A)(iii)(II), by striking "section 4049" in paragraph (2)(A)(iii)(II) and inserting "section 4022(c)", and by striking the last sentence of paragraph (3)(C)(i) effective as if included in P.L. 100-203, § 9312(c).

Prior to being stricken, the last sentence of clause (i) read as follows:

If the corporation concurs in the findings of the plan administrator (or the corporation itself makes such a finding) the corporation shall take the actions set forth in subparagraph (B)(ii)(II) relating to the trust established for purposes of section 4049.

P.L. 101-239, § 7881(g)(1):

Amended ERISA Sec. 4041(d)(1) by striking "sufficient for benefit commitments" and inserting "sufficient for benefit liabilities," effective as if included in P.L. 100-203, § 9313.

P.L. 101-239, § 7881(g)(2):

Amended ERISA Sec. 4041(c)(2)(B) by inserting "proposed" before "termination" in the parenthetical material in the second sentence, effective as if included in P.L. 100-203, § 9313.

P.L. 101-239, §7881(g)(3):

Amended ERISA Sec. 4041(c)(2)(A)(ii) by inserting new material before "certification," by inserting new material after "termination date" in subclause (I) and by striking "date" and inserting "dates" in subclauses (II) through (V), effective as if included in P.L. 100-203, § 9313(a)(2)(D).

P.L. 101-239, §7881(g)(4):

Amended ERISA Sec. 4041(b)(3)(B) by adding a period at the end, effective December 22, 1987.

P.L. 101-239, §7881(g)(5):

Amended P.L. 100-203, § 9313(b)(3) by inserting "each place it appears" before the period, effective December 22, 1987.

P.L. 101-239, §7893(d)(2):

Amended ERISA Sec. 4041(c)(3)(D)(ii)(I) by striking "of" and inserting "under," effective as if included in P.L. 99-272, § 11009(a).

P.L. 100-203, §9312(c)(1):

Amended ERISA Sec. 4041(c)(3)(B)(ii) by striking subclause (II); by striking "plan, and" at the end of subclause (I) and inserting "plan."; and by striking "available to it—"and all that follows through "the plan administrator" and inserting "available to it, the plan administrator" effective for

(A) plan terminations under section 4041(c) of ERISA with respect to which notices of intent to terminate are provided under section 4041(a)(2) of ERISA after December 17, 1987, and

(B) plan terminations with respect to which proceedings are instituted by the Pension Benefit Guaranty Corporation under section 4042 of ERISA after December 17, 1987.

Prior to amendment ERISA Sec. 4041(c)(3)(B)(ii)(II) read as follows:

(II) the corporation shall establish a separate trust in connection with the plan for purposes of section 4049.

P.L. 100-203, ERISA §9312(c)(2):

Amended ERISA Sec. 4041(c)(3)(B)(iii) by striking subclause (II); by striking "section 4042, and" at the end of subclause (I) and inserting "section 4042."; and by striking "available to it—"and all that follows through "the corporation" in subclause (I) and inserting "available to it, the corporation".

For the effective date, see Act Sec. 9312(c)(1), above. Prior to amendment, ERISA Sec. 4041(c)(3)(B)(iii)(II) read as follows:

(II) the corporation shall establish a separate trust in connection with the plan for purposes of section 4049 unless the corporation determines that all benefit commitments under the plan are benefits guaranteed by the corporation under section 4022.

P.L. 100-203, §9313(a)(1):

Amended ERISA Sec. 4041(b)(1)(D) by striking out "commitments" and inserting "liabilities" instead, to read as above.

P.L. 100-203, §9313(a)(2)(A):

Amended ERISA Sec. 4041(b)(2)(A), (2)(C), (2)(D), (3) by striking out "benefit commitments" and inserting "benefit liabilities" instead each place it appeared, to read as above.

P.L. 100-203, §9313(a)(2)(B):

Amended ERISA Sec. 4041(b)(2)(B)

(i) by striking out "the amount of such person's benefit commitments (if any)" and inserting in lieu thereof "the amount of the benefit liabilities (if any) attributable to such person"; and

(ii) by striking out "such benefit commitments" and inserting in lieu thereof "such benefit liabilities".

Prior to amendment, ERISA Sec. 4041(b)(2)(B) read as follows:

(B) Notice to Participants and Beneficiaries of Benefit Commitments.—No later than the date on which a notice is sent by the plan administrator under subparagraph (A), the plan administrator shall send a notice to each person who is a participant or beneficiary under the plan—

(i) specifying the amount of such person's benefit commitments (if any) as of the proposed termination date and the benefit form on the basis of which such amount is determined and

(ii) including the following information used in determining such benefit commitments:

(I) the length of service,

(II) the age of the participant or beneficiary,

(III) wages,

(IV) the assumptions, including the interest rate, and

(V) such other information as the corporation may require.

Such notice shall be written in such manner as is likely to be understood by the participant or beneficiary and as may be prescribed in regulations of the corporation.

P.L. 100-203, §9313(a)(2)(C)(i):

Amended ERISA Sec. 4041(b)(3)(A) by striking out clauses (i) and (ii) and inserting

"(i) purchase irrevocable commitments from an insurer to provide all benefit liabilities under the plan, or

"(ii) in accordance with the provisions of the plan and any applicable regulations, otherwise fully provide all benefit liabilities under the plan." instead, to read as above.

Prior to amendment, ERISA Sec. 4041(b)(3)(A) read as follows:

(3) Methods of Final Distribution of Assets.—

(A) In General.—In connection with any final distribution of assets pursuant to the standard termination of the plan under this subsection, the plan administrator shall distribute the assets in accordance with section 4044. In distributing such assets, the plan administrator shall—

(i) purchase irrevocable commitments from an insurer to provide the benefit commitments under the plan and all other benefits (if any) under the plan to which assets are required to be allocated under section 4044, or

(ii) in accordance with the provisions of the plan and any applicable regulations of the corporation, otherwise fully provide the benefit commitments under the plan and all other benefits (if any) under the plan to which assets are required to be allocated under section 4044.

P.L. 100-203, §9313(a)(2)(C)(ii):

Amended ERISA Sec. 4041(b)(3)(B) by striking out "so as to pay" and all that followed and inserting "so as to pay all benefit liabilities under the plan" instead, to read as above.

Prior to amendment, ERISA sec. 4041(b)(3)(B) read as follows:

(B) Certification to the Corporation of Final Distribution of Assets.—Within 30 days after the final distribution of assets is completed pursuant to the standard termination of the plan under this subsection, the plan administrator shall send a notice to the corporation certifying that the assets of the plan have been distributed in accordance with the provisions of subparagraph (A) so as to pay the benefit commitments under the plan and all other benefits under the plan to which assets are required to be allocated under section 4044.

P.L. 100-203, §9313(a)(2)(D):

Amended ERISA Secs. 4041(c)(2) and (3) by striking out "benefit commitment" each place it appears (including in any heading) and inserting in lieu thereof "benefit liabilities."

Prior to amendment, ERISA Secs. 4041(c)(2) and (3) read as follows:

(2) Termination Requirements.—

(A) Information Submitted to the Corporation.—As soon as practicable after the date on which the notice of intent to terminate is provided pursuant to subsection (a)(2), the plan administrator shall provide the corporation, in such form as may be prescribed by the corporation in regulations, the following information:

(i) such information as the corporation may prescribe by regulation as necessary to make determinations under subparagraph (B) and paragraph (3);

(ii) certification by an enrolled actuary of—

(I) the amount (as of the proposed termination date) of the current value of the assets of the plan,

(II) the actuarial present value (as of such date) of the benefit commitments under the plan,

(III) whether the plan is sufficient for benefit commitments as of such date,

(IV) the actuarial present value (as of such date) of benefits under the plan guaranteed under section 4022, and

(V) whether the plan is sufficient for guaranteed benefits as of such date;

(iii) in any case in which the plan is not sufficient for benefit commitments as of such date—

(I) the name and address of each participant and beneficiary under the plan as of such date, and

(II) such other information as shall be prescribed by the corporation by regulation as necessary to enable the corporation (or its designee under section 4049(b)) to be able to make payments to participants and beneficiaries required under section 4049, and

(iv) certification by the plan administrator that the information on which the enrolled actuary based the certifications under clause (ii) and the information provided to the corporation and under clauses (i) and (iii) are accurate and complete.

(B) Determination By the Corporation of Necessary Distress Criteria.—Upon receipt of the notice of intent to terminate required under subsection (a)(2) and the information required under subparagraph (A), the corporation shall determine whether the requirements of this subparagraph are met as provided in clause (i), (ii), or (iii). The requirements of this subparagraph are met if each person who is (as of the termination date) a contributing sponsor of such plan or a substantial member of such sponsor's controlled group meets the requirements of any of the following clauses:

(i) Liquidation in Bankruptcy or Insolvency Proceedings.—The requirements of this clause are met by a person if—

(I) such person has filed or has had filed against such person, as of the termination date, a petition seeking liquidation in a case under title 11, United States Code, or under any similar law of a State or political subdivision of a State, and

(II) such case has not, as of the termination date, been dismissed.

(ii) Reorganization in Bankruptcy or Insolvency Proceedings.—The requirements of this clause are met by a person if—

(I) such person has filed, or has had filed against such person, as of the termination date, a petition seeking reorganization in a case under title 11, United States Code, or under any similar law of a State or political subdivision of a State (or a case described in clause (i) filed by or against such person has been converted, as of such date, to such a case in which reorganization is sought),

(II) such case has not, as of the termination date, been dismissed, and

(III) the bankruptcy court (or other appropriate court in a case under such similar law of a State or political subdivision) approves the termination.

(iii) Termination Required to Enable Payment of Debts While Staying in Business or to Avoid Unreasonably Burdensome Pension Costs Caused by Declining Workforce.—The requirements of this clause are met by a person if such person demonstrates to the satisfaction of the corporation that—

(I) unless a distress termination occurs, such person will be unable to pay such person's debts when due and will be unable to continue in business, or

(II) the costs of providing pension coverage have become unreasonably burdensome to such person, solely as a result of a decline of such person's workforce covered as participants under all single-employer plans of which such person is a contributing sponsor.

(C) Substantial Member.—For purposes of subparagraph (B), the term "substantial member" of a controlled group means a person whose assets comprise 5 percent or more of the total assets of the controlled group as a whole.

(D) Notification of Determinations by the Corporation.—The corporation shall notify the plan administrator as soon as practicable of its determinations made pursuant to subparagraph (B).

(3) Termination Procedure.—

(A) Determinations by the Corporation Relating to Plan Sufficiency for Guaranteed Benefits and for Benefit Commitments.—If the corporation determines that the requirements for a distress termination set forth in paragraphs (1) and (2) are met, the corporation shall—

(i) determine that the plan is sufficient for guaranteed benefits (as of the termination date) or that the corporation is unable to make such determinations on the basis of information made available to the corporation,

(ii) determine that the plan is sufficient for benefit commitments (as of the termination date) or that the corporation is unable to make such determination on the basis of information made available to the corporation, and

(iii) notify the plan administrator of the determinations made pursuant to this subparagraph as soon as practicable.

(B) Implementation of Termination.—After the corporation notifies the plan administrator of its determinations under subparagraph (A), the termination of the plan shall be carried out as soon as practicable, as provided in clause (i), (ii), or (iii).

(i) Cases of Sufficiency for Benefit Commitments.—In any case in which the corporation determines that the plan is sufficient for benefit commitments, the plan administrator shall proceed to distribute the plan's assets, and make certification to the corporation with respect to such distribution, in the manner described in subsection (b)(3), and shall take such other actions as may be appropriate to carry out the termination of the plan.

(ii) Cases of Sufficiency for Guaranteed Benefits Without a Finding of Sufficiency for Benefit Commitments.—In any case in which the corporation determines that the plan is sufficient for guaranteed benefits, but further determines that it is unable to determine that the plan is sufficient for benefit commitments on the basis of the information made available to it—

(I) the plan administrator shall proceed to distribute the plan's assets in the manner described in subsection (b)(3), make certification to the corporation that the distribution has occurred, and take such actions as may be appropriate to carry out the termination of the plan, and

(II) the corporation shall establish a separate trust in connection with the plan for purposes of section 4049.

(iii) Cases Without Any Finding of Sufficiency.—In any case in which the corporation determines that it is unable to determine that the plan is sufficient for guaranteed benefits on the basis of the information made available to it—

(I) the corporation shall commence proceedings in accordance with section 4042, and

(II) the corporation shall establish a separate trust in connection with the plan for purposes of section 4049 unless the corporation determines that all benefit commitments under the plan are benefits guaranteed by the corporation under section 4022.

P.L. 100-203, §9313(a)(2)(E):

Amended ERISA Sec. 4041(d)(1) by striking out "no amount of unfunded benefit commitments" and inserting in lieu thereof "no amount of unfunded benefit liabilities", and by striking out "Benefit Commitments" in the paragraph heading and inserting in lieu thereof "Benefit Liabilities," to read as above.

Prior to amendment, ERISA Sec. 4041(d)(1) read as follows:

Act Sec. 4041. (d) Sufficiency.—For purposes of this section—

(1) Sufficiency for Benefit Commitments.—A single-employer plan is sufficient for benefit commitments if there is no amount of unfunded benefit commitments under the plan.

P.L. 100-203, §9313(b)(1):

Amended ERISA Sec. 4041(c)(2)(B) of ERISA by striking "a substantial member" in the matter preceding clause (i) and inserting "a member"; and by striking subparagraph (C) and by redesignating subparagraph (D) as subparagraph (C), to read as above.

P.L. 100-203, §9313(b)(2):

Amended ERISA Sec. 4041(c)(2)(B)(ii)(III) by striking "approves the termination" and inserting "determines that, unless the plan is terminated, such person will be unable to pay all its debts pursuant to a plan of reorganization and will be unable to continue in business outside the chapter 11 reorganization process and approves the termination."

P.L. 100-203, §9313(b)(3):

Amended ERISA Sec. 4041(c)(2)(B) by inserting "proposed" before "termination date", each place it appeared.

P.L. 100-203, §9313(b)(4):

Amended ERISA Sec. 4041(c)(2)(B)(i)(I) by inserting before the comma at the end the following: "(or a case described in clause (ii) filed by or against such person has been converted, as of such date, to a case in which liquidation is sought), to read as above.

P.L. 100-203, §9313(b)(5):

Amended ERISA Sec. 4041(c)(2)(B)(ii) by striking "and" at the end;

by redesignating subclause (III) as subclause (IV);

by inserting after subclause (II) the following new subclause:

"(III) such person timely submits to the corporation any request for the approval of the bankruptcy court (or other appropriate court in a case under such similar law of a State or political subdivision) of the plan termination, and";

and

in subclause (IV) (as redesignated), by striking "(or other" and all that follows through "subdivision)" and inserting "(or such other appropriate court)," to read as above.

The above amendments apply to plan terminations under ERISA Sec. 4041 with respect to which notices of intent to terminate are provided under ERISA Sec. 4041(a)(2) after December 17, 1987.

P.L. 100-203, §9314(a)(1):

Amended ERISA Sec. 4041(b)(2)(A)(iii) to read as above, effective December 22, 1987. Prior to amendment, subparagraph (iii) read as follows:

(iii) certification by the plan administrator that the information on which the enrolled actuary based the certification under clause (i) and the information provided to the corporation under clause (ii) are accurate and complete.

P.L. 100-203, §9314(a)(2):

Amended ERISA Sec. 4041(c)(2)(A)(iv) to read as above, effective December 22, 1987. Prior to amendment, Subparagraph (iv) read as follows:

(iv) certification by the plan administrator that the information on which the enrolled actuary based the certifications under clause (ii) and the information provided to the corporation under clauses (i) and (iii) are accurate and complete.

P.L. 99-272:

Act Sec. 11007(a) amended ERISA Sec. 4041 by striking out subsections (a) through (c) and inserting a new subsection (a) to read as above.

Act Sec. 11008(a) added a new subsection (b) to read as above.

Act Sec. 11009(a) added a new subsection (c) to read as above.

Act Sec. 11007(b) amended subsection (d) to read as above.

Act Sec. 11008(b) amended subsection (f) to read as above.

Act Sec. 11009(b) struck out subsection (e) and renumbered subsection (f) as subsection (e).

These amendments apply with respect to terminations pursuant to notices of intent filed with the PBGC on or after January 1, 1986 or proceedings begun on or after that date.

Prior to the above amendments, ERISA Secs. 4041(a) through (e) read as follows:

Sec. 4041. (a) Before the effective date of the termination of a single-employer plan, the plan administrator shall file a notice with the corporation that the plan is to be terminated on a proposed date (which may not be earlier than 10 days after the filing of the notice), and for a period of 90 days after the proposed termination date the plan administrator shall pay no amount pursuant to the termination procedure of the plan unless, before the expiration of such period, he receives a notice of sufficiency under subsection (b). Upon receiving such a notice, the plan administrator may proceed with the termination of the plan in a manner consistent with this subtitle.

Sec. 4041. (b) If the corporation determines that, after application of section 4044, the assets held under the plan are sufficient to discharge when due all obligations of the plan with respect to basic benefits, it shall notify the plan administrator of such determination as soon as practicable.

Sec. 4041. (c) If, within such 90-day period, the corporation finds that it is unable to determine that, if the assets of the plan are allocated in accordance with the provisions of section 4044, the assets held under the plan are sufficient to discharge when due all obligations of the plan with respect to basic benefits, it shall notify the plan administrator within such 90-day period of that finding. When the corporation issues a notice under this subsection, it shall commence proceedings in accordance with the provisions of section 4042. Upon receiving a notice under this subsection, the plan administrator shall refrain from taking any action under the proposed termination.

Sec. 4041. (d) The corporation and the plan administrator may agree to extend the 90-day period provided by this section by a written agreement signed by the corporation and the plan administrator before the expiration of the 90-day period, or the corporation may apply to an appropriate court (as defined in section 4042(g)) for an order extending the 90-day period provided by this section. The 90-day period shall be extended as provided in the agreement or in any court order obtained by the corporation. The 90-day period may be further extended by subsequent written agreements signed by the corporation and the plan administrator made before the expiration of a previously agreed upon extension of the 90-day period, or by subsequent order of the court. Any extension may be made upon such terms and conditions (including the payment of benefits) as are agreed upon by the corporation and the plan administrator or as specified in the court order.

Sec. 4041. (e) If, after the plan administrator has begun to terminate the plan as authorized by this section, the corporation or the plan administrator finds that the plan is unable, or will be unable, to pay basic benefits when due, the plan administrator shall notify the corporation of such finding as soon as practicable thereafter. If the corporation makes such a finding or concurs with the finding of the plan administrator, it shall institute appropriate proceedings under section 4042. The plan administrator terminating a plan shall furnish such reports to the corporation as it may require for purposes of its duties under this section.

P.L. 96-364, §403(g):

Amended ERISA Sec. 4041 by changing the title of the section to read as above (previously it read: "Termination by Plan Administrator"), amended subsection (a) by inserting "single-employer" after "termination of a" and by striking out subsection (g), effective September 26, 1980. Prior to its being stricken, subsection (g) read as follows:

"Notwithstanding any other provision of this title, a plan administrator or the corporation may petition the appropriate court for the appointment of a trustee in accordance with the provisions of section 4042 if the interests of the participants and beneficiaries would be better served by the appointment of the trustee."

Regulations

The following regulations were adopted by the Pension Benefit Guaranty Corporation on July 1, 1996 (61 FR 34002). Prior to July 1, 1996, PBGC regulations were under Chapter XXVI of Title 29 of the Code of Federal Regulations. Effective July 1, 1996, PBGC regulations were moved to Chapter XL, and were renumbered and reorganized. Reg. § 4041 was amended November 7, 1997 (62 FR 60424), effective January 1, 1998. Reg. § 4041.42 was amended May 28, 1998 (63 FR 29353), effective May 29, 1998. Reg §§ 4041.3 and 4041.5 were amended October 28, 2003 (68 FR 61344).

Subpart A—General Provisions

[¶ 15,440A]

§ 4041.1 **Purpose and scope.** This part sets forth the rules and procedures for terminating a single-employer plan in a standard or distress termination under section 4041 of ERISA, the exclusive means of voluntarily terminating a plan. [Amended 11/7/97 by 62 FR 60424.]

[¶ 15,440A-1]

§ 4041.2 **Definitions.** The following terms are defined in § 4001.2 of this chapter: affected party, annuity, benefit liabilities, Code, contributing sponsor, controlled group, distress termination, distribution date, EIN, employer, ERISA, guaranteed benefit, insurer, irrevocable commitment, IRS, mandatory employee contributions, normal retirement age, notice of intent to terminate, PBGC, person, plan administrator, plan year, PN, single-employer plan, standard termination, termination date, and title IV benefit. In addition, for purposes of this part:

Distress termination notice means the notice filed with the PBGC pursuant to § 4041.45.

Distribution notice means the notice issued to the plan administrator by the PBGC pursuant to § 4041.47(c) upon the PBGC's determination that the plan has sufficient assets to pay at least guaranteed benefits.

Majority owner means, with respect to a contributing sponsor of a single-employer plan, an individual who owns, directly or indirectly, 50 percent or more (taking into account the constructive ownership rules of section 414(b) and (c) of the Code) of—

(1) An unincorporated trade or business;

(2) The capital interest or the profits interest in a partnership; or

(3) Either the voting stock of a corporation or the value of all of the stock of a corporation.

Notice of noncompliance means a notice issued to a plan administrator by the PBGC pursuant to § 4041.31 advising the plan administrator that the requirements for a standard termination have not been satisfied and that the plan is an ongoing plan.

Notice of plan benefits means the notice to each participant and beneficiary required by § 4041.24.

Participant means—

(1) Any individual who is currently in employment covered by the plan and who is earning or retaining credited service under the plan, including any individual who is considered covered under the plan for purposes of meeting the minimum participation requirements but who, because of offset or similar provisions, does not have any accrued benefits;

(2) Any nonvested individual who is not currently in employment covered by the plan but who is earning or retaining credited service under the plan; and

(3) Any individual who is retired or separated from employment covered by the plan and who is receiving benefits under the plan or is entitled to begin receiving benefits under the plan in the future, excluding any such individual to whom an insurer has made an irrevocable commitment to pay all the benefits to which the individual is entitled under the plan.

Plan benefits means benefit liabilities determined as of the termination date (taking into account the rules in § 4041.8(a)).

Proposed termination date means the date specified as such by the plan administrator in the notice of intent to terminate or, if later, in the standard or distress termination notice.

Residual assets means the plan assets remaining after all plan benefits and other liabilities (e.g., PBGC premiums) of the plan have been satisfied (taking into account the rules in § 4041.8(b)).

Standard termination notice means the notice filed with the PBGC pursuant to § 4041.25.

State guaranty association means an association of insurers created by a State, the District of Columbia, or the Commonwealth of Puerto Rico to pay benefits and to continue coverage, within statutory limits, under life and health insurance policies and annuity contracts when an insurer fails. [Amended 11/7/97 by 62 FR 60424.]

[¶ 15,440A-2]

§ 4041.3 **Computation of time; filing and issuance rules.** (a) *Computation of time.* The PBGC applies the rules in subpart D of part 4000 of this chapter to compute any time period under this part. A proposed termination date may be any day, including a weekend or Federal holiday.

(b) *Filing with the PBGC.*

(1) *Method and date of filing.* The PBGC applies the rules in subpart A of part 4000 of this chapter to determine permissible methods of filing with the PBGC under this part. The PBGC applies the rules in subpart C of part 4000 of this chapter to determine the date that a submission under this part was filed with the PBGC.

(2) *Where to file.* See Sec. 4000.4 of this chapter for information on where to file.

(c) *Issuance to third parties.* The following rules apply to affected parties (other than the PBGC). For purposes of this paragraph (c), a person entitled to notice under the spin-off/termination transaction rules of Sec. 4041.23(c) or Sec. 4041.24(f) is treated as an affected party.

(1) *Method and date of issuance.* The PBGC applies the rules in subpart B of part 4000 of this chapter to determine permissible methods of issuance under this part. The PBGC applies the rules in subpart C of part 4000 of this chapter to determine the date that an issuance under this part was provided.

(2) *Omission of affected parties.* The failure to issue any notice to an affected party (other than any employee organization) within the specified time period will not cause the notice to be untimely if—

(i) *After-discovered affected parties.* The plan administrator could not reasonably have been expected to know of the affected party, and issues the notice promptly after discovering the affected party; or

(ii) *Unlocated participants.* The plan administrator could not locate the affected party after making reasonable efforts, and issues the notice promptly in the event the affected party is located.

(3) *Deceased participants.* In the case of a deceased participant, the plan administrator need not issue a notice to the participant's estate if the estate is not entitled to a distribution.

(4) *Form of notices to affected parties.* All notices to affected parties must be readable and written in a manner calculated to be understood by the average plan participant. The plan administrator may provide additional information with a notice only if the information is not misleading.

(5) *Foreign language* s. The plan administrator of a plan that (as of the proposed termination date) covers the numbers or percentages in § 2520.104b-10(e) of this title of participants literate only in the same non-English language must, for any notice to affected parties—

(i) Include a prominent legend in that common non-English language advising them how to obtain assistance in understanding the notice; or

(ii) Provide the notice in that common non-English language to those affected parties literate only in that language.

[Amended 11/7/97 by 62 FR 60424 and 10/28/2003 by 68 FR 61344.]

[¶ 15,440A-3]

§ 4041.4 **Disaster relief.** When the President of the United States declares that, under the Disaster Relief Act (42 U.S.C. 5121, 5122(2), 5141(b)), a major disaster exists, the Executive Director of the PBGC (or his or her designee) may, by issuing one or more notices of disaster relief, extend by up to 180 days any due date under this part. [Amended 11/7/97 by 62 FR 60424.]

§ 4041.5 **Record retention and availability**. (a) *Retention requirement*. (1) *Persons subject to requirement; records to be retained*. Each contributing sponsor and the plan administrator of a plan terminating in a standard termination, or in a distress termination that closes out in accordance with Sec. 4041.50, must maintain all records necessary to demonstrate compliance with section 4041 of ERISA and this part. If a contributing sponsor or the plan administrator maintains information in accordance with this section, the other(s) need not maintain that information.

(2) *Retention period*. The records described in paragraph (a)(1) of this section must be preserved for six years after the date when the post-distribution certification under this part is filed with the PBGC.

(3) *Electronic recordkeeping*. The contributing sponsor or plan administrator may use electronic media for maintenance and retention of records required by this part in accordance with the requirements of subpart E of part 4000 of this chapter.

(b) *Availability of records*. The contributing sponsor or plan administrator must make all records needed to determine compliance with section 4041 of ERISA and this part available to the PBGC upon request for inspection and photocopying (or, for electronic records, inspection, electronic copying, and printout) at the location where they are kept (or another, mutually agreeable, location) and must submit such records to the PBGC within 30 days after the date of a written request by the PBGC or by a later date specified therein.

[Amended 11/7/97 by 62 FR 60424 and 10/28/2003 by 68 FR 61344]

§ 4041.6 **Effect of failure to provide required information**. If a plan administrator fails to provide any information required under this part within the specified time limit, the PBGC may assess a penalty under section 4071 of ERISA of up to $1,100 a day for each day that the failure continues. The PBGC may also pursue any other equitable or legal remedies available to it under the law, including, if appropriate, the issuance of a notice of noncompliance under § 4041.31. [Amended 11/7/97 by 62 FR 60424.]

§ 4041.7 **Challenges to plan termination under collective bargaining agreement**. (a) *Suspension upon formal challenge to termination*. (1) Notice of formal challenge. (i) If the PBGC is advised, before its review period under § 4041.26(a) ends, or before issuance of a notice of inability to determine sufficiency or a distribution notice under § 4041.47(b) or (c), that a formal challenge to the termination has been initiated as described in paragraph (c) of this section, the PBGC will suspend the termination proceeding and so advise the plan administrator in writing.

(ii) If the PBGC is advised of a challenge described in paragraph (a)(1)(i) of this section after the time specified therein, the PBGC may suspend the termination proceeding and will so advise the plan administrator in writing.

(2) *Standard terminations*. During any period of suspension in a standard termination—

(i) The running of all time periods specified in ERISA or this part relevant to the termination will be suspended; and

(ii) The plan administrator must comply with the prohibitions in § 4041.22.

(3) *Distress terminations*. During any period of suspension in a distress termination—

(i) The issuance by the PBGC of any notice of inability to determine sufficiency or distribution notice will be stayed or, if any such notice was previously issued, its effectiveness will be stayed;

(ii) The plan administrator must comply with the prohibitions in § 4041.42; and

(iii) The plan administrator must file a distress termination notice with the PBGC pursuant to § 4041.45.

(b) *Existing collective bargaining agreement*. For purposes of this section, an existing collective bargaining agreement means a collective bargaining agreement that has not been made inoperative by a judicial ruling and, by its terms, either has not expired or is extended beyond its stated expiration date because neither of the collective bargaining parties took the required action to terminate it. When a collective bargaining agreement no longer meets these conditions, it ceases to be an "existing collective bargaining agreement," whether or not any or all of its terms may continue to apply by operation of law.

(c) *Formal challenge to termination*. A formal challenge to a plan termination asserting that the termination would violate the terms and conditions of an existing collective bargaining agreement is initiated when—

(1) Any procedure specified in the collective bargaining agreement for resolving disputes under the agreement commences; or

(2) Any action before an arbitrator, administrative agency or board, or court under applicable labor-management relations law commences.

(d) *Resolution of challenge*. Immediately upon the final resolution of the challenge, the plan administrator must notify the PBGC in writing of the outcome of the challenge, provide the PBGC with a copy of any award or order, and, if the validity of the proposed termination has been upheld, advise the PBGC whether the proposed termination is to proceed. The final resolution ends the suspension period under paragraph (a) of this section.

(1) *Challenge sustained*. If the final resolution is that the proposed termination violates an existing collective bargaining agreement, the PBGC will dismiss the termination proceeding, all actions taken to effect the plan termination will be null and void, and the plan will be an ongoing plan. In this event, in a distress termination, § 4041.42(d) will apply as of the date of the dismissal by the PBGC.

(2) *Termination sustained*. If the final resolution is that the proposed termination does not violate an existing collective bargaining agreement and the plan administrator has notified the PBGC that the termination is to proceed, the PBGC will reactivate the termination proceeding by sending a written notice thereof to the plan administrator, and—

(i) The termination proceeding will continue from the point where it was suspended;

(ii) All actions taken to effect the termination before the suspension will be effective;

(iii) Any time periods that were suspended will resume running from the date of the PBGC's notice of the reactivation of the proceeding;

(iv) Any time periods that had fewer than 15 days remaining will be extended to the 15th day after the date of the PBGC's notice, or such later date as the PBGC may specify; and

(v) In a distress termination, the PBGC will proceed to issue a notice of inability to determine sufficiency or a distribution notice (or reactivate any such notice stayed under paragraph (a)(3) of this section), either with or without first requesting updated information from the plan administrator pursuant to § 4041.45(c).

(e) *Final resolution of challenge*. A formal challenge to a proposed termination is finally resolved when—

(1) The parties involved in the challenge enter into a settlement that resolves the challenge;

(2) A final award, administrative decision, or court order is issued that is not subject to review or appeal; or

(3) A final award, administrative decision, or court order is issued that is not appealed, or review or enforcement of which is not sought, within the time for filing an appeal or requesting review or enforcement.

(f) *Involuntary termination by the PBGC*. Notwithstanding any other provision of this section, the PBGC retains the authority in any case to initiate a plan termination in accordance with the provisions of section 4042 of ERISA. [Amended 11/7/97 by 62 FR 60424.]

§ 4041.8 **Post-termination amendments**. (a) *Plan benefits*. A participant's or beneficiary's plan benefits are determined under the plan's provisions in effect on the plan's termination date. Notwithstanding the preceding sentence, an amendment that is adopted after the plan's termination date is taken into account with respect to a participant's or beneficiary's plan benefits to the extent the amendment—

Labor Laws & Regulations

(1) Does not decrease the value of the participant's or beneficiary's plan benefits under the plan's provisions in effect on the termination date; and

(2) Does not eliminate or restrict any form of benefit available to the participant or beneficiary on the plan's termination date.

(b) *Residual assets.* In a plan in which participants or beneficiaries will receive some or all of the plan's residual assets based on an allocation formula, the amount of the plan's residual assets and each participant's or beneficiary's share thereof is determined under the plan's provisions in effect on the plan's termination date. Notwithstanding the preceding sentence, an amendment adopted after the plan's termination date is taken into account with respect to a participant's or beneficiary's allocation of residual assets to the extent the amendment does not decrease the value of the participant's or beneficiary's allocation of residual assets under the plan's provisions in effect on the termination date.

(c) *Permitted decreases.* For purposes of this section, an amendment shall not be treated as decreasing the value of a participant's or beneficiary's plan benefits or allocation of residual assets to the extent—

(1) The decrease is necessary to meet a qualification requirement under section 401 of the Code;

(2) The participant's or beneficiary's allocation of residual assets is paid in the form of an increase in the participant's or beneficiary's plan benefits; or

(3) The decrease is offset by assets that would otherwise revert to the contributing sponsor or by additional contributions.

(d) *Distress terminations.* In the case of a distress termination, a participant's or beneficiary's benefit liabilities are determined as of the termination date in the same manner as plan benefits under this section. [Amended 11/7/97 by 62 FR 60424.]

Subpart B—Standard Termination Process

[¶ 15,440F]

§ 4041.21 **Requirements for a standard termination.** (a) *Notice and distribution requirements.* A standard termination is valid if the plan administrator—

(1) Issues a notice of intent to terminate to all affected parties (other than the PBGC) in accordance with § 4041.23;

(2) Issues notices of plan benefits to all affected parties entitled to plan benefits in accordance with § 4041.24;

(3) Files a standard termination notice with the PBGC in accordance with § 4041.25;

(4) Distributes the plan's assets in satisfaction of plan benefits in accordance with § 4041.28(a) and (c); and

(5) In the case of a spin-off/termination transaction (as defined in § 4041.23(c)), issues the notices required by § 4041.23(c), § 4041.24(f), and § 4041.27(a)(2) in accordance with such sections.

(b) *Plan sufficiency.* (1) *Commitment to make plan sufficient.* A contributing sponsor of a plan or any other member of the plan's controlled group may make a commitment to contribute any additional sums necessary to enable the plan to satisfy plan benefits in accordance with § 4041.28. A commitment will be valid only if—

(i) It is made to the plan;

(ii) It is in writing, signed by the contributing sponsor or controlled group member(s); and

(iii) In any case in which the person making the commitment is the subject of a bankruptcy liquidation or reorganization proceeding, as described in § 4041.41(c)(1) or (c)(2), the commitment is approved by the court before which the liquidation or reorganization proceeding is pending or a person not in bankruptcy unconditionally guarantees to meet the commitment at or before the time distribution of assets is required.

(2) *Alternative treatment of majority owner's benefit.* A majority owner may elect to forgo receipt of his or her plan benefits to the extent necessary to enable the plan to satisfy all other plan benefits in accordance with § 4041.28. Any such alternative treatment of the majority owner's plan benefits is valid only if—

(i) The majority owner's election is in writing;

(ii) In any case in which the plan would require the spouse of the majority owner to consent to distribution of the majority owner's receipt of his or her plan benefits in a form other than a qualified joint and survivor annuity, the spouse consents in writing to the election;

(iii) The majority owner makes the election and the spouse consents during the time period beginning with the date of issuance of the first notice of intent to terminate and ending with the date of the last distribution; and

(iv) Neither the majority owner's election nor the spouse's consent is inconsistent with a qualified domestic relations order (as defined in section 206(d)(3) of ERISA). [Amended 11/7/97 by 62 FR 60424.]

[¶ 15,440F-1]

§ 4041.22 **Administration of plan during pendency of termination process.** (a) *In general.* A plan administrator may distribute plan assets in connection with the termination of the plan only in accordance with the provisions of this part. From the first day the plan administrator issues a notice of intent to terminate to the last day of the PBGC's review period under § 4041.26(a), the plan administrator must continue to carry out the normal operations of the plan. During that time period, except as provided in paragraph (b) of this section, the plan administrator may not—

(1) Purchase irrevocable commitments to provide any plan benefits; or

(2) Pay benefits attributable to employer contributions, other than death benefits, in any form other than an annuity.

(b) *Exception.* The plan administrator may pay benefits attributable to employer contributions either through the purchase of irrevocable commitments or in a form other than an annuity if—

(1) The participant has separated from active employment or is otherwise permitted under the Code to receive the distribution;

(2) The distribution is consistent with prior plan practice; and

(3) The distribution is not reasonably expected to jeopardize the plan's sufficiency for plan benefits. [Amended 11/7/97 by 62 FR 60424.]

[¶ 15,440F-2]

§ 4041.23 **Notice of intent to terminate.** (a) *Notice requirement.* (1) *In general.* At least 60 days and no more than 90 days before the proposed termination date, the plan administrator must issue a notice of intent to terminate to each person (other than the PBGC) that is an affected party as of the proposed termination date. In the case of a beneficiary of a deceased participant or an alternate payee, the plan administrator must issue a notice of intent to terminate promptly to any person that becomes an affected party after the proposed termination date and on or before the distribution date.

(2) *Early issuance of NOIT.* The PBGC may consider a notice of intent to terminate to be timely under paragraph (a)(1) of this section if the notice was early by a de minimis number of days and the PBGC finds that the early issuance was the result of administrative error.

(b) *Contents of notice.* The PBGC's standard termination forms and instructions package includes a model notice of intent to terminate. The notice of intent to terminate must include—

(1) *Identifying information.* The name and PN of the plan, the name and EIN of each contributing sponsor, and the name, address, and telephone number of the person who may be contacted by an affected party with questions concerning the plan's termination;

(2) *Intent to terminate plan.* A statement that the plan administrator intends to terminate the plan in a standard termination as of a specified proposed termination date and will notify the affected party if the proposed termination date is changed to a later date or if the termination does not occur;

(3) *Sufficiency requirement.* A statement that, in order to terminate in a standard termination, plan assets must be sufficient to provide all plan benefits under the plan;

(4) *Cessation of accruals.* A statement (as applicable) that—

(i) Benefit accruals will cease as of the termination date, but will continue if the plan does not terminate;

(ii) A plan amendment has been adopted under which benefit accruals will cease, in accordance with section 204(h) of ERISA, as of the proposed termination date or a specified date before the proposed termination date, whether or not the plan is terminated; or

(iii) Benefit accruals ceased, in accordance with section 204(h) of ERISA, as of a specified date before the notice of intent to terminate was issued;

(5) *Annuity information.* If required under § 4041.27, the annuity information described therein;

(6) *Benefit information.* A statement that each affected party entitled to plan benefits will receive a written notification regarding his or her plan benefits;

(7) *Summary plan description.* A statement as to how an affected party entitled to receive the latest updated summary plan description under section 104(b) of ERISA can obtain it.

(8) *Continuation of monthly benefits.* For persons who are, as of the proposed termination date, in pay status, a statement (as applicable)—

(i) That their monthly (or other periodic) benefit amounts will not be affected by the plan's termination; or

(ii) Explaining how their monthly (or other periodic) benefit amounts will be affected under plan provisions); and

(9) *Extinguishment of guarantee.* A statement that after plan assets have been distributed in full satisfaction of all plan benefits under the plan with respect to a participant or a beneficiary of a deceased participant, either by the purchase of irrevocable commitments (annuity contracts) or by an alternative form of distribution provided for under the plan, the PBGC no longer guarantees that participant's or beneficiary's plan benefits.

(c) *Spin-off/termination transactions.* In the case of a transaction in which a single defined benefit plan is split into two or more plans and there is a reversion of residual assets to an employer upon the termination of one or more but fewer than all of the resulting plans (a "spin-off/termination transaction"), the plan administrator must, within the time period specified in paragraph (a) of this section, provide a notice describing the transaction to all participants, beneficiaries of deceased participants, and alternate payees in the original plan who are, as of the proposed termination date, covered by an ongoing plan. [Amended 11/7/97 by 62 FR 60424.]

[¶ 15,440F-3]

§ 4041.24 **Notices of plan benefits**. (a) *Notice requirement.* The plan administrator must, no later than the time the plan administrator files the standard termination notice with the PBGC, issue a notice of plan benefits to each person (other than the PBGC and any employee organization) who is an affected party as of the proposed termination date. In the case of a beneficiary of a deceased participant or an alternate payee, the plan administrator must issue a notice of plan benefits promptly to any person that becomes an affected party after the proposed termination date and on or before the distribution date.

(b) *Contents of notice.* The plan administrator must include in each notice of plan benefits—

(1) The name and PN of the plan, the name and EIN of each contributing sponsor, and the name, address, and telephone number of an individual who may be contacted to answer questions concerning plan benefits;

(2) The proposed termination date given in the notice of intent to terminate and any extended proposed termination date under § 4041.25(b);

(3) If the amount of plan benefits set forth in the notice is an estimate, a statement that the amount is an estimate and that plan benefits paid may be greater than or less than the estimate;

(4) Except in the case of an affected party in pay status for more than one year as of the proposed termination date—

(i) The personal data (if available) needed to calculate the affected party's plan benefits, along with a statement requesting that the affected party promptly correct any information he or she believes to be incorrect; and

(ii) If any of the personal data needed to calculate the affected party's plan benefits is not available, the best available data, along with a statement informing the affected party of the data not available and affording him or her the opportunity to provide it; and

(5) The information in paragraphs (c) through (e) of this section, as applicable.

(c) *Benefits of persons in pay status.* For an affected party in pay status as of the proposed termination date, the plan administrator must include in the notice of plan benefits—

(1) The amount and form of the participant's or beneficiary's plan benefits payable as of the proposed termination date;

(2) The amount and form of plan benefits, if any, payable to a beneficiary upon the participant's death and the name of the beneficiary; and

(3) The amount and date of any increase or decrease in the benefit scheduled to occur (or that has already occurred) after the proposed termination date and an explanation of the increase or decrease, including, where applicable, a reference to the pertinent plan provision.

(d) *Benefits of persons with valid elections or de minimis benefits.* For an affected party who, as of the proposed termination date, has validly elected a form and starting date with respect to plan benefits not yet in pay status, or with respect to whom the plan administrator has determined that a nonconsensual lump sum distribution will be made, the plan administrator must include in the notice of plan benefits—

(1) The amount and form of the person's plan benefits payable as of the projected benefit starting date, and what that date is;

(2) The information in paragraphs (c)(2) and (c)(3) of this section;

(3) If the plan benefits will be paid in any form other than a lump sum and the age at which, or form in which, the plan benefits will be paid differs from the normal retirement benefit—

(i) The age or form stated in the plan; and

(ii) The age or form adjustment factors; and

(4) If the plan benefits will be paid in a lump sum—

(i) An explanation of when a lump sum may be paid without the consent of the participant or the participant's spouse;

(ii) A description of the mortality table used to convert to the lump sum benefit (e.g., the mortality table published by the IRS in Revenue Ruling 95-6, 1995-1 C.B. 80) and a reference to the pertinent plan provisions;

(iii) A description of the interest rate to be used to convert to the lump sum benefit (e.g., the 30-year Treasury rate for the third month before the month in which the lump sum is distributed), a reference to the pertinent plan provision, and (if known) the applicable interest rate;

(iv) An explanation of how interest rates are used to calculate lump sums;

(v) A statement that the use of a higher interest rate results in a smaller lump sum amount; and

(vi) A statement that the applicable interest rate may change before the distribution date.

(e) *Benefits of all other persons not in pay status.* For any other affected party not described in paragraph (c) or (d) of this section (or described therein only with respect to a portion of the affected party's plan benefits), the plan administrator must include in the notice of plan benefits—

(1) The amount and form of the person's plan benefits payable at normal retirement age in any one form permitted under the plan;

(2) Any alternative benefit forms, including those payable to a beneficiary upon the person's death either before or after benefits commence;

(3) If the person is or may become entitled to a benefit that would be payable before normal retirement age, the amount and form

512

Labor Laws & Regulations

of benefit that would be payable at the earliest benefit commencement date (or, if more than one such form is payable at the earliest benefit commencement date, any one of those forms) and whether the benefit commencing on such date would be subject to future reduction; and

(4) If the plan benefits may be paid in a lump sum, the information in paragraph (d)(4) of this section.

(f) *Spin-off/termination transactions.* In the case of a spin-off/termination transaction (as defined in §4041.23(c)), the plan administrator must, no later than the time the plan administrator files the standard termination notice for any terminating plan, provide all participants, beneficiaries of deceased participants, and alternate payees in the original plan who are (as of the proposed termination date) covered by an ongoing plan with a notice of plan benefits containing the information in paragraphs (b) through (e) of this section. [Amended 11/6/97 by 62 FR 60424.]

[¶ 15,440F-4]

§4041.25 **Standard termination notice.** (a) *Notice requirement.* The plan administrator must file with the PBGC a standard termination notice, consisting of the PBGC Form 500, completed in accordance with the instructions thereto, on or before the 180th day after the proposed termination date.

(b) *Change of proposed termination date.* The plan administrator may, in the standard termination notice, select a proposed termination date that is later than the date specified in the notice of intent to terminate, provided it is not later than 90 days after the earliest date on which a notice of intent to terminate was issued to any affected party.

(c) *Request for IRS determination letter.* To qualify for the distribution deadline in §4041.28(a)(1)(ii), the plan administrator must submit to the IRS a valid request for a determination of the plan's qualification status upon termination ("determination letter") by the time the standard termination notice is filed. [Amended 11/7/97 by 62 FR 60424.]

[¶ 15,440F-5]

§4041.26 **PBGC review of standard termination notice.** (a) *Review period.* (1) *In general.* The PBGC will notify the plan administrator in writing of the date on which it received a complete standard termination notice at the address provided in the PBGC's standard termination forms and instructions package. If the PBGC does not issue a notice of noncompliance under §4041.31 during its 60-day review period following such date, the plan administrator must proceed to close out the plan in accordance with §4041.28.

(2) *Extension of review period.* The PBGC and the plan administrator may, before the expiration of the PBGC review period in paragraph (a)(1) of this section, agree in writing to extend that period.

(b) *If standard termination notice is incomplete.* (1) *For purposes of timely filing.* If the standard termination notice is incomplete, the PBGC may, based on the nature and extent of the omission, provide the plan administrator an opportunity to complete the notice. In such a case, the standard termination notice will be deemed to have been complete as of the date when originally filed for purposes of §4041.25(a), provided the plan administrator provides the missing information by the later of—

(i) The 180th day after the proposed termination date; or

(ii) The 30th day after the date of the PBGC notice that the filing was incomplete.

(2) *For purposes of PBGC review period.* If the standard termination notice is completed under paragraph (b)(1) of this section, the PBGC will determine whether the notice will be deemed to have been complete as of the date when originally filed for purposes of determining when the PBGC's review period begins under §4041.26(a)(1).

(c) *Additional information.* (1) *Deadline for providing additional information.* The PBGC may in any case require the submission of additional information relevant to the termination proceeding. Any such additional information becomes part of the standard termination notice and must be submitted within 30 days after the date of a written request by the PBGC, or within a different time period specified therein. The PBGC may in its discretion shorten the time period where

it determines that the interests of the PBGC or participants may be prejudiced by a delay in receipt of the information.

(2) *Effect on termination proceeding.* A request for additional information will suspend the running of the PBGC's 60-day review period. The review period will begin running again on the day the required information is received and continue for the greater of—

(i) The number of days remaining in the review period; or

(ii) Five regular business days. [Amended 11/7/97 by 62 FR 60424.]

[¶ 15,440F-6]

§4041.27 **Notice of annuity information.** (a) *Notice requirement.* (1) *In general.* The plan administrator must provide notices in accordance with this section to each affected party entitled to plan benefits other than an affected party whose plan benefits will be distributed in the form of a nonconsensual lump sum.

(2) *Spin-off/termination transactions.* The plan administrator must provide the information in paragraph (d) of this section to a person entitled to notice under §§4041.23(c) or 4041.24(f), at the same time and in the same manner as required for an affected party.

(b) *Content of notice.* The plan administrator must include, as part of the notice of intent to terminate—

(1) *Identity of insurers.* The name and address of the insurer or insurers from whom (if known), or (if not) from among whom, the plan administrator intends to purchase irrevocable commitments (annuity contracts);

(2) *Change in identity of insurers.* A statement that if the plan administrator later decides to select a different insurer, affected parties will receive a supplemental notice no later than 45 days before the distribution date; and

(3) *State guaranty association coverage information.* A statement informing the affected party—

(i) That once the plan distributes a benefit in the form of an annuity purchased from an insurance company, the insurance company takes over the responsibility for paying that benefit;

(ii) That all states, the District of Columbia, and the Commonwealth of Puerto Rico have established "guaranty associations" to protect policy holders in the event of an insurance company's financial failure;

(iii) That a guaranty association is responsible for all, part, or none of the annuity if the insurance company cannot pay;

(iv) That each guaranty association has dollar limits on the extent of its guaranty coverage, along with a general description of the applicable dollar coverage limits;

(v) That in most cases the policy holder is covered by the guaranty association for the state where he or she lives at the time the insurance company fails to pay; and

(vi) How to obtain the addresses and telephone numbers of guaranty association offices from the PBGC (as described in the applicable forms and instructions package).

(c) *Where insurer(s) not known.* (1) *Extension of deadline for notice.* If the identity-of-insurer information in paragraph (b)(1) of this section is not known at the time the plan administrator is required to provide it to an affected party as part of a notice of intent to terminate, the plan administrator must instead provide it in a supplemental notice under paragraph (d) of this section.

(2) *Alternative NOIT information.* A plan administrator that qualifies for the extension in paragraph (c)(1) of this section with respect to a notice of intent to terminate must include therein (in lieu of the information in paragraph (b) of this section) a statement that—

(i) Irrevocable commitments (annuity contracts) may be purchased from an insurer to provide some or all of the benefits under the plan;

(ii) The insurer or insurers have not yet been identified; and

(iii) Affected parties will be notified at a later date (but no later than 45 days before the distribution date) of the name and address

¶15,440F-4   Reg. §4041.24(e)(4)

of the insurer or insurers from whom (if known), or (if not) from among whom, the plan administrator intends to purchase irrevocable commitments (annuity contracts).

(d) *Supplemental notice.* The plan administrator must provide a supplemental notice to an affected party in accordance with this paragraph (d) if the plan administrator did not previously notify the affected party of the identity of insurer(s) or, after having previously notified the affected party of the identity of insurer(s), decides to select a different insurer. A failure to provide a required supplemental notice to an affected party will be deemed to be a failure to comply with the notice of intent to terminate requirements.

(1) *Deadline for supplemental notice.* The deadline for issuing the supplemental notice is 45 days before the affected party's distribution date (or, in the case of an employee organization, 45 days before the earliest distribution date for any affected party that it represents).

(2) *Content of supplemental notice.* The supplemental notice must include—

(i) The identity-of-insurer information in paragraph (b)(1) of this section;

(ii) The information regarding change of identity of insurer(s) in paragraph (b)(2) of this section; and

(iii) Unless the state guaranty association coverage information in paragraph (b)(3) of this section was previously provided to the affected party, such information and the extinguishment-of-guarantee information in § 4041.23(b)(9). [Amended 11/7/97 by 62 FR 60424.]

[¶ 15,440F-7]

§ 4041.28 **Closeout of plan.** (a) *Distribution deadline.* (1) *In general.* Unless a notice of noncompliance is issued under § 4041.31(a), the plan administrator must complete the distribution of plan assets in satisfaction of plan benefits (through priority category 6 under section 4044 of ERISA and part 4044 of this chapter) by the later of—

(i) 180 days after the expiration of the PBGC's 60-day (or extended) review period under § 4041.26(a); or

(ii) If the plan administrator meets the requirements of § 4041.25(c), 120 days after receipt of a favorable determination from the IRS.

(2) *Revocation of notice of noncompliance.* If the PBGC revokes a notice of noncompliance issued under § 4041.31(a), the distribution deadline is extended until the 180th day after the date of the revocation.

(b) *Assets insufficient to satisfy plan benefits.* If, at the time of any distribution, the plan administrator determines that plan assets are not sufficient to satisfy all plan benefits (with assets determined net of other liabilities, including PBGC premiums), the plan administrator may not make any further distribution of assets to effect the plan's termination and must promptly notify the PBGC.

(c) *Method of distribution.* (1) *In general.* The plan administrator must, in accordance with all applicable requirements under the Code and ERISA, distribute plan assets in satisfaction of all plan benefits by purchase of an irrevocable commitment from an insurer or in another permitted form.

(2) *Lump sum calculations.* In the absence of evidence establishing that another date is the "annuity starting date" under the Code, the distribution date is the "annuity starting date" for purposes of—

(i) Calculating the present value of plan benefits that may be provided in a form other than by purchase of an irrevocable commitment from an insurer (e.g., in selecting the interest rate(s) to be used to value a lump sum distribution); and

(ii) Determining whether plan benefits will be paid in such other form.

(3) *Selection of insurer.* In the case of plan benefits that will be provided by purchase of an irrevocable commitment from an insurer, the plan administrator must select the insurer in accordance with the fiduciary standards of Title I of ERISA.

(4) *Participating annuity contracts.* In the case of a plan in which any residual assets will be distributed to participants, a participating annuity contract may be purchased to satisfy the requirement that annuities be provided by the purchase of irrevocable commitments only if the portion of the price of the contract that is attributable to the participation feature—

(i) Is not taken into account in determining the amount of residual assets; and

(ii) Is not paid from residual assets allocable to participants.

(5) *Missing participants.* The plan administrator must distribute plan benefits to missing participants in accordance with part 4050.

(d) *Provision of annuity contract.* If plan benefits are provided through the purchase of irrevocable commitments—

(1) Either the plan administrator or the insurer must, within 30 days after it is available, provide each participant and beneficiary with a copy of the annuity contract or certificate showing the insurer's name and address and clearly reflecting the insurer's obligation to provide the participant's or beneficiary's plan benefits; and

(2) If such a contract or certificate is not provided to the participant or beneficiary by the date on which the post-distribution certification is required to be filed in order to avoid the assessment of penalties under § 4041.29(b), the plan administrator must, no later than that date, provide the participant and beneficiary with a notice that includes—

(i) A statement that the obligation for providing the participant's or beneficiary's plan benefits has transferred to the insurer;

(ii) The name and address of the insurer;

(iii) The name, address, and telephone number of the person designated by the insurer to answer questions concerning the annuity; and

(iv) A statement that the participant or beneficiary will receive from the plan administrator or insurer a copy of the annuity contract or a certificate showing the insurer's name and address and clearly reflecting the insurer's obligation to provide the participant's or beneficiary's plan benefits. [Amended 11/7/97 by 62 FR 60424.]

[¶ 15,440F-8]

§ 4041.29 **Post-distribution certification.** (a) *Deadline.* Within 30 days after the last distribution date for any affected party, the plan administrator must file with the PBGC a post-distribution certification consisting of the PBGC Form 501, completed in accordance with the instructions thereto.

(b) *Assessment of penalties.* The PBGC will assess a penalty for late filing of a post-distribution certification only to the extent the certification is filed more than 90 days after the distribution deadline (including extensions) under § 4041.28(a). [Amended 11/7/97 by 62 FR 60424.]

[¶ 15,440F-9]

§ 4041.30 **Requests for deadline extensions.** (a) *In general.* The PBGC may in its discretion extend a deadline for taking action under this subpart to a later date. The PBGC will grant such an extension where it finds compelling reasons why it is not administratively feasible for the plan administrator (or other persons acting on behalf of the plan administrator) to take the action until the later date and the delay is brief. The PBGC will consider—

(1) The length of the delay; and

(2) Whether ordinary business care and prudence in attempting to meet the deadline is exercised.

(b) *Time of extension request.* Any request for an extension under paragraph (a) of this section that is filed later than the 15th day before the applicable deadline must include a justification for not filing the request earlier.

(c) *IRS determination letter requests.* Any request for an extension under paragraph (a) of this section of the deadline in § 4041.25(c) for submitting a determination letter request to the IRS (in order to qualify for the distribution deadline in § 4041.28(a)(1)(ii)) will be deemed to be granted unless the PBGC notifies the plan administrator otherwise within 60 days after receipt of the request (or, if later, by the end of the PBGC's review period under § 4041.26(a)). The PBGC will notify the plan administrator in writing of the date on which it receives such request.

(d) *Statutory deadlines not extendable.* The PBGC will not—

(1) *Pre-distribution deadlines.* (i) Extend the 60-day time limit under § 4041.23(a) for issuing the notice of intent to terminate; or

(ii) Waive the requirement in § 4041.24(a) that the notice of plan benefits be issued by the time the plan administrator files the standard termination notice with the PBGC; or

(2) *Post-distribution deadlines.* Extend the deadline under § 4041.29(a) for filing the post-distribution certification. However, the PBGC will assess a penalty for late filing of a post-distribution certification only under the circumstances described in § 4041.29(b). [Amended 11/7/97 by 62 FR 60424.]

[¶ 15,440F-10]

§ 4041.31 **Notice of noncompliance.** (a) *Failure to meet pre-distribution requirements.* (1) *In general.* Except as provided in paragraphs (a)(2) and (c) of this section, the PBGC will issue a notice of noncompliance within the 60-day (or extended) time period prescribed by § 4041.26(a) whenever it determines that—

(i) The plan administrator failed to issue the notice of intent to terminate to all affected parties (other than the PBGC) in accordance with § 4041.23;

(ii) The plan administrator failed to issue notices of plan benefits to all affected parties entitled to plan benefits in accordance with § 4041.24;

(iii) The plan administrator failed to file the standard termination notice in accordance with § 4041.25;

(iv) As of the distribution date proposed in the standard termination notice, plan assets will not be sufficient to satisfy all plan benefits under the plan; or

(v) In the case of a spin-off/termination transaction (as described in § 4041.23(c)), the plan administrator failed to issue any notice required by § 4041.23(c), § 4041.24(f), or § 4041.27(a)(2) in accordance with such section.

(2) *Interests of participants.* The PBGC may decide not to issue a notice of noncompliance based on a failure to meet a requirement under paragraphs (a)(1)(i) through (a)(1)(iii) or (a)(1)(v) of this section if it determines that issuance of the notice would be inconsistent with the interests of participants and beneficiaries.

(3) *Continuing authority.* The PBGC may issue a notice of noncompliance or suspend the termination proceeding based on a failure to meet a requirement under paragraphs (a)(1)(i) through (a)(1)(v) of this section after expiration of the 60-day (or extended) time period prescribed by § 4041.26(a) (including upon audit) if the PBGC determines such action is necessary to carry out the purposes of Title IV.

(b) *Failure to meet distribution requirements.* (1) *In general.* If the PBGC determines, as part of an audit or otherwise, that the plan administrator has not satisfied any distribution requirement of § 4041.28(a) or (c), it may issue a notice of noncompliance.

(2) *Criteria.* In deciding whether to issue a notice of noncompliance under paragraph (b)(1) of this section, the PBGC may consider—

(i) The nature and extent of the failure to satisfy a requirement of § 4041.28(a) or (c);

(ii) Any corrective action taken by the plan administrator; and

(iii) The interests of participants and beneficiaries.

(3) *Late distributions.* The PBGC will not issue a notice of noncompliance for failure to distribute timely based on any facts disclosed in the post-distribution certification if 60 or more days have passed from the PBGC's receipt of the post-distribution certification. The 60-day period may be extended by agreement between the plan administrator and the PBGC.

(c) *Correction of errors.* The PBGC will not issue a notice of noncompliance based solely on the plan administrator's inclusion of erroneous information (or omission of correct information) in a notice required to be provided to any person under this part if—

(1) The PBGC determines that the plan administrator acted in good faith in connection with the error;

(2) The plan administrator corrects the error no later than—

(i) In the case of an error in the notice of plan benefits under § 4041.24, the latest date an election notice may be provided to the person; or

(ii) In any other case, as soon as practicable after the plan administrator knows or should know of the error, or by any later date specified by the PBGC; and

(3) The PBGC determines that the delay in providing the correct information will not substantially harm any person.

(d) *Reconsideration.* A plan administrator may request reconsideration of a notice of noncompliance in accordance with the rules prescribed in part 4003, subpart C.

(e) *Consequences of notice of noncompliance.* (1) *Effect on termination.* A notice of noncompliance ends the standard termination proceeding, nullifies all actions taken to terminate the plan, and renders the plan an ongoing plan. A notice of noncompliance is effective upon the expiration of the period within which the plan administrator may request reconsideration under paragraph (d) of this section or, if reconsideration is requested, a decision by the PBGC upholding the notice. However, once a notice is issued, the running of all time periods specified in ERISA or this part relevant to the termination will be suspended, and the plan administrator may take no further action to terminate the plan (except by initiation of a new termination) unless and until the notice is revoked. A plan administrator that still desires to terminate a plan must initiate the termination process again, starting with the issuance of a new notice of intent to terminate.

(2) *Effect on plan administration.* If the PBGC issues a notice of noncompliance, the prohibitions in § 4041.22(a)(1) and (a)(2) will cease to apply—

(i) Upon expiration of the period during which reconsideration may be requested or, if earlier, at the time the plan administrator decides not to request reconsideration; or

(ii) If reconsideration is requested, upon PBGC issuance of a decision on reconsideration upholding the notice of noncompliance.

(3) *Revocation of notice of noncompliance.* If a notice of noncompliance is revoked, unless the PBGC provides otherwise, any time period suspended by the issuance of the notice will resume running from the date of the revocation. In no case will the review period under § 4041.26(a) end less than 60 days from the date the PBGC received the standard termination notice.

(f) *If no notice of noncompliance is issued.* A standard termination is deemed to be valid if—

(1) The plan administrator files a standard termination notice under § 4041.25 and the PBGC does not issue a notice of noncompliance pursuant to § 4041.31(a); and

(2) The plan administrator files a post-distribution certification under § 4041.29 and the PBGC does not issue a notice of noncompliance pursuant to § 4041.31(b).

(g) *Notice to affected parties.* Upon a decision by the PBGC on reconsideration affirming the issuance of a notice of noncompliance or, if earlier, upon the plan administrator's decision not to request reconsideration, the plan administrator must notify the affected parties (other than the PBGC), and any persons who were provided notice under § 4041.23(c), in writing that the plan is not going to terminate or, if applicable, that the termination was invalid but that a new notice of intent to terminate is being issued. [Amended 11/7/97 by 62 FR 60424.]

Subpart C—Distress Termination Process

[¶ 15,440J]

§ 4041.41 **Requirements for a distress termination.** (a) *Distress requirements.* A plan may be terminated in a distress termination only if—

(1) The plan administrator issues a notice of intent to terminate to each affected party in accordance with § 4041.43 at least 60 days and (except with PBGC approval) not more than 90 days before the proposed termination date;

(2) The plan administrator files a distress termination notice with the PBGC in accordance with §4041.45 no later than 120 days after the proposed termination date; and

(3) The PBGC determines that each contributing sponsor and each member of its controlled group satisfy one of the distress criteria set forth in paragraph (c) of this section.

(b) *Effect of failure to satisfy requirements.* (1) Except as provided in paragraph (b)(2)(i) of this section, if the plan administrator does not satisfy all of the requirements for a distress termination, any action taken to effect the plan termination is null and void, and the plan is an ongoing plan. A plan administrator who still desires to terminate the plan must initiate the termination process again, starting with the issuance of a new notice of intent to terminate.

(2)(i) The PBGC may, upon its own motion, waive any requirement with respect to notices to be filed with the PBGC under paragraph (a)(1) or (a)(2) of this section if the PBGC believes that it will be less costly or administratively burdensome to the PBGC to do so. The PBGC will not entertain requests for waivers under this paragraph.

(ii) Notwithstanding any other provision of this part, the PBGC retains the authority in any case to initiate a plan termination in accordance with the provisions of section 4042 of ERISA.

(c) *Distress criteria.* In a distress termination, each contributing sponsor and each member of its controlled group must satisfy at least one (but not necessarily the same one) of the following criteria in order for a distress termination to occur:

(1) *Liquidation.* This criterion is met if, as of the proposed termination date—

(i) A person has filed or had filed against it a petition seeking liquidation in a case under title 11, United States Code, or under a similar federal law or law of a State or political subdivision of a State, or a case described in paragraph (e)(2) of this section has been converted to such a case; and

(ii) The case has not been dismissed.

(2) *Reorganization.* This criterion is met if—

(i) As of the proposed termination date, a person has filed or had filed against it a petition seeking reorganization in a case under title 11, United States Code, or under a similar law of a state or a political subdivision of a state, or a case described in paragraph (e)(1) of this section has been converted to such a case;

(ii) As of the proposed termination date, the case has not been dismissed;

(iii) The person notifies the PBGC of any request to the bankruptcy court (or other appropriate court in a case under such similar law of a state or a political subdivision of a state) for approval of the plan termination by concurrently filing with the PBGC a copy of the motion requesting court approval, including any documents submitted in support of the request; and

(iv) The bankruptcy court or other appropriate court determines that, unless the plan is terminated, such person will be unable to pay all its debts pursuant to a plan of reorganization and will be unable to continue in business outside the reorganization process and approves the plan termination.

(3) *Inability to continue in business.* This criterion is met if a person demonstrates to the satisfaction of the PBGC that, unless a distress termination occurs, the person will be unable to pay its debts when due and to continue in business.

(4) *Unreasonably burdensome pension costs.* This criterion is met if a person demonstrates to the satisfaction of the PBGC that the person's costs of providing pension coverage have become unreasonably burdensome solely as a result of declining covered employment under all single-employer plans for which that person is a contributing sponsor.

(d) *Non-duplicative efforts.* (1) If a person requests approval of the plan termination by a court, as described in paragraph (c)(2) of this section, the PBGC—

(i) Will normally enter an appearance to request that the court make specific findings as to whether the contributing sponsor or controlled group member meets the distress test in paragraph (c)(3) of this section, or state that it is unable to make such findings;

(ii) Will provide the court with any information it has that may be germane to the court's ruling;

(iii) Will, if the person has requested, or later requests, a determination by the PBGC under paragraph (c)(3) of this section, defer action on the request until the court makes its determination; and

(iv) Will be bound by a final and non-appealable order of the court.

(2) If a person requests a determination by the PBGC under paragraph (c)(3) of this section, the PBGC determines that the distress criterion is not met, and the person thereafter requests approval of the plan termination by a court, as described in paragraph (c)(2) of this section, the PBGC will advise the court of its determination and make its administrative record available to the court.

(e) *Non-recognition of certain actions.* If the PBGC finds that a person undertook any action or failed to act for the principal purpose of satisfying any of the distress criteria contained in paragraph (c) of this section, rather than for a reasonable business purpose, the PBGC will disregard such act or failure to act in determining whether the person has satisfied any of those criteria.

(f) *Requests for deadline extensions.* The PBGC may extend any deadline under this subpart in accordance with the rules described in section §4041.30, except that the PBGC will not extend—

(1) *Pre-distribution deadlines.* The 60-day time limit under §4041.43(a) for issuing the notice of intent to terminate; or

(2) *Post-distribution deadlines.* The deadline under §4041.50 for filing the post-distribution certification. [Amended 11/7/97 by 62 FR 60424.]

[¶ 15,440J-1]

§4041.42 Administration of plan during termination process. (a) *General rule.* Except to the extent specifically prohibited by this section, during the pendency of termination proceedings the plan administrator must continue to carry out the normal operations of the plan, such as putting participants into pay status, collecting contributions due the plan, and investing plan assets.

(b) *Prohibitions after issuing notice of intent to terminate.* The plan administrator may not make loans to plan participants beginning on the first day he or she issues a notice of intent to terminate, and from that date until a distribution is permitted pursuant to §4041.50, the plan administrator may not—

(1) Distribute plan assets pursuant to, or (except as required by this part) take any other actions to implement, the termination of the plan;

(2) Pay benefits attributable to employer contributions, other than death benefits, in any form other than as an annuity; or

(3) Purchase irrevocable commitments to provide benefits from an insurer.

(c) *Limitation on benefit payments on or after proposed termination date.* Beginning on the proposed termination date, the plan administrator must reduce benefits to the level determined under part 4022, subpart D, of this chapter.

(d) *Failure to qualify for distress termination.* In any case where the PBGC determines, pursuant to §4041.44(c) or §4041.46(c)(1), that the requirements for a distress termination are not satisfied—

(1) The prohibitions in paragraph (b) of this section, other than those in paragraph (b)(1), will cease to apply—

(i) Upon expiration of the period during which reconsideration may be requested under §§4041.44(e) and 4041.46(e) or, if earlier, at the time the plan administrator decides not to request reconsideration; or

(ii) If reconsideration is requested, upon PBGC issuance of its decision on reconsideration.

(2) Any benefits that were not paid pursuant to paragraph (c) of this section will be due and payable as of the effective date of the PBGC's determination, together with interest from the date (or dates)

on which the unpaid amounts were originally due until the date on which they are paid in full at the rate or rates prescribed under §4022.81(c)(3) of this chapter.

(e) *Effect of subsequent insufficiency.* If the plan administrator makes a finding of subsequent insufficiency for guaranteed benefits pursuant to §4041.49(b), or the PBGC notifies the plan administrator that it has made a finding of subsequent insufficiency for guaranteed benefits pursuant to §4041.40(d), the prohibitions in paragraph (b) of this section will apply in accordance with §4041.49(e). [Amended 11/7/97 by 62 FR 60424.]

[¶ 15,440J-2]

§4041.43 **Notice of intent to terminate.** (a) *General rules.* (1) At least 60 days and (except with PBGC approval) no more than 90 days before the proposed termination date, the plan administrator must issue a written notice of intent to terminate to each person who is an affected party as of the proposed termination date.

(2) The plan administrator must issue the notice of intent to terminate to all affected parties other than the PBGC at or before the time he or she files the notice with the PBGC.

(3) The notice to affected parties other than the PBGC must contain all of the information specified in paragraph (b) of this section.

(4) The notice to the PBGC must be filed on PBGC Form 600, Distress Termination, Notice of Intent to Terminate, completed in accordance with the instructions thereto.

(5) In the case of a beneficiary of a deceased participant or an alternate payee, the plan administrator must issue a notice of intent to terminate promptly to any person that becomes an affected party after the proposed termination date and on or before the date a trustee is appointed for the plan pursuant to section 4042(c) of ERISA (or, in the case of a plan that distributes assets pursuant to §4041.50, the distribution date).

(b) *Contents of notice to affected parties other than the PBGC.* The plan administrator must include in the notice of intent to terminate to each affected party other than the PBGC all of the following information:

(1) The name of the plan and of the contributing sponsor;

(2) The EIN of the contributing sponsor and the PN; if there is no EIN or PN, the notice must so state;

(3) The name, address, and telephone number of the person who may be contacted by an affected party with questions concerning the plan's termination;

(4) A statement that the plan administrator expects to terminate the plan in a distress termination on a specified proposed termination date;

(5) The cessation of accruals information in §4041.23(b)(4);

(6) A statement as to how an affected party entitled to receive the latest updated summary plan description under section 104(b) of ERISA can obtain it;

(7) A statement of whether plan assets are sufficient to pay all guaranteed benefits or all benefit liabilities;

(8) A brief description of what benefits are guaranteed by the PBGC (e.g., if only a portion of the benefits are guaranteed because of the phase-in rule, this should be explained), and a statement that participants and beneficiaries also may receive a portion of the benefits to which each is entitled under the terms of the plan in excess of guaranteed benefits; and

(9) A statement, if applicable, that benefits may be subject to reduction because of the limitations on the amounts guaranteed by the PBGC or because plan assets are insufficient to pay for full benefits (pursuant to part 4022, subparts B and D, of this chapter) and that payments in excess of the amount guaranteed by the PBGC may be recouped by the PBGC (pursuant to part 4022, subpart E, of this chapter).

(c) *Spin-off/termination transactions.* In the case of a spin-off/termination transaction (as described in §4041.23(c)), the plan administrator must provide all participants and beneficiaries in the original plan who are also participants or beneficiaries in the ongoing plan (as

of the proposed termination date) with a notice describing the transaction no later than the date on which the plan administrator completes the issuance of notices of intent to terminate under this section. [Amended 11/7/97 by 62 FR 60424.]

[¶ 15,440J-3]

§4041.44 **PBGC review of notice of intent to terminate.** (a) *General.* When a notice of intent to terminate is filed with it, the PBGC—

(1) Will determine whether the notice was issued in compliance with §4041.43; and

(2) Will advise the plan administrator of its determination, in accordance with paragraph (b) or (c) of this section, no later than the proposed termination date specified in the notice.

(b) *Tentative finding of compliance.* If the PBGC determines that the issuance of the notice of intent to terminate appears to be in compliance with §4041.43, it will notify the plan administrator in writing that—

(1) The PBGC has made a tentative determination of compliance;

(2) The distress termination proceeding may continue; and

(3) After reviewing the distress termination notice filed pursuant to §4041.45, the PBGC will make final, or reverse, this tentative determination.

(c) *Finding of noncompliance.* If the PBGC determines that the issuance of the notice of intent to terminate was not in compliance with §4041.43 (except for requirements that the PBGC elects to waive under §4041.41(b)(2)(i) with respect to the notice filed with the PBGC), the PBGC will notify the plan administrator in writing—

(1) That the PBGC has determined that the notice of intent to terminate was not properly issued; and

(2) That the proposed distress termination is null and void and the plan is an ongoing plan.

(d) *Information on need to institute section 4042 proceedings.* The PBGC may require the plan administrator to submit, within 20 days after the plan administrator's receipt of the PBGC's written request (or such other period as may be specified in such written request), any information that the PBGC determines it needs in order to decide whether to institute termination or trusteeship proceedings pursuant to section 4042 of ERISA, whenever—

(1) A notice of intent to terminate indicates that benefits currently in pay status (or that should be in pay status) are not being paid or that this is likely to occur within the 180-day period following the issuance of the notice of intent to terminate;

(2) The PBGC issues a determination under paragraph (c) of this section; or

(3) The PBGC has any reason to believe that it may be necessary or appropriate to institute proceedings under section 4042 of ERISA.

(e) *Reconsideration of finding of noncompliance.* A plan administrator may request reconsideration of the PBGC's determination of noncompliance under paragraph (c) of this section in accordance with the rules prescribed in part 4003, subpart C, of this chapter. Any request for reconsideration automatically stays the effectiveness of the determination until the PBGC issues its decision on reconsideration, but does not stay the time period within which information must be submitted to the PBGC in response to a request under paragraph (d) of this section.

(f) *Notice to affected parties.* Upon a decision by the PBGC affirming a finding of noncompliance or upon the expiration of the period within which the plan administrator may request reconsideration of a finding of noncompliance (or, if earlier, upon the plan administrator's decision not to request reconsideration), the plan administrator must notify the affected parties (and any persons who were provided notice under §4041.43(e)) in writing that the plan is not going to terminate or, if applicable, that the termination is invalid but that a new notice of intent to terminate is being issued. [Amended 11/7/97 by 62 FR 60424.]

[¶ 15,440J-4]

§ 4041.45 **Distress termination notice**. (a) *General rule*. The plan administrator must file with the PBGC a PBGC Form 601, Distress Termination Notice, Single-Employer Plan Termination, with Schedule EA-D, Distress Termination Enrolled Actuary Certification, that has been completed in accordance with the instructions thereto, on or before the 120th day after the proposed termination date.

(b) *Participant and benefit information*. (1) *Plan insufficient for guaranteed benefits*. Unless the enrolled actuary certifies, in the Schedule EA-D filed in accordance with paragraph (a) of this section, that the plan is sufficient either for guaranteed benefits or for benefit liabilities, the plan administrator must file with the PBGC the participant and benefit information described in PBGC Form 601 and the instructions thereto by the later of—

(i) 120 days after the proposed termination date, or

(ii) 30 days after receipt of the PBGC's determination, pursuant to § 4041.46(b), that the requirements for a distress termination have been satisfied.

(2) *Plan sufficient for guaranteed benefits or benefit liabilities*. If the enrolled actuary certifies that the plan is sufficient either for guaranteed benefits or for benefit liabilities, the plan administrator need not submit the participant and benefit information described in PBGC Form 601 and the instructions thereto unless requested to do so pursuant to paragraph (c) of this section.

(3) *Effect of failure to provide information*. The PBGC may void the distress termination if the plan administrator fails to provide complete participant and benefit information in accordance with this section.

(c) *Additional information*. The PBGC may in any case require the submission of any additional information that it needs to make the determinations that it is required to make under this part or to pay benefits pursuant to section 4061 or 4022(c) of ERISA. The plan administrator must submit any information requested under this paragraph within 30 days after receiving the PBGC's written request (or such other period as may be specified in such written request). [Amended 11/7/97 by 62 FR 60424.]

[¶ 15,440J-5]

§ 4041.46 **PBGC determination of compliance with requirements for distress termination**. (a) *General*. Based on the information contained and submitted with the PBGC Form 600 and the PBGC Form 601, with Schedule EA-D, and on any information submitted by an affected party or otherwise obtained by the PBGC, the PBGC will determine whether the requirements for a distress termination set forth in § 4041.41(c) have been met and will notify the plan administrator in writing of its determination, in accordance with paragraph (b) or (c) of this section.

(b) *Qualifying termination*. If the PBGC determines that all of the requirements of § 4041.41(c) have been satisfied, it will so advise the plan administrator and will also advise the plan administrator of whether participant and benefit information must be submitted in accordance with § 4041.45(b).

(c) *Non-qualifying termination*. (1) Except as provided in paragraph (c)(2) of this section, if the PBGC determines that any of the requirements of § 4041.41 have not been met, it will notify the plan administrator of its determination, the basis therefor, and the effect thereof (as provided in § 4041.41(b)).

(2) If the only basis for the PBGC's determination described in paragraph (c)(1) of this section is that the distress termination notice is incomplete, the PBGC will advise the plan administrator of the missing item(s) of information and that the information must be filed with the PBGC no later than the 120th day after the proposed termination date or the 30th day after the date of the PBGC's notice of its determination, whichever is later.

(d) *Reconsideration of determination of non-qualification*. A plan administrator may request reconsideration of the PBGC's determination under paragraph (c)(1) of this section in accordance with the rules prescribed in part 4003, subpart C, of this chapter. The filing of a request for reconsideration automatically stays the effectiveness of the determination until the PBGC issues its decision on reconsideration.

(e) *Notice to affected parties*. Upon a decision by the PBGC affirming a determination of non-qualification or upon the expiration of the period within which the plan administrator may request reconsideration of a determination of non-qualification (or, if earlier, upon the plan administrator's decision not to request reconsideration), the plan administrator must notify the affected parties (and any persons who were provided notice under § 4041.43(e)) in writing that the plan is not going to terminate or, if applicable, that the termination is invalid but that a new notice of intent to terminate is being issued. [Amended 11/7/97 by 62 FR 60424.]

[¶ 15,440J-6]

§ 4041.47 **PBGC determination of plan sufficiency/insufficiency**. (a) *General*. Upon receipt of participant and benefit information filed pursuant to § 4041.45(b)(1) or (c), the PBGC will determine the degree to which the plan is sufficient and notify the plan administrator in writing of its determination in accordance with paragraph (b) or (c) of this section.

(b) *Insufficiency for guaranteed benefits*. If the PBGC finds that it is unable to determine that a plan is sufficient for guaranteed benefits, it will issue a "notice of inability to determine sufficiency" notifying the plan administrator of this finding and advising the plan administrator that—

(1) The plan administrator must continue to administer the plan under the restrictions imposed by § 4041.42; and

(2) The termination will be completed under section 4042 of ERISA.

(c) *Sufficiency for guaranteed benefits or benefit liabilities*. If the PBGC determines that a plan is sufficient for guaranteed benefits but not for benefit liabilities or is sufficient for benefit liabilities, the PBGC will issue to the plan administrator a distribution notice advising the plan administrator—

(1) To issue notices of benefit distribution in accordance with § 4041.48;

(2) To close out the plan in accordance with § 4041.50;

(3) To file a timely post-distribution certification with the PBGC in accordance with § 4041.50(b); and

(4) That either the plan administrator or the contributing sponsor must preserve and maintain plan records in accordance with § 4041.5.

(d) *Alternative treatment of majority owner's benefit*. A majority owner may elect to forgo receipt of all or part of his or her plan benefits in connection with a distress termination. Any such alternative treatment—

(1) Is valid only if the conditions in § 4041.21(b)(2)(i) through (iv) are met (except that, in the case of a plan that does not distribute assets pursuant to § 4041.50, the majority owner may make the election and the spouse may consent any time on or after the date of issuance of the first notice of intent to terminate); and—

(2) Is subject to the PBGC's approval if the election—

(i) Is made after the termination date; and

(ii) Would result in the PBGC determining that the plan is sufficient for guaranteed benefits under paragraph (c). [Amended 11/7/97 by 62 FR 60424.]

[¶ 15,440J-7]

§ 4041.48 **Sufficient plans; notice requirements**. (a) *Notices of benefit distribution*. When a distribution notice is issued by the PBGC pursuant to § 4041.47, the plan administrator must issue notices of benefit distribution in accordance with the rules regarding notices of plan benefits in § 4041.24, except that—

(1) The deadline for issuing the notices of benefit distribution is the 60th day after receipt of the distribution notice; and

(2) With respect to the information described in § 4041.24(b) through (e), the term "plan benefits" is replaced with "title IV benefits" and the term "proposed termination date" is replaced with "termination date".

(b) *Certification to PBGC*. No later than 15 days after the date on which the plan administrator completes the issuance of the notices of benefit distribution, the plan administrator must file with the PBGC a certification that the notices were so issued in accordance with the requirements of this section.

(c) *Notice of annuity information*. (1) *In general*. Unless all title IV benefits will be distributed in the form of nonconsensual lump sums, the plan administrator must provide a notice of annuity information to each affected party other than—

(i) An affected party whose title IV benefits will be distributed in the form of a nonconsensual lump sum; and

(ii) The PBGC.

(2) *Spin-off/termination transactions*. The plan administrator must provide the information in paragraph (c)(4) of this section to a person entitled to notice under § 4041.43(c), at the same time and in the same manner as required for an affected party described in paragraph (c)(1) of this section.

(3) *Selection of different insurer*. A plan administrator that decides to select a different insurer after having previously notified the affected party of the identity of insurer(s) under this paragraph must provide another notice of annuity information.

(4) *Content of notice*. The notice must include—

(i) The identity-of-insurer information in § 4041.27(b)(1);

(ii) The information regarding change in identity of insurer(s) in § 4041.27(b)(2); and

(iii) Unless the state guaranty coverage information in § 4041.27(b)(3) was previously provided to the affected party, such information and the extinguishment-of-guaranty information in § 4041.23(b)(9) (replacing the term "plan benefits" with "title IV benefits").

(5) *Deadline for notice*. The plan administrator must issue the notice of annuity information to each affected party by the deadline in § 4041.27(d)(1).

(d) *Request for IRS determination letter*. To qualify for the distribution deadline in § 4041.28(a)(1)(ii) (as modified and made applicable by § 4041.50(c)), the plan administrator must submit to the IRS a valid request for a determination of the plan's qualification status upon termination ("determination letter") by the day on which the plan administrator completes the issuance of the notices of benefit distribution. [Amended 11/7/97 by 62 FR 60424.]

[¶ 15,440J-8]

§ 4041.49 **Verification of plan sufficiency prior to closeout**. (a) *General rule*. Before distributing plan assets pursuant to a closeout under § 4041.50, the plan administrator must verify whether the plan's assets are still sufficient to provide for benefits at the level determined by the PBGC, i.e., guaranteed benefits or benefit liabilities. If the plan administrator finds that the plan is no longer able to provide for benefits at the level determined by the PBGC, then paragraph (b) or (c) of this section, as appropriate, will apply.

(b) *Subsequent insufficiency for guaranteed benefits*. When a plan administrator finds that a plan is no longer sufficient for guaranteed

benefits, the plan administrator must promptly notify the PBGC in writing of that fact and may take no further action to implement the plan termination, pending the PBGC's determination and notice pursuant to paragraph (b)(1) or (b)(2) of this section.

(1) *PBGC concurrence with finding*. If the PBGC concurs with the plan administrator's finding, the distribution notice will be void, and the PBGC will—

(i) Issue the plan administrator a notice of inability to determine sufficiency in accordance with § 4041.47(b); and

(ii) Require the plan administrator to submit a new valuation, certified to by an enrolled actuary, of the benefit liabilities and guaranteed benefits under the plan, valued in accordance with §§ 4044.41 through 4044.57 of this chapter as of the date of the plan administrator's notice to the PBGC.

(2) *PBGC non-concurrence with finding*. If the PBGC does not concur with the plan administrator's finding, it will so notify the plan administrator in writing, and the distribution notice will remain in effect.

(c) *Subsequent insufficiency for benefit liabilities*. When a plan administrator finds that a plan is sufficient for guaranteed benefits but is no longer sufficient for benefit liabilities, the plan administrator must immediately notify the PBGC in writing of this fact, but must continue with the distribution of assets in accordance with § 4041.50.

(d) *Finding by PBGC of subsequent insufficiency*. In any case in which the PBGC finds on its own initiative that a subsequent insufficiency for guaranteed benefits has occurred, paragraph (b)(1) of this section will apply, except that the guaranteed benefits must be revalued as of the date of the PBGC's finding.

(e) *Restrictions upon finding of subsequent insufficiency*. When the plan administrator makes the finding described in paragraph (b) of this section or receives notice that the PBGC has made the finding described in paragraph (d) of this section, the plan administrator is (except to the extent the PBGC otherwise directs) subject to the prohibitions in § 4041.42. [Amended 11/7/97 by 62 FR 60424.]

[¶ 15,440J-9]

§ 4041.50 **Closeout of plan**. If a plan administrator receives a distribution notice from the PBGC pursuant to § 4041.47 and neither the plan administrator nor the PBGC makes the finding described in § 4041.49(b) or (d), the plan administrator must distribute plan assets in accordance with § 4041.28 and file a post-distribution certification in accordance with § 4041.29, except that—

(a) The term "plan benefits" is replaced with "title IV benefits";

(b) For purposes of applying the distribution deadline in § 4041.28(a)(1)(i), the phrase "after the expiration of the PBGC's 60-day (or extended) review period under § 4041.26(a)" is replaced with "the day on which the plan administrator completes the issuance of the notices of benefit distribution pursuant to § 4041.48(a)"; and

(c) For purposes of applying the distribution deadline in § 4041.28(a)(1)(ii), the phrase "the requirements of § 4041.25(c)" is replaced with "the requirements of § 4041.48(d)". [Amended 11/7/97 by 62 FR 60424.]

≫→ **Caution:** *Generally, for fully-funded, single-employer pension plans, which issued their first notice of intent to terminate before January 1, 1998, unamended regulation § 4041 applies. The regulations, prior to the amendments made by the PBGC on 11/7/97 (62 FR 60424), previously read:*

Subpart A—General Provisions

[¶ 15,441]

§ 4041.1 **Purpose and scope**. This part sets forth the rules and procedures for terminating a single-employer pension plan in a standard termination or in a distress termination under ERISA. Subpart A contains various general rules that apply to both standard terminations and distress terminations. Subpart B sets forth the specific steps that a plan administrator must follow in order to terminate a plan in a standard termination. Subpart C sets forth the specific steps that a plan administrator must follow in order to terminate a plan in a distress termination. This part applies to the termination of any single-employer plan covered under section 4021(a) of ERISA and not excluded by

section 4021(b). This part does not reflect the amendments to sections 4041(b)(2)(C)(i) (relating to the PBGC's authority not to nullify a termination if nullification would be inconsistent with the interests of participants and beneficiaries) or 4041(c)(2)(B)(i)(I) (relating to the liquidation criteria for a distress termination) that were contained in the Retirement Protection Act of 1994 (Pub. L. 103-465, section 778(a) and (b)).

[¶ 15,441A]

§ 4041.2 **Definitions**. The following terms are defined in § 4001.2 of this chapter: affected party, annuity, benefit liabilities, Code, contributing sponsor, controlled group, distress termination, distribution date, employer, ERISA, guaranteed benefit, insurer, irrevocable commitment, IRS, mandatory employee contributions, normal retirement age, notice of intent to terminate, PBGC, person, plan, plan administrator, plan year, single-employer plan, standard termination, termination date, and title IV benefit.

In addition, for purposes of this part:

Distress termination notice means the notice filed with the PBGC pursuant to section 4041(c)(2)(A) of ERISA and §4041.43. PBGC Form 601 (including Schedule EA-D) is the distress termination notice.

Distribution notice means the notice issued to the plan administrator by the PBGC pursuant to §4041.45(c) of this part upon the PBGC's determination that the plan has sufficient assets to pay at least guaranteed benefits.

Existing collective bargaining agreement means a collective bargaining agreement that—

(1) By its terms, either has not expired or is extended beyond its stated expiration date because neither of the collective bargaining parties took the required action to terminate it, and

(2) Has not been made inoperative by a judicial ruling. When a collective bargaining agreement no longer meets these conditions, it ceases to be an "existing collective bargaining agreement," whether or not any or all of its terms may continue to apply by operation of law.

Majority owner means, with respect to a contributing sponsor of a single-employer plan, an individual who owns, directly or indirectly, 50 percent or more of—

(1) An unincorporated trade or business,

(2) The capital interest or the profits interest in a partnership, or

(3) Either the voting stock of a corporation or the value of all of the stock of a corporation. For this purpose, the constructive ownership rules of section 414(b) and (c) of the Code shall apply.

Notice of benefit distribution means the notice to each participant and beneficiary required by §4041.46 of this part describing the benefit to be distributed to him or her.

Notice of noncompliance means a notice issued to a plan administrator by the PBGC pursuant to section 4041(b)(2)(C) of ERISA and §4041.26 of this part advising the plan administrator that the requirements for a standard termination have not been satisfied and that the plan is an ongoing plan.

Notice of plan benefits means the notice to each participant and beneficiary required by section 4041(b)(2)(B) of ERISA and §§4041.22 and 4041.23 of this part describing his or her plan benefits.

Participant means—

(1) Any individual who is currently in employment covered by the plan and who is earning or retaining credited service under the plan, including any individual who is considered covered under the plan for purposes of meeting the minimum participation requirements but who, because of offset or similar provisions, does not have any accrued benefits;

(2) Any nonvested individual who is not currently in employment covered by the plan but who is earning or retaining credited service under the plan; and

(3) Any individual who is retired or separated from employment covered by the plan and who is receiving benefits under the plan or is entitled to begin receiving benefits under the plan in the future, excluding any such individual to whom an insurer has made an irrevocable commitment to pay all the benefits to which the individual is entitled under the plan.

Plan benefits means the benefits to which a participant is, or may become, entitled under the plan's provisions in effect as of the termination date, based on the participant's accrued benefit under the plan as of that date. Each participant's "plan benefits" equals that participant's "benefit liabilities," and the sum of all "plan benefits" equals the plan's "benefit liabilities."

Proposed distribution date means the date chosen by the plan administrator as the tentative date for the distribution of plan assets pursuant to a standard termination. A proposed distribution date may not be earlier than the 61st day, nor later than the 240th day, following the day on which the plan administrator files a standard termination notice with the PBGC.

Proposed termination date means the date specified as such by the plan administrator in the notice of intent to terminate or, if later, in the standard termination notice or the distress termination notice. A proposed termination date specified in the notice of intent to terminate may not be earlier than the 60th day, nor later than the 90th day, after the issuance of the notice of intent to terminate. A proposed termination date becomes the 'termination date' if a plan terminates in a standard termination. A proposed termination date specified in the distress termination notice may not be earlier than the proposed termination date specified in the notice of intent to terminate, or (except with PBGC approval) later than the 90th day after the issuance of the notice of intent to terminate.

Residual assets means the plan assets remaining after all benefit liabilities and other liabilities of the plan have been satisfied.

Standard termination notice means the notice filed with the PBGC pursuant to section 4041(b)(2)(A) of ERISA and §4041.24 of this part advising the PBGC of a proposed standard termination. PBGC Form 500 (including Schedule EA-S) is the standard termination notice.

[¶ 15,441B]

§4041.3 **Requirements for a standard termination or a distress termination.** (a) *Exclusive means of voluntary plan termination.* A plan may be voluntarily terminated by the plan administrator only if all of the requirements for a standard termination set forth in paragraph (b) of this section are satisfied or all of the requirements for a distress termination set forth in paragraph (c) of this section are satisfied.

(b) *Requirements for a standard termination.* A plan may be terminated in a standard termination only if—

(1) The plan administrator issues a notice of intent to terminate to each affected party in accordance with §4041.21 at least 60 days and not more than 90 days before the proposed termination date;

(2) The plan administrator files a standard termination notice with the PBGC in accordance with §4041.24 no later than 120 days after the proposed termination date or, if applicable, no later than the due date established in an extension notice issued under §4041.8;

(3) The plan administrator issues notices of plan benefits to plan participants and beneficiaries in accordance with §§4041.22 and 4041.23 no later than the date that the standard termination notice is filed with the PBGC;

(4) The PBGC does not issue a notice of noncompliance to the plan administrator pursuant to §4041.26; and

(5) The plan administrator distributes plan assets in accordance with §4041.27(c) within the 180-day (or extended) distribution period under §4041.27(a), (e), and (f) (or, where applicable, within the time prescribed in part 4050 of this chapter), in satisfaction of all benefit liabilities under the plan.

(c) *Requirements for a distress termination.* A plan may be terminated in a distress termination only if—

(1) The plan administrator issues a notice of intent to terminate to each affected party in accordance with §4041.41 at least 60 days and not more than 90 days before the proposed termination date;

(2) The plan administrator files a distress termination notice with the PBGC in accordance with §4041.43 no later than 120 days after the proposed termination date or, if applicable, no later than the due date established in an extension notice issued under §4041.8; and

(3) The PBGC determines that each contributing sponsor and each member of its controlled group satisfy one of the distress criteria set forth in paragraph (e) of this section.

(d) *Effect of failure to satisfy requirements.* (1) If the plan administrator does not satisfy all of the requirements of paragraph (b) of this section for a standard termination or, except as provided in paragraph (d)(2)(i) of this section, all of the requirements of paragraph (c) of this section for a distress termination, any action taken to effect the plan termination shall be null and void, and the plan shall be an ongoing plan. A plan administrator who still desires to terminate the plan shall initiate the termination process again, starting with the issuance of a new notice of intent to terminate.

(2)(i) The PBGC may, upon its own motion, waive any requirement with respect to notices to be filed with the PBGC under paragraph (c)(1) or (c)(2) of this section if the PBGC believes that it will be less costly or administratively burdensome to the PBGC to do so. The PBGC will not entertain requests for waivers under this paragraph.

(ii) Notwithstanding any other provision of this part, the PBGC retains the authority in any case to initiate a plan termination in accordance with the provisions of section 4042 of ERISA.

(e) *Distress criteria.* In a distress termination, each contributing sponsor and each member of its controlled group shall satisfy at least one (but not necessarily the same one) of the following criteria in order for a distress termination to occur:

(1) *Liquidation.* This criterion is met if, as of the proposed termination date—

(i) A person has filed or had filed against it a petition seeking liquidation in a case under title 11, United States Code, or under a similar federal law or law of a State or political subdivision of a State, or a case described in paragraph (e)(2) of this section has been converted to such a case; and

(ii) The case has not been dismissed.

(2) *Reorganization.* This criterion is met if—

(i) As of the proposed termination date, a person has filed or had filed against it a petition seeking reorganization in a case under title 11, United States Code, or under a similar law of a state or a political subdivision of a state, or a case described in paragraph (e)(1) of this section has been converted to such a case;

(ii) As of the proposed termination date, the case has not been dismissed;

(iii) The person notifies the PBGC of any request to the bankruptcy court (or other appropriate court in a case under such similar law of a state or a political subdivision of a state) for approval of the plan termination by concurrently filing with the PBGC a copy of the motion requesting court approval, including any documents submitted in support of the request; and

(iv) The bankruptcy court or other appropriate court determines that, unless the plan is terminated, such person will be unable to pay all its debts pursuant to a plan of reorganization and will be unable to continue in business outside the reorganization process and approves the plan termination.

(3) *Inability to continue in business.* This criterion is met if a person demonstrates to the satisfaction of the PBGC that, unless a distress termination occurs, the person will be unable to pay its debts when due and to continue in business.

(4) *Unreasonably burdensome pension costs.* This criterion is met if a person demonstrates to the satisfaction of the PBGC that the person's costs of providing pension coverage have become unreasonably burdensome solely as a result of declining covered employment under all single-employer plans for which that person is a contributing sponsor.

(f) *Non-duplicative efforts.* (1) If a person requests approval of the plan termination by a court, as described in paragraph (e)(2) of this section, the PBGC—

(i) Will normally enter an appearance to request that the court make specific findings as to whether the contributing sponsor or controlled group member meets the distress test in paragraph (e)(3) of this section, or state that it is unable to make such findings;

(ii) Will provide the court with any information it has that may be germane to the court's ruling;

(iii) Will, if the person has requested, or later requests, a determination by the PBGC under paragraph (e)(3) of this section, defer action on the request until the court makes its determination; and

(iv) Will be bound by a final and non-appealable order of the court.

(2) If a person requests a determination by the PBGC under paragraph (e)(3) of this section, the PBGC determines that the distress criterion is not met, and the person thereafter requests approval of the plan termination by a court, as described in paragraph (e)(2) of this section, the PBGC will advise the court of its determination and make its administrative record available to the court.

(g) *Non-recognition of certain actions.* If the PBGC finds that a person undertook any action or failed to act for the principal purpose of satisfying any of the distress criteria contained in paragraph (e) of this section, rather than for a reasonable business purpose, the PBGC shall disregard such act or failure to act in determining whether the person has satisfied any of those criteria.

[¶ 15,441C]

§4041.4 **Administration of plan during pendency of termination proceedings.** (a) *General rule.* Except to the extent specifically prohibited by this section, during the pendency of termination proceedings the plan administrator shall continue to carry out the normal operations of the plan, such as putting participants into pay status, collecting contributions due the plan, investing plan assets, and, during the pendency of a standard termination, making loans to participants, in accordance with plan provisions and applicable law and regulations.

(b) *Prohibitions after issuance of notice of intent to terminate in a standard termination.* Except as provided in paragraph (d) of this section, during the period beginning on the first day the plan administrator issues a notice of intent to terminate and ending on the last day of the PBGC's 60-day (or extended) review period, as described in §4041.25(a), the plan administrator shall not—

(1) Distribute plan assets pursuant to or in furtherance of the termination of the plan;

(2) Pay benefits attributable to employer contributions, other than death benefits, in any form other than as an annuity; or

(3) Purchase irrevocable commitments to provide benefits from an insurer.

(c) *Prohibitions after issuing notice of intent to terminate in a distress termination.* The plan administrator shall not make loans to plan participants beginning on the first day he or she issues a notice of intent to terminate, and from that date until a distribution is permitted pursuant to §4041.48, the plan administrator shall not—

(1) Distribute plan assets pursuant to, or (except as required by this part) take any other actions to implement, the termination of the plan;

(2) Pay benefits attributable to employer contributions, other than death benefits, in any form other than as an annuity; or

(3) Purchase irrevocable commitments to provide benefits from an insurer.

(d) *Exceptions in a standard termination.* During the period set forth in paragraph (b) of this section, the plan administrator may pay benefits attributable to employer contributions either through the purchase of irrevocable commitments from an insurer or in a form other than an annuity if—

(1) The participant has separated from active employment;

(2) The distribution is consistent with prior plan practice; and

(3) The distribution is not reasonably expected to jeopardize the plan's sufficiency for benefit liabilities.

(e) *Effect of notice of noncompliance in a standard termination.* If the PBGC issues a notice of noncompliance pursuant to §4041.26, the prohibitions described in paragraphs (b)(2) and (b)(3) of this section shall cease to apply—

(1) Upon expiration of the period during which reconsideration may be requested under §4041.26(c) or, if earlier, at the time the plan administrator decides not to request reconsideration; or

(2) If reconsideration is requested, upon PBGC issuance of its decision on reconsideration.

(f) *Limitation on benefit payments on or after proposed termination date in a distress termination.* Beginning on the proposed termination date, the plan administrator shall reduce benefits to the level determined under part 4022, subpart D, of this chapter.

(g) *Failure to qualify for distress termination.* In any case where the PBGC determines, pursuant to §4041.42(c) or §4041.44(c)(1), that the requirements for a distress termination are not satisfied—

(1) The prohibitions in paragraph (c) of this section, other than those in paragraph (c)(1), shall cease to apply—

(i) Upon expiration of the period during which reconsideration may be requested under §§4041.42(e) and 4041.44(d) or, if earlier, at the time the plan administrator decides not to request reconsideration; or

(ii) If reconsideration is requested, upon PBGC issuance of its decision on reconsideration.

(2) Any benefits that were not paid pursuant to paragraph (f) of this section shall be due and payable as of the effective date of the PBGC's determination, together with interest from the date (or dates) on which the unpaid amounts were originally due until the date on which they are paid in full at the rate or rates prescribed under § 4022.81(d) of this chapter.

(h) *Effect of subsequent insufficiency.* If the plan administrator makes a finding of subsequent insufficiency for guaranteed benefits pursuant to § 4041.47(b), or the PBGC notifies the plan administrator that it has made a finding of subsequent insufficiency for guaranteed benefits pursuant to § 4041.47(d), the prohibitions in paragraph (c) of this section shall apply in accordance with § 4041.47(e).

[¶ 15,441D]

§ 4041.5 **Challenges to plan termination under collective bargaining agreement.** (a) *Suspension upon formal challenge to termination.* (1)(i) If the PBGC is advised, before the 60-day (or extended) period specified in § 4041.25 ends (in a standard termination) or before issuance of a notice of inability to determine sufficiency or a distribution notice pursuant to § 4041.45(b) or (c) (in a distress termination), that a formal challenge to the termination (as described in paragraph (b) of this section) has been initiated, the PBGC shall suspend the termination proceeding and shall so advise the plan administrator in writing.

(ii) If the PBGC is advised of a challenge described in paragraph (a)(1)(i) of this section after the 60-day (or extended) period specified in § 4041.25 ends (in a standard termination) or after issuance of a notice of inability to determine sufficiency or a distribution notice pursuant to § 4041.45(b) or (c) (in a distress termination) but before the termination procedure is concluded pursuant to this part, the PBGC may suspend the termination proceeding and, if it does, shall so advise the plan administrator in writing.

(2) The rules in paragraphs (a)(3) or (a)(4) (as appropriate) shall apply during a period of suspension beginning on the date of the PBGC's written notification to the plan administrator and ending with the final resolution of the challenge to the termination:

(3) *In a standard termination.* (i) The running of all time periods specified in ERISA or this part relevant to the termination shall be suspended; and

(ii) The plan administrator shall comply with the prohibitions in § 4041.4.

(4) *In a distress termination—*

(i) The suspension shall stay the issuance by the PBGC of any notice of inability to determine sufficiency or distribution notice or, if any such notice was previously issued, shall stay its effectiveness;

(ii) The plan administrator shall comply with the prohibitions in § 4041.4; and

(iii) The plan administrator shall file a distress termination notice with the PBGC in the manner and within the time specified in § 4041.43.

(b) *Formal challenge to termination.* For purposes of this section, a formal challenge to a plan termination is initiated when any of the following actions is taken, asserting that the termination would violate the terms and conditions of an existing collective bargaining agreement:

(1) The commencement of any procedure specified in the collective bargaining agreement for resolving disputes under the agreement; or

(2) The commencement of any action before an arbitrator, administrative agency or board, or court under applicable labor-management relations law.

(c) *Resolution of challenge.* Immediately upon the final resolution (as described in paragraph (d) of this section) of the formal challenge to the termination, the plan administrator shall notify the PBGC in writing of the outcome of the challenge, and shall provide the PBGC

with a copy of the award or order, if any. If the validity of the proposed termination has been upheld, the plan administrator also shall advise the PBGC whether the plan administrator wishes to continue the proposed termination.

(1) *Challenge sustained.* If the arbitrator, agency, board, or court has determined (or the parties have agreed) that the proposed termination violates an existing collective bargaining agreement, the PBGC shall dismiss the termination proceeding, all actions taken to effect the plan termination shall be null and void, and the plan shall be an ongoing plan. In this event, in a distress termination, § 4041.4(g) shall apply as of the date of the dismissal by the PBGC.

(2) *Termination sustained.* If the arbitrator, agency, board, or court has determined (or the parties have agreed) that the proposed termination does not violate an existing collective bargaining agreement and the plan administrator wishes to proceed with the termination, the PBGC shall reactivate the termination proceeding by sending a written notice thereof to the plan administrator, and the following rules shall apply:

(i) The termination proceeding shall continue from the point where it was suspended;

(ii) All actions taken to effect the termination before the suspension shall be effective;

(iii) Any time periods that were suspended shall resume running from the date of the PBGC's notice of the reactivation of the proceeding;

(iv) Any time periods that had fewer than 15 days remaining shall be extended to the 15th day after the date of the PBGC's notice, or such later date as the PBGC may specify, and

(v) In a distress termination, the PBGC shall proceed to issue a notice of inability to determine sufficiency or a distribution notice (or reactivate any such notice stayed under paragraph (a)(3) of this section), either with or without first requesting updated information from the plan administrator pursuant to § 4041.43(c).

(d) *Final resolution of challenge.* For purposes of this section, a formal challenge to a proposed termination is finally resolved when—

(1) The parties involved in the challenge enter into a settlement that resolves the challenge;

(2) A final award, administrative decision, or court order is issued that is not subject to review or appeal; or

(3) A final award, administrative decision, or court order is issued that is not appealed, or review or enforcement of which is not sought, within the time for filing an appeal or requesting review or enforcement.

(e) *Involuntary termination by the PBGC.* Notwithstanding any other provision of this section, the PBGC retains the authority in any case to initiate a plan termination in accordance with the provisions of section 4042 of ERISA.

[¶ 15,441E]

§ 4041.6 **Annuity requirements.** (a) *General rule.* Except as provided in paragraphs (b) and (d) of this section (or, where applicable, in part 4050 of this chapter), when a plan is closed out under § 4041.27 (in a standard termination) or § 4041.48 (in a distress termination), any benefit that is payable as an annuity under the provisions of the plan must be provided in annuity form through the purchase from an insurer of a single premium, nonparticipating, nonsurrenderable annuity contract that constitutes an irrevocable commitment by the insurer to provide the benefits purchased.

(b) *Exceptions to annuity requirement.* A benefit that is payable as an annuity under the provisions of a plan need not be provided in annuity form if the plan provides for an alternative form of distribution and either paragraph (b)(1) or (b)(2) of this section applies:

(1) The participant is not in pay status as of the distribution date, and the present value of the participant's total benefit under the plan, including amounts previously distributed to the participant, is $3,500 or less, determined in accordance with sections 411(a)(11) and 417(e)(3) of the Code and the regulations thereunder. The present value of such benefits shall be determined using the interest rate or rates as of—

(i) The date set forth in the plan for such purpose, provided that the plan provision is in accord with section 417(e)(3) of the Code and the regulations thereunder (substituting "distribution date" for "annuity starting date" wherever used in the plan); or

(ii) If the plan does not provide for such a date, the distribution date.

(2) The participant elected the alternative form of distribution in writing, with the written consent of his or her spouse, in accordance with the requirements of sections 401(a)(11), 411(a)(11), and 417 of the Code and the regulations thereunder.

(c) *Optional benefit forms.* Except as permitted by sections 401(a)(11), 411(d)(6), and 417 of the Code and the regulations thereunder, an annuity contract purchased to satisfy the annuity requirement shall preserve all applicable benefit options provided under the plan as of the termination date.

(d) *Participating annuities.* (1) *General rule.* Notwithstanding the requirement of paragraph (a) of this section that an annuity contract be nonparticipating, a participating annuity contract may be purchased to satisfy the annuity requirement if the plan can provide for all benefit liabilities and—

(i) All benefit liabilities will be guaranteed under the annuity contract as the unconditional, irrevocable, and noncancellable obligation of the insurer;

(ii) In no event, including unfavorable investment or actuarial experience, can the amounts payable to participants under the annuity contract decrease except to correct mistakes; and

(iii) As provided in paragraph (d)(2) of this section, no amount of residual assets to which participants(2) are entitled will be used to pay for the participation feature.

(2) *Plans with residual assets.* If all or a portion of the residual assets of a plan will be distributed to participants—

(i) The additional premium for the participation feature must be paid from the contributing sponsor's share, if any, of the residual assets or from assets of the contributing sponsor; and

(ii) If the plan provided for mandatory employee contributions, the amount of residual assets must be determined using the price of the annuities for all benefit liabilities without the participation feature.

[¶ 15,441F]

§ 4041.7 **Facilitating plan sufficiency in a standard termination**. (a) *Commitment to make plan sufficient—*

(1) *General rule.* At any time before a standard termination notice is filed with the PBGC, in order to enable the plan to terminate in that standard termination, a contributing sponsor or a member of a controlled group of a contributing sponsor may make a commitment to contribute any additional sums necessary to make the plan sufficient for all benefit liabilities. Any such commitment shall be treated as a plan asset for all purposes under this part. A sample commitment is included in the appendix to this part.

(2) *Requirements for valid commitment.* A commitment to make a plan sufficient for all benefit liabilities shall be valid for purposes of this part only if the commitment—

(i) Is made to the plan;

(ii) Is in writing, signed by the contributing sponsor and/or controlled group member(s); and

(iii) If the contributing sponsor or controlled group member is the subject of a bankruptcy liquidation or reorganization proceeding, as described in § 4041.3(e)(1) or (e)(2) of this part, is approved by the court before which the liquidation or reorganization proceeding is pending or is unconditionally guaranteed, by a person not in bankruptcy, to be met at or before the time distribution of assets is required in the standard termination.

(b) *Alternative treatment of majority owner's benefit.* (1) *General rule.* In order to facilitate the termination of the plan and distribution of assets in a standard termination, a majority owner may agree to forego receipt of all or part of his or her benefit until the benefit liabilities of all other plan participants have been satisfied.

(2) *Requirements for valid agreement.* Any agreement by a majority owner to an alternative treatment of his or her benefit is valid only if—

(i) The agreement is in writing;

(ii) In any case in which the total value of the benefit (determined in accordance with § 4041.6(b) of this part) is greater than $3,500, the spouse, if any, of the majority owner consents, in writing, to the alternative treatment of the benefit; and

(iii) The agreement is not inconsistent with a qualified domestic relations order (as defined in section 206(d)(3) of ERISA).

[¶ 15,441G]

§ 4041.8 **Disaster relief.** (a) Notwithstanding any other provision in this part, when the President of the United States declares that, under the Disaster Relief Act of 1974, as amended (42 U.S.C. 5121, 5122(2), 5141(b)), a major disaster exists, the Executive Director of the PBGC (or his or her designee) may, by issuing one or more notices of disaster relief, extend by up to 180 days the due date for—

(1) Filing the standard termination notice under § 4041.24;

(2) Completing the distribution of plan assets in a standard termination under § 4041.27;

(3) Filing the distress termination notice pursuant to § 4041.43;

(4) Issuing the notices of benefit distribution in a distress termination pursuant to § 4041.46(a)(1); or

(5) Completing the distribution of plan assets in a distress termination pursuant to § 4041.48.

(b) The due date extension or extensions described in paragraph (a) of this section shall apply only to plan terminations with respect to which the principal place of business of the contributing sponsor or the plan administrator, or the office of the service provider, bank, insurance company, or other person maintaining the information necessary to file the standard or distress termination notice, issue notices of plan benefits or benefit distribution, or complete the distribution of plan assets (as applicable), is within a designated disaster area.

(c) The standard or distress termination notice or the post-distribution certification shall identify the termination as being qualified for the due date extension.

[¶ 15,441H]

§ 4041.9 **Filing with the PBGC.** (a) *Date of filing.* Any document required or permitted to be filed with the PBGC under this part shall be deemed filed on the date that it is received at the PBGC, providing it is received no later than 4:00 p.m. on a day other than Saturday, Sunday, or a Federal holiday. Documents received after 4:00 p.m. or on Saturday, Sunday, or a Federal holiday shall be deemed filed on the next regular business day.

(b) *How to file.* Except as may otherwise be provided in applicable forms and instructions, any document to be filed under this part may be delivered by mail or by hand to: Reports Processing, Insurance Operations Department, Pension Benefit Guaranty Corporation, 1200 K Street NW., Washington, DC 20005-4026

[¶ 15,441I]

§ 4041.10 **Computation of time**. In computing any period of time prescribed or allowed by this part, the day of the act or event from which the designated period of time begins to run is not counted. The last day of the period so computed shall be included, unless it is a Saturday, Sunday, or Federal holiday, in which event the period runs until the end of the next day that is not a Saturday, Sunday, or Federal holiday. Notwithstanding the preceding sentence, a proposed termination date may be any day, including a Saturday, Sunday, or Federal holiday.

[¶ 15,441J]

§ 4041.11 **Maintenance of plan records**. Either the contributing sponsor or the plan administrator of a plan terminating in a standard termination or a plan terminating in a distress termination that closes out in accordance with § 4041.48 pursuant to a distribution notice issued under § 4041.45(c) shall maintain and preserve all records used to compute benefits with respect to each individual who is a plan participant or a beneficiary of a deceased participant as of the termination date in accordance with the following rules:

(a) The records to be maintained and preserved are those used to compute the benefit for purposes of distribution to each individual in accordance with § 4041.27(c) (in a standard termination) or § 4041.48 (in a distress termination) and include, but are not limited to, the plan documents and all underlying data, including worksheets prepared by or at the direction of the enrolled actuary, used in determining the amount, form, and value of benefits.

(b) All records subject to this section shall be preserved for six years after the date the post-distribution certification required under § 4041.27(h) (in a standard termination) or § 4041.48(b) (in a distress termination) is filed with the PBGC.

(c) The contributing sponsor or plan administrator, as appropriate, shall make records subject to this section available to the PBGC upon request for inspection and photocopying, and shall submit such records to the PBGC within 30 days after receipt of the PBGC's written request therefor (or such other period as may be specified in such written request).

[¶ 15,441K]

§ 4041.12 **Information collection**. The information collection requirements contained in this part have been approved by the Office of Management and Budget under control number 1212-0036.

Subpart B—Standard Termination Process

[¶ 15,442]

§ 4041.21 **Notice of intent to terminate**. (a) *General rule*. At least 60 days and no more than 90 days before the proposed termination date, the plan administrator shall issue to each person who is (as of the proposed termination date) an affected party (other than the PBGC) a written notice of intent to terminate containing all of the information specified in paragraph (d) of this section. Failure to comply with the requirements of this section shall nullify the proposed termination.

(b) *Discovery of other affected parties*. Notwithstanding the provisions of paragraph (a) of this section, if the plan administrator discovers additional affected parties after the expiration of the time period specified in paragraph (a) of this section, the failure to issue the notice of intent to terminate to such parties within the specified time period will not cause the notice to be untimely under paragraph (a) of this section if the plan administrator could not reasonably have been expected to know of the additional affected parties and if he or she promptly issues the notice to each additional affected party.

(c) *Issuance*. (1) *Method*. The plan administrator shall issue the notice of intent to terminate to each affected party (other than the PBGC) individually either by hand delivery or by first-class mail or courier service directed to the affected party's last known address.

(2) *When issued*. The notice of intent to terminate is deemed issued to each affected party on the date on which it is handed to the affected party or deposited with a mail or courier service (as evidenced by a postmark or written receipt).

(d) *Contents of notice*. The plan administrator shall include in the notice of intent to terminate all of the following information:

(1) The name of the plan and of the contributing sponsor;

(2) The employer identification number ("EIN") of the contributing sponsor and the plan number ("PN"); if there is no EIN or PN, the notice shall so state;

(3) The name, address, and telephone number of the person who may be contacted by an affected party with questions concerning the plan's termination;

(4) A statement that the plan administrator expects to terminate the plan in a standard termination on a proposed termination date that is either—

(i) A specific date set forth in the notice, or

(ii) A date to be determined that is dependent on the occurrence of some future event;

(5) If the proposed termination date is dependent on the occurrence of a future event, the nature of the event (such as the merger of the contributing sponsor with another entity), generally when the event

is expected to occur, and when the termination will occur in relation to the other event;

(6) A statement that benefit and service accruals will continue until the termination date or, if applicable, that benefit accruals were or will be frozen as of a specific date in accordance with section 204(h) of ERISA;

(7) A statement that, in order to terminate in a standard termination, plan assets must be sufficient to provide all benefit liabilities under the plan with respect to each participant and each beneficiary of a deceased participant;

(8) A statement that, after plan assets have been distributed to provide all benefit liabilities with respect to a participant or a beneficiary of a deceased participant, either by the purchase of an irrevocable commitment or commitments from an insurer to provide benefits or by an alternative form of distribution provided for under the plan, the PBGC's guarantee with respect to that participant's or beneficiary's benefit ends;

(9) If distribution of benefits under the plan may be wholly or partially by the purchase of irrevocable commitments from an insurer—

(i) The name and address of the insurer or insurers from whom, or (if not then known) the insurers from among whom, the plan administrator intends to purchase the irrevocable commitments; or

(ii) If the plan administrator has not identified an insurer or insurers at the time the notice of intent to terminate is issued, a statement that—

(A) Irrevocable commitments may be purchased from an insurer to provide some or all of the benefits under the plan,

(B) The insurer or insurers have not yet been identified, and

(C) Affected parties (other than the PBGC) will be notified at a later date (but no later than 45 days before the distribution date) of the name and address of the insurer or insurers from whom, or (if not then known) the insurers from among whom, the plan administrator intends to purchase the irrevocable commitments;

(10) A statement that if the termination does not occur, the plan administrator will notify the affected parties (other than the PBGC) in writing of that fact;

(11) A statement that each affected party, other than the PBGC or any employee organization, will receive a written notification of the benefits that the person will receive; and

(12) For retirees only, a statement that their monthly (or other periodic) benefit amounts will not be affected by the plan's termination.

(e) *Supplemental notice requirements*. (1) The plan administrator shall issue a supplemental notice (or notices) of intent to terminate to each affected party (other than the PBGC) in accordance with the rules in paragraph (e)(2) of this section if—

(i) The plan administrator has not yet identified an insurer or insurers at the time the notice of intent to terminate is issued; or

(ii) The plan administrator notifies affected parties (other than the PBGC) of the insurer or insurers from whom (or from among whom) he or she intends to purchase the irrevocable commitments, either in the notice of intent to terminate or in a later notice, but subsequently decides to select a different insurer.

(2) The plan administrator shall issue each supplemental notice in the manner provided in paragraph (c) of this section no later than 45 days before the distribution date and shall include the name and address of the insurer or insurers from whom, or (if not then known) the insurers from among whom, the plan administrator intends to purchase the irrevocable commitments.

(3) Any supplemental notice or notices meeting the requirements of paragraph (e)(2) of this section shall be deemed a part of the notice of intent to terminate.

(f) *Spin-off/termination transactions*. In the case of a spin-off/termination transaction, the plan administrator shall provide all participants in the original plan who are covered by the ongoing plan (as of the proposed termination date) with a notice describing the transaction no later than the date on which the plan administrator completes the issuance of notices of intent to terminate under this section. A spin-off/

termination is a transaction in which a single defined benefit plan is split into two or more plans, in conjunction with the termination of one or more of the plans, resulting in a reversion of residual assets to the employer.

[¶ 15,442A]

§ 4041.22 **Issuance of notices of plan benefits**. (a) *General rule.* No later than the date on which the plan administrator files the standard termination notice with the PBGC, as required by § 4041.24, the plan administrator shall issue to each person described in paragraph (b) of this section a notice of that individual's plan benefits. The notice shall be in the form and contain the information specified in § 4041.23. Failure to comply with the requirements of this section shall nullify the proposed termination.

(b) *Persons entitled to notice.* The plan administrator shall issue a notice of plan benefits to each person (other than the PBGC or any employee organization) who is an affected party as of the proposed termination date (and, in the case of a spin-off/termination transaction as described in § 4043.21(f), each person who is, as of the proposed termination date, a participant in the original plan who is covered by the ongoing plan).

(c) *Discovery of other affected parties.* Notwithstanding the provisions of paragraph (a) of this section, if the plan administrator discovers additional persons entitled to a notice of plan benefits after the expiration of the time period specified in paragraph (a) of this section, the failure to issue a notice of plan benefits to such persons within the specified time period will not cause such notices to be untimely under paragraph (a) of this section if the plan administrator could not reasonably have been expected to know of the additional persons and if he or she promptly issues, to each such additional person, a notice of plan benefits in the form and containing the information specified in § 4041.23.

(d) *Issuance.* (1) *Method.* The plan administrator shall issue a notice of plan benefits individually to each person described in paragraph (b) of this section, either by hand-delivery or by first-class mail or courier service directed to the person's last known address.

(2) *When issued.* A notice of plan benefits is deemed issued to each person on the date it is handed to the person or deposited with a mail or courier service (as evidenced by a postmark or written receipt).

[¶ 15,442B]

§ 4041.23 **Form and contents of notices of plan benefits**. (a) *Form of notices.* The plan administrator shall provide notices of plan benefits written in plain, non-technical English that is likely to be understood by the average participant or beneficiary. If technical terms must be used, their meaning shall be explained in non-technical language.

(b) *Foreign languages.* The plan administrator of a plan described in this paragraph shall comply with paragraph (a) of this section and also shall include in the notices a statement, prominently displayed, in the foreign language (or languages) common to the non-English speaking plan participants advising them of how they may obtain assistance in understanding the notice. The assistance need not involve written materials, but shall be adequate to reasonably ensure that the participants and beneficiaries understand the information contained in their notices and shall be provided through media and at times and places that are reasonably accessible to the participants and beneficiaries. A plan is described in this paragraph if, as of the proposed termination date, the plan either—

(1) Covers fewer than 100 participants and at least 25 percent of those participants speak only the same non-English language or

(2) Covers 100 or more participants and at least the lesser of 500 or 10 percent of those participants speak the same non-English language.

(c) *Contents of notice.* In addition to the information described in paragraph (d), (e), or (f) of this section, as applicable, the plan administrator shall include in each notice of plan benefits the following information:

(1) The name of the plan, the employer identification number ("EIN") of the contributing sponsor, and the plan number ("PN"); if there is no EIN or PN, the notice shall so state;

(2) The name, address, and telephone number of the person who may be contacted to answer questions concerning a participant's or beneficiary's benefit;

(3) The proposed termination date and, if applicable, a statement that this date is later than the proposed termination date given in the notice of intent to terminate; and

(4) If the amount of the plan benefits set forth in a notice is an estimate, a statement that the amount is an estimate and that benefits paid may be greater than or less than the estimate.

(d) *Benefits of persons in pay status.* The plan administrator shall include in the notice of plan benefits for a participant or beneficiary in pay status as of the proposed termination date the following information:

(1) The amount and form of the participant's plan benefits payable as of the proposed termination date;

(2) The amount and form of benefit, if any, payable to a beneficiary upon the participant's death and the name of the beneficiary;

(3) The amount and date of any increase or decrease in the benefit scheduled to occur after the proposed termination date (or that has already occurred) and an explanation of the increase or decrease, including, where applicable, a reference to the pertinent plan provision; and

(4) For benefits of participants or beneficiaries in pay status for one year or less as of the proposed termination date, the specific personal data used to calculate the plan benefits described in paragraphs (d)(1) and (d)(2) of this section, e.g., participant's age at retirement, spouse's age, participant's length of service, and including, for Social Security offset benefits, the participant's actual or, if unknown, estimated Social Security benefit and, for an estimated benefit, the assumptions used for the participant's earnings history.

(e) *Benefits of participants not in pay status but form and starting date known.* The plan administrator shall include in the notice of plan benefits for a participant who is not in pay status as of the proposed termination date, but who has, as of that date, elected to retire and has elected a form and starting date, or with respect to whom the plan administrator has determined a lump sum distribution will be made, the following information:

(1) The amount and form of the participant's plan benefits payable as of the projected benefit starting date, and what that date is;

(2) The amount and form of benefit, if any, payable to a beneficiary upon the participant's death and the name of the beneficiary;

(3) The amount and date of any increase or decrease in the benefit scheduled to occur after the proposed termination date (or that has already occurred) and an explanation of the increase or decrease, including, where applicable, a reference to the pertinent plan provision; and

(4) If the age at which, or form in which, the plan benefits will be paid differs from the age or form in which the participant's accrued benefit at normal retirement age is stated in the plan, the age or form stated in the plan and the age or form adjustment factors, including, in the case of a lump sum benefit, the interest rate used to convert to the lump sum benefit described in paragraph (e)(1) of this section and a reference to the pertinent plan provision;

(5) The specific personal data, as described in paragraph (d)(4) of this section, used to calculate the plan benefits (other than a lump sum benefit) described in paragraphs (e)(1) and (e)(2) of this section and, with respect to a benefit payable as a lump sum, the personal data used to calculate the underlying annuity; and

(6) If the plan benefits will be paid in a lump sum, an explanation of how the interest rate is used to calculate the lump sum; a statement that the higher the interest rate used, the smaller the lump sum amount; and, if applicable, a statement that the lump sum amount given is an estimate because the applicable interest rate may change before the distribution date.

(f) *Benefits of all other participants not in pay status.* The plan administrator shall include in the notice of plan benefits for any participant not described in paragraph (d) or (e) of this section, the following information:

(1) The amount and form of the participant's plan benefits payable at normal retirement age in any form permitted under the plan;

(2) The availability of any alternative benefit forms, including those payable to a beneficiary upon the participant's death either before or after retirement, and, for any benefits to which the participant is or may become entitled that would be payable before normal retirement age, the earliest benefit commencement date, the amount payable on and after such date, and whether the benefit would be subject to future reduction;

(3) The specific personal data, as described in paragraph (d)(4) of this section, used to calculate the plan benefits described in paragraph (f)(1) of this section and, with respect to a benefit that may be paid in a lump sum, the personal data used to calculate the underlying annuity; and

(4) If the plan benefits may be paid in a lump sum, an explanation of when a lump sum may be paid without a participant's consent; an explanation of how the interest rate is used to calculate the lump sum; and a statement that the higher the interest rate used, the smaller the lump sum amount.

[¶ 15,442C]

§ 4041.24 **Standard termination notice.** (a) *Form.* The plan administrator shall file with the PBGC a PBGC Form 500, Standard Termination Notice, Single-Employer Plan Termination, with Schedule EA-S, Standard Termination Certification of Sufficiency, that has been completed in accordance with the instructions thereto. Except as provided in § 4041.8, the plan administrator shall file the standard termination notice on or before the 120th day after the proposed termination date.

(b) *Supplemental notice requirement.* If any of the benefits of the terminating plan may be provided in annuity form through the purchase of irrevocable commitments from an insurer and either of the conditions in paragraph (b)(1) of this section is met, the plan administrator shall file a supplemental notice (or notices) with the PBGC in accordance with the provisions in paragraph (b)(2) of this section.

(1) The plan administrator shall file with the PBGC a supplemental notice (or notices) if—

(i) The insurer or insurers from whom the plan administrator intends to purchase irrevocable commitments is not identified in the standard termination notice filed with the PBGC, or

(ii) The plan administrator has notified the PBGC of the insurer or insurers from whom he or she intends to purchase irrevocable commitments, either in the standard termination notice or in a later notice pursuant to paragraph (b)(2) of this section, and subsequently decides to select a different insurer.

(2) The supplemental notice (or notices) may be filed at any time after the filing of the standard termination notice, but no later than 45 days before the distribution date, and shall—

(i) Be in writing addressed to: Reports Processing, Insurance Operations Department, Pension Benefit Guaranty Corporation, 1200 K Street NW., Washington, DC 20005-4026.

(ii) Give information identifying the contributing sponsor and the plan by name, address, employer identification and plan numbers ("EIN/PN"), and PBGC case number (if applicable); and

(iii) Give the name and address of the insurer or insurers from whom, or (if not then known) the insurers from among whom, the plan administrator intends to purchase the irrevocable commitments.

[¶ 15,442D]

§ 4041.25 **PBGC action upon filing of standard termination notice.** (a) *Review period upon filing of standard termination notice.* (1) *General rule.* After a complete standard termination notice has been filed in accordance with § 4041.9, the PBGC has 60 days to review the notice, determine whether to issue a notice of noncompliance pursuant to § 4041.26, and issue any such notice. The 60-day review period begins on the day following the filing of a complete standard termination notice and includes the 60th day. If the PBGC does not issue a notice of noncompliance by the last day of this 60-day period, the plan administrator shall proceed to close out the plan in accordance with § 4041.27.

(2) *Extension of review period.* The 60-day review period may be extended according to the following rules:

(i) The PBGC and the plan administrator may agree in writing, before the expiration of the 60-day review period, to extend the period for up to an additional 60 days;

(ii) More than one such extension may be made; and

(iii) Any extension may be made upon whatever terms and conditions are agreed to by the PBGC and the plan administrator.

(3) *Suspension of review period.* The 60-day review period shall be suspended in accordance with paragraph (d) of this section if the PBGC requests supplemental information.

(b) *Acknowledgment of complete standard termination notice.* The PBGC shall notify the plan administrator in writing of the date on which a complete standard termination notice was filed, so that the plan administrator may determine when the 60-day review period will expire.

(c) *Return of incomplete standard termination notice.* The PBGC shall return an incomplete standard termination notice and advise the plan administrator in writing of the missing item(s) of information and that the complete standard termination notice must be filed no later than the 120th day after the proposed termination date or the 20th day after the date of the PBGC notice, whichever is later.

(d) *Authority to request supplemental information.* Whenever the PBGC has reason to believe that any of the requirements of § § 4041.21 through 4041.24 of this part were not complied with, or in any proposed termination that will result in a reversion of residual assets to the contributing sponsor, the PBGC may require the submission of information supplementing that furnished pursuant to § 4041.24. A request for additional information under this paragraph shall be in writing and shall suspend the running of the 60-day (or extended) review period described in paragraph (a) of this section. That period shall begin running again on the day following the filing of the required information. If a plan administrator or contributing sponsor fails to submit information required under this paragraph within the period specified in the PBGC's request, the PBGC may issue a notice of noncompliance in accordance with § 4041.26 or take other appropriate action to enforce the requirements of Title IV of ERISA.

(e) *Authority to suspend or nullify proposed termination.* Notwithstanding any other provision of this part, the PBGC may, by written notice to the plan administrator, suspend or nullify a proposed termination after expiration of the 60-day (or extended) review period in any case in which it determines that such action is necessary to carry out the purposes of Title IV of ERISA.

[¶ 15,442E]

§ 4041.26 **Notice of noncompliance.** (a) *General.* (1) The PBGC shall issue to the plan administrator a written notice of noncompliance, within the period prescribed by § 4041.25, whenever it makes one of the following determinations:

(i) A determination that the plan administrator failed to issue the notice of intent to terminate in accordance with § 4041.21.

(ii) A determination that the plan administrator failed to issue notices of plan benefits in accordance with § § 4041.22 and 4041.23.

(iii) A determination that the standard termination notice, or any supplemental notice, was not filed in accordance with § 4041.24.

(iv) A determination that, as of the proposed distribution date, plan assets will not be sufficient to satisfy all benefit liabilities under the plan.

(2) The PBGC shall base any determination described in paragraph (a)(1) of this section on the information contained in the standard termination notice, including any supplemental submission under § 4041.25(d) and any supplemental notice under § 4041.24(b), or on information provided by any affected party or otherwise obtained by the PBGC.

(b) *Effect of notice of noncompliance.* A notice of noncompliance ends the standard termination proceeding, nullifies all actions taken to terminate the plan, and renders the plan an ongoing plan. The notice of noncompliance is effective upon the expiration of the period within which the plan administrator may request reconsideration pursuant to paragraph (c) of this section but, once a notice is issued, the plan administrator shall take no further action to terminate the plan (except by initiation of a new termination) unless and until the notice is revoked pursuant to a decision by the PBGC on reconsideration.

(c) *Reconsideration of notice of noncompliance.* A plan administrator may request reconsideration of a notice of noncompliance in accordance with the rules prescribed in part 4003, subpart C, of this chapter. Any request for reconsideration automatically stays the effectiveness of the notice of noncompliance until the PBGC issues its decision on reconsideration.

(d) *Notice to affected parties.* (1) *General rule.* Upon a decision by the PBGC on reconsideration affirming the issuance of a notice of noncompliance (or, if earlier, upon the plan administrator's decision not to request reconsideration), the plan administrator shall notify the affected parties (other than the PBGC), and any persons who were provided notice under §4041.21(f), in writing that the plan is not going to terminate or, if applicable, that the termination was invalid but that a new notice of intent to terminate is being issued.

(2) *Method of issuance.* The notices shall be delivered by first-class mail or by hand to each person described in paragraph (d)(1) who is an employee organization or a participant or beneficiary who is then in pay status. The notices to other participants and beneficiaries shall be provided in any manner reasonably calculated to reach those participants and beneficiaries. Reasonable methods of notification include, but are not limited to, posting the notice at participants' worksites or publishing the notice in an employee organization newsletter or newspaper of general circulation in the area or areas where participants and beneficiaries reside.

[¶ 15,442F]

§4041.27 **Closeout of plan.** (a) *General rules.* (1) *Distribution.* Except as provided in paragraphs (b), (e), and (f) of this section and §4041.8 of this part, if the PBGC does not issue a notice of noncompliance within the period specified in §4041.25 or, if a notice of noncompliance is issued and later revoked after reconsideration under §4041.26(c), the plan administrator shall complete the distribution of plan assets in accordance with paragraph (c) of this section within 180 days after the expiration of the review period specified in §4041.25 (or, if applicable, the date on which the PBGC revokes the notice of noncompliance) or, if applicable, within the time prescribed in part 4050 of this chapter.

(2) *Post-distribution requirements.* The plan administrator shall file with the PBGC a post-distribution certification in accordance with paragraph (h) of this section and, if any of the plan's benefit liabilities payable to a participant or beneficiary have been distributed through the purchase of irrevocable commitments, the plan administrator also shall provide such participant or beneficiary with a notice, contract, or certificate in accordance with paragraph (g) of this section.

(b) *Assets insufficient to satisfy benefit liabilities.* Before distributing plan assets to close out the plan, the plan administrator shall determine that plan assets are, in fact, sufficient to satisfy all benefit liabilities. In determining if plan assets are sufficient, the plan administrator shall subtract all liabilities (other than the future benefit liabilities that will be provided when assets are distributed), e.g., benefit payments due before the distribution date; PBGC premiums for all plan years through and including the plan year in which assets are distributed; expenses, fees, and other administrative costs. If plan assets are not sufficient to satisfy all benefit liabilities, the plan administrator shall not make any distribution of assets to effect the plan's termination. In the event of an insufficiency, the plan administrator shall promptly notify the PBGC.

(c) *Method of distribution.* The plan administrator shall distribute plan assets in accordance with §4041.6 by purchasing irrevocable commitments from an insurer in satisfaction of all benefit liabilities that must be provided in annuity form, and by otherwise providing all benefit liabilities that need not be provided in annuity form. The plan administrator shall comply with part 4050 of this chapter (dealing with missing participants), if applicable.

(d) *Failure to distribute within 180-day period.* Except as provided in paragraphs (e) and (f) of this section, failure to distribute assets in accordance with paragraph (c) of this section within the 180-day distribution period set forth in paragraph (a)(1) of this section, because of an insufficiency of plan assets as described in paragraph (b) of this section or for any other reason, shall nullify the termination. All actions taken to effect the plan's termination shall be null and void, and the plan shall be an ongoing plan. In this event, the plan administrator shall notify affected parties (other than the PBGC) in writing, in accordance with §4041.26(d), that the plan is not going to terminate or, if applicable, that the termination was invalid but that a new notice of intent to terminate is being issued.

(e) *Automatic extension of time for distribution.* (1) *Requirements for automatic extension.* The plan administrator shall be entitled to an automatic extension of the 180-day period in which to complete the distribution of plan assets if the plan administrator—

(i) Submits to the IRS a complete request for a determination with respect to the plan's tax-qualification status upon termination ("determination letter") on or before the date that the plan administrator files the standard termination notice with the PBGC;

(ii) Does not receive a determination letter at least 60 days before the expiration of the 180-day period; and

(iii) On or before the expiration of the 180-day period, notifies the PBGC in writing that an extension of the distribution deadline is required and certifies that the conditions in this paragraph have been met.

(2) *Extension period.* If the requirements in paragraph (e)(1) of this section are met, the time within which the plan administrator shall complete the distribution of plan assets is automatically extended until the 60th day after receipt of a favorable determination letter from the IRS.

(f) *Discretionary extension of time for distribution.* If the plan administrator will be unable to complete the distribution of plan assets within the 180-day (or extended) period for any reason other than an insufficiency described in paragraph (b) of this section, the plan administrator may request, and the PBGC shall grant or deny, in its discretion, an extension of time within which to complete the distribution according to the following rules:

(1) The plan administrator shall file a written request for a discretionary extension with the PBGC at least 30 days before the expiration of the 180-day (or extended) distribution period, explain the reason(s) for the request, and provide a date certain by which the distribution will be made if the extension is granted.

(2) The PBGC will not grant a discretionary extension based on failure to meet the requirements for an automatic extension under paragraph (e) of this section or failure to locate all participants or beneficiaries.

(3) The PBGC will grant a discretionary extension, in whole or in part, only if it is satisfied that the delay in making the distribution is not due to the action or inaction of the plan administrator or the contributing sponsor and that the distribution can in fact be completed by the date requested.

(g) *Notice of annuity contract.* In the case of the distribution of benefit liabilities through the purchase of irrevocable commitments—

(1) Either the plan administrator or the insurer shall, as soon as practicable, provide each participant and beneficiary with a copy of the annuity contract or certificate showing the insurer's name and address and clearly reflecting the insurer's obligation to provide the participant's or beneficiary's benefit;

(2) If such a contract or certificate is not available on or before the date on which the post-distribution certificate is required to be filed pursuant to paragraph (h) of this section, the plan administrator shall, no later than such date, provide each participant and beneficiary with a written notice stating—

(i) That the obligation for providing the participant's or beneficiary's plan benefits has transferred to the insurer;

(ii) The name and address of the insurer;

(iii) The name, address, and telephone number of the person designated by the insurer to answer questions concerning the annuity; and

(iv) That the participant or beneficiary will receive from the plan administrator or insurer a copy of the annuity contract or a certificate showing the insurer's name and address and clearly reflecting the insurer's obligation to provide the participant's or beneficiary's benefit; and

(3) The plan administrator shall certify to the PBGC, as part of the post-distribution certification required under paragraph (h) of this section, that the requirements in paragraph (g)(1) or (g)(2) of this section have been satisfied.

(h) *Post-distribution certification.* Within 30 days after the last distribution date, the plan administrator shall file with the PBGC a PBGC Form 501, Post-Distribution Certification for Standard Termination, that has been completed in accordance with the instructions thereto. This requirement shall be considered satisfied if, in accordance with §4050.6(a)(2) and (a)(3) of this chapter, the plan administrator files a preliminary post-distribution certification within 30 days after the last distribution date and, in addition, timely files an amended post-distribution certification that otherwise satisfies all applicable requirements.

Subpart C—Distress Termination Process

[¶ 15,443]

§ 4041.41 **Notice of intent to terminate.** (a) *General rules.* (1) At least 60 days and no more than 90 days before the proposed termination date, the plan administrator shall issue to each person who is (as of the proposed termination date) an affected party a written notice of intent to terminate.

(2) The plan administrator shall issue the notice of intent to terminate to all affected parties other than the PBGC at or before the time he or she files the notice with the PBGC.

(3) The notice to affected parties other than the PBGC shall contain all of the information specified in paragraph (d) of this section.

(4) The notice to the PBGC shall be filed on PBGC Form 600, Distress Termination, Notice of Intent to Terminate, completed in accordance with the instructions thereto.

(b) *Discovery of other affected parties.* Notwithstanding the provisions of paragraphs (a)(1) and (a)(2) of this section, if the plan administrator discovers additional affected parties after the expiration of the time period specified in paragraphs (a)(1) or (a)(2) of this section, the failure to issue the notice of intent to terminate to such parties within the specified time periods will not cause the notice to be untimely under paragraph (a) of this section if the plan administrator could not reasonably have been expected to know of the additional affected parties and if he or she promptly issues the notice to each additional affected party.

(c) *Issuance.* (1) *Method.* The plan administrator shall issue the notice of intent to terminate individually to each affected party. The notice to the PBGC shall be filed in accordance with §4041.9. The notice to each of the other affected parties shall be either hand delivered or delivered by first-class mail or courier service directed to the affected party's last known address.

(2) *When issued.* The notice of intent to terminate is deemed issued to the PBGC on the date on which it is filed and to any other affected party on the date on which it is handed to the affected party or deposited with a mail or courier service (as evidenced by a postmark or written receipt).

(d) *Contents of notice to affected parties other than the PBGC.* The plan administrator shall include in the notice of intent to terminate to each affected party other than the PBGC all of the following information:

(1) The name of the plan and of the contributing sponsor;

(2) The employer identification number ("EIN") of the contributing sponsor and the plan number ("PN"); if there is no EIN or PN, the notice shall so state;

(3) The name, address, and telephone number of the person who may be contacted by an affected party with questions concerning the plan's termination;

(4) A statement that the plan administrator expects to terminate the plan in a distress termination on a specified proposed termination date.

(5) A statement that benefit and service accruals will continue until the termination date or, if applicable, that benefit accruals were or will be frozen as of a specific date in accordance with section 204(h) of ERISA;

(6) A statement of whether plan assets are sufficient to pay all guaranteed benefits or all benefit liabilities;

(7) A brief description of what benefits are guaranteed by the PBGC (e.g., if only a portion of the benefits are guaranteed because of the phase-in rule, this should be explained), and a statement that participants and beneficiaries also may receive a portion of the benefits to which each is entitled under the terms of the plan in excess of guaranteed benefits; and

(8) A statement, if applicable, that benefits may be subject to reduction because of the limitations on the amounts guaranteed by the PBGC or because plan assets are insufficient to pay for full benefits (pursuant to part 4022, subparts B and D, of this chapter) and that payments in excess of the amount guaranteed by the PBGC may be recouped by the PBGC (pursuant to part 4022, subpart E, of this chapter).

(e) *Spin-off/termination transactions.* In the case of a spin-off/termination transaction (as described in §4041.21(f)), the plan administrator shall provide all participants and beneficiaries in the original plan who are also participants or beneficiaries in the ongoing plan (as of the proposed termination date) with a notice describing the transaction no later than the date on which the plan administrator completes the issuance of notices of intent to terminate under this section.

[¶ 15,443A]

§ 4041.42 **PBGC review of notice of intent to terminate.** (a) *General.* When a notice of intent to terminate is filed with it, the PBGC—

(1) Shall determine whether the notice was issued in compliance with §4041.41; and

(2) Shall advise the plan administrator of its determination, in accordance with paragraph (b) or (c) of this section, no later than the proposed termination date specified in the notice.

(b) *Tentative finding of compliance.* If the PBGC determines that the issuance of the notice of intent to terminate appears to be in compliance with §4041.41, it shall notify the plan administrator in writing that—

(1) The PBGC has made a tentative determination of compliance;

(2) The distress termination proceeding may continue; and

(3) After reviewing the distress termination notice filed pursuant to §4041.43, the PBGC will make final, or reverse, this tentative determination.

(c) *Finding of noncompliance.* If the PBGC determines that the issuance of the notice of intent to terminate was not in compliance with §4041.41 (except for requirements that the PBGC elects to waive under §4041.3(d)(2)(i) with respect to the notice filed with the PBGC), the PBGC shall notify the plan administrator in writing—

(1) That the PBGC has determined that the notice of intent to terminate was not properly issued; and

(2) That the proposed distress termination is null and void and the plan is an ongoing plan.

(d) *Information on need to institute section 4042 proceedings.* The PBGC may require the plan administrator to submit, within 20 days after the plan administrator's receipt of the PBGC's written request (or such other period as may be specified in such written request), any information that the PBGC determines it needs in order to decide whether to institute termination or trusteeship proceedings pursuant to section 4042 of ERISA, whenever—

(1) A notice of intent to terminate indicates that benefits currently in pay status (or that should be in pay status) are not being paid or that this is likely to occur within the 180-day period following the issuance of the notice of intent to terminate;

(2) The PBGC issues a determination under paragraph (c) of this section; or

(3) The PBGC has any reason to believe that it may be necessary or appropriate to institute proceedings under section 4042 of ERISA.

(e) *Reconsideration of finding of noncompliance.* A plan administrator may request reconsideration of the PBGC's determination of noncompliance under paragraph (c) of this section in accordance with the rules prescribed in part 4003, subpart C, of this chapter. Any request for reconsideration automatically stays the effectiveness of the determination until the PBGC issues its decision on reconsideration, but does not stay the time period within which information must be submitted to the PBGC in response to a request under paragraph (d) of this section.

(f) *Notice to affected parties.* Upon a decision by the PBGC affirming a finding of noncompliance or upon the expiration of the period within which the plan administrator may request reconsideration of a finding of noncompliance (or, if earlier, upon the plan administrator's decision not to request reconsideration), the plan administrator shall notify the affected parties (and any persons who were provided notice under §4041.41(e)) in writing that the plan is not going to terminate or, if applicable, that the termination is invalid but that a new notice of intent to terminate is being issued. The notice required by this paragraph shall be provided in the manner described in §4041.26(d)(2).

[¶ 15,443B]

§4041.43 **Distress termination notice.** (a) *General rule.* The plan administrator shall file with the PBGC a PBGC Form 601, Distress Termination Notice, Single-Employer Plan Termination, with Schedule EA-D, Distress Termination Enrolled Actuary Certification, that has been completed in accordance with the instructions thereto, on or before the 120th day after the proposed termination date or, if applicable, no later than the due date established in an extension notice issued under §4041.8.

(b) *Participant and benefit information.* (1) *Plan insufficient for guaranteed benefits.* Unless the enrolled actuary certifies, in the Schedule EA-D filed in accordance with paragraph (a) of this section, that the plan is sufficient either for guaranteed benefits or for benefit liabilities, the plan administrator shall file with the PBGC the participant and benefit information described in PBGC Form 601 and the instructions thereto by the later of—

(i) 120 days after the proposed termination date, or

(ii) 30 days after receipt of the PBGC's determination, pursuant to §4041.44(b), that the requirements for a distress termination have been satisfied.

(2) *Plan sufficient for guaranteed benefits or benefit liabilities.* If the enrolled actuary certifies that the plan is sufficient either for guaranteed benefits or for benefit liabilities, the plan administrator need not submit the participant and benefit information described in PBGC Form 601 and the instructions thereto unless requested to do so pursuant to paragraph (c) of this section.

(3) *Effect of failure to provide information.* The PBGC may void the distress termination if the plan administrator fails to provide complete participant and benefit information in accordance with this section.

(c) *Additional information.* The PBGC may in any case require the submission of any additional information that it needs to make the determinations that it is required to make under this part or to pay benefits pursuant to section 4061 or 4022(c) of ERISA. The plan administrator shall submit any information requested under this paragraph within 30 days after receiving the PBGC's written request (or such other period as may be specified in such written request).

(d) *Due date extension.* Notwithstanding the provisions of paragraphs (a), (b), and (c) of this section, the due date for filing PBGC

Form 601 or other information required under this section may be extended by a notice issued under §4041.8.

[¶ 15,443C]

§4041.44 **PBGC determination of compliance with requirements for distress termination.** (a) *General.* Based on the information contained in and submitted with the PBGC Form 600 and the PBGC Form 601, with Schedule EA-D, and on any information submitted by an affected party or otherwise obtained by the PBGC, the PBGC shall determine whether the requirements for a distress termination set forth in §4041.3(c) have been met and shall notify the plan administrator in writing of its determination, in accordance with paragraph (b) or (c) of this section.

(b) *Qualifying termination.* If the PBGC determines that all of the requirements of §4041.3(c) have been satisfied, it shall so advise the plan administrator and shall also advise the plan administrator of whether participant and benefit information must be submitted in accordance with §4041.43(b).

(c) *Non-qualifying termination.* (1) Except as provided in paragraph (c)(2) of this section, if the PBGC determines that any of the requirements of §4041.3(c) has not been met, it shall notify the plan administrator of its determination, the basis therefor, and the effect thereof (as provided in §4041.3(d)).

(2) If the only basis for the PBGC's determination described in paragraph (c)(1) of this section is that the distress termination notice is incomplete, the PBGC shall advise the plan administrator of the missing item(s) of information and that the information must be filed with the PBGC no later than the 120th day after the proposed termination date or the 30th day after the date of the PBGC's notice of its determination, whichever is later, or, if applicable, no later than the due date established in an extension notice issued under §4041.8.

(d) *Reconsideration of determination of non-qualification.* A plan administrator may request reconsideration of the PBGC's determination under paragraph (c)(1) of this section in accordance with the rules prescribed in part 4003, subpart C, of this chapter. The filing of a request for reconsideration automatically stays the effectiveness of the determination until the PBGC issues its decision on reconsideration.

(e) *Notice to affected parties.* Upon a decision by the PBGC affirming a determination of non-qualification or upon the expiration of the period within which the plan administrator may request reconsideration of a determination of non-qualification (or, if earlier, upon the plan administrator's decision not to request reconsideration), the plan administrator shall notify the affected parties (and any persons who were provided notice under §4041.41(e)) in writing that the plan is not going to terminate or, if applicable, that the termination is invalid but that a new notice of intent to terminate is being issued. The notice required by this paragraph shall be provided in the manner described in §4041.26(d)(2).

[¶ 15,443D]

§4041.45 **PBGC determination of plan sufficiency/insufficiency.** (a) *General.* Upon receipt of participant and benefit information filed pursuant to §4041.43(b)(1) or (c), the PBGC shall determine the degree to which the plan is sufficient and notify the plan administrator in writing of its determination in accordance with paragraph (b) or (c) of this section.

(b) *Insufficiency for guaranteed benefits.* If the PBGC finds that it is unable to determine that a plan is sufficient for guaranteed benefits, it shall issue a "notice of inability to determine sufficiency" notifying the plan administrator of this finding and advising the plan administrator that—

(1) The plan administrator shall continue to administer the plan under the restrictions imposed by §4041.4; and

(2) The termination shall be completed under section 4042 of ERISA.

(c) *Sufficiency for guaranteed benefits or benefit liabilities.* If the PBGC determines that a plan is sufficient for guaranteed benefits but not for benefit liabilities or is sufficient for benefit liabilities, the PBGC shall issue to the plan administrator a distribution notice advising the plan administrator—

(1) To issue notices of benefit distribution in accordance with §4041.46;

(2) To close out the plan in accordance with §4041.48;

(3) To file a timely post-distribution certification with the PBGC in accordance with §4041.48(b); and

(4) That either the plan administrator or the contributing sponsor must preserve and maintain plan records in accordance with §4041.11.

[¶ 15,443E]

§4041.46 **Notices of benefit distribution**. (a) *General rules*. When a distribution notice is issued by the PBGC pursuant to §4041.45(c), the plan administrator shall—

(1) No later than 60 days after receiving the distribution notice or, if applicable, no later than the due date established in an extension notice issued under §4041.8, issue a notice of benefit distribution in accordance with the rules described in paragraphs (c) and (d) of this section to each person (other than any employee organization or the PBGC) who is an affected party as of the termination date (and, in the case of a spin-off/termination transaction as described in §4041.21(f), each person who is, as of the termination date, a participant in the original plan and covered by the ongoing plan); and

(2) No later than 15 days after the date on which the plan administrator completes the issuance of the notices of benefit distribution, file with the PBGC a certification that the notices were so issued in accordance with the requirements of this section.

(b) *Discovery of other affected parties*. Notwithstanding the provisions of paragraph (a) of this section, if the plan administrator discovers additional persons entitled to a notice of benefit distribution after the expiration of the time period specified in paragraph (a)(1) of this section, the failure to issue the notices of benefit distribution to such persons within the specified time period will not cause such notices to be untimely under paragraph (a) of this section if the plan administrator could not reasonably have been expected to know of the additional persons and if he or she promptly issues, to each such additional person, a notice of benefit distribution in the form and containing the information specified in paragraph (d) of this section.

(c) *Issuance*. (1) *Method*. The plan administrator shall issue a notice of benefit distribution individually to each person, either by hand-delivery or by first-class mail or courier service directed to the person's last known address.

(2) *When issued*. A notice of benefit distribution is deemed issued to each person on the date it is handed to the person or deposited with a mail or courier service (as evidenced by a postmark or written receipt).

(d) *Form and content of notices*. The plan administrator shall provide notices of benefit distribution in the form described in §4041.23(a) and (b) of this part and shall include in each—

(1) The information described in §4041.23(c) of this part;

(2) The information described in §4041.23(d), (e), or (f) of this part, as applicable (replacing the term "plan benefits" with "Title IV benefits" and "proposed termination date" with "termination date".

(3) A statement that, after plan assets have been distributed to provide all of the Title IV benefits payable with respect to a participant or a beneficiary of a deceased participant, either by the purchase of an irrevocable commitment or commitments from an insurer to provide benefits or by an alternative form of distribution provided for under the plan, the PBGC's guarantee with respect to that participant's or beneficiary's benefit ends; and

(4) If distribution of benefits under the plan may be wholly or partially by the purchase of irrevocable commitments from an insurer—

(i) The name and address of the insurer or insurers from whom, or (if not then known) the insurers from among whom, the plan administrator intends to purchase the irrevocable commitments; or

(ii) If the plan administrator has not identified an insurer or insurers at the time the notice of distribution is issued, a statement that

the affected party to whom the notice is directed will be notified at a later date (but no later than 45 days before the distribution date) of the name and address of the insurer or insurers from whom, or (if not then known) the insurers from among whom, irrevocable commitments may be purchased.

(e) *Supplemental notice requirements*. (1) The plan administrator shall issue a supplemental notice (or notices) of distribution to each person in accordance with the rules in paragraph (e)(2) of this section if—

(i) The plan administrator has not yet identified an insurer or insurers at the time the notice of distribution is issued; or

(ii) The plan administrator included in the notice of distribution the name or names of the insurer or insurers from whom (or from among whom) he or she intends to purchase the irrevocable commitments, but subsequently decides to select a different insurer.

(2) The plan administrator shall issue each supplemental notice in the manner provided in paragraph (c) of this section no later than 45 days before the distribution date and shall include the name and address of the insurer or insurers from whom, or (if not then known) the insurers from among whom, the plan administrator intends to purchase the irrevocable commitments.

[¶ 15,443F]

§4041.47 **Verification of plan sufficiency prior to closeout**. (a) *General rule*. Before distributing plan assets pursuant to a closeout under §4041.48, the plan administrator shall verify whether the plan's assets are still sufficient to provide for benefits at the level determined by the PBGC, i.e., guaranteed benefits or benefit liabilities. If the plan administrator finds that the plan is no longer able to provide for benefits at the level determined by the PBGC, then paragraph (b) or (c) of this section, as appropriate, shall apply.

(b) *Subsequent insufficiency for guaranteed benefits*. When a plan administrator finds that a plan is no longer sufficient for guaranteed benefits, the plan administrator shall promptly notify the PBGC in writing of that fact and shall take no further action to implement the plan termination, pending the PBGC's determination and notice pursuant to paragraph (b)(1) or (b)(2) of this section.

(1) *PBGC concurrence with finding*. If the PBGC concurs with the plan administrator's finding, the distribution notice shall be void, and the PBGC shall—

(i) Issue the plan administrator a notice of inability to determine sufficiency in accordance with §4041.45(b); and

(ii) Require the plan administrator to submit a new valuation, certified to by an enrolled actuary, of the benefit liabilities and guaranteed benefits under the plan, valued in accordance with §§4044.41 through 4044.57 of this chapter as of the date of the plan administrator's notice to the PBGC.

(2) *PBGC non-concurrence with finding*. If the PBGC does not concur with the plan administrator's finding, it shall so notify the plan administrator in writing, and the distribution notice shall remain in effect.

(c) *Subsequent insufficiency for benefit liabilities*. When a plan administrator finds that a plan is sufficient for guaranteed benefits but is no longer sufficient for benefit liabilities, the plan administrator shall immediately notify the PBGC in writing of this fact, but shall continue with the distribution of assets in accordance with §4041.48.

(d) *Finding by PBGC of subsequent insufficiency*. In any case in which the PBGC finds on its own initiative that a subsequent insufficiency for guaranteed benefits has occurred, paragraph (b)(1) of this section shall apply, except that the guaranteed benefits shall be revalued as of the date of the PBGC's finding.

(e) *Restrictions upon finding of subsequent insufficiency*. When the plan administrator makes the finding described in paragraph (b) of this section or receives notice that the PBGC has made the finding described in paragraph (d) of this section, the plan administrator shall (except to the extent the PBGC otherwise directs) be subject to the prohibitions in §4041.4(c).

[¶ 15,443G]

§4041.48 **Closeout of plan**. (a) *General rules.* (1) *Distribution.* If a plan administrator receives a distribution notice from the PBGC pursuant to §4041.45(c) and neither the plan administrator nor the PBGC makes the finding described in §4041.47(b) or (d), the plan administrator shall distribute plan assets in accordance with §§4041.6 and 4041.27(c) of this part no earlier than the 61st day and (except as provided in §4041.8 or 4041.27(e) or (f)) no later than the 180th day following the day on which the plan administrator completes the issuance of the notices of benefit distribution pursuant to §4041.46(a), or, where applicable, within the time prescribed in part 4050 of this chapter. For purposes of applying §4041.27(e)(1)(i), the phrase "the date that the plan administrator files the standard termination notice with the PBGC" shall be replaced by "the date that the plan administrator completes issuance of the notices of benefit distribution."

(2) *Notice of annuity contract.* If any of the plan's benefit liabilities payable to a participant or beneficiary have been distributed through the purchase of irrevocable commitments, the plan administrator shall provide such participant or beneficiary with a notice, contract, or certificate in accordance with §4041.27(g).

(b) *Post-distribution certification.* Within 30 days after the last distribution date, the plan administrator shall file with the PBGC a PBGC Form 602, Post-Distribution Certification for Distress Termination, that has been completed in accordance with the instructions thereto. This requirement shall be considered satisfied if, in accordance with §4050.6 (a)(2) and (a)(3) of this chapter, the plan administrator files a preliminary post-distribution certification within 30 days after the last distribution date and, in addition, timely files an amended post-distribution certification that otherwise satisfies all applicable requirements.

[¶ 15,443H]

§4041.48 **Appendix to Part 4041: Agreement for Commitment To Make Plan Sufficient for Benefit Liabilities.**

This agreement, by and between [name of company] XXXXXXXXXX (the "Company") and [name of plan] XXXXXXXXXX (the "Plan") shall be effective as of the last date executed.

Whereas, the Plan is an employee pension benefit plan as described in section 3(2)(A) of the Employee Retirement Income Security Act of 1974 ("ERISA"), 29 U.S.C. 1001-1461; and

Whereas the Company is [describe entity, e.g., corporation, partnership] XXXXXXXXXX; and

Whereas, the Company is a contributing sponsor of the Plan, or a member of the contributing sponsor's controlled group, as described in section 4001(a)(13) and (14) of ERISA, 29 U.S.C. 1301(2)(13) and (14); and

Whereas, the Plan is covered by the termination insurance provisions of Title IV of ERISA, 29 U.S.C. 1301-1461; and

Whereas, the Plan administrator has issued or intends to issue to each affected party a notice of intent to terminate the Plan, pursuant to section 4041(a)(2) of ERISA, 29 U.S.C. 1341(a)(2); and

Whereas, the Company wishes the Plan to be sufficient for benefit liabilities, as described in section 4001(a)(16) of ERISA, 29 U.S.C. 1301(a)(16); and

Whereas, the parties understand that if the Plan is not able to satisfy all its obligations for benefit liabilities, it will not be able to terminate in a standard termination under section 4041(b) of ERISA, 29 U.S.C. 1341(b); and

Whereas, the Company is not a debtor in a bankruptcy or other insolvency proceeding.

[Alternative Paragraph]

Whereas, the Company is a debtor in a bankruptcy or other insolvency proceeding and the court before which the proceeding is pending approves this commitment.

Whereas, the Company is a debtor in a bankruptcy or other insolvency proceeding and this commitment is unconditionally guaranteed, by an entity or person not in bankruptcy, to be met at or before the time distribution is required in this standard termination.

Now Therefore, the parties hereto agree as follows:

1. The Company promises to pay to the Plan, on or before the date prescribed for distribution of Plan assets by the plan administrator, the amount necessary, if any, to ensure that, on the date the plan administrator distributes the assets of the Plan, the Plan is able to provide all benefit liabilities.

2. For the sole purpose of determining whether the Plan is sufficient to provide all benefit liabilities, an amount equal to the amount described in paragraph 1 shall be deemed a Plan asset available for allocation among the participants and beneficiaries of the Plan, in accordance with section 4044 of ERISA, 29 U.S.C. 1344.

3. This Agreement shall in no way relieve the Company of its obligations to pay contributions under the Plan.

Date:

By:

Company:

By:

Plan:

[¶ 15,449F]
TERMINATION OF MULTIEMPLOYER PLANS

Act Sec. 4041A. (a) Termination of a multiemployer plan under this section occurs as a result of—

(1) the adoption after the date of enactment of the Multiemployer Pension Plan Amendments Act of 1980 of a plan amendment which provides that participants will receive no credit for any purpose under the plan for service with any employer after the date specified by such amendment;

(2) the withdrawal of every employer from the plan, within the meaning of section 4203, or the cessation of the obligation of all employers to contribute under the plan; or

(3) the adoption of an amendment to the plan which causes the plan to become a plan described in section 4021(b)(1).

Act Sec. 4041A. (b)(1) The date on which a plan terminates under paragraph (1) or (3) of subsection (a) is the later of—

(A) the date on which the amendment is adopted, or

(B) the date on which the amendment takes effect.

(2) The date on which a plan terminates under paragraph (2) of subsection (a) is the earlier of—

(A) the date on which the last employer withdraws, or

(B) the first day of the first plan year for which no employer contributions were required under the plan.

Act Sec. 4041A. (c) Except as provided in subsection (f)(1), the plan sponsor of a plan which terminates under paragraph (2) of subsection (a) shall—

(1) limit the payment of benefits to benefits which are nonforfeitable under the plan as of the date of the termination, and

(2) pay benefits attributable to employer contributions, other than death benefits, only in the form of an annuity, unless the plan assets are distributed in full satisfaction of all nonforfeitable benefits under the plan.

Act Sec. 4041A. (d) The plan sponsor of a plan which terminates under paragraph (2) of subsection (a) shall reduce benefits and suspend benefit payments in accordance with section 4281.

Act Sec. 4041A. (e) In the case of a plan which terminates under paragraph (1) or (3) of subsection (a), the rate of an employer's contributions under the plan for each plan year beginning on or after the plan termination date shall equal or exceed the highest rate of employer contributions at which the employer had an obligation to contribute under the plan in the 5 preceding plan years ending on or before the plan termination date, unless the corporation approves a reduction in the rate based on a finding that the plan is or soon will be fully funded.

Act Sec. 4041A. (f)(1) The plan sponsor of a terminated plan may authorize the payment other than in the form of an annuity of a participant's entire nonforfeitable benefit attributable to employer contributions, other than a death benefit, if the value of the entire nonforfeitable benefit does not exceed $1,750. The corporation may authorize the payment of benefits under the terms of a terminated plan other than nonforfeitable benefits, or the payment other than in the form of an annuity of benefits having a value greater than $1,750, if the corporation determines that such payment is not adverse to the interest of the plan's participants and beneficiaries generally and does not unreasonably increase the corporation's risk of loss with respect to the plan.

(2) The corporation may prescribe reporting requirements for terminated plans, and rules and standards for the administration of such plans, which the corporation considers appropriate to protect the interests of plan participants and beneficiaries or to prevent unreasonable loss to the corporation.

Amendment:

P.L. 96-364, §103

Added new section 4041A, effective September 26, 1980.

Regulations

The following regulations were adopted by the Pension Benefit Guaranty Corporation on July 1, 1996 (61 FR 34002). Prior to July 1, 1996, PBGC regulations were under Chapter XXVI of Title 29 of the Code of Federal Regulations. Effective July 1, 1996, PBGC regulations were moved to Chapter XL, and were renumbered and reorganized. Reg. §4041A.43 was amended July 15, 1998 (63 FR38305), effective July 16, 1998. Reg. §4041A.3 was amended October 28, 2003 (68 FR 61344).

Subpart A—General Provisions

[¶ 15,449G]

§4041A.1 **Purpose and scope.** The purpose of this part is to establish rules for notifying the PBGC of the termination of a multiemployer plan and rules for the administration of multiemployer plans that have terminated by mass withdrawal. Subpart B prescribes the contents of and procedures for filing a Notice of Termination for a multiemployer plan. Subpart C prescribes basic duties of plan sponsors of mass-withdrawal-terminated plans. (Other duties are prescribed in part 4281 of this chapter.) Subpart D contains procedures for closing out sufficient plans. This part applies to terminated multiemployer plans covered by title IV of ERISA but, in the case of subparts C and D, only to plans terminated by mass withdrawal under section 4041A(a)(2) of ERISA (including plans created by partition pursuant to section 4233 of ERISA).

[¶ 15,449H]

§4041A.2 **Definitions.** The following terms are defined in §4001.1 of this chapter: annuity, ERISA, insurer, IRS, mass withdrawal, multiemployer plan, nonforfeitable benefit, PBGC, plan, and plan year.

In addition, for purposes of this part:

Available resources means, for a plan year, available resources as described in section 4245(b)(3) of ERISA.

Benefits subject to reduction means those benefits accrued under plan amendments (or plans) adopted after March 26, 1980, or under collective bargaining agreements entered into after March 26, 1980, that are not eligible for the PBGC's guarantee under section 4022A(b) of ERISA.

Financial assistance means financial assistance from the PBGC under section 4261 of ERISA.

Insolvency benefit level means the greater of the resource benefit level or the benefit level guaranteed by the PBGC for each participant and beneficiary in pay status.

Insolvency year means insolvency year as described in section 4245(b)(4) of ERISA.

Insolvent means that a plan is unable to pay benefits when due during the plan year. A plan terminated by mass withdrawal is not insolvent unless it has been amended to eliminate all benefits that are subject to reduction under section 4281(c) of ERISA, or, in the absence of an amendment, no benefits under the plan are subject to reduction under section 4281(c) of ERISA.

Nonguaranteed benefits means those benefits that are eligible for the PBGC's guarantee under section 4022A(b) of ERISA, but exceed the guarantee limits under section 4022A(c).

Resource benefit level means resource benefit level as described in section 4245(b)(2) of ERISA.

[¶ 15,449I]

§4041A.3 **Method and date of filing; where to file; computation of time; issuances to third parties.** (a) *Method and date of filing.* The PBGC applies the rules in subpart A of part 4000 of this chapter to determine permissible methods of filing with the PBGC under this part. The PBGC applies the rules in subpart C of part 4000 of this chapter to determine the date that a submission under this part was filed with the PBGC.

(b) *Where to file.* See Sec. 4000.4 of this chapter for information on where to file.

(c) *Computation of time.* The PBGC applies the rules in subpart D of part 4000 of this chapter to compute any time period for filing or issuance under this part.

(d) *Method and date of issuance.* The PBGC applies the rules in subpart B of part 4000 of this chapter to determine permissible methods of issuance under this part. The PBGC applies the rules in subpart C of part 4000 of this chapter to determine the date that an issuance under this part was provided. [Amended 10/28/2003 by 68 FR 61344.]

Subpart B—Notice of Termination

[¶ 15,449J]

§4041A.11 **Requirement of notice.** (a) *General.* A Notice of Termination shall be filed with the PBGC by a multiemployer plan when the plan has terminated as described in section 4041A(a) of ERISA.

(b) *Who shall file.* The plan sponsor or a duly authorized representative acting on behalf of the plan sponsor shall sign and file the Notice.

(c) *When to file.* (1) For a termination pursuant to a plan amendment, the Notice shall be filed with the PBGC within thirty days after the amendment is adopted or effective, whichever is later.

(2) For a termination that results from a mass withdrawal, the Notice shall be filed with the PBGC within thirty days after the last employer withdrew from the plan or thirty days after the first day of the first plan year for which no employer contributions were required under the plan, whichever is earlier.

(Approved by the Office of Management and Budget under control number 1212-0020)

[¶ 15,449K]

§4041A.12 **Contents of notice.** (a) *Information to be contained in notice.* Except to the extent provided in paragraph (d), each Notice shall contain:

(1) The name of the plan;

(2) The name, address and telephone number of the plan sponsor and of the plan sponsor's duly authorized representative, if any;

(3) The name, address, and telephone number of the person that will administer the plan after the date of termination, if other than the plan sponsor;

(4) A copy of the plan's most recent Form 5500 (Annual Report Form), including schedules; and

(5) The date of termination of the plan.

(b) *Information to be contained in a notice involving a mass withdrawal.* In addition to the information contained in paragraph (a) and except as provided in paragraph (d), the following information shall be contained in a Notice filed by a plan that has terminated by mass withdrawal:

(1) A copy of the plan document in effect 5 years prior to the date of termination and copies of any amendments adopted after that date.

(2) A copy (or copies) of the trust agreement (or agreements), if any, authorizing the plan sponsor to control and manage the operation and administration of the plan.

(3) A copy of the most recent actuarial statement and opinion (if any) relating to the plan.

(4) A statement of any material change in the assets or liabilities of the plan occurring after either the date of the actuarial statement referred to in item (5) or the date of the plan's Form 5500 submitted as part of the Notice.

(5) Complete copies of any letters of determination issued by the IRS relating to the establishment of the plan, any letters of determination relating to the disqualification of the plan and any subsequent requalification, and any letters of determination relating to the termination of the plan.

(6) A statement whether the plan assets will be sufficient to pay all benefits in pay status during the 12-month period following the date of termination.

(7) If plan assets on hand are sufficient to satisfy all nonforfeitable benefits under the plan, and if the plan sponsor intends to distribute such assets, a brief description of the proposed method of distributing the plan assets.

(8) If plan assets on hand are not sufficient to satisfy all nonforfeitable benefits under the plan, the name and address of any employer who contributed to the plan within 3 plan years prior to the date of termination.

(c) *Certification.* As part of the Notice, the plan sponsor or duly authorized representatives shall certify that all information and documents submitted pursuant to this section are true and correct to the best of the plan sponsor's or representative's knowledge and belief.

(d) *Avoiding duplication.* Information described in paragraphs (a) and (b) of this section need not be supplied if it duplicates information contained in Form 5500, or a schedule thereof, that a plan submits as part of the Notice.

(e) *Additional information.* In addition to the information described in paragraphs (a) and (b) of this section, the PBGC may require the submission of any other information which the PBGC determines is necessary for review of a Notice of Termination.

Subpart C—Plan Sponsor Duties

[¶ 15,449L]

§ 4041A.21 **General rule.** The plan sponsor of a multiemployer plan that terminates by mass withdrawal shall continue to administer the plan in accordance with applicable statutory provisions, regulations, and plan provisions until a trustee is appointed under section 4042 of ERISA or until plan assets are distributed in accordance with subpart D of this part. In addition, the plan sponsor shall be responsible for the specific duties described in this subpart.

[¶ 15,449M]

§ 4041A.22 **Payment of benefits.** (a) Except as provided in paragraph (b), the plan sponsor shall pay any benefit attributable to employer contributions, other than a death benefit, only in the form of an annuity.

(b) The plan sponsor may pay a benefit in a form other than an annuity if—

(1) The plan distributes plan assets in accordance with subpart D of this part;

(2) The PBGC approves the payment of the benefit in an alternative form pursuant to § 4041A.27; or

(3) The value of the entire nonforfeitable benefit does not exceed $1,750.

(c) Except to the extent provided in the next sentence, the plan sponsor shall not pay benefits in excess of the amount that is nonforfeitable under the plan as of the date of termination, unless authorized to do so by the PBGC pursuant to § 4041A.27. Subject to the restriction stated in paragraph (d) of this section, however, the plan sponsor may pay a qualified preretirement survivor annuity with respect to a participant who died after the date of termination.

(d) The payment of benefits subject to reduction shall be discontinued to the extent provided in § 4281.31 if the plan sponsor determines, in accordance with § 4041A.24, that the plan's assets are insufficient to provide all nonforfeitable benefits.

(e) The plan sponsor shall, to the extent provided in § 4281.41, suspend the payment of nonguaranteed benefits if the plan sponsor determines, in accordance with § 4041A.25, that the plan is insolvent.

(f) The plan sponsor shall, to the extent required by § 4281.42, make retroactive payments of suspended benefits if it determines under that section that the level of the plan's available resources requires such payments.

[¶ 15,449N]

§ 4041A.23 **Imposition and collection of withdrawal liability.** Until plan assets are distributed in accordance with subpart D of this part, or until the end of the plan year as of which the PBGC determines that plan assets (exclusive of claims for withdrawal liability) are sufficient to satisfy all nonforfeitable benefits under the plan, the plan sponsor shall be responsible for determining, imposing and collecting withdrawal liability (including the liability arising as a result of the mass withdrawal), in accordance with part 4219, subpart C, of this chapter and sections 4201 through 4225 of ERISA.

[¶ 15,449O]

§ 4041A.24 **Annual plan valuations and monitoring.** (a) *Annual valuation.* Not later than 150 days after the end of the plan year, the plan sponsor shall determine or cause to be determined in writing the value of nonforfeitable benefits under the plan and the value of the plan's assets, in accordance with part 4281, subpart B. This valuation shall be done as of the end of the plan year in which the plan terminates and each plan year thereafter (exclusive of a plan year for which the plan receives financial assistance from the PBGC under section 4261 of ERISA) up to but not including the plan year in which the plan is closed out in accordance with subpart D of this part.

(b) *Plan monitoring.* Upon receipt of the annual valuation described in paragraph (a) of this section, the plan sponsor shall determine whether the value of nonforfeitable benefits exceeds the value of the plan's assets, including claims for withdrawal liability owed to the plan. When benefits do exceed assets, the plan sponsor shall—

(1) If the plan provides benefits subject to reduction, amend the plan to reduce those benefits in accordance with the procedures in part 4281, subpart C, of this chapter to the extent necessary to ensure that the plan's assets are sufficient to discharge when due all of the plan's obligations with respect to nonforfeitable benefits; or

(2) If the plan provides no benefits subject to reduction, make periodic determinations of plan solvency in accordance with § 4041A.25.

(c) *Notices of benefit reductions.* The plan sponsor of a plan that has been amended to reduce benefits shall provide participants and beneficiaries and the PBGC notice of the benefit reduction in accordance with § 4281.32.

[¶ 15,449P]

§ 4041A.25 **Periodic determinations of plan solvency.** (a) *Annual insolvency determination.* The plan sponsor of a plan that has been amended to eliminate all benefits that are subject to reduction under section 4281(c) of ERISA shall determine in writing whether the plan is expected to be insolvent for the first plan year beginning after the effective date of the amendment and for each plan year thereafter. In the event that a plan adopts more than one amendment reducing benefits under section 4281(c) of ERISA, the initial determination shall be made for the first plan year beginning after the effective date of the amendment that effects the elimination of all such benefits, and a determination shall be made for each plan year thereafter. The plan sponsor of a plan under which no benefits are subject to reduction under section 4281(c) of ERISA as of the date the plan terminated shall determine in writing whether the plan is expected to be insolvent. The initial determination shall be made for the second plan year beginning after the first plan year for which it is determined under section 4281(b) of ERISA that the value of nonforfeitable benefits under the plan exceeds the value of the plan's assets. The plan sponsor shall also make a solvency determination for each plan year thereafter. A determination required under this paragraph shall be made no later than six months before the beginning of the plan year to which it applies.

(b) *Other determination of insolvency*. Whether or not a prior determination of plan solvency has been made under paragraph (a) of this section (or under section 4245 of ERISA), a plan sponsor that has reason to believe, taking into account the plan's recent and anticipated financial experience, that the plan is or may be insolvent for the current or next plan year shall determine in writing whether the plan is expected to be insolvent for that plan year.

(c) *Benefit suspensions*. If the plan sponsor determines that the plan is, or is expected to be, insolvent for a plan year, it shall suspend benefits in accordance with § 4281.41.

(d) *Insolvency notices*. If the plan sponsor determines that the plan is, or is expected to be, insolvent for a plan year, it shall issue notices of insolvency or annual updates and notices of insolvency benefit level of the PBGC and to plan participants and beneficiaries in accordance with part 4281, subpart D.

[¶ 15,449Q]

§ 4041A.26 **Financial assistance**. A plan sponsor that determines a resource benefit level under section 4245(b)(2) of ERISA that is below the level of guaranteed benefits or that determines that the plan will be unable to pay guaranteed benefits for any month during an insolvency year shall apply for financial assistance from the PBGC in accordance with § 4281.47.

[¶ 15,449R]

§ 4041A.27 **PBGC approval to pay benefits not otherwise permitted**. Upon written application by the plan sponsor, the PBGC may authorize the plan to pay benefits other than nonforfeitable benefits or to pay benefits valued at more than $1,750 in a form other than an annuity. The PBGC will approve such payments if it determines that the plan sponsor has demonstrated that the payments are not adverse to the interests of the plan's participants and beneficiaries generally and do not unreasonably increase the PBGC's risk of loss with respect to the plan.

Subpart D—Closeout of Sufficient Plans

[¶ 15,449S]

§ 4041A.41 **General rule**. If a plan's assets, excluding any claim of the plan for unpaid withdrawal liability, are sufficient to satisfy all obligations for nonforfeitable benefits provided under the plan, the plan sponsor may close out the plan in accordance with this subpart by distributing plan assets in full satisfaction of all nonforfeitable benefits under the plan.

[¶ 15,449T]

§ 4041A.42 **Method of distribution**. The plan sponsor shall distribute plan assets by purchasing from an insurer contracts to provide all benefits required by § 4041A.43 to be provided in annuity form and by paying in a lump sum (or other alternative elected by the participant) all other benefits.

[¶ 15,449U]

§ 4041A.43 **Benefit forms**. (a) *General rule*. Except as provided in paragraph (b) of this section, the sponsor of a plan that is closed out shall provide for the payment of any benefit attributable to employer contributions only in the form of an annuity.

(b) *Exceptions*. The plan sponsor may pay a benefit attributable to employer contributions in a form other than an annuity if:

(1) The present value of the participant's entire nonforfeitable benefit, determined using the interest assumption under § § 4044.41 through 4044.57, does not exceed $5,000.

(2) The payment is for death benefits provided under the plan.

(3) The participant elects an alternative form of distribution under paragraph (c) of this section.

(c) *Alternative forms of distribution*. The plan sponsor may allow participants to elect alternative forms of distribution in accordance with this paragraph. When a form of distribution is offered as an alternative to the normal form, the plan sponsor shall notify each participant, in writing, of the form and estimated amount of the participant's normal form of distribution. The notification shall also describe any risks attendant to the alternative form. Participants' elections of alternative forms shall be in writing.

[¶ 15,449V]

§ 4041A.44 **Cessation of withdrawal liability**. The obligation of an employer to make payments of initial withdrawal liability and mass withdrawal liability shall cease on the date on which the plan's assets are distributed in full satisfaction of all nonforfeitable benefits provided by the plan.

[¶ 15,450]
INSTITUTION OF TERMINATION PROCEEDINGS BY THE CORPORATION

Act Sec. 4042. (a) The corporation may institute proceedings under this section to terminate a plan whenever it determines that—

(1) the plan has not met the minimum funding standard required under section 412 of the Internal Revenue Code of 1986, or has been notified by the Secretary of the Treasury that a notice of deficiency under section 6212 of such Code has been mailed with respect to the tax imposed under section 4971(a) of such Code,

(2) the plan will be unable to pay benefits when due,

(3) the reportable event described in section 4043(c)(7) has occurred, or

(4) the possible long-run loss of the corporation with respect to the plan may reasonably be expected to increase unreasonably if the plan is not terminated.

The corporation shall as soon as practicable institute proceedings under this section to terminate a single-employer plan whenever the corporation determines that the plan does not have assets available to pay benefits which are currently due under the terms of the plan. The corporation may prescribe a simplified procedure to follow in terminating small plans as long as that procedure includes substantial safeguards for the rights of the participants and beneficiaries under the plans, and for the employers who maintain such plans (including the requirement for a court decree under subsection (c)). Notwithstanding any other provision of this title, the corporation is authorized to pool assets of terminated plans for purposes of administration, investment, payment of liabilities of all such terminated plans, and such other purposes as it determines to be appropriate in the administration of this title.

Act Sec. 4042. (b)(1) Whenever the corporation makes a determination under subsection (a) with respect to a plan or is required under subsection (a) to institute proceedings under this section, it may, upon notice to the plan, apply to the appropriate United States district court for the appointment of a trustee to administer the plan with respect to which the determination is made pending the issuance of a decree under subsection (c) ordering the termination of the plan. If within 3 business days after the filing of an application under this subsection, or such other period as the court may order, the administrator of the plan consents to the appointment of a trustee, or fails to show why a trustee should not be appointed, the court may grant the application and appoint a trustee to administer the plan in accordance with its terms until the corporation determines that the plan should be terminated or that termination is unnecessary. The corporation may request that it be appointed as trustee of a plan in any case.

(2) Notwithstanding any other provision of this title—

(A) upon the petition of a plan administrator or the corporation, the appropriate United States district court may appoint a trustee in accordance with the provisions of this section if the interests of the plan participants would be better served by the appointment of the trustee, and

(B) upon the petition of the corporation, the appropriate United States district court shall appoint a trustee proposed by the corporation for a multiemployer plan which is in reorganization or to which section 4041A(d) applies, unless such appointment would be adverse to the interests of the plan participants and beneficiaries in the aggregate.

(3) The corporation and plan administrator may agree to the appointment of a trustee without proceeding in accordance with the requirements of paragraphs (1) and (2).

Act Sec. 4042. (c) If the corporation is required under subsection (a) of this section to commence proceedings under this section with respect to a plan or, after issuing a notice under this section to a plan administrator, has determined that the plan should be terminated, it may, upon notice to the plan administrator, apply to the appropriate United States district court for a decree adjudicating that the plan must be terminated in order to protect the interests of the participants *or* to avoid any unreasonable deterioration of the financial condition of the plan or any unreasonable increase in the liability of the fund. If the trustee appointed under subsection (b) disagrees with the determination of the corporation under the preceding sentence he may intervene in the proceeding relating to the application for the decree, or make application for such decree himself. Upon granting a decree for which the corporation or trustee has applied under this subsection the court shall authorize the trustee appointed under subsection (b) (or appoint a trustee if one has not been appointed under such subsection and authorize him) to terminate the plan in accordance with the provisions of this subtitle. If the corporation and the plan administrator agree that a plan should be terminated and agree to the appointment of a trustee without proceeding in accordance with the requirements of this subsection (other than this sentence) the trustee shall have the power described in subsection (d)(1) and, in addition to any other duties imposed on the trustee under law or by agreement between the corporation and the plan administrator, the trustee is subject to the duties described in subsection (d)(3). Whenever a trustee appointed under this title is operating a plan with discretion as to the date upon which final distribution of the assets is to be commenced, the trustee shall notify the corporation at least 10 days before the date on which he proposes to commence such distribution.

(3) In the case of a proceeding initiated under this section, the plan administrator shall provide the corporation, upon the request of the corporation, the information described in clauses (ii), (iii), and (iv) of section 4041(c)(2)(A).

Act Sec. 4042.(d)(1)(A) A trustee appointed under subsection (b) shall have the power—

(i) to do any act authorized by the plan or this title to be done by the plan administrator or any trustee of the plan;

(ii) to require the transfer of all (or any part) of the assets and records of the plan to himself as trustee;

(iii) to invest any assets of the plan which he holds in accordance with the provisions of the plan, regulations of the corporation, and applicable rules of law;

(iv) to limit payment of benefits under the plan to basic benefits or to continue payment of some or all of the benefits which were being paid prior to his appointment;

(v) in the case of a multiemployer plan, to reduce benefits or suspend benefit payments under the plan, give appropriate notices, amend the plan, and perform other acts required or authorized by subtitle (E) to be performed by the plan sponsor or administrator;

(vi) to do such other acts as he deems necessary to continue operation of the plan without increasing the potential liability of the corporation if such acts may be done under the provisions of the plan; and

(vii) to require the plan sponsor, the plan administrator, any contributing or withdrawn employer, and any employee organization representing plan participants to furnish any information with respect to the plan which the trustee may reasonably need in order to administer the plan.

If the court to which application is made under subsection (c) dismisses the application with prejudice, or if the corporation fails to apply for a decree under subsection (c) within 30 days after the date on which the trustee is appointed under subsection (b), the trustee shall transfer all assets and records of the plan held by him to the plan administrator within 3 business days after such dismissal or the expiration of such 30-day period, and shall not be liable to the plan or any other person for his acts as trustee except for willful misconduct, or for conduct in violation of the provisions of part 4 of subtitle B of title I of this Act (except as provided in subsection (d)(1)(A)(v)). The 30-day period referred to in this subparagraph may be extended as provided by agreement between the plan administrator and the corporation or by court order obtained by the corporation.

(B) If the court to which an application is made under subsection (c) issues the decree requested in such application, in addition to the powers described in subparagraph (A), the trustee shall have the power—

(i) to pay benefits under the plan in accordance with the requirements of this title;

(ii) to collect for the plan any amounts due the plan, including but not limited to the power to collect from the persons obligated to meet the requirements of section 302 or the terms of the plan;

(iii) to receive any payment made by the corporation to the plan under this title;

(iv) to commence, prosecute, or defend on behalf of the plan any suit or proceeding involving the plan;

(v) to issue, publish, or file such notices, statements, and reports as may be required by the corporation or any order of the court;

(vi) to liquidate the plan assets;

(vii) to recover payments under section 4045(a); and

(viii) to do such other acts as may be necessary to comply with this title or any order of the court and to protect the interests of plan participants and beneficiaries.

(2) As soon as practicable after his appointment, the trustee shall give notice to interested parties of the institution of proceedings under this title to determine whether the plan should be terminated or to terminate the plan, whichever is applicable. For purposes of this paragraph, the term "interested party" means—

(A) the plan administrator,

(B) each participant in the plan and each beneficiary of a deceased participant,

(C) each employer who may be subject to liability under section 4062, 4063, or 4064,

(D) each employer who is or may be liable to the plan under section part 1 of subtitle E,

(E) each employer who has an obligation to contribute, within the meaning of section 4212(a), under a multiemployer plan, and

(F) each employee organization which, for purposes of collective bargaining, represents plan participants employed by an employer described in subparagraph (C), (D), or (E).

(3) Except to the extent inconsistent with the provisions of this Act, or as may be otherwise ordered by the court, a trustee appointed under this section shall be subject to the same duties as those of a trustee under section 704, title 11, United States Code, and shall be, with respect to the plan, a fiduciary within the meaning of paragraph (21) of section 3 of this Act and under section 4975(e) of the Internal Revenue Code of 1986 (except to the extent that the provisions of this title are inconsistent with the requirements applicable under part 4 of subtitle B of title I of this Act and of such section 4975).

Act Sec. 4042. (e) An application by the corporation under this section may be filed notwithstanding the pendency in the same or any other court of any bankruptcy, mortgage foreclosure, or equity receivership proceeding, or any proceeding to reorganize, conserve, or liquidate such plan or its property, or any proceeding to enforce a lien against property of the plan.

Act Sec. 4042. (f) Upon the filing of an application for the appointment of a trustee or the issuance of a decree under this section, the court to which an application is made shall have exclusive jurisdiction of the plan involved and its property wherever located with the powers, to the extent consistent with the purposes of this section, of a court of the United States having jurisdiction over cases under chapter 11 of title 11 of the United States Code. Pending an adjudication under subsection (c) such court shall stay, and upon appointment by it of a trustee, as provided in this section such court shall continue the stay of, any pending mortgage foreclosure, equity receivership, or other proceeding to reorganize, conserve, or liquidate the plan or its property and any other suit against any receiver, conservator, or trustee of the plan or its property. Pending such adjudication and upon the appointment by it of such trustee, the court may stay any proceeding to enforce a lien against property of the plan or any other suit against the plan.

Act Sec. 4042. (g) An action under this subsection may be brought in the judicial district where the plan administrator resides or does business or where any asset of the plan is situated. A district court in which such action is brought may issue process with respect to such action in any other judicial district.

Act Sec. 4042. (h) (1) The amount of compensation paid to each trustee appointed under the provisions of this title shall require the prior approval of the corporation, and, in the case of a trustee appointed by a court, the consent of that court.

(2) Trustees shall appoint, retain, and compensate accountants, actuaries, and other professional service personnel in accordance with regulations prescribed by the corporation.

Act Sec. 4042. (i) [Repealed]

Amendments:

P.L. 103-465, §771(e)(2):

Act Sec. 771(e)(2) amended ERISA Sec. 4042(a)(3) by striking "4043(b)(7)" and inserting "4043(c)(7)".

The above amendment is effective for events occurring 60 days or more after December 8, 1994.

P.L. 101-239, §7881(g)(7):

Amended P.L. 100-203, §9314(b) by striking "section 4042" and inserting "section 4042(a)" and by striking "third sentence" and inserting "last sentence," effective December 22, 1987.

P.L. 101-239, §7891(a)(1):

Titles I, III, and IV of ERISA (other than sections 3(37)(E), 301(a)(7), and 308, the last sentence of section 408(d), and sections 414(c), 4001(a)(3)(ii), and 4303) are each amended by striking "Internal Revenue Code of 1954" each place it appears and inserting "Internal Revenue Code of 1986" effective October 22, 1986.

P.L. 101-239, §7893(e):

Amended ERISA Sec. 4042(a) by inserting a period after "terms of the plan" in the matter following paragraph (4), effective as if included in P.L. 99-272, §11010(a)(1).

P.L. 100-203, §9312(c)(3):

Repealed ERISA Sec. 4042(i) effective for (A) plan terminations under section 4041(c) of ERISA with respect to which notices of intent to terminate are provided under section 4041(a)(2) of ERISA after December 17, 1987, and (B) plan termination with respect to which proceedings are instituted by the Pension Benefit Guaranty Corporation under section 4042 of ERISA after December 17, 1987.

Prior to repeal, ERISA Sec. 4042(i) read as follows:

(i) In any case in which a plan is terminated under this section in a termination proceeding initiated by the corporation pursuant to subsection (a), the corporation shall establish a separate trust in connection with the plan for purposes of section 4049, unless the corporation determines that all benefit commitments under the plan are benefits guaranteed by the corporation under section 4022 or that there is no amount of unfunded benefit commitments under the plan.

P.L. 100-203, §9314(b):

Amended ERISA Sec. 4042(a) by striking the last sentence and inserting a new last sentence, to read as above, effective December 22, 1987. Prior to amendment, ERISA Sec. 4042(a), last sentence, read as follows:

The corporation is authorized to pool the assets of terminated plans for purposes of administration and such other purposes, not inconsistent with its duties to the plan participants and the employer maintaining the plan under this title, as it determines to be required for the efficient administration of this title.

Amended ERISA Sec. 4042(c) by adding paragraph (3), to read as above, effective December 22, 1987.

P.L. 96-364, §402(a)(6):

Amended Sec. 4042 effective September 26, 1980 by: striking out "such small" in subsection (a) and inserting "terminated"; redesignating subsection (b) as subsection (b)(1) and inserting at the end thereof ERISA Secs. 4042(b)(2) and (3); striking out "and" after "interests of the participants" in subsection (c) and inserting "or"; striking out "further" each place it appears in subsection (c) and inserting "unreasonable"; in subsection (d)(1)(A), striking out "and" in clause (iv), redesignating clause (v) as clause (vi) and inserting new ERISA Sec. 4042(d)(1)(A)(v) and (vii); by striking out "allocation requirements of section 4044" in subsection (d)(1)(B)(i) and inserting "requirements of this title"; striking out ", except to the extent that the corporation is an adverse party in a suit or proceeding" in subsection (d)(1)(B)(iv); by striking out "and" in subsection (d)(2)(B); and striking out the period in subsection (d)(2)(C), inserting a comma, and inserting new ERISA Sec. 4042(d)(2)(D) through (F).

P.L. 95-598, §321(a):

Amended Sec. 4042, effective October 1, 1979, by striking out the word "bankruptcy" after the word "pending" in subsection (f) and by substituting the words "the United States having jurisdiction over cases under chapter 11 of title 11 of the United States Code" for the words "bankruptcy and of a court in a proceeding under chapter X of the Bankruptcy Act" in subsection (f).

P.L. 92-272, §11010(a)(1):

Amended ERISA Sec. 4042(a) by striking "is" in paragraph (2) and inserting "will be" and amended the matter following paragraph (4) by adding a new sentence at the beginning of the matter to read as above.

Act Sec. 11010(a)(2) amended ERISA Sec. 4042(b)(1) by inserting "or is required under subsection (a) to institute court proceedings under this section," after "to a plan" and amended ERISA Sec. 4042(c) by striking out "If the corporation has issued a notice under this section to a plan administrator and (whether or not a trustee has been appointed under subsection (b)) has determined" and inserted "If the corporation is required under subsection (a) of this section to commence court proceedings under this section with respect to a plan or, after issuing a notice under this section to a plan administrator, has determined in its place."

Act Sec. 11010(b) added ERISA Sec. 4042(i) to read as above.

Act Sec. 11010(c) amended the heading of ERISA Sec. 4042 to read as above.

The above amendments are effective with respect to notices of intent to terminate filed with the PBGC or with proceedings begun on or after January 1, 1986.

Act Sec. 11016(c)(10) amended ERISA Sec. 4042(d)(1)(B)(ii) by inserting after "amounts due the plan" ", including but not limited to the power to collect from the persons obligated to meet the requirements of section 302 or the terms of the plan." Act Sec. 11016(c)(11) added ERISA Sec. 4042(d)(3) to read as above, effective on April 7, 1986.

[¶ 15,460]
REPORTABLE EVENTS

Act Sec. 4043. (a) Within 30 days after the plan administrator or the contributing sponsor knows or has reason to know that a reportable event described in subsection (c) has occurred, he shall notify the corporation that such event has occurred, unless a notice otherwise required under this subsection has already been provided with respect to such event. The corporation is authorized to waive the requirement of the preceding sentence with respect to any or all reportable events with respect to any plan, and to require the notification to be made by including the event in the annual report made by the plan.

Act Sec. 4043. (b)(1) The requirements of this subsection shall be applicable to a contributing sponsor if, as of the close of the preceding plan year—

(A) the aggregate unfunded vested benefits (as determined under section 4006(a)(3)(E)(iii)) of plans subject to this title which are maintained by such sponsor and members of such sponsor's controlled groups (disregarding plans with no unfunded vested benefits) exceed $50,000,000, and

(B) the funded vested benefit percentage for such plans is less than 90 percent.

For purposes of subparapraph (B), the funded vested benefit percentage means the percentage which the aggregate value of the assets of such plans bears to the aggregate vested benefits of such plans (determined in accordance with section 4006(a)(3)(E)(iii)).

(2) This subsection shall not apply to an event if the contributing sponser, or the member of the contributing sponser's controlled group to which the event relates, is—

(A) a person subject to the reporting requirements of section 13 or 15(d) of the Securities Exchange Act of 1934, or

(B) a subsidiary (as defined for purposes of such Act) of a person subject to such reporting requirements.

(3) No later than 30 days prior to the effective date of an event described in paragraph (9), (10), (11), (12), or (13) of subsection (c), a contributing sponsor to which the requirements of this subsection apply shall notify the corporation that the event is about to occur.

(4) The corporation may waive the requirement of this subsection with respect to any or all reportable events with respect to any contributing sponsor.

Act Sec. 4043. (c) For purposes of this section a reportable event occurs—

(1) when the Secretary of the Treasury issues notice that a plan has ceased to be a plan described in section 4021(a)(2), or when the Secretary of Labor determines the plan is not in compliance with title I of this Act;

(2) when an amendment of the plan is adopted if, under the amendment, the benefit payable with respect to any participant may be decreased;

(3) when the number of active participants is less than 80 percent of the number of such participants at the beginning of the plan year, or is less than 75 percent of the number of such participants at the beginning of the previous plan year;

(4) when the Secretary of the Treasury determines that there has been a termination or partial termination of the plan within the meaning of section 411(d)(3) of the Internal Revenue Code of 1986, but the occurrence of such a termination or partial termination does not, by itself, constitute or require a termination of a plan under this title;

(5) when the plan fails to meet the minimum funding standards under section 412 of such Code (without regard to whether the plan is a plan described in section 4021(a)(2) of this Act) or under section 302 of this Act;

(6) when the plan is unable to pay benefits thereunder when due;

(7) when there is a distribution under the plan to a participant who is a substantial owner as defined in section 4022(b)(6) if—

(A) such distribution has a value of $10,000 or more;

(B) such distribution is not made by reason of the death of the participant; and

(C) immediately after the distribution, the plan has nonforfeitable benefits which are not funded;

(8) when a plan merges, consolidates, or transfers its assets under section 208 of this Act, or when an alternative method of compliance is prescribed by the Secretary of Labor under section 110 of this Act;

(9) when, as a result of an event, a person ceases to be a member of the controlled group;

(10) when a contributing sponsor or a member of a contributing sponsor's controlled group liquidates in a case under title 11, United States Code, or under any similar Federal law or law of a State or political subdivision of a State;

(11) when a contributing sponsor or a member of a contributing sponsor's controlled group declares an extraordinary dividend (as defined in section 1059(c) of the Internal Revenue Code of 1986) or redeems, in any 12-month period, an aggregate of 10 percent or more of the total combined voting power of all classes of stock entitled to vote, or an aggregate of 10 percent of [or] more of the total value of shares of all classes of stock, of a contributing sponsor and all members of its controlled group;

(12) when, in any 12-month period, an aggregate of 3 percent or more of the benefit liabilities of a plan covered by this title and maintained by a contributing sponsor or a member of its controlled group are transferred to a person that is not a member of the controlled group or to a plan or plans maintained by a person or persons that are not such a contributing sponsor or a member of its controlled group; or

(13) when any other event occurs that may be indicative of a need to terminate the plan and that is prescribed by the corporation in regulations.

For purposes of paragraph (7), all distributions to a participant within any 24 month period are treated as a single distribution.

Act Sec. 4043. (d) The Secretary of the Treasury shall notify the corporation—

(1) whenever a reportable event described in paragraph (1), (4), or (5) of subsection (c) occurs, or

(2) whenever any other event occurs which the Secretary of the Treasury believes indicates that the plan may not be sound.

Act Sec. 4043. (e) The Secretary of Labor shall notify the corporation—

(1) whenever a reportable event described in paragraph (1), (5), or (8) of subsection (c) occurs, or

(2) whenever any other event occurs which the Secretary of Labor believes indicates that the plan may not be sound.

Act Sec. 4043. (f) Any information or documentary material submitted to the corporation pursuant to this section shall be exempt from disclosure under section 552 of title 5, United States Code, and no such information or documentary material may be made public, except as may be relevant to any administrative or judicial action or proceeding. Nothing in this section is intended to prevent disclosure to either body of Congress or to any duly authorized committee or subcommittee of the Congress.

Amendments

P.L. 103-465, §771(a):

Act Sec. 771(a) amended ERISA Sec. 4043(a) by inserting in the first sentence "or the contributing sponsor" before "knows or has reason to know"; by inserting in the first sentence ", unless a notice otherwise required under this subsection has already been provided with respect to such event" before the period at the end; and by striking the last sentence. Prior to amendment, the last sentence of ERISA Sec. 4043(a) read as follows:

Whenever an employer making contributions under a plan to which section 4021 applies knows or has reason to know that a reportable event has occurred he shall notify the plan administrator immediately.

P.L. 103-465, §771(b):

Act Sec. 771(b) amended ERISA Sec. 4043 by redesignating subsection (b) as subsection (c) and by inserting after subsection (a) a new subsection (b) to read as above.

Act Sec. 771(b) amended ERISA Sec. 4043 by redesignating subsection (c) as subsection (d).

Act Sec. 771(b) amended ERISA Sec. 4043 by redesignating subsection (d) as subsection (e).

P.L. 103-465, §771(c):

Act Sec. 771(c) amended ERISA Sec. 4043(c) (as redesignated by Act Sec. 771(b)) by striking the "or" at the end of paragraph (8); by striking paragraph (9); and by inserting

after paragraph (8) new paragraphs (9)-(13) to read as above. Prior to amendment, ERISA Sec. 4043(b)(9) read as follows:

(9) when any other event occurs which the corporation determines may be indicative of a need to terminate the plan.

P.L. 103-465, §771(d):

Act Sec. 771(d) amended ERISA Sec. 4043 by adding at the end a new subsection (f) to read as above.

P.L. 103-465, §771(e)(1):

Act Sec. 771(e)(1) amended ERISA Sec. 4043(a) by striking "subsection (b)" and inserting "subsection (c)".

Act Sec. 771(e)(1) amended ERISA Sec. 4043(d) (as redesignated by Act Sec. 771(b)) by striking "subsection (b)" and inserting "subsection (c)".

The above amendments are effective for events occurring 60 days or more after December 8, 1994.

P.L. 101-239, §7891(a)(1):

Titles I, III, and IV of ERISA (other than sections 3(37)(E), 301(a)(7), and 308, the last sentence of section 408(d), and sections 414(c), 4001(a)(3)(ii), and 4303) are each amended by striking "Internal Revenue Code of 1954" each place it appears and inserting "Internal Revenue Code of 1986" effective October 22, 1986.

Regulations

The following regulations were adopted by the Pension Benefit Guaranty Corporation on December 2, 1996 (61 FR 63988), effective January 1, 1997. Reg. 4043.3 was amended effective August 11, 1997 (62 FR 36993). Reg. §§4043.5, 4043.6 and 4043.7 were amended October 28, 2003 (68 FR 61344).

Subpart A—General Provisions

[¶ 15,461]

§4043.1 **Purpose and scope.** This part prescribes the requirements for notifying the PBGC of a reportable event under section 4043 of ERISA or of a failure to make certain required contributions under section 302(f)(4) of ERISA or section 412(n)(4) of the Code. Subpart A contains definitions and general rules. Subpart B contains rules for post-event notice of a reportable event. Subpart C contains rules for advance notice of a reportable event. Subpart D contains rules for notifying the PBGC of a failure to make certain required contributions.

[¶ 15,461A]

§4043.2 **Definitions.** The following terms are defined in §4001.2 of this chapter: Code, contributing sponsor, controlled group, ERISA, fair market value, irrevocable commitment, multiemployer plan, notice of intent to terminate, PBGC, person, plan, plan administrator, proposed termination date, single-employer plan, and substantial owner.

In addition, for purposes of this part:

De minimis 10-percent segment means, in connection with a plan's controlled group, one or more entities that in the aggregate have for a fiscal year—

(1) Revenue not exceeding 10 percent of the controlled group's revenue;

(2) Annual operating income not exceeding the greatest of—

(i) 10 percent of the controlled group's annual operating income;

(ii) 5 percent of the controlled group's first $200 million in net tangible assets at the end of the fiscal year(s); or

(iii) $5 million; and

(3) Net tangible assets at the end of the fiscal year(s) not exceeding the greater of—

(i) 10 percent of the controlled group's net tangible assets at the end of the fiscal year(s); or

(ii) $5 million.

De minimis 5-percent segment has the same meaning as a de minimis 10-percent segment, except that "5 percent" is substituted for "10 percent" each time it appears.

Event year means the plan year in which the reportable event occurs.

Fair market value of the plan's assets means the fair market value of the plan's assets as of the testing date for the applicable plan year, including contributions attributable to the previous plan year for funding purposes under section 302(c)(10) of ERISA or section 412(c)(10) of the Code if made by the earlier of the due date or filing date of the variable rate premium for the applicable plan year, but not to the extent contributions are used to satisfy the quarterly contribution requirements under section 302(e) of ERISA or section 412(m) of the Code for the applicable plan year.

Foreign entity means a member of a controlled group that—

(1) Is not a contributing sponsor of a plan;

(2) Is not organized under the laws of (or, if an individual, is not a domiciliary of) any state (as defined in section 3(10) of ERISA); and

(3) For the fiscal year that includes the date the reportable event occurs, meets one of the following tests—

(i) Is not required to file any United States federal income tax form;

(ii) Has no income reportable on any United States federal income tax form other than passive income not exceeding $1,000; or

(iii) Does not own substantial assets in the United States (disregarding stock of a member of the plan's controlled group) and is not required to file any quarterly United States tax returns for employee withholding.

Foreign-linked entity means a person that—

(1) Is neither a foreign entity nor a contributing sponsor of a plan; and

(2) Is a member of the plan's controlled group only because of ownership interests in or by foreign entities.

Foreign parent means a foreign entity that is a direct or indirect parent of a person that is a contributing sponsor.

Form 5500 due date means the deadline (including extensions) for filing the annual report under section 103 of ERISA.

Notice date means the deadline (including extensions) for filing notice of the reportable event with the PBGC.

Participant means a participant as defined in §4006.2.

Public company means a person subject to the reporting requirements of section 13 or 15(d) of the Securities Exchange Act of 1934 or a subsidiary (as defined for purposes of the Securities Exchange Act of 1934) of a person subject to such reporting requirements.

Testing date means, with respect to a plan year—

(1) The last day of the prior plan year, except as provided in paragraphs (2) or (3) of this definition;

(2) In the case of a new or newly-covered plan (as defined in §4006.2 of this chapter), the first day of the plan year or, if later, the date on which the plan becomes effective for benefit accruals for future service; or

(3) In the case of a plan described in §4006.5(e)(2) of this chapter (relating to certain mergers or spinoffs), the first day of the plan year.

Ultimate parent means the parent at the highest level in the chain of corporations and/or other organizations constituting the parent-subsidiary controlled group.

Unfunded vested benefits means unfunded vested benefits determined in accordance with §4006.4 of this chapter, without regard to the exemptions and special rules in §4006.5(a)-(c) of this chapter. For purposes of subpart B only, unfunded vested benefits may be determined by subtracting the fair market value of the plan's assets from the plan's vested benefits amount.

Variable rate premium means the portion of the premium determined under section 4006(a)(3)(E) of ERISA and §4006.3(b) of this chapter.

Vested benefits amount means the vested benefits amount determined under §4006.4(b)(1) of this chapter.

[¶ 15,461B]

§4043.3 **Requirement of notice.** (a) *Obligation to file.* (1) *In general.* Each person that is required to file a notice under this part, or a

duly authorized representative, shall submit the information required by this part by the time specified in §4043.20 (for post-event notice), §4043.61 (for advance notice), or §4043.81 (for Form 200 filings). Any information previously filed with the PBGC may be incorporated by reference.

(2) *Multiple plans.* If a reportable event occurs for more than one plan, the filing obligation with respect to each plan is independent of the filing obligation with respect to any other plan.

(3) *Optional consolidated filing.* A filing by any person will be deemed to be a filing by all persons required to notify the PBGC under this part. If notices are required for two or more events, the notices may be combined in one filing.

(b) *Contents of reportable event notice.* A person required to file a reportable event notice shall provide, by the notice date, the following general information, along with any other information required for each reportable event under subpart B or C of this part:

(1) The name of the plan;

(2) The name, address, and telephone number of the contributing sponsor(s) and of an individual that should be contacted;

(3) The name, address, and telephone number of the plan administrator and of an individual that should be contacted;

(4) The EIN of the contributing sponsor and the EIN/PN of the plan;

(5) A brief statement of the pertinent facts relating to the reportable event;

(6) A copy of the plan document in effect, i.e., the last restatement of the plan and all amendments thereto;

(7) A copy of the most recent actuarial statement and opinion (if any) relating to the plan; and

(8) A statement of any material change in the assets or liabilities of the plan occurring after the date of the most recent actuarial statement and opinion.

(c) *Optional reportable event forms.* The PBGC shall issue optional reportable events forms, which may provide for reduced initial information submissions.

(d) *Requests for additional information.* The PBGC may, in any case, require the submission of additional information. Any such information shall be submitted for subpart B of this part within 30 days, and for subpart C or D of this part within 7 days, after the date of a written request by the PBGC, or within a different time period specified therein. The PBGC may in its discretion shorten the time period where it determines that the interests of the PBGC or participants may be prejudiced by a delay in receipt of the information.

(e) *Effect of failure to file.* If a notice (or any other information required under this part) is not provided within the specified time limit, the PBGC may assess against each person required to provide the notice a separate penalty under section 4071 of ERISA of up to $1,100 a day for each day that the failure continues. The PBGC may pursue any other equitable or legal remedies available to it under the law. [Amended by 62 FR 36993, effective August 11, 1997.]

[¶ 15,461C]

§4043.4 **Waivers and extensions.** (a) *Specific events.* For specific reportable events, waivers from reporting and information requirements and extensions of time are provided in subparts B and C of this part. If an occurrence constitutes two or more reportable events, reporting requirements for each event are determined independently. For example, any event reportable under more than one section will be exempt from reporting only if it satisfies the requirements for a waiver under each section.

(b) *Multiemployer plans.* The requirements of section 4043 of ERISA are waived with respect to multiemployer plans.

(c) *Terminating plans.* No notice is required from the plan administrator or contributing sponsor of a plan if the notice date is on or after the date on which—

(1) All of the plan's assets (other than any excess assets) are distributed pursuant to a termination; or

(2) A trustee is appointed for the plan under section 4042(c) of ERISA.

(d) *Other waivers and extensions*. The PBGC may extend any deadline or waive any other requirement under this part where it finds convincing evidence that the waiver or extension is appropriate under the circumstances. Any waiver or extension may be subject to conditions. A request for a waiver or extension must be filed in writing with the PBGC and must state the facts and circumstances on which the request is based.

[¶ 15,461D]

§ 4043.5 **How and where to file**. The PBGC applies the rules in subpart A of part 4000 of this chapter and the instructions to the applicable PBGC reporting form to determine permissible methods of filing with the PBGC under this part. See Sec. 4000.4 of this chapter for information on where to file.

[Amended 10/28/2003 by 68 FR 61344]

[¶ 15,461E]

§ 4043.6 **Date of filing**. (a) *Post-Event notice filings*. The PBGC applies the rules in subpart C of part 4000 of this chapter to determine the date that a submission under subpart B of this part was filed with the PBGC.

(b) *Advance notice and Form 200 filings*. Information filed under subpart C or D of this part is treated as filed on the date it is received by the PBGC. Subpart C of part 4000 of this chapter provides rules for determining when the PBGC receives a submission.

(c) *Partial electronic filing; deemed filing date*. A reportable event notice or Form 200 will be deemed timely filed if—

(1) An electronic transmission containing at least the minimum initial information (as specified in the instruction to the applicable form) is filed on or before the notice date; and

(2) The remaining initial information is received by the PBGC on or before—

(i) The first regular business day following the notice date, in the case of advance notice or a Form 200; or

(ii) The second regular business day following the notice date, in the case of post-event notice.

(d) *Receipt date*. Information received on a weekend or Federal holiday or after 5:00 p.m. on a weekday is considered filed on the next regular business day.

[Amended 10/28/2003 by 68 FR 61344]

[¶ 15,461F]

§ 4043.7 **Computation of time**. The PBGC applies the rules in subpart D of part 4000 of this chapter to compute any time period under this part.

[Amended 10/28/2003 by 68 FR 61344]

[¶ 15,461G]

§ 4043.8 **Confidentiality**. In accordance with section 4043(f) of ERISA and § 4901.21(a)(3) of this chapter, any information or documentary material that is not publicly available and is submitted to the PBGC pursuant to this part shall not be made public, except as may be relevant to any administrative or judicial action or proceeding or for disclosures to either body of Congress or to any duly authorized committee or subcommittee of the Congress.

Subpart B—Post-Event Notice of Reportable Events

[¶ 15,462]

§ 4043.20 **Post-event filing obligation**. The plan administrator and each contributing sponsor of a plan for which a reportable event under this subpart has occurred are required to notify the PBGC within 30 days after that person knows or has reason to know that the reportable event has occurred, unless a waiver or extension applies. If there is a change in plan administrator or contributing sponsor, the reporting obligation applies to the person who is the plan administrator or contributing sponsor of the plan on the 30th day after the reportable event occurs.

[¶ 15,462A]

§ 4043.21 **Tax disqualification and Title I Noncompliance**. (a) *Reportable event*. A reportable event occurs when the Secretary of the Treasury issues notice that a plan has ceased to be a plan described

in section 4021(a)(2) of ERISA, or when the Secretary of Labor determines that a plan is not in compliance with title I of ERISA.

(b) *Waivers*. Notice is waived for this event.

[¶ 15,462B]

§ 4043.22 **Amendment decreasing benefits payable**. (a) *Reportable event*. A reportable event occurs when an amendment to a plan is adopted under which the retirement benefit payable from employer contributions with respect to any participant may be decreased.

(b) *Waivers*. Notice is waived for this event.

[¶ 15,462C]

§ 4043.23 **Active participant reduction**. (a) *Reportable event*. A reportable event occurs when the number of active participants under a plan is reduced to less than 80 percent of the number of active participants at the beginning of the plan year, or to less than 75 percent of the number of active participants at the beginning of the previous plan year.

(b) *Initial information required*. In addition to the information in § 4043.3(b), the notice shall include—

(1) A statement explaining the cause of the reduction (e.g., facility shutdown or sale); and

(2) The number of active participants at the date the reportable event occurs, at the beginning of the plan year, and at the beginning of the prior plan year.

(c) *Waivers*. (1) *Small plan*. Notice is waived if the plan has fewer than 100 participants at the beginning of either the current or the previous plan year.

(2) *Plan funding*. Notice is waived if—

(i) *No variable rate premium*. No variable rate premium is required to be paid for the plan for the event year;

(ii) *$1 million unfunded vested benefits*. As of the testing date for the event year, the plan has less than $1 million in unfunded vested benefits; or

(iii) *No unfunded vested benefits*. As of the testing date for the event year, the plan would have no unfunded vested benefits if unfunded vested benefits were determined in accordance with the assumptions and methodology in § 4010.4(b)(2) of this chapter.

(3) *No facility closing event/80-percent funded*. Notice is waived if—

(i) The active participant reduction would not be reportable if only those active participant reductions resulting from cessation of operations at one or more facilities were taken into account; and

(ii) As of the testing date for the event year, the fair market value of the plan's assets is at least 80 percent of the plan's vested benefits amount.

(d) *Extensions*. The notice date is extended to the latest of—

(1) *Form 1 extension*. 30 days after the plan's variable rate premium filing due date for the event year if a waiver under any of paragraphs (c)(2)(i) through (c)(2)(iii) or (c)(3) of this section would apply if "the plan year preceding the event year" were substituted for "the event year";

(2) *Form 5500 extension*. 30 days after the plan's Form 5500 due date that next follows the date the reportable event occurs, provided the event would not be reportable counting only those participant reductions resulting from cessation of operations at a single facility; and

(3) *Form 1-ES extension*. The due date for the Form 1-ES for the plan year following the event year if—

(i) The plan is required to file a Form 1-ES for the plan year following the event year;

(ii) The event would not be reportable counting only those participant reductions resulting from cessation of operations at a single facility; and

(iii) The participant reduction represents no more than 20 percent of the total active participants (at the beginning of the plan year(s) in which the reduction occurs) in all plans maintained by any member of the plan's controlled group.

(e) *Determination of the number of active participants.* (1) *Determination date.* The number of active participants at the beginning of a plan year may be determined by using the number of active participants at the end of the previous plan year.

(2) *Active participant.* "Active participant" means a participant who—

(i) Is receiving compensation for work performed;

(ii) Is on paid or unpaid leave granted for a reason other than a layoff;

(iii) Is laid off from work for a period of time that has lasted less than 30 days; or

(iv) Is absent from work due to a recurring reduction in employment that occurs at least annually.

[¶ 15,462D]

§ 4043.24 **Termination or partial termination**. (a) *Reportable event.* A reportable event occurs when the Secretary of the Treasury determines that there has been a termination or partial termination of a plan within the meaning of section 411(d)(3) of the Code.

(b) *Waivers.* Notice is waived for this event.

[¶ 15,462E]

§ 4043.25 **Failure to make required minimum funding payment**. (a) *Reportable event.* A reportable event occurs when a required installment or a payment required under section 302 of ERISA or section 412 of the Code (including a payment required as a condition of a funding waiver) is not made by the due date for the payment. In the case of a payment needed to avoid a deficiency in the plan's funding standard account, the due date is the latest date such payment may be made under section 302(c)(10)(A) of ERISA or section 412(c)(10)(A) of the Code.

(b) *Initial information required.* In addition to the information in § 4043.3(b), the notice shall include—

(1) The due date and amount of the required minimum funding payment that was not made and of the next payment due;

(2) The name of each member of the plan's controlled group and its ownership relationship to other members of that controlled group; and

(3) For each other plan maintained by any member of the plan's controlled group, identification of the plan and its contributing sponsor(s) by name and EIN/PN or EIN, as appropriate.

(c) *Waiver.* Notice is waived if the required minimum funding payment is made by the 30th day after its due date.

(d) *Form 200 filed.* If, with respect to the same failure, a Form 200 has been completed and submitted in accordance with § 4043.81, the Form 200 filing shall satisfy the requirements of this section.

[¶ 15,462F]

§ 4043.26 **Inability to pay benefits when due**. (a) *Reportable event.* A reportable event occurs when a plan is currently unable or projected to be unable to pay benefits.

(1) *Current inability.* A plan is currently unable to pay benefits if it fails to provide any participant or beneficiary the full benefits to which the person is entitled under the terms of the plan, at the time the benefit is due and in the form in which it is due. A plan shall not be treated as being currently unable to pay benefits if its failure to pay is caused solely by the need to verify the person's eligibility for benefits; the inability to locate the person; or any other administrative delay if the delay is for less than the shorter of two months or two full benefit payment periods.

(2) *Projected inability.* A plan is projected to be unable to pay benefits when, as of the last day of any quarter of a plan year, the plan's "liquid assets" are less than two times the amount of the "disbursements from the plan" for such quarter. Liquid assets and disburse-

ments from the plan have the same meaning as under section 302(e)(5)(E) of ERISA and section 412(m)(5)(E) of the Code.

(b) *Initial information required.* In addition to the information in § 4043.3(b), the notice shall include—

(1) The date of any current inability and the amount of benefit payments not made;

(2) The next date on which the plan is expected to be unable to pay benefits, the amount of the projected shortfall, and the number of plan participants and beneficiaries expected to be affected by the inability to pay benefits;

(3) For a projected inability described in paragraph (a)(2), the amount of the plan's liquid assets at the end of the quarter, and the amount of its disbursements for the quarter; and

(4) The name, address, and phone number of the trustee of the plan (and of any custodian).

(c) *Waivers.* Notice is waived unless the reportable event occurs during a plan year for which the plan is described in section 302(d)(6)(A) of ERISA or section 412(l)(6)(A) of the Code.

[¶ 15,462G]

§ 4043.27 **Distribution to a substantial owner**. (a) *Reportable event.* A reportable event occurs for a plan when—

(1) There is a distribution to a substantial owner of a contributing sponsor of the plan;

(2) The total of all distributions made to the substantial owner within the one-year period ending with the date of such distribution exceeds $10,000;

(3) The distribution is not made by reason of the substantial owner's death; and

(4) Immediately after the distribution, the plan has nonforfeitable benefits (as provided in § 4022.5) that are not funded.

(b) *Initial information required.* In addition to the information in § 4043.3(b), the notice shall include—

(1) The name, address and telephone number of the substantial owner receiving the distribution(s); and

(2) The amount, form, and date of each distribution.

(c) *Waivers.* (1) *Distribution up to section 415 limit.* Notice is waived if the total of all distributions made to the substantial owner within the one-year period ending with the date of the distribution does not exceed the limitation (as of the date the reportable event occurs) under section 415(b)(1)(A) of the Code (as adjusted in accordance with section 415(d)) when expressed as an annual benefit in the form of a straight life annuity to a participant beginning at Social Security retirement age ($120,000 for calendar year 1996).

(2) *Plan funding.* Notice is waived if—

(i) *No variable rate premium.* No variable rate premium is required to be paid for the plan for the event year;

(ii) *No unfunded vested benefits.* As of the testing date for the event year, the plan would have no unfunded vested benefits if unfunded vested benefits were determined in accordance with the assumptions and methodology in § 4010.4(b)(2) of this chapter; or

(iii) *80-percent funded.* As of the testing date for the event year, the fair market value of the plan's assets is at least 80 percent of the plan's vested benefits amount.

(3) *Distribution up to one percent of assets.* Notice is waived if the sum of the values of all distributions that are made to the substantial owner within the one-year period ending with the date of the distribution is one percent or less of the end-of-year current value of the plan's assets (as required to be reported on the plan's Form 5500) for either of the two plan years immediately preceding the event year.

(d) *Form 1 extension.* The notice date is extended until 30 days after the plan's variable rate premium filing due date for the event year, provided that a waiver under any of paragraphs (c)(2)(i) through (c)(2)(iii) of this section would apply if "the plan year preceding the event year" were substituted for "the event year."

(e) *Determination rules.* (1) *Valuation of distribution.* The value of a distribution under this section is the sum of—

(i) The cash amounts actually received by the substantial owner;

(ii) The purchase price of any irrevocable commitment; and

(iii) The fair market value of any other assets distributed, determined as of the date of distribution to the substantial owner.

(2) *Date of substantial owner distribution.* The date of distribution to a substantial owner of a cash distribution is the date it is received by the substantial owner. The date of distribution to a substantial owner of an irrevocable commitment is the date on which the obligation to provide benefits passes from the plan to the insurer. The date of any other distribution to a substantial owner is the date when the plan relinquishes control over the assets transferred directly or indirectly to the substantial owner.

(3) *Determination date.* The determination of whether a participant is (or has been in the preceding 60 months) a substantial owner is made on the date when there has been a distribution that would be reportable under this section if made to a substantial owner.

[¶ 15,462H]

§ 4043.28 **Plan merger, consolidation, or transfer.** (a) *Reportable event.* A reportable event occurs when a plan merges, consolidates, or transfers its assets or liabilities under section 208 of ERISA or section 414(l) of the Code.

(b) *Waivers.* Notice is waived for this event. However, notice may be required under § 4043.29 (for a controlled group change) or § 4043.32 (for a transfer of benefit liabilities).

[¶ 15,462I]

§ 4043.29 **Change in contributing sponsor or controlled group.** (a) *Reportable event.* A reportable event occurs for a plan when there is a transaction that results, or will result, in one or more persons ceasing to be members of the plan's controlled group. For purposes of this section, the term "transaction" includes, but is not limited to, a legally binding agreement, whether or not written, to transfer ownership, an actual transfer of ownership, and an actual change in ownership that occurs as a matter of law or through the exercise or lapse of pre-existing rights. A transaction is not reportable if it will result solely in a reorganization involving a mere change in identity, form, or place of organization, however effected.

(b) *Initial information required.* In addition to the information in § 4043.3(b), the notice shall include—

(1) The name of each member of the plan's old and new controlled groups and the member's ownership relationship to other members of those groups;

(2) For each other plan maintained by any member of the plan's old or new controlled group, identification of the plan and its contributing sponsor(s) by name and EIN/PN or EIN, as appropriate; and

(3) A copy of the most recent audited (or if not available, unaudited) financial statements, and the most recent interim financial statements, of the plan's contributing sponsor (both old and new, in the case of a change in the contributing sponsor) and any persons that will cease to be in the plan's controlled group.

(c) *Waivers.* (1) *De minimis 10-percent segment.* Notice is waived if the person or persons that will cease to be members of the plan's controlled group represent a de minimis 10-percent segment of the plan's old controlled group for the most recent fiscal year(s) ending on or before the date the reportable event occurs.

(2) *Foreign entity.* Notice is waived if each person that will cease to be a member of the plan's controlled group is a foreign entity other than a foreign parent.

(3) *Plan funding.* Notice is waived if—

(i) *No variable rate premium.* No variable rate premium is required to be paid for the plan for the event year;

(ii) *$1 million unfunded vested benefits.* As of the testing date for the event year, the plan has less than $1 million in unfunded vested benefits; or

(iii) *No unfunded vested benefits.* As of the testing date for the event year, the plan would have no unfunded vested benefits if unfunded vested benefits were determined in accordance with the assumptions and methodology in § 4010.4(b)(2) of this chapter.

(4) *Public company/80-percent funded.* Notice is waived if—

(i) The plan's contributing sponsor before the effective date of the transaction is a public company; and

(ii) As of the testing date for the event year, the fair market value of the plan's assets is at least 80 percent of the plan's vested benefits amount.

(d) *Extensions.* The notice date is extended to the latest of—

(1) *Form 1 extension.* 30 days after the plan's variable rate premium filing due date for the event year if a waiver under any of paragraphs (c)(3)(i) through (c)(3)(iii) or (c)(4) of this section would apply if "the plan year preceding the event year" were substituted for "the event year";

(2) *Foreign parent and foreign-linked entities.* With respect to a transaction in which only foreign parents or foreign-linked entities will cease to be members of the plan's controlled group, 30 days after the plan's first Form 5500 due date after the person required to notify the PBGC has actual knowledge of the transaction and of the controlled group relationship; and

(3) *Press releases; Forms 10Q.* If the plan's contributing sponsor before the effective date of the transaction is a public company, 30 days after the earlier of—

(i) The first Form 10Q filing deadline that occurs after the transaction; or

(ii) The date (if any) when a press release with respect to the transaction is issued.

(e) *Examples.* The following examples assume that no waivers apply.

(1) *Controlled group breakup.* Plan A's controlled group consists of Company A (its contributing sponsor), Company B (which maintains Plan B), and Company C. As a result of a transaction, the controlled group will break into two separate controlled groups—one segment consisting of Company A and the other segment consisting of Companies B and C. Both Company A (Plan A's contributing sponsor) and the plan administrator of plan A are required to report that Companies B and C will leave plan A's controlled group. Company B (Plan B's contributing sponsor) and the plan administrator of Plan B are required to report that Company A will leave Plan B's controlled group. Company C is not required to report because it is not a contributing sponsor or a plan administrator.

(2) *Change in contributing sponsor.* Plan Q is maintained by Company Q. Company Q enters into a binding contract to sell a portion of its assets and to transfer employees participating in Plan Q, along with Plan Q, to Company R, which is not a member of Company Q's controlled group. There will be no change in the structure of Company Q's controlled group. On the effective date of the sale, Company R will become the contributing sponsor of Plan Q. A reportable event occurs on the date of the transaction (i.e., the binding contract), because as a result of the transaction, Company Q (and any other member of its controlled group) will cease to be a member of Plan Q's controlled group. If, on the 30th day after Company Q and Company R enter into the binding contract, the change in the contributing sponsor has not yet become effective, Company Q has the reporting obligation. If the change in the contributing sponsor has become effective by the 30th day, Company R has the reporting obligation.

(3) *Merger/consolidation within a controlled group.* Company X and Company Y are subsidiaries of Company Z, which maintains Plan Z. Company Y merges into Company X (only Company X survives). Company Z and the plan administrator of Plan Z must report that Company Y has ceased to be a member of Plan Z's controlled group.

[¶ 15,462J]

§4043.30 **Liquidation**. (a) *Reportable event*. A reportable event occurs for a plan when a member of the plan's controlled group—

(1) Is involved in any transaction to implement its complete liquidation (including liquidation into another controlled group member);

(2) Institutes or has instituted against it a proceeding to be dissolved or is dissolved, whichever occurs first; or

(3) Liquidates in a case under the Bankruptcy Code, or under any similar law.

(b) *Initial information required*. In addition to the information in §4043.3(b), the notice shall include—

(1) The name of each member of the plan's controlled group before and after the liquidation and its ownership relationship to other members of that controlled group; and

(2) For each other plan maintained by any member of the plan's controlled group, identification of the plan and its contributing sponsor(s) by name and EIN/PN or EIN, as appropriate.

(c) *Waivers*. (1) *De minimis 10-percent segment*. Notice is waived if—

(i) The person or persons that liquidate represent a de minimis 10percent segment of the plan's controlled group for the most recent fiscal year(s) ending on or before the date the reportable event occurs; and

(ii) Each plan that was maintained by the liquidating member is maintained by another member of the plan's controlled group after the liquidation.

(2) *Foreign entity*. Notice is waived if each person that liquidates is a foreign entity other than a foreign parent.

(3) *Plan funding*. Notice is waived if each plan that was maintained by the liquidating member is maintained by another member of the plan's controlled group after the liquidation and—

(i) *No variable rate premium*. No variable rate premium is required to be paid for the plan for the event year;

(ii) *$1 million unfunded vested benefits*. As of the testing date for the event year, the plan has less than $1 million in unfunded vested benefits; or

(iii) *No unfunded vested benefits*. As of the testing date for the event year, the plan would have no unfunded vested benefits if unfunded vested benefits were determined in accordance with the assumptions and methodology in §4010.4(b)(2) of this chapter.

(4) *Public company/80-percent funded*. Notice is waived if—

(i) The plan's contributing sponsor is a public company;

(ii) As of the testing date for the event year, the fair market value of the plan's assets is at least 80 percent of the plan's vested benefits amount; and

(iii) Each plan that was maintained by the liquidating member is maintained by another member of the plan's controlled group after the liquidation.

(d) *Extensions*. The notice date is extended to the latest of—

(1) *Form 1 extension*. 30 days after the plan's variable rate premium filing due date for the event year if a waiver under any of paragraphs (c)(3)(i) through (c)(3)(iii) or (c)(4) of this section would apply if "the plan year preceding the event year" were substituted for "the event year";

(2) *Foreign parent and foreign-linked entity*. 30 days after the plan's first Form 5500 due date after the person required to notify the PBGC has actual knowledge of the transaction and of the controlled group relationship, if the person liquidating is a foreign parent or foreign-linked entity; and

(3) *Press releases; Forms 10Q*. If the plan's contributing sponsor is a public company, 30 days after the earlier of—

(i) The first Form 10Q filing deadline that occurs after the transaction; or

(ii) The date (if any) when a press release with respect to the transaction is issued.

[¶ 15,462K]

§4043.31 **Extraordinary dividend or stock redemption**. (a) *Reportable event*. A reportable event occurs for a plan when any member of the plan's controlled group declares a dividend (as defined in paragraph (e)(3) of this section) or redeems its own stock, if the resulting distribution is reportable under this paragraph.

(1) *Cash distributions*. A cash distribution is reportable if—

(i) The distribution, when combined with any other cash distributions to shareholders previously made during the fiscal year, exceeds the adjusted net income (as defined in paragraph (e)(1) of this section) of the person making the distribution for the preceding fiscal year; and

(ii) The distribution, when combined with any other cash distributions to shareholders previously made during the fiscal year or during the three prior fiscal years, exceeds the adjusted net income (as defined in paragraph (e)(1) of this section) of the person making the distribution for the four preceding fiscal years.

(2) *Non-cash distributions*. A non-cash distribution is reportable if its net value (as defined in paragraph (e)(4) of this section), when combined with the net value of any other non-cash distributions to shareholders previously made during the fiscal year, exceeds 10 percent of the total net assets (as defined in paragraph (e)(6) of this section) of the person making the distribution.

(3) *Combined distributions*. If both cash and non-cash distributions to shareholders are made during a fiscal year, a distribution is reportable when the sum of the cash distribution percentage (as defined in paragraph (e)(2) of this section) and the non-cash distribution percentages (as defined in paragraph (e)(5) of this section) for the fiscal year exceeds 100 percent.

(b) *Information required*. In addition to the information in §4043.5(b), the notice shall include—

(1) Identification of the person making the distribution (by name and EIN); and

(2) The date and amount of any cash distribution during the fiscal year;

(3) A description of any non-cash distribution during the fiscal year, the fair market value of each asset distributed, and the date or dates of distribution; and

(4) A statement as to whether the recipient was a member of the plan's controlled group.

(c) *Waivers*. (1) *Extraordinary dividends and stock redemptions*. The reportable event described in section 4043(c)(11) of ERISA related to extraordinary dividends and stock redemptions is waived except to the extent reporting is required under this section.

(2) *De minimis 5-percent segment*. Notice is waived if the person making the distribution is a de minimis 5-percent segment of the plan's controlled group for the most recent fiscal year(s) ending on or before the date the reportable event occurs.

(3) *Foreign entity*. Notice is waived if the person making the distribution is a foreign entity other than a foreign parent.

(4) *Foreign parent*. Notice is waived if the person making the distribution is a foreign parent, and the distribution is made solely to other members of the plan's controlled group.

(5) *Plan funding*. Notice is waived if—

(i) *No variable rate premium*. No variable rate premium is required to be paid for the plan for the event year;

(ii) *$1 million unfunded vested benefits*. As of the testing date for the event year, the plan has less than $1 million in unfunded vested benefits;

(iii) *No unfunded vested benefits*. As of the testing date for the event year, the plan would have no unfunded vested benefits if unfunded vested benefits were determined in accordance with the assumptions and methodology in § 4010.4(b)(2) of this chapter; or

(iv) *80-percent funded*. As of the testing date for the event year, the fair market value of the plan's assets is at least 80 percent of the plan's vested benefits amount.

(d) *Extensions*. The notice date is extended to the latest of—

(1) *Form 1 extension*. 30 days after the plan's variable rate premium filing due date for the event year if a waiver under any of paragraphs (c)(5)(i) through (c)(5)(iv) of this section would apply if "the plan year preceding the event year" were substituted for "the event year";

(2) *Foreign parent and foreign-linked entity*. 30 days after the plan's first Form 5500 due date after the person required to notify the PBGC has actual knowledge of the distribution and the controlled group relationship, if the person making the distribution is a foreign parent or foreign-linked entity; and

(3) *Press releases; Forms 10Q*. If the plan's contributing sponsor is a public company, 30 days after the earlier of—

(i) The first Form 10Q filing deadline that occurs after the distribution; or

(ii) The date (if any) when a press release with respect to the distribution is issued.

(e) *Definitions*. (1) *Adjusted net income* means the net income before after-tax gain or loss on any sale of assets, as determined in accordance with generally accepted accounting principles and practices.

(2) *Cash distribution percentage* means, for a fiscal year, the lesser of—

(i) The percentage that all cash distributions to one or more shareholders made during that fiscal year bears to the adjusted net income (as defined in paragraph (e)(1) of this section) of the person making the distributions for the preceding fiscal year, or

(ii) The percentage that all cash distributions to one or more shareholders made during that fiscal year and the three preceding fiscal years bears to the adjusted net income (as defined in paragraph (e)(1) of this section) of the person making the distributions for the four preceding fiscal years.

(3) *Dividend* means a distribution to one or more shareholders. A payment by a person to a member of its controlled group is treated as a distribution to its shareholder(s).

(4) *Net value of non-cash distribution* means the fair market value of assets transferred by the person making the distribution, reduced by the fair market value of any liabilities assumed or consideration given by the recipient in connection with the distribution. A distribution of stock that one controlled group member holds in another controlled group member is disregarded. Net value determinations should be based on readily available fair market value(s) or independent appraisal(s) performed within one year before the distribution is made. To the extent that fair market values are not readily available and no such appraisals exist, the fair market value of an asset transferred in connection with a distribution or a liability assumed by a recipient of a distribution shall be deemed to be equal to 200 percent of the book value of the asset or liability on the books of the person making the distribution. Stock redeemed is deemed to have no value.

(5) *Non-cash distribution percentage* means the percentage that the net value of the non-cash distribution bears to one-tenth of the value of the total net assets (as defined in paragraph (e)(6) of this section) of the person making the distribution.

(6) *Total net assets* means, with respect to the person declaring a non-cash distribution—

(i) If all classes of the person's securities are publicly traded, the total market value (immediately before the distribution is made) of the publicly-traded securities of the person making the distribution;

(ii) If no classes of the person's securities are publicly traded, the excess (immediately before the distribution is made) of the book

value of the person's assets over the book value of the person's liabilities, adjusted to reflect the net value of the non-cash distribution; or

(iii) If some but not all classes of the person's securities are publicly traded, the greater of the amounts in paragraphs (e)(6)(i) or (ii) of this section.

[¶ 15,462L]

§ 4043.32 **Transfer of benefit liabilities**. (a) *Reportable event*. (1) *In general*. A reportable event occurs for a plan when—

(i) The plan or any other plan maintained by a person in the plan's controlled group makes a transfer of benefit liabilities to a person, or to a plan or plans maintained by a person or persons, that are not members of the transferor plan's controlled group; and

(ii) The amount of benefit liabilities transferred, in conjunction with other benefit liabilities transferred during the 12-month period ending on the date of the transfer, is 3 percent or more of the plan's total benefit liabilities. Both the benefit liabilities transferred and the plan's total benefit liabilities shall be valued as of any one date in the plan year in which the transfer occurs, using actuarial assumptions that comply with section 414(l) of the Code.

(2) *Date of transfer*. The date of transfer shall be determined on the basis of the facts and circumstances of the particular situation. For transfers subject to the requirements of section 414(l) of the Code, the date determined in accordance with 26 CFR 1.414(l)-1(b)(11) will be considered the date of transfer.

(b) *Initial information required*. In addition to the information required in § 4043.3(b), the notice shall include—

(1) Identification of the transferee(s) and each contributing sponsor of each transferee plan by name and EIN/PN or EIN, as appropriate;

(2) An explanation of the actuarial assumptions used in determining the value of benefit liabilities (and, if appropriate, the value of plan assets) for each transfer; and

(3) An estimate of the amounts of assets and liabilities being transferred, and the number of participants whose benefits are transferred.

(c) *Waivers*. (1) *Complete plan transfer*. Notice is waived if the transfer is a transfer of all of the transferor plan's benefit liabilities and assets to one other plan.

(2) *Transfer of less than 3 percent of assets*. Notice is waived if the value of the assets being transferred—

(i) Equals the present value of the accrued benefits (whether or not vested) being transferred, using actuarial assumptions that comply with section 414(l) of the Code; and

(ii) In conjunction with other assets transferred during the same plan year, is less than 3 percent of the assets of the transferor plan as of at least one day in that year.

(3) *Section 414(l) safe harbor*. Notice is waived if the transfer complies with section 414(l) of the Code using the actuarial assumptions prescribed for valuing benefits in trusteed plans under § 4044.51-57 of this chapter.

(4) *Fully funded plans*. Notice is waived if the transfer complies with section 414(l) of the Code using reasonable actuarial assumptions and, after the transfer, the transferor and transferee plans are fully funded (using the actuarial assumptions prescribed for valuing benefits in trusteed plans under § 4044.51-57) of this chapter.

(d) *Who must file*. Only the plan administrator and contributing sponsor of the plan that made the transfer described in paragraph (a)(1) of this section are required to file a notice of a reportable event under this section. Notice by any other contributing sponsor or plan administrator is waived.

[¶ 15,462M]

§ 4043.33 **Application for minimum funding waiver**. (a) *Reportable event*. A reportable event for a plan occurs when an application for a minimum funding waiver for the plan is submitted under section 303 of ERISA or section 412(d) of the Code.

(b) *Initial information required.* In addition to the information in § 4043.3(b), the notice shall include a copy of the waiver application, including all attachments.

[¶ 15,462N]

§ 4043.34 **Loan default.** (a) *Reportable event.* A reportable event occurs for a plan whenever there is a default by a member of the plan's controlled group with respect to a loan with an outstanding balance of $10 million or more, if—

(1) The default results from the debtor's failure to make a required loan payment when due (unless the payment is made within 30 days after the due date);

(2) The lender accelerates the loan; or

(3) The debtor receives a written notice of default from the lender (and does not establish the notice was issued in error) on account of:

(i) A drop in the debtor's cash reserves below an agreed-upon level;

(ii) An unusual or catastrophic event experienced by the debtor; or

(iii) A persisting failure by the debtor to attain agreed-upon financial performance levels.

(b) *Initial information required.* In addition to the information in § 4043.3(b), the notice shall include—

(1) A copy of the relevant loan documents (e.g., promissory note, security agreement);

(2) The due date and amount of any missed payment;

(3) A copy of any notice of default from the lender; and

(4) A copy of any notice of acceleration from the lender.

(c) *Waivers.* (1) *Default cured.* Notice is waived if the default is cured, or waived by the lender, within 30 days or, if later, by the end of any cure period provided by the loan agreement.

(2) *Foreign entity.* Notice is waived if the debtor is a foreign entity other than a foreign parent.

(3) *Plan funding.* Notice is waived if—

(i) *No variable rate premium.* No variable rate premium is required to be paid for the plan for the event year;

(ii) *$1 million unfunded vested benefits.* As of the testing date for the event year, the plan has less than $1 million in unfunded vested benefits;

(iii) *No unfunded vested benefits.* As of the testing date for the event year, the plan would have no unfunded vested benefits if unfunded vested benefits were determined in accordance with the assumptions and methodology in § 4010.4(b)(2) of this chapter; or

(iv) *80-percent funded.* As of the testing date for the event year, the fair market value of the plan's assets is at least 80 percent of the plan's vested benefits amount.

(d) *Notice date and extensions.*

(1) *In general.* Except as provided in paragraph (d)(2) or (d)(3) of this section, the notice date is 30 days after the person required to report knows or has reason to know of the occurrence of the default, without regard to the time of any other conditions required for the default to be reportable.

(2) *Cure period extensions.* The notice date is extended to one day after—

(i) The applicable cure period provided in the loan agreement (in the case of a reportable event described in paragraph (a)(1) of this section);

(ii) The date the loan is accelerated (in the case of a reportable event described in paragraph (a)(2) of this section); or

(iii) The date the debtor receives written notice of the default (in the case of a reportable event described in paragraph (a)(3) of this section).

(3) *Form 1 extension.* The notice date is extended to 30 days after the plan's variable rate premium filing due date for the event year, if a waiver under any of paragraphs (c)(3)(i) through (c)(3)(iv) of this section would apply if the "the plan year preceding the event year" were substituted for "the event year."

(4) *Foreign parent and foreign-linked entities.* With respect to a loan default involving only a foreign parent or a foreign-linked entity, the notice date is extended to 30 days after the plan's first Form 5500 due date after the person required to notify the PBGC has actual knowledge of the default and of the controlled group relationship.

(5) *Example.* Company A has a debt with an outstanding balance of $20 million, for which a payment is due on October 1. Under the terms of the loan, the default may be cured within 10 days. Company A does not make the payment until October 31. Because Company A has made the payment within 30 days of the due date, no reportable event has occurred. If Company A does not make the payment by October 31, a reportable event will have occurred on October 1, and notice will be due by October 31.

[¶ 15,462O]

§ 4043.35 **Bankruptcy or similar settlement.** (a) *Reportable event.* A reportable event occurs for a plan when any member of the plan's controlled group—

(1) Commences a bankruptcy case (under the Bankruptcy Code), or has a bankruptcy case commenced against it;

(2) Commences or has commenced against it any other type of insolvency proceeding (including, but not limited to, the appointment of a receiver);

(3) Commences, or has commenced against it, a proceeding to effect a composition, extension, or settlement with creditors;

(4) Executes a general assignment for the benefit of creditors; or

(5) Undertakes to effect any other nonjudicial composition, extension, or settlement with substantially all its creditors.

(b) *Initial information required.* In addition to the information in § 4043.3(b), the notice shall include—

(1) A copy of all papers filed in the relevant proceeding, including, but not limited to, petitions and supporting schedules;

(2) The last date for filing claims;

(3) The name, address, and phone number of any trustee or receiver (or similar person);

(4) The name of each member of the plan's controlled group and its ownership relationship to other members of that controlled group; and

(5) For each other plan maintained by any member of the plan's controlled group, identification of the plan and its contributing sponsor(s) by name and EIN/PN or EIN, as appropriate.

(c) *Waivers.* Notice is waived if the person described in paragraph (a) of this section is a foreign entity other than a foreign parent.

(d) *Extensions.* Unless the controlled group member described in paragraph (a) of this section is the contributing sponsor of the plan, the notice date is extended until 30 days after the person required to notify the PBGC has actual knowledge of the reportable event.

Subpart C—Advance Notice of Reportable Events

[¶ 15,463]

§ 4043.61 **Advance reporting filing obligation.** (a) *In general.* Unless a waiver or extension applies with respect to the plan, each contributing sponsor of a plan for which a reportable event under this subpart is going to occur is required to notify the PBGC no later than 30 days before the effective date of the reportable event if the contributing sponsor is subject to advance reporting. If there is a change in contributing sponsor, the reporting obligation applies to the person who is the contributing sponsor of the plan on the notice date.

(b) *Persons subject to advance reporting.* A contributing sponsor is subject to the advance reporting requirement under paragraph (a) of this section if—

(1) Neither the contributing sponsor nor the member of the plan's controlled group to which the event relates is a public company; and

(2) The contributing sponsor is a member of a controlled group maintaining one or more plans that, in the aggregate (disregarding plans with no unfunded vested benefits) have—

(i) Vested benefits amounts that exceed the actuarial values of plan assets by more than $50 million; and

(ii) A funded vested benefit percentage of less than 90 percent.

(c) *Funding determinations.* For purposes of paragraph (b)(2) of this section—

(1) *Actuarial value of assets.* The actuarial value of plan assets is determined in accordance with § 4006.4(b)(2) of this chapter;

(2) *Funded vested benefit percentage.* The aggregate funded vested percentage of one or more plans is the percentage that the total actuarial values of plan assets bears to the plans' total vested benefits amounts; and

(3) *Testing date.* Each plan's assets and vested benefits amount are determined as of that plan's testing date for the plan year that includes the effective date of the reportable event.

(d) *Shortening of 30-day period.* Pursuant to § 4043.3(d), the PBGC may, upon review of an advance notice, shorten the notice period to allow for an earlier effective date.

[¶ 15,463A]

§ 4043.62 **Change in contributing sponsor or controlled group.** (a) *Reportable event and information required.* Advance notice is required for a change in a plan's contributing sponsor or controlled group, as described in § 4043.29(a), and the notice shall include the information described in § 4043.29(b) and, if known, the expected effective date of the reportable event.

(b) *Waivers.* (1) *Small plan.* Notice is waived with respect to a change of contributing sponsor if the transferred plan has 500 or fewer participants.

(2) *De minimis 5-percent segment.* Notice is waived if the person or persons that will cease to be members of the plan's controlled group represent a de minimis 5-percent segment of the plan's old controlled group for the most recent fiscal year(s) ending on or before the effective date of the reportable event.

[¶ 15,463B]

§ 4043.63 **Liquidation.** (a) *Reportable event and information required.* Advance notice is required for a liquidation of a member of a plan's controlled group, as described in § 4043.30(a), and the notice shall include the information described in § 4043.30(b) and, if known, the expected effective date of the reportable event.

(b) *Waiver.* Notice is waived if the person that liquidates is a de minimis 5-percent segment of the plan's controlled group for the most recent fiscal year(s) ending on or before the effective date of the reportable event, and each plan that was maintained by the liquidating member is maintained by another member of the plan's controlled group.

[¶ 15,463C]

§ 4043.64 **Extraordinary dividend or stock redemption.** (a) *Reportable event and information required.* Advance notice is required for a distribution by a member of a plan's controlled group that would be described in § 4043.31(a) if both assets and liabilities were valued at fair market value. The notice shall include the information described in § 4043.31(b).

(b) *Waiver.* Notice is waived if the person making the distribution is a de minimis 5-percent segment of the plan's controlled group for the most recent fiscal year(s) ending on or before the effective date of the reportable event.

[¶ 15,463D]

§ 4043.65 **Transfer of benefit liabilities.** (a) *Reportable event and information required.* Advance notice is required for a transfer of benefit liabilities, as described in § 4043.32(a) (determined without regard to § 4043.32(d)), and the notice shall include the information described in § 4043.32(b).

(b) *Waivers.* Notice is waived—

(1) In the circumstances described in § 4043.32(c)(1), (c)(2), and (c)(4); and

(2) If the benefit liabilities of 500 or fewer participants are transferred, in the circumstances described in § 4043.32(c)(3).

[¶ 15,463E]

§ 4043.66 **Application for minimum funding waiver.** (a) *Reportable event and information required.* Advance notice is required for an application for a minimum funding waiver, as described in § 4043.33(a), and the notice shall include the information described in § 4043.33(b).

(b) *Extension.* The notice date is extended until 10 days after the reportable event has occurred.

[¶ 15,463F]

§ 4043.67 **Loan default.** (a) *Reportable event and information required.* Advance notice is required for a loan default, as described in § 4043.34(a) (or that would be so described if "10 days" were substituted for "30 days" in § 4043.34(a)(1)). The notice shall include the information described in § 4043.34(b).

(b) *Waivers.* Notice is waived if the reportable default is cured, or the lender waives the default, within 10 days or, if later, by the end of any cure period.

(c) *Extensions.* The notice date is extended to the later of—

(1) *10 days after default.* 10 days after the default occurs (without regard to the time of any other conditions required for the default to be reportable); and

(2) *One day after subsequent event.* One day after—

(i) The applicable cure period provided in the loan agreement (in the case of a default described in § 4043.34(a)(1));

(ii) The date the loan is accelerated (in the case of a default described in § 4043.34(a)(2)); and

(iii) The date the debtor receives written notice of the default (in the case of a default described in § 4043.34(a)(3)).

[¶ 15,463G]

§ 4043.68 **Bankruptcy or similar settlement.** (a) *Reportable event and information required.* Advance notice is required for a bankruptcy or similar settlement, as described in § 4043.35(a), and the notice shall include the information described in § 4043.35(b).

(b) *Extension.* The notice date is extended until 10 days after the reportable event has occurred.

Subpart D—Notice of Failure To Make Required Contributions

[¶ 15,464]

§ 4043.81 **PBGC Form 200, notice of failure to make required contributions; supplementary information.** (a) *General rules.* To comply with the notification requirement in section 302(f)(4) of ERISA and section 412(n)(4) of the Code, a contributing sponsor of a single-employer plan that is covered under section 4021 of ERISA and, if that contributing sponsor is a member of a parent-subsidiary controlled group, the ultimate parent must complete and submit in accordance with this section a properly certified Form 200 that includes all required documentation and other information, as described in the related filing instructions. Notice is required whenever the unpaid balance of a required installment or any other payment required under section 302 of ERISA and section 412 of the Code (including interest), when added to the aggregate unpaid balance of all preceding such installments or other payments for which payment was not made when due (including interest), exceeds $1 million.

(1) Form 200 must be filed with the PBGC no later than 10 days after the due date for any required payment for which payment was not made when due.

(2) If a contributing sponsor or the ultimate parent completes and submits Form 200 in accordance with this section, the PBGC will consider the notification requirement in section 302(f)(4) of ERISA and section 412(n)(4) of the Code to be satisfied by all members of a controlled group of which the person who has filed Form 200 is a member.

(b) *Supplementary information.* If, upon review of a Form 200, the PBGC concludes that it needs additional information in order to make decisions regarding enforcement of a lien imposed by section 302(f) of ERISA and section 412(n) of the Code, the PBGC may require any member of the contributing sponsor's controlled group to supplement the Form 200 in accordance with § 4043.3(d).

[¶ 15,470]
ALLOCATION OF ASSETS

Act Sec. 4044. (a) In the case of the termination of a single-employer plan, the plan administrator shall allocate the assets of the plan (available to provide benefits) among the participants and beneficiaries of the plan in the following order:

(1) First, to that portion of each individual's accrued benefit which is derived from the participant's contributions to the plan which were not mandatory contributions.

(2) Second, to that portion of each individual's accrued benefit which is derived from the participant's mandatory contributions.

(3) Third, in the case of benefits payable as an annuity—

(A) in the case of the benefit of a participant or beneficiary which was in pay status as of the beginning of the 3-year period ending on the termination date of the plan, to each such benefit, based on the provisions of the plan (as in effect during the 5-year period ending on such date) under which such benefit would be the least,

(B) in the case of a participant's or beneficiary's benefit (other than a benefit described in subparagraph (A)) which would have been in pay status as of the beginning of such 3-year period if the participant had retired prior to the beginning of the 3-year period and if his benefits had commenced (in the normal form of annuity under the plan) as of the beginning of such period, to each such benefit based on the provisions of the plan (as in effect during the 5-year period ending on such date) under which benefit would be the least.

For purposes of subparagraph (A), the lowest benefit in pay status during a 3-year period shall be considered the benefit in pay status for such period.

(4) Fourth—

(A) to all other benefits (if any) of individuals under the plan guaranteed under this title (determined without regard to section 4022B(a)), and

(B) to the additional benefits (if any) which would be determined under subparagraph (A) if section 4022(b)(5) did not apply.

For purposes of this paragraph, section 4021 shall be applied without regard to subsection (c) thereof.

(5) Fifth, to all other nonforfeitable benefits under the plan.

(6) Sixth, to all other benefits under the plan.

Act Sec. 4044. (b) For purposes of subsection (a)—

(1) The amount allocated under any paragraph of subsection (a) with respect to any benefit shall be properly adjusted for any allocation of assets with respect to that benefit under a prior paragraph of subsection (a).

(2) If the assets available for allocation under any paragraph of subsection (a) (other than paragraphs (5) and (6)) are insufficient to satisfy in full the benefits of all individuals which are described in that paragraph, the assets shall be allocated pro rata among such individuals on the basis of the present value (as of the termination date) of their respective benefits described in that paragraph.

(3) This paragraph applies if the assets available for allocation under paragraph (5) of subsection (a) are not sufficient to satisfy in full the benefits of individuals described in that paragraph.

(A) If this paragraph applies, except as provided in subparagraph (B), the assets shall be allocated to the benefits of individuals described in such paragraph (5) on the basis of the benefits of individuals which would have been described in such paragraph (5) under the plan as in effect at the beginning of the 5-year period ending on the date of plan termination.

(B) If the assets available for allocation under subparagraph (A) are sufficient to satisfy in full the benefits described in such subparagraph (without regard to this subparagraph), then for purposes of subparagraph (A), benefits of individuals described in such subparagraph shall be determined on the basis of the plan as amended by the most recent plan amendment effective during such 5-year period under which the assets available for allocation are sufficient to satisfy in full the benefits of individuals described in subparagraph (A) and any assets remaining to be allocated under such subparagraph shall be allocated under subparagraph (A) on the basis of the plan as amended by the next succeeding plan amendment effective during such period.

(4) If the Secretary of the Treasury determines that the allocation made pursuant to this section (without regard to this paragraph) results in discrimination prohibited by section 401(a)(4) of the Internal Revenue Code of 1986 then, if required to prevent the disqualification of the plan (or any trust under the plan) under section 401(a) or 403(a) of such Code, the assets allocated under subsection (a)(4)(B), (a)(5), and (a)(6) shall be reallocated to the extent necessary to avoid such discrimination.

(5) The term "mandatory contributions" means amounts contributed to the plan by a participant which are required as a condition of employment, as a condition of participation in such plan, or as a condition of obtaining benefits under the plan attributable to employer contributions. For this purpose, the total amount of mandatory contributions of a participant is the amount of such contributions reduced (but not below zero) by the sum of the amounts paid or distributed to him under the plan before its termination.

(6) A plan may establish subclasses and categories within the classes described in paragraphs (1) through (6) of subsection (a) in accordance with regulations prescribed by the corporation.

Act Sec. 4044. (c) Any increase or decrease in the value of the assets of a single-employer plan occurring during the period beginning on the later of (1) the date a trustee is appointed under section 4042(b) or (2) the date on which the plan is terminated is to be allocated between the plan and the corporation in the manner determined by the court (in the case of a court-appointed trustee) or as agreed upon by the corporation and the plan administrator in any other case. Any increase or decrease in the value of the assets of a single-employer plan occurring after the date on which the plan is terminated shall be credited to, or suffered by, the corporation.

Act Sec. 4044. (d)(1) Subject to paragraph (3), any residual assets of a single-employer plan may be distributed to the employer if,—

(A) all liabilities of the plan to participants and their beneficiaries have been satisfied,

(B) the distribution does not contravene any provision of law, and

(C) the plan provides for such a distribution in these circumstances.

(2)(A) In determining the extent to which a plan provides for the distribution of plan assets to the employer for purposes of paragraph (1)(C), any such provision, and any amendment increasing the amount which may be distributed to the employer, shall not be treated as effective before the end of the fifth calendar year following the date of the adoption of such provision or amendment.

(B) A distribution to the employer from a plan shall not be treated as failing to satisfy the requirements of this paragraph if the plan has been in effect for fewer than 5 years and the plan has provided for such a distribution since the effective date of the plan.

(C) Except as otherwise provided in regulations of the Secretary of the Treasury, in any case in which a transaction described in section 208 occurs, subparagraph (A) shall continue to apply separately with respect to the amounts of any assets transferred in such transaction.

(D) For purposes of this subsection, the term "employer" includes any member of the controlled group of which the employer is a member. For purposes of the preceding sentence, the term "controlled group" means any group treated as a single employer under subsection (b), (c), (m) or (o) of section 414 of the Internal Revenue Code of 1986.

(3)(A) Before any distribution from a plan pursuant to paragraph (1), if any assets of the plan attributable to employee contributions remain after satisfaction of all liabilities described in subsection (a), such remaining assets shall be equitably distributed to the participants who made such contributions or their beneficiaries (including alternate payees, within the meaning of section 206(d)(3)(K)).

(B) For purposes of subparagraph (A), the portion of the remaining assets which are attributable to employee contributions shall be an amount equal to the product derived by multiplying—

(i) the market value of the total remaining assets, by

(ii) a fraction—

(I) the numerator of which is the present value of all portions of the accrued benefits with respect to participants which are derived from participants' mandatory contributions (referred to in subsection (a)(2)), and

(II) the denominator of which is present value of all benefits with respect to which assets are allocated under paragraph (2) through (6) of subsection (a).

(C) For purposes of this paragraph, each person who is, as of the termination date—

(i) a participant under the plan, or

(ii) an individual who has received, during the 3-year period ending with the termination date, a distribution from the plan of such individual's entire nonforfeitable benefit in the form of a single sum distribution in accordance with section 203(e) or in the form of irrevocable commitments purchased by the plan from an insurer to provide such nonforfeitable benefit,

shall be treated as a participant with respect to the termination, if all or part of the nonforfeitable benefit with respect to such person is or was attributable to participants' mandatory contributions (referred to in subsection (a)(2)).

(4) Nothing in this subsection shall be construed to limit the requirements of section 4980(d) of the Internal Revenue Code of 1986 (as in effect immediately after the enactment of the Omnibus Budget Reconciliation Act of 1990) or section 404(d) of this Act with respect to any distribution of residual assets of a single-employer plan to the employer.

Amendments

P.L. 101-508, Sec. 12001(b)(2)(B):

Amended ERISA Sec. 4044(d) by adding a new paragraph (4) to read as above effective for reversions occurring after September 30, 1990 except for the provisions of Act Sec. 12003(b).

SEC. 12003. EFFECTIVE DATE.

* * *

(b) Exception.—The amendments made by this subtitle shall not apply to any reversion after September 30, 1990, if—

(1) in the case of plans subject to title IV of the Employee Retirement Income Security Act of 1974, a notice of intent to terminate under such title was provided to participants (or if no participants, to the Pension Benefit Guaranty Corporation) before October 1, 1990,

(2) in the case of plans subject to title I (and not to title IV) of such Act, a notice of intent to reduce future accruals under section 204(h) of such Act was provided to participants in connection with the termination before October 1, 1990,

(3) in the case of plans not subject to title I or IV of such Act, a request for a determination letter with respect to the termination was filed with the Secretary of the Treasury or the Secretary's delegate before October 1, 1990, or

(4) in the case of plans not subject to title I or IV of such Act and having only 1 participant, a resolution terminating the plan was adopted by the employer before October 1, 1990.

P.L. 101-239, §§ 7881(e)(1) and (4):

Amended P.L. 100-203, § 9311(a)(2) to read as below effective December 22, 1987.

P.L. 101-239, § 7881(e)(2):

Amended P.L. 100-203, § 9311(d) to read as below effective December 22, 1987.

P.L. 101-239, § 7894(g)(2):

Amended ERISA Sec. 4044(a)(1) by striking "accured" and inserting "accrued" effective September 2, 1974.

P.L. 101-239, § 7891(a)(1):

Titles I, III, and IV of ERISA (other than sections 3(37)(E), 301(a)(7), and 308, the last sentence of section 408(d), and sections 414(c), 4001(a)(3)(ii), and 4303) are each amended by striking "Internal Revenue Code of 1954" each place it appears and inserting "Internal Revenue Code of 1986" effective October 22, 1986.

P.L. 100-203, § 9311(a)(1):

Amended ERISA Sec. 4044(d) by redesignating paragraph (2) as (3) and adding a new paragraph (2) to read as above.

P.L. 100-203, § 9311(a)(2):

(2) Transitional rule.—The amendments made by paragraph (1) shall apply, in the case of plans which, as of December 17, 1987, have no provision relating to the distribution of residual plan assets upon termination only with respect to plan amendments providing for the distribution of plan assets to the employer which are adopted after December 17, 1988.

P.L. 100-203, § 9311(b)(1):

Amended ERISA Sec. 4044(d)(1) by striking "Any" and inserting "Subject to paragraph (3), any."

P.L. 100-203, § 9311(b)(2):

Amended ERISA Sec. 4044(d) by striking paragraph (3) (as redesignated) and adding a new paragraph (3) to read as above. Prior to being stricken paragraph (3) read as follows:

(3) Notwithstanding the provisions of paragraph (1), if any assets of the plan attributable to employee contributions remain after all liabilities of the plan to participants and their beneficiaries have been satisfied, such assets shall be equitably distributed to the employees who made such contributions (or their beneficaries) in accordance with their rate of contributions.

P.L. 100-203, § 9311(c):

Amended ERISA Sec. 4044(b)(4) by striking "section 401(a), 403(a), or 405(a)" and inserting "section 401(a) or 403(a)".

The above amendments are effective for: (1) plan terminations under section 4041(c) of ERISA for which notices of intent to terminate are provided under section 4041(a)(2) of ERISA after December 17, 1987, and (2) plan terminations for which proceedings are instituted by the Pension Benefit Guaranty Corporation under section 4042 of ERISA after December 17, 1987.

P.L. 100-203, § 9311(d):

(d) Effective date.—The amendments made by this section shall apply with respect to—

(1) plan terminations under section 4041 of ERISA with respect to which notices of intent to terminate are provided under section 4041(a)(2) of ERISA after December 17, 1987, and

(2) plan terminations with respect to which proceedings are instituted by the Pension Benefit Guaranty Corporation under section 4042 of ERISA after December 17, 1987.

Except as provided in subsection (a)(2), the amendments made by subsection (a) shall apply to any provision of the plan or plan amendment adopted after December 17, 1987.

P.L. 99-2762, § 11016(c)(12):

Amended ERISA Sec. 4044(a), first sentence, by deleting "defined benefit."

Act Sec. 11016(c)(13) amended ERISA Sec. 4044(a)(4)(A) by striking out "section 4022(b)(5)" and inserting "section 4022B(a)" and amended ERISA Sec. 4044(a)(4)(B) by striking out "section 4022(b)(6)" and inserting "section 4022(b)(5)," effective on April 7, 1986.

P.L. 96-364, § 402(a)(7):

Amended Sec. 4044 effective September 26, 1980 by: inserting "single-employer" before "defined benefit plan" in subsection (a); inserting "single-employer" before "plan occurring during" and before "plan occurring after" in subsection (c); and inserting "single-employer" before "plan may be distributed" in subsection (d)(1).

Regulations

The following regulations were adopted by the Pension Benefit Guaranty Corporation on July 1, 1996 (61 FR 34002). Prior to July 1, 1996, PBGC regulations were under Chapter XXVI of Title 29 of the Code of Federal Regulations. Effective July 1, 1996, PBGC regulations were moved to Chapter XL, and were renumbered and reorganized. Reg. § 4044.13 was officially corrected December 30, 1997 (62 FR 67728). Reg. §§ 4044.52 and 4044.54 were amended July 15, 1998 (63 FR 38305), effective July 16, 1998 and March 17, 2000 (65 FR 14751), effective May 1, 2000. Reg. § 4044.53 was amended March 17, 2000 (65 FR 14751), effective May 1, 2000. The Appendices to Part 4044 were amended on March 17, 2000 (65 FR 14751), effective May 1, 2000. Reg. § 4044.2 was amended and Reg. § 4044.13 was revised April 8, 2002 (67 FR 16949), effective June 1, 2002.

Note: Certain provisions of part 4044 have been superseded by legislative changes. For example, there are references to provisions formerly codified in 29 CFR part 2617, subpart C (and to the Notice of Sufficiency provided for thereunder) that no longer exist because of changes in the PBGC's plan termination regulations in response to the Single-Employer Pension Plan Amendments Act of 1986 and the Pension Protection Act of 1987. The PBGC intends to amend part 4044 at a later date to conform it to current statutory provisions.

Subpart A—Allocation of Assets

General Provisions

[¶ 15,471]

§ 4044.1 **Purpose and scope**. This part implements section 4044 of ERISA, which contains rules for allocating a plan's assets when the plan terminates. These rules have been in effect since September 2, 1974, the date of enactment of ERISA. This part applies to any single-employer plan covered by title IV of ERISA that submits a notice of intent to terminate, or for which PBGC commences an action to terminate the plan under section 4042 of ERISA.

(a) *Subpart A*. Sections 4044.1 through 4044.4 set forth general rules for applying §§ 4044.10 through 4044.17. Sections 4044.10 through 4044.17 interpret the rules and describe procedures for allocating plan assets to priority categories 1 through 6.

(b) *Subpart B*. The purpose of subpart B is to establish the method of determining the value of benefits and assets under terminating single-employer pension plans covered by title IV of ERISA. This valuation is needed for both plans trusteed under title IV and plans which are not trusteed. For the former, the valuation is needed to allocate plan assets in accordance with subpart A of this part and to determine the amount of any plan asset insufficiency. For the latter, the valuation is needed to allocate assets in accordance with subpart A and to distribute the assets in accordance with subpart B of part 4041 of this chapter.

(1) Section 4044.41 sets forth the general provisions of subpart B and applies to all terminating single-employer plans. Sections 4044.51 through 4044.57 prescribe the benefit valuation rules for plans that receive or that expect to receive a Notice of Inability to Determine Sufficiency from PBGC and are placed into trusteeship by PBGC, including (in §§ 4044.55 through 4044.57) the rules and procedures a plan administrator shall follow to determine the expected retirement age (XRA) for a plan participant entitled to early retirement benefits for whom the annuity starting date is not known as of the valuation date. This applies to all trusteed plans which have such early retirement benefits. The plan administrator shall determine an XRA under § 4044.55, § 4044.56 or § 4044.57, as appropriate, for each active participant or participant with a deferred vested benefit who is entitled to an early retirement benefit and who as of the valuation date has not selected an annuity starting date. [See Note at beginning of part 4044.]

(2) Sections 4044.71 through 4044.75 prescribe the benefit valuation rules for calculating the value of a benefit to be paid a participant or beneficiary under a terminating pension plan that is distributing assets where the plan has received a Notice of Sufficiency issued by PBGC pursuant to part 2617 of this chapter and has not been placed into trusteeship by PBGC. [See Note at beginning of part 4044.]

[¶ 15,471A]

§ 4044.2 **Definitions**. (a) The following terms are defined in § 4001.2 of this chapter: annuity, basic-type benefit, Code, distribution date, ERISA, fair market value, guaranteed benefit, insurer, IRS, irrevocable commitment, mandatory employee contributions, nonbasic-type benefit, nonforfeitable benefit, normal retirement age, notice of intent to terminate, PBGC, person, plan, plan administrator, single-employer plan, substantial owner, termination date, and voluntary employee contributions.

(b) For purposes of this part:

Deferred annuity means an annuity under which the specified date or age at which payments are to begin occurs after the valuation date.

Earliest retirement age at valuation date means the later of (a) a participant's age on his or her birthday nearest to the valuation date, or (b) the participant's attained age as of his or her Earliest PBGC Retirement Date (as determined under Sec. 4022.10 of this chapter). [Amended by 67 FR 16949, April 8, 2002.]

Early retirement benefit means an annuity benefit payable under the terms of the plan, under which the participant is entitled to begin receiving payments before his or her normal retirement age and which is not payable on account of the disability of the participant. It may be reduced according to the terms of the plan.

Expected retirement age (XRA) means the age, determined in accordance with §§ 4044.55 through 4044.57, at which a participant is expected to begin receiving benefits when the participant has not elected, before the allocation date, an annuity starting date. This is the age to which a participant's benefit payment is assumed to be deferred for valuation purposes. An XRA is equal to or greater than the participant's earliest retirement age at valuation date but less than his or her normal retirement age.

Non-trusteed plan means a single-employer plan which receives a Notice of Sufficiency from PBGC and is able to close out by purchasing annuities in the private sector in accordance with part 2617 of this chapter. [See Note at beginning of part 4044.]

Notice of Sufficiency means a notice issued by the PBGC that it has determined that plan assets are sufficient to discharge when due all obligations of the plan with respect to benefits in priority categories 1 through 4 after plan assets have been allocated to benefits in accordance with section 4044 of ERISA and this subpart. [See Note at beginning of part 4044.]

Priority category means one of the categories contained in sections 4044(a)(1) through (a)(6) of ERISA that establish the order in which plan assets are to be allocated.

Trusteed plan means a single-employer plan which has been placed into trusteeship by PBGC.

Unreduced retirement age (URA) means the earlier of the normal retirement age specified in the plan or the age at which an unreduced benefit is first payable.

Valuation date means (1) for non-trusteed plans, the date of distribution and (2) for trusteed plans, the date of termination.

(c) For purposes of subpart B of this part (unless otherwise required by the context):

Age means the participant's age at his or her nearest birthday and is determined by rounding the individual's exact age to the nearest whole year. Half years are rounded to the next highest year. This is also known as the "insurance age."

(d) For purposes of §§ 4044.55 through 4044.57:

Monthly benefit means the guaranteed benefit payable by PBGC.

(e) For purposes of §§ 4044.71 through 4044.75:

Lump sum payable in lieu of an annuity means a benefit that is payable in a single installment and is derived from an annuity payable under the plan.

Other lump sum benefit means a benefit in priority category 5 or 6, determined under subpart A of this part, that is payable in a single installment (or substantially so) under the terms of the plan, and that is not derived from an annuity payable under the plan. The benefit may be a severance pay benefit, a death benefit or other single installment benefit.

Qualifying bid means a bid obtained from an insurer in accordance with § 2617.14(b) of this chapter. [See Note at beginning of part 4044.]

[¶ 15,471B]

§ 4044.3 **General rule**. (a) *Asset allocation*. Upon the termination of a single-employer plan, the plan administrator shall allocate the plan assets available to pay for benefits under the plan in the manner prescribed by this subpart. Plan assets available to pay for benefits include all plan assets (valued according to § 4044.41(b)) remaining after the subtraction of all liabilities, other than liabilities for future benefit payments, paid or payable from plan assets under the provisions of the plan. Liabilities include expenses, fees and other administrative costs, and benefit payments due before the allocation date. Except as provided in § 4044.4(b), an irrevocable commitment by an insurer to pay a benefit, which commitment is in effect on the date of the asset allocation, is not considered a plan asset, and a benefit payable under such a commitment is excluded from the allocation process.

(b) *Allocation date.* For plans that close out pursuant to a Notice of Sufficiency under the provisions of subpart C of part 2617 of this chapter, assets shall be allocated as of the date plan assets are to be distributed. For other plans, assets shall be allocated as of the termination date. [See Note at beginning of part 4044.]

[¶ 15,471C]

§ 4044.4 **Violations.** (a) *General.* A plan administrator violates ERISA if plan assets are allocated or distributed upon plan termination in a manner other than that prescribed in section 4044 of ERISA and this subpart, except as may be required to prevent disqualification of the plan under the Code and regulations thereunder.

(b) *Distributions in anticipation of termination.* A distribution, transfer, or allocation of assets to a participant or to an insurance company for the benefit of a participant, made in anticipation of plan termination, is considered to be an allocation of plan assets upon termination, and is covered by paragraph (a) of this section. In determining whether a distribution, transfer, or allocation of assets has been made in anticipation of plan termination PBGC will consider all of the facts and circumstances including—

(1) Any change in funding or operation procedures;

(2) Past practice with regard to employee requests for forms of distribution;

(3) Whether the distribution is consistent with plan provisions; and

(4) Whether an annuity contract that provides for a cutback based on the guarantee limits in subpart B of part 4022 of this chapter could have been purchased from an insurance company.

Allocation of Assets to Benefit Categories

[¶ 15,472]

§ 4044.10 **Manner of allocation.** (a) *General.* The plan administrator shall allocate plan assets available to pay for benefits under the plan using the rules and procedures set forth in paragraphs (b) through (f) of this section, or any other procedure that results in each participant (or beneficiary) receiving the same benefits he or she would receive if the procedures in paragraphs (b) through (f) were followed.

(b) *Assigning benefits.* The basic-type and nonbasic-type benefits payable with respect to each participant in a terminated plan shall be assigned to one or more priority categories in accordance with §§ 4044.11 through 4044.16. Benefits derived from voluntary employee contributions, which are assigned only to priority category 1, are treated, under section 204(c)(4) of ERISA and section 411(d)(5) of the Code, as benefits under a separate plan. The amount of a benefit payable with respect to each participant shall be determined as of the termination date.

(c) *Valuing benefits.* The value of a participant's benefit or benefits assigned to each priority category shall be determined, as of the allocation date, in accordance with the provisions of subpart B of this part. The value of each participant's basic-type benefit or benefits in a priority category shall be reduced by the value of the participant's benefit of the same type that is assigned to a higher priority category. Except as provided in the next two sentences, the same procedure shall be followed for nonbasic-type benefits. The value of a participant's nonbasic-type benefits in priority categories 3, 5, and 6 shall not be reduced by the value of the participant's nonbasic-type benefit assigned to priority category 2. Benefits in priority category 1 shall neither be included in nor subtracted from lower priority categories. In no event shall a benefit assigned to a priority category be valued at less than zero.

(d) *Allocating assets to priority categories.* Plan assets available to pay for benefits under the plan shall be allocated to each priority category in succession, beginning with priority category 1. If the plan has sufficient assets to pay for all benefits in a priority category, the remaining assets shall then be allocated to the next lower priority category. This process shall be repeated until all benefits in priority

categories 1 through 6 have been provided or until all available plan assets have been allocated.

(e) *Allocating assets within priority categories.* Except for priority category 5, if the plan assets available for allocation to any priority category are insufficient to pay for all benefits in that priority category, those assets shall be distributed among the participants according to the ratio that the value of each participant's benefit or benefits in that priority category bears to the total value of all benefits in that priority category. If the plan assets available for allocation to priority category 5 are insufficient to pay for all benefits in that category, the assets shall be allocated, first, to the value of each participant's nonforfeitable benefits that would be assigned to priority category 5 under § 4044.15 after reduction for the value of benefits assigned to higher priority categories, based only on the provisions of the plan in effect at the beginning of the 5-year period immediately preceding the termination date. If assets available for allocation to priority category 5 are sufficient to fully satisfy the value of those benefits, assets shall then be allocated to the value of the benefit increase under the oldest amendment during the 5-year period immediately preceding the termination date, reduced by the value of benefits assigned to higher priority categories (including higher subcategories in priority category 5). This allocation procedure shall be repeated for each succeeding plan amendment within the 5-year period until all plan assets available for allocation have been exhausted. If an amendment decreased benefits, amounts previously allocated with respect to each participant in excess of the value of the reduced benefit shall be reduced accordingly. In the subcategory in which assets are exhausted, the assets shall be distributed among the participants according to the ratio that the value of each participant's benefit or benefits in that subcategory bears to the total value of all benefits in that subcategory.

(f) *Applying assets to basic-type or nonbasic-type benefits within priority categories.* The assets allocated to a participant's benefit or benefits within each priority category shall first be applied to pay for the participant's basic-type benefit or benefits assigned to that priority category. Any assets allocated on behalf of that participant remaining after satisfying the participant's basic-type benefit or benefits in that priority category shall then be applied to pay for the participant's nonbasic-type benefit or benefits assigned to that priority category. If the assets allocable to a participant's basic-type benefit or benefits in all priority categories are insufficient to pay for all of the participant's guaranteed benefits, the assets allocated to that participant's benefit in priority category 4 shall be applied, first, to the guaranteed portion of the participant's benefit in priority category 4. The remaining assets allocated to that participant's benefit in priority category 4, if any, shall be applied to the nonguaranteed portion of the participant's benefit.

(g) *Allocation to established subclasses.* Notwithstanding paragraphs (e) and (f) of this section, the assets of a plan that has established subclasses within any priority category may be allocated to the plan's subclasses in accordance with the rules set forth in § 4044.17.

[¶ 15,472A]

§ 4044.11 **Priority category 1 benefits.** (a) *Definition.* The benefits in priority category 1 are participants' accrued benefits derived from voluntary employee contributions.

(b) *Assigning benefits.* Absent an election described in the next sentence, the benefit assigned to priority category 1 with respect to each participant is the balance of the separate account maintained for the participant's voluntary contributions. If a participant has elected to receive an annuity in lieu of his or her account balance, the benefit assigned to priority category 1 with respect to that participant is the present value of that annuity.

[¶ 15,472B]

§ 4044.12 **Priority category 2 benefits.** (a) *Definition.* The benefits in priority category 2 are participants' accrued benefits derived from mandatory employee contributions, whether to be paid as an annuity benefit with a pre-retirement death benefit that returns mandatory employee contributions or, if a participant so elects under the terms of the plan and subpart A of part 4022 of this chapter, as a lump sum benefit. Benefits are primarily basic-type benefits although nonbasic-type benefits may also be included as follows:

(1) *Basic-type benefits.* The basic-type benefit in priority category 2 with respect to each participant is the sum of the values of the annuity benefit and the pre-retirement death benefit determined under the provisions of paragraph (c)(1) of this section.

(2) *Nonbasic-type benefits.* If a participant elects to receive a lump sum benefit and if the value of the lump sum benefit exceeds the value of the basic-type benefit in priority category 2 determined with respect to the participant, the excess is a nonbasic-type benefit. There is no nonbasic-type benefit in priority category 2 for a participant who does not elect to receive a lump sum benefit.

(b) *Conversion of mandatory employee contributions to an annuity benefit.* Subject to the limitation set forth in paragraph (b)(3) of this section, a participant's accumulated mandatory employee contributions shall be converted to an annuity form of benefit payable at the normal retirement age or, if the plan provides for early retirement, at the expected retirement age. The conversion shall be made using the interest rates and factors specified in paragraph (b)(2) of this section. The form of the annuity benefit (e.g., straight life annuity, joint and survivor annuity, cash refund annuity, etc.) is the form that the participant or beneficiary is entitled to on the termination date. If the participant does not have a nonforfeitable right to a benefit, other than the return of his or her mandatory contributions in a lump sum, the annuity form of benefit is the form the participant would be entitled to if the participant had a nonforfeitable right to an annuity benefit under the plan on the termination date.

(1) *Accumulated mandatory employee contributions.* Subject to any addition for the cost of ancillary benefits plus interest, as provided in the following sentence, the amount of the accumulated mandatory employee contributions for each participant is the participant's total nonforfeitable mandatory employee contributions remaining in the plan on the termination date plus interest, if any, under the plan provisions. Mandatory employee contributions, if any, used after the effective date of the minimum vesting standards in section 203 of ERISA and section 411 of the Code for costs or to provide ancillary benefits such as life insurance or health insurance, plus interest under the plan provisions, shall be added to the contributions that remain in the plan to determine the accumulated mandatory employee contributions.

(2) *Interest rates and conversion factors.* The interest rates and conversion factors used in the administration of the plan shall be used to convert a participant's accumulated mandatory contributions to the annuity form of benefit. In the absence of plan rules and factors, the interest rates and conversion factors established by the IRS for allocation of accrued benefits between employer and employee contributions under the provisions of section 204(c) of ERISA and section 411(c) of the Code shall be used.

(3) *Minimum accrued benefit.* The annuity benefit derived from mandatory employee contributions may not be less than the minimum accrued benefit under the provisions of section 204(c) of ERISA and section 411(c) of the Code.

(c) *Assigning benefits.* If a participant or beneficiary elects to receive a lump sum benefit, his or her benefit shall be determined under paragraph (c)(2) of this section. Otherwise, the benefits with respect to a participant shall be determined under paragraph (c)(1) of this section.

(1) *Annuity benefit and pre-retirement death benefit.* The annuity benefit and the pre-retirement death benefit assigned to priority category 2 with respect to a participant are determined as follows:

(i) The annuity benefit is the benefit computed under paragraph (b) of this section.

(ii) Except for adjustments necessary to meet the minimum lump sum requirements as hereafter provided, the pre-retirement death benefit is the benefit under the plan that returns all or a portion of the participant's mandatory employee contributions upon the death of the participant before retirement. A benefit that became payable in a single installment (or substantially so) because the participant died before the termination date is a liability of the plan within the meaning of §4044.3(a) and should not be assigned to priority category 2. A benefit payable upon a participant's death that is included in the

annuity form of the benefit derived from mandatory employee contributions (e.g., the survivor's portion of a joint and survivor annuity or the cash refund portion of a cash refund annuity) is assigned to priority category 2 as part of the annuity benefit under paragraph (c)(1)(i) of this section and is not assigned as a death benefit. The pre-retirement death benefit may not be less than the minimum lump sum required upon withdrawal of mandatory employee contributions by the IRS under section 204(c) of ERISA and section 411(c) of the Code.

(2) *Lump sum benefit.* Except for adjustments necessary to meet the minimum lump sum requirements as hereafter provided, if a participant elects to receive a lump sum benefit under the provisions of the plan, the amount of the benefit that is assigned to priority category 2 with respect to the participant is—

(i) The combined value of the annuity benefit and the pre-retirement death benefit determined according to paragraph (c)(1) (which constitutes the basic-type benefit) plus

(ii) The amount, if any, of the participant's accumulated mandatory employee contributions that exceeds the combined value of the annuity benefit and the pre-retirement death benefit (which constitutes the nonbasic-type benefit), but not more than

(iii) The amount of the participant's accumulated mandatory contributions.

(3) For purposes of paragraph (c)(2) of this section, accumulated mandatory contributions means the contributions with interest, if any, payable under plan provisions to the participant or beneficiary on termination of the plan or, in the absence of such provisions, the amount that is payable if the participant withdrew his or her contributions on the termination date. The lump sum benefit may not be less than the minimum lump required by the IRS under section 204(c) of ERISA and section 411(c) of the Code upon withdrawal of mandatory employee contributions.

[¶ 15,472C]
§ 4044.13 **Priority category 3 benefits.**

(a) *Definition.* The benefits in priority category 3 are those annuity benefits that were in pay status before the beginning of the 3-year period ending on the termination date, and those annuity benefits that could have been in pay status (then or as of the next payment date under the plan's rules for starting benefit payments) for participants who, before the beginning of the 3-year period ending on the termination date, had reached their Earliest PBGC Retirement Date (as determined under § 4022.10 of this chapter based on plan provisions in effect on the day before the beginning of the 3-year period ending on the termination date). Benefit increases that were effective throughout the 5-year period ending on the termination date, including automatic benefit increases during that period to the extent provided in paragraph (b)(5) of this section, shall be included in determining the priority category 3 benefit. Benefits are primarily basic-type benefits, although nonbasic-type benefits will be included if any portion of a participant's priority category 3 benefit is not guaranteeable under the provisions of subpart A of part 4022 and § 4022.21 of this chapter.

(b) *Assigning benefits.* The annuity benefit that is assigned to priority category 3 with respect to each participant is the lowest annuity that was paid or payable under the rules in paragraphs (b)(2) through (b)(6) of this section.

(1) *Eligibility of participants and beneficiaries.* A participant or beneficiary is eligible for a priority category 3 benefit if either of the following applies [Revised by 67 FR 16959, April 8, 2002]:

(i) The participant's (or beneficiary's) benefit was in pay status before the beginning of the 3-year period ending on the termination date.

(ii) Before the beginning of the 3-year period ending on the termination date, the participant was eligible for an annuity benefit that could have been in pay status and had reached his or her Earliest PBGC Retirement Date (as determined in § 4022.10 of this chapter, based on plan provisions in effect on the day before the beginning of the 3-year period ending on the termination date). Whether a participant was eligible to receive an annuity before the beginning of the 3-year period shall be determined using the plan provisions in effect on the day before the beginning of the 3-year period.

(iii) If a participant described in either of the preceding two paragraphs died during the 3-year period ending on the date of the plan termination and his or her beneficiary is entitled to an annuity, the beneficiary is eligible for a priority category 3 benefit. [Revised by 67 FR 16949, April 8, 2002.]

(2) *Plan provisions governing determination of benefit.* In determining the amount of the priority category 3 annuity with respect to a participant, the plan administrator shall use the participant's age, service, actual or expected retirement age, and other relevant facts as of the following dates:

(i) Except as provided in the next sentence, for a participant or beneficiary whose benefit was in pay status before the beginning of the 3-year period ending on the termination date, the priority category 3 benefit shall be determined according to plan provisions in effect on the date the benefit commenced. Benefit increases that were effective throughout the 5-year period ending on the termination date, including automatic benefit increases during that period to the extent provided in paragraph (b)(5) of this section, shall be included in determining the priority category 3 benefit. The form of annuity elected by a retiree is considered the normal form of annuity for that participant [Corrected by 67 FR 38003, May 31, 2002].

(ii) For a participant who was eligible to receive an annuity before the beginning of the 3-year period ending on the termination date but whose benefit was not in pay status, the priority category 3 benefit and the normal form of annuity shall be determined according to plan provisions in effect on the day before the beginning of the 3-year period ending on the termination date as if the benefit had commenced at that time.

(3) *General benefit limitations.* The general benefit limitation is determined as follows:

(i) If a participant's benefit was in pay status before the beginning of the 3-year period, the benefit assigned to priority category 3 with respect to that participant is limited to the lesser of the lowest annuity benefit in pay status during the 3-year period ending on the termination date and the lowest annuity benefit payable under the plan provisions at any time during the 5-year period ending on the termination date.

(ii) Unless a benefit was in pay status before the beginning of the 3-year period ending on the termination date, the benefit assigned to priority category 3 with respect to a participant is limited to the lowest annuity benefit payable under the plan provisions, including any reduction for early retirement, at any time during the 5-year period ending on the termination date. If the annuity form of benefit under a formula that appears to produce the lowest benefit differs from the normal annuity form for the participant under paragraph (b)(2)(ii) of this section, the benefits shall be compared after the differing form is converted to the normal annuity form, using plan factors. In the absence of plan factors, the factors in subpart B of part 4022 of this chapter shall be used.

(iii) For purposes of this paragraph, if a terminating plan has been in effect less than five years on the termination date, computed in accordance with paragraph (b)(6) of this section, the lowest annuity benefit under the plan during the 5-year period ending on the termination date is zero. If the plan is a successor to a previously established defined benefit plan within the meaning of section 4021(a) of ERISA, the time it has been in effect will include the time the predecessor plan was in effect.

(4) *Determination of beneficiary's benefit.* If a beneficiary is eligible for a priority category 3 benefit because of the death of a participant during the 3-year period ending on the termination date, the benefit assigned to priority category 3 for the beneficiary shall be determined as if the participant had died the day before the 3-year period began.

(5) *Automatic benefit increases.* If plan provisions adopted and effective on or before the first day of the 5-year period ending on the

termination date provided for automatic increases in the benefit formula for both active participants and those in pay status or for participants in pay status only, the lowest annuity benefit payable during the 5-year period ending on the termination date determined under paragraph (b)(3) of this section includes the automatic increases scheduled during the fourth and fifth years preceding termination, subject to the restriction that benefit increases for active participants in excess of the increases for retirees shall not be taken into account [Corrected by 67 FR 38003, May 31, 2002].

(6) *Computation of time periods.* For purposes of this section, a plan or amendment is "in effect" on the later of the date on which it is adopted or the date it becomes effective.

[¶ 15,472D]

§ 4044.14 **Priority category 4 benefits.** The benefits assigned to priority category 4 with respect to each participant are the participant's basic-type benefits that do not exceed the guarantee limits set forth in subpart B of part 4022 of this chapter, except as provided in the next sentence. The benefit assigned to priority category 4 with respect to a participant is not limited by the aggregate benefits limitations set forth in § 4022B.1 of this chapter for individuals who are participants in more than one plan or by the phase-in limitation applicable to substantial owners set forth in § 4022.26.

[¶ 15,472E]

§ 4044.15 **Priority category 5 benefits.** The benefits assigned to priority category 5 with respect to each participant are all of the participant's nonforfeitable benefits under the plan.

[¶ 15,472F]

§ 4044.16 **Priority category 6 benefits.** The benefits assigned to priority category 6 with respect to each participant are all of the participant's benefits under the plan, whether forfeitable or nonforfeitable.

[¶ 15,472G]

§ 4044.17 **Subclasses.** (a) *General rule.* A plan may establish one or more subclasses within any priority category, other than priority categories 1 and 2, which subclasses will govern the allocation of assets within that priority category. The subclasses may be based only on a participant's longer service, older age, or disability, or any combination thereof.

(b) *Limitation.* Except as provided in paragraph (c) of this section, whenever the allocation within a priority category on the basis of the subclasses established by the plan increases or decreases the cumulative amount of assets that otherwise would be allocated to guaranteed benefits, the assets so shifted shall be reallocated to other participants' benefits within the priority category in accordance with the subclasses.

(c) *Exception for subclasses in effect on September 2, 1974.* A plan administrator may allocate assets to subclasses within any priority category, other than priority categories 1 and 2, without regard to the limitation in paragraph (b) of this section if, on September 2, 1974, the plan provided for allocation of plan assets upon termination of the plan based on a participant's longer service, older age, or disability, or any combination thereof, and—

(1) Such provisions are still in effect; or

(2) The plan, if subsequently amended to modify or remove those subclasses, is re-amended to re-establish the same subclasses on or before July 28, 1981.

(d) *Discrimination under Code.* Notwithstanding the provisions of paragraphs (a) through (c) of this section, allocation of assets to subclasses established under this section is permitted only to the extent that the allocation does not result in discrimination prohibited under the Code and regulations thereunder.

Allocation of Residual Assets

[¶ 15,473]

§ 4044.30 **[Reserved].**

Subpart B—Valuation of Benefits and Assets

General Provisions

[¶ 15,474]

§ 4044.41 **General valuation rules.** (a) *Valuation of benefits—*

(1) *Trusteed plans.* The plan administrator of a plan that has been or will be placed into trusteeship by the PBGC shall value plan benefits in accordance with §§ 4044.51 through 4044.57.

(2) *Non-trusteed plans.* The plan administrator of a non-trusteed plan shall value plan benefits in accordance with § 4044.71 through 4044.75. If a plan with respect to which PBGC has issued a Notice of Sufficiency is unable to satisfy all benefits assigned to priority categories 1 through 4 on the distribution date, the PBGC will place it into trusteeship and the plan administrator shall re-value the benefits in accordance with §§ 4044.51 through 4044.57. [See Note at beginning of part 4044.]

(b) *Valuation of assets.* Plan assets shall be valued at their fair market value, based on the method of valuation that most accurately reflects such fair market value.

Trusteed Plans

[¶ 15,475]

§ 4044.51 **Benefits to be valued.** (a) *Form of benefit.* The plan administrator shall determine the form of each benefit to be valued in accordance with the following rules:

(1) If a benefit is in pay status as of the valuation date, the plan administrator shall value the form of the benefit being paid.

(2) If a benefit is not in pay status as of the valuation date but a valid election with respect to the form of benefit has been made on or before the valuation date, the plan administrator shall value the form of benefit so elected.

(3) If a benefit is not in pay status as of the valuation date and no valid election with respect to the form of benefit has been made on or before the valuation date, the plan administrator shall value the form of benefit that, under the terms of the plan, is payable in the absence of a valid election.

(b) *Timing of benefit.* The plan administrator shall value benefits whose starting date is subject to election using the assumption specified in paragraph (b)(1) or (b)(2) of this section.

(1) *Where election made.* If a valid election of the starting date of a benefit has been made on or before the valuation date, the plan administrator shall assume that the starting date of the benefit is the starting date so elected.

(2) *Where no election made.* If no valid election of the starting date of a benefit has been made on or before the valuation date, the plan administrator shall assume that the starting date of the benefit is the later of—

(i) The expected retirement age, as determined under §§ 4044.55 through 4044.57, of the participant with respect to whom the benefit is payable, or

(ii) The valuation date.

[¶ 15,475A]

§ 4044.52 **Valuation of benefits.** The plan administrator shall value all benefits as of the valuation date by—

(a) Using the mortality assumptions prescribed by Sec. 4044.53 and the interest assumptions prescribed in appendix B to this part;

(b) Using interpolation methods, where necessary, at least as accurate as linear interpolation;

(c) Using valuation formulas that accord with generally accepted actuarial principles and practices; and

(d) Adjusting the values to reflect loading expenses in accordance with appendix C to this part.

[Amended 3/17/00 by 65 FR 14751; 12/2/2005 by 70 FR 72207.]

[¶ 15,475B]

§ 4044.53 **Mortality assumptions.** (a) *General rule.* Subject to paragraph (b) of this section (regarding certain death benefits), the plan administrator shall use the mortality factors prescribed in paragraphs (c), (d), (e), (f), and (g) of this section to value benefits under § 4044.52.

(b) *Certain death benefits.* If an annuity for one person is in pay status on the valuation date, and if the payment of a death benefit after the valuation date to another person, who need not be identifiable on the valuation date, depends in whole or in part on the death of the pay status annuitant, then the plan administrator shall value the death benefit using—

(1) The mortality rates that are applicable to the annuity in pay status under this section to represent the mortality of the pay status annuitant; and

(2) The mortality rates under paragraph (c) of this section to represent the mortality of the death beneficiary.

(c) *Healthy lives.* If the individual is not disabled under paragraph (f) of this section, the plan administrator will value the benefit using—

(1) For male participants, the rates in Table 1 of Appendix A to this part projected from 1994 to the calendar year in which the valuation date occurs plus 10 years using Scale AA from Table 2 of Appendix A to this part; and

(2) For female participants, the rates in Table 3 of Appendix A to this part projected from 1994 to the calendar year in which the valuation date occurs plus 10 years using Scale AA from Table 4 of Appendix A to this part.

(d) *Social Security disabled lives.* If the individual is Social Security disabled under paragraph (f)(1) of this section, the plan administrator will value the benefit using—

(1) For male participants, the rates in Table 5 of Appendix A to this part; and

(2) For female participants, the rates in Table 6 of Appendix A to this part.

(e) *Non-Social Security disabled lives.* If the individual is non-Social Security disabled under paragraph (f)(2) of this section, the plan administrator will value the benefit at each age using—

(1) For male participants, the lesser of—

(i) The rate determined from Table 1 of Appendix A to this part projected from 1994 to the calendar year in which the valuation date occurs plus 10 years using Scale AA from Table 2 of Appendix A to this part and setting the resulting table forward three years, or

(ii) The rate in Table 5 of Appendix A to this part.

(2) For female participants, the lesser of—

(i) The rate determined from Table 3 of Appendix A to this part projected from 1994 to the calendar year in which the valuation date occurs plus 10 years using Scale AA from Table 4 of Appendix A to this part and setting the resulting table forward three years, or

(ii) The rate in Table 6 of Appendix A to this part.

(f) *Definitions of disability.* (1) *Social Security disabled.* A participant is Social Security disabled if, on the valuation date, the participant is less than age 65 and has a benefit in pay status that—

(i) Is being received as a disability benefit under a plan provision requiring either receipt of or eligibility for Social Security disability benefits, or

(ii) Was converted under the plan's terms from a disability benefit under a plan provision requiring either receipt of or eligibility for Social Security disability benefits to an early or normal retirement benefit for any reason other than a change in the participant's health status.

(2) *Non-Social Security disabled.* A participant is non-Social Security disabled if, on the valuation date, the participant is less than age 65, is not Social Security disabled, and has a benefit in pay status that—

(i) Is being received as a disability benefit under the plan, or

(ii) Was converted under the plan's terms from a disability benefit to an early or normal retirement benefit for any reason other than a change in the participant's health status.

(g) *Contingent annuitant mortality during deferral period.* If a participant's joint and survivor benefit is valued as a deferred annuity, the mortality of the contingent annuitant during the deferral period will be disregarded.

[Revised 12/2/2005 by 70 FR 72207.]

[¶ 15,475C]

§ 4044.54 **Removed and Reserved**. [Removed and Reserved 3/17/00 by 65 FR 14751.]

[¶ 15,475D]

§ 4044.55 **Expected Retirement Age**. XRA when a participant must retire to receive a benefit.—

(a) *Applicability.* Except as provided in § 4044.57, the plan administrator shall determine the XRA under this section when plan provisions or established plan practice require a participant to retire from his or her job to begin receiving an early retirement benefit.

(b) *Data needed.* The plan administrator shall determine for each participant who is entitled to an early retirement benefit—

(1) The amount of the participant's monthly benefit payable at unreduced retirement age in the normal form payable under the terms of the plan or in the form validly elected by the participant before the termination date;

(2) The calendar year in which the participant reaches unreduced retirement age ("URA");

(3) The participant's URA; and

(4) The participant's earliest retirement age at the valuation date.

(c) *Procedure.* (1) The plan administrator shall determine whether a participant is in the high, medium or low retirement rate category using the applicable Selection of Retirement Rate Category Table in appendix D, based on the participant's benefit determined under paragraph (b)(1) of this section and the year in which the participant reaches URA.

(2) Based on the retirement rate category determined under paragraph (c)(1), the plan administrator shall determine the XRA from Table II-A, II-B or II-C, as appropriate, by using the participant's URA and earliest retirement age at valuation date.

[¶ 15,475E]

§ 4044.56 **XRA when a participant need not retire to receive a benefit**. (a) *Applicability.* Except as provided in § 4044.57, the plan administrator shall determine the XRA under this section when plan provisions or established plan practice do not require a participant to retire from his or her job to begin receiving his or her early retirement benefit.

(b) *Data needed.* The plan administrator shall determine for each participant—

(1) The participant's URA; and

(2) The participant's earliest retirement age at valuation date.

(c) *Procedure.* Participants in this case are always assigned to the high retirement rate category and therefore the plan administrator shall use Table II-C of appendix D to determine the XRA. The plan administrator shall determine the XRA from Table II-C by using the participant's URA and earliest retirement age at termination date.

[¶ 15,475F]

§ 4044.57 **Special rule for facility closing**. (a) *Applicability.* The plan administrator shall determine the XRA under this section, rather than § 4044.55 or § 4044.56, when both the conditions set forth in paragraphs (a)(1) and (a)(2) of this section exist.

(1) The facility at which the participant is or was employed permanently closed within one year before the valuation date, or is in the process of being permanently closed on the valuation date.

(2) The participant left employment at the facility less than one year before the valuation date or was still employed at the facility on the valuation date.

(b) *XRA.* The XRA is equal to the earliest retirement age at valuation date.

Non-Trusteed Plans

[¶ 15,476]

§ 4044.71 **Valuation of annuity benefits**. The value of a benefit which is to be paid as an annuity is the cost of purchasing the annuity on the date of distribution from an insurer under the qualifying bid.

[¶ 15,476A]

§ 4044.72 **Form of annuity to be valued**. (a) When both the participant and beneficiary are alive on the date of distribution, the form of annuity to be valued is—

(1) For a participant or beneficiary already receiving a monthly benefit, that form which is being received, or

(2) For a participant or beneficiary not receiving a monthly benefit, the normal annuity form payable under the plan or the optional form for which the participant has made a valid election pursuant to § 2617.4(c) of this chapter. [See Note at beginning of part 4044.]

(b) When the participant dies after the date of plan termination but before the date of distribution, the form of annuity to be valued is determined under paragraph (b)(1) or (b)(2) of this section:

(1) For a participant who was entitled to a deferred annuity—

(i) If the form was a single or joint life annuity, no benefit shall be valued; or

(ii) If the participant had made a valid election of a lump sum benefit before he or she died, the form to be valued is the lump sum.

(2) For a participant who was eligible for immediate retirement, and for a participant who was in pay status at the date of termination—

(i) If the form was a single life annuity, no benefit shall be valued;

(ii) If the form was an annuity for a period certain and life thereafter, the form to be valued is an annuity for the certain period;

(iii) If the form was a joint and survivor annuity, the form to be valued is a single life annuity payable to the beneficiary, unless the beneficiary has also died, in which case no benefit shall be valued;

(iv) If the form was an annuity for a period certain and joint and survivor thereafter, the form to be valued is an annuity for the certain period and the life of the beneficiary thereafter, unless the beneficiary has also died, in which case the form to be valued is an annuity for the certain period;

(v) If the form was a cash refund annuity, the form to be valued is the remaining lump sum death benefit; or

(vi) If the participant had elected a lump sum benefit before he or she died, the form to be valued is the lump sum.

(c) When the participant is still living and the named beneficiary or spouse dies after the date of termination but before the date of distribution, the form of annuity to be valued is determined under paragraph (c)(1) or (c)(2) of this section:

(1) For a participant entitled to a deferred annuity—

(i) If the form was a joint and survivor annuity, the form to be valued is a single life annuity payable to the participant; or

(ii) If the form was an annuity for a period certain and joint and survivor thereafter, the form to be valued is an annuity for the certain period and the life of the participant thereafter.

(2) For a participant eligible for immediate retirement and for a participant in pay status at the date of termination—

(i) If the form was a joint and survivor annuity, the form to be valued is a single life annuity payable to the participant; or

(ii) If the form was an annuity for a period certain and joint survivor thereafter annuity, the form to be valued is an annuity for the certain period and for the life of the participant thereafter.

[¶ 15,476B]

§ 4044.73 **Lump sums and other alternative forms of distribution in lieu of annuities**. (a) *Valuation.* (1) The value of the lump sum or other alternative form of distribution is the present value of the normal form of benefit provided by the plan payable at normal retirement age, determined as of the date of distribution using reasonable actuarial assumptions as to interest and mortality.

(2) If the participant dies before the date of distribution, but had elected a lump sum benefit, the present value shall be determined as if the participant were alive on the date of distribution.

(b) *Actuarial assumptions.* The plan administrator shall specify the actuarial assumptions used to determine the value calculated under paragraph (a) of this section when the plan administrator submits the benefit valuation data to the PBGC pursuant to § 2617.12 of part 2617 of this chapter. The same actuarial assumptions shall be used for all such calculations. The PBGC reserves the right to review the actuarial assumptions used and to re-value the benefits determined by the plan administrator if the actuarial assumptions are found to be unreasonable.

[See Note at beginning of part 4044.]

[¶ 15,476C]

§ 4044.74 **Withdrawal of employee contributions**. (a) If a participant has not started to receive monthly benefit payments on the date of distribution, the value of the lump sum which returns mandatory employee contributions is equal to the total amount of contributions made by the participant, plus interest that is payable to the participant under the terms of the plan, plus interest on that total amount from the date of termination to the date of distribution. The rate of interest credited on employee contributions up to the date of termination shall be the greater of the interest rate provided under the terms of the plan or the interest rate required under section 204(c) of ERISA or section 411(c) of the IRC.

(b) If a participant has started to receive monthly benefit payments on the date of distribution, part of which are attributable to his or her contributions, the value of the lump sum which returns employee contributions is equal to the excess of the amount described in paragraph (b)(1) of this section over the amount computed in paragraph (b)(2) of this section.

(1) The amount of accumulated mandatory employee contributions remaining in the plan as of the date of termination plus interest from the date of termination to the date of distribution.

(2) The excess of benefit payments made from the plan between date of plan termination and the date of distribution, over the amount of payments that would have been made if the employee contributions had been paid as a lump sum on the date of plan termination, with interest accumulated on the excess from the date of payment to the date of distribution.

(c) *Interest assumptions.* The interest rate used under this section to credit interest between the date of termination to the date of distribution shall be a reasonable rate and shall be the same for both paragraphs (a) and (b).

[¶ 15,476D]

§ 4044.75 **Other lump sum benefits**. The value of a lump sum benefit which is not covered under § 4044.73 or § 4044.74 is equal to—

(a) The value under the qualifying bid, if an insurer provides the benefit; or

(b) The present value of the benefit as of the date of distribution, determined using reasonable actuarial assumptions, if the benefit is to be distributed other than by the purchase of the benefit from an insurer. The PBGC reserves the right to review the actuarial assumptions as to reasonableness and re-value the benefit if the actuarial assumptions are unreasonable.

[See Note at beginning of part 4044.]

[¶ 15,476E]

§ 4044.75 **Appendix A to Part 4044—Mortality Rate Tables**

The mortality tables in this appendix set forth for each age x the probability qX that an individual aged x (in 1994, when using Table 1 or Table 3) will not survive to attain age x + 1. The projection scales in this appendix set forth for each age x the annual reduction AAX in the mortality rate at age x.

TABLE 1.—MORTALITY TABLE FOR HEALTHY MALE PARTICIPANTS
[94 GAM basic]

Age x	q_x
15	0.000371
16	0.000421
17	0.000463
18	0.000495
19	0.000521
20	0.000545
21	0.000570
22	0.000598
23	0.000633
24	0.000671
25	0.000711
26	0.000749
27	0.000782
28	0.000811
29	0.000838
30	0.000862
31	0.000883
32	0.000902
33	0.000912
34	0.000913
35	0.000915
36	0.000927
37	0.000958
38	0.001010
39	0.001075
40	0.001153
41	0.001243
42	0.001346
43	0.001454
44	0.001568
45	0.001697
46	0.001852
47	0.002042
48	0.002260
49	0.002501
50	0.002773
51	0.003088
52	0.003455
53	0.003854
54	0.004278
55	0.004758
56	0.005322
57	0.006001
58	0.006774
59	0.007623
60	0.008576
61	0.009663
62	0.010911
63	0.012335
64	0.013914
65	0.015629
66	0.017462
67	0.019391
68	0.021354

Age x	q_x
69	0.023364
70	0.025516
71	0.027905
72	0.030625
73	0.033549
74	0.036614
75	0.040012
76	0.043933
77	0.048570
78	0.053991
79	0.060066
80	0.066696
81	0.073780
82	0.081217
83	0.088721
84	0.096358
85	0.104559
86	0.113755
87	0.124377
88	0.136537
89	0.149949
90	0.164442
91	0.179849
92	0.196001
93	0.213325
94	0.231936
95	0.251189
96	0.270441
97	0.289048
98	0.306750
99	0.323976
100	0.341116
101	0.358560
102	0.376699
103	0.396884
104	0.418855
105	0.440585
106	0.460043
107	0.475200
108	0.485670
109	0.492807
110	0.497189
111	0.499394
112	0.500000
113	0.500000
114	0.500000
115	0.500000
116	0.500000
117	0.500000
118	0.500000
119	0.500000
120	1.000000

TABLE 2.—PROJECTION SCALE AA FOR HEALTHY MALE PARTICIPANTS

Age x	AA_x
15	0.019
16	0.019
17	0.019
18	0.019
19	0.019
20	0.019
21	0.018
22	0.017
23	0.015
24	0.013
25	0.010
26	0.006
27	0.005
28	0.005
29	0.005
30	0.005
31	0.005
32	0.005
33	0.005
34	0.005
35	0.005
36	0.005
37	0.005
38	0.006
39	0.007
40	0.008
41	0.009
42	0.010
43	0.011
44	0.012
45	0.013
46	0.014
47	0.015
48	0.016
49	0.017
50	0.018
51	0.019
52	0.020
53	0.020
54	0.020
55	0.019
56	0.018
57	0.017
58	0.016
59	0.016
60	0.016
61	0.015
62	0.015
63	0.014
64	0.014
65	0.014
66	0.013
67	0.013
68	0.014
69	0.014

Age x	AA_x
70	0.015
71	0.015
72	0.015
73	0.015
74	0.015
75	0.014
76	0.014
77	0.013
78	0.012
79	0.011
80	0.010
81	0.009
82	0.008
83	0.008
84	0.007
85	0.007
86	0.007
87	0.006
88	0.005
89	0.005
90	0.004
91	0.004
92	0.003
93	0.003
94	0.003
95	0.002
96	0.002
97	0.002
98	0.001
99	0.001
100	0.001
101	0.000
102	0.000
103	0.000
104	0.000
105	0.000
106	0.000
107	0.000
108	0.000
109	0.000
110	0.000
111	0.000
112	0.000
113	0.000
114	0.000
115	0.000
116	0.000
117	0.000
118	0.000
119	0.000
120	0.000

TABLE 3.—MORTALITY TABLE FOR HEALTHY FEMALE PARTICIPANTS
[94 GAM Basic]

Age x	q_x
15	0.000233
16	0.000261
17	0.000281
18	0.000293
19	0.000301
20	0.000305
21	0.000308
22	0.000311
23	0.000313
24	0.000313
25	0.000313
26	0.000316
27	0.000324
28	0.000338
29	0.000356
30	0.000377
31	0.000401
32	0.000427
33	0.000454
34	0.000482
35	0.000514
36	0.000550
37	0.000593
38	0.000643
39	0.000701
40	0.000763
41	0.000826
42	0.000888
43	0.000943
44	0.000992
45	0.001046
46	0.001111
47	0.001196
48	0.001297
49	0.001408
50	0.001536
51	0.001686
52	0.001864
53	0.002051
54	0.002241
55	0.002466
56	0.002755
57	0.003139
58	0.003612
59	0.004154
60	0.004773
61	0.005476
62	0.006271
63	0.007179
64	0.008194
65	0.009286
66	0.010423
67	0.011574
68	0.012648

Age x	q_x
69	0.013665
70	0.014763
71	0.016079
72	0.017748
73	0.019724
74	0.021915
75	0.024393
76	0.027231
77	0.030501
78	0.034115
79	0.038024
80	0.042361
81	0.047260
82	0.052853
83	0.058986
84	0.065569
85	0.072836
86	0.081018
87	0.090348
88	0.100882
89	0.112467
90	0.125016
91	0.138442
92	0.152660
93	0.167668
94	0.183524
95	0.200229
96	0.217783
97	0.236188
98	0.255605
99	0.276035
100	0.297233
101	0.318956
102	0.340960
103	0.364586
104	0.389996
105	0.415180
106	0.438126
107	0.456824
108	0.471493
109	0.483473
110	0.492436
111	0.498054
112	0.500000
113	0.500000
114	0.500000
115	0.500000
116	0.500000
117	0.500000
118	0.500000
119	0.500000
120	1.000000

TABLE 4.—PROJECTION SCALE AA FOR HEALTHY FEMALE PARTICIPANTS

Age x	AA_x
15	0.016
16	0.015
17	0.014
18	0.014
19	0.015
20	0.016
21	0.017
22	0.017
23	0.016
24	0.015
25	0.014
26	0.012
27	0.012
28	0.012
29	0.012
30	0.010
31	0.008
32	0.008
33	0.009
34	0.010
35	0.011
36	0.012
37	0.013
38	0.014
39	0.015
40	0.015
41	0.015
42	0.015
43	0.015
44	0.015
45	0.016
46	0.017
47	0.018
48	0.018
49	0.018
50	0.017
51	0.016
52	0.014
53	0.012
54	0.010
55	0.008
56	0.006
57	0.005
58	0.005
59	0.005
60	0.005
61	0.005
62	0.005
63	0.005
64	0.005
65	0.005
66	0.005
67	0.005
68	0.005
69	0.005

Age x	AA$_x$
70	0.005
71	0.006
72	0.006
73	0.007
74	0.007
75	0.008
76	0.008
77	0.007
78	0.007
79	0.007
80	0.007
81	0.007
82	0.007
83	0.007
84	0.007
85	0.006
86	0.005
87	0.004
88	0.004
89	0.003
90	0.003
91	0.003
92	0.003
93	0.002
94	0.002
95	0.002
96	0.002
97	0.001
98	0.001
99	0.001
100	0.001
101	0.000
102	0.000
103	0.000
104	0.000
105	0.000
106	0.000
107	0.000
108	0.000
109	0.000
110	0.000
111	0.000
112	0.000
113	0.000
114	0.000
115	0.000
116	0.000
117	0.000
118	0.000
119	0.000
120	0.000

TABLE 5.—MORTALITY TABLE FOR SOCIAL SECURITY DISABLED MALE PARTICIPANTS

Age x	q$_x$
15	0.022010
16	0.022502
17	0.023001
18	0.023519
19	0.024045
20	0.024583
21	0.025133
22	0.025697
23	0.026269
24	0.026857
25	0.027457
26	0.028071
27	0.028704
28	0.029345
29	0.029999
30	0.030661
31	0.031331
32	0.032006
33	0.032689
34	0.033405
35	0.034184
36	0.034981
37	0.035796
38	0.036634
39	0.037493
40	0.038373
41	0.039272
42	0.040189
43	0.041122
44	0.042071
45	0.043033
46	0.044007
47	0.044993
48	0.045989
49	0.046993
50	0.048004
51	0.049021
52	0.050042
53	0.051067
54	0.052093
55	0.053120
56	0.054144
57	0.055089
58	0.056068
59	0.057080
60	0.058118
61	0.059172
62	0.060232
63	0.061303
64	0.062429
65	0.063669
66	0.065082
67	0.066724
68	0.068642

Age x	q_x	Age x	q_x
69	0.070834	24	0.011468
70	0.073284	25	0.011974
71	0.075979	26	0.012502
72	0.078903	27	0.013057
73	0.082070	28	0.013632
74	0.085606	29	0.014229
75	0.088918	30	0.014843
76	0.092208	31	0.015473
77	0.095625	32	0.016103
78	0.099216	33	0.016604
79	0.103030	34	0.017121
80	0.107113	35	0.017654
81	0.111515	36	0.018204
82	0.116283	37	0.018770
83	0.121464	38	0.019355
84	0.127108	39	0.019957
85	0.133262	40	0.020579
86	0.139974	41	0.021219
87	0.147292	42	0.021880
88	0.155265	43	0.022561
89	0.163939	44	0.023263
90	0.173363	45	0.023988
91	0.183585	46	0.024734
92	0.194653	47	0.025504
93	0.206615	48	0.026298
94	0.219519	49	0.027117
95	0.234086	50	0.027961
96	0.248436	51	0.028832
97	0.263954	52	0.029730
98	0.280803	53	0.030655
99	0.299154	54	0.031609
100	0.319185	55	0.032594
101	0.341086	56	0.033608
102	0.365052	57	0.034655
103	0.393102	58	0.035733
104	0.427255	59	0.036846
105	0.469531	60	0.037993
106	0.521945	61	0.039176
107	0.586518	62	0.040395
108	0.665268	63	0.041653
109	0.760215	64	0.042950
110	1.000000	65	0.044287
		66	0.045666
		67	0.046828
		68	0.048070
		69	0.049584
		70	0.051331

TABLE 6.—MORTALITY TABLE FOR SOCIAL SECURITY DISABLED FEMALE
PARTICIPANTS

Age x	q_x	Age x	q_x
		71	0.053268
15	0.007777	72	0.055356
16	0.008120	73	0.057573
17	0.008476	74	0.059979
18	0.008852	75	0.062574
19	0.009243	76	0.065480
20	0.009650	77	0.068690
21	0.010076	78	0.072237
22	0.010521	79	0.076156
23	0.010984		

Age x	q_x		Age x	q_x
80	0.080480		98	0.266289
81	0.085243		99	0.284758
82	0.090480		100	0.303433
83	0.096224		101	0.327385
84	0.102508		102	0.359020
85	0.109368		103	0.395842
86	0.116837		104	0.438360
87	0.124948		105	0.487816
88	0.133736		106	0.545886
89	0.143234		107	0.614309
90	0.153477		108	0.694884
91	0.164498		109	0.789474
92	0.176332		110	1.000000
93	0.189011			
94	0.202571			
95	0.217045			
96	0.232467			
97	0.248870			

[Revised 12/2/2005 by 70 FR 72208.]

[¶ 15,476F]

§ 4044.75 **Appendix B to Part 4044: Interest Rates Used To Value Benefits**.

[This table sets forth, for each indicated calendar month, the interest rates (denoted by i_1, i_2, ..., and referred to generally as i_t) assumed to be in effect between specified anniversaries of a valuation date that occurs within that calendar month; those anniversaries are specified in the columns adjacent to the rates. The last listed rate is assumed to be in effect after the last listed anniversary date.] [Amended 3/17/00 by 65 FR 14751]

The values of i_t are:

For valuation dates occurring in the month —	i_t for t =		i_t for t =		i_t for t =	
Nov. 1993	.0560	1-25	.0525	> 25	N/A	N/A
Dec. 1993	.0560	1-25	.0525	> 25	N/A	N/A
Jan. 1994	.0590	1-25	.0525	> 25	N/A	N/A
Feb. 1994	.0590	1-25	.0525	> 25	N/A	N/A
March 1994	.0580	1-25	.0525	> 25	N/A	N/A
April 1994	.0620	1-25	.0525	> 25	N/A	N/A
May 1994	.0650	1-25	.0525	> 25	N/A	N/A
June 1994	.0670	1-25	.0525	> 25	N/A	N/A
July 1994	.0690	1-25	.0525	> 25	N/A	N/A
Aug. 1994	.0700	1-25	.0525	> 25	N/A	N/A
Sep. 1994	.0690	1-25	.0525	> 25	N/A	N/A
Oct. 1994	.0700	1-25	.0525	> 25	N/A	N/A
Nov. 1994	.0730	1-25	.0525	> 25	N/A	N/A
Dec. 1994	.0750	1-25	.0525	> 25	N/A	N/A

The values of i_t are:

For valuation dates occurring in the month —	i_t for t =		i_t for t =		i_t for t =	
Jan. 1995	.0750	1-20	.0575	> 20	N/A	N/A
Feb. 1995	.0730	1-20	.0575	> 20	N/A	N/A
March 1995	.0730	1-20	.0575	> 20	N/A	N/A
April 1995	.0710	1-20	.0575	> 20	N/A	N/A
May 1995	.0690	1-20	.0575	> 20	N/A	N/A
June 1995	.0680	1-20	.0575	> 20	N/A	N/A
July 1995	.0630	1-20	.0575	> 20	N/A	N/A
Aug. 1995	.0620	1-20	.0575	> 20	N/A	N/A
Sep. 1995	.0640	1-20	.0575	> 20	N/A	N/A
Oct. 1995	.0630	1-20	.0575	> 20	N/A	N/A
Nov. 1995	.0620	1-20	.0575	> 20	N/A	N/A
Dec. 1995	.0600	1-20	.0575	> 20	N/A	N/A

The values of i_t are:

For valuation dates occurring in the month —	i_t for t =		i_t for t =		i_t for t =	
Jan. 1996	.0560	1-20	.0475	> 20	N/A	N/A
Feb. 1996	.0540	1-20	.0475	> 20	N/A	N/A
March 1996	.0550	1-20	.0475	> 20	N/A	N/A
April 1996	.0580	1-20	.0475	> 20	N/A	N/A
May 1996	.0600	1-20	.0475	> 20	N/A	N/A
June 1996	.0620	1-20	.0475	> 20	N/A	N/A
July 1996	.0620	1-20	.0475	> 20	N/A	N/A
Aug. 1996	.0630	1-20	.0475	> 20	N/A	N/A
Sep. 1996	.0630	1-20	.0475	> 20	N/A	N/A
Oct. 1996	.0630	1-20	.0475	> 20	N/A	N/A
Nov. 1996	.0620	1-20	.0475	> 20	N/A	N/A
Dec. 1996	.0600	1-20	.0475	> 20	N/A	N/A

The values of i_t are:

For valuation dates occurring in the month —	i_t for t =		i_t for t =		i_t for t =	
Jan. 1997	.0580	1-25	.0500	> 25	N/A	N/A
Feb. 1997	.0590	1-25	.0500	> 25	N/A	N/A
March 1997	.0620	1-25	.0500	> 25	N/A	N/A
April 1997	.0610	1-25	.0500	> 25	N/A	N/A
May 1997	.0630	1-25	.0500	> 25	N/A	N/A
June 1997	.0640	1-25	.0500	> 25	N/A	N/A
July 1997	.0630	1-25	.0500	> 25	N/A	N/A
Aug. 1997	.0610	1-25	.0500	> 25	N/A	N/A
Sep. 1997	.0570	1-25	.0500	> 25	N/A	N/A
Oct. 1997	.0590	1-25	.0500	> 25	N/A	N/A
Nov. 1997	.0570	1-25	.0500	> 25	N/A	N/A
Dec. 1997	.0560	1-25	.0500	> 25	N/A	N/A

The values of i_t are:

For valuation dates occurring in the month —	i_t for t =		i_t for t =		i_t for t =	
Jan. 1998	.0560	1-25	.0525	> 25	N/A	N/A
Feb. 1998	.0550	1-25	.0525	> 25	N/A	N/A
March 1998	.0550	1-25	.0525	> 25	N/A	N/A
April 1998	.0550	1-25	.0525	> 25	N/A	N/A
May 1998	.0560	1-25	.0525	> 25	N/A	N/A
June 1998	.0560	1-25	.0525	> 25	N/A	N/A
July 1998	.0550	1-25	.0525	> 25	N/A	N/A
Aug. 1998	.0540	1-25	.0525	> 25	N/A	N/A
Sep. 1998	.0540	1-25	.0525	> 25	N/A	N/A
Oct. 1998	.0540	1-25	.0525	> 25	N/A	N/A
Nov. 1998	.0530	1-25	.0525	> 25	N/A	N/A
Dec. 1998	.0540	1-25	.0525	> 25	N/A	N/A

The values of i_t are:

For valuation dates occurring in the month —	i_t for t =		i_t for t =		i_t for t =	
Jan. 1999	.0530	1-20	.0525	> 20	N/A	N/A
Feb. 1999	.0540	1-20	.0525	> 20	N/A	N/A
March 1999	.0530	1-20	.0525	> 20	N/A	N/A
April 1999	.0560	1-20	.0525	> 20	N/A	N/A
May 1999	.0570	1-20	.0525	> 20	N/A	N/A
June 1999	.0570	1-20	.0525	> 20	N/A	N/A

The values of i_t are:

For valuation dates occurring in the month —	i_t for $t =$		i_t for $t =$		i_t for $t =$	
July 1999	.0600	1-20	.0525	> 20	N/A	N/A
Aug. 1999	.0630	1-20	.0525	> 20	N/A	N/A
Sep. 1999	.0630	1-20	.0525	> 20	N/A	N/A
Oct. 1999	.0630	1-20	.0525	> 20	N/A	N/A
Nov. 1999	.0630	1-20	.0525	> 20	N/A	N/A
Dec. 1999	.0650	1-20	.0525	> 20	N/A	N/A

The values of i_t are:

For valuation dates occurring in the month —	i_t for $t =$		i_t for $t =$		i_t for $t =$	
Jan. 2000	.0690	1-25	.0625	> 25	N/A	N/A
Feb. 2000	.0710	1-25	.0625	> 25	N/A	N/A
March 2000	.0710	1-25	.0625	> 25	N/A	N/A
April 2000	.0710	1-25	.0625	> 25	N/A	N/A
May 2000	.0700	1-25	.0625	> 25	N/A	N/A
June 2000	.0710	1-25	.0625	> 25	N/A	N/A
July 2000	.0740	1-25	.0625	> 25	N/A	N/A
Aug. 2000[1]	.0710	1-25	.0625	> 25	N/A	N/A
Sep. 2000[2]	.0700	1-25	.0625	> 25	N/A	N/A
Oct. 2000[3]	.0700	1-25	.0625	> 25	N/A	N/A
Nov. 2000[4]	.0710	1-25	.0625	> 25	N/A	N/A
Dec. 2000[5]	.0700	1-25	.0625	> 25	N/A	N/A

The values of i_t are:

For valuation dates occurring in the month —	i_t for $t =$		i_t for $t =$		i_t for $t =$	
Jan. 2001[6]	.0670	1-20	.0625	> 20	N/A	N/A
Feb. 2001[7]	.0650	1-20	.0625	> 20	N/A	N/A
Mar. 2001[8]	.0640	1-20	.0625	> 20	N/A	N/A
Apr. 2001[9]	.0640	1-20	.0625	> 20	N/A	N/A
May 2001[10]	.0640	1-20	.0625	> 20	N/A	N/A
June 2001[11]	.0660	1-20	.0625	> 20	N/A	N/A
July 2001[12]	.0660	1-20	.0625	> 20	N/A	N/A
Aug. 2001[13]	.0640	1-20	.0625	> 20	N/A	N/A
Sep. 2001[14]	.0630	1-20	.0625	> 20	N/A	N/A
Oct. 2001[15]	.0610	1-20	.0625	> 20	N/A	N/A
Nov. 2001[16]	.0650	1-20	.0625	> 20	N/A	N/A
Dec. 2001[17]	.0610	1-20	.0625	> 20	N/A	N/A

The values of i_t are:

For valuation dates occurring in the month —	i_t for $t =$		i_t for $t =$		i_t for $t =$	
Jan. 2002[18]	.0580	1-25	.0425	> 25	N/A	N/A
Feb. 2002[19]	.0580	1-25	.0425	> 25	N/A	N/A
Mar. 2002[20]	.0560	1-25	.0425	> 25	N/A	N/A
Apr. 2002[21]	.0550	1-25	.0425	> 25	N/A	N/A
May 2002[22]	.0590	1-25	.0425	> 25	N/A	N/A
June 2002[23]	.0570	1-25	.0425	> 25	N/A	N/A
July 2002[24]	.0570	1-25	.0425	> 25	N/A	N/A
Aug. 2002[25]	.0550	1-25	.0425	> 25	N/A	N/A
Sep. 2002[26]	.0540	1-25	.0425	> 25	N/A	N/A
Oct. 2002[27]	.0530	1-25	.0425	> 25	N/A	N/A
Nov. 2002[28]	.0500	1-25	.0425	> 25	N/A	N/A
Dec. 2002[29]	.0530	1-25	.0425	> 25	N/A	N/A

The values of i_t are:

For valuation dates occurring in the month —	i_t for t =		i_t for t =		i_t for t =	
Jan. 2003[30]	.0530	1-20	.0525	> 20	N/A	N/A
Feb. 2003[31]	.0510	1-20	.0525	> 20	N/A	N/A
Mar. 2003[32]	.0510	1-20	.0525	> 20	N/A	N/A
Apr. 2003[33]	.0490	1-20	.0525	> 20	N/A	N/A
May 2003[34]	.0490	1-20	.0525	> 20	N/A	N/A
June 2003[35]	.0470	1-20	.0525	> 20	N/A	N/A
July 2003[36]	.0430	1-20	.0525	> 20	N/A	N/A
Aug. 2003[37]	.0440	1-20	.0525	> 20	N/A	N/A
Sep. 2003[38]	.0490	1-20	.0525	> 20	N/A	N/A
Oct. 2003[39]	.0490	1-20	.0525	> 20	N/A	N/A
Nov. 2003[40]	.04960	1-20	.0525	> 20	N/A	N/A
Dec. 2003[41]	.0470	1-20	.0525	> 20	N/A	N/A

The values of i_t are:

For valuation dates occurring in the month —	i_t for t =		i_t for t =		i_t for t =	
Jan. 2004[42]	.0420	1-20	.0500	> 20	N/A	N/A
Feb. 2004[43]	.0410	1-20	.0500	> 20	N/A	N/A
Mar. 2004[44]	.0410	1-20	.0500	> 20	N/A	N/A
Apr. 2004[45]	.0400	1-20	.0500	> 20	N/A	N/A
May 2004[46]	.0390	1-20	.0500	> 20	N/A	N/A
June 2004[47]	.0430	1-20	.0500	> 20	N/A	N/A
July 2004[48]	.0450	1-20	.0500	> 20	N/A	N/A
Aug. 2004[49]	.0430	1-20	.0500	> 20	N/A	N/A
Sep. 2004[50]	.0420	1-20	.0500	> 20	N/A	N/A
Oct. 2004[51]	.0400	1-20	.0500	> 20	N/A	N/A
Nov. 2004[52]	.0380	1-20	.0500	> 20	N/A	N/A
Dec. 2004[53]	.0380	1-20	.0500	> 20	N/A	N/A

The values of i_t are:

For valuation dates occurring in the month —	i_t for t =		i_t for t =		i_t for t =	
Jan. 2005[54]	.0410	1-20	.0475	> 20	N/A	N/A
Feb. 2005[55]	.0400	1-20	.0475	> 20	N/A	N/A
Mar. 2005[56]	.0380	1-20	.0475	> 20	N/A	N/A
Apr. 2005[57]	.0380	1-20	.0475	> 20	N/A	N/A
May 2005[58]	.0390	1-20	.0475	> 20	N/A	N/A
June 2005[59]	.0370	1-20	.0475	> 20	N/A	N/A
July 2005[60]	.0360	1-20	.0475	> 20	N/A	N/A
Aug. 2005[61]	.0340	1-20	.0475	> 20	N/A	N/A
Sep. 2005[62]	.0360	1-20	.0475	> 20	N/A	N/A
Oct. 2005[63]	.0350	1-20	.0475	> 20	N/A	N/A
Nov. 2005[64]	.0370	1-20	.0475	> 20	N/A	N/A
Dec. 2005[65]	.0400	1-20	.0475	> 20	N/A	N/A

The values of i_t are:

For valuation dates occurring in the month —	i_t for t =		i_t for t =		i_t for t =	
Jan. 2006[66]	.5700	1-20	.0475	> 20	N/A	N/A

[1] 65 FR 43694, 7/14/2000.
[2] 65 FR 49737, 8/15/2000.
[3] 65 FR 55896, 9/15/2000.
[4] 65 FR 60859, 10/13/2000.

[5] 65 FR 68892, 11/15/2000.
[6] 65 FR 78415, 12/15/2000.
[7] 66 FR 2822, 1/12/2001.
[8] 66 FR 10365, 2/15/2001.
[9] 66 FR 15031, 3/15/2001.
[10] 66 FR 19089, 4/13/2001.
[11] 66 FR 26791, 5/15/2001.
[12] 66 FR 32543, 6/15/2001.
[13] 66 FR 36702, 7/13/2001.
[14] 66 FR 42737, 8/15/2001.
[15] 66 FR 47885, 9/14/2001.
[16] 66 FR 52315, 10/15/2001.
[17] 66 FR 57369, 11/15/2001.
[18] 66 FR 64744, 12/14/2001.
[19] 67 FR 1861, 1/15/2002.
[20] 67 FR 7076, 2/15/2002.
[21] 67 FR 11572, 3/15/2002.
[22] 67 FR 18112, 4/15/2002.
[23] 67 FR 34610, 5/15/2002.
[24] 67 FR 40850, 6/14/2002.
[25] 67 FR 46376, 7/15/2002.
[26] 67 FR 53307, 8/15/2002.
[27] 67 FR 57949, 9/13/2002.
[28] 67 FR 63544, 10/15/2002.
[29] 67 FR 69121, 11/15/2002.
[30] 67 FR 76682, 12/13/2002.
[31] 68 FR 1965, 1/15/2003.
[32] 68 FR 7419, 2/14/2003.
[33] 68 FR 12303, 3/14/2003.
[34] 68 FR 18122, 4/15/2003.
[35] 68 FR 26206, 5/15/2003.
[36] 68 FR 35294, 6/13/2003.
[37] 68 FR 41714, 7/15/2003.
[38] 68 FR 48787, 8/15/2003.
[39] 68 FR 53880, 9/15/2003.
[40] 68 FR 59315, 10/15/2003.
[41] 68 FR 64525, 11/14/2003.
[42] 68 FR 69606, 12/15/2003.
[43] 69 FR 2299, 1/15/2004.
[44] 69 FR 7119, 2/13/2004.
[45] 69 FR 12072, 3/15/2004.
[46] 69 FR 20079, 4/15/2004.
[47] 69 FR 26769, 5/14/2004.
[48] 69 FR 33302, 6/15/2004.
[49] 69 FR 42333, 7/15/2004.
[50] 69 FR 50070, 8/13/2004.
[50] 69 FR 50070, 8/13/2004.
[51] 69 FR 55500, 9/15/2004.
[52] 69 FR 61150, 10/15/2004.
[53] 69 FR 65543, 11/15/2004.
[54] 69 FR 74973, 12/15/2004.
[55] 70 FR 2568, 1/14/2005.
[56] 70 FR 7651, 2/15/2005.
[57] 70 FR 12585, 3/15/2005.
[58] 70 FR 19890, 4/15/2005.
[59] 70 FR 25470, 5/13/2005.
[60] 70 FR 34655, 6/15/2005.
[61] 70 FR 40882, 7/15/2005.
[62] 70 FR 47725, 8/15/2005.
[63] 70 FR 54477, 9/15/2005.
[64] 70 FR 60002, 10/14/2005.
[65] 70 FR 69277, 11/15/2005.
[66] 70 FR 74200, 12/15/2005.

[¶ 15,476G]

§ 4044.75 Appendix C to Part 4044: Loading Assumptions.

If the total value of the plan's benefit liabilities (as defined in 29 U.S.C. Sec. 1301(a)(16)), exclusive of the loading charge, is—		The loading charge equals—
greater than	but less than or equal to	
$0	$200,000	5% of the total value of the plan's benefits, plus $200 for each plan participant.

If the total value of the plan's benefit liabilities (as defined in 29 U.S.C. Sec. 1301(a)(16)), exclusive of the loading charge, is—

greater than	but less than or equal to
$200,000	————

The loading charge equals—

$10,000, plus a percentage of the excess of the total value over $200,000, plus $200 for each plan participant; the percentage is equal to 1% + [(P%-7.50%)/10], where P% is the initial rate, expressed as a percentage, set forth in appendix B of this part for the valuation of benefits. [Amended 3/17/00 by 65 FR 14751.]

[¶ 15,476H]

§ 4044.75 **Appendix D to Part 4044: Tables Used To Determine Expected Retirement Age.**

TABLE I-06.—SELECTION OF RETIREMENT RATE CATEGORY
[For plans with valuation dates after December 31, 2005, and before January 1, 2007]

Participant reaches URA in year—	Participant's retirement rate category is—			
	Low[1] if monthly benefit at URA is less than—	Medium[2] if monthly benefit at URA is		High[3] if monthly benefit is greater than—
		From	To	
2007	500	500	2,113	2,113
2008	512	512	2,164	2,164
2009	524	524	2,216	2,216
2010	536	536	2,269	2,269
2011	549	549	2,324	2,324
2012	562	562	2,379	2,379
2013	576	576	2,437	2,437
2014	590	590	2,495	2,495
2015	604	604	2,555	2,555
2016 or later	618	618	2,616	2,616

[1] Table II-A.
[2] Table II-B.
[3] Table II-C.

Table II-A.—Expected Retirement Ages for Individuals in the Low Category

Participant's earliest retirement age at valuation date.	Unreduced retirement age										
	60	61	62	63	64	65	66	67	68	69	70
42	53	53	53	54	54	54	54	54	54	54	54
43	53	54	54	54	55	55	55	55	55	55	55
44	54	54	55	55	55	55	55	56	56	56	56
45	54	55	55	56	56	56	56	56	56	56	56
46	55	55	56	56	56	57	57	57	57	57	57
47	56	56	56	57	57	57	57	57	57	57	57
48	56	57	57	57	58	58	58	58	58	58	58
49	56	57	58	58	58	58	59	59	59	59	59
50	57	57	58	58	59	59	59	59	59	59	59
51	57	58	58	59	59	60	60	60	60	60	60
52	58	58	59	59	60	60	60	60	60	60	60
53	58	59	59	60	60	61	61	61	61	61	61
54	58	59	60	60	61	61	61	61	61	61	61
55	59	59	60	61	61	61	62	62	62	62	62
56	59	60	60	61	61	62	62	62	62	62	62
57	59	60	61	61	62	62	62	62	62	62	62
58	59	60	61	61	62	62	63	63	63	63	63
59	59	60	61	62	62	63	63	63	63	63	63
60	60	60	61	62	62	63	63	63	63	63	63
61		61	61	62	63	63	63	63	64	64	64
62			62	63	63	63	63	64	64	64	64
63				63	63	63	64	64	65	65	65

Participant's earliest retirement age at valuation date.	Unreduced retirement age										
	60	61	62	63	64	65	66	67	68	69	70
64	..	..	..	..	64	64	65	65	65	65	65
65	..	..	..	..	..	65	65	65	65	65	65
66	..	..	..	..	..	..	66	66	66	66	66
67	..	..	..	..	..	..	..	67	67	67	67
68	..	..	..	..	..	..	..	..	68	68	68
69	..	..	..	..	..	..	..	..	..	69	69
70	..	..	..	..	..	..	..	..	..	..	70

Table II-B.—Expected Retirement Ages for Individuals in the Medium Category

Participant's earliest retirement age at valuation date.	Unreduced retirement age										
	60	61	62	63	64	65	66	67	68	69	70
42	49	49	49	49	49	49	49	49	49	49	49
43	50	50	50	50	50	50	50	50	50	50	50
44	50	51	51	51	51	51	51	51	51	51	51
45	51	51	52	52	52	52	52	52	52	52	52
46	52	52	52	53	53	53	53	53	53	53	53
47	53	53	53	53	53	54	54	54	54	54	54
48	54	54	54	54	54	54	54	54	54	54	54
49	54	55	55	55	55	55	55	55	55	55	55
50	55	55	56	56	56	56	56	56	56	56	56
51	56	56	56	57	57	57	57	57	57	57	57
52	56	57	57	57	57	58	58	58	58	58	58
53	57	57	58	58	58	58	58	58	58	58	58
54	57	58	58	59	59	59	59	59	59	59	59
55	58	58	59	59	59	60	60	60	60	60	60
56	58	59	59	60	60	60	60	60	60	60	60
57	59	59	60	60	61	61	61	61	61	61	61
58	59	60	60	61	61	61	61	61	61	61	61
59	59	60	61	61	62	62	62	62	62	62	62
60	60	60	61	62	62	62	62	62	62	62	62
61	..	61	61	62	62	63	63	63	63	63	63
62	..	..	62	62	62	63	63	63	63	63	63
63	..	..	..	63	63	64	64	64	64	64	64
64	..	..	..	..	64	64	64	64	64	64	64
65	..	..	..	..	..	65	65	65	65	65	65
66	..	..	..	..	..	..	66	66	66	66	66
67	..	..	..	..	..	..	..	67	67	67	67
68	..	..	..	..	..	..	..	..	68	68	68
69	..	..	..	..	..	..	..	..	..	69	69
70	..	..	..	..	..	..	..	..	..	..	70

Table II-C.—Expected Retirement Ages for Individuals in the High Category

Participant's earliest retirement age at valuation date.	Unreduced retirement age										
	60	61	62	63	64	65	66	67	68	69	70
42	46	46	46	46	46	47	47	47	47	47	47
43	47	47	47	47	47	47	47	47	47	47	47
44	48	48	48	48	48	48	48	48	48	48	48
45	49	49	49	49	49	49	49	49	49	49	49
46	50	50	50	50	50	50	50	50	50	50	50
47	51	51	51	51	51	51	51	51	51	51	51
48	52	52	52	52	52	52	52	52	52	52	52
49	53	53	53	53	53	53	53	53	53	53	53
50	54	54	54	54	54	54	54	54	54	54	54
51	54	55	55	55	55	55	55	55	55	55	55
52	55	55	56	56	56	56	56	56	56	56	56

					Unreduced retirement age						
Participant's earliest retirement age at valuation date.	60	61	62	63	64	65	66	67	68	69	70
53	56	56	56	57	57	57	57	57	57	57	57
54	57	57	57	57	57	58	58	58	58	58	58
55	57	58	58	58	58	58	58	58	58	58	58
56	58	58	59	59	59	59	59	59	59	59	59
57	58	59	59	60	60	60	60	60	60	60	60
58	59	59	60	60	60	60	61	61	61	61	61
59	59	60	60	61	61	61	61	61	61	61	61
60	60	60	61	61	61	62	62	62	62	62	62
61		61	61	62	62	62	62	62	62	62	62
62			62	62	62	62	62	62	62	62	62
63				63	63	63	64	64	64	64	64
64					64	64	64	64	64	64	64
65						65	65	65	65	65	65
66							66	66	66	66	66
67								67	67	67	67
68									68	68	68
69										69	69
70											70

[¶ 15,480]
RECAPTURE OF CERTAIN PAYMENTS

Act Sec. 4045. (a) Except as provided in subsection (c), the trustee is authorized to recover for the benefit of a plan from a participant the recoverable amount (as defined in subsection (b)) of all payments from the plan to him which commenced within the 3-year period immediately preceding the time the plan is terminated.

Act Sec. 4045. (b) For purposes of subsection (a) the recoverable amount is the excess of the amount determined under paragraph (1) over the amount determined under paragraph (2).

(1) The amount determined under this paragraph is the sum of the amount of the actual payments received by the participant within the 3-year period.

(2) The amount determined under this paragraph is the sum of—

(A) the sum of the amount such participant would have received during each consecutive 12-month period within the 3 years if the participant received the benefit in the form described in paragraph (3),

(B) the sum for each of the consecutive 12-month periods of the lesser of—

(i) the excess, if any, of $10,000 over the benefit in the form described in paragraph (3), or

(ii) the excess of the actual payment, if any, over the benefit in the form described in paragraph (3), and

(C) the present value at the time of termination of the participant's future benefits guaranteed under this title as if the benefits commenced in the form described in paragraph (3).

(3) The form of benefit for purposes of this subsection shall be the monthly benefit the participant would have received during the consecutive 12-month period, if he had elected at the time of the first payment made during the 3-year period, to receive his interest in the plan as a monthly benefit in the form of a life annuity commencing at the time of such first payment.

Act Sec. 4045. (c) (1) In the event of a distribution described in section 4043(b)(7) the 3-year period referred to in subsection (b) shall not end sooner than the date on which the corporation is notified of the distribution.

(2) The trustee shall not recover any payment made from a plan after or on account of the death of a participant, or to a participant who is disabled (within the meaning of section 72(m)(7) of the Internal Revenue Code of 1986).

(3) The corporation is authorized to waive, in whole or in part, the recovery of any amount which the trustee is authorized to recover for the benefit of a plan under this section in any case in which it determines that substantial economic hardship would result to the participant or his beneficiaries from whom such amount is recoverable.

Amendment

P.L. 101-239, §7891(a)(1):

Titles I, III, and IV of ERISA (other than sections 3(37)(E), 301(a)(7), and 308, the last sentence of section 408(d), and sections 414(c), 4001(a)(3)(ii), and 4303) are each amended by striking "Internal Revenue Code of 1954" each place it appears and inserting "Internal Revenue Code of 1986" effective October 22, 1986.

[¶ 15,490]
REPORTS TO TRUSTEE

Act Sec. 4046. The corporation and the plan administrator of any plan to be terminated under this subtitle shall furnish to the trustee such information as the corporation or the plan administrator has and, to the extent practicable, can obtain regarding—

(1) the amount of benefits payable with respect to each participant under a plan to be terminated,

(2) the amount of basic benefits guaranteed under section 4022 or 4022A which are payable with respect to each participant in the plan,

(3) the present value, as of the time of termination, of the aggregate amount of basic benefits payable under section 4022 or 4022A (determined without regard to section 4022B),

(4) the fair market value of the assets of the plan at the time of termination,

(5) the computations under section 4044, and all actuarial assumptions under which the items described in paragraphs (1) through (4) were computed, and

(6) any other information with respect to the plan the trustee may require in order to terminate the plan.

Amendment

P.L. 96-364, §403(e):

Amended Sec. 4046 by inserting "or 4022A" after "4022" in paragraphs (2) and (3) and by inserting "basic" after "benefits" in paragraphs (2) and (3) and by inserting "4022B" in place of "4022(b)(5)" in paragraph (3), effective September 26, 1980.

[¶ 15,500]
RESTORATION OF PLANS

Act Sec. 4047. Whenever the corporation determines that a plan which is to be terminated under section 4041 or 4042, or which is in the process of being terminated under section 4041 or 4042, should not be terminated under section 4041 or 4042 as a result of such circumstances as the corporation determines to be relevant, the corporation is authorized to cease any activities undertaken to terminate the plan, and to take whatever action is necessary and within its power to restore the plan to its status prior to the determination that the plan was to be terminated under section 4041 or 4042. In the case of a plan which has been terminated under section 4041 or 4042 the corporation is authorized in any such case in which the corporation determines such action to be appropriate and consistent with its duties under this title, to take such action as may be necessary to restore the plan to its pretermination status, including, but not limited to, the transfer to the employer or a plan administrator of control of part or all of the remaining assets and liabilities of the plan.

Amendments

P.L. 101-239, §7893(g)(1):

Amended ERISA Sec. 4047 in the first sentence by striking "under this subtitle" effective April 7, 1986.

P.L. 99-272:

Act Sec. 11016(a)(3) amended ERISA Sec. 4047 by inserting "under section 4041 or 4042" after "terminated" each place it appears in the first sentence and by striking out "section 4042" and inserting "section 4041 or 4042" in the second sentence.

These changes take effect on April 7, 1986.

Regulations

The following regulations were adopted by the Pension Benefit Guaranty Corporation on July 1, 1996 (61 FR 34002). Prior to July 1, 1996, PBGC regulations were under Chapter XXVI of Title 29 of the Code of Federal Regulations. Effective July 1, 1996, PBGC regulations were moved to Chapter XL, and were renumbered and reorganized.

[¶ 15,501]

§4047.1 **Purpose and scope.** Section 4047 of ERISA gives the PBGC broad authority to take any necessary actions in furtherance of a plan restoration order issued pursuant to section 4047. This part (along with Treasury regulation 26 CFR 1.412(c)(1)-3) describes certain legal obligations that arise incidental to a plan restoration under section 4047. This part also establishes procedures with respect to these obligations that are intended to facilitate the orderly transition of a restored plan from terminated (or terminating) status to ongoing status, and to help ensure that the restored plan will continue to be ongoing consistent with the best interests of the plan's participants and beneficiaries and the single-employer insurance program. This part applies to terminated and terminating single-employer plans (except for plans terminated and terminating under ERISA section 4041(b)) with respect to which the PBGC has issued or is issuing a plan restoration order pursuant to ERISA section 4047.

[¶ 15,501A]

§4047.2 **Definitions.** The following terms are defined in §4001.2 of this chapter: *controlled group, ERISA, IRS, PBGC, plan, plan administrator, plan year,* and *single-employer plan.*

[¶ 15,501B]

§4047.3 **Funding of restored plan.** (a) *General.* Whenever the PBGC issues or has issued a plan restoration order under ERISA section 4047, it shall issue to the plan sponsor a restoration payment schedule order in accordance with the rules of this section. PBGC, through its Executive Director, shall also issue a certification to its Board of Directors and the IRS, as described in paragraph (c) of this section. If more than one plan is or has been restored, the PBGC shall issue a separate restoration payment schedule order and separate certification with respect to each restored plan.

(b) *Restoration payment schedule order.* A restoration payment schedule order shall set forth a schedule of payments sufficient to amortize the initial restoration amortization base described in paragraph (b) of 26 CFR 1.412(c)(1)-3 over a period extending no more than 30 years after the initial post-restoration valuation date, as defined in paragraph (a)(1) of 26 CFR 1.412(c)(1)-3. The restoration payment schedule shall be consistent with the requirements of 26 CFR 1.412(c)(1)-3 and may require payments at intervals of less than one year, as determined by the PBGC. The PBGC may, in its discretion, amend the restoration payment schedule at any time, consistent with the requirements of 26 CFR 1.412(c)(1)-3.

(c) *Certification.* The Executive Director's certification to the Board of Directors and the IRS pursuant to paragraph (a) of this section shall state that the PBGC has reviewed the funding of the plan, the financial condition of the plan sponsor and its controlled group members, the payments required under the restoration payment sched-ule (taking into account the availability of deferrals as permitted under paragraph (c)(4) of 26 CFR 1.412(c)(1)-3) and any other factor that the PBGC deems relevant, and, based on that review, determines that it is in the best interests of the plan's participants and beneficiaries and the single-employer insurance program that the restored plan not be reterminated.

(d) *Periodic PBGC review.* As long as a restoration payment schedule order issued under this section is in effect, the PBGC shall review annually the funding status of the plan with respect to which the order applies. As part of this review, the PBGC, through its Executive Director, shall issue a certification in the form described in paragraph (c) of this section. As a result of its funding review, PBGC may amend the restoration payment schedule, consistent with the requirements of paragraph (c)(2) of 26 CFR 1.412(c)(1)-3.

[¶ 15,501C]

§4047.4 **Payment of premiums.** (a) *General.* Upon restoration of a plan pursuant to ERISA section 4047, the obligation to pay PBGC premiums pursuant to ERISA section 4007 is reinstated as of the date on which the plan was trusteed under section 4042 of ERISA. Except as otherwise specifically provided in paragraphs (b) and (c) of this section, the amount of the outstanding premiums owed shall be computed and paid by the plan administrator in accordance with part 4006 of this chapter (Premium Rates) and the forms and instructions issued pursuant thereto, as in effect for the plan years for which premiums are owed.

(b) *Notification of premiums owed.* Whenever the PBGC issues or has issued a plan restoration order, it shall send a written notice to the plan administrator of the restored plan advising the plan administrator of the plan year(s) for which premiums are owed. PBGC will include with the notice the necessary premium payment forms and instructions. The notice shall prescribe the payment due dates for the outstanding premiums.

(c) *Methods for determining variable rate portion of the premium.* In general, the variable rate portion of the outstanding premiums shall be determined in accordance with the premium regulation and forms, as provided in paragraph (a) of this section, except that for any plan year following a plan year for which Form 5500, Schedule B was not filed because the plan was terminated, the alternative calculation method in §4006.4(c) of this chapter may not be used.

[¶ 15,501D]

§4047.5 **Repayment of PBGC payments of guaranteed benefits.** (a) *General.* Upon restoration of a plan pursuant to ERISA section 4047, amounts paid by the PBGC from its single-employer insurance fund (the fund established pursuant to ERISA section 4005(a)) to pay guaranteed benefits and related expenses under the plan while it was terminated are a debt of the restored plan. The terms and conditions for payment of this debt shall be determined by the PBGC.

(b) *Repayment terms.* The PBGC shall prescribe reasonable terms and conditions for payment of the debt described in paragraph (a) of this section, including the number, amount and commencement date of the payments. In establishing the terms, PBGC will consider the cash needs of the plan, the timing and amount of contributions owed to the plan, the liquidity of plan assets, the interests of the single-employer insurance program, and any other factors PBGC deems relevant. PBGC may, in its discretion, revise any of the payment terms and conditions,

upon written notice to the plan administrator in accordance with paragraph (c) of this section.

(c) *Notification to plan administrator.* Whenever the PBGC issues or has issued a plan restoration order, it shall send a written notice to the plan administrator of the restored plan advising the plan administrator of the amount owed the PBGC pursuant to paragraph (a) of this section. The notice shall also include the terms and conditions for payment of this debt, as established under paragraph (b) of this section.

[¶ 15,510]
DATE OF TERMINATION

Act Sec. 4048. (a) For purposes of this title, the termination date of a single-employer plan is—

(1) in the case of a plan terminated in a standard termination in accordance with the provisions of section 4041(b), the termination date proposed in the notice provided under section 4041(a)(2),

(2) in the case of a plan terminated in a distress termination in accordance with the provisions of section 4041(c), the date established by the plan administrator and agreed to by the corporation,

(3) in the case of a plan terminated in accordance with the provisions of section 4042, the date established by the corporation and agreed to by the plan administrator, or

(4) In the case of a plan terminated under section 4041(c) or 4042 in any case in which no agreement is reached between the plan administrator and the corporation (or the trustee), the date established by the court.

Act Sec. 4048. (b) For purposes of this title, the date of termination of a multiemployer plan is—

(1) in the case of a plan terminated in accordance with the provisions of section 4041A, the date determined under subsection (b) of that section; or

(2) in the case of a plan terminated in accordance with the provisions of section 4042, the date agreed to between the plan administrator and the corporation (or the trustee appointed under section 4042(b)(2), if any), or, if no agreement is reached, the date established by the court.

Amendments

P.L. 99-272:

Act Sec. 11016(a)(4) amended ERISA Sec. 4048(a) by redesignating paragraphs (1) through (3) as paragraphs (2) through (4) and adding new paragraph (1) to read as above; by striking out "date of termination" and inserting "termination date;" by inserting "in a distress termination" after "terminated" and by striking out "section 4041" and inserting "section 4041(c)" in paragraph (2); and by striking out "in accor-

dance with the provisions of either section" and inserting "under section 4041(c) or 4042" in paragraph (4).

These amendments take effect on April 7, 1986.

P.L. 96-364, § 402(a)(8):

Amended Sec. 4048, effective September 26, 1980 by: inserting "(a)" before "For"; inserting "of a single-employer plan" after "date of termination"; and added new subsection (b).

[¶ 15,520]
DISTRIBUTION TO PARTICIPANTS AND BENEFICIARIES OF LIABILITY PAYMENTS TO SECTION 4049 TRUST

Act Sec. 4049. [Repealed]

Amendments

P.L. 100-203, § 9312(a):

Repealed ERISA Sec. 4049 effective for (A) plan termination under section 4041(c) of ERISA for which notices of intent to terminate are provided under section 4041(a)(2) of ERISA after December 17, 1987, and (B) plan terminations for which proceedings are instituted by the Pension Benefit Guaranty Corporation under section 4042 of ERISA after December 17, 1987.

Prior to repeal, ERISA Sec. 4049 read as follows:

(a) Trust Requirements.—The requirements of this section apply to a trust established by the corporation in connection with a terminated plan pursuant to section 4041(c)(3)(B)(ii) or (iii) or 4042(i), the trust shall be used exclusively for—

(1) receiving liability payments under section 4062(c) from the persons who were (as of the termination date) contributing sponsors of the terminated plan and members of their controlled groups,

(2) making distributions as provided in this section to the persons who were (as of the termination date) participants and beneficiaries under the terminated plan, and

(3) defraying the reasonable administrative expenses incurred in carrying out responsibilities under this section.

The trust shall be maintained for such period of time as is necessary to receive all liability payments required to be made to the trust under section 4062(c) with respect to the terminated plan and to make all distributions required to be made to participants and beneficiaries under this section with respect to the terminated plan.

Reasonable administrative expenses incurred in carrying out the responsibilities under this section prior to the receipt of any liability payments under section 4062(c) shall be paid by the persons described in section 4062(a) in accordance with procedures which shall be prescribed by the corporation by regulation, and the amount of the liability determined under section 4062(c) shall be reduced by the amount of such expenses so paid.

(b) Designation of Fiduciary by the Corporation.—

(1) Purposes for Designation of Fiduciary.—

(A) Collection of Liability.—The corporation shall designate a fiduciary (within the meaning of section 3(21)) to serve as trustee of the trust for purposes of conducting negotiations and assessing and collecting liability pursuant to section 4062(c).

(B) Administration of Trust.—

(i) Corporation's Functions.—Except as provided in clause (ii), the corporation shall serve as trustee of the trust for purposes of administering the trust, including making distributions from the trust to participants and beneficiaries.

(ii) Designation of Fiduciary If Cost-Effective.—If the corporation determines that it would be cost-effective to do so, it may designate a fiduciary (within the meaning of

section 3(21)), including the fiduciary designated under subparagraph (A), to perform the functions described in clause (i).

(2) Fiduciary Requirements.—A fiduciary designated under paragraph (1) shall be—

(A) independent of each contributing sponsor of the plan and the members of such sponsor's controlled group, and

(B) subject to the requirements of part 4 of subtitle B of title I (other than section 406(a)) as if such trust were a plan subject to such part.

(c) Distribution From Trust.—

(1) In General.—Not later than 30 days after the end of each liability payment year (described in section 4062(e)(3)) with respect to a terminated single-employer plan, the corporation, or its designee under subsection (b), shall distribute from the trust maintained pursuant to subsection (a) to each person who was (as of the termination date) a participant or beneficiary under the plan—

(A) in any case not described in subparagraph (B), an amount equal to the outstanding amount of benefit commitments to such person under the plan (including interest calculated from the termination date), to the extent not previously paid under this paragraph, or

(B) in any case in which the balance in the trust at the end of such year which is in cash or may be prudently converted to cash (after taking into account liability payments received under subsection (a)(1) and administrative expenses paid under subsection (a)(3)) is less than the total of all amounts described in subparagraph (A) in connection with all persons who were (as of the termination date) participants and beneficiaries under the terminated plan, the product derived by multiplying—

(i) the amount described in subparagraph (A) in connection with each such person, by

(ii) a fraction—

(I) the numerator of which is such balance in the trust, and

(II) the denominator of which is equal to the total of all amounts described in subparagraph (A) in connection with all persons who were (as of the termination date) participants and beneficiaries under the terminated plan.

(2) Carry-Over of Minimal Payment Amounts.—The corporation, or its designee under subsection (b), may withhold a payment to any person under this subsection in connection with any liability payment year (other than the last liability payment year with respect to which payments under paragraph (1) are payable) if such payment does not exceed $100. In any case in which such a payment is so withheld, the payment to such person in connection with the next following liability payment year shall be increased by the amount of such withheld payment.

Act Sec. 4049. (d) Regulations.—The corporation may issue such regulations as it considers necessary to carry out the purposes of this section.

P.L. 100-203, § 9312(d)(2):

Amended ERISA Sec. 4049(a), as in effect prior to its repeal, by adding a new sentence at the end of the subsection, to read as above.

P.L. 99-514, § 1879(u)(2):

Amended Sec. 4049(a) by inserting "or 4042(i)" after "section 4041(c)(3)(B)(ii) or (iii)", effective on date of enactment.

P.L. 99-272:

Act Sec. 11012(a) added new ERISA Sec. 4049 to read as above, effective with respect to terminations pursuant to notices of intent filed with the PBGC on or after January 1, 1986 or proceedings begun on or after that date.

[¶ 15,530]
MISSING PARTICIPANTS

Act Sec. 4050.(a) General rule.—

(1) PAYMENT TO THE CORPORATION. A plan administrator satisfies section 4041(b)(3)(A) in the case of a missing participant only if the plan administrator—

(A) transfers the participant's designated benefit to the corporation or purchases an irrevocable commitment from an insurer in accordance with clause (i) of section 4041(b)(3)(A), and

(B) provides the corporation such information and certifications with respect to such designated benefits or irrevocable commitments as the corporation shall specify.

(2) TREATMENT OF TRANSFERRED ASSETS. A transfer to the corporation under this section shall be treated as a transfer of assets from a terminated plan to the corporation as trustee, and shall be held with assets of terminated plans for which the corporation is trustee under section 4042, subject to the rules set forth in that section.

(3) PAYMENT BY THE CORPORATION. After a missing participant whose designated benefit was transferred to the corporation is located—

(A) in any case in which the plan could have distributed the benefit of the missing participant in a single sum without participant or spousal consent under section 205(g), the corporation shall pay the participant or beneficiary a single sum benefit equal to the designated benefit paid the corporation plus interest as specified by the corporation, and

(B) in any other case, the corporation shall pay a benefit based on the designated benefit and the assumptions prescribed by the corporation at the time that the corporation received the designated benefit.

The corporation shall make payments under subparagraph (B) available in the same forms and at the same times as a guaranteed benefit under section 4022 would be available to be paid, except that the corporation may make a benefit available in the form of a single sum if the plan provided a single sum benefit (other than a single sum described in subsection (b)(2)(A)).

(b) Definitions. For purposes of this section—

(1) MISSING PARTICIPANT. The term "missing participant" means a participant or beneficiary under a terminating plan whom the plan administrator cannot locate after a diligent search.

(2) DESIGNATED BENEFIT. The term "designated benefit" means the single sum benefit the participant would receive—

(A) under the plan's assumptions, in the case of a distribution that can be made without participant or spousal consent under section 205(g);

(B) under the assumptions of the corporation in effect on the date that the designated benefit is transferred to the corporation, in the case of a plan that does not pay any single sums other than those described in subparagraph (A); or

(C) under the assumptions of the corporation or of the plan, whichever provides the higher single sum, in the case of a plan that pays a single sum other than those described in subparagraph (A).

(c) Regulatory authority. The corporation shall prescribe such regulations as are necessary to carry out the purposes of this section, including rules relating to what will be considered a diligent search, the amount payable to the corporation, and the amount to be paid by the corporation.

Amendment

P.L. 103-465, § 776(a):

Act Sec. 776(a) amended subtitle C of title IV of ERISA by adding a new section 4050 to read as above.

The above amendment is effective with respect to distributions that occur in plan years commencing after final regulations implementing the provision are prescribed by the Pension Benefit Guaranty Corporation.

Regulations

The following regulations were adopted by the Pension Benefit Guaranty Corporation on July 1, 1996 (61 FR 34002). Prior to July 1, 1996, PBGC regulations were under Chapter XXVI of Title 29 of the Code of Federal Regulations. Effective July 1, 1996, PBGC regulations were moved to Chapter XL, and were renumbered and reorganized. Reg. § 4051 was amended November 7, 1997 (62 FR 60424), effective January 1, 1998. Reg. § 4050.2 was amended May 28, 1998 (63 FR 29353), effective May 29, 1998. Reg. § § 4050.2 and 4050.5 were amended July 15, 1998 (63 FR 38305), effective August 17, 1998. Appendix A to Part 4050 was amended July 15, 1998 (63 FR 38305), effective August 17, 1998. Reg. § 4050.2 was amended March 17, 2000 (65 FR 14751), effective May 1, 2000. Reg. § 4050.6 was amended October 28, 2003 (68 FR 61344).

[¶ 15,530A]

§ 4050.1 **Purpose and scope.** This part prescribes rules for distributing benefits under a terminating single-employer plan for any individual whom the plan administrator has not located when distributing benefits under § 4041.28 of this chapter. This part applies to a plan if the plan's deemed distribution date (or the date of a payment made in accordance with § 4050.12) is in a plan year beginning on or after January 1, 1996. [Amended 11/7/97 by 62 FR 60424.]

[¶ 15,530B]

§ 4050.2 **Definitions.** The following terms are defined in § 4001.2 of this chapter: *annuity, Code, ERISA, insurer, irrevocable commitment, mandatory employee contributions, normal retirement age, PBGC, person, plan, plan administrator, plan year,* and *title IV benefit.*

In addition, for purposes of this part:

Deemed distribution date means—

(1) The last day of the period in which distribution may be made under part 4041 of this chapter; or

(2) If the plan administrator selects an earlier date that is no earlier than the date when all benefit distributions have been made under the plan except for distributions to missing participants whose designated benefits are paid to the PBGC, such earlier date.

Designated benefit means the amount payable to the PBGC for a missing participant pursuant to § 4050.5.

Designated benefit interest rate means the rate of interest applicable to underpayments of guaranteed benefits by the PBGC under § 4022.81(c) of this chapter.

Guaranteed benefit form means, with respect to a benefit, the form in which the PBGC would pay a guaranteed benefit to a participant or beneficiary in the PBGC's program for trusteed plans under subparts A and B of part 4022 of this chapter (treating the deemed distribution date as the termination date for this purpose).

Missing participant means a participant or beneficiary entitled to a distribution under a terminating plan whom the plan administrator has not located as of the date when the plan administrator pays the individual's designated benefit to the PBGC (or distributes the individual's benefit by purchasing an irrevocable commitment from an insurer). In the absence of proof of death, individuals not located are presumed living.

Missing participant annuity assumptions means the interest rate assumptions and actuarial methods for valuing benefits under Sec. 4044.52 of this chapter, applied—

(1) As if the deemed distribution date were the termination date;

(2) Using the mortality rates prescribed in Revenue Ruling 95-6, 1995-1 C.B. 80 (for availability, see 26 CFR 601.601(d));

(3) Without using the expected retirement age assumptions in Secs. 4044.55 through 4044.57 of this chapter;

(4) Without making the adjustment for expenses provided for in Sec. 4044.52(e) of this chapter; and

(5) By adding $300, as an adjustment (loading) for expenses, for each missing participant whose designated benefit without such adjustment would be greater than $5,000. [Amended 3/17/00 by 65 FR 14751.]

Missing participant forms and instructions means PBGC Forms 501 and 602, Schedule MP thereto, and related forms, and their instructions.

Missing participant lump sum assumptions means the interest rate and mortality assumptions and actuarial methods for determining the lump sum value of a benefit under Sec. 4022.7(d) of this chapter applied—

(1) As if the deemed distribution date were the termination date; and

(2) Without using the expected retirement age assumptions in Secs. 4044.55 through 4044.57 of this chapter. [Amended 3/17/00 by 65 FR 14751.]

Pay status means, with respect to a benefit under a plan, that the plan administrator has made or (except for administrative delay or a waiting period) would have made one or more benefit payments.

Post-distribution certification means the post-distribution certification required by § 4041.29 or § 4041.50 of this chapter.

Unloaded designated benefit means the designated benefit reduced by $300; except that the reduction does not apply in the case of a designated benefit determined using the missing participant annuity assumptions without adding the $300 load described in paragraph (5) of the definition of "missing participant annuity assumptions." [Amended 11/7/97 by 62 FR 60424.]

[¶ 15,530C]

§ 4050.3 **Method of distribution for missing participants.** The plan administrator of a terminating plan must distribute benefits for each missing participant by—

(a) Purchasing from an insurer an irrevocable commitment that satisfies the requirements of § 4041.28(c) or § 4041.50 of this chapter (whichever is applicable); or

(b) Paying the PBGC a designated benefit in accordance with §§ 4050.4 through 4050.6 (subject to the special rules in § 4050.12). [Amended 11/7/97 by 62 FR 60424.]

[¶ 15,530D]

§ 4050.4 **Diligent search.** (a) *Search required.* A diligent search must be made for each missing participant before information about the missing participant or payment is submitted to the PBGC pursuant to § 4050.6.

(b) *Diligence.* A search is a diligent search only if the search—

(1) Begins not more than 6 months before notices of intent to terminate are issued and is carried on in such a manner that if the individual is found, distribution to the individual can reasonably be expected to be made on or before the deemed distribution date;

(2) Includes inquiry of any plan beneficiaries (including alternate payees) of the missing participant whose names and addresses are known to the plan administrator; and

(3) Includes use of a commercial locator service to search for the missing participant (without charge to the missing participant or reduction of the missing participant's plan benefit). [Amended 11/7/97 by 62 FR 60424.]

[¶ 15,530E]

§ 4050.5 **Designated benefit.** (a) *Amount of designated benefit.* The amount of the designated benefit is the amount determined under paragraph (a)(1), (a)(2), (a)(3), or (a)(4) of this section (whichever is applicable) or, if less, the maximum amount that could be provided under the plan to the missing participant in the form of a single sum in accordance with section 415 of the Code.

(1) *Mandatory lump sum.* The designated benefit of a missing participant required under a plan to receive a mandatory lump sum as of the deemed distribution date is the lump sum payment that the plan administrator would have distributed to the missing participant as of the deemed distribution date.

(2) *De minimis lump sum.* The designated benefit of a missing participant not described in paragraph (a)(1) of this section whose benefit is not in pay status as of the deemed distribution date and whose benefit has a de minimis actuarial present value ($5,000 or less) as of the deemed distribution date under the missing participant lump sum assumptions is such value.

(3) *No lump sum.* The designated benefit of a missing participant not described in paragraph (a)(1) or (a)(2) of this section who, as of the deemed distribution date, cannot elect an immediate lump sum under the plan is the actuarial present value of the missing participant's benefit as of the deemed distribution date under the missing participant annuity assumptions.

(4) *Elective lump sum.* The designated benefit of a missing participant not described in paragraph (a)(1), (a)(2), or (a)(3) of this section is the greater of the amounts determined under the methodologies of paragraph (a)(1) or (a)(3) of this section.

(b) *Assumptions.* When the plan administrator uses the missing participant annuity assumptions or the missing participant lump sum assumptions for purposes of determining the designated benefit under paragraph (a) of this section, the plan administrator must value the most valuable benefit, as determined under paragraph (b)(1) of this section, using the assumptions described in paragraph (b)(2) or (b)(3) of this section (whichever is applicable).

(1) *Most valuable benefit.* For a missing participant whose benefit is in pay status as of the deemed distribution date, the most valuable benefit is the pay status benefit. For a missing participant whose benefit is not in pay status as of the deemed distribution date, the most valuable benefit is the benefit payable at the age on or after the deemed distribution date (beginning with the participant's earliest early retirement age and ending with the participant's normal retirement age) for which the present value as of the deemed distribution date is the greatest. The present value as of the deemed distribution date with respect to any age is determined by multiplying:

(i) The monthly (or other periodic) benefit payable under the plan; by

(ii) The present value (determined as of the deemed distribution date using the missing participant annuity assumptions) of a $1 monthly (or other periodic) annuity beginning at the applicable age.

(2) *Participant.* A missing participant who is a participant, and whose benefit is not in pay status as of the deemed distribution date, is assumed to be married to a spouse the same age, and the form of benefit that must be valued is the qualified joint and survivor annuity benefit that would be payable under the plan. If the participant's benefit is in pay status as of the deemed distribution date, the form and beneficiary of the participant's benefit are the form of benefit and beneficiary of the pay status benefit.

(3) *Beneficiary.* A missing participant who is a beneficiary, and whose benefit is not in pay status as of the deemed distribution date, is assumed not to be married, and the form of benefit that must be valued is the survivor benefit that would be payable under the plan. If the beneficiary's benefit is in pay status as of the deemed distribution date,

the form and beneficiary of the beneficiary's benefit are the form of benefit and beneficiary of the pay status benefit.

(4) *Examples*. See Appendix A to this part for examples illustrating the provisions of this section.

(c) *Missed payments*. In determining the designated benefit, the plan administrator must include the value of any payments that were due before the deemed distribution date but that were not made.

(d) *Payment of designated benefits*. Payment of designated benefits must be made in accordance with § 4050.6 and will be deemed made on the deemed distribution date. [Amended 11/7/97 by 62 FR 60424.]

[¶ 15,530F]

§ 4050.6 Payment and required documentation. (a) *Time of payment and filing*. The plan administrator must pay designated benefits, and file the information and certifications (of the plan administrator and the plan's enrolled actuary) specified in the missing participant forms and instructions, by the time the post-distribution certification is due. Except as otherwise provided in the missing participant forms and instructions, the plan administrator must submit the designated benefits, information, and certifications with the post-distribution certification.

(b) *Late charges*. (1) *Interest on late payments*. Except as provided in paragraph (b)(2) of this section, if the plan administrator does not pay a designated benefit by the time specified in paragraph (a) of this section, the plan administrator must pay interest as assessed by the PBGC for the period beginning on the deemed distribution date and ending on the date when the payment is received by the PBGC. Interest will be assessed at the rate provided for late premium payments in § 4007.7 of this chapter. Interest assessed under this paragraph will be deemed paid in full if payment of the amount assessed is received by the PBGC within 30 days after the date of a PBGC bill for such amount.

(2) *Assessment of interest and penalties*. The PBGC will assess interest for late payment of a designated benefit or a penalty for late filing of information only to the extent paid or filed beyond the time provided in § 4041.29(b).

(c) *Supplemental information*. Within 30 days after the date of a written request from the PBGC, a plan administrator required to provide the information and certifications described in paragraph (a) of this section must file supplemental information, as requested, for the purpose of verifying designated benefits, determining benefits to be paid by the PBGC under this part, and substantiating diligent searches.

(d) *Filing with the PBGC*. (1) *Method and date of filing*. The PBGC applies the rules in subpart A of part 4000 of this chapter to determine permissible methods of filing with the PBGC under this part. The PBGC applies the rules in subpart C of part 4000 of this chapter to determine the date that a submission under this part was filed with the PBGC.

(2) *Where to file*. See Sec. 4000.4 of this chapter for information on where to file.

(3) *Computation of time*. The PBGC applies the rules in subpart D of part 4000 of this chapter to compute any time period for filing under this part. However, for purposes of determining the amount of an interest charge under Sec. 4050.6(b) or Sec. 4050.12(c)(2)(iii), the rule in Sec. 4000.43(a) of this chapter governing periods ending on weekends or Federal holidays does not apply.

[Amended 11/7/97 by 62 FR 60424 and 10/28/2003 by 68 FR 61344]

[¶ 15,530G]

§ 4050.7 Benefits of missing participants—in general. (a) *If annuity purchased*. If a plan administrator distributes a missing participant's benefit by purchasing an irrevocable commitment from an insurer, and the missing participant (or his or her beneficiary or estate) later contacts the PBGC, the PBGC will inform the person of the identity of the insurer, the relevant policy number, and (to the extent known) the amount or value of the benefit.

(b) *If designated benefit paid*. If the PBGC locates or is contacted by a missing participant (or his or her beneficiary or estate) for whom a plan administrator paid a designated benefit to the PBGC, the PBGC will pay benefits in accordance with §§ 4050.8 through 4050.10 (subject to the limitations and special rules in §§ 4050.11 and 4050.12).

(c) *Examples*. See Appendix B to this part for examples illustrating the provisions of §§ 4050.8 through 4050.10. [Amended 11/7/97 by 62 FR 60424.]

[¶ 15,530H]

§ 4050.8 Automatic lump sum. This section applies to a missing participant whose designated benefit was determined under § 4050.5(a)(1) (mandatory lump sum) or § 4050.5(a)(2) (de minimis lump sum).

(a) *General rule*. (1) *Benefit paid*. The PBGC will pay a single sum benefit equal to the designated benefit plus interest at the designated benefit interest rate from the deemed distribution date to the date on which the PBGC pays the benefit.

(2) *Payee*. Payment will be made—

(i) To the missing participant, if located;

(ii) If the missing participant died before the deemed distribution date, and if the plan so provides, to the missing participant's beneficiary or estate; or

(iii) If the missing participant dies on or after the deemed distribution date, to the missing participant's estate.

(b) *De minimis annuity alternative*. If the guaranteed benefit form for a missing participant whose designated benefit was determined under § 4050.5(a)(2) (de minimis lump sum) (or the guaranteed benefit form for a beneficiary of such a missing participant) would provide for the election of an annuity, the missing participant (or the beneficiary) may elect to receive an annuity. If such an election is made—

(1) The PBGC will pay the benefit in the elected guaranteed benefit form, beginning on the annuity starting date elected by the missing participant (or the beneficiary), which may not be before the later of the date of the election or the earliest date on which the missing participant (or the beneficiary) could have begun receiving benefits under the plan; and

(2) The benefit paid will be actuarially equivalent to the designated benefit, i.e., each monthly (or other periodic) benefit payment will equal the designated benefit divided by the present value (determined as of the deemed distribution date under the missing participant lump sum assumptions) of a $1 monthly (or other periodic) annuity beginning on the annuity starting date. [Amended 11/7/97 by 62 FR 60424.]

[¶ 15,530I]

§ 4050.9 Annuity or elective lump sum—living missing participant. This section applies to a missing participant whose designated benefit was determined under § 4050.5(a)(3) (no lump sum) or § 4050.5(a)(4) (elective lump sum) and who is living on the date as of which the PBGC begins paying benefits.

(a) *Missing participant whose benefit was not in pay status as of the deemed distribution date*. The PBGC will pay the benefit of a missing participant whose benefit was not in pay status as of the deemed distribution date as follows.

(1) *Time and form of benefit*. The PBGC will pay the missing participant's benefit in the guaranteed benefit form, beginning on the annuity starting date elected by the missing participant (which may not be before the later of the date of the election or the earliest date on which the missing participant could have begun receiving benefits under the plan).

(2) *Amount of benefit*. The PBGC will pay a benefit that is actuarially equivalent to the unloaded designated benefit, i.e., each monthly (or other periodic) benefit payment will equal the unloaded designated benefit divided by the present value (determined as of the deemed distribution date under the missing participant annuity assumptions) of a $1 monthly (or other periodic) annuity beginning on the annuity starting date.

(b) *Missing participant whose benefit was in pay status as of the deemed distribution date.* The PBGC will pay the benefit of a missing participant whose benefit was in pay status as of the deemed distribution date as follows.

(1) *Time and form of benefit.* The PBGC will pay the benefit in the form that was in pay status, beginning when the missing participant is located.

(2) *Amount of benefit.* The PBGC will pay the monthly (or other periodic) amount of the pay status benefit, plus a lump sum equal to the payments the missing participant would have received under the plan, plus interest on the missed payments (at the plan rate up to the deemed distribution date and thereafter at the designated benefit interest rate) to the date as of which the PBGC pays the lump sum.

(c) *Payment of lump sum.* If a missing participant whose designated benefit was determined under § 4050.5(a)(4) (elective lump sum) so elects, the PBGC will pay his or her benefit in the form of a single sum. This election is not effective unless the missing participant's spouse consents (if such consent would be required under section 205 of ERISA). The single sum equals the designated benefit plus interest (at the designated benefit interest rate) from the deemed distribution date to the date as of which the PBGC pays the benefit. [Amended 11/7/97 by 62 FR 60424.]

[¶ 15,530J]

§ 4050.10 **Annuity or elective lump sum—beneficiary of deceased missing participant.** This section applies to a beneficiary of a deceased missing participant whose designated benefit was determined under § 4050.5(a)(3) (no lump sum) or § 4050.5(a)(4) (elective lump sum) and whose benefit is not payable under § 4050.9.

(a) *If deceased missing participant's benefit was not in pay status as of the deemed distribution date.* The PBGC will pay a benefit with respect to a deceased missing participant whose benefit was not in pay status as of the deemed distribution date as follows.

(1) *General rule.*

(i) *Beneficiary.* The PBGC will pay a benefit to the surviving spouse of a missing participant who was a participant (unless the surviving spouse has properly waived a benefit in accordance with section 205 of ERISA).

(ii) *Form and amount of benefit.* The PBGC will pay the survivor benefit in the form of a single life annuity. Each monthly (or other periodic) benefit payment will equal 50 percent of the quotient that results when the unloaded designated benefit is divided by the present value (determined as of the deemed distribution date under the missing participant annuity assumptions, and assuming that the missing participant survived to the deemed distribution date) of a $1 monthly (or other periodic) joint and 50 percent survivor annuity beginning on the annuity starting date, under which reduced payments (at the 50 percent level) are made only after the death of the missing participant during the life of the spouse (and not after the death of the spouse during the missing participant's life).

(iii) *Time of benefit.* The PBGC will pay the survivor benefit beginning at the time elected by the surviving spouse (which may not be before the later of the date of the election or the earliest date on which the surviving spouse could have begun receiving benefits under the plan).

(2) *If missing participant died before deemed distribution date.* Notwithstanding the provisions of paragraph (a)(1) of this section, if a beneficiary of a missing participant who died before the deemed distribution date establishes to the PBGC's satisfaction that he or she is the proper beneficiary or would have received benefits under the plan in a form, at a time, or in an amount different from the benefit paid under paragraph (a)(1)(ii) or (a)(1)(iii) of this section, the PBGC will make payments in accordance with the facts so established, but only in the guaranteed benefit form.

(3) *Elective lump sum.* Notwithstanding the provisions of paragraphs (a)(1) and (a)(2) of this section, if the beneficiary of a missing participant whose designated benefit was determined under § 4050.5(a)(4) (elective lump sum) so elects, the PBGC will pay his or

her benefit in the form of a single sum. The single sum will be equal to the actuarial present value (determined as of the deemed distribution date under the missing participant annuity assumptions) of the death benefit payable on the annuity starting date, plus interest (at the designated benefit interest rate) from the deemed distribution date to the date as of which the PBGC pays the benefit.

(b) *If deceased missing participant's benefit was in pay status as of the deemed distribution date.* The PBGC will pay a benefit with respect to a deceased missing participant whose benefit was in pay status as of the deemed distribution date as follows.

(1) *Beneficiary.* The PBGC will pay a benefit to the beneficiary (if any) of the benefit that was in pay status as of the deemed distribution date.

(2) *Form and amount of benefit.* The PBGC will pay a monthly (or other periodic) amount equal to the monthly (or other periodic) amount, if any, that the beneficiary would have received under the form of payment in effect, plus a lump sum payment equal to the payments the beneficiary would have received under the plan after the missing participant's death and before the date as of which the benefit is paid under paragraph (b)(4) of this section, plus interest on the missed payments (at the plan rate up to the deemed distribution date and thereafter at the designated benefit interest rate) to the date as of which the benefit is paid under paragraph (b)(4) of this section.

(3) *Lump sum payment to estate.* The PBGC will make a lump sum payment to the missing participant's estate equal to the payments that the missing participant would have received under the plan for the period before the missing participant's death, plus interest on the missed payments (at the plan rate up to the deemed distribution date and thereafter at the designated benefit interest rate) to the date when the lump sum is paid. Notwithstanding the preceding sentence, if a beneficiary of a missing participant other than the estate establishes to the PBGC's satisfaction that the beneficiary is entitled to the lump sum payment, the PBGC will pay the lump sum to such beneficiary.

(4) *Time of benefit.* The PBGC will pay the survivor benefit beginning when the beneficiary is located.

(5) *Spouse deceased.* If the PBGC locates the estate of the deceased missing participant's spouse under circumstances where a benefit would have been paid under this paragraph (b) if the spouse had been located while alive, the PBGC will pay to the spouse's estate a lump sum payment computed in the same manner as provided for in paragraph (b)(2) of this section based on the period from the missing participant's death to the death of the spouse. [Amended 11/7/97 by 62 FR 60424.]

[¶ 15,530K]

§ 4050.11 **Limitations.** (a) *Exclusive benefit.* The benefits provided for under this part will be the only benefits payable by the PBGC to missing participants or to beneficiaries based on the benefits of deceased missing participants.

(b) *Limitation on benefit value.* The total actuarial present value of all benefits paid with respect to a missing participant under §§ 4050.8 through 4050.10, determined as of the deemed distribution date, will not exceed the missing participant's designated benefit.

(c) *Guaranteed benefit.* If a missing participant or his or her beneficiary establishes to the PBGC's satisfaction that the benefit under §§ 4050.8 through 4050.10 (based on the designated benefit actually paid to the PBGC) is less than the minimum benefit in this paragraph (c), the PBGC will instead pay the minimum benefit. The minimum benefit is the lesser of:

(1) The benefit as determined under the PBGC's rules for paying guaranteed benefits in trusteed plans under subparts A and B of part 4022 of this chapter (treating the deemed distribution date as the termination date for this purpose); or

(2) The benefit based on the designated benefit that should have been paid under § 4050.5.

(d) *Limitation on annuity starting date.* A missing participant (or his or her survivor) may not elect an annuity starting date after the later of—

(1) The required beginning date under section 401(a)(9) of the Code; or

(2) The date when the missing participant (or the survivor) is notified of his or her right to a benefit. [Amended 11/7/97 by 62 FR 60424.]

[¶ 15,530L]

§ 4050.12 **Special rules.** (a) *Missing participants located quickly.* Notwithstanding the provisions of §§ 4050.8 through 4050.10, if the PBGC or the plan administrator locates a missing participant within 30 days after the PBGC receives the missing participant's designated benefit, the PBGC may in its discretion return the missing participant's designated benefit to the plan administrator, and the plan administrator must make distribution to the individual in such manner as the PBGC will direct.

(b) *Qualified domestic relations orders.* Plan administrators must and the PBGC will take the provisions of qualified domestic relations orders (QDROs) under section 206(d)(3) of ERISA or section 414(p) of the Code into account in determining designated benefits and benefit payments by the PBGC, including treating an alternate payee under an applicable QDRO as a missing participant or as a beneficiary of a missing participant, as appropriate, in accordance with the terms of the QDRO. For purposes of calculating the amount of the designated benefit of an alternate payee, the plan administrator must use the assumptions for a missing participant who is a beneficiary under § 4050.5(b).

(c) *Employee contributions.* (1) *Mandatory employee contributions.* Notwithstanding the provisions of § 4050.5, if a missing participant made mandatory contributions (within the meaning of section 4044(a)(2) of ERISA), the missing participant's designated benefit may not be less than the sum of the missing participant's mandatory contributions and interest to the deemed distribution date at the plan's rate or the rate under section 204(c) of ERISA (whichever produces the greater amount).

(2) *Voluntary employee contributions.* (i) *Applicability.* This paragraph (c)(2) applies to any employee contributions that were not mandatory (within the meaning of section 4044(a)(2) of ERISA) to which a missing participant is entitled in connection with the termination of a defined benefit plan.

(ii) *Payment to PBGC.* A plan administrator, in accordance with the missing participant forms and instructions, must pay the employee contributions described in paragraph (c)(2)(i) of this section (together with any earnings thereon) to the PBGC, and must file Schedule MP with the PBGC, by the time the designated benefit is due under § 4050.6. Any such amount must be in addition to the designated benefit and must be separately identified.

(iii) *Payment by PBGC.* In addition to any other amounts paid by the PBGC under §§ 4050.8 through 4050.10, the PBGC will pay any amount paid to it under paragraph (c)(2)(ii) of this section, with interest at the designated benefit interest rate from the date of receipt by the PBGC to the date of payment by the PBGC, in the same manner as described in § 4050.8 (automatic lump sums), except that if the missing participant died before the deemed distribution date and there is no beneficiary, payment will be made to the missing participant's estate.

(d) *Residual assets.* The PBGC will determine, in a manner consistent with the purposes of this part and section 4050 of ERISA, how the provisions of this part apply to any distribution (to participants and beneficiaries who cannot be located) of residual assets remaining after the satisfaction of plan benefits (as defined in § 4041.2 of this chapter) in connection with the termination of a defined benefit plan. Unless the PBGC otherwise determines, the payment of residual assets for a participant or beneficiary who cannot be located, and the submission to the PBGC of the related Schedule MP (or amended Schedule MP), must be made no earlier than the date when the post-distribution certification is filed with the PBGC, and no later than the later of—

(1) The 30th day after the date on which all residual assets have been distributed to all participants and beneficiaries other than those who cannot be located and for whom payment of residual assets is made to the PBGC, and

(2) The date when the post-distribution certification is filed with the PBGC.

(e) *Sufficient distress terminations.* In the case of a plan undergoing a distress termination (under section 4041(c) of ERISA) that is sufficient for at least all guaranteed benefits and that distributes its assets in the manner described in section 4041(b)(3) of ERISA, the benefit assumed to be payable by the plan for purposes of determining the amount of the designated benefit under § 4050.5 is limited to the title IV benefit plus any benefit to which funds under section 4022(c) of ERISA have been allocated.

(f) *Similar rules for later payments.* If the PBGC determines that one or more persons should receive benefits (which may be in addition to benefits already provided) in order for a plan termination to be valid (e.g., upon audit of the termination), and one or more of such individuals cannot be located, the PBGC will determine, in a manner consistent with the purposes of this part and section 4050 of ERISA, how the provisions of this part apply to such benefits.

(g) *Discretionary extensions.* Any deadline under this part may be extended in accordance with the rules described in § 4041.30 of this chapter.

(h) *Payments beginning after required beginning date.* If the PBGC begins paying an annuity under § 4050.9(a) or 4050.10(a) to a participant or a participant's spouse after the required beginning date under section 401(a)(9)(C) of the Code, the PBGC will pay to the participant or the spouse (or their respective estates) or both, as appropriate, the lump sum equivalent of the past annuity payments the participant and spouse would have received if the PBGC had begun making payments on the required beginning date. The PBGC will also pay lump sum equivalents under this paragraph (g) if the PBGC locates the estate of the participant or spouse after both are deceased. (Nothing in this paragraph (g) will increase the total value of the benefits payable with respect to a missing participant.) [Amended 11/7/97 by 62 FR 60424.]

[¶ 15,530M]

§ 4050.12 **Appendix A to Part 4050—Examples of Designated Benefit Determinations for Missing Participants Under § 4050.5 in Plans with Deemed Distributions Dates On and After August 17, 1998.** The calculation of the designated benefit under § 4050.5 is illustrated by the following examples.

Example 1. Plan A provides that any participant whose benefit has a value at distribution of $3,500 or less will be paid a lump sum, and that no other lump sums will be paid. P, Q, and R are missing participants.

(1) As of the deemed distribution date, the value of P's benefit is $3,000 under plan A's assumptions. Under § 4050.5(a)(1), the plan administrator pays the PBGC $3,000 as P's designated benefit.

(2) As of the deemed distribution date, the value of Q's benefit is $5,200 under plan A's assumptions and $4,700 under the missing participant lump sum assumptions. Under § 4050.5(a)(2), the plan administrator pays the PBGC $4,700 as Q's designated benefit.

(3) As of the deemed distribution date, the value of R's benefit is $4,900 under plan A's assumptions, $3,600 under the missing participant lump sum assumptions, and $4,950 under the missing participant annuity assumptions. Under § 4050.5(a)(3), the plan administrator pays the PBGC $4,950 as R's designated benefit.

Example 2. Plan B provides for a normal retirement age of 65 and permits early commencement of benefits at any age between 60 and 65, with benefits reduced by 5 percent for each year before age 65 that the benefit begins. The qualified joint and 50 percent survivor annuity payable under the terms of the plan requires in all cases a 16 percent reduction in the benefit otherwise payable. The plan does not provide for elective lump sums.

(1) M is a missing participant who separated from service under plan B with a deferred vested benefit. M is age 50 at the deemed distribution date, and has a normal retirement benefit of $1,000 per month payable at age 65 in the form of a single life annuity. M's benefit as of the deemed distribution date has a value greater than $5,000 using either plan assumptions or the missing participant lump sum assumptions.

Reg. § 4050.12   **¶ 15,530M**

Accordingly, M's designated benefit is to be determined under § 4050.5(a)(3).

(2) For purposes of determining M's designated benefit, M is assumed to be married to a spouse who is also age 50 on the deemed distribution date. M's monthly benefit in the form of the qualified joint and survivor annuity under the plan varies from $840 at age 65 (the normal retirement age) ($1,000 × (1-.16)) to $630 at age 60 (the earliest retirement age) ($1,000 × (1-5 × (.05)) × (1-.16)).

(3) Under § 4050.5(a)(3), M's benefit is to be valued using the missing participant annuity assumptions. The select and ultimate interest rates on Plan B's deemed distribution date are 7.50 percent for the first 20 years and 5.75 percent thereafter. Using these rates and the blended mortality table described in paragraph (2) of the definition of "missing participant annuity assumptions" in § 4050.2, the plan administrator determines that the benefit commencing at age 60 is the most valuable benefit (i.e., the benefit at age 60 is more valuable than the benefit at ages 61, 62, 63, 64 or 65). The present value as of the deemed distribution date of each dollar of annual benefit (payable monthly as a joint and 50 percent survivor annuity) is $5.4307 if the benefit begins at age 60. (Because a new spouse may succeed to the survivor benefit, the mortality of the spouse during the deferral period is ignored.) Thus, without adjustment (loading) for expenses, the value of the benefit beginning at age 60 is $41,056 (12 × $630 × 5.4307). The designated benefit is equal to this value plus an expense adjustment of $300, or a total of $41,356. [Amended 11/7/97 by 62 FR 60424.]

[¶ 15,530N]

§ 4050.12 **Appendix B to Part 4050—Examples of Benefit Payments for Missing Participants Under §§ 4050.8 Through 4050.10.** The provisions of §§ 4050.8 through 4050.10 are illustrated by the following examples.

Example 1. Participant M from Plan B (see Example 2 in Appendix A of this part) is located. M's spouse is ten years younger than M. M elects to receive benefits in the form of a joint and 50 percent survivor annuity commencing at age 62.

(1) M's designated benefit was $41,356. The unloaded designated benefit was $41,056. As of Plan B's deemed distribution date (and using the missing participant annuity assumptions), the present value per dollar of annual benefit (payable monthly as a joint and 50 percent survivor annuity commencing at age 62 and reflecting the actual age of M's spouse) is $4.7405. Thus, the monthly benefit to M at age 62 is $722 ($41,056 / (4.7405 × 12)). M's spouse will receive $361 (50 percent of $722) per month for life after the death of M.

(2) If M had instead been found to have died on or after the deemed distribution date, and M's spouse wanted benefits to commence when M would have attained age 62, the same calculation would be performed to arrive at a monthly benefit of $361 to M's spouse.

Example 2. Participant P is a missing participant from Plan C, a plan that allows elective lump sums upon plan termination. Plan C's administrator pays a designated benefit of $10,000 to the PBGC on behalf of P, who was age 30 on the deemed distribution date.

(1) P's spouse, S, is located and has a death certificate showing that P died on or after the deemed distribution date with S as spouse. S is the same age as P, and would like survivor benefits to commence immediately, at age 55 (as permitted by the plan). S's benefit is the survivor's share of the joint and 50 percent survivor annuity which is actuarially equivalent, as of the deemed distribution date, to $9,700 (the unloaded designated benefit).

(2) The select and ultimate interest rates on Plan C's deemed distribution date were 7.50 percent for the first 20 years and 5.75 percent thereafter. Using these rates and the blended mortality table described in paragraph (2) of the definition of "missing participant annuity assumptions" in § 4050.2, the present value as of the deemed distribution date of each dollar of annual benefit (payable monthly as a joint and 50 percent survivor annuity) is $2.4048 if the benefit begins when S and P would have been age 55. Thus, the monthly benefit to S commencing at age 55 is $168 (50 percent of $9,700 / (2.4048 × 12)). Since P could have elected a lump sum upon plan termination, S may elect a lump sum. S's lump sum is the present value as of the deemed distribution date (using the missing participant annuity assumptions) of the monthly benefit of $168, accumulated with interest at the designated benefit interest rate to the date paid. [Amended 11/7/97 by 62 FR 60424.]

»»→ *Caution: Generally, for fully-funded, single-employer pension plans, which issued their first notice of intent to terminate before January 1, 1998, unamended regulation § 4050 applies. The regulations, prior to the amendments made by the PBGC on 11/7/97 (62 FR 60424), previously read:*

[¶ 15,531]

§ 4050.1 **Purpose and scope.** This part prescribes rules for distributing benefits under a terminating single-employer plan for any individual whom the plan administrator has not located when distributing benefits under § 4041.27(c) of this chapter. This part applies to a plan if the plan's deemed distribution date (or the date of a payment made in accordance with § 4050.12) is in a plan year beginning on or after January 1, 1996.

[¶ 15,531A]

§ 4050.2 **Definitions.** The following terms are defined in § 4001.2 of this chapter: *annuity, benefit liabilities, Code, ERISA, insurer, irrevocable commitment, mandatory employee contributions, normal retirement age, PBGC, person, plan, plan administrator, plan year,* and *title IV benefit.*

In addition, for purposes of this part:

Deemed distribution date means the last day of the period in which distribution may be made (determined without regard to the provisions of this part) under § 4041.27(a) or § 4041.48(a) of this chapter (whichever applies) or such earlier date as may be selected by the plan administrator of a terminating plan that is on or after the date when all benefit distributions have been made under the plan except for distributions to—

(1) Late-discovered participants,

(2) Missing participants (including recently-missing participants) whose designated benefits are paid to the PBGC, and

(3) Recently-missing participants whose benefits are distributed by purchasing an irrevocable commitment from an insurer.

Designated benefit means the amount payable to the PBGC for a missing participant pursuant to § 4050.5.

Designated benefit interest rate means the rate of interest applicable to underpayments of guaranteed benefits by the PBGC under § 4022.81(d) of this chapter.

Guaranteed benefit form means, with respect to a benefit, the form in which the PBGC would pay a guaranteed benefit to a participant or beneficiary in the PBGC's program for trusteed plans under subparts A and B of part 4022 of this chapter (treating the deemed distribution date as the termination date for this purpose).

Late-discovered participant means a participant or beneficiary entitled to a distribution under a terminating plan whom the plan administrator locates before the plan administrator pays the individual's designated benefit to the PBGC (or distributes the individual's benefit by purchasing an irrevocable commitment from an insurer) and not more than 90 days before the deemed distribution date.

Missing participant means a participant or beneficiary entitled to a distribution under a terminating plan whom the plan administrator has not located as of the date when the plan administrator pays the individual's designated benefit to the PBGC (or distributes the individual's benefit by purchasing an irrevocable commitment from an insurer). In the absence of proof of death, individuals not located are presumed living.

Missing participant annuity assumptions means the interest rate assumptions and actuarial methods (using the interest rates for annuity valuations in Table I of appendix B to part 4044 of this chapter) for valuing a benefit to be paid by the PBGC as an annuity under subpart B of part 4044, applied—

(1) As if the deemed distribution date were the termination date;

(2) Using unisex mortality rates that are a fixed blend of 50 percent of the male mortality rates and 50 percent of the female mortality rates from the 1983 Group Annuity Mortality Table as prescribed in Rev. Rul. 95-6, 1995-1 C.B. 80 (Cumulative Bulletins are available from the Super-

intendent of Documents, Government Printing Office, Washington, DC 20402);

(3) Without using the expected retirement age assumptions in §§ 4044.55 through 4044.57 of this chapter;

(4) Without making the adjustment for expenses provided for in § 4044.52(a)(5) of this chapter; and

(5) By adding $300, as an adjustment (loading) for expenses, for each missing participant whose designated benefit without such adjustment would be greater than $3,500.

Missing participant forms and instructions means PBGC Forms 501 and 602, Schedule MP thereto, and related forms, and their instructions.

Missing participant lump sum assumptions means the interest rate assumptions and actuarial methods (using the interest rates for lump sum valuations in Table II of appendix B to part 4044 of this chapter) for valuing a benefit to be paid by the PBGC as a lump sum under subpart B of part 4044 of this chapter, applied—

(1) As if the deemed distribution date were the termination date;

(2) Using mortality assumptions from Table 3 of appendix A to part 4044 of this chapter; and

(3) Without using the expected retirement age assumptions in §§ 4044.55 through 4044.57 of this chapter.

Pay status means, with respect to a benefit under a plan, that the plan administrator has made or (except for administrative delay or a waiting period) would have made one or more benefit payments.

Post-distribution certification means the post-distribution certification required by § 4041.27(h) or § 4041.48(b) of this chapter.

Recently-missing participant means a participant or beneficiary whom the plan administrator discovers to be a missing participant on or after the 90th day before the deemed distribution date.

Unloaded designated benefit means the designated benefit reduced by $300; except that the reduction shall not apply in the case of a designated benefit determined using the missing participant annuity assumptions without adding the $300 load described in paragraph (5) of the definition of "missing participant annuity assumptions."

[¶ 15,531B]

§ 4050.3 **Method of distribution for missing participants.** The plan administrator of a terminating plan shall distribute benefits for each missing participant by—

(a) purchasing from an insurer an irrevocable commitment that satisfies the requirements of § 4041.27(c) or § 4041.48(a)(1) of this chapter (whichever is applicable); or

(b) paying the PBGC a designated benefit in accordance with §§ 4050.4 through 4050.6 (subject to the special rules in § 4050.12).

[¶ 15,531C]

§ 4050.4 **Diligent search.** (a) *Search required.* A diligent search shall be made for each missing participant whose designated benefit (or voluntary employee contributions under § 4050.12(d)(2)) is paid to the PBGC. The search shall be made before the payment is made.

(b) *Diligence.* A search is a diligent search only if the search—

(1) Begins not more than 6 months before notices of intent to terminate are issued and is carried on in such a manner that if the individual is found, distribution to the individual can reasonably be expected to be made on or before the deemed distribution date (or, in the case of a recently-missing participant, on or before the 90th day after the deemed distribution date);

(2) Includes inquiry of any plan beneficiaries (including alternate payees) of the missing participant whose names and addresses are known to the plan administrator; and

(3) Includes use of a commercial locator service to search for the missing participant (without charge to the missing participant or reduction of the missing participant's plan benefit).

[¶ 15,531D]

§ 4050.5 **Designated benefit.** (a) *Amount of designated benefit.* The amount of the designated benefit shall be the amount determined under paragraph (a)(1), (a)(2), (a)(3), or (a)(4) of this section (which-

ever is applicable) or, if less, the maximum amount that could be provided under the plan to the missing participant in the form of a single sum in accordance with section 415 of the Code.

(1) *Mandatory lump sum.* The designated benefit of a missing participant required under a plan to receive a mandatory lump sum as of the deemed distribution date shall be the lump sum payment that the plan administrator would have distributed to the missing participant as of the deemed distribution date.

(2) *De minimis lump sum.* The designated benefit of a missing participant not described in paragraph (a)(1) of this section whose benefit is not in pay status as of the deemed distribution date and whose benefit has a de minimis actuarial present value ($3,500 or less) as of the deemed distribution date under the missing participant lump sum assumptions shall be such value.

(3) *No lump sum.* The designated benefit of a missing participant not described in paragraph (a)(1) or (a)(2) of this section who, as of the deemed distribution date, cannot elect an immediate lump sum under the plan shall be the actuarial present value of the missing participant's benefit as of the deemed distribution date under the missing participant annuity assumptions.

(4) *Elective lump sum.* The designated benefit of a missing participant not described in paragraph (a)(1), (a)(2), or (a)(3) of this section shall be the greater of the amounts determined under the methodologies of paragraph (a)(1) or (a)(3) of this section.

(b) *Assumptions.* When the plan administrator uses the missing participant annuity assumptions or the missing participant lump sum assumptions for purposes of determining the designated benefit under paragraph (a) of this section, the plan administrator shall value the most valuable benefit, as determined under paragraph (b)(1) of this section, using the assumptions described in paragraph (b)(2) or (b)(3) of this section (whichever is applicable).

(1) *Most valuable benefit.* For a missing participant whose benefit is in pay status as of the deemed distribution date, the most valuable benefit is the pay status benefit. For a missing participant whose benefit is not in pay status as of the deemed distribution date, the most valuable benefit is the benefit payable at the age on or after the deemed distribution date (beginning with the participant's earliest early retirement age and ending with the participant's normal retirement age) for which the present value as of the deemed distribution date is the greatest. The present value as of the deemed distribution date with respect to any age is determined by multiplying:

(i) the monthly (or other periodic) benefit payable under the plan; by

(ii) the present value (determined as of the deemed distribution date using the missing participant annuity assumptions) of a $1 monthly (or other periodic) annuity beginning at the applicable age.

(2) *Participant.* A missing participant who is a participant, and whose benefit is not in pay status as of the deemed distribution date, is assumed to be married to a spouse the same age, and the form of benefit that must be valued is the qualified joint and survivor annuity benefit that would be payable under the plan. If the participant's benefit is in pay status as of the deemed distribution date, the form and beneficiary of the participant's benefit are the form of benefit and beneficiary of the pay status benefit.

(3) *Beneficiary.* A missing participant who is a beneficiary, and whose benefit is not in pay status as of the deemed distribution date, is assumed not to be married, and the form of benefit that must be valued is the survivor benefit that would be payable under the plan. If the beneficiary's benefit is in pay status as of the deemed distribution date, the form and beneficiary of the beneficiary's benefit are the form of benefit and beneficiary of the pay status benefit.

(4) *Examples.* See Appendix A to this part for examples illustrating the provisions of this section.

(c) *Missed payments.* In determining the designated benefit, the plan administrator shall include the value of any payments that were due before the deemed distribution date but that were not made.

(d) *Payment of designated benefits.* Payment of designated benefits shall be made in accordance with § 4050.6 and shall be deemed made on the deemed distribution date.

[¶ 15,531E]

§ 4050.6 **Payment and required documentation.** (a) *Time of payment and filing.* (1) *General rule.* The plan administrator shall pay designated benefits, and file the information and certifications (of the plan administrator and the plan's enrolled actuary) specified in the missing participant forms and instructions, by the time the post-distribution certification is due (determined in accordance with § 4041.9 of this chapter). Except as otherwise provided in the missing participant forms and instructions, the plan administrator shall submit the designated benefits, information, and certifications with the post-distribution certification.

(2) *Recently-missing participants.* For a recently-missing participant, the plan administrator shall either purchase an irrevocable commitment from an insurer not later than 90 days after the deemed distribution date or pay a designated benefit to the PBGC by the time the amended post-distribution certification is due under paragraph (a) (2) (ii) of this section. Except as otherwise provided in the missing participant forms and instructions—

(i) *Payment.* The plan administrator shall submit the designated benefit with the amended post-distribution certification described in paragraph (a) (2) (ii) of this section; and

(ii) *Filing.* If (in the case of a recently-missing participant for whom a designated benefit is to be paid to the PBGC) a diligent search has not been completed or (in the case of any other recently-missing participant) an irrevocable commitment has not been purchased when the plan administrator submits the filing described in paragraph (a) (1) of this section, the plan administrator shall so indicate in that filing and submit an amended filing (including an amended post-distribution certification) within 120 days after the deemed distribution date (subject to extension under § 4050.12(h)) in accordance with the missing participant forms and instructions.

(3) *Late-discovered participants.* When it is impracticable for the plan administrator to include complete and accurate final information on a late-discovered participant in a timely post-distribution certification, the plan administrator shall submit an amended post-distribution certification within 120 days after the deemed distribution date (subject to extension under § 4050.12(h)) in accordance with the missing participant forms and instructions.

(b) *Interest on late payments.* If the plan administrator does not pay a designated benefit by the time specified in paragraph (a) of this section, the plan administrator shall pay interest as assessed by the PBGC for the period beginning on the deemed distribution date and ending on the date when the payment is received by the PBGC. Interest will be assessed at the rate provided for late premium payments in § 4007.7 of this chapter. Interest assessed under this paragraph shall be deemed paid in full if payment of the amount assessed is received by the PBGC within 30 days after the date of a PBGC bill for such amount.

(c) *Supplemental information.* Within 30 days after the date of a written request from the PBGC, a plan administrator required to provide the information and certifications described in paragraph (a) of this section shall file supplemental information, as requested, for the purpose of verifying designated benefits, determining benefits to be paid by the PBGC under this part, and substantiating diligent searches.

(1) *Information mailed.* Supplemental information filed under this paragraph (c) is considered filed on the date of the United States postmark stamped on the cover in which the information is mailed, if—

(i) The postmark was made by the United States Postal Service; and

(ii) The information was mailed postage prepaid, properly addressed to the PBGC.

(2) *Information delivered.* When the plan administrator sends or transmits the information to the PBGC by means other than the United States Postal Service, the information is considered filed on the date it

is received by the PBGC. Information received on a weekend or Federal holiday or after 5:00 p.m. on a weekday is considered filed on the next regular business day.

[¶ 15,531F]

§ 4050.7 **Benefits of missing participants—in general.** (a) *If annuity purchased.* If a plan administrator distributes a missing participant's benefit by purchasing an irrevocable commitment from an insurer, and the missing participant (or his or her beneficiary or estate) later contacts the PBGC, the PBGC will inform the person of the identity of the insurer and the relevant policy number.

(b) *If designated benefit paid.* If the PBGC locates or is contacted by a missing participant (or his or her beneficiary or estate) for whom a plan administrator paid a designated benefit to the PBGC, the PBGC will pay benefits in accordance with § § 4050.8 through 4050.10 (subject to the limitations and special rules in § § 4050.11 and 4050.12).

(c) *Examples.* See Appendix B to this part for examples illustrating the provisions of § § 4050.8 through 4050.10.

[¶ 15,531G]

§ 4050.8 **Automatic lump sum.** This section applies to a missing participant whose designated benefit was determined under § 4050.5(a)(1) (mandatory lump sum) or § 4050.5(a)(2) (de minimis lump sum).

(a) *General rule.* (1) *Benefit paid.* The PBGC will pay a single sum benefit equal to the designated benefit plus interest at the designated benefit interest rate from the deemed distribution date to the date on which the PBGC pays the benefit.

(2) *Payee.* Payment shall be made—

(i) To the missing participant, if located;

(ii) If the missing participant died before the deemed distribution date, and if the plan so provides, to the missing participant's beneficiary or estate; or

(iii) If the missing participant dies on or after the deemed distribution date, to the missing participant's estate.

(b) *De minimis annuity alternative.* If the guaranteed benefit form for a missing participant whose designated benefit was determined under § 4050.5(a)(2) (de minimis lump sum) (or the guaranteed benefit form for a beneficiary of such a missing participant) would provide for the election of an annuity, the missing participant (or the beneficiary) may elect to receive an annuity. If such an election is made—

(1) The PBGC will pay the benefit in the elected guaranteed benefit form, beginning on the annuity starting date elected by the missing participant (or the beneficiary), which shall not be before the later of the date of the election or the earliest date on which the missing participant (or the beneficiary) could have begun receiving benefits under the plan; and

(2) The benefit paid will be actuarially equivalent to the designated benefit, i.e., each monthly (or other periodic) benefit payment will equal the designated benefit divided by the present value (determined as of the deemed distribution date under the missing participant lump sum assumptions) of a $1 monthly (or other periodic) annuity beginning on the annuity starting date.

[¶ 15,531H]

§ 4050.9 **Annuity or elective lump sum—living missing participant.** This section applies to a missing participant whose designated benefit was determined under § 4050.5(a)(3) (no lump sum) or § 4050.5(a)(4) (elective lump sum) and who is living on the date as of which the PBGC begins paying benefits.

(a) *Missing participant whose benefit was not in pay status as of the deemed distribution date.* The PBGC will pay the benefit of a missing participant whose benefit was not in pay status as of the deemed distribution date as follows.

(1) *Time and form of benefit.* The PBGC will pay the missing participant's benefit in the guaranteed benefit form, beginning on the annuity starting date elected by the missing participant (which shall not be before the later of the date of the election or the earliest date on

which the missing participant could have begun receiving benefits under the plan).

(2) *Amount of benefit.* The PBGC will pay a benefit that is actuarially equivalent to the unloaded designated benefit, i.e., each monthly (or other periodic) benefit payment will equal the unloaded designated benefit divided by the present value (determined as of the deemed distribution date under the missing participant annuity assumptions) of a $1 monthly (or other periodic) annuity beginning on the annuity starting date.

(b) *Missing participant whose benefit was in pay status as of the deemed distribution date.* The PBGC will pay the benefit of a missing participant whose benefit was in pay status as of the deemed distribution date as follows.

(1) *Time and form of benefit.* The PBGC will pay the benefit in the form that was in pay status, beginning when the missing participant is located.

(2) *Amount of benefit.* The PBGC will pay the monthly (or other periodic) amount of the pay status benefit, plus a lump sum equal to the payments the missing participant would have received under the plan, plus interest on the missed payments (at the plan rate up to the deemed distribution date and thereafter at the designated benefit interest rate) to the date as of which the PBGC pays the lump sum.

(c) *Payment of lump sum.* If a missing participant whose designated benefit was determined under §4050.5(a)(4) (elective lump sum) so elects, the PBGC will pay his or her benefit in the form of a single sum. This election is not effective unless the missing participant's spouse consents (if such consent would be required under section 205 of ERISA). The single sum equals the designated benefit plus interest (at the designated benefit interest rate) from the deemed distribution date to the date as of which the PBGC pays the benefit.

[¶ 15,531I]

§4050.10 Annuity or elective lump sum—beneficiary of deceased missing participant. This section applies to a beneficiary of a deceased missing participant whose designated benefit was determined under §4050.5(a)(3) (no lump sum) or §4050.5(a)(4) (elective lump sum) and whose benefit is not payable under §4050.9.

(a) *If deceased missing participant's benefit was not in pay status as of the deemed distribution date.* The PBGC will pay a benefit with respect to a deceased missing participant whose benefit was not in pay status as of the deemed distribution date as follows.

(1) *General rule.* (i) *Beneficiary.* The PBGC will pay a benefit to the surviving spouse of a missing participant who was a participant (unless the surviving spouse has properly waived a benefit in accordance with section 205 of ERISA).

(ii) *Form and amount of benefit.* The PBGC will pay the survivor benefit in the form of a single life annuity. Each monthly (or other periodic) benefit payment will equal 50% of the quotient that results when the unloaded designated benefit is divided by the present value (determined as of the deemed distribution date under the missing participant annuity assumptions, and assuming that the missing participant survived to the deemed distribution date) of a $1 monthly (or other periodic) joint and 50 percent survivor annuity beginning on the annuity starting date, under which reduced payments (at the 50 percent level) are made only after the death of the missing participant during the life of the spouse (and not after the death of the spouse during the missing participant's life).

(iii) *Time of benefit.* The PBGC will pay the survivor benefit beginning at the time elected by the surviving spouse (which shall not be before the later of the date of the election or the earliest date on which the surviving spouse could have begun receiving benefits under the plan).

(2) *If missing participant died before deemed distribution date.* Notwithstanding the provisions of paragraph (a)(1) of this section, if a beneficiary of a missing participant who died before the deemed distribution date establishes to the PBGC's satisfaction that he or she is the proper beneficiary or would have received benefits under the plan in a form, at a time, or in an amount different from the benefit paid under

paragraph (a)(1)(ii) or (a)(1)(iii) of this section, the PBGC will make payments in accordance with the facts so established, but only in the guaranteed benefit form.

(3) *Elective lump sum.* Notwithstanding the provisions of paragraphs (a)(1) and (a)(2) of this section, if the beneficiary of a missing participant whose designated benefit was determined under §4050.5(a)(4) (elective lump sum) so elects, the PBGC will pay his or her benefit in the form of a single sum. The single sum will be equal to the actuarial present value (determined as of the deemed distribution date under the missing participant annuity assumptions) of the death benefit payable on the annuity starting date, plus interest (at the designated benefit interest rate) from the deemed distribution date to the date as of which the PBGC pays the benefit.

(b) *If deceased missing participant's benefit was in pay status as of the deemed distribution date.* The PBGC will pay a benefit with respect to a deceased missing participant whose benefit was in pay status as of the deemed distribution date as follows.

(1) *Beneficiary.* The PBGC will pay a benefit to the beneficiary (if any) of the benefit that was in pay status as of the deemed distribution date.

(2) *Form and amount of benefit.* The PBGC will pay a monthly (or other periodic) amount equal to the monthly (or other periodic) amount, if any, that the beneficiary would have received under the form of payment in effect, plus a lump sum payment equal to the payments the beneficiary would have received under the plan subsequent to the missing participant's death and prior to the date as of which the benefit is paid under paragraph (b)(4) of this section, plus interest on the missed payments (at the plan rate up to the deemed distribution date and thereafter at the designated benefit interest rate) to the date as of which the benefit is paid under paragraph (b)(4) of this section.

(3) *Lump sum payment to estate.* The PBGC will make a lump sum payment to the missing participant's estate equal to the payments that the missing participant would have received under the plan for the period prior to the missing participant's death, plus interest on the missed payments (at the plan rate up to the deemed distribution date and thereafter at the designated benefit interest rate) to the date when the lump sum is paid. Notwithstanding the preceding sentence, if a beneficiary of a missing participant other than the estate establishes to the PBGC's satisfaction that the beneficiary is entitled to the lump sum payment, the PBGC will pay the lump sum to such beneficiary.

(4) *Time of benefit.* The PBGC will pay the survivor benefit beginning when the beneficiary is located.

(5) *Spouse deceased.* If the PBGC locates the estate of the deceased missing participant's spouse under circumstances where a benefit would have been paid under this paragraph (b) if the spouse had been located while alive, the PBGC shall pay to the spouse's estate a lump sum payment computed in the same manner as provided for in paragraph (b)(2) of this section based on the period from the missing participant's death to the death of the spouse.

[¶ 15,531J]

§4050.11 Limitations. (a) *Exclusive benefit.* The benefits provided for under this part shall be the only benefits payable by the PBGC to missing participants or to beneficiaries based on the benefits of deceased missing participants.

(b) *Limitation on benefit value.* The total actuarial present value of all benefits paid with respect to a missing participant under §§4050.8 through 4050.10, determined as of the deemed distribution date, shall not exceed the missing participant's designated benefit.

(c) *Guaranteed benefit.* If a missing participant or his or her beneficiary establishes to the PBGC's satisfaction that the benefit under §§4050.8 through 4050.10 (based on the designated benefit actually paid to the PBGC) is less than the minimum benefit in this paragraph (c), the PBGC shall instead pay the minimum benefit. The minimum benefit shall be the lesser of:

(1) The benefit as determined under the PBGC's rules for paying guaranteed benefits in trusteed plans under subparts A and B of part 4022 of this chapter (treating the deemed distribution date as the termination date for this purpose); or

(2) The benefit based on the designated benefit that should have been paid under § 4050.5.

(d) *Limitation on annuity starting date.* A missing participant (or his or her survivor) may not elect an annuity starting date after the later of—

(1) the required beginning date under section 401(a)(9) of the Code; or

(2) the date when the missing participant (or the survivor) is notified of his or her right to a benefit.

[¶ 15,531K]

§ 4050.12 **Special rules.** (a) *Late-discovered participants.* The plan administrator of a plan that terminates with one or more late-discovered participants shall (after issuing notices to each such participant in accordance with §§ 4041.21 and 4041.41 or 4041.46 of this chapter (whichever apply)), distribute each such late-discovered participant's benefit within the period (determined without regard to the provisions of this part) described in § 4041.27(a) or § 4041.48(a) of this chapter (whichever applies) if practicable or (if not) as soon thereafter as practicable, but not more than 90 days after the deemed distribution date (subject to extension under § 4050.12(h)).

(b) *Missing participants located quickly.* Notwithstanding the provisions of §§ 4050.8 through 4050.10, if the PBGC or the plan administrator locates a missing participant within 30 days after the PBGC receives the missing participant's designated benefit, the PBGC may in its discretion return the missing participant's designated benefit to the plan administrator, and the plan administrator shall treat the missing participant like a late-discovered participant.

(c) *Qualified domestic relations orders.* Plan administrators and the PBGC shall take the provisions of qualified domestic relations orders (QDROs) under section 206(d)(3) of ERISA or section 414(p) of the Code into account in determining designated benefits and benefit payments by the PBGC, including treating an alternate payee under an applicable QDRO as a missing participant or as a beneficiary of a missing participant, as appropriate, in accordance with the terms of the QDRO. For purposes of calculating the amount of the designated benefit of an alternate payee, the plan administrator shall use the assumptions for a missing participant who is a beneficiary under § 4050.5(b).

(d) *Employee contributions.* (1) *Mandatory employee contributions.* Notwithstanding the provisions of § 4050.5, if a missing participant made mandatory contributions (within the meaning of section 4044(a)(2) of ERISA), the missing participant's designated benefit shall not be less than the sum of the missing participant's mandatory contributions and interest to the deemed distribution date at the plan's rate or the rate under section 204(c) of ERISA (whichever produces the greater amount).

(2) *Voluntary employee contributions.*

(i) *Applicability.* This paragraph (d)(2) applies to any employee contributions that were not mandatory (within the meaning of section 4044(a)(2) of ERISA) to which a missing participant is entitled in connection with the termination of a defined benefit plan.

(ii) *Payment to PBGC.* A plan administrator, in accordance with the missing participant forms and instructions, shall pay the employee contributions described in paragraph (d)(2)(i) of this section (together with any earnings thereon) to the PBGC, and shall file Schedule MP with the PBGC, by the time the designated benefit is due under § 4050.6. Any such amount shall be in addition to the designated benefit and shall be separately identified.

(iii) *Payment by PBGC.* In addition to any other amounts paid by the PBGC under §§ 4050.8 through 4050.10, the PBGC shall pay any amount paid to it under paragraph (d)(2)(ii) of this section, with interest at the designated benefit interest rate from the date of receipt by the PBGC to the date of payment by the PBGC, in the same manner as described in § 4050.8 (automatic lump sums), except that if the missing participant died before the deemed distribution date and there is no beneficiary, payment shall be made to the missing participant's estate.

(e) *Residual assets.* The PBGC shall determine, in a manner consistent with the purposes of this part and section 4050 of ERISA, how the provisions of this part shall apply to any distribution, to participants and beneficiaries who cannot be located, of residual assets remaining after the satisfaction of benefit liabilities in connection with the termination of a defined benefit plan. Unless the PBGC otherwise determines, the deadline for payment of residual assets for a missing participant and for submission to the PBGC of a Schedule MP (or an amended Schedule MP) is the 30th day after the date on which all residual assets have been distributed to all participants and beneficiaries other than missing participants for whom payment of residual assets is made to the PBGC.

(f) *Sufficient distress terminations.* In the case of a plan undergoing a distress termination (under section 4041(c) of ERISA) that is sufficient for at least all guaranteed benefits and that distributes its assets in the manner described in section 4041(b)(3) of ERISA, the benefit assumed to be payable by the plan for purposes of determining the amount of the designated benefit under § 4050.5 shall be limited to the Title IV benefit plus any benefit to which funds under section 4022(c) of ERISA have been allocated.

(g) *Similar rules for later payments.* If the PBGC determines that one or more persons should receive benefits (which may be in addition to benefits already provided) in order for a plan termination to be valid (e.g., upon audit of the termination), and one or more of such individuals cannot be located, the PBGC shall determine, in a manner consistent with the purposes of this part and section 4050 of ERISA, how the provisions of this part shall apply to such benefits.

(h) *Discretionary extensions.* The PBGC may in its sole discretion extend the 120-day amended filing periods in § 4050.6(a)(2)(ii) and (3) and the 90-day distribution periods in § 4050.6(a)(2) and in paragraph (a) of this section—

(1) Where a recently-missing participant becomes a late-discovered participant,

(2) Where the PBGC returns the designated benefit of a missing participant who is located quickly to the plan administrator under § 4050.12(b), or

(3) In other unusual circumstances.

(i) *Payments beginning after age 70 1/2.* If the PBGC begins paying an annuity under § 4050.9(a) or 4050.10(a) to a participant or a participant's spouse after the January 1 following the date when the participant attained or would have attained age 70 1/2, the PBGC shall pay to the participant or the spouse (or their respective estates) or both, as appropriate, the lump sum equivalent of the past annuity payments the participant and spouse would have received if the PBGC had begun making payments on such January 1. The PBGC shall also pay lump sum equivalents under this paragraph (i) if the PBGC locates the estate of the participant or spouse after both are deceased. (Nothing in this paragraph (i) shall increase the total value of the benefits payable with respect to a missing participant.)

[¶ 15,531L]

§ 4050.13 **OMB control number.** The collection of information requirements contained in this part have been approved by the Office of Management under OMB Control Number 1212-0036.

[¶ 15,531M]

§ 4050.13 **Appendix A to part 4050—Examples of Designated Benefit Determinations for Missing Participants under § 4050.5**

The calculation of the designated benefit under § 4050.5 is illustrated by the following examples.

Example 1. Plan A provides that any participant whose benefit has a value at distribution of $1,750 or less will be paid a lump sum, and that no other lump sums will be paid. P, Q, and R are missing participants.

(1) As of the deemed distribution date, the value of P's benefit is $1,700 under plan A's assumptions. Under § 4050.5(a)(1), the plan administrator pays the PBGC $1,700 as P's designated benefit.

(2) As of the deemed distribution date, the value of Q's benefit is $3,700 under plan A's assumptions and $3,200 under the missing participant lump sum assumptions. Under § 4050.5(a)(2), the plan administrator pays the PBGC $3,200 as Q's designated benefit.

(3) As of the deemed distribution date, the value of R's benefit is $3,400 under plan A's assumptions, $3,600 under the missing participant lump sum assumptions, and $3,450 under the missing participant annuity assumptions. Under § 4050.5(a)(3), the plan administrator pays the PBGC $3,450 as R's designated benefit.

Example 2. Plan B provides for a normal retirement age of 65 and permits early commencement of benefits at any age between 60 and 65, with benefits reduced by 5 percent for each year before age 65 that the benefit begins. The qualified joint and 50 percent survivor annuity payable under the terms of the plan requires in all cases a 16 percent reduction in the benefit otherwise payable. The plan does not provide for elective lump sums.

(1) M is a missing participant who separated from service under plan B with a deferred vested benefit. M is age 50 at the deemed distribution date, and has a normal retirement benefit of $1,000 per month payable at age 65 in the form of a single life annuity. M's benefit as of the deemed distribution date has a value greater than $3,500 using either plan assumptions or the missing participant lump sum assumptions. Accordingly, M's designated benefit is to be determined under § 4050.5(a)(3).

(2) For purposes of determining M's designated benefit, M is assumed to be married to a spouse who is also age 50 on the deemed distribution date. M's monthly benefit in the form of the qualified joint and survivor annuity under the plan varies from $840 at age 65 (the normal retirement age) ($1,000 × (1 - .16)) to $630 at age 60 (the earliest retirement age) ($1,000 × (1 - 5 × (.05)) × (1 - .16)).

(3) Under § 4050.5(a)(3), M's benefit is to be valued using the missing participant annuity assumptions. The select and ultimate interest rates on Plan B's deemed distribution date are 7.50 percent for the first 20 years and 5.75 percent thereafter. Using these rates and the blended mortality table described in paragraph (2) of the definition of "missing participant annuity assumptions" in § 4050.2, the plan administrator determines that the benefit commencing at age 60 is the most valuable benefit (i.e., the benefit at age 60 is more valuable than the benefit at ages 61, 62, 63, 64 or 65). The present value as of the deemed distribution date of each dollar of annual benefit (payable monthly as a joint and 50 percent survivor annuity) is $5.4307 if the benefit begins at age 60. (Because a new spouse may succeed to the survivor benefit, the mortality of the spouse during the deferral period is ignored.) Thus, without adjustment (loading) for expenses, the value of the benefit beginning at age 60 is $41,056 (12 × $630 × 5.4307). The designated benefit is equal to this value plus an expense adjustment of $300, or a total of $41,356.

§ 4050.13 Appendix B to Part 4050—Examples of Benefit Payments for Missing Participants Under §§ 4050.8 Through 4050.10

The provisions of §§ 4050.8 through 4050.10 are illustrated by the following examples.

Example 1. Participant M from Plan B (see Example 2 in Appendix A of this part) is located. M's spouse is ten years younger than M. M elects to receive benefits in the form of a joint and 50 percent survivor annuity commencing at age 62.

(1) M's designated benefit was $41,356. The unloaded designated benefit was $41,056. As of Plan B's deemed distribution date (and using the missing participant annuity assumptions), the present value per dollar of monthly benefit (payable monthly as a joint and 50 percent survivor annuity commencing at age 62 and reflecting the actual age of M's spouse) is $4.7405. Thus, the monthly benefit to M at age 62 is $722 ($41,056 / (4.7405 x 12)). M's spouse will receive $361 (50 percent of $722) per month for life after the death of M.

(2) If M had instead been found to have died on or after the deemed distribution date, and M's spouse wanted benefits to commence when M would have attained age 62, the same calculation would be performed to arrive at a monthly benefit of $361 to M's spouse.

Example 2. Participant P is a missing participant from Plan C, a plan that allows elective lump sums upon plan termination. Plan C's administrator pays a designated benefit of $10,000 to the PBGC on behalf of P, who was age 30 on the deemed distribution date.

(1) P's spouse, S, is located and has a death certificate showing that P died on or after the deemed distribution date with S as spouse. S is the same age as P, and would like survivor benefits to commence immediately, at age 55 (as permitted by the plan). S's benefit is the survivor's share of the joint and 50 percent survivor annuity which is actuarially equivalent, as of the deemed distribution date, to $9,700 (the unloaded designated benefit).

(2) The select and ultimate interest rates on Plan C's deemed distribution date were 7.50 percent for the first 20 years and 5.75 percent thereafter. Using these rates and the blended mortality table described in paragraph (2) of the definition of "missing participant annuity assumptions" in § 4050.2, the present value as of the deemed distribution date of each dollar of annual benefit (payable monthly as a joint and 50 percent survivor annuity) is $2.4048 if the benefit begins when S and P would have been age 55. Thus, the monthly benefit to S commencing at age 55 is $168 (50 percent of $9,700 / (2.4048 x 12)). Since P could have elected a lump sum upon plan termination, S may elect a lump sum. S's lump sum is the present value as of the deemed distribution date (using the missing participant annuity assumptions) of the monthly benefit of $168, accumulated with interest at the designated benefit interest rate to the date paid.

Subtitle D—Liability

AMOUNTS PAYABLE BY THE CORPORATION

Act Sec. 4061. The corporation shall pay benefits under a single-employer plan terminated under this title subject to the limitations and requirements of subtitle B of this title. The corporation shall provide financial assistance to pay benefits under a multiemployer plan which is insolvent under section 4245 or 4281(d)(2)(A), subject to the limitations and requirements of subtitles B, C, and E of this title. Amounts guaranteed by the corporation under sections 4022 and 4022A shall be paid by the corporation only out of the appropriate fund. The corporation shall make payments under the supplemental program to reimburse multiemployer plans for uncollectible withdrawal liability only out of the fund established under section 4005(e).

Amendment

P.L. 96-364, § 403(f):

Amended Sec. 4061 to read as above, effective September 26, 1980. Prior to amendment, Sec. 4061 read as follows:

"The corporation shall pay benefits under a plan terminated under this title subject to the limitations and requirements of subtitle B of this title. Amounts guaranteed by the corporation under section 4022 shall be paid by the corporation out of the appropriate fund."

Regulations

The following regulations were adopted by the Pension Benefit Guaranty Corporation on July 1, 1996 (61 FR 34002). Prior to July 1, 1996, PBGC regulations were under Chapter XXVI of Title 29 of the Code of Federal Regulations. Effective July 1, 1996, PBGC regulations were moved to Chapter XL, and were renumbered and reorganized.

§ 4061.1 **Cross-references.** See part 4022 of this chapter regarding benefits payable under terminated single-employer plans and § 4281.47 of this chapter regarding financial assistance to pay benefits under insolvent multiemployer plans.

[¶ 15,620]
LIABILITY FOR TERMINATION OF SINGLE-EMPLOYER PLANS UNDER A DISTRESS TERMINATION OR A TERMINATION BY THE CORPORATION

Act Sec. 4062.(a) In General. In any case in which a single-employer plan is terminated in a distress termination under section 4041(c) or a termination otherwise instituted by the corporation under section 4042, any person who is, on the termination date, a contributing sponsor of the plan or a member of such a contributing sponsor's controlled group shall incur liability under this section. The liability under this section of all such persons shall be joint and several. The liability under this section consists of—

(1) liability to the corporation, to the extent provided in subsection (b), and

(2) liability to the trustee appointed under subsection (b) or (c) of section 4042, to the extent provided in subsection (c).

Act Sec. 4062. LIABILITY TO THE CORPORATION.—

(b)(1) Amount of liability.—

(A) In general. Except as provided in subparagraph (B), the liability to the corporation of a person described in subsection (a) shall be the total amount of the unfunded benefit liabilities (as to the termination date) to all participants and beneficiaries under the plan, together with interest (at a reasonable rate) calculated from the termination date in accordance with regulations prescribed by the corporation.

(B) Special rule in case of subsequent insufficiency. For purposes of subparagraph (A), in any case described in section 4041(c)(3)(C)(ii), actuarial present values shall be determined as of the date of the notice to the corporation (or the finding by the corporation) described in such section.

(2) Payment of liability.—

(A) In general. Except as provided in subparagraph (B), the liability to the corporation under this subsection shall be due and payable to the corporation as of the termination date, in cash or securities acceptable to the corporations.

(B) Special rule. Payment of so much of the liability under paragraph (1)(A) as exceeds 30 percent of the collective net worth of all persons described in subsection (a) (including interest)" shall be made under commercially reasonable terms prescribed by the corporation. The parties involved shall make a reasonable effort to reach the agreement on such commercially reasonable terms. Any such terms prescribed by the corporation shall provide for deferral of 50 percent of any amount of liability otherwise payable for any year under this subparagraph if a person subject to such liability demonstrates to the satisfaction of the corporation that no person subject to such liability has any individual pre-tax profits for such person's fiscal year ending during such year.

(3) Alternative arrangements. The corporation and any person liable under this section may agree to alternative arrangements for the satisfaction of liability to the corporation under this subsection.

Act Sec. 4062. LIABILITY TO SECTION 4042 TRUSTEE. (c) A person described in subsection (a) shall be subject to liability under this subsection to the trustee appointed under subsection (b) or (c). The liability of such person under this subsection shall consist of—

(1) the outstanding balance of the accumulated funding deficiencies (within the meaning of section 302(a)(2) of this Act and section 412(a) of the Internal Revenue Code of 1986) of the plan (if any) (which, for purposes of this subparagraph, shall include the amount of any increase in such accumulated funding deficiencies of the plan which would result if all pending applications for waivers of the minimum funding standard under section 303 of this Act or section 412(d) of such Code and for extensions of the amortization period under section 304 of this Act or section 412(e) of such Code with respect to such plan were denied and if no additional contributions (other than those already made by the termination date) were made for the plan year in which the termination date occurs or for any previous plan year),

(2) the outstanding balance of the amount of waived funding deficiencies of the plan waived before such date under section 303 of this Act or section 412(d) of such Code (if any), and

(3) the outstanding balance of the amount of decreases in the minimum funding standard allowed before such date under section 304 of this Act or section 412(e) of such Code (if any), together with interest (at a reasonable rate) calculated from the termination date in accordance with regulations prescribed by the corporation. The liability under this subsection shall be due and payable to such trustee as of the termination date, in cash or securities acceptable to such trustee.

Act Sec. 4062. DEFINITIONS.

(d)(1) Collective net worth of persons subject to liability.—

(A) In general. The collective net worth of persons subject to liability in connection with a plan termination consists of the sum of the individual net worths of all persons who—

(i) have individual net worths which are greater than zero, and

(ii) are (as of the termination date) contributing sponsors of the terminated plan or members of their controlled groups.

(B) Determination of net worth. For purposes of this paragraph, the net worth of a person is—

(i) determined on whatever basis best reflects, in the determination of the corporation, the current status of the person's operations and prospects at the time chosen for determining the net worth of the person, and

(ii) increased by the amount of any transfers of assets made by the person which are determined by the corporation to be improper under the circumstances, including any such transfers which would be inappropriate under title 11, United States Code, if the person were a debtor in a case under chapter 7 of such title.

(C) Timing of determination. For purposes of this paragraph, determinations of net worth shall be made as of a day chosen by the corporation (during the 120-day period ending with the termination date) and shall be computed without regard to any liability under this section.

(2) Pre-tax profits. The term "pre-tax profits" means—

(A) except as provided in subparagraph (B), for any fiscal year of any person, such person's consolidated net income (excluding any extraordinary charges to income and including any extraordinary credits to income) for such fiscal year, as shown on audited financial statements prepared in accordance with generally accepted accounting principles, or

(B) for any fiscal year of an organization described in section 501(c) of the Internal Revenue Code of 1954, the excess of income over expenses (as such terms are defined for such organizations under generally accepted accounting principles),

before provision for or deduction of Federal or other income tax, any contribution to any single-employer plan of which such person is a contributing sponsor at any time during the period beginning on the termination date and ending with the end of such fiscal year, and any amounts required to be paid for such fiscal year under this section. The corporation may by regulation require such information to be filed on such forms as may be necessary to determine the existence and amount of such pre-tax profits.

Act Sec. 4062. TREATMENT OF SUBSTANTIAL CESSATION OF OPERATIONS. (e) If an employer ceases operations at a facility in any location and, as a result of such cessation of operations, more than 20 percent of the total number of his employees who are participants under a plan established and maintained by him are separated from employment, the employer shall be treated with respect to that plan as if he were a substantial employer under a plan under which more than one employer makes contributions and the provisions of sections 4063, 4064, and 4065 shall apply.

Amendments

P.L. 101-239, § 7881(f)(2):

Amended ERISA Sec. 4062(a) by inserting "and" at the end of paragraph (1); by striking paragraph (2); by redesignating paragraph (3) as paragraph (2); and in paragraph (2) (as redesignated) by striking "subsection (d)" and inserting "subsection (c)." Prior to being stricken, paragraph (2) read as follows:

(2) liability to the trust established pursuant to section 4041(c)(3)(B)(ii) or (iii) or section 4042(i) to the extent provided in subsection (c), and

P.L. 101-239, § 7881(f)(10)(A):

Amended ERISA Sec. 4062(b)(2)(B) by striking "the liability under paragraph (1)(A)(ii)" and inserting "so much of the liability under paragraph (1)(A) as exceeds 30 percent of the collective net worth of all persons described in subsection (a) (including interest)."

P.L. 101-239, § 7881(f)(10)(B):

Amended P.L. 100-203, § 9312(b)(2)(B)(ii) to read as below.

The above amendments are effective as if included in P.L. 100-203, § 9312.

P.L. 101-239, § 7891(a)(1):

Titles I, III, and IV of ERISA (other than sections 3(37)(E), 301(a)(7), and 308, the last sentence of section 408(d), and sections 414(c), 4001(a)(3)(ii), and 4303) are each amended by striking "Internal Revenue Code of 1954" each place it appears and inserting "Internal Revenue Code of 1986" effective October 22, 1986.

P.L. 100-203, § 9312(b)(1)(A)

Repealed ERISA Sec. 4062(c) effective for (A) plan terminations under section 4041(c) of ERISA with respect to which notices of intent to terminate are provided under section 4041(a)(2) of ERISA after December 17, 1987, and (B) plan terminations with respect to which proceedings are instituted by the Pension Benefit Guaranty Corporation under section 4042 of ERISA after December 17, 1987.

Prior to repeal, ERISA Sec. 4062(c) read as follows:

Act Sec. 4062. (c) Liability to Section 4049 Trust.—

(1) Amount of Liability.—

(A) In General.—In any case in which there is an outstanding amount of benefit commitments under a plan terminated under section 4041(c) or 4042, a person described in subsection (a) shall be subject to liability under this subsection to the trust established under section 4041(c)(3)(B)(ii) or (iii) or section 4042(i) in connection with the terminated plan. Except as provided in subparagraph (B), the liability of such person under this subsection shall consist of the lesser of—

(i) 75 pecent of the total outstanding amount of benefit commitments under the plan, or

(ii) 15 percent of the actuarial present value (determined as of the termination date of the basis of assumptions prescribed by the corporation for purposes of section 4044) of all benefit commitments under the plan.

(B) Special Rule in Case of Subsequent Insufficiency.—For purposes of subparagraph (A)—

(i) Plan Insufficient for Guaranteed Benefits.—In any case described in section 4041(c)(3)(C)(ii), actuarial present values shall be determined as of the date of the notice to the corporation (or the finding by the corporation) described in such section.

(ii) Plans Sufficient for Guaranteed Benefits but Insufficient for Benefit Entitlement.—In any case described in section 4041(c)(3)(C)(i) but not described in section 4041(c)(3)(C)(ii), actuarial present values shall be determined as of the date on which the final distribution of assets is completed.

(2) Payment of Liability.—

(A) General Rule.—Except as otherwise provided in this paragraph, payment of a person's liability under this subsection shall be made for liability payment years under commercially reasonable terms prescribed by the fiduciary designated by corporation pursuant to section 4049(b)(1)(A). Such fiduciary and the liable persons assessed liability under this subsection shall make a reasonable effort to reach agreement on such commercially reasonable terms.

(B) Special Rule for Plans with Low Amounts of Liability.—In any case in which the amount described in paragraph (1)(A) is less than $100,000, the requirements of subparagraph (A) may be satisfied by payment of such liability over 10 liability payment years in equal annual installments (with interest at the rate determined under section 6621(b) of the Internal Revenue Code of 1954. The corporation may, by regulation, increase the dollar amount referred to in this subparagraph as it determines appropriate, taking into account reasonable administrative costs of trusts established under section 4041(c)(3)(B)(ii) or (iii) or section 4042(i).

(C) Deferral of Payments.—The terms of payment provided for under subparagraph (A) or (B) shall also provide for deferral of 75 percent of any amount of liability otherwise payable for any liability payment year if a person subject to such liability demonstrates to the satisfaction of the corporation that no person subject to such liability has any individual pre-tax profits for such person's fiscal year ending during such year. The amount of liability so deferred is payable only after payment in full of any amount of liability under subsection (b) in connection with the termination of the same plan which has been deferred pursuant to terms provided for under subsection (b)(2)(B).

P.L. 100-203, § 9312(b)(1)(B):

Amended ERISA Sec. 4062 by redesignating subsections (d), (e) and (f) as (c), (d) and (e). For the effective date, see Act Sec. 9312(b)(1)(A), above.

P.L. 100-203, § 9312(b)(2)(A):

Amended ERISA Sec. 4062(b)(1)(A) to read as above. For the effective date, see Act Sec. 9312(b)(1)(A), above. Prior to amendment, ERISA Sec. 4062(b)(1)(A) read as follows:

(A) In General.—Except as provided in subparagraph (B), the liability to the corporation of a person described in subsection (a) shall consist of the sum of—

(1) the lesser of—

(I) the total amount of unfunded guaranteed benefits (as of the termination date) of all participants and beneficiaries under the plan, or

(II) 30 percent of the collective net worth of all persons described in subsection (a), and

(ii) the excess (if any) of—

(I) 75 percent of the amount described in clause (i)(I), over

(II) the amount described in clause (i)(II), together with interest (at a reasonable rate) calculated from the termination date in accordance with regulations prescribed by the corporation.

P.L. 100-203, § 9312(b)(2)(B)(ii):

Amended ERISA Sec. 4062(d) by striking out paragraph 3. For the effective date, see Act Sec. 9312(b)(1)(A), above.

P.L. 99-272:

Act Sec. 11011(a) amended ERISA Sec. 4062 by redesignating section (e) as section (f), by striking out sections (a) through (d) and by adding new sections (a)-(e) to read as above. Subsection (f), as redesignated, was amended by Act Sec. 11011(b) to insert "Treatment of substantial cessation of operations.—"after(f).

The above amendments apply to payments made after January 1, 1986 in taxable years ending after that date.

Prior to amendment, ERISA Sec. 4062 read as follows:

LIABILITY OF EMPLOYER

Act Sec. 4062. (a) This section applies to any employer who maintained a single-employer plan at the time it was terminated, but does not apply—

(1) to an employer who maintained a plan with respect to which he paid the annual premium described in section 4006(a)(2)(B) for each of the 5 plan years immediately preceding the plan year during which the plan terminated unless the conditions imposed by the corporation on the payment of coverage under section 4023 do not permit such coverage to apply under the circumstances, or

(2) to the extent of any liability arising out of the insolvency of an insurance company with respect to an insurance contract.

Act Sec. 4062. (b) Any employer to which this section applies shall be liable to the corporation, in an amount equal to the lesser of—

(1) the excess of—

(A) the current value of the plan's benefits guaranteed under this title on the date of termination over

(B) the current value of the plan's assets allocable to such benefits on the date of termination, or

(2) 30 percent of the net worth of the employer determined as of a day, chosen by the corporation but not more than 120 days prior to the date of termination, computed without regard to any liability under this section.

Act Sec. 4062. (c) For purposes of subsection (b)(2) the net worth of an employer is—

(1) determined on whatever basis best reflects, in the determination of the corporation, the current status of the employer's operations and prospects at the time chosen for determining the net worth of the employer, and

(2) increased by the amount of any transfers of assets made by the employer determined by the corporation to be improper under the circumstances, including any such transfers which would be inappropriate under title 11 of the United States Code if the employer were a debtor in a case under chapter 7 of such title.

Act Sec. 4062. (d) For purposes of this section the following rules apply in the case of certain corporate reorganizations:

(1) If an employer ceases to exist by reason of a reorganization which involves a mere change in identity, form, or place of organization, however effected, a successor corporation resulting from such reorganization shall be treated as the employer to whom this section applies.

(2) If an employer ceases to exist by reason of a liquidation into a parent corporation, the parent corporation shall be treated as the employer to whom this section applies.

(3) If an employer ceases to exist by reason of a merger, consolidation, or division, the successor corporation or corporations shall be treated as the employer to whom this section applies.

Act Sec. 4062. (e) If an employer ceases operations at a facility in any location and, as a result of such cessation of operations, more than 20 percent of the total number of his employees who are participants under a plan established and maintained by him are separatd from employment, the employer shall be treated with respect to that plan as if he were a substantial employer under a plan under which more than one employer makes contributions and the provisions of sections 4063, 4064, and 4065 shall apply.

P.L. 96-364, § 403(g):

Amended Sec. 4062(a) by striking out "plan (other than a multiemployer plan)" and substituting "single-employer plan" in its place, effective September 26, 1980.

P.L. 95-598, § 321(b):

Amended Sec. 4062(c), effective October 1, 1979, by substituting "title 11 of the United States Code" for "Bankruptcy Act" and by substituting "a debtor in a case under chapter 7 of such title" for "the subject of a proceeding under that Act."

Regulations

The following regulations were adopted by the Pension Benefit Guaranty Corporation on July 1, 1996 (61 FR 34002). Prior to July 1, 1996, PBGC regulations were under Chapter XXVI of Title 29 of the Code of Federal Regulations. Effective July 1, 1996, PBGC regulations were moved to Chapter XL, and were renumbered and reorganized. Reg. §§ 4062.9 and 4062.10 were amended October 28, 2003 (68 FR 61344).

[¶ 15,621]

§ 4062.1 **Purpose and scope.** The purpose of this part is to set forth rules for determination and payment of the liability incurred, under section 4062(b) of ERISA, upon termination of any single-employer plan and, to the extent appropriate, determination of the liability incurred with respect to multiple employer plans under sections 4063 and 4064 of ERISA. The provisions of this part regarding the amount of liability to the PBGC that is incurred upon termination of a single-employer plan apply with respect to a plan for which a notice of intent to terminate under section 4041(c) of ERISA is issued or proceedings to terminate under section 4042 of ERISA are instituted after December 17, 1987. Those provisions also apply, to the extent described in paragraph (a) of this section, to the amount of liability for withdrawal from a multiple employer plan after that date.

[¶ 15,621A]

§ 4062.2 **Definitions.** The following terms are defined in § 4001.2 of this chapter: *benefit liabilities, Code, contributing sponsor, controlled group, ERISA, fair market value, guaranteed benefit, multiple employer plan, notice of intent to terminate, PBGC, person, plan, plan administrator, proposed termination date, single-employer plan,* and *termination date.*

In addition, for purposes of this part, the term *collective net worth of persons subject to liability in connection with a plan termination* means the sum of the individual net worths of all persons that have individual net worths which are greater than zero and that (as of the termination date) are contributing sponsors of the terminated plan or members of their controlled groups, as determined in accordance with section 4062(d)(1) of ERISA and § 4062.4 of this part.

[¶ 15,621B]

§ 4062.3 **Amount and payment of section 4062(b) liability.** (a) *Amount of liability.* (1) *General rule.* Except as provided in paragraph (a)(2) of this section, the amount of section 4062(b) liability is the total amount (as of the termination date) of the unfunded benefit liabilities (within the meaning of section 4001(a)(18) of ERISA) to all participants and beneficiaries under the plan, together with interest calculated from the termination date in accordance with § 4062.7.

(2) *Special rule in case of subsequent finding of inability to pay guaranteed benefits.* In any distress termination proceeding under section 4041(c) of ERISA and part 4041 of this chapter in which (as described in section 4041(c)(3)(C)(ii) of ERISA), after a determination that the plan is sufficient for benefit liabilities or for guaranteed benefits, the plan administrator finds that the plan is or will be insufficient for guaranteed benefits and the PBGC concurs with that finding, or the PBGC makes such a finding on its own initiative, actuarial present values shall be determined as of the date of the notice to, or the finding by, the PBGC of insufficiency for guaranteed benefits.

(b) *Payment of liability.* Section 4062(b) liability is due and payable as of the termination date, in cash or securities acceptable to the PBGC, except that, as provided in § 4062.8(c), the PBGC shall prescribe commercially reasonable terms for payment of so much of such liability as exceeds 30 percent of the collective net worth of persons subject to liability in connection with a plan termination. The PBGC may make alternative arrangements, as provided in § 4062.8(b).

[¶ 15,621C]

§ 4062.4 **Determinations of net worth and collective net worth.** (a) *General rules.* When a contributing sponsor, or member(s) of a contributing sponsor's controlled group, notifies and submits information to the PBGC in accordance with § 4062.6, the PBGC shall determine the net worth, as of the net worth record date, of that contributing sponsor and any members of its controlled group based on the factors

set forth in paragraph (c) of this section and shall include the value of any assets that it determines, pursuant to paragraph (d) of this section, have been improperly transferred. In making such determinations, the PBGC will consider information submitted pursuant to § 4062.6. The PBGC shall then determine the collective net worth of persons subject to liability in connection with a plan termination.

(b) *Partnerships and sole proprietorships.* In the case of a person that is a partnership or a sole proprietorship, net worth does not include the personal assets and liabilities of the partners or sole proprietor, except for the assets included pursuant to paragraph (d) of this section. As used in this paragraph, "personal assets" are those assets which do not produce income for the business being valued or are not used in the business.

(c) *Factors for determining net worth.* A person's net worth is equal to its fair market value and fair market value shall be determined on the basis of the factors set forth below, to the extent relevant; different factors may be considered with respect to different portions of the person's operations.

(1) A bona fide sale of, agreement to sell, or offer to purchase or sell the business of the person made on or about the net worth record date.

(2) A bona fide sale of, agreement to sell, or offer to purchase or sell stock or a partnership interest in the person, made on or about the net worth record date.

(3) If stock in the person is publicly traded, the price of such stock on or about the net worth record date.

(4) The price/earnings ratios and prices of stocks of similar trades or businesses on or about the net worth record date.

(5) The person's economic outlook, as reflected by its earnings and dividend projections, current financial condition, and business history.

(6) The economic outlook for the person's industry and the market it serves.

(7) The appraised value, including the liquidating value, of the person's tangible and intangible assets.

(8) The value of the equity assumed in a plan of reorganization of a person in a case under title 11, United States Code, or any similar law of a state or political subdivision thereof.

(9) Any other factor relevant in determining the person's net worth.

(d) *Improper transfers.* A person's net worth shall include the value of any assets transferred by the person which the PBGC determines were improperly transferred for the purpose, as inferred from all the facts and circumstances, and with the effect of avoiding liability under this part. Assets "improperly transferred" include but are not limited to assets sold, leased or otherwise transferred for less than adequate consideration and assets distributed as gifts, capital distributions and stock redemptions inconsistent with past practices of the employer. The word "transfer" includes but is not limited to sales, assignments, pledges, leases, gifts and dividends.

[¶ 15,621D]

§ 4062.5 **Net worth record date.** (a) *General.* Unless the PBGC establishes an earlier net worth record date pursuant to paragraph (b) of this section, the net worth record date, for all purposes under this part, is the plan's termination date.

(b) *Establishment of an earlier net worth record date.* At any time during a termination proceeding, the PBGC, in order to prevent undue loss to or abuse of the plan termination insurance system, may establish as the net worth record date an earlier date during the 120-day period ending with the termination date.

(c) *Notification.* Whenever the PBGC establishes an earlier net worth record date, it shall immediately give liable person(s) written notification of that fact. The written notice may also include a request for additional information, as provided in §4062.6(a)(3).

[¶ 15,621E]

§4062.6 **Net worth notification and information.** (a) *General.* (1) A contributing sponsor or member of the contributing sponsor's controlled group that believes section 4062(b) liability exceeds 30 percent of the collective net worth of persons subject to liability in connection with a plan termination shall—

(i) So notify the PBGC by the 90th day after the notice of intent to terminate is filed with the PBGC or, if no notice of intent to terminate is filed with the PBGC and the PBGC institutes proceedings under section 4042 of ERISA, within 30 days after the establishment of the plan's termination date in such proceedings; and

(ii) Submit to the PBGC the information specified in paragraph (b) of this section with respect to the contributing sponsor and each member of the contributing sponsor's controlled group (if any)—

(A) By the 120th day after the proposed termination date, or

(B) If no notice of intent to terminate is filed with the PBGC and the PBGC institutes proceedings under section 4042 of ERISA, within 120 days after the establishment of the plan's termination date in such proceedings.

(2) If a contributing sponsor or a member of its controlled group complies with the requirements of paragraph (a)(1) of this section, the PBGC will consider the requirements to be satisfied by all members of that controlled group.

(3) The PBGC may require any person subject to liability—

(i) To submit the information specified in paragraph (b) of this section within a shorter period whenever the PBGC believes that its ability to obtain information or payment of liability is in jeopardy, and

(ii) To submit additional information within 30 days, or a different specified time, after the PBGC's written notification that it needs such information to make net worth determinations.

(4) If a provision of paragraph (b) of this section or a PBGC notice specifies information previously submitted to the PBGC, a person may respond by identifying the previous submission in which the response was provided.

(b) *Net worth information.* The following information specifications apply, individually, with respect to each person subject to liability:

(1) An estimate, made in accordance with §4062.4, of the person's net worth on the net worth record date and a statement, with supporting evidence, of the basis for the estimate.

(2) A copy of the person's audited (or if not available, unaudited) financial statements for the 5 full fiscal years plus any partial fiscal year preceding the net worth record date. The statements must include balance sheets, income statements, and statements of changes in financial position and must be accompanied by the annual reports, if available.

(3) A statement of all sales and copies of all offers or agreements to buy or sell at least 25 percent of the person's assets or at least 5 percent of the person's stock or partnership interest, made on or about the net worth record date.

(4) A statement of the person's current financial condition and business history.

(5) A statement of the person's business plans, including projected earnings and, if available, dividend projections.

(6) Any appraisal of the person's fixed and intangible assets made on or about the net worth record date.

(7) A copy of any plan of reorganization, whether or not confirmed, with respect to a case under title 11, United States Code, or any similar law of a state or political subdivision thereof, involving the person and occurring within 5 calendar years prior to or any time after the net worth record date.

(c) *Incomplete submission.* If a contributing sponsor and/or members of the contributing sponsor's controlled group do not submit all of the information required pursuant to paragraph (a) of this section (other than the estimate described in paragraph (b)(1) of this section) with respect to each person subject to liability, the PBGC may base determinations of net worth and the collective net worth of persons subject to liability in connection with a plan termination on any such information that such person(s) did submit, as well as any other pertinent information that the PBGC may have. In general, the PBGC will view information as of a date further removed from the net worth record date as having less probative value than information as of a date nearer to the net worth record date.

[¶ 15,621F]

§4062.7 **Calculating interest on liability and refunds of overpayments.** (a) *Interest.* Whether or not the PBGC has granted deferred payment terms pursuant to §4062.8, the amount of liability under this part includes interest, from the termination date, on any unpaid portion of the liability. Such interest accrues at the rate set forth in paragraph (c) of this section until the liability is paid in full and is compounded daily. When liability under this part is paid in more than one payment, the PBGC will apply each payment to the satisfaction of accrued interest and then to the reduction of principal.

(b) *Refunds.* If a contributing sponsor or member(s) of a contributing sponsor's controlled group pays the PBGC an amount that exceeds the full amount of liability under this part, the PBGC shall refund the excess amount, with interest at the rate set forth in paragraph (c) of this section. Interest on an overpayment accrues from the later of the date of the overpayment or 10 days prior to the termination date until the date of the refund and is compounded daily.

(c) *Interest rate.* The interest rate on liability under this part and refunds thereof is the annual rate prescribed in section 6601(a) of the Code, and will change whenever the interest rate under section 6601(a) of the Code changes.

[¶ 15,621G]

§4062.8 **Arrangements for satisfying liability.** (a) *General.* The PBGC will defer payment, or agree to other arrangements for the satisfaction, of any portion of liability to the PBGC only when—

(1) As provided in paragraph (b) of this section, the PBGC determines that such action is necessary to avoid the imposition of a severe hardship and that there is a reasonable possibility that the terms so prescribed will be met and the entire liability paid; or

(2) As provided in paragraph (c) of this section, the PBGC determines that section 4062(b) liability exceeds 30 percent of the collective net worth of persons subject to liability in connection with a plan termination.

(b) *Upon request.* If the PBGC determines that such action is necessary to avoid the imposition of a severe hardship on persons that are or may become liable under section 4062, 4063, or 4064 of ERISA and that there is a reasonable possibility that persons so liable will be able to meet the terms prescribed and pay the entire liability, the PBGC, in its discretion and when so requested in accordance with paragraph (b)(2) of this section, may grant deferred payment or other terms for the satisfaction of such liability.

(1) In determining what, if any, terms to grant, the PBGC shall examine the following factors:

(i) The ratio of the liability to the net worth of the person making the request and (if different) to the collective net worth of persons subject to liability in connection with a plan termination.

(ii) The overall financial condition of persons that are or may become liable, including, with respect to each such person—

(A) The amounts and terms of existing debts;

(B) The amount and availability of liquid assets;

(C) Current and past cash flow; and

(D) Projected cash flow, including a projection of the impact on operations that would be caused by the immediate full payment of the liability.

(iii) The availability of credit from private sector sources to the person making the request and to other liable persons.

Reg. §4062.8(b)(1)(iii) **¶ 15,621G**

(2) A contributing sponsor or member of a contributing sponsor's controlled group may request deferred payment or other terms for the satisfaction of any portion of the liability under section 4062, 4063, or 4064 of ERISA at any time by filing a written request. The request must include the information specified in §4062.6(b), except that—

(i) If the request is filed one year or more after the net worth record date, references to "the net worth record date" in §4062.6(b) shall be replaced by "the most recent annual anniversary of the net worth record date"; and

(ii) Information that already has been submitted to the PBGC need not be submitted again.

(c) *Liability exceeding 30 percent of collective net worth.* If the PBGC determines that section 4062(b) liability exceeds 30 percent of the collective net worth of persons subject to the liability, the PBGC will, after making a reasonable effort to reach agreement with such persons, prescribe commercially reasonable terms for payment of so much of the liability as exceeds 30 percent of the collective net worth of such persons. The terms prescribed by the PBGC for payment of that portion of the liability (including interest) will provide for deferral of 50 percent of any amount otherwise payable for any year if a person subject to such liability demonstrates to the satisfaction of the PBGC that no person subject to such liability has any individual pre-tax profits (within the meaning of section 4062(d)(2) of ERISA) for such person's last full fiscal year ending during that year.

(d) *Interest.* Interest on unpaid liability is calculated in accordance with §4062.7(a).

(e) *Security during period of deferred payment.* As a condition to the granting of deferred payment terms, PBGC may, in its discretion, require that the liable person(s) provide PBGC with such security for its obligations as the PBGC deems adequate.

[¶ 15,621H]

§4062.9 **Method and date of filing; where to file.** (a) *Method of filing.* The PBGC applies the rules in subpart A of part 4000 of this chapter to determine permissible methods of filing with the PBGC under this part. Payment of liability must be clearly designated as such and include the name of the plan.

(b) *Filing date.* The PBGC applies the rules in subpart C of part 4000 of this chapter to determine the date that a submission under this part was filed with the PBGC.

(c) *Where to file.* See Sec. 4000.4 of this chapter for information on where to file.

[Amended 10/28/2003 by 68 FR 61344]

[¶ 15,621I]

§4062.10 **Computation of time.** The PBGC applies the rules in subpart D of part 4000 of this chapter to compute any time period under this part. However, for purposes of determining the amount of an interest charge under Sec. 4062.7, the rule in Sec. 4000.43(a) of this chapter governing periods ending on weekends or Federal holidays does not apply.

[Amended 10/28/2003 by 68 FR 61344]

[¶ 15,630]
LIABILITY OF SUBSTANTIAL EMPLOYER FOR WITHDRAWAL FROM SINGLE-EMPLOYER PLANS UNDER MULTIPLE CONTROLLED GROUPS

Act Sec. 4063. (a) Except as provided in subsection (d), the plan administrator of a single-employer plan which has two or more contributing sponsors at least two of whom are not under common control—

(1) shall notify the corporation of the withdrawal during a plan year of a substantial employer for such plan year from the plan, with 60 days after such withdrawal, and

(2) request that the corporation determine the liability of all persons with respect to the withdrawal of the substantial employer.

The corporation shall, as soon as practicable thereafter, determine whether there is liability resulting from the withdrawal of the substantial employer and notify the liable persons of such liability.

Act Sec. 4063. (b) Except as provided in subsection (c), any one or more contributing sponsors who withdraw, during a plan year for which they constitute a substantial employer, from a single-employer plan which has two or more contributing sponsors at least two of whom are not under common control, shall, upon notification of such contributing sponsors by the corporation as provided by subsection (a), be liable, together with the members of their controlled groups, to the corporation in accordance with the provisions of section 4062 and this section. The amount of such employer's liability shall be computed on the basis of an amount determined by the corporation to be the amount described in section 4062 for the entire plan, as if the plan had been terminated by the corporation on the date of the employer's withdrawal, multiplied by a fraction—

(1) the numerator of which is the total amount required to be contributed to the plan by such contributing sponsor for the last 5 years ending prior to the withdrawal, and

(2) the denominator of which is the total amount required to be contributed to the plan by all contributing sponsors for such last 5 years.

In addition to and in lieu of the manner prescribed in the preceding sentence, the corporation may also determine such liability of each such employer on any other equitable basis prescribed by the corporation in regulations. Any amount collected by the corporation under this subsection shall be held in escrow subject to disposition in accordance with the provisions of paragraph (2) and (3) of subsection (c).

Act Sec. 4063. (c)(1) In lieu of payment of contributing sponsor's liability under this section the contributing sponsor may be required to furnish a bond to the corporation in an amount not exceeding 150 percent of his liability to insure payment of his liability under this section. The bond shall have as surety thereon a corporate surety company which is an acceptable surety on Federal bonds under authority granted by the Secretary of the Treasury under sections 6 through 13 of title 6, United States Code. Any such bond shall be in a form or of a type approved by the Secretary including individual bonds or schedule or blanket forms of bonds which covers a group or class.

(2) If the plan is not terminated under section 4041(c) or 4042 within the 5-year period commencing on the day of withdrawal, the liability of such employer is abated and any payment held in escrow shall be refunded without interest to the employer (or the bond cancelled) in accordance with bylaws or rules prescribed by the corporation.

(3) If the plan terminates under section 4041(c) or 4042 within the 5-year period commencing on the day of withdrawal, the corporation shall—

(A) demand payment or realize on the bond and hold such amount in escrow for the benefit of the plan;

(B) treat any escrowed payments under this section as if they were plan assets and apply them in a manner consistent with this subtitle; and

(c) refund any amount to the contributing sponsor which is not required to meet any obligation of the corporation with respect to the plan.

Act Sec. 4063. (d) The provisions of this subsection apply in the case of a withdrawal described in subsection (a), and the provision of subsections (b) and (c) shall not apply, if the corporation determines that the procedure provided for under this subsection is consistent with the purposes of this section and section 4064 and is more appropriate in the particular case. Upon a showing by the plan administrator of the plan that the withdrawal from the plan by one or more contributing sponsors has resulted, or will result, in a significant reduction in the amount of aggregate contributions to or under the plan by employers, the corporation may—

(1) require the plan fund to be equitably allocated between those participants no longer working in covered service under the plan as a result of the withdrawal, and those participants who remain in covered service under the plan;

(2) treat that portion of the plan funds allocable under paragraph (1) to participants no longer in covered service as a termination; and

(3) treat that portion of the plan fund allocable to participants remaining in covered service as a separate plan.

Act Sec. 4063. (e) The corporation is authorized to waive the application of the provisions of subsections (b), (c), and (d) of this section to any employer or plan administrator whenever it determines that there is an indemnity agreement in effect among contributing sponsors under the plan which is adequate to satisfy the purposes of this section and of section 4064.

Amendments

P.L. 99-272:

Act Sec. 11016(a)(5)(A)(i)(I) amended ERISA Sec. 4063(a) by striking out "plan under which more than one employer makes contributions (other than a multiemployer plan)" and inserting "single-employer plan which has two or more contributing sponsors at least two of whom are not under common control."

Act Sec. 11016(a)(5)(A)(i)(II) amended ERISA Sec. 4063(a)(1) by striking out "withdrawal of a substantial employer" and inserting "withdrawal during the plan year of a substantial employer for such plan year."

Act Sec. 11016(a)(5)(A)(i)(III) amended ERISA Sec. 4063(a)(2) by striking out "of such employer" and inserting "of all persons with respect to the withdrawal of the substantial employer."

Act Sec. 11016(a)(5)(A)(i)(IV) amended ERISA Sec. 4063(a) by striking out "whether such employer is liable for any amount under this subtitle with respect to the withdrawal" and inserting "whether there is liability resulting from the withdrawal of the substantial employer."

Act Sec. 11016(a)(5)(A)(i)(V) amended ERISA Sec. 4063(a) by striking out "notify such employer" and inserting "notify the liable persons."

Act Sec. 11016(a)(5)(A)(ii)(I) amended ERISA Sec. 4063(b) by striking out "an employer who withdraws from a plan to which section 4021 applies, during a plan year for which he was a substantial employer, and who is notified by the corporation as provided by subsection (a), shall be liable" and by inserting *"any one or more contributing sponsors who withdraw, during a plan year for which they constitute a substantial employer, from a single-employer plan which has two or more contributing sponsors at least two of whom are not under common control, shall, upon notification of such contributing sponsors by the corporation as provided by subsection (a), be liable, together with the members of their controlled groups."*

Act Sec. 11016(a)(5)(A)(ii)(II) amended ERISA Sec. 4063(b) by striking out "such employer's."

Act Sec. 11016(a)(5)(A)(ii)(III) amended ERISA Sec. 4063(b) by striking out "the employer's withdrawal" and inserting "the withdrawal referred to in subsection (a)(1)."

Act Sec. 11016(a)(5)(A)(ii)(IV) amended ERISA Sec. 4063(b)(1) by striking out "such employer" and inserting "such contributing sponsors."

Act Sec. 11016(a)(5)(A)(ii)(V) amended ERISA Sec. 4063(b)(2) by striking out "all employers" and inserting "all contributing sponsors."

Act Sec. 11016(a)(5)(A)(ii)(VI) amended ERISA Sec. 4063(b) by striking out "the liability of each such employer" and inserting "such liability."

Act Sec. 11016(a)(5)(A)(iii)(I) amended ERISA Sec. 4063(c)(1) by striking out "In lieu of payment of his liability under this section the employer" and inserting "In lieu of payment of a contributing sponsor's liability under this section the contributing sponsor."

Act Sec. 11016(a)(5)(A)(iii)(II) amended ERISA Sec. 4063(c)(2) by inserting "under section 4041(c) or 4042" after "terminated;" by striking out "of such employer;" and, by striking out "to the employer (or his bond cancelled)" and inserting "(or the bond cancelled)."

Act Sec. 11016(a)(5)(A)(iii)(III) amended ERISA Sec. 4063(c)(3) by inserting "under section 4041(c) or 4042" after "terminates."

Act Sec. 11016(a)(5)(A)(iv)(I) amended ERISA Sec. 4063(d) by striking out "Upon a showing by the plan administrator of a plan (other than a multiemployer plan) that the withdrawal from the plan by any employer or employers has resulted" and inserting "Upon a showing by the plan administrator of the plan that the withdrawal from the plan by one or more contributing sponsors has resulted."

Act Sec. 11016(a)(5)(A)(iv)(II) amended ERISA Sec. 4063(d) by striking out "by employers."

Act Sec. 11016(a)(5)(A)(iv)(III) amended ERISA Sec. 4063(d)(1) by striking out "all other employers" and inserting "the."

Act Sec. 11016(a)(5)(A)(iv) amended ERISA Sec. 4063(d)(2) by striking out "termination" and inserting "plan termination under section 4042."

Act Sec. 11016(a)(5)(A)(v)(I) amended ERISA Sec. 4063(e) by striking out "to any employer or plan administrator."

Act Sec. 11016(a)(5)(A)(v)(II) amended ERISA Sec. 4063(e) by striking out "all other employers" and inserting "contributing sponsors."

Act Sec. 11016(a)(5)(A)(vi) amended the title to ERISA Sec. 4063 by adding at the end "From Single-Employer Plans Under Multiple Controlled Groups."

The above amendments take effect April 7, 1986.

P.L. 96-364, § 403(h):

Amended Sec. 4063 by adding "(other than a multiemployer plan)" in the first sentence in subsection (a) and the second sentence in subsection (d), effective September 26, 1980.

Regulations

The following regulations were adopted by the Pension Benefit Guaranty Corporation on July 1, 1996 (61 FR 34002). Prior to July 1, 1996, PBGC regulations were under Chapter XXVI of Title 29 of the Code of Federal Regulations. Effective July 1, 1996, PBGC regulations were moved to Chapter XL, and were renumbered and reorganized.

[¶ 15,631]

§ 4063.1 **Cross-references.** (a) Part 4062, subpart A, of this chapter sets forth rules for determination and payment of the liability incurred, under section 4062(b) of ERISA, upon termination of any single-employer plan and, to the extent appropriate, determination of the liability incurred with respect to multiple employer plans under sections 4063 and 4064 of ERISA.

(b) Part 4068 of this chapter includes rules regarding the PBGC's lien under section 4068 of ERISA with respect to liability arising under section 4062, 4063, or 4064.

[¶ 15,640]

LIABILITY ON TERMINATION OF SINGLE-EMPLOYER PLANS UNDER MULTIPLE CONTROLLED GROUPS

Act Sec. 4064. (a) This section applies to all contributing sponsors of a single-employer plan which has two or more contributing sponsors at least two of whom are not under common control at the time such plan is terminated under section 4041(c) or 4042 or who, at any time within the 5 plan years preceding the date of termination, made contributions under the plan.

Act Sec. 4064. (b) The corporation shall determine the liability with respect to each contributing sponsor and each member of its controlled group in a manner consistent with section 4062, except that the amount of liability determined under section 4062(b)(1) with respect to the entire plan shall be allocated to each controlled group by multiplying such amount by a fraction—

(1) the numerator of which is the amount required to be contributed to the plan for the last 5 plan years ending prior to the termination date by persons in such controlled group as contributing sponsors, and

(2) the denominator of which is the total amount required to be contributed to the plan for such last 5 years by all persons as contributing sponsors,

and section 4068(a) shall be applied separately with respect to each controlled group.

The corporation may also determine the liability of each such contributing sponsor and member of its controlled group on any other equitable basis prescribed by the corporation in regulations.

Amendments

P.L. 101-239, § 7881(f)(3)(A):

Amended ERISA Sec. 4064(b) by striking "and clauses (i)(II) and (ii) of section 4062(b)(1)(A)" and inserting "and section 4068(a)" effective as if included in P.L. 100-203, § 9312(b)(2).

P.L. 100-203, § 9312(b)(2)(C)(i):

Amended ERISA Sec. 4064(b) to read as above, effective for (A) plan terminations under section 4041(c) of ERISA with respect to which notices of intent to terminate are provided under section 4041(a)(2) of ERISA after December 17, 1987, and (B) plan terminations with respect to which proceedings are instituted by the Pension Benefit Guaranty Corporation under section 4042 of ERISA after December 17, 1987.

Prior to amendment, ERISA Sec. 4064(b), up to the second sentence, read as follows:

(b) The corporation shall determine the liability with respect to each contributing sponsor and each member of its controlled group in a manner consistent with section 4062, except that—

(1) the amount of the liability determined under section 4062(b)(1) with respect to the entire plan—

(A) shall be determined without regard to clauses (i)(II) and (ii) of section 4062(b)(1)(A), and

(B) shall be allocated to each controlled group by multiplying such amount by a fraction—

(i) the numerator of which is the amount required to be contributed to the plan for the last 5 plan years ending prior to the termination date by persons in such controlled group as contributing sponsors, and

(ii) the denominator of which is the total amount required to be contributed to the plan for such last 5 plan years by all persons as contributing sponsors,

and clauses (i)(II) and (ii) of section 4062(b)(1)(A) shall be applied separately with respect to each such controlled group, and

(2) the amount of the liability determined under section 4062(c)(1) with respect to the entire plan shall be allocated to each controlled group by multiplying such amount by the fraction described in paragraph (1)(B) in connection with such controlled group.

P.L. 99-272, § 11016(a)(5)(B)(i)(I), (II) and (ii):

Amended ERISA Sec. 4064(a) by striking out "all employers who maintain a plan under which more than one employer makes contributions (other than a multiemployer plan)" and inserting "all contributing sponsors of a single-employer plan which has two or more contributing sponsors at least two of whom are not under common control."

Amended ERISA Sec. 4064(a) by inserting "under section 4041(c) or 4042" after "terminated."

Amended ERISA Sec. 4064(b) to read as above.

Prior to amendment, ERISA Sec. 4064 read as follows:

Sec. 4064. (b) The corporation shall determine the liability of each such employer in a manner consistent with section 4062 except that the amount of the liability determined under section 4062(b)(1) with respect to the entire plan shall be allocated to each employer by multiplying such amounts by a fraction—

(1) the numerator of which is the amount required to be contributed to the plan by each employer for the last 5 plan years ending prior to the termination, and

(2) the denominator of which is the total amount required to be contributed to the plan by all such employers for such last 5 years, and the limitation described in section 4062(b)(2) shall be applied separately to each employer. The corporation may also determine the liability of each such employer on any other equitable basis prescribed by the corporation in regulations.

Act Sec. 11016(a)(5)(B)(iii) changed the heading of ERISA Sec. 4064 to read as above. Prior to amendment, the heading read as follows:

"Liability of Employers on Termination of Plan Maintained by More Than One Employer."

These amendments take effect on April 7, 1986.

P.L. 96-364, § 403(i)

Amended Sec. 4064(a), effective September 26, 1980, by adding "(other than a multiemployer plan)" after "plan under which more than one employer makes contributions".

Regulations

The following regulations were adopted by the Pension Benefit Guaranty Corporation on July 1, 1996 (61 FR 34002). Prior to July 1, 1996, PBGC regulations were under Chapter XXVI of Title 29 of the Code of Federal Regulations. Effective July 1, 1996, PBGC regulations were moved to Chapter XL, and were renumbered and reorganized.

[¶ 15,641]

§ 4064.1 **Cross-references.** (a) Part 4062, subpart A, of this chapter sets forth rules for determination and payment of the liability incurred under section 4062(b) of ERISA, upon termination of any single-employer plan and, to the extent appropriate, determination of the liability incurred with respect to multiple employer plans under sections 4063 and 4064 of ERISA.

(b) Part 4068 of this chapter includes rules regarding the PBGC's lien under section 4068 of ERISA with respect to liability arising under section 4062, 4063, or 4064.

[¶ 15,650]
ANNUAL REPORT OF PLAN ADMINISTRATOR

Act Sec. 4065. For each plan year for which section 4021 applies to a plan, the plan administrator shall file with the corporation, on a form prescribed by the corporation, an annual report which identifies the plan and plan administrator and which includes—

(1) a copy of each notification required under section 4063 with respect to such year,

(2) a statement disclosing whether any reportable event (described in section 4043(b)) occurred during the plan year except to the extent the corporation waives such requirement, and

(3) in the case of a multiemployer plan, information with respect to such plan which the corporation determines is necessary for the enforcement of subtitle E and requires by regulation, which may include—

(A) a statement certified by the plan's enrolled actuary of—

(i) the value of all vested benefits under the plan as of the end of the plan year, and

(ii) the value of the plan's assets as of the end of the plan year;

(B) a statement certified by the plan sponsor of each claim for outstanding withdrawal liability (within the meaning of section 4001(a)(12)) and its value as of the end of that plan year and as of the end of the preceding plan year; and

(C) the number of employers having an obligation to contribute to the plan and the number of employers required to make withdrawal liability payments.

The report shall be filed within 6 months after the close of the plan year to which it relates. The corporation shall cooperate with the Secretary of the Treasury and the Secretary of Labor in an endeavor to coordinate the timing and content, and possibly obtain the combination, of reports under this section with reports required to be made by plan administrators to such Secretaries.

Amendment

P.L. 96-364, § 106:

Amended section 4065(2) to read as above (by adding "except to the extent the corporation waives such requirement, and") and added new section 4065(3), effective September 26, 1980.

Regulations

The following regulations were adopted by the Pension Benefit Guaranty Corporation on July 1, 1996 (61 FR 34002). Prior to July 1, 1996, PBGC regulations were under Chapter XXVI of Title 29 of the Code of Federal Regulations. Effective July 1, 1996, PBGC regulations were moved to Chapter XL, and were renumbered and reorganized. Reg. § 4065.3 was amended December 2, 1996 (61 FR 63998), effective January 1, 1997.

[¶ 15,651]

§ 4065.1 **Purpose and scope.** The purpose of this part is to specify the form and content of the Annual Report required by section 4065 of ERISA. This part applies to all plans covered by title IV of ERISA.

[¶ 15,651A]

§ 4065.2 **Definitions.** The following terms are defined in § 4001.2 of this chapter: *ERISA, IRS, PBGC,* and *plan.*

[¶ 15,651B]

§ 4065.3 **Filing requirement.** (a) The requirement to report the occurrence of a reportable event under section 4043 of ERISA in the Annual Report is waived. (Added 12/2/96 by 61 FR 63998.)

(b) Plan administrators shall file the Annual Report on IRS/DOL/PBGC Forms 5500, 5500-C, 5500-K or 5500-R, as appropriate, in accordance with the instructions therein. (Approved by the Office of Management and Budget under control number 1212-0026.)

[¶ 15,660]
ANNUAL NOTIFICATION TO SUBSTANTIAL EMPLOYERS

Act Sec. 4066. The plan administrator of each single-employer plan which has at least two contributing sponsors at least two of whom are not under common control shall notify, within 6 months after the close of each plan year, any contributing sponsor of the plan who is described in section 4001(a)(2) that such contributing sponsor (alone or together with members of such contributing sponsor's controlled group) constitutes a substantial employer.

Amendments

P.L. 101-239, §7893(g)(2):

Amended ERISA Sec. 4066 by inserting "any" before "contributing sponsor" the first place it appears, effective April 7, 1986.

P.L. 99-272:

Act Sec. 11016(a)(5)(C) amended ERISA Sec. 4066 to read as above, effective on April 7, 1986.

Prior to amendment, ERISA Sec. 4066 read as follows:

Sec. 4066. The plan administrator of each plan under which contributions are made by more than one employer (other than a multiemployer plan) shall notify, within 6 months after the close of each plan year, any employer making contributions under that plan who is described in section 4001(a)(2) that he is a substantial employer for that year.

P.L. 96-364, §403(j):

Amended Sec. 4066 to read as above by adding "(other than a multiemployer plan)" after "contributions are made by more than one employer."

[¶ 15,661]
RECOVERY OF LIABILITY FOR PLAN TERMINATION

Act Sec. 4067. The corporation is authorized to make arrangements with contributing sponsors and members of their controlled groups who are or may become liable under section 4062, 4063, or 4064 for payment of their liability, including arrangements for deferred payment of amounts of liability to the corporation accruing as of the termination date on such terms and for such periods as the corporation deems equitable and appropriate.

Amendment

P.L. 100-203, §9313(b)(6):

Amended ERISA Sec. 4067 by striking "controlled groups who are" and inserting "controlled groups who are or may become", to read as above, effective with respect to notices of intent to terminate under ERISA Sec. 4041(a)(2) which are provided after December 17, 1987.

P.L. 99-272, §11016(a)(6)(A):

Amended ERISA Sec. 4067 to read as above, effective on April 7, 1986. Additionally the section's title was amended by the striking out of "EMPLOYER."

Prior to amendment, ERISA Sec. 4067 read as follows:

Sec. 4067. The corporation is authorized to make arrangements with employers who are liable under section 4062, 4063, or 4064 for payment of their liability, including arrangements for deferred payment on such terms and for such periods as the corporation deems equitable and appropriate.

Regulations

The following regulations were adopted by the Pension Benefit Guaranty Corporation on July 1, 1996 (61 FR 34002). Prior to July 1, 1996, PBGC regulations were under Chapter XXVI of Title 29 of the Code of Federal Regulations. Effective July 1, 1996, PBGC regulations were moved to Chapter XL, and were renumbered and reorganized.

[¶ 15,661A]

§4067.1 **Cross-reference.** Section 4062.8 of this chapter contains rules on deferred payment and other arrangements for satisfaction of liability to the PBGC after termination of single-employer plans.

[¶ 15,662]
LIEN FOR LIABILITY

Act Sec. 4068. (a) If any person liable to the corporation under section 4062, 4063, or 4064 neglects or refuses to pay, after demand, the amount of such liability (including interest), there shall be a lien in favor of the corporation in the amount of such liability (including interest) upon all property and rights to property, whether real or personal, belonging to such person, except that such lien may not be in an amount in excess of 30 percent of the collective net worth of all persons described in section 4062(a) upon all property and rights to property, whether real or personal, belonging to such person.

Act Sec. 4068. (b) The lien imposed by subsection (a) arises on the date of termination of a plan, and continues until the liability imposed under section 4062, 4063, or 4064 is satisfied or becomes unenforceable by reason of lapse of time.

Act Sec. 4068. (c)(1) Except as otherwise provided under this section, the priority of a lien imposed under subsection (a) shall be determined in the same manner as under section 6323 of the Internal Revenue Code of 1986 (as in effect on the date of the enactment of the Single-Employer Pension Plan Amendments Act of 1986). Such section 6323 shall be applied for purposes of this section by disregarding subsection (g)(4) and by substituting—

(A) "lien imposed by section 4068 of the Employee Retirement Income Security Act of 1974" for "lien imposed by section 6321" each place it appears in subsections (a), (b), (c)(1), (c)(4)(B), (d), (e), and (h)(5);

(B) "the corporation" for "the Secretary" in subsections (a) and (b)(9)(C);

(C) "the payment of the amount on which the section 4068(a) lien is based" for "the collection of any tax under this title" in subsection (b)(3);

(D) "a person whose property is subject to the lien" for "the taxpayer" in subsections (b)(8), (c)(2)(A)(i) (the first place it appears), (c)(2)(A)(ii), (c)(2)(B), (c)(4)(B), and (c)(4)(C) (in the matter preceding clause (i));

(E) "such person" for "the taxpayer" in subsections (c)(2)(A)(i) (the second place it appears) and (c)(4)(C)(ii);

(F) "payment of the loan value of the amount on which the lien is based is made to the corporation" for "satisfaction of a levy pursuant to section 6332(b)" in subsection (b)(9)(C);

(G) "section 4068(a) lien" for "tax lien" each place it appears in subsections (c)(1), (c)(2)(A), (c)(2)(B), (c)(3)(B)(iii), (c)(4)(B), (d), and (h)(5); and

(H) "the date on which the lien is first filed" for "the date of the assessment of the tax" in subsection (g)(3)(A).

(2) In a case under title 11 of the United States Code or in insolvency proceedings, the lien imposed under subsection (a) shall be treated in the same manner as a tax due and owing to the United States for purposes of title 11 of the United States Code or section 3713 of title 31 of the United States Code.

(3) For purposes of applying section 6323(a) of the Internal Revenue Code of 1986 to determine the priority between the lien imposed under subsection (a) and a Federal tax lien, each lien shall be treated as a judgment lien arising as of the time notice of such lien is filed.

(4) For purposes of this subsection, notice of the lien imposed by subsection (a) shall be filed in the same manner as under section 6323(f) and (g) of the Internal Revenue Code of 1986.

Act Sec. 4068. (d)(1) In any case where there has been a refusal or neglect to pay the liability imposed under section 4062, 4063, or 4064, the corporation may bring civil action in a district court of the United States to enforce the lien of the corporation under this section with respect to such liability or to subject any property, of whatever nature, of the liable person, or in which he has any right, title, or interest to the payment of such liability.

(2) The liability imposed by section 4062, 4063, or 4064 may be collected by a proceeding in court if the proceeding is commenced within 6 years after the date upon which the plan was terminated or prior to the expiration of any period for collection agreed upon in writing by the corporation and the liable person before the expiration of such 6-year period. The period of limitations provided under this paragraph shall be suspended for the period the assets of the liable person are in the control or custody of any court of the United States, or of any State, or of the District of Columbia, and for 6 months thereafter, and for any period during which the liable person is outside the United States if such period of absence is for a continuous period of at least 6 months.

Act Sec. 4068. (e) If the corporation determines that release of the lien or subordination of the lien to any other creditor of the liable person would not adversely affect the collection of the liability imposed under section 4062, 4063, or 4064, or that the amount realizable by the corporation from the property to which the lien attaches will ultimately be increased by such release or subordination, and that the ultimate collection of the liability will be facilitated by such release or subordination, the corporation may issue a certificate of release or subordination of the lien with respect to such property, or any part thereof.

Act Sec. 4068. DEFINITIONS. (f) For purposes of this section—

(1) The collective net worth of persons subject to liability in connection with a plan termination shall be determined as provided in section 4062(d)(1).

(2) The term "pre-tax profits" has the meaning provided in section 4062(d)(2).

Amendments

P.L. 101-239, § 7881(f)(3)(B):

Amended ERISA Sec. 4068(a), effective as if included in P.L. 100-203, § 9312(b)(2), by striking the last sentence which had read:

The preceding provisions of this subsection shall be applied in a manner consistent with the provisions of section 4064(d) relating to treatment of multiple controlled groups.

P.L. 101-239, § 7881(f)(10)(C):

Amended ERISA Sec. 4068 by adding a new subsection (f) to read as above. For the effective date, see P.L. 100-203, § 9312(b)(2)(B)(i).

P.L. 101-239, § 7881(f)(12):

Amended ERISA Sec. 4068(a) by striking "to the extent such amount does not exceed 30 percent of the collective net worth of all persons described in section 4062(a)" the first place it appeared; and by striking "to the extent such amount does not exceed 30 percent of the collective net worth of all persons described in section 4062(a)" the second place it appeared and all that followed and inserting the following: "in the amount of such liability (including interest) upon all property and rights to property, whether real or personal, belonging to such person, except that such lien may not be in an amount in excess of 30 percent of the collective net worth of all persons described in section 4062(a)." For the effective date, see P.L. 100-203, § 9312(b)(2)(B)(i).

P.L. 101-239, § 7891(a)(1):

Titles I, III, and IV of ERISA (other than sections 3(37)(E), 301(a)(7), and 308, the last sentence of section 408(d), and sections 414(c), 4001(a)(3)(ii), and 4303) are each amended by striking "Internal Revenue Code of 1954" each place it appears and inserting "Internal Revenue Code of 1986", effective October 22, 1986.

P.L. 101-239, § 7894(g)(4):

Amended ERISA Sec. 4068(c)(2) by striking "section 3466 of the Revised Statutes (31 U.S.C. 191)" and inserting "section 3713 of title 31 of the United States Code," effective as if included in P.L. 97-258, § 3.

P.L 100-203, § 9312(b)(2)(B)(i):

Amended ERISA Sec. 4068(a) by striking out "to the extent of an amount equal to the unpaid amount described in section 4062(b)(1)(A)(i)" each place it appears and inserting in lieu thereof "to the extent such amount does not exceed 30 percent of the collective net worth of all persons described in section 4062(a)", effective for (A) plan terminations under section 4041(c) of ERISA with respect to which notices of intent to terminate are provided under section 4041(a)(2) of ERISA after December 17, 1987, and (B) plan terminations with respect to which proceedings are instituted by the Pension Benefit Guaranty Corporation under section 4042 of ERISA after December 17, 1987.

P.L. 100-203, § 9312(b)(2)(C)(ii):

Amended ERISA Sec. 4068(a) by adding a new sentence at the end to read as above. For the effective date, see Act Sec. 9312(b)(2)(B)(i), above.

P.L. 99-272, § 11016(a)(6)(B)(i):

Amended ERISA Sec. 4068 by striking out "of Employer" in the heading.

Act Sec. 11016(a)(6)(B)(ii) amended ERISA Sec. 4068(a) by striking out "employer or employers" the first place it appeared and inserting "person"; by striking out "neglect or refuse" and inserting "neglects or refuses"; by inserting "to the extent of an amount equal to the unpaid amount described in section 4062(b)(1)(A)(i)" after "liability" and after "corporation" the second place it appears; and, by striking out "employer or employers" and inserting "person."

Act Sec. 11016(a)(B)(iii) amended ERISA Sec. 4068(d)(1) by striking out "employer" and inserting "liable person."

Act Sec. 11016(a)(6)(B)(iv) amended ERISA Sec. 4068(d)(2) by striking out "employer" and inserting "liable person."

Act Sec. 11016(a)(6)(B)(v) amended ERISA Sec. 4068(e) by striking out "employer or employers" and inserting "liable person."

Act Sec. 11016(a)(6)(B)(vi) amended ERISA Sec. 4068 by striking out subsection (c)(1) and inserting a new subsection (c)(1) to read as above. Prior to amendment, ERISA Sec. 4068(c)(1) read as follows:

Sec. 4068. (c)(1) Except as otherwise provided under this section, the priority of the lien imposed under subsection (a) shall be determined in the same manner as under section 6323 of the Internal Revenue Code of 1954. Such section 6323 shall be applied by substituting "lien imposed by sections 4068 of the Employee Retirement Income Security Act of 1974" for "lien imposed by section 6321"; "corporation" for "Secretary or his delegate"; "employer liability lien" for "tax lien"; "employer" for "taxpayer"; "lien arising under section 4068(a) of the Employee Retirement Income Security Act of 1974" for "assessment of the tax"; and "payment of the loan value is made to the corporation" for "satisfaction of a levy pursuant to section 6332(b)"; each place such terms appear.

Act Sec. 11016(c)(14) amended ERISA Sec. 4068(e) by striking out ", with the consent of the board of directors".

These amendments take effect on April 7, 1986.

P.L. 95-598, § 321(c):

Amended Sec. 4068(c)(2) effective October 1, 1979, by substituting "a case under title 11 of the United States Code or in" for "the case of bankruptcy or" and by substituting "title 11 of the United States Code" for "the Bankruptcy Act."

Regulations

The following regulations were adopted by the Pension Benefit Guaranty Corporation on July 1, 1996 (61 FR 34002). Prior to July 1, 1996, PBGC regulations were under Chapter XXVI of Title 29 of the Code of Federal Regulations. Effective July 1, 1996, PBGC regulations were moved to Chapter XL, and were renumbered and reorganized.

[¶ 15,662A]

§ 4068.1 **Purpose; cross-references.** This part contains rules regarding the PBGC's lien under section 4068 of ERISA with respect to liability arising under section 4062, 4063, or 4064 of ERISA.

[¶ 15,662B]

§ 4068.2 **Definitions.** The following terms are defined in § 4001.2 of this chapter: *ERISA, PBGC, person, plan,* and *termination date.*

Collective net worth of persons subject to liability in connection with a plan termination has the meaning in § 4062.2.

[¶ 15,662C]

§ 4068.3 **Notification of and demand for liability.** (a) *Notification of liability.* Except as provided in paragraph (c) of this section, when the PBGC has determined the amount of the liability under part 4062 and whether or not the liability has already been paid, the PBGC shall notify liable person(s) in writing of the amount of the liability. If the full liability has not yet been paid, the notification will include a request for payment of the full liability and will indicate that, as provided in § 4062.8, the PBGC will prescribe commercially reasonable terms for payment of so much of the liability as it determines exceeds 30 percent of the collective net worth of persons subject to liability in connection with a plan termination. In all cases, the notification will include a statement of the right to appeal the assessment of liability pursuant to part 4003.

(b) *Demand for liability.* Except as provided in paragraph (c) of this section, if person(s) liable to the PBGC fail to pay the full liability and no appeal is filed or an appeal is filed and the decision on appeal finds liability, the PBGC will issue a demand letter for the liability—

(1) If no appeal is filed, upon the expiration of time to file an appeal under part 4003; or

(2) If an appeal is filed, upon issuance of a decision on the appeal finding that there is liability under this part.

The demand letter will indicate that, as provided in § 4062.8, the PBGC will prescribe commercially reasonable terms for payment of so much of the liability as it determines exceeds 30 percent of the collective net worth of such persons.

(c) *Special rule.* Notwithstanding paragraphs (a) and (b) of this section, the PBGC may, in any case in which it believes that its ability to assert or obtain payment of liability is in jeopardy, issue a demand letter for the liability under this part immediately upon determining the liability, without first issuing a notification of liability pursuant to paragraph (a) of this section. When the PBGC issues a demand letter under this paragraph, there is no right to an appeal pursuant to part 4003 of this chapter.

[¶ 15,662D]

§ 4068.4 **Lien.** If any person liable to the PBGC under section 4062, 4063, or 4064 of ERISA fails or refuses to pay the full amount of such liability within the time specified in the demand letter issued under § 4068.3, the PBGC shall have a lien in the amount of the liability, including interest, arising as of the plan's termination date, upon all property and rights to property, whether real or personal, belonging to that person, except that such lien may not be in an amount in excess of 30 percent of the collective net worth of all persons described in section 4062(a) of ERISA and part 4062 of this chapter.

[¶ 15,662L]
TREATMENT OF TRANSACTIONS TO EVADE LIABILITY; EFFECT OF CORPORATE REORGANIZATION

Act Sec. 4069.(a) Treatment of Transactions to Evade Liability. If a principal purpose of any person in entering into any transaction is to evade liability to which such person would be subject under this subtitle and the transaction becomes effective within five years before the termination date of the termination on which such liability would be based, then such person and the members of such person's controlled group (determined as of the termination date) shall be subject to liability under this subtitle in connection with such termination as if such person were a contributing sponsor of the terminated plan as of the termination date. This subsection shall not cause any person to be liable under this subtitle in connection with such plan termination for any increases or improvements in the benefits provided under the plan which are adopted after the date on which the transaction referred to in the preceding sentence become effective.

Act Sec. 4069. Effect of Corporate Reorganization. (b) For purposes of this subtitle, the following rules apply in the case of certain corporate reorganizations:

(1) Change of Identity, Form, Etc.. If a person ceases to exist by reason of a reorganization which involves a mere change in identity, form, or place of organization, however effected, a successor corporation resulting from such reorganization shall be, treated as the person to whom this subtitle applies.

(2) Liquidation into Parent Corporation. If a person ceases to exist by reason of liquidation into a parent corporation, the parent corporation shall be treated as the person to whom this subtitle applies.

(3) Merger, Consolidation, or Division. If a person ceases to exist by reason of a merger, consolidation, or division, the successor corporation or corporations shall be treated as the person to whom this subtitle applies.

Amendment:

P.L. 99-272:

Act Sec. 11013(a) added new ERISA Sec. 4069 to read as above, effective for transactions which become effective on or after January 1, 1986.

[¶ 15,662R]
ENFORCEMENT AUTHORITY RELATING TO TERMINATIONS OF SINGLE-EMPLOYER PLANS

Act Sec. 4070.(a) In General. Any person who is with respect to a single-employer plan a fiduciary, contributing sponsor, member of a contributing sponsor's controlled group, participant, or beneficiary, and is adversely affected by an act or practice of any party (other than the corporation) in violation of any provision of section 4041, 4042, 4062, 4063, 4064, or 4069, or who is an employee organization representing such a participant so adversely affected for purposes of collective bargaining with respect to such plan, may bring an action—

(1) to enjoin such act or practice, or

(2) to obtain other appropriate equitable relief (A) to redress such violation or (B) to enforce such provision.

Act Sec. 4070. Status of Plan as Party to Action and With Respect to Legal Process. (b) A single-employer plan may be sued under this section as an entity. Service of summons, subpoena, or other legal process of a court upon a trustee or an administrator of a single-employer plan in such trustee's or administrator's capacity as such shall constitute service upon the plan. If a plan has not designated in the summary plan description of the plan an individual as agent for the service of legal process, service upon any contributing sponsor of the plan shall constitute such service. Any money judgment under this section against a single-employer plan shall be enforceable only against the plan as an entity and shall not be enforceable against any other person unless liability against such person is established in such person's individual capacity.

Act Sec. 4070. Jurisdiction and Venue. (c) The district courts of the United States shall have exclusive jurisdiction of civil actions under this section. Such actions may be brought in the district where the plan is administered, where the violation took place, or where a defendant resides or may be found, and process may be served in any other district where a defendant resides or may be found. The district courts of the United States shall have jurisdiction, without regard to the amount in controversy or the citizenship of the parties, to grant the relief provided for in subsection (a) in any action.

Act Sec. 4070. Right of Corporation to Intervene. (d) A copy of the complaint or notice of appeal in any action under this section shall be served upon the corporation by certified mail. The corporation shall have the right in its discretion to intervene in any action.

Act Sec. 4070. Awards of Costs and Expenses.—

(e)(1) General Rule. In any action brought under this section, the court in its discretion may award all or a portion of the costs and expenses incurred in connection with such action, including reasonable attorney's fees, to any party who prevails or substantially prevails in such action.

(2) Exemption for Plans. Notwithstanding the preceding provisions of this subsection, no plan shall be required in any action to pay any costs and expenses (including attorney's fees).

Act Sec. 4070. Limitation on Actions.—

(f)(1) In General. Except as provided in paragraph (3), an action under this section may not be brought after the later of—

(A) 6 years after the date on which the cause of action arose, or

(B) 3 years after the applicable date specified in paragraph (2).

(2) Applicable Date.—

(A) General Rule. Except as provided in subparagraph (B), the applicable date specified in this paragraph is the earliest date on which the plaintiff acquired or should have acquired actual knowledge of the existence of such cause of action.

(B) Special Rule for Plaintiffs Who Are Fiduciaries. In the case of a plaintiff who is a fiduciary bringing the action in the exercise of fiduciary duties, the applicable date specified in this paragraph is the date on which the plaintiff became a fiduciary with respect to the plan if such date is later than the date described in subparagraph (A).

(3) Cases of Fraud or Concealment. In the case of fraud or concealment, the period described in paragraph (1)(B) shall be extended to 6 years after the applicable date specified in paragraph (2).

Amendments

P.L. 101-239, § 7881(f)(8):

Amended ERISA Sec. 4070 by striking "4049," effective December 22, 1987.

P.L. 99-272:

Act Sec. 11014(a) added ERISA Sec. 4070 to read as above, effective with respect to terminations pursuant to notices of intent filed with the PBGC on or after January 1, 1986 or proceedings begun on or after that date.

[¶ 15,662U]
PENALTY FOR FAILURE TO TIMELY PROVIDE REQUIRED INFORMATION

Act Sec. 4071. The corporation may assess a penalty, payable to the corporation, against any person who fails to provide any notice or other material information required under this subtitle, subtitle A, B, or C as section 302(f)(4) or 307(e) or any regulations prescribed under any such subtitle or such section, within the applicable time limit specified therein. Such penalty shall not exceed $1,000 for each day for which such failure continues.

Amendment

P.L. 101-239, §7881(i)(3)(B):

Amended ERISA Sec. 4071 by striking "or subtitle A, B, or C" and inserting ", subtitle A, B, or C as section 302(f)(4) or 307(e)" and by inserting "or such section" after "such subtitle."

P.L. 100-203, §9314(c):

Added ERISA Sec. 4071, to read as above, effective December 22, 1987.

Regulations

The following regulations were adopted by the Pension Benefit Guaranty Corporation on July 10, 1997 (62 FR 36993) and are effective August 11, 1997.

[¶ 15,662V]

§4071.1 **Purpose and scope.** This part specifies the maximum daily amount of penalties that may be assessed by the PBGC under ERISA section 4071 for certain failures to provide notices or other material information, as such amount has been adjusted to account for inflation pursuant to the Federal Civil Monetary Penalty Inflation Adjustment Act of 1990, as amended by the Debt Collection Improvement Act of 1996.

[¶ 15,662W]

§4071.2 **Definitions.** The following terms are defined in §4001.2 of this chapter: *ERISA* and *PBGC.*

[¶ 15,662X]

§4071.3 **Penalty amount.** The maximum daily amount of the penalty under section 4071 of ERISA shall be $1,100.

Subtitle E—Special Provisions for Multiemployer Plans
Part 1—Employer Withdrawals

[¶ 15,663]
WITHDRAWAL LIABILITY ESTABLISHED

Act Sec. 4201. (a) If an employer withdraws from a multiemployer plan in a complete withdrawal or a partial withdrawal, then the employer is liable to the plan in the amount determined under this part to be the withdrawal liability.

Act Sec. 4201. (b) For purposes of subsection (a)—

(1) The withdrawal liability of an employer to a plan is the amount determined under section 4211 to be the allocable amount of unfunded vested benefits, adjusted—

    (A) first, by any de minimis reduction applicable under section 4209,

    (B) next, in the case of a partial withdrawal, in accordance with section 4206,

    (C) then, to the extent necessary to reflect the limitation on annual payments under section 4219(c)(1)(B), and

    (D) finally, in accordance with section 4225.

(2) The term "complete withdrawal" means a complete withdrawal described in section 4203.

(3) The term "partial withdrawal" means a partial withdrawal described in section 4205.

Amendment

P.L. 96-364, §104(2):

Added Sec. 4201, effective September 26, 1980 under ERISA Sec. 4402.

[¶ 15,664]
DETERMINATION AND COLLECTION OF LIABILITY; NOTIFICATION OF EMPLOYER

Act Sec. 4202. When an employer withdraws from a multiemployer plan, the plan sponsor, in accordance with this part, shall—

(1) determine the amount of the employer's withdrawal liability,

(2) notify the employer of the amount of the withdrawal liability, and

(3) collect the amount of the withdrawal liability from the employer.

Amendment

P.L. 96-364, §104(2):

Added Sec. 4202, effective September 26, 1980 under ERISA Sec. 4402.

[¶ 15,665]
COMPLETE WITHDRAWAL

Act Sec. 4203. (a) For purposes of this part, a complete withdrawal from a multiemployer plan occurs when an employer—

(1) permanently ceases to have an obligation to contribute under the plan, or

(2) permanently ceases all covered operations under the plan.

Act Sec. 4203. (b)(1) Notwithstanding subsection (a), in the case of an employer that has an obligation to contribute under a plan for work performed in the building and construction industry, a complete withdrawal occurs only as described in paragraph (2), if—

    (A) substantially all the employees with respect to whom the employer has an obligation to contribute under the plan perform work in the building and construction industry, and

    (B) the plan—

        (i) primarily covers employees in the building and construction industry, or

        (ii) is amended to provide that this subsection applies to employers described in this paragraph.

(2) A withdrawal occurs under this paragraph if—

    (A) an employer ceases to have an obligation to contribute under the plan, and

(B) the employer—

(i) continues to perform work in the jurisdiction of the collective bargaining agreement of the type for which contributions were previously required, or

(ii) resumes such work within 5 years after the date on which the obligation to contribute under the plan ceases, and does not renew the obligation at the time of the resumption.

(3) In the case of a plan terminated by mass withdrawal (within the meaning of section 4041A(a)(2)), paragraph (2) shall be applied by substituting "3 years" for "5 years" in subparagraph (B)(ii).

Act Sec. 4203.(c)(1) Notwithstanding subsection (a), in the case of an employer that has an obligation to contribute under a plan for work performed in the entertainment industry, primarily on a temporary or project-by-project basis, if the plan primarily covers employees in the entertainment industry, a complete withdrawal occurs only as described in subsection (b)(2) applied by substituting "plan" for "collective bargaining agreement" in subparagraph (B)(i) thereof.

(2) For purposes of this subsection, the term "entertainment industry" means—

(A) theater, motion picture (except to the extent provided in regulations prescribed by the corporation), radio, television, sound or visual recording, music, and dance, and

(B) such other entertainment activities as the corporation may determine to be appropriate.

(3) The corporation may by regulation exclude a group or class of employers described in the preceding sentence from the application of this subsection if the corporation determines that such exclusion is necessary—

(A) to protect the interest of the plan's participants and beneficiaries, or

(B) to prevent a significant risk of loss to the corporation with respect to the plan.

(4) A plan may be amended to provide that this subsection shall not apply to a group or class of employers under the plan.

Act Sec. 4203.(d)(1) Notwithstanding subsection (a), in the case of an employer who—

(A) has an obligation to contribute under a plan described in paragraph (2) primarily for work described in such paragraph, and

(B) does not continue to perform work within the jurisdiction of the plan,

a complete withdrawal occurs only as described in paragraph (3).

(2) A plan is described in this paragraph if substantially all of the contributions required under the plan are made by employers primarily engaged in the long and short haul trucking industry, the household goods moving industry, or the public warehousing industry.

(3) A withdrawal occurs under this paragraph if—

(A) an employer permanently ceases to have an obligation to contribute under the plan or permanently ceases all covered operations under the plan, and

(B) either—

(i) the corporation determines that the plan has suffered substantial damage to its contribution base as a result of such cessation, or

(ii) the employer fails to furnish a bond issued by a corporate surety company that is an acceptable surety for purposes of section 412, or an amount held in escrow by a bank or similar financial institution satisfactory to the plan, in an amount equal to 50 percent of the withdrawal liability of the employer.

(4) If, after an employer furnishes a bond or escrow to a plan under paragraph (3)(B)(ii), the corporation determines that the cessation of the employer's obligation to contribute under the plan (considered together with any cessations by other employers), or cessation of covered operations under the plan, has resulted in substantial damage to the contribution base of the plan, the employer shall be treated as having withdrawn from the plan on the date on which the obligation to contribute or covered operations ceased, and such bond or escrow shall be paid to the plan. The corporation shall not make a determination under this paragraph more than 60 months after the date on which such obligation to contribute or covered operations ceased.

(5) If the corporation determines that the employer has no further liability under the plan either—

(A) because it determines that the contribution base of the plan has not suffered substantial damage as a result of the cessation of the employer's obligation to contribute or cessation of covered operations (considered together with any cessation of contribution obligation, or of covered operations, with respect to other employers), or

(B) because it may not make a determination under paragraph (4) because of the last sentence thereof,

then the bond shall be cancelled or the escrow refunded.

(6) Nothing in this subsection shall be construed as a limitation on the amount of the withdrawal liability of any employer.

Act Sec. 4203. (e) For purposes of this part, the date of a complete withdrawal is the date of the cessation of the obligation to contribute or the cessation of covered operations.

Act Sec. 4203.(f)(1) The corporation may prescribe regulations under which plans in industries other than the construction or entertainment industries may be amended to provide for special withdrawal liability rules similar to the rules described in subsections (b) and (c).

(2) Regulations under paragraph (1) shall permit use of special withdrawal liability rules—

(A) only in industries (or portions thereof) in which, as determined by the corporation, the characteristics that would make use of such rules appropriate are clearly shown, and

(B) only if the corporation determines, in each instance in which special withdrawal liability rules are permitted, that use of such rules will not pose a significant risk to the corporation under this title.

Amendment

P.L. 96-364, § 104(2):

Added Sec. 4203, effective September 26, 1980 under ERISA Sec. 4402.

Regulations

The following regulations were adopted by the Pension Benefit Guaranty Corporation on July 1, 1996 (61 FR 34002). Prior to July 1, 1996, PBGC regulations were under Chapter XXVI of Title 29 of the Code of Federal Regulations. Effective July 1, 1996, PBGC regulations were moved to Chapter XL, and were renumbered and reorganized. Reg. § 4203.4 was amended October 28, 2003 (68 FR 61344).

[¶ 15,666]

§ 4203.1 **Purpose and scope.** (a) *Purpose.* The purpose of this part is to prescribe procedures whereby a multiemployer plan may, pursuant to sections 4203(f) and 4208(e)(3) of ERISA, request the PBGC to approve a plan amendment which establishes special complete or partial withdrawal liability rules.

(b) *Scope.* This part applies to a multiemployer pension plan covered by Title IV of ERISA.

[¶ 15,666A]

§ 4203.2 **Definitions.** The following terms are defined in § 4001.2 of this chapter: *complete withdrawal, employer, ERISA, multiemployer plan, PBGC, person, plan, plan sponsor,* and *plan year.*

[¶ 15,666B]

§ 4203.3 **Plan adoption of special withdrawal rules.** (a) *General rule.* A plan may, subject to the approval of the PBGC, establish by plan amendment special complete or partial withdrawal liability rules. A complete withdrawal liability rule adopted pursuant to this part shall be similar to the rules for the construction and entertainment industries described in section 4203(b) and (c) of ERISA. A partial withdrawal liability rule adopted pursuant to this part shall be consistent with the complete withdrawal rule adopted by the plan. A plan amendment adopted under this part may not be put into effect until it is approved by the PBGC.

(b) *Discretionary provisions of the plan amendment.* A plan amendment adopted pursuant to this part may—

(1) Cover an entire industry or industries, or be limited to a segment of an industry; and

(2) Apply to cessations of the obligation to contribute that occurred prior to the adoption of the amendment.

[¶ 15,666C]

§ 4203.4 **Requests for PBGC approval of plan amendments.** (a) *Filing of request.* (1) *In general.* A plan shall apply to the PBGC for approval of a plan amendment which establishes special complete or partial withdrawal liability rules. The request for approval shall be filed after the amendment is adopted. PBGC approval shall also be required for any subsequent modification of the plan amendment, other than a repeal of the amendment which results in employers being subject to the general statutory rules on withdrawal.

(2) *Method of filing.* The PBGC applies the rules in subpart A of part 4000 of this chapter to determine permissible methods of filing with the PBGC under this part.

[Amended 10/28/2003 by 68 FR 61344]

(b) *Who may request.* The plan sponsor, or a duly authorized representative acting on behalf of the plan sponsor, shall sign and submit the request.

(c) *Where to file.* See Sec. 4000.4 of this chapter for information on where to file.

[Amended 10/28/2003 by 68 FR 61344]

(d) *Information.* Each request shall contain the following information:

(1) The name and address of the plan for which the plan amendment is being submitted, and the telephone number of the plan sponsor or its authorized representative.

(2) A copy of the executed amendment, including the proposed effective date.

(3) A statement certifying that notice of the adoption of the amendment and the request for approval filed under this part has been given to all employers who have an obligation to contribute under the plan and to all employee organizations representing employees covered under the plan.

(4) A statement indicating how the withdrawal rules in the plan amendment would operate in the event of a sale of assets by a contrib-

uting employer or the cessation of the obligation to contribute or the cessation of covered operations by all employers.

(5) A copy of the plan's most recent actuarial valuation.

(6) For each of the previous five plan years, information on the number of plan participants by category (active, retired and separate vested) and a complete financial statement. This requirement may be satisfied by the submission for each of those years of Form 5500, including schedule B, or similar reports required under prior law.

(7) A detailed description of the industry to which the plan amendment will apply, including information sufficient to demonstrate the effect of withdrawals on the plan's contribution base, and information establishing industry characteristics which would indicate that withdrawals in the industry do not typically have an adverse effect on the plan's contribution base. Such industry characteristics include the mobility of employees, the intermittent nature of employment, the project-by-project nature of the work, extreme fluctuations in the level of an employer's covered work under the plan, the existence of a consistent pattern of entry and withdrawal by employers, and the local nature of the work performed.

(e) *Supplemental information.* In addition to the information described in paragraph (d) of this section, a plan may submit any other information it believes is pertinent to its request. The PBGC may require the plan sponsor to submit any other information the PBGC determines it needs to review a request under this part.

[¶ 15,666D]

§ 4203.5 **PBGC action on requests.** (a) *General.* The PBGC shall approve a plan amendment providing for the application of special complete or partial withdrawal liability rules upon a determination by the PBGC that the plan amendment—

(1) Will apply only to an industry that has characteristics that would make use of the special withdrawal rules appropriate; and

(2) Will not pose a significant risk to the insurance system.

(b) *Notice of pendency of request.* As soon as practicable after receiving a request for approval of a plan amendment containing all the information required under § 4203.4, the PBGC shall publish a notice of the pendency of the request in the Federal Register. The notice shall contain a summary of the request and invite interested persons to submit written comments to the PBGC concerning the request. The notice will normally provide for a comment period of 45 days.

(c) *PBGC decision on request.* After the close of the comment period, PBGC shall issue its decision in writing on the request for approval of a plan amendment. Notice of the decision shall be published in the Federal Register.

[¶ 15,666E]

§ 4203.6 **OMB control number.** The collections of information contained in this part have been approved by the Office of Management and Budget under OMB control number 1212-0050.

[¶ 15,667]
SALE OF ASSETS

Act Sec. 4204. (a)(1) A complete or partial withdrawal of an employer (hereinafter in this section referred to as the "seller") under this section does not occur solely because, as a result of a bona fide, arm's-length sale of assets to an unrelated party (hereinafter in this section referred to as the "purchaser"), the seller ceases covered operations or ceases to have an obligation to contribute for such operations, if—

(A) the purchaser has an obligation to contribute to the plan with respect to the operations for substantially the same number of contribution base units for which the seller had an obligation to contribute to the plan;

(B) the purchaser provides to the plan for a period of 5 plan years commencing with the first plan year beginning after the sale of assets, a bond issued by a corporate surety company that is an acceptable surety for purposes of section 412 of this Act, or an amount held in escrow by a bank or similar financial institution satisfactory to the plan, in an amount equal to the greater of—

(i) the average annual contribution required to be made by the seller with respect to the operations under the plan for the 3 plan years preceding the plan year in which the sale of the employer's assets occurs, or

(ii) the annual contribution that the seller was required to make with respect to the operations under the plan for the last plan year before the plan year in which the sale of the assets occurs, which bond or escrow shall be paid to the plan if the purchaser withdraws from the plan, or fails to make a contribution to the plan when due, at any time during the first 5 plan years beginning after the sale; and

(C) the contract for sale provides that, if the purchaser withdraws in a complete withdrawal, or a partial withdrawal with respect to operations, during such first 5 plan years, the seller is secondarily liable for any withdrawal liability it would have had to the plan with respect to the operations (but for this section) if the liability of the purchaser with respect to the plan is not paid.

(2) If the purchaser—

(A) withdraws before the last day of the fifth plan year beginning after the sale, and

(B) fails to make any withdrawal liability payment when due, then the seller shall pay to the plan an amount equal to the payment that would have been due from the seller but for this section.

(3)(A) If all, or substantially all, of the seller's assets are distributed, or if the seller is liquidated before the end of the 5 plan year period described in paragraph (1)(C), then the seller shall provide a bond or amount in escrow equal to the present value of the withdrawal liability the seller would have had but for this subsection.

(B) If only a portion of the seller's assets are distributed during such period, then a bond or escrow shall be required, in accordance with regulations prescribed by the corporation, in a manner consistent with subparagraph (A).

(4) The liability of the party furnishing a bond or escrow under this subsection shall be reduced, upon payment of the bond or escrow to the plan, by the amount thereof.

Act Sec. 4204. (b)(1) For the purposes of this part, the liability of the purchaser shall be determined as if the purchaser had been required to contribute to the plan in the year of the sale and the 4 plan years preceding the sale the amount the seller was required to contribute for such operations for such 5 plan years.

(2) If the plan is in reorganization in the plan year in which the sale of assets occurs, the purchaser shall furnish a bond or escrow in an amount equal to 200 percent of the amount described in subsection (a)(1)(B).

Act Sec. 4204. (c) The corporation may by regulation vary the standards in subparagraphs (B) and (C) of subsection (a)(1) if the variance would more effectively or equitably carry out the purposes of this title. Before it promulgates such regulations, the corporation may grant individual or class variances or exemptions from the requirements of such subparagraphs if the particular case warrants it. Before granting such an individual or class variance or exemption, the corporation—

(1) shall publish notice in the Federal Register of the pendency of the variance or exemption,

(2) shall require that adequate notice be given to interested persons, and

(3) shall afford interested persons an opportunity to present their views.

Act Sec. 4204. (d) For purposes of this section, the term "unrelated party" means a purchaser or seller who does not bear a relationship to the seller or purchaser, as the case may be, that is described in section 267(b) of the Internal Revenue Code of 1986, or that is described in regulations prescribed by the corporation applying principles similar to the principles of such section.

Amendments

P.L. 101-239, § 7891(a)(1):

Titles I, III, and IV of ERISA (other than sections 3(37)(E), 301(a)(7), and 308, the last sentence of section 408(d), and sections 414(c), 4001(a)(3)(ii), and 4303) are each amended by striking "Internal Revenue Code of 1954" each place it appears and inserting "Internal Revenue Code of 1986", effective October 22, 1986.

P.L. 96-364, § 104(2):

Added Sec 4204, effective September 26, 1980 under ERISA Sec. 4402.

Regulations

The following regulations were adopted by the Pension Benefit Guaranty Corporation on July 1, 1996 (61 FR 34002). Prior to July 1, 1996, PBGC regulations were under Chapter XXVI of Title 29 of the Code of Federal Regulations. Effective July 1, 1996, PBGC regulations were moved to Chapter XL, and were renumbered and reorganized. Reg. § 4204.11 and Reg. § 4204.21 were amended October 28, 2003 (68 FR 61344).

Subpart A—General

[¶ 15,668]

§ 4204.1 Purpose and scope. (a) *Purpose.* Under section 4204 of ERISA, an employer that ceases covered operations under a multiemployer plan, or ceases to have an obligation to contribute for such operations, because of a bona fide, arm's-length sale of assets to an unrelated purchaser does not incur withdrawal liability if certain conditions are met. One condition is that the sale contract provide that the seller will be secondarily liable if the purchaser withdraws from the plan within five years and does not pay its withdrawal liability. Another condition is that the purchaser furnish a bond or place funds in escrow, for a period of five plan years, in a prescribed amount. Section 4204 also authorizes the PBGC to provide for variances or exemptions from these requirements. Subpart B of this part provides variances and exemptions from the requirements for certain sales of assets. Subpart C of this part establishes procedures under which a purchaser or seller may, when the conditions set forth in subpart B are not satisfied or when the parties decline to provide certain financial information to the plan, request the PBGC to grant individual or class variances or exemptions from the requirements.

(b) *Scope.* In general, this part applies to any sale of assets described in section 4204(a)(1) of ERISA. However, this part does not apply to a sale of assets involving operations for which the seller is obligated to contribute to a plan described in section 404(c) of the Code, or a continuation of such a plan, unless the plan is amended to provide that section 4204 applies.

[¶ 15,668A]

§ 4204.2 Definitions. The following terms are defined in § 4001.2 of this chapter: *Code, employer, ERISA, IRS, multiemployer plan, PBGC, person, plan, plan administrator, plan sponsor,* and *plan year.*

In addition, for purposes of this part:

Date of determination means the date on which a seller ceases covered operations or ceases to have an obligation to contribute for such operations as a result of a sale of assets within the meaning of section 4204(a) of ERISA.

Net income after taxes means revenue minus expenses after taxes (excluding extraordinary and non-recurring income or expenses), as presented in an audited financial statement or, in the absence of such statement, in an unaudited financial statement, each prepared in conformance with generally accepted accounting principles.

Net tangible assets means tangible assets (assets other than licenses, patents copyrights, trade names, trademarks, goodwill, experimental or organizational expenses, unamortized debt discounts and expenses and all other assets which, under generally accepted accounting principles, are deemed intangible) less liabilities (other than pension liabilities). Encumbered assets shall be excluded from net tangible assets only to the extent of the amount of the encumbrance.

Purchaser means a purchaser described in section 4204(a)(1) of ERISA.

Seller means a seller described in section 4204(a)(1) of ERISA.

Subpart B—Variance of the Statutory Requirements

[¶ 15,668B]

§ 4204.11 Variance of the bond/escrow and sale-contract requirements. (a) *General rule.* A purchaser's bond or escrow under section 4204(a)(1)(B) of ERISA and the sale-contract provision under section 4204(a)(1)(C) are not required if the parties to the sale inform the plan in writing of their intention that the sale be covered by section 4204 of ERISA and demonstrate to the satisfaction of the plan that at least one of the criteria contained in § 4204.12 or § 4204.13(a) is satisfied.

(b) *Requests after posting of bond or establishment of escrow.* A request for a variance may be submitted at any time. If, after a purchaser has posted a bond or placed money in escrow pursuant to section 4204(a)(1)(B) of ERISA, the purchaser demonstrates to the satisfaction of the plan that the criterion in either § 4204.13(a)(1) or (a)(2) is satisfied, then the bond shall be cancelled or the amount in escrow shall be refunded. For purposes of considering a request after the bond or escrow is in place, the words "the year preceding the date of the variance request" shall be substituted for "the date of determination" for the first mention of that term in both § 4204.13 (a)(1) and (a)(2). In addition, in determining the purchaser's average net income after taxes under § 4204.13(a)(1), for any year included in the average for which the net income figure does not reflect the interest expense incurred with respect to the sale, the purchaser's net income shall be reduced by the amount of interest paid with respect to the sale in the fiscal year following the date of determination.

[Amended 10/28/2003 by 68 FR 61344]

(c) *Information required.* A request for a variance shall contain financial or other information that is sufficient to establish that one of the criteria in § 4204.12 or § 4204.13(a) is satisfied. A request on the basis of either § 4204.13(a)(1) or (a)(2) shall also include a copy of the purchaser's audited (if available) or (if not) unaudited financial statements for the specified time period.

(d) *Limited exemption during pendency of request.* Provided that all of the information required to be submitted is submitted before the first day of the first plan year beginning after the sale, a plan may not, pending its decision on the variance, require a purchaser to post a bond or place an amount in escrow pursuant to section 4204(a)(1)(B). In the event a bond or escrow is not in place pursuant to the preceding sentence, and the plan determines that the request does not qualify for a variance, the purchaser shall comply with section 4204(a)(1)(B) within 30 days after the date on which it receives notice of the plan's decision.

(Approved by the Office of Management and Budget under control number 1212—0021)

(e) *Method and date of issuance.* The PBGC applies the rules in subpart B of part 4000 of this chapter to determine permissible methods of issuance under this subpart. The PBGC applies the rules in subpart C of part 4000 of this chapter to determine the date that an issuance under this subpart was provided.

[Amended 10/28/2003 by 68 FR 61344]

(Approved by the Office of Management and Budget under control number 1212—0021)

[¶ 15,668C]

§ 4204.12 **De minimis transactions.** The criterion under this section is that the amount of the bond or escrow does not exceed the lesser of $250,000 or two percent of the average total annual contributions made by all employers to the plan, for the purposes of section 412(b)(3)(A) of the Code, for the three most recent plan years ending before the date of determination. For this purpose, "contributions made" shall have the same meaning as the term has under § 4211.12(a) of this chapter.

[¶ 15,668D]

§ 4204.13 **Net income and net tangible assets tests.** (a) *General.* The criteria under this section are that either—

(1) *Net income test.* The purchaser's average net income after taxes for its three most recent fiscal years ending before the date of determination (as defined in § 4204.12), reduced by any interest expense incurred with respect to the sale which is payable in the fiscal year following the date of determination, equals or exceeds 150 percent of the amount of the bond or escrow required under ERISA section 4204(a)(1)(B); or

(2) *Net tangible assets test.* The purchaser's net tangible assets at the end of the fiscal year preceding the date of determination (as defined in § 4204.12), equal or exceed—

(i) If the purchaser was not obligated to contribute to the plan before the sale, the amount of unfunded vested benefits allocable to the seller under section 4211 (with respect to the purchased operations), as of the date of determination, or

(ii) If the purchaser was obligated to contribute to the plan before the sale, the sum of the amount of unfunded vested benefits allocable to the purchaser and to the seller under ERISA section 4211 (with respect to the purchased operations), each as of the date of determination.

(b) *Special rule when more than one plan is covered by request.* For the purposes of paragraphs (a)(1) and (a)(2), if the transaction involves the assumption by the purchaser of the seller's obligation to contribute to more than one multiemployer plan, then the total amount of the bond or escrow or of the unfunded vested benefits, as applicable, for all of the plans with respect to which the purchaser has not posted a bond or escrow shall be used to determine whether the applicable test is met.

(c) *Non-applicability of tests in event of purchaser's insolvency.* A purchaser will not qualify for a variance under this subpart pursuant to paragraph (a)(1) or (a)(2) of this section if, as of the earlier of the date of the plan's decision on the variance request or the first day of the first plan year beginning after the date of determination, the purchaser is the subject of a petition under title 11, United States Code, or of a proceeding under similar provisions of state insolvency laws.

Subpart C—Procedures for Individual and Class Variances or Exemptions

[¶ 15,668E]

§ 4204.21 **Requests to PBGC for variances and exemptions.** (a) *Filing of request.* (1) *In general.* If a transaction covered by this part does not satisfy the conditions set forth in subpart B of this part, or if the parties decline to provide to the plan privileged or confidential financial information within the meaning of section 552(b)(4) of the Freedom of Information Act (5 U.S.C. 552), the purchaser or seller may request from the PBGC an exemption or variance from the requirements of section 4204(a)(1)(B) and (C) of ERISA.

(2) *Method of filing.* The PBGC applies the rules in subpart A of part 4000 of this chapter to determine permissible methods of filing with the PBGC under this subpart.

[Amended 10/28/2003 by 68 FR 61344]

(b) *Who may request.* A purchaser or a seller may file a request for a variance or exemption. The request may be submitted by one or more duly authorized representatives acting on behalf of the party or parties. When a contributing employer withdraws from a plan as a result of related sales of assets involving several purchasers, or withdraws from more than one plan as a result of a single sale, the application may request a class variance or exemption for all the transactions.

(c) *Where to file.* See Sec. 4000.4 of this chapter for information on where to file.

[Amended 10/28/2003 by 68 FR 61344]

(d) *Information.* Each request shall contain the following information:

(1) The name and address of the plan or plans for which the variance or exemption is being requested, and the telephone number of the plan administrator of each plan.

(2) For each plan described in paragraph (d)(1) of this section, the nine-digit Employer Identification Number (EIN) assigned by the IRS to the plan sponsor and the three-digit Plan Identification Number (PN) assigned by the plan sponsor to the plan, and, if different, also the EIN and PN last filed with the PBGC. If an EIN or PN has not been assigned, that should be indicated.

(3) The name, address and telephone number of the seller and of its duly authorized representative, if any.

(4) The name, address and telephone number of the purchaser and of its duly authorized representative, if any.

(5) A full description of each transaction for which the request is being made, including effective date.

(6) A statement explaining why the requested variance or exemption would not significantly increase the risk of financial loss to the plan, including evidence, financial or otherwise, that supports that conclusion.

(7) When the request for a variance or exemption is filed by the seller alone, a statement signed by the purchaser indicating its intention that section 4204 of ERISA apply to the sale of assets.

(8) A statement indicating the amount of the purchaser's bond or escrow required under section 4204(a)(1)(B) of ERISA.

(9) The estimated amount of withdrawal liability that the seller would otherwise incur as a result of the sale if section 4204 did not apply to the sale.

(10) A certification that a complete copy of the request has been sent to each plan described in paragraph (d)(1) of this section and each collective bargaining representative of the seller's employees by certified mail, return receipt requested.

(e) *Additional information.* In addition to the information described in paragraph (d) of this section, the PBGC may require the purchaser, the seller, or the plan to submit any other information the PBGC determines it needs to review the request.

(f) *Disclosure of information.* Any party submitting information pursuant to this section may include a statement of whether any of the information is of a nature that its disclosure may not be required under the Freedom of Information Act, 5 U.S.C. 552. The statement should specify the information that may not be subject to disclosure and the grounds therefor.

(Approved by the Office of Management and Budget under control number 1212-0021)

[¶ 15,668F]

§ 4204.22 **PBGC action on requests.** (a) *General.* The PBGC shall approve a request for a variance or exemption if PBGC determines that approval of the request is warranted, in that it—

(1) Would more effectively or equitably carry out the purposes of title IV of ERISA; and

(2) Would not significantly increase the risk of financial loss to the plan.

(b) *Notice of pendency of request.* As soon as practicable after receiving a variance or exemption request containing all the information specified in § 4204.21, the PBGC shall publish a notice of the pendency of the request in the Federal Register. The notice shall provide that any interested person may, within the period of time specified therein, submit written comments to the PBGC concerning the request. The notice will usually provide for a comment period of 45 days.

(c) *PBGC decision on request.* The PBGC shall issue a decision on a variance or exemption request as soon as practicable after the close of the comment period described in paragraph (b) of this section. PBGC's decision shall be in writing, and if the PBGC disapproves the request, the decision shall state the reasons therefor. Notice of the decision shall be published in the Federal Register.

[¶ 15,669]
PARTIAL WITHDRAWALS

Act Sec. 4205. (a) Except as otherwise provided in this section, there is a partial withdrawal by an employer from a plan on the last day of a plan year if for such plan year—

(1) there is a 70-percent contribution decline, or

(2) there is a partial cessation of the employer's contribution obligation.

Act Sec. 4205. (b) Purposes of subsection (a)—

(1) (A) There is a 70-percent contribution decline for any plan year if during each plan year in the 3-year testing period the employer's contribution base units do not exceed 30 percent of the employer's contribution base units for the high base year.

(B) For purposes of subparagraph (A)—

(i) The term "3-year testing period" means the period consisting of the plan year and the immediately preceding 2 plan years.

(ii) The number of contribution base units for the high base year is the average number of such units for the 2 plan years for which the employer's contribution base units were the highest within the 5 plan years immediately preceding the beginning of the 3-year testing period.

(2) (A) There is a partial cessation of the employer's contribution obligation for the plan year if, during such year—

(i) the employer permanently ceases to have an obligation to contribute under one or more but fewer than all collective bargaining agreements under which the employer has been obligated to contribute under the plan but continues to perform work in the jurisdiction of the collective bargaining agreement of the type for which contributions were previously required or transfers such work to another location, or

(ii) an employer permanently ceases to have an obligation to contribute under the plan with respect to work performed at one or more but fewer than all of its facilities, but continues to perform work at the facility of the type for which the obligation to contribute ceased.

(B) For purposes of subparagraph (A), a cessation of obligations under a collective bargaining agreement shall not be considered to have occurred solely because, with respect to the same plan, one agreement that requires contributions to the plan has been substituted for another agreement.

Act Sec. 4205. (c) (1) In the case of a plan in which a majority of the covered employees are employed in the retail food industry, the plan may be amended to provide that this section shall be applied with respect to such plan—

(A) by substituting "35 percent" for "70 percent" in subsections (a) and (b), and

(B) by substituting "65 percent" for "30 percent" in subsection (b).

(2) Any amendment adopted under paragraph (1) shall provide rules for the equitable reduction of withdrawal liability in any case in which the number of the plan's contribution base units, in the 2 plan years following the plan year of withdrawal of the employer, is higher than such number immediately after the withdrawal.

(3) Section 4208 shall not apply to a plan which has been amended under paragraph (1).

Act Sec. 4205. (d) In the case of a plan described in section 404(c) of the Internal Revenue Code of 1986, or a continuation thereof, the plan may be amended to provide rules setting forth other conditions consistent with the purposes of this Act under which an employer has liability for partial withdrawal.

<table>
<tr><td>Amendment</td><td></td></tr>
</table>

P.L. 101-239, § 7891(a)(1):

Titles I, III, and IV of ERISA (other than sections 3(37)(E), 301(a)(7), and 308, the last sentence of section 408(d), and sections 414(c), 4001(a)(3)(ii), and 4303) are each amended by striking "Internal Revenue Code of 1954" each place it appears and inserting "Internal Revenue Code of 1986", effective October 22, 1986.

P.L. 96-364, § 104(2):

Added Sec. 4205, effective September 26, 1980 under ERISA Sec. 4402, except that Sec. 4205(a)(1) does not apply to any plan year beginning before September 26, 1982, and Sec. 4205(a)(2) does not apply with respect to any cessation of contribution obligations occurring before September 26, 1980 (Sec. 108(d) of P.L. 96-364).

[¶ 15,670]
ADJUSTMENT FOR PARTIAL WITHDRAWAL

Act Sec. 4206. (a) The amount of an employer's liability for a partial withdrawal, before the application of sections 4219(c)(1) and 4225, is equal to the product of—

(1) the amount determined under section 4211, and adjusted under section 4209 if appropriate, determined as if the employer had withdrawn from the plan in a complete withdrawal—

(A) on the date of the partial withdrawal, or

(B) in the case of a partial withdrawal described in section 4205(a)(1) (relating to 70-percent contribution decline), on the last day of the first plan year in the 3-year testing period, multiplied by

(2) a fraction which is 1 minus a fraction—

(A) the numerator of which is the employer's contribution base units for the plan year following the plan year in which the partial withdrawal occurs, and

(B) the denominator of which is the average of the employer's contribution base units for—

(i) except as provided in clause (ii), the 5 plan years immediately preceding the plan year in which the partial withdrawal occurs, or

(ii) in the case of a partial withdrawal described in section 4205(a)(1) (relating to 70-percent contribution decline), the 5 plan years immediately preceding the beginning of the 3-year testing period.

Act Sec. 4206.(b)(1) In the case of an employer that has withdrawal liability for a partial withdrawal from a plan, any withdrawal liability of that employer for a partial or complete withdrawal from that plan in a subsequent plan year shall be reduced by the amount of any partial withdrawal liability (reduced by any abatement or reduction of such liability) of the employer with respect to the plan for a previous plan year.

(2) The corporation shall prescribe such regulations as may be necessary to provide for proper adjustments in the reduction provided by paragraph (1) for—

(A) changes in unfunded vested benefits arising after the close of the prior year for which partial withdrawal liability was determined,

(B) changes in contribution base units occurring after the close of the prior year for which partial withdrawal liability was determined, and

(C) any other factors for which it determines adjustment to be appropriate,

so that the liability for any complete or partial withdrawal in any subsequent year (after the application of the reduction) properly reflects the employer's share of liability with respect to the plan.

Amendment

P.L. 96-364, § 104(2):

Added Sec. 4206, effective September 26, 1980 under ERISA Sec. 4402.

Regulations

The following regulations were adopted by the Pension Benefit Guaranty Corporation on July 1, 1996 (61 FR 34002). Prior to July 1, 1996, PBGC regulations were under Chapter XXVI of Title 29 of the Code of Federal Regulations. Effective July 1, 1996, PBGC regulations were moved to Chapter XL, and were renumbered and reorganized.

[¶ 15,670A]

§ 4206.1 **Purpose and scope.** (a) *Purpose.* The purpose of this part is to prescribe rules, pursuant to section 4206(b) of ERISA, for adjusting the partial or complete withdrawal liability of an employer that previously partially withdrew from the same multiemployer plan. Section 4206(b)(1) provides that when an employer that has partially withdrawn from a plan subsequently incurs liability for another partial or a complete withdrawal from that plan, the employer's liability for the subsequent withdrawal is to be reduced by the amount of its liability for the prior partial withdrawal (less any waiver or reduction of that prior liability). Section 4206(b)(2) requires the PBGC to prescribe regulations adjusting the amount of this credit to ensure that the liability for the subsequent withdrawal properly reflects the employer's share of liability with respect to the plan. The purpose of the credit is to protect a withdrawing employer from being charged twice for the same unfunded vested benefits of the plan. The reduction in the credit protects the other employers in the plan from becoming responsible for unfunded vested benefits properly allocable to the withdrawing employer. In the interests of simplicity, the rules in this part provide for, generally, a one-step calculation of the adjusted credit under section 4206(b)(2) against the subsequent liability, rather than for separate calculations first of the credit under section 4206(b)(1) and then of the reduction in the credit under paragraph (b)(2) of that section. In cases where the withdrawal liability for the prior partial withdrawal was reduced by an abatement or other reduction of that liability, the adjusted credit is further reduced in accordance with § 4206.8 of this part.

(b) *Scope.* This part applies to multiemployer plans covered under Title IV of ERISA, and to employers that have partially withdrawn from such plans after September 25, 1980 and subsequently completely or partially withdraw from the same plan.

[¶ 15,670B]

§ 4206.2 **Definitions.** The following are defined in § 4001.2 of this chapter: *Code, employer, ERISA, multiemployer plan, PBGC, plan,* and *plan year.*

In addition, for purposes of this part:

Complete withdrawal means a complete withdrawal as described in section 4203 of ERISA.

Partial withdrawal means a partial withdrawal as described in section 4205 of ERISA.

[¶ 15,670C]

§ 4206.3 **Credit against liability for a subsequent withdrawal.** Whenever an employer that was assessed withdrawal liability for a partial withdrawal from a plan partially or completely withdraws from that plan in a subsequent plan year, it shall receive a credit against the new withdrawal liability in an amount greater than or equal to zero, determined in accordance with this part. If the credit determined under

§§ 4206.4 through 4206.9 is less than zero, the amount of the credit shall equal zero.

[¶ 15,670D]

§ 4206.4 **Amount of credit in plans using the presumptive method.** (a) *General.* In a plan that uses the presumptive allocation method described in section 4211(b) of ERISA, the credit shall equal the sum of the unamortized old liabilities determined under paragraph (b) of this section, multiplied by the fractions described or determined under paragraph (c) of this section. When an employer's prior partial withdrawal liability has been reduced or waived, this credit shall be adjusted in accordance with § 4206.8.

(b) *Unamortized old liabilities.* The amounts determined under this paragraph are the employer's proportional shares, if any, of the unamortized amounts as of the end of the plan year preceding the withdrawal for which the credit is being calculated, of—

(1) The plan's unfunded vested benefits as of the end of the last plan year ending before September 26, 1980;

(2) The annual changes in the plan's unfunded vested benefits for plan years ending after September 25, 1980, and before the year of the prior partial withdrawal; and

(3) The reallocated unfunded vested benefits (if any), as determined under section 4211(b)(4) of ERISA, for plan years ending before the year of the prior partial withdrawal.

(c) *Employer's allocable share of old liabilities.* The sum of the amounts determined under paragraph (b) are multiplied by the two fractions described in this paragraph in order to determine the amount of the old liabilities that was previously assessed against the employer.

(1) The first fraction is the fraction determined under section 4206(a)(2) of ERISA for the prior partial withdrawal.

(2) The second fraction is a fraction, the numerator of which is the amount of the liability assessed against the employer for the prior partial withdrawal, and the denominator of which is the product of—

(i) The amount of unfunded vested benefits allocable to the employer as if it had completely withdrawn as of the date of the prior partial withdrawal (determined without regard to any adjustments), multiplied by—

(ii) The fraction determined under section 4206(a)(2) of ERISA for the prior partial withdrawal.

[¶ 15,670E]

§ 4206.5 **Amount of credit in plans using the modified presumptive method.** (a) *General.* In a plan that uses the modified presumptive method described in section 4211(c)(2) of ERISA, the credit shall equal the sum of the unamortized old liabilities determined under paragraph (b) of this section, multiplied by the fractions described or determined under paragraph (c) of this section. When an employer's prior partial withdrawal liability has been reduced or waived, this credit shall be adjusted in accordance with § 4206.8.

(b) *Unamortized old liabilities.* The amounts described in this paragraph shall be determined as of the end of the plan year preceding the withdrawal for which the credit is being calculated, and are the employer's proportional shares, if any, of—

(1) The plan's unfunded vested benefits as of the end of the last plan year ending before September 26, 1980, reduced as if those obligations were being fully amortized in level annual installments over 15 years beginning with the first plan year ending on or after such date; and

(2) The aggregate post-1980 change amount determined under section 4211(c)(2)(C) of ERISA as if the employer had completely withdrawn in the year of the prior partial withdrawal, reduced as if those obligations were being fully amortized in level annual installments over the 5-year period beginning with the plan year in which the prior partial withdrawal occurred.

(c) *Employer's allocable share of old liabilities.* The sum of the amounts determined under paragraph (b) are multiplied by the two fractions described in this paragraph in order to determine the amount of old liabilities that was previously assessed against the employer.

(1) The first fraction is the fraction determined under section 4206(a)(2) of ERISA for the prior partial withdrawal.

(2) The second fraction is a fraction, the numerator of which is the amount of the liability assessed against the employer for the prior partial withdrawal, and the denominator of which is the product of—

(i) The amount of unfunded vested benefits allocable to the employer as if it had completely withdrawn as of the date of the prior partial withdrawal (determined without regard to any adjustments), multiplied by—

(ii) The fraction determined under section 4206(a)(2) of ERISA for the prior partial withdrawal.

[¶ 15,670F]

§ 4206.6 **Amount of credit in plans using the rolling-5 method.** In a plan that uses the rolling-5 allocation method described in section 4211(c)(3) of ERISA, the credit shall equal the amount of the liability assessed for the prior partial withdrawal, reduced as if that amount was being fully amortized in level annual installments over the 5-year period beginning with the plan year in which the prior partial withdrawal occurred. When an employer's prior partial withdrawal liability has been reduced or waived, this credit shall be adjusted in accordance with § 4206.8.

[¶ 15,670G]

§ 4206.7 **Amount of credit in plans using the direct attribution method.** In a plan that uses the direct attribution allocation method

described in section 4211(c)(4) of ERISA, the credit shall equal the amount of the liability assessed for the prior partial withdrawal, reduced as if that amount was being fully amortized in level annual installments beginning with the plan year in which the prior partial withdrawal occurred, over the greater of 10 years or the amortization period for the resulting base when the combined charge base and the combined credit base are offset under section 412(b)(4) of the Code. When an employer's prior partial withdrawal liability has been reduced or waived, this credit shall be adjusted in accordance with § 4206.8.

[¶ 15,670H]

§ 4206.8 **Reduction of credit for abatement or other reduction of prior partial withdrawal liability.** (a) *General.* If an employer's withdrawal liability for a prior partial withdrawal has been reduced or waived, the credit determined pursuant to § § 4206.4 through 4206.7 shall be adjusted in accordance with this section.

(b) *Computation.* The adjusted credit is calculated by multiplying the credit determined under the preceding sections of this part by a fraction—

(1) the numerator of which is the excess of the total partial withdrawal liability of the employer for all partial withdrawals in prior years (excluding those partial withdrawals for which the credit is zero) over the present value of each abatement or other reduction of that prior withdrawal liability calculated as of the date on which that prior partial withdrawal liability was determined; and

(2) the denominator of which is the total partial withdrawal liability of the employer for all partial withdrawals in prior years (excluding those partial withdrawals for which the credit is zero).

[¶ 15,670I]

§ 4206.9 **Amount of credit in plans using alternative allocation methods.** A plan that has adopted an alternative method of allocating unfunded vested benefits pursuant to section 4211(c)(5) of ERISA and part 4211 of this chapter shall adopt, by plan amendment, a method of calculating the credit provided by § 4206.3 that is consistent with the rules in § § 4206.4 through 4206.8 for plans using the statutory allocation method most similar to the plan's alternative allocation method.

[¶ 15,670J]

§ 4206.10 **Special rule for 70-percent decline partial withdrawals.** For the purposes of applying the rules in § § 4206.4 through 4206.9 in any case in which either the prior or subsequent partial withdrawal resulted from a 70-percent contribution decline (or a 35-percent decline in the case of certain retail food industry plans), the first year of the 3-year testing period shall be deemed to be the plan year in which the partial withdrawal occurred.

[¶ 15,671]
REDUCTION OR WAIVER OF COMPLETE WITHDRAWAL LIABILITY

Act Sec. 4207. (a) The corporation shall provide by regulation for the reduction or waiver of liability for a complete withdrawal in the event that an employer who has withdrawn from a plan subsequently resumes covered operations under the plan or renews an obligation to contribute under the plan, to the extent that the corporation determines that reduction or waiver of withdrawal liability is consistent with the purposes of this Act.

Act Sec. 4207. (b) The corporation shall prescribe by regulation a procedure and standards for the amendment of plans to provide alternative rules for the reduction or waiver of liability for a complete withdrawal in the event that an employer who has withdrawn from the plan subsequently resumes covered operations or renews an obligation to contribute under the plan. The rules may apply only to the extent that the rules are consistent with the purposes of this Act.

Amendment:

P.L. 96-364, § 104(2):

Added Sec. 4207, effective September 26, 1980 under ERISA Sec. 4402.

Regulations

The following regulations were adopted by the Pension Benefit Guaranty Corporation on July 1, 1996 (61 FR 34002). Prior to July 1, 1996, PBGC regulations were under Chapter XXVI of Title 29 of the Code of Federal Regulations. Effective July 1, 1996, PBGC regulations were moved to Chapter XL, and were renumbered and reorganized. Reg. § 4207.10 was revised and Reg. § 4207.11 was added October 28, 2003 (68 FR 61344).

[¶ 15,671A]

§ 4207.1 **Purpose and scope.** (a) *Purpose.* The purpose of this part is to prescribe rules, pursuant to section 4207(a) of ERISA, for reducing or waiving the withdrawal liability of certain employers that have completely withdrawn from a multiemployer plan and subsequently resume covered operations under the plan. This part prescribes rules pursuant to which the plan must waive the employer's obligation to make future liability payments with respect to its complete withdrawal and must calculate the amount of the employer's liability for a partial or

complete withdrawal from the plan after its reentry into the plan. This part also provides procedures, pursuant to section 4207(b) of ERISA, for plan sponsors of multiemployer plans to apply to PBGC for approval of plan amendments that provide for the reduction or waiver of complete withdrawal liability under conditions other than those specified in section 4207(a) of ERISA and this part.

(b) *Scope.* This part applies to multiemployer plans covered under title IV of ERISA, and to employers that have completely withdrawn from such plans after September 25, 1980, and that have not, as of the date of their reentry into the plan, fully satisfied their obligation to pay withdrawal liability arising from the complete withdrawal.

[¶ 15,671B]

§ 4207.2 Definitions. The following terms are defined in § 4001.2 of this chapter: *employer, ERISA, IRS, Multiemployer Act, multiemployer plan, nonforfeitable benefit, PBGC, plan,* and *plan year.*

In addition, for purposes of this part:

Complete withdrawal means a complete withdrawal as described in section 4203 of ERISA.

Eligible employer means the employer, as defined in section 4001(b) of ERISA, as it existed on the date of its initial partial or complete withdrawal, as applicable. An eligible employer shall continue to be an eligible employer notwithstanding the occurrence of any of the following events:

(1) A restoration involving a mere change in identity, form or place of organization, however effected;

(2) A reorganization involving a liquidation into a parent corporation;

(3) A merger, consolidation or division solely between (or among) trades or businesses (whether or not incorporated) of the employer; or

(4) An acquisition by or of, or a merger or combination with another trade or business.

Partial withdrawal means a partial withdrawal as described in section 4205 of ERISA.

Period of withdrawal means the plan year in which the employer completely withdrew from the plan, the plan year in which the employer reentered the plan and all intervening plan years.

[¶ 15,671C]

§ 4207.3 Abatement. (a) *General.* Whenever an eligible employer that has completely withdrawn from a multiemployer plan reenters the plan, it may apply to the plan for abatement of its complete withdrawal liability. Applications shall be filed by the date of the first scheduled withdrawal liability payment falling due after the employer resumes covered operations or, if later, the fifteenth calendar day after the employer resumes covered operations. Applications shall identify the eligible employer, the withdrawn employer, if different, the date of withdrawal, and the date of resumption of covered operations. Upon receiving an application for abatement, the plan sponsor shall determine, in accordance with paragraph (b) of this section, whether the employer satisfies the requirements for abatement of its complete withdrawal liability under § 4207.5, § 4207.9, or a plan amendment which has been approved by PBGC pursuant to § 4207.10. If the plan sponsor determines that the employer satisfies the requirements for abatement of its complete withdrawal liability, the provisions of paragraph (c) of this section shall apply. If the plan sponsor determines that the employer does not satisfy the requirements for abatement of its complete withdrawal liability, the provisions of paragraphs (d) and (e) of this section shall apply.

(b) *Determination of abatement.* As soon as practicable after an eligible employer that completely withdrew from a multiemployer plan applies for abatement, the plan sponsor shall determine whether the employer satisfies the requirements for abatement of its complete withdrawal liability under this part and shall notify the employer in writing of its determination and of the consequences of its determination, as described in paragraphs (c) or (d) and (e) of this section, as appropriate. If a bond or escrow has been provided to the plan under § 4207.4, the plan sponsor shall send a copy of the notice to the bonding or escrow agent.

(c) *Effects of abatement.* If the plan sponsor determines that the employer satisfies the requirements for abatement of its complete withdrawal liability under this part, then—

(1) The employer shall have no obligation to make future withdrawal liability payments to the plan with respect to its complete withdrawal;

(2) The employer's liability for a subsequent withdrawal shall be determined in accordance with § 4207.7 or § 4207.8, as applicable;

(3) Any bonds furnished under § 4207.4 shall be cancelled and any amounts held in escrow under § 4207.4 shall be refunded to the employer; and

(4) Any withdrawal liability payments due after the reentry and made by the employer to the plan shall be refunded by the plan without interest.

(d) *Effects of non-abatement.* If the plan sponsor determines that the employer does not satisfy the requirements for abatement of its complete withdrawal liability under this part, then—

(1) The bond or escrow furnished under § 4207.4 shall be paid to the plan within 30 days after the date of the plan sponsor's notice under paragraph (b) of this section;

(2) The employer shall pay to the plan within 30 days after the date of the plan sponsor's notice under paragraph (b) of this section, the amount of its withdrawal liability payment or payments, with respect to which the bond or escrow was furnished, in excess of the bond or escrow;

(3) The employer shall resume making its withdrawal liability payments as they are due to the plan; and

(4) The employer shall be treated as a new employer for purposes of any future application of the withdrawal liability rules in sections 4201-4225 of title IV of ERISA with respect to its participation in the plan after its reentry into the plan, except that in plans using the "direct attribution" method (section 4211(c)(4) of ERISA), the nonforfeitable benefits attributable to service with the employer shall include nonforfeitable benefits attributable to service prior to reentry that were not nonforfeitable at that time.

(e) *Collection of payments due and review of non-abatement determination.* The rules in part 4219, subpart C, of this chapter (relating to overdue, defaulted, and overpaid withdrawal liability) shall apply with respect to all payments required to be made under paragraphs (d)(2) and (d)(3) of this section. For this purpose, a payment required to be made under paragraph (d)(2) shall be treated as a withdrawal liability payment due on the 30th day after the date of the plan sponsor's notice under paragraph (b) of this section.

(1) *Review of non-abatement determination.* A plan sponsor's determination that the employer does not satisfy the requirements for abatement under this part shall be subject to plan review under section 4219(b)(2) of ERISA and to arbitration under section 4221 of ERISA, within the times prescribed by those sections. For this purpose, the plan sponsor's notice under paragraph (b) of this section shall be treated as a demand under section 4219(b)(1) of ERISA.

(2) *Determination of abatement.* If the plan sponsor or an arbitrator determines that the employer satisfies the requirements for abatement of its complete withdrawal liability under this part, the plan sponsor shall immediately refund the following payments (plus interest, except as indicated below, determined in accordance with § 4219.31(d) of this chapter as if the payments were overpayments of withdrawal liability) to the employer in a lump sum:

(i) The amount of the employer's withdrawal liability payment or payments, without interest, due after its reentry and made by the employer.

(ii) The bond or escrow paid to the plan under paragraph (d)(1) of this section.

(iii) The amount of the employer's withdrawal liability payment or payments in excess of the bond or escrow, paid to the plan under paragraph (d)(2) of this section.

(iv) Any withdrawal liability payment made by the employer to the plan pursuant to paragraph (d)(3) of this section after the plan sponsor's notice under paragraph (b) of this section.

[¶ 15,671D]

§ 4207.4 Withdrawal liability payments during pendency of abatement determination. (a) *General rule.* An eligible employer that completely withdraws from a multiemployer plan and subsequently reenters the plan may, in lieu of making withdrawal liability payments due after its reentry, provide a bond to, or establish an escrow account for, the plan that satisfies the requirements of paragraph (b) of this section or any plan rules adopted under paragraph (d) of this section, pending a determination by the plan sponsor under §4207.3(b) of whether the employer satisfies the requirements for abatement of its complete withdrawal liability. An employer that applies for abatement and neither provides a bond/escrow nor pays its withdrawal liability payments remains eligible for abatement.

(b) *Bond/escrow.* The bond or escrow allowed by this section shall be in an amount equal to 70 percent of the withdrawal liability payments that would otherwise be due. The bond or escrow relating to each payment shall be furnished before the due date of that payment. A single bond or escrow may be provided for more than one payment due during the pendency of the plan sponsor's determination. The bond or escrow agreement shall provide that if the plan sponsor determines that the employer does not satisfy the requirements for abatement of its complete withdrawal liability under this part, the bond or escrow shall be paid to the plan upon notice from the plan sponsor to the bonding or escrow agent. A bond provided under this paragraph shall be issued by a corporate surety company that is an acceptable surety for purposes of section 412 of ERISA.

(c) *Notice of bond/escrow.* Concurrently with posting a bond or establishing an escrow account under paragraph (b) of this section, the employer shall notify the plan sponsor. The notice shall include a statement of the amount of the bond or escrow, the scheduled payment or payments with respect to which the bond or escrow is being furnished, and the name and address of the bonding or escrow agent.

(d) *Plan amendments concerning bond/escrow.* A plan may, by amendment, adopt rules decreasing the amount specified in paragraph (b) of a bond or escrow allowed under this section. A plan amendment adopted under this paragraph may be applied only to the extent that it is consistent with the purposes of ERISA.

[¶ 15,671E]

§4207.5 **Requirements for abatement.** (a) *General rule.* Except as provided in §4207.9 (d) and (e) (pertaining to acquisitions, mergers and other combinations), an eligible employer that completely withdraws from a multiemployer plan and subsequently reenters the plan shall have its liability for that withdrawal abated in accordance with §4207.3(c) if the employer resumes covered operations under the plan, and the number of contribution base units with respect to which the employer has an obligation to contribute under the plan for the measurement period (as defined in paragraph (b) of this section) after it resumes covered operations exceeds 30 percent of the number of contribution base units with respect to which the employer had an obligation to contribute under the plan for the base year (as defined in paragraph (c) of this section).

(b) *Measurement period.* If the employer resumes covered operations under the plan at least six full months prior to the end of a plan year and would satisfy the test in paragraph (a) based on its contribution base units for that plan year, then the measurement period shall be the period from the date it resumes covered operations until the end of that plan year. If the employer would not satisfy this test, or if the employer resumes covered operations under the plan less than six full months prior to the end of the plan year, the measurement period shall be the first twelve months after it resumes covered operations.

(c) *Base year.* For purposes of paragraph (a) of this section, the employer's number of contribution base units for the base year is the average number of contribution base units for the two plan years in which its contribution base units were the highest, within the five plan years immediately preceding the year of its complete withdrawal.

[¶ 15,671F]

§4207.6 **Partial withdrawals after reentry.** (a) *General rule.* For purposes of determining whether there is a partial withdrawal of an eligible employer whose liability is abated under this part upon the employer's reentry into the plan or at any time thereafter, the plan sponsor shall apply the rules in section 4205 of ERISA, as modified by the rules in this section, and section 108 of the Multiemployer Act. A partial withdrawal of an employer whose liability is abated under this part may occur under these rules upon the employer's reentry into the plan. However, a plan sponsor may not demand payment of withdrawal liability for a partial withdrawal occurring upon the employer's reentry before the plan sponsor has determined that the employer's liability for

its complete withdrawal is abated under this part and has so notified the employer in accordance with §4207.3(b).

(b) *Partial withdrawal—70-percent contribution decline.* The plan sponsor shall determine whether there is a partial withdrawal described in section 4205(a)(1) of ERISA (relating to a 70-percent contribution decline) in accordance with the rules in section 4205 of ERISA and section 108 of the Multiemployer Act, as modified by the rules in this paragraph, and shall determine the amount of an employer's liability for that partial withdrawal in accordance with the rules in §4207.8(b).

(1) *Definition of "3-year testing period".* For purposes of section 4205(b)(1) of ERISA, the term "3-year testing period" means the period consisting of the plan year for which the determination is made and the two immediately preceding plan years, excluding any plan year during the period of withdrawal.

(2) *Contribution base units for high base year.* For purposes of section 4205(b)(1) of ERISA and except as provided in section 108(d)(3) of the Multiemployer Act, in determining the number of contribution base units for the high base year, if the five plan years immediately preceding the beginning of the 3-year testing period include a plan year during the period of withdrawal, the number of contribution base units for each such year of withdrawal shall be deemed to be the greater of—

(i) The employer's contribution base units for that plan year; or

(ii) The average of the employer's contribution base units for the three plan years preceding the plan year in which the employer completely withdrew from the plan.

(c) *Partial withdrawal—partial cessation of contribution obligation.* The plan sponsor shall determine whether there is a partial withdrawal described in section 4205(a)(2) of ERISA (relating to a partial cessation of the employer's contribution obligation) in accordance with the rules in section 4205 of ERISA, as modified by the rules in this paragraph, and section 108 of the Multiemployer Act. In making this determination, the sponsor shall exclude all plan years during the period of withdrawal. A partial withdrawal under this paragraph can occur no earlier than the plan year of reentry. If the sponsor determines that there was a partial withdrawal, it shall determine the amount of an employer's liability for that partial withdrawal in accordance with the rules in §4207.8(c).

[¶ 15,671G]

§4207.7 **Liability for subsequent complete withdrawals and related adjustments for allocating unfunded vested benefits.** (a) *General.* When an eligible employer that has had its liability for a complete withdrawal abated under this part completely withdraws from the plan, the employer's liability for that subsequent withdrawal shall be determined in accordance with the rules in sections 4201-4225 of title IV, as modified by the rules in this section, and section 108 of the Multiemployer Act. In the case of a combination described in §4207.9(d), the modifications described in this section shall be applied only with respect to that portion of the eligible employer that had previously withdrawn from the plan. In the case of a combination described in §4207.9(e), the modifications shall be applied separately with respect to each previously withdrawn employer that comprises the eligible employer. In addition, when a plan has abated the liability of a reentered employer, if the plan uses either the "presumptive" or the "direct attribution" method (section 4211(b) or (c)(4), respectively) for allocating unfunded vested benefits, the plan shall modify those allocation methods as described in this section in allocating unfunded vested benefits to any employer that withdraws from the plan after the reentry.

(b) *Allocation of unfunded vested benefits for subsequent withdrawal in plans using "presumptive" method.* In a plan using the "presumptive" allocation method under section 4211(b) of ERISA, the amount of unfunded vested benefits allocable to a reentered employer for a subsequent withdrawal shall equal the sum of—

(1) The unamortized amount of the employer's allocable shares of the amounts described in section 4211(b)(1), for the plan years preceding the initial withdrawal, determined as if the employer had not previously withdrawn;

(2) The sum of the unamortized annual credits attributable to the year of the initial withdrawal and each succeeding year ending prior to reentry; and

(3) The unamortized amount of the employer's allocable shares of the amounts-described in section 4211(b)(1)(A) and (C) for plan years ending after its reentry. For purposes of paragraph (b)(2), the annual credit for a plan year is the amount by which the employer's withdrawal liability payments for the year exceed the greater of the employer's imputed contributions or actual contributions for the year. The employer's imputed contributions for a year shall equal the average annual required contributions of the employer for the three plan years preceding the initial withdrawal. The amount of the credit for a plan year is reduced by 5 percent of the original amount for each succeeding plan year ending prior to the year of the subsequent withdrawal.

(c) *Allocation of unfunded vested benefits for subsequent withdrawal in plans using "modified presumptive" or "rolling-5" method.* In a plan using either the "modified presumptive" allocation method under section 4211(c)(2) of ERISA or the "rolling-5" method under section 4211(c)(3), the amount of unfunded vested benefits allocable to a reentered employer for a subsequent withdrawal shall equal the sum of—

(1) The amount determined under section 4211(c)(2) or (c)(3) of ERISA, as appropriate, as if the date of reentry were the employer's initial date of participation in the plan; and

(2) The outstanding balance, as of the date of reentry, of the unfunded vested benefits allocated to the employer for its previous withdrawal (as defined in paragraph (c)(2)(i) of this section) reduced as if that amount were being fully amortized in level annual installments, at the plan's funding rate as of the date of reentry, over the period described in paragraph (c)(2)(ii), beginning with the first plan year after reentry.

(i) The outstanding balance of the unfunded vested benefits allocated to an employer for its previous withdrawal is the excess of the amount determined under section 4211(c)(2) or (c)(3) of ERISA as of the end of the plan year in which the employer initially withdrew, accumulated with interest at the plan's funding rate for that year, from that year to the date of reentry, over the withdrawal liability payments made by the employer, accumulated with interest from the date of payment to the date of reentry at the plan's funding rate for the year of entry.

(ii) The period referred to in paragraph (c)(2) for plans using the modified presumptive method is the greater of five years, or the number of full plan years remaining on the amortization schedule under section 4211(c)(2)(B)(i) of ERISA. For plans using the rolling-5 method, the period is five years.

(d) *Adjustments applicable to all employers in plans using "presumptive" method.* In a plan using the "presumptive" allocation method under section 4211(b) of ERISA, when the plan has abated the withdrawal liability of a reentered employer pursuant to this part, the following adjustments to the allocation method shall be made in computing the unfunded vested benefits allocable to any employer that withdraws from the plan in a plan year beginning after the reentry:

(1) The sum of the unamortized amounts of the annual credits of a reentered employer shall be treated as a reallocated amount under section 4211(b)(4) of ERISA in the plan year in which the employer reenters.

(2) In the event that the 5-year period used to compute the denominator of the fraction described in section 4211(b)(2)(E) and (b)(4)(D) of ERISA includes a year during the period of withdrawal of a reentered employer, the contributions for a year during the period of withdrawal shall be adjusted to include any actual or imputed contributions of the employer, as determined under paragraph (b) of this section.

(e) *Adjustments applicable to all employers in plans using "direct attribution" method.* In a plan using the "direct attribution" method under section 4211(c)(4) of ERISA, when the plan has abated the withdrawal liability of a reentered employer pursuant to this part, the following adjustments to the allocation method shall be made in computing the unfunded vested benefits allocable to any employer that withdraws from the plan in a plan year beginning after the reentry:

(1) The nonforfeitable benefits attributable to service with a reentered employer prior to its initial withdrawal shall be treated as benefits that are attributable to service with that employer.

(2) For purposes of section 4211(c)(4)(D)(ii) and (iii) of ERISA, withdrawal liability payments made by a reentered employer shall be treated as contributions made by the reentered employer.

(f) *Plans using alternative allocation methods under section 4211(c)(5).* A plan that has adopted an alternative method of allocating unfunded vested benefits pursuant to section 4211(c)(5) of ERISA and part 4211 of this chapter shall adopt by plan amendment a method of determining a reentered employer's allocable share of the plan's unfunded vested benefits upon its subsequent withdrawal. The method shall treat the reentered employer and other withdrawing employers in a manner consistent with the treatment under the paragraph(s) of this section applicable to plans using the statutory allocation method most similar to the plan's alternative allocation method.

(g) *Adjustments to amount of annual withdrawal liability payments for subsequent withdrawal.* For purposes of section 4219(c)(1)(C)(i)(I) and (ii)(I) of ERISA, in determining the amount of the annual withdrawal liability payments for a subsequent complete withdrawal, if the period of ten consecutive plan years ending before the plan year in which the withdrawal occurs includes a plan year during the period of withdrawal, the employer's number of contribution base units, used in section 4219(c)(1)(C)(i)(I), or the required employer contributions, used in section 4219(c)(1)(C)(ii)(I), for each such plan year during the period of withdrawal shall be deemed to be the greater of—

(1) The employer's contribution base units or the required employer contributions, as applicable, for that year; or

(2) The average of the employer's contribution base units or of the required employer contributions, as applicable, for those plan years not during the period of withdrawal, within the ten consecutive plan years ending before the plan year in which the employer's subsequent complete withdrawal occurred.

[¶ 15,671H]

§ 4207.8 **Liability for subsequent partial withdrawals.** (a) *General.* When an eligible employer that has had its liability for a complete withdrawal abated under this part partially withdraws from the plan, the employer's liability for that subsequent partial withdrawal shall be determined in accordance with the rules in sections 4201-4225 of ERISA, as modified by the rules in § 4207.7(b) through (g) of this part and the rules in this section, and section 108 of the Multiemployer Act.

(b) *Liability for a 70-percent contribution decline.* The amount of an employer's liability under section 4206(a) (relating to the calculation of liability for a partial withdrawal), section 4208 (relating to the reduction of liability for a partial withdrawal) and section 4219(c)(1) (relating to the schedule of partial withdrawal liability payments) of ERISA, for a subsequent partial withdrawal described in section 4205(a)(1) of ERISA (relating to a 70-percent contribution decline) shall be modified in accordance with the rules in this paragraph.

(1) *Definition of "3-year testing period".* For purposes of sections 4206(a) and 4219(c)(1) of ERISA, and paragraphs (b)(2)-(b)(4) of this section, the term "3-year testing period" means the period consisting of the plan year for which the determination is made and the two immediately preceding plan years, excluding any plan year during the period of withdrawal.

(2) *Determination date of section 4211 allocable share.* For purposes of section 4206(a)(1)(B) of ERISA, the amount determined under section 4211 shall be determined as if the employer had withdrawn from the plan in a complete withdrawal on the last day of the first plan year in the 3-year testing period or the last day of the plan year in which the employer reentered the plan, whichever is later.

(3) *Calculation of fractional share of section 4211 amount.* For purposes of sections 4206(a)(2)(B)(ii) and 4219(c)(1)(E)(ii) of ERISA, if the five plan years immediately preceding the beginning of the 3-year testing period include a plan year during the period of withdrawal, then, in determining the denominator of the fraction described in

section 4206(a)(2), the employer's contribution base units for each such year of withdrawal shall be deemed to be the greater of—

(i) The employer's contribution base units for that plan year; or

(ii) The average of the employer's contribution base units for the three plan years preceding the plan year in which the employer completely withdrew from the plan.

(4) *Contribution base units for high base year.* If the five plan years immediately preceding the beginning of the 3-year testing period include a plan year during the period of withdrawal, then for purposes of section 4208(a) and (b)(1) of ERISA, the number of contribution base units for the high base year shall be the number of contribution base units determined under paragraph (b)(3) of this section.

(c) *Liability for partial cessation of contribution obligation.* The amount of an employer's liability under section 4206(a) (relating to the calculation of liability for a partial withdrawal) and section 4219(c)(1) (relating to the amount of the annual partial withdrawal liability payments) of ERISA, for a subsequent partial withdrawal described in section 4205(a)(2) of ERISA (relating to a partial cessation of the contribution obligation) shall be modified in accordance with the rules in this paragraph. For purposes of sections 4206(a)(2)(B)(i) and 4219(c)(1)(E)(ii) of ERISA, if the five plan years immediately preceding the plan year in which the partial withdrawal occurs include a plan year during the period of withdrawal, the denominator of the fraction described in section 4206(a)(2) shall be determined in accordance with the rule set forth in paragraph (b)(3) of this section.

[¶ 15,671I]

§4207.9 **Special rules.** (a) *Employer that has withdrawn and reentered the plan before the effective date of this part.* This part shall apply, in accordance with the rules in this paragraph, with respect to an eligible employer that completely withdraws from a multiemployer plan after September 25, 1980, and is performing covered work under the plan on the effective date of this part. Upon the application of an employer described in the preceding sentence, the plan sponsor of a multiemployer plan shall determine whether the employer satisfies the requirements for abatement of its complete withdrawal liability under this part. Pending the plan sponsor's determination, the employer may provide the plan with a bond or escrow that satisfies the requirements of §4207.4, in lieu of making its withdrawal liability payments due after its application for an abatement determination. The plan sponsor shall notify the employer in writing of its determination and the consequences of its determination as described in §4207.3 (c) or (d) and (e), as applicable. If the plan sponsor determines that the employer qualifies for abatement, only withdrawal liability payments made prior to the employer's reentry shall be retained by the plan; payments made by the employer after its reentry shall be refunded to the employer, with interest on those made prior to the application for abatement, in accordance with §4207.3(e)(2). If a bond or escrow has been provided to the plan in accordance with §4207.4, the plan sponsor shall send a copy of the notice to the bonding or escrow agent. Sections 4207.6 through 4207.8 shall apply with respect to the employer's subsequent complete withdrawal occurring on or after the effective date of this part, or partial withdrawal occurring either before or after that date. This paragraph shall not negate reasonable actions taken by plans prior to the effective date of this part under plan rules implementing section 4207(a) of ERISA that were validly adopted pursuant to section 405 of the Multiemployer Act.

(b) *Employer with multiple complete withdrawals that has reentered the plan before effective date of this part.* If an employer described in paragraph (a) of this section has completely withdrawn from a multiemployer plan on two or more occasions before the effective date of this part, the rules in paragraph (a) of this section shall be applied as modified by this paragraph.

(1) The plan sponsor shall determine whether the employer satisfies the requirements for abatement under §4207.5 based on the most recent complete withdrawal.

(2) If the employer satisfies the requirements for abatement, the employer's liability with respect to all previous complete withdrawals shall be abated.

(3) If the liability is abated, §§4207.6 and 4207.7 shall be applied as if the employer's earliest complete withdrawal were its initial complete withdrawal.

(c) *Employer with multiple complete withdrawals that has not reentered the plan as of the effective date of this part.* If an eligible employer has completely withdrawn from a multiemployer plan on two or more occasions between September 26, 1980 and the effective date of this part and is not performing covered work under the plan on the effective date of this regulation, the rules in this part shall apply, subject to the modifications specified in paragraphs (b)(1)-(b)(3) of this section, upon the employer's reentry into the plan.

(d) *Combination of withdrawn employer with contributing employer.* If a withdrawn employer merges or otherwise combines with an employer that has an obligation to contribute to the plan from which the first employer withdrew, the combined entity is the eligible employer, and the rules of §4207.5 shall be applied—

(1) By subtracting from the measurement period contribution base units the contribution base units for which the non-withdrawn portion of the employer was obligated to contribute in the last plan year ending prior to the combination;

(2) By determining the base year contribution base units solely by reference to the contribution base units of the withdrawn portion of the employer; and

(3) By using the date of the combination, rather than the date of resumption of covered operations, to begin the measurement period.

(e) *Combination of two or more withdrawn employers.* If two or more withdrawn employers merge or otherwise combine, the combined entity is the eligible employer, and the rules of §4207.5 shall be applied by combining the number of contribution base units with respect to which each portion of the employer had an obligation to contribute under the plan for its base year. However, the combined number of contribution base units shall not include contribution base units of a withdrawn portion of the employer that had fully paid its withdrawal liability as of the date of the resumption of covered operations.

[¶ 15,671J]

§4207.10 **Plan rules for abatement.** (a) *General rule.* Subject to the approval of the PBGC, a plan may, by amendment, adopt rules for the reduction or waiver of complete withdrawal liability under conditions other than those specified in §§4207.5 and 4207.9 (c) and (d), provided that such conditions relate to events occurring or factors existing subsequent to a complete withdrawal year. The request for PBGC approval shall be filed after the amendment is adopted. A plan amendment under this section may not be put into effect until it is approved by the PBGC. However, an amendment that is approved by the PBGC may apply retroactively to the date of the adoption of the amendment. PBGC approval shall also be required for any subsequent modification of the amendment, other than repeal of the amendment. Sections 4207.6, 4207.7, and 4207.8 shall apply to all subsequent partial withdrawals after a reduction or waiver of complete withdrawal liability under a plan amendment approved by the PBGC pursuant to this section.

(b) *Who may request.* The plan sponsor, or a duly authorized representative acting on behalf of the plan sponsor, shall sign and submit the request.

(c) *Where to file.* See Sec. 4000.4 of this chapter for information on where to file.

[Amended 10/28/2003 by 68 FR 61344]

(d) *Information.* Each request shall contain the following information:

(1) The name and address of the plan for which the plan amendment is being submitted and the telephone number of the plan sponsor or its duly authorized representative.

(2) The nine-digit Employer Identification Number (EIN) assigned to the plan sponsor by the IRS and the three-digit Plan Identification Number (PN) assigned to the plan by the plan sponsor, and, if different, the EIN and PN last filed with the PBGC. If no EIN or PN has been assigned, that should be indicated.

(3) A copy of the executed amendment, including—

(i) The date on which the amendment was adopted;

(ii) The proposed effective date; and

(iii) The full text of the rules on the reduction or waiver of complete withdrawal liability.

(4) A copy of the most recent actuarial valuation report of the plan.

(5) A statement certifying that notice of the adoption of the amendment and of the request for approval filed under this section has been given to all employers that have an obligation to contribute under the plan and to all employee organizations representing employees covered under the plan.

(e) *Supplemental information.* In addition to the information described in paragraph (d) of this section, a plan may submit any other information that it believes it pertinent to its request. The PBGC may require the plan sponsor to submit any other information that the PBGC determines it needs to review a request under this section.

(f) *Criteria for PBGC approval.* The PBGC shall approve a plan amendment authorized by paragraph (a) of this section if it determines that the rules therein are consistent with the purposes of ERISA. An abatement rule is not consistent with the purposes of ERISA if—

(1) Implementation of the rule would be adverse to the interest of plan participants and beneficiaries; or

(2) The rule would increase the PBGC's risk of loss with respect to the plan.

(Approved by the Office of Management and Budget under control number 1212-0044)

[¶ 15,671K]

§ 4207.11 **Method of filing; method and date of issuance.** (a) *Method of filing.* The PBGC applies the rules in subpart A of part 4000 of this chapter to determine permissible methods of filing with the PBGC under this part.

(b) *Method of issuance.* The PBGC applies the rules in subpart B of part 4000 of this chapter to determine permissible methods of issuance under this part.

(c) *Date of issuance.* The PBGC applies the rules in subpart C of part 4000 of this chapter to determine the date that an issuance under this part was provided.

[Added 10/28/2003 by 68 FR 61344]

[¶ 15,673]
REDUCTION OF PARTIAL WITHDRAWAL LIABILITY

Act Sec. 4208. (a)(1) If, for any 2 consecutive plan years following the plan year in which an employer has partially withdrawn from a plan under section 4205(a)(1) (referred to elsewhere in this section as the "partial withdrawal year"), the number of contribution base units with respect to which the employer has an obligation to contribute under the plan for each such year is not less than 90 percent of the total number of contribution base units with respect to which the employer had an obligation to contribute under the plan for the high base year (within the meaning of section 4205(b)(1)(B)(ii)), then the employer shall have no obligation to make payments with respect to such partial withdrawal (other than delinquent payments) for plan years beginning after the second consecutive plan year following the partial withdrawal year.

(2)(A) For any plan year for which the number of contribution base units with respect to which an employer who has partially withdrawn under section 4205(a)(1) has an obligation to contribute under the plan equals or exceeds the number of units for the highest year determined under paragraph (1) without regard to "90 percent of", the employer may furnish (in lieu of payment of the partial withdrawal liability determined under section 4206) a bond to the plan in the amount determined by the plan sponsor (not exceeding 50 percent of the annual payment otherwise required).

(B) If the plan sponsor determines under paragraph (1) that the employer has no further liability to the plan for the partial withdrawal, then the bond shall be cancelled.

(C) If the plan sponsor determines under paragraph (1) that the employer continues to have liability to the plan for the partial withdrawal, then—

(i) the bond shall be paid to the plan,

(ii) the employer shall immediately be liable for the outstanding amount of liability due with respect to the plan year for which the bond was posted, and

(iii) the employer shall continue to make the partial withdrawal liability payments as they are due.

Act Sec. 4208. (b) If—

(1) for any 2 consecutive plan years following a partial withdrawal under section 4205(a)(1), the number of contribution base units with respect to which the employer has an obligation to contribute for each such year exceeds 30 percent of the total number of contribution base units with respect to which the employer had an obligation to contribute for the high base year (within the meaning of section 4205(b)(1)(B)(ii)), and

(2) the total number of contribution base units with respect to which all employers under the plan have obligations to contribute in each of such 2 consecutive years is not less than 90 percent of the total number of contribution base units for which all employers had obligations to contribute in the partial withdrawal plan year;

then, the employer shall have no obligation to make payments with respect to such partial withdrawal (other than delinquent payments) for plan years beginning after the second such consecutive plan year.

Act Sec. 4208. (c) In any case in which, in any plan year following a partial withdrawal under section 4205(a)(1), the number of contribution base units with respect to which the employer has an obligation to contribute for such year equals or exceeds 110 percent (or such other percentage as the plan may provide by amendment and which is not prohibited under regulations prescribed by the corporation) of the number of contribution base units with respect to which the employer had an obligation to contribute in the partial withdrawal year, then the amount of the employer's partial withdrawal liability payment for such year shall be reduced pro rata, in accordance with regulations prescribed by the corporation.

Act Sec. 4208. (d)(1) An employer to whom section 4203(b) (relating to the building and construction industry) applies is liable for a partial withdrawal only if the employer's obligation to contribute under the plan is continued for no more than an insubstantial portion of its work in the craft and area jurisdiction of the collective bargaining agreement of the type for which contributions are required.

(2) An employer to whom section 4203(c) (relating to the entertainment industry) applies shall have no liability for a partial withdrawal except under the conditions and to the extent prescribed by the corporation by regulation.

Act Sec. 4208. (e)(1) The corporation may prescribe regulations providing for the reduction or elimination of partial withdrawal liability under any conditions with respect to which the corporation determines that reduction or elimination of partial withdrawal liability is consistent with the purposes of this Act.

(2) Under such regulations, reduction of withdrawal liability shall be provided only with respect to subsequent changes in the employer's contributions for the same operations, or under the same collective bargaining agreement, that gave rise to the partial withdrawal, and changes in the employer's contribution base units with respect to other facilities or other collective bargaining agreements shall not be taken into account.

(3) The corporation shall prescribe by regulation a procedure by which a plan may by amendment adopt rules for the reduction or elimination of partial withdrawal liability under any other conditions, subject to the approval of the corporation based on its determination that adoption of such rules by the plan is consistent with the purposes of this Act.

Amendment

P.L. 96-364, § 104(2):

Added Sec. 4208, effective September 26, 1980 under ERISA Sec. 4402.

Regulations

The following regulations were adopted by the Pension Benefit Guaranty Corporation on July 1, 1996 (61 FR 34002). Prior to July 1, 1996, PBGC regulations were under Chapter XXVI of Title 29 of the Code of Federal Regulations. Effective July 1, 1996, PBGC regulations were moved to Chapter XL, and were renumbered and reorganized. Reg. § 4208.9 was amended, and Reg. § 4208.10 was added, on October 28, 2003 (68 FR 61344).

[¶ 15,673A]

§ 4208.1 **Purpose and scope.** (a) *Purpose.* The purpose of this part is to establish rules for reducing or waiving the liability of certain employers that have partially withdrawn from a multiemployer pension plan.

(b) *Scope.* This part applies to multiemployer pension plans covered under title IV of ERISA and to employers that have partially withdrawn from such plans after September 25, 1980, and that have not, as of the date on which they satisfy the conditions for reducing or eliminating their partial withdrawal liability, fully satisfied their obligation to pay that partial withdrawal liability. This rule shall not negate reasonable actions taken by plans prior to the effective date of this part under plan rules implementing section 4208 of ERISA that were validly adopted pursuant to section 405 of the Multiemployer Act.

[¶ 15,673B]

§ 4208.2 **Definitions.** The following terms are defined in § 4001.2 of this chapter: *employer, ERISA, IRS, Multiemployer Act, multiemployer plan, PBGC, plan,* and *plan year.*

In addition, for purposes of this part:

Complete withdrawal means a complete withdrawal as described in section 4203 of ERISA.

Eligible employer means the employer, as defined in section 4001(b) of ERISA, as it existed on the date of its initial partial or complete withdrawal, as applicable. An eligible employer shall continue to be an eligible employer notwithstanding the occurrence of any of the following events:

(1) A restoration involving a mere change in identity, form or place of organization, however effected;

(2) A reorganization involving a liquidation into a parent corporation;

(3) A merger, consolidation or division solely between (or among) trades or businesses (whether or not incorporated) of the employer; or

(4) An acquisition by or of, or a merger or combination with another trade or business.

Partial withdrawal means a partial withdrawal as described in section 4205 of ERISA.

Partial withdrawal year means the third year of the 3-year testing period in the case of a partial withdrawal caused by a 70-percent contribution decline, or the year of the partial cessation in the case of a partial withdrawal caused by a partial cessation of the employer's contribution obligation.

[¶ 15,673C]

§ 4208.3 **Abatement.** (a) *General.* Whenever an eligible employer that has partially withdrawn from a multiemployer plan satisfies the requirements in § 4208.4 for the reduction or waiver of its partial withdrawal liability, it may apply to the plan for abatement of its partial withdrawal liability. Applications shall identify the eligible employer, the withdrawn employer (if different), the date of withdrawal, and the basis for reduction or waiver of its withdrawal liability. Upon receiving a complete application for abatement, the plan sponsor shall determine, in accordance with paragraph (b) of this section, whether the employer satisfies the requirements for abatement of its partial withdrawal liability under § 4208.4. If the plan sponsor determines that the employer satisfies the requirements for abatement of its partial withdrawal liability, the provisions of paragraph (c) of this section shall apply. If the plan sponsor determines that the employer does not satisfy the requirements for abatement of its partial withdrawal liability, the provisions of paragraphs (d) and (e) of this section shall apply.

(b) *Determination of abatement.* Within 60 days after an eligible employer that partially withdrew from a multiemployer plan applies for abatement in accordance with paragraph (a) of this section, the plan sponsor shall determine whether the employer satisfies the requirements for abatement of its partial withdrawal liability under § 4208.4 and shall notify the employer in writing of its determination and of the consequences of its determination, as described in paragraphs (c) or (d) and (e) of this section, as appropriate. If a bond or escrow has been provided to the plan under § 4208.5 of this part, the plan sponsor shall send a copy of the notice to the bonding or escrow agent.

(c) *Effects of abatement.* If the plan sponsor determines that the employer satisfies the requirements for abatement of its partial withdrawal liability under § 4208.4, then—

(1) The employer's partial withdrawal liability shall be eliminated or its annual partial withdrawal liability payments shall be reduced in accordance with § 4208.6, as applicable;

(2) The employer's liability for a subsequent withdrawal shall be determined in accordance with § 4208.7;

(3) Any bonds furnished under § 4208.5 shall be canceled and any amounts held in escrow under § 4208.5 shall be refunded to the employer; and

(4) Any withdrawal liability payments originally due and paid after the end of the plan year in which the conditions for abatement were satisfied, in excess of the amount due under this part after that date shall be credited to the remaining withdrawal liability payments, if any, owed by the employer, beginning with the first payment due after the revised payment schedule is issued pursuant to this paragraph. If the credited amount is greater than the outstanding amount of the employer's partial withdrawal liability, the amount remaining after satisfaction of the liability shall be refunded to the employer. Interest on the credited amount at the rate prescribed in part 4219, subpart C, of this chapter (relating to overdue, defaulted, and overpaid withdrawal liability) shall be added if the plan sponsor does not issue a revised payment schedule reflecting the credit or make the required refund within 60 days after receipt by the plan sponsor of a complete abatement application. Interest shall accrue from the 61st day.

(d) *Effects of non-abatement.* If the plan sponsor determines that the employer does not satisfy the requirements for abatement of its partial withdrawal liability under § 4208.4, then the employer shall take or cause to be taken the actions set forth in paragraphs (d)(1)-(d)(3) of this section. The rules in part 4219, subpart C, shall apply with respect to all payments required to be made under paragraphs (d)(2) and (d)(3). For this purpose, a payment required under paragraph (d)(2) shall be treated as a withdrawal liability payment due on the 30th day after the date of the plan sponsor's notice under paragraph (b) of this section.

(1) Any bond or escrow furnished under § 4208.5 shall be paid to the plan within 30 days after the date of the plan sponsor's notice under paragraph (b) of this section.

(2) The employer shall pay to the plan within 30 days after the date of the plan sponsor's notice under paragraph (b) of this section, the amount of its withdrawal liability payment or payments, with respect to which the bond or escrow was furnished, in excess of the bond or escrow.

(3) The employer shall resume or continue making its partial withdrawal liability payments as they are due to the plan.

(e) *Review of non-abatement determination.* A plan sponsor's determinations that the employer does not satisfy the requirements for abatement under § 4208.4 and of the amount of reduction determined under § 4208.6 shall be subject to plan review under section 4219(b)(2) of ERISA and to arbitration under section 4221 of ERISA and part 4221 of this chapter, within the times prescribed by those provisions. For this purpose, the plan sponsor's notice under paragraph (b) of this section shall be treated as a demand under section 4219(b)(1) of ERISA. If the plan sponsor upon review or an arbitrator determines that the employer satisfies the requirements for abatement of its partial withdrawal liability under § 4208.4, the plan sponsor shall immediately refund the amounts described in paragraph (e)(1) of this section if the liability is waived, or credit and refund the amounts described in paragraph (e)(2) if the annual payment is reduced.

(1) *Refund for waived liability.* If the employer's partial withdrawal liability is waived, the plan sponsor shall refund to the employer the payments made pursuant to paragraphs (d)(1)-(d)(3) of this section (plus interest determined in accordance with § 4219.31(d) of this chapter as if the payments were overpayments of withdrawal liability).

(2) *Credit for reduced annual payment.* If the employer's annual partial withdrawal liability payment is reduced, the plan sponsor shall credit the payments made pursuant to paragraphs (d)(1)-(d)(3) of this section (plus interest determined in accordance with § 4219.31(d) of this chapter as if the payments were overpayments of withdrawal liability) to future withdrawal liability payments owed by the employer, beginning with the first payment that is due after the determination, and refund any credit (including interest) remaining after satisfaction of the outstanding amount of the employer's partial withdrawal liability.

[¶ 15,673D]

§ 4208.4 **Conditions for abatement.** (a) *Waiver of liability for a 70-percent contribution decline.* An employer that has incurred a partial withdrawal under section 4205(a)(1) of ERISA shall have no obligation to make payments with respect to that partial withdrawal (other than delinquent payments) for plan years beginning after the second consecutive plan year in which the conditions of either paragraph (a)(1) or (a)(2) are satisfied for each of the two years:

(1) The number of contribution base units with respect to which the employer has an obligation to contribute under the plan for each year is not less than 90 percent of the total number of contribution base units with respect to which the employer had an obligation to contribute to the plan for the high base year (as defined in paragraph (d) of this section).

(2) The conditions of this paragraph are satisfied if—

(i) The number of contribution base units with respect to which the employer has an obligation to contribute for each year exceeds 30 percent of the total number of contribution base units with respect to which the employer had an obligation to contribute to the plan for the high base year (as defined in paragraph (d) of this section); and

(ii) The total number of contribution base units with respect to which all employers under the plan have obligations to contribute in each of the two years is not less than 90 percent of the total number of contribution base units for which all employers had obligations to contribute in the partial withdrawal year.

(b) *Waiver of liability for a partial cessation of the employer's contribution obligation.* Except as provided in § 4208.8, an employer that has incurred partial withdrawal liability under section 4205(a)(2) of ERISA shall have no obligation to make payments with respect to that partial withdrawal (other than delinquent payments) for plan years beginning after the second consecutive plan year in which the employer satisfies the conditions under either paragraph (b)(1) or (b)(2) of this section.

(1) *Partial restoration of withdrawn work.* The employer satisfies the conditions under this paragraph if, for each of two consecutive plan years—

(i) The employer makes contributions for the same facility or under the same collective bargaining agreement that gave rise to the partial withdrawal;

(ii) The employer's contribution base units for that facility or under that agreement exceed 30 percent of the contribution base units with respect to which the employer had an obligation to contribute for that facility or under that agreement for the high base year (as defined in paragraph (d) of this section); and

(iii) The total number of contribution base units with respect to which the employer has an obligation to contribute to the plan equals at least 90 percent of the total number of contribution base units with respect to which the employer had an obligation to contribute under the plan for the high base year (as defined in paragraph (d) of this section).

(2) *Substantial restoration of withdrawn work.* The employer satisfies the conditions under this paragraph if, for each of two consecutive plan years—

(i) The employer makes contributions for the same facility or under the same collective bargaining agreement that gave rise to the partial withdrawal;

(ii) The employer's contribution base units for that facility or under that agreement are not less than 90 percent of the contribution base units with respect to which the employer had an obligation to contribute for that facility or under that agreement for the high base year (as defined in paragraph (d) of this section); and

(iii) The total number of contribution base units with respect to which the employer has an obligation to contribute to the plan equals or exceeds the sum of—

(A) The number of contribution base units with respect to which the employer had an obligation to contribute in the year prior to the partial withdrawal year, determined without regard to the contribution base units for the facility or under the agreement that gave rise to the partial withdrawal; and

(B) 90 percent of the contribution base units with respect to which the employer had an obligation to contribute for that facility or under that agreement in either the year prior to the partial withdrawal year or the high base year (as defined in paragraph (d) of this section), whichever is less.

(c) *Reduction in annual partial withdrawal liability payment—*

(1) *Partial withdrawals under section 4205(a)(1).* An employer shall be entitled to a reduction of its annual partial withdrawal liability payment for a plan year if the number of contribution base units with respect to which the employer had an obligation to contribute during the plan year exceeds the greater of—

(i) 110 percent (or such lower number as the plan may, by amendment, adopt) of the number of contribution base units with respect to which the employer had an obligation to contribute in the partial withdrawal year; or

(ii) The total number of contribution base units with respect to which the employer had an obligation to contribute to the plan for the plan year following the partial withdrawal year.

(2) *Partial withdrawals under section 4205(a)(2).* An employer that resumes the obligation to contribute with respect to a facility or collective bargaining agreement that gave rise to a partial withdrawal, but does not qualify to have that liability waived under paragraph (b) of this section, shall have its annual partial withdrawal liability payment reduced for any plan year in which the total number of contribution base units with respect to which the employer has an obligation to contribute equals or exceeds the sum of—

(i) The number of contribution base units for the reentered facility or agreement during that year; and

(ii) The total number of contribution base units with respect to which the employer had an obligation to contribute to the plan for the year following the partial withdrawal year.

(d) *High base year.* For purposes of paragraphs (a) and (b)(1)(iii) of this section, the high base year contributions are the average of the total contribution base units for the two plan years for which the employer's total contribution base units were highest within the five plan years immediately preceding the beginning of the 3-year testing period defined in section 4205(b)(1)(B)(i) of ERISA, with respect to paragraph (a) of this section, or the partial withdrawal year, with respect to paragraph (b)(1)(iii) of this section. For purposes of paragraphs (b)(1)(ii) and (b)(2) of this section, the high base year contributions are the average number of contribution base units for the facility or under the agreement for the two plan years for which the employer's contribution base units for that facility or under that agreement were highest within the five plan years immediately preceding the partial withdrawal.

[¶ 15,673E]

§ 4208.5 **Withdrawal liability payments during pendency of abatement determination.** (a) *Bond/Escrow.* An employer that has satisfied the requirements of § 4208.4(a)(1) without regard to "90 percent of" or § 4208.4(b) for one year with respect to all partial withdrawals it incurred in a plan year may, in lieu of making scheduled withdrawal liability payments in the second year for those withdrawals, provide a bond to, or establish an escrow account for, the plan that satisfies the requirements of paragraph (b) of this section or any plan rules adopted under paragraph (d) of this section, pending a determination by the plan sponsor of whether the employer satisfies the requirements of § 4208.4 (a)(1) or (b) for the second consecutive plan year. An employer that applies for abatement and neither provides a bond/escrow nor makes its withdrawal liability payments remains eligible for abatement.

(b) *Amount of bond/escrow.* The bond or escrow allowed by this section shall be in an amount equal to 50 percent of the withdrawal liability payments that would otherwise be due. The bond or escrow relating to each payment shall be furnished before the due date of that payment. A single bond or escrow may be provided for more than one payment due during the pendency of the plan sponsor's determination. The bond or escrow agreement shall provide that if the plan sponsor determines that the employer does not satisfy the requirements for abatement of its partial withdrawal liability under § 4208.4 (a)(1) or (b), the bond or escrow shall be paid to the plan upon notice from the plan sponsor to the bonding or escrow agent. A bond provided under this paragraph shall be issued by a corporate surety company that is an acceptable surety for purposes of section 412 of ERISA.

(c) *Notice of bond/escrow.* Concurrently with posting a bond or establishing an escrow account under this section, the employer shall notify the plan sponsor. The notice shall include a statement of the amount of the bond or escrow, the scheduled payment or payments with respect to which the bond or escrow is being furnished, and the name and address of the bonding or escrow agent.

(d) *Plan amendments concerning bond/escrow.* A plan may, by amendment, adopt rules decreasing the amount of the bond or escrow specified in paragraph (b) of this section. A plan amendment adopted under this paragraph may be applied only to the extent that it is consistent with the purposes of ERISA. An amendment satisfies this requirement only if it does not create an unreasonable risk of loss to the plan.

(e) *Plan sponsor determination.* Within 60 days after the end of the plan year in which the bond/escrow is furnished, the plan sponsor shall determine whether the employer satisfied the requirements of § 4208.4 (a)(1) or (b) for the second consecutive plan year. The plan sponsor shall notify the employer and the bonding or escrow agent in writing of its determination and of the consequences of its determination, as described in § 4208.3 (c) or (d) and (e), as appropriate.

[¶ 15,673F]

§ 4208.6 **Computation of reduced annual partial withdrawal liability payment.** (a) *Amount of reduced payment.* An employer that satisfies the requirements of § 4208.4 (c)(1) or (c)(2) shall have its annual partial withdrawal liability payment for that plan year reduced in accordance with paragraph (a)(1) or (a)(2) of this section, respectively.

(1) The reduced annual payment amount for an employer that satisfies § 4208.4(c)(1) shall be determined by substituting the number of contribution base units in the plan year in which the requirements are satisfied for the number of contribution base units in the year following the partial withdrawal year in the numerator of the fraction described in section 4206(a)(2)(A) of ERISA.

(2) The reduced annual payment for an employer that satisfies § 4208.4(c)(2) shall be determined by adding the contribution base units for which the employer is obligated to contribute with respect to the reentered facility or agreement in the year in which the requirements are satisfied to the numerator of the fraction described in section 4206(a)(2)(A) of ERISA.

(b) *Credit for reduction.* The plan sponsor shall credit the account of an employer that satisfies the requirements of § 4208.4(c)(1) or (c)(2) with the amount of annual withdrawal liability that it paid in excess of the amount described in paragraph (a)(1) or (a)(2) of this section, as appropriate. The credit shall be applied, a revised payment schedule issued, refund made and interest added, all in accordance with § 4208.3(c)(4).

[¶ 15,673G]

§ 4208.7 **Adjustment of withdrawal liability for subsequent withdrawals.** The liability of an employer for a partial or complete withdrawal from a plan subsequent to a partial withdrawal from that plan in a prior plan year shall be reduced in accordance with part 4206 of this chapter.

[¶ 15,673H]

§ 4208.8 **Multiple partial withdrawals in one plan year.** (a) *General rule.* If an employer partially withdraws from the same multiemployer plan on two or more occasions during the same plan year, the rules of § 4208.4 shall be applied as modified by this section.

(b) *Partial withdrawals under section 4205(a)(1) and (a)(2) in the same plan year.* If an employer partially withdraws from the same multiemployer plan as a result of a 70-percent contribution decline and a partial cessation of the employer's contribution obligation in the same plan year, the employer shall not be eligible for abatement under § 4208.4 (b) or (c)(2) or under paragraph (c) of this section. The employer may qualify for abatement under § 4208.4(a) and (c)(1) and under any rules adopted by the plan pursuant to § 4208.9.

(c) *Multiple partial cessations of the employer's contribution obligation.* If an employer permanently ceases to have an obligation to contribute for more than one facility, under more than one collective bargaining agreement, or for one or more facilities and under one or more collective bargaining agreements, resulting in multiple partial withdrawals under section 4205(b)(2)(A) in the same plan year, the abatement rules in § 4208.4(b) shall be applied as modified by this paragraph. If an employer resumes work at all such facilities and under all such collective bargaining agreements, the determination of whether the employer qualifies for elimination of its liability under § 4208.4(b) shall be made by substituting the test set forth in paragraph (c)(1) of this section for that prescribed by § 4208.4 (b)(1)(ii) or (b)(2)(ii), as applicable. If the employer resumes work at or under fewer than all the facilities or collective bargaining agreements described in this paragraph, the employer cannot qualify for elimination of its liability under § 4208.4(b). However, the employer may qualify for a reduction in its partial withdrawal liability pursuant to paragraph (c)(2) of this section.

(1) *Resumption of work at all facilities and under all bargaining agreements.* The test under this paragraph is satisfied if for each of the two consecutive plan years referred to in § 4208.4(b), the employer's total contribution base units for the facilities and under the collective bargaining agreements with respect to which the employer incurred the multiple partial withdrawals exceed 30 percent of the total number of contribution base units with respect to which the employer had an obligation to contribute for those facilities and under those agreements for the base year (as defined in paragraph (d) of this section).

(2) *Resumption at fewer than all facilities or under fewer than all bargaining agreements.* If the employer satisfies the conditions in § 4208.4 (b)(1)(i) and (b)(1)(iii) and paragraph (c)(2)(i) of this section, or the conditions in § 4208.4 (b)(2)(i) and (b)(2)(iii) and paragraph (c)(2)(ii) of this section, as applicable, the employer's withdrawal liability shall be partially waived as set forth in paragraph (c)(2)(iii) of this section.

(i) With respect to a resumption of work under § 4208.4(b)(1), the condition under this paragraph is satisfied if, for the two consecutive plan years referred to in § 4208.4(b)(1), the employer's contribution base units for any reentered facility or agreement exceed 30 percent of the number of contribution base units with respect to which the employer had an obligation to contribute for that facility or under that agreement for the base year (as defined in paragraph (d) of this section).

(ii) With respect to a resumption of work under § 4208.4(b)(2), the condition under this paragraph is satisfied if, for the two consecutive plan years referred to in § 4208.4(b)(2), the employer's contribution base units for any reentered facility or agreement exceed 90 percent of the number of contribution base units with respect to which the employer had an obligation to contribute for that facility or under that agreement for the base year (as defined in paragraph (d) of this section).

(iii) The employer's reduced withdrawal liability and, if any, the reduced annual payments of the liability shall be determined by adding the average number of contribution base units that the employer is required to contribute for those two consecutive years for that facility(ies) or agreement(s) to the numerator of the fraction described in section 4206(a)(2)(A) of ERISA. The amount of any remaining partial withdrawal liability shall be paid over the schedule originally established starting with the first payment due after the revised payment schedule is issued under § 4208.3(c)(4).

(d) *Base Year.* For purposes of this section, the base year contribution base units for a reentered facility(ies) or under a reentered agreement(s) are the average number of contribution base units for the facility(ies) or under the agreement(s) for the two plan years for which the employer's contribution base units for that facility(ies) or under that agreement(s) were highest within the five plan years immediately preceding the partial withdrawal.

[¶ 15,673I]

§ 4208.9 Plan adoption of additional abatement conditions.
(a) *General rule.* A plan may by amendment, subject to the approval of the PBGC, adopt rules for the reduction or waiver of partial withdrawal liability under conditions other than those specified in § 4208.4, provided that such conditions relate to events occurring or factors existing subsequent to a partial withdrawal year. The request for PBGC approval shall be filed after the amendment is adopted. PBGC approval shall also be required for any subsequent modification of the amendment, other than repeal of the amendment. A plan amendment under this section may not be put into effect until it is approved by the PBGC. An amendment that is approved by the PBGC may apply retroactively.

(b) *Who may request.* The plan sponsor, or a duly authorized representative acting on behalf of the plan sponsor, shall sign and submit the request.

(c) *Where to file.* See Sec. 4000.4 of this chapter for information on where to file.

[Amended 10/28/2003 by 68 FR 61344]

(d) *Information.* Each request shall contain the following information:

(1) The name and address of the plan for which the plan amendment is being submitted and the telephone number of the plan sponsor or its duly authorized representative.

(2) The nine-digit Employer Identification Number (EIN) assigned to the plan sponsor by the IRS and the three-digit Plan Identification Number (PIN) assigned to the plan by the plan sponsor, and, if different, also the EIN-PIN last filed with the PBGC. If an EIN-PIN has not been assigned, that should be indicated.

(3) A copy of the executed amendment, including—

(i) the date on which the amendment was adopted;

(ii) the proposed effective date;

(iii) the full text of the rules on the reduction or waiver of partial withdrawal liability; and

(iv) the full text of the rules adjusting the reduction in the employer's liability for a subsequent partial or complete withdrawal, as required by section 4206(b)(1) of ERISA.

(4) A copy of the most recent actuarial valuation report of the plan.

(5) A statement certifying that notice of the adoption of the amendment and of the request for approval filed under this section has been given to all employers that have an obligation to contribute under the plan and to all employee organizations representing employees covered under the plan.

(e) *Supplemental information.* In addition to the information described in paragraph (d) of this section, a plan may submit any other information that it believes is pertinent to its request. The PBGC may require the plan sponsor to submit any other information that the PBGC determines that it needs to review a request under this section.

(f) *Criteria for PBGC approval.* The PBGC shall approve a plan amendment authorized by paragraph (a) of this section if it determines that the rules therein are consistent with the purposes of ERISA. An abatement amendment is not consistent with the purposes of ERISA unless the PBGC determines that—

(1) The amendment is not adverse to the interests of plan participants and beneficiaries in the aggregate; and

(2) The amendment would not significantly increase the PBGC's risk of loss with respect to the plan.

(Approved by the Office of Management and Budget under control no. 1212-0039)

[¶ 15,673J]

§ 4208.10 Method of filing; method and date of issuance.
(a) *Method of filing.* The PBGC applies the rules in subpart A of part 4000 of this chapter to determine permissible methods of filing with the PBGC under this part.

(b) *Method of issuance.* The PBGC applies the rules in subpart B of part 4000 of this chapter to determine permissible methods of issuance under this part.

(c) *Date of issuance.* The PBGC applies the rules in subpart C of part 4000 of this chapter to determine the date that an issuance under this part was provided.

[Added 10/28/2003 by 68 FR 61344]

[¶ 15,674]
DE MINIMIS RULE

Act Sec. 4209. (a) Except in the case of a plan amended under subsection (b), the amount of the unfunded vested benefits allocable under section 4211 to an employer who withdraws from a plan shall be reduced by the smaller of—

(1) ¾ of 1 percent of the plan's unfunded vested obligations (determined as of the end of the plan year ending before the date of withdrawal), or

(2) $50,000,

reduced by the amount, if any, by which the unfunded vested benefits allowable to the employer, determined without regard to this subsection, exceeds $100,000.

Act Sec. 4209. (b) A plan may be amended to provide for the reduction of the amount determined under section 4211 by not more than the greater of—

(1) the amount determined under subsection (a), or

(2) the lesser of—

(A) the amount determined under subsection (a)(1), or

(B) $100,000,

reduced by the amount, if any, by which the amount determined under section 4211 for the employer, determined without regard to this subsection, exceeds $150,000.

Act Sec. 4209. (c) This section does not apply—

(1) to an employer who withdraws in a plan year in which substantially all employers withdraw from the plan, or

(2) in any case in which substantially all employers withdraw from the plan during a period of one or more plan years pursuant to an agreement or arrangement to withdraw, to an employer who withdraws pursuant to such agreement or arrangement.

Act Sec. 4209. (d) In any action or proceeding to determine or collect withdrawal liability, if substantially all employers have withdrawn from a plan within a period of 3 plan years, an employer who has withdrawn from such plan during such period shall be presumed to have withdrawn from the plan pursuant to an agreement or arrangement, unless the employer proves otherwise by a preponderance of the evidence.

Amendment

P.L. 96-364, § 104(2):

Added Sec. 4209, effective September 26, 1980 under ERISA Sec. 4402.

[¶ 15,675]
NO WITHDRAWAL LIABILITY FOR CERTAIN TEMPORARY CONTRIBUTION OBLIGATION PERIODS

Act Sec. 4210.(a) An employer who withdraws from a plan in complete or partial withdrawal is not liable to the plan if the employer—

(1) first had an obligation to contribute to the plan after the date of the enactment of the Multiemployer Pension Plan Amendments Act of 1980,

(2) had an obligation to contribute to the plan for no more than the lesser of—

(A) 6 consecutive plan years preceding the date on which the employer withdraws, or

(B) the number of years required for vesting under the plan,

(3) was required to make contributions to the plan for each such plan year in an amount equal to less than 2 percent of the sum of all employer contributions made to the plan for each such year, and

(4) has never avoided withdrawal liability because of the application of this section with respect to the plan.

Act Sec. 4210. (b) Subsection (a) shall apply to an employer with respect to a plan only if—

(1) the plan is not a plan which primarily covers employees in the building and construction industry;

(2) the plan is amended to provide that subsection (a) applies;

(3) the plan provides, or is amended to provide, that the reduction under section 411(a)(3)(E) of the Internal Revenue Code of 1986 applies with respect to the employees of the employer; and

(4) the ratio of the assets of the plan for the plan year preceding the first plan year for which the employer was required to contribute to the plan to the benefit payments made during that plan year was at least 8 to 1.

Amendments

P.L. 101-239, § 7891(a)(1):

Titles 1, III, and IV of ERISA (other than sections 3(37)(E), 301(a)(7), and 308, the last sentence of section 408(d), and sections 414(c), 4001(a)(3)(ii), and 4303) are each amended by striking "Internal Revenue Code of 1954" each place it appears and inserting "Internal Revenue Code of 1986", effective October 22, 1986.

P.L. 96-364, § 104(2):

Added Sec. 4210, effective September 26, 1980 under ERISA Sec. 4402.

[¶ 15,676]
METHODS FOR COMPUTING WITHDRAWAL LIABILITY

Act Sec. 4211.(a) The amount of the unfunded vested benefits allocable to an employer that withdraws from a plan shall be determined in accordance with subsection (b), (c), or (d) of this section.

Act Sec. 4211.(b)(1) Except as provided in subsections (c) and (d), the amount of unfunded vested benefits allocable to an employer that withdraws is the sum of—

(A) the employer's proportional share of the unamortized amount of the change in the plan's unfunded vested benefits for plan years ending after September 25, 1980, as determined under paragraph (2);

(B) the employer's proportional share, if any, of the unamortized amount of the plan's unfunded vested benefits at the end of the plan year ending before September 26, 1980, as determined under paragraph (3); and

(C) the employer's proportional share of the unamortized amounts of the reallocated unfunded vested benefits (if any) as determined under paragraph (4).

If the sum of the amounts determined with respect to an employer under paragraphs (2), (3), and (4) is negative, the unfunded vested benefits allocable to the employer shall be zero.

(2)(A) An employer's proportional share of the unamortized amount of the change in the plan's unfunded vested benefits for plan years ending after September 25, 1980, is the sum of the employer's proportional shares of the unamortized amount of the change in unfunded vested benefits for each plan year in which the employer has an obligation to contribute under the plan ending—

(i) after such date, and

(ii) before the plan year in which the withdrawal of the employer occurs.

(B) The change in a plan's unfunded vested benefits for a plan year is the amount by which—

(i) the unfunded vested benefits at the end of the plan year exceeds

(ii) the sum of—

(I) the unamortized amount of the unfunded vested benefits for the last plan year ending before September 26, 1980, and

(II) the sum of the unamortized amounts of the change in unfunded vested benefits for each plan year ending after September 25, 1980, and preceding the plan year for which the change is determined.

(C) The unamortized amount of the change in a plan's unfunded vested benefits with respect to a plan year is the change in unfunded vested benefits for the plan year, reduced by 5 percent of such change for each succeeding plan year.

(D) The unamortized amount of the unfunded vested benefits for the last plan year ending before September 26, 1980, is the amount of the unfunded vested benefits as of the end of that plan year reduced by 5 percent of such amount for each succeeding plan year.

(E) An employer's proportional share of the unamortized amount of a change in unfunded vested benefits is the product of—

(i) the unamortized amount of such change (as of the end of the plan year preceding the plan year in which the employer withdraws); multiplied by

(ii) a fraction—

(I) the numerator of which is the sum of the contributions required to be made under the plan by the employer for the year in which such change arose and for the 4 preceding plan years, and

(II) the denominator of which is the sum for the plan year in which such change arose and the 4 preceding plan years of all contributions made by employers who had an obligation to contribute under the plan for the plan year in which such change arose reduced by the contributions made in such years by employers who had withdrawn from the plan in the year in which the change arose.

(3) An employer's proportional share of the unamortized amount of the plan's unfunded vested benefits for the last plan year ending before September 26, 1980, is the product of—

(A) such unamortized amount; multiplied by—

(B) a fraction—

(i) the numerator of which is the sum of all contributions required to be made by the employer under the plan for the most recent 5 plan years ending before September 26, 1980, and

(ii) the denominator of which is the sum of all contributions made for the most recent 5 plan years ending before September 26, 1980, by all employers—

(I) who had an obligation to contribute under the plan for the first plan year ending on or after such date, and

(II) who had not withdrawn from the plan before such date.

(4)(A) An employer's proportional share of the unamortized amount of the reallocated unfunded vested benefits is the sum of the employer's proportional shares of the unamortized amount of the reallocated unfunded vested benefits for each plan year ending before the plan year in which the employer withdrew from the plan.

(B) Except as otherwise provided in regulations prescribed by the corporation, the reallocated unfunded vested benefits for a plan year is the sum of—

(i) any amount which the plan sponsor determines in that plan year to be uncollectible for reasons arising out of cases or proceedings under Title 11, United States Code, or similar proceedings,

(ii) any amount which the plan sponsor determines in that plan year will not be assessed as a result of the operation of section 4209, 4219(c)(1)(B), or section 4225 against an employer to whom a notice described in section 4219 has been sent, and

(iii) any amount which the plan sponsor determines to be uncollectible or unassessible in that plan year for other reasons under standards not inconsistent with regulations prescribed by the corporation.

(C) The unamortized amount of the reallocated unfunded vested benefits with respect to a plan year is the reallocated unfunded vested benefits for the plan year, reduced by 5 percent of such reallocated unfunded vested benefits for each succeeding plan year.

(D) An employer's proportional share of the unamortized amount of the reallocated unfunded vested benefits with respect to a plan year is the product of—

(i) the unamortized amount of the reallocated unfunded vested benefits (as of the end of the plan year preceding the plan year in which the employer withdraws); multiplied by

(ii) the fraction defined in paragraph (2)(E)(ii).

Act Sec. 4211.(c)(1) A multiemployer plan, other than a plan which primarily covers employees in the building and construction industry, may be amended to provide that the amount of unfunded vested benefits allocable to an employer that withdraws from the plan is an amount determined under paragraph (2), (3), (4), or (5) of this subsection, rather than under subsection (b) or (d). A plan described in section 4203(b)(1)(B)(i) (relating to the building and construction industry) may be amended, to the extent provided in regulations prescribed by the corporation, to provide that the amount of the unfunded vested benefits allocable to an employer not described in section 4203(b)(1)(A) shall be determined in a manner different from that provided in subsection (b).

(2)(A) The amount of the unfunded vested benefits allocable to any employer under this paragraph is the sum of the amounts determined under subparagraphs (B) and (C).

(B) The amount determined under this subparagraph is the product of—

(i) the plan's unfunded vested benefits as of the end of the last plan year ending before September 26, 1980, reduced as if those obligations were being fully amortized in level annual installments over 15 years beginning with the first plan year ending on or after such date; multiplied by

(ii) a fraction—

(I) the numerator of which is the sum of all contributions required to be made by the employer under the plan for the last 5 plan years ending before September 26, 1980, and

(II) the denominator of which is the sum of all contributions made for the last 5 plan years ending before September 26, 1980, by all employers who had an obligation to contribute under the plan for the first plan year ending after September 25, 1980, and who had not withdrawn from the plan before such date.

(C) The amount determined under this subparagraph is the product of—

(i) an amount equal to—

(I) the plan's unfunded vested benefits as of the end of the plan year preceding the plan year in which the employer withdraws, less

(II) the sum of the value as of such date of all outstanding claims for withdrawal liability which can reasonably be expected to be collected, with respect to employers withdrawing before such year, and that portion of the amount determined under subparagraph (B)(i) which is allocable to employers who have an obligation to contribute under the plan in the plan year preceding the plan year in which the employer withdraws and who also had an obligation to contribute under the plan for the first plan year ending after September 25, 1980; multiplied by

(ii) a fraction—

(I) the numerator of which is the total amount required to be contributed under the plan by the employer for the last 5 plan years ending before the date on which the employer withdraws, and

(II) the denominator of which is the total amount contributed under the plan by all employers for the last 5 plan years ending before the date on which the employer withdraws, increased by the amount of any employer contributions owed with respect to earlier periods which were collected in those plan years, and decreased by any amount contributed by an employer who withdrew from the plan under this part during those plan years.

(D) The corporation may by regulation permit adjustments in any denominator under this section, consistent with the purposes of this title, where such adjustment would be appropriate to ease administrative burdens of plan sponsors in calculating such denominators.

(3) The amount of the unfunded vested benefits allocable to an employer under this paragraph is the product of—

(A) the plan's unfunded vested benefits as of the end of the plan year preceding the plan year in which the employer withdraws, less the value as of the end of such year of all outstanding claims for withdrawal liability which can reasonably be expected to be collected from employers withdrawing before such year; multiplied by

(B) a fraction—

(i) the numerator of which is the total amount required to be contributed by the employer under the plan for the last 5 plan years ending before the withdrawal, and

(ii) the denominator of which is the total amount contributed under the plan by all employers for the last 5 plan years ending before the withdrawal, increased by any employer contributions owed with respect to earlier periods which were collected in those plan years, and decreased by any amount contributed to the plan during those plan years by employers who withdrew from the plan under this section during those plan years.

(4)(A) The amount of the unfunded vested benefits allocable to an employer under this paragraph is equal to the sum of—

(i) the plan's unfunded vested benefits which are attributable to participants' service with the employer (determined as of the end of the plan year preceding the plan year in which the employer withdraws), and

(ii) the employer's proportional share of any unfunded vested benefits which are not attributable to service with the employer or other employers who are obligated to contribute under the plan in the plan year preceding the plan year in which the employer withdraws (determined as of the end of the plan year preceding the plan year in which the employer withdraws).

(B) The plan's unfunded vested benefits which are attributable to participants' service with the employer is the amount equal to the value of nonforfeitable benefits under the plan which are attributable to participants' service with such employer (determined under plan rules not inconsistent with regulations of the corporation) decreased by the share of plan assets determined under subparagraph (C) which is allocated to the employer as provided under subparagraph (D).

(C) The value of plan assets determined under this subparagraph is the value of plan assets allocated to nonforfeitable benefits which are attributable to service with the employers who have an obligation to contribute under the plan in the plan year preceding the plan year in which the employer withdraws, which is determined by multiplying—

(i) the value of the plan assets as of the end of the plan year preceding the plan year in which the employer withdraws, by

(ii) a fraction—

(I) the numerator of which is the value of nonforfeitable benefits which are attributable to service with such employers, and

(II) the denominator of which is the value of all nonforfeitable benefits under the plan as of the end of the plan year.

(D) The share of plan assets, determined under subparagraph (C), which is allocated to the employer shall be determined in accordance with one of the following methods which shall be adopted by the plan by amendment:

(i) by multiplying the value of plan assets determined under subparagraph (C) by a fraction—

(I) the numerator of which is the value of the nonforfeitable benefits which are attributable to service with the employer; and

(II) the denominator of which is the value of the nonforfeitable benefits which are attributable to service with all employers who have an obligation to contribute under the plan in the plan year preceding the plan year in which the employer withdraws:

(ii) by multiplying the value of plan assets determined under subparagraph (C) by a fraction—

(I) the numerator of which is the sum of all contributions (accumulated with interest) which have been made to the plan by the employer for the plan year preceding the plan year in which the employer withdraws and all preceding plan years; and

(II) the denominator of which is the sum of all contributions (accumulated with interest) which have been made to the plan (for the plan year preceding the plan year in which the employer withdraws and all preceding plan years) by all employers who have an obligation to contribute to the plan for the plan year preceding the plan year in which the employer withdraws; or

(iii) by multiplying the value of plan assets under subparagraph (C) by a fraction—

(I) the numerator of which is the amount determined under clause (ii)(I) of this subparagraph, less the sum of benefit payments (accumulated with interest) made to participants (and their beneficiaries) for the plan years described in such clause (ii)(I) which are attributable to service with the employer; and

(II) the denominator of which is the amount determined under clause (ii)(II) of this subparagraph, reduced by the sum of benefit payments (accumulated with interest) made to participants (and their beneficiaries) for the plan years described in such clause (ii)(II) which are attributable to service with respect to the employers described in such clause (ii)(II).

(E) The amount of the plan's unfunded vested benefits for a plan year preceding the plan year in which an employer withdraws, which is not attributable to service with employers who have an obligation to contribute under the plan in the plan year preceding the plan year in which such employer withdraws, is equal to—

(i) an amount equal to—

(I) the value of all nonforfeitable benefits under the plan at the end of such plan year; reduced by

(II) the value of nonforfeitable benefits under the plan at the end of such plan year which are attributable to participants' service with employers who have an obligation to contribute under the plan for such plan year; reduced by

(ii) an amount equal to—

(I) the value of the plan assets as of the end of such plan year; reduced by

(II) the value of plan assets as of the end of such plan year as determined under subparagraph (C); reduced by

(iii) the value of all outstanding claims for withdrawal liability which can reasonably be expected to be collected with respect to employers withdrawing before the year preceding the plan year in which the employer withdraws.

(F) The employer's proportional share described in subparagraph (A)(ii) for a plan year is the amount determined under subparagraph (E) for the employer, but not in excess of an amount which bears the same ratio to the sum of the amounts determined under subparagraph (E) for all employers under the plan as the amount determined under subparagraph (C) for the employer bears to the sum of the amounts determined under subparagraph (C) for all employers under the plan.

(G) The corporation may prescribe by regulation other methods which a plan may adopt for allocating assets to determine the amount of the unfunded vested benefits attributable to service with the employer and to determine the employer's share of unfunded vested benefits not attributable to service with employers who have an obligation to contribute under the plan in the plan year in which the employer withdraws.

(5)(A) The corporation shall prescribe by regulation a procedure by which a plan may, by amendment, adopt any other alternative method for determining an employer's allocable share of unfunded vested benefits under this section, subject to the approval of the corporation based on its determination that adoption of the method by the plan would not significantly increase the risk of loss to plan participants and beneficiaries or to the corporation.

(B) The corporation may prescribe by regulation standard approaches for alternative methods, other than those set forth in the preceding paragraphs of this subsection, which a plan may adopt under subparagraph (A), for which the corporation may waive or modify the approval requirements of subparagraph (A). Any alternative method shall provide for the allocation of substantially all of a plan's unfunded vested benefits among employers who have an obligation to contribute under the plan.

(C) Unless the corporation by regulation provides otherwise, a plan may be amended to provide that a period of more than 5 but not more than 10 plan years may be used for determining the numerator and denominator of any fraction which is used under any method authorized under this section for determining an employer's allocable share of unfunded vested benefits under this section.

(D) The corporation may by regulation permit adjustments in any denominator under this section, consistent with the purposes of this title, where such adjustment would be appropriate to ease administrative burdens of plan sponsors in calculating such denominators.

Act Sec. 4211. (d)(1) The method of calculating an employer's allocable share of unfunded vested benefits set forth in subsection (c)(3) shall be the method for calculating an employer's allocable share of unfunded vested benefits under a plan to which section 404(c) of the Internal Revenue Code of 1986, or a continuation of such a plan, applies, unless the plan is amended to adopt another method authorized under subsection (b) or (c).

(2) Sections 4204, 4209, 4219(c)(1)(B), and 4225 shall not apply with respect to the withdrawal of an employer from a plan described in paragraph (1) unless the plan is amended to provide that any of such sections apply.

Act Sec. 4211. (e) In the case of a transfer of liabilities to another plan incident to an employer's withdrawal or partial withdrawal, the withdrawn employer's liability under this part shall be reduced in an amount equal to the value, as of the end of the last plan year ending on or before the date of the withdrawal, of the transferred unfunded vested benefits.

Act Sec. 4211. (f) In the case of a withdrawal following a merger of multiemployer plans, subsection (b), (c), or (d) shall be applied in accordance with regulations prescribed by the corporation; except that, if a withdrawal occurs in the first plan year beginning after a merger of multiemployer plans, the determination under this section shall be made as if each of the multiemployer plans had remained separate plans.

Amendments

P.L. 101-239, § 7891(a)(1):

Titles I, III, and IV of ERISA (other than sections 3(37)(E), 301(a)(7), and 308, the last sentence of section 408(d), and sections 414(c), 4001(a)(3)(ii), and 4303) are each amended by striking "Internal Revenue Code of 1954" each place it appears and inserting "Internal Revenue Code of 1986", effective October 22, 1986.

P.L. 98-369, § 558(b):

Amended ERISA Secs. 4211(b) and (c) by striking out "April 28, 1980" each place it appeared and inserting "September 25, 1980" instead and by striking "April 29, 1980" each place it appeared and inserting "September 26, 1980" instead.

P.L. 96-364, § 104(2):

Added Sec. 4211, effective September 26, 1980 under ERISA Sec. 4402.

Regulations

The following regulations were adopted by the Pension Benefit Guaranty Corporation on July 1, 1996 (61 FR 34002). Prior to July 1, 1996, PBGC regulations were under Chapter XXVI of Title 29 of the Code of Federal Regulations. Effective July 1, 1996, PBGC regulations were moved to Chapter XL, and were renumbered and reorganized. Reg. § 4211.22 was amended October 28, 2003 (68 FR 61344).

Subpart A—General

[¶ 15,678]

§ 4211.1 **Purpose and scope.** (a) *Purpose.* Section 4211 of ERISA provides four methods for allocating unfunded vested benefits to employers that withdraw from a multiemployer plan: the presumptive method (section 4211(b)); the modified presumptive method (section 4211(c)(2)); the rolling-5 method (section 4211(c)(3)); and the direct attribution method (section 4211(c)(4)). With the minor exceptions covered in § 4211.3, a plan determines the amount of unfunded vested benefits allocable to a withdrawing employer in accordance with the presumptive method, unless the plan is amended to adopt an alternative allocative method. Generally, the PBGC must approve the adoption of an alternative allocation method. On September 25, 1984, 49 FR 37686, the PBGC granted a class approval of all plan amendments adopting one of the statutory alternative allocation methods. Subpart C sets forth the criteria and procedures for PBGC approval of nonstatutory alternative allocation methods. Section 4211(c)(5) of ERISA also permits certain modifications to the statutory allocation methods. The PBGC is to prescribe these modifications in a regulation, and plans may adopt them without PBGC approval. Subpart B contains the permissible modifications to the statutory methods. Plans may adopt other modifications subject to PBGC approval under subpart C. Finally, under section 4211(f) of ERISA, the PBGC is required to prescribe rules governing the application of the statutory allocation methods or modified methods by plans following merger of multiemployer plans. Subpart D sets forth alternative allocative methods to be used by merged plans. In addition, such plans may adopt any of the allocation methods or modifications described under subparts B and C in accordance with the rules under subparts B and C.

(b) *Scope.* This part applies to all multiemployer plans covered by title IV of ERISA.

[¶ 15,678A]

§ 4211.2 **Definitions.** The following terms are defined in § 4001.2 of this chapter: *Code, employer, IRS, multiemployer plan, nonforfeitable benefit, PBGC, plan,* and *plan year.*

In addition, for purposes of this part:

Initial plan year means a merged plan's first complete plan year that begins after the establishment of the merged plan.

Initial plan year unfunded vested benefits means the unfunded vested benefits as of the close of the initial plan year, less the value as of the end of the initial plan year of all outstanding claims for withdrawal liability that can reasonably be expected to be collected from employers that had withdrawn as of the end of the initial plan year.

Merged plan means a plan that is the result of the merger of two or more multiemployer plans.

Merger means the combining of two or more multiemployer plans into one multiemployer plan.

Prior plan means the plan in which an employer participated immediately before that plan became a part of the merged plan.

Unfunded vested benefits means an amount by which the value of nonforfeitable benefits under the plan exceeds the value of the assets of the plan.

Withdrawing employer means the employer for whom withdrawal liability is being calculated under section 4201 of ERISA.

Withdrawn employer means an employer who, prior to the withdrawing employer, has discontinued contributions to the plan or covered operations under the plan and whose obligation to contribute has not been assumed by a successor employer within the meaning of section 4204 of ERISA. A temporary suspension of contributions, including a suspension described in section 4218(2) of ERISA, is not considered a discontinuance of contributions.

[¶ 15,678B]

§ 4211.3 **Special rules for construction industry and IRC section 404(c) plans.** (a) *Construction plans.* Except as provided in §§ 4211.11(b) and 4211.21(b), a plan that primarily covers employees in the building and construction industry shall use the presumptive method for allocating unfunded vested benefits.

(b) *Section 404(c) plans.* A plan described in section 404(c) of the Code or a continuation of such a plan shall allocate unfunded vested benefits under the rolling-5 method unless the plan, by amendment, adopts an alternative method or modification.

Subpart B—Changes Not Subject to PBGC Approval

[¶ 15,678C]

§ 4211.11 **Changes not subject to PBGC approval.** (a) *General rule.* A plan, other than a plan that primarily covers employees in the building and construction industry, may adopt, by amendment, any of the statutory allocation methods and any of the modifications set forth in §§ 4211.12 and 4211.13, without the approval of the PBGC.

(b) *Building and construction industry plans.* A plan that primarily covers employees in the building and construction industry may adopt, by amendment, any of the modifications to the presumptive rule set forth in § 4211.12 without the approval of the PBGC.

[¶ 15,678D]

§ 4211.12 **Modifications to the presumptive, modified presumptive and rolling-5 methods.** (a) *"Contributions made" and "total amount contributed".* Each of the allocation fractions used in the presumptive, modified presumptive and rolling-5 methods is based on contributions that certain employers have made to the plan for a five-year period. For purposes of these methods, and except as provided in paragraph (b) of this section, "the sum of all contributions made" or "total amount contributed" by employers for a plan year means the amounts (other than withdrawal liability payments) considered contributed to the plan for the plan year for purposes of section 412(b)(3)(A) of the Code. For plan years before section 412 applies to the plan, "the sum of all contributions made" or "total amount contributed" means the amount reported to the IRS or the Department of Labor as total contributions for the plan year; for example, for plan years in which the plan filed the Form 5500, the amount reported as total contributions on that form. Employee contributions, if any, shall be excluded from the totals.

(b) *Changing the period for counting contributions.* A plan sponsor may amend a plan to modify the denominators in the presumptive, modified presumptive and rolling-5 methods in accordance with one of the alternatives described in this paragraph. Except as provided in paragraph (b)(4) of this section, any amendment adopted under this paragraph shall be applied consistently to all plan years. Contributions counted for one plan year may be not counted for any other plan year. If a contribution is counted as part of the "total amount contributed" for any plan year used to determine a denominator, that contribution may not also be counted as a contribution owed with respect to an earlier year used to determine the same denominator, regardless of when the plan collected that contribution.

(1) A plan sponsor may amend a plan to provide that "the sum of all contributions made" or "total amount contributed" for a plan year means the amount of contributions that the plan actually received during the plan year, without regard to whether the contributions are treated as made for that plan year under section 412(b)(3)(A) of the Code.

(2) A plan sponsor may amend a plan to provide that "the sum of all contributions made" or "total amount contributed" for a plan year means the amount of contributions actually received during the plan year, increased by the amount of contributions received during a specified period of time after the close of the plan year not to exceed the period described in section 412(c)(10) of the Code and regulations thereunder.

(3) A plan sponsor may amend a plan to provide that "the sum of all contributions made" or "total amount contributed" for a plan year means the amount of contributions actually received during the plan year, increased by the amount of contributions accrued during the plan year and received during a specified period of time after the close of the plan year not to exceed the period described in section 412(c)(10) of the Code and regulations thereunder.

(4) A plan sponsor may amend a plan to provide that—

(i) For plan years ending before September 26, 1980, "the sum of all contributions made" or "total amount contributed" means the amount of total contributions reported on Form 5500 and, for years before the plan was required to file Form 5500, the amount of total contributions reported on any predecessor reporting form required by the Department of Labor or the IRS; and

(ii) For subsequent plan years, "the sum of all contributions made" or "total amount contributed" means the amount described in paragraph (a) of this section, or the amount described in paragraph (b)(1), (b)(2) or (b)(3) of this section.

(c) *Excluding contributions of significant withdrawn employers.* Contributions of certain withdrawn employers are excluded from the denominator in each of the fractions used to determine a withdrawing employer's share of unfunded vested benefits under the presumptive, modified presumptive and rolling-5 methods. Except as provided in paragraph (c)(1) of this section, contributions of all employers that permanently cease to have an obligation to contribute to the plan or permanently cease covered operations before the end of the period of plan years used to determine the fractions for allocating unfunded vested benefits under each of those methods (and contributions of all employers that withdrew before September 26, 1980) are excluded from the denominators of the fractions.

(1) The plan sponsor of a plan using the presumptive, modified presumptive or rolling-5 method may amend the plan to provide that only the contributions of significant withdrawn employers shall be excluded from the denominators of the fractions used in those methods.

(2) For purposes of this paragraph (c), "significant withdrawn employer" means—

(i) An employer to which the plan has sent a notice of withdrawal liability under section 4219 of ERISA; or

(ii) A withdrawn employer that in any plan year used to determine the denominator of a fraction contributed at least $250,000 or, if less, 1% of all contributions made by employers for that year.

(3) If a group of employers withdraw in a concerted withdrawal, the plan shall treat the group as a single employer in determining whether the members are significant withdrawn employers under paragraph (c)(2) of this section. A "concerted withdrawal" means a cessation of contributions to the plan during a single plan year—

(i) By an employer association;

(ii) By all or substantially all of the employers covered by a single collective bargaining agreement; or

(iii) By all or substantially all of the employers covered by agreements with a single labor organization.

[¶ 15,678E]

§ 4211.13 **Modifications to the direct attribution method.** (a) *Error in direct attribution method.* The unfunded vested benefits allocated to a withdrawing employer under the direct attribution method are the sum of the employer's attributable liability, determined under section 4211(c)(4)(A)(i) and (B) of ERISA, and the employer's share of the plan's unattributable liability, determined under section 4211(c)(4)(E) and allocated to the employer under section 4211(c)(4)(F). Plan sponsors should allocate unattributable liabilities on the basis of the employer's share of the attributable liabilities. However, section 4211(c)(4)(F) of ERISA, which describes the allocation of unattributable liabilities, contains a typographical error. Therefore, plans adopting the direct attribution method shall modify the phrase "as the amount determined under subparagraph (C) for the employer bears to the sum of the amounts determined under subparagraph (C) for all employers under the plan" in section 4211(c)(4)(F) by substituting "subparagraph (B)" for "subparagraph (C)" in both places it appears.

(b) *Allocating unattributable liability based on contributions in period before withdrawal.* A plan that is amended to adopt the direct attribution method may provide that instead of allocating the unattributable liability in accordance with section 4211(c)(4)(F) of ERISA, the employer's share of the plan's unattributable liability shall be determined by multiplying the plan's unattributable liability determined under section 4211(c)(4)(E) by a fraction—

(1) The numerator of which is the total amount of contributions required to be made by the withdrawing employer over a period of consecutive plan years (not fewer than five) ending before the withdrawal; and

(2) The denominator of which is the total amount contributed under the plan by all employers for the same period of years used in paragraph (b)(1) of this section, decreased by any amount contributed by an employer that withdrew from the plan during those plan years.

Subpart C—Changes Subject to PBGC Approval

[¶ 15,678F]

§ 4211.21 **Changes subject to PBGC approval.** (a) *General rule.* Subject to the approval of the PBGC pursuant to this subpart, a plan, other than a plan that primarily covers employees in the building and construction industry, may adopt, by amendment, any allocation method or modification to an allocation method that is not permitted under subpart B of this part.

(b) *Building and construction industry plans.* Subject to the approval of the PBGC pursuant to this subpart, a plan that primarily covers employees in the building and construction industry may adopt, by amendment, any allocation method or modification to an allocation method that is not permitted under § 4211.12 if the method or modification is applicable only to its employers that are not construction industry employers within the meaning of section 4203(b)(1)(A) of ERISA.

(c) *Substantial overallocation not allowed.* No plan may adopt an allocation method or modification to an allocation method that results in a systematic and substantial overallocation of the plan's unfunded vested benefits.

(d) *Use of method prior to approval.* A plan may implement an alternative allocation method or modification to an allocation method that requires PBGC approval before that approval is given. However, the plan sponsor shall assess liability in accordance with this paragraph.

(1) *Demand for payment.* Until the PBGC approves the allocation method or modification, a plan may not demand withdrawal liability under section 4219 of ERISA in an amount that exceeds the lesser of the amount calculated under the amendment or the amount calculated under the allocation method that the plan would be required to use if the PBGC did not approve the amendment. The plan must inform each withdrawing employer of both amounts and explain that the higher amount may become payable depending on the PBGC's decision on the amendment.

(2) *Adjustment of liability.* When necessary because of the PBGC decision on the amendment, the plan shall adjust the amount demanded from each employer under paragraph (c)(1) of this section and the employer's withdrawal liability payment schedule. The length of the payment schedule shall be increased, as necessary. The plan shall notify each affected employer of the adjusted liability and payment schedule and shall collect the adjusted amount in accordance with the adjusted schedule.

[¶ 15,678G]

§ 4211.22 **Requests for PBGC approval.** (a) *Filing of request.* (1) *In general.* A plan shall submit a request for approval of an alternative allocation method or modification to an allocation method to the PBGC in accordance with the requirements of this section as soon as practicable after the adoption of the amendment.

(2) *Method of filing.* The PBGC applies the rules in subpart A of part 4000 of this chapter to determine permissible methods of filing with the PBGC under this subpart.

[Amended 10/28/2003 by 68 FR 61344]

(b) *Who shall submit.* The plan sponsor, or a duly authorized representative acting on behalf of the plan sponsor, shall sign the request.

(c) *Where to submit.* See Sec. 4000.4 of this chapter for information on where to file.

[Amended 10/28/2003 by 68 FR 61344]

(d) *Content.* Each request shall contain the following information:

(1) The name, address and telephone number of the plan sponsor, and of the duly authorized representative, if any, of the plan sponsor.

(2) The name of the plan.

(3) The nine-digit Employer Identification Number (EIN) that the Internal Revenue Service assigned to the plan sponsor and the three-digit Plan Identification Number (PIN) that the plan sponsor assigned to the plan, and, if different, also the EIN-PIN that the plan last filed with the PBGC. If the plan has no EIN-PIN, the request shall so indicate.

(4) The date the amendment was adopted.

(5) A copy of the amendment, setting forth the full text of the alternative allocation method or modification.

(6) The allocation method that the plan currently uses and a copy of the plan amendment (if any) that adopted the method.

(7) A statement certifying that notice of the adoption of the amendment has been given to all employers that have an obligation to contribute under the plan and to all employee organizations that represent employees covered by the plan.

(e) *Additional information.* In addition to the information listed in paragraph (d) of this section, the PBGC may require the plan sponsor to submit any other information that the PBGC determines is necessary for the review of an alternative allocation method or modification to an allocation method.

(Approved by the Office of Management and Budget under control number 1212-0035)

[¶ 15,678H]

§ 4211.23 **Approval of alternative method.** (a) *General.* The PBGC shall approve an alternative allocation method or modification to an allocation method if the PBGC determines that adoption of the method or modification would not significantly increase the risk of loss to plan participants and beneficiaries or to the PBGC.

(b) *Criteria.* An alternative allocation method or modification to an allocation method satisfies the requirements of paragraph (a) of this section if it meets the following three conditions:

(1) The method or modification allocates a plan's unfunded vested benefits, both for the adoption year and for the five subsequent plan years, to the same extent as any of the statutory allocation methods, or any modification to a statutory allocation method permitted under subpart B.

(2) The method or modification allocates unfunded vested benefits to each employer on the basis of either the employer's share of contributions to the plan or the unfunded vested benefits attributable to each employer. The method or modification may take into account differences in contribution rates paid by different employers and differences in benefits of different employers' employees.

(3) The method or modification fully reallocates among employers that have not withdrawn from the plan all unfunded vested benefits that the plan sponsor has determined cannot be collected from withdrawn employers, or that are not assessed against withdrawn employers because of sections 4209, 4219(c)(1)(B) or 4225 of ERISA.

(c) *PBGC action on request.* The PBGC's decision on a request for approval shall be in writing. If the PBGC disapproves the request, the decision shall state the reasons for the disapproval and shall include a statement of the sponsor's right to request a reconsideration of the decision pursuant to part 4003 of this chapter.

[¶ 15,678I]

§ 4211.24 **Special rule for certain alternative methods previously approved.** A plan may not apply to any employer withdrawing

on or after November 25, 1987, an allocation method approved by the PBGC before that date that allocates to the employer the greater of the amounts of unfunded vested benefits determined under two different allocation rules. Until a plan that has been using such a method is amended to adopt a valid allocation method, its allocation method shall be deemed to be the statutory allocation method that would apply if it had never been amended.

Subpart D—Allocation Methods for Merged Multiemployer Plans

[¶ 15,678J]

§ 4211.31 **Allocation of unfunded vested benefits following the merger of plans.** (a) *General Rule.* Except as provided in paragraphs (b) through (d) of this section, when two or more multiemployer plans merge, the merged plan shall adopt one of the statutory allocation methods, in accordance with subpart B of this part, or one of the allocation methods prescribed in §§ 4211.32 through 4211.35, and the method adopted shall apply to all employer withdrawals occurring after the initial plan year. Alternatively, a merged plan may adopt its own allocation method in accordance with subpart C of this part. If a merged plan fails to adopt an allocation method pursuant to this subpart or subpart B or C, it shall use the presumptive allocation method prescribed in § 4211.32. In addition, a merged plan may adopt any of the modifications prescribed in § 4211.36 or in subpart B of this part.

(b) *Construction plans.* Except as provided in the next sentence, a merged plan that primarily covers employees in the building and construction industry shall use the presumptive allocation method prescribed in § 4211.32. However, the plan may, with respect to employers that are not construction industry employers within the meaning of section 4203(b)(1)(A) of ERISA, adopt, by amendment, one of the alternative methods prescribed in §§ 4211.33 through 4211.35 or any other allocation method. Any such amendment shall be adopted in accordance with subpart C of this part. A construction plan may, without the PBGC's approval, adopt by amendment any of the modifications set forth in § 4211.36 or any of the modifications to the statutory presumptive method set forth in § 4211.12.

(c) *Section 404(c) plans.* A merged plan that is a continuation of a plan described in section 404(c) of the Code shall use the rolling-5 allocation method prescribed in § 4211.34, unless the plan, by amendment, adopts an alternative method. The plan may adopt one of the statutory allocation methods or one of the allocation methods set forth in §§ 4211.32 through 4211.35 without PBGC approval; adoption of any other allocation method is subject to PBGC approval under subpart B of this plan. The plan may, without the PBGC's approval, adopt by amendment any of the modifications set forth in § 4211.36 or in subpart B of this part.

(d) *Withdrawals before the end of the initial plan year.* For employer withdrawals after the effective date of a merger and prior to the end of the initial plan year, the amount of unfunded vested benefits allocable to a withdrawing employer shall be determined in accordance with § 4211.37.

[¶ 15,678K]

§ 4211.32 **Presumptive method for withdrawals after the initial plan year.** (a) *General rule.* Under this section, the amount of unfunded vested benefits allocable to an employer that withdraws from a merged plan after the initial plan year is the sum (but not less than zero) of—

(1) The employer's proportional share, if any, of the unamortized amount of the plan's initial plan year unfunded vested benefits, as determined under paragraph (b) of this section;

(2) The employer's proportional share of the unamortized amount of the change in the plan's unfunded vested benefits for plan years ending after the initial plan year, as determined under paragraph (c) of this section; and

(3) The employer's proportional share of the unamortized amounts of the reallocated unfunded vested benefits (if any) as determined under paragraph (d) of this section.

(b) *Share of initial plan year unfunded vested benefits.* An employer's proportional share, if any, of the unamortized amount of the plan's initial plan year unfunded vested benefits is the sum of the employer's share of its prior plan's liabilities (determined under paragraph (b)(1) of this section) and the employer's share of the adjusted initial plan year unfunded vested benefits (determined under paragraph (b)(2) of this section), with such sum reduced by five percent of the original amount for each plan year subsequent to the initial year.

(1) *Share of prior plan liabilities.* An employer's share of its prior plan's liabilities is the amount of unfunded vested benefits that would have been allocable to the employer if it had withdrawn on the first day of the initial plan year, determined as if each plan had remained a separate plan.

(2) *Share of adjusted initial plan year unfunded vested benefits.* An employer's share of the adjusted initial plan year unfunded vested benefits equals the plan's initial plan year unfunded vested benefits, less the amount that would be determined under paragraph (b)(1) of this section for each employer that had not withdrawn as of the end of the initial plan year, multiplied by a fraction—

(i) The numerator of which is the amount determined under paragraph (b)(1) of this section; and

(ii) The denominator of which is the sum of the amounts that would be determined under paragraph (b)(1) of this section for each employer that had not withdrawn as of the end of the initial plan year.

(c) *Share of annual changes.* An employer's proportional share of the unamortized amount of the change in the plan's unfunded vested for the plan years ending after the end of the initial plan year is the sum of the employer's proportional shares (determined under paragraph (c)(2) of this section) of the unamortized amount of the change in unfunded vested benefits (determined under paragraph (c)(1) of this section) for each plan year in which the employer has an obligation to contribute under the plan ending after the initial plan year and before the plan year in which the employer withdraws.

(1) *Change in plan's unfunded vested benefits.* The change in a plan's unfunded vested benefits for a plan year is the amount by which the unfunded vested benefits at the end of a plan year, less the value as of the end of such year of all outstanding claims for withdrawal liability that can reasonably be expected to be collected from employers that had withdrawn as of the end of the initial plan year, exceed the sum of the unamortized amount of the initial plan year unfunded vested benefits (determined under paragraph (c)(1)(i) of this section) and the unamortized amounts of the change in unfunded vested benefits for each plan year ending after the initial plan year and preceding the plan year for which the change is determined (determined under paragraph (c)(1)(ii) of this section).

(i) *Unamortized amount of initial plan year unfunded vested benefits.* The unamortized amount of the initial plan year unfunded vested benefits is the amount of those benefits reduced by five percent of the original amount for each succeeding plan year.

(ii) *Unamortized amount of the change.* The unamortized amount of the change in a plan's unfunded vested benefits with respect to a plan year is the change in unfunded vested benefits for the plan year, reduced by five percent of such change for each succeeding plan year.

(2) *Employer's proportional share.* An employer's proportional share of the amount determined under paragraph (c)(1) of this section is computed by multiplying that amount by a fraction—

(i) The numerator of which is the total amount required to be contributed under the plan (or under the employer's prior plan) by the employer for the plan year in which the change arose and the four preceding full plan years; and

(ii) The denominator of which is the total amount contributed under the plan (or under employer's prior plan) for the plan year in which the change arose and the four preceding full plan years by all employers that had an obligation to contribute under the plan for the plan year in which such change arose, reduced by any amount contributed by an employer that withdrew from the plan in the year in which the change arose.

(d) *Share of reallocated amounts.* An employer's proportional share of the unamortized amounts of the reallocated unfunded vested benefits, if any, is the sum of the employer's proportional shares (determined under paragraph (d)(2) of this section) of the unamortized amount of the reallocated unfunded vested benefits (determined under paragraph (d)(1) of this section) for each plan year ending before the plan year in which the employer withdrew from the plan.

(1) *Unamortized amount of reallocated unfunded vested benefits.* The unamortized amount of the reallocated unfunded vested benefits with respect to a plan year is the sum of the amounts described in paragraphs (d)(1)(i), (d)(1)(ii), and (d)(1)(iii) of this section for the plan year, reduced by five percent of such sum for each succeeding plan year.

(i) *Uncollectible amounts.* Amounts included as reallocable under this paragraph are those that the plan sponsor determines in that plan year to be uncollectible for reasons arising out of cases or proceedings under Title 11, United States Code, or similar proceedings, with respect to an employer that withdrew after the close of the initial plan year.

(ii) *Relief amounts.* Amounts included as reallocable under this paragraph are those that the plan sponsor determines in that plan year will not be assessed as a result of the operation of sections 4209, 4219(c)(1)(B), or 4225 of ERISA with respect to an employer that withdrew after the close of the initial plan year.

(iii) *Other amounts.* Amounts included as reallocable under this paragraph are those that the plan sponsor determines in that plan year to be uncollectible or unassessable for other reasons under standards not inconsistent with regulations prescribed by the PBGC.

(2) *Employer's proportional share.* An employer's proportional share of the amount of the reallocated unfunded vested benefits with respect to a plan year is computed by multiplying the unamortized amount of the reallocated unfunded vested benefits (as of the end of the year preceding the plan year in which the employer withdraws) by the allocation fraction described in paragraph (c)(2) of this section for the same plan year.

[¶ 15,678L]

§ 4211.33 **Modified presumptive method for withdrawals after the initial plan year**. (a) *General rule.* Under this section, the amount of unfunded vested benefits allocable to an employer that withdraws from a merged plan after the initial plan year is the sum of the employer's proportional share, if any, of the unamortized amount of the plan's initial plan year unfunded vested benefits (determined under paragraph (b) of this section) and the employer's proportional share of the unamortized amount of the unfunded vested benefits arising after the initial plan year (determined under paragraph (c) of this section).

(b) *Share of initial plan year unfunded vested benefits.* An employer's proportional share, if any, of the unamortized amount of the plan's initial plan year unfunded vested benefits is the sum of the employer's share of its prior plan's liabilities, as determined under § 4211.32(b)(1), and the employer's share of the adjusted initial plan year unfunded vested benefits, as determined under § 4211.32(b)(2), with such sum reduced as if it were being fully amortized in level annual installments over fifteen years beginning with the first plan year after the initial plan year.

(c) *Share of unfunded vested benefits arising after the initial plan year.* An employer's proportional share of the amount of the plan's unfunded vested benefits arising after the initial plan year is the employer's proportional share (determined under paragraph (c)(2) of this section) of the plan's unfunded vested benefits as of the end of the plan year preceding the plan year in which the employer withdraws, reduced by the amount of the plan's unfunded vested benefits as of the close of the initial plan year (determined under paragraph (c)(1) of this section).

(1) *Amount of unfunded vested benefits.* The plan's unfunded vested benefits as of the end of the plan year preceding the plan year in which the employer withdraws shall be reduced by the sum of—

(i) The value as of that date of all outstanding claims for withdrawal liability that can reasonably be expected to be collected, with respect to employers that withdrew before that plan year; and

(ii) The sum of the amounts that would be allocable under paragraph (b) of this section to all employers that have an obligation to contribute in the plan year preceding the plan year in which the employer withdraws and that also had an obligation to contribute in the first plan year ending after the initial plan year.

(2) *Employer's proportional share.* An employer's proportional share of the amount determined under paragraph (c)(1) of this section is computed by multiplying that amount by a fraction—

(i) The numerator of which is the total amount required to be contributed under the plan (or under the employer's prior plan) by the employer for the last five full plan years ending before the date on which the employer withdraws; and

(ii) The denominator of which is the total amount contributed under the plan (or under each employer's prior plan) by all employers for the last five full plan years ending before the date on which the employer withdraws, increased by the amount of any employer contributions owed with respect to earlier periods that were collected in those plan years, and decreased by any amount contributed by an employer that withdrew from the plan (or prior plan) during those plan years.

[¶ 15,678M]

§ 4211.34 Rolling-5 method for withdrawals after the initial plan year. (a) *General rule.* Under this section, the amount of unfunded vested benefits allocable to an employer that withdraws from a merged plan after the initial plan year is the sum of the employer's proportional share, if any, of the unamortized amount of the plan's initial plan year unfunded vested benefits (determined under paragraph (b) of this section) and the employer's proportional share of the unamortized amount of the unfunded vested benefits arising after the initial plan year (determined under paragraph (c) of this section).

(b) *Share of initial plan year unfunded vested benefits.* An employer's proportional share, if any, of the unamortized amount of the plan's initial plan year unfunded vested benefits is the sum of the employer's share of its prior plan's liabilities, as determined under § 4211.32(b)(1), and the employer's share of the adjusted initial plan year unfunded vested benefits, as determined under § 4211.32(b)(2), with such sum reduced as if it were being fully amortized in level annual installments over five years beginning with the first plan year after the initial plan year.

(c) *Share of unfunded vested benefits arising after the initial plan year.* An employer's proportional share of the amount of the plan's unfunded vested benefits arising after the initial plan year is the employer's proportional share determined under § 4211.33(c).

[¶ 15,678N]

§ 4211.35 Direct attribution method for withdrawals after the initial plan year. The allocation method under this section is the allocation method described in section 4211(c)(4) of ERISA.

[¶ 15,678O]

§ 4211.36 Modifications to the determination of initial liabilities, the amortization of initial liabilities, and the allocation fraction. (a) *General rule.* A plan using any of the allocation methods described in §§ 4211.32 through 4211.34 may, by plan amendment and without PBGC approval, adopt any of the modifications described in this section.

(b) *Restarting initial liabilities.* A plan may be amended to allocate the initial plan year unfunded vested benefits under § 4211.32(b), § 4211.33(b), or § 4211.34(b) without separately allocating to employers the liabilities attributable to their participation under their prior plans. An amendment under this paragraph must include an allocation fraction under paragraph (d) of this section for determining the employer's proportional share of the total unfunded benefits as of the close of the initial plan year.

(c) *Amortizing initial liabilities.* A plan may by amendment modify the amortization of initial liabilities in either of the following ways:

(1) If two or more plans that use the presumptive allocation method of section 4211(b) of ERISA merge, the merged plan may adjust the amortization of initial liabilities under § 4211.32(b) to amortize those unfunded vested benefits over the remaining length of the prior plans' amortization schedules.

(2) A plan that has adopted the allocation method under § 4211.33 or § 4211.34 may adjust the amortization of initial liabilities under § 4211.33(b) or § 4211.34(b) to amortize those unfunded vested benefits in level annual installments over any period of at least five and not more than fifteen years.

(d) *Changing the allocation fraction.* A plan may by amendment replace the allocation fraction under § 4211.32(b), § 4211.33(b), or § 4211.34(b) with any of the following contribution-based fractions—

(1) A fraction, the numerator of which is the total amount required to be contributed under the merged and prior plans by the withdrawing employer in the 60-month period ending on the last day of the initial plan year, and the denominator of which is the sum for that period of the contributions made by all employers that had not withdrawn as of the end of the initial plan year;

(2) A fraction, the numerator of which is the total amount required to be contributed by the withdrawing employer for the initial plan year and the four preceding full plan years of its prior plan, and the denominator of which is the sum of all contributions made over that period by employers that had not withdrawn as of the end of the initial plan year; or

(3) A fraction, the numerator of which is the total amount required to be contributed to the plan by the withdrawing employer since the effective date of the merger, and the denominator of which is the sum of all contributions made over that period by employers that had not withdrawn as of the end of the initial plan year.

[¶ 15,678P]

§ 4211.37 Allocating unfunded vested benefits for withdrawals before the end of the initial plan year. If an employer withdraws after the effective date of a merger and before the end of the initial plan year, the amount of unfunded vested benefits allocable to the employer shall be determined as if each plan had remained a separate plan. In making this determination, the plan sponsor shall use the allocation method of the withdrawing employer's prior plan and shall compute the employer's allocable share of the plan's unfunded vested benefits as if the day before the effective date of the merger were the end of the last plan year prior to the withdrawal.

[¶ 15,679]
OBLIGATION TO CONTRIBUTE; SPECIAL RULES

Act Sec. 4212. (a) For purposes of this part, the term "obligation to contribute" means an obligation to contribute arising—

(1) under one or more collective bargaining (or related) agreements, or

(2) as a result of a duty under applicable labor-management relations law, but does not include an obligation to pay withdrawal liability under this section or to pay delinquent contributions.

Act Sec. 4212. (b) Payments of withdrawal liability under this part shall not be considered contributions for purposes of this part.

Act Sec. 4212. (c) If a principal purpose of any transaction is to evade or avoid liability under this part, this part shall be applied (and liability shall be determined and collected) without regard to such transaction.

Amendment

P.L. 96-364, § 104(2):

Added Sec. 4212, effective September 26, 1980 under ERISA Sec. 4402.

[¶ 15,680]
ACTUARIAL ASSUMPTIONS, ETC.

Act Sec. 4213. (a) The corporation may prescribe by regulation actuarial assumptions which may be used by a plan actuary in determining the unfunded vested benefits of a plan for purposes of determining an employer's withdrawal liability under this part. Withdrawal liability under this part shall be determined by each plan on the basis of—

(1) actuarial assumptions and methods which, in the aggregate, are reasonable (taking into account the experience of the plan and reasonable expectations) and which, in combination, offer the actuary's best estimate of anticipated experience under the plan, or

(2) actuarial assumptions and methods sets forth in the corporation's regulations for purposes of determining an employer's withdrawal liability.

Act Sec. 4213. (b) In determining the unfunded vested benefits of a plan for purposes of determining an employer's withdrawal liability under this part, the plan actuary may—

(1) rely on the most recent complete actuarial valuation used for purposes of section 412 of the Internal Revenue Code of 1954 and reasonable estimates for the interim years of the unfunded vested benefits, and

(2) in the absence of complete data, rely on the data available or on data secured by a sampling which can reasonably be expected to be representative of the status of the entire plan.

Act Sec. 4213. (c) For purposes of this part, the term "unfunded vested benefits" means with respect to a plan, an amount equal to—

(A) the value of nonforfeitable benefits under the plan, less

(B) the value of the assets of the plan.

Amendment

P.L. 96-364, § 104(2):

Added Sec. 4213, effective September 26, 1980 under ERISA Sec. 4402.

[¶ 15,681]
APPLICATION OF PLAN AMENDMENTS

Act Sec. 4214. (a) No plan rule or amendment adopted after January 31, 1981, under section 4209 or 4211(c) may be applied without the employer's consent with respect to liability for a withdrawal or partial withdrawal which occurred before the date on which the rule or amendment was adopted.

Act Sec. 4214. (b) All plan rules and amendments authorized under this part shall operate and be applied uniformly with respect to each employer, except that special provisions may be made to take into account the creditworthiness of an employer. The plan sponsor shall give notice to all employers who have an obligation to contribute under the plan and to all employee organizations representing employees covered under the plan of any plan rules or amendments adopted pursuant to this section.

Amendment

P.L. 96-364, § 104(2):

Added Sec. 4214, effective September 26, 1980 under ERISA Sec. 4402.

[¶ 15,682]
PLAN NOTIFICATION TO CORPORATION OF POTENTIALLY SIGNIFICANT WITHDRAWALS

Act Sec. 4215. The corporation may, by regulation, require the plan sponsor of a multiemployer plan to provide notice to the corporation when the withdrawal from the plan by any employer has resulted, or will result, in a significant reduction in the amount of aggregate contributions under the plan made by employers.

Amendment

P.L. 96-364, § 104(2):

Added Sec. 4215, effective September 26, 1980 under ERISA Sec. 4402.

[¶ 15,683]
SPECIAL RULES FOR SECTION 404(c) PLANS

Act Sec. 4216. (a) In case of a plan described in subsection (b)—

(1) if an employer withdraws prior to a determination described in section 4041A(a)(2), the amount of withdrawal liability to be paid in any year by such employer shall be an amount equal to the greater of—

(A) the amount determined under section 4219(c)(1)(C)(i), or

(B) the product of—

(i) the number of contribution base units for which the employer would have been required to make contributions for the prior plan year if the employer had not withdrawn, multiplied by

(ii) the contribution rate for the plan year which would be required to meet the amortization schedules contained in section 4243(d)(3)(B)(ii) (determined without regard to any limitation on such rate otherwise provided by this title)

except that an employer shall not be required to pay an amount in excess of the withdrawal liability computed with interest; and

(2) the withdrawal liability of an employer who withdraws after December 31, 1983, as a result of a termination described in section 4041A(a)(2) which is agreed to by the labor organization that appoints the employee representative on the joint board of trustees which sponsors the plan, shall be determined under subsection (c) if—

(A) as a result of prior employer withdrawals in any plan year commencing after January 1, 1980, the number of contribution base units is reduced to less than 67 percent of the average number of such units for the calendar years 1974 through 1979; and

(B) at least 50 percent of the withdrawal liability attributable to the first 33 percent decline described in subparagraph (A) has been determined by the plan sponsor to be uncollectible within the meaning of regulations of the corporation of general applicability; and

(C) the rate of employer contributions under the plan for each year following the first plan year beginning after the date of enactment of the Multiemployer Pension Plan Amendments Act of 1980 and preceding the termination date equals or exceeds the rate described in section 4243(d)(3).

Act Sec. 4216. (b) A plan is described in this subsection if—

(1) it is a plan described in section 404(c) of the Internal Revenue Code of 1986 or a continuation thereof; and

(2) participation in the plan is substantially limited to individuals who retired prior to January 1, 1976.

Act Sec. 4216. (c)(1) The amount of an employer's liability under this paragraph is the product of—

(A) the amount of the employer's withdrawal liability determined without regard to this section, and

(B) the greater of 90 percent, or a fraction—

(i) the numerator of which is an amount equal to the portion of the plan's unfunded vested benefits that is attributable to plan participants who have a total of 10 or more years of signatory service, and

(ii) the denominator of which is an amount equal to the total unfunded vested benefits of the plan.

(2) For purposes of paragraph (1), the term "a year of signatory service" means a year during any portion of which a participant was employed for an employer who was obligated to contribute in that year, or who was subsequently obligated to contribute.

Amendments

P.L. 96-364, § 104(2):

Added Sec. 4216, effective September 26, 1980 under ERISA Sec. 4402.

[¶ 15,684]
APPLICATION OF PART IN CASE OF CERTAIN PRE-1980 WITHDRAWALS

Act Sec. 4217. (a) For the purpose of determining the amount of unfunded vested benefits allocable to an employer for a partial or complete withdrawal from a plan which occurs after September 25, 1980, and for the purpose of determining whether there has been a partial withdrawal after such date, the amount of contributions, and the number of contribution base units, of such employer properly allocable—

(1) to work performed under a collective bargaining agreement for which there was a permanent cessation of the obligation to contribute before September 26, 1980, or

(2) to work performed at a facility at which all covered operations permanently ceased before September 26, 1980, or for which there was a permanent cessation of the obligation to contribute before that date,

shall not be taken into account.

Act Sec. 4217. (b) A plan may, in a manner not inconsistent with regulations, which shall be prescribed by the corporation, adjust the amount of unfunded vested benefits allocable to other employers under a plan maintained by an employer described in subsection (a).

Amendments

P.L. 98-369, § 558(b):

Amended ERISA Sec. 4217(a) by striking out "April 28, 1980" each place it appeared and inserting "September 25, 1980" instead and by striking out "April 29, 1980" each place it appeared and inserting "September 26, 1980" instead.

P.L. 96-364, § 104(2):

Added Sec. 4217, effective September 26, 1980 under ERISA Sec. 4402.

[¶ 15,685]
WITHDRAWAL NOT TO OCCUR MERELY BECAUSE OF CHANGE IN BUSINESS FORM OR SUSPENSION OF CONTRIBUTIONS DURING LABOR DISPUTE

Act Sec. 4218. Notwithstanding any other provision of this part, an employer shall not be considered to have withdrawn from a plan solely because—

(1) an employer ceases to exist by reason of—

(A) a change in corporate structure described in section 4069(b) or

(B) a change to an unincorporated form of business enterprise,

if the change causes no interruption in employer contributions or obligations to contribute under the plan, or

(2) an employer suspends contributions under the plan during a labor dispute involving its employees.

For purposes of this part, a successor or parent corporation or other entity resulting from any such change shall be considered the original employer.

Amendments

P.L. 101-239, § 7862(b)(1)(c):

Added new paragraph (8) to P.L. 99-514, § 1879(u), effective September 26, 1980.

P.L. 101-239, § 7893(f):

Amended ERISA Sec. 4218(1)(A) by striking "section 4062(d)" and by inserting "section 4069(b)", effective September 26, 1980.

P.L. 99-514, § 1879(u):

Amended ERISA Sec. 4218(1)(A) by striking "section 4062(d)" and inserting "section 4069(b)."

P.L. 96-364, § 104(2):

Added Sec. 4218, effective September 26, 1980 under ERISA Sec. 4402.

[¶ 15,686]
NOTICE, COLLECTION, ETC., OF WITHDRAWAL LIABILITY

Act Sec. 4219. (a) An employer shall, within 30 days after a written request from the plan sponsor, furnish such information as the plan sponsor reasonably determines to be necessary to enable the plan sponsor to comply with the requirements of this part.

Act Sec. 4219. (b)(1) As soon as practicable after an employer's complete or partial withdrawal, the plan sponsor shall—

(A) notify the employer of—

(i) the amount of the liability, and

(ii) the schedule for liability payments, and

(B) demand payment in accordance with the schedule.

(2)(A) No later than 90 days after the employer receives the notice described in paragraph (1), the employer—

(i) may ask the plan sponsor to review any specific matter relating to the determination of the employer's liability and the schedule of payments,

(ii) may identify any inaccuracy in the determination of the amount of the unfunded vested benefits allocable to the employer, and

(iii) may furnish any additional relevant information to the plan sponsor.

(B) After a reasonable review of any matter raised, the plan sponsor shall notify the employer of—

(i) the plan sponsor's decision,

(ii) the basis for the decision, and

(iii) the reason for any change in the determination of the employer's liability or schedule of liability payments.

Act Sec. 4219. (c)(1)(A)(i) Except as provided in subparagraphs (B) and (D) of this paragraph and in paragraphs (4) and (5), an employer shall pay the amount determined under section 4211, adjusted if appropriate first under section 4209 and then under section 4206 over the period of years necessary to amortize the amount in level annual payments determined under subparagraph (C), calculated as if the first payment were made on the first day of the plan year following the plan year in which the withdrawal occurs and as if each subsequent payment were made on the first day of each subsequent plan year. Actual payment shall commence in accordance with paragraph (2).

(ii) The determination of the amortization period described in clause (i) shall be based on the assumptions used for the most recent actuarial valuation for the plan.

(B) In any case in which the amortization period described in subparagraph (A) exceeds 20 years, the employer's liability shall be limited to the first 20 annual payments determined under subparagraph (C).

(C)(i) Except as provided in subparagraph (E), the amount of each annual payment shall be the product of—

(I) the average annual number of contribution base units for the period of 3 consecutive plan years, during the period of 10 consecutive plan years ending before the plan year in which the withdrawal occurs, in which the number of contribution base units for which the employer had an obligation to contribute under the plan is the highest, and

(II) the highest contribution rate at which the employer had an obligation to contribute under the plan during the 10 plan years ending with the plan year in which the withdrawal occurs.

For purposes of the preceding sentence, a partial withdrawal described in section 4205(a)(1) shall be deemed to occur on the last day of the first year of the 3-year testing period described in section 4205(b)(1)(B)(i).

(ii)(I) A plan may be amended to provide that for any plan year ending before 1986 the amount of each annual payment shall be (in lieu of the amount determined under clause (i)) the average of the required employer contributions under the plan for the period of 3 consecutive plan years (during the period of 10 consecutive plan years ending with the plan year preceding the plan year in which the withdrawal occurs) for which such required contributions were the highest.

(II) Subparagraph (B) shall not apply to any plan year to which this clause applies.

(III) This clause shall not apply in the case of any withdrawal described in subparagraph (D).

(IV) If under a plan this clause applies to any plan year but does not apply to the next plan year, this clause shall not apply to any plan year after such next plan year.

(V) For purposes of this clause, the term "required contributions" means, for any period, the amounts which the employer was obligated to contribute for such period (not taking into account any delinquent contribution for any other period).

(iii) A plan may be amended to provide that for the first plan year ending on or after September 26, 1980, the number "5" shall be substituted for the number "10" each place it appears in clause (i) or clause (ii) (whichever is appropriate). If the plan is so amended, the number "5" shall be increased by one for each succeeding plan year until the number "10" is reached.

(D) In any case in which a multiemployer plan terminates by the withdrawal of every employer from the plan, or in which substantially all the employers withdraw from a plan pursuant to an agreement or arrangement to withdraw from the plan—

(i) the liability of each such employer who has withdrawn shall be determined (or redetermined) under this paragraph without regard to subparagraph (B), and

(ii) notwithstanding any other provision of this part, the total unfunded vested benefits of the plan shall be fully allocated among all such employers in a manner not inconsistent with regulations which shall be prescribed by the corporation.

Withdrawal by an employer from a plan, during a period of 3 consecutive plan years within which substantially all the employers who have an obligation to contribute under the plan withdraw, shall be presumed to be a withdrawal pursuant to an agreement or arrangement, unless the employer proves otherwise by a preponderance of the evidence.

(E) In the case of a partial withdrawal described in section 4205(a), the amount of each annual payment shall be the product of—

(i) the amount determined under subparagraph (C) (determined without regard to this subparagraph), multiplied by

(ii) the fraction determined under section 4206(a)(2).

(2) Withdrawal liability shall be payable in accordance with the schedule set forth by the plan sponsor under subsection (b)(1) beginning no later than 60 days after the date of the demand notwithstanding any request for review or appeal of determinations of the amount of such liability or of the schedule.

(3) Each annual payment determined under paragraph (1)(C) shall be payable in 4 equal installments due quarterly, or at other intervals specified by plan rules. If a payment is not made when due, interest on the payment shall accrue from the due date until the date on which the payment is made.

(4) The employer shall be entitled to prepay the outstanding amount of the unpaid annual withdrawal liability payments determined under paragraph (1)(C), plus accrued interest, if any, in whole or in part, without penalty. If the prepayment is made pursuant to a withdrawal which is later determined to be part of a withdrawal described in paragraph (1)(D), the withdrawal liability of the employer shall not be limited to the amount of the prepayment.

(5) In the event of a default, a plan sponsor may require immediate payment of the outstanding amount of an employer's withdrawal liability, plus accrued interest on the total outstanding liability from the due date of the first payment which was not timely made. For purposes of this section, the term "default" means—

(A) the failure of an employer to make, when due, any payment under this section, if the failure is not cured within 60 days after the employer receives written notification from the plan sponsor of such failure, and

(B) any other event defined in rules adopted by the plan which indicates a substantial likelihood that an employer will be unable to pay its withdrawal liability.

(6) Except as provided in paragraph (1)(A)(ii), interest under this subsection shall be charged at rates based on prevailing market rates for comparable obligations, in accordance with regulations prescribed by the corporation.

(7) A multiemployer plan may adopt rules for other terms and conditions for the satisfaction of an employer's withdrawal liability if such rules—

(A) are consistent with this Act, and

(B) are not inconsistent with regulations of the corporation.

(8) In the case of a terminated multiemployer plan, an employer's obligation to make payments under this section ceases at the end of the plan year in which the assets of the plan (exclusive of withdrawal liability claims) are sufficient to meet all obligations of the plan, as determined by the corporation.

Act Sec. 4219. (d) The prohibitions provided in section 406(a) do not apply to any action required or permitted under this part.

Amendments

P.L. 98-369, § 558(b):

Amended ERISA Sec. 4219(c)(1)(C)(iii) by striking out "April 29, 1980" and inserting "September 26, 1980" instead.

P.L. 96-364, § 104(2):

Added Sec. 4219, effective September 26, 1980 under ERISA Sec. 4402.

Regulations

The following regulations were adopted by the Pension Benefit Guaranty Corporation on July 1, 1996 (61 FR 34002). Prior to July 1, 1996, PBGC regulations were under Chapter XXVI of Title 29 of the Code of Federal Regulations. Effective July 1, 1996, PBGC regulations were moved to Chapter XL, and were renumbered and reorganized. Reg. § 4219.17 was amended and Reg. § 4219.19 was added October 28, 2003 (68 FR 61344).

Subpart A—General

[¶ 15,687]

§ 4219.1 Purpose and scope. (a) *Subpart A.* Subpart A of this part describes the purpose and scope of the provisions in this part and defined terms used in this part.

(b) *Subpart B.*

(1) *Purpose.* When a multiemployer plan terminates by the withdrawal of every employer from the plan, or when substantially all employers withdraw from a multiemployer plan pursuant to an agreement or arrangement to withdraw from the plan, section 4219(c)(1)(D)(i) of ERISA requires that the liability of such withdraw-

ing employers be determined (or redetermined) without regard to the 20-year limitation on annual payments established in section 4219(c)(1)(B) of ERISA. In addition, section 4219(c)(1)(D)(ii) requires that, upon the occurrence of a withdrawal described above, the total unfunded vested benefits of the plan be fully allocated among such withdrawing employers in a manner that is not inconsistent with PBGC regulations. Section 4209(c) of ERISA provides that the de minimis reduction established in sections 4209(a) and (b) of ERISA shall not apply to an employer that withdraws in a plan year in which substantially all employers withdraw from the plan, or to an employer that withdraws pursuant to an agreement to withdraw during a period of one or more plan years during which substantially all employers withdraw pursuant to an agreement or arrangement to withdraw. The purpose of subpart B of this part is to prescribe rules, pursuant to sections 4219(c)(1)(D) and 4209(c) of ERISA, for redetermining an employer's withdrawal liability and fully allocating the unfunded vested benefits of a multiemployer plan in either of two mass-withdrawal situations: the termination of a plan by the withdrawal of every employer and the withdrawal of substantially all employers pursuant to an agreement or arrangement to withdraw. Subpart B also prescribes rules for redetermining the liability of an employer without regard to section 4209(a) or (b) when the employer withdraws in a plan year in which substantially all employers withdraw, regardless of the occurrence of a mass withdrawal. (See part 4281 regarding the valuation of unfunded vested benefits to be fully allocated under subpart B, and parts 4041A and 4281 regarding the powers and duties of the plan sponsor of a plan terminated by mass withdrawal.)

(2) *Scope.* Subpart B applies to multiemployer plans covered by title IV of ERISA, with respect to which there is a termination by the withdrawal of every employer (including a plan created by a partition pursuant to section 4233 of ERISA) or a withdrawal of substantially all employers in the plan pursuant to an agreement or arrangement to withdraw from the plan, and to employers that withdraw from such multiemployer plans. The obligations of a plan sponsor of a masswithdrawal-terminated plan under subpart B shall cease to apply when the plan assets are distributed in full satisfaction of all nonforfeitable benefits under the plan. Subpart B also applies, to the extent appropriate, to multiemployer plans with respect to which there is a withdrawal of substantially all employers in a single plan year and to employers that withdraw from such plans in that plan year.

(c) *Subpart C.* Subpart C establishes the interest rate to be charged on overdue, defaulted and overpaid withdrawal liability under section 4219(c)(6) of ERISA, and authorizes multiemployer plans to adopt alternative rules concerning assessment of interest and related matters. Subpart C applies to multiemployer plans covered under title IV of ERISA, and to employers that have withdrawn from such plans after April 28, 1980 (May 2, 1979, for certain employers in the seagoing industry).

[¶ 15,687A]

§ 4219.2 **Definitions.** (a) The following terms are defined in section 4001.2 of this chapter: *employer, ERISA, IRS, mass withdrawal, multiemployer plan, nonforfeitable benefit, PBGC, plan,* and *plan year.*

(b) For purposes of this part:

Initial withdrawal liability means the amount of withdrawal liability determined in accordance with sections 4201 through 4225 of title IV without regard to the occurrence of a mass withdrawal.

Mass withdrawal liability means the sum of an employer's liability for de minimis amounts, liability for 20-year-limitation amounts, and reallocation liability.

Mass withdrawal valuation date means—

(1) In the case of a termination by mass withdrawal, the last day of the plan year in which the plan terminates; or

(2) in the case of a withdrawal of substantially all employers pursuant to an agreement or arrangement to withdraw, the last day of the plan year as of which substantially all employers have withdrawn.

Reallocation liability means the amount of unfunded vested benefits allocated to an employer in the event of a mass withdrawal.

Reallocation record date means a date selected by the plan sponsor, which shall be not earlier than the date of the plan's actuarial report for

the year of the mass withdrawal and not later than one year after the mass withdrawal valuation date.

Redetermination liability means the sum of an employer's liability for de minimis amounts and the employer's liability for 20-year-limitation amounts.

Unfunded vested benefits means the amount by which the present value of a plan's vested benefits exceeds the value of plan assets (including claims of the plan for unpaid initial withdrawal liability and redetermination liability), determined in accordance with section 4281 of ERISA and part 4281, subpart B.

(c) For purposes of subpart B—

Withdrawal means a complete withdrawal as defined in section 4203 of ERISA.

Subpart B—Redetermination of Withdrawal Liability Upon Mass Withdrawal

[¶ 15,687B]

§ 4219.11 **Withdrawal liability upon mass withdrawal.** (a) *Initial withdrawal liability.* The plan sponsor of a multiemployer plan that experiences a mass withdrawal shall determine initial withdrawal liability pursuant to section 4201 of ERISA of every employer that has completely or partially withdrawn from the plan and for whom the liability has not previously been determined and, in accordance with section 4202 of ERISA, notify each employer of the amount of the initial withdrawal liability and collect the amount of the initial withdrawal liability from each employer.

(b) *Mass withdrawal liability.* The plan sponsor of a multiemployer plan that experiences a mass withdrawal shall also—

(1) Notify withdrawing employers, in accordance with § 4219.16(a), that a mass withdrawal has occurred;

(2) Within 150 days after the mass withdrawal valuation date, determine the liability of withdrawn employers for de minimis amounts and for 20-year-limitation amounts in accordance with §§ 4219.13 and 4219.14;

(3) Within one year after the reallocation record date, determine the reallocation liability of withdrawn employers in accordance with § 4219.15;

(4) Notify each withdrawing employer of the amount of mass withdrawal liability determined pursuant to this subpart and the schedule for payment of such liability, and demand payment of and collect that liability, in accordance with § 4219.16; and

(5) Notify the PBGC of the occurrence of a mass withdrawal and certify, in accordance with § 4219.17, that determinations of mass withdrawal liability have been completed.

(c) *Extensions of time.* The plan sponsor of a multiemployer plan that experiences a mass withdrawal may apply to the PBGC for an extension of the deadlines contained in paragraph (b) of this section. The PBGC shall approve such a request only if it finds that failure to grant the extension will create an unreasonable risk of loss to plan participants or the PBGC.

[¶ 15,687C]

§ 4219.12 **Employers liable upon mass withdrawal.** (a) *Liability for de minimis amounts.* An employer shall be liable for de minimis amounts to the extent provided in section 4219(c)(1)(D) of ERISA if the employer's initial withdrawal liability was reduced pursuant to section 4209(a) or (b) of ERISA.

(b) *Liability for 20-year-limitation amounts.* An employer shall be liable for 20-year-limitation amounts to the extent provided in section 4219(c)(1)(D) of ERISA.

(c) *Liability for reallocation liability.* An employer shall be liable for reallocation liability if the employer withdrew pursuant to an agreement or arrangement to withdraw from a multiemployer plan from which substantially all employers withdrew pursuant to an agreement or arrangement to withdraw, or if the employer withdrew after the beginning of the second full plan year preceding the termination date from a plan that terminated by the withdrawal of every employer, and, as of the reallocation record date—

(1) The employer has not been completely liquidated or dissolved;

(2) The employer is not the subject of a case or proceeding under title 11, United States Code, or any case or proceeding under similar provisions of state insolvency laws, except that a plan sponsor may determine that such an employer is liable for reallocation liability if the plan sponsor determines that the employer is reasonably expected to be able to pay its initial withdrawal liability and its redetermination liability in full and on time to the plan; and

(3) The plan sponsor has not determined that the employer's initial withdrawal liability or its redetermination liability is limited by section 4225 of ERISA.

(d) *General exclusion.* In the event that a plan experiences successive mass withdrawals, an employer that has been determined to be liable under this subpart for any component of mass withdrawal liability shall not be liable as a result of the same withdrawal for that component of mass withdrawal liability with respect to a subsequent mass withdrawal.

(e) *Free-look rule.* An employer that is not liable for initial withdrawal liability pursuant to a plan amendment adopting section 4210(a) of ERISA shall not be liable for de minimis amounts or for 20-year-limitation amounts, but shall be liable for reallocation liability in accordance with paragraph (c) of this section.

(f) *Payment of initial withdrawal liability.* An employer's payment of its total initial withdrawal liability, whether by prepayment or otherwise, for a withdrawal which is later determined to be part of a mass withdrawal shall not exclude the employer from or otherwise limit the employer's mass withdrawal liability under this subpart.

(g) *Agreement presumed.* Withdrawal by an employer during a period of three consecutive plan years within which substantially all employers withdraw from a plan shall be presumed to be a withdrawal pursuant to an agreement or arrangement to withdraw unless the employer proves otherwise by a preponderance of the evidence.

[¶ 15,687D]

§ 4219.13 **Amount of liability for de minimis amounts**. An employer that is liable for de minimis amounts shall be liable to the plan for the amount by which the employer's allocable share of unfunded vested benefits for the purpose of determining its initial withdrawal liability was reduced pursuant to section 4209(a) or (b) of ERISA. Any liability for de minimis amounts determined under this section shall be limited by section 4225 of ERISA to the extent that section would have been limiting had the employer's initial withdrawal liability been determined without regard to the de minimis reduction.

[¶ 15,687E]

§ 4219.14 **Amount of liability for 20-year-limitation amounts**. An employer that is liable for 20-year-limitation amounts shall be liable to the plan for an amount equal to the present value of all initial withdrawal liability payments for which the employer was not liable pursuant to section 4219(c)(1)(B) of ERISA. The present value of such payments shall be determined as of the end of the plan year preceding the plan year in which the employer withdrew, using the assumptions that were used to determine the employer's payment schedule for initial withdrawal liability pursuant to section 4219(c)(1)(A)(ii) of ERISA. Any liability for 20-year-limitation amounts determined under this section shall be limited by section 4225 of ERISA to the extent that section would have been limiting had the employer's initial withdrawal liability been determined without regard to the 20-year limitation.

[¶ 15,687F]

§ 4219.15 **Determination of reallocation liability**. (a) *General rule.* In accordance with the rules in this section, the plan sponsor shall determine the amount of unfunded vested benefits to be reallocated and shall fully allocate those unfunded vested benefits among all employers liable for reallocation liability.

(b) *Amount of unfunded vested benefits to be reallocated.* For purposes of this section, the amount of a plan's unfunded vested benefits to be reallocated shall be the amount of the plan's unfunded vested benefits, determined as of the mass withdrawal valuation date, adjusted

to exclude from plan assets the value of the plan's claims for unpaid initial withdrawal liability and unpaid redetermination liability that are deemed to be uncollectible under § 4219.12(c)(1) or (c)(2).

(c) *Amount of reallocation liability.* An employer's reallocation liability shall be equal to the sum of the employer's initial allocable share of the plan's unfunded vested benefits, as determined under paragraph (c)(1) of this section, plus any unassessable amounts allocated to the employer under paragraph (c)(2), limited by section 4225 of ERISA to the extent that section would have been limiting had the employer's reallocation liability been included in the employer's initial withdrawal liability. If a plan is determined to have no unfunded vested benefits to be reallocated, the reallocation liability of each liable employer shall be zero.

(1) *Initial allocable share.* Except as otherwise provided in rules adopted by the plan pursuant to paragraph (d) of this section, and in accordance with paragraph (c)(3) of this section, an employer's initial allocable share shall be equal to the product of the plan's unfunded vested benefits to be reallocated, multiplied by a fraction—

(i) The numerator of which is the sum of the employer's initial withdrawal liability and the employer's redetermination liability, if any; and

(ii) The denominator of which is the sum of all initial withdrawal liabilities and all the redetermination liabilities of all employers liable for reallocation liability.

(2) *Allocation of unassessable amounts.* If after computing each employer's initial allocable share of unfunded vested benefits, the plan sponsor knows that any portion of an employer's initial allocable share is unassessable as withdrawal liability because of the limitations in section 4225 of ERISA, the plan sponsor shall allocate any such unassessable amounts among all other liable employers. This allocation shall be done by prorating the unassessable amounts on the basis of each such employer's initial allocable share. No employer shall be liable for unfunded vested benefits allocated under paragraph (c)(1) or this paragraph to another employer that are determined to be unassessable or uncollectible subsequent to the plan sponsor's demand for payment of reallocation liability.

(3) *Special rule for certain employers with no or reduced initial withdrawal liability.* If an employer has no initial withdrawal liability because of the application of the free-look rule in section 4210 of ERISA, then, in computing the fraction prescribed in paragraph (c)(1), the plan sponsor shall use the employer's allocable share of unfunded vested benefits, determined under section 4211 of ERISA at the time of the employer's withdrawal and adjusted in accordance with section 4225 of ERISA, if applicable. If an employer's initial withdrawal liability was reduced pursuant to section 4209(a) or (b) of ERISA and the employer is not liable for de minimis amounts pursuant to § 4219.13, then, in computing the fraction prescribed in paragraph (c)(1) of this section, the plan sponsor shall use the employer's allocable share of unfunded vested benefits, determined under section 4211 of ERISA at the time of the employer's withdrawal and adjusted in accordance with section 4225 of ERISA, if applicable.

(d) *Plan rules.* Plans may adopt rules for calculating an employer's initial allocable share of the plan's unfunded vested benefits in a manner other than that prescribed in paragraph (c)(1) of this section, provided that those rules allocate the plan's unfunded vested benefits to substantially the same extent the prescribed rules would. Plan rules adopted under this paragraph shall operate and be applied uniformly with respect to each employer. If such rules would increase the reallocation liability of any employer, they may be effective with respect to that employer earlier than three full plan years after their adoption only if the employer consents to the application of the rules to itself. The plan sponsor shall give a written notice to each contributing employer and each employee organization that represents employees covered by the plan of the adoption of plan rules under this paragraph.

[¶ 15,687G]

§ 4219.16 **Imposition of liability**. (a) *Notice of mass withdrawal.* Within 30 days after the mass withdrawal valuation date, the plan sponsor shall give written notice of the occurrence of a mass withdrawal to each employer that the plan sponsor reasonably expects may be a liable employer under § 4219.12. The notice shall include—

(1) The mass withdrawal valuation date;

(2) A description of the consequences of a mass withdrawal under this subpart; and

(3) A statement that each employer obligated to make initial withdrawal liability payments shall continue to make those payments in accordance with its schedule. Failure of the plan sponsor to notify an employer of a mass withdrawal as required by this paragraph shall not cancel the employer's mass withdrawal liability or waive the plan's claim for such liability.

(b) *Notice of redetermination liability*. Within 30 days after the date as of which the plan sponsor is required under § 4219.11(b)(2) to have determined the redetermination liability of employers, the plan sponsor shall issue a notice of redetermination liability in writing to each employer liable under § 4219.12 for de minimis amounts or 20-year-limitation amounts, or both. The notice shall include—

(1) The amount of the employer's liability, if any, for de minimis amounts determined pursuant to § 4219.13;

(2) The amount of the employer's liability, if any, for 20-year-limitation amounts determined pursuant to § 4219.14;

(3) The schedule for payment of the liability determined under paragraph (f) of this section;

(4) A demand for payment of the liability in accordance with the schedule; and

(5) A statement of when the plan sponsor expects to issue notices of reallocation liability to liable employers.

(c) *Notice of reallocation liability*. Within 30 days after the date as of which the plan sponsor is required under § 4219.11(b)(3) to have determined the reallocation liability of employers, the plan sponsor shall issue a notice of reallocation liability in writing to each employer liable for reallocation liability. The notice shall include—

(1) The amount of the employer's reallocation liability determined pursuant to § 4219.15;

(2) The schedule for payment of the liability determined under paragraph (f) of this section; and

(3) A demand for payment of the liability in accordance with the schedule.

(d) *Notice to employers not liable*. The plan sponsor shall notify in writing any employer that receives a notice of mass withdrawal under paragraph (a) of this section and subsequently is determined not to be liable for mass withdrawal liability or any component thereof. The notice shall specify the liability from which the employer is excluded and shall be provided to the employer not later than the date by which liable employers are to be provided notices of reallocation liability pursuant to paragraph (c) of this section. If the employer is not liable for mass withdrawal liability, the notice shall also include a statement, if applicable, that the employer is obligated to continue to make initial withdrawal liability payments in accordance with its existing schedule for payment of such liability.

(e) *Combined notices*. A plan sponsor may combine a notice of redetermination liability with the notice of and demand for payment of initial withdrawal liability. If a mass withdrawal and a withdrawal described in § 4219.18 occur concurrently, a plan sponsor may combine—

(1) A notice of mass withdrawal with a notice of withdrawal issued pursuant to § 4219.18(d); and

(2) A notice of redetermination liability with a notice of liability issued pursuant to § 4219.18(e).

(f) *Payment schedules*. The plan sponsor shall establish payment schedules for payment of an employer's mass withdrawal liability in accordance with the rules in section 4219(c) of ERISA, as modified by this paragraph. For an employer that owes initial withdrawal liability as of the mass withdrawal valuation date, the plan sponsor shall establish new payment schedules for each element of mass withdrawal liability by amending the initial withdrawal liability payment schedule in accor-

dance with the paragraph (f)(1) of this section. For all other employers, the payment schedules shall be established in accordance with paragraph (f)(2).

(1) *Employers owing initial withdrawal liability as of mass withdrawal valuation date*. For an employer that owes initial withdrawal liability as of the mass withdrawal valuation date, the plan sponsor shall amend the existing schedule of payments in order to amortize the new amounts of liability being assessed, i.e., redetermination liability and reallocation liability. With respect to redetermination liability, the plan sponsor shall add that liability to the total initial withdrawal liability and determine a new payment schedule, in accordance with section 4219(c)(1) of ERISA, using the interest assumptions that were used to determine the original payment schedule. For reallocation liability, the plan sponsor shall add that liability to the present value, as of the date following the mass withdrawal valuation date, of the unpaid portion of the amended payment schedule described in the preceding sentence and determine a new payment schedule of level annual payments, calculated as if the first payment were made on the day following the mass withdrawal valuation date using the interest assumptions used for determining the amount of unfunded vested benefits to be reallocated.

(2) *Other employers*. For an employer that had no initial withdrawal liability, or had fully paid its liability prior to the mass withdrawal valuation date, the plan sponsor shall determine the payment schedule for redetermination liability, in accordance with section 4219(c)(1) of ERISA, in the same manner and using the same interest assumptions as were used or would have been used in determining the payment schedule for the employer's initial withdrawal liability. With respect to reallocation liability, the plan sponsor shall follow the rules prescribed in paragraph (f)(1) of this section.

(g) *Review of mass withdrawal liability determinations*. Determinations of mass withdrawal liability made pursuant to this subpart shall be subject to plan review under section 4219(b)(2) of ERISA and to arbitration under section 4221 of ERISA within the times prescribed by those sections. Matters that relate solely to the amount of, and schedule of payments for, an employer's initial withdrawal liability are not matters relating to the employer's liability under this subpart and are not subject to review pursuant to this paragraph.

(h) *Cessation of withdrawal liability obligations*. If the plan sponsor of a terminated plan distributes plan assets in full satisfaction of all nonforfeitable benefits under the plan, the plan sponsor's obligation to impose and collect liability, and each employer's obligation to pay liability, in accordance with this subpart ceases on the date of such distribution.

(i) *Determination that a mass withdrawal has not occurred*. If a plan sponsor determines, after imposing mass withdrawal liability pursuant to this subpart, that a mass withdrawal has not occurred, the plan sponsor shall refund to employers all payments of mass withdrawal liability with interest, except that a plan sponsor shall not refund payments of liability for de minimis amounts to an employer that remains liable for such amounts under § 4219.18. Interest shall be credited at the interest rate prescribed in subpart C and shall accrue from the date the payment was received by the plan until the date of the refund.

[¶ 15,687H]

§ 4219.17 **Filings with PBGC**. (a) *Filing requirements*. (1) *In general*. The plan sponsor shall file with PBGC a notice that a mass withdrawal has occurred and separate certifications that determinations of redetermination liability and reallocation liability have been made and notices provided to employers in accordance with this subpart.

(2) *Method of filing*. The PBGC applies the rules in subpart A of part 4000 of this chapter to determine permissible methods of filing with the PBGC under this subpart.

(3) *Computation of time*. The PBGC applies the rules in subpart D of part 4000 of this chapter to compute any time period under this subpart for filing with the PBGC.

[Amended 10/28/2003 by 68 FR 61344]

(b) *Who shall file.* The plan sponsor or a duly authorized representative acting on behalf of the plan sponsor shall sign and file the notice and the certifications.

(c) *When to file.* A notice of mass withdrawal for a plan from which substantially all employers withdraw pursuant to an agreement or arrangement to withdraw shall be filed with the PBGC no later than 30 days after the mass withdrawal valuation date. A notice of mass withdrawal termination shall be filed within the time prescribed for the filing of that notice in part 4041A, subparts A and B, of this chapter. Certifications of liability determinations shall be filed with the PBGC no later than 30 days after the date on which the plan sponsor is required to have provided employers with notices pursuant to § 4219.16.

(d) *Where to file.* See Sec. 4000.4 of this chapter for information on where to file.

[Amended 10/28/2003 by 68 FR 61344]

(e) *Date of filing.* The PBGC applies the rules in subpart C of part 4000 of this chapter to determine the date that a submission under this subpart was filed with the PBGC.

[Amended 10/28/2003 by 68 FR 61344]

(f) *Contents of notice of mass withdrawal.* If a plan terminates by the withdrawal of every employer, a notice of termination filed in accordance with part 4041A, subparts A and B, of this chapter shall satisfy the requirements for a notice of mass withdrawal under this subpart. If substantially all employers withdraw from a plan pursuant to an agreement or arrangement to withdraw, the notice of mass withdrawal shall contain the following information:

(1) The name of the plan.

(2) The name, address and telephone number of the plan sponsor and of the duly authorized representative, if any, of the plan sponsor.

(3) The nine-digit Employer Identification Number (EIN) assigned by the IRS to the plan sponsor and the three-digit Plan Identification Number (PIN) assigned by the plan sponsor to the plan, and, if different, the EIN or PIN last filed with the PBGC. If no EIN or PIN has been assigned, the notice shall so indicate.

(4) The mass withdrawal valuation date.

(5) A description of the facts on which the plan sponsor has based its determination that a mass withdrawal has occurred, including the number of contributing employers withdrawn and the number remaining in the plan, and a description of the effect of the mass withdrawal on the plan's contribution base.

(g) *Contents of certifications.* Each certification shall contain the following information:

(1) The name of the plan.

(2) The name, address and telephone number of the plan sponsor and of the duly authorized representative, if any, of the plan sponsor.

(3) The nine-digit Employer Identification Number (EIN) assigned by the IRS to the plan sponsor and the three-digit Plan Identification Number (PIN) last assigned by the plan sponsor to the plan, and, if different, the EIN or PIN filed with the PBGC. If no EIN or PIN has been assigned, the notice shall so indicate.

(4) Identification of the liability determination to which the certification relates.

(5) A certification, signed by the plan sponsor or a duly authorized representative, that the determinations have been made and the notices given in accordance with this subpart.

(6) For reallocation liability certifications—

(i) A certification, signed by the plan's actuary, that the determination of unfunded vested benefits has been done in accordance with part 4281, subpart B; and

(ii) A copy of plan rules, if any, adopted pursuant to § 4219.15(d).

(h) *Additional information.* In addition to the information described in paragraph (g) of this section, the PBGC may require the plan sponsor to submit any other information the PBGC determines it needs in order to monitor compliance with this subpart.

[¶ 15,687I]

§ 4219.18 **Withdrawal in a plan year in which substantially all employers withdraw.** (a) *General rule.* An employer that withdraws in a plan year in which substantially all employers withdraw from the plan shall be liable to the plan for de minimis amounts if the employer's initial withdrawal liability was reduced pursuant to section 4209(a) or (b) of ERISA.

(b) *Amount of liability.* An employer's liability for de minimis amounts under this section shall be determined pursuant to § 4219.13.

(c) *Plan sponsor's obligations.* The plan sponsor of a plan that experiences a withdrawal described in paragraph (a) shall—

(1) Determine and collect initial withdrawal liability of every employer that has completely or partially withdrawn, in accordance with sections 4201 and 4202 of ERISA;

(2) Notify each employer that is or may be liable under this section, in accordance with paragraph (d) of this section;

(3) Within 90 days after the end of the plan year in which the withdrawal occurred, determine, in accordance with paragraph (b) of this section, the liability of each withdrawing employer that is liable under this section;

(4) Notify each liable employer, in accordance with paragraph (e) of this section, of the amount of its liability under this section, demand payment of and collect that liability; and

(5) Certify to the PBGC that determinations of liability have been completed, in accordance with paragraph (g) of this section.

(d) *Notice of withdrawal.* Within 30 days after the end of a plan year in which a plan experiences a withdrawal described in paragraph (a), the plan sponsor shall notify in writing each employer that is or may be liable under this section. The notice shall specify the plan year in which substantially all employers have withdrawn, describe the consequences of such withdrawal under this section, and state that an employer obligated to make initial withdrawal liability payments shall continue to make those payments in accordance with its schedule.

(e) *Notice of liability.* Within 30 days after the determination of liability, the plan sponsor shall issue a notice of liability in writing to each liable employer. The notice shall include—

(1) The amount of the employer's liability for de minimis amounts;

(2) A schedule for payment of the liability, determined under § 4219.16(f); and

(3) A demand for payment of the liability in accordance with the schedule.

(f) *Review of liability determinations.* Determinations of liability made pursuant to this section shall be subject to plan review under section 4219(b)(2) of ERISA and to arbitration under section 4221 of ERISA, subject to the limitations contained in § 4219.16(g).

(g) *Notice to the PBGC.* No later than 30 days after the notices of liability under this section are required to be provided to liable employers, the plan sponsor shall file with the PBGC a notice. The notice shall include the items described in § 4219.17(g)(1) through (g)(3), as well as the information listed below. In addition, the PBGC may require the plan sponsor to submit any further information that the PBGC determines it needs in order to monitor compliance with this section.

(1) The plan year in which the withdrawal occurred.

(2) A description of the effect of the withdrawal, including the number of contributing employers that withdrew in the plan year in which substantially all employers withdrew, the number of employers remaining in the plan, and a description of the effect of the withdrawal on the plan's contribution base.

(3) A certification, signed by the plan sponsor or duly authorized representative, that determinations have been made and notices given in accordance with this section.

[¶ 15,687J]

§ 4219.19 **Method and date of issuance; computation of time.** The PBGC applies the rules in subpart B of part 4000 of this chapter to determine permissible methods of issuance under this subpart. The

PBGC applies the rules in subpart C of part 4000 of this chapter to determine the date that an issuance under this subpart was provided. The PBGC applies the rules in subpart D of part 4000 of this chapter to compute any time period for issuances to third parties under this subpart.

[Added 10/28/2003 by 68 FR 61344]

[¶ 15,687J-1]

§ 4219.20 **Information collection**. The information collection requirements contained in §§ 4219.16, 4219.17, and 4219.18 have been approved by the Office of Management and Budget under control number 1212-0034.

Subpart C—Overdue, Defaulted, and Overpaid Withdrawal Liability

[¶ 15,687K]

§ 4219.31 **Overdue and defaulted withdrawal liability; overpayment**. (a) *Overdue withdrawal liability payment*. Except as otherwise provided in rules adopted by the plan in accordance with § 4219.33, a withdrawal liability payment is overdue if it is not paid on the date set forth in the schedule of payments established by the plan sponsor.

(b) *Default*.

(1) Except as provided in paragraph (c)(1), "default" means—

(i) The failure of an employer to pay any overdue withdrawal liability payment within 60 days after the employer receives written notification from the plan sponsor that the payment is overdue; and

(ii) Any other event described in rules adopted by the plan which indicates a substantial likelihood that an employer will be unable to pay its withdrawal liability.

(2) In the event of a default, a plan sponsor may require immediate payment of all or a portion of the outstanding amount of an employer's withdrawal liability, plus interest. In the event that the plan sponsor accelerates only a portion of the outstanding amount of an employer's withdrawal liability, the plan sponsor shall establish a new schedule of payments for the remaining amount of the employer's withdrawal liability.

(c) *Plan review or arbitration of liability determination*. The following rules shall apply with respect to the obligation to make withdrawal liability payments during the period for plan review and arbitration and with respect to the failure to make such payments:

(1) A default as a result of failure to make any payments shall not occur until the 61st day after the last of—

(i) Expiration of the period described in section 4219(b)(2)(A) of ERISA;

(ii) If the employer requests review under section 4219(b)(2)(A) of ERISA of the plan's withdrawal liability determination or the schedule of payments established by the plan, expiration of the period described in section 4221(a)(1) of ERISA for initiation of arbitration; or

(iii) If arbitration is timely initiated either by the plan, the employer or both, issuance of the arbitrator's decision.

(2) Any amounts due before the expiration of the period described in paragraph (c)(1) shall be paid in accordance with the schedule established by the plan sponsor. If a payment is not made when due under the schedule, the payment is overdue and interest shall accrue in accordance with the rules and at the same rate set forth in § 4219.32.

(d) *Overpayments*. If the plan sponsor or an arbitrator determines that payments made in accordance with the schedule of payments established by the plan sponsor have resulted in an overpayment of withdrawal liability, the plan sponsor shall refund the overpayment, with interest, in a lump sum. The plan sponsor shall credit interest on the overpayment from the date of the overpayment to the date on which the overpayment is refunded to the employer at the same rate as the rate for overdue withdrawal liability payments, as established under § 4219.32 or by the plan pursuant to § 4219.33.

[¶ 15,687L]

§ 4219.32 **Interest on overdue, defaulted and overpaid withdrawal liability**. (a) *Interest assessed*. The plan sponsor of a multiemployer plan—

(1) Shall assess interest on overdue withdrawal liability payments from the due date, as defined in paragraph (d) of this section, until the date paid, as defined in paragraph (e); and

(2) In the event of a default, may assess interest on any accelerated portion of the outstanding withdrawal liability from the due date, as defined in paragraph (d) of this section, until the date paid, as defined in paragraph (e).

(b) *Interest rate*. Except as otherwise provided in rules adopted by the plan pursuant to § 4219.33, interest under this section shall be charged or credited for each calendar quarter at an annual rate equal to the average quoted prime rate on short-term commercial loans for the fifteenth day (or next business day if the fifteenth day is not a business day) of the month preceding the beginning of each calendar quarter, as reported by the Board of Governors of the Federal Reserve System in Statistical Release H.15 ("Selected Interest Rates").

(c) *Calculation of interest*. The interest rate under paragraph (b) of this section is the nominal rate for any calendar quarter or portion thereof. The amount of interest due the plan for overdue or defaulted withdrawal liability, or due the employer for overpayment, is equal to the overdue, defaulted, or overpaid amount multiplied by:

(1) For each full calendar quarter in the period from the due date (or date of overpayment) to the date paid (or date of refund), one-fourth of the annual rate in effect for that quarter;

(2) For each full calendar month in a partial quarter in that period, one-twelfth of the annual rate in effect for that quarter; and

(3) For each day in a partial month in that period, one-three-hundred-sixtieth of the annual rate in effect for that month.

(d) *Due date*. Except as otherwise provided in rules adopted by the plan, the due date from which interest accrues shall be, for an overdue withdrawal liability payment and for an amount of withdrawal liability in default, the date of the missed payment that gave rise to the delinquency or the default.

(e) *Date paid*. Any payment of withdrawal liability shall be deemed to have been paid on the date on which it is received.

[¶ 15,687M]

§ 4219.33 **Plan rules concerning overdue and defaulted withdrawal liability**. Plans may adopt rules relating to overdue and defaulted withdrawal liability, provided that those rules are consistent with ERISA. These rules may include, but are not limited to, rules for determining the rate of interest to be charged on overdue, defaulted and overpaid withdrawal liability (provided that the rate reflects prevailing market rates for comparable obligations); rules providing reasonable grace periods during which late payments may be made without interest; additional definitions of default which indicate a substantial likelihood that an employer will be unable to pay its withdrawal liability; and rules pertaining to acceleration of the outstanding balance on default. Plan rules adopted under this section shall be reasonable. Plan rules shall operate and be applied uniformly with respect to each employer, except that the rules may take into account the creditworthiness of an employer. Rules which take into account the creditworthiness of an employer shall state with particularity the categories of creditworthiness the plan will use, the specific differences in treatment accorded employers in different categories, and the standards and procedures for assigning an employer to a category.

[¶ 15,688]
APPROVAL OF AMENDMENTS

Act Sec. 4220.(a) Except as provided in subsection (b), if an amendment to a multiemployer plan authorized by any preceding section of this part is adopted more than 36 months after the effective date of this section, the amendment shall be effective only if the corporation approves the amendment, or, within 90 days after the corporation receives notice and a copy of the amendment from the plan sponsor, fails to disapprove the amendment.

Act Sec. 4220. (b) An amendment permitted by section 4211(c)(5) may be adopted only in accordance with that section.

Act Sec. 4220. (c) The corporation shall disapprove an amendment referred to in subsection (a) or (b) only if the corporation determines that the amendment creates an unreasonable risk of loss to plan participants and beneficiaries or to the corporation.
Amendment

P.L. 96-364, § 104(2):

Added Sec. 4220, effective September 26, 1980 under ERISA Sec. 4402.

Regulations

The following regulations were adopted by the Pension Benefit Guaranty Corporation on July 1, 1996 (61 FR 34002). Prior to July 1, 1996, PBGC regulations were under Chapter XXVI of Title 29 of the Code of Federal Regulations. Effective July 1, 1996, PBGC regulations were moved to Chapter XL, and were renumbered and reorganized. Reg. § 4220.3 was amended October 28, 2003 (68 FR 61344).

[¶ 15,688A]

§ 4220.1 **Purpose and scope.** (a) *General.* This part establishes procedures under which a plan sponsor shall request the PBGC to approve a plan amendment under section 4220 of ERISA. This part applies to all multiemployer plans covered by title IV of ERISA that adopt amendments pursuant to the authorization of sections 4201-4219 of ERISA (except for amendments adopted pursuant to section 4211(c)(5)). (The covered amendments are set forth in paragraph (b) of this section.) The subsequent modification of a plan amendment adopted by authorization of those sections is also covered by this part. This part does not, however, cover a plan amendment that merely repeals a previously adopted amendment, returning the plan to the statutorily prescribed rule.

(b) *Covered amendments.* Amendments made pursuant to the following sections of ERISA are covered by this part:

(1) Section 4203(b)(1)(B)(ii).

(2) Section 4203(c)(4).

(3) Section 4205(c)(1).

(4) Section 4205(d).

(5) Section 4209(b).

(6) Section 4210(b)(2).

(7) Section 4211(c)(1).

(8) Section 4211(c)(4)(D).

(9) Section 4211(d)(1).

(10) Section 4211(d)(2).

(11) Section 4219(c)(1)(C)(ii)(I).

(12) Section 4219(c)(1)(C)(iii).

(c) *Exception.* Submission of a request for approval under this part is not required for a plan amendment for which the PBGC has published a notice in the Federal Register granting class approval.

[¶ 15,688B]

§ 4220.2 **Definitions.** The following terms are defined in § 4001.2 of this chapter: *employer, ERISA, IRS, multiemployer plan, PBGC, plan,* and *plan sponsor.*

[¶ 15,688C]

§ 4220.3 **Requests for PBGC approval.** (a) *Filing of request.* (1) *In general.* A request for approval of an amendment filed with the PBGC in accordance with this section shall constitute notice to the PBGC for purposes of the 90-day period specified in section 4220 of ERISA. A request is treated as filed on the date on which a request containing all information required by paragraph (d) of this section is received by the PBGC. Subpart C of part 4000 of this chapter provides rules for determining when the PBGC receives a submission.

(2) *Method of filing.* The PBGC applies the rules in subpart A of part 4000 of this chapter to determine permissible methods of filing with the PBGC under this part.

[Amended 10/28/2003 by 68 FR 61344]

(b) *Who may request.* The plan sponsor, or a duly authorized representative acting on behalf of a plan sponsor, shall sign and submit the request.

(c) *Where to file.* See Sec. 4000.4 of this chapter for information on where to file.

[Amended 10/28/2003 by 68 FR 61344]

(d) *Information.* Each request filed shall contain the following information:

(1) The name of the plan for which the amendment is being submitted, and the name, address and the telephone number of the plan sponsor or its duly authorized representative.

(2) The nine-digit Employer Identification Number (EIN) assigned by the IRS to the plan sponsor and the three-digit Plan Identification Number (PIN) assigned by the plan sponsor to the plan, and, if different, the EIN or PIN last filed with PBGC. If no EIN or PIN has been assigned, that fact must be indicated.

(3) A copy of the amendment as adopted, including its proposed effective date.

(4) A copy of the most recent actuarial valuation of the plan.

(5) A statement containing a certification that notice of the adoption of the amendment has been given to all employers who have an obligation to contribute under the plan and to all employee organizations representing employees covered by the plan.

(6) Any other information that the plan sponsor believes to be pertinent to its request.

(e) *Supplemental information.* The PBGC may require a plan sponsor to submit any other information that the PBGC determines to be necessary to review a request under this part. The PBGC may suspend the running of the 90-day period pursuant to § 4220.4(c), pending the submission of the supplemental information.

(f) *Computation of time.* The PBGC applies the rules in subpart D of part 4000 of this chapter to compute any time period under this part.

[Amended 10/28/2003 by 68 FR 61344]

(Approved by the Office of Management and Budget under control number 1212-0031)

[¶ 15,688D]

§ 4220.4 **PBGC action on requests.** (a) *General.* Upon receipt of a complete request, the PBGC shall notify the plan sponsor in writing of the date of commencement of the 90-day period specified in section 4220 of ERISA. Except as provided in paragraph (c) of this section, the PBGC shall approve or disapprove a plan amendment submitted to it under this part within 90 days after receipt of a complete request for approval. If the PBGC fails to act within the 90-day period, or within that period notifies the plan sponsor that it will not disapprove the amendment, the amendment may be made effective without the approval of the PBGC.

(b) *Decision on request.* The PBGC's decision on a request for approval shall be in writing. If the PBGC disapproves the plan amendment, the decision shall state the reasons for the disapproval. An approval by the PBGC constitutes its finding only with respect to the issue of risk as set forth in section 4220(c) of ERISA, and not with respect to whether the amendment is otherwise properly adopted in accordance with the terms of ERISA and the plan in question.

(c) *Suspension of the 90-day period.* The PBGC may suspend the running of the 90-day period referred to in paragraph (a) of this section if it determines that additional information is required under § 4220.3(e). When it does so, PBGC's request for additional information will advise the plan sponsor that the running of 90-day period has been suspended. The 90-day period will resume running on the date on which the additional information is received by the PBGC, and the PBGC will notify the plan sponsor of that date upon receipt of the information.

[¶ 15,689]
RESOLUTION OF DISPUTES

Act Sec. 4221. (a) (1) Any dispute between an employer and the plan sponsor of a multiemployer plan concerning a determination made under sections 4201 through 4219 shall be resolved through arbitration. Either party may initiate the arbitration proceeding within a 60-day period after the earlier of—

(A) the date of notification to the employer under section 4219(b)(2)(B), or

(B) 120 days after the date of the employer's request under section 4219(b)(2)(A). The parties may jointly initiate arbitration within the 180-day period after the date of the plan sponsor's demand under section 4219(b)(1).

(2) An arbitration proceeding under this section shall be conducted in accordance with fair and equitable procedures to be promulgated by the corporation. The plan sponsor may purchase insurance to cover potential liability of the arbitrator. If the parties have not provided for the costs of the arbitration, including arbitrator's fees, by agreement, the arbitrator shall assess such fees. The arbitrator may also award reasonable attorney's fees.

(3) (A) For purposes of any proceeding under this section, any determination made by a plan sponsor under sections 4201 through 4219 and section 4225 is presumed correct unless the party contesting the determination shows by a preponderance of the evidence that the determination was unreasonable or clearly erroneous.

(B) In the case of the determination of a plan's unfunded vested benefits for a plan year, the determination is presumed correct unless a party contesting the determination shows by a preponderance of evidence that—

(i) the actuarial assumptions and methods used in the determination were, in the aggregate, unreasonable (taking into account the experience of the plan and reasonable expectations), or

(ii) the plan's actuary made a significant error in applying the actuarial assumptions or methods.

Act Sec. 4221. (b) (1) If no arbitration proceeding has been initiated pursuant to subsection (a), the amounts demanded by the plan sponsor under section 4219(b)(1) shall be due and owing on the schedule set forth by the plan sponsor. The plan sponsor may bring an action in a State or Federal court of competent jurisdiction for collection.

(2) Upon completion of the arbitration proceedings in favor of one of the parties, any party thereto may bring an action, no later than 30 days after the issuance of an arbitrator's award, in an appropriate United States district court in accordance with section 4301 to enforce, vacate, or modify the arbitrator's award.

(3) Any arbitration proceedings under this section shall, to the extent consistent with this title, be conducted in the same manner, subject to the same limitations, carried out with the same powers (including subpoena power), and enforced in United States courts as an arbitration proceeding carried out under title 9, United States Code.

Act Sec. 4221. (c) In any proceeding under subsection (b), there shall be a presumption, rebuttable only by a clear preponderance of the evidence, that the findings of fact made by the arbitrator were correct.

Act Sec. 4221. (d) Payments shall be made by an employer in accordance with the determinations made under this part until the arbitrator issues a final decision with respect to the determination submitted for arbitration, with any necessary adjustments in subsequent payments for overpayments or underpayments arising out of the decision of the arbitrator with respect to the determination. If the employer fails to make timely payment in accordance with such final decision, the employer shall be treated as being delinquent in the making of a contribution required under the plan (within the meaning of section 515).

Act Sec. 4221. (e) If any employer requests in writing that the plan sponsor make available to the employer general information necessary for the employer to compute its withdrawal liability with respect to the plan (other than information which is unique to that employer), the plan sponsor shall furnish the information to the employer without charge. If any employer requests in writing that the plan sponsor make an estimate of such employer's potential withdrawal liability with respect to the plan or to provide information unique to that employer, the plan sponsor may require the employer to pay the reasonable cost of making such estimate or providing such information.

Act. Sec. 4221. Act sec. 4221 (f) Procedures Applicable to Certain Disputes.—

(1) In general. If—

(A) a plan sponsor of a plan determines that—

(i) a complete or partial withdrawal of an employer has occurred, or

(ii) an employer is liable for withdrawal liability payments with respect to the complete or partial withdrawal of an employer from the plan,

(B) such determination is based in whole or in part on a finding by the plan sponsor under section 4212(c) that a principal purpose of a transaction that occurred before January 1, 1999, was to evade or avoid withdrawal liability under this subtitle, and

(C) such transaction occurred at least 5 years before the date of the complete or partial withdrawal, then the special rules under paragraph (2) shall be used in applying subsections (a) and (d) of this section and section 4219(c) to the employer.

(2) Special rules.—

(A) Determination. Notwithstanding subsection (a)(3)—

(i) a determination by the plan sponsor under paragraph (1)(B) shall not be presumed to be correct, and

(ii) the plan sponsor shall have the burden to establish, by a preponderance of the evidence, the elements of the claim under section 4212(c) that a principal purpose of the transaction was to evade or avoid withdrawal liability under this subtitle.

Nothing in this subparagraph shall affect the burden of establishing any other element of a claim for withdrawal liability under this subtitle.

(B) Procedure. Notwithstanding subsection (d) and section 4219(c), if an employer contests the plan sponsor's determination under paragraph (1) through an arbitration proceeding pursuant to subsection (a), or through a claim brought in a court of competent jurisdiction, the employer shall not be obligated to make any withdrawal liability payments until a final decision in the arbitration proceeding, or in court, upholds the plan sponsor's determination..

Amendment

P.L. 108-218, §202(a):

Added subsection (f).

Act Sec. 202(b) provides:

Effective Date.—The amendments made by this section shall apply to any employer that receives a notification under section 4219(b)(1) of the Employee Retirement Income Security Act of 1974 (29 U.S.C. 1399(b)(1)) after October 31, 2003.

P.L. 96-364, §104(2):

Added Sec. 4221, effective September 26, 1980 under ERISA Sec. 4402.

Regulations

The following regulations were adopted by the Pension Benefit Guaranty Corporation on July 1, 1996 (61 FR 34002). Prior to July 1, 1996, PBGC regulations were under Chapter XXVI of Title 29 of the Code of Federal Regulations. Effective July 1, 1996, PBGC regulations were moved to Chapter XL, and were renumbered and reorganized. Reg. §4221.4, Reg. §4221.6, Reg. §4221.12, Reg. §4221.13, and Reg. §4221.14 were amended October 28, 2003 (68 FR 61344).

[¶ 15,689A]

§ 4221.1 **Purpose and scope.** (a) *Purpose.* The purpose of this part is to establish procedures for the arbitration, pursuant to section 4221 of ERISA, of withdrawal liability disputes arising under sections 4201 through 4219 and 4225 of ERISA.

(b) *Scope.* This part applies to arbitration proceedings initiated pursuant to section 4221 of ERISA and this part on or after September 26, 1985. On and after the effective date, any plan rules governing arbitration procedures (other than a plan rule adopting a PBGC-approved arbitration procedure in accordance with § 4221.14) are effective only to the extent that they are consistent with this part and adopted by the arbitrator in a particular proceeding.

[¶ 15,689B]

§ 4221.2 **Definitions.** The following terms are defined in § 4001.2 of this chapter: *ERISA, IRS, multiemployer plan, PBGC, plan,* and *plan sponsor.*

In addition, for purposes of this part:

Arbitrator means an individual or panel of individuals selected according to this part to decide a dispute concerning withdrawal liability.

Employer means an individual, partnership, corporation or other entity against which a plan sponsor has made a demand for payment of withdrawal liability pursuant to section 4219(b)(1) of ERISA.

Party or parties means the employer and the plan sponsor involved in a withdrawal liability dispute.

Withdrawal liability dispute means a dispute described in § 4221.1(a) of this chapter.

[¶ 15,689C]

§ 4221.3 **Initiation of arbitration.** (a) *Time limits—in general.* Arbitration of a withdrawal liability dispute may be initiated within the time limits described in section 4221(a)(1) of ERISA.

(b) *Waiver or extension of time limits.* Arbitration shall be initiated in accordance with this section, notwithstanding any inconsistent provision of any agreement entered into by the parties before the date on which the employer received notice of the plan's assessment of withdrawal liability. The parties may, however, agree at any time to waive or extend the time limits for initiating arbitration.

(c) *Establishment of timeliness of initiation.* A party that unilaterally initiates arbitration is responsible for establishing that the notice of initiation of arbitration was timely received by the other party. If arbitration is initiated by agreement of the parties, the date on which the agreement to arbitrate was executed establishes whether the arbitration was timely initiated.

(d) *Contents of agreement or notice.* If the employer initiates arbitration, it shall include in the notice of initiation a statement that it disputes the plan sponsor's determination of its withdrawal liability and is initiating arbitration. A copy of the demand for withdrawal liability and any request for reconsideration, and the response thereto, shall be attached to the notice. If a party other than an employer initiates arbitration, it shall include in the notice a statement that it is initiating arbitration and a brief description of the questions on which arbitration is sought. If arbitration is initiated by agreement, the agreement shall include a brief description of the questions submitted to arbitration. In no case is compliance with formal rules of pleading required.

(e) *Effect of deficient agreement or notice.* If a party fails to object promptly in writing to deficiencies in an initiation agreement or a notice of initiation of arbitration, it waives its right to object.

[¶ 15,689D]

§ 4221.4 **Appointment of the arbitrator.** (a) *Appointment of and acceptance by arbitrator.* The parties shall select the arbitrator within 45 days after the arbitration is initiated, or within such other period as is mutually agreed after the initiation of arbitration, and shall mail to the designated arbitrator a notice of his or her appointment. The notice of appointment shall include a copy of the notice or agreement initiating arbitration, a statement that the arbitration is to be conducted in accordance with this part, and a request for a written acceptance by the arbitrator. The arbitrator's appointment becomes effective upon his or her written acceptance, stating his or her availability to serve and

making any disclosures required by paragraph (b) of this section. If the arbitrator does not accept in writing within 15 days after the notice of appointment is mailed or delivered to him or her, he or she is deemed to have declined to act, and the parties shall select a new arbitrator in accordance with paragraph (d) of this section.

(b) *Disclosure by arbitrator and disqualification.* Upon accepting the appointment, the arbitrator shall disclose to the parties any circumstances likely to affect his or her impartiality, including any bias or any financial or personal interest in the result of the arbitration and any past or present relationship with the parties or their counsel. If any party determines that the arbitrator should be disqualified because of the information disclosed, that party shall notify all other parties and the arbitrator no later than 10 days after the arbitrator makes the disclosure required by this paragraph (but in no event later than the commencement of the hearing under § 4221.6). The arbitrator shall then withdraw, and the parties shall select another arbitrator in accordance with paragraph (d) of this section.

(c) *Challenge and withdrawal.* After the arbitrator has been selected, a party may request that he or she withdraw from the proceedings at any point before a final award is rendered on the ground that he or she is unable to render an award impartially. The request for withdrawal shall be served on all other parties and the arbitrator by hand or by certified or registered mail (or by any other method that includes verification or acknowledgment of receipt and meets (if applicable) the requirements of Sec. 4000.14 of this chapter) and shall include a statement of the circumstances that, in the requesting party's view, affect the arbitrator's impartiality and a statement that the requesting party has brought these circumstances to the attention of the arbitrator and the other parties at the earliest practicable point in the proceedings. If the arbitrator determines that the circumstances adduced are likely to affect his or her impartiality and have been presented in a timely fashion, he or she shall withdraw from the proceedings and notify the parties of the reasons for his or her withdrawal. The parties shall then select a new arbitrator in accordance with paragraph (d) of this section.

[Amended 10/28/2003 by 68 FR 61344]

(d) *Filling vacancies.* If the designated arbitrator declines his or her appointment or, after accepting his or her appointment, is disqualified, resigns, dies, withdraws, or is unable to perform his or her duties at any time before a final award is rendered, the parties shall select another arbitrator to fill the vacancy. The selection shall be made, in accordance with the procedure used in the initial selection, within 20 days after the parties receive notice of the vacancy. The matter shall then be reheard by the newly chosen arbitrator, who may, in his or her discretion, rely on all or any portion of the record already established.

(e) *Failure to select arbitrator.* If the parties fail to select an arbitrator within the time prescribed by this section, either party or both may seek the designation and appointment of an arbitrator in a United States district court pursuant to the provisions of title 9 of the United States Code.

[¶ 15,689E]

§ 4221.5 **Powers and duties of the arbitrator.** (a) *Arbitration hearing.* Except as otherwise provided in this part, the arbitrator shall conduct the arbitration hearing under § 4221.6 in the same manner, and shall possess the same powers, as an arbitrator conducting a proceeding under title 9 of the United States Code.

(1) *Application of the law.* In reaching his or her decision, the arbitrator shall follow applicable law, as embodied in statutes, regulations, court decisions, interpretations of the agencies charged with the enforcement of ERISA, and other pertinent authorities.

(2) *Prehearing discovery.* The arbitrator may allow any party to conduct prehearing discovery by interrogatories, depositions, requests for the production of documents, or other means, upon a showing that the discovery sought is likely to lead to the production of relevant evidence and will not be disproportionately burdensome to the other parties. The arbitrator may impose appropriate sanctions if he or she determines that a party has failed to respond to discovery in good faith or has conducted discovery proceedings in bad faith or for the purpose of harassment. The arbitrator may, at the request of any party or on his

or her own motion, require parties to give advance notice of expert or other witnesses that they intend to introduce.

(3) *Admissibility of evidence.* The arbitrator determines the relevance and materiality of the evidence offered during the course of the hearing and is the judge of the admissibility of evidence offered. Conformity to legal rules of evidence is not necessary. To the extent reasonably practicable, all evidence shall be taken in the presence of the arbitrator and the parties. The arbitrator may, however, consider affidavits, transcripts of depositions, and similar documents.

(4) *Production of documents or other evidence.* The arbitrator may subpoena witnesses or documents upon his or her own initiative or upon request by any party after determining that the evidence is likely to be relevant to the dispute.

(b) *Prehearing conference.* If it appears that a prehearing conference will expedite the proceedings, the arbitrator may, at any time before the commencement of the arbitration hearing under §4221.6, direct the parties to appear at a conference to consider settlement of the case, clarification of issues and stipulation of facts not in dispute, admission of documents to avoid unnecessary proof, limitations on the number of expert or other witnesses, and any other matters that could expedite the disposition of the proceedings.

(c) *Proceeding without hearing.* The arbitrator may render an award without a hearing if the parties agree and file with the arbitrator such evidence as the arbitrator deems necessary to enable him or her to render an award under §4221.8.

[¶ 15,689F]

§4221.6 **Hearing.** (a) *Time and place of hearing established.* Unless the parties agree to proceed without a hearing as provided in §4221.5(c), the parties and the arbitrator shall, no later than 15 days after the written acceptance by the arbitrator is mailed to the parties, establish a date and place for the hearing. If agreement is not reached within the 15-day period, the arbitrator shall, within 10 additional days, choose a location and set a hearing date. The date set for the hearing may be no later than 50 days after the mailing date of the arbitrator's written acceptance.

(b) *Notice.* After the time and place for the hearing have been established, the arbitrator shall serve a written notice of the hearing on the parties by hand, by certified or registered mail, or by any other method that includes verification or acknowledgment of receipt and meets (if applicable) the requirements of Sec. 4000.14 of this chapter.

[Amended 10/28/2003 by 68 FR 61344]

(c) *Appearances.* The parties may appear in person or by counsel or other representatives. Any party that, after being duly notified and without good cause shown, fails to appear in person or by representative at a hearing or conference, or fails to file documents in a timely manner, is deemed to have waived all rights with respect thereto and is subject to whatever orders or determinations the arbitrator may make.

(d) *Record and transcript of hearing.* Upon the request of either party, the arbitrator shall arrange for a record of the arbitration hearing to be made by stenographic means or by tape recording. The cost of making the record and the costs of transcription and copying are costs of the arbitration proceedings payable as provided in §4221.10(b) except that, if only one party requests that a transcript of the record be made, that party shall pay the cost of the transcript.

(e) *Order of hearing.* The arbitrator shall conduct the hearing in accordance with the following rules:

(1) *Opening.* The arbitrator shall open the hearing and place in the record the notice of initiation of arbitration or the initiation agreement. The arbitrator may ask for statements clarifying the issues involved.

(2) *Presentation of claim and response.* The arbitrator shall establish the procedure for presentation of claim and response in such a manner as to afford full and equal opportunity to all parties for the presentation of their cases.

(3) *Witnesses.* All witnesses shall testify under oath or affirmation and are subject to cross-examination by opposing parties. If testimony of an expert witness is offered by a party without prior notice to the other party, the arbitrator shall grant the other party a reasonable time to prepare for cross-examination and to produce expert witnesses on its own behalf. The arbitrator may on his or her own initiative call expert witnesses on any issue raised in the arbitration. The cost of any expert called by the arbitrator is a cost of the proceedings payable as provided in §4221.10(b).

(f) *Continuance of hearing.* The arbitrator may, for good cause shown, grant a continuance for a reasonable period. When granting a continuance, the arbitrator shall set a date for resumption of the hearing.

(g) *Filing of briefs.* Each party may file a written statement of facts and argument supporting the party's position. The parties' briefs are due no later than 30 days after the close of the hearing. Within 15 days thereafter, each party may file a reply brief concerning matters contained in the opposing brief. The arbitrator may establish a briefing schedule and may reduce or extend these time limits. Each party shall deliver copies of all of its briefs to the arbitrator and to all opposing parties.

[¶ 15,689G]

§4221.7 **Reopening of proceedings.** (a) *Grounds for reopening.* At any time before a final award is rendered, the proceedings may be reopened, on the motion of the arbitrator or at the request of any party, for the purpose of taking further evidence or rehearing or rearguing any matter, if the arbitrator determines that—

(1) The reopening is likely to result in new information that will have a material effect on the outcome of the arbitration;

(2) Good cause exists for the failure of the party that requested reopening to present such information at the hearing; and

(3) The delay caused by the reopening will not be unfairly injurious to any party.

(b) *Comments on and notice of reopening.* The arbitrator shall allow all affected parties the opportunity to comment on any motion or request to reopen the proceedings. If he or she determines that the proceedings should be reopened, he or she shall give all parties written notice of the reasons for reopening and of the schedule of the reopened proceedings.

[¶ 15,689H]

§4221.8 **Award.** (a) *Form.* The arbitrator shall render a written award that—

(1) States the basis for the award, including such findings of fact and conclusions of law (which need not be explicitly designated as such) as are necessary to resolve the dispute;

(2) Adjusts (or provides a method for adjusting) the amount or schedule of payments to be made after the award to reflect overpayments or underpayments made before the award was rendered or requires the plan sponsor to refund overpayments in accordance with §4219.31(d); and

(3) Provides for an allocation of costs in accordance with §4221.10.

(b) *Time of award.* Except as provided in paragraphs (c), (d), and (e) of this section, the arbitrator shall render the award no later than 30 days after the proceedings close. The award is rendered when filed or served on the parties as provided in §4221.13. The award is final when the period for seeking modification or reconsideration in accordance with §4221.9(a) has expired or the arbitrator has rendered a revised award in accordance with §4221.9(c).

(c) *Reopened proceedings.* If the proceedings are reopened in accordance with §4221.7 after the close of the hearing, the arbitrator shall render the award no later than 30 days after the date on which the reopened proceedings are closed.

(d) *Absence of hearing.* If the parties have chosen to proceed without a hearing, the arbitrator shall render the award no later than 30 days after the date on which final statements and proofs are filed with him or her.

(e) *Agreement for extension of time.* Notwithstanding paragraphs (b), (c), and (d), the parties may agree to an extension of time for the arbitrator's award in light of the particular facts and circumstances of their dispute.

(f) *Close of proceedings.* For purposes of paragraphs (b) and (c) of this section, the proceedings are closed on the date on which the last brief or reply brief is due or, if no briefs are to be filed, on the date on which the hearing or rehearing closes.

(g) *Publication of award.* After a final award has been rendered, the plan sponsor shall make copies available upon request to the PBGC and to all companies that contribute to the plan. The plan sponsor may impose reasonable charges for copying and postage.

[¶ 15,689I]

§ 4221.9 **Reconsideration of award.** (a) *Motion for reconsideration and objections.* A party may seek modification or reconsideration of the arbitrator's award by filing a written motion with the arbitrator and all opposing parties within 20 days after the award is rendered. Opposing parties may file objections to modification or reconsideration within 10 days after the motion is filed. The filing of a written motion for modification or reconsideration suspends the 30-day period under section 4221(b)(2) of ERISA for requesting court review of the award. The 30-day statutory period again begins to run when the arbitrator denies the motion pursuant to paragraph (c) of this section or renders a revised award.

(b) *Grounds for modification or reconsideration.* The arbitrator may grant a motion for modification or reconsideration of the award only if—

(1) There is a numerical error or a mistake in the description of any person, thing, or property referred to in the award; or

(2) The arbitrator has rendered an award upon a matter not submitted to the arbitrator and the matter affects the merits of the decision; or

(3) The award is imperfect in a matter of form not affecting the merits of the dispute.

(c) *Decision of arbitrator.* The arbitrator shall grant or deny the motion for modification or reconsideration, and may render an opinion to support his or her decision within 20 days after the motion is filed with the arbitrator, or within 30 days after the motion is filed if an objection is also filed.

[¶ 15,689J]

§ 4221.10 **Costs.** The costs of arbitration under this part shall be borne by the parties as follows:

(a) *Witnesses.* Each party to the dispute shall bear the costs of its own witnesses.

(b) *Other costs of arbitration.* Except as provided in § 4221.6(d) with respect to a transcript of the hearing, the parties shall bear the other costs of the arbitration proceedings equally unless the arbitrator determines otherwise. The parties may, however, agree to a different allocation of costs if their agreement is entered into after the employer has received notice of the plan's assessment of withdrawal liability.

(c) *Attorneys' fees.* The arbitrator may require a party that initiates or contests an arbitration in bad faith or engages in dilatory, harassing, or other improper conduct during the course of the arbitration to pay reasonable attorneys' fees of other parties.

[¶ 15,689K]

§ 4221.11 **Waiver of rules.** Any party that fails to object in writing in a timely manner to any deviation from any provision of this part is deemed to have waived the right to interpose that objection thereafter.

[¶ 15,689L]

§ 4221.12 **Calculation of periods of time.** The PBGC applies the rules in subpart D of part 4000 of this chapter to compute any time period under this part.

[Amended 10/28/2003 by 68 FR 61344]

[¶ 15,689M]

§ 4221.13 **Filing and issuance rules.** (a) *Method and date of filing.* The PBGC applies the rules in subpart A of part 4000 of this chapter to determine permissible methods of filing with the PBGC under this part. The PBGC applies the rules in subpart C of part 4000 of this chapter to determine the date that a submission under this part was filed with the PBGC.

(b) *Where to file.* See Sec. 4000.4 of this chapter for information on where to file.

(c) *Method and date of issuance.* The PBGC applies the rules in subpart B of part 4000 of this chapter to determine permissible methods of issuance under this part. The PBGC applies the rules in subpart C of part 4000 of this chapter to determine the date that an issuance under this part was provided.

[Amended 10/28/2003 by 68 FR 61344]

[¶ 15,689N]

§ 4221.14 **PBGC-approved arbitration procedures.** (a) *Use of PBGC-approved arbitration procedures.* In lieu of the procedures prescribed by this part, an arbitration may be conducted in accordance with an alternative arbitration procedure approved by the PBGC in accordance with paragraph (c) of this section. A plan may by plan amendment require the use of a PBGC-approved procedure for all arbitrations of withdrawal liability disputes, or the parties may agree to the use of a PBGC-approved procedure in a particular case.

(b) *Scope of alternative procedures.* If an arbitration is conducted in accordance with a PBGC-approved arbitration procedure, the alternative procedure shall govern all aspects of the arbitration, with the following exceptions:

(1) The time limits for the initiation of arbitration may not differ from those provided for by § 4221.3.

(2) The arbitrator shall be selected after the initiation of the arbitration.

(3) The arbitrator shall give the parties opportunity for prehearing discovery substantially equivalent to that provided by § 4221.5(a)(2).

(4) The award shall be made available to the public to at least the extent provided by § 4221.8(g).

(5) The costs of arbitration shall be allocated in accordance with § 4221.10.

(c) *Procedure for approval of alternative procedures.* The PBGC may approve arbitration procedures on its own initiative by publishing an appropriate notice in the Federal Register. The sponsor of an arbitration procedure may request PBGC approval of its procedures by submitting an application to the PBGC. The application shall include:

(1) A copy of the procedures for which approval is sought;

(2) A description of the history, structure and membership of the organization that sponsors the procedures; and

(3) A discussion of the reasons why, in the sponsoring organization's opinion, the procedures satisfy the criteria for approval set forth in this section.

[Amended 10/28/2003 by 68 FR 61344]

(d) *Criteria for approval of alternative procedures.* The PBGC shall approve an application if it determines that the proposed procedures will be substantially fair to all parties involved in the arbitration of a withdrawal liability dispute and that the sponsoring organization is neutral and able to carry out its role under the procedures. The PBGC may request comments on the application by publishing an appropriate notice in the Federal Register. Notice of the PBGC's decision on the application shall be published in the Federal Register. Unless the notice of approval specifies otherwise, approval will remain effective until revoked by the PBGC through a Federal Register notice.

[¶ 15,690]
REIMBURSEMENTS FOR UNCOLLECTIBLE WITHDRAWAL LIABILITY

Act Sec. 4222.(a) By May 1, 1982, the corporation shall establish by regulation a supplemental program to reimburse multiemployer plans for withdrawal liability payments which are due from employers and which are determined to be uncollectible for reasons arising out of cases or proceedings involving the employers under title 11, United States Code, or similar cases or proceedings. Participation in the supplemental program shall be on a voluntary basis, and a plan which elects coverage under the program shall pay premiums to the corporation in accordance with a premium schedule which shall be prescribed from time to time by the corporation. The premium schedule shall contain such rates and bases for the application of such rates as the corporation considers to be appropriate.

Act Sec. 4222. (b) The corporation may provide under the program for reimbursement of amounts of withdrawal liability determined to be uncollectible for any other reasons the corporation considers appropriate.

Act Sec. 4222. (c) The cost of the program (including such administrative and legal costs as the corporation considers appropriate) may be paid only out of premiums collected under such program.

Act Sec. 4222. (d) The supplemental program may be offered to eligible plans on such terms and conditions, and with such limitations with respect to the payment of reimbursements (including the exclusion of de minimis amounts of uncollectible employer liability, and the reduction or elimination of reimbursements which cannot be paid from collected premiums) and such restrictions on withdrawal from the program, as the corporation considers necessary and appropriate.

Act Sec. 4222. (e) The corporation may enter into arrangements with private insurers to carry out in whole or in part the program authorized by this section and may require plans which elect coverage under the program to elect coverage by those private insurers.

Amendment:

P.L. 96-364, § 104(2):

Added Sec. 4222, effective September 26, 1980 under ERISA Sec. 4402.

[¶ 15,691]
WITHDRAWAL LIABILITY PAYMENT FUND

Act Sec. 4223.(a) The plan sponsors of multiemployer plans may establish or participate in a withdrawal liability payment fund.

Act Sec. 4223. (b) For purposes of this section, the term "withdrawal liability payment fund", and the term "fund", mean a trust which—

(1) is established and maintained under section 501(c)(22) of the Internal Revenue Code of 1986,

(2) maintains agreements which cover a substantial portion of the participants who are in multiemployer plans which (under the rules of the trust instrument) are eligible to participate in the fund,

(3) is funded by amounts paid by the plans which participate in the fund, and

(4) is administered by a Board of Trustees, and in the administration of the fund there is equal representation of—

(A) trustees representing employers who are obligated to contribute to the plans participating in the fund, and

(B) trustees representing employees who are participants in plans which participate in the fund.

Act Sec. 4223.(c)(1) If an employer withdraws from a plan which participates in a withdrawal liability payment fund, then, to the extent provided in the trust, the fund shall pay to that plan—

(A) the employer's unattributable liability,

(B) the employer's withdrawal liability payments which would have been due but for section 4208, 4209, 4219, or 4225,

(C) the employer's withdrawal liability payments to the extent they are uncollectible.

(2) The fund may provide for the payment of the employer's attributable liability if the fund—

(A) provides for the payment of both the attributable and the unattributable liability of the employer in a single payment, and

(B) is subrogated to all rights of the plan against the employer.

(3) For purposes of this section, the term—

(A) "attributable liability" means the excess, if any, determined under the provisions of a plan not inconsistent with regulations of the corporation, of—

(i) the value of vested benefits accrued as a result of service with the employer, over

(ii) the value of plan assets attributed to the employer, and

(B) "unattributable liability" means the excess of withdrawal liability over attributable liability.

Such terms may be further defined, and the manner in which they shall be applied may be prescribed, by the corporation by regulation.

(4)(A) The trust of a fund shall be maintained for the exclusive purpose of paying—

(i) any amount described in paragraph (1) and paragraph (2), and

(ii) reasonable and necessary administrative expenses in connection with the establishment and operation of the trust and the processing of claims against the fund.

(B) The amounts paid by a plan to a fund shall be deemed a reasonable expense of administering the plan under sections 403(c)(1) and 404(a)(1)(A)(ii), and the payments made by a fund to a participating plan shall be deemed services necessary for the operation of the plan within the meaning of section 408(b)(2) or within the meaning of section 4975(d)(2) of the Internal Revenue Code of 1986.

Act Sec. 4223.(d)(1) For purposes of this part—

(A) only amounts paid by the fund to a plan under subsection (c)(1)(A) shall be credited to withdrawal liability otherwise payable by the employer, unless the plan otherwise provides, and

(B) any amounts paid by the fund under subsection (c) to a plan shall be treated by the plan as a payment of withdrawal liability to such plan.

(2) For purposes of applying provisions relating to the funding stand ard accounts (and minimum contribution requirements), amounts paid from the plan to the fund shall be applied to reduce the amount treated as contributed to the plan.

Act Sec. 4223. (e) The fund shall be subrogated to the rights of the plan against the employer that has withdrawn from the plan for amounts paid by a fund to a plan under—

(1) subsection (c)(1)(A), to the extent not credited under subsection (d)(1)(A), and

(2) subsection (c)(1)(C).

Act Sec. 4223. (f) Notwithstanding any other provision of this Act, a fiduciary of the fund shall discharge the fiduciary's duties with respect to the fund in accordance with the standards for fiduciaries prescribed by this Act (to the extent not inconsistent with the purposes of this section), and in accordance with the documents and instruments governing the fund insofar as such documents and instruments are consistent with the provisions of this Act (to the extent not inconsistent with the purposes of this section). The provisions of the preceding sentence shall supersede any and all State laws relating to fiduciaries insofar as they may now or hereafter relate to a fund to which this section applies.

Act Sec. 4223. (g) No payments shall be made from a fund to a plan on the occasion of a withdrawal or partial withdrawal of an employer from such plan if the employees representing the withdrawn contribution base units continue, after such withdrawal, to be represented under section 9 of the National Labor

Relations Act (or other applicable labor laws) in negotiations with such employer by the labor organization which represented such employees immediately preceding such withdrawal.

Act Sec. 4223. (h) Nothing in this section shall be construed to prohibit the purchase of insurance by an employer from any other person, to limit the circumstances under which such insurance would be payable, or to limit in any way the terms and conditions of such insurance.

Act Sec. 4223. (i) The corporation may provide by regulation rules not inconsistent with this section governing the establishment and maintenance of funds, but only to the extent necessary to carry out the purposes of this part (other than section 4222).

Amendments:

P.L. 101-239, § 7891(a)(1):

Titles I, III, and IV of ERISA (other than sections 3(37)(E), 301(a)(7), and 308, the last sentence of section 408(d), and sections 414(c), 4001(a)(3)(ii), and 4303) are each amended by striking "Internal Revenue Code of 1954" each place it appears and inserting "Internal Revenue Code of 1986", effective October 22, 1986.

P.L. 96-364, § 104(2):

Added Sec. 4223, effective September 26, 1980 under ERISA Sec. 4402.

[¶ 15,692]
ALTERNATIVE METHOD OF WITHDRAWAL LIABILITY PAYMENTS

Act Sec. 4224. A multiemployer plan may adopt rules providing for other terms and conditions for the satisfaction of an employer's withdrawal liability if such rules are consistent with this Act and with such regulations as may be prescribed by the corporation.

Amendment

P.L. 96-364, § 104(2):

Added Sec. 4224, effective September 26, 1980 under ERISA Sec. 4402.

[¶ 15,696]
LIMITATION ON WITHDRAWAL LIABILITY

Act Sec. 4225. (a)(1) In the case of bona fide sale of all or substantially all of the employer's assets in an arm's-length transaction to an unrelated party (within the meaning of section 4204(d)), the unfunded vested benefits allocable to an employer (after the application of all sections of this part having a lower number designation than this section), other than an employer undergoing reorganization under title 11, United States Code, or similar provisions of State law, shall not exceed the greater of—

(A) a portion (determined under paragraph (2)) of the liquidation or dissolution value of the employer (determined after the sale or exchange of such assets), or

(B) the unfunded vested benefits attributable to employees of the employer.

(2) For purposes of paragraph (1), the portion shall be determined in accordance with the following table:

If the liquidation or dissolution value of the employer after the sale or exchange is—	The portion is—
Not more than $2,000,000	30 percent of the amount.
More than $2,000,000, but not more than $4,000,000,	$600,000, plus 35 percent of the amount in excess of $2,000,000.
More than $4,000,000, but not more than $6,000,000,	$1,300,000, plus 40 percent of the amount in excess of $4,000,000.
More than $6,000,000, but not more than $7,000,000,	$2,100,000, plus 45 percent of the amount in excess of $6,000,000.
More than $7,000,000, but not more than $8,000,000,	$2,550,000, plus 50 percent of the amount in excess of $7,000,000.
More than $8,000,000, but not more than $9,000,000,	$3,050,000, plus 60 percent of the amount in excess of $8,000,000.
More than $9,000,000, but not more than $10,000,000,	$3,650,000, plus 70 percent of the amount in excess of $9,000,000.
More than $10,000,000.	$4,350,000, plus 80 percent of the amount in excess of $10,000,000.

Act Sec. 4225. (b) In the case of an insolvent employer undergoing liquidation or dissolution, the unfunded vested benefits allocable to that employer shall not exceed an amount equal to the sum of—

(1) 50 percent of the unfunded vested benefits allocable to the employer (determined without regard to this section), and

(2) that portion of 50 percent of the unfunded vested benefits allocable to the employer (as determined under paragraph (1)) which does not exceed the liquidation or dissolution value of the employer determined—

(A) as of the commencement of liquidation or dissolution, and

(B) after reducing the liquidation or dissolution value of the employer by the amount determined under paragraph (1).

Act Sec. 4225. (c) To the extent that the withdrawal liability of an employer is attributable to his obligation to contribute to or under a plan as an individual (whether as a sole proprietor or as a member of a partnership), property which may be exempt from the estate under section 522 of title 11, United States Code, or under similar provisions of law, shall not be subject to enforcement of such liability.

Act Sec. 4225. (d) For purposes of this section—

(1) an employer is insolvent if the liabilities of the employer, including withdrawal liability under the plan (determined without regard to subsection (b)), exceed the assets of the employer (determined as of the commencement of the liquidation or dissolution), and

(2) the liquidation or dissolution value of the employer shall be determined without regard to such withdrawal liability.

Act Sec. 4225. (e) In the case of one or more withdrawals of an employer attributable to the same sale, liquidation, or dissolution, under regulations prescribed by the corporation—

(1) all such withdrawals shall be treated as a single withdrawal for the purpose of applying this section, and

(2) the withdrawal liability of the employer to each plan shall be an amount which bears the same ratio to the present value of the withdrawal liability payments to all plans (after the application of the preceding provisions of this section) as the withdrawal liability of the employer to such plan (determined without regard to this section) bears to the withdrawal liability of the employer to all such plans (determined without regard to this section).

Amendment

P.L. 96-364, § 104(2):

Added Sec. 4225, effective September 26, 1980 under ERISA Sec. 4402.

Part 2—Merger or Transfer of Plan Assets or Liabilities

[¶ 15,700]
MERGERS AND TRANSFERS BETWEEN MULTIEMPLOYER PLANS

Act Sec. 4231. (a) Unless otherwise provided in regulations prescribed by the corporation, a plan sponsor may not cause a multiemployer plan to merge with one or more multiemployer plans, or engage in a transfer of assets and liabilities to or from another multiemployer plan, unless such merger or transfer satisfies the requirements of subsection (b).

Act Sec. 4231. (b) A merger or transfer satisfies the requirements of this section if—

(1) in accordance with regulations of the corporation, the plan sponsor of a multiemployer plan notifies the corporation of a merger with or transfer of plan assets or liabilities to another multiemployer plan at least 120 days before the effective date of the merger or transfer;

(2) no participant's or beneficiary's accrued benefit will be lower immediately after the effective date of the merger or transfer than the benefit immediately before that date;

(3) the benefits of participants and beneficiaries are not reasonably expected to be subject to suspension under section 4245; and

(4) an actuarial valuation of the assets and liabilities of each of the affected plans has been performed during the plan year preceding the effective date of the merger or transfer, based upon the most recent data available as of the day before the start of that plan year, or other valuation of such assets and liabilities performed under such standards and procedures as the corporation may prescribe by regulation.

Act Sec. 4231. (c) The merger of multiemployer plans or the transfer of assets or liabilities between multiemployer plans, shall be deemed not to constitute a violation of the provisions of section 406(a) or section 406(b)(2) if the corporation determines that the merger or transfer otherwise satisfies the requirements of this section.

Act Sec. 4231. (d) A plan to which liabilities are transferred under this section is a successor plan for purposes of section 4022A(b)(2)(B).

Amendment

P.L. 96-364, § 104(2):

Added Sec. 4231 effective September 26, 1980 under ERISA Sec. 4402.

Regulations

The following regulations were adopted by the Pension Benefit Guaranty Corporation on July 1, 1996 (61 FR 34002). Prior to July 1, 1996, PBGC regulations were under Chapter XXVI of Title 29 of the Code of Federal Regulations. Effective July 1, 1996, PBGC regulations were moved to Chapter XL, and were renumbered and reorganized. Amendments to regulations ERISA Secs. 4231.1—4231.10 were published on May 4, 1998 (63 FR 24421). Reg. § 4231.8 was amended October 28, 2003 (68 FR 61344).

[¶ 15,700A]

§ 4231.1 **Purpose and scope.** (a) *Purpose.* The purpose of this part is to prescribe notice requirements under section 4231 of ERISA for mergers and transfers of assets or liabilities among multiemployer pension plans. This part also interprets the other requirements of section 4231 and prescribes special rules for de minimis mergers and transfers. The collections of information in this part have been approved by the Office of Management and Budget under OMB control number 1212-0022.

(b) *Scope.* This part applies to mergers and transfers among multiemployer plans where all of the plans immediately before and immediately after the transaction are multiemployer plans covered by title IV of ERISA.

[¶ 15,700B]

§ 4231.2 **Definitions.** The following terms are defined in Sec. 4001.2 of this chapter: *Code, EIN, ERISA, fair market value, IRS, multiemployer plan, PBGC, plan, plan year,* and *PN.*

In addition, for purposes of this part:

Actuarial valuation means a valuation of assets and liabilities performed by an enrolled actuary using the actuarial assumptions used for purposes of determining the charges and credits to the funding standard account under section 302 of ERISA and section 412 of the Code.

Certified change of collective bargaining representative means a change of collective bargaining representative certified under the Labor-Management Relations Act of 1947, as amended, or the Railway Labor Act, as amended.

Fair market value of assets has the same meaning as the term has for minimum funding purposes under section 302 of ERISA and section 412 of the Code.

Merger means the combining of two or more plans into a single plan. For example, a consolidation of two plans into a new plan is a merger.

Significantly affected plan means a plan that—

(1) Transfers assets that equal or exceed 15 percent of its assets before the transfer,

(2) Receives a transfer of unfunded accrued benefits that equal or exceed 15 percent of its assets before the transfer,

(3) Is created by a spinoff from another plan, or

(4) Engages in a merger or transfer (other than a de minimis merger or transfer) either—

(i) After such plan has terminated by mass withdrawal under section 4041A(a)(2) of ERISA, or

(ii) With another plan that has so terminated.

Transfer and transfer of assets or liabilities mean a diminution of assets or liabilities with respect to one plan and the acquisition of these assets or the assumption of these liabilities by another plan or plans (including a plan that did not exist prior to the transfer). However, the shifting of assets or liabilities pursuant to a written reciprocity agreement between two multiemployer plans in which one plan assumes liabilities of another plan is not a transfer of assets or liabilities. In addition, the shifting of assets between several funding media used for a single plan (such as between trusts, between annuity contracts, or between trusts and annuity contracts) is not a transfer of assets or liabilities.

Unfunded accrued benefits means the excess of the present value of a plan's accrued benefits over the fair market value of its assets, determined on the basis of the actuarial valuation required under Sec. 4231.5(b).

[¶ 15,700C]

§ 4231.3 **Requirements for mergers and transfers.** (a) *General requirements.* A plan sponsor may not cause a multiemployer plan to merge with one or more multiemployer plans or transfer assets or liabilities to or from another multiemployer plan unless the merger or transfer satisfies all of the following requirements:

(1) No participant's or beneficiary's accrued benefit is lower immediately after the effective date of the merger or transfer than the benefit immediately before that date.

(2) Actuarial valuations of the plans that existed before the merger or transfer have been performed in accordance with Sec. 4231.5.

(3) For each plan that exists after the transaction, an enrolled actuary—

(i) Determines that the plan meets the applicable plan solvency requirement set forth in Sec. 4231.6; or

(ii) Otherwise demonstrates that benefits under the plan are not reasonably expected to be subject to suspension under section 4245 of ERISA.

(4) The plan sponsor notifies the PBGC of the merger or transfer in accordance with Sec. 4231.8.

(b) *Compliance determination.* If a plan sponsor requests a determination that a merger or transfer that may otherwise be prohibited by section 406(a) or (b)(2) of ERISA satisfies the requirements of section 4231 of ERISA, the plan sponsor must submit the information described in Sec. 4231.9 in addition to the information required by Sec. 4231.8. PBGC may request additional information if necessary to determine whether a merger or transfer complies with the requirements of section 4231 and this part. Plan sponsors are not required to request a compliance determination. Under section 4231(c) of ERISA, if the PBGC determines that the merger or transfer complies with section 4231 of ERISA and this part, the merger or transfer will not constitute a violation of the prohibited transaction provisions of section 406(a) and (b)(2) of ERISA.

(c) *Certified change in bargaining representative.* Transfers of assets and liabilities pursuant to a certified change in bargaining representative are governed by section 4235 of ERISA. Plan sponsors involved in such transfers are not required to comply with this part. However, under section 4235(f)(1) of ERISA, the plan sponsors of the plans involved in the transfer may agree to a transfer that complies with sections 4231 and 4234 of ERISA. Plan sponsors that elect to comply with sections 4231 and 4234 must comply with the rules in this part.

[¶ 15,700D]

§ 4231.4 Preservation of accrued benefits. Section 4231(b)(2) of ERISA and Sec. 4231.3(a)(1) require that no participant's or beneficiary's accrued benefit may be lower immediately after the effective date of the merger or transfer than the benefit immediately before the merger or transfer. A plan that assumes an obligation to pay benefits for a group of participants satisfies this requirement only if the plan contains a provision preserving all accrued benefits. The determination of what is an accrued benefit must be made in accordance with section 411 of the Code and the regulations thereunder.

[¶ 15,700E]

§ 4231.5 Valuation requirement. (a) *In general.* For a plan that is not a significantly affected plan, or that is a significantly affected plan only because the merger or transfer involves a plan that has terminated by mass withdrawal under section 4041A(a)(2) of ERISA, the actuarial valuation requirement under section 4231(b)(4) of ERISA and Sec. 4231.3(a)(2) is satisfied if an actuarial valuation has been performed for the plan based on the plan's assets and liabilities as of a date not more than three years before the date on which the notice of the merger or transfer is filed.

(b) *Significantly affected plans.* For a significantly affected plan, other than a plan that is a significantly affected plan only because the merger or transfer involves a plan that has terminated by mass withdrawal under section 4041A(a)(2) of ERISA, the actuarial valuation requirement under section 4231(b)(4) of ERISA and Sec. 4231.3(a)(2) is satisfied only if an actuarial valuation has been performed for the plan based on the plan's assets and liabilities as of a date not earlier than the first day of the last plan year ending before the proposed effective date of the transaction. The valuation must separately identify assets, contributions, and liabilities being transferred and must be based on the actuarial assumptions and methods that are expected to be used for the plan for the first plan year beginning after the transfer.

[¶ 15,700F]

§ 4231.6 Plan solvency tests. (a) *In general.* For a plan that is not a significantly affected plan, the plan solvency requirement of section 4231(b)(3) of ERISA and Sec. 4231.3(a)(3)(i) is satisfied if—

(1) The expected fair market value of plan assets immediately after the merger or transfer equals or exceeds five times the benefit payments for the last plan year ending before the proposed effective date of the merger or transfer; or

(2) In each of the first five plan years beginning on or after the proposed effective date of the merger or transfer, expected plan assets plus expected contributions and investment earnings equal or exceed expected expenses and benefit payments for the plan year.

(b) *Significantly affected plans.* The plan solvency requirement of section 4231(b)(3) of ERISA and Sec. 4231.3(a)(3)(i) is satisfied for a significantly affected plan if all of the following requirements are met:

(1) Expected contributions equal or exceed the estimated amount necessary to satisfy the minimum funding requirement of section 412(a) of the Code (including reorganization funding, if applicable) for the five plan years beginning on or after the proposed effective date of the transaction.

(2) The expected fair market value of plan assets immediately after the transaction equal or exceed the total amount of expected benefit payments for the first five plan years beginning on or after the proposed effective date of the transaction.

(3) Expected contributions for the first plan year beginning on or after the proposed effective date of the transaction equal or exceed expected benefit payments for that plan year.

(4) Expected contributions for the amortization period equal or exceed unfunded accrued benefits plus expected normal costs. The actuary may select as the amortization period either—

(i) The first 25 plan years beginning on or after the proposed effective date of the transaction, or

(ii) The amortization period for the resulting base when the combined charge base and the combined credit base are offset under section 412(b)(4) of the Code.

(c) *Rules for determinations.* In determining whether a transaction satisfies the plan solvency requirements set forth in this section, the following rules apply:

(1) Expected contributions after a merger or transfer must be determined by assuming that contributions for each plan year will equal contributions for the last full plan year ending before the date on which the notice of merger or transfer is filed with the PBGC. Contributions must be adjusted, however, to reflect—

(i) The merger or transfer,

(ii) Any change in the rate of employer contributions that has been negotiated (whether or not in effect), and

(iii) Any trend of changing contribution base units over the preceding five plan years or other period of time that can be demonstrated to be more appropriate.

(2) Expected normal costs must be determined under the funding method and assumptions expected to be used by the plan actuary for purposes of determining the minimum funding requirement under section 412 of the Code (which requires that such assumptions be reasonable in the aggregate). If the plan uses an aggregate funding method, normal costs must be determined under the entry age normal method.

(3) Expected benefit payments must be determined by assuming that current benefits remain in effect and that all scheduled increases in benefits occur.

(4) The expected fair market value of plan assets immediately after the merger or transfer must be based on the most recent data available immediately before the date on which the notice is filed.

(5) Expected investment earnings must be determined using the same interest assumption to be used for determining the minimum funding requirement under section 412 of the Code.

(6) Expected expenses must be determined using expenses in the last plan year ending before the notice is filed, adjusted to reflect any anticipated changes.

(7) Expected plan assets for a plan year must be determined by adjusting the most current data on fair market value of plan assets to reflect expected contributions, investment earnings, benefit payments and expenses for each plan year between the date of the most current data and the beginning of the plan year for which expected assets are being determined.

[¶ 15,700G]

§ 4231.7 De minimis mergers and transfers. (a) *Special plan solvency rule.* The determination of whether a de minimis merger or transfer satisfies the plan solvency requirement in Sec. 4231.6(a) may be made without regard to any other de minimis mergers or transfers that have occurred since the last actuarial valuation.

(b) *De minimis merger defined.* A merger is de minimis if the present value of accrued benefits (whether or not vested) of one plan is less than 3 percent of the fair market value of the other plan's assets.

(c) *De minimis transfer defined.* A transfer of assets or liabilities is de minimis if—

(1) The fair market value of the assets transferred, if any, is less than 3 percent of the fair market value of all the assets of the transferor plan;

(2) The present value of the accrued benefits transferred (whether or not vested) is less than 3 percent of the fair market value of all the assets of the transferee plan; and

(3) The transferee plan is not a plan that has terminated under section 4041A(a)(2) of ERISA.

(d) *Value of assets and benefits.* For purposes of paragraphs (b) and (c) of this section, the value of plan assets and accrued benefits may be determined as of any date prior to the proposed effective date of the transaction, but not earlier than the date of the most recent actuarial valuation.

(e) *Aggregation required.* In determining whether a merger or transfer is de minimis, the assets and accrued benefits transferred in previous de minimis mergers and transfers within the same plan year must be aggregated as described in paragraphs (e)(1) and (e)(2) of this section. For the purposes of those paragraphs, the value of plan assets may be determined as of the date during the plan year on which the total value of the plan's assets is the highest.

(1) A merger is not de minimis if the total present value of accrued benefits merged into a plan, when aggregated with all prior de minimis mergers of and transfers to that plan effective within the same plan year, equals or exceeds 3 percent of the value of the plan's assets.

(2) A transfer is not de minimis if, when aggregated with all previous de minimis mergers and transfers effective within the same plan year—

(i) The value of all assets transferred from a plan equals or exceeds 3 percent of the value of the plan's assets; or

(ii) The present value of all accrued benefits transferred to a plan equals or exceeds 3 percent of the plan's assets.

[¶ 15,700H]

§ 4231.8 **Notice of merger or transfer.** (a) *Filing of request.* (1) *When to file.* Except as provided in paragraph (f) of this section, a notice of a proposed merger or transfer must be filed not less than 120 days before the effective date of the transaction. For purposes of this part, the effective date of a merger or transfer is the earlier of—

(i) The date on which one plan assumes liability for benefits accrued under another plan involved in the transaction; or

(ii) The date on which one plan transfers assets to another plan involved in the transaction.

(2) *Method of filing.* The PBGC applies the rules in subpart A of part 4000 of this chapter to determine permissible methods of filing with the PBGC under this part.

(3) *Computation of time.* The PBGC applies the rules in subpart D of part 4000 of this chapter to compute any time period for filing under this part.

[Amended 10/28/2003 by 68 FR 61344]

(b) *Who must file.* The plan sponsors of all plans involved in a merger or transfer, or the duly authorized representative(s) acting on behalf of the plan sponsors, must jointly file the notice required by this section.

(c) *Where to file.* See Sec. 4000.4 of this chapter for information on where to file.

[Amended 10/28/2003 by 68 FR 61344]

(d) *Date of filing.* The PBGC applies the rules in subpart C of part 4000 of this chapter to determine the date that a submission under this part was filed with the PBGC. For purposes of paragraph (a) of this section, the notice is not considered filed until all of the information required by paragraph (e) of this section has been submitted.

[Amended 10/28/2003 by 68 FR 61344]

(e) *Information required.* Each notice must contain the following information:

(1) For each plan involved in the merger or transfer—

(i) The name of the plan;

(ii) The name, address and telephone number of the plan sponsor and of the plan sponsor's duly authorized representative, if any; and

(iii) The plan sponsor's EIN and the plan's PN and, if different, the EIN or PN last filed with the PBGC. If no EIN or PN has been assigned, the notice must so indicate.

(2) Whether the transaction being reported is a merger or transfer, whether it involves any plan that has terminated under section 4041A(a)(2) of ERISA, whether any significantly affected plan is involved in the transaction (and, if so, identifying each such plan), and whether it is a de minimis transaction as defined in Sec. 4231.7 (and, if so, including an enrolled actuary's certification to that effect).

(3) The proposed effective date of the transaction.

(4) A copy of each plan provision stating that no participant's or beneficiary's accrued benefit will be lower immediately after the effective date of the merger or transfer than the benefit immediately before that date.

(5) For each plan that exists after the transaction, one of the following statements, certified by an enrolled actuary:

(i) A statement that the plan satisfies the applicable plan solvency test set forth in Sec. 4231.6, indicating which is the applicable test.

(ii) A statement of the basis on which the actuary has determined that benefits under the plan are not reasonably expected to be subject to suspension under section 4245 of ERISA, including the supporting data or calculations, assumptions and methods.

(6) For each plan that exists before a transaction (unless the transaction is de minimis and does not involve any plan that has terminated under section 4041A(a)(2) of ERISA), a copy of the most recent actuarial valuation report that satisfies the requirements of Sec. 4231.5.

(7) For each significantly affected plan that exists after the transaction, the following information used in making the plan solvency determination under Sec. 4231.6(b):

(i) The present value of the accrued benefits and fair market value of plan assets under the valuation required by Sec. 4231.5(b), allocable to the plan after the transaction.

(ii) The fair market value of assets in the plan after the transaction (determined in accordance with Sec. 4231.6(c)(4)).

(iii) The expected benefit payments for the plan in the first plan year beginning on or after the proposed effective date of the transaction (determined in accordance with Sec. 4231.6(c)(3)).

(iv) The contribution rates in effect for the plan for the first plan year beginning on or after the proposed effective date of the transaction.

(v) The expected contributions for the plan in the first plan year beginning on or after the proposed effective date of the transaction (determined in accordance with Sec. 4231.6(c)(1)).

(f) *Waiver of notice.* The PBGC may waive the notice requirements of this section and section 4231(b)(1) of ERISA if—

(1) A plan sponsor demonstrates to the satisfaction of the PBGC that failure to complete the merger or transfer in less than 120 days after filing the notice will cause harm to participants or beneficiaries of the plans involved in the transaction;

(2) The PBGC determines that the transaction complies with the requirements of section 4231 of ERISA; or

(3) The PBGC completes its review of the transaction.

[¶ 15,700I]

§ 4231.9 **Request for compliance determination.** (a) *General.* The plan sponsor(s) of one or more plans involved in a merger or transfer, or the duly authorized representative(s) acting on behalf of the plan sponsor(s), may file a request for a determination that the transaction complies with the requirements of section 4231 of ERISA. The request must contain the information described in paragraph (b) or (c) of this section, as applicable.

(1) *The place of filing.* The request must be delivered to the address set forth in Sec. 4231.8(c).

(2) *Single request permitted for all de minimis transactions.* Because the plan solvency test for de minimis mergers and transfers is based on the most recent valuation (without adjustment for intervening de minimis transactions), a plan sponsor may submit a single request for a compliance determination covering all de minimis mergers or transfers that occur between one plan valuation and the next. However, the plan sponsor must still notify PBGC of each de minimis merger or transfer separately, in accordance with Sec. 4231.8. The single request for a compliance determination may be filed concurrently with any one of the notices of a de minimis merger or transfer.

(b) *Contents of request.* (1) *General.* A request for a compliance determination concerning a merger or transfer that is not de minimis must contain—

(i) A copy of the merger or transfer agreement;

(ii) A summary of the required calculations, including a complete description of assumptions and methods, on which the enrolled actuary based each certification that a plan involved in the merger or transfer satisfied a plan solvency test described in Sec. 4231.6; and

(iii) For each significantly affected plan, other than a plan that is a significantly affected plan only because the merger or transfer involves a plan that has terminated by mass withdrawal under section 4041A(a)(2) of ERISA, copies of all actuarial valuations performed within the 5 years preceding the date of filing the notice required under Sec. 4231.8.

(2) *De minimis merger or transfer.* A request for a compliance determination concerning a de minimis merger or transfer must contain one of the following statements for each plan that exists after the transaction, certified by an enrolled actuary:

(i) A statement that the plan satisfies one of the plan solvency tests set forth in Sec. 4231.6(a), indicating which test is satisfied.

(ii) A statement of the basis on which the actuary has determined that benefits under the plan are not reasonably expected to be subject to suspension under section 4245 of ERISA, including supporting data or calculations, assumptions and methods.

[¶ 15,700J]

§4231.10 **Actuarial calculations and assumptions.** (a) *Most recent valuation.* All calculations required by this part must be based on the most recent actuarial valuation as of the date of filing the notice, updated to show any material changes.

(b) *Assumptions.* All calculations required by this part must be based on methods and assumptions that are reasonable in the aggregate, based on generally accepted actuarial principles.

(c) *Updated calculations.* If the actual effective date of the merger or transfer is more than one year after the date the notice is filed with the PBGC, PBGC may require the plans involved to provide updated calculations and representations based on the actual effective date of the transaction.

[¶ 15,701]

TRANSFERS BETWEEN A MULTIEMPLOYER PLAN AND A SINGLE-EMPLOYER PLAN

Act Sec. 4232.(a) A transfer of assets or liabilities between, or a merger of, a multiemployer plan and a single-employer plan shall satisfy the requirements of this section.

Act Sec. 4232. (b) No accrued benefit of a participant or beneficiary may be lower immediately after the effective date of a transfer or merger described in subsection (a) than the benefit immediately before that date.

Act Sec. 4232.(c)(1) Except as provided in paragraphs (2) and (3), a multiemployer plan which transfers liabilities to a single-employer plan shall be liable to the corporation if the single-employer plan terminates within 60 months after the effective date of the transfer. The amount of liability shall be the lesser of—

(A) the amount of the plan asset insufficiency of the terminated single-employer plan, less 30 percent of the net worth of the employer who maintained the single-employer plan, determined in accordance with section 4062 or 4064, or

(B) the value, on the effective date of the transfer, of the unfunded benefits transferred to the single-employer plan which are guaranteed under section 4022.

(2) A multiemployer plan shall be liable to the corporation as provided in paragraph (1) unless, within 180 days after the corporation receives an application (together with such information as the corporation may reasonably require for purposes of such application) from the multiemployer plan sponsor for a determination under this paragraph—

(A) the corporation determines that the interests of the plan participants and beneficiaries and of the corporation are adequately protected, or

(B) fails to make any determination regarding the adequacy with which such interests are protected with respect to such transfer of liabilities.

If, after the receipt of such application, the corporation requests from the plan sponsor additional information necessary for the determination, the running of the 180-day period shall be suspended from the date of such request until the receipt by the corporation of the additional information requested. The corporation may by regulation prescribe procedures and standards for the issuance of determinations under this paragraph. This paragraph shall not apply to any application submitted less than 180 days after the date of enactment of the Multiemployer Pension Plan Amendments Act of 1980.

(3) A multiemployer plan shall not be liable to the corporation as provided in paragraph (1) in the case of a transfer from the multiemployer plan to a single-employer plan of liabilities which accrued under a single-employer plan which merged with the multiemployer plan, if the value of liabilities transferred to the single-employer plan does not exceed the value of the liabilities for benefits which accrued before the merger, and the value of the assets transferred to the single-employer plan is substantially equal to the value of the assets which would have been in the single-employer plan if the employer had maintained and funded it as a separate plan under which no benefits accrued after the date of the merger.

(4) The corporation may make equitable arrangements with multiemployer plans which are liable under this subsection for satisfaction of their liability.

Act Sec. 4232. (d) Benefits under a single-employer plan to which liabilities are transferred in accordance with this section are guaranteed under section 4022 to the extent provided in that section as of the effective date of the transfer and the plan is a successor plan.

Act Sec. 4232.(e)(1) Except as provided in paragraph (2), a multiemployer plan may not transfer liabilities to a single-employer plan unless the plan sponsor of the plan to which the liabilities would be transferred agrees to the transfer.

(2) In the case of a transfer described in subsection (c)(3), paragraph (1) of this subsection is satisfied by the advance agreement to the transfer by the employer who will be obligated to contribute to the single-employer plan.

Act Sec. 4232.(f)(1) The corporation may prescribe by regulation such additional requirements with respect to the transfer of assets or liabilities as may be necessary to protect the interests of plan participants and beneficiaries and the corporation.

(2) Except as otherwise determined by the corporation, a transfer of assets or liabilities to a single-employer plan from a plan in reorganization under section 4241 is not effective unless the corporation approves such transfer.

(3) No transfer to which this section applies, in connection with a termination described in section 4041A(a)(2) shall be effective unless the transfer meets such requirements as may be established by the corporation to prevent an increase in the risk of loss to the corporation.

Amendment

P.L. 96-364, §104(2):

Added Sec. 4232, effective September 26, 1980 under ERISA Sec. 4402.

[¶ 15,702]
PARTITION

Act Sec. 4233. (a) The corporation may order the partition of a multiemployer plan in accordance with this section.

Act Sec. 4233. (b) A plan sponsor may apply to the corporation for an order partitioning a plan. The corporation may not order the partition of a plan except upon notice to the plan sponsor and the participants and beneficiaries whose vested benefits will be affected by the partition of the plan, and upon finding that—

(1) a substantial reduction in the amount of aggregate contributions under the plan has resulted or will result from a case or proceeding under title 11, United States Code, with respect to an employer;

(2) the plan is likely to become insolvent;

(3) contributions will have to be increased significantly in reorganization to meet the minimum contribution requirement and prevent insolvency; and

(4) partition would significantly reduce the likelihood that the plan will become insolvent.

Act Sec. 4233. (c) The corporation may order the partition of a plan notwithstanding the pendency of a proceeding described in subsection (b)(1).

Act Sec. 4233. (d) The corporation's partition order shall provide for a transfer or no more than the nonforfeitable benefits directly attributable to service with the employer referred to in subsection (b)(1) and an equitable share of assets.

Act Sec. 4233. (e) The plan created by the partition is—

(1) a successor plan to which section 4022A applies, and

(2) a terminated multiemployer plan to which section 4041A(d) applies, with respect to which only the employer described in subsection (b)(1) has withdrawal liability, and to which section 4068 applies.

Act Sec. 4233. (f) The corporation may proceed under section 4042(c) through (h) for a decree partitioning a plan and appointing a trustee for the terminated portion of a partitioned plan. The court may order the partition of a plan upon making the findings described in subsection (b)(1) through (4), and subject to the conditions set forth in subsections (c) through (e).

Amendment

P.L. 96-364, § 104(2):

Added Sec. 4233, effective September 26, 1980 under ERISA Sec. 4402.

[¶ 15,703]
ASSET TRANSFER RULES

Act Sec. 4234. (a) A transfer of assets from a multiemployer plan to another plan shall comply with asset-transfer rules which shall be adopted by the multiemployer plan and which—

(1) do not unreasonably restrict the transfer of plan assets in connection with the transfer of plan liabilities, and

(2) operate and are applied uniformly with respect to each proposed transfer, except that the rules may provide for reasonable variations taking into account the potential financial impact of a proposed transfer on the multiemployer plan.

Plan rules authorizing asset transfers consistent with the requirements of section 4232(c)(3) shall be considered to satisfy the requirements of this subsection.

Act Sec. 4234. (b) The corporation shall prescribe regulations which exempt de minimis transfers of assets from the requirements of this part.

Act Sec. 4234. (c) This part shall not apply to transfers of assets pursuant to written reciprocity agreements, except to the extent provided in regulations prescribed by the corporation.

Amendment

P.L. 96-364, § 104(2):

Added Sec. 4234, effective September 26, 1980 under ERISA Sec. 4402.

[¶ 15,704]
TRANSFERS PURSUANT TO CHANGE IN BARGAINING REPRESENTATIVE

Act Sec. 4235. (a) In any case in which an employer has completely or partially withdrawn from a multiemployer plan (hereafter in this section referred to as the "old plan") as a result of a certified change of collective bargaining representative occurring after September 25, 1980, if participants of the old plan who are employed by the employer will, as a result of that change, participate in another multiemployer plan (hereafter in this section referred to as the "new plan"), the old plan shall transfer assets and liabilities to the new plan in accordance with this section.

Act Sec. 4235. (b)(1) The employer shall notify the plan sponsor of the old plan of a change in multiemployer plan participation described in subsection (a) no later than 30 days after the employer determines that the change will occur.

(2) The plan sponsor of the old plan shall—

(A) notify the employer of—

(i) the amount of the employer's withdrawal liability determined under part 1 with respect to the withdrawal,

(ii) the old plan's intent to transfer to the new plan the nonforfeitable benefits of the employees who are no longer working in covered service under the old plan as a result of the change of bargaining representative, and

(iii) the amount of assets and liabilities which are to be transferred to the new plan, and

(B) notify the plan sponsor of the new plan of the benefits, assets, and liabilities which will be transferred to the new plan.

(3) Within 60 days after receipt of the notice described in paragraph (2)(B), the new plan may file an appeal with the corporation to prevent the transfer. The transfer shall not be made if the corporation determines that the new plan would suffer substantial financial harm as a result of the transfer. Upon notification described in paragraph (2), if—

(A) the employer fails to object to the transfer within 60 days after receipt of the notice described in paragraph (2)(A), or

(B) the new plan either—

(i) fails to file such an appeal, or

(ii) the corporation, pursuant to such an appeal, fails to find that the new plan would suffer substantial financial harm as a result of the transfer described in the notice under paragraph (2)(B) within 180 days after the date on which the appeal is filed,

then the plan sponsor of the old plan shall transfer the appropriate amount of assets and liabilities to the new plan.

Act Sec. 4235. (c) If the plan sponsor of the old plan transfers the appropriate amount of assets and liabilities under this section to the new plan, then the amount of the employer's withdrawal liability (as determined under section 4201(b) without regard to such transfer and this section) with respect to the old plan shall be reduced by the amount by which—

(1) the value of the unfunded vested benefits allocable to the employer which were transferred by the plan sponsor of the old plan to the new plan, exceeds

(2) the value of the assets transferred.

Act Sec. 4235. (d) In any case in which there is a complete or partial withdrawal described in subsection (a), if—

    (1) the new plan files an appeal with the corporation under subsection (b)(3), and

    (2) the employer is required by section 4219 to begin making payments of withdrawal liability before the earlier of—

        (A) the date on which the corporation finds that the new plan would not suffer substantial financial harm as a result of the transfer, or

        (B) the last day of the 180-day period beginning on the date on which the new plan files its appeal,

then the employer shall make such payments into an escrow held by a bank or similar financial institution satisfactory to the old plan. If the transfer is made, the amounts paid into the escrow shall be returned to the employer. If the transfer is not made, the amounts paid into the escrow shall be paid to the old plan and credited against the employer's withdrawal liability.

Act Sec. 4235. (e)(1) Notwithstanding subsection (b), the plan sponsor shall not transfer any assets to the new plan if—

        (A) the old plan is in reorganization (within the meaning of section 4241(a)), or

        (B) the transfer of assets would cause the old plan to go into reorganization (within the meaning of section 4241(a)).

    (2) In any case in which a transfer of assets from the old plan to the new plan is prohibited by paragraph (1), the plan sponsor of the old plan shall transfer—

        (A) all nonforfeitable benefits described in subsection (b)(2), if the value of such benefits does not exceed the withdrawal liability of the employer with respect to such withdrawal, or

        (B) such nonforfeitable benefits having a value equal to the withdrawal liability of the employer, if the value of such benefits exceeds the withdrawal liability of the employer.

Act Sec. 4235. (f)(1) Notwithstanding subsections (b) and (e), the plan sponsors of the old plan and the new plan may agree to a transfer of assets and liabilities that complies with sections 4231 and 4234, rather than this section, except that the employer's liability with respect to the withdrawal from the old plan shall be reduced under subsection (c) as if assets and liabilities had been transferred in accordance with this section.

    (2) If the employer withdraws from the new plan within 240 months after the effective date of a transfer of assets and liabilities described in this section, the amount of the employer's withdrawal liability to the new plan shall be the greater of—

        (A) the employer's withdrawal liability determined under part 1 with respect to the new plan, or

        (B) the amount by which the employer's withdrawal liability to the old plan was reduced under subsection (c), reduced by 5 percent for each 12-month period following the effective date of the transfer and ending before the date of the withdrawal from the new plan.

Act Sec. 4235. (g) For purposes of this section—

    (1) "appropriate amount of assets" means the amount by which the value of the nonforfeitable benefits to be transferred exceeds the amount of the employer's withdrawal liability to the old plan (determined under part 1 without regard to section 4211(e)), and

    (2) "certified change of collective bargaining representative" means a change of collective bargaining representative certified under the Labor-Management Relations Act, 1947, or the Railway Labor Act.

Amendments

P.L. 98-369, § 558(b):

    Amended ERISA Sec. 4235(a) by striking out "April 28, 1980" and inserting "September 25, 1980" instead.

P.L. 96-364, § 104(2):

    Added Sec. 4235, September 26, 1980 under ERISA Sec. 4402.

Part 3—Reorganization; Minimum Contribution Requirement for Multiemployer Plans

[¶ 15,706]
REORGANIZATION STATUS

Act Sec. 4241. (a) A multiemployer plan is in reorganization for a plan year if the plan's reorganization index for that year is greater than zero.

Act Sec. 4241. (b)(1) A plan's reorganization index for any plan year is the excess of—

    (A) the vested benefits charge for such year, over

    (B) the net charge to the funding standard account for such year.

    (2) For purposes of this part, the net charge to the funding standard account for any plan year is the excess (if any) of—

        (A) the charges to the funding standard account for such year under section 412(b)(2) of the Internal Revenue Code of 1986, over

        (B) the credits to the funding standard account under section 412(b)(3)(B) of such Code.

    (3) For purposes of this part, the vested benefits charge for any plan year is the amount which would be necessary to amortize the plan's unfunded vested benefits as of the end of the base plan year in equal annual installments—

        (A) over 10 years, to the extent such benefits are attributable to persons in pay status, and

        (B) over 25 years, to the extent such benefits are attributable to other participants.

    (4)(A) The vested benefits charge for a plan year shall be based on an actuarial valuation of the plan as of the end of the base plan year, adjusted to reflect—

        (i) any—

            (I) decrease of 5 percent or more in the value of plan assets, or increase of 5 percent or more in the number of persons in pay status, during the period beginning on the first day of the plan year following the base plan year and ending on the adjustment date, or

            (II) at the election of the plan sponsor, actuarial valuation of the plan as of the adjustment date or any later date not later than the last day of the plan year for which the determination is being made,

        (ii) any change in benefits under the plan which is not otherwise taken into account under this subparagraph and which is pursuant to any amendment—

            (I) adopted before the end of the plan year for which the determination is being made, and

            (II) effective after the end of the base plan year and on or before the end of the plan year referred to in subclause (I), and

        (iii) any other event (including an event described in subparagraph (B)(i)(I)) which, as determined in accordance with regulations prescribed by the Secretary, would substantially increase the plan's vested benefit charge.

        (B)(i) In determining the vested benefits charge for a plan year following a plan year in which the plan was not in reorganization, any change in benefits which—

            (I) results from the changing of a group of participants from one benefit level to another benefit level under a schedule of plan benefits as a result of changes in a collective bargaining agreement, or

            (II) results from any other change in a collective bargaining agreement,

shall not be taken into account except to the extent provided in regulations prescribed by the Secretary of the Treasury.

(ii) Except as otherwise determined by the Secretary of the Treasury, in determining the vested benefits charge for any plan year following any plan year in which the plan was in reorganization, any change in benefits—

(I) described in clause (i)(I), or

(II) described in clause (i)(II) as determined under regulations prescribed by the Secretary of the Treasury, shall, for purposes of subparagraph (A)(ii), be treated as a change in benefits pursuant to an amendment to a plan.

(5)(A) For purposes of this part, the base plan year for any plan year is—

(i) if there is a relevant collective bargaining agreement, the last plan year ending at least 6 months before the relevant effective date, or

(ii) if there is no relevant collective bargaining agreement, the last plan year ending at least 12 months before the beginning of the plan year.

(B) For purposes of this part, a relevant collective bargaining agreement is a collective bargaining agreement—

(i) which is in effect for at least 6 months during the plan year, and

(ii) which has not been in effect for more than 36 months as of the end of the plan year.

(C) For purposes of this part, the relevant effective date is the earliest of the effective dates for the relevant collective bargaining agreements.

(D) For purposes of this part, the adjustment date is the date which is—

(i) 90 days before the relevant effective date, or

(ii) if there is no relevant effective date, 90 days before the beginning of the plan year.

(6) For purposes of this part, the term "person in pay status" means—

(A) a participant or beneficiary on the last day of the base plan year who, at any time during such year, was paid an early, late, normal, or disability retirement benefit (or a death benefit related to a retirement benefit), and

(B) to the extent provided in regulations prescribed by the Secretary of the Treasury, any other person who is entitled to such a benefit under the plan.

(7) For purposes of paragraph (3)—

(A) in determining the plan's unfunded vested benefits, plan assets shall first be allocated to the vested benefits attributable to persons in pay status, and

(B) the vested benefits charge shall be determined without regard to reductions in accrued benefits under section 4244A which are first effective in the plan year.

(8) For purposes of this part, any outstanding claim for withdrawal liability shall not be considered a plan asset, except as otherwise provided in regulations prescribed by the Secretary of the Treasury.

(9) For purposes of this part, the term "unfunded vested benefits" means with respect to a plan, an amount (determined in accordance with regulations prescribed by the Secretary of the Treasury) equal to—

(A) the value of nonforfeitable benefits under the plan, less

(B) the value of assets of the plan.

Act Sec. 4241. (c) Except as provided in regulations prescribed by the corporation, while a plan is in reorganization a benefit with respect to a participant (other than a death benefit) which is attributable to employer contributions and which has a value of more than $1,750 may not be paid in a form other than an annuity which (by itself or in combination with social security, railroad retirement, or workers' compensation benefits) provides substantially level payments over the life of the participant.

Act Sec. 4241. (d) Any multiemployer plan which terminates under section 4041A(a)(2) shall not be considered in reorganization after the last day of the plan year in which the plan is treated as having terminated.

Amendments

P.L. 101-239, § 7891(a)(1):

Titles I, III, and IV of ERISA (other than sections 3(37)(E), 301(a)(7), and 308, the last sentence of section 408(d), and sections 414(c), 4001(a)(3)(ii), and 4303) are each amended by striking "Internal Revenue Code of 1954" each place it appears and inserting "Internal Revenue Code of 1986", effective October 22, 1986.

P.L. 96-364, § 104(2):

Added Sec. 4241 effective on or after the earlier of the date on which the last collective bargaining agreement providing contributions under the plan, which was in effect on September 26, 1980, expires, without regard to extensions agreed to on or after September 26, 1980 or September 26, 1983 under ERISA Sec. 4402.

[¶ 15,708]
NOTICE OF REORGANIZATION AND FUNDING REQUIREMENTS

Act Sec. 4242. (a)(1) If—

(A) a multiemployer plan is in reorganization for a plan year, and

(B) section 4243 would require an increase in contributions for such plan year,

the plan sponsor shall notify the persons described in paragraph (2) that the plan is in reorganization and that, if contributions to the plan are not increased, accrued benefits under the plan may be reduced or an excise tax may be imposed (or both such reduction and imposition may occur).

(2) The persons described in this paragraph are—

(A) each employer who has an obligation to contribute under the plan (within the meaning of section 4201(h)(5)), and

(B) each employee organization which, for purposes of collective bargaining, represents plan participants employed by such an employer.

(3) The determination under paragraph (1)(B) shall be made without regard to the overburden credit provided by section 4244.

Act Sec. 4242. (b) The corporation may prescribe additional or alternative requirements for assuring, in the case of a plan with respect to which notice is required by subsection (a)(1), that the persons described in subsection (a)(2)—

(1) receive appropriate notice that the plan is in reorganization,

(2) are adequately informed of the implications of reorganization status, and

(3) have reasonable access to information relevant to the plan's reorganization status.

Amendment

P.L. 96-364, § 104(2):

Added Sec. 4242 effective on or after the earlier of the date on which the last collective bargaining agreement providing contributions under the plan, which was in effect on September 26, 1980, expires, without regard to extensions agreed to on or after September 26, 1980 or September 26, 1983 under ERISA Sec. 4402.

[¶ 15,709]
MINIMUM CONTRIBUTION REQUIREMENT

Act Sec. 4243. (a)(1) For any plan year for which a plan is in reorganization—

(A) the plan shall continue to maintain its funding standard account while it is in reorganization, and

(B) the plan's accumulated funding deficiency under section 302(a) for such plan year shall be equal to the excess (if any) of—

(i) the sum of the minimum contribution requirement for such plan year (taking into account any overburden credit under section 4244(a)) plus the plan's accumulated funding deficiency for the preceding plan year (determined under this section if the plan was in reorganization during such year or under section 302(a) if the plan was not in reorganization), over

(ii) amounts considered contributed by employers to or under the plan for the plan year (increased by any amount waived under subsection (f) for the plan year).

(2) For purposes of paragraph (1), withdrawal liability payments (whether or not received) which are due with respect to withdrawals before the end of the base plan year shall be considered amounts contributed by the employer to or under the plan if, as of the adjustment date, it was reasonable for the plan sponsor to anticipate that such payments would be made during the plan year.

Act Sec. 4243.(b)(1) Except as otherwise provided in this section, for purposes of this part the minimum contribution requirement for a plan year in which a plan is in reorganization is an amount equal to the excess of—

(A) the sum of—

(i) the plan's vested benefits charge for the plan year, and

(ii) the increase in normal cost for the plan year determined under the entry age normal funding method which is attributable to plan amendments adopted while the plan was in reorganization, over

(B) the amount of the overburden credit (if any) determined under section 4244 for the plan year.

(2) If the plan's current contribution base for the plan year is less than the plan's valuation contribution base for the plan year, the minimum contribution requirement for such plan year shall be equal to the product of the amount determined under paragraph (1) (after any adjustment required by this part other than this paragraph) and a fraction—

(A) the numerator of which is the plan's current contribution base for the plan year, and

(B) the denominator of which is the plan's valuation contribution base for the plan year.

(3)(A) If the vested benefits charge for a plan year of a plan in reorganization is less than the plan's cash-flow amount for the plan year, the plan's minimum contribution requirement for the plan year is the amount determined under paragraph (1) (determined before the application of paragraph (2)) after substituting the term "cash-flow amount" for the term "vested benefits charge" in paragraph (1)(A).

(B) For purposes of subparagraph (A), a plan's cash-flow amount for a plan year is an amount equal to—

(i) the amount of the benefits payable under the plan for the base plan year, plus the amount of the plan's administrative expenses for the base plan year, reduced by

(ii) the value of the available plan assets for the base plan year determined under regulations prescribed by the Secretary of the Treasury, adjusted in a manner consistent with section 4241(b)(4).

Act Sec. 4243.(c)(1) For purposes of this part, a plan's current contribution base for a plan year is the number of contribution base units with respect to which contributions are required to be made under the plan for that plan year, determined in accordance with regulations prescribed by the Secretary of the Treasury.

(2)(A) Except as provided in subparagraph (B), for purposes of this part a plan's valuation contribution base is the number of contribution base units for which contributions were received for the base plan year—

(i) adjusted to reflect declines in the contribution base which have occurred (or could reasonably be anticipated) as of the adjustment date for the plan year referred to in paragraph (1),

(ii) adjusted upward (in accordance with regulations prescribed by the Secretary of the Treasury) for any contribution base reduction in the base plan year caused by a strike or lockout or by unusual events, such as fire, earthquake, or severe weather conditions, and

(iii) adjusted (in accordance with regulations prescribed by the Secretary of the Treasury) for reductions in the contribution base resulting from transfers of liabilities.

(B) For any plan year—

(i) in which the plan is insolvent (within the meaning of section 4245(b)(1)), and

(ii) beginning with the first plan year beginning after the expiration of all relevant collective bargaining agreements which were in effect in the plan year in which the plan became insolvent,

the plan's valuation contribution base is the greater of the number of contribution base units for which contributions were received for the first or second plan year preceding the first plan year in which the plan is insolvent, adjusted as provided in clause (ii) or (iii) of subparagraph (A).

Act Sec. 4243.(d)(1) Under regulations prescribed by the Secretary of the Treasury, the minimum contribution requirement applicable to any plan for any plan year which is determined under subsection (b) (without regard to subsection (b)(2)) shall not exceed an amount which is equal to the sum of—

(A) the greater of—

(i) the funding standard requirement for such plan year, or

(ii) 107 percent of—

(I) if the plan was not in reorganization in the preceding plan year, the funding standard requirement for such preceding plan year, or

(II) if the plan was in reorganization in the preceding plan year, the sum of the amount determined under this subparagraph for the preceding plan year and the amount (if any) determined under subparagraph (B) for the preceding plan year, plus

(B) if for the plan year a change in benefits is first required to be considered in computing the charges under section 412(b)(2)(A) or (B) of the Internal Revenue Code of 1986, the sum of—

(i) the increase in normal cost for a plan year determined under the entry age normal funding method due to increases in benefits described in section 4241(b)(4)(A)(ii) (determined without regard to section 4241(b)(4)(B)(i)), and

(ii) the amount necessary to amortize in equal annual installments the increase in the value of vested benefits under the plan due to increases in benefits described in clause (i) over—

(I) 10 years, to the extent such increase in value is attributable to persons in pay status, or

(II) 25 years, to the extent such increase in value is attributable to other participants.

(2) For purposes of paragraph (1), the funding standard requirement for any plan year is an amount equal to the net charge to the funding standard account for such plan year (as defined in section 4241(b)(2)).

(3)(A) In the case of a plan described in section 4216(b), if a plan amendment which increases benefits is adopted after January 1, 1980—

(i) paragraph (1) shall apply only if the plan is a plan described in subparagraph (B), and

(ii) the amount under paragraph (1) shall be determined without regard to paragraph (1)(B).

(B) A plan is described in this subparagraph if—

(i) the rate of employer contributions under the plan for the first plan year beginning on or after the date on which an amendment increasing benefits is adopted, multiplied by the valuation contribution base for that plan year, equals or exceeds the sum of—

(I) the amount that would be necessary to amortize fully, in equal annual installments, by July 1, 1986, the unfunded vested benefits attributable to plan provisions in effect on July 1, 1977 (determined as of the last day of the base plan year); and

(II) the amount that would be necessary to amortize fully, in equal annual installments, over the period described in subparagraph (C), beginning with the first day of the first plan year beginning on or after the date on which the amendment is adopted, the unfunded vested benefits (determined as of the last day of the base plan year) attributable to each plan amendment after July 1, 1977; and

(ii) the rate of employer contributions for each subsequent plan year is not less than the lesser of—

(I) the rate which when multiplied by the valuation contribution base for that subsequent plan year produces the annual amount that would be necessary to complete the amortization schedule described in clause (i), or

(II) the rate for the plan year immediately preceding such subsequent plan year, plus 5 percent of such rate.

(C) The period determined under this subparagraph is the lesser of—

(i) 12 years, or

(ii) a period equal in length to the average of the remaining expected lives of all persons receiving benefits under the plan.

(4) Paragraph (1) shall not apply with respect to a plan, other than a plan described in paragraph (3), for the period of consecutive plan years in each of which the plan is in reorganization, beginning with a plan year in which occurs the earlier of the date of the adoption or the effective date of any amendment of the plan which increases benefits with respect to service performed before the plan year in which the adoption of the amendment occurred.

Act Sec. 4243. (e) In determining the minimum contribution requirement with respect to a plan for a plan year under subsection (b), the vested benefits charge may be adjusted to reflect a plan amendment reducing benefits under section 412(c)(8) of the Internal Revenue Code of 1986.

Act Sec. 4243. (f)(1) The Secretary of the Treasury may waive any accumulated funding deficiency under this section in accordance with the provisions of section 303(a).

(2) Any waiver under paragraph (1) shall not be treated as a waived funding deficiency (within the meaning of section 303(c)).

Act Sec. 4243. (g) For purposes of making any determination under this part, the requirements of section 302(c)(3) shall apply.

Amendments

P.L. 101-239, § 7891(a)(1):

Titles I, III, and IV of ERISA (other than sections 3(37)(E), 301(a)(7), and 308, the last sentence of section 408(d), and sections 414(c), 4001(a)(3)(ii), and 4303) are each amended by striking "Internal Revenue Code of 1954" each place it appears and inserting "Internal Revenue Code of 1986", effective October 22, 1986.

P.L. 96-364, § 104(2):

Added Sec. 4243 effective on or after the earlier of the date on which the last collective bargaining agreement providing contributions under the plan, which was in effect on September 26, 1980, expires, without regard to extensions agreed to on or after September 26, 1980 or September 26, 1983 under ERISA Sec. 4402.

[¶ 15,710]
OVERBURDEN CREDIT AGAINST MINIMUM CONTRIBUTION REQUIREMENT

Act Sec. 4244. (a) For purposes of determining the minimum contribution requirement under section 4243 (before the application of section 4243(b)(2) or (d)) the plan sponsor of a plan which is overburdened for the plan year shall apply an overburden credit against the plan's minimum contribution requirement for the plan year (determined without regard to section 4243(b)(2) or (d) and without regard to this section).

Act Sec. 4244. (b) A plan is overburdened for a plan year if—

(1) the average number of pay status participants under the plan in the base plan year exceeds the average of the number of active participants in the base plan year and the 2 plan years preceding the base plan year, and

(2) the rate of employer contributions under the plan equals or exceeds the greater of—

(A) such rate for the preceding plan year, or

(B) such rate for the plan year preceding the first year in which the plan is in reorganization.

Act Sec. 4244. (c) The amount of the overburden credit for a plan year is the product of—

(1) one-half of the average guaranteed benefit paid for the base plan year, and

(2) the overburden factor for the plan year.

The amount of the overburden credit for a plan year shall not exceed the amount of the minimum contribution requirement for such year (determined without regard to this section).

Act Sec. 4244. (d) For purposes of this section, the overburden factor of a plan for the plan year is an amount equal to—

(1) the average number of pay status participants for the base plan year, reduced by

(2) the average of the number of active participants for the base plan year and for each of the 2 plan years preceding the base plan year.

Act Sec. 4244. (e) For purposes of this section—

(1) The term "pay status participant" means, with respect to a plan, a participant receiving retirement benefits under the plan.

(2) The number of active participants for a plan year shall be the sum of—

(A) the number of active employees who are participants in the plan and on whose behalf contributions are required to be made during the plan year;

(B) the number of active employees who are not participants in the plan but who are in an employment unit covered by a collective bargaining agreement which requires the employees' employer to contribute to the plan, unless service in such employment unit was never covered under the plan or a predecessor thereof, and

(C) the total number of active employees attributed to employers who made payments to the plan for the plan year of withdrawal liability pursuant to part 1, determined by dividing—

(i) the total amount of such payments, by

(ii) the amount equal to the total contributions received by the plan during the plan year divided by the average number of active employees who were participants in the plan during the plan year.

The Secretary of the Treasury shall by regulation provide alternative methods of determining active participants where (by reason of irregular employment, contributions on a unit basis, or otherwise) this paragraph does not yield a representative basis for determining the credit.

(3) The term "average number" means, with respect to pay status participants for a plan year, a number equal to one-half the sum of—

(A) the number with respect to the plan as of the beginning of the plan year, and

(B) the number with respect to the plan as of the end of the plan year.

(4) The average guaranteed benefit paid is 12 times the average monthly pension payment guaranteed under section 4022A(c)(1) determined under the provisions of the plan in effect at the beginning of the first plan year in which the plan is in reorganization and without regard to section 4022A(c)(2).

(5) The first year in which the plan is in reorganization is the first of a period of 1 or more consecutive plan years in which the plan has been in reorganization not taking into account any plan years the plan was in reorganization prior to any period of 3 or more consecutive plan years in which the plan was not in reorganization.

Act Sec. 4244. (f)(1) Notwithstanding any other provision of this section, a plan is not eligible for an overburden credit for a plan year if the Secretary of the Treasury finds that the plan's current contribution base for the plan year was reduced, without a corresponding reduction in the plan's unfunded vested benefits attributable to pay status participants, as a result of a change in an agreement providing for employer contributions under the plan.

¶ 15,710   Act Sec. 4243(d)(3)(B)(i)(II)

(2) For purposes of paragraph (1), a complete or partial withdrawal of an employer (within the meaning of part 1) does not impair a plan's eligibility for an overburden credit, unless the Secretary of the Treasury finds that a contribution base reduction described in paragraph (1) resulted from a transfer of liabilities to another plan in connection with the withdrawal.

Act Sec. 4244. (g) Notwithstanding any other provision of this section, if 2 or more multiemployer plans merge, the amount of the overburden credit which may be applied under this section with respect to the plan resulting from the merger for any of the 3 plan years ending after the effective date of the merger shall not exceed the sum of the used overburden credit for each of the merging plans for its last plan year ending before the effective date of the merger. For purposes of the preceding sentence, the used overburden credit is that portion of the credit which does not exceed the excess of the minimum contribution requirement (determined without regard to any overburden requirement under this section) over the employer contributions required under the plan.

Amendment

P.L. 96-364, § 104(2):

Added Sec. 4244 effective on or after the earlier of the date on which the last collective bargaining agreement providing contributions under the plan, which was in effect on September 26, 1980, expires, without regard to extensions agreed to on or after September 26, 1980 or September 26, 1983 under ERISA Sec. 4402.

[¶ 15,712]
ADJUSTMENTS IN ACCRUED BENEFITS

Act Sec. 4244A. (a)(1) Notwithstanding sections 203 and 204, a multiemployer plan in reorganization may be amended in accordance with this section, to reduce or eliminate accrued benefits attributable to employer contributions which, under section 4022A(b), are not eligible for the corporation's guarantee. The preceding sentence shall only apply to accrued benefits under plan amendments (or plans) adopted after March 26, 1980, or under collective bargaining agreements entered into after March 26, 1980.

(2) In determining the minimum contribution requirement with respect to a plan for a plan year under section 4243(b), the vested benefits charge may be adjusted to reflect a plan amendment reducing benefits under this section or section 412(c)(8) of the Internal Revenue Code of 1986, but only if the amendment is adopted and effective no later than 2 ½ months after the end of the plan year, or within such extended period as the Secretary of the Treasury may prescribe by regulation under section 412(c)(10) of such Code.

Act Sec. 4244A. (b)(1) Accrued benefits may not be reduced under this section unless—

(A) notice has been given, at least 6 months before the first day of the plan year in which the amendment reducing benefits is adopted, to—

(i) plan participants and beneficiaries,

(ii) each employer who has an obligation to contribute (within the meaning of section 4212(a)) under the plan, and

(iii) each employee organization which, for purposes of collective bargaining, represents plan participants employed by such an employer,

that the plan is in reorganization and that, if contributions under the plan are not increased, accrued benefits under the plan will be reduced or an excise tax will be imposed on employers;

(B) in accordance with regulations prescribed by the Secretary of the Treasury—

(i) any category of accrued benefits is not reduced with respect to inactive participants to a greater extent proportionally than such category of accrued benefits is reduced with respect to active participants,

(ii) benefits attributable to employer contributions other than accrued benefits and the rate of future benefit accruals are reduced at least to an extent equal to the reduction in accrued benefits of inactive participants, and

(iii) in any case in which the accrued benefit of a participant or beneficiary is reduced by changing the benefit form or the requirements which the participant or beneficiary must satisfy to be entitled to the benefit, such reduction is not applicable to—

(I) any participant or beneficiary in pay status on the effective date of the amendment, or the beneficiary of such a participant, or

(II) any participant who has attained normal retirement age, or who is within 5 years of attaining normal retirement age, on the effective date of the amendment, or the beneficiary of any such participant; and

(C) the rate of employer contributions for the plan year in which the amendment becomes effective and for all succeeding plan years in which the plan is in reorganization equals or exceeds the greater of—

(i) the rate of employer contributions, calculated without regard to the amendment, for the plan year in which the amendment becomes effective, or

(ii) the rate of employer contributions for the plan year preceding the plan year in which the amendment becomes effective.

(2) The plan sponsors shall include in any notice required to be sent to plan participants and beneficiaries under paragraph (1) information as to the rights and remedies of plan participants and beneficiaries as well as how to contact the Department of Labor for further information and assistance where appropriate.

Act Sec. 4244A. (c) A plan may not recoup a benefit payment which is in excess of the amount payable under the plan because of an amendment retroactively reducing accrued benefits under this section.

Act Sec. 4244A. (d)(1)(A) A plan which has been amended to reduce accrued benefits under this section may be amended to increase or restore accrued benefits, or the rate of future benefit accruals, only if the plan is amended to restore levels of previously reduced accrued benefits of inactive participants and of participants who are within 5 years of attaining normal retirement age to at least the same extent as any such increase in accrued benefits or in the rate of future benefit accruals.

(B) For purposes of this subsection, in the case of a plan which has been amended under this section to reduce accrued benefits—

(i) an increase in a benefit, or in the rate of future benefit accruals, shall be considered a benefit increase to the extent that the benefit, or the accrual rate, is thereby increased above the highest benefit level, or accrual rate, which was in effect under the terms of the plan before the effective date of the amendment reducing accrued benefits, and

(ii) an increase in a benefit, or in the rate of future benefit accruals, shall be considered a benefit restoration to the extent that the benefit, or the accrual rate, is not thereby increased above the highest benefit level, or accrual rate, which was in effect under the terms of the plan immediately before the effective date of the amendment reducing accrued benefits.

(2) If a plan is amended to partially restore previously reduced accrued benefit levels, or the rate of future benefit accruals, the benefits of inactive participants shall be restored in at least the same proportions as other accrued benefits which are restored.

(3) No benefit increase under a plan may take effect in a plan year in which an amendment reducing accrued benefits under the plan, in accordance with this section, is adopted or first becomes effective.

(4) A plan is not required to make retroactive benefit payments with respect to that portion of an accrued benefit which was reduced and subsequently restored under this section.

Act Sec. 4244A. (e) For purposes of this section, "inactive participant" means a person not in covered service under the plan who is in pay status under the plan or who has a nonforfeitable benefit under the plan.

Act Sec. 4244A. (f) The Secretary of the Treasury may prescribe rules under which, notwithstanding any other provision of this section, accrued benefit reductions or benefit increases for different participant groups may be varied equitably to reflect variations in contribution rates and other relevant factors reflecting differences in negotiated levels of financial support for plan benefit obligations.

Amendments

P.L. 101-239, §7891(a)(1):

Titles I, III, and IV of ERISA (other than sections 3(37)(E), 301(a)(7), and 308, the last sentence of section 408(d), and sections 414(c), 4001(a)(3)(ii), and 4303) are each amended by striking "Internal Revenue Code of 1954" each place it appears and inserting "Internal Revenue Code of 1986", effective October 22, 1976.

P.L. 96-364, §104(2):

Added Sec. 4244A effective on or after the earlier of the date on which the last collective bargaining agreement providing contributions under the plan, which was in effect on September 26, 1980, expires, without regard to extensions agreed to on or after September 26, 1980 or September 26, 1983 under ERISA Sec. 4402.

[¶ 15,713]
INSOLVENT PLANS

Act Sec. 4245. (a) Notwithstanding sections 203 and 204, in any case in which benefit payments under an insolvent multiemployer plan exceed the resource benefit level, any such payments of benefits which are not basic benefits shall be suspended, in accordance with this section, to the extent necessary to reduce the sum of such payments and the payments of such basic benefits to the greater of the resource benefit level or the level of basic benefits, unless an alternative procedure is prescribed by the corporation under section 4022A(g)(5).

Act Sec. 4245. (b) For purposes of this section, for a plan year—

(1) a multiemployer plan is insolvent if the plan's available resources are not sufficient to pay benefits under the plan when due for the plan year, or if the plan is determined to be insolvent under subsection (d);

(2) "resource benefit level" means the level of monthly benefits determined under subsections (c)(1) and (3) and (d)(3) to be the highest level which can be paid out of the plan's available resources;

(3) "available resources" means the plan's cash, marketable assets, contributions, withdrawal liability payments, and earnings, less reasonable administrative expenses and amounts owed for such plan year to the corporation under section 4261(b)(2); and

(4) "insolvency year" means a plan year in which a plan is insolvent.

Act Sec. 4245. (c)(1) The plan sponsor of a plan in reorganization shall determine in writing the plan's resource benefit level for each insolvency year, based on the plan sponsor's reasonable projection of the plan's available resources and the benefits payable under the plan.

(2) The suspension of benefit payments under this section shall, in accordance with regulations prescribed by the Secretary of the Treasury, apply in substantially uniform proportions to the benefits of all persons in pay status (within the meaning of section 4241(b)(6)) under the plan, except that the Secretary of the Treasury may prescribe rules under which benefit suspensions for different participant groups may be varied equitably to reflect variations in contribution rates and other relevant factors including differences in negotiated levels of financial support for plan benefit obligations.

(3) Notwithstanding paragraph (2), if a plan sponsor determines in writing a resource benefit level for a plan year which is below the level of basic benefits, the payment of all benefits other than basic benefits must be suspended for that plan year.

(4)(A) If, by the end of an insolvency year, the plan sponsor determines in writing that the plan's available resources in that insolvency year could have supported benefit payments above the resource benefit level for that insolvency year, the plan sponsor shall distribute the excess resources to the participants and beneficiaries who received benefit payments from the plan in that insolvency year, in accordance with regulations prescribed by the Secretary of the Treasury.

(B) For purposes of this paragraph, the term "excess resources" means available resources above the amount necessary to support the resource benefit level, but no greater than the amount necessary to pay benefits for the plan year at the benefit levels under the plan.

(5) If, by the end of an insolvency year, any benefit has not been paid at the resource benefit level, amounts up to the resource benefit level which were unpaid shall be distributed to the participants and beneficiaries, in accordance with regulations prescribed by the Secretary of the Treasury, to the extent possible taking into account the plan's total available resources in that insolvency year.

(6) Except as provided in paragraph (4) or (5), a plan is not required to make retroactive benefit payments with respect to that portion of a benefit which was suspended under this section.

Act Sec. 4245. (d)(1) As of the end of the first plan year in which a plan is in reorganization, and at least every 3 plan years thereafter (unless the plan is no longer in reorganization), the plan sponsor shall compare the value of plan assets (determined in accordance with section 4243(b)(3)(B)(ii)) for that plan year with the total amount of benefit payments made under the plan for that plan year. Unless the plan sponsor determines that the value of plan assets exceeds 3 times the total amount of benefit payments, the plan sponsor shall determine whether the plan will be insolvent in any of the next 3 plan years.

(2) If, at any time, the plan sponsor of a plan in reorganization reasonably determines, taking into account the plan's recent and anticipated financial experience, that the plan's available resources are not sufficient to pay benefits under the plan when due for the next plan year, the plan sponsor shall make such determination available to interested parties.

(3) The plan sponsor of a plan in reorganization shall determine in writing for each insolvency year the resource benefit level and the level of basic benefits no later than 3 months before the insolvency year.

Act Sec. 4245. (e)(1) If the plan sponsor of a plan in reorganization determines under subsection (d)(1) or (2) that the plan may become insolvent (within the meaning of subsection (b)(1)), the plan sponsor shall—

(A) notify the Secretary of the Treasury, the corporation, the parties described in section 4242(a)(2), and the plan participants and beneficiaries of that determination, and

(B) inform the parties described in section 4242(a)(2) and the plan participants and beneficiaries that if insolvency occurs certain benefit payments will be suspended, but that basic benefits will continue to be paid.

(2) No later than 2 months before the first day of each insolvency year, the plan sponsor of a plan in reorganization shall notify the Secretary of the Treasury, the corporation, and the parties described in paragraph (1)(B) of the resource benefit level determined in writing for that insolvency year.

(3) In any case in which the plan sponsor anticipates that the resource benefit level for an insolvency year may not exceed the level of basic benefits, the plan sponsor shall notify the corporation.

(4) Notice required by this subsection shall be given in accordance with regulations prescribed by the corporation, except that notice to the Secretary of the Treasury shall be given in accordance with regulations prescribed by the Secretary of the Treasury.

(5) The corporation may prescribe a time other than the time prescribed by this section for the making of a determination or the filing of a notice under this section.

Act Sec. 4245. (f)(1) If the plan sponsor of an insolvent plan, for which the resource benefit level is above the level of basic benefits, anticipates that, for any month in an insolvency year, the plan will not have funds sufficient to pay basic benefits, the plan sponsor may apply for financial assistance from the corporation under section 4261.

(2) A plan sponsor who has determined a resource benefit level for an insolvency year which is below the level of basic benefits shall apply for financial assistance from the corporation under section 4261.

Amendment

P.L. 96-364, §104(2):

Added Sec. 4245, effective on or after the earlier of the date on which the last collective bargaining agreement provided contributions under the plan, which was in effect on September 26, 1980, expires, without regard to extensions agreed to on or after September 26, 1980 or September 26, 1983 under ERISA Sec. 4402.

Regulations

The following regulations were adopted by the Pension Benefit Guaranty Corporation on July 1, 1996 (61 FR 34002). Prior to July 1, 1996, PBGC regulations were under Chapter XXVI of Title 29 of the Code of Federal Regulations. Effective July 1, 1996, PBGC regulations were moved to Chapter XL, and were renumbered and reorganized. Reg. §§ 4245.3—4245.8 were amended October 28, 2003 (68 FR 61344).

[¶ 15,713A]

§ 4245.1 **Purpose and scope.** (a) *Purpose.* The purpose of this part is to prescribe notice requirements pertaining to insolvent multiemployer plans that are in reorganization.

(b) *Scope.* This part applies to multiemployer plans in reorganization covered by title IV of ERISA, other than plans that have terminated by mass withdrawal under section 4041A(a)(2) of ERISA.

[¶ 15,713B]

§ 4245.2 **Definitions.** The following terms are defined in § 4001.2 of this chapter: *employer, ERISA, IRS, multiemployer plan, nonforfeitable benefit, PBGC, person, plan,* and *plan year.*

In addition, for purposes of this part:

Actuarial valuation means a report submitted to the plan in connection with a valuation of plan assets and liabilities, which, in the case of a plan covered by subparts C and D of part 4281, shall be performed in accordance with subpart B of part 4281.

Available resources means, for a plan year, available resources as described in section 4245(b)(3) of ERISA.

Benefits subject to reduction means those benefits accrued under plan amendments (or plans) adopted after March 26, 1980, or under collective bargaining agreements entered into after March 26, 1980, that are not eligible for the PBGC's guarantee under section 4022A(b) of ERISA.

Financial assistance means financial assistance from the PBGC under section 4261 of ERISA.

Insolvency benefit level means the greater of the resource benefit level or the benefit level guaranteed by the PBGC for each participant and beneficiary in pay status.

Insolvency year means insolvency year as described in section 4245(b)(4) of ERISA.

Insolvent means that a plan is unable to pay benefits when due during the plan year. A plan terminated by mass withdrawal is not insolvent unless it has been amended to eliminate all benefits that are subject to reduction under section 4281(c) of ERISA, or, in the absence of an amendment, no benefits under the plan are subject to reduction under section 4281(c) of ERISA.

Reasonably expected to enter pay status means, with respect to plan participants and beneficiaries, persons (other than those in pay status) who, according to plan records, are disabled, have applied for benefits, or have reached or will reach during the applicable period the normal retirement age under the plan, and any others whom it is reasonable for the plan sponsor to expect to enter pay status during the applicable period.

Reorganization means reorganization under section 4241(a) of ERISA.

Resource benefit level means resource benefit level as described in section 4245(b)(2) of ERISA.

[¶ 15,713C]

§ 4245.3 **Notice of insolvency.** (a) *Requirement of notice.* A plan sponsor of a multiemployer plan in reorganization that determines under section 4245(b)(1), (d)(1) or (d)(2) of ERISA that the plan's available resources are or may be insufficient to pay benefits when due for a plan year shall so notify the PBGC and the interested parties, as defined in paragraph (e) of this section. A single notice may cover more than one plan year. The notices shall be delivered in the manner and within the time prescribed in this section and shall contain the information described in § 4245.4.

[Amended 10/28/2003 by 68 FR 61344]

(b) *When delivered.* A plan sponsor shall mail or otherwise deliver the notices of insolvency no later than 30 days after it determines that the plan is or may become insolvent, as described in paragraph (a) of this section. However, the notice to participants and beneficiaries in pay status may be delivered concurrently with the first benefit payment made more than 30 days after the determination of insolvency.

(c) *Delivery to PBGC.* (1) *Method of filing.* The PBGC applies the rules in subpart A of part 4000 of this chapter to determine permissible methods of filing the notice of insolvency with the PBGC under this part.

(2) *Filing date.* The PBGC applies the rules in subpart C of part 4000 of this chapter to determine the date that a notice of insolvency under this part was filed with the PBGC.

[Amended 10/28/2003 by 68 FR 61344]

(d) *Delivery to interested parties.* (1) *Method of issuance.* The PBGC applies the rules in subpart B of part 4000 of this chapter to determine permissible methods of issuance of the notice of insolvency to interested parties. In addition to the methods permitted under subpart B of part 4000, the plan sponsor may notify interested parties, other than participants and beneficiaries who are in pay status when the notice is required to be delivered, by posting the notice at participants' work sites or publishing the notice in a union newsletter or in a newspaper of general circulation in the area or areas where participants reside. Notice to a participant shall be deemed notice to that participant's beneficiary or beneficiaries.

(2) *Issuance date.* The PBGC applies the rules in subpart C of part 4000 of this chapter to determine the date that the notice of insolvency was issued.

[Amended 10/28/2003 by 68 FR 61344]

(e) *Interested parties.* For purposes of this part, the term "interested parties" means—

(1) Employers required to contribute to the plan;

(2) Employee organizations that, for collective bargaining purposes, represent plan participants employed by such employers; and

(3) Plan participants and beneficiaries.

[¶ 15,713D]

§ 4245.4 **Contents of notice of insolvency.** (a) *Notice to the PBGC.* A notice of insolvency required to be filed with the PBGC pursuant to § 4245.3 shall contain the information set forth below:

(1) The name of the plan.

(2) The name, address and telephone number of the plan sponsor and of the plan sponsor's duly authorized representative, if any.

(3) The nine-digit Employer Identification Number (EIN) assigned by the IRS to the plan sponsor and the three-digit Plan Identification Number (PIN) assigned by the plan sponsor to the plan, and, if different, the EIN or PIN last filed with the PBGC. If no EIN or PIN has been assigned, the notice shall so indicate.

(4) The IRS key district that has jurisdiction over determination letters with respect to the plan.

(5) The case number assigned to the plan by the PBGC. If the plan has no case number, the notice shall state whether the plan has previously filed a notice of insolvency with the PBGC and, if so, the date on which the notice was filed.

(6) The plan year or years for which the plan sponsor has determined that the plan is or may become insolvent.

(7) A copy of the plan document, including the last restatement of the plan and all subsequent amendments in effect, or to become effective, during the insolvency year or years. However, if a copy of the plan document was submitted to the PBGC with a previous notice of insolvency or notice of insolvency benefit level, only subsequent plan amendments need be submitted, and the notice shall state when the copy of the plan document was filed.

(8) A copy of the most recent actuarial valuation for the plan and a copy of the most recent Schedule B (Form 5500) filed for the plan, if the Schedule B contains more recent information than the actuarial valuation. If the actuarial valuation or Schedule B was previ-

ously submitted to the PBGC, it may be omitted, and the notice shall state the date on which the document was filed and that the information is still accurate and complete.

(9) The estimated amount of annual benefit payments under the plan (determined without regard to the insolvency) for each insolvency year.

(10) The estimated amount of the plan's available resources for each insolvency year.

(11) A certification, signed by the plan sponsor (or a duly authorized representative), that notices of insolvency have been given to all interested parties in accordance with the requirements of this part.

(b) *Notices to interested parties.* A notice of insolvency required under § 4245.3 to be given to interested parties, as defined in § 4245.3(e), shall contain the information set forth below:

(1) The name of the plan.

(2) The plan year or years for which the plan sponsor has determined that the plan is or may become insolvent.

(3) The estimated amount of annual benefit payment under the plan (determined without regard to the insolvency) for each insolvency year.

(4) The estimated amount of the plan's available resources for each insolvency year.

(5) A statement that, during the insolvency year, benefits above the amount that can be paid from available resources or the level guaranteed by the PBGC, whichever is greater, will be suspended, with a brief explanation of which benefits are guaranteed by the PBGC. The following statement may be included as an explanation of PBGC-guaranteed benefits:

Should the plan become insolvent, each participant's benefit guaranteed by the Pension Benefit Guaranty Corporation (PBGC) is determined as follows. Each participant's nonforfeitable monthly benefit payable under the plan at retirement is computed. This benefit is then divided by the participant's years of credited service under the plan. Of the resulting figure (the accrual rate), the first $5 is guaranteed at 100%. Any additional amount (up to $15) is either 75% or 65% guaranteed, depending on the past funding practices of the plan. Any remaining amount that exceeds $20 is not guaranteed. The PBGC guarantees the payment of a monthly benefit equal to this adjusted accrual rate times years of credited service. The PBGC does not guarantee benefits or benefit increases that have been in effect for fewer than 60 months before the plan becomes insolvent or is amended to reduce accrued benefits.

(6) The name, address, and telephone number of the plan administrator or other person designated by the plan sponsor to answer inquiries concerning benefits during the plan's insolvency.

[Amended 10/28/2003 by 68 FR 61344]

[¶ 15,713E]

§ 4245.5 **Notice of insolvency benefit level.** (a) *Requirement of notice.* Except as provided in paragraph (b) of this section, for each insolvency year the plan sponsor shall notify the PBGC and the interested parties, as defined in § 4245.3(e), of the level of benefits expected to be paid during the year (the "insolvency benefit level"). These notices shall be delivered in the manner and within the time prescribed in this section and shall contain the information described in § 4245.6.

[Amended 10/28/2003 by 68 FR 61344]

(b) *Waiver of notice to certain interested parties.* The notice of insolvency benefit level required under this section need not be given to interested parties, other than participants and beneficiaries who are in pay status or are reasonably expected to enter pay status during the insolvency year, for an insolvency year immediately following the plan year in which a notice of insolvency was required to be delivered pursuant to § 4245.3, provided that the notice of insolvency was in fact delivered.

(c) *When delivered.* The plan sponsor shall mail or otherwise deliver the required notices of insolvency benefit level no later than 60 days before the beginning of the insolvency year, except that if the determination of insolvency is made fewer than 120 days before the

beginning of the insolvency year, the notices shall be delivered within 60 days after the date of the plan sponsor's determination.

(d) *Delivery to PBGC.* (1) *Method of filing.* The PBGC applies the rules in subpart A of part 4000 of this chapter to determine permissible methods of filing a notice of insolvency benefit level with the PBGC under this part.

(2) *Filing date.* The PBGC applies the rules in subpart C of part 4000 of this chapter to determine the date that a notice of insolvency benefit level under this part was filed with the PBGC.

[Amended 10/28/2003 by 68 FR 61344]

(e) *Delivery to interested parties.* (1) *Method of issuance.* The PBGC applies the rules in subpart B of part 4000 of this chapter to determine permissible methods of issuance of the notice of insolvency benefit levels to interested parties. In addition to the methods permitted under subpart B of part 4000, the plan sponsor may notify interested parties, other than participants and beneficiaries who are in pay status or reasonably expected to enter pay status during the insolvency year for which the notice is given, by posting the notice at participants' work sites or publishing the notice in a union newsletter or in a newspaper of general circulation in the area or areas where participants reside. Notice to a participant shall be deemed notice to that participant's beneficiary or beneficiaries.

(2) *Issuance date.* The PBGC applies the rules in subpart C of part 4000 of this chapter to determine the date that the notice of insolvency benefit levels was issued.

[Amended 10/28/2003 by 68 FR 61344]

[¶ 15,713F]

§ 4245.6 **Contents of notice of insolvency benefit level.** (a) *Notice to the PBGC.* A notice of insolvency benefit level required to be filed with the PBGC pursuant to § 4245.5(a) shall contain the information set forth below, except as provided in the next sentence. The information required in paragraphs (a)(7) to (a)(10) need be submitted only if it is different from the information submitted to the PBGC with the notice of insolvency filed for that insolvency year (see § 4245.4 (a)(7) to (a)(10)) or the notice of insolvency benefit level filed for a prior year. When any information is omitted under this exception, the notice shall so state and indicate when the notice of insolvency or prior notice of insolvency benefit level was filed.

(1) The name of the plan.

(2) The name, address and telephone number of the plan sponsor and of the plan sponsor's authorized representative, if any.

(3) The nine-digit Employer Identification Number (EIN) assigned by the IRS to the plan sponsor and the three-digit Plan Identification Number (PIN) assigned by the plan sponsor to the plan, and, if different, the EIN or PIN last filed with the PBGC. If no EIN or PIN has been assigned, the notice shall so indicate.

(4) The IRS key district that has jurisdiction over determination letters with respect to the plan.

(5) The case number assigned to the plan by the PBGC.

(6) The plan year for which the notice is filed.

(7) A copy of the plan document, including any amendments, in effect during the insolvency year.

(8) A copy of the most recent actuarial valuation for the plan and a copy of the most recent Schedule B (Form 5500) filed for the plan, if the Schedule B contains more recent information than the actuarial valuation.

(9) The estimated amount of annual benefit payments under the plan (determined without regard to the insolvency) for the insolvency year.

(10) The estimated amount of the plan's available resources for the insolvency year.

(11) The estimated amount of the annual benefit payments guaranteed by the PBGC for the insolvency year.

(12) The amount of financial assistance, if any, requested from the PBGC.

(13) A certification, signed by the plan sponsor (or a duly authorized representative), that notices of insolvency benefit level have

been given to all interested parties in accordance with the requirements of this part.

When financial assistance is requested, the PBGC may require the plan sponsor to submit additional information necessary to process the request.

(b) *Notices to interested parties other than participants in or entering pay status.* A notice of insolvency benefit level required by §4245.5(a) to be delivered to interested parties, as defined in §4245.3(e), other than a notice to a participant or beneficiary who is in pay status or is reasonably expected to enter pay status during the insolvency year, shall include the information set forth below:

(1) The name of the plan.

(2) The plan year for which the notice is issued.

(3) The estimated amount of annual benefit payments under the plan (determined without regard to the insolvency) for the insolvency year.

(4) The estimated amount of the plan's available resources for the insolvency year.

(5) The amount of financial assistance, if any, requested from the PBGC.

[Amended 10/28/2003 by 68 FR 61344]

(c) *Notices to participants and beneficiaries in or entering pay status.* A notice of insolvency benefit level required by §4245.5(a) to be delivered to participants and beneficiaries who are in pay status or are reasonably expected to enter pay status during the insolvency year for which the notice is given, shall include the following information:

(1) The name of the plan.

(2) The plan year for which the notice is issued.

(3) A statement of the monthly benefit expected to be paid to the participant or beneficiary during the insolvency year.

(4) A statement that in subsequent plan years, depending on the plan's available resources, this benefit level may be increased or decreased but will not fall below the level guaranteed by the PBGC, and that the participant or beneficiary will be notified in advance of the new benefit level if it is less than his full nonforfeitable benefit under the plan.

(5) The name, address, and telephone number of the plan administrator or other person designated by the plan sponsor to answer inquiries concerning benefits during the plan's insolvency.

[¶ 15,713G]

§4245.7 **PBGC address.** See Sec. 4000.4 of this chapter for information on where to file.

[Amended 10/28/2003 by 68 FR 61344]

(Approved by the Office of Management and Budget under control number 1212-0033)

[¶ 15,713H]

§4245.8 **Computation of time.** The PBGC applies the rules in subpart D of part 4000 of this chapter to compute any time period for filing or issuance under this part.

[Added 10/28/2003 by 68 FR 61344]

Part 4—Financial Assistance

[¶ 15,714]
FINANCIAL ASSISTANCE

Act Sec. 4261.(a) If, upon receipt of an application for financial assistance under section 4245(f) or section 4281(d), the corporation verifies that the plan is or will be insolvent and unable to pay basic benefits when due, the corporation shall provide the plan financial assistance in an amount sufficient to enable the plan to pay basic benefits under the plan.

Act Sec. 4261.(b)(1) Financial assistance shall be provided under such conditions as the corporation determines are equitable and are appropriate to prevent unreasonable loss to the corporation with respect to the plan.

(2) A plan which has received financial assistance shall repay the amount of such assistance to the corporation on reasonable terms consistent with regulations prescribed by the corporation.

Act Sec. 4261. (c) Pending determination of the amount described in subsection (a), the corporation may provide financial assistance in such amounts as it considers appropriate in order to avoid undue hardship to plan participants and beneficiaries.

Amendment

P.L. 96-364, §104(2):

Added Sec. 4261 effective September 26, 1980 under ERISA Sec. 4402.

Regulations

The following regulations were adopted by the Pension Benefit Guaranty Corporation on July 1, 1996 (61 FR 34002). Prior to July 1, 1996, PBGC regulations were under Chapter XXVI of Title 29 of the Code of Federal Regulations. Effective July 1, 1996, PBGC regulations were moved to Chapter XL, and were renumbered and reorganized.

[¶ 15,714A]

§4261.1 **Cross-reference.** See §4281.47 for procedures for applying to the PBGC for financial assistance under section 4261 of ERISA.

Part 5—Benefits After Termination

[¶ 15,715]
BENEFITS UNDER CERTAIN TERMINATED PLANS

Act Sec. 4281.(a) Notwithstanding sections 203 and 204, the plan sponsor of a terminated multiemployer plan to which section 4041A(d) applies shall amend the plan to reduce benefits, and shall suspend benefit payments, as required by this section.

Act Sec. 4281.(b)(1) The value of nonforfeitable benefits under a terminated plan referred to in subsection (a), and the value of the plan's assets, shall be determined in writing, in accordance with regulations prescribed by the corporation, as of the end of the plan year during which section 4041A(d) becomes applicable to the plan, and each plan year thereafter.

(2) For purposes of this section, plan assets include outstanding claims for withdrawal liability (within the meaning of section 4001(a)(12)).

Act Sec. 4281.(c)(1) If, according to the determination made under subsection (b), the value of nonforfeitable benefits exceeds the value of the plan's assets, the plan sponsor shall amend the plan to reduce benefits under the plan to the extent necessary to ensure that the plan's assets are sufficient, as determined and certified in accordance with regulations prescribed by the corporation, to discharge when due all of the plan's obligations with respect to nonforfeitable benefits.

(2) Any plan amendment required by this subsection shall, in accordance with regulations prescribed by the Secretary of the Treasury—

(A) reduce benefits only to the extent necessary to comply with paragraph (1);

(B) reduce accrued benefits only to the extent that those benefits are not eligible for the corporation's guarantee under section 4022A(b);

(C) comply with the rules for and limitations on benefit reductions under a plan in reorganization, as prescribed in section 4244A, except to the extent that the corporation prescribes other rules and limitations in regulations under this section; and

(D) take effect no later than 6 months after the end of the plan year for which it is determined that the value of nonforfeitable benefits exceeds the value of the plan's assets.

Act Sec. 4281. (d)(1) In any case in which benefit payments under a plan which is insolvent under paragraph (2)(A) exceed the resource benefit level, any such payments which are not basic benefits shall be suspended, in accordance with this subsection, to the extent necessary to reduce the sum of such payments and such basic benefits to the greater of the resource benefit level or the level of basic benefits, unless an alternative procedure is prescribed by the corporation in connection with a supplemental guarantee program established under section 4022A(g)(2).

(2) For purposes of this subsection, for a plan year—

(A) a plan is insolvent if—

(i) the plan has been amended to reduce benefits to the extent permitted by subsection (c), and

(ii) the plan's available resources are not sufficient to pay benefits under the plan when due for the plan year; and

(B) "resource benefit level" and "available resources" have the meanings set forth in paragraphs (2) and (3), respectively, of section 4245(b).

(3) The plan sponsor of a plan which is insolvent (within the meaning of paragraph (2)(A)) shall have the powers and duties of the plan sponsor of a plan in reorganization which is insolvent (within the meaning of section 4245(b)(1)), except that regulations governing the plan sponsor's exercise of those powers and duties under this section shall be prescribed by the corporation, and the corporation shall prescribe by regulation notice requirements which assure that plan participants and beneficiaries receive adequate notice of benefit suspensions.

(4) A plan is not required to make retroactive benefit payments with respect to that portion of a benefit which was suspended under this subsection, except that the provisions of section 4245(c)(4) and (5) shall apply in the case of plans which are insolvent under paragraph (2)(A), in connection with the plan year during which such section 4041A(d) first became applicable to the plan and every year thereafter, in the same manner and to the same extent as such provisions apply to insolvent plans in reorganization under section 4245, in connection with insolvency years under such section 4245.

Amendment

P.L. 96-364, §104(2):

Added Sec. 4281, effective September 26, 1980 under ERISA Sec. 4402.

Regulations

The following regulations were adopted by the Pension Benefit Guaranty Corporation on July 1, 1996 (61 FR 34002). Prior to July 1, 1996, PBGC regulations were under Chapter XXVI of Title 29 of the Code of Federal Regulations. Effective July 1, 1996, PBGC regulations were moved to Chapter XL, and were renumbered and reorganized. Reg. §§ 4281.13 and 4281.14 were amended July 15, 1998 (63 FR 38305), effective August 17, 1998. Reg. § 4281.15 was removed and reserved July 15, 1998 (63 FR 38305), effective August 17, 1998. Reg. §4281.3, Reg. §4281.32, Reg. §4281.43, and Reg. §4281.45 were amended October 28, 2003 (68 FR 61344).

Subpart A—General Provisions

[¶ 15,715A]

§4281.1 **Purpose and scope.** (a) *General.* (1) *Purpose.* When a multiemployer plan terminates by mass withdrawal under section 4041A(a)(2) of ERISA, the plan's assets and benefits must be valued annually under section 4281(b) of ERISA, and plan benefits may have to be reduced or suspended to the extent provided in section 4281(c) or (d). This part implements the provisions of section 4281 and provides rules for applying for financial assistance from the PBGC under section 4261 of ERISA. The plan valuation rules in this part also apply to the determination of reallocation liability under section 4219(c)(1)(D) of ERISA and subpart B of part 4219 of this chapter for multiemployer plans that undergo mass withdrawal (with or without termination).

(2) *Scope.* This part applies to multiemployer plans covered by Title IV of ERISA that have terminated by mass withdrawal under section 4041A(a)(2) of ERISA (including plans created by partition pursuant to section 4233 of ERISA). Subpart B of this part also applies to covered multiemployer plans that have undergone mass withdrawal without terminating.

(b) *Subpart B.* Subpart B establishes rules for determining the value of multiemployer plan benefits and assets, including outstanding claims for withdrawal liability, for plans required to perform annual valuations under section 4281(b) of ERISA or allocate unfunded vested benefits under section 4219(c)(1)(D) of ERISA.

(c) *Subpart C.* Subpart C sets forth procedures under which the plan sponsor of a terminated plan shall amend the plan to reduce benefits subject to reduction in accordance with section 4281(c) of ERISA and §4041A.24(b) of this chapter. Subpart C applies to a plan for which the annual valuation required by §4041A.24(a) indicates that the value of nonforfeitable benefits under the plan exceeds the value of the plan's assets (including claims for withdrawal liability) if, at the end of the plan year for which that valuation was done, the plan provided any benefits subject to reduction. Benefit reductions required to be made under subpart C shall not apply to accrued benefits under plans or plan amendments adopted on or before March 26, 1980, or under collective bargaining agreements entered into on or before March 26, 1980.

(d) *Subpart D.* Subpart D sets forth the procedures under which the plan sponsor of an insolvent plan must suspend benefit payments and issue insolvency notices in accordance with section 4281(d) of ERISA and §4041A.25(c) and (d) of this chapter. Subpart D applies to a plan that has been amended under section 4281(c) of ERISA and subpart C of this part to eliminate all benefits subject to reduction and to a plan that provided no benefits subject to reduction as of the date on which the plan terminated.

[¶ 15,715B]

§4281.2 **Definitions.** The following terms are defined in section 4001.2 of this chapter: *annuity, employer, ERISA, fair market value, IRS, insurer, irrevocable commitment, mass withdrawal, multiemployer plan, nonforfeitable benefit, normal retirement age, PBGC, person, plan, plan administrator,* and *plan year.*

In addition, for purposes of this part:

Available resources means, for a plan year, available resources as described in section 4245(b)(3) of ERISA.

Benefits subject to reduction means those benefits accrued under plan amendments (or plans) adopted after March 26, 1980, or under collective bargaining agreements entered into after March 26, 1980, that are not eligible for the PBGC's guarantee under section 4022A(b) of ERISA.

Financial assistance means financial assistance from the PBGC under section 4261 of ERISA.

Insolvency benefit level means the greater of the resource benefit level or the benefit level guaranteed by the PBGC for each participant and beneficiary in pay status.

Insolvency year means insolvency year as described in section 4245(b)(4) of ERISA.

Insolvent means that a plan is unable to pay benefits when due during the plan year. A plan terminated by mass withdrawal is not insolvent unless it has been amended to eliminate all benefits that are subject to reduction under section 4281(c), or, in the absence of an amendment, no benefits under the plan are subject to reduction under section 4281(c) of ERISA.

Pro rata means that the required benefit reduction or payment shall be allocated among affected participants in the same proportion that each such participant's nonforfeitable benefits under the plan bear to all nonforfeitable benefits of those participants under the plan.

Reasonably expected to enter pay status means, with respect to plan participants and beneficiaries, persons (other than those in pay status) who, according to plan records, are disabled, have applied for benefits, or have reached or will reach during the applicable period the normal retirement age under the plan, and any others whom it is reasonable for the plan sponsor to expect to enter pay status during the applicable period.

Resource benefit level means resource benefit level as described in section 4245(b)(2) of ERISA.

Valuation date means the last day of the plan year in which the plan terminates and the last day of each plan year thereafter.

[¶ 15,715C]

§ 4281.3 **Filing and issuance rules**. (a) *Method of filing*. The PBGC applies the rules in subpart A of part 4000 of this chapter to determine permissible methods of filing with the PBGC under this part.

(b) *Method of issuance*. See Sec. 4281.32(c) for notices of benefit reductions, Sec. 4281.43(e) for notices of insolvency, and Sec. 4281.45(c) for notices of insolvency benefit level.

(c) *Date of filing*. The PBGC applies the rules in subpart C of part 4000 of this chapter to determine the date that a submission under this part was filed with the PBGC.

(d) *Date of issuance*. The PBGC applies the rules in subpart C of part 4000 of this chapter to determine the date that an issuance under this part was provided.

(e) *Where to file*. See Sec. 4000.4 of this chapter for information on where to file.

(f) *Computation of time*. The PBGC applies the rules in subpart D of part 4000 of this chapter to compute any time period for filing or issuance under this part.

[Amended 10/28/2003 by 68 FR 61344]

[¶ 15,715D]

§ 4281.4 **Collection of information**. The collection of information requirements contained in this part have been approved by the Office of Management and Budget under control number 1212-0032.

Subpart B—Valuation of Plan Benefits and Plan Assets

[¶ 15,715E]

§ 4281.11 **Valuation dates**. (a) *Annual valuations of mass-with-drawal-terminated plans*. The valuation dates for the annual valuation required under section 4281(b) of ERISA shall be the last day of the plan year in which the plan terminates and the last day of each plan year thereafter.

(b) *Valuations related to mass withdrawal reallocation liability*. The valuation date for determining the value of unfunded vested benefits (for purposes of allocation) under section 4219(c)(1)(D) of ERISA shall be—

(1) If the plan terminates by mass withdrawal, the last day of the plan year in which the plan terminates; or

(2) If substantially all the employers withdraw from the plan pursuant to an agreement or arrangement to withdraw from the plan, the last day of the plan year as of which substantially all employers have withdrawn from the plan pursuant to the agreement or arrangement.

[¶ 15,715F]

§ 4281.12 **Benefits to be valued**. (a) *Form of benefit*. The plan sponsor shall determine the form of each benefit to be valued, without regard to the form of benefit valued in any prior year, in accordance with the following rules:

(1) If a benefit is in pay status as of the valuation date, the plan sponsor shall value the form of benefit being paid.

(2) If a benefit is not in pay status as of the valuation date but a valid election with respect to the form of benefit has been made on or

before the valuation date, the plan sponsor shall value the form of benefit so elected.

(3) If a benefit is not in pay status as of the valuation date and no valid election with respect to the form of benefit has been made on or before the valuation date, the plan sponsor shall value the form of benefit that, under the terms of the plan or applicable law, is payable in the absence of a valid election.

(b) *Timing of benefit*. The plan sponsor shall value benefits whose starting date is subject to election—

(1) By assuming that the starting date of each benefit is the earliest date, not preceding the valuation date, that could be elected; or

(2) By using any other assumption that the plan sponsor demonstrates to the satisfaction of the PBGC is more reasonable under the circumstances.

[¶ 15,715G]

§ 4281.13 **Benefit valuation methods**. *General rule*. Except as otherwise provided in § 4281.16 (regarding plans that are closing out), the plan sponsor shall value benefits as of the valuation date by—

(a) Using the interest assumptions described in Table I of appendix B to part 4044 of this chapter;

(b) Using the mortality assumptions described in § 4281.14;

(c) Using interpolation methods, where necessary, at least as accurate as linear interpolation;

(d) Applying valuation formulas that accord with generally accepted actuarial principles and practices; and

(e) Adjusting the values to reflect the loading for expenses in accordance with appendix C to part 4044 of this chapter (substituting the term "benefits" for the term "benefit liabilities (as defined in 29 U.S.C. § 1301(a)(16))").

[¶ 15,715H]

§ 4281.14 **Mortality assumptions**. (a) *General rule*. Subject to paragraph (b) of this section (regarding certain death benefits), the plan administrator shall use the mortality factors prescribed in paragraphs (c), (d), and (e) of this section to value benefits under § 4281.13.

(b) *Certain death benefits*. If an annuity for one person is in pay status on the valuation date, and if the payment of a death benefit after the valuation date to another person, who need not be identifiable on the valuation date, depends in whole or in part on the death of the pay status annuitant, then the plan administrator shall value the death benefit using—

(1) the mortality rates that are applicable to the annuity in pay status under this section to represent the mortality of the pay status annuitant; and

(2) the mortality rates applicable to annuities not in pay status and to deferred benefits other than annuities, under paragraph (c) of this section, to represent the mortality of the death beneficiary.

(c) *Mortality rates for healthy lives*. The mortality rates applicable to annuities in pay status on the valuation date that are not being received as disability benefits, to annuities not in pay status on the valuation date, and to deferred benefits other than annuities, are,—

(1) For male participants, the rates in Table 1 of appendix A to part 4044 of this chapter, and

(2) For female participants, the rates in Table 1 of appendix A to part 4044 of this chapter, set back 6 years.

(d) *Mortality rates for disabled lives (other than Social Security disability)*. The mortality rates applicable to annuities in pay status on the valuation date that are being received as disability benefits and for which neither eligibility for, nor receipt of, Social Security disability benefits is a prerequisite, are,—

(1) For male participants, the rates in Table 1 of appendix A to part 4044 of this chapter, set forward 3 years, and

(2) For female participants, the rates in Table 1 of appendix A to part 4044 of this chapter, set back 3 years.

(e) *Mortality rates for disabled lives (Social Security disability)*. The mortality rates applicable to annuities in pay status on the valuation date that are being received as disability benefits and for which either eligibility for, or receipt of, Social Security disability benefits is a prerequisite, are the rates in Tables 2-M and 2-F of appendix A to part 4044 of this chapter.

§ 4281.15 **[Reserved.]**

§ 4281.16 **Benefit valuation methods—plans closing out**. (a) *Applicability*. For purposes of the annual valuation required by section 4281(b) of ERISA, the plan sponsor shall value the plan's benefits in accordance with paragraph (b) of this section if,—

(1) *Plans closed out before valuation*. Before the time when the valuation is performed, the plan has satisfied in full all liabilities for payment of nonforfeitable benefits, in a manner consistent with the terms of the plan and applicable law, by the purchase of one or more nonparticipating irrevocable commitments from one or more insurers, with respect to all benefits payable as annuities, and by the payment of single-sum cash distributions, with respect to benefits not payable as annuities; or

(2) *Plans to be closed out after valuation*. As of the time when the valuation is performed, the plan sponsor reasonably expects that the plan will close out before the next annual valuation date and the plan sponsor has a currently exercisable bid or bids to provide the irrevocable commitment(s) described in paragraph (a)(1) of this section and the total cost of the irrevocable commitment(s) under the bid, plus the total amount of the single-sum cash distributions described in paragraph (a)(1), does not exceed the value of the plan's assets, exclusive of outstanding claims for withdrawal liability, as determined under this subpart.

(b) *Valuation rule*. The present value of nonforfeitable benefits under this section is the total amount of single-sum cash distributions made or to be made plus the cost of the irrevocable commitment(s) purchased or to be purchased in order to satisfy in full all liabilities of the plan for nonforfeitable benefits.

§ 4281.17 **Asset valuation methods—in general**. (a) *General rule*. The plan sponsor shall value plan assets as of the valuation date, using the valuation methods prescribed by this section and § 4281.18 (regarding outstanding claims for withdrawal liability), and deducting administrative liabilities in accordance with paragraph (c) of this section.

(b) *Assets other than withdrawal liability claims*. The plan sponsor shall value any plan asset (other than an outstanding claim for withdrawal liability) by such method or methods as the plan sponsor reasonably believes most accurately determine fair market value.

(c) *Adjustment for administrative liabilities*. In determining the total value of plan assets, the plan sponsor shall subtract all plan liabilities, other than liabilities to pay benefits. For this purpose, any obligation to repay financial assistance received from the PBGC under section 4261 of ERISA is a plan liability other than a liability to pay benefits. The obligation to repay financial assistance shall be valued by determining the value of the scheduled payments in the same manner as prescribed in § 4281.18(a) for valuing claims for withdrawal liability.

§ 4281.18 **Outstanding claims for withdrawal liability**. (a) *Value of claim*. The plan sponsor shall value an outstanding claim for withdrawal liability owed by an employer described in paragraph (b) of this section in accordance with paragraphs (a)(1) and (a)(2) of this section:

(1) If the schedule of withdrawal liability payments provides for one or more series of equal payments, the plan sponsor shall value each series of payments as an annuity certain in accordance with the provisions of § 4281.13.

(2) If the schedule of withdrawal liability payments provides for one or more payments that are not part of a series of equal payments as described in paragraph (a)(1) of this section, the plan sponsor shall value each such unequal payment as a lump-sum payment in accordance with the provisions of § 4281.13.

(b) *Employers neither liquidated nor in insolvency proceedings*. The plan sponsor shall value an outstanding claim for withdrawal liability under paragraph (a) of this section if, as of the valuation date—

(1) The employer has not been completely liquidated or dissolved; and

(2) The employer is not the subject of any case or proceeding under title 11, United States Code, or any case or proceeding under similar provisions of state insolvency laws; except that the claim for withdrawal liability of an employer that is the subject of a proceeding described in this paragraph (b)(2) shall be valued under paragraph (a) of this section if the plan sponsor determines that the employer is reasonably expected to be able to pay its withdrawal liability in full and on time.

(c) *Claims against other employers*. The plan sponsor shall value at zero any outstanding claim for withdrawal liability owed by an employer that does not meet the conditions set forth in paragraph (b) of this section.

Subpart C—Benefit Reductions

§ 4281.31 **Plan amendment**. The plan sponsor of a plan described in § 4281.31 shall amend the plan to eliminate those benefits subject to reduction in excess of the value of benefits that can be provided by plan assets. Such reductions shall be effected by a pro rata reduction of all benefits subject to reduction or by elimination or pro rata reduction of any category of benefit. Benefit reductions required by this section shall apply only prospectively. An amendment required under this section shall take effect no later than six months after the end of the plan year for which it is determined that the value of nonforfeitable benefits exceeds the value of the plan's assets.

§ 4281.32 **Notices of benefit reductions**. (a) *Requirement of notices*. A plan sponsor of a multiemployer plan under which a plan amendment reducing benefits is adopted pursuant to section 4281(c) of ERISA shall so notify the PBGC and plan participants and beneficiaries whose benefits are reduced by the amendment. The notices shall be delivered in the manner and within the time prescribed, and shall contain the information described, in this section. The notice required in this section shall be filed in lieu of the notice described in section 4244A(b)(2) of ERISA.

(b) *When delivered*. The plan sponsor shall mail or otherwise deliver the notices of benefit reduction no later than the earlier of—

(1) 45 days after the amendment reducing benefits is adopted; or

(2) The date of the first reduced benefit payment.

(c) *Method of issuance to interested parties*. The PBGC applies the rules in subpart B of part 4000 of this chapter to determine permissible methods of issuance of the notice of benefit reduction to interested parties. In addition to the methods permitted under subpart B of part 4000, the plan sponsor may notify interested parties, other than participants and beneficiaries who are in pay status when the notice is required to be delivered or who are reasonably expected to enter pay status before the end of the plan year after the plan year in which the amendment is adopted, by posting the notice at participants' work sites or publishing the notice in a union newsletter or in a newspaper of general circulation in the area or areas where participants reside. Notice to a participant shall be deemed notice to that participant's beneficiary or beneficiaries.

[Amended 10/28/2003 by 68 FR 61344]

(d) *Contents of notice to the PBGC*. A notice of benefit reduction required to be filed with the PBGC pursuant to paragraph (a) of this section shall contain the following information:

(1) The name of the plan.

(2) The name, address, and telephone number of the plan sponsor and of the plan sponsor's duly authorized representative, if any.

(3) The nine-digit Employer Identification Number (EIN) assigned by the IRS to the plan sponsor and the three-digit Plan Number

(PN) assigned by the plan sponsor to the plan, and, if different, the EIN or PN last filed with the PBGC. If no EIN or PN has been assigned, the notice shall so state.

(4) The case number assigned by the PBGC to the filing of the plan's notice of termination pursuant to part 4041A, subpart B, of this chapter.

(5) A statement that a plan amendment reducing benefits has been adopted, listing the date of adoption and the effective date of the amendment.

(6) A certification, signed by the plan sponsor or its duly authorized representative, that notice of the benefit reductions has been given to all participants and beneficiaries whose benefits are reduced by the plan amendment, in accordance with the requirements of this section.

(e) *Contents of notice to participants and beneficiaries.* A notice of benefit reductions required under paragraph (a) of this section to be given to plan participants and beneficiaries whose benefits are reduced by the amendment shall contain the following information:

(1) The name of the plan.

(2) A statement that a plan amendment reducing benefits has been adopted, listing the date of adoption and the effective date of the amendment.

(3) A summary of the amendment, including a description of the effect of the amendment on the benefits to which it applies.

(4) The name, address, and telephone number of the plan administrator or other person designated by the plan sponsor to answer inquiries concerning benefits.

[¶ 15,715O]

§ 4281.33 **Restoration of benefits.** (a) *General.* The plan sponsor of a plan that has been amended to reduce benefits under this subpart shall amend the plan to restore those benefits before adopting any amendment increasing benefits under the plan. A plan is not required to make retroactive benefit payments with respect to any benefit that was reduced and subsequently restored in accordance with this section.

(b) *Notice to the PBGC.* The plan sponsor shall notify the PBGC in writing of any restoration under this section. The notice shall include the information specified in § 4281.32(d)(1) through (d)(4); a statement that a plan amendment restoring benefits has been adopted, the date of adoption, and the effective date of the amendment; and a certification, signed by the plan sponsor or its duly authorized representative, that the amendment has been adopted in accordance with this section.

Subpart D—Benefit Suspensions

[¶ 15,715P]

§ 4281.41 **Benefit suspensions.** If the plan sponsor determines that the plan is or is expected to be insolvent for a plan year, the plan sponsor shall suspend benefits to the extent necessary to reduce the benefits to the greater of the resource benefit level or the level of guaranteed benefits.

[¶ 15,715Q]

§ 4281.42 **Retroactive payments.** (a) *Erroneous resource benefit level.* If, by the end of a year in which benefits were suspended under § 4281.41, the plan sponsor determines in writing that the plan's available resources in that year could have supported benefit payments above the resource benefit level determined for that year, the plan sponsor may distribute the excess resources to each affected participant and beneficiary who received benefit payments that year on a pro rata basis. The amount distributed to each participant under this paragraph may not exceed the amount that, when added to benefit payments already made, brings the total benefit for the plan year up to the total benefit provided under the plan.

(b) *Benefits paid below resource benefit level.* If, by the end of a plan year in which benefits were suspended under § 4281.41, any benefit has not been paid at the resource benefit level, amounts up to the resource benefit level that were unpaid shall be distributed to each affected participant and beneficiary on a pro rata basis to the extent possible, taking into account the plan's total available resources in that year.

[¶ 15,715R]

§ 4281.43 **Notices of insolvency and annual updates.** (a) *Requirement of notices of insolvency.* A plan sponsor that determines that the plan is, or is expected to be, insolvent for a plan year shall issue notices of insolvency to the PBGC and to plan participants and beneficiaries. Once notices of insolvency have been issued to the PBGC and to plan participants and beneficiaries, no notice of insolvency needs to be issued for subsequent insolvency years. Notices shall be delivered in the manner and within the time prescribed in this section and shall contain the information described in § 4281.44.

(b) *Requirement of annual updates.* A plan sponsor that has issued notices of insolvency to the PBGC and to plan participants and beneficiaries shall thereafter issue annual updates to the PBGC and participants and beneficiaries for each plan year beginning after the plan year for which the notice of insolvency was issued. However, the p*lan sponsor need not issue an annual update to plan participants and beneficiaries who are issued notices of insolvency benefit level in accordance with § 4281.45 for the same insolvency year. A plan sponsor that, after issuing annual updates for a plan year, determines under § 4041A.25(b) that the plan is or may be insolvent for that plan year need not issue revised annual updates. Annual updates shall be delivered in the manner and within the time prescribed in this section and shall contain the information described in § 4281.44.

(c) *Notices of insolvency—when delivered.* Except as provided in the next sentence, the plan sponsor shall mail or otherwise deliver the notices of insolvency no later than 30 days after the plan sponsor determines that the plan is or may be insolvent. However, the notice to plan participants and beneficiaries in pay status may be delivered concurrently with the first benefit payment made after the determination of insolvency.

(d) *Annual updates—when delivered.* Except as provided in the next sentence, the plan sponsor shall mail or otherwise deliver annual updates no later than 60 days before the beginning of the plan year for which the annual update is issued. A plan sponsor that determines under § 4041A.25(b) that the plan is or may be insolvent for a plan year and that has not at that time issued annual updates for that year, shall mail or otherwise deliver the annual updates by the later of 60 days before the beginning of the plan year or 30 days after the date of the plan sponsor's determination under § 4041A.25(b).

(e) *Notices of insolvency—method of issuance to interested parties.* The PBGC applies the rules in subpart B of part 4000 of this chapter to determine permissible methods of issuance of the notice of insolvency. In addition to the methods permitted under subpart B of part 4000, the plan sponsor may notify interested parties, other than participants and beneficiaries who are in pay status when the notice is required to be delivered, by posting the notice at participants' work sites or publishing the notice in a union newsletter or in a newspaper of general circulation in the area or areas where participants reside. Notice to a participant shall be deemed notice to that participant's beneficiary or beneficiaries.

[Amended 10/28/2003 by 68 FR 61344]

(f) *Annual updates—method of issuance.* The PBGC applies the rules in subpart B of part 4000 of this chapter to determine permissible methods of issuance of the annual update to participants and beneficiaries. In addition to the methods permitted under subpart B of part 4000, the plan sponsor may notify interested parties by posting the notice at participants' work sites or publishing the notice in a union newsletter or in a newspaper of general circulation in the area or areas where participants reside. Notice to a participant shall be deemed notice to that participant's beneficiary or beneficiaries.

[Amended 10/28/2003 by 68 FR 61344]

[¶ 15,715S]

§ 4281.44 **Contents of notices of insolvency and annual updates.** (a) *Notice of insolvency to the PBGC.* A notice of insolvency required under § 4281.43(a) to be filed with the PBGC shall contain the following information:

(1) The name of the plan.

(2) The name, address, and telephone number of the plan sponsor and of the plan sponsor's duly authorized representative, if any.

(3) The nine-digit Employer Identification Number (EIN) assigned by the IRS to the plan sponsor and the three-digit Plan Number (PN) assigned by the plan sponsor to the plan, and, if different, the EIN or PN last filed with the PBGC. If no EIN or PN has been assigned, the notice shall so state.

(4) The IRS Key District that has jurisdiction over determination letters with respect to the plan.

(5) The case number assigned by the PBGC to the filing of the plan's notice of termination pursuant to part 4041A, subparts A and B, of this chapter.

(6) The plan year for which the plan sponsor has determined that the plan is or may be insolvent.

(7) A copy of the plan document currently in effect, i.e., a copy of the last restatement of the plan and all subsequent amendments. However, if a copy of the plan document was submitted to the PBGC with a previous filing, only subsequent plan amendments need be submitted, and the notice shall state when the copy of the plan document was filed.

(8) A copy of the most recent actuarial valuation for the plan (i.e., the most recent report submitted to the plan in connection with a valuation of plan assets and liabilities, which shall be performed in accordance with subpart B of this part). If the actuarial valuation was previously submitted to the PBGC, it may be omitted, and the notice shall state the date on which the document was filed and that the information is still accurate and complete.

(9) The estimated amount of annual benefit payments under the plan (determined without regard to the insolvency) for the insolvency year.

(10) The estimated amount of the plan's available resources for the insolvency year.

(11) The estimated amount of the annual benefits guaranteed by the PBGC for the insolvency year.

(12) A statement indicating whether the notice of insolvency is the result of an insolvency determination under §4041A.25(a) or (b).

(13) A certification, signed by the plan sponsor or its duly authorized representative, that notices of insolvency have been given to all plan participants and beneficiaries in accordance with this part.

(b) *Notice of insolvency to participants and beneficiaries.* A notice of insolvency required under §4281.43(a) to be issued to plan participants and beneficiaries shall contain the following information:

(1) The name of the plan.

(2) A statement of the plan year for which the plan sponsor has determined that the plan is or may be insolvent.

(3) A statement that benefits above the amount that can be paid from available resources or the level guaranteed by the PBGC, whichever is greater, will be suspended during the insolvency year, with a brief explanation of which benefits are guaranteed by the PBGC.

(4) The name, address, and telephone number of the plan administrator or other person designated by the plan sponsor to answer inquiries concerning benefits.

(c) *Annual update to the PBGC.* Each annual update required by §4281.43(b) to be filed with the PBGC shall contain the following information:

(1) The case number assigned by the PBGC to the filing of the plan's notice of termination pursuant to part 4041A, subparts A and B, of this chapter.

(2) A copy of the annual update to plan participants and beneficiaries, as described in paragraph (d) of this section, for the plan year.

(3) A statement indicating whether the annual update is the result of an insolvency determination under §4041A.25(a) or (b).

(4) A certification, signed by the plan sponsor or a duly authorized representative, that the annual update has been given to all plan participants and beneficiaries in accordance with this part.

(d) *Annual updates to participants and beneficiaries.* Each annual update required by §4281.43(b) to be issued to plan participants and beneficiaries shall contain the following information:

(1) The name of the plan.

(2) The date the notice of insolvency was issued and the insolvency year identified in the notice.

(3) The plan year to which the annual update pertains and the plan sponsor's determination whether the plan may be insolvent in that year.

(4) If the plan may be insolvent for the plan year, a statement that benefits above the amount that can be paid from available resources or the level guaranteed by the PBGC, whichever is greater, will be suspended during the insolvency year, with a brief explanation of which benefits are guaranteed by the PBGC.

(5) If the plan will not be insolvent for the plan year, a statement that full nonforfeitable benefits under the plan will be paid.

(6) The name, address, and telephone number of the plan administrator or other person designated by the plan sponsor to answer inquiries concerning benefits.

[¶ 15,715T]

§4281.45 **Notices of insolvency benefit level**. (a) *Requirement of notices.* For each insolvency year, the plan sponsor shall issue a notice of insolvency benefit level to the PBGC and to plan participants and beneficiaries in pay status or reasonably expected to enter pay status during the insolvency year. The notices shall be delivered in the manner and within the time prescribed in this section and shall contain the information described in §4281.46.

(b) *When delivered.* The plan sponsor shall mail or otherwise deliver the notices of insolvency benefit level no later than 60 days before the beginning of the insolvency year. A plan sponsor that determines under §4041A.25(b) that the plan is or may be insolvent for a plan year shall mail or otherwise deliver the notices of insolvency benefit level by the later of 60 days before the beginning of the insolvency year or 60 days after the date of the plan sponsor's determination under §4041A.25(b).

(c) *Method of issuance.* The notices of insolvency benefit level shall be delivered to the PBGC and to plan participants and beneficiaries in pay status or reasonably expected to enter pay status during the insolvency year. The PBGC applies the rules in subpart B of part 4000 of this chapter to determine permissible methods of issuance of the notice of insolvency benefit levels to interested parties.

[Amended 10/28/2003 by 68 FR 61344]

[¶ 15,715U]

§4281.46 **Contents of notices of insolvency benefit level**. (a) *Notice to the PBGC.* A notice of insolvency benefit level required by §4281.45(a) to be filed with the PBGC shall contain the information specified in §4281.44(a)(1) through (a)(5) and (a)(7) through (a)(11) and:

(1) The insolvency year for which the notice is being filed.

(2) The amount of financial assistance, if any, requested from the PBGC. (When financial assistance is requested, the plan sponsor shall submit an application in accordance with §4281.47.)

(3) A statement indicating whether the notice of insolvency benefit level is the result of an insolvency determination under §4041A.25(a) or (b).

(4) A certification, signed by the plan sponsor or its duly authorized representative, that a notice of insolvency benefit level has been sent to all plan participants and beneficiaries in pay status or reasonably expected to enter pay status during the insolvency year, in accordance with this part.

(b) *Notice to participants in or entering pay status.* A notice of insolvency benefit level required by §4281.45(a) to be delivered to plan participants and beneficiaries in pay status or reasonably expected to enter pay status during the insolvency year for which the notice is given, shall contain the following information:

(1) The name of the plan.

(2) The insolvency year for which the notice is being sent.

(3) The monthly benefit that the participant or beneficiary may expect to receive during the insolvency year.

(4) A statement that in subsequent plan years, depending on the plan's available resources, this benefit level may be increased or decreased but not below the level guaranteed by the PBGC, and that the participant or beneficiary will be notified in advance of the new benefit level if it is less than the participant's full nonforfeitable benefit under the plan.

(5) The amount of the participant's or beneficiary's monthly nonforfeitable benefit under the plan.

(6) The amount of the participant's or beneficiary's monthly benefit that is guaranteed by the PBGC.

(7) The name, address, and telephone number of the plan administrator or other person designated by the plan sponsor to answer inquiries concerning benefits.

[¶ 15,715V]

§ 4281.47 **Application for financial assistance.** (a) *General.* If the plan sponsor determines that the plan's resource benefit level for an insolvency year is below the level of benefits guaranteed by PBGC or that the plan will be unable to pay guaranteed benefits when due for any month during the year, the plan sponsor shall apply to the PBGC for financial assistance pursuant to section 4261 of ERISA. The application shall be filed within the time prescribed in paragraph (b) of this section. When the resource benefit level is below the guarantee level, the application shall contain the information set forth in paragraph (c) of this section. When the plan is unable to pay guaranteed benefits for any month, the application shall contain the information set forth in paragraph (d) of this section.

(b) *When to apply.* When the plan sponsor determines a resource benefit level that is less than guaranteed benefits, it shall apply for financial assistance at the same time that it submits its notice of insolvency benefit level pursuant to § 4281.45. When the plan sponsor determines an inability to pay guaranteed benefits for any month, it

shall apply for financial assistance within 15 days after making that determination.

(c) *Contents of application—resource benefit level below level of guaranteed benefits.* A plan sponsor applying for financial assistance because the plan's resource benefit level is below the level of guaranteed benefits shall file an application that includes the information specified in § 4281.44(a)(1) through (a)(5) and:

(1) The insolvency year for which the application is being filed.

(2) A participant data schedule showing each participant and beneficiary in pay status or reasonably expected to enter pay status during the year for which financial assistance is requested, listing for each—

(i) Name;

(ii) Sex;

(iii) Date of birth;

(iv) Credited service;

(v) Vested accrued monthly benefit;

(vi) Monthly benefit guaranteed by PBGC;

(vii) Benefit commencement date; and

(viii) Type of benefit.

(d) *Contents of application—unable to pay guaranteed benefits for any month.* A plan sponsor applying for financial assistance because the plan is unable to pay guaranteed benefits for any month shall file an application that includes the data described in § 4281.44(a)(1) through (a)(5), the month for which financial assistance is requested, and the plan's available resources and guaranteed benefits payable in that month. The participant data schedule described in paragraph (c)(2) of this section shall be submitted upon the request of the PBGC.

(e) *Additional information.* The PBGC may request any additional information that it needs to calculate or verify the amount of financial assistance necessary as part of the conditions of granting financial assistance pursuant to section 4261 of ERISA.

Part 6—Enforcement

[¶ 15,716]
CIVIL ACTIONS

Act Sec. 4301. (a)(1) A plan fiduciary, employer, plan participant, or beneficiary, who is adversely affected by the act or omission of any party under this subtitle with respect to a multiemployer plan, or an employee organization which represents such a plan participant or beneficiary for purposes of collective bargaining, may bring an action for appropriate legal or equitable relief, or both.

(2) Notwithstanding paragraph (1), this section does not authorize an action against the Secretary of the Treasury, the Secretary of Labor, or the corporation.

Act Sec. 4301. (b) In any action under this section to compel an employer to pay withdrawal liability, any failure of the employer to make any withdrawal liability payment within the time prescribed shall be treated in the same manner as a delinquent contribution (within the meaning of section 515).

Act Sec. 4301. (c) The district courts of the United States shall have exclusive jurisdiction of an action under this section without regard to the amount in controversy, except that State courts of competent jurisdiction shall have concurrent jurisdiction over an action brought by a plan fiduciary to collect withdrawal liability.

Act Sec. 4301. (d) An action under this section may be brought in the district where the plan is administered or where a defendant resides or does business, and process may be served in any district where a defendant resides, does business, or may be found.

Act Sec. 4301. (e) In any action under this section, the court may award all or a portion of the costs and expenses incurred in connection with such action, including reasonable attorney's fees, to the prevailing party.

Act Sec. 4301. (f) An action under this section may not be brought after the later of—

(1) 6 years after the date on which the cause of action arose, or

(2) 3 years after the earliest date on which the plaintiff acquired or should have acquired actual knowledge of the existence of such cause of action; except that in the case of fraud or concealment, such action may be brought not later than 6 years after the date of discovery of the existence of such cause of action.

Act Sec. 4301. (g) A copy of the complaint in any action under this section or section 4221 shall be served upon the corporation by certified mail. The corporation may intervene in any such action.

Amendment:

P. L. 96-364, § 104(2):

Added Sec. 4301 effective September 26, 1980 under ERISA Sec. 4402.

[¶ 15,717]
PENALTY FOR FAILURE TO PROVIDE NOTICE

Act Sec. 4302. Any person who fails, without reasonable cause, to provide a notice required under this subtitle or any implementing regulations shall be liable to the corporation in an amount up to $100 for each day for which such failure continues. The corporation may bring a civil action against any such person in the United States District Court for the District of Columbia or in any district court of the United States within the jurisdiction of which the plan assets are located, the plan is administered, or a defendant resides or does business, and process may be served in any district where a defendant resides, does business, or may be found.

Amendment

P. L. 96-364, § 104(2):

Added Sec. 4302 effective September 26, 1980 under ERISA Sec. 4402.

Regulations

The following regulations were adopted by the Pension Benefit Guaranty Corporation on July 10, 1997 (62 FR 36993) and are effective August 11, 1997.

[¶ 15,717A]

§ 4302.1 **Purpose and scope.** This part specifies the maximum daily amount of penalties for which a person may be liable to the PBGC under ERISA section 4302 for certain failures to provide multiemployer plan notices, as such amount has been adjusted to account for inflation pursuant to the Federal Civil Monetary Penalty Inflation Adjustment Act of 1990, as amended by the Debt Collection Improvement Act of 1996.

[¶ 15,717B]

§ 4302.2 **Definitions.** The following terms are defined in § 4001.2 of this chapter: *ERISA, multiemployer plan,* and *PBGC.*

[¶ 15,717C]

§ 4302.3 **Penalty amount.** The maximum daily amount of the penalty under section 4302 of ERISA shall be $110.

[¶ 15,718]
ELECTION OF PLAN STATUS

Act Sec. 4303. (a) Within one year after the date of the enactment of the Multiemployer Pension Plan Amendments Act of 1980, a multiemployer plan may irrevocably elect, pursuant to procedures established by the corporation, that the plan shall not be treated as a multiemployer plan for any purpose under this Act or the Internal Revenue Code of 1954, if for each of the last 3 plan years ending prior to the effective date of the Multiemployer Pension Plan Amendments Act of 1980—

(1) the plan was not a multiemployer plan because the plan was not a plan described in section 3(37) (A) (iii) of this Act and section 414(f) (1) (C) of the Internal Revenue Code of 1954 (as such provisions were in effect on the day before the date of the enactment of the Multiemployer Pension Plan Amendments Act of 1980); and

(2) the plan had been identified as a plan that was not a multiemployer plan in substantially all its filings with the corporation, the Secretary of Labor and the Secretary of the Treasury.

Act Sec. 4303. (b) An election described in subsection (a) shall be effective only if—

(1) the plan is amended to provide that it shall not be treated as a multiemployer plan for all purposes under this Act and the Internal Revenue Code of 1954, and

(2) written notice of the amendment is provided to the corporation within 60 days after the amendment is adopted.

Act Sec. 4303. (c) An election described in subsection (a) shall be treated as being effective as of the date of the enactment of the Multiemployer Pension Plan Amendments Act of 1980.

Amendment:

P.L. 96-364, § 105:

Added new section 4303, effective September 26, 1980, except that the prior definition of multiemployer plan will continue for plan years beginning before enactment.

Subtitle F—Transition Rules and Effective Dates

[¶ 15,719]
AMENDMENTS TO INTERNAL REVENUE CODE OF 1954

Act Sec. 4401 (a) Section 404 of the Internal Revenue Code of 1986 (relating to deduction for contributions of an employer to employees' trust or annuity plan in compensation under a deferred-payment plan) is amended by adding at the end thereof the following new subsection:

[Code Sec. 404(g)]

"(g) CERTAIN EMPLOYER LIABILITY PAYMENTS CONSIDERED AS CONTRIBUTIONS. For purposes of this section any amount paid by an employer under section 4062, 4063, or 4064 of the Employee Retirement Income Security Act of 1974 shall be treated as a contribution to which this section applies by such employer to or under a stock bonus, pension, profit-sharing, or annuity plan."

Act Sec. 4401 (b) Section 6511(d) of the Internal Revenue Code of 1986 (relating to special rules applicable to income taxes) is amended by adding at the end thereof the following new paragraph:

[Code Sec. 6511(d)(8)]

"(8) SPECIAL PERIOD OF LIMITATION WITH RESPECT TO AMOUNTS INCLUDED IN INCOME SUBSEQUENTLY RECAPTURED UNDER QUALIFIED PLAN TERMINATION. If the claim for credit or refund relates to an overpayment of tax imposed by subtitle A on account of the recapture, under section 4045 of the Employee Retirement Income Security Act of 1974, of amounts included in income for a prior taxable year, the 3-year period of limitation prescribed in subsection (a) shall be extended, for purposes of permitting a credit or refund of the amount of the recapture, until the date which occurs one year after the date on which such recaptured amount is paid by the taxpayer.".

[The above amendments to the Internal Revenue Code of 1986 are incorporated in place in the "Internal Revenue Code—Regulations."]

Amendments

P.L. 101-239, § 7891(a)(1):

Titles I, III, and IV of ERISA (other than sections 3(37) (E), 301(a) (7), and 308, the last sentence of section 408(d), and sections 414(c), 4001(a) (3) (ii), and 4303) are each amended by striking "Internal Revenue Code of 1954" each place it appears and inserting "Internal Revenue Code of 1986," effective October 22, 1986.

P.L. 96-364, § 108(a):

Renumbered Sec. 4081 to Sec. 4401, effective September 26, 1980.

[¶ 15,720]
EFFECTIVE DATE; SPECIAL RULES

Act Sec. 4402 (a) The provisions of this title take effect on the date of enactment of this Act.

Act Sec. 4402 (b) Notwithstanding the provisions of subsection (a), the corporation shall pay benefits guaranteed under this title with respect to any plan—

(1) which is not a multiemployer plan,

(2) which terminates after June 30, 1974, and before the date of enactment of this Act,

(3) to which section 4021 would apply if that section were effective beginning on July 1, 1974, and

(4) with respect to which a notice is filed with the Secretary of Labor and received by him not later than 10 days after the date of enactment of this Act, except that, for reasonable cause shown, such notice may be filed with the Secretary of Labor and received by him not later than October 31, 1974, stating that the plan is a plan described in paragraphs (1), (2), and (3).

The corporation shall not pay benefits guaranteed under this title with respect to a plan described in the preceding sentence unless the corporation finds substantial evidence that the plan was terminated for a reasonable business purpose and not for the purpose of obtaining the payment of benefits by the corporation under this title or for the purpose of avoiding the liability which might be imposed under subtitle D if the plan terminated on or after the date of enactment of this Act. The provisions of subtitle D do not apply in the case of such a plan which terminates before the date of enactment of this Act. For purposes of determining whether a plan is a plan described in paragraph (2), the provisions of section 4048 shall not apply, but the corporation shall make the determination on the basis of the date on which benefits ceased to accrue on or any other reasonable basis consistent with the purposes of this subsection.

Act Sec. 4402(c)(1) Except as provided in paragraphs (2), (3), and (4), the corporation shall not pay benefits guaranteed under this title with respect to a multiemployer plan which terminates before August 1, 1980. Whenever the corporation exercises the authority granted under paragraph (2) or (3), the corporation shall notify the Committee on Education and Labor and the Committee on Ways and Means of the House of Representatives, and the Committee on Labor and Public Welfare and the Committee on Finance of the Senate.

(2) The corporation may, in its discretion, pay benefits guaranteed under this title with respect to a multiemployer plan which terminates after the date of enactment of this Act and before August 1, 1980, if—

(A) the plan was maintained during the 60 months immediately preceding the date on which the plan terminates, and

(B) the corporation determines that the payment by the corporation of benefits guaranteed under this title with respect to that plan will not jeopardize the payments the corporation anticipates it may be required to make in connection with benefits guaranteed under this title with respect to multiemployer plans which terminate after July 31, 1980.

(3) Notwithstanding any provision of section 4021 or 4022 which would prevent such payments, the corporation, in carrying out its authority under paragraph (2), may pay benefits guaranteed under this title with respect to a multiemployer plan described in paragraph (2) in any case in which those benefits would otherwise not be payable if—

(A) the plan has been in effect for at least 5 years.

(B) the plan has been in substantial compliance with the funding requirements for a qualified plan with respect to the employees and former employees in those employment units on the basis of which the participating employers have contributed to the plan for the preceding 5 years, and

(C) the participating employers and employees organization or organizations had no reasonable recourse other than termination.

(4) If the corporation determines, under paragraph (2) or (3), that it will pay benefits guaranteed under this title with respect to a multiemployer plan which terminates before August 1, 1980, the corporation—

(A) may establish requirements for the continuation of payments which commenced before January 2, 1974, with respect to retired participants under the plan,

(B) may not, notwithstanding any other provision of this title, make payments with respect to any participant under such a plan who, on January 1, 1974, was receiving payment of retirement benefits, in excess of the amounts and rates payable with respect to such participant on that date,

(C) may not make any payments with respect to benefits guaranteed under this title in connection with such a plan which are derived, directly or indirectly, from amounts borrowed under section 4005(c), and

(D) shall review from time to time payments made under the authority granted to it by paragraphs (2) and (3), and reduce or terminate such payments to the extent necessary to avoid jeopardizing the ability of the corporation to make payments of benefits guaranteed under this title in connection with multiemployer plans which terminate after July 31, 1980, without increasing premium rates for such plans.

Act Sec. 4402 (d) Notwithstanding any other provision of this title, guaranteed benefits payable by the corporation pursuant to its discretionary authority under this section shall continue to be paid at the level guaranteed under section 4022, without regard to any limitation on payment under subparagraph (C) or (D) of subsection (c)(4).

Act Sec. 4402(e)(1) Except as provided in paragraphs (2), (3), and (4), the amendments to this Act made by the Multiemployer Pension Plan Amendments Act of 1980 shall take effect on the date of the enactment of that Act.

(2)(A) Except as provided in this paragraph, part 1 of subtitle E, relating to withdrawal liability, takes effect on September 26, 1980.

(B) For purposes of determining withdrawal liability under part 1 of subtitle E, an employer who has withdrawn from a plan shall be considered to have withdrawn from a multiemployer plan if, at the time of the withdrawal, the plan was a multiemployer plan as defined in section 4001(a)(3) as in effect at the time of the withdrawal.

(3) Sections 4241 through 4245, relating to multiemployer plan reorganization, shall take effect, with respect to each plan, of the first day of the first plan year beginning on or after the earlier of—

(A) the date on which the last collective bargaining agreement providing for employer contributions under the plan, which was in effect on the date of the enactment of the Multiemployer Pension Plan Amendments Act of 1980, expires, without regard to extensions agreed to on or after the date of the enactment of that Act, or

(B) 3 years after the date of the enactment of the Multiemployer Pension Plan Amendments Act of 1980.

(4) Section 4235 shall take effect on September 26, 1980.

Act Sec. 4402(f)(1) In the event that before the date of enactment of the Multiemployer Pension Plan Amendments Act of 1980, the corporation has determined that—

(A) an employer has withdrawn from a multiemployer plan under section 4063, and

(B) the employer is liable to the corporation under such section,

the corporation shall retain the amount of liability paid to it or furnished in the form of a bond and shall pay such liability to the plan in the event the plan terminates in accordance with section 4041A(a)(2) before the earlier of September 26, 1980, or the day after the 5-year period commencing on the date of such withdrawal.

(2) In any case in which the plan is not so terminated within the period described in paragraph (1), the liability of the employer is abated and any payment held in escrow shall be refunded without interest to the employer or the employer's bond shall be cancelled.

Act Sec. 4402(g)(1) In any case in which an employer or employers withdrew from a multiemployer plan before the effective date of part 1 of subtitle E, the corporation may—

(A) apply section 4063(d), as in effect before the amendments made by the Multiemployer Penson Plan Amendments Act of 1980, to such plan,

(B) assess liability against the withdrawn employer with respect to the resulting terminated plan,

(C) guarantee benefits under the terminated plan under section 4022, as in effect before such amendments, and

(D) if necessary, enforce such action through suit brought under section 4003.

(2) The corporation shall use the revolving fund used by the corporation with respect to basic benefits guaranteed under section 4022A in guaranteeing benefits under a terminated plan described in this subsection.

Act Sec. 4402.(h)(1) In the case of an employer who entered into a collective bargaining agreement—

(A) which was effective on January 12, 1979, and which remained in effect through May 15, 1982, and

(B) under which contributions to a multiemployer plan were to cease on January 12, 1982,

any withdrawal liability incurred by the employer pursuant to part 1 of subtitle E as a result of the complete or partial withdrawal of the employer from the multiemployer plan before January 16, 1982, shall be void.

(2) In any case in which—

(A) an employer engaged in the grocery wholesaling business—

(i) had ceased all covered operations under a multiemployer plan before June 30, 1981, and had relocated its operations to a new facility in another State, and

(ii) had notified a local union representative on May 14, 1980, that the employer had tentatively decided to discontinue operations and relocate to a new facility in another State, and

(B) all State and local approvals with respect to construction of and commencement of operations at the new facility had been obtained, a contract for construction had been entered into, and construction of the new facility had begun before September 26, 1980,

any withdrawal liability incurred by the employer pursuant to part 1 of subtitle E as a result of the complete or partial withdrawal of the employer from the multiemployer plan before June 30, 1981, shall be void.

Act Sec. 4402. (i) The preceding provisions of this section shall not apply with respect to amendments made to this title in provisions enacted after the date of the enactment of the Tax Reform Act of 1986.

Amendments

P.L. 101-239, § 7862(a):

Amended ERISA Sec. 4402(h)(1) by striking "January 12, 1982" the second place it appeared and inserting "January 16, 1982" effective July 18, 1984.

P.L. 101-239, § 7894(h)(5):

Amended ERISA Sec. 4402 by adding new subsection (i) to read as above.

P.L. 99-514, § 1852(i):

Added new Sec. 4402(h) to read as above, effective July 18, 1984.

P.L. 98-360, § 558(b):

Amended ERISA Secs. 4402(e) and (f)(1) by striking out "April 29, 1980" each place it appeared and inserting "September 26, 1980" instead.

P.L. 96-364, § 108:

Renumbered old sections 4081 and 4082 as 4401 and 4402. Amended section 4402(d) to read as above, struck out section 4402(e) and added new sections 4402(e), (f) and (g), effective September 26, 1980.

Prior to amendment, sections 4402(d) and (e) read:

"(d) The corporation shall present to the Committee on Education and Labor of the House of Representatives and the Committee on Human Resources and the Committee on Finance of the Senate a report which comprehensively addresses the anticipated financial condition of the program relating to mandatory coverage of multiemployer plans, including possible events which might cause the corporation to experience serious financial difficulty after July 1, 1979. Such report shall include an explanation of any alternative courses of action which might be taken by the corporation to insure proper coverage of multi-employer plans and the proper financing of the program relating to such plans. If the report contains recommendations for amendments to this title, such recommendations shall be fully explained, and shall be accompanied by explanations of other options for legislative change considered and rejected by the corporation. The report shall be presented by July 1, 1978."

"(e) Notwithstanding any provision of title IV of this Act to the contrary, the annual insurance premium payable to the Pension Benefit Guaranty Corporation for coverage of basic benefits guaranteed under section 4022 of this Act by plans that are not multiemployer plans shall be $2.60 for each participant in the plan. This subsection shall be effective for plan years beginning on or after January 1, 1978, and the premium prescribed by this subsection shall be deemed to be the rate imposed by title IV of this Act for non-multiemployer plans until the rate schedule for such plans is revised pursuant to the procedure set out in section 4006 of this Act."

P.L. 96-293:

Amended Secs. 4082(c)(1), 4082(c)(2), and 4082(c)(4) by substituting "August 1, 1980," for "July 1, 1980," each place it appeared.

Amended Secs. 4082(c)(2)(B) and 4082(c)(4)(D) by substituting "July 31, 1980," for June 30, 1980," each place it appeared.

P.L. 96-239:

Amended Secs. 4082(c)(1), 4082(c)(2), and 4082(c)(4) by substituting "July 1, 1980," for "May 1, 1980," each place it appeared.

Amended Secs. 4082(c)(2)(B) and 4082(c)(4)(D) by substituting "June 30, 1980," for "April 30, 1980," each place it appeared.

P.L. 96-24:

Amended Secs. 4082(c)(1), 4082(c)(2), and 4082(c)(4) by substituting "May 1, 1980" for "July 1, 1979" each place it appeared.

Amended Secs. 4082(c)(2)(B) and 4082(c)(4)(D) by substituting "April 30, 1980" for "June 30, 1979" each place it appeared.

P.L. 95-214:

Amended Secs. 4082(c)(1), 4082(c)(2) and 4082(c)(4) by substituting "July 1, 1979" for "January 1, 1978" each place it appeared.

Amended Secs. 4082(c)(2)(B) and 4082(c)(4)(D) by substituting "June 30, 1979" for "December 31, 1977" each place it appeared.

Added Sec. 4082(d), effective December 19, 1977.

Added Sec. 4082(e), effective December 19, 1977.

Regulations

The following regulations were adopted by the Pension Benefit Guaranty Corporation on July 1, 1996 (61 FR 34002). Prior to July 1, 1996, PBGC regulations were under Chapter XXVI of Title 29 of the Code of Federal Regulations. Effective July 1, 1996, PBGC regulations were moved to Chapter XL, and were renumbered and reorganized. PBGC Reg. Sec. 4902.9 was amended June 14, 2001, 66 FR 32221. Reg. § 4901.6, Reg. § 4901.11, Reg. § 4901.15, Reg. § 4901.33, Reg. § 4902.3, Reg. § 4902.5, Reg. § 4902.6, Reg. § 4902.7, Reg. § 4903.2, and Reg. § 4907.170 were amended, and Reg. § 4902.10 was added, on October 28, 2003 (68 FR 61344). Reg. § 4904.1 was removed on February 13, 2004 (69 FR 7120).

Subpart A—General

[¶ 15,720A]

§ 4901.1 **Purpose and scope.** This part contains the general rules of the PBGC implementing the Freedom of Information Act. This part sets forth generally the categories of records accessible to the public, the types of records subject to prohibitions or restrictions on disclosure, and the procedure whereby members of the public may obtain access to and inspect and copy information from records in the custody of the PBGC.

[¶ 15,720B]

§ 4901.2 **Definitions.** In addition to terminology in part 4001 of this chapter, as used in this part—

Agency, person, party, rule, rulemaking, order, and *adjudication* have the meanings attributed to these terms by the definitions in 5 U.S.C. 551, except where the context demonstrates that a different meaning is intended, and except that for purposes of the Freedom of Information Act the term agency as defined in 5 U.S.C. 551 includes any executive department, military department, Government corporation, Govern-ment controlled corporation, or other establishment in the executive branch of the Government (including the Executive Office of the President) or any independent regulatory agency.

Disclosure officer means the designated official in the Communications and Public Affairs Department, PBGC.

FOIA means the Freedom of Information Act, as amended (5 U.S.C. 552).

Working day means any weekday excepting Federal holidays.

[¶ 15,720C]

§ 4901.3 **Disclosure facilities.** (a) *Public reference room.* The PBGC will maintain a public reference room in its offices located at 1200 K Street NW., Washington, DC 20005-4026, wherein persons may inspect and copy all records made available for such purposes under this part.

(b) *No withdrawal of records.* No person may remove any record made available for inspection or copying under this part from the place where it is made available except with the written consent of the General Counsel of the PBGC.

[¶ 15,720D]

§ 4901.4 **Information maintained in public reference room.** The PBGC shall make available in its public reference room for inspection and copying without formal request—

(a) *Information published in the Federal Register.* Copies of Federal Register documents published by the PBGC, and copies of Federal Register indexes;

(b) *Information in PBGC publications.* Copies of informational material, such as press releases, pamphlets, and other material ordinarily made available to the public without cost as part of a public information program;

(c) *Rulemaking proceedings.* All papers and documents made a part of the official record in administrative proceedings conducted by the PBGC in connection with the issuance, amendment, or revocation of rules and regulations or determinations having general applicability or legal effect with respect to members of the public or a class thereof (with a register being kept to identify the persons who inspect the records and the times at which they do so);

(d) Except to the extent that deletion of identifying details is required to prevent a clearly unwarranted invasion of personal privacy (in which case the justification for the deletion shall be fully explained in writing)—

(1) *Adjudication proceedings.* Final opinions, orders, and (except to the extent that an exemption provided by FOIA must be asserted in the public interest to prevent a clearly unwarranted invasion of personal privacy or violation of law or to ensure the proper discharge of the functions of the PBGC) other papers and documents made a part of the official record in adjudication proceedings conducted by the PBGC,

(2) *Policy statements and interpretations.* Statements of policy and interpretations affecting a member of the public which have been adopted by the PBGC and which have not been published in the Federal Register, and

(3) *Staff manuals and instructions.* Administrative staff manuals and instructions to staff issued by the PBGC that affect any member of the public, and

(e) *Indexes to certain records.* Current indexes (updated at least quarterly) identifying materials described in paragraph (a)(2) of FOIA and paragraph (d) of this section.

[¶ 15,720E]

§ 4901.5 **Disclosure of other information.** (a) *In general.* Upon the request of any person submitted in accordance with subpart B of this part, the disclosure officer shall make any document (or portion thereof) from the records of the PBGC in the custody of any official of the PBGC available for inspection and copying unless exempt from disclosure under the provisions of subsection (b) of FOIA and subpart C of this part. The subpart B procedures must be used for records that are not made available in the PBGC's public reference room under § 4901.4 and may be used for records that are available in the public reference room. Records that could be produced only by manipulation of existing information (such as computer analyses of existing data), thus creating information not previously in being, are not records of the PBGC and are not required to be furnished under FOIA.

(b) *Discretionary disclosure.* Notwithstanding the applicability of an exemption under subsection (b) of FOIA and subpart C of this part (other than an exemption under paragraph (b)(1) or (b)(3) of FOIA and § 4901.21(a)(2) and (a)(3)), the disclosure officer may (subject to 18 U.S.C. 1905 and § 4901.21(a)(1)) make any document (or portion thereof) from the records of the PBGC available for inspection and copying if the disclosure officer determines that disclosure furthers the public interest and does not impede the discharge of any of the functions of the PBGC.

[¶ 15,720E-1]

§ 4901.6 **Filing rules; computation of time.** (a) *Filing rules.* (1) *Where to file.* See Sec. 4000.4 of this chapter for information on where to file a submission under this part with the PBGC.

(2) *Method of filing.* The PBGC applies the rules in subpart A of part 4000 of this chapter to determine permissible methods of filing with the PBGC under this part.

(3) *Date of filing.* The PBGC applies the rules in subpart C of part 4000 of this chapter to determine the date that a submission under this part was filed with the PBGC.

(b) *Computation of time.* The PBGC applies the rules in subpart D of part 4000 of this chapter to compute any time period under this part.

[Added 10/28/2003 by 68 FR 61344]

Subpart B—Procedure for Formal Requests

[¶ 15,720F]

§ 4901.11 **Submittal of requests for access to records.** A request to inspect or copy any record subject to this subpart shall be submitted to the Disclosure Officer, Pension Benefit Guaranty Corporation. Such a request may be sent to the Disclosure Officer or made in person between the hours of 9 a.m. and 4 p.m. on any working day in the Communications and Public Affairs Department, PBGC, 1200 K Street, NW., Suite 240, Washington, DC 20005-4026. To expedite processing, the request should be prominently identified as a "FOIA request."

[Amended 10/28/2003 by 68 FR 61344]

[¶ 15,720G]

§ 4901.12 **Description of information requested.** (a) *In general.* Each request should reasonably describe the record or records sought in sufficient detail to permit identification and location with a reasonable amount of effort. So far as practicable, the request should specify the subject matter of the record, the place where and date or approximate date when made, the person or office that made it, and any other pertinent identifying details.

(b) *Deficient descriptions.* If the description is insufficient to enable a professional employee familiar with the subject area of the request to locate the record with a reasonable amount of effort, the disclosure officer will notify the requester and, to the extent possible, indicate the additional information required. Every reasonable effort shall be made to assist a requester in the identification and location of the record or records sought. Records will not be withheld merely because it is difficult to find them.

(c) *Requests for categories of records.* Requests calling for all records falling within a reasonably specific category will be regarded as reasonably described within the meaning of this section and paragraph (a)(3) of FOIA if the PBGC is reasonably able to determine which records come within the request and to search for and collect them without unduly interfering with PBGC operations. If PBGC operations would be unduly disrupted, the disclosure officer shall promptly notify the requester and provide an opportunity to confer in an attempt to reduce the request to manageable proportions.

[¶ 15,720H]

§ 4901.13 **Receipt by agency of request.** The disclosure officer shall note the date and time of receipt on each request for access to records. A request shall be deemed received and the period within which action on the request shall be taken, as set forth in § 4901.14 of this part, shall begin on the next business day following such date, except that a request shall be deemed received only if and when the PBGC receives—

(a) A sufficient description under § 4901.12;

(b) Payment or assurance of payment if required under § 4901.33(b); and

(c) The requester's consent to pay substantial search, review, and/or duplication charges under subpart D of this part if the PBGC determines that such charges may be substantial and so notifies the requester. Consent may be in the form of a statement that costs under subpart D will be acceptable either in any amount or up to a specified amount. To avoid possible delay, a requester may include such a statement in a request.

[¶ 15,720I]

§ 4901.14 **Action on request.** (a) *Time for action.* Promptly and in any event within 10 working days after receipt of a disclosure request (subject to extension under §4901.16), the disclosure officer shall take action with respect to each requested item (or portion of an item) under either paragraph (b), (c), or (d) of this section.

(b) *Request granted.* If the disclosure officer determines that the request should be granted, the requester shall be so advised and the records shall be promptly made available to the requester.

(c) *Request denied.* If the disclosure officer determines that the request should be denied, the requester shall be so advised in writing with a brief statement of the reasons for the denial, including a reference to the specific exemption(s) authorizing the denial and an explanation of how each such exemption applies to the matter withheld. The denial shall also include the name and title or position of the person(s) responsible for the denial and outline the appeal procedure available.

(d) *Records not promptly located.* As to records that are not located in time to make an informed determination, the disclosure officer may deny the request and so advise the requester in writing with an explanation of the circumstances. The denial shall also include the name and title or position of the person(s) responsible for the denial, outline the appeal procedure available, and advise the requester that the search or examination will be continued and that the denial may be withdrawn, modified, or confirmed when processing of the request is completed.

[¶ 15,720J]

§4901.15 **Appeals from denial of requests.** (a) *Submittal of appeals.* If a disclosure request is denied in whole or in part by the disclosure officer, the requester may file a written appeal within 30 days from the date of the denial or, if later (in the case of a partial denial), 30 days from the date the requester receives the disclosed material. The appeal shall state the grounds for appeal and any supporting statements or arguments, and shall be addressed to the General Counsel, Pension Benefit Guaranty Corporation. See Sec. 4000.4 of this chapter for information on where to file. To expedite processing, the words "FOIA appeal" should appear prominently on the request.

[Amended 10/28/2003 by 68 FR 61344]

(b) *Receipt and consideration of appeal.* The General Counsel shall note the date and time of receipt on each appeal and notify the requester thereof. Promptly and in any event within 20 working days after receipt of an appeal (subject to extension under §4901.16), the General Counsel shall issue a decision on the appeal.

(1) The General Counsel may determine de novo whether the denial of disclosure was in accordance with FOIA and this part.

(2) If the denial appealed from was under §4901.14(d), the General Counsel shall consider any supplementary determination by the disclosure officer in deciding the appeal.

(3) Unless otherwise ordered by the court, the General Counsel may act on an appeal notwithstanding the pendency of an action for judicial relief in the same matter and, if no appeal has been filed, may treat such an action as the filing of an appeal.

(c) *Decision on appeal.* As to each item (or portion of an item) whose nondisclosure is appealed, the General Counsel shall either—

(1) Grant the appeal and so advise the requester in writing, in which case the records with respect to which the appeal is granted shall be promptly made available to the requester; or

(2) Deny the appeal and so advise the requester in writing with a brief statement of the reasons for the denial, including a reference to the specific exemption(s) authorizing the denial, an explanation of how each such exemption applies to the matter withheld, and notice of the provisions for judicial review in paragraph (a)(4) of FOIA. The General Counsel's decision shall be the final action of the PBGC with respect to the request.

(d) *Records of appeals.* Copies of both grants and denials of appeals shall be collected in one file available in the PBGC's public reference room under §4901.4(d)(1) and indexed under §4901.4(e).

[¶ 15,720K]

§4901.16 **Extensions of time.** In unusual circumstances (as described in subparagraph (a)(6)(B) of FOIA), the time to respond to a disclosure request under §4901.14(a) or an appeal under §4901.15(b) may be extended as reasonably necessary to process the request or appeal. The disclosure officer (with the prior approval of the General Counsel) or the General Counsel, as appropriate, shall notify the requester in writing within the original time period of the reasons for the extension and the date when a response is expected to be sent. The maximum extension for responding to a disclosure request shall be 10 working days, and the maximum extension for responding to an appeal shall be 10 working days minus the amount of any extension on the request to which the appeal relates.

[¶ 15,720L]

§4901.17 **Exhaustion of administrative remedies.** If the disclosure officer fails to make a determination to grant or deny access to requested records, or the General Counsel does not make a decision on appeal from a denial of access to PBGC records, within the time prescribed (including any extension) for making such determination or decision, the requester's administrative remedies shall be deemed exhausted and the requester may apply for judicial relief under FOIA. However, since a court may allow the PBGC additional time to act as provided in FOIA, processing of the request or appeal shall continue and the requester shall be so advised.

Subpart C—Restrictions on Disclosure

[¶ 15,720M]

§4901.21 **Restrictions in general.** (a) *Records not disclosable.* Records shall not be disclosed to the extent prohibited by—

(1) 18 U.S.C. 1905, dealing in general with commercial and financial information;

(2) Paragraph (b)(1) of FOIA, dealing in general with matters of national defense and foreign policy; or

(3) Paragraph (b)(3) of FOIA, dealing in general with matters specifically exempted from disclosure by statute, including information or documentary material submitted to the PBGC pursuant to sections 4010 and 4043 of ERISA.

(b) *Records disclosure of which may be refused.* Records need not (but may, as provided in §4901.5(b)) be disclosed to the extent provided by—

(1) Paragraph (b)(2) of FOIA, dealing in general with internal agency personnel rules and practices;

(2) Paragraph (b)(4) of FOIA, dealing in general with trade secrets and commercial and financial information;

(3) Paragraph (b)(5) of FOIA, dealing in general with inter-agency and intra-agency memoranda and letters;

(4) Paragraph (b)(6) of FOIA, dealing in general with personnel, medical, and similar files;

(5) Paragraph (b)(7) of FOIA, dealing in general with records or information compiled for law enforcement purposes;

(6) Paragraph (b)(8) of FOIA, dealing in general with reports on financial institutions; or

(7) Paragraph (b)(9) of FOIA, dealing in general with information about wells.

[¶ 15,720N]

§4901.22 **Partial disclosure.** If an otherwise disclosable record contains some material that is protected from disclosure, the record shall not for that reason be withheld from disclosure if deletion of the protected material is feasible. This principle shall be applied in particular to identifying details the disclosure of which would constitute an unwarranted invasion of personal privacy.

[¶ 15,720O]

§4901.23 **Record of concern to more than one agency.** If the release of a record in the custody of the PBGC would be of concern not only to the PBGC but also to another Federal agency, the record will be made available by the PBGC only if its interest in the record is the primary interest and only after coordination with the other interested agency. If the interest of the PBGC in the record is not primary, the request will be transferred promptly to the agency having the primary interest, and the requester will be so notified.

[¶ 15,720P]

§ 4901.24 **Special rules for trade secrets and confidential commercial or financial information submitted to the PBGC.** (a) *Application.* To the extent permitted by law, this section applies to a request for disclosure of a record that contains information that has been designated by the submitter in good faith in accordance with paragraph (b) of this section or a record that the PBGC has reason to believe contains such information, unless—

(1) Access to the information is denied;

(2) The information has been published or officially made available to the public;

(3) Disclosure of the information is required by law other than FOIA; or

(4) The designation under paragraph (b) of this section appears obviously frivolous, except that in such a case the PBGC will notify the submitter in writing of a determination to disclose the information within a reasonable time before the disclosure date (which shall be specified in the notice).

(b) *Designation by submitter.* To designate information as being subject to this section, the submitter shall, at the time of submission or by a reasonable time thereafter, assert that information being submitted is confidential business information and designate, with appropriate markings, the portion(s) of the submission to which the assertion applies. Any designation under this paragraph shall expire 10 years after the date of submission unless a longer designation period is requested and reasonable justification is provided therefor.

(c) *Notification to submitter of disclosure request.* When disclosure of information subject to this section may be made, the disclosure officer or (where disclosure may be made in response to an appeal) the General Counsel shall promptly notify the submitter, describing (or providing a copy of) the information that may be disclosed, and afford the submitter a reasonable period of time to object in writing to the requested disclosure. (The notification to the submitter may be oral or written; if oral, it will be confirmed in writing.) When a submitter is notified under this paragraph, the requester shall be notified that the submitter is being afforded an opportunity to object to disclosure.

(d) *Objection of submitter.* A submitter's statement objecting to disclosure should specify all grounds relied upon for opposing disclosure of any portion(s) of the information under subsection (b) of FOIA and, with respect to the exemption in paragraph (b)(4) of FOIA, demonstrate why the information is a trade secret or is commercial or financial information that is privileged or confidential. Facts asserted should be certified or otherwise supported. (Information provided pursuant to this paragraph may itself be subject to disclosure under FOIA.) Any timely objection of a submitter under this paragraph shall be carefully considered in determining whether to grant a disclosure request or appeal.

(e) *Notification to submitter of decision to disclose.* If the disclosure officer or (where disclosure is in response to an appeal) the General Counsel decides to disclose information subject to this section despite the submitter's objections, the disclosure officer (or General Counsel) shall give the submitter written notice, explaining briefly why the information is to be disclosed despite those objections, describing the information to be disclosed, and specifying the date when the information will be disclosed to the requester. The notification shall, to the extent permitted by law, be provided a reasonable number of days before the disclosure date so specified, and a copy shall be provided to the requester.

(f) *Notification to submitter of action to compel disclosure.* The disclosure officer or the General Counsel shall promptly notify the submitter if a requester brings suit seeking to compel disclosure.

Subpart D—Fees

[¶ 15,720Q]

§ 4901.31 **Charges for services.** (a) *Generally.* Pursuant to the provisions of FOIA, as amended, charges will be assessed to cover the direct costs of searching for, reviewing, and/or duplicating records requested under FOIA from the PBGC, except where the charges are limited or waived under paragraph (b) or (d) of this section, according to the fee schedule in § 4901.32 of this part. No charge will be assessed if the costs of routine collection and processing of the fee would be equal to or greater than the fee itself.

(1) "Direct costs" means those expenditures which the PBGC actually incurs in searching for and duplicating (and in the case of commercial requesters, reviewing) documents to respond to a request under FOIA and this part. Direct costs include, for example, the salary of the employee performing work (i.e., the basic rate of pay plus benefits) or an established average pay for a homogeneous class of personnel (e.g., all administrative/clerical or all professional/executive), and the cost of operating duplicating machinery. Not included in direct costs are overhead expenses such as costs of space, and heating or lighting the facility in which the records are stored.

(2) "Search" means all time spent looking for material that is responsive to a request under FOIA and this part, including page-by-page or line-by-line identification of materials within a document, if required, and may be done manually or by computer using existing programming. "Search" should be distinguished from "review" which is defined in paragraph (a)(3) of this section.

(3) "Review" means the process of examining documents located in response to a request under FOIA and this part to determine whether any portion of any document located is permitted or required to be withheld. It also includes processing any documents for disclosure, e.g., doing all that is necessary to excise them and otherwise prepare them for release. Review does not include time spent resolving general legal or policy issues regarding the application of exemptions.

(4) "Duplication" means the process of making a copy of a document necessary to respond to a request under FOIA and this part, in a form that is reasonably usable by the requester. Copies can take the form of paper copy, microform, audio-visual materials, or machine readable documentation (e.g., magnetic tape or disk), among others.

(b) *Categories of requesters.* Requesters who seek access to records under FOIA and this part are divided into four categories: commercial use requesters, educational and noncommercial scientific institutions, representatives of the news media, and all other requesters. The PBGC will determine the category of a requester and charge fees according to the following rules.

(1) *Commercial use requesters.* When records are requested for commercial use, the PBGC will assess charges, as provided in this subpart, for the full direct costs of searching for, reviewing for release, and duplicating the records sought. Fees for search and review may be charged even if the record searched for is not found or if, after it is found, it is determined that the request to inspect it may be denied under the provisions of subsection (b) of FOIA and this part.

(i) "Commercial use" request means a request from or on behalf of one who seeks information for a use or purpose that furthers the commercial, trade, or profit interests of the requester or the person on whose behalf the request is made.

(ii) In determining whether a request properly belongs in this category, the PBGC will look to the use to which a requester will put the documents requested. Moreover, where the PBGC has reasonable cause to doubt the use to which a requester will put the records sought, or where that use is not clear from the request itself, the PBGC will require the requester to provide clarification before assigning the request to this category.

(2) *Educational and noncommercial scientific institution requesters.* When records are requested by an educational or noncommercial scientific institution, the PBGC will assess charges, as provided in this subpart, for the full direct cost of duplication only, excluding charges for the first 100 pages.

(i) "Educational institution" means a preschool, a public or private elementary or secondary school, an institution of graduate higher education, an institution of undergraduate higher education, an institution of professional education, and an institution of vocational education, which operates a program or programs of scholarly research.

(ii) "Noncommercial scientific institution" means an institution that is not operated on a "commercial" basis as that term is defined in paragraph (b)(1)(i) of this section, and which is operated solely for the purpose of conducting scientific research the results of which are not intended to promote any particular product or industry.

(iii) To be eligible for inclusion in this category, requesters must show that the request is being made as authorized by and under the auspices of a qualifying institution and that the records are not sought for a commercial use, but are sought in furtherance of scholarly (if the request is from an educational institution) or scientific (if the request is from a noncommercial scientific institution) research.

(3) *Requesters who are representatives of the news media.* When records are requested by representatives of the news media, the PBGC will assess charges, as provided in this subpart, for the full direct cost of duplication only, excluding charges for the first 100 pages.

(i) "Representative of the news media" means any person actively gathering news for an entity that is organized and operated to publish or broadcast news to the public. The term "news" means information that is about current events or that would be of current interest to the public. Examples of news media entities include television or radio stations broadcasting to the public at large, and publishers of periodicals (but only in those instances when they can qualify as disseminators of "news") who make their products available for purchase or subscription by the general public. These examples are not intended to be all-inclusive. "Freelance" journalists may be regarded as working for a news organization if they can demonstrate a solid basis for expecting publication through that organization, even though not actually employed by it.

(ii) To be eligible for inclusion in this category, the request must not be made for a commercial use. A request for records supporting the news dissemination function of the requester who is a representative of the news media shall not be considered to be a request that is for a commercial use.

(4) *All other requesters.* When records are requested by requesters who do not fit into any of the categories in paragraphs (b)(1) through (b)(3) of this section, the PBGC will assess charges, as provided in this subpart, for the full direct cost of searching for and duplicating the records sought, with the exceptions that there will be no charge for the first 100 pages of duplication and the first two hours of manual search time (or its cost equivalent in computer search time). Notwithstanding the preceding sentence, there will be no charge for search time in the event of requests under the Privacy Act of 1974 from subjects of records filed in the PBGC's systems of records for the disclosure of records about themselves. Search fees, where applicable, may be charged even if the record searched for is not found.

(c) *Aggregation of requests.* If the PBGC reasonably believes that a requester or group of requesters is attempting to break a request down into a series of requests for the purpose of evading the assessment of fees, the PBGC will aggregate any such requests and charge accordingly. In no case will the PBGC aggregate multiple requests on unrelated subjects from one requester.

(d) *Waiver or reduction of charges.* Circumstances under which searching, review, and duplication facilities or services may be made available to the requester without charge or at a reduced charge are set forth in § 4901.34 of this part.

[¶ 15,720R]

§ 4901.32 **Fee schedule.** (a) *Charges for searching and review of records.* Charges applicable under this subpart to the search for and review of records will be made according to the following fee schedule:

(1) *Search and review time.* (i) Ordinary search and review by custodial or clerical personnel, $1.75 for each one-quarter hour or fraction thereof of employee worktime required to locate or obtain the records to be searched and to make the necessary review; and (ii) search or review requiring services of professional or supervisory personnel to locate or review requested records, $4.00 for each one-quarter hour or fraction thereof of professional or supervisory personnel worktime.

(2) *Additional search costs.* If the search for a requested record requires transportation of the searcher to the location of the records or transportation of the records to the searcher, at a cost in excess of $5.00, actual transportation costs will be added to the search time cost.

(3) *Search in computerized records.* Charges for information that is available in whole or in part in computerized form will include the cost of operating the central processing unit (CPU) for that portion of operating time that is directly attributable to searching for records responsive to the request, personnel salaries apportionable to the search, and tape or printout production or an established agency-wide average rate for CPU operating costs and operator/programmer salaries involved in FOIA searches. Charges will be computed at the rates prescribed in paragraphs (a) and (b) of this section.

(b) *Charges for duplication of records.* Charges applicable under this subpart for obtaining requested copies of records made available for inspection will be made according to the following fee schedule and subject to the following conditions.

(1) *Standard copying fee.* $0.15 for each page of record copies furnished. This standard fee is also applicable to the furnishing of copies of available computer printouts as stated in paragraph (a)(3) of this section.

(2) *Voluminous material.* If the volume of page copy desired by the requester is such that the reproduction charge at the standard page rate would be in excess of $50, the person desiring reproduction may request a special rate quotation from the PBGC.

(3) *Limit of service.* Not more than 10 copies of any document will be furnished.

(4) *Manual copying by requester.* No charge will be made for manual copying by the requesting party of any document made available for inspection under the provisions of this part. The PBGC shall provide facilities for such copying without charge at reasonable times during normal working hours.

(5) *Indexes.* Pursuant to paragraph (a)(2) of FOIA copies of indexes or supplements thereto which are maintained as therein provided but which have not been published will be provided on request at a cost not to exceed the direct cost of duplication.

(c) *Other charges.* The scheduled fees, set forth in paragraphs (a) and (b) of this section, for furnishing records made available for inspection and duplication represent the direct costs of furnishing the copies at the place of duplication. Upon request, single copies of the records will be mailed, postage prepaid, free of charge. Actual costs of transmitting records by special methods such as registered, certified, or special delivery mail or messenger, and of special handling or packaging, if required, will be charged in addition to the scheduled fees.

[¶ 15,720S]

§ 4901.33 **Payment of fees.** (a) *Medium of payment.* Payment of the applicable fees as provided in this subsection shall be made in cash, by U.S. postal money order, or by check payable to the PBGC. Postage stamps will not be accepted in lieu of cash, checks, or money orders as payment for fees specified in the schedule. Cash should not be sent by mail.

(b) *Advance payment or assurance of payment.* Payment or assurance of payment before work is begun or continued on a request may be required under the following rules.

(1) Where the PBGC estimates or determines that charges allowable under the rules in this subpart are likely to exceed $250, the PBGC may require advance payment of the entire fee or assurance of payment, as follows:

(i) Where the requester has a history of prompt payment of fees under this part, the PBGC will notify the requester of the likely cost and obtain satisfactory assurance of full payment; or

(ii) Where the requester has no history of payment for requests made pursuant to FOIA and this part, the PBGC may require the requester to make an advance payment of an amount up to the full estimated charges.

(2) Where the requester has previously failed to pay a fee charged in a timely fashion (i.e., within 30 days of the date of the billing), the PBGC may require the requester to pay the full amount owed plus any applicable interest as provided in paragraph (c) of this

section (or demonstrate that he has, in fact, paid the fee) and to make an advance payment of the full amount of the estimated fee.

(c) *Late payment interest charges.* The PBGC may assess late payment interest charges on any amounts unpaid by the 31st day after the date a bill is sent to a requester. Interest will be assessed at the rate prescribed in 31 U.S.C. 3717 and will accrue from the date the bill is sent.

[Amended 10/28/2003 by 68 FR 61344]

[¶ 15,720T]

§ 4901.34 **Waiver or reduction of charges**. (a) The disclosure officer may waive or reduce fees otherwise applicable under this subpart when disclosure of the information is in the public interest because it is likely to contribute significantly to public understanding of the operations or activities of the government and is not primarily in the commercial interest of the requester. A fee waiver request shall set forth full and complete information upon which the request for waiver is based.

(b) The disclosure officer may reduce or waive fees applicable under this subpart when the requester has demonstrated his inability to pay such fees.

[¶ 15,720U]

§ 4902.1 **Purpose and scope**. This part establishes procedures whereby an individual can determine whether the PBGC maintains any system of records that contains a record pertaining to the individual, procedures to effect access to an individual's record upon his or her request, and procedures for making requests to amend records, for making the initial determinations on such requests, and for appealing denials of such requests. This part also prescribes the fees for making copies of an individual's record. Finally, this part sets forth those systems of records that are exempted from certain disclosure and other provisions of the Privacy Act (5 U.S.C. 552a).

[¶ 15,720V]

§ 4902.2 **Definitions**. In addition to terminology in part 4001 of this chapter, as used in this part:

Disclosure officer means the designated official in the Communications and Public Affairs Department, PBGC.

Record means any item, collection, or grouping of information about an individual that is maintained by an agency, including, but not limited to, his or her education, financial transactions, medical history, and criminal or employment history and that contains his or her name, or the identifying number, symbol, or other identifying particular assigned to the individual, such as a finger or voice print or a photograph.

System of records means a group of any records under the control of any agency from which information is retrieved by the name of the individual or by some identifying number, symbol, or other identifying particular assigned to the individual.

Working day means any weekday excepting Federal holidays.

[¶ 15,720W]

§ 4902.3 **Procedures for determining existence of and requesting access to records**. (a) Any individual may submit a request to the Disclosure Officer, Pension Benefit Guaranty Corporation, for the purpose of learning whether a system of records maintained by the PBGC contains any record pertaining to the requestor or obtaining access to such a record. Such a request may be sent to the Disclosure Officer or made in person between the hours of 9 a.m. and 4 p.m. on any working day in the Communications and Public Affairs Department, PBGC, 1200 K Street, NW., Suite 240, Washington, DC 20005-4026.

[Amended 10/28/2003 by 68 FR 61344]

(b) Each request submitted pursuant to paragraph (a) of this section shall include the name of the system of records to which the request pertains and the requester's full name, home address and date of birth, and shall prominently state the words, "Privacy Act Request." If this information is insufficient to enable the PBGC to identify the record in question, or to determine the identity of the requester (to ensure the privacy of the subject of the record), the disclosure officer shall request such further identifying data as the disclosure officer deems necessary to locate the record or to determine the identity of the requester.

[Amended 10/28/2003 by 68 FR 61344]

(c) Unless the request is only for notification of the existence of a record and such notification is required under the Freedom of Information Act (5 U.S.C. 552), the requester shall be required to provide verification of his or her identity to the PBGC as set forth in paragraph (c) (1) or (2) of this section, as appropriate.

(1) If the request is made by mail, the requester shall submit a notarized statement establishing his or her identity.

(2) If the request is made in person, the requester shall show identification satisfactory to the disclosure officer, such as a driver's license, employee identification, annuitant identification or Medicare card.

(d) The disclosure officer shall respond to the request in writing within 10 working days after receipt of the request or of such additional information as may be required under paragraph (b) of this section. If a request for access to a record is granted, the response shall state when the record will be made available.

[¶ 15,720X]

§ 4902.4 **Disclosure of record to an individual**. (a) When the disclosure officer grants a request for access to records under § 4902.3, such records shall be made available when the requester is advised of the determination or as promptly thereafter as possible. At the requester's option, the record will be made available for the requester's inspection and copying at the Communications and Public Affairs Department, Pension Benefit Guaranty Corporation, 1200 K Street NW., Washington, DC 20005-4026, between the hours of 9 a.m. and 4 p.m. on any working day, or a copy of the record will be mailed to the requester.

(b) If the requester desires to be accompanied by another individual during the inspection and/or copying of the record, the requester shall, either when the record is made available or at any earlier time, submit to the disclosure officer a signed statement identifying such other individual and authorizing such other individual to be present during the inspection and/or copying of the record.

[¶ 15,720Y]

§ 4902.5 **Procedures for requesting amendment of a record**. (a) Any individual about whom the PBGC maintains a record contained in a system of records may request that the record be amended. Such a request shall be submitted in the same manner described in § 4902.3(a).

(b) Each request submitted under paragraph (a) of this section shall include the information described in § 4902.3(b) and a statement specifying the changes to be made in the record and the justification therefor. The disclosure officer may request further identifying data as described in § 4902.3(b).

(c) An individual who desires assistance in the preparation of a request for amendment of a record shall submit such request for assistance in writing to the Deputy General Counsel, Pension Benefit Guaranty Corporation. The Deputy General Counsel shall respond to such request as promptly as possible.

[Amended 10/28/2003 by 68 FR 61344]

[¶ 15,720Z]

§ 4902.6 **Action on request for amendment of a record**. (a) Within 20 working days after receipt by the PBGC of a request for amendment of a record under § 4902.5, unless for good cause shown the Executive Director of the PBGC extends such 20-day period, the disclosure officer shall notify the requester in writing whether and to what extent the request shall be granted. To the extent that the request is granted, the disclosure officer shall cause the requested amendment to be made promptly.

(b) When a request for amendment of a record is denied in whole or in part, the denial shall include a statement of the reasons therefor, the procedures for appealing such denial, and a notice that the requester has a right to assistance in preparing an appeal of the denial.

(c) An individual who desires assistance in preparing an appeal of a denial under this section shall submit a request to the Deputy General Counsel, Pension Benefit Guaranty Corporation. The Deputy General Counsel shall respond to the request as promptly as possible, but in no event more than 30 days after receipt.

[Amended 10/28/2003 by 68 FR 61344]

[¶ 15,721]

§ 4902.7 **Appeal of a denial of a request for amendment of a record**. (a) An appeal from a denial of a request for amendment of a record under Sec. 4902.6 shall be submitted, within 45 days of receipt of the denial, to the General Counsel, Pension Benefit Guaranty Corporation, unless the record subject to such request is one maintained by the Office of the General Counsel, in which event the appeal shall be submitted to the Deputy Executive Director, Pension Benefit Guaranty Corporation. The appeal shall state in detail the basis on which it is made and shall clearly state "Privacy Act Request" on the first page. In addition, the submission shall clearly state "Privacy Act Request" on the envelope (for mail, hand delivery, or commercial delivery), in the subject line (for e-mail), or on the cover sheet (for fax).

[Amended 10/28/2003 by 68 FR 61344]

(b) Within 30 working days after the receipt of the appeal, unless for good cause shown the Executive Director of the PBGC extends such 30-day period, the General Counsel or, where appropriate, the Deputy Executive Director, shall issue a decision in writing granting or denying the appeal in whole or in part. To the extent that the appeal is granted, the General Counsel or, where appropriate, the Deputy Executive Director, shall cause the requested amendment to be made promptly. To the extent that the appeal is denied, the decision shall include the reasons for the denial and a notice of the requester's right to submit a brief statement setting forth reasons for disputing the denial of appeal, to seek judicial review of the denial pursuant to 5 U.S.C. 552a(g)(1)(A), and to obtain further information concerning the provisions for judicial review under that section.

(c) An individual whose appeal has been denied in whole or in part may submit a brief summary statement setting forth reasons for disputing such denial. Such statement shall be submitted within 30 days of receipt of the denial of the appeal to the Disclosure Officer. Any such statement shall be made available by the PBGC to anyone to whom the record is subsequently furnished and may also be accompanied, at the discretion of the PBGC, by a brief statement summarizing the PBGC's reasons for refusing to amend the record. The PBGC shall also provide copies of the individual's statement of dispute to all prior recipients of the record with respect to whom an accounting of the disclosure of the record was maintained pursuant to 5 U.S.C. 552a(c)(1).

(d) To request further information concerning the provisions for judicial review, an individual shall submit such request in writing to the Deputy General Counsel, who shall respond to such request as promptly as possible.

[¶ 15,721A]

§ 4902.8 **Fees**. When an individual requests a copy of his or her record under § 4902.4, charges for the copying shall be made according to the following fee schedule:

(a) *Standard copying fee.* There shall be a charge of $0.15 per page of record copies furnished. Where the copying fee is less than $1.50, it shall not be assessed.

(b) *Voluminous material.* If the volume of page copy desired by the requester is such that the reproduction charge at the standard page rate would be in excess of $50, the individual desiring reproduction may request a special rate quotation from the PBGC.

(c) *Manual copying by requester.* No charge will be made for manual copying by the requester of any document made available for inspection under § 4902.4. The PBGC shall provide facilities for such copying without charge between the hours of 9 a.m. and 4 p.m. on any working day.

[¶ 15,721B]

§ 4902.9 **Specific exemptions**. (a) Under the authority granted by 5 U.S.C. 552a(k)(5), the PBGC hereby exempts the system of records entitled "Personnel Security Investigation Records—PBGC" from the provisions of 5 U.S.C. §§ 552a (c)(3), (d), (e)(1), (e)(4) (G), (H), and (I), and (f), to the extent that the disclosure of such material would reveal the identity of a source who furnished information to PBGC under an express promise of confidentiality or, before September 27, 1975, under an implied promise of confidentiality.

(b) The reasons for asserting this exemption are to insure the gaining of information essential to determining suitability and fitness for PBGC employment or for work for the PBGC as a contractor or as an employee of a contractor, access to information, and security clearances, to insure that full and candid disclosures are obtained in making such determinations, to prevent subjects of such determinations from thwarting the completion of such determinations, and to avoid revealing the identities of persons who furnish information to the PBGC in confidence. [Amended June 14, 2001, 66 FR 32221.]

[¶ 15,721B-1]

§ 4902.10 **Filing rules; computation of time**. (a) *Filing rules.* (1) *Where to file.* See Sec. 4000.4 of this chapter for information on where to file a submission under this part with the PBGC.

(2) *Method of filing.* The PBGC applies the rules in subpart A of part 4000 of this chapter to determine permissible methods of filing with the PBGC under this part.

(3) *Date of filing.* The PBGC applies the rules in subpart C of part 4000 of this chapter to determine the date that a submission under this part was filed with the PBGC.

(b) *Computation of time.* The PBGC applies the rules in subpart D of part 4000 of this chapter to compute any time period for filing under this part.

[Added 10/28/2003 by 68 FR 61344]

Subpart A—General

[¶ 15,721C]

§ 4903.1 **Purpose and scope**. (a) *Subpart A.* Subpart A of this part contains definitions and general provisions applicable to debt collection generally.

(b) *Subpart B.* Subpart B of this part prescribes procedures for debt collection by administrative offset, as authorized by the Federal Claims Collection Act (31 U.S.C. 3716), and consistent with applicable provisions of the Federal Claims Collection Standards. These procedures apply when the PBGC determines that collection by administrative offset of a claim that is liquidated or certain in amount is feasible and not otherwise prohibited or when another agency seeks administrative offset against a payment to be made by the PBGC.

(c) *Subpart C.* Subpart C of this part prescribes procedures for debt collection by tax refund offset, as authorized by section 3720A of subchapter II, chapter 37 of title 31 of the United States Code (31 U.S.C. 3720A) and in accordance with applicable IRS regulations (26 CFR 301-6402.6), including a related procedure for disclosure to a consumer reporting agency. These procedures apply to determinations that a debt of at least $25 is past-due and legally enforceable, to referrals by the PBGC of past-due, legally enforceable debts to the IRS for offset, and to any subsequent corrections of information contained in such referrals.

[¶ 15,721D]

§ 4903.2 **General**. (a) Certain PBGC efforts to obtain payment of debts arising out of activities under ERISA are authorized by and subject to requirements prescribed under other federal statutes. When, and to the extent, such requirements apply to collection of a debt by the PBGC, PBGC activities will be consistent with such requirements, as well as with any other applicable requirements (see, e.g., parts 4003, 4007, and 4062 of this chapter).

(b)(1) The Executive Director of the PBGC has delegated to the Director of the Financial Operations Department primary responsibility for PBGC debt collection activities. This delegation includes responsibility for procedures implementing requirements prescribed under federal statutes other than ERISA, and for coordinating the activities of other PBGC departments with functional responsibilities for different types of claims.

(2) PBGC departments are responsible for ascertaining indebtedness and other aspects of agency collection activities within their areas of functional responsibility.

(c) The PBGC applies the rules in subpart A of part 4000 of this chapter to determine permissible methods of filing with the PBGC under this part. The PBGC applies the rules in subpart C of part 4000 of this chapter to determine the date that a submission under this part was filed with the PBGC. See Sec. 4000.4 of this chapter for information on where to file.

[Added 10/28/2003 by 68 FR 61344]

(d) The PBGC applies the rules in subpart D of part 4000 of this chapter to compute any time period for filing under this part.

[Added 10/28/2003 by 68 FR 61344]

[¶ 15,721E]

§ 4903.3 **Definitions.** The following terms are defined in § 4001.2 of this chapter: *IRS, PBGC,* and *person.* In addition, for purposes of this part:

Administrative offset has the meaning set forth in 31 U.S.C. 3701(a)(1).

Agency means an executive or legislative agency (within the meaning of 31 U.S.C. 3701(a)(4)).

Claim and debt, as defined in the Federal Claims Collection Standards (4 CFR 101.2(a)), are used synonymously and interchangeably to refer to an amount of money or property which has been determined by an appropriate agency official to be owed to the United States from any person, organization, or entity, except another Federal agency.

Consumer reporting agency has the meaning set forth in 31 U.S.C. 3701(a)(3).

Federal Claims Collection Act means the Federal Claims Collection Act of 1966, as amended (31 U.S.C. 3701 et seq.).

Federal Claims Collection Standards means 4 CFR parts 101 through 105, which are regulations issued jointly by the Comptroller General of the United States and the Attorney General of the United States that implement the Federal Claims Collection Act.

Repayment agreement means a written agreement by a debtor to repay a debt to the PBGC.

Tax refund offset means the reduction by the IRS of a tax overpayment payable to a taxpayer by the amount of past-due, legally enforceable debt owed by that taxpayer to a federal agency that has entered into an agreement with the IRS with regard to its participation in the tax refund offset program, pursuant to IRS regulations (26 CFR 301.6402-6).

Subpart B—Administrative Offset

[¶ 15,721F]

§ 4903.21 **Application of Federal Claims Collection Standards.** The PBGC will determine the feasibility of collection by administrative offset, whether to accept a repayment agreement in lieu of offset, and how to apply amounts collected by administrative offset on multiple debts as provided in the Federal Claims Collection Standards (4 CFR 102.3).

(a) *Feasibility.* The PBGC will determine whether collection by administrative offset is feasible on a case-by-case basis in the exercise of sound discretion. In making such determinations, the PBGC will consider:

(1) Whether administrative offset can be accomplished, both practically and legally;

(2) Whether administrative offset is best suited to further and protect all governmental interests;

(3) In appropriate circumstances, the debtor's financial condition; and

(4) Whether offset would tend to interfere substantially with or defeat the purposes of the program authorizing the payments against which offset is contemplated.

(b) *Repayment agreements.* The PBGC will exercise its discretion in determining whether to accept a repayment agreement in lieu of offset, balancing the Government's interest in collecting the debt against fairness to the debtor. If the debt is delinquent (within the meaning of 4 CFR 101.2(b)) and the debtor has not disputed its existence or amount, the PBGC will accept a repayment agreement in lieu of offset only if the debtor is able to establish that offset would result in undue financial hardship or would be against equity and good conscience.

(c) *Multiple debts.* When the PBGC collects multiple debts by administrative offset, it will apply the recovered amounts to those debts in accordance with the best interests of the United States, as determined by the facts and circumstances of the particular case, paying special attention to applicable statutes of limitations.

[¶ 15,721G]

§ 4903.22 **Administrative offset procedures.** (a) *General.* Except as otherwise required by law or as provided in paragraph (e) of this section, the PBGC will not effect administrative offset against a payment to be made to a debtor prior to the completion of the procedures specified in paragraphs (b) and (c) of this section. However, the PBGC will not duplicate any notice or other procedural protection it previously provided in connection with the same debt under some other statutory or regulatory authority, such as part 4003 of this chapter.

(b) *Notice.* The PBGC will provide written notice informing the debtor of the following:

(1) The nature and amount of the debt, and the PBGC's intention to collect by offset;

(2) That the debtor may inspect and copy PBGC records pertaining to the debt in accordance with part 4901 or part 4902 of this chapter, as applicable (access under the Freedom of Information Act (5 U.S.C. 552) or the Privacy Act (5 U.S.C. 552a), respectively);

(3) How and from whom the debtor may obtain administrative review of a determination of indebtedness;

(4) The facts and circumstances that the PBGC will consider in determining whether to accept a repayment agreement in lieu of offset; and

(5) If the PBGC has not previously demanded payment of the debt, the date by which payment must be made to avoid further collection action.

(c) *Administrative review.* (1) A debtor may obtain review within the PBGC of a determination of indebtedness by submitting a written request for review, designated as such, to the PBGC official specified in the notice of indebtedness. Unless another regulation in this chapter specifies a different period of time, such a request must be submitted within 30 days after the date of a PBGC notice under paragraph (b) of this section.

(2) A request for review must:

(i) State the ground(s) on which the debtor disputes the debt; and

(ii) Reference all pertinent information already in the possession of the PBGC and include any additional information believed to be relevant.

(3) The PBGC will review a determination of indebtedness, when requested to do so in a timely manner. The PBGC will issue a written decision, based on the written record, and will notify the debtor of its decision.

(i) The review will be conducted by an official of at least the same level of authority as the person who made the determination of indebtedness.

(ii) The notice of the PBGC's decision on review will include a brief statement of the reason(s) why the determination of indebtedness has or has not been changed.

(4) Upon receipt of a request for administrative review, the PBGC may, in its discretion, temporarily suspend transactions in any of the debtor's accounts maintained by the PBGC. If the PBGC resolves the dispute in the debtor's favor, it will lift the suspension immediately.

(d) *Repayment agreement in lieu of offset.* (1) The PBGC will not consider entering a repayment agreement in lieu of offset unless a debtor submits a copy of the debtor's most recent audited (or if not available, unaudited) financial statement (with balance sheets, income statements, and statements of changes in financial position), to the extent such documents have been prepared, and other information regarding the debtor's financial condition (e.g., the types of information on assets, liabilities, earnings, and other factors specified in paragraphs (b)(3) through (b)(7) of § 4062.6 of this chapter).

(2) The PBGC may require appropriate security as a condition of accepting a repayment agreement in lieu of offset.

(e) *Exception.* (1) The PBGC may effect administrative offset against a payment to be made to the debtor prior to completing the procedures specified in paragraphs (b) and (c) of this section if:

(i) Failure to take the offset would substantially prejudice the government's ability to collect the debt; and

(ii) The time before the payment is to be made does not reasonably permit the completion of those procedures.

(2) The PBGC has determined that a case in which it applies the special rule in § 4068.3(c) of this chapter meets the criteria in paragraph (e)(1) of this section.

(3) If the PBGC effects administrative offset against a payment to be made to a debtor prior to completing the procedures specified in paragraphs (b) and (c) of this section, the PBGC—

(i) Will promptly complete those procedures; and

(ii) Will promptly refund any amounts recovered by offset but later found not to be owed to the Government.

[¶ 15,721H]

§ 4903.23 **PBGC requests for offset by other agencies.** (a) *General.* The PBGC may request that funds payable to its debtor by another agency be administratively offset to collect a debt owed to the PBGC by the debtor. A PBGC request for administrative offset against amounts due and payable from the Civil Service Retirement and Disability Fund will be made in accordance with 5 CFR part 831, subpart R (Agency Requests to OPM for Recovery of a Debt from the Civil Service Retirement and Disability Fund).

(b) *Certification.* In requesting administrative offset, the Director of the Financial Operations Department (or a department official designated by the Director) will certify in writing to the agency holding funds of the debtor—

(1) That the debtor owes the debt (including the amount) and that the PBGC has fully complied with the provisions of 4 CFR 102.3; and

(2) In a request for administrative offset against amounts due and payable from the Civil Service Retirement and Disability Fund, that the PBGC has complied with applicable statutes and the regulations and procedures of the Office of Personnel Management.

[¶ 15,721I]

§ 4903.24 **Requests for offset from other agencies.** (a) *General.* As provided in the Federal Claims Collections Standards (4 CFR 102.3(d)), the PBGC generally will comply with requests from other agencies to initiate administrative offset to collect debts owed to the United States unless the requesting agency has not complied with the applicable provisions of the Federal Claims Collection Standards or the offset would be otherwise contrary to law.

(b) *Submission of requests.* (1) Any agency may request that funds payable to its debtor by the PBGC be administratively offset to collect a debt owed to such agency by the debtor by submitting the certification described in paragraph (c) of this section.

(2) All such requests should be directed to the Director, Financial Operations Department. See Sec. 4000.4 of this chapter for additional information on where to file.

[Amended 10/28/2003 by 68 FR 61344]

(c) *Certification required.* The PBGC will not initiate administrative offset in response to a request from another agency until it receives written certification from the requesting agency, signed by an appropriate agency official, that the debtor owes the debt (including the amount) and that the requesting agency has fully complied with the provisions of 4 CFR 102.3 (with a citation to the agency's own administrative offset regulations).

Subpart C—Tax Refund Offset

[¶ 15,721J]

§ 4903.31 **Eligibility of debt for tax refund offset.** The PBGC will determine whether a debt is eligible for tax refund offset in accordance with IRS regulations (26 CFR 301.6402-6 (c) and (d)). The PBGC may refer a past-due, legally enforceable debt to the IRS for offset if:

(a) The debt is a judgment debt, or the PBGC's right of action accrued not more than 10 years earlier (unless the debt is specifically exempt from this requirement);

(b) The PBGC cannot currently collect the debt by salary offset (pursuant to 5 U.S.C. 5514(a)(1));

(c) The debt is ineligible for administrative offset (by reason of 31 U.S.C. 3716(c)(2)), or the PBGC cannot currently collect the debt by administrative offset (under 31 U.S.C. 3716 and subpart B of this part) against amounts payable by the debtor to the PBGC;

(d) The PBGC has notified, or attempted to notify, the debtor of its intent to refer the debt, given the debtor an opportunity to present evidence that all or part of the debt is not past-due or not legally enforceable, considered any evidence presented by the debtor in accordance with § 4903.32, and determined that the debt is past-due and legally enforceable;

(e) If the debt is a consumer debt and exceeds $100, the PBGC has disclosed the debt to a consumer reporting agency (as authorized by 31 U.S.C. 3711(f) and provided in § 4903.32), unless a consumer reporting agency would be prohibited from reporting information concerning the debt (by reason of 15 U.S.C. 1681c); and

(f) The debt is at least $25.

[¶ 15,721K]

§ 4903.32 **Tax refund offset procedures.** (a) *General.* Before referring a debt for tax refund offset, the PBGC will complete the procedures specified in paragraph (b) and, if applicable, paragraph (c) of this section. The PBGC may satisfy these requirements in conjunction with any other procedures that apply to the same debt, such as those prescribed in § 4903.22 or part 4003 of this chapter.

(b) *Notice, opportunity to present evidence, and determination of indebtedness.*

(1) The PBGC will notify, or make a reasonable attempt to notify, a person owing a debt (a "debtor") that a debt is past-due and if not repaid within 60 days, the PBGC will refer the debt to the IRS for offset against any overpayment of tax. For this purpose, compliance with IRS procedures (26 CFR 301.6402-6(d)(1)) constitutes a reasonable attempt to notify a debtor.

(2) A debtor will have at least 60 days to present evidence, for consideration by the PBGC, that all or part of a debt is not past-due or not legally enforceable.

(3) If evidence that all or part of a debt is not past-due or not legally enforceable is considered by an agent or person other than a PBGC employee acting on behalf of the PBGC, a debtor will have at least 30 days from the date of the determination on the debt to request review by the Director of the Financial Operations Department (or a department official designated by the Director).

(4) The PBGC will notify a debtor of its determination as to whether all or part of a debt is past-due and legally enforceable.

(c) *Consumer reporting agency disclosure.*

(1)(i) If a consumer debt exceeds $100, the Director of the Financial Operations Department (or a department official designated by the Director), after verifying the validity and overdue status of the debt and that section 605 of the Consumer Credit Protection Act (15 U.S.C. 1681c) does not prohibit a consumer reporting agency from reporting information concerning the debt because it is obsolete, will send the individual who owes the debt a written notice—

(A) That the debt is past-due;

(B) That the PBGC intends to disclose to a consumer reporting agency that the individual is responsible for the debt and the specific information to be disclosed; and

(C) How the individual may obtain an explanation of the debt, dispute the information in PBGC's records, and obtain administrative review of the debt.

(ii) If the PBGC does not have a current address for an individual, the Director of the Financial Operations Department (or a department official designated by the Director) will take reasonable action to locate the individual.

(2) The Director of the Financial Operations Department (or a department official designated by the Director) will disclose the debt if, within 60 days (or, at his or her discretion, more than 60 days) after

sending the notice described in paragraph (c)(1) of this section, the individual has not repaid the debt, or agreed to repay the debt under a written agreement, or requested administrative review of the debt.

[¶ 15,721L-1]

§ 4903.33 **Referral of debt for tax refund offset.** The Director of the Financial Operations Department (or a department official designated by the Director) will refer debts to the IRS for refund offset, and will correct referrals, in accordance with IRS regulations (26 CFR 301.6402-6(e) and (f)).

Subpart D—Salary Offset [Reserved]

[¶ 15,721M-1]

§ 4904.1 **Outside employment and other activity.** (a)-(e) [Removed on February 13, 2004, 69 FR 7120].

[¶ 15,721M-2]

§ 4905.1 **Purpose and scope.** (a) *Purpose.* This part sets forth the rules and procedures to be followed when a PBGC employee or former employee is requested or served with compulsory process to appear as a witness or produce documents in a proceeding in which the PBGC is not a party, if such appearance arises out of, or is related to, his or her employment with the PBGC. It provides a centralized decisionmaking mechanism for responding to such requests and compulsory process.

(b) *Scope.* (1) This part applies when, in a judicial, administrative, legislative, or other proceeding, a PBGC employee or former employee is requested or served with compulsory process to provide testimony concerning information acquired in the course of performing official duties or because of official status and/or to produce material acquired in the course of performing official duties or contained in PBGC files.

(2) This part does not apply to:

(i) Proceedings in which the PBGC is a party;

(ii) Congressional requests or subpoenas for testimony or documents; or

(iii) Appearances by PBGC employees in proceedings that do not arise out of, or relate to, their employment with PBGC (e.g., outside activities that are engaged in consistent with applicable standards of ethical conduct).

[¶ 15,721M-3]

§ 4905.2 **Definitions.** For purposes of this part:

Appearance means testimony or production of documents or other material, including an affidavit, deposition, interrogatory, declaration, or other required written submission.

Compulsory Process means any subpoena, order, or other demand of a court or other authority (e.g., an administrative agency or a state or local legislative body) for the appearance of a PBGC employee or former employee.

Employee means any officer or employee of the PBGC, including a special government employee.

Proceeding means any proceeding before any federal, state, or local court; federal, state, or local agency; state or local legislature; or other authority responsible for administering regulatory requirements or adjudicating disputes or controversies, including arbitration, mediation, and other similar proceedings.

Special government employee means an employee of the PBGC who is retained, designated, appointed or employed to perform, with or without compensation, for not to exceed one hundred and thirty days during any three hundred and sixty-five consecutive days, temporary duties either on a full-time or intermittent basis (18 U.S.C. 202).

[¶ 15,721M-4]

§ 4905.3 **General.** No PBGC employee or former employee may appear in any proceeding to which this part applies to testify and/or produce documents or other material unless authorized under this part.

[¶ 15,721M-5]

§ 4905.4 **Appearances by PBGC employees.** (a) Whenever a PBGC employee or former employee is requested or served with compulsory process to appear in a proceeding to which this part applies, he or she will promptly notify the General Counsel.

(b) The General Counsel or his or her designee will authorize an appearance by a PBGC employee or former employee if, and to the extent, he or she determines that such appearance is in the interest of the PBGC.

(1) In determining whether an appearance is in the interest of the PBGC, the General Counsel or his or her designee will consider relevant factors, including:

(i) What, if any, objective of the PBGC (and, where relevant, any federal agency, if the United States is a party) would be promoted by the appearance;

(ii) Whether the appearance would unnecessarily interfere with the employee's official duties;

(iii) Whether the appearance would result in the appearance of improperly favoring one litigant over another; and

(iv) Whether the appearance is appropriate under applicable substantive and procedural rules.

(2) If the General Counsel or his or her designee concludes that compulsory process is essentially a request for PBGC record information, it will be treated as a request under the Freedom of Information Act, as amended, in accordance with part 4901 of this chapter, except to the extent that the Privacy Act of 1974, as amended, and part 4902 of this chapter govern disclosure of a record maintained on an individual.

(c) If, in response to compulsory process in a proceeding to which this part applies, the General Counsel or his or her designee has not authorized an appearance by the return date, the employee or former employee shall appear at the stated time and place (unless advised by the General Counsel or his or her designee that process either was not validly issued or served or has been withdrawn), accompanied by a PBGC attorney, produce a copy of this part of the regulations, and respectfully decline to provide any testimony or produce any documents or other material. When the demand is under consideration, the employee shall respectfully request that the court or other authority stay the demand pending the employee's receipt of instructions from the General Counsel.

[¶ 15,721M-6]

§ 4905.5 **Requests for authenticated copies of PBGC records.** The PBGC will grant requests for authenticated copies of PBGC records, for purposes of admissibility under 28 U.S.C. 1733 and Rule 44 of the Federal Rules of Civil Procedure, for records that are to be disclosed pursuant to this part or part 4901 of this chapter. Appropriate fees will be charged for providing authenticated copies of PBGC records, in accordance with part 4901, subpart D, of this chapter.

[¶ 15,721M-7]

§ 4905.6 **Penalty.** A PBGC employee who testifies or produces documents or other material in violation of a provision of this part of the regulations shall be subject to disciplinary action.

[¶ 15,721N-1]

§ 4907.101 **Purpose.** This part effectuates section 119 of the Rehabilitation, Comprehensive Services, and Developmental Disabilities Amendments of 1978, which amended section 504 of the Rehabilitation Act of 1973 to prohibit discrimination on the basis of handicap in programs or activities conducted by Executive agencies or the United States Postal Service.

[¶ 15,721N-2]

§ 4907.102 **Application.** This part applies to all programs or activities conducted by the agency.

[¶ 15,721N-3]

§ 4907.103 **Definitions.** For purposes of this part, the term—

Assistant Attorney General means the Assistant Attorney General, Civil Rights Division, United States Department of Justice.

Auxiliary aids means services or devices that enable persons with impaired sensory, manual, or speaking skills to have an equal opportunity to participate in, and enjoy the benefits of, programs or activities conducted by the agency. For example, auxiliary aids useful for persons with impaired vision include readers, brailled materials, audio recordings, telecommunications devices and other similar services and devices. Auxiliary aids useful for persons with impaired hearing include telephone handset amplifiers, telephones compatible with hearing aids, telecommunication devices for deaf persons' (TDD's), interpreters, notetakers, written materials, and other similar services and devices.

Complete complaint means a written statement that contains the complainant's name and address and describes the agency's alleged discriminatory action in sufficient detail to inform the agency of the nature and date of the alleged violation of section 504. It shall be signed by the complainant or by someone authorized to do so on his or her behalf. Complaints filed on behalf of classes or third parties shall describe or identify (by name, if possible) the alleged victims of discrimination.

Facility means all or any portion of buildings, structures, equipment, roads, walks, parking lots, rolling stock or other conveyances, or other real or personal property.

Handicapped person means any person who has a physical or mental impairment that substantially limits one or more major life activities, has a record of such an impairment, or is regarded as having such an impairment.

As used in this definition, the phrase:

(1) Physical or mental impairment includes—

(i) Any physiological disorder or condition, cosmetic disfigurement, or anatomical loss affecting one or more of the following body systems: Neurological; musculoskeletal; special sense organs; respiratory, including speech organs; cardiovascular; reproductive; digestive; genitourinary; hemic and lymphatic; skin; and endocrine; or

(ii) Any mental or psychological disorder, such as mental retardation, organic brain syndrome, emotional or mental illness, and specific learning disabilities. The term "physical or mental impairment" includes, but is not limited to, such diseases and conditions as orthopedic, visual, speech, and hearing impairments, cerebral palsy, epilepsy, muscular dystrophy, multiple sclerosis, cancer, heart disease, diabetes, mental retardation, emotional illness, and drug addiction and alcoholism.

(2) Major life activities includes functions such as caring for one's self, performing manual tasks, walking, seeing, hearing, speaking, breathing, learning, and working.

(3) Has a record of such an impairment means has a history of, or has been misclassified as having, a mental or physical impairment that substantially limits one or more major life activities.

(4) Is regarded as having an impairment means—

(i) Has a physical or mental impairment that does not substantially limit major life activities but is treated by the agency as constituting such a limitation;

(ii) Has a physical or mental impairment that substantially limits major life activities only as a result of the attitudes of others toward such impairment; or

(iii) Has none of the impairments defined in subparagraph (1) of this definition but is treated by the agency as having such an impairment.

Historic preservation programs means programs conducted by the agency that have preservation of historic properties as a primary purpose.

Historic properties means those properties that are listed or eligible for listing in the National Register of Historic Places or properties designated as historic under a statute of the appropriate State or local government body.

Qualified handicapped person means—

(1) With respect to preschool, elementary, or secondary education services provided by the agency, a handicapped person who is a member of a class of persons otherwise entitled by statute, regulation, or agency policy to receive education services from the agency.

(2) With respect to any other agency program or activity under which a person is required to perform services or to achieve a level of accomplishment, a handicapped person who meets the essential eligibility requirements and who can achieve the purpose of the program or activity without modifications in the program or activity that the agency can demonstrate would result in a fundamental alteration in its nature;

(3) With respect to any other program or activity, a handicapped person who meets the essential eligibility requirements for participation in, or receipt of benefits from, that program or activity; and

(4) Qualified handicapped person is defined for purposes of employment in 29 CFR 1613.702(f), which is made applicable to this part by §4907.140.

Section 504 means section 504 of the Rehabilitation Act of 1973 (Pub. L. 93-112, 87 Stat. 394 (29 U.S.C. 794)), as amended by the Rehabilitation Act Amendments of 1974 (Pub. L. 93-516, 88 Stat. 1617), and the Rehabilitation, Comprehensive Services, and Developmental Disabilities Amendments of 1978 (Pub. L. 95-602, 92 Stat. 2955). As used in this part, section 504 applies only to programs or activities conducted by Executive agencies and not to federally assisted programs.

Substantial impairment means a significant loss of the integrity of finished materials, design quality, or special character resulting from a permanent alteration.

[¶ 15,721N-4]

§§4907.104-4907.109 **[Reserved.]**

[¶ 15,721N-10]

§4907.110 **Self-evaluation.** (a) The agency shall, by August 24, 1987, evaluate its current policies and practices, and the effects thereof, that do not or may not meet the requirements of this part, and, to the extent modification of any such policies and practices is required, the agency shall proceed to make the necessary modifications.

(b) The agency shall provide an opportunity to interested persons, including handicapped persons or organizations representing handicapped persons, to participate in the self-evaluation process by submitting comments (both oral and written).

(c) The agency shall, until three years following the completion of the self-evaluation, maintain on file and make available for public inspection:

(1) a description of areas examined and any problems identified, and

(2) a description of any modifications made.

[¶ 15,721N-11]

§4907.111 **Notice.** The agency shall make available to employees, applicants, participants, beneficiaries, and other interested persons such information regarding the provisions of this part and its applicability to the programs or activities conducted by the agency, and make such information available to them in such manner as the head of the agency finds necessary to apprise such persons of the protections against discrimination assured them by section 504 and this regulation.

[¶ 15,721N-12]

§§4907.112-4907.129 **[Reserved.]**

[¶ 15,721N-30]

§4907.130 **General prohibitions against discrimination.** (a) No qualified handicapped person shall, on the basis of handicap, be excluded from participation in, be denied the benefits of, or otherwise be subjected to discrimination under any program or activity conducted by the agency.

(b)(1) The agency, in providing any aid, benefit, or service, may not, directly or through contractual, licensing, or other arrangements, on the basis of handicap—

(i) Deny a qualified handicapped person the opportunity to participate in or benefit from the aid, benefit, or service;

(ii) Afford a qualified handicapped person an opportunity to participate in or benefit from the aid, benefit, or service that is not equal to that afforded others;

(iii) Provide a qualified handicapped person with an aid, benefit, or service that is not as effective in affording equal opportunity to obtain the same result, to gain the same benefit, or to reach the same level of achievement as that provided to others;

(iv) Provide different or separate aid, benefits, or services to handicapped persons or to any class of handicapped persons than is provided to others unless such action is necessary to provide qualified handicapped persons with aid, benefits, or services that are as effective as those provided to others;

(v) Deny a qualified handicapped person the opportunity to participate as a member of planning or advisory boards; or

(vi) Otherwise limit a qualified handicapped person in the enjoyment of any right, privilege, advantage, or opportunity enjoyed by others receiving the aid, benefit, or service.

(2) The agency may not deny a qualified handicapped person the opportunity to participate in programs or activities that are not separate or different, despite the existence of permissibly separate or different programs or activities.

(3) The agency may not, directly or through contractual or other arrangements, utilize criteria or methods of administration the purpose or effect of which would—

(i) Subject qualified handicapped persons to discrimination on the basis of handicap; or

(ii) Defeat or substantially impair accomplishment of the objectives of a program or activity with respect to handicapped persons.

(4) The agency may not, in determining the site or location of a facility, make selections the purpose or effect of which would—

(i) Exclude handicapped persons from, deny them the benefits of, or otherwise subject them to discrimination under any program or activity conducted by the agency; or

(ii) Defeat or substantially impair the accomplishment of the objectives of a program or activity with respect to handicapped persons.

(5) The agency, in the selection of procurement contractors, may not use criteria that subject qualified handicapped persons to discrimination on the basis of handicap.

(6) The agency may not administer a licensing or certification program in a manner that subjects qualified handicapped persons to discrimination on the basis of handicap, nor may the agency establish requirements for the programs or activities of licensees or certified entities that subject qualified handicapped persons to discrimination on the basis of handicap. However, the programs or activities of entities that are licensed or certified by the agency are not, themselves, covered by this part.

(c) The exclusion of nonhandicapped persons from the benefits of a program limited by Federal statute or Executive Order to handicapped persons or the exclusion of a specific class of handicapped persons from a program limited by Federal statute or Executive Order to a different class of handicapped persons is not prohibited by this part.

(d) The agency shall administer programs and activities in the most integrated setting appropriate to the needs of qualified handicapped persons.

[¶ 15,721N-31]
§§ 4907.131-4907.139 **[Reserved.]**

[¶ 15,721N-40]
§ 4907.140 **Employment**. No qualified handicapped person shall, on the basis of handicap, be subjected to discrimination in employment under any program or activity conducted by the agency. The definitions, requirements, and procedures of section 501 of the Rehabilitation Act of 1973 (29 U.S.C. 791), as established by the Equal Employment Opportunity Commission in 29 CFR part 1613, shall apply to employment in federally-conducted programs or activities.

[¶ 15,721N-41]
§§ 4907.141-4907.148 **[Reserved.]**

[¶ 15,721N-49]
§ 4907.149 **Program accessibility: Discrimination prohibited**. Except as otherwise provided in § 4907.150, no qualified handicapped person shall, because the agency's facilities are inaccessible to or unusable by handicapped persons, be denied the benefits of, be excluded from participation in, or otherwise be subjected to discrimination under any program or activity conducted by the agency.

[¶ 15,721N-50]
§ 4907.150 **Program accessibility: Existing facilities**. (a) *General*. The agency shall operate each program or activity so that the program

or activity, when viewed in its entirety, is readily accessible to and usable by handicapped persons. This paragraph does not—

(1) Necessarily require the agency to make each of its existing facilities accessible to and usable by handicapped persons;

(2) In the case of historic preservation programs, require the agency to take any action that would result in a substantial impairment of significant historic features of an historic property; or

(3) Require the agency to take any action that it can demonstrate would result in a fundamental alteration in the nature of a program or activity or in undue financial and administrative burdens. In those circumstances where agency personnel believe that the proposed action would fundamentally alter the program or activity or would result in undue financial and administrative burdens, the agency has the burden of proving that compliance with § 4907.150(a) would result in such alteration or burdens. The decision that compliance would result in such alteration or burdens must be made by the agency head or his or her designee after considering all agency resources available for use in the funding and operation of the conducted program or activity, and must be accompanied by a written statement of the reasons for reaching that conclusion. If an action would result in such an alteration or such burdens, the agency shall take any other action that would not result in such an alteration or such burdens but would nevertheless ensure that handicapped persons receive the benefits and services of the program or activity.

(b) *Methods*—

(1) *General*. The agency may comply with the requirements of this section through such means as redesign of equipment, reassignment of services to accessible buildings, assignment of aides to beneficiaries, home visits, delivery of services at alternate accessible sites, alteration of existing facilities and construction of new facilities, use of accessible rolling stock, or any other methods that result in making its programs or activities readily accessible to and usable by handicapped persons. The agency is not required to make structural changes in existing facilities where other methods are effective in achieving compliance with this section. The agency, in making alterations to existing buildings, shall meet accessibility requirements to the extent compelled by the Architectural Barriers Act of 1968, as amended (42 U.S.C. 4151-4157), and any regulations implementing it. In choosing among available methods for meeting the requirements of this section, the agency shall give priority to those methods that offer programs and activities to qualified handicapped persons in the most integrated setting appropriate.

(2) *Historic preservation programs*. In meeting the requirements of § 4907.150(a) in historic preservation programs, the agency shall give priority to methods that provide physical access to handicapped persons. In cases where a physical alteration to an historic property is not required because of § 4907.150(a)(2) or (a)(3), alternative methods of achieving program accessibility include—

(i) Using audio-visual materials and devices to depict those portions of an historic property that cannot otherwise be made accessible;

(ii) Assigning persons to guide handicapped persons into or through portions of historic properties that cannot otherwise be made accessible; or

(iii) Adopting other innovative methods.

(c) *Time period for compliance*. The agency shall comply with the obligations established under this section by October 21, 1986, except that where structural changes in facilities are undertaken, such changes shall be made by August 22, 1989, but in any event as expeditiously as possible.

(d) *Transition plan*. In the event that structural changes to facilities will be undertaken to achieve program accessibility, the agency shall develop, by February 23, 1987 a transition plan setting forth the steps necessary to complete such changes. The agency shall provide an opportunity to interested persons, including handicapped persons or organizations representing handicapped persons, to participate in the development of the transition plan by submitting comments (both oral and written). A copy of the transition plan shall be made available for public inspection. The plan shall, at a minimum—

(1) Identify physical obstacles in the agency's facilities that limit the accessibility of its programs or activities to handicapped persons;

(2) Describe in detail the methods that will be used to make the facilities accessible;

(3) Specify the schedule for taking the steps necessary to achieve compliance with this section and, if the time period of the transition plan is longer than one year, identify steps that will be taken during each year of the transition period; and

(4) Indicate the official responsible for implementation of the plan.

[¶ 15,721N-51]

§ 4907.151 **Program accessibility: New construction and alterations.** Each building or part of a building that is constructed or altered by, on behalf of, or for the use of the agency shall be designed, constructed, or altered so as to be readily accessible to and usable by handicapped persons. The definitions, requirements, and standards of the Architectural Barriers Act (42 U.S.C. 4151-4157), as established in 41 CFR 101-19.600 to 101-19.607, apply to buildings covered by this section.

[¶ 15,721N-52]

§§ 4907.152-4907.159 [Reserved.]

[¶ 15,721N-60]

§ 4907.160 **Communications.** (a) The agency shall take appropriate steps to ensure effective communication with applicants, participants, personnel of other Federal entities, and members of the public.

(1) The agency shall furnish appropriate auxiliary aids where necessary to afford a handicapped person an equal opportunity to participate in, and enjoy the benefits of, a program or activity conducted by the agency.

(i) In determining what type of auxiliary aid is necessary, the agency shall give primary consideration to the requests of the handicapped person.

(ii) The agency need not provide individually prescribed devices, readers for personal use or study, or other devices of a personal nature.

(2) Where the agency communicates with applicants and beneficiaries by telephone, telecommunication devices for deaf person (TDD's) or equally effective telecommunication systems shall be used.

(b) The agency shall ensure that interested persons, including persons with impaired vision or hearing, can obtain information as to the existence and location of accessible services, activities, and facilities.

(c) The agency shall provide signage at a primary entrance to each of its inaccessible facilities, directing users to a location at which they can obtain information about accessible facilities. The international symbol for accessibility shall be used at each primary entrance of an accessible facility.

(d) This section does not require the agency to take any action that it can demonstrate would result in a fundamental alteration in the nature of a program or activity or in undue financial and administrative burdens. In those circumstances where agency personnel believe that the proposed action would fundamentally alter the program or activity or would result in undue financial and administrative burdens, the agency has the burden of proving that compliance with § 4907.160 would result in such alteration or burdens. The decision that compliance would result in such alteration or burdens must be made by the agency head or his or her designee after considering all agency resources available for use in the funding and operation of the conducted program or activity, and must be accompanied by a written statement of the reasons for reaching that conclusion. If an action required to comply with this section would result in such an alteration or such burdens, the agency shall take any other action that would not result in such an alteration or such burdens but would nevertheless ensure that, to the maximum extent possible, handicapped persons receive the benefits and services of the program or activity.

[¶ 15,721N-61]

§ 4907.161-§ 4907.169 [Reserved.]

[¶ 15,721N-70]

§ 4907.170 **Compliance procedures.** (a) Except as provided in paragraph (b) of this section, this section applies to all allegations of discrimination on the basis of handicap in programs or activities conducted by the agency.

(b) The agency shall process complaints alleging violations of section 504 with respect to employment according to the procedures established by the Equal Employment Opportunity Commission in 29 CFR part 1613 pursuant to section 501 of the Rehabilitation Act of 1973 (29 U.S.C. 791).

(c) The Equal Opportunity Manager shall be responsible for coordinating implementation of this section.

(1) *Where to file.* See Sec. 4000.4 of this chapter for information on where to file complaints under this part.

(2) *Method of filing.* The PBGC applies the rules in subpart A of part 4000 of this chapter to determine permissible methods of filing with the PBGC under this part.

(3) *Date of filing.* The PBGC applies the rules in subpart C of part 4000 of this chapter to determine the date that a submission under this part was filed with the PBGC.

(4) *Computation of time.* The PBGC applies the rules in subpart D of part 4000 of this chapter to compute any time period under this part.

[Amended 10/28/2003 by 68 FR 61344]

(d) The agency shall accept and investigate all complete complaints for which it has jurisdiction. All complete complaints must be filed within 180 days of the alleged act of discrimination. The agency may extend this time period for good cause.

(e) If the agency receives a complaint over which it does not have jurisdiction, it shall promptly notify the complainant and shall make reasonable efforts to refer the complaint to the appropriate government entity.

(f) The agency shall notify the Architectural and Transportation Barriers Compliance Board upon receipt of any complaint alleging that a building or facility that is subject to the Architectural Barriers Act of 1968, as amended (42 U.S.C. 4151-4157), or section 502 of the Rehabilitation Act of 1973, as amended (29 U.S.C. 792), is not readily accessible to and usable by handicapped persons.

(g) Within 180 days of the receipt of a complete complaint for which it has jurisdiction, the agency shall notify the complainant of the results of the investigation in a letter containing—

(1) Findings of fact and conclusions of law;

(2) A description of a remedy for each violation found; and

(3) A notice of the right to appeal.

(h) Appeals of the findings of fact and conclusions of law or remedies must be filed by the complainant within 90 days of receipt from the agency of the letter required by § 4907.170(g). The agency may extend this time for good cause.

(i) Timely appeals shall be accepted and processed by the head of the agency.

(j) The head of the agency shall notify the complainant of the results of the appeal within 60 days of the receipt of the request. If the head of the agency determines that additional information is needed from the complainant, he or she shall have 60 days from the date of receipt of the additional information to make his or her determination on the appeal.

(k) The time limits cited in paragraphs (g) and (j) of this section may be extended with the permission of the Assistant Attorney General.

(l) The agency may delegate its authority for conducting complaint investigations to other Federal agencies, except that the authority for making the final determination may not be delegated to another agency.

[¶ 15,721N-71]

§§ 4907.171-4907.999 [Reserved.]

Economic Growth and Tax Relief Reconciliation Act of 2001

P.L. 107-16

Signed on June 7, 2001

[Reproduced below are sections of the Economic Growth and Tax Relief Reconciliation Act of 2001 which did not amend any sections of the Internal Revenue Code of 1986 or the Employee Retirement Income Security Act of 1974 (ERISA).]

[¶15,721R]

Act Sec. 1. SHORT TITLE; REFERENCES; TABLE OF CONTENTS.

(a) SHORT TITLE. This Act may be cited as the "Economic Growth and Tax Relief Reconciliation Act of 2001".

(b) AMENDMENT OF 1986 CODE. Except as otherwise expressly provided, whenever in this Act an amendment or repeal is expressed in terms of an amendment to, or repeal of, a section or other provision, the reference shall be considered to be made to a section or other provision of the Internal Revenue Code of 1986.

* * *

[¶15,721R-1]

Act Sec. 620. ELIMINATION OF USER FEE FOR REQUESTS TO IRS REGARDING PENSION PLANS.

(a) ELIMINATION OF CERTAIN USER FEES. The Secretary of the Treasury or the Secretary's delegate shall not require payment of user fees under the program established under section 10511 of the Revenue Act of 1987 for requests to the Internal Revenue Service for determination letters with respect to the qualified status of a pension benefit plan maintained solely by one or more eligible employers or any trust which is part of the plan. The preceding sentence shall not apply to any request—

(1) made after the later of—

(A) the fifth plan year the pension benefit plan is in existence; or

(B) the end of any remedial amendment period with respect to the plan beginning within the first 5 plan years; or

(2) made by the sponsor of any prototype or similar plan which the sponsor intends to market to participating employers.

(b) PENSION BENEFIT PLAN. For purposes of this section, the term "pension benefit plan" means a pension, profit-sharing, stock bonus, annuity, or employee stock ownership plan.

(c) ELIGIBLE EMPLOYER. For purposes of this section, the term "eligible employer" means an eligible employer (as defined in section 408(p)(2)(C)(i)(I) of the Internal Revenue Code of 1986) which has at least one employee who is not a highly compensated employee (as defined in section 414(q)) and is participating in the plan. The determination of whether an employer is an eligible employer under this section shall be made as of the date of the request described in subsection (a).

(d) DETERMINATION OF AVERAGE FEES CHARGED. For purposes of any determination of average fees charged, any request to which subsection (a) applies shall not be taken into account.

(e) EFFECTIVE DATE. The provisions of this section shall apply with respect to requests made after December 31, 2001.

* * *

[¶15,721R-2]

Act Sec. 634. MODIFICATION TO MINIMUM DISTRIBUTION RULES.

The Secretary of the Treasury shall modify the life expectancy tables under the regulations relating to minimum distribution requirements under sections 401(a)(9), 408(a)(6) and (b)(3), 403(b)(10), and 457(d)(2) of the Internal Revenue Code to reflect current life expectancy.

* * *

[¶15,721R-3]

Act Sec. 636. PROVISIONS RELATING TO HARDSHIP DISTRIBUTIONS.

(a) SAFE HARBOR RELIEF.—

(1) IN GENERAL. The Secretary of the Treasury shall revise the regulations relating to hardship distributions under section 401(k)(2)(B)(i)(IV) of the Internal Revenue Code of 1986 to provide that the period an employee is prohibited from making elective and employee contributions in order for a distribution to be deemed necessary to satisfy financial need shall be equal to 6 months.

(2) EFFECTIVE DATE. The revised regulations under this subsection shall apply to years beginning after December 31, 2001.

* * *

Subtitle D—Increasing Portability for Participants

* * *

[¶15,721R-4]

Act Sec. 645. TREATMENT OF FORMS OF DISTRIBUTION.

* * *

(b) REGULATIONS.—

* * *

(3) SECRETARY DIRECTED. Not later than December 31, 2003, the Secretary of the Treasury is directed to issue regulations under section 411(d)(6) of the Internal Revenue Code of 1986 and section 204(g) of the Employee Retirement Income Security Act of 1974, including the regulations required by the amendment made by this subsection. Such regulations shall apply to plan years beginning after December 31, 2003, or such earlier date as is specified by the Secretary of the Treasury.

* * *

Subtitle E—Strengthening Pension Security and Enforcement
PART I—GENERAL PROVISIONS

* * *

[¶15,721R-5]

Act Sec. 655. PROTECTION OF INVESTMENT OF EMPLOYEE CONTRIBUTIONS TO 401(k) PLANS.

(a) IN GENERAL. Section 1524(b) of the Taxpayer Relief Act of 1997 is amended to read as follows:

"(b) EFFECTIVE DATE.—

"(1) IN GENERAL. Except as provided in paragraph (2), the amendments made by this section shall apply to elective deferrals for plan years beginning after December 31, 1998.

"(2) NONAPPLICATION TO PREVIOUSLY ACQUIRED PROPERTY. The amendments made by this section shall not apply to any elective deferral which is invested in assets consisting of qualifying employer securities, qualifying employer real property, or both, if such assets were acquired before January 1, 1999.".

• • *TAXPAYER RELIEF ACT OF 1997 ACT SEC. 1524(b) BEFORE AMENDMENT*————————————————————————

ACT SEC. 1524. DIVERSIFICATION OF SECTION 401(k) PLAN INVESTMENTS.

* * *

(b) EFFECTIVE DATE. The amendments made by this section shall apply to elective deferrals for plan years beginning after December 31, 1998.

(b) EFFECTIVE DATE. The amendment made by this section shall apply as if included in the provision of the Taxpayer Relief Act of 1997 to which it relates.

* * *

[¶15,721R-6]

Act Sec. 657. AUTOMATIC ROLLOVERS OF CERTAIN MANDATORY DISTRIBUTIONS.

* * *

(c) FIDUCIARY RULES.—

* * *

(2) REGULATIONS.—

(A) AUTOMATIC ROLLOVER SAFE HARBOR. Not later than 3 years after the date of enactment of this Act, the Secretary of Labor shall prescribe regulations providing for safe harbors under which the designation of an institution and investment of funds in accordance with section 401(a)(31)(B) of the Internal Revenue Code of 1986 is deemed to satisfy the fiduciary requirements of section 404(a) of the Employee Retirement Income Security Act of 1974 (29 U.S.C. 1104(a)).

(B) USE OF LOW-COST INDIVIDUAL RETIREMENT PLANS. The Secretary of the Treasury and the Secretary of Labor may provide, and shall give consideration to providing, special relief with respect to the use of low-cost individual retirement plans for purposes of transfers under section 401(a)(31)(B) of the Internal Revenue Code of 1986 and for other uses that promote the preservation of assets for retirement income purposes.

* * *

[¶15,721R-7]

Act Sec. 658. CLARIFICATION OF TREATMENT OF CONTRIBUTIONS TO MULTIEMPLOYER PLAN.

(a) NOT CONSIDERED METHOD OF ACCOUNTING. For purposes of section 446 of the Internal Revenue Code of 1986, a determination under section 404(a)(6) of such Code regarding the taxable year with respect to which a contribution to a multiemployer pension plan is deemed made shall not be treated as a method of accounting of the taxpayer. No deduction shall be allowed for any taxable year for any contribution to a multiemployer pension plan with respect to which a deduction was previously allowed.

(b) REGULATIONS. The Secretary of the Treasury shall promulgate such regulations as necessary to clarify that a taxpayer shall not be allowed an aggregate amount of deductions for contributions to a multiemployer pension plan which exceeds the amount of such contributions made or deemed made under section 404(a)(6) of the Internal Revenue Code of 1986 to such plan.

(c) EFFECTIVE DATE. Subsection (a), and any regulations promulgated under subsection (b), shall be effective for years ending after the date of the enactment of this Act.

* * *

[¶15,721R-8]

Act Sec. 663. REPEAL OF TRANSITION RULE RELATING TO CERTAIN HIGHLY COMPENSATED EMPLOYEES.

(a) IN GENERAL. Paragraph (4) of section 1114(c) of the Tax Reform Act of 1986 is hereby repealed.

ACT SEC. 1114. **DEFENITION OF HIGHLY COMPENSATED EMPLOYEE.**

* * *

(c) EFFECTIVE DATE.—

* * *

(4) SPECIAL RULE FOR DETERMINING HIGHLY COMPENSATED EMPLOYEES. For purposes of sections 401(k) and 401(m) of the Internal Revenue Code of 1986, in the case of an employer incorporated on December 15, 1924, if more than 50 percent of its employees in the top-paid group (within the meaning of section 414(q)(4) of such Code) earn less than $25,000 (indexed at the same time and in the same manner as under section 415(d) of such Code), then the highly compensated employees shall include employees described in section 414(q)(1)(C) of such Code determined without regard to the level of compensation of such employees.

(b) EFFECTIVE DATE. The repeal made by subsection (a) shall apply to plan years beginning after December 31, 2001.

[¶15,721R-9]

Act Sec. 664. EMPLOYEES OF TAX-EXEMPT ENTITIES.

(a) IN GENERAL. The Secretary of the Treasury shall modify Treasury Regulations section 1.410(b)-6(g) to provide that employees of an organization described in section 403(b)(1)(A)(i) of the Internal Revenue Code of 1986 who are eligible to make contributions under section 403(b) of such Code pursuant to a salary reduction agreement may be treated as excludable with respect to a plan under section 401(k) or (m) of such Code that is provided under the same general arrangement as a plan under such section 401(k), if—

(1) no employee of an organization described in section 403(b)(1)(A)(i) of such Code is eligible to participate in such section 401(k) plan or section 401(m) plan; and

(2) 95 percent of the employees who are not employees of an organization described in section 403(b)(1)(A)(i) of such Code are eligible to participate in such plan under such section 401(k) or (m).

(b) EFFECTIVE DATE. The modification required by subsection (a) shall apply as of the same date set forth in section 1426(b) of the Small Business Job Protection Act of 1996.

TITLE IX—COMPLIANCE WITH CONGRESSIONAL BUDGET ACT

[¶15,721R-10]

Act Sec. 901. SUNSET OF PROVISIONS OF ACT.

(a) IN GENERAL. All provisions of, and amendments made by, this Act shall not apply—

(1) to taxable, plan, or limitation years beginning after December 31, 2010, or

(2) in the case of title V, to estates of decedents dying, gifts made, or generation skipping transfers, after December 31, 2010.

(b) APPLICATION OF CERTAIN LAWS. The Internal Revenue Code of 1986 and the Employee Retirement Income Security Act of 1974 shall be applied and administered to years, estates, gifts, and transfers described in subsection (a) as if the provisions and amendments described in subsection (a) had never been enacted.

IRS Restructuring and Reform Act of 1998

P.L. 105-206

Signed on July 22, 1998

[Reproduced below are sections of the IRS Restructuring and Reform Act of 1998 which did not amend any sections of the Internal Revenue Code of 1986 or the Employee Retirement Income Security Act of 1974 (ERISA).]

[¶15,721S]

Act Sec. 1. SHORT TITLE.

(a) SHORT TITLE. This Act may be cited as the "Internal Revenue Service Restructuring and Reform Act of 1998."

* * *

[¶15,721S-1]

Act Sec. 6015. AMENDMENTS RELATED TO TITLE XV OF 1997 ACT.

* * *

(b) AMENDMENT RELATED TO SECTION 1505 OF 1997 ACT.. Section 1505(d)(2) of the 1997 Act is amended by striking "(b)(12)" and inserting "(b)(12)(A)(i)".

(c) AMENDMENTS RELATED TO SECTION 1529 OF 1997 ACT.—

(1) Section 1529(a) of the 1997 Act is amended to read as follows:

"(a) GENERAL RULE. Amounts to which this section applies which are received by an individual (or the survivors of the individual) as a result of hypertension or heart disease of the individual shall be excludable from gross income under section 104(a)(1) of the Internal Revenue Code of 1986."

(2) Section 1529(b)(1)(B) of the 1997 Act is amended to read as follows:

"(B) under—

"(i) a State law (as amended on May 19, 1992) which irrebuttably presumed that heart disease and hypertension are work-related illnesses but only for employees hired before July 1, 1992; or

"(ii) any other statute, ordinance, labor agreement, or similar provision as a disability pension payment or in the nature of a disability pension payment attributable to employment as a police officer or fireman, but only if the individual is referred to in the State law described in clause (i); and".

[¶15,721S-2]

Act Sec. 6016. AMENDMENTS RELATED TO TITLE XVI OF 1997 ACT.

(a) AMENDMENTS RELATED TO SECTION 1601(d) OF 1997 ACT.—

* * *

(2) AMENDMENT TO SECTION 1601(d)(4). Section 1601(d)(4)(A) of the 1997 Act is amended—

(A) by striking "Section 403(b)(11)" and inserting "Paragraphs (7)(A)(ii) and (11) of section 403(b)", and

(B) by striking "403(b)(1)" in clause (ii) and inserting "403(b)(10)".

[¶15,721S-3]

Act Sec. 6018. AMENDMENTS RELATED TO SMALL BUSINESS JOB PROTECTION ACT OF 1996.

* * *

(c) AMENDMENT RELATING TO SECTION 1431. Subparagraph (E) of section 1431(c)(1) of the Small Business Job Protection Act of 1996 is amended to read as follows:

"(E) Section 414(q)(5), as redesignated by subparagraph (A), is amended by striking 'under paragraph (4) or the number of officers taken into account under paragraph (5)'".

Child Support Performance and Incentive Act of 1998

P.L. 105-200

Signed on July 16, 1998

[Reproduced below is a section of the Child Support Performance and Incentive Act of 1998 which did not amend any sections of the Internal Revenue Code of 1986 or the Employee Retirement Income Security Act of 1974 (ERISA).]

[¶15,721T]

Act Sec. 1. SHORT TITLE.

This Act may be cited as the "Child Support Performance and Incentive Act of 1998".

* * *

TITLE IV—MISCELLANEOUS

[¶15,721T-1]

Act Sec. 401. ELIMINATION OF BARRIERS TO THE EFFECTIVE ESTABLISHMENT AND ENFORCEMENT OF MEDICAL CHILD SUPPORT.

* * *

(f) **Qualified Medical Child Support Orders and National Medical Support Notices for Church Plans.—**

(1) In general. Each church group health plan shall provide benefits in accordance with the applicable requirements of any qualified medical child support order. A qualified medical child support order with respect to any participant or beneficiary shall be deemed to apply to each such group health plan which has received such order, from which the participant or beneficiary is eligible to receive benefits, and with respect to which the requirements of paragraph (4) are met.

(2) Definitions. For purposes of this subsection—

(A) Church group health plan. The term "church group health plan" means a group health plan which is a church plan.

(B) Qualified medical child support order. The term "qualified medical child support order" means a medical child support order—

(i) which creates or recognizes the existence of an alternate recipient's right to, or assigns to an alternate recipient the right to, receive benefits for which a participant or beneficiary is eligible under a church group health plan; and

(ii) with respect to which the requirements of paragraphs (3) and (4) are met.

(C) Medical child support order. The term "medical child support order" means any judgment, decree, or order (including approval of a settlement agreement) which—

(i) provides for child support with respect to a child of a participant under a church group health plan or provides for health benefit coverage to such a child, is made pursuant to a State domestic relations law (including a community property law), and relates to benefits under such plan; or

(ii) is made pursuant to a law relating to medical child support described in section 1908 of the Social Security Act (as added by section 13822 of the Omnibus Budget Reconciliation Act of 1993) with respect to a church group health plan,

if such judgment, decree, or order: (I) is issued by a court of competent jurisdiction; or (II) is issued through an administrative process established under State law and has the force and effect of law under applicable State law. For purposes of this paragraph, an administrative notice which is issued pursuant to an administrative process referred to in subclause (II) of the preceding sentence and which has the effect of an order described in clause (i) or (ii) of the preceding sentence shall be treated as such an order.

(D) Alternate recipient. The term "alternate recipient" means any child of a participant who is recognized under a medical child support order as having a right to enrollment under a church group health plan with respect to such participant.

(E) Group health plan. The term "group health plan" has the meaning provided in section 607(1) of the Employee Retirement Income Security Act of 1974.

(F) State. The term "State" includes the District of Columbia, the Commonwealth of Puerto Rico, the Virgin Islands, Guam, and American Samoa.

(G) Other terms. The terms "participant", "beneficiary", "administrator", and "church plan" shall have the meanings provided such terms, respectively, by paragraphs (7), (8), (16), and (33) of section 3 of the Employee Retirement Income Security Act of 1974.

(3) Information to be included in qualified order. A medical child support order meets the requirements of this paragraph only if such order clearly specifies—

(A) the name and the last known mailing address (if any) of the participant and the name and mailing address of each alternate recipient covered by the order, except that, to the extent provided in the order, the name and mailing address of an official of a State or a political subdivision thereof may be substituted for the mailing address of any such alternate recipient;

(B) a reasonable description of the type of coverage to be provided to each such alternate recipient, or the manner in which such type of coverage is to be determined; and

(C) the period to which such order applies.

(4) Restriction on new types or forms of benefits. A medical child support order meets the requirements of this paragraph only if such order does not require a church group health plan to provide any type or form of benefit, or any option, not otherwise provided under the plan, except to the extent necessary to meet the requirements of a law relating to medical child support described in section 1908 of the Social Security Act (as added by section 13822 of the Omnibus Budget Reconciliation Act of 1993).

(5) Procedural requirements.—

(A) Timely notifications and determinations. In the case of any medical child support order received by a church group health plan—

(i) the plan administrator shall promptly notify the participant and each alternate recipient of the receipt of such order and the plan's procedures for determining whether medical child support orders are qualified medical child support orders; and

(ii) within a reasonable period after receipt of such order, the plan administrator shall determine whether such order is a qualified medical child support order and notify the participant and each alternate recipient of such determination.

(B) Establishment of procedures for determining qualified status of orders. Each church group health plan shall establish reasonable procedures to determine whether medical child support orders are qualified medical child support orders and to administer the provision of benefits under such qualified orders. Such procedures—

(i) shall be in writing;

(ii) shall provide for the notification of each person specified in a medical child support order as eligible to receive benefits under the plan (at the address included in the medical child support order) of such procedures promptly upon receipt by the plan of the medical child support order; and

(iii) shall permit an alternate recipient to designate a representative for receipt of copies of notices that are sent to the alternate recipient with respect to a medical child support order.

(C) National medical support notice deemed to be a qualified medical child support order.—

(i) In general. If the plan administrator of any church group health plan which is maintained by the employer of a noncustodial parent of a child or to which such an employer contributes receives an appropriately completed National Medical Support Notice promulgated pursuant to subsection (b) of this section in the case of such child, and the Notice meets the requirements of paragraphs (3) and (4) of this subsection, the Notice shall be deemed to be a qualified medical child support order in the case of such child.

(ii) Enrollment of child in plan. In any case in which an appropriately completed National Medical Support Notice is issued in the case of a child of a participant under a church group health plan who is a noncustodial parent of the child, and the Notice is deemed under clause (i) to be a qualified medical child support order, the plan administrator, within 40 business days after the date of the Notice, shall—

(I) notify the State agency issuing the Notice with respect to such child whether coverage of the child is available under the terms of the plan and, if so, whether such child is covered under the plan and either the effective date of the coverage or any steps necessary to be taken by the custodial parent (or by the official of a State or political subdivision thereof substituted for the name of such child pursuant to paragraph (3)(A)) to effectuate the coverage; and

(II) provide to the custodial parent (or such substituted official) a description of the coverage available and any forms or documents necessary to effectuate such coverage.

(iii) Rule of construction. Nothing in this subparagraph shall be construed as requiring a church group health plan, upon receipt of a National Medical Support Notice, to provide benefits under the plan (or eligibility for such benefits) in addition to benefits (or eligibility for benefits) provided under the terms of the plan as of immediately before receipt of such Notice.

(6) Direct provision of benefits provided to alternate recipients. Any payment for benefits made by a church group health plan pursuant to a medical child support order in reimbursement for expenses paid by an alternate recipient or an alternate recipient's custodial parent or legal guardian shall be made to the alternate recipient or the alternate recipient's custodial parent or legal guardian.

(7) Payment to state official treated as satisfaction of plan's obligation to make payment to alternate recipient. Payment of benefits by a church group health plan to an official of a State or a political subdivision thereof whose name and address have been substituted for the address of an alternate recipient in a medical child support order, pursuant to paragraph (3)(A), shall be treated, for purposes of this subsection and part D of title IV of the Social Security Act, as payment of benefits to the alternate recipient.

(8) Effective date. The provisions of this subsection shall take effect on the date of the issuance of interim regulations pursuant to subsection (b)(4) of this section.

* * *

Taxpayer Relief Act of 1997

P.L. 105-34

Signed on August 5, 1997

[Reproduced below are sections of the Taxpayer Relief Act of 1997 which did not amend any sections of the Internal Revenue Code of 1986 or the Employee Retirement Income Security Act of 1974 (ERISA).]

[¶15,721U]

Act Sec. 1. SHORT TITLE.

(a) SHORT TITLE. This Act may be cited as the "Taxpayer Relief Act of 1997."

* * *

[¶15,721U-1]

Act Sec. 1508. MODIFICATION OF FUNDING REQUIREMENTS FOR CERTAIN PLANS.

(a) FUNDING RULES FOR CERTAIN PLANS. Section 769 of the Retirement Protection Act of 1994 is amended by adding at the end the following new subsection:

»»→ *Caution: Section 769(c) below was amended by the Pension Funding Equity Act of 2004. The amended section appears at ¶ 13,987A. The amendment applies to plan years beginning after December 31, 2003.*

(c) TRANSITION RULES FOR CERTAIN PLANS.—

(1) IN GENERAL. In the case of a plan that—

(A) was not required to pay a variable rate premium for the plan year beginning in 1996;

(B) has not, in any plan year beginning after 1995 and before 2009, merged with another plan (other than a plan sponsored by an employer that was in 1996 within the controlled group of the plan sponsor); and

(C) is sponsored by a company that is engaged primarily in the interurban or interstate passenger bus service,

the transition rules described in paragraph (2) shall apply for any plan year beginning after 1996 and before 2010.

(2) TRANSITION RULES. The transition rules described in this paragraph are as follows:

(A) For purposes of section 412(l)(9)(A) of the Internal Revenue Code of 1986 and section 302(d)(9)(A) of the Employee Retirement Income Security Act of 1974—

(i) the funded current liability percentage for any plan year beginning after 1996 and before 2005 shall be treated as not less than 90 percent if for such plan year the funded current liability percentage is at least 85 percent, and

(ii) the funded current liability percentage for any plan year beginning after 2004 and before 2010 shall be treated as not less than 90 percent if for such plan year the funded current liability percentage satisfies the minimum percentage determined according to the following table:

"In the case of a plan year beginning in:	The minimum percentage is:
2005	86 percent
2006	87 percent
2007	88 percent
2008	89 percent
2009 and thereafter	90 percent.

(B) Sections 412(c)(7)(E)(i)(I) of such Code and 302(c)(7)(E)(i)(I) of such Act shall be applied—

(i) by substituting '85 percent' for '90 percent' for plan years beginning after 1996 and before 2005, and

(ii) by substituting the minimum percentage specified in the table contained in subparagraph (A)(ii) for '90 percent' for plan years beginning after 2004 and before 2010.

(C) In the event the funded current liability percentage of a plan is less than 85 percent for any plan year beginning after 1996 and before 2005, the transition rules under subparagraphs (A) and (B) shall continue to apply to the plan if contributions for such a plan year are made to the plan in an amount equal to the lesser of—

(i) the amount necessary to result in a funded current liability percentage of 85 percent, or

(ii) the greater of—

(I) 2 percent of the plan's current liability as of the beginning of such plan year, or

(II) the amount necessary to result in a funded current liability percentage of 80 percent as of the end of such plan year.

For the plan year beginning in 2005 and for each of the 3 succeeding plan years, the transition rules under subparagraphs (A) and (B) shall continue to apply to the plan for such plan year only if contributions to the plan for such plan year equal at least the expected increase in current liability due to benefits accruing during such plan year.".

(b) EFFECTIVE DATE. The amendment made by this section shall apply to plan years beginning after December 31, 1996.

[¶15,721U-2]

Act Sec. 1509. CLARIFICATION OF DISQUALIFICATION RULES RELATING TO ACCEPTANCE OF ROLLOVER CONTRIBUTIONS.

The Secretary of the Treasury or his delegate shall clarify that, under the Internal Revenue Service regulations protecting pension plans from disqualification by reason of the receipt of invalid rollover contributions under section 402(c) of the Internal Revenue Code of 1986, in order for the administrator of the plan receiving any such contribution to reasonably conclude that the contribution is a valid rollover contribution it is not necessary for the distributing plan to have a determination letter with respect to its status as a qualified plan under section 401 of such Code.

[¶15,721U-3]

Act Sec. 1510. NEW TECHNOLOGIES IN RETIREMENT PLANS.

(a) IN GENERAL. Not later than December 31, 1998, the Secretary of the Treasury and the Secretary of Labor shall each issue guidance which is designed to—

(1) interpret the notice, election, consent, disclosure, and time requirements (and related recordkeeping requirements) under the Internal Revenue Code of 1986 and the Employee Retirement Income Security Act of 1974 relating to retirement plans as applied to the use of new technologies by plan sponsors and administrators while maintaining the protection of the rights of participants and beneficiaries, and

(2) clarify the extent to which writing requirements under the Internal Revenue Code of 1986 relating to retirement plans shall be interpreted to permit paperless transactions.

(b) APPLICABILITY OF FINAL REGULATIONS. Final regulations applicable to the guidance regarding new technologies described in subsection (a) shall not be effective until the first plan year beginning at least 6 months after the issuance of such final regulations.

* * *

[¶15,721U-5]

Act Sec. 1529. TREATMENT OF CERTAIN DISABILITY BENEFITS RECEIVED BY FORMER POLICE OFFICERS OR FIREFIGHTERS.

(a) GENERAL RULE. For purposes of determining whether any amount to which this section applies is excludable from gross income under section 104(a)(1) of the Internal Revenue Code of 1986, the following conditions shall be treated as personal injuries or sickness in the course of employment:

(1) Heart disease.

(2) Hypertension.

(b) AMOUNTS TO WHICH SECTION APPLIES. This section shall apply to any amount—

(1) which is payable—

(A) to an individual (or to the survivors of an individual) who was a full-time employee of any police department or fire department which is organized and operated by a State, by any political subdivision thereof, or by any agency or instrumentality of a State or political subdivision thereof, and

(B) under a State law (as amended on May 19, 1992) which irrebuttably presumed that heart disease and hypertension are work-related illnesses but only for employees separating from service before July 1, 1992; and

(2) which was received in calendar year 1989, 1990, or 1991.

(c) WAIVER OF STATUTE OF LIMITATIONS. If, on the date of the enactment of this Act (or at any time within the 1-year period beginning on such date of enactment), credit or refund of any overpayment of tax resulting from the provisions of this section is barred by any law or rule of law (including res judicata), then credit or refund of such overpayment shall, nevertheless, be allowed or made if claim therefore is filed before the date 1 year after such date of enactment.

* * *

Subtitle D—Provisions Relating to Plan Amendments

[¶15,721U-6]

Act Sec. 1541. PROVISIONS RELATING TO PLAN AMENDMENTS.

(a) IN GENERAL. If this section applies to any plan or contract amendment—

(1) such plan or contract shall be treated as being operated in accordance with the terms of the plan during the period described in subsection (b)(2)(A), and

(2) such plan shall not fail to meet the requirements of section 411(d)(6) of the Internal Revenue Code of 1986 or section 204(g) of the Employee Retirement Income Security Act of 1974 by reason of such amendment.

(b) AMENDMENTS TO WHICH SECTION APPLIES—

(1) IN GENERAL. This section shall apply to any amendment to any plan or annuity contract which is made—

(A) pursuant to any amendment made by this title or subtitle H of title X, and

(B) before the first day of the first plan year beginning on or after January 1, 1999.

In the case of a governmental plan (as defined in section 414(d) of the Internal Revenue Code of 1986), this paragraph shall be applied by substituting "2001" for "1999".

(2) CONDITIONS. This section shall not apply to any amendment unless—

(A) during the period—

(i) beginning on the date the legislative amendment described in paragraph (1)(A) takes effect (or in the case of a plan or contract amendment not required by such legislative amendment, the effective date specified by the plan), and

(ii) ending on the date described in paragraph (1)(B) (or, if earlier, the date the plan or contract amendment is adopted),

the plan or contract is operated as if such plan or contract amendment were in effect, and

(B) such plan or contract amendment applies retroactively for such period.

* * *

Balanced Budget Act of 1997

P.L. 105-33

Signed on August 5, 1997

[Reproduced below are sections of the Balanced Budget Act of 1997 which did not amend any sections of the Internal Revenue Code of 1986 or the Employee Retirement Income Security Act of 1974 (ERISA).]

[¶ 15,721V]

Act Sec. 1. SHORT TITLE.

(a) SHORT TITLE. This Act may be cited as the "Balanced Budget Act of 1997."

* * *

TITLE IV—MEDICARE, MEDICAID AND CHILDREN HEALTH PROVISIONS

* * *

Subtitle J—State Children's Health Insurance Programs

Chapter 1—State Children's Health Insurance Programs

[¶ 15,721V-1]

Act Sec. 4901. ESTABLISHMENT OF PROGRAM.

(a) Establishment. The Social Security Act is amended by adding at the end the following new title:

"Title XXI—State Children's Health Insurance Program

* * *

"SEC. 2109. MISCELLANEOUS PROVISIONS.

"(a) Relation to Other Laws.—

"(1) HIPAA. Health benefits coverage provided under section 2101(a)(1) (and coverage provided under a waiver under section 2105(c)(2)(B)) shall be treated as cretible coverage for purposes of part 7 of subtitle Bof Title II of the Employee Retirement Income Security Act of 1974, Title XXVII of the Public Health Service Act, and subtitle K of the Internal Revenue Code of 1986.

"(2) ERISA. Nothing in this title shall be construed as affecting or modifying section 514 of the Employee Retirement Income Security Act of 1974 (29) U.S.C. 1144) with respect to a group health plan (as defined in section 2791(a)(1) of the Public Health Service Act (42 U.S.C. 300gg-91(a)(1)).

* * *

Health Insurance Portability and Accountability Act of 1996

P.L. 104-191

Signed on August 21, 1996

[Reproduced below are sections of the Health Insurance Portability and Accountability Act of 1996 which did not amend any sections of the Internal Revenue Code of 1986 or the Employee Retirement Income Security Act of 1974 (ERISA).]

[¶15,721W]

Act Sec. 1. SHORT TITLE; TABLE OF CONTENTS.

(a) SHORT TITLE. This Act may be cited as the Health Insurance Portability and Accountability Act of 1996.

* * *

TITLE IV—APPLICATION AND ENFORCEMENT OF GROUP HEALTH PLAN REQUIREMENTS

* * *

Subtitle B—Clarification of Certain Continuation Coverage Requirements

[¶15,721W-1]

Act Sec. 421. COBRA CLARIFICATIONS.

* * *

(e) NOTIFICATION OF CHANGES. Not later than November 1, 1996, each group health plan (covered under title XXII of the Public Health Service Act, part 6 of subtitle B of title I of the Employee Retirement Income Security Act of 1974, and section 4980B(f) of the Internal Revenue Code of 1986) shall notify each qualified beneficiary who has elected continuation coverage under such title, part or section of the amendments made by this section.

* * *

Small Business Job Protection Act of 1996

P.L. 104-188

Signed on August 20, 1996

[Reproduced below are sections of the Small Business Job Protection Act of 1996 which did not amend any sections of the Internal Revenue Code of 1986 or the Employee Retirement Income Security Act of 1974 (ERISA).]

TITLE I—SMALL BUSINESS AND OTHER TAX PROVISIONS

[¶15,721X]

Act Sec. 1101. AMENDMENT OF 1986 CODE.

Except as otherwise expressly provided, whenever in this title an amendment or repeal is expressed in terms of an amendment to, or repeal of, a section or other provision, the reference shall be considered to be made to a section or other provision of the Internal Revenue Code of 1986.

[¶15,721X-1]

Act Sec. 1102. UNDERPAYMENTS OF ESTIMATED TAX.

No addition to the tax shall be made under section 6654 or 6655 of the Internal Revenue Code of 1986 (relating to failure to pay estimated tax) with respect to any underpayment of an installment required to be paid before the date of the enactment of this Act to the extent such underpayment was created or increased by any provision of this title.

* * *

Subtitle B—Extension of Certain Expiring Provisions

* * *

[¶15,721X-2]

Act Sec. 1202. EMPLOYER-PROVIDED EDUCATIONAL ASSISTANCE PROGRAMS.

* * *

(c) EFFECTIVE DATES.—

* * *

(3) EXPEDITED PROCEDURES. The Secretary of the Treasury shall establish expedited procedures for the refund of any overpayment of taxes imposed by the Internal Revenue Code of 1986 which is attributable to amounts excluded from gross income during 1995 or 1996 under section 127 of such Code, including procedures waiving the requirement that an employer obtain an employee's signature where the employer demonstrates to the satisfaction of the Secretary that any refund collected by the employer on behalf of the employee will be paid to the employee.

* * *

CHAPTER 2—INCREASED ACCESS TO RETIREMENT PLANS

Subchapter A—Simple Savings Plans

[¶15,721X-3]

Act Sec. 1421. ESTABLISHMENT OF SAVINGS INCENTIVE MATCH PLANS FOR EMPLOYEES OF SMALL EMPLOYERS.

* * *

(b) TAX TREATMENT OF SIMPLE RETIREMENT ACCOUNTS.—.

* * *

(8) EMPLOYMENT TAXES.—

* * *

(B) Section 209(a)(4) of the Social Security Act is amended by inserting "; or (J) under an arrangement to which section 408(p) of such Code applies, other than any elective contributions under paragraph (2)(A)(i) thereof" before the semicolon at the end thereof.

* * *

CHAPTER 3—NONDISCRIMINATION PROVISIONS

[¶15,721X-4]

Act Sec. 1431. DEFINITION OF HIGHLY COMPENSATED EMPLOYEES; REPEAL OF FAMILY AGGREGATION.

* * *

(c) CONFORMING AMENDMENTS.—

* * *

(2) Section 1114(c)(4) of the Tax Reform Act of 1986 is amended by adding at the end the following new sentence: "Any reference in this paragraph to section 414(q) shall be treated as a reference to such section as in effect on the day before the date of the enactment of the Small Business Job Protection Act of 1996.".

(d) EFFECTIVE DATE.—

(1) IN GENERAL. The amendments made by this section shall apply to years beginning after December 31, 1996, except that in determining whether an employee is a highly compensated employee for years beginning in 1997, such amendments shall be treated as having been in effect for years beginning in 1996.

Act Sec. 1431.   ¶15,721X-4

* * *

CHAPTER 4—MISCELLANEOUS PROVISIONS

* * *

[¶15,721X-5]

Act Sec. 1449. TRANSITION RULE FOR COMPUTING MAXIMUM BENEFITS UNDER SECTION 415 LIMITATIONS.

(a) IN GENERAL. Subparagraph (A) of section 767(d)(3) of the Uruguay Round Agreements Act is amended to read as follows:

"(A) EXCEPTION. A plan that was adopted and in effect before December 8, 1994, shall not be required to apply the amendments made by subsection (b) with respect to benefits accrued before the earlier of—

"(i) the later of the date a plan amendment applying the amendments made by subsection (b) is adopted or made effective, or

"(ii) the first day of the first limitation year beginning after December 31, 1999.

Determinations under section 415(b)(2)(E) of the Internal Revenue Code of 1986 before such earlier date shall be made with respect to such benefits on the basis of such section as in effect on December 7, 1994 (except that the modification made by section 1449(b) of the Small Business Job Protection Act of 1996 shall be taken into account), and the provisions of the plan as in effect on December 7, 1994, but only if such provisions of the plan meet the requirements of such section (as so in effect).".

* * *

(c) EFFECTIVE DATE. The amendments made by this section shall take effect as if included in the provisions of section 767 of the Uruguay Round Agreements Act.

(d) TRANSITIONAL RULE. In the case of a plan that was adopted and in effect before December 8, 1994, if—

(1) a plan amendment was adopted or made effective on or before the date of the enactment of this Act applying the amendments made by section 767 of the Uruguay Round Agreements Act, and

(2) within 1 year after the date of the enactment of this Act, a plan amendment is adopted which repeals the amendment referred to in paragraph (1), the amendment referred to in paragraph (1) shall not be taken into account in applying section 767(d)(3)(A) of the Uruguay Round Agreements Act, as amended by subsection (a).

* * *

[¶15,721X-6]

Act Sec. 1450. MODIFICATIONS OF SECTION 403(b).

(a) MULTIPLE SALARY REDUCTION AGREEMENTS PERMITTED.—

(1) GENERAL RULE. For purposes of section 403(b) of the Internal Revenue Code of 1986, the frequency that an employee is permitted to enter into a salary reduction agreement, the salary to which such an agreement may apply, and the ability to revoke such an agreement shall be determined under the rules applicable to cash or deferred elections under section 401(k) of such Code.

* * *

(3) EFFECTIVE DATE. This subsection shall apply to taxable years beginning after December 31, 1995.

(b) TREATMENT OF INDIAN TRIBAL GOVERNMENTS.—

(1) IN GENERAL. In the case of any contract purchased in a plan year beginning before January 1, 1995, section 403(b) of the Internal Revenue Code of 1986 shall be applied as if any reference to an employer described in section 501(c)(3) of the Internal Revenue Code of 1986 which is exempt from tax under section 501 of such Code included a reference to an employer which is an Indian tribal government (as defined by section 7701(a)(40) of such Code), a subdivision of an Indian tribal government (determined in accordance with section 7871(d) of such Code), an agency or instrumentality of an Indian tribal government or subdivision thereof, or a corporation chartered under Federal, State, or tribal law which is owned in whole or in part by any of the foregoing.

(2) ROLLOVERS. Solely for purposes of applying section 403(b)(8) of such Code to a contract to which paragraph (1) applies, a qualified cash or deferred arrangement under section 401(k) of such Code shall be treated as if it were a plan or contract described in clause (ii) of section 403(b)(8)(A) of such Code.

* * *

[¶15,721X-7]

Act Sec. 1457. SAMPLE LANGUAGE FOR SPOUSAL CONSENT AND QUALIFIED DOMESTIC RELATIONS FORMS.

(a) DEVELOPMENT OF SAMPLE LANGUAGE. Not later than January 1, 1997, the Secretary of the Treasury shall develop—

(1) sample language for inclusion in a form for the spousal consent required under section 417(a)(2) of the Internal Revenue Code of 1986 and section 205(c)(2) of the Employee Retirement Income Security Act of 1974 which—

(A) is written in a manner calculated to be understood by the average person, and

(B) discloses in plain form—

(i) whether the waiver to which the spouse consents is irrevocable, and

(ii) whether such waiver may be revoked by a qualified domestic relations order, and

(2) sample language for inclusion in a form for a qualified domestic relations order described in section 414(p)(1)(A) of such Code and section 206(d)(3)(B)(i) of such Act which—

(A) meets the requirements contained in such sections, and

(B) the provisions of which focus attention on the need to consider the treatment of any lump sum payment, qualified joint and survivor annuity, or qualified preretirement survivor annuity.

(b) PUBLICITY. The Secretary of the Treasury shall include publicity for the sample language developed under subsection (a) in the pension outreach efforts undertaken by the Secretary.

[¶15,721X-8]

Act Sec. 1458. TREATMENT OF LENGTH OF SERVICE AWARDS TO VOLUNTEERS PERFORMING FIRE FIGHTING OR PREVENTION SERVICES, EMERGENCY MEDICAL SERVICES, OR AMBULANCE SERVICES.

* * *

(b) EXEMPTION FROM SOCIAL SECURITY TAXES.—

* * *

(2) Section 209(a)(4) of the Social Security Act is amended by inserting "; or (K) under a plan described in section 457(e)(11)(A)(ii) of the Internal Revenue Code of 1986 and maintained by an eligible employer (as defined in section 457(e)(1) of such Code)" before the semicolon at the end thereof.

(c) EFFECTIVE DATE.—

* * *

(2) SUBSECTION (B). The amendments made by subsection (b) shall apply to remuneration paid after December 31, 1996.

* * *

[¶15,721X-9]

Act Sec. 1462. DEFINITION OF HIGHLY COMPENSATED EMPLOYEE FOR PRE-ERISA RULES FOR CHURCH PLANS.

* * *

(b) SAFEHARBOR AUTHORITY. The Secretary of the Treasury may design nondiscrimination and coverage safe harbors for church plans.

* * *

[¶15,721X-10]

Act Sec. 1465. DATE FOR ADOPTION OF PLAN AMENDMENTS.

If any amendment made by this subtitle requires an amendment to any plan or annuity contract, such amendment shall not be required to be made before the first day of the first plan year beginning on or after January 1, 1998, if—

(1) during the period after such amendment takes effect and before such first plan year, the plan or contract is operated in accordance with the requirements of such amendment, and

(2) such amendment applies retroactively to such period.

In the case of a governmental plan (as defined in section 414(d) of the Internal Revenue Code of 1986, this section shall be applied by substituting "2000" for "1998".

* * *

Uruguay Round Agreements Act

P.L. 103-465

Signed on December 8, 1994

[¶15,721Y]

Title VII—Revenue Provisions

* * *

[¶15,721Y-1]

Act Sec. 769 SPECIAL FUNDING RULES FOR CERTAIN PLANS.

(a) **Funding Rules Not to Apply to Certain Plans.** Any changes made by this Act to section 412 of the Internal Revenue Code of 1986 or to part 3 of subtitle B of title I of the Employee Retirement Income Security Act of 1974 shall not apply to—

(1) a plan which is, on the date of enactment of this Act, subject to a restoration payment schedule order issued by the Pension Benefit Guaranty Corporation that meets the requirements of section 1.412(c)(1)-3 of the Treasury Regulations, or

(2) a plan established by an affected air carrier (as defined under section 4001(a)(14)(C)(ii)(I) of such Act) and assumed by a new plan Sponsor pursuant to the terms of a written agreement with the Pension Benefit Guaranty Corporation dated January 5, 1993, and approved by the United States Bankruptcy Court for the District of Delaware on December 30, 1992.

(b) **Change in Actuarial Method.** Any amortization installments for bases established under section 412(b) of the Internal Revenue Code of 1986 and section 302(b) of the Employee Retirement Income Security Act of 1974 for plan years beginning after December 31, 1987, and before January 1, 1993, by reason of nonelective changes under the frozen entry age actuarial cost method shall not be included in the calculation of offsets under section 412(l)(1)(A)(ii) of such Code and section 302(d)(1)(A)(ii) of such Act for the 1st 5 plan years beginning after December 31, 1994.

* * *

(c) TRANSITION RULES FOR CERTAIN PLANS.—

(1) IN GENERAL. In the case of a plan that—

(A) was not required to pay a variable rate premium for the plan year beginning in 1996;

(B) has not, in any plan year beginning after 1995 and before 2009, merged with another plan (other than a plan sponsored by an employer that was in 1996 within the controlled group of the plan sponsor); and

(C) is sponsored by a company that is engaged primarily in the interurban or interstate passenger bus service,

except as provided in paragraph (3), the transition rules described in paragraph (2) shall apply for any plan year beginning after 1996 and before 2010.

(2) TRANSITION RULES. The transition rules described in this paragraph are as follows:

(A) For purposes of section 412(l)(9)(A) of the Internal Revenue Code of 1986 and section 302(d)(9)(A) of the Employee Retirement Income Security Act of 1974—

(i) the funded current liability percentage for any plan year beginning after 1996 and before 2005 shall be treated as not less than 90 percent if for such plan year the funded current liability percentage is at least 85 percent, and

(ii) the funded current liability percentage for any plan year beginning after 2004 and before 2010 shall be treated as not less than 90 percent if for such plan year the funded current liability percentage satisfies the minimum percentage determined according to the following table:

"In the case of a plan year beginning in:	The minimum percentage is:
2005	86 percent
2006	87 percent
2007	88 percent
2008	89 percent
2009 and thereafter	90 percent.

(B) Sections 412(c)(7)(E)(i)(I) of such Code and 302(c)(7)(E)(i)(I) of such Act shall be applied—

(i) by substituting '85 percent' for '90 percent' for plan years beginning after 1996 and before 2005, and

(ii) by substituting the minimum percentage specified in the table contained in subparagraph (A)(ii) for '90 percent' for plan years beginning after 2004 and before 2010.

(C) In the event the funded current liability percentage of a plan is less than 85 percent for any plan year beginning after 1996 and before 2005, the transition rules under subparagraphs (A) and (B) shall continue to apply to the plan if contributions for such a plan year are made to the plan in an amount equal to the lesser of—

(i) the amount necessary to result in a funded current liability percentage of 85 percent, or

(ii) the greater of—

(I) 2 percent of the plan's current liability as of the beginning of such plan year, or

(II) the amount necessary to result in a funded current liability percentage of 80 percent as of the end of such plan year.

For the plan year beginning in 2005 and for each of the 3 succeeding plan years, the transition rules under subparagraphs (A) and (B) shall continue to apply to the plan for such plan year only if contributions to the plan for such plan year equal at least the expected increase in current liability due to benefits accruing during such plan year."

(3) SPECIAL RULES. In the case of plan years beginning in 2004 and 2005, the following transition rules shall apply in lieu of the transition rules described in paragraph (2):

(A) For purposes of section 412(l)(9)(A) of the Internal Revenue Code of 1986 and section 302(d)(9)(A) of the Employee Retirement Income Security Act of 1974, the funded current liability percentage of any plan year shall be treated as not less than 90 percent.

(B) For purposes of section 412(m) of the Internal Revenue Code of 1986 and section 302(e) of the Employee Retirement Income Security Act of 1974, the funded current liability percentage for any plan year shall be treated as not less than 100 percent.

(C) For purposes of determining unfunded vested benefits under section 4006(a)(3)(E)(iii) of the Employee Retirement Income Security Act of 1974, the mortality table shall be the mortality table used by the plan.

Amendment

P.L. 108-218, § 201(a):

Amended Sec. 769(c) to read as above.

The amendment applies to plan years beginning after December 31, 2003.

Omnibus Budget Reconciliation Act of 1993

P.L. 103-66

Signed on August 10, 1993

[¶15,721Z]

Title XIII—Revenue, Health Care, Human Resources, Income Security, Customs and Trade, Food Stamp Program, and Timber Sale Provisions

Chapter 1—REVENUE PROVISIONS

[¶15,721Z-1]

Act Sec. 13001 SHORT TITLE; ETC.

(a) SHORT TITLE. This chapter may be cited as the "Revenue Reconciliation Act of 1993".

(b) AMENDMENT TO 1986 CODE. Except as otherwise expressly provided, whenever in this chapter an amendment or repeal is expressed in terms of an amendment to, or repeal of, a section or other provision, the reference shall be considered to be made to a section or other provision of the Internal Revenue Code of 1986.

* * *

(d) WAIVER OF ESTIMATED TAX PENALTIES. No addition to tax shall be made under section 6654 or 6655 of the Internal Revenue Code of 1986 for any period before April 16, 1994 (March 16, 1994, in the case of a corporation), with respect to any underpayment to the extent such underpayment was created or increased by any provision of this chapter.

* * *

Subchapter A—Training and Investment Incentives

Part I—Provisions Relating to Education and Training

[¶15,721Z-2]

Act Sec.13101 EMPLOYER-PROVIDED EDUCATIONAL ASSISTANCE.

(a) EXTENSION OF EXCLUSION.—

* * *

(2) CONFORMING AMENDMENT. Paragraph (2) of section 103(a) of the Tax Extension Act of 1991 is hereby repealed.

* * *

Part VI—Other Changes

* * *

[¶15,721Z-3]

Act Sec. 13174 TEMPORARY EXTENSION OF DEDUCTION FOR HEALTH INSURANCE COSTS OF SELF-EMPLOYED INDIVIDUALS.

(a) IN GENERAL.—

* * *

(2) CONFORMING AMENDMENT. Paragraph (2) of section 110(a) of the Tax Extension Act of 1991 is hereby repealed.

* * *

Unemployment Compensation Amendments of 1992

P.L. 102-318

Signed on July 3, 1992

[¶15,722A]

Act Sec. 1 SHORT TITLE.

This Act may be cited as the "Unemployment Compensation Amendments of 1992."

* * *

Title V—Revenue Provisions

[¶15,722A-1]

Act Sec. 501 AMENDMENT OF 1986 CODE.

Except as otherwise expressly provided, whenever in this title an amendment or repeal is expressed in terms of an amendment to, or repeal of, a section or other provision, the reference shall be considered to be made to a section or other provision of the Internal Revenue Code of 1986.

* * *

Subtitle B—Pension Distributions

[¶15,722A-2]

Act Sec. 521 TAXABILITY OF BENEFICIARY OF QUALIFIED PLAN.

* * *

(d) **Model Explanation**. The Secretary of the Treasury or his delegate shall develop a model explanation which a plan administrator may provide to a recipient in order to meet the requirements of section 402(f) of the Internal Revenue Code of 1986.

(e) **Effective Dates.—**

(1) IN GENERAL. The amendments made by this section shall apply to distributions after December 31, 1992.

(2) SPECIAL RULE FOR PARTIAL DISTRIBUTIONS. For purposes of section 402(a)(5)(D)(i)(II) of the Internal Revenue Code of 1986 (as in effect before the amendments made by this section), a distribution before January 1, 1993, which is made before or at the same time as a series of periodic payments shall not be treated as one of such series if it is not substantially equal in amount to other payments in such series.

[¶15,722A-3]

Act Sec. 522 REQUIREMENT THAT QUALIFIED PLANS INCLUDE OPTIONAL TRUSTEE-TO-TRUSTEE TRANSFERS OF ELIGIBLE ROLLOVER DISTRIBUTIONS.

* * *

(d) **Effective Dates.—**

(1) IN GENERAL. Except as provided in paragraph (2), the amendments made by this section shall apply to distributions after December 31, 1992.

(2) TRANSITION RULE FOR CERTAIN ANNUITY CONTRACTS. If, as of July 1, 1992, a State law prohibits a direct trustee-to-trustee transfer from an annuity contract described in section 403(b) of the Internal Revenue Code of 1986 which was purchased for an employee by an employer which is a State or a political subdivision thereof (or an agency or instrumentality of any 1 or more of either), the amendments made by this section shall not apply to distributions before the earlier of—

(A) 90 days after the first day after July 1, 1992, on which such transfer is allowed under state law, or

(B) January 1, 1994.

[¶15,722A-4]

Act Sec. 523 DATE FOR ADOPTION OF PLAN AMENDMENTS.

If any amendment made by this subtitle requires an amendment to any plan, such plan amendment shall not be required to be made before the first plan year beginning on or after January 1, 1994, if—

(1) during the period after such amendment takes effect and before such first plan year, the plan is operated in accordance with the requirements of such amendment, and

(2) such plan amendment applies retroactively to such period.

Comprehensive Deposit Insurance Reform and Taxpayer Protection Act of 1991

P.L. 102-242

Signed on December 19, 1991

[¶ 15,722B]

ACT SEC. 1 **SHORT TITLE.**

This Act may be cited as the "Federal Deposit Insurance Corporation Improvement Act of 1991".

* * *

TITLE IV—MISCELLANEOUS PROVISIONS

* * *

Subtitle I—Bank and Thrift Employee Provisions

[¶ 15,722B-1]

ACT SEC. 451(a) **Continuation Coverage.** The Federal Deposit Insurance Corporation—

(1) shall, in its capacity as a successor of a failed depository institution (whether acting directly or through any bridge bank), have the same obligation to provide a group health plan meeting the requirements of section 602 of the Employee Retirement Income Security Act of 1974 (relating to continuation coverage requirements of group health plans) with respect to former employees of such institution as such institution would have had but for its failure, and

(2) shall require that any successor described in subsection (b)(1)(B)(iii) provide a group health plan with respect to former employees of such institution in the same manner as the failed depository institution would have been required to provide but for its failure.

(b) **Definitions.** For purposes of this section—

    (1) SUCCESSOR. An entity is a successor of a failed depository institution during any period if—

        (A) such entity hold substantially all of the assets or liabilities of such institution, and

        (B) such entity is—

            (i) the Federal Deposit Insurance Corporation,

            (ii) any bridge bank, or

            (iii) an entity that acquires such assets or liabilities from the Federal Deposit Insurance Corporation or a bridge bank.

    (2) FAILED DEPOSITORY INSTITUTION. The term "failed depository institution" means any depository institution (as defined in section 3(c) of the Federal Deposit Insurance Act) for which a receiver has been appointed.

    (3) BRIDGE BANK. The term "bridge bank" has the meaning given such term by section 11(i) of the Federal Deposit Insurance Act.

(c) **No premium costs imposed on fdic.** Subsection (a) shall not be construed as requiring the Federal Deposit Insurance Corporation to incur, by reason of this section, any obligation for any premium under any group health plan referred to in such subsection.

(d) **Effective Date.** This section shall apply to plan years beginning on or after the date of the enactment of this Act, regardless of whether the qualifying event under section 603 of the Employee Retirement Income Security Act of 1974 occurred before, on, or after such date.

Revenue Reconciliation Act of 1990

P.L. 101-508

Signed on November 5, 1990

[Reproduced below are sections of the Revenue Reconciliation Act of 1990 (P.L. 101-508) that did not amend the Internal Revenue Code of 1986 or the Employee Retirement Income Security Act of 1974 (ERISA).]

[¶15,722C]

Act Sec. 11001 SHORT TITLE; ETC.

(a) SHORT TITLE. This title may be cited as the "Revenue Reconciliation Act of 1990".

(b) AMENDMENT OF 1986 CODE. Except as otherwise expressly provided, whenever in this title an amendment or repeal is expressed in terms of an amendment to, or repeal of, a section or other provision, the reference shall be considered to be made to a section or other provision of the Internal Revenue Code of 1986.

(c) SECTION 15 NOT TO APPLY. Except as otherwise expressly provided in this title, no amendment made by this title shall be treated as a change in a rate of tax for purposes of section 15 of the Internal Revenue Code of 1986.

* * *

[¶15,722C-1]

Act Sec. 11319 SHORT TITLE; ETC.

(a) SHORT TITLE. This title may be cited as the "Revenue Reconciliation Act of 1990".

(b) AMENDMENT OF 1986 CODE. Except as otherwise expressly provided, whenever in this title an amendment or repeal is expressed in terms of an amendment to, or repeal of, a section or other provision, the reference shall be considered to be made to a section or other provision of the Internal Revenue Code of 1986.

(c) SECTION 15 NOT TO APPLY. Except as otherwise expressly provided in this title, no amendment made by this title shall be treated as a change in a rate of tax for purposes of section 15 of the Internal Revenue Code of 1986.

* * *

Omnibus Budget Reconciliation Act of 1989

P.L. 101-239

Signed on December 19, 1989

Title VII—Revenue Measures

[¶15,722D]

Act Sec. 7001 SHORT TITLE; ETC.

(a) **Short Title.** This title may be cited as the "Revenue Reconciliation Act of 1989."

(b) **Amendment of 1986 Code.** Except as otherwise expressly provided, whenever in this title an amendment or repeal is expressed in terms of an amendment to, or repeal of, a section or other provision, the reference shall be considered to be made to a section or other provision of the Internal Revenue Code of 1986.

[¶15,722D-1]

Act Sec. 7812 AMENDMENT RELATED TO TITLE II OF THE 1988 ACT.

(a) **Amendment Related to Section 2001 of the 1988 Act.** Subparagraph (C) of section 2001(d)(7) of the 1988 Act is amended by striking "section 6427(g)(1)" and inserting "section 6427(f)(1)".

* * *

(d) **Amendment Related to Section 2005 of the 1988 Act.** Section 2005(e) of the 1988 Act is amended by inserting ", except that the amendment made by subsection (a)(1) shall take effect as if included in the amendment made by section 1131(c) of the Tax Reform Act of 1986".

Part V—Amendments Related to Pension Provisions

[¶15,722D-2]

Act Sec. 7851 DEFINITIONS.

For purposes of this part—

(1) REFORM ACT. Except where incompatible with the intent, the term "Reform Act" means the Tax Reform Act of 1986.

(2) ERISA. The term "ERISA" means the Employee Retirement Income Security Act of 1974.

[¶15,722D-3]

Act Sec. 7861 AMENDMENTS RELATED TO TAX REFORM ACT OF 1986

* * *

(b) **Amendment Related to Section 1132 of the Act.—**

(1) Notwithstanding any other provision of law, in the case of any qualified pension plan and welfare benefit plan described in paragraph (2), the assets of such pension plan in excess of its liabilities may be transferred to such welfare benefit plan upon the termination of such pension plan if such assets are to be used to provide retiree health benefits.

(2) For purposes of paragraph (1), a qualified pension plan and welfare benefit plan are described in this paragraph if—

(A) both such plans are jointly administered pursuant to a collective bargaining agreement between the employer maintaining such plans and one or more employee representatives,

(B) the welfare benefit plan provides retiree health benefits, and

(C) the qualified pension plan has assets in excess of liabilities (determined on a termination basis) and the welfare benefit plan has assets which are less than the present value of the benefits to be provided under the plan (determined as of the time of termination of the pension plan).

(3) For purposes of the Internal Revenue Code of 1986, any transfer of assets to which paragraph (1) applies shall be treated as a reversion of such assets to the employer maintaining the plan which is includible in the gross income of such employer and subject to the tax imposed by section 4980 of such Code.

TITLE X—MISCELLANEOUS AND TECHNICAL SOCIAL SECURITY ACT AMENDMENTS

* * *

Subtitle B—Technical Provisions

* * *

[¶15,722D-4]

Act Sec. 10208 INCLUSION OF CERTAIN DEFERRED COMPENSATION IN DETERMINATION OF WAGE-BASED ADJUSTMENTS.

(a) **In General.** Section 209 of the Social Security Act (42 U.S.C. 409) is amended by adding at the end the following new subsection:

"(k)(1) For purposes of sections 203(f)(8)(B)(ii), 213(d)(2)(B), 215(a)(1)(B)(ii), 215(b)(3)(A)(ii), 224(f)(2)(B), and 230(b)(2) (and 230(b)(2) as in effect immediately prior to the enactment of the Social Security Amendments of 1977), the term 'deemed average total wages' for any particular calendar year means the product of—

"(A) the SSA average wage index (as defined in section 215(i)(1)(G) and promulgated by the Secretary) for the calendar year preceding such particular calendar year, and

"(B) the quotient obtained by dividing—

"(i) the average of total wages (as defined in regulations of the Secretary and computed without regard to the limitation specified in subsection (a)(1) and by including deferred compensation amounts) reported to the Secretary of the Treasury or his delegate for such particular calendar year, by "(ii) the average of total wages (as so defined and computed) reported to the Secretary of the Treasury or his delegate for the calendar year preceding such particular calendar year.

"(2) For purposes of paragraph (1), the term 'deferred compensation amount' means—

"(A) any amount excluded from gross income under chapter 1 of the Internal Revenue Code of 1986 by reason of section 402(a)(8), 402(h)(1)(B), or 457(a) of such Code or by reason of a salary reduction agreement under section 403(b) of such Code,

"(B) any amount with respect to which a deduction is allowable under chapter 1 of such Code by reason of a contribution to a plan described in section 501(c)(18) of such Code, and

"(C) to the extent provided in regulations of the Secretary, deferred compensation provided under any arrangement, agreement, or plan referred to in subsection (i) or (j).".

(b) **Conforming Amendments.** (1) Sections 203(f)(8)(B)(ii), 215(b)(3)(A)(ii), and 230(b)(2)(A) of the Social Security Act (42 U.S.C. 403(f)(8)(B)(ii)(I), 415(b)(3)(A)(ii)(I), and 430(b)(2)(A)), as amended by subsection (d)(2)(A)(i), are each further amended—

(A) by striking "the average of the total wages (as defined in regulations of the Secretary and computed without regard to the limitations specified in section 209(a)(1)) reported to the Secretary of the Treasury or his delegate" and inserting "the deemed average total wages (as defined in section 209(k)(1))";

(B) by striking "the average of the total wages (as so defined and computed) reported to the Secretary of the Treasury or his delegate" and inserting "the deemed average total wages (as so defined)"; and

(C) in section 215(b)(3)(A)(ii)(I), by striking "(after 1976)".

(2) Sections 213(d)(2)(B), 215(b)(1)(B)(ii), and 224(f)(2)(B) of such Act (42 U.S.C. 413(d)(2)(B), 415(a)(1)(B)(ii), and 424a(f)(2)(B)), as amended by subsection (d)(2)(A)(i), as each further amended—

(A) by striking "the average of the total wages (as defined in regulations of the Secretary and computed without regard to the limitations specified in section 209(a)(1)) reported to the Secretary of the Treasury or his delegate" and inserting "the deemed average total wages (as defined in section 209(k)(1))";

(B) in section 213(d)(2)(B) and 215(a)(1)(B)(ii)(II), by striking "(as so defined and computed)" and inserting "(as defined in regulations of the Secretary and computed without regard to the limitations specified in section 209(a)(1))"; and

(C) in section 224(f)(2)(B)(ii), by inserting "(I)" after "(ii)", by striking "as so defined and computed)" and inserting "(as defined in regulations of the Secretary and computed without regard to the limitations specified in section 209(a)(1))", and by inserting after "disability)" the following: ", if such calendar year is before 1991, or (II) the deemed average total wages (as defined in section 209(k)(1)) for the calendar year before the year in which the reduction was first computed (but not counting any reduction made in benefits for a previous period of disability), if such calendar year is after 1990".

(3) Section 215(i)(1)(G) of such Act (42 U.S.C. 415(i)(1)(G)) is amended by striking "the average of the total wages reported to the Secretary of the Treasury or his delegate as determined for purposes of subsection (b)(3)(A)(ii)" and inserting "the amount determined for such calendar year under subsection (b)(3)(A)(ii)(I)."

(4) Section 215(a)(1)(C)(ii) of such Act (42 U.S.C. 415(a)(1)(C)(ii)) is amended by striking "change." and inserting "change (except that, for purposes of subsection (b)(2)(A) of such section 230 as so in effect, the reference therein to the average of the wages of all employees as reported to the Secretary of the Treasury for any calendar year shall be deemed a reference to the deemed average total wages (within the meaning of section 209(k)(1)) for such calendar year).".

(5) Section 230(d) of such Act (42 U.S.C. 430(d)) is amended by striking "change." and inserting "change (except that, for purposes of subsection (b)(2)(A) of such section 230 as so in effect, the reference therein to the average of the wages of all employees as reported to the Secretary of the Treasury for any calendar year shall be deemed a reference to the deemed average total wage (within the meaning of section 209(k)(1)) for such calendar year).".

(c) **Effective Date.**—

(1) IN GENERAL. The amendments made by subsections (a) and (b) shall apply with respect to the computation of average total wage amounts (under the amended provisions) for calendar years after 1990.

(2) TRANSITIONAL RULE. For purposes of determining the contribution and benefit base for 1990, 1991, and 1992 under section 230(b) of the Social Security Act (and section 230(b) of such Act as in effect immediately prior to enactment of the Social Security Amendments of 1977)—

(A) the average of total wages for 1988 shall be deemed to be equal to the amount which would have been determined with regard to this paragraph, plus 2 percent of the amount which has been determined to be the average of total wages for 1987,

(B) the average of total wages for 1989 shall be deemed to be equal to the amount which would have been determined without regard to this paragraph, plus 2 percent of the amount which would have been determined to the average of total wages for 1988 without regard to subparagraph (A), and

(C) the average of total wages reported to the Secretary of the Treasury for 1990 shall be deemed to be equal to the product of—

(i) the SSA average wage index (as defined in section 215(i)(1)(G) of the Social Security Act and promulgated by the Secretary) for 1989, and

(ii) the quotient obtained by dividing—

(I) the average of total wages (as defined in regulations of the Secretary and computed without regard to the limitations of section 209(a)(1) of the Social Security Act and by including deferred compensation amounts, within the meaning of section 209(k)(2) of such Act as added by this section) reported to the Secretary of the Treasury or his delegate for 1990, by

(II) the average of total wages (as so defined and computed without regard to the limitations specified in such section 209(a)(1) and by excluding deferred compensation amounts within the meaning of such section 209(k)(2)) reported to the Secretary of the Treasury or his delegate for 1989.

(3) DETERMINATION OF CONTRIBUTION AND BENEFIT BASE FOR 1993. For purposes of determining the contribution and benefit base for 1993 under section 230(b) of the Social Security Act (and section 230(b) of such Act as in effect immediately prior to enactment of the Social Security Amendments of 1977), the average of total wages for 1990 shall be determined without regard to subparagraph (C) of paragraph (2).

(4) REVISED DETERMINATION UNDER SECTION 230 OF THE SOCIAL SECURITY ACT. As soon as possible after the enactment of this Act, the Secretary of Health and Human Services shall revise and publish, in accordance with the provisions of this Act and the amendments made thereby, the contribution and benefit base under section 230 of the Social Security Act with respect to remuneration paid after 1989 and taxable years beginning after calendar year 1989.

* * *

Technical and Miscellaneous Revenue Act of 1988

P.L. 100-647

Signed on November 10, 1988

[Reproduced below are sections of the Technical and Miscellaneous Revenue Act of 1988 which did not amend any section of the Internal Revenue Code of 1986 or the Employee Retirement Income Security Act of 1974 (ERISA). Sections which amended the Internal Revenue Code of 1986 are reflected in the "Code & Regulations" divisions starting at ¶ 11,000. Sections which amended ERISA are reflected in the "Labor Laws and Regulations" division starting at ¶ 14,110.— CCH.]

TITLE I—TECHNICAL CORRECTIONS TO THE TAX REFORM ACT OF 1986

[¶ 15,722E]

Act Sec. 1 SHORT TITLE; ETC.

(a) **Short Title**. This Act may be cited as the "Technical and Miscellaneous Revenue Act of 1988".

(b) **Definitions**. For purposes of this Act—

(1) 1986 CODE. The term "1986 Code" means the Internal Revenue Code of 1986.

(2) REFORM ACT. Except where incompatible with the intent, the term "Reform Act" means the Tax Reform Act of 1986.

* * *

[¶ 15,722E-1]

Act Sec. 1011 AMENDMENTS RELATED TO PARTS I AND II OF SUBTITLE A OF TITLE XI OF THE REFORM ACT.

* * *

(c) **Amendments Related to Section 1105 of the Reform Act.—**

* * *

(6)(C) Section 1854(f)(4)(C) of the Reform Act is amended by striking out "section 402(g)" and inserting in lieu thereof "section 402(j)".

* * *

(8) Section 1105(c)(2)(A) of the Reform Act is amended by striking out "the last of such collective bargaining agreements" and inserting in lieu thereof "such agreement".

(9) Section 1105(c) of the Reform Act is amended by adding at the end thereof the following new paragraph:

"(6) REPORTING REQUIREMENTS. The amendments made by subsection (b) shall apply to calendar years beginning after December 31, 1986."

* * *

(d) **Amendments Related to Section 1106 of the Reform Act.—**

* * *

(5) Paragraph (4) of section 1106(i) of the Reform Act is amended by striking the period at the end thereof and inserting in lieu thereof "(determined as if the amendments made by this section were in effect for such year).".

* * *

(e) **Amendments Related to Section 1107 of the Reform Act.—**

* * *

(6) Section 1107(c)(3) of the Reform Act is amended—

(A) by striking out "eligible" each place it appears, and

(B) by inserting at the end of subparagraph (B) the following new sentence: "This subparagraph shall only apply to individuals who were covered under the plan and agreement on August 16, 1986."

(7) Paragraph (5) of section 1107(c) of the Reform Act is amended—

(A) by striking out "to employees on August 1, 1986, of",

(B) by striking out "a deferred compensation plan" in subparagraph (A) and inserting in lieu thereof "to employees on August 16, 1986,",

(C) by inserting "maintaining a deferred compensation plan" after "Alabama" in subparagraph (A), and

(D) by striking out "a deferred compensation plan" in subparagraph (B) and inserting in lieu thereof "to individuals eligible to participate on August 16, 1986, in a deferred compensation plan".

* * *

(f) **Amendments Related to Section 1108 of the Reform Act.—**

* * *

(7) Section 1108(h) of the Reform Act is amended to read as follows:

"(h) EFFECTIVE DATES.—

"(1) IN GENERAL. Except as provided in paragraph (2), the amendments made by this section shall apply to years beginning after December 31, 1986.

"(2) INTEGRATION RULES. Subparagraphs (D) and (E) of section 408(k)(3) of the Internal Revenue Code of 1954 (as in effect before the amendments made by this section) shall continue to apply for years beginning after December 31, 1986, and before January 1, 1989, except that employer contributions under an arrangement under section 408(k)(6) of the Internal Revenue Code of 1986 (as added by this section) may not be integrated under such subparagraphs."

(8) Section 209(e)(8) of the Social Security Act is amended to read as follows:

"(8) under a simplified employee pension (as defined in section 408(k)(1) of such Code), other than any contributions described in section 408(k)(6) of such Code,".

* * *

(g) Amendments Related to Section 1111 of the Reform Act.—

* * *

(4) Section 1111(c)(3) of the Reform Act is amended by striking out "benefits pursuant to, and individuals covered by, any such agreement in".

* * *

(h) Amendments Related to Section 1112 of the Reform Act.—

* * *

(6) Clause (iii) of section 1112(e)(3)(A) of the Reform Act is amended by striking out "a plan or merger" and inserting in lieu thereof "the plan".

(7) Section 1112(e)(2) of the Reform Act is amended by striking out "employees covered by such agreement in".

(8) Subsection (e) of section 1112 of the Reform Act is amended by striking out paragraph (3)(C) and by adding at the end of such subsection the following new paragraph:

"(4) SPECIAL RULE FOR PLANS WHICH MAY NOT TERMINATE. To the extent provided in regulations prescribed by the Secretary of the Treasury or his delegate, if a plan is prohibited from terminating under title IV of the Employee Retirement Income Security Act of 1974 before the 1st year to which the amendment made by subsection (b) would apply, the amendment made by subsection (b) shall only apply to years after the 1st year in which the plan is able to terminate."

(9) Subparagraph (B) of section 1112(e)(3) of the Reform Act is amended to read as follows:

"(B) INTEREST RATE FOR DETERMINING ACCRUED BENEFIT OF HIGHLY COMPENSATED EMPLOYEES FOR CERTAIN PURPOSES. In the case of a termination, transfer, or distribution of assets of a plan described in subparagraph (A)(ii) before the 1st year to which the amendment made by subsection (b) applies—

"(i) AMOUNT ELIGIBLE FOR ROLLOVER, INCOME AVERAGING, OR TAX-FREE TRANSFER. For purposes of determining any eligible amount, the present value of the accrued benefit of any highly compensated employee shall be determined by using an interest rate not less than the highest of—

"(I) the applicable rate under the plan's method in effect under the plan on August 16, 1986,

"(II) the highest rate (as of the date of the termination, transfer, or distribution) determined under any of the methods applicable under the plan at any time after August 15, 1986, and before the termination, transfer, or distribution in calculating the present value of the accrued benefit of an employee who is not a highly compensated employee under the plan (or any other plan used in determining whether the plan meets the requirements of section 401 of the Internal Revenue Code of 1986), or

"(III) 5 percent.

"(ii) ELIGIBLE AMOUNT. For purposes of clause (i), the term 'eligible amount' means any amount with respect to a highly compensated employee which—

"(I) may be rolled over under section 402(a)(5) of such Code,

"(II) is eligible for income averaging under section 402(e)(1) of such Code, or capital gains treatment under section 402(a)(2) or 403(a)(2) of such Code (as in effect before this Act), or

"(III) may be transferred to another plan without inclusion in gross income.

"(iii) AMOUNTS SUBJECT TO EARLY WITHDRAWAL OR EXCESS DISTRIBUTION TAX. For purposes of sections 72(t) and 4980A of such Code, there shall not be taken into account the excess (if any) of—

"(I) the amount distributed to a highly compensated employee by reason of such termination or distribution, over

"(II) the amount determined by using the interest rate applicable under clause (i).

"(iv) DISTRIBUTIONS OF ANNUITY CONTRACTS. If an annuity contract purchased after August 16, 1986, is distributed to a highly compensated employee in connection with such termination or distribution, there shall be included in gross income for the taxable year of such distribution an amount equal to the excess of—

"(I) the purchase price of such contract, over

"(II) the present value of the benefits payable under such contract determined by using the interest rate applicable under clause (i).

Such excess shall not be taken into account for purposes of sections 72(t) and 4980A of such Code.

"(v) HIGHLY COMPENSATED EMPLOYEE. For purposes of this subparagraph, the term 'highly compensated employee' has the meaning given such term by section 414(q) of such Code."

* * *

(k) Amendments Related to Section 1116 of the Reform Act.—

* * *

(3)(B) Section 1116(b)(4) of the Reform Act is amended by striking out "any" the first place it appears and inserting in lieu thereof "an".

* * *

(8) Subparagraph (B) of section 1116(f)(2) of the Reform Act is amended by adding at the end thereof the following new sentence: "If clause (i) or (ii) applies to any arrangement adopted by a governmental unit, then any cash or deferred arrangement adopted by such unit on or after the date referred to in the applicable clause shall be treated as adopted before such date."

* * *

(10) Clause (i) of section 1116(f)(2)(B) of the Reform Act is amended by striking out "(or political subdivision thereof)" and inserting in lieu thereof "or political subdivision thereof, or any agency or instrumentality thereof,".

(l) Amendments Related to Section 1117 of the Reform Act.—

* * *

(12) Subsection (d) of section 1117 of the Reform Act is amended by adding at the end thereof the following new paragraph:

"(4) DISTRIBUTIONS BEFORE PLAN AMENDMENT.—

"(A) IN GENERAL. If a plan amendment is required to allow a plan to make any distribution described in section 401(m)(6) of the Internal Revenue Code of 1986, any such distribution which is made before the close of the 1st plan year for which such amendment is required to be in effect under section 1140 shall be treated as made in accordance with the provisions of the plan.

"(B) DISTRIBUTIONS PURSUANT TO MODEL AMENDMENT.—

"(i) SECRETARY TO PRESCRIBE AMENDMENT. The Secretary of the Treasury or his delegate shall prescribe an amendment which allows a plan to make any distribution described in section 401(m)(6) of the Internal Revenue Code of 1986.

"(ii) ADOPTION BY PLAN. If a plan adopts the amendment prescribed under clause (i) and makes a distribution in accordance with such amendment, such distribution shall be treated as made in accordance with the provisions of the plan."

(m) Amendments Related to Section 1120 of the Reform Act.—

* * *

(3) Section 1120(c) of the Reform Act is amended to read as follows:

"(c) EFFECTIVE DATES.—

"(1) IN GENERAL. Except as provided in paragraph (2), the amendments made by this section shall apply to years beginning after December 31, 1988.

"(2) COLLECTIVE BARGAINING AGREEMENTS. In the case of a plan maintained pursuant to 1 or more collective bargaining agreements between employee representatives and 1 or more employers ratified before March 1, 1986, the amendments made by this section shall not apply to plan years beginning before the earlier of—

"(A) January 1, 1991, or

"(B) the later of—

"(i) January 1, 1989, or

"(ii) the date on which the last of such collective bargaining agreements terminates (determined without regard to any extension thereof after February 28, 1986)."

[¶15,722E-2]

Act Sec. 1011A AMENDMENTS RELATED TO PARTS III AND IV OF SUBTITLE A OF TITLE XI OF THE REFORM ACT.

(a) Amendments Related to Section 1121 of the Reform Act.—

* * *

(3) Section 1121(d) of the Reform Act is amended by adding at the end thereof the following new paragraph:

"(5) PLANS MAY INCORPORATE SECTION 401(a)(9) REQUIREMENTS BY REFERENCE. Notwithstanding any other provision of law, except as provided in regulations prescribed by the Secretary of the Treasury or his delegate, a plan may incorporate by reference the requirements of section 401(a)(9) of the Internal Revenue Code of 1986."

(4) Section 1121(d)(3) of the Reform Act is amended by striking out "plan years" and inserting in lieu thereof "years".

* * *

(b) Amendments Related to Section 1122 of the Reform Act.—

* * *

(11) Section 1122(h) of the Reform Act is amended by adding at the end thereof the following new paragraph:

"(9) SPECIAL RULE FOR STATE PLANS. In the case of a plan maintained by a State which on May 5, 1986, permitted withdrawal by the employee of employee contributions (other than as an annuity), section 72(e) of the Internal Revenue Code of 1986 shall be applied—

"(A) without regard to the phrase 'before separation from service' in paragraph (8)(D), and

"(B) by treating any amount received (other than as an annuity) before or with the 1st annuity payment as having been received before the annuity starting date."

(12) Subparagraph (B) of section 1122(h)(2) of the Reform Act is amended by inserting ", except that section 72(b)(3) of the Internal Revenue Code of 1986 (as added by such subsection) shall apply to individuals whose annuity starting date is after July 1, 1986" after "1986".

(13) Sections 1122(h)(3)(C) and (h)(4)(C) of the Reform Act are each amended by striking out "with respect to any other lump sum distribution" and inserting in lieu thereof "for purposes of such Code".

(14) Clause (i) of section 1122(h)(3)(C) of the Reform Act is amended—

(A) by striking out "individual" and inserting in lieu thereof "employee", and

(B) by inserting "or by an individual, estate, or trust with respect to such an employee" after "1986".

(15) Section 1122(h)(5) of the Reform Act is amended—

(A) by striking out "individual" and inserting in lieu thereof "employee",

(B) by inserting "and by including in gross income the zero bracket amount in effect under section 63(d) of such Code for such years" after "1986" in the last sentence, and

(C) by adding at the end thereof the following new sentence: "This paragraph shall also apply to an individual, estate, or trust which receives a distribution with respect to an employee described in this paragraph."

(c) Amendments Related to Section 1123 of the Reform Act.—

* * *

(11) Section 1123(e)(2) of the Reform Act is amended—

(A) by striking out "taxable", and

(B) by inserting ", but only with respect to distributions from contracts described in section 403(b) of the Internal Revenue Code of 1986 which are attributable to assets other than assets held as of the close of the last year beginning before January 1, 1989" after "1988".

(12) Section 1123(e) of the Reform Act is amended by adding at the end thereof the following new paragraph:

"(5) SPECIAL RULE FOR DISTRIBUTIONS UNDER AN ANNUITY CONTRACT. The amendments made by paragraphs (1), (2), and (3) of subsection (b) shall not apply to any distribution under an annuity contract if—

"(A) as of March 1, 1986, payments were being made under such contract pursuant to a written election providing a specific schedule for the distribution of the taxpayer's interest in such contract, and

"(B) such distribution is made pursuant to such written election."

* * *

(d) Amendments Related to Section 1124 of the Reform Act.—

(1) Section 1124(a) of the Reform Act is amended to read as follows:

"(a) IN GENERAL. If an employee dies, separates from service, or becomes disabled before 1987 and an individual, trust, or estate receives a lump-sum distribution with respect to such employee after December 31, 1986, and before March 16, 1987, on account of such death, separation from service, or disability, then, for purposes of the Internal Revenue Code of 1986, such individual, estate, or trust may treat such distribution as if it were received in 1986."

(2) Section 1124(b) of the Reform Act is amended—

(A) by striking out "employee" each place it appears and inserting in lieu thereof "individual, estate, or trust", and

(B) by inserting "with respect to an employee" after "receives".

(3) Section 1124 of the Reform Act is amended by adding at the end thereof the following new subsection:

"(c) LUMP SUM DISTRIBUTION. For purposes of this section, the term 'lump sum distribution' has the meaning given such term by section 402(e)(4)(A) of the Internal Revenue Code of 1986, without regard to subparagraph (B) or (H) of section 402(e)(4) of such Code."

(e) Amendments Related to Section 1131 of the Reform Act.—

* * *

(3) Section 1131(d) of the Reform Act is amended to read as follows:

"(d) EFFECTIVE DATES.—

"(1) IN GENERAL. Except as provided in paragraph (2), the amendments made by this section shall apply to taxable years beginning after December 31, 1986.

"(2) SPECIAL RULES FOR COLLECTIVE BARGAINING AGREEMENTS. In the case of a plan maintained pursuant to 1 or more collective bargaining agreements between employee representatives and 1 or more employers ratified before March 1, 1986, the amendments made by this section shall not apply to contributions pursuant to any such agreement for taxable years beginning before the earlier of—

"(A) January 1, 1989, or

"(B) the date on which the last of such collective bargaining agreements terminates (determined without regard to any extension thereof after February 28, 1986)."

* * *

(f) Amendments Related to Section 1132 of the Reform Act.—

* * *

(4) Subparagraph (B) of section 1132(c)(2) of the Reform Act is amended by striking out "November 19, 1978" and inserting in lieu thereof "September 19, 1978".

(5) Section 1132(c) of the Reform Act is amended by adding at the end thereof the following new paragraph:

"(5) SPECIAL RULE FOR EMPLOYEE STOCK OWNERSHIP PLANS. Section 4980(c)(3) of the Internal Revenue Code of 1986 (as added by subsection (a)) shall apply to reversions occurring after March 31, 1985."

* * *

(g) Amendments Related to Section 1133 of the Reform Act.—

* * *

(8) Paragraph (1) of section 1133(c) of the Reform Act is amended by inserting ", other than a distribution with respect to a decedent dying before January 1, 1987" after "1986".

* * *

(k) AMENDMENT RELATED TO SECTION 1139 OF THE REFORM ACT. Clause (i) of section 1139(d)(2)(A) of the Reform Act is amended by striking out "before January" and inserting in lieu thereof "after January".

* * *

[¶15,722E-3]

Act Sec. 1011B AMENDMENTS RELATED TO SUBTITLES B AND C OF TITLE XI OF THE REFORM ACT.

(a) Amendments Related to Section 1151 of the Reform Act.—

* * *

(22)(E) The third to the last sentence of section 209 of the Social Security Act is amended—

  (i) by striking out the period at the end of clause (2) and inserting in lieu thereof ", or", and

  (ii) by inserting after clause (2) the following new clause:

  "(3) Any amount required to be included in gross income under section 89 of the Internal Revenue Code of 1986."

* * *

(23)(B) Section 209(e)(9) of the Social Security Act is amended by inserting "if such payment would not be treated as wages without regard to such plan and it is reasonable to believe that (if section 125 applied for purposes of this section) section 125 would not treat any wages as constructively received" after "1986)".

(24) Section 1151(h)(3) of the Reform Act is amended by striking out "Section 6039B(c)" and inserting in lieu thereof "Section 6039D(c)".

(25) Paragraph (1) of section 1151(k) of the Reform Act is amended by adding at the end thereof the following new sentence: "Notwithstanding the preceding sentence, the amendments made by subsections (e)(1) and (i)(3)(C) shall, to the extent they relate to sections 106, 162(i)(2), and 162(k) of the Internal Revenue Code of 1986, apply to years beginning after 1986."

(26) Section 1151(k) of the Reform Act is amended by adding at the end thereof the following new paragraph:

"(6) CERTAIN PLANS MAINTAINED BY EDUCATIONAL INSTITUTIONS. If an educational organization described in section 170(b)(1)(A)(ii) of the Internal Revenue Code of 1986 makes an election under this paragraph with respect to a plan described in section 125(c)(2)(C) of such Code, the amendments made by this section shall apply with respect to such plan for plan years beginning after the date of the enactment of this Act."

* * *

(b) **Amendments Related to Section 1161 of the Reform Act.—**

* * *

(4) Section 211(a) of the Social Security Act is amended by inserting after paragraph (13) the following new paragraph:

"(14) The deduction under section 162(m) (relating to health insurance costs of self-employed individuals) shall not be allowed."

* * *

(f) **Amendments Related to Section 1168 of the Reform Act.—**

* * *

(4) Section 1168(c) of the Reform Act is amended by striking out "1986" and inserting in lieu thereof "1984".

(g) **Amendments Related to Section 1172 of the Reform Act.—**

(1) Section 1172(b)(1)(A) of the Reform Act is amended by inserting "each place it appears" before the comma.

* * *

(h) **Amendments Related to Section 1173 of the Reform Act.—**

* * *

(5)(B) Subparagraph (B) of section 1173(c)(2) of the Reform Act is amended to read as follows:

"(B) Section 133(b)(1)(A) of the Internal Revenue Code of 1986, as amended by subsection (b)(2), shall apply to any loan used (or part of a series of loans used) to refinance a loan which—

  "(i) was used to acquire employer securities after May 23, 1984, and

  "(ii) met the requirements of section 133 of the Internal Revenue Code of 1986 as in effect as of the later of—

   "(I) the date on which the loan was made, or

   "(II) July 19, 1984."

* * *

(i) **Amendments Related to Section 1174 of the Reform Act.—**

* * *

(2) Section 1174(a)(2) of the Reform Act is amended by striking out "plan terminations" and inserting in lieu thereof "distributions".

* * *

[¶15,722E-4]

Act Sec.1018 AMENDMENTS RELATED TO TITLE XVIII OF THE REFORM ACT.

* * *

(t) **Additional Amendments Related to Pension Plans.—**

* * *

(2) AMENDMENTS RELATED TO SECTION 1851 OF THE REFORM ACT.—

  (A) Section 1851(a) of the Reform Act is amended by striking out paragraph (4) thereof.

* * *

  (D) Subparagraph (B) of section 1851(a)(3) of the Reform Act is amended by inserting ", section 505, and section 4976(b)(1)(B)" after "section 419A".

(3) AMENDMENTS RELATED TO SECTION 1852 OF THE REFORM ACT.—

  (A) Paragraph (4) of section 1852(a) of the Reform Act is amended by adding at the end thereof the following new subparagraph:

"(C) An individual whose required beginning date would, but for the amendment made by subparagraph (A), occur after December 31, 1986, but whose required beginning date after such amendment occurs before January 1, 1987, shall be treated as if such individual had become a 5-percent owner during the plan year ending in 1986."

(B) Section 1852(h)(2) of the Reform Act is amended by striking out "section 416(l)" and inserting in lieu thereof "section 415(l)".

(C) Section 1852(h)(1) of the Reform Act is amended by striking out "Subsection" and inserting in lieu thereof "Effective for years beginning after December 31, 1985, subsection".

* * *

(4) AMENDMENTS RELATED TO SECTION 1854 OF THE REFORM ACT.—

* * *

(F) Section 1854(a)(3)(B) of the Reform Act is amended by striking out "1042(b)(3)" and inserting in lieu thereof "1042(b)".

(G) Subparagraph (C) of section 1854(a)(3) of the Reform Act is amended to read as follows:

"(C)(i) Except as provided in clause (ii), the amendments made by this paragraph shall apply to sales of securities after the date of the enactment of this Act.

"(ii) A taxpayer or executor may elect to have section 1042(b)(3) of the Internal Revenue Code of 1954 (as in effect before the amendment made by subparagraph (B)) apply to sales before the date of the enactments of this Act.

* * *

(u) **Additional Clerical Amendments.**—

(1) Paragraph (5) of section 104(b) of the Reform Act is amended by striking out "1222(b)" and inserting in lieu thereof "1122(b)".

(2) The amendment made by section 122(c)(2) of the Reform Act shall be applied as if it also struck out the comma at the end of section 274(b)(1)(B) of the 1986 Code.

* * *

(12) Subparagraph (B) of section 1851(a)(6) of the Reform Act is amended by striking out "Subsection (b)" and inserting in lieu thereof "Subsection (a)".

* * *

(34) Paragraph (14) of section 1114(b) of the Reform Act is amended—

(A) by striking out "section 501(c)(17)" and inserting in lieu thereof "section 501(c)(17)(A)", and

(B) by striking out "duties consists" and inserting in lieu thereof "duties consist".

* * *

(38) The amendment made by section 1221(b)(3)(B) of the Reform Act shall be construed as striking out paragraph (3) of section 954(e) of the 1986 Code.

* * *

(42) Paragraph (3) of section 1404(c) of the Reform Act is amended by striking out "section 6601" and inserting in lieu thereof "section 6601(b)".

* * *

(50) Section 13303(a) of Public Law 99-272 is amended (in the matter proposed to be inserted in section 3306(c) of the Internal Revenue Code of 1954),

* * *

[¶15,722E-5]

Act Sec. 1019 EFFECTIVE DATE.

(a) **General Rule.** Except as otherwise provided in this title, any amendment made by this title shall take effect as if included in the provision of the Reform Act to which such amendment relates.

(b) **Waiver of Estimated Tax Penalties.** No addition to tax shall be made under section 6654 or 6655 of the 1986 Code for any period before April 16, 1989, (March 16, 1989 in the case of a taxpayer subject to section 6655 of the 1986 Code) with respect to any underpayment to the extent such underpayment was created or increased by any provision of this title or title II.

TITLE II—AMENDMENTS RELATED TO TAX PROVISIONS IN OTHER LEGISLATION

* * *

[¶15,722E-6]

Act Sec. 2004 AMENDMENTS RELATED TO THE REVENUE ACT OF 1987.

(a) **Amendment Related to Section 10101 of the Act.** Section 10101(b) of the Revenue Act of 1987 is amended to read as follows:

"(b) **Effective Date.**—

"(1) IN GENERAL. The amendment made by subsection (a) shall apply to expenses paid in taxable years beginning after December 31, 1987.

"(2) SPECIAL RULE FOR CAFETERIA PLANS. For purposes of section 125 of the Internal Revenue Code of 1986, a plan shall not be treated as failing to be a cafeteria plan solely because under the plan a participant elected before January 1, 1988, to receive reimbursement under the plan for dependent care assistance for periods after December 31, 1987, and such assistance included reimbursement for expenses at a camp where the dependent stays overnight."

* * *

(c) **Amendment Related to Section 10103.** Paragraph (1) of section 10103(a) of the Revenue Act of 1987 is amended by inserting "in a plan established for its employees by the United States" after "participant".

(1) Paragraph (2) of section 10221(e) of the Revenue Act of 1987 is amended by striking out "amendments made by subsection (b)" and inserting in lieu thereof "amendments made by subsection (c)".

* * *

(j) **Amendments Related to Section 10222 of the Act.—**

* * *

(1)(B) Paragraph (2) of section 10222(a) of the Revenue Act of 1987 is amended by adding at the end thereof the following new subparagraph:

"(C) TREATMENT OF CERTAIN EXCESS LOSS ACCOUNTS.—

"(i) IN GENERAL. If—

"(I) any disposition on or before December 15, 1987, of stock resulted in an inclusion of an excess loss account (or would have so resulted if the amendments made by paragraph (1) had applied to such disposition), and

"(II) there is an unrecaptured amount with respect to such disposition,

the portion of such unrecaptured amount allocable to stock disposed of in a disposition to which the amendment made by paragraph (1) applies shall be taken into account as negative basis. To the extent permitted by the Secretary of the Treasury or his delegate, the preceding sentence shall not apply to the extent the taxpayer elects to reduce its basis in indebtedness of the corporation with respect to which there would have been an excess loss account.

"(ii) SPECIAL RULES. For purposes of this subparagraph—

"(I) UNRECAPTURED AMOUNT. The term 'unrecaptured amount' means the amount by which the inclusion referred to in clause (i)(I) would have been increased if the amendment made by paragraph (1) and applied to the disposition.

"(II) COORDINATION WITH BINDING CONTRACT EXCEPTION. A disposition shall be treated as occurring on or before December 15, 1987, if the amendment made by paragraph (1) does not apply to such disposition by reason of subparagraph (B)."

* * *

(4) Subparagraph (B) of section 10222(b)(2) of the Revenue Act of 1987 is amended to read as follows:

"(B) EXCEPTION. The amendment made by paragraph (1) shall not apply for purposes of determining gain or loss on any disposition of stock after December 15, 1987, and before January 1, 1989, if such disposition is pursuant to a written binding contract, governmental order, letter of intent or preliminary agreement, or stock acquisition agreement, in effect on or before December 15, 1987."

(k) **Amendments Related to Section 10223 of the Act.—**

* * *

(3) Paragraph (2) of section 10223(d) of the Revenue Act of 1987 is amended by adding at the end thereof the following new subparagraph:

"(D) TREATMENT OF CERTAIN MEMBERS OF AFFILIATED GROUP.—

"(i) IN GENERAL. For purposes of subparagraph (A), all corporations which were in existence on the designated date and were members of the same affiliated group which included the distributees on such date shall be treated as 1 distributee.

"(ii) LIMITATION TO STOCK HELD ON DESIGNATED DATE. Clause (i) shall not exempt any distribution from the amendments made by this section if such distribution is with respect to stock not held by the distributee (determined without regard to clause (i)) on the designated date directly or indirectly through a corporation which goes out of existence in the transaction.

"(iii) DESIGNATED DATE. For purposes of this subparagraph, the term 'designated date' means the later of—

"(I) December 15, 1987, or

"(II) the date on which the acquisition meeting the requirements of subparagraph (A) occurred."

(4) Subparagraph (B) of section 10223(d)(2) of the Revenue Act of 1987 is amended—

* * *

[¶ 15,722E-7]

Act Sec. 2005 AMENDMENTS RELATED TO PENSION PROTECTION ACT AND FULL FUNDING LIMITATIONS.

(a) **Amendment Related to Section 9303.—**

* * *

(2)(B) Subparagraph (C) of section 302(d)(3) of the Employee Retirement Income Security Act of 1974 is amended—

(i) by striking out "October 17, 1987" in clause (i) and inserting in lieu thereof "October 29, 1987", and

(ii) by striking out "October 16, 1987" in clause (iii) and inserting in lieu thereof "October 28, 1987".

* * *

(c) **Amendments Related to Section 9301.—**

* * *

(3)(A) Except as provided in subparagraph (B), the amendments made by this subsection shall apply with respect to transactions occurring after July 26, 1988.

(B) The amendments made by this subsection shall not apply to any transaction occurring after July 26, 1988, if on or before such date the board of directors of the employer, approves such transaction or the employer took similar binding action.

(d) **Other Provisions.—**

* * *

(2) Subparagraph (B) of section 302(d)(3) of the Employee Retirement Income Security Act of 1974 is amended—

(A) by striking out "October 17, 1987" in clause (i) and inserting in lieu thereof "October 29, 1987", and

(B) by striking out "October 16, 1987" in clause (iii) and inserting in lieu thereof "October 28, 1987".

* * *

[¶15,722E-8]

Act Sec. 3011 FAILURE TO SATISFY CONTINUATION COVERAGE REQUIREMENTS OF GROUP HEALTH PLANS.

* * *

(b) Technical Amendments.—

* * *

(7) Paragraph (1) of section 2208 of the Public Health Service Act is amended by the striking out "section 162(i)(3) of the Internal Revenue Code of 1954" and inserting in lieu thereof "section 162(i)(2) of the Internal Revenue Code of 1986".

* * *

Subtitle C—Employee Benefit Nondiscrimination Rules

[¶15,722E-9]

Act Sec. 3021 MODIFICATIONS TO DISCRIMINATION RULES APPLICABLE TO CERTAIN EMPLOYEE BENEFIT PLANS.

(a) Modification to Section 89.—

* * *

(2) TIME FOR TESTING.—

* * *

(B) DESIGNATIONS FOR 1989 NOT BINDING. Any designation of a testing day for a year beginning in 1989 shall be disregarded in determining the day which may be designated as the testing day for years beginning after 1989.

* * *

(c) Transitional Provisions for Purposes of Section 89.—

(1) TEMPORARY VALUATION RULES. In the case of testing years beginning before the later of January 1, 1991, or the date 1 year after the Secretary of the Treasury or his delegate first issues such valuation rules as are necessary to apply the provisions of section 89 of the 1986 Code to health plans (or if later the effective date of such rules)—

(A) Section 89(g)(3)(B) of the 1986 Code shall not apply.

(B)(i) Except as provided in clause (ii), the value of coverage under a health plan for purposes of section 89 of the 1986 Code shall be determined in substantially the same manner as costs under a health plan are determined under section 4980B(f)(4) of the 1986 Code.

(ii) For purposes of determining whether an employer meets the requirements of subsections (d), (e), and (f) of section 89 of the 1986 Code, value under clause (i) may be determined under any other reasonable method selected by the employer.

(2) FORMER EMPLOYEES. The amendments made by section 1151 of the Reform Act shall not apply to former employees who separated from service with the employer before January 1, 1989 (and were not reemployed on or after such date), and such former employees shall not be taken into account in determining whether the requirements of section 89 of the 1986 Code are met with respect to other former employees. The preceding sentence shall not apply to the extent that—

(A) the value of employer-provided benefits provided to any such former employee exceeds the value of such benefits which were provided under the terms of the plan as in effect on December 31, 1988, or

(B) the employer-provided benefits provided to such former employees are modified so as to discriminate in favor of such former employees who are highly compensated employees.

Any excess value under the preceding sentence shall be determined without regard to any increase required by Federal law, regulation or rule or any increase which is the same for employees separating on or before December 31, 1988, and employees separating after such date and which does not discriminate in favor of highly compensated employees who separated from service after December 31, 1988.

(3) WRITTEN PLAN REQUIREMENT. The requirements of section 89(k)(1)(A) of the 1986 Code shall be treated as met with respect to any testing year beginning in 1989, if—

(A) the plan is in writing before the close of such year,

(B) the employees had reasonable notice of the plan's essential features on or before the beginning of such year, and

(C) the provisions of the written plan apply for the entire year.

(4) RULES TO BE PRESCRIBED BEFORE NOVEMBER 15, 1988. Not later than November 15, 1988, the Secretary of the Treasury or his delegate shall issue such rules as may be necessary to carry out the provisions of section 89 of the 1986 Code.

* * *

TITLE III—ADDITIONAL SIMPLIFICATION AND CLARIFICATION PROVISIONS

Subtitle C—Pensions and Employee Benefits

* * *

[¶15,722E-10]

Act Sec. 6052 MODIFICATIONS OF DISCRIMINATION RULES APPLICABLE TO CERTAIN ANNUITY CONTRACTS.

* * *

(b) Sampling. In the case of plan years beginning in 1989, 1990, or 1991, determinations as to whether a plan meets the requirements of section 403(b)(12) of the 1986 Code may be made on the basis of a statistically valid random sample. The preceding sentence shall apply only if—

(1) the sampling is conducted by an independent person in a manner not inconsistent with regulations prescribed by the Secretary, and

(2) the statistical method and sample size result in a 95 percent probability that the results will have a margin of error not greater than 3 percent.

[¶15,722E-11]

Act Sec. 6056 STUDY OF EFFECT OF MINIMUM PARTICIPATION RULE ON EMPLOYERS REQUIRED TO PROVIDE CERTAIN RETIREMENT BENEFITS.

(a) **Study**. The Secretary of the Treasury or his delegate shall conduct a study on the application of section 401(a)(26) of the Internal Revenue Code of 1986 to Government contractors who—

    (1) are required by Federal law to provide certain employees specified retirement benefits, and

    (2) establish a separate plan for such employees while maintaining a separate plan for employees who are not entitled to such benefits.

Such study shall consider the Federal requirements with respect to employee benefits for employees of Government contractors, whether a special minimum participation rule should apply to such employees, and methods by which plans may be modified to satisfy minimum participation requirements.

(b) **Report**. The Secretary of the Treasury or his delegate shall report the results of the study under subsection (a) to the Committee on Finance of the Senate and the Committee on Ways and Means of the House of Representatives not later than September 1, 1989.

* * *

[¶15,722E-12]

Act Sec. 6061 LOANS TO ACQUIRE EMPLOYER SECURITIES.

Notwithstanding the last sentence of section 111B[1011B](h)(5)(A) of this Act, the amendments made by paragraphs (1) and (2) of section 111B[1011B](h) of this Act shall not apply to any loan used to refinance a loan described in section 133(b)(1)(A) of the 1986 Code which is made before October 22, 1986, if the terms of the refinanced loan do not extend the total commitment period beyond the later of—

    (1) the term of the original securities acquisition loan, or

    (2) the amortization period used to determine the regular payments (prior to any final or balloon payment) applicable to the original securities acquisition loan.

[¶15,722E-13]

Act Sec. 6062 EFFECTIVE DATE OF SECTION 415 LIMITATIONS OF COLLECTIVELY BARGAINED AGREEMENTS.

(a) **In General**. Paragraph (2) of section 1106(i) of the Reform Act is amended to read as follows:

"(2) COLLECTIVE BARGAINING AGREEMENTS. In the case of a plan in effect before March 1, 1986, pursuant to 1 or more collective bargaining agreements between employee representatives and 1 or more employers, the amendments made by this section (other than subsection (d)) shall not apply to contributions or benefits pursuant to such agreement in years beginning before October 1, 1991."

(b) **Effective Date**. The amendment made by this section shall take effect as if included in the provisions of section 1106 of the Reform Act.

[¶15,722E-14]

Act Sec. 6063 TREATMENT OF PRE-1989 ELECTIONS FOR DEPENDENT CARE ASSISTANCE UNDER CAFETERIA PLANS.

For purposes of section 125 of the 1986 Code, a plan shall not be treated as failing to be a cafeteria plan solely because under the plan a participant elected before January 1, 1989, to receive reimbursement under the plan for dependent care assistance for periods after December 31, 1988, and such assistance is includible in gross income under the provisions of the Family Support Act of 1988.

[¶15,722E-15]

Act Sec. 6064 SHORT TITLE; ETC.

(a) **Short Title**. This Act may be cited as the "Technical and Miscellaneous Revenue Act of 1988".

(b) **Definitions**. For purposes of this Act—

    (1) 1986 CODE. The term "1986 Code" means the Internal Revenue Code of 1986.

    (2) REFORM ACT. Except where incompatible with the intent, the term "Reform Act" means the Tax Reform Act of 1986.

* * *

[¶15,722E-16]

Act Sec. 6065 EXCEPTION FOR GOVERNMENTAL PLANS.

In the case of plan years beginning before January 1, 1993, section 401(a)(26) of the 1986 Code shall not apply to any governmental plan (within the meaning of section 414(d) of such Code) with respect to employees who were participants in such plan on July 14, 1988.

* * *

[¶15,722E-17]

Act Sec. 6067 SPECIAL RULE FOR APPLYING SPIN-OFF RULES TO BRIDGE BANKS.

* * *

(b) **Study**. The Secretary of the Treasury or his delegate, in consultation with the Federal Deposit Insurance Corporation, shall conduct a study with respect to the proper method of allocating assets in the case of a transaction to which the amendment made by this subsection applies. The Secretary of the Treasury shall not later than January 1, 1990, report the results of such study to the Committee on Ways and Means of the House of Representatives and to the Committee on Finance of the Senate.

* * *

[¶ 15,722E-18]

Act Sec. 6069 INCREASE IN EMPLOYER REVERSION TAX.

* * *

(b) **Effective Date.—**

(1) IN GENERAL. The amendment made by subsection (a) shall apply to reversions occurring on or after October 21, 1988.

(2) EXCEPTION. The amendment made by subsection (a) shall not apply to any reversion on or after October 21, 1988, pursuant to a plan termination if—

(A) with respect to plans subject to title IV of the Employee Retirement Income Security Act of 1974, a notice of intent to terminate required under such title was provided to participants (or if no participants, to the Pension Benefit Guaranty Corporation) before October 21, 1988,

(B) with respect to plans subject to title I of such Act, a notice of intent to reduce future accruals required under section 204(h) of such Act was provided to participants in connection with the termination before October 21, 1988,.

(C) with respect to plans not subject to title I or IV of such Act, the Board of Directors of the employer approved the termination or the employer took other binding action before October 21, 1988, or

(D) such plan termination was directed by a final order of a court of competent jurisdiction entered before October 21, 1988, and notice of such order was provided to participants before such date.

* * *

[¶ 15,722E-19]

Act Sec. 6072 STUDY OF TREATMENT OF CERTAIN TECHNICAL PERSONNEL.

The Secretary of the Treasury or his delegate shall conduct a study of the treatment provided by section 1706 of the Reform Act (relating to treatment of certain technical personnel). The report of such study shall be submitted not later than September 1, 1989, to the Committee on Ways and Means of the House of Representatives and the Committee on Finance of the Senate.

TITLE VIII—AMENDMENTS RELATING TO SOCIAL SECURITY ACT PROGRAMS

Subtitle A—Old-Age, Survivors, and Disability Insurance and Related Provisions

* * *

[¶ 15,722E-20]

Act Sec. 8013 EXCLUSION OF EMPLOYEES SEPARATED FROM EMPLOYMENT BEFORE JANUARY 1, 1989, FROM RULE INCLUDING AS WAGES TAXABLE UNDER FICA CERTAIN PAYMENTS FOR GROUP-TERM LIFE INSURANCE.

(a) **In General**. Subsection (b) of section 9003 of the Omnibus Budget Reconciliation Act of 1987 (101 Stat. 1330-287) is amended by striking "December 31, 1987." and inserting "December 31, 1987, except that such amendments shall not apply with respect to payments by the employer (or a successor of such employer) for group-term life insurance for such employer's former employees who separated from employment with the employer on or before December 31, 1988, to the extent that such payments are not for coverage for any such employee for any period for which such employee is employed by such employer (or a successor of such employer) after the date of such separation.".

(b) **Effective Date**. The amendment made by subsection (a) shall apply as if such amendment had been included or reflected in section 9003(b) of the Omnibus Budget Reconciliation Act of 1987 at the time of its enactment.

Omnibus Budget Reconciliation Act of 1987

P.L. 100-203

Signed on December 22, 1987

[Reproduced below are sections of the Omnibus Budget Reconciliation Act of 1987 which did not amend any sections of the Internal Revenue Code of 1986 or the Employee Retirement Income Security Act of 1974 (ERISA).]

[¶15,723]

Act Sec. 9301 FULL-FUNDING LIMITATION FOR DEDUCTIONS TO QUALIFIED PLANS

* * *

Act Sec. 9301(c)(2) Regulations. The Secretary of the Treasury or his delegate shall prescribe such regulations as are necessary to carry out the amendments made by this section no later than August 15, 1988.

(3) Study. The Secretary of the Treasury or his delegate shall study the effect of the amendments made by this section on benefit security under defined benefit pension plans and shall report the results of such study to the Committee on Ways and Means of the House of Representatives and to the Committee on Finance of the Senate no later than August 15, 1988.

[¶15,723A]

Act Sec. 9302 SHORT TITLE: DEFINITIONS

PART II—PENSION FUNDING AND TERMINATION REQUIREMENTS

Act Sec. 9302. (a) Short Title. This part may be cited as the "Pension Protection Act".

Act Sec. 9302. (b) Definitions. For purposes of this part—

(1) 1986 Code. The term "1986 Code" means the Internal Revenue Code of 1986.

(2) ERISA. The term "ERISA" means the Employee Retirement Income Security Act of 1974.

[¶15,723B]

Act Sec. 9303 ADDITIONAL FUNDING REQUIREMENTS

* * *

Act Sec. 9303. (c) Revision Of Valuation Regulations. Effective with respect to plan years beginning after December 31, 1987, the provisions of the regulations prescribed under section 412(c)(2) of the 1986 Code which permit asset valuations to be based on a range between 85 percent and 115 percent of average value shall have no force and effect with respect to plans other than multiemployer plans (as defined in section 414(f) of the 1986 Code). The Secretary of the Treasury or his delegate shall amend such regulations to carry out the purposes of the preceding sentence.

* * *

Act Sec. 9303. (e) Effective Date.—

(1) In General. Except as provided in this subsection, the amendments made by this section shall apply with respect to plan years beginning after December 31, 1988.

(2) Subsections (C) and (D). The amendments made by subsections (c) and (d) shall apply with respect to years beginning after December 31, 1987.

(3) Special Rule for Steel Companies.—

(A) In General. For any plan year beginning before January 1, 1994, any increase in the funding standard account under section 412(1) of the 1986 Code or section 302(d) of ERISA (as added by this section) with respect to any steel employee plan shall not exceed the sum of—

(i) the required percentage of the current liability under such plan, plus

(ii) the amount determined under subparagraph (C)(i) for such plan year.

(B) Required Percentage. For purposes of subparagraph (A), the term "required percentage" means, with respect to any plan year, the excess (if any) of—

(i) the sum of—

(I) the funded current liability percentage as of the beginning of the 1st plan year beginning after December 31, 1988 (determined without regard to any plan amendment adopted after June 30, 1987), plus

(II) 1 percentage point for the plan year for which the determination under this paragraph is being made and for each prior plan year beginning after December 31, 1988, over

(ii) the funded current liability percentage as of the beginning of the plan year for which such determination is being made.

(C) Special rules for Contingent Events. In the case of any unpredictable contingent event benefit with respect to which the event on which such benefits are contingent occurs after December 17, 1987—

(i) Amortization Amount. For purposes of subparagraph (A)(ii), the amount determined under this clause for any plan year is the amount which would be determined if the unpredictable contingent event benefit liability were amortized in equal annual installments over 10 plan years (beginning with the plan year in which such event occurs).

(ii) Benefit and Contributions Not Taken into Account. For purposes of subparagraph (B), in determining the funded current liability percentage for any plan year, there shall not be taken into account—

(I) the unpredictable contingent event benefit liability, or

(II) any amount contributed to the plan which is attributable to clause (i).

(D) Steel Employee Plan. For purposes of this paragraph, the term "steel employee plan" means any plan if—

    (i) such plan is maintained by a steel company, and

    (ii) substantially all of the employees covered by such plan are employees of such company.

(E) Other Definitions. For purposes of this paragraph—

    (i) Steel Company. The term "steel company" means any corporation described in section 806(b) of the Steel Import Stabilization Act.

    (ii) Other Definitions. The terms "current liability", "funded current liability percentage", and "unpredictable contingent event benefit" have the meanings given such terms by section 412(l) of the 1986 Code (as added by this section).

(F) Special Rule. The provisions of this paragraph shall apply in the case of a company which was originally incorporated on April 25, 1927, in Michigan and reincorporated on June 3, 1968, in Delaware in the same manner as if such company were a steel company.

[¶15,723C]

Act Sec. 9306 ACT SEC. 9306. FUNDING WAIVERS

* * *

Act Sec. 9306(f) Effective Dates.—

(1) In General. Except as provided in this subsection, the amendments made by this section shall apply in the case of—

    (A) any application submitted after December 17, 1987, and

    (B) any waiver granted pursuant to such an application.

(2) Special Rule for Application Requirement.—

    (A) In General. The amendments made by subsections (a)(1)(A) and (a)(2)(A) shall apply to plan years beginning after December 31, 1987.

    (B) Transitional rule for years beginning in 1988. In the case of any plan year beginning during calendar 1988, section 412(d)(4) of the 1986 Code and section 303(d)(1) of ERISA (as added by subsection (a)(1)) shall be applied by substituting "6th month" for "3rd month".

(3) Frequency of Waivers. In applying the second sentence of section 412(d) of the 1986 Code and section 303(a) of ERISA to plans other than multiemployer plans, the number of waivers which may be granted pursuant to applications submitted after December 17, 1987, shall be determined without regard to waivers granted with respect to plan years beginning before January 1, 1988.

(4) Subsection (d). The amendments made by subsection (d) shall apply to applications submitted more than 90 days after the date of the enactment of this Act.

[¶15,723D]

Act Sec. 9331 LIMITATIONS ON EMPLOYER REVERSIONS UPON PLAN TERMINATION

(a)(2) TRANSITIONAL RULE. The amendments made by paragraph (1) shall apply, in the case of plans which, as of December 17, 1987, have no provision relating to the distribution of plan assets to the employer for purposes of section 4044(d)(1)(C) of the Employee Retirement Income Security Act of 1974, only with respect to plan amendments providing for the distribution of plan assets to the employer which are adopted after 1 year after the effective date of such amendments made by paragraph (1). Such amendment shall not apply to any provision of the plan adopted on or before December 17, 1987, which provides for the distribution of plan assets to the employer.

[¶15,723E]

Act Sec. 9312 ACT SEC. 9312. ELIMINATION OF SECTION 4049 TRUST; INCREASE IN LIABILITY TO PENSION BENEFIT GUARANTY CORPORATION AND IN PAYMENTS BY CORPORATION TO PARTICIPANTS AND BENEFICIARIES

* * *

Act Sec. 9312(b) Conforming Amendments.

* * *

(3) Payment by Corporation to Participants and Beneficiaries of Recovery Percentage of Outstanding Amount of Benefit Liabilities.—

* * *

    (B) Transitional Rule.—

        (i) In General. In the case of any plan termination to which the amendments made by this section apply and with respect to which notices of intent to terminate were provided on or before December 17, 1990—

        (I) subparagraph (A) of section 4022(c)(1) of ERISA (as amended by this paragraph) shall not apply, and

        (II) subparagraph (B) of section 4022(c)(1) of ERISA (as so amended) shall apply irrespective of the outstanding amount of benefit liabilities under the plan.

        (ii) Limitation. Clause (i) shall not apply in the case of any plan termination referred to in clause (i) with respect to which the recovery ratio is not finally determined under section 4022(c)(1)(B) of ERISA (as so amended) as of December 17, 1990.

[¶15,723F]

Act Sec. 9331 ACT SEC. 9331. INCREASE IN PREMIUM RATES

* * *

Act Sec. 9331(f) Effective Date.—

(1) In General. The amendments made by this section shall apply to plan years beginning after December 31, 1987.

(2) Separate Accounting. The amendments made by subsection (d) shall apply to fiscal years after September 30, 1988.

[¶15,723G]

Act Sec. 9341 ACT SEC. 9341. SECURITY REQUIRED UPON ADOPTION OF PLAN AMENDMENT RESULTING IN SIGNIFICANT UNDERFUNDING

* * *

Act Sec. 9341(c) EFFECTIVE DATE.—

(1) In General. Except as provided in this subsection, the amendments made by this section shall apply to plan amendments adopted after the date of the enactment of this Act.

(2) Collective Bargaining Agreements. In the case of a plan maintained pursuant to 1 or more collective bargaining agreements between employee representatives and 1 or more employers ratified before the date of the enactment of this Act, the amendments made by this section shall not apply to plan amendments adopted pursuant to collective bargaining agreements ratified before the date of enactment.

[¶15,723H]

Act Sec. 9342 REPORTING REQUIREMENTS

(c) EFFECTIVE DATE.—

(1) In General. The amendments made by this section shall apply with respect to reports required to be filed after December 31, 1987.

(2) Regulations. The Secretary of Labor shall issue the regulations required to carry out the amendments made by subsection (c) not later than January 1, 1989.

[¶15,723I]

Act Sec. 9343 COORDINATION OF PROVISIONS OF THE INTERNAL REVENUE CODE OF 1986 WITH PROVISIONS OF THE EMPLOYEE RETIREMENT INCOME SECURITY ACT OF 1974

(a) INTERPRETATION OF INTERNAL REVENUE CODE. Except to the extent specifically provided in the Internal Revenue Code of 1986 or as determined by the Secretary of the Treasury, titles I and IV of the Employee Retirement Income Security Act of 1974 are not applicable in interpreting such Code.

[¶15,723J]

Act Sec. 9346 ACT SEC. 9346. INTEREST RATE ON ACCUMULATED CONTRIBUTIONS

* * *

Act Sec. 9346(c) EFFECTIVE DATE.—

(1) In General. The amendments made by this section shall apply to plan years beginning after December 31, 1987.

(2) Plan Amendments Not Required Until January 1, 1989. If any amendment made by this section requires an amendment to any plan, such plan amendment shall not be required to be made before the first plan year beginning on or after January 1, 1989, if—

(A) during the period after such amendments made by this section take effect and before such first plan year, the plan is operated in accordance with the requirements of such amendments or in accordance with an amendment prescribed by the Secretary of the Treasury and adopted by the plan, and

(B) such plan amendment applies retroactively to the period after such amendments take effect and such first plan year.

A plan shall not be treated as failing to provide definitely determinable benefits or contributions, or to be operated in accordance with the provisions of the plan, merely because it operates in accordance with this subsection.

[¶15,723K]

Act Sec. 10511 FEES FOR REQUESTS FOR RULING, DETERMINATIONS, AND SIMILAR LETTERS

(a) GENERAL RULE. The Secretary of the Treasury or his delegate (hereinafter in this section referred to as the "Secretary") shall establish a program requiring the payment of user fees for requests to the Internal Revenue Service for ruling letters, opinion letters, and determination letters and for similar requests.

(b) PROGRAM CRITERIA.—

(1) In General. The fees charged under the program required by subsection (a)—

(A) shall vary according to categories (or subcategories) established by the Secretary,

(B) shall be determined after taking into account the average time for (and difficulty of) complying with requests in each category (and subcategory), and

(C) shall be payable in advance.

(2) Exemptions, Etc.. The Secretary shall provide for such exemptions (and reduced fees) under such program as he determines to be appropriate.

(3) Average Fee Requirement. The average fee charged under the program required by subsection (a) shall be less than the amount determined under the following table:

Category	Average Fee
Employee plan ruling and opinion	$250
Exempt organization ruling	$350
Employee plan determination	$300

Category	Average Fee
Exempt organization determination	$275
Chief counsel ruling	$200

(c) APPLICATION OF SECTION. Subsection (a) shall apply with respect to requests made on or after the 1st day of the second calendar month beginning after the date of the enactment of this Act and before September 30, 1990. Subsection (a) shall also apply with respect to requests made after September 30, 1990, and before October 1, 2000.

Amendments

P.L. 103-465, § 743:

Act Sec. 743 amended OBRA '87 Act Sec. 10511(c) by striking "October 1, 1995" And inserting "October 1, 2000".

The above amendment is effective December 8, 1994.

P.L. 101-508, § 11319(a):

Act Sec. 11319(a) amended OBRA '87 Act Sec. 10511(c) by adding at the end thereof the following new sentence: "Subsection (a) shall also apply with respect to requests made after September 30, 1990, and before October 1, 1995."

The above amendment is effective September 29, 1990.

Omnibus Budget Reconciliation Act of 1985

P.L. 99-272

Signed on April 7, 1986

[Reproduced below are sections of the Omnibus Budget Reconciliation Act of 1985 which did not amend any sections of the Internal Revenue Code of 1954 or the Employee Retirement Income Security Act of 1974 (ERISA).]

[¶15,724]

Act Sec. 1 SHORT TITLE

This Act may be cited as the "Consolidated Omnibus Budget Reconciliation Act of 1985".

TABLE OF CONTENTS

* * *

[¶15,724A]

Act Sec. 10001 EMPLOYERS REQUIRED TO PROVIDE CERTAIN EMPLOYEES AND FAMILY MEMBERS WITH CONTINUED HEALTH INSURANCE COVERAGE AT GROUP RATES (INTERNAL REVENUE CODE AMENDMENTS).

* * *

(e) EFFECTIVE DATES.—

(1) GENERAL RULE. The amendments made by this section shall apply to plan years beginning on or after July 1, 1986.

(2) SPECIAL RULE FOR COLLECTIVE BARGAINING AGREEMENTS. In the case of a group health plan maintained pursuant to one or more collective bargaining agreements between employee representatives and one or more employers ratified before the date of the enactment of this Act, the amendments made by this section shall not apply to plan years beginning before the later of—

(A) the date on which the last of the collective bargaining agreements relating to the plan terminates (determined without regard to any extension thereof agreed to after the date of the enactment of this Act), or

(B) January 1, 1987.

For purposes of subparagraph (A), any plan amendment made pursuant to a collective bargaining agreement relating to the plan which amends the plan solely to conform to any requirement added by this section shall not be treated as a termination of such collective bargaining agreement.

[¶15,724B]

Act Sec. 10002 TEMPORARY EXTENSION OF COVERAGE AT GROUP RATES FOR CERTAIN EMPLOYEES AND FAMILY MEMBERS (ERISA AMENDMENTS).

* * *

(d) EFFECTIVE DATES.—

(1) GENERAL RULE. The amendments made by this section shall apply to plan years beginning on or after July 1, 1986.

(2) SPECIAL RULE FOR COLLECTIVE BARGAINING AGREEMENTS. In the case of a group health plan maintained pursuant to one or more collective bargaining agreements between employee representatives and one or more employers ratified before the date of the enactment of this Act, the amendments made by this section shall not apply to plan years beginning before the later of—

(A) the date on which the last of the collective bargaining agreements relating to the plan terminates (determined without regard to any extension thereof agreed to after the date of the enactment of this Act), or

(B) January 1, 1987.

For purposes of subparagraph (A), any plan amendment made pursuant to a collective bargaining agreement relating to the plan which amends the plan solely to conform to any requirement added by this section shall not be treated as a termination of such collective bargaining agreement.

(e) NOTIFICATION TO COVERED EMPLOYEES. At the time that the amendments made by this section apply to a group health plan (within the meaning of section 607(1) of the Employee Retirement Income Security Act of 1974), the plan shall notify each covered employee, and spouse of the employee (if any), who is covered under the plan at that time of the continuation coverage required under part 6 of subtitle B of title I of such Act. The notice furnished under this subsection is in lieu of notice that may otherwise be required under section 606(1) of such Act with respect to such individuals.

[¶15,724C]

Act Sec. 10003 CONTINUATION OF HEALTH INSURANCE FOR STATE AND LOCAL EMPLOYEES WHO LOST EMPLOYMENT-RELATED COVERAGE (PUBLIC HEALTH SERVICE ACT AMENDMENTS).

(a) IN GENERAL. The Public Health Service Act is amended by adding at the end the following new title:

"TITLE XXII—REQUIREMENTS FOR CERTAIN GROUP HEALTH PLANS FOR CERTAIN STATE AND LOCAL EMPLOYEES

"SEC. 2201. STATE AND LOCAL GOVERNMENTAL GROUP HEALTH PLANS MUST PROVIDE CONTINUATION COVERAGE TO CERTAIN INDIVIDUALS.

"(a) IN GENERAL. In accordance with regulations which the Secretary shall prescribe, each group health plan that is maintained by any State that receives funds under this Act, by any political subdivision, shall provide, in accordance with this title, that each qualified beneficiary who would lose coverage under the plan as a result of a qualifying event is entitled, under the plan, to elect, within the election period, continuation coverage under the plan.

"(b) EXCEPTION FOR CERTAIN PLANS. Subsection (a) shall not apply to—

"(1) any group health plan for any calendar year if all employers maintaining such plan normally employed fewer than 20 employees on a typical business day during the preceding calendar year, or

"(2) any group health plan maintained for employees by the government of the District of Columbia or any territory or possession of the United States or any agency or instrumentality.

Under regulations, rules similar to the rules of subsections (a) and (b) of section 52 of the Internal Revenue Code of 1954 (relating to employers under common control) shall apply for purposes of paragraph (1).

"SEC. 2202. CONTINUATION COVERAGE.

"For purposes of section 2201, the term 'continuation coverage' means coverage under the plan which meets the following requirements:

"(1) TYPE OF BENEFIT COVERAGE. The coverage must consist of coverage which, as of the time the coverage is being provided, is identical to the coverage provided under the plan to similarly situated beneficiaries under the plan with respect to whom a qualifying event has not occurred.

"(2) PERIOD OF COVERAGE. The coverage must extend for at least the period beginning on the date of the qualifying event and ending not earlier than the earliest of the following:

"(A) MAXIMUM PERIOD. In the case of—

"(i) a qualifying event described in section 2203(2) (relating to terminations and reduced hours), the date which is 18 months after the date of the qualifying event, and

"(ii) any qualifying event not described in clause (i), the date which is 36 months after the date of the qualifying event.

"(B) END OF PLAN. The date on which the employer ceases to provide any group health plan to any employee.

"(C) FAILURE TO PAY PREMIUM. The date on which coverage ceases under the plan by reason of a failure to make timely payment of any premium required under the plan with respect to the qualified beneficiary.

"(D) REEMPLOYMENT OR MEDICARE ELIGIBLITY. The date on which the qualified beneficiary first becomes, after the date of the election—

"(i) a covered employee under any other group health plan, or

"(ii) entitled to benefits under title XVIII of the Social Security Act.

"(E) REMARRIAGE OF SPOUSE. In the case of an individual who is a qualified beneficiary by reason of being the spouse of a covered employee, the date on which the beneficiary remarries and becomes covered under a group health plan.

"(3) PREMIUM REQUIREMENTS. The plan may require payment of a premium for any period of continuation coverage, except that such premium—

"(A) shall not exceed 102 percent of the applicable premium for such period, and

"(B) may, at the election of the payor, be made in monthly installments.

If an election is made after the qualifying event, the plan shall permit payment for continuation coverage during the period preceding the election to be made within 45 days of the date of the election.

"(4) NO REQUIREMENT OF INSURABILITY. The coverage may not be conditioned upon, or discriminate on the basis of lack of, evidence of insurability.

"(5) CONVERSION OPTION. In the case of a qualified beneficiary whose period of continuation coverage expires under paragraph (2)(A), the plan must, during the 180-day period ending on such expiration date, provide to the qualified beneficiary the option of enrollment under a conversion health plan otherwise generally available under the plan.

"SEC. 2203. QUALIFYING EVENT.

"For purposes of this title, the term 'qualifying event' means, with respect to any covered employee, any of the following events which, but for the continuation coverage required under this title, would result in the loss of coverage of a qualified beneficiary:

"(1) The death of the covered employee.

"(2) The termination (other than by reason of such employee's gross misconduct), or reduction of hours, of the covered employee's employment.

"(3) The divorce or legal separation of the covered employee from the employee's spouse.

"(4) The covered employee becoming entitled to benefits under title XVIII of the Social Security Act.

"(5) A dependent child ceasing to be a dependent child under the generally applicable requirements of the plan.

"SEC. 2204. APPLICABLE PREMIUM.

"For purposes of this title—

"(1) IN GENERAL. The term 'applicable premium' means, with respect to any period of continuation coverage of qualified beneficiaries, the cost to the plan for such period of the coverage for similarly situated beneficiaries with respect to whom a qualifying event has not occurred (without regard to whether such cost is paid by the employer or employee).

"(2) SPECIAL RULE FOR SELF-INSURED PLANS. To the extent that a plan is a self-insured plan—

"(A) IN GENERAL. Except as provided in subparagraph (B), the applicable premium for any period of continuation coverage of qualified beneficiaries shall be equal to a reasonable estimate of the cost of providing coverage for such period for similarly situated beneficiaries which—

"(i) is determined on an actuarial basis, and

"(ii) takes into account such factors as the Secretary may prescribe in regulations.

"(B) DETERMINATION ON BASIS OF PAST COST. If a plan administrator elects to have this subparagraph apply, the applicable premium for any period of continuation coverage of qualified beneficiaries shall be equal to—

"(i) the cost to the plan for similarly situated beneficiaries for the same period occurring during the preceding determination period under paragraph (3), adjusted by

"(ii) the percentage increase or decrease in the implicit price deflator of the gross national product (calculated by the Department of Commerce and published in the Survey of Current Business) for the 12-month period ending on the last day of the sixth month of such preceding determination period.

"(C) SUBPARAGRAPH (B) NOT TO APPLY WHERE SIGNIFICANT CHANGE. A plan administrator may not elect to have subparagraph (B) apply in any case in which there is any significant difference, between the determination period and the preceding determination period, in coverage under, or in employees covered by, the plan. The determination under the preceding sentence for any determination period shall be made at the same time as the determination under paragraph (3).

"(3) DETERMINATION PERIOD. The determination of any applicable premium shall be made for a period of 12 months and shall be made before the beginning of such period.

"SEC. 2205. ELECTION.

"For purposes of this title—

"(1) ELECTION PERIOD. The term 'election period' means the period which—

"(A) begins not later than the date on which coverage terminates under the plan by reason of a qualifying event,

"(B) is of at least 60 days' duration, and

"(C) ends not earlier than 60 days after the later of—

"(i) is of at least

"(ii) the date described in subparagraph (A), or

"(iii) in the case of any qualified beneficiary who receives notice under section 2206(4), the date of such notice.

"(2) EFFECT OF ELECTION ON OTHER BENEFICIARIES. Except as otherwise specified in an election, any election by a qualified beneficiary described in subparagraph (A)(i) or (B) of section 2208(3) shall be deemed to include an election of continuation coverage on behalf of any other qualified beneficiary who would lose coverage under the plan by reason of the qualifying event.

"SEC. 2206. NOTICE REQUIREMENTS.

"In accordance with regulations prescribed by the Secretary—

"(1) the group health plan shall provide, at the time of commencement of coverage under the plan, written notice to each covered employee and spouse of the employee (if any) of the rights provided under this subsection,

"(2) the employer of an employee under a plan must notify the plan administrator of a qualifying event described in paragraph (1), (2), or (4) of section 2203 within 30 days of the date of the qualifying event,

"(3) each covered employee or qualified beneficiary is responsible for notifying the plan administrator of the occurrence of any qualifying event described in paragraph (3) or (5) of section 2203, and

"(4) the plan administrator shall notify—

"(A) in the case of a qualifying event described in paragraph (1), (2) or (4) of section 2203, any qualified beneficiary with respect to such event, and

"(B) in the case of a qualifying event described in paragraph (3) or (5) of section 2203 where the covered employee notifies the plan administrator under paragraph (3), any qualified beneficiary with respect to such event, of such beneficiary's rights under this subsection.

For purposes of paragraph (4), any notification shall be made within 14 days of the date on which the plan administrator is notified under paragraph (2) or (3), whichever is applicable, and any such notification to an individual who is a qualified beneficiary as the spouse of the covered employee shall be treated as notification to all other qualified beneficiaries residing with such spouse at the time such notification is made.

"SEC. 2207. ENFORCEMENT.

"Any individual who is aggrieved by the failure of a State, political subdivision, or agency or instrumentality thereof, to comply with the requirements of this title may bring an action for appropriate equitable relief.

"SEC. 2208. DEFINITIONS.

"For purposes of this title—

"(1) GROUP HEALTH PLAN. The term 'group health plan' has the meaning given such term in section 162(i)(3) of the Internal Revenue Code of 1954.

"(2) COVERED EMPLOYEE. The term 'covered employee' means an individual who is (or was) provided coverage under a group health plan by virtue of the individual's employment or previous employment with an employer.

"(3) QUALIFIED BENEFICIARY.—

"(A) IN GENERAL. The term 'qualified beneficiary' means, with respect to a covered employee under a group health plan, any other individual who, on the day before the qualifying event for that employee, is a beneficiary under the plan—

"(i) as the spouse of the covered employee, or

"(ii) as the dependent child of the employee.

"(B) SPECIAL RULE FOR TERMINATIONS AND REDUCED EMPLOYMENT. In the case of a qualifying event described in section 2203(2), the term 'disqualified beneficiary' includes the covered employee.

"(4) PLAN ADMINISTRATOR. The term 'plan administrator' has the meaning given the term 'administrator' by section 3(16)(A) of the Employee Retirement Income Security Act of 1974."

"(b) EFFECTIVE DATES—

"(1) GENERAL RULE. The amendments made by this section shall apply to plan years beginning on or after July 1, 1986.

"(2) SPECIAL RULE FOR COLLECTIVE BARGAINING AGREEMENTS. In the case of a group health plan maintained pursuant to one or more collective bargaining agreements between employee representatives and one or more employerr satified before the date of the enactment of this Act, the amendments made by this section shall not apply to plan years beginning before the later of—

"(A) the date on which the last of the collective bargaining agreements relating to the plan terminates (determined without regard to any extension thereof agreed to after the date of the enactment of this Act), or

"(B) January 1, 1987.

For purposes of subparagraph (A), any plan amendment made pursuant to a collective bargaining agreement relating to the plan which amends the plan solely to conform to any requirement added by this section shall not be treated as a termination of such collective bargaining agreement.

   (c) NOTIFICATION TO COVERED EMPLOYEES. At the time that the amendments made by this section apply to a group health plan (covered under section 2201 of the Public Health Service Act), the plan shall notify each covered employee, and spouse of the employee (if any), who is covered under the plan at the time of the continuation coverage required under title XXII of such Act. The notice furnished under this subsection is in lieu of notice that may otherwise be required under section 2206(1) of such Act with respect to such individuals.

Single-Employer Pension Plan Amendments Act of 1986

P.L. 99-272

Signed on April 7, 1986

[Reproduced below are sections of the Single-Employer Pension Plan Amendments Act of 1986 which did not amend any sections of the Internal Revenue Code of 1954 or the Employee Retirement Income Security Act of 1974 (ERISA).]

TITLE XI—SINGLE-EMPLOYER PLAN TERMINATION INSURANCE SYSTEM AMENDMENTS

[¶15,724D]

Act Sec. 11001 SHORT TITLE AND TABLE OF CONTENTS.

This title may be cited as "Single-Employer Pension Plan Amendments Act of 1986".

TABLE OF CONTENTS

[¶15,724E]

Act Sec. 11002 FINDINGS AND DECLARATION OF POLICY.

(A) FINDINGS. The Congress finds that—

(1) single-employer defined benefit pension plans have a substantial impact on interstate commerce and are affected with a national interest;

(2) the continued well-being and retirement income security of millions of workers, retirees, and their dependents are directly affected by such plans;

(3) the existence of a sound termination insurance system is fundamental to the retirement income security of participants and beneficiaries of such plans; and

(4) the current termination insurance system in some instances encourages employers to terminate pension plans, evade their obligations to pay benefits, and shift unfunded pension liabilities onto the termination insurance system and the other premium-payers.

(b) ADDITIONAL FINDINGS. The Congress further finds that modification of the current termination insurance system and an increase in the insurance premium for single-employer defined benefit pension plans—

(1) is desirable to increase the likelihood that full benefits will be paid to participants and beneficiaries of such plans;

(2) is desirable to provide for the transfer of liabilities to the termination insurance system only in cases of severe hardship;

(3) is necessary to maintain the premium costs of such system at a reasonable level; and

(4) is necessary to finance properly current funding deficiencies and future obligations of the single-employer pension plan termination insurance system.

(c) DECLARATION OF POLICY. It is hereby declared to be the policy of this title—

(1) to foster and facilitate interstate commerce,

(2) to encourage the maintenance and growth of single-employer defined benefit pension plans,

(3) to increase the likelihood that participants and beneficiaries under single-employer defined benefit pension plans will receive their full benefits,

(4) to provide for the transfer of unfunded pension liabilities onto the single-employer pension plan termination insurance system only in cases of severe hardship,

(5) to maintain the premium costs of such system at a reasonable level; and

(6) to assure the prudent financing of current funding deficiencies and future obligations of the single-employer pension plan termination insurance system by increasing termination insurance premiums.

[¶15,724F]

Act Sec. 11003 AMENDMENT OF THE EMPLOYEE RETIREMENT INCOME SECURITY ACT OF 1974.

Whenever in this title an amendment or repeal is expressed in terms of an amendment to or repeal of a section or other provision, the reference is to a section or other provision of the Employee Retirement Income Security Act of 1974, unless otherwise specified.

[¶15,724G]

Act Sec. 11005 SINGLE-EMPLOYER PLAN TERMINATION INSURANCE PREMIUMS.

* * *

(e) TRANSITIONAL RULE.—

(1) NOTICE OF PREMIUM INCREASE. Not later than 30 days after the date of the enactment of this Act, the Pension Benefit Guaranty Corporation shall send a notice to the plan administrator of each single-employer plan affected by the premium increase established by the amendment made by subsection (a)(1). Such notice shall describe such increase and the requirements of this subsection.

(2) DUE DATE FOR UNPAID PREMIUMS. With respect to any plan year beginning during the period beginning on January 1, 1986, and ending 30 days after the date of the enactment of this Act, any unpaid amount of such premium increase shall be due and payable no later than the earlier of 60 days after the date of the enactment of this Act or 30 days after the date on which the notice required by paragraph (1) is sent, except that in no event shall the amount of the premium increase established under the amendment made by subsection (a)(1) be due and payable for a plan year earlier than the date on which premiums for the plan would have been due for such plan year had this Act not been enacted.

(3) ENFORCEMENT. For purposes of enforcement, the requirements of paragraphs (1) and (2) shall be considered to be requirements of sections 4006 and 4007 of the Employee Retirement Income Security Act of 1974 (29 U.S.C. 1306 and 1307.)

[¶15,724H]

Act Sec. 11006 NOTICE OF SIGNIFICANT REDUCTION IN BENEFIT ACCRUALS.

* * *

EFFECTIVE DATE.—The amendments made by subsection (a) shall apply with respect to plan amendments adopted on or after January 1, 1986, except that, in the case of plan amendments adopted on or after January 1, 1986, and on or before the date of the enactment of this Act, the requirements of section 204(h) of the Employee Retirement Income Security Act of 1974 (as added by this section) shall be treated as met if the written notice under such section 204(h) is provided before 60 days after the date of the enactment of this Act.

[¶15,724I]

Act Sec. 11008 STANDARD TERMINATION OF SINGLE-EMPLOYER PLANS.

* * *

(c) AUTHORITY FOR 60-DAY EXTENSION. In the case of a standard termination of a plan under section 4041(b) of the Employee Retirement Income Security Act of 1974 (as amended by this section) with respect to which a notice of intent to terminate is filed before 120 days after the date of the enactment of this Act, the Pension Benefit Guaranty Corporation may, without the consent of the plan administrator, extend the 60-day period under section 4041(b)(2)(C)(i) of such Act (as so amended) for a period not to exceed 60 days.

(d) SPECIAL TEMPORARY RULE.—

(1) REQUIREMENTS TO BE MET BEFORE FINAL DISTRIBUTION OF ASSETS. In the case of the termination of a single-employer plan described in paragraph (2) with respect to which the amount payable to the employer pursuant to section 4044(d) exceeds $1,000,000 (determined as of the proposed date of final distribution of assets), the final distribution of assets pursuant to such termination may not occur unless the Pension Benefit Guaranty Corporation—

(A) determines that the assets of the plan are sufficient for benefit commitments (within the meaning of section 4041(d)(1) of the Employee Retirement Income Security Act of 1974 (as amended by section 11007)) under the plan, and

(B) issues to the plan administrator a written notice setting forth the determination described in subparagraph (A).

(2) PLANS TO WHICH SUBSECTION APPLIES. A single-employer plan is described in this paragraph if—

(A) the plan administrator has filed a notice of intent to terminate with the Pension Benefit Guaranty Corporation, and—

(i) the filing was made before January 1, 1986, and the Corporation has not issued a notice of sufficiency for such plan before the date of the enactment of this Act, or

(ii) the filing is made on or after January 1, 1986, and before 60 days after the date of the enactment of this Act and the Corporation has not issued a notice of sufficiency for such plan before the date of the enactment of this Act, and

(B) of the persons who are (as of the termination date) paticipants in the plan, the lesser of 10 percent or 200 have filed complaints with the Corporation regarding such termination—

(i) in the case of plans described in subparagraph (A)(i), before 15 days after the date of the enactment of this Act, or

(ii) in any other case, before the later of 15 days after the date of the enactment of this Act or 45 days after the date of the filing of such notice.

(3) CONSIDERATION OF COMPLAINTS. The Corporation shall consider and respond to such complaints not later than 90 days after the date on which the Corportion makes the determination described in paragraph (1)(A). The Corporation may hold informal hearings to expedite consideration of such complaints. Any such hearing shall be exempt from the requirements of chapter 5 of title 5, United States Code.

(4) DELAY ON ISSUANCE OF NOTICE.—

(A) GENERAL RULE. Except as provided in subparagraph (B), the Corporation shall not issue any notice described in paragraph (1)(B) until 90 days after the date on which the Corporation makes the determination described in paragraph (1)(A).

(B) EXCEPTION IN CASES OF SUBSTANTIAL BUSINESS HARDSHIP. Except in the case of an acquisition, takeover, or leveraged buyout, the preceding provisions of this subsection shall not apply if the contributing sponsor demonstrates to the satisfaction of the Corporation that the contributing sponsor is experiencing substantial business hardship. For purposes of this subparagraph, a contributing sponsor shall be considered as experiencing substantial business hardship if the contributing sponsor has been operating, and can demonstrate that the contributing sponsor will continue to operate, at an economic loss.

[¶15,724J]

Act Sec. 11012 DISTRIBUTION TO PARTICIPANTS AND BENEFICIARIES OF LIABILITY PAYMENTS TO SECTION 4049 TRUST.

(d) Special Delayed Payment Rule. In the case of a distress termination under section 4041(c) of the Employee Retirement Income Security Act of 1974 (as amended by section 11009) pursuant to a notice of intent to terminate filed before January 1, 1987, no payment of liability otherwise payable as provided in section 4062(c)(2)(B) of such Act (as amended by this section) shall be required to be made before January 1, 1989.

[¶15,724K]

Act Sec. 11016 CONFORMING, CLARIFYING, TECHNICAL, AND MISCELLANEOUS AMENDMENTS.

(b)

* * *

(3) Transition rules. Any regulations, modifications or waivers which have been issued by the Secretary of Labor with respect to section 103(d)(6) of the Employee Retirement Income Security Act of 1974 (as in effect immediately before the date of the enactment of this Act) shall remain in full force and effect until modified by any regulations with respect to such section 103(d)(6) prescribed by the Pension Benefit Guaranty Corporation.

* * *

(d) Studies by Comptroller General.—

(1) In general. The Comptroller General of the United States may, pursuant to the request of any Member of Congress, study employee benefit plans, including the effect of such plans on employees, participants, and their beneficiaries.

(2) Access to books, documents, etc. For the purpose of conducting studies under this subsection, the Comptroller General, or any of his duly authorized representatives, shall have access to and the right to examine and copy any books, documents, papers, records, or other recorded information—

(A) within the possession or control of the administrator, sponsor, or employer of and persons providing services to any employee benefit plan, and

(B) which the Comptroller General or his representative finds, in his own judgment, pertinent to such study.

The Comptroller General shall not disclose the identity of any individual or employer in making any information obtained under this subsection available to the public.

(3) Definitions. For purposes of this subsection, the terms "employee benefit plan," "participant," "administrator," "beneficiary," "plan sponsor," "employee," and "employer" are defined in section 3 of the Employee Retirement Income Security Act of 1974.

(4) Effective date. The preceding provisions of this subsection shall be effective on the date of the enactment of this Act.

(e) Amendments to the Table of Contents of ERISA. The table of contents in section 1 is amended—

(1) by striking out the item relating to section 4004;

(2) by striking out the item relating to section 4042 and inserting in lieu thereof the following new item:

"Sec. 4042.   Institution of termination proceedings by the corporation.";

(3) by inserting after the item relating to section 4048 the following new item:

"Sec. 4049.   Distribution to participants and beneficiaries of liability payments to section 4049 trust."; and

(4) by striking out the items relating to subtitle D of title IV and inserting in lieu thereof the following new items:

"Subtitle D—Liability

"Sec. 4061.	Amounts payable by the corporation.
"Sec. 4062.	Liability for termination of single-employer plans under a distress termination or a termination by the corporation.
"Sec. 4063.	Liability of substantial employer for withdrawal from single-employer plans under multiple controlled groups.
"Sec. 4064.	Liability on termination of single-employer plans under multiple controlled groups.
"Sec. 4065.	Annual report of plan administrator.
"Sec. 4066.	Annual notification of substantial employers.
"Sec. 4067.	Recovery of liability for plan termination.
"Sec. 4068.	Lien for liability.
"Sec. 4069.	Treatment of transactions to evade liability; effect of corporate reorganization.
"Sec. 4070.	Enforcement authority relating to terminations of single-employer plans."

[¶15,724L]

Act Sec. 11017 STUDIES.

(a) Single-Employer Pension Plan Termination Insurance Premium Study.—

(1) In general. As soon as practicable after the date of the enactment of this Act, the Pension Benefit Guaranty Corporation shall conduct a study of the premiums established under the single-employer pension plan termination insurance program under title IV of the Employee Retirement Income Security Act of 1974.

(2) Matters to be studied. The Corporation shall specifically consider in its study the following matters:

(A) the effect of the amendments made by this title on the long-term stability of the single-employer pension plan termination insurance program under title IV of the Employee Retirement Income Security Act of 1974,

(B) alternatives to the current statutory mechanism with respect to pro-proposals for changes in the premium levels under such program,

(C) the methods currently used by the Corporation in projecting future program costs of the single employer pension plan termination insurance program,

(D) alternative methods of projecting such future program costs and an evaluation of each such alternative method,

(E) the methods currently used by the Corporation in determining premiums needed to allocate and adequately fund such future program costs,

(F) alternative methods of making such premium determinations and an evaluation of such alternative method, and

(G) alternative premium bases upon which some or all of such projected future program costs would be allocated on an exposure-related or risk-related computation, which may take into account the different exposures or risks imposed on the Corporation by plan sponsors with different histories and under different circumstances.

(3) SUBMISSION OF CORPORATION'S REPORT. Not later than one year after the date of the enactment of this Act, the Corporation shall report the results of its study, together with any recommendations for statutory change, to an advisory council, to be appointed by the chairman of the Committee on Education and Labor and the Committee on Ways and Means of the House of Representatives and the Committee on Labor and Human Resources and the Committee on Finance of the Senate. The advisory council shall be composed of representatives of single-employer plan sponsors, employee organizations representing single-employer plan participants, and members of the general public who are experts in the matters to be considered in the study. The members of the advisory council shall serve without compensation.

(4) SUBMISSION OF COUNCIL'S REPORT TO CONGRESS. Not later than 180 days after the date of the submission of the Corporation's report to the advisory council under paragraph (3), the advisory council shall submit the results of the Corporation's study and the Corporation's recommendations, together with the recommendations of the council, to the Speaker of the House of Representatives and the President pro tempore of the Senate.

(5) COOPERATION BY THE PENSION BENEFIT GUARANTY CORPORATION AND OTHER FEDERAL AGENCIES. The Corporation shall cooperate with the advisory council in reviewing the results of the Corporation's study and recommendations. In order to avoid unnecessary expense and duplication, to the extent not otherwise prohibited by law, the Corporation and any other Federal agency shall provide to the advisory council any data, analysis, or other relevant information related to the matters under review.

(b) OVERFUNDED PENSION PLAN STUDY.—

(1) IN GENERAL. As soon as practicable after the date of enactment of this Act, the Secretary of Labor shall conduct a study of terminations resulting in residual assets under section 4044(d) of the Employee Retirement Income Security Act of 1974.

(2) REPORT. No later than May 1, 1986, the Secretary of Labor shall submit a report on the study conducted under paragraph (1), together with any recommendations for statutory changes, to the chairmen of the Committee on Education and Labor and the Committee on Ways and Means of the House of Representatives and the Committee on Labor and Human Resources and the Committee on Finance of the Senate.

[¶15,724M]

Act Sec. 11018 LIMITATION ON REGULATIONS.

(a) REGULATORY TREATMENT OF ASSETS OF REAL ESTATE ENTITIES.—

(1) IN GENERAL. Except as a defense, no rule or regulation adopted pursuant to the Secretary's proposed regulation defining "plan assets" for purposes of the Employee Retirement Income Security Act of 1974 (50 Fed. Reg. 961, January 8, 1985, as modified by 50 Fed. Reg. 6361, February 15, 1985), or any reproposal thereof prior to the adoption of the regulations required to be issued in accordance with subsection (d), shall apply to any asset of a real estate entity in which a plan, account, or arrangement subject to such Act invests if—

(A) any interest in the entity is first offered to a plan, account, or arrangement subject to such Act investing in the entity (hereinafter in this section referred to as a "plan investor") on or before the date which is 120 days after the date of publication of such rule or regulation as a final rule or regulation;

(B) no plan investor acquires an interest in the entity from an issuer or underwriter at any time on or after the date which is 270 days after the date of publication of such rule or regulation as a final rule or regulation (except pursuant to a contract or subscription binding on the plan investor and entered into, or tendered, before the expiration of such 270-day period, or pursuant to the exercise, on or before December 31, 1990, of a warrant which was the subject of an effective registration under the Securities Act of 1933 (15 U.S.C. 77q et seq.) prior to the date of the enactment of this section); and

(C) every interest in the entity acquired by a plan investor (or contracted for or subscribed to by a plan investor) before the expiration of such 270-day period is a security—

(i) which is part of an issue or class of securities which upon such acquisition or at any time during the offering period is held by 100 or more persons;

(ii) the economic rights of ownership in respect of which are freely transferable;

(iii) which is registered under the Securities Act of 1933; and

(iv) which is part of an issue or class of securities which is registered under the Securities Exchange Act of 1934 (15 U.S.C. 78a et seq.) (or is so registered within three years of the effective date of the registration statement of such securities for purposes of the Securities Act of 1933: *Provided,* That the issue provides plan investors with such reports with respect to the offering period as are required with respect to such period by the Securities and Exchange Commission under such Acts and the rules and regulations promulgated thereunder).

In the case of partnerships organized prior to enactment of this section, the requirements of subparagraphs (iii) and (iv) shall not apply to initial limited partnership interests in an entity otherwise described above: *Provided,* That such entity was the subject of an effective registration under the Securities Act of 1933 prior to the date of the enactment of this section, such interests were issued solely for partnership organizational purposes in compliance with State limited partnership laws, and such interest has a value as of the date of issue of less than $20,000 and represents less than one percent of the total interests outstanding as of the completion of the offering period.

(2) MAINTENANCE OF CURRENT REGULATORY TREATMENT. No asset of any real estate entity described in paragraph (1) shall be treated as an asset of any plan investor for any purpose of the employee Retirement Income Security Act of 1974 if the assets of such entity would not have been assets of such plan investor under the provisions of—

(A) Interpretive Bulletin 75-2 (29 CFR 2509 750-2); or

(B) the regulations proposed by the Secretary of Labor and published—

(i) on August 28, 1979, at 44 Fed. Reg. 50363;

(ii) on June 6, 1980, at 45 Fed. Reg. 38084;

    (iii) on January 8, 1985, at 50 Fed. Reg. 961; or

    (iv) on February 15, 1985, at 50 Fed. Reg. 6361,

without regard to any limitation of any effective date proposed therein.

(b) DEFINITIONS AND SPECIAL RULES. For purposes of this section—

    (1) The term "real estate entity" means an entity which, at any time within two years after the closing of its offering period has invested or has contracted to invest at least 75 percent of the value of its net assets available for investment in direct or indirect ownership of "real estate assets" or "interests in real property".

    (2) The term "real estate asset" means real property (including an interest in real property) and any share of stock or beneficial interest, partnership interest, depository receipt, or any other interest in any other real estate entity.

    (3) The term "interest in real property" includes, directly or indirectly, the following:

        (A) the ownership or co-ownership of land or improvements thereon;

        (B) any mortgage (including an interest in or co-ownership of any mortgage, leasehold mortgage, pool of mortgages, deed of trust, or similar instrument) on land or improvements thereon,

        (C) any leasehold of land or improvements thereon; and

        (D) any option to acquire any of the foregoing, but does not include any mineral, oil, or gas royalty interest.

    (4) Whether the economic rights of ownership with respect to a security are "freely transferable" shall be determined based upon all the facts and circumstances, but ordinarily none of the following, alone or in any combination, shall cause the economic rights of ownership to be considered not freely transferable—

        (A) any requirement that not less than a minimum number of shares or units of such security be transferred or assigned by any investor: *Provided,* That such requirement does not prevent transfer of all of the then remaining shares or units held by an investor;

        (B) any prohibition against transfer or assignment of such security or rights in respect thereof to an ineligible or unsuitable investor;

        (C) any restriction on or prohibition against any transfer or assignment which would either result in a termination or reclassification of the entity for Federal or State tax purposes or which would violate any State or Federal statute, regulation, court order judicial decree, or rule of law;

        (D) any requirement that reasonable transfer or administrative fees be paid in connection with a transfer or assignment;

        (E) any requirement that advance notice of a transfer or assignment be given to the entity and any requirement regarding execution of documentation evidencing such transfer or assignment (including documentation setting forth representation from either or both of the transferor or transferee as to compliance with any restriction or requirement described in this section or requiring compliance with the entity's governing instruments);

        (F) any restriction or substitution of an assignee as a limited partner of a partnership, including a general partner consent requirement: *Provided,* That the economic benefits of ownership of the assignor may be transferred or assigned without regard to such restriction or consent (other than compliance with any other restriction described in this section);

        (G) any administrative procedure which establishes an effective date, or an event such as the completion of the offering, prior to which a transfer or assignment will not be effective; and

        (H) any limitation or restriction on transfer or assignment which is not created or imposed by the issuer or any person acting for or on behalf of such issuer.

(c) NO EFFECT ON SECRETARY'S AUTHORITY OTHER THAN AS PROVIDED. Except as provided in subsection (a), nothing in this section shall limit the authority of the Secretary of Labor to issue regulations or otherwise interpret section 3(21) of the Employee Retirement Income Security Act of 1974.

(d) TIME LIMIT FOR FINAL REGULATIONS. The Secretary of Labor shall adopt final regulations defining "plan assets" by December 31, 1986.

(e) EFFECTIVE DATE. The preceding provisions of this section shall take effect on the date of the enactment of this Act.

[¶15,724N]

Act Sec. 11019 EFFECTIVE DATE OF TITLE; TEMPORARY PROCEDURES.

(a) IN GENERAL. Except as otherwise provided in this title, the amendments shall not apply with respect to terminations for which—

    (1) notices of intent to terminate were filed with the Pension Benefit Guaranty Corporation under section 4041 of the Employee Retirement Income Security Act of 1974 before such date, or

    (2) proceedings were commenced under section 4042 of such Act before such date.

(b) TRANSITIONAL RULES.—

    (1) IN GENERAL. In the case of a single-employer plan termination for which a notice of intent to terminate was filed with the Pension Benefit Guaranty Corporation under section 4041 of the Employee Retirement Income Security Act of 1974 (as in effect before the amendments made by this title) on or after January 1, 1986, but before the date of the enactment of this Act, the amendments made by this title shall apply with respect to such termination, as modified by paragraphs (2) and (3).

    (2) DEEMED COMPLIANCE WITH NOTICE REQUIREMENTS. The requirements of subsections (a)(2), (b)(1)(A), and (c)(1)(A) of section 4041 of the Employee Retirement Income Security Act of 1974 (as amended by this title) shall be considered to have been met with respect to a termination described in paragraph (1) if—

        (A) the plan administrator provided notice to the participants in the plan regarding the termination in compliance with applicable regulations of the Pension Benefit Guaranty Corporation as in effect on the date of the notice, and

        (B) the notice of intent to terminate provided to the Pension Benefit Guaranty Corporation in connection with the termination was filed with the Corporation not less than 10 days before the proposed date of termination specified in the notice.

For purposes of section 4041 of such Act (as amended by this title), the proposed date of termination specified in the notice of intent to terminate referred to in subparagraph (B) shall be considered the proposed termination date.

    (3) SPECIAL TERMINATION PROCEDURES.—

        (A) IN GENERAL. This paragraph shall apply with respect to any termination described in paragraph (1) if, within 90 days after the date of enactment of this Act, the plan administrator notifies the Corporation in writing—

(i) that the plan administrator wishes the termination to proceed as a standard termination under section 4041(b) of the Employee Retirement Income Security Act of 1974 (as amended by this title) in accordance with subparagraph (B),

(ii) that the plan administrator wishes the termination to proceed as a distress termination under section 4041(c) of such Act (as amended by this title) in accordance with subparagraph (C), or

(iii) that the plan administrator wishes to stop the termination proceedings in accordance with subparagraph (D).

(B) TERMINATIONS PROCEEDING AS STANDARD TERMINATION.—

(i) TERMINATIONS FOR WHICH SUFFICIENCY NOTICES HAVE NOT BEEN ISSUED.—

(I) IN GENERAL. In the case of a plan termination described in paragraph (1) with respect to which the Corporation has been provided the notification described in subparagraph (A)(i) and with respect to which a notice of sufficiency has not been issued by the Corporation before the date of the enactment of this Act, if, during the 90-day period commencing on the date of the notice required in subclause (II), all benefit commitments under the plan have been satisfied, the termination shall be treated as a standard termination under section 4041(b) of such Act (as amended by this title).

(II) SPECIAL NOTICE REGARDING SUFFICIENCY FOR TERMINATIONS FOR WHICH NOTICES OF SUFFICIENCY HAVE NOT BEEN ISSUED AS OF DATE OF ENACTMENT. In the case of a plan termination described in paragraph (1) with respect to which the Corporation has been provided the notification described in subparagraph (A)(i) and with respect to which a notice of sufficiency has not been issued by the Corporation before the date of the enactment of this Act, the Corporation shall make the determinations described in section 4041(c)(3)(A)(i) and (ii) (as amended by this title) and notify the plan administrator of such determinations as provided in section 4041(c)(3)(A)(iii) (as amended by this title).

(ii) TERMINATIONS FOR WHICH NOTICES OF SUFFICIENCY HAVE BEEN ISSUED. In the case of a plan termination described in paragraph (1) with respect to which the Corporation has been provided the notification described in subparagraph (A)(i) and with respect to which a notice of sufficiency has been issued by the Corporation before the date of the enactment of this Act, clause (i)(I) shall apply, except that the 90-day period referred to in clause (i)(I) shall begin on the date of the enactment of this Act.

(C) TERMINATIONS PROCEEDING AS DISTRESS TERMINATION. In the case of a plan termination described in paragraph (1) with respect to which the Corporation has been provided the notification described in subparagraph (A)(ii), if the requirements of section 4041(c)(2)(B) of such Act (as amended by this title) are met, the termination shall be treated as a distress termination under section 404(c) of such Act (as amended by this title).

(D) TERMINATION OF PROCEEDINGS BY PLAN ADMINISTRATOR.—

(i) IN GENERAL. Except as provided in clause (ii), in the case of a plan termination described in paragraph (1) with respect to which the Corporation has been provided the notification described in subparagraph (A)(iii), the termination shall not take effect.

(ii) TERMINATIONS WITH RESPECT TO WHICH FINAL DISTRIBUTION OF ASSETS HAS COMMENCED. Clause (i) shall not apply with respect to a termination with respect to which the final distribution of assets has commenced before the date of the enactment of this Act unless, within 90 days after the date of the enactment of this Act, the plan has been restored in accordance with procedures issued by the Corporation pursuant to subsection (c).

(E) AUTHORITY OF CORPORATION TO EXTEND 90-DAY PERIODS TO PERMIT STANDARD TERMINATION. The Corporation may, on a case-by-case basis in accordance with subsection (c), provide for extensions of the applicable 90-day period referred to in clause (i) or (ii) of subparagraph (B) if it is demonstrated to the satisfaction of the Corporation that—

(i) the plan could not otherwise, pursuant to the preceding provisions of this paragraph, terminate in a termination treated as a standard termination under section 4041(b) of the Employee Retirement Income Security Act of 1974 (as amended by this title), and

(ii) the extension would result in a greater likelihood that benefit commitments under the plan would be paid in full,

except that any such period may not be so extended beyond one year after the date of the enactment of this Act.

(c) AUTHORITY TO PRESCRIBE TEMPORARY PROCEDURES. The Pension Benefit Guaranty Corporation may prescribe temporary procedures for purposes of carrying out the amendments made by this title during the 180-day period beginning on the date described in subsection (a).

[¶15,724O]

Act Sec. 13207 APPLICATION OF FRINGE BENEFIT RULES TO AIRLINES AND THEIR AFFILIATES.

* * *

(c) TRANSITIONAL RULE FOR DETERMINATION OF LINE OF BUSINESS IN CASE OF AFFILIATED GROUP OPERATING AIRLINE. If, as of September 12, 1984—

(1) an individual—

(A) was an employee (within the meaning of section 132 of the Internal Revenue Code of 1954, including subsection (f) thereof) of one member of an affiliated group (as defined in section 1504 of such Code), hereinafter referred to as the "first corporation", and

(B) was eligible for no-additional-cost service in the form of air transportation provided by another member of such affiliated group, hereinafter referred to as the "second corporation",

(2) at least 50 percent of the individuals performing service for the first corporation were or had been employees of, or had previously performed services for, the second corporation, and

(3) the primary business of the affiliated group was air transportation of passengers,

then, for purposes of applying paragraphs (1) and (2) of section 132(a) of the Internal Revenue Code of 1954, with respect to no-additional-cost services and qualified employee discounts provided after December 31, 1984, for such individual by the second corporation, the first corporation shall be treated as engaged in the same air transportation line of business as the second corporation. For purposes of the preceding sentence, an employee of the second corporation who is performing services for the first corporation shall also be treated as an employee of the first corporation.

(d) SPECIAL RULE FOR SERVICES RELATED TO PROVIDING AIR TRANSPORTATION. Section 531 of the Tax Reform Act of 1984 is amended by redesignating subsections (g) and (h) as subsections (h) and (i), respectively, and by inserting after subsection (f) the following new subsection:

"(g) SPECIAL RULE FOR CERTAIN SERVICES RELATED TO AIR TRANSPORTATION.—

"(g)(1) IN GENERAL. If—

"(g)(1)(A) an individual performs services for a qualified air transportation organization, and

"(g)(1)(B) such services are performed primarily for persons engaged in providing air transportation and are of the kind which (if performed on September 12, 1984) would qualify such individual for no-additional-cost services in the form of air transportation,

then, with respect to such individual, such qualified air transportation organization shall be treated as engaged in the line of business of providing air transportation.

"(g)(2) QUALIFIED AIR TRANSPORTATION ORGANIZATION. For purposes of paragraph (1), the term 'qualified air transportation organization' means any organization—

"(g)(2)(A) if such organization (or a predecessor) was in existence on September 12, 1984,

"(g)(2)(B) if—

"(g)(2)(B)(i) such organization is described in section 501(c)(6) of the Internal Revenue Code of 1954 and the membership of such organization is limited to entities engaged in the transportation by air if individuals or property for compensation or hire, or

"(g)(2)(B)(ii) such organization is a corporation all the stock of which is owned entirely by entities referred to in clause (i), and

"(g)(2)(C) if such organization is operated in furtherance of the activities of its members or owners.".

Tax Reform Act of 1986

P.L. 99-514

Signed on October 22, 1986

[Reproduced below are sections of the Tax Reform Act of 1986 which did not amend any sections of the Internal Revenue Code of 1986 or the Employee Retirement Income Security Act of 1974 (ERISA).]

[¶15,725]

Act Sec. 1 SHORT TITLE; TABLE OF CONTENTS.

(a) SHORT TITLE. This Act may be cited as the "Tax Reform Act of 1986".

* * *

[¶15,725A]

Act Sec. 2 INTERNAL REVENUE CODE OF 1986.

(a) REDESIGNATION OF 1954 CODE. The Internal Revenue Title enacted August 16, 1954, as heretofore, hereby, or hereafter amended, may be cited as the "Internal Revenue Code of 1986".

(b) REFERENCES IN LAWS, ETC. Except when inappropriate, any reference in any law, Executive order, or other document—

(1) to the Internal Revenue Code of 1954 shall include a reference to the Internal Revenue Code of 1986, and

(2) to the Internal Revenue Code of 1986 shall include a reference to the provisions of law formerly known as the Internal Revenue Code of 1954.

[¶15,725B]

Act Sec. 3 AMENDMENT OF 1986 CODE; COORDINATION WITH SECTION 15.

(a) AMENDMENT OF 1986 CODE. Except as otherwise expressly provided, whenever in this Act an amendment or repeal is expressed in terms of an amendment to, or repeal of, a section or other provision, the reference shall be considered to be made to a section or other provision of the Internal Revenue Code of 1986.

* * *

[¶15,725C]

Act Sec. 1140 PLAN AMENDMENTS NOT REQUIRED UNTIL JANUARY 1, 1989.

(a) IN GENERAL. If any amendment made by this subtitle or subtitle C requires an amendment to any plan, such plan amendment shall not be required to be made before the first plan year beginning on or after January 1, 1989, if—

(1) during the period after such amendment takes effect and before such first plan year, the plan is operated in accordance with the requirements of such amendment or in accordance with an amendment prescribed by the Secretary and adopted by the plan, and

(2) such plan amendment applies retroactively to the period after such amendment takes effect and such first plan year.

A pension plan shall not be treated as failing to provide definitely determinable benefits or contributions, or to be operated in accordance with the provisions of the plan, merely because it operates in accordance with this provision.

(b) MODEL AMENDMENT.—

(1) SECRETARY TO PRESCRIBE AMENDMENT. The Secretary of the Treasury or his delegate shall prescribe an amendment or amendments which allow a plan to meet the requirements of any amendment made by this subtitle, subtitle C, or title XVIII of this Act—

(A) which requires an amendment to such plan, and

(B) is effective before the first plan year beginning after December 31, 1988.

(2) ADOPTION BY PLAN. If a plan adopts the amendment or amendments prescribed under paragraph (1) and operates in accordance with such amendment or amendments, such plan shall not be treated as failing to provide definitely determinable benefits or contributions or to be operated in accordance with the provisions of the plan.

(c) SPECIAL RULE FOR COLLECTIVELY BARGAINED PLANS. In the case of a plan maintained pursuant to 1 or more collective bargaining agreements between employee representatives and 1 or more employers ratified before March 1, 1986, subsection (a) shall be applied by substituting for the first plan year beginning on or after January 1, 1989, the first plan year after the later of

(1) December 31, 1988, or

(2) the earlier of—

(A) December 31, 1990, or

(B) the date on which the last of such collective bargaining agreements terminate (without regard to any extension after February 28, 1986).

For purposes of paragraph (1)(B) and any other provision of this title, an agreement shall not be treated as terminated merely because the plan is amended pursuant to such agreement to meet the requirements of any amendment made by this title or title XVIII of this Act.

Amendments

P.L. 101-239, §7861(c)(1):

Amended Sec. 1140(b)(1) of P.L. 99-514 by striking "or subtitle C" and inserting ", subtitle C, or title XVIII of this Act".

P.L. 101-239, §7861(c)(2):

Amended Sec. 1140(c) of P.L. 99-514 by striking the end of the sentence following "the first plan year beginning" and inserting new material to read as above.

P.L. 101-239, §7861(c)(3):

Amended Sec. 1140(c) of P.L. 99-514 by adding a new flush sentence at the end to read as above.

The above amendments are effective as if included in the provisions of the Tax Reform Act of 1986 they amend.

[¶15,725D]

Act Sec. 1141 ISSUANCE OF FINAL REGULATIONS.

The Secretary of the Treasury or his delegate shall issue before February 1, 1988, such final regulations as may be necessary to carry out the amendments made by—

(1) section 1111, relating to application of nondiscrimination rules to integrated plans,

(2) section 1112, relating to coverage requirements for qualified plans,

(3) section 1113, relating to minimum vesting standards,

(4) section 1114, relating to the definition of highly compensated employee,

(5) section 1115, relating to separate lines of business and the definition of compensation,

(6) section 1116, relating to rules for section 401(k) plans,

(7) section 1117, relating to nondiscrimination requirements for employer matching and employer contribution,

(8) section 1120, relating to nondiscrimination requirements for tax sheltered annuities, and

(9) section 1133, relating to tax on excess distributions.

[¶15,725E]

Act Sec. 1142 SECRETARY TO ACCEPT APPLICATIONS WITH RESPECT TO SECTION 401(K) PLANS.

The Secretary of the Treasury or his delegate shall, not later than May 1, 1987, begin accepting applications for opinion letters with respect to master and prototype plans for qualified cash or deferred arrangements under section 401(k) of the Internal Revenue Code of 1986.

[¶15,725F]

Act Sec. 1145 REQUIREMENT OF JOINT AND SURVIVOR ANNUITIES AND PRERETIREMENT SURVIVOR ANNUITIES NOT TO APPLY TO CERTAIN PLAN.

* * *

(b) AMENDMENTS TO THE EMPLOYEE RETIREMENT INCOME SECURITY ACT OF 1974. Section 205(b) of the Employee Retirement Income Security Act of 1974 (29 U.S.C. 1082(b)) is amended by adding at the end thereof the following new paragraph:

"(3) This section shall not apply to a plan which the Secretary of the Treasury or his delegate has determined is a plan described in section 404(c) of the Internal Revenue Code of 1986 (or a continuation thereof) in which participation is substantially limited to individuals who, before January 1, 1976, ceased employment covered by the plan."

(c) AMENDMENTS TO RETIREMENT EQUITY ACT. Section 303 of the Retirement Equity Act of 1984 is amended by adding at the end thereof the following new subsection:

"(f) The amendments made by section 301 of this Act shall not apply to the termination of a defined benefit plan if such termination—

"(1) is pursuant to a resolution directing the termination of such plan which was adopted by the Board of Directors of a corporation on July 17, 1984, and

"(2) occurred on November 30, 1984."

* * *

[¶15,725G]

Act Sec. 1151 NONDISCRIMINATION RULES FOR COVERAGE AND BENEFITS UNDER CERTAIN STATUTORY EMPLOYEE BENEFIT PLANS.

* * *

(d) COORDINATION WITH CAFETERIA PLANS.—

* * *

(2) APPLICATION WITH EMPLOYMENT TAXES.—

* * *

(C) Section 209(e) of the Social Security Act is amended by inserting before the semicolon at the end thereof the following: ", or (9) under a cafeteria plan (within the meaning of section 125 of the Internal Revenue Code of 1986)."

* * *

[¶15,725H]

Act Sec. 1167 EXTENSION OF DUE DATE FOR STUDY OF WELFARE BENEFIT PLANS.

Section 560(b) of the Tax Reform Act of 1984 is amended by striking out "February 1, 1985" and inserting in lieu thereof "the date which is 1 year after the date of the enactment of the Tax Reform Act of 1986".

[¶15,725I]

Act Sec. 1851 AMENDMENTS RELATED TO WELFARE BENEFIT PLAN PROVISIONS.

(a) AMENDMENTS RELATED TO SECTION 511 OF THE ACT.—

* * *

(12) CLARIFICATION OF EFFECTIVE DATE. Subsection (e) of section 511 of the Tax Reform Act of 1984 is amended by adding at the end thereof the following new paragraphs:

"(6) Amendments Related to Tax on Unrelated Business Income. The amendments made by subsection (b) shall apply with respect to taxable years ending after December 31, 1985. For purposes of section 15 of the Internal Revenue Code of 1954, such amendments shall be treated as a change in the rate of a tax imposed by chapter 1 of such Code.

"(7) Amendments Related to Excise Taxes on Certain Welfare Benefit Plans. The amendments made by subsection (c) shall apply to benefits provided after December 31, 1985.

* * *

(14) Clerical Amendment. Paragraph (2) of section 511(e) of the Tax Reform Act of 1984 is amended by striking out "and section 514".

[¶15,725J]

Act Sec. 1852 AMENDMENTS RELATED TO PENSION PLAN PROVISIONS.

* * *

(b) Amendments Related to Section 522 of the Act.—

* * *

(9) Subsection (e) of section 522 of the Tax Reform Act of 1984 is amended by striking out "the date of the amendment" and inserting in lieu thereof "the date of the enactment".

* * *

(e) Amendments Related to Section 525 of the Act.—

* * *

(3) Section 525(b) of the Tax Reform Act of 1984 is amended by adding at the end thereof the following new paragraph:

"(4) Irrevocable election. For purposes of paragraph (2) and section 245(c) of the Tax Equity and Fiscal Responsibility Act of 1982, an individual who—

"(A) separated from service before January 1, 1985, with respect to paragraph (2), or January 1, 1983, with respect to section 245(c) of the Tax Equity and Fiscal Responsibility Act of 1982, and

"(B) meets the requirements of such paragraph or such section other than the requirement that there be an irrevocable election, and that the individual be in pay status,

shall be treated as having made an irrevocable election and as being in pay status within the time prescribed with respect to a form of benefit if such individual does not change such form of benefit before death."

(f) Amendment Related to Section 526 of the Act. Paragraph (2) of section 526(d) of the Tax Reform Act of 1984 is amended by striking out "paragraph (6)" and inserting in lieu thereof "paragraph (7)".

* * *

[¶15,725K]

Act Sec. 1853 AMENDMENTS RELATED TO FRINGE BENEFIT PROVISIONS.

* * *

(b) Amendments to Section 125.—

* * *

(2) Transitional Rule. Paragraph (5) of section 531(b) of the Tax Reform Act of 1984 (relating to exception for certain cafeteria plans and benefits) is amended by adding at the end thereof the following new subparagraph:

"(D) Collective bargaining agreements. In the case of any cafeteria plan in existence on February 10, 1984, and maintained pursuant to 1 or more collective bargaining agreements between employee representatives and 1 or more employers, the date on which the last of such collective bargaining agreements terminates (determined without regard to any extension thereof agreed to after July 18, 1984) shall be substituted for 'January 1, 1985' in subparagraph (A) and for 'July 1, 1985' in subparagraph (B). For purposes of the preceding sentence, any plan amendment made pursuant to a collective bargaining agreement relating to the plan which amends the plan solely to conform to any requirement added by this section (or any requirement in the regulations under section 125 of the Internal Revenue Code of 1954 proposed on May 6, 1984) shall not be treated as a termination of such collective bargaining agreement."

(3) Special Rule Where Contributions or Reimbursements Suspended. Paragraph (5) of section 531(b) of the Tax Reform Act of 1984 is amended by adding at the end thereof the following new subparagraph:

"(E) Special rule where contributions or reimbursements suspended. For purposes of subparagraphs (A) and (B), a plan shall not be treated as not continuing to fail to satisfy the rules referred to in such subparagraphs with respect to any benefit provided in the form of a flexible spending arrangement merely because contributions or reimbursements (or both) with respect to such plan were suspended before January 1, 1985."

* * *

(d) Treatment of Telephone Concession Service for Certain Retirees. Section 559 of the Tax Reform Act of 1984 is amended by adding at the end thereof the following subsection:

"(e) Telephone Service for Pre-Divestiture Retirees. In the case of an employee who, by reason of retirement or disability, separated before January 1, 1984, from the service of an entity subject to the modified final judgment—

"(1) all entities subject to the modified final judgment shall be treated as a single employer in the same line of business for purposes of determining whether telephone service provided to the employee is a no-additional-cost service as defined in section 132 of the Internal Revenue Code of 1954; and

"(2) payment by an entity subject to the modified final judgment of all or part of the cost of local telephone service provided to the employee by a person other than an entity subject to the modified final judgment (including rebate of the amount paid by the employee for the service and payment to the person providing the service) shall be treated as telephone service provided to the employee by such single employer for purposes of determining whether the telephone service is a no-additional-cost service as defined in section 132 of the Internal Revenue Code of 1954.

For purposes of this subsection, the term 'employee' has the meaning given to such term by section 132(f) of the Internal Revenue Code of 1954."

* * *

[¶15,725L]

Act Sec. 1855 AMENDMENTS RELATED TO MISCELLANEOUS EMPLOYEE BENEFIT PROVISIONS.

(a) SECTION 555 OF THE ACT. Subsection (c) of section 555 of the Tax Reform Act of 1984 (relating to technical amendments to the incentive stock option provisions) is amended—

(1) by striking out "subsection (a)" in paragraph (1) and inserting in lieu thereof "subsection (a)(1)",

(2) by striking out "subsection (b)" in paragraph (2) and inserting in lieu thereof "subsection (a)(2)",

(3) by striking out "after March 20, 1984," in paragraph (2), and

(4) by striking out "subsection (c)" in paragraph (3) and inserting in lieu thereof "subsection (b)".

(b) AMENDMENT RELATED TO SECTION 556 OF THE ACT. Section 556 of the Tax Reform Act of 1984 is amended by striking out so much of such section as precedes paragraph (1) thereof and inserting in lieu thereof the following:

" SEC. 556. TIME FOR MAKING CERTAIN SECTION 83(B) ELECTIONS.

"In the case of any transfer of property in connection with the performance of services on or before November 18, 1982, the election permitted by section 83(b) of the Internal Revenue Code of 1954 may be made, notwithstanding paragraph (2) of such section 83(b), with the income tax return for any taxable year ending after July 18, 1984, and beginning before the date of the enactment of the Tax Reform Act of 1986 if—".

* * *

[¶15,725M]

Act Sec. 1875 AMENDMENTS RELATED TO TITLE VII OF THE ACT.

* * *

(c) AMENDMENTS RELATED TO SECTION 713.—

* * *

(2) Section 713(c) of the Tax Reform Act of 1984 is amended by adding at the end thereof the following new paragraph:

"(4) EFFECTIVE DATE FOR PARAGRAPH (3). The amendment made by paragraph (3) shall apply to distributions after July 18, 1984."

* * *

(5) Section 713(d)(1) of the Tax Reform Act of 1984 is amended by striking out "Paragraph" and inserting in lieu thereof "Effective with respect to contributions made in taxable years beginning after December 31, 1983, paragraph".

* * *

[¶15,725N]

Act Sec. 1879 MISCELLANEOUS PROVISIONS.

* * *

(p) AMENDMENT RELATED TO SECTION 252 OF THE ECONOMIC RECOVERY TAX ACT OF 1981.—

(1) Notwithstanding subsection (c) of section 252 of the Economic Recovery Tax Act of 1981, the amendment made by subsection (a) of such section 252 (and the provisions of subsection (b) of such section 252) shall apply to any transfer of stock to any person if—

(A) such transfer occurred in November or December of 1973 and was pursuant to the exercise of an option granted in November or December of 1971,

(B) in December 1973 the corporation granting the option was acquired by another corporation in a transaction qualifying as a reorganization under section 368 of the Internal Revenue Code of 1954,

(C) the fair market value (as of July 1, 1974) of the stock received by such person in the reorganization in exchange for the stock transferred to him pursuant to the exercise of such option was less than 50 percent of the fair market value of the stock so received (as of December 4, 1973),

(D) in 1975 or 1976 such person sold substantially all of the stock received in such reorganization, and

(E) such person makes an election under this section at such time and in such manner as the Secretary of the Treasury or his delegate shall prescribe.

(2) LIMITATION ON AMOUNT OF BENEFIT. Subsection (a) shall not apply to transfers with respect to any employee to the extent that the application of subsection (a) with respect to such employee would (but for this subsection) result in a reduction in liability for income tax with respect to such employee for all taxable years in excess of $100,000 (determined without regard to any interest).

(3) STATUTE OF LIMITATIONS.—

(A) OVERPAYMENTS. If refund or credit of any overpayments of tax resulting from the application of subsection (a) is prevented on the date of the enactment of this Act (or at any time within 6 months after such date of enactment) by the operation of any law or rule of law, refund or credit of such overpayment (to the extent attributable to the application of subsection (a)) may, nevertheless, be made or allowed if claim therefor is filed before the close of such 6-month period.

(B) DEFICIENCIES. If the assessment of any deficiency of tax resulting from the application of subsection (a) is prevent on the date of the enactment of this Act (or at any time within 6 months after such date of enactment) by the operation of any law or rule of law, assessment of such deficiency (to the extent attributable to the application of subsection (a)) may, nevertheless, be made within such 6-month period.

[¶15,725O]

Act Sec. 1898 TECHNICAL CORRECTIONS TO THE RETIREMENT EQUITY ACT OF 1984.

* * *

(g) AMENDMENT RELATED TO SECTION 302 OF THE ACT. Paragraph (2) of section 302(b) of the Retirement Equity Act of 1984 is amended by striking out "January 1, 1987" and inserting in lieu thereof "July 1, 1988".

(h) AMENDMENTS RELATED TO SECTION 303 OF THE ACT.—

(1)(A) Subsection (c) of section 303 of the Retirement Equity Act of 1984 (relating to transitional rule for requirement of joint and survivor annuity and preretirement survivor annuity) is amended by adding at the end thereof the following new paragraph:

"(4) ELIMINATION OF DOUBLE DEATH BENEFITS.—

"(A) IN GENERAL. In the case of a participant described in paragraph (2), death benefits (other than a qualified joint and survivor annuity or a qualified preretirement survivor annuity) payable to any beneficiary shall be reduced by the amount payable to the surviving spouse of such participant by reason of paragraph (2). The reduction under the preceding sentence shall be made on the basis of the respective present values (as of the date of the participant's death) of such death benefits and the amount so payable to the surviving spouse.

"(B) SPOUSE MAY WAIVE PROVISIONS OF PARAGRAPH (2). In the case of any participant described in paragraph (2), the surviving spouse of such participant may waive the provisions of paragraph (2). Such waiver shall be made on or before the close of the second plan year to which the amendments made by section 103 of this Act apply. Such a waiver shall not be treated as a transfer of property for purposes of chapter 12 of the Internal Revenue Code of 1954 and shall not be treated as an assignment or alienation for purposes of section 401(a)(13) of the Internal Revenue Code of 1954 or section 206(d) of the Employee Retirement Income Security Act of 1974."

* * *

(2) Subparagraph (A) of section 303(e)(2) of the Retirement Equity Act of 1984 (relating to treatment of certain participants who perform services on or after January 1, 1976) is amended by striking out "in the first plan year" and inserting in lieu thereof "in any plan year".

(3) Paragraph (2) of section 303(c) of the Retirement Equity Act is amended by adding at the end thereof the following new sentence: "In the case of a profit-sharing or stock bonus plan to which this paragraph applies, the plan shall be treated as meeting the requirements of the amendments made by sections 103 and 203 with respect to any participant if the plan made a distribution in a form other than a life annuity to the surviving spouse of the participant of such participant's nonforfeitable benefit."

* * *

Retirement Equity Act of 1984

P.L. 98-397

Signed on August 23, 1984

[Reproduced below are sections of the Retirement Equity Act of 1984 which did not amend any sections of the Internal Revenue Code of 1954 or the Employee Retirement Income Security Act of 1974 (ERISA).]

[¶15,725P]

An Act

To amend the Employee Retirement Income Security Act of 1974 and the Internal Revenue Code of 1954 to improve the delivery of retirement benefits and provide for greater equity under private pension plans for workers and their spouses and dependents by taking into account changes in work patterns, the status of marriage as an economic partnership, and the substantial contribution to that partnership of spouses who work both in and outside the home, and for other purposes.

Be it enacted by the Senate and House of Representatives of the United States of America in Congress assembled,

Act Sec. 1 SHORT TITLE.

This Act may be cited as the "Retirement Equity Act of 1984".

* * *

[¶15,725Q]

Act Sec. 302 GENERAL EFFECTIVE DATES.

(a) IN GENERAL. Except as otherwise provided in this section or section 303, the amendments made by this Act shall apply to plan years beginning after December 31, 1984.

(b) SPECIAL RULE FOR COLLECTIVE BARGAINING AGREEMENTS. In the case of a plan maintained pursuant to 1 or more collective bargaining agreements between employee representatives and 1 or more employers ratified before the date of the enactment of this Act, except as provided in subsection (d) or section 303, the amendments made by this Act shall not apply to plan years beginning before the earlier of—

(1) the date on which the last of the collective bargaining agreements relating to the plan terminates (determined without regard to any extension thereof agreed to after the date of the enactment of this Act), or

(2) January 1, 1987.

For purposes of paragraph (1), any plan amendment made pursuant to a collective bargaining agreement relating to the plan which amends the plan solely to conform to any requirement added by title I or II shall not be treated as a termination of such collective bargaining agreement.

(c) NOTICE REQUIREMENT. The amendments made by section 207 shall apply to distributions after December 31, 1984.

(d) SPECIAL RULES FOR TREATMENT OF PLAN AMENDMENTS.—

(1) IN GENERAL. Except as provided in paragraph (2), the amendments made by section 301 shall apply to plan amendments made after July 30, 1984.

(2) SPECIAL RULE FOR COLLECTIVE BARGAINING AGREEMENTS. In the case of a plan maintained pursuant to 1 or more collective bargaining agreements entered into before January 1, 1985, which are—

(A) between employee representatives and 1 or more employers, and

(B) successor agreements to 1 or more collective bargaining agreements which terminate after July 30, 1984, and before January 1, 1985,

the amendments made by section 301 shall not apply to plan amendments adopted before April 1, 1985, pursuant to such successor agreements (without regard to any modification or reopening after December 31, 1984).

[¶15,725R]

Act Sec. 303 TRANSITIONAL RULES.

(a) AMENDMENTS RELATING TO VESTING RULES; BREAKS IN SERVICE; MATERNITY OR PATERNITY LEAVE.—

(1) MINIMUM AGE FOR VESTING. The amendments made by sections 102(b) and 202(b) shall apply in the case of participants who have at least 1 hour of service under the plan on or after the first day of the first plan year to which the amendments made by this Act apply.

(2) BREAK IN SERVICE RULES. If, as of the day before the first day of the first plan year to which the amendments made by this Act apply, section 202(a) or (b) or 203(b) of the Employee Retirement Income Security Act of 1974 or section 410(a) or 411(a) of the Internal Revenue Code of 1954 (as in effect on the day before the date of the enactment of this Act) would not require any service to be taken into account, nothing in the amendments made by subsections (c) and (d) of section 102 of this Act and subsections (c) and (d) of section 202 of this Act shall be construed as requiring such service to be taken into account under such section 202(a) or (b), 203(b), 410(a), or 411(a); as the case may be.

(3) MATERNITY OR PATERNITY LEAVE. The amendments made by sections 102(e) and 202(e) shall apply in the case of absences from work which begin on or after the first day of the first plan year to which the amendments made by this Act apply.

(b) SPECIAL RULE FOR AMENDMENTS RELATING TO MATERNITY OR PATERNITY ABSENCES. If a plan is administered in a manner which would meet the amendments made by sections 102(e) and 202(e) (relating to certain maternity or paternity absences not treated as breaks in service), such plan need not be amended to meet such requirements until the earlier of—

(1) the date on which such plan is first otherwise amended after the date of the enactment of this Act, or

(2) the beginning of the first plan year beginning after December 31, 1986.

(c) REQUIREMENT OF JOINT AND SURVIVOR ANNUITY AND PRERETIREMENT SURVIVOR ANNUITY.—

(1) REQUIREMENT THAT PARTICIPANT HAVE AT LEAST 1 HOUR OF SERVICE OR PAID LEAVE ON OR AFTER DATE OF ENACTMENT. The amendments made by sections 103 and 203 shall apply only in the case of participants who have at least 1 hour of service under the plan on or after the date of the enactment of this Act or have at least 1 hour of paid leave on or after such date of enactment.

(2). Requirement that preretirement survivor annuity be provided in case of certain participants dying on or after date of enactment. In the case of any participant.

   (A) who has at least 1 hour of service under the plan on or after the date of the enactment of this Act or has at least 1 hour of paid leave on or after such date of enactment,

   (B) who dies before the annuity starting date, and

   (C) who dies on or after the date of the enactment of this Act and before the first day of the first plan year to which the amendments made by this Act apply,

the amendments made by sections 103 and 203 shall be treated as in effect as of the time of such participant's death.

(3) Spousal consent required for certain elections after December 31, 1984. Any election after December 31, 1984, and before the first day of the first plan year to which the amendments made by this Act apply not to take a joint and survivor annuity shall not be effective unless the requirements of section 205(c)(2) of the Employee Retirement Income Security Act of 1974 (as amended by section 103 of this Act) and section 417(a)(2) of the Internal Revenue Code of 1954 (as added by section 203 of this Act) are met with respect to such election.

(d) Amendments Relating to Assignments in Divorce, Etc., Proceedings. The amendments made by sections 104 and 204 shall take effect on January 1, 1985, except that in the case of a domestic relations order entered before such date, the plan administrator—

   (1) shall treat such order as a qualified domestic relations order if such administrator is paying benefits pursuant to such order on such date, and

   (2) may treat any other such order entered before such date as a qualified domestic relations order even if such order does not meet the requirement of such amendments.

(e) Treatment of Certain Participants Who Separate From Service Before Date of Enactment.—

   (1) Joint and survivor annuity provisions of employee retirement income security act of 1974 apply to certain participants. If—

   (A) a participant had at least 1 hour of service under the plan on or after September 2, 1974,

   (B) section 205 of the Employee Retirement Income Security Act of 1974 and section 401(a)(11) of the Internal Revenue Code of 1954 (as in effect on the day before the date of the enactment of this Act) would not (but for this paragraph) apply to such participant.

   (C) the amendments made by sections 103 and 203 of this Act do not apply to such participant, and

   (D) as of the date of the enactment of this Act, the participant's annuity starting date has not occurred and the participant is alive,

then such participant may elect to have section 205 of the Employee Retirement Income Security Act of 1974 and section 401(a)(11) of the Internal Revenue Code of 1954 (as in effect on the day before the date of the enactment of this Act) apply.

   (2) Treatment of certain participants who perform service on or after January 1, 1976. If—

   (A) a participant had at least 1 hour of service in the first plan year beginning on or after January 1, 1976,

   (B) the amendments made by sections 103 and 203 would not (but for this paragraph) apply to such participant,

   (C) when such participant separated from service, such participant had at least 10 years of service under the plan and had a nonforfeitable right to all (or any portion) of such participant's accrued benefit derived from employer contributions, and

   (D) as of the date of the enactment of this Act, such participant's annuity starting date has not occurred and such participant is alive,

then such participant may elect to have the qualified preretirement survivor annuity requirements of the amendments made by sections 103 and 203 apply.

   (3) Period during which election may be made. An election under paragraph (1) or (2) may be made by any participant during the period—

   (A) beginning on the date of the enactment of this Act, and

   (B) ending on the earlier of the participant's annuity starting date or the date of the participant's death.

   (4) Requirement of notice.—

   (A) In general.—

      (i) Time and manner. Every plan shall give notice of the provisions of this subsection at such time or times and in such manner or manners as the Secretary of the Treasury may prescribe.

      (ii) Penalty. If any plan fails to meet the requirements of clause (i), such plan shall pay a civil penalty to the Secretary of the Treasury equal to $1 per participant for each day during the period beginning with the first day on which such failure occurs and ending on the day before notice is given by the plan; except that the amount of such penalty imposed on any plan shall not exceed $2,500.

   (B) Responsibilities of Secretary of Labor. The Secretary of Labor shall take such steps (by public announcements and otherwise) as may be necessary or appropriate to bring to public attention the provisions of this subsection.

(f) The amendments made by section 301 of this Act shall not apply to the termination of a defined benefit plan if such termination—

   (1) is pursuant to a resolution directing the termination of such plan which was adopted by the Board of Directors of a corporation on July 17, 1984, and

   (2) occurred on November 30, 1984.

Amendments

P.L. 101-239, § 7861(d)(1):

Amended Sec. 303(f) of P.L. 98-397 by striking "July 24, 1984" and inserting "July 17, 1984."

P.L. 99-514, § 1145(c):

Amended Sec. 303 of P.L. 98-397 by adding a new subsection (f) to read as above.

[¶15,725S]

Act Sec. 304 STUDY BY COMPTROLLER GENERAL OF THE UNITED STATES

(a) General Rule. The Comptroller General of the United States shall conduct a detailed study (based on a reliable scientific sample of typical pension plans of various designs and sizes) of the effect on women of participation, vesting, funding, integration, survivorship features, and other relevant plan and Federal pension rules.

(b) General Accounting Office Access to Records. For the purpose of conducting the study under subsection (a), the Comptroller General, or any of his duly authorized representatives, shall have access to and the right to examine and copy—

(1) any pension plan books, documents, papers, records, or other recorded information within the possession or control of the plan administrator or sponsor, or any person providing services to the plan, and

(2) any payroll, employment, or other related records within the possession or control of any employer contributing to or sponsoring a pension plan,

that is pertinent to such study. The Comptroller General shall not disclose the identity of any individual or employer in making any information obtained under this subsection available to the public.

(c) DEFINITIONS. For purposes of this section, the terms "pension plan", "administrator", "plan sponsor", and "employer" are defined in section 3 of the Employee Retirement Income Security Act of 1974, as amended.

(d) COOPERATION WITH OTHER FEDERAL AGENCIES. In conducting the study under subsection (a), the Comptroller General shall consult with the Internal Revenue Service, the Department of Labor, and other interested Federal agencies so as to prevent any duplication of data compilation or analysis.

(e) REPORT. Not later than January 1, 1990, the Comptroller General shall submit a report on the study conducted under this section to the Committee on Ways and Means of the House of Representatives, the Committee on Education and Labor of the House of Representatives, the Committee on Finance of the Senate, the Committee on Labor and Human Resources of the Senate, and the Joint Committee on Taxation.

Tax Reform Act of 1984

P.L. 98-369

Signed on July 18, 1984

[Reproduced below are sections of the Tax Reform Act of 1984 that did not amend any sections of the Internal Revenue Code of 1954 or the Employee Retirement Income Security Act of 1974.]

An Act

To provide for tax reform, and for deficit reduction.

Be it enacted by the Senate and House of Representatives of the United States of America in Congress assembled,

[¶15,726]

Act Sec. 1 Short Title.

(a) SHORT TITLE. This Act may be cited as the "Deficit Reduction Act of 1984".

(b) ACT DIVIDED INTO 2 DIVISIONS. This Act consists of 2 divisions as follows:

(1) DIVISION A. Tax Reform Act of 1984.

(2) DIVISION B. Spending Reduction Act of 1984.

DIVISION A—TAX REFORM ACT OF 1984

[¶15,726A]

Act Sec. 5 SHORT TITLE; ETC.

(a) SHORT TITLE. This division may be cited as the "Tax Reform Act of 1984".

(b) AMENDMENT OF 1954 CODE. Except as otherwise expressly provided, whenever in this division an amendment or repeal is expressed in terms of an amendment to, or repeal of, a section or other provision, the reference shall be considered to be made to a section or other provision of the Internal Revenue Code of 1954.

* * *

[¶15,726B]

Act Sec. 553 DISTRIBUTION REQUIREMENTS FOR ACCOUNTS AND ANNUITIES OF AN INSURER IN A REHABILITATION PROCEEDING.

(a) IN GENERAL. For purposes of sections 401(a)(9), 408(a)(6) and (7), and 408(b)(3) and (4) of the Internal Revenue Code of 1954—

(1) a trust, custodial account, or annuity or other contract forming part of a pension or profit-sharing plan, or a retirement annuity, or

(2) a grantor of an individual retirement account or an individual retirement annuity.

shall not be treated as failing to meet the requirements of such sections if such account, annuity, or contract, was issued by an insurance company which, on March 15, 1984, was a party to a rehabilitation proceeding under the applicable State insurance law.

(b) LIMITATION. Subsection (a) shall apply only during the period during which—

(1) the insurance company continues to be a party to the proceeding described in subsection (a), and

(2) distributions under the trust, custodial account, or annuity or other contract may not be made by reason of such proceeding.

* * *

[¶15,726C]

Act Sec. 558 ELIMINATION OF RETROACTIVE APPLICATION OF AMENDMENTS MADE BY MULTIEMPLOYER PENSION PLAN AMENDMENTS ACT OF 1980.

(a) IN GENERAL.—

(1) LIABILITY. Any withdrawal liability incurred by an employer pursuant to part 1 of subtitle E of title IV of the Employee Retirement Income Security Act of 1974 (29 U.S.C. 1381 et seq.) as a result of the complete or partial withdrawal of such employer from a multiemployer plan before September 26, 1980, shall be void.

(2) REFUNDS. Any amounts paid by an employer to a plan sponsor as a result of such withdrawal liability shall be refunded by the plan sponsor to the employer with interest (in accordance with section 401(a)(2)), less a reasonable amount for administrative expenses incurred by the plan sponsor (other than legal expenses incurred with respect to the plan) in calculating, assessing, and refunding such amounts.

(b) CONFORMING AMENDMENTS.—

(1) * * *

(2) MULTIEMPLOYER PENSION PLAN AMENDMENTS ACT OF 1980. Section 108(d) of the Multiemployer Pension Plan Amendments Act of 1980 (29 U.S.C. 1385 note) is amended—

(A) by striking out "April 29, 1982" in paragraph (1) and inserting in lieu thereof "September 26, 1982"; and

(B) by striking out "April 29, 1980" each place it appears in paragraphs (2) and (3) and inserting in lieu thereof "September 26, 1980".

(c) NO INCREASE IN LIABILITY. The amendments made by this section shall be construed to increase the liability incurred by any employer pursuant to part 1 of subtitle E of title IV of the Employee Retirement Income Security Act of 1974 (29 U.S.C. 1381 et seq.), as in effect immediately before the amendments made by subsection (b), as a result of the complete or partial withdrawal of such employer from a multiemployer plan prior to September 26, 1980.

(d) SPECIAL RULE FOR CERTAIN BINDING AGREEMENTS. In the case of an employer who, on September 26, 1980, has a binding agreement to withdraw from a multiemployer plan, subsection (a)(1) shall be applied by substituting "December 31, 1980" for "September 26, 1980".

[¶15,726D]

Act Sec. 559 TELECOMMUNICATION EMPLOYEES.

(a) EMPLOYEE PROTECTION. Notwithstanding any provisions of the divestiture interchange agreement to the contrary, in the case of any change in employment on or after January 1, 1985, by a covered employee, the recognition of service credit, and enforcement of such recognition, shall be governed in the same manner and to [the] same extent as provided under the divestiture interchange agreement for a change in employment by a covered employee during calendar year 1984.

(b) EMPLOYEES COVERED. For purposes of this section, a covered employee is an individual—

(1) who is an employee of an entity subject to the modified final judgment,

(2) who is serving in an eligible position, and

(3) who—

(A) on December 31, 1983, was an employee of any such entity serving in an eligible position, or

(B) was a former employee with rehire or recall rights on such date and is rehired during the period of the employee's rehire or recall rights.

(c) DEFINITIONS. For purposes of this section—

(1) The term "service credit" means service credit for benefit accrual, vesting, and eligibility for benefits under any pension plan, or any other employee benefits, including the interchange and treatment of associated benefit obligations and assets.

(2) The term "change in employment" means the commencement of employment of a covered employee by an entity subject to the modified final judgment after the termination of employment (with or without break in service) of such individual from an eligible position within another entity subject to the modified final judgment.

(3) The term "eligible position" means any position (A) which is not a supervisory position, within the meaning of section 2(11) of the National Labor Relations Act (29 U.S.C. 152(11)) or (B) the annual base pay rate for which is not more than $50,000, adjusted by the percentage increase in the consumer price index since December 31, 1983.

(4) The term "modified final judgment" means the judgment of the United States District Court for the District of Columbia in the case, United States against Western Electric, et alia, No. 82-0192, as modified.

(5) The term "entity subject to the modified final judgment" means—

(A) any carrier divested as a result of the modified final judgment,

(B) the corporation owning such carrier before divestiture,

(C) any other communications common carrier owned, in whole or in part, by such corporation on December 31, 1983, or

(D) any Interchange Company (as defined in the divestiture interchange agreement) excluding any subsidiary of such company other than any such subsidiary—

(i) which was established as of December 31, 1983, and

(ii) which participates in a defined benefit pension plan maintained by such Interchange Company.

(6) The term "divestiture interchange agreement" refers to the agreement between entities subject to the modified final judgment which was executed as of November 1, 1983, and which provides for mutual reciprocal recognition of service credit.

(7) The term "consumer price index" means the Consumer Price Index (all items—United States city average) published monthly by the Bureau of Labor Statistics.

(d) COORDINATION WITH OTHER BENEFIT-RELATED PROVISIONS. Nothing in this section shall be construed to limit benefits which would otherwise be available to any individual, whether provided under the modified final judgment, under applicable law, or otherwise.

[¶15,726E]

Act Sec. 560 STUDY OF EMPLOYEE WELFARE BENEFIT PLANS.

(a) IN GENERAL. The Secretary of the Treasury shall make a study of the problems relating to the use of employee welfare benefit plans for the provision of benefits to current and retired employees. Such study shall include a study of the need for participation, vesting, and funding standards.

(b) REPORT. A report of the study conducted under subsection (a), together with such recommendations for legislation as the Secretary deems appropriate, shall be made to the Congress by not later than February 1, 1985.

* * *

Tax Equity and Fiscal Responsibility Act of 1982

P.L. 97-248

Signed on September 3, 1982

[Reproduced below are sections of the Tax Equity and Fiscal Responsibility Act of 1982 which did not amend any sections of the Internal Revenue Code of 1954.]

An Act

To provide for tax equity and fiscal responsibility, and for other purposes.

Be it enacted by the Senate and House of Representatives of the United States of America in Congress assembled,

[¶15,727]

Act Sec. 1 SHORT TITLE; TABLE OF CONTENTS; AMENDMENT OF 1954 CODE.

(a) SHORT TITLE. This Act may be cited as the "Tax Equity and Fiscal Responsibility Act of 1982".

(b) TABLE OF CONTENTS.—

* * *

[¶15,727A]

Act Sec. 247 EXISTING PERSONAL SERVICE CORPORATIONS MAY LIQUIDATE UNDER SECTION 333 DURING 1983 OR 1984.

(a) IN GENERAL. In the case of a complete liquidation of a personal service corporation (within the meaning of section 535(c)(2)(B) of the Internal Revenue Code of 1954) during 1983 or 1984, the following rules shall apply with respect to any shareholder other than a corporation:

(1) The determination of whether section 333 of such Code applies shall be made without regard to whether the corporation is a collapsible corporation to which section 341(a) of such Code applies.

(2) No gain or loss shall be recognized by the liquidating corporation on the distribution of any unrealized receivable in such liquidation.

(3)(A) Except as provided in subparagraph (C), any disposition by a shareholder of any unrealized receivable received in the liquidation shall be treated as a sale at fair market value of such receivable and any gain or loss shall be treated as ordinary gain or loss.

(B) For purposes of subparagraph (A), the term "disposition" includes—

(i) failing to hold the property in the trade or business which generated the receivables, and

(ii) failing to hold a continuing interest in such trade or business.

(C) For purposes of subparagraph (A), the term "disposition" does not include transmission at death to the estate of the decedent or transfer to a person pursuant to the right of such person to receive such property by reason of the death of the decedent or by bequest, devise, or inheritance from the decedent.

(4) Unrealized receivables distributed in the liquidation shall be treated as having a zero basis.

(5) For purposes of computing earnings and profits, the liquidating corporation shall not treat unrealized receivables distributed in the liquidation as an item of income.

(b) UNREALIZED RECEIVABLES DEFINED. For purposes of this section, the term "unrealized receivables" has the meaning given such term by the first sentence of section 751(c) of such Code.

* * *

[¶15,727B]

Act Sec. 252 DEFERRED COMPENSATION PLANS FOR STATE JUDGES.

Subsection (c) of section 131 of the Revenue Act of 1978 is amended by adding at the end thereof the following new paragraph:

"(3) DEFERRED COMPENSATION PLANS FOR STATE JUDGES.—

"(A) IN GENERAL. The amendments made by this section shall not apply to any qualified State judicial plan.

"(B) QUALIFIED STATE JUDICIAL PLAN. For purposes of subparagraph (A), the term 'qualified State judicial plan' means any retirement plan of a State for the exclusive benefit of judges or their beneficiaries if—

"(i) such plan has been continuously in existence since December 31, 1978,

"(ii) under such plan, all judges eligible to benefit under the plan—

"(I) are required to participate, and

"(II) are required to contribute the same fixed percentage of their basic or regular rate of compensation as judge,

"(iii) under such plan, no judge has an option as to contributions or benefits the exercise of which would affect the amount of includible compensation,

"(iv) the retirement payments of a judge under the plan are a percentage of the compensation of judges of that State holding similar positions, and

"(v) the plan during any year does not pay benefits with respect to any participant which exceed the limitations of section 415(b) of the Internal Revenue Code of 1954."

* * *

[¶15,727C]

Act Sec. 334 WITHHOLDING ON PENSIONS, ANNUITIES, AND CERTAIN OTHER DEFERRED INCOME.

* * *

(e) EFFECTIVE DATES.—

* * *

(6) WAIVER OF PENALTY. No penalty shall be assessed under section 6672 with respect to any failure to withhold as required by the amendments made by this section if such failure was before July 1, 1983, and if the person made a good faith effort to comply with such withholding requirements.

Multiemployer Pension Plan Amendments Act of 1980

P.L. 96-364

Signed on September 26, 1980

[Reproduced below are sections of the Multiemployer Pension Plan Amendments Act of 1980 which did not amend any sections of the Internal Revenue Code of 1954 or the Employee Retirement Income Security Act of 1974 (ERISA).]

[¶ 15,728]

AN ACT

To amend the Employee Retirement Income Security Act of 1974 and the Internal Revenue Code of 1954 to improve retirement income security under private multiemployer pension plans by strengthening the funding requirements for those plans, to authorize plan preservation measures for financially troubled multiemployer pension plans, and to revise the manner in which the pension plan termination insurance provisions apply to multiemployer plans, and for other purposes.

Be it enacted by the Senate and House of Representatives of the United States of America in Congress assembled,

[¶ 15,728A]

Act Sec. 1 SHORT TITLE.

This Act may be cited as the "Multiemployer Pension Plan Amendments Act of 1980".

[¶ 15,728B]

Act Sec. 2 TABLE OF CONTENTS.

The table of contents is as follows:

TABLE OF CONTENTS

[¶15,728C]

Act Sec. 3 FINDINGS AND DECLARATION OF POLICY.

Act Sec. 3. (a) The Congress finds that—

(1) multiemployer pension plans have a substantial impact on interstate commerce and are affected with a national public interest;

(2) multiemployer pension plans have accounted for a substantial portion of the increase in private pension plan coverage over the past three decades;

(3) the continued well-being and security of millions of employees, retirees, and their dependents are directly affected by multiemployer pension plans; and

(4)(A) withdrawals of contributing employers from a multiemployer pension plan frequently result in substantially increased funding obligations for employers who continue to contribute to the plan, adversely affecting the plan, its participants and beneficiaries, and labor-management relations, and

(B) in a declining industry, the incidence of employer withdrawals is higher and the adverse effects described in subparagraph (A) are exacerbated.

Act Sec. 3. (b) The Congress further finds that—

(1) it is desirable to modify the current multiemployer plan termination insurance provisions in order to increase the likelihood of protecting plan participants against benefit losses; and

(2) it is desirable to replace the termination insurance program for multiemployer pension plans with an insolvency-based benefit protection program that will enhance the financial soundness of such plans, place primary emphasis on plan continuation, and contain program costs within reasonable limits.

Act Sec. 3. (c) It is hereby declared to be the policy of this Act—

(1) to foster and facilitate interstate commerce,

(2) to alleviate certain problems which tend to discourage the maintenance and growth of multiemployer pension plans,

(3) to provide reasonable protection for the interests of participants and beneficiaries of financially distressed multiemployer pension plans, and

(4) to provide a financially self-sufficient program for the guarantee of employee benefits under multiemployer plans.

* * *

[¶15,728D]

Act Sec. 108 TRANSITION RULES AND EFFECTIVE DATES.

* * *

Act Sec. 108. (c)(2)(A) For the purpose of applying section 4205 of the Employee Retirement Income Security Act of 1974 in the case of an employer described in subparagraph (B)—

(i) "more than 75 percent" shall be substituted for "70 percent" in subsections (a) and (b) of such section,

(ii) "25 percent or less" shall be substituted for "30 percent" in subsection (b) of such section, and

(iii) the number of contribution units for the high base year shall be the average annual number of such units for calendar years 1970 and 1971.

(B) An employer is described in this subparagraph if—

(i) the employer is engaged in the trade or business of shipping bulk cargoes in the Great Lakes Maritime Industry, and whose fleet consists of vessels the gross registered tonnage of which was at least 7,800, as stated in the American Bureau of Shipping Record, and

(ii) whose fleet during any 5 years from the period 1970 through and including 1979 has experienced a 33 percent or more increase in the contribution units as measured from the average annual contribution units for the calendar years 1970 and 1971.

Act Sec. 108. (c)(3)(A) For the purpose of determining the withdrawal liability of an employer under title IV of the Employee Retirement Income Security Act of 1974 from a plan that terminates while the plan is insolvent (within the meaning of section 4245 of such Act), the plan's unfunded vested benefits shall be reduced by an amount equal to the sum of all overburden credits that were applied in determining the plan's accumulated funding deficiency for all plan years preceding the first plan year in which the plan is insolvent, plus interest thereon.

(B) The provisions of subparagraph (A) apply only if—

(i) the plan would have been eligible for the overburden credit in the last plan year beginning before the date of the enactment of this Act, if section 4243 of the Employee Retirement Income Security Act of 1974 had been in effect for that plan year, and

(ii) the Pension Benefit Guaranty Corporation determines that the reduction of unfunded vested benefits under subparagraph (A) would not significantly increase the risk of loss to the corporation.

Act Sec. 108. (c)(4) In the case of an employer who withdrew before the date of enactment of this Act from a multiemployer plan covering employees in the seagoing industry (as determined by the corporation), sections 4201 through 4219 of the Employee Retirement Income Security Act of 1974, as added by this Act, are effective as of May 3, 1979. For the purpose of applying section 4217 for purposes of the preceding sentence, the date "May 2, 1979," shall be substituted for "April 28, 1980," and the date "May 3, 1979" shall be substituted for "April 29, 1980". For purposes of this paragraph, terms which are used in title IV of the Employee Retirement Income Security Act of 1974, or in regulations prescribed under that title, and which are used in the preceding sentence have the same meaning as when used in that Act or those regulations. For purposes of this paragraph, the term "employer" includes only a substantial employer covering employees in the seagoing industry (as so determined) in connection with ports on the West Coast of the United States, but does not include an employer who withdrew from a plan because of a change in the collective bargaining representative.

Act Sec. 108. (d) For purposes of section 4205 of the Employee Retirement Income Security Act of 1974—

(1) subsection (a)(1) of such section shall not apply to any plan year beginning before September 26, 1982,

(2) subsection (a)(2) of such section shall not apply with respect to any cessation of contribution obligations occurring before September 26, 1980, and

(3) in applying subsection (b) of such section, the employer's contribution base units for any plan year ending before September 26, 1980, shall be deemed to be equal to the employer's contribution base units for the last plan year ending before such date.

Amendment:

P.L. 98-369, §558(b)(2):

Amended Sec. 108(d) by striking out "April 29, 1982" in paragraph (1) and inserting "September 26, 1982" and by striking out "April 29, 1980" in paragraphs (2) and (3) inserting "September 26, 1980."

Act Sec. 108. (e)(1) In the case of a partial withdrawal under section 4205 of the Employee Retirement Income Security Act of 1974, an employer who—

(A) before December 13, 1979, had publicly announced the total cessation of covered operations at a facility in a State (and such cessation occurred within 12 months after the announcement),

(B) had not been obligated to make contributions to the plan on behalf of the employees at such facility for more than 8 years before the discontinuance of contributions, and

(C) after the discontinuance of contributions does not within 1 year after the date of the partial withdrawal perform work in the same State of the type for which contributions were previously required,

shall be liable under such section with respect to such partial withdrawal in an amount not greater than the amount determined under paragraph (2).

(2) The amount determined under this paragraph is the excess (if any) of—

(A) the present value (on the withdrawal date) of the benefits under the plan which—

(i) were vested on the withdrawal date (or, if earlier, at the time of separation from service with the employer at the facility),

(ii) were accrued by employees who on December 13, 1979 (or, if earlier, at the time of separation from service with the employer at the facility), were employed at the facility, and

(iii) are attributable to service with the withdrawing employer, over (B)(i) the sum of—

(I) all employer contributions to the plan on behalf of employees at the facility before the withdrawal date,

(II) interest (to the withdrawal date) on amounts described in subclause (I), and

(III) $100,000, reduced by

(ii) the sum of—

(I) the benefits paid under the plan on or before the withdrawal date with respect to former employees who separated from employment at the facility, and

(II) interest (to the withdrawal date) on amount described in subclause (I).

(3) For purposes of paragraph (2)—

(A) actuarial assumptions shall be those used in the last actuarial report completed before December 13, 1979,

(B) the term "withdrawal date" means the date on which the employer ceased work at the facility of the type for which contributions were previously required, and

(C) the term "facility" means the facility referred to in paragraph (1).

* * *

[¶15,728E]

Act Sec. 210 EFFECTIVE DATE.

Act Sec. 210. (a) Except as otherwise provided in this section, the amendments made by this title shall take effect on the date of the enactment of this Act.

Act Sec. 210. (b) Subpart C of part I of subchapter D of chapter 1 of such Code (as added by this Act) shall take effect, with respect to each plan, on the first day of the first plan year beginning on or after the earlier of—

(1) the date on which the last collective-bargaining agreement providing for employer contributions under the plan, which was in effect on the date of the enactment of this Act, expires, without regard to extensions agreed to after such date of enactment, or

(2) 3 years after the date of the enactment of this Act.

Act Sec. 210. (c) The amendments made by section 209 shall apply to taxable years ending after the date of the enactment of this Act.

* * *

[¶15,728F]

Act Sec. 405 ACTION TAKEN BEFORE REGULATIONS ARE PRESCRIBED.

Act Sec. 405. (a) Except as otherwise provided in the amendments made by this Act and in subsection (b), if the way in which any such amendment will apply to a particular circumstance is to be set forth in regulations, any reasonable action during the period before such regulations take effect shall be treated as complying with such regulations for such period.

Act Sec. 405. (b) Subsection (a) shall not apply to any action which violates any instruction issued, or temporary rule prescribed, by the agency having jurisdiction but only if such instruction or rule was published, or furnished to the party taking the action, before such action was taken.

* * *

[¶15,728G]

Act Sec. 408 DEDUCTIBILITY OF PAYMENTS TO PLAN BY A CORPORATION OPERATING PUBLIC TRANSPORTATION SYSTEM ACQUIRED BY A STATE.

Act Sec. 408. (a) For purposes of subsection (g) of section 404 of the Internal Revenue Code of 1954 (relating to certain employer liability payments considered as contributions), as amended by section 205 of this Act, any payment made to a plan covering employees of a corporation operating a public transportation system shall be treated as a payment described in paragraph (1) of such subsection if—

(1) such payment is made to fund accrued benefits under the plan in conjunction with an acquisition by a State (or agency or instrumentality thereof) of the stock or assets of such corporation, and

(2) such acquisition is pursuant to a State public transportation law enacted after June 30, 1979, and before January 1, 1980.

Act Sec. 408. (b) The provisions of this section shall apply to payments made after June 29, 1980.

* * *

[¶15,728H]

Act Sec. 412 STUDIES BY PENSION BENEFIT GUARANTY CORPORATION AND SECRETARY OF LABOR.

Act Sec. 412. (a)(1) The Pension Benefit Guaranty Corporation shall conduct a separate study with respect to—

(A) the advantages and disadvantages of establishing a graduated premium rate schedule under section 4006 of the Employee Retirement Income and Security Act of 1974 which is based on risk, and

(B) the necessity of adopting special rules in cases of union-mandated withdrawal from multiemployer pension plans.

(2) The Corporation shall report to the Congress the results of the studies conducted under paragraph (1), including its recommendations with respect thereto.

Act Sec. 412. (b)(1) The Secretary of Labor shall study the feasibility of requiring collective bargaining on both the issues of contributions to, and benefits from, multiemployer plans.

(2) The Secretary shall submit a report on the study conducted under paragraph (1) to the Congress within 3 years of the date of the enactment of this Act.

[¶15,728I]

Act Sec. 413 STUDY BY GENERAL ACCOUNTING OFFICE; HEARINGS REQUIRED.

Act Sec. 413. (a)(1) The Comptroller General of the United States shall conduct a study of the effects of the amendments made by, and the provisions of, this Act on—

(A) participants, beneficiaries, employers, employer organizations, and other parties affected by this Act, and

(B) the self-sufficiency of the fund established under section 4005 of the Employee Retirement Income Security Act of 1974 with respect to benefits guaranteed under section 4022A of such Act, taking into account the financial conditions of multiemployer plans and employers.

(2)(A) The Comptroller General shall report to the Congress no later than June 30, 1985, the results of the study conducted under paragraph (1), including his recommendations with respect thereto.

(B) The report submitted under subparagraph (A) shall be made available to the public.

Act Sec. 413. (b) In conducting the study under subsection(a)(1), the Comptroller General shall consult with the Committees on Finance and Labor and Human Resources of the Senate and the Committees on Education and Labor and Ways and Means of the House of Representatives.

Act Sec. 413. (c) The committees described in subsection (b) shall conduct hearings on the report and recommendations submitted under subsection (a)(2).

Act Sec. 413. (d) For purposes of conducting the study required by this section, the Comptroller General, or any of his duly authorized representatives, shall have access to and the right to examine and copy any books, documents, papers, records, or other recorded information—

(1) within the possession or control of the administrator or the sponsor of any plan, and

(2) which the Comptroller General or his representative finds, in his own judgment, pertinent to such study.

The Comptroller General shall not disclose the identity of any individual in making any information obtained under this subsection available to the public.

* * *

[¶15,728J]

Act Sec. 415 INCREASE IN LENGTH OF SERVICE IN ARMED FORCES REQUIRED FOR EX-SERVICEMEN TO BE ELIGIBLE FOR UNEMPLOYMENT BENEFITS.

Act Sec. 415. (a) GENERAL RULE. Subparagraph (A) of section 8521(a)(1) of title 5 of the United States Code is amended by striking out "90 days or more" and inserting in lieu thereof "365 days or more".

Act Sec. 415. (b) EFFECTIVE DATE. The amendment made by subsection (a) shall apply with respect to determinations of Federal service in the case of individuals filing claims for unemployment compensation on or after October 1, 1980.

[¶15,728K]

Act Sec. 416 CESSATION OF EXTENDED BENEFITS WHEN PAID UNDER AN INTERSTATE CLAIM IN A STATE WHERE EXTENDED BENEFIT PERIOD IS NOT IN EFFECT.

Act Sec. 416. (a) GENERAL RULE. Section 202 of the Federal-State Extended Unemployment Compensation Act of 1970 is amended by adding at the end thereof the following new subsection:

"Cessation of Extended Benefits When Paid Under an Interstate Claim in a State Where Extended Benefit Period Is Not in Effect

"(c)"(c)(1) Except as provided in paragraph (2), payment of extended compensation shall not be made to any individual for any week if—

"(c)(1)(A) extended compensation would (but for this subsection) have been payable for such week pursuant to an interstate claim filed in any State under the interstate benefit payment plan, and

"(c)(1)(B) an extended benefit period is not in effect for such week in such State.

"(c)(2) Paragraph (1) shall not apply with respect to the first 2 weeks for which extended compensation is payable (determined without regard to this subsection) pursuant to an interstate claim filed under the interstate benefit payment plan to the individual from the extended compensation account estabished for the benefit year.

"(c)(3) Section 3304(a)(9)(A) of the Internal Revenue Code of 1954 shall not apply to any denial of compensation required under this subsection."

Act Sec. 416. (b) EFFECTIVE DATE.—

(1) IN GENERAL. The amendment made by subsection (a) shall apply to weeks of unemployment beginning after October 1, 1980; except that such amendment shall not be a requirement of any State law under section 3304(a)(11) of the Internal Revenue Code of 1954 for any week which begins before June 1, 1981.

(2) SPECIAL RULE FOR CERTAIN STATES. In the case of any State the legislature of which does not meet in a regular session which begins during calendar year 1981 and before April 1, 1981, paragraph (1) shall be applied by substituting "June 1, 1982" for "June 1, 1981".

Age Discrimination in Employment Act of 1967, As Amended

(Act of December 6, 1967, P.L. 90-202, 81 Stat. 609, 29 U.S.C., 1964 Ed., Supplement IV, Chapter 14, Sections 621-634, effective June 12, 1968, as amended by P.L. 93-259, effective May 1, 1974, and as further amended by P.L. 95-256, effective January 1, 1979; by P.L. 97-248, effective January 1, 1983; by P.L. 98-459, effective October 9, 1984; by P.L. 99-509, effective January 1, 1988; by P.L. 99-592, effective January 1, 1987; by P.L. 101-239, effective December 19, 1989; by P.L. 101-433, effective November 5, 1990; by P.L. 101-521, effective November 5, 1990; and by P.L. 102-166, effective November 21, 1991.)

[¶ 15,731]

Act Sec. 1 TITLE OF ACT.

This Act may be cited as the "Age Discrimination in Employment Act of 1967."

[¶ 15,732]

Act Sec. 2 STATEMENT OF FINDINGS AND PURPOSE.

(a) The Congress hereby finds and declares that—

(1) in the face of rising productivity and affluence, older workers find themselves disadvantaged in their efforts to retain employment, and especially to regain employment when displaced from jobs;

(2) the setting of arbitrary age limits regardless of potential for job performance has become a common practice, and certain otherwise desirable practices may work to the disadvantage of older persons;

(3) the incidence of unemployment, especially long-term unemployment with resultant deterioration of skill, morale, and employer acceptability, is, relative to the younger ages, high among older workers; their numbers are great and growing; and their employment problems grave;

(4) the existence in industries affecting commerce of arbitrary discrimination in employment because of age burdens commerce and the free flow of goods in commerce.

(b) It is therefore the purpose of this Act to promote employment of older persons based on their ability rather than age; to prohibit arbitrary age discrimination in employment; to help employers and workers find ways of meeting problems arising from the impact of age on employment.

[¶ 15,733]

Act Sec. 3 EDUCATION AND RESEARCH PROGRAM.

(a) The Secretary of Labor shall undertake studies and provide information to labor unions, management, and the general public concerning the needs and abilities of older workers, and their potentials for continued employment and contribution to the economy. In order to achieve the purposes of this Act, the Secretary of Labor shall carry on a continuing program of education and information, under which he may, among other measures—

(1) undertake research, and promote research, with a view to reducing barriers to the employment of older persons, and the promotion of measures for utilizing their skills;

(2) publish and otherwise make available to employers, professional societies, the various media of communication, and other interested persons the findings of studies and other materials for the promotion of employment;

(3) foster through the public employment service system and through cooperative effort the development of facilities of public and private agencies for expanding the opportunities and potentials of older persons;

(4) sponsor and assist State and community informational and educational programs.

(b) Not later than six months after the effective date of this Act, the Secretary shall recommend to the Congress any measures he may deem desirable to change the lower or upper age limits set forth in section 12.

[¶ 15,734]

Act Sec. 4 PROHIBITION OF AGE DISCRIMINATION.

(a) It shall be unlawful for an employer—

(1) to fail or refuse to hire or to discharge any individual or otherwise discriminate against any individual with respect to his compensation, terms, conditions, or privileges of employment, because of such individual's age;

(2) to limit, segregate, or classify his employees in any way which would deprive or tend to deprive any individual of employment opportunities or otherwise adversely affect his status as an employee, because of such individual's age; or

(3) to reduce the wage rate of any employee in order to comply with this Act.

(b) It shall be unlawful for an employment agency to fail or refuse to refer for employment, or otherwise to discriminate against, any individual because of such individual's age, or to classify or refer for employment any individual on the basis of such individual's age.

(c) It shall be unlawful for a labor organization—

(1) to exclude or to expel from its membership, or otherwise to discriminate against, any individual because of his age;

(2) to limit, segregate, or classify its membership, or to classify or fail or refuse to refer for employment any individual, in any way which would deprive or tend to deprive any individual of employment opportunities, or would limit such employment opportunities or otherwise adversely affect his status as an employee or as an applicant for employment, because of such individual's age;

(3) to cause or attempt to cause an employer to discriminate against an individual in violation of this section.

(d) It shall be unlawful for an employer to discriminate against any of his employees or applicants for employment, for an employment agency to discriminate against any individual, or for a labor organization to discriminate against any member thereof or applicant for membership, because such individual, member or applicant for membership has opposed any practice made unlawful by this section, or because such individual, member, or applicant for membership has made a charge, testified, assisted, or participated in any manner in an investigation, proceeding, or litigation under this Act.

(e) It shall be unlawful for an employer, labor organization, or employment agency to print or publish, or cause to be printed or published, any notice or advertisement relating to employment by such an employer or membership in or any classification or referral for employment by such a labor organization, or relating to any classification or referral for employment by such an employment agency, indicating any preference, limitation, specification, or discrimination, based on age.

(f) It shall not be unlawful for an employer, employment agency, or labor organization—

(1) to take any action otherwise prohibited under subsections (a), (b), (c), or (e) of this section where age is a bona fide occupational qualification reasonably necessary to the normal operation of the particular business, or where the differentiation is based on reasonable factors other than age, or where

such practices involve an employee in a workplace in a foreign country, and compliance with such subsections would cause such employer, or a corporation controlled by such employer, to violate the laws of the country in which such workplace is located.

(2) to take any action otherwise prohibited under subsection (a), (b), (c), or (e) of this section—

(A) to observe the terms of a bona fide seniority system that is not intended to evade the purposes of this Act, except that no such seniority system shall require or permit the involuntary retirement of any individual specified by section 12(a) because of the age of such individual; or

(B) to observe the terms of a bona fide employee benefit plan—

(i) where, for each benefit or benefit package, the actual amount of payment made or cost incurred on behalf of an older worker is no less than that made or incurred on behalf of a younger worker, as permissible under section 1625.10, title 29, Code of Federal Regulations (as in effect on June 22, 1989); or

(ii) that is a voluntary early retirement incentive plan consistent with the relevant purpose or purposes of this Act.

Notwithstanding clause (i) or (ii) of subparagraph (B), no such employee benefit plan or voluntary early retirement incentive plan shall excuse the failure to hire any individual, and no such employee benefit plan shall require or permit the involuntary retirement of any individual specified by section 12(a), because of the age of such individual. An employer, employment agency, or labor organization acting under subparagraph (A), or under clause (i) or (ii) of subparagraph (B), shall have the burden of proving that such actions are lawful in any civil enforcement proceeding brought under this Act; or

(3) to discharge or otherwise discipline an individual for good cause.

(g) [Repealed]

(h)(1) If an employer controls a corporation whose place of incorporation is in a foreign country, any practice by such corporation prohibited under this section shall be presumed to be such practice by such employer.

(2) The prohibitions of this section shall not apply where the employer is a foreign person not controlled by an American employer.

(3) For the purpose of this subsection the determination of whether an employer controls a corporation shall be based upon the—

(A) interrelation of operations,

(B) common management,

(C) centralized control of labor relations, and

(D) common ownership or financial control,

of the employer and the corporation.

(i)(1) Except as otherwise provided in this subsection, it shall be unlawful for an employer, an employment agency, a labor organization, or any combination thereof to establish or maintain an employee pension benefit plan which requires or permits—

(A) in the case of a defined benefit plan, the cessation of an employee's benefit accrual, or the reduction of the rate of an employee's benefit accrual, because of age, or

(B) in the case of a defined contribution plan, the cessation of allocations to an employee's account, or the reduction of the rate at which amounts are allocated to an employee's account, because of age.

(2) Nothing in this section shall be construed to prohibit an employer, employment agency, or labor organization from observing any provision of an employee pension benefit plan to the extent that such provision imposes (without regard to age) a limitation on the amount of benefits that the plan provides or a limitation on the number of years of service or years of participation which are taken into account for purposes of determining benefit accrual under the plan.

(3) In the case of any employee who, as of the end of any plan year under a defined benefit plan, has attained normal retirement age under such plan—

(A) if distribution of benefits under such plan with respect to such employee has commenced as of the end of such plan year, then any requirement of this subsection for continued accrual of benefits under such plan with respect to such employee during such plan year shall be treated as satisfied to the extent of the actuarial equivalent of in-service distribution of benefits, and

(B) if distribution of benefits under such plan with respect to such employee has not commenced as of the end of such year in accordance with section 206(a)(3) of the Employee Retirement Income Security Act of 1974 and section 401(a)(14)(C) of the Internal Revenue Code of 1986, and the payment of benefits under such plan with respect to such employee is not suspended during such plan year pursuant to section 203(a)(3)(B) of the Employee Retirement Income Security Act of 1974 or section 411(a)(3)(B) of the Internal Revenue Code of 1986, then any requirement of this subsection for continued accrual of benefits under such plan with respect to such employee during such plan year shall be treated as satisfied to the extent of any adjustment in the benefit payable under the plan during such plan year attributable to the delay in the distribution of benefits after the attainment of normal retirement age.

The provisions of this paragraph shall apply in accordance with regulations of the Secretary of the Treasury. Such regulations shall provide for the application of the preceding provisions of this paragraph to all employee pension benefit plans subject to this subsection and may provide for the application of such provisions, in the case of any such employee, with respect to any period of time within a plan year.

(4) Compliance with the requirements of this subsection with respect to an employee pension benefit plan shall constitute compliance with the requirements of this section relating to benefit accrual under such plan.

(5) Paragraph (1) shall not apply with respect to any employee who is a highly compensated employee (within the meaning of section 414(q) of the Internal Revenue Code of 1986) to the extent provided in regulations prescribed by the Secretary of the Treasury for purposes of precluding discrimination in favor of highly compensated employees within the meaning of subchapter D of chapter 1 of the Internal Revenue Code of 1986.

(6) A plan shall not be treated as failing to meet the requirements of paragraph (1) solely because the subsidized portion of any early retirement benefit is disregarded in determining benefit accruals or it is a plan permitted by subsection (m) of this section.

(7) Any regulations prescribed by the Secretary of the Treasury pursuant to clause (v) of section 411(b)(1)(H) of the Internal Revenue Code of 1986 and subparagraphs (C) and (D) of section 411(b)(2) of such Code shall apply with respect to the requirement of this subsection in the same manner and to the same extent as such regulations apply with respect to the requirements of such sections 411(b)(1)(H) and 411(b)(2).

(8) A plan shall not be treated as failing to meet the requirements of this section solely because such plan provides a normal retirement age described in section 3(24)(B) of the Employee Retirement Income Security Act of 1974 and section 411(a)(8)(B) of the Internal Revenue Code of 1986.

(9) For purposes of this subsection—

(A) The terms "employee pension benefit plan", "defined benefit plan", "defined contribution plan", and "normal retirement age" have the meanings provided such terms in section 3 of the Employee Retirement Income Security Act of 1974 (29 U.S.C. 1002).

(B) The term "compensation" has the meaning provided by section 414(s) of the Internal Revenue Code of 1986.

(j) It shall not be unlawful for an employer which is a State, a political subdivision of a State, an agency or instrumentality of a State or a political subdivision of a State, or an interstate agency to fail or refuse to hire or to discharge any individual because of such individual's age if such action is taken—

(1) with respect to the employment of an individual as a firefighter or as a law enforcement officer, the employer has complied with section 3(d)(2) of the Age Discrimination in Employment Amendments of 1996 if the individual was discharged after the date described in such section, and the individual has attained—

    (A) the age of hiring or retirement, respectively, in effect under applicable State or local law on March 3, 1983, or

    (B)(i) if the individual was not hired, the age of hiring in effect on the date of such failure or refusal to hire under applicable State or local law after September 30, 1996; or

      (ii) if applicable State or local law was enacted after September 30, 1996, and the individual was discharged, the higher of—

        (I) the age of retirement in effect on the date of such discharge under such law; and

        (II) age 55; and

(2) pursuant to a bona fide hiring or retirement plan that is not a subterfuge to evade the purposes of this chapter.

(k) A seniority system or employee benefit plan shall comply with this Act regardless of the date of adoption of such system or plan.

(l) Notwithstanding clause (i) or (ii) of subsection (f)(2)(B)—

(1) It shall not be a violation of subsection (a), (b), (c), or (e) solely because—

    (A) an employee pension benefit plan (as defined in section 3(2) of the Employee Retirement Income Security Act of 1974 (29 U.S.C. 1002(2))) provides for the attainment of a minimum age as a condition of eligibility for normal or early retirement benefits; or

    (B) a defined benefit plan (as defined in section 3(35) of such Act) provides for—

      (i) payments that constitute the subsidized portion of an early retirement benefit; or

      (ii) social security supplements for plan participants that commence before the age and terminate at the age (specified by the plan) when participants are eligible to receive reduced or unreduced old-age insurance benefits under title II of the Social Security Act (42 U.S.C. 401 et seq.), and that do not exceed such old-age insurance benefits.

(2)(A) It shall not be a violation of subsection (a), (b), (c) or (e) solely because following a contingent event unrelated to age—

      (i) the value of any retiree health benefits received by an individual eligible for an immediate pension;

      (ii) the value of any additional pension benefits that are made available solely as a result of the contingent event unrelated to age and following which the individual is eligible for not less than an immediate and unreduced pension; or

      (iii) the values described in both clauses (i) and (ii)

are deducted from severance pay made available as a result of the contingent event unrelated to age.

    (B) For an individual who receives immediate pension benefits that are actuarially reduced under subparagraph (A)(i), the amount of the deduction available pursuant to subparagraph (A)(i) shall be reduced by the same percentage as the reduction in the pension benefits.

    (C) For purposes of this paragraph, severance pay shall include that portion of supplemental unemployment compensation benefits (as described in section 501(c)(17) of the Internal Revenue Code of 1986) that—

      (i) constitutes additional benefits of up to 52 weeks;

      (ii) has the primary purpose and effect of continuing benefits until an individual becomes eligible for an immediate and unreduced pension; and

      (iii) is discontinued once the individual becomes eligible for an immediate and unreduced pension.

    (D) For purposes of this paragraph and solely in order to make the deduction authorized under this paragraph, the term "retiree health benefits" means benefits provided pursuant to a group health plan covering retirees, for which (determined as of the contingent event unrelated to age)—

      (i) the package of benefits provided by the employer for the retirees who are below age 65 is at least comparable to benefits provided under title XVIII of the Social Security Act (42 U.S.C. 1395 et seq.);

      (ii) the package of benefits provided by the employer for the retirees who are age 65 and above is at least comparable to that offered under a plan that provides a benefit package with one-fourth the value of benefits provided under title XVIII of such Act

      (iii) the package of benefits provided by the employer is as described in clauses (i) and (ii).

    (E)(i) If the obligation of the employer to provide retiree health benefits is of limited duration, the value for each individual shall be calculated at a rate of $3,000 per year for benefit years before age 65, and $750 per year for benefit years beginning at age 65 and above.

      (ii) If the obligation of the employer to provide retiree health benefits is of unlimited duration, the value for each individual shall be calculated at a rate of $48,000 for individuals below age 65, and $24,000 for individuals age 65 and above.

      (iii) The values described in clauses (i) and (ii) shall be calculated based on the age of the individual as of the date of the contingent event unrelated to age. The values are effective on the date of enactment of this subsection, and shall be adjusted on an annual basis, with respect to a contingent event that occurs subsequent to the first year after the date of enactment of this subsection, based on the medical component of the Consumer Price Index for all-urban consumers published by the Department of Labor.

      (iv) If an individual is required to pay a premium for retiree health benefits, the value calculated pursuant to this subparagraph shall be reduced by whatever percentage of the overall premium the individual is required to pay.

    (F) If an employer that has implemented a deduction pursuant to subparagraph (A) fails to fulfill the obligation described in subparagraph (E), any aggrieved individual may bring an action for specific performance of the obligation described in subparagraph (E). The relief shall be in addition to any other remedies provided under Federal or State law.

(3) It shall not be a violation of subsection (a), (b), (c), or (e) solely because an employer provides a bona fide employee benefit plan or plans under which long-term disability benefits received by a individual are reduced by any pension benefits (other than those attributable to employee contributions)—

    (A) paid to the individual that the individual voluntarily elects to receive; or

    (B) for which an individual who has attained the later of age 62 or normal retirement age is eligible.

(m) Notwithstanding subsection (f)(2)(B) of this section, it shall not be a violation of subsection (a), (b), (c), or (e) of this section solely because a plan of an institution of higher education (as defined in section 1001 of title 20) offers employees who are serving under a contract of unlimited tenure (or similar arrangement providing for unlimited tenure) supplemental benefits upon voluntary retirement that are reduced or eliminated on the basis of age, if—

(1) such institution does not implement with respect to such employees any age-based reduction or cessation of benefits that are not such supplemental benefits, except as permitted by other provisions of this chapter;

(2) such supplemental benefits are in addition to any retirement or severance benefits which have been offered generally to employees serving under a contract of unlimited tenure (or similar arrangement providing for unlimited tenure), independent of any early retirement or exit-incentive plan, within the preceding 365 days; and

(3) any employee who attains the minimum age and satisfies all non-age-based conditions for receiving a benefit under the plan has an opportunity lasting not less than 180 days to elect to retire and to receive the maximum benefit that could then be elected by a younger but otherwise similarly situated employee, and the plan does not require retirement to occur sooner than 180 days after such election.

Amendments

P.L. 105-244, Act Sec. 941(b) amended ADEA Sec. 4(i)(6), by inserting "or it is a plan permitted by subsection (m)" following "benefit accruals".

P.L. 105-244, Act Sec. 941(a) amended ADEA Sec. 4(j)(1) to read as above.

P.L. 105-244, Act Sec. 941(a) added ADEA Sec. 4(m).

P.L. 101-521, Act Sec. (1) amended ADEA Sec. 4(1)(2)(A), as added by P.L. 101-433, by striking "and" at the end of clause (i), by striking the comma at the end of clause (ii) and inserting "; or" and by inserting new clause (iii) to read as above, effective November 5, 1990. See also Act Sec. 105, below.

P.L. 101-521, Act Sec. (2) amended ADEA Sec. 4(1)(2)(D), as added by P.L. 101-433, by inserting "and solely in order to make the deduction authorized under this paragraph" after "For purposes of this paragraph," by striking "and" at the end of clause (i), by striking the period at the end of clause (ii) and inserting "; or" and by inserting new clause (iii) to read as above, effective November 5, 1990. See also Act Sec. 105, below.

P.L. 101-433, Sec. 103(1) amended ADEA Sec. 4(f) by striking paragraph (2) and inserting new paragraph (2) to read as above, effective with respect to any employee benefits established or modified after October 16, 1990, and other conduct occurring after April 14, 1991. See also Act Sec. 105, below. Prior to amendment, paragraph (2) read as follows:

"(2) to observe the terms of a bona fide seniority system or any bona fide employee benefit plan such as a retirement, pension, or insurance plan, which is not a subterfuge to evade the purposes of this Act, except that no such employee benefit plan shall excuse the failure to hire any individual or permit the involuntary retirement of any individual specified by section 12(a) of this Act because of the age of such individual;"

P.L. 101-433, Sec. 103(2) redesignated ADEA Sec. 4(i) [the second (i)] as (j), effective with respect to any employee benefits established or modified after October 16, 1990, and other conduct occurring after April 14, 1991. See also Act Sec. 105, below.

P.L. 101-433, Sec. 103(3) amended ADEA Sec. 4 by adding new paragraph (k) to read as above, effective with respect to any employee benefits established or modified after October 16, 1990, and other conduct occurring after April 14, 1991. See also Act Sec. 105, below.

P.L. 101-433, Sec. 103(3) amended ADEA Sec. 4 by adding new paragraph (l) to read as above, effective with respect to any employee benefits established or modified after October 16, 1990, and other conduct occurring after April 14, 1991. See also Act Sec. 105, below.

P.L. 101-433, Act. Sec. 105 provides:

SEC. 105. EFFECTIVE DATE.—(a) IN GENERAL.—Except as otherwise provided in this section, this title and the amendments made by this title shall apply only to—

(1) any employee benefit established or modified on or after the date of enactment of this Act; and

(2) other conduct occurring more than 180 days after the date of enactment of this Act.

(b) COLLECTIVELY BARGAINED AGREEMENTS.—With respect to any employee benefits provided in accordance with a collective bargaining agreement—

(1) that is in effect as of the date of enactment of this Act;

(2) that terminates after such date of enactment;

(3) any provision of which was entered into by a labor organization (as defined by section 6(d)(4) of the Fair Labor Standards Act of 1938 (29 U.S.C. 206(d)(4))); and

(4) that contains any provision that would be superseded (in whole or part) by this title and the amendments made by this title, but for the operation of this section,

this title and the amendments made by this title shall not apply until the termination of such collective bargaining agreement or June 1, 1992, whichever occurs first.

(c) STATES AND POLITICAL SUBDIVISIONS.—

(1) IN GENERAL.—With respect to any employee benefits provided by an employer—

(A) that is a State or political subdivision of a State or any agency or instrumentality of a State or political subdivision of a State; and

(B) that maintained an employee benefit plan at any time between June 23, 1989, and the date of enactment of this Act that would be superseded (in whole or part) by this title and the amendments made by this title but for the operation of this subsection, and which plan may be modified only through a change in applicable State or local law,

this title and the amendments made by this title shall not apply until the date that is 2 years after the date of enactment of this Act.

(2) ELECTION OF DISABILITY COVERAGE FOR EMPLOYEES HIRED PRIOR TO EFFECTIVE DATE.—

(A) IN GENERAL.—An employer that maintains a plan described in paragraph (1)(B) may, with regard to disability benefits provided pursuant to such a plan—

(i) following reasonable notice to all employees, implement new disability benefits that satisfy the requirements of the Age Discrimination in Employment Act of 1967 (as amended by this title); and

(ii) then offer to each employee covered by a plan described in paragraph (1)(B) the option to elect such new disability benefits in lieu of the existing disability benefits, if—

(I) the offer is made and reasonable notice provided no later than the date that is 2 years after the date of enactment of this Act; and

(II) the employee is given up to 180 days after the offer in which to make the election.

(B) PREVIOUS DISABILITY BENEFITS.—If the employee does not elect to be covered by the new disability benefits, the employer may continue to cover the employee under the previous disability benefits even though such previous benefits do not otherwise satisfy the requirements of the Age Discrimination in Employment Act of 1967 (as amended by this title).

(C) ABROGATION OF RIGHT TO RECEIVE BENEFITS.—An election of coverage under the new disability benefits shall abrogate any right the electing employee may have had to receive existing disability benefits. The employee shall maintain any years of service accumulated for purposes of determining eligibility for the new benefits.

(3) STATE ASSISTANCE.—The Equal Employment Opportunity Commission, the Secretary of Labor, and the Secretary of the Treasury shall, on request, provide to States assistance in identifying and securing independent technical advice to assist in complying with this subsection.

(4) DEFINITIONS.—For purposes of this subsection:

(A) EMPLOYER AND STATE.—The terms "employer" and "State" shall have the respective meanings provided such terms under subsections (b) and (i) of section 11 of the Age Discrimination in Employment Act of 1967 (29 U.S.C. 630).

(B) DISABILITY BENEFITS.—The term "disability benefits" means any program for employees of a State or political subdivision of a State that provides long-term disability benefits, whether on an insured basis in a separate employee benefit plan or as part of an employee pension benefit plan.

(C) REASONABLE NOTICE.—The term "reasonable notice" means, with respect to notice of new disability benefits described in paragraph (2)(A) that is given to each employee, notice that—

(i) is sufficiently accurate and comprehensive to apprise the employee of the terms and conditions of the disability benefits, including whether the employee is immediately eligible for such benefits; and

(ii) is written in a manner calculated to be understood by the average employee eligible to participate.

(d) DISCRIMINATION IN EMPLOYEE PENSION BENEFIT PLANS.—Nothing in this title, or the amendments made by this title, shall be construed as limiting the prohibitions against discrimination that are set forth in section 4(j) of the Age Discrimination in Employment Act of 1967 (as redesignated by section 103(2) of this Act).

(e) CONTINUED BENEFIT PAYMENTS.—Notwithstanding any other provision of this section, on and after the effective date of this title and the amendments made by this title (as determined in accordance with subsections (a), (b), and (c)), this title and the amendments made by this title shall not apply to a series of benefit payments made to an individual or the individual's representative that began prior to the effective date and that continue after the effective date pursuant to an arrangement that was in effect on the effective date, except that no substantial modification to such arrangement may be made after the date of enactment of this Act if the intent of the modification is to evade the purposes of this Act.

P.L. 101-239, §6202(b)(3)(C) amended ADEA Sec. 4(g) by striking section 4(g) effective for items and services furnished after December 19, 1989.

P.L. 99-592, Sec. 2 (a), amended ADEA Sec. 4(g)(1) by striking out "through 69" each place it appears and inserting in lieu thereof "or older." Sec. 2(b) amended ADEA Sec. 4(g) by striking out "(g)(1)" and inserting in lieu thereof "(h)(1)." It should be noted that these amendments had already been made by P.L. 99-272.

P.L. 99-592, Sec. 3(a), added ADEA Sec. 4(i). P.L. 99-509 also added an ADEA Sec. 4(i). ADEA Sec. 4(i), as added by P.L. 99-592, had been designated as Sec 4(i)[j]. Sec. 3(b) provides that the amendment made by Sec. 3(a), which adds the measure in Sec. 4(i)[j] concerning firefighters and law enforcement officers, is repealed December 31, 1993.

P.L. 99-592, Sec. 7, provides:

"SEC. 7. EFFECTIVE DATE; APPLICATION OF AMENDMENTS.—(a) IN GENERAL.—Except as provided in subsection (b), this Act and the amendments made by this Act shall take effect on January 1, 1987, except that with respect to any employee who is subject to a collective-bargaining agreement—

"(1) which is in effect on June 30, 1986,

"(2) which terminates after January 1, 1987,

"(3) any provision of which was entered into by a labor organization (as defined by section 6(d)(4) of the Fair Labor Standards Act of 1938 (29 U.S.C. 206(d)(4)), and

"(4) which contains any provision that would be superseded by such amendments, but for the operation of this section, such amendments shall not apply until the termination of such collective bargaining agreement or January 1, 1990, whichever occurs first.

"(b) EFFECT ON EXISTING CAUSES OF ACTION.—The amendments made by sections 3 and 4 of this Act shall not apply with respect to any cause of action arising under the Age Discrimination in Employment Act of 1967 as in effect before January 1, 1987."

P.L. 99-592, Sec. 5, provides:

"SEC. 5. STUDY AND PROPOSED GUIDELINES RELATING TO POLICE OFFICERS AND FIREFIGHTERS.—(a) STUDY.—Not later than 4 years after the date of enactment of this Act, the Secretary of Labor and the Equal Employment Opportunity Commission, jointly, shall—

"(1) conduct a study—

"(A) to determine whether physical and mental fitness tests are valid measurements of the ability and competency of police officers and firefighters to perform the requirements of their jobs,

"(B) if such tests are found to be valid measurements of such ability and competency, to determine which particular types of tests most effectively measure such ability and competency, and

"(C) to develop recommendations with respect to specific standards that such tests, and the administration of such tests should satisfy, and

"(2) submit a report to the Speaker of the House of Representatives and the President pro tempore of the Senate that includes—

"(A) a description of the results of such study, and

"(B) a statement of the recommendations developed under paragraph (1)(C).

"(b) CONSULTATION REQUIREMENT.—The Secretary of Labor and the Equal Employment Opportunity Commission shall, during the conduct of the study required under subsection (a) and prior to the development of recommendations under paragraph (1)(C), consult with the United States Fire Administration, the Federal Emergency Management Agency, organizations representing law enforcement officers, firefighters, and their employers, and organizations representing older Americans.

"(c) PROPOSED GUIDELINES.—Not later than 5 years after the date of the enactment of this Act, the Equal Employment Opportunity Commission shall propose, in accordance with subchapter II of chapter 5 of title 5 of the United States Code, guidelines for the administration and use of physical and mental fitness tests to measure the ability and competency of police officers and firefighters to perform the requirements of their jobs."

P.L. 99-509, Sec. 9201, added ADEA Sec. 4(i). The relevant portion of Sec. 9204 of P.L. 99-509, concerning effective dates and regulations, provides as follows:

"SEC. 9204. EFFECTIVE DATE; REGULATIONS.—

"(a) APPLICABILITY TO EMPLOYEES WITH SERVICE AFTER 1988.—

"(1) IN GENERAL.—The amendments made by sections 9201 and 9202 shall apply only with respect to plan years beginning on or after January 1, 1988, and only to employees who have 1 hour of service in any plan year to which such amendments apply.

"(2) SPECIAL RULE FOR COLLECTIVELY BARGAINED PLANS.—In the case of a plan maintained pursuant to 1 or more collective bargaining agreements between employee representatives and 1 or more employers ratified before March 1, 1986, paragraph (1) shall be applied to benefits pursuant to, and individuals covered by, any such agreement by substituting for 'January 1, 1988' the date of the commencement of the first plan year beginning on or after the earlier of—

"(A) the later of—

"(i) January 1, 1988, or

"(ii) the date on which the last of such collective bargaining agreements terminates (determined without regard to any extension thereof after February 28, 1986), or

"(B) January 1, 1990.

* * *

"(c) PLAN AMENDMENTS.—If any amendment made by this subtitle requires an amendment to any plan, such plan amendment shall not be required to be made before the first plan year beginning on or after January 1, 1989, if—

"(1) during the period after such amendment takes effect and before such first plan year, the plan is operated in accordance with the requirements of such amendment, and

"(2) such plan amendment applies retroactively to the period after such amendment takes effect and such first plan year. A pension plan shall not be treated as failing to provide definitely determinable benefits or contributions, or to be operated in accordance with the provisions of the plan, merely because it operates in accordance with this subsection.

"(d) INTERAGENCY COORDINATION.—The regulations and rulings issued by the Secretary of Labor, the regulations and rulings issued by the Secretary of the Treasury, and the regulations and rulings issued by the Equal Employment Opportunity Commission pursuant to the amendments made by this subtitle shall each be consistent with the others. The Secretary of Labor, the Secretary of the Treasury, and the Equal Employment Opportunity Commission shall each consult with the other to the extent necessary to meet the requirements of the preceding sentence.

"(e) FINAL REGULATIONS.—The Secretary of Labor, the Secretary of the Treasury, and the Equal Employment Opportunity Commission shall each issue before February 1, 1988, such final regulations as may be necessary to carry out the amendments made by this subtitle."

P.L. 99-272, Sec. 9201(b)(1) amended ADEA Sec. 4(g)(1) by striking out "through 69" each place it appeared and inserting "or older" in its place. P.L. 99-272, Sec. 9201(b)(3) redesignated the second subsection (g), added by P.L. 98-459, Sec. 802(b)(2), as subsection (h).

P.L. 98-459, Sec. 802(b)(1) amended ADEA Sec. 4(f)(1) to read as above, effective October 9, 1984. Sec. 802(b)(2) added new ADEA Sec. 4(g) to read as above, effective October 9, 1984. Sec. 4(g) was later redesignated 4(h) by P.L. 99-272.

P.L. 98-369, Sec. 2301(b) amended Sec. 4(g), effective January 1, 1985, (1) by inserting ", and any employee's spouse aged 65 through 69," after "aged 65 through 69"; and (2) by inserting ", and the spouse of such employee," after "same conditions as any employee".

P.L. 97-248; Sec. 116(a), added Sec. 4(g), effective January 1, 1983.

Prior to amendment by P.L. 95-256, Sec. 4(f)(2) read as follows: "(2) to observe the terms of a bona fide seniority system or any bona fide employee benefit plan such as a retirement, pension, or insurance plan, which is not a subterfuge to evade the purposes of this Act, except that no such employee benefit plan shall excuse the failure to hire any individual; or".

[¶15,735]

Act Sec. 5 STUDY BY SECRETARY OF LABOR.

(a)(1) The Secretary of Labor is directed to undertake an appropriate study of institutional and other arrangements giving rise to involuntary retirement, and report his findings and any appropriate legislative recommendations to the President and to the Congress.

Such study shall include—

(A) an examination of the effect of the amendment made by section 3(a) of the Age Discrimination in Employment Act Amendments of 1978 in raising the upper age limitation established by section 12(a) of this Act to 70 years of age;

(B) a determination of the feasibility of eliminating such limitation;

(C) a determination of the feasibility of raising such limitation above 70 years of age; and

(D) an examination of the effect of the exemption contained in section 12(c), relating to certain executive employees, and the exemption contained in section 12(d), relating to tenured teaching personnel.

(a)(2) The Secretary may undertake the study required by paragraph (1) of this subsection directly or by contract or other arrangement.

(b) The report required by subsection (a) of this section shall be transmitted to the President and to the Congress as an interim report not later than January 1, 1981, and in final form not later than January 1, 1982.

Amendments

Prior to amendment by P.L. 95-256, entire Sec. 5 read as follows: "Sec. 5. The Secretary of Labor is directed to undertake an appropriate study of institutional and other arrangements giving rise to involuntary retirement, and report his findings and any appropriate legislative recommendations to the President and to the Congress."

[¶15,736]

Act Sec. 6 ADMINISTRATION.

The Secretary shall have the power—

(a) to make delegations, to appoint such agents and employees, and to pay for technical assistance on a fee-for-service basis, as he deems necessary to assist him in the performance of his functions under this Act;

(b) to cooperate with regional, State, local, and other agencies, and to cooperate with and furnish technical assistance to employers, labor organizations, and employment agencies to aid in effectuating the purposes of this Act.

[¶15,737]

Act Sec. 7 RECORDKEEPING, INVESTIGATION AND ENFORCEMENT.

(a) The Secretary shall have the power to make investigations and require the keeping of records necessary or appropriate for the administration of this Act in accordance with the powers and procedures provided in sections 9 and 11 of the Fair Labor Standards Act of 1938, as amended (29 U.S.C. 209 and 211).

(b) The provisions of this Act shall be enforced in accordance with the powers, remedies, and procedures provided in section 11(b), 16 (except for subsection (a) thereof), and 17 of the Fair Labor Standards Act of 1938, as amended (29 U.S.C. 211(b), 216, 217), and subsection (c) of this section. Any act prohibited under section 4 of this Act shall be deemed to be a prohibited act under section 15 of the Fair Labor Standards Act of 1938, as amended (29 U.S.C. 215). Amounts owing to a person as a result of a violation of this Act shall be deemed to be unpaid minimum wages or unpaid overtime compensation for purposes of sections 16 and 17 of the Fair Labor Standards Act of 1938, as amended (29 U.S.C. 216, 217): *Provided,* That liquidated damages shall be payable only in cases of willful violations of this Act. In any action brought to enforce this Act the court shall have jurisdiction to grant such legal or equitable relief as may be appropriate to effectuate the purposes of this Act, including without limitation judgments compelling employment, reinstatement or promotion, or enforcing the liability for amounts deemed to be unpaid minimum wages or unpaid overtime compensation under this section. Before instituting any action under this section, the Secretary shall attempt to eliminate the discriminatory practice or practices alleged, and to effect voluntary compliance with the requirements of this Act through informal methods of conciliation, conference, and persuasion.

(c)(1) Any person aggrieved may bring a civil action in any court of competent jurisdiction for such legal or equitable relief as will effectuate the purposes of this Act: *Provided,* That the right of any person to bring such action shall terminate upon the commencement of an action by the Secretary to enforce the right of such employee under this Act.

(c)(2) In an action brought under paragraph (1), a person shall be entitled to a trial by jury of any issue of fact in any such action for recovery of amounts owing as a result of a violation of this Act, regardless of whether equitable relief is sought by any party in such action.

(d) No civil action may be commenced by an individual under this section until 60 days after a charge alleging unlawful discrimination has been filed with the Secretary. Such a charge shall be filed—

(1) within 180 days after the alleged unlawful practice occurred;

(2) in a case to which section 14(b) applies, within 300 days after the alleged unlawful practice occurred, or within 30 days after receipt by an individual of notice of termination of proceedings under State law, whichever is earlier.

Upon receiving such a charge, the Secretary shall promptly notify all persons named in such charge as prospective defendants in the action and shall promptly seek to eliminate any alleged unlawful practice by informal methods of conciliation, conference, and persuasion.

»»→ Caution: [The statute of limitations under Sec. 7(e) has been extended under P.L. 100-283—See Historical Comment.]

(e) Section 10 of the Portal-to-Portal Act of 1947 shall apply to actions under this Act. If a charge filed with the Commission under this Act is dismissed or the proceedings of the Commission are otherwise terminated by the Commission, the Commission shall notify the person aggrieved. A civil action may be brought under this section by a person defined in section 11(a) against the respondent named in the charge within 90 days after the date of the receipt of such notice.

(f)(1) An individual may not waive any right or claim under this Act unless the waiver is knowing and voluntary. Except as provided in paragraph (2), a waiver may not be considered knowing and voluntary unless at a minimum—

(A) the waiver is part of an agreement between the individual and the employer that is written in a manner calculated to be understood by such individual, or by the average individual eligible to participate;

(B) the waiver specifically refers to rights or claims arising under this Act;

(C) the individual does not waive rights or claims that may arise after the date the waiver is executed;

(D) the individual waives rights or claims only in exchange for consideration in addition to anything of value to which the individual already is entitled;

(E) the individual is advised in writing to consult with an attorney prior to executing the agreement;

(F)(i) the individual is given a period of at least 21 days within which to consider the agreement; or

(ii) if a waiver is requested in connection with an exit incentive or other employment termination program offered to a group or class of employees, the individual is given a period of at least 45 days within which to consider the agreement;

(G) the agreement provides that for a period of at least 7 days following the execution of such agreement, the individual may revoke the agreement, and the agreement shall not become effective or enforceable until the revocation period has expired;

(H) if a waiver is requested in connection with an exit incentive or other employment termination program offered to a group or class of employees, the employer (at the commencement of the period specified in subparagraph (F)) informs the individual in writing in a manner calculated to be understood by the average individual eligible to participate, as to—

(i) any class, unit, or group of individuals covered by such program, any eligibility factors for such program, and any time limits applicable to such programs; and

(ii) the job titles and ages of all individuals eligible or selected for the program, and the ages of all individuals in the same job classification or organizational unit who are not eligible or selected for the program.

(2) A waiver in settlement of a charge filed with the Equal Employment Opportunity Commission, or an action filed in court by the individual or the individual's representative, alleging age discrimination of a kind prohibited under section 4 or 15 may not be considered knowing and voluntary unless at a minimum—

(A) subparagraphs (A) through (E) of paragraph (1) have been met; and

(B) the individual is given a reasonable period of time within which to consider the settlement agreement.

(3) In any dispute that may arise over whether any of the requirements, conditions, and circumstances set forth in subparagraph (A), (B), (C), (D), (E), (F), (G), or (H) of paragraph (1), or subparagraph (A) or (B) of paragraph (2), have been met, the party asserting the validity of a waiver shall have the burden of proving in a court of competent jurisdiction that a waiver was knowing and voluntary pursuant to paragraph (1) or (2).

(4) No waiver agreement may affect the Commission's rights and responsibilities to enforce this Act. No waiver may be used to justify interfering with the protected right of an employee to file a charge or participate in an investigation or proceeding conducted by the Commission.

Amendments

P.L. 102-166, Sec. 115, amended ADEA Sec. 7(e) by eliminating the text of paragraph (2), deleting references to paragraphs (1) and (2), and deleting a reference to Sec. 6 of the Portal-to-Portal Act to read as above, effective November 21, 1991. Prior to amendment, Sec. 7(e) read as follows:

"(e)(1) Sections 6 and 10 of the Portal-to-Portal Act of 1947 shall apply to actions under this Act.

(2) For the period during which the Secretary is attempting to effect voluntary compliance with requirements of this Act through informal methods of conciliation, conference, and persuasion pursuant to subsection (b), the statute of limitations as provided in section 6 of the Portal-to-Portal Act of 1947 shall be tolled, but in no event for a period in excess of one year."

P.L. 101-433, Sec. 201, amended ADEA Sec. 7 by adding a new subsection (f) to read as above, effective for waivers other than those that occur before October 16, 1990.

P.L. 101-433, Act Sec. 202(B), provides:

(b) RULE ON WAIVERS.—Effective on the date of enactment of this Act, the rule on waivers issued by the Equal Employment Opportunity Commission and contained in section 1627.16(c) of title 29, Code of Federal Regulations, shall have no force and effect.

P.L. 100-283, approved by the President on April 12, 1988, temporarily extended the statute of limitations under Sec. 7(e) although it did not directly amend the section. The Act provides as follows:

SECTION 1. SHORT TITLE.

This Act may be cited as the "Age Discrimination Claims Assistance Act of 1988."

SEC. 2. FINDINGS.

The Congress finds that—

(1) the Equal Employment Opportunity Commission (hereafter in this Act referred to as the "Commission") has failed to process an undetermined number of charges filed under the Age Discrimination in Employment Act of 1967 (29 U.S.C. 621-634) before the running of the statute of limitations applicable to bringing civil actions in the Federal courts under such Act, and

(2) many persons who filed such charges with the Commission have lost the right to bring civil actions with respect to the unlawful practices alleged in such charges.

SEC. 3. EXTENSION OF STATUTE OF LIMITATIONS.

Notwithstanding section 7(e) of the Age Discrimination in Employment Act of 1967 (29 U.S.C. 626(e)), a civil action may be brought under section 7 of such Act by the Commission or an aggrieved person, during the 540-day period beginning on the date of enactment of this Act (April 12, 1988) if—

(1) with respect to the alleged unlawful practice on which the claim in such civil action is based, a charge was timely filed under such Act with the Commission after December 31, 1983,

(2) the Commission did not, within the applicable period set forth in section 7(e) either—

(A) eliminate such alleged unlawful practice by informal methods of conciliation, conference, and persuasion, or

(B) notify such persons, in writing, of the disposition of such charge and of the right of such person to bring a civil action on such claim,

(3) the statute of limitations applicable under such section 7(e) to such claim ran before the date of enactment of this Act, and

(4) a civil action on such claim was not brought by the Commission or such person before the running of the statute of limitations.

SEC. 4. NOTICE OF STATUTE OF LIMITATIONS.

(a) NOTICE REGARDING CLAIMS FOR WHICH STATUTE OF LIMITATIONS IS EXTENDED.—Not later than 60 days after the date of enactment of this Act (April 12, 1988), the Commission shall provide the notice specified in subsection (b) to each person who has filed a charge to which section 3 applies.

(b) CONTENTS OF NOTICE.—The notice required to be provided under subsection (a) to a person shall be in writing and shall include the following information:

(1) The rights and benefits to which such person is entitled under the Age Discrimination in Employment Act of 1967.

(2) The date (which is 540 days after the date of the enactment of this Act [April 12, 1988]) on which the statute of limitations applicable to such person's claim will run.

(3) That such person may bring a civil action on such claims before the date specified in paragraph (2).

SEC. 5. REPORTS.

(a) CONTENTS OF REPORTS.—For each 180-day period in the 540-day period beginning on the date of enactment of this Act (April 12, 1988), the Commission shall submit a written report that includes all of the following information:

(1) The number of persons who have claims to which section 3 applies and the dates charges based on such claims were filed with the Commission.

(2) The number of persons to whom notice was provided in accordance with section 4(a) and the date the notice was provided.

(3) With respect to alleged unlawful practices on which claims affected by section 3 are based, the number of such alleged unlawful practices that the Commission has attempted to eliminate by informal methods of conciliation, conference, and persuasion in the 180-day period for which the report is submitted.

(4) The number of alleged unlawful practices referred to in paragraph (3) that were so eliminated in such period.

(5) The number of civil actions filed by the Commission on behalf of persons to whom notice was sent under section 4.

(b) SUBMISSION OF REPORTS.—Each report required by subsection (a) shall be submitted by the Commission to—

(1) the Committee on Education and Labor, and the Select Committee on Aging, of the House of Representatives, and

(2) the Committee on Labor and Human Resources, and the Special Committee on Aging, of the Senate,

not later than 30 days after the expiration of the 180-day period for which such report is required.

Prior to amendment by P.L. 95-256, Sec. 7(d) read as follows:

"(d) No civil action may be commenced by any individual under this section until the individual has given the Secretary not less than sixty days' notice of an intent to file such action. Such notice shall be filed—

"(1) within one hundred and eighty days after the alleged unlawful practice occurred, or

"(2) in a case to which section 14(b) applies, within three hundred days after the alleged unlawful practice occurred or within thirty days after receipt by the individual of notice of termination of proceedings under State law, whichever is earlier.

"Upon receiving a notice of intent to sue, the Secretary shall promptly notify all persons named therein as prospective defendants in the action and shall promptly seek to eliminate any alleged unlawful practice by informal methods of conciliation, conference, and persuasion."

[¶15,738]

Act Sec. 8 NOTICES TO BE POSTED.

Every employer, employment agency, and labor organization shall post and keep posted in conspicuous places upon its premises a notice to be prepared or approved by the Secretary setting forth information as the Secretary deems appropriate to effectuate the purposes of this Act.

[¶15,739]

Act Sec. 9 RULES AND REGULATIONS.

In accordance with the provisions of subchapter II of chapter 5, United States Code, the Secretary of Labor may issue such rules and regulations as he may consider necessary or appropriate for carrying out this Act, and may establish such reasonable exemptions to and from any or all provisions of this Act as he may find necessary and proper in the public interest.

Amendments

P.L. 101-433, Act Sec. 104 provides:

SEC. 104. RULES AND REGULATIONS.—Notwithstanding section 9 of the Age Discrimination in Employment Act of 1967 (29 U.S.C. 628), the Equal Employment Opportunity Commission may issue such rules and regulations as the Commission may consider necessary or appropriate for carrying out this title, and the amendments made by this title, only after consultation with the Secretary of the Treasury and the Secretary of Labor.

[¶15,740]

Act Sec. 10 CRIMINAL PENALTIES.

Whoever shall forcibly resist, oppose, impede, intimidate, or interfere, with a duly authorized representative of the Secretary while he is engaged in the performance of duties under this Act shall be punished by a fine of not more than $500 or by imprisonment for not more than one year, or by both: *Provided, however,* That no person shall be imprisoned under this section except when there has been a prior conviction hereunder.

[¶15,741]

Act Sec. 11 DEFINITIONS.

For the purposes of this Act—

(a) The term "person" means one or more individuals, partnerships, associations, labor organizations, corporations, business trusts, legal representatives, or any organized groups of persons.

(b) The term "employer" means a person engaged in an industry affecting commerce who has twenty or more employees for each working day in each of twenty or more calendar weeks in the current or preceding calendar year: *Provided,* That prior to June 30, 1968, employers having fewer than fifty employees shall not be considered employers. The term also means (1) any agent of such a person, and (2) a State or political subdivision of a State and any agency or instrumentality of a State or a political subdivision of a State, and any interstate agency, but such term does not include the United States, or a corporation wholly owned by the Government of the United States.

(c) The term "employment agency" means any person regularly undertaking with or without compensation to procure employees for an employer and includes an agent of such a person; but shall not include an agency of the United States.

(d) The term "labor organization" means a labor organization engaged in an industry affecting commerce, and any agent of such an organization, and includes any organization of any kind, any agency, or employee representation committee, group, association, or plan so engaged in which employees participate and which exists for the purpose, in whole or in part, of dealing with employers concerning grievances, labor disputes, wages, rates of pay, hours, or other terms or conditions of employment, and any conference, general committee, joint or system board, or joint council so engaged which is subordinate to a national or international labor organization.

(e) A labor organization shall be deemed to be engaged in an industry affecting commerce if (1) it maintains or operates a hiring hall or hiring office which procures employees for an employer or procures for employees opportunities to work for an employer, or (2) the number of its members (or, where it is a labor organization composed of other labor organizations or their representatives, if the aggregate number of the members of such other labor organization) is fifty or more prior to July 1, 1968, or twenty-five or more on or after July 1, 1968, and such labor organization—

(1) is the certified representative of employees under the provisions of the National Labor Relations Act, as amended, or the Railway Labor Act, as amended; or

(2) although not certified, is a national or international labor organization or a local labor organization recognized or acting as the representative of employees of an employer or employers engaged in an industry affecting commerce; or

(3) has chartered a local labor organization or subsidiary body which is representing or actively seeking to represent employees of employers within the meaning of paragraph (1) or (2); or

(4) has been chartered by a labor organization representing or actively seeking to represent employees within the meaning of paragraph (1) or (2) as the local or subordinate body through which such employees may enjoy membership or become affiliated with such labor organization; or

(5) is a conference, general committee, joint or system board, or joint council subordinate to a national or international labor organization, which includes a labor organization engaged in an industry affecting commerce within the meaning of any of the preceding paragraphs of this subsection.

(f) The term "employee" means an individual employed by any employer except that the term "employee" shall not include any person elected to public office in any State or political subdivision of any State by the qualified voters thereof, or any person chosen by such officer to be on such officer's personal staff, or an appointee on the policy-making level or an immediate adviser with respect to the exercise of the constitutional or legal powers of the office. The exemption set forth in the preceding sentence shall not include employees subject to the civil service laws of a State government, governmental agency, or political subdivision. The term "employee" includes any individual who is a citizen of the United States employed by an employer in a workplace in a foreign country.

(g) The term "commerce" means trade, traffic, commerce, transportation, transmission, or communication among the several States; or between a State and any place outside thereof; or within the District of Columbia, or a possession of the United States; or between points in the same State but through a point outside thereof.

(h) The term "industry affecting commerce" means any activity, business, or industry in commerce or in which a labor dispute would hinder or obstruct commerce or the free flow of commerce and includes any activity or industry "affecting commerce" within the meaning of the Labor-Management Reporting and Disclosure Act of 1959.

(i) The term "State" includes a State of the United States, the District of Columbia, Puerto Rico, the Virgin Islands, American Samoa, Guam, Wake Island, the Canal Zone, and Outer Continental Shelf lands defined in the Outer Continental Shelf Lands Act.

(j) The term "firefighter" means an employee, the duties of whose position are primarily to perform work directly connected with the control and extinguishment of fires or the maintenance and use of firefighting apparatus and equipment, including an employee engaged in this activity who is transferred to a supervisory or administrative position.

(k) The term "law enforcement officer" means an employee, the duties of whose position are primarily the investigation, apprehension, or detention of individuals suspected or convicted of offenses against the criminal laws of a State, including an employee engaged in this activity who is transferred to a supervisory or administrative position. For the purpose of this subsection, "detention" includes the duties of employees assigned to guard individuals incarcerated in any penal institution.

(l) The term "compensation, terms, conditions, or privileges of employment" encompasses all employee benefits, including such benefits provided pursuant to a bona fide employee benefit plan.

Amendments

P.L. 101-433, Sec. 102:

Amended ADEA Sec. 11 by adding new subsection (1) to read as above, effective with respect to any employee benefits established or modified after October 16, 1990 and other conduct occurring after April 14, 1991. See also Act Sec. 105 under Historical Comment to Act Sec. 104.

P.L. 99-592, Sec. 4, added ADEA Secs. 11(j) and 11(k). The amendment is generally effective on January 1, 1987. For additional details on the effective date, see the Historical comment following ADEA Sec. 4.

P.L. 98-459, sec. 801(a) amended ADEA Sec. 11(f) to read as above, by adding a new sentence at the end, effective October 9, 1984.

Prior to amendment by P.L. 95-256, Secs. 11(b), 11(c) and 11(f) read as follows:

"(b) The term 'employer' means a person engaged in an industry affecting commerce who has twenty-five or more employees for each working day in each of twenty or more calendar weeks in the current or preceding calendar year: *Provided,* That prior to June 30, 1968, employers having fewer than fifty employees shall not be considered employers. The term also means any agent of such a person, but such term does not include the United States, a corporation wholly owned by the Government of the United States, or a State or political subdivision thereof."

"(c) The term 'employment agency' means any person regularly undertaking with or without compensation to procure employees for an employer and includes an agent of such a person; but shall not include an agency of the United States, or an agency of a State or political subdivision of a State, except that such term shall include the United States Employment Service and the system of State and local employment services receiving Federal assistance.

"(f) The term 'employee' means an individual employed by an employer."

[¶ 15,742]

Act Sec. 12 AGE LIMITATION.

(a) The prohibitions in this Act shall be limited to individuals who are at least 40 years of age.

(b) In the case of any personnel action affecting employees or applicants for employment which is subject to the provisions of section 15 of this Act, the prohibitions established in section 15 of this act shall be limited to individuals who are at least 40 years of age.

(c)(1) Nothing in this Act shall be construed to prohibit compulsory retirement of any employee who has attained 65 years of age and who, for the 2-year period immediately before retirement, is employed in a bona fide executive or a high policy-making position, if such employee is entitled to an immediate nonforfeitable annual retirement benefit from a pension, profit-sharing, savings, or deferred compensation plan, or any combination of such plans, of the employer of such employee, which equals, in the aggregate, at least $44,000.

(c)(2) In applying the retirement benefit test of paragraph (1) of this subsection, if any such retirement benefit is in a form other than a straight life annuity (with no ancillary benefits), or if employees contribute to any such plan or make rollover contributions, such benefit shall be adjusted in accordance with regulations prescribed by the Secretary, after consultation with the Secretary of the Treasury, so that the benefit is the equivalent of a straight life annuity (with no ancillary benefits) under a plan to which employees do not contribute and under which no rollover contributions are made.

(d) Nothing in this Act shall be construed to prohibit compulsory retirement of any employee who has attained 70 years of age, and who is serving under a contract of unlimited tenure (or similar arrangement providing for unlimited tenure) at an institution of higher education (as defined by section 1201(a) of the Higher Education Act of 1965).

Amendments

P.L. 101-239, § 6202(b)(3)(C) amended ADEA Sec. 12(a) by striking "except the provisions of section 4(g))", effective for items and services furnished after December 19, 1989.

P.L. 99-592, Sec. 2(c)(1), amended ADEA Sec. 12(a) by striking out "but less than seventy years of age" after the words "40 years of age." Sec. 2(c) amended ADEA sec. 12(c)(2) by striking out "but not seventy years of age," after the words "65 years of age." The amendment is generally effective on January 1, 1987. For greater details on the effective date, see the Historical comment with respect to P.L. 99-592 following Sec. 4 of the ADEA.

P.L. 99-592, Sec. 6(a), added ADEA Sec. 12(d). The provision is generally effective on January 1, 1987. Additional details relating to the effective date of P.L. 99-592 are in the Historical comment following Sec. 4 of the ADEA. Sec. 6(b) of the Act provides that the amendment of Sec. 6(a), adding ADEA Sec. 12(d), relating to college professors, is repealed on December 31, 1993.

P.L. 99-592, Sec. 6(c), provides:

"(c) STUDY REQUIRED.—(1) The Equal Employment Opportunity Commission shall, not later than 12 months after the date of enactment of this Act, enter into an agreement with the National Academy of Sciences for the conduct of a study to analyze the potential consequences of the elimination of mandatory retirement on institutions of higher education.

"(2) The study required by paragraph (1) of this subsection shall be conducted under the general supervision of the National Academy of Sciences by a study panel composed of 9 members. The study panel shall consist of—

"(A) 4 members who shall be administrators at institutions of higher education selected by the National Academy of Sciences after consultation with the American Council of Education, the Association of American Universities, and the National Association of State Universities and Land Grant Colleges;

"(B) 4 members who shall be teachers or retired teachers at institutions of higher education (who do not serve in an administrative capacity at such institutions), selected by the National Academy of Sciences after consultation with the American Federation of Teachers, the National Education Association, the American Association of University Professors, and the American Association of Retired Persons; and

"(C) one member selected by the National Academy of Sciences.

"(3) The results of the study shall be reported, with recommendations, to the President and to the Congress not later than 5 years after the date of enactment of this Act [October 31, 1991].

"(4) The expenses of the study required by this subsection shall be paid from funds available to the Equal Employment Opportunity Commission.

P.L. 99-272, Sec. 9201(b)(2) amended ADEA Sec. 12(a) by inserting "(except the provisions of section 4(g))" after "Act."

P.L. 98-459, sec. 802(c)(1) amended ADEA Sec. 12(c)(1) by striking out "$27,000" and inserting "$44,000" instead, effective October 9, 1984 except that the amendment does not apply with respect to any individual who retires or is compelled to retire before October 9, 1984.

P.L. 95-256 added Sec. 12(d), effective January 1, 1979, automatically repealed July 1, 1982. Prior to repeal, the provision read as follows: "(d) Nothing in this Act shall be construed to prohibit compulsory retirement of any employee who has attained 65 years of age but not 70 years of age, and who is serving under a contract of unlimited tenure (or similar arrangement providing for unlimited tenure) at an institution of higher education (as defined by section 1201(a) of the Higher Education Act of 1965)."

[¶15,743]

Act Sec. 13 ANNUAL REPORT.

The Secretary shall submit annually in January a report to the Congress covering his activities for the preceding year and including such information, data, and recommendations for further legislation in connection with the matters covered by this Act as he may find advisable. Such report shall contain an evaluation and appraisal by the Secretary of the effect of the minimum and maximum ages established by this Act, together with his recommendations to the Congress. In making such evaluation and appraisal, the Secretary shall take into consideration any changes which may have occurred in the general age level of the population, the effect of the Act upon workers not covered by its provisions, and such other factors as he may deem pertinent.

[¶15,744]

Act Sec. 14 FEDERAL-STATE RELATIONSHIP.

(a) Nothing in this Act shall affect the jurisdiction of any agency of any State performing like functions with regard to discriminatory employement practices on account of age except that upon commencement of action under this Act such action shall supersede any State action.

(b) In the case of an alleged unlawful practice occurring in a State which has a law prohibiting discrimination in employment because of age and establishing or authorizing a State authority to grant or seek relief from such discriminatory practice, no suit may be brought under section 7 of this Act before the expiration of sixty days after proceedings have been commenced under the State law, unless such proceedings have been earlier terminated: *Provided,* That such sixty-day period shall be extended to one hundred and twenty days during the first year after the effective date of such State law. If any requirement for the commencement of such proceedings is imposed by a State authority other than a requirement of the filing of a written and signed statement of the facts upon which the proceeding is based, the proceeding shall be deemed to have been commenced for the purposes of this subsection at the time such statement is sent by registered mail to the appropriate State authority.

[¶15,745]

Act Sec. 15 FEDERAL EMPLOYEES.

(a) All personnel actions affecting employees or applicants for employment who are at least 40 years of age (except personnel actions with regard to aliens employed outside the limits of the United States) in military departments as defined in section 102 of title 5, United States Code, in executive agencies as defined in section 105 of title 5, United States Code (including employees and applicants for employment who are paid from nonappropriated funds), in the United States Postal Service and the Postal Rate Commission, in those units in the government of the District of Columbia having positions in the competitive service, and in those units of the legislative and judicial branches of the Federal Government having positions in the competitive service, and in the Library of Congress shall be made free from any discrimination based on age.

(b) Except as otherwise provided in this subsection, the Civil Service Commission is authorized to enforce the provisions of subsection (a) through appropriate remedies, including reinstatment or hiring of employees with or without backpay, as will effectuate the policies of this section. The Civil Service Commission shall issue such rules, regulations, orders, and instructions as it deems necessary and appropriate to carry out its responsibilities under this section. The Civil Service Commission shall—

(1) be responsible for the review and evaluation of the operation of all agency programs designed to carry out the policy of this section, periodically obtaining and publishing (on at least a semi-annual basis) progress reports from each such department, agency, or unit;

(2) consult with and solicit the recommendations of interested individuals, groups, and organizations relating to nondiscrimination in employment on account of age; and

(3) provide for the acceptance and processing of complaints of discrimination in Federal employment on account of age.

The head of each such department, agency, or unit shall comply with such rules, regulations, orders, and instructions of the Civil Service Commission which shall include a provision that an employee or applicant for employment shall be notified of any final action taken on any complaint of discrimination filed by him thereunder. Reasonable exemptions to the provisions of this section may be established by the Commission but only when the Commission has established a maximum age requirement on the basis of a determination that age is a bona fide occupational qualification necessary to the performance of the duties of the position. With respect to employment in the Library of Congress, authorities granted in this subsection to the Civil Service Commission shall be exercised by the Librarian of Congress.

(c) Any persons aggrieved may bring a civil action in any Federal district court of competent jurisdiction for such legal or equitable relief as will effectuate the purposes of this Act.

(d) When the individual has not filed a complaint concerning age discrimination with the Commission, no civil action may be commenced by the individual under this section until the individual has given the Commission not less than thirty days' notice of an intent to file such action. Such notice shall be filed within one hundred and eighty days after the alleged unlawful practice occurred. Upon receiving a notice of intent to sue, the Commission shall promptly notify all persons named therein as prospective defendants in the action and take any appropriate action to assure the elimination of any unlawful practice.

(e) Nothing contained in this section shall relieve any Government agency or official of the responsibility to assure nondiscrimination on account of age in employment as required under any provision of Federal law.

(f) Any personnel action of any department, agency or other entity referred to in subsection (a) of this section shall not be subject to, or affected by, any provision of this Act, other than the provisions of section 12(b) of this Act and the provisions of this section.

(g)(1) The Civil Service Commission shall undertake a study relating to the effects of the amendments made to this section by the Age Discrimination in Employment Act Amendments of 1978, and the effects of section 12(b) of this Act, as added by the Age Discrimination in Employment Act Amendments of 1978.

(g)(2) The Civil Service Commission shall transmit a report to the President and to the Congress containing the findings of the Commission resulting from the study of the Commission under paragraph (1) of this subsection. Such report shall be transmitted no later than January 1, 1980.

P.L. 93-259 added Section 15(a) through (e) as a new provision.

P.L. 95-256 amended Sec. 15(a) by adding "who are at least 40 years of age" after the word "employment."

[¶15,746]

Act Sec. 16 EFFECTIVE DATE.

This Act shall become effective one hundred and eighty days after enactment, except (a) that the Secretary of Labor may extend the delay in effective date of any provision of this Act up to an additional ninety days thereafter if he finds that such time is necessary in permitting adjustments to the provisions hereof, and (b) that on or after the date of enactment the Secretary of Labor is authorized to issue such rules and regulations as may be necessary to carry out its provisions.

Amendments

Prior to amendment by P.L. 93-259, Sec. 16 was designated as Section 15 of the Age Discrimination in Employment Act.

[¶15,747]

Act Sec. 17 APPROPRIATIONS.

There are hereby authorized to be appropriated such sums as may be necessary to carry out this Act.

Amendments

Prior to amendment by P.L. 95-256, Sec. 17 contained an annual appropriation limit of $5,000,000.

Prior to amendment by P.L. 93-259, Sec. 17 was designated Sec. 16.

Age Discrimination in Employment Regulations
(Equal Employment Opportunity Commission)

[¶ 15,750]

Equal Employment Opportunity Commission regulations under the Age Discrimination in Employment Act—Reproduced below are excerpts from the regulations promulgated by the EEOC on the Age Discrimination in Employment Act. Reg. § 1625.6 (46 FR 47724) relates to bona fide occupational qualifications. Reg. § 1625.7 (46 FR 47724) concerns differentiations based on factors other than age. Reg. § 1625.8 (46 FR 47724) discusses bona fide seniority systems. Reg. § 1625.9 (46 FR 47724) reflects the EEOC's interpretation of ADEA Sec. 4(f)(2)'s prohibition against involuntary retirement because of age. Pursuant to ADEA Sec. 12(c), an executive may be subject to compulsory retirement, if, among other requirements, he is entitled to an annual retirement benefit of at least $27,000. Reg. § 1625.10 (formerly Reg. § 860.120) relates costs and benefits under employee benefit plans. Reg. § 1625.12 (44 FR 66791) sets forth the EEOC's interpretative statements regarding the exemption. Reg. § 1627.17 (44 FR 66791) indicates how the $27,000 annual retirement benefit is to be calculated under specified circumstances. Reg. § 1625.20 is a final and interim rule on group health insurance benefits for employees age 65-69, which awaits OMB approval and publication in the Federal Register. Reg. § 1625.21 (61 FR 15378), added April 8, 1996, discusses age limitations for apprenticeship programs. The recordkeeping requirements are set forth in Reg. §§ 1627.2—1627.16 (44 FR 38459). Former Reg. § 1627.16(c), allowing unsupervised waivers, was removed by 57 FR 4158 on February 4, 1992. Former Reg. § 1625.13 on age limitations for apprentices was removed by 61 FR 15378 on April 8, 1996 (having been replaced by Reg. § 1625.21).

Reg. §§ 1625.8, 1625.9(c) and (d), 1625.10(f), and 1625.12(a) were amended by 53 FR 5971 on February 29, 1988. Reg. § 1625.23 was added by 65 FR 77437 on December 11, 2000.

Also previously reproduced here was Reg. § 860.120(f)(1)(iv)(B) which stated that the ADEA permits employers to cease contributions and accruals to pension and retirement plans for employees who continue to work past normal retirement age. It was rescinded pursuant to *American Association of Retired Persons, et al. v. EEOC,* (CCH Pension Plan Guide, ¶ 23,723K). The notice of rescission was published in the *Federal Register* on March 18, 1987 (52 FR 8448), (CCH Pension Plan Guide, ¶ 23,725A).

EQUAL EMPLOYMENT OPPORTUNITY COMMISSION

29 CFR Parts 1625 and 1627

Age Discrimination in Employment; Final
Interpretations

[¶ 15,750A]

§ 1625.1 Definitions. The Equal Employment Opportunity Commission is hereinafter referred to as the "Commission". The terms "person", "employer", "employment agency", "labor organization", and "employee" shall have the meanings set forth in Section 11 of the Age Discrimination in Employment Act of 1967, as amended, 29 U.S.C. 621 *et seq.,* hereinafter referred to as the "Act". References to "employers" in this part state principles that are applicable not only to employers but also to labor organizations and to employment agencies.

[¶ 15,750B]

§ 1625.6 Bona fide occupational qualifications. (a) Whether occupational qualifications will be deemed to be "bona fide" to a specific job and "reasonably necessary to the normal operation of the particular business," will be determined on the basis of all the pertinent facts surrounding each particular situation. It is anticipated that this concept of a bona fide occupational qualification will have limited scope and application. Further, as this is an exception to the Act it must be narrowly construed.

(b) An employer asserting a BFOQ defense has the burden of proving that (1) the age limit is reasonably necessary to the essence of the business, and either (2) that all or substantially all individuals excluded from the job involved are in fact disqualified, or (3) that some of the individuals so excluded possess a disqualifying trait that cannot be ascertained except by reference to age. If the employer's objective in asserting a BFOQ is the goal of public safety, the employer must prove that the challenged practice does indeed effectuate that goal and that there is no acceptable alternative which would better advance it or equally advance it with less discriminatory impact.

(c) Many State and local governments have enacted laws or administrative regulations which limit employment opportunities based on age. Unless these laws meet the standards for the establishment of a valid bona fide occupational qualification under section 4(f)(1) of the Act, they will be considered in conflict with and effectively superseded by the ADEA.

[¶ 15,750C]

§ 1625.7 Differentiations based on reasonable factors other than age. (a) Section 4(f)(1) of the Act provides that

* * * it shall not be unlawful for an employer, employment agency, or labor organization * * * to take any action otherwise prohibited under paragraphs (a), (b), (c), or (e) of this section * * * where the differentiation is based on reasonable factors other than age * * *.

(b) No precise and unequivocal determination can be made as to the scope of the phrase "differentiation based on reasonable factors other than age." Whether such differentiations exist must be decided on the basis of all the particular facts and circumstances surrounding each individual situation.

(c) When an employment practice uses age as a limiting criterion, the defense that the practice is justified by a reasonable factor other than age is unavailable.

(d) When an employment practice, including a test, is claimed as a basis for different treatment of employees or applicants for employment on the grounds that it is a "factor other than" age, and such a practice has an adverse impact on individuals within the protected age group, it can only be justified as a business necessity. Tests which are asserted as "reasonable factors other than age" will be scrutinized in accordance with the standards set forth at Part 1607 of this Title.

(e) When the exception of "a reasonable factor other than age" is raised against an individual claim of discriminatory treatment, the employer bears the burden of showing that the "reasonable factor other than age" exists factually.

(f) A differentiation based on the average cost of employing older employees as a group is unlawful except with respect to employee benefit plans which qualify for the section 4(f)(2) exception to the Act.

[¶ 15,750D]

§ 1625.8 Bona fide seniority systems. Section 4(f)(2) of the Act provides that

* * * It shall not be unlawful for an employer, employment agency, or labor organization * * * to observe the terms of a bona fide seniority system * * * which is not a subterfuge to evade the purposes of this Act except that no such seniority system * * * shall require or permit the involuntary retirement of any individual specified by section 12(a) of this Act because of the age of such individual. * * *

(a) Though a seniority system may be qualified by such factors as merit, capacity, or ability, any bona fide seniority system must be based on length of service as the primary criterion for the equitable allocation of available employment opportunities and prerogatives among younger and older workers.

(b) Adoption of a purported seniority system which gives those with longer service lesser rights, and results in discharge or less favored treatment to those within the protection of the Act, may, depending upon the circumstances, be a "subterfuge to evade the purposes" of the Act.

(c) Unless the essential terms and conditions of an alleged seniority system have been communicated to the affected employees and can be shown to be applied uniformly to all of those affected, regardless of age, it will not be considered a bona fide seniority system within the meaning of the Act.

(d) It should be noted that seniority systems which segregate, classify, or otherwise discriminate against individuals on the basis of race, color, religion, sex, or national origin, are prohibited under Title VII of the Civil Rights Act of 1964, where that Act otherwise applies. The "bona fides" of such a system will be closely scrutinized to ensure that such a system is, in fact, bona fide under the ADEA. (Amended by 53 FR 5971 on February 29, 1988 and by 53 FR 15673 on May 3, 1988).

[¶ 15,750E]

§ 1625.9 Prohibition of involuntary retirement. (a) (1) As originally enacted in 1967, section 4(f)(2) of the Act provided: "It shall not be unlawful * * * to observe the terms of a bona fide seniority system or any bona fide employee benefit plan such as a retirement, pension, or insurance plan, which is not a subterfuge to evade the purposes of this Act, except that no such employee benefit plan shall excuse the failure to hire any individual * * *." The Department of Labor interpreted the provision as "Authoriz[ing] involuntary retirement irrespective of age; *Provided,* That such retirement is pursuant to the terms of a retirement or pension plan meeting the requirements of section 4(f)(2)." The Department took the position that in order to meet the requirements of section 4(f)(2), the involuntary retirement provision had to be (i) contained in a bona fide pension or retirement plan, (ii) required by the terms of the plan and not optional, and (iii) essential to the plan's economic survival or to some other legitimate business purpose—i.e., the provision was not in the plan as the result of arbitrary discrimination on the basis of age.

(2) As revised by the 1978 amendments, section 4(f)(2) was amended by adding the following clause at the end: "and no such seniority system or employee benefit plan shall require or permit the involuntary retirement of an individual specified by section 12(a) of this Act because of the age of such individual * * *." The Conference Committee Report expressly states that this amendment is intended "to make absolutely clear one of the original purposes of this provision, namely, that the exception does not authorize an employer to require or permit involuntary retirement of an employee within the protected age group on account of age" (H.R. Rept. No. 95-950, p. 8).

(b)(1) The amendment applies to all new and existing seniority systems and employee benefit plans. Accordingly, any system or plan provision requiring or permitting involuntary retirement is unlawful, regardless of whether the provision antedates the 1967 Act or the 1978 amendments.

(2) Where lawsuits pending on the date of enactment (April 6, 1978) or filed thereafter challenge involuntary retirements which occurred either before or after that date, the amendment applies.

(c)(1) The amendment protects all individuals covered by section 12(a) of the Act. Section 12(a) was amended in October of 1986 by the Age Discrimination in Employment Amendments of 1986, Pub. L. 99-592, 100 Stat. 3342 (1986), which removed the age 70 limit. Section 12(a) provides that the Act's prohibitions shall be limited to individuals who are at least forty years of age. Accordingly, unless a specific exemption applies, an employer can no longer force retirement or otherwise discriminate on the basis of age against an individual because (s)he is 70 or older.

(2) The amendment to section 12(a) of the Act became effective on January 1, 1987, except with respect to any employee subject to a collective bargaining agreement containing a provision that would be superseded by such amendment that was in effect on June 30, 1986, and which terminates after January 1, 1987. In that case, the amendment is effective on the termination of the agreement or January 1, 1990, whichever comes first.

(d) Neither section 4(f)(2) nor any other provision of the Act makes it unlawful for a plan to permit individuals to elect early retirement at a specified age at their own option. Not is it unlawful for a plan to require early retirement for reasons other than age. (Amended by 53 FR 5971 on February 29, 1988).

[¶ 15,750F]

§ 1625.10 Costs and benefits under employee benefit plans. (a)(1) *General.* Section 4(f)(2) of the Act provides that it is not unlawful for an employer, employment agency, or labor organization "to observe the terms of * * * any bona fide employee benefit plan such as a retirement, pension, or insurance plan, which is not a subterfuge to evade the purposes of this Act, except that no such employee benefit plan shall excuse the failure to hire any individual and no such * * * employee benefit plan shall require or permit the involuntary retirement of any individual specified by section 12(a) of this Act because of the age of such individuals." The legislative history of this provision indicates that its purpose is to permit age-based reductions in employee benefit plans where such reductions are justified by significant cost considerations. Accordingly, section 4(f)(2) does not apply, for example, to paid vacations and uninsured paid sick leave, since reductions in these benefits would not be justified by significant cost considerations. Where employee benefit plans do meet the criteria in section 4(f)(2), benefit levels for older workers may be reduced to the extent necessary to achieve approximate equivalency in cost for older and younger workers. A benefit plan will be considered in compliance with the statute where the actual amount of payment made, or cost incurred, in behalf of an older worker is equal to that made or incurred in behalf of a younger worker, even though the older worker may thereby receive a lesser amount of benefits or insurance coverage. Since section 4(f)(2) is an exception from the general nondiscrimination provisions of the Act, the burden is on the one seeking to invoke the exception to show that every element has been clearly and unmistakably met. The exception must be narrowly construed. The following sections explain three key elements of the exception: (i) What a "bona fide employee benefit plan" is; (ii) what it means to "observe the terms" of such a plan; and (iii) what kind of plan, or plan provision, would be considered "a subterfuge to evade the purposes of [the] Act." There is also a discussion of the application of the general rules governing all plans with respect to specific kinds of employee benefit plans.

(2) *Relation of section 4(f)(2) to sections 4(a), 4(b) and 4(c).* Sections 4(a), 4(b) and 4(c) prohibit specified acts of discrimination on the basis of age. Section 4(a) in particular makes it unlawful for an employer to "discriminate against any individual with respect to his compensation, terms, conditions, or privileges of employment, because of such individual's age * * *." Section 4(f)(2) is an exception to this general prohibition. Where an employer under an employee benefit plan provides the same level of benefits to older workers as to younger workers, there is no violation of section 4(a), and accordingly the practice does not have to be justified under section 4(f)(2).

(b) *"Bona fide employee benefit plan".* Section 4(f)(2) applies only to bona fide employee benefit plans. A plan is considered "bona fide" if its terms (including cessation of contributions or accruals in the case of retirement income plans) have been accurately described in writing to all employees and if it actually provides the benefits in accordance with the terms of the plan. Notifying employees promptly of the provisions and changes in an employee benefit plan is essential if they are to know how the plan affects them. For these purposes, it would be sufficient under the ADEA for employers to follow the disclosure requirements of ERISA and the regulations thereunder. The plan must actually provide the benefits its provisions describe, since otherwise the notification of the provisions to employees is misleading and inaccurate. An "employee benefit plan" is a plan, such as a retirement, pension, or insurance plan, which provides employees with what are frequently referred to as "fringe benefits." The term does not refer to wages or salary in cash; neither section 4(f)(2) nor any other section of the Act excuses the payment of lower wages or salary to older employees on account of age. Whether or not any particular employee benefit plan may lawfully provide lower benefits to older employees on account of age depends on whether all of the elements of the exception have been met. An "employee-pay-all" employee benefit plan is one of the "terms, conditions, or privileges of employment" with respect to which discrimination on the basis of age is forbidden under section 4(a)(1). In such a plan, benefits for older workers may be reduced only to the extent and according to the same principles as apply to other plans under section 4(f)(2).

(c) *"To observe the terms" of a plan.* In order for a bona fide employee benefit plan which provides lower benefits to older employees on account of age to be within the section 4(f)(2) exception, the lower benefits must be provided in "observ[ance of] the terms of" the plan. As this statutory text makes clear, the section 4(f)(2) exception is limited to otherwise discriminatory actions which are actually prescribed by the terms of a bona fide employee benefit plan. Where the employer, employment agency, or labor organization is not required by the express provisions of the plan to provide lesser benefits to older workers, section 4(f)(2) does not apply. Important purposes are served by this requirement. Where a discriminatory policy is an express term of a benefit plan, employees presumably have some opportunity to know of the policy and to plan (or protest) accordingly. Moreover, the requirement that the discrimination actually be prescribed by a plan assures that the particular plan provision will be equally applied to all employees of the same age. Where a discriminatory provision is an optional term of the plan, it permits individual, discretionary acts of discrimination, which do not fall within the section 4(f)(2) exception.

(d) *"Subterfuge".* In order for a bona fide employee benefit plan which prescribes lower benefits for older employees on account of age to be within the section 4(f)(2) exception, it must not be "a subterfuge to evade the purposes of [the] Act." In general, a plan or plan provision which prescribes lower benefits for older employees on account of age is not a "subterfuge" within the meaning of section 4(f)(2), provided that the lower level of benefits is justified by age-related cost considerations. (The only exception to this general rule is with respect to certain retirement plans. See paragraph (f)(4) of this section.) There are certain other requirements that must be met in order for a plan not to be a subterfuge. These requirements are set forth below.

(1) *Cost data—General.* Cost data used in justification of a benefit plan which provides lower benefits to older employees on account of age must be valid and reasonable. This standard is met where an employer has

cost data which show the actual cost to it of providing the particular benefit (or benefits) in question over a representative period of years. An employer may rely [on] cost data for its own employees over such a period, or on cost data for a larger group of similarly situated employees. Sometimes, as a result of experience rating or other causes, an employer incurs costs that differ significantly from costs for a group of similarly situated employees. Such an employer may not rely on cost data for the similarly situated employees where such reliance would result in significantly lower benefits for its own older employees. Where reliable cost information is not available, reasonable projections made from existing cost data meeting the standard set forth above will be considered acceptable.

(2) *Cost data—Individual benefit basis and "benefit package" basis.* Cost comparisons and adjustments under section 4(f)(2) must be made on a benefit-by-benefit basis or on a "benefit package" basis, as described below.

(i) *Benefit-by-benefit basis.* Adjustments made on a benefit-by-benefit basis must be made in the amount or level of a specific form of benefit for a specific event or contingency. For example, higher group term life insurance costs for older workers would justify a corresponding reduction in the amount of group term life insurance coverage for older workers, on the basis of age. However, a benefit-by-benefit approach would not justify the substitution of one form of benefit for another, even though both forms of benefit are designed for the same contingency, such as death. See paragraph (f)(1) of this section.

(ii) *"Benefit package" basis.* As an alternative to the benefit-by-benefit basis, cost comparisons and adjustments under section 4(f)(2) may be made on a limited "benefit package" basis. Under this approach, subject to the limitations described below, cost comparisons and adjustments can be made with respect to section 4(f)(2) plans in the aggregate. This alternative basis provides greater flexibility than a benefit-by-benefit basis in order to carry out the declared statutory purpose "to help employers and workers find ways of meeting problems arising from the impact of age on employment." A "benefit package" approach is an alternative approach consistent with this purpose and with the general purpose of section 4(f)(2) only if it is not used to reduce the cost to the employer or the favorability to the employees of overall employee benefits for older employees. A "benefit package" approach used for either of these purposes would be a subterfuge to evade the purposes of the Act. In order to assure that such a "benefit package" approach is not abused and is consistent with the legislative intent, it is subject to the limitations described in paragraph (f), which also includes a general example.

(3) *Cost data—Five year maximum basis.* Cost comparisons and adjustments under section 4(f)(2) may be made on the basis of age brackets of up to 5 years. Thus a particular benefit may be reduced for employees of any age within the protected age group by an amount no greater than that which could be justified by the additional cost to provide them with the same level of the benefit as younger employees within a specified five-year age group immediately preceding theirs. For example, where an employer chooses to provide unreduced group term life insurance benefits until age 60, benefits for employees who are between 60 and 65 years of age may be reduced only to the extent necessary to achieve approximate equivalency in costs with employees who are 55 to 60 years old. Similarly, any reductions in benefit levels for 65 to 70 year old employees cannot exceed an amount which is proportional to the additional costs for their coverage over 60 to 65 year old employees.

(4) *Employee contributions in support of employee benefit plans—*

(i) *As a condition of employment.* An older employee within the protected age group may not be required as a condition of employment to make greater contributions than a younger employee in support of an employee benefit plan. Such a requirement would be in effect a mandatory reduction in take-home pay, which is never authorized by section 4(f)(2), and would impose an impediment to employment in violation of the specific restrictions in section 4(f)(2).

(ii) *As a condition of participation in a voluntary employee benefit plan.* An older employee within the protected age group may be required as a condition of participation in a voluntary employee benefit plan to make a greater contribution than a younger employee only if the older employee is not thereby required to bear a greater proportion of the total premium cost (employer-paid and employee-paid) than the younger employee. Otherwise the requirement would discriminate against the older employee by making compensation in the form of an employer contribution available on less favorable terms than for the younger employee and denying that contribution altogether to an older employee unwilling or unable to meet the less favorable terms. Such discrimination is not authorized by section 4(f)(2).

This principle applies to three different contribution arrangements as follows:

(A) *Employee-pay-all plans.* Older employees, like younger employees, may be required to contribute as a condition of participation up to the full premium cost for their age.

(B) *Non-contributory ("employer-pay-all") plans.* Where younger employees are not required to contribute any portion of the total premium cost, older employees may not be required to contribute any portion.

(C) *Contributory plans.* In these plans employers and participating employees share the premium cost. The required contributions of participants may increase with age so long as the *proportion* of the total premium required to be paid by the participants does not increase with age.

(iii) *As an option in order to receive an unreduced benefit.* An older employee may be given the option, as an individual, to make the additional contribution necessary to receive the same level of benefits as a younger employee (provided that the contemplated reduction in benefits is otherwise justified by section 4(f)(2)).

(5) *Forfeiture clauses.* Clauses in employee benefit plans which state that litigation or participation in any manner in a formal proceeding by an employee will result in the forfeiture of his rights are unlawful insofar as they may be applied to those who seek redress under the Act. This is by reason of section 4(d) which provides that it is unlawful for an employer, employment agency, or labor organization to discriminate against any individual because such individual "has made a charge, testified, assisted, or participated in any manner in an investigation, proceeding, or litigation under this Act."

(6) *Refusal to hire clauses.* Any provision of an employee benefit plan which requires or permits the refusal to hire an individual specified in section 12(a) of the Act on the basis of age is a subterfuge to evade the purposes of the Act and cannot be excused under section 4(f)(2).

(7) *Involuntary retirement clauses.* Any provision of an employee benefit plan which requires or permits the involuntary retirement of any individual specified in section 12(a) of the Act on the basis of age is a subterfuge to evade the purpose of the Act and cannot be excused under section 4(f)(2).

(e) *Benefits provided by the Government.* An employer does not violate the Act by permitting certain benefits to be provided by the Government, even though the availability of such benefits may be based on age. For example, it is not necessary for an employer to provide health benefits which are otherwise provided to certain employees by Medicare. However, the availability of benefits from the Government will not justify a reduction in employer-provided benefits if the result is that, taking the employer-provided and Government-provided benefits together, an older employee is entitled to a lesser benefit of any type (including coverage for family and/or dependents) than a similarly situated younger employee. For example, the availability of certain benefits to an older employee under Medicare will not justify denying an older employee a benefit which is provided to younger employees and is not provided to the older employee by Medicare.

(f) *Application of section 4(f)(2) to various employee benefit plans.*

(1) *Benefit-by-benefit approach.* This portion of the interpretation discusses how a benefit-by-benefit approach would apply to four of the most common types of employee benefit plans.

(i) *Life insurance.* It is not uncommon for life insurance coverage to remain constant until a specified age, frequently 65, and then be reduced. This practice will not violate the Act (even if reductions start before age 65), provided that the reduction for an employee of a particular age is no greater than is justified by the increased cost of coverage for that employee's specific age bracket encompassing no more than five years. It should be noted that a total denial of life insurance, on the basis of age, would not be justified under a benefit-by-benefit analysis. However, it is not unlawful for life insurance coverage to cease upon separation from service.

(ii) *Long-term disability.* Under a benefit-by-benefit approach, where employees who are disabled at younger ages are entitled to long-term disability benefits, there is no cost-based justification for denying such benefits altogether, on the basis of age, to employees who are disabled at older ages. It is not unlawful to cut off long-term disability benefits and coverage on the basis of some non-age factor, such as recovery from disability. Reductions on the basis of age in the level or duration of benefits available for disability are justifiable only on the basis of age-related cost considerations as set forth elsewhere in this section. An employer which provides long-term disability coverage to all employees may avoid any increases in the cost to it that such coverage for older employees would entail by reducing the level of benefits available to older employees. An employer may also avoid such cost increases by reducing the duration of benefits available to employees who become disabled at older ages, without reducing the level of benefits. In this connection, the Department would not assert a violation where the level of benefits is not reduced and the duration of benefits is reduced in the following manner:

(A) With respect to disabilities which occur at age 60 or less, benefits cease at age 65.

(B) With respect to disabilities which occur after age 60, benefits cease 5 years after disablement. Cost data may be produced to support other patterns of reduction as well.

(iii) *Retirement plans.* (A) *Participation.* No employee hired prior to normal retirement age may be excluded from a defined contribution plan. With respect to defined benefit plans not subject to the Employee Retirement Income Security Act (ERISA), Pub. L. 93-406, 29 U.S.C. 1001, 1003(a) and (b), an employee hired at an age more than 5 years prior to normal retirement age may not be excluded from such a plan unless the exclusion is justifiable on the basis of cost considerations as set forth elsewhere in this section. With respect to defined benefit plans subject to ERISA, such an exclusion would be unlawful in any case. An employee hired less than 5 years prior to normal retirement age may be excluded from a defined benefit plan, regardless of whether or not the plan is covered by ERISA. Similarly, any employee hired after normal retirement age may be excluded from a defined benefit plan.

(2) *"Benefit Package" Approach*

A "benefit package" approach to compliance under section 4(f)(2) offers greater flexibility than a benefit-by-benefit approach by permitting deviations from a benefit-by-benefit approach so long as the overall result is no lesser cost to the employer *and* no less favorable benefits for employees. As previously noted, in order to assure that such an approach is used for the benefit of older workers and not to their detriment, and is otherwise consistent with the legislative intent, it is subject to limitations as set forth below:

(i) *A benefit package approach shall apply only to employee benefit plans which fall within section 4(f)(2).*

(ii) *A benefit package approach shall not apply to a retirement or pension plan.* The 1978 legislative history sets forth specific and comprehensive rules governing such plans, which have been adopted above. These rules are not tied to actuarially significant cost considerations but are intended to deal with the special funding arrangements of retirement or pension plans. Variations from these special rules are therefore not justified by variations from the cost-based benefit-by-benefit approach in other benefit plans, nor may variations from the special rules governing pension and retirement plans justify variations from the benefit-by-benefit approach in other benefit plans.

(iii) *A benefit package approach shall not be used to justify reductions in health benefits greater than would be justified under a benefit-by-benefit approach.* Such benefits appear to be of particular importance to older workers in meeting "problems arising from the impact of age" and were of particular concern to Congress. Therefore, the "benefit package" approach may not be used to reduce health insurance benefits by more than is warranted by the increase in the cost to the employer of those benefits alone. Any greater reduction would be a subterfuge to evade the purpose of the Act.

(iv) *A benefit reduction greater than would be justified under a benefit-by-benefit approach must be offset by another benefit available to the same employees.* No employees may be deprived because of age of one benefit without an offsetting benefit being made available to them.

(v) *Employers who wish to justify benefit reductions under a benefit package approach must be prepared to produce data to show that those reductions are fully justified.* Thus employers must be able to show that deviations from a benefit-by-benefit approach do not result in lesser cost to them or less favorable benefits to their employees. A general example consistent with these limitations may be given. Assume two employee benefit plans, providing Benefit "A" and Benefit "B." Both plans fall within section 4(f)(2), and neither is a retirement or pension plan subject to special

rules. Both benefits are available to all employees. Age-based cost increases would justify a 10% decrease in both benefits on a benefit-by-benefit basis. The affected employees would, however, find it more favorable—that is, more consistent with meeting their needs—for no reduction to be made in Benefit "A" and a greater reduction to be made in Benefit "B." This "trade-off" would not result in reduction in health benefits. The "trade-off" may therefore be made. The details of the "trade-off" depend on data on the relative cost to the employer of the two benefits. If the data show that Benefit "A" and Benefit "B" cost the same, Benefit "B" may be reduced up to 20% if Benefit "A" is unreduced. If the data show that Benefit "A" costs only half as much as Benefit "B," however, Benefit "B" may be reduced up to only 15% if Benefit "A" is unreduced, since a greater reduction in Benefit "B" would result in an impermissible reduction in total benefit costs.

(g) *Relation of ADEA to State laws.* The ADEA does not preempt State age discrimination in employment laws. However, the failure of the ADEA to preempt such laws does not affect the issue of whether section 514 of the Employee Retirement Income Security Act (ERISA) preempts State laws which related to employee benefit plans. [Redesignated Reg. § 1625.10 by 52 FR 23811 on June 25, 1987].

[¶ 15,750H]

§1625.12 Exemption for bona fide executive or high policymaking employees.—

(a) Section 12(c)(1) of the Act, added by the 1978 amendments and as amended in 1984 and 1986, provides: "Nothing in this Act shall be construed to prohibit compulsory retirement of any employee who has attained 65 years of age, and who, for the 2-year period immediately before retirement, is employed in a bona fide executive or higher policymaking position, if such employee is entitled to an immediate nonforfeitable annual retirement benefit from a pension, profit-sharing, savings, or deferred compensation plan, or any combination of such plans, of the employer of such employee which equals, in the aggregate, at least $44,000."

(b) Since this provision is an exemption from the non-discrimination requirements of the Act, the burden is on the one seeking to invoke the exemption to show that every element has been clearly and unmistakably met. Moreover, as with other exemptions from the Act, this exemption must be narrowly construed.

(c) An employee within the exemption can lawfully be forced to retire on account of age at age 65 or above. In addition, the employer is free to retain such employees, either in the same position or status or in a different position or status. For example, an employee who falls within the exemption may be offered a position of lesser status or a part-time position. An employee who accepts such a new status or position, however, may not be treated any less favorably, on account of age, than any similarly situated younger employee.

(d)(1) In order for an employee to qualify as a "bona fide executive," the employer must initially show that the employee satisfies the definition of a bona fide executive set forth in § 541.1 of this chapter. Each of the requirements in paragraphs (a) through (e) of § 541.1 must be satisfied, regardless of the level of the employee's salary or compensation.

(2) Even if an employee qualifies as an executive under the definition in § 541.1 of this chapter, the exemption from the ADEA may not be claimed unless the employee also meets the further criteria specified in the Conference Committee Report in the form of examples (see H.R. Rept. No. 95-950, p. 9). The examples are intended to make clear that the exemption does not apply to middle-management employees, no matter how great their retirement income, but only to a very few top level employees who exercise substantial executive authority over a significant number of employees and a large volume of business. As stated in the Conference Report (H.R. Rept. No. 95-950, p. 9):

"Typically the head of a significant and substantial local or regional operation of a corporation [or other business organization], such as a major production facility or retail establishment, but not the head of a minor branch, warehouse or retail store, would be covered by the term "bona fide executive." Individuals at higher levels in the corporate organizational structure who possess comparable or greater levels of responsibility and authority as measured by established and recognized criteria would also be covered.

"The heads of major departments or divisions of corporations [or other business organizations] are usually located at corporate or regional headquarters. With respect to employees whose duties are associated with corporate headquarters operations, such as finance, marketing, legal, production and manufacturing (or in a corporation organized on a product line basis, the management of product lines), the definition would cover employees who head those divisions.

"In a large organization the immediate subordinates of the heads of these divisions sometimes also exercise executive authority, within the meaning of this exemption. The conferees intend the definition to cover such employees if they possess responsibility which is comparable to or greater than that possessed by the head of a significant and substantial local operation who meets the definition."

(e) The phrase "high policymaking position," according to the Conference Report (H.R. Rept. No. 95-950, p. 10), is limited to "* * * certain top level employees who are not 'bona fide executives' * * *." Specifically, these are:

"* * * individuals who have little or no line authority but whose position and responsibility are such that they play a significant role in the development of corporate policy and effectively recommend the implementation thereof.

"For example, the chief economist or the chief research scientist of a corporation typically has little line authority. His duties would be primarily intellectual as opposed to executive or managerial. His responsibility would be to evaluate significant economic or scientific trends and issues, to develop and recommend policy direction to the top executive officers of the corporation, and he would have a significant impact on the ultimate decision on such policies by virtue of his expertise and direct access to the decisionmakers. Such an employee would meet the definition of a 'high policymaking' employee."

On the other hand, as this description makes clear, the support personnel of a "high policymaking" employeee would not be subject to the exemption even if they supervise the development, and draft the recommendation, of various policies submitted by their supervisors.

(f) In order for the exemption to apply to a particular employee, the employee must have been in a "bona fide executive or high policymaking position," as those terms are defined in this section, for the two-year period immediately before retirement. Thus, an employee who holds two or more different positions during the two-year period is subject to the exemption only if each such job is an executive or high policymaking position.

(g) The Conference Committee Report expressly states that the exemption is not applicable to Federal employees covered by section 15 of the Act (H.R. Rept. No. 95-950, p. 10).

(h) The "annual retirement benefit," to which covered employees must be entitled, is the sum of amounts payable during each one-year period from the date on which such benefits first become receivable by the retiree. Once established, the annual period upon which calculations are based may not be changed from year to year.

(i) The annual retirement benefit must be immediately available to the employee to be retired pursuant to the exemption. For purposes of determining compliance, "immediate" means that the payment of plan benefits (in a lump sum or the first of a series of periodic payments) must occur not later than 60 days after the effective date of the retirement in question. The fact that an employee will receive benefits only after expiration of the 60-day period will not preclude his retirement pursuant to the exemption, if the employee could have elected to receive benefits within that period.

(j)(1) The annual retirement benefit must equal, in the aggregate, at least $27,000. The manner of determining whether this requirement has been satisfied is set forth in § 1627.17(c).

(2) In determining whether the aggregate annual retirement benefit equals at least $27,000, the only benefits which may be counted are those authorized by and provided under the terms of a pension, profitsharing, savings, or deferred compensation plan. (Regulations issued pursuant to section 12(c)(2) of the Act, regarding the manner of calculating the amount of qualified retirement benefits for purposes of the exemption, are set forth in § 1627.17 of this Chapter.)

(k)(1) The annual retirement benefit must be "nonforfeitable." Accordingly, the exemption may not be applied to any employee subject to plan provisions which could cause the cessation of payments to a retiree or result in the reduction of benefits to less than $27,000 in any one year. For example, where a plan contains a provision under which benefits would be suspended if a retiree engages in litigation against the former employer, or obtains employment with a competitor of the former employer, the retirement benefit will be deemed to be forfeitable. However, retirement benefits will not be deemed forfeitable solely because the benefits are discontinued or suspended for reasons permitted under section 411(a)(3) of the Internal Revenue Code.

(2) An annual retirement benefit will not be deemed forfeitable merely because the minimum statutory benefit level is not guaranteed against the possibility of plan bankruptcy or is subject to benefit restrictions in the event of early termination of the plan in accordance with Treasury Regulation 1.401-4(c). However, as of the effective date of the retirement in question, there must be at least a reasonable expectation that the plan will meet its obligations.

* * *

[¶ 15,750I]

§ 1625.21 Apprenticeship programs. All apprenticeship programs, including those apprenticeship programs created or maintained by joint labor-management organizations, are subject to the prohibitions of sec. 4 of the Age Discrimination in Employment Act of 1967, as amended, 29 U.S.C.

623. Age limitations in apprenticeship programs are valid only if excepted under sec. 4(f)(1) of the Act, 29 U.S.C. 623(f)(1), or exempted by the Commission under sec. 9 of the Act, 29 U.S.C. 628, in accordance with the procedures set forth in 29 CFR 1627.15.

[¶ 15,750J]

§ 1625.22 Waivers of rights and claims under the ADEA.

(a) *Introduction.*

(1) Congress amended the ADEA in 1990 to clarify the prohibitions against discrimination on the basis of age. In Title II of OWBPA, Congress addressed waivers of rights and claims under the ADEA, amending section 7 of the ADEA by adding a new subsection (f).

(2) Section 7(f)(1) of the ADEA expressly provides that waivers may be valid and enforceable under the ADEA only if the waiver is "knowing and voluntary". Sections 7(f)(1) and 7(f)(2) of the ADEA set out the minimum requirements for determining whether a waiver is knowing and voluntary.

(3) Other facts and circumstances may bear on the question of whether the waiver is knowing and voluntary, as, for example, if there is a material mistake, omission, or misstatement in the information furnished by the employer to an employee in connection with the waiver.

(4) The rules in this section apply to all waivers of ADEA rights and claims, regardless of whether the employee is employed in the private or public sector, including employment by the United States Government.

(b) *Wording of Waiver Agreements.*

(1) Section 7(f)(1)(A) of the ADEA provides, as part of the minimum requirements for a knowing and voluntary waiver, that:

The waiver is part of an agreement between the individual and the employer that is written in a manner calculated to be understood by such individual, or by the average individual eligible to participate.

(2) The entire waiver agreement must be in writing.

(3) Waiver agreements must be drafted in plain language geared to the level of understanding of the individual party to the agreement or individuals eligible to participate. Employers should take into account such factors as the level of comprehension and education of typical participants. Consideration of these factors usually will require the limitation or elimination of technical jargon and of long, complex sentences.

(4) The waiver agreement must not have the effect of misleading, misinforming, or failing to inform participants and affected individuals. Any advantages or disadvantages described shall be presented without either exaggerating the benefits or minimizing the limitations.

(5) Section 7(f)(1)(H) of the ADEA, relating to exit incentive or other employment termination programs offered to a group or class of employees, also contains a requirement that information be conveyed "in writing in a manner calculated to be understood by the average participant." The same standards applicable to the similar language in section 7(f)(1)(A) of the ADEA apply here as well.

(6) Section 7(f)(1)(B) of the ADEA provides, as part of the minimum requirements for a knowing and voluntary waiver, that "the waiver specifically refers to rights or claims under this Act." Pursuant to this subsection, the waiver agreement must refer to the Age Discrimination in Employment Act (ADEA) by name in connection with the waiver.

(7) Section 7(f)(1)(E) of the ADEA requires that an individual must be "advised in writing to consult with an attorney prior to executing the agreement."

(c) *Waiver of future rights.*

(1) Section 7(f)(1)(C) of the ADEA provides that:

A waiver may not be considered knowing and voluntary unless at a minimum . . . the individual does not waive rights or claims that may arise after the date the waiver is executed.

(2) The waiver of rights or claims that arise following the execution of a waiver is prohibited. However, section 7(f)(1)(C) of the ADEA does not bar, in a waiver that otherwise is consistent with statutory requirements, the enforcement of agreements to perform future employment-related actions such as the employee's agreement to retire or otherwise terminate employment at a future date.

(d) *Consideration.*

(1) Section 7(f)(1)(D) of the ADEA states that:

A waiver may not be considered knowing and voluntary unless at a minimum * * * the individual waives rights or claims only in exchange for consideration in addition to anything of value to which the individual already is entitled.

(2) "Consideration in addition" means anything of value in addition to that to which the individual is already entitled in the absence of a waiver.

(3) If a benefit or other thing of value was eliminated in contravention of law or contract, express or implied, the subsequent offer of such benefit or thing of value in connection with a waiver will not constitute "consideration" for purposes of section 7(f)(1) of the ADEA. Whether such elimination as to one employee or group of employees is in contravention of law or

contract as to other employees, or to that individual employee at some later time, may vary depending on the facts and circumstances of each case.

(4) An employer is not required to give a person age 40 or older a greater amount of consideration than is given to a person under the age of 40, solely because of that person's membership in the protected class under the ADEA.

(e) *Time periods.*

(1) Section 7(f)(1)(F) of the ADEA states that:

A waiver may not be considered knowing and voluntary unless at a minimum * * *

(i) The individual is given a period of at least 21 days within which to consider the agreement; or

(ii) If a waiver is requested in connection with an exit incentive or other employment termination program offered to a group or class of employees, the individual is given a period of at least 45 days within which to consider the agreement.

(2) Section 7(f)(1)(G) of the ADEA states:

A waiver may not be considered knowing and voluntary unless at a minimum . . . the agreement provides that for a period of at least 7 days following the execution of such agreement, the individual may revoke the agreement, and the agreement shall not become effective or enforceable until the revocation period has expired.

(3) The term "exit incentive or other employment termination program" includes both voluntary and involuntary programs.

(4) The 21 or 45 day period runs from the date of the employer's final offer. Material changes to the final offer restart the running of the 21 or 45 day period; changes made to the final offer that are not material do not restart the running of the 21 or 45 day period. The parties may agree that changes, whether material or immaterial, do not restart the running of the 21 or 45 day period.

(5) The 7 day revocation period cannot be shortened by the parties, by agreement or otherwise.

(6) An employee may sign a release prior to the end of the 21 or 45 day time period, thereby commencing the mandatory 7 day revocation period. This is permissible as long as the employee's decision to accept such shortening of time is knowing and voluntary and is not induced by the employer through fraud, misrepresentation, a threat to withdraw or alter the offer prior to the expiration of the 21 or 45 day time period, or by providing different terms to employees who sign the release prior to the expiration of such time period. However, if an employee signs a release before the expiration of the 21 or 45 day time period, the employer may expedite the processing of the consideration provided in exchange for the waiver.

(f) *Informational requirements.*

(1) *Introduction.*

(i) Section 7(f)(1)(H) of the ADEA provides that:

A waiver may not be considered knowing and voluntary unless at a minimum . . . if a waiver is requested in connection with an exit incentive or other employment termination program offered to a group or class of employees, the employer (at the commencement of the period specified in subparagraph (F)) [which provides time periods for employees to consider the waiver] informs the individual in writing in a manner calculated to be understood by the average individual eligible to participate, as to:

(i) Any class, unit, or group of individuals covered by such program, any eligibility factors for such program, and any time limits applicable to such program; and

(ii) The job titles and ages of all individuals eligible or selected for the program, and the ages of all individuals in the same job classification or organizational unit who are not eligible or selected for the program.

(ii) Section 7(f)(1)(H) of the ADEA addresses two principal issues: to whom information must be provided, and what information must be disclosed to such individuals.

(iii)(A) Section 7(f)(1)(H) of the ADEA references two types of "programs" under which employers seeking waivers must make written disclosures: "exit incentive programs" and "other employment termination programs." Usually an "exit incentive program" is a voluntary program offered to a group or class of employees where such employees are offered consideration in addition to anything of value to which the individuals are already entitled (hereinafter in this section, "additional consideration") in exchange for their decision to resign voluntarily and sign a waiver. Usually "other employment termination program" refers to a group or class of employees who were involuntarily terminated and who are offered additional consideration in return for their decision to sign a waiver.

(B) The question of the existence of a "program" will be decided based upon the facts and circumstances of each case. A "program" exists when an employer offers additional consideration for the signing of a waiver pursuant to an exit incentive or other employment termination (e.g., a reduction in force) to two or more employees. Typically, an involuntary termination program is a standardized formula or package of benefits that is available to two or more employees, while an exit incentive program typi-

cally is a standardized formula or package of benefits designed to induce employees to sever their employment voluntarily. In both cases, the terms of the programs generally are not subject to negotiation between the parties.

(C) Regardless of the type of program, the scope of the terms "class," "unit," "group," "job classification," and "organizational unit" is determined by examining the "decisional unit" at issue. (See paragraph (f)(3) of this section, "The Decisional Unit.")

(D) A "program" for purposes of the ADEA need not constitute an "employee benefit plan" for purposes of the Employee Retirement Income Security Act of 1974 (ERISA). An employer may or may not have an ERISA severance plan in connection with its OWBPA program.

(iv) The purpose of the informational requirements is to provide an employee with enough information regarding the program to allow the employee to make an informed choice whether or not to sign a waiver agreement.

(2) *To whom must the information be given.* The required information must be given to each person in the decisional unit who is asked to sign a waiver agreement.

(3) *The decisional unit.*

(i)(A) The terms "class," "unit," or "group" in section 7(f)(1)(H)(i) of the ADEA and "job classification or organizational unit" in section 7(f)(1)(H)(ii) of the ADEA refer to examples of categories or groupings of employees affected by a program within an employer's particular organizational structure. The terms are not meant to be an exclusive list of characterizations of an employer's organization.

(B) When identifying the scope of the "class, unit, or group," and "job classification or organizational unit," an employer should consider its organizational structure and decision-making process. A "decisional unit" is that portion of the employer's organizational structure from which the employer chose the persons who would be offered consideration for the signing of a waiver and those who would not be offered consideration for the signing of a waiver. The term "decisional unit" has been developed to reflect the process by which an employer chose certain employees for a program and ruled out others from that program.

(ii)(A) The variety of terms used in section 7(f)(1)(H) of the ADEA demonstrates that employers often use differing terminology to describe their organizational structures. When identifying the population of the decisional unit, the employer acts on a case-by-case basis, and thus the determination of the appropriate class, unit, or group, and job classification or organizational unit for purposes of section 7(f)(1)(H) of the ADEA also must be made on a case-by-case basis.

(B) The examples in paragraph (f)(3)(iii), of this section demonstrate that in appropriate cases some subgroup of a facility's work force may be the decisional unit. In other situations, it may be appropriate for the decisional unit to comprise several facilities. However, as the decisional unit is typically no broader than the facility, in general the disclosure need be no broader than the facility. "Facility" as it is used throughout this section generally refers to place or location. However, in some circumstances terms such as "school," "plant," or "complex" may be more appropriate.

(C) Often, when utilizing a program an employer is attempting to reduce its workforce at a particular facility in an effort to eliminate what it deems to be excessive overhead, expenses, or costs from its organization at that facility. If the employer's goal is the reduction of its workforce at a particular facility and that employer undertakes a decision-making process by which certain employees of the facility are selected for a program, and others are not selected for a program, then that facility generally will be the decisional unit for purposes of section 7(f)(1)(H) of the ADEA.

(D) However, if an employer seeks to terminate employees by exclusively considering a particular portion or subgroup of its operations at a specific facility, then that subgroup or portion of the workforce at that facility will be considered the decisional unit.

(E) Likewise, if the employer analyzes its operations at several facilities, specifically considers and compares ages, seniority rosters, or similar factors at differing facilities, and determines to focus its workforce reduction at a particular facility, then by the nature of that employer's decision-making process the decisional unit would include all considered facilities and not just the facility selected for the reductions.

(iii) The following examples are not all-inclusive and are meant only to assist employers and employees in determining the appropriate decisional unit. Involuntary reductions in force typically are structured along one or more of the following lines:

(A) *Facility-wide:* Ten percent of the employees in the Springfield facility will be terminated within the next ten days;

(B) *Division-wide:* Fifteen of the employees in the Computer Division will be terminated in December;

(C) *Department-wide:* One-half of the workers in the Keyboard Department of the Computer Division will be terminated in December;

(D) *Reporting:* Ten percent of the employees who report to the Vice President for Sales, wherever the employees are located, will be terminated immediately;

(E) *Job Category:* Ten percent of all accountants, wherever the employees are located, will be terminated next week.

(iv) In the examples in paragraph (f)(3)(iii) of this section, the decisional units are, respectively:

(A) The Springfield facility;

(B) The Computer Division;

(C) The Keyboard Department;

(D) All employees reporting to the Vice President for Sales; and

(E) All accountants.

(v) While the particular circumstances of each termination program will determine the decisional unit, the following examples also may assist in determining when the decisional unit is other than the entire facility:

(A) A number of small facilities with interrelated functions and employees in a specific geographic area may comprise a single decisional unit;

(B) If a company utilizes personnel for a common function at more than one facility, the decisional unit for that function (i.e., accounting) may be broader than the one facility;

(C) A large facility with several distinct functions may comprise a number of decisional units; for example, if a single facility has distinct internal functions with no employee overlap (i.e., manufacturing, accounting, human resources), and the program is confined to a distinct function, a smaller decisional unit may be appropriate.

(vi)(A) For purposes of this section, higher level review of termination decisions generally will not change the size of the decisional unit unless the reviewing process alters its scope. For example, review by the Human Resources Department to monitor compliance with discrimination laws does not affect the decisional unit. Similarly, when a regional manager in charge of more than one facility reviews the termination decisions regarding one of those facilities, the review does not alter the decisional unit, which remains the one facility under consideration.

(B) However, if the regional manager in the course of review determines that persons in other facilities should also be considered for termination, the decisional unit becomes the population of all facilities considered. Further, if, for example, the regional manager and his three immediate subordinates jointly review the termination decisions, taking into account more than one facility, the decisional unit becomes the populations of all facilities considered.

(vii) This regulatory section is limited to the requirements of section 7(f)(1)(H) and is not intended to affect the scope of discovery or of substantive proceedings in the processing of charges of violation of the ADEA or in litigation involving such charges.

(4) *Presentation of information.*

(i) The information provided must be in writing and must be written in a manner calculated to be understood by the average individual eligible to participate.

(ii) Information regarding ages should be broken down according to the age of each person eligible or selected for the program and each person

Job Title		
(1) Mechanical Engineers, I		
(2) Mechanical Engineers, II		
(3) Structural Engineers, I		
(4) Structural Engineers, II		
(5) Purchasing Agents		

(g) *Waivers settling charges and lawsuits.*

(1) Section 7(f)(2) of the ADEA provides that:

A waiver in settlement of a charge filed with the Equal Employment Opportunity Commission, or an action filed in court by the individual or the individual's representative, alleging age discrimination of a kind prohibited under section 4 or 15 may not be considered knowing and voluntary unless at a minimum:

(A) Subparagraphs (A) through (E) of paragraph (1) have been met; and

(B) The individual is given a reasonable period of time within which to consider the settlement agreement.

not eligible or selected for the program. The use of age bands broader than one year (such as "age 20-30") does not satisfy this requirement.

(iii) In a termination of persons in several established grade levels and/or other established subcategories within a job category or job title, the information shall be broken down by grade level or other subcategory.

(iv) If an employer in its disclosure combines information concerning both voluntary and involuntary terminations, the employer shall present the information in a manner that distinguishes between voluntary and involuntary terminations.

(v) If the terminees are selected from a subset of a decisional unit, the employer must still disclose information for the entire population of the decisional unit. For example, if the employer decides that a 10% RIF in the Accounting Department will come from the accountants whose performance is in the bottom one-third of the Division, the employer still must disclose information for all employees in the Accounting Department, even those who are the highest rated.

(vi) An involuntary termination program in a decisional unit may take place in successive increments over a period of time. Special rules apply to this situation. Specifically, information supplied with regard to the involuntary termination program should be cumulative, so that later terminees are provided ages and job titles or job categories, as appropriate, for all persons in the decisional unit at the beginning of the program and all persons terminated to date. There is no duty to supplement the information given to earlier terminees so long as the disclosure, at the time it is given, conforms to the requirements of this section.

(vii) The following example demonstrates one way in which the required information could be presented to the employees. (This example is not presented as a prototype notification agreement that automatically will comply with the ADEA. Each information disclosure must be structured based upon the individual case, taking into account the corporate structure, the population of the decisional unit, and the requirements of section 7(f)(1)(H) of the ADEA): Example: Y Corporation lost a major construction contract and determined that it must terminate 10% of the employees in the Construction Division. Y decided to offer all terminees $20,000 in severance pay in exchange for a waiver of all rights. The waiver provides the section 7(f)(1)(H) of the ADEA information as follows:

(A) The decisional unit is the Construction Division.

(B) All persons in the Construction Division are eligible for the program. All persons who are being terminated in our November RIF are selected for the program.

(C) All persons who are being offered consideration under a waiver agreement must sign the agreement and return it to the Personnel Office within 45 days after receiving the waiver. Once the signed waiver is returned to the Personnel Office, the employee has 7 days to revoke the waiver agreement.

(D) The following is a listing of the ages and job titles of persons in the Construction Division who were and were not selected for termination and the offer of consideration for signing a waiver:

Age	No. Selected	No. not selected
25	21	48
26	11	73
63	4	18
64	3	11
28	3	10
29	11	17
Etc., for all ages		
21	5	8
Etc., for all ages		
23	2	4
Etc., for all ages		
26	10	11
Etc., for all ages		

(2) The language in section 7(f)(2) of the ADEA, "discrimination of a kind prohibited under section 4 or 15" refers to allegations of age discrimination of the type prohibited by the ADEA.

(3) The standards set out in paragraph (f) of this section for complying with the provisions of section 7(f)(1) (A)-(E) of the ADEA also will apply for purposes of complying with the provisions of section 7(f)(2)(A) of the ADEA.

(4) The term "reasonable time within which to consider the settlement agreement" means reasonable under all the circumstances, including whether the individual is represented by counsel or has the assistance of counsel.

(5) However, while the time periods under section 7(f)(1) of the ADEA do not apply to subsection 7(f)(2) of the ADEA, a waiver agreement under

this subsection that provides an employee the time periods specified in section 7(f)(1) of the ADEA will be considered "reasonable" for purposes of section 7(f)(2)(B) of the ADEA.

(6) A waiver agreement in compliance with this section that is in settlement of an EEOC charge does not require the participation or supervision of EEOC.

(h) *Burden of proof.* In any dispute that may arise over whether any of the requirements, conditions, and circumstances set forth in section 7(f) of the ADEA, subparagraph (A), (B), (C), (D), (E), (F), (G), or (H) of paragraph (1), or subparagraph (A) or (B) of paragraph (2), have been met, the party asserting the validity of a waiver shall have the burden of proving in a court of competent jurisdiction that a waiver was knowing and voluntary pursuant to paragraph (1) or (2) of section 7(f) of the ADEA.

(i) *EEOC's enforcement powers.*

(1) Section 7(f)(4) of the ADEA states:

No waiver agreement may affect the Commission's rights and responsibilities to enforce [the ADEA]. No waiver may be used to justify interfering with the protected right of an employee to file a charge or participate in an investigation or proceeding conducted by the Commission.

(2) No waiver agreement may include any provision prohibiting any individual from:

(i) Filing a charge or complaint, including a challenge to the validity of the waiver agreement, with EEOC, or

(ii) Participating in any investigation or proceeding conducted by EEOC.

(3) No waiver agreement may include any provision imposing any condition precedent, any penalty, or any other limitation adversely affecting any individual's right to:

(i) File a charge or complaint, including a challenge to the validity of the waiver agreement, with EEOC, or

(ii) Participate in any investigation or proceeding conducted by EEOC.

(j) *Effective date of this section.*

(1) This section is effective July 6, 1998.

(2) This section applies to waivers offered by employers on or after the effective date specified in paragraph (j)(1) of this section.

(3) No inference is to be drawn from this section regarding the validity of waivers offered prior to the effective date.

(k) *Statutory authority.* The regulations in this section are legislative regulations issued pursuant to section 9 of the ADEA and Title II of OWBPA.

[FR Doc. 98-14908 Filed 6-4-98; 8:45 am]

[¶ 15,750K]

§ 1625.23 Waivers of rights and claims: Tender back of consideration.—

(a) An individual alleging that a waiver agreement, covenant not to sue, or other equivalent arrangement was not knowing and voluntary under the ADEA is not required to tender back the consideration given for that agreement before filing either a lawsuit or a charge of discrimination with EEOC or any state or local fair employment practices agency acting as an EEOC referral agency for purposes of filing the charge with EEOC. Retention of consideration does not foreclose a challenge to any waiver agreement, covenant not to sue, or other equivalent arrangement; nor does the retention constitute the ratification of any waiver agreement, covenant not to sue, or other equivalent arrangement.

(b) No ADEA waiver agreement, covenant not to sue, or other equivalent arrangement may impose any condition precedent, any penalty, or any other limitation adversely affecting any individual's right to challenge the agreement. This prohibition includes, but is not limited to, provisions requiring employees to tender back consideration received, and provisions allowing employers to recover attorneys' fees and/or damages because of the filing of an ADEA suit. This rule is not intended to preclude employers from recovering attorneys' fees or costs specifically authorized under federal law.

(c) *Restitution, recoupment, or setoff.*

(1) Where an employee successfully challenges a waiver agreement, covenant not to sue, or other equivalent arrangement, and prevails on the merits of an ADEA claim, courts have the discretion to determine whether an employer is entitled to restitution, recoupment or setoff (hereinafter, "reduction") against the employee's monetary award. A reduction never can exceed the amount recovered by the employee, or the consideration the employee received for signing the waiver agreement, covenant not to sue, or other equivalent arrangement, whichever is less.

(2) In a case involving more than one plaintiff, any reduction must be applied on a plaintiff-by-plaintiff basis. No individual's award can be reduced based on the consideration received by any other person.

(d) No employer may abrogate its duties to any signatory under a waiver agreement, covenant not to sue, or other equivalent arrangement, even if one or more of the signatories or the EEOC successfully challenges the validity of that agreement under the ADEA [Added 12-11-00 by 65 FR 77437].

29 CFR Parts 850, 1627—Records to Be Made or Kept Relating to Age; Notices to Be Posted; Administrative Exemptions; Recodification of 29 CFR Part 850

* * *

Subpart B—Records to Be Made or Kept Relating to Age; Notices to Be Posted

[¶ 15,751]

§ 1627.2 Forms of records. No particular order or form of records is required by the regulations in this Part 1627. It is required only that the records contain in some form the information specified. If the information required is available in records kept for other purposes, or can be obtained readily by recomputing or extending data recorded in some other form, no further records are required to be made or kept on a routine basis by this Part 1627.

[¶ 15,752]

§ 1627.3 Records to be kept by employers. (a) Every employer shall make and keep for three years payroll or other records for each of his employees which contain: (1) Name; (2) Address; (3) Date of birth; (4) Occupation; (5) Rate of pay; and (6) Compensation earned each week.

(b)(1) Every employer who, in the regular course of his business, makes, obtains, or uses, any personnel or employment records related to the following, shall, except as provided in subparagraphs (3) and (4) of this paragraph, keep them for a period of 1 year from the date of the personnel action to which any records relate:

* * *

(2) Every employer shall keep on file any employee benefit plans such as pension and insurance plans, as well as copies of any seniority systems and merit systems which are in writing, for the full period the plan or system is in effect, and for at least 1 year after its termination. If the plan or system is not in writing, a memorandum fully outlining the terms of such plan or system and the manner in which it has been communicated to the affected employees, together with notations relating to any changes or revisions thereto, shall be kept on file for a like period.

* * *

(4) When an enforcement action is commenced under section 7 of the Act regarding a particular applicant or employee, the Commission or its authorized representative may require the employer to retain any record required to be kept under subparagraph (1), (2), or (3) of this paragraph which is relative to such action until the final disposition thereof.

* * *

[¶ 15,753]

§ 1627.6 Availability of records for inspection. (a) *Place records are to be kept.* The records required to be kept by this part shall be kept safe and accessible at the place of employment or business at which the individual to whom they relate is employed or has applied for employment or membership, or at one or more established central recordkeeping offices.

(b) *Inspection of records.* All records required by this part to be kept shall be made available for inspection and transcription by authorized representatives of the Commission during business hours generally observed by the office at which they are kept or in the community generally. Where records are maintained at a central recordkeeping office pursuant to paragraph (a) of this section, such records shall be made available at the office at which they would otherwise be required to be kept within 72 hours following request from the Commission or its authorized representative.

[¶ 15,754]

§ 1627.7 Transcriptions and reports. Every person required to maintain records under the Act shall make such extension, recomputation or transcriptions of his records and shall submit such reports concerning actions taken and limitations and classifications of individuals set forth in records as the Commission or its authorized representative may request in writing.

[¶ 15,755]

§1627.10 Notices to be posted. Every employer, employment agency, and labor organization which has an obligation under the Age Discrimination in Employment Act of 1967 shall post and keep posted in conspicuous places upon its premises the notice pertaining to the applicability of the Act prescribed by the Commission or its authorized representative. Such a notice must be posted in prominent and accessible places where it can readily be observed by employees, applicants for employment and union members.

[¶ 15,756]

§1627.11 Petitions for recordkeeping exceptions. (a) *Submission of petitions for relief.* Each employer, employment agency, or labor organization who for good cause wishes to maintain records in a manner other than required in this part, or to be relieved of preserving certain records for the period or periods prescribed in this part, may submit in writing a petition to the Commission requesting such relief setting forth the reasons therefor and proposing alternative recordkeeping or record-retention procedures.

(b) *Action on petitions.* If, on review of the petition and after completion of any necessary or appropriate investigation supplementary thereto, the Commission shall find that the alternative procedure proposed, if granted, will not hamper or interfere with the enforcement of the Act, and will be of equivalent usefulness in its enforcement, the Commission may grant the petition subject to such conditions as it may determine appropriate and subject to revocation. Whenever any relief granted to any person is sought to be revoked for failure to comply with the conditions of the Commission, that person shall be notified in writing of the facts constituting such failure and afforded an opportunity to achieve or demonstrate compliance.

(c) *Compliance after submission of petitions.* The submission of a petition or any delay of the Commission in acting upon such petition shall not relieve any employer, employment agency, or labor organization from any obligations to comply with this part. However, the Commission shall give notice of the denial of any petition with due promptness.

Subpart C—Administrative Exemptions

[¶ 15,757]

§1627.15 Administrative exemptions; procedures. (a) Section 9 of the Act provides that, "In accordance with the provisions of subchapter II of chapter 5, of title 5, United States Code, the Secretary of Labor * * * may establish such reasonable exemptions to and from any or all provisions of this Act as he may find necessary and proper in the public interest."

(b) The authority conferred on the Commission by section 9 of the Act to establish reasonable exemptions will be exercised with caution and due regard for the remedial purpose of the statute to promote employment of older persons based on their ability rather than age and to prohibit arbitrary age discrimination in employment. Administrative action consistent with this statutory purpose may be taken under this section, with or without a request therefor, when found necessary and proper in the public interest in accordance with the statutory standards. No formal procedures have been prescribed for requesting such action. However, a reasonable exemption from the Act's provisions will be granted only if it is decided, after notice published in the FEDERAL REGISTER giving all interested persons an opportunity to present data, views, or arguments, that a strong and affirmative showing has been made that such exemption is in fact necessary and proper in the public interest. Request for such exemption shall be submitted in writing to the Commission.

[¶ 15,758]

§1627.16 Specific exemptions. (a) Pursuant to the authority contained in section 9 of the Act and in accordance with the procedure provided therein and in §1627.15(b) of this part, it has been found necessary and proper in the public interest to exempt from all prohibitions of the Act all activities and programs under Federal contracts or grants, or carried out by the public employment services of the several States, designed exclusively to provide employment for, or to encourage the employment of, persons with special employment problems, including employment activities and programs under the Manpower Development and Training Act of 1962, as amended, and the Economic Opportunity Act of 1964, as amended, for persons among the long-term unemployed, handicapped, members of minority groups, older workers, or youth. Questions concerning the application of this exemption shall be referred to the Commission for decision.

(b) Any employer, employment agency, or labor organization the activities of which are exempt from the prohibitions of the Act under paragraph

(a) of this section shall maintain and preserve records containing the same information and data that is required of employers, employment agencies, and labor organizations under §§1627.3, 1627.4, and 1627.5, respectively.

Subpart D—Statutory Exemption

[¶ 15,758A]

§1627.17 Calculating the amount of qualified retirement benefits for purposes of the exemption for bona fide executives or high policymaking employees. (a) Section 12(c)(1) of the Act, added by the 1978 amendments and amended in 1984 and 1986, provides: "Nothing in this Act shall be construed to prohibit compulsory retirement of any employee who has attained 65 years of age, and who, for the 2-year period immediately before retirement, is employed in a bona fide executive or high policymaking position, if such employee is entitled to an immediate nonforfeitable annual retirement benefit from a pension, profitsharing, savings, or deferred compensation plan, or any combination of such plans, of the employer of such employee, which equals, in the aggregate, at least $44,000." The Commission's interpretative statements regarding this exemption are set forth in section 1625 of this chapter.

(b) Section 12(c)(2) of the Act provides:

In applying the retirement benefit test of paragraph (a) of this subsection, if any such retirement benefit is in a form other than a straight life annuity (with no ancillary benefits), or if employees contribute to any such plan or make rollover contributions, such benefit shall be adjusted in accordance with regulations prescribed by the Commission, after consultation with the Secretary of the Treasury, so that the benefit is the equivalent of a straight life annuity (with no ancillary benefits) under a plan to which employees do not contribute and under which no rollover contributions are made.

(c)(1) The requirement that an employee be entitled to the equivalent of a $27,000 straight life annuity (with no ancillary benefits) is satisfied in any case where the employee has the option of receiving, during each year of his or her lifetime following retirement, an annual payment of at least $27,000, or periodic payments on a more frequent basis which, in the aggregate, equal at least $27,000 per year: *Provided, however,* That the portion of the retirement income figure attributable to Social Security, employee contributions, rollover contributions and contributions of prior employers is excluded in the manner described in paragraph (e) of this section. (A retirement benefit which excludes these amounts is sometimes referred to herein as a "qualified" retirement benefit.)

(2) The requirement is also met where the employee has the option of receiving, upon retirement, a lump sum payment with which it is possible to purchase a single life annuity (with no ancillary benefits) yielding at least $27,000 per year as adjusted.

(3) The requirement is also satisfied where the employee is entitled to receive, upon retirement, benefits whose aggregate value, as of the date of the employee's retirement, with respect to those payments which are scheduled to be made within the period of life expectancy of the employee, is $27,000 per year as adjusted.

(4) Where an employee has one or more of the options described in paragraphs (c)(1)-(3) of this section, but instead selects another option (or options), the test is also met. On the other hand, where an employee has no choice but to have certain benefits provided after his or her death, the value of these benefits may not be included in this determination.

(5) The determination of the value of those benefits which may be counted towards the $27,000 requirement must be made on the basis of reasonable actuarial assumptions with respect to mortality and interest. For purposes of excluding from this determination any benefits which are available only after death, it is not necessary to determine the life expectancy of each person on an individual basis. A reasonable actuarial assumption with respect to mortality will suffice.

(6) The benefits computed under paragraphs (c)(1), (2) and (3) of this section shall be aggregated for purposes of determining whether the $27,000 requirement has been met.

(d) The only retirement benefits which may be counted towards the $27,000 annual benefit are those from a pension, profit-sharing, savings, or deferred compensation plan, or any combination of such plans. Such plans include, but are not limited to, stock bonus, thrift and simplified employee pensions. The value of benefits from any other employee benefit plans, such as health or life insurance, may not be counted.

(e) In calculating the value of a pension, profit-sharing, savings, or deferred compensation plan (or any combination of such plans), amounts attributable to Social Security, employee contributions, contributions of prior employers, and rollover contributions must be excluded. Specific rules are set forth below.

(1) *Social Security.* Amounts attributable to Social Security must be excluded. Since these amounts are readily determinable, no specific rules are deemed necessary.

(2) *Employee contributions.* Amounts attributable to employee contributions must be excluded. The regulations governing this requirement are based on section 411(c) of the Internal Revenue Code and Treasury Regulations thereunder (§ 1.411(c)-(1)), relating to the allocation of accrued benefits between employer and employee contributions. Different calculations are needed to determine the amount of employee contributions, depending upon whether the retirement income plan is a defined contribution plan or a defined benefit plan. Defined contribution plans (also referred to as individual account plans) generally provide that each participant has an individual account and the participant's benefits are based solely on the account balance. No set benefit is promised in defined contribution plans, and the final amount is a result not only of the actual contributions, but also of other factors, such as investment gains and losses. Any retirement income plan which is not an individual account plan is a defined benefit plan. Defined benefit plans generally provide a definitely determinable benefit, by specifying either a flat monthly payment or a schedule of payments based on a formula (frequently involving salary and years of service), and they are funded according to actuarial principles over the employee's period of participation.

(i) *Defined contribution plans.* (A) *Separate accounts maintained.* If a separate account is maintained with respect to an employee's contributions and all income, expenses, gains and losses attributable thereto, the balance in such an account represents the amount attributable to employee contributions.

(B) *Separate accounts not maintained.* If a separate account is not maintained with respect to an employee's contributions and the income, expenses, gains and losses attributable thereto, the proportion of the total benefit attributable to employee contributions is determined by multiplying that benefit by a fraction—

(1) The numerator of which is the total amount of the employee's contributions under the plan (less withdrawals), and

(2) The denominator of which is the sum of the numerator and the total contributions made under the plan by the employer on behalf of the employee (less withdrawals).

Example: A defined contribution plan does not maintain separate accounts for employee contributions. An employee's annual retirement benefit under the plan is $40,000. The employee has contributed $96,000 and the employer has contributed $144,000 to the employee's individual account; no withdrawals have been made. The amount of the $40,000 annual benefit attributable to employee contributions is $40,000 × $96,000/$96,000 + $144,000 = $16,000. Hence the employer's share of the $40,000 annual retirement benefit is $40,000 minus $16,000 or $24,000—too low to fall within the exemption.

(ii) *Defined benefit plans.* (A) *Separate accounts maintained.* If a separate account is maintained with respect to an employee's contributions and all income, expenses, gains and losses attributable thereto, the balance in such an account represents the amount attributable to employee contributions.

(B) *Separate accounts not maintained.* If a separate account is not maintained with respect to an employee's contributions and the income, expenses, gains and losses attributable thereto, all of the contributions made by an employee must be converted actuarially to a single life annuity (without ancillary benefits) commencing at the age of forced retirement. An employee's accumulated contributions are the sum of all contributions (mandatory and, if not separately accounted for, voluntary) made by the employee, together with interest on the sum of all such contributions compounded annually at the rate of 5 percent per annum from the time each

such contribution was made until the date of retirement. *Provided, however,* That prior to the date any plan became subject to section 411(c) of the Internal Revenue Code, interest will be credited at the rate (if any) specified in the plan. The amount of the employee's accumulated contribution described in the previous sentence must be multiplied by an "appropriate conversion factor" in order to convert it to a single life annuity (without ancillary benefits) commencing at the age of actual retirement. The appropriate conversion factor depends upon the age of retirement. In accordance with Rev. Rul. 76-47, 1976-2 C.B. 109, the following conversion factors shall be used with respect to the specified retirement ages:

Retirement age:	Conversion factor percent
65 through 66	10
67 through 68	11
69	12

Example: An employee is scheduled to receive a pension from a defined benefit plan of $50,000 per year. Over the years he has contributed $150,000 to the plan, and at age 65 this amount, when contributions have been compounded at appropriate annual interest rates, is equal to $240,000. In accordance with Rev. Rul. 76-47, 10 percent is an appropriate conversion factor. When the $240,000 is multiplied by this conversion factor, the product is $24,000, which represents that part of the $50,000 annual pension payment which is attributable to employee contributions. The difference— $26,000—represents the employer's contribution, which is too low to meet the test in the exemption.

(3) *Contributions of prior employers.* Amounts attributable to contributions of prior employers must be excluded.

(i) *Current employer distinguished from prior employers.* Under the section 12(c) exemption, for purposes of excluding contributions of prior employers, a prior employer is every previous employer of the employee except those previous employers which are members of a "controlled group of corporations" with, or "under common control" with, the employer which forces the employee to retire, as those terms are used in sections 414(b) and 414(c) of the Internal Revenue Code, as modified by section 414(h) (26 U.S.C. 414(b), (c) and (h)).

(ii) *Benefits attributable to current employer and to prior employers.* Where the current employer maintains or contributes to a plan plan which is separate from plans maintained or contributed to by prior employers, the amount of the employee's benefit attributable to those prior employers can be readily determined. However, where the current employer maintains or contributes to the same plan as prior employers, the following rule shall apply. The benefit attributable to the current employer shall be the total benefit received by the employee, reduced by the benefit that the employee would have received from the plan if he or she had never worked for the current employer. For purposes of this calculation, it shall be assumed that all benefits have always been vested, even if benefits accrued as a result of service with a prior employer had not in fact been vested.

(4) *Rollover contributions.* Amounts attributable to rollover contributions must be excluded. For purposes of § 1627.17(e), a rollover contribution (as defined in sections 402(a)(5), 403(a)(4), 408(d)(3) and 409(b)(3)(C) of the Internal Revenue Code) shall be treated as an employee contribution. These amounts have already been excluded as a result of the computations set forth in § 1627.17(e)(2). Accordingly, no separate calculation is necessary to comply with this requirement.

[¶ 15,759]

[**Reserved.** Reg. §§ 860.110 and 860.120 formerly appeared at this paragraph. However, 29 CFR Part 860 was rendered obsolete and removed from the Code of Federal Regulations (52 FR 23812) on June 25, 1987. Reg. § 860.120 was redesignated within Part 1625 as Reg. § 1625.10 (CCH PENSION PLAN GUIDE, ¶ 15,750F).]

Criminal Code

[¶16,201]

SEC. 664. THEFT OR EMBEZZLEMENT FROM EMPLOYEE BENEFIT PLAN

Any person who embezzles, steals, or unlawfully and willfully abstracts or converts to his own use or to the use of another, any of the moneys, funds, securities, premiums, credits, property, or other assets of any employee welfare benefit plan or employee pension benefit plan, or of any fund connected therewith, shall be fined not more than $10,000, or imprisoned not more than five years, or both.

As used in this section, the term "any employee welfare benefit plan or employee pension benefit plan" means any employee benefit plan subject to any provision of Title I of the Employee Retirement Income Security Act of 1974.

.01 Historical Comment.

P.L. 93-406 amended Sec. 664, effective January 1, 1975, except that in the case of a plan which has a plan year which begins before January 1, 1975, and ends after December 31, 1974, the Secretary of Labor may postpone by regulation the effective date of the repeal of any provision of the Welfare and Pension Plans Disclosure Act until the beginning of the first plan year of the plan wich begins after January 1, 1975. Prior to the amendment, the language which reads "any employee benefit plan subject to any provision of Title I of the Employee Retirement Security Act of 1974" read "any such plan subject to the provisions of the Welfare and Pension Plans Disclosure Act."

Source: P.L. 87-420, approved March 20, 1962, effective June 18, 1962.

[¶16,202]

SEC. 1027. FALSE STATEMENTS AND CONCEALMENT OF FACTS IN RELATION TO DOCUMENTS REQUIRED BY THE EMPLOYEE RETIREMENT INCOME SECURITY ACT OF 1974

Whoever, in any document required by Title I of the Employee Retirement Income Security Act of 1974 (as amended from time to time) to be published, or kept as part of the records of any employee welfare benefit plan or employee pension benefit plan, or certified to the administrator of any such plan, makes any false statement or representation of fact, knowing it to be false, or knowingly conceals, covers up, or fails to disclose any fact the disclosure of which is required by such title or is necessary to verify, explain, clarify or check for accuracy and completeness any report required by such title to be published or any information required by such title to be certified, shall be fined not more than $10,000, or imprisoned not more than five years, or both.

.01 Historical Comment.

P.L. 93-406 amended Sec. 1027 effective January 1, 1975, except that in the case of a plan which has a plan year which begins before January 1, 1975 and ends after December 31, 1974, the Secretary of Labor may postpone by regulation the effective date of the repeal of any provision of the Welfare and Pension Plans Disclosure Act until the beginning of the first plan year of the plan which begins after January 1, 1975. Prior to amendment, the heading of Section 1027 read "False Statements and Concealment of Facts in Relation to Documents Required by the Welfare and Pension Plans Disclosure Act."

After amendment "Welfare and Pension Plans Disclosure Act" was sticken and replaced by "Employee Retirement Income Security Act of 1974." Wherever the word "title" appears in the present section, the word "Act" formerly appeared. The words "Whoever, in any document required by title I of the Employee Retirement Income Security Act of 1974 (as amended from time to time)" formerly read "Whoever, in any document required by the Welfare and Pension Plans Disclosure Act (as amended from time to time)."

Source: P.L. 87-420, approved March 20, 1962, effective June 18, 1962.

[¶16,203]

SEC. 1954 OFFER, ACCEPTANCE, OR SOLICITATION TO INFLUENCE OPERATIONS OF EMPLOYEE BENEFIT PLAN

Whoever being—

(1) an administrator, officer, trustee, custodian, counsel, agent, or employee of any employee welfare benefit plan or employee pension benefit plan; or

(2) an officer, counsel, agent, or employee of an employer or an employer any of whose employees are covered by such plan; or

(3) an officer, counsel, agent, or employee of an employee organization any of whose members are covered by such plan; or

(4) a person who, or an officer, counsel, agent, or employee of an organization which, provides benefit plan services to such plan

receives or agrees to receive or solicits any fee, kickback, commission, gift, loan, money, or thing of value because of or with intent to be influenced with respect to, any of his actions, decisions, or other duties relating to any question or matter concerning such plan or any person who directly or indirectly gives or offers, or promises to give or offer, any fee, kickback, commission, gift, loan, money, or thing of value prohibited by this section, shall be fined not more than $10,000 or imprisoned not more than three years, or both: *Provided,* That this section shall not prohibit the payment to or acceptance by any person of bona fide salary, compensation, or other payments made for goods or facilities actually furnished or for services actually performed in the regular course of his duties as such person, administrator, officer, trustee, custodian, counsel, agent, or employee of such plan, employer, employee organization, or organization providing benefit plan services to such plan.

As used in this section, the term (a) "any employee welfare benefit plan" or "employee pension benefit plan" means any employee welfare benefit plan or employee pension benefit plan, respectively, subject to any provision of Title I of the Employee Retirement Income Security Act of 1974 and (b) "employee organization" and "administrator" as defined respectively in sections 3(4) and 3(16) of the Employee Retirement Income Security Act of 1974.

.01 Historical Comment.

P.L. 93-406 amended Sec. 1954, effective January 1, 1975, except that in the case of a plan which has a plan year which begins before January 1, 1975 and ends after December 31, 1974, the Secretary may postpone by regulation the effective date of the repeal of any provision of the Welfare and Pension Plans Disclosure Act until the beginning of the first plan year of the plan which begins after January 1, 1975. Section 1954 was amended by striking out "any plan subject to the provisions of the Welfare and Pension Plans Disclosure Act, as amended" and inserting in lieu thereof "any employee welfare benefit plan or employee pension benefit plan, respectively, subject to any provision of title I of the Employee Retirement Income Security Act of 1974"; and by striking out "sections 3(3) and 5(b)(1) and (2) of the Welfare and Pension Plans Disclosure Act, as amended" and inserting in lieu thereof "sections 3(4) and (3)(16) of the Employee Retirement Income Security Act of 1974".

P.L. 91-452, Title II, Sec. 225, effective October 31, 1970. Section 1954 was amended by striking "(a) Whoever" and inserting in lieu thereof "Whoever" and by striking subsection (b) thereof.

Source: P.L. 87-420, approved March 20, 1962, effective September 16, 1962.

National Credit Union Administration Regulations

[¶ 16,400]

National Credit Union Administration Regulations: Employee Retirement Benefit Plans.—The following regulations authorize federal credit unions to act as trustees and custodians of certain qualified retirement plans and individual retirement accounts.

The regulations were published in the *Federal Register* of June 17, 1975 (40 FR 25582). The regulations were amended effective July 7, 1978 (43 FR 29270), October 6, 1981 (46 FR 49107), and December 13, 1983 (48 FR 55423). The regulations were further amended, by interim final regulations, to permit federal credit unions to become trustees or custodians of Education IRAs and Roth IRAs. Savings Incentive Match Plan for Employees (SIMPLE) accounts and Medical Savings Accounts (MSAs) were not specifically addressed in the regulations because SIMPLE accounts are already covered by the NCUA regulations regarding IRAs and amendments regarding MSAs will be considered more thoroughly by the NCUA at a later time. The interim final regulations were effective March 24, 1998 (63 FR 14025) and were later adopted, September 29, 1998, as final regulations without any changes except to make the interim final rules retroactively effective as of January 1, 1998 in order to protect those federal credit unions that began acting as trustees of Roth IRAs and Education IRAs between January 1, 1998 and March 23, 1998. The final regulations adopting the interim amendments were published in the *Federal Reg*ister on September 30, 1998 (63 FR 52146), and were revised by 65 FR 10933, March 1, 2000.

As to Section 701.19, proposed rules were issued on December 20, 2001 (66 FR 65662) and September 25, 2002 (67 FR 60184), and a final rule was issued on April 30, 2003 (68 FR 23025), effective May 30, 2003. The final rule is set forth at ¶ 16,401 below; the preamble to the final rule is set forth at ¶ 24,806K.

The introductory comments to the regulations provide in part: "BYLAW CHANGE—In order for a Federal credit union to establish Keogh and IRA trust accounts under the new regulations, it will be necessary for the board of directors to adopt new bylaw provisions. The Administrator will provide all Federal credit unions with preapproved amendments and the procedure and forms necessary for this purpose.

"The new provisions will serve two purposes. First, they expressly provide for the issuance of shares in either revocable or irrevocable trusts, including specific reference to shares issued pursuant to pension plans authorized by regulation. Secondly, the new provisions eliminate problems which have resulted from the present language in Article XVII. Therefore, even though the bylaw changes are directly tied in with the new pension regulations, they are also designed to relieve restrictions imposed by the present bylaw provisions which affect all Federal credit unions, whether or not they intend to offer Keogh or IRA accounts."

Reg. Sec. 721.3 (¶ 16,401F), Reg. Sec. 724.1(¶ 16,402) and Reg. Sec. 724.2 (¶ 16,402A) were amended on July 29, 2004 (69 FR 45237). The corresponding regulation preamble is set forth at ¶ 24,806N.

[¶ 16,401]

§701.19 Benefits for Employees of Federal Credit Unions.

(a) *General authority*. A federal credit union may provide employee benefits, including retirement benefits, to its employees and officers who are compensated in conformance with the Act and the bylaws, individually or collectively with other credit unions. The kind and amount of these benefits must be reasonable given the federal credit union's size, financial condition, and the duties of the employees.

(b) *Plan trustees and custodians*. Where a federal credit union is the benefit plan trustee or custodian, the plan must be authorized and maintained in accordance with the provisions of part 724 of this chapter. Where the benefit plan trustee or custodian is a party other than a federal credit union, the benefit plan must be maintained in accordance with applicable laws governing employee benefit plans, including any applicable rules and regulations issued by the Secretary of Labor, the Secretary of the Treasury, or any other federal or state authority exercising jurisdiction over the plan.

(c) *Investment authority*. A federal credit union investing to fund an employee benefit plan obligation is not subject to the investment limitations of the Act and part 703 or, as applicable, part 704, of this chapter and may purchase an investment that would otherwise be impermissible if the investment is directly related to the federal credit union's obligation or potential obligation under the employee benefit plan and the federal credit union holds the investment only for as long as it has an actual or potential obligation under the employee benefit plan.

(d) *Defined benefit plans*. Under paragraph (c) of this section, a federal credit union may invest to fund a defined benefit plan if the investment meets the conditions provided in that paragraph. If a federal credit union invests to fund a defined benefit plan that is not subject to the fiduciary responsibility provisions of part 4 of the Employee Retirement Income Security Act of 1974, it should diversify its investment portfolio to minimize the risk of large losses unless it is clearly prudent not to do so under the circumstances.

(e) *Liability insurance*. No federal credit union may occupy the position of a fiduciary, as defined in the Employee Retirement Income Security Act of 1974 and the rules and regulations issued by the Secretary of Labor, unless it has obtained appropriate liability insurance as described and permitted by Section 410(b) of the Employee Retirement Income Security Act of 1974.

(f) *Definitions*. For this section, defined benefit plan has the same meaning as in 29 U.S.C. 1002(35) and employee benefit plan has the same meaning as in 29 U.S.C. 1002(3).

[¶ 16,401A]

§701.35 Share, share draft and share certificate accounts.

(a) Federal credit unions may offer share, share draft, and share certificate accounts in accordance with section 107(6) of the Act (12 U.S.C. 1757(6)) and the board of directors may declare dividends on such accounts as provided in section 117 of the Act, (12 U.S.C. 1763).

(b) A Federal credit union shall accurately represent the terms and conditions of its share, share draft, and share certificate accounts in all advertising, disclosures, or agreements, whether written or oral.

(c) A Federal credit union may, consistent with this section, parts 707 and 740 of this subchapter, other federal law, and its contractual obligations, determine the types of fees or charges and other matters affecting the opening, maintaining and closing of a share, share draft or share certificate account. State laws regulating such activities are not applicable to federal credit unions.

(d) For purposes of this section, "state law" means the constitution, statutes, regulations, and judicial decisions of any state, the District of Columbia, the several territories and possessions of the United States, and the Commonwealth of Puerto Rico.

[¶ 16,401F]

§721.3 What categories of activities are preapproved as incidental powers necessary or requisite to carry on a credit union's business?

* * *

(1) *Trustee or custodial services*. Trustee or custodial services are services in which you are authorized to act under any written trust instrument or custodial agreement created or organized in the United States and forming part of a tax-advantaged savings plan, as authorized under the Internal Revenue Code. These services may include acting as a trustee or custodian for member retirement, education and health savings accounts. [Amended by 69 FR 45237, 7/29/04.]

[¶ 16,402]

§724.1 Federal credit unions acting as trustees and custodians of certain tax-advantaged savings plans.

A federal credit union is authorized to act as trustee or custodian, and may receive reasonable compensation for so acting, under any written trust instrument or custodial agreement created or organized in the United States and forming part of a tax-advantaged savings plan which qualifies or qualified for specific tax treatment under sections 223, 401(d), 408, 408A and 530 of the Internal Revenue Code (26 U.S.C. 223, 401(d), 408, 408A and 530), for its members or groups of its members, provided the funds of such plans are invested in share accounts or share certificate accounts of the Federal credit union. Federal credit unions located in a territory, including the trust territories, or a possession of the United States, or the Commonwealth of Puerto Rico, are also authorized to act as trustee or custodian for such plans, if authorized under sections 223, 401(d), 408, 408A and 530 of the Internal Revenue Code as applied to the territory or possession under similar provisions of territorial law. All funds held in a trustee or custodial capacity must be maintained in accordance with applicable laws and rules and regulations as may be promulgated by the Secretary of Labor, the Secretary of the Treasury, or any other authority exercising jurisdiction over such trust or custodial accounts. The federal credit union shall maintain individual records for each participant which show in detail all transactions relating to the funds of each participant or beneficiary. [Amended by 63 FR 14025, 3/24/98. Revised by 65 FR 10933, 3/1/00. Amended by 69 FR 45237, 7/29/04.]

[¶ 16,402A]

§724.2 Self-directed plans.

A federal credit union may facilitate transfers of plan funds to assets other than share and share certificates of the credit union, provided the conditions of §724.1 are met and the following additional conditions are met:

(a) All contributions of funds are initially made to a share or share certificate account in the Federal credit union;

(b) Any subsequent transfer of funds to other assets is solely at the direction of the member and the Federal credit union exercises no investment discretion and provides no investment advice with respect to plan assets (i.e., the credit union performs only custodial duties); and

(c) The member is clearly notified of the fact that National Credit Union Share Insurance Fund coverage is limited to funds held in share or share certificate accounts of NCUSIF-insured credit unions. [Amended by 69 FR 45237, 7/29/04.]

[¶ 16,402B]

§724.3 Appointment of successor trustee or custodian.

Any plan operated pursuant to this part shall provide for the appointment of a successor trustee or custodian by a person, committee, corporation or organization other than the Federal credit union or any person acting in his capacity as a director, employee or agent of the Federal credit union upon notice from the Federal credit union or the Board that the Federal credit union is unwilling or unable to continue to act as trustee or custodian.

[¶ 16,403]

§745.9-2 IRA/Keogh accounts.

(a) The present vested ascertainable interest of a participant or designated beneficiary in a trust or custodial account maintained pursuant to a pension or profit-sharing plan described under section 401(d) (Keogh account), section 408(a) (IRA) and section 408A (Roth IRA) of the Internal Revenue Code (26 U.S.C. 401(d), 408(a) and 408A) will be insured up to $100,000 separately from other accounts of the participant or designated beneficiary. For insurance purposes, IRA and Roth IRA accounts will be combined together and insured in the aggregate up to $100,000. A Keogh account will be separately insured from an IRA account, Roth IRA account or, where applicable, aggregated IRA and Roth IRA accounts. [Revised by 65 FR 10933, 3/1/00 and by 65 FR 34921, 6/1/00.]

(b) Upon liquidation of the credit union, any share insurance payment shall be made by the NCUA Board to the trustee or custodian, or the successor trustee or custodian, unless otherwise directed in writing by the plan participant or beneficiary.

[¶ 16,403A]

§745.9-3 Deferred compensation accounts.

Funds deposited by an employer pursuant to a deferred compensation plan (including section 401(K) of the Internal Revenue Code) shall be insured up to $100,000 as to the interest of each plan participant who is a member, separately from other accounts of the participant or employer.

[¶ 16,404]

Appendix to Part 745—Examples of Insurance Coverage Afforded Accounts in Credit Unions Insured by the National Credit Union Share Insurance Fund

* * *

G. How Are Trust Accounts and Retirement Accounts Insured?

* * *

* * * Although credit unions may serve as trustees or custodians for self-directed IRA, Roth IRA and Keogh accounts, once the funds in those accounts are taken out of the credit union, they are no longer insured. [Added June 1, 2000, by 65 FR 34921.]

* * *

Uniformed Services Employment and Reemployment Rights Act of 1994

P.L. 103-353

Signed on October 22, 1994

[¶16,451]

CHAPTERS 43—EMPLOYMENT AND REEMPLOYMENT RIGHTS OF MEMBERS OF THE ARMED FORCES

* * *

[¶16,452]

Act SEC. 4317. Health plans. (a)(1)(A) Subject to paragraphs (2) and (3), in any case in which a person (or the person's dependents) has coverage under a health plan in connection with the person's position of employment, including a group health plan (as defined in section 607(1) of the Employee Retirement Income Security Act of 1974), and such person is absent from such position of employment by reason of service in the uniformed services, the plan shall provide that the person may elect to continue such coverage as provided in this subsection. The maximum period of coverage of a person and the person's dependents under such an election shall be the lesser of —

    (i) the 24-month period beginning on the date on which the person's absence begins; or

    (ii) the day after the date on which the person fails to apply for or return to a position of employment, as determined under section 4312(e).

    (B) A person who elects to continue health-plan coverage under this paragraph may be required to pay not more than 102 percent of the full premium under the plan (determined in the same manner as the applicable premium under section 4980B(f)(4) of the Internal Revenue Code of 1986) associated with such coverage for the employer's other employees, except that in the case of a person who performs service in the uniformed services for less than 31 days, such person may not be required to pay more than the employee share, if any, for such coverage.

    (C) In the case of a health plan that is a multiemployer plan, as defined in section 3(37) of the Employee Retirement Income Security Act of 1974, any liability under the plan for employer contributions and benefits arising under this paragraph shall be allocated—

        (i) by the plan in such manner as the plan sponsor shall provide; or

        (ii) if the sponsor does not provide—

            (I) to the last employer employing the person before the period served by the person in the uniformed services, or

            (II) if such last employer is no longer functional, to the plan.

(b)(1) Except as provided in paragraph (2), in the case of a person whose coverage under a health plan was terminated by reason of service in the uniformed services, an exclusion or waiting period may not be imposed in connection with the reinstatement of such coverage upon reemployment under this chapter if an exclusion or waiting period would not have been imposed under a health plan had coverage of such person by such plan not been terminated as a result of such service. This paragraph applies to the person who is reemployed and to any individual who is covered by such plan by reason of the reinstatement of the coverage of such person.

    (2) Paragraph (1) shall not apply to the coverage of any illness or injury determined by the Secretary of Veterans Affairs to have been incurred in, or aggravated during, performance of service in the uniformed services.

.01 Historical Comment

P.L. 103-353, §2(a), Oct. 13, 1994, 108 Stat. 3161, as amended by

P.L. 108-454, December 10, 2004.

[¶16,453]

Act SEC. 4318. Employee pension benefit plans. (a)(1)(A) Except as provided in subparagraph (B), in the case of a right provided pursuant to an employee pension benefit plan (including those described in sections 3(2) and 3(33) of the Employee Retirement Income Security Act of 1974), or a right provided under any Federal or State law governing pension benefits for governmental employees, the right to pension benefits of a person reemployed under this chapter shall be determined under this section.

    (B) In the case of benefits under the Thrift Savings Plan, the rights of a person reemployed under this chapter shall be those rights provided in section 6432b of title 5. The first sentence of this subparagraph shall not be construed to affect any other right or benefit under this chapter.

    (2)(A) A person reemployed under this chapter shall be treated as not having incurred a break in service with the employer or employers maintaining the plan by reason of such person's period or periods of service in the uniformed services.

    (B) Each period served by a person in the uniformed services shall, upon reemployment under this chapter, be deemed to constitute service with the employer or employers maintaining the plan for the purpose of determining the nonforfeitability of the person's accrued benefits and for purpose of determining the accrual of benefits under the plan.

(b)(1) An employer reemploying a person under this chapter shall, with respect to a period of service described in subsection (a)(2)(B), be liable to an employee pension benefit plan for funding any obligation of the plan to provide the benefits described in subsection (a)(2) and shall allocate the amount of any employer contribution for the person in the same manner and to the same extent the allocation occurs for other employees during the period of service. For purposes of determining the amount of such liability and any obligation of the plan, earnings and forfeitures shall not be included. For purposes of determining the amount of such liability and for purposes of section 515 of the Employee Retirement Income Security Act of 1974 or any similar Federal or State law governing pension benefit for governmental employees, service in the uniformed services that is deemed under subsection (a) to be service with the employer shall be deemed to be service with the employer under the terms of the plan or any applicable collective bargaining agreement. In the case of a multiemployer plan, as defined in section 3(37) of the Employee Retirement Income Security Act of 1974, any liability of the plan described in this paragraph shall be allocated.

    (A) by the plan in such manner as the sponsor maintaining the plan provider; or

    (B) if the sponsor does not provide—

        (i) to the last employer employing the person before the period served by the person in the uniformed services, or

        (ii) if such last employer is no longer functional, to the plan.

    (2) A person reemployed under this chapter shall be entitled to accrued benefits pursuant to subsection (a) that are contingent on the making of, or derived from, employee contributions or elective deferrals (as defined in section 402(g)(3) of the Internal Revenue Code of 1966) only to the extent the person makes payment to the plan with respect to such contributions or deferrals. No such payment may exceed the amount the person would have been permitted or required to contribute had the person remained continuously employed by the employer throughout the period of service described in

subsection (a)(2)(B). Any payment to the plan described in this paragraph shall be made during the period beginning with the date of reemployment and whose duration is three times the period of the person's service in the uniformed services, not to exceed five years.

(3) For purposes of computing an employer's liability under paragraph (1) or the employee's contributions under paragraph (2), the employee's compensation during the period of service described in subsection (a)(2)(B) shall be computed—

(A) at the rate the employee would have received but for the period of service described in subsection (a)(2)(B), or

(B) in the case that the determination of such rate is not reasonably certain, on the basis of the employee's average rate of compensation during the 12-month period immediately preceding such period (or, if shorter, the period of employment immediately preceding such period).

(C) Any employer who reemploys a person under this chapter and who is an employer contributing to a multiemployer plan, as defined in section 3(37) of the Employee Retirement Income Security Act of 1974, under which benefits are or may be payable to such person by reason of the obligations set forth in this chapter, shall, within 30 days after the date of such reemployment, provide information, in writing, of such reemployment to the administrator of such plan.

.01 Historical Comment

P.L. 103-353, Sec. 8(h) provides:

(h) Employer Pension Benefit Plans.—(1) Nothing in this Act shall be construed to relieve an employer of an obligation to provide contributions to a pension plan (or provide pension benefits), or to relieve the obligation of a pension plan to provide pension benefits, which is required by the provisions of chapter 43 of title 38, United States Code, in effect on the day before this Act takes effect.

(2) If any employee pension benefit plan is not in compliance with section 4318 of such title or paragraph (1) of this subsection on the date of enactment of this Act, such plan shall have two years to come into compliance with such section and paragraph.

Final Regulations

Reproduced below are relevant sections of the final Department of Labor regulations that implement the Uniformed Services Employment and Reemployment Rights Act (USERRA). The regulations were published in the *Federal Register* on March 10, 2005 (70 FR 12105) and on December 19, 2005 (70 FR 75246 and 75313).

[¶ 16,453A]

ACT SEC. 1002.1 PART 1002

Subpart A——Introduction to the Regulations under the Uniformed Services Employment and Reemployment Rights Act of 1994

General Provisions

§ 1002.1 What is the purpose of this part?

§ 1002.2 Is USERRA a new law?

§ 1002.3 When did USERRA become effective?

§ 1002.4 What is the role of the Secretary of Labor under USERRA?

§ 1002.5 What definitions apply to USERRA?

§ 1002.6 What types of service in the uniformed services are covered by USERRA?

§ 1002.7 How does USERRA relate to other laws, public and private contracts, and employer practices?

Subpart B——Anti-Discrimination And Anti-Retaliation

Protection from Employer Discrimination and Retaliation

§ 1002.18 What status or activity is protected from employer discrimination by USERRA?

§ 1002.19 What activity is protected from employer retaliation by USERRA?

§ 1002.20 Does USERRA protect an individual who does not actually perform service in the uniformed services?

§ 1002.21 Do the Act's prohibitions against discrimination and retaliation apply to all employment positions?

§ 1002.22 Who has the burden of proving discrimination or retaliation in violation of USERRA?

§ 1002.23 What must the individual show to carry the burden of proving that the employer discriminated or retaliated against him or her?

Subpart C——Eligibility For Reemployment

General Eligibility Requirements for Reemployment

§ 1002.32 What criteria must the employee meet to be eligible under USERRA for reemployment after service in the uniformed services?

§ 1002.33 Does the employee have to prove that the employer discriminated against him or her in order to be eligible for reemployment?

Coverage of Employers and Positions

§ 1002.34 Which employers are covered by USERRA?

§ 1002.35 Is a successor in interest an employer covered by USERRA?

§ 1002.36 Can an employer be liable as a successor in interest if it was unaware that an employee may claim reemployment rights when the employer acquired the business?

§ 1002.37 Can one employee be employed in one job by more than one employer?

§ 1002.38 Can a hiring hall be an employer?

§ 1002.39 Are States (and their political subdivisions), the District of Columbia, the Commonwealth of Puerto Rico, and United States territories, considered employers?

§ 1002.40 Does USERRA protect against discrimination in initial hiring decisions?

§ 1002.41 Does an employee have rights under USERRA even though he or she holds a temporary, parttime, probationary, or seasonal employment position?

§ 1002.42 What rights does an employee have under USERRA if he or she is on layoff, on strike, or on a leave of absence?

§ 1002.43 Does an individual have rights under USERRA even if he or she is an executive, managerial, or professional employee?

§ 1002.44 Does USERRA cover an independent contractor?

Coverage of Service in the Uniformed Services

§ 1002.54 Are all military fitness examinations considered "service in the uniformed services?"

§ 1002.55 Is all funeral honors duty considered "service in the uniformed services?"

§ 1002.56 What types of service in the National Disaster Medical System are considered "service in the uniformed services?"

§ 1002.57 Is all service as a member of the National Guard considered "service in the uniformed services?"

§ 1002.58 Is service in the commissioned corps of the Public Health Service considered "service in the uniformed services?"

§ 1002.59 Are there any circumstances in which special categories of persons are considered to perform "service in the uniformed services?"

§ 1002.60 Does USERRA cover an individual attending a military service academy?

§ 1002.61 Does USERRA cover a member of the Reserve Officers Training Corps?

§ 1002.62 Does USERRA cover a member of the Commissioned Corps of the National Oceanic and Atmospheric Administration, the Civil Air Patrol, or the Coast Guard Auxiliary?

Absence from a Position of Employment Necessitated by Reason of Service in the Uniformed Services

§ 1002.73 Does service in the uniformed services have to be an employee's sole reason for leaving an employment position in order to have USERRA reemployment rights?

§ 1002.74 Must the employee begin service in the uniformed services immediately after leaving his or her employment position in order to have USERRA reemployment rights?

Requirement of Notice

§ 1002.85 Must the employee give advance notice to the employer of his or her service in the uniformed services?

§ 1002.86 When is the employee excused from giving advance notice of service in the uniformed services ?

§ 1002.87 Is the employee required to get permission from his or her employer before leaving to perform service in the uniformed services?

§ 1002.88 Is the employee required to tell his or her civilian employer that he or she intends to seek reemployment after completing uniformed service before the employee leaves to perform service in the uniformed services?

Period of Service

§ 1002.99 Is there a limit on the total amount of service in the uniformed services that an employee may perform and still retain reemployment rights with the employer?

§ 1002.100 Does the fiveyear service limit include all absences from an employment position that are related to service in the uniformed services?

§ 1002.101 Does the fiveyear service limit include periods of service that the employee performed when he or she worked for a previous employer?

§ 1002.102 Does the fiveyear service limit include periods of service that the employee performed before USERRA was enacted ?

§ 1002.103 Are there any types of service in the uniformed services that an employee can perform that do not count against USERRA's fiveyear service limit?

§ 1002.104 Is the employee required to accommodate his or her employer's needs as to the timing, frequency or duration of service?

APPLICATION FOR REEMPLOYMENT

§ 1002.115 Is the employee required to report to or submit a timely application for reemployment to his or her preservice employer upon completing the period of service in the uniformed services?

§ 1002.116 Is the time period for reporting back to an employer extended if the employee is hospitalized for, or convalescing from, an illness or injury incurred in, or aggravated during, the performance of service?

§ 1002.117 Are there any consequences if the employee fails to report for or submit a timely application for reemployment?

§ 1002.118 Is an application for reemployment required to be in any particular form?

§ 1002.119 To whom must the employee submit the application for reemployment?

§ 1002.120 If the employee seeks or obtains employment with an employer other than the pre service employer before the end of the period within which a reemployment application must be filed, will that jeopardize reemployment rights with the preservice employer?

§ 1002.121 Is the employee required to submit documentation to the employer in connection with the application for reemployment?

§ 1002.122 Is the employer required to reemploy the employee if documentation establishing the employee's eligibility does not exist or is not readily available?

§ 1002.123 What documents satisfy the requirement that the employee establish eligibility for reemployment after a period of service of more than thirty days?

CHARACTER OF SERVICE

§ 1002.134 What type of discharge or separation from service is required for an employee to be entitled to reemployment under USERRA?

§ 1002.135 What types of discharge or separation from uniformed service will make the employee ineligible for reemployment under USERRA?

§ 1002.136 Who determines the characterization of service?

§ 1002.137 If the employee receives a disqualifying discharge or release from uniformed service and it is later upgraded, will reemployment rights be restored?

§ 1002.138 If the employee receives a retroactive upgrade in the characterization of service, will that entitle him or her to claim back wages and benefits lost as of the date of separation from service?

EMPLOYER STATUTORY DEFENSES

§ 1002.139 Are there any circumstances in which the preservice employer is excused from its obligation to reemploy the employee following a period of uniformed service? What statutory defenses are available to the employer in an action or proceeding for reemployment benefits?

SUBPART D —RIGHTS, BENEFITS, AND OBLIGATIONS OF PERSONS ABSENT FROM EMPLOYMENT DUE TO SERVICE IN THE UNIFORMED SERVICES

FURLOUGH AND LEAVE OF ABSENCE

§ 1002.149 What is the employee's status with his or her civilian employer while performing service in the uniformed services?

§ 1002.150 Which nonseniority rights and benefits is the employee entitled to during a period of service?

§ 1002.151 If the employer provides full or partial pay to the employee while he or she is on military leave, is the employer required to also provide the nonseniority rights and benefits ordinarily granted to similarly situated employees on furlough or leave of absence?

§ 1002.152 If employment is interrupted by a period of service in the uniformed services, are there any circumstances under which the employee is not entitled to the nonseniority rights and benefits ordinarily granted to similarly situated employees on furlough or leave of absence?

§ 1002.153 If employment is interrupted by a period of service in the uniformed services, is the employee permitted upon request to use accrued vacation, annual or similar leave with pay during the service? Can the employer require the employee to use accrued leave during a period of service?

HEALTH PLAN COVERAGE

§ 1002.163 What types of health plans are covered by USERRA?

§ 1002.164 What health plan coverage must the employer provide for the employee under USERRA?

§ 1002.165 How does the employee elect continuing health plan coverage?

§ 1002.166 How much must the employee pay in order to continue his or her health plan coverage?

§ 1002.167 What actions may a plan administrator take if the employee does not elect or pay for continuing coverage in a timely manner?

§ 1002.168 If the employee's coverage was terminated at the beginning of or during service, does his or her coverage have to be reinstated upon reemployment?

§ 1002.169 Can the employee elect to delay reinstatement of health plan coverage until a date after the date he or she is reemployed?

§ 1002.170 In a multiemployer health plan, how is liability allocated for employer contributions and benefits arising under USERRA's health plan provisions?

§1002.171 How does the continuation of health plan coverage apply to a multiemployer plan that provides health plan coverage through a health benefits account system?

SUBPART E —REEMPLOYMENT RIGHTS AND BENEFITS

PROMPT REEMPLOYMENT

§ 1002.180 When is an employee entitled to be reemployed by his or her civilian employer?

§ 1002.181 How is "prompt reemployment" defined?

REEMPLOYMENT POSITION

§ 1002.191 What position is the employee entitled to upon reemployment?

§ 1002.192 How is the specific reemployment position determined?

§ 1002.193 Does the reemployment position include elements such as seniority, status, and rate of pay?

§ 1002.194 Can the application of the escalator principle result in adverse consequences when the employee is reemployed?

§ 1002.195 What other factors can determine the reemployment position?

§ 1002.196 What is the employee's reemployment position if the period of service was less than 91 days?

§ 1002.197 What is the reemployment position if the employee's period of service in the uniformed services was more than 90 days?

§ 1002.198 What efforts must the employer make to help the employee become qualified for the reemployment position?

§ 1002.199 What priority must the employer follow if two or more returning employees are entitled to reemployment in the same position?

SENIORITY RIGHTS AND BENEFITS

§1002.210 What seniority rights does an employee have when reemployed following a period of uniformed service?

§ 1002.211 Does USERRA require the employer to use a seniority system?

§ 1002.212 How does a person know whether a particular right or benefit is a senioritybased right or benefit?

§ 1002.213 How can the employee demonstrate a reasonable certainty that he or she would have received the seniority right or benefit if he or she had remained continuously employed during the period of service?

DISABLED EMPLOYEES

§ 1002.225 Is the employee entitled to any specific reemployment benefits if he or she has a disability that was incurred in, or aggravated during, the period of service?

§ 1002.226 If the employee has a disability that was incurred in, or aggravated during, the period of service, what efforts must the employer make to help him or her become qualified for the reemployment position?

RATE OF PAY

§ 1002.236 How is the employee's rate of pay determined when he or she returns from a period of service?

PROTECTION AGAINST DISCHARGE

§ 1002.247 Does USERRA provide the employee with protection against discharge?

§ 1002.248 What constitutes cause for discharge under USERRA?

PENSION PLAN BENEFITS

§ 1002.259 How does USERRA protect an employee's pension benefits?

§ 1002.260 What pension benefit plans are covered under USERRA?

§ 1002.261 Who is responsible for funding any plan obligation to provide the employee with pension benefits?

§ 1002.262 When is the employer required to make the plan contribution that is attributable to the employee's period of uniformed service?

§ 1002.263 Does the employee pay interest when he or she makes up missed contributions or elective deferrals?

§ 1002.264 Is the employee allowed to repay a previous distribution from a pension benefits plan upon being reemployed?

§ 1002.265 If the employee is reemployed with his or her preservice employer, is the employee's pension benefit the same as if he or she had remained continuously employed?

§ 1002.266 What are the obligations of a multiemployer pension benefit plan under USERRA?

§ 1002.267 How is compensation during the period of service calculated in order to determine the employee's pension benefits, if benefits are based on compensation?

SUBPART F —COMPLIANCE ASSISTANCE, ENFORCEMENT AND REMEDIES

COMPLIANCE ASSISTANCE

§ 1002.277 What assistance does the Department of Labor provide to employees and employers concerning employment, reemployment, or other rights and benefits under USERRA?

INVESTIGATION AND REFERRAL

§ 1002.288 How does an individual file a USERRA complaint?

§ 1002.289 How will VETS investigate a USERRA complaint?

§ 1002.290 Does VETS have the authority to order compliance with USERRA?

§ 1002.291 What actions may an individual take if the complaint is not resolved by VETS?

§ 1002.292 What can the Attorney General do about the complaint?

ENFORCEMENT OF RIGHTS AND BENEFITS AGAINST A STATE OR PRIVATE EMPLOYER

§ 1002.303 Is an individual required to file his or her complaint with VETS?

§ 1002.304 If an individual files a complaint with VETS and VETS' efforts do not resolve the complaint, can the individual pursue the claim on his or her own?

§ 1002.305 What court has jurisdiction in an action against a State or private employer?

§ 1002.306 Is a National Guard civilian technician considered a State or Federal employee for purposes of USERRA?

§ 1002.307 What is the proper venue in an action against a State or private employer?

§ 1002.308 Who has legal standing to bring an action under USERRA?

§ 1002.309 Who is a necessary party in an action under USERRA?

§ 1002.310 How are fees and court costs charged or taxed in an action under USERRA?

§ 1002.311 Is there a statute of limitations in an action under USERRA?

§ 1002.312 What remedies may be awarded for a violation of USERRA?

§ 1002.313 Are there special damages provisions that apply to actions initiated in the name of the United States?

§ 1002.314 May a court use its equity powers in an action or proceeding under the Act?

ATHORITY: section 4331(a) of USERRA (Pub. L. 103353, 108 Stat. 3150, 38 U.S.C. 4331(a)).

Subpart A—Introduction to the Regulations under the Uniformed Services Employment and Reemployment Rights Act of 1994

GENERAL PROVISIONS

§ 1002.1 What is the purpose of this part?

This part implements the Uniformed Services Employment and Reemployment Rights Act of 1994 ("USERRA" or "the Act"). 38 U.S.C. 43014334. USERRA is a law that establishes certain rights and benefits for employees, and duties for employers. USERRA affects employment, reemployment, and retention in employment, when employees serve or have served in the uniformed services. There are five subparts to these regulations. Subpart A gives an introduction to the USERRA regulations. Subpart B describes USERRA's antidiscrimination and antiretaliation provisions. Subpart C explains the steps that must be taken by a uniformed service member who wants to return to his or her previous civilian employment. Subpart D describes the rights, benefits, and obligations of persons absent from employment due to service in the uniformed services, including rights and obligations related to health plan coverage. Subpart E describes the rights, benefits, and obligations of the returning veteran or service member. Subpart F explains the role of the Department of Labor in enforcing and giving assistance under USERRA. These regulations implement USERRA as it applies to States, local governments, and private employers. Separate regulations published by the Federal Office of Personnel Management implement USERRA for Federal executive agency employers and employees.

§ 1002.2 Is USERRA a new law?

USERRA is the latest in a series of laws protecting veterans' employment and reemployment rights going back to the Selective Training and Service Act of 1940. USERRA's immediate predecessor was commonly referred to as the Veterans' Reemployment Rights Act (VRRA), which was enacted as section 404 of the Vietnam Era Veterans' Readjustment Assistance Act of 1974. In enacting USERRA, Congress emphasized USERRA's continuity with the VRRA and its intention to clarify and strengthen that law. Congress also emphasized that Federal laws protecting veterans' employment and reemployment rights for the past fifty years had been successful and that the large body of case law that had developed under those statutes remained in full force and effect, to the extent it is consistent with USERRA. USERRA authorized the Department of Labor to publish regulations implementing the Act for State, local government, and private employers. USERRA also authorized the Office of Personnel Management to issue regulations implementing the Act for Federal executive agencies (other than some Federal intelligence agencies). USERRA established a separate program for employees of some Federal intelligence agencies.

§ 1002.3 When did USERRA become effective?

USERRA became law on October 13, 1994. USERRA's reemployment provisions apply to members of the uniformed services seeking civilian reemployment on or after December 12, 1994. USERRA's antidiscrimination and antiretaliation provisions became effective on October 13, 1994.

§ 1002.4 What is the role of the Secretary of Labor under USERRA?

(a) USERRA charges the Secretary of Labor (through the Veterans' Employment and Training Service) with providing assistance to any person with respect to the employment and reemployment rights and benefits to which such person is entitled under the Act. More information about the Secretary's role in providing this assistance is contained in Subpart F.

(b) USERRA also authorizes the Secretary of Labor to issue regulations implementing the Act with respect to States, local governments, and private employers. These regulations are issued under this authority.

(c) The Secretary of Labor delegated authority to the Assistant Secretary for Veterans' Employment and Training for administering the veterans' reemployment rights program by Secretary's Order 183 (February 3, 1983) and for carrying out the functions and authority vested in the Secretary pursuant to USERRA by memorandum of April 22, 2002 (67 FR 31827).

§ 1002.5 What definitions apply to USERRA?

(a) *Attorney General*

means the Attorney General of the United States or any person designated by the Attorney General to carry out a responsibility of the Attorney General under USERRA.

(b) *Benefit, benefit of employment, or rights and benefits*

means any advantage, profit, privilege, gain, status, account, or interest (other than wages or salary for work performed) that accrues to the employee because of an employment contract, employment agreement, or employer policy, plan, or practice. The term includes rights and benefits under a pension plan, health plan, or employee stock ownership plan, insurance coverage and awards, bonuses, severance pay, supplemental unemployment benefits, vacations, and the opportunity to select work hours or the location of employment.

(c) *Employee*

means any person employed by an employer. The term also includes any person who is a citizen, national or permanent resident alien of the United States who is employed in a workplace in a foreign country by an employer that is an entity incorporated or organized in the United States, or that is controlled by an entity organized in the United States. "Employee" includes the former employees of an employer.

(d)(1) *Employer,*

except as provided below in paragraphs (2) and (3), means any person, institution, organization, or other entity that pays salary or wages for work performed, or that has control over employment opportunities, including—

(i) a person, institution, organization, or other entity to whom the employer has delegated the performance of employmentrelated responsibilities, except in the case that such entity has been delegated functions that are purely ministerial in nature, such as maintenance of personnel files or the preparation of forms for submission to a government agency;

(ii) the Federal Government;

(iii) a State;

(iv) any successor in interest to a person, institution, organization, or other entity referred to in this definition; and,

(v) a person, institution, organization, or other entity that has denied initial employment in violation of 38 U.S.C. 4311, USERRA's antidiscrimination and antiretaliation provisions.

(2) In the case of a National Guard technician employed under 32 U.S.C. 709, the term "employer" means the adjutant general of the State in which the technician is employed.

(3) An employee pension benefit plan as described in section 3(2) of the Employee Retirement Income Security Act of 1974 (ERISA) (29 U.S.C. 1002(2)) is considered an employer for an individual that it does not actually employ only with respect to the obligation to provide pension benefits.

(e) *Health plan*

means an insurance policy, insurance contract, medical or hospital service agreement, membership or subscription contract, or other arrangement under which health services for individuals are provided or the expenses of such services are paid.

(f) *National Disaster Medical System (NDMS)*

is an agency within the Federal Emergency Management Agency, Department of Homeland Security, established by the National Disaster Medical System (NDMS) is an agency within the Federal Emergency Management Agency, Department of Homeland Security, established by the Public Health Security and Bioterrorism Preparedness and Response Act of 2002, P.L. 107188 . *The NDMS* provides medicalrelated assistance to respond to the needs of victims of public health emergencies. Participants in the NDMS are volunteers who serve as intermittent Federal employees when activated. For purposes of USERRA coverage only, these persons are treated as members of the uniformed services when they are activated to provide assistance in response to a public health emergency or to be present for a short period of time when there is a risk of a public health emergency, or when they are participating in authorized training. *See* 42 U.S.C. 300hh11(e).

(g) *Notice*

when the employee is required to give advance notice of service, means any written or verbal notification of an obligation or intention to perform service in the uniformed services provided to an employer by the employee who will perform such service, or by the uniformed service in which the service is to be performed.

(h) *Qualified*

with respect to an employment position, means having the ability to perform the essential tasks of the position.

(i) *Reasonable efforts*

in the case of actions required of an employer, means actions, including training provided by an employer that do not place an undue hardship on the employer.

(j) *Secretary*

means the Secretary of Labor or any person designated by the Secretary of Labor to carry out an activity under USERRA and these regulations, unless a different office is expressly indicated in the regulation.

(k) *Seniority*

means longevity in employment together with any benefits of employment that accrue with, or are determined by, longevity in employment.

(l) *Service in the uniformed services*

means the performance of duty on a voluntary or involuntary basis in a uniformed service under competent authority. Service in the uniformed services includes active duty, active and inactive duty for training, National Guard duty under Federal statute, and a period for which a person is absent from a position of employment for an examination to determine the fitness of the person to perform such duty. The term also includes a period for which a person is absent from employment to perform funeral honors duty as authorized by law (10 U.S.C. 12503 or 32 U.S.C. 115). The Public Health Security and Bioterrorism Preparedness and Response Act of 2002, P.L. 107188, provides that service as an intermittent disasterresponse appointee upon activation of the National Disaster Medical System (NDMS) or as a participant in an authorized training program is deemed "service in the uniformed services." 42 U.S.C. 300hh11(e)(3).

(m) *State*

means each of the several States of the United States, the District of Columbia, the Commonwealth of Puerto Rico, Guam, the Virgin Islands, and other territories of the United States (including the agencies and political subdivisions thereof); however, for purposes of enforcement of rights under 38 U.S.C. 4323, a political subdivision of a State is a private employer.

(n) *Undue hardship*

in the case of actions taken by an employer, means an action requiring significant difficulty or expense, when considered in light of—

(1) the nature and cost of the action needed under USERRA and these regulations;

(2) the overall financial resources of the facility or facilities involved in the provision of the action; the number of persons employed at such facility; the effect on expenses and resources, or the impact otherwise of such action upon the operation of the facility;

(3) the overall financial resources of the employer; the overall size of the business of an employer with respect to the number of its employees; the number, type, and location of its facilities; and,

(4) the type of operation or operations of the employer, including the composition, structure, and functions of the work force of such employer;

the geographic separateness, administrative, or fiscal relationship of the facility or facilities in question to the employer.

(o) *Uniformed services*

means the Armed Forces; the Army National Guard and the Air National Guard when engaged in active duty for training, inactive duty training, or fulltime National Guard duty; the commissioned corps of the Public Health Service; and any other category of persons designated by the President in time of war or national emergency. For purposes of USERRA coverage only, service as an intermittent disaster response appointee of the NDMS when federally activated or attending authorized training in support of their Federal mission is deemed "service in the uniformed services," although such appointee is not a member of the "uniformed services" as defined by USERRA.

§ 1002.6 What types of service in the uniformed services are covered by USERRA?

USERRA's definition of "service in the uniformed services" covers all categories of military training and service, including duty performed on a voluntary or involuntary basis, in time of peace or war. Although most often understood as applying to National Guard and reserve military personnel, USERRA also applies to persons serving in the active components of the Armed Forces. Certain types of service specified in 42 U.S.C. 300hh11 by members of the National Disaster Medical System are covered by USERRA.

§ 1002.7 How does USERRA relate to other laws, public and private contracts, and employer practices?

(a) USERRA establishes a floor, not a ceiling, for the employment and reemployment rights and benefits of those it protects. In other words, an employer may provide greater rights and benefits than USERRA requires, but no employer can refuse to provide any right or benefit guaranteed by USERRA.

(b) USERRA supersedes any State law (including any local law or ordinance), contract, agreement, policy, plan, practice, or other matter that reduces, limits, or eliminates in any manner any right or benefit provided by USERRA, including the establishment of additional prerequisites to the exercise of any USERRA right or the receipt of any USERRA benefit. For example, an employment contract that determines seniority based only on actual days of work in the place of employment would be superseded by USERRA, which requires that seniority credit be given for periods of absence from work due to service in the uniformed services.

(c) USERRA does not supersede, nullify or diminish any Federal or State law (including any local law or ordinance), contract, agreement, policy, plan, practice, or other matter that establishes an employment right or benefit that is more beneficial than, or is in addition to, a right or benefit provided under the Act. For example, although USERRA does not require an employer to pay an employee for time away from work performing service, an employer policy, plan, or practice that provides such a benefit is permissible under USERRA.

(d) If an employer provides a benefit that exceeds USERRA's requirements in one area, it cannot reduce or limit other rights or benefits provided by USERRA. For example, even though USERRA does not require it, an employer may provide a fixed number of days of paid military leave per year to employees who are members of the National Guard or Reserve. The fact that it provides such a benefit, however, does not permit an employer to refuse to provide an unpaid leave of absence to an employee to perform service in the uniformed services in excess of the number of days of paid military leave.

Subpart B—Anti-Discrimination And Anti-Retaliation

Protection from Employer Discrimination and Retaliation

§ 1002.18 What status or activity is protected from employer discrimination by USERRA?

An employer must not deny initial employment, reemployment, retention in employment, promotion, or any benefit of employment to an individual on the basis of his or her membership, application for membership, performance of service, application for service, or obligation for service in the uniformed services.

§ 1002.19 What activity is protected from employer retaliation by USERRA?

An employer must not retaliate against an individual by taking any adverse employment action against him or her because the individual has taken an action to enforce a protection afforded any person under USERRA; testified or otherwise made a statement in or in connection with a proceeding under USERRA; assisted or participated in a USERRA investigation: or, exercised a right provided for by USERRA.

§ 1002.20 Does USERRA protect an individual who does not actually perform service in the uniformed services?

Yes. Employers are prohibited from taking actions against an individual for any of the activities protected by the Act, whether or not he or she has performed service in the uniformed services.

§ 1002.21 Do the Act's prohibitions against discrimination and retaliation apply to all employment positions?

The prohibitions against discrimination and retaliation apply to all covered employers (including hiring halls and potential employers, see sections 1002.36 and .38) and employment positions, including those that are for a brief, nonrecurrent period, and for which there is no reasonable expectation that the employment position will continue indefinitely or for a significant period. However, USERRA's reemployment rights and benefits do not apply to such brief, nonrecurrent positions of employment.

§ 1002.22 Who has the burden of proving discrimination or retaliation in violation of USERRA?

The individual has the burden of proving that a status or activity protected by USERRA was one of the reasons that the employer took action against him or her, in order to establish that the action was discrimination or retaliation in violation of USERRA. If the individual succeeds in proving that the status or activity protected by USERRA was one of the reasons the employer took action against him or her, the employer has the burden to prove the affirmative defense that it would have taken the action anyway.

§ 1002.23 What must the individual show to carry the burden of proving that the employer discriminated or retaliated against him or her?

(a) In order to prove that the employer discriminated or retaliated against the individual, he or she must first show that the employer's action was motivated by one or more of the following:

(1) membership or application for membership in a uniformed service;

(2) performance of service, application for service, or obligation for service in a uniformed service;

(3) action taken to enforce a protection afforded any person under USERRA;

(4) testimony or statement made in or in connection with a USERRA proceeding;

(5) assistance or participation in a USERRA investigation; or,

(6) exercise of a right provided for by USERRA.

(b) If the individual proves that the employer's action was based on one of the prohibited motives listed in paragraph (a) of this section, the employer has the burden to prove the affirmative defense that the action would have been taken anyway absent the USERRAprotected status or activity.

Subpart C—Eligibility For Reemployment

General Eligibility Requirements for Reemployment

§ 1002.32 What criteria must the employee meet to be eligible under USERRA for reemployment after service in the uniformed services?

(a) In general, if the employee has been absent from a position of civilian employment by reason of service in the uniformed services, he or she will be eligible for reemployment under USERRA by meeting the following criteria:

(1) the employer had advance notice of the employee's service;

(2) the employee has five years or less of cumulative service in the uniformed services in his or her employment relationship with a particular employer;

(3) the employee timely returns to work or applies for reemployment; and,

(4) the employee has not been separated from service with a disqualifying discharge or under other than honorable conditions.

(b) These general eligibility requirements have important qualifications and exceptions, which are described in detail in §§ 1002.73 through 1002.138. If the employee meets these eligibility criteria, then he or she is eligible for reemployment unless the employer establishes one of the defenses described in § 1002.139. The employment position to which the employee is entitled is described in §§ 1002.191through 1002.199.

§ 1002.33 Does the employee have to prove that the employer discriminated against him or her in order to be eligible for reemployment?

No. The employee is not required to prove that the employer discriminated against him or her because of the employee's uniformed service in order to be eligible for reemployment.

Coverage of Employers and Positions

§ 1002.34 Which employers are covered by USERRA?

(a) USERRA applies to all public and private employers in the United States, regardless of size. For example, an employer with only one employee is covered for purposes of the Act.

(b) USERRA applies to foreign employers doing business in the United States. A foreign employer that has a physical location or branch in the United States (including U.S. territories and possessions) must comply with USERRA for any of its employees who are employed in the United States.

(c) An American company operating either directly or through an entity under its control in a foreign country must also comply with USERRA for all its foreign operations, unless compliance would violate the law of the foreign country in which the workplace is located.

§ 1002.35 Is a successor in interest an employer covered by USERRA?

USERRA's definition of "employer" includes a successor in interest. In general, an employer is a successor in interest where there is a substantial continuity in operations, facilities, and workforce from the former employer. The determination whether an employer is a successor in interest must be made on a casebycase basis using a multifactor test that considers the following:

(a) whether there has been a substantial continuity of business operations from the former to the current employer;

(b) whether the current employer uses the same or similar facilities, machinery, equipment, and methods of production;

(c) whether there has been a substantial continuity of employees;

(d) whether there is a similarity of jobs and working conditions;

(e) whether there is a similarity of supervisors or managers; and,

(f) whether there is a similarity of products or services.

§ 1002.36 Can an employer be liable as a successor in interest if it was unaware that an employee may claim reemployment rights when the employer acquired the business?

Yes. In order to be a successor in interest, it is not necessary for an employer to have notice of a potential reemployment claim at the time of merger, acquisition, or other form of succession.

§ 1002.37 Can one employee be employed in one job by more than one employer?

Yes. Under USERRA, an employer includes not only the person or entity that pays an employee's salary or wages, but also includes a person or entity that has control over his or her employment opportunities, including a person or entity to whom an employer has delegated the performance of employmentrelated responsibilities. For example, if the employee is a security guard hired by a security company and he or she is assigned to a work site, the employee may report both to the security company and to the site owner. In such an instance, both employers share responsibility for compliance with USERRA. If the security company declines to assign the employee to a job because of a uniformed service obligation (for example, National Guard duties), then the security company could be in violation of the reemployment requirements and the antidiscrimination provisions of USERRA. Similarly, if the employer at the work site causes the employee's removal from the job position because of his or her uniformed service obligations, then the work site employer could be in violation of the reemployment requirements and the antidiscrimination provisions of USERRA.

§ 1002.38 Can a hiring hall be an employer?

Yes. In certain occupations (for example, longshoreman, stagehand, construction worker), the employee may frequently work for many different employers. A hiring hall operated by a union or an employer association typically assigns the employee to the jobs. In these industries, it may not be unusual for the employee to work his or her entire career in a series of shortterm job assignments. The definition of "employer" includes a person, institution, organization, or other entity to which the employer has delegated the performance of employmentrelated responsibilities. A hiring hall therefore is considered the employee's employer if the hiring and job assignment functions have been delegated by an employer to the hiring hall. As the employer, a hiring hall has reemployment responsibilities to its employees. USERRA's antidiscrimination and antiretaliation provisions also apply to the hiring hall.

§ 1002.39 Are States (and their political subdivisions), the District of Columbia, the Commonwealth of Puerto Rico, and United States territories, considered employers?

Yes. States and their political subdivisions, such as counties, parishes, cities, towns, villages, and school districts, are considered employers under USERRA. The District of Columbia, the Commonwealth of Puerto Rico, Guam, the Virgin Islands, and territories of the United States, are also considered employers under the Act.

§ 1002.40 Does USERRA protect against discrimination in initial hiring decisions?

Yes. The Act's definition of employer includes a person, institution, organization, or other entity that has denied initial employment to an individual in violation of USERRA's anti discrimination provisions. An employer need not actually employ an individual to be his or her "employer" under the Act, if it has denied initial employment on the basis of the individual's membership, application for membership, performance of service, application for service, or obligation for service in the uniformed services. Similarly, the employer would be liable if it denied initial employment on the basis of the individual's action taken to enforce a protection afforded to any person under USERRA, his or her testimony or statement in connection with any USERRA proceeding, assistance or other participation in a USERRA investigation, or the exercise of any other right provided by the Act. For example, if the individual has been denied initial employment because of his or her obligations as a member of the National Guard or Reserves, the company or entity denying employment is an employer for purposes of USERRA. Similarly, if an entity withdraws an offer of employment because the individual is called upon to fulfill an obligation in the uniformed services, the entity withdrawing the employment offer is an employer for purposes of USERRA.

§ 1002.41 Does an employee have rights under USERRA even though he or she holds a temporary, parttime, probationary, or seasonal employment position?

USERRA rights are not diminished because an employee holds a temporary, parttime, probationary, or seasonal employment position. However, an employer is not required to reemploy an employee if the employment he or she left to serve in the uniformed services was for a brief, nonrecurrent period and there is no reasonable expectation that the employment would have continued indefinitely or for a significant period. The employer bears the burden of proving this affirmative defense.

§ 1002.42 What rights does an employee have under USERRA if he or she is on layoff, on strike, or on a leave of absence?

(a) If an employee is laid off with recall rights, on strike, or on a leave of absence, he or she is an employee for purposes of USERRA. If the employee is on layoff and begins service in the uniformed services, or is laid off while performing service, he or she may be entitled to reemployment on return if the employer would have recalled the employee to employment during the period of service. Similar principles apply if the employee is on strike or on a leave of absence from work when he or she begins a period of service in the uniformed services.

(b) If the employee is sent a recall notice during a period of service in the uniformed services and cannot resume the position of employment because of the service, he or she still remains an employee for purposes of the Act. Therefore, if the employee is otherwise eligible, he or she is entitled to reemployment following the conclusion of the period of service even if he or she did not respond to the recall notice.

(c) If the employee is laid off before or during service in the uniformed services, and the employer would not have recalled him or her during that period of service, the employee is not entitled to reemployment following the period of service simply because he or she is a covered employee. Reemployment rights under USERRA cannot put the employee in a better position than if he or she had remained in the civilian employment position.

§ 1002.43 Does an individual have rights under USERRA even if he or she is an executive, managerial, or professional employee?

Yes. USERRA applies to all employees. There is no exclusion for executive, managerial, or professional employees.

§ 1002.44 Does USERRA cover an independent contractor?

(a) No. USERRA does not provide protections for an independent contractor.

(b) In deciding whether an individual is an independent contractor, the following factors need to be considered:

(1) the extent of the employer's right to control the manner in which the individual's work is to be performed;

(2) the opportunity for profit or loss that depends upon the individual's managerial skill;

(3) any investment in equipment or materials required for the individual's tasks, or his or her employment of helpers;

(4) whether the service the individual performs requires a special skill;

(5) the degree of permanence of the individual's working relationship; and,

(6) whether the service the individual performs is an integral part of the employer's business.

(c) No single one of these factors is controlling, but all are relevant to determining whether an individual is an employee or an independent contractor.

Coverage of Service in the Uniformed Services

§ 1002.54 Are all military fitness examinations considered "service in the uniformed services?"

Yes. USERRA's definition of "service in the uniformed services" includes a period for which an employee is absent from a position of employment for the purpose of an examination to determine his or her fitness to perform duty in the uniformed services. Military fitness examinations can address more than physical or medical fitness, and include evaluations for mental, educational, and other types of fitness. Any examination to determine an employee's fitness for service is covered, whether it is an initial or recurring examination. For example, a periodic medical examination required of a Reserve component member to determine fitness for continued service is covered.

§ 1002.55 Is all funeral honors duty considered "service in the uniformed services?"

(a) USERRA's definition of "service in the uniformed services" includes a period for which an employee is absent from employment for the purpose of performing authorized funeral honors duty under 10 U.S.C. 12503 (members of Reserve ordered to perform funeral honors duty) or 32 U.S.C. 115 (Member of Air or Army National Guard ordered to perform funeral honors duty).

(b) Funeral honors duty performed by persons who are not members of the uniformed services, such as members of veterans' service organizations, is not "service in the uniformed services."

§ 1002.56 What types of service in the National Disaster Medical System are considered "service in the uniformed services?"

Under a provision of the Public Health Security and Bioterrorism Preparedness and Response Act of 2002, 42 U.S.C. 300hh 11(e)(3), "service in the uniformed services" includes service performed as an intermittent disasterresponse appointee upon activation of the National Disaster Medical System or participation in an authorized training program, even if the individual is not a member of the uniformed services.

§ 1002.57 Is all service as a member of the National Guard considered "service in the uniformed services?"

The National Guard has a dual status. It is a Reserve component of the Army, or, in the case of the Air National Guard, of the Air Force. Simultaneously, it is a State military force subject to callup by the State Governor for duty not subject to Federal control, such as emergency duty in cases of floods or riots. National Guard members may perform service under either Federal or State authority, but only Federal National Guard service is covered by USERRA.

(a) National Guard service under Federal authority is protected by USERRA. Service under Federal authority includes active duty performed under Title 10 of the United States Code. Service under Federal authority also includes duty under Title 32 of the United States Code, such as active duty for training, inactive duty training, or fulltime National Guard duty.

(b) National Guard service under authority of State law is not protected by USERRA. However, many States have laws protecting the civilian job rights of National Guard members who serve under State orders. Enforcement of those State laws is not covered by USERRA or these regulations.

§ 1002.58 Is service in the commissioned corps of the Public Health Service considered "service in the uniformed services?"

Yes. Service in the commissioned corps of the Public Health Service (PHS) is "service in the uniformed services" under USERRA.

§ 1002.59 Are there any circumstances in which special categories of persons are considered to perform "service in the uniformed services?"

Yes. In time of war or national emergency the President has authority to designate any category of persons as a "uniformed service" for purposes of USERRA. If the President exercises this authority, service as a member of that category of persons would be "service in the uniformed services" under USERRA.

§ 1002.60 Does USERRA cover an individual attending a military service academy?

Yes. Attending a military service academy is considered uniformed service for purposes of USERRA. There are four service academies: The United States Military Academy (West Point, New York), the United States Naval Academy (Annapolis, Maryland), the United States Air Force Academy (Colorado Springs, Colorado), and the United States Coast Guard Academy (New London, Connecticut).

§ 1002.61 Does USERRA cover a member of the Reserve Officers Training Corps?

Yes, under certain conditions.

(a) Membership in the Reserve Officers Training Corps (ROTC) or the Junior ROTC is not "service in the uniformed services." However, some Reserve and National Guard enlisted members use a college ROTC program as a means of qualifying for commissioned officer status. National Guard and Reserve members in an ROTC program may at times, while participating in that program, be receiving active duty and inactive duty training service credit with their unit. In these cases, participating in ROTC training sessions is considered "service in the uniformed services," and qualifies a person for protection under USERRA's reemployment and anti discrimination provisions.

(b) Typically, an individual in a College ROTC program enters into an agreement with a particular military service that obligates such individual to either complete the ROTC program and accept a commission or, in case he or she does not successfully complete the ROTC program, to serve as an enlisted member. Although an individual does not qualify for reemployment protection, except as specified in (a) above, he or she is protected under USERRA's antidiscrimination provisions because, as a result of the agreement, he or she has applied to become a member of the uniformed service and has incurred an obligation to perform future service.

§ 1002.62 Does USERRA cover a member of the Commissioned Corps of the National Oceanic and Atmospheric Administration, the Civil Air Patrol, or the Coast Guard Auxiliary?

No. Although the Commissioned Corps of the National Oceanic and Atmospheric Administration (NOAA) is a "uniformed service" for some purposes, it is not included in USERRA's definition of this term. Service in the Civil Air Patrol and the Coast Guard Auxiliary similarly is not considered "service in the uniformed services" for purposes of USERRA. Consequently, service performed in the Commissioned Corps of the National Oceanic and Atmospheric Administration (NOAA), the Civil Air Patrol, and the Coast Guard Auxiliary is not protected by USERRA.

Absence from a Position of Employment Necessitated by Reason of Service in the Uniformed Services

§ 1002.73 Does service in the uniformed services have to be an employee's sole reason for leaving an employment position in order to have USERRA reemployment rights?

No. If absence from a position of employment is necessitated by service in the uniformed services, and the employee otherwise meets the Act's eligibility requirements, he or she has reemployment rights under USERRA, even if the employee uses the absence for other purposes as well. An employee is not required to leave the employment position for the sole purpose of performing service in the uniformed services. For example, if the employee is required to report to an out of State location for military training and he or she spends offduty time during that assignment moonlighting as a security guard or visiting relatives who live in that State, the employee will not lose reemployment rights simply because he or she used some of the time away from the job to do something other than attend the military training. Also, if an employee receives advance notification of a mobilization order, and leaves his or her employment position in order to prepare for duty, but the mobilization is cancelled, the employee will not lose any reemployment rights.

§ 1002.74 Must the employee begin service in the uniformed services immediately after leaving his or her employment position in order to have USERRA reemployment rights?

No. At a minimum, an employee must have enough time after leaving the employment position to travel safely to the uniformed service site and arrive fit to perform the service. Depending on the specific circumstances, including the duration of service, the amount of notice received, and the location of the service, additional time to rest, or to arrange affairs and report to duty, may be necessitated by reason of service in the uniformed services. The following examples help to explain the issue of the period of time between leaving civilian employment and beginning of service in the uniformed services:

(a) If the employee performs a full overnight shift for the civilian employer and travels directly from the work site to perform a full day of uniformed service, the employee would not be considered fit to perform the uniformed service. An absence from that work shift is necessitated so that the employee can report for uniformed service fit for duty.

(b) If the employee is ordered to perform an extended period of service in the uniformed services, he or she may require a reasonable period of time off from the civilian job to put his or her personal affairs in order, before beginning the service. Taking such time off is also necessitated by the uniformed service.

(c) If the employee leaves a position of employment in order to enlist or otherwise perform service in the uniformed services and, through no fault of his or her own, the beginning date of the service is delayed, this delay does not terminate any reemployment rights.

Requirement of Notice

§ 1002.85 Must the employee give advance notice to the employer of his or her service in the uniformed services?

(a) Yes. The employee, or an appropriate officer of the uniformed service in which his or her service is to be performed, must notify the employer that the employee intends to leave the employment position to perform service in the uniformed services, with certain exceptions described below. In cases in which an employee is employed by more than one employer, the employee, or an appropriate office of the uniformed service in which his or her service is to be performed, must notify each employer that the employee intends to leave the employment position to perform service in the uniformed services, with certain exceptions described below.

(b) The Department of Defense USERRA regulations at 32 C.F.R. 104.3 provide that an "appropriate officer" can give notice on the employee's behalf. An "appropriate officer" is a commissioned, warrant, or noncommissioned officer authorized to give such notice by the military service concerned.

(c) The employee's notice to the employer may be either verbal or written. The notice may be informal and does not need to follow any particular format.

(d) Although USERRA does not specify how far in advance notice must be given to the employer, an employee should provide notice as far in advance as is reasonable under the circumstances. In regulations promulgated by the Department of Defense under USERRA, 32 C.F.R. § 104.6(a)(2)(i)(B), the Defense Department "strongly recommends that advance notice to civilian employers be provided at least 30 days prior to departure for uniformed service when it is feasible to do so."

§ 1002.86 When is the employee excused from giving advance notice of service in the uniformed services?

The employee is required to give advance notice of pending service unless giving such notice is prevented by military necessity, or is otherwise impossible or unreasonable under all the circumstances.

(a) Only a designated authority can make a determination of "military necessity," and such a determination is not subject to judicial review. Guidelines for defining "military necessity" appear in regulations issued by the Department of Defense at 32 C.F.R. 104.3. In general, these regulations cover situations where a mission, operation, exercise or requirement is classified, or could be compromised or otherwise adversely affected by public knowledge. In certain cases, the Secretary of Homeland Security, in consultation with the Secretary of Defense, can make a determination that giving of notice by intermittent disasterresponse appointees of the National Disaster Medical System is precluded by "military necessity." *See* 42 U.S.C. § 300hh11(e)(3)(B).

(b) It may be impossible or unreasonable to give advance notice under certain circumstances. Such circumstances may include the unavailability of the employee's employer or the employer's representative, or a requirement that the employee report for uniformed service in an extremely short period of time.

§ 1002.87 Is the employee required to get permission from his or her employer before leaving to perform service in the uniformed services?

No. The employee is not required to ask for or get his or her employer's permission to leave to perform service in the uniformed services. The employee is only required to give the employer notice of pending service.

§ 1002.88 Is the employee required to tell his or her civilian employer that he or she intends to seek reemployment after completing uniformed service before the employee leaves to perform service in the uniformed services?

No. When the employee leaves the employment position to begin a period of service, he or she is not required to tell the civilian employer that he or she intends to seek reemployment after completing uniformed service. Even if the employee tells the employer before entering or completing uniformed service that he or she does not intend to seek reemployment after completing the uniformed service, the employee does not forfeit the right to reemployment after completing service. The employee is not required to decide in advance of leaving the civilian employment position whether he or she will seek reemployment after completing uniformed service.

Period of Service

§ 1002.99 Is there a limit on the total amount of service in the uniformed services that an employee may perform and still retain reemployment rights with the employer?

Yes. In general, the employee may perform service in the uniformed services for a cumulative period of up to five (5) years and retain reemployment rights with the employer. The exceptions to this rule are described below.

§ 1002.100 Does the fiveyear service limit include all absences from an employment position that are related to service in the uniformed services?

No. The fiveyear period includes only the time the employee spends actually performing service in the uniformed services. A period of absence from employment before or after performing service in the uniformed services does not count against the fiveyear limit. For example, after the employee completes a period of service in the uniformed services, he or she is provided a certain amount of time, depending upon the length of service, to report back to work or submit an application for reemployment. The period between completing the uniformed service and reporting back to work or seeking reemployment does not count against the fiveyear limit.

§ 1002.101 Does the fiveyear service limit include periods of service that the employee performed when he or she worked for a previous employer?

No. An employee is entitled to a leave of absence for uniformed service for up to five years with each employer for whom he or she works. When the employee takes a position with a new employer, the fiveyear period begins again regardless of how much service he or she performed while working in any previous employment relationship. If an employee is employed by more than one employer, a separate fiveyear period runs as to each employer independently, even if those employers share or codetermine the employee's terms and conditions of employment.

§ 1002.102 Does the fiveyear service limit include periods of service that the employee performed before USERRA was enacted ?

It depends. USERRA provides reemployment rights to which an employee may become entitled beginning on or after December 12, 1994, but any uniformed service performed before December 12, 1994, that was counted against the service limitations of the previous law (the Veterans Reemployment Rights Act), also counts against USERRA's fiveyear limit.

§ 1002.103 Are there any types of service in the uniformed services that an employee can perform that do not count against USERRA's fiveyear service limit?

(a) USERRA creates the following exceptions to the fiveyear limit on service in the uniformed services:

(1) Service that is required beyond five years to complete an initial period of obligated service. Some military specialties require an individual to serve more than five years because of the amount of time or expense involved in training. If the employee works in one of those specialties, he or she has reemployment rights when the initial period of obligated service is completed;

(2) If the employee was unable to obtain orders releasing him or her from service in the uniformed services before the expiration of the fiveyear period, and the inability was not the employee's fault;

(3)(i) Service performed to fulfill periodic National Guard and Reserve training requirements as prescribed by 10 U.S.C. 10147 and 32 U.S.C. 502(a) and 503; and,

(ii) Service performed to fulfill additional training requirements determined and certified by a proper military authority as necessary for the employee's professional development, or to complete skill training or retraining;

(4) Service performed in a uniformed service if he or she was ordered to or retained on active duty under:

(i) 10 U.S.C. 688 (involuntary active duty by a military retiree);

(ii) 10 U.S.C. 12301(a) (involuntary active duty in wartime);

(iii) 10 U.S.C. 12301(g) (retention on active duty while in captive status);

(iv) 10 U.S.C. 12302 (involuntary active duty during a national emergency for up to 24 months);

(v) 10 U.S.C. 12304 (involuntary active duty for an operational mission for up to 270 days);

(vi) 10 U.S.C. 12305 (involuntary retention on active duty of a critical person during time of crisis or other specific conditions);

(vii) 14 U.S.C. 331 (involuntary active duty by retired Coast Guard officer);

(viii) 14 U.S.C. 332 (voluntary active duty by retired Coast Guard officer);

(ix) 14 U.S.C. 359 (involuntary active duty by retired Coast Guard enlisted member);

(x) 14 U.S.C. 360 (voluntary active duty by retired Coast Guard enlisted member);

(xi) 14 U.S.C. 367 (involuntary retention of Coast Guard enlisted member on active duty); and

(xii) 14 U.S.C. 712 (involuntary active duty by Coast Guard Reserve member for natural or manmade disasters).

(5) Service performed in a uniformed service if the employee was ordered to or retained on active duty (other than for training) under any provision of law because of a war or national emergency declared by the President or the Congress, as determined by the Secretary concerned;

(6) Service performed in a uniformed service if the employee was ordered to active duty (other than for training) in support of an operational mission for which personnel have been ordered to active duty under 10 U.S.C. 12304, as determined by a proper military authority;

(7) Service performed in a uniformed service if the employee was ordered to active duty in support of a critical mission or requirement of the uniformed services as determined by the Secretary concerned; and,

(8) Service performed as a member of the National Guard if the employee was called to respond to an invasion, danger of invasion, rebellion, danger of rebellion, insurrection, or the inability of the President with regular forces to execute the laws of the United States.

(b) Service performed to mitigate economic harm where the employee's employer is in violation of its employment or reemployment obligations to him or her.

§ 1002.104 Is the employee required to accommodate his or her employer's needs as to the timing, frequency or duration of service?

No. The employee is not required to accommodate his or her employer's interests or concerns regarding the timing, frequency, or duration of uniformed service. The employer cannot refuse to reemploy the employee because it believes that the timing, frequency or duration of the service is unreasonable. However, the employer is permitted to bring its concerns over the timing, frequency, or duration of the employee's service to the attention of the appropriate military authority. Regulations issued by the Department of Defense at 32 CFR 104.4 direct military authorities to provide assistance to an employer in addressing these types of employment issues. The military authorities are required to consider requests from employers of National Guard and Reserve members to adjust scheduled absences from civilian employment to perform service.

Application for Reemployment

§ 1002.115 Is the employee required to report to or submit a timely application for reemployment to his or her preservice employer upon completing the period of service in the uniformed services?

Yes. Upon completing service in the uniformed services, the employee must notify the preservice employer of his or her intent to return to the employment position by either reporting to work or submitting a timely application for reemployment. Whether the employee is required to report to work or submit a timely application for reemployment depends upon the length of service, as follows:

(a) *Period of service less than 31 days or for a period of any length for the purpose of a fitness examination.* If the period of service in the uniformed services was less than 31 days, or the employee was absent from a position of employment for a period of any length for the purpose of an examination to determine his or her fitness to perform service, the employee must report back to the employer not later than the beginning of the first full regularlyscheduled work period on the first full calendar day following the completion of the period of service, and the expiration of eight hours after a period allowing for safe transportation from the place of that service to the employee's residence. For example, if the employee completes a period of service and travel home, arriving at ten o'clock in the evening, he or she cannot be required to report to the employer until the beginning of the next full regularlyscheduled work period that begins at least eight hours after arriving home, i.e., no earlier than six o'clock the next morning. If it is impossible or unreasonable for the employee to report within such time period through no fault of his or her own, he or she must report to the employer as soon as possible after the expiration of the eighthour period.

(b) *Period of service more than 30 days but less than 181 days.* If the employee's period of service in the uniformed services was for more than 30 days but less than 181 days, he or she must submit an application for reemployment (written or verbal) with the employer not later than 14 days after completing service. If it is impossible or unreasonable for the employee to apply within 14 days through no fault of his or her own, he or she must submit the application not later than the next full calendar day after it becomes possible to do so.

(c) *Period of service more than 180 days.* If the employee's period of service in the uniformed services was for more than 180 days, he or she must submit an application for reemployment (written or verbal) not later than 90 days after completing service.

§ 1002.116 Is the time period for reporting back to an employer extended if the employee is hospitalized for, or convalescing from, an illness or injury incurred in, or aggravated during, the performance of service?

Yes. If the employee is hospitalized for, or convalescing from, an illness or injury incurred in, or aggravated during, the performance of service, he or she must report to or submit an application for reemployment to the employer at the end of the period necessary for recovering from the illness or injury. This period may not exceed two years from the date of the completion of service, except that it must be extended by the minimum time necessary to accommodate circumstances beyond the employee's control that make reporting within the period impossible or unreasonable. This period for recuperation and recovery extends the time period for reporting to or submitting an application for reemployment to the employer, and is not applicable following reemployment.

§ 1002.117 Are there any consequences if the employee fails to report for or submit a timely application for reemployment?

(a) If the employee fails to timely report for or apply for reemployment, he or she does not automatically forfeit entitlement to USERRA's reemployment and other rights and benefits. Rather, the employee becomes subject to the conduct rules, established policy, and general practices of the employer pertaining to an absence from scheduled work.

(b) If reporting or submitting an employment application to the employer is impossible or unreasonable through no fault of the employee, he or she may report to the employer as soon as possible (in the case of a period of service less than 31 days) or submit an application for reemployment to the employer by the next full calendar day after it becomes possible to do so (in the case of a period of service from 31 to 180 days), and the employee will be considered to have timely reported or applied for reemployment.

§ 1002.118 Is an application for reemployment required to be in any particular form?

An application for reemployment need not follow any particular format. The employee may apply orally or in writing. The application should indicate that the employee is a former employee returning from service in the uniformed services and that he or she seeks reemployment with the preservice employer. The employee is permitted but not required to identify a particular reemployment position in which he or she is interested.

§ 1002.119 To whom must the employee submit the application for reemployment?

The application must be submitted to the preservice employer or to an agent or representative of the employer who has apparent responsibility for receiving employment applications. Depending upon the circumstances, such a person could be a personnel or human resources officer, or a firstline supervisor. If there has been a change in ownership of the employer, the application should be submitted to the employer's successo,rininterest.

§ 1002.120 If the employee seeks or obtains employment with an employer other than the pre service employer before the end of the period within which a reemployment application must be filed, will that jeopardize reemployment rights with the preservice employer?

No. The employee has reemployment rights with the preservice employer provided that he or she makes a timely reemployment application to that employer. The employee may seek or obtain employment with an employer other than the preservice employer during the period of time within which a reemployment application must be made, without giving up reemployment rights with the preservice employer. However, such alternative employment during the application period should not be of a type that would constitute cause for the employer to discipline or terminate the employee following reemployment. For instance, if the employer forbids employees from working concurrently for a direct competitor during employment, violation of such a policy may constitute cause for discipline or even termination.

§ 1002.121 Is the employee required to submit documentation to the employer in connection with the application for reemployment?

Yes, if the period of service exceeded 30 days and if requested by the employer to do so. If the employee submits an application for reemployment after a period of service of more than 30 days, he or she must, upon the request of the employer, provide documentation to establish that:

(a) the reemployment application is timely;

(b) the employee has not exceeded the fiveyear limit on the duration of service (subject to the exceptions listed at § 1002.103); and,

(c) the employee's separation or dismissal from service was not disqualifying.

§ 1002.122 Is the employer required to reemploy the employee if documentation establishing the employee's eligibility does not exist or is not readily available?

Yes. The employer is not permitted to delay or deny reemployment by demanding documentation that does not exist or is not readily available. The employee is not liable for administrative delays in the issuance of military documentation. If the employee is reemployed after an absence from employment for more than 90 days, the employer may require that he or she submit the documentation establishing entitlement to reemployment before treating the employee as not having had a break in service for pension purposes. If the documentation is received after reemployment and it shows that the employee is not entitled to reemployment, the employer may terminate employment and any rights or benefits that the employee may have been granted.

§ 1002.123 What documents satisfy the requirement that the employee establish eligibility for reemployment after a period of service of more than thirty days?

(a) Documents that satisfy the requirements of USERRA include the following:

(1) DD (Department of Defense) 214 Certificate of Release or Discharge from Active Duty;

(2) (2) Copy of duty orders prepared by the facility where the orders were fulfilled carrying an endorsement indicating completion of the described service;

(3) Letter from the commanding officer of a Personnel Support Activity or someone of comparable authority;

(4) Certificate of completion from military training school;

(5) Discharge certificate showing character of service; and,

(6) Copy of extracts from payroll documents showing periods of service;

(7) Letter from National Disaster Medical System (NDMS) Team Leader or Administrative Officer verifying dates and times of NDMS training or Federal activation .

(b) The types of documents that are necessary to establish eligibility for reemployment will vary from case to case. Not all of these documents are available or necessary in every instance to establish reemployment eligibility.

Character of Service

§ 1002.134 What type of discharge or separation from service is required for an employee to be entitled to reemployment under USERRA?

USERRA does not require any particular form of discharge or separation from service. However, even if the employee is otherwise eligible for reemployment, he or she will be disqualified if the characterization of service falls within one of four categories. USERRA requires that the employee not have received one of these types of discharge.

§ 1002.135 What types of discharge or separation from uniformed service will make the employee ineligible for reemployment under USERRA?

Reemployment rights are terminated if the employee is:

(a) separated from uniformed service with a dishonorable or bad conduct discharge;

(b) separated from uniformed service under other than honorable conditions, as characterized by regulations of the uniformed service;

(c) a commissioned officer dismissed as permitted under 10 U.S.C. 1161(a) by sentence of a general courtmartial; in commutation of a sentence of a general courtmartial; or, in time of war, by order of the President; or,

(d) a commissioned officer dropped from the rolls under 10 U.S.C. 1161(b) due to absence without authority for at least three months; separation by reason of a sentence to confinement adjudged by a courtmartial; or, a sentence to confinement in a Federal or State penitentiary or correctional institution.

§ 1002.136 Who determines the characterization of service?

The branch of service in which the employee performs the tour of duty determines the characterization of service.

§ 1002.137 If the employee receives a disqualifying discharge or release from uniformed service and it is later upgraded, will reemployment rights be restored?

Yes. A military review board has the authority to prospectively or retroactively upgrade a disqualifying discharge or release. A retroactive upgrade would restore reemployment rights providing the employee otherwise meets the Act's eligibility criteria.

§ 1002.138 If the employee receives a retroactive upgrade in the characterization of service, will that entitle him or her to claim back wages and benefits lost as of the date of separation from service?

No. A retroactive upgrade allows the employee to obtain reinstatement with the former employer, provided the employee otherwise meets the Act's eligibility criteria. Back pay and other benefits such as pension plan credits attributable to the time period between discharge and the retroactive upgrade are not required to be restored by the employer in this situation.

Employer Statutory Defenses

§ 1002.139 Are there any circumstances in which the preservice employer is excused from its obligation to reemploy the employee following a period of uniformed service? What statutory defenses are available to the employer in an action or proceeding for reemployment benefits?

(a) Even if the employee is otherwise eligible for reemployment benefits, the employer is not required to reemploy him or her if the employer establishes that its circumstances have so changed as to make reemployment impossible or unreasonable. For example, an employer may be excused from reemploying the employee where there has been an intervening reduction in force that would have included that employee. The employer may not, however, refuse to reemploy the employee on the basis that another employee was hired to fill the reemployment position during the employee's absence, even if reemployment might require the termination of that replacement employee;

(b) Even if the employee is otherwise eligible for reemployment benefits, the employer is not required to reemploy him or her if it establishes that assisting the employee in becoming qualified for reemployment would impose an undue hardship, as defined in § 1002.5(n) and discussed in § 1002.198, on the employer; or,

(c) Even if the employee is otherwise eligible for reemployment benefits, the employer is not required to reemploy him or her if it establishes that the employment position vacated by the employee in order to perform service in

the uniformed services was for a brief, nonrecurrent period and there was no reasonable expectation that the employment would continue indefinitely or for a significant period.

(d) The employer defenses included in this section are affirmative ones, and the employer carries the burden to prove by a preponderance of the evidence that any one or more of these defenses is applicable.

Subpart D—Rights, Benefits, and Obligations of Persons Absent from Employment Due to Service in the Uniformed Services

Furlough and Leave of Absence

§ 1002.149 What is the employee's status with his or her civilian employer while performing service in the uniformed services?

During a period of service in the uniformed services, the employee is deemed to be on furlough or leave of absence from the civilian employer. In this status, the employee is entitled to the nonseniority rights and benefits generally provided by the employer to other employees with similar seniority, status, and pay that are on furlough or leave of absence. Entitlement to these nonseniority rights and benefits is not dependent on how the employer characterizes the employee's status during a period of service. For example, if the employer characterizes the employee as "terminated" during the period of uniformed service, this characterization cannot be used to avoid USERRA's requirement that the employee be deemed on furlough or leave of absence, and therefore entitled to the nonseniority rights and benefits generally provided to employees on furlough or leave of absence.

§ 1002.150 Which nonseniority rights and benefits is the employee entitled to during a period of service?

(a) The nonseniority rights and benefits to which an employee is entitled during a period of service are those that the employer provides to similarly situated employees by an employment contract, agreement, policy, practice, or plan in effect at the employee's workplace. These rights and benefits include those in effect at the beginning of the employee's employment and those established after employment began. They also include those rights and benefits that become effective during the employee's period of service and that are provided to similarly situated employees on furlough or leave of absence.

(b) If the nonseniority benefits to which employees on furlough or leave of absence are entitled vary according to the type of leave, the employee must be given the most favorable treatment accorded to any comparable form of leave when he or she performs service in the uniformed services. In order to determine whether any two types of leave are comparable, the duration of the leave may be the most significant factor to compare. For instance, a two-day funeral leave will not be "comparable" to an extended leave for service in the uniformed service. In addition to comparing the duration of the absences, other factors such as the purpose of the leave and the ability of the employee to choose when to take the leave should also be considered.

(c) As a general matter, accrual of vacation leave is considered to be a nonseniority benefit that must be provided by an employer to an employee on a military leave of absence only if the employer provides that benefit to similarly situated employees on comparable leaves of absence.

§ 1002.151 If the employer provides full or partial pay to the employee while he or she is on military leave, is the employer required to also provide the nonseniority rights and benefits ordinarily granted to similarly situated employees on furlough or leave of absence?

Yes. If the employer provides additional benefits such as full or partial pay when the employee performs service, the employer is not excused from providing other rights and benefits to which the employee is entitled under the Act.

§ 1002.152 If employment is interrupted by a period of service in the uniformed services, are there any circumstances under which the employee is not entitled to the nonseniority rights and benefits ordinarily granted to similarly situated employees on furlough or leave of absence?

If employment is interrupted by a period of service in the uniformed services and the employee knowingly provides written notice of intent not to return to the position of employment after service in the uniformed services, he or she is not entitled to those nonseniority rights and benefits. The employee's written notice does not waive entitlement to any other rights to which he or she is entitled under the Act, including the right to reemployment after service.

§ 1002.153 If employment is interrupted by a period of service in the uniformed services, is the employee permitted upon request to use accrued vacation, annual or similar leave with pay during the service? Can the employer require the employee to use accrued leave during a period of service?

(a) If employment is interrupted by a period of service, the employee must be permitted upon request to use any accrued vacation, annual, or similar leave with pay during the period of service, in order to continue his or her civilian pay. However, the employee is not entitled to use sick leave that accrued with the civilian employer during a period of service in the uniformed services, unless the employer allows employees to use sick leave for any reason, or allows other similarly situated employees on comparable furlough or leave of absence to use accrued paid sick leave. Sick leave is usually not comparable to annual or vacation leave; it is generally intended to provide income when the employee or a family member is ill and the employee is unable to work.

(b) The employer may not require the employee to use accrued vacation, annual, or similar leave during a period of service in the uniformed services.

Health Plan Coverage

§ 1002.163 What types of health plans are covered by USERRA?

(a) USERRA defines a health plan to include an insurance policy or contract, medical or hospital service agreement, membership or subscription contract, or arrangement under which the employee's health services are provided or the expenses of those services are paid.

(b) USERRA covers group health plans as defined in the Employee Retirement Income Security Act of 1974 (ERISA) at 29 U.S.C. 1191b(a). USERRA applies to group health plans that are subject to ERISA, and plans that are not subject to ERISA, such as those sponsored by State or local governments or religious organizations for their employees.

(c) USERRA covers multiemployer plans maintained pursuant to one or more collective bargaining agreements between employers and employee organizations. USERRA applies to multiemployer plans as they are defined in ERISA at 29 U.S.C. 1002(37). USERRA contains provisions that apply specifically to multiemployer plans in certain situations.

§ 1002.164 What health plan coverage must the employer provide for the employee under USERRA?

If the employee has coverage under a health plan in connection with his or her employment, the plan must permit the employee to elect to continue the coverage for a certain period of time as described below:

(a) When the employee is performing service in the uniformed services, he or she is entitled to continuing coverage for himself or herself (and dependents if the plan offers dependent coverage) under a health plan provided in connection with the employment. The plan must allow the employee to elect to continue coverage for a period of time that is the lesser of:

(1) the 24-month period beginning on the date on which the employee's absence for the purpose of performing service begins; or,

(2) the period beginning on the date on which the employee's absence for the purpose of performing service begins, and ending on the date on which he or she fails to return from service or apply for a position of employment as provided under sections 1002.115-123 of these regulations.

(b) USERRA does not require the employer to establish a health plan if there is no health plan coverage in connection with the employment, or, where there is a plan, to provide any particular type of coverage.

(c) USERRA does not require the employer to permit the employee to initiate new health plan coverage at the beginning of a period of service if he or she did not previously have such coverage.

§ 1002.165 How does the employee elect continuing health plan coverage?

USERRA does not specify requirements for electing continuing coverage. Health plan administrators may develop reasonable requirements addressing how continuing coverage may be elected, consistent with the terms of the plan and the Act's exceptions to the requirement that the employee give advance notice of service in the uniformed services. For example, the employee cannot be precluded from electing continuing health plan coverage under circumstances where it is impossible or unreasonable for him or her to make a timely election of coverage.

§ 1002.166 How much must the employee pay in order to continue health plan coverage?

(a) If the employee performs service in the uniformed service for fewer than 31 days, he or she cannot be required to pay more than the regular employee share, if any, for health plan coverage.

(b) If the employee performs service in the uniformed service for 31 or more days, he or she may be required to pay no more than 102% of the full premium under the plan, which represents the employer's share plus the employee's share, plus 2% for administrative costs.

(c) USERRA does not specify requirements for methods of paying for continuing coverage. Health plan administrators may develop reasonable procedures for payment, consistent with the terms of the plan.

§ 1002.167 What actions may a plan administrator take if the employee does not elect or pay for continuing coverage in a timely manner?

The actions a plan administrator may take regarding the provision or cancellation of an employee's continuing coverage depend on whether the employee is excused from the requirement to give advance notice, whether the plan has established reasonable rules for election of continuation coverage, and whether the plan has established reasonable rules for the payment for continuation coverage.

(a) *No notice of service and no election of continuation coverage:*. If an employer provides employment-based health coverage to an employee who leaves employment for uniformed service without giving advance notice of service, the plan administrator may cancel the employee's health plan coverage upon the employee's departure from employment for uniformed service. However, in cases in which an employee's failure to give advance notice of service was excused under the statute because it was impossible, unreasonable, or precluded by military necessity, the plan administrator must reinstate the employee's health coverage retroactively upon his or her election to continue coverage and payment of all unpaid amounts due, and the employee must incur no administrative reinstatement costs. In order to qualify for an exception to the requirement of timely election of continuing health care, an employee must first be excused from giving notice of service under the statute.

(b) *Notice of service but no election of continuing coverage:*. Plan administrators may develop reasonable rules addressing how continuing coverage may be elected. Where health plans are also covered under the Consolidated Omnibus Budget Reconciliation Act of 1985, 26 U.S.C. 4980B (COBRA), it may be reasonable for a health plan administrator to adopt COBRA-compliant rules regarding election of continuing coverage, as long as those rules do not conflict with any provision of USERRA or this rule. If an employer provides employment-based health coverage to an employee who leaves employment for uniformed service for a period of service in excess of 30 days after having given advance notice of service but without making an election regarding continuing coverage, the plan administrator may cancel the employee's health plan coverage upon the employee's departure from employment for uniformed service, but must reinstate coverage without the imposition of administrative reinstatement costs under the following conditions:

(1) Plan administrators who have developed reasonable rules regarding the period within which an employee may elect continuing coverage must permit retroactive reinstatement of uninterrupted coverage to the date of departure if the employee elects continuing coverage and pays all unpaid amounts due within the periods established by the plan;

(2) In cases in which plan administrators have not developed rules regarding the period within which an employee may elect continuing coverage, the plan must permit retroactive reinstatement of uninterrupted coverage to the date of departure upon the employee's election and payment of all unpaid amounts at any time during the period established in section 1002.164(a).

(c) *Election of continuation coverage without timely payment:*. Health plan administrators may adopt reasonable rules allowing cancellation of coverage if timely payment is not made. Where health plans are covered under COBRA, it may be reasonable for a health plan administrator to adopt COBRA-compliant rules regarding payment for continuing coverage, as long as those rules do not conflict with any provision of USERRA or this rule.

§ 1002.168 If the employee's coverage was terminated at the beginning of or during service, does his or her coverage have to be reinstated upon reemployment?

(a) If health plan coverage for the employee or a dependent was terminated by reason of service in the uniformed services, that coverage must be reinstated upon reemployment. An exclusion or waiting period may not be imposed in connection with the reinstatement of coverage upon reemployment, if an exclusion or waiting period would not have been imposed had coverage not been terminated by reason of such service.

(b) USERRA permits a health plan to impose an exclusion or waiting period as to illnesses or injuries determined by the Secretary of Veterans Affairs to have been incurred in, or aggravated during, performance of service in the uniformed services. The determination that the employee's illness or injury was incurred in, or aggravated during, the performance of service may only be made by the Secretary of Veterans Affairs or his or her representative. Other coverage, for injuries or illnesses that are not servicer-elated (or for the employee's dependents, if he or she has dependent coverage), must be reinstated subject to paragraph (a) of this section.

§ 1002.169 Can the employee elect to delay reinstatement of health plan coverage until a date after the date he or she is reemployed?

USERRA requires the employer to reinstate health plan coverage upon request at reemployment. USERRA permits but does not require the employer to allow the employee to delay reinstatement of health plan coverage until a date that is later than the date of reemployment.

§ 1002.170 In a multiemployer health plan, how is liability allocated for employer contributions and benefits arising under USERRA's health plan provisions?

Liability under a multiemployer plan for employer contributions and benefits in connection with USERRA's health plan provisions must be allocated either as the plan sponsor provides, or, if the sponsor does not provide, to the employee's last employer before his or her service. If the last employer is no longer functional, liability for continuing coverage is allocated to the health plan.

§ 1002.171 How does the continuation of health plan benefits apply to a multiemployer plan that provides health plan coverage through a health benefits account system?

(a) Some employees receive health plan benefits provided pursuant to a multiemployer plan that utilizes a health benefits account system in which an employee accumulates prospective health benefit eligibility, also commonly referred to as "dollar bank," "credit bank," and "hour bank" plans. In such cases, where an employee with a positive health benefits account balance elects to continue the coverage, the employee may further elect either option below:

(1) The employee may expend his or her health account balance during an absence from employment due to service in the uniformed services in lieu of paying for the continuation of coverage as set out in section 1002.166. If an employee's health account balance becomes depleted during the applicable period provided for in section 1002.164(a), the employee must be permitted, at his or her option, to continue coverage pursuant to section 1002.166. Upon reemployment, the plan must provide for immediate reinstatement of the employee as required by section 1002.168, but may require the employee to pay the cost of the coverage until the employee earns the credits necessary to sustain continued coverage in the plan.

(2) The employee may pay for continuation coverage as set out in section 1002.166, in order to maintain intact his or her account balance as of the beginning date of the absence from employment due to service in the uniformed services. This option permits the employee to resume usage of the account balance upon reemployment.

(b) Employers or plan administrators providing such plans should counsel employees of their options set out in this subsection.

Subpart E—Reemployment Rights and Benefits

Prompt Reemployment

§ 1002.180 When is an employee entitled to be reemployed by his or her civilian employer?

The employer must promptly reemploy the employee when he or she returns from a period of service if the employee meets the Act's eligibility criteria as described in Subpart C of these regulations.

§ 1002.181 How is "prompt reemployment" defined?

"Prompt reemployment" means as soon as practicable under the circumstances of each case. Absent unusual circumstances, reemployment must occur within two weeks of the employee's application for reemployment. For example, prompt reinstatement after a weekend National Guard duty generally means the next regularly scheduled working day. On the other hand, prompt reinstatement following several years of active duty may require more time, because the employer may have to reassign or give notice to another employee who occupied the returning employee's position.

Reemployment Position

§ 1002.191 What position is the employee entitled to upon reemployment?

As a general rule, the employee is entitled to reemployment in the job position that he or she would have attained with reasonable certainty if not for the absence due to uniformed service. This position is known as the escalator position. The principle behind the escalator position is that, if not for the period of uniformed service, the employee could have been promoted (or, alternatively, demoted, transferred, or laid off) due to intervening events. The escalator principle requires that the employee be reemployed in a position that reflects with reasonable certainty the pay, benefits, seniority, and other job perquisites, that he or she would have attained if not for the period of service. Depending upon the specific circumstances, the employer may have the option, or be required, to reemploy the employee in a position other than the escalator position.

§ 1002.192 How is the specific reemployment position determined?

In all cases, the starting point for determining the proper reemployment position is the escalator position, which is the job position that the employee would have attained if his or her continuous employment had not been interrupted due to uniformed service. Once this position is determined, the employer may have to consider several factors before determining the appropriate reemployment position in any particular case. Such factors may include the employee's length of service, qualifications, and disability, if any. The reemployment position may be either the escalator position; the preservice position; a position comparable to the escalator or preservice position; or, the nearest approximation to one of these positions.

§ 1002.193 Does the reemployment position include elements such as seniority, status, and rate of pay?

(a) Yes. The reemployment position includes the seniority, status, and rate of pay that an employee would ordinarily have attained in that position given his or her job history, including prospects for future earnings and advancement. The employer must determine the seniority rights, status, and rate of pay as though the employee had been continuously employed during the period of service. The seniority rights, status, and pay of an employment position include those established (or changed) by a collective bargaining agreement, employer policy, or employment practice. The sources of seniority rights, status, and pay include agreements, policies, and practices in effect at the beginning of the employee's service, and any changes that may have occurred during the period of service. In particular, the employee's status in the reemployment position could include opportunities for advancement, general working conditions, job location, shift assignment, rank, responsibility, and geographical location.

(b) If an opportunity for promotion, or eligibility for promotion, that the employee missed during service is based on a skills test or examination, then the employer should give him or her a reasonable amount of time to adjust to the employment position and then give a skills test or examination. No fixed amount of time for permitting adjustment to reemployment will be deemed reasonable in all cases. However, in determining a reasonable amount of time to permit an employee to adjust to reemployment before scheduling a makeup test or examination, an employer may take into account a variety of factors, including but not limited to the length of time the returning employee was absent from work, the level of difficulty of the test itself, the typical time necessary to prepare or study for the test, the duties and responsibilities of the reemployment position and the promotional position, and the nature and responsibilities of the service member while serving in the uniformed service. If the employee is successful on the makeup exam and, based on the results of that exam, there is a reasonable certainty that he or she would have been promoted, or made eligible for promotion, during the time that the employee served in the uniformed service, then the promotion or eligibility for promotion must be made effective as of the date it would have occurred had employment not been interrupted by uniformed service.

§ 1002.194 Can the application of the escalator principle result in adverse consequences when the employee is reemployed?

Yes. The Act does not prohibit lawful adverse job consequences that result from the employee's restoration on the seniority ladder. Depending on the circumstances, the escalator principle may cause an employee to be reemployed in a higher or lower position, laid off, or even terminated. For example, if an employee's seniority or job classification would have resulted in the employee being laid off during the period of service, and the layoff continued after the date of reemployment, reemployment would reinstate the employee to layoff status. Similarly, the status of the reemployment position requires the employer to assess what would have happened to such factors as the employee's opportunities for advancement, working conditions, job location, shift assignment, rank, responsibility, and geographical location, if he or she had remained continuously employed. The reemployment position may involve transfer to another shift or location, more or less strenuous working conditions, or changed opportunities for advancement, depending upon the application of the escalator principle.

§ 1002.195 What other factors can determine the reemployment position?

Once the employee's escalator position is determined, other factors may allow, or require, the employer to reemploy the employee in a position other than the escalator position. These factors, which are explained in §§ 1002.196 through 1002.199, are:

(a) the length of the employee's most recent period of uniformed service;

(b) the employee's qualifications; and,

(c) whether the employee has a disability incurred or aggravated during uniformed service.

§ 1002.196 What is the employee's reemployment position if the period of service was less than 91 days?

Following a period of service in the uniformed services of less than 91 days, the employee must be reemployed according to the following priority:

(a) The employee must be reemployed in the escalator position. He or she must be qualified to perform the duties of this position. The employer must make reasonable efforts to help the employee become qualified to perform the duties of this position.

(b) If the employee is not qualified to perform the duties of the escalator position after reasonable efforts by the employer, the employee must be reemployed in the position in which he or she was employed on the date that the period of service began. The employee must be qualified to perform the duties of this position. The employer must make reasonable efforts to help the employee become qualified to perform the duties of this position.

(c) If the employee is not qualified to perform the duties of the escalator position or the preservice position, after reasonable efforts by the employer, he or she must be reemployed in any other position that is the nearest approximation first to the escalator position and then to the preservice position. The employee must be qualified to perform the duties of this position. The employer must make reasonable efforts to help the employee become qualified to perform the duties of this position.

§ 1002.197 What is the reemployment position if the employee's period of service in the uniformed services was more than 90 days?

Following a period of service of more than 90 days, the employee must be reemployed according to the following priority:

(a) The employee must be reemployed in the escalator position or a position of like seniority, status, and pay. He or she must be qualified to perform the duties of this position. The employer must make reasonable efforts to help the employee become qualified to perform the duties of this position.

(b) If the employee is not qualified to perform the duties of the escalator position or a like position after reasonable efforts by the employer, the employee must be reemployed in the position in which he or she was employed on the date that the period of service began or in a position of like seniority, status, and pay. The employee must be qualified to perform the duties of this position. The employer must make reasonable efforts to help the employee become qualified to perform the duties of this position.

(c) If the employee is not qualified to perform the duties of the escalator position, the preservice position, or a like position, after reasonable efforts by the employer, he or she must be reemployed in any other position that is the nearest approximation first to the escalator position and then to the preservice position. The employee must be qualified to perform the duties of this position. The employer must make reasonable efforts to help the employee become qualified to perform the duties of this position.

§ 1002.198 What efforts must the employer make to help the employee become qualified for the reemployment position?

The employee must be qualified for the reemployment position. The employer must make reasonable efforts to help the employee become qualified to perform the duties of this position. The employer is not required to reemploy the employee on his or her return from service if he or she cannot, after reasonable efforts by the employer, qualify for the appropriate reemployment position.

(a)(1) "Qualified" means that the employee has the ability to perform the essential tasks of the position. The employee's inability to perform one or more nonessential tasks of a position does not make him or her unqualified.

(2) Whether a task is essential depends on several factors, and these factors include but are not limited to:

(i) the employer's judgment as to which functions are essential;

(ii) written job descriptions developed before the hiring process begins;

(iii) the amount of time on the job spent performing the function;

(iv) the consequences of not requiring the individual to perform the function;

(v) the terms of a collective bargaining agreement;

(vi) the work experience of past incumbents in the job; and/or

(vii) the current work experience of incumbents in similar jobs.

(b) Only after the employer makes reasonable efforts, as defined in § 1002.5(i), may it determine that the employee is not qualified for the reemployment position. These reasonable efforts must be made at no cost to the employee.

§ 1002.199 What priority must the employer follow if two or more returning employees are entitled to reemployment in the same position?

If two or more employees are entitled to reemployment in the same position and more than one employee has reported or applied for employment in that position, the employee who first left the position for uniformed service has the first priority on reemployment in that position. The remaining employee (or employees) is entitled to be reemployed in a position similar to that in which the employee would have been reemployed according to the rules that normally determine a reemployment position, as set out in §§ 1002.196 through 1002.197.

Seniority Rights and Benefits

§ 1002.210 What seniority rights does an employee have when reemployed following a period of uniformed service?

The employee is entitled to the seniority and senioritybased rights and benefits that he or she had on the date the uniformed service began, plus any seniority and senioritybased rights and benefits that the employee would have attained if he or she had remained continuously employed. In determining entitlement to seniority and senioritybased rights and benefits, the period of absence from employment due to or necessitated by uniformed service is not considered a break in employment. The rights and benefits protected by USERRA upon reemployment include those provided by the employer and those required by statute. For example, under USERRA, a reemployed service member would be eligible for leave under the Family and Medical Leave Act of 1993, 29 U.S.C. 26012654 (FMLA), if the number of months and the number of hours of work for which the service member was employed by the civilian employer, together with the number of months and the number of hours of work for which the service member would have been employed by the civilian employer during the period of uniformed service, meet FMLA's eligibility requirements. In the event that a service member is denied FMLA leave for failing to satisfy the FMLA's hours of work requirement due to absence from employment necessitated by uniformed service, the service member may have a cause of action under USERRA but not under the FMLA.

§ 1002.211 Does USERRA require the employer to use a seniority system?

No. USERRA does not require the employer to adopt a formal seniority system. USERRA defines seniority as longevity in employment together with any employment benefits that accrue with, or are determined by, longevity in employment. In the absence of a formal seniority system, such as one established through collective bargaining, USERRA looks to the custom and practice in the place of employment to determine the employee's entitlement to any employment benefits that accrue with, or are determined by, longevity in employment.

§ 1002.212 How does a person know whether a particular right or benefit is a senioritybased right or benefit?

A senioritybased right or benefit is one that accrues with, or is determined by, longevity in employment. Generally, whether a right or benefit is senioritybased depends on three factors:

(a) whether the right or benefit is a reward for length of service rather than a form of shortterm compensation for work performed;

(b) whether it is reasonably certain that the employee would have received the right or benefit if he or she had remained continuously employed during the period of service; and,

(c) whether it is the employer's actual custom or practice to provide or withhold the right or benefit as a reward for length of service. Provisions of an employment contract or policies in the employee handbook are not controlling if the employer's actual custom or practice is different from what is written in the contract or handbook.

§ 1002.213 How can the employee demonstrate a reasonable certainty that he or she would have received the seniority right or benefit if he or she had remained continuously employed during the period of service?

A reasonable certainty is a high probability that the employee would have received the seniority or senioritybased right or benefit if he or she had been continuously employed. The employee does not have to establish that he or she would have received the benefit as an absolute certainty. The employee can demonstrate a reasonable certainty that he or she would have received the seniority right or benefit by showing that other employees with seniority similar to that which the employee would have had if he or she had remained continuously employed received the right or benefit. The employer cannot withhold the right or benefit based on an assumption that a series of unlikely events could have prevented the employee from gaining the right or benefit.

Disabled Employees

§ 1002.225 Is the employee entitled to any specific reemployment benefits if he or she has a disability that was incurred in, or aggravated during, the period of service?

Yes. A disabled service member is entitled, to the same extent as any other individual, to the escalator position he or she would have attained but for uniformed service. If the employee has a disability incurred in, or aggravated during, the period of service in the uniformed services, the employer must make reasonable efforts to accommodate that disability and to help the employee become qualified to perform the duties of his or her reemployment position. If the employee is not qualified for reemployment in the escalator position because of a disability after reasonable efforts by the employer to accommodate the disability and to help the employee to become qualified, the employee must be reemployed in a position according to the following priority. The employer must make reasonable efforts to accommodate the employee's disability and to help him or her to become qualified to perform the duties of one of these positions:

(a) a position that is equivalent in seniority, status, and pay to the escalator position; or,

(b) a position that is the nearest approximation to the equivalent position, consistent with the circumstances of the employee's case, in terms of seniority, status, and pay. A position that is the nearest approximation to the equivalent position may be a higher or lower position, depending on the circumstances.

§ 1002.226 If the employee has a disability that was incurred in, or aggravated during, the period of service, what efforts must the employer make to help him or her become qualified for the reemployment position?

(a) USERRA requires that the employee be qualified for the reemployment position regardless of any disability. The employer must make reasonable efforts to help the employee to become qualified to perform the duties of this position. The employer is not required to reemploy the employee on his or her return from service if he or she cannot, after reasonable efforts by the employer, qualify for the appropriate reemployment position.

(b) "Qualified" has the same meaning here as in § 1002.198.

Rate of Pay

§ 1002.236 How is the employee's rate of pay determined when he or she returns from a period of service?

The employee's rate of pay is determined by applying the same escalator principles that are used to determine the reemployment position, as follows:

(a) If the employee is reemployed in the escalator position, the employer must compensate him or her at the rate of pay associated with the escalator position. The rate of pay must be determined by taking into account any pay increases, differentials, step increases, merit increases, or periodic increases that the employee would have attained with reasonable certainty had he or she remained continuously employed during the period of service. In addition, when considering whether merit or performance increases would have been attained with reasonable certainty, an employer may examine the returning employee's own work history, his or her history of merit increases, and the work and pay history of employees in the same or similar position. For example, if the employee missed a merit pay increase while performing service, but qualified for previous merit pay increases, then the rate of pay should include the merit pay increase that was missed. If the merit pay increase that the employee missed during service is based on a skills test or examination, then the employer should give the employee a reasonable amount of time to adjust to the reemployment position and then give him or her the skills test or examination. No fixed amount of time for permitting adjustment to reemployment will be deemed reasonable in all cases. However, in determining a reasonable amount of time to permit an employee to adjust to reemployment before scheduling a makeup test or examination, an employer may take into account a variety of factors, includ-

ing but not limited to the length of time the returning employee was absent from work, the level of difficulty of the test itself, the typical time necessary to prepare or study for the test, the duties and responsibilities of the reemployment position and the promotional position, and the nature and responsibilities of the service member while serving in the uniformed service. The escalator principle also applies in the event a pay reduction occurred in the reemployment position during the period of service. Any pay adjustment must be made effective as of the date it would have occurred had the employee's employment not been interrupted by uniformed service.

(b) If the employee is reemployed in the preservice position or another position, the employer must compensate him or her at the rate of pay associated with the position in which he or she is reemployed. As with the escalator position, the rate of pay must be determined by taking into account any pay increases, differentials, step increases, merit increases, or periodic increases that the employee would have attained with reasonable certainty had he or she remained continuously employed during the period of service.

Protection Against Discharge

§ 1002.247 Does USERRA provide the employee with protection against discharge?

Yes. If the employee's most recent period of service in the uniformed services was more than 30 days, he or she must not be discharged except for cause -

(a) for 180 days after the employee's date of reemployment if his or her most recent period of uniformed service was more than 30 days but less than 181 days; or,

(b) for one year after the date of reemployment if the employee's most recent period of uniformed service was more than 180 days.

§ 1002.248 What constitutes cause for discharge under USERRA?

The employee may be discharged for cause based either on conduct or, in some circumstances, because of the application of other legitimate nondiscriminatory reasons.

(a) In a discharge action based on conduct, the employer bears the burden of proving that it is reasonable to discharge the employee for the conduct in question, and that he or she had notice, which was express or can be fairly implied, that the conduct would constitute cause for discharge.

(b) If, based on the application of other legitimate nondiscriminatory reasons, the employee's job position is eliminated, or the employee is placed on layoff status, either of these situations would constitute cause for purposes of USERRA. The employer bears the burden of proving that the employee's job would have been eliminated or that he or she would have been laid off.

Pension Plan Benefits

§ 1002.259 How does USERRA protect an employee's pension benefits?

On reemployment, the employee is treated as not having a break in service with the employer or employers maintaining a pension plan, for purposes of participation, vesting and accrual of benefits, by reason of the period of absence from employment due to or necessitated by service in the uniformed services.

(a) Depending on the length of the employee's period of service, he or she is entitled to take from one to ninety days following service before reporting back to work or applying for reemployment (*See* § 1002.115). This period of time must be treated as continuous service with the employer for purposes of determining participation, vesting and accrual of pension benefits under the plan.

(b) If the employee is hospitalized for, or convalescing from, an illness or injury incurred in, or aggravated during, service, he or she is entitled to report to or submit an application for reemployment at the end of the time period necessary for him or her to recover from the illness or injury. This period, which may not exceed two years from the date the employee completed service, except in circumstances beyond his or her control, must be treated as continuous service with the employer for purposes of determining the participation, vesting and accrual of pension benefits under the plan.

§ 1002.260 What pension benefit plans are covered under USERRA?

(a) The Employee Retirement Income Security Act of 1974 (ERISA) defines an employee pension benefit plan as a plan that provides retirement income to employees, or defers employee income to a period extending to or beyond the termination of employment. Any such plan maintained by the employer or employers is covered under USERRA. USERRA also covers certain pension plans not covered by ERISA, such as those sponsored by a State, government entity, or church for its employees.

(b) USERRA does not cover pension benefits under the Federal Thrift Savings Plan; those benefits are covered under 5 U.S.C. 8432b.

§ 1002.261 Who is responsible for funding any plan obligation to provide the employee with pension benefits?

With the exception of multiemployer plans, which have separate rules discussed below, the employer is liable to the pension benefit plan to fund any obligation of the plan to provide benefits that are attributable to the employee's period of service. In the case of a defined contribution plan, once the employee is reemployed, the employer must allocate the amount of its makeup contribution for the employee, if any; his or her makeup employee contributions, if any; and his or her elective deferrals, if any; in the same manner and to the same extent that it allocates the amounts for other employees during the period of service. In the case of a defined benefit plan, the employee's accrued benefit will be increased for the period of service once he or she is reemployed and, if applicable, has repaid any amounts previously paid to him or her from the plan and made any employee contributions that may be required to be made under the plan.

§ 1002.262 When is the employer required to make the plan contribution that is attributable to the employee's period of uniformed service?

(a) The employer is not required to make its contribution until the employee is reemployed. For employer contributions to a plan in which the employee is not required or permitted to contribute, the employer must make the contribution attributable to the employee's period of service no later than ninety days after the date of reemployment, or when plan contributions are normally due for the year in which the service in the uniformed services was performed, whichever is later. If it is impossible or unreasonable for the employer to make the contribution within this time period, the employer must make the contribution as soon as practicable.

(b) If the employee is enrolled in a contributory plan he or she is allowed (but not required) to make up his or her missed contributions or elective deferrals. These makeup contributions or elective deferrals must be made during a time period starting with the date of reemployment and continuing for up to three times the length of the employee's immediate past period of uniformed service, with the repayment period not to exceed five years. Makeup contributions or elective deferrals may only be made during this period and while the employee is employed with the postservice employer.

(c) If the employee's plan is contributory and he or she does not make up his or her contributions or elective deferrals, he or she will not receive the employer match or the accrued benefit attributable to his or her contribution because the employer is required to make contributions that are contingent on or attributable to the employee's contributions or elective deferrals only to the extent that the employee makes up his or her payments to the plan. Any employer contributions that are contingent on or attributable to the employee's makeup contributions or elective deferrals must be made according to the plan's requirements for employer matching contributions.

(d) The employee is not required to make up the full amount of employee contributions or elective deferrals that he or she missed making during the period of service. If the employee does not make up all of the missed contributions or elective deferrals, his or her pension may be less than if he or she had done so.

(e) Any vested accrued benefit in the pension plan that the employee was entitled to prior to the period of uniformed service remains intact whether or not he or she chooses to be reemployed under the Act after leaving the uniformed service.

(f) An adjustment will be made to the amount of employee contributions or elective deferrals the employee will be able to make to the pension plan for any employee contributions or elective deferrals he or she actually made to the plan during the period of service.

§ 1002.263 Does the employee pay interest when he or she makes up missed contributions or elective deferrals?

No. The employee is not required or permitted to make up a missed contribution in an amount that exceeds the amount he or she would have been permitted or required to contribute had he or she remained continuously employed during the period of service.

§ 1002.264 Is the employee allowed to repay a previous distribution from a pension benefits plan upon being reemployed?

Yes, provided the plan is a defined benefit plan. If the employee received a distribution of all or part of the accrued benefit from a defined benefit plan in connection with his or her service in the uniformed services before he or she became reemployed, he or she must be allowed to repay the withdrawn amounts when he or she is reemployed. The amount the employee must repay includes any interest that would have accrued had the monies not been withdrawn. The employee must be allowed to repay these amounts during a time period starting with the date of reemployment and continuing for up to three times the length of the employee's immediate past period of uniformed service, with the repayment period not to exceed five years (or such longer time as may be agreed to between the employer and the employee), provided the employee is employed with the postservice employer during this period.

§ 1002.265 If the employee is reemployed with his or her preservice employer, is the employee's pension benefit the same as if he or she had remained continuously employed?

The amount of the employee's pension benefit depends on the type of pension plan.

(a) In a noncontributory defined benefit plan, where the amount of the pension benefit is determined according to a specific formula, the employee's benefit will be the same as though he or she had remained continuously employed during the period of service.

(b) In a contributory defined benefit plan, the employee will need to make up contributions in order to have the same benefit as if he or she had remained continuously employed during the period of service.

(c) In a defined contribution plan, the benefit may not be the same as if the employee had remained continuously employed, even though the employee and the employer make up any contributions or elective deferrals attributable to the period of service, because the employee is not entitled to forfeitures and earnings or required to experience losses that accrued during the period or periods of service.

§ 1002.266 What are the obligations of a multiemployer pension benefit plan under USERRA?

A multiemployer pension benefit plan is one to which more than one employer is required to contribute, and which is maintained pursuant to one or more collective bargaining agreements between one or more employee organizations and more than one employer. The Act uses ERISA's definition of a multiemployer plan. In addition to the provisions of USERRA that apply to all pension benefit plans, there are provisions that apply specifically to multiemployer plans, as follows:

(a) The last employer that employed the employee before the period of service is responsible for making the employer contribution to the multiemployer plan, if the plan sponsor does not provide otherwise. If the last employer is no longer functional, the plan must nevertheless provide coverage to the employee.

(b) An employer that contributes to a multiemployer plan and that reemploys the employee pursuant to USERRA must provide written notice of reemployment to the plan administrator within 30 days after the date of reemployment. The returning service member should notify the reemploying employer that he or she has been reemployed pursuant to USERRA. The 30day period within which the reemploying employer must provide written notice to the multiemployer plan pursuant to this subsection does not begin until the employer has knowledge that the employee was reemployed pursuant to USERRA.

(c) The employee is entitled to the same employer contribution whether he or she is reemployed by the preservice employer or by a different employer contributing to the same multiemployer plan, provided that the preservice employer and the postservice employer share a common means or practice of hiring the employee, such as common participation in a union hiring hall.

§ 1002.267 How is compensation during the period of service calculated in order to determine the employee's pension benefits, if benefits are based on compensation?

In many pension benefit plans, the employee's compensation determines the amount of his or her contribution or the retirement benefit to which he or she is entitled.

(a) Where the employee's rate of compensation must be calculated to determine pension entitlement, the calculation must be made using the rate of pay that the employee would have received but for the period of uniformed service.

(b)(1) Where the rate of pay the employee would have received is not reasonably certain, such as where compensation is based on commissions earned, the average rate of compensation during the 12month period prior to the period of uniformed service must be used.

(2) Where the rate of pay the employee would have received is not reasonably certain and he or she was employed for less than 12 months prior to the period of uniformed service, the average rate of compensation must be derived from this shorter period of employment that preceded service.

Subpart F—Compliance Assistance, Enforcement and Remedies

Compliance Assistance

§ 1002.277 What assistance does the Department of Labor provide to employees and employers concerning employment, reemployment, or other rights and benefits under USERRA?

The Secretary, through the Veterans' Employment and Training Service (VETS), provides assistance to any person or entity with respect to employment and reemployment rights and benefits under USERRA. This assistance includes a wide range of compliance assistance outreach activities, such as responding to inquiries; conducting USERRA briefings and Webcasts; issuing news releases; and, maintaining the elaws USERRA Advisor (located at *http://www.dol.gov/elaws/userra.htm*), the eVETS Resource Advisor and other webbased materials (located at http://www.dol.gov/vets), which are designed to increase awareness of the Act among affected persons, the media, and the general public. In providing such assistance, VETS may request the assistance of other Federal and State agencies, and utilize the assistance of volunteers.

Investigation and Referral

§ 1002.288 How does an individual file a USERRA complaint?

If an individual is claiming entitlement to employment rights or benefits or reemployment rights or benefits and alleges that an employer has failed or refused, or is about to fail or refuse, to comply with the Act, the individual may file a complaint with VETS or initiate a private legal action in a court of law (see § 1002.303 below). A complaint may be filed with VETS either in writing, using VETS Form 1010, or electronically, using VETS Form e1010 (instructions and the forms can be accessed at http://www.dol.gov/elaws/vets/userra/1010.asp). A complaint must include the name and address of the employer, a summary of the basis for the complaint, and a request for relief.

§ 1002.289 How will VETS investigate a USERRA complaint?

(a) In carrying out any investigation, VETS has, at all reasonable times, reasonable access to and the right to interview persons with information relevant to the investigation. VETS also has reasonable access to, for purposes of examination, the right to copy and receive any documents of any person or employer that VETS considers relevant to the investigation.

(b) VETS may require by subpoena the attendance and testimony of witnesses and the production of documents relating to any matter under investigation. In case of disobedience of or resistance to the subpoena, the Attorney General may, at VETS' request, apply to any district court of the United States in whose jurisdiction such disobedience or resistance occurs for an order enforcing the subpoena. The district courts of the United States have jurisdiction to order compliance with the subpoena, and to punish failure to obey a subpoena as a contempt of court. This paragraph does not authorize VETS to seek issuance of a subpoena to the legislative or judicial branches of the United States.

§ 1002.290 Does VETS have the authority to order compliance with USERRA?

No. If VETS determines as a result of an investigation that the complaint is meritorious, VETS attempts to resolve the complaint by making reasonable efforts to ensure that any persons or entities named in the complaint comply with the Act. If VETS' efforts do not resolve the complaint, VETS notifies the person who submitted the complaint of:

(a) the results of the investigation; and,

(b) the person's right to proceed under the enforcement of rights provisions in 38 U.S.C. 4323 (against a State or private employer), or 38 U.S.C. 4324 (against a Federal executive agency or the Office of Personnel Management (OPM)).

§ 1002.291 What actions may an individual take if the complaint is not resolved by VETS?

If an individual receives a notification from VETS of an unsuccessful effort to resolve his or her complaint relating to a State or private employer, the individual may request that VETS refer the complaint to the Attorney General.

§ 1002.292 What can the Attorney General do about the complaint?

(a) If the Attorney General is reasonably satisfied that an individual's complaint is meritorious, meaning that he or she is entitled to the rights or benefits sought, the Attorney General may appear on his or her behalf and act as the individual's attorney, and initiate a legal action to obtain appropriate relief.

(b) If the Attorney General determines that the individual's complaint does not have merit, the Attorney General may decline to represent him or her.

Enforcement of Rights and Benefits Against a State or Private Employer

§ 1002.303 Is an individual required to file his or her complaint with VETS?

No. The individual may initiate a private action for relief against a State or private employer if he or she decides not to apply to VETS for assistance.

§ 1002.304 If an individual files a complaint with VETS and VETS' efforts do not resolve the complaint, can the individual pursue the claim on his or her own?

Yes. If VETS notifies an individual that it is unable to resolve the complaint, the individual may pursue the claim on his or her own. The individual may choose to be represented by private counsel whether or not the Attorney General decides to represent him or her as to the complaint.

§ 1002.305 What court has jurisdiction in an action against a State or private employer?

(a) If an action is brought against a State or private employer by the Attorney General, the district courts of the United States have jurisdiction over the action. If the action is brought against a State by the Attorney General, it must be brought in the name of the United States as the plaintiff in the action.

(b) If an action is brought against a State by a person, the action may be brought in a State court of competent jurisdiction according to the laws of the State.

(c) If an action is brought against a private employer or a political subdivision of a State by a person, the district courts of the United States have jurisdiction over the action.

(d) An action brought against a State Adjutant General, as an employer of a civilian National Guard technician, is considered an action against a State for purposes of determining which court has jurisdiction.

§ 1002.306 Is a National Guard civilian technician considered a State or Federal employee for purposes of USERRA?

A National Guard civilian technician is considered a State employee for USERRA purposes, although he or she is considered a Federal employee for most other purposes.

§ 1002.307 What is the proper venue in an action against a State or private employer?

(a) If an action is brought by the Attorney General against a State, the action may proceed in the United States district court for any district in which the State exercises any authority or carries out any function.

(b) If an action is brought against a private employer, or a political subdivision of a State, the action may proceed in the United States district court for any district in which the employer maintains a place of business.

§ 1002.308 Who has legal standing to bring an action under USERRA?

An action may be brought only by the United States or by the person, or representative of a person, claiming rights or benefits under the Act. An employer, prospective employer or other similar entity may not bring an action under the Act.

§ 1002.309 Who is a necessary party in an action under USERRA?

In an action under USERRA only an employer or a potential employer, as the case may be, is a necessary party respondent. In some circumstances, such as where terms in a collective bargaining agreement need to be interpreted, the court may allow an interested party to intervene in the action.

§ 1002.310 How are fees and court costs charged or taxed in an action under USERRA?

No fees or court costs may be charged or taxed against an individual if he or she is claiming rights under the Act. If the individual obtains private counsel for any action or proceeding to enforce a provision of the Act, and prevails, the court may award reasonable attorney fees, expert witness fees, and other litigation expenses.

§ 1002.311 Is there a statute of limitations in an action under USERRA?

USERRA does not have a statute of limitations, and it expressly precludes the application of any State statute of limitations. At least one court, however, has held that the fouryear general Federal statute of limitations, 28 U.S.C. 1658, applies to actions under USERRA. *Rogers v. City of San Antonio*, 2003 WL 1566502 (W.D. Texas), *reversed on other grounds*, 392 F.3d 758 (5th Cir. 2004). *But see Akhdary v. City of Chattanooga*, 2002 WL 32060140 (E.D. Tenn.). In addition, if an individual unreasonably delays asserting his or her rights, and that unreasonable delay causes prejudice to the employer, the courts have recognized the availability of the equitable doctrine of *laches* to bar a claim under USERRA. Accordingly, individuals asserting rights under USERRA should determine whether the issue of the applicability of the Federal statute of limitations has been resolved and, in any event, act promptly to preserve their rights under USERRA.

§ 1002.312 What remedies may be awarded for a violation of USERRA?

In any action or proceeding the court may award relief as follows:

(a) The court may require the employer to comply with the provisions of the Act;

(b) The court may require the employer to compensate the individual for any loss of wages or benefits suffered by reason of the employer's failure to comply with the Act;

(c) The court may require the employer to pay the individual an amount equal to the amount of lost wages and benefits as liquidated damages, if the court determines that the employer's failure to comply with the Act was willful. A violation shall be considered to be willful if the employer either knew or showed reckless disregard for whether its conduct was prohibited by the Act.

(d) Any wages, benefits, or liquidated damages awarded under paragraphs (b) and (c) of this section are in addition to, and must not diminish, any of the other rights and benefits provided by USERRA (such as, for example, the right to be employed or reemployed by the employer).

§ 1002.313 Are there special damages provisions that apply to actions initiated in the name of the United States?

Yes. In an action brought in the name of the United States, for which the relief includes compensation for lost wages, benefits, or liquidated damages, the compensation must be held in a special deposit account and must be paid, on order of the Attorney General, directly to the person. If the compensation is not paid to the individual because of the Federal Government's inability to do so within a period of three years, the compensation must be converted into the Treasury of the United States as miscellaneous receipts.

§ 1002.314 May a court use its equity powers in an action or proceeding under the Act?

Yes. A court may use its full equity powers, including the issuance of temporary or permanent injunctions, temporary restraining orders, and contempt orders, to vindicate the rights or benefits guaranteed under the Act.

[¶ 16,453B]

ACT SEC. 1002. PART 1002—REGULATIONS UNDER THE UNIFORMED SERVICES EMPLOYMENT AND REEMPLOYMENT RIGHTS ACT OF 1994

Appendix to Part 1002—Your Rights Under USERRA

Pursuant to 38 U.S.C. 4334(a), each employer shall provide to persons entitled to rights and benefits under USERRA a notice of the rights, benefits, and obligations of such persons and such employers under USERRA. The requirement for the provision of notice under this section may be met by the posting of one of the following notices where employers customarily place notices for employees. The following texts are provided by the Secretary of Labor to employers pursuant to 38 U.S.C. 4334(b). Text A is appropriate for use by employers in the private sector and for State government employers. Text B is appropriate for use by Federal Executive Agencies.

Text A—For Use by Private Sector and State Government Employers
Your Rights Under USERRA

The Uniformed Services Employment and Reemployment Rights Act

USERRA protects the job rights of individuals who voluntarily or involuntarily leave employment positions to undertake military service or certain types of service in the National Disaster Medical System. USERRA also prohibits employers from discriminating against past and present members of the uniformed services, and applicants to the uniformed services.

Reemployment Rights

You have the right to be reemployed in your civilian job if you leave that job to perform service in the uniformed service and:

• You ensure that your employer receives advance written or verbal notice of your service;

• You have five years or less of cumulative service in the uniformed services while with that particular employer;

• You return to work or apply for reemployment in a timely manner after conclusion of service; and

• You have not been separated from service with a disqualifying discharge or under other than honorable conditions.

If you are eligible to be reemployed, you must be restored to the job and benefits you would have attained if you had not been absent due to military service or, in some cases, a comparable job.

Right To Be Free From Discrimination and Retaliation

If you:

• Are a past or present member of the uniformed service;

• Have applied for membership in the uniformed service;

or

• Are obligated to serve in the uniformed service; then an employer may not deny you

• Initial employment;

• Reemployment;

• Retention in employment;

• Promotion; or

• Any benefit of employment.

because of this status.

In addition, an employer may not retaliate against anyone assisting in the enforcement of USERRA rights, including testifying or making a statement in connection with a proceeding under USERRA, even if that person has no service connection.

Health Insurance Protection

• If you leave your job to perform military service, you have the right to elect to continue your existing employer-based health plan coverage for you and your dependents for up to 24 months while in the military.

• Even if you don't elect to continue coverage during your military service, you have the right to be reinstated in your employer's health plan when you are reemployed, generally without any waiting periods or exclusions (e.g., pre-existing condition exclusions) except for service-connected illnesses or injuries.

Enforcement

• The U.S. Department of Labor, Veterans' Employment and Training Service (VETS) is authorized to investigate and resolve complaints of USERRA violations.

For assistance in filing a complaint, or for any other information on USERRA, contact VETS at 1-866-4-USA-DOL or visit its Web site at *http://frwebgate.access.gpo.gov/cgi-bin/leaving.cgi?from=leavingFR.html&log=linklog&to=http://www.dol.gov/vets* An interactive online USERRA Advisor can be viewed at *http://frwebgate.access.gpo.gov/cgi-bin/leaving.cgi?from=leavingFR.html&log=linklog&to=http://www.dol.gov/elaws/userra.htm.*

• If you file a complaint with VETS and VETS is unable to resolve it, you may request that your case be referred to the Department of Justice for representation.

• You may also bypass the VETS process and bring a civil action against an employer for violations of USERRA.

The rights listed here may vary depending on the circumstances. The text of this notice was prepared by VETS, and may be viewed on the Internet at this address: *http://frwebgate.access.gpo.gov/cgi-bin/leaving.cgi?from=leavingFR.html&log=linklog&to=http://www.dol.gov/vets/programs/userra/poster.htm.*

Federal law requires employers to notify employees of their rights under USERRA, and employers may meet this requirement by displaying the text of this notice where they customarily place notices for employees.

Text B—For Use by Federal Executive Agencies
Your Rights Under USERRA

The Uniformed Services Employment and Reemployment Rights Act

USERRA protects the job rights of individuals who voluntarily or involuntarily leave employment positions to undertake military service or certain types of service in the National Disaster Medical System. USERRA also prohibits employers from discriminating against past and present members of the uniformed services, and applicants to the uniformed services.

Reemployment Rights

You have the right to be reemployed in your civilian job if you leave that job to perform service in the uniformed service and:

• You ensure that your employer receives advance written or verbal notice of your service;

• You have five years or less of cumulative service in the uniformed services while with that particular employer;

• You return to work or apply for reemployment in a timely manner after conclusion of service; and

• You have not been separated from service with a disqualifying discharge or under other than honorable conditions.

If you are eligible to be reemployed, you must be restored to the job and benefits you would have attained if you had not been absent due to military service or, in some cases, a comparable job.

Right To Be Free From Discrimination and Retaliation

If you:

• Are a past or present member of the uniformed service;

• Have applied for membership in the uniformed service; or

• Are obligated to serve in the uniformed service; then an employer may not deny you

• Initial employment;

• Reemployment;

• Retention in employment;

• Promotion; or

• Any benefit of employment.

because of this status.

In addition, an employer may not retaliate against anyone assisting in the enforcement of USERRA rights, including testifying or making a statement in connection with a proceeding under USERRA, even if that person has no service connection.

Health Insurance Protection

• If you leave your job to perform military service, you have the right to elect to continue your existing employer-based health plan coverage for you and your dependents for up to 24 months while in the military.

• Even if you don't elect to continue coverage during your military service, you have the right to be reinstated in your employer's health plan when you are reemployed, generally without any waiting periods or exclusions (e.g., pre-existing condition exclusions) except for service-connected illnesses or injuries.

Enforcement

• The U.S. Department of Labor, Veterans' Employment and Training Service (VETS) is authorized to investigate and resolve complaints of USERRA violations.

For assistance in filing a complaint, or for any other information on USERRA, contact VETS at 1-866-4-USA-DOL or visit its Web site at *http://frwebgate.access.gpo.gov/cgi-bin/leaving.cgi?from=leavingFR.html&log=linklog&to=http://www.dol.gov/vets* An interactive online USERRA Advisor can be viewed at *http://frwebgate.access.gpo.gov/cgi-bin/leaving.cgi?from=leavingFR.html&log=linklog&to=http://www.dol.gov/elaws/userra.htm*.

• In some cases involving USERRA claims against Federal executive agencies, a complaint filed with VETS before September 30, 2007, may be transferred to the Office of Special Counsel for investigation and resolution pursuant to a demonstration project established under Section 204 of the Veterans Benefits Improvement Act of 2004, Public Law 108-454 (Dec. 10, 2004).

• If VETS is unable to resolve a complaint that has not been transferred for investigation under the demonstration project, you may request that your case be referred to the Office of Special Counsel for representation.

• You may also bypass the VETS process and bring a civil action against an employer for violations of USERRA.

The rights listed here may vary depending on the circumstances. The text of this notice was prepared by VETS, and may be viewed on the Internet at this address: *http://frwebgate.access.gpo.gov/cgi-bin/leaving.cgi?from=leavingFR.html&log=linklog&to=http://www.dol.gov/vets/* programs/userra/poster.htm. Federal law requires employers to notify employees of their rights under USERRA, and employers may meet this requirement by displaying the text of this notice where they customarily place notices for employees.

U.S. Department of Labor, Veterans' Employment and Training Service, 1-866-487-2365.

Bankruptcy Abuse Prevention and Consumer Protection Act of 2005

P.L. 109-8

Signed on April 20, 2005

[Reproduced below are excerpts from the Bankruptcy Abuse Prevention and Consumer Protection Act of 2005 (P.L. 109-8) that pertain to pensions and employee benefits.]

TITLE II—ENHANCED CONSUMER PROTECTION

SUBTITLE C—OTHER CONSUMER PROTECTIONS

[¶16,456]

ACT SEC. 224. PROTECTION OF RETIREMENT SAVINGS IN BANKRUPTCY. (a) *In general*. Section 522 of title 11, United States Code, is amended—

(1) in subsection (b)—

(A) in paragraph (2)—

(i) in subparagraph (A), by striking 'and' at the end;

(ii) in subparagraph (B), by striking the period at the end and inserting '; and';

(iii) by adding at the end the following:

'(C) retirement funds to the extent that those funds are in a fund or account that is exempt from taxation under section 401, 403, 408, 408A, 414, 57, or 501(a) of the Internal Revenue Code of 1986.'; and

(iv) by striking '(2)(A) any property' and inserting:

'(3) Property listed in this paragraph is—

'(A) any property';

(B) by striking paragraph (1) and inserting:

'(2) Property listed in this paragraph is property that is specified under subsection (d), unless the State law that is applicable to the debtor under paragraph (3)(A) specifically does not so authorize.';

(C) by striking '(b) Notwithstanding' and inserting '(b)(1) Notwithstanding';

(D) by striking 'paragraph (2)' each place it appears and inserting 'paragraph (3)';

(E) by striking 'paragraph (1)' each place it appears and inserting 'paragraph (2)';

(F) by striking 'Such property is—'; and

(G) by adding at the end the following:

'(4) For purposes of paragraph (3)(C) and subsection (d)(12), the following shall apply:

'(A) If the retirement funds are in a retirement fund that has received a favorable determination under section 7805 of the Internal Revenue Code of 1986, and that determination is in effect as of the date of the filing of the petition in a case under this title, those funds shall be presumed to be exempt from the estate.

'(B) If the retirement funds are in a retirement fund that has not received a favorable determination under such section 7805, those funds are exempt from the estate if the debtor demonstrates that—

'(i) no prior determination to the contrary has been made by a court or the Internal Revenue Service; and

'(ii)(I) the retirement fund is in substantial compliance with the applicable requirements of the Internal Revenue Code of 1986; or

'(II) the retirement fund fails to be in substantial compliance with the applicable requirements of the Internal Revenue Code of 1986 and the debtor is not materially responsible for that failure.

'(C) A direct transfer of retirement funds from 1 fund or account that is exempt from taxation under section 401, 403, 408, 408A, 414, 457, or 501(a) of the Internal Revenue Code of 1986, under section 401(a)(31) of the Internal Revenue Code of 1986, or otherwise, shall not cease to qualify for exemption under paragraph (3)(C) or subsection (d)(12) by reason of such direct transfer.

'(D)(i) Any distribution that qualifies as an eligible rollover distribution within the meaning of section 402(c) of the Internal Revenue Code of 1986 or that is described in clause (ii) shall not cease to qualify for exemption under paragraph (3)(C) or subsection (d)(12) by reason of such distribution.

'(ii) A distribution described in this clause is an amount that—

'(I) has been distributed from a fund or account that is exempt from taxation under section 401, 403, 408, 408A, 414, 457, or 501(a) of the Internal Revenue Code of 1986; and

'(II) to the extent allowed by law, is deposited in such a fund or account not later than 60 days after the distribution of such amount.'; and

(2) in subsection (d)—

(A) in the matter preceding paragraph (1), by striking 'subsection (b)(1)' and inserting 'subsection (b)(2)'; and

(B) by adding at the end the following:

'(12) Retirement funds to the extent that those funds are in a fund or account that is exempt from taxation under section 401, 403, 408, 408A, 414, 457, or 501(a) of the Internal Revenue Code of 1986.'.

(b) *Automatic stay*. Section 362(b) of title 11, United States Code, is amended—

(1) in paragraph (17), by striking 'or' at the end;

(2) in paragraph (18), by striking the period and inserting a semicolon; and

(3) by inserting after paragraph (18) the following:

'(19) under subsection (a), of withholding of income from a debtor's wages and collection of amounts withheld, under the debtor's agreement authorizing that withholding and collection for the benefit of a pension, profit-sharing, stock bonus, or other plan established under section 401, 403, 408, 408A, 414, 457, or 501(c) of the Internal Revenue Code of 1986, that is sponsored by the employer of the debtor, or an affiliate, successor, or predecessor of such employer—

'(A) to the extent that the amounts withheld and collected are used solely for payments relating to a loan from a plan under section 408(b)(1) of the Employee Retirement Income Security Act of 1974 or is subject to section 72(p) of the Internal Revenue Code of 1986; or

'(B) a loan from a thrift savings plan permitted under subchapter III of chapter 84 of title 5, that satisfies the requirements of section 8433(g) of such title; but nothing in this paragraph may be construed to provide that any loan made under a governmental plan under section 414(d), or a contract or account under section 403(b), of the Internal Revenue Code of 1986 constitutes a claim or a debt under this title;'.

(c) *Exceptions to discharge.* Section 523(a) of title 11, United States Code, as amended by section 215, is amended by inserting after paragraph (17) the following:

'(18) owed to a pension, profit-sharing, stock bonus, or other plan established under section 401, 403, 408, 408A, 414, 457, or 501(c) of the Internal Revenue Code of 1986, under—

'(A) a loan permitted under section 408(b)(1) of the Employee Retirement Income Security Act of 1974, or subject to section 72(p) of the Internal Revenue Code of 1986; or

'(B) a loan from a thrift savings plan permitted under subchapter III of chapter 84 of title 5, that satisfies the requirements of section 8433(g) of such title; but nothing in this paragraph may be construed to provide that any loan made under a governmental plan under section 414(d), or a contract or account under section 403(b), of the Internal Revenue Code of 1986 constitutes a claim or a debt under this title; or'.

(d) *Plan contents.* Section 1322 of title 11, United States Code, is amended by adding at the end the following:

'(f) A plan may not materially alter the terms of a loan described in section 362(b)(19) and any amounts required to repay such loan shall not constitute 'disposable income' under section 1325.'.

(e) *Asset limitation.* (1) *Limitation.* Section 522 of title 11, United States Code, is amended by adding at the end the following:

'(n) For assets in individual retirement accounts described in section 408 or 408A of the Internal Revenue Code of 1986, other than a simplified employee pension under section 408(k) of such Code or a simple retirement account under section 408(p) of such Code, the aggregate value of such assets exempted under this section, without regard to amounts attributable to rollover contributions under section 402(c), 402(e)(6), 403(a)(4), 403(a)(5), and 403(b)(8) of the Internal Revenue Code of 1986, and earnings thereon, shall not exceed $1,000,000 in a case filed by a debtor who is an individual, except that such amount may be increased if the interests of justice so require.'.

(2) *Adjustment of dollar amounts.* Paragraphs (1) and (2) of section 104(b) of title 11, United States Code, are amended by inserting '522(n),' after '522(d),'.

[¶16,457]

ACT SEC. 225 PROTECTION OF EDUCATION SAVINGS IN BANKRUPTCY. (a) *Exclusions.* Section 541 of title 11, United States Code, is amended—

(1) in subsection (b)—

(A) in paragraph (4), by striking 'or' at the end;

(B) by redesignating paragraph (5) as paragraph (9); and

(C) by inserting after paragraph (4) the following:

'(5) funds placed in an education individual retirement account (as defined in section 530(b)(1) of the Internal Revenue Code of 1986) not later than 365 days before the date of the filing of the petition in a case under this title, but—

'(A) only if the designated beneficiary of such account was a child, stepchild, grandchild, or stepgrandchild of the debtor for the taxable year for which funds were placed in such account;

'(B) only to the extent that such funds—

'(i) are not pledged or promised to any entity in connection with any extension of credit; and

'(ii) are not excess contributions (as described in section 4973(e) of the Internal Revenue Code of 1986); and

'(C) in the case of funds placed in all such accounts having the same designated beneficiary not earlier than 720 days nor later than 365 days before such date, only so much of such funds as does not exceed $5,000;

'(6) funds used to purchase a tuition credit or certificate or contributed to an account in accordance with section 529(b)(1)(A) of the Internal Revenue Code of 1986 under a qualified State tuition program (as defined in section 529(b)(1) of such Code) not later than 365 days before the date of the filing of the petition in a case under this title, but—

'(A) only if the designated beneficiary of the amounts paid or contributed to such tuition program was a child, stepchild, grandchild, or stepgrandchild of the debtor for the taxable year for which funds were paid or contributed;

'(B) with respect to the aggregate amount paid or contributed to such program having the same designated beneficiary, only so much of such amount as does not exceed the total contributions permitted under section 529(b)(7) of such Code with respect to such beneficiary, as adjusted beginning on the date of the filing of the petition in a case under this title by the annual increase or decrease (rounded to the nearest tenth of 1 percent) in the education expenditure category of the Consumer Price Index prepared by the Department of Labor; and

'(C) in the case of funds paid or contributed to such program having the same designated beneficiary not earlier than 720 days nor later than 365 days before such date, only so much of such funds as does not exceed $5,000;'; and

(2) by adding at the end the following:

'(e) In determining whether any of the relationships specified in paragraph (5)(A) or (6)(A) of subsection (b) exists, a legally adopted child of an individual (and a child who is a member of an individual's household, if placed with such individual by an authorized placement agency for legal adoption by such individual), or a foster child of an individual (if such child has as the child's principal place of abode the home of the debtor and is a member of the debtor's household) shall be treated as a child of such individual by blood.'.

(b) *Debtor's duties.* Section 521 of title 11, United States Code, as amended by section 106, is amended by adding at the end the following:

'(c) In addition to meeting the requirements under subsection (a), a debtor shall file with the court a record of any interest that a debtor has in an education individual retirement account (as defined in section 530(b)(1) of the Internal Revenue Code of 1986) or under a qualified State tuition program (as defined in section 529(b)(1) of such Code).'.

* * *

¶16,457   ACT SEC. 225

TITLE III.—DISCOURAGING BANKRUPTCY ABUSE

[¶16,458]

ACT SEC. 323 EXCLUDING EMPLOYEE BENEFIT PLAN PARTICIPANT CONTRIBUTIONS AND OTHER PROPERTY FROM THE ESTATE. Section 541(b) of title 11, United States Code, as amended by section 225, is amended by adding after paragraph (6), as added by section 225(a)(1)(C), the following:

'(7) any amount—

'(A) withheld by an employer from the wages of employees for payment as contributions—

'(i) to—

'(I) an employee benefit plan that is subject to title I of the Employee Retirement Income Security Act of 1974 or under an employee benefit plan which is a governmental plan under section 414(d) of the Internal Revenue Code of 1986;

'(II) a deferred compensation plan under section 457 of the Internal Revenue Code of 1986; or

'(III) a tax-deferred annuity under section 403(b) of the Internal Revenue Code of 1986; except that such amount under this subparagraph shall not constitute disposable income as defined in section 1325(b)(2); or

'(ii) to a health insurance plan regulated by State law whether or not subject to such title; or

'(B) received by an employer from employees for payment as contributions—

'(i) to—

'(I) an employee benefit plan that is subject to title I of the Employee Retirement Income Security Act of 1974 or under an employee benefit plan which is a governmental plan under section 414(d) of the Internal Revenue Code of 1986;

'(II) a deferred compensation plan under section 457 of the Internal Revenue Code of 1986; or

'(III) a tax-deferred annuity under section 403(b) of the Internal Revenue Code of 1986; except that such amount under this subparagraph shall not constitute disposable income, as defined in section 1325(b)(2); or

'(ii) to a health insurance plan regulated by State law whether or not subject to such title;'.

* * *

[¶16,459]

ACT SEC. 329. CLARIFICATION OF POSTPETITION WAGES AND BENEFITS. Section 503(b)(1)(A) of title 11, United States Code, is amended to read as follows:

'(A) the actual, necessary costs and expenses of preserving the estate including—

'(i) wages, salaries, and commissions for services rendered after the commencement of the case; and

'(ii) wages and benefits awarded pursuant to a judicial proceeding or a proceeding of the National Labor Relations Board as back pay attributable to any period of time occurring after commencement of the case under this title, as a result of a violation of Federal or State law by the debtor, without regard to the time of the occurrence of unlawful conduct on which such award is based or to whether any services were rendered, if the court determines that payment of wages and benefits by reason of the operation of this clause will not substantially increase the probability of layoff or termination of current employees, or of nonpayment of domestic support obligations, during the case under this title;'.

* * *

[¶16,459A]

ACT SEC. 331. LIMITATION ON RETENTION BONUSES, SEVERANCE PAY, AND CERTAIN OTHER PAYMENTS. Section 503 of title 11, United States Code, is amended by adding at the end the following:

'(c) Notwithstanding subsection (b), there shall neither be allowed, nor paid—

'(1) a transfer made to, or an obligation incurred for the benefit of, an insider of the debtor for the purpose of inducing such person to remain with the debtor's business, absent a finding by the court based on evidence in the record that—

'(A) the transfer or obligation is essential to retention of the person because the individual has a bona fide job offer from another business at the same or greater rate of compensation;

'(B) the services provided by the person are essential to the survival of the business; and

'(C) either—

'(i) the amount of the transfer made to, or obligation incurred for the benefit of, the person is not greater than an amount equal to 10 times the amount of the mean transfer or obligation of a similar kind given to nonmanagement employees for any purpose during the calendar year in which the transfer is made or the obligation is incurred; or

'(ii) if no such similar transfers were made to, or obligations were incurred for the benefit of, such nonmanagement employees during such calendar year, the amount of the transfer or obligation is not greater than an amount equal to 25 percent of the amount of any similar transfer or obligation made to or incurred for the benefit of such insider for any purpose during the calendar year before the year in which such transfer is made or obligation is incurred;

'(2) a severance payment to an insider of the debtor, unless—

'(A) the payment is part of a program that is generally applicable to all full-time employees; and

'(B) the amount of the payment is not greater than 10 times the amount of the mean severance pay given to nonmanagement employees during the calendar year in which the payment is made; or

'(3) other transfers or obligations that are outside the ordinary course of business and not justified by the facts and circumstances of the case, including transfers made to, or obligations incurred for the benefit of, officers, managers, or consultants hired after the date of the filing of the petition.'.

[¶16,459B]

ACT SEC. 332. FRAUDULENT INVOLUNTARY BANKRUPTCY. (a) *Short title.* This section may be cited as the 'Involuntary Bankruptcy Improvement Act of 2005'.

(b) *Involuntary cases.* Section 303 of title 11, United States Code, is amended by adding at the end the following:

'(l)(1) If—

'(A) the petition under this section is false or contains any materially false, fictitious, or fraudulent statement;

'(B) the debtor is an individual; and

'(C) the court dismisses such petition, the court, upon the motion of the debtor, shall seal all the records of the court relating to such petition, and all references to such petition.

'(2) If the debtor is an individual and the court dismisses a petition under this section, the court may enter an order prohibiting all consumer reporting agencies (as defined in section 603(f) of the Fair Credit Reporting Act (15 U.S.C. 1681a(f))) from making any consumer report (as defined in section 603(d) of that Act) that contains any information relating to such petition or to the case commenced by the filing of such petition.

'(3) Upon the expiration of the statute of limitations described in section 3282 of title 18, for a violation of section 152 or 157 of such title, the court, upon the motion of the debtor and for good cause, may expunge any records relating to a petition filed under this section.'.

(c) *Bankruptcy fraud.* Section 157 of title 18, United States Code, is amended by inserting ', including a fraudulent involuntary bankruptcy petition under section 303 of such title' after 'title 11'.

* * *

TITLE IV.—GENERAL AND SMALL BUSINESS BANKRUPTCY PROVISIONS

SUBTITLE B—SMALL BANKRUPTCY PROVISIONS

[¶16,459C]

ACT SEC. 446. DUTIES WITH RESPECT TO A DEBTOR WHO IS A PLAN ADMINISTRATOR OF AN EMPLOYEE BENEFIT PLAN. (a) *In general.* Section 521(a) of title 11, United States Code, as amended by sections 106 and 304, is amended—

(1) in paragraph (5), by striking 'and' at the end;

(2) in paragraph (6), by striking the period at the end and inserting '; and'; and

(3) by adding after paragraph (6) the following:

'(7) unless a trustee is serving in the case, continue to perform the obligations required of the administrator (as defined in section 3 of the Employee Retirement Income Security Act of 1974) of an employee benefit plan if at the time of the commencement of the case the debtor (or any entity designated by the debtor) served as such administrator.'.

(b) *Duties of trustees.* Section 704(a) of title 11, United States Code, as amended by sections 102 and 219, is amended—

(1) in paragraph (10), by striking 'and' at the end; and

(2) by adding at the end the following:

'(11) if, at the time of the commencement of the case, the debtor (or any entity designated by the debtor) served as the administrator (as defined in section 3 of the Employee Retirement Income Security Act of 1974) of an employee benefit plan, continue to perform the obligations required of the administrator; and'.

(c) *Conforming amendment.* Section 1106(a)(1) of title 11, United States Code, is amended to read as follows:

'(1) perform the duties of the trustee, as specified in paragraphs (2), (5), (7), (8), (9), (10), and (11) of section 704;'.

* * *

TITLE XIII.—TECHNICAL AMENDMENTS

[¶16,459D]

ACT SEC. 1202. ADJUSTMENT OF DOLLAR AMOUNTS. Section 104(b) of title 11, United States Code, as amended by this Act, is further amended—

(1) by inserting '101(19A),' after '101(18),' each place it appears;

(2) by inserting '522(f)(3) and 522(f)(4),' after '522(d),' each place it appears;

(3) by inserting '541(b), 547(c)(9),' after '523(a)(2)(C),' each place it appears;

(4) in paragraph (1), by striking 'and 1325(b)(3)' and inserting '1322(d), 1325(b), and 1326(b)(3) of this title and section 1409(b) of title 28'; and

(5) in paragraph (2), by striking 'and 1325(b)(3) of this title' and inserting '1322(d), 1325(b), and 1326(b)(3) of this title and section 1409(b) of title 28'.

* * *

[¶16,459E]

ACT SEC. 1208. ALLOWANCE OF ADMINISTRATIVE EXPENSES. Section 503(b)(4) of title 11, United States Code, is amended by inserting 'subparagraph (A), (B), (C), (D), or (E) of' before 'paragraph (3)'.

[¶16,459F]

ACT SEC. 1209. EXCEPTIONS TO DISCHARGE. Section 523 of title 11, United States Code, as amended by sections 215 and 314, is amended—

(1) by transferring paragraph (15), as added by section 304(e) of Public Law 103-394 (108 Stat. 4133), so as to insert such paragraph after subsection (a)(14A);

(2) in subsection (a)(9), by striking 'motor vehicle' and inserting 'motor vehicle, vessel, or aircraft'; and

(3) in subsection (e), by striking 'a insured' and inserting 'an insured'.

* * *

TITLE XIV.—PREVENTING CORPORATE BANKRUPTCY ABUSE

[¶16,459G]

ACT SEC. 1401. EMPLOYEE WAGE AND BENEFIT PRIORITIES. Section 507(a) of title 11, United States Code, as amended by section 212, is amended—

(1) in paragraph (4) by striking '90' and inserting '180', and

(2) in paragraphs (4) and (5) by striking '$4,000' and inserting '$10,000'.

[¶16,459H]

ACT SEC. 1402. FRAUDULENT TRANSFERS AND OBLIGATIONS. Section 548 of title 11, United States Code, is amended—

(1) in subsections (a) and (b) by striking 'one year' and inserting '2 years',

(2) in subsection (a)—(A) by inserting '(including any transfer to or for the benefit of an insider under an employment contract)' after 'transfer' the 1st place it appears, and

(B) by inserting '(including any obligation to or for the benefit of an insider under an employment contract)' after 'obligation' the 1st place it appears, and

(3) in subsection (a)(1)(B)(ii)—

(A) in subclause (II) by striking 'or' at the end,

(B) in subclause (III) by striking the period at the end and inserting'; or', and

(C) by adding at the end the following:

'(IV) made such transfer to or for the benefit of an insider, or incurred such obligation to or for the benefit of an insider, under an employment contract and not in the ordinary course of business.'.

(4) by adding at the end the following:

'(e)(1) In addition to any transfer that the trustee may otherwise avoid, the trustee may avoid any transfer of an interest of the debtor in property that was made on or within 10 years before the date of the filing of the petition, if—

'(A) such transfer was made to a self-settled trust or similar device;

'(B) such transfer was by the debtor;

'(C) the debtor is a beneficiary of such trust or similar device; and

'(D) the debtor made such transfer with actual intent to hinder, delay, or defraud any entity to which the debtor was or became, on or after the date that such transfer was made, indebted.

'(2) For the purposes of this subsection, a transfer includes a transfer made in anticipation of any money judgment, settlement, civil penalty, equitable order, or criminal fine incurred by, or which the debtor believed would be incurred by—

'(A) any violation of the securities laws (as defined in section 3(a)(47) of the Securities Exchange Act of 1934 (15 U.S.C. 78c(a)(47))), any State securities laws, or any regulation or order issued under Federal securities laws or State securities laws; or

'(B) fraud, deceit, or manipulation in a fiduciary capacity or in connection with the purchase or sale of any security registered under section 12 or 15(d) of the Securities Exchange Act of 1934 (15 U.S.C. 78l and 78o(d)) or under section 6 of the Securities Act of 1933 (15 U.S.C. 77f).'.

* * *

[¶16,459I]

ACT SEC. 1403. PAYMENT OF INSURANCE BENEFITS TO RETIRED EMPLOYEES. Section 1114 of title 11, United States Code, is amended—

(1) by redesignating subsection (l) as subsection (m), and

(2) by inserting after subsection (k) the following:

'(l) If the debtor, during the 180-day period ending on the date of the filing of the petition—

'(1) modified retiree benefits; and

'(2) was insolvent on the date such benefits were modified; the court, on motion of a party in interest, and after notice and a hearing, shall issue an order reinstating as of the date the modification was made, such benefits as in effect immediately before such date unless the court finds that the balance of the equities clearly favors such modification.'.

* * *

[¶16,459J]

ACT SEC. 1406. EFFECTIVE DATE; APPLICATION OF AMENDMENTS. (a) *Effective date.* Except as provided in subsection (b), this title and the amendments made by this title shall take effect on the date of the enactment of this Act.

(b) *Application of amendments.* (1) *In general.* ***except as provided in paragraph (2), the amendments made by this title shall apply only with respect to cases commenced under title 11 of the United States Code on or after the date of the enactment of this Act.

(2) *Avoidance period.* The amendment made by section 1402(1) shall apply only with respect to cases commenced under title 11 of the United States Code more than 1 year after the date of the enactment of this Act.

TITLE XV—GENERAL EFFECTIVE DATE; APPLICATION OF AMENDMENTS

[¶16,459K]

ACT SEC. 1501. EFFECTIVE DATE; APPLICATION OF AMENDMENTS. (a) *Effective date.* Except as otherwise provided in this Act, this Act and the amendments made by this Act shall take effect 180 days after the date of enactment of this Act.

(b) *Application of amendments.* (1) *In general.* Except as otherwise provided in this Act and paragraph (2), the amendments made by this Act shall not apply with respect to cases commenced under title 11, United States Code, before the effective date of this Act.

(2) *Certain limitation applicable to debtors.* The amendments made by sections 308, 322, and 330 shall apply with respect to cases commenced under title 11, United States Code, on or after the date of the enactment of this Act.

[¶16,459L]

ACT SEC. 1502. TECHNICAL CORRECTIONS. (a) *Conforming amendments to Title 11 of the United States Code.* Title 11 of the United States Code, as amended by the preceding provisions of this Act, is amended—

(1) in section 507—

   (A) in subsection (a)—

      (i) in paragraph (5)(B)(ii) by striking 'paragraph (3)' and inserting 'paragraph (4)'; and

      (ii) in paragraph (8)(D) by striking 'paragraph (3)' and inserting 'paragraph (4)';

   (B) in subsection (b) by striking 'subsection (a)(1)' and inserting 'subsection (a)(2)'; and

   (C) in subsection (d) by striking 'subsection (a)(3)' and inserting 'subsection (a)(1)';

(2) in section 523(a)(1)(A) by striking '507(a)(2)' and inserting '507(a)(3)';

(3) in section 752(a) by striking '507(a)(1)' and inserting '507(a)(2)';

(4) in section 766—

   (A) in subsection (h) by striking '507(a)(1)' and inserting '507(a)(2)'; and

   (B) in subsection (i) by striking '507(a)(1)' each place it appears and inserting '507(a)(2)';

(5) in section 901(a) by striking '507(a)(1)' and inserting '507(a)(2)';

(6) in section 943(b)(5) by striking '507(a)(1)' and inserting '507(a)(2)';

(7) in section 1123(a)(1) by striking '507(a)(1), 507(a)(2)' and inserting '507(a)(2), 507(a)(3)';

(8) in section 1129(a)(9)—

   (A) in subparagraph (A) by striking '507(a)(1) or 507(a)(2)' and inserting '507(a)(2) or 507(a)(3)'; and

   (B) in subparagraph (B) by striking '507(a)(3)' and inserting '507(a)(1)';

(9) in section 1226(b)(1) by striking '507(a)(1)' and inserting '507(a)(2)'; and

(10) in section 1326(b)(1) by striking '507(a)(1)' and inserting '507(a)(2)'.

(b) *Related conforming amendment.* Section 6(e) of the Securities Investor Protection Act of 1970 (15 U.S.C. 78fff(e)) is amended by striking '507(a)(1)' and inserting '507(a)(2)'.

Katrina Emergency Tax Relief Act

P.L. 109-73

Signed on September 21, 2005

[Reproduced below are excerpts from the Katrina Emergency Tax Relief Act (P.L. 109-73) that pertain to pensions and employee benefits. The Act provides emergency tax relief for victims of Hurricane Katrina. **NOTE:** The provisions at ¶ 16,460C—¶ 16,460F, ¶ 16,460H, ¶ 16,460K (in part) and ¶ 16,460L were repealed by P.L. 109-135 (Gulf Opportunity Zone Act of 2005), Sec. 201(b)(4). See ¶ 13,475.]

[¶16,460A]

ACT SEC. 1. SHORT TITLE, ETC. (a) *Short title.* This Act may be cited as the "Katrina Emergency Tax Relief Act of 2005".

* * *

[¶16,460B]

ACT SEC. 2. HURRICANE KATRINA DISASTER AREA. For purposes of this Act—

(1) *Hurricane Katrina disaster area.* The term "Hurricane Katrina disaster area" means an area with respect to which a major disaster has been declared by the President before September 14, 2005, under section 401 of the Robert T. Stafford Disaster Relief and Emergency Assistance Act by reason of Hurricane Katrina.

(2) *Core disaster area.* The term "core disaster area" means that portion of the Hurricane Katrina disaster area determined by the President to warrant individual or individual and public assistance from the Federal Government under such Act.

TITLE I.—SPECIAL RULES FOR USE OF RETIREMENT FUNDS FOR RELIEF RELATING TO HURRICANE KATRINA

[¶16,460C]

ACT SEC. 101. TAX-FAVORED WITHDRAWALS FROM RETIREMENT PLANS FOR RELIEF RELATING TO HURRICANE KATRINA. (a) *In general.* Section 72(t) of the Internal Revenue Code of 1986 shall not apply to any qualified Hurricane Katrina distribution.

(b) *Aggregate dollar limitation.*—

(1) *In general.* For purposes of this section, the aggregate amount of distributions received by an individual which may be treated as qualified Hurricane Katrina distributions for any taxable year shall not exceed the excess (if any) of—

(A) $100,000, over

(B) the aggregate amounts treated as qualified Hurricane Katrina distributions received by such individual for all prior taxable years.

(2) *Treatment of plan distributions.* If a distribution to an individual would (without regard to paragraph (1)) be a qualified Hurricane Katrina distribution, a plan shall not be treated as violating any requirement of the Internal Revenue Code of 1986 merely because the plan treats such distribution as a qualified Hurricane Katrina distribution, unless the aggregate amount of such distributions from all plans maintained by the employer (and any member of any controlled group which includes the employer) to such individual exceeds $100,000.

(3) *Controlled group.* For purposes of paragraph (2), the term "controlled group" means any group treated as a single employer under sub-section (b), (c), (m), or (o) of section 414 of such Code.

(c) *Amount distributed may be repaid.*—

(1) *In general.* Any individual who receives a qualified Hurricane Katrina distribution may, at any time during the 3-year period beginning on the day after the date on which such distribution was received, make one or more contributions in an aggregate amount not to exceed the amount of such distribution to an eligible retirement plan of which such individual is a beneficiary and to which a rollover contribution of such distribution could be made under section 402(c), 403(a)(4), 403(b)(8), 408(d)(3), or 457(e)(16) of such Code, as the case may be.

(2) *Treatment of repayments of distributions from eligible retirement plans other than IRAs.* For purposes of such Code, if a contribution is made pursuant to paragraph (1) with respect to a qualified Hurricane Katrina distribution from an eligible retirement plan other than an individual retirement plan, then the taxpayer shall, to the extent of the amount of the contribution, be treated as having received the qualified Hurricane Katrina distribution in an eligible rollover distribution (as defined in section 402(c)(4) of such Code) and as having transferred the amount to the eligible retirement plan in a direct trustee to trustee transfer within 60 days of the distribution.

(3) *Treatment of repayments for distributions from IRAs.* For purposes of such Code, if a contribution is made pursuant to paragraph (1) with respect to a qualified Hurricane Katrina distribution from an individual retirement plan (as defined by section 7701(a)(37) of such Code), then, to the extent of the amount of the contribution, the qualified Hurricane Katrina distribution shall be treated as a distribution described in section 408(d)(3) of such Code and as having been transferred to the eligible retirement plan in a direct trustee to trustee transfer within 60 days of the distribution.

(d) *Definitions.*—For purposes of this section—

(1) *Qualified Hurricane Katrina distribution* . Except as provided in subsection (b), the term "qualified Hurricane Katrina distribution" means any distribution from an eligible retirement plan made on or after August 25, 2005, and before January 1, 2007, to an individual whose principal place of abode on August 28, 2005, is located in the Hurricane Katrina disaster area and who has sustained an economic loss by reason of Hurricane Katrina.

(2) *Eligible retirement plan.* The term "eligible retirement plan" shall have the meaning given such term by section 402(c)(8)(B) of such Code.

(e) *Income inclusion spread over 3 year period for qualified Hurricane Katrina distributions.*—

(1) *In general.* In the case of any qualified Hurricane Katrina distribution, unless the taxpayer elects not to have this subsection apply for any taxable year, any amount required to be included in gross income for such taxable year shall be so included ratably over the 3-taxable year period beginning with such taxable year.

(2) *Special rule.* For purposes of paragraph (1), rules similar to the rules of subparagraph (E) of section 408A(d)(3) of such Code shall apply.

ACT SEC. 101.   ¶16,460C

(f) *Special rules.—*

(1) *Exemption of distributions from trustee to trustee transfer and withholding rules.* For purposes of sections 401(a)(31), 402(f), and 3405 of such Code, qualified Hurricane Katrina distributions shall not be treated as eligible rollover distributions.

(2) *Qualified Hurricane Katrina distributions treated as meeting plan distribution requirements.* For purposes of such Code, a qualified Hurricane Katrina distribution shall be treated as meeting the requirements of sections 401(k)(2)(B)(i), 403(b)(7)(A)(ii), 403(b)(11), and 457(d)(1)(A) of such Code. [**NOTE:** Act Sec. 101 was repealed by P.L. 109-135, Act Sec. 201(b)(4).]

[¶16,460D]

ACT SEC. 102. RECONTRIBUTIONS OF WITHDRAWALS FOR HOME PURCHASES CANCELLED DUE TO HURRICANE KATRINA. (a) *Recontributions.—*

(1) *In general.* Any individual who received a qualified distribution may, during the period beginning on August 25, 2005, and ending on February 28, 2006, make one or more contributions in an aggregate amount not to exceed the amount of such qualified distribution to an eligible retirement plan (as defined in section 402(c)(8)(B) of the Internal Revenue Code of 1986) of which such individual is a beneficiary and to which a rollover contribution of such distribution could be made under section 402(c), 403(a)(4), 403(b)(8), or 408(d)(3) of such Code, as the case may be.

(2) *Treatment of repayments.* Rules similar to the rules of paragraphs (2) and (3) of section 101(c) of this Act shall apply for purposes of this section.

(b) *Qualified distribution defined.* For purposes of this section, the term "qualified distribution" means any distribution—

(1) described in section 401(k)(2)(B)(i)(IV), 403(b)(7)(A)(ii) (but only to the extent such distribution relates to financial hardship), 403(b)(11)(B), or 72(t)(2)(F) of such Code,

(2) received after February 28, 2005, and before August 29, 2005, and

(3) which was to be used to purchase or construct a principal residence in the Hurricane Katrina disaster area, but which was not so purchased or constructed on account of Hurricane Katrina. [**NOTE:** Act Sec. 102 was repealed by P.L. 109-135, Act Sec. 201(b)(4).]

[¶16,460E]

ACT SEC. 103. LOANS FROM QUALIFIFED PLANS FOR RELIEF RELATING TO HURRICANE KATRINA. (a) *Increase in limit on loans not treated as distributions.* In the case of any loan from a qualified employer plan (as defined under section 72(p)(4) of the Internal Revenue Code of 1986) to a qualified individual made after the date of enactment of this Act and before January 1, 2007—

(1) clause (i) of section 72(p)(2)(A) of such Code shall be applied by substituting "$100,000" for "$50,000", and

(2) (2) clause (ii) of such section shall be applied by substituting "the present value of the nonforfeitable accrued benefit of the employee under the plan" for "one-half of the present value of the nonforfeitable accrued benefit of the employee under the plan".

(b) *Delay of repayment.* In the case of a qualified individual with an outstanding loan on or after August 25, 2005, from a qualified employer plan (as defined in section 72(p)(4) of such Code)—

(1) if the due date pursuant to subparagraph (B) or (C) of section 72(p)(2) of such Code for any repayment with respect to such loan occurs during the period beginning on August 25, 2005, and ending on December 31, 2006, such due date shall be delayed for 1 year,

(2) any subsequent repayments with respect to any such loan shall be appropriately adjusted to reflect the delay in the due date under paragraph (1) and any interest accruing during such delay, and

(3) in determining the 5-year period and the term of a loan under subparagraph (B) or (C) of section 72(p)(2) of such Code, the period described in paragraph (1) shall be disregarded.

(c) *Qualified individual.* For purposes of this section, the term "qualified individual" means an individual whose principal place of abode on August 28, 2005, is located in the Hurricane Katrina disaster area and who has sustained an economic loss by reason of Hurricane Katrina. [**Note:** Act Sec. 103 was repealed by P.L. 109-135, Act Sec. 201(b)(4).]

[¶16,460F]

ACT SEC. 104. PROVISIONS RELATING TO PLAN AMENDMENTS. (a) *In general.* If this section applies to any amendment to any plan or annuity contract, such plan or contract shall be treated as being operated in accordance with the terms of the plan during the period described in subsection (b)(2)(A).

(b) *Amendments to which section applies.—*

(1) *In general.* This section shall apply to any amendment to any plan or annuity contract which is made—

(A) pursuant to any amendment made by this title, or pursuant to any regulation issued by the Secretary of the Treasury or the Secretary of Labor under this title, and

(B) on or before the last day of the first plan year beginning on or after January 1, 2007, or such later date as the Secretary of the Treasury may prescribe.

In the case of a governmental plan (as defined in section 414(d) of the Internal Revenue Code of 1986), subparagraph (B) shall be applied by substituting the date which is 2 years after the date otherwise applied under subparagraph (B).

(2) *Conditions.* This section shall not apply to any amendment unless—

(A) during the period—

(i) beginning on the date the legislative or regulatory amendment described in paragraph (1)(A) takes effect (or in the case of a plan or contract amendment not required by such legislative or regulatory amendment, the effective date specified by the plan), and

(ii) ending on the date described in paragraph (1)(B) (or, if earlier, the date the plan or contract amendment is adopted),

the plan or contract is operated as if such plan or contract amendment were in effect; and

(B) (iii) such plan or contract amendment applies retroactively for such period. [**NOTE:** Act Sec. 104 was repealed by P.L. 109-135, Act Sec. 201(b)(4).]

¶16,460D ACT SEC. 102.

TITLE II.—EMPLOYMENT RELIEF

[¶16,460G]

ACT SEC. 201. WORK OPPORTUNITY TAX CREDIT FOR HURRICANE KATRINA EMPLOYEES. (a) *In general*. For purposes of section 51 of the Internal Revenue Code of 1986, a Hurricane Katrina employee shall be treated as a member of a targeted group.

(b) *Hurricane Katrina Employee*. For purposes of this section, the term "Hurricane Katrina employee" means—

(1) any individual who on August 28, 2005, had a principal place of abode in the core disaster area and who is hired during the 2-year period beginning on such date for a position the principal place of employment of which is located in the core disaster area, and

(2) any individual who on such date had a principal place of abode in the core disaster area, who is displaced from such abode by reason of Hurricane Katrina, and who is hired during the period beginning on such date and ending on December 31, 2005.

(c) *Reasonable identification acceptable*. In lieu of the certification requirement under subparagraph (A) of section 51(d)(12) of such Code, an individual may provide to the employer reasonable evidence that the individual is a Hurricane Katrina employee, and subparagraph (B) of such section shall be applied as if such evidence were a certification described in such subparagraph.

(d) *Special rules for determining credit*. For purposes of applying subpart F of part IV of subchapter A of chapter 1 of such Code to wages paid or incurred to any Hurricane Katrina employee—

(1) section 51(c)(4) of such Code shall not apply, and

(2) section 51(i)(2) of such Code shall not apply with respect to the first hire of such employee as a Hurricane Katrina employee, unless such employee was an employee of the employer on August 28, 2005.

[¶16,460H]

ACT SEC. 202. EMPLOYEE RETENTION CREDIT FOR EMPLOYERS AFFECTED BY HURRICANE KATRINA. (a) *In general*. In the case of an eligible employer, there shall be allowed as a credit against the tax imposed by chapter 1 of the Internal Revenue Code of 1986 for the taxable year an amount equal to 40 percent of the qualified wages with respect to each eligible employee of such employer for such taxable year. For purposes of the preceding sentence, the amount of qualified wages which may be taken into account with respect to any individual shall not exceed $6,000.

(b) *Definitions*. For purposes of this section—

(1) *Eligible employer*. The term "eligible employer" means any employer—

(A) which conducted an active trade or business on August 28, 2005, in a core disaster area, and

(B) with respect to whom the trade or business described in subparagraph (A) is inoperable on any day after August 28, 2005, and before January 1, 2006, as a result of damage sustained by reason of Hurricane Katrina.

(2) *Eligible employee*. The term "eligible employee" means with respect to an eligible employer an employee whose principal place of employment on August 28, 2005, with such eligible employer was in a core disaster area.

(3) *Qualified wages*. The term "qualified wages" means wages (as defined in section 51(c)(1) of such Code, but without regard to section 3306(b)(2)(B) of such Code) paid or incurred by an eligible employer with respect to an eligible employee on any day after August 28, 2005, and before January 1, 2006, which occurs during the period—

(A) beginning on the date on which the trade or business described in paragraph (1) first became inoperable at the principal place of employment of the employee immediately before Hurricane Katrina, and

(B) ending on the date on which such trade or business has resumed significant operations at such principal place of employment.

Such term shall include wages paid without regard to whether the employee performs no services, performs services at a different place of employment than such principal place of employment, or performs services at such principal place of employment before significant operations have resumed.

(c) *Credit not allowed for large businesses*. The term "eligible employer" shall not include any trade or business for any taxable year if such trade or business employed an average of more than 200 employees on business days during the taxable year.

(d) *Certain rules to appl* y. For purposes of this section, rules similar to the rules of sections 51(i)(1), 52, and 280C(a) of such Code shall apply.

(e) *Employee not taken into account more than once*. An employee shall not be treated as an eligible employee for purposes of this section for any period with respect to any employer if such employer is allowed a credit under section 51 of such Code with respect to such employee for such period.

(f) *Credit to be part of general business credit*. The credit allowed under this section shall be added to the current year business credit under section 38(b) of such Code and shall be treated as a credit allowed under subpart D of part IV of subchapter A of chapter 1 of such Code. [**NOTE:** Act Sec. 202 was repealed by P.L. 109-135, Act Sec. 201(b)(4).]

TITLE III.—CHARITABLE GIVING INCENTIVES

[¶16,460I]

ACT SEC. 303. INCREASE IN STANDARD MILEAGE RATE FOR CHARITABLE USE OF VEHICLES. Notwithstanding section 170(i) of the Internal Revenue Code of 1986, for purposes of computing the deduction under section 170 of such Code for use of a vehicle described in subsection (f)(12)(E)(i) of such section for provision of relief related to Hurricane Katrina during the period beginning on August 25, 2005, and ending on December 31, 2006, the standard mileage rate shall be 70 percent of the standard mileage rate in effect under section 162(a) of such Code at the time of such use. Any increase under this section shall be rounded to the next highest cent.

[¶16,460J]

ACT SEC. 304. MILEAGE REIMBURSEMENTS TO CHARITABLE VOLUNTEERS EXCLUDED FROM GROSS INCOME. (a) *In general*. For purposes of the Internal Revenue Code of 1986, gross income of an individual for taxable years ending on or after August 25, 2005, does not include amounts received, from an organization described in section 170(c) of such Code, as reimbursement of operating expenses with respect to use of a passenger automobile

ACT SEC. 304.   ¶16,460J

for the benefit of such organization in connection with providing relief relating to Hurricane Katrina during the period beginning on August 25, 2005, and ending on December 31, 2006. The preceding sentence shall apply only to the extent that the expenses which are reimbursed would be deductible under chapter 1 of such Code if section 274(d) of such Code were applied—

(1) by using the standard business mileage rate in effect under section 162(a) at the time of such use, and

(2) as if the individual were an employee of an organization not described in section 170(c) of such Code.

(b) *Application to volunteer services only.* Subsection (a) shall not apply with respect to any expenses relating to the performance of services for compensation.

(c) *No double benefit.* No deduction or credit shall be allowed under any other provision of such Code with respect to the expenses excludable from gross income under subsection (a).

* * *

TITLE IV.—ADDITIONAL TAX RELIEF PROVISIONS

[¶16,460K]

ACT SEC. 403. REQUIRED EXERCISE OF AUTHORITY UNDER SECTION 7508A FOR TAX RELIEF RELATING TO HURRICANE KATRINA. (a) *Authority includes suspension of payment of employment and excise taxes.* Subparagraphs (A) and (B) of section 7508(a)(1) of the Internal Revenue Code of 1986 are amended to read as follows:

"(A) Filing any return of income, estate, gift, employment, or excise tax;

"(B) Payment of any income, estate, gift, employment, or excise tax or any installment thereof or of any other liability to the United States in respect thereof;".

(b) *Application with respect to Hurricane Katrina.* In the case of any taxpayer determined by the Secretary of the Treasury to be affected by the Presidentially declared disaster relating to Hurricane Katrina, any relief provided by the Secretary of the Treasury under section 7508A of the Internal Revenue Code of 1986 shall be for a period ending not earlier than February 28, 2006, and shall be treated as applying to the filing of returns relating to, and the payment of, employment and excise taxes. [**NOTE:** Act Sec. 403(b) was repealed by P.L. 109-135, Act Sec. 201(b)(4).]

(c) *Effective date.* The amendment made by subsection (a) shall apply for any period for performing an act which has not expired before August 25, 2005.

* * *

[¶16,460L]

ACT SEC. 407. SECRETARIAL AUTHORITY TO MAKE ADJUSTMENTS REGARDING TAXPAYER AND DEPENDENCY STATUS. With respect to taxable years beginning in 2005 or 2006, the Secretary of the Treasury or the Secretary's delegate may make such adjustments in the application of the internal revenue laws as may be necessary to ensure that taxpayers do not lose any deduction or credit or experience a change of filing status by reason of temporary relocations by reason of Hurricane Katrina. Any adjustments made under the preceding sentence shall ensure that an individual is not taken into account by more than one taxpayer with respect to the same tax benefit. [**NOTE:** Act Sec. 407 was repealed by P.L. 109-135, Act Sec. 201(b)(4).]

* * *

¶ 16,830 TEXT OF ERISA REORGANIZATION PLAN

Following is the text of Reorganization Plan No. 4 of 1978 (the ERISA Reorganization Plan).

Prepared by the President and transmitted to the Senate and the House of Representatives in Congress assembled, August 10, 1978, pursuant to the provisions of chapter 9 of title 5 of the United States Code.

EMPLOYEE RETIREMENT INCOME SECURITY ACT TRANSFERS

[¶ 16,831]

Section 101. Transfer to the Secretary of the Treasury

Except as otherwise provided in sections 104 and 106 of this Plan, all authority of the Secretary of Labor to issue the following described documents pursuant to the statutes hereinafter specified is hereby transferred to the Secretary of the Treasury:

(a) regulations, rulings, opinions, variances and waivers under Parts 2 and 3 of subtitle B of title I and subsection 1012(c) of title II of the Employee Retirement Income Security Act of 1974 (29 U.S.C. 1001 note) (hereinafter referred to as "ERISA"), *except* for sections and subsections 201, 203(a)(3)(B), 209, and 301(a) of ERISA;

(b) such regulations, ruling, and opinions which are granted to the Secretary of Labor under Sections 404, 410, 411, 412, and 413 of the Internal Revenue Code of 1954, as amended, (hereinafter referred to as the "Code"), *except* for subsection 411(a)(3)(B) of the Code and the definitions of "collectively bargained plan" and "collective bargaining agreement" contained in subsections 404(a)(1)(B) and (a)(1)(C), 410(b)(2)(A) and (b)(2)(B), and 413(a)(1) of the Code; and

(c) regulations, rulings, and opinions under subsections 3(19), 3(22), 3(23), 3(24), 3(25), 3(27), 3(28), 3(29), 3(30), and 3(31) of subtitle A of title I of ERISA.

[¶ 16,832]

Section 102. Transfers to the Secretary of Labor

Except as otherwise provided in section 105 of this plan, all authority of the Secretary of the Treasury to issue the following described documents pursuant to the statutes hereinafter specified is hereby transferred to the Secretary of Labor:

(a) regulations, rulings, opinions, and exemptions under section 4975 of the Code, *except* for (i) subsections 4975(a), (b), (c)(3), (d)(3), (e)(1), and (e)(7) of the Code; (ii) to the extent necessary for the continued enforcement of subsections 4975(a) and (b) by the Secretary of the Treasury, subsections 4975(f)(1), (f)(2), (f)(4), (f)(5), and (f)(6) of the Code; and (iii) exemptions with respect to transactions that are exempted by subsection 404(c) of ERISA from the provisions of part 4 of subtitle B of title I of ERISA; and

(b) regulations, rulings, and opinions under subsection 2003(c) of ERISA, *except* for subsection 2003(c)(1)(B).

[¶ 16,833]

Section 103. Coordination Concerning Certain Fiduciary Actions

In the case of fiduciary actions which are subject to part 4 of subtitle B of title I of ERISA, the Secretary of the Treasury shall notify the Secrtary of Labor prior to the time of commencing any proceeding to determine whether the action violates the exclusive benefit rule of subsection 401(a) of the Code, but not later than prior to issuing a preliminary notice of intent to disqualify under that rule, and the Secretary of the Treasury shall not issue a determination that a plan or trust does not satisfy the requirements of subsection 401(a) by reason of the exclusive benefit rule of subsection 401(a), unless within 90 days after the date on which the Secretary of the Treasury notifies the Secretary of Labor of pending action, the Secretary of Labor certifies that he has no objection to the disqualification or the Secretary of Labor fails to respond to the Secretary of the Treasury. The requirements of this paragraph do not apply in the case of any termination or jeopardy assessment under section 6851 or 6861 of the Code that has been approved in advance by the Commissioner of Internal Revenue, or as delegated, the Assistant Commissioner for Employee Plans and Exempt Organizations.

[¶ 16,834]

Section 104. Enforcement by the Secretary of Labor

The transfers provided for in section 101 of this plan shall not affect the ability of the Secretary of Labor, subject to the provisions of title III of ERISA relating to jurisdiction, administration, and enforcement, to engage in enforcement under section 502 of ERISA or to exercise the authority set forth under title III of ERISA, including the ability to make interpretations necessary to engage in such enforcement or to exercise such authority. However, in bringing such actions and in exercising such authority with respect to parts 2 and 3 of subtitle B of title I of ERISA and any definitions for which the authority of the Secretary of Labor is transferred to the Secretary of the Treasury as provided in section 101 of this plan, the Secretary of Labor shall be bound by the regulations, rulings, opinions, variances, and waivers issued by the Secretary of the Treasury.

[¶ 16,835]

Section 105. Enforcement by the Secretary of the Treasury

The transfers provided for in section 102 of this plan shall not affect the ability of the Secretary of the Treasury, subject to the provisions of title III of ERISA relating to jurisdiction, administration, and enforcement, (a) to audit plans and employers and to enforce the excise tax provisions of subsections 4975(a) and 4975(b) of the Code, to exercise the authority set forth in subsections 502(b)(1) and 502(h) of ERISA, or to exercise the authority set forth in title III of ERISA, including the ability to make interpretations necessary to audit, to enforce such taxes, and to exercise such authority; and (b) consistent with the coordination requirements under section 103 of this plan, to disqualify, under section 401 of the Code, a plan subject to part 4 of subtitle B of title I of ERISA, including the ability to make the interpretations necessary to make such disqualification. However, in enforcing such excise taxes and, to the extent applicable, in disqualifying such plans the Secretary of the Treasury shall be bound by the regulations, rulings, opinions, and exemptions issued by the Secretary of Labor pursuant to the authority transferred to the Secretary of Labor as provided in section 102 of this plan.

[¶ 16,836]

Section 106. Coordination for Section 101 Transfers

(a) The Secretary of the Treasury shall not exercise the functions transferred pursuant to section 101 of this plan to issue in proposed or final form any of the documents described in subsection (b) of this Section in any case in which such documents would significantly impact on or substantially affect collectively bargained plans unless, within 100 calendar days after the Secretary of the Treasury notifies the Scretary of Labor of such proposed action, the Secretary of Labor certifies that he has no objection or he fails to respond to the Secretary of the Treasury. The fact of such a notification, except for such notification for documents described in subsection (b)(iv) of this Section, from the Secretary of the Treasury to the Secretary of Labor shall be announced by the Secretary of Labor to the public within ten days following the date of receipt of the notification by the Secretary of Labor.

(b) The documents to which this Section applies are:

(i) amendments to regulations issued pursuant to subsections 202(a)(3), 203(b)(2) and (3)(A), 204(b)(3)(A), (C), and (E), and 210(a)(2) of ERISA, and subsections 410(a)(3) and 411(a)(5), (6)(A), and (b)(3)(A), (C), and (E), 413(b)(4) and (c)(3) and 414(f) of the Code;

(ii) regulations issued pursuant to subsections 204(b)(3)(D), 302(c)(8), and 304(a) and (b)(2)(A) of ERISA, and subsections 411(b)(3)(D), 412(c)(8), (e), and (f)(2)(A) of the Code; and

(iii) revenue rulings (within the meaning of 26 CFR section 601.201(a)(6)), revenue procedures, and similar publications, if the rulings, procedures and publications are issued under one of the statutory provisions listed in (i) and (ii) of this subsection; and

(iv) rulings (within the meaning of 26 CFR section 601.201(a)(2)) issued prior to the issuance of a published regulation under one of the statutory provisions listed in (i) and (ii) of this subsection and not issued under a published Revenue Ruling.

(c) For those documents described in subsections (b)(i), (b)(ii) and (b)(iii) of this section, the Secretary of Labor may request the Secretary of the Treasury to initiate the actions described in this section 106 of this plan.

[¶ 16,837]

Section 107. Evaluation

On or before January 31, 1980, the President will submit to both Houses of the Congress an evaluation of the extent to which this reorganization plan has alleviated the problems associated with the present administrative structure under ERISA, accompanied by specific legislative recommendations for a long-term administrative structure under ERISA.

[¶ 16,838]

Section 108. Incidental Transfers

So much of the personnel, property, records, and unexpended balances of appropriations, allocations and other funds employed, used, held, available, or to be made available in connection with the functions transferred under this plan, as the Director of the Office of Management and Budget shall determine, shall be transferred to the appropriate agency, or component at such time or times as the Director of the Office of Management and Budget shall provide, except that no such unexpended balances transferred shall be used for purposes other than those for which the appropriation was originally made. The Director of the Office of Management and Budget shall provide for terminating the affairs of any agencies abolished herein and for such further measures and dispositions as such Director deems necessary to effectuate the purposes of this reorganization plan.

[¶ 16,839]

Section 109. Effective Date

The provisions of this reorganization plan shall become effective at such time or times, on or before April 30, 1979, as the President shall specify, but not sooner than the earliest time allowable under section 906 of title 5 United States Code. [The provisions of the Reorganization Plan went into effect on December 31, 1978, under Executive Order 12108, December 18, 1978 (44 FR 1065)].

Proposed Regulations—Internal Revenue Code

¶ 20,118B

Proposed regulations: Individual retirement plans: Annual reporting requirements.—Reproduced below is the text of proposed regulations that require annual reporting of information relating to individual retirement plans. The regulations affect trustees of individual retirement accounts and issuers of individual retirement annuities as well as individuals who own or benefit from such plans. In particular, the proposed regulations reflect changes made by Internal Revenue Service News Release IR-83-88 (CCH PENSION PLAN GUIDE, ¶ 17,019G) and the Tax Reform Act of 1984.

The proposed regulations were published in the Federal Register on November 16, 1984 (49 FR 45450).

Department of the Treasury

Internal Revenue Service

[26 CFR Part 1]

[EE-65-83]

Annual Information Reports of Trustees and Issuers of Individual Retirement Plans

Notice of Proposed Rulemaking

AGENCY: Internal Revenue Service, Treasury.

ACTION: Notice of proposed rulemaking.

SUMMARY: This document contains proposed regulations that require annual reporting of information relating to individual retirement plans. The regulations reflect changes made to the applicable reporting requirements by both News Release IR-83-88 and the Tax Reform Act of 1984. The regulations affect trustees of individual retirement accounts and issuers of individual retirement annuities (including accounts and annuities that are simplified employee pensions), and individuals who oen or benefit from such individual retirement plans.

DATES: Written comments and requests for a public hearing must be delivered or mailed by January 15, 1985. The amendments are proposed to be effective for reports relating to calendar years beginning after 1982.

ADDRESS: Send comments and requests for a public hearing to: Commissioner of Internal Revenue, Attention: CC:LR:T

(EE-65-83), 1111 Constitution Avenue, N.W., Washington, D.C. 20224.

FOR FURTHER INFORMATION CONTACT: Philip R. Bosco of the Employee Plans and Exempt Organization Division, Office of the Chief Counsel, Internal Revenue Service, 1111 Constitution Avenue, N.W., Washington, D.C. 20224 (Attention: CC:LR:T), 202-566-3430 (not a toll-free number).

SUPPLEMENTARY INFORMATION: BACKGROUND

Section 408 of the Internal Revenue Code of 1954 defines various individual retirement plans, including individual retirement accounts, individual retirement annuities, and simplified employee pensions. Section 408(i) of the Code provides that the trustee of an individual retirement account or the issuer of an individual retirement annuity (including an account or annuity that is a simplified employee pension) shall make such reports regarding the status of an account or annuity as the Secretary may require under regulations.

Section 1.408-5(c)(1) of the Income Tax Regulations (26 CFR Part 1) under section 408 of the Code requires that an annual report must be furnished to each participant, i.e., the individual for whose benefit the account was established or in whose name the annuity was purchased (or the beneficiary of such individual). The report must contain the following information for transactions occurring during the calendar year: the amount of contributions; the amount of distributions; in the case of an endowment contract, the amount of the premium paid allocable to the cost of life insurance; and the name and address of the trustee or issuer. The report must be furnished on or before June 30 following the calendar year for which the report is required. Paragraph (c)(2) of § 1.408-5 provides that the Commissioner may require the annual report to be filed with the Service at the time the Commissioner specifies.

On June 28, 1983, the Service issued News Release IR-83-88 relating to the filing requirement permissible under § 1.408-5(c)(2). Beginning with the 1983 calendar year, the annual reports required by § 1.408-5 must also be filed with the Service. New Form 5498, Individual Retirement Arrangement Information, has been developed for this purpose. The form, a copy of which may be utilized to satisfy the existing reporting requirement of § 1.408-5, must contain the following information for transactions occurring during the calendar year: the amount of

contributions (exclusive of rollover contributions for calendar years after 1983); the amount of rollover contributions (for calendar years after 1983); and the name and address of the trustee or issuer. For the 1983 calendar year, the form must be filed with the Service, and the annual report furnished to the participant, on or before June 30, 1984. Finally, IR-83-88 stated that, for calendar year 1984, the form must be filed with the Service on or before February 28, 1985, and the annual report must be furnished to the participant on or before June 30, 1985.

On July 18, 1984, section 147 of the Tax Reform Act of 1984 (Pub. L. 98-369) amended section 408(i) to provide that the information reports required by such section identify the taxable year to which individual retirement plan contributions relate. This amendment is effective for contributions made after December 31, 1984.

The proposed regulations contained in this document amend § 1.408-5 to conform such section to both the new filing requirements announced in News Release IR-83-88 and the new reporting requirement added by the Tax Reform Act of 1984. The amendments are to be issued under the authority contained in sections 408(i) and 7805 of the Code (88 Stat. 964, 26 U.S.C. 408(i); 68A Stat. 917, 26 U.S.C. 7805, respectively).

As proposed, the regulations necessarily modify the requirements of IR-83-88 for calendar years 1984 and thereafter. Beginning with calendar year 1984, Form 5498 shall be filed with the Service and the statement to the participant shall be furnished to such person on or before May 31 following the calendar year for which such reports are required. For calendar year 1984, this is a change of the due dates originally announced in IR-83-88. Beginning with calendar year 1985, both Form 5498 and the statement to the participant must report, as the amount of contributions for the calendar year, the amount of contributions made during or after the calendar year that relate to such calendar year. Also beginning with calendar year 1985, both Form 5498 and the statement to the participant must report, in the case of an endowment contract premium allocable to the cost of life insurance, that amount of the premium paid either during or after the calendar year that relates to such calendar year.

Finally, the proposed regulations contain special transitional requirements for the 1985 calendar year reports. For that calendar year both Form 5498 and the statement to the participant must report, as a separate entry, the amount of contributions made during 1985 that relate to 1984. This requirement also applies to the statement to the participant in the case of an endowment contract premium allocable to the cost of life insurance paid during 1985 that relates to 1984.

SPECIAL ANALYSIS

The Commissioner of Internal Revenue has determined that these proposed rules are not major rules as defined in either Executive Order 12291 or the Treasury and OMB implementation of that Order dated April 29, 1983. Accordingly, a Regulatory Impact Analysis is not required.

Although this document is a notice of proposed rulemaking that solicits public comments, the Internal Revenue Service has concluded that the regulations proposed herein are interpretative and that the notice and public procedure requirements of 5 U.S.C. 553 do not apply. Accordingly, these proposed regulations do not constitute regulations subject to the Regulatory Flexibility Act (5 U.S.C. Chapter 6).

COMMENTS AND REQUEST FOR A PUBLIC HEARING

Before adopting these proposed regulations, consideration will be given to any written comments that are submitted (preferably seven copies) to the Commissioner of Internal Revenue. All comments will be available for public inspection and copying. A public hearing will be held upon written request to the Commissioner by any person who has submitted written comments. If a public hearing is held, notice of the time and place will be published in the *Federal Register*.

The collection of information requirements contained in this notice of proposed rulemaking have been submitted to the Office of Management and Budget (OMB) for review under section 3504(h) of the

Paperwork Reduction Act of 1980. Comments on these requirements should be sent to the Office of Information and Regulatory Affairs of OMB, Attention: Desk Office for Internal Revenue Service, New Executive Office Building, Washington, D.C. 20503. The Internal Revenue Service requests that persons submitting comments on these requirements to OMB also send copies of those comments to the Service.

DRAFTING INFORMATION

The principal author of these proposed regulations is Philip R. Bosco of the Employee Plans and Exempt Organizations Division of the Office of Chief Counsel, Internal Revenue Service. However, personnel from other offices of the Internal Revenue Service and Treasury Department participated in developing the regulations, on matters of both substance and style.

LIST OF SUBJECTS IN 26 CFR 1.401-1—1.425-1

Employee benefit plans, pensions, individual retirement accounts.

Proposed amendments to the regulations

The proposed amendments to 26 CFR Part 1 are as follows:

Section 1.408-5 is amended by revising the section to read as follows:

§ 1.408-5 Annual reports by trustees and issuers.

(a) *Requirement and form of report.* The trustee of an individual retirement account or the issuer of an individual retirement annuity (including an account or annuity that is a simplified employee pension) shall make annual calendar year reports on Form 5498 concerning the status of the account or annuity. The report shall contain the following information for transactions occurring during or after the calendar year that relate to such calendar year:

(1) The name, address and identifying number of the trustee or issuer;

(2) The name, address, and identifying number of the participant (the individual on whose behalf the account is established or in whose name the annuity is purchased (or the beneficiary of the individual or owner));

(3) The amount of contributions (exclusive of rollover contributions) made during or after the calendar year that relate to such calendar year;

(4) The amount of rollover contributions made during the calendar year;

(5) In the case of an endowment contract, the amount of the premium allocable to the cost of life insurance paid either during or after the calendar year that relates to such calendar year; and

(6) Such other information as the Commissioner may require.

(b) *Manner and time for filing.* The report on Form 5498 shall be filed, accompanied by transmittal Form 1096, with the appropriate Internal Revenue Service Center. The report shall be filed on or before May 31 following the calendar year for which the report is required.

(c) *Statement of participants.* (1) Each trustee or issuer required to file Form 5498 under this section shall furnish the participant a state-ment containing the information required to be furnished on Form 5498 plus the value of the account or annuity at the end of the calendar year. A copy of Form 5498, containing the additional information specified in the previous sentence, may be used to satisfy the statement requirement of this paragraph. If a copy of Form 5498 is not used to satisfy the statement requirement of this paragraph, the statement shall contain the following language: "This information is being furnished to the Internal Revenue Service."

(2) Each statement required by this paragraph to be furnished to participants shall be furnished to such person on or before May 31 following the calendar year for which the report on Form 5498 is required.

(d) *Penalties.* Section 6693 prescribes penalties for failure to file an annual report required by this section.

(e) *Effective date.* In general, this section applies to reports for calendar years beginning with 1983. For additional requirements relating to the 1985 calendar year reports, see paragraph (f) of this section. For special requirements relating to the 1983 and 1984 calendar year reports, see paragraph (g) of this section. For requirements relating to pre-1983 calendar year reports, see 26 C.F.R. § 1.408-5 (1983).

(f) *Reports for calendar year 1985.* For calendar year 1985, both Form 5498 and the statement to the participant must report, as a separate entry, the amount of contributions made during the 1985 calendar year that relate to the 1984 calendar year. This also applies, in the case of the statement to the participant, to endowment contract premiums allocable to the cost of life insurance that are paid during the 1985 calendar year but that relate to the 1984 calendar year.

(g) *Reports for calendar years 1983 and 1984.* (1) For calendar years 1983 and 1984, neither Form 5498 nor the statement to the participant need identify the calendar year to which a contribution relates. The form and statement need only report the amount of contributions actually made during the calendar year. This also applies to endowment contract premiums allocable to the cost of life insurance and paid during the calendar year.

(2) For calendar years 1983 and 1984, Form 5498 need not report (but the statement to the participant must report), in the case of an endowment contract, the amount of !he premium allocable to the cost of life insurance paid during the calendar year.

(3) For calendar year 1983, neither Form 5498 nor the statement to the participant need separately report rollover contributions made during the calendar year. Rollover contributions are to be aggregated with the amount of other contributions made during the calendar year.

(4) For calendar year 1983, the statement to the participant need not contain the language required by paragraph (c)(1) of this section.

(5) For calendar year 1983, Form 5498 shall be filed, and the statement to the participant shall be furnished, on or before June 30, 1984.

(h) *Related reports by trustees and issuers.* See § 1.408-7 for reports relating to distributions from individual retirement plans.

(signed) Roscoe L. Egger, Jr.

Commissioner of Internal Revenue

[¶ 20,118C Reserved.—Proposed regulations relating to the deduction of employer liability payments were formerly reproduced at this point. The final regulations are at ¶ 11,869A.]

¶ 20,118D

Proposed regulations: Limits on contributions to and reserves of welfare benefit funds maintained pursuant to a collective bargaining agreement: Cross reference to temporary regulations.—The Internal Revenue Service has issued temporary regulations relating to contributions to and reserves of welfare benefit funds maintained pursuant to a collective bargaining agreement. The text of those temporary regulations (CCH PENSION PLAN GUIDE, ¶ 12,970) serves as the common document for this notice of proposed rulemaking which follows.

These regulations appeared in the *Federal Register* on July 3, 1985.

AGENCY: Internal Revenue Service, Treasury.

ACTION: Notice of proposed rulemaking by cross reference to temporary regulations.

SUMMARY: In the Rules and Regulations portion of this issue of the Federal Register, the Internal Revenue Service is issuing temporary regulations relating to contributions to and reserves of welfare benefit funds maintained pursuant to a collective bargaining agreement. The text of those temporary regulations [CCH PENSION PLAN GUIDE, ¶ 12,970] also serves as the comment document for this notice of proposed rulemaking.

DATES: Written comments and requests for a public hearing must be delivered or mailed by September 3, 1985. The regulations are proposed to be effective for contributions paid or accrued after December 31, 1985.

ADDRESS: Send comments and requests for a public hearing to Commissioner of Internal Revenue, Attn: CC:LR:T (EE-66-84), 1111 Constitution Avenue N.W., Washington D.C. 20224.

FOR FURTHER INFORMATION CONTACT: John T. Ricotta of the Employee Plans and Exempt Organizations Division, Office of Chief Counsel, Internal Revenue Service, 1111 Constitution Ave., N. W.,

Washington, D.C. 20224, Attention: CC:LR:T (EE-66-84), telephone: 202-566-4396 (not a toll-free number).

SUPPLEMENTARY INFORMATION: BACKGROUND

The temporary regulations provide guidance concerning the limits on contributions to and the reserves of welfare benefit funds maintained pursuant to a collective bargaining agreement under section 419A(f)(5) of the Internal Revenue Code of 1954 (Code), as added to the Code by section 511 of the Tax Reform Act of 1984 (26 U.S.C. §419A). The proposed regulations are issued under the authority contained in section 7805 of the Code (26 U.S.C. §7805). For the text of the temporary regulations, see F.R. Doc. [—] published in the Rules and Regulations portion of this issue of the FEDERAL REGISTER.

SPECIAL ANALYSES

The Commissioner of Internal Revenue has determined that this proposed rule is not a major rule as defined in Executive Order 12291 and that a Regulatory Impact Analysis is therefore not required. Although this document is a notice of proposed rulemaking which solicits public comment, the Internal Revenue has concluded that the regulations proposed herein are interpretative and that the notice and public procedure requirements of 5 U.S.C. 553 do not apply. Accordingly, these proposed regulations do not constitute regulations subject to the Regulatory Flexibility Act (5 U.S.C. Chapter 6).

COMMENTS AND REQUESTS FOR A PUBLIC HEARING

Before adopting the temporary regulations referred to in this document as final regulations, consideration will be given to any written comments that are submitted (preferably 8 copies) to the Commissioner of Internal Revenue. All comments will be available for public inspection and copying. A public hearing will be held upon written request to the Commissioner by any person who has submitted written comments. If a public hearing is held, notice of the time and place will be published in the FEDERAL REGISTER.

LIST OF SUBJECTS IN 26 CFR §§1.401-0—1.425-1

Income Taxes, Employee Benefit Plans, Pensions, Stock Options, Individual Retirement Accounts, Employee Stock Ownership Plans.

M. Eddie Heironimus

Acting Commissioner of Internal Revenue

[¶ 20,118E Reserved.—Proposed regulations requiring employers filing information returns on certain forms to use magnetic media instead of paper forms were formerly reproduced at this point. The final regulations appear at ¶ 13,649D.]

[¶ 20,118F Reserved.—Proposed regulations which include new unisex annuity tables used to compute the portion of an amount received as an annuity that is includible in gross income were formerly reproduced at this point. The final regulations appear at ¶ 11,194—11,197, 11,199, 11,201, and 11,803.]

¶ 20,118G

Proposed regulations: Employee achievement awards: Tax Reform Act of 1986.—Reproduced below is the text of proposed regulations that would amend the regulations (CCH PENSION PLAN GUIDE, ¶ 11,357) on the excludability and deductibility of certain employee awards. These amendments, if adopted, will provide guidance needed to comply with the Tax Reform Act of 1986.

The proposed regulations were established in the *Federal Register* on January 9, 1989 (54 FR 627).

DEPARTMENT OF THE TREASURY

Internal Revenue Service

26 CFR Part 1

[IA-111-86]

Income Tax; Taxable Years Beginning After December 31, 1986; Changes With Respect to Prizes and Awards and Employee Achievement Awards

AGENCY: Internal Revenue Service.

ACTION: Notice of proposed rulemaking.

SUMMARY: This document contains proposed amendments to the regulations relating to the excludability of certain prizes and awards and to the deductibility of certain employee awards. Changes to the applicable tax law were made by the Tax Reform Act of 1986. These amendments, if adopted, will provide the public with the guidance needed to comply with the Act.

DATES: Written comments and requests for a public hearing must be delivered or mailed by March 10, 1989. The amendments are proposed to be effective after December 31, 1986.

ADDRESS: Send comments and requests for a public hearing to: Commissioner of Internal Revenue, Internal Revenue Service, 1111 Constitution Avenue, NW., Washington, DC 20224; Attention: CC:CORP:T:R, IA-111-86.

FURTHER INFORMATION CONTACT: Johnnel St. Germain of the Office of Assistant Chief Counsel (Income Tax and Accounting), Internal Revenue Service, 1111 Constitution Avenue, NW., Washington, DC 20224; Attention: CC:CORP:T:R, IA-111-86. Telephone 202-566-4509 (not a toll-free call).

SUPPLEMENTARY INFORMATION:

Paperwork Reduction Act

The collections of information contained in this notice of proposed rulemaking have been submitted to the Office of Management and Budget for review in accordance with the Paperwork Reduction Act of 1980 (44 U.S.C. 3504(h)). Comments on the collections of information should be sent to the Office of Information and Regulatory Affairs, Office of Management and Budget, Washington, DC 20503, attention: Desk Officer for the Internal Revenue Service. Copies of comments should also be sent to the Internal Revenue Service at the address previously specified.

The collections of information in this regulation are in 26 CFR 1.74-1(c). This information is required by the Internal Revenue Service in order to verify that the proper amount of income is reported by taxpayers on their returns of tax. The likely respondents are individuals.

Estimated total annual reporting burden: 1,275 hours.

Estimated average annual burden per respondent: 15 minutes.

Estimated number of respondents: 5,100.

Background

This document contains proposed amendments to the Income Tax Regulations (26 CFR Part 1) under sections 74, 102, and 274 of the Internal Revenue Code (Code). The amendments are proposed to conform the regulations to section 122 of the Tax Reform Act of 1986 (Pub. L. 99-514). The proposed amendments, if adopted, will be issued under the authority contained in section 7805 of the Code (68A Stat. 917; 26 U.S.C. 7805).

General Information

Prior to the 1986 Code, section 74 stated that prizes and awards, other than certain types of fellowship grants and scholarships, were includible in gross income unless they were made primarily in recognition of religious, charitable, scientific, educational, artistic, literary, or civic achievement. To qualify for the exclusion, the recipient must have been selected without any action on his part and could not be required to render substantial services as a condition to receiving the prize or award.

Within the context of a business relationship, prizes and awards that would otherwise be includible in a recipient's gross income were excludable if they qualified as gifts under section 102. In general, section 274(b) disallowed an employer a business deduction for gifts to an employee to the extent that the total cost of all gifts of cash, tangible personal property, and other items to the same individual during the taxable year exceeded $25. A special exception to the $25 limitation was allowed for items of tangible personal property awarded to an employee for length of service, safety achievement, or productivity. The employer could deduct the cost of such an award up to $400. If the item was provided under a qualified award plan, the deductibility limitation was increased to $1600, provided the average cost of all plan awards made during the year did not exceed $400. A de minimis fringe benefit under section 132(e) was, and continues to be, excludable from gross income and is not subject to the requirements imposed upon prizes and awards under sections 74 and 274.

Explanation of Provisions

These proposed amendments relate to the includability of certain prizes and awards and to the deductibility of certain employee awards and reflect the substantial changes made by the Tax Reform Act of 1986 (the Act) to sections 74, 102 and 274 of the Internal Revenue Code (Code). Changes to the applicable sections of the Code and regulations, amended or newly incorporated by this document, are effective for awards made after December 31, 1986.

Under the Act, the section 74(b) exclusion for prizes or awards received in recognition of charitable achievement is available only if the payor transfers the prize or award to one or more entities described in paragraph (1) and/or (2) of section 170(c) pursuant to the direction of the recipient.

Section 1.74-1(c) of the proposed regulations requires that recipients of prizes and awards clearly designate, in writing, within 45 days of the date the item is granted that they wish to have the prize or award transferred to one or more qualifying donee organizations. The proposed regulations set forth requirements which, in certain instances, determine whether a qualifying designation has been made.

Section 1.74-1(d) of the proposed regulations clarifies that the exclusion under section 74(b) will not be available unless the prize or award is transferred by the payor to one or more qualified donee organizations before the recipient, or any person other than the grantor or a qualified donee organization, uses the item. In general, a transfer may be accomplished by any method that results in receipt of the prize or award by, or on behalf of, one or more qualified donee organizations.

Section 1.74-1(e) further clarifies the requirements of section 74(b) by defining certain terms. Definitions are included which determine what constitutes a "qualified donee organization," when a "disqualifying use" has taken place, and when an item is considered "granted."

Section 1.74-1(f) provides that neither the payor nor the recipient of the prize or award may claim a charitable contribution deduction for the value of any prize or award for which an exclusion is allowed under section 74(b).

All of the requirements of section 74(b) in existence prior to passage of the Act remain in effect and must be met in order for the award recipient to be eligible for the exclusion. Accordingly, rules and regulations governing these additional requirements, to the extent they are not inconsistent with the proposed regulations, will remain in effect.

New Code section 74(c) excludes certain employee achievement awards from gross income. The exclusion applies, subject to certain limitations, to the value of awards made by the employer for safety achievement or length of service achievement. The amount of the exclusion generally corresponds with the deduction given the employer under new section 274(j) for these "employee achievement awards." Thus, in general, the employee must include these awards in income to the extent that the fair market value of the award, or, if greater, the cost of the award to the employer, exceeds the amount deductible under section 274(j). The exclusion allows an employee to exclude the full fair market value of the award where the cost of the award is fully deductible by the employer.

Section 1.74-2(d) of the proposed regulations provides special rules for employee achievement awards applicable to sole-proprietors and tax-exempt employers.

Section 1.74-2(e) clarifies that an employee award, whether or not an employee achievement award, may be excludible from gross income as a de minimis fringe benefit under section 132(e).

Section 102(c) of the Code clarifies that, with the exception of employee achievement awards under section 74(c) and de minimis

fringe benefits under section 132(e), an employee shall not exclude from gross income any amount transferred to the employee (or for the employee's benefit) by, or on behalf of, the employer in the form of a gift, bequest, devise, or inheritance. Therefore, while awards satisfying the requirements of section 74(c) and de minimis fringe benefits qualifying under section 132(e) will be excluded from gross income under those sections, no amounts (except in certain narrowly defined circumstances) transferred by, or on behalf of, an individual's employer will be excludable from gross income under section 102.

Section 1.102-1(f)(2) of the proposed regulations provides that for purposes of section 102(c), extraordinary transfers to the natural objects of one's bounty will not be considered transfers for the benefit of an employee if it can be shown that the transfer was not made in recognition of the transferee's employment. Thus, the rules set out in *Comm. v. Duberstein,* 363 U.S. 278 (1960), formerly applicable in the determination of whether all property transferred inter-vivos from an employer to an employee constitutes a gift, will only be applicable where the transferee employee would be the natural object of the employer's bounty.

From an employer's perspective, the Act substantially modifies an employer's ability to deduct the cost of certain employee awards. New section 274(j) defines deductible "employee achievement awards" to include only those awards made for length of service or safety achievement. In addition, an employee achievement award must be an item of tangible personal property awarded as part of a meaningful presentation and made under conditions and circumstances that do not create a significant likelihood of the payment of disguised compensation.

Section 274(j) also establishes a limit on the amount that may be deducted by an employer. The annual deduction limitation per employee is $400 for employee achievement awards that are not awarded as part of a qualified award plan. The annual deduction limitation per employee is $1,600 for employee achievement awards that are awarded as part of a qualified award plan. In no event may an employer deduct more than $1,600 per employee for all employee achievement awards made during the year. An award is not a qualified plan award where the average cost of all employee achievement awards made by the employer pursuant to a plan exceeds $400 during the taxable year.

Section 1.274-8(b) of the proposed regulations clarifies that the $1,600 deduction limitation applies in the aggregate, so that the $1,600 limitation for qualified plan awards and the $400 limitation for employee achievement awards that are not qualified plan awards cannot be added together to allow deductions exceeding $1,600 for employee achievement awards made to an employee in a taxable year.

Section 1.274-8(c)(2) of the proposed regulations provides that tangible personal property does not include cash or any gift certificate other than a nonnegotiable gift certificate conferring only the right to receive tangible personal property. The proposed regulations also give examples of what will be considered to create a significant likelihood of the payment of disguised compensation. For example, the providing of employee achievement awards in a manner that discriminates in favor of highly paid employees will be considered to be a payment of disguised compensation.

Section 1.274-8(c)(5) of the proposed regulations defines a "qualified plan award" as an employee achievement award presented pursuant to an established written award plan or program of the employer that does not discriminate as to eligibility or benefits.

Section 1.274-8(d)(1) of the proposed regulations states that the deduction limitations shall apply to a partnership as well as to each member of the partnership. Paragraph (d)(2) provides that the cost of length of service achievement awards (other than awards excludable under section 132(e)) may only be deducted by the employer if the employee has at least 5 years of service with the employer and has not received a length of service achievement award during that year or any of the 4 prior years. In addition, this paragraph clarifies that although a retirement award will be treated as having been provided for length of service achievement, it may also qualify for treatment as a de minimis fringe benefit under section 132(e) of the Code. Paragraph (d)(3) provides guidance with respect to safety achievement awards. An employer may deduct the cost of safety achievement awards only when presented to no more than 10 percent of an employer's eligible employees. Eligible employees include any employee who has worked for the employer in full time capacity for at least one year and who is not a manager, administrator, clerical employee, or other professional employee. Special rules clarify that in the case where more than 10 percent of an employer's eligible employees receive a safety achievement award, no award will be considered to be awarded for safety achievement if it cannot be determined that the award was presented before the 10 percent limitation was exceeded.

The Act specifically excludes awards qualifying as de minimis fringe benefits under section 132(e) from the requirements for length of service achievement and safety achievement. As a result, employers are not required to consider section 132(e) awards in determining whether employee achievement awards comply with the 5 year limitations for length of service achievement and the 10 percent eligible employee limitations for safety achievement.

Special Analyses

The Commissioner of Internal Revenue has determined that this proposed rule is not a major rule as defined in Executive Order 12291. Accordingly, a Regulatory Impact Analysis is not required. The Internal Revenue Service has concluded that although this document is a notice of proposed rulemaking that solicits public comment, the regulations proposed herein are interpretative and the notice and public procedure requirements of 5 U.S.C. 553 do not apply. Accordingly, no Regulatory Flexibility Analysis is required for this rule.

Comments and Requests for a Public Hearing

Before adopting these proposed regulations, consideration will be given to any written comments that are submitted (preferably eight copies) to the Commissioner of Internal Revenue. All comments will be available for public inspection and copying. A public hearing will be held upon written request to the Commissioner by any person who has submitted written comments. If a public hearing is held, notice of time and place will he published in the **Federal Register.**

Drafting Information

The principal author of these proposed regulations is Christopher J. Wilson, formerly of the Legislation and Regulations Division of the Office of Chief Counsel, Internal Revenue Service. However, personnel from other offices of the Internal Revenue Service and Treasury Department participated in developing the regulations, on matters of both substance and style.

List of Subjects in 26 CFR Parts 1.61-1 Through 1.281-4

Income taxes, Taxable income, Deductions, Exemptions.

Proposed Amendments to the Regulations

The proposed amendments to 26 CFR Part 1 are as follows:

[* * *]

§ 1.274-3 [Amended].

Par. 6. Section 1.274-3 is amended as follows:

(a) The last sentence of paragraph (b)(1) is amended by substituting "subsections (b) and (c) of section 74" for "section 74(b)".

(b) The language "recipient, or" at the end of paragraph (b)(2)(ii) is replaced by the language "recipient."

(c) Subdivisions (iii) and (iv) of paragraph (b)(2) are removed.

(d) The first, second, and fourth sentences of the flush material immediately following subdivision (iv) are removed and the last sentence is amended by substituting "sections 61, 74, 102, and 132" for "sections 61, 74, and 102".

(e) Paragraph (d) is removed and paragraphs (e), (f), and (g) are redesignated as paragraphs (d), (e), and (f).

§ 1.274-8 [Redesignated as § 1.274-9].

Par. 7. Section 1.274-8 is redesignated as § 1.274-9 and a new § 1.274-8 is added immediately following § 1.274-7 to read as set forth below.

§ 1.274-8 Disallowance of certain employee achievement award expenses.

(a) *In general.* No deduction is allowable under section 162 or 212 for any portion of the cost of an employee achievement award (as defined in section 274(j)(3)(A)) in excess of the deduction limitations of section 274(j)(2).

(b) *Deduction limitations.* The deduction for the cost of an employee achievement award made by an employer to an employee: (1) Which is not a qualified plan award, when added to the cost to the employer for all other employee achievement awards made to such employee during the taxable year which are not qualified plan awards, shall not exceed $400, and (2) which is a qualified plan award, when added to the cost to the employer for all other employee achievement awards made to such employee during the taxable year (including employee achievement awards which are not qualified plan awards), shall not exceed $1,600. Thus, the $1,600 limitation is the maximum amount that may be deducted by an employer for all employee achievement awards granted to any one employee during the taxable year.

(c) *Definitions*—(1) *Employee achievement award.* The term "employee achievement award", for purposes of this section, means an item of tangible personal property that is transferred to an employee by reason of the employee's length of service or safety achievement. The item must be awarded as part of a meaningful presentation, and under conditions and circumstances that do not create a significant likelihood of the payment of disguised compensation. For purposes of section 274(j), an award made by a sole proprietorship to the sole proprietor is not an award made to an employee.

(2) *Tangible personal property.* For purposes of this section, the term "tangible personal property" does not include cash or a certificate (other than a nonnegotiable certificate conferring only the right to receive tangible personal property). If a certificate entitles an employee to receive a reduction of the balance due on his account with the issuer of the certificate, the certificate is a negotiable certificate and is not tangible personal property for purposes of this section. Other items that will not be considered to be items of tangible personal property include vacations, meals, lodging, tickets to theater and sporting events, and stocks, bonds, and other securities.

(3) *Meaningful presentation.* Whether an award is presented as part of a meaningful presentation is determined by a facts and circumstances test. While the presentation need not be elaborate, it must be a ceremonious observance emphasizing the recipient's achievement in the area of safety or length of service.

(4) *Disguised compensation.* An award will be considered disguised compensation if the conditions and circumstances surrounding the award create a significant likelihood that it is payment of compensation. Examples include the making of employee achievement awards at the time of annual salary adjustments or as a substitute for a prior program of awarding cash bonuses, the providing of employee achievement awards in a manner that discriminates in favor of highly paid employees, or, with respect to awards the cost of which would otherwise be fully deductible by the employer under the deduction limitations of section 274(j)(2), the making of an employee achievement award the cost of which to the employer is grossly disproportionate to the fair market value of the item.

(5) *Qualified plan awards*—(i) *In general.* Except as provided in paragraph (c)(5)(ii) of this section, the term "qualified plan award" means an employee achievement award that is presented pursuant to an established written plan or program that does not discriminate in terms of eligibility or benefits in favor of highly compensated employees. See section 414(q) of the Code for the definition of highly compensated employees. Whether an award plan is established shall be determined from all the facts and circumstances of the particular case, including the frequency and timing of any changes to the plan. Whether or not an award plan is discriminatory shall be determined from all the facts and circumstances of the particular case. An award plan may fail to qualify because it is discriminatory in its actual operation even though the written provisions of the award plan are nondiscriminatory.

(ii) *Items not treated as qualified plan awards.* No award presented by an employer during the taxable year will be considered a qualified plan award if the average cost of all employee achievement awards presented during the taxable year by the taxpayer under any plan described in paragraph (c)(5)(i) of this section exceeds $400. The average cost of employee achievement awards shall be computed by dividing (A) the sum of the costs to the employer for all employee achievement awards (without regard to the deductibility of those costs) by (B) the total number of employee achievement awards presented. For purposes of the preceding sentence, employee achievement awards of nominal value shall not be taken into account in the computation of average cost. An employee achievement award that costs the employer $50 or less shall be considered an employee achievement award of nominal value.

(d) *Special rules*—(1) *Partnerships.* Where employee achievement awards are made by a partnership, the deduction limitations of section 274(j)(2) shall apply to the partnership as well as to each member thereof.

(2) *Length of service awards.*—An item shall not be treated as having been provided for length of service achievement if the item is presented for less than 5 years employment with the taxpayer or if the award recipient received a length of service achievement award (other than an award excludable under section 132(e)(1)) during that year or any of the prior 4 calendar years. An award presented upon the occasion of a recipient's retirement is a length of service award subject to the rules of this section. However, under appropriate circumstances,

a traditional retirement award will be treated as a de minimis fringe. For example, assume that an employer provides a gold watch to each employee who completes 25 years of service with the employer. The value of the gold watch is excluded from gross income as a de minimis fringe. However, if the employer provides a gold watch to an employee who has not completed lengthy service with the employer or on an occasion other than retirement, the value of the watch is not excludable from gross income under section 132(e).

(3) *Safety achievement awards*—(i) *In general.* An item shall not be treated having been provided for safety achievement if—

(A) During the taxable year, employee achievement awards (other than awards excludable under section 132(e)(1)) for safety achievement have previously been awarded by the taxpayer to more than 10 percent of the eligible employees of the taxpayer, or

(B) Such item is awarded to a manager, administrator, clerical employee, or other professional employee.

(ii) *"Eligible employee" defined.* An eligible employee is one not described in paragraph (d)(3)(i)(B) of this section and who has worked in a full-time capacity for the taxpayer for a minimum of one year

immediately preceding the date on which the safety achievement award is presented.

(iii) *Special rules.* Where safety achievement awards are presented to more than 10 percent of the taxpayer's eligible employees, only those awards presented to eligible employees before 10 percent of the taxpayer's eligible employees are exceeded shall be treated as having been provided for safety achievement. Where the only safety achievement awards presented by an employer consist of items that are presented at one time during the calendar year, then, if safety achievement awards are presented to more than 10 percent of the taxpayer's eligible employees, the taxpayer may deduct an amount equal to the product of the cost of the item (subject to the applicable deduction limitation) and 10 percent of the taxpayer's eligible employees. Except as provided in the preceding sentence, no award shall be treated as having been provided for safety achievement except to the extent that it can be reasonably demonstrated that that award was made before the 10 percent limitation was exceeded.

Lawrence B. Gibbs,

Commissioner of Internal Revenue.

[FR Doc. 89-368 Filed 1-6-89; 8:45 am]

[¶ 20,118H Reserved.—Proposed regulations on the minimum participation standards under Code Sec. 401(a)(26) were formerly reproduced at this paragraph. They were withdrawn by the IRS and replaced by new proposed regulations published in the *Federal Register* dated May 14, 1990 (55 FR 19935) and corrected on June 22, 1990 (55 FR 25673). The new proposed regulations appear at ¶ 20,121B.]

¶ 20,118I

Proposed regulations: Fringe benefits: Nondiscrimination rules.—Reproduced below are proposed regulations regarding cafeteria plans. The proposals may be relied upon by taxpayers as current working authority. The proposals affect accident and health plans, group-term life insurance and other welfare benefit plans. Note: Q-6 has been republished and A-6(c) and A-6(d) have been revised in proposed regulations reproduced at ¶ 20,227. Q-6 was also republished and A-6(b)(2), A-6(c) and A-6(d) amended in proposed regulations reproduced at ¶ 20,247. Additionally, A-6(f) has been withdrawn and replaced by Temp. Reg. § 1.125-4T(j) at ¶ 11,288E. A-6(c), A-6(c), and A-6(d) were again amended in proposed regulations reproduced at ¶ 20,258. The revised proposed regulations were published in the *Federal Register* on November 7, 1997 (62 FR 60196), March 23, 2000 (65 FR 15587), and January 10, 2001 (66 FR 1923)..

Proposed regulations on compliance with Code Sec. 89 nondiscrimination rules, which were issued along with the proposals under Code Sec. 125, have been removed because Code Sec. 89 was retroactively repealed by P.L. 101-140.

The proposed regulations were published in the Federal Register on March 7, 1989 (54 FR 9460).

Benefits Provided Under Certain Employee Benefit Plans

AGENCY: Internal Revenue Service, Treasury.

ACTION: Notice of proposed rulemaking.

SUMMARY: This document contains proposed regulations relating to benefits provided under certain employee benefit plans under sections 89 and 125 of the Internal Revenue Code of 1986. The regulations reflect changes made by the Revenue Act of 1978, the Tax Reform Act of 1984, the Tax Reform Act of 1986, and the Technical and Miscellaneous Revenue Act of 1988. The regulations provide the public with guidance on the nondiscrimination and qualification requirements for certain employee benefit plans and affect sponsors of, and participants in, a variety of types of plans, including accident and health plans, group-term life insurance, and dependent care assistance programs.

DATES: Written comments and requests for a public hearing must be delivered or mailed on or before [SIXTY DAYS AFTER THE DATE OF PUBLICATION OF THIS NOTICE OF PROPOSED RULEMAKING IN THE FEDERAL REGISTER]. The amendments are generally proposed to apply to plan years beginning after December 31, 1988.

ADDRESS: Send comments and requests for a public hearing to: Commissioner of Internal Revenue, Attention: CC:CORP:T:R (EE-130-86), Washington, DC 20224.

FOR FURTHER INFORMATION CONTACT: Felix Zech or David Munroe of the Office of the Assistant Chief Counsel, Employee Benefits and Exempt Organizations, Internal Revenue Service, 1111 Cons31tution Avenue, N.W., Washington, DC 20224 (Attention: CC:CORP:T:R (EE-130-86)) ((202) 535-3818) (not a toll-free number).

SUPPLEMENTARY INFORMATION:

Paperwork Reduction Act

The collections of information contained in this notice of proposed rulemaking have been submitted to the Office of Management and Budget for review in accordance with the Paperwork Reduction Act of 1980 (44 U.S.C. 3504(h)). Comments on the collections of information should be sent to the Office of Management and Budget, Paperwork Reduction Project, Washington, DC 20503, with copies to the Internal

Revenue Service, Attention: IRS Reports Clearance Officer TR:FP, Washington, DC 20224.

The collections of information in these regulations are in § 1.89(a)-1 and § 1.89(k)-1. Certain of this information is required by the Internal Revenue Service to memorialize the method of testing used by the employer in determining whether it meets the requirements of section 89(a) and correctly reports an employee's wages on the Form W-2. Additional requirements include the preparation of a written plan document, a notice relating to benefits (both required under section 89(k)). The likely respondents/recordkeepers are employers who provide welfare benefit programs to their employees.

These estimates are an approximation of the average time expected to be necessary for a collection of information. They are based on such information as is available to the Internal Revenue Service. Individual recordkeepers may require more or less time, depending on their particular circumstances.

The burden estimates represent an estimation of the actual time for recordkeeping, learning about the law, computations and testings.

The estimated total annual reporting and/or recordkeeping burden: 9,000,000 hours. With respect to learning about the law, testing and making any written elections, the estimated annual burden per respondent/recordkeeper varies from 1 hour to 40 hours, depending on individual circumstances, with an estimated average of 10 hours. The estimated number of respondents and/or recordkeepers: 750,000. With respect to physically preparing the written plan, notice and statement relating to employees, the estimated annual burden per respondent/recordkeeper varies from 30 minutes to 4 hours, depending on individual circumstances, with an estimated average of 2 hours. The estimated number of respondents and/or recordkeepers: 750,000. Estimated annual frequency of response (for reporting requirements only): as necessary.

Background

This document contains proposed additions to the Income Tax Regulations (26 CFR Part 1) under sections 89 and 125 of the Internal Revenue Code of 1986 (Code). The additions with respect to section 89 are proposed to conform the regulations to section 1151 of the Tax

Reform Act of 1986 (TRA '86) (100 Stat. 2494), and section 3021 of the Technical and Miscellaneous Revenue Act of 1988 (TAMRA '88) (102 Stat. 3625). The additions with respect to section 125 are proposed pursuant to section 134 of the Revenue Act of 1978 (92 Stat. 2763), section 101 of the Technical Corrections Act of 1979 (92 Stat. 2227), section 226 of the Miscellaneous Revenue Act of 1980 (94 Stat. 3525), section 531(b)(4) of the Tax Reform Act of 1984 (96 Stat. 494), section 1151 of the Tax Reform Act of 1986 (TRA '86) (100 Stat. 2494), and section 1011B of the Technical and Miscellaneous Revenue Act of 1988 (TAMRA '88) (102 Stat. 3485).

Section 89 was intended, in part, to discourage employers from offering health plans and other welfare benefits that disproportionately favor highly compensated employees either as to coverage or extent of benefits. A principal objective of this legislation was to extend health coverage for employees not now covered. The sanction for failing to meet nondiscrimination criteria outlined in the statute and this implementing rule is the taxation of the excess value of highly compensated employees' benefits.

To help provide an improved basis for evaluation of the specific content and effect of the statute and these regulations, comments are invited on changes in plan provisions, the numbers and types of employees eligible for plans affected by these regulations, and employee participation rates that may be associated with one or more changes proposed in these regulations. Information indicating the effect on particular groups of employees identified by wage levels, occupations, industries or other characteristics would be especially useful. Comments also are invited on the expected effect on costs to employers and health providers which result from particular requirements.

Explanation Of Rules

The proposed regulations include guidance in three general areas. First, they provide information with respect to miscellaneous matters relating to the nondiscrimination rules of section 89(a). Second, the proposed regulations contain detailed guidance with respect to the qualification requirements of section 89(k). Finally, the proposed regulations include questions and answers relating to section 125 (cafeteria plans) and supplementing the existing proposed regulations contained at § 1.125-1 (49 FR 19321). The proposed regulations include a variety of special rules to facilitate the application of and compliance with sections 89 and 125, particularly for plan years beginning in 1989.

* * *

Miscellaneous matters relating to section 125.

Proposed § 1.125-2 contains seven questions and answers that supplement and, in part, update the questions and answers contained in proposed regulations under § 1.125-1 that were published on May 7, 1984 (49 FR 19321), and amended on December 31, 1984 (49 FR 50733). Q&A-1 of proposed § 1.125-2 provides that Q&A-2 through Q&A-6 of that section are generally effective in accordance with the effective date provisions of section 89 (generally plan years commencing after December 31, 1988). In addition, Q&A-1 provides that Q&A-7 of proposed § 1.125-2 (relating to flexible spending arrangements subject to sections 106 and 105) applies to plan years beginning after December 31, 1989.

Many of the questions and answers under § 1.125-2 clarify previously proposed § 1.125-1 as well as § 1.125-2T of the Temporary Regulations published on February 4, 1986 (51 FR 4318). To the extent the provisions of proposed § 1.125-2 clarify the provisions of proposed § 1.125-1 or § 1.125-2T and are less restrictive, the Service will apply them as if contained in those regulations. However, consistent with the statement in the preamble to the May 7, 1984 Notice of Proposed Rulemaking, to the extent that the provisions of proposed § 1.125-2 clarify the provisions of proposed § 1.125-1 and § 1.125-2T and are more restrictive, the Service will apply them only as set forth in Q&A-1 of proposed § 1.125-2.

Q&A-2 and Q&A-3 of the proposed regulation under § 1.125-2 restate the general requirements of section 125. Q&A-4 sets forth what benefits are treated as qualified benefits and what benefits constitute cash under a cafeteria plan. For example, Q&A-4 provides that a benefit that is taxable because it is determined to be an excess benefit under section 89(b) or because the plan fails to satisfy section 89(k) remains a qualified benefit under section 125. As a result of this provision a cafeteria plan may provide such taxable benefits.

The proposed regulation provides further guidance with regard to the rule that a cafeteria plan may not operate to defer compensation. Thus, under Q&A-5, to the extent that a benefit carries over to the following plan year, such benefit may not be offered under a cafeteria plan. For example, life or health insurance with a savings or investment feature (e.g., so-called whole-life or whole-health insurance) may not be

offered in a cafeteria plan. Q&A-5 also contains a rule to determine the extent to which the inclusion of elective vacation days under a cafeteria plan operates to permit the deferral of compensation.

A cafeteria plan may permit employees to make elective contributions under a qualified cash or deferred arrangement described in section 401(k). Similarly, a cafeteria plan does not impermissibly allow the deferral of compensation merely because, as an option under the plan, employees may make after-tax employee contributions under a qualified plan that is subject to section 401(m). Finally, the deferred compensation prohibition does not prevent an employer from providing employer matching contributions subject to section 401(m) with respect to elective contributions under section 401(k) or after-tax employee contributions subject to section 401(m).

Q&A-6 clarifies and expands the rule contained in proposed § 1.125-1 concerning when an employee may revoke a benefit election and make a new election under a cafeteria plan. In general, Q&A-6 provides that a plan may allow such a revocation and subsequent election in the following circumstances: when a third-party health care insurer or provider significantly increases the cost to the employee of coverage or significantly curtails or ceases coverage; when the participant has a change in family status; or when the participant has separated from service. In addition, a cafeteria plan may provide that a benefit ceases if the participant has ceased making required premium payments. Finally, a cafeteria plan may allow a revocation or modification with respect to elective contributions subject to section 401(k) and after-tax employee contributions subject to section 401(m), to the extent such modification or revocation is permitted under section 401(k) or 401(m).

Q&A-7 contains special rules applicable to health plans that are flexible spending arrangements (FSAs). These rules are intended to protect the integrity of the distinction between the taxable treatment of personal medical expenses (subject to the rules of section 213) and the more favorable tax treatment of employer-provided health plan coverage and benefits under section 106 or 105, including benefits received under employee-purchased accident or health coverage under section 104.

In general, if a health plan has a low maximum limitation on benefits and the amount of the premium for coverage is the same or similar to this limitation on benefits, there is a significant concern that the plan operates primarily to exclude from income amounts paid for personal medical expenses that would otherwise only be deductible under section 213 to the extent that they exceed 7.5 percent of adjusted gross income. This concern is greater if, with respect to such plan, there is no person, such as an employer or insurance company, who bears a risk of experience loss with respect to the health plan and thus has an interest in regulating the arrangement to minimize adverse selection and substantiate claimed expenses. In order to limit the extent to which health FSAs effectively operate to exclude amounts paid for personal medical expenses, Q&A-7 applies requirements to health FSAs that are similar to the requirements that an independent health insurer with a meaningful risk of loss would apply to protect against adverse selection and the inappropriate reimbursement of expenses. Thus, the requirements in the proposed regulation are consistent with those features that are commonly associated with arrangements that exhibit the basic risk-shifting and risk-spreading characteristics of insurance.

Q&A-7 clarifies that an employee's salary reduction contributions under a health FSA are payments of a premium by the employee for health coverage with respect to which the maximum reimbursement amount is the same or similar to the amount of the required premium. Therefore, health FSAs are bona fide plans and are not separate, employee-by-employee, health expense reimbursement accounts that operate in a manner similar to employee-funded, defined contribution plans. The maximum amount of reimbursement available under a health FSA at any particular time with respect to an individual cannot be based on the amount of premium that the individual has paid as of such time. Rather, the maximum reimbursement amount must be uniform throughout the coverage period. In addition, health FSAs cannot reimburse employees for premiums for other health coverage. Finally, because there is no party directly involved in an FSA with an interest in assuring that claims are bona fide, the proposed regulation imposes certain claims substantiation requirements for FSAs.

Under the proposed regulation, experience gains under health FSAs (i.e., premiums in excess of claims paid plus expenses) may be treated as gains under bona fide health plans. Thus, such gains may be available to pay reasonable and bona fide dividends or premium refunds to the premium payers. Similarly, experience gains may be used to reduce required premiums for coverage in future years. For example, experience gains for one year may be used in a second year to permit the health FSA to charge all eligible employees only a $490 premium for coverage with a $500 reimbursement maximum. In no case, however, may the treatment of experience gains under a health FSA have the effect, directly or indirectly, of reimbursing employees based on their individual claims.

Reliance On These Proposed Regulations

Taxpayers may rely on these proposed regulations for guidance pending the issuance of final regulations. Because these proposed regulations are generally effective for years beginning after December 31, 1988, the Service will apply these proposed regulations in issuing rulings and in examining returns with respect to taxpayers and plans after that date. If future regulations are more restrictive than these proposed regulations, such regulations will be applied without retroactive effect.

Special Analyses

The Commissioner of Internal Revenue has determined that this proposed rule is not a major rule as defined in Executive Order 12291 and that a regulatory impact analysis is therefore not required. Although this document is a notice of proposed rulemaking which solicits public comments, the Internal Revenue Service has concluded that the regulations proposed herein are interpretative and that the notice and public procedure requirements of 5 U.S.C. 553 do not apply. Accordingly, the proposed regulations do not constitute regulations subject to the Regulatory Flexibility Act (5 U.S.C. Chapter 6).

Comments And Requests For Public Hearing

Before adopting these proposed regulations, consideration will be given to any written comments that are submitted (preferably eight copies) to the Commissioner of Internal Revenue. All comments will be available for public inspection and copying. A public hearing will be held upon written request to the Commissioner by any person who has submitted written comments. If a public hearing is held, notice of the time and place will be published in the FEDERAL REGISTER.

Drafting Information

The principal authors of the proposed regulations are Felix Zech, David Munroe, and Steven Miller of the Office of the Assistant Chief Counsel (Employee Benefits and Exempt Organizations). However, personnel from other offices of the Internal Revenue Service and Treasury Department participated in developing the proposed regulations on matters of both substance and style.

Table Of Contents

* * *

§ 1.125-1 Questions and answers relating to cafeteria plans.

* * *

Q-30: Are there additional rules for cafeteria plans?

§ 1.125-2 Miscellaneous Cafeteria Plan questions and answers.

Q-1: What are the effective dates for these cafeteria plan rules?

Q-2: What does section 125 of the Code provide?

Q-3: What is a cafeteria plan under section 125?

§ 1.125-1 Questions and Answers relating to cafeteria plans.

* * *

Q-30: Are there additional rules for cafeteria plans?

A-30: Yes. Additional rules for cafeteria plans are contained in § 1.125-2 and take effect as set forth in Q&A-1 of § 1.125-2. To the extent that § 1.125-2 and this § 1.125-1 are inconsistent, § 1.125-2 supersedes this § 1.125-1. See ¶ 20,137Q and 20,137R.

§ 1.125-2. Miscellaneous Cafeteria Plan Questions and Answers.—The following is a list of the questions addressed in this section.

Q-1: What are the effective dates of these cafeteria plan rules?

Q-2: What does section 125 of the Code provide?

Q-3: What is a cafeteria plan under section 125?

Q-4: What benefits constitute qualified benefits and what benefits constitute cash under a cafeteria plan?

Q-5: May a cafeteria plan include a benefit that defers the receipt of compensation?

Q-6: In what circumstances may participants revoke existing elections and make new elections under a cafeteria plan?

Q-7: How do the rules governing the tax-favored treatment of employer-provided benefits apply to plans that are flexible spending arrangements?

Q-1: What are the effective dates of these cafeteria plan rules?

A-1: Q&A-1 through Q&A-6 of this § 1.125-2 apply to plan years of cafeteria plans as set forth in Q&A-10 of § 1.89(a)-1 (regarding the effective date of section 89).[1] Q&A-7 of this § 1.125-2 (relating to

---

[1] Q-10: What are the effective dates of the section 89 nondiscrimination and qualification rules?

A-10: (a) *Effective date*—(1) *In general.* Except as otherwise provided in this Q&A-10, the nondiscrimination rules of sections 89(a)-(j) and 89(l)-(m) and the qualification rules of section 89(k) apply for plan years beginning after December 31, 1988.

(2) *Collectively bargained plans*—(i) *In general.* In the case of a collectively bargained plan that is adopted pursuant to one or more collective bargaining agreements ratified prior to March 1, 1986, section 89 does not apply to such plan with respect to employees included in a unit of employees covered by any of such collective bargaining agreements in years beginning before the earlier of January 1, 1991, or the date on which the last collective bargaining agreement relating to the plan expires (determined without regard to extensions after February 28, 1986).

(ii) *Definition of collectively bargained plan.* A collectively bargained plan is a plan covering only eligible individuals who are included in a unit of employees covered by an agreement that is a collective bargaining agreement entered into between employee representatives and one or more employers (as determined under section 7701(a)(46)). A plan that is maintained pursuant to two or more collective bargaining agreements is treated as two or more collectively bargained plans to the extent that the employer-provided benefits provided pursuant to the agreements are not uniform. Thus, for example, if a multiemployer plan is maintained pursuant to three collective bargaining agreements, two of which provide for an identical benefit structure and one of which provides for a different benefit structure, the plan is treated as two separate, collectively bargained plans for purposes of this paragraph (a)(2).

(iii) *Plans benefiting non-collectively bargained employees.* If a plan provides employer-provided benefits to employees who are included in a unit of employees covered by a collective bargaining agreement and to employees who are not included in any such unit of employees (i.e., non-collectively bargained employees), the non-collectively bargained employees are treated as covered by a plan that is not a collectively bargained plan for purposes of this paragraph (a)(2). Thus, the delayed effective date of paragraph (a)(2)(i) of this Q&A-10 is available only with respect to the portion of the plan that provides employer-provided benefits to the collectively bargained employees.

(iv) *Treatment of collectively bargained employees as excludable employees.* Unless the employer elects otherwise, employees who receive employer-provided benefits under a collectively bargained plan to which section 89 does not yet apply by reason of this paragraph (a)(2) are to be treated as excludable employees (i.e., as though they were described in section 89(h)) for purposes of applying the nondiscrimination tests of section 89 to plans that are subject to section 89. However, an employer may elect in writing not to treat such collectively bargained employees as excludable employees for purposes of applying section 89 to plans that are subject to section 89. Such an election must be made with respect to all collectively bargained employees, regardless of bargaining unit, and once made applies to all subsequent testing years. Such an election does not accelerate the

otherwise applicable effective date with respect to the application of the qualification rules of section 89(k) to such collectively bargained plan or plans. However, if the employer makes an election under this paragraph (a)(2)(iv), then the nondiscrimination rules of section 89 are effective with respect to such plan or plans and thus a highly compensated employee within the group of otherwise excludable employees (i.e., nonexcludable by reason of such election), may have an excess benefit under section 89(b).

(v) *Examples.* The provisions of this paragraph (a)(2) are illustrated by the following examples:

Example 1. A collective bargaining agreement ratified in January 1986 is scheduled to expire on December 31, 1992. Such agreement provides for contributions by an employer to a multiemployer plan providing health coverage. Assuming that no employee who is included in the collective bargaining unit receives health coverage from the employer other than coverage under the multiemployer plan, the collective bargaining employees and their health coverage may be disregarded by the employer in applying the section 89 nondiscrimination tests for any period before January 1, 1991.

Example 2. Employer X maintains two health plans, Plan A (covering non-collectively bargained employees) and Plan B (covering collectively bargained employees). Plan B is a multiemployer plan that has an effective date for purposes of section 89 of January 1, 1991. Plan A is an insurance plan with a policy that expires on June 30, 1989. The collectively bargained employees receiving benefits under Plan B may be treated as excludable employees until January of 1991 and their health coverage may be disregarded by Employer X in applying the nondiscrimination tests of section 89 until that date. However, before that date, Employer X may elect to take such collectively bargained employees (and their employer-provided benefits) into account for purposes of testing Plan A for periods prior to January of 1991.

(b) *Definition of plan year*—(1) *In general.* Except as provided in paragraph (b)(2) or (b)(3) of this Q&A-10, for purposes of determining the applicable effective date of section 89 with respect to a plan, the plan year is the year that is designated as the plan year in the written plan. For plans other than health and group-term life insurance plans, if there is no such designation, the plan year is the calendar year. For purposes of this rule, the designation of a plan year solely for purposes of filing the Form 5500 is to be disregarded.

(2) *Certain health and group-term life insurance plans*—(i) *Insured plans.* If a health or group-term life insurance plan's plan year is not clearly ascertainable from a written plan document adopted and in existence on January 1, 1989, and the plan is provided under an arrangement through an insurance company, the policy year is the applicable plan year for effective date purposes. If there is no policy year, the employer may elect in writing either the limit/deductible year, the calendar year, or the employer's fiscal year as the applicable plan year for effective date purposes. If the employer does not make such an election, the applicable plan year is the calendar year. An arrangement is not provided through an insurance company for purposes of this paragraph (b) if the insurance company provides merely administrative services under the arrangement.

flexible spending arrangements) applies to plan years beginning after December 31, 1989.

Q-2: What does section 125 of the Code provide?

A-2: In general, an employee who has an election among nontaxable benefits and taxable benefits (including cash) must include in gross income any taxable benefits that the employee could have actually received pursuant to the employee's election. The amount of these benefits is included in the employee's income in the year in which the employee would have actually received the taxable benefits if the employee had elected such benefits. This generally is the result even if the employee's election between the nontaxable benefits and taxable benefits is made prior to the year in which the employee would have actually received the taxable benefits. However, section 125 provides that cash (including certain taxable benefits) provided under a nondiscriminatory cafeteria plan will not be included in a participant's gross income merely because the participant has the opportunity, before the cash becomes currently available to the participant, to choose among cash and the nontaxable benefits under the cafeteria plan.

Q-3: What is a cafeteria plan under section 125?

A-3: A cafeteria plan is a plan maintained by an employer for the benefit of its employees that satisfies the requirements of section 89(k), under which all participants are employees, and under which each participant has the opportunity to choose among cash and qualified benefits. Additionally, a cafeteria plan satisfies the written plan document requirement of clause (v) of Q&A-3 of § 1.125-1 only if the plan describes the maximum amount of elective contributions available to any employee under the plan either by stating the maximum dollar amount or maximum percentage of compensation that may be contributed as elective contributions under the plan by employees or by stating the method for determining the maximum amount or percentage of elective contributions that employees may make under the plan. The meaning of "elective contributions" under a cafeteria plan is the same as the meaning of "salary reduction contributions" under a cafeteria plan. See also paragraph (a)(2) of Q&A-8 of § 1.89(a)-1.[2]

Q-4: What benefits constitute qualified benefits and what benefits constitute cash under a cafeteria plan?

A-4: (a) *Qualified benefits*—(1) *In general.* A benefit is a qualified benefit under a cafeteria plan if the benefit does not defer the receipt of compensation and the benefit is not includible in an employee's gross income by reason of an express provision of Chapter 1 of the Code. In the case of insurance-type benefits, such as benefits provided under accident or health plans (sections 106 and 105) and group-term life insurance plans (section 79), the benefit is the coverage under the plan.

(2) *Items that constitute qualified benefits*—(i) *Accident or health plans.* Coverage under an accident or health plan is a qualified benefit to the extent that such coverage is excludable from income under section 106. Thus, for example, coverage under a long-term disability plan and coverage under an accidental death and dismemberment policy may be qualified benefits.

(ii) *Group-term life insurance.* Group-term life insurance coverage that is excludable from gross income under section 79 and group-term life insurance coverage that is includible in gross income solely because the death benefit payable thereunder is in excess of the dollar limit of section 79 are qualified benefits.

(iii) *Certain discriminatory benefits.* Accident or health plan coverage, group-term life insurance coverage, and benefits under a dependent care assistance program do not fail to be qualified benefits under a cafeteria plan merely because they are includible in gross income solely because of section 89 or any other applicable nondiscrimination requirement (e.g., section 129(d)).

(iv) *Certain dependent care assistance benefits.* Benefits under a dependent care assistance program that would have been excludable from gross income under section 129 but for the elimination of overnight camp expenses from dependent care assistance under such section (effective January 1, 1988) or the reduction of the age limit on children qualifying as dependents under such section (effective January 1, 1989) do not fail to be qualified benefits merely because such changes in law cause such benefits to be taxable. However, the preceding sentence applies only if the benefits are provided under a program that otherwise qualifies as a dependent care assistance program under section 129, are taxable to the employee upon receipt, and are provided by the December 31 next following the effective date of the applicable change in law. After such date, such benefits will not constitute qualified benefits but may be treated as cash pursuant to paragraph (b) of this Q&A-4.

(Footnote Continued)

(ii) *Self-insured plans.* If a health or group-term life insurance plan's plan year is not clearly ascertainable from a written plan document adopted and in existence on January 1, 1989, and the coverage under such plan is not provided under an arrangement through an insurance company, the employer may elect in writing either the limit/deductible year, the calendar year, or the employer's fiscal year as the applicable plan year for effective date purposes. If the employer does not make such an election, the applicable plan year is the calendar year.

(iii) *Limit/deductible year.* The limit/deductible year is the year with respect to which the plan's benefit and deductible limits are applied, except that if different years are used for benefit limit purposes and for deductible limit purposes, it means the limit or deductible year that commences earlier in the calendar year.

(3) *Special rule to prevent delay of the section 89 effective date*—(i) *In general.* Notwithstanding paragraphs (b)(1) and (b)(2) of this Q&A-10, in the case of a health or group-term life insurance plan with respect to which the first day of the first plan year beginning after December 31, 1988 (determined under paragraphs (b)(1) and (b)(2)), is later during the calendar year than the first day of the first plan year (also determined under such paragraphs) beginning in 1988, the first plan year beginning after December 31, 1988, is deemed to begin on the day that is 12 months after the first day of the plan's first plan year beginning in 1988. Thus, section 89 becomes effective with respect to such plan on the first anniversary date of the plan's first plan year beginning in 1988. In addition, for purposes of this Q&A-10, a plan's last plan year beginning in 1988 is not treated as longer than 12 months in duration. Thus, for example, an agreement between an employer and insurance company to extend for longer than 12 months the last plan year of a health plan beginning in 1988 is not recognized for purposes of determining the applicable section 89 effective date with respect to such plan. Such plan is treated as commencing a new plan year on the day that is 12 months after the first day of the last plan year commencing in 1988.

(ii) *Exceptions*—(A) *In general.* Except as provided in paragraph (b)(3)(iii) of this Q&A-10, paragraph (b)(3)(i) of this Q&A-10 does not apply to the extent that any of the tests described in this paragraph (b)(3)(ii)(B) through (D) are satisfied.

(B) *Three-month rule.* A plan is a health plan and the first day of the plan's first plan year beginning after December 31, 1988, is not more than 3 months later during the calendar year than the first day of the plan's first plan year beginning in 1988 and the selection of the new plan year was for bona fide business reasons unrelated to section 89 (e.g., by reason of a merger or acquisition).

(C) *New carrier rule.* A plan is a health plan and the health coverage for the plan's first plan year beginning after December 31, 1988, is provided through an insurance arrangement with an insurance company unrelated to any insurance company that provided health coverage under the plan for the first day of the plan's first plan year beginning in 1988 and such change in insurance carriers and the selection of the new plan year were for bona fide business reasons unrelated to section 89.

(D) *Uniform plan year.* The first day of the plan's first plan year beginning after December 31, 1988, is the same day during the calendar year on which commenced in 1988 the plan year or years of the plan or plans of the same type that provided, in the aggregate, at least 25 percent of the total employer-provided benefits provided under all plans of the same type during 1988 and the selection of the new plan year was for bona fide business reasons unrelated to section 89. This rule may be applied in the case of a merger or acquisition by treating such transaction as having occurred on December 31, 1987.

(iii) *Retroactive plan year changes.* This paragraph (b)(3) is to be applied by disregarding any change in a plan year that is made after the commencement of such plan year.

(iv) *Additional rules.* The Commissioner may, through revenue rulings, notices, and other guidance of general applicability, provide such additional exceptions to paragraph (b)(3)(i) of this Q&A-10 as are appropriate if such exceptions do not have the effect of permitting employers to delay significantly the effective date of section 89 with respect to their plans without any significant, independent business reason.

(4) *New plans.* For purposes of this Q&A-10, a plan is not treated as a new plan commencing in calendar year 1989, unless such plan provides coverage and benefits that are substantially different from the coverage and benefits previously provided by a plan in calendar year 1988.

(5) *Certain dispositions or acquisitions.* If a person becomes or ceases to be a member of a group described in section 414(b), (c), (m) or (o) on or before December 31, 1988, the transitional rule of section 89(j)(8) is not applicable with respect to any plan of such person or of any member of such group unless the requirements of section 89 were met immediately before such change in the group. This determination is to be made as though section 89 (and this section) were effective with respect to all such plans of such person. Alternatively, for testing years beginning in 1989, the nondiscrimination rules of section 89 may be applied separately to the separate portions of the group under section 414(b), (c), (m) and (o) involved in the change of the group as if such portions did not become part of the same group until December 31, 1989.

[2] Q-8: How are salary reduction contributions treated for purposes of the section 89 nondiscrimination tests?

A-8: (a) *Treatment of salary reduction contributions*—

* * *

(2) *Definition of salary reduction contributions.* The term "salary reduction contributions" means all employer contributions that are excludable from the gross income of an employee by reason of section 125. Thus, all elective contributions under a cafeteria plan described in section 125 that are excludable from employees' gross incomes are salary reduction contributions, even if such amounts are available in cash or other taxable benefits only if the employee satisfies a specified condition under the plan (e.g., the completion of a statement that the employee has other health plan coverage). This is the case regardless of the manner in which such contributions are described under a plan. For example, amounts that are described as employer or company credits under a cafeteria plan are salary reduction contributions to the extent that such amounts are available to employees in cash or other taxable benefits under the plan, even if, for example, the plan defines salary reduction contributions as only those contributions that are directly and explicitly deducted from employees' regular salaries.

(b) *Currently taxable benefits treated as cash.* In general, a benefit is treated as cash if such benefit does not defer the receipt of compensation and an employee who receives such benefit purchases such benefit with after-tax employee contributions or is treated, for all purposes under the Code (including, for example, reporting and withholding purposes), as receiving, at the time that such benefit is received, cash compensation equal to the full value of such benefit at such time and then purchasing such benefit with after-tax employee contributions. Thus, for example, long-term disability coverage is treated as cash if the cafeteria plan provides that an employee may purchase the coverage under the plan with after-tax employee contributions, or provides that the employee receiving such coverage is treated as having received cash compensation equal to the value of the coverage and then as having purchased the coverage with after-tax employee contributions. Any taxable benefit that is not described in paragraph (a) of this Q&A-4 and is not treated as cash under this paragraph (b) may not be included in a cafeteria plan.

(c) *Qualified cash or deferred arrangements.* Elective contributions to a qualified cash or deferred arrangement (section 401(k)) are permitted under a cafeteria plan. In addition, after-tax employee contributions under a qualified plan subject to section 401(m) are permitted under a cafeteria plan. The right to make such contributions will not cause a plan to fail to be a cafeteria plan merely because, under the qualified plan, employer matching contributions are made with respect to elective or after-tax employee contributions.

(d) *Benefits that do not constitute qualified benefits or cash.* Benefits of the type described in section 117 or 132 do not constitute qualified benefits or cash and thus may not be included in a cafeteria plan regardless of whether any such benefit is purchased with after-tax employee contributions or on any other basis. Thus, for example, health diagnostic or examination plans are qualified benefits under a cafeteria plan because such plans are accident or health plans that are eligible for the exclusion under section 106 and are not, in any case, eligible for the exclusion under section 132.

Q-5: May a cafeteria plan include a benefit that defers the receipt of compensation?

A-5: (a) *In general.* A cafeteria plan may not include any plan that offers a benefit that defers the receipt of compensation. In addition, a cafeteria plan may not operate in a manner that enables employees to defer compensation. For example, a plan that permits employees to carry over unused elective contributions or plan benefits (e.g., accident or health plan coverage) from one plan year to another operates to defer compensation. This is the case regardless of how the contributions or benefits are used by the employee in the subsequent plan year (e.g., whether they are automatically or electively converted into another taxable or nontaxable benefit in the subsequent plan year or used to provide additional benefits of the same type). Similarly, a cafeteria plan operates to permit the deferral of compensation if the plan permits participants to use contributions for one plan year to purchase a benefit that will be provided in a subsequent plan year (e.g., life, health, disability, or long-term care insurance coverage with a savings or investment feature, such as whole life insurance). For example, a cafeteria plan operates to permit the deferral of compensation if the cafeteria plan includes a health plan that is a flexible spending arrangement (as defined in Q&A-7 of this section) and such health plan may reimburse participants' premium payments for other accident or health coverage extending beyond the end of the plan year. See Q&A-7 of this section for the treatment of experience gains under a health plan that is a flexible spending arrangement.

(b) *Exceptions.* A plan does not fail to be a cafeteria plan merely because the plan permits participants to make elective contributions under a qualified cash or deferred arrangement under section 401(k) or permits participants employed by certain educational institutions to purchase retiree group-term life insurance. Similarly, a cafeteria plan does not include a benefit that defers the receipt of compensation merely because the cafeteria plan provides the opportunity to make after-tax employee contributions subject to section 401(m) under a qualified plan. In addition, a cafeteria plan will not be treated as including a benefit that defers the receipt of compensation merely because, under the qualified plan, employer matching contributions (as defined in section 401(m)(4)(A)) are made with respect to such elective contributions or after-tax employee contributions. Finally, reasonable premium rebates or policy dividends paid with respect to benefits provided under a cafeteria plan do not constitute impermissible deferred compensation if such rebates or dividends are paid before the close of the 12-month period immediately following the plan year to which such rebates and dividends relate.

(c) *Treatment of paid vacation days under a cafeteria plan*—(1) *In general.* A cafeteria plan may include elective, paid vacation days by permitting participants to receive either additional or fewer paid vacation days than the employer otherwise provides to the employees on a nonelective basis, if the inclusion of elective vacation days under the plan does not operate to permit the deferral of compensation.

(2) *Ordering of elective and nonelective vacation days.* In determining whether a plan that provides for paid vacation days operates to permit the deferral of compensation, and thus fails to be a cafeteria plan, a participant is deemed to use nonelective vacation days (i.e., the vacation days with respect to which the employee had no election) before elective vacation days.

(3) *Cashing out unused elective vacation days.* A plan does not operate to permit the deferral of compensation merely because the plan permits a participant who has not used all elective, paid vacation days for a plan year to receive in cash the value of such unused days in exchange for such days if the participant receives the cash on or before the earlier of the last day of the plan year of the cafeteria plan or the last day of the employee's taxable year to which the elective contributions used to purchase the unused days relate.

(4) *Examples.* The following examples illustrate the rules of this paragraph (c):

Example 1. Assume that an employer provides an employee with 2 weeks of paid vacation for each calendar year and maintains a calendar year cafeteria plan that permits the employee to "purchase," with elective contributions, an additional week of paid vacation. Assume further that Employee A, with a calendar tax year, purchases 1 additional week of vacation. If Employee A uses only 2 weeks of vacation during the year, the employee is treated as having used the 2 nonelective weeks and as having retained the 1 elective week. If the 1 remaining week (i.e., the elective week) may be carried over to the next year (or the value thereof used for any other purpose in the next year), the plan operates to permit the deferral of compensation and thus is not a cafeteria plan. However, the cafeteria plan may permit the employee to receive the value of the unused elective vacation week in cash before the end of the applicable calendar year.

Example 2. The facts are the same as set forth in Example 1, except that Employee A uses only 1 week of vacation during the year. Thus, Employee A is treated as having used 1 nonelective week and as having retained 1 nonelective week as well as 1 elective week of vacation. Because the nonelective vacation days are not part of the cafeteria plan (i.e., the employer or plan does not permit participants to exchange regular vacation days for other benefits), Employee A may be permitted to carry over the 1 nonelective week of vacation to the next year. In addition, under the terms of the cafeteria plan, Employee A must either forfeit the remaining elective vacation week or receive in cash the value of such unused days before the end of the applicable calendar year.

→ **Caution: Q-6 has been republished and A-6(c) and A-6(d) have been revised in proposed regulations reproduced at ¶ 20,227. Additionally, A-6(f) has been withdrawn and replaced by Temp. Reg. § 1.125-4T(j) at ¶ 11,288E. Additionally, Q-6 has been republished and A-6(b)(2), A-6(c) and A-6(d) have been amended in proposed regulations reproduced at ¶ 20,247.**

Q-6: In what circumstances may participants revoke existing elections and make new elections under a cafeteria plan?

A-6: (a) *In general.* A plan is not a cafeteria plan unless the plan requires that participants make elections among the benefits offered under the plan. In general, an election will not be deemed to have been made if, after a participant has elected and begun to receive a benefit under the plan, the participant is permitted to revoke the election during the period of coverage under the plan, even if the revocation relates only to the remaining portion of the coverage period with respect to the benefit and even if the revocation is in response to a change in the tax treatment of such benefit. However, in the circumstances specified in paragraphs (b) through (g) of this Q&A-6, notwithstanding Q&A-8 of § 1.125-1, the terms of a cafeteria plan may permit a participant to revoke an existing election and, in some cases, to make a new election with respect to the remaining portion of the period of coverage. If a new election is permitted under this Q&A-6, then such new election must be consistent with the reason that such change was permitted. In addition, a cafeteria plan may permit an election change to the extent required under paragraph (c)(6) of Q&A-3 of § 1.89(a)-1.[3]

---

[3] Q-3: Under what circumstances may employees be disregarded for purposes of section 89 when the employees receive health coverage from other employers or when employees do not have a family or have a family whose members receive health coverage from another employer?

Such election changes will not cause taxable benefits offered under the cafeteria plan to be treated as currently available to employees. See Q&A-7 of this section for certain additional limits on election changes that relate to certain flexible spending arrangements.

(b) *Significant cost or coverage changes—* (1) *Cost changes.* If the cost of a health plan provided by an independent, third-party provider under a cafeteria plan increases or decreases during a plan year and under the terms of the cafeteria plan, employees are required to make a corresponding change in their premium payments, the cafeteria plan may, on a reasonable and consistent basis, automatically increase or decrease, as the case may be, all affected participants' elective contributions or after-tax employee contributions for such health plan. Alternatively, if the premium amount significantly increases, a cafeteria plan may permit participants either to make a corresponding change in their premium payments or to revoke their elections and, in lieu thereof, to receive on a prospective basis, coverage under another health plan with similar coverage. No elective adjustments of participants' contributions or revocations of participants' elections other than those provided for in the preceding sentence may be permitted under a cafeteria plan on account of changes in the cost of a health plan.

→ **Caution: A-6(b)(2) has been amended in proposed regulations reproduced at ¶ 20,247.**

(2) *Coverage changes.* If the coverage under a health plan provided by an independent, third-party provider is significantly curtailed or ceases during a period of coverage, a cafeteria plan may permit all affected participants to revoke their elections of the health plan and, in lieu thereof, to receive on a prospective basis coverage under another health plan with similar coverage.

→ **Caution: A-6(c) has been revised in proposed regulations reproduced at ¶ 20,227 and ¶ 20,247.**

(c) *Certain changes in family status.* A cafeteria plan may permit a participant to revoke a benefit election during a period of coverage and to make a new election for the remaining portion of the period if the revocation and new election are both on account of a change in family status and are consistent with such change in family status. For purposes of this paragraph (d), examples of changes in family status for which a benefit election change may be permitted include the marriage or divorce of the employee, the death of the employee's spouse or a dependent, the birth or adoption of a child of the employee, the termination of employment (or the commencement of employment) of the employee's spouse, the switching from part-time to full-time employment status or from full-time to part-time status by the employee or the employee's spouse, and the taking of an unpaid leave of absence by the employee or the employee's spouse. Election changes are also permitted where there has been a significant change in the health coverage of the employee or spouse attributable to the spouse's employment. Benefit election changes are consistent with family status changes only if the election changes are necessary or appropriate as a result of the family status changes.

→ **Caution: A-6(d) has been revised in proposed regulations reproduced at ¶ 20,227 and ¶ 20,247.**

(d) *Separation from service.* A cafeteria plan may permit an employee who separates from the service of the employer during a period of coverage to revoke existing benefit elections and terminate the receipt of benefits for the remaining portion of the coverage period. However, in such case, the plan must prohibit the employee, if the employee should return to service for the employer, from making new benefit elections for the remaining portion of the period of coverage.

(e) *Cessation of required contributions.* A cafeteria plan may provide that a benefit will cease to be provided to an employee if the employee fails to make the required premium payments with respect to the benefit (e.g., employee ceases to make premium payments for health

plan coverage after a separation from service). However, in such case, the plan must prohibit the employee from making a new benefit election for the remaining portion of the period of coverage.

→ **Caution: A-6(f) has been withdrawn and replaced by Temp. Reg. § 1.125-4T(j) at ¶ 11,288E.**

(f) *Elective contributions under a qualified cash or deferred arrangement.* A cafeteria plan may permit a participant who has elected to make elective contributions under a qualified cash or deferred arrangement (within the meaning of section 401(k)) to modify or revoke the election as permitted under section 401(k). Similarly, a cafeteria plan may permit a participant who has elected to make after-tax employee contributions subject to section 401(m) to modify or revoke the election as permitted under section 401(m). Thus, for example, a cafeteria plan may include a benefit option providing for elective contributions under a qualified cash or deferred arrangement which requires that, as a condition of a hardship distribution, the employee receiving the distribution cease making elective contributions under the arrangement for a specified period.

Q-7: How do the rules governing the tax-favored treatment of employer-provided benefits apply to plans that are flexible spending arrangements?

A-7: (a) *In general.* Health plans that are flexible spending arrangements as defined in paragraph (c) of this Q&A-7 (health FSAs) must conform to the generally applicable rules under sections 105 and 106 in order for the coverage and reimbursements under such plans to qualify for tax-favored treatment under such sections. Thus, health FSAs must qualify as accident or health plans. This means that, in general, while the health coverage under the FSA need not be provided through a commercial insurance contract, health FSAs must exhibit the risk-shifting and risk-distribution characteristics of insurance. Similarly, reimbursements under health FSAs must be paid specifically to reimburse the participant for medical expenses incurred previously during the period of coverage. Furthermore, a health FSA cannot operate under a cafeteria plan in a manner that enables participants to receive coverage only for periods for which the participants expect to incur medical expenses if such periods constitute less than a plan year. A reimbursement is not paid specifically to reimburse the participant for medical expenses if the participant is entitled to these amounts, in the form of cash or any other taxable or nontaxable benefit (including health coverage for an additional period), without regard to whether or not the employee incurs medical expenses during the period of coverage. A health FSA will not qualify for tax-favored treatment under sections 105 and 106 of the Code if the effect of the reimbursement arrangement eliminates all, or substantially all, risk of loss to the employer maintaining the plan or other insurer. These rules apply with respect to a health plan without regard to whether the plan is provided through a cafeteria plan. See Q&A-17 of § 1.125-1.

(b) *Special requirements—*(1) *In general.* A health FSA must satisfy the requirements set forth in this paragraph (b) in order for the employer-provided health coverage provided through the health FSA to qualify for the exclusion from income under section 106 and for the reimbursements and other benefits pursuant to the health FSA coverage to qualify for the exclusion from income under section 105.

(2) *Uniform coverage throughout coverage period.* The maximum amount of reimbursement under a health FSA must be available at all times during the period of coverage (properly reduced as of any particular time for prior reimbursements for the same period of coverage). Thus, the maximum amount of reimbursement at any particular time during the period of coverage cannot relate to the extent to which the participant has paid the required premiums for coverage under the health FSA for the coverage period. Similarly, the payment schedule for the required premiums for coverage under a health FSA may not be

---

(Footnote Continued)

***
(c) *75 percent benefits test and 80 percent coverage test.—*

***

(6) *Certain nonhighly compensated employees.* A nonhighly compensated employee may not be disregarded under paragraph (c)(3) of this Q&A-3 because of other core health coverage unless, at the time such other coverage ceases, such employee is eligible to elect coverage under any core health plan of the employer for which the employee was eligible (through election or otherwise) during the immediately preceding period in which the employee could have elected coverage (e.g. an open season). The election period for purposes of the rule in this paragraph (c)(6) must be no shorter than 30 days. This paragraph (c)(6) applies without regard to the reason for the cessation of the employee's other core health coverage and without regard to whether the employer's health plans otherwise permit employees to commence coverage at other than an open season. Similarly, a nonhighly compensated employee may not be disregarded as having no family or having a family with other coverage under paragraph (c)(3) of this Q&A-3 unless such

employee is eligible to elect (on the same conditions set forth in the preceding two sentences) family-only coverage, upon a change in family status in which the employee acquires a family or upon a loss of such other coverage for a member of the family. This paragraph (c)(6) does not require that an employee be eligible to participate under a plan for which the employee would not previously have been eligible. In addition, any otherwise applicable eligibility conditions that would have barred participation during the immediately preceding open season, such as insurability, may continue to be applied with respect to eligibility resulting under this paragraph (c)(6) but only if such conditions exist at the time the other core health coverage ceases and such conditions are applied on a uniform, consistent and nondiscriminatory basis. However, in no event may an employer impose conditions on eligibility that were not previously applicable to such employee during the immediately preceding open season. Conditions that were previously applicable, may be applied with regard to the facts in existence either at the time of previous eligibility or at the time the other core coverage ceases, as long as such application is on a uniform, consistent and nondiscriminatory basis. This paragraph (c)(6) is applicable only for plan years beginning after December 31, 1990.

based on the rate or amount of covered claims incurred during the coverage period. Reimbursement will be deemed to be available at all times if it is paid at least monthly or when the total amount of the claims to be submitted is at least a specified, reasonable minimum amount (e.g., $50). If the employee revokes existing elections, the employer must reimburse the employee for any amount previously paid for coverage or benefits relating to the period after the date of the employee's separation from service regardless of the employee's claims or reimbursements as of such date. The following examples illustrate the rules of this paragraph (b)(2):

Example 1. Assume that an employee elects coverage under a health FSA providing coverage of up to $300 in medical expenses and the annual premium for a calendar year of coverage is $300. Assume also that the employee is permitted to pay the $300 premium through salary reduction of $25 per month throughout the coverage period. The employee must be eligible to receive the maximum amount of reimbursement of $300 at all times throughout the coverage period (reduced by prior reimbursements). Thus, if the employee incurs $250 of medical expenses in January, the full $250 must be available for reimbursement even though the employee has made only one premium payment. If the employee incurs another $50 in health expenses in February, the remaining $50 of the $300 maximum must be available for reimbursement. The employer or plan may not provide for an acceleration of the required premium payments based on the employee's incurred claims and reimbursements.

Example 2. Assume that an employee elects coverage under a health FSA with a maximum reimbursement limit of $500 for a calendar year of coverage and is required to pay the $450 premium for such coverage in two equal $225 installments, one at the beginning of the period of coverage and the second installment by the beginning of the sixth month of coverage. Assume further that the employee incurs a $400 medical expense in February and the FSA makes a $400 reimbursement to the employee in March. The employee does not incur any additional medical expenses before the end of June, at which time the employee separates from service. If the employee fails to make the second premium installment, the employee's coverage under the FSA may be terminated as of the end of June so that medical expenses incurred after June are not covered. If the employee pays the second premium installment, the employee's coverage under the FSA must continue, so that additional medical expenses (up to the remaining $100) incurred before the end of December are covered.

(3) *Twelve-month period of coverage.* The period of coverage under a health FSA must be 12 months or, in the case of a short first plan year or a short plan year of a cafeteria plan where the plan year is being changed, the entire short plan year. Election changes to increase or decrease the level of coverage under a health FSA during the 12-month period of coverage are not permitted with respect to health FSAs. However, a cafeteria plan may permit participants to make health FSA election changes for the remaining portion of the 12-month period of coverage on account of and consistent with certain family status changes. See Q&A-6 of this section. In addition, a cafeteria plan may provide that the period of coverage under a health FSA terminates if the employee ceases to make required premium payments; however, such employee may not be permitted to make a new health FSA benefit election for the remaining portion of the original coverage period. Also, a cafeteria plan may permit an employee who separates from the service of the employer during a period of coverage to revoke existing benefit elections and terminate receipt of benefits, including coverage under the health FSA. For the application of the health care continuation rules of section 4980B of the Code to health FSAs, see the regulations under section 4980B or its predecessor section 162(k) of the Code. The requirements of this paragraph (b)(3) are illustrated by the following example:

Example. Assume that an employee has elected a $300 calendar year health FSA, with monthly premium payments of $25 during the 12-month period of coverage. Such employee separates from service for the employer at the end of June and ceases to make additional premium payments. The cafeteria plan may provide that the FSA's period of coverage does not extend beyond June if the employee does not continue to make the required premium payments. However, if the employee makes the total premium payment for the 12-month period of coverage, the cafeteria plan may not terminate the FSA's period of coverage merely because the employee separated from service before the end of the coverage period.

(4) *Prohibited reimbursement.* A health FSA can only reimburse medical expenses as defined in section 213. Thus, for example, a health FSA cannot reimburse dependent care expenses. In addition, a health FSA may not treat participants' premium payments for other health coverage as reimbursable expenses. Thus, for example, a health FSA may not reimburse participants for premiums paid for other health plan

coverage, including premiums paid for health coverage under a plan maintained by the employer of the employee's spouse or dependent. (See also Q&A-5 of this section with respect to whether the reimbursement of other premiums constitutes impermissible deferred compensation.) This paragraph (b)(4) does not prevent premiums for current health plan coverage (including coverage under a health FSA) from being paid on a salary reduction basis through the ordinary operation of the cafeteria plan.

(5) *Claims substantiation.* A health FSA may reimburse a medical expense only if the participant provides a written statement from an independent third party stating that the medical expense has been incurred and the amount of such expense and the participant provides a written statement that the medical expense has not been reimbursed or is not reimbursable under, any other health plan coverage. Thus, for example, as with any other flexible spending arrangement, a health FSA cannot make advance reimbursements of future or projected expenses. In determining whether, under all the facts and circumstances, employees are being reimbursed for inadequately substantiated claims, special scrutiny will be given to other arrangements such as employer-to-employee loans that are related to the employee premium payments or actual or projected employee claims.

(6) *Claims incurred.* Medical expenses reimbursed under a health FSA must be incurred during the participant's period of coverage under the FSA. Expenses are treated as having been incurred when the participant is provided with the medical care that gives rise to the medical expenses, and not when the participant is formally billed or charged for, or pays for the medical care. Also, expenses are not treated as incurred during a period of FSA coverage if such expenses are incurred before the later of the date the health FSA is first in existence or the participant first becomes enrolled under the health FSA.

(7) *FSA experience gains.* If a health FSA has an experience gain with respect to a year of coverage, the excess of the premiums paid (e.g., employer contributions, including salary reduction contributions and after-tax employee contributions) and income (if any) of the FSA over the FSA's total claims reimbursements and reasonable administrative costs for the year may be used to reduce required premiums for the following year or may be returned to the premium payers (the participants for premiums paid by salary reduction or employee contributions) as dividends or premium refunds. Such experience gains must be allocated among premium payers on a reasonable and uniform basis. It is permissible to allocate such amounts based on the different coverage levels under the FSA received by the premium payers. However, in no case may the experience gains be allocated among premium payers based (directly or indirectly) on their individual claims experience. The requirements of this paragraph (b)(7) are illustrated in the following example:

Example. Assume that an employer maintains a cafeteria plan under which its 1,200 employees may elect one of several different annual coverage levels under a health FSA in $100 increments from $500 to $2,000. For a plan year, 1,000 employees elect levels of coverage under the health FSA. For such year, the FSA has an experience gain of $5,000 (i.e., premium payments for the year exceed reimbursed claims plus administrative costs by $5,000). The $5,000 may be allocated to all premium payers for the year, as a premium refund, on a per capita basis weighted to reflect the participants' elected levels of coverage. Alternatively, the $5,000 may be used to reduce the required premiums under the health FSA for all eligible employees for the next plan year (e.g., a $500 health FSA for the next year might be priced at $480) or to reimburse claims incurred above the elective limit in such year as long as such reimbursements are made in a nondiscriminatory manner.

(8) *Dependent care assistance.* Analogous rules to this paragraph (b), with the exception of paragraph (b)(2) relating to uniform coverage throughout the coverage period, are applicable to dependent care assistance provided under section 129. See Q&A-18 of § 1.125-1.

(c) *Definition of flexible spending arrangement.* A flexible spending arrangement (FSA) generally is a benefit program that provides employees with coverage under which specified, incurred expenses may be reimbursed (subject to reimbursement maximums and any other reasonable conditions) and under which the maximum amount of reimbursement that is reasonably available to a participant for a period of coverage is not substantially in excess of the total premium (including both employee-paid and employer-paid portions of the premium) for such participant's coverage. A maximum amount of reimbursement is not substantially in excess of the total premium if such maximum amount is less than 500 percent of the premium. A single FSA may provide participants with different levels of coverage and maximum amounts of reimbursement. However, for purposes of section 89, each different level of coverage under a FSA is a separate plan.

(d) *Effective date.* This Q&A-7 is effective for plan years beginning after December 31, 1989.

(e) *Authority to issue additional requirements.* The Commissioner, in revenue rulings, notices and other publications of general applicability, may make any modification to, or issue such additional requirements for the application of, the rules contained in this Q&A-7 as may be necessary to insure proper compliance with the intent of such rules.

(f) *Example.* The provisions of paragraph (c) of this Q&A-7 are illustrated by the following example:

Example 1. Assume that an employer with 1,000 employees maintains a cafeteria plan under which the employees may elect among several benefit options, including insured health plans and HMOs. The plan provides that the required premiums or contributions for the benefits are to be made by salary reduction. Even though the plan may characterize employees' premium payments and other contributions as flexible spending contributions or credits, the operation of a cafeteria plan to permit employees' contributions to be made on a salary reduction basis does not, standing alone, cause the plan (or any benefit thereunder) to be treated as a flexible spending arrangement.

Example 2. Assume that an employer with 1,000 employees maintains a cafeteria plan under which the employees may elect, among other benefits, a level of coverage under an arrangement that will reimburse medical expenses incurred during a year up to the specified amount elected by the employee. The maximum amount of reimbursement that can be deducted for a year is $5,000. Each employee's premium for such coverage is equal to the maximum reimbursement amount selected by the employee. Such an arrangement is a health FSA. [Reg. § 1.125-2.]

[¶ 20,119 Reserved.—Proposed Reg. §§ 1.406-1 and 1.407-1, relating to plans of certain subsidiaries, were formerly reproduced at this point. The final regulations appear at ¶ 11,961 and 12,011.]

[¶ 20,120 Reserved.—Proposed Reg. §§ 1.46-1, 1.50A-1, 1.72-17, 1.72-17A, 1.401-13, 1.401-14, 1.401(e)-1, 1.401(e)-2, 1.401(e)-3, 1.401(e)-4, 1.401(e)-5, 1.401(e)-6, 1.404(e)-1 and 1.404(e)-1A, relating to contributions to pension, profit-sharing, etc., plans on behalf of self-employed individuals and shareholder-employees were formerly reproduced at this point. The final regulations appear at ¶ 11,207, 11,207A, 11,713, 11,724, 11,724A, 11,724B, 11,724C, 11,724D, 11,724E, 11,868, and 11,869.]

¶ 20,121

Proposed regulations— Treatment of certain lump sum distributions.—Reproduced below are proposed amendments to conform regulations under sections 62, 72, 101, 122, 402, 403, 405, 652, and 1304 of the Internal Revenue Code of 1954 to the provisions of the Employee Retirement Income Security Act (P.L. 93-406), relating to taxation of certain lump sum distributions. The proposed regulations will provide a method of computing the capital gain portion of a lump sum distribution and will impose a separate tax on the ordinary income portion of a lump sum distribution. The ordinary income portion of a distribution to a recipient will be deductible from gross income equal to the amount of the ordinary income portion of the distribution included in the recipient's gross income. The proposed changes also provide a special method for computing tax on a distribution which includes an annuity contract. Under the proposed changes, a distribution to multiple recipients cannot qualify as a lump sum distribution unless the amount of the distribution is otherwise includible in the income of the individual in respect of whom the distribution was made under the judicial doctrines of assignment of income or constructive receipt. Finally, the proposed regulations redefine "active participation," as it relates to an employee in a particular plan who receives a lump sum distribution.

The proposed regulations were published in the Federal Register of April 30, 1975 at 40 F.R. 18798. Official corrections, published in the Federal Register of May 23, 1975 (40 F.R. 22548), have been made in place in the proposed regulations.

Back references: ¶ 3736 and 3754.

Notice is hereby given that the regulations set forth in tentative form [below] are proposed to be prescribed by the Commissioner of Internal Revenue, with the approval of the Secretary of the Treasury or his delegate. Prior to the final adoption of such regulations, consideration will be given to any comments pertaining thereto which are submitted in writing (preferably six copies) to the Commissioner of Internal Revenue, Attention: CC:LR:T, Washington, D.C. 20224, by June 16, 1975. Pursuant to 26 CFR 601.601(b), designations of material as confidential or not to be disclosed, contained in such comments, will not be accepted. Thus, a person submitting written comments should not include therein material that he considers to be confidential or inappropriate for disclosure to the public. It will be presumed by the Internal Revenue Service that every written comment submitted to it in response to this notice of proposed rule making is intended by the person submitting it to be subject in its entirety to public inspection and copying in accordance with the procedures of 26 CFR 601.702(d)(9). Any person submitting written comments who desires an opportunity to comment orally at a public hearing on these proposed regulations should submit his request, in writing, to the Commissioner by June 16, 1975. In such case, a public hearing will be held, and notice of the time, place, and date will be published in a subsequent issue of the Federal Register unless the person or persons who have requested a hearing withdraw their requests for a hearing before notice of the hearing has been filed with the Office of the Federal Register. The proposed regulations are to be issued under the authority contained in sections 402(a)(2), 402(e) and 7805 of the Internal Revenue Code of 1954 (88 Stat. 990, 987 and 68A Stat. 917; 26 U.S.C. 402(a)(2), 402(e), 7805).

(Signed) Donald C. Alexander

Commissioner of Internal Revenue

Preamble

This document proposes amendments to the Income Tax Regulations (26 CFR Part 1) in order to conform the regulations under sections 62, 72, 101, 122, 402, 403, 405, 652, and 1304 of the Internal Revenue Code of 1954 to the provisions of section 2005 of the Employee Retirement Income Security Act of 1974 (Public Law 93-406, 88 Stat. 987), relating to taxation of certain lump sum distributions.

The amendments proposed relating to sections 62, 72, 101, 122, 403, 405, 652, and 1304 of the Code merely conform the regulations under those sections to the changes in the taxation of a lump sum distribution under section 402 of the Code, as amended by section 2005(a) of the Act.

Under section 402(a)(2) of the Code, as amended, a method of computing the capital gain portion of a lump sum distribution is provided. In general, the capital gain portion of a lump sum distribution will be an amount equal to the product of the total taxable amount of the lump sum distribution and a fraction, the numerator of which is the number of calendar years of active participation before January 1, 1974, and the denominator of which is the total number of calendar years of active participation.

Under section 402(e)(1) of the Code, as amended, a separate tax is imposed on the ordinary income portion of a lump sum distribution.

Under section 402(e)(2) of the Code, as amended, a special rule is provided for computing the separate tax on the ordinary income portion of a lump sum distribution if there have been one or more lump sum distributions after December 31, 1973, made with respect to the recipient within the 6-taxable-year period ending on the last day of the taxable year of the recipient in which the distribution is made.

Under section 402(e)(3) of the Code, as amended, a deduction is allowed from gross income equal to the amount of the ordinary income portion of the distribution included in the recipient's gross income.

Under section 402(e)(4) of the Code, as amended, definitions and special rules are provided for computing the separate tax, including the definition of a lump sum distribution and the computation of the ordinary income portion of a lump sum distribution.

Under proposed § 1.402(e)-2(c)(1), a special method for computing the separate tax on a distribution including an annuity contract is provided. In such a case, the adjusted total taxable amount must be determined. For taxable years beginning before January 1, 1975, the adjusted total taxable amount is defined as the sum of the total taxable amount of the lump sum distribution for the taxable year, and the current actuarial value of annuity contracts distributed to the recipient reduced by the portion of the net amount contributed by the employee which is allocable to the annuity contract. For taxable years beginning after December 31, 1974, the adjusted total taxable amount is defined as the sum of the total taxable amount of the lump sum distribution for the taxable year, and the current actuarial value of annuity contracts distributed to the recipient reduced by the excess of the net amount contributed by the employee over the cash and other property distributed.

Under proposed § 1.402(e)-2(d)(1) a distribution to multiple recipients (except a payment or distribution solely to two or more trusts) cannot qualify as a lump sum distribution unless the amount of the distribution is otherwise includible in the income of the individual in respect of whom the distribution was made under the judicial doctrines of assignment of income or constructive receipt of income.

Under proposed § 1.402(e)-2(d)(3), the term "active participation" is defined so that active participation commences with the first month in which an employee becomes a participant under the plan and ends with the earliest of (1) the month in which the employee receives a lump sum distribution under the plan, (2) in the case of an employee without regard to section 401(e)(1), the month in which the employee separates from the service of the employer, (3) the month in which the employee dies, or (4) in the case of a self-employed individual who receives a lump sum distribution on account of disability, the first month in which he becomes disabled.

It is contemplated that upon adoption of the proposed amendments the Temporary Income Tax Regulations under section 402(e)(4)(B) (§ 11.402(e)(4)(B-1) will be revoked.

Proposed amendments to the regulations

In order to conform the Income Tax Regulations (26 CFR Part 1) to the provisions of section 2005 of the Employee Retirement Income Security Act of 1974 (Public Law 93-406, 88 Stat. 987), such regulations are amended as follows:

[INCOME TAX REGULATIONS]

Paragraph 1. Section 1.62 is amended by adding a new paragraph (11) at the end thereof and revising the historical note. These added and revised provisions read as follows:

* * *

[Asterisks represent 1954 Code Sec. 62 as amended by sec. 7(b), Self-Employed Individuals Tax Retirement Act 1962 (76 Stat. 828); sec. 213(b) Rev. Act 1964 (78 Stat. 52); sec. 2005(c)(9) Employee Retirement Income Security Act 1974 (88 Stat. 992)]

Par. 2 Reserved. Proposed Reg. § 1.62-1(c)(14), on the deduction for the ordinary income portion of lump-sum distributions, was formerly reproduced at this point. The final regulation appears at ¶ 11,181.

Par. 3. Subdivision (i) of § 1.72-4(a)(1) is amended by deleting "72(o)" and inserting in lieu thereof "72(n)". As amended, § 1.724(a)(1)(i) reads as follows:

§ 1.72-4 Exclusion ratio.

(a) *General rule.* (1)(i) To determine the proportionate part of the total amount received each year as an annuity which is excludable from the gross income of a recipient in the taxable year of receipt (other than amounts received under (A) certain employee annuities described in section 72(d) and § 1.72-13, or (B) certain annuities described in section 72(n) and § 1.122-1), an exclusion ratio is to be determined for each contract. In general, this ratio is determined by dividing the investment in the contract as found under § 1.72-6 by the expected return under such contract as found under § 1.72-5. Where a single consideration is given for a particular contract which provides for two or more annuity elements, an exclusion ratio shall be determined for the contract as a whole by dividing the investment in such contract by the aggregate of the expected returns under all the annuity elements provided thereunder. However, where the provisions of paragraph (b)(3) of § 1.72-2 apply to payments received under such a contract, see paragraph (b)(3) of § 1.72-6.

Par. 4. Section 1.72-13(e)(3) is amended by deleting "72(o)" and inserting in lieu thereof "72(n)". As amended § 1.72-13(e)(3) reads as follows:

§ 1.72-13 Special rule for employee contributions recoverable in three years.

* * *

(e) *Inapplicability of section 72(d) and this section.* Section 72(d) and this section do not apply to: * * *

(3) Amounts paid to an annuitant under chapter 73 of title 10 of the United States Code with respect to which section 72(n) and § 1.122-1 apply.

Par. 5. Section 1.101 is amended by revising subsection (b)(2)(B) and the historical note. As amended, these revised provisions read as follows:

* * *

[Asterisks represent 1954 Code Sec. 101 as amended by sec. 23(d), Technical Amendments Act 1958 (72 Stat. 1622); sec. 7(c), Self-Employed Individuals Tax Retirement Act 1962 (80 Stat. 32); sec. 101(j)(1), Tax Reform Act 1969 (Public Law 91-172, 83 Stat. 655); sec. 2005(c)(15), Employee Retirement Income Security Act 1974 (88 Stat. 992)]

Par. 6. Paragraph (d) of § 1.101-2 is amended by revising subparagraph (3)(i) and examples (2), (3), and (4) of subparagraph (ii) to read as follows:

§ 1.101-2 Employees' death benefits.

* * *

(d) *Nonforfeitable rights.* * * *

(3)(i) Notwithstanding the rule stated in subparagraph (d)(1) of this paragraph and illustrated in subparagraph (2) of this section, the exclusion from gross income provided by section 101(b) applies to a lump sum distribution (as defined in section 402(e)(4)(A) and the regulations thereunder) with respect to which the deceased employee possessed, immediately before his death, a nonforfeitable right to receive the amounts while living (see section 101(b)(2)(B)(i) and (ii)). See paragraph (d)(4) of this section relating to the exclusion of amounts which are received under annuity contracts purchased by certain exempt organizations and with respect to which the deceased employee possessed, immediately before his death, a nonforfeitable right to receive the amounts while living.

(ii) The application of the provisions of paragraph (d)(3)(i) of this section may be illustrated by the following examples:

Example (2). The trustee of the X Corporation noncontributory, "qualified," profit-sharing plan is required under the provisions of the plan to pay to the beneficiary of B, an employee of the X Corporation who died on July 1, 1974, the benefit due on account of the death of B. The provisions of the profit-sharing plan give each participating employee, in case of termination of employment, a 10 percent vested interest in the amount accumulated in his account for each of the first 10 years of participation in the plan, but, in case of death, the entire balance to the credit of the participant's account is to be paid to his beneficiary. At the time of B's death he had been a participant for five years. The accumulation in his account was $8,000 and the amount which would have been distributable to him in the event of termination of employment was $4,000 (50 percent of $8,000). After his death, $8,000 is paid to his beneficiary in a lump sum. (it may be noted that these are the same facts as in example (5) of subparagraph (2) of this paragraph except that the employee has been a participant for five years instead of three and the plan is a "qualified" plan.) It is immaterial that the employee had a nonforfeitable right to $4,000 because the payment of the $8,000 to the beneficiary is the payment of a lump sum distribution to which subdivision (i) of this subparagraph applies. Assuming no other death benefits are involved, the beneficiary may exclude $5,000 of the $8,000 payment from gross income.

Example (3). The facts are the same as in example (2) except that the beneficiary is entitled to receive only the $4,000 to which the employee had a nonforfeitable right and elects, 30 days after B's death, to receive it over a period of ten years. Because the distribution is not a lump sum distribution and because B's interest is nonforfeitable, no exclusion from gross income is allowable with respect to the $4,000.

Example (4). The X Corporation instituted a trust, forming part of a "qualified" profit-sharing plan for its employees, the cost thereof being borne entirely by the corporation. The plan provides, in part, that if an employee leaves the employ of the corporation, either voluntarily or involuntarily, before retirement, 10 percent of the account balance provided for the employee in the trust fund will be paid to the employee for each of the first 10 years of service. The plan further provides that if an employee dies before reaching retirement age, his beneficiary will receive a percentage of the account balance provided for the employee in the trust fund, on the same basis as shown in the preceding sentence. A, an employee of the X Corporation for 5 years, died before attaining retirement age while in the employ of the corporation. At the time of his death, $15,000 was the account balance provided for him in the trust fund. His beneficiary receives $7,500 in a lump sum, an amount equal to 50 percent of the account balance provided for A's retirement. The beneficiary may exclude from gross income (assuming no other death benefits are involved) $5,000 of the $7,500, since the latter amount constitutes a lump sum distribution to which subdivision (i) of this subparagraph applies.

Par. 7. Section 1.122 is amended by deleting "72(o)" in section 122(b)(2) and inserting in lieu thereof "72(n)". As amended, §1.122(b)(2) reads as follows:

* * *

[Asterisks represent 1954 Code Sec. 122 as added by Sec. 1(a)(1), Act of Mar. 8, 1966 (80 Stat. 32); as amended by sec. 2005(c)(10), Employed Retirement Income Security Act 1974 (88 Stat. 992)]

Par. 8. Section 1.122-1 is amended by deleting "72(o)" each place it appears and inserting in lieu thereof "72(n)". As amended, §1.122-1(b)(2)(ii) and examples (2) and (3) of §1.122-1(d) read as follows:

§ *1.122-1 Applicable rules relating to certain reduced uniformed services retirement pay.*

* * *

(b) *Rule applicable after December 31, 1965*

(2)

(ii) Upon the death of a member or former member of the uniformed services, where the "consideration for the contract" (as described in paragraph (b)(2)(iii) of this section) has not been excluded in whole or in part from gross income under section 122(b) and (b)(2)(i) of this section, the survivor of such member who is receiving an annuity under chapter 73 of title 10 of the United States Code shall, after December 31, 1965, exclude from gross income under section 72(n) and this subdivision such annuity payments received after December 31, 1965, until there has been so excluded annuity payments equalling the portion of the "consideration for the contract" not previously excluded under paragraph (b)(2)(i) of this section.

* * *

(d) *Examples.* The rules discussed in paragraph (a) of this section may be illustrated by the following examples:

* * *

Example (2). Assume the facts in Example (1) except that A retires on disability resulting from active service and his disability is rated at 40 percent. The entire amount of disability retirement pay, prior to and including 1966, is excludable from gross income under sections 104(a)(4) and 105(d), and in 1966, section 122(a). Assume further that A attains retirement age on December 31, 1966, dies on January 1, 1967, and his widow then begins receiving a survivor annuity under the Retired Serviceman's Family Protection Plan (10 U.S.C. 1431). A's widow may exclude from gross income in 1967 and 1968 under section 72(n) and paragraph (b)(2)(ii) of this section, the $1,800 of "consideration for the contract" i.e., the reductions in 1963, 1964, and 1965 to provide the survivor annuity. Thus, A's widow will exclude all of the survivor annuity she receives in 1967 ($1,350) and $450 of the $1,350 annuity received in 1968. In addition, if A had not attained retirement age at the time of his death, his widow would, under section 101 and paragraph (a)(2) of §1.101-2, exclude up to $5,000 subject to the limitations of paragraph (b)(2)(ii) of this section.

Example (3). Assume, in the previous example, that A dies on January 1, 1965, and his widow then begins receiving a survivor annuity. Assume further that A's widow is entitled to exclude under section 72(b) $1,000 of the $1,350 she received in 1965. Under section 72(n) and paragraph (b)(2)(ii) of this section, A's widow for 1966 will exclude the $200 remaining consideration for the contract ($1,200 – $1,000) and will include $1,150 of the survivor annuity in gross income.

* * *

Par. 9. Section 1.402(a) is amended by revising subparagraph (2) and the historical note. As amended, these revised provisions read as follows:

* * *

[Asterisks represent 1954 Code Sec. 402(a) as amended by Sec. 4(c) Self-Employed Individuals Tax Retirement Act 1962 (76 Stat. 825); sec. 221(c)(1), Rev. Act 1964 (78 Stat. 75); sec. 2005(b)(1), Employee Retirement Income Security Act 1974 (88 Stat. 990)]

Par. 10. Section 1.402(a)-1 is amended by revising paragraphs (a)(1)(ii), (a)(1)(iii), (a)(2), (a)(5), (a)(6), (a)(7), (a)(9), and (b)(1) to read as follows:

§ *1.402(a)-1 Taxability of beneficiary under a trust which meets the requirements of section 401(a).*

(a) *In general.* (1) * * *

(ii) The provisions of section 402(a) relate only to distribution by a trust which is described in section 401(a) and which is exempt under section 501(a) for the taxable year of the trust in which the distribution is made. With three exceptions, the distribution from such an exempt trust when received or made available is taxable to the distributee or recipient to the extent provided in section 72 (relating to annuities). First, for taxable years beginning before January 1, 1964, section 72(e)(3) (relating to the treatment of certain lump sums), as in effect before such date, shall not apply to such distributions. For taxable years beginning after December 31, 1963, such distributions may be taken into account in computations under sections 1301 through 1305 (relating to income averaging). For treatment of such total distributions, see paragraph (a)(6) of this section. Secondly, if the taxable year ends after December 31, 1969 and begins before January 1, 1974, the portion of the distribution treated as long-term capital gain is subject to the limitation under section 402(a)(5), as in effect on December 31, 1973. Thirdly, for taxable years beginning after December 31, 1973, a certain portion, described in section 402(a)(2), of a lump sum distribution, as defined in section 402(e)(4)(A) is taxable as long-term capital gain and a certain portion, described in section 402(e)(4)(E), may be taxable under section 402(e). For the treatment of such lump sum distributions, see paragraph (a)(9) of this section. Under certain circumstances, an amount representing the unrealized appreciation in the value of the securities of the employer is excludable from gross income for the year of distribution. For the rules relating to such exclusion, see paragraph (b) of this section. Furthermore, the exclusion provided by section 105(b) is applicable to a distribution from a trust described in section 401(a) and exempt under section 501(a) if such distribution constitutes wages or payments in lieu of wages for a period during which an employee is absent from work on account of a personal injury or sickness. See §1.72-15 for the rules relating to the tax treatment of accident or health benefits received under a plan to which section 72 applies.

(iii) Except as provided in paragraph (b) of this section, a distribution of property (other than an annuity contract) by a trust described in section 401(a) and exempt under section 501(a) shall be taken into account by the recipient at its fair market value. For valuation of an annuity contract, see §1.402(e)-2(c)(1)(ii)(F).

(2) If a trust described in section 401(a) and exempt under section 501(a) purchases an annuity contract for an employee and distributes it to the employee in a year for which the trust is exempt, and the contract contains a cash surrender value which may be available to an employee by surrendering the contract, such cash surrender value will not be considered income to the employee unless and until the contract is surrendered. For the rule as to nontransferability of annuity contracts issued after 1962, see paragraph (b)(1) of §1.401-9. However, the distribution of an annuity contract must be treated as a lump sum distribution under section 402(e) for purposes of determining the separate tax imposed under section 402(e)(1)(A). If, however, the contract distributed by such exempt trust is a retirement income, endowment, or other life insurance contract and is distributed after October 26, 1956, the entire cash value of such contract at the time of distribution must be included in the distributee's income in accordance with the provisions of section 402(a), except to the extent that, within 60 days after the distribution of such contract, (i) all or any portion of such value is irrevocably converted into a contract under which no part of any proceeds payable on death at any time would be excludable under section 101(a) (relating to life insurance proceeds), or (ii) such contract is treated as a rollover contribution under section 402(a)(5), as in effect after December 31, 1973. If the contract distributed by such trust is a transferable annuity contract issued after 1962, or a retirement income, endowment, or other life insurance contract which is distributed after 1962 (whether or not transferable), then notwithstanding the preceding sentence the entire cash value of the contract is includible in the distributee's gross income, unless within such 60 days such contract is also made nontransferable.

(5) If pension or annuity payments or other benefits are paid or made available to the beneficiary of a deceased employee or a deceased retired employee by a trust described in section 401(a) which is exempt under section 501(a), such amounts are taxable in accordance with the rules of section 402(a) and this section. In case such amounts are taxable under section 72, the "investment in the contract" shall be determined by reference to the amount contributed by the employee and by applying the applicable rules of sections 72 and 101(b)(2)(D). In case the amounts paid to, or includible in the gross income of, the beneficiaries of the deceased employee or deceased retired employee constitute a distribution to which paragraph (6) or (9) (whichever

applies) of this section is applicable the extent to which the distribution is taxable is determined by reference to the contributions of the employee, by reference to any prior distributions which were excludable from gross income as a return of employee contributions, and by applying the applicable rules of sections 72 and 101(b).

(6) This subparagraph applies in the case of a total distribution made in a taxable year of the distributee or payee ending before January 1, 1970.

(i) If the total distributions payable with respect to any employee under a trust described in section 401(a) which in the year of distribution is exempt under section 501(a) are paid to, or includible in the gross income of, the distributee within one taxable year of the distributee on account of the employee's death or other separation from the service, or death after such separation from service, the amount of such distribution, to the extent it exceeds the net amount contributed by the employee, shall be considered a gain from the sale or exchange of a capital asset held for more than six months. The total distributions payable are includible in the gross income of the distributee within one taxable year if they are made available to such distributee and the distributee fails to make a timely election under section 72(h) to receive an annuity in lieu of such total distributions. The "net amount contributed by the employee" is the amount actually contributed by the employee plus any amounts considered to be contributed by the employee under the rules of section 72(f), 101(b), and paragraph (a)(3) of this section, reduced by any amounts theretofore distributed to him which were excludable from gross income as a return of employee contributions. See, however, paragraph (b) of this section for rules relating to the exclusion of amounts representing net unrealized appreciation in the value of securities of the employer corporation. In addition, all or part of the amount otherwise includible in gross income under this paragraph by a nonresident alien individual in respect of a distribution by the United States under a qualified pension plan may be excludable from gross income under section 402(a)(4). For rules relating to such exclusion, see paragraph (c) of this section. For additional rules relating to the treatment of total distributions described in this subdivision in the case of a nonresident alien individual, see sections 871 and 1441 and the regulations thereunder.

(7) The capital gains treatment provided by section 402(a)(2), as in effect for taxable years beginning before January 1, 1974, and subparagraph (a)(6) of this section is not applicable to distributions paid during such years to a distributee to the extent such distributions are attributable to contributions made on behalf of an employee while he was a self-employed individual in the business with respect to which the plan was maintained. For the taxation of such amounts, see §1.72-18. For the rules for determining the amount attributable to contributions on behalf of an employee while he was self-employed, see paragraphs (b)(4) and (c)(2) of such section.

* * *

(9) For taxable years beginning after December 31, 1973, in the case of a lump sum distribution (as defined in section 402(e)(4)(A)) made to a recipient which is an individual, estate, or trust, so much of the total taxable amount (as defined in section 402(e)(4)(D) and §1.402(e)-2(d)(2)) of such lump sum distribution as is equal to the product of such total taxable amount multiplied by a fraction—

(i) The numerator of which is the number of calendar years of active participation (as determined under §1.402(e)-2(d)(3)(ii)) by the employee in such plan before January 1, 1974, and

(ii) The denominator of which is the number of calendar years of active participation (as determined under §1.402(e)-2(d)(3)(ii)) by the employee in such plan, shall be treated as gain from the sale or exchange of a capital asset held for more than six months. For purposes of this subparagraph, in the case of an individual who at no time during his participation under the plan is an employee within the meaning of section 401(c)(1), determination of whether any distribution is a lump sum distribution shall be made without regard to the requirement that an election be made under section 402(e)(4)(B) and §1.402(e)-3.

(b) *Distributions including securities of the employer corporation*—(1) *In general.* (i) If a trust described in section 401(a) which is exempt under section 501(a) makes a distribution to a distributee, and such distribution includes securities of the employer corporation, the amount of any net unrealized appreciation in such securities shall be excluded from the distributee's income in the year of such distribution to the following extent:

(A) If the distribution constitutes a total distribution to which the regulations of paragraph (a)(6) of this section are applicable, or if the distribution would constitute a lump sum distribution as defined in

section 402(e)(4)(A) (without regard to section 402(e)(4)(H)), the amount to be excluded is the entire net unrealized appreciation attributable to that part of the distribution which consists of securities of the employer corporation; and

(B) If the distribution is other than a total distribution to which paragraph (a)(6) of this section is applicable, or if the distribution is other than a lump sum distribution as defined in section 402(e)(4)(A) (without regard to section 402(e)(4)(H)), the amount to be excluded is that portion of the net unrealized appreciation in the securities of the employer corporation which is attributable to the amount considered to be contributed by the employee to the purchase of such securities.

The amount of net unrealized appreciation which is excludable under the regulations of (b)(1)(i)(A) and (B) of this section shall not be included in the basis of the securities in the hands of the distributee at the time of distribution for purposes of determining gain or loss on their subsequent disposition. Further, the amount of net unrealized appreciation which is not included in the basis of the securities in the hands of the distributee at the time of distribution shall be considered as a gain from the sale or exchange of a capital asset held for more than six months to the extent that such appreciation is realized in a subsequent taxable transaction. However, if the net gain realized by the distributee in a subsequent taxable transaction exceeds the amount of the net unrealized appreciation at the time of distribution, such excess shall constitute a long-term or short-term capital gain depending upon the holding period of the securities in the hands of the distributee.

(ii) (A) For purposes of section 402(a) and of this section, the term "securities" means only shares of stock and bonds or debentures issued by a corporation with interest coupons or in registered form, and the term "securities of the employer corporation" includes securities of a parent or subsidiary corporation (as defined in subsections (e) and (f) of section 425) of the employer corporation.

(B) For purposes of this paragraph, for taxable years beginning after December 31, 1973, the term "distributee means recipient".

Par. 11. Section 1.402(e) is amended to read as follows:

* * *

[Asterisks represent 1954 Code Sec. 402]

Par. 12. There are added immediately after §1.402(e)-1 the following new sections:

§1.402(e)-2 *Treatment of certain lump sum distributions made after 1973.*

(a) *In general.* (1) *Tax imposed; deduction allowed.* For a taxable year, at the election of the recipient of a lump sum distribution, the ordinary income portion of such distribution is subject to the tax imposed by section 402(e)(1)(A) (hereinafter referred to as the "separate tax") and, under section 402(e)(3), an amount equal to such portion is allowable as a deduction from gross income (see section 62 (11), as added by sec. 2005(c)(9) of Pub. L. No. 93-406, and the regulations thereunder) to the extent such portion is included in the gross income of the taxpayer for such year. The separate tax imposed by section 402(e)(1)(A) is an addition to the tax otherwise imposed under chapter 1 of the Code and may be elected whether or not the tax otherwise imposed by such chapter is computed under part I of subchapter Q of such chapter (relating to income averaging). This section applies with respect to distributions or payments made, or made available, to a recipient after December 31, 1973, in taxable years of the recipient beginning after that date.

(2) *Cross references*—(i) *Computation; ordinary method.* Paragraph (b) of this section provides rules with respect to a distribution which is not a multiple distribution, and does not include an annuity contract.

(ii) *Computation; special method (distribution including an annuity contract).* Paragraph (c)(1) of this section provides rules with respect to a distribution which is not a multiple distribution and which includes an annuity contract.

(iii) *Computation; special method (multiple distribution).* Paragraph (c)(2) of this section provides rules with respect to a distribution which is a multiple distribution.

(iv) *Lump sum distribution.* For the definition of the term "lump sum distribution", see paragraph (d)(1) of this section.

(v) *Total taxable amount.* For the definition of the term "total taxable amount," see paragraph (d)(2) of this section.

(vi) *Ordinary income portion.* For the definition of the term "ordinary income portion," see paragraph (d)(3) of this section.

(vii) *Multiple distribution.* For the definition of the term "multiple distribution," see paragraph (c)(2)(ii)(E) of this section.

(viii) *Election.* For rules relating to the election of lump sum distribution treatment under this section, see §1.402(e)-3.

(b) *Ordinary method*—(1) *In general.* In the case of a distribution which is not included in a multiple distribution, and which does not include an annuity contract, if the recipient elects (under §1.402(e)-3) to treat such distribution as a lump sum distribution under this section, the tax imposed by section 402(e)(1)(A) for the recipient's taxable year is an amount equal to the initial separate tax determined under subparagraph (2) of this paragraph) for such taxable year, multiplied by a fraction—

(i) The numerator of which is the ordinary income portion (determined under paragraph (d)(3) of this section) of such lump sum distribution for such taxable year, and

(ii) The denominator of which is the total taxable amount (determined under paragraph (d)(2) of this section) of such lump sum distribution for such taxable year.

(2) *Computation of initial separate tax.* For purposes of subparagraph (1) of this paragraph, the initial separate tax is an amount equal to 10 times the tax which would be imposed by section 1(c) (relating to unmarried individuals (other than surviving spouses and heads of households)) if the recipient were an individual referred to in such section and the taxable income referred to in such section were an amount equal to one-tenth of the excess of—

(i) The total taxable amount (determined under paragraph (d)(2) of this section) of the lump sum distribution, over

(ii) The minimum distribution allowance (determined under paragraph (b)(3) of this section).

(3) *Computation of minimum distribution allowance.* For purposes of paragraph (b)(2)(ii) of this section, the minimum distribution allowance is the lesser of—

(i) $10,000, or

(ii) One-half of the total taxable amount of the lump sum distribution for the taxable year,

reduced (but not below zero) by 20 percent of the excess (if any) of such total taxable amount over $20,000.

(4) *Example.* The application of this paragraph is illustrated by the following example:

Example. (i) On December 22, 1975, A separates from the service of the M Corporation and receives a lump sum distribution of $65,000 from the M Corporation's contributory qualified plan. A's contributions to the plan as an employee were $15,000. A has been an active participant in the plan since February 20, 1966. A and his wife, B, are each age 50. Neither received an annuity contract from a qualified plan in 1974 or 1975. Neither received a lump sum distribution in 1974. A and B file a joint return for the calendar year 1975. Their income for 1975 consists of A's salary of $15,000 from the M Corporation and of $5,000 from the N Corporation. Their deductions for 1975 (other than deductions attributable to the distribution) consist of itemized deductions of $3,000. Their average base period income (determined under section 1302(b)(1)) for the four preceding taxable years (1971 through 1974) is $14,000. Assuming there are no changes in the applicable tax law after 1974, A and B's income tax liability for 1975 is computed as follows.

(ii) A and B's gross income for 1975 is $70,000, computed by adding the total taxable amount of the lump sum distribution (determined under paragraph (d)(2) of this section) to their otherwise computed gross income [$15,000 + $5,000 + ($65,000 − $15,000)]. Their adjusted gross income for 1975 is $40,000 [$70,000 − ($10,000 + $20,000)] computed by reducing their gross income by the sum of the lump sum distribution deduction allowed by section 402(e)(3) with respect to the ordinary income portion of the distribution [$50,000 x 24/120] and the deduction allowed by section 1202 with respect to the capital gains portion of the distribution [($50,000 × 96/120) x 0.5]. A and B's joint taxable income is $35,500 (their itemized deductions are $3,000 and their personal exemptions total $1,500). A and B choose to apply the income averaging rules of section 1301 for 1975. Thus, A and B's income tax liability not including the separate tax on the ordinary income portion of the distribution is $8,828.

(iii) The minimum distribution allowance with respect to A's distribution is $4,000 [$10,000 − (($50,000 − $20,000) × 0.2)]. The initial separate tax on A's distribution is 10 times the tax imposed by section 1(c), computed as if the taxable income therein described were

$4,600   [$50,000 − $4,000].
—————————————
10

Thus, A's initial separate tax is $8,160. The separate tax on A's distribution is computed by multiplying the initial separate tax and the quotient of the ordinary income portion divided by the total taxable amount. Thus, the separate tax on A's distribution is $1,632 [$8,160 × $10,000/$50,000].

(iv) A and B's total income tax liability for 1975 is the sum of the income tax as otherwise determined and the separate tax. Thus, A and B's total income tax liability for 1975 is $10,460 [$8,828 + $1,632].

(c) *Special method*—(1) *Computation of separate tax on distribution including annuity contract and lump sum distribution*—(i) *Computation.* In the case of a distribution which is not included in a multiple distribution and which includes an annuity contract, if the recipient elects (under §1.402(e)-3) to treat the portion of such distribution not consisting of an annuity contract as a lump sum distribution under this section, the separate tax imposed by section 402(e)(l)(A) of the recipient's taxable year is the excess (if any) of the adjusted separate tax over the tax attributable to the annuity contract (determined under paragraph (c)(1)(iii) of this section).

(ii) *Definitions.* For purposes of this section—

(A) *Adjusted separate tax.* The adjusted separate tax is an amount equal to the adjusted initial separate tax multiplied by a fraction—

(*1*) The numerator of which is the ordinary income portion of the distribution, and

(*2*) The denominator of which is the total taxable amount (determined under paragraph (d)(2) of this section) of the lump sum distribution.

(B) *Adjusted initial separate tax.* The adjusted initial separate tax is an amount equal to 10 times the tax which would be imposed by section 1(c) (relating to unmarried individuals (other than surviving spouses and heads of households)) if the recipient were an individual referred to in such section and the taxable income referred to in such section were an amount equal to one-tenth of the excess of—

(*1*) the adjusted total taxable amount of the lump sum distribution, over

(*2*) the adjusted minimum distribution allowance.

(C) *Adjusted total taxable amount.* (*1*) For taxable years beginning before January 1, 1975, the adjusted total taxable amount is the sum of—

(*i*) The excess (if any) of the current actuarial value of annuity contracts distributed to the recipient, over the portion of the net amount contributed by the employee which is allocable to the contract, and

(*ii*) The total taxable amount (determined under paragraph (d)(2) of this section) of the lump sum distribution for the taxable year. For purposes of (c)(1)(ii)(C)(*1*)(*i*) of this section (*1*), the net amount contributed by the employee which is allocable to the contract is an amount equal to the amounts considered contributed by the employee under the plan (determined by applying sections 72(f) and 101(b), and paragraph (b) of §1.72-16) reduced by any amount theretofore distributed to the employee which were [sicl not includible in his gross income multiplied by a fraction, the numerator of which is the current actuarial value of the contract, and the denominator of which is the sum of such current actuarial value and the value of other property (including cash) distributed.

(*2*) For taxable years beginning after December 31, 1974, the adjusted total taxable amount is the sum of—

(*i*) The current actuarial value of annuity contracts distributed to the recipient, reduced by the excess, if any, of the net amount contributed by the employee (as defined in paragraph (d)(2)(ii)(A) of this section) over the cash and other property distributed, and

(*ii*) The total taxable amount (determined under paragraph (d)(2) of this section) of the lump sum distribution for the taxable year.

(D) *Adjusted ordinary income portion.* The adjusted ordinary income portion of a lump sum distribution is the amount which would be computed under (3) of paragraph (d)(3) of this section if "adjusted total taxable amount" is substituted for "total taxable amount" in such subparagraph.

(E) *Adjusted minimum distribution allowance.* The adjusted minimum distribution allowance is the lesser of—

(*1*) $10,000, or

(*2*) one-half of the adjusted total taxable amount of the lump sum distribution for the taxable year, reduced (but not below zero) by 20 percent of the excess (if any) of the adjusted total taxable amount over $20,000.

(F) *Current actuarial value.* The current actuarial value of an annuity contract is the greater of—

(1) The cash value of the annuity contract (determined without regard to any loans under the contract) on the date of distribution, or

(2) The amount determined under the appropriate tables contained in publication No. 861, entitled "Annuity Factors for Lump Sum Distributions."

(iii) *Tax attributable to an annuity contract.* For purposes of subdivision (i) of this subparagraph, the tax attributable to an annuity contract is the product of—

(A) The quotient of the adjusted ordinary income portion (determined under paragraph (c)(1)(ii)(D) of this section) of the lump sum distribution divided by the adjusted total taxable amount (determined under paragraph (c)(1)(ii)(C) of this section), and

(B) 10 times the tax which would be imposed by section 1(c) (relating to unmarried individuals (other than surviving spouses and heads of households)) if the recipient were an individual referred to in such section and the taxable income were an amount equal to one-tenth of the excess of—

(1) The current actuarial value of the annuity contract, over

(2) The adjusted minimum distribution allowance multiplied by a fraction—

(i) The numerator of which is the current actuarial value of the annuity contract, and

(ii) The denominator of which is the adjusted total taxable amount (determined under paragraph (c)(1)(ii) of this section).

(iv) *Examples.* The application of this subparagraph is illustrated by the following examples:

Example (1). (i) On December 29, 1975, A separates from the service of the M Corporation and receives a distribution of the balance to the credit of his account under the M Corporation's noncontributory qualified plan. The distribution consists of cash of $44,000, and an annuity contract with a current actuarial value of $6,000. A has been a participant in the plan since March 26, 1966. A and his wife, B, are each age 50. Neither received a previous distribution from a qualified plan. A and B file a joint return for 1975. Their income for 1975, other than the distribution, consists of A's salary from the M Corporation of $15,000 and of $5,000 from the N Corporation. Their deductions (other than deductions attributable to the distribution) consist of itemized deductions of $3,000. They are not otherwise permitted to use income averaging for 1975 under section 1301. Assuming there are no changes in the applicable tax law after 1974, A and B's income tax liability for 1975 is computed as follows.

(ii) A and B's gross income for 1975 is $64,000, computed by adding the total taxable amount (determined under paragraph (d)(2) of this section) of the lump sum distribution to their otherwise computed gross income [$15,000 + $5,000 + $44,000]. Their adjusted gross income for 1975 is $37,600 [$64,000 − ($8,800 + $17,600)], computed by reducing their gross income by the sum of the lump sum distribution deduction allowed by section 4o2(e)(3) with respect to the ordinary income portion of the distribution [$44,000 × 24/120] and the deduction allowed by section 1202 with respect to the capital gains portion of the distribution [($44,000 × 96/120) × 0.5]. A and B's taxable income for 1975 is $33.100 (their itemized deductions are $3,000 and their personal exemptions total $1,500).

Thus, A and B's income tax liability not including the separate tax on the ordinary income portion of the distribution is $9,122.

(iii) The adjusted total taxable amount of A's distribution is the sum of the current actuarial value of the annuity contract distributed and the total taxable amount of the lump sum distribution. Thus, the adjusted total taxable amount of A's distribution is $50,000 [$6,000 + $44,000]. The adjusted minimum distribution allowance with respect to A's distribution is the lesser of $10,000 or Y2 of the adjusted total taxable amount, reduced by 20 percent of the excess (if any) of the adjusted total taxable amount over $20,000. Thus, the adjusted minimum distribution allowance with respect to A's distribution is $4000 [$10,000 − (($50,000 − $20,000) x 0.2)1. The adjusted initial separate tax on A's distribution is computed by multiplying 10 times the tax imposed by section 1(c) computed as if the taxable income therein described were $4,600 [($50,000 − $4,000)/10]. Thus, A's adjusted initial separate tax is $3,160. The adjusted separate tax on A's distribution is computed by multiplying the adjusted initial separate tax by the quotient of the ordinary income portion divided by tide total taxable amount. Thus, the

adjusted separate tax on A's distribution is $1,632 ($8,160 × $8,800/$44,000). The tax attributable to the annuity contract is 10 times the tax that would be imposed by section 1(c) computed as if the taxable income of a person described therein were

$$\frac{\$552 \quad [\$6,000 - (\$4,000 \times (\$6,000/\$50,000))]}{10}$$

multiplied by the quotient described in the second preceding sentence. Thus, the tax attributable to the annuity contract is $156 [$778 × $8,800/$44,000]. The separate tax on A's distribution is computed by reducing the adjusted separate tax by the tax attributable to the annuity contract. Thus, the separate tax on A's distribution is $1,476 [$1,632 − $156].

(iv) A and B's total income tax liability for 1975 is the sum of their income tax liability, as otherwise determined, and the separate tax. Thus A and B's total income tax liability for 1975 is $10,598 [$9,122 + $1,476].

Example (2). (i) Assume the same facts as in example (1) except that the M Corporation's qualified plan is contributory and that A's contributions under the plan as an employee were $1,760, and the current actuarial value of the annuity contract which is distributed is $5,760.

(ii) A and B's gross income for 1975 is $62,240. computed by adding the total taxable amount (determined tinder paragraph (d)(2) of this section) of the lump sum distribution to their otherwise computed gross income [$15,000 + $5,000 + ($44.000 − $1.760)]. Their adjusted gross income for 1975 is $36,896 [$62,240 − ($8,448 + $16,896)1, computed by reducing their gross income by the sum of the lump sum distribution deduction allowed by section 402 (e)(3) with respect to the ordinary income portion of the distribution [$42,240 x 24/120] and the deduction allowed by section 1202 with respect to the capital gains portion of the distribution. [($42,240 × 96/120) x 0.5]. A and B's taxable income for 1975 is $32,396 (their itemized deductions are $3,000 and their personal exemptions total $1,500). Thus A and B's income tax liability not including the separate tax on the ordinary income portion of the distribution is $8,826.

(iii) The adjusted total taxable amount of A's distribution is the sum of the current actuarial value of the annuity contract distributed and the total taxable amount of the lump sum distribution. Thus, the adjusted total taxable amount of A's distribution is $48,000 [$5,760 + ($44,000 − $1,760)]. The adjusted minimum distribution allowance with respect to A's distribution is the lesser of $10,000 or 1/2 of the adjusted total taxable amount, reduced by 20 percent of the excess of the adjusted total taxable amount over $20,000. Thus, the adjusted minimum distribution allowance with respect to A's distribution is $4,400 [$10,000 − (($48,000 − $20,000) × 0.2)1. The adjusted initial separate tax on A's distribution is 10 times the tax imposed by section 1(c) computed as if the taxable income therein described were

$$\frac{\$4,360 \quad [(\$48,000 - \$4,400)].}{10}$$

Thus, A's adjusted initial separate tax is $7,656. The adjusted separate tax on A's distribution is computed by multiplying the adjusted initial separate tax by the quotient of the ordinary income portion divided by the total taxable amount. Thus, the adjusted separate tax on A's distribution is $1,531 [$7,656 x $8,448/$42,240I. The tax attributable to the annuity contract is 10 times the tax that would be imposed by section 1(c) computed as if the taxable income of a person therein described were

$$\frac{\$523 \quad [\$5,760 - (\$4,400 \text{ x } (\$5,760/\$48,000))]}{10}$$

multiplied by the quotient described in the second preceding sentence. Thus, the tax attributable to the annuity contract is $147 [$735 × $8,443/$42,240]. The separate tax on A's distribution is computed by reducing the adjusted separate tax by the tax attributable to the annuity contract. Thus, the separate tax on A's distribution is $1,384 [$1,531 − $147].

(iv) A and B's total income tax liability for 1975 is the sum of their income tax liability, as otherwise determined, and the separate tax. Thus A and B's total income tax liability for 1975 is $10,210 [$1,384 + $8,826].

Example (3). (i) On December 7, 1974 C separates from the service of P Corporation and receives a distribution of the balance to the credit of his account under the P Corporations contributory qualified plan. The distribution consists of cash of $44,000, and an annuity contract with a current actuarial value of $6,000. C has been a participant in the plan since February 20. 1965. C's contributions under the plan as an employee were $2.000. C and his wife, D, are each age 50. Neither received a previous distribution from a qualified plan. C and D file a joint return for 1974. Their income for 1974, other than the distribution, consists of C's salary from the P Corporation of $20,000. Their deductions (other than deductions attributable to the distribution) consist of itemized deductions of $3,000. They are not otherwise permitted to use income averaging for 1974 under section 1301. C and D's income tax liability for 1974 is computed as follows.

(ii) C and D's gross income for 1974 is $62,240, computed by adding the total taxable amount (determined under paragraph (d)(2) of this section) of the lump sum distribution to their otherwise computed gross income [$20,000 + ($44,000 – $1,760)] Their adjusted gross income for 1974 is $39,008 [$62,240 – ($4,224 + $19,008)], computed by reducing their gross income by the sum of the lump sum distribution deduction allowed by section 402(e)(3) with respect to the ordinary income portion of the distribution [$42,240 × 12/120] and the deduction allowed by section 1202 with respect to the capital gains portion of the distribution [($42,240 × 108/120) × 0.5]. C and D's taxable income for 1974 is $34,508 (their itemized deductions are $3,000 and their personal exemptions total $1,500). C and D's income tax liability for 1974 not including the separate tax on the ordinary income portion of the distribution is $9,713.

(iii) The adjusted total taxable amount of C's distribution is the sum of the current actuarial value of the annuity contract distributed and the total taxable amount of the lump sum distribution. Thus, the adjusted total taxable amount of C's distribution is $48.000 [($6,000 – $240) + ($44,000 – $1,760)]. The adjusted minimum distribution allowance with respect to C's distribution is the lesser of $10,000 or ½ of the adjusted total taxable amount, reduced by 20 percent of the excess of the adjusted total taxable amount over $20,000. Thus, the adjusted minimum distribution allowance with respect to C's distribution is $4,400 [$10,000 – (($48,000 – $20,000) × 0.2)]. The adjusted initial separate tax on C's distribution is 10 times the tax imposed by section 1(c) computed as if the taxable income therein described were

$$\$4,360 \qquad \frac{[(\$48,000 - \$4,400)]}{10}$$

Thus, C's adjusted 10 initial separate tax is $7,656. The adjusted separate tax on C's distribution is computed by multiplying the adjusted initial separate tax by the quotient of the ordinary income portion divided by the total taxable amount Thus, the adjusted separate tax on C's distribution is $766 ($7,656 x $4,224/$42,240). The tax attributable to the annuity contract is 10 times the tax imposed by section 1(c) computed as if the taxable income therein described were

$$\$360 \qquad \frac{[\$5,760 - (\$4,400 \times (\$5,760/\$48,000))]}{10},$$

multiplied by the quotient described in the second preceding sentence. Thus, the amount attributable to the annuity contract is $74 [$735 × ($4,224/$42,240)]. The separate tax on C's distribution is computed by reducing the adjusted separate tax by the tax attributable to the annuity contract. Thus, the separate tax on C's distribution is $692 ($766 – $74).

(iv) C and D's total income tax liability for 1974 is the sum of their income tax liability, as otherwise determined, and the separate tax. Thus, C and D's total income tax liability for 1974 is $10,405 [$9,713 + $692].

(2) *Computation of separate tax in case of multiple distribution—(i) Computation.* In the case of a payment or distribution which is included in a multiple distribution, the separate tax imposed on such multiple distribution by section 402(e)(1)(A) for the recipient's taxable year is the excess (if any) of the modified separate tax, over the sum of

(A) The aggregate amount of the separate tax imposed by section 402(e)(1)(A) paid during the lookback period, and

(B) The modified tax attributable to the annuity contract.

(ii) *Definitions.* For purposes of this section—(A) *Modified separate tax.* The term "modified separate tax" means an amount equal to the modified initial separate tax multiplied by a fraction

(1) The numerator of which is the sum of the ordinary income portions of the lump sum distributions made within the lookback period, and

(2) The denominator of which is the sum of the total taxable amounts of the lump sum distributions made within the lookback period.

(B) *Modified initial separate tax.* The modified initial separate tax is an amount equal to 10 times the tax which would be imposed by section 1(c) (relating to unmarried individuals (other than surviving

spouses and heads of households)) if the recipient were an individual referred to in such section and the taxable income referred to in such section were an amount equal to one-tenth of the excess of—

(1) The modified total taxable amount of the lump sum distribution. over

(2) The modified minimum distribution allowance.

(C) *Modified total taxable amount.* The modified total taxable amount is the sum of the total taxable amounts (determined under paragraph (d)(2) of this section) of the distributions made during the lookback period and, in the case of a distribution made during such period to which subparagraph (C)(1) of this section applied, the amount specified in paragraph (C)(1)(ii) (C)(1)(i) or (2)(i) of this paragraph, which ever is applicable.

(D) *Modified minimum distribution allowance.* The modified minimum distribution allowance is the lesser of

(1) $10,000, or

(2) one-half of the modified total taxable amount, reduced (but not below zero) by 20 percent of the excess of the modified total taxable amount over $20,000.

(E) *Multiple distribution.* A distribution or payment received during a taxable year of the recipient which begins with or within a lookback period and after December 31, 1973, is included in a multiple distribution for such lookback period if—

(*1*) Any part of such distribution or payment (i) is treated as a lump sum distribution under this section or (ii) consists of a contract which would constitute all or a part of a lump sum distribution (determined without regard to section 402(e)(4)(B) and §1.402(e)-3), except for the fact that it is an annuity contract, and

(*2*) a distribution or payment received in another such taxable year is treated as a lump sum distribution under this section. For purposes of this subdivision (E), if the recipient of a lump sum distribution is a trust and if a beneficiary of such trust is an employee with respect to the plan under which the distribution is made, or treated as the owner of such trust for purposes of subpart E of part I of subchapter J of chapter 1 of the Code (relating to grantors and others treated as substantial owners), then such employee or owner shall be treated as the sole recipient of the lump sum distribution. For purposes of this subdivision (E), the term "an employee with respect to the plan under which the distribution is made" means an individual who immediately before the distribution is made, is a participant in the plan under which the distribution is made.

(F) *Lookback period.* The lookback period with respect to any recipient is a period of 6 consecutive taxable years ending on the last day of the taxable year of the recipient in which a payment or distribution which is a multiple distribution is made.

(iii) *Modified tax attributable to an annuity contract.* For purposes of subdivision (i) of this subparagraph, the modified tax attributable to an annuity contract is equal to the product of—

(A) The quotient of the sum of the ordinary income portions (determined under paragraph (d)(3)) of the lump sum distributions received during the lookback period divided by the sum of the total taxable amounts (determined under paragraph (d)(2)) of the distributions made during the lookback period, and

(B) 10 times the tax which would be imposed by section 1(c) (relating to unmarried individuals (other than surviving spouses and heads of households)) if the recipient were an individual referred to in such section and the taxable income were an amount equal to one-tenth of the excess of—

(*1*) The sum of the amounts described in paragraph C (1)(ii)(C)(1)(i) or (2)(i) of this section in respect of the annuity contracts distributed during the lookback period, over

(2) the modified minimum distribution allowance multiplied by a fraction—

(i) The numerator of which is the sum of the amounts described in paragraph C(2)(iii)(B) in (1) of this section, and

(ii) the denominator of which is the modified total taxable amount (determined under paragraph (C)(2)(ii)(C) of this section).

(iv) The application of this subparagraph is illustrated by the following examples:

Example (1). (i) On December 7, 1976, A separates from the service of N Corporation and receives a distribution of the balance to the credit of his account under the N Corporation's noncontributory qualified plan. The distribution consists of cash of $4,000 and an annuity contract with a current actuarial value of $6,000. A has been a participant in the plan since October 13, 1967. A and his wife, B, are each age 50. A and B file a joint return for 1976. Their income for 1976, other than the distribution, consists of A's salary from N Corporation of $25,000 and interest income of $3,000. Their deductions (other than deductions attributable to the distribution) consist of itemized deductions of $2,100. They are not otherwise permitted to use income averaging for 1976 under section 1301. A received a distribution in 1975 from the M Corporation and elected lump sum treatment for such distribution. The ordinary income portion of such distribution was $10,000; the total taxable amount of such distribution was $50,000; the adjusted ordinary income portion and the adjusted total taxable amount of such distribution are the same as the ordinary income portion and the total taxable amount; and they paid a separate tax on such distribution of $1,632. Assuming there are no changes in the applicable tax law after 1974, A and B's income tax liability for 1976 is computed as follows:

(ii) A and B's gross income for 1976 is $32,000, computed by adding the total taxable amount (determined under paragraph (d)(2) of this section) of the lump sum distribution to their otherwise computed gross income [$25,000 + $3,000 + $4,000]. Their adjusted gross income for 1976 is $29,400 [$32,000 – ($1,200 + $1,400)], computed by reducing their gross income by the sum of the lump sum distribution deduction allowed by section 402(e)(3) with respect to the ordinary income portion of the distribution [$4,000 × 36/120] and the deduction allowed by section 1202 with respect to the capital gains portion of the distribution [($4,000 × (84/120)) × 0.5]. A and B's taxable income for 1976 is $25,800 (their itemized deductions are $2,100 and their personal exemptions total $1,500). Thus, A and B's income tax liability for 1976, not including the separate tax on the ordinary income portion of the distribution, is $6,308.

(iii) The adjusted total taxable amount of A's distribution for 1976 is the sum of the current actuarial value of the annuity contract distributed and the total taxable amount of the lump sum distribution. Thus, the adjusted total taxable amount of A's 1976 distribution is $10,000 [$6,000 + $4,000]. The modified total taxable amount is $60,000 [$50,000 + $10,000]. The modified minimum distribution allowance with respect to A's 1976 distribution is the lesser of $10,000 or 1/2 of the modified total taxable amount, reduced by 20 percent of the excess (if any) of the modified total taxable amount over $20,000. Thus, the modified minimum distribution allowance with respect to A's 1976 distribution is $2,000 [$10,000 – (($60,000 – $20,000) × 0.2)]. The modified initial separate tax on A's 1976 distribution is computed by multiplying 10 times the tax imposed by section 1(c) computed as if the taxable income therein described were $5,800

$$[\frac{[(\$60,000 - \$2,000)]}{10}]$$

Thus, A's modified initial separate tax is $10,680. The modified separate tax on A's 1976 distribution is computed by multiplying the modified initial separate tax by the quotient of the sum of the ordinary income portions of the lump sum distributions received during the lookback period divided by the sum of the total taxable amounts of each lump sum distribution made during such period. Thus, the modified separate tax on A's 1976 distribution is $2,215 [$10,680 × ($10,000 + $1,200)/ ($50,000 + $4,000)]. The modified tax attributable to the annuity contract is 10 times the tax imposed by section 1(c) computed as if the taxable income of a person described therein were $580

$$[\frac{[\$6,000 - ((\$6,000/\$60,000) \times \$2,000)]}{10}]$$

multiplied by the quotient described in the second preceding sentence. Thus, the modified tax attributable to the annuity contract is $170 [$820 × ($10,000 + $1,200)/($50,000 + $4,000)]. The separate tax on A's 1976 distribution is computed by reducing the modified separate tax by the sum of the separate tax paid during the lookback period, and the modified tax attributable to the annuity contract. Thus, the separate tax on A's 1976 distribution is $413 [$2,215 ($1,632 + $170)].

(iv) A and B's total income tax liability for 1976 is the sum of their income tax liability as otherwise determined, and the separate tax. Thus, A and B's total income tax liability for 1976 is $6,721 [$6,308 + $413].

Example (2). (i) Assume the same facts as in example (1) except that the N Corporation's qualified plan was contributory and that A's contributions under the plan as an employee were $800, and the current actuarial value of the annuity contract which is distributed is $4,800.

(ii) A and B's gross income for 1976 is $31,200, computed by adding the total taxable amount (determined under paragraph (d)(2) of this section) of the lump sum distribution to their otherwise computed

gross income [$25,000 + $3,000 + ($4,000 – $800)]. Their adjusted gross income for 1976 is $29,120 [$31,200 – ($960 + $1,120)] computed by reducing their gross income by the sum of the lump sum distribution deduction allowed by section 402(e)(3) with respect to the ordinary income portion of the distribution [$3,200 × 36/120] and the deduction allowed by section 1202 with respect to the capital gains portion of the distribution [($3,200 × 84/120) × 0.5]. A and B's taxable income for 1976 is $25,520, their itemized taxable deductions are $2,100 and their personal exemptions total $1,500. Thus, A and B's income tax liability for 1976, not including the separate tax on the ordinary income portion of the distribution, is $6,207.

(iii) The adjusted total taxable amount of A's distribution for 1976 is the sum of the current actuarial value of the annuity contract distributed and the total taxable amount of the lump sum distribution. Thus, the adjusted total taxable amount of A's 1976 distribution is $8,000 [$4,800 + ($4,000 – $800)]. The modified total taxable amount is $58,000 [$50,000 + $8,000]. The modified minimum distribution allowance with respect to A's 1976 distribution is the lesser of $10,000 or 1/2 of the modified total taxable amount reduced by the excess, if any, of such modified total taxable amount over $20,000. Thus, the modified minimum distribution allowance with respect to A's 1976 distribution is $2,400 [$10,000 – [(($8,000 + $50,000) – $20,000) × 0.2]]. The modified initial separate tax on A's 1976 distribution is 10 times the tax imposed by section 1(c) computed as if the taxable income therein described were $5,560

$$[\frac{(\$58,000 - \$2,400) \$2,000)]}{10}]$$

Thus, A's modified initial separate tax is $10,176. The modified separate tax on A's 1976 distribution is computed by multiplying the modified initial separate tax by the quotient of the sum of the ordinary income portions of each lump sum distribution received during the lookback period divided by the sum of the total taxable amounts of each lump sum distribution made during such period. Thus, the modified separate tax on A's 1976 distribution is $2,096 [$10,176 × ($10,000 + $960)/ ($50,000 + $3,200)]. The modified tax attributable to the annuity contract is 10 times the tax imposed by section 1(c) computed as if the taxable income therein described were $460

$$\$4,800 - [\frac{(\$2,400 \times (\$4,800/\$58,000))}{10}]$$

multiplied by the quotient described in the second preceding sentence. Thus, the modified tax attributable to the annuity contract is $133 [$644 × ($10,000 + $960)/($50,000 + $3,200)]. The separate tax on A's 1976 distribution is computed by reducing the modified separate tax by the sum of the separate tax paid during the lookback period, and the modified tax attributable to the annuity contract. Thus, the separate tax on A's 1976 distribution is $331 [$2,096 – ($1,632 + $133)].

(iv) A and B's total income tax liability for 1976 is the sum of their income tax liability as otherwise determined, and the separate tax. Thus, A and B's total income tax liability for 1976 is $6,538 [$6,207 + $331].

Example (3). (i) Assume the same facts as in example (1) except that the distribution on December 7, 1976, from the N Corporation's non-contributory qualified plan consists only of an annuity contract with a current actuarial value of $6,000.

(ii) A and B's gross income for 1976 is $28,000, computed by adding the total taxable amount (determined under paragraph (d)(2) of this section) of the lump sum distribution to their otherwise computed gross income [$25,000 + $3,000 + 0]. Their adjusted gross income for 1976 is $28,000 [$28,000 – ($0 + $0)], computed by reducing their gross income by the sum of the lump sum distribution deduction allowed by section 402(e)(3) with respect to the ordinary income portion of the distribution [$0 × 36/120] and the deduction allowed by section 1202 with respect to the capital gains portion of the distribution [($0 x 84/120) × 0.5]. Their taxable income for 1976 is $24,000 (their itemized deductions are $2,100 and their personal exemptions total $1,500). Thus, A and B's income tax liability for 1976, not including the separate tax on the distribution, is $5,804.

(iii) The adjusted total taxable amount of A's distribution for 1976 is the sum of the current actuarial value of the annuity contract distributed and the total taxable amount of the lump sum distribution. Thus, the adjusted total taxable amount of A's 1976 distribution is $6,000 [$6,000 + $0]. The modified total taxable amount is $56,000 [$6,000 + $50,000]. The modified minimum distribution allowance with respect to A's 1976 distribution is the lesser of $10,000 or 1/2 of the modified total taxable amount, reduced by 20 percent of the excess (if any) of the modified total taxable amount over $20,000. Thus, the modified minimum distribution allowance with respect to A's 1976 distribution is $2,800 [$10,000 − (($56,000 − $20,000) × 0.2)]. The modified initial separate tax on A's 1976 distribution is computed by multiplying 10 times the tax imposed by section 1(c) computed as if the taxable income therein described were $5,320

$$\left[\frac{\$56,000 - \$2,800}{10} \right]$$

Thus, A's modified initial separate tax is $9,672. The modified separate tax on A's 1976 distribution is computed by multiplying the modified initial separate tax by the quotient of she sum of the ordinary income portions of the lump sum distributions received during the lookback period divided by the sum of the total taxable amounts of each lump sum distribution made during such period. Thus, the modified separate tax on A's 1976 distribution is $1,934 [$9,672 × ($10,000 + $0)/($50,000 + $0)]. The modified tax attributable to the annuity contract is 10 times the tax imposed by section 1(c) computed as if the taxable income of a person described therein were $570

$$\frac{[\$6,000 - ((\$6,000/\$56,000) \times \$2,800)]}{10}$$

multiplied by the quotient described in the second preceding sentence. Thus, the modi-fied tax attributable to the annuity contract is $161 [$805 × ($10,000 + $0)/($50,000 + $0)]. The separate tax on A's 1976 distribution is computed by reducing the modified separate tax by the sum of the separate tax paid during the lookback period, and the modified tax attributable to the annuity contract. Thus, the separate tax on A's 1976 distribution is $141 [$1,934 − ($1,632 + $161)].

(iv) A and B's total income tax liability for 1976 is the sum of their income tax liability as otherwise determined, and the separate tax. Thus, A and B's total income tax liability for 1976 is $5,945 [$5,804 + $141].

Example (4). (i) Assume the same facts as in example (3) except that the N Corporation's qualified plan was contributory and that A's contributions under the plan as an employee were $2,000.

(ii) A and B's gross income for 1976 is $28,000, computed by adding the total taxable amount (determined under paragraph (d)(2) of this section) of the lump sum distribution to their otherwise computed gross income [$25,000 + $3,000 + 0]. Their adjusted gross income for 1976 is $28,000 [$28,000 − ($0 + $0)], computed by reducing their gross income by the sum of the lump sum distribution deduction allowed by section 402(e)(3) with respect to the ordinary income portion of the distribution [$0 × 36/120] and the deduction allowed by section 1202 with respect to the capital gains portion of the distribution [($0 × 84/120) × 0.5]. Their taxable income for 1976 is $24,400 (their itemized deductions are $2,100 and their personal exemptions total $1,500). Thus, A and B's income tax liability for 1976, not including the separate tax on the distribution is $5,804.

(iii) The adjusted total taxable amount of A's distribution for 1976 is the sum of the current actuarial value of the annuity contract distributed, reduced by the excess of the net amount contributed by the employee over the cash and other property distributed, and the total taxable amount of the lump sum distribution. Thus, the adjusted total taxable amount of A's 1976 distribution is $4,000 [($6,000 − $2,000) + $0]. The modified total taxable amount is $54,000 [$50,000 + $4,000.] The modified minimum distribution allowance with respect to A's 1976 distribution is the lesser of $10,000 or 1/2 of the modified total taxable amount, reduced by 20 percent of the excess (if any) of the modified total taxable amount over $20,000. Thus, the modified minimum distribution allowance with respect to A's 1976 distribution is $3,200 [$10,000 − (($54,000 − $20,000) × 0.2)]. The modified initial separate tax on A's 1976 distribution is computed by multiplying 10 times the tax imposed by section 1(c) computed as if the taxable income therein described were $5,080

$$\frac{[\$54,000 - \$3,200].}{10}$$

Thus, A's modified initial separate tax is $9,168. The modified separate tax on A's 1976 distribution is computed by multiplying the modified initial separate tax by the quotient of the sum of the ordinary income portions of the lump sum distribution received during the lookback period divided by the sum of the total taxable amounts of each lump sum distribution made during such period. Thus, the modified separate tax on A's 1976 distribution is $1,833 [$9,168 × ($10,000 + $0)/($50,000 + $0)]. The modified tax attributable to the annuity contract is 10 times the tax imposed by section 1(c) computed as if the taxable income therein described were $376

$$\frac{[\$4,000 - ((\$4,000/\$54,000) \times \$3,200)]}{10}$$

multiplied by the quotient described in the second preceding sentence. Thus, the modified tax attributable to the annuity contract is $105 [$526 × ($10,000 + $0)/($50,000 + $0)]. The separate tax on A's 1976 distribution is computed by reducing the modified separate tax by the sum of the separate tax paid during the lookback period, and the modified tax attributable to the annuity contract. Thus, the separate tax on A's 1976 distribution is $96 [$1,833 − ($1,632 + $105)].

(iv) A and B's total income tax liability for 1976 is the sum of their income tax liability as otherwise determined and the separate tax. Thus, A and B's total income tax liability for 1976 is $5,900 [$5,804 + $96].

(d) *Definitions.* For purposes of this section and §1.402(e)-3—(1) *Lump sum distribution.* (i) For taxable years of a recipient beginning after December 31, 1973, the term "lump sum distribution" means the distribution or payment within one taxable year of the recipient of the balance under the plan to the credit of an employee which becomes payable, or is made available, to the recipient—

(A) On account of the employee's death,

(B) After the employee attains age 59 ½,

(C) In the case of an employee who at no time during his participation in the plan was an employee within the meaning of section 401(c)(1), on account of the employee's separation from the service, or

(D) In the case of an employee within the meaning of section 401(c)(1), after the employee has become disabled within the meaning of section 72(m)(7) and paragraph (f) of §1.72-17,

from a trust forming part of a plan described in section 401(a) and which is exempt from tax under section 501(a) or from a plan described in section 403(a). Although periodic payments made under an annuity contract distributed under a plan described in the preceding sentence are taxed under section 72, solely for purposes of determining the adjusted total taxable amount or the modified total taxable amount, an annuity contract distributed from a plan described in the preceding sentence shall be treated as a lump sum distribution.

(ii) (A) A distribution or payment is not a lump sum distribution unless it constitutes the balance to the credit of the employee at the time the distribution or payment commences. For purposes of the preceding sentence, the time at which a distribution or payment commences shall be the date on which the requirements of subdivision (A), (B), (C), or (D) (whichever is applicable) of paragraph (d)(1)(i) of this section are satisfied, disregarding any previous distribution which constituted the balance to the credit of the employee.

(B) A distribution made before the death of an employee (for example, annuity payments received by the employee after retirement) will not preclude an amount paid on account of the death of the employee from being treated as a lump sum distribution by the recipient. Further, if a distribution or payment constitutes the balance to the credit of the employee, such distribution or payment shall not be treated as other than a lump sum distribution merely because an additional amount, attributable to the last or a subsequent year of service, is credited to the account of the employee and distributed.

(C) The application of this subdivision may be illustrated by the following example:

Example. A, an individual who is a calendar year taxpayer, retires from services with the M Corporation on October 31, 1975 after attaining age 59-1/2. A begins to receive monthly annuity payments under the M Corporation's qualified plan on November 1, 1975. On February 3, 1976, A takes the balance to his credit under the M Corporation's plan in lieu of any future annuity payments. The balance to the credit of A under the M Corporation's plan is distributed to him on February 3, 1976, and as of such date he had not previously received any amount constituting a lump sum distribution. Such payments and distributions are not to be treated as a lump sum distribution because they are not paid within 1 taxable year of the recipient.

(iii) A payment or distribution described in paragraph (d)(1)(i) of this section which is made to more than one person (except a payment or distribution made solely to two or more trusts), shall not be treated as a lump sum distribution, unless the entire amount paid or distributed is included in the income of the employee in respect of whom the payment or distribution is made. Thus, for example, a distribution of the balance to the credit of the employee after the death of the employee made to the surviving spouse and his children cannot be treated as a lump sum distribution by the surviving spouse and children. However, a distribution to the employee's estate can be treated as a lump sum distribution even though the estate subsequently distributes the amount received to the surviving spouse and children.

(iv) The term "balance to the credit of the employee" does not include United States Retirement Plan Bonds held by a trust to the credit of an employee. Thus, a distribution or payment by a plan described in subdivision (i) of this subparagraph may constitute a lump sum distribution with respect to an employee even though the trust retains retirement plan bonds registered in the name of such employee. Similarly, the proceeds of a retirement plan bond received as a part of the balance to the credit of an employee will not be entitled to be treated as a lump sum distribution. See section 405(e) and paragraph (a)(4) of § 1.405-3.

(v) The term "balance to the credit of the employee" includes any amount to the credit of the employee under any plan which is required to be aggregated under the provisions of section 402(e)(4)(C) and paragraph (e)(1) of this section.

(vi) The term "balance to the credit of the employee" does not include any amount which has been placed in a separate account for the funding of medical benefits described in section 401(h) as defined in paragraph (a) of § 1.401-14. Thus, a distri-bution or payment by a plan described in subdivision (i) of this subparagraph may constitute the "balance to the credit of the employee" with respect to an employee even though the trust retains amounts attributable to the funding of medical benefits described in section 401(h).

(vii) The term "balance to the credit of the employee" includes any amount which is not forfeited under the plan as of the close of the taxable year of the recipient within which the distribution is made except that in the case of an employee who has separated from the service and incurs a break in service (within the meaning of section 411), such term does not include an amount which is forfeited at the close of the plan year, beginning with or within such taxable year, by reason of such break in service.

(viii) The balance to the credit of the employee is includible in the gross income of the recipient if the recipient fails to make a timely election under section 72(h) to receive an annuity in lieu of such balance.

(2) *Total taxable amount.* (i) The term "total taxable amount" means, with respect to a lump sum distribution described in the first sentence of paragraph (d)(1)(i) of this section, the amount of such lump sum distribution which exceeds the sum of—

(A) The net amount contributed by the employee, and

(B) The net unrealized appreciation attributable to that part of the distribution which consists of the securities of the employer corporation so distributed.

(ii) For purposes of paragraph (d)(2)(i)(A) of this section, the term "net amount contributed by the employee" means—

(A) For taxable years beginning after December 31, 1974, the amount actually contributed by the employee plus any amounts considered to be contributed by the employee under the rules of sections 72(f) and 101(b), and paragraph (b) of § 1.72-16, reduced by any amounts theretofore distributed to him which were excludable from gross income as a return of employee contributions.

(B) For taxable years beginning before January 1, 1975, an amount equal to the product of the amounts considered contributed by the employee under the plan (determined by applying section 72(f) and 101(b), and paragraph (b) of § 1.72-16) reduced by any amounts theretofore distributed to the employee which were not includible in his gross income, multiplied by a fraction—

(i) The numerator of which is the excess, if any, of the sum of the current actuarial value of the annuity contract distributed and the value of the other property (including cash) distributed, over such current actuarial value, and

(ii) The denominator of which is the sum of the current actuarial value of the annuity contract distributed and the value of other property (including cash) distributed.

(iii) The provisions of this subparagraph may be illustrated by the following examples:

Example (1). A, age 60, receives a lump sum distribution from the N Corporation's noncontributory qualified plan on November 24, 1975. The distribution of $25,000 consists of cash and M Corporation securities with net unrealized appreciation of $15,000. The total taxable amount of the distribution to A is $10,000.

Example (2). B, age 60, receives a lump sum distribution from the N Corporation's contributory qualified plan on December 29, 1975. The distribution consists of $25,000 in cash. B's contributions under the plan as an employee are $5,000. The total taxable amount of the distribution to B is $20,000.

Example (3). W receives a lump sum distribution on April 1, 1975, from the M Corporation's noncontributory qualified plan as beneficiary of H on account of H's death. The distribution consists of $25,000 in cash. The total taxable amount of distribution to W is $20,000 if W is otherwise allowed a $5,000 exclusion under section 101(b).

(3) *Ordinary income portion* (i) The ordinary income portion of a lump sum distribution is the product of the total taxable amount of the lump sum distribution, multiplied by a fraction—

(A) the numerator of which is the number of calendar years of active participation by the employee in the plan after December 31, 1973, under which the lump sum distribution is made, and

(B) the denominator of which is the total number of calendar years of active participation by the employee in such plan.

(ii) For purposes of computing the fraction described in subdivision (i) of this subparagraph, the number of calendar years of active participation shall be the number of calendar months during the period beginning with the first month in which the employee became a participant under the plan and ending with the earliest of—

(A) The month in which the employee receives a lump sum distribution under the plan,

(B) In the case of an employee who is not an employee within the meaning of section 401(c)(1), the month in which the employee separates from the service,

(C) The month in which the employee dies, or

(D) In the case of an employee within the meaning of section 401(c)(1) who receives a lump sum distribution on account of disability, the first month in which he becomes disabled within the meaning of section 72(m)(?) and paragraph (f) of § 1.72-17.

In computing the month. of active participation, in the case of active participation before January 1, 1974, a pout of a calendar year in which the employee was an active participant under the plan shall be counted as 12 months, and in the case of active participation after December 31, 1973 a part of a calendar month in which an individual is an active participant under the plan shall be counted as 1 month. Thus, for example, if A, an individual, became an active participant under a plan on December 31, 1965, and continued to be an active participant under the plan until May 7, 1976, A has 108 (12×9) months of active participation under the plan before January 1, 1974, and A has 29 ($12 + 12 + 5$) months of active participation after December 31, 1973. For special rule[s] in case of aggregation of plans, see paragraph (e)(1)(ii) of this section.

(4) *Employee; employer.* The term "employee" includes an employee within the meaning of section 401(c)(1) and the employer of such individual is the person treated as his employer under section 401(c)(4).

(5) *Securities.* The terms "securities" and "securities of the employer corporation shall have the meanings provided in sections 402(a)(3)(A) and 402(a)(3)(B), respectively.

(e) *Special rules—(1) Aggregation. (i) Aggregation of trusts and plans*—(A) For purposes of determining the balance to the credit of an employee, all trusts described in section 401(a) and which are exempt from tax under section 501(a) and which are part of a plan shall be treated as a single trust; all pension plans described in section 401(a) maintained by an employer shall be treated as a single plan; all profit-sharing plans described in section 401(a) maintained by an employer shall he treated as a single plan; and all stock bonus plans described in section 401(a) maintained by an employer shall be treated as a single plan. For purposes of this subdivision (i), an annuity contract shall be considered to be a trust.

(B) Trusts which are not described in section 401(a) or which are not exempt from tax under section 501(a), and annuity contracts which do not satisfy the requirements of section 404(a)(2) shall not be taken into account for purposes of subdivision (i) of this subparagraph.

(ii) *Computation of ordinary income portion.* The ordinary income portion of a distribution from two or more plans (which are treated as a single plan under subdivision (i) of this subparagraph) shall be computed by aggregating all of the amounts which would constitute the ordinary income portion of a lump sum distribution if each plan maintained by the employer were not subject to the application of subdivision (i) of this subparagraph.

(iii) *Examples.* The application of this subparagraph is illustrated by the following examples:

Example (1). M Corporation maintains a qualified profit-sharing plan and a qualified defined benefit pension plan. A, who has participated in each plan for 5 years and is age 55, separates from the service on December 5, 1975. On December 5, 1975, A receives a distribution of the balance to the credit of his account under the profit-sharing plan. Payment of his pension benefits, however, will not commence until he attains age 65. A is entitled to treat his profit-sharing distribution as a lump sum distribution.

Example (2). Assume the same facts as in example (1) except bat instead of a profit-sharing plan, M Corporation maintains a qualified money purchase pension plan. A is not entitled to have the amount received from the money purchase pension plan treated as a lump sum distribution.

Example (3). Assume the same facts as in example (2) except that the trust forming part of the defined benefit pension maintained by M Corporation is not a qualified trust. A is entitled to have the amount received from the money purchase plan treated as a lump sum distribution.

Example (4). N Corporation maintains profit-sharing plan X and profit-scaring plan Y which plans are qualified and are noncontributory. A is a participant in each plan. A has been a participant in the profit-sharing plan X since October 13, 1966 and a participant in profit-sharing plan Y since its inception on May 9, 1968. A, age 55, separates from the service on December 5, 1975. He receives the balance to his credit from each plan upon separation. He receives $50,000 from profit-sharing plan X and $60,000 from profit-sharing plan Y. The ordinary income portion of his distribution from the N Corporation plans is $25,000 [($50,000 × (24/120)) + ($60,000 × (24/96))].

(2) *Community property laws*. (i) Except as provided in paragraph (e)(2)(ii) of this section, the provisions of this section shall be applied without regard to community property laws.

(ii) In applying the provisions of section 402(e)(3), relating to the allowance of a deduction from gross income of the ordinary income portion of a lump sum distribution, community property laws shall not be disregarded. Thus, for example, if A, a married individual subject to the community property laws of a jurisdiction, receives a lump sum distribution of which the ordinary income portion is $10,000, and he and his wife, B, file separate returns for the taxable year, generally, one half of the total taxable amount of the lump sum distribution is includible in A's gross income, and he will be entitled to a deduction under section 402(e)(3) of $5,000. In this case, the other half of the total taxable amount is includible in B's gross income, and she will be entitled to a deduction of $5,000. The entire amount of the lump sum distribution, however, must be taken into account by A in computing the separate tax imposed by section 402(e)(1)(A).

(3) *Minimum period of service*. For purposes of computing the separate tax imposed by section 402(e)(1)(A), no amount distributed or paid to an employee may be treated as a lump sum distribution under section 402(e>(4)(A) and this section unless he has been a participant in the plan for at least 5 full taxable years of such employee (preceding his taxable year in which such amount is distributed or paid). Thus, for example, if an amount, which would otherwise be a lump sum distribution, is distributed to A, an employee who has completed only 4 of his taxable years of participation in the plan before the first day of the taxable year in which the amount is distributed, A is not. entitled to use the provisions of section 402(e) to compute the tax on the ordinary income portion of the amount distribution. If the amount were distributed to A's beneficiary on account of A's death, however, Ax beneficiary could treat the distribution as a lump sum distribution under section 402(e) and this section.

(4) *Amounts subject to penalty*. Section 402(e) and this section do not apply to an amount described in section 72(m)(5)(A) (ii) and §1.72-17(e)(1)(i)(b) to the extent the provisions of section 72(m)(5) apply to such amount.

(5) *Distributions including securities of the employer corporation*. For rules relating to distributions including securities of the employer corporation, see §1.402(a)-1(b).

(6) *Liability for tax*. (i) Except as provided in subdivision (ii) of this subparagraph the recipient shall be liable for the tax imposed by section 402(e)(1)(A).

(ii) (A) In any case in which the recipient of a lump sum distribution is a trust, if a beneficiary of such trust is—

(1) An employee with respect to the plan under which the distribution is made, or

(2) Treated as the owner of such trust for purposes of subpart E of part I of subchapter J of chapter 1 of the Code (relating to grantors and others treated as substantial owners),

then such employee or the owner shall be treated as the sole recipient of the lump sum distribution. For purposes of (1) of this subdivision, the term "an employee with respect to the plan under which the distribution is made" means an individual who immediately before the distribution is made, is a participant in the plan under which the distribution is made.

(B)(1) In any case in which a lump sum distribution is made within a taxable year with respect to an individual only to two or more trusts, if a beneficiary of any one of such trusts is not treated as the sole recipient of the distribution by reason of the application of (A) of this subdivision (ii) the separate tax imposed by section 402(e)(1). (A) shall be computed as if the distribution were made to a single recipient consisting of all of such trusts, but the liability for such separate tax shall be allocated among the trusts according to the relative portions of the total taxable amount of the distribution received by each trust.

(2) In any case in which a lump sum distribution is made in a succeeding taxable year in a lookback period with respect to a trust described in (1) of this subdivision (B), the separate tax imposed by section 402[(e)](1)(A) shall be computed as if the amount described in section 402(e)(2)(A) (relating to the amount of tax imposed by section 402(e)(1)(A) paid with respect to other distributions in a lookback period) includes the separate tax determined in (1) of this subdivision (B) (without regard to the allocation described therein).

(7) *Change in exempt status of trust*. For principles applicable in making appropriate adjustments if the trust was not exempt for one or more years before the year of distribution, see §1.402(a)-1(a)(1)(iv).

(f) *Reporting—(1) Information required*. An employer who maintains a, plan described in section 401(a) or 403(a), under which a distribution or payment which may be treated as a lump sum distribution is made in a taxable year of the recipient beginning after December 31, 1973, shall communicate (or cause to be communicated) in writing, to the recipient on Form 1099 R the following information (where applicable):

(i) The gross amount of such distribution (including the value of any United States retirement plan bonds distributed to or held for the recipient);

(ii) The total taxable amount of such distribution;

(iii) The ordinary income portion and capital gain element of such distribution;

(iv) The net amount contributed by the employee (within the meaning of paragraph (d)(2)(ii) of this section);

(v) The portions of such distribution excludable from the gross income of the recipient under paragraph (c) of §1.72-16 and paragraph (b) of §1.402(a)-1;

(vi) The value of any United States retirement plan bonds distributed to or held for the recipient in excess of the net amount contributed by the employee (within the meaning of paragraph (d)(2)(ii) of this section) included in the basis of such bonds;

(vii) The current actuarial value of any annuity contract distributed as part of the balance to the credit of the employee in excess of the net amount contributed by the employee (within the meaning of paragraph (d)(2)(ii) of this section) considered to be an investment in the contract;

(viii) The net unrealized appreciation on any securities of the employer corporation.

(2) *Alternate method of communication*. The obligation of the employer to communicate the information described in subparagraph (1) of this paragraph to the recipient shall be satisfied if the fiduciary of the trust or the payer of such distribution communicates the information to the recipient.

(3) *Taxable year of recipient*. The report required by this paragraph may be prepared, at the option of the employer as if the taxable year of each employee were the calendar year.

(4) *Failure to satisfy requirements*. In the event that the requirements of this paragraph are not satisfied, the information required to be furnished under this paragraph shall be furnished as part of the return required to be filed under section 6058 and the regulations thereunder.

§ 1.402(e)-3 Election to treat an amount as a lump sum distribution.

* * *

(a) *In general*. For purposes of sections 402, 403, and this section, an amount which is described in section 402(e)(4)(A) and which is not an annuity contract may be treated as a lump sum distribution under section 402(e)(4)(A) only if the taxpayer elects for ?he taxable year to have all such amounts received during such year so treated. Not more than one election may be made under this section with respect to an employee after such employee has attained age 59V2.

(b) *Taxpayers eligible to make the election.* Individuals, estates, and trusts are the only taxpayers eligible to make the election provided by this section. In the case of a lump sum distribution made with respect to an employee to 2 or more trusts, the election provided by this section shall be made by the employee or by the personal representative of a deceased employee.

(c) *Procedure for making election—(1) Time and scope of election.* An election under this section shall be made for each taxable year to which such election is to apply. The election shall be made before the expiration of the period (including extensions thereof) prescribed in section 6511 for making a claim for credit or refund of the assessed tax imposed by chapter 1 of subtitle A of the Code for such taxable year.

(2) *Manner of making election.* An election by the taxpayer with respect to a tax-able year shall be made by filing Form 4972 as a part of the taxpayer's income tax return or amended return for the taxable year.

(3) *Revocation of election.* An election made pursuant to this section may be revoked within the time prescribed in subparagraph (1) of this paragraph for making an election, only if there is filed, within such time, an amended income tax return for such taxable year, which includes a statement revoking the election and is accompanied by payment of any tax attributable to the revocation. If an election for a taxable year is revoked, another election may be made for that taxable year under paragraphs (c)(1) and (2) of this section.

(4) *Eject of election on subsequent distribution.* An election made pursuant to this section shall be an election to treat an annuity contract distributed after December 31, 1973, in a lookback period (as defined in § 1.402(e)-2(c)(2)(iii)(F)) beginning after such date as a lump sum distribution in the taxable year of the recipient in which such contract is distributed.

Par. 13. Section 1.403(a) is amended by amending paragraph (A)(2)(iii) thereof and by revising the historical note. As amended, these revised provisions read as follows:

§ *1.403(a) Statutory provisions; taxation of employee annuities; qualified annuity plan.*

* * *

[Asterisks represent 1954 Code Sec. 403(a) as amended by Sec. 23(b), Technical Amendments Act 1958 (72 Stat. 1622); sec. 4(d), Self-Employed Individuals Tax Retirement Act 1962 (76 Stat. 825); sec. 232(e)(4), Rev. Act 1964 (78 Stat. 111); sec. 2005 (b)(2), Employee Retirement Income Security Act 1974 (88 Stat. 991)]

Par. 14. Section 1.403(a)-1(b)(1) and (2) are amended to read as follows:

§ *1.403(a)-1 Taxability of beneficiary under a qualified annuity plan.*

* * *

(b) The amounts received by or made available to any employee referred to in paragraph (a) of this section under an annuity contract shall be included in the gross income of the employee for the taxable year in which received on made available, as provided in section 72 (relating to annuities), except that—

(1) For taxable years beginning before January 1, 1970, certain total distributions described in section 403(a)(2)(as in effect for such years) are taxable as long-term capital gains (see § 1.403(a)-2 for rules applicable to such amounts), and

(2) For taxable years beginning after December 31, 1973, a portion of a lump sum distribution (as defined by section 402 (e)(4)(A)) is treated as long-term capital gains (see paragraph (d) of § 1.403(a)-2 for rules applicable to such portion and see § 1.402(e)-2 for the computation of the separate tax on the portion of a lump sum distribution not treated as long-term capital gains).

For taxable years beginning before January 1, 1964, section 72(e)(3) (relating to treatment of certain lump sums), as in effect before such date, shall not apply to an amount described in this paragraph. For taxable years beginning after December 31, 1963, such amounts may be taken into account in computations under section 1301 through 1305 (relating to income averaging)

* * *

Par. 15. Section 1.403(a)-2(a)(1) and (b) are amended; (c) is revised, (d) and (e) are added to read as follows:

§ *1.403(a)-2. Capital gains treatment for certain distributions.*

(a) For taxable years beginning before January 1, 1970, if the total amounts payable with respect to any employee for whom an annuity contract has been purchased by an employer under a plan which—

(1) Is a plan described in section 403(a) (1) and § 1.403(a)-1, and

* * *

(b) For taxable years beginning before January 1, 1970—

(1) The term "total amounts" means the balance to the credit of an employee with respect to all annuities under the annuity plan which becomes payable to the payee by reason of the employee's death or other separation from the service, or by reason of his death after separation from the service. If an employee commences to receive annuity payments on retirement and then a lump sum payment is made to his widow upon his death, the capital gains treatment applies to the lump sum payment, but it does not apply to amounts received before the time the "total amounts" become payable. However, if the total amount to the credit of the employee at the time of his death or other separation from the service or death after separation from the service is paid or includible in the gross income of the payee within one taxable year of the payee, such amount is entitled to the capital gains treatment notwithstanding that in a later taxable year an additional amount is credited to the employee and paid to the payee.

* * *

(c) For taxable years beginning before January 1, 1970, the provisions of this section are not applicable to any amounts paid to a payee to the extent such amounts are attributable to contributions made on behalf of an employee while he was a self-employed individual in the business with respect to which the plan was established. For the taxation of such amounts, see § 1.72-18. For such years for the rules for determining the amount attributable to contributions on behalf of an employee while he was self-employed, see paragraphs (b)(4) and (c)(2) of such section.

(d) For taxable years ending after December 31, 1969, and beginning before January 1, 1974, the portion of the total amounts described in paragraph (b)(1) of this section treated as gain from the sale or exchange of a capital asset held for more than six months is subject to the limitation of section 403(a)(2)(C), as in effect on December 31, 1973.

(e) For taxable years beginning after December 31, 1973—

(1) If a lump sum distribution (as defined in section 402(e)(4)(A) and the regulations thereunder) is received by, or made available to, the recipient under an annuity contract described in subparagraph (2)(i) of this paragraph, the ordinary income portion (as defined in section 402(e)(4)(E) and the regulations thereunder) of such distribution shall be taxable in accordance with the provisions of section 402(e) and the regulations thereunder and the portion of such distribution determined under paragraph (3) of this section shall be treated in accordance with the provisions of subparagraph (2) of this section.

(2) If—

(i) An annuity contract is purchased by an employer for an employee under a plan described in section 403(a)(1) and § 1.403 (a)-1,

(ii) Such plan requires that refunds of contributions with respect to annuity contracts purchased under the plan be used to reduce subsequent premiums on the contracts under the plan, and

(iii) A lump sum distribution (as define in section 402(e)(4)(A) and the regulations' thereunder) is paid to the recipient, the amount described in paragraph (e)(3) of this section shall be treated as gain from the sale or exchange of a capital asset held for more than 6 months.

(3) For purposes of paragraph (e)(2) of this section, the portion of a lump sum distribution treated as gain from the sale or exchange of a capital asset held for more than 6 months is an amount equal to the total taxable amount of the lump sum distribution (as defined in section 402(e)(4) (D) and the regulations thereunder) multiplied by a fraction—

(i) The numerator of which is the number of calendar years of active participation (as determined under § 1.402(e)-2(d)(3)(ii)) by the employee in such plan before January 1, 1974, and

(ii) The denominator of which is the number of calendar years of active participation (as determined under § 1.402(e)-2 (d)(3)(ii)) by the employee in such plan.

(4) For the purposes of this paragraph—

(i) In the case of an employee who is an employee without regard to section 401(c) (1), the determination of whether or not an amount is a lump sum distribution shall be made without regard to the requirements of section 402(e)(4)(B) and § 1.402(e)-3.

(ii) No distribution to any taxpayer other than an individual, estate, or trust may be treated as a lump sum distribution under this section.

Par. 16. Section 1.405 is amended by deleting "Section 72(n) and section 402(a)(2)" in subsection (e) and inserting in lieu thereof "Subsection(a)(2) and (e) of section 402"

and revising the historical note. These amended, and revised provisions read as follows:

* * *

[Asterisks represent 1954 Code] Sec. 405 as added by sea 5, Self-Employed Individuals Tax Retirement Act 1962 (76 Stat. 826) and as amended by Sec. 106(d)(5), Social Security Amendments 1965 (79 Stat. 337); sea 515(c)(1) Tax Reform Act 1969 (83 Stat. 654); sec. 2005(c)(11) Employee Retirement Income Security Act 1974 (88 Stat. 992)1

Par. 17. Paragraph (4) of § 1.405-3(a) is revised to read as follows:

§ 1.405.3 Taxation of retirement bonds.

(a) *In general.* * * *

(4) The provisions of section 402(a)(2) and (e) are not applicable to a retirement bond. In general, section 402(a)(2) provides for capital gains treatment of a portion of a lump sum distribution as defined in section 402(e)(4)(A) and section 402(e) provides a special I0year averaging of the ordinary income portion of much a lump sum distribution. The proceeds of a retirement bond received upon redemption will not be entitled to such capital gains treatment or 10-year averaging even though the bond is received as part of, or as the entire, balance to the credit of the employee. Nor will such a bond be taken into consideration in determining the balance to the credit of the employee. Thus, a distribution by a qualified trust may constitute a lump sum distribution for purposes of section 402(a)(2) and (e) even though the trust retains retirement bonds registered in the name of the employee.

Par. 18. Section 1.652(b)-1is amended by deleting "72(n)" and inserting in lieu thereof "402(a)(2)". As amended, § 1.652(b)-1 reads as follows:

§ 1.652(b)-1 Character of amounts.

In determining the gross income of a beneficiary, the amounts includible under § 1.652(a)-1 have the same character in the hands of the beneficiary as in the hands of the trust. For example, to the extent that the amounts specified in § 1.652(a)-1 consist of income exempt from tax under section 103, such amounts are not included in the beneficiary's gross income. Similarly, dividends distributed to a beneficiary retain their original character in the beneficiary's hands for purposes of determining the availability to the beneficiary of the dividends received credit under section 34 (for dividends received on or before December 31, 1964) and the dividend exclusion under section 116. Also, to the extent that the amounts specified in § 1.652(a)-1 consist of "earned income" in the hands of the trust under the provisions of section 1348 such amount shall be treat-A under section 1348 as "earned income" in the hands of the beneficiary. Similarly, to the extent the amounts specified in § 1.652(a)-1 consist of an amount received as a part of a lump sum distribution from a qualified plan and to which the provisions of section 402(a)(2) would apply in the hands of the trust, such amount shall be treated as subject to such section in the hands of the beneficiary except where such amount is deemed under section 666(a) to have been distributed in a preceding taxable year of the trust and the partial tax described in section 668 (a)(2) is determined under section 668 (b)(1)(B). The tax treatment of amounts determined under § 1.652(a)-1 depends upon the beneficiary's status with respect to them, not upon the status of the trust. Thus, if a beneficiary is deemed to have received foreign income of a foreign trust, the includibility of such income in his gross income depends upon his taxable status with respect to that income.

Par. 19. Section 1.1304 is amended by deleting paragraph (b)(2) and redesignating paragraphs (3), (4), (5), and (6) as paragraphs (2), (3), (4), and (5), respectively, and revising the historical note. These amended and revised provisions read as follows:

* * *

[[Asterisks represent 1954 Code] Sec. 1304 as amended by sec. 232(a), Rev. Act 1964 (78 Stat. 105); secs. 311(c) and (d), 515 (c)(4), 802(c)(5), and 803(d)(8), Tax Reform Act 1969 (83 Stat. 537, 646, 678, 684); sec. 2005(c)(6) Employee Retirement Income Security Act 1974 (88 Stat. 991)]

Par. 20. Paragraph (a) of § 1.1304-2 is amended to read as follows:

§ 1.1304-2 Provisions inapplicable if income averaging is chosen.

(a) *Provisions inapplicable.* If a taxpayer chooses the benefits of income averaging for any taxable year, pursuant to section 1304(a) and § 1.1304-1, the following sections of the Code will not apply for such year: * * *

(2) In taxable years beginning before January 1, 1974, section 72(n)(2) (relating to limitation of tax in case of certain distributions with respect to contributions by self-employed individuals).

* * *

[Temporary income tax regulations under the Employee Retirement Income Security Act of 1974]

Par. 21. Section 11.402(e)(4)(B)-1 is revoked.

[¶ 20,121A Reserved.—Proposed regulations under Code Secs. 401(a)(4) and 410(b) were formerly reproduced here. The final regulations are reproduced at ¶ 11,720W-14 and 12,165.]

[¶ 20,121B Reserved.—Proposed regulations relating to minimum participation requirements under Code Sec. 401(a)(26) were formerly reproduced here. The final regulations are now at ¶ 11,720Z-31 through ¶ 11,720Z-40.]

[¶ 20,121C Reserved.—Proposed rules relating to the $200,000 compensation limit under Code Sec. 401(a)(17) were formerly reproduced here. The final regulations are at ¶ 11,720Z-11.]

¶ 20,121D

Proposed regulations: Compensation: Definition.—Temporary and proposed regulations have been issued by the IRS to provide guidance with respect to definitions of compensation.

The temporary and proposed regulations were published in the Federal Register on May 14, 1990 (55 FR 19945).

AGENCY: Internal Revenue Service, Treasury.

ACTION: Notice of proposed rulemaking by cross-reference to temporary regulations.

SUMMARY: In the Rules and Regulations portion of this issue of the Federal Register, the Internal Revenue Service is issuing temporary regulations relating to the scope and meaning of the term "compensation" in section 414(s) of the Internal Revenue Code of 1986. They reflect changes made by the Tax Reform Act of 1986 (TRA '86) and by the Technical and Miscellaneous Revenue Act of 1988 (TAMRA). The text of those temporary regulations also serves as the text for this Notice of Proposed Rulemaking. These regulations will provide the public with guidance necessary to comply with the law and will affect sponsors of, and participants in, pension, profit-sharing and stock bonus plans, and certain other employee benefit plans.

DATES: Written comments must be received by July 13, 1990. Requests to speak (with outlines of oral comments) at a public hearing scheduled for Wednesday, September 26, 1990, at 10:00 a.m., and continuing at 10:00 a.m. each day, if necessary, on Thursday, September 27, 1990, and Friday, September 28, 1990, must received by Wednesday, September 12, 1990. See the notice of hearing published elsewhere in this issue of the Federal Register.

ADDRESSES: Send comments and requests to speak (with outlines of oral comments) at the public hearing to: Internal Revenue Service, P.O.

Box 7604, Ben Franklin Station, Attn: CC:CORP:T:R (EE-129-86), Room 4429, Washington, D.C. 20044.

FOR FURTHER INFORMATION CONTACT: Concerning the regulation, Marjorie Hoffman, Office of the Assistant Chief Counsel (Employee Benefits and Exempt Organizations), at 202-343-6954 (not a toll-free number). Concerning the hearing, Carol Savage, Regulations Unit, at 202-343-0232 or 202-343-0232 or 202-566-3935 (not toll free numbers).

SUPPLEMENTARY INFORMATION:

Background

The temporary regulations in the Rules and Regulations portion of this issue of the Federal Register amend 26 CFR by amending § 1.414(s)-1T and § 1.415-2(d) to provide guidance with respect to definitions of compensation within the meaning of section 414(s) and section 415(c)(3) of the Internal Revenue Code (Code). The regulations are proposed to be issued under the authority contained in sections 414(s) and 7805 of the Code (100 Stat. 2453, 68A Stat. 917; 26 U.S.C. 414(s), 7805). For the text of the temporary regulations, see T.D. 8301 published in the Rules and Regulations portion of this issue of the Federal Register.

Special analyses

It has been determined that these proposed rules are not major rules as defined in Executive order 12291. Therefore, a Regulatory Impact Analysis is not required. It has been determined that section 553(b) of the Administrative Procedure Act (5 U.S.C. Chapter 5) and the Regulatory Flexibility Act (5 U.S.C. Chapter 6) do not apply to these regulations, and therefore, an initial Regulatory Flexibility Analysis is not required. Pursuant to section 7805(f) of the Internal Revenue Code, the proposed regulations are being sent to the Administrator of the Small Business Administration for comment on their impact on small business.

Comments and requests for public hearing

Before adopting these proposed regulations, consideration will be given to any written comments that are submitted (preferably a signed original and eight copies) to the Commissioner of Internal Revenue. All comments will be available for public inspection and copying in their entirety. Because the Treasury Department expects to issue final regulations on this matter as soon as possible, a public hearing will be held at 10:00 a.m. on September 26, 1990, and continued, if necessary, on September 27 and 28, 1990, in the I.R.S. Auditorium, Seventh Floor, 7400 Corridor, Internal Revenue Building, 1111 Constitution Ave., N.W., Washington, D.C. Comments must be received by July 13, 1990. Requests to speak (with outlines of oral comments) must be received by Wednesday, September 12, 1990. See the notice of hearing published elsewhere in this issue of the Federal Register.

Drafting information

The principal author of these proposed regulations is Marjorie Hoffman, Office of the Assistant Chief Counsel (Employee Benefits and Exempt Organizations). However, other personnel from the Service and Treasury Department participated in their development.

List of Subjects

26 CFR 1.401-0—1.425-1

Employee benefit plans, Employee stock ownership plans, Income taxes, Individual retirement accounts, Pensions, Stock options.

[¶ 20,122 Reserved.—Proposed Reg. §§ 1.7476-1, 1.7476-2, and 301.7476-1, relating to notification of interested parties regarding qualification of certain retirement plans, were formerly reported at this point. The final regulations now appear at ¶ 13,913, 13,914 and 13,916.]

[¶ 20,123 Reserved.—Proposed Reg. § 1.7476-3 relating to notice of determination was formerly reported at this point. The final regulation now appears at ¶ 13,915.]

[¶ 20,124 Reserved.—Proposed Reg. § 54.4975-9, relating to the definition of "fiduciary," was formerly reported at this point. The final regulation now appears at ¶ 13,647.]

[¶ 20,125 Reserved.—Proposed Reg. §§ 20.2039-1(a) and 20.2039-2(d), relating to the exclusion of annuity interests created by community property laws, were formerly reported at this point. The final regulations now appear at ¶ 13,501 and 13,502.]

[¶ 20,126 Reserved.—Proposed Reg. § 1.514(b)-1, relating to the definition of debt-financed property and the determination of interest on a refund of taxes on property acquired for prospective exempt use, was formerly reported at this point. The final regulation now appears at ¶ 13,233.]

[¶ 20,127 Reserved.—The discussion draft of proposed Reg. § 1.61-16 and proposed amendments of Reg. § 1.61-2 relating to treatment of fringe benefits was withdrawn in the Federal Register of December 28, 1976 (41 FR 56334). The announcement of the withdrawal appears in a Treasury Department News Release at ¶ 17,070T.]

[¶ 20,128 Reserved.—Proposed Reg. §§ 1.512(a)-1 and 1.512(a)-4, relating to the treatment of unrelated business income of war veteran organizations, were formerly reproduced at this point. The final regulations appear at ¶ 13,211 and 13,212B.]

[¶ 20,129 Reserved.—Proposed Reg. §§ 1.414(f)-1 and 1.414(g)-1, concerning the definitions of "multiemployer plan" and "plan administrator," were formerly reproduced at this point. The final regulations appear at ¶ 12,361 and ¶ 12,362.]

[¶ 20,130 Reserved.—Proposed Reg. § 1.401(a)-11, relating to qualified joint and survivor annuities, was formerly reproduced at this point. The final regulation appears at ¶ 11,719.]

[¶ 20,131 Reserved.—Proposed Reg. §§ 1.410(a)-1—1.410(a)-6, 1.410(b)-1, 1.410(d)-1, 1.413-1(a) and 1.413-2(a), relating to minimum participation standards, were formerly reproduced at this point. Reg. §§ 1.413-1(a) and 1.413-2(a) were renumbered §§ 1.413-1(b) and 1.413-2(b). The final regulations appear at ¶ 12,156—12,161, 12,163, 12,171, 12,311, and 12,312.]

[¶ 20,132 Reserved.—Proposed Reg. § 1.401(a)-14, relating to the commencement of benefits under qualified trusts, was formerly reproduced at this point. The final regulation appears at ¶ 11,720.]

[¶ 20,133 Reserved.—Proposed Reg. §§ 1.401-5 and 1.401(b)-1, relating to certain retroactive amendments of employee plans, were formerly reproduced at this point. The final regulations appear at ¶ 11,705 and 11,721.]

[¶ 20,134 Reserved.—Proposed Reg. § 1.401(a)-15, relating to the requirement that plan benefits are not decreased on account of certain social security increases, was formerly reproduced at this point. The final regulation appears at ¶ 11,720A.]

[¶ 20,135 Reserved.—Proposed Reg. § 1.401-12, relating to nonbank trustees of pension and profit-sharing trusts benefiting owner-employees, was formerly reproduced at this point. The final regulation appears at ¶ 11,712.]

[¶ 20,136 Reserved.—Proposed regulations §§ 1.401-8 and 1.401-8A, relating to custodial accounts and annuity contracts under qualified pension, profit-sharing, and stock bonus plans, were formerly reproduced at this point. The final regulations appear at ¶ 11,707A and 11,708.]

[¶ 20,137 Reserved.—Proposed regulations under Code Secs. 401(a)-19, 404(a), 406, 407, 411, and 805, relating to minimum vesting standards, were formerly reproduced at this point. The final regulations appear at ¶ 11,700A, 11,720O, 11,859, 12,211—12,231, 12,311, 12,312, and 13,302.]

[¶ 20,137A Reserved.—Proposed regulations under Code Secs. 2039 and 2517, relating to the estate and gift tax treatment of amounts payable under qualified employee retirement plans, were formerly reproduced at this point. The final regulations appear at ¶ 13,502, 13,502A, 13,502B, 13,502C and 13,521.]

¶ 20,137B

Proposed regulations relating to individual retirement plans and simplified employee pensions.—Reproduced below is the text of proposed regulations under Code Secs. 62, 219, 220, 404, 408, 409, 2503, 3121, 3306, 4973, 4974, and 6693, relating to individual retirement plans and simplified employee pensions (SEPs.) The proposed regulations were filed with the *Federal Register* on July 13, 1981 and published on July 14, 1981.

DEPARTMENT OF THE TREASURY

Internal Revenue Services

26 CFR Parts 1, 25, 31, 54, and 301

[EE-7-78]

Individual Retirement Plans and Simplified Employee Pensions

AGENCY: Internal Revenue Service, Treasury.

ACTION: Notice of proposed rulemaking.

SUMMARY: This document contains proposed regulations relating to individual retirement plans and simplified employee pensions. Changes to the applicable law were made by the Employee Retirement Income Security Act of 1974, the Tax Reform Act of 1976, the Revenue Act of 1978 and the Technical Corrections Act of 1979. The regulations would provide the public with the guidance needed to comply with these Acts and would affect institutions which sponsor individual retirement plans and simplified employee pensions. The regulations also affect employers and individuals who use these plans for retirement income.

DATES: Written comments and requests for a public hearing must be delivered or mailed by September 14, 1981. The amendments would have varying effective dates. The provisions relating to spousal individual retirement plans are generally effective for taxable years beginning after December 31, 1976. The provisions relating to simplified employee pensions are generally effective for taxable years beginning after December 31, 1978. The provisions defining "active participant" for individuals covered by defined benefit offset plans are effective for taxable years beginning after December 31, 1980.

ADDRESS: Send comments and requests for a public hearing to: Commissioner of Internal Revenue, Attention: CC:LR:T (EE-7-78), Washington, D.C. 20224.

FOR FURTHER INFORMATION CONTACT: William D. Gibbs of the Employee Plans and Exempt Organizations Division, Office of the Chief Counsel, Internal Revenue Service, 1111 Constitution Avenue, N.W., Washington, D.C. 20224 (Attention: CC:LR:T) (202-566-3430) (not a toll-free number).

SUPPLEMENTARY INFORMATION:

Background

This document contains proposed amendments to the Income Tax Regulations (26 CFR Part 1), the Gift Tax Regulations (26 CFR Part 31), the Regulations on Pension Excise Taxes (26 CFR Part 54) and the Procedure and Administration Regulations (26 CFR Part 301) under section 62, 219, 220, 404, 408, 409, 2503, 3121, 3306, 4973, 4974,, and 6693 of the Internal Revenue Code of 1954. These amendments are proposed to conform the regulations to section 2002(d) of the Employee Retirement Income Security Act of 1974 (88 Stat. 966), section 1501 of the Tax Reform Act of 1976 (90 Stat. 1734), section 152, 156(c) and 157 of the Revenue Act of 1978 (90 Stat. 1734), sections 152, 156(c) and 157 of the Revenue Act of 1978 (92 Stat. 2797, 2802, 2803), and sections 101(a)(10), (101)(a)(14)(A), 101(a)(B), and 101(a)(14)(E)(ii) of the Technical Corrections Act of 1979 (94 Stat. 201-205). These regulations are to be issued under the authority contained in section

7805 of the Internal Revenue Code of 1954 (68A Stat. 917; 26 U.S.C. 7805).

On August 8, 1980, the Federal Register published final regulations relating to individual retirement plans under the Income Tax Regulations (26 CFR Part 1) under section 219, 409, 409 and under the Pension Excise Taxes (26 CFR Part 54) under section 4974 (45 FR 52782). Also, because of subsequent statutory provisions, some of the proposed regulations published on February 21, 1975 (40 FR 7661) were withdrawn in connection with those final regulations. The preamble to those final regulations indicated that regulations under other statutory provisions relating to retirement plans would be reproposed at a later date. This document contains these reproposed amendments, other than those relating to the rollover rules under Code sections 402 and 403. The Service intends to repropose these rules at a later date in connection with the regulations under Code sections 402(a) (5), (6) and (7), and 403(a) (4), (6) and (8).

Spousal Individual Retirement Plans

Internal Revenue Code section 220 allows an individual to deduct amounts contributed to an individual retirement plan maintained for the individual's benefit and an individual retirement plan maintained for the benefit of the individual's non-employed spouse. The proposed regulations set forth the type of funding arrangements which must be used and additional limitations and restrictions the individual and spouse must meet in order for the individual to obtain this deduction.

Simplified Employees Pensions

Internal Revenue Code section 408(k) sets forth rules for simplified employee pension ("SEP's"). The proposed regulations, §§ 1.408-7 through -9, indicate to employers and sponsoring institutions what requirements these arrangements must meet. Section 1.404(h)-1 of the proposed regulations sets forth the special deduction limitations for employers under Code section 404(h). Section 1.219-1(d)(4) and 1.219-3 of the proposed regulations set forth the rules governing the inclusion/deduction rules for employees for employer contributions to SEP's.

An employee will be allowed to deduct an employer contribution to a simplified employee pension. In general, the maximum amount the employee will be allowed to deduct is the lesser of 15 percent of compensation includible in gross income or $7,500. Proposed § 1.219-3 makes it clear that the deduction and the compensation are computed separately with respect to each employer's arrangement. Thus, an employee who has two or more employers can use only the compensation from the employer maintaining the simplified employee pension arrangement in computing the section 219(b)(7) limitation. On the other hand, if two or more employers of an employee each maintain a simplified employee will be allowed to deduct each employer's contribution, up to the compensation and dollar limit applied separately to each employer. Special limitations apply to certain related employers under Code section 414(b) and (c) and to self-employed individuals.

Certain rules have been included to make SEP arrangements more administrable by employers and the Service. Under proposed § 1.408-7(d)(1)(iii) and employer is not required to make a contribution to the SEP of an otherwise eligible employee who receives less than $200 compensation for a calendar year. This relieves employers of the burden of setting up SEP's to which very shall amounts of money will be contributed (the maximum deductible contribution would equal $30 (15% or $200)). This rule was published by the Service in Announcement 80-112, 1980-36 I.R.B. 35.

Further, under proposed § 1.408-7(d)(2), employers may execute necessary documents on behalf of employees who are unwilling or unable to execute those documents or whom the employer is unable to locate. This remedial rule prevents an employer's SEP arrangement from being disqualified because of a recalcitrant employee or one who has left the employer's service and is unable to be located by the employer. (See also proposed § 1.408-9(c) for possible reporting requirements in this instance.) Comments are requested as to what alternative remedial action, in lieu of execution on behalf of employees, employer would wish to take to avoid disqualification of their SEP arrangements. Comments also are requested on this proposed rule as to whether in a particular State there is any law that would preclude this action by the employer on the employee's behalf.

Employer contributions which exceed the amounts called for under the written allocation formula for the SEP arrangement are treated as if made to the employee's individual retirement account or individual retirement annuity, maintained outside the employee's SEP. It is contemplated that the employer, when it discovers the erroneous contribution, will notify the employee of the amount of the non-SEP contribution made in excess of the allocation formula. Because this amount may result in an excess contribution when made the employee may wish to take appropriate action in order to avoid IRA penalties. The normal IRA rules under Code section 219 apply in such a situation. This rule is proposed in order to prevent the entire SEP arrangement from being disqualified due to an inadvertent error on the part of the employer, such as an incorrect calculation of employee compensation. Under Code section 408(k), the entire SEP arrangement could be disqualified on account of the excess contribution. This rule is proposed to provide relief in such cases. See proposed § 1.408-7(f) and the example of how the rule would operate in a particular case.

Proposed § 1.408-7(c)(2) contains a special rule clarifying the relationship between SEP's and salary reduction agreements. This rule makes it clear that employer contributions to an employee's individual retirement account or annuity that are made under a salary reduction agreement between the employer and employee are not treated as employer contributions to an employee's simplified employee pension. Thus, if the employee may elect either an contribution or current compensation, the contribution is treated as an employee contribution and, therefore, is not eligible for the favorable SEP arrangement rules.

Similarly, other contributions such as voluntary contributions made by the employee, or on behalf of the employee by the employer as the agent for the employee (such as by payroll withholding), are treated as employee contributions.

Even though the employer picks the institution or substantially influences the employee's choice of the institution to which the employer makes the SEP contribution and which serves as trustee or sponsor for the employee's DEP, the SEP arrangement remains qualified under the Code. Further, this action by the employer is not a prohibition on withdrawal of funds within the meaning of Code section 408(k)(4)(B). The employer should, however, be aware that the Department of Labor may require special reporting for such action. (See 29 CFR 2520.104-48 (1980) and 29 CFR 2520.104-49 (1981).)

Proposed § 1.408-9 contains reporting requirements for SEP's. Employer who use the Service's Model Simplified Employee Pension Arrangement (Form 5305-SEP) and furnish the Model to their employees will satisfy the disclosure requirements relating to adoption of the SEP arrangement. Further, if the employer reports the amount of the SEP contribution on an employee's W-2, the annual reporting requirements will be satisfied. The Department of Labor also has reporting requirements for SEP's, which are in addition to the requirements of the Internal Revenue Service. (See 29 CFR 2520.104-48 (1980) and 29 CFR 2520.104-49 (1981).)

Employers who failed to make required contributions on behalf of employees for calendar year 1979 because the employees were no longer employed at the end of the employer's taxable year may make such "make up" contributions before January 1, 1981. This conforms to Announcement 80-112, 1980-36 I.R.B. 35. This relief is given because employers may not have anticipated the rules contained in that announcement and § 1.408-7(d)(1), (2) and (3), relating to which employees are entitled to receive an allocation. It is expected that employers who make such contributions will comply with the reporting requirements of § 1.408-9(b) and file amended tax returns. Likewise, employees who receive such contributions are expected to file amended tax returns.

Other Amendments

Conforming and technical amendments made by the Tax Reform Act of 1976, the Revenue Act of 1978, and the Technical Corrections Act of 1979 have been made to the regulations under Code sections 62, 219, 220, 404, 408, 409, 415, 3121, 3306, 4973, 4974, and 6693.

Also, regulations are proposed which define "active participant" under section 219(b)(2) for individuals who are covered with Federal or State benefits such as social security benefits. These rules were requested by commentators at the public hearing held July 19, 1979, on the reproposed active participant rules, and in other written comments on those proposed regulations published in the **Federal Register** on March 23, 1979 (44 FR 17754). This proposed rule allows employees to make IRA contributions when, in effect, they get no benefit from their employers' plans.

Regulatory Flexibility Act

Although this document is a notice of proposed rulemaking which solicits public comment, the Internal Revenue Service has concluded that the regulations proposed herein are interpretative and that the notice and public procedure requirements of 5 U.S.C. 553 do not apply. Accordingly, these proposed regulations do not constitute regulations subject to the Regulatory Flexibility Act (5 U.S.C. chapter 6).

Comments and Requests for a Public Hearing

Before adopting these proposed regulations, consideration will be given to any written comments that are submitted (preferably six copies) to the Commissioner of Internal Revenue. All comments will be available for public inspection and copying. A public hearing will be held upon written request to the Commissioner by any person who has submitted written comments. If a public hearing is held, notice of the time and place will be published in the **Federal Register**.

Drafting Information

The principal author of these proposed regulations is William D. Gibbs of the Employee Plans and Exempt Organizations Division of the Office of Chief Counsel, Internal Revenue Service. However, personnel from other offices of the Internal Revenue Service and Treasury Department participated in developing the regulation, both on matters of substance and style.

Proposed Amendments to the Regulations

The proposed amendments to 26 CFR Parts 1, 25, 31, 54, and 301 are as follows:

Income Tax Regulations (26 CFR Part 1)

PART 1—INCOME TAX; TAXABLE YEARS BEGINNING AFTER DECEMBER 31, 1953

Paragraph 1. Section 1.62-1 is amended by revising paragraphs (c)(13) to read as follows:

§ 1.62-1 Adjusted gross income.

* * *

(c) * * *

(13) Deductions allowed by sections 219 and 220 for contributions to an individual retirement account described in section 408(a), for an individual retirement annuity described in section 408(b), or for a retirement bond described in section 409;

Par. 2. Section 1.219-1 is revised by adding: (1) a new subdivision (iv) to paragraph (b)(2), and (2) new paragraphs (d) and (e) to read as follows:

§ 1.219-1 Deduction for retirement savings.

* * *

(b) Limitations and restrictions. * * *

(2) Restrictions. * * *

(iv) Alternative deduction. No deduction is allowed under subsection (a) for the taxable year if the individual claims the deduction allowed by section 220 (relating to retirement savings for certain married individuals) for the taxable year.

* * *

(d) Time when contributions deemed made—(1) Taxable years beginning before January 1, 1978. For taxable years beginning before January 1, 1977, a taxpayer must make a contribution to an individual retirement plan during a taxable year in order to receive a deduction for such taxable year. For taxable years beginning after December 31,

1976, and before January 1, 1978, a taxpayer shall be deemed to have made a contribution on the last day of the preceding taxable year if the contribution is made on account of such taxable year and is made not later than 45 days after the end of such taxable year. A contribution made not later than 45 days after the end of a taxable year shall be treated as made on account of such taxable year if the individual specifies in writing to the trustee, insurance company, or custodian that the amounts contributed are for such taxable year.

(2) *Taxable years beginning after December 31, 1977.* For taxable years beginning after December 31, 1977, a taxpayer shall be deemed to have made a contribution on the last day of the preceding taxable year if the contribution is made on account of such taxable year and is made not later than the time prescribed by law for filing the return for such taxable year (including extensions thereof). A contribution made not later than the time prescribed by law for filing the return for a taxable year (including extensions thereof) shall be treated as made on account of such taxable year if it is irrevocably specified in writing to the trustee, insurance company, or custodian that the amounts contributed are for such taxable year.

(3) *Time when individual retirement plan must be established.* For purposes of this paragraph, an individual retirement plan need not be established until the contribution is made.

(4) *Year of inclusion in income.* Any amount paid by an employer to an individual retirement account, for an individual retirement annuity or for an individual retirement bond (including an individual retirement account or individual retirement annuity maintained as part of a simplified employee pension plan) shall be included in the gross income of the employee for the taxable year for which the contribution is made.

(e) *Excess contributions treated as contribution made during subsequent year for which there is an unused limitation*—(1) *In general.* If for the taxable year the maximum amount allowable as a deduction under this section exceeds the amount contributed, then the taxpayer, whether or not a deduction is actually claimed, shall be treated as having made an additional contribution for the taxable year in an amount equal to the lesser of—

(i) The amount of such excess, or

(ii) The amount of the excess contributions for such taxable year (determined under section 4973(b)(2) without regard to subparagraph (C) thereof).

(2) *Amount contributed.* For purposes of this paragraph, the amount contributed—

(i) Shall be determined without regard to this paragraph, and

(ii) Shall not include any rollover contribution.

(3) *special rule where excess deduction was allowed for closed year.* Proper reduction shall be made in the amount allowable as a deduction by reason of this paragraph for any amount allowed as a deduction under this section or section 220 for a prior taxable year for which the period for assessing a deficiency has expired if the amount so allowed exceeds the amount which should have been allowed for such prior taxable year.

(4) *Effective date.* (i) This paragraph shall apply to the determination of deductions for taxable years beginning after December 31, 1975.

(ii) If, but for this subdivision, an amount would be allowable as a deduction by reason of section 219(c)(5) for a taxable year beginning before January 1, 1978, such amount shall be allowable only for the taxpayer's first taxable year beginning in 1978.

(5) *Examples.* The provisions of this paragraph may be illustrated by the following examples. (Assume in each example, unless otherwise stated, that it is less than age 70 ½ and is not covered by a simplified employee pension or a plan described in section 219(b)(2).)

Example (1). (i) B, a calendar-year taxpayer, earns $8,000 in compensation includible in gross income for 1979. On December 1, 1979, B establishes an individual retirement account (IRA) and contributes $1,500 to the account. B does not withdraw any money from the IRA after the initial contribution. Under section 219(b)(i), the maximum amount that B can deduct for 1979 is 15% of $8,000 or $1,200. B has an excess contribution for 1979 of $300.

(ii) For 1980, B has compensation includible in gross income of $12,000. B makes a $1,000 contribution to his IRA for 1980.

(iii) Although B made only a $1,000 contribution to his IRA for 1980, under the rules contained in this paragraph, B is treated as having made an additional contribution of $300 for 1980 and will be allowed to deduct $1,300 as his 1980 IRA contribution.

Example (2). (i) For 1979, the facts are the same as in *Example (1).*

(ii) For 1980, B has compensation includible in gross income of $12,000. B makes a $1,500 contribution to his IRA for 1980.

(iii) B will be allowed a $1,500 deduction for 1980 (the amount of his contribution). B will not be allowed a deduction for the $300 excess contribution made in 1979 because the maximum amount allowable for 1980 does not exceed the amount contributed.

Example (3). (i) For 1979, the facts are the same as in *Example (1).*

(ii) For 1980, B has compensation includible in gross income of $12,000. B makes a $1,400 contribution to his IRA for 1980.

(iii) For 1980, B will be allowed to deduct his contribution of $1,400 and $100 of the excess contribution made for 1979. He will not be allowed to deduct the remaining $200 of the excess contribution made for 1979 because that would make his deduction for 1980 more than $1,500, his allowable deduction for 1980.

(iv) For 1981, B has compensation includible in gross income of $15,000. B makes a $1,300 contribution to his IRA for 1981.

(v) B will be allowed to deduct the remaining $200 and his $1,300 contribution for 1981.

Example (4). (i) For 1979, the facts are the same as in *Example (1).*

(ii) For 1980, B has compensation includible in gross income of $12,000. B makes a $1,000 contribution to his IRA for 1980. B is allowed to deduct the $300 excess contribution for 1980 but fails to do so on his return. Consequently, B deducts only $1,000 for 1980.

(iii) Under no circumstances will B be allowed to deduct the $300 excess contribution made for 1979 for any taxable year after 1980 because B is treated as having made the contribution for 1980.

Example (5). (i) For 1979, the facts are the same as *Example (1).*

(ii) For 1980, B has compensation includible in gross income of $15,000 and is an active participant in a plan described in section 219(b)(2)(A).

(iii) B will not be allowed to deduct for 1980 the $300 excess contribution for 1979 because the maximum amount allowable as a deduction under sections 219(b)(1) and 219(b)(2) is $0.

Par. 3. Section 1.219-2 is amended by: (1) revising the first sentence of paragraph (b)(1); (2) renumbering paragraph (b)(2), (3), and (4) as paragraph (b)(3), (4) and (5), respectively, and adding a new paragraph (b)(2) before the renumbered paragraph (b)(3), (4) and (5); (3) revising paragraph (f) and (4) adding new examples (3), (4) and (5) after *Example (2)* in paragraph (h). These revised and added provisions read as follows:

§ 1.219-2 Definition of active participant.

* * * * *

(b) *Defined benefit plans*—(1) *In general.* Except as provided in subparagraphs (2), (3), (4) and (5) of this paragraph, an individual is an active participant in a defined benefit plan if for any portion of the plan year ending with or within such individual's taxable year he is not excluded under the eligibility provisions of this plan. * * *

(2) *Special rule for offset plans.* For taxable years beginning after December 31, 1980, an individual who satisfies the eligibility requirements of a plan under which benefits are offset by Social Security or Railroad Retirement benefits is not considered an active participant by virtue of participation in such plan for a particular plan year if such individual's compensation for the calendar year during which such plan year ends does not exceed the offset plan's breakpoint compensation amount for such plan year. Breakpoint compensation is the maximum compensation determined for the plan for a plan year that any participant could earn and have a projected benefit from the offset plan of $0. For purposes of determining the projected plan benefit, the following assumptions are made: plan participation begins at age 25 and maximum credited service is earned for participation from age 25 to age 65 regardless of the participant's actual participation; plan benefits, including the offset, are based on W-2 earnings from the employer for such calendar year regardless of the definition of compensation on which plan benefits are based; and the projected Social Security Primary Insurance Amount (PIA) is computed under a formula that the Commissioner may, from time to time, prescribed for this purpose.

* * * * *

(f) *Certain individuals not active participants*—(1) *Election out of plan.* For purposes of this section, an individual who elects pursuant to the plan not to participate in the plan will be considered to be ineligible for participation for the period to which the election applies, in the case of a defined benefit plan, such as an election shall be effective no earlier than the first plan year commencing after the date of the election.

(2) *Members of reserve components.* A member of a reserve component of the armed forces (as defined in section 261(a) of Title 10 of the United States Code) is not considered to be an active participant in a plan described in section 219(b)(2)(A)(iv) for a taxable year solely because he is a member of a reserve component unless he has served in excess of 90 days on active duty (other than military duty for training) during the year.

(3) *Volunteer firefighters.* An individual whose participation in a plan described in section 219(b)(2)(A)(iv) is based solely upon his activity as a volunteer firefighter and whose accrued benefit as of the beginning of the taxable year is not more than an annual benefit of $1,800 (when expressed as a single life annuity commencing at age 65) is not considered to be an active participant in such a plan for the taxable year.

* * * * *

(h) *Examples.* * * *

Example (3). (i) For plan year X the annual projected Social Security PIA is determined as follows:

Compensation range[1]	PIA formula[1]
$0 to $1,626	PIA = $1,484.
$1,627 to $2,160	PIA = .90 (compensation).
$2,161 to $13,020	PIA = .32 (compensation) + $1,253.
$13,021 to $22,900	PIA = 15 (compensation) + $3,466.
$22,901 and over	PIA = $6,901.

[1] These numbers are for illustrative purposes only.

(ii) V is a defined benefit plan which provides a normal retirement benefit of 1.5% of high five-year average earnings excluding overtime pay, minus 2% of Social Security PIA, the difference multiplied by years of plan participation up to a maximum of 30 years. V provides that individuals commence plan participation on their date of employment. Normal retirement age is 62. V's breakpoint compensation for the plan year ending in year X can be determined as follows:

I. *Determine V's projected benefits:*

An individual credited with 40 years of service (from age 25 to 65) would have a projected benefit of:

(30) (1.5% (compensation) –2% (PIA))

or

45% (compensation) –60% (PIA).

Note that in the determination of the projected benefit, the normal retirement age is assumed to be age 65 rather than the actual normal retirement age of 62, the participant is assumed to have 40 years of credited service, and the plan definition of compensation is assumed to be the same as is used to compute the Social Security benefit.

II. *Determine V's formula compensation changepoints.* The formula compensation changepoints are amounts where the projected benefit formula, expressed in terms of compensation, changes:

Since V's benefit formula applies uniformly to all compensation, the compensation changepoints are determined by the PIA portion only, and are

a. $1,626,

b. 2,160.

c. 13,020.

d. 22,900.

III. *Determine which of the formula compensation changepoints first produces a projected benefit greater than 0.* This can be done by testing the projected benefit for compensation amounts equal to V's compensation changepoints:

a. Formula compensation changepoint equal to $1,626.

i. Projected benefit = 45% × 1,626 – 60% × 1.464 = 0.

V's compensation breakpoint, therefore, exceeds $1,626.

b. Formula compensation changepoint equal to $2,160.

i. Projected benefit = 45% × 2,160 – 60% × (90 × 2,160) = 0.

V's compensation breakpoint, therefore, exceeds $2,160.

c. Formula compensation changepoint equal to $13,020.

i. Projected benefit = 45% × 13,020 – 60% × (.32 × 13,020 + 1,253) = 2,607.

V's compensation breakpoint is, therefore, in the compensation range $2,161 to $13,020.

IV. *Determine V's compensation breakpoint within the $2,161 to $13,020 compensation range.*

V's compensation breakpoint can be determined by finding the greatest compensation that will result in a projected benefit of 0 for this compensation range:

a. 45% × compensation – 60% × (.32 × compensation + 1,253) = 0.

b. Eliminate the parentheses in equation a by multiplying each of the terms within the parentheses by – 60%. 45% × compensation – 19.2% × compensation – 751.80 = 0.

c. Add 751.80 to both sides of equation in b and combine the first two terms. 25.8% × compensation = 751.80.

d. Dividing both sides of the equation in c by 25.8%, V's breakpoint compensation for 1979 = $2,914.

V. Therefore, individuals whose W-2 earnings from the employer do not exceed $2,914 in year X are not considered active participants by virtue of participating in Plan V.

Example (4). For year X the annual projected Social Security PIA is determined as in *Example (3).*

T is defined benefit plan which provides a normal retirement benefit equal to 20% of final average earnings plus 10% of such earnings in excess of $2,000 minus 45% of PIA, the net result reduced pro-rata for participation less than 15 years. Participation commences upon attainment of age 20. Normal retirement age is 65.

I. *Determine T's projected benefit for year X.*

An individual credited with 40 years of service (from age 25 to 65) would have projected benefit of:

20% of compensation plus 10% of compensation in excess of $2,000, if any

minus

45% of PIA

II. *Determine T's formula compensation changepoints.*

$2,000 is a formula compensation changepoint, in addition to the four PIA changepoints, since T's benefit formula changes at this compensation amount. The five formula compensation changepoints are:

a. $1,626.

b. 2,000.

c. 2,160.

d. 13,020.

e. 22,900.

III. *Determine which of T's formula compensation changepoints first produces a projected benefit greater than 0.*

a. Compensation changepoint equal to $1,626.

i. Projected benefit = 20% × 1,626 + 10% × 0 – 45% × 1.424 = 0.

T's compensation changepoint, therefore, exceeds $1,626.

b. Compensation changepoint equal to $2,000.

i. Projected benefit = 20% × 2,000 + 10% × 0 – 45% × (.90 × 2,000) = 0.

T's compensation changepoint, therefore, exceeds $2,000.

c. Compensation changepoint equal to $2,160.

i. Projected benefit = 20% × 2,160 + 10% × (2,160 – 2,000) – 45% × (.90 × 2,160) = 0.

T's compensation breakpoint, therefore, exceeds $2,160.

d. Compensation changepoint equal to $13,020.

i. Projected benefit = 20% × 13,020 + 10% (13,020 – 2,000) – 45% × (.32 × 13,020 + 1,253) = 1,267.

T's compensation breakpoint, therefore, in the compensation range $2,160 to $13,020.

IV. *Determine T's breakpoint compensation within the $2,160 to $13,020 range.*

T's compensation breakpoint can be determined by finding the greatest compensation that will result in a projected benefit of 0 for this range:

a. 20% × comp. + 10% × (comp. – 2,000) – 45% × (.32 × comp. + 1.253) = 0.

b. Eliminating both parenthesis in equation a. by multiplying each of the terms within by the appropriate percentage.

$20\% \times \text{comp.} + 10\% \times \text{comp.} - 200 - 14.4\% \times \text{comp.} - 563.85 = 0.$

c. Add 763.85 to both sides of equation and combine remaining terms in equation b.

$15.6\% \times \text{comp.} = 763.85.$

d. Dividing each side of equation c. by 15.6%, T's breakpoint compensation for year X = $4,896.

V. Therefore, individuals whose W-2 earnings do not exceed $4,896 in year X are not considered active participants by virtue of participating in Plan T.

Example (5). Assume the same facts as *Example (4),* except that T also provides a minimum monthly benefit of $100 for participants with 15 or more years of plan participation. There is no compensation amount which will produce a projected benefit of $0. Therefore, all individuals who satisfy T's eligibility requirements are considered active participants.

Par. 4. There are added after § 1.219-2 the following new sections:

§ 1.219-3 Limitation on simplified employee pension deductions.

(a) *General rule*—(1) *In general.* Under section 219(b)(7), if an employer contribution is made on behalf of an employee to a simplified employee pension described in section 408(k), the limitations of this action, and not section 219(b)(1) and § 1.219-1(b)(1), shall apply for purposes of computing the maximum allowable deduction for that individual employee. The other rules of section 219 and §§ 1.219-1 and 1.219-2 apply for purposes of computing an individual's deduction except as modified by this section.

(2) *Employer limitation.* The maximum deduction limitation under section 219(a) for an employee with respect to an employer contribution to the employee's simplified employee pension under that employer's arrangement cannot exceed an amount equal to the lesser of—

(i) 15 percent of the employee's compensation from that employer (determined without regard to the employer contribution to the simplified employee pension) includible in the employee's gross income for the taxable year, or

(ii) The amount contributed by that employer to the employee's simplified employee pension and included in gross income (but not in excess of $7,500).

(3) *Special rules*—(i) *Compensation.* Compensation referred to in paragraph (a)(2)(i) has the same meaning as under § 1.219-1(c)(1) except that it includes only the compensation from the employer making the contribution to the simplified employee pension. Thus, if an individual earns $50,000 from employer A and $20,000 from employer B and employer B contributes $4,000 to a simplified employee pension on behalf of the individual, the maximum amount the individual will be able to deduct under section 219(b)(7) is 15 percent of $20,000, or $3,000.

(ii) *Special rule for officers, shareholders, and owner-employees.* In the case of an employee who is an officer, shareholder, or owner-employee described in section 408(k)(3) with respect to a particular employer, the $7,500 amount referred to in paragraph (a)(2)(ii) shall be reduced by the amount of tax taken into account with respect to such individual under section 408(k)(3)(D).

(iii) *More than one employer arrangement.* Except as provided in paragraph (c), below, the maximum deduction under paragraph (a)(2) for an individual who receives simplified employee pension contributions under two or more employers' simplified employee pension arrangements cannot exceed the sum of the maximum deduction limitations computed separately for that individual under each such employer's arrangement.

(iv) *Section 408 rules.* Under section 408(j), for purposes of applying the $7,500 limitations under section 408(a)(1), (b)(1), (b)(2)(B) and (d)(5) (§ 1.408-2(b)(1), § 1.408-3(b)(2) and § 1.408-4(h)(3)(i), respectively), the $7,500 limitations shall be applied separately with respect to each employer's contributions to a individual's simplified employee pension.

(b) *Limitations not applicable to SEP contributions*—(1) *Active participant.* The limitations on coverage by certain other plans in section 219(b)(2) and § 1.219-1(b)(2)(i) shall not apply with respect to the employer contribution to a simplified employee pension. Thus, an employee is allowed a deduction for an employer's contribution to a simplified employee pension even though he is an active participant in an employer's qualified plan.

(2) *Contributions to simplified employee pensions after age 70 ½.* The denial of deductions for contributions after age 70 ½ contained in section 219(b)(3) and § 1.219-1(b)(2)(ii) shall not apply with respect to the employer contribution to a simplified employee pension.

(c) *Multiple employer, etc. limitations*—(1) *Section 414(b) and (c) employers.* In the case of a controlled group of employers within the meaning of section 414(b) or (c), the maximum deduction limitation for an employee under paragraph (a)(2) shall be computed by treating such employers as one employer maintaining a single simplified pension arrangement and by treating the compensation of that employee from such employers as if from one employer. Thus, for example, for a particular employee the 15 percent limitation on compensation would be determined with regard to the compensation from all employers within such group. Further, the maximum deduction with respect to such group could not exceed $7,500.

(2) *Self-employed individuals.* In the case of an employee who is a self-employed individual within the meaning of section 401(c)(1) with respect to more than one trade or business, the maximum deduction limitation for such an employee under paragraph (a)(2) shall not exceed the lesser of the sum of such limitation applied separately with respect to the simplified employee pension arrangement of each trade or business or such limitation determined by treating such trades or businesses as if they constituted a single employer.

(d) *Additional deduction for employee contributions.* If the maximum allowable deduction for an individual employee determined under paragraph (a) for employer contributions to that individual's simplified employee pensions is less than $1,500, the individual shall be entitled to an additional deduction for contributions to individual retirement programs maintained on his behalf. The additional deduction shall equal the excess, if any, of the section 219(b)(1) and § 1.219-1(b)(1) maximum deduction limitation over the maximum deduction limitation determined under paragraph (a). For purpose of determining the compensation limit of section 219(b)(1), employer simplified employee pension contributions shall not be taken into account. Thus, for example, if $1,000 is deductible by individual A for employer contributions under a simplified employee pension arrangement and A's compensation, not including the $1,000 SEP contribution, is $10,000, than A would be entitled to an additional deduction of $500.

(e) *Examples.* The provisions of this section may be illustrated by the following examples:

Example (1). Corporation X is a calendar-year, cash basis taxpayer. It adopts a simplified employee pension agreement in 1980 and wishes to contribute the maximum amount on behalf of each employee for 1980. Individual E is a calendar-year taxpayer who is employed solely by Corporation X in 1980. Beginning in June 1980, Corporation X pays $100 each month into a simplified employee pension maintained on behalf of E. X makes a total payment to E's simplified employee pension during the year of $700. E's other compensation from X for the year totals $15,000. The maximum amount which E will be allowed to deduct as a simplified employee pension contribution is 15% of $15,000, or $2,250. Therefore, X may make an additional contribution for 1980 to E's simplified employee pension of $1,550. X makes this additional contribution to E's simplified employee pension in February of 1981. E's total compensation for 1980 includible in gross income is $15,000 ♦ $2,250 or $17,250.

Example (2). (i) Corporation G is a calendar-year taxpayer which does not maintain an integrated plan as defined in section 408(k)(3)(E). It adopts a simplified employee pension agreement for 1980. It wishes to contribute 15% of compensation on behalf of each employee reduced by its tax under section 3111(a). The corporation has 4 employees, A, B, C, and D. D is a shareholder. The compensation for these employees for 1980 is as follows:

A ✓ $10,000

B ✓ 20,000

C ✓ 30,000

D ✓ 60,000

(ii) The amount of money which the corporation will be allowed to contribute on behalf of each employee under this allocation formula and the amount of the employer contribution each employee will be allowed to deduct is set forth in the following table:

Employee	Compensation	Lesser of $7500 or 15% of Comp.	3111(a)[1]Tax	SEP[2] Contribution	Sec. 219(b)(7) deduction
A	$10,000	$1,500	$508.00	$992.00	$992.00
B	20,000	3,000	1,016.00	1,984.00	1,984.00
C	30,000	4,500	1,315.72	1,184.28	1,184.28
D	60,000	7,500	1,315.72	6,184.28	6,184.28

[1] The section 3111(a) tax is computed by multiplying compensation up to the taxable wage base ($25,900 for 1980) by the tax rate (5.08% for 1980).
[2] Simplified Employee Pension.

Example (3). Corporations A and B are calendar year taxpayers. Corporations A and B are not members of a controlled group of employers within the meaning of section 414(b) or (c). Individual M is employed full-time by Corporation A and part-time by Corporation B. Corporation A adopts a simplified employee pension agreement for calendar year 1980 and agrees to contribute 15% of compensation for each participant. M is a participant under Corporation A's simplified employee pension agreement and earns $15,000 for 1980 from Corporation A before A's contribution to his simplified employee pension. M also earns $5,000 as a part-time employee of Corporation B for 1980. Corporation A contributes $2,500 to M's simplified employee pension. The maximum amount that M will be allowed to deduct under Section 219(b)(7) for 1980 is 15% of $15,000 or $2,250. The remaining $250 is an excess contribution because M cannot consider the compensation earned from Corporation B under § 1.219-3(a)(3)(i).

Example (4). Individual P is employed by Corporation H and Corporation O. Corporation H and O are not members of a controlled group of employers within the meaning of section 414(b) or (c). Both Corporation H and Corporation O maintain a simplified employee pension arrangement and contribute 15 percent of compensation on behalf of each employee. P earns $50,000 from Corporation H and $60,000 from Corporation O. Corporation H and O each contributes $7,500 under its simplified employee pension arrangement to an individual retirement account maintained on behalf of P. P will be allowed to deduct $15,000 for employer contributions to simplified employee pensions because each employer has a simplified employee pension arrangement and the SEP contributions by Corporation H and O do not exceed the applicable $7,500 ← 15 percent limitation.

§ 1.220-1 Deduction for retirement savings for certain married individuals.

(a) *In general.* Subject to the limitations and restrictions of paragraphs (c), (d) and (e) and the special rules of paragraph (f) of this section, there shall be allowed a deduction under section 62 from gross income of amounts paid for the taxable year of an individual by or on behalf of such individual for the benefit of himself and his spouse to an individual retirement account described in section 408(a), for an individual retirement annuity described in section 408(b), or for an individual retirement bond described in section 409. The amounts contributed to an individual retirement account, for an individual retirement annuity, or for an individual retirement bond by or on behalf of an individual for the benefit of himself and his spouse shall be deductible only by such individual. The first sentence of this paragraph shall apply only in the case of a contribution of cash; a contribution of property other than cash is not allowable as a deduction. In the case of an individual retirement bond, a deduction will not be allowed if the bond is redeemed within 12 months of its issue date.

(b) *Definitions*—(1) *Compensation.* For purposes of this section, the term "compensation" has the meaning set forth in § 1.219-1(c)(1).

(2) *Active participant.* For purposes of this section, the term "active participant" has the meaning set forth in § 1.219-2.

(3) *Individual retirement subaccount.* For purposes of this section, the term individual retirement subaccount is that part of an individual retirement account maintained for the exclusive benefit of the individual or the individual's spouse and which meets the following requirements:

(i) The individual or spouse for whom the subaccount is maintained has exclusive control over the subaccount after deposits have been made,

(ii) The subaccount, by itself, meets the requirements of section 408(a), except that it is not a separate trust,

(iii) The trustee or custodian maintains records indicating the ownership of the funds, and

(iv) The individual and spouse do not jointly own the individual retirement account of which the subaccount is a part.

(c) *Types of funding arrangements permitted.* The deduction under paragraph (a) of this section shall be allowed only if one of the following types of funding arrangements is used:

(1) A separate individual retirement account, individual retirement annuity, or individual retirement bond is established or purchased for the benefit of the individual and a separate individual retirement account, individual retirement annuity or individual retirement bond is established or purchased for the individual's spouse.

(2) A single individual retirement account described in section 408(a) is established or purchased and such account has an individual retirement subaccount for the benefit of the individual and an individual retirement subaccount for the benefit of the spouse. The single individual retirement account cannot be owned jointly by the husband and wife.

(3) An individual retirement account described in section 408(c) is maintained by an employer or employee association and such account has arrangements described in subparagraphs (1) or (2).

(d) *Maximum deduction.* The amount allowable as a deduction under section 220(a) to an individual for any taxable year may not exceed—

(1) Twice the amount paid (including prior excess contributions) to the account, subaccount, annuity, or for the bond, established for the individual or for the spouse to or for which the lesser amount was paid for the taxable year.

(2) An amount equal to 15 percent of the compensation includible in the individual's gross income for the taxable year, or

(3) $1,750

whichever is the smallest amount.

(e) *Limitations and restrictions*—(1) *Alternative deduction.* No deduction is allowable under section 220(a) for the taxable year if the individual claims the deduction allowed by section 219(a) for the taxable year.

(2) *Individual or spouse covered by certain other plans.* No deduction is allowable under section 220(a) to an individual for the taxable year if for any part of such year—

(i) He or his spouse was an active participant (as defined in § 1.219-2), or

(ii) Amounts were contributed by his employer, or his spouse's employer, on the individual's or spouse's behalf for an annuity contract described in section 403(b) (whether or not his, or his spouse's, rights in such contract are nonforfeitable).

(3) *Contributions after age 70 ½.* No deduction is allowable under section 220(a) with respect to any payment which is made for a taxable year of an individual if either the individual or his spouse has attained age 70 ½ before the close of such taxable year.

(4) *Recontributed amounts.* No deduction is allowable under section 220(a) for any taxable year of an individual with respect to a rollover contribution described in section 402(a)(5), 402(a)(7), 403(a)(4), 403(b)(8), 408(d)(3), or 409(b)(3)(C).

(5) *Amounts contributed under endowment contracts.* The rules for endowment contracts under section 220 are the same as the provisions for such contracts under § 1.219-1(b)(3).

(6) *Employed spouses.* No deduction is allowable under section 220(a) if the spouse of the individual has any compensation (as defined in § 1.219-1(c)(1) determined without regard to section 911) for the taxable year of such spouse ending with or within the taxable year of the individual.

(f) *Special rules*—(1) *Community property.* Section 220 is to be applied without regard to any community property laws.

(2) *Time when contributions deemed made.* The time when contributions are deemed made is determined in the same manner as under section 219(c)(3). See § 1.219-1(d).

(g) *Excess contributions treated as contribution made during subsequent year for which there is an unused limitation*—(1) *In general.* If for the taxable year the maximum amount allowable as a deduction under this section exceeds the amount contributed, then the taxpayer, whether or not a deduction is actually claimed, shall be treated as having made an additional contribution for the taxable year in an amount equal to the lesser of—

(i) The amount of such excess, or

(ii) The amount of the excess contributions for such taxable year (determined under section 4973(b)(2) without regard to subparagraph (C) thereof).

For purposes of computing the maximum deduction under section 220(b)(1), the excess contribution for a previous year shall be treated as made for the current year.

(2) *Amount contributed.* For purposes of this paragraph, the amount contributed—

(i) Shall be determined without regard to this paragraph, and

(ii) Shall not include any rollover contribution.

(3) *Special rule where excess contribution was allowed for closed year.* Proper reduction shall be made in the amount allowable as a deduction by reason of this paragraph for any amount allowed as a deduction under this section or section 219 for a prior taxable year for which the period for assessing a deficiency has expired if the amount so allowed exceeds the amount which should have been allowed for such prior taxable year.

(4) *Examples.* The provisions of this paragraph may be illustrated by the following examples:

Example (1). (i) H, a calendar-year taxpayer, earns $10,000 in compensation includible in gross income for 1979. H is married to W, also a calander-year taxpayer, who has no compensation for 1979. For 1979, neither H nor W is covered by certain other plans within the meaning of section 220(b)(3). On November 24, 1979, H establishes an individual retirement account (IRA) for himself and an individual retirement account for W. H contributes $850 to each account. Neither H nor W withdraws any money from either account after the initial contribution. Under section 220(b)(1) the maximum amount that H can deduct for 1979 is 15 percent of the compensation includible in his gross income or $1,500. H has made an excess contribution of $200 for 1979.

(ii) for 1980, H has compensation includible in gross income of $12,000. W has no compensation for 1980. For 1980, neither H nor W is covered by certain other plans, within the meaning of section 220(b)(3). No contributions are made to the IRA of H or W for 1980.

(iii) Although H made no contributions to either his or W's IRA for 1980, under the rules contained in this paragraph, H is treated as having made an additional contribution of $100 to his IRA and $100 to W's IRA for 1980 and will be allowed to deduct $200 as his 1980 IRA contribution.

Example (2). (i) For 1979, the facts are the same as in *Example (1).*

(ii) For 1980, H has compensation of $15,000 includible in gross income and is not covered by any other plans within the meaning of section 219(b)(2). W also goes to work in 1980 and has compensation of $6,000, but is not covered by certain other plans within the meaning of section 219(b)(2). H will not be treated as having made a deductible contribution of a previous year's excess contribution within the meaning of section 220(c)(6) because W has compensation for 1980. However, both H and W now meet the deduction standards of section 219 and each will be treated as having made a deductible contribution of $100 to their separate IRA's for 1980 under section 219(c)(5).

Example (3). (i) For 1979, the facts are the same as in *Example (1).*

(ii) For 1980, H has compensation of $15,000 includible in gross income and is covered by certain other plans within the meaning of section 220(b)(3). W has no compensation for 1980 and is not covered by certain other plans within the meaning of section 220(b)(3). H will not be treated as having made a deductible contribution of a previous year's excess contribution within the meaning of section 219(c)(5) or 220(c)(6) because H is covered by other plans for 1980 and has no allowable deduction under section 219 or 220.

(iii) W will not be treated as having made a deductible contribution of a previous year's excess contribution within the meaning of section 219(c)(5) because W has no compensation for 1980 and thus no allowable deduction under section 219.

(h) *Effective date.* (1) This section is effective for taxable years beginning after December 31, 1976.

(2) If, but for this subparagraph, an amount would be allowable as a deduction by reason of section 220(c)(6) and paragraph (g) for a taxable year beginning before January 1, 1978, such amount shall be allowable only for the taxpayer's first taxable year beginning in 1978.

Par. 5. There is added after § 1.404(e)-1A the following new section:

§ 1.404(h)(1) Special rules for simplified employee pensions.

(a) *In general.* (1) Employer contributions to a simplified employee pension shall be treated as if they are made to a plan subject to the requirements of section 404. Employer contributions to a simplified employee pension are subject to the limitations of subparagraphs (2), (3), (4) and (5). For purposes of this paragraph participants means those employees who satisfy the age, service and other requirements to participate in a simplified employee pension. For purposes of this paragraph, "compensation" means all of the compensation paid by the employer except either that for which a deduction is allowable under section 404(h) for simplified employee pension or that for which a deduction is allowable under a plan that qualifies under section 401(a), including a plan that qualifies under section 404(a)(2) or 405.

(2) Employer contributions made for a calendar year are deductible for the taxable year of the employer with which or within which the calendar year ends.

(3) Contributions made within 3 ½ months after the close of a calendar year are treated as if they were made on the last day of such calendar year if they are made on account of such calendar year.

(4) The amount deductible for a taxable year for a simplified employee pension shall not exceed 15 percent of the compensation paid to the employees who are participants during the calendar year ending with or within the taxable year.

(5) The excess of the amount contributed over the amount deductible for a taxable year shall be deductible in the succeeding taxable years in order of time subject to the 15 percent limit of subparagraph (4).

(b) *Effect on stock bonus and profit-sharing trust.* For any taxable year for which the employer has a deduction under section 404(h)(1), the otherwise applicable limitations in section 404(a)(3)(A) shall be reduced by the amount of the allowable deductions under section 404(h)(1) with respect to participants in the stock bonus or profit-sharing trust.

(c) *Effect on limit on deductions.* For any taxable year for which the employer has an allowable deduction under section 404(h)(1), the otherwise applicable 25 percent limitations in section 404(a)(7) shall be reduced by the amount of the allowable deductions under section 404(h)(1) with respect to participants in the stock bonus or profit-sharing trust.

(d) *Effect on self-employed individuals or shareholder-employee.* The limitations described in paragraphs (1), (2)(A), and (4) of section 404(e) or described in section 1379(b)(1) for any taxable year shall be reduced by the amount of the allowable deductions under section 404(h)(1) with respect to an employee within the meaning of section 401(c)(1) or a shareholder-employee (as defined in section 1379(d)).

(e) *Examples.* The provisions of this section may be illustrated by the following examples:

Example (1). Corporation X is a calendar-year taxpayer. On January 2, 1980, it adopts a simplified employee pension arrangement. At the end of 1980, if determines that it has paid $230,000 to all of its employees. Eight of its employees met its eligibility provisions for contributions to simplified employee pensions and their compensation totaled $140,000 before any contributions were made to their simplified employee pensions. Corporation X will be allowed to deduct its contributions to its employees' simplified employee pensions, not to exceed 15% of $140,000 or $21,000.

Example (2). Corporation Y is a calendar-year taxpayer which maintains a simplified employee pension agreement and a profit-sharing plan. The corporation has 100 employees. For the taxable year of 1980, it makes contributions to the simplified employee pensions of 75 of its employees. These contributions are 10 percent of compensation received in 1980. These same 75 employees are also participants in the corporation's profit-sharing plan. These 75 employees had total compensation paid during 1980 of $1,125,000. The corporation can deduct $112,500 under section 404(h) as its contributions to the simplified employee pension agreement. The corporation must reduce the otherwise applicable allowable deduction for contributions to the profit-sharing plan on behalf of these employees by the $112,500.

Example (3). Corporation Z is a calendar-year taxpayer which maintains a simplified employee pension arrangement and a profit-sharing plan. The corporation has 100 employees. For the taxable year of 1980, it makes contributions to the simplified employee pensions of 75 of its employees. These contributions are 10 percent of compensation received in 1980. Twenty-five of these employees are also participants in the corporation's profit-sharing plan. Each of these 75 employees had compensation for the year of $15,000, or total compensation of $1,125,000. The corporation deducts $112,500 under section 404(h) as its contribution to the simplified employee pension arrangement. The corporation must reduce the otherwise applicable allowable deduction for contributions to the profit-sharing plan on behalf of the 25 employees by $37,500, the amount contributed to the simplified employee pensions on behalf of employees covered by the profit-sharing plan.

Example (4). Corporation K is a taxpayer with a taxable year of December 1—November 30. On December 15, 1979, it adopts a simplified employee pension arrangement for its employees. It would like to make contributions to the plan on behalf of its employees for calendar year 1979. In order to make contributions to its employees' simplified employee pensions for calendar year 1979, the corporation must make the contributions by April 15, 1980. In order to receive a deduction for its taxable year ending November 30, 1980, for the contributions for calendar year 1979, the corporation must make the contributions by April 15, 1980.

Par. 6. Section 1.408-2 is amended by revising paragraph (c)(3) to read as follows:

§ 1.408-2 Individual retirement accounts.

* * * * *

(c) * * *

(3) *Special requirement*. There must be a separate accounting for the interest of each employee or member (or spouse of an employee or member).

* * * * *

Par. 7. Section 1.408-3 is revised by adding new paragraphs (b)(6) and (f). These added provisions read as follows:

§ 1.408-3 Individual retirement annuities.

* * * * *

(b) * * *

(6) *Flexible premium*. (i) In the case of annuity contracts issued after November 6, 1978, the premiums under such contracts are not fixed. See paragraph (f) for the definition of an annuity contract under which "the premiums are not fixed."

(ii) In the case of a fixed premium individual retirement annuity or individual retirement endowment contract issued before November 7, 1978, the issuer of such contract may offer the holder of the contract the option of exchanging such contract for a flexible premium contract. If such an exchange is made before January 1, 1981, the exchange shall not constitute a distribution and shall be nontaxable.

* * * * *

(f) *Flexible premium annuity contract*—(1) *In general*. A flexible premium retirement annuity contract shall be considered a contract under which "the premiums are not fixed" if it provides the following.

(i) At no time after the initial premium for the contract has been paid is there a specified renewal premium required.

(ii) The contract must allow for the continuance of the contract (as a paid-up annuity) under its nonforfeiture provision if premium payments cease altogether.

(iii) The contract, if being continued on a paid-up basis (*i.e.*, if it has not been terminated by a payment in cash), will be reinstated at any date prior to its maturity date upon payment of a premium to the insurer.

(2) *Exceptions*. (i) The insurer may require that if a premium is remitted, it will be accepted only if the amount remitted is some stated amount, not in excess of $50.

(ii) The contract may provide that if no premiums have been received under the contract for two (2) full years and the paid-up annuity benefit at maturity of the plan stipulated in the contract arising from the premium paid prior to such two-year period would be less than $20 a month, the insurer may, at its option, terminate the contract by payment in cash of the then present value of the paid-up benefit (computed on the same basis specified in the contract for determining the paid-up benefit).

(3) *Permissible provisions*. A flexible premium contract will not be considered to have fixed premiums merely because—

(i) A maximum limit (which may be expressed as a multiple of the premium paid in the first year of the contract) is placed on the amount of the premium that the insurer will accept in any year,

(ii) An annual charge is made against the policy value,

(iii) A fee (which may be composed of a flat dollar amount plus an amount equal to the required premium tax imposed by the state government) is charged upon the acceptance of each premium by the insurer, or

(iv) The contract requires a level annual premium for a supplementary benefit, such as a waiver of premium benefit.

Par. 8. Section 1.408-4 is amended by: (1) Adding new paragraphs (b)(3), (b)(4)(ii), and (c)(3)(ii); and (2) adding a new paragraph (h). These added provisions read as follows:

§ 1.408-4 Treatment of distributions from individual retirement arrangements.

* * * * *

(b) *Rollover Contribution.* * * *

(3) *To section 403(b) contract.*

Paragraph (a)(1) of this section does not apply to any amount paid or distributed from an individual retirement account or individual retirement annuity to the individual for whose benefit the account or annuity is maintained if—

(i) The entire amount received (including money and other property) represents the entire interest in the account or the entire value of the annuity,

(ii) No amount in the account and no part of the value of the annuity is attributable to any source other than a rollover contribution from an annuity contract described in section 403(b) and any earnings on such rollover,

(iii) The entire amount thereof is paid into an annuity contract described in section 403(b) (for the benefit of such individual) not later than the 60th day after the receipt of the payment or distribution, and

(iv) The distribution or transfer is made in a taxable year beginning after December 31, 1978.

(4) * * *

(ii) For taxable years beginning after December 31, 1977, paragraph (b)(1) of this section does not apply to any amount received by an individual from an individual retirement account, individual retirement annuity or retirement bond if at any time during the 1-year period ending on the day of receipt, the individual received any other amount from the individual retirement account, individual retirement annuity or retirement bond which was not includible in his gross income because of the application of paragraph (b)(1) of this section. This rule applies to each separate individual retirement account, individual retirement annuity, or retirement bond maintained by an individual. Thus, if an individual maintains two individual retirement accounts, IRA-1 and IRA-2, and rolls over the assets of IRA-1 into IRA-3, he is not precluded by this subdivision from making a tax-free rollover from IRA-2 to IRA-3 or any other IRA within one year after the rollover from IRA-1 to IRA-3.

(c) * * *

(3) *Time of inclusion.* * * *

(ii) For taxable years beginning after December 31, 1976, the amount of net income determined under subparagraph (2) is includible in the gross income of the individual in the taxable year in which such excess contribution is made. The amount of net income thus distributed is subject to the tax imposed by section 408(f)(1) for the year includible in gross income.

(h) *Certain deductions of excess contributions after due date of return for taxable year*—(1) *general rule*. In the case of any individual, if the aggregate contributions (other than valid rollover contributions) paid for any taxable year to an individual retirement account or for an individual retirement annuity do not exceed $1,750, section 408(d)(1) shall not apply to the distribution of any such contribution to the extent that such contribution exceeds the amount allowable as a deduction under section 219 or 220 for the taxable year for which the contribution was paid—

(i) If such distribution is received after the date described in section 408(d)(4),

(ii) But only to the extent that no deduction has been allowed under section 219 or 220 with respect to such excess contribution.

(2) *Excess rollover contribution attributable to erroneous information.* If the taxpayer reasonably relies on information supplied pursuant to subtitle F of the Internal Revenue Code of 1954 for determining the amount of a rollover contribution, but such information was erroneous, subparagraph (1) of this paragraph shall be applied by increasing the dollar limit set forth therein by that portion of the excess contribution which was attributable to such information.

(3) *Special rule for contributions to simplified employee pension.* If employer contributions on behalf of the individual are paid for the taxable year to a simplified employee pension, the dollar limitation of subparagraph (1) shall be the lesser of the amount of such contributions or $7,500. See § 1.219-3(a)(3)(iv) for a special rule where there is more than one employer.

(4) *Effective date.* (1) Subparagraphs (1) and (2) of this paragraph shall apply to distributions in taxable years beginning after December 31, 1975.

(ii) In the case of contributions for taxable years beginning before January 1, 1978, paragraph (5) of section 408(d) of the Internal Revenue Code of 1954 shall be applied as if such paragraph did not contain any dollar limitation.

(4) *Examples.* The provisions of this paragraph may be illustrated by the following examples:

Example (1). T, a calendar-year taxpayer, had been a participant in a government pension plan for 6 years prior to separation from service on July 31, 1976. The plan required T to make mandatory contributions and as of July 31, 1976, these mandatory contributions totaled $6,000. Upon T's separation from service, she was given the option of receiving back all of her mandatory contributions or leaving them with the plan. T elected to receive her mandatory contributions and attempted to roll over these amounts into an individual retirement account (IRA) in August of 1976. The trustee of the IRA accepted these funds and IRA was established. In March of 1977, T discovered that the funds she received from the government plan did not qualify for rollover treatment because they were employee contributions and withdrew all of the money from her IRA. T will not have to include any of the money withdrawn from the IRA in gross income for 1977 because the transitional rule of paragraph (h)(3)(ii) permits the withdrawal of all contributions which have not been allowed as deductions under section 219 or 220 made to IRA's for taxable years beginning before January 1, 1978, regardless of the amount of the contribution.

Example (2). (i) On April 1, 1980, A, a calendar-year taxpayer, receives a lump sum distribution satisfying the requirements of section 402(e)(4)(A) and (C) under the plan of A's employer. The distribution consists of $50,000 case. A made contributions under the plan totaling $8,000, and has received no prior distributions under the plan. However, on the form furnished to A by the employer on account of the distribution, A's contributions under the plan are listed as totaling only $4,500. A reasonably relied on this information.

(ii) A desires to establish an individual retirement account (as described in section 408(a)) with the cash received in the distribution. A desires to contribute the maximum amount permitted under the rollover rules. Under sections 402(a)(5)(B) and 402(a)(5)(D)(ii), A determines that the maximum rollover amount is $45,500, the total of the distribution ($50,000), less the amount listed as A's contributions under the plan ($4,500). The actual maximum rollover amount is $42,000, the total of the distribution ($50,000), less A's actual contribution under the plan ($8,000).

(iii) On May 23, 1980, A contributes $45,500 to an individual retirement account as a rollover contribution.

(iv) On May 1, 1981, A's employer furnishes A a corrected statement indicating that A's contributions under the plan were $8,000. On June 1, 1981, A withdraws $3,500 from the individual retirement account to correct the mistaken contribution. A will not have to include the $3,500 withdrawn from the individual retirement account due to erroneous information furnished by the employer and reasonably relied upon by A and thus falls under the exception provided in section 408(d)(5)(B) to section 406(d)(1).

Par 9. Section 1.406-6 is amended by removing paragraph (d)(4)(xi) and adding a new paragraph (b) to read as follows:

§ 1.408-6 Disclosure statements for individual retirement arrangements.

* * *

(b) *Disclosure statements for spousal individual retirement arrangements.* The trustee of an individual retirement account and the issuer of an individual retirement annuity shall furnish to the benefited individual of a spousal individual retirement arrangement a disclosure statement in accordance with paragraph (d). In the case of a spousal individual retirement arrangement that uses subaccounts, the benefited individual includes both the working and non-working spouse.

Par. 10. There are added after § 1.408-6 the following new sections:

§ 1.408-7 Simplified employee pension.

(a) *In general.* The term "simplified employee pension" means an individual retirement account or individual retirement annuity described in section 408(a), (b) or (c) with respect to which the requirements of paragraphs (b), (d), (e), (g), and (h) of this section are met and the requirements of § 1.408-8 are met with respect to any calendar year.

(b) *Establishment of simplified employee pension.* In order to establish a simplified employee pension, the employer must execute a written instrument (hereinafter referred to as the simplified employee pension arrangement) within the time prescribed for making deductible contributions. This instrument shall include: the name of the employer, the requirements for employee participation, the signature of a responsible official, and the definite allocation formula specified in section 408(k)(5) and paragraph (f) of this section.

(c) *Variation in contribution*—(1) *Permitted variations.* An employer's total contributions to its employees' simplified employee pensions may vary annually at the employer's discretion.

(2) *Salary reduction.* Contributions made to a simplified employee pension under an arrangement under which the contribution will be made only if the employee receives a reduction in compensation or forgoes a compensation increase shall be treated as employer contributions to a simplified employee pension only if the arrangement precludes an individual election by the employee. If there is an individual election, then the contribution shall be treated as an employee contribution.

(d) *Participation requirements*—(1) *Age and service requirements.* This paragraph is satisfied with respect to a simplified employee pension arrangement for a calendar year only if for such year the employer contributes to the simplified employee pension on behalf of each individual who is an employee at any time during the calendar year who has—

(i) Attained age 25,

(ii) Performed service for the employer during at least 3 of the immediately preceding 5 calendar years, and

(iii) Received at least $200 compensation from the employer for the calendar year.

(2) *Execution of documents.* The employer may execute any necessary documents on behalf of an employee who is entitled to a contribution to a simplified employee pension if the employee is unable or unwilling to execute such documents or the employer is unable to locate the employee.

(3) *Required employment.* An employer may not require that an employee be employed as of a particular date in order to receive a contribution for a calendar year.

(4) *Nonresident aliens and employees covered by collective-bargaining agreements.* An employer may exclude from participation in the simplified employee pension arrangement employees described in section 410(b)(2)(A) or 410(b)(2)(C).

(5) *Example.* The provisions of this paragraph may be illustrated by the following example:

Example. Corporation X maintains a simplified employee pension arrangement for its employees. Individual J worked for Corporation X while in graduate school in 1976, 1977, and 1978. J began to work for corporation X on a full-time basis. J earned $5,000 from Corporation X for 1979. J became 25 on December 31, 1979. Corporation X must make a contribution to a simplified employee pension maintained on behalf of J for 1979 because as of December 31, 1979, J had met the minimum age requirement of section 408(k)(2), had performed service for Corporation X in 3 of the 5 calendar years preceding 1979, and met the minimum compensation requirements of paragraph (d)(1)(iii).

(e) *Requirement of written allocation formula*—(1) *Requirement of definite written allocation formula.* Employer contributions to a simplified employee pension must be made under a definite written allocation formula which specifies—

(i) The requirements which an employee must satisfy to share in an allocation, and

(ii) The manner in which the amount allocated to each employee's account is computed.

(2) *Employer may vary formula.* An employer may vary the definite written allocation formula from year to year provided the simplified employee pension arrangement is amended by the permissible date for making contributions to indicate the new formula.

(f) *Treatment of contributions which exceed the written allocation formula—*

(1) *General rule.* To the extent that employer contributions do not satisfy § 1.408—7(e)(1), the contributions shall be deemed to be contributions which are not made under a simplified employee pension arrangement except for purposes of section 408(a)(1), (b)(2)(B) and (d)(5). These contribution shall be deemed made to an individual retirement account or individual retirement annuity not maintained as part of a simplified employee pension arrangement.

(2) *Example.* This paragraph is illustrated by the following example:

Example. (i) Assume that in 1979 Corporation X adopts a simplified employee pension arrangement ("SEP Arrangement"). The arrangement calls for Corporation X to contribute the same percentage of each participant's compensation exclusive of SEP contributions to a simplified employee pension (Allocation Compensation). X has three employees, A, B, and C, who satisfy the participation requirements of the SEP Arrangement. The compensation, the contributions to the individual simplified employee pension ("SEP") for A, B and C and the varying treatment of the contributions are set forth as follows:

Employee	Gross income	Net compensation before contribution	SEP-IRA contribution	Ratio of SEP-IRA contributions to net compensation (percent)
A	$110,000	$10,000	$1,000	10
B	11,500	10,000	1,500	15
C	57,500	50,000	7,500	15
Totals	80,000	$70,000	$10,000	

(ii) Under the special rule of this paragraph, because only 10 percent of compensation was allocated to A, and the allocation formula provides that the same percentage will be allocated to each participant, a certain portion of the contribution to B and C under the SEP shall be deemed made to IRA's that are not part of the SEP Arrangement.

(iii) To determine A's and B's Allocation Compensation the respective total compensation included in A's and B's gross income must be divided by 1.10 (1 plus the percentage of Allocation Compensation contributed to A under the SEP Arrangement). The excess of compensation included in gross income over Allocation Compensation is considered as a contribution under the SEP. The following table shows the result of this calculation:

Employee	Gross income	Allocation compensation[1]	SEP-IRA contribution	Deemed IRA contribution[2]
A	$11,000	$10,000	$1,000	$0
B	11,500	10,455	1,045	455
C	57,500	52,273	5,227	2,273
Totals	80,000	72,728	7,272	2,728

[1] Gross income divided by 1.10.
[2] Also included in Allocation Compensation.

(iv) Under section 404(h) for purposes of computing Corporation X's deduction, only the $7,272 is considered as a contribution to a SEP Arrangement described in section 409(k) under the special rule. The allowable 404(h) deduction equals $10,900 (15% of the excess of total compensation of $80,000 over the SEP contribution of $7,272 or 15% of $72,728). The other $2,728 is payment of compensation and subject to the deduction rules of section 162 or 212. Similarly, the $2,728 would not be considered as an employer SEP contribution for purposes of exemption from FICA and FUTA taxes under sections 3121 and 3306.

(v) The effect of treating the $2,273 as a contribution to SEP's for purposes of section 408(a)(1), (b)(2)(B) and (d)(5) is to not disqualify the individual retirement arrangement of C for accepting non-SEP contributions in excess of $1,500 and to allow C to withdraw the excess contribution of $2,273 without including that amount in income under section 404(d)(1).

(g) *Permitted withdrawals.* A simplified employee pension meets the requirements of this paragraph only if—

(1) Employer contributions thereto are not conditioned on the retention in such pension of any portion of the amount contributed, and

(2) There is no prohibition imposed by the employer on withdrawals from the simplified employee pension.

See section 408(d) for rules concerning the taxation of withdrawals from individual retirement accounts and annuities. See section 408(f)(1) for penalties for premature withdrawals from individual retirement accounts and annuities.

(h) *Section 401(j) plan.* The requirements of this paragraph are met with respect to a simplified employee pension for a calendar year unless the employer maintains during any part of such year a plan—

(1) Some or all of the active participants in which are employees (within the meaning of section 4012(c)(1)) or shareholder-employees (as defined in section 1379(d)), and

(2) To which section 401(j) applies.

§ 1.408-8 Nondiscrimination requirements for simplified employee pensions.

(a) *In general.* The requirements of this section are met with respect to a simplified employee pension for a calendar year if for such year the contributions made by the employer to simplified employee pensions of its employees do not discriminate in favor of any employee who is—

(1) An officer,

(2) A shareholder, within the meaning of paragraph (b)(2),

(3) A self-employed individual, or

(4) Highly compensated.

(b) *Special rules.* (1) For purposes of this section, employees described in subparagraph (A) or (C) of section 410 (b)(2) shall be excluded from consideration.

(2) An individual shall be considered a shareholder if he owns (with the application of section 318) more than 10 percent of the value of the stock of the employer.

(c) *Contributions must bear a uniform relationship to total compensation—*(1) *General rule.* Contributions shall be considered discriminatory unless employer contributions to its employees' simplified employee pensions bear a uniform relationship to the total compensation (not in excess of the first $100,000) of each employee maintaining a simplified employee pension. A rate of contribution which decreases as compensation increases shall be considered uniform.

(2) *Definition of compensation.* For purposes of this section, the term "compensation" has the meaning set forth in §1.219-1, and is determined without regard to the employer contributions to the simplified employee pension arrangement.

(3) *Example.* The provisions of this paragraph may be illustrated by the following example:

Example. Corporation X maintains a simplified employee pension arrangement which allocates employer contributions in the manner described below. First, contributions made by June 30 of each year are allocated in proportion to compensation paid from January 1 to June 30. Second, contributions made between July 1 and December 31 are allocated in proportion to compensation paid during the same period.

In 1980, the salaries paid, and contributions allocated are shown below:

Participant	Compensation[1]	Allocation[2]	Compensation[3]	Allocation[4]
A	10,000	500	10,000	1,000
B	10,000	500	1,000	100
C	10,000	500	15,000	1,500

[1] Jan. 1, 1980 to June 30, 1980.
[2] June 30, 1980.
[3] July 1, 1980 to Dec. 31, 1980.
[4] Dec. 31, 1980.

For 1980, A, B, and C received allocations equal to 7.5 percent, 5.45 percent, and 8 percent of compensation, respectively. These contributions are discriminatory because they do not bear a uniform relationship to total compensation.

(d) *Treatment of certain contributions and taxes—*(1) *General rule.* (i) Except as provided in this paragraph, employer contributions do not meet the requirements of this section unless such contributions meet the requirements of this section without taking into account contributions or benefits under Chapter 2 of the Internal Revenue Code (relating to tax on self-employment income), Chapter 21 (relating to Federal Insurance Contribution Act), Title II of the Social Security Act, or any other Federal or State law ("Social Security Taxes"). If the employer does not maintain an integrated plan at any time during the taxable year, taxes paid under section 3111(a) (relating to tax on employers) with respect to an employe may, for purposes of this section, be taken into account as a contribution by the employer to an employee's simplified employee pension. If contributions are made to the simplified employee pension of an owner-employee, the preceding sentence shall not apply unless paid by an such owner-employees under section 1401(a), and the taxes which would be payable under section 1401(a) by such owner-employees but for paragraphs (4) and (5) of section 1402(c), are taken into account as contributions by the employer on behalf of such owner-employee. The amount of such taxes shall be determined in a manner consistent with § 1.401-12(h)(3).

(ii) If contributions are made to the simplified employee pension of a self-employed individual who is not an owner-employee, the arrangement may be integrated. In such a case, the portion of the earned income of such individual which does not exceed the maximum amount which may be treated as self-employment income under section 1402(b)(1) shall be treated as "wages" under section 3121(a)(1) subject to the tax imposed by section 3111(a) and such tax shall be taken into account as employer contributions.

(iii) An employer may take into account as contributions amounts not in excess of such Social Security taxes. Thus, an employer may integrate using a rate less than the maximum rate of tax under section 3111(a) or compensation less than the maximum amount specified as wages under section 3121(a).

(2) *Integrated plan defined.* For purposes of subparagraph (1), the term "integrated plan" means a plan which meets the requirements on section 401(a), 403(a), or 405(a) but would not meet such requirements if contributions or benefits under Chapter 2 (relating to tax on self-employment income), Chapter 21 (relating to Federal Insurance Contributions Act), Title II of the Social Security Act, or any other Federal or State law were not taken into account.

(e) *Examples.* The provisions of this section may be illustrated by the following examples:

Example (1). Corporation M adopts a simplified employee pension arrangement. The corporation would like to contribute 7.5% of an employee's first $10,000 in compensation and 5% of all compensation above $10,000. The simplified employee pension arrangement which Corporation M adopts will not be considered discriminatory within the meaning of paragraph (c) of this section because the rate of contribution decreases as compensation increases.

Example (2). Corporation L adopts a simplified employee pension plan. It wishes to contribute to the simplified employee pension of each employee who is currently performing service. The corporation would like to contribute to the simplified employee pensions 5% of the total compensation of each employee who has completed up to 5 years of service and 7% of the total compensation of each employee who has completed more than 5 years of service. The simplified employee pension plan which Corporation L adopts will be considered discriminatory within the meaning of paragraph (c) of this section because the employer contributions do not bear a uniform relationship to each employee's total compensation.

§ 1.408-9 Reports for simplified employee pensions.

(a) *Information to be furnished upon adoption of plan.* (1) An employer who adopts a definite written allocation formula for making contributions to an employee's simplified employee pension shall furnish the employee in writing the following information:

(i) A notice that the simplified employee pension arrangement has been adopted,

(ii) The requirements which an employee must meet in order to receive a contribution under the agreement,

(iii) The basis upon which the employer's contribution will be allocated to employees, and

(iv) Such other information that the Commissioner may require.

(2) The information in subparagraph (1) must be furnished to an employee no later than a reasonable time after the later of the time the employee becomes employed or the time of the adoption of the simplified employee pension arrangement.

(3) The Commissioner may relieve employers from furnishing any or all of the information specified in subparagraph (1).

(b) *Information to be furnished for a calendar year.* (1) For each calendar year, the employer shall furnish to the employee a written statement indicating the amount of employer contributions made to the employee's individual retirement account or individual retirement annuity under the simplified employee pension arrangement. This requirement is satisfied if the information is on the employee's W-2 for the calendar year for which the contribution is made. Amounts described in § 1.408-7(f)(1) which are not considered made under the simplified employee pension arrangement should not be included.

(2) The information required to be furnished by subparagraph (1) shall be furnished to the employee no later than the later of 30 days after the contribution or January 31 following the calendar year for which the contribution was made.

(c) The Internal Revenue Service may require reports to be filed with the Service with respect to employees who cannot be located by the employer (see § 1.408-7(d)(2)). Such reports shall include such information and shall be filed in the time and manner as the Commissioner specifies.

(d) *Effective date.* The provisions of this section are effective for calendar years beginning after December 31, 1978.

Par. 11. Section 1.409-1 is amended by adding "or 220" after 219 each place it appears and by revising paragraph (c) to read as follows:

§ 1.409-1 Retirement bonds.

* * * * *

(c) *Rollover.* The first sentence of paragraph (b)(1) of this section shall not apply in any case in which a retirement bond is redeemed by the registered owner before the close of the taxable year in which he attains the age of 70 ½ if he transfers the entire amount of the proceeds of such redemption to—

(1) An individual retirement account described in section 408(a) or an individual retirement annuity described in section 408(b) (other than an endowment contract described in § 1.408-3(e)), or

(2) An employees' trust which is described in section 401(a) which is exempt from tax under section 501(a), an annuity plan described in section 403 (a), or an annuity contract described in section 403(b), for the benefit of the registered owner,

on or before the 60th day after the day on which he received the proceeds of such redemption. This paragraph does not apply in the case of a transfer to such an employees' trust or such an annuity plan unless no part of the value of such proceeds is attributable to any source other than a rollover contribution from such an employees' trust or annuity plan (other than an annuity plan or a trust forming part of a plan under which the individual was an employee within the meaning of section 401(c)(1) at the time contributions were made on his behalf under the plan). This paragraph does not apply in the case of a transfer to an annuity contract described in section 403(b) unless no part of the value of such proceeds is attributable to any source other than a rollover contribution from such annuity contract.

Par. 12. Section 1.415-8 is amended by adding at the end thereof new paragraph (i).

§ 1.415-8 Combing and aggregating plans.

* * * * *

(i) *Special aggregation rule for simplified employee pension.* For purposes of section 415 and this section, any contribution made by an employer to a simplified employee pension (as defined in section 408(k)) of an individual for a calendar year shall be treated as an employer contribution to a defined contribution plan maintained by that employer. This paragraph shall apply to taxable years beginning after December 31, 1980.

Gift Tax Regulations

26 CFR Part 25

PART 25—GIFT TAX; GIFTS MADE AFTER DECEMBER 31, 1954

Par. 13. There is added after § 25.2503-4 the following new section:

§ 25.2503-5 Individual retirement plan for spouse.

(a) *In general.* For purposes of section 2503(b), and payment made by an individual for the benefit of his or her spouse—

(1) To individual retirement account described in section 408(a).

(2) To an individual retirement subaccount described in § 1.220-1(b)(3),

(3) For an individual retirement annuity described in section 408(b), or

(4) For a retirement bond described in section 409,

shall not be considered a gift of a future interest in property to the extent that such payment is allowable as a deduction under section 220 for the taxable year for which the contribution is made. Thus, for example, if individual A paid $900 to an individual retirement account for 1980 on behalf of A's spouse, B, of which $875 was deductible, $875 would not be a gift of a future interest.

(b) *Effective date.* Paragraph (a) of this section is effective for transfers made after December 31, 1976.

Employment Tax Regulations

26 CFR Part 31

PART 31—EMPLOYMENT TAXES; APPLICABLE ON AND AFTER JANUARY 1, 1955

Par. 14. Section 31.3121(a)(5)-1 is amended by adding at the end thereof a new paragraph (d). This new paragraph reads as follows:

§ 31.3121(a)(5)-1 Payments from or to certain tax-exempt trusts, or under or to certain annuity plans or bond purchase plans.

* * * * *

(d) *Payments to a simplified employee pension.* The term "wages" does not include any payment made after December 31, 1978 by an employer on behalf of an employee to a simplified employee pension described in section 408(k) if at the time of the payment it is reasonable to believe that the employee will be entitled to a deduction under section 219 for such payment.

Par. 15. Section 31.3306(b)(5)-1 is amended by adding at the end thereof a new paragraph (d). This new paragraph reads as follows:

§ 31.3306(b)(5)-1 Payments from or to certain tax-exempt trusts, or under or to certain annuity plans or bond purchase plans.

* * * * *

(d) *Payments to a simplified employee pension.* The term "wages" does not include any payment made after December 31, 1978 by an employer on behalf of an employee to a simplified employee pension described in section 40B(k) if at the time of the payment it is reasonable to believe that the employee will be entitled to a deduction under section 219 for such payment.

Pension Excise Tax Regulations

26 CFR Part 54

PART 54—PENSION EXCISE TAXES

Par. 16. There is inserted in the appropriate place the following new section:

§ 54.4973-1 Excess contributions to certain accounts, contracts and bonds.

(a) *In general.* Under section 4973, in the case of an individual retirement account (described in section 408(a)), an individual retirement annuity (described in section 498(b)), a custodial account treated as an annuity contract under section 403(b)(7)(A), or an individual retirement bond described in section 409. a tax equal to 6 percent of the amount of excess contributions (as defined in paragraph (c) or (d) of this section) to such account, annuity or bond is imposed.

(b) *Individual liable for tax*—(1) *Individual retirement plans.* In the case of an individual retirement account, individual retirement annuity or individual retirement bond the tax imposed by section 4973 shall be paid by the individual to whom a deduction is or would be allowed with respect to contributions for the taxable year under section 219 (determined without regard to subsection (b)(1) thereof) or section 220 (determined without regard to subsection (b)(1) thereof), whichever is appropriate.

(2) *Custodial accounts under section 403(b)(7)(A).* In the case of a custodial account treated as an annuity contract under section 403(b)(7)(A), the tax imposed by section 4973 shall be paid by the individual for whose benefit the account is maintained.

(c) *Excess contributions defined for individual retirement plans.* For purposes of section 4973, in the case of individual retirement accounts, individual retirement annuities, or individual retirement bonds, the term "excess contributions" means the sum of—

(1) The excess (if any) of—

(i) The amount contributed for the taxable year to the accounts or for the annuities or bonds (other than a valid rollover contribution described in section 402(a)(5), 402(a)(7), 403(a)(4), 403(b)(8), 408(d)(3), 409(b)(3)(C)), over

(ii) The amount allowable as a deduction under section 219 or 220 for such contributions, and

(2) The amount determined under his subsection for the preceding taxable year, reduced by the sum of—

(i) The distributions out of the account for the taxable year which were included in the gross income of the payee under section 408(d)(1).

(ii) The distributions out of the account for the taxable bear to which section 408(d)(5) applies. and

(iii) The excess (if any) of the minimum amount allowable as a deduction under section 219 or 220 for the taxable year over the amount contributed (determined without regard to sections 219(c)(5) and 220(c)(6)) to the accounts or for the annuities or bonds for the taxable year. For purposes of this paragraph, any contribution which is distributed from the individual retirement account, individual retirement annuity, or bond in a distribution to which section 408(d)(4) applies shall be treated as an amount not contributed.

(d) *Excess contributions defined for custodial accounts under section 403(b)(7)(A).* For purposes of section 4973, in the case of a custodial account referred to in paragraph (b)(2) of this section, the term "excess contributions" means the sum of—

(1) The excess (if any) of the amount contributed for the taxable year to such account (other than a valid rollover contribution described in section 403(b)(8), 408(d)(3)(A)(iii), or 409(b)(3)(C)), over the lesser of the amount excludable from gross income under section 403(b) or the amount permitted to be contributed under the limitations contained in section 415 (or under whichever such section is applicable, if only one is applicable), and

(2) The amount determined under this subsection for the preceding taxable year, reduced by—

(i) The excess (if any) of the lesser of (A) the amount excludable from gross income under section 403(b) or (B) the amount permitted to be contributed under the limitations contained in section 415 over the amount contributed to the account for the taxable year (or under whichever such section is applicable, if only one is applicable), and

(ii) The sum of the distributions out of the account (for the taxable year) which are included in gross income under section 72(e).

(e) *Special rules.* (1) The tax imposed by section 4973 cannot exceed 6 percent of the value (determined as of the close of the individuals taxable year) of the account, annuity or bond.

(2) In the case of an endowment contract described in section 408(b), the tax imposed by section 4973 is not applicable to any amount allocate under § 1.219-1(b)(3) to the cost of life insurance under the contract.

(f) *Examples.* The provisions of this section may be illustrated by the following examples;

Example (1). On April 20, 1979, A, a single individual, establishes an individual retirement account (IRA) and contributes $1,500. On January 11, 1980, A determines he has compensation for 1979 within the meaning of section 219(c) and the regulations thereafter of $8,000. Under section 219. the maximum amount allowable as a deduction for retirement savings available to A is $1,200. On April 15, 1980, A files his income tax return for 1979 taking a deduction of $1,200 for his contribution to his IRA, and as of such date there had been no distribution from the IRA. Under section 4973. A would have $300 of excess contribution in his account for 1979 [($1,500-$1,200) + 0] and A would be liable for an excise tax of $18 on such excess contribution.

Example (2) Assume the same facts as in Example (1). Assume further that on July 1, 1980, A contributes $1,500 to his account. On January 9, 1981, A determines that he has compensation for 1980 of $12,000. Under section 219, the maximum amount allowable to A as a deduction for retirement savings is $1,500 for 1980. On April 15, 1981. A files his income tax return for 1980 taking a deduction of $1,500 for his contribution to his IRA. As of such date, there had been no distribution from the account. Under section 4973, A would have $300 of excess contributions in his IRA for 1980 ($1,500 - $1,500) + ($300 - $0)] and would be liable for an excise tax of $18 on such excess contribution.

Example (3) Assume the same facts as in Example (1) and (2). Assume further that on July 1, 1981, A contributes $1,000 to his account. On January 9, 1982, A determines that he has compensation for 1981 of $15,000. Under section 219, the maximum amount allowable as a deduction to A as a deduction for retirement savings is $1,500 for 1981. On April 15, 1982. A files his income tax return for 1981 taking a deduction of $1,000 for his 1981 contribution to his IRA and an additional deduction of $300 under section 219(c)(5). A will have no excess contributions in his IRA for 1981 because he made no excess contributions for 1981 and the previous year's excess contribution has been eliminated by the underutilization (section 4973(b)(2)(C)) of 1981's allowable contribution.

Example (4) Assume the same facts as in Examples (1) and (2). Assume further that on July 1, 1981, A contributes $1,500 to his account. On December 1, 1981, A withdraws $300 from his IRA. On January 9. 1982. A determines that he has compensation for 1981 of $15,000. Under section 219. the maximum amount allowable as a deduction to A as a deduction for retirement savings is $1,500 for 1981. On April 15, 1982, A files his income tax return for 1981 taking a deduction of $1,500 for his 1981 contribution to his IRA. A will have no excess contributions in his IRA for 1981 because he made no excess contributions for 1981 and the previous year's excess contribution has been eliminated in a distribution described in section 408(d)(5).

Example (5) On February 1, 1979, H, an individual, establishes an IRA for himself and one for his nonworking spouse W. He contributes $875 to his account and $775 to his wife's account. On January 31, 1980. H determines that he has compensation for 1979 within the meaning of section 220(c) and the regulations thereunder of $20,000. Under Section 220(b)(1). the maximum amount allowable as a deduction for retirement savings to A is $1,550. On April 15, 1980. H files a Joint income tax return for 1979 and takes a deduction of $1,550 for his contribution to the IRA of himself and his spouse. As of such date, there had been no distribution from either IRA. Under section 4973, H would have $100 of excess contributions in his account for 1979 [($1,650 – $1,550) + 0] and H would be liable for an excise tax of $6 on such excess contribution.

Example (6) Assume the same facts as in Example (5). Assume further that on June 1, 1980, H contributes $875 to his account and $875 to his wife's account. On January 31, 1981, H determines that he has compensation for 1980 within the meaning of section 220(c) and the regulations thereunder of $20,000. Under section 220(b)(1), the maximum amount allowable as a deduction for retirement savings is $1,750. On April 15, 1981, H files his income tax return for 1980 taking a deduction of $1,750 for his contribution to the individual retirement account of himself and his wife. As of such date, there had been no distribution from either account. Under section 4973, H would have $100 of excess contributions in his account for 1980 and would be liable for an excise tax of $6 for such excess contribution.

Example (7) Assume the same facts as in Example (5). Assume further that on June 1, 1980, A contributes $1,000 to his account and nothing to his wife's account. On January 31, 1981, A determines that he has compensation for 1980 within the meaning of section 219(c) of $22,000. On April 15, 1981, H files his income tax return for 1980 and takes a $1,000 deduction under section 219(a) for the 1980 contribution to his IRA and a $100 deduction under section 219(c)(5) for the 1979 excess contribution Under section 4973. H would have $0 excess contributions for 1980 because the previous year's excess contribution has been eliminated under section 4973(b)(2)(C).

Example (8) On March 1, 1979, a custodial account under section 403(b)(7)(A) is established for the benefit of T who is otherwise

eligible to have such an account established and a contribution of $7,000 is made to such account by A's employer which is a tax-exempt organization described in section 501(c)(3). The amount excludible from T's gross income in 1979 under section 403(b) is $4,000 and the amount permitted to be contributed for 1979 under section 415 is $5,000. Under section 4973, T would have an excess contribution of $3,000 [($7,000 – $4,000) + 0] in his account for 1979 and would be liable for an excise tax of $180.

Par. 17. A new paragraph (d) is added to §54.474-1 to read as follows:

§54.4974-1 Excise tax on accumulations in individual retirement accounts or annuities.

* * *

(d) *Waiver of tax in certain cases*—(1) In general. If the payee described in section 4974(a) establishes to the satisfaction of the Commissioner that—

(i) The shortfall described in section 4974(a) in the amount distributed during any taxable year was due to reasonable error, and

(ii) Reasonable steps are being taken to remedy the shortfall, the tax imposed by section 4974(a) may be waived.

(2) *Reasonable error.* Examples of reasonable error leading to an underdistribution include: erroneous advice from the sponsoring organization or other pension advisors or organizations which misled the payee, attempts by the payee to apply the required formula which led to a miscalculation, or misunderstanding of the formula.

Procedure and Administration Regulations

26 CFR Part 301

PART 301—PROCEDURE AND ADMINISTRATION

Par. 18. Section 301.6693-1 is revised by changing its title, adding after paragraph (a)(2) a new paragraph (a)(3), and amending paragraph (e). Section 301.6693-1, as revised, reads as follows:

§301.6693-1 Penalty for failure to provide reports and documents concerning individual retirement accounts, individual retirement annuities and simplified employee pensions.

(a) *In general.* * * *

(3) *Simplified employee pensions.* An employer who makes a contribution on behalf of an employee to a simplified employee pension who fails to furnish or file a report or any other document required under section 408(1) or §1.406-9 within the time and in the manner prescribed for furnishing or filing such item shall pay a penalty of $10 for each failure unless it is shown that such failure is due to reasonable cause.

* * *

(e) *Effective date.* This section shall take effect on January 1, 1975, except for paragraph (a)(3) which is effective for years beginning after December 31, 1978.

Roscoe L. Egger, Jr.,

Commissioner of Internal Revenue.

[FR Doc. 81-20505 filed 7-13-81; 8:45 am]

[¶ **20,137C** Reserved.—**Formerly reproduced at this paragraph were proposed regulations relating to disclosures of returns and return information to officers and employees of the Labor Department and the Pension Benefit Guaranty Corporation. The regulations were finalized on September 9, 1983, by T.D. 7911 and appear at ¶ 13,763.**]

¶ 20,137D

Proposed regulations— Qualified joint and survivor annuities—*BBS Associates, Inc. v. Commissioner.*—Reproduced below are proposed regulations that are designed to conform the rules on qualified joint and survivor annuities with the holdings of the Tax Court and the U.S. Court of Appeals for the Third Circuit in *BBS Associates, Inc. v. Commissioner.* The proposed regulations were published in the Federal Register on October 27, 1982 (47 FR 47600).

DEPARTMENT OF THE TREASURY INTERNAL REVENUE SERVICE

[26 CFR Part 1]

[EE-52-78]

QUALIFIED JOINT AND SURVIVOR ANNUITY

NOTICE OF PROPOSED RULEMAKING

AGENCY: Internal Revenue Service, Treasury.

ACTION: Notice of proposed rulemaking.

SUMMARY: This document contains proposed regulations relating to qualified joint and survivor annuities required to be provided under certain retirement plans. Changes to the present regulations are being made to conform them to *BBS Associates, Inc. v. Commissioner of Internal Revenue,* 74 T.C. 1118 (1980), *aff'd* No. 80-2851 (3d Cir. July 29, 1981) and to simplify them. The regulations would affect sponsors of, administrators of and participants in certain retirement plans.

DATES: Written comments and requests for a public hearing must be delivered or mailed by December 27, 1982. The regulations are generally effective for plan years beginning after December 31, 1975.

ADDRESS: Send comments and requests for a public hearing to: Commissioner of Internal Revenue, Attention: CC:LR:T (EE-52-78), Washington, D.C. 20224.

FOR FURTHER INFORMATION CONTACT: William D. Gibbs of the Employee Plans and Exempt Organizations Division, Office of the Chief Counsel, Internal Revenue Service, 1111 Constitution Avenue, N.W., Washington, D.C. 20224 (Attention: CC:LR:T) (202-566-3430) (not a toll-free number).

SUPPLEMENTARY INFORMATION:

Background

This document contains proposed amendments to the Income Tax Regulations (26 CFR Part 1) under section 401(a)(11) of the Internal Revenue Code of 1954. These amendments are proposed to conform the regulations to *BBS Associates, Inc. v. Commissioner of Internal Revenue,* 74 T.C. 1118 (1980), *aff'd.* No. 80-2851 (3d Cir. July 29, 1981) and to simplify them. These regulations are to be issued under the authority contained in section 7805 of the Internal Revenue Code of 1954 (68A Stat. 917; 26 U.S.C. 7805).

Qualified Joint and Survivor Annuity

Section 401(a)(11) provides that if a trust provides for the payment of benefits in the form of an annuity, such trust must provide for the payment of annuity benefits in a form having the effect of a qualified joint and survivor annuity in order for the trust to be qualified under section 401.

The existing regulations under section 401(a)(11) interpret this provision to require a plan offering a life annuity benefit as a benefit option to provide that the automatic form of benefit payment be a qualified joint and survivor annuity.

The Tax Court and the Court of Appeals for the Third Circuit rejected the Service's interpretation in *BBS Associates, Inc. v. Commissioner of Internal Revenue,* 74 T.C. 1118 (1980), *aff'd.* No. 80-2851 (3d Cir. July 29, 1981). The court held that sections 401(a)(11)(A) and 401(a)(11)(E) do not require that the automatic form of benefit distribution be a qualified joint and survivor annuity merely because a plan offers a life annuity as an optional form of benefit. The court also held that *Example 1* of § 1.401(a)-11(a)(3), which illustrated the Service's position, was invalid.

In Notice 82-4, 1982-8 I.R.B. 36, the Service stated that it would not file a petition for a writ of certiorari in the *BBS* case and that the invalidated regulations would be amended.

This notice of proposed rulemaking conforms § 1.401(a)-11 to the *BBS* decision. The proposed regulations require that, in order for a plan to qualify under section 401(a), if the plan offers benefits payable as a life annuity, such life annuity benefits must be paid in the form of a qualified joint and survivor annuity unless the participant elects otherwise.

Approval of Benefit Options

The court also held in the *BBS* decision that section 401(a)(11) was not violated by a plan provision requiring administrative committee consent before forms of benefit payment other than a lump sum could be elected. The proposed regulations clarify that such a procedure is permissible. However, it is made clear that such a procedure can not result in the denial of benefit payments required by section 401(a)(11). The regulations illustrate a method whereby a plan may use an administrative committee and satisfy the requirements of section 401(a)(11).

Changes to Simplify Administration

The proposed changes to the regulations under section 401(a)(11) also include several changes that are intended to ease the administrative burdens of complying with the joint and survivor annuity requirements.

The regulations require the plan administrator, to provide certain information to participants concerning their ability to elect out of a joint and survivor annuity and to elect an early survivor annuity. The pro-

posed amendments make it clear that it is permissible to provide this information by posting it, as opposed to mailing or hand delivering it to individual plan participants.

The regulations currently allow defined contribution plans to satisfy the requirement that election of an early survivor annuity be permitted by automatically paying a survivor benefit equal to the vested portion of the account balance. The proposed amendments allow defined benefit plans to adopt a similar procedure if the plan pays a survivor benefit equal to the present value of the vested benefit.

Executive Order 12291 and Regulatory Flexibility Act

The Commissioner has determined than this proposed regulation is not a major regulation for purposes of Executive Order 12291. Accordingly, a regulatory impact analysis is not required.

Although this document is a notice of proposed rulemaking which solicits public comments, the Internal Revenue Service has concluded that the regulations proposed herein are interpretative and that the notice and public procedure requirements of 5 U.S.C. 553 do not apply. Accordingly, these proposed regulations do not constitute regulations subject to the Regulatory Flexibility Act (5 U.S.C. chapter 6).

Comments and Requests for a Public Hearing

Before adopting these proposed regulations, consideration will be given to any written comments that are submitted (preferably six copies) to the Commissioner of Internal Revenue. All comments will be available for public inspection and copying. A public hearing will be held upon written request to the Commissioner by any person who has submitted written comments. If a public hearing is held, notice of the time and place will be published in the Federal Register.

Drafting Information

The principal author of these proposed regulations is William D. Gibbs of the Employee Plans and Exempt Organizations Division of the Office of Chief Counsel, Internal Revenue Service. However, personnel from other offices of the Internal Revenue Service and Treasury Department participated in developing the regulation, both on matters of substance and style.

List of Subjects in 26 CFR

1.401-0—1.425-1

Income taxes, Employee benefit plan, Pensions, Stock options, Individual retirement accounts, Employee stock ownership plans.

Proposed amendments to the regulations

The proposed amendments to 26 CFR Part 1 are as follows:

Section 1.401(a)-(11) is amended by—

1. Striking out in paragraphs (a)(1)(i), (ii) and (iii) "such benefits" and inserting in lieu thereof "life annuity benefits".

2. Revising paragraph (a)(3) *Example* (1).

3. Revising paragraph (c)(2)(i)(C).

4. Revising the first two sentences of paragraph (c)(3)(ii).

5. Revising paragraph (d)(1) and adding a new paragraph (d)(5).

These revised and added provisions read as follows:

§ *1.401(a)-11 Qualified joint and survivor annuities.*

(a) *General rule—* * * *

(3) *Illustrations* * * *

Example (1). The X Corporation Defined Contribution Plan was established in 1960. As in effect on January 1, 1974, the plan provided that, upon his retirement, a participant could elect to receive the balance of his individual account in the form of (1) a lump-sum cash payment, (2) a lump-sum distribution consisting of X Corporation stock, (3) five equal annual cash payments, (4) a life annuity, or (5) a combination of options (1) through (4). The plan also provided that, if a participant did not elect another form of distribution, the balance of his individual account would be distributed to him in the form of a lump-sum cash payment upon his retirement. Assume that section 401(a)(11) and this section became applicable to the plan as of its plan year beginning January 1, 1976, with respect to persons who were active participants in the plan as of such date (see paragraph (f) of this section). If the X Corporation Defined Contribution Plan continues to allow the life annuity payment option, it must be amended to provide that if a participant elects a life annuity option the life annuity benefit will be paid in a form having the effect of a qualified joint and survivor annuity, except to the extent that the participant elects another form of benefit payment. However, the plan can continue to provide that, if no election is made, the balance will be paid as a lump-sum cash payment. If the trust is not so amended, it will fail to qualify under section 401(a).

* * *

(c) *Elections.* * * *

(2) *Election of early survivor annuity*—(i) *In general.* * * *

(C) A plan is not required to provide an election under this subparagraph if—

(*1*) The plan provides that an early survivor annuity is the only form of benefit payable under the plan with respect to a married participant who dies while employed by an employer maintaining the plan,

(*2*) in the case of a defined contribution plan, the plan provides a survivor benefit at least equal in value to the vested portion of the participant's account balance, if the participant dies while in active service with an employer maintaining the plan, or

(*3*) in the case of a defined benefit plan, the plan provides a survivor benefit at least equal in value to the present value of the vested portion of the participant's accrued benefit (determined immediately prior to death), if the participant dies while in active service with an employer maintaining the plan. Any present values must be determined in accordance with actuarial assumptions or factors specified in the plan.

* * *

(3) *Information to be provided by plan administrator.* * * *

(ii) The method or methods used to provide the information described in subdivision (i) of this subparagraph may vary. Posting which meets the requirements of § 1.7476-2(c)(1) may be used; see § 1.7476-2(c)(i) for examples of other methods which may be used. * * *

(d) *Permissible additional plan provisions*— (1) *In general.* A plan will not fail to meet the requirements of section 401(a)(11) and this section merely because it contains one or more of the provisions described in paragraph (d)(2) through (5) of this section.

* * *

(5) *Benefit option approval by third party.* (i) A plan may provide that optional forms of benefit payment elected by a participant are subject to the approval of an administrative committee or similar third party. However, the administrative committee cannot deny a participant any of the benefits required by section 401(a)(11). For example, if a plan offers a life annuity option, the committee may deny the participant a qualified joint and survivor annuity only by denying the participant access to all life annuity options without knowledge of whether the participant wishes to receive a qualified joint and survivor annuity. Alternatively, if the committee knows which form of life annuity the participant has chosen before it makes its decision, the committee cannot withhold its consent for payment of a qualified joint and survivor annuity even though it denies all other life annuity options.

(ii) The provisions of this subparagraph may be illustrated by the following example:

Example. Plan M provides that the automatic form of benefit payout will be a single sum distribution. The plan also permits, subject to approval by the administrative committee, the election of several optional forms of life annuity. On the election form that is reviewed by the administrative committee the participant indicates whether any life annuity option is preferred, without indicating the particular life annuity chosen. Thus, the committee approves or disapproves the election without knowledge of whether a qualified joint and survivor annuity will be elected. The administrative committee approval provision in Plan M does not cause the plan to fail to satisfy this section. On the other hand, if the form indicates which form of life annuity is preferred, committee disapproval of any election of the qualified joint and survivor annuity would cause the plan to fail to satisfy this section.

* * *

(signed) Roscoe L. Egger, Jr.

Commissioner of Internal Revenue

¶ 20,137E

Proposed regulations on minimum funding standards and the excise taxes imposed for failure to meet the funding standards.— Reproduced below are proposed regulations relating to the minimum funding requirements under Code Sec. 412 and the excise taxes imposed under Code Sec. 4971 for failure to meet the minimum funding standards. The proposed regulations address issues affecting funding standard accounts, such as charges and credits, amortization amounts, the treatment of interest, unreasonable assumptions or funding methods, and plan termination. Also discussed are questions relating to money purchase plans, bond valuation elections, frequency of actuarial valuations, timing of contributions, and alternative minimum funding standard accounts.

The proposed regulations were published in the *Federal Register* on December 1, 1982 (47 FR 54093).

Notice Of Proposed Rulemaking

AGENCY: Internal Revenue Service, Treasury.

ACTION: Notice of proposed rulemaking.

SUMMARY: This document contains proposed regulations relating to the minimum funding requirements for employee pension benefit plans, and to excise taxes for failure to meet the minimum funding standards. Changes to the applicable tax law were made by the Employee Retirement Income Security Act of 1974. The regulations would provide the public with guidance needed to comply with that Act and would affect all pension plans subject to the provisions of the Act.

DATES: Written comments and requests for public hearing must be delivered or mailed by January 28, 1983. The proposed amendments would apply generally for plan years beginning after 1975, but earlier (or later) in the case of some plans as provided for meeting the minimum funding requirements under the Act. The proposed rules pertaining to the frequency of actuarial valuations, and to the time for making contributions, generally would not be effective prior to the publication of final regulations.

ADDRESS: Send comments and requests for a public hearing to: Commissioner of Internal Revenue, Attention: CC:LR:T (EE-99-78), Washington, D.C. 20224.

FOR FURTHER INFORMATION CONTACT: Eric A. Raps of the Employee Plans and Exempt Organizations Division, Office of the Chief Counsel, Internal Revenue Service, 1111 Constitution Avenue, N.W., Washington, D.C. 20224 (Attention: CC:LR T) (202-566-6212, not a toll-free call).

SUPPLEMENTARY INFORMATION

Background

This document contains proposed amendments to the Income Tax Regulations (26 CFR Part 1) under section 412 of the Internal Revenue Code of 1954. These amendments are proposed to conform the regulations to section 1013(a) of the Employee Retirement Income Security Act of 1974 (ERISA) (88 Stat. 914). The proposed amendments would also apply for purposes of sections 302 and 305 of ERISA (88 Stat. 869, 873).

The proposed amendments would be issued under the authority of section 302(b)(4), (b)(5), (c)(2)(B), (c)(9) and (c)(10) of ERISA (88 Stat. 870, 871, and 872; 29 U.S.C. 1082) and sections 412(b)(4), (b)(5), (c)(2)(B), (c)(9) and (c)(10) and 7805 of the Internal Revenue Code of 1954 (88 Stat. 915, 916, and 917; 68A Stat. 917; 26 U.S.C. 412(b)(4), (b)(5), (c)(2)(B), (c)(9), and (c)(10) and 7805).

This document also contains proposed amendments to the Income Tax Regulations (26 CFR Part 1) and the Pension Excise Tax Regulations (26 CFR Part 54) under section 413(b)(6) and (c)(5) and section 4971 of the Internal Revenue Code of 1954. These regulations are proposed primarily to conform the regulations to section 1013(b) of the Employee Retirement income Security Act of 1974 (ERISA) (88 Stat. 920). They are to be issued under the authority of section 413(b)(6) and (c)(5) and section 7805 of the Internal Revenue Code of 1954 (88 Stat. 924, 925, 68A Stat. 917; 26 U.S.C. 413(b)(6) and (c)(5), 7805).

The proposed regulations do not reflect changes to the second-level excise tax made by the Act of Dec. 24, 1980, Pub. L. 96-596 (94 Stat. 3469), or amendments to sections 412 and 4971 made by the Multiemployer Pension Plan Amendments Act of 1980, Pub. L 96-364 (94 Stat. 1208).

Purpose And Scope

The proposed amendments address the remaining statutory provisions not yet addressed by regulations relating to the minimum funding requirements with respect to which either regulatory guidance is required by law or interpretative assistance would be helpful in applying the law. These proposed amendments, together with proposed or final regulations previously issued under section 412 of the Code, generally constitute the regulatory guidance to be provided with respect to the minimum funding requirements, with the exception of rules relating to mergers. However, comments noting additional issues with respect to which regulatory guidance might be helpful will be considered along with comments addressing issues that arise under the proposed amendments.

The provisions under section 4971 of the Code contain sanctions for enforcing the minimum funding requirements. The sanctions are two excise taxes. The initial tax is 5 percent of an accumulated funding deficiency, and an additional tax of 100 percent is imposed if the deficiency is not corrected. Generally, the employer responsible for contributing to the plan is liable for these taxes.

Section 3002(b) of ERISA provides special rules regarding the section 4971 taxes and coordination of matters regarding these taxes with the Secretary of Labor.

Funding Standard Account

Under section 412(b) of the Code, a plan must maintain a funding standard account. The mechanics for reflecting charges and credits to the account appear in section 412(b)(2) and (3). The proposed amendments address a number of key issues arising under the funding standard account provisions.

Money Purchase Plans

Under the proposed amendments, a money purchase pension plan is, like other plans, required to maintain a funding standard account. However, the accounting under such a plan for funding purposes is limited to charges for the contribution required under the formula provided by the plan, credits for amounts actually contributed, and charges and credits to amortize certain bases.

Normally, the need to create an amortization base does not exist under a money purchase plan. However, such a base would be created, for example, with the issuance of a waiver of the minimum funding standard for a plan.

Combining And Offsetting

The proposed amendments would provide rules, as required under section 412(b)(4) of the Code, for combining and offsetting amortization amounts determined under the funding standard account. The proposed method for combining and offsetting these amounts is described in the legislative history of ERISA. (See H.R. Rep. No. 93-807, 93rd Cong., 2d Sess. 86-87 (1974), 1974-3 C.B. Supp. 321-322.)

Treatment Of Interest

The proposed amendments would provide rules, as required by section 412(b)(5) of the Code, for treating interest charges and credits under the funding standard account.

Generally under the proposed amendments, charges and credits are made as of an assumed accounting date under the plan. There must be an interest charge or credit, as the case may be, for the period between this assumed date and the end of the plan year.

A contribution made during the "grace period" between the last day of a plan year and the day determined under section 412(c)(10) is treated as having been made on the last day of the plan year.

Retroactive Changes

The proposed amendments provide for reflecting in the funding standard account retroactive changes required by the Commissioner to adjust for the use of unreasonable assumptions or funding methods.

Plan Termination

The proposed amendments relating to the effect of plan termination on the funding standard account are substantially identical to the provisions of Rev. Rul. 79-237, 1979-2 C.B. 190.

Bond Valuation Election

The proposed amendments would provide rules, as required by section 412(c)(2)(B) of the Code, for the election of a special valuation rule applicable to bonds and other evidences of indebtedness. The proposed amendments would be substantially identical to temporary regulations published in 1974 with respect to the bond valuation election. However, the proposed amendments would clarify the temporary rules by providing that certain convertible debt instruments are treated as debt until converted into equity securities. The rules concerning valuation of convertible debt would be effective only for debt instruments acquired after the date on which the proposal is adopted as a final regulation. For debt instruments acquired before that date, a valuation method will be considered acceptable if it is applied on a consistent basis.

Actuarial Valuation

The proposed amendments would provide rules, as required by section 412(c)(9) of the Code, relating to the frequency of actuarial valuations for plans. These rules would identify situations in which valuations may be required more frequently than once every 3 years. Comments are requested as to the appropriateness of requiring more frequent valuations under the situations described in the proposed amendments. Comments are also requested as to any additional circumstances where valuations should be required more frequently than once every 3 years. The rules also would describe how the funding standard account is to be maintained for years when there is no valuation.

Timing Of Contributions

The proposed amendments would provide rules, as required by section 412(c)(10) of the Code, relating to the time for making contributions for purposes of section 412. Unlike the temporary regulations published in 1976, these rules would not contain an automatic six-month extension of the two and one-half month grace period set forth as a general rule under the statute for meeting the minimum funding requirements. The Commissioner may approve applications for an extension of the grace period of up to six months. This more restrictive approach would be applied prospectively from a date after the publication of final regulations. However, a transitional rule is provided to phase in the two and one-half month period over the first three plan years following a date after publication of final regulations, and extensions may be approved by the Commissioner.

Alternative Funding Standard Account

The proposed amendments contain rules that would apply to plans maintaining the alternative minimum funding standard account. These rules would reflect section 412(g)(1) by limiting the use of the alternative account to plans using a funding method that requires contributions in all years at least equal to those required under the entry age normal funding method. Thus, only plans that use the entry age normal funding method may use the alternative account.

Allocation Of Excise Tax Liability

The proposed amendments would contain rules to allocate excise tax liability under section 4971 of more than one employer, but they would permit allocation in a reasonable manner that is not inconsistent with the rules provided.

Uner the proposed amendments, the tax liability of each employer would generally be based on the obligation of each employer to contribute to the plan. To the extent that a funding deficiency would be attributable to the delinquent contribution of an individual employer, that employer would be liable for the tax. To the extent that a funding deficiency is not attributable to a delinquent contribution, each employer would share liability in proportion to its share of required contributions to the plan.

Allocations For Related Employers

The general rules for allocating tax liability would not apply to certain related employers. To the extent that an accumulated funding deficiency is attributable to related employers, those employers would be jointly and severally liable for the excise tax with respect to that deficiency. This rule would apply to related employers maintaining a plan of their own or in conjunction with other employers.

Employer Withdrawal

The proposed amendments would generally provide that an employer withdrawing from a plan remains liable for tax imposed with respect to the portion of an accumulated funding deficiency attributable to that employer for years prior to withdrawal. The remaining employers would be liable for the tax attributable to the accumulated funding deficiency for years after an employer's withdrawal, even if the deficiency is attributable to prior years.

Temporary Regulations Superseded

The proposed amendments contain rules that would supersede the following temporary regulations: § 11.412(c)-7, relating to the election to treat certain retroactive plan amendments as made on the first day of the plan year; § 11.412(c)-11, relating to the election with respect to bonds; and § 11.412(c)-12, relating to the extension of time to make contributions to satisfy requirements of section 412.

Executive Order 12291 And Regulatory Flexibility Act

The Commissioner of Internal Revenue has determined that this proposed regulation is not a major regulation for purposes of Executive Order 12291. Accordingly, a regulatory impact analysis is not required.

Although this document is a notice of proposed rule making which solicits public comments, the Internal Revenue Service has concluded that the regulations proposed herein are interpretative and that the notice and public procedure requirements of 5 U.S.C. 553 do not apply. Accordingly, these proposed regulations do not constitute regulations subject to the Regulatory Flexibility Act (5 U.S.C. chapter 6).

Comments And Requests For A Public Hearing

Before adopting these proposed regulations, consideration will be given to any written comments that are submitted (preferably eight copies) to the Commissioner of Internal Revenue. It is requested that persons submitting comments use professional letterhead stationery only if the comment represents the position of the firm or a named client, rather than the views of the writer. All comments are available for public inspection and copying. A public hearing will be held upon written request to the Commissioner by any person who has submitted written comments. If a public hearing is held, notice of the time and place will be published in the FEDERAL REGISTER.

Drafting Information

The principal author of these proposed regulations is Joel E. Horowitz of the Employee Plans and Exempt Organizations Division of the Office of Chief Counsel, Internal Revenue Service. However, personnel from other offices of the Internal Revenue Service and Treasury Department participated in developing the regulations, both on matters of substance and style.

List Of Subjects In 26 CFR 1.401-0—1.425-1

Income taxes, Employee benefit plans, Pensions.

Proposed amendments to the regulations

The proposed amendments to 26 CFR Parts 1, 11, and 54 are as follows:

Income Tax Regulations

(26 CFR Part 1)

Paragraph 1. The Income Tax Regulations, 26 CFR Part 1, are amended by adding the following new sections immediately after § 1.411(d)-3:

§ 1.412(a)-1 General scope of minimum funding standard requirements.

(a) *General rule.* Section 412 of the Code provides minimum funding requirements for plans that include a trust qualified under section 401(a) and for plans that meet the requirements of section 403(a) or section 405(a). Generally, such plans include defined benefit pension plans, money purchase pension plans (including target benefit plans), qualified annuity plans, and qualified bond purchase plans. The minimum funding requirements continue to apply to any plan that was qualified under, or was determined to have met the requirements of, these sections for any plan year beginning on or after the effective date described in paragraph (d) of this section for the plan. Also, under section 302 of the Employee Retirement Income Security Act of 1974 ("ERISA"), the minimum funding requirements apply to employee pension benefit plans described in section 301(a) of that Act. The regulations prescribed under this section and the following sections with respect to section 412 also apply for purposes of sections 302 and 305 of ERISA. These topics are among those discussed in the following sections: maintenance of a funding standard account (including rules for combining and offsetting amounts to be amortized, rules for computing interest on amounts charged and credited to the account, rules relating to the treatment of gains and losses, and rules relating to retroactive changes in the funding standard account required by the Commissioner), § 1.412(b)-1; amortization of experience gains in connection with group deferred annuity contracts, § 1.412(b)-2; funding standard account adjustments for plan mergers and spinoffs, § 1.412(b)-3; plan terminations, § 1.412(b)-4; election of the alternative amortization method of funding, § 1.412(b)-5; determinations to be

made under funding method, § 1.412(c)(1)-2; valuation of plan assets and reasonable valuation methods, § 1.412(c)(2); bond valuation election, § 1.412(c)(2)-2; reasonable funding methods, § 1.412(c)(3)-1 and -2; certain changes in accrued liability, § 1.412(c)(4)-1; changes in funding method or plan year, § 1.412(c)(5)-1; full funding and the full funding limitation, § 1.412(c)(6)-1 and § 1.412(c)(7)-1; retroactive plan amendment, § 1.412(c)(8)-1; frequency of actuarial valuations, § 412(c)(9)-1; time for making contributions to satisfy section 412, § 1.412(c)(10)-1; and maintenance of an alternative funding standard account, § 1.412(g)-1.

(b) *Exceptions.* See section 412(h) for a list of plans not subject to the requirements of section 412. These excepted plans include profit-sharing or stock bonus plans; certain insurance contract, government, and church plans; and certain plans that do not provide for employer contributions.

(c) *Failure to meet minimum funding standards.* A plan fails to meet the minimum funding standards for a plan year if, as of the end of that year, there is an accumulated funding deficiency as defined in section 412(a) and § 54.4971-1(d). See regulations to taxes for failure to meet the minimum funding standards.

(d) *Effective date*—(1) *In general.* Unless otherwise provided, this section and the following sections providing regulations under section 412 apply to any plan year to which section 412 applies. For a plan in existence on January 1, 1974, section 412 generally applies to plan years beginning in 1976. However, this time is extended by special transitional rules under section 1017(c)(2) of ERISA for such existing plans under collective bargaining agreements. For a plan not in existence on January 1, 1974, section 412 generally applies for plan years beginning after September 2, 1974.

(2) *date when plan is in existence.* See § 1.410(a)-2(c) for rules concerning the date when a plan is considered to be in existence.

(3) *Early application of section 412.* See § 1.410(a)-2(d) for rules permitting plans in existence on January 1, 1974, to elect to have section 412, as well as other provisions added by section 1013 of ERISA, apply to plan year beginning after September 4, 1974, and before the effective date of the provision otherwise applicable to the plan.

(4) *Transitional rule.* The regulations issued under sections § 1.412(b)-1, § 1.412)b)-3, § 1.412(b)-4, § 1.41'2(c)(2)-2, § 1.412(c)(4)-1, § 1.412(c)(5)-1, § 1.412(c)(6)-1, § 1.412(c)(7)-1, § 1.412(c)(8)-1, § 1.412(c)(9)-1, § 1.412 (c)(10)-1, and § 1.412(g)-1, unless otherwise indicated are effective with respect to a particular plan when section 412 first applies to that plan. However, for plan years beginning on or before [INSERT DATE 60 DAYS AFTER PUBLICATION OF THESE REGULATIONS AS A TREASURY DECISION IN THE FEDERAL REGISTER] the plan may rely on the prior published position of the Internal Revenue Service with respect to the application of section 412. Other effective dates are included in § 1.412(b)-2, § 1.412(c)(1)-2, § 1.412(c)(2)-1, § 1.412(c)(3)-2 and § 1.412(i)-1.

§ 1.412(b)-1 Funding standard account.

(a) *General rule.* Generally, for each single plan subject to the minimum funding standards there must be maintained a funding standard account as prescribed by section 412(b). (See § 1.414(1)-1(b)(1) for definition of "single plan".) Such an account for a money purchase pension plan reflects charges for contributions required under the plan, credits for amounts contributed, and charges and credits for amortization bases described in paragraph (b)(3) of this section,.

(b) *Definitions and special rules.*—(1) *Accounting date*—(i) *In general.* Each charge or credit to the funding standard account is charged or credited as of an accounting date. The accounting date for an item depends on the nature of the item and must be consistent with the computation of the amount of that item.

(ii) *Specific accounting dates.* The accounting date for each individual charge for normal cost or any charge or credit for the amortization of an amortization base is the date as of which the charge or credit is computed as due during the plan year. The last day of the plan year is the accounting date for any credit described in section 412(b)(3)(C). The first day of the plan year is the accounting date for any credit described in section 412(b)(3)(D) or for any accumulated funding deficiency or credit balance existing as of the end of the prior plan year. The accounting date for each contribution is made or, if made during the period described in section 412(c)(10) the last day of the plan year. Further, any contribution made must be credited as of the accounting date.

(2) *Valuation rate.* The term "valuation rate" means the assumed interest rate used to value plan liabilities.

(3) *Amortization base.* For purposes of this section, the term "amortization base" means any amount established under section 412(b)(2)(B), (C), or (D) to be amortized as a charge to the funding standard account, under section 412(b)(3)(B) to be amortized as a credit to the funding standard account, any other base resulting from a combination of offset of bases or any shortfall gain or loss base under § 1.412(c)(1)-2. Any base required by the Commissioner to be established pursuant to any approved change in funding method is also an amortization base. Each amortization base established under one of the provisions enumerated above with respect to a particular year is referred to as an "individual base."

(4) *Amortization period.* The amortization period for a base is the period of years stated in section 412(b)(2) or (3) over which a particular base is to be amortized. See § 1.412(c)(1)-2(g)(2) and (h)(2) for amortization periods under the shortfall method. See section 412(b)(2) and (3) for amortization periods for bases described in those sections. See paragraph (d) of this section for amortization periods of bases resulting from a combination or offset of bases. If the number of years in the amortization period is not an integer, the charge or credit in the last year will not be for the entire amortization amount but will be for the outstanding balance of the base at the time of the charge or credit.

(5) *Outstanding balance.* The outstanding balance of a base as of the end of a plan year equals the difference between two amounts:

(i) The first amount is the outstanding balance of the base as of the beginning of the plan year (or, if later, the date as of which the base is required to be established) increased by interest at the valuation rate.

(ii) The second amount is the charge (or credit) for that year for the base increased by interest at the valuation rate. For purposes of testing the basic funding formula in § 1.412(c)(3)-1(b)(1) the outstanding balance of amortizable bases must be computed as of the valuation date (the same date as of which the present value of future benefits and the present value of normal costs over the future working lifetime of participants are determined), rather than as of the end of the plan year. In testing the basic funding formula, the outstanding balance as of a valuation date equals the difference two amounts. The first amount is the outstanding balance as of the preceding valuation date (or, if later, the date as of which the base is required to be established) increased by interest at the valuation rate. The second amount is the charge (or credit) for the plan year preceding the plan year to which the current valuation refers increased by interest at the valuation rate.

(6) *Remaining amortization period.* The remaining amortization period for an amortization base is the difference between the amortization period and the number of years (including whole and fractional years) for which the base has been reduced by charging or crediting the funding standard account, as the case may be, with the amortization payment for each year.

(7) *Amortization amount.* The amortization amount is the amount of the charge or credit to the funding standard account required with respect to an amortization base for a plan year.

(8) *True and absolute values.* See § 1.404(a)-14(b)(4) for a definition of the terms "absolute value."

(9) *Immediate gain type funding method.* A funding method is an immediate gain type method if, under the method—

(i) The accrued liability may be determined solely from the computations with respect to the liabilities;

(ii) The accrued liability is an integral part of the funding method; and

(iii) The accrued liability is the excess of the present value, as of any valuation date, of the projected future benefit costs for all plan participants and beneficiaries over the present value of future contributions for the normal cost of all current plan participants.

Examples of the immediate gain type of funding method are the unit credit method, the entry-age normal cost method, and the individual level premium method.

(10) *Spread gain type funding method.* A funding method is a spread gain type method if it is not an immediate gain type method. Examples of the spread gain type of funding method are the aggregate cost method, the frozen initial liability cost method and the attained age normal cost method.

(11) *Actual unfunded liability for immediate gain funding methods.*—(1) *In general.* For a funding method of the immediate gain type, the actual unfunded liability as of any valuation date is the excess, if any, of the accrued liability over the actuarial value of assets as of that date.

(ii) *Accrued liability.* The accrued liability is equal to the present value of future benefits less the present value of future normal costs.

Generally, for purposes of computing costs for a plan year and gains and losses for a plan year, the normal cost for the plan year to which the valuation refers is considered to be a future normal cost and is not included in the accrued liability.

(iii) *Actuarial value of assets.* The value of assets must be determined in a manner consistent with section 412(c)(2) of the Code and § 1.412(c)(2)-1. Furthermore, for the purposes of computing costs for a plan year and gains and losses for a plan year, the assets must be treated in a manner that is consistent with the method of calculation of the accrued liability. If, in determining the accrued liability, the normal cost for the plan year to which valuation refers is treated as a future normal cost, then the assets used to compute the unfunded accrued liability should not include contributions that are credited to the funding standard account for the plan year to which the valuation refers or for any plan year thereafter.

(12) *Actual unfunded liability for spread gain funding methods.* For a funding method of the spread gain type that maintains an unfunded liability, the actual unfunded liability equals the expected unfunded liability.

(13) *Expected unfunded liability.* The expected unfunded liability as of any valuation date is determined as:

(i) The actual unfunded liability as of the prior valuation date increased with interest at the valuation rate to this later valuation date, plus

(ii) Normal costs representing accrued liabilities that were not included in determining the accrued liability as of the prior valuation date (*i.e.,* such costs as of the prior valuation date) but that are included (*i.e.,* are not considered future normal costs) in determining the accrued liability as of this later valuation date, plus interest at the valuation rate from the date as of which the normal costs were assumed payable to this valuation date, minus

(iii) The amount considered contributed by the employer to or under the plan for the plan year that was not included in the calculation of the actual unfunded liability as of the prior valuation date and was included in the calculation of the actual unfunded liability as of this later valuation date, plus interest at the valuation rate from the date on which the contribution was made if during the plan year, or under section 412(C)(10) was deemed to have been made if made after the plan year, to this later valuation date.

(14) *Plan year to which a valuation refers.* The plan year for which the funding standard account is charged with the first normal cost determined by a valuation is the plan year to which the valuation refers. See also § 1.412(c)(9)-1(b) concerning the date of a valuation.

(c) *Establishment and maintenance of amortization bases.*—(1) *Immediate gain type funding methods.* Under a plan using an immediate gain type funding method, a new amortization base must be established to reflect each change in unfunded past service liability arising from a plan amendment, net experience gain or loss, and change in unfunded past service liability arising from a change in funding method or actuarial assumptions.

(2) *Spread gain type funding methods*—(i) *In general.* Under a plan using a spread gain type funding method, amortization bases may be established to reflect changes in unfunded past service liability arising from plan amendments or changes in actuarial assumptions. Alternatively, these changes in unfunded liability may be reflected in the normal cost. Whether these changes are reflected in amortization bases or in the normal cost is part of the funding method. Thus, any change from past practice constitutes a change in funding method and must be approved under section 412(c)(5). Furthermore, the method must treat increases and decreases due to any type of event consistently.

(ii) *Experience gain or loss.* An amortization base may not be established to reflect a new experience gain or loss under a plan using a spread gain type funding method.

(3) *Special amortization bases.* Any amortization base established to amortize a waived funding deficiency under section 412(b)(2)(C) must continue to maintained regardless of the type of funding method used by the plan. Also see § 1.412(b)-1(d)(1).

(d) *Combining and offsetting amounts to be amortized*—(1) *In general.* Under section 412(b)(4), individual bases, with the exception of bases under section 412(b)(2)(C), may be combined and offset to form a single base. This single base is computed under the provisions of paragraph (d) that follow. However, any number of amortization bases having the same remaining amortization period may be combined and offset simply by adding the outstanding balances of the individual bases, using true rather than absolute values, without regard to the computations under paragraph (d) of this section that follow. Bases under section 412(b)(2)(C) may not be combined with any bases not established under section 412(b)(2)(C).

(2) *Combine outstanding balances of bases for charges and for credits.* Except as provided in subparagraph (1) the outstanding balances of any individual bases established for the purpose of charging the funding standard account may be combined as of any date by adding the outstanding balance of each base to be combined as of that date. Likewise, the outstanding balances of any bases for crediting the account may be combined.

(3) *Determine remaining amortization period of each combined base.* The remaining amortization period of a combined base is determined as follows:

(i) Add the amortization amounts, based on the same mode of payment, for the individual bases being combined. Amortization amounts are of the same mode of payment if they are charged or credited on the same day of the plan year, or on the same days if charged or credited in installments during the plan year.

(ii) Divide the outstanding balance of the combined base by the combined amortization amount determined under subdivision (i).

(iii) Compute the period of years for which the amount determined under subdivision (ii) provides an annuity certain of $1 per year at the valuation rate. This number, the remaining amortization period, must be computed in terms of fractional years, if necessary. Standard present value tables may be used together with linear interpolation.

(iv) As an alternative, the amortization period may be rounded to the next lowest integer (if charge bases) or next highest integer (if credit bases) and the amortization amount must then be recomputed by dividing the outstanding balance of the combined based by the present value of annuity certain of $1 per year at the valuation rate for the rounded amortization period.

(4) *Offset.* Combined bases may be offset only if all charge and credit bases have been combined (except those that may not be combined pursuant to subparagraph (1)). The combined charge base and the combined credit base are offset by subtracting the lesser outstanding balance from the greater outstanding balance. The difference between these two outstanding balances is amortized over the remaining amortization period for the greater of the two outstanding balances, whether for charges or for credits. The amortization amount (charge or credit) for this offset base is the level amount payable for each plan year to reduce the outstanding balance of the base to zero over the remaining amortization period at the valuation rate. However, see paragraph (d)(3)(iv) of this section concerning an alternative method of computing the remaining amortization period.

(5) *Example.* Assume that at the beginning of a plan year the actuary for a plan decides to combine and offset the amortization bases as reflected in the plan's funding standard account. No funding deficiency of the plan has been waived. All amortization amounts are due at the end of the plan year. The valuation rate is 5 percent. Based on pertinent information from the plan records, all amortization bases, A and B for charges and C and D for credits, are combined and offset as follows:

Base	Outstanding balance (beginning of year)	Amortization amount (due end of year)	Remaining amortization period
(i) Individual bases.			
A	$165,468	$10,000	36
B	8,863	1,000	12
C	(4,153)	(500)	11
D	(30,745)	(2,000)	30
(i) Combined bases.			
AB	$174,331	$11,000	32.23
CD	(34,898)	(2,500)	24.53
(i) Offset base.			
ABCD	$139,433	$8,798	32.23

(iv) The outstanding balanes of the charge and credit bases were combined in step (ii) by adding the outstanding balances of the like bases (165,468 + 8,863 = 174,331 and 4,153 + 30,745 = 34,898). The charge and credit base amortization amounts were similarly computed (10,000 + 1,000 = 11,000 and 500 + 2,000 = 2,500). The remaining amortization periods were derived from standard present value tables and linear interpolation as the amount having a present value at the 5 percent valuation rate for a $1 per year annuity certain equal to the ration of the outstanding balance to the amortization amount.

(v) The combined bases were offset in step (iii) by subtracting base CD from AB to obtain the $139,433 outstanding balance, using the 32.23 remaining amortization period for base AB, and computing the $8,798 amortization amount as the level annual amount necessary to amortize the base fully over 32.23 years. (Alternatively, the amortization period may be rounded to 32 years. The amortization charge corresponding to that amortization period is $8,823.)

(e) *Interest.*—(1) *General rule.* The funding standard account is charged or credited with interest at the valuation rate for the time between the accounting date for the item giving rise to the interest charge or credit and the end of the plan year.

(2) *Change of interest rate.* A change of the assumed interest rate under a plan does not affect the outstanding balance or the remaining amortization period of any existing base. However, the amortization amount for each base is increased to reflect an increase in interest and decrease to reflect a decrease in interest so that the present value of future amortization amounts equal the outstanding balance of the base. This chane is made in addition to creating any new base required by § 1.412(b)-1(c).

(f) *Gains and losses.*—(1) *Amortization requirements*—(i) *Immediate gain type funding method.* A plan that uses an immediate gain type of funding method separately amortizes experience gains and losses over the period prescribed in section 412(b)(2)(B)(iv) and (3)(B)(ii). The first year of the amortization of an experience gain or less determined as of particular valuation date is the plan year to which the valuation refers.

(ii) *Spread gain type funding method.* A plan that uses a spread gain type of funding method spreads experience gains and losses over

future periods as part of the plan's normal cost. These gains and losses are reflected in the amount charged to the funding standard account under section 412(b)(2)(A) and are not separately amortized.

(2) *Amount of experience gain or loss.*—(i) *In general.* For an immediate gain type of funding method the experience gain determined as of a valuation late is the excess of the expected unfunded liability described in § 1.412(b)-1(b)(13) over the actual unfunded liability described in § 1.412(b)-1(b)(11). The experience loss is the excess of the actual unfunded liability described in § 1.412(b)-1(b)(11) over the expected unfunded liability described in § 1.412(b)-1(b)(13).

(ii) *Special rule.* Paragraph (f)(2)(ii) of this section applies to an immediate gain funding method if there are no other amortization charges (under section 412(b)(2(B), (C), or (D)) or credits (under section 412(b)(3)(B) for the first plan year in which the loss will be amortized. The experience loss as of the valuation date is the sum of—

(A) The actual unfunded liability as of the valuation date, plus

(B) Any credit balance (or minus any funding deficiency) in the funding standard account as of the first day of the first plan year in which the loss will be amortized adjusted with interest at the valuation rate to the valuation date.

(g) *Certain retroactive changes required by Commissioner.* Under section 412(c)(3), all costs liabilities, rates of interest, and other factors under the plan must be determined on the basis on actuarial assumptions and methods which, in th aggregate, are reasonable. Assumptions and methods are established in the first Schedule B (Form 5500) that is filed with respect to a plan year and may not be changed for that plan year. However, upon a determination by the Commissioner that the the actuarial asssumptions and methods used by a plan are not reasonable in the aggregate, the Commissioner may require certain retroactive adjustments to the funding standard account of the plan. The funding standard account must reflect these changes as required by the Commissioner.

(h) *Reasonable actuarial assumptions.*—(1) *In general.* The determination whether actuarial assumptions are reasonable in the aggregate is generally based upon the experience under the plan, unless it is established that past experience is not likely to recur and thus is not a good indication of future experience. In addition, assumptions may be considered unreasonable in the circumstances described in paragraphs (h)(2)-(4) of this section.

(2) *Noncounterbalancing assumptions.* Assumptions may be considered unreasonable if an assumption used by the plan is not yet reflected in the experience of the plan, is not reasonable under the circumstances of the plan, and is not counterbalanced by another assumption. For example, isn a plan with one participant who has not yet attained the normal retirement age, an assumption of an unreasonable annuity purchase rate could be counter balanced by a change in the plan interest rate.

(3) *Inconsistent with benefit structure.* As assumptions may be unreasonable if use of an assumption is inconsistent with the benefit structure of the plan. For example, a plan which provides benefits not based on compensation may not assume a salary increase if it spreads the present value of future normal costs over the present value of future compensation.

(4) *Inconsistent assumptions.* Assumptions may be considered unreasonable in the aggregate if one plan assumption is inconsistent with other assumptions used by the plan. For example, an assumption which projects benefits based on a salary increase of 5-percent per year may cause assumptions to be unreasonable in the aggregate in a plan which spreads normal costs over future years' compensation using an assumption of 8-percent annual compensation increases.

Par. 2. The Income Tax Regulations, 26 CFR Part 1, are amended by adding the following new sections after § 1.412(b)-2.

§ 1.412(b)-3 *Funding standard account adjustments for plan mergers and spinoffs.* [RESERVED]

§ 1.412(b)-4 *Plan termination and plan years of less than twelve months.*

(a) *General rules.* The minimum funding standard under section 412 applies to a plan under the end of the plan year in which the plan terminates. Therefore, the funding standard account (or the alternative funding standard account, as the case may be) must be maintained until the end of the plan year in which the plan terminates even though the plan terminates before the last day of the plan year.

(b) *Defined benefit plan.* In the case of a defined benefit plan, the charges and credits to the funding standard account are adjusted ratably to reflect the portion of the plan year before the date of plan termination. Similarly, annual charges and adjusted for a short plan year. However, this ratable adjustment is not made for credits under section 412(b)(2)(C), and (D), for interest charges and credits under section 412(b)(5), and for credits under section 412(c)(6).

(c) *Money purchase pension plans*—(1) *General rule for termination.* In the case of a money purchase pension plan, the minimum funding standard requires the funding standard account to be charged with the entire amount of any contribution due on or before the date of plan termination however, it does not require a charge for contributions due after that date.

(2) *General rule for short plan year.* In the case of a money purchase pension plan, the minimum funding standard requires the funding standard account to be charged with the entire amount of any contribution due as of a date within a short plan year.

(3) *Due date of contributions.* For the purposes of paragraphs (c)(1) and (2) of this section, a contribution is due as of the earlier of—

(i) The date specified in the plan, or

(ii) The date as of which the contribution is required to be allocated.

(4) *Date for allocation of contribution.* For purposes of paragraph (c)(3)(ii) of this section, a contribution is required to be allocated as of a date if all the requirements for the allocation have been satisfied as of that date.

(d) *Date of plan termination*—(1) *Title IV plans.* In the case of a plan subject to Title IV of ERISA, the date of plan termination is generally the date described in section 40489 of ERISA. However, if that date precedes the tenth day after the date on which notice of intent to terminate is filed, and if any contributions made or required by Code section 412 to avoid an accumulated funding deficiency for the period ending on such tenth day would increase any participant's benefits upon termination (taking benefits guaranteed by the Pension Benefit Guaranty Corporation into account), the date of termination will be the tenth day after the date on which notice of intent to terminate is filed.

(2) *Other plans.* In the case of a plan not subject to Title IV of ERISA, the date of plan termination occurs no earlier than the date on which the actions necessary to effect the plan termination are taken. The determination of this date is based on the facts and circumstances of each case.

(e) *Partial terminations.* This section does not apply to a partial plan termination within the meaning of section 411(d)(3)(A).

(f) *Funding excise taxes.* See § 54.4971-3(d) of the Pension Excise Tax Regulations (26 CFR Part 54) for the effect of plan termination on an employer's liability for taxes imposed by section 4971(a) and (b).

Par. 3. The Income Tax Regulations, 26 CFR Part 1, are amended by adding the following new section after § 1.412(c)(2)-1:

§ 1.412(c)(2)-2 *Bond valuation election.*

(a) *Scope of election.*—(1) *In general.* The election described in section 412(c)(2)(B) with respect to bonds generally applies to all bonds and evidences of indebtedness including those acquired by merger. The election applies only to defined benefit plans. A defined contribution plan must value bonds and other evidences of indebtedness on the basis of fair market value.

(2) *Exception.* The election does not apply to bonds or evidences of indebtedness at any time that they are in default as to principal or interest.

(3) *Convertible debt.* For purposes of this section, a debut instrument which is convertible into an equity security and acquired after [THE DATE 90 DAYS AFTER THE DATE ON WHICH § 1.412(c)(2)-2 IS ADOPTED AS A TREASURY DECISION] is treated as an evidence of indebtedness until the conversion occurs.

(b) *Effect of election.*—(1) *In general.* The effect of the election is that bonds and other evidences of indebtedness included among the plan assets are valued on an amortized basis rather than on a fair market value basis.

(2) *Amount amortized.*—(i) *In general.* The amount amortized with respect to a bond or other evidence of indebtedness is generally the difference between its initial cost when acquired by the plan and its redemption value at the end of the amortization period. In the case of a bond or other evidence of indebtedness that was acquired by the plan in a plan year before the plan year for which the election was made, the amortized value for each year must be determined as though the election had always been in effect with respect to the bond or other evidence of indebtedness.

(ii) *Spinoffs.* The amount amortized after a spinoff is based on the initial cost to the plan which acquired the bond or other evidence of indebtedness and not the value to the plan after the spinoff.

(iii) *Mergers.* The amount amortized after a merger is based on the cost of the plan which first elected to value the bonds and other evidences of indebtedness on an amortized basis. In the case of a bond or other evidence of indebtedness that was acquired by any merging plan before the election was first made with respect to the bond or other evidence of indebtedness, the premium or discount shall be amortized as provided in paragraph (b)(2)(i).

(3) *Amortization period.* The amortization period is the time from the date on which the plan acquires the bond or other evidence of indebtedness to its maturity date (or, in the case of a debt instrument that is callable prior to maturity, the earliest call date).

(c) *Effect of default.* Once the election is made, it applies to each debt instrument held or acquired that is not in default as to principal or interest. While in default, the instrument is subject to the fair market value requirements of section 412(c)(2)(A).

(d) *Manner of making election.* The plan administrator makes the election by preparing a statement that the election described in section 412(c)(2)(B) is being made and by filing the statement attached to the annual return required under section 6058 for the first plan year for which the election is to apply.

(e) *Revocation of election.*—(1) *Effect.* Once consent to the revocation of the election is obtained as prescribed in paragraph (e)(2) of this section, all plan assets are valued under section 412(c)(2)(A).

(2) *Consent.* Consent for the revocation of the election must be obtained in the manner prescribed by the Commissioner for obtaining permission to change funding methods under section 412(c)(5) and § 1.412(c)(5)-1.

(3) *Mergers.* A plan which has acquired a bond or other evidence of indebtedness by merger must obtain the consent of the Commissioner to value bonds and other evidences of indebtedness on a basis other than amortized value if an election under section 412(c)(2)(B) with respect to the asset acquired had been made prior to the merger.

Par. 4. The Income Tax Regulations, 26 CFR Part 1, are amended by adding the following new sections after § 1.412(c)(3)-2:

§ 1.412(c)(4)-1 Certain changes in accrued liability.

(a) *In general.* In the case of immediate gain type funding methods, section 412(c)(4) treats certain increases and decreases in the accrued liability under a plan as an experience gain or loss. Plans using a spread gain type of funding method will reflect the gain or loss in determining the normal cost under the plan. Under section 412(b)(2) and (3), plans which are valued using a funding method of the immediate gain type will amortize the amount treated as an experience gain or loss in equal amounts over the period described in section 412(b). See § 1.412(b)-1(b)(9) and (10) for examples of spread gain type and immediate gain type funding methods.

(b) *Applicable changes.* A change treated as an experience gain or loss under section 412(c)(4) includes an increase or decrease in accrued liability caused by:

(1) A change in benefits under the Social Security Act,

(2) A change in other retirement benefits created under Federal or State law,

(3) A change in the definition of "wages" under section 3121, or

(4) A change in the amount of wages under section 3121 that are taken into account for purposes of section 401(a)(5) and the regulations thereunder.

§ 1.412(c)(5)-1 Change in plan year or funding method.

Approval given under section 412(c)(5) authorizes a change in plan year or funding method. Written requests for approval are to be submitted, as directed by the Commissioner, to Commissioner of Internal Revenue, Attention: OP:E:A:P, 1111 Constitution Avenue, N.W., Washington, D.C. 29224, Such a request must be submitted before the close of the plan year of which the change is to be effective unless an extension of time for filing request is granted.

§ 1.412(c)(6)-1 Full funding and full funding limitation.

(a) *In general.* This section provides rules relating to full funding and the full funding limitation under section 412(c)(6) and (7). The full funding limitation for a plan year is the excess, if any, of the accrued liability under the plan plus the normal cost of the plan year over the value of the plan's assets.

(b) *Valuation.*—(1) *Timing rule.* For purposes of this section, assets and accrued liabilities are to be valued at the usual time used by the plan for valuations.

(2) *Interest adjustments.* If the valuation is performed before the end of the plan year, the assets and accrued liabilities (including normal cost) are projected to the end of the plan year. The projection is based on the valuation rate.

(c) *Calculation of accrued liability.* The accrued liability of a plan is determined under the funding method used by the plan. However, if the funding method used by the plan is not an immediate gain method and, thus, does not directly calculate an accrued liability, the calculation of the accrued liability is made under the entry age normal funding method.

(d) *Calculation of normal cost.* In general the normal cost is the normal cost determined under the funding method used by the plan. However, if under paragraph (c) accrued liability is calculated under the entry age normal cost method, then the normal cost is also calculated under the entry age normal cost method.

(e) *Calculation of assets.* The value of plan assets used to determine the full funding limitation is the lesser of the fair market value of the assets or the actuarial value of the assets, if different. The value of plan assets must be reduced by any credit balance existing on the first day of the plan year.

(f) *Effect of full funding on deduction limits.* See § 404(a)-14(k) for provisions relating to the effect of the full funding limitation on the maximum deductible contribution limitations and 10-year amortization bases under section 404(a).

(g) *Effect of the full funding limitation on the funding standard account.*—(1) *General rule.* If, as of the end of any plan year, the accumulated funding deficiency (calculated without regard to any credit balance for the plan year or any contributions made for that plan year) exceeds the full funding limitation of section 412(c)(7) calculated as the valuation date and projected, if necessary, to the end of the plan year, then the following adjustments are made:

(i) The amount of such excess is credited to the funding standard account for the plan year.

(ii) As of the end of that plan year, all the amounts described in paragraphs (2)(B), (C), (D), and (3)(B) of section 412(b) which are required to be amortized shall be considered fully amortized.

(2) *Example.* The principles of section 412(c)(6) and of paragraph (e) of this section are illustrated in the following example:

Example. Assume that a single employer plan is established on January 1, 1976, with a calendar plan year. The funding method is the accrued benefit cost method (unit credit method), the interest assumption is 5 percent, and both the normal cost and the amortization charges and credits are calculated on the basis of payment at the beginning of the year. The annual charge to the funding standard account due to the amortization (over 30 years) of the initial past service liability is $200, and the annual credit due to the amortization (over 15 years) of a 1979 experience gain is $10. A valuation is performed as of January 1, 1985, to determine costs for the 1985 plan year. There was a credit balance of $100 in the funding standard account on December 31, 1984. As of January 1, 1985, plan assets (determined in accordance with section 412(c)(7)(B) and reduced by the $100 credit balance as of January 1, 1985) were $10,400; the accrued liability under the plan was $10,000; the normal cost (for the 1985 plan year) was $1,200; and the 1985 employer contribution (made as of January 1, 1985) was $1,000. The accumulated funding deficiency (calculated ignoring the credit balance and employer contribution) as of December 31, 1985, is $1,459.50, determined as the excess of charges of $1,470 ($1,200 normal cost, plus $200 amortization charge, plus $70 interest) over the credits of $10.50 ($10 amortization credit, plus, $.50 interest). The full limitation as of the valuation date (January 1, 1985) is $800, determined as the excess of the sum of the accrued liability ($10,000) plus normal cost ($1,200) over the adjusted plan assets ($10,400). The value of this $800 as of the end of the year (i.e., December 31, 1985) is $800 plus $40 interest, or $840.00. The excess, as of the end of the 1985 plan year, of the accumulated funding deficiency over the full funding limitation is thus $1,459.50 minus $840.00, or $619.50. The funding standard account is charged and credited as follows:

Charges

Normal cost	$1,200.00
Amortization charge	200.00
Interest	70.00
Total	$1,470.00

Credits

Credit balance	$100.00
Contribution	1,000.00
Amortization credit	10.00
Interest	55.50
Sec. 412(c)(6) credit	619.50
Total	$1,784.50

Credit balance December 31, 1985	$314.50

§ 1.412(c)(7)-1 Full funding limitation.

See § 1.412(c)(6)-1 for rules relating both to full funding under section 412(c)(6) and to the full funding limitation under section 412(c)(7).

§ 1.412(c)(8)-1 Election to treat certain retroactive plan amendments as made on first day of a plan year.

The function of the Secretary of Labor described in section 412(c)(8) was transferred to the Secretary of Treasury as of December 31, 1978, by Reorganization Plan No. 4 of 1978, 197901 C.B. 480. Therefore, the material described in section 412(c)(8) now must be filed as directed by the Secretary of Treasury.

§ 1.412(c)(9)-1 Frequency of actuarial valuations.

(a) *Required valuation.* Section 412(c)(9) requires an actuarial valuation not less frequently than once every three years. Paragraph (b) of this section provides general rules for performing valuations. Paragraph (d) describes certain situations in which the Commissioner may require an actuarial valuation more frequently than once every three years. These rules may be waived at the discretion of the Commissioner and do not apply to mutiemployer plans within the meaning of section 414(f).

(b) *General rules for valuations.*—(1) *Dates of valuation.* Except as provided by the Commissioner, the valuation must be as of a date within the plan year to which the valuation refers or within the one month prior to that year. All assets and liabilities must be valued as of the same date. The valuation must us data as of the valuation data; it is not permissible to use adjusted data from a prior or subsequent year.

(2) *Use of prior valuations.* A plan may not use a valuation for any subsequent plan year if that valuation was not also used for the year to which it refers. Also, a prior valuation may not be used if the plan has used any subsequent valuation for another plan year.

(c) *Funding standard account rules for years when there is no valuation.*—(1) *Amortization of bases.* After an amortization amount of that base is charged or credit in each plan year, whether or not a valuation is performed for the year, until the outstanding balance of the base is zero. However, see § 1.412(c)(6)-1 for rules for years after a full funding limitation credit and § 1.412(b)-1 for combining and offsetting bases.

(2) *Normal cost.* If valuations are performed less frequently than every year, then any valuation computes the normal cost for the year to which the valuation refers and for subsequent years until another valuation applies. In those subsequent years, the normal cost is—

(i) If the funding method computes normal cost as a level dollar amount, the same dollar amount as for the year to which the valuation refers;

(ii) If the funding method computes normal cost as a level percentage pay, the same percentage of current pay as for the year to which the valuation refers, or

(iii) If the funding method computes normal cost as an amount equal to the present value of benefits accruing under the method for the year, under any reasonable method.

The rules in subdivisions (i) and (ii) apply whether the funding method computes normal cost on either an individual or an aggregate basis.

(d) *Situations when more frequent valuations are required.*—(1) *Amendments is increas ing actuarial costs*—(i) *General rule.* A valuation is required for any plan year when a plan amendment first increases the actuarial costs of a plan. For this purpose, actuarial costs consist of the plan's normal costs under section 412(b)(2)(A), amortization charges under section 412(b)(2)(B), and amortization credits under section 412(b)(3)(B).

(ii) *Exception.* No valuation will be required under paragraph (d)(1)(i) of this section if two conditions are met: first, the plan actuary estimates that the cost increase attributable to the amendment is less than 5 percent of the actuarial cost determined without regard to the amendment; and second, the actuary files a signed statement to that effect with the annual return required under section 6058 for the year of the amendment.

(2) *Certain changes in number of participants*—(i) *General rule.* A valuation is required for a plan year when the actual number of plan participants that would be considered in the current valuations differs from the number of participants that were considered in the prior valuation by more than 20 percent of that number.

(ii) *Exception.* Notwithstanding subdivision (i), no valuation will be required merely because of a change in the number of estimated participants under a plan that determines normal cost as a level percentage of payroll (on either an individual or aggregate basis) or as a level dollar amount per individual.

(iii) *Plans using shortfall method.* No valuation will be required merely because of a change in the number of estimated participants under a plan which uses the shortfall method described in § 1.412(c)(1)-2. However, a valuation is required for a plan year if the estimated units of service or production ("estimated base units" under § 1.412(c)(1)-2(e)) for the prior plan exceeds the actual number of units of service or production for that plan year be more than 20 percent.

(3) *Change in actuarial funding method or assumptions.* A valuation is required for any plan year with respect to which a change in the funding method or actuarial assumptions of a plan is made.

(4) *Mergers and spinoffs*— (i) *General rule.* A valuation is required for any plan merger or spinoff occurs.

(ii) *Safe harbor for mergers.* In the case of a merger, no valuation will be required under paragraph (d)(4) of this section if the *de minimis* rule in § 1.414(l)-1(h) is satisfied.

(iii) *Safe harbor for spinoffs.* In the case of a spinoff, no valuation will be required under paragraph (d)(4) of this section if the present value of all the benefits being spun off from the plan during the plan year is less than 3 percent of the plan's assets as of the beginning of the year.

(5) *Change in average age of participant s*— (i) *General rule.* A valuation is required for any plan year with respect to which the average age of plan participants changes significantly, within the meaning of subdivisions (i) and (iii), from the average age of plan participants at the last valuation.

(ii) *Rule for large plans.* For a plan with 100 or more participants, an increase or decrease in average age of more than two years is a significant change.

(iii) *Rule for small plans.* For a plan with fewer than 100 participants, an increase or decrease in average age of more than four years is a significant change.

(6) *Alternative minimum funding standard account.* A valuation is required for each year for which the plan uses the alternative minimum funding standard account.

(7) *Deductibility considerations.* A valuation is required when it appears that the full funding limitation has been reached for purposes of determining the maximum deductible contribution limitations of section 404(a).

(8) *Other situations.* The Commissioner may require valuations in other situations as the facts and circumstances warrant.

§ 1.412(c)(10)-1 Time for making contributions to satisfy section 412.

(a) *General rule.* Under section 412(c)(10), a contribution made after the end of a plan year but no later than two and one-half months after the end of that year is deemed to have been made on the last day of that year.

(b) *Extension of general rule*—(1) *Plan years ending before* [*90 DAYS AFTER PUBLICATION DATE OF FINAL REGULATIONS*]. For plan years ending before [90 DAYS AFTER PUBLICATION OF FINAL REGULATIONS], for purposes of section 412 a contribution for such a plan year that is made not later than eight and one-half months after the end of that plan year is deemed to have been made on the last day of that year.

(2) *Plan years ending on or after* [*90 DAYS AFTER PUBLICATION OF FINAL REGULATIONS*]—(I) *Transitional rule.* The two and one-half month period provided in section 412(c)(10) and § 1.410(c)(10)-1(a) is extended for each of the first three plan years ending after [90 DAYS AFTER PUBLICATION OF FINAL REGULATIONS]. For the first plan year ending after [90 DAYS AFTER PUBLICATION OF FINAL REGULATIONS], a contribution made not later then eight and one-half months after the end of that plan year is deemed to have been made on the last day of that year. For the second year, the two and one-half month period is extended to six and one-half months, and for the third year, the two and one-half period is extended to four and one-half months.

(ii) *Extensions of general and transitional periods.* The time for making contributions under the general rule described in paragraph (a) and transitional rule of paragraph (b)(2)(i) of this section may be extended to a date not beyond eight and one-half months after the end of the plan year. Extensions of the two and one-half month period and transitional years' periods are granted on an individual basis by the Commissioner. A request for extension should be submitted to the Commissioner of Internal Revenue, 1111 Constitution Avenue, N.W., Washington, D.C. 20224 (Attention OP:E:A).

(c) *Effect on section 404.* The rules of this section, relating to the timing of contributions for purposes of section 412, operate independently from the rules under section 404(a)(6), relating to the timing of contributions for purposes of claiming a deduction under section 404.

§ 1.412(g)-1 Alternative maximum funding standard account.

(a) *In general.* A plan that maintains an alternative minimum funding standard account (" ASA ") for any plan year under section 412(g) must satisfy the requirements of this section. To use the ASA, a plan must use a funding method that requires contributions for all years that are not less than those required under the entry age normal cost method of funding. A funding method does not affect cost of plan benefits but only the incidence of contributions in different years. Thus, any funding method that requires a contribution in one year that exceeds that required by the entry age normal method (EAN) for that year must require a lesser contribution in another year. Hence, only a plan which uses the EAN cost method may use the ASA.

(b) *Special rules*—(1) *Dual accounting.* While maintaining an ASA, a plan must maintain the funding standard account under section 412(b) for each plan year.

(2) *Change of method.* For any plan year, the choice of whether to use the ASA is independent of whether the ASA or funding standard account was used in the prior year. Any change from the choice made in the prior year does not require approval of the Commissioner. Further, a plan which has filed for a plan year the actuarial report described in section 6059(b) using the ASA to determine its minimum funding requirement may change to use the funding standard account to determine the funding requirement for that year. However, a plan may not switch to the ASA for a plan year after having filed the actuarial report for that year using the funding standard account.

(3) *PBGC Valuation.* In determining charges and credits to the ASA under paragraphs (b) and (c) of this section (other than the amount in paragraph (c)(2)(i)), a plan must value its assets and liabilities on a termination basis as provided in regulations issued by the Pension Benefit Guaranty Corporation (PBGC) under sections 4041 and 4062 of the Employee Retirement Income Security Act of 1974 ("ERISA") for plans placed in trusteeship by PBGC.

(4) *Cumulative nature of account.* When the ASA is used for a plan year after a plan year for which the ASA was not used, the credit balance and charge balance as of the first day of the year equal zero. However, during any continuous period of years for which the ASA is used, the credit or charge balance as of the end of any ASA year are carried forward as beginning balances in the next ASA year.

(c) *Charges*—(1) *In general.* The GSA is charged with the amounts described in paragraph (c) of this section.

(2) *Normal cost.* The ASA is charged with the normal cost of the plan for a plan year. This amount is the normal cost for that plan year computed—

(i) Under the method of funding and actuarial assumptions used for purposes of maintaining the plan's funding standard account or, if less,

(ii) As the present value of benefits expected, on a termination basis, to accrue during the plan year.

(3) *Unfunded accrued benefits.* The ASA is charged with the unfunded accrued benefits of the plan for a plan year. This amount is the excess of—

(i) The present value of accrued benefits under the plan, determined as of the valuation date for the plan year, over

(ii) The fair market value of plan assets, determined as of the valuation date for the plan year.

Because fair market value is used, any election to value evidences of indebtedness at amortized value does not apply in computing this value.

(4) *Credit balance from prior plan year.* The ASA is charged as of the first day of a plan year with any ASA credit balance carried forward from the prior plan year.

(5) *Interest.* The ASA is charged with interest on the amounts charged to the ASA under paragraph (b)(2), (b)(3) and (b)(4) of this section, as generally prescribed for the funding standard account under §1.412(b)-1(e).

(d) *Credits*—(1) *In general.* The ASA is credited with the amounts described in paragraph (d) of this section.

(2) *Employer contributions.* The ASA is credited with the amount of contributions made by the employer to the plan for the plan year.

(3) *Interest.* The ASA is credited with the interest on the amount credited under paragraph (d)(2), determined as of the end of the plan year as generally prescribed for the funding standard account under §1.412(b)-1(e).

Par. 5. The Income Tax Regulations, 26 CFR Part 1, are further amended by adding new paragraphs (f) and (g) of §1.413-1 to read as follows:

§ 1.413-1 Special rules for collectively bargained plans.

* * *

(f) *Minimum funding standard.* The minimum funding standard for a collectively bargained plan shall be determined as if all participants in the plan were employed by a single employer.

(g) *Liability for funding tax.* See §54.4971-3 of the Pension Excise Tax Regulations, 26 CFR Part 54, for rules under section 413(b)(6), relating to liability for excise tax on failure to meet minimum funding standards with respect to collectively bargained plans.

* * *

Par. 6. The Income Tax Regulations, 26 CFR Part 1, are further amended by adding new paragraphs (e) and (f) of §1.413-2 to read as follows:

§ 1.413-2 Special rules for plans maintained by more than one employer.

* * *

(e) *Minimum funding standard.* The minimum funding standard for a plan maintained by more than one employer shall be determined as if all participants in the plan were employed by a single employer.

(f) *Liability for funding tax.* See §54.4971-3 of the Pension Excise Tax Regulations, 26 CFR Part 54, for rules under section 413(c)(5), relating to liability for excise tax on failure to meet minimum funding standards with respect to plans maintained by more than one employer.

Temporary Income Tax Regulations Under The Employee Retirement Income Security Act Of 1974

(26 CFR Part 54)

Par. 7. The Temporary Regulations under the Employee Retirement Income Security Act of 1974, 26 CFR Part 11, are amended by removing the following sections: §11.412(c)-7, §11.412(c)-11, and §11.412(c)-12.

Pension Excise Tax Regulations

(26 CFR Part 54)

Par. 8. The Pension Excise Tax Regulations, 26 CFR Part 54, are amended by adding in the appropriate place the following new sections:

§54.4971-1 General rules relating to excise tax on failure to meet minimum funding standards.

(a) *Scope.* This section and §§54.4971-1 and 54.4971-3 provide rules for the imposition of tax on a failure to meet the minimum funding standards of section 412. General rules appear in this section. Operational rules and special definitions appear in §54.4971-2 Rules relating to tax liability appear in §54.4971-3.

(b) *Initial tax*—(1) *General rule.* Section 4971(a) imposes an initial tax on an employer who maintains a plan to which section 412 applies for each taxable year in which there is an accumulated funding deficiency as of the end of the plan year ending with or within such taxable year.

(2) *Amount of tax.* The initial tax is 5 percent of the accumulated funding deficiency determined under section 412 as of the end of the plan year ending with or within the taxable year of the employer.

(c) *Additional tax.* [Reserved]

(d) *Accumulated funding deficiency*—(1) *In general.* The accumulated funding deficiency of a plan for a plan year is the lesser of the amounts described in paragraphs (d)(2) and (d)(3). Paragraph (d)(3) only applies for a year if the actuarial report described in section 6059(b) was filed using the alternative funding standard account for that year.

(2) *Funding standard account method.* The accumulated funding deficiency under this subparagraph is equal to the excess, as of the end of the plan year, of the total charges to the funding standard account under section 412 for all plan years to which section 412 applies over the total credits to that account under section 412 for those years.

(3) *Alternative funding standard account method.* The accumulated funding deficiency under this subparagraph is equal to the excess, as of the end of the plan year, of the total charges to the alternative minimum funding standard account under section 412(g) for that plan years over the total credits to the account under section 412(g) for that year.

§54.4971-2 Operational rules and special definitions relating to excise tax on failure to meet minimum funding standards.

(a) *Correction*—(1) *General rule.* To correct an accumulated funding deficiency for a plan year, a contribution must be made to the plan that reduces the deficiency, as of the end of that plan year, to zero. To reduce the deficiency to zero, the contribution must include interest at the plan's actuarial valuation rate for the period between the end of the plan year and the date of the contribution.

(2) *Corrective effect of certain retroactive amendments.* Certain retroactive plan amendments that meet the requirements of section 412(c)(8) may reduce an accumulated funding deficiency for a plan year to zero.

(3) *Optional corrective actions when employers withdraw from certain plans.* See § 54.4971-3(e)(2) for correcting deficiencies attributable to certain withdrawing employers.

(b) *No deduction.* Under section 275(a)(6), no deduction is allowed for a tax imposed under section 4971(a) or (b).

(c) *Waiver of imposition of tax.* Under section 3002(b) of the Employee Retirement Income Security Act of 1974 (ERISA), the Commissioner may waive the imposition of the additional tax under section 4971(b) in appropriate cases. This authority does not extend to the imposition of the initial tax under section 4971(a).

(d) *Notification of the Secretary of Labor*— (1) *In general.* Except as provided in paragraph (d)(2) of this section, before issuing a notice of deficiency with respect to the tax imposed under section 4971(a) or (b), the Commissioner must notify the Secretary of Labor that the Internal Revenue Servicer proposes to assess the tax. The purpose of this notice is to give the Secretary of labor a reasonable opportunity to obtain a correction of the accumulated funding deficiency or to comment on the imposition of the tax. (See section 4971(d) and section 3002(b) of ERISA.) The Commissioner may issue a notice of deficiency with respect to the tax imposed under section 4971(a) or (b) 60 days after the mailing of the notice of proposed deficiency to the Secretary of Lab or. Any action taken by the Secretary of Labor will not affect the imposition of the 5-percent initial tax imposed by section 4971(a). See paragraph (c) of this section, however, concerning the Commissioner's authority to waive the 100-percent additional tax imposed by section 4971(b).

(2) *Jeopardy assessments.* The Commissioner may determine that the assessment or collection of the tax imposed under section 4971(a) or (b) will be jeopardized by delay. If the Commissioner makes this determination, the Internal Revenue Service may immediately assess a deficiency under section 6861 without prior notice to the Secretary of Labor. Abatement of the assessment may be granted upon correction of the deficiency. See section 6861 and § 301.6861-1 concerning abatement of assessments.

(e) *Requests for investigation with respect to tax imposed under section 4971.* Under section 3002(b) of ERISA, upon receiving a written request from the Secretary of Labor or from the Pension Benefit Guaranty Corporation, the Commissioner will investigate whether the taxes under section 4971(a) and (b) should be imposed on any employer referred to in the request.

§ 54.4971-3 *Rules relating to liability for excise tax on failure to meet minimum funding standards.*

(a) *General rule*—(1) *One employer.* An excise tax imposed under section 4971(a) or (b) with respect to a plan to or under which only one employer is responsible for contributing must be paid by that employer.

(2) *More than one employer.* An excise tax imposed under section 4971(a) or (b) with respect to a plan to or under which more than one employer is responsible for contributing must be allocated between these employers under paragraph (b) of this section.

(3) *Related employers.* Related corporations, trades, and businesses described in section 414(b) and (c) are "related employers" for purposes of this section. All related employers are treated as one employer for purposes of paragraph (b) of this section. The tax liability of each such related employer is determined separately by allocations under paragraph (c) of this section.

(b) *Allocation of tax liability*—(1) *In general.* Section 413(b)(6) and (c)(5) and section 414(b) and (c) discuss liability for tax under section 4971(a) or (b) with respect to collectively bargained plans and plans of more than one employer. Each employer's tax liability relates to an accumulated funding deficiency under a plan. However, the funding deficiency is determined with respect to a plan as a whole, not with respect to individual employers adopting the plan. Therefore, the deficiency must be allocated among employers adopting or maintaining the plan to determine their individual liability for a tax. Except as otherwise provided in paragraphs (c) and (d) of this section, this liability must be determined in a reasonable manner that is not inconsistent with the requirements of this paragraph (b).

(2) *Failure of individual employer to meet obligation under plan or contract*—(i) *Single delinquency.* An accumulated funding deficiency may be attributable, in whole or in part, to a delinquent contribution, that is, the failure of an individual employer to contribute to the plan as required by its terms or by the terms of a collectively bargained agreement pursuant to which the plan is maintained. To the extent that an accumulated funding deficiency is attributable to a delinquent contribution, the delinquent employer is solely liable for the resulting tax imposed under section 4971(a) or (b).

(ii) *Multiple delinquency.* If an accumulated funding deficiency is attributable to more than one delinquent employer, liability for tax is allocated in proportion to each employer's share of the delinquency.

(iii) *Further liability.* A delinquent employer may also be liable for the portion of tax determined by an allocation under paragraph (b)(3) of this section.

(3) *Failure of employers in the aggregate to avoid accumulated funding deficiency*—(1) *Aggregate failure.* An accumulated funding deficiency may be attributable, in whole or in part, to the failure of employers in the aggregate to contribute to the plan a sufficient amount to avoid an accumulated funding deficiency. To the extent that a deficiency for a plan year is not attributable to a delinquent contribution for that year, the deficiency is attributable to an aggregate failure described in this subparagraph (3). Thus, for example, if 10 percent of the deficiency results from a delinquent contribution described in paragraph (b)(2) of this section 90 percent results from failures described in this subparagraph (3). The allocation of tax liability to an individual employer for such an aggregate failure to avoid an accumulated funding deficiency is made under paragraph (b)(3)(ii) of this section.

(ii) *Allocation rule for aggregate failure.* An individual employer's liability for tax attributable to an aggregate failure described in this subparagraph (3) is the product of the tax attributable to the aggregate failure times a fraction. The numerator of this fraction is the contribution the employer is required to make for the plan year under the plan or under the collectively bargained agreement pursuant to which plan is maintained. The denominator of this fraction is the total contribution all employers are required to make for the plan year under the plan or under the collectively bargained agreement pursuant to which the plan is maintained. Thus, for example, if an employer is responsible for one-half of a plan's required contribution and 90 percent of an accumulated funding deficiency arises under this subparagraph (3), that employer is liable under this subparagraph (3) for 45 percent of the tax under section 4971(a) or (b), as the case may be, with respect to that deficiency.

(c) *Allocation rules for related employers*—(1) *In general.* To the extent that an accumulated funding deficiency is attributable to related employers, those employers are jointly and severally liable for an excise tax imposed under section 4971(a) or (b) with respect to that deficiency.

(2) *Plans not solely maintained by related employers.* A plan that is not solely maintained by related employers first allocates tax liability under paragraph (b) of this section by treating the related employers as a single employer. The related employers are jointly and severally liable for the tax liability so allocated to any of the related employers.

(d) *Effect of plan termination on employer's tax liability.* No tax is imposed under section 4971(a) for years after the plan year in which a plan terminates. An employer is liable only for unpaid 5-percent initial taxes under section 4971(a) and any additional tax which has been imposed under section 4971(b).

(e) *Effect of employer withdrawal from plan*—(1) *General rule.* An employer that withdraws from a plan remains liable for tax imposed with respect to the portion of an accumulated funding deficiency attributable to that employer for plan years before withdrawal.

(2) *Years subsequent to withdrawal.* For any plan year with an accumulated funding deficiency, the tax is allocated between the employers responsible for contributing to the plan for that plan year in accordance with paragraphs (b) or (c) even if the deficiency in that year is attributable to an uncorrected deficiency from a prior year.

(f) *Examples.* The provisions of paragraphs (a)-(c) of this section may be illustrated by the following examples:

Example (1). Employers W, X, Y, and Z maintain a collectively bargained plan. Y and Z are related employers under paragraph (a)(3). W and X are each unrelated to any other employer. For plan year 1982, the employers are obligated, under the collectively bargained agreement, to contribute the following amount: W—$10x; X—$20x; Y—$30x; Z—$40x. As of the last date for making plan contributions, there is a delinquency of $10x attributable to W and $30x attributable to Y. Under paragraph (b)(2)(ii), W is liable for 10/40 of the tax imposed for 1982.

Under paragraphs (b)(2)(ii) and (c)(2), *Y* and *Z* are jointly and severally liable for 30/40 of the tax.

Example (2). Assume the same facts as in Example (1). For plan year 1983, the minimum funding requirement is $145x. Contributions totalling $110x are made for 1983 in the amounts provided by the agreement: *W*— $15x; *X*—$20x; *Y*—$30x; *Z*—$45x. Under paragraph (b)(3)(i) of this section, there is an aggregate failure to avoid an accumulated funding deficiency, as the minimum funding requirement exceeds plan contributions by $35x. The tax attributable to the aggregate failure is allocated under paragraphs (b)(3)(ii) and (c)(2) as follows: *W* is liable for 15/110, or 13.6 percent of the tax; *X* is liable for 20/110, or 18.2 percent. *Y* and *Z* are jointly and severally liable for 75/110, or 68.2 percent.

Example (3). Assume the same facts as in Example (1). For 1984, the minimum funding requirement is $210x and employers are obligated under the agreement to contribute $130x: *W*—$15x; *X*—$25x; *Y*—

$30x; *Z*— $60x. There is a funding deficiency due in part to a delinquency attributable to *Y*. Under paragraph (b)(3)(i), the remaining deficiency is an aggregate failure. Under paragraphs (b)(2)(i) and (c), *Y* and *Z* are jointly and severally liable for the 23 percent (30/130) of the excise tax attributable to the delinquency. The remaining 76.9 percent of the tax is allocated as follows: *W*—15/130 (11.5 percent) of the 76.9 percent; *X*—25/130 (19.2 percent) of the aggregate failure tax; *Y* and *Z*, combined under paragraph (c)(2)—90/130 (69.2 percent) of the aggregate failure tax. *Y* and *Z* are jointly and severally liable for approximately 76.3 percent of the total tax under section 4971 for the year: 23.1 percent attributable to *Y*'s delinquency and 53.2 percent (69.2 × 76.9 attributable to the aggregate failure under paragraph (b)(3).

Roscoe L. Egger, Jr.

Commissioner.

[FR Doc. 82-32582 Filed 11-30-82; 8:45 am]

[¶ 20,137F Reserved.—Proposed regulations providing rules governing the deductibility by employers of expenses for awards to employees formerly were reproduced here. The final regulations are at ¶ 11,357.]

¶ 20,137G

Proposed regulations— Affiliated service groups—Two or more separate service organizations.—Reproduced below are proposed regulations prescribing rules for determining whether two or more separate service groups constitute an affiliated service group. The proposed regulations were published in the *Federal Register* on February 28, 1983 (48 FR 8293).

Affiliated Service Groups; Proposed Rulemaking

AGENCY: Internal Revenue Service, Treasury.

ACTION: Notice of proposed rulemaking.

SUMMARY: This document contains proposed regulations prescribing rules for determining whether two or more separate service organizations constitute an affiliated service group, and detailing how certain requirements are satisfied by a qualified retirement plan maintained by a member of an affiliated service group. Changes to the applicable tax law were made by the Miscellaneous Revenue Act of 1980. The regulations would provide the public with additional guidance needed to comply with that Act and would affect all employers that maintain qualified retirement plans and that are members of an affiliated service group.

DATES: Written comments and requests for a public hearing must be delivered or mailed by April 29, 1983. For plans that were not in existence on November 30 1980, the amendments is proposed to be effective for plan years ending after that date. For plans in existence on November 30, 1980, the amendments is proposed to be effective for plan years beginning after that date.

ADDRESS: Send comments and requests for a public hearing to: Commissioner of Internal Revenue, Attention: CC:LR:T (EE-3-81), Washington, D.C. 20224.

FOR FURTHER INFORMATION CONTACT: Patricia K. Keesler of the Employee Plans and Exempt Organizations Division, Office of Chief Counsel, Internal Revenue Service, 1111 Constitution Avenue, NW., Washington, D.C. 20224 (Attention: CC:LR:T) (202/566-3430) (not a toll-free number).

SUPPLEMENTARY INFORMATION:

Background

This document contains proposed amendments to the Income Tax Regulations (26 CFR Part 1) under section 414(m) of the Internal Revenue Code of 1954. These amendments are proposed to conform the regulations to section 201 of the Miscellaneous Revenue Act of 1980 (94 Stat. 3526) and section 5 of Pub. L. 96-613 (94 Stat. 3580). These regulations do not reflect amendments made to section 414(m) under the Tax Equity and Fiscal Responsibility Act of 1982. These regulations are to be issued under the authority contained in section 414(m) and in section 7805 of the Internal Revenue Code of 1954 (94 Stat. 3526, 94 Stat. 3580, 68A Stat. 917; 26 U.S.C. 414(m), 7805).

Statutory Provisions

Section 414(m)(1) of the Code provides that, for purposes of certain employee benefit requirements listed in section 414(m)(4), except to the extent otherwise provided in regulations, all employees of the members of an affiliated service group shall be treated as employed by a single employer.

Section 414(m)(2) defines an affiliated service group as a First Service Organization and one or more of the following: (A) Any service organization (A Organization) that is a shareholder or partner in the

First Service Organization and that regularly performs services for the First Service Organization or is regularly associated with the First Service Organization in performing services for third persons; and (B) any other organization (B Organization) if a significant portion of the business of that organization is the performance of services for the First Service Organization, for A Organizations, or both, of a type historically performed by employees in the service field of the First Service Organization or the A Organizations, and ten percent or more of the interests in the organization is held by persons who are officers, highly compensated employees, or owners of the First Service Organization or of the A Organizations.

Section 414(m)(3) defines a service organization as an organization the principal business of which is the performance of services.

Section 414(m)(5)(A) provides that the term "organization" means a corporation, partnership, or other organization. Section 414(m)(5)(B) provides that principles of section 267(c) apply in determining ownership.

Section 414(m)(6) provides that the Secretary of the Treasury or his delegate shall prescribe such regulations as may be necessary to prevent the avoidance of the employee benefit requirements listed in section 414(m)(4) through the use of separate service organizations.

Prior Guidelines

Initial guidelines under section 414(m) were set forth in Revenue Ruling 81-105, 1981-1 C.B. 256. Rev. Rul. 81-105 provided illustrations of how the provisions of section 414(m) operate by way of three examples. The rules set forth in Rev. Rul. 81-105 remain operative and are not affected by the promulgation of these proposed regulations.

Revenue Procedure 81-12, 1981-1 C.B. 652, prescribes procedures for (1) obtaining a ruling on whether two or more organizations are members of an affiliated service group, and (2) obtaining determination letters on the qualification, under section 401(a) or 403(a), of an employee's pension, profit-sharing, stock bonus, annuity, or bond purchase plan established by a member or of an affiliated service group.

Administrative Exemptions

Several parties have expressed concern that aggregation may be required under the rules of section 414(m)(2)(A) and (B) in situations where there has been no attempt to avoid the employee benefit requirements listed in section 414(m)(4).

Those parties noted that an organization qualifies as an A Organization whenever it is a shareholder or partner in the First Service Organization and regularly performs services for the First Service Organization or is regularly associated with the First Service Organization in performing services for third persons. Thus, aggregation will be required regardless of how small the interest is that the A Organization holds in the First Service Organization, irrespective of whether the services performed by the A Organization are of a type historically performed by employees in the service field of the First Service Organization, and even if the services performed for the First Service Organization only constitute an insignificant portion of the business of the A Organization.

However, section 414(m)(1) grants authority to promulgate regulations that specify when all the employees of an affiliated service group will not be treated as employed by a single employer. Accordingly, proposed Treasury Regulation § 1.414(m)-1(c) provides that a corporation, other than a professional service corporation, will not be treated as a First Service Organization for purposes of section 414(m)(2)(A). Professional service corporations are not excepted from treatment as First Service Organizations for purposes of section 414(m)(2)(A) because the legislative history indicates that such corporations were intended to be covered. A special definition of professional service corporations is provided in the proposed regulation.

A corporation will still be treated as a First Service Organization for purposes of section 414(m)(2)(B). Thus, two corporations, neither of which is a professional service organization, will be aggregated only if one of the corporations satisfies the more stringent tests to be classified as a B Organization.

However, the Commissioner may determine that, in practice, the exception in the A Organization test for corporations, other than professional service corporations, results in an avoidance of the requirements of section 414(m) that circumvents Congressional intent. If such avoidance is found in a significant number of cases, this exception may be removed from the regulations.

Similarly, several parties have mentioned that aggregation may be required under section 414(m)(2)(B) whenever the owner of the potential B Organization acquires an interest in the First Service Organization (or in an A Organization), even though this interest is minimal and even though the owner does not have any other significant connection with the First Service Organization (*i.e.*, the owner is not an officer or highly compensated employee of the First Service Organization).

Pursuant to the authority contained in section 414(m)(1), a special rule is provided for determining whether ten percent or more of the interests in the potential B Organization is held by officers, highly compensated employees, or owners of the First Service Organization (or of an A Organization). For this purpose, the interests held by persons who are owners of the First Service Organization and the B Organization (but who are not also officers or highly compensated employees of the First Service Organization), will be taken into account as owners of the First Service Organization only if they hold, in the aggregate, three percent or more of the interests in such First Service Organization.

There may be other situations, not covered by the special rules of the regulations, where aggregation should not be required although the organizations are described in the literal language of either section 414(m)(2)(A) or (B). Comments are solicited from the public as to what these rules should be.

Significant Portion

Proposed Treasury Regulation § 1.414(m)-2(c)(2) provides that the determination of whether providing services for the First Service Organization, for one or more A Organizations determined with respect to the First Service Organization, or for both, is a significant portion of the business of the potential B Organization will generally be based on the facts and circumstances. However, two specific rules are provided.

A safe harbor rule is provided under which the performance of services for the First Service Organization, for one or more A Organizations, or for both, will not be considered a significant portion of the business of a potential B Organization if the Service Receipts Percentage is less than five percent. The Service Receipts Percentage is the ratio of the gross receipts of the organization derived from performing services for the First Service Organization, for one or more A Organizations, or for both, to the total gross receipts of the organization derived from performing services. This ratio is the greater of the ratio for the year for which the determination is being made or for the three year period including that year and the two preceding years (or the period of existence of the organizations, if less).

Except for a situation described in the preceding paragraph, the performance of services for the First Service Organization, for one or more A Organizations, or for both, will be considered a significant portion of the business of the potential B Organization if the Total Receipts Percentage is ten percent or more. The Total Receipts Percentage is calculated in the same manner as the Service Receipts Percentage, except that gross receipts in the denominator are determined without regard to whether they were derived from performing services.

Comments from the public are requested regarding these significant portion tests.

Historically Performed

Proposed Treasury Regulation § 1.414(m)-2(c)(3) provides that services will be considered of a type historically performed by employees in a particular service field if it was not unusual for the services to be performed by employees of organizations in that service field in the United States on December 13, 1980 (the date of enactment of section 414(m)).

Constructive Ownership

Proposed Treasury Regulation § 1.414(m)-2(d)(2) provides that in determining ownership for purposes of section 414(m), an individual's interest under a plan that qualifies under section 401(a) will be taken into account. Comments from the public are requested concerning appropriateness of this rule in cases in which the investment in employer securities by the plan results from an independent decision of the plan trustee.

Organization

Proposed Treasury Regulation § 1.414(m)-2(e) provides that the term "organization" includes a sole proprietorship. The proposed regulations do not consider the impact of sections 414(b) (controlled group of corporations) or 414(c) (group of trades or businesses under common control) on the definition of "organization" in § 1.414(m)-2(e)(1). Specifically, the regulations do not consider the situation in which a particular organization is potentially part of both an affiliated service group and either a controlled group of corporations or a group of trades or businesses under common control. In such a situation, issues arise as to the order in which the determinations are made as to what constitutes a single employer. For example, whereas an individual corporation may be a service organization, the controlled group of which that corporation is a part may not be a service organization (or vice versa). Comments from the public are requested regarding the treatment of a controlled group of corporations or a group of trades or businesses under common control in this respect.

Service Organization

Proposed Treasury Regulation § 1.414(m)-2(f) provides that the principal business of an organization will be considered the performance of services if capital is not a material income-producing factor for the organization. The test for determining whether or not capital is a material income-producing factor is similar to the test in Treasury Regulation § 1.1348-3(a)(3)(ii), as in effect on February 28, 1983.

Numerous fields are listed in proposed Treasury Regulation § 1.414(m)-2(f) as being service fields. Organizations engaged in a field not listed therein and in which capital is a material income-producing factor will not be considered to be service organizations until the first day of the first plan year beginning at least 180 days after the date of the publication of an official document (such as a revenue ruling) giving notice to the contrary. The Commissioner of Internal Revenue is granted authority to determine that certain organizations, or types of organizations, should not be considered as being subject to the requirements of section 414(m) even though the organizations are engaged in a field listed in the proposed regulation. Comments are requested from the public as to examples of organizations that should or should not be considered as being service organizations subject to the provisions of section 414(m).

Multiple Affiliated Service Groups

Proposed Treasury Regulation § 1.414(m)-2(g) provides rules for multiple affiliated service groups. Two or more affiliated service groups will not be aggregated simply because an organization is an A Organization or a B Organization with respect to each affiliated service group. However, if an organization is a First Service Organization with respect to two or more A Organizations or two or more B Organizations, or both, all of the organizations will be considered to constitute a single affiliated service group.

Special Qualification Requirements

Pursuant to the authority granted in section 414(m)(6), proposed Treasury Regulation § 1.414(m)-3(b) provides that if a plan maintained by a member of an affiliated service group covers an employee described in section 401(c)(1) (self-employed individual), an owner-employee (as described in section 401(c)(3)), or a shareholder-employee (as described in section 1379(d)), the plan must also satisfy the special requirements relating to plans that cover those types of employees, to the extent those requirements apply, even though that individual is not employed by the member maintaining the plan. This provision only applies if such an employee's earned income or compensation received as a shareholder-employee is taken into account in computing contributions or benefits under the plan.

Multiple Employer Plans

Proposed Treasury Regulation § 1.414(m)-3(c) provides that if a plan maintained by a member of an affiliated service group covers an individual who is not an employee of that member, but who is an employee of another member of that affiliated service group, the plan will be considered to be maintained by more than one employer for purposes of several provisions of section 413(c) (relating to plans maintained by more than one employer). This rule allows a member of the affiliated service group to deduct contributions on behalf of individuals who are not employed by that member.

However, this multiple employer plan rule does not apply in the case of a controlled group of corporations (as described in section 414(b)) or a group of trades or businesses under common control (as described in section 414(c)). Those situations will be governed by the special rules of section 414(b) or (c), respectively.

Discrimination

Proposed Treasury Regulation § 1.414(m)-3(d) provides that in testing for discrimination under section 401(a)(4) (requiring that contributions or benefits do not discriminate in favor of employees who are officers, shareholders, or highly compensated) all of the compensation paid to an individual must be considered in determining the contributions or benefits on behalf of the individual under a plan maintained by a member of an affiliated service group without regard to the percentage of the organization employing the individual owned by the member maintaining the plan.

Effective Dates

In the case of a plan that was not in existence on November 30, 1980, section 414(m) applies to plan years ending after that date. In the case of a plan that was in existence on November 30, 1980, section 414(m) applies to plan years beginning after that date.

Proposed Treasury Regulation § 1.414(m)-4(b)(1) provides that a defined contribution plan in existence on November 30, 1980 that fails to satisfy the requirements for qualification under section 401(a) solely because of the application of section 414(m) will be treated as continuing to satisfy the requirements of section 401(a) after the effective date of section 414(m) if the plan is terminated and all amounts are distributed to participants within 180 days after the latest of:

(i) [the date of the publication of this regulation in the *Federal Register* as a Treasury decision]

(ii) The date on which notice of the final determination with respect to a request for a determination letter is issued by the Internal Revenue Service, such request is withdrawn, or such request is finally disposed of by the Internal Revenue Service, provided the request for a determination letter was pending on [the date of the publication of this regulation in the *Federal Register* as a Treasury decision] or, in the case of a request for a determination letter on the plan termination, was made within 60 days after [the date of the publication of this regulation in the *Federal Register* as a Treasury decision], or

(iii) If a petition is timely filed with the United States Tax Court for a declaratory judgment under section 7476 with respect to the final determination (or the failure of the Internal Revenue Service to make a final determination) in response to such request, the date on which the decision of the United States Tax Court in such proceeding becomes final.

Proposed Treasury Regulation § 1.414(m)-4(b)(2) provides that a defined benefit plan in existence on November 30, 1980 that fails to satisfy the requirements for qualification under section 401(a) solely because of the application of section 414(m) will be treated as continuing to satisfy the requirements of section 401(a) after the effective date of section 414(m) if the plan is terminated and all amounts are distributed within the same period as that provided for defined contribution plans. However, deductions for contributions to the plan for plan years after the effective date of section 414(m) are limited to those necessary to satisfy the minimum funding standards of section 412.

Reliance on Proposed Regulations

Pending the adoption of final regulations, taxpayers may rely on the rules contained in this notice of proposed rulemaking and the Internal Revenue Service will issue determination, opinion, and ruling letters based on these rules. If any provisions of the final regulations are less favorable to taxpayers than these proposed rules, those provisions only will be effective for periods after adoption of final regulations.

Comments and Requests for a Public Hearing

Before adopting these proposed regulations, consideration will be given to any written comments that are submitted (preferably seven copies) to the Commissioner of Internal Revenue. All comments will be available for public inspection and copying. A public hearing will be held upon written request to the Commissioner by any person who has submitted written comments. If a public hearing is held, notice of the time and place will be published in the *Federal Register*.

Executive Order 12291 and Regulatory Flexibility Act

The Commissioner has determined that this proposed regulation is not a major regulation for purposes of Executive Order 12291. Accordingly, a regulatory impact analysis is not required.

Although this document is a notice of proposed rulemaking which solicits public comments, the Internal Revenue Service has concluded that the regulations proposed herein are interpretative and that the notice and public procedure requirements of 5 U.S.C. 553 do not apply. Accordingly, these proposed regulations do not constitute regulations subject to the Regulatory Flexibility Act (5 U.S.C. chapter 6).

Drafting Information

The principal authors of these proposed regulations are Kirk F. Maldonado and Mary M. Levontin of the Employee Plans and Exempt Organizations Division of the Office of Chief Counsel, Internal Revenue Service and Treasury Department, participated in developing these regulations, both on matters of substance and style.

List of Subjects in 26 CFR 1.401-0-1.425-1

Income taxes, Employee benefit plans, Pensions.

Proposed Amendments to the Regulations

PART 1—[AMENDED]

The proposed amendments to 26 CFR Part 1 are as follows:

§ 1.105-11 [Amended]

Paragraph 1. Paragraph (f) of § 1.105-11 is amended by striking out "section 414(b) and (c)" and inserting in lieu thereof "section 414(b), (c), or (m)."

Par. 2. The following new sections are added at the appropriate place:

§ 1.414(m)-1. Affiliated service groups.

(a) *In general.* Section 414(m) provides rules that require, in some circumstances, employees of separate organizations to be treated as if they were employed by a single employer for purposes of certain employee benefit requirements. For other rules requiring aggregation of employees of different organizations, see section 414(b) (relating to controlled groups of corporations) and section 414(c) (relating to trades or businesses under common control). If aggregation is required under either of the preceding provisions and also under section 414(m), the requirements with respect to all of the applicable provisions must be satisfied.

(b) *Aggregation.* Except as provided in paragraph (c), all the employees of the members of an affiliated service group shall be treated as if they were employed by a single employer for purposes of the employee benefit reuirements listed in § 1.414(m)-3.

(c) *Aggregation not required.* Pursuant to the authority contained in section 414(m)(1), a corporation, other than a professional service corporation, shall not be treated as a First Service Organization (see § 1.414(m)-2) for purposes of section 414(m)(2)(A). Also, a special rule is provided in § 1.414(m)-2(c)(4) for determining ownership under section 414(m)(2)(B). For purposes of this paragraph, a professional service corporation is a corporation that is organized under state law for the principal purpose of providing professional services and has at least one shareholder who is licensed or otherwise legally authorized to render the type of services for which the corporation is organized. "Professional services" means the services performed by certified or other public accountants, actuaries, architects, attorneys, chiropodists, chiropractors, medical doctors, dentists, professional engineers, optometrists, osteopaths, podiatrists, psychologists, and veterinarians. The Commissioner may expand the list of services in the preceding sentence. However, no such expansion will be effective with respect to any organization until the first day of the first plan year beginning at least 180 days after the publication of such change.

§ 1.414(m)-2 Definitions.

(a) *Affiliated service group.* "Affiliated service group" means a group consisting of a service organization (First Service Organization) and

(1) One or more A Organizations described in paragraph (b), or

(2) One or more B Organizations described in paragraph (c), or

(3) One or more A Organizations described in paragraph (b) and one or more B Organizations described in paragraph (c).

(b) *A Organizations*—(1) *General rule.* A service organization is an A Organization if it:

(i) Is a partner or shareholder in the First Service Organization (regardless of the percentage interest it owns in the First Service Organization but determined with regard to the constructive ownership rules of paragraph (d)); and

(ii) Regularly performs services for the First Service Organization, or is regularly associated with the First Service Organization in performing services for third persons. It is not necessary that any of the employees of the organization directly perform services for the First Service Organization; it is sufficient that the organization is regularly associated with the First Service Organization in performing services for third persons.

(2) *Regularly performs services for.* The determination of whether a service organization regularly performs services for the First Service Organization or is regularly associated with the First Service Organization in performing services for third persons shall be made on the basis of the facts and circumstances. One factor that is relevant in making this determination is the amount of the earned income that the organization derives from performing services for the First Service Organization, or from performing services for persons in association with the First Service Organization.

(3) *Examples.* The provisions of this paragraph may be illustrated by the following examples.

Example (1). A Organization. (i) Attorney N is incorporated, and the corporation is a partner in a law firm. Attorney N and his corporation are regularly associated with the law firm in performing services for third persons.

(ii) Considering the law firm as a First Service Organization, the corporation is an A Organization because it is a partner in the law firm and it is regularly associated with the law firm in performing services for third persons. Accordingly, the corporation and the law firm constitute an affiliated service group.

Example (2). Corporation. (i) Corporation F is a service organization that is a shareholder in Corporation G, another service organization. F regularly provides services for G. Neither corporation is a professional service corporation within the meaning of subsection (1)(c).

(ii) Neither corporation may be considered a First Service Organization for purposes of this paragraph and, thus, aggregation will not be required by operation of the A Organization test. However, G or F may be treated as a First Service Organization and the other organization may be a B Organization under the rules of subsection (2)(c).

Example (3). Regularly associated with (i) R, S & T is a law partnership with offices in numerous cities. The office in the city of D is incorporated, and the corporation is a partner in the law firm. All of the employees of the corporation work directly for the corporation, and none of them work directly for any of the other offices of the law firm.

(ii) Considering the law firm as a First Service Organization, the corporation is an A Organization because it is a partner in the First Service Organization and is regularly associated with the law firm in performing services for third persons. Accordingly, the corporation and the law firm constitute an affiliated service group.

(c) *B Organizations*—(1) *General rule.* An organization is a B Organization if:

(i) A significant portion of the business of the organization is the performance of services for the First Service Organization, for one or more A Organizations determined with respect to the First Service Organization, or for both.

(ii) Those services are of a type historically performed by employees in the service field of the First Service Organization or the A Organizations, and

(iii) Ten percent or more of the interests in the organization is held, in the aggregate, by persons who are designated group members (as defined in subparagraph (4)) of the First Service Organization or of the A Organizations, determined using the constructive ownership rules of paragraph (d).

(2) *Significant portion*—(i) *General rule.* Except as provided in paragraphs (c)(2)(ii) and (iii), the determination of whether providing services for the First Service Organization, for one or more A Organizations, or for both, is a significant portion of the business of an organization will be based on the facts and circumstances. Wherever it appears in this paragraph (c)(2), "one or more A organizations" means one or

more A organizations determined with respect to the First Service Organization.

(ii) *Service Receipts safe harbor.* The performance of services for the First Service Organizations, for one or more A Organizations, or for both, will not be considered a significant portion of the business of an organization if the Service Receipts Percentage is less than five percent.

(iii) *Total Receipts threshold test.* The performance of services for the First Service Organization, for one or more A Organizations, or for both, will be considered a significant portion of the business of an organization if the Total Receipts Percentage is ten percent or more.

(iv) *Service Receipts Percentage.* The Service Receipts Percentage is the ratio of the gross receipts of the organization derived from performing services for the First Service Organization, for one or more A Organizations, or for both, to the total gross receipts of the organization derived from performing services. This ratio is the greater of the ratio for the year for which the determination is being made or for the three year period including that year and the two preceding years (or the period of the organization's existence, if less).

(v) *Total Receipts Percentage.* The Total Receipts Percentage is calculated in the same manner as the Service Receipts Percentage, except that gross receipts in the denominator are determined without regard to whether they were derived from performing services.

(3) *Historically performed.* Services will be considered of a type historically performed by employees in a particular service field if it was not unusual for the services to be performed by employees of organizations in that service field (in the United States) on December 13, 1980.

(4) *Designated group*—(i) *Definition.* "Designated group" members are the officers, the highly compensated employees, and the common owners of an organization (as defined in paragraph (c)(4)(ii)). However, even though a person is not a common owner, the interests the person holds in the potential B Organization will be taken into account if the person is an officer or a highly compensated employee of the First Service Organization or of an A Organization.

(ii) *Common owner.* A person who is an owner of a First Service Organization or of an A Organization is a common owner if at least three percent of the interests in the organization is, in the aggregate, held by persons who are owners of the potential B organization (determined using the constructive ownership rules of paragraph (d)).

(5) *Owner.* The term "owner" includes organizations that have an ownership interest described in paragraph (c).

(6) *Aggregation of ownership interests.* It is not necessary that a single designated group member of the First Service Organization or of an A Organization own ten percent or more of the interests, determined using the constructive ownership rules of paragraph (d), in the organization for the organization to be a B Organization. It is sufficient that the sum of the interests, determined using the constructive ownership rules of paragraph (d), held by all of the designated group members of the First Service Organization, and the designated group members of the A Organizations, is ten percent or more of the interests in the organizations.

(7) *Non-service organization.* An organization may be a B Organization even though it does not qualify as a service organization under paragraph (f).

(8) *Examples.* The provisions of this paragraph may be illustrated by the following examples.

Example (1). B Organization. (i) R is a service organization that has 11 partners. Each partner of R owns one percent of the stock in Corporation D. The corporation provides services to the partnership of a type historically performed by employees in the service field of the partnership. A significant portion of the business of the corporation consists of providing services to the partnership.

(ii) Considering the partnership as a First Service Organization, the corporation is a B organization because a significant portion of the business of the corporation is the performance of services for the partnership of a type historically performed by employees in the service field of the partnership, and more than ten percent of the interests in the corporation is held, in the aggregate, by the designated group members (consisting of the 11 common owners of the partnership). Accordingly, the corporation and the partnership constitute an affiliated service group.

(iii) A similar result would be obtained if no more than 8 percent of the 11 percent ownership in Corporation D were held by highly compensated employees of R who were not owners of R (even though no one group of the three preceding groups held 10 percent or more of the stock of Corporation D).

Example (2). Other aggregation rules. (i) C, an individual, is a 60 percent partner in D, a service organization, and regularly performs services for D. C is also an 80 percent partner in F. A significant portion of the gross receipts of F are derived from providing services to D of a type historically performed by employees in the service field of D.

(ii) Viewing D as a First Service Organization, F is a B Organization because a significant portion of gross receipts of F are derived from performing services for D of a type historically performed by employees in that service field, and more than ten percent of the interest in F is held by the designated group member C (who is a common owner of D). Accordingly, D and F constitute an affiliated service group. Additionally, the employees of D and F are aggregated under the rules of section 414(c). Thus, any plan maintained by a member of the affiliated service group must satisfy the aggregation rules of sections 414(c) and 414(m).

Example (3). Common owner. (i) Corporation T is a service organization. The sole function of Corporation W is to provide services to Corporation T of a type historically performed by employees in the service field of Corporation T. Individual C owns all of the stock of Corporation W and two percent of the stock of Corporation T. C is not an officer or a highly compensated employee of Corporation T.

(ii) Considering Corporation T as a First Service Organization, Corporation W is not a B Organization because it is not 10 percent owned by designated group members. Because C owns less than 3 percent of Corporation T, C is not a common owner of T.

Example (4). B Organization. (i) Individual M owns one-third of an employee benefit consulting firm. M also owns one-third of an insurance agency. A significant portion of the business of the consulting firm consists of assisting the insurance agency in developing employee benefit packages for sale to third persons and providing services to the insurance company in connection with employee benefit programs sold to other clients of the insurance agency. Additionally, the consulting firm frequently provides services to clients who have purchased insurance arrangements from the insurance company for the employee benefit plans they maintain. The insurance company frequently refers clients to the consulting firm to assist them in the design of their employee benefit plans. The percentage of the total gross receipts of the consulting firm that represent gross receipts from the performance of these services for the insurance agency is 20 percent.

(ii) Considering the insurance agency as a First Service Organization, the consulting firm is a B Organization because a significant portion of the business of the consulting firm (as determined under the Total Receipts Percentage Test) is the performance of services for the insurance agency of a type historically performed by employees in the service field of insurance, and more than 10 percent of the interests in the consulting firm is held by owners of the insurance agency. Thus, the insurance agency and the consulting firm constitute an affiliated service group.

Example (5). B Organization. (i) Attorney T is incorporated, and the corporation is a 6% shareholder in a law firm (which is also incorporated). All of the work of Corporation T is performed for the law firm.

(ii) Under the principles of section 267(c), T is deemed to own the shares of the law firm owned by T Corporation. Thus, T is a common owner of the law firm. Considering the law firm as a First Service Organization, Corporation T is a B Organization because a significant portion of the business of Corporation T consists of performing services for the law firm of a type historically performed by employees, and 100 percent of Corporation T is owned by a common owner of the law firm.

Example (6). Significant portion. (i) The income of Corporation X is derived from both performing services and other business activities. The amount of its receipts derived from performing services for, and its total receipts derived from, Corporation Z and the total for all other customers is set forth below.

	Origin of income	Corpora- tion Z	All cus- tomers
Year 1	Services	$4	$100
	Total		120
Year 2	Services	9	150
	Total		180
Year 3	Services	42	200
	Total		240

(ii) In year 1 (the first year of existence of Corporation X), the Service Receipts Percentage for Corporation X (for its business with Corporation Z) is less than five percent ($4/$100, or 4%). Thus performing services for Corporation Z will not be considered a significant portion of the business of Corporation X.

(iii) In year 2, the Service Receipts Percentage is the greater of the ratio for that year ($9/$150, or 6%) or for years 1 and 2 combined ($13/$250, or 5.2%), which is six percent. The Total Receipts Percentage is the greater of the ratio for that year ($9/$180, or 5%) or for years 1 and 2 combined ($13/$300, or 4.3%), which is five percent. Because the Service Receipts Percentage is greater than five percent and the Total Receipts Percentage is less than ten percent, whether performing services for Corporation Z constitutes a significant portion of the business of Corporation X is determined by the facts and circumstances.

(iv) In year 3, the Service Receipts Percentage is the greater of the ratio for that year ($42/$200, or 21%) or for years 1, 2, and 3 combined ($55/$450, or 12.2%), which is 21 percent. The Total Receipts Percentage is the greater of the ratio for that year ($42/$240, or 17.5%) or for years 1, 2, and 3 combined ($55/$540, or 10.1%), which is 17.5 percent. Because the Total Receipts Percentage is greater than ten percent and the Service Receipts Percentage is not less than five percent, a significant portion of the business of Corporation X is considered to be the performance of services for Corporation Z.

(d) *Ownership*—(1) *Constructive ownership.* Except as otherwise provided in the regulations under section 414(m), the principles of section 267(c) (relating to constructive ownership of stock) shall apply in determining ownership for purposes of section 414(m). Accordingly, the rules of section 267(c) shall apply to partnership interests as well as to stock.

(2) *Qualified plans.* In determining ownership for purposes of section 414(m), an individual's interest under a plan that qualifies under section 401(a) will be taken into account.

(3) *Special rules.* For purposes of section 414(m):

(i) Stock or partnership interests owned, directly or indirectly, by or for a corporation, partnership, estate, or trust shall be considered as being owned proportionately by or for its shareholders, partners, or beneficiaries;

(ii) An individual shall be considered as owning the stock or partnership interests owned, directly or indirectly, by or for his family;

(iii) An individual owning (otherwise than by the application of paragraph (d)(3)(ii)) any stock in a corporation or interest in a partnership shall be considered as owning the stock or partnership interests owned, directly or indirectly, by or for his partner;

(iv) The family of an individual shall include only his brothers and sisters (whether by the whole or half blood), spouse, ancestors, and lineal descendants; and

(v) Stock or partnership interests constructively owned by a person by reason of the application of paragraph (d)(3)(i) shall, for the purpose of applying paragraph (d)(3)(i), (ii), or (iii), be treated as actually owned by such person, but stock or partnership interests constructively owned by an individual by reason of the application of paragraph (d)(3)(ii) or (iii) shall not be treated as owned by him for the purpose of again applying either of such subdivisions in order to make another the constructive owner of such stock or partnership interests.

(4) *Examples.* The provisions of this paragraph may be illustrated by the following examples.

Example (1). Constructive ownership. (i) Individual K is incorporated as K Corporation, and K Corporation is a partner in a management consulting firm K & F. K regularly performs services for the management consulting firm K & F. The secretarial services for the consulting firm are performed by Corporation M. A significant portion of the business of the secretarial corporation, M, consists of providing services to the consulting firm. All of the stock of the secretarial corporation, M, is owned by individual K.

(ii) Considering the consulting firm as a First Service Organization, Corporation K is an A Organization because it is a partner in the consulting firm and regularly performs services for the firm or is regularly associated with the firm in performing services for third persons.

(iii) Under the principles of section 267(c), individual K is deemed to own the partnership interest in the consulting firm that is held by K Corporation. Thus, K is considered to be an owner of the consulting firm.

(iv) Considering the consulting firm as a First Service Organization, the secretarial corporation is a B Organization because a significant portion of its business consists of performing services for the consulting firm or for Corporation K of a type historically performed by employees in the service field of management consulting, and at least ten percent of the interests in the secretarial corporation, M, is held by individual K, an owner of the consulting firm.

Example (2). Constructive ownership. (i) J is the office manager and highly compensated employee of an accounting partnership, H & H. The secretarial services for the partnership are provided by Corporation W. J owns fifty percent of the stock of the secretarial corporation. A significant portion of the business of the secretarial corporation consists of providing services to the partnership.

(ii) Considering the partnership as a First Service Organization, the secretarial corporation is a B Organization because a significant portion of the business of the secretarial corporation is the performance of services for the partnership of a type historically performed by employees of accounting firms, and more than ten percent of the interests in the corporation is held by a highly compensated employee of the partnership.

(iii) Under the principles of section 267(c), the result would be the same, for example, if the stock were held (instead of by J) by the spouse of J, the children of J, the parents or grandparents of J, a trust for the benefit of J's children, or by a combination of such relatives.

Example (3). Qualified plan. (i) T is the chief executive officer of W Corporation, which is the consulting firm. T is also a participant in the W Corporation Profit-Sharing Plan, which qualifies under section 401(a). T's account balance in the plan is $150,000, and it consists of 25 percent of the stock of X Corporation. The sole function of X Corporation is to provide secretarial services to W Corporation.

(ii) Considering W Corporation as a First Service Organization, X Corporation is a B Organization because a significant portion of the business of X Corporation consists of providing secretarial services to W Corporation, secretarial services are of a type historically performed by employees in the field of consulting, and 25 percent of the stock of X Corporation is considered to be owned by T, a highly compensated employee of W Corporation, using the principles of section 267(c). Accordingly, W Corporation and X Corporation constitute an affiliated service group.

(e) *Organization*—(1) *General rule.* The term "organization" includes a sole proprietorship, partnership, corporation, or any other type of entity regardless of its ownership format.

(2) *Special rule.* [Reserved]

(f) *Service organization*—(1) *Noncapital intensive organizations.* The principal business of an organization will be considered the performance of services if capital is not a material income-producing factor for the organization, even though the organization is not engaged in a field listed in subparagraph (2). Whether capital is a material income-producing factor must be determined by reference to all the facts and circumstances of each case. In general, capital is a material income-producing factor if a substantial portion of the gross income of the business is attributable to the employment of capital in the business, as reflected, for example, by a substantial investment in inventories, plant, machinery, or other equipment. Additionally, capital is a material income-producing factor for banks and similar institutions. However, capital is not a material income-producing factor if the gross income of the business consists principally of fees, commissions, or other compensation for personal services performed by an individual.

(2) *Specific fields.* Regardless of whether subparagraph (1) applies, an organization engaged in any one or more of the following fields is a service organization:

(i) Health;

(ii) Law;

(iii) Engineering;

(iv) Architecture;

(v) Accounting;

(vi) Actuarial science;

(vii) Performing arts;

(viii) Consulting; and

(ix) Insurance.

Notwithstanding the preceding sentence, an organization will not be considered to be performing services merely because it is engaged in the manufacture or sale of equipment or supplies used in the above fields, or merely because it is engaged in performing research or publishing in the above fields. An organization will not be considered to be a service organization under this subparagraph (2) merely because an employee provides one of the enumerated services to the organiza-

tion or to other employees of the organization unless the organization is also engaged in the performance of the same services for third parties.

(3) *Other organizations.* Organizations engaged in performing services and that are not described in subparagraph (1) or (2) shall not be considered to be service organizations. The Commissioner may expand the list of fields contained in subparagraph (2). However, no such expansion will be effective until the first day of the first plan year beginning at least 180 days after the publication of such change.

(4) *Exempted organizations.* The Commissioner may determine that certain organizations, or types of organizations, should not be considered as subject to the requirements of section 414(m), even though the organizations are described in subparagraph (1) or (2).

(g) *Multiple affiliated service groups*—(1) *Multiple First Service Organizations.* Two or more affiliated service groups will not be aggregated simply because an organization is an A Organization or a B Organization with respect to each affiliated service group.

(2) *Multiple A or B Organizations.* If an organization is a First Service Organization with respect to two or more A Organizations or two or more B Organizations, or both, all of the organizations shall be considered to constitute a single affiliated service group.

(3) The provisions of this paragraph may be illustrated by the following examples.

Example (1).—Multiple First Service Organizations. (i) Corporation P provides secretarial service to numerous dentists in a medical building, each of whom maintains his own separate unincorporated practice. Dentist T owns 20 percent of the secretarial corporation and accounts for 20 percent of its gross receipts. Dentist W owns 25 percent of the corporation and accounts for 25 percent of its gross receipts.

(ii) Considering Dentist T as a First Service Organization, the secretarial corporation, P, is a B Organization because 20 percent of the gross receipts of the corporation are derived from performing services for Dentist T of a type historically performed by employees of dentists, and 20 percent of the interests in the corporation is owned by Dentist T. Accordingly, Dentist T and the corporation constitute an affiliated service group.

(iii) Considering Dentist W as a First Service Organization, the secretarial corporation, P, is a B Organization, because 25 percent of the gross receipts of the corporation are derived from performing services for Dentist W of a type historically performed by employees of dentists, and 25 percent of the interests in the corporation is owned by Dentist W. Accordingly, Dentist W and the corporation constitute an affiliated service group. However, this affiliated service group does not include Dentist T even though the secretarial corporation, P, is a B Organization with respect to both dentists. Thus, there are two affiliated service groups.

Example (2).— Multiple B Organizations. (i) Doctor N is incorporated as Corporation N. Secretarial services are provided to Corporation N by Corporation Q. Corporation N owns 20 percent of the interests in the secretarial corporation and provides 20 percent of its gross receipts. Nursing services are provided to Corporation N by Corporation R. Corporation N owns 25 percent of the interests in the nursing corporation and provides 25 percent of its gross receipts.

(ii) Considering Corporation N as a First Service Organization, the secretarial corporation, Q, is a B Organization because 20 percent of the gross receipts of the secretarial corporation, Q, are derived from performing services for Corporation N of a type historically performed by employees of doctors, and 20 percent of the secretarial corporation is owned by the owner of Corporation N. Accordingly, Corporation N and the secretarial corporation, Q, constitute an affiliated service group.

(iii) Considering Corporation N as a First Service Organization, the nursing corporation, R, is a B Organization because 25 percent of the gross receipts of the nursing corporation, R, are derived from performing services for Corporation N of a type historically performed by employees of doctors, and 25 percent of the nursing corporation is owned by the owner of Corporation N. Accordingly, Corporation N and the nursing corporation constitute an affiliated service group.

(iv) For purposes of section 414(m), there will be considered to be one affiliated service group consisting of Corporation N, the secretarial corporation, Q, and the nursing corporation, R.

§ 1.414(m)-3 Employee benefit requirements.

(a) *Employee benefit requirements affected.* All of the employees of the members of an affiliated service group shall be treated as employed by a single employer for purposes of the following employee benefit requirements:

(1) Sections 401(a)(3) and 410 (relating to minimum participation requirements);

(2) Section 401(a)(4) (requiring that contributions or benefits do not discriminate in favor of employees who are officers, shareholders, or highly compensated);

(3) Sections 401(a)(7) and 411 (relating to minimum vesting standards);

(4) Sections 401(a)(16) and 415 (relating to limitations on contributions and benefits);

(5) Section 408(k) (relating to simplified employee pensions);

(6) Section 105(h) (relating to self-insured medical reimbursement plans);

(7) Section 125 (relating to cafeteria plans); and

(8) Pursuant to the authority granted in section 414(m)(6), section 401(a)(10) (relatingg to plans providing contributions or benefits to owner-employees).

(b) *Special requirements.* If a plan maintained by a member of an affiliated service group covers an employee described in section 401(c)(1) (self-employed individual), an owner-employee within the meaning of section 401(c)(3), or a shareholder-employee within the meaning of section 1379(d), the plan must also satisfy the following requirements to the extent they apply:

(1) Section 401(a)(9) (relating to special distribution requirements for plans benefiting self-employed individuals);

(2) Section 401(a)(10) (relating to special requirements for plans benefiting owner-employees);

(3) Section 401(a)(17) (relating to a limitation on the compensation base of plans benefiting self-employed individuals or shareholder-employees); and

(4) Section 401(a)(18) (relating to special requirements for defined benefit plans benefiting self-employed individuals or shareholder-employees).

Pursuant to the authority granted in section 414(m)(6), a plan that covers a self-employed individual, an owner-employee, or a shareholder-employee will be subject to the preceding requirements, even though that individual is not employed by the member of the affiliated service group maintaining the plan. These requirements apply only if the earned income of the self-employed individual or owner-employee or the compensation received as a shareholder-employee is taken into account in computing contributions or benefits under the plan.

(c) *Multiple employer plans*—(1) *General rule.* If a plan maintained by a member of an affiliated service group covers an individual who is not an employee of that member, but who is an employee of another member of that affiliated service group, the plan will be considered to be maintained by the member that does employ that individual. Thus, the plan will be considered to be maintained by more than one employer for purposes of section 413(c)(2) (relating to the exclusive benefit rule), (4) (relating to funding), (5) (relating to liability for funding tax), and (6) (relating to deductions). Therefore, a member of an affiliated service group may deduct contributions on behalf of individuals who are not employees of that member, if the individuals are employed by another member of that affiliated service group.

(2) *Special rule.* The multiple employer plan rule contained in paragraph (c)(1) shall not apply in the case of a controlled group of corporations (as described in section 414(b)) or a group of trades or businesses under common control (as described in section 414(c)).

(d) *Discrimination.* In testing for discrimination under section 401(a)(4) (requiring that contributions or benefits do not discriminate in favor of employees who are officers, shareholders, or highly compensated), all of the compensation paid to an employee must be considered in determining the contributions or benefits under a plan maintained by a member of an affiliated service group, without regard to the percentage of the organization employing the individual owned by the member maintaining the plan.

(e) *Example.* The provisions of this section may be illustrated by the following example.

(1) T is incorporated and Corporation T is a partner in a service organization. Corporation T employs only its sole shareholder and maintains a retirement plan. W and Z, the other partners in the service

organization, are not incorporated. Each partner has a one-third interest in the service organization. The partnership has eight common law employees.

(2) Considering the partnership as a First Service Organization, Corporation T is an A Organization because it is a partner in the First Service Organization and regularly performs services for the partnership or is regularly associated with the partnership in performing services for third persons. Accordingly, the partnership and Corporation T constitute an affiliated service group.

(3) If the retirement plan maintained by Corporation T covers any of the common law employees of the partnership, it will be benefiting individuals who are not employees of the member of the affiliated service group maintaining the plan (Corporation T). As such, the plan will be considered to be maintained by more than one employer, and will be subject to the rules of section 413(c)(2), (4), (5), and (6) and the regulations thereunder. Thus, contributions by Corporation T on behalf of these individuals will not fail to be deductible under section 404 merely because they are not employees of Corporation T. In testing for discrimination under section 401(a)(4), all of the compensation paid to the employees of the partnership must be taken into account in determining their contributions or benefits under the plan, without regard to the percentage of the partnership owned by Corporation T.

(4) If the plan maintained by Corporation T covers partners W and Z, the plan must also satisfy the requirements listed in paragraph (b), to the extent they are applicable.

§ 1.414(m)-4 Effective dates.

(a) *Effective dates*—(1) *New plans.* In the case of a plan that was not in existence on November 30, 1980, section 414(m) and the regulations thereunder apply to plan years ending after November 30, 1980.

(2) *Existing plans.* In the case of a plan in existence on November 30, 1980, section 414(m) and the regulations thereunder shall apply to plan years beginning after November 30, 1980.

(b) *Frozen plans*—(1) *Defined contribution plans.* In the case of a defined contribution plan in existence on November 30, 1980, that fails to satisfy the requirements of section 401(a) solely because of the application of section 414(m), the trust shall be treated as continuing to satisfy the requirements of section 401(a) after the effective date of section 414(m) if the plan is terminated and all amounts are distributed to the participants within 180 days after the latest of:

(i) [The date of the publication of this regulation in the *Federal Register* as a Treasury decision],

(ii) The date on which notice of the final determination with respect to a request for a determination letter is issued by the Internal Revenue Service, such request is withdrawn, or such request is finally disposed of by the Internal Revenue Service, provided the request for a determination letter was pending on [the date of the publication of this regulation in the *Federal Register* as a Treasury decision] or, in the case of a request for a determination letter on the plan termination, was made within 60 days after the [date of the publication of this regulation in the *Federal Register* as a Treasury decision].

(iii) If a petition is timely filed with the United States Tax Court for a declaratory judgment under section 7476 with respect to the final determination (or the failure of the Internal Revenue Service to make a final determination) in response to such request, the date on which the decision of the United States Tax Court in such proceeding becomes final.

(2) *Defined benefit plans.* In the case of a defined benefit plan in existence on November 30, 1980, that fails to satisfy the requirements of section 401(a) solely because of the application of section 414(m), the trust shall be treated as continuing to satisfy the requirements of section 414(m) if the plan is terminated within 180 days after the latest of the dates determined in a manner consistent with paragraph (b)(1). However, deductions for contributions to the plan for plan years after the effective date of section 414(m) are limited to those necessary to satisfy the minimum funding standards of section 412.

§ 1.415-8 [Amended]

Par. 3. Paragraph (c) of § 1.415-8 is amended by adding "or by an affiliated service group (within the meaning of section 414(m)" before the words "is deemed maintained."

Roscoe L. Egger, Jr.,

Commissioner of Internal Revenue.

[FR Doc. 83-5045 Filed 2-25-83; 8:45 am]

[¶ 20,137H Reserved.—Proposed Regs. §§ 1.401(b)-1 and 1.416-1, relating to top-heavy pension, profit-sharing, and stock bonus plans were formerly reproduced at this point. The final regulations appear at ¶ 11,721 and 12,503.]

¶ 20,137I

Proposed regulations: Multiemployer plans.—Reproduced below were proposed regulations relating, in the case of multiemployer plans, to the return of employer contributions or withdrawal liability overpayments which were made due to a mistake of fact or law. The proposed regulations were published in the *Federal Register* on March 11, 1983 (48 FR 10374). Final regulations, which were published in the *Federal Register* on July 22, 2002 (67 FR 47692), are reproduced at ¶ 11,720W-12. The preamble appears at ¶ 24,506R.

¶ 20,137J

Proposed regulation— Personal service corporations—Reallocation of income, deductions, credits and exclusions.—Following are proposed regulations relating to the reallocation of income, deductions, credits, and exclusions between a personal service corporation and its employee-owners if the corporation was formed primarily to avoid or evade federal income taxes. The proposed regulations were published in the *Federal Register* on March 31, 1983 (48 FR 13438).

DEPARTMENT OF THE TREASURY

Internal Revenue Service

26 CFR Part 1

[LR-188-82]

Personal Service Corporations; Proposed Income Tax Regulations

AGENCY: Internal Revenue Service, Treasury.

ACTION: Notice of proposed rulemaking.

SUMMARY: This document provides proposed regulations relating to the reallocation of income, deductions, credits and exclusions between a personal service corporation and its employee-owners if the corporation was formed or availed primarily to evade or avoid Federal income taxes. Changes to the applicable tax law were made by section 250 of the Tax Equity and Fiscal Responsibility Act of 1982 (TEFRA), which added new section 269A to the Internal Revenue Code of 1954. These regulations would affect all employee-owners and their personal service corporations if the personal service corporation provides substantially all of its services for or on behalf of one other entity, but only if the corporation was formed or availed of primarily to evade or avoid Federal income taxes. These regulations would provide affected persons with the guidance to comply with the law.

DATES: Written comments and requests for a public hearing must be delivered or mailed by May 31, 1983. The regulations provided by this document are proposed to be generally effective for taxable years of personal service corporations beginning after December 31, 1982.

ADDRESS: Send comments and requests for a public hearing to: Commissioner of Internal Revenue, Attention: CC:LR:T (LR-188-82) Washington, D.C. 20224.

FOR FURTHER INFORMATION CONTACT: Phoebe A. Mix or Philip R. Bosco of Legislation and Regulations Division, Office of Chief Counsel, Internal Revenue Service, 1111 Constitution Avenue, N.W., Washington, D.C. 20224, Attention: CC:LR:T, (202) 566-3238, not a toll-free call.

SUPPLEMENTARY INFORMATION:

Background

Section 269A was added to the Internal Revenue Code by the Tax Equity and Fiscal Responsibility Act of 1982. Section 269A permits the Secretary to allocate all income, deductions, credits, exclusions, and other tax benefits between a personal service corporation and its employee-owners in order to prevent the avoidance or evasion of Federal income taxes or to reflect clearly the income of the personal service corporation or any of its employee-owners if substantially all of the services are performed for one other entity and if the principal purpose for forming, or availing of, the corporation is the avoidance or evasion of Federal income taxes. Avoidance or evasion of Federal income taxes may be either the reduction of income of an employee-owner through the use of the corporation or the securing of one or more tax benefits that would not otherwise be available. These regulations define benefits that would not otherwise be available as benefits that would not be available to a taxpayer providing services as an unincorporated individual.

These regulations also provide a safe-harbor, excluding from the application of section 269A those situations in which the Federal income tax liability of each employee-owner is reduced by not more than 10 percent of $2,500, whichever is less.

Prior to "parity" between qualified retirement plans of corporations and those of noncorporate employers (effective generally for taxable years beginning after December 31, 1983), an employee-owner can make larger contributions to a corporate qualified retirement plan than could have been made to a Keogh or H.R. 10 plan had the corporation not been in existence. For corporations in existence before the date of enactment of TEFRA (September 3, 1982), qualified retirement plans available to corporations generally will not be taken into account for purposes of determining the corporation's principal purpose. Thus, a corporation created principally to take advantage of the higher contributions to corporate plans may still have an impermissible purpose if its principal purpose (other than qualified retirement plan benefit) was to reduce income or secure one or more tax benefits. If a corporation is found to have an impermissible principal purpose, the contributions to the qualified retirement plan will neither be reallocated to the employee-owner nor reduced as a result of reallocation of other income to the employee-owner. For corporations formed after the date of enactment of TEFRA, this protection is not available for contributions or benefits that would not have been available to the employee-owner absent the corporation. In that case, contributions to a qualified retirement plan will be considered in determining the corporation's principal purpose and may be reallocated or reduced through application of section 269A.

Section 269A does not override other sections of the Code or existing tax law principles. Nothing in these regulations, including the safe-harbor provision, precludes application of any other Code section (*e.g.*, sections 61 or 482) or principle of tax law (*e.g.*, assignment of income doctrine) to reallocate or reapportion income, deductions, credits or any other tax benefits if such reallocation is necessary to reflect the true earner of the income.

The regulations provide guidance regarding certain specific section 269A issues determined to be of major interest. No inference should be drawn regarding issues not included in the regulations, or as to why some issues, and not others, are addressed.

Special Analysis

The Commissioner of Internal Revenue has determined that these proposed regulations are not a major rule as defined in Executive Order 12291. Accordingly, a Regulatory Impact Analysis is not required. Although this document is a notice of proposed rulemaking that solicits public comment, the Internal Revenue Service has concluded that the notice and public procedure requirements of 5 U.S.C. 553 do not apply because the rules proposed are interpretative. Accordingly, a Regulatory Flexibility Analysis is not required.

Comments and Requests for a Public Hearing

Before adopting these proposed regulations, consideration will be given to any written comments that are submitted (preferably seven copies) to the Commissioner of Internal Revenue. All comments will be available for public inspection and copying. A public hearing will be held upon written request to the Commissioner by any person who has submitted written comments. If a public hearing is held, notice of the time and place will be published in the Federal Register.

Drafting Information

The principal authors of these proposed regulations are Phoebe A. Mix and Philip R. Bosco of the Legislation and Regulations Division of the Office of Chief Counsel, Internal Revenue Service. However, personnel from other offices of the Internal Revenue Service and Treasury participated in developing the regulations, both on matters of substance and style.

List of Subjects in 26 CFR 1.296A-1

Income taxes, Personal service corporations.

PART I—[AMENDED]

Proposed Amendments to the Regulations

The Income Tax Regulations (26 CFR Part 1) are proposed to be amended by adding the new § 1.269A-1, in the appropriate place:

§ 1.269A Personal service corporations.

(a) *In general.* Section 269A permits the Internal Revenue Service to reallocate income and tax benefits between personal service corporations and their employee-owners to prevent evasion or avoidance of Federal income taxes or to reflect clearly the income of the personal service corporation or any of its employee-owners, if:

(1) Substantially all of the services of the personal service corporation are performed for or on behalf of one other entity, and

(2) The principal purpose for which the corporation was formed or availed of is the evasion or avoidance of Federal income tax. Such purpose is evidenced when use of the corporation either reduces the income of any employee-owner, or secures for any employee-owner one or more tax benefits which would not otherwise be available.

(b) *Definitions.* For purposes of section 269A and the regulations thereunder, the following definitions will apply:

(1) *Personal service corporation.* The term "personal service corporation" means a corporation the principal activity of which is the performance of personal services that are substantially performed by employee-owners.

(2) *Employee-owner.* The term "employee-owner" means an employee who owns, directly or indirectly, on any day of the corporation's taxable year, more than 10 percent of the outstanding stock of the personal service corporation. Section 318 will apply to determine indirect stock ownership, except that "5 per cent" is to be substituted for "50 percent" in section 318(a)(2)(C).

(3) *Entity.* The term "entity" means a corporation, partnership, or other entity. All persons related to such entity will be treated as one entity. A related person is a related person within the meaning of section 103(b)(6)(C).

(4) *Not otherwise be available.* The term "not otherwise be available" refers to any tax benefit that would not be available to an employee-owner had such employee-owner performed the personal services in an individual capacity.

(5) *Qualified employer plan.* The term "qualified employer plan" means a qualified employer plan as defined in section 219(e)(3).

(6) *Tax benefits.* The term "tax benefits" means any expense, deduction, credit, exclusion or other allowance which would not otherwise be available. The term includes, but is not limited to: multiple surtax exemptions being claimed by the owners of a single integrated business operation conducted through multiple corporate entities, accumulation of income by the corporation, the corporate dividends received deduction under section 213, deferral of income of an employee-owner through the use of a corporation with a fiscal year or accounting method differing from that of such employee-owner, the use of multiple classes of stock to deflect income to taxpayers in lower tax brackets, group-term life insurance (section 79), certain accident and health plans (section 105 and 106), certain employee death benefits (section 101), meals and lodging furnished for the convenience of the employer (section 119), and qualified transportation expenses (section 124). Except as otherwise provided in paragraph (d)(2)(ii) of this section, the term "tax benefits" does not include contributions to a qualified employer plan.

(c) *Safe harbor.* In general, a personal service corporation will be deemed not to have been formed or availed of for the principal purpose of avoiding or evading Federal income taxes if the Federal income tax liability of the employee-owner is reduced in a 12 month period by more than the lesser of (1) $2,500 or (2) 10 percent of the Federal income tax liability of the employee-owner that would have resulted in that 12 month period had the employee-owner performed the personal services in an individual capacity. For purposes of the computation required by this paragraph, and current corporate tax liability incurred for that 12 month period by the personal service corporation will be considered to be the tax liability of the employee-owners in proportion to the employee-owners stock holding in the personal service corporation.

(d) *Special rules relating to qualified employer plans.*—(1) *In general.* Contributions to, and benefits under, qualified employer plans will not be taken into account in determining the presence or absence of a principal purpose of the personal service corporation for purposes of paragraph (c) of this section, except as provided in this paragraph.

(2) *Taxable years beginning before January 1, 1984.* For taxable years beginning before January 1, 1984.

(i) *Corporations in existence on or before September 3, 1982.* For corporations in existence on or before September 3, 1982, the general rule provided in paragraph (d)(1) of this section will apply unless:

(A) The corporation adopts a new qualified employer plan after September 3, 1982, that has a plan year differing from either the taxable year of the corporation or the calendar year, or

(B) The corporation changes the plan year of an existing qualified employer plan, or its taxable year, after September 3, 1982, in a manner that would extend the period during which section 416 (relating to restrictions on "top heavy" plans), or section 269A (if this (B) did not apply) would be inapplicable to such corporation.

If (A) or (B) applies, the corporation will be treated as a corporation formed after September 3, 1982 for purposes of this paragraph.

(ii) *Corporations formed after September 3, 1982.* For corporations formed after September 3, 1982, contributions to, and benefits under, a qualified employer plan that are in excess of those that would have been available to an employee-owner performing the personal services in an individual capacity are to be taken into account in determining the principal purpose of the personal service corporation and will be considered to be tax benefits.

(e) *Effective dates.*—(1) *In general.* In general, section 269A and this section are effective for taxable years of personal service corporations beginning after December 31, 1982. Taxable years of employee-owners generally are not considered for purposes of this paragraph.

(2) *Exceptions.* If a personal service corporation changes its taxable year or qualified employer plan year after September 3, 1982, in a manner that would delay the effective date of section 416 (relating to restrictions on top-heavy plans), or section 269A (but for this (2)), section 269A will be applied to the corporation and its employee-owners on the earlier of the first day of the first taxable year of the corporation or any of its employee-owners beginning after December 31, 1982.

(f) *Effect on section 269A on other sections.* Nothing in section 269A or the regulations thereunder, including the safe harbor provided in paragraph (c) of this section, precludes application with respect to personal service corporations or their employee-owners of any other Code section (*e.g.,* sections 61 or 482) or tax law principle (*e.g.,* assignment of income doctrine) to reallocate or reapportion income, deductions, credits, etc., so as to reflect the true earner of income.

Roscoe L. Egger, Jr.,

Commissioner of Internal Revenue.

[¶ 20,137K Reserved.—Proposed regulations relating to uniform premium rates for group-term life insurance were formerly reproduced here. The final regulations appear at ¶ 11,231 and 11,233.]

[¶ 20,137L Reserved.—Proposed regulations relating to tables for valuing annuities, life estates, terms for years, remainders, and reversions for purposes of federal income, estate, and gift taxation were formerly reproduced here. The final regulations appear at ¶ 11,252, 12,365, 13,497, 13,498, and 13,498A.]

[¶ 20,137M Reserved.—Proposed regulations relating to the definition of brother-sister controlled group of corporations or businesses were formerly reproduced at this paragraph. The final regulations are at ¶ 12,355 and 12,358.]

[¶ 20,137N Reserved.—Formerly reproduced at this paragraph were proposed regulations on transactions in which property is transferred in connection with the performance of services under Code Sec. 83. The IRS withdrew the regulations when it later issued proposed regulations on Code Sec. 83 in 1994. See ¶ 20,203.]

¶ 20,137O

Proposed regulations: IRAs: SEPs: QVECs: Changes made by ERTA.—Reproduced below are proposed regulations reflecting changes relating to IRAs, SEPs and QVECs made by the Economic Recovery Tax Act of 1981 under Code Secs. 219, 408, 415, 2039 and 6652.

The proposed regulations were published in the *Federal Register* on January 23, 1984 (49 FR 2794). The proposed revision of Reg. § 1.409-1(b)(2)(i) was withdrawn on January 8, 1996 (61 FR 552).

Note that these regulations were proposed prior to changes made by the Tax Reform Act of 1986.

[4830-01]

[Final draft of 9/14/82]

DEPARTMENT OF THE TREASURY INTERNAL REVENUE SERVICE

[26 CFR Parts 1, 20, 25, and 301]

[EE-148-81]

Individual Retirement Plans, Simplified Employee Pensions, And Qualified Voluntary Employee Contributions

AGENCY: Internal Revenue Service, Treasury.

ACTION: Notice of proposed rulemaking.

SUMMARY: This document contains proposed regulations relating to individual retirement plans, simplified employee pensions, and qualified voluntary employee contributions. Changes to the applicable law were made by the Economic Recovery Tax Act of 1981. The regulations would provide the public with the guidance needed to comply with the Act. The regulations would affect: institutions which sponsor individual retirement plans and simplified employee pensions, employers and individuals who use individual retirement plans and simplified employee pensions for retirement income, employers who maintain plans which accept qualified voluntary employee contributions and employees who make qualified voluntary employee contributions.

DATES: Written comments and requests for a public hearing must be delivered or mailed by March 23, 1984. The regulations would be generally effective for taxable years beginning after December 31, 1981.

ADDRESS: Send comments and requests for a public hearing to: Commissioner of Internal Revenue, Attention: CC:LR:T (EE-148-81), Washington, D.C. 20224.

FOR FURTHER INFORMATION CONTACT: William D. Gibbs of the Employee Plans and Exempt Organizations Division, Office of the Chief Counsel, Internal Revenue Service, 1111 Constitution Avenue, N.W., Washington, D.C. 20224 (Attention: CC:LR:T) (202-566-3430) (not a toll-free number).

SUPPLEMENTARY INFORMATION:

Background

This document contains proposed amendments to the Income Tax Regulations (26 CFR Part 1), the Estate Tax Regulations (26 CFR Part 20), the Gift Tax Regulations (26 CFR Part 25), and the Procedure and Administration Regulations (26 CFR Part 301) under sections 219, 408, 409, 415, 2039, 2517, and 6652 of the Internal Revenue Code of 1954. These amendments are proposed to conform the regulations to sections 311 (except subsection (b)) and 314(b) of the Economic Recovery Tax Act of 1981 (95 Stat. 274, 286). These regulations are to be issued under the authority contained in section 7805 of the Internal Revenue Code of 1954 (68A Stat. 917; 26 U.S.C. 7805).

Individual Retirement Plans

Section 219, as amended by the Economic Recovery Tax Act of 1981, allows an individual a deduction of up to the lesser of $2,000 or compensation includible in gross income for contributions to an individual retirement plan. Unlike old section 219, an individual is allowed this deduction whether or not he is an "active participant" in an employer's plan. The deduction for individual retirement plan contributions is reduced, however, by amounts which the employee contributes to an employer's plan and treats as qualified voluntary employee contributions. The remainder of the individual retirement plan rules are similar to those under prior law.

Spousal Individual Retirement Accounts

Code section 220 was deleted by the Economic Recovery Tax Act of 1981. In its place is new section 219(c), which allows an individual and his nonworking spouse to contribute up to the lesser of compensation includible in the working spouse's gross income or $2,250 to individual retiremnet accounts. The spouses must file a joint return to obtain this additional $250 deduction. No deduction is allowed if the spouse for whose benefit the individual retirement plan is maintained has attained age 70 ½ before the close of the taxable year.

There is no requirement, as under old law, that equal amounts be contributed to the individual retirement accounts of both spouses. However, no more than $2,000 may be contributed to the individual retirement account of either spouse.

Simplified Employee Pensions

The Economic Recovery Tax Act of 1981 increased the maximum deduction for contributions to simplified employee pensions to the lesser of 15% of compensation from the employer maintaining the simplified employee pension arrangement or the amount contributed by the employer to the simplified employee pension and included in gross income (but not in excess of $15,000). An employer may also contribute and deduct the lesser of $2,000 or compensation includible in gross income regardless of the employer's contribution to the simplified employee pension.

Qualified Voluntary Employee Contributions

Section 219, as amended by the Economic Recovery Tax Act of 1981, allows an individual a deduction for qualified voluntary employee contributions (QVEC's). QVEC's are voluntary contributions made by an individual as an employee under an employer's plan. The employer's plan must allow employees to make contributions which may be treated as QVEC's.

The maximum amount which can be deducted as a QVEC is the lesser of $2,000 or the compensation includible in gross income from the employer which maintains the plan which accepts the QVEC's.

Proposed § 1.219(a)-5(a) sets forth the type of plans which can accept qualified voluntary employee contributions.

Proposed § 1.219(a)-5(c) sets forth the rules a plan must follow to receive qualified voluntary employee contributions.

Additional rules for QVEC's are set forth in proposed § 1.219(a)-5(d), (e), and (f).

The reporting rules for qualified voluntary employee contributions are in proposed § 1.219(e)-5(g). This provision gives the Commissioner discretionary authority to modify the reporting requirements for these contributions. Any such modification of the reporting requirements would be subject to review by the Office of Management and Budget under the Paperwork Reduction Act of 1980.

Other Amendments

Conforming and technical amendments made by the Economic Recovery Tax Act of 1981 have been made to the regulations under Code sections 408, 409, 415, 2039, 2517, and 6652.

Although the Treasury Department stopped selling retirement bonds in early 1982, the regulations contain references to Code sections 405 and 409. These references apply to retirement bonds sold through early 1982 and to retirement bonds that may be sold subsequently.

These proposed regulations do not reflect amendments made to the Code by the Tax Equity and Fiscal Responsibility Act of 1982. These proposed regulations reflect changes in the applicable statutory provisions made by the Technical Corrections Act of 1982.

Executive Order 12291 And Regulatory Flexibility Act

The Commissioner has determined that this proposed regulation is not a major regulation for purposes of Executive Order 12291. Accordingly, a regulatory impact analysis is not required.

Although this document is a notice of proposed rulemaking which solicits public comment, the Internal Revenue Service has concluded that the regulations proposed herein are interpretative and that the notice and public procedure requirements of 5 U.S.C. 553 do not apply. Accordingly, these proposed regulations do not constitute regulations subject to the Regulatory Flexibility Act (5 U.S.C. chapter 6).

Comments and Requests for a Public Hearing

Before adopting these proposed regulations, consideration will be given to any written comments that are submitted (preferably seven copies) to the Commissioner of Internal Revenue. All comments will be available for public inspection and copying. A public hearing will be held upon written request to the Commissioner by any person who has submitted written comments. If a public hearing is held, notice of the time and place will be published in the FEDERAL REGISTER.

The collection of information requirements contained in this notice of proposed rulemaking have been submitted to the Office of Management and Budget (OMB) for review under section 3504(h) of the Paperwork Reduction Act of 1980. Comments on these requirements should be sent to the Office of Information and Regulatory Affairs of OMB, Attention: Desk Office for Internal Revneue Service, New Executive Office Building, Washington, D.C. 20503. The Internal Revenue Service requests that persons submitting comments on these requirements to OMB also send copies of those comments to the Service.

Drafting Information

The principal author of these proposed regulations is William D. Gibbs of the Employee Plans and Exempt Organizations Division of the Office of Chief Counsel, Internal Revenue Service. However, personnel from other offices of the Internal Revenue Service and Treasury Department participated in developing the regulation, both on matters of substance and style.

List of Subjects in 26 CFR 1.61-1-1.281-4

Income taxes, Taxable income, Deductions, Exemptions.

List of Subjects in 26 CFR 1.401-0-1.425-1

Income taxes, Employee benefit plan, Pensions, Stock options, Individual retirement accounts, Employee stock ownership plans.

List of Subjects in 26 CFR Part 20

Estate taxes.

List of Subjects in 26 CFR Part 25

Gift taxes.

List of Subjects in 26 CFR Part 301

Administrative practice and procedure, Bankruptcy, Courts, Crime, Employment taxes, Estate taxes, Excise taxes, Gift taxes, Income taxes, Investigations, Law enforcement, Penalties, Pensions, Statistics, Taxes, Disclosure of information, Filing requirements.

Proposed amendments to the regulations

The proposed amendments to 26 CFR Parts 1, 20, 25, and 301 are as follows:

Income Tax Regulations [26 CFR Part 1]

Paragraph 1. There are added after proposed § 1.219-3, 46 FR 36202 (1981), the following new sections 1.219(a)-1 through 1.219(a)-6:

§ 1.219(a)-1 Deduction for contributions to individual retirement plans and employer plans under the Economic Recovery Tax Act of 1981.

(a) *In general.* Under section 219, as amended by the Economic Recovery Tax Act of 1981, an individual is allowed a deduction from gross income for amounts paid on his behalf to an individual retirement plan or to certain employer retirement plans. The following table indicates the location of the rules for deductions on behalf of individuals to individual retirement plans or employer plans.

§ 1.219(a)-2: Individual retirement plans.

§ 1.219(a)-3: Spousal individual retirement accounts.

§ 1.219(a)-4: Simplified employee pensions.

§ 1.219(a)-5: Employer plans.

§ 1.219(a)-6: Divorced individuals.

(b) *Definitions.* The following is a list of terms and their definitions to be used for purposes of this section and § § 1.219(a)-2 through 1.219(a)-6:

(1) *Individual retirement plan.* The term "individual retirement plan" means an individual retirement account described in section 408(a), an individual retirement annuity described in section 408(b), and a retirement bond described in section 409.

(2) *Simplified employee pension.* The term "simplified employee pension" has the meaning set forth in § 1.408-7(a).

(3) *Compensation.* The term "compensation" means wages, salaries, professional fees, or other amounts derived from or received for personal service actually rendered (including, but not limited to, commissions paid salesmen, compensation for services on the basis of a percentage of profits, commissions on insurance premiums, tips, and bonuses), but does not include amounts derived from or received as earnings or profits from property (including, but not limited to, interest and dividends) or amounts not includible in gross income such as amounts excluded under section 911. Compensation includes earned income, as defined in section 401(c)(2), reduced by amounts deductible under sections 404 and 405. Compensation does not include amounts received as deferred compensation, including any pension or annuity payment. Compensation does not include unemployment compensation within the meaning of section 85(c).

(4) *Qualified voluntary employee contribution.* The term "qualified voluntary employee contribution" means any employee contribution which is not a mandatory contribution within the meaning of section 411(c)(2)(C) made by an individual as an employee under qualified employer plan or government plan, which plan allows an employee to make such contribution, and which the individual has not designated as a contribution other than a qualified voluntary employee contribution. Thus, if employee contributions are required as a condition of plan participation, they are mandatory contributions within the meaning of section 411(c)(2)(C) and cannot be treated as qualified voluntary employee contributions.

(5) *Qualified retirement contribution.* The term "qualified retirement contribution" means any amount paid in cash for the taxable year by or on behalf of an individual for his benefit to an individual retirement plan and any qualified voluntary employee contribution paid in cash by the individual for the taxable year.

(6) *Deductible employee contribution.* The term "deductible employee contribution" means any qualified voluntary employee contribution made after December 31, 1981, in a taxable year beginning after such date and allowable as a deduction under section 219(a) for such taxable year.

(7) *Qualified employer plan.* The term "qualified employer plan" means—

(i) A plan described in section 401(a) which includes a trust exempt from tax under section 501(a),

(ii) An annuity plan described in section 403(a),

(iii) A qualified bond purchase plan described in section 405(a), and

(iv) A plan under which amounts are contributed by an individual's employer for an annuity contract described in section 403(b).

(8) *Government plan.* The term "government plan" means any retirement plan, whether or not qualified, established and maintained for its employees by the United States, by a State or political subdivision thereof, or by an agency or instrumentality of any of the foregoing.

(c) *Effective date.* This section and § § 1.219(a)-2 through 1.219(a)-6 are effective **for taxable years of individuals beginning after December 31, 1981.**

§ 1.219(a)-2 Deduction for contributions to individual retirement plans under the Economic Recovery Tax Act of 1981.

(a) *In general.* Subject to the limitations and restrictions of paragraph (b) and the special rules of paragraph (c)(3) of this section, there shall be allowed a deduction under section 62 from gross income of amounts paid for the taxable year of an individual by or on behalf of such individual to an individual retirement plan. The deduction described in the preceding sentence shall be allowed only to the individual on whose behalf such individual retirement plan is maintained and only in the case of a contribution of cash. No deduction is allowable under this section for a contribution of property other than cash. In the case of a retirement bond, no deduction is allowed if the bond is redeemed within 12 months of its issue date.

(b) *Limitations and restrictions*—(1) *Maximum deduction.* The amount allowable as a deduction for contributions to an individual retirement plan to an individual for any taxable year cannot exceed the lessor of—

(i) $2,000, or

(ii) An amount equal to the compensation includible in the individual's gross income for the taxable year, reduced by the amount of the individual's qualified voluntary employee contributions for the taxable year.

(2) *Contributions after age 70 ½.* No deduction is allowable for contributions to an individual retirement plan to an individual for the taxable year of the individual if he has attained the age of 70 ½ before the close of such taxable year.

(3) *Rollover contributions.* No deduction is allowable under § 1.219(a)-2(a) for any taxable year of an individual with respect to a rollover contribution described in section 402(a)(5), 402(a)(7), 403(a)(4), 403(b)(8), 405(d)(3), 408(d)(3), or 409(b)(3)(C).

(4) *Amounts contributed under endowment contracts.* (i) For any taxable year, no deduction is allowable under § 1.219(a)-2(a) for amounts paid under an endowment contract described in § 1.408-3(e) which is allocable under subdivision (ii) of this subparagraph to the cost of life insurance.

(ii) For any taxable year, the cost of current life insurance protection under an endowment contract described in paragraph (b)(4)(i) of this section is the product of the net premium cost, as determined by the commissioner, and the excess, if any, of the death benefit payable under the contract during the policy year beginning in the taxable year over the cash value of the contract at the end of such policy year.

(c) *Special rules*—(1) *Separate deduction for each individual.* The maximum deduction allowable for contributions to an individual retirement plan is computed separately for each individual. Thus, if a husband and wife each has compensation of $15,000 for the taxable year, the maximum amount allowable as a deduction on their joint return is $4,000. See § 1.219(a)-3 for the maximum deduction for a spousal individual retirement plan when one spouse has no compensation.

(2) *Community property.* Section 219 is to be applied without regard to any community property laws. Thus, if, for example, a husband and wife live in a community property jurisdiction, the husband has compensation of $30,000 for the taxable year, and the wife has no compensation for the taxable year, then the maximum amount allowable as a deduction for contributions to an individual retirement plan, other than a spousal individual retirement plan, is $2,000.

(3) *Employer contributions.* For purposes of this chapter, any amount paid by an employer to an individual retirement plan of an employee (other than a self-employed individual who is an employee within the meaning of section 401(c)(1)) constitutes the payment of compensation to the employee. The payment is includible in the employee's gross income, whether or not a deduction for such payment is allowable under section 219 to this employee. An employer will be entitled to a deduction for compensation paid to an employee for amounts the employer contributes on the employee's behalf to an individual retirement plan if such deduction is otherwise allowable under section 162. See § 1.404(h)-1 for certain limitations on this deduction in the case of employer contributions to a simplified employee pension.

(4) *Year of inclusion in income.* Any amount paid by an employer to an individual retirement plan (including an individual retirement account or individual retirement annuity maintained as part of a simplified employee pension arrangement) shall be included in the gross income of the employee for the taxable year for which the contribution was made.

(5) *Time when contributions deemed made.* A taxpayer shall be deemed to have made a contribution on the last day of the preceding taxable year if the contribution is made on account of the taxable year which includes such last day and is made not later than the time prescribed by law for filing the return for such taxable year (including extensions thereof). A contribution made not later than the time prescribed by law for filing the return for a taxable year (including extensions thereof) shall be treated as made on account of such taxable year if it is irrevocably specified in writing to the trustee, insurance company, or custodian that the amounts contributed are for such taxable year.

(d) *Excess contributions treated as contribution made during subsequent year for which there is an unused limitation*—(1) *In general.* This paragraph sets forth rules for the possible deduction of excess contributions made to an individual retirement plan for the taxable years

following the taxable year of the excess contribution. If for a taxable year subsequent to the taxable year for which the excess contribution was made, the maximum amount allowable as a deduction for contributions to an individual retirement plan exceeds the amount contributed, then the taxpayer, whether or not a deduction is actually claimed, shall be treated as having made an additional contribution for the taxable year in an amount equal to the lesser of—

(i) The amount of such excess, or

(ii) The amount of the excess contributions for such taxable year (determined under section 4973(b)(2) without regard to subparagraph (C) thereof).

(2) *Amount contributed.* For purposes of this paragraph, the amount contributed—

(i) Shall be determined without regard to this paragraph, and

(ii) Shall not incude any rollover contribution.

(3) *Special rule where excess deduction was allowed for closed year.* Proper reduction shall be made in the amount allowable as a deduction by reason of this paragraph for any amount allowed as a deduction for contributions to an individual retirement plan for a prior taxable year for which the period for assessing a deficiency has expired if the amount so allowed exceeds the amount which should have been allowed for such prior taxable year.

(4) *Excise tax consequences.* See section 4973 and the regulations thereunder for the excise tax applicable to excess contributions made to individual retirement plans.

(5) *Examples.* The provisions of this paragraph may be illustrated by the following examples. (Assume in each example, unless otherwise stated, that T is less than age 70 ½ and is not married.)

Example (1). (i) T, a calendar-year taxpayer, earns $1,500 in compensation includible in gross income for 1982. On December 1, 1982, T establishes an individual retirement account (IRA) and contributes $2,000 to the account. T does not withdraw any money from the IRA after the initial contribution. Under section 219(b)(1), the maximum amount that T can deduct for 1982 is $1,500. T has an excess contribution for 1982 of $500.

(ii) For 1983, T has compensation includible in gross income of $12,000. T makes a $1,000 contribution to his IRA for 1983.

(iii) Although T made only a $1,000 contribution to his IRA for 1983, under the rules contained in this paragraph, T is treated as having made an additional contribution of $500 for 1983 and will be allowed to deduct $1,500 as his 1983 IRA contribution.

Example (2). (i) For 1982, the facts are the same as in *Example (1)*.

(ii) For 1983, T has compensation includible in gross income of $12,000. T makes a $2,000 contribution to his IRA for 1983.

(iii) T will be allowed a $2,000 deduction for 1983 (the amount of his contribution). T will not be allowed a deduction for the $500 excess contribution made in 1982 because the maximum amount allowable for 1983 does not exceed the amount contributed.

Example (3). (i) For 1982, the facts are the same as in *Example (1)*.

(ii) For 1983, T has compensation includible in gross income of $12,000. T makes a $1,800 contribution to his IRA for 1983.

(iii) For 1983, T will be allowed to deduct his contribution of $1,800 and $200 of the excess contribution made for 1982. He will not be allowed to deduct the remaining $300 of the excess contribution made for 1982 because his deduction for 1983 would then exceed $2,000, his allowable deduction for 1983.

(iv) For 1984, T has compensation includible in gross income of $15,000. T makes a $1,300 contribution to his IRA for 1984.

(v) T will be allowed to deduct both his $1,300 contribution for 1984 and the remaining $300 contribution made for 1982.

Example (4). (i) For 1982, the facts are the same as in *Example (1)*.

(ii) For 1983, T has compensation includible in gross income of $12,000. T makes a $1,000 contribution to his IRA for 1983. T is allowed to deduct the $500 excess contribution for 1983 but fails to do so on his return. Consequently, T deducts ony $1,000 for 1983.

(iii) Under no circumstances will T be allowed to deduct the $500 excess contribution made for 1982 for any taxable year after 1983 because T is treated as having made the contribution for 1983.

Example (5). (i) For 1982, the facts are the same as in *Example (1)*.

(ii) For 1983, T has no compensation includible in gross income.

(iii) T will not be allowed to deduct for 1983 the $500 excess contribution for 1982 because the maximum amount allowable as a deduction under section 219(b)(1) is $0.

§ 1.219(a)-3 Deduction for retirement savings for certain married individuals.

(a) *In general.* Subject to the limitations and restrictions of paragraphs (c) and (d) and the special rules of paragraph (e) of this section, there shall be allowed a deduction under section 62 from gross income of amounts paid for the taxable year of an individual by or on behalf of such individual for the benefit of his spouse to an individual retirement plan. The amounts contributed to an individual retirement plan by or on behalf of an individual for the benefit of his spouse shall be deductible only by such individual and only in the case of a contribution of cash. No deduction is allowable under this section for a contribution of property other than cash. In the case of an individual retirement bond, no deduction is allowed if the bond is redeemed within 12 months of its issue date.

(b) *Definition of compensation.* For purposes of this section, the term "compensation" has the meaning set forth in § 1.219(a)-1(b)(3).

(c) *Maximum deduction.* The amount allowable as a deduction under this section to an individual for any taxable year may not exceed the smallest of—

(1) $2,000,

(2) An amount equal to the compensation includible in the individual's gross income for the taxable year less the amount allowed as a deduction under section 219(a) (determined without regard to contributions to a simplified employee pension allowed under section 219(b)(2)), § 1.219(a)-2 and § 1.219(a)-5 for the taxable year, or

(3) $2,250 less the amount allowed as a deduction under section 219(a) (determined without regard to contributions to a simplified employee pension allowed under section 219(b)(2)), § 1.219(a)-2 and § 1.219(a)-5 for the taxable year.

(d) *Limitations and restrictions*—(1) *Requirement to file joint return.* No deduction is allowable under this section for a taxable year unless the individual and his spouse file a joint return under section 6013 for the taxable year.

(2) *Employed spouses.* No deduction is allowable under this section if the spouse of the individual has any compensation for the taxable year of such spouse ending with or within the taxable year of the individual. For purposes of this subparagraph, compensation has the meaning set forth in § 1.219(a)-1(b)(3), except that compensation shall include amounts excluded under section 911.

(3) *Contributions after age 70 ½.* No deduction is allowable under this section with respect to any payment which is made for a taxable year of an individual if the individual for whose benefit the individual retirement plan is maintained has attained age 70 ½ before the close of such taxable year.

(4) *Recontributed amounts.* No deduction is allowable under this section for any taxable year of an individual with respect to a rollover contribution described in section 402(a)(5), 402(a)(7), 403(a)(4), 403(b)(8), 405(d)(3), 408(d)(3), or 409(b)(3)(C).

(5) *Amounts contributed under endowment contracts.* The rules for endowment contracts under this section are the same as the provisions for such contracts under § 1.219(a)-2(b)(4).

(e) *Special rules*—(1) *Community Property.* This section is to be applied without regard to any community property laws.

(2) *Time when contributions deemed made.* The time when contributions are deemed made is determined under section 219(f)(3). See § 1.219(a)-2(c)(5).

§ 1.219(a)-4 Deduction for contributions to simplified employee pensions.

(a) *General rule*—(1) *In general.* Under section 219(b)(2), if an employer contribution is made on behalf of an employee to a simplified employee pension described in section 408(k), the limitations of this section, and not section 219(b)(1) and § 1.219(a)-2, shall apply for purposes of computing the maximum allowable deduction with respect to that contribution for that individual employee.

(2) *Employer limitation.* The maximum deduction under section 219(b)(2) for an employee with respect to an employer contribution to the employee's simplified employee pension under that employer's arrangement cannot exceed an amount equal to the lesser of—

(i) 15 percent of the employee's compensation from the employer (determined without regard to the employer contribution to the simpli-

fied employee pension) includible in the employee's gross income for the taxable year, or

(ii) The amount contributed by that employer to the employee's simplified employee pension and included in gross income (but not in excess of $15,000).

(3) *Special rules*—(i) *Compensation.* Compensation referred to in paragraph (a)(2)(i) has the same meaning as under § 1.219(a)-1(b)(3) except that it includes only the compensation from the employer making the contribution to the simplified employee pension. Thus, if an individual earns $50,000 from employer A and $20,000 from employer B and employer B contributes $4,000 to a simplified employee pension on behalf of the individual, the maximum amount the individual will be able to deduct under section 219(b)(2) is 15 percent of $20,000, or $3,000.

(ii) *Special rule for officers, shareholders, and owner-employees.* In the case of an employee who is an officer, shareholder, or owner-employee described in section 408(k)(3) with respect to a particular employer, the $15,000 amount referred to in paragraph (a)(2)(ii) shall be reduced by the amount of tax taken into account with respect to such individual under section 408(k)(3)(D).

(iii) *More than one employer arrangement.* Except as provided in paragraph (c), below, the maximum deduction under paragraph (a)(2) for an individual who receives simplified employee pension contributions under two or more employers' simplified employee pension arrangements cannot exceed the sum of the maximum deduction limitations computed separately for that individual under each such employer's arrangement.

(iv) *Section 408 rules.* Under section 408(j), the limitations under section 408(a)(1) and (b)(2)(B) (§ 1.408-2(b)(1) and § 1.408-3(b)(2)), shall be applied separately with respect to each employer's contributions to an individual's simplified employee pension.

(4) *Additional deduction for individual retirement plan and qualified voluntary employee contribution.* The deduction under this paragraph is in addition to any deduction allowed under section 219(a) to the individual for qualified retirement contributions.

(b) *Contributions to simplified employee pensions after age 70 ½.* The denial of deductions for contributions after age 70 ½ contained in section 219(d)(1) and § 1.219(a)-2(b)(2) shall not apply with respect to employer contributions to a simplified employee pension.

(c) *Multiple employer, etc. limitations*—(1) *Section 414(b), (c) and (m) employers.* In the case of a controlled group of employers within the meaning of section 414(b) or (c) or employers aggregated under section 414(m), the maximum deduction limitation for an employee under paragraph (a)(2) shall be computed by treating such employers as one employer maintaining a single simplified employee pension arrangement and by treating the compensation of that employee from such employers as if from one employer. Thus, for example, for a particular employee the 15 percent limitation on compensation would be determined with regard to the compensation from all employers within such group. Further, the maximum deduction with respect to contributions made by employers included within such group could not exceed $15,000.

(2) *Self-employed individuals.* In the case of an employee who is a self-employed individual within the meaning of section 401(c)(1) with respect to more than one trade or business, the maximum deduction limitation for such an employee under paragraph (a)(2) shall not exceed the lesser of the sum of such limitation applied separately with respect to the simplified employee pension arrangement of each trade or business or such limitation determined by treating such trades or businesses as if they constituted a single employer.

(d) *Examples.* The provisions of this section may be illustrated by the following examples:

Example (1). Corporation X is a calendar-year, cash-basis taxpayer. It adopts a simplified employee pension agreement in 1982 and wishes to contribute the maximum amount on behalf of each employee for 1982. Individual E is a calendar-year taxpayer who is employed solely by Corporation X in 1982. Beginning in June, 1982, Corporation X pays $100 each month into a simplified employee pension maintained on behalf of E. X makes a total payment to E's simplified employee pension during the year of $700. E's other compensation from X for the year totals $15,000. The maximum amount which E will be allowed to deduct as a simplified employee pension contribution is 15% of $15,000, or $2,250. Therefore, X may make an additional contribution for 1982 to E's simplified employee pension of $1,550. X makes this additional contribution to E's simplified employee pension in February of 1983. E's total compensation includible in gross income for 1982 is $15,000 + $2,250 or $17,250.

Example (2). (i) Corporation G is a calendar-year taxpayer which adopts a simplified employee pension agreement for 1982. It does not maintain an integrated plan as defined in section 408(k)(3)(E). It wishes to contribute 15% of compensation on behalf of each employee reduced by its tax under section 3111(a). The corporation has 4 employees, A, B, C, and D. D is a shareholder. The compensation for these employees for 1982 is as follows:

A = $10,000

B = 20,000

C = 30,000

D = 120,000

(ii) The amount of money which the corporation will be allowed to contribute on behalf of each employee under this allocation formula and the amount of the employer contribution each employee will be allowed to deduct is set forth in the following table:

Employee	Compensation	Lesser of $15,000 or 15% of Comp.	3111(a)[1] Tax	SEP[2] Contribution	Sec. 219 (b) (2) Deduction
A	$10,000	$1,500	$540.00	$960.00	$960.00
B	20,000	3,000	1,080.00	1,920.00	1,920.00
C	30,000	4,500	1,620.00	2,880.00	2,880.00
D	120,000	15,000	1,749.60	13,250.40	13,250.40

[1] The section 3111(a) tax is computed by multiplying compensation up to the taxable wage base ($32,400 for 1982) by the tax rate (5.40% for 1982).
[2] Simplified Employee Pension.

Example (3). Corporations A and B are calendar year taxpayers. Corporations A and B are not aggregated employers under section 414(b), (c) or (m). Individual M is employed full-time by Corporation A and part-time by Corporation B. Corporation A adopts a simplified employee pension agreement for calendar year 1982 and agrees to contribute 15% of compensation for each participant. M is a participant under Corporation A's simplified employee pension agreement and earns $15,000 for 1982 from Corporation A before A's contribution to his simplified employee pension. M also earns $5,000 as a part-time employee of Corporation B for 1982. Corporation A contributes $2,500 to M's simplified employee pension. The maximum amount that M will be allowed to deduct under section 219(b)(2) for 1982 is 15% of $15,000 or $2,250. In addition, M would be allowed to deduct the remaining $250 under section 219(a) for qualified retirement contributions.

Example (4). Individual P is employed by Corporation H and Corporation O. Corporations H and O are not aggregated employers under section 414(b), (c) or (m). Both Corporation H and Corporation O maintain a simplified employee pension arrangement and contribute 15 percent of compensation on behalf of each employee, up to a maximum of $15,000. P earns $100,000 from Corporation H and $120,000 from Corporation O. Corporation H and O each contribute $15,000 under its simplified employee pension arrangement to an individual retirement account maintained on behalf of P. P will be allowed to deduct $30,000 for employer contributions to simplified employee pensions because each employer has a simplified employee pension arrangement and the SEP contributions by Corporation H and O do not exceed the applicable $15,000-15 percent limitation with respect to compensation received from each employer. In addition, P would be allowed to deduct $2,000 under section 219(a) for qualified retirement contributions.

§ 1.219(a)-5 Deduction for employee contributions to employer plans.

(a) *Deduction allowed.* In the case of an individual, there is allowed as a deduction amounts contributed in cash to a qualified employer plan or government plan (as defined, respectively, in paragraphs (b)(7) and (b)(8) of § 1.219(a)-1) and designated as qualified voluntary employee contributions. If an employee transfers an amount of cash from one account in a plan to the qualified voluntary employee contribution account, such transfer is a distribution for purposes of sections 72, 402 and 403, and the amounts are considered recontributed as qualified voluntary employee contributions. No deduction will be allowed for a contribution of property other than cash.

(b) *Limitations*—(1) *Maximum amount of deduction.* The amount allowable as a deduction under paragraph (a) to any individual for any taxable year shall not exceed the lesser of $2,000 or an amount equal to the compensation (from the employer who maintains the plan) includible in the individual's gross income for such taxable year.

(2) *Contributions after age 70 ½.* No deduction is allowable for contributions under paragraph (a) to an individual for the taxable year of the individual if he has attained the age of 70 ½ before the close of such taxable year.

(3) *Rollover contributions.* No deduction is allowable under paragraph (a) for any taxable year of an individual with respect to a rollover contribution described in section 402(a)(5), 402(a)(7), 403(a)(4), 403(b)(8), 405(d)(3), 408(d)(3), or 409(b)(3)(C).

(c) *Rules for plans accepting qualified voluntary employee contributions*—(1) *Plan provision, etc.* (i) No plan may receive qualified voluntary employee contributions unless the plan document provides for acceptance of voluntary contributions. No plan may receive qualified voluntary employee contributions unless either the plan document provides for acceptance of qualified voluntary employee contributions

or the employer or the plan administrator manifests an intent to accept such contributions. Such intention must be communicated to the employees. Any manner of communication that satisfies § 1.7476-2(c)(1) shall satisfy the requirements of this subparagraph.

(ii) If the plan document provides for the acceptance of voluntary contributions, but does not specifically provide for acceptance of qualified voluntary employee contributions, the plan qualification limitation on voluntary contributions (the limit of 10 percent of the employee's cumulative compensation less prior voluntary contributions) would apply to both qualified voluntary employee contributions and other voluntary contributions. On the other hand, if the plan document provides for acceptance of both qualified voluntary employee contributions and other voluntary contributions, the plan qualification limitation on voluntary contributions would apply only to the contributions other than the qualified voluntary employee contributions.

(2) *Plans accepting only qualified voluntary employee contributions.* A qualified pension plan or stock bonus plan may be estabished that provides only for qualified voluntary employee contributions. Similarly, a government plan may be established that provides only for qualified voluntary employee contributions. A plan that provides only for qualified voluntary employee contributions would not satisfy the qualification requirements for a profit-sharing plan.

(3) *Recordkeeping provisions.* Separate accounting for qualified voluntary employee contributions that are deductible under this section is not required as a condition for receiving qualified voluntary employee contributions. However, failure to properly account for such contributions may result in adverse tax consequences to employees upon subsequent plan distributions and reporting and recordkeeping penalties for employers. See section 72(o) for rules for accounting for such contributions.

(4) *Status as employee.* An amount will not be considered as a qualified voluntary employee contribution on behalf of an individual unless the individual is an employee of the employer at some time during the calendar year for which the voluntary contribution is made. See section 415(c) concerning the effect of a nondeductible voluntary employee contribution on plan qualification.

(5) *Contribution before receipt of compensation.* A plan may allow an individual to make a qualified voluntary employee contribution greater than the amount he has received in compensation from the employer at the time the contribution is made. However, see paragraph (f) of this section.

(d) *Designations, procedures, etc.*—(1) *Plan procedures.* (i) A plan which accepts qualified voluntary employee contributions may adopt procedures by which an employee can designate the character of the employee's voluntary contributions as either qualified voluntary employee contributions or other employee contributions. Such procedures may, but need not, be in the plan document.

(ii) In the absence of such plan procedures, all voluntary employee contributions shall be deemed to be qualified voluntary employee contributions unless the employee notifies the employer that the contributions are not qualified voluntary employee contributions. Such notification must be received by April 15 following the calendar year for which such contributions were made. If such notification is not received, contributions are deemed to be qualified voluntary employee contributions for the prior year.

(2) *Characterization procedures, etc.* (i) The plan procedures may allow an employee to elect whether or not an employee contribution is to be treated as a qualified voluntary employee contribution or as other voluntary contributions. This election can be required either prior to or

after the contribution is made. If a contribution may be treated under such procedures as a qualified voluntary employee contribution or other voluntary contribution for a calendar year and the employee has not by April 15 of the subsequent calendar year designated the character of the contribution, the contribution must be treated as a qualified voluntary employee contribution for the calendar year. An employer may allow the election to be irrevocable or revocable. A procedure allowing revocable elections may limit the time within which an election may be revoked. The revocation of an election after April 15 following the calendar year for which the contribution was made is deemed to be ineffective in changing the character of employee contributions.

(ii) For purposes of this section, if the plan procedures allow employees to make contributions on account of the immediately preceding calendar year, a taxpayer shall be deemed to have made a qualified voluntary employee contribution to such plan on the last day of the preceding calendar year if the contribution is on account of such year and is made by April 15 of the calendar year or such earlier time as provided by the plan procedure.

(e) *Nondiscrimination requirements*—(1) *General rule.* Plans subject to the nondiscrimination requirements of section 401(a)(4) which accept qualified voluntary employee contributions must permit such contributions in a nondiscriminatory manner in order to satisfy section 401(a)(4). If a plan permits participants to make qualified voluntary employee contributions, the opportunity to make such contributions must be reasonably available to a nondiscriminatory group of employees. The availability standard will be satisfied if a nondiscriminatory group of employees is eligible to make qualified voluntary employee contributions under the terms of the plan and if a nondiscriminatory group of employees actually has the opportunity to make qualified voluntary employee contributions when plan restrictions are taken into account.

(2) *Eligible employees.* A nondiscriminatory group of employees is eligible to make qualified voluntary employee contributions under the terms of the plan if the group either meets the percentage requirements of section 410(b)(1)(A) or comprises a classification of employees that does not discriminate in favor of employees who are officers, shareholders, or highly compensated, as provided in section 410(b)(1)(B).

(3) *Plan restrictions.* In some cases, an employee may not be permitted to make qualified voluntary employee contributions until a plan restriction (such as making a certain level of mandatory employee contributions) is satisfied. In this case, it is necessary to determine whether a nondiscriminatory group of employees actually has the opportunity to make qualified voluntary employee contributions. For this purpose, only employees who have satisfied the plan restriction will be considered to have the opportunity to make deductible contributions. Thus, for example, if a plan requires an employee to make mandatory contributions of 6 percent of compensation in order to make qualified voluntary employee contributions and if only a small percentage of employees make the 6 percent mandatory contributions, then the group of employees who have the opportunity to make qualified voluntary employee contributions may not satisfy either test under section 410(b). A similar rule is applicable to integrated plans: employees who are not permitted to make qualified voluntary employee contributions to such a plan because they earn less than the integration level amount will be considered as employees who do not have the opportunity to make qualified voluntary employee contributions.

(4) *Permissible contributions.* If the availability standards are met, and if the qualified voluntary employee contributions permitted are not higher, as a percentage of compensation, for officers, shareholders or highly compensated employees than for other participants, the qualified voluntary employee contribution feature will meet the requirement that contributions or benefits not discriminate in favor of employees who are officers, shareholders, or highly compensated. This is so because the contributions are made by the employee, not the employer.

(5) *Acceptable contributions.* A plan may accept qualified voluntary employee contributions in an amount less than the maximum deduction allowable to an individual.

(f) *Excess qualified voluntary employee contributions.* Voluntary employee contributions which exceed the amount allocable as a deduction under paragraph (b) of this section will be treated as nondeductible voluntary employee contributions to the plan. See § 1.415-6(b)(8).

(g) *Reports*—(1) *Requirements.* Each employer who maintains a plan which accepts qualified voluntary employee contributions must furnish to each employee—

(i) A report showing the amount of qualified voluntary employee contributions the employee made for the calendar year, and

(ii) A report showing the amount of withdrawals made by the employee of qualified voluntary employee contributions during the calendar year.

(2) *Times.* (i) The report required by paragraph (g)(1)(i) of this section must be furnished by the later of January 31 following the year for which the contribution was made or the time the contribution is made.

(ii) The report required by paragraph (g)(1)(ii) of this section must be furnished by January 31 following the year of withdrawal.

(3) *Authority for additional reports.* The Commissioner may require additional reports to be given to individuals or to be filed with the Service. Such reports shall be furnished at the time and in the manner that the Commissioner specifies.

(4) *Authority to modify reporting requirements.* The Commissioner may, in his discretion, modify the reporting requirements of this paragraph. Such modification may include: the matters to be reported, the forms to be used for the reports, the time when the reports must be filed or furnished, who must receive the reports, the substitution of the plan administrator for the employer as the person required to file or furnish the reports, and the deletion of some or all of the reporting requirements. The Commissioner may, in his discretion, relieve employers from making the reports required by section 219(f)(4) and this paragraph (g). This discretion includes the ability to relieve categories of employers (but not individual employers) from furnishing or filing any report required by section 219(f)(4) and this paragraph (g).

(5) *Effective date.* This paragraph shall apply to reports for calendar years after 1982.

§ 1.219(a)-6 Alternative deduction for divorced individuals.

(a) *In general.* A divorced individual may use the provisions of this section rather than § 1.219(a)-2 in computing the maximum amount he may deduct as a contribution to an individual retirement plan. A divorced individual is not required to use the provisions of this section; he may use the provisions of § 1.219(a)-2 in computing the maximum amount he may deduct as a contribution to an individual retirement plan.

(b) *Individuals who may use this section.* An individual may compute the deduction for a contribution to an individual retirement plan under this section if—

(1) An individual retirement plan was established for the benefit of the individual at least five years before the beginning of the calendar year in which the decree of divorce or separate maintenance was issued, and

(2) For at least three of the former spouse's most recent five taxable years ending before the taxable year in which the decree was issued, such former spouse was allowed a deduction under section 219(c) (or the corresponding provisions of prior law) for contributions to such individual retirement plan.

(c) *Limitations*—(1) *Amount of deduction.* An individual who computes his deduction for contributions to an individual retirement plan under this section may deduct the smallest of—

(i) The amount contributed to the individual retirement plan for the taxable year,

(ii) $1,125, or

(iii) The sum of the amount of compensation includible in the individual's gross income for the taxable year and any qualifying alimony received by the individual during the taxable year.

(2) *Contributions after age 70 ½.* No deduction is allowable for contributions to an individaul retirement plan to an individual for the taxable year of the individual if he has attained the age of 70 ½ before the close of such taxable year.

(3) *Rollover contributions.* No deduction is allowable under this section for any taxable year of an individual with respect to a rollover contribution described in section 402(a)(5), 402(a)(7), 403(a)(4), 403(b)(8), 405(d)(3), 408(d)(3), or 409(b)(3)(C).

(d) *Qualifying alimony.* For purposes of this section, the term "qualifying alimony" means amounts includible in the individual's gross income under section 71(a)(1) (relating to a decree of divorce or separate maintenance).

Par. 2. Section 1.408-2 is amended by revising paragraph (b)(1) to read as follows:

§ 1.408-2 Individual retirement accounts.

* * *

(b) * * *

(1) *Amount of acceptable contributions.* Except in the case of a contribution to a simplified employee pension described in section 408(k) and a rollover contribution described in section 408(d)(3), 402(a)(5), 402(a)(7), 403(a)(4), 403(b)(8), 405(d)(3), or 409(b)(3)(C), the trust instrument must provide that contributions may not be accepted by the trustee for the taxable year in excess of $2,000 on behalf of any individual for whom the trust is maintained. An individual retirement account maintained as a simplified employee pension may provide for the receipt of up to the limits specified in section 408(j) for a calendar year.

* * *

Par. 3. Section 1.408-3 is amended by revision paragraph (b)(2) to read as follows:

§ 1.408-3 Individual retirement annuities.

* * *

(b) * * *

(2) *Annual premium.* Except in the case of a contribution to a simplified employee pension described in section 408(k), the annual premium on behalf of any individual for the annuity cannot exceed $2,000. Any refund of premiums must be applied before the close of the calendar year following the year of the refund toward the payment of future premiums or the purchase of additional benefits. An individual retirement annuity maintained as a simplified employee pension may provide for an annual premium of up to the limits specified in section 408(j).

* * *

Par. 4. There is added after proposed § 1.408-9, 46 FR 36209 (1981), the following new section 1.408-10:

§ 1.408-10 Investment in collectibles.

(a) *In general.* The acquisition by an individual retirement account or by an individually-directed account under a plan described in section 401(a) of any collectble shall be treated (for purposes of sections 402 and 408) as a distribution from such account in an amount equal to the cost to such account of such collectible.

(b) *Collectible defined.* For purposes of this section, the term "collectible" means—

(1) Any work of art,

(2) Any rug or antique,

(3) Any metal or gem,

(4) Any stamp or coin,

(5) Any alcoholic beverage,

(6) Any musical instrument,

(7) Any historical objects (documents, clothes, etc.), or

(8) Any other tangible personal property which the Commissioner determines is a "collectible" for purposes of this section.

(c) *Individually-directed account.* For purposes of this section, the term "individually-directed account" means an account under a plan that provides for individual accounts and that has the effect of permitting a plan participant to invest or control the manner in which the account will be invested.

(d) *Acquisition.* For purposes of this section, the term acquisition includes a purchase, exchange, contribution, or any method by which an individual retirement account or individually-directed account may directly or indirectly acquire a collectible.

(e) *Cost.* For purposes of this section, cost means fair market value.

(f) *Premature withdrawal penalty.* The ten percent penalty described in sections 72(m)(5) and 408(f)(1) shall apply in the case of a deemed distribution from an individual retirement account described in paragraph (a) of this section.

(g) *Amounts subsequently distributed.* When a collectible is actually distributed from an individual retirement account or an individually-directed account, any amounts included in gross income because of this section shall not be included in gross income at the time when the collectible is actually distributed.

¶ 20,137O

(h) *Effective date.* This section applies to property acquired after December 31, 1981, in taxable years ending after such date.

* * *

Par. 6. Section 1.415-1 is amended by removing paragraph (c) and paragraph (f)(3).

Par. 7. Section 1.415-2 is amended by removing paragraph (b)(8).

Par. 8. Section 1.415-6 is amended by: (1) Revising paragraph (b)(3) to read as set forth below, (2) removing paragraph (b)(7)(iv), and (3) adding a new paragraph (b)(8) to read as set forth below.

§ 1.415-6 Limitation for defined contribution plans.

* * *

(b) *Annual additions.* * * *

(3) *Employee contributions.* For purposes of subparagraph (1)(ii) of this paragraph, the term "annual additions" includes, to the extent employee contributions would otherwise be taken into account under this section as an annual addition, mandatory employee contributions (as defined in section 411(c)(2)(C) and the regulations thereunder) as well as voluntary employee contributions. The term "annual additions" does not include—

(i) Rollover contributions (as defined in sections 402(a)(5), 403(a)(4), 403(b)(8), 405(d)(3), 408(d)(3) and 409(b)(3)(C)),

(ii) Repayments of loans made to a participant from the plan,

(iii) Repayments of amounts described in section 411(a)(7)(B) (in accordance with section 411(a)(7)(C)) and section 411(a)(3)(D) (see § 1.411(a)-7(d)(6)(iii)(B)),

(iv) The direct transfer of employee contributions from one qualified plan to another,

(v) Employee contributions to a simplified employee pension allowable as a deduction under section 219(a), or

(vi) Deductible employee contributions within the meaning of section 72(o)(5).

However, the Commissioner may in an appropriate case, considering all of the facts and circumstances, treat transactions between the plan and the employee or certain allocations to participants' accounts as giving rise to annual additions.

* * *

(8) *Qualified voluntary employee contributions.* This subparagraph provides rules for qualified voluntary employee contributions that are eligible for the deduction under section 219(a). This subparagraph is applicable only if the total of such contributions for the year is not in excess of $2,000. If such contributions are not deductible under section 219, and result in an annual addition that causes the section 415 limits to be exceeded, they will not be treated as annual additions to the extent that the portion of the contribution exceeding the limitation (and earnings thereon) is returned to the employee as soon as administratively feasible after the employer knows or has reason to know that such contributions are not deductible employee contributions within the meaning of section 72(o)(5).

* * *

Par. 9. Section 1.415-7 is amended by: (1) Removing paragraph (c)(2)(iii), (2) redesignating paragraph (c)(2)(iv) as paragraph (c)(2)(iii), and (3) removing paragraph (i).

Estate Tax Regulations

[26 CFR Part 20]

Par. 10. Section 20.2039-2 is amended by adding a new subdivision (ix) to paragraph (c)(1) to read as follows:

§ 20.2039-2 Annuities under "qualified plans" and section 403(b) annuity contracts.

* * *

(c) *Amounts excludable from the gross estate.*

(1) * * *

(ix) Any deductible employee contributions (within the meaning of section 72(o)(5)) are considered amounts contributed by the employer.

Par. 11. Section 20.2039-4 is amended by adding a new paragraph (h) to read as follows:

§ 20.2039-4 Lump sum distributions from "qualified plans;" decedents dying after December 31, 1978.

* * *

(h) *Accumulated deductible employee contributions.* For purposes of this section, a lump sum distribution includes an amount attributable to accumulated deductible employee contributions (as defined in section 72(o)(5)(B)) in any qualified plan taken into account for purposes of determining whether any distribution from that qualified plan is a lump sum distribution as determined under paragraph (b) of this section. Thus, amounts attributable to accumulated deductible employee contributions in a qualified plan under which amounts are payable in a lump sum distribution are not excludable from the decedent's gross estate under § 20.2039-2, unless the recipient makes the section 402(a)/403(c) taxation election with respect to a lump sum distribution payable from that qualified plan.

Gift Tax Regulations

[26 CFR Part 25]

Par. 12. Section 25.2517-1 is amended by adding a new subdivision (viii) to paragraph (c)(1) to read as follows:

§ 25.2517-1 Employees' annuities.

* * *

(c) *Limitation on amount excludable from gift.*

(1) * * *

(vii) Any deductible employee contributions (within the meaning of section 72(o)(5)) are considered amounts contributed by the employer.

* * *

Procedure and Administration Regulations

[26 CFR Part 301]

Par. 13. There is added after § 301.6652-3 the following new section:

§ 301.6652-4 Failure to file information with respect to qualified voluntary employee contributions.

(a) *Failure to make annual reports to employees.* In the case of a failure to make an annual report required by § 1.219(a)-5(g) which contains the information required by such section on the date prescribed therefore, there shall be paid (on notice and demand by the Secretary and in the same manner as tax) by the person failing to make such annual report an amount equal to $25 for each participant with respect to when there was a failure to make such report, multiplied by the number of years during which such failure continues.

(b) *Limitation.* The total amount imposed under this section on any person shall not exceed $10,000 with respect to any calendar year.

(signed) Roscoe L. Egger, Jr.

Commissioner of Internal Revenue

[¶ 20,137P Reserved.—Proposed Regs. §§ 53.4941(e)-1, 53.4961-1, 53.4961-2, 53.4963-1, 53.4971-1, 53.4975-1, 141.4975-13 and 301.7422-1, relating to second-tier excise taxes were formerly reproduced at this point. The final regulations appear at ¶ 13,584, 13,593F, 13,593G, 13,597F, 13,600D, 13,642, 13,648 and 13,905.]

¶ 20,137Q

Proposed regulations: Tax treatment of cafeteria plans.—Reproduced below are proposed regulations on the tax treatment of cafeteria plans set forth in a question and answer format. Note: Q&A-21 has been replaced by a new Q&A-21 in proposed regulations at ¶ 20,137R. Additional Q&As providing transition rules in accordance with changes made by the Tax Reform Act of 1984 also appear at that paragraph. In addition, Q-8 has been republished and A-8 has been revised in proposed regulations reproduced at ¶ 20,227. A-8 was also amended in proposed regulations reproduced at ¶ 20,247 and in proposed regulations reproduced at ¶ 20,258. The revised proposed regulations were published in the *Federal Register* on November 7, 1997 (62 FR 60196), March 23, 2000 (65 FR 15587), and January 10, 2001 (66 FR 1923).

The proposed regulations were published in the *Federal Register* on May 7, 1984 (49 FR 19321).

DEPARTMENT OF THE TREASURY

Internal Revenue Service

26 CFR Part 1

[EE-16-79]

Tax Treatment of Cafeteria Plans

AGENCY: Internal Revenue Service, Treasury.

ACTION: Notice of proposed rulemaking.

SUMMARY: This document contains proposed regulations relating to the tax treatment of cafeteria plans. Changes to the applicable tax law were made by the Revenue Act of 1978, by the Technical Corrections Act of 1979 and by the Miscellaneous Revenue Act of 1980. The proposed regulations would provide the public with the guidance needed to comply with those Acts and would affect employees who participate in cafeteria plans.

DATES: Written comments and requests for a public hearing must be delivered or mailed by July 6, 1984. The regulations are generally proposed to be effective for plan years beginning after December 31, 1978, except with respect to certain provisions set forth in Q&A-21 which would be effective as of September 4, 1984. In addition, transitional relief is provided with respect to employer contributions made before June 1, 1984, pursuant to certain "flexible spending arrangements" that satisfy specified conditions. Also, the provision relating to qualified cash or deferred arrangements would be effective for plan years beginning after December 31, 1980.

ADDRESS: Send comments and requests for a public heating to: Commissioner of Internal Revenue, Attention: CC:LT:T(EE-16-79), Washington, D.C. 20224.

FOR FURTHER INFORMATION CONTACT: Harry Beker of the Employee Plans and Exempt Organizations Division, Office of the Chief Counsel, Internal Revenue Service, 1111 Constitution Avenue, NW., Washington, D.C. 20224 (Attention: CC:EE) (202-566-6212) (not a toll-free call).

SUPPLEMENTARY INFORMATION:

Background

This document contains proposed Income Tax Regulations (26 CFR Part 1) under section 125 of the Internal Revenue Code of 1954. These proposed regulations are to be issued pursuant to section 134 of the Revenue Act of 1978 (92 Stat. 2763), section 101 of the Technical Corrections Act of 1979 (92 Stat. 2227), section 226 of the Miscellaneous Revenue Act of 1980 (94 Stat. 3529) and under the authority contained in section 7805 of the Code (68A Stat. 917, 26 U.S.C. 7805).

Format

These proposed regulations are presented in the form of questions and answers. The questions and answers do not address various issues regarding the application of the discrimination standards under section 125. Written comments are requested specifically with respect to the application of these discrimination standards. In particular, comments are requested regarding tests that a plan may use to determine whether it is nondiscrimination, and test to assure that the pricing of benefits under a cafeteria plan is not discriminatory.

The guidance provided by these questions and answers may be relied upon to comply with provisions of section 125 and will be applied by the Internal Revenue Service in resolving issues arising under cafeteria plans and related Code sections. However, pending the issuance of final regulations, advance determinations and rulings regarding whether a cafeteria plan is or is not discriminatory will not be issued; determination regarding discrimination will be made only on audit.

If final regulations are more restrictive than the guidance in this Notice, the regulations will not be applied retroactively. No inference, however, should be drawn regarding issues not expressly raised that may be suggested by a particular question or answer or by the inclusion or exclusion of certain questions.

Nonapplicability of Executive Order 12291

The Treasury Department has determined that this Regulation is not subject to review under Executive Order 12291 or the Treasury and

Office of Management and Budget implementation of the Order dated April 28, 1982.

Regulatory Flexibility Act

Although this document is a notice of proposed rulemaking which solicits public comments, the Internal Revenue Service has concluded that the regulations proposed herein are interpretative and that the notice and public procedure requirements of 5 U.S.C. 553 do not apply. Accordingly, these proposed regulations do not constitute regulations subject to the Regulatory Flexibility Act (5 U.S.C. chapter 6).

Comments and Requests for a Public Hearing

Before adopting these proposed regulations, consideration will be given to any written comments that are submitted (preferably seven copies) to the Commissioner of Internal Revenue. All comments will be available for public inspection and copying. A public hearing will be heal on a date announced in the notice of public hearing appearing elsewhere in this *Federal Register*.

Drafting Information

The principal author of these proposed regulations is Harry Beker of the Employee Plans and Exempt Organizations Division of the Office of Chief Counsel, Internal Revenue Service. However, personnel from other offices of the Internal Revenue Service and Treasury Department participated in developing the regulations, both on matters of substance and style.

List of Subjects in 26 CFR Parts 1.61-1—1.1281-4

Income taxes, Taxable income.

PART 1—[AMENDED]

Proposed Amendments to the Regulations

Accordingly, it is proposed to amend the Income Tax Regulations, 26 CFR Part 1, by adding the following new section:

§ 1.125-1 *Questions and answers relating to cafeteria plans.*

Q-1: What does section 125 of the Internal Revenue Code provide?

A-1: Section 125 provides that a participant in a nondiscriminatory cafeteria plan will not be treated as having received the taxable benefits offered under the plan solely because the participant has the opportunity, before the benefits become currently available to the participant, to choose among the taxable and nontaxable benefits offered under the plan.

Q-2: What is a "cafeteria plan" under section 125?

A-2: A "cafeteria plan" is a separate written benefit plan maintained by an employer for the benefit of its employees, under which all participants are employees and each participant has the opportunity to select the particular benefits that he desires. A cafeteria plan may offer participants the opportunity to select among various taxable benefits and nontaxable benefits, but a plan must offer at least one taxable benefit and at least one nontaxable benefit. For example, if participants are given the opportunity to elect only among two or more nontaxable benefits, the plan is not a cafeteria plan.

Q-3: What must the written cafeteria plan document contain?

A-3: The written document embodying a cafeteria plan must contain at least the following information: (i) A specific description of each of the benefits available under the plan, including the periods during which the benefits are provided (i.e., the periods of coverage), (ii) the plan's eligibility rules governing participation, (iii) the procedures governing participants' elections under the plan, including the period during which elections may be made, the extent to which elections are irrevocable, and the periods with respect to which elections are effective, (iv) the manner in which employer contributions may be made under the plan, such as by salary reduction agreement between the participant and the employer or by nonelective employer contributions to the plan, (v) the maximum amount of employer contributions available to any participant under the plan, and (vi) the plan year on which the cafeteria plan operates.

In describing the benefits available under the cafeteria plan, the plan document need not be self-contained. For example, the plan document may include by reference benefits established under other "separate written plans," such as coverage under a qualified group legal services plan (section 120) or under a dependent care assistance program (section 129), without describing in full the benefits established under these other plans. But, for example, if the plan offers different maximum levels of coverage under a dependent care assistance program, the descriptions must specify the available maximums. In addition, an

arrangement under which a participant is provided with coverage under a dependent care assistance program for dependent care expenses incurred during the period of coverage up to a specified amount (e.g., $500) and the right to receive, either directly or indirectly in the form of cash or any other benefit, any portion of the specified amount that is not reimbursed for such expenses will be considered a single benefit and must be fully described as such in the plan document. This also is the case with other benefits, such as coverage under an accident or health plan and coverage under a qualified group legal services plan. See Q&A-17 and Q&A-18 regarding the taxability of such benefit arrangements.

Q-4: What does the term "employees" mean under section 125?

A-4: The term "employees" includes present and former employees of the employer. All employees who are treated as employed by a single employer under subsections (b), (c), or (m) of section 414 are treated as employed by a single employer for purposes of section 125. The term "employees" does not, however, include self-employed individuals described in section 401(c) of the Code. Even though former employees generally are treated as employees, a cafeteria plan may not be established predominantly for the benefit of former employees of the employer.

In addition, even though the spouses and other beneficiaries of participants may not be participants in a cafeteria plan, a plan may provide benefits to spouses and beneficiaries of participants. For example, the spouse of a participant may not be permitted to participate actively in a cafeteria plan (i.e., the spouse may not be given the opportunity to select or purchase benefits offered by the plan), but the spouse of a participant may benefit from the participant's selection of family medical insurance coverage or of coverage under a dependent care assistance program. A participant's spouse will not be treated as actively participating in a cafeteria plan merely because the spouse has the right, upon the death of the participant, to select among various settlement options available with respect to a death benefit selected by the participant under the cafeteria plan or to elect among permissible distribution options with respect to the deceased participant's benefits under a cash or deferred arrangement that is part of the cafeteria plan.

Q-5: What benefits may be offered to participants under a cafeteria plan?

A-5: With the exception of benefits that defer the receipt of compensation (see Q&A-7), a cafeteria plan may offer participants the opportunity to select among certain taxable benefits and nontaxable benefits described in the plan document. The term "taxable benefit" means cash, property, or other benefits attributable to employer contributions that are currently taxable to the participant under the Internal Revenue Code upon receipt by the participant. The term "nontaxable benefit" means any benefit attributable to employer contributions to the extent that such benefit is not currently taxable to the participant under the Internal Revenue Code upon receipt of the benefit. Thus, a cafeteria plan may offer participants the following benefits, which will be nontaxable when provided in accordance with the applicable provisions of the Internal Revenue Code: group-term life insurance up to $50,000 (section 79), coverage under an accident or health plan (section 106), coverage under a qualified group legal services plan (section 120), and coverage under a dependent care assistance program (section 129). Also, amounts received by participants under one of these benefits may or may not be taxable depending upon whether such amounts qualify for an exclusion from gross income. See Q&A-17 and Q&A-18 regarding the inclusion of an accident or health plan, dependent care assistance program, or qualified group legal services plan in a cafeteria plan. Also, see Q&A-7 regarding the inclusion of deferred compensation benefits in a cafeteria plan.

In addition, a cafeteria plan may offer benefits that are nontaxable because they are attributable to after-tax employee contributions. For example, a cafeteria plan may offer participants the opportunity to purchase, with after-tax employee contributions, coverage under an accident or health plan providing for the payment of disability benefits. A participant's receipt of coverage under such an accident or health plan would not trigger taxable income because the coverage would be purchased with after-tax employee contributions. Similarly, any amounts paid to a participant under such an accident or health plan on account of disability incurred during the year of coverage may be nontaxable under section 104(a)(3).

Q-6: May employer contributions to a cafeteria plan be made pursuant to a salary reduction agreement between the participant and employer?

A-6: Yes. The term "employer contributions" means amounts that have not been actually or constructively received (after taking section 125 into account) by the participant and have been specified in the plan document as available to a participant for the purpose of selecting or "purchasing" benefits under the plan. A plan document may provide that the employer will make employer contributions, in whole or in part, pursuant to salary reduction agreements under which participants elect to reduce their compensation or to forego increases in compensation and to have such amounts contributed, as employer contributions, by the employer on their behalf. A salary reduction agreement will have the effect of causing the amounts contributed thereunder to be treated as employer contributions under a cafeteria plan only to the extent the agreement relates to compensation that has not been actually or constructively received by the participant as of the date of the agreement (after taking section 125 into account) and, subsequently, does not become currently available to the participant. In addition, a plan document also may provide that the employer will make employer contributions on behalf of participants equal to specified amounts (or specified percentages of compensation) and that such nonelective contributions will be available to participants for the selection or purchase of benefits under the plan.

Q-7: May a cafeteria plan offer a benefit that defers the receipt of compensation?

A-7: No. A cafeteria plan does not include any plan that offers a benefit that defers the receipt of compensation, with the exception of the opportunity for participants to make elective contributions under a qualified cash or deferred arrangement defined in section 401(k). Thus, employer contributions made at a participant's election to a profit-sharing plan containing a qualified cash or deferred arrangement will be treated as nontaxable benefits under a cafeteria plan.

In addition, a cafeteria plan does not include a plan that operates in a manner that enables participants to defer the receipt of compensation. Generally, a plan that permits participants to carry over unused benefits or contributions from one plan year to a subsequent plan year operates to enable participants to defer the receipt of compensation. This is the case regardless of whether the plan permits participants to convert the unused contributions or benefits into another benefit in the subsequent plan year. For example, a plan that offers participants the opportunity to purchase vacation days (or to receive cash or other benefits under the plan in lieu of vacation days) will not be a cafeteria plan if participants who purchase the vacation days for a plan year are allowed to use any unused days in a subsequent plan year. This is the case even though the plan does not permit the participant to convert, in the subsequent plan year, the unused vacation days into any other benefit.In determining whether a plan permits participants to carry over unused vacation days, a participant will be deemed to have used his nonelective vacation days (i.e., the vacation days with respect to which the participant had no election under the plan) before his elective vacation days. For example, assume that an employer provides a participant with three weeks of vacation for a year and, under the plan, the participant is permitted to receive cash or other benefits in lieu of one of these three weeks. Assume that the participant elects not to exchange the one elective week of vacation for another benefit. If the participant uses two weeks of vacation during the year, he will be treated as having used the two nonelective weeks of vacation. Thus, if the participant is permitted to carry the one unused week over to the next year, the plan will be treated as operating to enable participants to defer the receipt of compensation. Thus, the plan will fail to be a cafeteria plan and the section 125 exception to the constructive receipt rules will not apply.

In addition, a plan that allows participants to use employer contributions for one plan year to purchase a benefit that will be provided in a subsequent plan year operates to enable participants to defer the receipt of compensation.

→ **Caution: Q-8 has been republished and A-8 has been revised in proposed regulations at ¶ 20,227 and at ¶ 20,247.**

Q-8: What requirements apply to participants' elections under a cafeteria plan?

A-8: A plan is not a cafeteria plan unless the plan requires that participants make elections among the benefits offered under the plan. A plan may provide that elections may be made at any time. However, benefit elections under a cafeteria plan should be made in accordance with certain guidelines (see Q&A-15) in order for participants to qualify for the protections of the section 125 exception to the constructive receipt rules. An election will not be deemed to have been made if, after a participant has elected and begun to receive a benefit under the plan, the participant is permitted to revoke the election, even if the revocation relates only to that portion of the benefit that has not yet been provided to the participant. For example, a plan that permits a participant to revoke his election of coverage under a dependent care assistance program or of coverage under an accident or health plan after the period of coverage has commenced will not be a cafeteria plan. However, a cafeteria plan may permit a participant to revoke a benefit

election after the period of coverage has commenced and to make a new election with respect to the remainder of the period of coverage if both the revocation and new election are on account of and consistent with a change in family status (e.g., marriage, divorce, death of spouse or child, birth or adoption of child, and termination of employment of spouse).

Q-9: What is the tax treatment of benefits offered under a nondiscriminatory cafeteria plan?

A-9: A participant in a nondiscriminatory cafeteria plan will not be treated as having received taxable benefits offered under the plan and thus will not be required to include the benefits in gross income solely because the plan offers the participants the opportunity, before the benefits become currently available to the participant, to elect to receive or not to receive the benefits. Section 125 thus provides an exception to the constructive receipt rules that apply with respect to employee elections among nontaxable benefits (including cash). These constructive receipt rules generally provide that an individual will be required to include in gross income the taxable benefits that he could have elected to receive if the individual had the opportunity to elect to receive or not to receive the benefits even though both the opportunity to make this election occurs and the actual election is made before the benefits become currently available to the individual. Section 125 does not, however, alter the application of the constructive receipt rules to a situation in which benefits become currently available to an individual even though the individual elects not to receive and does not actually receive the benefits. Thus, if taxable benefits become currently available to a participant in a nondiscriminatory cafeteria plan, the participant will be taxable on the benefits, even though the participant has elected or subsequently elects not to receive the benefits and does not actually receive the benefits.

Q-10: What is the tax treatment of benefits offered under a discriminatory cafeteria plan?

A-10: The section 125 exception to the constructive receipt rules is not available to the highly compensated participants in a cafeteria plan that is discriminatory for a plan year. Thus, a highly compensated participant in a cafeteria plan that is discriminatory for a plan year will be taxable on the combination of the taxable benefits with the greatest aggregate value that he could have selected for the plan year. The section 125 exception to the constructive receipt rules remains available to participants who are not highly compensated without regard to whether the cafeteria plan is discriminatory.

Q-11: How are the amounts taxable to a highly compensated participant because a cafeteria plan is discriminatory for a plan year to be allocated among the benefits actually selected by the participant for the plan year?

A-11: A highly compensated participant in a discriminatory cafeteria plan is taxable on the maximum taxable benefits that he could have selected for the plan year. For example, assume that a cafeteria plan provides a highly compensated participant with the opportunity to select, for a plan year, benefits costing $1300 from among the following: up to $300 in cash, coverage under an accident or health plan providing medical expense reimbursement (cost of $600), coverage under an accident or health plan providing disability benefits (cost of $200), coverage under a qualified legal services plan (cost of $400), and coverage under a dependent care assistance program (cost of $400). For the plan year in question, the participant elects to receive $100 in cash, coverage under both the accident or health plans ($600 and $200), and coverage under the dependent care assistance program ($400). If the cafeteria plan is discriminatory for the plan year, the participant will be taxable on the $100 cash benefit actually selected and on the $200 cash benefit that the participant could have selected. This $300 will be allocated, first, to the taxable benefits actually selected by the participant and, second, on a pro rata basis to the nontaxable benefits actually selected by the participant. Thus, $100 is allocated to the $100 cash benefit actually received and the $200 is allocated as employee contributions among the nontaxable benefits actually selected as follows: $100 to coverage under the accident or health plan for medical care, $33.33 to the coverage under the accident or health plan for disability benefits, and $66.67 to the coverage under the dependent care assistance program.

This allocation would not affect the nontaxable status of any of these benefits—the purchase of coverage under any of these plans with employee contributions would not trigger taxable income—but it may affect the taxability of amounts received under any of the plans. In addition, depending upon whether other conditions are satisfied, the participant may be able to deduct under section 213 some or all of the employee cost of the coverage under the accident or health plan for medical care. Thus, reimbursements received by the participant for medical care expenses incurred during the year of coverage may be nontaxable under either section 104(a)(3) or section 105(b), depending upon whether the reimbursements are attributable to after-tax employee or pre-tax employer contributions. Also, if the participant became disabled during the year of coverage, benefits provided under the accident or health plan would be nontaxable to the participant under section 104(a)(3) to the extent that the benefits were attributable to the portion of the coverage purchased with the after-tax employee contributions. Finally, any reimbursements received under the dependent care assistance program for the year of coverage will be nontaxable under section 129 if the requirements of that section are satisfied.

Q-12: When must a highly compensated participant in a discriminatory cafeteria plan include in gross income amounts attributable to the taxable benefits that the participants could have selected, but did not in fact select?

A-12: Amounts required to be included in gross income by a highly compensated participant because a cafeteria plan does not satisfy the applicable nondiscrimination standards for a plan year will be treated as received or accrued in the participant's taxable year within which ends the plan year with respect to which an election was or could have been made.

Q-13: Who are highly compensated participants under section 125?

A-13: The term "highly compensated participant" means a participant who is an officer, a shareholder owning more than 5 percent of the voting power or value of all classes of stock of the employer, or highly compensated. The classification of a participant as highly compensated for this purpose will be made on the basis of the facts and circumstances of each case. A spouse or a dependent (within the meaning of section 152) of sny such "highly compensated participant" will be treated as highly compensated.

Q-14: When will a benefit be treated as currently available to a participant in a cafeteria plan?

A-14: A benefit is treated as currently available to a participant if the participant is free to receive the benefit currently at his discretion or the participant could receive the benefit currently if an election or notice of an intent to receive the benefit were given. A benefit will not be treated as not currently available merely because a requirement that the participant must elect or give notice of intent to receive the benefit in advance of receipt of the benefit. However, a benefit is not currently available to a participant if there is a substantial limitation or restriction on the participant's receipt of the benefit. A benefit will not be treated as currently available if the participant may under no circumstances receive the benefit before a particular time in the future and there is a substantial risk that, if the participant does not fulfill specified conditions during the period proceding this time, the participant will not receive the benefit.

Q-15: What procedures with respect to benefit elections should a cafeteria plan adopt in order to assure that participants are not subject to tax, under the constructive receipt rules, on taxable benefits that the participants have elected not to receive?

A.15: Generally, in order for participants to avoid constructive receipt with respect to taxable benefits offered under a cafeteria plan, the taxable benefits must at no time become currently available to the participants. Thus, a cafeteria plan should require participants to elect the specific benefits that they will receive before the taxable benefits become currently available. A benefit will not be treated as currently available as of the time of the election if the election specifies the future period for which the benefit will be provided and the election is made before the beginning of this period.

In addition, after the beginning of the specified period for which the benefits are provided, the taxable benefits must not become currently aviailable to the participants. After the commencement of this period, taxable benefits will be treated as currently available if participants have the right to revoke their elections of nontaxable benefits and instead to receive the taxable benefits for such period, without regard to whether the participants actually revoke their elections. For example, assume that a cafeteria plan offers each participant the opportunity to elect, for a plan year, between coverage under a dependent care assistance program for up to $2000 of the dependent care expenses incurred by the participant during the plan year or a cash benefit of $2000 for the year. If the plan requires participants to elect between these benefits before the beginning of the plan year and, after the year has commenced, the participants are prohibited from revoking their elections, participants who elected coverage under the dependent care assistance program will not be taxable on the cash benefit of $2000. But if, after the beginning of the plan year, participants have the right to revoke their elections of coverage under the dependent care assistance program and thereby to receive the cash benefit, the participants will be treated as having received the $2000 in cash even though they do not revoke their elections. The same result would obtain even though the cash benefit is not payable until the end of the plan year. See Q&A-8, however, regarding the revocation of elections on account of changes in family status.

Q-16: Do the rules of section 125 affect whether any particular benefit offered under a cafeteria plan is a taxable or non-taxable benefit?

A-16: Generally, no. A benefit that is nontaxable under its Internal Revenue Code when offered separately is treated as a nontaxable benefit under a cafeteria plan only if the rules providing for the exclusion of the benefit from gross income continue to be satisfied when the benefit is offered under the cafeteria plan. For example, if $50,000 in group-term life insurance is offered under a cafeteria plan and the rules under section 79(a) governing the exclusion of the cost of this benefit from gross income are satisfied, the rules of section 79(d) still apply to determine the status of the benefit as taxable or nontaxable for key employees who participate in the plan. See Q&A-17 and Q&A-18, however, regarding the inclusion of coverage under an accident or health plan, dependent care assistance program, or qualified group legal services plan in a cafeteria plan.

Similarly, if a cafeteria plan offers benefits that are nontaxable under the Internal Revenue Code when offered outside of a cafeteria plan, but are prohibited from inclusion in a cafeteria plan, the benefits will be treated as taxable benefits under the cafeteria plan. Thus, coverage under a qualified transportation plan (section 124) and coverage under an educational assistance program (section 127) will be treated as taxable benefits if offered under a cafeteria plan. Also, any benefits (either reimbursement for expenses or in kind benefits) received by a participiant under a qualified transportation plan or an educational assistance program will be taxable if the benefits are provided under a cafeteria plan.

Finally, if a benefit that is taxable under the Internal Revenue Code when offered separately is offered under a cafeteria plan, the benefit will continue to be a taxable benefit under the cafeteria plan. For example, if a cafeteria plan offers a participant the opportunity to direct the employer to make charitable contributions or contributions to an individual retirement account on behalf of the participant, such contributions must be included in the participant's gross income for income and employment tax purposes without regard to whether the plan satisfies section 125 and without regard to whether the contributions are deductible by the participant.

Q-17: How are the specific rules of section 105, providing an income exclusion for amounts received as reimbursement for medical care expenses under an accident or heaalth plan, to be applied when coverage under an accident or health plan is offered as a benefit under a cafeteria plan?

A-17: Section 105(b) provides an exclusion from gross income for amounts that are paid to an employee under an employer-funded accident or health plan specifically to reimburse the employee for certain medical care expenses incurred by the employee during the period for which the benefit is provided to the employee, i.e., the period during which the employee is covered under the accident or health plan. Section 105(h) provides that the exclusion provided by section 105(b) is not available with respect to certain amounts received by a highly compensated individual (as defined in section 105(h)(5) under a discriminatory plan. Several rules are of particular importance when coverage under an accident or health plan is a benefit offered under a cafeteria plan.

First, in order for medical care reimbursments paid to a participant under a cafeteria plan to be treated as nontaxable under section 105(b), the reimbursements must be paid pursuant to an employer-funded "accident or health plan," as defined in section 105(e) and § 1.105-5. This means that, although the reimbursements need not be provided under a commercial insurance contract, the reimbursements must be provided under a benefit that exhibits the risk-shifting and risk-distribution characteristics of insurance. A benefit will not exhibit the required risk-shifting and risk-distribution characteristics, even though the benefit is provided under a commercial insurance contract, if the ordinary actuarial risk of the insurer is negated either under the terms of the benefit or by any related benefit or arrangement (including arrangements formally outside of the cafeteria plan).

Second, a cafeteria plan benefit under which a participant will receive reimbursements of medical expenses is a benefit within sections 106 and 105(b) only if, under the benefit, reimbursments are paid specifically to reimburse the participant for medical expenses incurred during the period of coverage. Amounts paid to a participant as reimbursement are not treated as paid specifically to reimburse the participant for medical expenses, if, under the benefit, the participant is entitled to the amounts, in the form of cash (e.g., routine payment of salary) or any other taxable or nontaxable benefit, irrespective of whether or not he incurs medical expenses during the period of coverage, even if the participant will not receive the amounts not used for expense reimbursement until the end of the period. A benefit under which participants will receive reimbursement for medical expenses up to a specified amount, if they incur non expenses, will receive cash or any other benefit in lieu of the reimbursements is not a benefit that qualifies for the exclusions under sections 106 and 105(b). See § 1.105-2. This is the case without regard to whether the benefit was purchased with contributions made at the employer's discretion, at the participant's discretion (such as pursuant to a salary reduction agreement), or pursuant to a collective bargaining agreement. For example, if a cafeteria plan offers participants coverage under an employer-funded plan that provides for the reimbursement of medical expenses incurred during the plan year up to a specified amount (e.g., $1,000) and the participants are entitled to receive, in the form of any other taxable or nontaxable benefits (including deferrals under a cash or deferred arrangement), any portion of the specified amount that is not paid as reimbursement for medical expenses, the employer contributions used to purchase the coverage will not qualify for the section 106 exclusion and any reimbursements paid to participants for expense incurred during the year of coverage will not be eligible for the section 105(b) exception. Arrangements formally outside of the cafeteria plan that provide for the adjustment of a participant's compensation or a participant's receipt of any other benefits on the basis of the expenses incurred or reimbursements received by the participant will be considered in determining whether the reimbursments are provided under a benefit eligible for the exclusions under sections 106 and 105(b).

Third, the medical expenses that are reimbursed under an accident or health plan must have been incurred during the period for which the participant is actually covered by the accident or health plan in order for the reimbursements to be excluded from gross income under section 105(b). For purposes of this rule, expenses are treated as having been incurred when the participant is provided with the medical care that gives rise to the medical expenses, and not when the participant is formally billed, charged for, or pays for the medical care. Also, for purposes of this rule, medical expenses that are incurred before the later of the date the plan is in existence and the date the participant is enrolled in the plan will not be treated as having been incurred during the period for which the participiant is covered by the plan. Thus, in order for reimbursements to be excluded from gross income under section 105(b), the accident or health plan must provide a participant the right to reimbursement for medical expenses incurred during a specified period of plan coverage. Reimbursements of expenses incurred prior to or after the specified period of coverage will not be excluded under section 105(b). However, the actual reimbursement of covered medical care expenses may be made after the applicable period of coverage.

Fourth, in order for reimbursements under an accident or health plan to qualify for the section 105(b) exclusion, the cafeteria plan may not operate in a manner that enables participants to purchase coverage under the accident or health plan only for periods during which the participants expect to incur medical care. For example, if a cafeteria plan permits participants to purchase coverage under an accident or health plan on a month-by-month or an expense-by-expense basis, reimbursements under the accident or health plan will not qualify for the section 105(b) exclusion. If, however, the period of coverage under an accident or health plan offered in a cafeteria plan is twelve months (or, in the case of a cafeteria plan's initial plan year, at least equal to the plan year) and the plan does not permit a participant to select specific amounts of coverage, reimbursement, or salary reduction for less than twelve months, the cafeteria plan will be deemed not to operate to enable participants to purchase coverage only for periods during which medical care will be incurred. See Q & A—8 regarding the revocation of elections during a period of coverage on account of changes in family status.

Fifth, in order for reimbursements to a highly compensated individual under a self-insured accident or health plan to be treated as nontaxable under a cafeteria plan, the discrimination rules of section 105(h) must be satisfied. For purposes of these rules, coverage under a self-insured accident or health plan offered by a cafeteria plan will be treated as an optional benefit (even if only one level and type of coverage is offered) and, for purposes of the optional benefit rule in § 1.105-11(c)(3)(i), employer contributions will be treated as employee contributions to the extent that taxable benefits are offered by the plan. In addition, the accident or health plan offered by the cafeteria plan must provide for the non-discriminatory reimbursement of expenses on a per capita basis, rather than as a proportion of compensation.

Q-18: How are the specific rules of section 129, providing an income exclusion for dependent care assistance provided under a dependent care assistance program, to be applied when coverage under a dependent care assistance program is offered as a benefit under a cafeteria plan?

A-18: Section 129(a) provides an employee with an exclusion from gross income both for employer-funded coverage under a dependent care assistance program and for amounts paid or incurred by the employer for dependent care assistance provided to the employee if the amounts are paid or incurred under a dependent care assistance program. A program under which participants receive reimbursements of dependent care expenses up to a specified amount and are entitled to receive, in the form of any other taxable or nontaxable benefits, any portion of the specified amount not used for reimbursement is to be treated as a single benefit that is not a dependent care assistance program within the scope of section 129. Thus, dependent care assistance provided under a cafeteria plan will be treated as provided under a dependent care assistance porogram only if, after the participant has elected coverage under the program and the period of coverage has commenced, the participant does not have the right to receive amounts under the program other than as reimbursements for dependent care expenses. This is the case without regard to whether coverage under the program was purchased with contributions made at the employer's discretion, at the participant's discretion, or pursuant to a collective bargaining agreement. For example, assume a cafeteria plan allows participants to elect to receive, for a particular plan year, either the right to reimbursements of dependent care expenses incurred dcuring the year up to $2,000 or a cash benefit of $2,000. If the participant elects the right to receive reimbursements of dependent care expenses, the reimbursements will not be treated as made under a dependent care assistance program if, after the period of coverage has commenced, the participant has the right to revoke his election of this benefit and instead to receive the cash or if, under the terms of the program itself, the participant is entitled to receive, in the form of cash (e.g., routine payment of salary) or any other benefit, any amounts not reimbursed for dependent care provided during the period of coverage. Arrangements formally outside of the cafeteria plan that provide for the adjustment on a participant's compensation or a participant's receipt of any other benefits on the basis of the assistance or reimbursements received by the participants will be considered in determining whether a dependent care benefit is a dependent care assistance program under section 129.

Moreover, in order for dependent care assistance to be treated as provided under a dependent care assistance program eligible for the section 129 exclusion, the care must be provided to or on behalf of the participant during the period for which the participant is covered by the program. For example, if a participant elects coverage for a plan year under a dependent care assistance program that provides for the reimbursement of dependent care expenses, only reimbursements for dependent care expenses incurred during that plan year will be treated as having been provided under a dependent care assistance program within the scope of section 129. For purposes of this rule, dependent care expenses will be treated as having been incurred when the dependent care is provided, and not when the participant is formally billed, charged for, or pays for the dependent care. Also, for purposes of this rule, expenses that are incurred before the later of the date the program is in existence and the date the participant is enrolled in the program will not be treated as having been incurred during the period for which the participant is covered by the program. Similarly, if the dependent care assistance program furnishes the dependent care in kind (e.g., under an employer-maintained child care facility), only dependent care provided during the plan year of coverage will be treated as having been provided under a dependent care assistance program within scope of section 129.

In addition, in order for dependent care assistance under a cafeteria plan to be treated as provided under a dependent care assistance program eligible for the section 129 exclusion, the plan may not operate in a manner that enables participants to purchase coverage under the program only for periods during which the participants expect to receive dependent care assistance. If the period of coverage under a dependent care assistance program offered by a cafeteria plan is twelve months (or, in the case of a cafeteria plan's initial plan year, at least equal to the plan year) and the plan does not permit a participant to select specific amounts of coverage, reimbursement, or salary reduction for less than twelve months, the plan will be deemed not to operate to enable participants to purchase coverage only for periods during which dependent care assistance will be received. See Q&A-8 regarding the revocation of elections during the period of coverage on account of changes in family status.

Finally, if coverage under a dependent care assistance program is a benefit offered under a cafeteria plan, the rules of section 129 will determine the status of the benefit as a taxable or nontaxable benefit. As a result, coverage under a dependent care assistance program in a cafeteria plan will be nontaxable for a plan year only if, among other requirements, the principal shareholder and owner discrimination test contained in section 129(d)(4) is satisfied with respect to employer contributions actually used to provide participants with dependent care assistance during the plan year. In addition, amounts paid or incurred by the employer under a dependent care assistance program are excludable from gross income only to the extent that these amounts do not exceed the lesser of the participant's earned income or the participant's spouse's earned income.

Rules similar to the rules applicable to dependent care assistance program apply with respect to coverage under a qualified group legal services plan (section 120) offered as a benefit under a cafeteria plan.

Q-19: What are the rules governing whether a cafeteria plan is discriminatory?

A-19: The applicable discrimination rules under section 125 provide that, in order to be treated as nondiscriminatory for a plan year, a cafeteria plan must not discriminate in favor of highly compensated participants as to benefits and contributions for that plan year. Generally, this discrimination determination will be made on the basis of the facts and circumstances of each case. Section 125(c) provides that a cafeteria plan does not discriminate where either (i) total nontaxable benefits and total benefits or (ii) employer contributions allocable to total nontaxable benefits and employer contributions allocable to total benefits do not discriminate in favor of highly compensated participants. A cafeteria plan must satisfy section 125(c) with respect to both benefit availability and benefit selection. Thus, a plan must give each participant an equal opportunity to select nontaxable benefits, and the actual selection of nontaxable benefits under the plan must not be discriminatory, i.e., highly compensated participants do not disproportionately select nontaxable benefits while other participants select taxable benefits.

In addition to not discriminating as to either benefit availability or benefit selection, a cafeteria plan must not discriminate in favor of highly compensated participants in actual operation. A plan may be discriminatory in actual operation if the duration of the plan (or of a particular nontaxable benefit offered under the plan) coincides with the period during which highly compensated participants utilize the plan (or the benefit).

Q-20: May nontaxable benefits provided under a cafeteria plan be counted as "compensation" under section 401(a)(5) for purposes of determining whether a qualified pension, profit-sharing, or stock bonus plan discriminates under section 410(a)(4), or under section 415 for purposes of the limitations contained in that section?

A-20: A qualified pension, profit-sharing, or stock bonus plan will not be treated as discriminatory within the meaning of section 401(a)(4) merely because, for purposes of allocating contributions to the participant or calculating the participant's benefit under the plan, the plan considers nontaxable benefits provided to a participant as compensation. For example, if a participant in a cafeteria plan elects coverage under an accident or health plan, the value of such coverage may be considered as compensation under a qualified plan for purposes of calculating the participant's allocation or benefit under the qualified plan. Nontaxable reimbursements under the accident or health plan, however, generally may not be treated as compensation under a qualified plan. Similarly, the value of coverage under a dependent care assistance program may be counted as compensation under a qualified plan for allocation and benefit purposes, but nontaxable reimbursements of dependent care expenses under the program generally may not be treated as compensation for these purposes. On the other hand, a qualified plan will not be treated as discriminatory under section 401(a)(4) merely because the plan does not consider nontaxable benefits, such as coverage under an accident or health plan or coverage under a dependent care assistance program, as compensation for allocation or benefit purposes under the plan.

For purposes of section 415, "compensation" does not include amounts that are excluded from gross income, such as premiums for group-term life insurance under section 79 or employer contributions to an accident or health plan excluded under section 106.

→ **Caution: Q&A-21 have been replaced by a new Q&A-21 in proposed regulations at ¶ 20,137R.**

Q-21: What are the effective dates of the rules contained in these questions and answers?

A-21: These rules contained in questions and answers relating to section 125 generally shall apply to plan years of cafeteria plans beginning after December 31, 1978. However, a cafeteria plan that failed to satisfy one or more of the following rules for plan years beginning before May 7, 1984 will not be deemed thereby to have failed to satisfy section 125 for such plan years if, by September 4, 1984, the plan is amended to operate in accordance with these rules: (i) the rules requiring certain information to be included in the cafeteria plan document (Q&A-3), (ii) the rules governing the active participating of a participant's spouse in a cafeteria plan (Q&A-4), (iii) only in the case of a plan under which participants were permitted neither to carry over unused benefits for more than one plan year nor to convert, into any benefits, any unused benefits that had been carried over to a subsequent plan year, the rules prohibiting the carryover of any unused contribution or benefit from one plan year to a subsequent plan year (Q&A-7), and (iv) the rules limiting the revocability of benefit elections (Q&A-8). A cafeteria plan may treat the portion of its current plan year remaining after September 4, 1984 as a new period of coverage for purposes of satisfying the rules governing benefit elections (Q&A-8). Also, a benefit offering participants the opportunity to make elective contributions under a qualified cash or deferred arrangement may be included in a cafeteria plan only in plan years beginning after December 31, 1980.

The rules contained in Q&A-17 governing the taxability of coverage and benefits under an accident or health plan relate specifically to sections 105 and 106 and thus generally are effective with respect to all taxable years beginning after December 31, 1953. The rules contained in Q&A-18 governing the taxability of coverage and benefits under a dependent care assistance program relate specifically to section 129 and thus generally are effective with respect to all taxable years beginning after December 31, 1981. The rules contained in Q&A-18 governing the taxability of coverage and benefits under a qualified group legal services plan relate specifically to section 120 and thus generally are effective with respect to all taxable years beginning after December 31, 1976. However, if coverage under an accident or health plan, dependent care assistance program, or qualified group legal services plan was offered as a benefit under a cafeteria plan as such benefit failed to satisfy, before May 7, 1984, the rule prohibiting a plan from operating to enable a participant to elect coverage under an accident or health plan, a dependent care assistance program, or a qualified group legal services plan only for periods during which the participant expects to receive medical care, dependent care, or legal services (Q&A-17 and Q&A-18), such benefit will not be deemed solely on account of such failure to have failed to satisfy the statutory rules providing for the income exclusion of such coverage or of any benefits provided thereunder, if, by September 4, 1984, the cafeteria plan is amended to operate in accordance with such election of coverage rule. A cafeteria plan may treat the portion of its current plan year remaining after September 4, 1984 as a new period of coverage and as an initial plan year for purposes of satisfying the rule prohibiting a plan from operating to enable participants to elect coverage under an accident or health plan, dependent care assistance program, or qualified group legal services plan only for periods during which they expect to receive medical care, dependent care, or legal services (Q&A-17 and Q&A-18).

In addition, if the conditions set forth below are satisfied, employer contributions (including elective and nonelective contributions) made before June 1, 1984, under an arrangement described in the next sentence which is part of a cafeteria plan, will not be treated as having been made to an accident or health plan, dependent care assistance program, or qualified group legal services plan that fails to satisfy the rules contained in the second and third paragraph of Q&A-17 and the first paragraph of Q&A-18, merely because, for a plan year, a participant was entitled to receive, in the form of cash or any other taxable or nontaxable benefit, amounts available for reimbursement under the arrangement without regard to whether covered expenses are incurred. An arrangement is described in this sentence only if, under the arrangement,

(i) An account was actually established on behalf of the participant by the employer, by an entry of the employer's books or in similar fashion, prior to the beginning of the plan year (or prior to the date on which an individual first becomes eligible to participate under the arrangement in the case of an individual who first becomes eligible to participate, on account of years of employment, during the plan year);

(ii) The amount (or specific rate) of contributions to the account under the arrangement was fixed prior to the beginning of the plan year,

(iii) Neither the participant nor the employer possessed the right to increase or decrease contributions to the account during the plan year (but a plan may provide that contributions could be terminated during the year on account of the participant's (a) separation from service or

(b) cessation of participation under the arrangement for the remainder of the plan year);

(iv) Contributions were actually deposited in or credited to the account before being made available for reimbursement; and

(v) Distributions were not available for reasons other than reimbursement of covered expenses until the end of the plan year (but a plan may provide that a single distribution of the unreimbursed balance may be made on account of the participant's (a) separation from service or (b) cessation of participation under the arrangement for the remainder of the plan year).

A cafeteria plan may operate on a plan year other than the calendar year for purposes of this transitional rule, so long as terms of the plan permit contributions to a plan to be fixed only once during, and a distribution of the unreimbursed amount to be received, only once for any plan year, provided that contributions may be fixed for a short plan year of the plan's first period of operation. This transitional rule does not affect or alter the requirement of Q&A-17 and -18 that expenses that are reimbursed under an arrangement must have been incurred during the period for which the participant actually is covered by the arrangement.

Roscoe L. Egger, Jr.,

Commissioner of Internal Revenue.

[FR Doc. 84-12263 Filed 5-2-84; 2:49 pm]

¶ 20,137R

Proposed regulations: Cafeteria plans: Transition rules.—Reproduced below is the text of proposed regulations that amend portions of previously issued proposed regulations (¶ 20,137Q) relating to the tax treatment of cafeteria plans. The proposed regulations also provide transition rules relieving certain cafeteria plans from requirements of the earlier proposed regulations. The proposed regulations were filed with the Federal Register on December 26, 1984. They were published in the Federal Register on December 31, 1984 (49 FR 50733).

Back references: ¶ 9111, 9113, 9114, 9115, and 9118.

INTERNAL REVENUE SERVICE

[26 CFR Part 1]

[EE-16-79]

TAX TREATMENT OF CAFETERIA PLANS

(TRANSITION RULES) NOTICE OF PROPOSED RULEMAKING

AGENCY: Internal Revenue Service, Treasury.

ACTION: Amendment of notice of proposed rulemaking.

SUMMARY: This document contains proposed amendments to a notice of proposed rulemaking which was published in the Federal Register on May 7, 1984 (49 F.R. 19321). That notice contained proposed regulations relating to the tax treatment of cafeteria plans. Changes to the applicable tax law necessitating the proposed amendments were made by section 531(b)(5) of the Tax Reform Act of 1984. The proposed amendments relate to general and special transition relief under the proposed regulations and provide the public with the guidance needed to comply with that Act.

DATES: Written comments and requests for a public hearing must be delivered or mailed by January 30, 1985. The proposed regulations are generally to be effective for plan years beginning after December 31, 1978, but are subject to the general and special transition rules.

ADDRESS: Send comments and requests for a public hearing to: Commissioner of Internal Revenue, Attention: CC:LR:T (EE-16-79), Washington, D.C. 20224.

FOR FURTHER INFORMATION CONTACT: Harry Beker of the Employee Plans and Exempt Organizations Division, Office of the Chief Counsel, Internal Revenue Service, 1111 Constitution Avenue, N.W., Washington, D.C. 20224 (Attention: CC:EE) (202-566-6212) (not a toll-free call).

SUPPLEMENTAL INFORMATION:

Background

This document contains proposed amendments to the notice of proposed rulemaking under section 125 of the Internal Revenue Code of 1954. On May 7, 1984, the Federal Register published proposed regulations relating to the tax treatment of cafeteria plans (49 FR 19321). The regulations in this document are being proposed in order to replace portions of these earlier proposed regulations which have been rendered obsolete by section 531(b)(5) of the Tax Reform Act of 1984 (98 Stat. 494). The proposed regulations are issued under the authority contained in section 7805 of the Internal Revenue Code of 1954 (68A Stat. 917, 26 U.S.C. 7805).

On February 10, 1984, the Internal Revenue Service issued a news release (IR-84-22) which stated that so-called "flexible spending arrangements" do not provide employees with nontaxable benefits under the Code because, under such arrangements, employees are assured of receiving the benefit of what they would have received had no covered expenses been incurred.

On May 7, 1984, proposed regulations in question and answer form were published in the Federal Register. Q&A-21 provided that the proposed regulations were generally to be effective for cafeteria plan years beginning after December 31, 1978. However, as to particular rules in the proposed regulations, a cafeteria plan could be amended by September 4, 1984, to meet those particular rules and thus the requirements of the proposed regulations. In addition, as to benefits provided under a flexible spending arrangement which was part of a cafeteria plan, if such arrangement met specified conditions, the benefits (funded by employer contributions made before June 1, 1984) qualified for the statutory exclusion notwithstanding that a cash-out of unused contributions was available at the end of the plan year.

General Rules

The Tax Reform Act of 1984 renders Q&A-21 obsolete and provides both general and special transition relief from certain of the rules in the proposed regulations for certain cafeteria plans and flexible spending arrangements. First, as to plans and arrangements which were in existence on or before February 10, 1984 (or for which substantial implementation costs had been incurred before such date) and which failed on or before such date and continued to fail thereafter to satisfy the proposed regulations, general transition relief is provided until January 1, 1985, provided that the plans or arrangements are not modified after February 10, 1984, to allow additional benefits.

Second, as to flexible spending arrangements which qualify for general transition relief through December 31, 1984, under which an employee must fix the amount of contributions before the beginning of the period of coverage and under which unused contributions generally are not available to the employee before July 1, 1985, special transition relief is available until July 1, 1985, provided there are no modifications after December 31, 1984, which allow for additional benefits.

Section 7805(b) Relief for Amended and Suspended Plans and Benefits

Section 531(b)(5)(A) of the Tax Reform Act grants general transition relief only to cafeteria plans and benefits (including benefits that are provided through flexible spending arrangements) that failed on or before February 10, 1984, and "continued to fail thereafter" to satisfy the rules in the proposed regulations. In addition, general transition relief is available only until the effective date, after February 10, 1984, "of any modification to provide additional benefits."

A plan or benefit that has been modified (by amendment or otherwise) after February 10, 1984, so that the plan or benefit no longer continues to fail one or more of the rules of the proposed regulations (a "conforming modification") does not "continue to fail thereafter" and therefore does not meet the requirement of the statute for continued general transition relief with respect to the rule or rules in question. For example, if contributions or reimbursements (or both) under a flexible spending arrangement have been suspended, the benefit provided through the flexible spending arrangement does not satisfy the statute for continued relief. Furthermore, a modification to restore a plan or benefit to its condition before a conforming modification (e.g., a reactivation of contributions or reimbursements or both under a suspended flexible spending arrangement) would be a "modification to provide additional benefits." Therefore, as to a plan or benefit which, after February 10, 1984, was modified so that it no longer failed to satisfy one or more of the rules in the proposed regulations, general transition relief is available only until the effective date of the modification but not thereafter with respect to the rule or rules in question. These statutory requirements are reflected in Q&A-25.

The Internal Revenue Service has determined, however, that participants in plans or benefits that were modified, after February 10, 1984, so that they no longer fail to satisfy one or more of the rules in the proposed regulations should not be disadvantaged because of such conforming modifications. In order to limit any adverse effect upon those participants, the Internal Revenue Service has determined to grant such plans and benefits relief under section 7805(b) of the Internal Revenue Code (see Q&A-26). Accordingly, the rules delineated in Q&A-27 generally do not become effective with respect to such plans or benefits until January 1, 1985.

Pursuant to the grant of section 7805(b) relief, a plan or benefit that has been modified, after February 10, 1984, so that it no longer fails to satisfy one or more of the rules in the proposed regulations may be further modified and continue in operation until December 31, 1984, but only under the same terms that applied immediately before the conforming modification. However, because such modified plans or benefits do not qualify for general transition relief through December 31, 1984, special transition relief is not available to such plans or benefits.

In addition, pursuant to the grant of section 7805(b) relief, certain relief is available, as set forth in Q&A-29, for cafeteria plans or benefits that were eligible for transition relief under the regulations proposed on May 7, 1984, but are not eligible for general transition relief under Q&A-25.

Nonapplicability of Executive Order 12291

The Treasury Department has determined that this regulation is not subject to review under Executive Order 12291 or the Treasury and Office of Management and Budget implementation of the Order dated April 29, 1983.

Regulatory Flexibility Act

Although this document is a notice of proposed rulemaking which solicits public comment, the Internal Revenue Service has concluded that the regulations proposed herein are interpretative and that the notice and public procedure requirements of 5 U.S.C. 533 do not apply. Accordingly, these proposed regulations do not constitute regulations subject to the Regulatory Flexibility Act (5 U.S.C. chapter 6).

Comments and Request for a Public Hearing

Before adopting these proposed regulations, consideration will be given to any written comments that are submitted (preferably seven copies) to the Commissioner of Internal Revenue. All comments will be available for public inspection and copying. A public hearing will be held upon request to the Commissioner by any person who has submitted written comments. If a public hearing is held, notice of the time and place will be published in the Federal Register.

Drafting Information

The principal author of these proposed regulations is Harry Beker of the Employee Plans and Exempt Organizations Division of the Office of Chief Counsel, Internal Revenue Service. However, personnel from other offices of the Internal Revenue Service and Treasury Department participated in developing the regulations, both on matters of substance and style.

List of Subjects in 26 CFR §§ 1.61-1-1.281-4

Income taxes, Taxable income.

Proposed amendments to the regulations

The proposed amendments to 26 CFR Part 1 are as follows:

Paragraph 1. Q & A-21 of proposed § 1.125-1 as published in the Federal Register on May 7, 1984 (43 FR 19328-19329) is removed.

Par. 2. New Qs & As of proposed § 1.125-1 are substituted to read as follows:

§ 1.125-1 Questions and Answers Relating to Cafeteria Plans

* * *

Q-21: What are the general effective dates of the rules in Q & A-1 through Q & A-20?

A-21: The rules in Q & A-1 through Q & A-20 relating to section 125 generally apply to plan years of cafeteria plans beginning after December 31, 1978.

The rules in Q & A-17 governing the taxability of coverage and benefits received under an accident or health plan relate specifically to sections 105 and 106 and thus generally are effective with respect to all taxable years beginning after December 31, 1953. The rules in Q & A-18 governing the taxability of coverage and benefits received under a

dependent care assistance program relate specifically to section 129 and thus generally are effective with respect to all taxable years beginning after December 31, 1981. The rules in Q & A-18 governing the taxability of coverage and benefits received under a qualified group legal services plan relate specifically to section 120 and thus generally are effective with respect to all taxable years beginning after December 31, 1976.

See Q & A-22 through Q & A-28 for the general and special transition rules, which provide delayed effective dates with respect to certain of these rules. See also Q & A-29 for certain relief that is available for cafeteria plans or benefits that were eligible for transition relief under the regulations proposed on May 7, 1984, but are not eligible for general transition relief under Q & A-25.

Q-22: Which cafeteria plans and benefits provided under cafeteria plans are eligible for the general and special transition relief?

A-22: There are two transition rules providing delayed effective dates with respect to certain of the rules in Q & A-1 through Q & A-20. First, general transition relief, as described in Q & A-25 and Q & A-27, is provided to cafeteria plans that were in existence on or before February 10, 1984, and to benefits (including benefits that are provided through flexible spending arrangements) in existence on or before such day. Second, special transition relief, as described in Q & A-28, is provided to certain benefits (including benefits that are provided through flexible spending arrangements) that (i) were in existence on or before February 10, 1984, and (ii) qualify for general transition relief through December 31, 1984. See Q & A-23 and Q & A-24 for the rules for determining whether a cafeteria plan or a benefit was in existence on or before February 10, 1984.

Flexible spending arrangements are used to pay benefits, such as medical, legal, or dependent care assistance, that are intended to qualify as nontaxable under the applicable rules of the Code. Generally, under the flexible spending arrangement form of a benefit, a participant is assured of receiving, in salary, cash or some other form, amounts that are available for expense reimbursement during the period of coverage without regard to whether the participant incurs covered expenses during the period.

Plans or arrangements that are not cafeteria plans because of a failure to satisfy one or more of the rules specified in Q & A-27 will be treated as cafeteria plans solely for purposes of the transition relief set forth in Q & A-21 through Q & A-29. For example, a plan providing only a medical benefit through a flexible spending arrangement will be treated as a cafeteria plan for purposes of the transition relief only. Also, a plan under which a participant may elect among two or more benefits, each of which would be nontaxable but for the failure of one of the benefits to satisfy certain of the requirements in Q & A-17 or Q & A-18, will be treated as a cafeteria plan to determine eligibility for transition relief under Q & A-21 through Q & A-29.

Q-23: What rules apply to determine whether a cafeteria plan or a benefit was in existence on or before February 10, 1984?

A-23: A cafeteria plan will be treated as existence on or before February 10, 1984, if on or before such day (i) the plan was reduced to writing and communicated to employees in written form and (ii) amounts were contributed with respect to benefits provided under the plan.

A cafeteria plan will be treated as having been reduced to writing if the available benefits and the operation of such plan have been fully described in written form (e.g., by summary plan description or plan brochure), even though a formal plan document may not have been written. Amounts will be treated as having been contributed with respect to benefits provided under the plan if the employer made contributions (including contributions pursuant to salary reduction agreements) to purchase or provide benefits elected under the plan.

A cafeteria plan that was not actually in existence on or before February 10, 1984, nevertheless will be treated as in existence on or before such day if the employer incurred "substantial implementation costs" with respect to that particular plan. See Q & A-24 for a discussion of the rules applicable to the "substantial implementation cost" determination.

A benefit will be treated as in existence on or before February 10, 1984, only if on or before such day (i) the benefit was part of a cafeteria plan that was in existence on or before February 10, 1984, (ii) the benefit was fully described in written form and communicated to employees in such form (e.g., as part of the summary plan description or plan brochure), and (iii) amounts were contributed with respect to the benefit under the plan. A benefit that was not actually in existence on or before February 10, 1984, is not eligible for general transition relief.

Q-24: What rules apply in determining whether an employer has incurred "substantial implementation costs" with respect to a particular plan?

A-24: A cafeteria plan that was not actually in existence on or before February 10, 1984, will be treated as in existence on or before such day only if the employer incurred "substantial implementation costs" with respect to that particular plan. An employer will be treated as having incurred "substantial implementation costs" with respect to a particular plan only if, before February 10, 1984, it incurred either more than $15,000 of implementation costs for that plan or more than one-half of the total costs of implementing that plan.

In determining when an implementation cost has been incurred, the time of the performance of the services or production of the product giving rise to the cost, rather than the formal billing or payment of the cost, shall control. Thus, if before February 10, 1984, an employer has paid for services or a product that have not been performed or produced before such day, such cost will not be treated as having been incurred before such day.

Only the costs of designing and installing computer programs and manual accounting systems for the operation of the plan and the costs of printing brochures, descriptions, and election forms for the plan are eligible for treatment as substantial implementation costs. Other cost items (e.g., amounts expended for fees or salaries for feasibility and legal opinions and for designing the plan) are not implementation costs for these purposes.

In order for costs to be treated as implementation costs with respect to a particular cafeteria plan, the costs must be specifically allocable to such plan. As a result, before February 10, 1984, an employer must have intended to establish the particular plan, and the costs in question must be directly related to that plan. An employer's intent to establish a cafeteria plan will be evidenced only if the design specifications for the plan have been developed and agreed upon by February 10, 1984. In addition, costs will not be specifically allocable to a plan if the costs would have been incurred by the employer without regard to whether the plan in question was established. For example, the cost of designing and installing a computer program will be treated as an implementation cost with respect to a particular plan only if such program was specifically designed and installed for that plan as evidenced by plan design specifications developed by February 10, 1984. However, an employer that incurred implementation costs with respect to a particular cafeteria plan may not treat such costs as implementation costs with respect to another plan that had not actually been designed when such costs were incurred.

However, if an employer incurred costs with respect to two cafeteria plans, both of which had been specifically designed and agreed-upon (but not installed) as of the time such costs were incurred, and these costs are not specifically allocable between the plans, the costs are to be allocated on the basis of the number of participants in the two plans. For example, by February 10, 1984, an employer incurred $10,000 for the design of computer programs for the administration of two cafeteria plans—Plan A and Plan B—each of which had been specifically designed as of such day. Because Plan A will cover 25 percent of the employer's workforce and Plan B will cover 75 percent of the workforce, $2500 of the $10,000 is allocable to Plan A and $7500 is allocable to Plan B.

Q-25: What relief is provided under the general transition rule?

A-25: In the case of a cafeteria plan or a benefit in a cafeteria plan that qualifies for general transition relief, the general effective dates in Q & A-21 do not apply with respect to the rules specified in Q & A-27. In lieu of the otherwise applicable general effective date, the effective date with respect to the application of a particular rule to a cafeteria plan or a benefit in a cafeteria plan under the general transition rule is the earliest of the following dates: (i) January 1, 1985, (ii) the effective date, after February 10, 1984, of a modification to the particular plan or benefit in question to provide an additional benefit, (iii) the effective date of the termination or elimination of the particular plan or benefit in question, and (iv) the effective date, after February 10, 1984, of a modification to the particular plan or benefit in question that causes such plan or benefit no longer to fail to satisfy the particular rule in question ("conforming modification").

Modifications to Provide Additional Benefits

The addition of a new benefit to a cafeteria plan will not be treated as a modification to provide an additional benefit if, as of February 10, 1984, it was the employer's intention, as evidenced in writing and communicated to employees, that the benefit become effective under the plan as of the particular date of addition. For example, if by February 10, 1984, an employer had announced to employees, in writing, that a new medical benefit would become available to partici-

pants on November 1, 1984, the addition of the medical benefit on such day will not be treated as a modification to provide additional benefits. However, if the new medical benefit was not actually in existence on February 10, 1984, general transition relief would not be available with respect to the new benefit.

If, after February 10, 1984, an employer modifies a flexible spending arrangement under a cafeteria plan to provide employees with additional rights, such modification would be a modification to such benefit to provide an additional benefit. Examples of additional rights are the right to make additional contributions, make more frequent changes in the amount of their contributions, receive reimbursements for expenses for which reimbursements previously had not been available, receive taxable cash under the arrangement more frequently than had been permitted, and receive new or different treatment of amounts that were available but unused for expense reimbursements (e.g., a cash-out in lieu of or in addition to a carryover). Similarly, if either contributions or reimbursements (or both) with respect to a benefit provided through a flexible spending arrangement were suspended, reactivating contributions or reimbursements (even under the same terms that applied immediately before the suspension) will be treated as a modification to provide additional benefits.

A modification that permits a plan or benefit to conform to the general and special transition rules will not be treated as a modification to provide additional benefits. For example, an extension, from December 15, 1984, until January 15, 1985, of the cut off date by which expense reimbursement claims must be submitted under a flexible spending arrangement for expenses incurred during the period ending on December 31, 1984, will not be a modification to provide an additional benefit. Similarly, an alteration to a flexible spending arrangement so that a period of coverage scheduled to end on February 28, 1985, will end on December 31, 1984, and a new period will run from January 1, 1985, through June 30, 1985, will not be a modification to provide an additional benefit.

A modification, after February 10, 1984, to a plan or benefit that causes the plan or benefit to fail one or more of the rules in the regulations generally will be treated as a provision of an additional benefit. For example, if a medical benefit, which satisfies the applicable rules in sections 105 and 106 and in these regulations, is converted, on May 15, 1984, into a flexible spending arrangement, such conversion will be a modification to provide an additional benefit.

A modification, after February 10, 1984, to permit participation by employees who would not otherwise have become eligible to participate in the plan will be treated as a modification to provide an additional benefit. However, the addition of individuals who first become eligible to participate in a cafeteria plan under the eligibility and participation rules in effect on February 10, 1984, will not be treated as a modification to provide an additional benefit.

Terminations

A benefit will be treated as terminated if the plan is amended to eliminate the benefit and the amendment has taken effect. The rules delineated in Q&A-27 will become effective with respect to the benefit that has been terminated on the effective date of the termination. However, a benefit provided under a flexible spending arrangement will be treated as suspended, rather than terminated, if (i) the employer communicated to employees that either contributions or reimbursements (or both) with respect to the arrangement were being suspended, but might be permitted in the future, and (ii) amounts under the arrangement were not made available to employees during the period of suspension for reasons other than the reimbursement of covered expenses, unless such amounts were otherwise available under the terms of the arrangement in effect immediately before the suspension.

Conforming Modifications

A modification (by amendment or otherwise) that becomes effective after February 10, 1984, and causes a cafeteria plan or a benefit (including a benefit provided through a flexible spending arrangement) no longer to fail to satisfy one or more of the rules in the Q&A-1 through Q&A-20, will be treated as a "conforming modification" that cuts off general transition relief for the particular rule or rules in question; such rule or rules will become effective with respect to the particular plan or benefit on the effective date of the conforming modification. However, notwithstanding that a conforming modification has been made with respect to one or more of the rules in Q&A-1 through Q&A-20, general transition relief remains available to that particular plan or benefit with respect to the rule or rules which have not been so modified. Conforming modifications include both amendments that bring a plan or benefit into conformity with one or more of the rules in Q&A-1 through Q&A-20, and suspensions of contributions or reimbursements (or both) with respect to benefits provided through flexible spending arrangements. But see Q&A-26 for certain additional relief that is provided to plans or benefits with respect to which conforming modifications have been made.

Q-26: What additional relief is available to cafeteria plans or benefits with respect to which conforming modifications have been made?

A-26: In the case of a plan or benefit that has been modified, after February 10, 1984, so that it no longer fails to satisfy one or more of the rules in the proposed regulations, general transition relief with respect to the rule or rules in question is available only until the effective date of such conforming modification but not thereafter (although general transition relief remains available with respect to the rule or rules not so modified). However, pursuant to the authority contained in Section 7805(b) of the Internal Revenue Code, the particular rule or rules in question, if delineated in Q&A-27, shall not become effective with respect to such plan or benefit until January 1, 1985.

Such a plan or benefit may therefore be further modified and continue in operation through December 31, 1984, but only under the same terms that applied immediately before the conforming modification. For example, assume that, effective April 1, 1984, a flexible spending arrangement was modified by plan amendment to provide that amounts available for medical reimbursement would no longer be available to the employee without regard to whether the employee incurred medical care during the period of coverage. Assuming that such amendment is a conforming modification, the flexible spending arrangement may be further modified to continue in operation through December 31, 1984, under the same terms that applied immediately before the conforming modification.

Because such a modified plan or benefit does not qualify for general transition relief and is permitted to operated through December 31, 1984, only through a grant of section 7805(b) relief, special transition relief as set forth in Q&A-28 is not available to such plan or benefit.

Q-27: Which of the rules in Q&A-1 through Q&A-20 are subject to the general transition rule?

A-27: Relief under the general transition rule is provided with respect to both the cafeteria plan rules and with respect to the rules governing the taxability of benefits.

Cafeteria Plan Rules

The following cafeteria plan rules are subject to general transition relief: (i) the rules requiring that specific information be included in the written cafeteria plan document (Q&A-3); (ii) the rules governing the active participation of a participant's spouse in a cafeteria plan (Q&A-4); (iii) the rules governing the information that must be included in the written plan document with respect to salary reduction (Q&A-6) (but the availability of salary reduction must have nevertheless been fully described in written form and communicated to employees in such form); (iv) the rules precluding a plan from operating in a manner that enables participants to defer the receipt of compensation, such as by permitting the carryover of unused benefits from one plan year to another plan year (Q&A-7); (v) the rules limiting the revocability of benefit elections (Q&A-8); and (vi) as described in the following paragraph, the rules governing the scope of the section 125 exception to the generally applicable constructive receipt rules (Q&A-9, Q&A-14, and Q&A-15).

Generally, the general transition rule does not alter the scope of the section 125 exception to the general constructive receipt rules. Thus, an employee will be taxable on taxable benefits, salary or other compensation that he has actually received or that has become currently available (as described in Q&A-14 and without regard to these general transition rules), even though the employee currently or subsequently elects not to receive and actually does not receive such taxable benefits. For example, an employee in a flexible spending arrangement under which otherwise taxable compensation actually received is recharacterized as a nontaxable expense reimbursement will be taxable on such recharacterized amount. However, for purposes of general transition relief, the section 125 exception will provide that (i) an employee will not be treated as having constructively received a taxable benefit (including cash) under a cafeteria plan merely because the employee may revoke an election of a particular benefit with respect to a future period and instead receive the taxable benefit for such period, and (ii) an employee will not be treated as having constructively received amounts that have been set aside subject to a fixed distribution or withdrawal right under an arrangement.

The cafeteria plan rules not delineated in the preceding paragraphs are effective with respect to a plan or benefit as determined under the general effective date rules in Q&A-21.

Notwithstanding the application of the effective dates under the general transition rule, a plan may permit an employee to carry over unused amounts from a period of coverage or a plan year ending December 31, 1984, to a period of coverage or plan year beginning on January 1, 1985, without failing the rule precluding a cafeteria plan from operating in a manner to permit participants to defer the receipt of compensation.

Rules Governing the Taxability of Benefits

The following rules governing the taxability of a benefit are subject to the general transition relief: (i) in order to qualify for the section 105(b) exclusion from gross income, medical expense reimbursements must be provided under a medical benefit that exhibits the risk-shifting and risk-distribution characteristics of insurance (Q&A-17); (ii) in order to qualify for the section 105(b), 120, or 129 exclusion from gross income, the medical, dependent care, or legal expense reimbursements must be provided under a benefit with respect to which the participant is not entitled to receive, in the form of cash or some other benefit, the amounts available for reimbursement irrespective of whether the participant incurs covered expenses during the period of coverage (Q&A-17 and Q&A-18); (iii) in order to qualify for the section 105(b), 120, or 129 exclusion from gross income, the medical, dependent care, or legal expense reimbursements must be for medical care, dependent care, or legal care incurred during the period for which the participant is actually covered by the benefit (Q&A-17 and Q&A-18); (iv) medical care, dependent care, and legal care are treated as having been incurred when the participant is provided with the care that gives rise to the covered expenses, rather than when the participant is formally billed, charged for, or pays for the care (Q&A-17 and Q&A-18); and (v) in order for medical, dependent care, or legal expense reimbursements to qualify for the section 105(b), 120, or 129 exclusion from gross income, the cafeteria plan does not operate in a manner that enables participants to purchase coverage under the benefit only for periods during which the participants expect to incur covered expenses (Q&A-17 and Q&A-18).

Notwithstanding the application of the effective dates under the general transition rule, a plan may permit an employee to carry over or receive, after December 31, 1984, a cash-out of amounts available but unused under a flexible spending arrangement as of December 31, 1984. Similarly, expense reimbursements under a flexible spending arrangement may be made after December 31, 1984, if such reimbursements relate to expenses incurred and contributions made on or before December 31, 1984. Finally, a plan will not be treated as operating to permit participants to elect coverage only for periods in which the participants expect to incur covered expenses merely because the period of coverage with respect to a flexible spending arrangement is terminated on December 31, 1984.

Q-28: What relief is provided under the special transition rule?

A-28: Except as provided below, for purposes of the application of the rules set forth in the following paragraph to a benefit in a cafeteria plan (including a benefit that is provided through a flexible spending arrangement) that qualifies for the general transition rule through December 31, 1984, the otherwise applicable effective dates under the general transition rule, set forth in Q&A-25, will be applied by substituting July 1, 1985, in lieu of January 1, 1985.

The special transition rule applies with respect to the following rules: (i) in order to qualify for the section 105(b) exclusion from gross income, medical expense reimbursements must be provided under a medical benefit that exhibits the risk-shifting and risk-distribution characteristics of insurance (Q&A-17), and (ii) in order to qualify for the section 105(b), 120, or 129 exclusion from gross income, the medical, dependent care, or legal expense reimbursements must be provided under a benefit with respect to which a participant is not entitled to receive, in the form of cash or some other benefit, amounts available for reimbursement without regard to whether the participant incurs covered expenses during the period of coverage (Q&A-17 and Q&A-18). For purposes of the special transition rule, a period of coverage from January 1, 1985, through June 30, 1985, will satisfy the rules, in Q&A-17 and Q&A-18, precluding a cafeteria plan from operating to permit participants to purchase coverage only for periods during which the participants expect to incur covered expenses.

Notwithstanding the foregoing paragraphs, the otherwise applicable effective date set forth in Q&A-25 will not be modified by substituting July 1, 1985, in lieu of January 1, 1985, unless the particular benefit in question satisfies the following conditions: (i) the amount or specific rate of employer contributions (including salary reduction contributions) to be made with respect to the benefit is fixed prior to January 1, 1985 (or, if later, prior to the date on which the individual first becomes eligible to participate under the benefit); (ii) the employer contributions are deposited in or credited to an account (including an entry on the employer's books) established on behalf of the participant by the employer before being made available for expense reimbursement; (iii) neither the participant nor the employer have the right to increase or decrease contributions to the account during the period between January 1, 1985 (or, if later, the date on which the individual first becomes eligible to participate under the benefit), and July 1, 1985 (but contributions may be terminated during this period on account of the participant's separation from the service of the employer, and contributions may be terminated or increased or decreased on account of and consistent with certain changes in family status, as set forth in Q&A-8, or with a change in employment status from full-time to part-time or from part-time to full-time); and (iv) distributions are not available with respect to contributions made after December 31, 1984, for reasons other than the reimbursement of covered expenses before the earlier of July 1, 1985, or the participant's separation from the service of the employer.

Amounts available but unused, as of June 30, 1985, for reimbursement under a benefit in a cafeteria plan qualifying for special transition relief may be (i) used to reimburse covered expenses incurred before July 1, 1985, (ii) distributed in cash to participants, (iii) used to provide the participants with any other taxable or nontaxable benefits (e.g., contribution to a qualified profit-sharing plan), or (iv) made available for the reimbursement of covered expenses incurred after June 30, 1985. If amounts unused as of June 30, 1985, remain available for the reimbursement of expenses incurred before July 1, 1985, and are not made available for the reimbursement of covered expenses incurred after June 30, 1985, the post-June reimbursements of pre-July expenses will not fail to qualify for the section 105(b), 120, or 129 exclusion from gross income merely because any amounts unused for such pre-July expenses are provided in the form of cash or some other benefit, to participants before December 31, 1985. If, however, amounts unused as of June 30, 1985, for the reimbursement of covered expenses incurred before July 1, 1985, are made available for the reimbursement of expenses incurred after June 30, 1985, the rules in Q&A-17 and Q&A-18 must be satisfied with respect to such amounts.

Q-29: What relief is available for cafeteria plans of benefits that were eligible for transition relief under the regulations proposed on May 7, 1984, but are not eligible for general transition relief as set forth in Q&A-25?

A-29: Q&A-25 provides general transition relief only to those plans or benefits in existence on or before February 10, 1984. The proposed regulations originally provided transition relief for those plans or benefits in existence on or before May 7, 1984. Thus, plans or benefits which were not in existence on or before February 10, 1984, but were in existence on or before May 7, 1984, would have been eligible for transition relief under the regulations as originally proposed but are not eligible for general transition relief under Q&A-25. With respect to such plans and benefits, the following relief is provided:

Cafeteria Plan Rules

A cafeteria plan that failed to satisfy one or more of the following rules for plan years beginning on or before May 7, 1984 will not be deemed thereby to have failed to satisfy section 125 for such plan years if, by September 4, 1984, the plan was amended to operate in accordance with these rules: (i) the rules requiring certain information to be included in the cafeteria plan document (Q&A-3), (ii) the rules governing the active participation of a participant's spouse in a cafeteria plan (Q&A-4), (iii) only in case of a plan under which participants were permitted neither to carry over unused benefits for more than one plan year nor to convert, into any other benefits, any unused benefits that had been carried over to a subsequent plan year, the rules prohibiting the carryover of any unused contribution or benefit from one plan year to a subsequent plan year (Q&A-7), and (iv) the rules limiting the revocability of benefit elections (Q&A-8). A cafeteria plan may treat the portion of its current plan year remaining after September 4, 1984 as a new period of coverage for purposes of satisfying the rules governing benefit elections (Q&A-8). Also, a benefit offering participants the opportunity to make elective contributions under a qualified cash or deferred arrangement may be included in a cafeteria plan only in plan years beginning after December 31, 1980.

Rules Governing the Taxability of Benefits

If the coverage under an accident or health plan, dependent care assistance program, or qualified group legal services plan was offered as a benefit under a cafeteria plan and such benefit failed to satisfy, on or before May 7, 1984, the rule prohibiting a plan from operating to enable a participant to elect coverage under an accident or health plan, a dependent care assistance program, or a qualified group legal services plan only for periods during which the participant expects to receive medical care, dependent care, or legal services (Q&A-17 and Q&A-18), such benefit will not be deemed solely on account of such failure to have failed to satisfy the statutory rules providing for the income exclusion of such coverage or of any benefits provided thereunder, if, by September 4, 1984, the cafeteria plan was amended to operate in accordance with such election of coverage rule. A cafeteria plan may treat the portion of its current plan year remaining after September 4, 1984 as a new period of coverage and as an initial plan year for purposes of satisfying the rule prohibiting a plan from operating to enable participants to elect coverage under an accident or health plan, dependent care assistance program, or qualified group legal services plan only for periods during which they expect to receive medical care, dependent care, or legal services (Q&A-17 and Q&A-18).

In addition, if the conditions set forth below are satisfied, employer contributions (including elective and nonelective contributions) made before June 1, 1984, under an arrangement described in the next sentence which is part of a cafeteria plan, will not be treated as having been made to an accident or health plan, dependent care assistance program, or qualified group legal services plan that fails to satisfy the rules contained in the second and third paragraphs of Q&A-17 and the first paragraph of Q&A-18, merely because, for the period beginning with the plan year and ending no later than December 31, 1984, a participant was entitled to receive, in the form of cash or any other taxable or nontaxable benefit, amounts available for reimbursement under the arrangement without regard to whether covered expenses are incurred. An arrangement is described in this sentence only if, under the arrangement,

(i) An account was actually established on behalf of the participant by the employer, by an entry on the employer's books or in similar fashion prior to the beginning of the plan year (or prior to the date on which an individual first becomes eligible to participate under the arrangement in the case of an individual who first becomes eligible to participate, on account of years of employment, during the plan year);

(ii) The amount (or specific rate) of contributions to the account under the arrangement was fixed prior to the beginning of the plan year;

(iii) Neither the participant nor the employer possessed the right to increase or decrease contributions to the account during the plan year (but a plan may provide that contributions could be terminated during the year on account of the participant's (a) separation from service or (b) cessation of participation under the arrangement for the remainder of the plan year);

(iv) Contributions were actually deposited in or credited to the account before being made available for reimbursement; and

(v) Distributions were not available for reasons other than reimbursement of covered expenses until the end of the plan year or until December 31, 1984, whichever is earlier (but a plan may provide that a single distribution of the unreimbursed balance may be made on account of the participant's (a) separation from service or (b) cessation of participation under the arrangement for the remainder of the plan year).

A cafeteria plan may operate on a plan year other than the calendar year for purposes of this transitional rule, so long as the terms of the plan permit contributions to a plan to be fixed only once during, and a distribution of the unreimbursed amount to be received only once for the period beginning with the plan year and ending no later than December 31, 1984, provided that contributions may be fixed for a short plan year of the plan's first period of operation. This transitional rule does not affect or alter the requirement of Q&A-17 and -18 that expenses that are reimbursed under an arrangement must have been incurred during the period for which the participant actually is covered by the arrangement.

¶ 20,137S

Proposed regulations: Taxation of fringe benefits.—Reproduced below is the text of proposed regulations concerning the treatment of taxable and nontaxable fringe benefits. The proposed regulations were published in the Federal Register on February 20, 1985 (50 FR 7073). The proposed regulations were also issued as temporary regulations under T.D. 8009 and are reproduced at ¶ 11,172A, 11,289N, 11,306, 13,530A, 13,551, 13,576, and 13,648E. Portions of the proposed regulations dealing with Temp. Reg. §§ 1.132-1T Q/A 4a, 1.274-5T, and 1.274-6T have been withdrawn to reflect the repeal of the contemporaneous recordkeeping requirements (

¶ 23,694E). **Proposed regulations which are also temporary regulations, contain the new rules on the substantiation of business expenses (¶ 20,137U).**

DEPARTMENT OF THE TREASURY INTERNAL REVENUE SERVICE

26 CFR Parts 1, 31, and 54

[LR-216-84]

Taxation of Fringe Benefits; Withdrawal of Previous Notice of Proposed Rulemaking and Notice of Proposed Rulemaking by Cross-Reference to Temporary Regulations

AGENCY: Internal Revenue Service, Treasury.

ACTION: Withdrawal of previous notice of proposed rulemaking and notice of proposed rulemaking by cross-reference to temporary regulations.

SUMMARY: This document withdraws the notice of proposed rulemaking by cross-reference to temporary regulations that was published in the *Federal Register* on January 7, 1985 (50 FR 836), relating to the taxation of fringe benefits. Temporary regulations also published on January 7, 1985 (50 FR 747) served as the comment document for the withdrawn notice of rulemaking. In the Rules and Regulations portion of this issue of the *Federal Register,* the Internal Revenue Service is amending those temporary regulations. The text of the temporary regulations, as amended, serves as the comment document for a new notice of proposed rulemaking contained in this document.

DATES: Written comments must be delivered or mailed by April 8, 1985. The regulations are proposed to be effective as of January 1, 1985. One amendment that is published elsewhere in this issue of the *Federal Register* is proposed to be effective as of March 22, 1985.

ADDRESS: Send comments to: Commissioner of Internal Revenue, Attention: CC:LR:T (LR-216-84), Washington, D.C. 20224.

FOR FURTHER INFORMATION CONTACT: Annette J. Guarisco of the Legislation and Regulations Division, Office of Chief Counsel, Internal Revenue Service, 1111 Constitution Avenue, NW., Washington, D.C. 20224, Attention CC:LR:T (202) 566-3918 (not toll-free call).

SUPPLEMENTARY INFORMATION:

Background

Temporary regulations published in the *Federal Register* on January 7, 1985 (50 FR 747) amended Parts 1, 31, and 54 of Title 26 of the Code of Federal Regulations, relating to the taxation of fringe benefits. Those temporary regulations are amended by a Treasury decision published in the Rules and Regulations portion of this issue of the *Federal Register.*

The regulations as amended provide guidance on the treatment of taxable and nontaxable fringe benefits, including the valuation of taxable fringe benefits for purposes of income and employment tax withholding. In particular, the regulations provide special rules for valuing employer-provided automobiles, use of employer-provided automobiles or other vehicles for commuting, flights on employer-provided airplanes, and free or discounted flights on commercial airlines. In addition, the regulations provide guidance concerning when and in what manner employers must collect and pay income and employment taxes.

Sections 61, 3121, 3231, 3306, 3401, and 3501 of the Internal Revenue Code of 1954 (Code) were amended, and sections 132 and 4977 were added to the Code, by section 531 of the Tax Reform Act of 1984 (98 Stat. 877). The regulations are to be issued under the authority contained in sections 132 and 7805 of the Code (98 Stat. 878; 68A Stat. 917). The preamble to the temporary regulations published on January 7, 1985, and the preamble to the amendments published in this issue of the *Federal Register* contain a detailed explanation of the provisions of the regulations. The temporary regulations, as amended, will remain in effect until superseded by final regulations which are proposed to be based on the temporary regulations.

Comments

Before adopting these proposed regulations, consideration will be given to any written comments that are submitted (preferably eight copies) to the Commissioner of Internal Revenue. All comments will be available for public inspection and copying. Comments submitted with respect to the withdrawn notice of proposed rulemaking remain on file and need not be resubmitted. Notice of the time and place of the public hearing is published in this *Federal Register.*

Comments are invited concerning the administrability and appropriateness of the special rules contained in the temporary regulations relating to valuing employer-provided automobiles, use of employer-provided automobiles or other vehicles for commuting, flights on employer-provided airplanes, and free or discounted flights on commercial airlines. In particular, comments are requested on the manner in which employers and employees should elect to use these special valuation rules, including any necessary reporting requirements.

To use the special rule for valuing the availability of an employer-provided vehicle for commuting, the employer must require the employee to commute in the vehicle for bona fide noncompensatory business reasons. Examples of these reasons may include:

(1) The availability of an employee to respond at any time to a radio dispatch or similar call (for example, a utility company truck equipped with tools necessary to respond to a power emergency),

(2) The elimination of a significant expense for the employer because of the need to provide security for, or to garage, the vehicle (for example, the danger of vandalism in the case of a vehicle parked overnight on a construction site), and

(3) The attendant public benefit derived from such requirement (for example, a police automobile parked in public view). Suggestions of other reasons are invited.

Comments are requested relating to the allocation by employers of the income attributable to personal use of vehicles that are available to more than one employee during a period. Comments are invited concerning the appropriateness of requiring employers to allocate income attributable to personal use or, in the alternative, providing that employees may determine, together with their employer, the allocation of income attributable to personal use.

Comments are also requested concerning the definition of "officer" for purposes of determining whether an employee is a "key employee." In particular, comments are invited regarding the circumstances under which employees of certain employers, such as banks and thrift institutions, should or should not be considered officers.

Comments are also requested relating to the need for special rules for valuing other taxable fringe benefits, such as the use of an employer-subsidized eating facility that does not meet the statutory exclusion requirements, because for example, it is not available on a nondiscriminatory basis to all employees or it derives revenue that normally equals or exceeds the costs of operating the facility. In addition, comments are invited concerning the need for a special rule for valuing the use of an employer-operated athletic facility that is not eligible for an exclusion from income because, for example, substantially all the use of the facility is not by employees and their spouses and dependent children. Comments should also focus on the need for special rules for valuing international flights on employer-provided airplanes and use of employer-provided automobiles in foreign countries.

Comments are also requested relating to the definition of "employee" for purposes of the section 4977 election concerning the line-of-business restriction in section 132. Specifically, comments are requested as to whether, and to what extent, retirees should be included in the definition of employee.

Comments are also requested concerning the circumstances under which retirees should be treated as officers, owners, or highly compensated employees for purposes of the nondiscrimination rules contained in section 132.

The collection of information requirements contained in these regulations have been submitted to the Office of Management and Budget (OMB) in accordance with the requirements of the Paperwork Reduction Act of 1980. Comments on those requirements should be sent to the Office of Information and Regulatory Affairs of OMB, Attention: Desk Officer for Internal Revenue Service, New Executive Office Building, Washington, D.C. 20503. The Internal Revenue Service requests that persons submitting comments on these requirements to OMB also send copies to the Service.

Special Analyses

The Commissioner of Internal Revenue has determined that this proposed rule is not a major rule as defined in Executive Order 12291. Accordingly, a Regulatory Impact Analysis is not required.

Although this document is a notice of proposed rulemaking that solicits public comments, the Internal Revenue Service has concluded that the regulations proposed herein are interpretative and that the notice and public procedure requirements of 5 U.S.C. 553 do not apply.

Accordingly, no Regulatory Flexibility Analysis is required by Chapter 6 of Title 5, United States Code.

Drafting Information

The principal author of these regulations is Annette J. Guarisco of the Legislation and Regulations Division of the Office of Chief Counsel, Internal Revenue Service. However, personnel from other offices of the Internal Revenue Service and Treasury Department participated in developing the regulations, on matters of both substance and style.

List of Subjects

26 CFR 1.61-1.281-4

Income taxes, Taxable income, Deductions, Exemptions.

26 CFR Part 31

Employment taxes, Income taxes, Lotteries, Railroad Retirement, Social Security, Unemployment tax, Withholding.

26 CFR Part 54

Excise taxes, Pensions.

The notice of proposed rulemaking by cross-reference to temporary regulations that was published in the *Federal Register* on January 7, 1985 (50 FR 836), relating to the taxation of fringe benefits, is hereby withdrawn. The withdrawn notice of proposed rulemaking is superseded by the notice of proposed rulemaking by cross-reference to temporary regulations that is contained in this document.

Roscoe L. Egger, Jr.,

Commissioner of Internal Revenue.

[FR Doc. 85-4138 Filed 2-15-85; 8:45 am]

[The proposed regulations were also issued as temporary regulations and are reproduced at ¶ 11,172A, 11,289N, 11,306, 13,530A, and 13,648E.]

¶ 20,137T

Proposed regulations: Cost recovery deductions and investment tax credit: Automobiles used in trade or business: Use of "listed property" for business and personal purposes.—Reproduced below is the text of proposed regulations relating to the limitation on the amount of cost recovery deductions and investment tax credit allowed to taxpayers who purchase passenger automobiles for use in a trade or business or for use in the production of income, and to the limitations on cost recovery deductions and the investment tax credit allowed to taxpayers who use "listed property" for both business and personal purposes. The proposed regulations, which are also temporary regulations, were published in the Federal Register on February 20, 1985 (50 FR 7071). Temporary regulations which serve as the text for these proposals are at ¶ 11,357G, 11,357H and 11,358A—11,358D. Portions of the proposed regulations dealing with Temp. Reg. §§ 1.132-1T Q/A 4a, 1.274-5T, and 1.274-6T have been withdrawn to reflect the repeal of the contemporaneous recordkeeping requirements (¶ 23,694E). Proposed regulations, which are also temporary regulations, contain the new rules on the substantiation of business expenses (¶ 20,137V).

DEPARTMENT OF THE TREASURY

Internal Revenue Service

26 CFR Part 1

[LR-145-84]

Limitation on Amount of Depreciation and Investment Tax Credit for Luxury Automobiles; Limitation When Certain Property Is Used For Personal Purposes

AGENCY: Internal Revenue Service, Treasury.

ACTION: Withdrawal of previous notice of proposed rulemaking and notice of proposed rulemaking by cross-reference to temporary regulations.

SUMMARY: This document withdraws the notice of proposed rulemaking by cross-reference to temporary regulations that was published in the *Federal Register* on October 24, 1984 (49 FR 42743), relating to the limitation on the amount of cost recovery deductions and investment tax credit allowed to taxpayers who purchase passenger automobiles for use in a trade or business or for use in the production of income, and to the limitations on cost recovery deductions and the investment tax credit allowed to taxpayers who use "listed property" for both business and personal purposes. The text of temporary income tax regulations under sections 274 and 280F of the Internal Revenue Code of 1954, also published on that date (49 FR 41701), served as the comment document for the withdrawn notice of proposed rulemaking. In the Rules and Regulations portion of this issue of the *Federal Register,* the Internal Revenue Service is amending the temporary regulations under sections 274 and 280F that were published on October 24, 1984, and issuing a new temporary regulation under section 274. The text of the new and amended temporary regulations serves as the comment document for a new notice of proposed rulemaking contained in this document.

DATES: Proposed effective dates. The regulations relating to the limitations on the investment tax credit and recovery deductions are proposed to be effective in general for "listed property" placed in service or leased after June 18, 1984. Those regulations would not apply to certain property acquired or leased pursuant to a binding contract in effect on June 18, 1984. The regulations relating to substantiation requirements for the use of "listed property" are proposed to be effective for taxable years beginning after December 31, 1984.

Dates for comments. Written comments must be delivered or mailed by April 8, 1985.

ADDRESS: Send comments to: Commissioner of Internal Revenue. Attention: CC:LR:T (LR-145-84), Washington, D.C. 20224.

FOR FURTHER INFORMATION CONTACT: George T. Magnatta (with respect to cost recovery deduction questions) (202-566-6456), Michel A. Daze (with respect to investment tax credit or leasing questions) (202-566-3829), or Cynthia E. Grigsby (with respect to definitional or substantiation questions (202-566-3935), of the Legislation and Regulations Division, Office of the Chief Counsel, Internal Revenue Service, 1111 Constitution Avenue, NW., Washington, D.C. 20224 (Attention: CC:LR:T).

SUPPLEMENTARY INFORMATION:

Background

Temporary regulations published in the *Federal Register* on October 24, 1984 (49 FR 42701) amended the Income Tax Regulations (26 CFR Part 1) to reflect amendments to section 274 of the Internal Revenue Code of 1954, relating to substantiation requirements, and the addition to the Code of section 280F, relating to limitations on cost recovery deductions and the investment tax credit for certain property. Those temporary regulations are amended and a new temporary regulation under section 274 is added by a Treasury decision published in the Rules and Regulations portion of this issue of the *Federal Register.* The preamble to the temporary regulations published on October 24, 1984, and the preamble to the amendments published in this issue of the *Federal Register* contain a detailed explanation of the provisions of the regulations. The temporary regulations, as amended, will remain in effect until superseded by final regulations which are proposed to be based on the temporary regulations and issued under the authority contained in sections 280F and 7805 of the Internal Revenue Code of 1954 (98 Stat. 494, 26 U.S.C. 280F; 68A Stat. 917, 26 U.S.C. 7805).

Comments

Before these proposed amendments are adopted, consideration will be given to any written comments that are submitted (preferably eight copies) to the Commissioner of Internal Revenue. All comments will be available for public inspection and copying. Comments submitted with respect to the withdrawn notice or proposed rulemaking remain on file and need not be resubmitted.

Certain types of vehicles are excluded from the definition of "passenger automobile" including, *inter alia,* any truck or van, if the regulations so specify. Comments are invited as to the types of trucks or vans that should be excluded from the definition of "passenger automobile."

Comments are also invited with respect to the manner of allocating the use of "listed property" between the business and personal use of the property. Specifically, the Internal Revenue Service is interested in suggestions as to whether different measures of business and personal use other than those provided in the temporary regulations are appropriate.

¶20,137T

The temporary regulations (§ 1.274-6T) published in this issue of the *Federal Register* prescribed certain methods that a taxpayer may use to satisfy the "adequate contemporaneous record" requirement of section 274(d)(4). For example, if an employer provides an automobile for use by an employee who spends most of a normal business day using the automobile in connection with the employer's business, the employer may treat the automobile as used 70 percent for business and 30 percent for personal purposes. The employer must also determine an amount to be included in the employee's income for the availability of the automobile for personal use. It is thought that the employee should have the opportunity to document a greater amount of business use and thus reduce the amount of the taxable fringe benefit. Comments are requested as to whether the regulations should require an employer to notify an employee if the employer is using one of the methods prescribed in § 1.274-6T. Comments are also welcome on whether the regulations should establish a procedure for employers and employees to elect the same method at the beginning of each calendar year.

In the case of a fleet of vehicles owned or leased by an employer and used by employees for most of a normal business day in connection with the employer's trade or business, the Service is considering an alternative method for the employer to satisfy its "adequate contemporaneous record" requirement. In lieu of using the percentages prescribed in § 1.274-6T(b)(3) of the temporary regulations, an employer would be able to establish different percentages for direct use of a vehicle in the employer's trade or business and personal use by employees by a method similar to the following:

(1) The employer would identify a class of at least 100 vehicles that are physically similar and that are used in a similar fashion.

(2) In each taxable year, the employer would choose a random sample of the class of vehicles using accepted sampling techniques.

(3) The sample size would preferably be at least 250 vehicles, or one-half the class in the case of fleets of less than 500 vehicles, and

(4) The percentage of average business use of the vehicles in the sample would apply to the class if determined from records of actual use kept for these vehicles. Comments are invited with respect to this alternative method of satisfying the "adequate contemporaneous record" requirement.

A public hearing had been scheduled to be held on February 5, 1985, at the national office of the Internal Revenue Service. That hearing is postponed and will be rescheduled at a later time in order to provide the public an opportunity to consider the amendments proposed by this notice. Notice of the time and place of the hearing is published in this *Federal Register*.

The collection of information requirements contained in the temporary regulations have been submitted to the Office of Management and Budget (OMB) for review under Section 3504(h) of the Paperwork Reduction Act. Comments on these requirements should be sent to the Office of Information and Regulatory Affairs of OMB, Attention: Desk Officer for Internal Revenue Service, New Executive Office Building, Washington, D.C. 20503. The Internal Revenue Service requests that persons submitting comments on the requirements to OMB also send copies of those comments to the Service.

Executive Order 12291 and Regulatory Flexibility Act

The Commissioner of Internal Revenue has determined that this proposed rule is not a major rule as defined in Executive Order 12291 and that a Regulatory Impact Analysis is therefore not required.

Although this document is a notice of proposed rulemaking which solicits public comment, the Internal Revenue Service has concluded that the regulations proposed herein are interpretative and that the notice and public procedure requirements of 5 U.S.C. 553 do not apply. Accordingly, these proposed regulations do not constitute regulations subject to the Regulatory Flexibility Act (5 U.S.C. Chapter 6).

List of Subjects in 26 CFR 1.61-1 Through 1.281-4.

Income taxes, Taxable income, Deductions, Exemptions. The notice of proposed rulemaking by cross-reference to temporary regulations that was published in the *Federal Register* on October 24, 1984 (49 FR 42743), relating to the limitation on the amount of cost recovery deductions and investment tax credit allowed for passenger automobiles and to the limitations on cost recovery deductions and the investment tax credit allowed for "listed property", is hereby withdrawn. The withdrawn notice of proposed rulemaking is superseded by the notice of proposed rulemaking by cross-reference to temporary regulations that is contained in this document.

Roscoe L. Egger, Jr.,

Commissioner of Internal Revenue.

[FR Doc. 85-4137 Filed 2-15-85; 8:45 am]

¶ 20,137U

Proposed regulations: Taxation of fringe benefits-.—Reproduced below is the text of proposed regulations dealing with rules for valuing the commuting use of employer-provided vehicles and rules relating to working condition fringe exclusions. The proposed regulations were published in the Federal Register on November 6, 1985 (50 FR 46087). The proposed regulations were also issued as temporary regulations under T.D. 8061 and are reproduced at ¶ 11,172A and 11,289N.

[4830-01]

[Final draft of 9-18-85]

DEPARTMENT OF THE TREASURY INTERNAL REVENUE SERVICE

[26 CFR PART 1]

[LR-216-84]

Taxation of Fringe Benefits; Notice of Proposed Rulemaking

AGENCY: Internal Revenue Service, Treasury.

ACTION: Notice of proposed rulemaking by cross-reference to temporary regulations.

SUMMARY: In the Rules and Regulations portion of this issue of the FEDERAL REGISTER, the Internal Revenue Service is issuing temporary income tax regulations under section 61 and 132. The temporary regulations under section 61 provide rules for valuation of the commuting use of employer-provided vehicles. The temporary regulations under section 132 provide rules relating to working condition fringe exclusions. The text of the temporary regulations serves as the comment document for the notice of proposed rulemaking contained in this document.

DATES: Proposed effective date: The regulations are generally proposed to be effective as of January 1, 1985.

Dates for comments and requests for a public hearing: Written comments and requests for a public hearing must be delivered or mailed by January 5, 1986.

ADDRESS: Send comments and requests for a public hearing to Commissioner of Internal Revenue, 1111 Constitution Ave., N.W., Washington, D.C. 20224 Attention: CC:LR:T (LR-216-84).

FOR FURTHER INFORMATION CONTACT: Annette J. Guarisco of the Legislation and Regulations Division, Office of Chief Counsel, Internal Revenue Service, (202) 566-3918 (not a toll-free number).

SUPPLEMENTARY INFORMATION:

Background

The temporary regulations in the Rules and Regulations portion of this issue of the *Federal Register* amend Part 1 of Title 26 of the Code of Federal Regulations. The temporary regulations are designated by a "T" following their section citation. The final regulations, which this document proposes to base on those temporary regulations, would amend Part 1 of Title 26 of the Code of Federal Regulations.

Section 61 was amended and section 132 was added to the Internal Revenue Code of 1954 ("Code") by section 531 of the Tax Reform Act of 1984 (Pub. Law 98-369, 98 Stat. *877*). Section 274(d) of the Code was amended by section 179 of the Tax Reform Act of 1984 (99 Stat. 494) and section 1(a) of the Repeal of Contemporaneous Recordkeeping Requirements (Pub. Law 99-44, 99 Stat. 77). Because of the relationship between sections 274(d) and 132 of the Code, the temporary regulations under section 132 are amended.

Comments and Requests for a Public Hearing

Before these proposed amendments are adopted, consideration will be given to any written comments that are submitted (preferably eight copies) to the Commissioner of Internal Revenue. All comments will be available for public inspection and copying.

A public hearing will be held upon written request to the Commissioner by any person who has submitted written comments. If a public hearing is held, notice of the time and place will be published in the *Federal Register.*

The collection of information requirements contained in the temporary regulations have been submitted to the Office of Management and Budget (OMB) for review under the Paperwork Reduction Act of 1980. Comments on those requirements should be sent to the Office of Information and Regulatory Affairs, Attention: Desk Officer for Internal Revenue Service, New Executive Office Building, Washington, D.C. 20503. The Internal Revenue Service requests that persons submitting comments on the requirements to OMB also send copies of those comments to the Service.

Executive Order 12291 and Regulatory Flexibility Act

The Commissioner of Internal Revenue has determined that this proposed rule is not a major rule as defined in Executive Order 12291 and that a Regulatory Impact Analysis is therefore not required.

Although this document is a notice of proposed rulemaking which solicits public comments, the Internal Revenue Service has concluded that the regulations proposed herein are interpretative and that the notice and public procedure requirements of 5 U.S.C. 553 do not apply. Accordingly, these proposed regulations do not constitute regulations subject to the Regulatory Flexibility Act (5 U.S.C. Chapter 6).

Drafting Information

The principal author of this document is Annette J. Guarisco of the Legislation and Regulations Division of the Office of Chief Counsel, Internal Revenue Service. However, personnel from other offices of the Internal Revenue Service and Treasury Department participated in developing the regulations on matters of both substance and style.

List of Subjects in 26 CFR 1.61-1—1.281-4

Income taxes, Taxable income, Deductions, Exemptions.

Roscoe L. Egger, Jr.

Commissioner of Internal Revenue

¶ 20,137V

Proposed regulations: Taxation of fringe benefits.—Reproduced below is the text of proposed regulations concerning rules for the substantiation of deductions or credit claims with respect to traveling away from home, certain entertainment expenditures, business-related gifts, and "listed property". The proposed regulations were published in the *Federal Register* on November 6, 1985 (50 FR 46088). The proposed regulations were also issued as temporary regulations under T.D. 8061 and are reproduced at ¶ 11,306, 11,357G, 11,357H, 11,358B, and 11,358D.

[4830-01]

[Final Draft of 9-17-85]

DEPARTMENT OF THE TREASURY INTERNAL REVENUE SERVICE

[26 CFR Parts 1 and 602]

[LR-145-84]

Limitation on Amount of Depreciation and Investment Tax Credit for Luxury Automobiles; Limitation When Certain Property Is Used for Personal Purposes

Notice of Proposed Rulemaking

AGENCY: Internal Revenue Service, Treasury.

ACTION: Notice of proposed rulemaking by cross-reference to temporary regulations.

SUMMARY: In the Rules and Regulations portion of this issue of the *Federal Register,* the Internal Revenue Service is issuing temporary income tax regulations under section 274 and amending other temporary regulations under sections 162 and 280F. The temporary regulations under section 274 provide rules for the substantiation of any deduction or credit claimed with respect to traveling away from home, certain entertainment expenditures, business-related gifts, and "listed property." The amendment to the temporary regulations under section 162 relate to the deductibility of certain expenses incurred by employers and employees with respect to noncash fringe benefits. The amendments to the temporary regulations under section 280F provide new limitations on the deductions of lessees of passenger automobiles. The text of the new and amended temporary regulations serves as the comment document for the notice of proposed rulemaking contained in this document.

DATES: Proposed effective dates: The regulations under section 162 are proposed to be effective as of January 1, 1985. The regulations under section 274 relating to the substantiation of deductions and credits claimed with respect to certain business expenditures are proposed to be effective generally for taxable years beginning after December 31, 1985. The amendments relating to the limitations on the deductions of lessees of passenger automobiles are proposed to be effective generally for automobiles leased after April 2, 1935.

Dates for comments and requests for a public hearing: Written comments and requests for a public hearing must be delivered or mailed by January 5, 1986.

ADDRESS: Send comments and requests for a public hearing to Commissioner of Internal Revenue, Attention: CC:LR:T (LR-145-84), Washington, D.C. 20224.

FOR FURTHER INFORMATION CONTACT: Michel A. Daz'e of the Legislation and Regulations Division, Office of the Chief Counsel,

Internal Revenue Service, 1111 Constitution Avenue, N.W., Washington, D.C. 20224 (202-566-6456, not a toll-free call).

SUPPLEMENTARY INFORMATION:

Background

The temporary regulations published in the Rules and Regulations portion of this issue of the *Federal Register* amend the Income Tax Regulations (26 CFR Part 1) to reflect amendments to section 274 of the Internal Revenue Code of 1954, relating to substantiation requirements, and to section 280F relating to limitations on cost recovery deductions and the investment tax credit allowed for passenger automobiles. The temporary regulations issued under section 274 reflect amendments to section 274(d) by section 179 of the Tax Reform Act of 1984 (Pub. L. 98-369, 98 Stat. 494) and by sections 1(a) and 2 of the Repeal of Contemporaneous Recordkeeping Requirements (Pub. L. 99-44, 99 Stat. 77). The amendments to the temporary regulations under section 280F reflect amendments to that section by section 4 of Public Law 99-44. The preamble to the temporary regulations contains an explanation of the provisions of those regulations. The temporary regulations will remain in effect until superseded by final regulations which are proposed to be based on the temporary regulations.

Before amendment by the Tax Reform Act of 1984 and Public Law 99-44, section 274(d) required that any deduction for expenses incurred for (1) traveling away from home, (2) entertainment, amusement, or recreation activities or the use of a facility in connection with those activities, or (3) business-related gifts be substantiated by adequate records or sufficient evidence corroborating a taxpayer's own statement. Section 274(d) did not apply to vehicles when used in local travel. Instead, the more general substantiation standards under section 162 were applicable. As amended, section 274(d) requires, for taxable years beginning after December 31, 1985, that any deduction or credit claimed for the expenses described above and for expenses incurred with respect to "listed property" be substantiated by adequate records or sufficient evidence corroborating a taxpayer's own statement. Section 274(d) will then apply to vehicles used in local travel.

First adopted by Treasury decision in 1962, § 1.274-5 of the Income Tax Regulations reflects the addition of section 274(d) to the Code. Amendments to § 1.274-5 are proposed to conform the regulations to the 1984 Act and to Public Law 99-44. For the convenience of taxpayers who must comply with the section 274(d) substantiation requirements, the proposed amendments are incorporated into § 1.274-5 and published in full in the format of a temporary regulation. New material is indicated by underlining.

Comments and Requests for a Public Hearing

Before these proposed amendments are adopted, consideration will be given to any written comments that are submitted (preferably eight copies) to the Commissioner of Internal Revenue. All comments will be available for public inspection and copying.

Comments are invited, however, on only those portions of new temporary § 1.274-5T that are amendments to § 1.274-5 to reflect the recent legislation. Specifically, comments are invited on the following provisions that are included among those amendments:

Paragraph (b)(6), the elements of an expenditure or use with respect to listed property,

Paragraph (c)(2)(ii)(C), substantiation of business use,

Paragraph (c)(3)(ii), sampling rule for the substantiation of business use,

Paragraph (c)(6)(i)(C), aggregation of business use,

Paragraph (d)(2) and (3), disclosure on tax returns of certain information with respect to the use of listed property,

Paragraph (e), substantiation of working condition fringe exclusions and certain employee deductions, and

Paragraph (k), other vehicles that may be designated as qualified nonpersonal use vehicles.

Comments are also invited on the provisions of § 1.162-25T and § 1.274-6T and the amendments to the temporary regulations under section 280F. Comments have been received previously on the limitations applicable to lessees contained in § 1.280F-5T of those temporary regulations. The comments have pointed out that separate limitations are not applicable to lessees to whom lessors have elected to pass through the investment credit. The Internal Revenue Service intends to issue an announcement in the near future providing separate limitations for these lessees.

In the case of a fleet of vehicles owned or leased by an employer and used by employees in connection with the employer's business, the Service is considering an alternative method for the employer to satisfy its substantiation requirements. An employer would be able to establish the business use of each vehicle in the fleet and the personal use by an employee by a method similar to the following:

(1) The employer would identify a class of at least 100 vehicles that are physically similar and that are used in a similar fashion,

(2) No vehicle in the class would have a fair market value greater than $16,500,

(3) At the beginning of each taxable year, the employer would select from the class a random sample using accepted sampling techniques,

(4) The sample size would preferably be at least 250 vehicles, or one-half the class in the case of fleets of less than 500 vehicles (but in no event less than 50 vehicles),

(5) The taxpayer would determine the business use of each vehicle in the sample from adequate records maintained for each vehicle, and

(6) The average of the business use of each vehicle in the sample would be the business use of each vehicle in the class.

Comments are invited with respect to this alternative method of satisfying the substantiation requirements of section 274(d).

A public hearing will be held upon written request to the Commissioner by any person who submits written comments. If a public hearing is held, notice of the time and place will be published in the FEDERAL REGISTER.

The collection of information requirements contained in the temporary regulations have been submitted to the office of Management and Budget (OMB) for review under section 3504(b) of the Paperwork Reduction Act. Comments on these requirements should be sent to the Office of Information and Regulatory Affairs, Attention: Desk Officer for Internal Revenue Service, New Executive Office Building, Washington, D.C. 20503. The Internal Revenue Service requests that persons submitting comments on the requirements to OMB also send copies of those comments to the Service.

Executive Order 12291 and Regulatory Flexibility Act

The Commissioner of Internal Revenue has determined that this proposed rule is not a major rule as defined in Executive Order 12291 and that a Regulatory Impact Analysis is therefore not required.

Although this document is a notice of proposed rulemaking which solicits public comment, the Internal Revenue Service has concluded that the regulations proposed herein are interpretative and that the notice and public procedure requirements of 5 U.S.C. 553 do not apply. Accordingly, these proposed regulations do not constitute regulations subject to the Regulatory Flexibility Act (5 U.S.C. Chapter 6).

Drafting Information

The principal author of this document is Michel A. Dazé of the Legislation and Regulations Division of the Office of Chief Counsel, Internal Revenue Service. However, personnel from other offices of the Internal Revenue Service and Treasury Department participated in developing the regulations on matters of both substance and style.

List of Subjects

26 CFR 1.61-1—1.281-4

Income taxes, Taxable income, Deductions, Exemptions.

List of Subjects

26 CFR Part 602

Reporting and recordkeeping requirements.

Roscoe L. Egger, Jr.

Commissioner of Internal Revenue

[¶ 20,137W Reserved.—Proposed regulations relating to taxation of fringe benefits, were formerly reproduced at this point. The final regulations are at ¶ 11,172, 11,172A, 11,176, 11,289N-1—11,289N-8, 11,289O-11,289O-8.]

[¶ 20,137X Reserved.—Proposed regulations relating to certain restrictions on an employee's right to receive optional forms of benefit under qualified plans were formerly reproduced here. The final regulations appear at ¶ 11,716E and 12,233.]

¶ 20,137Y

Proposed regulations: Employee benefit provisions of the Tax Reform Act of 1984.—Following is the text of proposed regulations on the employee benefit provisions of the Tax Reform Act of 1984. The proposed regulations concern vacation pay, the economic performance requirement for certain employee benefits, group-term life insurance, welfare benefit plans, unfunded deferred benefits, requirements for exempt organizations, roll-overs, distributions, the estate tax exclusion, collective bargaining agreements, ESOPs, and treatment of employer and employee benefit associations. The proposed regulations were also issued as temporary regulations under T.D. 8073 and are reproduced at ¶ 11,209, 11,234, 11,288C, 11,289S, 11,304A, 11,751A, 11,851A, 11,859A, 11,865A, 11,867, 11,870, 12,905, 12,969, 13,154E, 13,156, 13,194, 13,212C, 13,383, 13,502D, 13,648C, 13,648G. The effective dates of the temporary regulations and the introductory material preceding the temporary regulations are at ¶ 23,698Y. The proposed regulations were published in the *Federal Register* on February 4, 1986 (51 FR 4391).

¶ 20,137W

[4830-01]

[Final Draft of 9-27-85]

DEPARTMENT OF THE TREASURY
INTERNAL REVENUE SERVICE

[26 CFR Parts 1, 20, 54, 301 and 602]

[EE-96-85]

Effective Dates And Other Issues Arising Under The Employee Benefit Provisions Of The Tax Reform Act Of 1984

Notice Of Proposed Rulemaking

AGENCY: Internal Revenue Service, Treasury.

ACTION: Notice of proposed rulemaking by cross reference to temporary regulations.

SUMMARY: In the Rules and Regulations portion of this issue of the *Federal Register,* the Internal Revenue Service is issuing temporary regulations relating to effective dates and certain other issues arising under the employee benefit provisions of the Tax Reform Act of 1984. The text of those temporary regulations also serves as the comment document for this notice of proposed rulemaking.

DATES: Written comments and requests for a public hearing must be delivered or mailed by April 7, 1986. The regulations are proposed to be effective on varying date provided in the temporary regulations.

ADDRESS: Send comments and requests for a public hearing to Commissioner of Internal Revenue, Attn: CC:LR:T (EE-96-85), 1111 Constitution Avenue N.W., Washington, D.C. 20224.

FOR FURTHER INFORMATION CONTACT: John T. Ricotta of the Employee Plans and Exempt Organizations Division, Office of Chief Counsel, Internal Revenue Service, 1111 Constitution Ave., N.W., Washington, D.C. 20224, Attention: CC:LR:T (EE-96-85), telephone: 202-566-3544 (not a toll-free number).

SUPPLEMENTARY INFORMATION

Background

The temporary regulations provide guidance concerning the economic performance requirement for certain employee benefits under section 461(h) of the Internal Revenue Code of 1954 (Code), as added by section 91 of the Tax Reform Act of 1984 (Act) (P.L. 98-369, 98 Stat. 598); the transitional rule for vested accrued vacation pay under section 463 of the Code, as amended by section 91(i) of the Act (P.L. 98-369, 98 Stat. 609); the treatment of group-term life insurance purchased for employees under section 79 of the Code, as amended by section 223 of the Act (P.L. 98-369, 98 Stat. 775); the treatment of funded welfare benefit plans under sections 419 and 419A of the Code, as added by section 511 of the Act (P.L. 98-369, 98 Stat. 854); the treatment of unfunded deferred benefits under sections 404(b) and 162 of the Code, as amended by section 512 of the Act (P.L. 98-369, 98 Stat. 862); additional requirements for tax-exempt status of certain organizations under section 505 of the Code, as added by section 513 of the Act

(P.L. 98-369, 98 Stat. 863); rollovers of partial distributions under sections 402 and 403 of the Code, as amended by section 522 of the Act (P.L. 98-369, 98 Stat. 868); distributions where substantially all contributions are employee contributions under section 72 of the Code, as amended by section 523 of the Act (P.L. 98-369, 98 Stat. 871); repeal of the estate tax exclusion for qualified plan benefits under section 2039 of the Code, as amended by section 525 of the Act (P.L. 98-369, 98 Stat. 873); determination of whether there is a collective bargaining agreement under section 7701(a)(46) of the Code, as added by section 526(c) of the Act (P.L. 98-369, 98 Stat. 881); nonrecognition of gain on stock sold to an employee stock ownership plan (ESOP) under section 1042 of the Code, as added by section 541 of the Act (P.L. 98-369, 98 Stat. 887); deductibility of dividends relating to ESOPs under sections 404 and 3405 of the Code, as amended by section 542 of the Act (P.L. 98-369, 98 Stat. 890); exclusion of interest on ESOP loans under section 133 of the Code, as added by section 543 of the Act (P.L. 98-369, 98 Stat. 894); treatment of an employer and an employee benefit association as related under section 1239 of the Code, as amended by section 557 of the Act (P.L. 98-369, 98 Stat. 898); and technical corrections to the pension provisions of the Tax Equity and Fiscal Responsibility Act of 1982 under sections 713 and 715 of the Act (P.L. 98-369, 98 Stat. 955, 966). The proposed regulations are issued under the authority contained in section 7805 of the Code (26 U.S.C. § 7805). For the text of the temporary regulations, see F.R. Doc. (—) published in the Rules and Regulations portion of this issue of the Federal Register.

Special Analysis

The Commissioner of Internal Revenue has determined that this proposed rule is not a major rule as defined in Executive Order 12291 and that a Regulatory Impact Analysis is therefore not required. Although this document is a notice of proposed rulemaking which solicits public comment, the Internal Revenue Service has concluded that the regulations proposed herein are interpretative and that the notice and public procedure requirements of 5 U.S.C. 553 do not apply. Accordingly, these proposed regulations do not constitute regulations subject to the Regulatory Flexibility Act (5 U.S.C. Chapter 6).

Comments and Requests for a Public Hearing

Before the adoption of these proposed regulations, consideration will be given to any written comments that are submitted (preferably eight copies) to the Commissioner of Internal Revenue. All comments will be available for public inspection and copying. A public hearing will be held upon written request to the Commissioner by any person who has submitted written comments. If a public hearing is held, notice of the time and place will be published in the Federal Register. The collection of information requirements contained herein have been submitted to the Office of Management and Budget (OMB) for review under section 3504(h) of the Paperwork Reduction Act. Comments on the requirements should be sent to the Office of Information and Regulatory Affairs, of OMB, Attention: Desk Officer for Internal Revenue Service, New Executive Office Building, Washington, D.C. 20503. The Internal Revenue Service requests persons submitting comments to OMB also to send copies of the comments to the Service.

Roscoe L. Egger, Jr.

Commissioner of Internal Revenue

¶ 20,137Z

Proposed regulations: Mortality table: Deferred payments of life insurance proceeds: Exclusion from gross income of deferred payments.—Following is the text of proposed regulations on the mortality table to be used in determining the extent to which deferred payments of life insurance proceeds are excluded from gross income. The proposed regulations were also issued as temporary regulations under T.D. 8161 and are reproduced at ¶ 11,256D. The introductory material preceding the temporary regulations is at ¶ 23,735Z. The proposed regulations were published in the *Federal Register* on September 21, 1987 (52 FR 35447).

DEPARTMENT OF THE TREASURY

INTERNAL REVENUE SERVICE

[26 CFR Part 1]

[LR-I35-86]

Mortality Table Used to Determine Exclusion for Deferred Payments of Life Insurance Proceeds

Notice of Proposed Rulemaking

AGENCY: Internal Revenue Service, Treasury.

ACTION: Notice of proposed rulemaking by cross-reference to temporary regulations.

SUMMARY: In the Rules and Regulations portion of this issue of the FEDERAL REGISTER, the Internal Revenue Service is issuing temporary regulations that prescribe the mortality table to be used in determining the extent to which deferred payments of life insurance proceeds are excluded from gross income. The text of the temporary regulations also serves as the comment document for this notice of proposed rulemaking.

DATES: Written comments and requests for a public hearing must be delivered or mailed by [60 DAYS AFTER DATE OF PUBLICATION OF THIS DOCUMENT IN THE FEDERAL REGISTER]. The regulations are proposed to be effective on October 23, 1986, and to apply to amounts received with respect to deaths occurring after October 22, 1986, in taxable years ending after October 22, 1986.

ADDRESS: Send comments and requests for a public hearing to: Commissioner of Internal Revenue, Attention: CC:LR:T (LR-135-86), Washington, D.C. 20224.

FOR FURTHER INFORMATION CONTACT: Sharon L. Hall of the Legislation and Regulations Division, Office of Chief Counsel, Internal Revenue Service, 1111 Constitution Avenue, N.W., Washington, D.C. 20224 (Attention: CC:LR:T), (202) 566-3288 (not a toll-free call).

SUPPLEMENTARY INFORMATION

Background

The temporary regulations (designated by a "T" following the section citation) in the Rules and Regulations section of this issue of the FEDERAL REGISTER amend the Income Tax Regulations (26 CFR Part 1) to provide rules under sections 101(d) of the Internal Revenue Code of 1986, as amended by section 1001(b) of the Tax Reform Act of 1986 (100 Stat. 2387). This document proposes to adopt those temporary regulations as final regulations. Accordingly, the text of the temporary regulations serves as the comment document for this notice of proposed rulemaking. The preamble to the temporary regulations provides a discussion of the proposed and temporary rules.

For the text of the temporary regulations, see FR Doc. (T.D. 8161) published in the Rules and Regulations section of this issue of the FEDERAL REGISTER.

Special Analysis

The Commissioner of Internal Revenue has determined that this proposed rule is not a major rule as defined in Executive Order 12291 and that a regulatory impact analysis therefore is not required. Al-though this document is a notice of proposed rulemaking that solicits public comment, the Internal Revenue Service has concluded that the regulations proposed herein are interpretative and that the notice and public procedure requirements of 5 U.S.C. 553 do not apply. Accordingly, these proposed regulations do not constitute regulations subject to the Regulatory Flexibility Act (5 U.S.C. chapter 6).

Comments and Requests for a Public Hearing

Before these proposed regulations are adopted, consideration will be given to any written comments that are submitted (preferably eight copies) to the Commissioner of Internal Revenue. All comments will be available for public inspection and copying. A public hearing will be held upon written request to the Commissioner by any person who has submitted written comments. If a public hearing is held, notice of the time and place will be published in the FEDERAL REGISTER.

Drafting Information

The principal author of these proposed regulations is Sharon L. Hall of the Legislation and Regulations Division of the Office of Chief Counsel, Internal Revenue Service. However, personnel from other offices of the Internal Revenue Service and Treasury Department participated in developing the regulations on matters of both substance and style.

List of Subjects in 26 CFR 1.61-1—1.281-4

Income taxes, Taxable income, Deductions, Exemptions.

(signed) Lawrence B. Gibbs

Commissioner of Internal Revenue

[¶ 20,138 Reserved.—Proposed regulations relating to employees of organizations under common control were formerly reproduced at this paragraph. The final regulations are at ¶ 12,353—12,358.]

[¶ 20,138A Reserved.—A notice of proposed rulemaking by cross-reference to temporary regulations related to notice, election, and consent rules under the Retirement Equity Act of 1984 was formerly reproduced at this paragraph. The temporary regulations were removed by T.D. 8219 (53 FR 31837).]

[¶ 20,138B Reserved.—Proposed and temporary regulations under Code Sec. 401 relating to effective dates, transitional rules, restrictions on distributions, and other issues arising under the Retirement Equity Act of 1984 were formerly reproduced here. The temporary regulations, which served as the text of the proposed regulations, were removed by T.D. 8219 (53 FR 31837).]

[¶ 20,138C Reserved.—Proposed regulations relating to cash or deferred arrangements under Code Sec. 401(k) and new nondiscrimination rules for employee contributions and matching contributions made to employee plans were formerly reproduced here. The final regulations now appear at ¶ 11,720J, 11,730, 11,731, 11,732, 11,732A, 11,732B, 11,751, 11,755-3, 11,755-4, 12,214, 12,233V, 12,406, 12,503, 13,648K and 13,648K-1.]

[¶ 20,139 Reserved.—Proposed Reg. §1.408-2(b)(2)(ii), relating to certain trustees of individual retirement accounts, was formerly reproduced here. The final regulation appears at ¶ 12,054.]

[¶ 20,140 Reserved.—Proposed Reg. §31.3401(a)-1, relating to federal income tax withholding on remuneration paid in the form of wage continuation payments, was formerly reproduced at this point. The final regulation appears at ¶ 13,551.]

[¶ 20,141 Reserved.—Proposed Reg. §1.408-1(d)(4) (redesignated as Reg. §1.408-6(d)(4) by T.D. 7714), relating to individual retirement account disclosure statements, was formerly reproduced at this point. The final regulation appears at ¶ 12,058.]

[¶ 20,142 Reserved.—Proposals to conform the regulations to provisions of section 101(j) of the Tax Reform Act of 1969 (83 Stat. 526) and section 2003(b) of the Pension Reform Act of 1974 were formerly reported at this point. The final regulations now appear at ¶ 11,252, 11,701, 11,712, 13,161, 13,162, 13,181—13,189, 13,502 and 13,521.]

[¶ 20,142A Reserved.—Proposed regulations relating to the minimum participation standards for qualified retirement plans were formerly reproduced at this point. The final regulations are at ¶ 12,156 and 12,163.]

[¶ 20,142B Reserved.—Proposed Regs. §§31.3401(a)(12)-1 and 301.6693-1, prescribing withholding tax rules for individual retirement plans and penalties for failure to furnish information in connection with such plans, were formerly reproduced at this point. The final regulations appear at ¶ 13,553 and 13,852.]

[¶ 20,142C Reserved.—Proposed regs. §§1.401(k)-1 and 1.402(a)-1(d), relating to cash or deferred arrangements, were formerly reproduced here. The final regulations now appear at ¶ 11,721, 11,730, 11,731, and 11,751.]

[¶ 20,142D Reserved.—Proposed Reg. §§1.401(a)-50 and 1.501(a)-1, relating to treatment of Puerto Rican retirement income plans, were formerly reproduced at this point. The final regulations appear at ¶ 11,720V and 13,161.]

¶20,138

[¶ 20,142E Reserved.—Proposed Reg. §§ 1.127-1, 1.127-2, 31.3121(a)(18)-1, 31.3306(b)(13)-1 and 31.3401(a)(19)-1, relating to educational assistance programs, were formerly reproduced at this point. The final regulations appear at ¶ 11,289A, 11,289B, 13,534M, and 13,553G.]

[¶ 20,142F Reserved.—Formerly reproduced at this paragraph were proposed regulations relating to the limitation of benefits in the event of an early termination of certain qualified plans. The proposed regulations were finalized by T.D. 7934 on January 9, 1984, and appear at ¶ 11,704.]

[¶ 20,142G Reserved.—Formerly reproduced at this paragraph were proposed regulations on withholding from amounts paid under accident or health plans. The proposed regulations were finalized by T.D. 7888 on April 22, 1983 (48 FR 17586) and appear at ¶ 13,551.]

¶ 20,142H

Proposed regulations— Withholding social security tax from sick pay.—Following are proposed regulations that relate to withholding of social security or railroad retirement taxes from sick pay. The regulations that are being proposed are also issued as temporary regulations and are reproduced at ¶ 13,535. Temp. Reg. § 32.2, which relates to withholding of railroad retirement taxes, is not reproduced because it is not pertinent to the PENSION PLAN GUIDE.

These regulations appeared in the *Federal Register* on July 6, 1982.

DEPARTMENT OF THE TREASURY

Internal Revenue Service

26 CFR Part 31

[LR-23-82]

Withholding Social Security or Railroad Retirement Tax from Sick Pay

AGENCY: Internal Revenue Service, Treasury.

ACTION: Notice of proposed rulemaking by cross-reference to temporary regulations.

SUMMARY: In the Rules and Regulations portion of this *Federal Register,* the Internal Revenue Service is publishing temporary regulations that relate to withholding social security or railroad retirement tax from sick pay. The text of those temporary regulations also serves as the comment document for this proposed rulemaking.

DATES: Written comments and requests for a public hearing must be delivered by September 7, 1982. The regulations are proposed to be effective with respect to sick pay payments made on or after January 1, 1982.

ADDRESS: Send comments and requests for a public hearing to: Commissioner of Internal Revenue, Attention: CC:LR:T (LR-23-82), Washington, D.C. 20224.

FOR FURTHER INFORMATION CONTACT: Pamela F. Olson of the Legislation and Regulations Division, Office of the Chief Counsel, Internal Revenue Service, 1111 Constitution Avenue, N.W., Washington, D.C. 20224 (Attention: CC:LR:T) (202-566-3459).

SUPPLEMENTARY INFORMATION:

Background

The temporary regulations in the Rules and Regulations portion of this issue of the *Federal Register* add a new Part 32 to Title 26 of the Code of Federal Regulations. The final regulations, which this document proposes are based on those temporary regulations, would be added to Part 31 of Title 26 of the Code of Federal Regulations. Section 32.1 would become § 31.3121(a)(2)-2, § 32.2 would become § 31.3231(e)-2, and Part 32 would be deleted.

The regulations would require an employer or third party making a payment on account of sickness or accident disability on or after January 1, 1982, to withhold, deposit, and pay the applicable social security or railroad retirement taxes based on the amount of the payment and provide a receipt of the amount of any such payment to the employee pursuant to section 6051. The regulations would allow third parties to transfer to the employer liability for paying the employer portion of the tax and responsibility for providing a receipt to the employee if they promptly (1) withhold the employee share of the tax, (2) deposit such portion pursuant to section 6302, and (3) notify the employer for whom services are normally rendered of the amount of the payment. Notification of the employer would be considered to be prompt if such notice is mailed on or before the required date for the deposit of the employee share of the tax by the third party. For purposes of the employer's paying the employer portion of the tax, payment to the employee would be deemed to have been made on the date that the employer receives notice of such payment from the third party.

The proposed regulations define "employer for whom services are normally rendered" as the last employer for whom the employee worked. Alternatives to this rule were considered for multiemployer plans. These alternatives included (1) allowing each plan to establish its own definition of "employer for whom services are normally rendered," (2) allocating the burden among all of the employers for whom the employee performed services over some period prior to the disability, (3) defining "employer for whom services are normally rendered" as the employer for whom the employee worked the most hours over some period prior to the disability, and (4) providing no definition of "employer for whom services are normally rendered." All of these alternatives were rejected in favor of the last employer rule because it was believed to be the rule which was most feasible administratively for the multiemployer plans, the employers, and the Service. For purposes of multiemployer plans which have purchased insurance to provide benefits to covered employees, the trust fund would be considered to be the third party making payments on account of sickness or accident disability provided the insurer withholds and deposits the tax imposed on the employee and notifies the plan of the payments. In order to relieve itself of liability, any such notified multiemployer plan which would itself be treated as the third party payer must, within 6 days of receipt of notification from the insurance company, notify the last employer for whom the employee worked.

The proposed regulations would not apply to a payment which is made under a workmen's compensation law, the Railroad Retirement Act, the Railroad Unemployment Insurance Act for days of sickness related to on-the-job injury, or which is unrelated to absence from work, is made after the expiration of six calendar months following the last calendar month in which the employee worked, or is attributable to a contribution by the employee.

The proposed regulations would allow a third party to request and rely on certain information from the employer in order to avoid overpayment of tax with respect to any employee receiving a payment on account of sickness or accident disability.

Employees of State and local governments may or may not be participants in the social security system. State and local governments that have elected to become part of the social security system do so by means of an agreement with the Secretary of Health and Human Services. Under these agreements, State governments make contributions equivalent to the social security tax which are deposited in Federal Reserve banks and accounted for to the Social Security Administration. Third parties making payments to employees of State and local governments should, therefore, contact the State or local government to determine the proper procedures to follow to insure correct and timely deposits and accurate wage reports.

The regulations are necessary because of the amendments made to section 3121(a) and 3231(e) by Pub. L. 97-123 (95 Stat. 1659). These statutory changes are effective with respect to payments made on or after January 1, 1982, on account of sickness or accident disability. These regulations are proposed to be issued under the authority contained in sections 3121(a) and 3231(e) (95 Stat. 1662 and 1663; 26 U. S. C. 3121(a) and 3231(e)) and 7805 (68A Stat. 917; 26 U. S. C. 7805) of the Internal Revenue Code of 1954.

Non-Applicability of Executive Order 12291

The Treasury Department has determined that this proposed regulation is not subject to review under Executive Order 12291 or the Treasury and OMB implementation of the Order dated April 28, 1982.

Regulatory Flexibility Act

Although this document is a notice of proposed rulemaking which solicits public comment, the Internal Revenue Service has concluded that the regulations proposed herein are interpretative and that the notice and public procedure requirements of 5 U. S. C. 553 do not apply. Accordingly, these proposed regulations do not constitute regulations subject to the Regulatory Flexibility Act (5 U. S. C. Chapter 6).

Comments and Requests for a Public Hearing

Before adopting these proposed regulations, consideration will be given to any written comments that are submitted (preferably six copies) to the Commissioner of Internal Revenue. All comments will be available for public inspection and copying. A public hearing will be held upon written request to the Commissioner by any person who has submitted written comments. If a public hearing is held, notice of the time and place will be published in the *Federal Register.*

Roscoe L. Egger, Jr.

Commissioner of Internal Revenue.

[FR Doc. 82-18185; Filed 6-30-82; 4:00 pm]

[¶ 20,142I Reserved.—Proposed Reg. §§ 20.20394(d) and (e), relating to the method for receiving an estate tax exclusion for lump-sum distributions from qualified plans, were formerly reproduced at this point. The final regulations appear at ¶ 13,502B.]

¶ 20,142J

Proposed regulations: Reclassification of investment arrangements: Multiple classes of ownership.—Reproduced below is the text of proposed regulations that relate to the classification for tax purposes of investment arrangements with multiple classes of ownership. The proposed regulations clarify that certain investment arrangements would be classified as associations or partnerships rather than trusts.

The proposed regulations were published in the Federal Register on May 2, 1984 (49 FR 18741).

26 CFR Part 301

[LR-68-84]

Classification of Investment Arrangements With Multiple Classes of Ownership

AGENCY: Internal Revenue Service, Treasury.

ACTION: Notice of proposed rulemaking.

SUMMARY: This document contains proposed regulations relating to the classification for federal tax purposes of investment arrangements with multiple classes of ownership. The proposed regulations are designed to clarify the meaning of the term "fixed investment trust" and the application of the classification rules to investment arrangements with multiple classes of ownership. The regulations would provide guidance to taxpayers and Internal Revenue Service personnel.

DATES: *Proposed effective date.* The amendments to the regulations are proposed to apply with respect to arrangements, any interests in which are initially issued after April 27, 1984.

Date for comments. Written comments must be delivered or mailed by July 2, 1984.

Date for public hearing. A public hearing on the proposed regulations will be held on July 31, 1984; for further information, see the notice of public hearing published elsewhere in this issue of the *Federal Register.* [CCH PENSION PLAN GUIDE, ¶ 23,653E].

ADDRESS: Send comments to Commissioner of Internal Revenue. Attention: CC:LR:T [LR-68-84], Washington, D.C. 20224.

FOR FURTHER INFORMATION CONTACT: Cynthia Grigsby of the Legislation and Regulations Division, Office of the Chief Counsel, Internal Revenue Service, 1111 Constitution Avenue NW., Washington. D.C. 20224 (Attention: CC:LR:T) (202-566-3935).

SUPPLEMENTARY INFORMATION:

Background

This document contains proposed amendments to the Regulations on Procedure and Administration (26 CFR Part 301) under section 7701 of the Internal Revenue Code of 1954. The proposed amendments relate to the definition of the term "trust" for federal tax purposes. These amendments to the regulations are proposed to be issued under the authority contained in section 7805 of the Internal Revenue Code of 1954 (68A Stat. 917; 26 U.S.C. 7805).

Explanation of Amendments

Existing § 301.7701-4(c) of the Regulations on Procedure and Administration provides guidance as to the classification for federal tax purposes of certain "investment" trusts. Under that regulation an entity of the type "commonly known as a fixed investment trust" is classified as a trust or an association (taxable as a corporation), depending upon the existence of a power under the agreement to vary the investment of the certificate holders. The question has been raised whether the rules for fixed investment trusts apply to an investment arrangement under which investors may choose among different classes of ownership with varying investment attributes.

The entities commonly known as fixed investment trusts at the time that the existing regulations were first promulgated in 1945 has only one class of certificates, with each certificate representing an undivided interest in trust property. "The investor [in a fixed trust] * * * has a beneficial undivided interest in specific deposited securities or property. * * * In the fixed trust * * * only one class of security is issued—the certificate of beneficial interest which is, in form, a receipt issued by the trustee for the deposited property" [Investment Trusts and Investment Companies, H.R. Doc. No. 567, 76th Cong., 3d Sess. 8-9 (1940) (footnote omitted).] The purpose of a fixed investment trust was to provide a convenient vehicle to enable investors to acquire undivided beneficial interests in a diversified investment portfolio. Thus, entities with multiple classes of ownership were not commonly known as fixed investment trusts at the time that the regulations were promulgated.[1] Consequently, the "fixed investment trust" rules were not intended to apply to such entities. In contrast, at the time the regulations were issued, multiple classes of ownership, such as preferred and common stock, often were associated with "management companies." H.R. Doc. No. 567 at 8-9. A "management trust," which is one type of management company, is classified for tax purposes as an association taxable as a corporation. Treas. Reg. § 301.7701-4(c).

In recent months new arrangements have been created that are claimed to be fixed investment trusts. In one such arrangement, a mortgage pool was formed to allow various groups of investors with different investment objectives to join together in a financial arrangement in which different rights and risks associated with a pool of mortgages are allocated among three classes of certificates. The first class of certificates provides for a priority in distributions from the pool and represents a short term interest while the second and third classes of certificates represent interests with longer maturities. The owner of a certificate in any of the three classes is not entitled to distributions of principal and interest on any specific mortgage or mortgages, but merely the right to certain distributions from the pool. Because there are multiple classes of ownership, this arrangement is not a fixed investment trust. Moreover, a significant objective of the arrangement is to shift to the first class of certificate holders the risk that mortgages in the pool will be prepaid, so that the holders of the second and third classes of certificates will have "call protection" (freedom from premature termination of their interests on account of prepayments.) This arrangement was not intended to protect and conserve property for the beneficiaries. Rather, the certificate holders, through this arrangement, associated together to fulfill their diverse profit-making objectives. The certificate holders must be viewed, therefore, as association in a joint enterprise for the conduct of business for profit, and the arrangement is classified as an association or a partnership under § 301.7701-2 of the regulations.

---

[1] In *Commissioner v. Chase National Bank,* 122 F.2d 540 (2d Cir. 1941). the court held that a trust having certificates with detachable coupons evidencing the bearer's rights to receive semiannual distributions from the trust paid out of dividends and other income from stocks held by the trust was a fixed investment trust. The court found, however, that the purpose underlying the arrangement was to enable investors to acquire undivided beneficial interests in the stocks held in the arrangement. 122 F.2d at 541. The detachable coupons were a convenience to facilitate distributions and there was no apparent intention for the coupons to be detached and actively traded prior to their maturity. Thus, there was no intention to create a second class of ownership.

A second new type of arrangement provides a vehicle for investors to divide the income and appreciation elements inherent in a share of common stock. In this arrangement, a custodian accepts shares of stock in a single corporation and issues to the depositor one certificate for each share deposited. The certificate is perforated and can be separated by the depositor into two parts, with one part representing the right to receive an amount referable to the current value of the share of stock and the right to dividends from the stock, and the other part representing the right to the future appreciation on the share above the amount allocated to holders of the first part. The purpose of the arrangement is to allow investors to separate the certificate, retain the portion that suits their objectives and sell the other portion in the market. Buying one of the two parts enables investors to fulfill their specific profit-making objectives. Although only one type or class of certificate is issued by the custodian, the effect of the arrangement is to create two classes of interests. Thus, the arrangement is not a fixed investment trust. Moreover, as with the type of arrangement described above, the investors have associated together to divide the burdens and benefits inherent in the contributed shares and must be viewed as associates with an objective to carry on a business and divide the gains therefrom. Thus, this arrangement is also classified as an association or a partnership under § 301.7701-2 of the regulations.

In a third type of arrangement, a custodian holds one or more issues of bonds and issues certificates representing the right to specific interest or principal payments on the bonds. Although this arrangement is similar to the described above, it is distinguishable in that the division of the property is only between the bonds and specific interest coupons thereon. In section 1232B of the Code, Congress has provided a method for taxing transactions involving such "stripped bonds" and "stripped coupons." Thus, it would be inconsistent with section 1232B to treat typical "coupon stripping" arrangements in which bonds are held by a custodian and interests in specifically identifiable stripped coupons or bonds are sold as either associations or partnerships.

The proposed amendments to the regulations clarify the meaning of "fixed investment trust" under the regulations. The existing regulations, in focusing on the power of the trustee to vary the investment of the certificate holders, reflect the issue that was of primary concern at the time the regulations were drafted. With the development of multiple class investment arrangements, however, there is a need for further elaboration on the definition of the term "fixed investment trust" and the essential elements of this type of entity. In providing this definition, the proposed amendments impose a limitation not expressly stated in the existing regulations, and thus it was decided that the amendments should be prospective from April 27, 1984. The proposed rules for classification will apply to investment arrangements, any interests in which are initially issued after April 27, 1984.

Special Analyses

The Commissioner of Internal Revenue has determined that this proposed rule is not a major rule as defined in Executive Order 12291 and that a Regulatory Impact Analysis is therefore not required.

Although this document is a notice of proposed rulemaking that solicits public comments, the Internal Revenue Service has concluded that the regulations proposed therein are interpretative and that the notice and public procedure requirements of 5 U.S.C. 553 do not apply. Accordingly, no Regulatory Flexibility Analysis is required by chapter 6 of title 5, United States Code.

Comments and Public Hearing

Before adoption of these proposed regulations, consideration will be given to any written comments that are submitted (preferably seven copies) to the Commissioner of Internal Revenue. All comments will be available for public inspection and copying.

A public hearing on the proposed regulations will be held on July 31, 1984. For further information about the public hearing, see the notice of hearing that appears elsewhere in this issue of the **Federal Register.**

Drafting Information

The principal author of these proposed regulations is Paul A. Francis of the Legislation and Regulations Division of the Office of Chief Counsel, Internal Revenue Service. However, personnel from other offices of the Internal Revenue Service and Treasury Department participated in developing the regulations, on matters of both substance and style.

List of Subjects in 26 CFR Part 301

Administrative practice and procedure, Bankruptcy, Courts, Crime, Employment taxes, Estate taxes, Excise taxes, Gift taxes, Income taxes, Investigations, Law enforcement, Penalties, Pensions, Statistics, Taxes, Disclosure of information, Filing requirements.

Proposed Amendments to the Regulations

PART 301—[AMENDED]

Accordingly, it is proposed to amend 26 CFR Part 301 as follows: Paragraph (c) of § 301.7701-4 is revised to read as follows:

§ 301.7701-4 Trusts.

* * *

(c) *Certain investment trusts*—(1) An "investment" trust of the type commonly known as a management trust is an association, and a trust of the type commonly known as a fixed investment trust is an association if there is power under the trust agreement to vary the investment of the certificate holders. See *Commissioner v. North American Bond Trust,* 122 F.2d 545 (2d Cir. 1941), *cert. denied* 314 U.S. 701 (1942). However, if there is no power under the trust agreement to vary the investment of the certificate holders, such fixed investment trust shall be classified as a trust.

(2) A trust commonly known as a fixed investment trust is an arrangement in which legal title to property is conveyed to a trustee for the benefit of a group of investors. Each investor in such a trust has an undivided beneficial interest in the property held in trust, typically represented by certificates of beneficial interest issued to the investor; there is only one class of ownership interest. An arrangement having more than one class of ownership interest is not a fixed investment trust because an investor, rather than having an undivided beneficial interest in each asset of the trust, has a participating interest that differs from the interest held by an investor of another class. Because an arrangement with multiple classes of ownership enable investors to fulfill varying profit-making objectives through the division of rights and the sharing of risks in certain assets, the arrangement is considered to have associates and an objective to carry on business and divide the gains therefrom. Such an arrangement, therefore, is classified as an association or a partnership under § 301.7701-2.

(3) The requirement that a fixed investment trust have only one class of undivided interests has no application to mere custodial arrangements formed to allow investors to own specifically identifiable stripped coupons or stripped bonds within the meaning of section 1232B.

(4) The provisions of paragraph (c)(2) of this section may be illustrated by the following examples:

Example (1). A corporation purchases a portfolio of residential mortgages (or participations in residential mortgages) and transfers the mortgages to a bank under a custody agreement. At the same time, the bank as custodian delivers to the corporation certificates evidencing rights to payments from the pooled mortgages; the corporation sells the certificates to the public. The custodian holds legal title to the mortgages in the pool for the benefit of the certificate holders but has no power to reinvest proceeds attributable to the mortgages in the pool or to vary investments in the pool in any other manner. There are two classes of certificates. Holders of class A certificates are entitled to all payments of mortgage principal, both scheduled and prepaid, until their certificates are retired; holders of class B certificates receive payments of principal only after all class A certificates have been retired. This arrangement has two classes of ownership and is therefore, not a fixed investment trust, such an arrangement is considered to have associates and an objective to carry on business for profit and divide the gains there from. Therefore, it is classified as an association or a partnership under § 301.7701-2.

Example (2). A promoter formed a trust in which shareholders of a publicly traded corporation could deposit their stock. For each share of stock deposited with the trust, the participant receives a certificate that can be separated into two parts. One part represents the right to dividends and the value of the underlying stock up to a specified amount, the other part represents the right to appreciation above the specified amount. The two parts are traded separately on the open market. There are two classes of ownership in this arrangement and it is, therefore, not a fixed investment trust. Such an arrangement is considered to have associates and an objective to carry on business for profit and divide the gains therefrom. Therefore, it is classified as an association or a partnership under § 301.7701-2.

* * *

Roscoe L. Egger, Jr.,

Commissioner of Internal Revenue.

[FR Doc. 84-11865 Filed 4-27-84; 4:57 am]

[¶ 20,143 Reserved.—§1.1441-2(a) and 1.1441-2(b)(2)(ii) were previously reproduced at this paragraph. The regulations were removed by subsequently proposed regulations that are at ¶ 20,216.]

[¶ 20,144 Reserved.—Proposed Reg. §§54.4975-7, 54.4975-11, and 54.4975-12, relating to employee stock ownership plans, were formerly reproduced at this point. The final regulations appear at ¶ 13,644, 13,647B, and 13,647C.]

[¶ 20,145 Reserved.—Proposed Reg. §§54.4975-6 and 54.4975-15, relating to exemption from excise tax for provision of services and office space to plans, were formerly reported at this point. The final regulations now appear at ¶ 13,643 and 13,647B.]

[¶ 20,146 Reserved.—Proposed Reg. §§1.46-7 and 1.46-8 were formerly reproduced at this point. Some of the proposals were revised and adopted as final regulations and appear at ¶ 11,123 and 11,124.]

¶ 20,146A

Proposed regulations— Election to treat no portion of a lump sum distribution from an employee benefit plan as long-term capital gain—Election to treat pre-1974 plan participation as post-1973 participation ("the 402(e)(4)(L) election").—Reproduced below is the text of proposed regulations under Code Secs. 402 and 403 relating to the taxation of lump sum distributions from qualified pension, profit-sharing, stock bonus and annuity plans which conform to previously proposed amendments (40 FR 18798, PENSION PLAN GUIDE, ¶ 20,121) to the Tax Reform Act of 1976. The proposed regulations were published in the Federal Register of May 31, 1979 (44 FR 31228).

DEPARTMENT OF THE TREASURY

Internal Revenue Service

[26 CFR Part 1]

[EE-16-78]

Income Tax; Election to Treat Pre-1974 Plan Participation as Post-1973 Participation

AGENCY: Internal Revenue Service, Treasury.

ACTION: Notice of proposed rulemaking.

SUMMARY: This document contains proposed regulations relating to the election to treat no portion of a lump sum distribution from an employee benefit plan as long-term capital gain. Changes in the applicable tax law were made by the Tax Reform Act of 1976. The regulations would provide the public with the guidance needed to comply with that Act and would affect any recipient of a lump sum distribution.

DATES: Written comments and requests for a public hearing must be delivered or mailed by July 30, 1979. The amendments are proposed to be effective for distributions received in taxable years of the recipient beginning after December 31, 1975.

ADDRESS: Send comments and requests for a public hearing to: Commissioner of Internal Revenue, Attention:

CC:LR:T:EE-16-78, Washington, D. C. 20224.

FOR FURTHER INFORMATION CONTACT:

Richard L. Johnson of the Employee Plans and Exempt Organizations Division, Office of the Chief Counsel, Internal Revenue Service, 1111 Constitution Avenue, NW., Washington, D. C. 20224. Attention: CC:LR:T, 202-566-3544 (Not a toll-free number).

SUPPLEMENTARY INFORMATION:

Background

On April 30, 1975, the Federal Register published at 40 FR 18798 proposed amendments to the Income Tax Regulations (26 CFR Part 1) under sections 402(a), 402(e), 403(a) and other sections of the Internal Revenue Code of 1954, relating to the taxation of lump sum distributions from qualified pension, profit-sharing, stock bonus and annuity plans. A correction notice was published in the Federal Register on May 23, 1975, at 40 FR 22548. The amendments were proposed to conform the regulations to section 2005 of the Employee Retirement Income Security Act of 1974 (88 Stat. 987). Proposed amendments contained in paragraphs 1 and 2 of the appendix to that notice of proposed rulemaking were adopted by Treasury decision 7399 published in the Federal Register on February 3, 1976, at 41 FR 5099. The remainder of the amendments proposed in the appendix to the notice of proposed rulemaking of April 30, 1975, have not yet been adopted.

This document contains further proposed amendments to the Income Tax Regulations (26 CFR Part 1) under Code sections 402(a)(2), 402(e) and 403(a)(2) to conform the regulations to Code section 402(e)(4)(L), as added by section 1512 of the Tax Reform Act of 1976 (90 Stat. 1742). The proposed regulations are to be issued under the authority contained in sections 402(e)(4)(L) and 7805 of the Internal Revenue Code of 1954 (90 Stat. 1742; 68A Stat. 917; 26 U. S. C. 402(e)(4)(L), 7805).

Pre-1974 and Post-1973 Plan Participation

Under Code section 402(a)(2) or 403(a)(2), a portion of a lump sum distribution from a qualified pension, profit sharing, stock bonus or annuity plan is taxable as long-term capital gain. If the employee has been a participant in the plan for at least 5 years, and if the recipient is eligible to make the required election, the portion of the distribution not taxable as long-term capital gain is taxable under the 10-year averaging provisions of Code section 402(e). The portion of a lump sum distribution taxable as long-term capital gain is determined by taking into account the number of calendar years of participation by the employee in the plan before January 1, 1974. The portion taxable under Code section 402(e) represents participation in the plan after December 31, 1973.

Ordinary Income Election

Under Code section 402(e)(4)(L), a recipient may elect, under certain circumstances, to treat all calendar years of the employee's participation in all plans before January 1, 1974, as calendar years of participation after December 31, 1973. In such a case, no portion of the lump sum distribution is taxable as long-term capital gain. If the distribution is otherwise eligible for application of Code section 402(e), the total taxable amount of the distribution is taxable under the 10-year averaging pro. visions.

Comments and Requests for a Public Hearing

Before adopting these proposed regulations, consideration will be given to any written comments that are submitted (preferably eight copies) to the Commissioner of Internal Revenue. All comments will be available for public inspection and copying. A public hearing will be held upon written request to the Commissioner by any person who has submitted written comments. If a public hearing is held, notice of the time and place will be published in the Federal Register.

Drafting Information

The principal author of these proposed regulations is Richard L. Johnson of the Employee Plans and Exempt Organizations Division of the Office of Chief Counsel, Internal Revenue Service. However, personnel from other offices of the Internal Revenue Service and Treasury Department participated in developing the regulation, both on matters of substance and style.

Proposed Amendments to the Regulations

The proposed amendments to the regulations are as follows:

Paragraph 1. Section 1.402(a)-1(a)(9), as set forth in paragraph 10 of the appendix to the notice of proposed rulemaking of April 30, 1975, is revised by adding a new sentence at the end thereof to read as follows:

§ 1.402(a)-1 Taxability of beneficiary under a trust which meets the requirements of section 401(a).

(a) *In general.* * * *

(9) * * * In the case of a lump sum distribution received by or made available to a recipient in a taxable year of the recipient beginning after December 31, 1975, the recipient may elect, in accordance with section 402(e)(4)(L) and §1.402(e)-14, to treat all calendar years of an employee's active participation in all plans in which the employee has been an active participant as years of active participation after December 31, 1973. If a recipient makes the election, no portion of any distribution received by or made available to the recipient with respect to the employee (whether in the recipient's taxable year for which the election is made, or thereafter) is taxable to the recipient as long-term capital gain under section 402(a)(2) and this subparagraph.

Par. 2. Section 1.402(e)-2(d)(3) as set forth in paragraph 12 of the appendix to the notice of proposed rulemaking of April 30, 1975, is revised by adding a new subdivision (iii) to read as follows:

§ 1.402(e)-2 Treatment of certain lump sum distributions made after 1973.

* * *

(d) *Definitions.* * * *

(3) *Ordinary income portion.* * * *

(iii) In the case of a lump sum distribution received in a taxable year of the recipient beginning after December 31, 1975, the recipient may elect, in accordance with section 402(e)(4)(L) and §1.402(e)-14, to treat all calendar years of an employee's active participation in all plans in which the employee has been an active participant as years of active participation after December 31, 1973. If a recipient makes the election, the ordinary income portion of any lump sum distribution received by the recipient with respect to the employee (whether in the recipient's taxable year for which the election is made, or thereafter) is equal to the total taxable amount of the distribution.

* * *

Par. 3. The following new section is added in the appropriate place:

§ 1.402(e)-14 Election to treat pre-1974 participation as post-1973 participation (the "402(e)(4)(L) election").

(a) *In general.* Under section 402(e)(4)(L) and this section, the recipient of a lump sum distribution may elect to treat all calendar years of an employee's active participation in all plans in which the employee has been an active participant as years of active participation after December 31, 1973. This election is the "402(e)(4)(L) election." For rules relating to the treatment of distributions made on behalf of an employee with respect to whom the election is made, see §1.402(a)-1(a)(9) (relating to the capital gains portion of a lump sum distribution) and §1.402(e)-2(d)(3)(iii) (relating to the ordinary income portion of a lump sum distribution). For purposes of this section the term "lump sum distribution" means a lump sum distribution as defined in section 402(e)(4)(A), without regard to section 402(e)(4)(B).

(b) *Taxpayers not eligible to make the election.* A taxpayer may not make the 402(e)(4)(L) election with respect to a lump sum distribution made on behalf of an employee, if—

(1) The taxpayer received a prior lump sum distribution made on behalf of the employee in a taxable year of the employee (or in a year that would have been a taxable year of the employee, but for the death of the employee) beginning after December 31, 1975, and

(2) A portion of that prior lump sum distribution was treated as long-term capital gain under section 402(a)(2) or 403(a)(2).

(c) *Time and scope of election*—(1) *In general.* The 402(e)(4)(L) election shall be made for the first lump sum distribution made with respect to an employee to which the election is to apply. The election does not apply to a lump sum distribution received by the recipient with respect to an other employee. The 402(e)(4)(L) election is irrevocable. A revocation under §1.402(e)-3 of the election to apply the separate tax to a lump sum distribution will not revoke a 402(e)(4)(L) election.

(2) *Application of separate tax.* Nothing in this section 402(e)(4)(L) and this section changes the requirements which must be satisfied in order for a lump sum distribution to be eligible for application of the separate tax under section 402(e). Accordingly, a lump sum distribution is not taxable under section 402(e) merely because the 402(e)(4)(L) election is made with respect to, or otherwise applies to, the distribution.

(3) *Example.* The provisions of subparagraph (2) of this paragraph may be illustrated by the following example:

Example. (i) A, a calendar year taxpayer aged 59 ½, separates from the service of A's employer, the M Corporation, on October 31, 1976. On December 15, 1976, A receives a distribution of the balance to A's credit under the M Corporation qualified profit sharing plan. A has been an active participant in the plan since January 1, 1971. The distribution is a lump sum distribution within the meaning of section 402(e)(4)(A) which satisfies the requirements of section 402(e)(4)(C), relating to the aggregation of certain trusts and plans, and section 402(e)(4)(H), relating to a minimum period of participation in the plan.

(ii) A makes the 402(e)(4)(L) election with respect to the distribution. Under section 402(e)(4)(L), all years of A's active participation in all plans in which A has been an active participant are treated as years of active participation after December 31, 1973. Accordingly, no portion of the distribution is taxable as long-term capital gain under section 402(a)(2), and the total taxable amount of the distribution is "ordinary income" for purposes of section 402(e). A also makes the section 402(e)(4)(B) election for A's taxable year in which A receives the distribution. Accordingly, the total taxable amount of the distribution is taxable under the 10-year averaging provisions of section 402(e) (the separate tax).

(iii) On January 15, 1977, A receives a distribution of the balance of A's credit under the M Corporation-qualified pension plan. A has been an active participant in the plan since January 1, 1958. The distribution is a lump sum distribution within the meaning of section 402(e)(4)(A) which satisfies the requirements of section 402 (e)(4)(C), relating to the aggregation of certain trusts and plans, and section 402 (e)(4)(H), relating to a minimum period of participation in the plan. No portion of the distribution is taxable as long-term capital gain under section 402(a)(2) because A made the 402(e)(4)(L) election with respect to A's 1976 distribution. In addition, no portion of the distribution is taxable under the 10-year averaging provisions of section 402(e) because A made a prior election under section 402(e)(4)(B) with respect to a distribution made on A's behalf and after A was age 59 ½ (the 1976 distribution).

(d) *Manner of making election.* The 402 (e)(4)(L) election shall be made in the manner indicated on the form filed pursuant to section 402(e)(4)(B) and §1.402(e)-3 (c)(2) before the expiration of the period prescribed in §1.402(e)-3 for making the election to apply the separate tax to the ordinary income portion of a lump sum distribution.

(e) *Effective date.* Taxpayers eligible under this section to make the 402(e)(4)(L) election may make the election with respect to a lump sum distribution received after December 31, 1975, and in a taxable year of the recipient beginning after that date.

Par. 4. Section 1.403(a)-2(e)(3), as set forth in paragraph 15 of the appendix to the notice of proposed rulemaking of April 30, 1975, is revised by adding, immediately after subdivision (ii) thereof, a new sentence to read as follows:

§ 1.403(a)-2 Capital gains treatment for certain distributions.

* * *

(e) * * *

(3) * * *

(i) * * *

(ii) * * *

In the case of a lump sum distribution received by or made available to a recipient in a taxable year of the recipient beginning after December 31, 1975, the recipient may elect, in accordance with section 402(e)(4)(L), and §1.402(e)-14, to treat all calendar years of an employee's active participation in all plans in which the employee has been an active participant as years of active participation after December 31, 1973. If a recipient makes the election, no portion of any distribution received by or made available to the recipient with respect to the employee (whether in the recipient's taxable year for which the election is made, or thereafter) is taxable to the recipient as long-term capital gain under section 403 (a)(2) and this subparagraph.

* * *

Jerome Kurtz,

Commissioner of Internal Revenue.

[FR Doc. 79-16949 Filed 5-30-79; 8:45am]

[¶ 20,146B Reserved.—Proposed Reg. §1.46-9, relating to investment credit employee stock ownership plans (TRASOPs) that provide for an extra one-half percent credit, was formerly reproduced at this point. The final regulation now appears at ¶ 11,124A.]

[¶ 20,147 Reserved.—Proposed Reg. §54.4975-14, relating to the election to pay an excise tax for certain pre-1975 prohibited transactions, was formerly reported at this point. The final regulation now appears at ¶ 13,647A.]

[¶ 20,148 Reserved.—Proposed Reg. §1.401(a)-13, relating to assignment or alienation of benefits, was formerly reported at this point. The final regulations appear at ¶ 11,719B.]

[¶ 20,149 Reserved.—Proposed Regs. §§1.79-1(b)(1)(ii), 1.79-1(b)(ii)(a) and 1.79-3 (d), relating to the qualification of group-term life insurance coverage for favorable tax treatment and which were formerly reported at this point, were withdrawn by the IRS.]

¶ 20,149A

[Note: The proposed regulations issued on June 15, 1987 (below) and January 7, 1998 (CCH P ENSION PLAN GUIDE ¶ 20,231), will remain in effect until the proposed regulations and the final regulations, issued on February 3, 1999, become effective for plan years beginning on or after January 1, 2000.—CCH.]

Proposed regulations: Continuation coverage of group health plans. Reproduced below is the text of proposed regulations relating to the requirement that a group health plan offer continuation coverage to people who would otherwise lose coverage as the result of a "qualifying event." The proposed regulations were published in the Federal Register on June 15, 1987 (52 FR 22716).

DEPARTMENT OF THE TREASURY INTERNAL REVENUE SERVICE

[26 CFR Part I]

[EE-143-86]

Income Tax; Continuation Coverage Requirements Of Group Health Plans

AGENCY: Internal Revenue Service, Treasury.

ACTION: Notice of proposed rulemaking.

SUMMARY: This document contains proposed regulations relating to the requirement that a group health plan offer continuation coverage to people who would otherwise lose coverage as a result of certain events. They reflect changes made by the Consolidated Omnibus Budget Reconciliation Act of 1985 (COBRA) and the Tax Reform Act of 1986. The regulations will generally affect sponsors of and participants in group health plans, and they provide plan sponsors with guidance necessary to comply with the law.

DATES: Written comments and requests for a public hearing must be delivered or mailed on or before August 14, 1987. These regulations are proposed to be effective when final regulations are published in the FEDERAL REGISTER as a Treasury decision.

ADDRESS: Send comments and requests for a public hearing to: Commissioner of Internal Revenue, Attention: CC:LR:T (EE-143-86) Washington, D.C. 20224.

FOR FURTHER INFORMATION CONTACT: Mark Schwimmer of the Employee Plans and Exempt Organizations Division, Office of Chief Counsel, Internal Revenue Service, 1111 Constitution Avenue, N.W., Washington, D.C. 20224 (Attention: CC:LR:T). Telephone 202-566-6212 (not a toll-free number).

SUPPLEMENTARY INFORMATION

Background

This document contains proposed amendments to the Income Tax Regulations (26 CFR Part 1) under sections 106(b), 162(i)(2), and 162(k) of the Internal Revenue Code of 1986 (Code). The proposed regulations conform the regulations to section 10001 of the Consolidated Omnibus Budget Reconciliation Act of 1985 (COBRA) (100 Stat. 222) and to section 1895(d) of the Tax Reform Act of 1986 (100 Stat. 2936), which made technical corrections to the COBRA provisions.

COBRA added a new section 162(k) of the Code to specify continuation coverage requirements for employer-provided group health plans. In general, a group health plan must offer each "qualified beneficiary" who would otherwise lose coverage under the plan as a result of a "qualifying event" an opportunity to elect continuation of the coverage being received immediately before the qualifying event. A qualified beneficiary who properly elects continuation coverage can be charged an amount no greater than 102 percent of the "applicable premium." The "applicable premium" is based on the plan's cost of providing coverage.

If a group health plan fails to comply with these continuation coverage requirements, the employer will be unable to deduct contributions made to that or any other group health plan (section 162(i)(2)), and certain highly compensated individuals will be unable to exclude from income any employer-provided coverage under that or any other group health plan (section 106(b)).

In addition, there may be non-tax consequences if a group health plan fails to comply with parallel requirements that section 10002 of COBRA added to Title I of the Employee Retirement Income Security Act of 1974 (ERISA). Title I of ERISA is administered by the Department of Labor. Governmental plans (as defined in section 414(d) of the Code) are exempt from both the tax and ERISA provisions. However, State and local governmental group health plans are subject to parallel requirements that section 10003 of COBRA added to the Public Health Service Act, which is administered by the Department of Health and Human Services.

The proposed regulations do not refelct section 9501 of the Omnibus Budget Reconciliation Act of 1986, which extended the COBRA continuation coverage requirements to certain individuals receiving retiree medical benefits from employers that are involved in bankruptcy proceedings. The changes made by that act will be addressed in a later issuance.

The proposed regulations clarify which plans must offer COBRA continuation coverage and the tax consequences of failing to do so. They also provide guidance on a variety of details, including the scope of the continuation coverage, who is a qualified beneficiary, what is a qualifying event, how elections are made, and when payment must be made. Rules regarding computation of the applicable premium under section 162(k)(4) will be addressed in a later issuance.

Section 414(t) as added by the Tax Reform Act of 1986 extends the employer aggregation rules of sections 414(b), (c), (m), and (o) to a variety of employee benefit provisions. The list of those provisions includes section 106 (denying an income exclusion to highly compensated employees of an employer maintaining a group health plan that fails to comply with section 162(k)), but does not include section 162(i)(2) (denying deductions to such an employer) or section 162(k) itself. A technical correction to add sections 162(i)(2) and 162(k) to the list was included in H. Con. Res. 395. Although the 99th Congress adjourned without enacting that concurrent resolution, the correction was identical in both House and Senate versions. Accordingly, the proposed regulations set forth employer aggregation rules that anticipate a similar technical correction with retroactive effect being enacted in the current session of Congress.

There is no connection between the proposed regulations and section 89 of the Code. For example, the definitions set forth in the proposed regulations will not affect the meaning of "core benefits," "non-core benefits," or any other terms for purposes of section 89. Also, the computation of applicable premiums for COBRA continuation coverage will not affect the determination of the value of group health plan benefits for purposes of section 89.

Effective Date

The regulations are proposed to be effective when final regulations are published in the *Federal Register* as a Treasury decision. Group health plans become subject to the COBRA continuation coverage requirements at different times, however, depending on the plan year of a plan and whether the plan is a collectively bargained plan. With respect to qualifying events that occur on or after the date that a plan became or becomes subject to those requirements and before the effective date of final regulations, the plan and the employer must operate in good faith compliance with a reasonable interpretation of the statutory requirements (i.e., title X of COBRA). For the period before the effective date of final regulations, the Internal Revenue Service will consider compliance with the terms of these proposed regulations to constitute good faith compliance with a reasonable interpretation of the statutory requirements (other than the statutory requirements regarding the computation of the applicable premium or the treatment, under section 9501 of the Omnibus Budget Reconciliation Act of 1986, of certain bankruptcies as qualifying events, which are not addressed in these proposed regulations). Moreover, plans and employers will be considered to be in compliance with the terms of these proposed regulations if, between June 15, 1987 and September 14, 1987, they operate in good faith compliance with a reasonable interpretation of the statutory requirements and, from September 15, 1987 until the effective date of final regulations, they operate in compliance with the terms of these proposed regulations. In addition, the Internal Revenue Service will not consider actions inconsistent with the terms of these proposed regulations necessarily to constitute a lack of good faith compliance with a reasonable interpretation of the statutory requirements; whether there has been good faith compliance with a reasonable interpretation of the statutory requirements will depend on all the facts and circumstances of each case.

Special Analyses

The Commissioner of Internal Revenue has determined that this proposed rule is not a major rule as defined in Executive Order 12291. Therefore, a Regulatory Impact Analysis is not required. Although this document is a notice of proposed rulemaking which solicits public comment, the Internal Revenue Service has concluded that the regulations proposed herein are interpretative and that the notice and public procedure requirements of 5 U.S.C. 553 do not apply. Accordingly, these proposed regulations do not constitute regulations subject to the Regulatory Flexibility Act (5 U.S.C. chapter 6).

Comments and Requests for Public Hearing

Before adopting these proposed regulations, consideration will be given to any written comments that are submitted (preferably eight copies) to the Commissioner of Internal Revenue. All comments will be available for public inspection and copying. A public hearing will be held upon written request to the Commissioner by any person who has submitted written comments. If a public hearing is held, notice of the time and place will be published in the *Federal Register.*

Drafting Information

The principal author of these proposed regulations is Mark Schwimmer of the Employee Plans and Exempt Organizations Division of the Office of Chief Counsel, Internal Revenue Service. However, personnel from other offices of the Internal Revenue Service and Treasury Department participated in developing the regulations, both on matters of substance and style.

List of Subjects in 26 CFR 1.61-1-1.281-4

Income taxes, Taxable income, Deductions, Exemptions

Proposed amendments to the regulations

The proposed amendments to 26 CFR Part 1 are as follows:

Paragraph 1. The authority citation for Part 1 is amended by adding the following citation:

Authority: 26 U.S.C. 7805. * * * Sections 1.106-1 and 1.162-26 also issued under 26 U.S.C. 106(b), 162(i)(2), and 162(k).

Par. 2. Section 1.106-1 is amended by redesignating the existing text as paragraph (a), revising the first sentence of paragraph (a), and adding a new paragraph (b). The revised and added provisions read as follows:

§ 1.106-1. Contributions by employer to accident and health plans.

(a) Except as set forth in paragraph (b) of this section, the gross income of an employee does not include contributions which his employer makes to an accident or health plan for compensation (through insurance or otherwise) to the employee for personal injuries or sickness incurred by him, his spouse, or his dependents, as defined in section 152. * * *

(b) In situations involving group health plans that do not comply with section 162(k), the exclusion described in paragraph (a) of this section is not available to highly compensated employees (as defined in section 414(q)). See § 1.162-26 (regarding continuation coverage requirements of group health plans).

Par. 3. A new section 1.162-26 is added immediately after § 1.162-25T to read as follows:

§ 1.162-26. Continuation coverage requirements of group health plans.

Table of Contents

List of Questions

COBRA in General

Q-1: What are the new health care continuation coverage requirements added to the Internal Revenue Code by the Consolidated Omnibus Budget Reconciliation Act of 1985 ("COBRA")?

Q-2: What is the effect of a group health plan's failure to comply with section 162(k)?

Q-3: How are employer deductions affected by a group health plan's failure to comply with section 162(k)?

Q-4: How is the gross income of certain individuals affected by a group health plan's failure to comply with section 162(k)?

Q-5: What is the employer?

Q-6: How does COBRA apply to a group health plan before the effective date of this section?

Which Plans Must Comply and When

Q-7: What is a group health plan?

Q-8: What group health plans are subject to COBRA?

Q-9: What is a small-employer plan?

Q-10: When is an arrangement considered to be two or more separate group health plans rather than a single group health plan?

Q-11: When must group health plans comply with section 162(k)?

Q-12: What is a collectively bargained group health plan?

Q-13: What is the plan year of a group health plan?

Q-14: How do the COBRA continuation coverage requirements apply to cafeteria plans and other flexible benefit arrangements?

Qualified Beneficiaries

Q-15: Who is a qualified beneficiary?

Q-16: Who is a covered employee?

Q-17: Other than those individuals who are qualified beneficiaries as of the day before a qualifying event, can any other person (such as a newborn or adopted child or a new spouse) obtain qualified beneficiary status for COBRA continuation coverage purposes?

Qualifying Events

Q-18: What is a qualifying event?

Q-19: Can a qualifying event result from a voluntary termination of employment?

Q-20: Can a qualifying event occur before the effective date of section 162(k) (as described in Q&A-11 of this section)?

Q-21: Can a qualifying event occur while a group health plan is excepted from COBRA (see Q&A-8 of this section)?

COBRA Continuation Coverage

Q-22: What is COBRA continuation coverage?

Q-23: How is COBRA continuation coverage affected by changes in the coverage that is provided to similarly situated beneficiaries with respect to whom a qualifying event has not occurred?

Q-24: Can a group health plan require a qualified beneficiary who wishes to receive COBRA continuation coverage to elect to receive a continuation of all of the coverage that he or she was receiving under the plan immmediately before the qualifying event?

Q-25: What is core coverage?

Q-26: Must a qualified beneficiary be given an opportunity to elect core coverage plus only one of two non-core coverages that the qualified beneficiary had under the plan immediately before the qualifying event?

Q-27: Must a qualified beneficiary who is covered under a single plan providing both core coverage and non-core coverage be offered the opportunity to elect non-core coverage only?

Q-28: What deductibles apply if COBRA continuation coverage is elected?

Q-29: How do a plan's limits apply to COBRA continuation coverage?

Q-30: Can a qualified beneficiary who elects COBRA continuation coverage ever change from the coverage received by that individual immediately before the qualifying event?

Q-31: Aside from open enrollment periods, can a qualified beneficiary who has elected COBRA continuation coverage choose to cover individuals (such as newborn children, adopted children, or new spouses) who join the qualified beneficiary's family on or after the date of the qualifying event?

Electing COBRA Continuation Coverage

Q-32: What is the minimum period during which a group health plan must allow a qualified beneficiary to elect COBRA continuation coverage (i.e., the election period)?

Q-33: Must a covered employee or qualified beneficiary inform the employer or plan administrator of the occurrence of a qualifying event?

Q-34: During the election period and before the qualified beneficiary has made an election, must coverage by provided?

Q-35: Is a waiver before the end of the election period effective to end a qualified beneficiary's election rights?

Q-36: Can an employer withhold money or other benefits owed to a qualified beneficiary until the qualified beneficiary either waives COBRA continuation, coverage, elects and pays for such coverage, or allows the election period to expire?

Q-37: Can each qualified beneficiary make an independent election under COBRA?

Duration of COBRA Continuation Coverage

Q-38: How long must COBRA continuation coverage be available to a qualified beneficiary?

Q-39: When does the maximum coverage period end?

Q-40: Can the maximum coverage period ever be expanded?

Q-41: If coverage is provided to a qualified beneficiary after a qualifying event without regard to COBRA continuation coverage (e.g., as a result of State or local law, industry practice, a collective bargaining agreement, or plan procedure), will such alternative coverage extend the maximum coverage period?

Q-42: How can an event that occurs before a group health plan becomes subject to section 162(k) affect the maximum coverage period when a later, qualifying event occurs?

Q-43: Must a qualified beneficiary be given the right to enroll in a conversion health plan at the end of the maximum coverage period for COBRA continuation coverage?

Paying for COBRA Continuation Coverage

Q-44: Can a qualified beneficiary be required to pay for COBRA continuation coverage?

Q-45: After a qualified beneficiary has elected COBRA continuation coverage under a group health plan, can the plan increase the amount that the qualified beneficiary must pay for COBRA continuation coverage?

Q-46: Must a qualified beneficiary be allowed to pay for COBRA continuation coverage in installments?

Q-47: Can a qualified beneficiary choose to have the first payment for COBRA continuation coverage applied prospectively only?

Q-48: What is timely payment for COBRA continuation coverage?

COBRA in General

Q-1: What are the new health care continuation coverage requirements added to the Internal Revenue Code by the Consolidated Omnibus Budget Reconciliation Act of 1985 ("COBRA")?

A-1: Section 10001 of COBRA added a new section 162(k) to the Code to provide generally that a group health plan must offer each qualified beneficiary who would otherwise lose coverage under the plan as a result of a qualifying event an opportunity to elect, within the applicable election period, continuation coverage under the plan. That continuation coverage is referred to in this section as "COBRA continuation coverage" and a group health plan that is subject to section 162(k) is referred to as being "subject to COBRA" (see Q&A-8 of this section). A qualified beneficiary can be required to pay for COBRA continuation coverage. A qualified beneficiary is defined in Q&A-15 of this section. A qualifying event is defined in Q&A-18 of this section. The election procedures are described in Q&A-32 through Q&A-37 of this section. COBRA continuation coverage is described in Q&A-22 through Q&A-31 of this section. Payment for COBRA continuation coverage is addressed in Q&A-44 through Q&A-48 of this section. Unless otherwise specified, any reference in this section to "COBRA" refers to section 10001 of COBRA and to section 162(k) of the Code as added by COBRA (as amended).

Q-2: What is the effect of a group health plan's failure to comply with section 162(k)?

A-2: If a group health plan subject to COBRA fails to comply with section 162(k), certain deductions are disallowed to the employer under section 162(i)(2) (see Q&A-3 of this section) and the income exclusion under section 106(a) is denied to certain highly compensated employees of the employer under section 106(b)(1) (see Q&A-4 of this section). There may be additional non-tax consequences if the plan fails to comply with parallel requirements that were added by section 10002 of COBRA to Title I of the Employee Retirement Income Security Act of 1974 (ERISA), which is administered by the Department of Labor. Although governmental plans are not subject to section 162(k) because they are not "subject to COBRA" (see Q&A-8 of this section), certain governmental plans are subject to parallel requirements that were added by section 10003 of COBRA to the Public Health Service Act, which is administered by the Department of Health and Human Services.

Q-3: How are employer deductions affected by a group health plan's failure to comply with section 162(k)?

A-3: (a) Under section 162(i)(2), if a group health plan subject to COBRA fails to comply with section 162(k), each employer maintaining the plan is denied a deduction for any contributions or other expenses paid or incurred in connection with any group health plan that it maintains. The deduction is denied for any taxable year of the taxpayer during which there are one or more days on which the plan is not in compliance with section 162(k). Thus, if a failure to comply with section 162(k) arises in one taxable year of a taxpayer and is not corrected until after the beginning of the following taxable year, the deduction for contributions or expenses for both of those taxable years is denied. Section 162(i)(2) operates each taxable year to permanently deny a deduction for amounts paid or incurred in that year, and is applied before applying any provision of the Code that governs the timing of an otherwise available deduction. Examples of such provisions include sections 263A (capitalization and inclusion in inventory costs), 419 (treatment of funded welfare benefit plans), and 460 (special rules for long-term contracts). In addition, section 162(i)(2) operates with respect to each employer maintaining the group health plan, without regard to whether the employers are treated as a single employer (see Q&A-5 of this section) and without regard to whether the failure to satisfy section 162(k) occurs with respect to only an employee of one of the employers. See Q&A-10 of this section regarding when an arrangement is treated as two or more separate group health plans.

(b) A failure of a group health plan to comply with section 162(k) that occurs before, and is not corrected by, the date that an employer maintaining the plan and another entity are first treated as a single employer under Q&A-5 of this section ("the combination date") will not result in a denial of a deduction to the other entity under paragraph (a) of this Q&A-3, so long as (1) the other entity did not also maintain the plan before the combination date, and (2) the failure is corrected before the end of the first taxable year of the other entity that begins after the combination date.

(c) The rules of this Q&A-3 are illustrated by the following examples:

Example 1: Plan A is a group health plan subject to COBRA that is maintained by two unrelated employers, X and Y. Section 162(k) became effective with respect to plan A before April 1, 1988. The taxable year of employer X ends on March 31, and the taxable year of employer Y ends on April 30. If Plan A fails to comply with section 162(k) on April 1, 1988, by not offering COBRA continuation coverage to a qualified beneficiary of an employee of employer X, and the failure is not corrected until June 1, 1988, both employers X and Y are disallowed deductions for their contributions and other expenses relating to all their group health plans (including any group health plan that is maintained only by employer X or only by employer Y) for each taxable year that includes one or more days of noncompliance. Thus, the disallowance applies to employer X for its taxable year ending March 31, 1989, and to employer Y for both its taxable year ending April 30, 1988, and its taxable year ending April 30, 1989. (However, see Q&A-10 of this section regarding when an arrangement is considered to be two or more separate group health plans.)

Example 2: Assume that companies Z and W are treated as a single employer under section 414(b) at all relevant times (see Q&A-5 of this section), that Z maintains group health plans P and Q, that W maintains group health plans R and S, and that none of these plans is excepted from COBRA (see Q&A-8 of this section). Assume further that the taxable year of company Z ends on May 31, that the taxable year of company W ends on July 31, and that section 162(k) becomes effective with respect to the group health plans as follows: for plan P on February 1, 1987; for plan Q on April 1, 1987; and for plans R and S on June 1, 1987. If at any time during February through May of 1987 plan P is not in compliance with section 162(k), then company Z is disallowed all deductions with respect to plans P and Q for its taxable year ending May 31, 1987, and Company W is disallowed all deductions with respect to plans R and S for its taxable year ending July 31, 1987.

Example 3: Assume that a group health plan maintained only by M, a calendar year employer, is subject to COBRA and fails to comply with section 162(k) during February of 1988, that the failure is corrected during April of 1988, and that on June 1, 1988 employer M becomes a wholly owned subsidiary of N, a previously unrelated corporation with a taxable year ending July 31. For 1988, M is disallowed a deduction for all its contributions with respect to any group health plan. Because M and N were not treated as a single employer (see Q&A-5 of this section) during the period of noncompliance by M's plan (i.e., February to April of 1988), the failure of M's plan to comply with section 162(k) during that period will not result in a disallowance of any deductions to N, the new parent corporation. Even if the failure to comply that arises in February of 1988 is not corrected until after June 1, 1988, it will not result in a disallowance of any deductions to N, so long as the failure to comply is corrected by July 31, 1989 (the end of N's first taxable year that begins after June 1, 1988). However, if the failure is not corrected until August of 1989, N will be disallowed a deduction for all its contributions with respect to any group health plan for its taxable years ending on July 31 of 1988, 1989, and 1990. Also, if another failure of M's plan to comply with section 162(k) arises on or after June 1, 1988, that second failure will result in a disallowance of deductions to N.

Example 4: Assume that a calendar year employer maintaining a group health plan through a welfare benefit fund contributes $800,000 to the fund in 1988 and $500,000 in 1989. Assume further that only $600,000 of the 1988 contribution would be deductible under section 419 for 1988, and that the remaining $200,000 would be deemed to be contributed in 1989 and deductible under section 419 for 1989 along with the $500,000 actually contributed in that year. However, the deduction under section 419 is only available if these amounts are otherwise deductible under section 162. Therefore, if at any time during 1988 the group health plan is not in compliance with section 162(k), the $800,000 contributed in 1988 is disallowed in full as a deduction for 1988 and for all later years. However, if the plan does comply with section 162(k) throughout 1988 but at some time during 1989 is not in compliance, the $600,000 deduction for 1988 is unaffected while the $700,000 otherwise deductible for 1989 is permanently disallowed.

Q-4: How is the gross income of certain individuals affected by a group health plan's failure to comply with section 162(k)?

A-4: (a) Under section 106(a), employer-provided coverage under an accident or health plan is generally excluded from the gross income of an employee. Under section 106(b), however, if a group health plan that is subject to COBRA fails to comply with section 162(k), certain individuals shall have certain employer-provided coverage included in their gross income for each of their taxable years during which the plan is not in compliance, even if the coverage would otherwise be excludable from income under section 106(a). The individuals referred to in the preceding sentence consist of each person who is, at any time during which the plan is not in compliance with section 162(k), a highly compensated employee (within the meaning of section 414(q) and the regulations under that section) of any employer maintaining the plan. The coverage included in the individual's gross income for each such taxable year shall consist of all coverage provided by the employer to the individual and his or her spouse and dependent children during that taxable year under any group health plan (other than a plan that is excepted from COBRA—see Q&A-8 of this section). For purposes of section 106(b) and this Q&A-4, whether an individual is a highly

compensated employee shall be determined on the basis of plan years or any alternative period permitted under section 414(q) and the regulations under that section. As used in the preceding sentence, "plan year" means the plan year as defined in Q&A-13 of this section.

(b) A failure of a group health plan to comply with section 162(k) that occurs before, and is not corrected by, the date that an employer maintaining the plan and another entity are first treated as a single employer under Q&A-5 of this section ("the combination date") will not result in an income inclusion for highly compensated employees of the other entity under paragraph (a) of this Q&A-4, so long as (1) the other entity did not also maintain the plan before the combination date, and (2) the failure is corrected before the end of the first taxable year of the other entity that begins after the combination date.

(c) The rules of this Q&A-4 are illustrated by the following examples, in which it is assumed that all individuals are calendar year taxpayers:

Example 1: Employer Z maintains group health plan T, and maintains no other group health plans. If plan T fails to comply with section 162(k) on November 10, 1988, and the failure is not correct until February 15, 1989, each individual who is a highly compensated employee of Z at any time from November 10, 1988, through February 15, 1989, shall have coverage included in gross income for that individual's 1988 and 1989 taxable years. If the individual was covered under plan T throughout those years, the coverage included in 1988 is all coverage provided by employer Z under plan T on behalf of the individual and the individual's family during 1988, and the coverage included in 1989 is the coverage provided by employer Z under plan T on behalf of the individual and the individual's family during 1989.

Example 2: The facts are the same as in Example 1, except that employer Z's highly compensated employees are covered under plan U. Even if plan U complies with section 162(k) at all times, each individual who is a highly compensated employee of Z at any time from November 10, 1988, through February 15, 1989 (the period of plan T's noncompliance), shall have coverage included in gross income for that individual's 1988 and 1989 taxable years. If the individual was covered under plan U throughout those years, the coverage included in 1988 is all coverage provided by employer Z under plan U on behalf of the individual and the individual's family during 1988, and the coverage included in 1989 is all coverage provided by employer Z under plan U on behalf of the individual and the individual's family during 1989.

Example 3: The facts are the same as in Example 1, except that the failure to comply with section 162(k) is corrected on December 20, 1988, rather than on February 15, 1989. The income inclusion for highly compensated employees applies only for the 1988 taxable year and only to those individuals who are highly compensated employees of Z at some time from November 10 to December 20, 1988.

Example 4: The facts are the same as in Example 1. In addition, employer W maintains group health plan V, and maintains no other group health plans. Employer W's taxable year ends on May 31. Employer W becomes a wholly-owned subsidiary of employer Z on December 1, 1988. Plan T's failure to comply with section 162(k) that arises on November 10, 1988, does not result in an income inclusion to any of employer W's highly compensated employees because the failure is corrected on February 15, 1989, which is before May 31, 1990 (the end of employer W's first taxable year that begins after December 1, 1988). However, if another failure of Plan T to comply with section 162(k) arises on December 15, 1988, and that failure to comply is also corrected on February 15, 1989, each employee of employer W who is a highly compensated employee at any time from December 15, 1988, through February 15, 1989, is also subject to the income inclusion set forth in this Q&A-4.

Q-5: What is the employer?

A-5: For purposes of this § 1.162-26 and sections 106(b), 162(i), and 162(k), the term "employer" refers to the employer and any entity that is a member of a group described in section 414(b), (c), (m), or (o) that includes the employer, and to any successor of either the employer or such an entity. However, the rule of this Q&A-5 does not apply for purposes of determining whether a group health plan is a small-employer plan (see Q&A-9 of this section).

Q-6: How does COBRA apply to a group health plan before the effective date of this section?

A-6: This section is proposed to be effective when final regulations that include it are published in the FEDERAL REGISTER as a Treasury decision. Group health plans become subject to the COBRA continuation coverage requirements at different times, however, as set forth in Q&A-11 of this section. With respect to qualifying events that occur on or after the date that a plan became or becomes subject to those requirements and before the effective date of final regulations, the plan and the employer must operate in good faith compliance with a reasonable interpretation of the statutory requirements (i.e., title X of COBRA). For the period before the effective date of final regulations, the Internal Revenue Service will consider compliance with the terms of these proposed regulations to constitute good faith complaince with a reasonable interpretation of the statutory requirements (other than the statutory requirements regarding the computation of the applicable premium or the treatment, under section 9501 of the Omnibus Budget Reconciliation Act of 1986, of certain bankruptcies as qualifying events, which are not addressed in these proposed regulations). Moreover, plans and employers will be considered to be in compliance with the terms of these proposed regulations if, between June 15, 1987 and September 14, 1987, they operate in good faith compliance with a reasonable interpretation of the statutory requirements and, from September 15, 1987 until the effective date of final regulations, they operate in compliance with the terms of these proposed regulations. In addition, the Internal Revenue Service will not consider actions inconsistent with the terms of these proposed regulations necessarily to constitute a lack of good faith compliance wtih a reasonable interpretation of the statutory requirements; whether there has been good faith compliance with a reasonable interpretation of the statutory requirements will depend on all the facts and circumstances of each case.

Which Plans Must Comply and When

Q-7: What is a group health plan?

A-7: (a) A group health plan is any plan maintained by an employer to provide medical care (as defined in section 213(d)) to the employer's employees, former employees, or the families of such employees or former employees, whether directly or through insurance, reimbursement, or otherwise, and whether or not provided through an on-site facility (except as set forth in paragraph (e) of this Q & A-7), or through a cafeteria plan (as defined in section 125) or other flexible benefit arrangement. For purposes of this Q & A-7, insurance includes not only group insurance policies but also one or more individual insurance policies in any arrangement that involves the provision of medical care to two or more employees. A plan "maintained by an employer," is any plan of, or contributed to (directly or indirectly), by an employer. Thus, a group health plan is "maintained by an employer," regardless of whether the employer contributes to it, if coverage under the plan would not be available at the same cost to an employee in the event that he or she were not employed by the employer. However, a plan that is maintained by an employee representative is not "maintained by an employer" if the employer does not contribute to the plan and has no involvement (e.g., payroll checkoff) in the operation of the plan. See Q & A-10 of this section for rules governing when a single arrangement is considered to be two or more separate group health plans.

(b) Medical care (as defined in section 213(d)) includes the diagnosis, cure, mitigation, treatment, or prevention of disease, and any other undertaking for the purposes of affecting any structure or function of the body. Medical care also includes transportation primarily for and essential to medical care as described in the preceding sentence. However, medical care does not include anything that is merely beneficial to the general health of an individual, such as a vacation. Thus, if an employer maintains a program that furthers general good health, but the program does not relate to the relief or alleviation of health or medical problems and is generally accessible to and used by employees without regard to their physical condition or state or health, that program is not considered a program that provides medical care and so is not a group health plan for purposes of this section.

(c) For example, if an employer maintains a spa, swimming pool, or exercise/fitnesss program that is normally accessible to and used by employees for reasons other than relief of health or medical problems, such a facility would not constitute medical care. In contrast, if the employer maintains a drug or alcohol treatment program or a health clinic, or any other facility or program that is intended to relieve or alleviate a physical condition or health problem (whether the condition or problem is chronic or acute), the facility or program is considered to be under the provision of medical care and so is considered a group health plan for purposes of this section.

(d) Whether a benefit provided to employees constitutes medical care is not affected by whether the benefit is excludable from income under section 132 (relating to certain fringe benefits). For example, if a department store provides its employees discounted prices on all merchandise, including health care items such as drugs or eyeglasses, the mere fact that the discounted prices also apply to health care items will not cause the program to be a plan providing medical care, so long as the discount program would normally be accessible to and used by employees without regard to health needs or physical condition. If, however, the employer maintaining the discount program is a health

clinic, so that the program is used exclusively by employees with health or medical needs, the program is considered as a plan providing medical care and so is considered a group health plan for purposes of this section.

(e) The provision of medical care at a facility that is located on the premises of an employer does not constitute a group health plan if (1) the medical care consists primarily of first aid that is provided during the employer's working hours for treatment of a health condition, illness, or injury that occurs during those working hours, (2) the medical care is available only to the employer's current employees, and (3) employees are not charged for the use of the facility.

Q-8: What group health plans are subject to COBRA?

A-8: (a) All group health plans are subject to COBRA (i.e., subject to section 162(k)) except group health plans described in section 106(b)(2). However, a group health plan is not subject to COBRA before the effective date prescribed for that plan in Q & A-11 of this section.

(b) The following group health plans are described in section 106(b)(2): (1) Small-employer plans (see Q & A-9 of this section), (2) church plans (within the meaning of section 414(e)), and (3) governmental plans (within the meaning of section 414(d)). Plans that are described in section 106(b)(2) are referred to in this §1.162-26 as "excepted from COBRA." The income inclusion rule of section 106(b)(1), the deduction denial rule of section 162(i), and the continuation coverage requirements of section 162(k) do not apply with respect to group health plans that are excepted from COBRA. Certain governmental plans, however, are governed by parallel requirements that were added by section 10003 of COBRA to the Public Health Service Act, which is administered by the Department of Health and Human Services.

Q-9: What is a "small-employer plan?"

A-9: (a) A "small-employer plan" is a group health plan maintained by one or more employers where each of the employers maintaining the plan for a calendar year normally employed fewer than 20 employees during the preceding calendar year. For purposes of this definition, each employer maintaining the plan shall, in combination with all other entities under common control with that employer (as determined under section 52(a) and (b)), be considered a single employer. See Q & A-10 of this section for rules governing when a single arrangement is considered to be two or more separate group health plans.

(b) An employer is considered as having normally employed fewer than 20 employees during a particular calendar year if, and only if, it had fewer than 20 employees on at least 50 percent of its working days during that year.

(c) In determining the number of its employees, an employer shall treat as employees all full-time and part-time employees, and all employees within the meaning of section 401(c)(1). For example, partners in a law firm are treated as employees for this purposes. An employer shall also treat as employees for this purpose all agents and independent contractors (and their employees, agents, and independent contractors, if any), and all directors (in the case of a corporation), but only if such individuals are eligible to participate in a group health plan maintained by the employer.

(d) The determination of whether a plan is a small-employer plan on any particular date depends on which employers are maintaining the plan on that date and on the workforce of those employers during the preceding calendar year. If a plan that is otherwise subject to COBRA ceases to be a small-employer plan because of the addition during a calendar year of an employer that did not normally employ fewer than 20 employees on a typical business day during the preceding calendar year, the plan ceases to be excepted from COBRA and section 162(k) becomes effective with respect to it immediately upon the addition of the new employer. In contrast, if the plan ceases to be a small-employer plan by reason of an increase during a calendar year in the workforce of an employer maintaining the plan, the plan ceases to be excepted from COBRA and section 162(k) becomes effective with respect to it on the January 1 immediately following the calendar year in which the employer's workforce increased. However, a plan described in the preceding sentence will be treated as not having become subject to section 162(k) on that January 1 (i.e., still expected from COBRA) if all the employers who did not normally employ fewer than 20 employees in the preceding calendar year have ceased to maintain the plan by February 1 immediately following that January 1. For example, if each employer maintaining a group health plan normally employs fewer than 20 employees during each of 1986 and 1987 but two of the employers do not normally employ fewer than 20 employees during 1988, the entire plan becomes subject to COBRA and must begin to comply with section 162(k) on January 1, 1989, even if the plan year is not a calendar year, unless those two employers depart from the plan before February 1, 1989.

Q-10: When is an arrangement considered to be two or more separate group health plans rather than a single group health plan?

A-10: (a) The rules below in paragraphs (b) through (g) of this Q&A-10 determine when an arrangement is considered to be two or more separate group health plans. If more than one of those paragraphs applies to a particular arrangement, the paragraphs are applied in succession to break the arrangements into the smallest possible group health plans. For example, if an arrangement offers high option and low option benefit schedules (see paragraph (c)) and constitutes a multiple employer welfare arrangement maintained by three different employers (see paragraph (d)), the arrangement consists of six separate group health plans: Three high-option plans (one for each employer) and three low-option plans (one for each employer).

(b) The rules in this Q&A-10 apply without regard to whether the arrangement is maintained by one or more than one employer. Moreover, the fact that a particular arrangement has been traditionally referred to as a single plan or has reported as a single plan (e.g., by filing a single Form 5500) is not controlling in the determination of whether the arrangement will be considered as two or more separate plans for purposes of section 162(k). All references elsewhere in this section to a "group health plan" are references to a separate group health plan as determined under this Q&A-10. The identification of separate group health plans is relevant to determinations such as those involving which coverage must be separately electable, the effective date of section 162(k), which employers will be denied deductions in the event of a failure to comply with section 162(k), the costs of continuation coverage, and the availability of the exception for small-employer plans (see Q&A-9 of this section). The relevance of treating an arrangement as two or more separate group health plans is illustrated by the following examples:

Example 1: If an employee is covered under more than one group health plan at the time of a qualifying event, the qualified beneficiaries must be offered an opportunity to elect COBRA continuation coverage with respect to each of the plans. In contrast, if the arrangement in which the employee participates is treated as a single group health plan with several features, no individual features of the plan would have to be made available to a qualified beneficiary unless the qualified beneficiary elects coverage under the entire plan. (But see Q&A-24 of this section regarding the election to receive only core coverage.)

Example 2: If an arrangement that involves many employers is considered to be a single group health plan, that plan will fail to qualify for the small-employer plan exception if any one of those employers had too many employees during the preceding calendar year. However, if the arrangement is considered to be a separate plan with respect to each employer, then the exception would be available for each of those particular employers that normally employed fewer than 20 employees during the preceding calendar year.

Example 3: An arrangement covering the employees of unrelated employers A and B fails to comply with section 162(k) by failing to offer COBRA continuation coverage to an employee of employer A, but complies with section 162(k) in all other respects. If the arrangement consists of two separate group health plans, one covering the employees of A and one covering the employees of B, employer A will lose deductions under section 162(i) and A's highly compensated employees will lose the benefit of the section 106(a) exclusion, but employer B and its employees will be unaffected. In contrast, if the arrangement consists of a single group health plan, the consequences of failing to comply with section 162(k) will apply to both employers A and B.

(c) Each different benefit package or option offered under an arrangement is treated as a separate group health plan. For this purpose, self-only coverage and self-and-family coverage are not considered to be separate packages or options. The rule of this paragraph (c) is illustrated by the following examples:

Example 1: If an arrangement offers "high option" and "low option" benefit schedules and the alternatives of self-only and self-and-family coverage, the arrangement is considered to be two separate plans: One offering high option coverage (whether self-only or self-and-family), and one offering low option coverage (whether self-only or self-and-family).

Example 2: If two types of coverage differ only because one has a $100 deductible and the other has a $250 deductible, or because one has a $1500 catastrophic limit and the other has a $2500 catastrophic limit, each type of coverage is a different benefit package and so is treated as a separate group health plan.

Example 3: An arrangement has a deductible equal to 1 percent of compensation, but consists of a single plan in all other respects. The fact that employees with different levels of compensation will have different deductibles will not cause the arrangement to be treated as separate group health plans for each resulting deductible.

Example 4: If an arrangement consists of a single plan in all respects except that an employee can choose to have either hospital benefits or hospital benefits combined with mental health benefits, there are two separate plans: One providing hospital coverage, and one providing hospital-and-mental-health coverage. If an employee could instead choose independently whether to have hospital benefits and whether to have mental-health benefits, there would also be two separate plans: One providing hospital-only coverage and one providing mental-health-only coverage. In such a case an employee receiving both hospital and mental-health benefits would be covered under two separate group health plans and would have separate COBRA election rights under each plan.

(d) An arrangement that constitutes a multiple employer welfare arrangement as defined in section 3(40) of the Employee Retirement Income Security Act of 1974 (ERISA), is considered a separate group health plan with respect to each employer maintaining the arrangement. Solely for purposes of this paragraph (d), the rules of section 3(40)(B) of ERISA (regarding trades or businesses under common control) shall apply in determining whether two or more employers are treated as a single employer.

(e) In the case of an insured arrangement, if two or more groups of employees are covered under separate contracts between a participating employer or employers and an insurer or insurers, each separate contract is considered a separate group health plan, even if the coverage under the separate contracts is identical.

(f) In the case of a self-funded arrangement, each segregated portion of the arrangement shall be considered a separate group health plan. A portion of an arrangement is a segregated portion if and only if (1) assets available to pay benefits under that portion are unavailable to pay benefits under any other portion, and (2) assets available to pay benefits under any other portion are unavailable to pay benefits out of that portion. For example, if several employers contribute to a trust that provides medical benefits but each employee's benefits are payable only out of contributions (and earnings on contributions) made by that employee's employer, each employer's portion of the arrangement is considered a separate group health plan. The rule of this paragraph (f) shall apply whether or not a trust is used, and whether or not the arrangement is partially insured through stop-loss insurance, insurance for some but not all benefits, or some other method.

(g) Arrangements providing medical benefits are broken down as described in Q&A-12 of this section into their collectively bargained portion (if any) and non-collectively-bargained portion (if any), each of which is considered a separate group health plan.

Q-11: When must group health plans comply with section 162(k)?

A-11: (a) Non-collectively bargained plans: For plans that are not excepted from COBRA (see Q&A-8 of this section) and that do not constitute collectively bargained group health plans (see Q&A-12 of this section), the requirements of section 162(k) apply as of the first day of the first plan year beginning on or after July 1, 1986. For example, if such a plan has a February 1 to January 31 plan year, it must begin to comply with section 162(k) by February 1, 1987.

(b) Collectively bargained plans: For plans that are not excepted from COBRA and that constitute collectively bargained group health plans (see Q&A-12 of this section), the requirements of section 162(k) apply as of the first day of the first plan year beginning on or after the later of (1) January 1, 1987, or (2) the date on which the last of the collective bargaining agreements relating to the plan terminates (determined without regard to any extension thereof agreed to after April 7, 1986). This rule is illustrated by the following example:

Example: Assume that the plan year of a collectively bargained group health plan is the calendar year and that, as of April 7, 1986, the plan is maintained pursuant to three collective bargaining agreements having expiration dates in October 1987, February 1988, and July 1988. The plan must comply with section 162(k) beginning on January 1, 1989. Of course, the plan must begin to comply by January 1, 1987, with respect to a collective bargaining unit that was not, as of April 7, 1986, covered by one of those three agreements.

Q-12: What is a collectively bargained group health plan?

A-12: (a) A collectively bargained group health plan is a group health plan covering only employees and former employees (and their families) who are covered by an agreement that is a collective bargaining agreement entered into between employee representatives and one or more employers (as determined under section 7701(a)(46)). Thus, if an arrangement that would otherwise be considered to be a single group health plan under the standards set out in Q&A-10 of this section covers both (1) employees and former employees (and their families) who are covered by a collective bargaining agreement described in the preceding sentence and (2) employees and former employees (and their families) who are not covered by such an agreement, the arrangement consists of two separate group health plans: One plan that is a collectively bargained group health plan and one that is not. The plan that is collectively bargained will have an effective date determined under paragraph (b) of Q&A-11 of this section, and the other plan will have an effective date determined under paragraph (a) of Q&A-11 of this section. For example, if the plan year is the calendar year and the only collective bargaining agreement in effect as of April 7, 1986, expires March 31, 1988, the effective date of section 162(k) is January 1, 1989, for the plan covering bargaining-unit employees and their families, and January 1, 1987, for the plan covering the other employees and their families.

(b) For purposes of this Q&A-12, employees of an employee representative that is a party to a collective bargaining agreement described in paragraph (a) of this Q&A-12, and employees of a trust or fund maintained to pay benefits to individuals covered by the collective bargaining agreement, are considered to be employees covered by that collective bargaining agreement. Thus, a plan that is otherwise considered a single, collectively bargained plan will not fail to be a single, collectively bargained plan merely because it also covers employees or former employees (and their families) of the employee representative or of a trust or fund from which the benefits are paid.

Q-13: What is the plan year of a group health plan?

A-13: (a) For purposes of determining when a group health plan must begin to comply with section 162(k) (see Q&A-11 of this section), the plan year of a group health plan is the year that is designed as the plan year in the plan document. However, if the plan document does not designate a plan year, or if there is no plan document, the plan year is determined under paragraph (b) of this Q&A-13. The designation of a plan year on a Form 5500 filed by a group health plan is not controlling in the determination of the plan year under this Q&A-13.

(b) If the plan year of a group health plan is determined under this paragraph (b), the plan year is the plan's limit/deductible year except that (1) in the case of an insured group health plan, the plan year is the policy year if that is later than the limit/deductible year or if the plan has no limit/deductible year, and (2) in the case of a self-funded group health plan having no limit/deductible year, the plan year is the later of the calendar year or the employer's taxable year. For purposes of this paragraph (b), a plan's "limit/deductible year" means the year that is used by the plan in applying benefit limits and deductibles, except that if different years are used for benefit limits and for deductibles, it means the later of those years. For purposes of this paragraph (b), one year is "later" than another if it begins later in relation to the underlying date from which the effective date of section 162(k) is determined for the plan under Q&A-11 of this section. Compare, for example, a year that begins on March 1 with a year that begins on December 1. The March 1 year is later than a December 1 year in the case of a non-collectively-bargained plan, because the first March 1 occurring on or after July 1, 1986, is March 1, 1987, which is later than December 1, 1986 (the first December 1 occurring on or after July 1, 1986). If, however, the plan is a collectively bargained plan and becomes subject to section 162(k) for the first plan year beginning on or after February 1, 1987, a December 1 year is later than a March 1 year.

Q-14: How do the COBRA continuation coverage requirements apply to cafeteria plans and other flexible benefit arrangements?

A-14: The provision of medical care through a cafeteria plan (as defined in section 125) or other flexible benefit arrangement constitues a group health plan. However, the COBRA continuation coverage requirements of section 162(k) apply only to those medical benefits under the cafeteria plan or other arrangement that a covered employee has actually chosen to receive (if any). The application of this rule to a cafeteria plan is illustrated by the following examples:

Example 1: Under the terms of a cafeteria plan, employees can choose among life insurance coverage, membership in a Health Maintenance Organization (HMO), coverage for medical expenses under an indemnity arrangement, and cash compensation. Of these available choices, the HMO and the indemnity arrangement constitute separate group health plans. Assume that these group health plans are subject to COBRA (see Q&A-8 of this section) and that the employer does not provide any group health plan outside of the cafeteria plan. Assume further that B and C are unmarried employees, that B has chosen the life insurance coverage, and that C has chosen the indemnity arrangement. B does not have to be offered COBRA continuation coverage

upon terminating employment, nor must a subsequent open enrollment period for active employees be made available to B. However, if C terminates employment and the termination constitutes a qualifying event, C must be offered an opportunity to elect COBRA continuation coverage under the indemnity arrangement. If C makes such an election and an open enrollment period for active employees occurs while C is still receiving the COBRA continuation coverage, C must be offered the opportunity to switch from the indemnity arrangement to the HMO (but not to the life insurance coverage because that does not constitute a group health plan).

Example 2: An employer maintains a group health plan under which all employees receive employer-paid coverage. Employees can arrange to cover their families by paying an additional amount. The employer also maintains a cafeteria plan, under which one of the options is to pay part or all of the charge for family coverage under the group health plan. Thus, an employee might pay for family coverage under the group health plan partly with before-tax dollars and partly with after-tax dollars. If an employee's family is receiving coverage under the group health plan when a qualifying event occurs, each of the qualified beneficiaries must be offered an opportunity to elect COBRA continuation coverage, regardless of how that qualified beneficiary's coverage was paid for before the qualifying event.

Example 3: One of the choices available under a cafeteria plan is an individual medical expense reimbursement arrangement. At the beginning of each calendar year, an employee can choose, instead of being paid a specified dollar amount of compensation, to have that amount placed in an account to be used for reimbursement of medical expenses incurred during the year by the employee or the employee's spouse or dependent children. Any amount remaining in the account as of the end of the year is forfeited. The reimbursement of medical expenses through these arrangements constitutes a group health plan.

Qualified Beneficiaries

Q-15: Who is a qualified beneficiary?

A-15: (a) Except as set forth in paragraphs (b) through (d) of this Q&A-15, a qualified beneficiary is an individual who, on the day before a qualifying event, is covered under a group health plan maintained by the employer of a covered employee by virtue of being on that day either (1) the covered employee, (2) the spouse of the covered employee, or (3) the dependent child of the covered employee.

(b) An individual is not a qualified beneficiary if, on the day before the qualifying event referred to in paragraph (a) of this Q&A-15, the individual (1) is covered under the group health plan by reason of another individual's election of COBRA continuation coverage and is not already a qualified beneficiary by reason of a prior qualifying event, or (2) is entitled to Medicare benefits under Title XVIII of the Social Security Act.

(c) A covered employee can be a qualified beneficiary only in connection with a qualifying event that consists of the termination (other than by reason of the covered employee's gross misconduct), or reduction of hours, of the covered employee's employment.

(d) An individual is not a qualified beneficiary if the individual's status as a covered employee is attributable to a period in which the individual was a nonresident alien who received no earned income (within the meaning of section 911(d)(2)) from the individual's employer that constituted income from sources within the United States (within the meaning of section 861(a)(3)). If, pursuant to the preceding sentence, an individual is not a qualified beneficiary, then a spouse or dependent child of the individual shall not be considered a qualified beneficiary by virtue of the relationship to the individual.

Q-16: Who is a covered employee?

A-16: (a) A covered employee is any individual who is (or was) provided coverage under a group health plan (other than a plan that is excepted from COBRA on the date of the qualifying event; see Q&A-8 of this section) by virtue of the individual's employment or previous employment with an employer. For example, a retiree or former employee who is covered by such a group health plan is a covered employee if the coverage results in whole or in part from his or her previous employment. An individual (whether a present or former employee) who is merely eligible for coverage under a group health plan is not a covered employee if the individual is not and has not been actually covered under the plan. The reason for an individual's lack of actual coverage (such as the individual's having declined participation in the plan or failed to satisfy the plan's conditions for participation) is not relevant for this purpose.

(b) The following individuals are also covered employees, but only if they are (or were) actually covered under a group health plan by virtue of their relationship to an employer maintaining the plan, and only if that plan or some other group health plan maintained by the employer covers one or more common-law employees of the employer: (1) employees within the meaning of section 401(c)(1), (2) agents and independent contractors (and their employees, agents, and independent contractors), and (3) directors (in the case of a corporation). The rule of this paragraph (b) is illustrated by the following example:

Example: A law firm maintains a group health plan for its common-law employees. If the firm also provides group health coverage for its partners, the partners are covered employees regardless of whether their coverage is provided under the same group health plan as the common-law employees or under a separate plan. In contrast, if the partners are the only individuals who receive any health coverage, they are not covered employees.

Q-17: Other than those individuals who are qualified beneficiaries as of the day before a qualifying event, can any other person (such as a newborn or adopted child or a new spouse) obtain qualified beneficiary status for COBRA continuation coverage purposes?

A-17: (a) No. The group of qualified beneficiaries entitled to elect COBRA continuation coverage as a result of a qualifying event is closed as of the day before the qualifying event. Thus, newborn children, adopted children, and spouses who join the family of a qualified beneficiary after that day do not become qualified beneficiaries. The new family members do not themselves become qualified beneficiaries even if they become covered under the plan. (For situations in which a plan is required to make coverage available to new family members of a qualified beneficiary who is receiving COBRA continuation coverage, see Q&A-31 of this section and paragraph (c) of Q&A-30 of this section.)

(b) A qualified beneficiary who fails to elect COBRA continuation coverage in connection with a qualifying event ceases to be a qualified beneficiary at the end of the election period (see Q&A-32 of this section). Thus, for example, if such a former qualified beneficiary is later added to a covered employee's coverage (e.g., during an open enrollment period) and then another qualifying event occurs with respect to the covered employee, the former qualified beneficiary will not be treated as a qualified beneficiary.

(c) The rules of this Q&A-17 are illustrated by the following examples:

Example 1: Assume that A is a single employee who voluntarily terminates employment and properly elects COBRA continuation coverage under a group health plan. Under the terms of the plan, a covered employee who marries can choose to have his or her spouse covered under the plan as of the date of marriage. One month after electing COBRA continuation coverage, A marries and chooses to cover A's spouse under the plan. A's spouse is not a qualified beneficiary. Thus, if A dies during the period of COBRA continuation coverage, the plan does not have to offer A's surviving spouse an opportunity to elect COBRA continuation coverage.

Example 2: Assume that B is a married employee who terminates employment, B properly elects COBRA continuation coverage for B but not B's spouse, and B's spouse declines to elect such coverage. B's spouse thus ceases to be a qualified beneficiary. Later, at the next open enrollment period, B adds the spouse as a beneficiary under the plan. The addition of the spouse during the open enrollment period does not make the spouse a qualified beneficiary. The plan will thus not have to offer the spouse an opportunity to elect COBRA continuation coverage upon a later divorce from or death of B.

Example 3: Assume that, under the terms of a group health plan, a covered employee's child ceases to be a dependent eligible for coverage upon attaining age 18. At that time, the child must be offered an opportunity to elect COBRA continuation coverage. If the child elects COBRA continuation coverage, the child marries during the period of the COBRA continuation coverage, and the child's spouse becomes covered under the group health plan, the child's spouse would not become a qualified beneficiary upon a later qualifying event as a result of that coverage.

Example 4: Assume that C is a single employee who, upon retirement, is given the opportunity to elect COBRA continuation coverage but declines it in favor of an alternative offer of 12 months of employer-paid retiree health benefits. C ceases to be a qualified beneficiary and will not have to be given another opportunity to elect COBRA continuation coverage at the end of those 12 months. Assume further that C marries D during the period of retiree health coverage and, under the terms of that coverage, D becomes covered under the plan. If a divorce from or death of C will result in D's losing coverage, D will be a qualified beneficiary because D's coverage under the plan on the day before the qualifying event (i.e., the divorce) will have been by reason of C's acceptance of 12 months of employer-paid coverage after the prior qualifying event (C's retirement) rather than by reason of an election of COBRA continuation coverage.

Example 5: Assume the same facts as in Example 4 except that, under the terms of the plan, the divorce or death does not cause D to lose coverage so that D continues to be covered for the balance of the original 12-month period. D does not have to be allowed to elect COBRA continuation coverage because the divorce or death does not constitute a qualifying event. See Q&A-18 of this section.

Qualifying Events

Q-18: What is a qualifying event?

A-18: (a) A qualifying event is an event that satisfies paragraphs (b), (c), and (d) of this Q&A-18.

(b) An event satisfies this paragraph (b) if the event is either (1) the death of a covered employee, (2) the termination (other than by reason of the employee's gross misconduct), or reduction of hours, of a covered employee's employment, (3) the divorce or legal separation of a covered employee from the employee's spouse, (4) a covered employee becoming entitled to Medicare benefits under Title XVIII of the Social Security Act, or (5) a dependent child ceasing to be a dependent child of the covered employee under the generally applicable requirements of the plan. In the case of a covered employee who is not a common-law employee, termination of "employment" for this purpose means termination of the relationship (e.g., directorship of a corporation or membership in a partnership) giving rise to the individual's treatment as a covered employee under paragraph (b) of Q&A-16 of this section.

(c) An event satisfies this paragraph (c) if, under the terms of the group health plan, the event causes the covered employee, or the spouse or a dependent child of the covered employee, to lose coverage under the plan. For this purpose, to "lose coverage" means to cease to be covered under the same terms and conditions as in effect immediately before the qualifying event. If coverage is reduced or eliminated in anticipation of an event, the reduction or elimination is disregarded in determining whether the event causes a loss of coverage. Moreover, for purposes of this paragraph (c), a loss of coverage need not occur immediately after the event, so long as the loss of coverage will occur before the end of the maximum coverage period (see Q&A-39 and Q&A-40 of this section). However, if neither the covered employee nor the spouse or a dependent child of the covered employee will lose coverage before the end of what would be the maximum coverage period, the event does not satisfy this paragraph (c).

(d) An event satisfies this paragraph (d) if it occurs while the plan is subject to COBRA. Thus, an event will not satisfy this paragraph (d) if it occurs before the plan becomes subject to section 162(k) (see Q&A-11 of this section) or while the plan is excepted from COBRA (see Q&A-8). See Q&A-20 and Q&A-21 of this section.

(e) The rules of this Q&A-18 are illustrated by the following examples, each of which assumes that paragraph (d) is satisfied:

Example 1: If an employee who is covered by a group health plan terminates employment (other than by reason of the employee's gross misconduct) and, as of the date of separation, is given 3 months of employer-paid coverage under the same terms and conditions as before that date, the termination is a qualifying event because it satisfies both paragraphs (b) and (c) of this Q&A-18.

Example 2: Upon the retirement of an employee who, along with the employee's spouse, has been covered under a group health plan, the employee is given identical coverage for life but the spousal coverage will not be continued beyond 6 months unless premiums are then paid by the employee or spouse. The spouse will "lose coverage" 6 months after the employee's retirement when the premium requirement takes effect, so the retirement is a qualifying event and the spouse must be given an opportunity to elect COBRA continuation coverage.

Example 3: F is a covered employee who is married to G, and both are covered under a group health plan maintained by F's employer. F and G are divorced and, under the terms of the plan, the divorce will cause G to lose coverage. The divorce is a qualifying event. If G elects COBRA continuation coverage and then remarries during the period of COBRA continuation coverage, G's new spouse might become covered under the plan. (See Q&A-31 of this section and paragraph (c) of Q&A-30 of this section.) However, G's later death or divorce from G's new spouse will not be a qualifying event because G is not a covered employee.

Q-19: Can a qualifying event result from a voluntary termination of employment?

A-19: Yes. Apart from gross misconduct, the facts surrounding a termination or reduction of hours are irrelevant. It does not matter whether the employee voluntarily terminated or was discharged. For example, a strike or walkout is a termination or reduction of hours that constitutes a qualifying event if the strike or walkout results in a loss of coverage as described in paragraph (c) of Q&A-18 of this section. Similarly, a layoff that results in such a loss of coverage is a qualifying event.

Q-20: Can a qualifying event occur before the effective date of section 162(k) (as described in Q&A-11 of this section)?

A-20: No. An event that occurs before section 162(k) becomes effective for a group health plan does not satisfy paragraph (d) of the definition of qualifying event in Q&A-18 of this section. A group health plan does not have to offer individuals whose coverage ends as a result of such an event the opportunity to elect COBRA continuation coverage. For example, if an employee terminated employment on July 15, 1986, and the plan covering the employee had a November 1 to October 31 plan year (so that the plan became subject to section 162(k) on November 1, 1986), the plan does not have to permit the employee to elect COBRA continuation coverage. Even if that employee is given 6 months of additional coverage from the July 15, 1986, termination date (whether merely as a result of the terms of the plan, or pursuant to state or local law or otherwise) so that the coverage extends beyond the November 1 effective date, the employee does not have to be given the opportunity to elect COBRA continuation coverage at the end of the 6 months' coverage because there will no qualifying event at that time. In contrast, if the employee's spouse is covered by the 6 months' coverage and, as a result of the employee's death after the November 1 effective date and before the end of the 6-month period, the spouse will lose coverage for the balance of the 6-month period, the death will constitute a qualifying event and the spouse will be a qualified beneficiary entitled to elect COBRA continuation coverage. See Q&A-42 of this section regarding the maximum coverage period in such a case.

Q-21: Can a qualifying event occur while a group health plan is excepted from COBRA (see Q&A-8 of this section)?

A-21: No. An event that occurs while a group health plan is excepted from COBRA does not satisfy paragraph (d) of the definition of qualifying event in Q&A-18 of this section. Even if the plan later becomes subject to COBRA, it does not have to provide COBRA election rights to anyone whose coverage ends as a result of such an event. For example, if a group health plan is excepted from COBRA as a small-employer plan during 1988 (see Q&A-9 of this section) and an employee terminates employment on December 31, 1988, the termination is not a qualifying event and the plan does not have to permit the employee to elect COBRA continuation coverage. This is the case even if the plan ceases to be a small-employer plan as of January 1, 1989. Also, the same result will follow even if the employee is given 3 months of coverage beyond December 31 (i.e., through March of 1989), because there will be no qualifying event as of the termination of coverage in March. However, if the employee's spouse is initially provided with the 3-month coverage through March 1989, but the spouse divorces the employee before the end of the 3 months and loses coverage as a result of the divorce, the divorce will constitute a qualifying event during 1989 and so entitle the spouse to elect COBRA continuation coverage. See Q&A-42 of this section regarding the maximum coverage period in such a case.

COBRA Continuation Coverage

Q-22: What is COBRA continuation coverage?

A-22: If a qualifying event occurs, each qualified beneficiary (other than a qualified beneficiary for whom the qualifying event will not result in any immediate or deferred loss of coverage) must be offered an opportunity to elect to continue to receive the group health plan coverage that he or she received immediately before the qualifying event. This continued coverage is "COBRA continuation coverage." Except as set forth in Q&A-23 through Q&A-31 of this section, if the continuation coverage offered differs in any way from the coverage enjoyed immediately before the qualifying event, the coverage offered does not constitute COBRA continuation coverage and the group health plan is not in compliance with section 162(k) unless other coverage that does constitute COBRA continuation coverage is also offered. Any elimination or reduction of coverage in anticipation of a qualifying event is disregarded for purposes of this Q&A-22 and for purposes of any other reference in this section to coverage in effect immediately before (or on the day before) a qualifying event. COBRA continuation coverage must not be conditioned upon, or discriminate on the basis of lack of, evidence of insurability.

Q-23: How is COBRA continuation coverage affected by changes in the coverage that is provided to similarly situated beneficiaries with respect to whom a qualifying event has not occurred?

A-23: COBRA continuation coverage must generally be the same as the group health plan coverage enjoyed by the qualified beneficiary immediately before the qualifying event. However, if the coverage provided to similarly situated active employees is changed or eliminated but the employer continues to maintain one or more group health plans (so that the qualified beneficiary's COBRA continuation coverage cannot be terminated at that time—see Q&A-37 of this section), the employer must permit the qualified beneficiary receiving COBRA continuation coverage to elect to be covered under any of the remaining group health plans maintained by the employer for similarly situated active employees. If the coverage of the qualified beneficiary was subject to deductibles and the change in coverage occurs before the end of the prescribed period for accumulating such deductibles, the new coverage selected by the qualified beneficiary must credit him or her with the amounts incurred under the original coverage. The rule in the preceding sentence also applies to those limits that are in the nature of deductibles, such as co-payment limits or catastrophic limits on a covered individual's out-of-pocket expenses. The qualified beneficiary can be charged the amount determined under Q&A-44 of this section for the coverage selected.

Q-24: Can a group health plan require a qualified beneficiary who wishes to receive COBRA continuation coverage to elect to receive a continuation of all of the coverage that he or she was receiving under the plan immediately before the qualifying event?

A-24: (a) In general, no. A qualified beneficiary who, immediately before the qualifying event, is covered by a plan that provides both core coverage and non-core coverage must be able to elect to receive either (1) the coverage that he or she had immediately before the qualifying event (including the core coverage and any non-core coverage), or (2) the core coverage only. However, there are two exceptions to this rule, as set forth in paragraphs (b) and (c) of this Q&A-24.

(b) If the applicable premium for core coverage would be at least 95 percent of the applicable premium for core coverage and non-core coverage combined, the plan does not have to offer qualified beneficiaries the opportunity to elect core coverage only. (See Q&A-44 of this section regarding the applicable premium.)

(c) If an employer maintaining a group health plan that includes non-core coverage also maintains at least one other group health plan for similarly situated active employees that does not provide any non-core coverage, the plan that includes non-core coverage does not have to offer a qualified beneficiary an opportunity to elect core coverage only. However, the qualified beneficiary must instead be offered the opportunity to elect coverage under any other group health plan maintained by the employer for similarly situated active employees.

Q-25: What is core coverage?

A-25: (a) "Core coverage" means all of the coverage that a qualified beneficiary was receiving under the group health plan immediately before a qualifying event that gives rise to the qualified beneficiary's COBRA election rights, other than "non-core coverage." Non-core coverage" means coverage for vision benefits and dental benefits. However, coverage for vision benefits or dental benefits that must be provided under applicable law is core coverage.

(b) For purposes of this Q&A-25, vision benefits include only those benefits related to vision care of a type that is not required under local law to be performed by a physician.

(c) For purposes of this Q&A-25, dental benefits does not include any benefits for dental care or oral surgery in connection with an accidental injury.

(d) The definitions in this Q&A-25 apply only for purposes of this § 1.162-26 and sections 106, 162(i)(2), and 162(k) of the Code.

Q-26: Must a qualified beneficiary be given an opportunity to elect core coverage plus only one of two non-core coverages that the qualified beneficiary had under the plan immediately before the qualifying event?

A-26: No. A group health plan is required only to offer qualified beneficiaries the right to elect (a) core coverage, or (b) core coverage plus all non-core coverages that the qualified beneficiary had immediately before the qualifying event. Thus, a qualified beneficiary who has core coverage plus vision and dental coverage upon the occurrence of a qualifying event must be offered the opportunity to continue either the core coverage or the core coverage and both dental and vision coverage. Such a qualified beneficiary would not have to be offered the opportunity to elect core coverage plus vision coverage only or core coverage plus dental coverage only. Of course, if the vision and dental coverage are provided under two separate plans that are independent of the core plan, a qualified beneficiary would be able to continue one or both of the coverages. Assume, for example, that an employer maintains three group health plans—a core plan, a vision plan, and a dental plan—and that each active employee can elect to be covered under one or more of the three plans. (Thus, an employee could have vision-only, dental-only, or core-only coverage, or any combination of the three.) A qualified beneficiary who is covered under all three plans at the time of a qualifying event would have separate election rights with respect to each plan, and so would be able to elect coverage under the dental-only and core-only plans.

Q-27: Must a qualified beneficiary who is covered under a single plan providing both core coverage and non-core coverage be offered the opportunity elect non-core coverage only?

A-27: No. A qualified beneficiary who is covered by a single plan providing both core coverage and non-core coverage need not be offered the opportunity to elect only non-core coverage. Of course, if immediately before the qualifying event the qualified beneficiary is covered by a group health plan that provides non-core coverage but no core coverage, the qualified beneficiary must be offered the opportunity to continue that non-core coverage. Moreover, such an individual generally would not have to be given the opportunity to elect core coverage. (But see Q&A-30 of this section regarding open enrollment periods.)

Q-28: What deductibles apply if COBRA continuation coverage is elected?

A-28: (a) Qualified beneficiaries electing COBRA continuation coverage are generally subject to the same deductibles as similarly situated employees for whom a qualifying event has not occurred. If a qualified beneficiary's COBRA continuation coverage begins before the end of the prescribed period for accumulating amounts toward deductibles, the qualified beneficiary must retain credit for expenses incurred toward those deductibles before the beginning of COBRA continuation coverage as though the qualifying event had not occurred. The specific application of this rule depends on the type of deductible, as set forth in paragraphs (b) through (d) of this Q&A-28. Special rules are set forth in paragraphs (e) and (f), and examples appear in paragraph (g).

(b) If a deductible is computed separately for each individual receiving coverage under the plan, each individual's remaining deductible amount (if any) on the date that COBRA continuation coverage begins is equal to that individual's remaining deductible amount immediately before that date.

(c) If a deductible is computed on a family basis, the deductible for each new family unit after the beginning of COBRA continuation coverage (or the existing family unit, in the case of a qualifying event that does not result in there being more than one family unit) is computed as follows: On the date that COBRA continuation coverage begins, the remaining deductible amount for each new family unit (or the remaining number of individual deductibles, in the case of a family deductible that is satisfied by completing a specified number of individual deductibles) is equal to the preexisting family unit's remaining deductible amount (or remaining number of individual deductibles, as applicable) immediately before that date. This rule applies regardless of whether the plan provides that the family deductible is an alternative to individual deductibles or an additional requirement.

(d) Deductibles that are not described in paragraphs (b) or (c) of this Q&A-28 must be treated in a manner consistent with the principles set forth in those paragraphs.

(e) If a deductible is computed on the basis of a covered employee's compensation instead of being a fixed dollar amount, the plan can treat the employee's compensation as frozen for the duration of the COBRA continuation coverage at the level that was used to compute the deductible in effect immediately before the COBRA continuation coverage began.

(f) If a single deductible is prescribed for core coverage and non-core coverage and a qualified beneficiary electing COBRA continuation coverage elects to receive core coverage only, the treatment of expenses for non-core coverage depends on when the expenses were incurred, as follows: if the expenses were incurred before the beginning of COBRA continuation coverage, they must continue to be counted toward satisfaction of the deductible, but they need not be counted if they were incurred after the beginning of COBRA continuation coverage.

(g) The rules of this Q&A-28 are illustrated by the following examples; in each example it is assumed that deductibles are determined on a calendar year basis:

Example 1: A group health plan applies a separate $100 annual deductible to each individual whom it covers. The plan provides that the spouse and dependent children of a covered employee will lose coverage on the last day of the month after the month of the covered employee's death. A covered employee dies on June 11, 1988. The spouse and the two dependent children elect COBRA continuation coverage, which will begin on August 1, 1988. As of July 31, 1988, the spouse has incurred $80 of covered expenses, the older child has incurred no covered expenses, and the younger one has incurred $120 (i.e., already satisfied the deductible). At the beginning of COBRA continuation coverage on August 1, the spouse has a remaining deductible of $20, the older child still has the full $100 deductible, and the younger one has no further deductible.

Example 2: A group health plan applies a separate $200 annual deductible to each individual whom it covers, except that each family member will be treated as having satisfied the individual deductible once the family has incurred $500 of covered expenses during the year. The plan provides that upon the divorce of a covered employee, coverage will end immediately for the employee's spouse and any children who do not remain in the employee's custody. Assume that a covered employee with four dependent children is divorced, that the spouse obtains custody of the two oldest children, and that the spouse and those children all elect COBRA continuation coverage to begin immediately. Assume also that the family had accumulated $420 of covered expenses before the divorce, as follows: $70 by each parent, $200 by the oldest child, $80 by the youngest child, and none by the other two children. Each new family unit after the divorce (i.e., the employee plus two children, still receiving regular coverage under the plan, and the spouse plus two children, receiving COBRA continuation coverage) has a remaining family deductible amount of $80 ($500 minus $420).

Example 3: The facts are the same as in Example 2, except that the family deductible is defined as two individual $200 deductibles instead of a $500 aggregate (i.e., the plan disregards all remaining individual deductibles after the satisfaction of any two individual deductibles). Before the divorce, the family has satisfied one individual deductible (the oldest child's). At the beginning of COBRA continuation coverage, therefore, each new family unit is treated as having already satisfied one individual deductible even though the oldest child is included in only one of the new family units.

Example 4: Each year a group health plan pays 70 percent of the cost of an individual's psychotherapy after that individual's first three visits. A qualified beneficiary who elects COBRA continuation coverage beginning August 1, 1988, and has already made two visits as of that date need only pay for one more visit before the plan must begin to pay 70 percent of the cost of the remaining visits during 1988.

Example 5: A group health plan has a $250 annual deductible per covered individual. The plan provides that if the deductible is not satisfied in a particular year, expenses incurred during October through December of that year are credited toward satisfaction of the deductible in the next year. A qualified beneficiary who has incurred covered expenses of $150 from January through September of 1988 and $40 during October elects COBRA continuation coverage beginning November 1, 1988. The remaining deductible amount for this qualified beneficiary is $60 at the beginning of the COBRA continuation coverage. If this individual incurs covered expenses of $50 in November and December of 1988 combined (so that the $250 deductible for 1988 is not satisfied), the $90 incurred from October through December of 1988 are credited toward satisfaction of the deductible amount for 1989.

Q-29: How do a plan's limits apply to COBRA continuation coverage?

A-29: (a) Limits are treated in the same way as deductibles (see Q&A-28 of this section). This rule applies both to limits on plan benefits (e.g., a maximum number of hospital days or dollar amount of reimbursable expenses) and limits that are in the nature of deductibles (e.g., a copayment limit, or a catastrophic limit on a covered employee's out-of-pocket expenses). This rule applies equally to annual and lifetime limits.

(b) The rule of this Q&A-29 is illustrated by the following examples; in each example it is assumed that limits are determined on a calendar year basis:

Example 1: A group health plan pays for a maximum of 150 days of hospital confinement per individual per year. A covered employee who has had 20 days of hospital confinement as of May 1, 1989, terminates employment and elects COBRA continuation coverage as of that date. During the remainder of 1989 the plan need only pay for a maximum of 130 days of hospital confinement for this individual.

Example 2: A group health plan reimburses a maximum of $20,000 of covered expenses per family per year, and the same $20,000 limit applies to unmarried covered employees. A covered employee and spouse who have no children divorce on May 1, 1989, and the spouse elects COBRA continuation coverage as of that date. If the employee and spouse together incurred $15,000 of reimbursable expenses during January through April of 1989, each of these individuals has a $5,000 maximum benefit for the remainder of 1989, regardless who incurred what portion of the $15,000.

Example 3: A group health plan pays for 80 percent of covered expenses after satisfaction of a $100-per-individual deductible, and 100 percent of them after a family has incurred out-of-pocket costs of $2,000. An employee and spouse with three dependent children divorce on June 1, 1989, and one of the children remains with the employee. The spouse elects COBRA continuation coverage as of that date for the spouse and the other two children. During January through May of 1989, all five individual deductibles were satisfied and the family incurred $4,000 of covered expenses, resulting in out-of-pocket expenses totalling $1,200 (five $100 deductibles, plus the non-reimbursed 20 percent of the other $3,500, or $700). For the remainder of 1989, each new family unit has an out-of-pocket limit of $800.

Q-30: Can a qualified beneficiary who elects COBRA continuation coverage ever change from the coverage received by that individual immediately before the qualifying event?

A-30: (a) In general, a qualified beneficiary need only be given an opportunity to continue the coverage that he or she was receiving immediately before the qualifying event. This is true regardless of whether the coverage received by the qualified beneficiary before the qualifying event ceases to be of value to the qualified beneficiary, such as in the case of a qualified beneficiary covered under a region-specific Health Maintenance Organization (HMO) who leaves the HMO's service region. The only situations in which a qualified beneficiary must be allowed to change from the coverage received immediately before the qualifying event are as set forth in paragraphs (b) and (c) of this Q&A-30, in Q&A-24 of this section (regarding core coverage), and in Q&A-23 of this section (regarding changes to or elimination of the coverage provided to similarly situated active employees).

(b) If a qualified beneficiary participates in a region-specific plan (such as an HMO or an on-site clinic) that will not service his or her health needs in the area to which he or she is relocating (regardless of the reason for the relocation) and the employer has employees in the area to which the qualified beneficiary relocates, the qualified beneficiary must be given an opportunity to elect alternative coverage if (and on the same basis as) a similarly situated active employee who transfers to that new location while continuing to work for the employer would be given the opportunity to elect alternative coverage at the time of transfer.

(c) If an employer maintains more than one group health plan and an open enrollment period is available to similarly situated active employees with respect to whom a qualifying event has not occurred, the same open enrollment period rights must be available to each qualified beneficiary receiving COBRA continuation coverage. An open enrollment period means a period during which an employee covered under a plan can choose to be covered under another group health plan, or to add or eliminate coverage of family members.

(d) The rules of this Q&A-30 are illustrated by the following examples:

Example 1: Assume that (1) E is an employee who works for an employer that maintains several group health plans; (2) under the terms of the plans, if an employee chooses to cover any family members under a plan, all family members must be covered by the same plan and that plan must be the same as the plan covering the employee; (3) immediately before E's termination of employment (for reasons other than gross misconduct), E is covered along with E's spouse and children by a plan that provides only core coverage, and (4) the coverage under that plan will end as a result of the termination of employment. Upon E's termination of employment, each of the four family members is a qualified beneficiary. Even though the employer maintains various other plans and options, it is not necessary for the qualified beneficiaries to be allowed to switch to a new plan when E terminates employment. Assume further that none of the four family members declines to elect COBRA continuation coverage, and that 3 months after E's termination of employment there is an open enrollment period during which similarly situated active employees are offered an opportunity to choose to be covered under a new plan or to add or eliminate family coverage. During the open enrollment period, each of the four qualified beneficiaries must be offered the opportunity to switch to another plan (as though each beneficiary were an individual employee). For example, each member of E's family could choose coverage under a separate plan, even though the family members of employed individuals could not choose coverage under separate plans. Of course, if each family member chooses COBRA continuation coverage under a separate plan, each family member can be required to pay an amount for that coverage that is based on the applicable premium for individual coverage under that separate plan. See Q&A-44 of this section.

Example 2: The facts are the same as in Example 1, except that E's family members are not covered under E's group health plan when E terminates employment. Although the family members do not have to be given an opportunity to elect COBRA continuation coverage, E must be allowed to add them to E's COBRA continuation coverage during the open enrollment period. This is true even though the family members are not, and cannot become, qualified beneficiaries (see Q&A-17 of this section).

Q-31: Aside from open enrollment periods, can a qualified beneficiary who has elected COBRA continuation coverage choose to cover individuals (such as newborn children, adopted children, or new spouses) who join the qualified beneficiary's family on or after the date of the qualifying event?

A-31: If the plan covering the qualified beneficiary provides that such new family members of active employees can become covered (either automatically or upon an appropriate election) before the next open enrollment period, then the same right must be extended to the new family members of a qualified beneficiary. Of course, if the addition of a new family member will result in a higher applicable premium (e.g., if the qualified beneficiary was previously receiving COBRA continuation as an individual, or if the applicable premium for family coverage depends on family size), the plan can require the qualified beneficiary to pay a correspondingly higher amount for the COBRA continuation coverage. See Q&A-44 of this section.

Electing COBRA Continuation Coverage

Q-32: What is the minimum period during which a group health plan must allow a qualified beneficiary to elect COBRA continuation coverage (i.e., the election period)?

A-32: A group health plan can condition the availability of COBRA continuation coverage upon a qualified beneficiary's timely election of such coverage. An election of COBRA continuation coverage is a timely election if it is made during the election period. The election period must begin on or before the date that the qualified beneficiary would lose coverage on account of the qualifying event. (See paragraph (c) of Q&A-18 of this section for the meaning of "lose coverage.") The election period must not end before the date that is 60 days after the later of (a) the date that the qualified beneficiary would lose coverage on account of the qualifying event, or (b) the date that the qualified beneficiary is sent notice of his or her right to elect COBRA continuation coverage. An election is considered to be made on the date that it is sent to the employer or plan administrator. The rules of this Q&A-32 are illustrated by the following example:

Example: An unmarried employee who is receiving employer-paid coverage under a group health plan voluntarily terminates employment on June 1, 1988. *Case 1:* If the plan provides that the employer-paid coverage ends immediately upon the termination of employment, the election period must begin on or before June 1, 1988, and must not end earlier than July 31, 1988. If the notice of the right to elect COBRA continuation coverage is not sent to the employee until June 15, 1988, the election period must not end earlier than August 14, 1988. *Case 2:* If the plan provides that the employer-paid coverage does not end until 6 months after the termination of employment, the employee does not lose coverage until December 1, 1988. The election period can therefore begin as late as December 1, 1988, and must not end before January 30, 1989. *Case 3:* If employer-paid coverage for 6 months after the termination of employment is offered only to those qualified beneficiaries who waive COBRA continuation coverage, the employee "loses coverage" on June 1, 1988, so the election period is the same as in Case 1. The difference between Case 2 and Case 3 is that in Case 2 the employee can receive 6 months of employer-paid coverage and then elect to pay for up to an additional 12 months of COBRA continuation coverage, while in Case 3 the employee must choose between 6 months of employer-paid coverage and paying for up to 18 months of COBRA continuation coverage. In all three cases, COBRA continuation coverage need not be provided for more than 18 months after the termination of employment (see Q&A-39 of this section), and in certain circumstances might be provided for a shorter period (see Q&A-38 of this section).

Q-33: Must a covered employee or qualified beneficiary inform the employer or plan administrator of the occurrence of a qualifying event?

A-33: In general, the employer or plan administrator must determine when a qualifying event has occurred. However, each covered employee or qualified beneficiary is responsible for notifying the employer or other plan administrator of the occurrence of a qualifying event that is either a dependent child ceasing to be a dependent child of the covered employee or a divorce or legal separation of a covered employee. If the notice is not sent to the employer or other plan administrator within 60 days after the later of (a) the date of the qualifying event, or (b) the date that the qualified beneficiary would lose coverage on account of the qualifying event, the group health plan does not have to offer the qualified beneficiary an opportunity to elect COBRA continuation coverage. For purposes of this Q&A-33, if more than one qualified beneficiary would lose coverage on account of a divorce or legal separation of a covered employee, a timely notice of the divorce or legal separation that is sent by the covered employee or any one of those qualified beneficiaries will be sufficient to preserve the election rights of all of the qualified beneficiaries.

Q-34: During the election period and before the qualified beneficiary has made an election, must coverage be provided?

A-34: (a) In general, each qualified beneficiary has until at least 60 days after the date that the qualifying event would cause him or her to lose coverage to decide whether to elect COBRA continuation coverage. If the election is made during that period, coverage must be provided from the date that coverage would otherwise have been lost (but see Q&A-35 of this section). This can be accomplished as described in paragraph (b) or (c) of this Q&A-34.

(b) In the case of an indemnity or reimbursement arrangement, the employer can provide for plan coverage during the election period or, if the plan allows retroactive reinstatement, the employer can drop the qualified beneficiary from the plan and reinstate him or her when the election is made. Of course, claims incurred by a qualified beneficiary during the election period do not have to be paid before the election (and, if applicable, payment for the coverage) is made.

(c) In the case of a group health plan that provides health services (such as a Health Maintenance Organization or a walk-in clinic), the plan can require that a qualified beneficiary who has not yet elected and paid for COBRA continuation coverage choose between (1) electing and paying for the coverage or (2) paying the reasonable and customary charge for the plan's services, but only if a qualified beneficiary who chooses to pay for the services will be reimbursed for that payment within 30 days after electing COBRA continuation coverage (and, if applicable, paying any balance due for the coverage). In the alternative, the plan can provide continued coverage and treat the qualified beneficiary's use of the facility as a constructive election. In such a case, the qualified beneficiary is obligated to pay any applicable charge for the coverage, but only if the qualified beneficiary is informed of the meaning of the constructive election before using the facility.

Q-35: Is a waiver before the end of the election period effective to end a qualified beneficiary's election rights?

A-35: A qualified beneficiary who, during the election period, waives COBRA continuation coverage can revoke the waiver at any time before the end of the election period. However, if a qualified beneficiary who waives COBRA continuation coverage later revokes the waiver, coverage need not be provided retroactively (i.e., from the date of the loss of coverage until the waiver is revoked). Waivers and revocations of waivers are considered made on the date that they are sent to the employer or plan administrator, as applicable.

Q-36: Can an employer withhold money or other benefits owed to a qualified beneficiary until the qualified beneficiary either waives COBRA continuation coverage, elects and pays for such coverage, or allows the election period to expire?

A-36: No. An employer must not withhold anything to which a qualified beneficiary is otherwise entitled (by operation of law or other agreement) in order to compel payment for COBRA continuation coverage or to coerce the qualified beneficiary to give up rights to COBRA continuation coverage (including the right to use the full election period to decide whether to elect such coverage). Such a withholding constitutes a failure to comply with section 162(k), and any purported waiver obtained by means of such a withholding is invalid.

Q-37: Can each qualified beneficiary make an independent election under COBRA?

A-37: Yes. Each qualified beneficiary must be offered the opportunity to make an independent election to receive COBRA continuation coverage and, if applicable, an independent election (a) to receive COBRA continuation coverage that is limited to core coverage and (b) to switch to another group health plan during an open enrollment period. However, if a qualified beneficiary who is either a covered employee or the spouse of a covered employee makes an election to provide any other qualified beneficiary with COBRA continuation coverage (whether for core coverage only or core plus non-core coverage), the election shall be binding on that other qualified beneficiary. An election on behalf of a minor child can be made by the child's parent or legal guardian. An election on behalf of a qualified beneficiary who is incapacitated or dies can be made by the legal representative of the qualified beneficiary or

the qualified beneficiary's estate, as determined under applicable state law, or by the spouse of the qualified beneficiary. The rules of this Q&A-37 are illustrated by the following examples:

Example 1: Assume that employee H and H's spouse are covered under a group health plan immediately before H's termination of employment (for reasons other than gross misconduct), the plan provides only core coverage, and the coverage under the plan will end as a result of the termination of employment. Upon H's termination of employment both H and H's spouse are qualified beneficiaries and each must be allowed to elect COBRA continuation coverage. Thus, H might elect COBRA continuation coverage while the spouse declines to elect such coverage. However, if H elects to provide COBRA continuation coverage for both of them, that election is binding on the spouse, and the spouse cannot decline COBRA continuation coverage. In contrast, H cannot decline COBRA continuation coverage on behalf of H's spouse. Thus, if H does not elect COBRA continuation coverage on behalf of the spouse, the spouse must still be allowed to elect COBRA continuation coverage.

Example 2: The facts are the same as in Example 1, except that coverage under the plan includes both core coverage and non-core coverage, and H and H's spouse have two dependent children who are also covered under the plan immediately before H's termination of employment. All four family members are qualified beneficiaries, each of whom must be offered the opportunity to elect COBRA continuation coverage either with or without non-core coverage. One possible result, therefore, is for the children to continue their full coverage while the parents continue only core coverage. This result can be achieved in a variety of ways, including separate elections by each family member, or a single election by H that binds the entire family.

Duration of COBRA Continuation Coverage

Q-38: How long must COBRA continuation coverage be available to a qualified beneficiary?

A-38: Except for an interruption of coverage in connection with a waiver as described in Q&A-35 of this section, COBRA continuation coverage that has been elected by a qualified beneficiary must extend for at least the period beginning on the date of the qualifying event and ending not before the earliest of the following dates: (a) the last day of the maximum coverage period (see Q&A-39 of this section); (b) the first day for which timely payment is not made to the plan with respect to the qualified beneficiary (see Q&A-48 of this section); (c) the date upon which the employer ceases to maintain any group health plan (including successor plans); (d) the first date after the date of the election upon which the qualified beneficiary is covered (i.e., actually covered, rather than merely eligible to be covered) under any other group health plan that is not maintained by the employer, even if that other coverage is less valuable to the qualified beneficiary than COBRA continuation coverage (e.g., if the other coverage provides no benefits for preexisting conditions); or (e) the date that the qualified beneficiary is entitled to Medicare benefits under Title XVIII of the Social Security Act. However, a group health plan can terminate for cause the coverage of a qualified beneficiary receiving COBRA continuation coverage on the same basis that the plan terminates for cause the coverage of similarly situated active employees with respect to whom a qualifying event has not occurred. For purposes of the preceding sentence, termination for cause does not include termination based on a failure to make timely payment to the plan. (See Q&A-48 of this section regarding timely payment.)

Q-39: When does the maximum coverage period end?

A-39: The maximum coverage period ends (a) 18 months after the qualifying event, if the qualifying event that gives rise to COBRA continuation coverage election rights is a termination or reduction of hours; and (b) 36 months after the qualifying event, for any other type of qualifying event. The end of the maximum coverage period is measured from the date of the qualifying event even if the qualifying event does not result in a loss of coverage under the plan until some later date. See also Q&A-40 of this section in the case of multiple qualifying events. Nothing in section 162(k) or this section prohibits a group health plan from providing coverage that continues beyond the end of the maximum coverage period.

Q-40: Can the maximum coverage period ever be expanded?

A-40: No, with one exception. The exception involves a qualifying event that gives rise to an 18-month maximum coverage period and is followed, within that 18-month period, by a second qualifying event (e.g., a death or divorce). In such a case, the original 18-month period is expanded to 36 months, but only for those individuals who were qualified beneficiaries under the group health plan as of the first qualifying event and were covered under the plan at the time of the second qualifying event. No qualifying event can give rise to a maxi-

884 Proposed Regulations

mum coverage period that ends more than 36 months after the date of the first qualifying event. For example, if an employee covered by a group health plan that is subject to COBRA terminates employment (for reasons other than gross misconduct) on December 31, 1987, the termination is a qualifying event giving rise to a maximum coverage period that extends for 18 months to June 30, 1989. If the employee dies after the employee and the employee's spouse and dependent children have elected COBRA continuation coverage and before June 30, 1989, the spouse and children (except anyone among them whose COBRA continuation coverage had already ended for some other reason) will be able to elect COBRA continuation coverage through December 31, 1990.

Q-41: If coverage is provided to a qualified beneficiary after a qualifying event without regard to COBRA continuation coverage (e.g., as a result of state or local law, industry practice, a collective bargaining agreement, or plan procedure), will such alternative coverage extend the maximum coverage period?

A-41: (a) The alternative coverage will not extend the maximum coverage period. The end of the maximum coverage period is measured solely from the date of the qualifying event, as described in Q&A-39 and Q&A-40 of this section.

(b) If the alternative coverage does not satisfy all the requirements for COBRA continuation coverage, the group health plan covering the qualified beneficiary immediately before the qualifying event is not in compliance with section 162(k) unless the qualified beneficiary receiving the alternative coverage was also offered the opportunity to elect COBRA continuation coverage and rejected COBRA continuation coverage in favor of the alternative coverage. At the end of that alternative coverage, the individual need not be offered a COBRA election. However, if the individual is a covered employee and the spouse or a dependent child of the individual would lose that alternative coverage as a result of a qualifying event (such as the death of the covered employee), the spouse or dependent child must be given an opportunity to elect to continue that alternative coverage, with a maximum coverage period of 36 months measured from the date of that qualifying event.

(c) If the alternative coverage does satisfy the requirements for COBRA continuation coverage, it can be credited toward satisfaction of the 18- or 36-month maximum coverage period. Moreover, in the case of a covered employee who receives more than 18 months of alternative coverage that satisfies the requirements for COBRA continuation coverage, if the spouse or a dependent child of the covered employee loses coverage as a result of a second qualifying event (such as the death of the covered employee) that occurs after the 18-month period, that spouse or dependent child need not be given an election to continue coverage.

Q-42: How can an event that occurs before a group health plan becomes subject to section 162(k) affect the maximum coverage period when a later, qualifying event occurs?

A-42: (a) If there are two events that satisfy the conditions set forth in paragraph (b) of this Q&A-42, then the first event is treated as though it were a qualifying event that occurred on the date that the plan became subject to section 162(k) (i.e., with a maximum coverage period that began on that date), so that the second event is not merely a qualifying event but a second qualifying event. This treatment applies solely for purposes of determining the maximum coverage period under Q&A-39 through Q&A-41 of this section in connection with that second qualifying event. It does not give rise to any right to elect COBRA continuation coverage in connection with the first event.

(b) The conditions referred to in paragraph (a) of this Q&A-42 are as follows: (1) the first event is listed in paragraph (b) of Q&A-18 of this section (regarding what is a qualifying event) but occurs before the date that the plan becomes subject to section 162(k), (2) the plan provides coverage to a qualified beneficiary after the first event that continues to or beyond the date that the plan becomes subject to section 162(k), and (3) a second event then occurs and is a qualifying event.

(c) The rule of this Q & A-42 is illustrated by the following examples:

Example 1: Assume that a group health plan became subject to section 162(k) on January 1, 1987. Employee F, who was covered by the plan, voluntarily terminated employment on January 1, 1986, and was given employer-paid coverage that would continue for 5 more years. F's spouse was also to be covered for the 5 years, except that the spouse's coverage would terminate upon divorce or F's death. F dies on January 1, 1988. F's death is a qualifying event, so F's spouse can elect COBRA continuation coverage (unless the election is precluded for some independent reason, such as the spouse's entitlement to Medicare benefits). F's termination of employment on January 1, 1986, is

treated as though it were a qualifying event that occurred on January 1, 1987. F's death is thus a *second* qualifying event, for which the spouse's maximum coverage period ends on January 1, 1990 (i.e., 36 months after the first qualifying event). The spouse can thus elect up to 24 months of COBRA continuation coverage.

Example 2: Assume the same facts as in Example 1, except that F's death occurs after January 1, 1990. The plan does not have to give F's spouse an opportunity to elect COBRA continuation coverage.

Q-43: Must a qualified beneficiary be given the right to enroll in a conversion health plan at the end of the maximum coverage period for COBRA continuation coverage?

A-43: If a qualified beneficiary's COBRA continuation coverage under a group health plan ends as a result of the expiration of the maximum coverage period, the group health plan must, during the 180-day period that ends on that expiration date, provide the qualified beneficiary the option of enrolling under a conversion health plan if such an option is otherwise generally available to similarly situated active employees under the group health plan. If such a conversion option is not otherwise generally available, COBRA does not require that it be made available to qualified beneficiaries.

Paying for COBRA Continuation Coverage

Q-44: Can a qualified beneficiary be required to pay for COBRA continuation coverage?

A-44: Yes. For any period of COBRA continuation coverage, a group health plan can require a qualified beneficiary to pay an amount that does not exceed 102 percent of the applicable premium for that period. The "applicable premium" is defined in section 162(k)(4) of the Code. A group health plan can terminate a qualified beneficiary's COBRA continuation coverage as of the first day of any period for which timely payment is not made to the plan with respect to that qualified beneficiary (see Q&A-28 of this section). For the meaning of "timely payment," see Q&A-48 of this section.

Q-45: After a qualified beneficiary has elected COBRA continuation coverage under a group health plan, can the plan increase the amount that the qualified beneficiary must pay for COBRA continuation coverage?

A-45: Yes, if the applicable premium increases. However, the applicable premium for each determination period must be computed and fixed by the plan before the determination period begins. A determination period is any 12-month period selected by the plan, but it must be applied consistently from year to year. Thus, each qualified beneficiary does not have a separate determination period beginning on the date (or anniversaries of the date) that COBRA continuation coverage begins for that qualified beneficiary.

Q-46: Must a qualified beneficiary be allowed to pay for COBRA continuation coverage in installments?

A-46: Yes. A group health plan must allow a qualified beneficiary to pay for COBRA continuation coverage in monthly installments. A group health plan can also allow qualified beneficiaries the alternative of paying for COBRA continuation coverage at other intervals (e.g., quarterly or semiannually).

Q-47: Can a qualified beneficiary choose to have the first payment for COBRA continuation coverage applied prospectively only?

A-47: No. The first payment for COBRA continuation coverage is applied to the period of coverage beginning immediately after the date that coverage under the plan would have been lost on account of the qualifying event. Of course, if the group health plan allows a qualified beneficiary to waive COBRA continuation coverage for any period before electing to receive COBRA continuation coverage, the first payment is not applied to period of the waiver.

Q-48: What is timely payment for COBRA continuation coverage?

A-48: (a) If a qualified beneficiary's election of COBRA continuation coverage is made after the date of the qualifying event, timely payment for any COBRA continuation coverage during the period before the date of the election means payment that is made to the plan within 45 days after the date of the election. Timely payment for any other period of COBRA continuation coverage is governed by paragraph (b) of this Q&A-48.

(b) In general, timely payment for a period of COBRA continuation coverage under a group health plan means payment that is made to the plan by the date that is 30 days after the first day of that period. However, payment that is made to the plan by a later date is also considered timely payment if either (1) under the terms of the plan, covered employees or qualified beneficiaries are allowed until that later date to pay for their coverage during the period, or (2) under the terms

¶20,149A

of an arrangement between the employer and an insurance company, Health Maintenance Organization, or other entity that provides plan benefits on the employer's behalf, the employer is allowed until that later date to pay for coverage of similarly situated employees during the period.

Lawrence B. Gibbs

Commissioner of Internal Revenue

J. Roger Mentz,

Assistant Secretary of the Treasury.

[FR Doc. 87-13366 Filed 6-10-87; 12:21 p.m.]

¶ 20,149B

Proposed regulations: Affiliated service groups: Employee leasing.—Reproduced below is the text of proposed regulations which prescribe rules for determining: (1) when a management organization and the organization for which the management organization performs management services constitute an affiliated service group; (2) when leased employees are treated as employees of the lessee organization for purposes of certain employee benefit provisions; and (3) when arrangements involving separate organizations, employee leasing, or other arrangements will be ignored in order to prevent the avoidance of certain employee benefit requirements.

These regulations appeared in the *Federal Register* on August 27, 1987.

[NOTE: Reg. §§1.414(m)-5; 1.414(m)-6; 1.414(n)-1 through 1.414(n)-4; 1.414(o)-1(c) through 1.414(o)-1(k)(1); 1.414(o)-1(k)(3); and 1.414(o)(k)(4) were withdrawn by the IRS on April 27, 1993 (58 F.R. 25587).]

DEPARTMENT OF THE TREASURY

Internal Revenue Service

26 CFR Part 1

[EE-111-82]

Affiliated Service Groups, Employee Leasing, and Other Arrangements

AGENCY: Internal Revenue Service, Treasury.

ACTION: Notice of proposed rulemaking.

SUMMARY: This document provides proposed regulations prescribing rules for determining: (1) When a management organization and the organization for which the management organization performs management services constitute an affiliated service group; (2) when leased employees are treated as employees of the lessee organization for purposes of certain employee benefit provisions; and (3) when arrangements involving separate organizations, employee leasing, or other arrangements will be ignored in order to prevent the avoidance of certain employee benefit requirements.

Changes to the applicable tax law were made by the Tax Equity and Fiscal Responsibility Act of 1982, the Tax Reform Act of 1984, and the Tax Reform Act of 1986. The regulations provide the public with guidance needed to comply with those Acts and would affect employers that maintain, and participants in, qualified plans.

DATES: Written comments and requests for a public hearing must be delivered or mailed by October 26, 1987. The regulations provided by this document are proposed to be generally effective for tax years beginning after December 31, 1983.

ADDRESS: Send comments and requests for a public hearing to: Commissioner of Internal Revenue, Attention: CC:LR:T (EE-111-82), Washington, DC 20224.

FOR FURTHER INFORMATION CONTACT: Michael Garvey of the Employee Plans and Exempt Organizations Division, Office of Chief Counsel, Internal Revenue Service, 1111 Constitution Avenue, NW., Washington, DC 20224, Attention: CC:LR:T, (202) 566-3903, not a toll-free call.

SUPPLEMENTARY INFORMATION:

Background

This document contains proposed amendments to the Income Tax Regulations (26 CFR Part 1) under sections 414(m)(5), 414(n), and 414(o) of the Internal Revenue Code. These amendments are proposed to conform the regulations to sections 246 and 248 of the Tax Equity and Fiscal Responsibility Act of 1982 (26 U.S.C. 414(m)(5), 414(n)), section 526 of the Tax Reform Act of 1984 (26 USC 414(n)(2), 414(o)), and section 1146 of the Tax Reform Act of 1986 (26 U.S.C. 414(n), 414(o)). Other sections of the Tax Reform Act of 1986 that relate to section 414(n) are not reflected in this document.

Organizations Performing Management Functions

Section 414(m)(5) of the Code expands the definition of an affiliated service group that is to be treated as a single employer under section 414(m) for purposes of certain employee benefit requirements. Pursuant to section 414(m)(5), an affiliated service group includes a management organization and a recipient organization (i.e., the organization (and related organizations) for which the management organization performs management functions). An organization is a management

organization if the principal business of the organization is the performing of, on a regular and continuing basis, management functions for a recipient organization.

Employee Leasing

Section 414(n) provides that, under certain circumstances, an individual ("leased employee") who performs services for a person ("recipient") through another person ("leasing organization") shall be treated as the employee of the recipient for purposes of certain employee benefit requirements. If the services being provided by an individual to a recipient are pursuant to an agreement between the recipient and the leasing organization, and the individual performs such services for the recipient on a substantially full-time basis for a period of at least one year, and the services are of a type historically performed by employees, then the individual is a leased employee and, therefore, shall be treated as an employee of the recipient.

Section 414(n)(5) provides, however, that if the leasing organization maintains a safe-harbor plan with respect to a leased employee, such individual will generally not be treated as an employee of the recipient. Section 414(n)(5), as originally enacted, required that a safe-harbor plan must be a qualified money purchase pension plan with provision for nonintegrated employer contributions of at least 7 ½ percent, immediate participation, and full and immediate vesting.

The Tax Reform Act of 1986 amended several provisions relating to sections 414(n) and 414(o). These amendments include the following:

(1) The definition of a safe-harbor plan under section 414(n)(5) has been amended to require a contribution rate of 10 percent and to require that the plan must cover all employees of the leasing organization (other than employees who perform substantially all of their services for the leasing organization (and not for recipients) and employees whose compensation from the leasing organization is less than $1,000 during the plan year and during each of the 3 prior plan years).

(2) Under section 414(n)(5), a leased employee will be treated as an employee of the recipient, regardless of the existence of a safe-harbor plan, if more than 20 percent of the recipient's nonhighly compensated workforce are leased employees (as specially defined for this purpose).

(3) A recordkeeping exception from the section 414(n) employee leasing provisions is provided under section 414(o) in the case of an employer that has no section 416(g) top-heavy plans and that uses the services of nonemployees only for an insignificant percentage of the employer's total workload.

(4) The scope of the section 414(n) employee leasing provisions has been expanded to include a number of non-pension employee benefit requirements (listed under section 414(n)(3)), including group-term life insurance, accident and health plans, qualified group legal services, cafeteria plans, etc. In addition, the employee leasing provisions will apply to these non-pension employee benefit requirements regardless of the existence of a safe-harbor plan.

Except for the amendments relating to the non-pension employee benefit requirements, the proposed regulations reflect the Tax Reform Act of 1986 amendments described above. Guidance relating to the non-pension employee benefit requirements, and other relevant amendments made by the Tax Reform Act of 1986, will be forthcoming.

Avoidance of Certain Employee Benefits Requirements

Section 414(o) provides that the Secretary shall prescribe such regulations as may be necessary to prevent the avoidance of any employee benefit requirement listed in sections 414(m)(4) or 414(n)(3) through the use of separate organizations, employee leasing, or other arrangements. Specifically, the Secretary has the authority to provide rules in addition to the rules contained in sections 414(m) and 414(n).

Pursuant to section 414(o), the proposed regulations provide rules relating to several arrangements that may result in the avoidance of the listed employee benefit requirements. These arrangements include the leasing of certain owners, the leasing of certain managers, the creation of successive organizations in time, expense sharing arrangements, plans maintained by certain corporate directors, and plans covering certain five-percent owners.

Effective Data

The amendments made to section 414 by the Tax Equity and Fiscal Responsibility Act of 1982 are effective for tax years of a recipient or of a member of an affiliated service group that begin after December 31, 1983.

The amendments made to section 414 by the Tax Reform Act of 1984 are effective as of July 18, 1984. The regulations promulgated under section 414(o), however, are variously effective for (1) plan years beginning more than six months after this document is published in the *Federal Register*, (2) plan years beginning more than sixty days after this document is published in the *Federal Register* as a Treasury decision, and (3) plan years beginning during or after the first tax year of a recipient beginning after December 31, 1983. (To the extent that the regulations under section 414(o) aggregate plans for purposes of section 415 that were not previously aggregated, the rules of § 1.415-10 apply.)

The amendments made to section 414 by the Tax Reform Act of 1986 are generally effective with respect to services performed after December 31, 1986. The recordkeeping exception from section 414(n), provided under section 414(o), and certain clarifying amendments under section 414(n) are effective as if originally enacted as part of the section 414 amendments made by the Tax Equity and Fiscal Responsibility Act of 1982. The section 414(n)(3) amendments relating to the non-pension employee benefit requirements are generally effective when section 89 applies to such non-pension employee benefits (see section 1151(k) of the Tax Reform Act of 1986).

Special Analysis

The Commissioner of Internal Revenue has determined this rule is not a major rule as defined in Executive Order 12291. Therefore, a Regulatory Impact Analysis is not required. Although this document is a notice of proposed rulemaking that solicits public comment, the Internal Revenue Service has concluded that the regulations proposed are interpretative and that the notice and public procedure requirements of 5 U.S.C. 553(b) do not apply. Accordingly, these proposed regulations do not constitute regulations subject to the Regulatory Flexibility Act (5 U.S.C. chapter 6).

Comments and Requests for a Public Hearing

Before adopting these proposed regulations, consideration will be given to any written comments that are submitted (preferably eight copies) to the Commissioner or Internal Revenue. All comments will be available for public inspection and copying. A public hearing will be held upon written request to the Commissioner by any person who has submitted written comments. If a public hearing is held, notice of the time and place will be published in the *Federal Register*.

Drafting Information

The principal author of these proposed regulations is Philip R. Bosco of the Employee Plans and Exempt Organizations Division of the Office of Chief Counsel, Internal Revenue Service. However, personnel from other offices of the Internal Revenue Service and Treasury participated in developing the regulations, both on matters of substance and style.

List of Subjects in 26 CFR 1.401-1-1.425-1

Employee benefit plans, Pensions.

Proposed Amendment to the Regulations

The Income Tax Regulations (26 CFR Part 1) are proposed to be amended as follows:

Paragraph 1. The authority citation for Part 1 is amended by adding the following citation:

Authority: 26 U.S.C. 7805. * * * Section 1.414(n)-1 also issued under 26 U.S.C. 414(n). Section 1.414(o)-1 also issued under 26 U.S.C. 414(o).

Par. 2. The following new sections are added immediately following § 1.414(m)-4 and read as follows:

§ 1.414(m)-5 Organizations performing management functions. [Withdrawn.]

* * *

§ 1.414(m)-6 Application of section 414(o) to section 414(m). [Withdrawn.]

* * *

§ 1.414(n)-1 Employee leasing. [Withdrawn.]

* * *

§ 1.414(n)-2 Qualified plan coverage of leased employees. [Withdrawn.]

* * *

§ 1.414(n)-3 Employee benefit requirements, recordkeeping, and effective dates. [Withdrawn.]

* * *

§ 1.414(n)-4 Application of section 414(o) to section 414(n). [Withdrawn.]

* * *

§ 1.414(o)-1 Avoidance of employee benefit requirements through the use of separate organizations, employee leasing, or other arrangements.

(a) *In general.* (1) Pursuant to section 414(o), this section provides rules, in addition to the rules contained in sections 414(m) and 414(n) and the regulations thereunder, to prevent the avoidance of any employee benefit requirement listed in either § 1.414(m)-3 or § 1.414(n)-3, through the use of separate organizations, employee leasing, or other arrangements.

(2) For the definition of the terms "person" and "leased employee", see § 1.414(n)-1(b). For the definition of the term "organization", see § 1.414(m)-5(a)(2). For the definition of the terms "management functions" and "management activities or services", see § 1.414(m)-5(c).

(3) For purposes of this section, the term "plan" means a stock bonus, pension, or profit-sharing plan qualified under section 401(a) or a simplified employee pension under section 408(k).

(4) For purposes of this section, the term "employee" includes a "self-employed individual" as defined in section 401(c)(1).

(5) For purposes of this section, the term "maintained", when used in the context of a plan maintained by any person, means "maintained at any time."

(6) For purposes of this section, services performed for a person other than as an employee of such person means services performed directly or indirectly for such person.

(b) *Services performed by leased owners—* (1) *In general.* (i) If an individual is a leased owner with respect to a recipient, then for purposes of determining whether any qualified plan actually maintained by the recipient and whether any qualified plan maintained by a leasing organization in which the leased owner is a participant (or in which the leased owner has or had an accrued benefit) satisfies the employee benefit requirements of section 1.41 4(n)-3(a) (except for paragraph (a)(6) of that section) for a plan year, the leased owner's interest in the leasing organization's qualified plan attributable to services performed by the leased owner for the recipient is to be treated as provided under a separate qualified plan maintained by the recipient covering only the leased owner and the leased owner is to be treated as an employee of the recipient. If a separate qualified plan is treated as maintained by the recipient with respect to a leased owner and such leased owner also participates in a qualified plan actually maintained by the recipient, the leased owner's interest in the leasing organization's qualified plan attributable to the leased owner's performance of services for the recipient that is treated as provided to the leased owner under a separate qualified plan of the recipient is to be treated as provided to the leased owner under the qualified plan actually maintained by the recipient for purposes of determining whether such qualified plan satisfies the applicable employee benefit requirements. If either the separate qualified plan for the leased owner that is treated as maintained by the recipient or any qualified plan that is actually maintained by the recipient fails to satisfy any of the applicable employee benefit requirements, then except as provided in paragraphs (b)(1)(ii) and (b)(1)(iii) of this section, the following qualified plans shall be treated as not satisfying such requirements: any qualified plan actually maintained by the recipient in which the leased owner is a participant (or has or had an accrual benefit) and any qualified plan that is actually maintained by a leasing organization in which the leased owner has an interest that is attributable to the leased owner's performance of services for the recipient.

(ii) The Commissioner will not apply paragraph (b)(1)(i) of this section so as to disqualify a plan actually maintained by a recipient unless the Commissioner determines that, taking into account all the facts and circumstances, the disqualification of a leasing organization's plan would be ineffective as a means of securing compliance with the applicable employee benefit requirements. For example, it may be appropriate to disqualify the recipient's plan where a leasing organization's plan was terminated or substantial assets were removed therefrom in a year for which the statute of limitations has run with respect to the employer, employee, or trust.

(iii) If pursuant to paragraph (b)(1)(i) of this section, more than one leasing organization plan is subject to disqualification and at least one of the plans would not be disqualified if another plan or plans were disqualified first, all affected plan sponsors may, by agreement, elect the plan or plans subject to disqualification, provided that such election is not inconsistent with the purposes of this paragraph (b), such as where the plan or plans elected were terminated or substantial assets were removed therefrom in a year for which the statute of limitations has run with respect to the employer, employee, or trust. In the absence of such an election, the Commissioner, taking into account all the facts and circumstances, shall have the discretion to determine which plan or plans shall be disqualified.

(2) *Leased owner.* (i) For purposes of this paragraph (b), an individual is a "leased owner" with respect to a recipient if during the plan year of a plan maintained by a leasing organization the individual (A) performs any services for a recipient other than as an employee of the recipient and (B) is, at the time such services are performed, a five-percent owner of the recipient. The fact that an individual may also perform services as an employee of the recipient does not affect his status as a leased owner. If an individual becomes a leased owner with respect to a recipient, such individual is from that point on always to be considered a leased owner with respect to the recipient, notwithstanding anything in this paragraph (b) to the contrary, even if subsequently all services performed by the individual for the recipient are performed as an employee of the recipient.

(ii) Except as provided in paragraph (b)(2)(iii) of this section, and notwithstanding the first sentence of paragraph (b)(2)(i) of this section to the contrary, an individual is not a leased owner with respect to a recipient for purposes of a plan year of a plan maintained by a leasing organization if, during each calendar year containing at least one day of such plan year, less than 25 percent of his total hours actually worked for substantial compensation are for all recipients with respect to which he is a leased owner (but for the application of this paragraph (b)(2)(ii)) and less than 25 percent of his total compensation is derived from performing services for all such recipients. For purposes of this paragraph (b)(2)(ii), performing services for the recipient includes services performed as an employee of the recipient and in any other capacity. For purposes of this paragraph (b)(2)(ii), the term "compensation" means (A) with respect to services performed as a common-law employee, compensation reportable on Form W-2, and (B) with respect to services performed other than as a common-law employee, earned income as defined in section 401(c)(2). See section 414(s) for the definition of "compensation" for years beginning after December 31, 1986.

(iii) Paragraph (b)(2)(ii) of this section does not apply to an individual who (A) is a leased owner with respect to a recipient pursuant to the application of the first sentence of paragraph (b)(2)(i) of this section, and (B) performs professional services (as defined in § 1.414(m)-1(c)) for the recipient, whether or not as an employee of the recipient, during the plan year of the plan maintained by the leasing organization, of the same type as the professional services performed by the recipient for third parties.

(3) *Recipient.* For purposes of this paragraph (b), the term "recipient" has the same meaning as in paragraphs (b)(2) and (b)(6) of § 1.414(n)-1, except that "leased owner" is substituted for "leased employee".

(4) *Leasing organization.* For purposes of this paragraph (b), the term "leasing organization" has the same meaning as in § 1.414(n)-1(b)(1), except that "leased owner" is substituted for "leased employee" and that "or provided" is added after "provides".

(5) *Five-percent owner.* For purposes of this paragraph (b), an individual is a 5-percent owner of a recipient if such individual is a 5-percent owner (as defined in section 416(i)) of any person included in the recipient.

(6) *Contributions, benefit, etc., provided to a leased owner.* For purposes of this paragraph (b), a leased owner's interest in a leasing organization (as defined in § 1.414(n)-2(b)(1)(ii) and in a leasing organization's qualified plan, as defined in § 1.414(n)-2(b)(1)(i), to the extent attributable to services for the recipient by the leased owner, is, for purposes of the applicable employee benefit requirements, treated as provided by the recipient or under a plan of the recipient. For rules relating to the application of this requirement, see paragraph (b)(2) of § 1.414(n)-2.

(7) *Effect on employee rules.* To the extent that a leased owner performs services for a recipient other than in the capacity of an employee, a leased owner is not an employee of the recipient and may not be actually covered by a plan of the recipient. Such leased owner may, however, qualify as a leased employee under section 414(n) and the regulations thereunder.

[NOTE: Reg. § 1.414(o)-1(c) through 1.414(o)-1(k)(1) withdrawn.]

* * *

(k) *Effective dates.* * * *.

(2) The provisions of paragraph (b) of this section are effective for tax years of recipients beginning after December 31, 1983. Therefore, the provisions of paragraph (b) apply to plan years beginning during and after the first tax year of a recipient beginning after December 31, 1983. For purposes of applying paragraph (b) of this section to plan years beginning during and after the first tax year of a recipient beginning after December 31, 1983, contributions, forfeitures and benefits provided during any plan year beginning prior to the first tax year of a recipient beginning after December 31, 1983, shall be taken into account if they would have been taken into account had paragraph (b) been effective for such prior plan year.

[NOTE: Reg. § 1.414(o)-1(k)(3) and 1.414(o)-1(k)(4) withdrawn.]

* * *

James I. Owens,

Acting Commissioner.

[FR Doc. 87-19579 Filed 8-26-87; 8:45 a.m.]

¶ 20,149C

Proposed regulations: Benefit accruals beyond normal retirement age: Employee benefit plans: Minimum vesting standards: Plan qualification.—Reproduced below is the text of proposed regulations relating to the requirement for the continued accrual of benefits beyond normal retirement age under employee pension benefit plans as provided for in the Omnibus Budget Reconciliation Act of 1986. The proposed regulations were published in the Federal Register on April 11, 1988 (53 FR 11876).

DEPARTMENT OF THE TREASURY

Internal Revenue Service

26 CFR Part 1

[EE-184-86]

Income Taxes; Continued Accruals Beyond Normal Retirement Age

AGENCY: Internal Revenue Service, Treasury.

ACTION: Notice of proposed rulemaking.

SUMMARY: This document contains proposed regulations relating to the requirement for continued accruals beyond normal retirement age under employee pension benefit plans. Changes to the applicable tax law were made by the Omnibus Budget Reconciliation Act of 1986. These regulations will provide the public with guidance needed to comply with the minimum participation and vesting standards and affect employers maintaining employee retirement plans.

DATES: Written comments and request for a public hearing must be delivered or mailed by June 10, 1988. These amendments generally apply to plan years beginning after December 31, 1987, except as otherwise specified in the Omnibus Budget Reconciliation Act of 1986.

ADDRESS: Send comments and requests for a public hearing to: Commissioner of Internal Revenue, Attention: CC:LR:T (EE-184-86) Washington, D.C. 20224.

FOR FURTHER INFORMATION CONTACT: Michael C. Garvey of the Employee Benefits and Exempt Organizations Division, Office of Chief Counsel, Internal Revenue Service, 1111 Constitution Avenue N.W.,

Washington, D.C. 20224 (Attention: CC:LR:T) (202-566-6271) (not a toll-free number).

SUPPLEMENTARY INFORMATION:

Background

This document contains proposed amendments to the Income Tax Regulations (26 CFR Part 1) under sections 410 and 411 of the Internal Revenue Code of 1986. These amendments are proposed to conform the regulations to sections 9201 through 9204, Subtitle C (Older Americans Pension benefits) of Title IX of the Omnibus Budget Reconciliation Act of 1986 (Pub. L. 99-509) (OBRA 1986) (100 Stat. 1874, 1973).

Explanation of Provisions

Section 9202(b)(1) of OBRA 1986 added subparagraph (H) to section 411(b)(1) of the Internal Revenue Code (Code) to provide rules for continued benefit accruals under defined benefit plans without regard to the attainment of any age. Section 9202 (b)(2) of OBRA 1986 redesignated paragraphs (2) and (3) of Code section 411(b) as paragraphs (3) and (4) and added a new paragraph (2) to Code section 411(b) to provide rules for allocations to the accounts of employees in defined contribution plans without regard to the attainment of any age.

Effective with respect to plan years beginning after December 31, 1987, section 411(b)(1)(H)(i) provides the general rule that a defined benefit plan will not be treated as meeting the minimum vesting standards of section 411 (and, accordingly, will not constitute a qualified plan under section 401(a)) if under the plan an employee's benefit accrual is ceased, or the rate of an employee's benefit accrual is reduced, because of the attainment of any age. Effective for plan years beginning after December 31, 1987, section 411(b)(2) provides that a defined contribution plan will not be treated as satisfying the minimum vesting standards of section 411 (and, accordingly, will not constitute a qualified plan under section 401(a)) if allocations to an employee's account are ceased, or the rate of allocations to an employee's account is reduced, because of the attainment of any age.

The proposed regulations provide that reductions or cessations of account allocations or benefit accruals that are based on factors other than age will not affect the qualification of the plan under section 411(b)(1)(H) or (b)(2). The proposed regulations also provide that benefits under a defined benefit plan may accrue at different rates without violating section 411(b)(1)(H), provided the difference in the rate of benefit accrual is determined without regard to the attainment of any age.

Section 411(b)(1)(H)(ii) provides that a plan will not be treated as failing to satisfy the general rule in section 411(b)(1)(H)(i) merely because the plan contains a limitation (determined without regard to age) on the maximum number of years of service or participation that are taken into account in determining benefits under the plan or merely because the plan contains a limitation on the amount of benefits an employee will receive under the plan. The proposed regulations provide that these limitations are permitted in both defined benefit plans and defined contributions plans (including target benefit plans).

Section 411(b)(1)(H)(iii) provides that, with respect to an employee who, as of the end of a plan year, has attained normal retirement age under a defined benefit plan, certain adjustments may be made to the benefit accrual for the plan year if the plan distributes benefits to the employee or if the plan adjusts the amount of the benefits payable to take into account delayed payment. The continued benefit accrual rules of section 411(b)(1)(H) operate in conjunction with the suspension of benefit payment rules under section 203(a)(3)(B) of the Employee Retirement Income Security Act of 1974 (ERISA) and the proposed regulations do not change the rules relating to the suspension of pension benefit payments under section 203(a)(3)(B) of ERISA and the regulations thereunder issued by the Department of Labor. However, the proposed regulations provide rules under which benefit accruals required under section 411(b)(1)(H)(i) may be reduced or offset either by the value of actuarial adjustments in an employee's normal retirement benefit or by the value of benefit distributions made to an employee.

Section 411(b)(1)(H)(iv) provides that a defined benefit plan will not be treated as failing to satisfy the general rule of section 411(b)(1)(H)(i) merely because the subsidized portion of an early retirement benefit provided under the plan (whether provided on a permanent or temporary basis) is disregarded in determining benefit accruals under the plan. The proposed regulations also provide that a plan will not be treated as failing to satisfy the general rule of section 411(b)(1)(H)(i) merely because a social security supplemental benefit or a qualified disability benefit is disregarded in determining benefit accruals under the plan.

The proposed regulations provide that the rate of an employee's benefit accrual under a defined benefit plan or the rate of allocations to an employee's account under a defined contribution plan will be considered to be reduced on account of the attainment of a specified age if optional forms of benefits, ancillary benefits or other benefits, rights or features under a plan that are provided with respect to benefits or allocations prior to such age are not provided (on terms that are at least as favorable to employees) with respect to benefits or allocations after such age. Thus, for example, under the proposed regulations, a plan may not make a lump sum option available only with respect to benefits or allocations attributable to service prior to a specified age. Similarly, a plan may not use actuarial assumptions that are less favorable to employees for determining lump sum benefits payable after a specified age than are used for determining lump sum benefits payable prior to such age. However, the proposed regulations provide that the accrual rate under a defined benefit plan will not be considered to be reduced merely because the subsidized portion of an early retirement benefit, a qualified disability benefit or a social security supplemental benefit provided under the plan ceases to be provided to an employee or is provided on a reduced basis to an employee by a plan on account of the employee's attainment of a specified age.

Section 411(b)(1)(H)(v) and (b)(2)(D) provide that the Secretary shall prescribe regulations coordinating the requirements of section 411(b)(1)(H) and (b)(2) with the requirements of sections 411(a), 404, 410, 415 and the antidiscrimination provisions of subchapter D of Chapter 1 (Code sections 401 through 425). The proposed regulations provide that no allocation to the account of an employee in a defined contribution plan and no benefit accrual on behalf of an employee in a defined benefit plan are required under section 411(b)(1)(H) or (b)(2) if such allocation or benefit accrual would cause the plan to (1) exceed the section 415 limitations on benefits and contributions, or (2) discriminate in favor of highly compensated employees within the meaning of section 401(a)(4).

Section 9203(a)(2) of OBRA 1986 amended Code section 410(a)(2) to provide that a plan will not constitute a qualified plan under section 401(a) if the plan excludes from participation (on the basis of age) an employee who has attained a specified age. The proposed regulations provide that, effective for plan years beginning after December 31, 1987, a plan may not apply a maximum age provision to any employee who has at least one hour of service for the employer on or after January 1, 1988, regardless of when the employee first performed an hour of service for the employer.

In the case of an employee who was ineligible to participate in a plan before the effective date of amended Code section 410(a)(2) because of a maximum age condition and who is eligible to participate in the plan on or after the effective date of such section, hours of service and years of service credited to the employee before the first plan year beginning on or after January 1, 1988, shall be taken into account in accordance with section 411 and the regulations thereunder and in accordance with 29 CFR Part 2530 for purposes of determining the employee's nonforfeitable right to the employee's accrued benefit. However, with respect to an employee described in the preceding sentence, hours of service and years of service credited to the employee before the first plan year beginning on or after January 1, 1988, are not required to be taken into account for purposes of determining the employee's accrued benefit under the plan for plan years beginning on or after January 1, 1988. See, also, section 411(a)(4) and § 1.411(a)-5 for rules relating to service that must be taken into account in determining an employee's nonforfeitable right to the employee's accrued benefit.

Section 9203(b)(2) of OBRA 1986 amended Code section 411(a)(8)(B) to provide rules relating to the determination of a participant's normal retirement age under a defined benefit plan and a defined contribution plan. Because section 203(e) of the pending Technical Corrections Act of 1987 (H.R. 2636) would change the definition of normal retirement age from the definition now set forth in section 411(a)(8)(B) (as amended by OBRA 1986), the proposed regulations do not set forth any rules under section 411(a)(8)(B) (as amended by OBRA 1986).

Section 9202(b) of OBRA 1986 amended Code section 411(B)(2)(C) to require the Secretary to provide by regulations for the application of the continued allocation rules of section 411(b)(2) to target benefit plans. The proposed regulations do not provide detailed special rules applicable to target benefit plans. Target benefit plans are subject to the rules applicable to defined contribution plans. The Commissioner will prescribe such additional rules relating to the continued allocation of contributions and accrual of benefits under target benefit plans as may be necessary or appropriate.

Effective Date

Section 9204(a)(1) of OBRA 1986 provides that the amendments made with regard to section 411(b)(1)(H) and (b)(2) "shall apply only with respect to plan years beginning on or after January 1, 1988, and only to employees who have 1 hour of service in any plan year to which such amendments apply." The proposed regulations provide that section 411(b)(1)(H) and (b)(2) does not apply to an employee who does not have at least 1 hour of service for the employer in a plan year beginning on or after January 1, 1988.

However, the proposed regulations provide that section 411(b)(1)(H) and (b)(2) applies with respect to all years of service completed by an employee who has at least 1 hour of service in a plan year beginning on or after January 1, 1988. Accordingly, under section 411(b)(1)(H)(i), the proposed regulations provide that, for plan years beginning on or after January 1, 1988, in determining the benefit payable under a defined benefit plan to a participant who has at least 1 hour of service in a plan year beginning on or after January 1, 1988, the plan does not satisfy section 411(a) if the plan disregards, because of the participant's attainment of any age, any year of service completed by the participant or any compensation earned by the participant after attaining such age, including years of service completed and compensation earned before the first plan year beginning on or after January 1, 1988. Under the proposed regulations, section 411(b)(2) does not require allocations to the accounts of employees under a defined contribution plan for any plan year beginning before January 1, 1988. However, the proposed regulations provide that, for plan years beginning on or after January 1, 1988, in determining the allocation to the account of a participant (who has at least 1 hour of service in a plan year beginning on or after January 1, 1988) under a defined contribution plan that determines allocations under a service related allocation formula, the plan does not satisfy section 411(a) if the plan disregards, because of the participant's attainment of any age, any year of service completed by the participant.

Under the proposed regulations, a defined benefit plan and a defined contribution plan will not be treated as impermissibly disregarding, because of the participant's attainment of any age, a year of service completed by the participant before the first plan year beginning before January 1, 1988, merely because the participant was not eligible under the plan to make mandatory or voluntary employee contributions (as well as contributions under a cash or deferred arrangement described in section 401(k)) for such year.

Title I of ERISA and OBRA 1986

Under section 101 of Reorganization Plan No. 4 of 1978 (43 FR 47713), the Secretary of the Treasury has jurisdiction over the subject matter addressed in the OBRA 1986 regulations. Therefore, under section 104 of the Reorganization Plan, these regulations apply when the Secretary of Labor exercises authority under Title I of ERISA (as amended, including the amendments made by Title IX of OBRA 1986 and the amendments by the Tax Reform Act of 1986). Thus, the requirements also apply to employee plans subject to Part 2 of Title I of ERISA.

Under section 9201 of OBRA 1986, these regulations also apply for purposes of applying comparable provisions under section 4(i)(7) of the Age Discrimination in Employment Act of 1967 (29 U.S.C. 623) as amended. No interference is intended under the proposed regulations as to the application of the Age Discrimination in Employment Act of 1967, as in effect prior to its amendment by OBRA 1986, to employees who are not credited with at least 1 hour of service in a plan year beginning on or after January 1, 1988.

Reliance on These Proposed Regulations

Taxpayers may rely on these proposed regulations for guidance pending the issuance of final regulations. Because these regulations are generally effective for plan years beginning after 1987, the Service will apply these proposed regulations in issuing rulings and in examining returns with respect to taxpayers and plans. If future guidance is more restrictive, such guidance will be applied without retroactive effect.

Time of Plan Amendments

The proposed regulations provide rules relating to the postponement of the deadline for amending plans to comply with the provisions of OBRA 1986. Plan amendments required to conform the plan to the changes contained in OBRA 1986 need not be made until the dates specified in section 1140 of the Tax Reform Act of 1986 (in general, the last day of the first plan year commencing on or after January 1, 1989). This deferred amendment date is available only if: (1) The plan is operated in accordance with the applicable provisions of OBRA 1986 for the period beginning with the effective date of the provision with respect to the plan; (2) the plan amendments adopted are retroactive to

such effective date; and (3) the plan amendments adopted are consistent with plan operation during the retroactive effective period.

Special Analyses

The Commissioner of Internal Revenue has determined that this proposed rule is not a major rule as defined in Executive Order 12291 and that a regulatory impact analysis is not required.

Although this document is a notice of proposed rulemaking which solicits public comments, the Internal Revenue Service has concluded that the regulations proposed herein are interpretative and that the notice and public procedure requirements of 5 U.S.C. 553 do not apply. Accordingly, these proposed regulations do not constitute regulations subject to the Regulatory Flexibility Act (5 U.S.C. Chapter 6).

Comments and Requests for a Public Hearing

Before adopting these proposed regulations, consideration will be given to any written comments that are submitted (preferably eight copies) to the Commissioner of Internal Revenue. All comments will be available for public inspection and copying. A public hearing will be held upon written request to the Commissioner by any person who has submitted comments. If a public hearing is held, notice of the time and place will be published in the *Federal Register*.

Drafting Information

The principal author of these proposed regulations is Michael C. Garvey of the Employee Benefits and Exempt Organizations Division of the Office of Chief Counsel, Internal Revenue Service. However, personnel from other offices of the Internal Revenue Service and Treasury Department participated in developing the regulations, both on matters of substance and style.

List of Subjects in 26 CFR 1.401-0-1.425-1

Income taxes, Employee benefits plans, Pensions.

Proposed Amendments to the Regulations

The proposed amendments to 26 CFR Part 1 are as follows:

PART 1—[AMENDED]

Income Tax Regulations

Paragraph 1. The authority citation for Part 1 is amended by adding the following citation:

Authority: 26 U.S.C. 7805 * * * Section 1.411(b)-2 is also issued under 26 U.S.C. 411(b)(1)(H) and 411(b)(2).

Par. 2. A new § 1.410(a)-4A is added immediately after § 1.410(a)-4 to read as follows:

§ 1.410(a)-4A. Maximum age conditions after 1987.

(a) *Maximum age conditions.* Under section 410(a)(2), a plan is not a qualified plan (and a trust forming a part of such plan is not a qualified trust) if the plan, either directly or indirectly, excludes any employee from participation on the basis of attaining a maximum age.

(b) *Effective date and transitional rule.* If a plan contains a provision that excludes an employee from participation on the basis of attaining a maximum age, the provision may not be applied in a plan year beginning on or after January 1, 1988, to any employee (regardless of when the employee first performed an hour of service for the employer) who is credited with at least 1 hour of service on or after January 1, 1988. For purposes of determining when such an employee (who is not otherwise ineligible to participate in the plan) must become eligible to participate in the plan under section 410(a)(1)(A)(ii), section 410(a)(1)(B) and the provisions of the plan, hours of service and years of service credited to the employee before the first plan year beginning on or after January 1, 1988, are taken into account in accordance with section 410 and the regulations thereunder and in accordance with 29 CFR Part 2530. Any employee who would be eligible to participate in the plan taking such service into account and whose entry date would be prior to the first day of the first plan year beginning on or after January 1, 1988, must participate in the plan as of the first day of such plan year.

(c) *Examples.* The provisions of this section may be illustrated by the following examples:

Example (1). Employer X maintains a defined benefit plan that uses a 12-month period beginning July 1 and ending June 30 as its plan year and that specifies a normal retirement age of 65. The plan provides that each employee of X is eligible to become a participant in the plan on the first entry date on or after the employee completes 1 year of service for X. The plan has 2 entry dates, July 1 and January 1. However, prior to the plan year beginning July 1, 1988, the plan contained a provision that excluded from participation any employee first hired within 5 years of attaining the plan's specified normal retirement age of 65. Employee A was hired by X on August 1, 1986 at age 62. A completes 1 year of service for X by August 1, 1987. If A performs at least one hour of service for X on or after January 1, 1988, the plan, in order to meet the requirements of section 410(a)(2), may not apply the maximum age provision to A on or after July 1, 1988, and A must be eligible to become a participant in the plan in accordance with the other eligibility rules contained in the plan, taking into account A's service with X performed prior to July 1, 1988 to the extent required under the terms of the plan or under section 410 and the regulations thereunder and under regulations in 29 CFR Part 2530. Accordingly, if A is still employed by X on July 1, 1988, A must become a participant in the plan on that date.

Example (2). Employer Y maintains a defined benefit plan that uses the calendar year as its plan year and that specifies a normal retirement age of 65. Employee B is first hired by Y in 1988 when B is age 66. In order for the plan to meet the requirements of section 410(a)(2), B may not be excluded from plan participation on the basis of B having attained a specified age.

Par. 3. Section 1.411(a)-1 is amended by revising paragraph (a)(3) to read as follows:

§ 1.411(a)-1. Minimum vesting standards; general rules.

(a) *In general.* * * *

(3) The plan satisfies the requirements of—

(i) Section 411(a)(2) and § 1.411(a)-3 (relating to vesting in accrued benefit derived from employer contributions),

(ii) In the case of a defined benefit plan, section 411(b)(1) and (3) (see §§ 1.411(b)-1 and 1.411(b)-2, relating to accrued benefit requirements, separate accounting and accruals and allocations after a specified age), and

(iii) In the case of a defined contribution plan, section 411(b)(2) and (3) (see §§ 1.411(b)-1(e)(2) and 1.411(b)-2, relating to accruals and allocations after a specified age and separate accounting).

* * *

Par. 4. Section 1.411(a)-7 is amended by adding a new paragraph (b)(3) to read as follows:

§ 1.411(a)-7. Definitions and special rules.

* * *

(b) *Normal retirement age.* * * *

(3) *Effect of Omnibus Budget Reconciliation Act of 1986 (OBRA).* [Reserved]

* * *

Par. 5. A new § 1.411(b)-2 is added after § 1.411(b)-1 to read as follows:

§ 1.411(b)-2. Accruals and allocations after a specified age.

(a) *In general.* Section 411(b)(1)(H) provides that a defined benefit plan does not satisfy the minimum vesting standards of section 411(a) if, under the plan, benefit accruals on behalf of a participant are discontinued or the rate of benefit accrual on behalf of a participant is reduced because of the participant's attainment of any age. Section 411(b)(2) provides that a defined contribution plan does not satisfy the minimum vesting standards of section 411(a) if, under the plan, allocations to a participant's account are reduced or discontinued or the rate of allocations to a participant's account is reduced because of the participant's attainment of any age. A defined benefit plan is not considered to discontinue benefit accruals or reduce the rate of benefit accrual on behalf of a participant because of the attainment of any age in violation of section 411(b)(1)(H) and a defined contribution plan is not considered to reduce or discontinue allocations to a participant's account or reduce the rate of allocations to a participant's account because of the attainment of any age in violation of section 411(b)(2) solely because of a positive correlation between increased age and a reduction or discontinuance in benefit accruals or account allocations under a plan. Thus, for example, if a defined benefit plan or a defined contribution plan provides for reduced or discontinued benefit accruals or account allocations on behalf of participants who have completed a specified number of years of credited service, the plan will not thereby fail to satisfy section 411(b)(1)(H) or (b)(2) solely because of a positive correlation between increased age and completion of the specified number of years of credited service. See paragraph (b)(2) of this section for rules relating to benefit and service limitations under defined benefit plans and paragraph (c)(2) of this section for rules

relating to limitations on allocations under defined contribution plans. Also, if benefit accruals or the rate of benefit accrual on behalf of a participant in a defined benefit plan or allocations or the rate of allocations to the account of a participant in a defined contribution plan are reduced or discontinued under the plan and the reason for the reduction or discontinuance is neither directly nor indirectly related to the participant's attainment of a specified age, the plan does not thereby fail to satisfy the requirements of section 411(b)(1)(H) or (b)(2). Thus, for example, if a defined benefit plan is amended to cease or reduce the rate of benefit accrual for all plan participants, such cessation or reduction does not fail to satisfy the requirements of section 411(b)(1)(H).

(b) *Defined benefit plans*—(1) *In general.* (i) A defined benefit plan does not satisfy the minimum vesting standards of section 411(a) if, either directly or indirectly, because of the attainment of any age—

(A) A participant's accrual of benefits is discontinued or the rate of a participant's accrual of benefits is decreased, or

(B) A participant's compensation after the attainment of such age is not taken into account in determining the participant's accrual of benefits.

(ii) In determining whether a defined benefit plan satisfies paragraph (b)(1)(i) of this section, the subsidized portion of an early retirement benefit (whether provided on a temporary or permanent basis), a social security supplement (as defined in § 1.411(a)-7(c)(4)(ii)) and a qualified disability benefit (as defined in § 1.411(a)-7(c)(3)) are disregarded in determining the rate of a participant's accrual of benefits under the plan.

(iii) The provisions of paragraph (b)(1)(i) of this section may be illustrated by the following example. In the example, assume that the participant completes the hours of service in a plan year required under the plan to accrue a full benefit for the plan year.

Example. Employer X maintains a defined benefit plan that provides a normal retirement benefit of 1% of a participant's average annual compensation, multiplied by the participant's years of credited service under the plan. Normal retirement age under the plan is age 65. The plan contains no limitations (other than the limitations imposed by section 415) on the maximum amount of benefits the plan will pay to any participant or on the maximum number of years of credited service taken into account under the plan for purposes of determining the amount of any participant's normal retirement benefit. Participant A became a participant in the plan at age 25 and worked continuously for X until A retired at age 70. The plan will satisfy the requirements of section 411(b)(1)(H) and paragraph (b)(2) of this section if, under the plan's benefit formula, upon A's retirement, A has an accrued normal retirement benefit of at least 45% of A's average annual compensation (1% per year × 45 years).

(2) *Benefit and service limitations*—(i) *In general.* A defined benefit plan does not fail to satisfy section 411(b)(1)(H) and paragraph (b) of this section solely because the plan limits the amount of benefits a participant may accrue under the plan or limits the number of years of service or years of participation taken into account for purposes of determining the accrual of benefits under the plan (credited service). For this purpose, a limitation that is expressed as a percentage of compensation (whether averaged over a participant's total years of credited service for the employer or over a shorter period) and a limitation of the type described in section 401(a)(5)(D) are treated as permissible limitations on the amount of benefits a participant may accrue under the plan. However, in applying a limitation on the number of years of credited service that are taken into account under a plan, the plan may not take into account any year of service that is disregarded in determining the accrual of benefits under the plan (prior to the effective date of section 411(b)(1)(H) and this section) because of the attainment of any age.

(ii) *Limitation not based on age.* Any limitation on the amount of benefits a participant may accrue under the plan and any limitation on the number of years of credited service taken into account under the plan may not be based, directly or indirectly, on the attainment of any age. A limitation that is determined by reference to age or that is not determinable except by reference to age is considered a limitation directly based on age. Thus, a plan provision that, for purposes of benefit accrual, disregards years of service completed after a participant becomes eligible to receive social security benefits is considered a limitation directly based on age. Similarly, a plan provision that, for purposes of benefit accrual, disregards years of service completed after the sum of a participant's age and the participant's number of years of credited service equals a specified number, is considered a limitation directly based on age. Whether a limitation is indirectly based on age is determined with reference to all the facts and circumstances.

(iii) *Examples.* The provisions of paragraph (b)(2) of this section may be illustrated by the following examples. In each example, assume that the participant completes the hours of service in a plan year required under the plan to accrue a full benefit for the plan year.

Example (1). Assume the same facts as in the example set forth in paragraph (b)(1)(ii) of this section, except that the plan provides that not more than 35 years of credited service will be taken into account in determining a participant's normal retirement benefit under the plan. Upon A's retirement at age 70, A will have a normal retirement benefit under the plan's benefit formula of 35% of A's average annual compensation (1% per year × 35 years. The plan will not fail to satisfy the requirements of section 411(b)(1)(H) and this paragraph (b) merely because the plan provides that the final 10 years of A's service under the plan is not taken into account in determining A's normal retirement benefit. The result would be the same if the plan provided that no participant could accrue a normal retirement benefit in excess of 35% of the participant's average annual compensation.

Example (2). Employer Y maintains a defined benefit plan that provides a normal retirement benefit of 50% of a participant's final average compensation. Normal retirement age under the plan is age 65. Other than the limitations imposed by section 415, the plan contains no provision that limits the accrual of the benefit payable to a participant who has less than a specified number of years of credited service for Y. Participant A is hired by Y at age 66 and commences participation in the plan at age 67. Under the plan's benefit formula, if A completes one year of credited service under the plan, A will be entitled to receive (subject to the limitations of section 415) a normal retirement benefit equal to 50% of A's final average compensation.

(3) *Different rates of benefit accrual*—(i) *In general.* A defined benefit plan does not fail to satisfy the requirements of section 411(b)(1)(H) and paragraph (b) of this section solely because the plan provides for the accrual of benefits at different rates with respect to participants under the plan. Accordingly, a plan under which a participant's accrued benefit is determined in accordance with the fractional rule described in section 411(b)(1)(C) and § 1.411(b)-1(b)(3) will not fail to satisfy the requirements of section 411(b)(1)(H) and paragraph (b) of this section solely because the rate at which a participant's normal retirement benefit accrues differs depending on the number of years of credited service a participant would have between the date of commencement of participation and the attainment of normal retirement age. In addition, a plan will not be treated as failing to satisfy section 411(b)(1)(H) and paragraph (b) of this section solely because the plan's benefit formula provides, on a uniform and consistent basis, a normal retirement benefit equal to, for example, 2% of average annual compensation multiplied by a participant's first 15 years of credited service and 1% of average annual compensation multiplied by a participant's years of credited service in excess of 15 years. The preceding sentence applies regardless of when the participant's normal retirement age occurs.

(ii) *Differences not based on age.* Any differences in the rate of benefit accrual described in paragraph (b)(3)(i) of this section may not be based, directly or indirectly, on the attainment of any age.

(4) *Certain adjustments for delayed retirement*—(i) *In general.* Under section 411(b)(1) (H)(iii), a plan may provide that benefit accruals that would otherwise be required under section 411(b)(1)(H)(i) and paragraph (b) of this section for a plan year are reduced (but not below zero) as set forth in paragraph (b)(4)(ii) and (iii) of this section. This paragraph (b)(4) applies for a plan year to a participant who, as of the end of the plan year, has attained normal retirement age under the plan.

(ii) *Distribution of benefits.* (A) A plan may provide that the benefit accrual otherwise required under section 411(b)(1)(H)(i) and paragraph (b) of this section for a plan year is reduced (but not below zero) by the actuarial equivalent of total plan benefit distributions (as determined under this paragraph (b)(4)(ii)) made to the participant by the close of the plan year.

(B) The plan benefit distributions described in this paragraph (b)(4)(ii) are limited to distributions made to the participant during plan years and periods with respect to which section 411(b)(1)(H)(i) and this section apply (including plan years and periods beginning before January 1, 1988) for which the plan could (without regard to section 401(a)(9) and the regulations thereunder) provide for the suspension of the participant's plan benefits in accordance with section 203(a)(3)(B) of the Employee Retirement Income Security Act of 1974 (ERISA) and regulations issued thereunder by the Department of Labor.

(C) For purposes of determining the total amount of plan benefit distributions that may be taken into account under this paragraph (b)(4)(ii) as of the close of a plan year, distributions shall be disre-

garded to the extent the total amount of distributions made to the participant by the close of the plan year exceeds the total amount of the distributions the participant would have received by the close of the plan year if the distributions had been made in accordance with the plan's normal form of benefit distribution. Accordingly, the plan is required to accrue a benefit for the plan year on behalf of a participant in accordance with the plan's benefit formula, taking into account all of the participant's years of credited service, reduced (but not below the participant's normal retirement benefit for the prior plan year) by the actuarial equivalent of total benefit distributions (taken into account under this paragraph (b)(4)(ii)) made to the participant by the close of the plan year. If, by the close of the plan year, the actuarial equivalent of total plan benefit distributions made to the participant and taken into account under this paragraph (b)(4)(ii) is greater than the total benefit accruals required under section 411(b)(1)(H)(i) and paragraph (b) of this section for the plan years during which such distributions were made, the plan is not required under section 411(b)(1)(H)(i) and paragraph (b) of this section to accrue any benefit on behalf of the participant for the plan year.

(iii) *Adjustment in benefits payable.* (A) A plan may provide that the benefit accrual otherwise required under section 411(b)(1)(H)(i) and paragraph (b) of this section for the plan year is reduced (but not below zero) by the amount of any actuarial adjustment under the plan in the benefit payable for the plan year with respect to the participant because of a delay in the payment of plan benefits after the participant's attainment of normal retirement age.

(B) For purposes of paragraph (b)(4)(iii)(A) of this section, the actuarial adjustment may be taken into account for a plan year only to the extent it is made to the greater of the participant's retirement benefit as of the close of the prior plan year, including any actuarial adjustment made under the plan for the prior plan year, and the participant's normal retirement benefit as of the close of the prior plan year determined by including benefit accruals required by section 411(b)(1)(H)(i) and paragraph (b) of this section. If the retirement benefit, as actuarially adjusted for the plan year in accordance with this paragraph (b)(4)(iii) for delayed payment, exceeds the normal retirement benefit, as determined by including benefit accruals required for the plan year by section 411(b)(1)(H)(i) and paragraph (b) of this section, the plan shall be required to provide the retirement benefit, as actuarially adjusted in accordance with this paragraph (b)(4)(iii) under the plan. Notwithstanding the provisions of this paragraph (b)(4)(iii)(B), in the case of a plan that suspends benefit payments in accordance with section 203(a)(3)(B) of the Employee Retirement Income Security Act of 1974 and the regulations issued thereunder by the Department of Labor, the plan does not fail to satisfy the requirements of section 411(b)(1)(H) and paragraph (b) of this section solely because the plan provides that the retirement benefit to which a participant is entitled as of the close of a plan year ending after the participant attains normal retirement age under the plan is the greater of the benefit payable at normal retirement age (not including benefit accruals otherwise required by section 411(b)(1)(H) and paragraph (b) of this section) actuarially adjusted under the plan to the close of the plan year for delayed payment, and the retirement benefit determined under the plan as of the close of the plan year determined by section 411(b)(1)(H) and paragraph (b) of this section and determined without regard to any offset that would otherwise be applicable under this paragraph (b)(4)(iii).

(iv) *Examples.* The provisions of paragraph (b)(4) of this section may be illustrated by the following examples. In each example, assume that the participant completes the hours of service in a plan year required under the plan to accrue a full benefit for the plan year and assume that the participant is not married unless otherwise specified.

Example (1). Employer Y maintains a defined benefit plan that provides a normal retirement benefit of $20 per month multiplied by the participant's years of credited service. The plan contains no limit on the number of years of credited service taken into account for purposes of determining the normal retirement benefit provided by the plan. Participant A attains normal retirement age of 65 and continues in the full time service of Y. At age 65, A has 30 years of credited service under the plan and could receive a normal retirement benefit of $600 per month ($20 × 30 years) if A retires. The plan provides for the suspension of A's normal retirement benefit (in accordance with section 203(a)(3)(B) of the Employee Retirement Income Security Act of 1974 (ERISA) and regulations thereunder issued by the Department of Labor) during the period of A's continued employment with Y. Accordingly, the plan does not provide for an actuarial adjustment of A's normal retirement benefit because of delayed payment and the plan does not pay A's normal retirement benefit while A remains in the full time service of Y. If A retires at age 67, after completing two additional years of credited service for Y, A must receive additional accruals for the two years of credited service completed after attaining normal retirement age in order for the plan to satisfy section 411(b)(1)(H)(i). Accordingly, A is entitled to receive a normal retirement benefit of $640 per month ($20 × 32 years).

Example (2). Assume the same facts as in *Example (1)*, except that the plan provides that at the time A's normal retirement benefit becomes payable, the amount of A's normal retirement benefit (determined as of A's normal retirement age and each year thereafter) will be actuarially increased for delayed retirement. The plan offsets this actuarial increase against benefit accruals in plan years ending after A's attainment of normal retirement age, as permitted by paragraph (b)(4)(iii) of this section. Accordingly, the plan does not provide for the suspension of normal retirement benefits (in accordance with section 203(a)(3)(B) of ERISA and regulations thereunder issued by the Department of Labor). Under section 411(b)(1)(H), the plan must provide A with a benefit of at least $620 per month after A completes 31 years of credited service for Y. However, under paragraph (b)(4)(iii) of this section, the plan is not required to provide A with a benefit accrual for A's additional year of credited service for Y because, under the plan, A will be entitled to receive, upon retirement at age 66 after completing 1 additional year of credited service for Y, an actuarially increased benefit of $672 per month. This monthly benefit of $672 is the greater of A's normal retirement benefit at normal retirement age ($20 × 30 years = $600) actuarially adjusted for delayed payment and A's normal retirement benefit ($20 × 31 years = $620) determined by taking into account A's year of credited service after attaining normal retirement age. Under the plan, A will be entitled to receive, upon retirement at age 67 after completing 2 additional years of credited service for Y after attaining normal retirement age, an actuarially increased benefit of $756 per month. This monthly benefit of $756 is the greater of A's actuarially adjusted normal retirement benefit at age 66 ($672) actuarially adjusted to $756 for delayed payment to age 67 and A's normal retirement benefit ($20 × 32 years = $640) determined by taking into account A's years of credited service after attaining normal retirement age.

Example (3). Assume the same facts as in *Example (1)*, except that the plan neither provides for the suspension of normal retirement benefit payments (in accordance with section 203(a)(3)(B) of ERISA and regulations thereunder issued by the Department of Labor) nor provides for an actuarial increase in benefit payments because of delayed payment of benefits. Consequently, the plan provides that the normal retirement benefit will be paid to a participant, beginning at age 65 (normal retirement age) even though the participant remains in the service of Y and offsets the value of the benefit distributions against benefit accruals in plan years ending after the participant's attainment of normal retirement age, as permitted by paragraph (b)(4)(ii) of this section. Participant B (who remains in the full time service of Y) receives 12 monthly benefit payments prior to attainment of age 66. The total monthly benefit payments of $7,200 ($600 × 12 payments) have an actuarial value at age 66 of $7,559 (reflecting interest and mortality) which would produce a monthly benefit of $72 commencing at age 66. The benefit accrual for the year of credited service B completed after attaining normal retirement age is $20 per month ($20 × 1 year). Because the actuarial value (determined as a monthly benefit of $72) of the benefit payments made during the one year of credited service after B's attainment of normal retirement age exceeds the benefit accrual for the one year of credited service after B's attainment of normal retirement age, the plan is not required to accrue benefits on behalf of B for the one year of credited service after B's attainment of normal retirement age and the plan is not required to increase B's monthly benefit payment of $600 at age 66.

Assume B receives 24 monthly benefit payments prior to B's retirement at age 67. The total monthly benefit payments of $14,400 ($600 ×

24 payments) have an actuarial value at age 67 of $15,839 (reflecting interest and mortality) which would produce a monthly benefit payment of $156 commencing at age 67. The benefit accrual for the two years of credited service B completed after attaining normal retirement age is $40 per month ($20 × 2 years). Because the actuarial value (determined as a monthly benefit of $156) of the benefit payments made during the two years of credited service after B's normal retirement age exceeds the benefit accrual for the two years of credited service after B's normal retirement age ($20 × 2 years = $40), the plan is not required to accrue benefits on behalf of B for the second year of credited service B completed after attaining normal retirement age and the plan is not required to increase B's monthly benefit payment of $600.

Example (4). Assume that Employer Z maintains a defined benefit plan that provides a normal retirement benefit of 2% of the average of a participant's high three consecutive years of compensation multiplied by the participant's years of credited service under the plan. The plan contains no limit on the number of years of credited service taken into account for purposes of determining the normal retirement benefit provided by the plan. Participant C, who has attained normal retirement age (age 65) under the plan, continues in the full time service of Z. At normal retirement age, C has average compensation of $20,000 for C's high three consecutive years and has 10 years of credited service under the plan. Thus, at normal retirement age, C is entitled to receive an annual normal retirement benefit of $4,000 ($20,000 × .02 × 10 years). Assume further that the plan provides for the suspension of N's normal retirement benefit (in accordance with section 203(a)(3)(B) of ERISA and regulations issued thereunder by the Department of Labor) during the period of C's continued employment with Z. Accordingly, the plan does not provide for the actuarial increase of C's normal retirement benefit because of delayed payment and the plan does not pay C's normal retirement benefit while C remains in the full time service of Z. At age 70, when C retires, C has average annual compensation for C's high three consecutive years of $35,000. Under section 411(b)(1)(H), C must be credited with 15 years of credited service for Z and C's increased compensation after attaining normal retirement age must be taken into account for purposes of determining C's normal retirement benefit. At age 70, C is entitled to receive an annual normal retirement benefit of $10,500 ($35,000 × .02 × 15 years).

Example (5). Assume the same facts as in *Example (4)*, except that the payment of C's retirement benefit is not suspended (in accordance with section 203(a)(3)((B) of ERISA and regulations issued thereunder by the Department of Labor) and, accordingly, the plan provides that retirement benefits that commence after a participant's normal retirement age will be actuarially increased for late retirement. The plan offsets this actuarial increase against benefit accruals in plan years ending after C's attainment of normal retirement age, as permitted by paragraph (b)(4)(iii) of this section. Under this provision, at the close of each plan year after C's attainment of normal retirement age, C's retirement benefit is actuarially increased. Under this provision, the actuarial increase for the plan year is made to the greater of C's normal retirement benefit at the close of the prior plan year (including previous actuarial adjustments) and C's normal retirement benefit at the close of the prior plan year determined by including all benefit accruals. Accordingly, at the close of each plan year, C is entitled to receive an annual normal retirement benefit equal to the greater of C's normal retirement benefit (adjusted actuarially under the plan from the benefit to which C was entitled at the close of the prior plan year) determined at the close of the plan year and C's normal retirement benefit determined at the close of the plan year by taking into account C's years of credited service and benefit accruals after C's attainment of normal retirement age. The foregoing is illustrated in the following table with respect to certain years of credited service performed by C after attaining normal retirement age 65.

Age	Years of credited service	Average compensation for high three consecutive years	Normal retirement benefit with additional accruals (.02 × column 2 × column 3)	Retirement benefit, as actuarially increased under the plan from the benefit at prior age (column 6)	Normal retirement benefit to which C is entitled (greater of column 4 and column 5)
1	2	3	4	5	6
65	10	$20,000	$4,000	N/A	$4,000
66	11	21,000	4,620	$4,482	4,620
67	12	29,000	6,960	5,192	6,960
68	13	30,000	7,800	7,848	7,848
69	14	33,000	9,240	8,880	9,240
70	15	35,000	10,500	10,494	10,500

Example (6). Assume the same facts as in *Example (4)*, except that C does not retire at age 70, but continues in the full time service of Z. Upon C's attainment of age 70, the plan commences benefit payments to C. The annual benefit paid to C in the first plan year is $10,500 ($35,000 × .02 × 15 years). In determining the annual benefit payable to C in each subsequent plan year, the plan offsets the value of benefit distributions made to the participant by the close of the prior plan year against benefit accruals in plan years during which such distributions were made, as permitted by paragraph (b)(4)(ii) of this section. Ac-

cordingly, for each subsequent plan year, C is entitled under the plan to receive benefit payments based on C's benefit (at the close of the prior plan year) determined under the plan formula by taking into account all of C's years of credited service, reduced (but not below C's normal retirement benefit for the prior plan year) by the value of total benefit distributions made to C by the close of the prior plan year. The foregoing is illustrated in the following table with respect to certain years of credited service performed by C while benefits were being distributed to C.

Years of benefit distributions	Years of credited service (as of close of the year)	Average compensation for high three years	Normal retirement benefit with additional accruals (.02 × column 2 × column 3)	Suspendible benefit distributions made during the year
1	2	3	4	5
N/A	15	$35,000	$10,500	N/A
1	16	35,000	11,200	$10,500
2	17	45,000	15,300	10,500
3	18	50,000	18,000	12,091

Years of benefit distributions	Cumulative suspendible benefit distributions made as of close of the year	Annual benefit that is actuarial equivalent of cumulative suspendible benefit distributions made as of close of the year	Retirement benefit to which C is entitled at close of the year (column 4 – column 7, but not less than column 8 for prior year)
1	6	7	8
N/A	N/A	N/A	$10,500
1	$10,500	$1,472	10,500
2	21,000	3,209	12,091
3	33,091	5,510	12,490

(c) *Defined contribution plans*—(1) *In general.* A defined contribution plan (including a target benefit plan described in § 1.410(a)-4(a)(1)) does not satisfy the minimum vesting standards of section 411(a) if, either directly or indirectly, because of the attainment of any age—

(i) The allocation of employer contributions or forfeitures to the accounts of participants is discontinued, or

(ii) The rate at which the allocation of employer contributions or forfeitures is made to the accounts of participants is decreased.

(2) *Limitations on allocations.* (i) A defined contribution plan (including a target benefit plan described in § 1.410(a)-4(a)(1)) does not fail to satisfy the minimum vesting standards of section 411(a) solely because the plan limits the total amount of employer contributions and forfeitures that may be allocated to a participant's account (for a particular plan year or for the participant's total years of credited service under the plan) or solely because the plan limits the total number of years of credited service for which a participant's account may receive allocations of employer contributions and forfeitures. The limitations described in the preceding sentence may not be applied with respect to the allocation of gains, losses or income of the trust to the account of a participant. Furthermore, a defined contribution plan (including a target benefit plan) does not fail to satisfy section 411(a) solely because the plan limits the number of years of credited service that may be taken into account for purposes of determining the amount of, or the rate at which, employer contributions and forfeitures are allocated to a participant's account for a particular plan year. However, in applying a credited service limitation described in this paragraph (c)(2)(i), the plan may not take into account any year of service (prior to the effective date of section 411(b)(2) and paragraph (c) of this section) that is disregarded in determining allocations to a participant's account because of the participant's attainment of any age.

(ii) Any limitation described in paragraph (c)(2)(i) of this section may not be based, directly or indirectly, on the attainment of any age. The provisions of paragraph (b)(2)(ii) of this section shall also apply for purposes of this paragraph (c).

(iii) The Commissioner shall provide such additional rules as may be necessary or appropriate with respect to the application of section 411(b)(2) and this section to target benefit plans.

(d) *Benefits and forms of benefits subject to requirements* —(1) *General rule.* Except as provided in paragraph (d)(2) of this section, section 411(b)(1)(H) and (b)(2) and paragraphs (b) and (c) of this section apply to all benefits (and forms of benefits) provided under a defined benefit plan and a defined contribution plan, including accrued benefits, benefits described in section 411(d)(6), ancillary benefits and other rights and features provided under the plan. Accordingly, except as provided in paragraph (d)(2) of this section, benefit accruals under a defined benefit plan and allocations under a defined contribution plan

will be considered to be reduced on account of the attainment of a specified age if optional forms of benefits, ancillary benefits, or other rights or features under the plan provided with respect to benefits or allocations attributable to credited service prior to the attainment of such age are not provided (on at least as favorable a basis to participants) with respect to benefits or allocations attributable to credited service after such age. Thus, for example, a plan may not provide a lump sum payment only with respect to benefits attributable to years of credited service before the attainment of a specified age. Similarly, except as provided in paragraph (d)(2) of this section, if an optional form of benefit is available under the plan at a specified age, the availability of such form of benefit, or the method for determining the manner in which such benefit is paid, may not, directly or indirectly, be denied or provided on terms less favorable to participants because of the attainment of any higher age. Similarly, if the method for determining the amount or the rate of the subsidized portion of a joint and survivor annuity or the subsidized portion of a preretirement survivor annuity is less favorable with respect to participants who have attained a specified age than with respect to participants who have not attained such age, benefit accruals or account allocations under the plan will be considered to be reduced on account of the attainment of such age.

(2) *Special rule for certain benefits.* A plan will not fail to satisfy section 411(b)(1)(H) or paragraph (b) of this section merely because the following benefits, or the manner in which such benefits are provided under the plan, vary because of the attainment of any higher age.

(i) The subsidized portion of an early retirement benefit (whether provided on a temporary or permanent basis),

(ii) A qualified disability benefit (as defined in § 1.411(a)-7(c)(3)); and

(iii) A social security supplement (as defined in § 1.411(a)-7(c)(4)(ii)).

(e) *Coordination with certain provisions.* Notwithstanding section 441(b)(1)(H), (b)(2) and the preceding paragraphs of this section, the following rules shall apply.

(1) *Section 415 limitations.* No allocation to the account of a participant in a defined contribution plan (including a target benefit plan described in § 1.410(a)-4(a)(1)) shall be required for a limitation year by section 411(b)(2) and no benefit accrual with respect to a participant in a defined benefit plan shall be required for a limitation year by section 411(b)(1)(H)(i) to the extent that the allocation of accrual would cause the plan to exceed the limitations of section 415(b), (c), or (e) applicable to the participant for the limitation year.

(2) *Prohibited discrimination.* (i) No allocation to the account of a highly compensated employee in a defined contribution plan (including a target benefit plan) shall be required for a plan year by section

411(b)(2) to the extent the allocation would cause the plan to discriminate in favor of highly compensated employees within the meaning of section 401(a)(4).

(ii) No benefit accrual on behalf of a highly compensated employee in a defined benefit plan shall be required for a plan year by section 411(b)(1)(H)(i) to the extent such benefit accrual would cause the plan to discriminate in favor of highly compensated employees within the meaning of section 410(a)(4).

(iii) The Commissioner may provide additional rules relating to prohibited discrimination in favor of highly compensated employees.

(3) *Permitted disparity.* In the case of a plan that would fail to satisfy section 401(a)(4) except for the application of section 401(a), no allocation to the account of a participant in a defined contribution plan and no benefit accrual on behalf of a participant in a defined benefit plan shall be required under section 411(b)(1)(H) or (b)(2) for a plan year to the extent such allocation or accrual would cause the plan to fail to satisfy the requirements of section 401(1) and the regulations thereunder for the plan year.

(f) *Effective dates*—(1) *Noncollectively bargained plans*—(i) *In general.* Except as otherwise provided in paragraph (f)(2) of this section, section 411(b)(1)(H) and (b)(2) and paragraphs (b) and (c) of this section are effective for plan years beginning on or after January 1, 1988, with respect to a participant who is credited with at least 1 hour of service in a plan year beginning on or after January 1, 1988. Section 411(b)(1)(H) and (b)(2) and paragraphs (b) and (c) of this section are not effective with respect to a participant who is not credited with at least 1 hour of service in a plan year beginning on or after January 1, 1988.

(ii) *Defined benefit plans.* In the case of a participant who is credited with at least 1 hour of service in a plan year beginning on or after January 1, 1988, section 411(b)(1)(H) and paragraph (b) of this section are effective with respect to all years of service completed by the participant, including years of service completed before the first plan year beginning on or after January 1, 1998. Accordingly, in the case of a participant described in the preceding sentence, a defined benefit plan does not satisfy section 411(b)(1)(H) and paragraph (b) of this section for a plan year beginning on or after January 1, 1988, if the plan disregards, because of the participant's attainment of any age, any year of service completed by the participant or any compensation earned by the participant after attaining such age. However, a defined benefit plan is not required under section 411(b)(1)(H) and paragraph (b) of this section to take into account for benefit accrual purposes any year of service completed before an employee becomes a participant in the plan. See paragraph (b)(2) of this section for rules relating to benefit and service limitations that may be imposed by a defined benefit plan.

(iii) *Defined contribution plans.* Section 411(b)(2) and paragraph (c) of this section are not applicable with respect to allocations of employer contributions or forfeitures to the accounts of participants under a defined contribution plan for a plan year beginning before January 1, 1988. However, in the case of a defined contribution plan under which allocations to the accounts of participants for a plan year are determined on the basis of an allocation formula that takes into account service or compensation for the employer during prior plan years, section 411(b)(2) and paragraph (c) of this section are effective for plan years beginning on or after January 1, 1988, with respect to all years of service completed by the participant, including years of service completed before the first plan year beginning on or after January 1, 1988. Accordingly, in the case of a participant who has at least 1 hour of service in a plan year beginning on or after January 1, 1988, a defined contribution plan containing an allocation formula described in the preceding sentence does not satisfy section 411(b)(2) and paragraph (c) of this section with respect to allocations for a plan year beginning on or after January 1, 1988, if the plan disregards, because of the participant's attainment of any age, any year of service completed by the participant. See paragraph (c)(2) of this section for the rules relating to limitations on allocations to the accounts of participants that may be imposed by a defined contribution plan.

(iv) *Employee contributions.* In applying paragraph (f)(1)(i), (ii) and (iii) of this section to plan years beginning on or after January 1, 1988, a year of service completed before the first plan year beginning on or after January 1, 1988, will not be treated as being disregarded under a plan on account of a participant's attainment of a specified age solely because such year of service is disregarded under the plan because the participant was not eligible to make voluntary or mandatory employee contributions (as well as contributions under a cash or deferred arrangement described in section 401(k)) under the plan for such year. A plan is not required to permit a participant to make voluntary or mandatory employee contributions (as well as contributions under a cash or deferred arrangement described in section 401(k)) for a plan year beginning before January 1, 1988, in order to satisfy section

411(b)(1)(H) or (b)(2) or paragraph (b) or (c) of this section for a plan year beginning on or after January 1, 1988.

(v) *Hour of service.* For purposes of this paragraph (f)(1), one hour of service means one hour of service recognized under the plan or required to be recognized under the plan by section 410 (relating to minimum participation standards) or section 411 (relating to minimum vesting standards). In the case of a plan that does not determine service on the basis of hours of service, one hour of service means any service recognized under the plan or required to be recognized under the plan by section 410 (relating to minimum participation standards) or section 411 (relating to minimum vesting standards).

(vi) *Examples.* The provisions of paragraph (f)(1) of this section may be illustrated by the following examples. In each example, assume that the participant completes the hours of service in a plan year required under the plan to accrue a full benefit or receive an allocation for the plan year.

Example (1). Employer X maintains a noncontributory defined benefit plan (that is not a collectively bargained plan) that provides a normal retirement benefit equal to 1% of a participant's average annual compensation for the participant's three consecutive years of highest compensation, multiplied by the participant's years of credited service under the plan. The plan contains no limit on the number of years of credited service taken into account for purposes of determining the normal retirement benefit provided by the plan. The plan uses the calendar year as its plan year. The plan specifies a normal retirement age of 65 and provides (prior to January 1, 1988) that no compensation earned and no service performed by a participant after attainment of normal retirement age will be taken into account in determining the participant's normal retirement benefit. Participant A attains normal retirement age on December 15, 1985. A continues in the full time service of X and has at least 1 hour of service for X during the plan year beginning on January 1, 1988. As of the plan year ending December 31, 1985, A had 35 years of credited service under the plan. In accordance with the plan provisions in effect prior to January 1, 1988, A's service and compensation during the 1986 and 1987 plan years is not taken into account in determining A's normal retirement benefit for those plan years. Beginning on January 1, 1988, the plan provisions that compensation earned and years of service completed after normal retirement age are not taken into account in determining a participant's normal retirement benefit may not be applied to A. Thus, as of the plan year beginning January 1, 1988, A's normal retirement benefit under the plan must be determined without regard to those provisions. Accordingly, beginning on January 1, 1988, the plan is required to take into account A's service for X and A's compensation from X during the 1986 and 1987 plan years for purposes of determining A's normal retirement benefit in order to satisfy section 411(b)(1)(H) and paragraph (b) of this section.

Example (2). Assume the same facts as in *Example (1),* except that the plan provides that, in determining a participant's normal retirement benefit under the plan (a) not more than 35 years of credited service will be taken into account and (b) no compensation earned after 35 years of credited service have been completed will be taken into account. Accordingly, the plan is not required to take into account A's service for X or A's compensation from X during the 1986 and 1987 plan years for purposes of determining A's normal retirement benefit in order to satisfy section 411(b)(1)(H) and paragraph (b) of this section.

Example (3). Assume the same facts as in *Example (1),* except that A retires on December 5, 1987 and does not perform any hours of service for X after A's retirement. Accordingly, the plan is not required to take into account A's service for X and A's compensation from X during the 1986 and 1987 plan years for purposes of determining A's normal retirement benefit in order to satisfy section 411(b)(1)(H) and paragraph (b) of this section.

Example (4). Assume the same facts as in *Example (1),* except that the plan requires, as a condition to accruing benefits attributable to employer contributions under the plan, that a participant make employee contributions under the plan. The plan provides that a participant is not eligible to make employee contributions in a plan year beginning after the plan year in which the participant attains normal retirement age under the plan. Accordingly, A does not make employee contributions during the 1986 and 1987 plan years and, therefore, does not accrue in those plan years a benefit attributable to employer contributions. The plan is not required to take into account A's service for X and A's compensation from X during the 1986 and 1987 plan years in order to satisfy section 411(b)(1)(H) and paragraph (b) of this section. In addition, the plan is not required to permit A to make employee contributions to the plan for the 1986 and 1987 plan years in order to satisfy section 411(b)(1)(H) and paragraph (b) of this section.

Example (5). Employer Y maintains a profit-sharing plan (that is not a collectively bargained plan). The plan is the only qualified plan maintained by Y and uses the calendar year as its plan year. The formula under the plan for allocating employer contributions and forfeitures to the accounts of participants contains a years of service factor. Pursuant to the allocation formula containing the years of service factor, employer contributions and forfeitures for the plan year are allocated among the accounts of participants on the basis of one unit for each full $200 of compensation for the participant for the plan year and one unit for each year of credited service for Y completed by the participant. The plan contains no limit on the number of years of credited service taken into account for purposes of determining the allocation to the account of a participant for the plan year under the plan's allocation formula. The plan specifies a normal retirement age of 65 and provides (prior to January 1, 1988) that no service performed by a participant in a plan year beginning after the attainment of normal retirement age will be taken into account in determining the allocation to the participant's account for a plan year. Participant B attains normal retirement age on December 15, 1985. B continues in the full time service of Y and has at least 1 hour of service for Y during the plan year beginning January 1, 1988. As of the plan year ending December 31, 1985, B had 35 years of credited service under the plan. In accordance with the plan provisions in effect prior to January 1, 1988, B's service during the 1986 and 1987 plan year is not taken into account in determining the allocation of employer contributions and forfeitures to B's account for the 1986 and 1987 plan years. As of the plan year beginning January 1, 1988, the plan provision that years of service in plan years beginning after attainment of normal retirement age are not taken into account in determining the allocation of employer contributions and forfeitures to the accounts of participants may not be applied to B. Thus, the allocation of employer contributions and forfeitures to B's account for the 1988 plan year must be determined under the allocation formula contained in the plan without regard to that provision. Accordingly, the plan is required to take into account B's service for Y during the 1986 and 1987 plan years for purposes of determining the allocation of employer contributions and forfeitures to B's account for the 1988 plan year in order to satisfy section 411(b)(2) and paragraph (c) of this section. However, the plan is not required to provide any additional allocations to B's account under the plan for the 1986 or 1987 plan year in order to satisfy section 411(b)(2) and paragraph (c) of this section.

Example (6). Assume the same facts as in *Example (5)*, except that the plan provides that, in determining the allocation of employer contributions and forfeitures to the account of a participant for a plan year, not more than 35 years of credited service for Y will be taken into account. Accordingly, the plan is not required to take into account B's service for Y during the 1986 or 1987 plan years for purposes of determining the allocation of employer contributions and forfeitures to B's account for the 1988 plan year under the allocation formula contained in the plan.

(2) *Collectively bargained plans*. (i) In the case of a plan maintained pursuant to 1 or more collective bargaining agreements between employee representatives and 1 or more employers, ratified before March 1, 1986, section 411(b)(1)(H) and (b)(2) is effective for benefits provided under, and employees covered by, any such agreement with respect to plan years beginning on or after the later of—

(A) January 1, 1988, or

(B) The date on which the last of such collective bargaining agreements terminates (determined without regard to any extension of any such agreement occurring on or after March 1, 1986).

However, notwithstanding the preceding sentence, section 411(b)(1)(H) and (b)(2) shall be effective for benefits provided under, and employees covered by, any agreement described in this paragraph

(f)(2)(i) no later than with respect to the first plan year beginning on or after January 1, 1990.

(ii) The effective date provisions of paragraph (f)(1) of this section shall apply in paragraph (f)(2)(i) of this section, except that the effective date determined under paragraph (f)(2)(i) of this section shall be substituted for the effective date determined under paragraph (f)(1) of this section.

(iii) In accordance with the provisions of paragraph (f)(2)(i) of this section, a plan described therein may be subject to different effective dates under section 411(b)(1)(H) and (b)(2) for employees who are covered by a collective bargaining agreement and employees who are not covered by a collective bargaining agreement.

(iv) For purposes of paragraph (f)(2)(i) of this section, the service crediting rules of paragraph (f)(1) of this section shall apply to a plan described in paragraph (f)(2)(i) of this section, except that in applying such rules the effective date determined under paragraph (f)(2)(i) of this section shall be substituted for the effective date determined under paragraph (f)(1) of this section. See paragraph (f)(1)(v) of this section for rules relating to the recognition of an hour of service.

(3) *Amendments to plans*. (i) Except as provided in paragraph (f)(3)(ii) of this section, plan amendments required by section 411(b)(1)(H) and (b)(2) (the applicable sections) shall not be required to be made before the first plan year beginning on or after January 1, 1989, if the following requirements are met—

(A) The plan is operated in accordance with the requirements of the applicable section for all periods before the first plan year beginning on or after January 1, 1989, for which such section is effective with respect to the plan; and

(B) Such plan amendments are adopted no later than the last day of the first plan year beginning on or after January 1, 1989, and are made effective retroactively for all periods for which the applicable section is effective with respect to the plan.

(ii) In the case of a collectively bargained plan described in paragraph (f)(2)(i) of this section that satisfies the requirements of paragraph (f)(3)(i) of this section (as modified by this paragraph (f)(3)(ii)), paragraph (f)(3)(i) shall be applied by substituting for "the first plan year beginning on or after January 1, 1989, "the first plan year beginning on or after the later of—

(A) January 1, 1989, or

(B) The date on which the last of such collective bargaining agreements terminates (determined without regard to any extension of any such agreement occurring on or after March 1, 1986).

However, notwithstanding the preceding sentence, section 411(b)(1)(H) and (b)(2) shall be applicable to plans described in this paragraph (f)(3)(ii) no later than the first plan year beginning on or after January 1, 1990.

Par. 6. Section 1.411(c)-1 is amended by revising paragraph (f)(2) to read as follows:

§ 1.411(c)-1 Allocation of accrued benefits between employer and employee contributions.

* * *

(f) *Suspension of benefits, etc.* * * *

(2) *Employment after retirement*. Except as permitted by paragraph (f)(1) of this section, a defined benefit plan must make an actuarial adjustment to an accrued benefit the payment of which is deferred past normal retirement age. See, also, section 411(b)(1)(H) (relating to continued accruals after normal retirement age) and § 1.411(b)-2.

Lawrence B. Gibbs,

Commissioner of Internal Revenue.

[FR Doc. 88-7880 Filed 4-8-88; 8:45 am]

[¶ 20,150 Reserved.—Proposed Reg. § 1.414(e)-1, relating to the definition of "church plan", was formerly reproduced at this point. The final regulation is ¶ 12,360.]

[¶ 20,150A Reserved.—Proposed regulations relating to the exclusion of certain disability payments from gross income were formerly reproduced at this paragraph. The regulations were withdrawn by the Internal Revenue Service in a withdrawal notice on January 13, 1987 (52 FR 2724).]

[¶ 20,150B Reserved.—Proposed regulations relating to the requirements for the filing of returns by employee plans were formerly reproduced at this paragraph. The final regulations appear at ¶ 13,649A, 13,650A, 13,651, 13,662, 13,789 and 13.905.]

¶ 20,150C

Proposed regulations on 26 CPR Part 301.—Reproduced below is the text of proposed regulations which clarify the significance, for classification purposes, of a power in the limited partners to remove a general partner, and provide that references in the classification rules to the Uniform Limited Partnership Act refer to that Act both as originally promulgated and as revised in 1976.

The proposed regulations were published in the Federal Register on October 27, 1980 (45 FR 70909).

DEPARTMENT OF THE TREASURY

Internal Revenue Service

26 CFR Part 301

[LR-232-78]

Revision of Rules on Tax Classification of Limited Partnerships in Light of Certain Recent Legislative Developments

AGENCY: Internal Revenue Service, Treasury.

ACTION: Notice of proposed rulemaking.

SUMMARY: This document contains proposed regulations relating to the classification, for federal tax purposes, of limited partnerships. The proposed regulations provide that references in the classification rules to the Uniform Limited Partnership Act (ULPA) refer to that Act both as originally promulgated and as revised in 1976. The proposed regulations also clarify the significance, for classification purposes, of a power in the limited partners to remove a general partner.

DATES: Written comments and requests for a public hearing must be delivered or mailed by December 26, 1980. The amendments are proposed to be effective for taxable years beginning after 1953.

ADDRESS: Send comments and requests for a public hearing to: Commissioner of Internal Revenue, Attention: CC:LR:T (LR-232-78), Washington, D.C. 20224.

FOR FURTHER INFORMATION CONTACT: Paul A. Francis (202-566-6640).

SUPPLEMENTARY INFORMATION:

Background

This document contains proposed amendments to the Regulations on Procedure and Administration (26 CFR Part 301) under section 7701 of the Internal Revenue Code of 1954. These regulations are proposed to make clear the application of certain tax classification rules to limited partnerships and are to be issued under the authority contained in section 7805 of the Internal Revenue Code of 1954 (68A Stat. 917; 26 U.S.C. 7805).

References to the ULPA

For federal tax purposes various entities may be classified as associations (which are taxable as corporations), partnerships, or trusts. Section 7701(a)(2) and (3) of the Code and §§ 301.7701-1 through 301.7701-4 of the Regulations on Procedure and Administration set forth the definitions and rules that control the tax classification of entities. Section 301.7701-2 provides that the classification of an entity depends upon the presence or absence of corporate characteristics. That section also includes certain special rules for determining whether an entity organized under a statute corresponding to the ULPA possesses or lacks the corporate characteristics of continuity of life, centralization of management, and limited liability.

The National Conference of Commissioners on Uniform State Laws revised the ULPA in 1976. The proposed regulations provide that references in § 301.7701-2 to the ULPA shall be deemed to refer to that Act both as originally promulgated and as revised in 1976. Thus, the same classification rules will apply to entities organized under a statute corresponding to the revised ULPA as apply to entities organized under a statute corresponding to the original ULPA.

Power to Remove General Partner

The proposed regulations provide that all the facts and circumstances must be taken into account in determining whether the characteristic of centralized management is found in a limited partnership whose limited partners may remove the general partner. The proposed regulations note that a substantially restricted removal power would not itself cause the partnership to possess centralized management.

Comments and Requests for a Public Hearing

Before adopting these proposed regulations, consideration will be given to any written comments that are submitted (preferably six copies) to the Commissioner of Internal Revenue. All comments will be available for public inspection and copying. A public hearing will be held upon written request to the Commissioner by any person who has submitted written comments. If a public hearing is held, notice of the time and place will be published in the Federal Register.

Drafting Information

The principal author of these proposed regulations was Paul A. Francis of the Legislation and Regulations Division of the Office of Chief Counsel, Internal Revenue Service. However, personnel from other offices of the Internal Revenue Service and Treasury Department participated in developing the regulation, both on matters of substance and style.

Proposed amendments to the regulations

For the reasons stated, it is proposed to amend § 301.7701-2 of the Regulations on Procedure and Administration (26 CFR Part 301) by adding a new subparagraph (5) at the end of paragraph (a) and by adding two new sentences at the end of paragraph (c)(4). These added provisions read as follows:

§ 301.7701-2 Associations.

(a) Characteristics of corporations.

* * *

(5) All references in this section to the Uniform Limited Partnership Act shall be deemed to refer both to the original Uniform Limited Partnership Act (adopted in 1916) and to the revised Uniform Limited Partnership Act (adopted by the National Conference of Commissioners on Uniform State Laws in 1976).

* * *

(e) Centralization of management.

* * *

(4) * * * Furthermore, if all or a specified group of the limited partners may remove a general partner, all the facts and circumstances must be taken into account in determining whether the partnership possesses centralized management. A substantially restricted right of the limited partners to remove the general partner (e. g., in the event of the general partner's gross negligence, self-dealing, or embezzlement) will not itself cause the partnership to possess centralized management.

* * *

Jerome Kurtz,

Commissioner of Internal Revenue.

[¶ 20,150D Reserved.—Proposed regulations relating to the tax treatment of insurance provided to employees under policies that are not underwritten on a group basis were formerly reproduced at this paragraph. The regulations were withdrawn by the Internal Revenue Service in a withdrawal notice on January 13, 1987 (52 FR 2724).]

¶ 20,150E

Proposed regulations: Incentive stock options.—Reproduced below are proposed regulations that explain the incentive stock option (ISO) rules enacted by the Economic Recovery Tax Act of 1981. The proposed regulations set forth the requirements for receiving special tax treatment for ISOs, the conditions that must be met for an option to qualify as an incentive stock option, and the rules for converting existing options to ISOs.

The proposed regulations were published in the Federal Register on February 7, 1984 (49 FR 4504). They were withdrawn by the IRS on June 9, 2003 (see ¶ 20,260W).

For statutory options granted on or before June 9, 2003, taxpayers may rely on these 1984 proposed regulations, the 2003 proposed regulations (¶ 20,260W), or on final regulations in T.D. 9144 issued on August 3, 2004 (see ¶ 24,507Q), until the earlier of January 1, 2006, or the first regularly scheduled stockholders meeting of the granting corporation occurring six months after August 3, 2004.

DEPARTMENT OF THE TREASURY

Internal Revenue Service

26 CFR Part 1

[LR-279-81]

Incentive Stock Options; Proposed Rulemaking

AGENCY: Internal Revenue Service, Treasury.

ACTION: Notice of proposed rulemaking.

SUMMARY: This document contains proposed regulations relating to incentive stock options. Changes to the applicable tax law were made by the Economic Recovery Tax Act of 1982. The regulations would affect certain taxpayers who participate in the transfer of stock pursuant to the exercise of incentive stock options and provide them with guidance to comply with the law.

DATES: Written comments and requests for a public hearing must be delivered or mailed by April 9, 1984. The amendments are proposed to be effective on the date they are published in the *Federal Register* as final regulations. In general, they apply to options granted after August 12, 1981, but they also provide transitional rules applicable to certain options granted after December 31, 1975, and before August 13, 1981.

ADDRESS: Send comments and requests for a public hearing to: Commissioner of Internal Revenue, Attention: CC:LR:T [LR-279-81], 1111 Constitution Avenue, NW., Washington, D.C. 20224.

FOR FURTHER INFORMATION CONTACT: Bruce H. Jurist of the Legislation and Regulations Division, Office of Chief Counsel, Internal Revenue Service, 1111 Constitution Ave, NW., Washington, D.C. 20224 (Attention: CC:LR:T), 202-566-3238, not a toll-free call.

SUPPLEMENTARY INFORMATION

Background

Prior to August 13, 1981, the tax treatment of employee stock options generally was governed by section 83 of the Code and the regulations thereunder. Under those rules, the value of a stock option constituted ordinary income to the employee when granted, only if the option itself had a readily ascertainable fair market value at that time. If the option did not have a readily ascertainable value when granted, it did not constitute ordinary income until exercised. At the time of exercise, the difference between the value of the stock received and the option price constituted ordinary income to the employee. An employer who granted a stock option generally was allowed a business expense deduction equal to the amount includible in the employee's income in its corresponding taxable year.

Changes to the applicable tax law were made by section 251 of the Economic Recovery Tax Act of 1981 (95 Stat. 172) (ERTA), which added new section 422A to the Code entitled "Incentive Stock Options," and provided a set of transitional rules for the conversion of certain options granted prior to the August 13, 1981 date of enactment. Related technical changes to section 251 of ERTA were made by section 102(j) of the Technical Corrections Act of 1982 (Pub. L. 97-448). Finally, section 201(b)(1)(C) of the Tax Equity and Fiscal Responsibility Act of 1982 (96 Stat. 324) (TEFRA), amended section 57(a) of the Code to include as an item of tax preference the spread (*i. e.,* the amount by which the fair market value of the stock at the time of exercise exceeds the option price) at the time an incentive stock option is exercised. Section 201(b)(1)(C) of TEFRA is effective for taxable years beginning after December 31, 1982.

Section 422A provides for a new statutory stock option under which pursuant to section 421, there will be no tax consequences when such option is either granted or exercised (except for potential minimum tax consequences), and the employee will be taxed at capital gain rates when and if the stock received on exercise of the option is sold. Similarly, no business expense deduction will be allowed to the employer with respect to such an option.

On December 21, 1981, the Internal Revenue Service published § 14a.422A-1, temporary regulations relating to the transitional rules provided by section 251(c) of ERTA (46 FR 61839). The temporary regulations provided guidance to taxpayers who wanted to convert certain existing stock options into incentive stock options. The regulations were drafted in a question and answer format so as to both facilitate their timely publication and limit their scope to the transitional period issues.

The proposed regulations contained in this document represent the complete set of regulations to be promulgated under section 422A. Accordingly, the information contained in the previously published temporary regulations has been incorporated into these proposed regulations. The proposed regulations are to be issued under the authority contained in section 7805 of the Internal Revenue Code of 1954 (68A Stat. 917; 26 U.S.C. 7805).

Requirements to Receive Special Tax Treatment

Section 1.422A-1 of the proposed regulations provides that an individual, in order to receive the special tax treatment available to incentive stock options under section 421(a), must meet the following two conditions:

(1) The individual must not dispose of the stock acquired pursuant to the exercise of an incentive stock option within two years after the option is granted and must hold the stock itself for at least one year. An exception to the above holding period requirements is provided with respect to certain transfers by insolvent individuals.

(2) For the entire time from the date of granting the option until three months (one year if employment ceased because the individual is disabled within the meaning of either section 105(d)(4) or section 37(e)(3)) before the date of exercise, the individual must be an employee either on the corporation granting the option, a parent or subsidiary of that corporation, or a corporation (or parent or subsidiary of that corporation) which has assumed the option of another corporation as a result of a corporate reorganization, liquidation, etc.

In the case of the death of the individual, both the holding period requirements and the employment requirement are waived.

If all requirements other than the above holding period requirements are met, tax is deferred until disposition of the stock, but gain (to the extent the value of the stock at exercise of the option exceeds the option price) is treated as ordinary income rather than capital gain, and the employer is allowed a deduction for that amount. In the case of certain dispositions where the amount realized on disposition is less than the stock's value at exercise, the amount of ordinary income, and the amount of the employer's deduction, are limited to the difference between the amount realized on the sale and the option price.

Incentive Stock Option Defined

Section 1.422A-2 of the proposed regulations provides that for an option to qualify as an incentive stock option, the following conditions must be met:

(1) The option must be granted under a plan specifying the aggregate number of shares of stock which may be issued and the employees or class of employees eligible to receive the options. This plan must be approved by the stockholders of the granting corporation within 12 months before or after the plan is adopted.

(2) The option must be granted within ten years from the date the plan is adopted or the date the plan is approved by the stockholders, whichever is earlier.

(3) The option must by its terms be exercisable only within ten years of the date it is granted.

(4) The option price must equal or exceed the fair market value of the stock at the time the option is granted. This requirement will be deemed satisfied if there has been a good faith attempt to value the stock accurately, even if the option price is less than the stock value.

(5) The option by its terms must be nontransferable other than at death and, during the employee's lifetime, must not be exercisable by any other person.

(6) The employee must not, at the time the option is granted, own stock representing more than ten percent of the voting power of all classes of stock of the employer corporation or its parent or subsidiary. However, the stock ownership limitation will not apply if the option price is at least 110 percent of the fair market value (at the time the option is granted) of the stock subject to the option and the option by its terms is not exercisable more than five years from the date it is granted.

(7) The option by its terms is not exercisable while there is outstanding any incentive stock option which was granted to the employee at an earlier time. For this purpose, an option which has not been exercised in full is outstanding until the expiration of the period during which it could have been exercised under its initial terms. Thus, the cancella-

tion of an earlier option will not enable a subsequent option to be exercised any sooner.

(8) In the case of options granted after 1980, the terms of the plan must limit the aggregate fair market value of the stock (determined at the time of the grant of the option) for which any employee may be granted incentive stock options in any calendar year to not more than $100,000 plus a carryover amount. The carryover amount for an employee from any year after 1980 is one-half of the amount by which $100,000 exceeds the value at time of grant of the stock for which incentive stock options were granted in such prior year. Amounts may be carried over three years. Options granted in any year use up the $100,000 current year limitation first and then the carryover amount from the earliest year. Amounts may be carried over from calendar years after 1980 whether or not the corporation had an incentive stock option plan in effect for the ealier year provided the individual was employed by the corporation (or subsidiary, parent, or predecessor corporation) for some part of the earlier year.

Permissible Provisions

Section 1.422A-2 of the proposed regulations also provides that an option will qualify as an incentive stock option even if any of the following provisions are present:

(1) Stock acquired on exercise of an incentive stock option may be paid for with stock of the corporation granting the option.

(2) The employee has the right to receive additional compensation (in cash or other property) at the time of exercise of the option so long as the additional amount is includible in income under the provisions of sections 61 and 83. Thus, the employer corporation may pay the employee additional amounts (whether or not the amount of additional compensation is determined by reference to the price of the stock and/or the option price) when the employee exercises the option.

(3) The option is subject to a condition not inconsistent with the qualification requirements of section 422A(b). For example, an employee's right to receive a taxable payment of cash or other property (including employer stock) in an amount equal to the difference between the then fair market value of the stock and the option price in exchange for the cancellation or surrender of the option (at a time when it is otherwise exercisable) does not disqualify the option. This applies where the exercise of this alternative right has the same economic and tax consequences as the exercise of the option followed by an immediate sale of the stock to the employer (which would be taxed as ordinary income under section 421(b)). However, an option that includes an alternative right is not an incentive stock option if the requirements of section 422A(b) amy be avoided by exericise of the alternative right. For example, an alternative right extending the option term beyond ten years, setting a price below fair market value, permitting transferability, or allowing nonsequential exercise, will prevent an option from qualifying as an incentive stock option.

Incentive Stock Option Transitional Rules

Section 1.422A-3 of the proposed regulations provides special rules relating to the conversion of certain existing options into incentive stock options. Pursuant to section 251(c) of ERTA, the proposed regulation provides the following guidelines for the conversion of options:

(1) Only options originally granted after December 31, 1975, will be eligible for conversion into incentive stock options.

(2) Options granted during the years 1976 through 1980 will be eligible for conversion only if the option was outstanding on January 1, 1981, and the granting corporation elects to convert the option. The aggregate value (determined at the time of grant) of stock the options for which may be converted into incentive stock options by such an election may not exceed $50,000 per calendar year and $200,000 in the aggregate for the five-year period 1976-1980. The election may be made with respect to those options (or portions of options) which the granting corporation selects. The taxation of options with respect to which no election is made will not be affected.

(3) In the case of an option granted after December 31, 1975, and outstanding on August 13, 1981, the option terms (or the terms of the plan under which the option was granted) may be changed, or shareholder approval obtained, to conform to the incentive stock option rules, by August 13, 1982, without the change giving rise to a new option requiring the setting of an option price based on the valuation of the stock on the date of change. All such changes relate back to the time of grant of the original option.

(4) Generally, an exercised option must have met the incentive stock option qualification requirements of section 422A(b), at the time it was exercised, to be eligible for conversion into an incentive stock option.

(5) For incentive stock options exercised prior to 1983, the difference between the option price and the value of the stock on the date of exercise is not an item of tax preference. However, for incentive stock options exercised after 1982 (which are not later subject to a disqualifying disposition), such difference is an item of tax preference subject to the alternative minimum tax under section 55 of the Code.

Technical and Conforming Amendments

Finally, because new section 422A interacts directly with other sections of the Code, the proposed regulations provide technical and conforming amendments to a number of existing regulations under sections 421, 425, and 6039.

Special Analyses

The Commissioner of Internal Revenue has determined that these proposed rules are not major rules as defined in either Executive Order 12291 or the Treasury and OMB implementation of that order dated April 29, 1983. Accordingly, a Regulatory Impact Analysis is not required. Although this document is a notice of proposed rulemaking that solicits public comment, the Internal Revenue Service has concluded that the notice and public procedure requirements of 5 U.S.C. 553 do not apply because the rules proposed are interpretative. Accordingly, these proposed regulations do not constitute regulations subject to the Regulatory Flexibility Act (5 U.S.C. chapter 6).

Comments and Request for a Public Hearing

Before adopting these proposed regulations, consideration will be given to any written comments that are submitted (preferably seven copies) to the Commissioner of Internal Revenue. All comments will be available for public inspection and copying. A public hearing will be held upon written request to the Commissioner by any person who has submitted written comments. If a public hearing is held, notice of the time and place will be published in the *Federal Register*.

The collection of information requirements contained in this notice of proposed rulemaking have been submitted to the Office of Management and Budget (OMB) for review under section 3504(h) of the Paperwork Reduction Act of 1980. Comments on these requirements should be sent to the Office of Information and Regulatory Affairs of OMB, Attention: Desk Office for Internal Revenue Service, New Executive Office Building, Washington D.C. 20503. The Internal Revenue Service requests that persons submitting comments on these requirements to OMB also send copies of those comments to the Service.

Drafting Information

The principal author of these proposed regulations is Philip R. Bosco of the Legislation and Regulations Division of the Office of Chief Counsel, Internal Revenue Service. However, other personnel in the Internal Revenue Service and Treasury Department participated in developing the regulations on matters of both substances and style.

List of Subjects in 26 CFR 1.401-1—1.425-1

Income taxes, Employee benefit plans, Pensions, Stock options, Individual retirement accounts, Employee stock ownership plans.

PART 1—[AMENDED]

Proposed Amendments to the Regulations

The proposed amendments to 26 CFR Part 1 are as follows:

Paragraph 1. Section 1.422A-1 is added to read as follows:

§ 1.422A-1 Incentive stock options—general rules.

(a) *Applicability of section 421(a)*. (1)(i) Section 421(a) applies with respect to the transfer of a share of stock to an individual pursuant to the exercise of an incentive stock option if the following conditions are satisfied—

(A) The individual makes no disposition of such share before the later of the expiration of the 2-year period beginning on the day of the grant of the option pursuant to which such share was transferred, or the expiration of the 1-year period beginning on the day of the transfer of such share, and

(B) At all times during the period beginning on the day of the grant of the option and ending on the day 3 months before the date of such exercise, the individual was an employee of either the corporation granting the option, a related corporation of such corporation, or a corporation (or a related corporation of such corporation) issuing or assuming a stock option in a transaction to which section 425(a) applies.

(ii) For rules relating to the disposition of shares of stock, see paragraph (c) of §1.425-1. For rules relating to the requisite employment relationship, see paragraph (h) of §1.421.7.

(2)(i) The holding period requirement of section 422A(a)(1), set forth in paragraph (a)(1)(i)(A) of this section, does not apply to certain transfers by insolvent individuals. If an insolvent individual holds a share of stock acquired pursuant to the exercise of an incentive stock option, and if such share is transferred to a trustee, receiver, or other similar fiduciary in any proceeding under the Bankruptcy Act or any other similar insolvency proceeding, neither such transfer, nor any other transfer of such share for the benefit of the insolvent individual's creditors in such proceeding shall constitute a disposition of such share for the purpose of section 422A(a)(1). For the purpose of this paragraph (a)(2) an individual is an insolvent only if his liabilities exceed his assets, or if the individual is unable to satisfy his liabilities as they become due.

(ii) A transfer by the trustee or other fiduciary that is not treated as a disposition for the purpose of section 422A(a)(1) may be a sale or exchange for purposes of recognizing capital gain or loss with respect to the share transferred. For example, if the trustee transfers the share to a creditor in the insolvency proceeding in complete or partial satisfaction of such creditor's claim against the insolvent individual, capital gain or loss must be recognized by the insolvent individual to the extent of the difference between the amount realized from such transfer and the adjusted basis of such share. To the extent any transfer by the trustee or other fiduciary (other than a transfer back to the insolvent individual) is not for the exclusive benefit of the creditors in the insolvency proceeding, such transfer will be treated as a disposition for purposes of section 422A(a)(1). Similarly, if the trustee or other fiduciary transfers the share back to the insolvent individual, any subsequent disposition of the share which is not made in respect of the insolvency proceeding and for the exclusive benefit of the creditors in such proceeding will be treated as a disposition for purposes of section 422A(a)(1).

(3) If the employee exercising an option ceased employment because of permanent and total disability within the meaning of either section 37(e)(3) or section 105(d)(4), 1 year is substituted for 3 months in the employment period requirement of section 422A(a)(2) and paragraph (a)(1)(i)(B) of this section.

(b) *Failure to satisfy holding period requirement.* (1) A disqualifying disposition of a share of stock acquired by the exercise of an incentive stock option (*i.e.,* a disposition before the expiration of the holding periods as determined under section 422A(a)(1) and paragraph (a)(1)(i)(A) of this section) makes section 421(A) inapplicable to the transfer of such share. Pursuant to section 421(b), the income attributable to such transfer shall be treated by the individual as income received in the taxable year in which such disqualifying disposition occurs. Similarly, a deduction under section 162 attributable to the transfer of the share of stock pursuant to the exercise of the option shall be allowable for the taxable year in which such disqualifying disposition occurs to the employer corporation (or to a corporation issuing or assuming the option in a transaction to which section 425(a) applies). In such cases, no amount shall be treated as income, and no amount shall be allowed as a deduction, for any taxable year other than the taxable year in which the disqualifying disposition occurs. Except as provided by section 421(b) and paragraph (b) of this section, the effects of a disqualifying disposition shall be determined pursuant to section 83 and the regulations thereunder.

(2) If an individual makes a disqualifying disposition of a share of stock acquired by the exercise of an incentive stock option, and if such disposition is a sale or exchange with respect to which a loss (if sustained) would be recognized to the individual, then, under section 422A(c)(2), the amount includible in the gross income of such individual, and deductible from the income of the employer corporation (or of a corporation issuing or assuming the option in a transaction to which section 425(a) applies) as compensation attributable to the exercise of such option, shall not exceed the excess (if any) of the amount realized on such sale or exchange over the adjusted basis of such share. Thus, the limitation does not apply when the disqualifying disposition is a sale described in section 1091 (relating to loss from wash sales of stock or securities), a gift, or a sale described in section 267(a)(1) (relating to sales between related persons), since a loss sustained in any such transaction would not be recognized. Subject to the limitation provided by section 422A(c)(1) and this paragraph (b)(2), the amount of compensation attributable to the exercise of the option is determined under §1.83-7.

(3) The application of this paragraph may be illustrated by the following examples:

Example (1). On June 1, 1982, X Corporation grants an incentive stock option to A, an employee of X Corporation, entitling A to purchase one share of X Corporatiom stock. On August 1, 1982, A exercises the option and the share of X Corporation stock is transferred to A on that date. In order to meet the holding period requirements of section 422A(a)(1), A must not dispose of the share acquired by exericse of the incentive stock option before June 1, 1984.

Example (2). Assume the same facts as in example (1) except that A exercises the option on June 1, 1983, and the share of X Corporation stock is transferred to A on June 10, 1983. In order to meet the holding period requirements of section 422A(a)(1), A must not dispose of the share acquired by exercise of the incentive stock option before June 10, 1984.

Example (3). Assume the same facts as in example (1) and assume further that the option price was $100, the fair market value of X Corporation stock on June 1, 1982, and that the fair market value of X Corporation stock was $200 on August 1, 1982, the date of exercise. Assume further that the share of X Corporation stock transferred to A was transferable and not subject to a substantial risk of forfeiture. A makes a disqualifying disposition by selling the share on June 1, 1983, for $250. Under section 83(a) and paragraph (a) of §1.83-7 (relating to options to which section 421 does not apply) the amount of compensation attributable to A's exercise is $100 (the difference between the fair market value of the share at the date of exercise, $200, and the amount paid for the share, $100). Because the amount realized, $250, is greater than the value of the stock at exercise, section 422A(c)(2) does not apply and thus does not affect the amount includible as compensation in A's gross income and deductible by X. A must include in gross income for the taxable year in which the sale occurred $100 as compensation and $50 as capital gain ($250, the amount realized from the sale, less A's basis of $200 (the $100 paid for the share plus the $100 increase in basis resulting from the inclusion of that amount in A's gross income as compensation attributable to the exercise of the option)). For its taxable year in which the disqualifying disposition occurs, X Corporation is allowed a deduction of $100 for compensation attributable to A's exercise of the incentive stock option provided the withholding requirements of §1.83-6 are met.

Example (4). Assume the same facts as in example (3), except that A sells the share for $150. Under section 422A(c)(2), A must include only $50 (the excess of the amount realized on such sale, $150, over the adjusted basis of the share, $100) in gross income as compensation attributable to the exercise of the incentive stock option instead of the $100 which otherwise would have been includible as compensation under section 83(a). A realizes no capital gain or loss as a result of the sale, since A's basis for the share is $150 (the $100 which A paid for the share, plus the $50 increase in basis resulting from the inclusion of that amount in A's gross income as compensation attributable to the exercise of the option). For its taxable year in which the disqualifying disposition occurs, X Corporation is allowed a deduction of $50 for compensation attributable to A's exercise of the stock option provided the withholding requirements of §1.83-6 are met.

Example (5). Assume the same facts as example (3), except that A sells the share for $50. The limitation of section 422A(c)(2) applies and A is not required to include any amount in gross income as compensation attributable to the exercise of the incentive stock option. A is allowed a capital loss of $50 (the difference between the amount realized on the sale, $50, and the adjusted basis of the share, $100). X Corporation is not allowed any deduction for compensation attributable to A's exercise of the incentive stock option and disqualifying disposition.

Example (6). Assume the same facts as in example (4) except that A sells the share to A's son for $150. Under section 267, a loss sustained in such a sale would not be recognized. Therefore, the limitation of section 422A(c)(2) does not apply. Accordingly, under section 83(a), A must include $100 (the difference between the fair market value of the share at date of exercise, $200, and the amount paid for the share, $100) in gross income as compensation attributable to the exercise of the incentive stock option in the taxable year in which the disqualifying disposition occurred. A will recognize no capital gain or loss on the transaction X Corporation will be allowed a $100 deduction for compensation paid to A in its taxable year in which the disqualifying disposition occurred provided the withholding requirements of §1.83-6 are met.

Example (8). Assume the same facts as in example (3), except that the share of X Corporation stock transferred to A is subject to a substantial risk of forfeiture and not transferable for a period of six months after such transfer. Assume further that the fair market value of X Corporation stock was $225 on February 1, 1983, the date the six-month restriction lapsed. Under section 83(a) and paragraph (a) of §1.83-7, the amount of compensation attributable to A's exercise of the option and subsequent disqualifying disposition is $125 (the difference between the fair market value of the share on the date the restriction lapsed, $225, and the amount paid for the share, $100). A must include in gross income for the taxable year in which the sale occurred $125 as compensation and $25 as capital gain ($250, the amount realized from the sale, less A's basis of $225 (the $100 paid for the share plus the $125 increase in basis resulting from the inclusion of that amount in A's gross income as compensation attributable to the exercise of the option)). For its taxable year in which the disqualifying disposition occurs, X Corporation is allowed a deduction of $125 for compensation attributable to A's exercise of the option provided the withholding requirements of § 1.83-6 are met.

(c) *Failure to satisfy employment requirement.* Section 421 does not apply to the transfer of a share of stock acquired by the exercise of an incentive stock option if the employment requirement as determined under section 422A(a)(2) and paragraph (a)(1)(i)(B) of this section is not met at the time of transfer. Consequently, the effects of such a transfer shall be determined pursuant to section 83 and the regulations thereunder.

Par. 2. Section 1.422A-2 is added after § 1.422A-1 to read as follows:

§ 1.422A-2 Incentive stock options defined.

(a) *Incentive stock option defined.* (1)(i) In general, the term "incentive stock option" means an option that meets the requirements of section 422A(b) and this section at the time of grant and that is granted to an individual after August 13, 1981. In addition, certain stock options granted to an individual after December 31, 1975, that were not incentive stock options at the time of grant, may be converted into incentive stock options. See § 1.422A-3 for special rules relating to such options. Section 422A(b)(1) requires that an incentive stock option be granted pursuant to a plan which meets certain requirements. See paragraph (b) of this section. Section 422A(b)(2) provides that in order for an option to be an incentive stock option it must be granted within 10 years of the adoption of the plan or the date of stockholder approval, whichever is earlier. See paragraph (c) of this section. In order to grant incentive stock options after the expiration of such 10-year period, a new plan must be adopted and approved. Such new plan may retain all of the terms of the old plan or may include new terms. Paragraphs (3), (4), (5), and (7) of section 422A(b) establish certain requirements which must be met by the terms of an incentive stock option. An option which, when granted, does not by its terms meet these requirements cannot be an incentive stock option. See paragraphs (d), (e), (f), and (g) of this section. However, an amendment of the terms of an option at any time to permit such option to meet the requirement of section 422A(b)(5) will be given retroactive effect. See section 425(h)(3)(B) and paragraph (e)(5)(iii) of § 1.425-1. Section 422A(b)(6) generally bars the grant of an incentive stock option to any employee whose stock ownership exceeds the limits provided by such section. An option granted to an employee whose stock ownership exceeds such limits cannot be an incentive stock option unless the special rule of section 422A(c)(8) applies. See paragraph (h) of this section. Section 422A(b)(8) bars the grant of an incentive stock option to any employee whose annual grants of incentive stock options exceed the limits provided by such section. An option granted to an employee whose annual grants exceed such limits cannot be an incentive stock option. See paragraph (b)(4) of this section. Section 422A(c)(5) provides that an incentive stock option may contain a number of permissible provisions that will not affect the option's status as an incentive stock option. See paragraph (i) of this section.

(ii) Whether a particular option is an incentive stock option is determined at the time such option is granted. Accordingly, except as otherwise specifically provided by sections 421 through 425 and the regulations thereunder, events subsequent to the grant of an option cannot affect the status of the option. For example, an option which is granted at a fair market value option price to an employee whose stock ownership exceeds the limitation provided by section 422A(b)(6) is not an incentive stock option when granted and can never become an incentive stock option, even if the individual's stock ownership is within the limitation at the time such option is exercised.

(iii) Except as otherwise specifically provided by sections 421 through 425 and the regulations thereunder, an incentive stock option must meet the requirements of section 422A(b) and this section at all times during the period beginning on the date of the granting of the option and ending on the date of the exercise or expiration of the option. Accordingly, such requirements must be met even during periods when section 421(a) would not apply to the transfer of stock on exercise of the option. For example, an option which provides that the sequential exercised restriction of section 422A(b)(7) will cease to have effect 3 months and a day after an optionee terminates employment is

not an incentive stock option when granted and can never become an incentive stock option.

(iv) An option granted after April 9, 1984, which meets the requirements of section 422A(b) and this section at the time of grant is an incentive stock option irrespective of any option or plan labeling to the contrary.

(2) Section 422A and this section do not apply to an option which is a restricted or qualified stock option.

(b) *Option plan.* (1) An incentive stock option must be granted pursuant to a written plan which meets the requirements of section 422A(b) and this paragraph (b). The authority to grant other stock options or rights pursuant to the plan, where the exercise of such other options or rights does not affect the exercise of incentive stock options granted pursuant to the plan, will not disqualify such incentive stock options.

(2) The plan required by section 422A must be approved by the stockholders of the granting corporation within 12 months before or after the date such plan is adopted. Ordinarily, a plan is adopted when approved by the board of directors and the date of such board action will be the reference point for determining whether stockholder approval occurs within the 12-month period. However, if the board's action is subject to a condition, such as stockholder approval, or the happening of a particular event, the plan is adopted on the date the condition is met or the event occurs, unless the board's resolution fixes the date of approval as the date of the board's action. The approval of stockholders must comply with all applicable provisions of the corporate charter, bylaws and applicable State law prescribing the method and degree of stockholder approval required for the granting of incentive stock options. Absent any such prescribed method and degree of stockholder approval, an incentive stock option must be approved by a simple majority vote of stockholders, voting either in person or by proxy, at a duly held stockholders' meeting.

(3)(i) The plan required by section 422A must designate the aggregate number of shares which may be issued under the plan and the employees or class of employees eligible to receive options under the plan. Unless otherwise specified, the terms designated shall apply to all options that may be granted under the plan, including options other than incentive stock options. If options other than incentive stock options may be granted, the plan may separately designate terms for each type of option. If individuals other than employees may be granted options, the plan must separately designate the employees or class of employees eligible to receive incentive stock options.

(ii) A plan which merely provides that the number of shares which may be issued under options shall not exceed a stated percentage of the shares outstanding at the time of each offering or grant under the plan will not satisfy the requirement that the plan state the aggregate number of shares which may be issued under the plan may be stated in terms of a percentage of either the authorized, issued or outstanding shares at the date of the adoption of the plan.

(iii) The requirement that the plan as adopted and approved must indicate the class of employees (or the employees) eligible to receive options will be considered satisfied by a general designation of the class of employees eligible to receive options under the plan. Thus, such designations as "key employees of the grantor corporation," "all salaried employees of the grantor corporation and its subsidiaries, including subsidiaries which become such after adoption of the plan" or "all employees of the corporation" will meet this requirement. Moreover, this requirement will be considered satisfied although the board of directors or another group is given authority to select the particular employees who are to receive options from a described class and to determine the number of shares to be optioned to each such employee.

(iv) The provisions relating to the aggregate number of shares to be issued under the plan and the class of employees (or the employees) eligible to receive options under the plan are the only provisions of a stock option plan which require stockholder approval for purposes of section 422A(b)(1). Any increase in the aggregate number of shares which may be issued under the plan (other than an increase merely reflecting a change in capitalization such as a stock dividend or stock split), or change in the designation of the employees or class of employees eligible to receive options under the plan will be considered as the adoption of a new plan requiring stockholder approval within the prescribed 12-month period. Any other changes in the terms of an incentive stock option plan are not considered the adoption of a new plan.

An option intended by the grantor corporation to be an incentive stock option will be treated as having been granted pursuant to a plan notwithstanding that the terms of the option conflict with terms of the plan unless such option is granted to an employee not eligible to receive options under the plan or options have been granted on stock in excess of the aggregate number of shares which may be issued under the plan.

(4)(i) The plan required by section 422A must, by its terms, provide that the aggregate fair market value (determined at the time of grant of the option) of stock for which an employee may be granted incentive stock options in any calendar year after 1980, under all such plans of the employer corporation (or its parent or subsidiary corporations, or a predecessor corporation (as defined in paragraph (f)(2) of this section) of any such corporation), shall not exceed $100,000 plus any unused limit carryover to such year.

(ii) The unused limit carryover is an amount determined for a calendar year after 1980 equal to one-half of the amount by which $100,000 exceeds the aggregate fair market value (determined at the time of grant of the option) of stock for which an employee was granted incentive stock options in such calendar year. The unused limit carryover for a calendar year may be applied to each of the 3 succeeding calendar years, reduced each calendar year by the amount of such carryover which was used in a prior calendar year. For purposes of this paragraph, the amount of incentive stock options granted during any calendar year shall be treated as first using up the $100,000 limit for such calendar year, and then any unused limit carryover to such calendar year in the order in which the carryovers arose.

(iii) Amounts may be carried over from calendar years after 1980 whether or not the granting corporation had an incentive stock option plan in effect for the year of the unused limit carryover, provided that the individual was employed by such corporation (or its parent or subsidiary corporations, or a predecessor corporation (as defined in paragraph (f)(2) of this section) of any such corporation) for some part of such year.

(iv) If an option intended to be an incentive stock option is granted to an employee, but such option gives the employee the right to buy stock in excess of the amount permitted by this paragraph (b)(4), no portion of such option is an incentive stock option. However, if the amount permitted has been exceeded because there was a failure of an attempt, made in good faith, to meet the option price requirements of section 422A(b)(4) and paragraph (e)(1) of this section, the requirements of this paragraph (b)(4) shall be considered to have been met. To determine whether there was a good-faith attempt to meet the option price requirements of section 422A(b)(4) and paragraph (e)(1) of this section, see paragraph (e)(2)(ii) of this section.

(c) *Duration of option grants under the plan.* An incentive stock option must be granted within 10 years from the date the plan required by section 422A is adopted, or the date such plan is approved by the stockholders, whichever is earlier.

(d) *Period for exercising options.* An incentive stock option by its terms must not be exercisable after the expiration of 10 years from the date the option is granted. An option which does not contain such a provision when granted cannot be an incentive stock option.

(e) *Option price.* (1) Except as provided by section 422A(c)(1) and paragraph (e)(2) of this section, the option price of an incentive stock option must not be less than the fair market value of the stock subject to the option at the time the option is granted. For general rules relating to the option price, see paragraph (e) of § 1.421-7. For rules relating to the determination of when an option is granted, see paragraph (c) of § 1.421-7. The option price may be determined in any manner so long as the minimum price possible under the terms of the option cannot be less than the fair market value of the stock at the date of grant.

(2)(i) Under section 422A(c)(1), if a share of stock is transferred to an individual pursuant to the exercise of an option which would fail to qualify as an incentive stock option because there was a failure of an attempt, made in good faith, to meet the requirements of section 422A(b)(4) and paragraph (e)(1) of this section, the requirements of such section and paragraph shall be considered to have been met.

(ii) Whether there was a good-faith attempt to set the option price at not less than the fair market value of the stock subject to the option at the time the option was granted depends on the facts and circumstances surrounding the case. For example, in the case of a publicly held stock that was actively traded in an established market at the time the option was granted, determining the fair market value of such stock by any reasonable method using market quotations would establish that a good-faith attempt to meet the requirements of section 422A(b)(4) and this paragraph was made. On the other hand, in the case of a stock which is not publicly traded, it is shown, for example, that the fair market value of the stock at the date of grant was based

upon an average of the fair market values as of such date set forth in the opinions of completely independent and well-qualified experts, such a showing will establish that there was a good-faith attempt to meet the requirements of section 422A(b)(4) and this paragraph. However, amounts treated as unstated interest under section 483 and the regulations thereunder, and amounts paid as interest under a deferred payment arrangement are not includible as part of the "option price." See paragraph (e)(1) of § 1.421-7. An attempt to set the option price at not less than fair market value will not be regarded as made in good faith where an adjustment of the option price to allow for the application of section 483 results in the option price being lower than the fair market value on which the option price was based.

(f) *Prior outstanding options.* (1)(i) Section 422A(b)(7) provides that an incentive stock option must, by its terms, not be exercisable while there is outstanding any incentive stock option which was granted, before the granting of the new incentive stock option, to the individual to purchase stock in the employer corporation, or in a corporation which, at the time of the granting of the new incentive stock option, is a parent or subsidiary corporation of the employer corporation, or a predecessor corporation of any of such corporations. Thus, in general, under section 422A(b)(7), an incentive stock option must not be exercisable until all incentive stock options which were previously granted to the individual by the grantor corporation, or by related or predecessor corporations, have been exercised in full or have expired solely by reason of the lapse of time. The limitation of section 422A(b)(7) applies irrespective of whether the transfer of stock pursuant to such prior outstanding incentive stock options can qualify for the special tax treatment of section 421. The exercisability of an incentive stock option is not affected by options which are not incentive stock options.

(ii) The restriction imposed by section 422A(b)(7) must be set forth in the terms of the option unless the individual in fact has no prior outstanding incentive stock options to purchase stock of the grantor corporation, a related corporation, or a predecessor corporation of any of such corporations at the time the new incentive stock option is granted. An option which incorporates by reference the provision of a plan containing the restrictions required by section 422A(b)(7) will be treated as an option which by its terms sets forth such restrictions. Except as provided by this paragraph (f)(2)(ii), an option which does not contain the restriction imposed by section 422A(b)(7), either expressly or incorporated by reference, cannot be an incentive-stock option, irrespective of whether such restriction is in fact complied with at the time the option is exercised and irrespective of whether the plan under which the option is granted contains the restriction required by section 422A(b)(7).

(iii) For purposes of section 422A(b)(7) and this paragraph (f), options granted or exercised on the same day are considered simultaneously granted or exercised.

(2) For purposes of section 422A(b)(7) and this paragraph (f), the term "predecessor corporation" means a corporation which was a party to a transaction described in section 425(a) (or which would be so described if a substitution or assumption under such section had been effected) with the grantor corporation, or a corporation which, at the time the new incentive stock option is granted, is a related corporation of the grantor corporation, or a predecessor corporations of any of such corporations.

(3) Except as is otherwise provided by this paragraph (f)(3), for purposes of section 422A(b)(7), an incentive stock option is treated as outstanding according to its original terms until such option is exercised in full or expires by reason of the lapse of time. Thus, for example, if an option outstanding according to its terms for 10 years is revised to shorten to 1 year the period during which it may be exercised, such option is treated as outstanding for 10 years from the original date of grant for purposes of section 422A(b)(7), notwithstanding the revision. If any portion of such an option is not exercised, such portion will be treated as outstanding until the expiration of the maximum period during which such portion, according to the terms of the option when granted, could have been exercised under any circumstances. An incentive stock option previously held by an individual and replaced in a transaction to which section 425(a) applies will not thereafter be treated as outstanding. However, if an incentive stock option is modified and under section 425(h) such modification is considered as the granting of a new option (even though for other purposes only one option is regarded as being in existence), the original incentive stock option continues for the purposes of section 422A(b)(7) to be outstanding, and may prevent an exercise of the new incentive stock option until the original option has, by its original terms, expired.

(4) The application of this paragraph may be illustrated by the following examples:

Example (1). S Corporation is a subsidiary of P Corporation. In 1982, E was an employee of S Corporation and was granted an incentive stock option by S to buy S stock. In June of 1983, E left S and became an employee of X Corporation, where he was granted an incentive stock option to purchase X stock. X Corporation is neither a related nor predecessor corporation of P or S. On June 1, 1984, E leaves X to become an employee of P Corporation, and on such date E is granted an incentive stock option by P to purchase P stock. Both E's incentive stock option on S stock and his incentive stock option on X stock are outstanding on June 1, 1984. In order to meet the requirements of Section 422A(b)(7), E's incentive stock option on P stock must, by its terms, not be exercisable until E's incentive stock option on S stock is exercised in full or expires solely by reason of the lapse of time. This requirement must be met even though at the time E's incentive stock option on P stock is granted, E's incentive stock option on S stock no longer qualifies for the special tax treatment or section 421.

Example (2). E is an employee of P Corporation. E holds an incentive stock option granted June 1, 1982, and an incentive stock option granted June 1, 1983. Both options were granted to him by P to purchase P stock. E has been granted no other incentive stock options by P, a related corporation, or a predecessor corporation of any of such corporations. On November 30, 1984, P cancels E's 1982 incentive stock option and in exchange therefor issues a new incentive stock option to E. Assume that each incentive stock option runs 10 years from grant. The 1982 incentive stock option, according to its terms when granted, would have expired solely by reason of the lapse of time at the close of business on May 31, 1992. Under section 422A(b)(7) and (c)(7), E's 1982 incentive stock option is treated as outstanding according to its original terms when granted, and E cannot exercise any of his incentive stock options until June 1, 1992 (the first day after the expiration of the original period for which E's 1982 incentive stock option was granted). On June 1, 1992, E's 1983 incentive stock option will be fully exercisable. E's 1984 incentive stock option will not be exercisable until after the full exercise or expiration of E's 1983 incentive stock option.

Example (3). Assume the same facts as in example (2). On June 1, 1986, P Corporation sells all of its assets to M Corporation, and on such date E becomes an employee of M Corporation. Assume further that M Corporation substitutes new options to purchase M stock for those options held by E in a transaction to which section 425(a) applies. For purposes of section 422A(b)(7), each M Corporation option received by E in substitution for a P Corporation option will be treated as outstanding to the same extent and in the same manner as the P option which it replaces. Thus, none of the M options received by E in substitution for his P options may be exercisable before June 1, 1992, and the M option issued in substitution for E's 1984 P option may be exercisable only after the full exercise or expiration of the M option issued in substitution for E's 1983 P option. If, in 1987, E is granted another incentive stock option by M Corporation, such option may be exercisable only after the full exercise or expiration of the incentive stock options granted by M to E in 1986 in substitution for E's options to purchase P stock. The options to purchase P stock which were replaced by M in the transaction to which section 425(a) applied will not be treated as outstanding for any purposes under section 422A(b)(7).

Example (4). Assume the same facts as in example (3) except assume that M does not effect a substitution or assumption of E's P Corporation incentive stock options under section 425(a). Although P is neither a parent nor subsidiary of M, for purposes of Section 422A(b)(7), P is a predecessor corporation of M Corporation. Accordingly, any incentive stock options granted to E by M (or its parent or subsidiary corporations, or a predecessor corporation of any of such corporations) must, by their terms, not be exercisable until the expiration of the option periods for all of E's incentive stock options granted to E by P Corporation.

Example (5). F is an employee of N Corporation. On January 1, 1982, N granted an incentive stock option to F to purchase 100 shares of N Corporation stock at a price of $100 per share. The option is exercisable in installments as follows: 20 shares on or after June 1, 1983; another 40 shares on or after June 1, 1984; and the last 40 shares on or after June 1, 1985. Under section 422A(c)(7), the entire option is treated as being outstanding as of the January 1, 1982 date of grant. Thus, under the facts given, any incentive stock options granted to F after January 1, 1982, may not be exercised until the full exercise or expiration of all installments of F's January 1, 1982 incentive stock option.

Example (6). F is an employee of N Corporation. On January 1, 1982, N grants F an incentive stock option to purchase 100 shares of N Corporation stock at a price of $100 a share at any time prior to January 1, 1992. The stock is then selling at $100 a share. On January 1, 1983, when the stock was selling at $95 a share, N modified the option to

permit F to purchase 100 shares of N Corporation stock at a price of $95 a share and to exercise the option at any time prior to January 1, 1993. Under section 425(n) N's modification is treated as the granting of a new option to F. Although for other purposes F, after the modification, has one option to purchase 100 shares of N Corporation stock at a price of $95 a share at any time prior to January 1, 1993, for purposes of section 422A(b)(7), F is regarded as having two options. Thus, F may not exercise the modified option until January 1, 1992, because until that date the original option is regarded as outstanding. If the option period had not been extended, F would never have been able to exercise the modified option because of the limitation of section 422A(b)(7) and the existence, for the purposes of that section, of a prior outstanding option having the same expiration date as the new option.

(g) *Restriction on transferability.* An incentive stock option, by its terms, must not be transferable by the individual to whom it is granted otherwise than by will or the laws of descent and distribution, and, during the lifetime of such individual, must not be exercisable by any other person. For general rules relating to the restriction on transferability required by section 422A(b)(5), are paragraph (b)(2) of § 1.421-7 and paragraph (c) of § 1.421-8. For a limited exception to the requirement of section 422A(b)(5), see section 425(h)(3).

(h) *Options granted to certain shareholders.* (1)(i). Except as provided in paragraph (h)(2) of this section, an option is not an incentive stock option if, immediately before such option is granted, the optionee owns stock possessing more than 10 percent of the total combined voting power of all classes of stock either of the employer corporation or of its parent or subsidiary corporation. In applying the limitation of section 422A(b)(6), the rules of section 425(d) (relating to attribution of stock ownership) shall apply in determining the stock ownership of the individual, and stock that the individual may purchase under outstanding options shall not be treated as stock owned by the individual.

(ii) The determination of the percentage of the total combined voting power of all classes of stock of the employer corporation (or of its parent or subsidiary corporations) that is owned by the individual is made with respect to each such corporation in the related group by comparing the voting power of the shares owned (or treated as owned) by the individual to the aggregate voting power of all shares actually issued and outstanding immediately before the grant of the option to such individual. The aggregate voting power of all shares actually issued and outstanding immediately before the grant of the option does not include the voting power of treasury shares or shares authorized for issue under outstanding options held by the individual or any other person.

(2) Paragraph (h)(1) of this section does not apply to an option if the time such option is granted the option price is at least 110 percent of the fair market value at such time of the stock subject to the option and such option by its terms is not exercisable after the expiration of 5 years from the date such option is granted. The rules of paragraph (e)(2) of this section relating to option price shall not apply to the determination of the minimum option price for purposes of this paragraph (h)(2).

(3) The application of this paragraph may be illustrated by the following examples:

Example (1). E, an employee of M Corporation, owns 15,000 shares of the common stock of M Corporation, the only class of M stock outstanding. M has 100,000 shares of its common stock outstanding. Since E owns stock comprising more than 10 percent of the total combined voting power of all classes of M Corporation stock, M cannot grant an incentive stock option to E unless such option is granted at an option price of at least 110 percent of the fair market value of the stock subject to the option and such option would expire no later than 5 years from its date of grant. An option is granted to E which purports to be an incentive stock option but which fails to meet the above option-price and term requirements. Such option is not an incentive stock option and is, therefore, subject to section 83(a). If E's father and brother each owned 7,500 shares of M Corporation stock, and E owned no M stock in E's own name, the result in this case would be the same, since under section 425(d) a person is treated as owning stock held by parents and siblings.

Example (2). Assume the same facts as in example (1) and assume further that M is a subsidiary corporation of P Corporation. Irrespective of whether E owns any P stock and irrespective of the number of P shares outstanding, an option granted to E by P Corporation which purports to be an incentive stock option, but which fails to meet the 110-percent-option-price and 5-year-term requirements, is not an incentive stock option. This results from E's ownership of more than 10 percent of the total combined voting power of all classes of stock of a subsidiary of P Corporation (*i.e.,* M Corporation). Thus, an individual who owns (or is treated as owning) stock in excess of the limitation of section 422A(b)(6), in any corporation in a group of corporations consisting of the employer corporation and its parent and subsidiary corporations, cannot receive an incentive stock option from any corporation in the group unless such option meets the 110-percent-option-price and 5-year-term requirements of section 422A(b)(6).

Example (3). F is an employee of R Corporation. R has only one class of stock, of which 100,000 shares are issued and outstanding. F owns no stock in R Corporation or in any parent or subsidiary of R Corporation for purposes of section 422A(b)(6). On January 1, 1983, R grants a 10-year incentive stock option to F to purchase 50,000 shares of R stock at $1 per share, the fair market value of R stock on the date of grant of the option. On April 1, 1983, F exercises half of the January option and receives 25,000 shares of R stock. On July 1, 1983, R grants a second 50,000 shares option to F which purports to be an incentive stock option. All of the terms of the July option are identical to the terms of the January option, including an option price of $1 per share, the fair market value of R stock on the date of grant of the second option. Pursuant to section 422A(b)(6), the July option is not an incentive stock option because on the date such option was granted F owned 20 percent (25,000 shares owned by F divided by 125,000 shares of R stock issued and outstanding) of the total combined voting power of all classes of R Corporation stock. The unexercised portion of the January option, because it was an incentive stock option on the date it was granted, remains an incentive stock option regardless of changes in the employee's percentage of stock ownership after grant of the option.

Example (4). Assume the same facts as in example (3) except that the partial exercise of the January incentive stock option on April 1, 1983, was for only 10,000 shares. Under these circumstances, the July option is an incentive stock option because on the date such option was granted, F did not own more than 10 percent of the total combined voting power of all classes of R Corporation stock.

(i) *Permissible provisions.* (1)(i) Pursuant to section 422A(c)(5)(A), an option which otherwise meets the requirements of section 422A(b) and this section will be an incentive stock option even if the employee has the right to exercise the option with previously acquired stock of the corporation which granted the option. For special rules relating to the transfer of statutory option stock as payment in connection with the exercise of an incentive stock option, see section 425(c) and the regulations thereunder.

(ii) All stock transferred pursuant to the exercise of an incentive stock option is subject to the holding period requirements of section 422A(a)(1) and paragraph (a) of § 1.422A-1, and the disqualifying disposition rules of section 421(b) and paragraph (b) of § 1.422A-1, regardless of whether such option is exercised with previously acquired stock of the corporation which granted the option. If an incentive stock option is exercised with previously acquired stock of the corporation which granted the option, and such exercise results in the basis allocation described in paragraph (i)(1)(iii) of this section, a disqualifying disposition of stock transferred pursuant to such exercise will be a disqualifying disposition of the stock with the lowest basis.

(iii) If the exercise of an incentive stock option with previously acquired stock of the corporation which granted the option is comprised in part of an exchange to which section 1036 (and so much of section 1031 as relates to section 1036) applies, then—

(A) The employee's basis in the incentive stock option stock transferred pursuant to the section 1036 exchange shall be the same as the employee's basis in the stock exchanged increased, if applicable, by any amount included in gross income as compensation pursuant to either sections 421 through 425 or section 83. Except for purposes of section 422A(a)(1) and paragraph (a) of § 1.422A-1, the holding period of the stock shall be determined pursuant to section 1223. For purposes of section 421(b), paragraph (b) of § 1.422A-1, and section 83 and the regulations thereunder, the amount paid for the stock shall be the fair market value of such stock on the date of the exchange.

(B) The employee's basis in the incentive stock option stock not transferred pursuant to the section 1036 exchange shall be zero. For all purposes, the holding period of the stock shall begin as of the date such stock is transferred. For purposes of section 421(b), paragraph (b) of § 1.422A-1, and section 83 and the regulations thereunder, the amount paid for the stock shall be zero.

(2) Pursuant to section 422(c)(5)(B), an option which otherwise meets the requirements of section 422A(b) and this section will be an incentive stock option even if the employee has the right to receive additional compensation, whether in cash or other property, at the time the option is exercised, provided such additional compensation is includible in income under the provisions of sections 61 and 83. The additional compensation may be determined in any manner including

by reference to the fair market value of the stock at the time of exercise, or by reference to the option price.

(3)(i) Pursuant to section 422A(c)(5)(C), an option which otherwise meets the requirements of section 422A(b) and this section will be an incentive stock option even if the option is subject to a condition, or grants a right, not inconsistent with the requirements of section 422A(b) and this section.

(ii) An option that includes an alternative right is not an incentive stock option if the requirements of section 422A(b) and this section may be avoided by exercise of the alternative right. For example, an alternative right extending the option term beyond ten years, setting a price below fair market value, permitting transferability, or allowing nonsequential exercise, will prevent an option from qualifying as an incentive stock option. If either of two options can be exercised, but not both, each such option is a disqualifying alternative right with respect to the other even though one or both options would individually satisfy the requirements of section 422A(b) and this section.

(iii) An alternative right to receive a taxable payment of cash and/or other property in exchange for the cancellation or surrender of the option does not disqualify the option as an incentive stock option if the right is exercisable only when the then fair market value of the stock exceeds the exercise price of the option and the option is otherwise exercisable, the right is transferable only when the option is otherwise transferable, and the exercise of the right has the same economic and tax consequences as the exercise of the option followed by an immediate sale of the stock. For this purpose, the exercise of the alternative right does not have the same economic and tax consequences if the payment exceeds the difference between the then fair market value of the stock and the exercise price of the option. If the above conditions have been met, the exercise of the alternative right will be considered to be the exercise of the option for purposes of the sequencing provisions of section 422A(b)(7).

(iv) Section 425(h)(1) shall not apply to the amendment of an alternative right described in paragraph (i)(3)(iii) of this section in order to conform the terms of the alternative right to the technical requirements of such paragraph. This paragraph (iv) shall apply only to options granted after August 13, 1981, and before January 21, 1982, that are amended before [insert date 60 days after this document is published in the Federal Register as final regulations].

(4) The application of this paragraph may be illustrated by the following examples:

Example (1). On June 1, 1984, X Corporation grants an incentive stock option to A, an employee of X Corporation, entitling A to purchase 100 shares of X Corporation common stock at $10 per share. The option provides that A may exercise the option with previously acquired X Corporation common stock. X Corporation has only one class of common stock outstanding. The stock transferable to A pursuant to the exercise of the incentive stock option is transferable and not subject to a substantial risk of forfeiture. On June 1, 1985, when the fair market value of X Corporation stock is $25 per share, A exercises the option and the 100 shares are transferred to A on that date. To exercise the option, A transferred to X Corporation 40 shares of X Corporation common stock that A had purchased on the open market on June 1, 1982, for $5 per share. After exercising the option, A owns 100 shares of incentive stock option stock. Pursuant to section 1036 (and so much of section 1031 as relates to section 1036), 40 shares have a $200 carryover basis and a three-year holding period, and 60 shares have a zero basis and a holding period beginning June 1, 1985.

Example (2). Assume the same facts as in example (1) and assume further that A sells 75 shares of the incentive stock option stock on September 1, 1985, for $30 per share. On that date, A has made a disqualifying disposition of the 75 shares of stock. Pursuant to paragraph (i)(1)(ii) of this Section, A has sold all 60 of the non-section-1036 shares and 15 of the 40 section-1036 shares. Therefore, pursuant to paragraph (i)(1)(iii) of this section and section 83(a), the amount of compensation attributable to A's exercise of the option and subsequent disqualifying disposition of 75 shares is $1,500 (the difference between the fair market value of the stock on the date of exercise, $1,875 (75 shares at $25 per share), and the amount paid for the stock, $375 (60 shares at $0 per share plus 15 shares at $25 per share)). In addition, A must recognize a long-term capital gain of $375 ($450, the amount realized from the sale of 15 shares, less A's basis of $75), and a short-term capital gain of $300 ($1,800, the amount realized from the sale of 60 shares, less A's basis of $1,500 resulting from the inclusion of that amount in income as compensation). Accordingly, A must include in gross income for the taxable year in which the sale occurs $1,500 as compensation, $375 as long-term capital gain, and $300 as short-term capital gain. For its taxable year in which the disqualifying disposition occurs, X Corporation is allowed a deduction of $1,500 for compensation paid to A provided the withholding requirements of § 1.83-6 are met.

Example (3). Assume the same facts as in example (2), except that instead of selling the 75 shares of incentive stock option stock on September 1, 1985, A uses those shares to exercise a second incentive stock option. The second option was granted to A by X Corporation on January 1, 1985, entitling A to purchase 100 shares of X Corporation common stock at $22.50 per share. As in example (2), A has made a disqualifying disposition of the 75 shares of stock. Pursuant to paragraph (i)(1)(ii) of this section, A has disposed of all 60 of the non-section-1036 shares and 15 of the 40 section-1036 shares. Therefore, pursuant to paragraph (i)(1)(iii) of this section and section 83(a), the amount of compensation attributable to A's exercise of the first option and subsequent disqualifying disposition of 75 shares is $1,500 (the difference between the fair market value of the stock on the date of exercise, $1,875 (75 shares at $25 per share), and the amount paid for the stock, $375 (60 shares at $0 per share plus 15 shares at $25 per share)). Unlike example (2), A does not recognize any capital gain as a result of exercising the second option because, for all purposes other than the determination of whether the exercise is a disposition pursuant to section 425(c), such exercise is an exchange to which section 1036 applies. Accordingly, A must include in gross income for the taxable year in which the disqualifying disposition occurs $1,500 as compensation. For its taxable year in which the disqualifying disposition occurs, X Corporation is allowed a deduction of $1,500 for compensation paid to A provided the withholding requirements of § 1.83-6 are met. After exercising the second option, A owns a total of 125 shares of incentive stock option stock. Pursuant to section 1036 (and so much of section 1031 as relates to section 1036), the 100 "new" shares of incentive stock option stock have the following bases and holding periods: 15 shares have a $74 carryover basis and a three-year-and-three-month holding period. 60 shares have a $1,500 basis resulting from the inclusion of that amount in income as compensation and a three-month holding period, and 25 shares have a zero basis and a holding period beginning September 1, 1985.

Example (4). Assume the same facts as in example (2), except that instead of selling the 75 shares of incentive stock option stock on September 1, 1985, A uses those shares to exercise a non-statutory stock option. The non-statutory stock option was granted to A by X Corporation on January 1, 1985, entitling A to purchase 100 shares of X Corporation common stock at $22.50 per share. Unlike example (3), A has not made a disqualifying disposition of the 75 shares of stock. After exercising the nonstatutory stock option, A owns a total of 100 shares of incentive stock option stock and 25 shares of non-statutory stock option stock. Pursuant to section 1036 (and so much of section 1031 as relates to section 1036), the 75 "new" shares of incentive stock option stock have the same basis and holding period as the 75 "old" shares used to exercise the non-statutory stock option. The additional 25 shares of stock received upon exercise of the non-statutory stock option are compensation for services pursuant to section 83(a). Accordingly, A must include in gross income for the taxable year in which the transfer of such shares occurs $750 (25 shares at $30 per share) as compensation. A's basis in such shares is the same as the amount included in gross income. For its taxable year in which the transfer occurs, X Corporation is allowed a deduction of $750 for compensation paid to A provided the withholding requirements of § 1.83-6 are met.

Example (5). Assume the same facts in example (1), except that the stock transferred pursuant to the exercise of the incentive stock option is subject to a substantial risk of forfeiture and not transferable for a period of six months after such transfer. Assume further that the shares that A uses to exercise the incentive stock option are similarly restricted. Such shares were transferred to A on January 1, 1985, pursuant to the exercise of a non-statutory stock option granted to A on January 1, 1984. A paid $5 per share for the stock when its fair market value was $22.50 per share. A did not file a section 83(b) election to include the $700 spread (the difference between the option price and the fair market value of the stock on date of exercise of the option) in gross income as compensation. After exercising the incentive stock option with the 40 shares of restricted stock, A owns 100 shares of restricted incentive stock option stock. Section 1036 (and so much of section 1031 as relates to section 1036) applies to the 40 shares exchanged in exercise of the incentive stock option. However, pursuant to section 83(g), the stock received in such exchange, because it is incentive stock option stock, is not subject to restrictions and conditions substantially similar to those to which the stock given in such exchange was subject. For purposes of section 83(a) & § 1.83-1(b)(1), therefore, A has disposed of the 40 shares of restricted stock on June 1, 1985, and must include in gross income as compensation $800 (the difference between the amount realized upon such disposition, $1,000, and the amount paid for the stock, $200). Accordingly, 40 shares of the incentive stock option stock have a $1,000 basis (the $200 original basis

plus the $800 included in income as compensation) and 60 shares of the incentive stock option stock have a zero basis. For its taxable year in which the disposition of the restricted stock occurs, X Corporation is allowed a deduction of $800 for compensation paid to A provided the withholding requirements of § 1.83-6 are met.

Par. 3. Section 1.422A-3 is added after § 1.422A-2 to read as follows:

§ 1.422A-3 Incentive stock option transitional rules.

(a) *In general.* (1) This section provides special rules pursuant to section 251(c) of the Economic Recovery Tax Act of 1981 (95 Stat. 172) for converting stock options into incentive stock options. These special rules apply to stock options granted after December 31, 1975, and either exercised on or after January 1, 1981, or outstanding on such date, if such stock options—

(i) Were granted prior to January 1, 1981;

(ii) Were exercised before January 21, 1982 and did not meet the requirements of section 422A(b) and § 1.422A-2 at the time of exercise;

(iii) Did not meet the requirements of section 422A(b) and § 1.422A-2 when granted and were outstanding on August 13, 1981; or

(iv) Were granted after December 31, 1980, and before August 14, 1981, and otherwise met the requirements of section 422A(b) and § 1.422A-2 when granted.

(2) Stock options granted before January 1, 1981, may be converted into incentive stock options, but only if the corporation that granted such options makes an election under paragraph (b) of this section. The aggregate fair market value of stock the options for which may be converted into incentive stock options by such an election is subject to an annual and a cumulative restriction. Such aggregate fair market value (determined as of the time the options were granted) may not exceed $50,000 per employee for options granted in any calendar year and $200,000 per employee for all options granted in the 5-year period ending December 31, 1980.

(3) Stock options that were exercised before January 21, 1982, and that did not meet certain requirements of section 422A(b) and § 1.422A-2 at the time of exercise may be converted into incentive stock options if the requirements of paragraph (c)(3) of this section are met.

(4) Stock options that did not meet the requirements of section 422A(b) and § 1.422-2 when granted and that were outstanding on August 13, 1981, may be converted into incentive stock options in accordance with paragraph (d) of this section. Section 425(h)(1) relating to the modification of statutory stock options) shall not apply to any change in the terms of an option (or the terms of the plan under which the option was granted) or shareholder approval of such a change required to convert such option into an incentive stock option if such change or shareholder approval occurs on or before August 13, 1982.

(5) Stock options that were granted after December 31, 1980, and before August 14, 1981, are incentive stock options if they otherwise meet the requirements of section 422A(b) and § 1.422A-2 when granted. No election is necessary to convert such options into incentive stock options.

(b) *Election procedure and requirements.* (1) A corporation may make only one election to convert stock options granted before 1981 into incentive stock options and such election must include all options granted by the corporation before 1981 that are to be converted into incentive stock options. Thus, a corporation that makes an election with respect to certain options granted before 1981 may not make any subsequent election with respect to other options granted before 1981. An election shall be made by attaching an election statement to the granting corporation's income tax return either for the first taxable year during which an incentive stock option (including an option treated as an incentive stock option by reason of the election or the other provisions of this section) is exercised, or for any prior taxable year. An election shall be made no later than the due date (taking extensions into account) of the income tax return. If such due date occurs before August 14, 1982, the granting corporation will be permitted to make the election at any time prior to August 14, 1982, on an election statement attached to an amended return. In any event, no election will be permitted after the due date (taking extensions into account) of the income tax return for the taxable year including December 31, 1982. The election statement must—

(i) Contain the name, address, and taxpayer identification number of the corporation;

(ii) Identify the election as an election under section 251(c)(1)(B) of the Economic Recovery Tax Act of 1981; and

(iii) Specify, by employee, the options to which the election applies and state, for each such option, the date of original grant (and, if applicable, date of most recent modification) and total exercise price (*i.e.,* the total number of shares subject to the option multiplied by the price per share). All options to which the election applies must meet the section 422A qualification requirements (other than the requirement of securing stockholder approval) at the time the election statement is filed.

(2) In its election under this paragraph, a corporation may generally select any eligible option (or portion of such option). The selection is, however, subject to the $50,000 annual and $200,000 cumulative limits applicable to each employee, and also subject to any existing plan requirements relating to who must be benefited under such plan as among different classes of employees. Eligible options (or portions of such options) may be selected on an option-by-option basis and/or an employee-by-employee basis. If only a portion of an option is selected and such portion is not exercised prior to January 21, 1982, the option must be amended prior to the exercise of such portion so as to clearly identify it as an incentive stock option. Whenever such a dual option is exercised, separate stock certificates must be issued (or reissued). See § 1.422A-3(c)(3)(iv) for the deadlines for amending options.

(c) *Eligibility issues: Pre-enactment modifications, dollar limitations.* (1) An option is not eligible for incentive stock option conversion unless it was originally granted after December 31, 1975. A modification, extension, or renewal on or after January 1, 1976, of an option originally granted prior to that date, will not make such option eligible for conversion into an incentive stock option, regardless of whether the option as so modified, extended, or renewed would be treated as newly granted within the meaning of section 425(h).

(2) An amendment to an otherwise eligible option (or plan) prior to August 13, 1981, will be subject to the rules of section 425(h). If, pursuant to section 425(h), the amendment is a modification, extension, or renewal of the option, such amendment shall be considered as the grant of a new option. Such an option is not eligible for conversion into an incentive stock option unless the option (and plan) comply with the section 422A qualification requirements. Since the option will be considered to have been granted on the date it was amended, the option price cannot be less than the fair market value of the stock on that date. If the option price is less than the fair market value of the stock on the date the option was amended, the corporation may qualify the option by adjusting the option price, so long as such adjustment occurs prior to the earliest of the exercise of the option, the date of the election under paragraph (b) of this section (if applicable), or August 14, 1982. If the corporation wishes to retain the original grant price (and grant date) of the option, the corporation may do so by rescinding the amendment, so long as such rescission occurs prior to the earliest of the exercise of the option, the date of the election under paragraph (b) of this section (if applicable), or August 14, 1982. If only a portion of an option is to become an incentive stock option, the adjustment of the option price or the rescission of the amendment need apply only to that portion. If an amendment is rescinded as to only a portion of an option so as to restore the original date of grant for that portion, the balance of the option is not eligible for conversion into an incentive stock option. For example, in the case of a $100,000 option granted in 1978 and amended in 1980, the corporation could not rescind the modification as to only half of the option, and then elect to convert into incentive stock options both the $50,000 portion of the option treated as granted in 1978 and the $50,000 portion of the option treated as granted in 1980.

(3)(i) Except as provided in this paragraph (c)(3), and an option is eligible for incentive stock option conversion only if, at the time of exercise, such option (and its plan) conform to all of the section 422A qualification requirements and the transitional rule limitations. It is not possible to amend an exercised option retroactively to correct nonconforming or missing terms, or to rescind an improper exercise.

(ii) An option exercised prior to January 21, 1982, may be converted into an incentive stock option even if the option does not contain the sequential exercise restriction required by section 422A(b)(7). Incentive stock option conversion will be available, however, only if the employee in fact had no prior outstanding incentive stock options at the time the option in question was exercised. An option exercised on or after January 21, 1982, without containing the sequential exercise restriction may not be converted into an incentive stock option unless the employee in fact had no prior outstanding incentive stock options at the time the option in question was granted. In order to identify prior outstanding incentive stock options it will be necessary to take into account all options elected or amended to become incentive stock options and all options granted as incentive stock options.

(iii) An option granted after 1980 and exercised prior to January 21, 1982, may be converted into an incentive stock option even if the plan does not contain at the time of exercise the $100,000 annual plus carryover limit required by section 422A(b)(8). Incentive stock option

conversion will be available, however, only for exercised amounts that do not exceed such limit. Where the limit has been exceeded, separate stock certificates must be issued (or reissued) no later than March 15, 1982. An option exercised on or after January 21, 1982, and before the plan has been amended to include the $100,000 annual plus carryover limit, may not be converted into an incentive stock option. Incentive stock option conversion is not available for such an option regardless of whether the limit is exceeded. An option exercised on or after January 21, 1982, and after the plan has been amended to include the $100,000 annual plus carryover limit, may not be converted into an incentive stock option where such limit has been exceeded. An option in excess of the limit must be amended, before it is exercised, so as clearly to identify that portion of the option intended to become an incentive stock option. Upon exercise of the option, separate stock certificates must be issued. An amended option that was required by its original terms to be exercised in full, must still be required to be exercised in full after it is amended.

(iv) An option granted before 1981 and exercised prior to January 21, 1982, may be converted into an incentive stock option even if the $50,000 annual limit or the $200,000 cumulative limit of paragraph (a)(2) of this section was exceeded. Incentive stock option conversion will be available, however, only for exercised amounts that do not exceed such limits. If either limit has been exceeded, separate stock certificates must be issued (or re-issued) no later than March 15, 1982. An option exercised on or after January 21, 1982, where either the $50,000 annual limit or the $200,000 cumulative limit was exceeded, may not be converted into an incentive stock option. An option in excess of such limits must be amended, before it is exercised, so as clearly to identify that portion of the option intended to become an incentive stock option. Upon exercise of the option, separate stock certificates must be issued. An amended option that was required by its original terms to be exercised in full, must still be required to be exercised in full after it is amended.

(4) The $50,000 annual and the $200,000 cumulative limits apply only to options granted prior to 1981 that are converted into incentive stock options by reason of an election under paragraph (b) of this section. Additionally, the limits relate only to the year of grant of an option, not the year in which an option vests (as in the case of an installment option) or the year of exercise. Unlike the $100,000 annual limit for options granted after 1980, the $50,000 annual limit does not incorporate an unused limit carryover from prior years. Both the $50,000 and the $200,000 limits apply to the fair market value of the stock at the time the options are granted, not to the option price of the options granted. Thus, in the case of an employee who is a 10 percent stockholder, an election would be permitted with respect to an option to purchase $50,000 worth of stock at an option price of $55,000. The requirement that options for which the election is made not exceed the $50,000 annual limit and the $200,000 cumulative limit will be deemed to have been satisfied if, at the time of grant, there was a good-faith attempt to value the stock accurately even if such valuation should subsequently prove to be in error.

(d) *Required option and plan amendments.* (1) The transitional rule waives the applicability of section 425(h) with respect to amendments of an option or a plan that are necessary to meet the minimum qualification requirements of section 422A. An amendment to add, modify, or delete a permissible term that is not necessary to meet such minimum qualification requirements does not fall within the waiver of section 425(h).

(2) The transitional rule waives the applicability of section 425(h) with respect to option and plan amendments only with respect to options outstanding on August 13, 1981. An option granted after August 13, 1981, and amended prior to exercise so as to qualify it as an incentive stock option, does not fall within the waiver of section 425(h). Such an option, therefore, will be treated as having been granted on the date it was amended. Consequently, the option price cannot be less than the fair market value of the stock as of the date of amendment. The option as originally granted, since it was not an incentive stock option at that time, will not be treated as still outstanding for purposes of the sequential exercise restriction of section 422A(b)(7).

(3) Amendments to an option plan, so as to meet the qualification requirements of section 422A, will apply to previously granted and outstanding options only if such amendments, by their terms, are clearly intended to have retroactive effect. Even if such amendments are intended to have retroactive effect, they need not apply to all previously granted options.

(4) The grant of an incentive stock option in exchange for the cancellation of an outstanding nonincentive stock option will not violate either the qualification requirements of section 422A or the transitional rules, provided the outstanding option is cancelled prior to the grant of

the incentive stock option. The cancelled option will not be treated as still outstanding for purposes of the sequential exercise restriction of section 422A(b)(7).

(e) *Stockholder approval issues.* (1) If an option plan received stockholder approval within 12 months before or after the date such plan was originally adopted and it is amended so as to qualify it as an incentive stock option plan, new stockholder approval will be required only if the original plan either did not specify the aggregate number of shares which may be issued under the plan or did not identify the employees or class of employees eligible to receive options under the plan, or if either of such terms is modified. The amendment of an option plan to add the $100,000 annual plus carryover limit, applicable to incentive stock options granted after 1980, will not require new stockholder approval.

(2) If a plan never received stockholder approval, or did not receive such approval within 12 months before or after such plan was adopted, the plan will qualify as an incentive stock option plan if stockholder approval is obtained prior to August 14, 1982, but only if an option granted pursuant to the plan was outstanding on August 13, 1981, and such option is to become an incentive stock option. If no option granted pursuant to the plan was outstanding on August 13, 1981, or no option outstanding on August 13, 1981, is to become an incentive stock option, the plan must be re-adopted by the granting corporation and, if necessary, amended to meet the qualification requirements of section 422A. Stockholder approval must be obtained within 12 months before or after the plan is re-adopted. Consequently, any option granted after August 13, 1981, and before the date the plan is re-adopted, that is to become an incentive stock option will be treated as having been granted on the date of re-adoption of the plan. The option price of such an option, therefore, cannot be less than the fair market value of the stock as of the date of re-adoption of the plan. The option as originally granted, since it was not an incentive stock option at that time, will not be treated as still outstanding for purposes of the sequential exercise restriction of section 422A(b)(7).

(3) If an option was granted pursuant to no plan at all and such option was outstanding on August 13, 1981, a plan may be adopted and stockholder approval obtained in order to qualify the option as an incentive stock option. The adoption of an incentive stock option plan and the obtaining of stockholder approval will be treated as amendments permitted under the transitional rules if they occur prior to August 14, 1982.

(4) Options granted under a plan that must be approved by stockholders to qualify as an incentive stock option plan and outstanding on August 13, 1981, are eligible to become incentive stock options even if they are exercised prior to the obtaining of stockholder approval provided stockholder approval is obtained before August 14, 1982.

(5) If, pursuant to paragraph (e) of this section, new stockholder approval is required in order to qualify a plan as an incentive stock option plan, see paragraph (b)(2) of § 1.422A-2 for the prescribed method and degree of stockholder approval.

(f) *Sequential exercise issues.* (1) The original grant dates (or later grant dates for options with pre-enactment modifications) of options that are converted into incentive stock options will determine the sequencing order for purposes of the sequential exercise restriction of section 422A(b)(7). For example, in the case of options granted in 1977, 1978, and 1979, assume that in 1980 the 1978 option was amended to add a term beneficial to the employee. Such an amendment would be a modification under the rules of section 425(h) and would cause the option to be treated as newly granted in 1980. If the 1977, 1978 (as modified), and 1979 options are converted into incentive stock options, the sequencing order would be as follows: the 1977 option must be exercised first, the 1979 option second, and the 1978 option (as modified) third.

(2) Options granted prior to 1981 that are converted into incentive stock options must be exercised prior to the exercise of any incentive stock options granted after 1980. For example, assume that an option granted and exercised during January of 1982 automatically qualifies, by its terms, as an incentive stock option. During February of 1982, the employer elected to convert an option granted to the employee during 1978 into an incentive stock option. For purposes of this section only, such an election will retroactively disqualify the 1982 option as an incentive stock option. If the 1982 option is to qualify as an incentive stock option, it cannot be exercised prior to the exercise or expiration of all incentive stock options previously granted and outstanding on the date the 1982 option was granted. When the 1982 option was granted during January of 1982, the 1978 option was already granted and outstanding for purposes of the sequential exercise restriction of section 422A(b)(7).

(3) The existence (or exercise) of stock options that are not converted into incentive stock options will not prevent the exercise of an incentive stock option because of the sequential exercise restriction of section 422A(b)(7). However, if an option that is converted into an incentive stock option contains other sequencing restrictions, the option will continue to be burdened by such restrictions. The deletion of such sequencing restrictions is not an amendment necessary in order to qualify the option as an incentive stock option. Consequently, the rules of section 425(h) would apply to such an amendment.

Par. 4. Section 1.421-7 is amended by revising paragraphs (b)(1), (b)(2), (d), (e)(1), (e)(2), and (h)(2) to read as follows:

§ 1.421-7 Meaning and use of certain terms.

* * *

(b) *Statutory options.* (1) The term "statutory options", used for purposes of convenience hereinafter in this section and in §§ 1.421-8 through 1.425-1, means a qualified stock option, as defined by section 422(b) and § 1.422-2; an incentive stock option, as defined by section 422A(b) and § 1.422A-2; an option granted under an employee stock purchase plan, as defined by section 423(b) and § 1A23-2; and a restricted stock option, as defined in section 424(b) and § 1.424-2.

(2) An option may qualify as a statutory option only if the option is not transferable (other than by will or by the laws of descent and distribution) by the individual to whom it is granted, and is exercisable, during the lifetime of such individual, only by him. See sections 422(b)(6), 422A(b)(5), 423(b)(9), and 424(b)(2). Accordingly, an option which is transferable by the individual to whom it is granted during his lifetime, or is exercisable during such individual's lifetime by another person, is not a statutory option. However, in case the option or the plan under which the option was granted contains a provision permitting the individual to whom the option was granted to designate the person who may exercise the option after his death, neither such provision, nor a designation pursuant to such provision, disqualifies the option as a statutory option.

* * *

(d) *Stock and voting stock.* For purposes of sections 421 through 425, the term "stock" means capital stock of any class, including voting or nonvoting common or preferred stock. Except as otherwise provided, the term includes both treasury stock and stock of original issue. Special classes of stock authorized to be issued to and held by employees are within the scope of the term "stock" as used in such sections, provided such stock otherwise possesses the rights and characteristics of capital stock. For purposes of determining what constitutes voting stock in ascertaining whether a plan has been approved by stockholders or whether the limitations pertaining to voting power contained in sections 422(b)(7), 422A(b)(6), 423(b)(3) and 424(b)(3) and the regulations thereunder have been met, stock which does not have voting rights until the happening of an event, such as the default in the payment of dividends on preferred stock, is not voting stock until the happening of the specified event. Moreover, stock which does not possess a general voting power, and may vote only on particular questions, is not voting stock. However, if such stock is entitled to vote on whether a stock option plan is to be adopted, it is voting stock for the purpose of ascertaining whether the plan has been approved by the shareholders.

(e) *Option price.* (1) For purposes of sections 421 through 425, the term "option price" or "price paid under the option" means the consideration in money or other property which, pursuant to the terms of the option, is the price at which the stock subject to the option is purchased. The term "option price" does not include amounts paid as interest under a deferred payment arrangement or treated as unstated interest under section 483 and the regulations thereunder. Thus, for example, section 483 is applicable in determining whether the pricing requirements of section 422(b)(4), 422A(b)(4) and (c)(8), 423(b)(6), 424(b)(1), or 424(c) are met and is applicable in determining the basis of any stock acquired pursuant to the exercise of a statutory option. However, with respect to statutory options granted prior to January 1, 1965, the determination of whether the applicable proving requirements are met shall be made without regard to section 483, but section 483 shall be taken into consideration in determining basis for purposes of determining gain or loss,

(2) In the case of a statutory option, any reasonable valuation method may be used for the purpose of determining whether at the time the option is granted the option price satisfies the pricing requirements of section 422(b)(4) relating to qualified stock options), section 422A(b)(4) and (c)(8) (relating to incentive stock options), section 423(b)(6) relating to employee stock purchase plans), or section 424(b)(1) relating to restricted stock options), whichever is applicable, with respect to the stock subject to the option. Such methods include

the valuation methods described in § 20.2031-2 of this chapter (Estate Tax Regulations).

* * *

(h) *Employment relationship.* * * *

(2) In order to qualify for the special tax treatment of section 421, in addition to meeting the requirements of subparagraph (1) of this paragraph, an individual exercising a qualified stock option, an incentive stock option, or an option granted under an employee stock purchase plan must, at all times during the period beginning with the date of the granting of such option and ending at the time of such exercise or on the day 3 months before the date of such exercise, be an employee of either the corporation granting such option, a related corporation of such corporation, or a corporation or a related corporation of such corporation issuing or assuming a stock option in a transaction to which section 425(a) applies. For this purpose, the employment relationship in respect of an option granted in accordance with the requirements of subparagraph (1) of this paragraph will be treated as continuing intact while the individual is on military, sick leave or other bona fide leave of absence (such as temporary employment by the Government) if the period of such leave does not exceed 90 days, or, if longer, so long as the individual's right to reemployment with the corporation granting the option (or a related corporation of such corporation, or a corporation, or a related corporation of such corporation issuing or assuming a stock option in a transaction to which section 425(a) applies) is guaranteed either by statute or by contract. Where the period of leave exceeds 90 days and where the individual's right to reemployment is not guaranteed either by statute or by contract, the employment relationship will be deemed to have terminated on the 91st day of such leave.

* * *

Par. 5. Section 1.421-8 is amended by revising paragraphs (a)(1), (b)(1), and (b)(2), adding new paragraph (b)(4), and revising paragraphs (c)(1) and (d) to read as follows:

§ 1.421-8 General rules.

(a) *Effect of qualifying transfer.* (1) If a share of stock is transferred to an individual pursuant to his exercise of a statutory option, and if the requirements of section 422(a) (relating to qualified stock options), section 422A(a) (relating to incentive stock options) section 423(a) (relating to employee stock purchase plans), or section 424(a) (relating to restricted stock option), whichever is applicable, are met, then—

(i) Except as provided in section 422(c)(1) (relating to exercise of option when price is less than value of stock), and paragraph (e)(2) of § 1.422-2, no income shall result at the time of the transfer of such share to the individual upon his exercise of the option with respect to such share;

(ii) No deduction under section 162 or the regulations thereunder (relating to trade or business expenses) shall be allowable at any time to the employer corporation, a related corporation of such corporation, or a corporation issuing or assuming a stock option in a transaction to which section 425(a) and paragraph (a) of § 1.425-1 (relating to corporate reorganizations, liquidations, etc.) applies, with respect to the share so transferred; and

(iii) No amount other than the price paid under the option shall be considered as received by any of such corporations for the share so transferred.

* * *

(b) *Effect of disqualifying disposition.* (1) The disposition of a share of stock, acquired by the exercise of a statutory option before the expiration of the applicable holding period as determined under section 422(a)(1), 422A(a)(1), 423(a)(1), or 424(a)(1), makes section 421 inapplicable to the transfer of such share. The income attributable to such transfer shall be treated by the individual as income received in the taxable year in which such disposition occurs. Similarly, a deduction under section 162 attributable to the transfer of the share of stock pursuant to the exercise of the option shall be allowable for the taxable year in which such disposition occurs to the employer corporation, its parent or subsidiary corporation or a corporation issuing or assuming a stock option in a transaction to which section 425(a) applies. In such cases, no amount shall be treated as income, and no amount shall be allowed as a deduction, for any taxable year other than the taxable year in which the disposition occurs. If the stock was transferred pursuant to the exercise of the option in a taxable year other than the taxable year or the disposition, the amount of the deduction shall be determined as if the employee had been paid compensation at the time provided in paragraph (d) of § 1.421-6.

(2) Section 421 is not made inapplicable by a transfer before the expiration of the applicable holding period as determined under section 422(a)(1), 422A(a)(1), 423(a)(1), or 424(a)(1), if such transfer is not a disposition of the stock as defined in section 425(c) and paragraph (c) of § 1.425-1, for example, a transfer from the decedent to his estate or a transfer by bequest or inheritance. Similarly, a disposition by the executor, administrator, heir, or legatee is not a disposition by the decedent. In case a statutory option is exercised by the estate of the individual to whom the option was granted, or by a person who acquired the option by bequest or inheritance or by reason of the death of such individual, see paragraph (c) of this section.

* * *

(4) For special rules relating to a disqualifying disposition of a share of stock acquired by exercise of an incentive stock option, see paragraph (b) of § 1.422A-1.

(c) *Exercise by estate.* (1) If a statutory option is exercised by the estate of the individual to whom the option was granted, or by any person who acquired such option by bequest or inheritance or by reason of the death of such individual, section 421(a) applies to such exercise in the same manner as if such option had been exercised by such deceased individual. Consequently, except as provided by section 422(c)(1) and paragraph (e)(2) of § 1.422-2, neither the estate nor such person is required to include any amount in gross income as a result of a transfer of stock pursuant to such exercise of the option. Nor does section 421(a) become inapplicable if such executor, administrator, or person disposes of the stock so acquired before the expiration of the applicable holding period as determined under section 422(a)(1), 422A(a)(1), 423(a)(1), or 424(a)(1). This special rule does not affect the applicability of section 1222, relating to what constitutes a short-term and long-term capital gain or loss. The executor, administrator, or such person need not exercise the option within three months after the death of the individual to whom the option was granted for section 421(a) to be applicable. However, the exercise of the option must be pursuant to the terms of the option, and any change in the terms of the option is subject to the rules of paragraph (e) of § 1.425-1, relating to the modification, extension, or renewal of the option. Section 421(a) is applicable even though such executor, administrator, or person is not employed by the corporation granting the option, or a related corporation, either when the option is exercised or at any time. However, section 421(a) is not applicable to an exercise of the option by the estate or by such person, unless the individual to whom the option was granted met the employment requirements of section 422(a)(2), 422A(a)(2), 423(a)(2), or 424(a)(2), whichever is applicable, either at the time of his death or within three months before such time. If the option is exercised by a person other than the executor or administrator, or other than a person who acquired the option by bequest or inheritance or by reason of the death of such deceased individual, section 421(a) is not applicable to the exercise. For example, if the option is sold by the estate, section 421(a) does not apply to an exercise of the option by such buyer; but if the option is distributed by the administrator to an heir as part of the estate, section 421(a) is applicable to an exercise of the option by such heir.

* * *

(d) *Exercise by deceased employee during lifetime.* If a statutory option is exercised by an individual to whom the option was granted and the individual dies before the expiration of the applicable holding period as determined under section 422(a)(1), 422A(a)(1), 423(a)(1), or 424(a)(1), section 421(a) does not become inapplicable if the executor or administrator of the estate of such individual, or any person who acquired such stock by bequest or inheritance or by reason of the death of such individual, disposes of such stock before the expiration of such applicable holding period. This rule does not affect the applicability of section 1222, relating to what constitutes a short-term and long-term capital gain or loss.

* * *

Par. 6. Section 1.425-1 is amended by revising paragraph (a)(6), redesignating paragraph (c)(3) as paragraph (c)(4) and revising paragraph (c)(4), adding new paragraph (c)(3), and revising paragraphs (d), (e)(1), (e)(5)(i) and (iii) and (e)(6) to read as follows:

§ 1.425-1 Definitions and special rules applicable to statutory options.

(a) *Corporate reorganizations, liquidations, etc.* * * *

(6) In order to have a substitution of an option under section 425(a) the optionee must, in connection with the corporate transaction, lose his rights under the old option. There cannot be a substitution of a new option for an old option within the meaning of section 425(a) if it is contemplated that the optionee may exercise both the old option and the new option. It is not necessary, however, to have a complete

substitution of a new option for the old option. However, if the old option was a qualified, incentive, or restricted stock option, any portion of such option which is not substituted or assumed in a transaction to which section 425(a) applies will be treated as an outstanding option to purchase stock of a predecessor corporation of the new employer or grantor corporation. See section 422(b)(5) and (c)(2) and paragraph (f) of §1.422-2, and section 422A(b)(7) and (c)(7) and paragraph (f) of §1.422A-2. For example, assume that X Corporation forms a new corporation, Y Corporation, by a transfer of certain assets and distributes the stock of X Corporation to the shareholders of X Corporation. Assume further that E, an employee of X Corporation, is thereafter an employee of both X Corporation and Y Corporation. Y Corporation wishes to substitute an option to purchase some of its stock for the statutory option which E has entitling him to purchase 100 shares of the stock of X Corporation. The option to purchase the stock of X Corporation, at $50 a share, was granted when the stock had a fair market value of $50 a share, and the stock was worth $100 a share just before the distribution of the new corporation's stock to the shareholders of X Corporation. The stock of X Corporation and of Y Corporation is worth $50 a share just after such distribution, which also is the time of the substitution. On these facts an option to purchase 200 shares of stock of Y Corporation at $25 a share could be given to the employee in complete substitution for the old option. It would also be permissible to give the employee an option to purchase 100 shares of stock of Y Corporation at $25 a share in substitution for his right to purchase 5O of the shares covered by the old option. However, if the option to purchase X stock was a qualified, incentive, or restricted stock option, then to the extent the old option is not assumed or a new option issued in substitution therefor in a transaction to which section 4Z5(a) applies, such old option will be treated as an outstanding option under either section 422(c)(2) for purposes of section 422(b)(5), or section 422A(c)(7) for purposes of section 422A(b)(7). See paragraph (f) of §1.422-2 and paragraph (f) of §1.422A-2.

* * *

(c) *Disposition of stock.* * * *

(3)(i) If there is a transfer of statutory option stock in connection with the exercise of any incentive stock option, and the applicable holding period requirements (under section 422(a)(1), 422A(a)(1), 423(a)(1), or 424(a)(1) are not met before such transfer, then no section referred to in paragraph (c)(1)(ii) of this section shall apply to such transfer for purposes of determining whether there has been a disposition of such stock.

(ii) For purposes of this paragraph (c)(3), the term "statutory option stock" means any stock acquired through the exercise of a qualified stock option, an incentive stock option, an option granted under an employee stock purchase plan, or a restricted stock option.

(iii) This paragraph (c)(3) applies only with respect to transfers of statutory option stock in connection with the exercise of an incentive stock option occurring after March 15, 1982.

(4) * * *

Example (7). On January 1, 1982, the X Corporation grants to E, an employee, an incentive stock option to purchase 100 shares of X Corporation stock at $100 per share, the fair market value of X Corporation stock on that date. According to the terms of the option, E can exercise the option by using previously acquired X Corporation stock. On January 1, 1983, while employed by X Corporation, E exercises part of the option and pays X Corporation $5,000 in cash. On that day, X Corporation transfers to E 50 shares of its stock having a fair market value of $6,000. Before January 1, 1984, E makes no disposition of the 50 shares so purchased. E realizes no income with respect to the transfer of the 50 shares of X Corporation stock on January 1, 1983. X Corporation is not entitled to any deduction at any time with respect to its transfer to E of the stock. E's basis for such 50 shares is $5,000.

Example (8). Assume the same facts as in example (7), except assume that on December 1, 1983, one year and 11 months after the grant of the incentive stock option and 11 months after the transfer of the 50 shares, E transfers 25 of the shares, having a fair market value of $5,000, to X Corporation as payment for the balance of the incentive stock option still outstanding. On that day, X Corporation transfers to E 50 shares of its stock having a fair market value of $10,000. The special rules of section 421(a) are not applicable to the transfer of 25 of the shares transferred on January 1, 1983, because disposition of such shares was made by E within two years of grant of the option and one year of exercise of the option.

(d) *Attribution of stock ownership.* Section 425(d) provides that in determining the amount of stock owned by an individual for purposes of applying the percentage limitations of section 422(b)(7), 422A(b)(6), 423(b)(3), and 424(b)(3), stock of the employer corporation or of a

related corporation which is owned (directly or indirectly) by or for such individual's brothers and sisters (whether by the whole or half blood), spouse, ancestors, and lineal descendants, shall be considered as owned by such individual. Also, for such purpose, if a domestic or foreign corporation, partnership, estate, or trust owns (directly or indirectly) stock of the employer corporation or of its parent or subsidiary, such stock shall be considered as being owned proportionately by or for the shareholders, partners, or beneficiaries of the corporation, partnership, estate, or trust.

(e) *Modification, extension, or renewal of option.* (1) Section 425(h) provides the rules for determining whether a share of stock transferred to an individual upon his exercise of an option, after the terms thereof have been modified, extended, or renewed, is transferred pursuant to the exercise of a statutory option. Such rules and the rules of this section are applicable to modifications, extensions, or renewals (or to changes which are not treated as modifications) of an option in any taxable year of the optionee which begins after December 31, 1963, except that section 425(h)(1) and this paragraph shall not apply to any change made before January 1, 1965, in the terms of an option granted after December 31, 1963, to permit such option to meet the requirements of section 422(b)(3), (4), or (5), and the regulations thereunder. See paragraphs (d), (e), and (f), of §1.422-2, relating to period for exercising options, option price, and prior outstanding options, respectively, in the case of qualified stock options. In addition, section 425(h)(1) and this paragraph shall not apply to any change made after August 13, 1981, and before August 14, 1982, in thc terms of an option granted after December 31, 1975, and outstanding on August 13, 1981, necessary to permit such option to meet the requirements of section 422A and the regulations thereunder. See §1.422A-3 for special rules relating to the conversion of existing options into incentive stock options.

* * *

(5)(i) The time or date when an option is modified, extended, or renewed shall be determined, insofar as applicable, in accordance with the rules governing determination of the time or date of granting an option provided in paragraph (c) of §1.421-7. For purposes of sections 421 through 425, the term "modification" means any change in the terms of the option (or change in the terms of the plan pursuant to which the option was granted) which gives the optionee additional benefits under the option regardless of whether the optionee in fact benefits from the change in the terms. For example, a change in the terms of the option, which shortens the period during which the option is exercisable, is not a modification. However, any one of the following changes is a modification: A change which provides more favorable terms for payment for the stock purchased under the option, such as the right to tender previously acquired stock; a change which provides an extension of the period during which an option may be exercised, such as after termination of employment; a change which provides an additional benefit upon exercise of the option, such as the payment of a cash bonus; and a change which provides an alternative to the exercise of the option, such as a stock appreciation right. Finally, a change which provides, either by its terms or in substance, that the optionee may receive an additional benefit under the option at the future discretion of the grantor, is a modification both at the time the option is changed and at the time the benefit is actually granted. Where an option is amended solely to increase the number of shares subject to the option, such increase shall not be considered as a modification of the option, but shall be treated as the grant of a new option for the additional shares.

* * *

(iii) Any change in the terms of an option for the purpose of qualifying the option as a statutory option grants additional benefits and, therefore, is a modification. However, if the terms of an option are changed to provide that the optionee cannot transfer the option except by will or by the laws of descent and distribution in order to meet the requirements of section 422(b)(6), 422A(b)(5), 423(b)(9), or 424(b)(2), such change is not a modification, provided that in any case where the purpose of the change is to meet the requirements of section 424(b)(2) the option is at the same time changed so that it is not exercisable after the expiration of ten years from the date the option was granted. Where an option is not immediately exercisable in full, a change in the terms of such option to accelerate the time at which the option (or any portion thereof) may be exercised is not a modification for purposes of section 425(h) and this section. A modification results where an option is revised to insert the language required by section 422(c)(6)(B).

* * *

(6) A statutory option may, as a result of a modification, extension, or renewal, thereafter cease to be a statutory option, or any option may, by modification, extension, or renewal, thereafter become a statutory op-

tion. Moreover, a qualified option after a modification may not be exercisable in accordance with its terms because of the requirements of section 422(b)(5) and section 422(c)(6). See paragraph (f)(3)(i) of § 1.422-2 and examples (8) and (9) of paragraph (f)(4) of § 1.422-2. Similarly, an incentive stock option after a modification may not be exercisable in accordance with its terms because of section 422A(b)(7). See paragraph (f)(3) of § 1.422A-2 and example (6) of paragraph (f)(4) of § 1.422A-2.

Par. 7. Section 1.6039-1 is amended by revising that part of paragraph (a) preceding paragraph (a)(1), and by revising that part of paragraph (b)(1) preceding paragraph (b)(1)(i) to read as follows:

§ 1.6039-1. Information returns required of corporations with respect to certain stock option transactions occurring on or after January 1, 1964.

(a) *Requirement of return under section 6039(a)(1)*. Every corporation which transfers stock to any person before January 1, 1980, pursuant to such person's exercise on or after January 1, 1964, of a qualified stock option described in section 422(b), or a restricted stock option described in section 424(b), shall make, for each calendar year in which such a transfer occurs, an information return on Form 3921 with respect to each transfer made during such year. The return shall include the following information:

* * *

(b) *Requirement of return under section 6039(a)(2)*. (1) Every corporation which records, or has by its agent recorded, before January 1, 1980, a transfer of the title to stock acquired by the transferor pursuant to his exercise on or after January 1, 1964, of—

* * *

Par. 8. Section 1.6039-2 is amended by revising paragraph (a), redesignating paragraphs (b) and (c) as paragraphs (c) and (e), respectively, and adding new paragraphs (b) and (d) to read as follows:

§ 1.6039-2 Statements to persons with respect to whom information is furnished.

(a) *Requirement of statement under section 6039(a)(1)*. Every corporation which transfers stock to any person after December 31, 1979, pursuant to such person's exercise of a qualified stock option described in section 422(b), an incentive stock option described in section 422A(b), or a restricted stock option described in section 424(b), shall furnish to such transferee, for each calendar year in which such a transfer occurs, a written statement with respect to the transfer or transfers made during such year. This statement shall include the following information:

(1) The name, address, and employer identification number of the corporation transferring the stock;

(2) The name, address, and identifying number of the person to whom the share or shares of stock were transferred;

(3) The name and address of the corporation the stock of which is the subject of the option (if other than the corporation transferring the stock);

(4) The date the option was granted;

(5) The date the shares were transferred to the person exercising the option;

(6) The fair market value of the stock at the time the option was exercised;

(7) The number of shares of stock transferred pursuant to the option;

(8) The type of option under which the transferred shares were acquired; and

(9) The total cost of all the shares.

(b) *Requirement of statement under section 6039(a)(2)*. (1) Every corporation which records, or has by its agent recorded, a transfer after December 31, 1979, of the title to stock acquired by the transferor pursuant to the transferor's exercise on or after January 1, 1964, or—

(i) An option granted under an employee stock purchase plan which meets the requirements of section 423(b), and with respect to which the special rule of section 423(c) applied, or

(ii) A restricted stock option which meets the requirements of section 424(b) and with respect to which the special rule of section 424(c)(i) applies.

shall furnish to such transferor, for each calendar year in which such a recorded transfer of title to such stock occurs, a written statement with respect to the transfer or transfers containing the information required by paragraph (b)(2) of this section.

(2) The statement required by paragraph (b)(1) of this section shall contain the following information:

(i) The name and address of the corporation whose stock is being transferred;

(ii) The name, address and identifying number of the transferor;

(iii) The date such stock was transferred to the transferor;

(iv) The number of shares to which title is being transferred; and

(v) The type of option under which the transferred shares were acquired.

(3) If the statement required by this paragraph is made by the authorized "transfer agent" of the corporation, it shall be deemed to have been made by the corporation. The term "transfer agent," as used in this paragraph, means any designee authorized to keep the stock ownership records of a corporation and to record a transfer of title of the stock of such corporation on behalf of such corporation.

(4) A statement is required by reason of a transfer described in section 6039(a)(2) of a share only with respect to the first transfer of such share by the person who exercised the option. Thus, for example, if the owner has record title to a share or shares of stock transferred to a recognized broker or financial institution and the stock is subsequently sold by such broker or institution (on behalf of the owner) the corporation is only required to furnish a written statement to the owner relating to the transfer of record title to the broker or financial institution. Similarly, a written statement is required when a share of stock is transferred by the optionee to himself and another person (or persons) as joint tenants, tenants by the entireties or tenants in common. However, when stock is originally issued to the optionee and another person (or persons) as joint tenants, or as tenants by the entirety, the written statement required by this paragraph shall be furnished (at such time and in such manner as is provided by this section) with respect to the first transfer of the title to such stock by the optionee.

(c) *Time for furnishing statements.*—(1) *In general.* Each statement required by this section to be furnished to any person for a calendar year shall be furnished to such person on or before January 31 of the year following the year for which the statement is required.

(2) *Extension of time.* For good cause shown upon written application of the corporation required to furnish statements under this section, the district director may grant an extension of time not exceeding 30 days in which to furnish such statements. The application shall be addressed to the district director with whom the income tax returns of the applicant-corporation are filed and shall contain a full recital of the reasons for requesting the extension to aid the district director in determining the period of the extension, if any, which will be granted. Such a request in the form of a letter to the district director signed by the applicant (or its agent) will suffice as an application. The application shall be filed on or before the date prescribed in subparagraph (1) of this paragraph for furnishing the statements required by this section.

(3) *Last day for furnishing statement.* For provisions relating to the time for performance of an act when the last day prescribed for performance falls on Saturday, Sunday, or a legal holiday, see § 301.7503.1 of this chapter (Regulations on Procedure and Administration).

(d) *Statements furnished by mail.* For purposes of this section, a statement shall be considered to be furnished to a person if it is mailed to such person's last known address.

(e) *Penalty.* For provisions relating to the penalty provided for failure to furnish a statement under this section, see § 301.6678-1 of this chapter (Regulations on Procedure and Administration).

James I. Owens,

Acting Commissioner of Internal Revenue.

[FR Doc. 84-3336 Filed 2-3-84; 9:47 am]

[¶ 20,151 Reserved.—Proposed Regs. §§ 301.6110-1 through 301.6110-7, relating to public inspection of written determinations, were formerly reproduced at this point. The final regulations appear at ¶ 13,786A—13,786G.]

[¶ 20,151A Reserved.—Proposed amendments to regulations clarifying that a partnership would lack the continuity of life if dissolution of the partnership occurred due not only to the retirement, death or insanity of a general partner but also from other types of withdrawal from the partnership by a general partner were formerly reproduced here. The final amendments are reproduced at ¶ 13,922.]

[¶ 20,152 Reserved.—Proposed Regs. §§ 1.401(a)-12 and 1.414(l)-1, relating to mergers and consolidations of retirement plans and transfers of plan assets or liabilities, were formerly reproduced here. The final regulations appear at ¶ 11,719A and 12,364.]

[¶ 20,153 Reserved.—Proposed amendments to Reg. § 54.4975-11, relating to requirements for stock ownership plans, were formerly reproduced at this point. The final regulations appear at ¶ 13,647B.]

[¶ 20,153A Reserved.—Proposed regulations on procedure and administration relating to the disclosure of returns and return information to various government departments and agencies were formerly reproduced at this point. The final regulations are at ¶ 13,761—13,763.]

[¶ 20,154 Reserved.]

[¶ 20,155 Reserved.—Proposed Reg. §§ 1.83-6(e) and (f) and 1.83-7(c), relating to the reporting requirements for nonqualified stock options, formerly reproduced at this point, have been withdrawn. The notice of withdrawal was published in the *Federal Register* on June 27, 1983 (48 FR 29538).]

[¶ 20,156 Reserved.—Proposed regulations on public inspection of written determinations were formerly reported at this point. The final regulations are at ¶ 13,786F.]

[¶ 20,157 Reserved.—Proposed regulations on group-term life insurance were formerly reproduced at this point. The final regulations are at ¶ 11,172, 13,511, 13,721 and 13,733.]

[¶ 20,157A Reserved.—Proposed regulations on the requirements for filing an actuarial report were formerly reproduced at this point. The final regulations are at ¶ 13,750B and 13,845.]

[¶ 20,157B Reserved.—Proposed Reg. § 301.6109-1, which modified the current information and reporting requirements for certain grantor trusts, was formerly reproduced here. The proposed regulation was pubished in the *Federal Register* of October 24, 1980 (45 FR 70478). The final regulation is reproduced at ¶ 13,782.]

[¶ 20,158 Reserved.—Proposed Reg. §§ 301.6057-1, 301.6057-2, 301.6057-3, and 301.6690-1, concerning annual report information relating to plan participants who separate from service with vested retirement benefits, were formerly reproduced here. The proposed regulations were published in the *Federal Register* of January 20, 1978 (43 FR 2892). The final regulations are reproduced at ¶ 13,733, 13,734, 13,803 and 13,883.]

[¶ 20,158A Reserved.—Proposed Reg. §§ 1.422-2 and 1.424-2 concerning qualified stock options granted after May 20, 1976 were formerly reproduced at this point. The final regulations appear at ¶ 13,122 and 13,142.]

[¶ 20,158B Reserved.—Proposed regulations on the definition of employee stock purchase plans and the coverage requirements of employee stock purchase plans were formerly reproduced at this point. The final regulations are at ¶ 13,132.]

[¶ 20,158C Reserved.—Proposed Reg. § 1.412(c)(3)-1, concerning reasonable funding methods designed to assure the equitable character and financial soundness of plans that must meet the minimum funding requirements of ERISA, formerly was reproduced here. The final regulations are reported at ¶ 12,250M.]

¶ 20,159

Proposed regulations on tax treatment of compensatory payments which are deferred under certain nonqualified compensation reduction plans or arrangements.—The proposed regulations would provide that if a taxpayer (whether or not an employee) individually chooses to have payment of some portion of his current compensation or an amount of an increase in compensation deferred and paid in a later year, the amount will nevertheless be treated as received by the taxpayer in the earlier taxable year.

The proposed regulations were published in the Federal Register of February 3, 1978 (43 FR 4638).

DEPARTMENT OF THE TREASURY INTERNAL REVENUE SERVICE

[26 CFR Part 1]

[LR-194-77]

Amounts Payments of Which are Deferred Under Certain Compensation Reduction Plans or Arrangements

Notice of Proposed Rulemaking

AGENCY: Internal Revenue Service, Treasury.

ACTION: Notice of proposed rulemaking.

SUMMARY: This document contains proposed regulations relating to the tax treatment of amounts of compensatory payments which are deferred under certain nonqualified compensation reduction plans or arrangements. The regulations would reflect a change in the Internal Revenue Service position relating to these plans or arrangements and provide the public with needed guidance.

DATES: Written comments and requests for a public hearing must be delivered or mailed by April 4, 1978. The amendments are proposed to be effective in the case of compensatory payments which the taxpayer has chosen to defer if the amount would have been payable, but for the taxpayer's exercise of the option to defer receipt, on or after a date 30 days following publication of this regulation as a Treasury decision in the FEDERAL REGISTER.

ADDRESS: Send comments and requests for a public hearing to: Commissioner of Internal Revenue, Attention: CC:LR:T (LR-194-77), Washington, D.C. 20224.

FOR FURTHER INFORMATION CONTACT: William E. Mantle of the Legislation and Regulations Division, Office of the Chief Counsel, Internal Revenue Service, 1111 Constitution Avenue, N.W., Washington, D.C. 20224 (Attention: CC:LR:T) (202-566-3734).

SUPPLEMENTARY INFORMATION:

Background

This document contains a proposed amendment to the Income Tax Regulations (26 CFR Part 1) under section 61 of the Internal Revenue Code of 1954. The amendment is proposed in order to change the Internal Revenue Service position on certain nonqualified compensation reduction plans or arrangements and is to be issued under the authority contained in section 7805 of the Internal Revenue Code of 1954 (68A Stat. 917; 26 U.S.C. 7805).

General Rule

The new regulation provides that if a taxpayer (whether or not an employee) individually chooses to have payment of some portion of his current compensation or an amount of an increase in compensation deferred and paid in a later year, the amount will nevertheless be treated as received by the taxpayer in the earlier taxable year. The taxpayer's exercise of the option to defer payment must be under a plan or arrangement other than one described in section 401(a), 403(a) or (b), or 405(a) of the Internal Revenue Code of 1954 (relating respectively to qualified pension, profit-sharing, and stock bonus plans; taxation of employee annuities; and qualified bond purchase plans).

Definition of Compensation

Under the proposed amendment, a taxpayer's compensation includes, in addition to basic or regular compensation fixed by contract, statute, or otherwise, a supplement, such as a bonus, and increases in basic or regular compensation.

Exception

An exception to the general rule is proposed to provide that it does not apply to the amount of any payment which the taxpayer has chosen to defer under an existing plan or arrangement if the amount would have been payable, but for the taxpayer's exercise of the option to defer receipt, before a date 30 days following publication of this regulation as a Treasury decision in the FEDERAL REGISTER.

Effect on Present IRS Published Positions

If this regulation is published as a Treasury decision, Rev. Rul. 67-449, 1967-2 C.B. 173, Rev. Rul. 68-86, 1968-1 C.B. 184, Rev. Rul. 69-650, 1969-2 C.B. 106, and Rev. Rul. 71-419, 1971-2 C.B. 220 would no longer be applied and present Service acquiescences in the decisions in *James F. Oates,* 18 T.C. 570 (1952) and *Ray S. Robinson,* 44 T.C. 20 (1965) would be reconsidered. Further, it would be necessary to examine the facts and circumstances of cases similar to those described in several other published revenue rulings (such as Examples (1) and (3) of Rev. Rul. 60-31, 1960-1 C.B. 174, Rev. Rul. 68-99, 1968-1 C.B. 193, and Rev. Rul. 72-25, 1972-1 C.B. 127) to determine whether the deferral of payment of compensation was in fact at the individual option of the taxpayer who earned the compensation.

On September 7, 1977, the Service announced in IR-1881 that it had suspended the issuance of rulings dealing with the income tax treatment of certain nonqualified deferred compensation plans established by State and local governments and other employers pending completion of a review of this area. The plans reviewed permit the employee to individually elect to defer a portion of his or her salary. This proposed amendment represents conclusions reached as a result of this review.

Comments and Requests for a Public Hearing

Before adopting these proposed regulations, consideration will be given to any written comments that are submitted (preferably six copies) to the Commissioner of Internal Revenue. All comments will be available for public inspection and copying. A public hearing will be held upon written request to the Commissioner by any person who has submitted written comments. If a public hearing is held, notice of the time and place will be published in the FEDERAL REGISTER.

Drafting Information

The principal author of these proposed regulations was William E. Mantle of the Legislation and Regulations Division of the Office of Chief Counsel, Internal Revenue Service. However, personnel from other offices of the Internal Revenue Service and Treasury Department participated in developing the regulation, both on matters of substance and style.

Proposed Amendments to the Regulations

26 CFR Part 1 is amended by adding a new § 1.61-16 immediately after § 1.61-15. The new section reads as follows:

§ 1.61-16 Amounts payments of which are deferred under certain compensation reduction plans or arrangements.—(a) *In general.* Except as otherwise provided in paragraph (b) of this section, if under a plan or arrangement (other than a plan or arrangement described in section 401(a), 403(a) or (b), or 405(a)) payment of an amount of a taxpayer's basic or regular compensation fixed by contract, statute, or otherwise (or supplements to such compensation, such as bonuses, or increases in such compensation) is, at the taxpayer's individual option, deferred to a taxable year later than that in which such amount would have been payable but for his exercise of such option, the amount shall be treated as received by the taxpayer in such earlier taxable year. For purposes of this paragraph, it is immaterial that the taxpayer's rights in the amount payment of which is so deferred become forfeitable by reason of his exercise of the option to defer payment.

(b) *Exception.* Paragraph (a) of this section shall not apply to an amount payment of which is deferred as described in paragraph (a) under a plan or arrangement in existence on February 3, 1978 if such amount would have been payable, but for the taxpayer's exercise of the option, at any time prior to [date 30 days following publication of this section as a Treasury decision]. For purposes of this paragraph, a plan or arrangement in existence on February 3, 1978 which is significantly amended after such date will be treated as a new plan as of the date of such amendment. Examples of significant amendments would be extension of coverage to an additional class of taxpayers or an increase in the maximum percentage of compensation subject to the taxpayer's option.

S.B. Wolfe

Acting Commissioner of Internal Revenue

¶ 20,159A

Proposed regulations: Payment of excise tax: Reversion of qualified plan assets to employer.—Reproduced below is the text of proposed regulations regarding the payment of the excise tax by employers receiving (directly or indirectly) reversions of qualified plan assets required by the Tax Reform Act of 1986. The regulations that are proposed are also issued as temporary regulations and are reproduced at ¶ 13,649B.

The proposed regulations were published in the *Federal Register* on April 3, 1987.

DEPARTMENT OF THE TREASURY

Internal Revenue Service

[26 CFR Parts 54 and 602]

[EE-151-86]

Payment of Excise Tax On Reversion of Qualified Plan Assets to Employer

Notice of Proposed Rulemaking

AGENCY: Internal Revenue Service, Treasury.

ACTION: Notice of proposed rulemaking by cross-reference to temporary regulations.

SUMMARY: This document provides regulations regarding the payment of the excise tax by employers receiving (directly or indirectly) reversions of qualified plan assets required by the Tax Reform Act of 1986. In the Rules and Regulations portion of this FEDERAL REGISTER, the Internal Revenue Service is issuing temporary regulations relating to the payment of the excise tax; the text of these temporary regulations also serves as the comment document for this notice of proposed rulemaking.

DATES: Written comments and requests for a public hearing must be delivered or mailed by June 1, 1987. These amendments are proposed to be applicable to reversions occurring after December 31, 1985.

ADDRESS: Please mail or deliver comments to: Commissioner of Internal Revenue, Attention: CC:LR:T (EE-151-86), 1111 Constitution Avenue, N.W., Washington, D.C. 20224.

FOR FURTHER INFORMATION CONTACT: Suzanne K. Tank of the Employee Plans and Exempt Organizations Division, Office of Chief Counsel, Internal Revenue Service, 1111 Constitution Avenue, N.W.,

Washington, D.C. 20224 (Attention: CC:LR:T) (202-566-3938, not a toll-free number).

SUPPLEMENTARY INFORMATION

Background

The temporary regulations in the Rules and Regulations portion of this issue of the FEDERAL REGISTER amend Part 54 of the Code of Federal Regulations. New §54.6011-1T [CCH PENSION PLAN GUIDE, ¶ 13,649B] and new §54.6071-1T [CCH PENSION PLAN GUIDE, ¶ 13,649C] are added to Part 54 of Title 26 of the Code of Federal Regulations. When §54.6011-1T is promulgated as final regulations, §54.6011-1 will be revised to reflect the new provision. For the text of the temporary regulations, see FR Doc. 87-7306 (TD 8133) published in the Rules and Regulations portion of this issue of the FEDERAL REGISTER. The preamble to the temporary regulations [CCH PENSION PLAN GUIDE, ¶ 23,725B] explains this addition to the Pension Excise Tax Regulations.

Nonapplicability of Executive Order 12291

The Commissioner of Internal Revenue has determined that this proposed rule is not a major rule as defined in Executive Order 12291 and that a regulatory impact analysis therefore is not required.

Regulatory Flexibility Act

The Secretary of the Treasury has certified that this rule will not have a significant impact on a substantial number of small entities. First, most small businesses maintain defined contribution plans. The regulations do not generally affect defined contribution plans. Hence, small businesses would not generally be affected by the regulation. Second, very few businesses with defined benefit plans will be terminating their plans and receiving a reversion in any calendar quarter or year. A Regulatory Flexibility Analysis, therefore, is not required under the Regulatory Flexibility Act (5 U.S.C. 605(b)).

Paperwork Reduction Act

The collection of information requirements contained in this regulation have been submitted to the Office of Management and Budget (OMB) for review under section 3504(h) of the Paperwork Reduction Act of 1980. Comments on these requirements should be sent to the Office of Information and Regulatory Affairs of OMB, Attention: Desk Officer for Internal Revenue Service, New Executive Office Building, Washington, D.C. 20503. The Internal Revenue Service requests that persons submitting comments on the requirements to OMB also send copies of these comments to the Service.

Drafting Information

The principal author of these proposed regulations is Suzanne K. Tank of the Employee Plans and Exempt Organizations Division of the Office of Chief Counsel, Internal Revenue Service. However, personnel from other offices of the Internal Revenue Service and the Treasury Department participated in developing the regulations, on matters of both substance and style.

Comments and Requests for a Public Hearing

Before adoption of these proposed regulations, consideration will be given to any written comments that are submitted (preferably eight copies) to the Commissioner of Internal Revenue. All comments will be available for public inspection and copying. A public hearing will be held upon written request to the Commissioner by any person who has submitted written comments. If a public hearing is held, notice of the time and place will be published in the FEDERAL REGISTER.

Lawrence B. Gibbs,

Commissioner of Internal Revenue.

¶ 20,159B

Fringe benefits: Employer-provided vehicle and fuel: Personal use: Valuation.—The IRS has updated previous guidance concerning the valuation of an employee's personal use of employer-provided fuel when an employer-provided automobile is valued under the automobile lease valuation rule. The proposals affect employees receiving this fringe benefit.

The proposed regulations were filed with the *Federal Register* on October 8, 1992, and published in the *Federal Register* on October 9, 1992 (57 FR 46525).

DEPARTMENT OF THE TREASURY

Internal Revenue Service

26 CFR Part 1

[EE-101-91]

RIN 1545-AQ28

Taxation of Fringe Benefits and Exclusions From Gross Income of Certain Fringe Benefits

AGENCY: Internal Revenue Service, Treasury.

ACTION: Notice of proposed rulemaking

SUMMARY: This document contains proposed amendments relating to the taxation and valuation of fringe benefits under section 61 of the Internal Revenue Code. These proposed amendments update previous guidance concerning the valuation of an employee's personal use of employer-provided fuel when an employer-provided automobile is valued pursuant to the automobile lease valuation rule. The proposed regulations affect employees receiving this fringe benefit and provide guidance to employers and employees to help determine their federal tax liability.

DATES: Written comments and requests for a public hearing must be received by November 9, 1992.

ADDRESSES: Send comments and requests for a public hearing to: Internal Revenue Service, P.O. Box 7604, Ben Franklin Station, Attention: CC:CORP:T:R (EE-l0l-91), Room 5228, Washington, D.C. 20044.

FOR FURTHER INFORMATION CONTACT: Marianna Dyson, at 202-622-4606 (not a toll-free number).

SUPPLEMENTARY INFORMATION:

Background

This document contains proposed amendments to the Income Tax Regulations (26 CFR part 1) under section 61 of the Internal Revenue Code of 1986 (Code). The amendments pertain to the valuation of employer-provided fuel under the automobile lease valuation rule of §1.61-21(d) of the regulations.

Explanation of Provisions

The final fringe benefit regulations issued in July 1989 and effective for benefits furnished on or after January 1, 1989, provide that in valuing the personal use of automobiles under §1.61-21(d) of the regulations, the Annual Lease Values do not include the fair market value of fuel provided by the employer. Thus, fuel consumed for any personal miles driven must be valued separately for inclusion in income. Section 1.61-21(d)(3)(ii)(A).

Under §1.61-21(d)(3)(ii)(B), employer-paid fuel provided *in kind* to employees for personal use may be valued at fair market value or, in the alternative, at 5.5 cents per mile. If the cost of the fuel is reimbursed by or charged to an employer, the value of the fuel is its fair market value, which is generally the amount of the actual reimbursement or amount charged, provided the purchase of the fuel is at arm's-length. Section 1.61-21(d)(3)(ii)(C).

For employers with fleets of at least 20 automobiles, §1.61-21(d)(3)(ii)(D) sets forth two additional methods for valuing fuel for personal use. The general method provides that employers who reimburse employees for the cost of fuel or allow employees to charge the employer for the cost of fuel may value the fuel by reference to the employer's "fleet-average cents-per-mile fuel cost." The fleet-average cents-per-mile fuel cost is equal to the fleet-average per-gallon fuel cost divided by the fleet-average miles-per-gallon rate. The average per-gallon fuel cost and the miles-per-gallon rate are determined by averaging the per-gallon fuel costs and miles-per-gallon rates of a representative sample of the automobiles in the fleet equal to the greater of ten percent of the automobiles in the fleet or 20 automobiles for a representative period. Section 1.61-21(d)(3)(ii)(D).

In lieu of calculating the "fleet-average cents-per-mile fuel cost" under the general method of paragraph (d)(3)(ii)(D) of §1.61-21, employers with fleets of at least 20 automobiles that use the fleet-average valuation rule of paragraph (d)(5)(D) may use the 5.5 cents-per-mile option of paragraph (d)(3)(ii)(B), if determining the amount of the actual reimbursement or the amount charged for the purchase of fuel would impose unreasonable administrative burdens on the employer ("the alternative method").

In no event, however, may an employer with a fleet of at least 20 automobiles use either the general or alternative method of paragraph (d)(3)(ii)(D) of §1.61-21 unless the requirements of paragraph (d)(5)(v)(D) are also met. This paragraph contains the rules for using a fleet-average value in calculating the Annual Lease Values of the automobiles in the fleet. In particular, it specifies that the fair market value of each vehicle in the fleet may not exceed $16,500 (as adjusted pursuant to section 280F(d)(7) of the Code).

For calendar years prior to 1991, Notice 89-110, 1989-2 C.B. 447, expanded the availability of the 5.5 cents-per-mile option to employers with fleets of at least 20 automobiles that satisfy the requirements of paragraph (d)(5)(v)(D), regardless of whether they are actually using the fleet-average valuation rule of paragraph (d)(5)(v). Notice 91-41, 1991-51 I.R.B. 63, provides that the 5.5 cents-per-mile option as provided in Notice 89-110 is available in calendar year 1991.

Notice 89-110 did not eliminate the requirement that the employer must demonstrate that it is using the 5.5 cents-per-mile option because determining the amount of the actual reimbursement or the amount charged for the purchase of fuel would impose unreasonable administrative burdens on the employer. As a practical matter, however, it is believed that fleet operators with at least 20 automobiles would have little difficulty in demonstrating the existence of unreasonable administrative burdens.

The proposed amendments to §1.61-21(d)(3)(ii) provide that, for calendar year 1992, employers with fleets of at least 20 automobiles may continue to use the 5.5 cents-per-mile rate as provided in Notice 89-110 and extended in Notice 91-41. In addition, the proposed amendments provide that employers with fleets of at least 20 automobiles may value fuel that is reimbursed by or charged to the employer by reference to the alternative cents-per-mile rate without regard to the rules in paragraph (d)(5)(v)(D) concerning the value of automobiles in the fleet, and without the necessity of demonstrating the existence of administrative burdens.

Finally, the proposed amendments provide that for calendar years subsequent to 1992 the Service will announce the appropriate cents-per-mile rate for valuing fuel that is provided in kind or that is reimbursed by or charged to employers with fleets of at least 20 automobiles. The announcement will appear in the annual revenue procedure concerning the optional standard mileage rates used in computing deductible costs of operating a passenger automobile for business.

The rules under paragraph (d)(3)(ii) of §1.61-21, as amended by this Notice, will enable employers with fleets of at least 20 automobiles to value the personal use of employer-paid fuel in any of the following ways: (1) fuel provided in kind may be valued at fair market value based on all the facts and circumstances; (2) fuel that is provided in kind may be valued at the cents-per-mile rate applicable to the particular year; (3) fuel, the cost of which is reimbursed by or charged to the employer, may be valued based on the amount of the actual reimbursement or the amount charged; (4) fuel, the cost of which is reimbursed by or charged to the employer, may be valued based on the fleet-average cents-per-mile fuel cost; or (5) fuel, the cost of which is reimbursed by or charged to the employer, may be valued based on the applicable cents-per-mile rate without regard to the fair market value of any automobile in the fleet or the administrative burdens requirement.

The amendments are proposed to be effective for benefits provided in calendar years beginning after December 31, 1992. However, because of the number of inquiries the Service has received from taxpayers expressing uncertainty as to the scope of the guidance in Notice 89-110 concerning employer-provided fuel, the amendments may be relied upon as if they had been included in the final regulations published on July 6, 1989.

Special Analyses

It has been determined that these rules are not major rules as defined in Executive Order 12291. Therefore, a Regulatory Impact Analysis is not required. It has also been determined that section 553(b) of the Administrative Procedure Act (5 U.S.C. chapter 5) and the Regulatory Flexibility Act (5 U.S.C. chapter 6) do not apply to these regulations, and, therefore, an initial Regulatory Flexibility Analysis is not required. Pursuant to section 7805(f) of the Internal Revenue Code, these regulations will be submitted to the Chief Counsel for Advocacy of the Small Business Administration for comment on their impact on small business.

Comments and Requests to Appear at a Public Hearing

Before adopting these proposed regulations, consideration will be given to any written comments that are submitted (preferably a signed original and eight copies) to the Internal Revenue Service. All comments will be available for public inspection and copying in their entirety. A public hearing will be held upon written request to the Commissioner by any person who has submitted written comments. Written comments and requests for a hearing must be received by November 9, 1992. If a public hearing is held, notice of the time and place will be published in the Federal Register.

Drafting Information

The principal author of these regulations is Marianna Dyson, Office of the Associate Chief Counsel (Employee Benefits and Exempt Organizations), Internal Revenue Service. However, personnel from other offices of the Service and Treasury Department participated in their development.

Par. 2. Section 1.61-21 is amended by revising paragraphs (d)(3)(ii)(A), (B), and (D) as follows:

* * *

(d) * * *

(3) * * *

(ii) *Fuel excluded*—(A) *In general.* The Annual Lease Values do not include the fair market value of fuel provided by the employer, whether fuel is provided in kind or its cost is reimbursed by or charged to the employer. Thus, if an employer provides fuel for the employee's personal use, the fuel must be valued separately for inclusion in income.

(B) *Valuation of fuel provided in kind.* Fuel provided in kind may be valued at fair market value based on all the facts and circumstances or, in the alternative, may be valued at 5.5 cents per mile for all miles driven by the employee in calendar years 1989 through 1992. For subsequent calendar years, the applicable cents-per-mile rate is the amount specified in the annual Revenue Procedure concerning the optional standard mileage rates used in computing deductible costs of operating a passenger automobile for business. However, fuel provided in kind may not be valued at the alternative cents-per-mile rate for miles driven outside the United States, Canada, or Mexico.

* * *

(D) *Additional methods available to employers with fleets of at least 20 automobiles*— (*1*) *Fleet-average cents-per-mile fuel cost.* If an employer with a fleet of at least 20 automobiles (regardless of whether the requirements of paragraph (d)(5)(v)(D) of this section are met) reimburses employees for the cost of fuel or allows employees to charge the employer for the cost of fuel, the fair market value of fuel provided to those automobiles may be determined by reference to the employer's fleet-average cents-per-mile fuel cost. The fleet-average cents-per-mile fuel cost is equal to the fleet-average per-gallon fuel cost divided by the fleet-average miles-per-gallon rate. The averages described in the preceding sentence must be determined by averaging the per-gallon fuel costs and miles-per-gallon rates of a representative sample of the automobiles in the fleet equal to the greater of ten percent of the automobiles in the fleet or 20 automobiles for a representative period, such as a two-month period.

(*2*) *Alternative cents-per-mile method.* In lieu of determining the fleet-average cents-per-mile fuel cost under paragraph (d)(3)(ii)(D)(*1*) of this section, an employer with a fleet of at least 20 automobiles may value the fuel provided for these automobiles by reference to the cents-per-mile rate set forth in paragraph (d)(3)(ii)(B) of this section (regardless of whether the requirements of paragraph (d)(5)(v)(D) of this section are met).

* * *

[¶ 20,160 Reserved.—Proposed regulations on custodial accounts for regulated investment company stock were formerly reproduced at this paragraph. The regulations were withdrawn by the Internal Revenue Service in a withdrawal notice on January 13, 1987 (51 FR 2724).]

[¶ 20,161 Reserved.—Proposed Reg. §§ 1.404(a)-2A, 1.6033-2, 1.6047-1, 301.6058-1, and 301.6652-3 on annual returns for employee retirement benefit plans were formerly reproduced at this point. The final regulations appear at ¶ 11,853, 13,662, 13,691, 13,745, and 13,803.]

[¶ 20,161A Reserved.—Proposed regulations on amortization of experience gains by plans funded by group deferred annuity contracts formerly appeared at this point. The final regulations appear at ¶ 12,250C.]

[¶ 20,162 Reserved.—Proposed regulations on the deduction limitations on contributions to defined benefit pension plans formerly appeared at this point. The final regulations appear at ¶ 11,864A.]

¶ 20,162A

Foreign deferred compensation plans: Qualified funded plans: Qualified reserve plans: Deductions or reductions of earnings and profits or accumulated profits: Elections.—The IRS has issued proposed regulations dealing with limitations on deductions and reductions in earnings and profits (or accumulated profits) with respect to certain foreign deferred compensation plans maintained by certain foreign corporations or by foreign branches of domestic corporations. Proposed regulations that were issued on April 8, 1985 have been withdrawn.

These regulations appeared in the *Federal Register* on May 7, 1993.

DEPARTMENT OF THE TREASURY

Internal Revenue Service

26 CFR Part 1

[EE-14-81]

RIN 1545-AD81

AGENCY: Internal Revenue Service, Treasury.

ACTION: Withdrawal of previous proposed rules and notice of proposed rulemaking.

SUMMARY: This document contains proposed regulations relating to the limitations on deductions and adjustments to earnings and profits (or accumulated profits) with respect to certain foreign deferred compensation plans. These new proposed regulations reflect changes to the applicable law made by the Act of December 28, 1980, as amended by the Technical Corrections Act of 1982, by the Tax Reform Act of 1986, and by the Technical and Miscellaneous Revenue Act of 1988. The new proposed regulations will affect employers (and shareholders of employers) that provide deferred compensation directly or indirectly to foreign employees and will provide the public and Internal Revenue Service personnel with the guidance needed to comply with section 404A of the Internal Revenue Code of 1986. These new proposed regulations supersede the prior proposed regulations published in the Federal Register on April 8, 1985 (50 FR 13821).

DATES: Written comments must be received by [*INSERT DATE THAT IS 60 DAYS AFTER THE DATE OF PUBLICATION OF THESE PROPOSED REGULATIONS IN THE FEDERAL REGISTER*]. Requests to speak (with outlines of oral comments) at a public hearing scheduled for October 5, 1993, at 10:00 a.m., must be received by September 14, 1993. See notice of hearing published elsewhere in this issue of the Federal Register.

ADDRESSES: Send comments, requests to appear at the public hearing, and outlines of comments to be presented to: Internal Revenue Service, P.O. Box 7604, Ben Franklin Station, Attention: CC:CORP:T:R (EE-14-81), Room 5228, Washington, D.C. 20044.

FOR FURTHER INFORMATION CONTACT: Concerning the proposed regulations, Elizabeth A. Purcell, Office of the Associate Chief Counsel (Employee Benefits and Exempt Organizations) at (202) 622-6080 (not a toll-free number). Concerning the hearing, Carol Savage, Regulations Unit, at (202) 622-8452 (not a toll-free number).

SUPPLEMENTARY INFORMATION:

Statutory Authority

This document contains proposed amendments to the Income Tax Regulations (26 CFR part 1) under sections 404A and 7805(a) of the Internal Revenue Code (Code).

Paperwork Reduction Act

The collection of information requirement contained in this notice of proposed rulemaking has been submitted to the Office of Management and Budget for review in accordance with the Paperwork Reduction Act of 1980 (44 U.S.C. 3504(h)). Comments on the collection of information should be sent to the Office of Management and Budget, Attention: Desk Officer for the Department of the Treasury, Office of Information and Regulatory Affairs, Washington, D.C. 20503, with copies to the Internal Revenue Service, Attention: IRS Reports Clearance Officer T:FP, Washington, D.C. 20224.

The collection of information requirement in these regulations is in §§ 1.404A-5, 1.404A-6 and 1.404A-7. This information is required by the Internal Revenue Service to determine accurately the correct deductions and reductions in earnings and profits for foreign deferred compensation. The likely respondents are businesses or other for-profit institutions.

These estimates are an approximation of the average time expected to be necessary for a collection of information. They are based on such information as is available to the Internal Revenue Service. Individual respondents may require greater or less time, depending on their particular circumstances. The estimated total annual reporting burden is 633,200 hours. The estimated annual reporting burden per respondent varies from 5 hours to 1,000 hours, depending on individual circumstances, with an estimated average of 506 hours. The estimated number of respondents is 1,250. The estimated annual frequency: once.

Background

On April 8, 1985, the Internal Revenue Service published in the Federal Register proposed amendments to the Income Tax Regulations under section 404A of the Internal Revenue Code of 1954 (now 1986) (50 FR 13821). Comments were requested and received, and a public hearing was held on September 20, 1985. After consideration of the comments received, the Service has determined that, rather than promulgate final regulations, it is more appropriate to withdraw the original proposed regulations and propose new regulations. This determination is based on a number of factors, including the number of significant substantive changes made to the prior proposed rules, changes to the underlying statute and other relevant Code provisions, and a need to reorganize the regulations. For a general discussion of section 404A and description of the prior proposed regulations, see the preamble to the prior proposed regulations published in the Federal Register on April 8, 1985.

The significant differences (or, where appropriate, the significant similarities) between these new proposed regulations and the prior proposed regulations are discussed, section by section, in the remainder of this preamble. Prior proposed § 1.404A-1 remains new proposed § 1.404A-1. However, the rules found in § 1.404A-2 of the prior proposed regulations are now incorporated in new proposed §§ 1.404A-6 and 1.404A-7. Prior proposed §§ 1.404A-3, 1.404A-4, 1.404A-5 and 1.404A-6 are redesignated §§ 1.404A-2, 1.404A-3, 1.404A-4 and 1.404A-5, respectively.

§ 1.404A-1: General rules concerning deductions and adjustments to earnings and profits for foreign deferred compensation plans.

90-percent test

As a condition to electing treatment as a qualified foreign plan, section 404A(e)(2) requires that 90 percent or more of the amounts taken into account for a taxable year under the plan be attributable to services performed by nonresident aliens, the compensation for which is not subject to United States federal income tax. Prior proposed § 1.404A-1(c) provided that, in determining whether the 90-percent test is satisfied, accrued benefits may be calculated under any reasonable method. It also provided that the rules for calculating the present value of accrued benefits at normal retirement age (except for the actuarial assumption safe harbor) under § 1.416-1 (concerning the determination whether a retirement plan is top-heavy) are presumed to be reasonable for this purpose.

Many commentators suggested that these rules for calculating accrued benefits for purposes of the 90-percent test are extremely burdensome and disproportionately expensive. They also suggested that the calculations require a degree of precision and accuracy that in many cases is unwarranted by the circumstances (i.e., where very few plan participants are United States citizens or residents and little compensation of the plan participants is subject to United States federal income tax). To give taxpayers in those cases a less burdensome and less expensive means of demonstrating compliance with the 90-percent requirement, a safe harbor provision has been provided in paragraph (c)(2) of new proposed §1.404A-1. It provides that the 90-percent requirement of §1.404A-1(a)(3) will be deemed satisfied with respect to a plan if the participants' benefits under the plan increase generally in proportion to their compensation taken into account under the plan, and the sum of (1) the compensation of United States citizens and residents taken into account under the plan, and (2) any other compensation subject to United States federal income tax taken into account under the plan, does not exceed five percent of all compensation taken into account under the plan for the plan year. This safe harbor provision does not apply, however, if the Commissioner determines that a significant purpose of the plan is to provide benefits not otherwise eligible for tax benefits under the Internal Revenue Code for participants who are United States citizens or residents. An example is provided in new proposed §1.404A-1(c)(4) to illustrate the application of this safe harbor provision.

Termination indemnity plans

Many commentators suggested that the regulations be revised to provide specifically that certain termination indemnity plans are considered deferred compensation plans for purposes of section 404A. The laws of many countries require employers to maintain termination indemnity plans to pay termination benefits. Some of these termination indemnities are payable solely upon involuntary discharge (other than by reason of mandatory retirement) and thus may be viewed as dismissal wage plans under United States tax principles. However, other termination indemnity plans are akin to deferred compensation plans. For example, one commentator noted that, in one European country, employers are required by law to provide severance benefits equal to one month's pay (final pay) for each year of service. These benefits are fully vested and payable upon all events of termination, including retirement.

Because the provisions of termination indemnity plans may vary widely, paragraph (iii) of the definition of deferred compensation in paragraph (e) of new proposed §1.404A-1 provides guidelines for determining whether such a plan provides deferred compensation. A termination indemnity plan is considered to provide deferred compensation if: (1) a major purpose of the plan is to provide for the payment of retirement benefits, (2) it has a benefit formula providing for payment based at least in part upon length of service, (3) it provides for the payment of benefits to employees (or their beneficiaries) after the employee's retirement, death or other termination of employment, and (4) it meets such other requirements as may be prescribed by the Commissioner with respect to termination indemnity plans. An example is provided under the definition of deferred compensation in paragraph (e) of new proposed §1.404A-1 to illustrate this provision. Any plan that meets these requirements is treated as providing deferred compensation, whether or not it is called a termination indemnity plan.

Equivalent of a trust

Section 404A(b)(5)(A) provides that, in order for a contribution to be taken into account in the case of a qualified funded plan, it must be paid to a trust or the "equivalent of a trust". The reference to the equivalent of a trust recognizes that, in some foreign countries, the common law concept of a trust does not exist. Thus, in those countries, the arrangement used to fund deferred compensation benefits for purposes of section 404A(b)(5)(A) must be functionally equivalent to a trust. The essential function of a trust in the context of a United States deferred compensation plan is to provide an entity separate from an employer through which deferred compensation benefits may be secured and liabilities funded. The four elements necessary to accomplish this function are provided in the definition of "equivalent of a trust" in paragraph (e) of new proposed §1.404A-1. These elements have been revised to allow an employer some latitude to insulate corpus and income from the claims of an employer's creditors, and to remove the concept of legal and beneficial ownership. Finally, the concept of fiduciary duty has been replaced with legally enforceable duty.

Some commentators urged the Service to endorse as the equivalent of a trust the so-called "Security Contract" or "Security Concept" developed in Germany. As explained by those commentators, the Security Contract combines a book reserve commitment by an employer with a pledge and guaranty. First, an employer establishes a book reserve for

its pension liabilities for which it receives a tax deduction under German law. It then establishes a wholly-owned subsidiary to which it transfers assets to fund its pension liabilities. As such, the corpus and income of the subsidiary are separately identifiable from an employer's general assets. This arrangement, without more, would not satisfy the requirements of the equivalent of a trust because the assets held by the subsidiary are not protected from the claims of an employer's creditors in the event of bankruptcy or receivership. Under the Security Contract concept, however, the subsidiary also pledges its assets irrevocably to a custodian who then gives a guaranty to the employees to pay the benefits up to the assets pledged to the custodian in the event an employer declares bankruptcy or goes into receivership. The custodian's guaranty is intended to place a prior lien on the assets pledged and protect them from the claims of an employer's creditors in the event of bankruptcy or receivership.

As one commentator asserted, however, it is unclear under German law that the arrangement provides such protection. According to that commentator, in the event of bankruptcy or receivership, the German Pension Guaranty Corporation is required by law to settle an employer's book reserve commitment. The Pension Guaranty Corporation then becomes a non-privileged creditor in the bankruptcy process and exercises any rights the employees have under the plan. As a non-privileged creditor, the Pension Guaranty Corporation is not entitled to all the assets pledged to the custodian, but is limited to a percentage of employer assets that is consistent with its general bankruptcy quota. Thus, it appears that the subsidiary's assets may be subject to the claims of an employer's creditors before all claims of the Pension Guaranty Corporation, exercising the rights of the employees under the plan, are settled.

Until the Service is satisfied that the corpus and income of the subsidiary are to be used to satisfy the claims of the employees and their beneficiaries (or those exercising their rights under the plan) before those of an employer's creditors, the Service cannot endorse this arrangement as the equivalent of a trust.

Exclusive means for deduction or reduction in earnings and profits

For foreign plans that fail to satisfy the requirements of section 404A, section 404 governs deductions for deferred compensation expense. For plans that are not qualified under section 401, section 404(a)(5) generally provides that the employer's deduction for contributions is delayed until amounts attributable to the employer's contribution are includible in the plan participant's gross income. In addition, under section 404(a)(5), deductions are denied altogether unless separate accounts are maintained for each participant. The Service took this position with respect to a foreign plan in Private Letter Ruling 7904042 (Oct. 25, 1978), available in the Freedom of Information Reading Room, Room 1569, Internal Revenue Service, 1111 Constitution Avenue, N.W., Washington, D.C. 20224. This position is reflected, in part, in paragraph (a) of new proposed §1.404A-1.

Prior proposed §1.404A-1(e) provided that earnings and profits (or accumulated profits) may be reduced with respect to payments by an employer to a funded foreign deferred compensation plan that are not deductible under section 404(a) even where an election under section 404A has not been made. Upon reexamination of the Congressional intent underlying the enactment of section 404A, however, the Service now believes that the position reflected in the prior proposed regulations is inconsistent with the purposes of section 404A (and the limitations thereunder). Thus, in accordance with the Secretary's section 404A(h) authority to prescribe regulations necessary to carry out the purposes of section 404A, paragraph (a) of new proposed §1.404A-1 provides that section 404A provides the exclusive means by which an employer may reduce earnings and profits for deferred compensation in situations other than those in which a reduction of earnings and profits is permitted under section 404. See also the discussion below of the relevance of sections 61, 671 through 679, and 1001 in this context.

Request for comments concerning foreign corporations that are not controlled

The Service is considering whether simplified or alternative methods of determining allowable earnings and profits reductions under section 404A might be appropriate for foreign corporations that are not controlled. Suggestions are invited on this matter.

§ 1.404A-2: Rules for qualified funded plans.

Substantiality of payments to trust

A commentator suggested that the focus of the flush language of paragraph (b) of prior proposed §1.404A-3 (requiring a trust to have "substantiality") should be on the substantiality of payments to a trust (or the equivalent of a trust) rather than on the substantiality of a trust (or the equivalent of a trust), because the determination with respect to the latter can be made under the standards set forth in prior proposed § 1.404A-1(g)(9). Accordingly, new proposed § 1.404A-2(b)(2)(i) provides that employer contributions must have substance. For example, contributions may not be made in the form of a promissory note. This also means that the contributions must be accumulated in the trust (or the equivalent of a trust) in order to be distributed as benefits under a deferred compensation plan. Whether contributions are being accumulated in the trust (or the equivalent of a trust) to be distributed as benefits will depend on the facts and circumstances. The example in paragraph (b)(5) of new proposed § 1.404A-2 reflects this change.

Exclusive benefit rule

Section 404A(b)(5)(A) provides that, in the case of a qualified funded plan, a contribution is taken into account only if it is paid to a trust (or the equivalent of a trust) that meets the requirements of section 401(a)(2). Section 401(a)(2) provides generally that it must be impossible, at any time prior to the satisfaction of all liabilities with respect to employees and their beneficiaries under the trust, for any part of the corpus or income to be used for, or diverted to, purposes other than the exclusive benefit of the employees or their beneficiaries. Thus, in effect, section 404A(b)(5)(A) reemphasizes, with regard to qualified funded plans, the general rule found in section 404A(e) that any "qualified foreign plan" must be for the exclusive benefit of an employer's employees or their beneficiaries. (As stated in the Senate Finance Committee Report, "[f]irst, the plan must be for the exclusive benefit of an employer's employees or their beneficiaries." S. Rep. No. 1039, 96th Cong., 2d Sess. 13 (1980).)

To reflect this emphasis, new proposed § 1.404A-2(b)(2) provides that one important factor that is taken into account in determining whether a trust has or has not been operated in a manner consistent with the exclusive benefit rule is whether it has not or has been involved in a transaction that would be described in section 4975(c)(1) if the plan were the type of plan subject to those rules. For example, a loan from the trust to an employer, on any terms, ordinarily would be a circumstance that strongly suggests noncompliance with section 404A(b)(5)(A). Similarly, a sale, exchange, or lease of any property between the trust and an employer would generally violate this provision. These rules, as set forth in new proposed § 1.404A-2(b)(2), apply prospectively.

Contributions deemed made before payment

Paragraph (c) of new proposed § 1.404A-2 clarifies the circumstances under which a payment made after the last day of an employer's taxable year is deemed to have been made on that last day.

Frequency of actuarial valuations

The new proposed regulations generally continue the requirement in the prior proposed regulations that an actuarial valuation be made no less frequently than once every three years for a qualified funded plan. However, for interim years, they require a reasonable actuarial determination to be made of whether the full funding limit in § 1.404A-5(c)(2) applies to the plan, and provide that the Commissioner may require an actuarial valuation in interim years under appropriate circumstances. It is anticipated that the Commissioner will not exercise this authority except in situations similar to those described in § 1.412(c)(9)-1(d) of the proposed regulations.

Shareholder-level consequences

A sentence in paragraph (d)(1) of prior proposed § 1.404A-3 provided that, where a foreign corporation maintained a qualified funded plan, the deductible amount was taken into account for the shareholder's taxable year in which or with which an employer's taxable year ended. This sentence has been deleted because section 404A does not govern the time at which adjustments to earnings and profits of a foreign employer corporation for a particular year are taken into account at the shareholder level.

§ 1.404A-3: Rules for qualified reserve plans.

The new proposed regulations have modified in several ways the guidance on the calculation of the amount that may be taken into account under a qualified reserve plan. First, the presentation has been changed in order to parallel the components of net periodic pension cost used in Statement of Financial Accounting Standards No. 87 "Employer's Accounting for Pensions" (1985), available from the Financial Accounting Standards Board, 401 Merritt 7, Norwalk, CT 06856. Thus, the amount taken into account for a year is based on the sum of a type of "service cost", "interest cost" and the amortization of the increase or decrease in the reserve from other sources. As part of this change, the steps for determining the actuarial gain or loss have been

made explicit. In addition, as discussed below, certain increases or decreases in the reserve that were subject to amortization under the old proposed regulations are now included in the reasonable addition to the reserve.

Ten-Year amortization

Section 404A(c)(4) provides for the spreading over ten years of certain increases and decreases in reserves on account of various events including a catch-all category of "such other factors as may be prescribed by regulations". The Senate Finance Committee Report includes two suggestions of possible items that could be included in this category: "adjustments in the reserve resulting from changes in levels of compensation on which benefits depend or the vesting in one year of a benefit which was accrued in a prior year." S. Rep. No. 1039, 96th Cong. 2d. Sess. 14 (1980).

Some commentators criticized the rule in paragraph (d) of prior proposed § 1.404A-4 providing for the amortization of changes in the reserve arising from these two sources. They suggested that the ten-year amortization requirement for increases or decreases to the reserve on account of changes in the level of compensation upon which plan benefits depend, and for vesting of benefits accrued in prior years, was unnecessary because those items are ongoing costs of the plan that are specifically contemplated by the plan and will arise periodically as each participant's circumstances dictate. Thus, those increases or decreases can be expected to occur regularly in the aggregate and will not create the "bunching" that section 404A(c)(4) was designed to avoid.

The new proposed regulations respond to commentators' concerns by incorporating certain increases in the reserve (as described below) into the definition of the reasonable addition to a reserve, subject to an anti-abuse rule. The effect of this change is to allow immediate recognition, rather than ten-year amortization, of these changes. Under normal circumstances this immediate recognition will not result in significant bunching of income or deductions. Further, to the extent bunching occurs, abuse potential is limited because the bunching is the result of a deferral of deductions rather than the recognition of these items. Finally, as discussed below, for taxable years beginning after December 31, 1986, the indirect foreign tax credit is determined using post-1986 earnings and profits (i.e., aggregated for all post-1986 years). Use of a multi-year earnings and profits pool diminishes the effect of bunching on the foreign tax credit.

The increases in reserve that are now included in the reasonable addition to the reserve are those increases that result from expected changes in compensation and from the increase in vesting for employees whose liabilities were included in the reserve as of the beginning of the year. Thus, for example, the reasonable addition to the reserve may reflect an expected increase in compensation of five percent and expected changes in the vesting percentage in the current year for all employees in the reserve as of the beginning of the year. By contrast, any increase in reserve that results from compensation changes that are greater than expected or from the inclusion of newly-vested employees who were not included in the prior year's reserve are categorized as actuarial losses subject to ten-year amortization.

§ 1.404A-4: United States and foreign law limitations on amounts taken into account for qualified foreign plans.

§ 404A(d) limitation—pooling of earnings and profits

Section 404A(d)(3) provides that, in determining the earnings and profits (and accumulated profits) of any foreign corporation with respect to a qualified foreign plan, the amount determined under section 404A with respect to any plan for any taxable year must not exceed the amount allowed as a deduction under the appropriate foreign law for such taxable year. As the legislative history makes clear, this limitation was imposed in response to "the possibilities for distortion of a taxpayer's indirect foreign tax credit which are presented by the present annual system for determining the amount of the foreign taxes paid by a subsidiary which are attributable to dividends paid to U.S. shareholders." S. Rep. No. 1039, 96th Cong., 2d Sess. 15 (1980). The legislative history further makes clear that "[t]his potential for distortion might be eliminated if the indirect credit were computed with reference to the subsidiary's accumulated foreign taxes and undistributed accumulated profits for all years." *Id.*

Section 1202(a) of the Tax Reform Act of 1986 amended section 902 to provide for computation of the indirect foreign tax credit by pooling all post-1986 earnings and profits and all post-1986 creditable foreign taxes. These amendments to section 902 prevent the distortion at which section 404A(d)(3) was aimed. Section 1012(b)(4) of the Technical and Miscellaneous Revenue Act of 1988 added specific regulatory authority to section 404A(d)(3) (retroactive to enactment of the Tax

Reform Act of 1986), to take this change in the law into account. Accordingly, pursuant to that grant of regulatory authority, new proposed §1.404A-4 provides that, for taxable years beginning after December 31, 1986, the reduction of earnings and profits of a foreign corporation with respect to a qualified foreign plan is determined without regard to the tax deduction under foreign law for that year. This new rule allows any amount that is disallowed for a year (because the foreign tax deduction for that year is greater than the amount allowed under section 404A(b) or (c)) to be carried forward to a future year, in which it may increase the amount allowable under section 404A.

Section 404A(d) limitation

Section 404A(d)(1) provides that the annual amount allowable under section 404A "shall equal" the lesser of the cumulative United States amount or the cumulative foreign amount, reduced by the aggregate amount. Prior proposed §1.404A-5 (a) provided that the annual amount allowable "shall not exceed" these cumulative amounts. The new proposed regulations adopt the language of the statute. See new proposed §1.404A-4 (b).

Foreign currency rules

One commentator requested guidance with respect to a number of foreign currency issues. Sections 985-989 were subsequently enacted by the Tax Reform Act of 1986. These sections, effective for taxable years beginning after December 31, 1986, address many of the problems identified by the commentator. Paragraph (d)(1) in new proposed §1.404A-4 clarifies that, for taxable years beginning after December 31, 1986, income or loss of foreign branches and earnings and profits (or deficits in earnings and profits) of foreign corporations are determined in functional currency as defined in section 985. For taxable years beginning before January 1, 1987, paragraph (d)(2) in new proposed §1.404A-4 provides that the rules in effect for those taxable years determine the amount of income or loss or earnings and profits (or deficit in earnings and profits) for the foreign branch or subsidiary. A new paragraph (d)(3) provides special rules for those circumstances where the net worth method of accounting is used.

§ 1.404A-5: Additional limitations on amounts taken into account for qualified foreign plans.

New proposed §1.404A-5 clarifies the evidentiary requirements and rules on actuarial assumptions. No significant changes are made to the rules in prior proposed §1.404A-6, which are now contained in new proposed §1.404A-5.

§ 1.404A-6: Elections under section 404A and other changes in accounting method.

Time and manner for making elections

Paragraph (b)(5) of prior proposed §1.404A-2 provided that elections made under section 404A must be made no later than the time prescribed by law for filing the United States tax return for a United States taxpayer's taxable year. For a qualified foreign plan maintained by a foreign corporation, the regulations have been modified to conform the filing requirements to the general rules applicable to tax accounting elections on behalf of foreign corporations under section 964. For example, under the new proposed regulations, a section 404A election need not be made before the United States shareholder's tax liability is affected by the earnings and profits of the foreign corporation. Such an effect on the United States shareholder's tax liability may occur as the result of any of the following: a dividend distribution, an income inclusion under section 951(a), a section 1248 transaction, a section 864(e) basis adjustment by earnings and profits, or an inclusion in income of the earnings of a qualified electing fund under section 1293(a)(1).

The prior proposed regulations provided that, in order for "protective" or "Method (2)" elections to be effective, taxpayers who made those elections had to file amended returns no later than 90 days after the date on which the final regulations were published in the Federal Register. See Ann. 81-114, Ann. 81-148 and Ann. 82-128, reproduced as an appendix to this preamble. Otherwise, the elections would have no effect. Numerous commentators suggested that the 90-day period is inadequate for taxpayers to evaluate the final regulations, collect the required data, make the appropriate actuarial calculations, decide whether the election is beneficial, and file the required returns. Thus, the deadlines for perfecting retroactive elections and making or perfecting certain other elections in new proposed §1.404A-7 have generally been extended to 365 days after the publication of final regulations.

Single plan

As originally proposed, §1.404A-2(b)(6)(i) provided that an election may be made with respect to each plan that qualifies as a "single plan". The term "single plan" has for this purpose the same definition as it has in §1.414(l)-1(b). Commentators asked for an illustration of the application of this single plan rule to an existing deferred compensation plan that is split into two single plans for purposes of section 404A. Thus, a new example has been added in paragraph (a)(2) of new proposed §1.404A-6.

Section 481(a) adjustment

New proposed §1.404A-6(a) addresses the adoption of methods of accounting and changes in methods of accounting with respect to a foreign deferred compensation plan for which an election under section 404A has been made. It clarifies, for example, that an initial election with respect to a pre-existing plan, termination of an election, revocation of an election, and a change in actuarial funding method, constitute changes in methods of accounting under section 446(e) and section 481(a). To compute the section 481(a) adjustment upon a change in method of accounting under section 404A, §1.404A-6(f)(6) of the prior proposed regulations required a historical computation. Taxpayers were to compute contributions, deductions or reductions in earnings and profits from the establishment of the plan to the first day of the first year in which a section 404A election was made. Commentators argued that this historical approach was unduly burdensome.

The new proposed regulations respond to commentators' concerns by generally replacing the historical computation requirement with a "snapshot" approach to determining the amount of the section 481(a) adjustment for purposes of section 404A. As illustrated below, the snapshot approach is adopted in the proposed regulations in an effort to reduce substantially taxpayers' recordkeeping and compliance burdens.

The snapshot approach is generally intended to compare (i) the extent to which an employer has accelerated deductions (or reductions in earnings and profits) under its old method of accounting for deferred compensation with (ii) the acceleration (if any) that would have been allowed under its new method of accounting. In the interest of avoiding historical calculations and other complexities, the snapshot approach generally attempts to compare the old and new methods of accounting based, to the extent possible, on actual reserve or fund balances existing at the time of the change. These balances generally have been reduced for amounts actually paid to plan participants and beneficiaries. However, amounts actually paid to participants and beneficiaries would be the same under both an employer's old method and its new method of accounting. Therefore, deductions attributable to such payments can be eliminated from consideration in determining both the old and the new method amounts that are compared.

In other words, in the case of both the old method and the new method of accounting, the extent of acceleration is measured by reference to a common baseline: the amount actually paid to plan participants and beneficiaries (i.e., a pay-as-you-go method). Thus, the snapshot approach generally measures the extent to which an employer, under its old method of accounting, has claimed deductions (or reductions in earnings and profits) that exceed the amount actually paid to plan participants and beneficiaries as of the change in accounting method. This amount (generally referred to as the "Old Method Closing Amount") is then compared to the deductions (or reductions in earnings and profits) in excess of the amount actually paid to plan participants and beneficiaries that the employer would have claimed for the same period under its new method of accounting (generally referred to as the "New Method Opening Amount"). The section 481(a) adjustment is equal to the difference between the Old Method Closing Amount and the New Method Opening Amount. The comparison is based on the status of the plan as of the beginning of the year of a change in accounting method.

To illustrate, if the employer has used a funded method of accounting for deferred compensation, the Old Method Closing Amount equals the amount of the fund balance as of the beginning of the year that the accounting method is changed. In determining the amount of the section 481(a) adjustment for purposes of section 404A, this fund balance is compared with a New Method Opening Amount. The New Method Opening Amount will depend on which new method of accounting the employer elects. If the employer makes a qualified funded plan election, the New Method Opening Amount generally will equal the amount of the fund balance, adjusted as appropriate to reflect the limitations in section 404A(b) and (d) on prior contributions to the fund that could have been taken into account under section 404A. If, however, the employer makes a qualified reserve plan election, the New Method Opening Amount generally will be the amount of the reserve under section 404A(c). Alternatively, if the new method of accounting is a non-section 404A method (i.e., a pay-as-you-go method), the New Method Opening Amount generally will be zero.

As the foregoing discussion indicates, the new method will not necessarily be a section 404A method (a qualified funded plan method or qualified reserve plan method), and the old method will not necessarily be a non-section 404A method. The section 481(a) adjustment and the proposed snapshot approach to computing the adjustment apply whether the employer is changing to or from a section 404A method or from one section 404A method to another. For example, assume that a foreign branch has a qualified funded plan with a trust fund balance of 15 of functional currency (as defined in section 985(b)). Assume that this fund balance resulted from FC10 of deductible contributions to the fund under section 404A, plus FC5 of net investment income earned within the fund. Under the snapshot approach, the Old Method Closing Amount upon a change to qualified reserve plan treatment is FC15. Assuming that the reserve under the qualified reserve plan method is FC20 as of the date of the method change, the New Method Opening Amount is FC20, and the amount of the section 481(a) adjustment under section 404A is a negative FC5.

By using the amount of the fund balance in determining both the Old Method Closing Amount and the New Method Opening Amount, the proposed regulations require consideration of both the deductions previously taken by the employer and the accumulated net income (or inside build-up) of a fund in calculating the amount of the section 481(a) adjustment for purposes of section 404A. The Service believes that, in addition to permitting the adoption of a simplified method for determining the section 481(a) adjustment, consideration of a fund's accumulated net income under the snapshot approach avoids additional complexities that might result from the application of sections 61 and 1001 at the time of an election under section 404A. For example, consider an employer that makes a qualified funded plan election after having used a funded method of accounting for a foreign deferred compensation plan that is not a qualified funded plan. Ordinarily, the value of the fund (which is used to satisfy the employer's plan liabilities) will exceed the employer's contributions to the fund (net of the fund's previous payments to plan participants and beneficiaries). If the snapshot method were not applied, arguably sections 61 and 1001 would result in a recognition of income (or increase in earnings and profits) by the employer at the time of the election equal to the excess of the value of the fund over the employer's basis in the fund. This result is consistent with the treatment of a change in method of accounting that consists of a qualified funded plan election as involving a change in the status of the fund from a grantor trust (defined and treated in accordance with sections 671 through 679) to a non-grantor trust (treated in a manner analogous to the treatment of a trust under a section 401(a) tax-qualified plan). The Service solicits comments from interested parties on this analysis and on the utility of the snapshot approach in reducing taxpayer burden.

Effect of section 404A(d)(1) limits on section 481(a) adjustment computation

Since the limitations of section 404A(d)(1) are part of the section 404A method of accounting under the new proposed regulations, the snapshot section 481(a) adjustment calculation must take into account the cumulative foreign amount limitation in section 404A(d) and new proposed § 1.404A-4. This is a departure from § 1.404A-6(f)(9) in the prior proposed regulations. The snapshot approach includes a simplified method to make this adjustment in computing the section 481(a) adjustment. More specifically, paragraph (g) of new proposed § 1.404A-6 allows taxpayers to use the snapshot approach to compute the initial cumulative United States and foreign law limitations under section 404A(d) as of the beginning of a year of change in method of accounting. The rules to initialize the cumulative United States amount, cumulative foreign amount and the aggregate amount rely on the constant relationship between these three amounts (i.e., the aggregate amount always equals the lesser of the two cumulative amounts).

Section 481(a) adjustment period

As required by section 404A(g)(5), the period for taking into account the section 481(a) adjustment arising from an election or a re-election under section 404A is 15 years. Additionally, new proposed § 1.404A-6(e)(2)(iii) provides for a six-year section 481(a) adjustment period for a change in method of accounting arising from the termination or revocation of an election under section 404A, and for any other change in accounting method under section 404A. This new paragraph also requires netting of any section 481(a) adjustment remaining from a previous change in method in determining the amount to be taken into account during the six-year section 481(a) adjustment period. The example in new proposed § 1.404A-6(e)(4) illustrates this netting rule.

Examples in the new proposed regulations illustrate the principle under section 446(e) and its underlying administrative procedures that the District Director may modify a taxpayer's calculated section 481(a) adjustment under section 404A if the District Director (1) determines that the taxpayer used an erroneous method of accounting in an open year prior to the year in which the taxpayer's qualified funded plan or qualified reserve plan election is effective, and (2) requires the taxpayer to change its erroneous method of accounting in that earlier open year. For example, if a taxpayer erroneously deducted FC100 for amounts accrued under a reserve plan in an open year prior to the effective date of a qualified reserve plan election under section 404A, the District Director could require the taxpayer to change its method of accounting in that earlier open year and to take a positive FC100 section 481(a) adjustment into account entirely in that earlier open year (rather than permitting the positive FC100 amount to be netted against any New Method Opening Amount under the snapshot approach and spread prospectively over a 15-year section 481(a) adjustment period). See section 2.02 of Rev. Proc. 92-20, 1992-1 C.B. 685.

§ 1.404A-7: Effective date and retroactive application.

Prior proposed § 1.404A-2(c), relating to retroactive elections, has been moved to § 1.404A-7. This change was made because the rules relating to retroactive elections are relatively discrete and thus logically should be set apart from the general election rules. Because the importance of these rules will greatly diminish within a few years, their placement at the end of the regulations will improve the clarity of the remainder of the regulations for the future. Other specific changes to the retroactive election rules are discussed below.

All-or-nothing rule

Many commentators criticized the rule in paragraph (c)(2)(ii) of prior proposed § 1.404A-2 as an improper interpretation of section 2(e)(2) of the Act of December 28, 1980 (Pub. L. 96-603). Prior proposed § 1.404A-2(c)(2)(i) provided that a taxpayer could elect, during its "open period," for section 404A to apply to a qualified foreign plan maintained by a foreign subsidiary. However, prior proposed § 1.404A-2(c)(2)(i) conditioned that election for any plan on a taxpayer electing to apply section 404A with respect to all written plans of every foreign subsidiary (whether or not wholly owned) that defer the receipt of compensation and that satisfy the requirements of section 404A(e)(1) and (2). Commentators argued that the "all-or-nothing rule" of section 2(e)(2) of the Act of December 28, 1980, simply provides that a taxpayer may elect to have section 404A apply for certain prior years, and that such an election must be made for all of a taxpayer's foreign subsidiaries. It does not, however, require that a taxpayer make an election under section 404A for any of its foreign subsidiaries' plans. According to this view, once the election is made to have section 404A apply to the foreign subsidiaries for prior years, the consequences of making or not making an election under section 404A will be determined as though section 404A had been in effect for those years.

After further consideration, the proposed regulations adopt the commentators' view of section 2(e)(2) of the Act of December 28, 1980. Thus, if a taxpayer makes an election to have section 404A apply retroactively to its foreign subsidiaries during its open period, the election to have section 404A apply must be made for all of a taxpayer's foreign subsidiaries (whether or not wholly owned) during a taxpayer's open period. Accordingly, if a taxpayer elects to have section 404A apply during a taxpayer's open period, it may not rely on any other law or rule of law to reduce earnings and profits (or accumulated profits) of any foreign subsidiary with respect to deferred compensation expenses, regardless of whether the taxpayer elects to apply section 404A to any specific deferred compensation plan. Paragraph (b) of new § 1.404A-7 reflects this view, and paragraph (c)(5) illustrates this rule with an example.

Making, perfecting and revoking retroactive elections

New proposed § 1.404A-7 provides rules for making, perfecting and revoking retroactive effective date elections as well as retroactive plan-by-plan elections for qualified foreign plans maintained by foreign subsidiaries and for qualified funded plans maintained by foreign branches. Taxpayers are afforded 365 days after publication of the final regulations to decide whether to perfect or revoke retroactive elections or to make, revoke or re-elect in intervals of six or more years, effective for taxable years in the open period (as defined in new proposed § 1.404A-7(g)(6)) and continuing after taxable years beginning after December 31, 1979. Taxpayers must file amended returns and attach statements in order to perfect a retroactive election and to conform all items to the treatment consistent with election or revocation. If the amended returns and statements are not timely filed, the retroactive elections will be deemed revoked.

Alternative to contemporaneous evidence requirement

Many commentators criticized the rule in prior proposed § 1.404A-2(c)(4)(iii) prohibiting a retroactive election if a taxpayer was unable to calculate the requisite section 481(a) adjustment based upon actual data, because, in effect, it unduly restricted taxpayers' ability to make retroactive elections. The commentators were concerned that many taxpayers would lack "actual data", and thus be unable to make the election, and that, even if such data were technically available, its retrieval would be prohibitively burdensome. After further consideration, the Service has altered this requirement. Accordingly, new proposed § 1.404A-7(f) provides that the section 481(a) adjustment must be made based upon contemporaneous substantiation quality data. If contemporaneous substantiation quality data is not readily available, however, the adjustment may be based on data which are combinations of actual contemporaneous evidence and reasonable actuarial backward projections of substantiation quality data.

For the convenience of taxpayers, Ann. 81-114, 1981 I.R.B. 21, Ann. 81-148, 1981-39 I.R.B. 15, and Ann. 82-128, 1982-39 I.R.B. 103, concerning Method (1) and Method (2) elections, are reproduced below.

Appendix

Announcement 81-114, 1981-28 I.R.B. 21

This announcement provides guidance relating to section 404A of the Internal Revenue Code. Until proposed regulations are published, taxpayers may rely on the guidance provided below.

Section 404A, added by the Act of December 28, 1980, Pub. L. 96-603 (1981-5 I.R.B. 31), allows taxpayers to make certain elections concerning deductions for amounts paid or accrued by an employer under qualified foreign plans. The two types of qualified foreign plans are qualified funded plans and qualified reserve plans. A qualified foreign plan is any written plan which defers the receipt of compensation and which satisfies two requirements. First, the plan must be for the exclusive benefit of the employer's employees or their beneficiaries. Second, 90 percent or more of the amounts taken into account for the taxable year under the plan must be attributable to services performed by nonresident aliens, the compensation for which is not subject to federal income tax. In addition, the employer must properly elect to have section 404A apply to such plan. If an employer does not make such an election, deductions (or reductions in earnings and profits) are allowed only as provided under section 404 for plans and trusts meeting the requirements of that section.

The rules of section 404A are applicable for taxable years beginning after December 31, 1979, and for certain prior years to the extent the taxpayer elects to have the provisions of section 404A of the Code apply retroactively. Pending the issuance of regulations relating to such elections, the elections referred to in section 404A(e)(3) and (f)(2) of the Code may be made either by (1) claiming the permissible deduction or credit on the taxpayer's income tax return for the first taxable year ending on or after December 31, 1980, including extensions (or an amended return that is filed no later than the end of the extended time period prescribed in section 6081, whether or not such time is actually extended for filing the taxpayer's return), or (2) attaching a statement of election to the taxpayer's income tax return within the time period described in the first method. If the election is made by attaching a statement of election under method (2), the taxpayer's current return would not include deductions or in the case of foreign subsidiaries, take into account reductions in earnings and profits that relate to foreign deferred compensation plans. Deductions or credits consistent with the election would be included on an amended return, to be filed no later than the deadline (described below) for revoking the election. Under either method, the taxpayer must attach to the return a list of plans with respect to which the elections are made. Method (1) or method (2) may also be used for the elections described in section 2(e) of Pub. L. 96-603. When method (2) is used in connection with section 2(e) of Pub. L. 96-603, taxpayers need not amend past returns until regulations are issued.

A taxpayer must determine the amount deductible under section 404A(d) based, in part, on the cumulative foreign amount as defined in section 404A(d)(2)(B). No deduction is allowable under section 404A unless the cumulative foreign amount is established in one of the documents described in section 404A(g)(2)(A)(i), (ii) or (iii) of the Code. Section 404A(g)(2)(A)(iii) authorizes the Secretary to promulgate regulations that would accept certain unspecified statements or evidence as being sufficient to establish the amount of the deduction under foreign law. Until such time as regulations are promulgated under section 404A(g)(2)(A)(iii), the requirements of that section will be considered to be satisfied by a statement prepared at or before the time the return is filed, which lists separately for each plan the cumulative foreign amount and which states that such cumulative foreign

amount has been determined pursuant to the requirements of the appropriate foreign tax law. The statement must be prepared by the U.S. taxpayer or a person authorized to practice before the Service. While a taxpayer need not attach any of these documents to its tax return, the taxpayer must furnish the documents for examination upon request of the Internal Revenue Service.

Taxpayers that have made the elections described in section 404A and/or section 2(e) of Pub. L. 96-603 under method (2) need not prepare the statement, described in the immediately preceding paragraph, until they amend their returns. In addition, taxpayers that have made the election described in section 404A for taxable years beginning after December 31, 1979, under Method (1), and have made the election described in section 2(e) of Pub. L. 96-603 under method (2) will satisfy section 404A(g)(2)(A)(iii) if the cumulative foreign amount in the statement reflects the aggregate foreign deductions allowed under foreign law for taxable years commencing after December 31, 1979.

Taxpayers that have already made an election, referred to in this announcement, that does not conform with the requirements stated herein may perfect that election on an amended return filed by the later of September 23, 1981 or by the due date of the taxpayer's income tax return for the first taxable year beginning after December 31, 1979, including extensions. These taxpayers may also satisfy section 404A(g)(2)(A)(iii), to the extent applicable as previously described in this announcement, by preparing the required statement within the same time limits for perfecting the elections under sections 404A(e)(3) and (f)(2).

The qualified reserve plan election, including any retroactive election described in section 2(e)(2) of Pub. L. 96-603, may be revoked on an amended return for the first taxable year ending on or after December 31, 1980, without the consent of the Commissioner until 90 days after the publication of final regulations regarding such elections. Similarly, the qualified foreign plan election and the retroactive election described in section 2(e)(3) may be revoked within the same period.

It is anticipated that the effective date of the final regulations generally will be for taxable years beginning after December 31, 1979, and such prior years as may be affected by an election under section 2(e) of Pub. L. 96-603. Accordingly, taxpayers may be required to amend their tax returns to the extent that deductions or credits claimed are inconsistent with final regulations.

Announcement 81-148, 1981-39 I.R.B. 15

On June 24, 1981, the Internal Revenue Service issued Announcement 81-114, 1981-28 I.R.B. 21. The announcement was intended to provide pre-regulation guidance to taxpayers concerning recent legislation under section 404A. Taxpayers have expressed concern with respect to a statement in that announcement, with respect to reductions of earnings and profits if section 404A is not elected. Announcement 81-114 is clarified as follows:

The decision not to elect section 404A will not affect the computation of earnings and profits with respect to contributions to plans as allowed under prior law. In the case of an accrued liability to a reserve plan, however, such accrued liability reduces earnings and profits only as provided in section 404A with respect to the taxable years described in section 2(e) of Pub. L. 96-603, 1980-2 C.B. 684.

Announcement 82-128, 1982-39 I.R.B. 103

Taxpayers that are interested in making the elections referred to in section 404A(e)(3) and (f)(2) of the Internal Revenue Code may continue to use the "method (1)" or "method (2)" election described in Announcement 81-114, 1981-28 I.R.B. 21 for taxable years beginning after December 31, 1979, until further guidance is made available. Pending the issuance of regulations under section 404A, qualified foreign plans must comply with the reporting requirements and other rules contained in Announcement 81-114.

Effective dates

The amendments are proposed generally to apply to taxable years beginning after December 31, 1979. The prohibited transaction rules in § 1.404A-2(a) are proposed to be effective May 6, 1993. If a taxpayer elected pursuant to section 2(e)(2) of the Act of December 28, 1980, the amendments are proposed to apply to certain prior taxable years beginning after December 31, 1970.

Special Analyses

It has been determined that these proposed rules are not major rules as defined in Executive Order 12291. Therefore, a Regulatory Impact Analysis is not required. It has also been determined that section 553(b) of the Administrative Procedure Act (5 U.S.C. chapter 5) and the Regulatory Flexibility Act (5 U.S.C. chapter 6) do not apply to these proposed regulations and, therefore, an initial Regulatory Flexibility Analysis is not required. Pursuant to section 7805(f) of the Internal Revenue Code, these proposed regulations will be submitted to the Chief Counsel for Advocacy of the Small Business Administration for comment on their impact on small business.

Comments and Requests to Appear at the Public Hearing

Before adopting these proposed regulations, consideration will be given to any written comments that are submitted (preferably a signed original and eight copies) to the Commissioner of Internal Revenue. All comments will be available for public inspection and copying in their entirety. Because the Treasury Department expects to issue final regulations on this matter as soon as possible, a public hearing will be held at 10:00 a.m. on October 5, 1993, in Room 2615, Internal Revenue Building, 1111 Constitution Ave., N.W., Washington, D.C. Written comments must be received by July 6, 1993. Requests to speak (with outlines of oral comments) at the public hearing must be received by September 14, 1993. See notice of hearing published elsewhere in this issue of the Federal Register.

Drafting Information

The principal author of these proposed regulations is Elizabeth A. Purcell of the Office of the Associate Chief Counsel (Employee Benefits and Exempt Organizations), Internal Revenue Service. However, personnel from other offices of the Service and Treasury Department participated in their development.

List of Subjects in 26 CFR 1.401-0 Through 1.419A-2T

Bonds, Employee benefit plans, Income taxes, Pensions, Reporting and recordkeeping requirements, Securities, Trusts and trustees.

Withdrawal of Proposed Amendments

The proposed amendments to 26 CFR part 1, relating to §§ 1.404A-0, 1.404A-1, 1.404A-2, 1.404A-3, 1.404A-4, 1.404A-5 and 1.404A-6, published in the **Federal Register** for April 8, 1985 (50 FR 13821), are withdrawn.

Proposed Amendments to the Regulations

Accordingly, the proposed amendments to 26 CFR part 1 are added to read as follows:

PART 1—INCOME TAX; TAXABLE YEARS BEGINNING AFTER DECEMBER 31, 1953

Paragraph 1. The authority citation for part 1 is amended by adding the following citations to read as follows:

Authority: 26 U.S.C. 7805 * * * §§ 1.404A-1, 1.404A-2, 1.404A-3, 1.404A-4, 1.404A-5, 1.404A-6 and 1.404A-7 also issued under 26 U.S.C. 404A. * * *

Par. 2. Sections 1.404A-0 through 1.404A-7 are added as follows:

§ 1.404A-0. Table of Contents, EE-14-81, 5/6/93.

This section 1.404A-0 lists the major headings that appear in §§ 1.404A-1 through 1.404A-7.

§ 1.404A-1 General rules concerning deductions and adjustments to earnings and profits for foreign deferred compensation plans.

(a) In general.

(b) 90-percent test.

(1) Reserve plans.

(2) Funded plans.

(c) Calculation of 90 percent amounts.

(1) In general.

(2) Safe harbor.

(3) Anti-abuse rule.

(4) Example.

(d) Deductions and reductions of earnings and profits.

(e) Definitions.

Actuarial present value.

Aggregate amount.

Appropriate foreign tax law.

Authorized officer.

Carryover contributions.

Change in method of accounting.

Closing year.

Contributions accumulated to pay deferred compensation.

Contributions to a trust.

Controlled foreign corporation.

Cumulative foreign amount.

Cumulative limitation.

Cumulative United States amount.

Deductible limit

Deductions.

Deferred compensation

Earnings and profits.

Employer.

Equivalent of a trust.

Erroneous deduction.

Exclusive benefit.

Fixed or determinable benefits.

Full funding limitation.

Functional currency.

Funded method.

Initial aggregate amount.

Initial Cumulative foreign amount.

Initial Cumulative United States amount.

Initial section 404A(d) amounts.

Liability.

Majority domestic corporate shareholders.

Method of accounting.

Method (1) election.

Method (2) election.

New Method Opening Amount.

Noncontrolled foreign corporation.

Nonqualified individual.

Nonqualified plan.

Old Method Closing Amount.

Open period.

Open years.

Opening reserve.

Opening year.

Pay-as-you-go method.

Period of adjustment.

Permitted plan year.

Plan year.

Primary evidence.

Prior deduction.

Protective election.

Qualified business unit.

Qualified foreign plan.

Qualified funded plan.

Qualified reserve plan.

Reasonable actuarial assumptions.

Reductions in earnings and profits.

Reserve method.

Retirement annuity.

Retroactive effective date election.

Retroactive period

Retroactive plan-by-plan election.

Revocation of election.

Secondary evidence.

Separate funding entity.

Short taxable year.

Single plan.

Substantial risk of forfeiture.

Substantiation quality data.

Taxable year of a controlled foreign corporation.

Taxable year of a noncontrolled foreign corporation.

Taxpayer.

Termination of election.

Transition period.

Trust.

Unit credit method.

United States tax significance.

Written plan.

(f) Application of other Code requirements.

(1) Deductibility requirement.

(2) Section 461 requirements.

1.404A-2 Rules for qualified funded plans.

(a) In general.

(b) Payment to a trust.

(1) Contribution requirements.

(2) Trust requirements.

(3) Retirement annuity.

(4) Effect of reversion of overfunded contributions.

(5) Example.

(c) Contribution deemed made before payment.

(1) Time of payment to trust.

(2) Time of designation.

(3) Irrevocable designation.

(d) Limitation for qualified funded plans.

(1) Plans with fixed or determinable benefits.

(2) Plans without fixed or determinable benefits.

(3) Limitations where more than one type of plan is maintained.

(4) Carryover contributions.

(5) Additional rules.

(e) Examples.

1.404A-3 Rules for qualified reserve plans.

(a) Amounts taken into account with respect to qualified reserve plans.

(1) General rule.

(2) Amounts less than zero.

(3) Exclusive rules for qualified reserve plans.

(b) Reasonable addition to a reserve for liabilities.

(1) General rule.

(2) Unit credit method required.

(3) Timing of valuation.

(4) Permissible actuarial assumptions.

(c) Ten-year amortization for certain changes in reserves.

(1) Actuarial valuation.

(2) Expected value of reserve.

(3) Special rule for certain cost of living adjustments.

(4) Anti-abuse rule.

(d) Examples.

1.404A-4 United States and foreign law limitations on amounts taken into account for qualified foreign plans.

(a) In general.

(b) Cumulative limitation.

(c) Special rule for foreign corporations in pre-pooling years.

(d) Rules relating to foreign currency.

(1) Taxable years beginning after December 31, 1986.

(2) Taxable years beginning before January 1, 1987.

(3) Special rules for the net worth method of accounting.

(e) Maintenance of more than one type of qualified foreign plan by an employer.

(f) United States and foreign law limitations not applicable.

(g) Definitions.

(1) Cumulative United States amount.

(2) Cumulative foreign amount.

(3) Appropriate foreign tax law.

(4) Aggregate amount.

(h) Examples.

1.404A-5 Additional limitations on amounts taken into account for qualified foreign plans.

(a) Restrictions for nonqualified individuals.

(1) General rule.

(2) Determination of service attribution.

(b) Records to be provided by taxpayer.

(1) In general.

(2) Primary evidence.

(3) Additional requirements.

(4) Secondary evidence.

(5) Foreign language.

(6) Additional information required by District Director.

(7) Authorized officer to complete documents.

(8) Transitional rules.

(c) Actuarial requirements.

(1) Reasonable actuarial assumptions.

(2) Full funding limitation.

1.404A-6 Elections under section 404A and changes in methods of accounting.

(a) Elections, changes in accounting methods, and changes in plan years.

(1) In general.

(2) Single plan.

(b) Initial elections under section 404A.

(1) In general.

(2) Time for making election.

(3) Manner in which election is to be made.

(4) Other requirements for election.

(c) Termination of election when a plan ceases to be a qualified foreign plan.

(1) In general.

(2) Rules for changing method of accounting upon termination of election.

(d) Other changes in methods of accounting and changes in plan year.

(1) Application for consent.

(2) Procedures for other changes in method of accounting.

(3) Plan year.

(e) Application of section 481.

(1) In general.

[Reg. § 1.404A-0.]

§ 1.404A-1. *General rules concerning deductions and adjustments to earnings and profits for foreign deferred compensation plans*, EE-14-81, 5/6/93.

(a) *In general.* Section 404A provides the exclusive means by which an employer may take a deduction or reduce earnings and profits for deferred compensation in situations other than those in which a deduction or reduction of earnings and profits is permitted under section 404. A deduction or reduction of earnings and profits is permitted under section 404A for amounts paid or accrued by an employer under a foreign deferred compensation plan, in the taxable year in which the amounts are properly taken into account under §§ 1.404A-1 through 1.404A-7, if each of the following requirements is satisfied:

(1) The plan is a written plan maintained by the employer that provides deferred compensation.

(2) The plan is maintained for the exclusive benefit of the employer's employees or their beneficiaries.

(3) 90 percent or more of the amounts taken into account under the plan are attributable to services performed by nonresident aliens, the compensation for which is not subject to United States federal income tax.

(4) An election under § 1.404A-6 or 1.404A-7 is made to treat the plan as either a qualified funded plan or a qualified reserve plan and to select a plan year.

(b) *90-percent test*—(1) *Reserve plans.* Paragraph (a)(3) of this section is not satisfied by a reserve plan unless 90 percent or more of the actuarial present value of the total vested benefits (i.e., benefits not subject to substantial risk of forfeiture) accrued under the plan is attributable to services performed by nonresident aliens, the compensation for which is not subject to United States federal income tax.

(2) *Funded plans*—(i) *Individual account plans.* Paragraph (a)(3) of this section is not satisfied by a funded plan with individual accounts unless 90 percent or more of the amounts allocated to individual accounts (as described in section 414(i)) under the plan are allocated to the accounts of nonresident aliens and are attributable to services the compensation for which is not subject to United States federal income tax.

(ii) *Plans without individual accounts.* Paragraph (a)(3) of this section is not satisfied by a funded plan not described in paragraph (b)(2)(i) of this section unless 90 percent or more of the actuarial present value of the total benefits accrued under the plan is attributable to services performed by nonresident aliens the compensation for which is not subject to United States federal income tax.

(c) *Calculation of 90 percent amounts*—(1) *In general.* In determining whether the tests described in paragraphs (b)(1) and (b)(2)(ii) of this section are satisfied, accrued benefits and the actuarial present values of accrued benefits may be calculated under any reasonable method. See § 1.404A-5(a) for rules describing the calculation of accrued benefits attributable to services for which the compensation is subject to United States federal income tax.

(2) *Safe harbor.* The requirement of paragraph (a)(3) of this section will be deemed satisfied with respect to a plan if—

(i) The participants' benefits under the plan increase generally in proportion to their compensation taken into account under the plan; and

(ii) The sum of the following amounts does not exceed five percent of all compensation taken into account under the plan for the plan year—

(A) The compensation of United States citizens and residents taken into account under the plan; and

(B) Any other compensation subject to United States federal income tax taken into account under the plan.

(3) *Anti-abuse rule.* Notwithstanding paragraph (c)(2) of this section, the requirement of paragraph (a)(3) of this section will not be deemed satisfied under paragraph (c)(2) of this section if the Commissioner determines that a significant purpose of the plan is to secure benefits not otherwise eligible for tax benefits under the Internal Revenue Code to participants who are United States citizens or residents.

(4) *Example.* The principles of paragraphs (c)(2) and (c)(3) of this section are illustrated by the following example:

Example. A foreign branch of a domestic corporation maintains a deferred compensation plan under which benefits are based upon a participant's average compensation for the last five consecutive years of employment. The significant purposes of the plan do not include the provision of benefits otherwise unavailable under the Code to participants who are United States citizens or residents. The foreign branch maintains its books and records in its functional currency (FC). The taxpayer's taxable year and the plan year are coterminous with the calendar year. During the plan year in question, the compensation taken into account under the plan for all plan participants totals FC200 million. Of the FC200 million, FC6 million of the compensation taken into account under the plan is compensation for United States citizens and residents or otherwise subject to United States federal income tax. Because the FC6 million is less than five percent of all compensation taken into account under the plan for the plan year, the 90-percent requirement of paragraph (a)(3) of this section is deemed satisfied for this taxable year.

(d) *Deductions and reductions of earnings and profits.* Deductions and reductions of earnings and profits for amounts paid by an employer to a plan that provides deferred compensation that does not meet the requirements of paragraph (a) of this section are governed exclusively by section 404, without regard to whether the plan benefits foreign employees.

(e) *Definitions.* The following definitions apply for purposes of section 404A and §§ 1.404A-1 through 1.404A-7:

Actuarial present value. "Actuarial present value" is defined in § 1.401(a)(4)-12.

Aggregate amount. "Aggregate amount" is defined in § 1.404A-4(g)(4).

Appropriate foreign tax law. "Appropriate foreign tax law" is defined in § 1.404A-4(g)(3).

Authorized officer. "Authorized officer" is defined in § 1.404A-5(b)(7).

Carryover contributions. "Carryover contributions" are defined in § 1.404A-2(d)(4).

Change in method of accounting. "Change in method of accounting" is defined in § 1.404A-6(a).

Closing year. "Closing year" is defined in § 1.404A-6(f)(4)(ii).

Contributions accumulated to pay deferred compensation. "Contributions accumulated to pay deferred compensation" are defined in § 1.404A-2(b)(2).

Contributions to a trust. "Contributions to a trust" are defined in § 1.404A-2(b)(1).

Controlled foreign corporation. "Controlled foreign corporation" means a controlled foreign corporation as defined in sections 953(c)(1)(B) and 957.

Cumulative foreign amount. "Cumulative foreign amount" is defined in § 1.404A-4(g)(2).

Cumulative limitation. "Cumulative limitation" is defined in § 1.404A-4(b).

Cumulative United States amount. "Cumulative United States amount" is defined in § 1.404A-4(g)(1).

Deductible limit. "Deductible limit" is defined in § 1.404A-2(d)(1)(i).

Deductions. "Deductions" are defined in § 1.404A-1(f)(1).

Deferred compensation—(i) In general. "Deferred compensation" means any item the deductibility of which is determined by reference to section 404, without regard to whether section 404 permits a deduction and without regard to whether elections are made under § 1.404A-6 or 1.404A-7. Deferred compensation, as described in the preceding sentence, does not include deferred benefits described in section 404(b)(2)(B).

(ii) *Social security.* A plan under which a foreign government (including a political subdivision, agency or instrumentality thereof) makes a contribution or a direct payment to a participant (or the participant's beneficiary) does not provide deferred compensation to the extent of such contributions or payments. Thus, for example, a foreign country's social security system generally will not be considered as providing deferred compensation. However, the fact that employers are required to maintain the plan by reason of foreign law, or the fact that the plan supplements social security benefits provided by a foreign country, or provides benefits in lieu of such social security benefits, does not prevent a plan from providing deferred compensation.

(iii) *Termination indemnity plans.* The determination of whether a plan (including a termination indemnity plan) provides deferred compensation must generally be made under paragraph (i) of this definition in light of all of the facts and circumstances. Benefits paid under a plan, including a plan denominated a termination indemnity plan will generally be treated as deferred compensation if—

(A) A major purpose of the plan is to provide for the payment of retirement benefits;

(B) The plan has a benefit formula providing for payment based at least in part upon length of service;

(C) The plan provides for the payment of benefits to employees (or their beneficiaries) after the employee's retirement, death or other termination of employment; and

(D) It meets such other requirements as may be prescribed by the Commissioner in guidance of general applicability with respect to termination indemnity plans.

(iv) *Example.* The definition of deferred compensation is illustrated by the following example:

Example. A domestic corporation maintains a branch operation in foreign country *F. F* requires that all employers doing business in its country provide benefits to employees under a termination indemnity plan insured by *F*'s government. The plan provides for payments to employees who terminate employment for any reason, including retirement, death, voluntary resignation and discharge for cause (other than for gross misconduct) and permits withdrawals for certain hardship conditions. Upon separation, the employee (or his or her beneficiary) receives an amount equal to the accumulation on the employer's books of one-thirteenth of his or her annual salary for each year of employment, with specified adjustments for interest and inflation. This termination indemnity plan provides deferred compensation as described in paragraph (e) of this section.

Earnings and profits. "Earnings and profits" means earnings and profits computed in accordance with sections 312 and 964(a) and, for taxable years beginning after December 31, 1986, section 986 and the regulations thereunder; and for purposes of section 902 in taxable years beginning before January 1, 1987, accumulated profits within the meaning of section 902(c) as in effect on the day before the enactment of the Tax Reform Act of 1986.

Employer. "Employer" means a person that maintains a plan for the payment of deferred compensation for services provided to it by its employees. "Employer" for purposes of the acceleration of the section 481(a) adjustment is defined in § 1.404A-6(e)(2)(iv).

Equivalent of a trust. "Equivalent of a trust" means a fund—

(i) The corpus and income of which is separately identifiable and segregated, through a separate legal entity, from the general assets of the employer;

(ii) The corpus and income of which is not subject, under the applicable foreign law, to the claims of the employer's creditors prior to the claims of employees and their beneficiaries under the plan;

(iii) The corpus and income of which, by law or by contract, cannot at any time prior to the satisfaction of all liabilities with respect to employees under the plan be used for, or diverted to, any purpose other than providing benefits under the plan; and

(iv) The corpus and income of which is held by a person who has a legally enforceable duty to operate the fund prudently.

Erroneous deduction. "Erroneous deduction" is defined in § 1.404A-7(d)(3)(ii).

Exclusive benefit. "Exclusive benefit" has the same meaning as in §§ 1.401-2 and 1.413-1(d).

Fixed or determinable benefits. "Fixed or determinable benefits" are defined in § 1.404A-2(d)(1)(i).

Full funding limitation. "Full funding limitation" is defined in § 1.404A-5(c)(2).

Functional currency. "Functional currency" (abbreviated as FC) means the functional currency of a taxpayer or a qualified business unit determined in accordance with section 985(b) and the regulations thereunder, or, for taxable years beginning before January 1, 1987, the currency in which the employer's books and records were maintained for United States tax purposes.

Funded method. "Funded method" is defined in § 1.404A-6(f)(2)(iv).

Initial aggregate amount. "Initial aggregate amount" is defined in § 1.404A-6(g)(2)(iii).

Initial Cumulative foreign amount. "Initial Cumulative foreign amount" is defined in § 1.404A-6(g)(2)(ii).

Initial Cumulative United States amount. "Initial Cumulative United States amount" is defined in § 1.404A-6(g)(2)(i).

Initial section 404A(d) amounts. "Initial section 404A(d) amounts" are defined in § 1.404A-6(g).

Liability. "Liability" is defined in § 1.404A-1 (f) (2).

Majority domestic corporate shareholders. "Majority domestic corporate shareholders" are defined in § 1.404A-6 (c) (2) (ii) (C).

Method of accounting. "Method of accounting" is defined in § 1.404A-6 (a) (1).

Method (1) election. "Method (1) election" is defined in § 1.404A-7 (g) (1).

Method (2) election. "Method (2) election" is defined in § 1.404A-7 (g) (2).

New Method Opening Amount. "New Method Opening Amount" is defined in § 1.404A-6 (f) (3).

Noncontrolled foreign corporation. "Noncontrolled foreign corporation" means a foreign corporation other than a controlled foreign corporation.

Nonqualified individual. "Nonqualified individual" is defined in § 1.404A-5 (a) (1).

Nonqualified plan. "Nonqualified plan" is defined in § 1.404A-6 (f) (3) (iii).

Old Method Closing Amount. "Old Method Closing Amount" is defined in § 1.404A-6 (f) (2).

Open period. "Open period" is defined in § 1.404A-7 (g) (6).

Open years. "Open years" are defined in § 1.404A-7 (g) (3).

Opening reserve. "Opening reserve" is defined in § 1.404A-6 (f) (3) (i).

Opening year. "Opening year" is defined in § 1.404A-6 (f) (4) (i).

Pay-as-you-go method. "Pay-as-you-go method" is defined in § 1.404A-6 (f) (2) (iii).

Period of adjustment. "Period of adjustment" is defined in § 1.404A-6 (e) (2).

Permitted plan year. "Permitted plan year" means the plan year of a plan providing deferred compensation ending with or within the employer's taxable year.

Plan year. "Plan year" means the annual accounting period of a plan providing deferred compensation.

Primary evidence. "Primary evidence" is defined in § 1.404A-5 (b) (2).

Prior deduction. "Prior deduction" is defined in § 1.404A-7 (d) (3) (i).

Protective election. "Protective election" is defined in § 1.404A-7 (g) (2).

Qualified business unit. "Qualified business unit" is defined in section 989 (a).

Qualified foreign plan. "Qualified foreign plan" means a plan that meets the requirements of paragraph (a) of this section.

Qualified funded plan. "Qualified funded plan" means a qualified foreign plan for which an election has been made under § 1.404A-6 or 1.404A-7 by the taxpayer to treat the plan as a qualified funded plan.

Qualified reserve plan. "Qualified reserve plan" means a qualified foreign plan for which an election has been made by the taxpayer under § 1.404A-6 or 1.404A-7 to treat the plan as a qualified reserve plan.

Reasonable actuarial assumptions. "Reasonable actuarial assumptions" are defined in § 1.404A-5 (c).

Reductions in earnings and profits. "Reductions in earnings and profits" are defined in § 1.404A-1 (f) (1).

Reserve method. "Reserve method" is defined in § 1.404A-6 (f) (2) (ii).

Retirement annuity. "Retirement annuity" is defined in § 1.404A-2 (b) (3).

Retroactive effective date election. "Retroactive effective date election" is defined in § 1.404A-7 (b) (1).

Retroactive period. "Retroactive period" is defined in § 1.404A-7 (g) (4).

Retroactive plan-by-plan election. "Retroactive plan-by-plan election" is defined in § 1.404A-7 (c) (1) and (d) (1).

Revocation of election. "Revocation of election" is defined in § 1.404A-6 (d) (1).

Secondary evidence. "Secondary evidence" is defined in § 1.404A-5 (b) (4).

Separate funding entity. "Separate funding entity" is defined in § 1.404A-6 (f) (4) (iii).

Short taxable year. "Short taxable year" is defined in § 1.404A-7 (d) (2).

Single plan. "Single plan" is defined in § 1.404A-6 (a) (2).

Substantial risk of forfeiture. "Substantial risk of forfeiture" is defined in § 1.404A-3 (b) (2).

Substantiation quality data. "Substantiation quality data" means less than precise data that is nevertheless the best data available for the plan year at reasonable expense.

Taxable year of a controlled foreign corporation. "Taxable year of a controlled foreign corporation" means the taxable year as defined in sections 441 (b) and 7701 (a) (23), subject to section 898.

Taxable year of a noncontrolled foreign corporation. "Taxable year of a noncontrolled foreign corporation" means the taxable year as defined in sections 441 (b) and 7701 (a) (23).

Taxpayer. "Taxpayer" is defined in section 7701 (a) (14).

Termination of election. "Termination of election" is defined in § 1.404A-6 (c) (1).

Transition period. "Transition period" is defined in § 1.404A-7 (g) (5).

Trust. "Trust" means a trust (as defined in § 301.7701-4 (a) of this chapter) or the equivalent of a trust.

Unit credit method. "Unit credit method" is defined in § 1.404A-3 (b) (2).

United States tax significance. "United States tax significance" is defined in § 1.404A-6 (b) (2) (ii).

Written plan. "Written plan" means a plan that is defined by plan instruments or required under the law of a foreign country, or both. An insurance contract can constitute a written plan.

(f) *Application of other Code requirements*—(1) *Deductibility requirement*—(i) *In general.* In order to deduct amounts under section 404A, amounts contributed to a qualified funded plan or properly added to a reserve with respect to a qualified reserve plan must otherwise be deductible. The standards under section 404 are to be used in determining whether an amount would otherwise be deductible for this purpose. Thus, amounts may be taken into account under section 404A only to the extent that they are ordinary and necessary expenses during the taxable year in carrying on a trade or business and are compensation for personal services actually rendered before the end of the year. Similarly, in order to reduce earnings and profits under section 404A by amounts contributed to a qualified funded plan or properly added to a reserve with respect to a qualified reserve plan, earnings and profits must otherwise be able to be reduced by such amounts under the general principles of sections 312, 901, 902, 960, and 964.

(ii) *Capitalization requirements.* In determining if an amount would otherwise be deductible (or able to be used to reduce earnings and profits) for purposes of paragraph (g) (1) (i) of this section, the fact that the amount is required to be capitalized (e.g., under section 263A) is ignored. Additionally, while section 404A and §§ 1.404A-1 through 1.404A-7 refer generally to permissible deductions or reductions of earnings and profits for deferred compensation, those references are intended to refer both to situations under which amounts may be taken into account as deductions or reductions of earnings and profits and to situations under which amounts may be taken into account through inclusion in the basis of inventory or through capitalization.

(2) *Section 461 requirements.* In determining whether any amount of deferred compensation may be taken into account under section 404A by an accrual method taxpayer, the conditions for accrual under section 461 must be met with respect to the amount by the last day of the taxable year. For this purpose, an amount determined under §§ 1.404A-1 through 1.404A-7 establishes the fact of the liability and determines the amount of the liability with reasonable accuracy. See § 1.461-4 (d) (2) (iii), which generally provides that the economic performance requirement of section 461 (h) is satisfied to the extent that any amount is otherwise properly taken into account under §§ 1.404A-1 through 1.404A-7. [Reg. § 1.404A-1.]

§ 1.404A-2. *Rules for qualified funded plans,* EE-14-81, 5/6/93.

(a) *In general.* Except as provided in this section and in §§ 1.404A-4 and 1.404A-5, the amount taken into account for a taxable year with respect to a qualified funded plan is the amount of the contributions paid by the employer to the trust in that year (regardless of whether the employer uses an accrual method of accounting). Accretions in a trust are not considered contributions to a plan.

(b) *Payment to a trust*—(1) *Contribution requirements.* Contributions paid under a qualified funded plan may not be taken into account unless they are—

(i) Paid to a trust which is operated in accordance with the requirements of section 401(a)(2);

(ii) Paid for a retirement annuity under which retirement benefits are provided and which is for the exclusive benefit of the employer's employees or their beneficiaries; or

(iii) Paid directly to a participant or beneficiary (rather than a trust).

(2) *Trust requirements—(i) General rule.* A contribution does not satisfy paragraph (b)(1)(i) of this section unless it is accumulated in the trust for the purpose of being distributed as deferred compensation. Whether a contribution is being accumulated in the trust for the purpose of being distributed as deferred compensation depends on the facts and circumstances. For purposes of paragraph (b)(1)(i) of this section, the fact that a trust has been (or has not been) involved in transactions that would be described in section 4975(c)(1) (and not exempted under section 4975(c)(2) or 4975(d)), e.g., contributions made in the form of a promissory note, if the plan were subject to section 4975(c)(1), is an important factor in determining whether the trust is not (or is) considered to be operated in accordance with the requirements of section 401(a)(2). In addition, a contribution to a trust does not satisfy paragraph (b)(1)(i) of this section unless it has substance.

(ii) *Effective date.* The section 4975(c)(1) factor in determining compliance with section 401(a)(2) provided in this paragraph (b)(2) is taken into account for all transactions entered into after May 6, 1993.

(3) *Retirement annuity.* A retirement annuity means a retirement annuity (as defined in section 404(a)(2)) except that the retirement annuity need not be part of a plan that meets the requirements of section 401(a) or 401(d). Notwithstanding the preceding sentence, the retirement annuity described therein need not be issued by an insurance company qualified to do business in a State in the United States if the taxpayer(s) and/or sponsoring employer(s) of the plan have shifted the risk of making payments under the plan to an entity that is qualified to do business in the country (or countries) where the plan is maintained.

(4) *Effect of reversion of overfunded contributions.* If any portion of a contribution to a trust may revert to the benefit of the employer before the satisfaction of all liabilities to employees or their beneficiaries covered by the trust, no amount of the contribution may be taken into account under this section.

(5) *Example.* The principles of paragraph (b) of this section are illustrated by the following example:

Example. A foreign subsidiary of a domestic corporation maintains a deferred compensation plan for its employees. The foreign subsidiary makes annual contributions under the plan to a trust. Each year after the contribution is made to the trust, the trustee lends the contribution back to the foreign subsidiary maintaining the plan. The foreign subsidiary executes promissory notes obligating it to repay the borrowed funds (at a reasonable rate of interest) to the trust and to pay any benefits due under the plan. Notwithstanding that the taxpayer may have designated the plan as a qualified funded plan, amounts may not be taken into account under section 404A with respect to contributions to the trust because the loans cause the trust to fail the requirements of section 401(a)(2). Even if the loans do not cause the trust to violate section 401(a)(2), the portion of any contribution that is loaned to the foreign subsidiary could not be taken into account because, to the extent of the loan (or loans), the contribution lacks substance and is not accumulated in the trust.

(c) *Contribution deemed made before payment—(1) Time of payment to trust.* Regardless of whether an employer uses the cash or an accrual method of accounting, for purposes of this section, a contribution to a trust that is paid after the close of an employer's taxable year is deemed to have been paid on the last day of that taxable year if—

(i) The payment is made on account of the taxable year and is made not later than the 15th day of the ninth month after the close of the taxable year;

(ii) The payment is treated by the plan in the same manner that the plan would treat a payment actually received on the last day of the taxable year; and

(iii) Either—

(A) The employer notifies the plan administrator or trustee in writing that the payment to the plan is designated on account of the taxable year;

(B) The taxpayer claims the payment as a deduction on its tax return for the taxable year; or

(C) The employer reduces earnings and profits with respect to the payment.

(2) *Time of designation.* Any designation of a payment pursuant to paragraph (c)(1)(iii)(A) of this section must occur not later than the time described in paragraph (c)(1)(i) of this section.

(3) *Irrevocable designation.* After a payment has been designated or claimed on a return in the manner provided in paragraph (c)(1)(iii)(A) of this section as being on account of a taxable year, the designation or claim may not be retracted or changed.

(d) *Limitation for qualified funded plans—(1) Plans with fixed or determinable benefits—(i) Limit on amount taken into account.* Contributions made to a qualified funded plan under which the benefits are fixed or determinable are not taken into account under this section to the extent they exceed the amount that would be taken into account under section 404(a)(1)(A)(ii) and (iii) (determined without regard to the last sentence of paragraph (A) of section 404(a)(1) and without regard to whether the trust is exempt under section 501(a)). Benefits are considered fixed or determinable for this purpose if either benefits under or contributions to the plan are definitely determinable within the meaning of § 1.401-1(b)(1)(i). The limit described in the first sentence of this paragraph (d)(1)(i) is determined on the basis of the permitted plan year of the qualified foreign plan. Thus, the limit for the employer's taxable year is the limit for the plan year ending with or within the employer's taxable year.

(ii) *Actuarial valuation requirements.* In determining the amount to be taken into account under this section, an actuarial valuation must be made not less frequently than once every three years. However, an actuarial valuation must be made for the first plan year of the plan for which an election under § 1.404A-6 is in effect. For interim years, a reasonable actuarial determination of whether the full funding limit in § 1.404A-5(c)(2) applies to the qualified funded plan must be made. The Commissioner may require a full actuarial valuation in an interim year under appropriate circumstances. See § 1.404A-6 for rules on changes in methods of accounting.

(2) *Plans without fixed or determinable benefits.* Contributions made to a qualified funded plan under which the benefits are not fixed or determinable may not be taken into account under this section to the extent they exceed the limitations of section 404(a)(3) (determined without regard to whether the payment is made to a trust that is exempt under section 501(a)).

(3) *Limitations where more than one type of plan is maintained.* Where payments are made for a taxable year to more than one type of qualified funded plan, the amounts that may be taken into account for the taxable year with respect to the payments are subject to the limitations of section 404(a)(7). The amount that is taken into account under this paragraph (d)(3) is determined without regard to whether the payment satisfies the minimum funding standard described in section 412.

(4) *Carryover contributions.* In the event that the aggregate amount of contributions paid during an employer's taxable year in which an election under section 404A is in effect (reduced by an amount described in section 404A(g)(1)) exceeds the amount that may be taken into account under section 404A(a) and this section (computed without regard to section 404A(d) and § 1.404A-4), the excess contributions are treated as an amount paid in the succeeding taxable year with respect to that qualified foreign plan. A carryover contribution is also taken into account in determining whether a carryover contribution exists for a succeeding taxable year.

(5) *Additional rules.* The Commissioner may prescribe additional rules for determining the amount that may be taken into account under this paragraph (d) in guidance of general applicability.

(e) *Examples.* The principles of this section are illustrated by the following examples:

Example 1. A qualified funded plan under which benefits are not fixed or determinable is maintained by a foreign branch of a domestic corporation. The foreign branch computes its income in units of local currency, the FC. The taxpayer's taxable year and the plan year are coterminous with the calendar year. The plan was established in 1985, and the taxpayer made an election to apply section 404A, a qualified funded plan election as described in § 1.404A-6. For the 1985 taxable year, the employer made a FC25,000 contribution under the plan, and FC15,000 of that contribution could be taken into account under paragraph (d)(2) of this section. The cumulative foreign amount for the 1985 taxable year was FC20,000. The amount of the excess contribution carried forward was FC10,000 (FC25,000–FC15,000), because the amount of the carryover contribution is determined without regard to section 404A(d) and § 1.404A-4.

Example 2. Assume the same facts as in *Example 1*, except that the entire FC25,000 contribution made under the plan may be taken into account under paragraph (d)(2) of this section. The amount of the excess contribution carried forward was zero, even though the cumulative United States amount may have exceeded the cumulative foreign amount for the taxable year, because the amount of the excess contribution is determined without regard to section 404A(d) and § 1.404A-4.

Example 3. P, a domestic corporation, owns all of the one class of stock of foreign corporation S. The taxable year for P is the calendar year. The taxable year for S is the fiscal year beginning on June 1. S made a contribution to its qualified funded plan on February 15, 1983, and notified the plan's trustee in writing that S designated the contribution as a payment on account of S's preceding taxable year (ending May 31, 1982). The contribution is taken into account in computing S's earnings and profits for S's taxable year ending May 31, 1982.

[Reg. § 1.404A-2.]

§ 1.404A-3. *Rules for qualified reserve plans*, EE-14-81, 5/6/93.

(a) *Amounts taken into account with respect to qualified reserve plans*—(1) *General rule.* Except as provided in §§ 1.404A-4 and 1.404A-5, the amount taken into account for a taxable year with respect to a qualified reserve plan equals the sum of—

(i) The reasonable addition during the permitted plan year to a reserve for liabilities under the plan as described in paragraph (b) of this section; and

(ii) The amortization of certain increases or decreases in the plan reserve over ten years, as described in paragraph (c) of this section.

(2) *Amounts less than zero.* If the amount to be taken into account under this section is less than zero, that amount must be treated as an increase in income and earnings and profits for the taxable year.

(3) *Exclusive rules for qualified reserve plans.* No amounts may be taken into account with respect to a qualified reserve plan except as provided for in this section. Thus, for example, no deduction is allowed for benefit payments from the reserve. Similarly, no amount may be taken into account for any payments made by the employer that are used either to reinsure the liabilities or benefits under a qualified reserve plan or to fund separately all or a portion of the benefits under a qualified reserve plan. These amounts may, however, be taken into account as contributions to a qualified funded plan to the extent the requirements of § 1.404A-2 are satisfied.

(b) *Reasonable addition to a reserve for liabilities*—(1) *General rule.* Except as provided in § 1.404A-7(f)(2), the reasonable addition to a reserve for a plan year equals the increase in the reserve, determined under the unit credit method as described in paragraph (b)(2) of this section, that arises from the passage of time and from additional service and expected changes in compensation in the current plan year for employees who were included in the reserve as of the end of the prior plan year. Thus, the reasonable addition to the reserve includes an element of interest on the reserve as of the beginning of the plan year (less the interest on the benefit payments during the plan year) and the actuarial present value of the expected increase in vested benefits accrued during the current plan year for employees who were included in the reserve as of the end of the prior plan year, determined without reference to any plan amendment during the plan year.

(2) *Unit credit method required.* The reserve for the employer's liability must be determined under the unit credit method. Thus, the reserve must be the actuarial present value of the employer's liability, taking into account service and compensation only through the valuation date. In determining the reserve under this section, benefits that are subject to a substantial risk of forfeiture may not be taken into account. The term "substantial risk of forfeiture" has the meaning stated in section 83, except that the term "property" in all events includes benefits accrued under a qualified reserve plan.

(3) *Timing of valuation.* The determination of the reserve and the reasonable addition to the reserve must be made as of the last day of the plan year.

(4) *Permissible actuarial assumptions*—(i) *Interest rates*—(A) *In general.* Notwithstanding any other provision of §§ 1.404A-1 through 1.404A-7, no amount may be taken into account under section 404A with respect to a qualified reserve plan unless the rate (or rates) of interest for the plan that are selected by the employer are within the permissible range. The interest rate selected by the employer for the plan under this paragraph must remain in effect for that plan until the first plan year for which that rate is no longer within the permissible range. At that time, a new rate of interest must be selected by the employer from within the permissible range applicable at that time.

(B) *Permissible range.* For purposes of this paragraph (b)(4), the term "permissible range" means a rate of interest that is not more than 1.2 and not less than the product of 0.8 multiplied by the average rate of interest for the highest quality long-term corporate bonds denominated in the functional currency of the qualified business unit of the employer whose books reflect the plan's liabilities for the 15-year period ending on the last day before the beginning of the employer's taxable year. If there is no market in long-term corporate bonds denominated in the relevant functional currency, or if the qualified business unit computes its income or earnings and profits in dollars under § 1.985-3, the employer must use a rate that can be demonstrated clearly to reflect income, based on all relevant facts and circumstances, including appropriate rates of inflation and commercial practices.

(ii) *Plan benefits.* Except as otherwise provided by the Commissioner, changes in plan benefits or applicable foreign law that become effective (whether or not retroactively) in a future plan year may not be taken into account until the plan year the change is effective. Notwithstanding the above, the reserve calculation may take into account cost-of-living adjustments that are part of the employee's vested accrued benefit, using assumptions regarding cost-of-living adjustments that are consistent with the interest rate assumptions described in paragraph (b)(4)(i) of this section and the terms of the plan. Thus, for example, a cost-of-living adjustment that does not require any future service on the part of the employee and is not subject to employer discretion may be taken into account.

(c) *Ten-year amortization for certain changes in reserves*—(1) *Actuarial valuation.* Each plan year an actuarial valuation must be made as of the end of the plan year, comparing the actual reserve with the expected value of the reserve. Any difference between the actual reserve determined as of the end of the plan year and the expected value of the reserve as of that date must be amortized in level amounts of principal over ten years, beginning in the plan year of the actuarial valuation. This amortization applies regardless of whether the difference is attributable to changes in employee population, changes in plan provisions, or changes in actuarial assumptions.

(2) *Expected value of reserve.* The expected value of the reserve as of the end of the plan year is equal to the sum of the reserve as of the end of the prior plan year plus the reasonable addition to the reserve for the plan year described in paragraph (b) of this section less the benefit payments during the plan year. Thus, the expected value of the reserve is generally determined on the basis of the plan in effect and the actuarial assumptions used as of the end of the prior plan year, but, because it includes the reasonable addition to the reserve, includes the effect of expected changes in compensation, service and vesting during the current plan year.

(3) *Special rule for certain cost of living adjustments.* Notwithstanding the general rule that the increase in liability from a plan amendment is amortized over ten years, if under foreign law a shorter period for amortization is required, that shorter period shall be substituted for ten years in this paragraph (c) if the amendment is a cost of living adjustment that either—

(i) Relates primarily to retirees; or

(ii) Is for employees of a foreign corporation in a taxable year beginning before [INSERT DATE THAT IS 90 DAYS AFTER THE DATE OF PUBLICATION OF FINAL REGULATIONS IN THE FEDERAL REGISTER].

(4) *Anti-abuse rule.* The Commissioner may reclassify any item included by a taxpayer as a reasonable addition to a reserve as instead subject to amortization over ten years if the Commissioner determines that the taxpayer's classification of that item circumvents the intent of section 404A(c)(4). Thus, for example, if the Commissioner determines that the vesting provisions of the plan cause the increase in vested benefits to be unreasonably large in a single plan year, the reasonable addition under paragraph (b) of this section must be calculated without recognizing any changes in vesting for the plan year.

(d) *Examples.* The principles of this section are illustrated by the following examples:

Example 1. S, a foreign subsidiary of P, a domestic corporation, contributes funds to an irrevocable trust which is used to pay benefits provided under S's reserve plan. The trust does not satisfy the requirements of section 401(a), 404(a)(4), or 404(a)(5). The funds are not used to provide benefits in addition to those provided by the reserve plan. In 1984, the year the plan was adopted, S elected to treat the plan as a qualified reserve plan. In 1984, S also contributed an amount to the irrevocable trust. The fact that S contributed an amount to the trust has no effect on the computation of the amount that S is entitled to take into account under this section in 1984 (or in any other year). Furthermore, no additional amount may be taken into account for the amount of the contribution to the trust beyond the amount permitted to be taken into account under this section.

Example 2. (a) Employer Y hired 10,000 employees in 1980, each of whom was age 40 at the beginning of the year and earned FC10,000. The employees immediately commenced participation in the plan. The plan provided that the accrued benefit at the end of X years equaled: (X multiplied by one percent) multiplied by the highest one year's compensation. The plan vesting was 20 percent per year starting after two years of service with the employer. Under the plan, once an employee was vested in a benefit, the benefit could not be forfeited for any reason other than the death of the employee. Employees who terminate

Year	End of Year Age
1980	41
1981	42
1982	43
1983	44
1984	45

Year	Compensation for Each Employee
1980	10,000
1981	10,000
1982	10,000
1983	12,000
1984	12,000

Year	Benefit Payments
1980	0
1981	0
1982	0
1983	369
1984	6,396

(b) *Computation of amounts taken into account for 1980.* The amount taken into account for 1980 was zero because there was no reasonable addition to the reserve (i.e., no increase in the reserve on account of the passage of time, additional service or expected changes in compensation for employees who were included in the reserve at the end of the prior year) and there were no amounts that are subject to ten-year amortization under paragraph (c) of this section.

(c) *Computation of amounts taken into account for 1981.* There was no amount taken into account for 1981 for the same reason as in 1980.

(d) *Computation of amount taken into account for 1982.* The amount taken into account in 1982 was the sum of the reasonable addition to the reserve determined under paragraph (b) of this section and the amortization of certain increases in the plan reserve over ten years determined under paragraph (c) of this section. There was no reasonable addition to the reserve (i.e., no increase in the reserve on account of the passage of time, additional service or expected changes in compensation for employees who were included in the reserve at the end of the prior year) for the 1982 year because no employee was included in the reserve as of the end of 1981. There were no benefits paid during 1981. Thus, the expected value of the reserve at the end of 1982 was zero. However, the actual value of the reserve at the end of 1982 was FC733,134 (9,931 employees × 60 × 1.230380). The difference between the expected and actual values of the reserve was taken into account over ten years beginning in 1982. Thus, the total amount taken into account for 1982 was FC73,313.

(e) *Computation of amount taken into account for 1983.* Using the employee data as of the end of 1982 and the expected rate of compensation increase for 1983, each employee's accrued benefit was expected to be 420 (10,500 × 4 years × .01) as of the end of 1983. 40 percent of this accrued benefit, or 168, was expected to be vested. Thus, the expected increase in each employee's vested accrued benefit was 108 (the difference between 168 and the vested accrued benefit as of the end of the prior year (60) for those employees who were included in the reserve as of the end of the prior year). There were 9,931 employees included in the reserve as of the end of the prior year and 9,931 × p $_{43}$ were expected to be in the reserve as of the end of 1983. The actuarial present value factor for a deferred annuity of FC1 commencing at age 65 payable monthly is 1.332564. Thus, the actuarial present value of the expected increase in vested accrued benefits as of the end of the year was FC1,425,212 (9,931 employees × p $_{43}$ × 108 × 1.332564). The reasonable addition to the reserve also included an element of interest

employment for reasons other than death or retirement receive an immediate single sum distribution in an amount equal to the actuarial present value (calculated at eight percent interest) of the vested accrued benefit (where the actuarial present value and the vested accrued benefit are determined as of the end of the prior plan year). Reserves and expected increases in the reserve were determined using eight percent interest, five percent assumed compensation increases, the UP-84 mortality table and assuming no pre-retirement terminations other than death. However as set forth in the relevant data below, the actual experience differed from these assumptions (e.g., the actual compensation did not increase five percent each year and the mortality and termination experience were different than assumed).

Number of Deaths	Number of Terminations	Number of Employees Remaining
16	5	9,979
18	5	9,956
20	5	9,931
25	5	9,901
30	25	9,846

End of Year Accrued Benefit for Each Employee	End of Year Vested Accrued Benefit for Each Employee
100	0
200	0
300	60
480	192
600	360

End of Year Actuarial Factor	End of Year Reserve for Vested Benefits
1.049706	0
1.136328	0
1.230380	733,134
1.332564	2,533,194
1.443638	5,117,062

on the reserve as of the end of the prior year equal to FC58,651 (8 percent × 733,134) that is offset by the interest attributable to the actual benefits paid during the year (FC15, which is interest on the benefits paid during the year (FC369) from the date of payment through the end of the year). Thus, the reasonable addition to the reserve for 1983 was FC1,483,848 (1,425,212 + 58,651 − 15) and the expected reserve at the end of the year was FC2,216,613 (733,134 + 1,483,848 − 369). The actual reserve at the end of 1983 is FC2,533,194, so there was an actuarial loss of FC316,581 (2,533,194 − 2,216,613) which was amortized over 10 years beginning in 1983. Thus, the total amount taken into account in 1983 was FC1,588,819 (1,483,848 + 73,313 + 10 percent of 316,581).

(f) *Computation of amount taken into account for 1984.* Using the employee data as of the end of 1983 and the expected rate of compensation increase for 1984, each employee's accrued benefit was expected to be 630 (12,600 × 5 years × .01) as of the end of 1984. 60 percent of this accrued benefit, or 378, was expected to be vested. Thus, the expected increase in each employee's vested accrued benefit was 186 (the difference between 378 and the vested accrued benefit as of the end of the prior year (192) for those employees who were included in the reserve as of the end of the prior year). There were 9,901 employees included in the reserve as of the end of the prior year and 9,901 × p $_{44}$ were expected to be in the reserve as of the end of 1984. The actuarial present value factor for a deferred annuity of FC1 commencing at age 65 payable monthly is 1.443638. Thus, the actuarial present value of the expected increase in vested accrued benefits as of the end of the year was FC2,650,355 (9,901 employees × p $_{44}$ × 186 × 1.443638). The reasonable addition to the reserve also included an element of interest on the reserve as of the end of the prior year equal to FC202,656 (8 percent × 2,533,194), offset by interest attributable to the actual benefits paid during the year (FC256, which is interest on the benefits paid during the year (FC6,396) from the date of payment through the end of the year). Thus, the reasonable addition to the reserve for 1984 was FC2,852,755 (2,650,355 + 202,656 − 256) and the expected reserve at the end of the year is FC5,379,553 (2,533,194 + 2,852,755 − 6,396). The actual reserve at the end of 1984 was FC5,117,062, so there was an actuarial gain of FC262,491 (5,379,553 − 5,117,062) which was amortized over 10 years beginning in 1984. Thus, the total amount taken into account in 1984 was FC2,931,477 (2,852,755 + 73,313 + 31,658 − 10 percent of 262,491).

(g) *Alternative computation method.* The amounts taken into account for 1982, 1983 and 1984 may also be illustrated as follows—

Worksheet for Calculating Amount Taken Into Account For Qualified Reserve Plans Under
§ 404A

(1)	Reserve at end of Prior Year	0
(2)	Interest on (1) to end of Current Year	0
(3)	Present Value of the Expected Increase in Vested Accrued Benefits for employees who were included in the reserve as of the end of the prior year.	0
(4)	Benefit Payments during current year	0
(5)	Interest on (4) from date of payment through end of Current year	0
(6)	Reasonable addition to the reserve (2) + (3) − (5)	0
(7)	Expected value of reserve (1) + (6) − (4)	0
(8)	Actual value of reserve	733,134
(9)	Amount to be amortized (8) − (7)	733,134
(10)	Remaining 10 Percent Bases from Prior Years (original amounts) (Item 12 from Prior Year)	0
(11)	10 percent Bases whose 10 years ended last year	0
(12)	(9) + (10) − (11)	733,134
(13)	10 percent of (12)	73,313
(14)	Amount Taken Into Account for Current Year [(6) + (13)]	73,313

1983

Worksheet For Calculating Amount Taken Into Account For Qualified Reserve Plans Under
§ 404A

(1)	Reserve at end of Prior Year	733,134
(2)	Interest on (1) to end of Current Year	58,651
(3)	Present Value of the Expected Increase in Vested Accrued Benefits for employees who were included in the reserve as of the end of the prior year	1,425,212
(4)	Benefit Payments during current year	369
(5)	Interest on (4) from date of payment through end of Current year	15
(6)	Reasonable addition to the reserve (2) + (3) − (5)	1,483,848
(7)	Expected value of reserve (1) + (6) − (4)	2,216,613
(8)	Actual value of reserve	2,533,194
(9)	Amount to be amortized (8) − (7)	316,581
(10)	Remaining 10 Percent Bases from Prior Years (original amounts) (Item 12 from Prior Year)	733,134
(11)	10 percent Bases whose 10 years ended last year	0
(12)	(9) + (10) − (11)	1,049,715
(13)	10 percent of (12)	104,971
(14)	Amount Taken Into Account for Current Year [(6) + (13)]	1,588,819

1984

Worksheet For Calculating Amount Taken Into Account For Qualified Reserve Plans Under
§ 404A

(1)	Reserve at end of Prior Year	2,533,194
(2)	Interest on (1) to end of Current Year	202,656
(3)	Present Value of the Expected Increase in Vested Accrued Benefits for employees who were included in the reserve as of the end of the prior year.	2,650,355
(4)	Benefit Payments during current year	6,396
(5)	Interest on (4) from date of payment through end of Current year	256
(6)	Reasonable addition to the reserve (2) + (3) − (5)	2,852,755
(7)	Expected value of reserve (1) + (6) − (4)	5,379,553
(8)	Actual value of reserve	5,117,062
(9)	Amount to be amortized (8) − (7)	(262,491)
(10)	Remaining 10 Percent Bases from Prior Years (original amounts) (Item 12 from Prior Year)	1,049,715
(11)	10 percent Bases whose 10 years ended last year	0
(12)	(9) + (10) − (11)	787,224

(13)	10 percent of (12)	78,722
(14)	Amount Taken Into Account for Current Year [(6) + (13)]	2,931,477

Example 3. (a) The facts are the same as in *Example 2*, except that the interest rate used to determine the reserve as of the end of 1984 has been decreased to 7%.

(b) The amount taken into account for 1984 under the alternative calculation method is determined as follows:

1984

Worksheet For Calculating Amount Taken Into Account For Qualified Reserve Plans Under
§ 404A

(1)	Reserve at end of Prior Year	2,533,194
(2)	Interest on (1) to end of Current Year	202,656
(3)	Present Value of the Expected Increase in Vested Accrued Benefits for employees who were included in the reserve as of the end of the prior year.	3,402,637
(4)	Benefit Payments during current year	6,396
(5)	Interest on (4) from date of payment through end of Current year	256
(6)	Reasonable addition to the reserve (2) + (3) − (5)	3,605,037
(7)	Expected value of reserve (1) + (6) − (4)	6,131,835
(8)	Actual value of reserve	6,569,498
(9)	Amount to be amortized (8) − (7)	437,663
(10)	Remaining 10 Percent Bases from Prior Years (original amounts) (Item 12 from Prior Year)	1,049,715
(11)	10 percent Bases whose 10 years ended last year	0
(12)	(9) + (10) − (11)	1,487,378
(13)	10 percent of (12)	148,738
(14)	Amount Taken Into Account for Current Year [(6) + (13)]	3,753,775

[Reg. § 1.404A-3.]

§ 1.404A-4. United States and foreign law limitations on amounts taken into account for qualified foreign plans, EE-14-81, 5/6/93.

(a) *In general.* Section 404A(d) and this section place two limits on the amount taken into account for a taxable year with respect to a qualified foreign plan under section 404A(b) and (c) and §§ 1.404A-2 and 1.404A-3. First, as set forth in paragraph (b) of this section, the cumulative amounts that are or have been taken into account under section 404A through the end of the current year may not exceed the cumulative amounts deductible under foreign law in that period. Because the foreign law deduction is cumulative, however, amounts previously disallowed under this rule are taken into account in later years as the amount deductible under foreign law increases. Second, for taxable years beginning before January 1, 1987, or such later year determined under section 902(c)(3)(A), the rule in paragraph (c) of this section further limits the amount taken into account during those taxable years. Because section 404A(d) and this section apply solely to amounts that would otherwise be taken into account under § 1.404A-2 or 1.404A-3, these limitations are applied without regard to amounts taken into account under section 481 (i.e., without regard to the portion of a section 481(a) adjustment that is taken into account during any taxable year within the section 481(a) adjustment period, as defined in § 1.404A-6(e)(2)). See § 1.404A-6, however, for rules applying the section 404A(d) limitations to the calculation of the section 481(a) adjustment.

(b) *Cumulative limitation.* The amount taken into account with respect to a qualified foreign plan for any taxable year equals—

(1) The lesser of—

(i) The cumulative United States amount; or

(ii) The cumulative foreign amount;

(2) Reduced by the aggregate amount.

(c) *Special rule for foreign corporations in pre-pooling years.* For a taxable year of a foreign corporation beginning before January 1, 1987, or such later year determined under section 902(c)(3)(A), the reduction in earnings and profits determined under paragraph (b) of this section with respect to a qualified foreign plan may not exceed the amount allowed as a deduction under the appropriate foreign tax laws for such taxable year. See *Example 3* of paragraph (h) of this section for an illustration of this rule.

(d) *Rules relating to foreign currency—*(1) *Taxable years beginning after December 31, 1986.* For taxable years beginning after December

31, 1986, the cumulative United States amount, the cumulative foreign amount, and the aggregate amount must be computed in the employer's functional currency. See generally section 964 and sections 985 through 989 for rules applicable to determining and translating into dollars the amount of income or loss of foreign branches and earnings and profits (or deficits in earnings and profits) of foreign corporations.

(2) *Taxable years beginning before January 1, 1987.* For taxable years beginning before January 1, 1987, the cumulative United States amount, the cumulative foreign amount, and the aggregate amount must be computed in the currency in which the foreign branch or foreign subsidiary kept its books and records. See Rev. Rul. 75-106, 1975-1 C.B. 31 (see § 601.601(d)(2)(ii)(b) of this chapter), for rules for determining the amount of income or loss of foreign branches using a net worth method of accounting. See Rev. Rul. 75-107, 1975-1 C.B. 32 (see § 601.601(d)(2)(ii)(b) of this chapter), for rules for determining the amount of income or loss of foreign branches using a profit and loss method of accounting. See sections 312, 902, and 1248 and the regulations thereunder for rules for determining the earnings and profits of noncontrolled foreign corporations. See section 964 and the regulations thereunder for rules for determining the earnings and profits of foreign corporations for purposes of subpart F.

(3) *Special rules for the net worth method of accounting.* For purposes of § 1.964-1(e)(4), an amount of deduction that is accrued but not paid at the end of the employer's taxable year with respect to a qualified funded plan must be treated as a short-term liability. In the case of a qualified reserve plan, for purposes of § 1.964-1(e), the amount of the reserve taken into account as a liability on the balance sheet as of the beginning of the taxable year must be limited to the aggregate amount, and the amount of the reserve taken into account as a liability on the balance sheet as of the close of the taxable year must be limited to the sum of the aggregate amount and the amount taken into account for the taxable year. For purposes of § 1.964-1(e)(4), each annual increase in the aggregate amount must be treated as a long-term liability incurred on the last day of the employer's taxable year to which the increase relates. As of the close of each taxable year, a portion of the aggregate amount equal to the amount of benefits expected to be paid during the succeeding taxable year must be reclassified as a short-term liability. The reclassified amount must be allocated to the annual increases in the aggregate amount on a first-in-first-out basis. Similar rules apply for purposes of determining the amount of reserve taken into account by a foreign branch using the net worth method of accounting for taxable years beginning before January 1, 1987, and by a qualified business unit that uses the United States dollar approximate

separate transactions method of accounting under § 1.985-3 in a taxable year beginning after December 31, 1986.

(e) *Maintenance of more than one type of qualified foreign plan by an employer.* In determining the deduction or reduction in earnings and profits when an employer maintains one plan for purposes of foreign law that is treated as two separate plans for purposes of § 1.404A-6(a)(2), the cumulative United States amount for each plan must be combined for purposes of paragraphs (a) and (b) of this section. See *Example 5* of paragraph (h) of this section for an illustration of this rule.

(f) *United States and foreign law limitations not applicable.* The limitations set forth in this section do not apply to the adjustments required by section 481, section 446(e) and section 2(e)(3)(A) of Public Law 96-603.

(g) *Definitions*—(1) *Cumulative United States amount.* The term "cumulative United States amount" means (with respect to a qualified foreign plan) the amount determined under section 404A (without regard to section 404A(d)) for the taxable year of the employer and for all consecutive prior taxable years for which an election under section 404A was in effect for the plan plus the "initial section 404A amount" within the meaning of § 1.404A-6(g)(2)(i).

(2) *Cumulative foreign amount.* The term "cumulative foreign amount" means (with respect to a qualified foreign plan) the cumulative amount allowed as a deduction under the appropriate foreign tax law for the taxable year of the employer and for all consecutive prior taxable years for which an election under section 404A was in effect for the plan plus the initial section 404A amount within the meaning of § 1.404A-6(g)(2)(ii).

(3) *Appropriate foreign tax law.* The appropriate foreign tax law is the income tax law of the country (other than the United States) that is the principal place of business of the qualified business unit of the employer whose books reflect the plan liabilities.

(4) *Aggregate amount.* The term "aggregate amount" means (with respect to a qualified foreign plan) amounts permitted to be taken into account under section 404A(d)(1) for all consecutive prior taxable years for which an election under section 404A was in effect for the plan plus the initial section 404A amount required by § 1.404A-6(g)(2)(iii).

(h) *Examples.* The principles of this section are illustrated by the following examples:

Example 1. X, a foreign subsidiary of a domestic corporation, maintains its main office in foreign country A, and a branch, Y, in foreign country B. The functional currency of X is the FC. Y's functional currency is the local currency, LC. X maintains a qualified foreign plan for the benefit of X's employees in B. In the year the plan was adopted, a section 404A election was made for the plan. The appropriate foreign tax law is the tax law of B because all the employees covered by the plan are in B and plan liabilities are accounted for on Y's books. The tax law of B permits X to deduct contributions to the plan. The cumulative amount allowed as a deduction under the tax law of B is LC80. The cumulative United States amount with respect to the plan is LC100. Therefore, the cumulative limitation is LC80. The earnings and profits of X include the profit and loss for Y (reflecting a reduction for contributions to the plan, computed in LC and translated into FC under the principles of section 987).

Example 2. A qualified reserve plan is maintained by a foreign branch of a domestic corporation. The foreign branch computes its income under the profit and loss method of Rev. Rul. 75-107, 1975-1 C.B. 32 (see § 601.601(d)(2)(ii)(b) of this chapter), in units of the local currency, the FC. The foreign branch established the qualified reserve plan in 1985 and the taxpayer made the elections described in § 1.404A-6. The taxpayer's taxable year and the plan year is the calendar year. The assumed amounts taken into account under section 404A and appropriate foreign tax law for selected years and the computations under this section which follow from the amounts, in units of FC, are shown in the following table—

		1985	1986	1987	1988
(1)	Amount determined with respect to the plan under section 404A for the taxable year without regard to section 404A(d) .	800,000	900,000	300,000	1,000,000
(2)	Cumulative United States amount	800,000	1,700,000	2,000,000	3,000,000
(3)	Cumulative foreign amount	1,000,000	1,600,000	2,000,000	2,200,000
(4)	Lesser of cumulative United States or cumulative foreign amount	800,000	1,600,000	2,000,000	2,200,000
(5)	Reduced by aggregate amount (cumulative sum of (6) for prior years)	(0)	(800,000)	(1,600,000)	(2,000,000)
		800,000	800,000	400,000	200,000
(6)	Amount taken into account for the taxable year	800,000	800,000	400,000	200,000

Example 3. Assume the same facts as in *Example 2* for all taxable years, except that the qualified reserve plan is maintained by a foreign subsidiary of a domestic corporation. The foreign subsidiary computes its earnings and profits in units of the local currency, the FC. The foreign subsidiary's taxable year and the plan year are calendar years.

The assumed amounts taken into account under section 404A and appropriate foreign law for selected years, and the computations under this section which follow from the amounts, in units of FC, are shown in the following table—

		1985	1986	1987	1988
(1)	Amount determined with respect to the plan under section 404A for the taxable year without regard to section 404A(d) .	800,000	900,000	300,000	1,000,000
(2)	Amount allowed as a deduction under the appropriate foreign tax laws for the taxable year	1,000,000	600,000	400,000	200,000
(3)	Cumulative United States amount	800,000	1,700,000	2,000,000	3,000,000
(4)	Cumulative foreign amount	1,000,000	1,600,000	2,000,000	2,200,000
(5)	Lesser of cumulative United States or cumulative foreign amount	800,000	1,600,000	2,000,000	2,200,000
(6)	Reduced by aggregate amount (cumulative sum of (7) or (8), whichever is applicable, for prior years)	(0)	(800,000)	(1,400,000)	(2,000,000)
		800,000	800,000	600,000	200,000
(7)	Amount taken into account for taxable years before 1987 (lesser of (2) and (6)) .	800,000	600,000	n/a	n/a
(8)	Amount taken into account for taxable years after 1986 (same as (6)) .	n/a	n/a	600,000	200,000

Example 4. Z, a domestic corporation, maintains a retirement plan for employees employed in its foreign branch office. The foreign branch computes its income under the profit and loss method Rev. Rul. 75-107, 1975-1 C.B. 32 (see § 601.601(d)(2)(ii)(b) of this chapter), in units of local currency, the FC. The plan is a combination book reserve and funded plan, but is considered a single plan under foreign law. The total retirement benefits that a participant is eligible to receive is the

sum of the benefits provided by the qualified reserve plan and the qualified funded plan. Pursuant to § 1.404A-6, in the year the plan was adopted, Z made a separate qualified reserve plan and funded plan election with respect to each portion of the foreign plan. The assumed deductions under section 404A and appropriate foreign law for selected years, and the computations under this section which follow from the deductions, are shown in the following table—

	Qualified funded plan		Qualified reserve plan		Combined amount—qualified foreign plans	
	1984	1985	1984	1985	1984	1985
(1) Amount determined with respect to the qualified foreign plans under section 404A for the taxable year without regard to section 404A(d)	40,000	90,000	30,000	80,000		
(2) Amount allowed as a deduction under the appropriate foreign tax laws for the taxable year					60,000	185,000
(3) Cumulative United States amount	40,000	130,000	30,000	110,000		
(4) Combined cumulative United States amount (cumulative sum of (3))					70,000	240,000
(5) Cumulative foreign amount (cumulative sum of (2))					60,000	245,000
(6) Aggregate amount					0	60,000
(7) Lesser of combined cumulative United States amount or cumulative foreign amount ((4) or (5))					60,000	240,000
(9) Reduced by the aggregate amount for the qualified funded and reserve plan (cumulative sum of (10) for prior years)					(0)	(60,000)
(10) Amount taken into account for taxable year					60,000	180,000

Example 5. A qualified reserve plan is maintained by *M*, the foreign subsidiary of *N*, a domestic corporation. *M* computes its earnings and profits in units of the local currency, the FC. The taxable years of *M* and *N* and the plan year are the calendar year. *M* established the qualified reserve plan in 1984 and *N* made the elections described in § 1.404A-6. In that year, the reasonable addition to the plan reserve under § 1.404A-3 was FC750,000. However, the amount allowed as a deduction under the appropriate foreign tax laws for the taxable year was FC650,000. The difference between the amount taken into account under § 1.404A-3 and the deduction under the appropriate foreign tax laws, FC100,000, could not be taken into account for any succeeding taxable year under § 1.404A-3, but it may later reduce *M*'s earnings and profits pursuant to paragraph (a) of this section.

[Reg. § 1.404A-4.]

§ 1.404A-5. Additional limitations on amounts taken into account for qualified foreign plans, EE-14-81, 5/6/93.

(a) *Restrictions for nonqualified individuals*—(1) *General rule.* Notwithstanding any other provisions of §§ 1.404A-1 through 1.404A-7, no amount may be taken into account under section 404A for any contribution or amount accrued that is attributable to services performed either in the current or in a prior taxable year—

(i) By a citizen or resident of the United States who is a highly compensated [employee] (within the meaning of section 414(q)) (or, for taxable years beginning before January 1, 1989, by a citizen or resident of the United States who is an officer, shareholder, or highly compensated (within the meaning of § 1.410(b)-1(d)); or

(ii) In the United States, the compensation for which is subject to tax under chapter 1 of subtitle A of the Internal Revenue Code.

(2) *Determination of service attribution*— (i) *Not limited to actual service.* Service performed by individuals described in paragraph (a)(1)(i) of this section includes service credited to those individuals. Service performed in the United States includes service credited in relation (directly or indirectly) to any United States service.

(ii) *Amounts attributable to service performed in the United States.* The accrued benefit attributable to services described in this paragraph (a) is the excess, if any, of the total accrued benefit over the accrued benefit determined without credit for time spent performing services described in this paragraph (a) and without regard to the compensation levels for that time.

(b) *Records to be provided by taxpayer*—(1) *In general.* Notwithstanding any other provisions of §§ 1.404A-1 through 1.404A-7, no amount may be taken into account under section 404A for any contribution or amount accrued unless the taxpayer attaches a statement to its United States income tax return for any taxable year for which a qualified foreign plan maintained by an employer has United States tax significance. This statement must specify the name and type of qualified foreign plan; the cumulative United States amount, the cumulative foreign amount, and the aggregate amount with respect to the plan; the

name and country of organization of the employer; and any other information the Commissioner may prescribe by forms and accompanying instructions or by revenue procedure.

(2) *Primary evidence.* The statement described in paragraph (b)(1) of this section and any required forms must be completed in good faith with all of the information called for and with the calculations referenced in paragraph (b)(1) of this section. Except as provided in paragraph (b)(4) of this section, one of the following documents must be attached to the United States income tax return—

(i) A statement from the foreign tax authorities specifying the amount of the deduction allowed in computing taxable income under the appropriate foreign tax law for the relevant year or years with respect to the qualified foreign plan; or

(ii) If the return under the appropriate foreign tax law shows the deduction for plan contributions or plan reserves as a separate identifiable item, a copy of the foreign tax return for the relevant year or years with respect to the qualified foreign plan.

(3) *Additional requirements.* The statement or return attached pursuant to paragraph (b)(2) of this section may be either the original, a duplicate original, a duly certified or authenticated copy, or a sworn copy. If only a sworn copy of a receipt or return is attached, there must be kept readily available for comparison on request the original, a duplicate original, or a duly certified or authenticated copy.

(4) *Secondary evidence.* Where the statement or return described in paragraph (b)(2)(i) or (b)(2)(ii) of this section is not available, all of the following information must be attached to the United States income tax return—

(i) A certified statement setting forth the cumulative foreign amount for each taxable year to which section 404A applies;

(ii) The excerpts from the employer's books and records showing either the change in the reserve or contributions made with respect to the plan for the taxable year to which section 404A applies; and

(iii) The computations of the foreign deduction relating to the plan to be established by data such as excerpts from the foreign law, assessment notices, or other documentary evidence.

(5) *Foreign language.* If the relevant returns, books, records or computations are not maintained in the English language, the taxpayer must furnish, upon request, a certified translation that is satisfactory to the District Director.

(6) *Additional information required by District Director.* If the taxpayer upon request of the District Director fails, without justification, to furnish any additional information that is significant, the provisions of section 982 will apply.

(7) *Authorized officer to complete documents.* The documents required by this section and by §§ 1.404A-6 and 1.404A-7 must be signed by an authorized officer of the taxpayer (as defined in section 6062 or 6063) who must verify under penalty of perjury that the statement and all

other documents submitted are true and correct to his knowledge and belief.

(8) *Transitional rule—good faith effort.* For taxable years ending before [*INSERT DATE THAT IS 90 DAYS AFTER THE DATE OF PUBLICATION OF FINAL REGULATIONS IN THE FEDERAL REGIS-TER*] a taxpayer will be treated as satisfying this paragraph (b) if it makes a good faith effort to provide reasonable documentation.

(c) *Actuarial requirements—(1) Reasonable actuarial assumptions.* Except as otherwise specifically provided in §§ 1.404A-2 and 1.404A-3 and this paragraph (c), in the case of a qualified reserve plan or a qualified funded plan under which benefits are fixed or determinable, no amount may be taken into account under section 404A unless costs, liabilities, rates of interest, and other factors under the plan are determined on the basis of actuarial assumptions and methods each of which is reasonable (taking into account the experience of the plan and reasonable expectations), or which, in the aggregate, result in an amount being taken into account that is equivalent to that which would be determined if each such assumption and method were reasonable, and that, in combination, offer the actuary's best estimate of anticipated experience under the plan. For plan years beginning before January 1, 1988, the preceding sentence is satisfied if costs, liabilities, rates of interest, and other factors under the plan are determined on the basis of actuarial assumptions and methods that are reasonable in the aggregate (taking into account the experience of the plan and reasonable expectations) and that, in combination, offer the actuary's best estimate of anticipated experience under the plan. Except to the extent required under that paragraph, the interest rate determined under § 1.404A-3(b)(4) may not be considered in determining whether other actuarial assumptions are reasonable in the aggregate for this purpose.

(2) *Full funding limitation.* Notwithstanding any other provisions of §§ 1.404A-1 through 1.404A-7, no amount may be taken into account under section 404A if the amount causes the assets in the trust (in the case of a qualified funded plan) or if taking into account the amount causes the amount of the reserve (in the case of a qualified reserve plan) to exceed the amount described in section 412(c)(7)(A)(i). [Reg. § 1.404A-5.]

§ 1.404A-6. Elections under section 404A and changes in methods of accounting, EE-14-81, 5/6/93.

(a) *Elections, changes in accounting methods, and changes in plan years—(1) In general—(i) Methods of accounting.* An election under section 404A with respect to a qualified foreign plan constitutes the adoption of a method of accounting if the election is made in the taxable year in which the plan is adopted. Any election under section 404A with respect to a pre-existing plan, however, constitutes a change in method of accounting requiring the Commissioner's consent under section 446 (e) and an adjustment under section 481(a). Additionally, any other change in the method used to determine the amount taken into account under section 404A(a), as well as the revocation of any election under section 404A, constitutes a change in accounting method subject to the consent and adjustment requirements of sections 446(e) and 481(a). This section provides procedures for obtaining the Commissioner's consent to make certain changes in methods of accounting under section 404A. Additionally, § 1.404A-7 provides special procedural rules applicable (along with the rules under this section) for retroactive and transition-period elections under section 404A.

(ii) *Changes not involving accounting methods.* Any change in treatment, adjustment, or correction described in § 1.446-1(e)(2)(ii)(b) (e.g., correction of computational errors) is not a change in accounting method. While a retroactive qualified funded plan election under § 1.404A-7(c) constitutes a change in method of accounting, a mere election to apply the effective date of section 404A under § 1.404A-7(b) retroactively does not necessarily result in a change in accounting method. Additionally, a retroactive election for funded foreign branch plans under § 1.404A-7(d) will not be treated as a change in method of accounting, except to the extent that the taxpayer took erroneous deductions under its method of accounting prior to the beginning of its open period. Finally, a change of actuarial assumptions will not be treated as a change in method of accounting for purposes of this section.

(2) *Single plan—(i) General rule.* Except as otherwise provided, the rules of this section regarding elections, revocations, and re-elections, and the adoption or change of a plan year, apply separately (i.e., on a plan-by-plan basis) to each plan that qualifies as a single plan (as defined in § 1.414(l)-1(b)). For purposes of this definition, a separate reserve maintained by an employer exclusively for its liability under a plan is considered a plan asset that is available exclusively to pay benefits to employees who are covered by the plan and to their beneficiaries. Although a plan may be treated as a reserve plan under

foreign law, this treatment is not binding for purposes of section 404A and this section.

(ii) *Example.* The principles of this paragraph (a)(2) are illustrated by the following example:

Example. S is a wholly-owned foreign subsidiary of *P*, a domestic corporation. *S* maintains a deferred compensation plan under local law to provide benefits to its employees upon retirement based upon years of service and the highest five-year average salary. *S* decided to account for 70 percent of its deferred compensation liabilities through an unfunded book reserve (Plan One), and to account for the remaining 30 percent through a trust equivalent (Plan Two). All of the assets of Plan One and Plan Two were available for payment of liabilities under their respective plans, and were only available for payment of liabilities under their respective plans. Thus, when deferred compensation was paid to *S*'s employees, within the meaning of this paragraph (a)(2), 70 percent of the amount was paid by check drawn against the general assets of *S* and 30 percent of the amount paid was paid by check drawn on the assets of the trust equivalent. Pursuant to this section, *P* made a qualified reserve plan election for Plan One, which it defined as a plan of deferred compensation with liability for 70 percent of the amount of deferred compensation owing to each employee under *S*'s deferred compensation plan. In addition, it made a qualified funded plan election for Plan Two, which it defined as a plan of deferred compensation with liability for the remaining 30 percent. Because *S*'s reserve for its liability was treated as a plan asset with respect to 70 percent of the liability and the assets of the trust, Plan One met the requirements of a "single plan" under § 1.414(l)-1(b), and Plan Two was a separate "single plan". Thus, *S* could take into account only 70 percent of its liability to each employee under its deferred compensation plan when calculating the reasonable additions to the reserve under section 404A(c) for Plan One. Similarly, the full funding limitation and other calculations with respect to Plan Two may only be made with respect to 30 percent of *S*'s liability to each employee under the foreign deferred compensation plan.

(b) *Initial elections under section 404A—(1) In general.* The Commissioner's consent to elect initially under section 404A to treat a single plan as a qualified funded plan or as a qualified reserve plan is granted automatically if the taxpayer complies with the requirements of this paragraph (b). Except as provided in § 1.404A-7, an initial election under this section with respect to any qualified foreign plan may be made only for a taxable year beginning after December 31, 1979.

(2) *Time for making election—(i) Foreign branch plans.* Except as provided in § 1.404A-7, the initial election for a qualified foreign plan maintained by a foreign branch must be made no later than the time prescribed by law for filing the United States return (including extensions) for the first taxable year for which the election is to be effective.

(ii) *Foreign corporation plans.* Except as provided in § 1.404A-7, the initial election for a qualified foreign plan maintained by a foreign corporation must be made no later than the time allowed for making elections under §§ 1.964-1 and 1.964-1T. Thus, the election under section 404A may be deferred until the earnings and profits of the foreign corporation have United States tax significance, as defined in §§ 1.964-1 and 1.964-1T. United States tax significance may occur in a number of ways, including, for example, a dividend distribution, an income inclusion under section 951(a), a section 1248 transaction, a step-up of basis by earnings and profits for purposes of valuing assets for interest allocation purposes under section 864(e), or an inclusion in income of the earnings of a qualified electing fund under section 1293(a)(1).

(3) *Manner in which election is to be made—(i) Foreign branch plans.* In the case of a qualified foreign plan maintained by a domestic corporation, the initial election must be made by the taxpayer by attaching a list of plans for which section 404A treatment is desired to a return filed within the time prescribed in paragraph (b)(2)(i) of this section.

(ii) *Controlled foreign corporation plans.* If a qualified foreign plan is maintained by a controlled foreign corporation, the initial election under this section must be made in the manner prescribed by §§ 1.964-1 and 1.964-1T and must include a list of all plans for which the election is made.

(iii) *Noncontrolled foreign corporation plans.* If a qualified foreign plan is maintained by a noncontrolled foreign corporation, the initial election under this section must be made in the manner prescribed by §§ 1.964-1 and 1.964-1T and must include a list of all plans for which the election is made, as if the noncontrolled foreign corporation were a controlled foreign corporation. In applying the rules of §§ 1.964-1 and 1.964-1T, the term "majority domestic corporate shareholders" is substituted for the term "controlling United States shareholders" wherever it appears in §§ 1.964-1 and 1.964-1T. The term "majority domestic corporate shareholders" has the meaning set forth in § 1.985-2(c)(3)(i).

(4) *Other requirements for election.* For each plan listed, pursuant to paragraph (b)(3) of this section, the taxpayer must designate whether it elects to treat the plan as a qualified funded plan or qualified reserve plan, and must designate a plan year. Additionally, for each plan listed, the taxpayer must disclose the amount of any section 481(a) adjustment, as well as the initial cumulative United States amount, the initial cumulative foreign amount, and the initial aggregate amount defined in paragraph (g) of this section. See § 1.404A-5(b) for rules on additional information required, signing and verifying required statements, and notices and forms necessary to elect under section 404A. Additionally, see § 1.404A-7(d)(1) for required agreement to assessment of tax for retroactive elections for funded foreign branch plans.

(c) *Termination of election when a plan ceases to be a qualified foreign plan*—(1) *In general.* An election under section 404A with respect to a foreign deferred compensation plan is terminated if at any time on or after the first day of the first taxable year for which the election is effective the plan ceases to be a qualified foreign plan by reason of a failure to satisfy the conditions of section 404A(e)(1) or (2). Thus, for example, the election is terminated (subject to the consent of the Commissioner) if more than 10 percent of the amounts taken into account under the plan are attributable to services performed by employees subject to United States federal income tax. As used in this section, the term "termination" refers only to situations under which a plan ceases to be a qualified foreign plan by reason of a failure to satisfy the conditions of section 404(e)(1) or (2). Thus, the term is distinguished from a voluntary revocation of an election (i.e., under paragraph (d)(1) of this section), which also causes a plan to cease to be a qualified foreign plan. Upon termination of an election under section 404A, a change in method of accounting is required. The conditional advance consent of the Commissioner is granted for this change in method of accounting. This conditional consent may be withdrawn, however, if the District Director determines that tax avoidance was a purpose of the termination or if the procedures in paragraph (c)(2) of this section are not satisfied.

(2) *Rules for changing method of accounting upon termination of election*—(i) *Time for making change*—(A) *Foreign branch plans.* Except as provided in § 1.404A-7, in the case of a plan of a foreign branch the change in method of accounting required upon termination of a section 404A election must be made no later than the time prescribed by law for filing the United States return (including extensions) for the taxable year in which the plan ceases to satisfy the requirements of section 404A(e)(1) or (2).

(B) *Foreign corporation plans.* Except as provided in § 1.404A-7, in the case of a plan of a foreign corporation the change in method of accounting required upon termination of a section 404A election shall be made no later than the first year after the termination in which the earnings and profits of the foreign corporation have United States tax significance, as defined in §§ 1.964-1 and 1.964-1T. See paragraph (b)(2)(ii) of this section for United States tax significance examples.

(ii) *Procedures for changing method of accounting upon termination of election*—(A) *Foreign branch plans.* The change in method of accounting required upon termination of a section 404A election with respect to a foreign branch plan must be made by attaching a statement to the return described in paragraph (c)(2)(i)(A) of this section disclosing the amount of any section 481(a) adjustment (required under paragraph (e) of this section and computed in accordance with paragraph (f) of this section) arising upon the change.

(B) *Controlled foreign corporation plans.* The change in method of accounting required upon termination of a section 404A election with respect to a controlled foreign corporation plan must be made in the manner prescribed by §§ 1.964-1 and 1.964-1T and must include disclosure of the amount of any section 481(a) adjustment (required under paragraph (e) of this section and computed in accordance with paragraph (f) of this section) arising upon the change.

(C) *Noncontrolled foreign corporation plans.* The change in method of accounting required upon termination of a section 404A election with respect to a noncontrolled foreign corporation plan must be made in the manner prescribed by §§ 1.964-1 and 1.964-1T and must include disclosure of the amount of any section 481(a) adjustment (required under paragraph (e) of this section and computed in accordance with paragraph (f) of this section) arising upon the change. In applying the rules of §§ 1.964-1 and 1.964-1T, the term "majority domestic corporate shareholders" is substituted for the term "controlling United States shareholders" wherever it appears in §§ 1.964-1 and 1.964-1T. The term "majority domestic corporate shareholders" has the meaning set forth in § 1.985-2(c)(3)(i).

(d) *Other changes in methods of accounting and changes in plan year*—(1) *Application for consent.* Except as provided in paragraph (c) of this section or in § 1.404A-7, once an initial election under section 404A is effective with respect to a plan, the taxpayer must separately apply to obtain the express consent of the Commissioner prior to changing any method of accounting with respect to a foreign deferred compensation plan. Application for the consent of the Commissioner is required whether or not the method being changed is proper or permitted under the Internal Revenue Code and regulations thereunder. Any change in method of accounting not described in this paragraph (d)(1) must be made in accordance with the requirements of section 446(e) and the regulations thereunder. The procedures prescribed in this paragraph (d), however, are the exclusive procedures for making the following changes in method of accounting—

(i) Revocation of a section 404A election;

(ii) Re-election under section 404A following termination or revocation of a section 404A election;

(iii) Changing the treatment of a plan from a qualified funded plan to a qualified reserve plan (or the converse); or

(iv) Changing the actuarial funding method used to determine costs under a qualified funded plan.

(2) *Procedures for other changes in method of accounting*—(i) *Foreign branch plans.* To request consent to a change in method of accounting described in paragraph (d)(1) of this section, the taxpayer must file an application on Form 3115 with the Commissioner generally within 180 days after the beginning of the taxable year in which the change is requested to be effective. In the case of a revocation of an election under section 404A, however, the 180-day period in the preceding sentence is extended to the time prescribed by law for filing the United States return for the taxable year of the change.

(ii) *Foreign corporation plans.* For a controlled foreign corporation or a noncontrolled foreign corporation, a request for consent to revocation or to another change in method of accounting must be made in accordance with the rules of §§ 1.964-1 and 1.964-1T.

(3) *Plan year.* A taxpayer must secure the consent of the Commissioner to change the plan year of a qualified foreign plan. Termination or revocation of a section 404A election will not effect a change in the plan year of the plan.

(e) *Application of section 481*—(1) *In general.* A change in method described in this section constitutes a change in method of accounting to which section 481 applies. Except as otherwise provided in this paragraph and in paragraph (f) of this section, this adjustment must be made in accordance with section 481 and the regulations thereunder in those circumstances. For purposes of section 481(a)(2), any change in method described in this section is considered a change in method of accounting initiated by the taxpayer.

(2) *Period of adjustment*—(i) *In general.* The section 481(a) adjustment period is determined under the rules of this paragraph (e)(2).

(ii) *Election or re-election.* In the case of an election or a re-election following termination or revocation, the section 481(a) adjustment required by paragraph (e)(1) of this section must be taken into account ratably over a 15-year period, beginning with the first taxable year for which the election or re-election is effective. This section 481(a) adjustment period also applies to a change from a qualified funded plan to a qualified reserve plan.

(iii) *Termination or revocation of election and all other changes in method.* The adjustment required by paragraph (e)(1) of this section for all changes in method (other than those described in paragraph (e)(2)(ii) of this section), including changes in election from a qualified reserve plan to a qualified funded plan, must be taken into account ratably over a six-year period, beginning with the first taxable year for which the change is effective. If an unamortized section 481(a) adjustment amount (e.g., from a previous change) remains at the end of a change in method of accounting to which this paragraph (e)(2)(iii) applies, the net amount of all of the section 481(a) adjustments must be taken into account ratably over this six-year section 481(a) adjustment period.

(iv) *Acceleration of section 481(a) adjustment.* If the employer ceases to engage in the relevant trade or business at any time prior to the expiration of the applicable section 481(a) adjustment period provided in paragraph (e)(2)(ii) or (e)(2)(iii) of this section, the employer must take into account, in the taxable year of cessation, the balance of any section 481(a) adjustment not previously taken into account in computing taxable income (in the case of a branch) or earnings and profits (in the case of a foreign corporation). For purposes of this paragraph (e)(2)(iv), whether or not an employer ceases to engage in the trade or business is to be determined under administrative procedures issued under § 1.446-1(e). In applying those procedures, "employer" is to be defined in the same manner as "taxpayer" is defined under those procedures.

(3) *Allocation and source.* The amount of any net negative section 481(a) adjustment determined under this section and taken into account for a taxable year must be allocated and apportioned under § 1.861-8 in the same manner as a deduction or reduction in earnings and profits under section 404A. Any net positive section 481(a) adjustment that is taken into account for a taxable year first must be reduced by directly allocating to such adjustment the employer's section 404A expense that is subject to apportionment (including any amount that otherwise would be capitalized); to the extent a net positive section 481(a) adjustment exceeds the amount of the employer's section 404A expense for the taxable year, such excess must be sourced or otherwise classified in the same manner as section 404A deductions or reductions in earnings and profits are allocated and apportioned.

Negative 1985 section 481(a) adjustment	(FC150,000)
Less: 1985, 1986 & 1987 amounts taken into account	30,000
Subtotal	(120,000)
Positive 1988 section 481(a) adjustment	132,000
Net positive section 481(a) adjustment	12,000
Section 481(a) adjustment period	÷ 6
Net amount taken into account annually during section 481(a) adjustment period	FC2,000

(f) *Computation of section 481(a) adjustment*—(1) *In general.* For purposes of section 404A, except as provided in § 1.404A-7(f)(1)(ii)(C), the amount of the section 481(a) adjustment required under paragraph (e)(1) of this section equals—

(i) The Old Method Closing Amount; less

(ii) The New Method Opening Amount.

(2) *Old Method Closing Amount*—(i) *In general.* Except as otherwise provided in paragraph (f)(2)(ii), (iii), or (iv) of this section (or as otherwise prescribed by the Commissioner), the Old Method Closing Amount equals—

(A) The total of all past deductions taken with respect to liabilities under the plan; plus

(B) The net income earned directly or indirectly by any separate funding entity (e.g., account or trust) with respect to the plan, but only to the extent that such net income has not previously been taken into account in determining taxable income (in the case of a foreign branch) or earnings and profits (in the case of a foreign corporation); minus

(C) The total of all past payments under the plan made to plan participants and beneficiaries by the employer, the trust, or the separate funding entity.

(ii) *Taxpayer formerly using a reserve method*—(A) *In general.* If a taxpayer has consistently taken amounts with respect to the plan into account under a reserve method, the Old Method Closing Amount equals the closing reserve balance at the end of the closing year calculated under the taxpayer's reserve method. For purposes of the preceding sentence, a reserve method means a method of accrual based on the actuarial present value of expected future plan benefits.

(B) *Former qualified reserve plan.* To request the Commissioner's consent in the case of a former qualified reserve plan, the closing reserve balance must be adjusted for any unamortized increases or decreases to the reserve described in § 1.404A-3(c) that have not yet been taken into account. For example, if the closing reserve balance is FC100,000, but FC10,000 of the closing reserve balance consists of an unamortized increase in the reserve that has not previously been taken into account due to the ten-year amortization requirements of § 1.404A-3(c), the Old Method Closing Amount is FC90,000.

(iii) *Taxpayer formerly using pay-as-you-go method.* If the taxpayer has consistently taken amounts into account with respect to the plan based only on actual payments of plan benefits to participants and beneficiaries, the Old Method Closing Amount equals zero.

(iv) *Taxpayer formerly using a funded method*—(A) *Payment to separate funding entity.* If the taxpayer has consistently taken amounts into account with respect to the plan based only on actual payments to a separate funding entity and on payments by the employer (but not by the funding entity) to plan participants or beneficiaries, the Old Method Closing Amount equals the balance in the separate funding entity at the

(4) *Example.* The principles of this paragraph (e) are illustrated by the following example:

Example. X, a domestic corporation, made an initial election under section 404A to treat an existing deferred compensation plan maintained by its foreign branch as a qualified reserve plan, effective beginning in *X*'s 1985 taxable year. *X*'s foreign branch maintains its books and records in FC, the functional currency. Previously, *X* had consistently used a permissible method of accounting with respect to the plan. The section 481(a) adjustment arising from *X*'s change in accounting method upon its section 404A election was a negative FC150,000. Beginning with its 1985 taxable year, *X* took into account a negative FC10,000 each year (FC150,000/15). Effective beginning in *X*'s 1988 taxable year, *X* received the Commissioner's express consent to change from a qualified reserve plan to a qualified funded plan. The section 481(a) adjustment attributable solely to the 1988 change was a positive FC132,000. Beginning with its 1988 taxable year, and for each of the five succeeding taxable years, *X* took into account a positive FC2,000, as computed below.

end of the closing year, including amounts attributable, directly or indirectly, to net investment income that has not previously been taken into account in determining taxable income (in the case of a foreign branch) or earnings and profits (in the case of a foreign corporation).

(B) *Former qualified funded plan.* In the case of a former qualified funded plan, the Old Method Closing Amount generally equals the amount described in paragraph (f)(2)(iv)(A) of this section, adjusted, however, by—

(*1*) Reducing the amount properly to reflect any net limitations under section 404A(b) and (g) (e.g., the full funding limitation for a qualified funded plan) that were applied in determining amounts taken into account under the former section 404A method of accounting; and

(*2*) Increasing the amount properly to reflect any amounts that are not paid during the closing year but that are permitted to be taken into account in the closing year under section 404A(b)(2) (relating to payments made after the close of the taxable year).

(v) *Section 404A(d) limitation.* In computing the Old Method Closing Amount upon the termination or revocation of an election under section 404A, the limitations of section 404A(d) and § 1.404A-4 must be taken into account. Thus, if the Old Method Closing Amount is determined under paragraph (f)(2)(ii)(B) or (f)(2)(iv)(B) of this section, the amount otherwise determined under those paragraphs shall be reduced by applying the section 404A(d) and § 1.404A-4 limitations to the extent the cumulative United States amount under § 1.404A-4 exceeds the cumulative foreign amount under § 1.404A-4.

(3) *New Method Opening Amount*—(i) *Qualified reserve plan.* In the case of an election to treat a plan as a qualified reserve plan, the New Method Opening Amount equals the balance of the reserve as of the end of the last day of the closing year, calculated under the rules of section 404A(c) and § 1.404A-3 based on plan information and data as of that date. The New Method Opening Amount must be reduced (or increased) for any unamortized increases (or decreases) to the reserve described in section 404A(c)(4) and § 1.404A-3(c).

(ii) *Qualified funded plan.* In the case of an election to be treated as a qualified funded plan, the New Method Opening Amount equals the amount of funds in the trust as of the beginning of the first day of the opening year, adjusted as necessary to take into account the rules of section 404A(b) and (g). If the separate funding entity does not qualify as a trust under § 1.404A-1(e), the New Method Opening Amount in the case of a qualified funded plan is zero because there is no balance in a trust as defined in § 1.404A-1(e).

(iii) *Nonqualified plan.* In the case of any plan that ceases to be a qualified foreign plan (either by reason of the termination or revocation of a section 404A election), the New Method Opening Amount is zero.

(iv) *Section 404A(d) limitation.* In computing the New Method Opening Amount upon an election under section 404A, the limitation on deductions of section 404A(d) and § 1.404A-4 must be taken into account. Thus, if the New Method Opening Amount is determined under paragraph (f)(2)(i) or (f)(2)(ii) of this section, the amount otherwise determined must be reduced to the extent the cumulative United States amount computed under §1.404A-4 exceeds the cumulative foreign amount computed under §1.404A-4. See paragraph (g) of this section for initialization of amounts taken into account under section 404A(d).

(4) *Definitions and special rules*—(i) *Opening year.* For purposes of this section, the opening year is the first taxable year for which the new method of accounting is effective with respect to a plan. For example, in the case of an election to treat a foreign corporation plan as a qualified reserve plan beginning in 1989, the opening year is 1989, even though the election may not be made until 1994 pursuant to paragraph (b)(2)(ii) of this section.

(ii) *Closing year.* For purposes of this section, the closing is the taxable year immediately preceding the opening year.

(iii) *Separate funding entity.* A separate funding entity described in paragraphs (f)(2)(i)(B) and (f)(2)(iv) of this section is any entity that satisfies the first requirement in the definition of the equivalent of a trust in §1.404A-1(e) (segregation in a separate legal entity) and, in practice, also satisfies the third requirement in that definition (dedication to payment of plan benefits) with respect to benefits under the relevant plan.

(iv) *Special rules for certain foreign corporation plans.* In the case of a foreign corporation's plan for which no method has been used for some or all prior taxable years because no calculation of earnings and profits has been necessary for those years (see, e.g., paragraph (b)(2)(ii) of this section), the employer may assume that the old method has been consistent with any method actually used consistently in immediately prior years. If no calculation of earnings and profits has been made for prior years, in determining the Old Method Closing Amount, the taxpayer may assume the method used was a method described in paragraph (f)(2)(iii) of this section. This assumed method used in the calculation of the Old Method Closing Amount must actually be used by the taxpayer for all the prior taxable years to the extent reductions of earnings and profits for those years are ever determined with respect to the plan.

(v) *Reference to rules applicable in the case of failure to consider net investment income in computing section 481(a) adjustment.* The treatment of net investment income earned by a funding vehicle that has not previously taken into account by the taxpayer in determining taxable income (in the case of a foreign branch) or earnings and profits (in the case of a foreign corporation), and that is not properly considered (as required under paragraphs (f)(2)(i)(B) and (f)(2)(iv)(A) of this section) in determining the amount of the section 481(a) adjustment for purposes of section 404A, is determined under other applicable provisions, which may include sections 61, 671 through 679, and 1001.

(vi) *Certain section 481(a) adjustments treated as carryover contributions.* In the case of an election for a plan to be treated as a qualified funded plan, any net positive section 481(a) adjustment is treated as a carryover contribution (within the meaning of §1.404A-2(d)(4)) to the extent that the adjustment is attributable to limits (that would be taken into account under §1.404A-2(d)(4)) on the amounts previously contributed to the trust under the plan that could be taken into account under section 404A.

(5) *Examples.* The principles of paragraph (f) of this section are illustrated by the following examples:

Example 1. Nonqualified reserve plan to qualified reserve plan. A foreign subsidiary of a domestic corporation established an irrevocable balance sheet reserve for pension expenses in 1981. The subsidiary maintains its books and records in FC, the functional currency. From 1981 through 1987, the taxpayer reduced earnings and profits of the foreign subsidiary by FC150,000, the amount of the pension liability which had accrued under the plan. This method of accounting was never challenged or changed by the District Director prior to the expiration of the statute of limitations for the 1981 through 1987 taxable years. Through December 31, 1987, the last day of the closing year, actual pension payments totalled FC15,000. For the 1988 taxable year, the taxpayer made an election for the plan to be treated as a qualified reserve plan. The reserve calculated under section 404A as of the first day of the 1988 taxable year, the opening year, and based upon employee census data as of that date, was FC175,000. The Old Method Closing Amount was FC135,000 (FC150,000 less FC15,000). The New Method Opening Amount was FC175,000. The section 481(a) adjustment was a negative FC40,000 (FC135,000 less FC175,000). This adjustment is to be taken into account over the 15-year section 481(a) adjustment period prescribed in paragraph (e)(2)(ii) of this section.

Example 2. Nonqualified reserve plan to qualified reserve plan. Assume the same facts as in *Example 1*, except that the reserve calculated

under section 404A as of the first day of the 1988 taxable year and based upon employee census data as of that date was FC75,000. The Old Method Closing Amount was FC135,000 (FC150,000 less FC15,000). The New Method Opening Amount was FC75,000. The section 481(a) adjustment was a positive FC60,000 (FC135,000 less FC75,000). This adjustment is to be taken into account over the 15-year section 481(a) adjustment period prescribed in paragraph (e)(2)(ii) of this section.

Example 3. Nonqualified funded plan to qualified reserve plan. M, a domestic corporation, wholly owns N, a foreign corporation. N maintains its books and records in FC, the local currency. From 1981 through 1988, N maintained a nonqualified funded plan. During this period, N contributed FC55,000 to the separate funding entity administering the plan and reduced earnings and profits by FC55,000. The separate funding entity realized net income of FC17,000 from investment of plan assets and paid nothing to participants. None of the FC17,000 net investment income earned in the separate funding entity was taken into account in computing N's earnings and profits. As of the last day of N's 1988 taxable year, the closing year, the plan's fund balance was FC72,000, comprised of FC55,000 (excess contributions) and FC17,000 (investment income). The reserve calculated under section 404A as of the first day of the 1989 taxable year, the opening year, was FC100,000. Effective for M's 1989 taxable year, M elected under section 404A to treat N's funded plan as a qualified reserve plan. The Old Method Closing Amount was FC72,000. The New Method Opening Amount was FC100,000; thus, if, in the future, N pays FC100,000 to plan participants or beneficiaries, that FC100,000 will not again reduce N's earnings and profits. The section 481(a) adjustment was a negative FC28,000 (FC72,000 less FC100,000). However, if the District Director later challenges and requires N to change its method of accounting for foreign deferred compensation used in determining its 1981 through 1988 earnings and profits in a taxable year prior to the 1989 taxable year, the section 481(a) adjustment could be changed from a negative FC28,000 to a negative FC100,000. Pursuant to the administrative procedures under section 446(e), the District Director, upon challenging the treatment of foreign deferred compensation in years prior to 1989, could require any necessary positive section 481(a) adjustment to be taken into account in one taxable year.

Example 4. Nonqualified funded plan to qualified funded plan. Y, a domestic corporation, wholly owns X, a foreign corporation. X maintains its books and records in FC, the local currency. From 1981 through 1988, X maintained a nonqualified funded plan. During this period, X reduced earnings and profits by contributions of FC55,000 to the plan. The plan paid participants FC30,000. As of the last day of Y's 1988 taxable year, the plan's fund balance was FC29,000, comprised of FC25,000 (net contributions) and FC4,000 (interest income that was never previously taken into account in determining earnings and profits). Effective for Y's 1989 taxable year, Y elected under section 404A to treat X's funded plan as a qualified funded plan. The Old Method Closing Amount was FC29,000. The New Method Opening Amount was FC29,000. The section 481(a) adjustment was zero (FC29,000 less FC29,000). See *Example 3*, however, for the effects on the section 481(a) adjustment of a successful challenge to X's method of accounting for foreign deferred compensation in years prior to 1989 by the District Director.

Example 5. Z, the wholly owned foreign subsidiary of Y, a domestic corporation, has maintained a reserve plan for its employees, beginning in 1981. Z maintains its books and records in FC, the local currency. Effective for 1984, Y elected under section 404A to treat the plan as a qualified reserve plan. The only section 481(a) adjustment required was to take into account the limitation under section 404A(d). In 1981 through 1983, prior to the section 404A election, Z's earnings and profits were reduced by additions to the reserve. This method of accounting was never challenged or changed by the District Director prior to the expiration of the statute of limitations for the 1981 through 1983 taxable years. Thus, the Old Method Closing Amount equaled the balance in the reserve, which was FC300. To compute the New Method Opening Amount, the opening reserve took into account the lesser of the cumulative United States amount (FC300) or the cumulative foreign amount (FC90) as of the first day of 1984, the opening year. Thus, the New Method Opening Amount was FC90. The section 481(a) adjustment was therefore a positive FC210 (FC300—FC90); 1/15 of this amount, FC14 (FC210/15), is being taken into account as an increase in earnings and profits each year over the 15-year section 481(a) adjustment period that began in 1984.

Example 6. Nonqualified reserve plan to qualified reserve plan. Assume the same facts as in *Example 5* for all taxable years and the annual United States reduction, foreign reduction, cumulative United States amount, cumulative foreign amount and the section 481(a) adjustment shown below. The total annual reduction (or increase) in Z's earnings and profits was as follows—

	1984	1985	1986	1987	1988	1989	1990
Amount determined under U.S. law with respect to the plan under section 404A for the taxable year without regard to section 404A(d)	FC(40)	FC(50)	FC(60)	FC(70)	FC(80)	FC(90)	FC(100)
Amount allowed as a deduction for the taxable year under the appropriate foreign tax laws	(70)	(260)	(50)	(40)	(30)	(20)	(10)
Cumulative U.S. amount	(340)	(390)	(450)	(520)	(600)	(690)	(790)
Cumulative foreign amount	(160)	(420)	(470)	(510)	(540)	(560)	(570)
Lesser of cumulative U.S. or foreign amount	(160)	(390)	(450)	(510)	(540)	(560)	(570)
Reduced by the aggregate amount	90	160	390	440	510	540	560
	(70)	(230)	(60)	(70)	(30)	(20)	(10)
Amount taken into account for the taxable year*	(70)	(230)	(50)	(70)	(30)	(20)	(10)
Positive section 481 adjustment	14	14	14	14	14	14	14
Total increase (reduction) in earnings and profits taken into account for the taxable year	FC(56)	FC(216)	FC(36)	FC(56)	FC(16)	FC(6)	FC(4)

(g) *Initial section 404A(d) amounts*—(1) *In general.* By making an election under section 404A, a taxpayer adopts section 404A(d) as part of its method of accounting. Section 1.404A-4 provides rules to apply the limitations of section 404A(d) in taxable years when an election under section 404A is in effect. This paragraph (g) provides rules to compute initial amounts under section 404A(d) in the opening year. These rules are based on the rules to compute the New Method Opening Amount in paragraph (f)(3) of this section.

(2) *Computation of amounts.* As of the first day of the opening year, the initial section 404A(d) amounts are as follows:

(i) The initial cumulative United States amount equals the New Method Opening Amount without regard to any reduction under paragraph (f)(3)(iv) of this section.

(ii) The initial cumulative foreign amount equals the New Method Opening Amount computed as though the appropriate foreign tax law were the new method of accounting and without regard to paragraph (f)(3)(iv) of this section.

(iii) The initial aggregate amount equals the lesser of—

(A) The initial cumulative United States amount; and

(B) The initial cumulative foreign amount.

(3) *Example.* The principles of paragraph (g) of this section are illustrated by the following example:

Example. A foreign subsidiary of a domestic corporation maintains its books and records in FC, the local currency. The subsidiary established a funded deferred compensation plan in 1983 but reduced earnings and profits on a pay-as-you-go basis. The plan year and the taxable year of the domestic corporation and the subsidiary are the calendar year. For the 1990 taxable year, the domestic corporation elected to treat the plan as a qualified reserve plan. The balance in the separate funding entity as of January 1, 1990, the first day of the opening year, was FC90,000. The initial United States cumulative amount (the opening reserve) was FC150,000. The initial foreign cumulative amount (the balance in the separate funding entity) was FC90,000. The initial aggregate amount was FC90,000 (the lesser of FC90,000 or FC150,000). Since the subsidiary reduced earnings and profits on the pay-as-you-go method, the Old Method Closing Amount was zero. The section 481(a) adjustment was a negative FC90,000 (zero less FC90,000 (the lesser of FC150,000 or FC90,000)).

[Reg. § 1.404A-6.]

§ 1.404A-7. *Effective date, retroactive elections, and transition rules, EE-14-81, 5/6/93.*

(a) *In general*—(1) *Effective date.* Except as otherwise provided in this section, section 404A applies to taxable years beginning after December 31, 1979.

(2) *Overview of retroactive elections for taxable years beginning before January 1, 1980*— (i) *Plans of foreign subsidiaries.* Section 2(e)(2) of Public Law 96-603 permitted a taxpayer to make section 404A apply retroactively for all of its foreign subsidiaries. Paragraph (b) of this section describes and provides the time and manner to make, perfect,

or revoke this retroactive effective date election. If a retroactive effective date election was made, the taxpayer was also eligible to make a qualified funded plan election or a qualified reserve plan election effective retroactively for any of its subsidiaries' plans that met the requirements of § 1.404A-1(a) (other than paragraph (4) thereof) for the relevant period. Paragraph (c) of this section describes and provides the time and manner to make, perfect, or revoke these retroactive plan-by-plan elections for foreign subsidiaries.

(ii) *Plans of foreign branches.* Section 2(e)(3) of Public Law 96-603 permitted a taxpayer to make a qualified funded plan election retroactively for any plans maintained by a foreign branch that met the requirements of § 1.404A-1(a) (other than paragraph (4) thereof) for the relevant period. Paragraph (d) of this section describes and provides the time and manner to make this retroactive plan-by-plan qualified funded plan election for plans maintained by foreign branches.

(3) *Overview of special transition rules for election, revocation, and re-election.* Paragraph (e) of this section provides the time and manner to make and revoke qualified funded plan and qualified reserve plan elections for a taxpayer's transition period.

(b) *Retroactive effective date elections for foreign subsidiaries*—(1) *In general.* Section 2(e)(2) of Public Law 96-603 permitted a taxpayer to make section 404A effective during the taxpayer's open period. If the election was made, the taxpayer accepted section 404A (including, for example, § 1.404A-1(d)) as the operative law for all foreign subsidiaries (whether or not controlled foreign corporations) during the taxpayer's entire open period. If the election was made, section 404A applies to all distributions from accumulated profits (or earnings and profits) earned after December 31, 1970 (unless the election is revoked pursuant to paragraph (b)(3) of this section, if applicable). If accumulated profits were earned prior to January 1, 1971, a change in method of accounting is required for the foreign subsidiary's taxable year that ends with or within the first taxable year in the taxpayer's open period. A section 481(a) adjustment is required for amounts taken into account prior to the beginning of the foreign subsidiary's year of change and must be computed applying the rules of § 1.404A-6(f).

(2) *Time and manner to make, perfect, or revoke election.* The retroactive effective date election described in paragraph (b)(1) of this section is not effective unless the election was actually made no later than the time prescribed by law for filing the United States return for the first taxable year ending on or after December 31, 1980, including extensions (whether or not the time was actually extended for filing the taxpayer's return), and unless the taxpayer perfects the election by filing a statement indicating the taxpayer's agreement to perfect the election with an amended return for the first taxable year ending on or after December 31, 1980, on or before [*INSERT DATE THAT IS 365 DAYS AFTER THE DATE OF PUBLICATION OF FINAL REGULATIONS IN THE* FEDERAL REGISTER]. In order to be effective, the perfection must be made in the manner provided in § 1.404A-6(b)(3)(ii) or (iii). An election that is not perfected is considered retroactively revoked.

(3) *Requirement to amend returns*—(i) *In general.* In addition to the amended return required by paragraph (b)(2) of this section, the taxpayer must file any other amended United States returns that are

---

* The limitation in § 1.404A-4(c) applies to taxable years 1984, 1985 and 1986. In 1986, the amount deductible under the appropriate foreign tax law was less than the lower of (1) the cumulative U.S. amount, or, (2) the cumulative foreign amount (then reduced by the aggregate amount).

necessary to conform the treatment of all items affected by the election or revocation to the treatment consistent with the election or revocation within the time period described in paragraph (b)(2) of this section. If no adjustments are necessary, the amended return required by paragraph (b)(2) of this section must contain a statement to that effect.

(ii) *Required statements.* All amended returns required by this paragraph (b)(3) must be accompanied by a statement containing—

(A) The open years, open period and retroactive period of the taxpayer;

(B) The taxable year for which the election is perfected or revoked;

(C) A statement that the election (or elections) are perfected or revoked pursuant to the authority contained in § 1.404A-7; and

(D) A signature and verification as provided in § 1.404A-5(b)(7).

(c) *Retroactive plan-by-plan elections for foreign subsidiaries*—(1) *In general.* Any taxpayer that makes a retroactive effective date election described in paragraph (a)(2)(i) of this section under the rules of paragraph (b) of this section may, at its option, also elect to treat any foreign plan of a subsidiary that met the requirements of § 1.404A-1(a) (other than paragraph (4) thereof) for the relevant period as a qualified funded plan or as a qualified reserve plan under section 404A, beginning in any taxable year of the foreign subsidiary that ends with or within the taxpayer's open period (or for any earlier taxable year beginning after December 31, 1971, for which earnings and profits of the subsidiary had no United States tax significance). Alternatively, the taxpayer may decide to make no such plan-by-plan election with respect to any particular plan or plans of any of its foreign subsidiaries. Rules similar to those contained in § 1.404A-6 (including, where applicable, the requirement to obtain the consent of the Commissioner) are used to effect such plan-by-plan elections. If the plan existed in a taxable year beginning prior to the first year for which the election was effective, a change in method of accounting is required for the year of the election. The year of change for purposes of computing the section 481(a) adjustment is the first year that the election is effective.

(2) *Time and manner to make, perfect, or revoke election.* A taxpayer that is eligible to make a plan-by-plan election described in paragraph (c)(1) of this section may make or perfect such an election by attaching a statement to that effect on an amended return for the year that the election is to be effective on or before [*INSERT DATE THAT IS 365 DAYS AFTER THE DATE OF PUBLICATION OF FINAL REGULATIONS IN THE* FEDERAL REGISTER]. In order to be effective, the perfection of a plan-by-plan election must be made in the manner

Taxable year	
1978	....
1979	....
Total reduction in earnings and profits	....
Total reduction in earnings and profits	
S	....
T	....

(ii) In 1981, P made a retroactive effective date election pursuant to section 2(e)(2) of Public Law 96-603 and paragraph (b) of this section for taxable years beginning after December 31, 1977, and ending before January 1, 1980, P's open period. Thus, with respect to its open period, P has made section 404A the operative law for all distributions of earnings and profits (or accumulated profits) earned after December 31, 1970 for S and T. The consequences of making or not making the retroactive plan-by-plan election under section 404A for each foreign plan will be determined as though section 404A had been in effect for those years. Accordingly, earnings and profits of S and T may not be reduced with respect to amounts accrued under their respective plans unless the plans met the requirements of § 1.404A-1(a) for those years in the open period.

(iii) P made a retroactive plan-by-plan election to treat S's Plan 1 as a qualified reserve plan for P's retroactive period. The amount taken into account under § 1.404A-3 for S's Plan 1 calculated under section 404A was FC25,000 for 1978 and FC35,000 for 1979. No election under

provided in § 1.404A-6(b)(3)(ii) or (iii). An election that is not perfected is considered retroactively revoked. Any election made or perfected under this paragraph (c) will continue in effect for taxable years beginning after the taxpayer's open period, unless revoked under paragraph (c)(4) or (e) of this section or § 1.404A-6.

(3) *Requirement to amend returns.* In addition to the amended return required by paragraph (c)(2) of this section, the taxpayer must file any other amended United States returns that are necessary to conform the treatment of all items affected by the election or revocation to the treatment consistent with the election or revocation. All amended returns must be accompanied by the statement described in paragraph (b)(3)(ii) of this section (substituting "made, perfected, or revoked" for "perfected or revoked" where applicable) and all of the information required by § 1.404A-6(b)(4) (and § 1.404A-6(c)(2)(ii), if applicable, in the case of a termination). If no adjustments are necessary, the amended return required by paragraph (c)(2) of this section must contain a statement to that effect.

(4) *Revocation after initial election and re-election permitted.* Any taxpayer that makes an initial election for any plan under paragraph (c)(2) of this section may, under the rules of that paragraph, revoke the election for any taxable year after the sixth consecutive taxable year for which the election is effective, and may re-elect for any taxable year after the sixth consecutive taxable year for which the election is not in effect (regardless of whether the election is not in effect due to revocation or termination of the election as defined in § 1.404A-6(c)(1)). The consecutive changes in method of accounting described in the first sentence of this paragraph (c)(3) must be made under the rules in § 1.404A-6 regarding the section 481(a) adjustment period. The Commissioner may approve a letter ruling request (see § 601.201 of this chapter) to shorten the six-year waiting period upon a showing of extraordinary circumstances.

(5) *Examples.* The principles of paragraphs (b) and (c) of this section are illustrated by the following examples:

Example 1. P, a domestic corporation, wholly owns two foreign subsidiaries, S and T. S and T maintain their books and records in FC, the local currency. Since 1978, S and T have maintained unfunded pension plans for their respective employees. S maintained two plans, Plan 1 and Plan 2, and T maintained one plan. The plan years and the taxable years of all three corporations are the calendar year.

(i) For 1978 and 1979, P reduced the earnings and profits of S and T by the amount of the pension liability that had accrued under the plans as follows—

	S's Plan 1	S's Plan 2	T's plan
	FC30,000	FC5,000	FC70,000
	50,000	15,000	80,000
	FC80,000	FC20,000	FC150,000
S	FC100,000		
T	FC150,000		

section 404A was made for S's Plan 2 or for T's plan. Thus, no amount of the accrued but unpaid pension liability attributable to S's Plan 2 or to T's plan may reduce S's or T's respective 1978 and 1979 earnings and profits. P amended its tax returns for 1978 and 1979 to reflect the correct reduction of earnings and profits of FC25,000 and FC35,000 with respect to S's Plan 1 and no reduction for those years with respect to S's Plan 2 or T's plan. Since S's and T's plans were established during the open period, no section 481(a) adjustment is required.

Example 2. Q, a domestic corporation, has wholly owned R, a foreign subsidiary, since R's formation in 1968. R maintains its books and records in FC, the local currency. Since 1968, R maintained an unfunded pension plan for its employees. The plan year and the taxable year of both corporations is the calendar year. R, since 1968, used a method of accounting under which it reduced earnings and profits by its accrued pension liability.

(i) R's earnings and profits were earned and distributed to Q as follows—

Taxable year	Earnings and profits	Distribution of earnings and profits
1968	FC10,000	
1969	20,000	
1970	20,000	
Subtotal		50,000

Taxable year	Earnings and profits	Distribution of earnings and profits
1971	30,000	
1972	30,000	
1973	30,000	
1974	30,000	
1975	30,000	FC200,000
Subtotal	150,000	
1976	40,000	
1977	40,000	
1978	40,000	
1979	40,000	
1980	40,000	
1981	50,000	
Subtotal	250,000	
Total	FC450,000	

(ii) In 1981, Q made a retroactive effective date election pursuant to section 2(e)(2) of Public Law 96-603 and paragraph (b)(1) of this section for its open period. As of December 31, 1980, Q's open period included the taxable years 1975 through 1979. Thus, with respect to those taxable years, Q has made section 404A the operative law for R. The consequences of making or not making the retroactive plan-by-plan election under section 404A for R's foreign plan will be determined as though section 404A had been in effect for those taxable years. Thus, the earnings and profits of R may not be reduced with respect to amounts accrued under R's plan, unless the plan met the requirements of § 1.404A-1(a) for those taxable years.

Q made a retroactive plan-by-plan election to treat R's plan as a qualified reserve plan effective beginning in 1971. Of the distribution of FC200,000 to Q in 1975, section 404A applies to FC150,000, because these accumulated profits (or earnings and profits) were earned in taxable years beginning after December 31, 1970 and were also distributed in 1975, within Q's open period. However, section 404A does not apply to the FC50,000 distribution made from accumulated profits earned before December 31, 1970. Since R's plan was established before Q's open period, a section 481(a) adjustment is required. This section 481(a) adjustment must be taken into account in determining earnings and profits beginning with the 1971 year of change.

(d) *Retroactive plan-by-plan qualified funded plan elections for certain plans of foreign branches*—(1) *In general.* Section 2(e)(3) of Public Law 96-603 permitted a taxpayer to make a qualified funded plan election retroactively for any plans maintained by a foreign branch that met the requirements of § 1.404A-1(a) (other than paragraph (4) thereof) for the relevant period. As a condition of making this election, a taxpayer is required to agree to the assessment of all deficiencies (including interest thereon) arising during those taxable years within the open period (even those taxable years that are not open years as defined in paragraph (g)(4) of this section) to the extent that the deficiencies arise from erroneous deductions claimed by the taxpayer with respect to all of the taxpayer's foreign branches that maintained a deferred compensation plan. For a taxpayer that agrees to the assessment of tax in an election under this paragraph (d), a change in method of accounting is necessary (and a section 481(a) adjustment is required in accordance with the provisions of § 1.404A-6) with respect to any erroneous deductions claimed by the taxpayer under its method of accounting in taxable years ending prior to the beginning of the open period. For such a change in method of accounting, the year of change is the first taxable year in the open period, and the method of accounting to which the taxpayer is required to change is the method permitted during the open period under this paragraph (d).

(2) *Amounts allowed as a deduction.* If an election under section 2(e)(3) of Public Law 96-603 was made under the rules of this paragraph (d), the aggregate of the taxpayer's prior deductions is allowed as a deduction ratably over a 15-year period, beginning with the taxpayer's first taxable year beginning after December 31, 1979. A fractional part of a year which is a taxable year (as defined in sections 441(b) and 7701(a)(23)) is a taxable year for purposes of the 15-year period.

(3) *Definitions*—(i) *Prior deduction*—(A) *In general.* The term "prior deduction" means a deduction with respect to a qualified funded plan (i.e., a plan that met the requirements of § 1.404A-1(a) for the relevant period, and with respect to which a qualified funded plan election was made under the rules of this paragraph (d)) maintained by a foreign branch of a taxpayer for a taxable year beginning before January 1, 1980—

(*1*) That the taxpayer claimed;

(*2*) That was not allowable under the law in effect prior to the enactment of section 404A;

(*3*) With respect to which, on December 1, 1980, the assessment of a deficiency was not barred by any law or rule of law; and

(*4*) That would have been allowable if section 404A applied to taxable years beginning before January 1, 1980.

(B) *Application of section 404A(d).* Because the prior deductions are limited by the amounts that may be taken into account under section 404A, the computation of those prior deductions for the relevant taxable years is subject to the limitations described in section 404A(d) and § 1.404A-4. However, once the aggregate of prior deductions is calculated, the aggregate, or any portion thereof permitted to be taken into account over the 15-year period of paragraph (d)(2) of this section, is not subject to the limitations prescribed by section 404A(d) and § 1.404A-4.

(ii) *Erroneous deduction.* The term "erroneous deduction" means an amount that is not deductible under section 404(a) (including section 404(a)(5)), that was deducted on a taxpayer's income tax return with respect to a foreign deferred compensation plan.

(4) *Time and manner to make, perfect, or revoke election*—(i) *In general.* A plan-by-plan election described in paragraph (d)(1) of this section is not effective unless the election was actually made no later than the time prescribed by law for filing the United States return for the first taxable year ending on or after December 31, 1980, including extensions (whether or not the time was actually extended for filing the taxpayer's return), and unless the taxpayer perfects the election by filing a statement indicating the taxpayer's agreement to perfect the election with an amended return for the first taxable year ending on or after December 31, 1980, on or before [*INSERT DATE THAT IS 365 DAYS AFTER THE DATE OF PUBLICATION OF FINAL REGULATIONS IN THE FEDERAL REGISTER*]. In order to be effective, the perfection must be made in the manner provided in § 1.404A-6(b)(3)(ii) or (iii). An election that is not perfected is considered retroactively revoked. Any election under this paragraph (d) will continue in effect for taxable years beginning after the taxpayer's open period, unless revoked under paragraph (e) of this section or § 1.404A-6.

(ii) *Requirement to amend returns.* In addition to the amended return required by paragraph (d)(4)(i) of this section, the taxpayer must file any other amended United States returns that are necessary to conform the treatment of all items affected by the election or revocation to the treatment consistent with the election or revocation under this paragraph (d) within the time period described in paragraph (d)(4)(i) of this section. All amended returns must be accompanied by the statement described in paragraph (b)(3)(ii) of this section and all of the information required by § 1.404A-6(b)(4) (and § 1.404A-6(c)(2)(ii), if applicable, in the case of a termination). If no adjustments are necessary, the amended return required by paragraph (d)(4)(i) of this section must contain a statement to that effect.

(5) *Examples.* The principles of this paragraph (d) are illustrated by the following examples:

Example 1. (i) During its open taxable years 1977 through 1979, X, a domestic corporation, maintained a nonqualified funded plan for the employees of its foreign branch. In 1981, X made a retroactive effective date election and a retroactive plan-by-plan election to treat this plan as a qualified funded plan. The amounts deducted on X's tax returns, the amount deductible under sections 404(a) and 404A (expressed in FC, the local currency) are as follows—

¶ 20,162A

	1977	1978	1979	Total
Amount deducted on tax return	FC100	FC100	FC100	FC300
Amount deductible under section 404(a)	20	20	20	FC60
Amount deductible under section 404A	90	90	90	FC270

(ii) The assessment (including interest) for the open years 1977 through 1979 is based on adjustments to the erroneous deductions of FC240 (FC300 less FC60).

(iii) The amount of the prior deductions taken into account ratably over 15 years as provided in paragraph (d)(2) of this section, beginning in 1981, is a negative FC210 (FC60 less FC270).

(iv) No section 481(a) adjustment is required because *X* took no deductions with respect to the plan prior to the beginning of its open period.

Example 2. (i) *Z*, a domestic corporation, maintained a nonqualified funded foreign branch plan for its foreign employees, beginning in its 1965 (calendar) taxable year. In 1981, *Z* made a retroactive effective date election and a retroactive plan-by-plan election to treat this plan as a qualified funded plan. As of December 31, 1980, *Z*'s 1965 taxable year was closed, but its 1978 taxable year was open. The amounts deducted on *Z*'s tax returns, the amount deductible under sections 404(a) and 404A (expressed in FC, the local currency) are as follows—

	1965	1978	Total
Amount deducted on tax return	FC20	FC80	FC100
Amount deductible under section 404(a)	5	6	FC11
Amount deductible under section 404A	10	40	FC60

(ii) Under paragraph (d)(1) of this section, *Z* agreed to an assessment of deficiencies for its 1978 taxable year based on its FC74 (FC80—FC6) of erroneous deductions as defined in paragraph (d)(3)(ii) of this section.

(iii) The FC34 (FC40—FC6) of prior deductions is permitted to be taken into account as a deduction over the 15-year period beginning with its 1980 taxable year as provided in paragraph (d)(2) of this section.

(iv) Additionally, because *Z* took erroneous deductions under its method of accounting prior to the beginning of its open period, it is required to change to the method of accounting permitted during the open period, and must take a section 481(a) adjustment (determined under the snapshot method of § 1.404A-6(f)) into account over the 15-year section 481(a) adjustment period of § 1.404A-6(e)(2)(ii) beginning in its 1978 year of change. See paragraph (d)(1) of this section.

Example 3. A foreign branch which computes its income under the profit and loss method of Rev. Rul. 75-107, 1975-1 C.B. 32 (see § 601.601(d)(2)(ii)(*b*) of this chapter), in units of local currency, the FC, maintains a qualified funded plan. In 1980, the taxpayer was eligible to make the elections described in this section, and did so during the 1980 taxable year. The amount determined under paragraph (d)(3)(i) of this section after taking into account the limitations prescribed [by] § 1.404A-4(a) for the open period was FC1,500,000. For the 1980 taxable year, and as provided in paragraph (d) of this section, FC100,000 of the prior deductions were deductible. The prior deductions allowed to be taken into account in the 1980 through 1994 taxable years are determined without regard to, and thus are not subject to, the limitations prescribed by § 1.404A-4(a).

(e) *Special transition rules for election, revocation and re-election*—(1) *In general.* This paragraph (e) provides the time and manner for making and revoking qualified funded plan and qualified reserve plan elections for a taxpayer's transition period. A taxpayer may make an election, revoke an election, and re-elect to treat any plan that met the

Plan-by-plan election effective
1971—1974
1982—1987

(ii) A section 481(a) adjustment is required for the years of change 1975, 1982 and 1988.

(f) *Special data rules for retroactive elections*—(1) *Retroactive calculation of section 481(a) adjustments*—(i) *General rule.* Retroactive elections may be made only if the taxpayer calculates the section 481(a) adjustment required by § 1.404A-6 based on substantiation quality data. Substantiation quality data generally must be current as of the date of the change in method of accounting. Nevertheless, if contemporaneous substantiation quality data is not readily available, the taxpayer may calculate the section 481(a) adjustment based on backward projections

requirements of § 1.404A-1(a) (other than paragraph (4) thereof) for the relevant period as a qualified funded plan or a qualified reserve plan under this paragraph (e) for the transition period without regard to whether a retroactive election is made under paragraph (b), (c), or (d) of this section. However, an election made under paragraph (c) or (d) of this section is deemed to continue in effect for taxable years beginning after December 31, 1979, unless revoked under paragraph (c)(4) of this section or this paragraph (e) or terminated or revoked under § 1.404A-6(f). See paragraphs (c)(2) and (d)(4)(i) of this section.

(2) *Time and manner initially to elect and revoke*—(i) *In general.* Taxpayers that wish to make an election under this paragraph (e) may have, but were not required to have, made a Method (1) or Method (2) election for the taxable year for which an election is made under this paragraph (e). Those taxpayers that wish to make (or perfect) an election under this paragraph (e) must attach a statement to that effect on an amended return for the year the election is to be effective on or before [*INSERT DATE THAT IS 365 DAYS AFTER THE DATE OF PUBLICATION OF FINAL REGULATIONS IN THE FEDERAL REGISTER*]. An election previously made that is not perfected is considered retroactively revoked.

(ii) *Requirement to amend returns.* In addition to the amended return required by paragraph (e)(2)(i) of this section, the taxpayer must file any other amended United States returns that are necessary to conform the treatment of all items affected by the election or revocation to the treatment consistent with the election or revocation under this paragraph (e) within the time period described in paragraph (e)(2)(i) of this section. All amended returns must be accompanied by the statement described in paragraph (b)(3)(ii) of this section (substituting "made, perfected, or revoked" for "perfected or revoked" where applicable) and all of the information required by § 1.404A-6(b)(4) (and § 1.404A-6(c)(2)(ii), if applicable, in the case of a termination). If no adjustments are necessary, the amended return required by paragraph (e)(2)(i) of this section must contain a statement to that effect.

(3) *Revocation after initial election and re-election permitted.* Any taxpayer that makes an initial election for any plan under paragraph (e)(2) of this section may, under the rules of that paragraph, revoke the election for any taxable year after the sixth consecutive taxable year for which the election is effective, and may re-elect for any taxable year after the sixth consecutive taxable year for which the election is not in effect (whether the election is not in effect due to either revocation or termination of the election as defined in § 1.404A-6(c)(1)). The consecutive changes in method of accounting described in the first sentence of this paragraph (e)(3) must be made under the rules in § 1.404A-6 regarding the section 481(a) adjustment period. The Commissioner may approve a letter ruling request to shorten the six-year waiting period upon a showing of extraordinary circumstances.

(4) *Example.* The principles of paragraph (e)(3) of this section are illustrated by the following example:

Example. (i) *L*, a domestic corporation, has wholly owned foreign subsidiary *M*, since *M*'s formation in 1971. *M* maintained a funded plan for its employees from 1971 through 1991. The taxable year of *L* and *M* is the calendar year. In 1981, *L* made a Method (2) election. Within 365 days after the publication of the final regulations in the Federal Register, *L* perfected its retroactive effective date election for all its foreign subsidiaries. *L*'s election terminated in 1975 due to its plan's violation of the requirements of section 404A(e)(2). Additionally, *L* perfected, revoked and re-elected on a plan-by-plan basis its election for *M*'s plan, as follows—

Plan-by-plan election terminated or revoked
1975—1981
1988—1993

to earlier years from the first taxable year beginning before January 1, 1980, for which sufficient contemporaneous substantiation quality data is readily available. However, such projections must satisfy the substantiation requirements in paragraph (f)(1)(ii) of this section. Furthermore, the taxpayer may not use any of the approaches provided for under this paragraph (f) if circumstances indicate that the overall result is a material distortion of the amounts allowable.

(ii) *Substantiation requirement for retroactive reserves*—(A) *In general.* Although reasonable actuarial estimates and projections may be used, the calculation of the opening balance of the reserve for the first year for which a qualified reserve plan election under paragraph (c)(1) of this section is effective must nonetheless be based on some actual contemporaneous evidence. Thus, the opening balance may be based on actual aggregate covered payroll, the actual number of covered employees, or a contemporaneous actuarial valuation that used reasonable actuarial methods. For example, if the taxpayer has contemporaneous records of the number of covered employees and the aggregate covered payroll, it may estimate other actuarial information, such as average age and marital status, based on reasonable actuarial methods (e.g., using substantiation quality data as of another date and adjusting for actual or expected changes for the interim years). The resulting combination of actual contemporaneous evidence and reasonably estimated data may be used to calculate the opening reserve. If a contemporaneous actuarial valuation is used as the basis of an opening reserve, the results of the valuation must be adjusted to reflect any difference between the actuarial method used in that actuarial valuation and the unit credit method, as required by section 404A(c) and §1.404A-3(b).

(B) *Interpolation.* In cases where a taxpayer can meet the substantiation requirement of paragraph (f)(1)(ii)(A) of this section for some years, but cannot meet that requirement in intervening years (including the year of the change in method of accounting), the taxpayer may interpolate a reserve balance for the intervening years based on reasonable actuarial methods. In the absence of evidence to the contrary, it is assumed that a pro rata allocation of amounts to those intervening years is a reasonable actuarial method. This paragraph (f)(1)(ii)(B) does not authorize any interpolation for years in which other evidence indicates that it would cause a material distortion (such as a year during which the work force was on strike and no deferred compensation benefits were accrued). In addition, this paragraph (f)(1)(ii)(B) does not authorize extrapolation of reserve balances to years that are not intervening years between years that meet the substantiation requirements of paragraph (f)(1)(ii)(A) of this section.

(C) *Extrapolation.* If the first year for which the taxpayer is able to meet the substantiation requirements of paragraph (f)(1)(ii)(A) of this section ("the substantiation year") is later than the year of the change in method of accounting, a taxpayer may use the approach described in this paragraph (f)(1)(ii)(C) to determine the section 481(a) adjustments described in §1.404A-6(f) in years prior to the substantiation year. Under this approach, the taxpayer's closing balance under its prior method as of the date of the change in the method of accounting is compared with the opening balance in the substantiation year. If the closing balance exceeds the opening balance, the excess is the amount to be used in calculating the adjustment under section 481, as required by §1.404A-6. However, if the closing balance of the taxpayer's reserve under its method used for years prior to the election under section 404A is less than the opening balance for the substantiation year, the opening balance as of the date of the change in method in accounting is assumed to be equal to the closing balance. Thus, if the closing balance is less than the opening balance for the substantiation year, there is no adjustment under section 481. In such a case, the difference between the opening balance as of the date of the change in method of accounting and the opening balance for the substantiation year is allocated to the years prior to the substantiation year based on reasonable actuarial methods using all available information.

(2) *Determination of reasonable addition to a reserve in interim years.* In the case of a qualified reserve plan that is using the interpolation option of paragraph (f)(1)(ii)(B) of this section or that is described in the last sentence in paragraph (f)(1)(ii)(C) of this section, none of the

increase in the reserve in the intervening year is considered a reasonable addition to the reserve under §1.404A-3(b). Thus, the entire amount of the increase must be considered an amount to be amortized over ten years under §1.404A-3(c).

(3) *Protective elections.* For those taxpayers that relied on the prior position of the Internal Revenue Service by making a Method (1) election under which the section 481(a) adjustment was computed in a manner inconsistent with this section or by making a Method (2) election under which no section 481(a) adjustment was reflected in the original return, appropriate adjustments required by section 404A and its underlying regulations must be made on an amended return filed no later than [*INSERT DATE THAT IS 365 DAYS AFTER THE DATE OF PUBLICATION OF FINAL REGULATIONS IN THE FEDERAL REGISTER*] for the first year the election is effective and for all subsequent affected years for which a return has been filed. If no adjustments are necessary, an amended return should be filed for the first year stating that no adjustments are necessary.

(g) *Definitions and special rules*—(1) *Method (1) election.* The term "Method (1) election" means an election that was made under Method (1) (as defined in Ann. 81-114, 1981-28 I.R.B. 21) (see §601.601(d)(2)(ii)(*b*) of this chapter) by claiming the deduction or credit allowable under section 404A on the taxpayer's income tax return for the first taxable year ending on or after December 31, 1980, including extensions (or an amended return filed no later than the end of the extended time period prescribed in section 6081, whether or not such time was actually extended for filing the taxpayer's return).

(2) *Protective or Method (2) election.* The term "protective election" or "Method (2) election" means an election that was made under Method (2) (as defined in Ann. 81-114, 1981-28 I.R.B. 21) (see §601.601(d)(2)(ii)(*b*) of this chapter) without claiming deductions attributable to a qualified foreign plan on the taxpayer's income tax return (or, in the case of foreign subsidiaries, without taking into account reductions of earnings and profits).

(3) *Open years of the taxpayer.* The term "open years of the taxpayer" means open taxable years beginning after December 31, 1971, and for which, on December 31, 1980, the making of a refund, or the assessment of a deficiency, was not barred by any law or rule of law.

(4) *Retroactive period.* The term "retroactive period" means a taxpayer's taxable year (whether or not the making of a refund, or the assessment of a deficiency, was barred by any law or rule of law for any taxable year) in the following range—

(i) Any taxable year selected by the taxpayer between taxable years beginning after December 31, 1970 and before January 1, 1980 (the beginning taxable year); and

(ii) The last taxable year beginning before January 1, 1980 (the ending taxable year).

(5) *Transition period.* The term "transition period" means taxable years beginning after December 31, 1979, and before [*INSERT THE DATE OF PUBLICATION OF FINAL REGULATIONS IN THE FEDERAL REGISTER*].

(6) *Open period.* For purposes of this section, the term "open period" means, with respect to any taxpayer, all taxable years beginning after December 31, 1971, and beginning before January 1, 1980, and for which, on December 31, 1980, the making of a refund, or the assessment of a deficiency, was not barred by any law or rule of law. [Reg. §1.404A-7.]

¶ 20,162B

Proposed regulations: Required distribution rules: Qualified plans: IRAs: Trust as beneficiary.—The IRS has issued proposed regulations under Code Sec. 401(a)(9) that make changes to the required distribution rules that apply if a trust is named as beneficiary of an employee's benefit under a qualified plan or IRA. The proposed regulations amend the existing proposed rules that were issued in 1987 (CCH PENSION PLAN GUIDE ¶ 20,163B) and, like the existing proposed rules, may be relied on until final regulations are issued.

The proposed regulations were published in the Federal Register on December 30, 1997 (62 FR 67780). The proposed regulations were amended March 25, 1998 (63 FR 14391).

DEPARTMENT OF THE TREASURY

Internal Revenue Service

26 CFR Part 1

[REG-209463-82]

RIN 1545-AV82

Required Distributions from Qualified Plans and Individual Retirement Plans

AGENCY: Internal Revenue Service (IRS), Treasury.

ACTION: Notice of proposed rulemaking.

SUMMARY: This document contains amendments to the existing proposed regulations under section 401(a)(9) that make changes to the rules that apply if a trust is named as a beneficiary of an employee's benefit under a retirement plan. These proposed regulations will affect administrators of, participants in, and beneficiaries of qualified plans, institutions which sponsor and individuals who administer individual retirement plans, individuals who use individual retirement plans, simplified employee pensions and SIMPLE Savings Plans for retirement income and beneficiaries of individual retirement plans; and employees for whom amounts are contributed to section 403(b) annuity contracts, custodial accounts, or retirement income accounts and beneficiaries of such contracts and accounts.

DATES: Written comments and requests for a public hearing must be received by March 30, 1998.

ADDRESSES: Send submissions to CC:DOM:CORP:R (REG-209463-82), room 5226, Internal Revenue Service, POB 7604, Ben Franklin Station, Washington, DC 20044. Submissions may be hand delivered between the hours of 8 a.m. and 5 p.m. to CC:DOM:CORP:R (REG-209463-82), Courier's Desk, Internal Revenue Service, 1111 Constitution Avenue NW., Washington, DC. Alternatively, taxpayers may submit comments electronically via the Internet by selecting the "Tax Regs" option on the IRS Home Page, or by submitting comments directly to the IRS Internet site at http://www.irs.ustreas.gov/prod/tax_regs/comments.html

FOR FURTHER INFORMATION CONTACT: Thomas Foley at (202) 622-6030 (not a toll-free number).

SUPPLEMENTARY INFORMATION:

Paperwork Reduction Act

The collection of information contained in this notice of proposed rulemaking has been submitted to the Office of Management and Budget for review in accordance with the Paperwork Reduction Act of 1995 (44 U.S.C. 3507(d)). Comments on the collection of information should be sent to the **Office of Management and Budget**, Attn: Desk Officer for the Department of the Treasury, Office of Information and Regulatory Affairs, Washington, DC 20503, with copies to the **Internal Revenue Service**, Attn: IRS Reports Clearance Officer, T:FP, Washington, DC 20224. Comments on the collection of information should be received by March 2, 1998. Comments are specifically requested concerning:

Whether the proposed collection of information is necessary for the proper performance of the functions of the **Internal Revenue Service**, including whether the information will have practical utility;

The accuracy of the estimated burden associated with the proposed collection of information (see below);

How the quality, utility, and clarity of the information to be collected may be enhanced;

How the burden of complying with the proposed collection of information may be minimized, including through the application of automated collection techniques or other forms of information technology; and

Estimates of capital or start-up costs and costs of operation, maintenance, and purchase of services to provide information.

The collection of information in this proposed regulation is in Question and Answer D-7 of §1.401(a)(9)-1. This information is required for a taxpayer who wants to name a trust and treat the underlying beneficiaries of the trust as designated beneficiaries of the taxpayer's benefit under a retirement plan or an individual retirement plan ("IRA"). The taxpayer must provide a copy of the trust instrument or IRA trustee, custodian, or issuer, or provide a list of all the beneficiaries of the trust, certify that, to the best of the taxpayer's knowledge, this list is correct and complete, and agree to provide a copy of the trust instrument upon demand. In addition, other related requirements for the beneficiaries of the trust to be treated as designated beneficiaries must be satisfied. If the trust instrument is amended at any time in the future, the taxpayer must, within a reasonable time, provide a copy of each such amendment, or provide corrected certifications to the extent that the amendment changes the information previously certified. In addition, by the end of the ninth month after the death of the taxpayer, the trustee of the trust must provide a copy of the trust to the plan administrator or IRA trustee, custodian, or issuer, or provide a list of all the beneficiaries of the trust, certify that, to the best of the taxpayer's knowledge, this list is correct and complete, and agrees to provide a copy of the trust instrument upon demand. The collection of information is required to obtain a benefit. The likely respondents are individuals or households.

Estimated total annual reporting hours is 333 hours.

The estimated average burden per respondent is 20 minutes.

The estimated total number of respondents is 1,000.

An agency may not conduct or sponsor, and a person is not required to respond to, a collection of information unless it displays a valid control number assigned by the Office of Management and Budget.

Books or records relating to a collection of information must be retained as long as their contents may become material in the adminis-

tration of any internal revenue law. Generally, tax returns and tax return information are confidential, as required by 26 U.S.C. 6103.

Background

On July 27, 1987, Proposed Regulations (EE-113-82) under sections 401(a)(9), 403(b), 408, and 4974 of the Internal Revenue Code of 1986 were published in the **Federal Register** (52 FR 28070) Those proposed regulations provide guidance for complying with the rules relating to required distributions from qualified plans, individual retirement plans, and section 403(b) annuity contracts, custodial accounts, and retirement income accounts. This document contains amendments to proposed §1.401(a)(9)-1 (hereinafter referred to as the Existing Proposed Regulations) that was included in EE-113-82. Specifically this document contains amendments to Q&As D-5 and Q&A D-6 of the Existing Proposed Regulations which prescribe specific requirements that must be met when a trust is named as a beneficiary of an employee's benefit under a plan, and adds a new Q&A D-7 to the Existing Proposed Regulations. Proposed §§1.408-8 and 1.403(b)-2 (also included in EE-113-82) provide that the provisions of proposed §1.401(a)(9)-1 generally apply to individual retirement plans, and section 403(b) annuity contracts, custodial accounts, and retirement income accounts. Accordingly, these amendments and additions also generally apply to such plans, contracts, and accounts.

The amendments and additions to the Existing Proposed Regulations in these proposed regulations are issued in response to comments and questions received regarding the Existing Proposed Regulations with respect to section 401(a)(9). Treasury and the IRS continue to welcome additional comments concerning the Existing Proposed Regulations and the other sections of EE-113-82.

As in the case of the Existing Proposed Regulations and the other sections of EE-113-82, taxpayers may rely on these proposed regulations for guidance pending the issuance of final regulations. If, and to the extent, future guidance is more restrictive than the guidance in these proposed regulations, the future guidance will be applied without retroactive effect.

Explanation of provisions

Overview

Section 401(a)(9)(A) provides that, in order for a plan to be qualified under section 401(a), distributions of each employee's interest in the plan must commence no later than the "required beginning date" for the employee and must be distributed over a period not to exceed the joint lives or joint life expectancy of the employee and the employee's designated beneficiary. Section 401(a)(9)(B) provides that if distribution does not commence prior to death in accordance with section 401(a)(9)(A), distributions of the employee's interest must be made within 5 years of the employee's death or, generally, commence within one year of the employee's death and be made over the life or life expectancy of the designated beneficiary.

Section 401(a)(9)(E) defines the term "designated beneficiary" as an individual designated as a beneficiary by the employee. The Existing Proposed Regulations provide that, for purposes of section 401(a)(9), only individuals may be designated beneficiaries. A beneficiary who is not an individual, such as the employee's estate, may not be a designated beneficiary for purposes of determining the minimum required distribution, but nevertheless may be designated as the employee's beneficiary under the plan. If a beneficiary who is not an individual is designated to receive an employee's benefit after death, the employee is treated as having no designated beneficiary when determining the required minimum distribution. In that case, under section 401(a)(9), distributions commencing before death must be made over the employee's single life or life expectancy and distributions commencing after death must be made within 5 years of the employee's death.

However, the Existing Proposed Regulations provide that if a trust is named as a beneficiary of an employee's benefit under the plan, the underlying beneficiaries of the trust may be treated as designated beneficiaries for purposes of section 401(a)(9) if certain requirements are satisfied. In response to comments, these proposed regulations modify these trust beneficiary requirements as explained below by:

• Permitting the designated beneficiary of a revocable trust to be treated as the designated beneficiary for purposes of determining the minimum distribution under section 401(a)(9), provided that the trust becomes irrevocable upon the death of the employee.

• Providing relief from the requirement that the plan be provided with a copy of the trust document if certain certification requirements are met.

Irrevocability of trust

The Existing Proposed Regulations generally provide that a trust must be irrevocable as of the employee's required beginning date in order for the beneficiaries of the trust to be treated as designated beneficiaries under the plan for purposes of determining the distribution period under section 401(a)(9)(A). Commentators have indicated that most trusts established for estate planning purposes and designated as the beneficiary of an employee's plan benefits are revocable instruments prior to the death of the employee. In response to those comments, these proposed regulations provide that a trust named as beneficiary of an employee's interest in a retirement plan be permitted to be revocable while the employee is alive, provided that it becomes irrevocable, by its terms, upon the death of the employee. The requirements in the Existing Proposed Regulations that the trust be valid under state law (or would be but for the fact that there is no corpus) and that the beneficiaries be identifiable from the trust instrument are retained.

Information to Plan Administrator

In order to permit the plan administrator to substantiate that the requirements for treating the beneficiaries of the trust as designated beneficiaries under the plan are satisfied, the Existing Proposed Regulations require that a copy of the trust instrument be provided to the plan administrator by the earlier of the required beginning date or the date of the employee's death. In response to comments, this proposed regulation permits an alternative method of substantiation.

As under the Existing Proposed Regulations, a copy of the trust instrument may be provided to the plan administrator. However, because the trust need not be irrevocable, under this method, the employee must also agree that if the trust instrument is amended at any time in the future, the employee will, within a reasonable time, provide a copy of each such amendment.

Alternatively, the employee may provide a list of all of the beneficiaries of the trust (including contingent beneficiaries) with a description of the portion to which they are entitled and any conditions on their entitlement, and certify that, to the best of the employee's knowledge, this list is correct and complete and that the other requirements for the beneficiaries of the trust to be treated as designated beneficiaries are satisfied. Under the second method, the employee must also agree to provide corrected certifications to the extent that the amendment changes the information previously certified. Finally, the employee must agree to provide a copy of the trust instrument to the plan administrator upon demand.

In addition, these proposed regulations provide that, if the minimum required distributions after death are determined by treating the beneficiaries of the trust as designated beneficiaries, a final certification as to the beneficiaries of the trust instrument must be provided to the plan administrator by the end of the ninth month after the death of the employee. This rule applies even if a copy of the trust instrument were provided to the plan administrator before the employee's death. Alternatively, an updated trust instrument may be provided.

The proposed regulations also provide that a plan will not fail to satisfy section 401(a)(9) merely because the terms of the actual trust instrument are inconsistent with the information in the certifications or trust instruments previously provided to the plan administrator if the plan administrator reasonably relies on the information provided in the certifications or trust instruments. However, the minimum required distributions for years after the year in which the discrepancy is discovered must be determined based on the actual terms of the trust instrument. For those years, the minimum required distribution will be determined by treating the beneficiaries of the employee as having been changed in the year in which the year the discrepancy was discovered to conform to the corrected information and by applying the change in beneficiary provisions found under the Existing Proposed Regulations. However, for purposes of determining the amount of the excise tax under section 4974 (including application of a waiver, if any, for reasonable error under section 4974), the minimum required distribution is determined for any year based on the actual terms of the trust in effect during the year.

Special Analyses

It has been determined that this notice of proposed rulemaking is not a significant regulatory action as defined in EO 12866. Therefore, a regulatory assessment is not required. It also has been determined that section 553(b) of the Administrative Procedure Act (5 U.S.C. chapter 5) does not apply to these regulations. Moreover, it hereby certified that the regulations in this document will not have a significant economic impact on a substantial number of small entities. This certification is based on the fact that the reporting burden is primarily on the plan

participant to supply the information rather than on the entity maintaining the retirement plan and the fact that the number of participants per plan to whom the burden applies is insignificant. Accordingly, a regulatory flexibility analysis under the Regulatory Flexibility Act (5 U.S.C. chapter 6) is not required. Pursuant to section 7805(f) of the Internal Revenue Code, this notice of proposed rulemaking will be submitted to the Chief Counsel for Advocacy of the Small Business Administration for comment on its impact on small business.

Comments and Requests for a Public Hearing

Before these proposed regulations are adopted as final regulations, consideration will be given to any written comments (preferably a signed original and eight (8) copies) or comments transmitted via Internet that are submitted timely to the IRS. All comments will be available for public inspection and copying. A public hearing may be scheduled if requested in writing by a person that timely submits written comments. If a public hearing is scheduled, notice of the date, time, and place for the hearing will be published in the **Federal Register**.

Drafting Information

The principal author of these regulations is Cheryl Press, Office of the Associate Chief Counsel (Employee Benefits and Exempt Organizations), IRS. However, other personnel from the IRS and Treasury Department participated in their development.

List of Subjects in 26 CFR Part 1

Income taxes, Reporting and recordkeeping requirements.

Amendments to the Previously Proposed Regulations

Accordingly, 26 CFR part 1 is proposed to be amended as follows:

PART 1—INCOME TAXES

Paragraph 1. The authority citation for part 1 continues to read in part as follows:

Authority: 26 U.S.C. 7805 ***

Par. 2. Section 1.401(a)(9)-1, as proposed to be added at 52 FR 28075, July 27, 1987, is amended by:

1. Revising Q&A D-5

2. Revising Q&A D-6.

3. Adding Q&A D-7

The additions and revisions read as follows:

§ 1.401(a)(9)-1 Required distributions from trust and plans.
*****

D. Determination of the Designated Beneficiary.
*****

D-5. Q. If a trust is named as a beneficiary of an employee, will the beneficiaries of the trust with respect to the trust's interest in the employee's benefit be treated as having been designated as beneficiaries of the employee under the plan for purposes of determining the distribution period under section 401(a)(9)(A)(ii)?

A. (a) Pursuant to D-2A of this section, only an individual may be a designated beneficiary for purposes of determining the distribution period under section 401(a)(9)(A)(ii). Consequently, a trust itself may not be the designated beneficiary even though the trust is named as a beneficiary. However, if the requirements of paragraph (b) of this D-5 are met, distributions made to the trust will be treated as paid to the beneficiaries of the trust with respect to the trust's interest in the employee's benefit, and the beneficiaries of the trust will be treated as having been designated as beneficiaries of the employee under the plan for purposes of determining the distribution period under section 401(a)(9)(A)(ii). If, as of any date on or after the employee's required beginning date, a trust is named as a beneficiary of the employee and the requirements in paragraph (b) of this D-5 are not met, the employee will be treated as not having a designated beneficiary under the plan for purposes of section 401(a)(9)(A)(ii). Consequently, for calendar years beginning after that date, distribution must be made over the employee's life (or over the period which would have been the employee's remaining life expectancy determined as if no beneficiary had been designated as of the employee's required beginning date). [Amended by 63 FR 14391, March 25, 1998.]

(b) The requirements of this paragraph (b) are met if, as of the later of the date on which the trust is named as a beneficiary of the employee, or the employee's required beginning date, and as of all subsequent periods during which the trust is named as a beneficiary, the following requirements are met:

(1) The trust is a valid trust under state law, or would be but for the fact that there is no corpus.

(2) The trust is irrevocable or will, by its terms, become irrevocable upon the death of the employee.

(3) The beneficiaries of the trust who are beneficiaries with respect to the trust's interest in the employee's benefit are identifiable from the trust instrument within the meaning of D-2 of this section.

(4) The documentation described in D-7 of this section has been provided to the plan administrator.

(c) In the case of payments to a trust having more than one beneficiary, see E-5 of this section for the rules for determining the designated beneficiary whose life expectancy will be used to determine the distribution period. If the beneficiary of the trust named as beneficiary is another trust, the beneficiaries of the other trust will be treated as having been designated as beneficiaries of the employee under the plan for purposes of determining the distribution period under section 401(a)(9)(A)(ii), provided that the requirements of paragraph (b) of this D-5 are satisfied with respect to such other trust in addition to the trust named as beneficiary. [Amended by 63 FR 14391, March 25, 1998.]

D-6. Q. If a trust is named as a beneficiary of an employee, will the beneficiaries of the trust with respect to the trust's interest in the employee's benefit be treated as designated beneficiaries under the plan with respect to the employee for purposes of determining the distribution period under section 401(a)(9)(B)(iii) and (iv)?

A. (a) If a trust is named as a beneficiary of an employee and the requirements of paragraph (b) of D-5 of this section are satisfied as of the date of the employee's death or, in the case of the documentation described in D-7 of this section, by the end of the ninth month beginning after the employee's date of death, then distributions to the trust for purposes of section 401(a)(9) will be treated as being paid to the appropriate beneficiary of the trust with respect to the trust's interest in the employee's benefit, and all beneficiaries of the trust with respect to the trust's interest in the employee's benefit will be treated as designated beneficiaries of the employee under the plan for purposes of determining the distribution period under section 401(a)(9)(B)(iii) and (iv). If the beneficiary of the trust named as beneficiary is another trust, the beneficiaries of the other trust will be treated as having been designated as beneficiaries of the employee under the plan for purposes of determining the distribution period under section 401(a)(9)(B)(iii) and (iv), provided that the requirements of paragraph (b) of D-5 of this section are satisfied with respect to such other trust in addition to the trust named as beneficiary. If a trust is named as a beneficiary of an employee and if the requirements of paragraph (b) of D-5 of this section are not satisfied as of the dates specified in the first sentence of this paragraph, the employee will be treated as not having a designated beneficiary under the plan. Consequently, distribution must be made in accordance with the five-year rule in section 401(a)(9)(B)(ii). [Amended by 63 FR 14391, March 25, 1998.]

(b) The rules of D-5 of this section and this D-6 also apply for purposes of applying the provisions of section 401(a)(9)(B)(iv)(II) if a trust is named as a beneficiary of the employee's surviving spouse. In the case of payments to a trust having more than one beneficiary, see E-5 of this section for the rules for determining the designated beneficiary whose life expectancy will be used to determine the distribution period.

D-7. Q. If a trust is named as a beneficiary of an employee, what documentation must be provided to the plan administrator so that the beneficiaries of the trust who are beneficiaries with respect to the trust's interest in the employee's benefit are identifiable to the plan administrator?

A. (a) *Required distributions commencing before death.* In order to satisfy the requirement of paragraph (b)(4) of D-5 of this section for distributions required under section 401(a)(9) to commence before the death of an employee, the employee must comply with either paragraph (a)(1) or (2) of this D-7:

(1) The employee provides to the plan administrator a copy of the trust instrument and agrees that if the trust instrument is amended at any time in the future, the employee will, within a reasonable time, provide to the plan administrator a copy of each such amendment.

(2) The employee—

(i) Provides to the plan administrator a list of all of the beneficiaries of the trust (including contingent and remainderman beneficiaries with a description of the conditions on their entitlement);

(ii) Certifies that, to the best of the employee's knowledge, this list is correct and complete and that the requirements of paragraphs (b)(1), (2), and (3) of D-5 of this section are satisfied;

(iii) Agrees to provide corrected certifications to the extent that an amendment changes any information previously certified; and

(iv) Agrees to provide a copy of the trust instrument to the plan administrator upon demand. [Amended by 63 FR 14391, March 25, 1998.]

(b) *Required distributions after death.* In order to satisfy the documentation requirement of this D-7 for required distributions after death, by the end of the ninth month beginning after the death of the employee, the trustee of the trust must either

(1) Provide the plan administrator with a final list of all of the beneficiaries of the trust (including contingent and remainderman beneficiaries with a description of the conditions on their entitlement) as of the date of death; certify that, to the best of the trustee's knowledge, this list is correct and complete and that the requirements of paragraph (b)(1), (2), and (3) of D-5 of this section are satisfied as of the date of death; and agree to provide a copy of the trust instrument to the plan administrator upon demand; or

(2) Provide the plan administrator with a copy of the actual trust document for the trust that is named as a beneficiary of the employee under the plan as of the employee's date of death. [Amended by 63 FR 14391, March 25, 1998.]

(c) *Relief for discrepancy between trust instrument and employee certifications or earlier trust instruments.* (1) If required distributions are determined based on the information provided to the plan administrator in certifications or trust instruments described in paragraph (a)(1), (a)(2) or (b) of this D-7, a plan will not fail to satisfy section 401(a)(9) merely because the actual terms of the trust instrument are inconsistent with the information in those certifications or trust instruments previously provided to the plan administrator, but only if the plan administrator reasonably relied on the information provided and the minimum required distributions for calendar years after the calendar year in which the discrepancy is discovered are determined based on the actual terms of the trust instrument. For purposes of determining whether the plan satisfies section 401(a)(9) for calendar years after the calendar year in which the discrepancy is discovered, if the actual beneficiaries under the trust instrument are different from the beneficiaries previously certified or listed in the trust instrument previously provided to the plan administrator, or the trust instrument specifying the actual beneficiaries does not satisfy the other requirements of paragraph (b) of D-5 of this section, the minimum required distribution will be determined by treating the beneficiaries of the employee as having been changed in the calendar year in which the discrepancy was discovered to conform to the corrected information and by applying the change in beneficiary provisions of E-5 of this section.

(2) For purposes of determining the amount of the excise tax under section 4974, the minimum required distribution is determined for any year based on the actual terms of the trust in effect during the year. [Amended by 63 FR 14391, March 25, 1998.]

*****

Michael P. Dolan

Deputy Commissioner of Internal Revenue

[¶ 20,163 Reserved.—Proposed regulations on defined benefit plans for self-employed individuals and shareholder-employees formerly were reproduced at this paragraph. The final regulations appear at ¶ 11,720C and 11,729—11,729E.]

[¶ 20,163A Reserved.—Proposed regulations relating to the limitations on deductions and adjustments to earnings and profits with respect to certain foreign deferred compensation plans formerly were reproduced at this paragraph. These proposals were withdrawn by the IRS on May 9, 1993 (57 FR 27219) and replaced by new proposed regulations which appear at ¶ 20,162A.]

¶ 20,163B

Proposed regulations: Required distribution rules: Qualified plans: IRAs: Tax-sheltered annuities: Custodial accounts: Retirement income accounts: Minimum distribution incidental benefit requirement.—Reproduced below is the text of proposed regulations relating to required distributions from qualified plans, individual retirement plans, Code Sec. 403(b) annuity contracts, custodial accounts, and retirement income accounts.

The proposed regulations were published in the *Federal Register* on July 27, 1987 (52 FR 28070). On December 30, 1997, the IRS issued proposed regulations, amending Q&As D-5 and D-6 and adding Q&A D-7 (see ¶ 20,162B).

DEPARTMENT OF THE TREASURY

Internal Revenue Service

[26 CFR Part 1]

[26 CFR Part 54]

[EE-113-82]

Required Distributions From Qualified Plans And Individual Retirement Plans Notice Of Proposed Rulemaking

AGENCY: Internal Revenue Service, Treasury.

ACTION: Notice of proposed rulemaking.

SUMMARY: This document contains proposed regulations relating to required distributions from qualified plans, individual retirement plans, and section 403(b) annuity contracts, custodial accounts, and retirement income accounts. Changes to the applicable tax law were made by the Tax Reform Act of 1986, the Tax Reform Act of 1984 and the Tax Equity and Fiscal Responsibility Act of 1982. These regulations will provide the public with guidance necessary to comply with the law and will affect administrators of, participants in, and beneficiaries of qualified plans; institutions which sponsor and individuals who administer individual retirement plans, individuals who use individual retirement plans and simplified employee pensions for retirement income and beneficiaries of individual retirement plans; and employees for whom accounts are contributed to section 403(b) annuity contracts, custodial accounts, or retirement income accounts and beneficiaries of such contracts and accounts.

DATES: Written comments and requests for a public hearing must be delivered or mailed by September 25, 1987. These amendments generally apply to calendar years beginning after December 31, 1984, except as otherwise specified in the applicable Act.

ADDRESS: Send comments and requests for a public hearing to: Commissioner of Internal Revenue, Attention: CC:LR:T (EE-113-82) Washington, D.C. 20224.

FOR FURTHER INFORMATION CONTACT: Marjorie Hoffman of the Employee Plans and Exempt Organizations Division, Office of the Chief Counsel, Internal Revenue Service, 111 Constitution Avenue, N.W., Washington, D.C. 20224 (Attention: CC:LR:T) (202-566-3903) (not a toll-free number).

SUPPLEMENTARY INFORMATION

Background

This document contains proposed amendments to the Income Tax Regulations (26 CFR Part 1) and to the Pension Excise Taxes Regulations (26 CFR Part 54) under sections 401, 403, 408, and 4974 of the Internal Revenue Code of 1986. These amendments are proposed to conform the regulations to sections 1121 and 1852 of the Tax Reform Act of 1986 (TRA of 1986) (100 Stat. 2464 and 2864), sections 521 and 713 of the Tax Reform Act of 1984 (TRA of 1984) (98 Stat. 865 and 955), and sections 242 and 243 of the Tax Equity and Fiscal Responsibility Act of 1982 (TEFRA) (96 Stat. 521).

Description of Distribution Rules

The basic principles of these regulations are illustrated by the following description of the rules for distributions made from an individual retirement account before the IRA owner's death. (Special rules in the regulations apply to distributions made after the IRA owner's death.) A distribution must be made for the year in which the IRA owner attains age 70 ½ (the 70 ½ year) and for each year thereafter. Essentially, the minimum distribution for each year is determined by dividing the account balance by the lesser of the applicable life expectancy or the applicable divisor. All calculations are based on calendar years.

The minimum distribution for the 70 ½ year must be made by April 1 of the following year. A further distribution must be made by December 31 of each year after the 70 ½ year. Thus, if no distribution is made in the calendar year in which the IRA owner attains age 70 ½, distributions for two years must be calculated and made in the year after the 70 ½ year (one by April 1 and one by December 31).

In general, the account balance used to determine the minimum distribution for a calendar year is the account balance as of the close of business on the last day of the previous calendar year. The account balance as of the close of business on the last day of the calendar year preceding the 70 ½ year is therefore used to determine the minimum distribution that must be made for the 70 ½ year, even if the actual distribution is made in the year following the 70 ½ year. However, if the distribution for the 70 ½ year is deferred until the first quarter of the subsequent year (January 1 through April 1), the account balance used to determine the second minimum distribution that must be made in that year is calculated by subtracting from the account balance as of the close of business on the last day of the 70 ½ year any distribution made in the first quarter of the subsequent year in order to satisfy the minimum distribution requirement for the 70 ½ year.

The applicable divisor is the divisor under the table in Q&A-4 of 1.401(a)(9)-2 used for purposes of satisfying the minimum distribution incidental benefit requirement. If the IRA has only one beneficiary other than the IRA owner, the applicable life expectancy is the joint life and last survivor expectancy of the IRA owner and the beneficiary. To determine this life expectancy, the first step is to determine the ages of the IRA owner and beneficiary as of their attained ages on their birthdays in the 70 ½ year. The individual's life expectancy may or may not be recalculated. If life expectancy is not recalculated, the applicable life expectancy for years after the 70 ½ year is the initial joint life and last survivor expectancy reduced by one for each subsequent calendar year.

If life expectancy is recalculated, the method of recalculation depends on whether the beneficiary is the IRA owner's spouse. If the spouse is the beneficiary, the applicable life expectancy for each year subsequent to the 70 ½ year is the joint life and last survivor expectancy of the IRA owner and spouse based on their attained ages on their birthdays in each subsequent year. If the beneficiary is not the IRA owner's spouse, the method of recalculation is explained in Question and Answer E-8 of § 1.401(a)(9)-1 and the examples therein. Also, as explained in Question and Answer E-8, if either life expectancy is being recalculated, distributions may be accelerated upon the death of the individual whose life expectancy is being recalculated.

In general, the rules applicable to minimum distributions from qualified plans are identical to those for IRAs. However, the employee's benefit under the plan is used in place of the account balance as of December 31 of the preceding calendar year. As explained in Question and Answer F-5 of § 1.401(a)(9)-1, the benefit is valued as of the last valuation date in the previous calendar year and is adjusted for contributions and forfeitures allocated and distributions made after that date.

The regulations also contain rules for special situations that affect the amount of the required minimum distribution from an IRA or a qualified plan, examples of which are the following:

1. *Multiple beneficiaries and changes in beneficiaries.* See Question and Answer E-5 of § 1.401(a)(9)-1.

2. *Death of the IRA owner (or employee) after the date distributions are required to commence.* See Questions and Answers B-4 through B-6 of § 1.401(a)(9)-1.

3. *Death of the IRA owner (or employee) before the date on which distributions are required to commence.* See Questions and Answers C-1 through C-6 of § 1.401(a)(9)-1.

4. *Distribution in the form of an annuity.* See Questions and Answers F-3 and F-4 of § 1.401(a)(9)-1.

5. *A trust being named as a beneficiary.* See Questions and Answers D-5 and D-6 of § 1.401(a)(9)-1.

6. *Rollovers or transfers from one IRA (or plan) to another.* See Questions and Answers G-1 through G-5 of § 1.401(a)(9)-1.

7. *A division of the benefit (or IRA) into separate accounts with or without different beneficiaries for each account.* See Questions and Answers H-1 through H-2A of § 1.401(a)(9)-1.

8. *A portion of an employee's benefit being payable to an alternate payee pursuant to a qualified domestic relations order.* See Question and Answer H-4 of § 1.401(a)(9)-1.

p31

Simplification of Required Distribution Rules

The Service is concerned that the regulations implementing the required distribution rules for qualified plans, IRAs, and tax-sheltered annuity contracts not cause practitioners, plan and IRA administrators, and taxpayers unnecessary difficulty. These statutory rules reflect an important policy objective. However, due to the inherent difficulty of the statutory rules, we believe that these regulations should provide as certain and simple rules as possible. In the preparation of these proposed regulations, the Service reviewed all available materials to identify issues that required resolution. The proposed regulations thus address as many of these issues as possible. Furthermore, the proposed regulations attempt to simplify compliance with the required distribution rules in several ways (e.g., by integrating the incidental benefit distribution requirement into the required distribution rules and by providing two alternative methods for calculating the distributions for 1985 and 1986 that must be made by the end of 1987). These efforts have added to the length of the proposed regulations, but should provide administrators and taxpayers with important certainty as to the requirements and thus should simplify compliance with the statutory rules.

Because of the time that many administrators will need to implement the required distributions rules, it is important that practitioners, administrators, and taxpayers provide the Service with comments on the proposed regulations at the earliest possible time. In particular, the Service specifically requests that comments consider further simplification to the rules contained in the proposed regulations, including alternative methods of complying with the statutory rules (including administrative safe harbors, particularly for IRAs). The Service will promptly review any comments and proposed alternatives so that any necessary modifications to these regulations applicable for 1987 can be announced well in advance of the end of 1987.

Transition Rules

Transition rules for determining the amounts of the minimum distributions required for qualified plans and IRAs for calendar years 1985, 1986, and 1987 are contained in Questions and Answers I-1 through I-15 of §1.401(a)(9)-1 and Questions and Answers B-1 through B-11 of §1.408-8. In accordance with Notice 86-14, 1986-48 IRB 10, these transition rules provide that minimum distributions for calendar years 1985 and 1986 are not required to be made from qualified plans and IRAs until December 31, 1987.

Incidental Benefit Requirement

Section 401(a)(9)(G), added by section 1852 of TRA of 1986 and effective for years after 1984, provides that distributions must be made in accordance with the incidental benefit requirements in order to satisfy section 401(a)(9). Section 403(b)(10), as added, and section 408(a)(6) and (b)(3), as amended by section 1852 of TRA of 1986, provide that requirements similar to the incidental benefit requirements of section 401(a) apply to annuity contracts, custodial accounts, and retirement income accounts described in section 403(b) and to IRAs.

Section 1.401(a)(9)-2 provides rules for satisfying the minimum distribution incidental benefit requirement (MDIB requirement). §1.401(a)-1 is proposed to be amended to incorporate the provisions of §1.401(a)(9)-2 and the existing incidental benefit requirement in §1.401-1(b)(1)(i) and (ii). For calendar years before 1989, the rules in existing revenue rulings continue to apply for purposes of determining whether distributions satisfy the MDIB requirement. For calendar year after 1988, revised MDIB requirements apply for purposes of determining whether distributions satisfy this requirement. For calendar years before 1989, the MDIB requirement will also be satisfied if distributions are made in accordance with the revised requirements.

The revised requirements provide objective rules for determining whether the amount distributed for a calendar year satisfies the MDIB requirement. These revised requirements have been developed to be integrated with the other minimum distribution requirements in section 401(a)(9). Consequently, taxpayers can apply both of these requirements, which are designed to work together, to determine on an annual basis whether plan distributions for a year are acceptable. The example in Question and Answer F-3A of 1.401(a)(9)-1 illustrate how these requirements work together.

Essentially, the revised rules provide that, where the spouse is not the designated beneficiary, the amount of the payments to be made to the employee before death must be determined in accordance with the principles of section 401(a)(9) using a hypothetical individual not more than 10 years younger than the employee as the employee's designated beneficiary. Where the distribution is in the form of a joint and survivor annuity, the revised rules were developed using an interest rate of eight percent. In general, if an employee's spouse is the employee's beneficiary, the MDIB requirement will be satisfied if distributions are made in accordance with section 401(a)(9), without regard to the MDIB requirement.

While these new objective rules are based on the principles in the existing rulings, they reach different results in certain cases. Thus, on an individual basis the operation of the new rules may require more or less to be distributed for a calendar year depending on the circumstances, such as the date the employee separated from service and the earliest retirement date under the plan.

Existing revenue rulings continue to provide guidance with respect to the application of the incidental benefit requirements to pre-retirement distributions in the form of permissible nonretirement benefits such as life, accident, or health insurance.

Amount to Be Distributed by the Required Beginning Date

As indicated above in the description of the distribution rules, the amount required to be distributed by an employee's or IRA owner's required beginning date is treated as the amount required to be distributed for the immediately preceding year, the year the employee or IRA owner attained age 70 ½ or retired, whichever is applicable. Under section 401(a)(9) as amended by TEFRA, distributions were required to commence by the end of the taxable year in which an employee either retired or attained age 70 ½. Under TRA of 1984, the date by which distribution must commence was extended to the April 1 of the calendar year following the calendar year in which the employee either attains age 70 ½ or retires. The required commencement date was not extended to the end of the calendar year following the calendar year in which the employee either attains age 70 ½ or retires. Thus, the extension to April 1 is merely an extension of the time to make the distribution previously required under TEFRA to be made by the end of the year in which the employee either attains age 70 ½ or retires. This extension was intended to solve the administrative problems that a plan would have faced if it were required to make a December 31 distribution to an employee who retires in December. There is no indication that the extension to April 1 for the first distribution was intended to provide a full additional year of tax deferral. Thus, the distribution for the calendar year after the employee attains age 70 ½ (or retires if applicable) must still be made by the end of that year.

When Distributions Have Begun in Accordance With Section 401(a)(9)(A)

Section 401(a)(9) provides different rules for determining the minimum distributions required after an employee's death depending on whether or not distributions have begun in accordance with section 401(a)(9) before the employee's death. Question and Answer B-5 of §1.401(a)(9)-1 generally provides that distributions are not treated as having begun until the employee's required beginning date even though payments were made before that date. However, Question and Answer B-5 provides an exception for certain distributions in the form of an annuity which commence before the required beginning date.

This interpretation was adopted because it is more administrable than other possible interpretations and places the least burden on plan administrators. If another interpretation had been adopted, additional rules would be required to determine when distributions made before the required beginning date are in accordance with section 401(a)(9)(A)(ii), placing both a burden on plan administrators to conform earlier distributions to such rules and on the Service to administer the additional rules. Further other interpretations considered would have provided that distributions commencing under a distribution option before the required beginning date would be required to be made in accordance with section 401(a)(9) both before and after the required beginning date in order to satisfy section 401(a)(9). This interpretation would have reduced the flexibility in choosing benefit options which plans may provide to employees without violating section 401(a)(9).

Use of Unisex Annuity Tables

The unisex expected return multiples in Table V and VI of §1.72-9 as amended by Treasury Decision 8115 published in the Federal Register on December 19, 1986 (51 F.R. 45690) must be used to compute life expectancies for purposes of determining required distribution under section 401(a)(9). Thus, these tables must be used for determining the amount of minimum distributions required for calendar years after 1984. The July 1, 1986 effective date, provided in Treasury Decision 8115 for using these tables does not apply to §1.401(a)(9)-1.

Designated Beneficiaries

In general, designated beneficiaries who may be taken into account under section 401(a)(9) are limited to those individuals who are designated as beneficiaries under the plan. Question and Answer D-2 of

§ 1.401(a)(9)-1 further provides that a beneficiary under the plan is an individual who is entitled to a portion of an employee's benefit, contingent on the employee's death or another specified event. Thus, a distribution such as that described in Rev. Rul. 72-240, 1972-1 CB 108, will not satisfy section 401(a) unless the same individual is both the beneficiary under the plan and the person whose life is being used to measure the payment period under the survivor portion of the joint and survivor annuity.

Amendment of Qualified Plans

Although minimum distributions are required to be made from qualified plans under section 401(a)(9) in order to retain a plan's tax-qualified status for calendar years after 1984, a plan will not be disqualified solely because it is not amended for section 401(a)(9) and the regulations thereunder prior to the amendment period contained in section 1140 of TRA of 1986 if the plan amendments are adopted retroactively to the effective date of section 401(a)(9) and the regulations thereunder. See Question and Answer A-4 of § 1.401 (a)(9)-1. However, distributions must satisfy the distribution requirements in section 401(a)(9) and the regulations thereunder in operation beginning with calendar year 1985 notwithstanding the absence of plan provisions.

Amendment of IRAs

In general, the minimum distribution rules in section 401(a)(9) and § 1.401(a)(9)-1 will apply to IRAs, beginning with calendar year 1985. The minimum distribution incidental benefit requirement in § 1.401(a)(9)-2 will apply to distributions from IRAs, beginning with calendar year 1989. The trust instrument or custodial agreement for an IRA with a favorable opinion letter need not be amended to provide the distribution rules in section 408(a)(6) and (b)(3) and these regulations

until the later of December 31, 1988, or such time as the Commissioner prescribes. See Question and Answer B-5 of § 1.408-8. (The date prescribed by the Commissioner will be established after the Service has published sample language for IRAs, including IRAs used for funding simplified employee pensions (SEPs), that, if adopted, will satisfy section 408(a)(6) and (b)(3).) Existing IRAs or newly established IRAs, established by executing Form 5305 or Form 5305A, may be the current (Rev. 11-83) editions of those forms until such time as the Commissioner prescribes. An IRA which does not have a favorable opinion letter and which is not established by executing Form 5305 or Form 5305A will satisfy section 408(a)(6) and 408(b)(3) until the date as of which IRAs with a favorable opinion letter must be amended if such IRA contains the statutory provisions in section 401(a)(9) applicable to IRAs. Notwithstanding the absence of trust provisions, Question and Answer B-5 of § 1.408-8 provides that distributions must satisfy the additional distribution requirements in 1.408-8 in operation.

Reliance on these Proposed Regulations

Taxpayers may rely on these proposed regulations for guidance pending the issuance of final regulations. Because these regulations are generally effective for calendar years after 1984, the Service will apply the questions and answers in these proposed regulations in issuing determination letters, opinion letters, and other rulings and in auditing returns with respect to taxpayers and plans. If future guidance is more restrictive, such guidance will be applied without retroactive effect.

PART 1—[AMENDED]

Index for Proposed Regulations

The following index is provided to assist taxpayers in using these proposed regulations.

§ 1.401(a)(9)-2. Minimum distribution incidental benefit requirements.

Special Analyses

The Commissioner of Internal Revenue has determined that this proposed rule is not a major rule as defined in Executive Order 12291 and that a regulatory impact analysis is not required.

Although this document is a notice of proposed rulemaking which solicits public comments, the Internal Revenue Service has concluded that the regulations proposed herein are interpretative and that the notice and public procedure requirements of 5 U. S. C. 553 do not apply. Accordingly, these proposed regulations do not constitute regulations subject to the Regulatory Flexibility Act (5 U. S. C. chapter 6).

Comments And Request For A Public Hearing

Before adopting these proposed regulations, consideration will be given to any written comments that are submitted (preferably eight copies) to the Commissioner of Internal Revenue. All comments will be available for public inspection and copying. A public hearing will be held upon written request to the Commissioner by any person who has submitted comments. If a public hearing is held, notice of the time and place will be published in the Federal Register. The collection of information requirements contained herein have been submitted to the Office of Management and Budget (OMB) for review under section 3504(h) of the Paperwork Reduction Act. Comments on the requirements should be sent to the Office of Information and Regulatory Affairs, of OMB, Attention: Desk Officer for Internal Revenue Service, New Executive Office Building, Washington, D. C. 20503. The Internal Revenue Service requests persons submitting copies of the comments to OMB also to send copies of the comments to the Service.

Drafting Information

The principal author of these proposed regulations is Marjorie Hoffman of the Employee Plans and Exempt Organizations Division of the Office of Chief Counsel, Internal Revenue Service. However, personnel from other offices of the Internal Revenue Service and Treasury Department participated in developing the regulation, both on matters of substance and style.

LIST OF SUBJECTS IN

26 CFR 1.401-0-1.425-1

Income taxes, Employee benefit

plans, Pensions.

26 CFR Part 54

Excise taxes

Proposed amendments to the regulations

The proposed amendments to 26 CFR Parts 1 and 54 are as follows:

Income Tax Regulations

(26 CFR Part 1)

Paragraph 1. The authority citation for Part 1 is amended by adding the following citation:

Authority: 26 U.S.C. 7805 * * * Section 1.401(a)(9)-1 is also issued under 26 U. S. C. §§401(a)(9), 408(a)(6), 408(b)(3), and 403(b)(10). Section 1.408-8 is also issued under 26 U.S.C. §§408(a)(6) and 408(b)(3). Section 1.403(b)-2 is also issued under 26 U.S.C. 403(b)(10).

Par. 2. Section 1.401(a)-1 is amended by adding a new paragraph (c) to read as follows:

§ 1.401(a)-1 Post-ERISA qualified plans and qualified trusts; in general.

* * * * *

(c) *Incidental death benefit requirement.* In order for a pension, stock bonus, or profit-sharing plan to be a qualified plan under section 401(a), distributions under the plan must satisfy the incidental death benefit requirement. Section 1.401-1(b)(1), a pre-ERISA regulation, and § 1.401(a)(9)-2 provide rules applicable to this requirement.

Par. 3. There are added §§ 1.401(a)(9)-1 and 1.401(a)(9)-2 after § 1.401(a)-2 to read as follows:

§ 1.401(a)(9)-1 Required distributions from trusts and plans.

The following questions and answers relate to the distribution rules for qualified plans provided in section 401(a)(9) of the Internal Revenue Code of 1986 and section 401(a)(9) of the Internal Revenue Code of 1954, as amended by section 521 of the Tax Reform Act of 1984 (Pub. L. 98-369) (TRA of 1984) and by section 1121 and 1852 of the Tax Reform Act of 1986 (TRA of 1986) (Pub. L. 99-514):

Table of Contents

A. In general.

B. Distributions commencing before an employee's death.

C. Distributions commencing after an employee's death.

D. Determination of the designated beneficiary.

E. Determination of life expectancy.

F. Determination of the amount which must be distributed each year.

G. Rollovers and transfers.

H. Special rules

I. Transitional rules.

J. Election under section 242(b)(2) of TEFRA.

A. *In General*

A-1. Q. What plans are subject to the new distributions rules in section 401(a)(9) of the Internal Revenue Code of 1986, as amended by section 521 of the Tax Reform Act of 1984, and by sections 1121 and 1852 of the Tax Reform Act of 1986, and the regulations thereunder?

A. All stock bonus, pension, and profit-sharing plans qualified under section 401(a) and annuity contracts described in section 403(a) are subject to the distribution rules in section 401(a)(9) of the Internal Revenue Code of 1986 and section 401(a)(9) of the Internal Revenue Code of 1954 as amended by section 521 of the Tax Reform Act of 1984 (TRA of 1984), and by sections 1121 and 1852 of the Tax Reform Act of 1986 (TRA of 1986) and the regulations thereunder. See § 1.403(b)-2 for the distribution rules applicable to annuity contracts or custodial accounts described in section 403(b), and see § 1.408-8 for the distribution rules applicable to individual retirement plans described in section 408. See also section 457(d)(2)(A) for distribution rules applicable to certain deferred compensation plans.

A-2. Q. Which employee account balances and benefits held under qualified trusts and plans are subject to the distribution rules of section 401(a)(9) of the Internal Revenue Code of 1986 and section 401(a)(9) of the Internal Revenue Code of 1954, as amended?

A. The distribution rules of section 401(a)(9) of the Internal Revenue Code of 1986 and 401(a)(9) of the Internal Revenue Code of 1954, as amended, apply to all account balances and benefits in existence on or after January 1, 1985. The new rules apply to such balances and benefits even though the employee has retired or died, or distributions have commenced prior to that time. However, section 521(e)(4) and (5) of TRA of 1984 provided delayed effective dates for governmental plans and plans maintained pursuant to collective bargaining agreements. Also see J-1 through J-5 concerning designations made pursuant to section 242(b)(5) of the Tax Equity and Fiscal Responsibility Act of 1982 (TEFRA).

A-3. Q. What specific provisions must a plan contain in order to satisfy section 401(a)(9)?

A. (a) *Required provisions.* In order to satisfy section 401(a)(9), the plan must include several written provisions reflecting section 401(a)(9). First, the plan must generally set forth the statutory rules of section 401(a)(9), including the incidental death benefit requirement in section 401 (a)(9)(G). Second, the plan must provide that distributions will be made in accordance with the regulations under section 401(a)(9), including § 1.401(a)(9)-2. The plan document must also provide that the provisions reflecting section 401(a)(9) override any distribution options in the plan inconsistent with section 401(a)(9). Finally, the plan must include any other provisions reflecting section 401(a)(9) as are prescribed by the Commissioner.

(b) *Optional provisions.* The plan may also include written provisions regarding any optional provisions governing plan distributions that do not conflict with section 401(a)(9) and the regulations thereunder.

(b) *Absence of optional provisions.* (1) Plan distributions will be required to be made under the default provisions set forth in this section unless the plan document contains optional provisions that override such default provisions. (2) For example, if distributions have not commenced to the employee at the time of the employee's death, distributions after the death of an employee are to be made automatically in accordance with the default provisions in C-4(a) unless the plan either (i) specifies in accordance with C-4(b) the method under which distributions will be made or (ii) provides for elections by the employee (or beneficiary) (in accordance with C-4(c)) and such elections are made by the employee or beneficiary. (3) Similarly, life expectancies of employees and spouses of employees automatically will be recalculated pursuant to E-7(a) unless the plan either (i) specifies in accordance with E-7(b) that life expectancies of employees and spouses of employees will not be calculated or (ii) provides for elections by the employee (or spouse) in accordance with E-7(c) (in which case life expectancy will not be recalculated if there is such an election or if a plan default provision so provides).

A-4. Q. When must plans be amended to satisfy section 401(a)(9) and how must they operate prior to such amendment?

A. (a) *Form requirements before 1989.* A plan will not be disqualified solely because it is not amended for section 401(a)(9) and the regulations thereunder prior to the end of the amendment period contained in section 1140 of TRA of 1986 if the plan amendments are adopted retroactively to the effective date of section 401(a)(9) and the regulations thereunder.

(b) *Operational requirements before 1989.* For plan years beginning in calendar years after 1984, a plan must satisfy section 401(a)(9) and the applicable regulations of section 401(a) in operation in order to meet the qualification requirements of section 401(a). Therefore, distributions for calendar years after 1984 must be made in accordance with the provisions of section 401(a)(9) and the regulations thereunder notwithstanding any provisions of the plan to the contrary. For plan years before the plan year in which the plan is required to be amended pursuant to paragraph (a), the plan will not fail to satisfy either the requirement that a plan be operated in accordance with its terms or the requirement that a pension plan provide definitely determinable benefits (or the requirement that a profit-sharing plan provide a definite predetermined formula for distributing the funds accumulated under the plan) merely because distributions are made to comply with section 401(a)(9) and the regulations thereunder rather than in accordance with the terms of the plan.

(c) *Default provisions.* For calendar years ending in plan years before the plan year in which the plan is required to be amended pursuant to paragraph (a), notwithstanding A-3(b), a plan will not be subject to the default provisions in this section if benefits are distributed in accordance with this section in a reasonable and consistent manner. For example, for purposes of determining pursuant to C-4 whether the five-year rule in section 401(a)(9)(B)(ii) or the exception to the five-year rule in section 401(a)(9)(B)(iii) and (iv) applies, a plan does not have to make distributions in accordance with the default provisions in C-4(a) if the plan administrator establishes a consistent policy of either (1) distributing benefits under one method or the other or (2) distributing benefits pursuant to an election by an employee or beneficiary (or in the absence of an election under one method or the other). Similarly, for purposes of determining whether or not the life expectancies of an employee and the employee's spouse will be recalculated pursuant to section 401(a)(9)(D) and E-7, a plan does not have to recalculate life expectancies of employees or their spouses if the plan administrator establishes a policy of either not recalculating such life expectancies or of allowing elections by employees or spouses. In the latter case, a plan does not have to recalculate the employee or the employee's spouse's life expectancy if the employee or spouse elects not to recalculate life expectancy (or in the absence of an election, of not recalculating life expectancies). However, if a plan administrator adopts a policy of not distributing in accordance with one of the default provisions, when the plan is amended to comply with section 401(a)(9), the amendment must be consistent with the policy established.

A-5. Q. To what extent will a plan be treated as failing to satisfy the qualification requirements of section 401(a) if the plan in operation fails to make distributions in accordance with section 401(a)(9)?

A. A plan will not satisfy the qualification requirements of section 401(a) with respect to a plan year unless all distributions required under section 401(a)(9) are made for the calendar year ending with or within such plan year. Notwithstanding the preceding sentence, for plan years beginning after December 31, 1988, a plan will not fail to satisfy the qualification requirements of section 401(a) because there are isolated instances when the minimum distribution requirements of section 401(a)(9) are not satisfied in operation. However, a pattern or regular practice of failing to meet the minimum distribution requirements of section 401(a)(9) with respect to one or more employees will not be considered an isolated instance even if each instance is de minimis.

B. *Distributions commencing before an employee's death.*

B-1. Q. In the case of distributions before an employee's death, how must the employee's entire interest be distributed in order to satisfy section 401(a)(9)(A)?

A. (a) In order to satisfy section 401(a)(9)(A), the entire interest of each employee (1) must be distributed to such employee not later than the required beginning date, or (2) must be distributed, beginning not later than the required beginning date, over the life of such employee or over the lives of such employee and the designated beneficiary (or over a period not extending beyond life expectancy of such employee or the joint life and last survivor expectancy of such employee and the designated beneficiary).

(b) See 13-2 and 13-3 for the definition of required beginning date. See D-1 through D-4 for the determination of the designated beneficiary of the employee. See E-1 and E-3 through E-8 for the rules for calculating the life expectancy of the employee (and the designated beneficiary). See F-1 through F-7 for the rules for determining the amount of the minimum distribution to be made each year.

B-2. Q. For purposes of section 401(a)(9)(C), what does the term "required beginning date" mean?

A. (a) For an employee who attains age 70½ after December 31, 1987 (i.e., age 70 after June 30, 1987), the term "required beginning date" means April 1 of the calendar year following the calendar year in which the employee attains age 70½.

(b) For an employee who attains age 70½ before January 1, 1988 (i. e., age 70 before July 1, 1987) and is not a "5-percent owner" (as defined in paragraph (d)), the term "required beginning date" means April 1 of the calendar year following the later of (1) the calendar year in which the employee attains age 70½ or (2) the calendar year in which the employee retires.

(c) For an employee who attains age 70½ before January 1, 1988 and is a "5-percent owner" (as defined in paragraph (d)), the term "required beginning date" means April 1 of the calendar year following the later of (1) the calendar year in which the employee attains age 70½, or (2) the earlier of (i) the calendar year with or within which ends the plan year in which the employee becomes a "5-percent owner," or (ii) the calendar year in which the employee retires.

(d)(1) An employee is treated as a "5-percent owner" for purposes of this Q&A, if such employee is a "5-percent owner" (as defined in section 416(i)) at any time during the plan year ending with or within the calendar year in which such owner attains age 66½ or any subsequent plan year. Once an employee is described in this subparagraph, distributions must continue to such employee even if such employee ceases to own more than 5 percent of the employer in a subsequent year.

(2) The determination of whether or not an employee is a 5-percent owner will be made in accordance with section 416 but will be made without regard to whether the plan is top-heavy.

(3) An employee's required beginning date is determined under paragraph (c) if the employee is a 5-percent owner during any plan year beginning after December 31, 1979. For example, if an employee attains age 66½ within calendar year 1980 and is a 5-percent owner during the plan year ending within calendar year 1980, but is not a 5-percent owner at any time during any other plan year, the employee is considered a 5-percent owner and the employee's required beginning date is determined under paragraph (c) and this paragraph.

B-3. Q. When does an employee attain age 70½?

A. An employee attains age 70½ as of the date six months after the 70th anniversary of the employee's birth. For example, if an employee's date of birth was June 30, 1919, the 70th anniversary of such employee's birth is June 30, 1989. Such employee attains age 70½ on December 30, 1989. Consequently, such employee's required beginning date is April 1, 1990. However, if the employee's date of birth was July 1, 1919, the 70th anniversary of such employee's birth would be July 1, 1989. Such employee would then attain age 70½ on January 1, 1990.

B-3A. Q. Must distributions made before the employee's required beginning date satisfy section 401(a)(9)?

A. Lifetime distributions made before the employee's required beginning date for calendar years before the employee's first distribution calendar year, as defined in F-1, need not be made in accordance with section 401(a)(9). However, if distributions commence under a particular distribution option, such as in the form of an annuity, before the employee's required beginning date for the employee's first distribution calendar year, the distribution option will fail to satisfy section 401(a)(9) at the time distributions commence if, under the particular distribution option, distributions to be made for the employee's first distribution calendar year or any subsequent distribution calendar year will not satisfy section 401(a)(9).

B-4. Q. if distributions have begun to an employee before the employee's death (in accordance with section 401(a)(9)(A)(ii)), how must distributions be made after an employee's death?

A. Section 401(a)(9)(B)(i) provides that if the distribution of the employee's interest has begun in accordance with section 401(a)(9)(A)(ii) and the employee dies before his entire interest has been distributed to him, the remaining portion of such interest must be distributed at least as rapidly as under the distribution method being used under section 401(a)(9)(A)(ii) as of the date of his death. As explained further in D-3, in the case of distributions which began before the employee's death and which are being paid over the lives of the employee and a designated beneficiary (or over a period not exceeding the joint life and last survivor expectancy), the designated beneficiary whose life or life expectancy was being used to determine the period described in section 401(a)(9)(A)(ii) must be the beneficiary of such remaining portion unless otherwise provided in E-5.

B-5. Q. For purposes of section 401(a)(9)(B), when are distributions considered to have begun to the employee in accordance with section 401(a)(9)(A)(ii)?

A. (a) *General rule.* Except as provided in paragraph (b), distributions are treated as having begun to the employee in accordance with section 401(a)(9)(A)(ii) on the employee's required beginning date, even though payments may actually have been made before that date. For example, if employee A upon retirement in 1990 at age 65½ begins receiving installment distributions from a profit-sharing plan over a period not exceeding the joint life and last survivor expectancy of A and A's beneficiary, benefits are not treated as having begun in accordance with section 401(a)(9)(A)(ii) until April 1, 1996 (the April 1 following the calendar year in which A attains age 70 ½). Consequently, if such employee dies before April 1, 1996 (A's required beginning date), distributions to be made after A's death must be made in accordance with section 401(a)(9)(B)(ii) or (iii) and (iv). This is the case even though the plan has distributed the minimum distribution for the first distribution calendar year (as defined in F-1) before A's death.

(b) *Annuities.* If distributions irrevocably (except for acceleration) commence to an employee on a date before the employee's required beginning date over a period permitted under section 401(a)(9)(A)(ii) and the distribution form is an annuity under which distributions are made in accordance with the provisions of F-3 (and if applicable F-4), distributions will be considered to have begun on the actual commencement date in accordance with section 401(a)(9)(A)(ii) even if the employee dies before the employee's required beginning date. Thus, pursuant to section 401(a)(9)(B)(i), after the employee's death, the remaining portion of the employee's interest must continue to be distributed at least as rapidly as under the method of distribution in effect as of the employee's date of death and the rules in section 401(a)(9)(B)(ii) or (iii) and (iv) do not apply. See D-3 and E-1 for special rules for determining the employee's designated beneficiary and for determining life expectancy.

(c) *Cross reference.* See F-3A for rules for satisfying the requirement that the employee's remaining interest be distributed at least as rapidly as under the method being used under section 401(a)(9)(A)(ii) as of the date of the employee's death.

C. *Distributions commencing after an employee's death.*

C-1. Q. In the case in which an employee dies before distributions are treated as having begun to the employee for purposes of section 401(a)(9)(A)(ii), how must the employee's entire interest be distributed in order to satisfy section 401(a)(9)?

A. (a) In the case in which an employee dies before distributions are treated as having begun to an employee in accordance with section 401(a)(9)(A)(ii), section 401(a)(9)(B) provides two methods for distributing the employee's interest. In order to satisfy section 401(a)(9), distributions must be made under one of these two methods. The first method (the five-year rule in section 401(a)(9)(B)(ii)) requires that the entire interest of the employee be distributed within 5 years of the employee's death regardless of to whom or to what entity the distribution is made. The second method (the exception to the five-year rule in section 401(a)(9)(B)(iii)) requires that any portion of an employee's interest which is payable to (or for the benefit of) a designated beneficiary be distributed, commencing within one year of the employee's death, over the life of such beneficiary (or over a period not extending beyond the life expectancy of such beneficiary). Section 401(a)(9)(B)(iv) provides special rules where the designated beneficiary is the surviving spouse of the employee, including a special commencement date for distribution under section 401(a)(9)(B)(iii) to the surviving spouse.

(b) See C-2 to determine when the five-year period in section 401(a)(9)(B)(ii) ends. See C-3 to determine when distribution under the exception to the five-year rule in section 401(a)(9)(13)(iii) and (iv) must commence. See C-4 for the rules for determining which of the methods described in paragraph (a) applies. See D-1, D-2, and D-4 in order to determine the designated beneficiary under section 401(a)((9)(B)(iii) and (iv). See E-2 through E-8 for the rules for calculating the designated beneficiary's life expectancy. See F-l through F-7 for the rules for determining the amount of the minimum distribution to be distributed each year.

C-2. Q. As of what date must the employee's entire interest be distributed in order to satisfy the five-year rule in section 401(a)(9)(B)(ii)?

A. In order to satisfy the five-year rule in section 401(a)(9)(B)(ii), the employee's entire interest must be distributed as of December 31 of the calendar year which contains the fifth anniversary of the date of the employee's death. For example, if an employee dies on January 1 of 1990, the entire interest must be distributed by December 31, 1995, in order to satisfy the five-year rule in section 401(a)(9)(B)(ii).

C-3. Q. When are distributions required to commence in order to satisfy the exception to the five-year rule in section 401(a)(9)(B)(iii) and (iv)?

A. (a) *Nonspousal beneficiary.* In order to satisfy the rule in section 401(a)(B)(iii) (the exception to the five-year rule for nonspouse beneficiaries), if the designated beneficiary is not the employee's surviving spouse, distributions must commence on or before December 31 of the calendar year immediately following the calendar year in which the employee died. This rule also applies to the distribution of the entire remaining benefit if, as of the employee's date of death, an individual is

designated as a beneficiary in addition to the employee's surviving spouse. See H-2 and H-2A, however, if the employee's benefit is divided into separate accounts (or segregated shares, in the case of a defined benefit plan).

(b) *Spousal beneficiary.* In order to satisfy the rule in section 401(a)(9)(B)(iii) and (iv), if the designated beneficiary is the employee's surviving spouse, distributions must commence on or before the later of (1) December 31 of the calendar year immediately following the calendar year in which the employee died and (2) December 31 of the calendar year in which the employee would have attained age 70 ½.

C-4. Q. How is it determined whether the five-year rule in section 401(a)(9)(B)(ii) or the exception to the five-year rule in section 401(a)(9)(B)(iii) and (iv) applies to a distribution?

A. (a) *No plan provision.* If a plan does not adopt an optional provision specifying the methods of distribution after the death of an employee, distribution must be made as follows:

(1) In the case in which the surviving spouse of an employee is a beneficiary of the employee, distributions are to be made in accordance with the exception to the five-year rule in section 401(a)(9)(B)(iii) and (iv).

(2) In all other cases, distributions are to be made in accordance with the five-year rule in section 401(a)(9)(B)(ii).

(b) *Optional methods.* The plan may adopt a provision specifying which of the two methods apply to distributions after the death of an employee. For example, the plan may specify that distribution in every case will be made in accordance with the exception to the five-year rule in section 401(a)(9)(B)(iii) and (iv). Further, a plan need not have the same method of distribution for the benefits of all employees, e.g., a plan may have one method of distribution for benefits of employees whose beneficiaries are not surviving spouses and another method of distribution for the benefits of employees whose beneficiaries are surviving spouses, so long as there is a single method with respect to the benefit of each employee. (If an employee's benefit is divided into separate accounts, see H-2 and H-2A).

(c) *Employee Elections.* A plan may adopt a provision that permits employees (or beneficiaries) to elect on an individual basis whether the five-year rule in section 401(a)(9)(B)(ii) or the exception to the five-year rule in section 401(a)(9)(B)(iii) and (iv) applies to distributions. In operation, such an election must be made no later than the earlier of (1) December 31 of the calendar year in which distribution would be required to commence in order to satisfy the requirements for the exception to the five-year rule in section 401(a)(9)(B)(iii) and (iv) (see C-3 for the determination of such calendar year), or (2) December 31 of the calendar year which contains the fifth anniversary of the date of death of the employee. As of such date, the election must be irrevocable with respect to the beneficiary (and all subsequent beneficiaries) and must apply to all subsequent years. If a plan provides for elections, the plan may also specify, pursuant to paragraph (b), which method of distribution applies if neither the employee nor the beneficiary makes the election. If neither the employee nor the beneficiary elects a method and the plan does not specify which rule applies, distribution must be made in accordance with paragraph (a).

(d) *Other requirements.* A plan must satisfy other distribution requirements under the Code. For example, plan distributions must satisfy the survivor annuity requirements of sections 401(a)(11) and 417, except as otherwise provided in this section. These requirements may mandate a particular method of distribution to a surviving spouse. Any plan provision described in paragraphs (b) and (c), or method of distribution elected pursuant to paragraph (c), must satisfy these other distribution rules.

C-5. Q. If the employee's surviving spouse is the employee's designated beneficiary and such spouse dies after the employee, but before distributions have begun to the surviving spouse under section 401(a)(9)(B)(iii) and (iv), how is the employee's interest to be distributed?

A. Pursuant to section 401(a)(9)(B)(iv)(II), if the surviving spouse dies after the employee, but before distributions to such spouse have begun under section 401(a)(9)(B)(iii) and (iv), the five-year rule in section 401(a)(9)(B)(ii) and the exception to the five-year rule in section 401(a)(9)(B)(iii) are to be applied as if the surviving spouse were the employee. In applying this rule, the date of death of the surviving spouse shall be substituted for the date of death of the employee. However, in such case, the rules in section 401(a)(9)(B)(iv) are not available to the surviving spouse of the deceased employee's surviving spouse.

C-6. For purposes of section 401(a)(9)(B)(iv)(II), when are distributions considered to have begun to the surviving spouse?

A. (a) *General rule.* Except as otherwise provided in paragraph (b), distributions are considered to have begun to the surviving spouse of an employee, for purposes of section 401(a)(9)(B)(iv)(II), on the date, determined in accordance with C-3, on which distributions are required to commence to the surviving spouse, even though payments have actually been made before that date. See paragraph (b) for special rule for annuities.

(b) *Annuity.* If distributions commence irrevocably (except for acceleration) to the surviving spouse of an employee over a period permitted under section 401(a)(9)(B)(iii)(II) before the date on which distributions are required to commence and the distribution form is an annuity under which distributions are made as of the date distributions commence in accordance wit's the provisions of F-3 (and F-4 if applicable), distributions will be considered to have begun on the actual commencement date for purposes of section 401(a)(9)(B)(iv)(II). Consequently, in such case, section 401(a)(9)(B)(ii) and (iii) will not apply upon the death of the surviving spouse as though the surviving spouse were the employee even if the spouse dies before the date, determined in accordance with C-3, on which distributions are required to commence to the surviving spouse. Instead, the annuity distributions must continue to be made, in accordance with the provisions of F-3 or F-4, at least as rapidly as under the method of distribution being used as of the date of the surviving spouse's death. The rules of F-3A shall apply in determining whether distributions are being made at least as rapidly as under the method of distribution being used as of the date of the surviving spouse's death.

D. *Determination of the designated beneficiary.*

D-1. Q. Must an employee (or the employee's spouse) make an affirmative election specifying a beneficiary for a person to be a designated beneficiary under section 401(a)(9)(E)?

A. No. A person's status as designated beneficiary is not dependent upon being selected by an employee (or by the employee's surviving spouse, in the case of certain distributions under section 401(a)(9)(B)(iv)(II)). Thus, for example, if the terms of the plan specify the beneficiary, then whoever is so specified is the designated beneficiary and is treated for purposes of section 401(a)(9) as having been designated by the employee (or the employee's surviving spouse). The choice of beneficiary is subject to the requirements of sections 401(a)(11), 414(p), and 417.

D-2. Q. May an individual who is not designated as a beneficiary under the plan be considered a designated beneficiary for purposes of determining the minimum distribution required under section 401(a)(9)?

A. (a)(1) Except to the extent provided in E-5 with respect to former beneficiaries, designated beneficiaries are only individuals who are designated as beneficiaries under the plan. An individual may be designated as a beneficiary under the plan either by the terms of the plan or, if the plan provides, by an affirmative election by the employee (or the employee's surviving spouse) specifying the beneficiary. A beneficiary designated as such under the plan is an individual who is entitled to a portion of an employee's benefit, contingent on the employee's death or another specified event. For example, if a distribution is in the form of a joint and survivor annuity over the life of the employee and another individual, the plan does not satisfy section 401(a)(9) unless such other individual is a designated beneficiary under the plan. A designated beneficiary need not be specified by name in the plan or by the employee to the plan in order to be a designated beneficiary so long as the individual who is to be the beneficiary is identifiable under the plan as of the employee's required beginning date, or as of the date of the employee's death (in the case of distributions governed by section 401(a)(9)(B)(iii) and (iv)), and at all subsequent times. The members of a class of beneficiaries capable of expansion or contraction will be treated as being identifiable if it is possible at the applicable time to identify the class member with the shortest life expectancy. The fact that an employee's interest under the plan passes to a certain individual under applicable state law does not make such individual a designated beneficiary unless such individual is designated as a beneficiary under the plan.

(2) This paragraph (a) is illustrated by the following example.

Example. Employee X attains age 70½ in calendar year 1990. As of April 1, 1991, X designates as his beneficiaries under the plan his spouse and his children. X does not specify them by name. Even though X did not specify his spouse and his children by name, they are identifiable based on their relationship to X as of his required beginning date. Further, it is irrelevant that additional children of X may be born after his required beginning date and thus that the class of beneficiaries is capable of expansion.

(b) See E-5 for the rules which apply if there is a change in beneficiaries under the plan with respect to an employee.

D-2A. Q. May a person other than an individual be considered to be a designated beneficiary for purposes of section 401(a)(9)?

A. (a) No. Only individuals may be designated beneficiaries for purposes of section 401(a)(9). A person who is not an individual, such as the employee's estate, may not be a designated beneficiary. However, see D-5 and D-6 for special rules which apply to trusts.

(b) Except as otherwise provided in D-5, D-6, and E-5(e)(1), if a person other than an individual is designated as a beneficiary of an employee's benefit, the employee will be treated as having no designated beneficiary for purposes of section 401(a)(9). In such case, distribution under section 401(a)(9)(A)(ii) must be made over the employee's life or over a period not exceeding the employee's life expectancy. Further, in such case, if upon the employee's death section 401(a)(9)(B)(i) does not apply, distribution must be made in accordance with the 5-year rule in section 401(a)(9)(B)(ii).

D-3. Q. For purposes of calculating the distribution period described in section 401(a)(9)(A)(ii) (for distributions before death), when is the designated beneficiary determined?

A. (a) *General rule required beginning date.* For purposes of calculating the distribution period described in section 401(a)(9)(A)(ii) (for distributions before death), except as otherwise provided in paragraphs (b) through (d), the designated beneficiary will be determined as of the employee's required beginning date. If, as of that date, there is no designated beneficiary under the plan to receive the employee's benefit upon the employee's death, the distribution period described in section 401(a)(9)(A)(ii) is limited to the employee's life (or a period not extending beyond the employee's life expectancy). (If there is a beneficiary (other than a beneficiary whose rights are contingent on the death of another beneficiary) who is not designated in accordance with D-2, there is deemed to be no designated beneficiary for purposes of section 401(a)(9)(A)(ii).)

(b) *Exception for first distribution year.* Except to the extent that B-5(b) is applicable, if a designated beneficiary is added or replaces another designated beneficiary during the calendar year in which the employee's required beginning date occurs, but on or before the employee's required beginning date (January 1 through April 1 of such calendar year), the designated beneficiary of the employee for purposes of calculating the minimum distribution for the employee's first distribution calendar year (as defined in F-1) may be determined as of any date after December 31 of the employee's first distribution calendar year and before the employee's required beginning date. Thus, e.g., for purposes of determining the minimum distribution for the employee's first distribution calendar year, either designated beneficiary may be used to determine the joint life and last survivor expectancy of the employee and designated beneficiary. However, for purposes of determining the minimum distribution for subsequent distribution calendar years (including the distribution calendar year in which the employee's required beginning date occurs), the designated beneficiary will be determined as of the employee's required beginning date.

(c) *Annuity form.* If annuity payments commence to an employee (either on or before the employee's required beginning date), the employee's designated beneficiary may be determined as of any date during the 90 days before the date on which the annuity payments commence.

(d) *Multiple and substitute beneficiaries.* Notwithstanding anything in this D-3 to the contrary, the rules in E-5 apply if more than one beneficiary is designated with respect to an employee as of the applicable date (in paragraphs (a), (b), or (c)), on which the employee's designated beneficiary is determined or if a beneficiary is added or replaces another beneficiary (due to death or any other reason) after such date.

D-4. Q. For purposes of calculating the distribution period described in section 401(a)(9)(B)(iii) or (iv) (for distributions beginning after death in accordance with the exception to the five-year rule), when is the designated beneficiary determined?

A. (a) *Employee.* Except as provided in paragraph (b), for purposes of calculating the distribution period described in section 401(a)(9)(B)(iii) or (iv), the designated beneficiary will be determined as of the employee's date of death. If, as of the date of the employee's death, there is no designated beneficiary under the plan with respect to that employee, distribution must be made in accordance with the five-year rule in section 401(a)(9)(B)(ii). (If there is a beneficiary (other than a beneficiary whose rights are contingent on the death of another beneficiary) who is not designated in accordance with D-2, there is deemed to be no designated beneficiary for purposes of section 401(a)(9)(B)(iii) and (iv).)

(b) *Surviving spouse.* As provided in C-5, in the case in which the employee's spouse is the designated beneficiary as of the date of the employee's death for distributions under section 401(a)(9)(B)(iii) and the surviving spouse dies after the employee and before the date on which distributions have begun to the spouse under section 401(a)(9)(B)(iii) and (iv), the rule in section 401(a)(9)(B)(iv)(II) will apply. Thus the relevant designated beneficiary for determining the distribution period is the designated beneficiary of the surviving spouse. Such designated beneficiary will be determined as of the surviving spouse's date of death (rather than the employee's date of death). If, as of the date of the surviving spouse's death, there is no designated beneficiary under the plan with respect to that surviving spouse, distribution must be made in accordance with the 5-year rule in section 401(a)(9)(B)(ii). (If there is a beneficiary (other than a beneficiary whose rights are contingent on the death of another beneficiary) who is not designated in accordance with D-2, there is deemed to be no designated beneficiary for purposes of section 401(a)(9)(B)(iii).)

(c) *Multiple beneficiaries.* Notwithstanding anything in this D-4 to the contrary, the rules in E-5 apply if more than one beneficiary is designated with respect to an employee as of the date determined in accordance with paragraphs (a) and (b) on which the designated beneficiary is to be determined.

D-5. Q. In the case in which a trust is named as a beneficiary of an employee, are the beneficiaries of the trust with respect to the trust's interest in the employee's benefit treated as having been designated as beneficiaries of the employee under the plan for purposes of determining the distribution period under section 401(a)(9)(A)(ii)?

A. (a) In the case in which a trust is named as a beneficiary of an employee, all beneficiaries of the trust with respect to the trust's interest in the employee's benefit are treated as having been designated as beneficiaries of the employee under the plan for purposes of determining the distribution period under section 401(a)(9)(A)(ii) if, as of the later of the date on which the trust is named as a beneficiary of the employee, or the employee's required beginning date, and as of all subsequent periods during which the trust is named as a beneficiary, the following requirements are met.

(1) The trust is a valid trust under state law, or would be but for the fact that there is no corpus.

(2) The trust is irrevocable.

(3) The beneficiaries of the trust who are beneficiaries with respect to the trust's interest in the employee's benefit are identifiable from the trust instrument within the meaning of D-2.

(4) A copy of the trust instrument is provided to the plan.

(b) Pursuant to D-2A, only an individual may be a designated beneficiary. Consequently, a trust itself may not be the designated beneficiary even though the trust is named as a beneficiary. However, if the requirements in paragraph (a) are met, for purposes of section 401(a)(9), distributions made to the trust will be treated as paid to the beneficiaries of the trust with respect to the trust's interest in the employee's benefit. If, as of any date on or after the employee's required beginning date, a trust is named as a beneficiary of the employee and the requirements in paragraph (a) are not met, the employee will be treated as not having a designated beneficiary under the plan for purposes of section 401(a)(9)(A)(ii). Consequently, for calendar years subsequent to such date, distribution must be made over the employee's life (or over the period which would have been the employee's remaining life expectancy determined as if no beneficiary had been designated as of the employee's required beginning date). In the case of payments to a trust having more than one beneficiary, see E-5 for the rules for determining the designated beneficiary whose life expectancy will be used to determine the distribution period.

D-6. Q. In the case in which a trust is named as a beneficiary of an employee, are beneficiaries of the trust with respect to the trust's interest in the employee's benefit treated as designated beneficiaries under the plan with respect to the employee for purposes of determining the distribution period under section 401(a)(9)(B)(iii) and (iv)?

A. (a) In the case in which a trust is named as a beneficiary of an employee, all beneficiaries of the trust with respect to the trust's interest in the employee's benefit are treated as designated beneficiaries of the employee under the plan for purposes of determining the distribution period under section 401(a)(9)(B)(iii) and (iv) if the requirements in paragraph (a) of D-5 are satisfied as of the date of the employee's death. If the requirements in paragraph (a) of D-5 are satisfied as of the date of the employee's death, distributions to the trust for purposes of section 401(a)(9) will be treated as being paid to

the appropriate beneficiary of the trust with respect to the trust's interest in the employee's benefit. However, if a trust is named as a beneficiary of an employee and if, as of the date of the employee's death, the requirements of D-5 are not satisfied, the employee will be treated as not having a designated beneficiary under the plan. Consequently, distribution must be made in accordance with the five-year rule in section 401(a)(9)(B)(ii).

(b) The rules of D-5 and this D-6 also apply for purposes of applying the provisions of section 401(a)(9)(B)(iv)(II) if a trust is named as a beneficiary of the employee's surviving spouse.

E. Determination of life expectancy.

E-1. Q. For required distributions under section 401(a)(9)(A), what age (or ages) is used to calculate the employee's life expectancy (or the joint life and last survivor expectancy of the employee and a designated beneficiary)?

A. (a) Except as otherwise provided in paragraph (b), for required distributions under section 401(a)(9)(A), life expectancies are calculated using the employee's (and the designated beneficiary's) attained age as of the employee's birthday (and the designated beneficiary's birthday) in the calendar year in which the employee attains age 70 ½. If life expectancy is being recalculated pursuant to E-6 through E-8, the life expectancy of the employee or spouse (or the joint life and last survivor expectancy of the employee and spouse) will be recalculated using the employee's (and the spouse's) attained age as of the employee's birthday (and the surviving spouse's birthday) in each succeeding calendar year in which recalculation is provided for purposes of calculating the minimum distribution for that distribution calendar year.

(b) If, pursuant to B-2(b), an employee's required beginning date is April 1 of the calendar year following the calendar year in which the employee retires or becomes a 5-percent owner, such calendar year is substituted in paragraph (a) for the calendar year in which the employee attains age 70 ½.

(c) If, in accordance with B-5(b), annuity payments commence to an employee before the employee's required beginning date, the calendar year in which the annuity payments commence is substituted in paragraph (a) for the calendar year in which the employee attains age 70 ½.

E-2. Q. In the case of any distribution under section 401(a)(9)(B)(iii) and (iv) what age is used to calculate the beneficiary's life expectancy?

A. (a) In the case of any distribution under section 401(a)(9)(B)(iii) and (iv), the life expectancy of any designated beneficiary is calculated based on the beneficiary's attained age as of the beneficiary's birthday in the calendar year in which distributions are required to commence to such beneficiary in order to satisfy section 401(a)(9)(B)(iii) and (iv). For example, if an unmarried participant (A) dies at age 50 on January 31, 1987, A's designated beneficiary is A's brother (B), and B will receive A's interest over B's life expectancy, the date on which distributions are required to commence to B in order to satisfy section 401(a)(9)(B)(iii) is December 31, 1988 (see C-3). Therefore, B's life expectancy is calculated based on B's attained age as of B's birthday in calendar year 1988. This rule also applies to a designated beneficiary of a surviving spouse where such surviving spouse is treated as the employee for purposes of applying section 401(a)(9)(B)(iii). If the life expectancy of the surviving spouse is being recalculated pursuant to E-6 through E-8, the life expectancy of the surviving spouse will be recalculated using the surviving spouse's attained age as the surviving spouse's birthday in each succeeding calendar year in which recalculation is provided, for purposes of calculating the minimum distribution for that distribution calendar year.

(b) If distribution under section 401(a)(9)(B)(iii) and (iv) commences irrevocably (except for acceleration) over a period described in section 401(a)(9)(B)(iii)(II) in a calendar year prior to the calendar year in which distributions are required to commence and distribution is an annuity under which distributions are made in accordance with the provisions of F-3 (and if applicable F-4), the designated beneficiary's life expectancy (where applicable) is based on the designated beneficiary's attained age as of the designated beneficiary's birthday in the calendar year in which distribution commences.

(c) If a designated beneficiary of the employee, other than the employee's surviving spouse, dies after the employee but before the designated beneficiary's birthday in the calendar year in which life expectancy is determined under paragraphs (a) and (b), such beneficiary will be treated as being alive on such date for purposes of calculating the designated beneficiary's life expectancy. (See C-5 for the special rule which applies if the surviving spouse dies after the employee but before the date on which distributions have begun to the surviving spouse.)

E-3 & 4. Q. What life expectancies must be used for purposes of determining required distributions under section 401(a)(9)?

A. Life expectancies for purposes of determining required distributions under section 401(a)(9) must be computed by use of the expected return multiples in Tables V and VI of § 1.72-9.

E-5. Q. If an employee has more than one designated beneficiary or if a designated beneficiary is added or replaces another designated beneficiary after the date for determining the designated beneficiary, which designated beneficiary's life expectancy will be used to determine the distribution period?

A. (a) *General rule.* (1) Except as otherwise provided in paragraph (f), if more than one individual is designated as a beneficiary with respect to an employee as of the applicable date for determining the designated beneficiary, the designated beneficiary with the shortest life expectancy will be the designated beneficiary for purposes of determining the distribution period. However, except as otherwise provided in D-5, D-6, and paragraph (e)(1) of this E-5, if a person other than an individual is designated as a beneficiary, the employee will be treated as not having any designated beneficiaries for purposes of section 401(a)(9) even if there are also individuals designated as beneficiaries. The date for determining the designated beneficiary (under D-3 or D-4, whichever is applicable) is the applicable date. The period described in section 401(a)(9)(A)(ii) (for distributions commencing before the employee's death) or section 401(a)(9)(B)(iii) (for distributions over a life expectancy commencing after the employee's death), whichever is applicable, is the distribution period.

(2) See H-2 for special rules which apply if an employee's benefit under a plan is divided into separate accounts (or segregated shares in the case of a defined benefit plan) and the beneficiaries with respect to a separate account differ from the beneficiaries of another separate account.

(b) *Contingent beneficiary.* Except as provided in paragraph (e)(1), if a beneficiary's entitlement to an employee's benefit is contingent on an event other than the employee's death (e.g., death of another beneficiary), such contingent beneficiary is considered to be a designated beneficiary for purposes of determining which designated beneficiary has the shortest life expectancy under paragraph (a).

(c) *New beneficiary.* (1) Except as provided in paragraph (e)(2) (in the case of the death of a beneficiary), if, after the applicable date for determining the designated beneficiary, a new designated beneficiary with a life expectancy shorter than the life expectancy of the designated beneficiary whose life expectancy is being used to determined [*sic*] the distribution period is added or replaces a designated beneficiary, the new designated beneficiary is treated as the designated beneficiary for purposes of determining the distribution period. In such case, the new beneficiary's life expectancy will be used to calculate the distribution period in subsequent calendar years. In determining the beneficiary with the shorter life expectancy, the life expectancies will be calculated as of the applicable birthdays in the calendar year specified in and in the manner provided in E-1 through E-4. Consequently, the old distribution period must be replaced by a new distribution period. The new distribution period equals the period which would have been the remaining joint life and last survivor expectancy of the employee and the designated beneficiary if the new designated beneficiary had been designated as of the applicable date. If, instead, the new designated beneficiary has a life expectancy longer than the life expectancy of the designated beneficiary whose life expectancy is being used to determine the distribution period, the life expectancy of the old designated beneficiary will continue to be used for purposes of determining the distribution period even though such old designated beneficiary is no longer a beneficiary under the plan.

(2) If a new beneficiary who is not an individual is added or replaces a designated beneficiary after the applicable date, unless otherwise provided in D-5 and D-6, the employee will be treated as not having designated a beneficiary. Further, except as provided in paragraph (e)(2) in the case of the death of a designated beneficiary, if at any point in time after the applicable date there is no beneficiary designated with respect to the employee, the employee will also be treated as not having a designated beneficiary. In either case, the new distribution period described in subparagraph (1) will equal the period which would have been the employee's remaining life expectancy if no beneficiary had been designated as of the applicable date.

(3) Any adjustment described in this paragraph will only affect distributions for calendar years after the calendar year in which the new designated beneficiary is added or replaces the prior beneficiary, or there is no beneficiary designated with respect to the employee.

(d) *Recalculation for spouse.* For purposes of determining the distribution period in accordance with paragraph (a) or (c)(1), if any designated beneficiary involved is the employee's spouse and the life expectancy of the spouse is being recalculated, the life expectancy of the spouse as recalculated will be compared in each calendar year to the remaining life expectancy of the other applicable designated beneficiary or beneficiaries, not recalculated, and the shortest life expectancy will be used for determining the minimum distribution required for that calendar year.

(e) *Death contingency.* (1) If a beneficiary's entitlement to an employee's benefit is contingent on the death of a prior beneficiary, such contingent beneficiary will not be considered a beneficiary for purposes of determining who is the designated beneficiary with the shortest life expectancy under paragraph (a) or whether a beneficiary who is not an individual is a beneficiary. This rule does not apply if the death occurs prior to the applicable date for determining the designated beneficiary.

(2) If the designated beneficiary whose life expectancy is being used to calculate the distribution period dies on or after the applicable date, such beneficiary's remaining life expectancy will be used to determine the distribution period whether or not a beneficiary with a shorter life expectancy receives the benefits. However, in accordance with E-8, if the designated beneficiary is the employee's spouse, the spouse's life expectancy is being recalculated, and the spouse dies, the spouse does not have any remaining life expectancy; therefore, in the calendar year following the spouse's death, the spouse's life expectancy will be reduced to zero.

(3) This paragraph is illustrated by the following example:

Example. The designated beneficiary of an unmarried participant (X) as of X's required beginning date on April 1, 1988, is X's sister (A), but X has specified that, in the event of A's death, X's brother (B) will become the beneficiary. A's life expectancy as of A's birthday in calendar year 1987 is 25 years. B's life expectancy as of B's birthday in calendar year 1987 is 10 years. On X's required beginning date, A is the designated beneficiary because B entitlement to benefits is contingent on A's death. A dies on May 1, 1988. A's remaining life expectancy will continue to be used to determine the distribution period with respect to X for purposes of determining the minimum distribution for the 1988 distribution calendar year and each succeeding distribution calendar year. This is true even though, upon A's death, B will become X's beneficiary and B's life expectancy as of B's birthday in calendar year 1987 is shorter than A's life expectancy as of A's birthday in that calendar year. However, if B's entitlement was not contingent on A's death but was contingent for another reason, B would be the designated beneficiary for purposes of determining the period described in section 401(a)(9)(A)(ii), even during the period in which his entitlement is contingent, because B's life expectancy, as of B's birthday in calendar year 1987, is shorter than A's life expectancy, as of A's birthday in that calendar year.

(f) *Designations by beneficiaries.* If the plan provides (or allows the employee to specify) that, after the employee's death any person or persons have the discretion to change the beneficiaries of the employee, then, for purposes of determining the dis-tribution period for both distributions before and after the employee's death, the employee will be treated as not having designated a beneficiary. However, such discretion will not be found to exist merely because the employee's surviving spouse may designate a beneficiary for distributions pursuant to section 401(a)(9)(B)(iv)(II).

E-6. Q. After life expectancy has been determined as of the date provided in E-1 or E-2, may life expectancy be recalculated?

A. Pursuant to section 401(a)(9)(D), after life expectancy has been determined as of the date provided in E-1 and E-2, life expectancy of an employee and the employee's spouse (other than in the case of a life annuity) may be recalculated in accordance with E-7 and E-8 but not more frequently than annually.

E-7. Q. How is it determined whether or not the life expectancies of the employee and the employee's spouse will be recalculated pursuant to section 401(a)(9)(D)?

A. (a) If the plan does not adopt an optional provision specifying whether life expectancies will be determined with or without regard to the permissive recalculation rule of section 401(a)(9)(D) and the employee or spouse has not made an election pursuant to paragraph (c), the life expectancy of the employee or spouse (or the joint life and last survivor expectancy of the employee and spouse) must be recalculated annually as provided in section 401(a)(9)(D) for purposes of determining all distributions required under section 401(a)(9).

(b) The plan may adopt a provision specifying whether life expectancies will be determined with or without regard to the permissive recalculation rule of section 401(a)(9)(D). The life expectancy of the employee may be recalculated even though the life expectancy of the spouse is not recalculated and, correspondingly, the life expectancy of the spouse may be recalculated even though the life expectancy of the employee is not recalculated.

(c) The plan may adopt a provision that permits the employee (or spouse, in the case of distributions described in section 401(a)(9)(B)(iii) and (iv)) to elect the applicability or inapplicability of section 401(a)(9)(D). If such election is permitted, the employee (or spouse) must elect whether or not life expectancy will be recalculated no later than the time of the first required distribution under section 401(a)(9). As of the date of the first required distribution under section 401(a)(9), a method (either recalculation of life expectancy or no recalculation of life expectancy) which is in effect with respect to an employee (or spouse) must be irrevocable with respect to the employee (or spouse) and must apply to all subsequent years. The plan may specify, pursuant to paragraph (b), whether or not life expectancy will be recalculated in the event that the employee (or spouse) fails to make the election. Absent such a plan provision, the life expectancy of the employee (and the spouse) must be recalculated annually pursuant to paragraph (a) in the event that the employee (or spouse) fails to make the election.

E-8 Q. How are life expectancies recalculated annually under section 401(a)(9)(D)?

A. (a) An employee's life expectancy (or the joint life and last survivor expectancy of the employee and spouse) is recalculated annually by redetermining the employee's life expectancy (or the joint life and last survivor expectancy of the employee and spouse) in each distribution calendar year using the employee's (and spouse's) attained age as of the employee's birthday (and the spouse's birthday) in that distribution calendar year. Upon the death of the employee (or the employee's spouse), the recalculated life expectancy of the employee (or the employee's spouse) will be reduced to zero in the calendar year following the calendar year of death. In any calendar year in which the last applicable life expectancy is reduced to zero, the plan must distribute the employee's entire remaining interest prior to the last day of such year in order to satisfy section 401(a)(9).

(b) If the designated beneficiary is not the employee's spouse (or if the spouse's life expectancy is not being recalculated) and the life expectancy of the employee is being recalculated annually, the applicable life expectancy for determining the minimum distribution for each distribution calendar year will be determined by recalculating the employee's life expectancy but not recalculating the beneficiary's life expectancy. Such applicable life expectancy is the joint life and last survivor expectancy using the employee's attained age as of the employee's birthday in the distribution calendar year and an adjusted age of the designated beneficiary. The adjusted age of the designated beneficiary is determined as follows: First, the beneficiary's applicable life expectancy is calculated based on the beneficiary's attained age as of the beneficiary's birthday in the calendar year described in E-1, reduced by one for each calendar year which has elapsed since that calendar year. The age (rounded if necessary to the higher age) in Table V of § 1.72-9 is then located which corresponds to the designated beneficiary's applicable life expectancy. Such age is the adjusted age of the designated beneficiary. As provided in paragraph (a), upon the death of the employee, the life expectancy of the employee is reduced to zero in the calendar year following the calendar year of the employee's death. Thus, for determining the minimum distribution for such calendar year and subsequent calendar years, the applicable life expectancy is the applicable life expectancy of the designated beneficiary determined under this paragraph.

(c) This Question and Answer is illustrated by the following examples:

Example 1. (a) A participant in a qualified profit-sharing plan retires on January 1, 1987. The benefit for determining the 1987 calendar year minimum distribution (determined in accordance with F-5) is $100,000. As of the participant's birthday in calendar year 1987, the participant, who was born December 31, 1916 is age 71. The participant's spouse died some years earlier and the participant designates his brother as his sole beneficiary on his retirement date and his brother is still designated as his sole beneficiary as of April 1, 1988. As of his brother's birthday in calendar year 1987, his brother, who was born on July 2, 1920, is age 67. The plan does not provide that life expectancies will not be recalculated and does not permit employees to elect not to recalculate life expectancy. Thus, pursuant to E-7(a), the life expectancy of the participant will be recalculated.

(b) For calendar year 1987, the payment that is to be made pursuant to section 401(a)(9) is the benefit of $100,000 divided by the joint and last survivor life expectancy of the participant and his brother calculated using their ages as of their birthdays in calendar year 1987. Pursuant to Table VI of § 1.72-9, such joint life and last survivor

expectancy is 21.7 years. The payment required for 1987 is therefore $4,608.30 ($100,000 divided by 21.7). $4,608.30 is distributed on April 1, 1988.

(c) The benefit for determining the 1988 minimum distribution (determined in accordance with F-5) before adjustment for the distribution on April 1, 1987 is $109,515.71. The amount of the minimum distribution for 1988 distributed on April 1, 1988 is then subtracted from that amount. (109,515.71 – 4,608.30 = 104,907.41.) Thus, $104,907.41 is the benefit to be used to determine the 1988 minimum distribution. The minimum payment for 1988 is determined by dividing the benefit of $104,907.41 by a recalculated joint life and last survivor expectancy of the participant and his brother. Such joint life and last survivor expectancy is recalculated as follows:

(1)	Life expectancy of brother (using age as of birthday in calendar year 1987, from Table V of § 1.72-9)	=	18.4	years
(2)	Number of years elapsed since calendar year 1987	=	1	year
(3)	Remaining period of life expectancy of brother, (1) – (2)	=	17.4	years
(4)	Age in Table V of § 1.72-9 corresponding to life expectancy of 17.4 years (rounding to higher age)	=	69	
(5)	Age of participant (age determined as of birthday in calendar year 1988)	=	72	
(6)	Joint life and last survivor expectancy using the age in (4) and (5) from Table VI of § 1.72-9	=	20.3	

The minimum payment for 1988 is therefore $5,167.85 ($104,907.41 divided by 20.3). This must be paid by December 31, 1988, to the participant.

(d) The benefit for determining the 1989 minimum distribution (determined in accordance with F-5) is $109,714.00. The minimum payment for 1989 is determined by dividing the benefit of $109,714.00 by the recalculated joint life and last survivor expectancy of the participant and his brother; such joint life and last survivor expectancy is recalculated as follows:

(1)	Life expectancy of brother (using age as of birthday in calendar year 1987 from Table V of § 1.72-9)	=	18.4	years
(2)	Number of years elapsed since 1987	=	2	years
(3)	Remaining period of life expectancy of brother (1) – (2) .	=	16.4	years
(4)	Age in Table V of § 1.72-9 corresponding to life expectancy of 16.4 years rounding to higher age)	=	70	
(5)	Age of participant (age determined using age as of birthday in calendar year 1989)	=	73	
(6)	Joint life and last survivor expectancy using the ages in (4) and (5) from Table VI of § 1.72-9 years	=	19.4	

The minimum payment for 1989 is therefor $5,655.36 ($109,714.00 divided by 19A). This must be paid by December 31, 1989, to the participant.

Example 2. Assume the same facts as in Example 1, except that the participant dies in 1988 after the participant's required beginning date. The recalculation of life expectancy for the participant and the calculation of the minimum payment for 1988 will be the same as in Example 1. The participant's life expectancy is not reduced to zero until the calendar year following the year of death. The calculation of the minimum payment for 1989 is as follows:

(1)	Life expectancy of brother (using age as of birthday in calendar year 1988 from Table V of § 1.79-9)	=	18.4 years
(2)	Number of elapsed years since 1987	=	2 years
(3)	Remaining period, (1) – (2)	=	16.4 years
(4)	Benefit for determining 1989 minimum distribution . . .	=	$109,714.00
(5)	Minimum payment for 1989, (4) divided by (3)	=	$ 6,689.88

Example 3. Assume the same facts in Example 1, except the brother (rather than the participant) dies in 1988 after the participant's required beginning date. The redetermination of life expectancy for the participant and the calculation of the minimum payment for 1988 and 1989 will be the same as in Example 1; the brother's life expectancy was fixed at the time benefits commenced and is used even after the brother dies.

F. Determination of the amount which must be distributed each year.

F-1. Q. If an employee's benefit is in the form of an individual account, what is the amount required to be distributed for each calendar year in the case of either (1) distributions to an employee before death over a period described in section 401(a)(9)(A)(ii) or (2) to a beneficiary after the employee's death over a period described in section 401(a)(9)(B)(iii)?

A. (a) *General rule.* If an employee's benefit is in the form of an individual account and is to be distributed over (1) a period not extending beyond the life expectancy of the employee or the joint life and last survivor expectancy of the employee and the designated beneficiary (as described in section 401(a)(9)(A)(ii)) or (2) over a period not extending beyond the life expectancy of the designated beneficiary (as described in section 401(a)(9)(B)(iii)), the amount required to be distributed for each calendar year, beginning with the first calendar year for which distributions are required and then for each succeeding calendar year, must at least equal the quotient obtained by dividing the employee's benefit by the applicable life expectancy. The minimum amount which is required to be distributed on or before an employee's required beginning date is always determined under this F-1 and not section 401(a)(9)(A)(i). The amount described in section 401(a)(9)(A)(i) will always exceed the amount determined under this F-1. See paragraph (e) for purchases of annuity contracts. Also, see F-4A and Q&A-4 of § 1.401(a)(9)-2 for additional limits under the minimum distribution incidental benefit requirement on the divisor which must be used to determine the minimum required distribution.

(b) *Distribution calendar year.* A calendar year for which a minimum distribution is required is a distribution calendar year. The first calendar year for which a distribution is required is an employee's first distribution calendar year. In the case of distributions required before death under section 401(a)(9)(A), if an employee's required beginning date is April 1 of the calendar year following the calendar year in which the employee attains age 70 ½, the employee's first distribution calendar year is the year the employee attains age 70 ½. However, if, pursuant to B-2(b), an employee's required beginning date is April 1 of the calendar year following the calendar year in which the employee retires or becomes a 5-percent owner, the calendar year in which the employee retires or becomes a 5-percent owner is the employee's first distribution calendar year. In the case of distributions to be made in accordance with the exception to the five-year rule in section 401(a)(9)(B)(iii) and (iv), the first distribution calendar year is the calendar year containing the date described in C-3(a) or C-3(b), whichever is applicable.

(c) *Time for distributions.* The distribution required to be made on or before the employee's required beginning date shall be treated as the distribution required for the employee's first distribution calendar year (as defined in paragraph (b)). The minimum distribution for other distribution calendar years, including the minimum distribution for the distribution calendar year in which the employee's required beginning date occurs, must be made on or before December 31 of that distribution calendar year.

(d) *Life expectancy.* The applicable life expectancy is the life expectancy (or joint life and last survivor expectancy) determined in accordance with E-1 through E-5, reduced by one for each calendar year which has elapsed since the date on which the life expectancy (or joint and last survivor expectancy) was calculated. However, pursuant to E-6 through E-8, life expectancy is recalculated, the applicable life expectancy will be the life expectancy as so recalculated.

(e) *Annuity contracts.* (1) Instead of satisfying F-1, the minimum distribution requirement may be satisfied by purchase with the employee's benefit of an annuity contract from an insurance company in accordance with F-4. Only a purchase of an annuity contract will insure that distribution can be made over the employee's or a beneficiary's life, or joint lives if applicable.

(2) If an annuity is purchased on or before the date when distributions are required to commence (the required beginning date, in the case of distributions before death, or the date determined under C-3, in the case of distributions after death), distribution under the annuity contract purchased will satisfy section 401(a)(9) if payments under the annuity contract are made in accordance with F-3.

(3) As explained in F-3A(b) with reference to distributions after death which must be made at least as rapidly as under the method used under section 401(a)(9)(A)(ii), unless life expectancy is being recalculated, if the annuity contract is purchased after the date on which distributions are required to commence, the annuity contract purchased may not be a life annuity and must be payable for a term certain not exceeding the remaining applicable life expectancy. The remaining applicable life expectancy is the applicable life expectancy described in paragraph (d) which would have been used, if the annuity contract had not been purchased, to determine the minimum distribution in accordance with paragraphs (a) through (c) for the first distribution calendar year in which the annuity contract is purchased.

(4) If the annuity contract is purchased after the date on which distributions are required to commence and life expectancy is being recalculated, distribution under the contract will satisfy section 401(a)(9) if the contract is a life annuity payable either (i) over the life (or lives) of the individual (or individuals) whose life expectancy is being recalculated (with or without a period certain that meets the requirements of subparagraph (3)) or (ii) for a term certain determined under subparagraph (3).

(5) If an annuity is purchased on or after the employee's required beginning date with a period certain feature, the period certain may not be lengthened after the date of the initial purchase by exchanging the annuity contract for an annuity contract with a longer period certain even if the original period certain was shorter than the maximum permitted.

F-2. Q. If an employee's benefit is in the form of an individual account and in any calendar year the amount distributed exceeds the minimum required, will credit be given in subsequent years for such excess distribution?

A. If, in any calendar year, the amount distributed exceeds the minimum required, no credit will be given in subsequent years for such excess distribution. However, in the case in which the employee's first distribution calendar year is the calendar year immediately preceding the employee's required beginning date, amounts distributed in the employee's first distribution calendar year will be credited toward the distribution required to be made on or before the employee's required beginning date for the employee's first distribution calendar year.

F-3. Q. How must annuity distributions under a defined benefit plan be paid in order to satisfy section 401(a)(9)?

A. (a) In order to satisfy section 401(a)(9), annuity distributions under a defined benefit plan must be paid in periodic payments made at intervals not longer than one year (payment intervals) for a life (or lives), or over a period certain not longer than a life expectancy (or joint life and last survivor expectancy) described in section 401(a)(9)(A)(ii) or section 401(a)(9)(B)(iii), whichever is applicable. The life expectancy (or joint life and last survivor expectancy) for purposes of determining the length of the period certain will be determined in accordance with E-1 through E-5, without recalculation of life expectancy. Once payments have commenced over a period certain, the period certain may not be lengthened even if the period certain is shorter than the maximum permitted. Payments must be either nonincreasing or increase only as follows:

(1) With any percentage increase in a specified and generally recognized cost-of-living index,

(2) To the extent of the reduction in the amount of the employee's payments to provide for a survivor benefit upon death, but only if the beneficiary whose life was being used to determine the period described in section 401(a)(9)(A)(ii) over which payments were being made dies and the payments continue otherwise in accordance with that section over the life of the employee,

(3) To provide cash refunds of employee contributions upon the employee's death, or

(4) Because of an increase in benefits under the plan. Also see FAA for additional requirements for distributions in the form of an annuity which must be satisfied in order for the distribution to satisfy the minimum distribution incidental benefit. If distribution is permitted to be made over the lives of the employee and the designated beneficiary, references to a life annuity herein include a joint and survivor annuity for purposes of section 401(a)(9).

(b) The annuity may be a life annuity with a period certain if the life (or lives, if applicable) and period certain each meet the requirements of paragraph (a).

(c) Distributions under a variable life annuity (or a life annuity with a period certain) will not be found to be increasing merely because the amount of the payments vary with the investment performance of the underlying assets. However, the Commissioner may prescribe additional requirements applicable to such variable life annuities.

(d)(1) If the annuity is a life annuity (or a life annuity with a period certain not exceeding 20 years), the following rule will apply. The first payment which must be made on or before the employee's required beginning date must be the payment which is required for one payment interval. The second payment need not be made until the end of the next payment interval even if that payment interval ends in the next calendar year. Similarly, in the case of distributions commencing after death in accordance with section 401(a)(9)(B)(iii) and (iv), the first payment that must be made on or before the date determined under C-3(a) or (b) (whichever is applicable) must be the payment which is required for one payment interval. Payment intervals are the periods for which payments are received, e.g., bimonthly, monthly, semi-annually, or annually.

(2) If the annuity is a period certain annuity without a life contingency (or is a life annuity with a period certain exceeding 20 years), periodic payments for each distribution calendar year (as defined in F-1(b)) will be combined and treated as an annual amount. Such annual amount must meet the requirements of paragraph (a). The amount

which is required to be distributed on or before the employee's required beginning date is the annual amount for the employee's first distribution calendar year (as defined in F-1(b)). The annual amount for other distribution calendar years, including the annual amount which is for the calendar year in which the employee's required beginning date occurs, must be distributed on or before December 31 of the calendar year for which the distribution is required. Similarly, in the case of such distributions commencing after death in accordance with section 401(a)(9)(B)(iii) and (iv), the amount which is required to be distributed on or before the date determined under C-3(a) or (b), whichever is applicable, is the annual amount for the beneficiary's first distribution calendar year.

(3) This paragraph is illustrated by the following examples:

Example (1). A defined benefit plan (Plan X) provides monthly annuity payments of $500 for the life of unmarried participants with a 10 year period certain. An unmarried participant (A) in the plan (Z) attains age 70 ½ in 1990. In order to meet the requirements of this paragraph, the first payment which must be made on or before April 1, 1991 will be $500 and the payments must continue to be made in monthly payments of $500 thereafter for the life and 10 year certain period.

Example (2). The facts are the same as in *Example (1),* except that the annuity is an optional form of payment elected by Z which provides for annuity payments of $700 a month for a 10 year period certain, without a life contingency. In such case, in order to meet the requirements of this paragraph, the monthly payments of $700 a month for each calendar year will be combined and treated as an annual amount of $8,400 a year. On or before April 1, 1987, Z must be paid $8,400, the annual amount for 1986. The annual amount for calendar year 1987 of $8,400 must be distributed on or before December 31, 1987.

(e) If distributions from a defined benefit plan are not in the form of an annuity, the employee's benefit will be treated as an individual account for purposes of determining the minimum distribution. See F-1 to determine the minimum distribution if distribution is being made over life expectancy.

F-3A. Q. How must distributions be made after the employee's death in order to be considered to satisfy the requirement that the employee's remaining interest be distributed at least as rapidly as under the distribution method being used under section 401(a)(9)(A)(ii) as of the date of the employee's death?

A: (a) *General rule.* After the employee's death, the requirement that the employee's remaining interest be distributed at least as rapidly as under the method of distribution being used under section 401(a)(9)(A)(ii) as of the date of the employee's death will be considered to be satisfied if the employee's remaining interest is distributed in accordance with either paragraph (b) or (c).

(b) *Individual account—General rule.* (1) Except as otherwise provided in subparagraph (2), if the employee's benefit is in the form of an individual account and, as of the date of the employee's death, distributions had commenced in accordance with F-1, the employee's remaining interest must continue to be distributed in accordance with F-1. If, before the employee's death, the divisor being used to determine the amount which was required to be distributed was the applicable divisor pursuant to Q&A4 of §1.401(a)(9)-2 rather than the applicable life expectancy determined under F-1, the required distributions after the employee's death may be determined without regard to §1.401(a)(9)-2 using the applicable life expectancy determined under F-1 as the relevant divisor.

(2) *Purchased annuity contract.* (i) The employee's remaining interest will be treated as distributed in accordance with F-1 if it (A) is distributed under an immediate annuity contract that makes payments for a period certain that satisfy F-3 and (B) is purchased at any time with the employee's remaining benefits. The period over which the annuity contract makes payments may not exceed the applicable life expectancy that would have been used to determine the minimum distribution under F-1 for the distribution calendar year in which the annuity is purchased (purchase year). Further, in the purchase year, the amount distributed (when combined with amounts distributed in the purchase year before the immediate annuity contract is purchased) must equal (or exceed) the lesser of (C) the amount required to be distributed for such purchase year under F-1 or (D) the amount of the annual amount for the purchase year determined under F-3(d)(2). If the employee's life expectancy is being recalculated in the purchase year, the applicable life expectancy is the life expectancy (or joint life and last survivor expectancy) as recalculated, in accordance with E-8, after the employee's death.

(ii) If the designated beneficiary is the surviving spouse and the spouse's life expectancy is being recalculated, the annuity contract must satisfy (i) except that it may be a life annuity (with or without a period certain) payable over the remaining life of the surviving spouse.

(c) *Existing annuity.* If, as of the date of the employee's death, the employee's benefit was being distributed as an annuity in accordance with F-3 (and F-4, if applicable), annuity distribution of the employee's remaining benefit must continue to be made (except for acceleration) in accordance with F-3 (and F-4, if applicable) for the remainder of the period under the annuity as of the date of the employee's death.

(d) *Examples.* This F-3A is illustrated by the following examples:

Example (1). (a) An employee (X) was born February 1, 1919. His required beginning date is April 1, 1990. As permitted by the plan, he elects not to recalculate life expectancy. Pursuant to E-1, life expectancy is determined using X's and X's designated beneficiary's attained ages as of their birthdays in calendar year 1989. The joint life and last survivor expectancy using such ages is 22 years under Table VI of §1.72-9. X dies on January 1, 1991 after receiving his minimum distribution from X's account for calendar year 1989 on April 1, 1990, and his minimum distribution from X's account for calendar year 1990 on December 31, 1990. His remaining benefit, determined in accordance with F-5, for purposes of determining the minimum distribution for calendar year 1991 is $20,000. Distribution of his benefit, after his death, must continue to be distributed in accordance with F-1 over the remaining 20 years of the joint life and last survivor expectancy of X and X's designated beneficiary. The minimum distribution for calendar year 1989 is $1,000 ($20,000 divided by 20).

(b) Alternatively, in calendar year 1991, the plan may distribute to X's designated beneficiary an immediate annuity contract purchased with X's remaining benefit which makes payments for a term certain not exceeding 20 years provided that the payments satisfy F-3. Assuming no amount is distributed in 1991 prior to the distribution of the annuity contract, the amount paid under the annuity contract in 1991 must equal or exceed the lesser of (1) $1,000 or (2) the annual amount payable under the annuity contract. If instead of purchasing an annuity in 1991 the plan distributed the $1,000 minimum distribution for calendar year to X's designated beneficiary, the plan may still distribute an immediate annuity in calendar year 1992. However, in such case, any period certain under the annuity contract must be for no more than 19 years.

Example (2). The facts are the same as in *Example (1)* except that Plan B is a defined benefit plan. On April 1, 1990, annuity distributions commence to X under a life annuity for the life of X with a 10 year term certain. After X's death the annuity distributions must continue to be made over the remaining years in the 10 year certain period even though the term certain originally could have been for 22 years and still have satisfied section 401(a)(9)(A)(ii).

F-4. Q. May distributions be made from an annuity contract which is purchased from an insurance company?

A. Yes. Distributions may be made from an annuity contract which is purchased by the plan from an insurance company with the employee's benefit and which makes payments that satisfy the provisions of F-3. However, if the payments actually made under the annuity contract do not meet the requirements of section 401(a)(9), the plan fails to satisfy section 401(a)(9).

F-4A. Q. Must distributions be made in accordance with the minimum distribution incidental benefit requirement under §1.401(a)(9)-2 in order to satisfy section 401(a)(9)?

A. Yes. Section 401(a)(9)(G) provides that any distribution required under the incidental benefit requirements of section 401(a) shall be treated as a distribution required under section 401(a)(9). Consequently, in order to satisfy section 401(a)(9), distributions must be made in accordance with minimum distribution incidental benefit requirement (MDIB requirement) in §1.401(a)(9)-2 in addition to the minimum distribution requirements in this §1.401(a)(9)-1.

(b) This Question and Answer is illustrated by the following example.

Example

(a) Employee (X) is a participant in a qualified profit-sharing plan (Plan A). Plan A provides that life expectancies are not recalculated. X, born December 1, 1918 is age 71 as of his birthday in the calendar year he attains age 70 ½. As of April 1, 1990, X's only beneficiary designated to the plan is his granddaughter (Y), born January 1, 1979. X's benefit under Plan A to be used to determine the minimum distribution for 1989 (determined under F-5) is $25,300.00.

(b) In order to satisfy the MDIB requirement in §1.401(a)(9)-2 and the minimum distribution requirements in this §1.401(a)(9)-1, distribution of X's entire interest must be distributed as follows. Distribution must commence not later than April 1, 1990 (X's required beginning date determined under B-2 and B-3). The distribution for 1989 (X's first distribution calendar year determined under F-1) must be calculated by dividing X's benefit of $25,300 by the lesser of (1) the applicable divisor from the table in Q&A-4 of § 1.401(a)(9)-2 and (2) the applicable life expectancy determined under F-1. The applicable divisor from the table in Q&A-4 of § 1.401(a)(9)-2 for an employee age 71 is 25.3. The applicable life expectancy is 71.8 (the joint life and last survivor expectancy from Table IV of § 1.72-9 of X and Y using their attained ages as of their birthdays in 1989 (the year X obtained age 70 ½) of 71 and 10). Thus, the minimum distribution for 1989 is $1,000 (25,300 divided by 25.3). $1,000 is distributed to X by Plan A on April 1, 1990.

(c) X's benefit to be used to determine the minimum distribution for 1990 (determined under F-5 including the adjustment for the distribution on April 1, 1990) is $26,803.00. The minimum distribution for 1990 must be made by December 31, 1990. The minimum distribution from 1990 is determined by dividing X's benefit of 26,803.00 by the lesser of (1) the applicable divisor from the table in Q&A-4 of § 1.401(a)(9)-2 for an employee age 72 and (2) the applicable life expectancy determined under F-1. The applicable divisor from the table in Q&A-4 of § 1.401(a)(9)-2 for an employee age 72 is 24.4. The applicable life is 70.8 (71.8 reduced by one, the number of years elapsed since the calendar year X attained age 70 ½). Thus the minimum distribution for 1990 is $1098.48 (26,803.00 divided by 24.4).

F-5. Q. What benefit is used for determining the employee's minimum distribution in the case of an individual account?

A. (a) In the case of an individual account, the benefit used in determining the minimum distribution for a distribution calendar year is the account balance as of the last valuation date in the calendar year immediately preceding any distribution calendar year (valuation calendar year) adjusted as set forth below.

(b) The account balance is increased by the amount of any contributions or forfeitures allocated to the account balance as of dates in the valuation calendar year after the valuation date. Contributions include contributions made after the close of the valuation calendar year which are allocated as of dates in the valuation calendar year.

(c)(1) The account balance is decreased by distributions made in the valuation calendar year after the valuation date.

(2)(i) The following rule applies if any portion of the minimum distribution for the first distribution calendar year is made in the second distribution calendar year (i.e., generally, the distribution calendar year in which the required beginning date as defined in section 401(a)(9)(C) occurs). In such case, for purposes of determining the account balance to be used for determining the minimum distribution for the second distribution calendar year, distributions described in paragraph (c)(1) shall include an additional amount. This additional amount is equal to the amount of any distribution made in the second distribution calendar year on or before the required beginning date that is not in excess (when added to the amounts distributed in the first calendar year) of the amount required to meet the minimum distribution for the first distribution calendar year.

(ii) This paragraph (c)(2) is illustrated by the following example:

Example. (a) Employee (X), born October 1, 1918, is a participant in a qualified defined contribution plan (Plan Z). X attains age 70 ½ in calendar year 1989. X's required beginning date is April 1, 1990. As of the last valuation date under Plan Z in calendar year 1988, which was on December 31, 1988, the value of X's account balance was $24,000. No contributions are made or amounts forfeited after such date which are allocated in calendar year 1988. No rollover amounts are received after such date by Plan Z on X's behalf which were distributed by a qualified plan or IRA in calendar years 1988, 1989, or 1990. The joint life and last survivor expectancy is 24 years. The required minimum distribution for calendar year 1989 is $1,000 ($24,000 divided by 24). That amount is distributed to X on April 1, 1990. On the same date, X elects not to recalculate life expectancy, as permitted by the plan.

(b) The value of X's account balance as of December 31, 1989 (the last valuation date under Plan Z in calendar year 1989) is $26,400. No contributions are made or amounts forfeited after such date which are allocated in calendar year 1989. In order to determine the benefit to be used in calculating the minimum distribution for calendar year 1990, the account balance of $26,400 will be reduced by $1,000, the amount of the minimum distribution for calendar year 1989 made on April 1, 1990. Consequently, the benefit for purposes of determining the minimum distribution for calendar year 1990 is $25,400.

(c) If, instead of $1,000 being distributed to X, $20,000 is distributed, the account balance of $26,400 would still be reduced by $1,000 in order to determine the benefit to be used in calculating the minimum

distribution for calendar year 1990. The amount of the distribution made on April 1, 1990, in order to meet the minimum distribution for 1989 would still be $1,000. The remaining $19,000 ($20,000 – $1,000) of the distribution is not the minimum distribution for 1989. Instead, the remaining $19,000 of the distribution satisfies the minimum distribution requirement with respect to X for calendar year 1990. The amount which is required to be distributed for calendar year 1990 is $1,104.35 ($25,400 divided by 23). Consequently, no additional amount is required to be distributed to X in 1990 because $19,000 exceeds $1,105.26. However, pursuant to F-2, the remaining $17,895.65 ($19,000 – $1,104.35) may not be used to satisfy the minimum distribution requirements for calendar year 1991 or any subsequent calendar years.

(d) If an amount is distributed by one plan and rolled over to another plan (receiving plan), G-2 provides additional rules for determining the benefit and minimum distribution under the receiving plan. If an amount is transferred from one plan (transferor plan) to another plan (transferee plan), G-3 and G-4 provide additional rules for determining the minimum distribution and the benefit under both the transferor and transferee plans.

F-6. Q. If a portion of an employee's benefit is not vested as of the employee's required beginning date, how is the determination of the minimum required distribution affected?

A. (a) If the employee's benefit is in the form of an individual account, the benefit used to determine the minimum distribution required for any distribution calendar year will be determined in accordance with F-5 without regard to whether or not any portion of the employee's benefit is not vested. If any portion of the employee's benefit is not vested, distributions will be treated as being paid from the vested portion of the benefit first. If, as of the end of a distribution calendar year (or as of the employee's required beginning date, in the case of the employee's first distribution calendar year), the total amount of the employee's vested benefit is less than the minimum distribution required for the calendar year, only the vested portion of the employee's benefit is required to be distributed by the end of the calendar year (or, if applicable, by the employee's required beginning date). Further, if no portion of the employee's benefit is vested as of that date, no distribution is required as of that date. However, in the calendar year when an amount becomes vested, the amount required to be distributed in such calendar year will include the additional amount. Such additional amount will equal the lesser of (1) the vested portion of the employee's benefit, and (2) the sum of amounts not distributed in prior calendar years because the employee's vested benefit was less than the minimum required distribution. In such case, an adjustment for the additional amount distributed which corresponds to the adjustment described in F-5(c)(2) will be made to the benefit used to determine the minimum distribution for that calendar year.

(b) In the case of annuity distributions from a defined benefit plan, if any portion of the employee's benefit is not vested as of December 31 of a distribution calendar year (or as of the employee's required beginning date in the case of the employee's first distribution calendar year), the portion which is not vested as of such date will be treated as not having accrued for purposes of determining the minimum distribution for that distribution calendar year. When an additional portion of the employee's benefit becomes vested, such portion will be treated as an additional accrual. See F-7 for the rules for distributing benefits which accrue under a defined benefit plan after the employee's required beginning date.

F-7. Q. In the case of annuity distributions under a defined benefit plan, how must additional benefits which accrue after the employee's required beginning date be distributed in order to satisfy section 401(a)(9)?

A. In the case of annuity distributions under a defined benefit plan, if any additional benefits accrue after the employee's required beginning date, distribution of such amount as a separate identifiable component must commence in accordance with F-3 beginning with the first payment interval ending in the calendar year immediately following the calendar year in which such amount accrues.

G. Rollovers and Transfers

G-1. Q. If an amount is distributed by one plan (distributing plan) and is rolled over to another plan, is the benefit or the minimum distribution under the distributing plan affected by the rollover?

A. No. If an amount is distributed by one plan and is rolled over to another plan, the amount distributed is still treated as a distribution by the distributing plan, notwithstanding the rollover.

G-1A. Q. If the amount is distributed by a plan in a distribution calendar year of that plan and rolled over to another plan, what amount will be treated as a minimum distribution required under section

401(a)(9) which may not be rolled over pursuant to section 402(a)(5)(G)?

A. (a) Except as otherwise provided in paragraphs (b) and (c), all amounts distributed in a distribution calendar year will be treated for purposes of section 402(a)(5)(G) as being required under section 401(a)(9) until the total amount distributed in such calendar year exceeds the total amount which is required to be distributed for such distribution calendar year in order to satisfy section 401(a)(9).

(b) In the case of any distribution in an employee's second distribution calendar year, the amounts distributed in such calendar year which will be treated for purposes of section 402(a)(5)(G) as being required under section 401(a)(9) will include the sum of (1) the amount required to be distributed for the second distribution calendar year and (2) the amount required to be distributed for the employee's first distribution calendar year (to the extent such amount is not distributed in the first distribution calendar year).

(c) If in any calendar year the minimum amount required to be distributed under section 401(a)(9) is not distributed, such amount will be treated as an amount which is required to be distributed in the next calendar year for purposes of section 402(a)(5)(G).

(d) If the employee's entire benefit is distributed in the employee's first and second distribution calendar year but before the employee's required beginning date, the amount distributed which will be treated as an amount which is required to be distributed under section 401(a)(9) for purposes of section 402(a)(5)(G) will be determined using the designated beneficiary of the employee, if any, under the plan (or individual retirement plan) receiving the rollover contribution.

G-1B. What are the tax consequences under section 402(a) and 408(d) to an employee who rolls over an amount which is required under section 401(a)(9)?

A. The tax consequences under section 402(a) and 408(d) to an employee who rolls over an amount which is required to be distributed under section 401(a)(9) are as follows:

(a) The amount which is required to be distributed under section 401(a)(9) is taxable under section 72 in the taxable year in which distributed without regard to the rollover.

(b) If the amount which is required to be distributed under section 401(a)(9) is contributed to an individual retirement plan as a rollover contribution, such amount will be treated as a contribution to an individual retirement plan which is not a rollover contribution and thus will be an excess contribution for purposes of section 4973 if the amount is not deductible under section 219 or may not be treated as a nondeductible contribution under section 408(o). Of course, if the amount is an excess contribution, it may be withdrawn with earnings from the account before the due date of the employee's return pursuant to section 408(d)(4) in order to avoid imposition of the excise tax under section 4973.

G-2. Q. If an amount is distributed by one plan (distributing plan) and is rolled over to another plan (receiving plan), how are the benefit and the minimum distribution under the receiving plan affected?

A. (a) Except as otherwise provided in paragraph (b), if an amount is distributed by one plan (distributing plan) and is rolled over to another plan (receiving plan), the benefit of the employee under the receiving plan is increased by the amount rolled over. However, the distribution has no impact on the minimum distribution required to be made by the receiving plan for the calendar year in which the rollover is received. But, if a minimum distribution is required to be made by the receiving plan for the following calendar year, the rollover amount must be considered to be part of the employee's benefit under the receiving plan. Consequently, for purposes of determining any minimum distribution for the calendar year immediately following the calendar year in which the amount rolled over is received by the receiving plan, in the case in which the amount rolled over is received after the last valuation date in the calendar year under the receiving plan, the benefit of the employee as of such valuation date, adjusted in accordance with F-5, will be increased by the rollover amount valued as of the date of receipt. For purposes of calculating the benefit under the receiving plan pursuant to the preceding sentence, if the amount rolled over is received by the receiving plan in a different calendar year from the calendar year in which it is distributed by the distributing plan, the amount rolled over is deemed to have been received by the receiving plan in the calendar year in which it was distributed by the distributing plan.

(b) If an amount is distributed by the distributing plan after the employee's required beginning date under both the distributing plan and the receiving plan, and the designated beneficiary of the employee under the receiving plan is a designated beneficiary with a life expec-

tancy that is longer than the life expectancy of the designated beneficiary under the distributing plan, the following rule will apply. In such case, the receiving plan must separately account for the amount rolled over and treat it as a separate benefit. It must then begin distribution of such separate benefit in the calendar year following the calendar year in which the amount rolled over was distributed by the distributing plan. The separate benefit attributable to the rollover amount must be distributed over a period not exceeding the period (including any adjustments for recalculation under section 401(a)(9)(D), if applicable) used by the distributing plan to determine the employee's minimum distribution with respect to the benefit attributable to the amount rolled over. For purposes of determining the life expectancies or lives used to determine the minimum distribution under the receiving plan, the designated beneficiary under the distributing plan will be the designated beneficiary under the receiving plan (with respect to the benefit attributable to the amount rolled over). If such beneficiary is changed under the receiving plan to a different beneficiary from the designated beneficiary under the distributing plan, or a beneficiary is added who was not a beneficiary under the distributing plan, the rules in E-5 applicable to changes in beneficiaries will be used to determine the period over which distributions must be made by the receiving plan.

G-3. Q. In the case of a transfer of an amount of an employee's benefit from one plan (transferor plan) to another plan (transferee plan), are there any special rules for satisfying the minimum distribution requirement or determining the employee's benefit under the transferor plan?

A. (a) In the case of a transfer of an amount of an employee's benefit from one plan to another, the transfer is not treated as a distribution by the transferor plan for purposes of section 401(a)(9). Instead, the benefit of the employee under the transferor plan is decreased by the amount transferred. However, if any portion of an employee's benefit is transferred in a distribution calendar year with respect to that employee, in order to satisfy section 401(a)(9), the transferor plan must determine the amount of the minimum distribution with respect to that employee for the calendar year of the transfer using the employee's benefit under the transferor plan before the transfer. Additionally, if any portion of an employee's benefit is transferred in the employee's second distribution calendar year but on or before the employee's required beginning date, in order to satisfy section 401(a)(9), the transferor plan must determine the amount of the minimum distribution requirement for the employee's first distribution calendar year based on the employee's benefit under the transferor plan before the transfer. The transferor plan may satisfy the minimum distribution requirement for the calendar year of the transfer (and the prior year if applicable) by segregating the amount which must be distributed from the employee's benefit and not transferring that amount. Such amount may be retained by the transferor plan and distributed on or before the date required or paid to an escrow account which in turn distributes such amount on or before the date required.

(b) For purposes of determining any minimum distribution for the calendar year immediately following the calendar year in which the transfer occurs, in the case of a transfer after the last valuation date for the calendar year of the transfer under the transferor plan, the benefit of the employee as of such valuation date, adjusted in accordance with F-5, will be decreased by the amount transferred valued as of the date transferred.

G-3A. Q. What are the excise tax consequences for an employee (or other distributee) if, before transferring a portion of an employee's benefit in a distribution calendar year, the transferor plan does not satisfy the minimum distribution requirement for the calendar year of the transfer (and, if applicable, the prior calendar year)?

A. If the transferor plan does not satisfy the minimum distribution for the calendar year of transfer (and, if applicable, the prior calendar year) in accordance with G-3, the amount required to be distributed to satisfy the minimum distribution requirement for the calendar year of the transfer (and, if applicable, the prior calendar year) will be treated for purposes of section 4974 as a minimum distribution that was not distributed. Consequently, the payee with respect to such amount will be subject to the excise tax imposed under section 4974.

G-4. Q. If an amount of an employee's benefit is transferred from one plan (transferor plan) to another plan (transferee plan), how are the benefit and the minimum distribution under the transferee plan affected?

A. (a) Except as otherwise provided in paragraph (b), in the case of a transfer from one plan (transferor plan) to another (transferee plan), the general rule is that the benefit of the employee under the transferee plan is increased by the amount transferred. The transfer has no impact on the minimum distribution required to be made by the transferee plan in the calendar year in which the transfer is received. However, if a minimum distribution is required from the transferee plan for the following calendar year, the transferred amount must be considered to be part of the employee's benefit under the transferee plan. Consequently, for purposes of determining any minimum distribution for the calendar year immediately following the calendar year in which the transfer occurs, in the case of a transfer after the last valuation date of the transferee plan in the transfer calendar year, the benefit of the employee under the receiving plan valued as of such valuation date, adjusted in accordance with F-5, will be increased by the amount transferred valued as of the date transferred.

(b) If an amount is transferred after the employee's required beginning date under both the transferor plan and the transferee plan, and the designated beneficiary of the employee under the transferee plan is a designated beneficiary with a life expectancy that is longer than the life expectancy of the designated beneficiary under the transferor plan, the following rule will apply. The transferee plan must separately account for the amount rolled over and treat it as a separate benefit. The transferee plan must then begin distribution of such separate benefit in the calendar year following the calendar year in which the amount was transferred. This benefit attributable to the transferred amount must be distributed over a period not exceeding the period (including any adjustments for recalculation under section 401(a)(9)(D), if applicable) used by the transferor plan to determine the employee's minimum distribution with respect to the benefit attributable to the amount transferred. For purposes of determining the life expectancies or lives used to determine the minimum distribution under the transferee plan, the designated beneficiary under the transferor plan will be the designated beneficiary under the transferee plan (with respect to the benefit attributable to the amount transferred). If such beneficiary is changed under the transferee plan to a different beneficiary from the designated beneficiary under the transferor plan or a beneficiary is added who was not a beneficiary under the transferor plan, the rules in E-5, applicable to changes in beneficiaries, will be used to determine the period over which distributions must be made by the transferee plan.

G-5. Q. How are a spinoff, merger or consolidation (as defined in § 1.414(l)-1) treated for purposes of determining an employee's benefit and minimum distribution under section 401(a)(9)?

A. For purposes of determining an employee's benefit and minimum distribution under section 401(a)(9), a spinoff, a merger, or a consolidation (as defined in § 1.414(l)) will be treated as a transfer of the benefits of the employees involved. Consequently, the benefit and minimum distribution of each employee involved under the transferor and transferee plans will be determined in accordance with G-3 and G-4.

H. *Special rules*

H-1. Q. What distribution rules apply if an employee is a participant in more than one plan?

A. If an employee is a participant in more than one plan, the plans in which the employee participates may not be aggregated for purposes of testing whether or not the distribution requirements of section 401(a)(9) are met. The distribution of the benefit of the employee under each plan must separately meet the requirements of section 401(a)(9).

H-2. Q. If an employee's benefit under a plan is divided into separate accounts (or segregated shares in the case of a defined benefit plan), do the distribution rules in section 401(a)(9) and these regulations apply separately to each separate account (or segregated share)?

A. (a) Except as otherwise provided in paragraphs (b) and (c), if an employee's benefit under a plan is divided into separate accounts (or segregated shares in the case of a defined benefit plan), the separate accounts (or segregated shares) will be aggregated for purposes of satisfying the rules in section 401(a)(9). Thus, except as otherwise provided in paragraphs (b) and (c), all separate accounts, including a separate account for nondeductible employee contributions (under section 72(e)(9)) or for qualified voluntary employee contributions (as defined in section 219(e)(2)), will be aggregated for purposes of section 401(a)(9).

(b) If, as of an employee's required beginning date or, in the case of distributions under section 401(a)(9)(B)(ii) or (iii) and (iv), as of the employee's (or spouse's where applicable) date of death, the beneficiaries with respect to a separate account (or segregated share in the case of a defined benefit plan) differ from the beneficiaries with respect to the other separate accounts (or segregate shares) of the employee, such separate account (or segregated share) need not be aggregated with other separate accounts (or segregated shares) in order to determine whether the distributions from such separate account (or segregated share) satisfy section 401(a)(9). Instead, the rules in section 401(a)(9) may separately apply to such separate account (or segre-

gated share). Thus, for example, if the employee designated a different beneficiary for each separate account (or segregated share), each separate account (or segregated share) may be distributed over the joint life (or joint life and last survivor expectancy) of the employee and the designated beneficiary (or the life or life expectancy of the designated beneficiary in the case of any distribution described in section 401(a)(9)(B)(iii) and (iv)) for that separate account (or segregated share). Further, for example, if, in the case of a distribution described in section 401(a)(9)(B)(iii) and (iv), the only designated beneficiary of a separate account (or segregated share) is the employee's surviving spouse, and beneficiaries other than the surviving spouse are designated with respect to the other separate accounts of the employee, distribution of the spouse's separate account (or segregated share) need not commence until the date determined under the first sentence in C-3(b) even if distribution of the other separate accounts (or segregated shares) must commence at an earlier date. Also, for example, in the case of a distribution after the death of an employee to which section 401(a)(9)(B)(i) does not apply, distribution from a separate account (or segregated share) of an employee may be made over a beneficiary's life expectancy in accordance with section 401(a)(9)(B)(iii) and (iv) even though distributions from other separate accounts (or segregated shares) with different beneficiaries are being made in accordance with the five-year rule in section 401(a)(9)(B)(ii).

(c) See G-2 through G-4 for special rules which apply to the distribution from separate accounts maintained because of a transfer or rollover.

H-2A. What is a separate account or segregated share for purposes of section 401(a)(9)?

A. (a) For purposes of section 401(a)(9) a separate account in an individual account is a portion of an employee's benefit determined by an acceptable separate accounting including allocating investment gains and losses, and contributions and forfeitures, on a pro rata basis in a reasonable and consistent matter between such portion and any other benefits. Further, the amounts of each such portion of the benefit will be separately determined for purposes of determining the amount of the minimum distribution in accordance with F-5.

(b) A benefit in a defined benefit plan is separated into segregated shares if it consists of separate identifiable components which may be separately distributed.

H-3. Q. Must a distribution that is required by section 401(a)(9) to be made by the required beginning date to the participant or that is required by section 401(a)(9)(B)(ii) to be made by the required time to a designated beneficiary who is a surviving spouse be made notwithstanding the failure of the participant, or spouse where applicable, to consent to a distribution while a benefit is immediately distributable?

A. Yes. Section 411(a)(11) and section 417(e) (see § 1.411(a)(11)-1T(c)(2) and § 1.417(e)-1T(c)) require participant and spousal consent to certain distributions of plan benefits while such benefits are immediately distributable. If a participant's normal retirement age is later than the required beginning date for the commencement of distributions under section 401(a)(9) and, therefore, benefits are still immediately distributable, the plan must, nevertheless, distribute plan benefits to the participant (or where applicable, to the spouse) in a manner that satisfies the requirements of section 401(a)(9). Section 401(a)(9) must be satisfied even though the participant (or spouse, where applicable) fails to consent to the distribution. In such a case, the plan may distribute in the form of a qualified joint and survivor annuity (QJSA) or in the form of a qualified preretirement survivor annuity (QPSA) and the consent requirements of sections 411(a)(11) and 417(e) are deemed to be satisfied if the plan has made reasonable efforts to obtain consent from the participant (or spouse if applicable) and if the distribution otherwise meets the requirements of section 417. If, because of section 401(a)(11)(B), the plan is not required to distribute in the form of a QJSA to a participant or a QPSA to a surviving spouse, the plan may distribute the minimum amount required at the time required to satisfy section 401(a)(9) and the consent requirements of sections 411(a)(11) and 417(e) are deemed to be satisfied if the plan has made reasonable efforts to obtain consent from the participant (or spouse if applicable) and if the distribution otherwise meets the requirements of section 417.

H-3A. Who is an employee's spouse or surviving spouse for purposes of section 401(a)(9)?

A. Except as otherwise provided in H-4(a) in the case of distributions of a portion of an employee's benefit payable to a former spouse of an employee pursuant to a qualified domestic relations order, for purposes of section 401(a)(9), an individual is a spouse or surviving spouse of an employee if such individual is treated as the employee's spouse under applicable state law as of the following dates, whichever is applicable. Sections 401(a)(11)(D) and 417(d) do not apply for purposes of determining who is an employee's spouse or surviving spouse under section 401(a)(9). In the case of distributions before the death of an employee under section 401(a)(9)(A)(ii), for purposes of determining whether the designated beneficiary's life expectancy may be recalculated, the spouse of the employee is determined as of the employee's required beginning date. In the case of distributions after the death of an employee, for purposes of determining whether, under the exception to the five-year rule in section 401(a)(9)(B)(iii) and (iv), the provisions of clause (iv) apply, the spouse of the employee is determined as of the date of death of the employee.

H-4. Q. In order to satisfy section 401(a)(9), are there any special rules which apply to the distribution of all or a portion of an employee's benefit payable to an alternate payee pursuant to a qualified domestic relations order as defined in section 414(p) (QDRO)?

A. (a) A former spouse to whom all or a portion of the employee's benefit is payable pursuant to a QDRO will be treated as a spouse (including a surviving spouse) of the employee for purposes of section 401(a)(9).

(b)(1) If a QDRO provides that an employee's benefit is to be divided and a portion is to be allocated to an alternate payee, such portion will be treated as a separate account (or segregated share) which separately must satisfy the requirements of section 401(a)(9) and may not be aggregated with other separate accounts (or segregated shares) of the employee for purposes of satisfying section 401(a)(9). Except as otherwise provided in subparagraph (2), distribution of such separate account allocated to an alternate payee pursuant to a QDRO must be made in accordance with section 401(a)(9). For example, in general, distribution of such account will satisfy section 401(a)(9)(A) if such account will be distributed, beginning not later than the employee's required beginning date over the life of the employee or over the lives of the employee and the alternate payee (or over a period not extending beyond the life expectancy of such employee or the joint life and last survivor expectancy of such employee and alternate payee). Distribution of the separate account will not satisfy section 401(a)(9)(A)(ii) if it is distributed over the joint lives of the alternate payee and a designated beneficiary (other than the employee). The determination of whether distribution from such account after the death of the employee to the alternate payee will be made in accordance with section 401(a)(9)(B)(i) or section 401(a)(9)(B)(ii) or (iii) and (iv) will depend on whether distributions have begun as determined under B-5 (which provides, in general, that distributions are not treated as having begun until the employee's required beginning date even though payments may actually have begun before that date). Further, for example, if the alternate payee dies before the date on which the designated beneficiary is determined under D-3 or D-4 and distribution of the separate account allocated to the alternate payee pursuant to the QDRO is to be made to the alternate payee's beneficiary, such beneficiary may be treated as a designated beneficiary for purposes of determining the minimum distribution required from such account if the beneficiary of the alternate payee is an individual and if such beneficiary is a beneficiary under the plan or specified to or in the plan. (Specification in the QDRO will also be treated as specification to the plan.)

(2) Distribution of the separate account allocated to an alternative payee pursuant to a QDRO will satisfy section 401(a)(9)(A) even though distributions are made to the alternate payee rather than the employee if the distribution otherwise meets the requirements of section 401(a)(9)(A). Distribution of the separate account allocated to an alternate payee pursuant to a QDRO will also meet the requirements of section 401(a)(9)(A)(ii) if such account is to be distributed, beginning not later than the employee's required beginning date, over the life of the alternate payee (or over a period not extending beyond the life expectancy of the alternative payee). If the plan permits the employee to elect not to recalculate life expectancies (life expectancies of the employee and the employee's spouse) pursuant to E-7(c), such election is to be made only by the alternate payee for purposes of distributing the separate account allocated to such alternative payee pursuant to the QDRO. Also, if the plan permits the employee to elect whether distribution upon the death of the employee will be made in accordance with the five-year rule in section 401(a)(9)(B)(ii) or the exception to the five-year rule in section 401(a)(9)(B)(iii) and (iv) pursuant to C-4(c), such election is to be made only by the alternate payee for purposes of distributing the separate account allocated to the alternate payee pursuant to the QDRO. If the alternate payee dies after distribution of the separate account allocated to the alternate payee pursuant to a QDRO has begun (determined under B-5), distribution of the remaining portion of that portion of the benefit allocated to the alternate payee must be made at least as rapidly (determined under B-6) as under the

method of distributions being used as of the date of the alternate payee's death. As provided in § 1.401(a)(9)-2, distribution of the separate account allocated to an alternate payee pursuant to a QDRO need not satisfy the minimum distribution incidental benefit rule as long as the distribution of such account otherwise satisfies section 401(a)(9).

(c) If a QDRO does not provide that an employee's benefit is to be divided but merely provides that a portion of an employee's benefit (otherwise payable to the employee) is to be paid to an alternate payee, such portion will not be treated as a separate account (or segregated share) of the employee. Instead, such portion will be aggregated with any amount distributed to the employee and will be treated as having been distributed to the employee for purposes of determining whether the minimum distribution requirement has been satisfied with respect to that employee.

H-5. Q. Will a plan fail to qualify as a pension plan within the meaning of section 401(a), solely because the plan permits distributions to commence to an employee on or after April 1 of the calendar year following the calendar year in which the employee attains age 70 ½ even though the employee has not retired or attained the normal retirement age under the plan as of the date on which such distributions commence?

A. No. A plan will not fail to qualify as a pension plan within the meaning of section 401(a), solely because the plan permits distributions to commence to an employee on or after April 1 of the calendar year following the calendar year in which the employee attains age 70 ½ even though the employee has not retired or attained the normal retirement age under the plan as of the date on which such distributions commence. This rule applies without regard to whether or not the employee is a 5-percent owner with respect to the plan year ending in the calendar year in which distributions commence.

H-6. Q. Is the distribution of an annuity contract a distribution for purposes of section 401(a)(9)?

A. No. The distribution of an annuity contract is not a distribution for purposes of section 401(a)(9).

H-7. Will a payment by a plan after the death of an employee fail to be treated as a distribution for purposes of section 401(a)(9) solely because it is made to an estate or a trust?

A. A payment by a plan after the death of an employee will not fail to be treated as a distribution for purposes of section 401(a)(9) solely because it is made to an estate or a trust. As a result, the estate or trust which receives a payment from a plan after the death of an employee need not distribute the amount of such payment to the beneficiaries of the estate or trust in accordance with section 401(a)(9)(B). However, pursuant to D-2A, distribution to the estate must satisfy the five-year rule in section 401(a)(9)(B)(iii) if the distribution to the employee had not begun (as defined in B-5) as of the employee's date of death, and pursuant to D-2A, an estate may not be a designated beneficiary. See D-5 and D-6 for provisions under which beneficiaries of a trust with respect to the trust's interest in an employee's benefit are treated as having been designated as beneficiaries of the employee under the plan.

H-8. Will a plan fail to satisfy section 411 if the plan is amended to eliminate benefit options that do not satisfy section 401(a)(9)?

A. Nothing in section 401(a)(9) permits a plan to eliminate for all participants a benefit option that could not otherwise be eliminated pursuant to section 411(d)(6). However, a plan must provide that, notwithstanding any other plan provisions, it will not distribute benefits under any option that does not satisfy section 401(a)(9). See A-3. Thus, the plan, notwithstanding section 411(d)(6), must prevent participants from electing benefit options that do not satisfy section 401(a)(9).

H-9. Does section 401(a)(4) prevent a plan from distributing benefits in any manner otherwise permitted under section 401(a)(9)?

A. A plan may not distribute benefits to any employee in any manner which results in discrimination prohibited under section 401(a)(4) even if the distribution otherwise satisfies section 401(a)(9).

I. *Transition Rules*

I-1. Q. Are there any special distribution rules for calendar years before 1988?

A. Yes. Minimum distributions required for calendar years 1985 and 1986 are not required to be made until December 31, 1987. Further, there are special rules for determining the amount that is required to be distributed for 1985 and 1986 (and with respect to certain employees for 1987). There are also special rules for determining the first distribution calendar year with respect to certain employees. In the case of an employee whose required beginning date is on or before April 1, 1987 and who is alive on December 31, 1987, see I-2 through I-5. In the case of an employee who dies before January 1, 1988, see I-6 through I-13. See I-14 through I-16 for other special transition rules.

I-2. Q. If an employee's required beginning date (see Q&A B-2 & 3) is on or before April 1, 1987 and such employee is alive on December 31, 1987, what is the first calendar year for which a distribution is required?

A. Except as provided in I-4 (special rule for certain life annuities), the following rules apply for purposes of determining the first distribution calendar year of an employee with a required beginning date on or before April 1, 1987 if such employee is alive on December 31, 1987:

(a) *Pre-1987 required beginning date.* If an employee's required beginning date was on or before April 1, 1986, the first distribution calendar year is 1985. However, under these transition rules, the minimum distribution for 1985 is not required to be made by April 1, 1986, and the minimum distribution for 1986 is not required to be made by December 31, 1986. Instead, the minimum distributions for calendar years 1985 and 1986 are required to be made by December 31, 1987. Thus, the minimum distributions for 1985, 1986, and 1987 must be made by December 31, 1987.

(b) *1987 required beginning date.* If an employee's required beginning date is April 1, 1987, the first distribution calendar year is 1986. However, under these transition rules, the minimum distribution for 1986 is not required to be made by April 1, 1987. Instead, the minimum distribution for 1986 is required to be made by December 31, 1987. Thus, the minimum distribution for 1986 and 1987 must be made by December 31, 1987.

I-3. Q. If (1) the employee is alive on December 31, 1987 and (2) the employee's first distribution calendar year is 1985 or 1986 (as determined under I-2), how is the amount of the minimum required distribution determined for calendar years 1985, 1986, and 1987?

A. (a) *In general.* If (1) the employee is alive on December 31, 1987 and (2) the employee's first distribution calendar year is 1985 or 1986 (as determined under I-2), the amount of the minimum distribution for calendar years 1985, 1986, and 1987 is to be determined under one of the three methods described in paragraphs (b), (c), and (d). The plan administrator is to determine which method, including the credit rules under paragraphs (b)(4) and (c)(3), is to be used. The same method used under this I-3 and I-8 must be used with respect to all such employees covered by the plan. See I-4 for a special amount of distribution rule for certain life annuities.

(b) *Life expectancy method.* Under the life expectancy method, the total amount of the minimum distribution required for calendar years 1985, 1986, and 1987 is determined as follows:

(1) *Designated beneficiary and life expectancy.* The designated beneficiary of the employee will be determined on any date in 1987. The applicable life expectancy (either the life expectancy of the employee or the joint life and last survivor expectancy of the employee and the employee's designated beneficiary, whichever is applicable) is determined using attained ages as of birthdays in 1987. In the case of a beneficiary who is not alive on his birthday in 1987, the beneficiary is treated as being alive on that date for purposes of determining life expectancy.

(2) *Benefit determination.* The benefit of the employee is determined using the account balance as of the last valuation date under the plan in 1986, adjusted in accordance with F-5 with the following further modifications. First, the benefit adjustment for distributions after the valuation date under F-5(c) is not made. Second, the benefit is increased by any distribution made in 1985 or 1986 before the valuation date for which credit is being taken under subparagraph (4).

(3) *Required distribution.* The total amount which must be distributed for calendar years 1985, 1986, and 1987 using the life expectancy method is determined by dividing the benefit determined under subparagraph (2) by the applicable life expectancy determined under subparagraph (1) and multiplying the quotient by:

(i) 2.8, in the case of an employee with respect to whom the first distribution calendar year is 1985, or

(ii) 1.9, in the case of an employee with respect to whom the first distribution calendar year is 1986.

(4) *Credit for distributions.* In determining whether the total amount which must be distributed for calendar years 1985, 1986 and 1987 has been distributed, credit may be taken (as determined by the plan administrator) for any amount distributed in a distribution calendar year of the employee. Consequently, to determine the amount which is required to be distributed in calendar year 1987, the plan administrator may reduce the total amount which must be distributed in 1987 for

calendar years 1985, 1986, and 1987 (determined under (3)) by the amounts distributed in:

(i) 1985 and 1986, in the case of an employee with respect to whom the first distribution calendar year is 1985, or

(ii) 1986, in the case of an employee with respect to whom the first distribution calendar year is 1986. However, in the case of distributions before the last valuation date in 1986, credit may only be taken for amounts which were used to increase the benefit pursuant to subparagraph (2).

(c) *Percentage method.* Under the percentage method, the total amount of the minimum distribution required for calendar years 1985, 1986, and 1987 is determined as follows:

(1) *Benefit determination.* The benefit of the employee is determined in the same manner as under paragraph (b)(2).

(2) *Required distribution.* The total amount required to be distributed for calendar years 1985, 1986, and 1987 is the following percentage of the benefit (determined in accordance with subparagraph (1)):

(i) 15%, in the case of an employee with respect to whom the first distribution calendar year is 1985, or

(ii) 10%, in the case of an employee with respect to whom the first distribution calendar year is 1986.

(3) *Credits.* Credits for distributions may be taken in the same manner as under paragraph (b)(4).

(d) *Regular method.* Under the regular method, the sum of the minimum distributions required for each calendar year 1985, 1986, and 1987, calculated separately, is determined under section 401(a)(9) and this section with appropriate adjustments. However, in determining the amount of the minimum distribution required for calendar years 1985, 1986, and 1987, the rule in F-2 does not apply. Also, credit (with an appropriate gross-up) may be taken toward the minimum distribution required for the 1986 or 1987 distribution calendar year for distributions in the 1985 or 1986 distribution calendar years that exceeded the minimum required distribution for such year. If distribution is being made in the form of an annuity and the annuity either is not a life annuity or is a life annuity with a period certain exceeding 20 years, the amount which must be distributed by December 31, 1987 is the aggregate of annual amounts (see F-3(d)(2)) for each calendar year for which a distribution is required before 1988, determined under I-2.

(e) This Q&A is illustrated by the following example:

Example.

(a) An employee (X), born February 1, 1914, is a participant in a profit-sharing plan (Plan Z). X retired December 31, 1979. Consequently his required beginning date occurred on or before April 1, 1986. Thus X's first distribution calendar year is 1985. As of January 1, 1987, X's spouse (Y), born March 1, 1920 is X's only beneficiary under Plan Z. As of December 31, 1986, the last valuation date under Plan Z in 1986, X's benefit is $198,000. In 1985, X received distributions from Plan Z totaling $5,000. In 1986 (before December 31), X received distributions from Plan Z totaling $7,000.

(b) Under the life expectancy method, X's minimum distribution required for 1985, 1986, and 1987 which must be distributed in 1987 by December 31 is determined as follows:

(1)	Benefit under Plan Z as of the last valuation date in 1986.	$198,000
(2)	Distributions in 1985.	$5,000
(3)	Distributions in 1986 before 12/31/86.	$7,000
(4)	Benefit to be used. (sum of (1), (2), and (3))	$210,000
(5)	X's attained age as of X's birthday in 1987.	73
(6)	Y's attained age as of Y's birthday in 1987.	67
(7)	Joint life and last survivor of X and Y (determined under Table VI of 1.72-9 using ages in (5) and (6)).	21
(8)	Benefit ((line 4) divided by the applicable life expectancy (line 7)).	$10,000
(9)	The total amount which must be distributed for 1985, 1986, and 1987. (2.8 × 10,000)	$28,000
(10)	Distribution in 1985 and 1986 for which credit may be taken (Sum of lines (2) and (3)).	$12,000
(11)	Amount required to be distributed in 1987. (Line 9 minus line 10)	$16,000

(c) Under the percentage method, X's minimum distribution required for 1985, 1986, and 1987 which must be distributed in 1987 by December 31 is determined as follows:

(1)	Benefit under Plan Z as of the last valuation date in 1986.	$198,000
(2)	Distributions in 1985.	$5,000
(3)	Distributions in 1986 before 12/31/86.	$7,000
(4)	Benefit to be used (sum of (1), (2), and (3)).	$210,000

(5) Total amount which must be distributed for 1985, 1986, and 1987 (15% of line (4)). $31,500

(6) Distribution in 1985 and 1986 for which credit may be taken (Sum of lines (2) and (3)). $12,000

(7) Amount required to be distributed in 1987. (Line 5 minus line 6) $19,500

I-4. Q. If (a) the employee's benefit is to be distributed in the form of a life annuity (or a life annuity with a period certain not exceeding 20 years), (b) the employee's required beginning date is on or before April 1, 1987, and (c) the employee is alive on December 31, 1987, then as of what date must distributions be made and how is the amount which must be distributed by that date determined?

A. (a) If the three conditions set forth in the question above are satisfied, and if the employee's required beginning date is on or before April 1, 1986, the first period for which a distribution is required is the last payment interval (as defined in F-3) ending on or before April 1, 1986. However, under these transition rules, no distribution is required to be made by April 1, 1986. Instead, distribution of an amount equal to the aggregate of the payments for all payment intervals from the last payment interval ending on or before April 1, 1986 through the last payment interval ending on or before December 31, 1987 must be made by December 31, 1987. Consequently, the total amount that must be distributed by December 31, 1987 will equal the total amount that would have been distributed by December 31, 1987, if annuity payments made in accordance with F-3 had begun on or before April 1, 1986.

(b) If the three conditions set forth above are satisfied and the employee's required beginning date is April 1, 1987, the first period for which a distribution is required is the last payment interval (as defined in F-3) ending on or before April 1, 1987. However, under these transition rules, no distribution is required to be made by April 1, 1987. Instead, distribution of an amount equal to the aggregate of the payments for all payment intervals from the last payment interval ending on or before April 1, 1987 through the last payment interval ending on or before December 31, 1987 must be made by December 31, 1987. Consequently, the total amount which must be distributed by December 31, 1987 will equal the total amount which would have been distributed by December 31, 1987, if annuity payments made in accordance with F-3 had begun on or before April 1, 1987.

(c) In the case of distributions in the form of a joint and survivor annuity, the designated beneficiary for purposes of determining the aggregate amount that is required to be distributed by December 31, 1987 may be determined as of any date during the 90 day period ending on the date on which annuity payments commence but not later than the earlier of (1) the date annuity distributions commence or (2) December 31, 1987.

(d) The provisions of this Question and Answer must be satisfied even if the employee and spouse do not consent to any catch-up distribution required by paragraph (a) or (b). The spouse's consent is not required even if as a result of making distributions required by paragraph (a) or (b), the amount payable after the death of the employee to the employee's surviving spouse is reduced. If (1) the plan has made reasonable efforts to obtain consent from the employee and the employee's spouse, (2) the requirement of section 417 that plan benefits be provided in the form of a qualified joint and survivor annuity is otherwise satisfied, and (3) the distribution otherwise meets the requirement of section 417, then the consent requirements of section 411(a)(11) and 417(e) are deemed to be satisfied with respect to the distribution.

(e) The amount of the catch-up distributions described in paragraphs (a) and (b) may be determined using either the normal form of qualified joint and survivor annuity under the terms of the plan or a benefit option, if any, selected by the employee as long as the distribution satisfies section 401(a)(9). Thus, if the employee has not elected a benefit option, the plan may determine the amount of the catch-up distribution using the qualified joint and survivor option under the plan (as long as such form of benefit provides for distributions that satisfy section 401(a)(9)).

(f) This Question and Answer is illustrated by the following example:

Example.

Plan Y, a defined benefit pension plan, provides that monthly annuity payments are to be made to an unmarried employee (X) for life with a 10 year period certain X's required beginning date is April 1, 1986 but X received no distributions before December 31, 1987. If annuity distributions had begun to X on April 1, 1986, he would have been entitled under the terms of Plan Y to receive a monthly benefit of $100. Thus if annuity distributions had begun on April 1, 1986, by December 31, 1987, the plan would have distributed $2100 to X, an amount equal to the aggregate of the payments for all payment intervals from the last

payment interval ending on or before April 1, 1986 through the last payment interval ending on or before December 31, 1987. This is the amount that the plan must distribute to X by December 31, 1987. (Annuity payments made after December 31, 1987 will be adjusted for interest on $2100 due to the delay in commencing distributions.)

I-5. Q. If an employee's required beginning date is on or before April 1, 1987, are there any special rules for determining the minimum distribution for calendar years after 1987?

A. (a) Except as otherwise provided in paragraphs (b) and (c), if an employee's required beginning date is on or before April 1, 1987 and if the employee's benefit is in the form of an individual account, the amount of the minimum distribution required for calendar years after 1987 will be determined in a manner consistent with the use of December 31, 1987 as the employee's required beginning date. Consequently, for example, the employee must elect, if such election is permitted by the plan administrator, no later than December 31 1987 whether or not life expectancy will be recalculated for purposes of determining the minimum distribution required for calendar years after 1987. Further, for example, the designated beneficiary of an employee will be determined as of December 31, 1987 for purposes of determining the minimum distribution required for calendar years after 1987.

(b) If an employee's required beginning date is on or before April 1, 1987 and if the employee's benefit is in the form of an individual account, the following rule applies for determining life expectancies for purposes of determining the minimum distribution for calendar years after 1987. If an employee's life expectancy is being recalculated, the joint life and last-survivor expectancy of the employee and the designated beneficiary (other than the employee's spouse) will be determined using the attained age of the employee as of the employee's birthday in the calendar year for which the minimum distribution is being determined and the attained age of the designated beneficiary as of the beneficiary's birthday in 1987, adjusted in accordance with E-8, for purposes of determining the minimum distribution required for calendar years after 1987. If an employee's life expectancy is not being recalculated, the joint life and last survivor expectancy of the employee and the designated beneficiary will be determined based on the attained ages of the employee and designated beneficiary as of their birthdays in 1987. Such joint life and last survivor expectancy is then reduced by one for each calendar year that has elapsed since 1987. In such case if the designated beneficiary is not alive on his birthday in 1987, such beneficiary will be treated as alive on that date for purposes of determining life expectancy. If the employee's designated beneficiary is the employee's spouse, and the life expectancy of the employee and spouse are being recalculated, the joint life and last survivor expectancy of the employee and spouse will be calculated using their attained ages as of their birthdays in the calendar year for which the minimum distribution is being determined.

(c) If any employee's required beginning date is on or before April 1, 1987 and if an employee's benefit is being distributed in the form of annuity payments, for determining the minimum distribution for calendar years after 1987, the following rules will apply. The designated beneficiary may be determined as of any date during the 90 day period ending on the date on which such annuity payments commence. Life expectancy will be determined using the attained ages of the employee and the employee's designated beneficiary as of their birthdays in the calendar year in which the annuity payments commence.

I-6. Q. If an employee dies before January 1, 1988, are distributions to be made in accordance with section 401(a)(9)(B)(i) or in accordance with section 401(a)(9)(B)(ii) or (iii) and (iv)?

A. (a) *General rule.* If an employee dies before January 1, 1988, distributions must be made in accordance with either the five year rule in section 401(a)(9)(B)(ii) or the exception to the five-year rule in section 401(a)(9)(B)(iii) and (iv), whichever is applicable. (See A-4 and C-4.) If an employee dies before January 1, 1986, and distribution is being made over the life or life expectancy of a designated beneficiary in accordance with section 401(a)(9)(B)(iii) and (iv), see I-7 through I-9 for the rules concerning (1) which calendar year is the first calendar year for which a distribution is required (or in the case of certain life annuities which period is the first payment interval for which a distribution is required), (2) as of what date distributions are required to commence, and (3) how the amount which is required to be distributed by such date is determined.

(b) *Certain distributions treated as having begun.* Except as otherwise provided in paragraph (c), if an employee's required beginning date is (or would have been) on or before April 1, 1987 and such employee dies in calendar year 1985, 1986 or 1987, but on or after the first day of the employee's first distribution calendar year, the plan administrator may, under these transition rules, treat distributions as having begun in accordance with section 401(a)(9)(A)(ii) before the employee died for purposes of section 401(a)(9)(B)(i). The plan administrator may make such determination on an individual by individual basis. Distributions may be treated as having begun for purposes of section 401(a)(9)(B)(i) even though payments were not actually made before the employee died. If, under this transition rule, distributions are treated as having begun before the employee died, distribution of the employee's benefit for calendar years 1985 (if applicable), 1986, 1987, and subsequent calendar years will be made to the employee's beneficiaries over a period described in section 401(a)(9)(A)(i) pursuant to section 401(a)(9)(B)(i) rather than in accordance with section 401(a)(9)(B)(ii) or (iii) and (iv). (See C-4.) If distributions are thus treated as having begun, the amount any minimum distribution required for calendar years 1985, 1986 or 1987 will be determined in accordance with I-2 through I-5 treating the employee as alive on December 31, 1987. If such amount was not paid to the employee before the employee's death, it must be paid to the beneficiaries of the employee on or before December 31, 1987. Further, in such case, the designated beneficiary of the employee will be determined as of any date in 1987. The applicable life expectancies are determined using birthdays in 1987, and by treating the employee and designated beneficiary as alive. Except as otherwise provided in these transition rules, the employee's life expectancy will not be recalculated. However, if the employee's spouse is a beneficiary, such spouse's life expectancy will be recalculated unless either (1) the plan administrator establishes a policy that spouses' life expectancies are not recalculated or (2) the spouse elects not to have life expectancy recalculated.

(c) *Distributions to the employee's spouse.* Except as otherwise provided in I-9(c) plan distributions must satisfy the survivor requirements of sections 401(a)(11) and 417 notwithstanding the rules in paragraph (b). These requirements may mandate a particular method of distribution to a surviving spouse or require spousal consent. Further, the rules in paragraph (b) allowing a plan administrator to treat distributions as having begun do not apply for purposes of determining under section 401(a)(11) and 417 whether distribution must be in the form of a qualified preretirement survivor annuity or a qualified joint and survivor annuity.

(d) *Example.* This I-6 is illustrated by the following example:

Example.

(a) An employee (X), born May 2, 1915, is a participant in Plan Y (a profit-sharing plan). X retired December 31, 1985. X died March 1, 1986. As of X's date of death, X's sole beneficiary under Plan Y was X's spouse. The plan administrator of Plan Y has established no policy concerning recalculation of life expectancy or of permitting elections of such recalculation. (Thus, any default provisions in this section of the regulations apply.)

(b) If X had survived, X's required beginning date would have been April 1, 1986 and X's first distribution calendar year would have been 1985. Because X died on or after January 1, 1985 and before December 31, 1987, the plan may distribute either (1) to X's spouse in accordance with the exception to the five year rule in section 401(a)(9)(B)(iii) and (iv) or (2) treat distributions as having begun to X before death pursuant to paragraph (b) of this I-6.

(c) If Plan Y distributes to X's spouse in accordance with the exception to the five-year rule in section 401(a)(9)(B)(iii) and (iv), the first distribution calendar year is 1987 and distributions must commence by December 31, 1987. If instead Plan Y treats distributions as having begun, X's first distribution calendar year is 1985. Under these transition rules, minimum distributions for 1985, 1986, and 1987 would then be required to be made by December 31, 1987. In accordance with paragraph (b) of this I-6, X's life expectancy will not be recalculated but, in accordance with E-7(a), X's spouse's life expectancy will be recalculated.

I-7. Q. If an employee died prior to January 1, 1986 and distributions are being made over the life expectancy of a designated beneficiary in accordance with section 401(a)(9)(B)(iii) and (iv), which is the first calendar year for which a distribution is required and when must distribution commence?

A. Except as otherwise provided in I-9 (special rule for certain life annuities), if an employee died prior to January 1, 1986 and distributions are being made over the life expectancy of a designated beneficiary in accordance with section 401(a)(9)(B)(iii) and (iv), the first distribution calendar year for which a minimum distribution is required is the later of (1) the calendar year which contains the required commencement date determined under C-3(a) or (b), whichever is applicable, or (2) calendar year 1985. However, under these transitional rules, if the first distribution calendar year is 1985, the minimum distribution for 1985 is not required to be made by December 31, 1985. Similarly, under these transition rules, if the first (or second) distribu-

tion calendar year is 1986, the minimum distribution for 1980 is not required to be made by December 31, 1986. Instead, in such case, the minimum distribution required for 1985 (if applicable), 1986, and 1987 is required to be made by December 31, 1987.

I-8. Q. If (a) distributions after the death of an employee are being made over the life expectancy of a designated beneficiary in accordance with section 401(a)(9)(B)(iii) and (iv), and (b) the first distribution calendar year is 1985 or 1986 (determined under I-3), then how is the amount of the minimum distribution determined for calendar years 1985, 1986, and 1987?

A. (a) *In general.* (1) If the two conditions set forth in the Question are satisfied, the amount of the minimum distribution for calendar years 1985, 1986, and 1987 is to be determined under one of the three methods described in paragraphs (b), (c), and (d). The plan administrator is to determine which method, including the credit rules under paragraph (b)(4) and (c)(3), is to be used. The same method used under this I-8 and I-2 must be used with respect to all such employees.

(2) See I-9 for a special rule for distributions in the form of a life annuity.

(b) *Life expectancy method.* Under the life expectancy method, the total amount of the minimum distribution required for calendar years 1985, 1986, and 1987 is determined as follows:

(1) *Designated beneficiary and life expectancy.* The designated beneficiary of the employee will be determined as of any date in 1987. The applicable life expectancy will be the designated beneficiary's life expectancy using attained age as of his birthday in 1987. In the case of a beneficiary who is not alive on his birthday in 1987, such beneficiary will be treated as being alive on his birthday in 1987 for purposes of determining life expectancy under this transitional rule.

(2) *Benefit determination.* The benefit of the employee is determined using the account balance as of the last valuation date under the plan in 1986, adjusted in accordance with F-5 with the following modifications. First, the benefit adjustment for distributions after the valuation date under F-5(c) is not made. Second, the benefit is increased by any distribution made in 1985 or 1986 before the valuation date described in subparagraph (2) for which credit is being taken under subparagraph (4).

(3) *Required distribution.* The total amount which must be distributed for calendar years 1985, 1986, and 1987 using the life expectancy method will be determined by dividing the benefit determined under subparagraph (2) by the applicable life expectancy determined under subparagraph (1) and multiplying the quotient by:

(i) 2.8, in the case of an employee with respect to whom the first distribution calendar year is 1985, or

(ii) 1.9, in the case of an employee with respect to whom the first distribution calendar year is 1986.

(4) *Credit for distributions.* In determining whether the total amount which must be distributed for calendar years 1985, 1986, and 1987 has been distributed credit may be taken (as determined by the plan administrator) for any amount distributed in a distribution calendar year of the employee (1985 through 1987). Consequently, to determine the amount which is required to be distributed in calendar year 1987, the plan administrator may reduce the total amount which must be distributed in 1987 for calendar years 1985, 1986, and 1987 (determined under subparagraph (3)) by the amounts distributed in:

(i) 1985 and 1986, in the case of an employee with respect to whom the first distribution calendar year is 1985, or

(ii) 1986, in the case of an employee with respect to whom the first distribution calendar year is 1986.

However, in the case of distributions before the last valuation date in 1986, credit may only be taken for amounts which were used to increase the benefit pursuant to subparagraph (2).

(c) *Percentage method.* Under the percentage method, the total amount of the minimum distribution required for calendar years 1985, 1986, and 1987 is determined as follows:

(1) *Benefit determination.* The benefit of the employee is determined in the same manner as under paragraph (b)(2).

(2) *Required distribution.* The total amount required to be distributed for calendar years 1985, 1986, and 1987 is the following percentage of the benefit (determined in accordance with subparagraph (1)):

(i) 15%, in the case of an employee with respect to whom the first distribution calendar year is 1985, or

(ii) 10%, in the case of an employee with respect to whom the first distribution calendar year is 1986.

(3) *Credits.* Credits for distributions may be taken in the same manner as under paragraph (b)(4).

(d) *Regular method.* Under the regular method, the sum of the minimum distributions required for each calendar year 1985, 1986, and 1987, calculated separately, is determined under section 401(a)(9) and this section with appropriate adjustments. However, the rule in F-2 does not apply. Also, credit (with an appropriate gross-up) may be taken toward the minimum required distribution for the 1986 or 1987 distribution calendar year for distributions in 1985 or 1986 distribution calendar years that exceeded the minimum required distribution for such year. If distribution is being made in the form of an annuity and the annuity is not a life annuity (or is a life annuity with a period certain exceeding 20 years), the amount which must be distributed by December 31, 1987 is the aggregate of annual amounts (see F-3 (d)(2)) for each calendar year for which a distribution is required before 1988, determined under I-2.

I-9. Q. If (a) the employee died prior to January 1, 1986, (b) distribution is to be made in accordance with the exception to the five-year rule in section 401(a)(9)(B)(iii) and (iv), and (c) the employees benefit is to be distributed in the form of a life annuity (or a life annuity with a period certain not exceeding 20 years), then as of what date must distributions be made, and how is the amount which must be distributed by that date determined?

A. (a) If the three conditions set forth in the Question are satisfied, the first period for which a distribution is required is the last payment interval (as defined in F-5) ending on or before the later of (1) the required commencement date determined under C-3(a) or (b), whichever is applicable, and (2) December 31, 1985. However, if such date is before December 31, 1987, under these transition rules, no distribution is required to be made on such date. Instead, distribution of an amount equal to the aggregate of the payments for all payment intervals from the last payment interval ending on or before that date through the last payment interval ending on or before December 31, 1987 must be made by December 31, 1987. Consequently, the total amount which must be distributed by December 31, 1987 will equal the total amount that which would have been distributed by December 31, 1987 if annuity payments made in accordance with C-3 had begun on or before the later of (1) the required commencement date determined under C-3(a) or (b), whichever is applicable, and (2) December 31, 1985.

(b) The designated beneficiary may be determined as of any date during the 90 day period ending on the earlier of (1) the date annuity distributions commence or (2) December 31, 1987.

(c) The provisions of this Question and Answer must be satisfied even if the surviving spouse does not consent to any catch-up distribution required under paragraph (a), and even if, as a result of such catch-up distribution, the amount payable after December 31, 1987 to the employee's surviving spouse under a qualified preretirement survivor annuity is reduced. In such case, if (1) the plan has made reasonable efforts to obtain consent from the employee's surviving spouse, (2) the requirement of section 417 that plan benefits be provided in the form of a qualified preretirement annuity is otherwise satisfied, and (3) the distribution otherwise meets the requirement of section 417, then the consent requirements of section 417 are deemed to be satisfied with respect to the distribution.

I-10. Q. If an employee died prior to January 1, 1986 and distributions are being made over the life expectancy of a designated beneficiary in accordance with section 401(a)(9)(B)(iii) and (iv), as of what date is the designated beneficiary determined, and what age is used to determine the designated beneficiary's life expectancy, for purposes of determining the minimum distribution for calendar years after 1987?

A. (a) If an employee died prior to January 1, 1986 and distributions are being made over the life expectancy of a designated beneficiary in accordance with section 401(a)(9)(B)(iii) and (iv), the designated beneficiary will be determined as of any date in 1987 for purposes of determining the minimum distribution for calendar years after 1987. The life expectancy of the designated beneficiary (other than the employee's surviving spouse whose life expectancy is being recalculated) will be determined using the attained age of the designated beneficiary as of such beneficiary's birthday in calendar year 1987, reduced by one for each calendar year which has elapsed after 1987. In such case if the designated beneficiary is not alive on his birthday in 1987, such beneficiary will be treated as being alive on that date for purposes of determining life expectancy. If the employee's surviving spouse is a designated beneficiary and such spouse's life expectancy is being recalculated, the life expectancy of spouse will be calculated using the attained age of the spouse as of such spouse's birthday in the calendar year for which the minimum distribution is being determined.

(b) If an employee died prior to January 1, 1986 and distributions are being made over the life expectancy of a designated beneficiary in accordance with section 401(a)(9)(B)(iii) and (iv) in the form of annuity payments, the designated beneficiary will be determined as of any date during the 90 day period ending on the date such annuity payments commence. The designated beneficiary's life expectancy will be determined using the attained age of the designated beneficiary as of such beneficiary's birthday in the calendar year in which the annuity payments commence.

I-11. Q. In the case of the surviving spouse of an employee for whom the first calendar year for which a distribution is required to be made is 1985 or 1986, when must the employee's spouse elect whether or not life expectancy will be recalculated?

A. If an employee for whom the first calendar year for which a distribution is required to be made is calendar year 1985 or 1986, any election, if permitted by the plan administrator, concerning recalculation of life expectancy must be made by December 31, 1987.

I-12. Q. When must the election described in C-4 (concerning whether distribution will be made in accordance with the five year rule in section 401(a)(9)(B)(ii) or the exception to the five-year rule in section 401(a)(9)(B)(iii) and (iv)) be made by a beneficiary otherwise required to make such election on or before December 31, 1985 or December 31, 1986?

A. The election described in C-4 (concerning whether distribution will be made in accordance with the five-year rule in section 401(a)(9)(B)(ii) or the exception to the five year rule in section 401(a)(9)(B)(iii) and (iv)), if otherwise required to have been made on or before December 31, 1985 or December 31, 1986, must, if permitted by the plan administrator, be made by December 31, 1987.

I-13. Q. If an employee died prior to January 1, 1985 and distribution is to be made in accordance with the five-year rule contained in section 401(a)(9)(B)(ii), as of what date must the employee's entire interest be distributed?

A. If an employee died prior to January 1, 1985 and distribution is to be made in accordance with the five-year rule contained in section 401(a)(9)(B)(ii), the employee's entire interest must be distributed as of the later of: (a) December 31 of the calendar year which contains the fifth anniversary of the employee's death or (b) December 31, 1987.

I-14. Q. If any portion of the minimum distribution required for calendar years 1985, 1986, or 1987 (which is required to be distributed by December 31, 1987) is distributed by a plan and rolled over to another plan (receiving plan) before such date, how does receipt of such rollover amount affect the qualification under section 401(a) of the plan accepting it?

A. If any portion of the minimum distribution required for calendar years 1985, 1986, or 1987 which is required to be distributed by December 31, 1987 is distributed by a plan and rolled over to another plan (receiving plan) before such date, under these transitional rules, the qualification under section 401(a) of the receiving plan is not affected by the receipt of such amount. However, see G-1B for the tax consequences to the distributee who rolls over the amount (including, if the amount is rolled over to an individual retirement plan, the rule for avoiding certain tax consequences). Certain tax consequences may be avoided by the distributee who rolls over to another qualified plan in either of two ways: (a) the receiving plan may distribute by December 31, 1987 that portion of the amount rolled over which is the minimum distribution from the distributing plan for calendar years 1985, 1986 or 1987 or (b) the distributing plan may distribute by December 31, 1987 an additional amount equal to that portion of the amount rolled over which is the minimum distribution from such plan for calendar years 1985, 1986 or 1987.

I-15. Q. In the case of a transfer in 1985, 1986, or 1987 of all or a portion of an employee's benefit from one plan (transferor plan) to another plan (transferee plan), is the amount transferred treated as an amount distributed for purposes of section 401(a)(9)?

A. (a) Except as otherwise provided in paragraph (b), in the case of a transfer in 1985, 1986, or 1987 but before [60 days after this notice is published] of all or a portion of an employee's benefit from one plan (transferor plan) to another plan (transferee plan) before the minimum amount required to be distributed by the transferor plan for such calendar year has been distributed, the transferor plan may treat the amount transferred as a distribution for purposes of section 401(a)(9).

(b) If all or a portion of an employee's benefit is transferred from one plan (transferor plan) to another plan (transferee plan) in 1985, 1986, or 1987 before [60 days after this notice is published] and before the minimum amount required to be distributed by the transferor plan for such calendar year has been distributed and the employee is a 5-percent owner (as defined in B-2) with respect to the employer maintaining either the transferor plan or the transferee plan, the transferee plan must distribute by December 31, 1987 any portion of the minimum distribution required to be distributed with respect to the portion of the benefit transferred but not distributed by the transferor plan for calendar years 1985, 1986, or 1987.

(c) In the case of a transfer in 1987 on or after [60 days after this notice is published], the rules in G-3 apply.

I-16. Q. What are the distribution requirements applicable to qualified plans that cover self-employed individuals described in section 401(c)(1) (HR 10 plans) for 1984?

A. For 1984, HR 10 plans are subject to the distribution requirements of section 401(a)(9) as in effect on September 2, 1982 (prior to such section's replacement by section 242(a) of TEFRA. (The after-death distribution rules in section 401(d)(7) applicable to owner-employees in HR 10 plans were repealed by section 237 of TEFRA and were not reinstated for 1984 by TRA of 1984.) An HR 10 plan that does not satisfy section 401(a)(9) (as in effect on September 2, 1982) in 1984 will not be considered to fail to qualify under section 401(a) or 403(a) solely for that reason if, in operation, the aggregate amount distributed by December 31, 1987 equals or exceeds the amount required to satisfy section 401(a)(9) prior to its amendment by TEFRA plus the amount required to satisfy section 401(a)(9) after its amendment by TRA of 1984 for calendar years 1985, 1986, and 1987. Thus, plan amendments to reflect the law for 1984 are not required in order to satisfy the old HR 10 requirement.

I-17. Q. In the case of a plan covering self-employed individuals to which the minimum distribution rules in §1.401-11(e) apply, if the aggregate amounts distributed with respect to an employee in calendar years prior to 1985 for which minimum distributions were required pursuant to §1.401-11(e) exceeded the aggregate amount required for such calendar years, may credit be given for such amount for purposes of satisfying the minimum distribution requirement for calendar years 1985 through 1987?

A. Yes. In the case of a plan covering self-employed individuals to which the minimum distribution rules in §1.401-11(e) apply, if the aggregate amounts distributed with respect to an employee in calendar years prior to 1985 for which minimum distributions were required pursuant to §1.401-11(e) exceed the aggregate amount required, credit may be taken for the difference between the aggregate amount distributed in calendar years before 1985 and the aggregate amount required to be distributed for such calendar years. Such excess amount will be treated as an amount distributed in calendar year 1985 for purposes of determining the amount which is required to be distributed by December 31, 1987 under I-3.

J. *Elections under section 242(b)(2) of TEFRA.*

J-1. Q. Is a plan disqualified merely because it pays benefits under a designation made before January 1, 1984, in accordance with section 242(b)(2) of TEFRA?

A. No. Even though the distribution requirements added by TEFRA were retroactively repealed by TRA of 1984, the transitional election rule in section 242(b) was preserved. Notice 83-23, 1983-2 CB 418, provides guidance for distributions permitted by this transitional rule. Satisfaction of the spousal consent requirements of section 417(a) and (e) (added by the Retirement Equity Act of 1984) will not be considered a revocation of the pre-1984 designation under that Notice. However, sections 401(a)(11) and 417 must be satisfied with respect to any distribution subject to such section. The election provided in section 242(b) is hereafter referred to as a section 242(b)(2) election.

J-2 Q. In the case in which an amount is transferred from one plan (transferor plan) to another plan (transferee plan), may the transferee plan distribute the amount transferred in accordance with a section 242(b)(2) election made under either the transferor plan or under the transferee plan?

A. (a) In the case in which an amount is transferred from one plan to another plan, the amount transferred may be distributed in accordance with a section 242(b)(2) election made under the transferor plan if the employee did not elect to have the amount transferred and if the amount transferred is separately accounted for by the transferee plan. However, only the benefit attributable to the amount transferred, plus earnings thereon, may be distributed in accordance with the section 242(b)(2) election made under the transferor plan. If the employee elected to have the amount transferred, the transfer will be treated as a distribution and rollover of the amount transferred for purposes of this J-2 and J-3.

(b) In the case in which an amount is transferred from one plan to another plan, the amount transferred may not be distributed in accor-

dance with a section 242(b)(2) election made under the transferee plan. If a section 242(b)(2) election was made under the transferee plan, the amount transferred must be separately accounted for. If the amount transferred is not separately accounted for under the transferee plan, the section 242(b)(2) election under the transferee plan is revoked and section 401(a)(9) will apply to subsequent distributions by the transferee plan.

(c) A merger, spinoff, or consolidation, as defined in 1.414(l)-1(b), will be treated as a transfer for purposes of the section 242(b)(2) election.

J-3. Q. If an amount is distributed by one plan (distributing plan) and rolled over into another plan (receiving plan), may the receiving plan distribute the amount rolled over in accordance with a section 242(b)(2) election made under either the distributing plan or the receiving plan?

A. No. If an amount is distributed by one plan and rolled over into another plan, the receiving plan must distribute the amount rolled over in accordance with section 401(a)(9) whether or not the employee made a section 242(b)(2) election under the distributing plan. Further, if the amount rolled over was not distributed in accordance with the election, the election under the distributing plan is revoked and section 401(a)(9) will apply to all subsequent distributions by the distributing plan. Finally, if the employee made a section 242(b)(2) election under the receiving plan and such election is still in effect, the amount rolled over must be separately accounted for under the receiving plan and distributed in accordance with section 401(a)(9). If amounts rolled over are not separately accounted for, any section 242(b)(2) election under the receiving plan is revoked and section 401(a)(9) will apply to subsequent distributions by the receiving plan.

J-4. Q. May a section 242(b)(2) election be revoked after the date by which distributions are required to commence in order to satisfy section 401(a)(9) and this section of the regulations?

A. Yes. A section 242(b)(2) election may be revoked after the date by which distributions are required to commence in order to satisfy section 401(a)(9) and this section of the regulations. However, if the section 242(b)(2) election is revoked after the date by which distributions are required to commence in order to satisfy section 401(a)(9) and this section of the regulations and the total amount of the distributions which would have been required to be made prior to the date of the revocation in order to satisfy section 401(a)(9), but for the section 242(b)(2) election, have not been made, the trust must distribute by the end of the calendar year following the calendar year in which the revocation occurs the total amount not yet distributed which was required to have been distributed to satisfy the requirements of section 401(a)(9) and continue distributions in accordance with such requirements. Further, an additional amount may be required to be distributed to satisfy the minimum distribution incidental death benefit requirement. See §1.401(a)(9)-2.

J-5. Q. May the distribution of amounts otherwise required to be distributed in 1985, 1986, or 1987 before December 31, 1987, pursuant to a section 242(b)(2) election be deferred until December 31, 1987 under the transition rule in I-1 or through J-15?

A. The transition rules in I-1 through I-15 do not apply to distributions to be made pursuant to a section 242(b)(2) election. Failure to make any distribution of an amount specified at the time specified under the method of distribution provided in a section 242(b)(2) election will be treated as a change in the election and thus a revocation of the election. In the event of such a revocation before December 31, 1987, the transition rules in I-1 through I-15 will apply to any distributions otherwise required to be made before December 31, 1987. Accordingly, in the event of such a revocation before December 31, 1987, any distribution otherwise required under section 401(a)(9) and this section of the regulations to be made before December 31, 1987 may be delayed until that date.

§1.401(a)(9)-2 Minimum distribution incidental benefit requirement.

Q-1. What is the incidental benefit requirement?

A. The incidental benefit requirement has two components, the minimum distribution incidental benefit requirement (MDIB requirement) and the pre-retirement incidental benefit requirement. The pre-retirement incidental benefit requirement applies to limit pre-retirement distributions in the form of nonretirement benefits such as life, accident, or health insurance. Both the MDIB requirement and the pre-retirement incidental benefit requirement requires that death and other nonretirement benefits payable under a pension, stock bonus, or profit-sharing plan be incidental to the primary purpose of the plan which is to provide retirement benefits (in the case of a pension plan) or deferred compensation (in the case of a profit-sharing plan) to the employee. Thus, the relationship of an employee's total benefits under the plan to the retirement benefits or deferred compensation payable to the employee must be such that the primary purpose of the plan is to provide retirement benefits or deferred compensation to the employee. See § 1.401-1(b)(1). Also, see section 401(a)(9)(G), as added by section 1852(a)(6) of the Tax Reform Act of 1986 (TRA of 1986) which provides that any distribution required to satisfy the incidental benefit requirement is also a required distribution under section 401(a)(9). Further, see section 403(b)(10), added by section 1852(a)(3)(A) of TRA of 1986, which codified the application of the incidental benefit requirement to annuity contracts and custodial contracts described in section 403(b). See section 408(a)(6) and (b)(3), as amended by section 1852(a)(1) of TRA of 1986, which extends the incidental benefit requirement to distribution from IRAs. Finally, see section 457(d)(2)(A), added by section 1107(a) of TRA of 1986, which provides that an eligible deferred compensation plan must satisfy section 401(a)(9) and thus the incidental benefit requirement.

Q-1A. How is the MDIB requirement satisfied?

A. (a) *Operational requirements.* Distributions under a plan in each calendar year must satisfy the MDIB requirement in order for the plan to be qualified under section 401(a) in operation. If any distributions for a calendar year fail to satisfy the MDIB requirement, the plan will not satisfy section 401(a) for the plan year beginning with or within that calendar year.

(b) *Required plan provisions.* See A-3 of § 1.401(a)(9)-1, which provides that the plan must include certain written provisions reflecting section 401(a)(9). Section 401(a)(9) includes the MDIB requirement.

Q-2. For calendar years beginning before January 1, 1989, how must benefits be distributed in order to satisfy the MDIB requirement?

A. For calendar years beginning before January 1, 1989, distribution of benefits must satisfy either the rules in effect as of [date of publication of this notice] interpreting § 1.401-1(b)(1)(i) or the rules in Q&A-3 through Q&A-7 in order to satisfy the MDIB requirement.

Q-3. For calendar years beginning after December 31, 1988, how must an employee's benefits be distributed in order to satisfy the MDIB requirement?

A. For calendar years beginning after December 31, 1988, distributions of an employee's benefit must commence not later than the employee's required beginning date as defined in section 401(a)(9)(C) and be made in accordance with the rules in Q&A-4 through Q&A-7 in order to satisfy the MDIB requirement. The amount required to be distributed to satisfy the MDIB requirement for a calendar year may be greater than the amount required to satisfy the other minimum distribution requirements in section 401(a)(9). Distributions made before the employee's required beginning date for calendar years before the employee's first distribution calendar year, as defined in F-1 of § 1.401(a)(9)-1, need not be made in accordance with the MDIB requirement. However, if distributions commence under a particular distribution option, such as in the form of an annuity, before the beginning of the employee's first distribution calendar year, the distribution option will fail to satisfy the MDIB requirement at the time distributions commence if, under the particular distribution option, distributions to be made for the employee's first distribution calendar year or any subsequent distribution calendar year will not satisfy the MDIB requirement. The MDIB requirement does not apply to distributions after the employee's death although distributions to be made after the death of the employee must be taken into account in determining whether distributions before the employee's death satisfy the MDIB requirement. Q&A-4 provides rules which apply to nonannuity distributions from an individual account. Q&A-5 provides rules which apply to distributions in the form of an annuity for a period certain without a life contingency. Q&A-6 provides rules which apply to distributions in the form of a life annuity or a joint and survivor annuity. Q&A-7 provides special rules which apply if the employee's beneficiary is the employee's spouse. Q&A-8 provides a special rule for annuity distributions commencing before January 1, 1988.

Q-4. For calendar years after 1988, if an employee's benefit is in the form of an individual account, how must the employee's benefit be distributed in order to satisfy the MDIB requirement?

A. (a) *General rule—(1) Explanation of rule.* If an employee's benefit is in the form of an individual account, distribution must be made for each distribution calendar year (determined under F-1 of § 1.401(a)(9)-1) of the employee in accordance with the following rules in order to satisfy the MDIB requirement. The first year for which a distribution must be made to satisfy the MDIB requirement is the employee's first distribution calendar year, determined under F-1 of § 1.401(a)(9)-1. The minimum amount that must be distributed for each distribution calendar year of the employee to satisfy the MDIB require-

ment is the amount determined by dividing the employee's benefit by the applicable divisor under the table below. The applicable divisor is determined using the attained age of the employee as of the employee's birthday in that distribution calendar year. The employee's benefit must be determined under F-5 of § 1.401(a)(9)-1. As under F-1 of § 1.401(a)(9)-1, the distribution required to be made by the employee's required beginning date is for the employee's first distribution calendar year, and in the case of distributions for other distribution calendar years, the distribution must be made by the end of such calendar year.

(2) *Table for determining applicable divisor*

Age of the employee	Applicable divisor
70	26.2
71	25.3
72	24.4
73	23.5
74	22.7
75	21.8
76	20.9
77	20.1
78	19.2
79	18.4
80	17.6
81	16.8
82	16.0
83	15.3
84	14.5
85	13.8
86	13.1
87	12.4
88	11.8
89	11.1
90	10.5
91	9.9
92	9.4
93	9.8
94	9.3
95	7.8
96	7.3
97	6.9
98	6.5
99	6.1
100	5.7
101	5.3
102	5.0
103	4.7
104	4.4
105	4.1
106	3.8
107	3.6
108	3.3
109	3.1
110	2.8
111	2.6
112	2.4
113	2.2
114	2.0
115 and older	1.8

(b) *Annuity contract.* If an employee's benefit is in the form of an individual account and the employee's benefit is used to purchase an annuity contract from an insurance company, the MDIB requirement is not satisfied unless the annuity distributions under the contract are made in accordance with Q&A-5 or Q&A-6.

Q-5. For calendar years after 1988, if an employee's benefit is being distributed in the form of a period certain annuity without a life contingency (e.g., installment payout), how must the benefit be distributed in order to satisfy the MDIB requirement?

A. (a) *General rule.* If an employee's benefit is being distributed in the form of a period certain annuity without a life contingency, the period certain may not exceed the applicable period determined using the table below. In general, the applicable period is determined using the attained age of the employee as of the employee's birthday in the calendar year in which the annuity payments commence. However, if distributions commence after the end of the employee's first distribution calendar year and on or before the employee's required beginning date, the applicable period is determined using the attained age of the employee as of the employee's birthday in the employee's first distribution calendar year. Further, if distributions commence before January 1 of the employee's first distribution calendar year under a benefit option which provides for distributions in the form of a period certain annuity without a life contingency, the MDIB requirement will not be satisfied as of the date distributions commence unless the benefit option provides that, as of the beginning of the employee's first distribution calendar year, the remaining period under the annuity (including such calendar year) will not exceed the period determined under the table below using the attained age of the employee as of the employee's birthday in the employee's first distribution calendar year. For example, if distributions commence to an employee (X), born May 5, 1930, on January 1, 1990, and the benefit option provides for distribution in the form of a period certain annuity for 37 years, the MDIB requirement is not satisfied when the distributions commence because the remaining period certain as the beginning of X's first distribution calendar year (year 2000) will be 27 years (37 minus 10) which exceeds 26.2. However, the benefit could provide for an automatic shortening of the period at age 70 ½ to conform to the MDIB requirement. Additionally, the amount of the annuity payments must satisfy F-3 of § 1.401(a)(9)-1 in order to satisfy the MDIB requirement. Of course, if the annuity payments commence after the employee's required beginning date, distributions before the annuity payments commence must satisfy Q&A-4.

(b) *Table*

Age of employee	Maximum period certain
70	26.2
71	25.3
72	24.4
73	23.5
74	22.7
75	21.8
76	20.9
77	20.1
78	19.2
79	18.4
80	17.6
81	16.8
82	16.0
83	15.3
84	14.5
85	13.8
86	13.1
87	12.4
88	11.8
89	11.1
90	10.5
91	9.9
92	9.4
93	8.8
94	8.3
95	7.8
96	7.3
97	6.9
98	6.5
99	6.1
100	5.7
101	5.3
102	5.0
103	4.7
104	4.4
105	4.1
106	3.8
107	3.6
108	3.3
109	3.1
110	2.8
111	2.6
112	2.4
113	2.2
114	2.0
115 and older	1.8

Q-6. For calendar years after 1988, how must distributions in the form of a life (or joint and survivor) annuity be made in order to satisfy the MDIB requirement?

A. (a) *Annuity for employee.* If the employee's benefit is payable in the form of a life annuity for the life of the employee satisfying section 401(a)(9), the MDIB requirement will be satisfied.

(b) *Joint and survivor annuity, nonspouse beneficiary-*(1) *Explanation of rule.* If distributions commence under a distribution option that is in the form of a joint and survivor annuity for the joint lives of the employee and a beneficiary, other than the employee's spouse, the MDIB requirement will not be satisfied as of the date distributions commence unless the distribution option provides that annuity payments to be made to the employee on and after the employee's required beginning date will satisfy the conditions of this paragraph. The periodic annuity payment payable to the survivor must not at any time on and after the employee's required beginning date exceed the applicable percentage of the annuity payment for such period payable to the employee using the table below. Thus, this requirement must be satisfied with respect to any benefit increase after such date, including increases to reflect increases in the cost of living. The applicable percentage is based on the excess of the age of the employee over the age of the beneficiary as of their attained ages as of their birthdays in the employee's first distribution calendar year. If the employee has more than one beneficiary, the applicable percentage will be the percentage using the age of the youngest beneficiary. Further, if a beneficiary replaces another beneficiary under the annuity or a beneficiary is added, and the new beneficiary is younger than the beneficiary being used to determine the applicable percentage, the employee's benefit must be adjusted in the calendar year following the calendar year of the change. The employee's benefit must be adjusted so that the periodic benefit payable to the survivor does not exceed the applicable percentage of the annuity payment for such period payable to the employee using the age of the employee and the new younger beneficiary. Additionally, the amount of the annuity payments must satisfy F-3 of § 1.401(a)(9)-1.

(2) *Table.*

Excess of age of employee over age of beneficiary	Applicable percentage
10 years or less	100%
11	96%
12	93%
13	90%
14	87%
15	84%
16	82%
17	79%
18	77%
19	75%
20	73%
21	72%
22	70%
23	68%
24	67%
25	66%
26	64%
27	63%
28	62%
29	61%
30	60%
31	59%
32	59%
33	58%
34	57%
35	56%
36	56%
37	55%
38	55%
39	54%
40	54%
41	53%
42	53%
43	53%
44 and greater	52%

(3) *Example.* This paragraph is illustrated by the following example.

Example. Distributions commence on January 1, 1993 to an employee (Z), born March 1, 1927, after retirement at age 65. Z's granddaughter (Y), born February 5, 1967, is Z's beneficiary. The distributions are in the form of a joint and survivor annuity for the lives of Z and Y with payments of $500 a month to Z and upon Z's death of $500 a month to Y, *i.e.* the projected monthly payment to Y is 100 percent of the monthly amount payable to Z. There is no provision under the option for a change in the projected payments to Y as of April 1, 1998, Z's required beginning date. Consequently, as of January 1, 1993, the date annuity distributions commence, the plan does not satisfy the

MDIB requirement in operation because, as of such date, the distribution option provides that, as of Z's required beginning date, the monthly payment to Y upon Z's death will exceed 54 percent of Z's monthly payment (the maximum percentage for a difference of ages of 40).

(c) *Period certain and annuity features.* If a distribution form includes a life annuity and a period certain, the amount of the annuity payments payable to the employee must satisfy either paragraph (a) or (b), whichever is applicable, and the period certain may not exceed the period determined under Q&A-4.

Q-7. For calendar years after 1988, if the employee's beneficiary is the employee's spouse, how must distributions be made in order to satisfy the MDIB requirement?

A. (a) *General rule.* If the employee's beneficiary, as of the employee's required beginning date, is the employee's spouse and the distributions satisfy section 401(a)(9) without regard to the MDIB requirement, the distributions to the employee will be deemed to satisfy the MDIB requirement. For example, if an employee's benefit is being distributed in the form of a joint and survivor annuity for the lives of the employee and the employee's spouse and the spouse is the employee's beneficiary, the amount of the periodic payment payable to the spouse may always be 100 percent of the annuity payment payable to the employee. However, under section 401(a)(9) the amount of the payments under the annuity must be nonincreasing unless specifically permitted under F-3 of § 1.401(a)(9)-1. A former spouse to whom all or a portion of an employee's benefit is payable pursuant to a qualified domestic relations order as defined in section 414(p) will be treated as a spouse of the employee for purposes of the MDIB requirement.

(b) *Multiple beneficiaries.* If the employee has more than one beneficiary, the special rule in paragraph (a) will only apply to the portion of the employee's benefit of which the spouse is the sole beneficiary. However, in order for the special requirement in paragraph (a) to apply to the distribution of the portion of the employee's benefit of which the spouse is the sole beneficiary, such portion must be a separate account (or segregated share, in the case of a defined benefit plan), as defined in H-2A of § 1.401(a)(9)-1.

(c) *Changes in beneficiaries.* (1) If, after the employee's required beginning date, the employee's spouse ceases to be the employee's sole beneficiary because the spouse dies before the employee, distributions after the death of the spouse to the employee will continue to satisfy the MDIB requirement if such distributions satisfy section 401(a)(9), without regard to the MDIB requirement. See paragraph (d)(2) if the employee's spouse dies before the employee's required beginning date.

(2) If, after the employee's required beginning date, the employee's spouse ceases to be the employee's sole beneficiary for a reason other than the death of the spouse, if the portion of the employee's benefit of which the employee's spouse is the beneficiary ceases to be maintained as a separate account or segregated share, or the spouse ceases to be the sole beneficiary of such separate account or segregated share for a reason other than the death of the spouse, the following rules apply. In the case of distributions from an individual account not in the form of an annuity, distributions in calendar years following the calendar year in which the spouse ceases to be the beneficiary must satisfy Q&A-4. If distribution is in the form of an annuity for a period certain, the remaining period of the period certain as of the calendar year following the calendar year of the change may not exceed the period which would have remained if annuity payments had commenced in accordance with Q&A-5 on the employee's required beginning date and the spouse was not the beneficiary. If the employee's benefit is being distributed in the form of a joint and survivor annuity, the amount of the periodic payment payable to the employee beginning in the calendar year following the calendar year of the change must be redetermined. The new amount may not exceed the applicable percentage under Q&A-6 using the excess of the age of the employee over the age of the new beneficiary using their attained ages as of their birthdays in the calendar year of the redetermination.

(d) *Change in status*—(1) *After the employee's required beginning date.* If a beneficiary of the employee is the employee's spouse as of the employee's required beginning date, such beneficiary will continue to be treated as a spouse of the employee for purposes of the MDIB requirement for all distribution calendar years of the employee even if such beneficiary ceases to be the employee's spouse by reason of divorce, and such beneficiary remains the employee's sole beneficiary.

(2) *Before the employee's required beginning date.* Generally, the special rule in paragraph (a) only applies if a beneficiary is the employee's spouse as of the employee's required beginning date. However, if distributions commence irrevocably (except for acceleration) to the employee before the employee's required beginning date over a period described in section 401(a)(9)(A)(ii), if the distribution form is an annuity under which distributions are made in accordance with the provisions of F-3 (and F-4, if applicable) of § 1.401(a)(9)-1, and if the employee's beneficiary with respect to the annuity payments is the employee's spouse, the following rules will apply. If the employee's spouse dies before the employee's required beginning date, distributions may continue over any remaining period certain under the annuity even if, as of the beginning of the employee's first distribution calendar year, such period exceeds the period permitted under Q&A-4. If such beneficiary ceases to be the employee's spouse by reason of divorce, such beneficiary will continue to be treated as a spouse of the employee for purposes of the MDIB requirement if such beneficiary continues to be the employee's beneficiary with respect to the annuity payments after the employee's required beginning date.

Q-8. For calendar years after 1988, is there any special rule for distributions in the form of an annuity that commence prior to January 1, 1989?

A. Yes. If distributions in the form of an annuity (from a defined benefit plan or under an annuity contract purchased from an insurance company) commence in accordance with F-3 (and F-4 if applicable) of § 1.401(a)(9)-1 prior to January 1, 1989, the annuity distributions in each calendar year (including calendar years after 1988) will satisfy the MDIB requirement if distributions are made in accordance with Q&A-2. This rule applies whether the annuity is a life (or joint and survivor) annuity or an annuity for a period certain, or a combination thereof, and without regard to whether the annuity form of payment is irrevocable. This special rule applies to a deferred annuity contract distributed to or owned by the employee prior to January 1, 1989 unless additional contributions are made under the plan by the employer with respect to such contract.

Q-9. Is there a special rule which applies to distributions under a designation of a method of distribution made before January 1, 1984, in accordance with section 242(b)(2) of the Tax Equity and Fiscal Responsibility Act (TEFRA)?

A. Yes. Distributions (including distributions in calendar years after 1988) under a designation of a method of distribution made before January 1, 1984, in accordance with section 242(b)(2) of TEFRA will satisfy the MDIB requirement if such distributions are made in accordance with Q&A-2. However, if the designation is revoked, distributions in calendar years after 1988, except as otherwise provided in Q&A-8, must satisfy the rules in Q&A-3 through Q&A-7. Further, if the revocation occurs in a calendar year after 1988, the trust must distribute by the end of the calendar year following the calendar year in which the revocation occurs the total amount which was required to be distributed under Q&A-3 through Q&A-7 for the calendar years that have elapsed since 1988.

Q-10. Will a plan fail to satisfy section 411 if the plan is amended to eliminate benefit options that do not satisfy the MDIB requirement?

A. Nothing in section 401(a)(9) permits a plan to eliminate for all participants a benefit option that could not otherwise be eliminated pursuant to section 411(d)(6). However, a plan must provide that, notwithstanding any other plan provisions, it will not distribute benefits under any option that does not satisfy section 401(a)(9), including the MDIB requirement. See A-3 of § 1.401(a)(9)-1. Thus, the plan, notwithstanding section 411(d)(6), must prevent participants from electing benefit options that do not satisfy the MDIB requirement.

Q-11. Does the MDIB requirement apply to distributions to an alternate payee pursuant to a qualified domestic relations order as defined in section 414(p) (QDRO)?

A. If a QDRO provides that an employee's benefit is to be divided and a portion allocated to an alternate payee, the MDIB requirement will not apply to the distribution of the portion of the employee's benefit allocated to the alternate payee. However, if the QDRO does not provide that an employee's benefit is to be divided but merely provides that a portion of an employee's benefit (otherwise payable to the employee) is to be paid to an alternate payee, the MDIB requirement will apply to the distribution of the employee's entire benefit (including the portion payable to the alternative payee). Also, see Q&A-7 with respect to distributions to a former spouse pursuant to the QDRO.

Par. 4. There is added the following new section after § 1.403(b)-1 to read as follows:

§ 1.403(b)-2 Required distributions from annuity contracts purchased, or custodial accounts or retirement income accounts established by, a section 501(c)(3) organizations or public schools.

Q-1. Are annuity contracts described in section 403(b)(1), custodial accounts described in section 403(b)(7), and retirement income accounts described in section 403(b)(9) subject to the distribution rules provided in section 401(a)(9)?

A. (a) Yes. Annuity contracts described in section 403(b)(1), custodial accounts described in section 403(b)(7), and retirement income accounts described in section 403(b)(9) are subject to the distribution rules provided in section 401(a)(9) for calendar years after 1986. Hereinafter, annuity contracts described in section 403(b)(1), custodial accounts described in section 403(b)(7), and retirement income accounts described in section 403(b)(9) will be referred to as section 403(b) contracts.

(b) For purposes of applying the distribution rules in section 401(a)(9), section 403(b) contracts will be treated as individual retirement annuities described in section 408(b) and individual retirement accounts described in section 408(a), respectively (IRAs). Consequently, except as otherwise provided in paragraph (c), the distribution rules in section 401(a)(9) will be applied to section 403(b) contracts in accordance with the provisions in § 1.408-8.

(c) The transitional rule in § 1.401(a)(9)-1 B-2(b) will apply to distributions from section 403(b) contracts even though such transitional rule does not apply to distributions from IRAs. Thus, for an employee who attained 70 ½ before January 1, 1988, the required beginning date is April 1, of the calendar year following the later of (1) the calendar year in which the employed attains 70 ½ or (2) the calendar year in which the employee retires. The concept of 5-percent owner has no application iii the case of employees of employers described in section 403(b)(1)(A).

Q-2. To what benefits under section 403(b) contracts, do the distribution rules provided in section 401(a)(9) and § 1.401(a)(9)-1 apply?

A. (a) The distribution rules provided in section 401(a)(9) and § 1.401(a)(9)-1 apply to all benefits under section 403(b) contracts accruing after December 31, 1986 (post-'86 account balance). The distribution rules provided in section 401(a)(9) and § 1.401(a)(9)-1 do not apply to the value of the account balance under the section 403(b) contract valued as of December 31, 1986, exclusive of subsequent earnings (pre-'87 account balance). Consequently, the post-'86 account balance includes earnings after December 31, 1986, on contributions made before January 1, 1987, in addition to contributions made after December 31, 1986 and earnings thereon. The issuer or custodian of the section 403(b) contract must keep records that enable it to identify the pre-'87 account balance and subsequent changes as set forth in paragraph (b) and provide such information upon request to the relevant employee or beneficiaries with respect to the contract. If the issuer does not keep such records, the entire account balance will be treated as subject to section 401(a)(9).

(b) In applying the distribution rules in section 401(a)(9), only the post-'86 account balance is used to calculate the minimum distribution required for a calendar year. The amount of any distribution required to satisfy the minimum distribution requirement for a calendar year will be treated as being paid from the post-'86 account balance. Any amount distributed in a calendar year in excess of the minimum distribution requirement for a calendar year will be treated as paid from the pre-'87 account balance. The pre-'87 account balance for the next calendar year will be permanently reduced by the deemed distributions from the account.

(c) The pre-'86 account balance and the post-'87 account balance have no relevance for purposes of determining the amount includible in income under section 72.

Q-3. Must the value of the account balance under a section 403(b) contract as of December 31, 1986 be distributed in accordance with the incidental benefit requirement?

A. Distributions of the entire account balance of a section 403(b) contract, including the value of the account balance under the contract or account as of December 31, 1986, must satisfy the minimum distribution incidental benefit requirement (MDIB requirement) in Q&A-2 of § 1.401 (a)(9)-2. Distributions required to satisfy the MDIB requirement in Q&A-2 of § 1.401(a)(9)-2 reduce the pre-'87 account balance as set forth in Q&A-2 of this section of the regulations. The MDIB requirement in Q&A-3 through Q&A-7 of § 1.401(a)(9)-2, applicable to calendar years after 1988, need only be satisfied for distributions from the post-'86 account.

Par. 5. There is added the following new section after § 1.408-7 to read as follows:

§ 1.408-8 Distribution requirements for individual retirement plans.

The following questions and answers relate to the distribution rules for IRAs provided in section 408(a)(6) and section 408(b)(3), as added by section 521(b) of the Tax Reform Act of 1984 (Pub. L. 98-369) (TRA

of 1984) and amended by section 1852(a) of the Tax Reform Act of 1986 (Pub. L. 99-514) (TRA of 1986).

Table of Contents

A. General rules

B. Effective dates and transitional rules

A. *General rules.*

A-1. Q. Are individual retirement plans (IRAs) subject to the distribution rules provided in section 401(a)(9) and § 1.401(a)(9)-1 for qualified plans?

A. Yes. Except as otherwise provided in this section, IRAs are subject to the distribution rules provided in section 401 (a)(9) and § 1.401(a)(9)-1 for qualified plans. The distribution rules in § 1.408-2 (b)(6) and (7) (as in effect on December 31, 1983) no longer apply to IRAs. For example, (a) the amount of the minimum distribution for each calendar year will be determined in accordance with § 1.401(a)(9)-1 F-1 through F-4A, (b) in the event that the individual for whom an IRA is maintained (individual) changes or adds beneficiaries after the distributions are required to commence, the maximum distribution period will be determined in accordance with § 1.401(a)(9)-1 E-5, (c) pursuant to § 1.401(a)(9)-1 H-1, the rules in section 401(a)(9) apply separately to each IRA maintained for an individual's benefit, and (d) the rules in § 1.401(a)(9)-1 E-6 through E-8 concerning recalculation of life expectancy apply to IRAs. However, the effective date and transitional rules for the distribution rules applicable to IRAs are determined under this § 1.408-8 and not § 1.401(a)(9)-1.

A-2. Q. Are employer contributions under a simplified employee pension (defined in section 408(k)) treated as contributions to an IRA?

A. Yes. IRAs that receive employer contributions under a simplified employee pension (defined in section 408(k)) are treated as IRAs and are, therefore, subject to the distribution rules in this section.

A-3. Q. In the case of distributions from an IRA, what does the term "required beginning date" mean?

A. In the case of distributions from an IRA, the term "required beginning date" means April 1, of the calendar year following the calendar year in which the individual attains age 70 ½. The transition rule in § 1.401(a)(9)-1 B-2(b) does not apply to distributions from IRAs.

A-3A. Q. Will an IRA lose its tax-exempt status for failing in operation to make minimum distributions in accordance with section 408(a)(6) and (b)(3).

A. An IRA will not lose its tax-exempt status for isolated instances of failing in operation to make minimum distributions in accordance with section 408(a)(8) and (b)(3). A pattern or regular practice of failing to meet the minimum distribution requirements of section 408(a)(6) and (b)(3) with respect to the individual (or of the individual's beneficiaries) will not be treated as an isolated instance even if each instance is de minimis.

A-4. Q. May an individual's beneficiary elect to treat such beneficiary's entire interest in the trust upon the death of the individual (or the remaining part of such interest if distribution to the beneficiary has commenced) as the beneficiary's own account?

A. (a) In the case of an individual who died before January 1, 1984, the provisions of § 1.408-2(b)(7)(ii) (as in effect on December 31, 1983) continue to apply to the distribution of such individual's account. Thus, any beneficiary (whether or not the beneficiary is the individual's surviving spouse) may treat his interest in such individual's account as the beneficiary's own account in accordance with § 1.408-2(b)(7)(ii), regardless of whether or not distribution to the beneficiary has commenced.

(b) In the case of an individual dying after December 31, 1983, the only beneficiary of the individual who may elect to treat the beneficiary's entire interest in the trust (or the remaining part of such interest if distribution thereof has commenced to the beneficiary) as the beneficiary's own account is the individual's surviving spouse. If the surviving spouse makes such an election, the spouse's interest in the account would then be subject to the distribution requirements of section 401(a)(9)(A), rather than those of section 401(a)(9)(B). An election will be considered to have been made by the surviving spouse if either of the following occurs: (1) any required amounts in the account (including any amounts that have been rolled over or transferred, in accordance with the requirements of section 408(d)(3)(A)(i), into an individual retirement account or individual retirement annuity for the benefit of such surviving spouse) have not been distributed within the appropriate time period applicable to the decedent under section 401(a)(9)(B), or (2) any additional amounts are contributed to the account (or to the account or annuity to which the surviving spouse has rolled such amounts over, as described in (1) above) which are subject, or deemed to be subject, to the distribution requirements of section 401(a)(9)(A). The result of such an election is that the surviving spouse shall then be considered the individual for whose benefit the trust is maintained.

A-5. Q. How is the benefit determined for purposes of calculating the minimum distribution from an IRA?

A. For purposes of determining the minimum distribution required to he made from an IRA in any calendar year, the account balance of the IRA as of the December 31 of the calendar year immediately preceding the calendar year for which distributions are being made will be substituted in § 1.401(a)(9)-1 F-1 for the benefit of the employee. The account balance as of December 31 of such calendar year is the value of the IRA upon close of business on such December 31. However, for purposes of determining the minimum distribution for the second distribution calendar year for an individual, the account balance as of December 31 of such calendar year must be reduced by any distribution (as described in § 1.401(a)(9)-1 F-5(c)(2)) made to satisfy the minimum distribution requirements for the individual's first distribution calendar year after such date.

A-6. Q. What rules apply in the case of a rollover to an IRA of an amount distributed by a qualified plan or another IRA?

A. If the surviving spouse of an employee rolls over a distribution from a qualified plan, such surviving spouse may elect to treat the IRA as the spouse's own IRA in accordance with the provisions in A-4. In the event of any other rollover to an IRA of an amount distributed by a qualified plan or another IRA, the rules in § 1.401(a)(9)-1 will apply for purposes of determining the account balance for the receiving IRA and the minimum distribution from the receiving IRA. Thus, for example, certain amounts rolled over to a plan must be separately accounted for and the minimum distribution with respect to such amounts must be separately determined, as described in G-2. However, because the value of the account balance is determined as of December 31 of the year preceding the year for which the minimum distribution is being determined and not as of a valuation date in the preceding year, the account balance of the receiving IRA need not be adjusted for the amount received as provided in § 1.401(a)(9)-1 G-2(a) in order to determine the minimum distribution for the calendar year following the calendar year in which the amount rolled over is received, unless the amount received is deemed to have been received in the immediately preceding year, pursuant to § 1.401(a)(9)-1 G-2(a) or (b)(7). In that case, for purposes of determining the minimum distribution for the calendar year in which such amount is actually received, either the account balance of the receiving IRA as of December 31 of the preceding year must be adjusted by the amount received in accordance with § 1.401(a)(9)-1 G-2(a) or the amount received will be treated as a separate account balance, in accordance with § 1.401(a)(9)-1 G-2(b).

A-7. Q. What rules apply in the case of a transfer from one IRA to another?

A. In the case of a transfer from one IRA to another IRA, the rules in § 1.401(a)(9)-1 G-3 and G-4 will apply for purposes of determining the account balance of, and the minimum distribution from, the IRA involved. Thus, the transferor IRA must distribute in the year of the transfer any amount required with respect to the portion of the account transferred; certain amounts transferred must be separately accounted for by the transferee IRA; and the minimum distribution with respect to such amounts must be separately determined by the transferee IRA. However, for purposes of determining the account balance of the transferee IRA and the transferor IRA, the account balance need not be adjusted for the amount transferred as provided in § 1.401(a)(9)-1 G-4(a) in order to calculate the minimum distribution for the calendar year following the calendar year of the transfer, because the account balance is determined as of December 31 of the calendar year immediately preceding the calendar year for which the minimum distribution is being determined.

A-8. Q. Can a qualified trust or plan described in section 401(a) or an annuity described in section 403(a) or 403(b) make a transfer to an IRA that is not a rollover contribution described in section 402(a)(7), 403(a)(4) or 403(b)(8)?

A. (a) No. A qualified trust or plan described in section 401(a) or an annuity described in section 403(a) or 403(b) can not make a transfer to an IRA. However, an IRA may accept a rollover contribution that satisfies the requirements of section 402(a)(5), 402(a)(7), 403(a)(4) or 403(b)(8) even if such contribution is distributed by a qualified trust, plan, or annuity directly to the IRA at the direction of the employee (or the employee's surviving spouse). Such contribution will not be treated as a transfer to an IRA. Instead, such contribution will be treated as

though it was distributed by the qualified trust, plan, or annuity to the employee (or the employee's surviving spouse) and subsequently rolled over to an IRA within the requisite 60 day period.

(b) Transfers directly from such a qualified trust or plan described in section 401(a) or annuity described in section 403(a) or 403(b) to an IRA may adversely affect both the qualified status of the trust, plan or annuity from which the transfer is made and the qualified status of the IRA which receives the transfer.

B. *Effective date and transition rules.*

B-1. Q. When are the distribution rules for IRAs in A-1 through A-8 effective?

A. The new distribution rules in A-1 through A-8 are effective for calendar years after calendar year 1984. However, distributions for calendar years 1985 and 1986 are not required to be made until December 31, 1987. If an individual attained age 70 ½ in calendar year 1986 or a prior calendar year and is alive on December 31, 1987, B-2 and B-3 provide special rules for determining the minimum distribution required for calendar years 1985 through 1987, and B-4 provides special rules for determining the minimum distribution required for calendar years after 1987. In the case of an individual who dies before January 1, 1988, B-4 through B-11 provide special rules for determining the minimum distribution required for calendar years 1985 through 1987 and for subsequent calendar years. See B-12 to determine when the IRA trust instrument must be amended. See B-13 to determine when the incidental death benefit rule applies to IRAs.

B-2. Q. If an individual attained age 70 ½ in calendar year 1986 or a prior calendar year and is alive on December 31, 1987, as of what date must the required distributions for calendar years 1985 through 1987 be made?

A. (a) *In general.* This B-2 determines when distributions must be made if an individual attained age 70 ½ in calendar year 1986 or a prior calendar year and is alive on December 31, 1987. Paragraph (d) provides a special rule which applies if distributions under certain annuity contracts which commenced not later than [30 days after publication of this notice].

(b) *70 ½ in a calendar year before 1985.* If an individual attained age 70 ½ in a calendar year prior to 1985, under these transition rules, the minimum distribution for 1985 is not required to be made by December 31, 1985 and the minimum distribution for calendar year 1986 is not required to be made by December 31, 1986. Instead, the minimum distribution for calendar years 1985 and 1986 are required to be made by December 31, 1987. Thus, the minimum distributions for calendar years 1985, 1986, and 1987 must be made by December 31, 1987.

(c) *70 ½ in 1985.* If an individual attained age 70 ½ in calendar year 1985, under these transition rules, the minimum distribution for calendar year 1985 is not required to be made by April 1, 1986, and the minimum distribution for calendar year 1986 is not required to be made by December 31, 1986. Instead, the minimum distributions for calendar years 1985 and 1986 are required to be made by December 31, 1987. Thus, the minimum distributions for calendar years 1985, 1986, and 1987 must be made by December 31, 1987.

(d) *70 ½ in 1986.* If an individual attained age 70 ½ in 1986, the minimum distribution required for calendar year 1986 is not required to be made by April 1, 1987. Instead, the minimum distribution for 1986 is required to be made by December 31, 1987. Thus, the minimum distributions for calendar years 1986 and 1987 must be made by December 31, 1987.

(e) *Certain annuity payments.* In the case of an individual described in paragraph (a) to whom nonincreasing annuity payments from one or more annuity contracts purchased from an insurance company commence not later than August 26, 1987 and to whom such annuity payments continue through December 31, 1987, no additional amount is required under these transition rules to be distributed for 1985, 1986, and 1987 from such annuity contracts. However, this rule only applies if such payments comply with § 1.401(a)(9)-1F-3 and F-4. If such payments commenced after the individual's required beginning date and if the individual has other IRAs (from which annuity payments as described above are not being made), any additional amount required to be distributed from such annuity contracts, under these transition rules, for 1985, 1986, and 1987 must be distributed to the extent available from such other IRAs. In determining whether an additional amount is required to be distributed from another IRA, the cash surrender value of the annuity contract as of the close of business on December 31, 1986 will be treated as the account balance of the annuity contract as of December 31, 1986.

B-3. Q. If (a) the individual attained age 70 ½ in calendar year 1986 or a prior calendar year and (b) the individual is alive on December 31,

1987, then how is the amount of the minimum required distribution from the individual's IRAs determined for calendar years 1985, 1986, and 1987?

A. (a) *In general.* If (1) the individual attained age 70 ½ in calendar year 1986 or a prior calendar year and (2) the individual is alive on December 31, 1987, for calendar years 1985, 1986, and 1987, the amount of the minimum distribution from the individual's IRAs is to be determined under one of the three methods: the life expectancy method, the percentage method, or the regular method. The individual will select which method is to be used. Under the life expectancy method and the percentage method, the total amount of the minimum distribution required for calendar years 1985, 1986, and 1987 is determined by aggregating the account balances under all of an individual's IRAs.

(b) *Life expectancy method.* Under the life expectancy method, the minimum distribution for 1985, 1986, and 1987 is determined as follows:

(1) *Designated beneficiary and life expectancy.* The designated beneficiary with respect to the individual under all IRAs will be determined as of any date in 1987. The beneficiary under all of the individual's IRAs as of such date with the longest life expectancy is the designated beneficiary that must be used to determine the aggregate minimum distribution. The applicable life expectancy (either the life expectancy of the individual or joint life and last survivor expectancy of the individual and the individual's designated beneficiary, whichever is applicable) is determined using ages as of birthdays in 1987. In the case of any beneficiary who is not alive on his birthday in 1987, such beneficiary is treated as being alive on that birthday for purposes of determining life expectancy.

(2) *Account balance.* The account balance is the aggregate of the account balances of all IRAs of the individual as of close of business December 31, 1986 with the following modifications. First, the aggregated account balance is increased by any amounts not reflected in an IRA as of such date due to withdrawal to make a rollover contribution to another IRA. Second, the aggregate account balance is then increased by any amount distributed in 1985 or 1986 for which credit is being taken under subparagraph (4).

(3) *Required distribution.* The total amount which must be distributed for calendar years 1985, 1986, and 1987 is determined by dividing the aggregate account balance determined under subparagraph (2) by the applicable life expectancy and multiplying the quotient by:

(i) 2.8, in the case of an individual with respect to whom the first distribution calendar year is 1985 (or a prior calendar year), or

(ii) 1.9, in the case of an individual with respect to whom the first distribution calendar year is 1986.

(4) *Credits for distributions.* In determining whether the total amount which must be distributed for calendar years 1985, 1986, and 1987 has been distributed, credit may be taken for any amount distributed in a distribution calendar year of the individual after 1984. However, in the case of any distribution in 1985 or 1986, credit may only be taken for amounts which were used to increase the aggregate account balance pursuant to subparagraph (2). See paragraph (e) for a special rule if an individual received excess distributions in a calendar year before 1985.

(c) *Percentage method.* Under the percentage method, the total amount of the minimum distribution required for calendar years 1985, 1986, and 1987 is determined as follows:

(1) *Account balance.* The account balance is determined in the same manner as under paragraph (b)(2).

(2) *Required distribution.* The total aggregate amount required to be distributed from all IRAs of the individual (which may be aggregated pursuant to this paragraph) is the following percentage of the aggregate account balance determined under subparagraph (1):

(i) 15%, in the case of an individual with respect to whom the first distribution calendar year under section 401(a)(9) is 1985, or

(ii) 10%, in the case of an individual with respect to whom the first distribution calendar year is 1986.

(3) *Credit for distributions.* Credits for distributions may be taken in the same manner as under paragraph (b)(4).

(d) *Regular method.* Under the regular method, the sum of the minimum distributions required for calendar years 1985, 1986, and 1987, calculated separately, is determined under section 408(a)(6) and (b)(3) and this section with appropriate adjustments. However, in determining the minimum distribution required for calendar years 1985, 1986, and 1987, the rule in § 1.401(a)(9)-1 F-2 does not apply. Also, credit (with an appropriate gross up) may be taken toward the minimum distribution required for the 1986 or 1987 distribution calendar year for distributions in the 1985 or 1986 distribution calendar years that exceeded the minimum required distribution for such year.

(e) *Credits.* Credit may be taken under the life expectancy method, the percentage method, and the regular method for excess distributions from IRAs in calendar years before 1985 to the extent that the aggregate amount distributed by the end of 1984 by all IRAs of the individual exceeded the aggregate of the minimum amounts required by 1.408-2(b)(6)(v) to have been distributed by the end of 1984. Such excess distributions will be treated as amounts distributed in 1985 for purposes of determining the amount which is required to be distributed by determining the amount which is required to be distributed by December 31, 1987 under each of those methods.

(f) *Example.* This Q&A is illustrated by the following example:

Example.

(a) An individual (X), born March 1, 1915, has three TRAs (IRA 1, IRA 2, and IRA 3) as of January 1, 1987. Each IRA has a different designated beneficiary. X's spouse, born January 15, 1920 is the sole designated beneficiary of IRA 1. X's daughter, born May 5, 1939, is the sole designated beneficiary of IRA 2. X's son, born April 2, 1941, is the sole designated beneficiary of IRA 3. X's account balance in IRA 1 as of December 31, 1986 is $53,000. X's account balance in IRA 2 as of December 31, 1986 is $25,000. X's account balance in IRA 3 as of December 31, 1986 is $24,000. Distributions in 1985 and 1986 from X's IRAs are as follows: $3,000 from IRA 1 in 1985, $1,500 from IRA 2 in 1986, and $2,500 from IRA 3 in 1986.

(b) Under the life expectancy method, X's required minimum distribution in 1987 (required to be made by December 31, 1987) is determined as follows:

(1)		Account balances as of December 31, 1986	
	(a)	IRA 1	$53,000.00
	(b)	IRA 2	$25,000.00
	(c)	IRA 3	$24,000.00
(2)		Aggregate account balances of X as of December 31, 1986	$102,000.00
(3)		Distribution in 1985	$3,000.00
(4)		Distribution in 1986 ($1,500 plus $2,500)	$4,000.00
(5)		Account balance to be used to determine minimum distribution (sum of lines 2, 3, and 4)	$109,000.00
(6)		Attained age of beneficiary with longest life expectancy (youngest—X's son) as of birthday in 1987	46.00
(7)		X's attained age as of X's birthday in 1987	72.00
(8)		Joint life and last survivor expectancy of X and X's son (using Table VI of § 1.72-9) using ages on lines 6 and 7	37.30
(9)		Account balance (line 5) divided by the applicable life expectancy (line 8)	$2,922.25
(10)		Total amount which must be distributed for 1985, 1986, and 1987 (line 9 multiplied by 2.8)	$8,182.30
(11)		Distributions in 1985 and 1986 for which credit may be taken (sum of lines (3) and (4))	$7,000.00
(12)		Amount required to be distributed in 1987 (line 10 minus line 11)	$1,182.30

(c) Under the percentage method, X's required minimum distribution in 1987 (required to be made by December 31, 1987) is determined as follows:

(1)		Account balances as of December 31, 1986:	
	(a)	IRA 1	$53,000
	(b)	IRA 2	$25,000
	(c)	IRA 3	$24,000
(2)		Aggregate account balances of X as of December 31, 1986	$102,000

(3)	Distribution in 1985	$3,000
(4)	Distribution in 1986 ($1,500 plus $2,500)	$4,000
(5)	Account balance to be used to determine minimum distribution (sum of lines 2, 3, and 4)	$109,000
(6)	Total amount which must be distributed for 1985, 1986, and 1987 (15% of line 5)	$16,350
(7)	Distributions in 1985 and 1986 for which credit may be taken (sum of lines 3 and 4)	$7,000
(8)	Amount required to be distributed in 1987 (line 6 minus line 7)	$9,350

B-4. Q. If an individual attained age 70 ½ in 1986 or in a prior calendar year, are there any special rules for determining the minimum distribution for calendar years after 1987?

A. (a) *Required beginning date.* If an individual attained age 70 ½ in 1986 or in a prior calendar year, the amount of the minimum distribution required for calendar years after 1987 will be determined in a manner consistent with the use of December 31, 1987 as the individual's required beginning date. Consequently, for example, if any election is permitted by the IRA trustee, the individual must elect no later than December 31, 1987 whether or not life expectancy will be recalculated for purposes of determining the minimum distribution required for calendar years after 1987. Further, for example, the designated beneficiary of the individual under each IRA will be determined as of December 31, 1987 for purposes of determining the minimum distribution required for calendar years after 1987.

(b) *Life expectancies.* If an individual attained age 70 ½ in 1986 or in a prior calendar year, for purposes of determining the minimum distribution for calendar years after 1987, life expectancies shall be determined for each IRA as follows. If the individual's designated beneficiary is the individual's spouse, and the life expectancy of the individual and spouse are being recalculated, the joint life and last survivor expectancy of the individual and spouse is calculated using their attained ages as of their birthdays in the calendar year for which the minimum distribution is being determined. If the individual's designated beneficiary is not the individual's spouse and life expectancy is being recalculated, the joint life and last survivor expectancy of the individual and the designated beneficiary (other than the individual's spouse) is determined using the attained age of the individual as of the individual's birthday in the calendar year for which the minimum distribution is being determined and the attained age of the designated beneficiary as of the beneficiary's birthday in 1987, adjusted in accordance with E-8. If an individual's life expectancy is not being recalculated, the joint life and last survivor expectancy of the individual and the designated beneficiary will be determined based on the attained ages of the individual and designated beneficiary as of their birthdays in 1987, reduced by one for each calendar year that has elapsed since 1987. For purposes of this paragraph (b), if the designated beneficiary is not alive on his birthday in 1987, such beneficiary will be deemed to be alive on that date for purposes of determining life expectancy.

(c) *Normal rules.* For years after 1987, the requirement that each IRA separately satisfy the minimum distribution requirement applies. Thus, except as noted in this section, the rules in H-1 through H-2A of § 1.401(a)(9)-1 apply.

B-5. Q. If an individual dies before January 1, 1988, are distributions to be made in accordance with section 401(a)(9)(B)(i) or in accordance with section 401(a)(9)(B)(ii) or (iii) and (iv)?

A. If an individual dies prior to January 1, 1988 (including deaths before January 1, 1985), the IRA must be distributed in accordance with section 401(a)(9)(B)(ii) or (iii) and (iv), whichever is applicable (see B-12 and § 1.401(a)(9)-1 C-4). If an individual dies prior to January 1, 1986, see B-6 and B-7 for rules concerning which calendar year is the first calendar year for which distributions must be made in accordance with section 401(a)(9), when such distributions are required to commence, and how the amount which is required to be distributed by such date is determined.

B-6. Q. If an individual died prior to January 1, 1986 and distributions are being made over the life expectancy of a designated beneficiary in accordance with section 401(a)(9)(B)(iii) and (iv), what is the first calendar year for which a distribution is required and when must distributions commence?

A. (a) *General rule.* If an individual died prior to January 1, 1986 and distributions are being made over the life expectancy of a designated beneficiary in accordance with section 401(a)(9)(B)(iii) and (iv), the first calendar year for which a minimum distribution under section 401(a)(9) is required is the later of: (1) the calendar year which contains the required commencement date determined under § 1.401(a)(9)-1 C-3(a) or (b), whichever is applicable, or (2) calendar year 1985. However, under these transition rules, if the first distribution calendar year for which minimum distributions must be determined in accordance with section 401(a)(9) is 1985, such minimum distribution is not required to be made by December 31, 1985. Similarly, under these transition rules, if the first (or second) distribution

calendar year (for which minimum distributions must be determined in accordance with section 401(a)(9)) is 1986, the minimum distribution for 1986 is not required to be made by December 31, 1986. Instead, in such case, the minimum distributions for 1985 (if applicable), 1986, and 1987, must be made by December 31, 1987. Paragraph (b) provides a special rule made by December 31, 1987. Paragraph (b) provides a special rule for certain annuity payments.

(b) *Certain annuity payments.* In the case of a beneficiary described in paragraph (a) to whom nonincreasing annuity payments from one or more annuity contracts purchased from an insurance company commenced not later than [30 days after the publication of this notice] and to whom such annuity payments continue through December 31, 1987, no additional amount is required under these transition rules to be distributed for 1985, 1986, and 1987 from such annuity contracts. However, this rule only applies if such annuity payments comply with § 1.401(a)(9)-1 F-3 and F-4. If such payments commenced after the last day of the distribution calendar year determined under paragraph (a), and if such beneficiary is also the sole beneficiary of other IRAs (from which annuity payments as described above are not being made) that were inherited from the same individual from whom such annuity contracts were inherited, any additional amount required to be distributed from such annuity contract, under these transition rules, for 1985, 1986, and 1987 must be distributed to the extent available from such other IRAs. In determining whether an additional amount is required to be distributed from another IRA, the cash surrender value of the annuity contract as of the close of business December 31, 1986 will be treated as the account balance of the annuity contract as of December 31, 1986.

B-7. Q. If (a) distributions are being made over the life expectancy of a designated beneficiary in accordance with section 401(a)(9)(B)(iii) and (iv) and (b) the first distribution calendar year is 1985 or 1986 (determined under B-6(a)), then how is the amount of the minimum distribution determined for calendar years 1985, 1986, and 1987?

A. (a) *In general.* If the two conditions set forth in the question are met, the amount of the minimum distribution for calendar years 1985, 1986, and 1987 is to be determined under one of three methods, the life and the regular method, the life expectancy method and the percentage method. IRAs which were inherited from the same individual and which have the same beneficiaries will be aggregated. The beneficiary (or beneficiaries) of the aggregated IRAs will select which of the three methods is to be used.

(b) *Life expectancy method.* Under the life expectancy method, the minimum distribution for 1985, 1986, and 1987 will then be determined as follows:

(1) *Designated beneficiary and life expectancy.* The designated beneficiary with respect to an individual for IRAs being aggregated will be determined as of any date in 1987. The applicable life expectancy will be the life expectancy of the designated beneficiary using the designated beneficiary's age as of his birthday in 1987. In the case of a beneficiary who is not alive on his birthday in 1987, the beneficiary will be treated as being alive on that date for purposes of determining life expectancy under this transition rule.

(2) *Account balance.* The account balance is the aggregate of the account balances of all the IRAs to be aggregated (determined under paragraph (a)) as of close of business December 31, 1986 with the following modifications. First, the aggregated account balance is increased by any amounts not reflected in an IRA as of such date due to withdrawal to make a rollover contribution to another IRA. Second, the aggregate account balance is then increased by any amount distributed in 1985 or 1986 for which credit is being taken under subparagraph (4).

(3) *Required distribution.* The total amount which must be distributed for calendar years 1985, 1986, and 1987 will be determined by dividing the account balance determined under subparagraph (2) by the applicable life expectancy determined under subparagraph (1) and multiplying the quotient by:

(i) 2.8, in the case of an individual with respect to whom the first distribution calendar year is 1985, or

(ii) 1.9, in the case of an individual with respect to whom the first distribution calendar year is 1986.

(4) *Credit for distributions.* In determining whether the total amount which must be distributed for calendar years 1985, 1986, and 1987 has

been distributed, credit may be taken for any amount distributed in a distribution calendar year of the individual after 1984. However, in the case of any distribution in 1985 or 1986, credit may only be taken for amounts which were used to increase the aggregate account balance pursuant to subparagraph (2).

(c) *Percentage method.* Under the percentage method, the total amount of the minimum distribution required for calendar years 1985, 1986, and 1987 is determined as follows:

(1) *Account balance.* The account balance is determined in the same manner as under paragraph (b)(2).

(2) *Required distribution.* The total aggregate amount required to be distributed from all the IRAs to be aggregated determined under paragraph (a) is the following percentage of the aggregate account balance determined under subparagraph (1):

(i) 15%, in the case of an individual with respect to whom the first distribution calendar year is 1985, or

(ii) 10%, in the case of an individual with respect to whom the first distribution calendar year is 1986.

(3) *Credit for distributions.* Credits for distributions may be taken in the same manner as under paragraph (b)(3).

(d) *Regular method.* Under the regular method, the sum of the minimum distributions required for calendar years 1985, 1986, and 1987, calculated separately, is determined under section 408(a)(6) and (b)(3) and this section with the appropriate adjustments. However, the rule in § 1.401(a)(9)-1 F-2 does not apply. Also credit (with an appropriate gross-up) may be taken toward the minimum distributions required for the 1986 or 1987 distribution calendar year for distributions in the 1985 or 1986 distribution calendar years which exceeded the minimum required distribution for such year.

B-8. Q. If distributions are being made with respect to an individual over the life expectancy of a designated beneficiary in accordance with section 401(a)(9)(B)(iii) and (iv), as of what date is the designated beneficiary determined, and as of what date is the life expectancy of the designated beneficiary determined, for purposes of determining the minimum distribution for calendar years after 1987?

A. If distributions are being made over the life expectancy of a designated beneficiary in accordance with section 401(a)(9)(B)(iii) and (iv), the designated beneficiary will be determined as of any date in 1987. The life expectancy of the designated beneficiary (other than an individual's surviving spouse whose life expectancy is being recalculated) will be determined using the attained age of the designated beneficiary as of such beneficiary's birthday in calendar year 1987, reduced by one for each calendar year which has elapsed after 1987. If the designated beneficiary is not alive on his birthday in 1987, such beneficiary will be treated as alive on that date for purposes of determining life expectancy. If the individual's surviving spouse is a designated beneficiary and such spouse's life expectancy is being recalculated, the life expectancy of such spouse will be calculated using the attained age of the spouse as of such spouse's birthday in the calendar year for which the minimum distribution is being determined.

B-9 Q. In the case of an individual's surviving spouse for whom a distribution is required to be made for 1985 or 1986, when must any election concerning recalculation of life expectancy be made by the spouse?

A. In the case of an individual's surviving spouse for whom a distribution is required to be made for 1985 or 1986, any election concerning recalculation of life expectancy must be made by December 31, 1987.

B-10. Q. When must the election described in § 1.401(a)(9)-1 C-4 (concerning whether distribution will be made in accordance with the five-year rule in section 401(a)(9)(B)(ii) or the exception to the five-year rule in section 401(a)(9)(B)(iii)) be made by a beneficiary otherwise required to make such election on or before December 31, 1986?

A. The election described in § 1.401(a) (9)-1 C-4 (concerning whether distribution will be made in accordance with the five-year rule in section 401(a)(9)(B)(ii) or the exception to the five-year rule in section 401(a)(9)(B)(iii)) if otherwise required to make such election on or before December 31, 1986 must be made by December 31, 1987.

B-11. Q. If an individual died prior to January 1, 1985, and distribution is to be made in accordance with the five-year rule contained in section 401(a)(9)(B)(ii), as of what date must the individual's entire interest be distributed?

A. If an individual died prior to January 1, 1985 and distribution is to be made in accordance with the five-year rule contained in section 401(a)(9)(b)(ii), the individual's entire interest must be distributed as

of the later of: (a) December 31 of the calendar year which contains the fifth anniversary of the employee's death or (b) December 31, 1987.

B-12. Q. When must the trust instrument for an IRA be amended to provide the distribution rules in section 408(a)(6) or

A. (a) The trust instrument for an IRA with a favorable opinion letter need not be amended until the later of December 31, 1988 or such time as the Commissioner prescribes (after publication of sample language for IRAs, including IRAs used for funding simplified employee pensions (SEPs)). In the case of an existing IRA or a newly established IRA which is established by executing Form 5305 or Form 5305A, the current (Rev. 11-83) editions of those forms may be used until such time as the Commissioner prescribes. Prior to the date when the trust instrument must be amended, an IRA with a favorable opinion letter or an IRA established by executing Form 5305 or Form 5305A will not be considered to fail to be described in section 408(a) or (b) merely because it fails in form to satisfy section 408(a)(6) or (b)(3) and this section of the regulations. However, distributions must satisfy section 408(a)(6) or 408(b)(3) and the regulations thereunder in operation, notwithstanding the absence of provisions in the trust instrument beginning with calendar year 1985.

(b) An IRA which does not have a favorable opinion letter and which is not established by executing Form 5305 or Form 5305A will satisfy section 408(a)(6) and 408(b)(3) until the date prescribed in paragraph (a) as of which IRAs with a favorable opinion letter must be amended if such IRA contains the statutory provisions in section 401(a)(9) applicable to IRAs. Not all provisions in section 401(a)(9) apply to IRAs. For example, pursuant to A-3, the transitional rule in § 1.401(a)(9)-1 B-2(b) does not apply to distributions from IRAs.

(c) For calendar years before the calendar year in which IRAs must be amended pursuant to this B-5, an IRA will not be subject to the default provisions of § 1.401(a)(9)-1 if distributions under each IRA are otherwise made in accordance with these regulations in a reasonable and consistent manner. For example, for purposes of determining, pursuant to § 1.401(a)(9)-1 C-4, whether the exception to the five-year rule in section 401(a)(9)(B)(iii) and (iv) applies, an IRA will be found to comply with section 408(a)(6) or (b)(3) in operation even though distributions are not made in accordance with the default provisions in § 1.401(a)(9)-1 C-4(a) if the IRA trustee decides with respect to an IRA to either distribute benefits under one method or the other or distribute benefits pursuant to the election by an individual or the individual's beneficiary (or in the absence of an election, under one or the other of such methods). Similarly, for calendar years before the calendar year in which IRAs must be amended pursuant to B-5, for purposes of determining whether or not the life expectancies off the individual and the individual's spouse will be recalculated pursuant to section 401(a)(9)(D) and § 1.401(a)(9)-1 E-7, an IRA will be found to comply with section 408(a)(6) or (b)(3) and this section of the regulations in operation even though the life expectancies of the individual and the individual's spouse are not recalculated if the trustee decides not to recalculate such life expectancies, if the IRA trustee allows elections by the individual or spouse and the individual or spouse elects not to recalculate life expectancy, or if the IRA trustee decides not to recalculate life expectancy in the absence of an election to recalculate life expectancy.

B-13. Q. Must distributions from IRAs for calendar years before 1989 satisfy the incidental benefit rule in § 1.401(a)(9)-2?

A. No. Distributions from IRAs for calendar years before 1989 are not required to satisfy the incidental benefit rule in § 1.401(a)(9)-2. However, for calendar years after 1988, distributions must satisfy the incidental benefit rule in § 1.401(a)(9)-2 which applies to calendar years after 1988.

B-14. Q. What are the distribution rules applicable to individual retirement plans (IRAs) in 1984?

A. For calendar year 1984, IRAs arc subject to the distribution requirements of section 408(a)(6) and (7) and section 408(b)(3) and (4), as in effect immediately prior to the enactment of the Tax Reform Act of 1984 (TRA of 1984). With respect to individuals who died prior to January 1, 1984, the law in effect immediately prior to the enactment of TRA of 1984 is the law in effect immediately prior to the enactment of the Tax Equity and Fiscal Responsibility Act (TEFRA). Section 243(b) of (TEFRA) (as amended by section 713(g) of TRA of 1984) denies deductions for contributions to, and rollover treatment for distributions to or from, inherited IRAs (as defined in section 408(d)(3)(c)(ii)) with respect to individuals dying after December 31, 1983.

Pension Excise Tax Regulations (26 CFR Part 54)

Par. 6. The authority citation for Part 54 is amended by adding the following citation:

Authority: 26 U. S. C. 7305 * * * Section 54.4974-2 is also issued under 26 U. S. C. 4974.

Par. 7. There is added the following new section after § 54.4974-1 to read as follows:

§ 54.49742. Excise tax on accumulations in qualified retirement plans.

Q-1. Is any tax imposed on a payee under any qualified retirement plan or any eligible deferred compensation plan (as defined in section 457(b)) to whom an amount is required to be distributed for a taxable year if the amount distributed during the taxable year is less than the minimum required distribution?

A. Yes. If the amount distributed to a payee under any qualified retirement plan or any eligible deferred compensation plan (as defined in section 457(b)) for a calendar year is less than the minimum required distribution for such year, an excise tax is imposed on such payee under section 4974 for the taxable year beginning with or within the calendar year during which the amount is required to be distributed. The tax is equal to 50 percent of the amount by which such minimum required distribution exceeds the actual amount distributed during the calendar year. Section 4974 provides that this tax shall be paid by the payee. For purposes of section 4974, the term "minimum required distribution" means the minimum amount required to be distributed pursuant to section 401(a)(9), 403(b)(10), 408(a)(6), 408(b)(3), or 457(d)(2), as the case may be, and the regulations thereunder. Except as otherwise provided in Q&A-6, the minimum required distribution for a calendar year is the minimum amount required to be distributed during the calendar year. Q&A-6 provides a special rule for amounts required to be distributed by an employee's (or individual's) required beginning date.

Q-2. For purposes of section 4974, what is a qualified retirement plan?

A. For purposes of section 4974, each of the following is a qualified retirement plan:

(a) A plan described in section 401(a) which includes a trust exempt from tax under section 501(a),

(b) An annuity plan described in section 403(a),

(c) An annuity contract, custodial account, or retirement income account described in 403(b),

(d) An individual retirement account described in section 408(a),

(e) An individual retirement annuity described in section 408(b), or

(f) Any other plan, contract account, or annuity that, at any time, has been treated as a plan, account, or annuity described in (a) through (e), whether or not such plan, contract, account, or annuity currently satisfies the applicable qualification requirements.

Q-3. If a payee's interest under a qualified retirement plan is in the form of an individual account, how is the minimum required distribution for a given calendar year determined for purposes of section 4974?

A. (a) *General rule.* If a payee's interest under a qualified retirement plan is in the form of an individual account and distribution of such account is not being made under an annuity contract purchased in accordance with § 1.401(a)(9)-1 F-4, the amount of the minimum required distribution for any calendar year for purposes of section 4974 is the minimum amount required to be distributed for such calendar year in order to satisfy the minimum distribution requirements in §§ 1.401(a)(9)-1 and 1.401(a)(9)-2 as provided in the following (whichever is applicable):

(1) Section 401(a)(9) and §§ 1.401(a)(9)-1 and 1.401(a)(9)-2 (in the case of a plan described in section 401(a) which includes a trust exempt under section 501(a) or an annuity plan described in section 403(a)),

(2) Section 403(b)(10) and § 1.403(b)-2 (in the case of an annuity contract or custodial account described in section 403(b)), or

(3) Section 408(a)(6) or (b)(3) and § 1.408-8 (in the case of an individual retirement account or annuity described in section 498(a) or

(b) *Default provisions.* Unless otherwise provided under the qualified retirement plan (or, if applicable, the governing instrument of the qualified retirement plan), the default provisions in § 1.401(a)(9)-1 apply in determining the minimum required distribution for purposes of section 4974. For example, if the amount of the minimum required distribution for purposes of section 4974 is to be determined using the life expectancies of the employee (or IRA owner), the employee's spouse (or IRA owner's spouse), or both, the life expectancy of such individuals must be recalculated in order to determine the minimum required distribution unless the exceptions in § 1.401(a)(9)-1 E-7 apply. Similarly, if the rules in § 1.401(a)(9)-1 C-1 through C-6 (after death

distribution rules) apply to a payee, the minimum required distribution for any given calendar year to satisfy the applicable section enumerated in paragraph (a) will be determined using the default provisions in § 1.401(a)(9) C-4 unless an exception stated therein applies.

(c) *Five year rule.* If the five-year rule in section 401(a)(9)(3)(ii) applies to the distribution to a payee, no amount is required to be distributed for any calendar year to satisfy the applicable enumerated section in paragraph (a) until the calendar year which contains the date five years after the date of the employee's death. For the calendar year which contains the date five years after the employee's death, the minimum amount required to be distributed to satisfy the applicable enumerated section is the payee's entire remaining interest in the qualified retirement plan.

Q-4. If a payee's interest in a qualified retirement plan is being distributed in the form of an annuity, how is the amount of the minimum required distribution determined for purposes of section 4974?

A. If a payee's interest in a qualified retirement plan is being distributed in the form of an annuity (either directly from the plan, in the case of a defined benefit plan, or under an annuity contract purchased from an insurance company), the amount of the minimum required distribution for purposes of section 4974 will be determined as follows:

(a) *Permissible annuity distribution option.* A permissible annuity distribution option is an annuity contract (or, in the case of annuity distributions from a defined benefit plan, a distribution option) which specifically provides for distributions which, if made as provided, would for every calendar year equal or exceed the minimum amount required to be distributed to satisfy the applicable section enumerated in paragraph (a) of Q-4 for every calendar year. If the annuity contract (or, in the case of annuity distributions from a defined benefit plan, a distribution option) under which distributions to the payee are being made is a permissible annuity distribution option, the minimum required distribution for a given calendar year will equal the amount which the annuity contract (or distribution option) provides is to be distributed for that calendar year.

(b) *Impermissible annuity distribution option.* An impermissible annuity distribution option is an annuity contract (or, in the case of annuity distributions from a defined benefit plan, a distribution option) under which distributions to the payee are being made specifically provides for distributions which, if made as provided, would for any calendar year be less than the minimum amount required to be distributed to satisfy the applicable section enumerated in paragraph (a) of Q-4. If the annuity contract (or, in the case of annuity distributions from a defined benefit plan, the distribution option) under which distributions to the payee are being made is an impermissible annuity distribution option, the minimum required distribution for each calendar year will be determined as follows:

(1) If the qualified retirement plan under which distributions are being made is a defined benefit plan, the minimum amount required to be distributed each year will be the amount which would have been distributed under the plan if the distribution option under which distributions to the payee were being made was the following permissible annuity distribution option:

(i) In the case of distributions commencing before the death of the employee, if there is a designated beneficiary under the impermissible annuity distribution option for purposes of section 401(a)(9), the permissible annuity distribution option is the joint and survivor annuity option under the plan for the lives of the employee and the designated beneficiary which provides for the greatest level amount payable to the employee determined on an annual basis. If the plan does not provide such an option or there is no designated beneficiary under the impermissible distribution option for purposes of section 401(a)(9), the permissible annuity distribution option is the life annuity option under the plan payable for the life of the employee in level amounts with no survivor benefit.

(ii) In the case of distributions commencing after the death of the employee, if there is a designated beneficiary under the impermissible annuity distribution option for purposes of section 401(a)(9), the permissible annuity distribution option is the life annuity option under the plan payable for the life of the designated beneficiary in level amounts. If there is no designated beneficiary, the five year rule in section 401(a)(9)(B)(ii) applies. See subparagraph (3).

The determination of whether or not there is a designated beneficiary and the determination of which designated beneficiary life is to be used in the case of multiple beneficiaries will be made in accordance with § 1.401(a)(9)-1. See D-1 through D-3, D-5, E-1, and E-5 of § 1.401(a)(9)-1. If the defined benefit plan does not provide for distribution in the form of the applicable permissible distribution option, the minimum required distribution for each calendar year will be an amount as determined by the Commissioner.

(2) If the qualified retirement plan under which distributions are being made is a defined contribution plan and the impermissible annuity distribution option is an annuity contract purchased from an insurance company, the minimum amount required to be distributed each year will be the amount which would have been distributed in the form of an annuity contract under the permissible annuity distribution option under the plan determined in accordance with subparagraph (1) for defined benefit plans. If the defined contribution plan does not provide the applicable permissible annuity distribution option, the minimum required distribution for each calendar year will be the amount which would have been distributed under an annuity described below purchased with the employee's or individual's account used to purchase the annuity contract which is the impermissible annuity distribution option.

(i) In the case of distributions commencing before the death of the employee, if there is a designated beneficiary under the impermissible annuity distribution option for purposes of section 401(a)(9), the annuity is a joint and survivor annuity for the lives of the employee and the designated beneficiary which provides level annual payments and which would have been a permissible annuity distribution option. However, the amount of the periodic payment which would have been payable to the survivor will be the applicable percentage under the table in Q&A-6 of §1-401(a)(9)-2 of the amount of the periodic payment which would have been payable to the employee or individual. If there is no designated beneficiary under the impermissible distribution option for purposes of section 401(a)(9), the annuity is a life annuity for the life of the employee with no survivor benefit which provides level annual payments and which would have been a permissible annuity distribution option.

(ii) In the case of a distribution commencing after the death of the employee, if there is a designated beneficiary under the impermissible annuity distribution option for purposes of section 401(a)(9), the annuity option is a life annuity for the life of the designated beneficiary which provides level annual payments and which would have been a permissible annuity distribution option. If there is no designated beneficiary, the five year rule in section 401(a)(9)(B)(ii) applies. See subparagraph (3).

The amount of the payments under the annuity contract will be determined using the interest and mortality tables specified in §20.2031-7 of the Estate Tax Regulations. The determination of whether or not there is a designated beneficiary and the determination of which designated beneficiary's life is to be used in the case of multiple beneficiaries will be made in accordance with §1.401(a)(9)-1. See D-1 through D-3, D-5, and E-5 of §1.401(a)(9)-1.

(3) If the five-year rule in section 401(a)(9)(B)(ii) applies to the distribution to the payee under the contract (or distribution option), no amount is required to be distributed to satisfy the applicable enumerated section in paragraph (a) until the calendar year which contains the date five years after the date of the employee's death. For the calendar year which contains the date five years after the employee's death, the minimum amount required to be distributed to satisfy the applicable enumerated section is the payee's entire remaining interest in the annuity contract (or under the plan in the case of distributions from a defined benefit plan).

Q-4A. If there is any remaining benefit with respect to an employee (or IRA owner) after any calendar year in which the entire remaining benefit is required to be distributed under section, what is the amount of the minimum required distribution for each calendar year subsequent to such calendar year?

A. If there is any remaining benefit with respect to an employee (or IRA owner) after the calendar year in which the entire remaining benefit is required to be distributed, the minimum required distribution for each calendar year subsequent to such calendar year is the entire remaining benefit. For example, if there is any remaining benefit with respect to an employee (or IRA owner), for which the minimum required distribution is being determined under paragraph (b) of Q&A-4, after the calendar year in which the life (or lives) described therein expire, the minimum required distribution for each subsequent calendar year is the entire remaining benefit.

Q-5. If a payee has an interest under an eligible deferred compensation plan (as defined in section 457(b)), how is the minimum required distribution for a given taxable year of the payee determined for purposes of section 4974?

A. If a payee has an interest under an eligible deferred compensation plan (as defined in section 457(b)), the minimum required distribution for a given taxable year of the payee determined for purposes of section 4974 is determined under section 457(d).

Q-6. With respect to which calendar year is the excise tax under section 4974 imposed in the case in which the amount not distributed is an amount required to be distributed by April 1 of a calendar year (by the employee's or individual's required beginning date)?

A. In the case in which the amount not paid is an amount required to be paid by April 1 of a calendar year, such amount is a minimum required distribution for the previous calendar year, i.e., for the employee's or the individual's first distribution calendar year. However, the excise tax under section 4974 is imposed for the calendar year containing the last day by which the amount is required to be distributed, i.e., the calendar year containing the employee's or individual's required beginning date, even though the preceding calendar year is the calendar year for which the amount is required to be distributed. Pursuant to F-2 of §1.401(a)(9)-1, amounts distributed in the employee's or individual's first distribution calendar year will reduce the amount required to be distributed in the next calendar year by the employee's or individual's required beginning date. There is also a minimum required distribution for the calendar year which contains the employee's required beginning date. Such distribution is also required to be made during the calendar year which contains the employee's required beginning date.

Q-7. For what taxable years is the excise tax imposed under section 4974 effective?

A. The excise tax imposed under section 4974 as amended by 1121 of the Tax Reform Act of 1986 (TRA '86) is effective for payees' taxable years beginning after December 31, 1988. Consequently, with respect to qualified plans described in section 401(a), annuity contracts and custodial accounts described in section 403(b), and an eligible deferred compensation plans (as defined in section 457(b)), the excise tax imposed under section 4974 only applies for taxable years beginning after December 31, 1988. However, with respect to individual retirement plans described in section 408, an excise tax is also imposed under section 4974 for taxable years beginning before January 1, 1989.

Q-8. Are there any circumstances when the excise tax under section 4974 for a taxable year may be waived?

A. The tax under section 4974(a) may be waived if the payee described in section 4974(a) establishes to the satisfaction of the Commissioner the following:

(a) The shortfall described in section 4974(a) in the amount distributed in any taxable year was due to reasonable error, and

(b) Reasonable steps are being taken to remedy the shortfall.

Lawrence B. Gibbs,

Commissioner of Internal Revenue.

¶ 20,163C

Qualification of plans and trusts: Highly compensated employees: Definitions.—The IRS has issued temporary regulations (¶ 12,364E) that also serve as proposed regulations relating to the scope and meaning of the term "highly compensated employee" in Code Sec. 414(q). The proposed IRS regulations were published in the Federal Register on February 1, 1991 (56 FR 3976).

DEPARTMENT OF THE TREASURY

Internal Revenue Service

[26 CFR Part 1]

[EE-129-86]

RIN 1545-A066

Definition of highly compensated employee.

AGENCY: Internal Revenue Service, Treasury.

ACTION: Notice of proposed rulemaking by cross-reference to temporary regulations.

SUMMARY: In the Rules and Regulations portion of this issue of the Federal Register, the Internal Revenue Service is issuing temporary regulations relating to the scope and meaning of the term "highly compensated employee" in section 414(q) of the Internal Revenue

Code of 1986. They reflect changes made by the Tax Reform Act of 1986 (TRA '86). The text of those temporary regulations also serves as the text for this Notice of Proposed Rulemaking. These regulations will provide the public with guidance necessary to comply with the law and will affect sponsors of, and participants in, pension, profit-sharing and stock bonus plans, and certain other employee benefit plans.

DATES: Written comments must be reeived by April 2, 1991. Requests to speak (with outlines of oral comments) at a public hearing scheduled for Thursday, May 16, 1991, at 10:00 a.m., and continued, if necessary, on Friday, May 17, 1991, must be received by May 2, 1991. See the notice of hearing published elsewhere in this issue of the Federal Register.

ADDRESSES: Send comments and requests to speak (with outlines of oral comments) at the public hearing to: Internal Revenue Service, P.O. Box 7604, Ben Franklin Station, Attn: CC:CORP:T:R (EE-129-86), Room 4429, Washington, D.C. 20044.

FOR FURTHER INFORMATION CONTACT: Concerning the regulation, Thomas G. Schendt or Rhonda G. Migdail, Office of the Assistant Chief Counsel (Employee Benefits and Exempt Organizations), at 202-633-0849 (not a toll-free number). Concerning the hearing, Robert Boyer, Regulations Unit, at 202-566-3935 (not a toll free number).

SUPPLEMENTARY INFORMATION:

Background

The temporary regulations in the Rules and Regulations portion of this issue of the Federal Register amend 26 CFR by amending § 1.414(q)-1T to provide guidance with respect to the definition of a highly compensated employee within the meaning of section 414(q) of the Internal Revenue Code (Code). The regulations are proposed to be issued under the authority contained in sections 414(q) and 7805 of the Code 100 Stat. 2448, 68A Stat. 917; 26 U.S.C. 414(q), 7805. For the text of the temporary regulations, see T.D. 8334 published in the Rules and Regulations portion of this issue of the Federal Register.

Special analyses

It has been determined that these proposed rules are not major rules as defined in Executive Order 12291. Therefore, a Regulatory Impact Analysis is not required. It has been determined that section 553(b) of the Administrative Procedure Act (5 U.S.C. Chapter 5) and the Regulatory Flexibility Act (5 U.S.C. Chapter 6) do not apply to these regulations, and therefore, an initial Regulatory Flexibility Analysis is not required. Pursuant to section 7805(f) of the Internal Revenue Code, the proposed regulations are being sent to the Chief Counsel on Advocacy of the Small Business Administration for comment on their impact on small business.

Comments and requests for public hearing

Before adopting these proposed regulations, consideration will be given to any written comments that are submitted (preferably a signed original and eight copies) to the Commissioner of Internal Revenue. All comments will be available for public inspection and copying in their entirety. Because the Treasury Department expects to issue final regulations on this matter as soon as possible, a public hearing will be held at 10:00 a.m. on May 16, 1991, and continued, if necessary, on Friday, May 17, 1991, in the I.R.S. Auditorium, Seventh Floor, 7400 Corridor, Internal Revenue Building, 1111 Constitution Ave., N.W., Washington, D.C. 20224.

List of Subjects

26 CFR 1.401-0—1.425-1

Employee benefit plans, Employee stock ownership plans, Income taxes, Individual retirement accounts, Pensions, Stock options.

Michael J. Murphy

Acting Commissioner of Internal Revenue

[¶ 20,164 Reserved.—Proposed regulation under Code Sec. 120, relating to the application for recognition as a qualified group legal services plan, was formerly reproduced at this point. The final regulation is at ¶ 11,285.]

¶ 20,164A

Proposed regulations on qualified group legal services plans.—Reproduced below is the text of proposed Reg. §§ 1.1201, 1.1202, and 1.501(c)(20)-1, which provide guidance for complying with the Tax Reform Act of 1976. The proposed regulations were published in the Federal Register of April 29, 1980 (45 FR 28360).

DEPARTMENT OF THE TREASURY

Internal Revenue Service

26 CFR Part 1

[EE-5-78]

Income Tax; Qualified Group Legal Services Plans

AGENCY: Internal Revenue Service, Treasury.

ACTION: Notice of proposed rulemaking.

SUMMARY: This document contains proposed regulations relating to qualified group legal services plans. Changes to the applicable tax law were made by the Tax Reform Act of 1976. The regulations would provide the public with the guidance needed to comply with that Act and would affect both employers who establish group legal services plans and employees and their spouses and dependents who receive benefits under these plans.

DATES: Written comments and requests for a public hearing must be delivered or mailed by June 30, 1980. The amendments are generally proposed to be effective for taxable years beginning after December 31, 1976, and ending before January 1, 1982.

ADDRESS: Send comments and requests for a public hearing to: Commissioner of Internal Revenue, Attention: CC:LR:T:EE-5-78, Washington, D.C. 20224.

FOR FURTHER INFORMATION CONTACT: Richard L. Johnson of the Employee Plans and Exempt Organizations Division, Office of the Chief Counsel, Internal Revenue Service, 1111 Constitution Avenue, NW., Washington, D.C. 20224, Attention CC:LR:T:EE-5-78, 202-566-3544 (Not a toll-free number).

SUPPLEMENTARY INFORMATION:

Background

This document contains proposed amendments to the Income Tax Regulations (26 CFR Part 1) under sections 120 and 501(c)(20) of the Internal Revenue Code of 1954, as added by section 2134 of the Tax Reform Act of 1976 (90 Stat. 1926). The amendments are to be issued under the authority contained in sections 120 and 7805 of the Internal Revenue Code of 1954 (90 Stat. 1926, 68A Stat. 917; 26 U. S. C. 120, 7805).

Prepaid Legal Services

Code section 120(a) excludes from the gross income of an employee, and the employee's spouse or dependent, employer contributions made on their behalf to a qualified group legal services plan. The value of legal services provided, or amounts paid for legal services, under the plan are also excluded from gross income.

Qualified Group Legal Services Plans

In order for a group legal services plan to be a qualified plan, the plan must satisfy certain requirements relating principally to nondiscrimination in employer contributions, plan benefits and eligibility for participation, the limitation on employer contributions for participants who are shareholders or owners, and the means by which the plan is funded. If the plan is funded by means of a trust, subject to certain requirements, the trust is exempt from tax.

Deletion of Regulations Under Repealed Code Provision

Existing § 1.120-1 of the Income Tax Regulations provides regulations under Code section 120, relating to statutory subsistence allowance received by police, which was repealed by section 3 of the Technical Amendments Act of 1958 (72 Stat. 1607). This section is being deleted.

Comments and Requests for a Public Hearing

Before adopting these proposed regulations, consideration will be given to any written comments that are submitted (pre-ferably six copies) to the Commissioner of Internal Revenue. All comments will be available for public inspection and copying. A public hearing will be held upon written request to the Commissioner by any person who has submitted written comments. If a public hearing is held, notice of the time and place will be published in the *Federal Register*.

Drafting Information

The principal author of these proposed regulations is Richard L. Johnson of the Employee Plans and Exempt Organizations Division of the Office of Chief Counsel, Internal Revenue Service. However, personnel from other offices of the Internal Revenue Service and Treasury Department participated in developing the regulation, both on matters of substance and style.

Proposed Amendments to the Regulations

The proposed amendments to 26 CFR Part 1 are as follows:

§ 1.120-1 [Deleted]

Paragraph 1. Section 1.120-1, relating to statutory subsistence allowances received by police, is deleted.

Par. 2. New §§ 1.120-1 and 1.120-2 are added in the appropriate place:

§ 1.120-1 Amounts received under a qualified group legal services plan.

(a) *Exclusion from gross income.* The gross income of an employee, or the employee's spouse or dependent, does not include—

(1) Amounts contributed by an employer on behalf of the employee, spouse, or dependent under a qualified group legal services plan described in § 1.120-2,

(2) The value of legal services provided the employee, spouse or dependent under the plan, or

(3) Amounts paid to the employee, spouse or dependent under the plan as reimbursement for the cost of personal legal services provided to the employee, spouse or dependent.

(b) *Definitions.* For rules relating to the meaning of the terms "employee," "employer," "spouse," and "dependent" see paragraph (d)(3) and (4) and paragraph (i) of § 1.120-2.

(c) *Effective date.* This section is effective with respect to employer contributions made on behalf of, and legal services provided to, an employee, spouse or dependent on or after the first day of the period of plan qualification (as determined under § 1.120-3(d)) and in taxable years of the employee, spouse or dependent beginning after December 31, 1976, and ending before January 1, 1982.

§ 1.120-2 Qualified group legal services plan.

(a) *In general.* In general, a qualified group legal services plan is a plan established and maintained by an employer under which the employer provides employees, or their spouses or dependents, personal legal services by prepaying, or providing in advance for, all or part of the legal fees for the services. To be a qualified plan, the plan must satisfy the requirements described in paragraphs (b) through (h) of this section and be recognized as a qualified plan by the Internal Revenue Service. Section 1.120-3 provides rules under which a plan must apply to the Internal Revenue Service for recognition as a qualified plan.

(b) *Separate written plan.* The plan must be a separate written plan of the employer. For purposes of this section—

(1) *Plan.* The term "plan" implies a permanent as distinguished from a temporary program. Thus, although the employer may reserve the right to change or terminate the plan, and to discontinue contributions thereunder, the abandonment of the plan for any reason other than a business necessity soon after it has taken effect will be evidence that the plan from its inception was not a *bona fide* plan for the benefit of employees generally (see paragraph (d) of this section). Such evidence will be given special weight if, for example, a plan is abandoned soon after extensive benefits are provided to persons with respect to whom discrimination in plan benefits is prohibited (see paragraph (e) of this section).

(2) *Separate plan.* The requirement that the plan be a separate plan means that the plan may not provide benefits which are not personal legal services within the meaning of paragraph (c) of this section. For example, the requirement for a separate plan is not satisfied if personal legal services are provided under an employee benefit plan that also

provides pension, disability, life insurance, medical or other such non-legal benefits. The requirement for a separate plan does not, however, preclude a single plan from being adopted by more than one employer.

(c) *Personal legal services*—(1) *In general.* In general, benefits under the plan must consist of, or be provided with respect to, only personal legal services that are specified in the plan. The plan must specifically prohibit a diversion or use of any funds of the plan for purposes other than the providing of personal legal services for the participants. In general, a personal legal service is a legal service (within the meaning of subparagraph (3) of this paragraph) provided to a participant employee, spouse or dependent which is not directly connected with or pertaining to—

(i) A trade or business of the employee, spouse or dependent,

(ii) The management, conservation or preservation of property held by the employee, spouse or dependent for the production of income, or

(iii) The production or collection of income by the employee, spouse or dependent.

(2) *Certain personal legal services.* Notwithstanding subparagraph (1)(ii) and (iii) of this paragraph, the following (if legal services within the meaning of subparagraph (3)) are considered personal legal services—

(i) A legal service provided to a participant with respect to securing, increasing or collecting alimony under a decree of divorce (or payments in lieu of alimony) or the division or redivision of community property under the community property laws of the State,

(ii) A legal service provided to a participant as heir or legatee of a decedent, or as beneficiary under a testamentary trust, in protecting or asserting rights to property of a decedent, or

(iii) A legal service provided to a participant with respect to the participant's claim for damages, other than compensatory damages, for personal injury.

(3) *Legal services*—(i) *Services of a lawyer.* In general, a legal service is a service performed by a lawyer if the performing of the service constitutes the practice of law.

(ii) *Services of a person not a lawyer.* A legal service may include a service performed by a person who is not a lawyer, if the service is performed under the direction or control of a lawyer, in conection with a legal service (within the meaning of subdivision (i)) performed by the lawyer, and the fee for the service is included in the legal fee of the lawyer. Examples of services to which this subdivision (ii) may apply are the services of an accountant, a researcher, a paralegal, a law clerk, an investigator or a searcher of title to real property.

(iii) *Court fees.* Amounts payable to a court in connection with the presentation, litigation or appeal from a matter before a court is considered the cost of a legal service. For example, benefits under the plan may be provided with respect to a court filing fee, a fee for service of summons or other process, the cost of a transcript of trial or the posting of bail bond.

(iv) *Other fees or charges.* An amount payable to a competent governmental authority (for example, the United States, a State or any subdivision thereof) is considered the cost of a legal service, if the amount is payable with respect to the filing or registration of a legal document (for example, a deed or will). However, any amount payable directly or indirectly to a governmental authority is not the cost of a legal service, if the amount is in the nature of a tax. For example, although a plan may provide for payment of an amount payable to a county for the filing or registration of a deed to real property, a plan may not provide for payment of an amount in the nature of a tax on the transfer of title to real property.

(4) *Limited initial consultation.* A plan is not other than a qualified plan merely because, in connection with providing personal legal services, the plan provides a specified "limited initial consultation" benefit without restricting the benefit to personal legal services. An "initial consultation" is a consultation, the purpose of which is to determine whether a plan participant is in need of a personal legal service and, if so, whether the required personal legal service may be provided under the plan. An initial consultation must not include document preparation or review, or representation of the participant. An initial consultation benefit is "limited", if under the plan it is limited either in time (*e.g.,* no more than 4 hours of initial consultation during any year) or number (*e.g.,* no more than 4 initial consultations during any year).

(d) *Exclusive benefit* —(1) *In general.* The plan must benefit only employees of the employer, including individuals who are employees within the meaning of paragraph (i)(1) of this section, or the spouses or dependents of employees.

(2) *Plans to which more than one employer contributes.* In the case of a plan to which more than one employer contributes, in determining whether the plan is for the exclusive benefit of an employer's employees, or their spouses or dependents, the employees of any employer who maintains the plan are considered the employees of each employer who maintains the plan.

(3) *Spouses of employees.* In general, for purposes of determining whether a plan is for the exclusive benefit of an employer's employees, or their spouses or dependents, the determination of whether an individual is a spouse of an employee is made at the time the legal services are provided to the individual. The term "spouse" includes a surviving spouse of a deceased employee. Although, in general, the term "spouse" does not include a person legally spearated from an employee under a decree of divorce or separate maintenance, a legal service provided to an employee's former spouse after the issuing of a decree of divorce, annulment or separate maintenance from the employee is considered a service provided to the spouse of an employee, if the service relates to the divorce, annulment or separation. For purposes of this section and § 1.120-1, the term "spouse" includes an individual to whom benefits may be provided under this subparagraph.

(4) *Dependents of employees.* For purposes of determining whether a plan is for the exclusive benefit of an employer's employees, or their spouses or dependents, benefits provided to the following individuals are considered benefits provided to a dependent of an employee:

(i) An individual who is a dependent of an employee within the meaning of section 152 for the taxable year of the employee within which the legal services are provided to the individual;

(ii) An individual who is described in paragraph (h)(2) of this section (relating to certain surviving dependents) at the time the legal services are provided to the individual; or

(iii) An individual who is a dependent of an employee within the meaning of section 152 for the taxable year of the employee ending on the date of the employee's death, under age 21 on the date of the employee's death, and under age 21 at the time the legal services are provided to the individual.

For purposes of this section and § 1.120-1, the term "dependent" means an individual to whom benefits may be provided under this subparagraph.

(5) *Estates of employees.* A plan is for the exclusive benefit of the employer's employees, or their spouses or dependents, notwithstanding that the plan provides benefits to the personal representative of a deceased employee, or spouse or dependent, with respect to the estate of the deceased.

(e) *Prohibited discrimination*—(1) *In general.* The plan must benefit the employer's employees generally. Among those benefited may be employees who are officers, shareholders, self-employed or highly compensated. A plan is not for the benefit of employees generally, however, if the plan discriminates in favor of employees described in the preceding sentence, or their spouses or dependents, in eligibility requirements (see subparagraph (2) of this paragraph) or in contributions or benefits (see subparagraph (3) of this paragraph).

(2) *Eligibility to participate.* A plan need not provide benefits for all employees (or their spouses or dependents). A plan must, however, benefit those employees (or their spouses or dependents) who qualify under a classification of employees set up by the employer which is found by the Internal Revenue Service not to discriminate in favor of employees who are officers, shareholders, self-employed or highly compensated, or their spouses or dependents. In general, this determination shall be made by applying the same standards as are applied under section 410(b)(1)(B) (relating to qualified pension, profit-sharing and stock bonus plans), without regard to section 401(a)(5). For purposes of making this determination, there shall be excluded from consideration employees not covered by the plan who are included in a unit of employees covered by an agreement which the Secretary of Labor finds to be a collective bargaining agreement between employee representatives and one or more employers, if the Internal Revenue Service finds that group legal services plan benefits were the subject of good faith bargaining between the employee representatives and the employer or employers. For purposes of determining whether such bargaining occurred, it is not material that the employees are not covered by another plan or that the employer's present plan was not considered in the bargaining.

(3) *Contributions and benefits*—(i) *In general.* Employer contributions under the plan or benefits provided under the plan must not discriminate in favor of employees who are officers, shareholders, self-employed or highly compensated, or their spouses or dependents, as against other employees, or their spouses or dependents, covered by

the plan. This does not mean that contributions or benefits may not vary. Variations in contributions or benefits may be provided so long as the plan, viewed as a whole for the benefit of employees in general, with all its attendant circumstances, does not discriminate in favor of those with respect to whom discrimination is prohibited. Thus, contributions or benefits which vary by reason of a formula which takes into account years of service with the employer, or other factors, are not prohibited unless those factors discriminate in favor of employees who are officers, shareholders, self-employed or highly compensated, or their spouses or dependents. Under this subparagraph (3), if a plan covers employees who are highly compensated, and benefits under the plan uniformly increase as compensation increases, the plan is not a qualified plan.

(ii) *Relative utilization of plan benefits.* Not only must a plan not discriminate on its face in employer contributions or plan benefits in favor of employees who are officers, shareholders, self-employed or highly compensated, or their spouses or dependents, the plan also must not discriminate in favor of such employees, or their spouses or dependents, in actual operation. Accordingly, the extent to which such employees, or their spouses or dependents, as a group, utilize plan benefits must be compared to the extent to which all other employees, or their spouses or dependents, as a group, utilize plan benefits. A plan is not other than a qualified plan for a plan year merely because, relative to their number, those employees, or their spouses or dependents, with respect to whom discrimination is prohibited utilize plan benefits to a greater extent than do other employees, or their spouses or dependents. However, a persistent pattern of greater relative utilization of plan benefits by the group of employees who are officers, shareholders, self-employed or highly compensated, or their spouses or dependents, may be evidence that the plan discriminates in favor of such employees and is not for the benefit of employees generally. Such evidence will be considered, together with all other pertinent facts and circumstances, to determine whether the plan improperly discriminates in actual operation.

(f) *Contribution limitation*—(1) *In general.* Under section 120(c)(3), a plan is a qualified plan for a plan year only if no more than 25% of the amount contributed by the employer under the plan for the plan year is contributed on behalf of the limitation class described in subparagraph (2). A plan satisfies the requirements of section 120(c)(3) for a plan year (as determined under the plan) if either—

(i) The plan satisfies the requirements of subparagraph (3), or

(ii) The percentage determined under subparagraph (4) is 25% or less, and the plan is not other than a qualified plan by reason of subparagraph (5).

(2) *Limitation class.* The limitation class consists of—

(i) *Shareholders.* Individuals who, on any day of the plan year, own more than 5% of the total number of shares of outstanding stock of the employer, or

(ii) *Owners.* In the case of an employer's trade or business, which is not incorporated, individuals who on any day of the plan year, own more than 5% of the capital or profits interest in the employer, and

(iii) *Spouses and dependents.* Individuals who are spouses or dependents of shareholders or owners described in subdivision (i) or (ii). For purposes of determining stock ownership, the attribution rules described in paragraph (i)(4) of this section apply. The regulations prescribed under section 414(c) are applicable in determining an individual's interest in the capital or profits of an unincorporated trade or business.

(3) *Disregarding allocation rules*—(i) *Plans providing legal services directly.* If a plan is one under which legal services are provided directly to a participant, the plan will satisfy the requirements of section 120(c)(3), without regard to the allocation rules described in subparagraphs (4) and (5) of this paragraph, if the plan satisfies the following requirement. The plan must provide and be operated so that no legal service may be provided to a member of the limitation class if to provide the service would cause the fair market value of legal services provided to date during the plan year to members of the limitation class to exceed 25% of the fair market value of the legal services provided under the plan to date during the plan year.

(ii) *Plans providing reimbursement for the cost of legal services.* If a plan is one under which a participant is reimbursed for the cost of legal services, the plan will satisfy the requirements of section 120(c)(3), without regard to the allocation rules described in subparagraphs (4) and (5) of this paragraph, if the plan satisfies the following requirement. The plan must provide and be operated so that no amount may be paid to a member of the limitation class if the payment would cause amounts paid to date during the plan year to members of the limitation class to exceed 25% of the amounts paid under the plan to date during the plan year.

(iii) *Limitation class; special rule.* For purposes of this subparagraph (3) an individual is a member of the limitation class only if the individual is a member (within the meaning of subparagraph (2)) on or before the date on which the determination described in subdivision (ii) or (iii) is required to be made.

(iv) *Example.* The provisions of subdivision (iii) of this subparagraph may be illustrated by the following example:

Example. (A) Plan X is a qualified group legal services plan under which plan participants are reimbursed for the cost of personal legal services specified in the plan. The plan includes a provision satisfying the requirements of subdivision (ii) of this subparagraph. The plan year is the calendar year.

(B) A, an individual, is a participant in Plan X. On March 18, 1981, A is paid an amount under the plan. On June 21, 1981, A purchases shares of stock of the employer maintaining the plan. As a result of the purchase A owns more than 5% of the total number of shares of outstanding stock of the employer. Accordingly, under subparagraph (2) of this paragraph, A is a member of the limited class for the plan year 1981. On August 14, 1981, A sells the shares of stock purchased on June 21, 1981, and no longer owns more than 5% of the total number of shares of outstanding stock of the employer. On October 9, 1981, A is paid an additional amount under the plan.

(C) For purposes of the determination required by subdivision (ii) of this subparagraph, if the determination is made for a date after March 17, 1981, and before June 21, 1981, the amount paid to A on March 18, 1981, is not considered an amount paid to a member of the limitation class. If the determination is made for a date after June 20, 1981, the amount paid to A on March 18, 1981, is considered an amount paid to a member of the limitation class. With respect to a determination made for a date after October 8, 1981, the amount paid to A on October 9, 1981, is considered an amount paid to a member of the limitation class.

(4) *Contribution allocation*—(i) *Equal benefits.* In general, if under a plan the same benefits are made available to each participant, the percentage of the amount contributed by the employer for a plan year that is considered contributed on behalf of the limitation class is equal to the number of participants who are members of the limitation class at any time during the plan year, divided by the number of individuals who are participants in the plan at any time during the plan year.

(ii) *Unequal benefits.* In general, if under the plan different benefits are made available to different participants or different classes of participants, the percentage of the amount contributed by the employer for a plan year that is considered contributed on behalf of the limitation class is equal to the fair market value (as of the first day of the plan year) of those benefits available under the plan to participants who are members of the limitation class at any time during the plan year, divided by the fair market value (as of the first day of the plan year) of those benefits available under the plan to all individuals who are participants in the plan at any time during the plan year.

(iii) *Individual premiums.* Notwithstanding subdivision (i) or (ii) of this subparagraph, if benefits are provided under the plan in exchange for the employer's prepayment or payment of a premium, and the amount of the prepayment or premium is determined by taking into account the circumstances of individual participants or classes of participants, the percentage of the amount contributed by the employer for a plan year that is considered contributed on behalf of the limitation class is equal to the sum of the prepayments or premiums paid for the plan year on behalf of participants who are members of the limitation class at any time during the plan year, divided by the sum of the prepayments or premiums paid for the plan year. A prepayment or premium is paid for the plan year if it is paid with respect to legal services provided or made available during the plan year. This subdivision (iii) will apply if, for example, equal benefits are provided each participant under the plan in exchange for the employer's payment of a premium with respect to each participant employee, and the amount of the premium varies, taking into account the employee's income level, the number and ages of the employee's dependents or other such factors.

(5) *Relative utilization of plan benefits*—(i) *Application.* The extent to which members of the limitation class, as a class, utilize plan benefits shall be taken into account in determining the percentage of amounts contributed by the employer that is considered contributed on behalf of the limitation class. The rules described in this subparagraph (5) are in addition to those described in subparagraph (4) of this paragraph, and a plan may be other than a qualified plan by reason of the application of this subparagraph (5), notwithstanding that the percentage determined under subparagraph (4) is 25% or less.

(ii) *Computation.* Under this subparagraph (5), if during any three successive plan years, benefits paid to or with respect to the limitation class (as determined for each plan year) exceed 25% of all benefits paid under the plan during the three years, the plan is not a qualified plan for the next succeeding plan year.

(iii) *Reapplication for recognition as a qualified plan.* A plan that is not a qualified plan for a plan year by reason of this subparagraph (5), may reapply under § 1.120-3 for recognition as a qualified plan for any plan year following the first plan year for which it is not a qualified plan. A plan so reapplying will be recognized as a qualified plan for any plan year for which recognition is sought only if the plan is a qualified plan under this subparagraph (5) for the first plan year for which such recognition is sought and otherwise satisfies the requirements of section 120 and this section.

(g) *Employer contributions*—(1) *In general.* Employer contributions under the plan may be made only—

(i) To insurance companies, or to organizations or persons that provide personal legal services, or indemnification against the cost of personal legal services, in exchange for a prepayment or payment of a premium,

(ii) To organizations or trusts described in section 501(c)(20),

(iii) To organizations described in section 510(c) that are permitted by that section to receive payments from an employer for support of a qualified group legal services plan, except that the organization shall pay or credit the contribution to an organization or trust described in section 501(c)(20),

(iv) As prepayment to providers of legal services under the plan, or

(v) A combination of the above.

(2) *Prepayment required.* For purposes of subparagraph (1)(i) and (iv), employer contributions are considered prepayments or premiums only if a contribution made with respect to benefits reasonably anticipated to be provided under the plan during any month is made on or before the tenth day of the month.

(h) *Employee contributions*—(1) *In general.* A plan is not a qualified plan if it permits participants to contribute under the plan other than as described in subparagraphs (2) and (3) of this paragraph.

(2) *Certain separated employees and surviving spouses and dependents.* A plan will not be other than a qualified plan merely because the plan allows—

(i) A separated former employee,

(ii) A surviving spouse of a deceased employee, or

(iii) An individual who is a dependent of an employee within the meaning of section 152 for the taxable year of the employee ending on the date of the death of the employee, to elect to continue as a participant under the plan on a self-contributory basis for a period not to exceed one year after the separation or death.

(3) *Certain employee contributions in lieu of employer contributions.* This subparagraph (3) applies with respect to a plan that—

(i) Is maintained pursuant to an agreement that the Secretary of Labor finds to be a collective bargaining agreement between employee representatives and one or more employers, and

(ii) Provides that an employer is required to contribute (or contribute in full) on behalf of a participant employee only if the employee completes a minimum number of hours of service with the employer within a stated period ending on or before the date the contribution is otherwise required to be made by the employer.

Such a plan is not other than a qualified plan merely because it permits a participant employee to contribute under the plan an amount not required to he contributed by the employer because the employee fails to complete the minimum number of hours. However, no amount may be contributed by an employee under this subparagraph (3) unless employer contributions on behalf of participant employees are required to be made monthly or more often, and at least one employer contribution is made on behalf of the employee under the plan before the contribution by the employee is made under the plan. In addition, a plan shall not be a qualified plan for a plan year by reason of this subparagraph (3), if amounts contributed by employees under this subparagraph (3) during the plan year exceed 5% of the total amount contributed wider the plan during the plan year.

(i) *Definitions.* For purposes of this section, § 1.120-1 and § 1.120-3—

(1) *Employee.* The term "employee" includes—

(i) A retired, disabled or, laid-off employee,

(ii) A present employee who is on leave, as, for example, in the Armed Forces of the United States,

(iii) An individual who is self-employed within the meaning of section 401(c)(1), or

(iv) A separated former employee who is covered by the plan by reason of paragraph (h)(2)(i) of this section (relating to employee contributions).

(2) *Employer.* An individual who owns the entire interest in an unincorporated trade or business is treated as his or her own employer. A partnership is treated as the employer of each partner who is an employee within the meaning of section 401(c)(1).

(3) *Officer.* An officer is an individual who is an officer within the meaning of regulations prescribed under section 414(c).

(4) *Shareholder.* The term "shareholder" includes an individual who is a shareholder as determined by the attribution rules under section 1563(d) and (e), without regard to section 1563(e)(3)(C).

(5) *Highly compensated.* The term "highly compensated" has the same meaning as it does for purposes of section 410(b)(1)(B).

Par. 3. There is added in the appropriate place the following new section:

§ 1.501(c)(20)-1 *Qualified group legal services plan trust.*

(a) *Qualified group legal services plan.* For purposes of this section, a "qualified group legal services plan" is a plan that satisfies the requirements of section 120(b) and § 1.120-2.

(b) *General requirements for exemption.* Under section 501(c)(20), an organization or trust created or organized in the United States is exempt as provided in section 501(a) if the exclusive function of the organization or trust is to form part of a qualified group legal services plan or plans.

(c) *Exception for trust associated with section 501(c) organization.* As described in section 120(c)(5)(C), employer contributions under a qualified group legal services plan may be paid to an organization described in section 501(c) if that organization is permitted by section 501(c) to receive payments from an employer for support of a qualified group legal services plan. However, that organization must, in turn, pay or credit the contributions to an organization or trust described in section 501(c)(20). In such a case, the organization or trust to which the contributions are finally paid or credited is considered to satisfy the require-ment that the *exclusive* function of the organization or trust be to form part of a qualified group legal services plan or plans, notwithstanding that the organization or trust provides legal services or indemnification against the cost of legal services unassociated with such a qualified plan. This exception applies, however, only if any such legal service or indemnification is provided under a program established and maintained by the organization described in section 501(c) to which the employer contributions under a qualified group legal services plan are first paid under section 120(c)(5)(C). Whether providing legal services or indemnification against the cost of legal services unassociated with a qualified group legal services plan is a permissible activity of an organization described in section 501(c) is determined under the rules under that paragraph of section 501(c) in which the organization is described.

Jerome Kurtz,

Commissioner of Internal Revenue.

[FR Doc. 80-13072 Filed 4-28-80; 8:45 am]

[¶ 20,165 Reserved.—Proposed regulations defining the term "reasonable actuarial method of valuation" for purposes of computing the minimum funding standard for pension plans were formerly reproduced at this point. The final regulations are at ¶ 12,250U.]

[¶ 20,165A Reserved.—Proposed regulations relating to the procedure for electing an alternative amortization method of funding certain pension plans formerly appeared at this point. The final regulations are at ¶ 12,250G.]

¶ 20,165B

Proposed regulations prescribing rules for determining if the vesting schedule of a qualified plan discriminates in favor of employees who are officers, shareholders, or highly compensated.—Reproduced below is the text of proposed Reg. § 1.411(d)-1(c)(2) which modifies previously proposed regulations (CCH Pension Plan Guide, ¶ 20,172). The proposed regulations also withdraw § 1.411(d)-(d) of the previously proposed regulation. The proposed regulations were filed with the Federal Register on June 9, 1980.

DEPARTMENT OF THE TREASURY

Internal Revenue Service

[26 CFR Part 1]

[EE-164-78]

Coordination Of Vesting And Discrimination Requirements For Qualified Plans

Notice Of Proposed Rulemaking

AGENCY: Internal Revenue Service, Treasury.

ACTION: Notice of proposed rulemaking.

SUMMARY: This document contains modifications to proposed regulations, published in the FEDERAL REGISTER for April 9, 1980 (45 FR 24201), relating to coordination of vesting and discrimination requirements for qualified pension, etc. plans. These modifications to the proposed regulations have been prepared in response to the comments received on the proposed regulation. The test for determining the existence of discriminatory vesting is reproposed in modified form and the "safe harbors" against a finding of discriminatory vesting are withdrawn.

DATES: A public hearing on the notice of proposed rulemaking published April 9, 1980, has been scheduled for July 10, 1980. A notice of the public hearing was published in the FEDERAL REGISTER on May 2, 1980. Outlines of oral comments for the public hearing must be delivered or mailed by June 26, 1980. Written comments on the modifications set forth in this notice must be delivered or mailed by [60 days after publication of this notice in the FEDERAL REGISTER].

ADDRESS: Send comments to: Commissioner of Internal Revenue, Attention: CC:LR:T (EE-164-78), Washington, D. C. 20224.a favorable advance determination letter. If a plan failed to satisfy these tests, a favorable determination letter was not issued unless the plan adopted the accelerated vesting schedule set forth in the Procedure (so-called "4/40 vesting").

Revenue Procedure 76-11, 1976-1 C.B. 550, was issued pending reconsideration of Revenue Procedure 75-49. That Procedure adopted two new alternative means of satisfying the requirements of section 411(d)(1) in order to secure a favorable advance determination letter, in addition to the tests contained in Revenue Procedure 75-49.

One of the new alternatives contained in Revenue Procedure 76-11 is to establish that the plan had previously received a favorable advance determination letter which had not been revoked, and that the percentage of vesting of each participant under the plan as amended is not less (at every point) than that provided under the vesting schedule of the plan when it received the most recent favorable prior determination letter.

The other new alternative contained in Revenue Procedure 76-11 is a demonstration, on the basis of all of the facts and circumstances that there have not been, and that there is no reason to believe there will be, any discriminatory accruals.

Revenue Procedure 76-11 also provided that a plan could secure a favorable determination letter without regard to whether the vesting is nondiscriminatory.

However, the determination letters processed in this manner contained a caveat to the effect that such letter is not a determination as to whether the vesting provisions of the plan satisfy the nondiscrimination requirements of section 401(a)(4).

The tests of Revenue Procedures 75-49 and 76-11 are applied only with respect to whether a plan could receive a favorable advance determination letter. The determination letter, by its terms, provided that the approval of the plan's qualified status by the Internal Revenue Service did not separate tests for determining discrimination in vesting where necessary with respect to the issuance of a determination letter and with respect to testing the operation of the plan's vesting schedule.

Thus, an employer could receive a favorable advance determination letter, but would have no protection against a finding that the plan's vesting schedule was discriminatory in operation. The proposed rules remove this separate testing of form and operation, and provide that the test for discriminatory vesting shall be made, in both situations, on the basis of the facts and circumstances. Thus, if a plan has a favorable advance determination letter based on the facts and circumstances test of the proposed rules, this determination will protect the plan from a finding of discriminatory vesting in operation, provided the facts and circumstances have not materially changed since the determination letter was issued.

Additionally, plans which currently possess certain types of favorable determination letters will be treated as if their determination letter was processed under the facts and circumstances test contained in the proposed rules. The plans which will be given this treatment are those which received their favorable determination letter based on their satisfying one or more of the following tests:

1. the key employee and/or the turnover test of Revenue Procedure 75-49;

2. the prior letter tests of Revenue Procedure 76-11; or

3. the facts and circumstances test of Revenue Procedure 76-11. Thus, a plan described above would also be protected against a finding of discriminatory vesting in operation, based on its outstanding favorable determination letter, provided the facts and circumstances have not materially changed.

Safe Harbors

Paragraph (d) of proposed regulation § 1.411(d)-1, as published in the FEDERAL REGISTER on April 9, 1980, sets forth two safe harbors against a finding of discriminatory vesting. Both of the safe harbors required the adoption of a vesting schedule substantially more rapid than 4/40 vesting. many of the commentators viewed this as an attempt to require that all plans adopt either one of these accelerated vesting schedules. Because that was not the intent of the proposed rules, the portion of the proposed regulation containing the safe harbors is withdrawn.

However, this deletion should not be interpreted as meaning that 4/40 vesting is a safe harbor. Comments are requested from the public as to the desirability of reinstating a safe harbor and, if so, on what basis.

Test For Discriminatory Vesting

Paragraph (c)(2) of proposed regulation § 1.411(d)-1, as published in the FEDERAL REGISTER on April 9, 1980, sets forth certain factors to be considered in applying the facts and circumstances test for discriminatory vesting. These factors were included simply to reflect current Internal Revenue Service practice and to provide greater guidance to both employers and to Internal Revenue Service personnel. The factors were not intended to create new standards.

Nevertheless, many commentators interpreted the recital of specific factors as substantially increasing their burden of establishing that the plan's vesting schedule is nondiscriminatory. Accordingly, the list of specific factors is deleted in the reproposed test for discriminatory vesting.

The determination of whether the vesting schedule of a plan is discriminatory, under the reproposed rules, shall be made on the basis of the facts and circumstances of each case. The reproposed rules now specifically provide that a plan's vesting schedule is nondiscriminatory if the disparity between the vested benefits provided to the prohibited group and the vested benefits provided to all other employees is reasonable.

Additional Guidance

It is anticipated that additional guidance regarding the application of the facts and circumstances test for discriminatory vesting will be provided in revenue rulings and procedures issued at the time the regulations are published in final form. Accordingly, comments are requested as to whether the following examples are appropriate for this purpose:

Example 1. A plan has the "10 year cliff" vesting schedule described in section 411(a)(2)(A) for all employees. Employment turnover among

member of the prohibited group is less than that for all other employees because the prohibited group tends to stay longer with the company. Nevertheless, the present value of the vested benefits for the officers and 5% shareholders (determined using the attribution rules of section 1563(e), without regard to section 1563(e)(3)(C)), is less than the present value of the vested benefits of all other employees. Because the vested benefits provided employees who are not officers or shareholders are greater than that provided officers and shareholders, the plan's vesting schedule is not considered to be discriminatory.

Example 2. The facts are the same as in *Example 1,* except that there has been no comparison of the pr3esent values of the vested benefits of each group of employees. However, it is clear that the class of employees who have bested benefits, considering those employees alone and not any nonvested employees, would satisfy the nondiscriminatory classification test of section 410(b)(1)(B) by covering a reasonable cross section. Because a reasonable cross section of all employees under the plan have bested benefits, the vesting schedule of the plan is not considered to be discriminatory. [When the example is published, specific facts along the lines of Revenue Ruling 70-200, 1970-1 C.B. 101, Revenue Ruling 74-255, 1974-1 C.B. 93, and Revenue Ruling 74-256, 1974-1 C.B. 94, will be included to illustrate the reasonable cross section test.]

Example 3. Company B has a plan that satisfies the minimum participation requirements of section 410. The plan provides for 4/40 vesting. In its six years of operation the plan has always covered five employees. Because of the high rate of employee turnover, the only employee, past or present, to earn vested benefit under the plan is X. X is the sole shareholder of Company B. Absent a showing of other facts and circumstances, the vesting schedule of the plan is discriminatory.

Comments And Public Hearing

Before adopting these proposed regulations, consideration will be given to any written comments that are submitted (preferably eight copies) to the Commissioner of Internal Revenue. All comments will be available for public inspection and copying. As indicated above, a public hearing has already been scheduled on the proposed regulations published April 9, 1980. Anyone wishing to comment on these modifications may do so at the hearing.

Drafting Information

The principal author of this regulation is Kirk F. Maldonado of the Employee Plans and Exempt Organizations Division of the Office of Chief Counsel, Internal Revenue Service. however, personnel from other offices of the Internal Revenue Service and the Treasury Department participated in developing the regulation, both on matters of substance and style.

Proposed Amendments To The Regulations

Accordingly, the notice of proposed rulemaking published in the FEDERAL REGISTER for April 9, 1980 (45 FR 24201) is modified as follows:

1. Paragraph (d) of § 1.411(d)-1, as set forth in the notice of proposed rulemaking published in the FEDERAL REGISTER for April 9, 1980 (45 FR 24201) is withdrawn.

2. Paragraph (c)(2) of § 1.411(d)-1, as set forth in the notice of proposed rulemaking published in the FEDERAL REGISTER for April 9, 1980 (45 FR 24201) is modified to read as follows:

§ 1.411(d)-1 Coordination of vesting and discrimination requirements.

* * *

(c) *Discriminatory vesting.* * * *

(2) *Test for discriminatory vesting.* The determination of whether there is, or there is reason to believe there will be, discriminatory vesting shall be made on the basis of the facts and circumstances of each case. A reasonable disparity between the vested benefits paid to or accrued by the prohibited group and the vested benefits paid to or accrued by other employees will not result in a finding that there is discriminatory vesting.

Commissioner of Internal Revenue

¶ 20,165C

Proposed regulations: Minimum vesting standards for qualified employee plans.—Reproduced below is the text of proposed regulations relating to the minimum vesting standards for qualified employee plans. The proposed regulations amend current regulations to reflect changes made by the Tax Reform Act of 1986. The proposed regulations were published in the Federal Register on January 6, 1988 (53 FR 261). The proposed regulations were also issued as temporary regulations under T.D. 8170 and are reproduced at

¶ 12,158A, 12,162H, 12,162I, 12,213A, 12,214A, and 12,218A. The effective dates of the temporary regulations and the introductory material preceding the temporary regulations are at ¶ 23,743T.

DEPARTMENT OF THE TREASURY

INTERNAL REVENUE SERVICE

[26 CFR Part 1]

[EE-167-86]

MINIMUM VESTING STANDARDS

NOTICE OF PROPOSED RULEMAKING

AGENCY: Internal Revenue Service, Treasury.

ACTION: Notice of proposed rulemaking by cross reference to temporary regulations.

SUMMARY: This document provides proposed regulations relating to the minimum vesting standards for qualified employee plans. Changes to the applicable laws were made by the Tax Reform Act of 1986. These proposed regulations amend the current regulations to reflect the changes. In the Rules and Regulations portion of this issue of the FEDERAL REGISTER, the Internal Revenue Service is issuing temporary regulations relating to the minimum vesting standards. The text of these temporary regulations also serves as the comment document for this notice of proposed rulemaking.

DATES: Written comments and requests for a public hearing must be delivered or mailed by March 7, 1988. The amendments are proposed to be generally effective for plan years beginning after December 31, 1988.

ADDRESS: Send comments and requests for a public hearing to: Commissioner of Internal Revenue, Attention: CC:LR:T (EE-167-86), 1111 Constitution Avenue, N.W., Washington, D.C. 20224.

FOR FURTHER INFORMATION CONTACT: V. Moore of the Employee Plans and Exempt Organizations Division, Office of Chief Counsel, Internal Revenue Service, 1111 Constitution Avenue, N.W., Washington, D.C. 20224 (Attention: CC:LR:T) (202-566-3938, not a toll-free call).

SUPPLEMENTARY INFORMATION:

Background

The temporary regulations in the Rules and Regulations portion of this issue of the FEDERAL REGISTER amend Part 1 of the Code of Federal Regulations. New § 1.410(a)-3T, § 1.410(a)-8T, § 1.410(a)-9T, § 1.411(a)-3T, § 1411(a)-4T, and § 1.411(a)-8T are added to Part 1 of Title 26 of the Code of Federal Regulations. When these temporary regulations are promulgated as final regulations, § 1.410(a)-3, § 1.410(a)-5, § 1.410(a)-7, § 1.411(a)-3, § 1.411(a)-4, and § 1.411(a)-8 will be revised to reflect the new provisions. For the text of the temporary regulations, see T.D. 8170 published in the Rules and Regulations portion of this issue of the FEDERAL REGISTER. The preamble to the temporary regulations explains the amendments to the Income Tax Regulations.

Regulatory Flexibility Act And Executive Order 12291

Although this document is a notice of proposed rulemaking which solicits public comment, the Internal Revenue Service has concluded that the regulations proposed herein are interpretative and that the notice and public procedure requirements of 5 U.S.C. 553 do not apply. Accordingly, these proposed regulations do not constitute regulations subject to the Regulatory Flexibility Act (5 U.S.C. chapter 6).

The Commissioner of Internal Revenue has determined that this proposed rule is not a major rule as defined in Executive Order 12291 and that a regulatory impact analysis therefore is not required.

Comments And Request For A Public Hearing

Before adopting these proposed regulations, consideration will be given to any written comments that are submitted (preferably eight copies) to the Commissioner of Internal Revenue. All comments will be available for public inspection and copying. A public hearing will be held upon written request to the Commissioner by any person who has submitted written comments. If a public hearing is held, notice of the time and place will be published in the FEDERAL REGISTER.

Drafting Information

The principal author of these proposed regulations is V. Moore of the Employee Plans and Exempt Organizations Division of the Office of Chief Counsel. Other offices of the Internal Revenue Service and Treasury Department participated in developing the regulations, both on matters of substance and style.

Lawrence B. Gibbs

Commissioner of Internal Revenue

¶ 20,165D

Proposed regulations: Highly compensated employee: Compensation: Tax Reform Act of 1986.—Reproduced below is the text of proposed regulations on the scope and meaning of the terms "highly compensated employee" in Code Sec. 414(q) and "compensation" in Code Sec. 414(s). They reflect changes made by the Tax Reform Act of 1986. The proposed regulations were also issued as temporary regulations under T.D. 8173 and are reproduced at ¶ 12,364E and 12,364G. The introductory material preceding the temporary regulations is at ¶ 23,746V. The proposed regulations were published in the Federal Register on February 19, 1988 (53 FR 4999).

DEPARTMENT OF THE TREASURY

Internal Revenue Service

[26 CFR Part 1]

[EE-129-86]

Definitions Of "Highly Compensated Employee" And "Compensation"

Notice Of Proposed Rulemaking

AGENCY: Internal Revenue Service, Treasury.

ACTION: Notice of proposed rulemaking by cross-reference to temporary regulations.

SUMMARY: In the Rules and Regulations portion of this issue of the Federal Register, the Internal Revenue Service is issuing temporary regulations relating to the scope and meaning of the terms "highly compensated employee" in section 414(q) and "compensation" in section 414(s) of the Internal Revenue Code of 1986. They reflect changes made by the Tax Reform Act of 1986 (TRA '86). The text of those temporary regulations also serves as the text for this Notice of Proposed Rulemaking. These regulations will provide the public with guidance necessary to comply with the law and would affect sponsors of, and participants in, pension, profit-sharing and stock bonus plans, and certain other employee benefit plans.

DATES: Written comments and requests for a public hearing must be delivered or mailed [60 DAYS AFTER DATE OF PUBLICATION OF NOTICE OF PROPOSED RULEMAKING]. In general, these regulations apply to years beginning on or after January 1, 1987, except as otherwise specified in TRA '86.

ADDRESS: Send comments and requests for a public hearing to: Commissioner of Internal Revenue, Attention: CC:LR:T (EE-129-86), Washington, D.C. 20224.

FOR FURTHER INFORMATION CONTACT: Nancy J. Marks of the Employee Plans and Exempt Organizations Division, Office of the Chief Counsel, Internal Revenue Service, 1111 Constitution Avenue, N.W., Washington, D.C. 20224 (Attention: CC:LR:T), (202-566-3938) (not a toll-free number).

SUPPLEMENTARY INFORMATION

Background

The temporary regulations in the Rules and Regulations portion of this issue of the Federal Register amend 26 CFR by adding a new section 1.414(q)-1T under Part 1 to provide guidance with respect to the definitions of highly compensated employee and compensation within the meaning of Code section 414(q) and (s). The regulations are proposed to be issued under the authority contained in sections 414(s) and 7805 of the Code (100 Stat. 2453, 68A Stat. 917; 26 U.S.C. 414(s), 7805). For the text of the temporary regulations, see F.R. Doc. (T.D. —) published in the Rules and Regulations portion of this issue of the Federal Register.

Special Analyses

The Commissioner of Internal Revenue has determined that this proposed rule is not a major rule as defined in Executive Order 12291 and that a regulatory impact analysis is not required.

Although this document is a notice of proposed rulemaking which solicits public comment, the Internal Revenue Service has concluded that the regulations proposed herein are interpretative and that the notice and public procedure requirements of 5 U.S.C. 553 do not apply. Accordingly, these proposed regulations do not constitute regulations subject to the Regulatory Flexibility Act (5 U.S.C. chapter 6).

Comments And Requests For Public Hearing

Before adopting these proposed regulations, consideration will be given to any written comments that are submitted (preferably eight copies) to the Commissioner of Internal Revenue. All comments will be available for public inspection and copying. A public hearing will be held upon written request to the Commissioner by any person who has submitted written comments. If a public hearing is held, notice of the time and place will be published in the FEDERAL REGISTER.

Drafting Information

The principal author of these proposed regulations is Nancy J. Marks of the Employee Plans and Exempt Organizations Division of the Office of Chief Counsel, Internal Revenue Service. However, personnel from other offices of the Internal Revenue Service and Treasury Department participated in developing the regulations, both on matters of substance and style.

List Of Subjects In 26 CFR 1.401-0-1.425-1

Income taxes, Employee benefit plans, Pensions.

Lawrence B. Gibbs,

Commissioner of Internal Revenue.

[¶ 20,166 Reserved.—Proposed regulations under Code Sec. 413, relating to collectively bargained plans and plans maintained by more than one employer were formerly reproduced at this point. The final regulations appear at ¶ 12,311 and 12,312.]

[¶ 20,166A Reserved.—Proposed regulations relating to the permitted disparity in employer contributions and employer-derived benefits for highly compensated employees in employee benefit plans and the determination of whether certain disparities resulted in prohibited discrimination were formerly reproduced here. The final regulations are at ¶ 11,731P—11,731P-6.]

[¶ 20,167 Reserved.—Proposed regulations on tax treatment of certain option income of exempt organizations formerly appeared at this point. The final regulations are at ¶ 13,213 and 13,233.]

[¶ 20,168 Reserved.—Proposed regulations requesting comments on temporary TRASOP regulations were formerly reproduced at this paragraph. The temporary regulations were finalized and appear at ¶ 11,124.]

[¶ 20,169 Reserved.—Proposed Reg. §§1.219-1(c) and 1.219-2(a)-(i), defining the term "active participant" for purposes of determining who can make deductible contributions to an individual retirement account, were formerly reproduced here. The final regulations appear at ¶ 11,331 and 11,332.]

[¶ 20,170 Reserved.—Proposed regulations relating to excise taxes imposed on excess contributions to Keogh plans were formerly reproduced at this point. The final regulations are at ¶ 13,611.]

[¶ 20,171 Reserved.—Proposed regulations under Code Secs. 401, 403, and 415, relating to limitations on benefits and contributions under qualified plans, were formerly reproduced at this point. The final regulations are at ¶ 11,702, 11,708, 11,715, 11,716, 11,720B, 11,725, 11,803, 11,901, and 12,401—12,410.]

¶ 20,172

Proposed regulations prescribing rules for determining if the vesting schedule of a qualified plan discriminates in favor of employees who are officers, shareholders, or highly compensated.—Reproduced below is the text of proposed Reg. § 1.411(d)-1, which sets forth guidelines for determining if a plan's vesting schedule discriminates in favor of prohibited groups.

The proposed regulations were published in the *Federal Register* of April 9, 1980 (45 FR 24201).

DEPARTMENT OF THE TREASURY

Internal Revenue Service

[26 CFR Part 1]

[EE-164-78]

Coordination Of Vesting And Discrimination Requirements For Qualified Plans

AGENCY: Internal Revenue Service, Treasury.

ACTION: Notice of proposed rulemaking.

SUMMARY: This document contains proposed regulations prescribing rules for determining if the vesting schedule of a qualified plan discriminates in favor of employees who are officers, shareholders, or highly compensated. Changes to the applicable tax law were made by the Employee Retirement Income Security Act of 1974. The regulations would provide the public with additional guidance needed to comply with that Act and would affect all employers maintaining qualified plans.

DATES: Written comments and requests for a public hearing must be delivered or mailed by June 9, 1980. The amendments are proposed to be effective for plan years beginning 30 days after the publication of this regulation in the FEDERAL REGISTER as a Treasury decision.

ADDRESS: Send comments and requests for a public hearing to: Commissioner of Internal Revenue, Attention: CC:LR:T (EE-164-78), Washington, D.C. 20224.

FOR FURTHER INFORMATION CONTACT: Kirk F. Maldonado of the Employee Plans and Exempt Organizations Division, Office of the Chief Counsel, Internal Revenue Service, 1111 Constitution Avenue, N.W., Washington, D.C. 20224 (Attention: CC:LR:T) (202-566-3430) (not a toll-free number).

SUPPLEMENTARY INFORMATION:

Background

This document contains proposed amendments to the Income Tax Regulations (26 CFR Part 1) under section 411(d)(1) of the Internal Revenue Code of 1954. These amendments are proposed to conform the regulations to section 1012(a) of the Employee Retirement Income Security Act of 1974 (88 Stat. 901) and these regulations are to be issued under the authority contained in section 7805 of the Internal Revenue Code of 1954 (68A Stat. 917; 26 U.S.C. 7805).

Statutory Provisions

Section 401(a)(4) of the Code provides that a plan which discriminates in favor of employees who are officers, shareholders, or highly compensated (hereinafter referred to as "prohibited group") is not a qualified plan under section 401(a). Section 411(d)(1) provides that the vesting schedule of a plan which satisfies the requirements of section 411 shall be considered as satisfying any vesting requirements resulting from the application of section 401(a)(4) except in two situations. One situation, as set forth in section 411(d)(1)(A), is a pattern of abuse under the plan which tends to discriminate in favor of the prohibited group (pattern of abuse). The other situation, as detailed in section

411(d)(1)(B), is where there have been, or there is reason to believe there will be, an accrual of benefits or forfeitures tending to discriminate in favor of the prohibited group (hereinafter referred to as "discriminatory vesting").

Prior Guidelines

Initial guidelines under section 411(d)(1) were set forth in Revenue Procedure 75-49, 1975-2 C.B. 584. That procedure established several alternative tests, with respect to vesting, that a plan must satisfy to secure a favorable advance determination letter. If a plan fails to satisfy these tests, a favorable advance determination letter will not be issued unless the plan adopts accelerated vesting (so-called "4/40 vesting").

Revenue Procedure 75-49 was modified in Revenue Procedure 76-11, 1976-1 C.B. 550. That procedure adopted alternative ways of satisfying the requirements of section 411(d)(1) in order to secure a favorable advance determination letter, in addition to the tests contained in Revenue Procedure 75-49.

The tests of Revenue Procedures 75-49 and 76-11 were applied only with respect to whether a plan could receive a favorable advance determination letter. The determination letter by its terms provided that the approval of the plan's qualified status by the Service did not extend to the plan in operation. Therefore, separate tests for determining discrimination in vesting were necessary with respect to the issuance of a determination letter and with respect to testing the operation of the plan's vesting schedule.

In addition, the tests described in Revenue Procedures 75-49 and 76-11 were generally mechanical. Objections were raised by plan administrators and sponsors when they were required to accept 4/40 vesting as a minimum schedule, and yet 4/40 vesting did not reflect the policies of ERISA if applied as a maximum vesting schedule. At the same time, it is recognized that there is a value in allowing safe harbors for plan administrators who seek a determination letter with respect to the qualified status of a plan. Therefore, although a facts and circumstances test more accurately reflects the vesting antidiscrimination provisions of the Code, and the policies of ERISA, it is recognized that some forms of safe harbor are appropriate for certainty purposes.

The rules contained in the proposed regulations attempt to accommodate both goals. On the one hand, a facts and circumstances test is described. This description is amplified by a list of factors which may be included in applying the test. It is anticipated that these factors will offer substantial guidance to plan administrators in reviewing the vesting provisions applicable both with respect to a determination letter application and with respect to the status of a plan in operation. On the other hand, two safe harbor tests are provided which would insulate a plan against a finding of discriminatory vesting under the plan.

After this regulation is adopted, it is anticipated that the tests and vesting schedule contained in Revenue Procedures 75-49 and 76-11 will no longer be applied. While plans having determination letters based on 4/40 vesting need not apply for a new determination letter on the basis of the plan's vesting schedule, plan administrators should be aware that the tests included in these regulations will be applied in testing the operation of each plan's vesting schedule and are cautioned to review each plan accordingly. Because of the guidance to be provided by this regulation after it is adopted, the concerns voiced by plan administrators under prior rules regarding how a plan's operation with respect to vesting would be judged should be alleviated. In addition, when a plan is submitted to the Internal Revenue Service for a determination letter it is anticipated that the rules in these regulations will be applied for purposes of issuing such letters.

Discrimination In Vesting

The proposed rules provide that the determination of whether there is a pattern of abuse or discriminatory vesting under a plan shall be determined on the facts and circumstances of each case. Several criteria are set forth as factors to be used in making such a determination.

Two safe harbors are provided against a finding of discriminatory vesting under the plan. One safe harbor requires full vesting after an employee has three years of service. The other safe harbor requires full vesting after ten years of service, and the sum of the vested percentages for the employee's service prior to the completion of ten years of service must equal or exceed 700.

Comments And Requests For A Public Hearing

Before adopting these proposed regulations, consideration will be given to any written comments that are submitted (preferably eight copies) to the Commissioner of Internal Revenue. All comments will be available for public inspection and copying. A public hearing will be held upon written request to the Commissioner by any person who has submitted written comments. If a public hearing is held, notice of the time and place will be published in the *Federal Register*.

Drafting Information

The principal author of these proposed regulations is Kirk F. Maldonado of the Employee Plans and Exempt Organizations Division of the Office of Chief Counsel, Internal Revenue Service. However, personnel from other offices of the Internal Revenue Service and Treasury Department participated in developing these regulations, both on matters of substance and style.

Proposed amendment to the regulations

It is proposed to amend 26 CFR Part 1 by adding the following new section at the appropriate place.

§ 1.411(d)-1 Coordinaation of vesting and discrimination requirements.

(a) *General rule.* A plan which satisfies the requirements of section 411(a)(2) shall be treated as satisfying any vesting schedule requirements resulting from the appliciation of section 401(a)(4) unless the plan is discriminatory within the meaning of section 411(d)(1) and this section. A plan is discriminatolry if there is a pattern of abuse or there is discriminatory vesting as determined under paragraphs (b) and (c) of this section, respectively. Under section 401(a)(4), a plan which discriminates in favor of employees who are officers, shareholders, or highly compensated (hereinafter referred to as "prohibited group") is not a qualified plan under section 401(a).

(b) *Pattern of abuse*—(1) *Definition.* A plan is discriminatory under section 411(d)(1)(A) and shall not be considered to satisfy the requirements of section 401(a)(4) if there has been a pattern of abuse under the plan tending to discriminate in favor of the prohibited group (hereinafter referred to as "pattern of abuse").

(2) *Test for pattern of abuse.* The determination of whether there has been a pattern of abuse shall be made on the basis of the facts and circumstances of each case. An example of a pattern of abuse is the systematic dismissal of employees before their accrued benefits vest.

(c) *Discriminatory vesting*—(1) *Definition.* A plan is discriminatory under section 411(d)(1)(B) and shall not be considered to satisfy the requirements of section 401(a)(4) if there have been, or there is reason to believe there will be, an accrual of benefits or forfeitures tending to discriminate in favor of the prohibited group by operation of the vesting schedule (hereinafter referred to as "discriminatory vesting").

》》→ *Proposed Reg. § 1.411(d)-1(c)(2) was modified by new Proposed Reg. § 1.414(d)-1(c)(2) at ¶ 20,165B.*

(2) *Test for discriminatory vesting.* Unless paragraph (d) applies, the determination of whether there is, or there is reason to believe there will be, discriminatory vesting shall be made on the basis of the facts and circumstances of each case. An unfavorable comparison based on one of the following factors does not require a finding that there is discriminatory vesting. Factors which are relevant to this determination include, but are not limited to, comparisons betwen the prohibited group and all other employees covered by the plan of:

(i) The employment turnover rate. The term "employment turnover rate" means the annual rate of turnover for employees.

(ii) The average percentage of vesting of each employee currently employed by the employer maintaining the plan.

(iii) The average percentage of vesting of each employee whose employment is terminated. For purposes of this subparagraph, a "termination of employment" occurs when the employee leaves by reason of a quit, discharge, retirement, or any other means.

(iv) The average number of years remaining for each employee until that employee becomes fully vested.

(v) In the case of a plan amendment which increases the length of service required for any particular level of vesting, the percentage of employees satisfying the new length of service requirement at the time it becomes effective.

》》→ *Proposed Reg. § 1.411(d)-1(d) was withdrawn. See ¶ 20,165B.*

(d) *Safe harbor test*—(1) *General rule.* A plan whose vesting schedule satisfies the requirements of subparagraph (2) or (3) of this paragraph shall be deemed not to be discriminatory under paragraph (c) of this section.

(2) *Three year rule.* A plan satisfies the requirements of this subparagraph if any employee who has completed 3 years of service has a 100%

nonforfeitable right to the accrued benefit derived from employer contributions.

(3) *Ten year rule.* A plan satisfies the requirements of this subparagraph if any employee who has completed 10 years of service has a 100% nonforfeitable right to the accrued benefit derived from employer contributions, and the sum of the 10 relevant percentages of the employee's nonforfeitable rights equals or exceeds 700. The relevant percentages to be added are the employee's vested percentage (if any) prior to the completion of the first year of service, and the vested percentages after the completion of each of the first 9 years of service.

(4) *Determination of years of service.* For purposes of this paragraph, the term "years of service" means years of service required to be taken into account for purposes of section 411(a)(2), determined without regard to subparagraphs (A), (B), and (C) of section 411(a)(4).

(5) *Examples.* The rules provided by this paragraph are illustrated by the following examples:

Example (1). (i) Plan A provides that years of service for purposes of vesting are calculated under section 411(a)(2) without regard to subparagraphs (A), (B), and (C) of section 411(a)(4). Under the plan, an employee is 100% vested in the accrued benefit derived from employer contributions after three years of service.

(ii) The vesting schedule of Plan A can be illustrated by the following table:

Completed years of service	Nonforfeitable percentage
less than 1	0
1 but less than 2	0
2 but less than 3	0
3 but less than 4	100
4 but less than 5	100
5 but less than 6	100
6 but less than 7	100
7 but less than 8	100
8 but less than 9	100
9 but less than 10	100
	700

(iii) Plan A satisfies the requirements of subparagraph (2) of this paragraph because an employee is 100% vested after three years of service. Plan A also satisfies the requirements of subparagraph (3) of this paragraph because the sum of the 10 relevant percentages equals 700 and an employee is 100% vested after 10 years of service. Therefore, Plan A is deemed to be nondiscriminatory under paragraph (c) of this section.

Example (2). (i) Plan B provides that years of service for purposes of vesting are calculated under section 411(a)(2), without regard to subparagraphs (A), (B), and (C) of section 411(a)(4). Under the plan, an employee is 20% vested after one year of service, 40% after two years, 60% after three years, 80% after four years, and 100% after five years.

(ii) The vesting schedule of Plan B can be illustrated by the following table:

Completed years of service	Nonforfeitable percentage
less than 1	0
1 but less than 2	20
2 but less than 3	40
3 but less than 4	60
4 but less than 5	80
5 but less than 6	100
6 but less than 7	100

Completed years of service	Nonforfeitable percentage
7 but less than 8	100
8 but less than 9	100
9 but less than 10	100
	700

(iii) Plan B does not satisfy the requirements of subparagraph (2) of this paragraph because an employee is not 100% vested after 3 years of service. However, Plan B satisfies the requirements of subparagraph (3) of this paragraph because the sum of the 10 relevant percentages equals 700 and an employee is 100% vested after 10 years of service. Therefore, Plan B is deemed to be nondiscriminatory under paragraph (c) of this section.

Example (3). (i) Plan C provides that years of service for purposes of vesting are calculated under section 411(a)(2), with regard to subparagraphs (A), (B), and (C) of section 411(a)(4). Under the plan, an employee's right to the accrued benefit derived from employer contributions vest as provided in section 411(a)(2)(A).

(ii) The vesting schedule of Plan C can be illustrated by the following table:

Completed years of service	Nonforfeitable percentage
less than 1	0
1 but less than 2	0
2 but less than 3	0
3 but less than 4	0
4 but less than 5	0
5 but less than 6	0
6 but less than 7	0
7 but less than 8	0
8 but less than 9	0
9 but less than 10	0
10 or more	100
	700

(iii) Plan C does not meet the requirements of subparagraph (2) of this paragraph because the employee is not 100% vested after 3 years of service. Plan C does not meet the requirements of subparagraph (3) of this paragraph because the sum of the 10 relevant percentages does not equal 700, although an employee is 100% vested after 10 years of service. Also, Plan C fails to meet the requirements of subparagraph (4) of this paragraph because an employee's service for vesting purposes is calculated using all of the subparagraphs of section 411(a)(4) instead of disregarding subparagraphs (A), (B), and (C) thereof.

(iv) Even though Plan C does not satisfy the requirements of subparagraph (2) or (3) of this paragraph, it may be found to be nondiscriminatory under paragraph (c) of this section if it satisfies the facts and circumstances test set forth in paragraph (c)(2) of this section.

(e) *Defined benefit plans.* A defined benefit plan which satisfies the benefit accrual requirements of section 411(b) shall still be subject to the nondiscrimination requirements of section 401(a)(4) with regard to its benefit accrual rates. Thus, even though a plan satisfies the section 411(b) requirements, the plan may still be discriminatory under section 401(a)(4) with respect to its benefit accruals.

(f) *Effective date.* This section shall apply to plan years beginning 30 days after the publication of this section in the FEDERAL REGISTER as a Treasury decision.

(Signed) Jerome Kurtz

Commissioner of Internal Revenue

[¶ 20,173 Reserved.—Proposed Reg. §§301.6104(a)-1 through 301.6104(a)-6, relating to public inspection of applications for tax exemption, applications for determination of the qualification of pension and other plans, and other related material, were formerly reproduced here. The finalized regulations now appear at ¶ 13,771—13,776.]

[¶ 20,174 Reserved.—Proposed regulations amending proposed rulemaking relating to custodial accounts for regulated investment company stock were formerly reproduced at this paragraph. The regulations were withdrawn by the Internal Revenue Service in a withdrawal notice on January 13, 1987 (52 FR 2724).]

[¶ 20,175 Reserved.—Proposed regulations relating to deferred compensation plans maintained by state and local governments and rural electric cooperatives were formerly reproduced at this paragraph. The final regulations are at ¶ 11,251, 11,252, 11,803, and 13,154—13,154C.]

[¶ 20,176 Reserved.—Proposed regulations concerning the diversification requirements for variable annuity, endowment, and life insurance contracts were formerly reproduced here. The final regulations are at ¶ 13,312B.]

¶ 20,177

Proposed regulations: Excess distributions: Excise tax: Qualified plans, IRAs, annuities, custodial accounts.—Reproduced below is the text of a notice of proposed rulemaking relating to the excise tax on excess distributions from qualified plans, individual retirement accounts, 403(b) annuity contracts, custodial accounts, and retirement income accounts. Temporary regulations, which serve as the text for these proposed regulations, appear at ¶ 13,648V. The proposed regulations were published in the *Federal Register* on December 10, 1987 (52 FR 46747).

DEPARTMENT OF THE TREASURY

Internal Revenue Service

26 CFR Parts 54 and 602

[EE-162-86]

Excise Tax on Excess Distributions from Retirement Plans; Proposed Rulemaking

AGENCY: Internal Revenue Service, Treasury.

ACTION: Notice of proposed rulemaking by cross-reference to temporary regulations.

SUMMARY: In the Rules and Regulations portion of this issue of the *Federal Register,* the Internal Revenue Service is issuing temporary regulations relating to the excise tax on excess distributions from retirement plans under section 1133 of the Tax Reform Act of 1986. The text of those temporary regulations also serves as the text for this Notice of Proposed Rulemaking.

DATES: Written comments and requests for a public hearing must be delivered or mailed before February 8, 1988.

ADDRESS: Send comments and requests for a public hearing to: Commissioner of Internal Revenue, Attention: CC:LR:T (EE-162-86), Washington, DC 20224.

FOR FURTHER INFORMATION CONTACT: Marjorie Hoffman of the Employee Plans and Exempt Organizations Division, Office of Chief Counsel, Internal Revenue Service, 1111 Constitution Avenue, NW., Washington, DC 20224, Attention: CC:LR:T (EE-162-86), 202-566-3903 (not a toll-free number).

SUPPLEMENTARY INFORMATION:

Background

The temporary regulations in the Rules and Regulations portion of this issue of the *Federal Register* amend 26 CFR by adding a new §54.4981A-1T under Part 54 to provide guidance so taxpayers can comply with section 4981A of the Internal Revenue Code. The final regulations which are proposed to be based on the temporary regulations would amend Part 54 of Title 26 of the Code of Federal Regulations by adding similar sections to Part 54 (Pension Excise Tax Regulations). The regulations are proposed to be issued under the authority contained in sections 4981A and 7805 of the Code (100 Stat. 2841, 26 U.S.C. 4981A; 68A Stat. 917, 26 U.S.C. 7805). For the text of the temporary regulations, see F.R. Doc. 87-28401 (T.D. 8165) published in the Rules and Regulations of this issue of the *Federal Register.*

Special Analyses

The Commissioner of Internal Revenue has determined that this proposed rule is not a major rule as defined in Executive Order 12291 and that a Regulatory Impact Analysis is therefore not required. Although this document is a notice of proposed rulemaking which solicits public comment, the Internal Revenue Service has concluded that the regulations proposed herein are interpretative and that the notice and public procedure requirements of 5 U.S.C. 553 do not apply. Accordingly, these proposed regulations do not constitute regulations subject to the Regulatory Flexibility Act (5 U.S.C. Chapter 6).

Comments and Request for Public Hearing

Before adopting these proposed regulations, consideration will be given to any written comments that are submitted (preferably 8 copies) to the Commissioner of Internal Revenue. All comments will be available for public inspection and copying. A public hearing will be held upon written request to the Commissioner by any person who has submitted written comments. If a public hearing is held, notice of the time and place will be published in the *Federal Register.* The collection of information requirements contained herein have been submitted to the Office of Management and Budget (OMB) for review under section 3504(h) of the Paperwork Reduction Act. Comments on the requirements should be sent to the Office of Information and Regulatory Affairs of OMB, Attention: Desk Officer for the Internal Revenue Service, New Executive Office Building, Washington, DC 20503. The Internal Revenue Service requests persons submitting comments to OMB also to send copies of the comments to the Service.

Drafting Information

The principal author of these proposed regulations is Marjorie Hoffman of the Employee Plans and Exempt Organizations Division of the Office of Chief Counsel, Internal Revenue Service. However, personnel from other offices of the Internal Revenue Service and Treasury Department participated in developing the regulations, both on matters of substance and style.

List of Subjects

26 CFR 54

Excise taxes, Pensions.

26 CFR 602

Reporting and recordkeeping requirements.

Lawrence B. Gibbs,

Commissioner of Internal Revenue.

[FR Doc. 87-28402 Filed 12-9-87; 8:45 am]

¶ 20,178

Proposed regulations: Golden parachute payments.—Reproduced below is the text of proposed regulations on golden parachute payments relating to exempt parachute payments, disqualified individuals, changes in corporate ownership or control, and reasonable compensation.

The proposed regulations were published in the *Federal Register* on May 5, 1989 (54 FR 19390).

The proposed regulations were amended by the proposed regulations at ¶ 20,260G, published in the *Federal Register* on February 20, 2002 (67 FR 7630). Under the new proposed regulations, the IRS clarified that the 1989 proposed regulations could be applied to any payments that are contingent on a change in ownership or control occurring prior to January 1, 2004.

AGENCY: Internal Revenue Service, Treasury.

ACTION: Notice of proposed rulemaking.

SUMMARY: This document contains proposed regulations relating to golden parachute payments. Changes to the applicable tax law were made by the Tax Reform Act of 1984, the Tax Reform Act of 1986, and the Technical and Miscellaneous Revenue Act of 1988. The regulations will provide guidance to taxpayers who must comply with section 280G of the Internal Revenue Code of 1986.

DATES: Written comments and requests for a public hearing must be delivered or mailed by July 5, 1989. Generally, these regulations are proposed to be effective for payments made under agreements entered into or renewed after June 14, 1984. These regulations also are proposed to be effective for certain payments under agreements entered into on or before June 14, 1984, and amended or supplemented in significant relevant respect after that date.

ADDRESS: Send comments and requests for a public hearing to: Internal Revenue Service, Attention: CC:CORP:T:R (PS217-84), Room 4429, Washington, D.C. 20024.

FOR FURTHER INFORMATION CONTACT: Stuart G. Wessler, 202-566-6016, or Robert Misner, 202-566-4752 (not toll-free numbers).

SUPPLEMENTARY INFORMATION:

Background

This document contains proposed amendments to the Income Tax Regulations (26 CFR Part 1) under section 280G of the Internal Revenue Code. These amendments are proposed to conform the Income Tax Regulations to section 67 of the Tax Reform Act of 1984 (Pub. L. No. 98-369; 98 Stat. 585), which added sections 280G and 4999 to the Code and amended Code sections 275(a)(6) and 3121(v)(2)(A), and to section 1804(j) of the Tax Reform Act of 1986 (Pub. L. No. 99-514; 100 Stat. 2807) and section 1018(d)(6)-(8) of the Technical and Miscellaneous Revenue Act of 1988 (Pub. L. No. 100-647; 102 Stat. 3581), which amended Code section 280G. These provisions relate to golden parachute payments. Specifically, section 280G denies a deduction for any "excess parachute payment," section 4999 imposes a 20-percent excise tax on the recipient of any excess parachute payment, section 275(a)(6) denies a deduction for the section 4999 excise tax, and section 3121(v)(2)(A) relates to FICA.

Overview of Statutory Provisions

In applying the golden parachute provisions, the first step is to identify payments that constitute "parachute payments." Section 280G(b)(2)(A) defines a "parachute payment" as any payment that meets all of the following four conditions: (a) the payment is in the nature of compensation; (b) the payment is to, or for the benefit of, a disqualified individual; (c) the payment is contingent on a change in the ownership of a corporation, the effective control of a corporation, or the ownership of a substantial portion of the assets of a corporation ("change in ownership or control"); and (d) the payment has (together with other payments described above in (a), (b), and (c) with respect to the same individual) an aggregate present value of at least 3 times the individual's base amount.

For this purpose, an individual's base amount is, in general, the individual's average annualized includible compensation for the most recent 5 taxable years ending before the change in ownership or control.

Section 280G(b)(2)(B) provides that the term "parachute payment" also includes any payment in the nature of compensation to, or for the benefit of, a disqualified individual if the payment is pursuant to an agreement that violates any generally enforced securities laws or regulations ("securities violation parachute payment").

Once payments are identified as "parachute payments", the next step is to determine any "excess" portion of the payments. Section 280G(b)(1) defines the term "excess parachute payment" as an amount equal to the excess of any parachute payment over the portion of the disqualified individual's base amount that is allocated to such payment. For this purpose, the portion of the base amount allocated to a parachute payment is the amount that bears the same ratio to the base amount as the present value of the parachute payment bears to the aggregate present value of all such payments to the same disqualified individual.

Generally, excess parachute payments may be reduced by certain amounts of reasonable compensation. Section 280G(b)(4)(B) provides that except in the case of securities violation parachute payments, the amount of an excess parachute payment is reduced by any portion of the payment that the taxpayer establishes by clear and convincing evidence is reasonable compensation for personal services actually rendered by the disqualified individual before the date of change in ownership or control. Such reasonable compensation is first offset against the portion of the base amount allocated to the payment.

Exempt Payments

Section 280G specifically exempts several types of payments from the definition of the term "parachute payment."

Deductions for payments exempt from the definition of "parachute payment" are not disallowed by section 280G, and such exempt payments are not subject to the 20-percent excise tax of section 4999. In addition, such exempt payments are not taken into account in applying the three-times-base-amount test of section 280G(b)(2)(A)(ii).

Section 280G(b)(5) provides an exemption for payments with respect to certain corporations. Pursuant to that section, the term "parachute payment" does not include any payment made to a disqualified individ-

ual with respect to a corporation which, immediately before the change in ownership or control, was a small business corporation (as defined in section 1361(b) but without regard to paragraph (1)(C) thereof). In addition, the term "parachute payment" does not include any payment made with respect to a corporation if, immediately before the change in ownership or control, no stock in the corporation was readily tradable on an established securities market (or otherwise) and certain shareholder approval requirements are met with respect to the payment. For this purpose, stock that is described in section 1504(a)(4) is not treated as being readily tradable on an established securities market if the payment does not adversely affect the shareholder's redemption and liquidation rights. The proposed regulations provide guidance on applying the exemptions contained in section 280G(b)(5).

Section 280G(b)(6) exempts certain payments under a qualified plan. Pursuant to that section, the term "parachute payment" does not include any payment to or from: (a) a plan described in section 401(a) which includes a trust exempt from tax under section 501(a); (b) an annuity plan desecribed in section 403(a); or (c) a simplified employee pension as defined in section 408(k).

Finally, section 280G(b)(4)(A) exempts certain payments of reasonable compensation. Pursuant to that section, except in the case of securities violation parachute payments, the term "parachute payment" does not include the portion of any payment which the taxpayer establishes by clear and convincing evidence is reasonable compensation for personal services to be rendered on or after the date of the change in ownership or control. The proposed regulations provide guidance for rdetermining amounts of reasonable compensation.

Disqualified Individuals

To be a parachute payment, a payment must be made to (or for the benefit of) a "disqualified individual." Section 280G(c) defines the term "disqualified individual" to include any individual who (a) is an employee or independent contractor who performs personal services for a corporation, and (b) is an officer, shareholder, or highly-compensated individual. The proposed regulations provide guidance on who will be treated as an "officer," a "shareholder," and a "highly-compensated individual" for this purpose.

Section 280G(c) provides that a "highly-compensated individual" with respect to a corporation only includes an individual who is (or would be if the individual were an employee) a member of the group consisting of the highest paid 1 percent of the employees of the corporation or, if less, the 250 highest paid employees of the corporation. The proposed regulations provide rules for applying this definition. In addition, the proposed regulations provide that no individual whose annual compensation is less than $75,000 will be treated as a highly compensated individual. The proposed regulations also provide an exception to the definition of "highly-compensated individual" to prevent fees earned by independent service providers (such as independent brokers, attorneys, and investment bankers) from becoming subject to section 280G when they perform services in connection with a change in ownership or control.

With respect to who will be treated as a "shareholder" for purposes of section 280G(c), the proposed regulations provide a *de minimis* rule. Pursuant to this rule, only an individual who owns stock of a corporation having a value that exceeds the lesser of $1 million, or 1 percent of the total value of the outstanding shares of all classes of the corporation's stock, is treated as a disqualified individual with respect to the corporation by reason of stock ownership. For purposes of determining the amount of the stock owned by an individual, the constructive ownership rules of section 318(a) shall apply.

The proposed regulations also limit the number of employees who will be treated as disqualified individuals with respect to a corporation by reason of being "officers" of the corporation. The proposed regulations provide that no more than 50 employees (or, if less, the greater of 3 employees or 10 percent of the employees of the corporation) will be treated as disqualified individuals with respect to a corporation by reason of being an officer of the corporation. In the case of an affiliated group treated as one corporation, the previous sentence will be applied to each member of such group.

Contingent on Change

To be a parachute payment, a payment must be contingent on a change in ownership or control. The proposed regulations provide rules on when a payment will be treated as so "contingent."

In general, a payment will be treated as contingent on a change in ownership or control if the payment would not in fact have been made had no change in ownership or control occurred. A payment generally will be treated as one which would not in fact have been made in the absence of a change in ownership or control unless it is substantially certain, at the time of the change, that the payment would have been made whether or not the change occurred. In addition, a payment generally is treated as contingent on a change in ownership of control if (a) the payment is contingent on an event that is closely associated with such a change, (b) a change in ownership or control actually occurs, and (c) the event is materially related to the change in ownership or control. Some types of events that are considered closely associated with a change in ownership or control are the onset of a tender offer, the termination of the disqualified individual's employment, and a significant reduction in the disqualified individual's job responsibilities.

Moreover, a payment will be treated as contingent on a change in ownership or control if the change accelerates the time at which the payment is made. However, if it is substantially certain at the time of the change that the payment would have been made whether or not the change occurred, but the payment is treated as contingent on the change solely because the change accelerates the time at which the payment is made, only a portion of the payment will be treated as contingent on the change. In such case, the portion of the payment that will be treated as contingent on the change is the amount by which the amount of the accelerated payment exceeds the present value of the payment absent the acceleration. In addition, if a payment is accelerated by a change in ownership or control and the payment is substantially certain, at the time of the change, to have been made without regard to such change provided that the disqualified individual had continued to perform services for the corporation for a specified period of time, only a portion of the payment is treated as contingent on the change. The proposed regulations provide rules for determining the portion of the payment so treated. The proposed regulations provide that payments made pursuant to an agreement that is entered into after a change in ownership or control will not be treated as contingent on the change. However, for this purpose, an agreement that is executed after a change in ownership or control pursuant to a legally enforceable agreement that was entered into before the change will be considered to have been entered into before the change.

Presumption That Payment Is Contingent on Change

Section 280G(b)(2)(C) provides a presumption that certain payments are contingent on a change in ownership or control. Specifically, this provision provides that any payment pursuant to an agreement (or an amendment of a previous agreement) that is entered into within one year before a change in ownership or control is presumed to be contingent on such change unless the contrary is established by clear and convincing evidence.

The proposed regulations provide that an amendment of a previous agreement triggers this presumption only if the previous agreement is amended "in any significant respect." The proposed regulations also provide that when the presumption is triggered by an amendment, only the portion of a payment that exceeds the amount of such payment that would have been made in the absence of the amendment is presumed, by reason of the amendment, to be contingent on the change in ownership or control.

In addition, the proposed regulations provide that if an agreement is entered into within one year before the date of a change in ownership or control, clear and convincing evidence that the agreement is (a) a nondiscriminatory employee plan or program; (b) a contract that replaces a prior contract entered into by the same parties more than one year before the change in ownership or control (if the new contract meets certain requirements); or (c) a contract between a corporation and a disqualified individual who did not perform services for the corporation prior to the individual's taxable year in which the change in ownership or control occurs (if the contract meets certain requirements); generally will rebut the presumption that payments under the agreement are contingent on the change.

Change in Ownership or Control

The proposed regulations also provide guidance on when a change in ownership or control will be considered to occur. The regulations provide that a change in the ownership of a corporation occurs when any one person, or more than one person acting as a group, acquires ownership of stock of the corporation that, together with stock held by such person or group, has more than 50 percent of the total fair market value or voting power of all of the corporation's outstanding stock. Section 318(a) will apply in determining stock ownership for this purpose.

The proposed regulations provide that a change in the ownership of a substantial portion of the assets of a corporation occurs when any one person, or more than one person acting as a group, acquires (or has acquired during the 12 months ending on the date of the most recent acquisition by such person or persons) assets from the corporation that

have a total fair market value equal to or more than one third of the total fair market value of all of the assets of the corporation immediately prior to such acquisition or acquisitions. However, the proposed regulations provide that a transfer of assets by a corporation will not be treated as a change in ownership if the assets are transferred to certain shareholders of the corporation or to an entity at least 50 percent of the total value or voting power of which is owned by the corporation.

Under the proposed regulations, a change in the effective control of a corporation is presumed to occur when either of the following events occurs: (a) any one person, or more than one person acting as a group acquires (or has acquired during the 12 month period ending on the date of the most recent acquisition) ownership of stock of the corporation possessing 20 percent or more of the total voting power of the stock of the corporation; or (b) a majority of the members of the corporation's board of directors is replaced during any 12-month period by directors whose appointment or election is not endorsed by a majority of the members of the corporation's board of directors prior to the appointment or election.

Under the proposed regulations, a taxpayer may rebut the presumption described in the preceding paragraph by establishing that such acquisition or acquisitions of the corporation's stock, or such replacement of the majority of the members of the corporation's board of directors, does not transfer the power to control (directly or indirectly) the management and policies of the corporation from any one person or group to another person or group.

Securities Violation Parachute Payments

The proposed regulation implement section 280G(b)(2)(B) by providing that the term "parachute payment" also includes any payment in the nature of compensation to (or for the benefit of) a disqualified individual if such payment is made (a) pursuant to an agreement that violates any generally enforced federal or state securities law or regulation, and (b) in connection with a potential or actual change in ownership or control. However, a violation will not be taken into account for this purpose if it is merely technical in character or is not materially prejudicial to shareholders or potential shareholders. Generally, a securities violation will be presumed not to exist unless the existence of the violation has been determined or admitted in a civil or criminal action (or an administrative action by a regulatory body charged with enforcing the particular securities law or regulation) which has been resolved by adjudication or consent.

Reasonable Compensation

As previously mentioned, section 280G(b)(4)(A) provides that except in the case of securities violation parachute payments, the amount of a payment treated as a parachute payment shall not include the portion of such payment which the taxpayer establishes by clear and convincing evidence is reasonable compensation for personal services to be rendered on or after the date of the change in ownership or control.

Section 280G(b)(4)(B) provides that except in the case of securities violation parachute payments, the amount of a payment treated as an excess parachute payment is reduced by any portion of the payment that the taxpayer establishes by clear and convincing evidence is reasonable compensation for personal services actually rendered by the disqualified individual before the date of the change in ownership or control. Such reasonable compensation is first offset against the portion of the base amount allocated to the payment.

The proposed regulations provide criteria for determining whether payments are reasonable compensation. In general, whether payments are reasonable compensation is determined on the basis of all the facts and circumstances in the particular case. Factors relevant to such a determination include the nature of the services rendered or to be rendered, the individual's historic compensation for performing such services, and the compensation of individuals performing comparable services in situations where the compensation is not contingent on the change. The proposed regulations also provide that payments made under certain nondiscriminatory employee plans or programs will generally be considered to be clear and convincing evidence that the payments are reasonable compensation.

Generally, clear and convincing evidence of reasonable compensation for personal services to be rendered on or after the change in ownership or control will not exist if the individual does not, in fact, perform the services. However, the proposed regulations provide that damages paid for the breach of an employment contract may be reasonable compensation for such services if certain factors are shown. One of these factors is that the damages must be reduced by mitigation. For this purpose, damages will be treated as being mitigated if the damages are reduced (or any payment of such damages is returned) to the extent of the disqualified individual's earned income during the remainder of the contract term. The proposed regulations do not provide a rule concerning the method of establishing mitigation of damages in other situations, such as where the disqualified individual does not accept alternative employment during the remainder of the contract term or where the individual and the corporation considered mitigation in determining the amount of a lump-sum settlement agreement, because the Service is concerned about the administrability of such a rule. Accordingly, the Service solicits comment on how a rule which would allow damages to be treated as mitigated in such cases could be administered.

Finally, the proposed regulations provide that for purposes of section 280G, severance payments will not be considered as reasonable compensation.

Issues on Which Comments are Requested

In addition to the issue concerning mitigation of damages, the Service solicits comment on the following issues:

(a) How the present value of a payment to be made in the future should be determined if such value depends on some uncertain future event or condition (and what adjustments, if any, are to be made if the amount of the actual payment differs from the amount used in determining present value). See Q/A-31, Q/A-32, and Q/A-33 of the proposed regulations.

(b) How the special rules of section 280G should interact with special income deferral rules such as those contained in section 83. See Q/A-12 and Q/A-13 of the proposed regulations.

(c) Whether the rules for identifying the disqualified individuals of a corporation (including the rules relating to the time period that should be utilized to determine who the disqualified individuals are and how the compensation for such a time period should be determined) could be simplified. See Q/A-20 and Q/A-21 of the proposed regulations.

(d) How severance payments should be treated. See Q/A-44 of the proposed regulations.

(e) Whether any of the rules contained in the proposed regulations should be given only prospective effect.

Special Analyses

The Commissioner of Internal Revenue has determined that this proposed rule is not a major rule as defined in Executive Order 12291 and that a Regulatory Impact Analysis is therefore not required.

Although this document is a notice of proposed rulemaking which solicits public comments, the Internal Revenue Service has concluded that the regulations proposed herein are interpretative and that the notice and public procedure requirements of 5 U.S.C. 553 do not apply. Accordingly, these proposed regulations do not constitute regulations subject to the Regulatory Flexibility Act (5 U.S.C. Chapter 6).

Comments and Requests for a Public Hearing

Before these proposed regulations are adopted consideration will be given to any written comments that are submitted to the Commissioner of Internal Revenue. All comments will be available for public inspection and copying. A public hearing will be held upon written request to the Commissioner by any person who has submitted written comments. If a public hearing is held, notice of the time and place will be published in the FEDERAL REGISTER.

Drafting Information

The principal author of these proposed regulations is Stuart G. Wessler of the Office of Chief Counsel, Internal Revenue Service. However, personnel from other offices of the Service and Treasury Department participated in their development.

List of Subjects

26 CFR §§ 1.61-1—1.281-4

Income taxes, Taxable income, Deductions, Exemptions.

Proposed amendments to the regulations

The proposed amendments to 26 CFR Part 1 are as follows:

PART 1—INCOME TAX; TAXABLE YEARS BEGINNING AFTER DECEMBER 31, 1986

Paragraph 1. The authority for Part 1 is amended by adding the following citation:

Authority: 26 U.S.C. 7805. * * * Section 1.280G-1 also issued under 26 U.S.C. 280G(b) and (e).

Par. 2. A new § 1.280G-1 is added after § 1.280F-6T to read as follows:

§ 1.280G-1. Golden parachute payments.—The following questions and answers relate to the treatment of golden parachute payments under section 280G of the Internal Revenue Code of 1986, as added by section 67 of the Tax Reform Act of 1984 (Pub. L. No. 98-369; 98 Stat. 585) and amended by section 1804(j) of the Tax Reform Act of 1986 (Pub. L. No. 99-514; 100 Stat. 2807) and section 1018(d)(6)-(8) of the Technical and Miscellaneous Revenue Act of 1988 (Pub. L. No. 100-647; 102 Stat. 3581).

The following is a table of contents for this section:

Overview

Q-1: What is the effect of Code section 280G?

A-1: Section 280G disallows a deduction for any "excess parachute payment" paid or accrued. For rules relating to the imposition of a nondeductible 20-percent excise tax on the recipient of any excess parachute payment, see Code sections 4999, 275(a)(6), and 3121(v)(2)(A).

Q-2: What is a "parachute payment" for purposes of section 280G?

A-2: (a) The term "parachute payment" means any payment (other than a payment with respect to certain corporations exempted under Q/A-6 of this section, a payment under a qualified plan exempted under Q/A-8 of this section, or a payment of reasonable compensation exempted under Q/A-9 of this section) that—

(1) Is in the nature of compensation;

(2) Is made or is to be made to (or for the benefit of) a "disqualified individual;"

(3) Is contingent on a change—

(i) In the ownership of a corporation,

(ii) In the effective control of a corporation, or

(iii) In the ownership of a substantial portion of the assets of a corporation; and

(4) Has (together with other payments described in paragraph (a)(1), (2), and (3) of this A-2 with respect to the same disqualified individual) an aggregate present value of at least 3 times the individual's "base amount."

Hereinafter, a change referred to in paragraph (a)(3) of this A-2 is referred to as a "change in ownership or control." For a discussion of the application of paragraph (a)(1), see Q/A-11 through Q/A-14; paragraph (a)(2), Q/A-15 through Q/A-21; paragraph (a)(3), Q/A-22 through Q/A-29; and paragraph (a)(4), Q/A-30 through Q/A-36.

(b) The term "parachute payment" also includes any payment in the nature of compensation to (or for the benefit of) a disqualified individual that is pursuant to an agreement that violates a generally enforced securities law or regulation. This type of parachute payment is referred to in this section as a "securities violation parachute payment." See Q/A-37 for the definition and treatment of securities violation parachute payments.

Q-3: What is an "excess parachute payment" for purposes of section 280G?

A-3: The term "excess parachute payment" means an amount equal to the excess of any parachute payment over the portion of the "base amount" allocated to such payment. Subject to certain exceptions and limitations, an excess parachute payment is reduced by any portion of the payment which the taxpayer establishes by clear and convincing evidence is reasonable compensation for personal services actually rendered by the disqualified individual before the date of the change in ownership or control. For a discussion of the computation of excess parachute payments and their reduction by reasonable compensation, see Q/A-38 through Q/A-44. For a discussion of the nonreduction of a securities violation parachute payment by reasonable compensation, see Q/A-37.

Q-4: What is the effective date of section 280G and this section?

A-4: In general, section 280G and this section apply to payments under agreements entered into or renewed after June 14, 1984. Section 280G and this section also apply to certain payments under agreements entered into on or before June 14, 1984, and amended or supplemented in significant relevant respect after that date. For a discussion of the application of the effective date, see Q/A-47 through Q/A-52.

Exempt Payments

Q-5: Are some types of payments exempt from the definition of the term "parachute payment"?

A-5: Yes. The following four types of payments are exempt from the definition of "parachute payment": (a) payments with respect to a small business corporation (described in Q/A-6 of this section); (b) certain payments with respect to a corporation no stock in which is readily tradable on an established securities market (or otherwise) (described in Q/A-6 of this section); (c) payments to or from a qualified plan (described in Q/A-8 of this section); and (d) certain payments of reasonable compensation (described in Q/A-9 of this section). Deductions for payments exempt from the definition of "parachute payment" are not disallowed by section 280G, and such exempt payments are not subject to the 20-percent excise tax of section 4999. In addition, such exempt payments are not taken into account in applying the three-times-base-amount test of Q/A-30 of this section.

Q-6: Which payments with respect to a corporation referred to in paragraph (a) or (b) of A-5 of this section are exempt from the definition of "parachute payment"?

A-6: (a) The term "parachute payment" does not include—

(1) Any payment to a disqualified individual with respect to a corporation which (immediately before the change in ownership or control) was a small business corporation (as defined in section 1361(b) but without regard to paragraph (1)(C) thereof), or

(2) Any payment to a disqualified individual with respect to a corporation (other than a small business corporation described in paragraph (a)(1) of this A-6) if—

(i) Immediately before the change in ownership or control, no stock in such corporation was readily tradable on an established securities market or otherwise, and

(ii) The shareholder approval requirements described in Q/A-7 of this section are met with respect to such payment.

(b) For purposes of paragraph (a)(1) of this A-6, the members of an affiliated group are not treated as one corporation.

(c) The requirements of paragraph (a)(2)(i) of this A-6 are not met if a substantial portion of the assets of any entity consists (directly or indirectly) of stock in such corporation and any ownership interest in such entity is readily tradable on an established securities market or otherwise. For this purpose, such stock constitutes a substantial portion of the assets of an entity if the total fair market value of the stock is equal to or more than one third of the total fair market value of all of the assets of the entity. If a corporation is a member of an affiliated group (which group is treated as one corporation under A-46 of this section), the requirements of paragraph (a)(2)(i) of this A-6 are not met if any stock in any member of such group is readily tradable on an established securities market or otherwise.

(d) For purposes of paragraph (a)(2)(i) of this A-6, the term "stock" does not include stock described in section 1504(a)(4) if the payment does not adversely affect the redemption and liquidation rights of any shareholder owning such stock.

(e) For purposes of paragraph (a)(2)(i) of this A-6, stock shall be treated as readily tradable if it is regularly quoted by brokers or dealers making a market in such stock.

(f) For purposes of paragraph (a)(2)(i) of this A-6, the term "established securities market" means an established securities market as defined in § 1.897-1(m).

(g) The following examples illustrate the application of this exemption:

Example (1). A small business corporation (within the meaning of paragraph (a)(1) of this section) operates two businesses. The corporation sells the assets of one of its businesses, and these assets represent a substantial portion of the assets of the corporation. Because of the sale, the corporation terminates its employment relationship with persons employed in the business the assets of which are sold. Several of these employees are highly-compensated individuals to whom the owners of the corporation make severance payments in excess of 3 times each employee's base amount. Since the corporation is a small business corporation immediately before the change in ownership or control, the payments are not parachute payments.

Example (2). Assume the same facts as in example (1), except that the corporation is not a small business corporation within the meaning of paragraph (a)(1) of this section. If no stock in the corporation is readily tradable on an established securities market (or otherwise) immediately before the change in ownership or control and the shareholder approval requirements described in Q/A-7 of this section are met, the payments are not parachute payments.

Example (3). Seventy percent of the stock of Corporation S is owned by Corporation P, stock in which is readily tradable on an established securities market. The Corporation S stock represents a substantial portion of the assets of Corporation P. Corporation P sells all of its stock in Corporation S to Corporation X. Because of the sale, Corporation S makes severance payments to several of its highly-compensated individuals in excess of 3 times each individual's base amount. Since stock in Corporation P is readily tradable on an established securities market, the payments are not exempt from the definition of "parachute payments" under this A-6.

Q-7: How are the shareholder approval requirements referred to in paragraph (a)(2)(ii) of A-6 of this section met?

A-7: (a) The shareholder approval requirements referred to in paragraph (a)(2)(ii) of A-6 of this section are met with respect to any payment if—

(1) Such payment was approved by a separate vote of the persons who owned, immediately before the change in ownership or control, more than 75 percent of the voting power of all outstanding stock of the corporation, and

(2) There was adequate disclosure, to all persons entitled to vote under paragraph (a)(1) of this A-7, of all material facts concerning all

material payments which (but for Q/A-6 of this section) would be parachute payments with respect to a disqualified individual.

The vote described in paragraph (a)(1) of this A-7 must determine the right of the disqualified individual to receive the payment, or, in the case of a payment made before the vote, the right of the disqualified individual to retain the payment.

(b) Approval of a payment by any shareholder that is not an individual ("entity shareholder") generally must be made by the person authorized by the entity shareholder to approve the payment. However, if a substantial portion of the assets of an entity shareholder consists (directly or indirectly) of stock in the corporation undergoing the change in ownership or control, approval of the payment by that entity shareholder must be made by a separate vote of the persons who hold, immediately before the change in ownership or control, more than 75 percent of the voting power of the entity shareholder. The preceding sentence does not apply if the value of the stock of the corporation owned, directly or indirectly, by or for the entity shareholder does not exceed 1 percent of the total value of the outstanding stock of the corporation. Where approval of a payment by an entity shareholder must be made by a separate vote of the owners of the entity shareholder, the normal voting rights of the entity shareholder determine which owners shall vote.

(c) In determining the persons who comprise the "more than 75 percent" group referred to in paragraph (a)(1) of this A-7, stock is not counted as outstanding stock if the stock is actually owned or constructively owned under section 318(a) by or for a disqualified individual who receives (or is to receive) payments that would be parachute payments if the shareholder approval requirements described in paragraph (a) of this A-7 were not met. Likewise, stock is not counted as outstanding stock if the owner is considered under section 318(a) to own any part of the stock owned directly or indirectly by or for a disqualified individual described in the preceding sentence. However, if all persons who hold voting power in the corporation or the entity shareholder are disqualified individuals or related persons described in either of the two preceding sentences, then stock owned by such persons is counted as outstanding stock.

(d) To be adequate disclosure for purposes of paragraph (a)(2) of this A-7, disclosure must be full and truthful disclosure of the material facts and such additional information as is necessary to make the disclosure not materially misleading at the time the disclosure was made. An omitted fact is considered a material fact if there is a substantial likelihood that a reasonable shareholder would consider it important.

(e) The following examples illustrate the application of this A-7:

Example (1). Corporation S has two shareholders—Corporation P, which owns 76 percent of the stock of Corporation S, and A, an individual, who owns the remaining 24 percent. No stock of Corporation P is readily tradable on an established securities market (or otherwise). Stock of Corporation S represents a substantial portion of the assets of Corporation P. All of the stock of Corporation S is sold to Corporation M. Contingent on the change in ownership of Corporation S, severance payments are made to the officers of Corporation S in excess of 3 times each officer's base amount. If the payments are approved by a separate vote of the persons who hold, immediately before the sale, more than 75 percent of the voting power of the outstanding stock of Corporation P and the disclosure rules of paragraph (a)(2) of this A-7 are compiled [complied] with, the shareholder approval requirements of this A-7 are met, and the payments are exempt from the definition of "parachute payment" pursuant to A-6 of this section [amended on June 20, 1989 (54 FR 25879)].

Example (2). Corporation M is wholly owned by Partnership P, no interest in which is readily tradable on an established securities market (or otherwise). Stock of Corporation M represents a substantial portion of the assets of Partnership P. Partnership P has one general partner and 200 limited partners. None of the limited partners are entitled to vote on issues involving the management of the partnership investments. If the payments are approved by the general partner and the disclosure rules of paragraph (a)(2) of this A-7 are complied with, the shareholder approval requirements of this A-7 are met, and the payments are exempt from the definition of "parachute payment" pursuant to A-6 of this section.

Q-8: Which payments under a qualified plan are exempt from the definition of "parachute payment"?

A-8: The term "parachute payment" does not include any payment to or from—

(a) A plan described in section 401(a) which includes a trust exempt from tax under section 501(a),

(b) An annuity plan described in section 403(a), or

(c) A simplified employee pension (as defined in section 408(k)).

Q-9: Which payments of reasonable compensation are exempt from the definition of "parachute payment"?

A-9: Except in the case of securities violation parachute payments, the term "parachute payment" does not include any payment (or portion thereof) which the taxpayer establishes by clear and convincing evidence is reasonable compensation for personal services to be rendered by the disqualified individual on or after the date of the change in ownership or control. See Q/A-38 through Q/A-44 for rules on determining amounts of reasonable compensation. See Q/A-37 for the definition and treatment of securities violation parachute payments.

Payor of Parachute Payments

Q-10: Who may be the payor of parachute payments?

A-10: Parachute payments within the meaning of Q/A-2 of this section may be paid directly or indirectly by the corporation referred to in paragraph (a)(3) of A-2 of this section, by a person acquiring ownership or effective control of that corporation or ownership of a substantial portion of that corporation's assets, or by any person whose relationship to such corporation or other person is such as to require attribution of stock ownership between the parties under section 318(a).

Payments in the Nature of Compensation

Q-11: What types of payments are in the nature of compensation?

A-11: (a) In general, for purposes of this section, all payments—in whatever form—are payments in the nature of compensation if they arise out of an employment relationship or are associated with the performance of services. For this purpose, the performance of services includes holding oneself out as available to perform services and refraining from performing services (such as under a covenant not to compete or similar arrangement). Payments in the nature of compensation include (but are not limited to) wages and salary, bonuses, severance pay, fringe benefits, and pension benefits and other deferred compensation (including any amount characterized by the parties as interest thereon). However, payments in the nature of compensation do not include attorney's fees or court costs paid or incurred in connection with the payment of any amount described in paragraph (a)(1), (2), and (3) of A-2 of this section.

(b) Transfers of property are treated as payments for purposes of this A-11. See Q/A-12 for rules on determining when such payments are considered made and the amount of such payments. See Q/A-13 for special rules on transfers of nonqualified stock options.

Q-12: If a property transfer to a disqualified individual is a payment in the nature of compensation, when is the payment considered made (or to be made), and how is the amount of the payment determined?

A-12: (a) Except as provided in this A-12 and A-13 of this section, a transfer of property is considered a payment made (or to be made) in the taxable year in which the property transferred is includible in the gross income of the disqualified individual under section 83 and the regulations thereunder. Thus, in general, such a payment is considered made (or to be made) when the property is transferred (as defined in §1.83-3(a)) to the disqualified individual and becomes substantially vested (as defined in §1.83-3(b)) in such individual. In such case, the amount of the payment is determined under section 83 and the regulations thereunder. Thus, in general, the amount of the payment is equal to the excess of the fair market value of the transferred property (determined without regard to any lapse restriction, as defined in §1.83-3(i) at the time that the property becomes substantially vested, over the amount (if any) paid for the property.

(b) An election made by a disqualified individual under section 83(b) with respect to transferred property will not apply for purposes of this A-12. Thus, even if such an election is made with respect to a property transfer that is a payment in the nature of compensation, the payment is generally considered made (or to be made) when the property is transferred to and becomes substantially vested in such individual.

(c) See Q/A-13 for rules on applying this A-12 to transfers of nonqualified stock options.

(d) *Example.* On January 1, 1986, Corporation M gives to A, a disqualified individual, in connection with his performance of services to Corporation M, a bonus of 100 shares of Corporation M stock. Under the terms of the bonus arrangement A is obligated to return the Corporation M stock to Corporation M unless the earnings of Corporation M double by January 1, 1989, or there is a change in ownership or control of Corporation M before that date. A's rights in the stock are treated as substantially nonvested (within the meaning of §1.83-3(b)) during that period because A's rights in the stock are subject to a substantial risk of forfeiture (within the meaning of § 1.83-3(c)) and are nontransferable (within the meaning of § 1.83-3(d)). On January 1, 1988, a change in the ownership of Corporation M occurs. On that day, the fair market value of the Corporation M stock is $250 per share. Since A's rights in the Corporation M stock become substantially vested (within the meaning of § 1.83-3(b)) on that day, the payment is considered made on that day, and the amount of the payment for purposes of this section is equal to $25,000 (100 × $250). See Q/A-39 for rules relating to the reduction of the excess parachute payment by the portion of the payment which is established to be reasonable compensation for personal services actually rendered before the date of a change in ownership or control.

Q-13: How are nonqualified stock options treated?

A-13: (a) For purposes of this section, if an option to which section 421 (relating generally to certain qualified and other options) does not apply has an ascertainable fair market value (whether or not readily ascertainable as defined in § 1.83-7(b)) at the time the option becomes substantially vested (as defined in § 1.83-3(b), the option shall be treated as property that is transferred not later than the time at which the option becomes substantially vested. Thus, for purposes of this section, the vesting of such an option is treated as a payment in the nature of compensation. The value of an option with a readily ascertainable fair market value at the time the option vests shall be determined by applying the rules set forth in § 1.83-7(b). The value of an option with an ascertainable fair market value at the time the option vests is determined under all the facts and circumstances in the particular case. Factors relevant to such a determination include, but are not limited to: (1) the difference between the option's exercise price and the value of the property subject to the option [at] the time of vesting; (2) the probability of the value of such property increasing or decreasing; and (3) the length of the period during which the option can be exercised. See Q/A-33 for the treatment of options the vesting of which is contingent on a change in ownership or control and that do not have an ascertainable fair market value at the time of vesting.

(b) Any money or other property transferred to the disqualified individual upon the exercise, or as consideration upon the sale or other disposition, of an option described in paragraph (a) of this A-14 after the time such option vests is not treated as a payment in the nature of compensation to the disqualified individual under A-11 of this section. Nonetheless, the amount of the otherwise allowable deduction under section 162 or 212 with respect to such transfer shall be reduced by the amount of the payment described in paragraph (a) of this section treated as an excess parachute payment.

(c) (The issue of whether an option to which section 421 applies will be treated as a payment for purposes of this section at the time of grant or at a later time is reserved for future regulations.)

Q-14: Are payments in the nature of compensation reduced by consideration paid by the disqualified individual?

A-14: Yes. To the extent not otherwise taken into account under Q/A-12 and Q/A-13 of this section, the amount of any payment in the nature of compensation is reduced by the amount of any money or the fair market value of any property (owned by the disqualified individual without restriction) that is (or will be) transferred by the disqualified individual in exchange for the payment. For purposes of the preceding sentence, the fair market value of property is determined as of the date the property is transferred by the disqualified individual.

Disqualified Individuals

Q-15: Who is a "disqualified individual"?

A-15: For purposes of this section, an individual is a disqualified individual with respect to a corporation if, at any time during the "disqualified individual determination period" (as defined in Q/A-20 of this section), the individual is an employee or independent contractor of the corporation and is, with respect to the corporation—

(a) A shareholder (but see Q/A-17),

(b) An officer (see Q/A-18), or

(c) A highly-compensated individual (see Q/A-19).

Q-16: Is a personal service corporation treated as an individual?

A-16: (a) Yes. For purposes of this section, a personal service corporation (as defined in section 269A (b) (1)), or a noncorporate entity that would be a personal service corporation if it were a corporation, is treated as an individual.

(b) *Example.* Corporation N, a personal service corporation (as defined in section 269A (b) (1)), has a single individual as its sole shareholder and employee. Corporation N performs personal services

for Corporation M as an independent contractor. The compensation paid to Corporation N by Corporation M puts Corporation N within the group of the highly-compensated individuals of Corporation M as determined under A-18 of this section. Hence, Corporation N is treated as a highly-compensated individual with respect to Corporation M.

Q-17: Are all shareholders of a corporation considered shareholders for purposes of paragraph (a) of A-15 of this section?

A-17: No. Only an individual who owns stock of a corporation having a fair market value that exceeds the lesser of $1 million, or 1 percent of the total fair market value of the outstanding shares of all classes of the corporation's stock, is treated as a disqualified individual with respect to the corporation by reason of stock ownership. An individual who owns a lesser amount of stock may, however, be a disqualified individual with respect to the corporation by reason of being an officer or highly-compensated individual with respect to the corporation. For purposes of determining the amount of stock owned by an individual, the constructive ownership rules of section 318 (a) shall apply.

Q-18: Who is an officer?

A-18: (a) For purposes of this section, whether an individual is an officer with respect to a corporation is determined upon the basis of all the facts and circumstances in the particular case (such as the source of the individual's authority, the term for which the individual is elected or appointed, and the nature and extent of the individual's duties). Generally, the term "officer" means an administrative executive who is in regular and continued service. The term "officer" implies continuity of service and excludes those employed for a special and single transaction. An individual who merely has the title of officer but not the authority of an officer is not considered an officer for purposes of this section. Similarly, an individual who does not have the title of officer but has the authority of an officer is an officer for purposes of this section.

(b) An individual who is an officer with respect to any member of an affiliated group that is treated as one corporation pursuant to Q/A-46 of this section is treated as an officer of such one corporation.

(c) No more than 50 employees (or, if less, the greater of 3 employees, or 10 percent of the employees (rounded up to the nearest integer)) of the corporation (in the case of an affiliated group treated as one corporation, each member of the affiliated group) shall be treated as disqualified individuals with respect to a corporation by reason of being an officer of the corporation. For purposes of the preceding sentence, the number of employees of the corporation is the greatest number of employees the corporation has during the disqualified individual determination period (as defined in Q/A-20 of this section). If the number of officers of the corporation exceeds the number of employees who may be treated as officers under the first sentence of this paragraph (c), then the employees who are treated as officers for purposes of this section are the highest paid 50 employees (or, if less, the greater of 3 employees, or 10 percent of the employees (rounded up to the nearest integer)) of the corporation when ranked on the basis of compensation (as determined under Q/A-21 of this section) paid during the disqualified individual determination period.

Q-19: Who is a "highly-compensated individual"?

A-19: (a) For purposes of this section, a "highly-compensated individual" with respect to a corporation is any individual who is, or would be if the individual were an employee, a member of the group consisting of the lesser of (1) the highest paid 1 percent of the employees of the corporation (rounded up to the nearest integer), or (2) the highest paid 250 employees of the corporation, when ranked on the basis of compensation (as determined under Q/A-21 of this section) paid during the disqualified individual determination period (as defined in Q/A-20 of this section). However, no individual whose annualized compensation during the disqualified individual determination period is less than $75,000 will be treated as a highly-compensated individual.

(b) An individual who is not an employee of the corporation is not treated as a highly-compensated individual with respect to the corporation on account of compensation received for performing services (such as brokerage, legal, or investment banking services) in connection with a change in ownership or control of the corporation, if the services are performed in the ordinary course of the individual's trade or business and the individual performs similar services for a significant number of clients unrelated to the corporation.

(c) In determining the total number of employees of a corporation for purposes of this A-19, employees are not counted if they normally work less than 17 1/2 hours per week (as defined in section 414 (q) (8) (B) and the regulations thereunder) or if they normally work during not more than 6 months during any year (as defined in section 414 (q) (8) (C) and the regulations thereunder). However, an employee who is not counted for purposes of the preceding sentence may still be a highly-compensated individual.

Q-20: What is the "disqualified individual determination period"?

A-20: (a) The "disqualified individual determination period" is the portion of the year of the corporation ending on the date of the change in ownership or control of the corporation (the "change in ownership period") and the twelve month period immediately preceding such change in ownership period. For purpose of this A-20, a corporation may elect to use its taxable year or the calendar year. For this purpose, the taxable year of an affiliated group treated as one corporation pursuant to Q/A-46 of this section is the taxable year of the common parent.

(b) The provisions of this A-20 may be illustrated by the following examples:

Example (1). A change in ownership of Corporation M, a calendar year corporation, takes place on June 12, 1988. The disqualified individual determination period of Corporation M begins on January 1, 1987 and ends on June 12, 1988.

Example (2). Assume the same facts as example (1), except that Corporation M is a fiscal year taxpayer with a taxable year ending on May 31. Corporation M may elect as its disqualified individual determination period either the period beginning on January 1, 1987, and ending on June 12, 1988, or the period beginning on June 1, 1987, and ending on June 12, 1988.

Q-21: How is "compensation" defined?

A-21: (a) For purposes of this section, the term "compensation" is the compensation which was payable by the corporation with respect to which the change in ownership or control occurs ("changed corporation"), by a predecessor entity, or by a related entity. Such compensation shall be determined without regard to sections 125, 402 (a) (8), and 402 (h) (1) (B), and in the case of employer contributions made pursuant to a salary reduction agreement, without regard to section 403 (b). Thus, for example, compensation includes elective or salary reduction contributions to a cafeteria plan, cash or deferred arrangement or tax-sheltered annuity.

(b) For purposes of this section, a "predecessor entity" is any entity which, as a result of a merger, consolidation, purchase or acquisition of property or stock, corporate separation, or other similar business transaction transfers some or all of its employees to the changed corporation or to a related entity or to a predecessor entity of the changed corporation. The term "related entity" includes: (1) all members of a controlled group of corporations (as defined in section 414(b)) that includes the changed corporation or a predecessor entity; (2) all trades or business (whether or not incorporated) that are under common control (as defined in section 414(c)) if such group includes the changed corporation or a predecessor entity; (3) all members of an affiliated service group (as defined in section 414(m)) that includes the changed corporation or a predecessor entity; and (4) any other entities required to be aggregated with the changed corporation or a predecessor entity pursuant to section 414(o) and the regulations thereunder (except leasing organizations as defined in section 414(n)).

(c) For purposes of Q/A-18 and Q/A-19 of this section, compensation that was contingent on the change in ownership or control and that was payable in the year of the change shall not be treated as compensation.

Contingent on Change in Ownership or Control

Q-22: When is a payment "contingent" on a change in ownership or control?

A-22: (a) In general, a payment is treated as "contingent" on a change in ownership or control if the payment would not, in fact, have been made had no change in ownership or control occurred. A payment generally is to be treated as one which would not, in fact, have been made in the absence of a change in ownership or control unless it is substantially certain, at the time of the change, that the payment would have been made whether or not the change occurred. (But see Q/A-23 of this section regarding payments under agreements entered into after a change in ownership or control.) Property that becomes substantially vested (as defined in § 1.83-3 (b)) as a result of a change in ownership or control will not be treated as a payment which was substantially certain to have been made whether or not the change occurred.

(b) A payment is also generally treated as contingent on a change in ownership or control if—

(1) The payment is contingent on an event that is closely associated with a change in ownership or control,

(2) A change in ownership or control actually occurs, and

(3) The event is materially related to the change in ownership or control.

For purposes of paragraph (b) (1) of this A-22, a payment is treated as contingent on an event that is closely associated with a change in ownership or control unless it is substantially certain, at the time of the event, that the payment would have been made whether or not the event occurred. An event is considered closely associated with a change in ownership or control if the event is of a type often preliminary or subsequent to, or otherwise closely associated with, a change in ownership or control. For example, the following events are considered closely associated with a change in the ownership or control of a corporation: the onset of a tender offer with respect to the corporation; a substantial increase in the market price of the corporation's stock that occurs within a short period (but only if such increase occurs prior to a change in ownership or control); the cessation of the listing of the corporation's stock on an established securities market; the acquisition of more than 5 percent of the corporation's stock by a person (or more than one person acting as a group) not in control of the corporation; the voluntary or involuntary termination of the disqualified individual's employment; and a significant reduction in the disqualified individual's job responsibilities. Whether other events will be treated as closely associated with a change in ownership or control will be based on all the facts and circumstances of the particular case. For purposes of paragraph (b) (3) of this A-22, an event will be presumed to be materially related to a change in ownership or control if the event occurs within the period beginning one year before and ending one year after the date of change in ownership or control. If such event occurs outside of the period beginning one year before and ending one year after the date of change in ownership or control, the event will be presumed not to be materially related to the change in ownership or control.

(c) A payment that would in fact have been made had no change in ownership or control occurred is treated as contingent on a change in ownership or control if the change accelerates the time at which the payment is made. Thus, for example, if a change in ownership or control accelerates the time of payment of vested deferred compensation, the payment may be treated as contingent on the change. See Q/A-24 regarding the portion of a payment that is so treated. See also Q/A-8 regarding the exemption for certain payments under qualified plans and Q/A-40 regarding treatment of a payment as reasonable compensation.

(d) A payment is treated as contingent on a change in ownership or control even if the employment or independent contractor relationship of the disqualified individual is not terminated (voluntarily or involuntarily) as a result of the change.

(e) The following examples illustrate the principles of this A-22:

Example (1). A contract between a corporation and A, a disqualified individual, provides that a payment will be made to A if his employment with the corporation is terminated at any time over the succeeding 3 years. Eighteen months later, a change in the ownership of the corporation occurs. Six months after the change in ownership, A's employment is terminated and the payment is made to A. It was not substantially certain, at the time of A's termination, that the payment would have been made had A's employment not been terminated. Termination of employment is considered closely associated with a change in ownership or control. Because the termination occurred within one year after the date of the change in ownership the termination of A's employment is presumed to be materially related to the change in ownership. If this presumption is not rebutted, the payment will be treated as contingent on the change in ownership.

Example (2). A contract between a corporation and a disqualified individual provides that a payment will be made to the individual upon the onset of a tender offer for shares of the corporation's stock. A tender offer is made on December 1, 1988, and the payment is made to the disqualified individual. Although the tender offer is unsuccessful, it leads to a negotiated merger with another entity on June 1, 1989, which results in a change in the ownership of the corporation. It was not substantially certain, at the time of the onset of the tender offer, that the payment would have been made had no tender offer taken place. The onset of a tender offer is considered closely associated with a change in ownership or control. Because the tender offer occurred within one year before the date of the change in ownership of the corporation, the onset of the tender offer is presumed to be materially related to the change in ownership. If this presumption is not rebutted, the payment will be treated as contingent on the change in ownership. If no change in ownership or control had occurred, the payment would not be treated as contingent on a change in ownership or control; however, the payment still could be a parachute payment under Q/A-37 of this section if the contract violated a generally enforced securities law or regulation.

Example (3). A contract between a corporation and a disqualified individual provides that a payment will be made to the individual if the corporation's level of product sales or profits reaches a specified level. At the time the contract was entered into, the parties had no reason to believe that such an increase in the corporation's level of product sales or profits would be preliminary or subsequent to, or otherwise closely associated with, a change in ownership or control of the corporation. Eighteen months later, a change in the ownership of the corporation occurs and within one year after the date of the change, the corporation's level of product sales or profits reaches the specified level. Under these facts and circumstances (and in the absence of contradictory evidence), the increase in product sales or profits of the corporation is not an event closely associated with the change in ownership or control of the corporation. Accordingly, even if the increase is materially related to the change, the payment will not be treated as contingent on a change in ownership or control.

Q-23: May a payment be treated as contingent on a change in ownership or control if the payment is made under an agreement entered into after the change?

A-23: (a) No. Payments are not treated as contingent on a change in ownership or control if they are made (or to be made) pursuant to an agreement entered into after the change. For this purpose, an agreement that is executed after a change in ownership or control, pursuant to a legally enforceable agreement that was entered into before the change, will be considered to have been entered into before the change. (See Q/A-9 regarding the exemption for reasonable compensation for services rendered on or after a change in ownership or control.)

(b) The following examples illustrate the principles of this A-23:

Example (1). Assume that a disqualified individual is an employee of a corporation. A change in control of the corporation occurs, and thereafter the individual enters into an employment agreement with the acquiring company. Since the agreement is entered into after the change in control occurs, payments to be made under agreement are not treated as contingent on the change.

Example (2). Assume the same facts as in example (1), except that the agreement between the disqualified individual and the acquiring company is executed after the change in control, pursuant to a legally enforceable agreement entered into before the change. Payments to be made under the agreement may be treated as contingent on the change in control pursuant to Q/A-22 of this section. However, see Q/A-9 regarding the exemption from the definition of parachute payment for certain amounts of reasonable compensation.

Q-24: If a payment is treated as contingent on a change in ownership or control, is the full amount of the payment so treated?

A-24: (a) Generally, yes. However, in certain circumstances, described in paragraphs (b) and (c) of this A-24, only a portion of the payment is treated as contingent on the change.

(b) This paragraph (b) applies if it is substantially certain, at the time of the change, that the payment would have been made whether or not the change occurred, but the payment is treated as contingent on the change solely because the change accelerates the time at which the payment is made. In such case, the portion of the payment that is treated as contingent on the change in ownership or control is the amount by which the amount of the accelerated payment exceeds the present value of the payment absent the acceleration. If the amount of such a payment absent the acceleration is not reasonably ascertainable, and the acceleration of the payment does not significantly increase the present value of the payment absent the acceleration, the present value of the payment absent the acceleration shall be treated as equal to the amount of the accelerated payment. For rules on determining present value, see paragraph (d) of this A-24, and Q/A-32 and Q/A-33.

(c)(1) This paragraph (c) applies in the case of a payment that is accelerated by a change in ownership or control and that was substantially certain, at the time of the change, to have been made without regard to the change if the disqualified individual had continued to perform services for the corporation for a specified period of time. In such case, the portion of the payment that is treated as contingent on the change in ownership or control is the lesser of—

(i) The amount of the accelerated payment; or

(ii) The amount by which the amount of the accelerated payment exceeds the present value of the payment that was expected to be made absent the acceleration (determined without regard to the risk of forfeiture for failure to continue to perform services), plus an amount,

as determined in paragraph (c)(2) of this A-24, to reflect the lapse of the obligation to continue to perform services.

If the value of the payment that was expected to be made absent the acceleration is not reasonably ascertainable, the future value of such payment shall be deemed to be equal to the amount of the accelerated payment.

(2) The amount reflecting the lapse of the obligation to continue to perform services (described in paragraph (c)(1)(ii) of this A-24) will depend on all of the facts and circumstances. In no event, however, shall such amount be less than 1 percent of the amount of the accelerated payment multiplied by the number of full months between the date that the individual's right to receive the payment is not subject to any requirement or condition which would be treated as resulting in a substantial risk of forfeiture (within the meaning of § 1.83-3 (c)) and the date that, absent the acceleration the individual's right to receive the payment would not have been subject to any requirement or condition which would be treated as resulting in a substantial risk of forfeiture.

(d) For purposes of this A-24, the present value of a payment is determined as of the date on which the accelerated payment is made.

(e) The following examples illustrate the principles of this A-24:

Example (1). A corporation and a disqualified individual enter into a contract providing that, if a change in the ownership or control of the corporation occurs, all of the nonforfeitable deferred compensation the individual has earned prior thereto will be paid immediately. The deferred compensation otherwise will be paid when the individual reaches age 60. A change in the ownership of the corporation occurs, and the deferred compensation is immediately paid. Since the payment would have been made in any event when the individual reached age 60, it is substantially certain, at the time of the change, that the payments would have been made whether or not the change occurred. The payment is treated as contingent on the change in ownership or control solely because the change accelerates the time at which the payments are made. Therefore, the portion of the payment treated as contingent on the change is the amount by which the amount of the accelerated payment (*i.e.*, the amount paid to the individual because of the change in ownership or control) exceeds the present value of the payment absent the acceleration (*i.e.*, the value of the deferred compensation at the time of the change in ownership or control, if the compensation had remained nonpayable until age 60).

Example (2). A corporation grants a stock appreciation right to a disqualified individual. After the stock appreciation right vests and becomes exercisable, a change in the ownership of the corporation occurs, and the individual exercises the right. Neither the granting nor the vesting of the stock appreciation right was treated as a payment in the nature of compensation. Even if the change in ownership accelerates the time at which the right is exercised, no portion of the payment received upon exercise of the right is treated as contingent on the change, since the amount of the accelerated payment does not exceed the present value of the payment absent the acceleration.

Example (3). As a result of a change in the effective control of a corporation, a disqualified individual with respect to the corporation receives payment of his vested account balance in a nonqualified individual account plan. Actual interest and other earnings on the plan assets are credited to each account as earned and before distribution. Investment of the plan assets is not restricted in such a manner as would prevent the earning of a market rate of return on the plan assets. The date on which the individual would have received his vested account balance absent the change in control is uncertain, and the rate of earnings on the plan assets is not fixed. Thus, the amount of the payment absent the acceleration is not reasonably ascertainable. Under these facts, acceleration of the payment does not significantly increase the present value of the payment absent the acceleration, and the present value of the payment absent the acceleration shall be treated as equal to the amount of the accelerated payment. Accordingly, no portion of the payment is treated as contingent on the change.

Example (4). As a result of a change in the effective control of a corporation, a disqualified individual with respect to the corporation receives payment of the individual's vested benefits under a nonqualified pension plan which the individual otherwise would have received upon retirement. The amount of the benefits is not actuarially reduced to reflect its earlier payment. The payment is treated as contingent on the change in control solely because the change accelerates the time at which the payment is made. Therefore, the portion of the payment treated as contingent on the change is the amount by which the amount of the accelerated payment exceeds the present value of the payment absent the acceleration.

Example (5). On January 15, 1986, a corporation and a disqualified individual enter into a contract providing for a cash payment of

$500,000 to be made to the individual on January 15, 1991. The payment is to be forfeited by the individual if he does not remain employed by the corporation for the entire 5-year period. However, the full amount of the payment is to be made immediately upon a change in the ownership or control of the corporation during the 5-year period. On January 15, 1989, a change in the ownership of the corporation occurs and the full amount of the payment ($500,000) is made on that date to the individual. Since the payment would have been made in the absence of the change if the individual had continued to perform services for the corporation until the end of the five year period, it is substantially certain, at the time of the change, that the payment would have been made in the absence of the change if the individual had continued to perform services for the corporation for a specified period of time. Therefore, only a portion of the payment is treated as contingent on the change. The portion of the payment that is treated as contingent on the change is the amount by which the amount of the accelerated payment (*i.e.*, $500,000, the amount paid to the individual because of the change in ownership) exceeds the present value of the payment that was expected to have been made absent the acceleration (*i.e.*, $406,838, the present value on January 15, 1989, of a $500,000 payment on January 15, 1991), plus an amount reflecting the lapse of the obligation to continue to perform services. Such amount will depend on all the facts and circumstances but in no event will such amount be less than $115,000 (1% × 23 months × $500,000). Accordingly, the minimum amount of the payment treated as contingent on the change in ownership or control is $208,162 ([$500,000 – $406,838] + $115,000). This result is not changed if the individual actually remains employed until the end of the 5-year period [amended on June 20, 1989 (54 FR 25879)].

Example (6). (i) On January 15, 1986, a corporation gives to a disqualified individual, in connection with his performance of services to the corporation, a bonus of 1,000 shares of the corporation's stock. Under the terms of the bonus arrangement, the individual is obligated to return the stock to the corporation if she terminates her employment for any reason prior to January 15, 1991. However, if there is a change in the ownership or effective control of the corporation prior to January 15, 1991, she ceases to be obligated to return the stock. The individual's rights in the stock are treated as substantially nonvested (within the meaning of § 1.83-3 (b)) during that period. On January 15, 1989, a change in the ownership of the corporation occurs. On that day, the fair market value of the stock is $500,000.

(ii) Since the stock would have become substantially vested in the individual in the absence of the change if she had continued to perform services for the corporation through January 15, 1991, it is substantially certain, at the time of the change, that the payment would have been made in the absence of the change if the individual had continued to perform services for the corporation for a specified period of time. Thus, only a portion of the payment is treated as contingent on the change in ownership or control. The portion of the payment that is treated as contingent on the change is the amount by which the amount of the accelerated payment on January 15, 1989 ($500,000), exceeds the present value of the payment that was expected to have been made on January 15, 1991, plus an amount reflecting the lapse of the obligation to continue to perform services. Assuming that, at the time of the change, it cannot be reasonably ascertained what the value of the stock would have been on January 15, 1991, the future value of such stock on January 15, 1991, is deemed to be $500,000, the amount of the accelerated payment. The present value on January 15, 1989, of a $500,000 payment to be made on January 15, 1991, is $406,838. Thus, the portion of the payment treated as contingent on the change is $93,162 ($500,000 – $406,838), plus an amount reflecting the lapse of the obligation to continue to perform services. Such amount will depend on all the facts and circumstances but in no event will such amount be less than $115,000 [1% × 23 months × $500,000] [amended on June 20, 1989 (54 FR 25879)].

Example (7). (i) On January 15, 1986, a corporation grants to a disqualified individual nonqualified stock options to purchase 30,000 shares of the corporation's stock. The options do not have a readily ascertainable fair market value at the time of grant. The options will be forfeited by the individual if he fails to perform personal services for the corporation until January 15, 1989. The options will, however, substantially vest in the individual at an earlier date if there is a change in ownership or control of the corporation. On January 16, 1988, a change in the ownership of the corporation occurs and the options become substantially vested in the individual. On January 16, 1988, the options have an ascertainable fair market value of $600,000.

(ii) At the time of the change, it is substantially certain that the payment of the options to purchase 30,000 shares would have been made in the absence of the change if the individual had continued to perform services for the corporation until January 15, 1989. Therefore,

only a portion of the payment is treated as contingent on the change. The portion of the payment that is treated as contingent on the change is the amount by which the amount of the accelerated payment on January 16, 1988 ($600,000) exceeds the present value on January 16, 1988, of the payment that was expected to have been made on January 15, 1989, absent the acceleration, plus an amount reflecting the lapse of the obligation to continue to perform services. Assuming that, at the time of the change, it cannot be reasonably ascertained what the value of the options would have been on January 15, 1989, the value of such options on January 16, 1988, is deemed to be $600,000, the amount of the accelerated payment. The present value on January 16, 1988, of a $600,000 payment to be made on January 15, 1989, is $549,964.13. Thus, the portion of the payment treated as contingent on the change is $50,035.87 ($600,000 – $549,964.13), plus an amount reflecting the lapse of the obligation to continue to perform services. Such amount will depend on all the facts and circumstances but in no event will such amount be less than $66,000 (1% × 11 months × $600,000) [amended on June 20, 1989 (54 FR 25879)].

Example (8). (i) The facts are the same as in example (7), except that the options become substantially vested periodically (absent a change in ownership of control), with one-third of the options vesting on January 15, 1987, 1988, and 1989, respectively. Thus, options to purchase 20,000 shares vest independently of the January 16, 1988, change in ownership and the options to purchase the remaining 10,000 shares vest as a result of the change.

(ii) At the time of the change, it is substantially certain that the payment of the options to purchase 10,000 shares would have been made without regard to the change if the individual had continued to perform services for the corporation until January 15, 1989. Therefore, only a portion of the payment is treated as contingent on the change. The portion of the payment that is treated as contingent on the change is the amount by which the amount of the accelerated payment on January 16, 1988 ($200,000) exceeds the present value on January 16, 1988, of the payment that was expected to have been made on January 15, 1989, absent the acceleration, plus an amount reflecting the lapse of the obligation to continue to perform services. Assuming that, at the time of the change, it cannot be reasonably ascertained what the value of the options would have been on January 15, 1989, the value of such options on January 16, 1988, is deemed to be $200,000, the amount of the accelerated payment. The present value on January 16, 1988, of a $200,000 payment to be made on January 15, 1989, is $183,328.38. Thus, the portion of the payment treated as contingent on the change is $16,671.62 ($200,000 – $183,328.38), plus an amount reflecting the lapse of the obligation to continue to perform services. Such amount will depend on all the facts and circumstances but in no event will such amount be less than $22,000 (1% × 11 months × $200,000) [amended on June 20, 1989 (54 FR 25879)].

Example (9). Assume the same facts as in example (7), except that the option agreement provides that the options will vest either upon the corporation's level of profits reaching a specified level, or if earlier, on the date on which there is a change in ownership or control of the corporation. The corporation's level of profits do not reach the specified level prior to January 16, 1988. In such case, the full amount of the payment, $600,000, is treated as contingent on the change because it was not substantially certain, at the time of the change, that the payment would have been made in the absence of the change if the individual had continued to perform services for the corporation for a specified period of time. See Q/A-39 for rules relating to the reduction of the excess parachute payment by the portion of the payment which is established to be reasonable compensation for personal services actually rendered before the date of a change in ownership or control.

Presumption That Payment Is Contingent on Change

Q-25: Is there a presumption that certain payments are contingent on a change in ownership or control?

A-25: Yes. For purposes of this section, any payment pursuant to—

(a) An agreement entered into within one year before the date of a change in ownership or control, or

(b) An amendment that modifies a previous agreement in any significant respect, if the amendment is made within one year before the date of a change in ownership or control,

is presumed to be contingent on such change unless the contrary is established by clear and convincing evidence. In the case of an amendment described in paragraph (b) of this A-25, only the portion of any payment that exceeds the amount of such payment that would have been made in the absence of the amendment is presumed, by reason of the amendment, to be contingent on the change in ownership or control.

Q-26: How may the presumption described in Q/A-25 of this section be rebutted?

A-26: (a) To rebut the presumption described in Q/A-25 of this section, the taxpayer must establish by clear and convincing evidence that the payment is not contingent on the change in ownership or control. Whether the payment is contingent on such change is determined on the basis of all the facts and circumstances of the particular case. Factors relevant to such a determination include, but are not limited to: (1) the content of the agreement or amendment; and (2) the circumstances surrounding the execution of the agreement or amendment, such as whether it was entered into at a time when a takeover attempt had commenced and the degree of likelihood that a change in ownership or control would actually occur.

(b) In the case of an agreement described in paragraph (a) of A-25 of this section, clear and convincing evidence that the agreement is one of the three following types will generally rebut the presumption that payments under the agreement are contingent on the change in ownership or control:

(1) A "nondiscriminatory employee plan or program" as defined in paragraph (c) of this A-26;

(2) A contract between a corporation and an individual that replaces a prior contract entered into by the same parties more than one year before the change in ownership or control, if the new contract does not provide for increased payments (apart from normal increases attributable to increased responsibilities or cost of living adjustments), accelerate the payment of amounts due at a future time, or modify (to the individual's benefit) the terms or conditions under which payments will be made; or

(3) A contract between a corporation and an individual who did not perform services for the corporation prior to the individual's taxable year in which the change in ownership or control occurs, if the contract does not provide for payments that are significantly different in amount, timing, terms, or conditions from those provided under contracts entered into by the corporation (other than contracts that themselves were entered into within one year before the change in ownership or control and in contemplation of the change) with individuals performing comparable services.

However, even if the presumption is rebutted with respect to an agreement, payments under the agreement still may be contingent on the change in ownership or control pursuant to Q/A-22 of this section.

(c) For purposes of this section, the term "nondiscriminatory employee plan or program" means: a group term life insurance plan that meets the requirements of section 79(d); an employee benefit plan that meets the requirements of section 89(d) and (e); a self insured medical reimbursement plan that meets the requirements of section 105(h); a qualified group legal services plan (within the meaning of section 120); a cafeteria plan (within the meaning of section 125); an educational assistance program (within the meaning of section 127); and a dependent care assistance program (within the meaning of section 129). Payments under certain other plans are exempt from the definition of "parachute payment" under Q/A-8 of this section.

(d) The following examples illustrate the application of the presumption:

Example (1). A corporation and a disqualified individual who is an employee of the corporation enter into an employment contract. The contract replaces a prior contract entered into by the same parties more than one year before the change and the new contract does not provide for any increased payments other than a cost of living adjustment, does not accelerate the payment of amounts due at a future time, and does not modify (to the individual's benefit) the terms or conditions under which payments will be made. Clear and convincing evidence of these facts rebuts the presumption described in A-25 of this section. However, payments under the contract still may be contingent on the change in ownership or control pursuant to Q/A-22 of this section.

Example (2). Assume the same facts as in example (1), except that the contract is entered into after a tender offer for the corporation's stock had commenced and it was likely that a change in ownership would occur and the contract provides for a substantial bonus payment to the individual upon his signing the contract. The individual has performed services for the corporation for many years, but previous employment contracts between the corporation and the individual did not provide for a similar signing bonus. One month after the contract is entered into, a change in the ownership of the corporation occurs. All payments under the contract are presumed to be contingent on the change in ownership even though the bonus payment would have been legally required even if no change had occurred. Clear and convincing

evidence of these facts rebuts the presumption described in A-25 of this section with respect to all of the payments under the contract with the exception of the bonus payment (which is treated as contingent on the change). However, such payments under the contract still may be contingent on the change in ownership or control pursuant to Q/A-22 of this section.

Change in Ownership or Control

Q-27: When does a change in the ownership of a corporation occur?

A-27: (a) For purposes of this section, a change in the ownership or control of a corporation occurs on the date that any one person, or more than one person acting as a group, acquires ownership of stock of the corporation that, together with stock held by such person or group, possesses more than 50 percent of the total fair market value or total voting power of the stock of such corporation. However, if any one person, or more than one person acting as a group, is considered to own more than 50 percent of the total fair market value or total voting power of the stock of a corporation, the acquisition of additional stock by the same person or persons is not considered to cause a change in the ownership of the corporation (or to cause a change in the effective control of the corporation (within the meaning of Q/A-28 of this section)). An increase in the percentage of stock owned by any one person, or persons acting as a group, as a result of a transaction in which the corporation acquires its stock in exchange for property will be treated as an acquisition of stock for purposes of this section.

(b) For purposes of paragraph (a) of this A-27, persons will not be considered to be "acting as a group" merely because they happen to purchase or own stock of the same corporation at the same time, or as a result of the same public offering. However, persons will be considered to be "acting as a group" if they are owners of an entity that enters into a merger, consolidation, purchase or acquisition of stock, or similar business transaction with the corporation.

(c) For purposes of this A-27, section 318(a) shall apply in determining stock ownership.

(d) The following examples illustrate the principles of this A-27:

Example (1). Corporation M has owned stock having a fair market value equal to 19 percent of the value of the stock of Corporation N (an otherwise unrelated corporation) for many years prior to 1986. Corporation M acquires additional stock having a fair market value equal to 15 percent of the value of the stock of Corporation N on January 1, 1986, and an additional 18 percent on February 21, 1987. As of February 21, 1987, Corporation M has acquired stock having a fair market value greater than 50 percent of the value of the stock of Corporation N. Thus, a change in the ownership of Corporation N is considered to occur on February 21, 1987 (assuming that Corporation M did not have effective control of Corporation N immediately prior to the acquisition on that date).

Example (2). All of the corporation's stock is owned by the founders of the corporation. The board of directors of the corporation decides to offer shares of the corporation to the public. After the public offering, the founders of the corporation own a total of 40 percent of the corporation's stock, and members of the public own 60 percent. If no one person (or more than one person acting as a group) owns more than 50 percent of the corporation's stock (by value or voting power) after the public offering, there is no change in the ownership of the corporation.

Example (3). Corporation P merges into Corporation O (a previously unrelated corporation). In the merger, the shareholders of Corporation P receive Corporation O stock in exchange for their Corporation P stock. Immediately after the merger, the former shareholders of Corporation P own stock having a fair market value equal to 60 percent of the value of the stock of Corporation O, and the former shareholders of Corporation O own stock having a fair market value equal to 40 percent of the value of the stock of Corporation O. The former shareholders of Corporation P will be treated as "acting as a group" in their acquisition of Corporation O stock. Thus, a change in the ownership of Corporation O occurs on the date of the merger.

Example (4). A, an individual, owns stock having a fair market value equal to 20 percent of the value of the stock of Corporation Q. On January 1, 1987, Corporation Q acquires in a redemption for cash all of the stock held by shareholders other than A. Thus, A is left as the sole shareholder of Corporation Q. A change in ownership of Corporation Q is considered to occur on January 1, 1987 (assuming that A did not have effective control of Corporation Q immediately prior to the redemption) [amended on June 20, 1989 (54 FR 25879)].

Example (5). Assume the same facts as in example (4), except that A owns stock having a fair market value equal to 51 percent of the value of all the stock of Corporation Q immediately prior to the redemption.

There is no change in the ownership of Corporation Q as a result of the redemption.

Q-28: When does a change in the effective control of a corporation occur?

A-28: (a) For purposes of this section, a change in the effective control of a corporation is presumed to occur on the date that either—

(1) Any one person, or more than one person acting as a group, acquires (or has acquired during the 12 month period ending on the date of the most recent acquisition by such person or persons) ownership of stock of the corporation possessing 20 percent or more of the total voting power of the stock of such corporation; or

(2) A majority of members of the corporation's board of directors is replaced during any 12-month period by directors whose appointment or election is not endorsed by a majority of the members of the corporation's board of directors prior to the date of the appointment or election.

This presumption may be rebutted by establishing that such acquisition or acquisitions of the corporation's stock, or such replacement of the majority of the members of the corporation's board of directors, does not transfer the power to control (directly or indirectly) the management and policies of the corporation from any one person (or more than one person acting as a group) to another person (or group). For purposes of this section, in the absence of an event described in paragraph (a)(1) or (2) of this A-28, a change in the effective control of a corporation is presumed not to have occurred.

(b) If any one person, or more than one person acting as a group, is considered to effectively control a corporation (within the meaning of this A-28), the acquisition of additional control of the corporation by the same person or persons is not considered to cause a change in the effective control of the corporation (or to cause a change in the ownership of the corporation within the meaning of Q/A-27 of this section).

(c) For purposes of this A-28, persons will not be considered to be "acting as a group" merely because they happen to purchase or own stock of the same corporation at the same time, or as a result of the same public offering. However, persons will be considered as "acting as a group" if they are owners of an entity that enters into a merger, consolidation, purchase or acquisition of stock, or similar business transaction with the corporation.

(d) Section 318(a) shall apply in determining stock ownership for purposes of this A-28.

(e) The following examples illustrate the principles of this A-28:

Example (1). Shareholder A acquired the following percentages of the voting stock of Corporation M (an otherwise unrelated corporation) on the following dates: 16 percent on January 1, 1985; 10 percent on January 10, 1986; 8 percent on February 10, 1986; 11 percent on March 1, 1987; and 8 percent on March 10, 1987. Thus, on March 10, 1987, A owns a total of 53 percent of M's voting stock. Since A did not acquire 20 percent or more of M's voting stock during any 12-month period, there is no presumption of a change in effective control pursuant to paragraph (a)(1) of this A-28. In addition, under these facts there is a presumption that no change in the effective control of Corporation M occurred. If this presumption is not rebutted (and thus no change in effective control of Corporation M is treated as occurring prior to March 10, 1987), a change in the ownership of Corporation M will be treated as having occurred on March 10, 1987 (pursuant to Q/A-27 of this section) since A had acquired more than 50 percent of Corporation M's voting stock as of that date.

Example (2). A minority group of shareholders of a corporation opposes the practices and policies of the corporation's current board of directors. A proxy contest ensues. The minority group presents its own slate of candidates for the board at the next annual meeting of the corporation's shareholders, and candidates of the minority group are elected to replace a majority of the current members of the board. A change in the effective control of the corporation is presumed to have occurred on the date the election of the new board of directors becomes effective.

Q-29: When does a change in the ownership of a substantial portion of a corporation's assets occur?

A-29: (a) For purposes of this section, a change in the ownership of a substantial portion of a corporation's assets occurs on the date that any one person, or more than one person acting as a group, acquires (or has acquired during the 12-month period ending on the date of the most recent acquisition by such person or persons) assets from the corporation that have a total fair market value equal to or more than

one third of the total fair market value of all of the assets of the corporation immediately prior to such acquisition or acquisitions.

(b) A transfer of assets by a corporation is not treated as a change in the ownership of such assets if the assets are transferred to—

(1) A shareholder of the corporation (immediately before the asset transfer) in exchange for or with respect to its stock,

(2) An entity, 50 percent or more of the total value or voting power of which is owned, directly or indirectly, by the corporation,

(3) A person, or more than one person acting as a group, that owns, directly or indirectly, 50 percent or more of the total value or voting power of all the outstanding stock of the corporation, or

(4) An entity, at least 50 percent of the total value or voting power is owned, directly or indirectly, by a person described in paragraph (b)(3) of this A-29.

For purposes of this paragraph (b) (except as otherwise provided), a person's status is determined immediately after the transfer of the assets. For example, a transfer of assets pursuant to a complete liquidation of a corporation, a redemption of a shareholder's interest, or a transfer to a majority-owned subsidiary of the corporation is not treated as a change in the ownership of the assets of the transferor corporation.

(c) For purposes of this A-29, section 318(a) shall apply in determining stock ownership.

(d) The following examples illustrate the principles of this A-29:

Example (1). Corporation M acquires assets having a fair market value of $500,000 from Corporation N (an unrelated corporation) on January 1, 1986. The total fair market value of Corporation N's assets immediately prior to the acquisition was $3 million. Since the value of the assets acquired by Corporation M is less than one third of the fair market value of Corporation N's total assets immediately prior to the acquisition, the acquisition does not represent a change in the ownership of a substantial portion of Corporation N's assets.

Example (2). Assume the same facts as in example (1). Also assume that on November 1, 1986, Corporation M acquires from Corporation N additional assets having a fair market value of $700,000. Thus, Corporation M has acquired from Corporation N assets worth a total of $1.2 million during the 12-month period ending on November 1, 1986. Since $1.2 million is more than one third of the total fair market value of all of Corporation N's assets immediately prior to the earlier of these acquisitions ($3 million), a change in the ownership of a substantial portion of Corporation N's assets is considered to have occurred on November 1, 1986.

Example (3). All of the assets of Corporation P are transferred to Corporation O (an unrelated corporation). In exchange, the shareholders of Corporation P receive Corporation O stock. Immediately after the transfer, the former shareholders of Corporation P own 60 percent of the fair market value of the outstanding stock of Corporation O and the former shareholders of Corporation O own 40 percent of the fair market value of the outstanding stock of Corporation O. Because Corporation O is an entity more than 50 percent of the fair market value of the outstanding stock of which is owned by the former shareholders of Corporation P, the transfer of assets is not treated as a change in ownership of a substantial portion of the assets of Corporation P.

"Three Times Base Amount Test" for Parachute Payments

Q-30: Are all payments that are in the nature of compensation, are made to a disqualified individual, and are contingent on a change in ownership or control, parachute payments?

A-30: (a) No. To determine whether such payments are parachute payments, they must be tested against the individual's "base amount" (as defined in Q/A-34 of this section). To do this, the aggregate present value of all payments in the nature of compensation that are made or to be made to (or for the benefit of) the same disqualified individual and are contingent on the change in ownership or control must be determined. If this aggregate present value equals or exceeds the amount equal to 3 times the individual's base amount, the payments are parachute payments. If this aggregate present value is less than the amount equal to 3 times the individual's base amount, no portion of the payments is a parachute payment. See Q/A-31, Q/A-32, and Q/A-33 for rules on determining present value. Parachute payments that are securities violation parachute payments are not included in the foregoing computation if they are not contingent on a change in ownership or control. See Q/A-37 for the definition and treatment of securities violation parachute payments.

(b) The following examples illustrate the principles of this A-30:

Example (1). A is a disqualified individual with respect to Corporation M. A's base amount is $100,000. Payments totalling $400,000 that are in the nature of compensation and contingent on a change in the ownership of Corporation M are made to A on the date of the change. The payments are parachute payments since they have an aggregate present value at least equal to 3 times A's base amount of $100,000 (3 × $100,000 = $300,000).

Example (2). Assume the same facts as in example (1), except that the payments contingent on the change in the ownership of Corporation M total $290,000. Since the payments do not have an aggregate present value at least equal to 3 times A's base amount, no portion of the payments is a parachute payment.

Q-31: As of what date is the present value of a payment determined?

A-31: Except as provided in this section, the present value of a payment is determined as of the date on which the change in ownership or control occurs, or, if a payment is made prior to such date, the date on which the payment is made.

Q-32: What discount rate is to be used to determine present value?

A-32: For purposes of this section, present value generally is determined by using a discount rate equal to 120 percent of the applicable Federal rate (determined under section 1274(d) and the regulations thereunder) compounded semiannually. The applicable Federal rate to be used for this purpose is the Federal rate that is in effect on the date as of which the present value is determined. See Q/As 24 and 31. However, for any payment, the corporation and the disqualified individual may elect to use the applicable Federal rate that is in effect on the date that the contract which provides for the payment is entered into, if such election is made in the contract [amended on June 20, 1989 (54 FR 25879) and on July 11, 1989 (54 FR 29061)].

Q-33: If the present value of a payment to be made in the future is contingent on an uncertain future event or condition, how is the present value of the payment determined?

A-33: (a) In certain cases, it may be necessary to apply the 3-times-base-amount test of Q/A-30 of this section or to allocate a portion of the base amount to a payment described in paragraph (a)(1), (2), and (3) of A-2 of this section at a time when the aggregate present value of all such payments cannot be determined with certainty because the time, amount, or right to receive one or more such payments is contingent on the occurrence of an uncertain future event or condition. For example, a disqualified individual's right to receive a payment may be contingent on the involuntary termination of such individual's employment with the corporation. In such a case, a reasonable estimate of the time and amount of the future payment shall be made, and the present value of the payment will be determined on the basis of this estimate. For purposes of making this estimate, an uncertain future event or condition that may reduce the present value of a payment will be taken into account only if the possibility of the occurrence of the event or condition can be determined on the basis of generally accepted actuarial principles or can be otherwise estimated with reasonable accuracy.

(b) Whenever a payment described in paragraph (a) of this A-33 is actually made or becomes certain not to be made, the 3-times-base-amount test described in Q/A-30 of this section shall be reapplied (and the portion of the base amount allocated to previous payments shall be reallocated (if necessary) to such payments) to reflect the actual time and amount of the payment. Whenever the 3-times-base-amount test is applied (or whenever the base amount is allocated), the aggregate present value of the payments received or to be received by the disqualified individual is redetermined as of the date described in A-31 of this section, using the discount rate described in A-32 of this section. This redetermination may affect the amount of any excess parachute payment for a prior taxable year.

(c) The following examples illustrate the principles of this A-33:

Example (1). A, a disqualified individual with respect to Corporation M, has a base amount of $100,000. Under his employment agreement with Corporation M, A is entitled to receive a payment in the nature of compensation in the amount of $250,000 contingent on a change in the ownership of Corporation M. In addition, the agreement provides that if A's employment is terminated within 1 year after the change in ownership, A will receive an additional payment in the nature of compensation in the amount of $150,000, payable 1 year after the date of the change in ownership. A and Corporation M are calendar year taxpayers. A change in the ownership of Corporation M occurs and A receives the first payment of $250,000. At the time Corporation M files its income tax return for the year of the change in ownership, it reasonably estimates that there is a 50-percent probability that, as a result of the change, A's employment will be terminated within 1 year of the date of the change. For purposes of applying the 3-times-base-

amount test (and if the first payment is determined to be a parachute payment, for purposes of allocating a portion of A's base amount to that payment), Corporation M shall assume that an additional payment of $75,000 (.5 × $150,000) will be made to A as a result of the change in ownership. The present value of the additional payment is determined under Q/A-31 and Q/A-32 of this section.

Example (2). B, a disqualified individual with respect to Corporation N, has a base amount of $100,000. Under her employment agreement with Corporation N, B is entitled to receive payments in the nature of compensation in the amount of $20,000 per month for a period of 24 months if B terminates employment with Corporation N as a result of a change in ownership of Corporation N. Such monthly payments are to be reduced by the amount of any compensation earned by B from unrelated employers during the 24-month period. B and Corporation N are calendar year taxpayers. On June 1, 1988, there is a change in the ownership of Corporation N. As a result of the change, B voluntarily terminates employment with Corporation N and begins to receive monthly payments under the agreement. Assume that the present value, determined as of June 1, 1988, of a stream of 24-monthly payments of $20,000, is $438,134. At the time Corporation N files its income tax return for 1988, it cannot be determined with reasonable accuracy whether B will earn any compensation from unrelated employers during the 24-month period. Accordingly, the present value of the payments to be received by B ($438,134) exceeds 3 times B's base amount ($300,000) and a portion of each of the 1988 payments will be treated as an excess parachute payment for the 1988 taxable year.

Example (3). Assume the same facts as in example (2), except that in April 1989 B becomes employed by an employer unrelated to Corporation N. At the time Corporation N files its income tax return for 1989, it has become certain that, due to the compensation earned by B from unrelated employers, the present value, determined as of June 1, 1988, of the stream of payments from Corporation N will not exceed $192,060. Because it has been redetermined that the present value of the payments received or to be received by B does not equal or exceed 3 times B's base amount, no portion of the payments made in 1988 or 1989 will be treated as excess parachute payments.

Q-34: What is the "base amount"?

A-34: (a) The base amount of a disqualified individual is the average annual compensation (as defined in Q/A-21 of this section) which was includible in the gross income of such individual for taxable years in the "base period" (or either was excludible from such gross income as "foreign earned income" within the meaning of section 911, or would have been includible in such gross income if such person had been a United States citizen or resident.) See Q/A-35 for the definition of "base period" and for examples of base amount computations.

(b) If the base period of a disqualified individual includes a short taxable year or less than all of a taxable year, compensation for such short or incomplete taxable year must be annualized before determining the average annual compensation for the base period. In annualizing compensation, the frequency with which payments are expected to be made over an annual period must be taken into account. Thus, any amount of compensation for such a short or incomplete taxable year that represents a payment that will not be made more often than once per year is not annualized.

(c) Because the base amount includes only compensation that is includible in gross income, the base amount does not include certain items that constitute parachute payments. For example, payments in the form of untaxed fringe benefits are not included in the base amount but may be treated as parachute payments.

Q-35: What is the "base period"?

A-35: (a) The "base period" of a disqualified individual is the most recent 5 taxable years of the individual ending before the date of the change in ownership or control. However, if the disqualified individual was not an employee or independent contractor of the corporation with respect to which the change in ownership or control occurs (or a predecessor entity or a related entity as defined in A-21 of this section) for this entire 5-year period, the individual's base period is the portion of such 5-year period during which the individual performed personal services for the corporation or predecessor entity or related entity.

(b) The following examples illustrate the principles of Q/A-34 of this section and this Q/A-35:

Example (1). A disqualified individual was employed by a corporation for 2 years and 4 months preceding his taxable year in which a change in ownership or control of the corporation occurs. The individual's includible compensation income from the corporation was $30,000 for the 4-month period, $120,000 for the first full year, and $150,000 for the second full year. The individual's base amount is $120,000

$$[(3 \times \$30,000) + \$120,000 + \$150,000].$$

$$[\qquad \qquad 3 \qquad \qquad]$$

Example (2). Assume the same facts as in example (1), except that the individual also received a $60,000 "sign-up" bonus when his employment with the corporation commenced at the beginning of the 4-month period. The individual's base amount is $140,000

$$[(\$60,000 + (3 + \$30,000) + \$120,000 + \$150,000].$$

$$[\qquad \qquad 3 \qquad \qquad]$$

Since the bonus will not be paid more often than once per year, the amount of the bonus is not increased in annualizing the individual's compensation for the 4-month period.

Q-36: How is the base amount determined in the case of a disqualified individual who did not perform services for the corporation (or a predecessor entity or a related entity as defined in A-21 of this section), prior to the individual's taxable year in which the change in ownership or control occurs?

A-36: (a) In such a case, the individual's base amount is the annualized compensation (as defined in Q/A-21 of this section) which—

(1) Was includible in the individual's gross income for that portion, prior to such change, of the individual's taxable year in which the change occurred (or either was excludible from such gross income as "foreign earned income" within the meaning of section 911, or would have been includible in such gross income if such person had been a United States citizen or resident),

(2) Was not contingent on the change in ownership or control, and

(3) Was not a securities violation parachute payment.

(b) The following examples illustrate the principles of this A-36:

Example (1). On January 1, 1986, A, an individual whose taxable year is the calendar year, enters into a 4-year employment contract with Corporation M as an officer of the corporation. A has not previously performed services for Corporation M (or any predecessor entity or related entity as defined in A-21 of this section). Under the employment contract, A is to receive an annual salary of $120,000 for each of the 4 years that he remains employed by Corporation M with any remaining unpaid balance to be paid immediately in the event that A's employment is terminated without cause. On July 1, 1986, after A has received compensation of $60,000, a change in the ownership of Corporation M occurs. Because of the change, A's employment is terminated without cause, and he receives a payment of $420,000. It is established by clear and convincing evidence that the $60,000 in compensation is not contingent on the change in ownership or control, but the presumption of Q/A-25 of this section is not rebutted with respect to the $420,000 payment. Thus, the payment of $420,000 is treated as contingent on the change in ownership of Corporation M. In this case, A's base amount is $120,000 (2 × $60,000). Since the present value of the payment which is contingent on the change in ownership of Corporation M ($420,000) is more than 3 times A's base amount of $120,000 (3 × $120,000 = $360,000), the payment is a parachute payment.

Example (2). Assume the same facts as in example (1), except that A also receives a "sign-up" bonus of $50,000 from Corporation M on January 1, 1986. It is established by clear and convincing evidence that the bonus is not contingent on the change in ownership. When the change in ownership occurs on July 1, 1986, A has received compensation of $110,000 (the $50,000 bonus plus $60,000 in salary). In this case, A's base amount is $170,000 [$50,000 + (2 × $60,000)]. Since the $50,000 bonus will not be paid more than once per year, the amount of the bonus is not increased in annualizing A's compensation. The present value of the potential parachute payment ($420,000) is less than 3 times A's base amount of $170,000 (3 × $170,000 = $510,000), and therefore no portion of the payment is a parachute payment.

Securities Violation Parachute Payments

Q-37: Must a payment be contingent on a change in ownership or control in order to be a parachute payment?

A-37: (a) No. The term "parachute payment" also includes any payment (other than a payment exempted under Q/A-6 or Q/A-8 of this section) that is in the nature of compensation and is to (or for the benefit of) a disqualified individual, if such payment is made or to be made—

(1) Pursuant to an agreement that violates any generally enforced Federal or State securities laws or regulations, and

(2) In connection with a potential or actual change in ownership or control.

A violation is not taken into account under paragraph (a)(1) of this A-37 if it is merely technical in character or is not materially prejudicial to shareholders or potential shareholders. Moreover, a violation will be presumed not to exist unless the existence of the violation has been determined or admitted in a civil or criminal action (or an administrative action by a regulatory body charged with enforcing the particular securities law or regulation) which has been resolved by adjudication or consent. Parachute payments described in this A-37 are referred to in this section as "securities violation parachute payments."

(b) Securities violation parachute payments that are not contingent on a change in ownership or control within the meaning of Q/A-22 of this section are not taken into account in applying the 3-times-base-amount test of Q/A-30 of this section. Such payments are considered parachute payments regardless of whether such test is met with respect to the disqualified individual. Moreover, the amount of a securities violation parachute payment treated as an excess parachute payment shall not be reduced by the portion of such payment that is reasonable compensation for personal services actually rendered before the date of a change in ownership or control if such payment is not contingent on such change. Likewise, the amount of a securities violation parachute payment shall include the portion of such payment that is reasonable compensation for personal services to be rendered on or after the date of a change in ownership or control if such payment is not contingent on such change.

(c) The rules in paragraph (b) of this A-37 also apply to securities violation parachute payments that are contingent on a change in ownership or control if the application of these rules results in greater total excess parachute payments with respect to the disqualified individual than would result if the payments were treated simply as payments contingent on a change in ownership or control (and hence were taken into account in applying the 3-times-base-amount test and were reduced by, or did not include, any applicable amount of reasonable compensation).

(d) The following examples illustrate the principles of this A-37:

Example (1). A, a disqualified individual with respect to Corporation M, receives two payments in the nature of compensation that are contingent on a change in the ownership or control of Corporation M. The present value of the first payment is equal to A's base amount and is not a securities violation parachute payment. The present value of the second payment is equal to 1.5 times A's base amount and is a securities violation parachute payment. Neither payment includes any reasonable compensation. If the second payment is treated simply as a payment contingent on a change in ownership or control, the amount of A's total excess parachute payments is zero because the aggregate present value of the payments does not equal or exceed 3 times A's base amount. If the second payment is treated as a securities violation parachute payment subject to the rules of paragraph (b) of this A-37, the amount of A's total excess parachute payments is 0.5 times A's base amount. Thus, the second payment is treated as a securities violation parachute payment.

Example (2). Assume the same facts as in example (1), except that the present value of the first payment is equal to 2 times A's base amount. If the second payment is treated simply as a payment contingent on a change in ownership or control, the total present value of the payments is 3.5 times A's base amount, and the amount of A's total excess parachute payments is 2.5 times A's base amount. If the second payment is treated as a securities violation parachute payment, the amount of A's total excess parachute payments is 0.5 times A's base amount. Thus, the second payment is treated simply as a payment contingent on a change in ownership or control.

Example (3). B, a disqualified individual with respect to Corporation N, receives two payments in the nature of compensation that are contingent on a change in the control of Corporation N. The present value of the first payment is equal to 4 times B's base amount and is a securities violation parachute payment. The present value of the second payment is equal to 2 times B's base amount and is not a securities violation parachute payment. B establishes by clear and convincing evidence that the entire amount of the first payment is reasonable compensation for personal services to be rendered after the change in control. If the first payment is treated simply as a payment contingent on a change in ownership or control, it is exempt from the definition of "parachute payment" pursuant to Q/A-9 of this section. Thus, the amount of B's total excess parachute payment is zero because the present value of the second payment does not equal or exceed three times B's base amount. However, if the first payment is treated as a securities violation parachute payment, the amount of B's total excess parachute payments is 3 times B's base amount. Thus, the first payment is treated as a securities violation parachute payment.

Example (4). Assume the same facts as in example (3), except that B does not receive the second payment and B establishes by clear and convincing evidence that the first payment is reasonable compensation for services actually rendered before the change in the control of Corporation N. If the payment is treated simply as a payment contingent on a change in ownership or control, the amount of B's excess parachute payment is zero because the amount treated as an excess parachute payment is reduced by the amount that B establishes as reasonable compensation. However, if the payment is treated as a securities violation parachute payment, the amount of B's excess parachute payment is 3 times B's base amount. Thus, the payment is treated as a securities violation parachute payment.

Computation and Reduction of Excess Parachute Payments

Q-38: How is the amount of an excess parachute payment computed?

A-38: (a) The amount of an excess parachute payment is the excess of the amount of any parachute payment over the portion of the disqualified individual's base amount that is allocated to such payment. For this purpose, the portion of the base amount allocated to any parachute payment is the amount that bears the same ratio to the base amount as the present value of such parachute payment bears to the aggregate present value of all parachute payments made or to be made to (or for the benefit of) the same disqualified individual. Thus, the portion of the base amount allocated to any parachute payment is determined by multiplying the base amount by a fraction, the numerator of which is the present value of such parachute payment and the denominator of which is the aggregate present value of all such payments. See Q/A-31, Q/A-32, and Q/A-33 for rules on determining present value and Q/A-34 for the definition of "base amount".

(b) *Example*. An individual with a base amount of $100,000 is entitled to receive two parachute payments, one of $200,000 and the other of $400,000. The $200,000 payment is made at the time of the change in ownership or control, and the $400,000 payment is to be made at a future date. The present value of the $400,000 payment is $300,000 on the date of the change in ownership or control. The portions of the base amount allocated to these payments are $40,000 ([$200,000/$500,000] × $100,000) and $60,000 ([$300,000/$500,000] × $100,000), respectively. Thus, the amount of the first excess parachute payment is $160,000 ($200,000 – $40,000) and that of the second is $340,000 ($400,000 – $60,000).

Q-39: May the amount of an excess parachute payment be reduced by reasonable compensation for personal services actually rendered before the change in ownership or control?

A-39: (a) Generally, yes. Except in the case of payments treated as securities violation parachute payments, the amount of an excess parachute payment is reduced by any portion of the payment that the taxpayer establishes by clear and convincing evidence is reasonable compensation for personal services actually rendered by the disqualified individual before the date of the change in ownership or control. Services reasonably compensated for by payments that are not parachute payments (either because the payments are not contingent on a change in ownership or control and are not securities violation parachute payments, or because the payments are made pursuant to a contract entered into before June 15, 1984, which has not been renewed, or amended or supplemented in significant relevant respect after June 14, 1984) are not taken into account for this purpose. The portion of any parachute payment that is established as reasonable compensation is first reduced by the portion of the disqualified individual's base amount that is allocated to such parachute payment; any remaining portion of the parachute payment established as reasonable compensation then reduces the excess parachute payment.

(b) Reasonable compensation for personal services to be rendered by the disqualified individual on or after the date of the change in ownership or control is exempt from the definition of "parachute payment" pursuant to Q/A-9 of this section. For rules on determining amounts of reasonable compensation, see Q/A-40 through Q/A-43.

(c) The following examples illustrate the principles of this A-39:

Example (1). Assume that a parachute payment of $600,000 is made to a disqualified individual, and the portion of the individual's base amount that is allocated to the parachute payment is $100,000. Also assume that $300,000 of the $600,000 parachute payment is established as reasonable compensation for personal services actually rendered by the disqualified individual before the date of the change in ownership or control. Before the reasonable compensation is taken into account, the amount of the excess parachute payment is $500,000 ($600,000 – $100,000). In reducing the excess parachute payment by reasonable compensation, the portion of the parachute payment that is established as reasonable compensation ($300,000) is first reduced by the portion of the disqualified individual's base amount that is allocated to the

parachute payment ($100,000), and the remainder ($200,000) then reduces the excess parachute payment. Thus, in this case, the excess parachute payment of $500,000 is reduced by $200,000 of reasonable compensation.

Example (2). Assume the same facts as in example (1), except that the full amount of the $600,000 parachute payment is established as reasonable compensation. In this case, the excess parachute payment of $500,000 is reduced to zero by $500,000 of reasonable compensation. As a result, no portion of any deduction for the payment is disallowed by section 280G, and no portion of the payment is subject to the 20-percent excise tax of section 4999.

Determination of Reasonable Compensation

Q-40: How is it determined whether payments are reasonable compensation?

A-40: In general, whether payments are reasonable compensation for personal services actually rendered, or to be rendered, by the disqualified individual is determined on the basis of all the facts and circumstances of the particular case. Factors relevant to such a determination include, but are not limited to, the following:

(a) The nature of the services rendered or to be rendered;

(b) The individual's historic compensation for performing such services; and

(c) The compensation of individuals performing comparable services in situations where the compensation is not contingent on a change in ownership or control.

Q-41: Is any particular type of evidence generally considered clear and convincing evidence of reasonable compensation for personal services?

A-41: Yes. A showing that payments are made under a nondiscriminatory employee plan or program (as defined in Q/A-26 of this section) generally is considered to be clear and convincing evidence that the payments are reasonable compensation. This is true whether the personal services for which the payments are made are actually rendered before, or to be rendered on or after, the date of the change in ownership or control. Q/A-46 of this section (relating to the treatment of an affiliated group as one corporation) does not apply for purposes of this A-41. No determination of reasonable compensation is needed in order for payments under qualified plans to be exempt from the definition of "parachute payment" under Q/A-8 of this section.

Q-42: Is any particular type of evidence generally considered clear and convincing evidence of reasonable compensation for personal services to be rendered on or after the date of a change in ownership or control?

A-42: (a) Yes. If payments are made or to be made to (or on behalf of) a disqualified individual for personal services to be rendered on or after the date of a change in ownership or control, a showing that—

(1) The payments were made or are to be made only for the period the individual actually performs such personal services, and

(2) The individual's annual compensation for such services is not significantly greater than such individual's annual compensation prior to the change in ownership or control, apart from normal increase attributable to increased responsibilities or cost of living adjustments (or is not significantly greater than the annual compensation customarily paid by the employer or by comparable employers to persons performing comparable services),

generally is considered to be clear and convincing evidence that the payments are reasonable compensation for services to be rendered on or after the date of change in ownership or control. However, except as provided in paragraph (b) of this A-42, such clear and convincing evidence will not exist if the individual does not, in fact, perform the services.

(b) If the employment of a disqualified individual is involuntarily terminated before the end of a contract term and the individual is paid damages for the breach of the contract, a showing of the following factors generally is considered clear and convincing evidence that the payment is reasonable compensation for personal services to be rendered on or after the date of change in ownership or control:

(1) The contract was not entered into, amended, or renewed in contemplation of the change in ownership or control;

(2) The compensation the individual would have received under the contract would qualify as reasonable compensation under section 162;

(3) The damages do not exceed the present value (determined as of the date of receipt) of the compensation the individual would have received under the contract if the individual had continued to perform services for the employer until the end of the contract term;

(4) The damages are received because an offer to provide personal services was made by the disqualified individual but was rejected by the employer; and

(5) The damages are reduced by mitigation.

Mitigation will be treated as occurring when such damages are reduced (or any payment of such damages is returned) to the extent of the disqualified individual's earned income (within the meaning of section 911(d)(2)(A)) during the remainder of the period in which the contract would have been in effect. See Q/A-44 for rules regarding damages for a failure to make severance payments.

(c) The following examples illustrate the principles of this A-42:

Example (1). A, a disqualified individual, has a three-year employment contract with Corporation M, a publicly traded corporation. Under this contract, A is to receive a salary for $100,000 for the first year of the contract and, for each succeeding year, an annual salary that is 10 percent higher than his prior year's salary. During the third year of the contract, Corporation N acquires all the stock of Corporation M. Prior to the change in ownership, Corporation N arranges to retain A's services by entering into an employment contract with him that is essentially the same as A's contract with Corporation M. Under the new contract, Corporation N is to fulfill Corporation M's obligations for the third year of the old contract, and, for each of the succeeding years, pay A an annual salary that is 10 percent higher than his prior year's salary. Amounts are payable under the new contract only for the portion of the contract term during which A remains employed by Corporation N. A showing of the facts described above (and in the absence of contradictory evidence) is regarded as clear and convincing evidence that all payments under the new contract are reasonable compensation for personal services to be rendered on or after the date of the change in ownership. Therefore, the payments under this agreement are exempt from the definition of "parachute payment" pursuant to Q/A-9 of this section.

Example (2). Assume the same facts as in example (1), except that the employment contract with Corporation N does not provide that amounts are payable under the contract only for the portion of the term for which A remains employed by Corporation N. Shortly after the change in ownership, and despite A's request to remain employed by Corporation N, A's employment with Corporation N is involuntarily terminated. Shortly thereafter, A obtains employment with Corporation 0. A commences a civil action against Corporation N, alleging breach of the employment contract. In settlement of the litigation, A receives an amount equal to the present value of the compensation A would have received under the contract with Corporation N, reduced by the amount of compensation A otherwise receives from Corporation 0 during the period that the contract would have been in effect. A showing of the facts described above (and in the absence of contradictory evidence) is regarded as clear and convincing evidence that the amount A receives as damages is reasonable compensation for personal services to be rendered on or after the date of the change in ownership. Therefore, the amount received by A is exempt from the definition of "parachute payment" pursuant to Q/A-9 of this section.

Q-43: Is any particular type of payment generally considered reasonable compensation for personal services actually rendered before the date of a change in ownership or control?

A-43: (a) Yes. Payments of compensation earned before the date of a change in ownership or control generally are considered reasonable compensation for personal services actually rendered before the date of a change in ownership or control if they qualify as reasonable compensation under section 162.

Q-44: May severance payments be treated as reasonable compensation?

A-44: No. Severance payments are not treated as reasonable compensation for personal services actually rendered before, or to be rendered on or after, the date of a change in ownership or control. Moreover, any damages paid for a failure to make severance payments are not treated as reasonable compensation for personal services actually rendered before, or to be rendered on or after, the date of such change. For purposes of this section, the term "severance payment" means any payment that is made to (or for the benefit of) a disqualified individual on account of the termination of such individual's employment prior to the end of a contract term, but shall not include any payment that otherwise would be made to (or for the benefit of) such individual upon the termination of such individual's employment, whenever occurring.

Miscellaneous Rules

Q-45: How is the term "corporation" defined?

A-45: For purposes of this section, the term "corporation" has the meaning prescribed by section 7701(a)(3) and shall include a publicly traded partnership treated as a corporation under section 7704(a).

Q-46: How is an affiliated group treated?

A-46: For purposes of this section, and except as otherwise provided in this section, all members of the same affiliated group (as defined in section 1504, determined without regard to section 1504(b)) are treated as one corporation. Rules affected by this treatment of an affiliated group include (but are not limited to) rules relating to exempt payments of certain corporations (Q/A-6, Q/A-7 (except as provided therein)), payor of parachute payments (Q/A-10), disqualified individuals (Q/A-15 through Q/A-21 (except as provided therein)), rebuttal of the presumption that payments are contingent on a change (Q/A-26 except as provided therein), change in ownership or control (Q/A-27, 28, 29), and reasonable compensation (Q/A-42, Q/A-43, and 44).

Effective Date

Q-47: What is the general effective date of section 280G and this section?

A-47: In general, section 280G and this section apply to payments under agreements entered into or renewed after June 14, 1984. Any agreement that is entered into before June 15, 1984, and is renewed after June 14, 1984, is to be treated as a new contract entered into on the day the renewal takes effect. (See Q/A-48 regarding application of section 280G and this section with respect to contracts entered into on or before June 14, 1984, and amended or supplemented after that date.)

Q-48: How is a contract that is cancellable at will treated for purposes of the effective date of section 280G and this section?

A-48: (a) For this purpose, a contract that is terminable or cancellable unconditionally at will by either party to the contract without the consent of the other, or by both parties to the contract, is treated as a new contract entered into on the date any such termination or cancellation, if made, would be effective. However, a contract is not treated as so terminable or cancellable if it can be terminated or cancelled only by terminating the employment relationship or independent contractor relationship of the disqualified individual.

(b) The following examples illustrate the principles of this A-48:

Example (1). Before June 15, 1984, a corporation and a disqualified individual enter into a contract providing for payments to the individual contingent on a change in the ownership or control of the corporation. The corporation may cancel the contract unconditionally at will by giving 3 months notice. Thus, the earliest date that any such cancellation after June 14, 1984, could be effective is September 15, 1984. The contract is treated as a new contract entered into on September 15, 1984, whether or not it is in fact cancelled. Therefore, section 280G and this section apply to all payments made or to be made under the contract in taxable years of the individual that end on or after September 15, 1984.

Example (2). On January 1, 1984, a corporation and a disqualified individual enter into a contract providing for payments to the individual contingent on a change in the ownership or control of the corporation. The corporation has a right to terminate the employment of the individual with or without cause, and the individual has the right to cease working for the corporation; otherwise, the contract is not terminable by either party. Since the contract is terminable only by terminating the employment relationship between the parties, it is not treated as terminable at will. Thus, since the contract was entered into on or before June 14, 1984, no payments under the contract are subject to section 280G or this section.

Q-49: Do section 280G and this section apply to payments under some agreements entered into on or before June 14, 1984, that are not renewed after this date?

A-49: Yes. Section 280G and this section apply to payments under a contract entered into on or before June 14, 1984, if the contract is amended or supplemented after June 14, 1984, in significant relevant respect. For this purpose, a "supplement" to a contract is defined as a new contract entered into after June 14, 1984, that affects the trigger, amount, or time of receipt of a payment under an existing contract.

Q-50: Under what circumstances is a contract considered to be amended or supplemented in significant relevant respect?

A-50: Except as otherwise provided in Q/A-51 of this section, a contract is considered to be amended or supplemented in significant relevant respect if provisions for payments contingent on a change in ownership or control ("parachute provisions"), or provisions in the nature of parachute provisions, are added to the contract, or are amended or supplemented to provide significant additional benefits to the disqualified individual. Thus, for example, a contract generally is treated as amended or supplemented in significant relevant respect if it is amended or supplemented:

(a) To add or modify, to the disqualified individual's benefit, a change in ownership or control trigger;

(b) To increase amounts payable that are contingent on a change in ownership or control (or, where payment is to be made under a formula, to modify the formula to the disqualified individual's advantage); or

(c) To accelerate, in the event of a change in ownership or control, the payment of amounts otherwise payable at a later date.

For purposes of this A-50, a payment will not be treated as being accelerated in the event of a change in ownership or control if the acceleration does not increase the present value of the payment.

Q-51: Will normal adjustments in an employment contract cause the contract to be treated as amended or supplemented in significant relevant respect?

A-51: No. A contract entered into on or before June 14, 1984, will not be treated as amended or supplemented in significant relevant respect merely by reason of normal adjustments in the terms of employment relationship or independent contractor relationship of the disqualified individual. Whether an adjustment in the terms of such a relationship is considered normal for this purpose depends on all of the facts and circumstances of the particular case. Relevant factors include, but are not limited to, the following:

(a) the length of time between the adjustment and the change in ownership or control;

(b) the extent to which the corporation, at the time of the adjustment, viewed itself as a likely takeover candidate;

(c) a comparison of the adjustment with historical practices of the corporation;

(d) the extent of overlap between the group receiving the benefits of the adjustment and those members of that group who are the beneficiaries of pre-June 15, 1984, parachute contracts; and

(e) the size of the adjustment, both in absolute terms and in comparison with the benefits provided to other members of the group receiving the benefits of the adjustment.

Q-52: What are some examples illustrating the principles of Q/A-49, Q/A-50, and Q/A-51 of this section?

A-52: The following examples illustrate these principles:

Example (1). Corporation M grants a nonqualified stock option to a disqualified individual before June 15, 1984. After June 14, 1984, at a time when the option is currently vested and exercisable by the individual regardless of whether a change in ownership or control occurs, Corporation M amends the option to permit the individual to surrender it for cash or other property equal to the fair market value of the stock that would have been received if the option had been exercised (minus the exercise price of the option). Since the individual could have exercised the option and then sold the stock received upon the exercise, the amendment does not provide significant additional benefits to the individual. Hence, the amendment does not cause payments under the option to become subject to section 280G and this section.

Example (2). Corporation N and A, a disqualified individual, enter into an employment contract before June 15, 1984, that provides for a payment, contingent on a change in the ownership or control of Corporation N, equal to 4 times A's base amount. After June 14, 1984, and at a time when Corporation N did not view itself as a likely takeover candidate, Corporation N increases A's annual compensation by 25 percent to reflect additional managerial responsibilities. Such increase is consistent with the historical practices of Corporation N. Although the amount payable to A contingent on a change in ownership is increased, the employment contract is not treated as amended in significant relevant respect because, under these facts (and in the absence of contrary evidence), the amendment to the contract is treated as a normal adjustment in the terms of the employment relationship.

Example (3). Before June 15, 1984, Corporation 0 enters into contracts with disqualified individuals A, B, and C, providing for payments contingent on a change in the ownership of Corporation 0 equal to 4 times each individual's base amount. After June 14, 1984, Corporation 0, consistent with its historical practices, grants identical nonvested stock options to numerous disqualified individuals, including A, B, and C. All of these new options provide that the vesting of all such options will be accelerated if a change in the ownership or control of Corporation 0 occurs. Section 280G and this section apply to payments under the options granted after June 14, 1984. However, the granting of these options does not cause the contracts that were entered into before June 15, 1984, to be treated as amended or supplemented in significant relevant respect because, under these facts (and in the absence of contrary evidence), the granting of options is treated as a normal adjustment in the terms of the employment relationship. [Reg. § 1.280G-1.]

[¶ 20,179 Reserved.—Proposed regulations relating to minimum participation requirements under Code Sec. 401(a)(26) were formerly reproduced here. The final regulations are now at ¶ 11,720Z-32, 11,720Z-34, and 11,720Z-39.]

[¶ 20,180 Reserved.—Introductory material to proposed rulemaking concerning the uniform premium table used to calculate the cost of group-term life insurance coverage was formerly reproduced here. The final regulation is reproduced at ¶ 11,233.]

[¶ 20,181 Reserved.—Amendments to proposed regulations under Code Sec. 410(a)(4) and Code Sec. 410(b), relating to the requirement that contributions or benefits may not discriminate in favor of highly compensated employees and to minimum coverage requirements, were formerly reproduced here. The final regulations are now at ¶ 11,720W-11,720W-13 and 12,163-12,163J.]

[¶ 20,182 Reserved.—Temporary regulations that also served as proposed regulations applying the minimum funding standards to terminated pension plans that were restored by the PBGC were formerly reproduced here. The final regulations are now at ¶ 12,250J.]

[¶ 20,183 Reserved.—Amendments to proposed regulations under Code Sec. 401(a)(4) and Code Sec. 410(b), relating to the requirement that contributions or benefits may not discriminate in favor of highly compensated employees and to minimum coverage requirements, were formerly reproduced here. The final regulations are now at ¶ 11,720W-11,720W-13 and 12,163-12,163J.]

¶ 20,184

Proposed regulations: Employee business expense reimbursements: Reporting and withholding.—The IRS has issued temporary regulations (¶ 11,181, 11,182, 13,551 and 13,551B) that also serve as proposed regulations relating to deductions allowable in computing adjusted gross income that consist of expenses paid or incurred by an employee under a reimbursement or other expense allowance arrangement. The proposed IRS regulations were published in the Federal Register on December 17, 1990 (55 FR 51688).

Reg. § 1.62-1T

DEPARTMENT OF THE TREASURY

Internal Revenue Service

26 CFR PART 1

EE-8-89

RIN 1545-AP29

Employee Business Expenses—Reporting and Withholding on Employee Business Expense Reimbursements and Allowances.

AGENCY: Internal Revenue Service, Treasury.

ACTION: Notice of proposed rulemaking by cross-reference to temporary regulations.

SUMMARY: In the Rules and Regulations portions of this issue of the Federal Register, the Internal Revenue Service is issuing a temporary regulation relating to deductions allowable in computing adjusted gross income that consist of expenses paid or incurred by an employee under a reimbursement or other expense allowance arrangement with his or her employer. The text of the temporary regulation also serves as the comment document for this notice of proposed rulemaking.

DATES: Written comments and requests for a public hearing must be delivered or mailed before [Insert date that is 60 days after publication of this document in the Federal Register].

ADDRESSES: Send comments and requests for a public hearing to Internal Revenue Service, P.O. Box 7604, Ben Franklin Station, Attention: CC:CORP:T:R (EE-8-89), Room 4425, Washington, D.C. 20044.

FOR FURTHER INFORMATION CONTACT: Richard Pavel at telephone 202-377-9372 (not a toll-free number).

SUPPLEMENTARY INFORMATION:

Background

The text of the temporary regulation amends 26 CFR by amending paragraphs (c)(2) and (f) of § 1.62-1T with respect to deductions allowable in computing adjusted gross income that consist of expenses paid or incurred by an employee under a reimbursement or other expense allowance arrangement with his or her employer. For the text of the temporary regulation, see T.D. 8324 published in the Rules and Regulations portion of this issue of the Federal Register.

Special Analyses

It has been determined that these proposed rules are not major rules as defined in Executive Order 12291. Therefore, a Regulatory Impact Analysis is not required. It has also been determined that section 553(b) of the Administrative Procedure Act (5 U.S.C. chapter 5) and the Regulatory Flexibility Act (5 U.S.C. chapter 6) do not apply to these regulations, and, therefore, an initial Regulatory Flexibility Analysis is not required. Pursuant to section 7805(f) of the Internal Revenue Code, these regulations will be submitted to the Administrator of the Small Business Administration for comment on their impact on small business.

Comments and Requests for a Public Hearing

Before these proposed regulations are adopted, consideration will be given to any written comments that are submitted (preferably nine copies) to the Internal Revenue Service. All comments will be available for public inspection and copying. A public hearing will be held upon written request to the Internal Revenue Service by any person who also submits written comments. If a public hearing is held, notice of the time and place will be published in the Federal Register.

Drafting Information

The principal author of these regulations is Richard Pavel of the Office of the Assistant Chief Counsel (Employee Benefits and Exempt Organizations), Internal Revenue Service. However, personnel from other offices of the Service and Treasury Department participated in their development.

[¶ 20,185 Reserved.—Proposed regulations relating to employer-provided transportation and transit passes for employees were formerly reproduced here. The final regulations are now at ¶ 11,176 and ¶ 11,2890-6.]

[¶ 20,186 Reserved.—Proposed regulations relating to employer-provided transportation and benefits for volunteers of exempt organizations were formerly reproduced here. The final regulations are now at ¶ 11,172A, 11,176, 11,2890, 11,2890-1 and 11,2890-5.

¶ 20,187

Proposed regulations: VEBAs: Single geographical locale requirement: Employment-related common bond.—The IRS has issued proposed amendments to regulations under Code Sec. 509(c)(9) which provide supplemental rules, including a safe harbor, that define the geographic area within which unrelated employers must be engaged in the same line of business in order for employees to be members of a tax-exempt voluntary employees' beneficiary association (VEBA). Employees of one or more unrelated employers engaged in the same line of business in the same geographic locale are considered to share an employment-related common bond for purposes of eligibility for membership in a VEBA. The proposed amendments were published in the Federal Register on August 7, 1992 (57 FR 34886).

AGENCY: Internal Revenue Service, Treasury.

ACTION: Notice of proposed rulemaking and notice of public hearing.

SUMMARY: This document contains proposed regulations about the qualification of voluntary employees' beneficiary associations (VEBAs) under section 501(c)(9) of the Internal Revenue Code (Code). The proposed regulations supplement the existing regulations with rules for determining whether the membership of an organization consists of employees of employers engaged in the same line of business in the same geographic locale. The proposed regulations will provide the public with guidance necessary to comply with the law in the case of an organization that does not consist exclusively of the employees of a single employer or the members of a single labor union. They will affect entities seeking to sponsor VEBAs covering the employees of more than one unrelated employer, as well as those employees.

DATES: Written comments must be received by October 6, 1992. Requests to speak (with outlines of oral comments) at a public hearing scheduled for December 3, 1992, at 1:00 p.m. must be received by November 12, 1992.

ADDRESSES: Send all submissions to: Internal Revenue Service, P.O. Box 7604, Ben Franklin Station, Attention: CC:CORP:T:R (EE-23-92) Washington, D.C. 20044.

FOR FURTHER INFORMATION CONTACT: Michael J. Roach at 202-622-6060 concerning the regulations; Carol Savage at 202-622-8452 concerning the hearing (not toll-free numbers).

SUPPLEMENTARY INFORMATION:

Background

The existing regulations at §1.501(c)(9)-2(a)(1) contain general rules for determining when an association qualifies as a voluntary employees' beneficiary association (VEBA) eligible for exemption from income tax under section 501(c)(9) of the Internal Revenue Code. Under those regulations, the members of the association must share an employment-related common bond. The members are deemed to share

an employment-related common bond if membership in the association is open only to persons whose eligibility for membership is based on employment by a single employer or affiliated group of employers, or is based on membership in one or more locals of a national or international labor union, or is based on coverage under one or more collective bargaining agreements. In addition, under the existing regulations, employees of one or more employers engaged in the same line of business in the same geographic locale are considered to share an employment-related common bond.

Questions have arisen about the geographic extent of a single "geographic locale." In its report on the Deficit Reduction Act of 1984, Pub. L. No. 98-369, 98 Stat. 494, the House Ways and Means Committee described the effect of the geographic locale restriction affecting VEBAs as follows:

Under [the] standards [prescribed in the regulations], for example, a group of car dealers in the same city or other similarly restricted geographical locale could form a VEBA to provide permissible benefits to their employees.

H.R. Rep. No. 432, Part II, 98th Cong., 2d Sess. 1285.

Administratively, the Internal Revenue Service has treated employers located in any one state as located in the same geographic locale. The Service has also treated a single standard metropolitan statistical area (SMSA), as defined by the Bureau of the Census, as a single geographic locale, even though the boundaries of some SMSAs include portions of more than one state.

In 1986, the United States Court of Appeals for the Seventh Circuit held the geographic locale restriction invalid in *Water Quality Association Employees' Benefit Corp. v. United States*, 795 F.2d 1303 (7th Cir. 1986). The court agreed with the Government's argument that the existence of an employment-related common bond is the essential factor that distinguishes a tax-exempt VEBA from a taxable insurance company, but concluded that restricting VEBAs covering employees of unrelated employers to those employers located in the same geographic locale did not enhance the employment-related bond of the employees participating in the organization.

The preamble to the final regulations published as T.D. 7750, 1981-1 C.B. 338 (46 F. R. 1719 (January 7, 1981)), explains the reason why the Secretary decided to retain the geographic locale restriction despite comments from the public requesting its deletion from the final regulations. In relevant part, the preamble states:

First, section 501(c)(9) provides for the exemption of associations of employees who enjoy some employment related bond. Allowing section 501(c)(9) to be used as a tax-exempt vehicle for offering insurance products to unrelated individuals scattered throughout the country would undermine those provisions of the Internal Revenue Code that prescribe the income tax treatment of insurance companies. Second, it is the position of the Internal Revenue Service that where an organization such as a national trade association or business league exempt from taxation under section 501(c)(6) operates a group insurance program for its members, the organization is engaged in an unrelated trade or business. *See* Rev. Rul. 66-151, 1966-1 C.B. 152; Rev. Rul. 73-386, 1973-2 C.B. 191; Rev. Rul. 78-52, 1978-1 C.B. 166. To allow trade associations to provide insurance benefits through a trust exempt under section 501(c)(9) would simply facilitate circumvention of the unrelated trade or business income tax otherwise applicable to such organizations.

These restrictions are consistent with the history of section 501(c)(9) of the Code. As Kenneth W. Gideon, then Assistant Secretary of the Treasury for Tax Policy, said in testimony before the Subcommittee on Taxation of the Senate Finance Committee on September 10, 1991, the VEBA tax exemption was originally intended to benefit associations formed and managed by employees of a single employer, or of small local groups of employers, to provide certain welfare benefits to their members in situations where such benefits would not otherwise have been available. *Tax Simplification Bills: Hearings on S. 1364, S. 1394, and H.R. 2777 Before the Subcommittee on Taxation of the Senate Committee on Finance*, 102d Cong., 1st Sess., 260-261. In 1928, when the predecessor of section 501(c)(9) of the Code was enacted as section 103(16) of the Revenue Act of 1928, 45 Stat; 791, ch. 852, the prevalent form of "mutual benefit association" that provided welfare benefits to employees was an organization providing benefits to the employees of a single establishment, such as an industrial plant. National Industrial Conference Board, *The Present Status of Mutual Benefit Associations*, 1-2, 50-51 (1931). At the time, there was concern that, although these organizations performed valuable social functions, they might not be able to continue to exist without a tax exemption. By contrast, larger associations covering employees of unrelated employers in different geographic areas are more likely to be viable without a tax exemption, and the benefits they provide are more likely to be available through commercial insurance. *Tax Simplification Bills, supra*, at 260. In general, when Congress exempts a class of organizations from income tax, it is deemed to have referred to the existing organizations of that class at the time the exemption was adopted. *United States v. Cambridge Loan and Building Co.*, 278 U.S. 55, 58 (1928). Thus, the absence of large regional or national organizations among the class of organizations known as VEBAs or "mutual benefit associations" that were dedicated to providing welfare benefits to employees in 1928 is relevant in determining the proper scope of the exemption granted by section 501(c)(9) of the Code.

The factors cited in the preamble to the 1981 regulations for imposing a geographic locale restriction on the membership of VEBAs that include employees of unrelated employers are matters of continuing concern today. Because of these factors and the history of section 501(c)(9), the proposed regulations limit the geographic region within which unrelated employers must be engaged in the same line of business in order for employees of those lines of business to participate in a single VEBA to the minimum area that is consistent with enabling all employees of employers engaged in a particular line of business to participate in an economically feasible VEBA. If VEBA participation were always limited to employees of employers located in the same state or SMSA, however, the diversity of regional population density and employment patterns in the United States could make it infeasible in many cases for benefits to be provided through a VEBA. Accordingly, the proposed regulations afford a safe harbor that treats any three contiguous states as a single geographic locale, and they authorize the Commissioner of Internal Revenue to recognize larger areas as a single geographic locale on a case-by-case basis upon application by an organization seeking recognition as a VEBA. Thus, the Commissioner may recognize an organization as a VEBA under section 501(c)(9), even though its members are employed by unrelated employers engaged in the same line of business located in any number of states, whether or not contiguous. To obtain recognition as a VEBA under this discretionary authority, the applicant must show (1) that it

would not be economically feasible to cover employees of employers engaged in that line of business in the states to be included in the proposed VEBA under two or more separate VEBAs, and (2) either that the states to be included are all contiguous, or that there are legitimate reasons supporting the inclusion of those particular states.

During the drafting of these proposed regulations consideration was given to a rule that would allow an area to be treated as a single geographic locale even though it included areas outside the United States. It is not clear, however, whether it is necessary or desirable to include such a rule. Comments are invited about the extent, if any, to which the regulations should allow the inclusion of areas outside the United States in a single geographic locale.

Proposed Effective Date

These regulations are proposed to be effective on August 7, 1992; however, taxpayers may treat the rules as applicable to prior years.

Special Analyses

It has been determined that these rules are not major rules as defined in Executive Order 12291. Therefore, a Regulatory Impact Analysis is not required. It has also been determined that section 553(b) of the Administrative Procedure Act (5 U.S.C. chapter 5) and the Regulatory Flexibility Act (5 U.S.C. chapter 6) do not apply to these proposed regulations and, therefore, an initial Regulatory Flexibility Analysis is not required. Pursuant to section 7805(f) of the Internal Revenue Code, these regulations will be submitted to the Chief Counsel for Advocacy of the Small Business Administration for comment on their impact on small business.

Comments and Public Hearing

Before these proposed regulations are adopted as final regulations, consideration will be given to any written comments that are submitted timely (preferably an original and eight copies) to the Internal Revenue Service. All comments will be available for public inspection and copying.

A public hearing will be held on Thursday, December 3, 1992, at 1:00 p.m. in the Internal Revenue Service Auditorium, Internal Revenue Building, 1111 Constitution Avenue, N.W. Washington, DC. The rules of § 601.601(a)(3) of the "Statement of Procedural Rules" (26 CFR part 601) shall apply to the public hearing.

Persons who have submitted written comments by October 6, 1992, and who also desire to present oral comments at the hearing on the proposed regulations, should submit, not later than November 12, 1992, a request to speak and an outline of the oral comments to be presented at the hearing stating the time they wish to devote to each subject.

Each speaker (or group of speakers representing a single entity) will be limited to 10 minutes for an oral presentation exclusive of the time consumed by the questions from the panel for the government and answers thereto.

Because of controlled access restrictions, attendees cannot be admitted beyond the lobby of the Internal Revenue Building before 12:45 p.m.

An agenda showing the scheduling of the speakers will be made after outlines are received from the persons testifying. Copies of the agenda will be available free of charge at the hearing.

Drafting Information

The principal author of these proposed regulations is Michael J. Roach, Office of the Associate Chief Counsel (Employee Benefits and Exempt Organizations), Internal Revenue Service. However, personnel from other offices of the Service and the Treasury Department participated in their development.

List of Subjects

26 CFR 1.501(a)-1 through 1.505(c)-1T

Income taxes, Nonprofit organizations, Reporting and recordkeeping requirements.

Proposed Amendment to the Regulations

Accordingly, the proposed amendment to 26 CFR part 1 is as follows:

PART 1—INCOME TAX; TAXABLE YEARS BEGINNING AFTER DECEMBER 31, 1953

Paragraph 1. The authority citation for part 1 continues to read in part as follows:

Authority: 26 U.S.C. 7805 * * *

Par. 2. In § 1.501(c)(9)-2, paragraph (a)(1) is amended by adding a sentence between the fourth and fifth sentences, and a new paragraph (d) is added, to read as follows:

(a) * * *

(1) *In general.* * * * (See paragraph (d) of this section for the meaning of geographic locale.) * * *

* * * * *

(d) *Meaning of geographic locale*—(1) *Three-state safe harbor.* An area is a single geographic locale for purposes of paragraph (a)(1) of this section if it does not exceed the boundaries of three contiguous states, *i.e.,* three states each of which shares a land or river border with at least one of the others. For this purpose, Alaska and Hawaii are deemed to be contiguous with each other and with each of the following states: Washington, Oregon, and California.

(2) *Discretionary authority to recognize larger areas as geographic locales.* In determining whether an organization covering employees of employers engaged in the same line of business is a voluntary employees' beneficiary association (VEBA) described in section 501(c)(9), the Commissioner may recognize an area that does not satisfy the three-state safe harbor in paragraph (d)(1) of this section as a single geographic locale if—

(i) It would not be economically feasible to cover employees of employers engaged in that line of business in that area under two or more separate VEBAs each extending over fewer states; and

(ii) Employment characteristics in that line of business, population characteristics, or other regional factors support the particular states included. This paragraph (d)(2)(ii) is deemed satisfied if the states included are contiguous.

(3) *Examples.* The following examples illustrate this paragraph (d).

Example 1. The membership of the W Association is made up of employers whose business consists of the distribution of produce in Virginia, North Carolina, and South Carolina. Because Virginia and South Carolina each share a land border with North Carolina, the three states are contiguous states and form a single geographic locale.

Example 2. The membership of the X Association is made up of employers whose business consists of the retail sale of computer software in Montana, Wyoming, North Dakota, South Dakota, and Nebraska, which are contiguous states. X establishes the X Trust to provide life, sick, accident, or other benefits for the employees of its members. The X Trust applies for recognition of exemption as a VEBA, stating that it intends to permit employees of any employer that is a member of X to join the proposed VEBA. In its application, the X Trust provides summaries of employer data and economic analyses showing that no division of the region into smaller groups of states would enable X to establish two or more separate VEBAs each with enough members to make the formation of those separate VEBAs economically feasible. Furthermore, although some possible divisions of the region into three-state or four-state areas could form an economically feasible VEBA, any such division of the five-state region covered by X would

leave employees of X's employer-members located in at least one state without a VEBA. The Commissioner may, as a matter of administrative discretion, recognize the X Trust as a VEBA described in section 501(c)(9) based on its showing that the limited number of employees in each state would make any division of the region into two or more VEBAs economically infeasible.

Example 3. The membership of the Y Association is made up of employers whose business consists of shipping freight by barge on the Mississippi and Ohio Rivers. Some of the members of Y conduct their business out of ports in Louisiana, while others operate out of ports in Arkansas, Missouri, and Ohio. Y establishes the Y Trust to provide life, sick, accident, or other benefits to the employees of its members. The Y Trust applies for recognition of exemption as a VEBA, stating that it intends to permit the employees of any employer that is a member of Y to join the proposed VEBA. In its application, the Y Trust sets forth facts tending to show that there are so few members of Y in each of the four states that any division of those states into two or more separate regions would result in creating VEBAs that would be too small to be economically feasible, that all of the members of Y are engaged in river shipping between inland and Gulf ports that are united by the existence of a natural waterway, and that the labor force engaged in providing transportation by river barge is distinct from that engaged in providing other means of transportation. Even though Ohio, Louisiana, Arkansas, and Missouri are not contiguous, because Ohio does not share a land or river border with any of the other three states, the Commissioner may, as a matter of administrative discretion, recognize the Y Trust as a VEBA described in section 501(c)(9) based on its showing that the establishment of separate VEBAs would not be economically feasible and that the characteristics of the river shipping business justify permitting a VEBA to cover the scattered concentrations of employees in that business located in Louisiana, Arkansas, Missouri, and Ohio.

Example 4. The membership of the Z Association is made up of employers whose business consists of the retail sale of agricultural implements in the states west of the Mississippi River except California, Alaska, and Hawaii. There are 21 states in the region covered by Z. Z establishes the Z1 Trust, the Z2 Trust, and the Z3 Trust to provide life, sick, accident or other benefits to the employees of its members. The trusts cover different subregions which were formed by dividing the Z region into three areas each consisting of seven contiguous states. Each trust applies for recognition of exemption as a VEBA, stating that it intends to permit the employees of any employer that is a member of Z located within its subregion to join its proposed VEBA. Each trust sets forth facts in its application tending to show that four states within its particular subregion would be needed to create a VEBA large enough to be economically feasible, so that any further division of its seven-state subregion would leave employees of at least some of Z's employer-members located in the subregion in an area too small to support an economically feasible VEBA. The applications contain no justification for the choice of three seven-state subregions. Since the applicants have not shown that it would not be economically feasible to divide the Z region into smaller subregions (*e.g.,* four containing four states and one containing five states), the applicants have not satisfied paragraph (d)(2)(i) of this section, and the Commissioner does not have the discretion to recognize the Z1, Z2, and Z3 Trusts as VEBAs described in section 501(c)(9).

[¶ 20,188 Reserved.—Proposed regulations to delay the effective date of final regulations under Code Secs. 401(a)(4), 410(b), and related nondiscrimination requirements, were formerly reproduced at this paragraph. The final nondiscrimination regulations, as revised, appear at ¶ 11,720W-14, 11,720X-5, 11,720Z-11, 11,731Q, 12,165, 12,364F-11—12,364F-22, and 12,364K.]

[¶ 20,189 Reserved.—Proposed regulations dealing with eligible rollover distributions from qualified retirement plans and tax-free annuities under Code Sec. 403(b) were formerly reproduced at this paragraph. The final regulations now appear at ¶ 11,720Z-50; 11,753-10; 11,755-2F; 11,830-10 and 13,566-10. The introductory material proceding the final regulations is at ¶ 23,911W.]

¶ 20,190

Proposed regulations: Valuations: Annuities: Estate tax.—The IRS has issued proposed amendments to regulations under the Code relating to the valuation of annuities, interests for life or a term of years, or remainder or reversionary interests for estate tax purposes. The amendments are required because Code Sec. 7520, added by the Technical and Miscellaneous Revenue Act of 1988, provides a new method of valuing these interests after April 30, 1989. The IRS has included actuarial tables in the proposed amendments. The proposed amendments were published in the *Federal Register* on November 2, 1992 (57 FR 49514).

[¶ 4830-01]

DEPARTMENT OF THE TREASURY

Internal Revenue Service

26 CFR Parts 1, 20, 25 and 602

RIN 1545-AM81

Valuation Tables

AGENCY: Internal Revenue Service, Treasury.

ACTION: Notice of proposed rulemaking.

SUMMARY: This document contains proposed amendments to the regulations under the Internal Revenue Code relating to the valuation of any annuity, any interest for life or a term of years, or any remainder or reversionary interest. These amendments are necessary because section 7520, which provides a new method for valuing these interests after April 30, 1989, was added to the Internal Revenue Code (the Code) by section 5031 of the Technical and Miscellaneous Revenue Act of 1988 (the Act). These proposed regulations would affect all transfers of such interests in property. The proposed regulations do not apply for purposes of section 72 of the Code (relating to the income taxation of life insurance, endowments, and annuities), for purposes of sections 401 through 419A, 457, 3121(v), 3306(r), and 6058 (relating to deferred compensation arrangements), for purposes of section 7872 (relating to income and gift taxation of interest-free and below-market interest rate loans), for purposes of certain property interests under sections 83 and 451, or for purposes of certain transfers under Chapter 14.

DATES: Written comments, requests to appear and outlines of comments to be presented at a public hearing must be received by November 30, 1992.

ADDRESSES: All submissions should be sent to: Internal Revenue Service, P.O. Box 7604, Ben Franklin Station, Attention: CC:CORP:T:R (PS-100-88), Room 5228, Washington, D.C. 20044.

FOR FURTHER INFORMATION CONTACT: William L. Blodgett, telephone 202-622-3090 (not a toll-free number).

SUPPLEMENTARY INFORMATION:

Paperwork Reduction Act

The collection of information contained in this notice of proposed rulemaking has been submitted to the Office of Management and Budget for review in accordance with the Paperwork Reduction Act of 1980 (44 U.S.C. 3504(h)). Comments on the collection of information should be sent to the Office of Management and Budget, Attention: Desk Officer for the Department of the Treasury, Office of Information and Regulatory Affairs, Washington, D.C. 20503, with copies to the Internal Revenue Service, Attn: IRS Reports Clearance Officer T:FP, Washington, D.C. 20224.

The collection of information in this proposed rulemaking is in §§ 20.7520-1 through 20.7520-4. This information is required to compute the present value of any annuity, any interest for life or a term of years, or any remainder or reversionary interest for income, gift, estate, and generation-skipping transfer tax purposes. The likely respondents are individuals, estates, trusts, and nonprofit institutions.

These estimates are an approximation of the average time expected to be necessary for a collection of information. They are based on such information as is available to the Internal Revenue Service. Individual respondents may require greater or less time, depending on their particular circumstances. Estimated total annual reporting burden: 4,500 hours. The estimated annual burden per respondent varies from 30 minutes to one hour, depending on individual circumstances, with an estimated average of 45 minutes. Estimated number of respondents: 6,000. Estimated annual frequency of responses: one.

Background

This document provides proposed regulations (26 CFR 20.7520) for the valuation of certain partial interests in property under section 7520 of the Internal Revenue Code of 1986 (the Code); as added by section 5031 of the Technical and Miscellaneous Revenue Act of 1988 (the Act).

In General

Section 7520 provides that the value of an annuity, an interest for life or a term of years, and a remainder or reversionary interest is to be determined under tables published by the Internal Revenue Service based on a discount rate (rounded to the nearest two-tenths of one percent) equal to 120 percent of the applicable Federal mid-term rate in effect under section 1274(d)(1) for the month in which the valuation date falls. These tables have been published in Internal Revenue Service Publications 1457 "Actuarial Values, Alpha Volume" and 1458 "Actuarial Values, Beta Volume." Those publications also contain special factors to make necessary adjustments for frequency and time of payments when the value of the interest is based upon recurring payments, along with examples of computations. The tables will be revised at least once every 10 years to reflect the most recent mortality experience available. Certain tables contained in those publications are included in these regulations so that taxpayers and their advisers can have more ready access to the tables.

To compute the present value of the property interest being transferred, it is necessary to use the interest rate that is 120 percent of the applicable Federal mid-term rate compounded annually and that is published in the Internal Revenue Bulletin for the month in which the valuation date falls. This rate must be rounded to the nearest two-tenths of one percent. However, if an income, estate, or gift tax charitable deduction is allowable for any part of the property transferred, the transferor may elect to use an interest rate that is 120 percent of the applicable Federal mid-term rate for either of the two months preceding the month in which the valuation date falls.

Section 7520 does not apply for purposes of section 72 of the Code (involving the income taxation of life insurance, endowments, and annuities), for purposes of sections 401 through 419A, 457, 3121(v), 3306(r), and 6058 (relating to deferred compensation arrangements), for purposes of section 7872 (relating to income and gift taxation of interest-free and below-market interest rate loans), for purposes of certain property interests under sections 83 and 451, or for purposes of certain transfers under chapter 14 of the Code.

During the 5 and ½ year period before the enactment of section 7520 of the Code, the present value of an annuity, an interest for life or a term of years, or a remainder or reversionary interest was computed using an interest rate of 10 percent, based on tables contained in regulations under section 2031 (estate tax), section 2512 (gift tax), section 2624 (generation-skipping transfer tax), section 664 (charitable remainder trusts), and section 642 (pooled income funds). The regulations under each of these sections are amended to provide that transfers of such interests with respect to which the valuation date falls on or after May 1, 1989, are valued under section 7520.

The following is a chart that summarizes the periods of time, the interest rates, and the applicable regulation sections under the existing and proposed regulations.

Valuation Period	Interest Rate	Prior Section	Revised Section
	* * *		
§ 2031:			
Valuation, in general	—	—	20.2031-7
05/01/89 - present	§ 7520	none	20.2031-7(e)
before - 01/01/52	4%	none	20.2031-7A(a)
01/01/52 - 12/31/70	3.5%	none	20.2031-7A(b)
01/01/71 - 11/30/83	6%	20.2031-10	20.2031-7A(c)
12/01/83 - 04/30/89	10%	20.2031-7	20.2031-7A(d)
	* * *		

With respect to transfers to pooled income funds, the proposed regulations provide rules for determining the rate of return for purposes of valuing charitable remainder gifts in pooled income funds described in section 642. In general, the rate of return for a pooled income fund is equal to the highest annual rate of return of the fund for the 3 taxable years immediately preceding the year in which the transfer of property to the fund is made. For a pooled income fund that has been in existence for less than 3 years, § 1.642(c)-6(b)(2) of the existing regulations provides a deemed rate of return of 9 percent for funds created between December 1, 1983, and April 30, 1989. This deemed rate was 1 percent less than general interest rate of 10 percent that was prescribed by the regulations for that period. Notice 89-60, 1989-1 C.B. 700 (See § 601.601(d)(2)(ii)(b) of the Statement of Procedural Rules), announced a method of determining the deemed rate of return for pooled income funds created after April 30, 1989. Under the Notice, the deemed rate is equal to 1 percent less than the highest average annual rate (120 percent of the applicable Federal mid-term rate rounded to the nearest two-tenths of one percent) for the 3 years preceding the date the fund is created. The proposed regulation provides that the deemed rate for pooled income funds created after April 30, 1989, is 90 percent of the same highest average annual rate for the 3 years preceding the creation of the fund. In the case of funds created in 1989 (after April 30), 1990, 1991, and 1992, the method in the proposed regulation yields the same deemed rate of return as the method in Notice 89-60. Although the proposed regulation applies to pooled income funds created after April 30, 1989, for transfers to pooled income funds created prior to November 2, 1992, a transferor can rely on the Notice.

Transitional Rules

Under section 5031 of the Act, section 7520 is effective where the valuation date with respect to a transfer occurs on or after May 1, 1989. These proposed regulations provide certain transitional rules intended to alleviate any adverse consequences resulting from the statutory change. Several principal provisions of the proposed regulations were announced in Notice 89-24, 1989-1 C.B. 660 (which announced the change from the 10 percent fixed rate of interest to the section 7520 floating rate of interest), and Notice 89-60 (which announced the change in mortality tables) (see § 601.601(d)(2)(ii)(b) of the Statement of Procedural Rules). A transitional rule in the proposed regulation provides that, for valuation dates of transfers after April 30, 1989, and before November 2, 1992, a transferor can rely on Notice 89-24 or

Notice 89-60 in valuing the transferred interest. For gift tax purposes, a transitional rule provides that if, after December 31, 1988, but before May 1, 1989, a donor transferred an interest in property, retaining an interest in the same property, and the donor later transferred the retained interest in the property after April 30, 1989, and before January 1, 1990, the donor may elect to value the transfer of the retained interest under either the 10 percent tables or the section 7520 tables (whichever is more beneficial). For estate tax purposes, a transitional rule provides that a decedent's estate may elect to value the property interest included in the gross estate under either set of tables if the decedent was under a mental incapacity that existed on May 1, 1989, and continued uninterrupted until the decedent's death. For determining the value of the remainder interest in a testamentary charitable remainder unitrust or annuity trust, a transitional rule provides that the interest rate of either 10 percent or the rate under section 7520 may be used if the decedent was mentally incompetent on May 1, 1989, and (1) such incompetency continued uninterrupted until death or (2) the decedent died within 90 days of first regaining competency after April 30, 1989.

Election Requirements

These regulations specify the time and manner of making the election to use the applicable Federal mid-term rate for either of the two months preceding the month in which the valuation date falls when a charitable deduction is allowable for part of the interest transferred. The election must be made with the first income, estate, or gift tax return that is filed after the transfer. Generally, the person required to file the return is also required to make the election. Any election may be revoked if revocation occurs within the period of limitations on assessment and collection under section 6501. If, in addition to the charitable interest, another interest in the same property is transferred and the taxpayer elects to use an interest rate from one of the two preceding months, the taxpayer must use the same rate to determine the value of each interest transferred. A cross-reference is provided in the proposed regulations to § 301.9100-8(a)(1), which provides interim rules for this election, which was enacted under the Technical and Miscellaneous Revenue Act of 1988.

Special Analyses

It has been determined that these proposed rules are not major rules as defined in Executive Order 12291. Therefore, a Regulatory Impact

Analysis is not required. It has also been determined that section 553(b) of the Administrative Procedure Act (5 U.S.C. chapter 5) and the Regulatory Flexibility Act (5 U.S.C. chapter 6) do not apply to these regulations, and, therefore, an initial Regulatory Flexibility Analysis is not required. Pursuant to section 7805(f) of the Internal Revenue Code, these proposed regulations will be submitted to the Chief Counsel for Advocacy of the Small Business Administration for comment on their impact on small business.

Comments and Requests for a Public Hearing

Before adopting these proposed regulations, consideration will be given to any written comments that are submitted timely (preferably a signed original and 8 copies) to the Internal Revenue Service. All comments will be available for public inspection and copying in their entirety. See the notice of public hearing published elsewhere in this issue of the **Federal Register.**

Drafting Information

The principal author of these regulations is William L. Blodgett of the Office of Assistant Chief Counsel (Passthroughs and Special Industries), Internal Revenue Service. However, personnel from other offices of the Internal Revenue Service and Treasury Department participated in their development.

List of Subjects

* * *

26 CFR Part 20

Estate taxes, Reporting and recordkeeping requirements.

26 CFR Part 25

* * *

Proposed amendments to the regulations

Accordingly, 26 CFR parts 1, 20, 25, and 602 are proposed to be amended as follows:

Parts 1, 20 and 25 [Amended]

Paragraph 1. In the list below, for each section indicated in the left column, remove the language in the middle column and add the language in the right column:

Section	Remove	Add
* * *		
1.101-2(e)(1)(iii)(b)(3)	paragraph (f) of	—
1.101-2(e)(2), *Example (1)* (ii)	paragraph (f) of	—
* * *		
1.170A-5(b), *Example 5,* fifth sentence	Table A(1) in § 20.2031-10(f)	§ 20.2031-7A(c)
* * *		
1.414(c)-2(b)(2)(ii), second sentence	or § 20.2031-10 (Estate Tax Regulations), whichever is appropriate,	—
1.414(c)-4(b)(3)(i), last sentence	or § 20.2031-10 (Estate Tax Regulations), whichever is appropriate,	—
* * *		
20.2031-7(a)(2) first and second sentences	paragraph (f)	paragraph (d)(6)
20.2031-7(a)(2)	paragraph (e)	paragraph (d)(5)
20.2031-7(b)(1)	paragraph (b)(1)	paragraph (d)(2)(i)
20.2031-7(b)(2)	paragraph (b)(2)	paragraph (d)(2)(ii)
20.2031-7(b)(2) (in the *Example*)	paragraph (b)(1)	paragraph (d)(2)(i)
20.2031-7(b)(3)(i)	paragraphs (b)(1) or (2)	paragraphs (d)(2)(i) or (ii)
20.2031-7(b)(3)(i)	paragraph (b)(3)(i)	paragraph (d)(2)(iii)(A)
20.2031-7(b)(3)(i) (in the *Example*)	paragraph (b)(2)	paragraph (d)(2)(ii)
20.2031-7(b)(3)(ii)	paragraph (b)(3)(ii)	paragraph (d)(2)(iii)(B)
20.2031-7(c)	paragraph (c)	paragraph (d)(3)
20.2031-7(d)	paragraph (d)	paragraph (d)(4)
20.2031-7(e)	paragraph (f)	paragraph (d)(6)
* * *		
20.2039-2(c)(1)(viii)	through 20.2031-10	
20.2039-5(c)(1)	through 20.2031-10	
20.2039-5(c)(2)	through 20.2031-10	
* * *		

PART 1—INCOME TAX; TAXABLE YEARS BEGINNING AFTER DECEMBER 31, 1953

Par. 2. The authority citation for part 1 continues to read in part:

Authority: 26 U.S.C. 7805 * * *

PART 20—ESTATE TAX; ESTATES OF DECEDENTS DYING AFTER AUGUST 16, 1954

Par. 12. The general authority citation for part 20 is revised to read as follows:

Authority: 26 U.S.C. 7805.

* * *

Par. 14. Section 20.2031-0 is added to read as follows:

§ 20.2031-0 Table of contents.

This section lists the section headings that appear in the regulations under section 2031.

§ 20.2031-1 Definition of gross estate; valuation of property.

§ 20.2031-2 Valuation of stocks and bonds.

§ 20.2031-3 Valuation of interests in businesses.

§ 20.2031-4 Valuation of notes.

§ 20.2031-5 Valuation of cash on hand or on deposit.

§ 20.2031-6 Valuation of household and personal effects.

§ 20.2031-7 Valuation of annuities, life estates, terms for years, remainders, and reversions after April 30, 1989.

§ 20.2031-7A Valuation of annuities, life estates, terms for years, remainders, and reversions before May 1, 1989.

§ 20.2031-8 Valuation of certain life insurance and annuity contracts; valuation of shares in an open-end investment company.

§ 20.2031-9 Valuation of other property.

Par. 15. Immediately following § 20.2046-1 an undesignated center heading and § 20.2031-7A are added to read as follows:

Actuarial tables applicable before May 1, 1989, § 20.2031-7A Valuation of annuities, life estates, terms for years, remainders, and reversions for estates of decedents who died before May 1, 1989—(a) Valuation of annuities, life estates, terms for years, remainders, and reversions for estates of decedents who died before January 1, 1952. Except as otherwise provided in § 20.2031-7(c), if the decedent died before January 1, 1952, the present value of annuities, life estates, terms for years, remainders, and reversions is their present value determined under this section. If the valuation of the interest involved is dependent upon the continuation or termination of one or more lives or upon a term certain concurrent with one or more lives, the factor for the present value is computed on the basis of interest at the rate of 4 percent a year, compounded annually, and life contingencies as to each life involved from values that are based on the Actuaries' or Combined Experience Table of Mortality, as extended. This table and related factors are described in former § 81.10 (as contained in CFR edition revised as of April 1, 1958). The present value of an interest measured by a term for years is computed on the basis of interest at the rate of 4 percent a year.

(b) *Valuation of annuities, life estates, terms for years, remainders, and reversions for estates of decedents who died after December 31, 1951, and before January 1, 1971.* Except as otherwise provided in § 20.2031-7(c), if the decedent died after December 31, 1951, and before January 1, 1971, the present value of annuities, life estates, terms for years,

Old CFR unit number in § 20.2031-7
§ 20.2031-7 heading
(a)
(a) (1)
(a) (2)
(a) (3)
(b)
(b) (1)
(b) (2)
(b) (3) (i)
(b) (3) (ii)
(c) through (f)

2. The paragraph heading for (d) is revised.

3. Paragraph (d) (1) (i) is revised.

4. Paragraph (d) (1) (iii) is revised.

5. Paragraph (d) (5), third and fourth sentences are revised.

6. The revised provisions read as follows:

§ 20.2031-7A Valuation of annuities, life estates, terms for years, remainders, and reversions before May 1, 1989.

* * * * *

(d) *Valuation of annuities, life estates, terms for years, remainders, and reversions for estates of decedents who died after November 30, 1983, if the valuation date for the gross estate is before May 1, 1989—* (1) *In general.* (i) Except as otherwise provided in § 20.2031-7(c), if the decedent died after November 30, 1983, and the valuation date for the gross estate is before May 1, 1989, the fair market value of annuities, life estates, terms for years, remainders, and reversions is their present value determined under this section. If a decedent died after November 30, 1983, and before August 9, 1984, or, in cases where the valuation date

remainders, and reversions is their present value determined under this section. If the valuation of the interest involved is dependent upon the continuation or termination of one or more lives, or upon a term certain concurrent with one or more lives, the factor for the present value is computed on the basis of interest at the rate of 3 ½ percent a year, compounded annually, and life contingencies as to each life involved are taken from U.S. Life Table 38. This table and related factors are set forth in former § 20.2031-7 (as contained in CFR edition revised as of April 1, 1984). Special factors involving one and two lives may be found in or computed with the use of tables contained in the publication entitled "Actuarial Values for Estate and Gift Tax," Publication Number 11 (Rev. 5-59). A copy of this publication may be purchased from the Superintendent of Documents, United States Printing Office, Washington, D.C. 20402. The present value of an interest measured by a term for years is computed on the basis of interest at the rate of 3 ½ percent a year.

(c) *Valuation of annuities, life estates, terms for years, remainders, and reversions for estates of decedents who died after December 31, 1970, and before December 1, 1983.* Except as otherwise provided in § 20.2031-7(c), if the decedent died after December 31, 1970, and before December 1, 1983, the present value of annuities, life estates, terms for years, remainders, and reversions is their present value determined under this section. If the valuation of the interest involved is dependent upon the continuation of or termination of one or more lives or upon a term certain concurrent with one or more lives, the factor for the present value is computed on the basis of interest at the rate of 6 percent a year, compounded annually, and life contingencies are determined as to each male and female life involved, from values that are set forth in Table LN. Table LN contains values that are taken from the life table for total males and the life table for total females appearing as Tables 2 and 3, respectively in United States Life Tables: 1959-1960, published by the Department of Health and Human Services, Public Health Service. Table LN and related factors are set forth in former § 20.2031-10 (as contained in CFR edition revised as of April 1, 1992). Special factors involving one and two lives may be found in or computed with the use of tables contained in Internal Revenue Service Publication 723E, "Actuarial Values I: Valuation of Last Survivor Charitable Remainders," (12-70), and Publication 723A, "Actuarial Values II: Factors at 6 Percent Involving One and Two Lives," (12-70). A copy of this publication may be purchased from the Superintendent of Documents, United States Printing Office, Washington, D.C. 20402.

Par. 16. Section 20.2031-7 is redesignated as § 20.2031-7A paragraph (d) and amended as follows:

1. The following redesignation table indicates the old CFR unit numbers for § 20.2031-7 and the corresponding new CFR unit numbers for § 20.2031-7A(d):

Corresponding new number in § 20.2031-7A
paragraph (d) heading
(d) (1)
(d) (1) (i)
(d) (1) (ii)
(d) (1) (iii)
(d) (2)
(d) (2) (i)
(d) (2) (ii)
(d) (2) (iii) (A)
(d) (2) (iii) (B)
(d) (3) through (d) (6)

of the decedent's gross estate is before May 1, 1989, if, on December 1, 1983, the decedent was mentally incompetent so that the disposition of the decedent's property could not be changed, and the decedent died on or after December 1, 1983, without having regained competency to dispose of the decedent's property, or if the decedent died within 90 days of the date on which the decedent first regained competency, the fair market value of annuities, life estates, terms for years, remainders, and reversions included in the estate of such decedent is their present value determined under either this section or § 20.2031-7A(c), at the option of the taxpayer. The value of annuities issued by companies regularly engaged in their sale, and of insurance policies on the lives of persons other than the decedent is determined under § 20.2031-8. The fair market value of a remainder interest in a charitable remainder unitrust as defined in § 1.664-3 is its present value determined under § 1.664-4. The fair market value of a life interest or term for years in a charitable remainder unitrust is the fair market value of the property as of the date of valuation less the fair market value of the remainder interest on such date determined under § 1.664-4. The fair market value of the interests in a pooled income fund, as defined in § 1.642(c)-5, is their value determined under § 1.642(c)-6.

* * * * *

(iii) In all examples set forth in this section, the decedent is assumed to have died on or after August 9, 1984, with the valuation date of the decedent's gross estate falling before May 1, 1989, and to have been competent to change the disposition of the property on December 1, 1983.

* * * * *

(5) *Actuarial computations by the Internal Revenue Service.* * * * Table LN contains values of *lx* taken from the life table for the total population appearing as Table 1 of United States Life Tables: 1969-71, published by the Department of Health and Human Services, Public Health Service. Many special factors involving one and two lives may be found in or computed with the use of tables contained in Internal Revenue Service publication 723E, "Actuarial Values II: Factors at 10 Percent Involving One and Two Lives," (12-83). A copy of this publication may be purchased from the Superintendent of Documents, United States Printing Office, Washington, D.C. 20402 * * *

* * * * *

Par. 17. New § 20.2031-7 is added to read as follows: *§ 20.2031-7 Valuation of annuities, life estates, terms for years, remainders, and reversions after April 30, 1989*—(a) *In general.* Except as otherwise provided in paragraph (c) of this section, the fair market value of annuities, life estates, terms for years, remainders, and reversions for

Decedent's Date of Death (or Alternate Valuation Date)		Applicable Section
After	Before	
—	01-01-52	20.2031-7A (a)
12-31-51	01-01-71	20.2031-7A(b)
12-31-70	12-01-83	20.2031-7A(c)
11-30-83	05-01-89	20.2031-7A(d)

(e) *Valuation of annuities, life estates, terms for years, remainders, and reversions for estates of decedents who died after April 30, 1989*—(1) *In general.* Except as otherwise provided in paragraph (c) of this section and § 20.7520-3, if the valuation date for the gross estate of the decedent is after April 30, 1989, the fair market value of annuities, life estates, terms for years, remainders, and reversions is their present value determined by use of the tables in paragraph (e)(6) of this section and the interest rate component described in § 20.7520-1(b)(1). The tables are also contained in Internal Revenue Service Publication 1457, "Actuarial Values, Alpha Volume," (8-89). A copy of this publication may be purchased from the Superintendent of Documents, United States Printing Office, Washington, D.C. 20402. If the valuation date is after April 30, 1989, and before November 2, 1992, a taxpayer can rely on Notice 89-24, 1989-1 C.B. 660, or Notice 89-60, 1989-1 C.B. 700 (See § 601.601(d)(2)(ii)(*b*) of this chapter).

(2) *Certain Interests*—(i) *Charitable Interests.* The fair market value of a remainder interest in a pooled income fund, as defined in § 1.642(c)-5, is its value determined under § 1.642(c)-6(e). The fair market value of a remainder interest in a charitable remainder annuity trust, as defined in § 1.664-2(a), is its present value determined under § 1.664-2(c). The fair market value of a remainder interest in a charitable remainder unitrust, as defined in § 1.664-3, is its present value determined under § 1.664-4(e). The fair market value of a life interest or term for years in a charitable remainder unitrust is the fair market value of the property as of the date of valuation less the fair market value of the remainder interest on that date determined under § 1.664-4(e).

(ii) *Annuities.* (A) The present value of an annuity may be determined by use of the appropriate table containing remainder factors. If an annuity is payable annually at the end of each year for the life of an individual, the aggregate amount payable annually is multiplied by an annuity factor derived from Table S (remainder factors for one life) in paragraph (e)(6) of this section based on the interest rate component on the valuation date. If an annuity is payable until the death of the survivor of two individuals, the aggregate amount payable annually is multiplied by an annuity factor derived from Table R(2) (remainder factors for two lives) in Publication 1457. A copy of this publication may be purchased from the Superintendent of Documents, United States Government Printing Office, Washington, D.C. 20402. In the case of an annuity that is payable at the end of each year for a term of years, the aggregate amount payable annually is multiplied by an annuity factor derived from Table B (remainder factors for a term of years) in paragraph (e)(6) of this section based on the interest rate component on the valuation date. The annuity factor is obtained by subtracting the remainder factor in Table S, Table R(2), or Table B, whichever is appropriate, under the appropriate interest rate component opposite the number of years nearest the age of the individual or individuals (or

estates of decedents is the present value of such interests determined under paragraph (d) of this section.

(b) *Actuarial computations by the Internal Revenue Service.* The regulations in this and in related sections provide tables with actuarial factors and examples that illustrate how to use the tables to compute the value of annuity, life, and remainder interests in property. These sections also refer to government publications that provide additional tables of factors and examples of computations for more complex situations. Some older publications are no longer available. If the executor of a decedent's estate requires a special factor or computation, the executor may request a ruling on the matter. A request for a ruling must comply with the instructions for requesting a ruling published periodically in the Internal Revenue Bulletin (see § 601.601(d)(2)(ii)(*b*) of this chapter) and include payment of the required user fee.

(c) *Commercial annuities and insurance contracts.* The value of annuities issued by companies regularly engaged in their sale, and of insurance policies on the lives of persons other than the decedent is determined under § 20.2031-8. See § 20.2042-1 with respect to insurance policies on the decedent's life.

(d) *Valuation.* The present value of annuities, life estates, terms for years, remainders, and reversions for estates of decedents who died after April 30, 1989, is determined under paragraph (e) of this section. The present value of annuities, life estates, terms for years, remainders, and reversions for estates of decedents who died before May 1, 1989, is determined under the following sections:

the term of years representing the duration of the annuity), from 1.00 and then dividing the result by the appropriate interest rate component expressed as a decimal number. Alternatively, annuity factors for the life of one individual have been published and are contained in column (2) of the appropriate Table S in publication 1457. Annuity factors for a term of years have been published and are contained in column (2) of the appropriate Table B in Publication 1457. If the annuity is payable at the end of semiannual, quarterly, monthly, or weekly periods, the product obtained by multiplying the annuity factor by the aggregate amount payable annually is then multiplied by the applicable adjustment factor set forth in Table K for payments made at the end of the specified periods. The provisions of this paragraph (e) are illustrated by the following example:

Example. At the time of the decedent's death in January 1990, the annuitant, age 72, is entitled to receive an annuity of $15,000 a year payable in equal monthly installments at the end of each period. The rate that is 120 percent of the applicable Federal mid-term rate for January 1990 is 9.57 percent. This rate is rounded to 9.6 percent. Under Table S, the remainder factor at 9.6 percent for an individual aged 72 is .40138. By converting the remainder factor to an annuity factor, as described above, the annuity factor at 9.6 percent for an individual aged 72 is 6.2356 (1.00 minus .40138, divided by .096). Under Table K, the adjustment factor under the column for payments made at the end of each monthly period at the rate of 9.6 percent is 1.0433. The aggregate annual amount, $15,000, is multiplied by the factor 6.2356 and the product multiplied by 1.0433. The present value of the annuity at the date of the decedent's death is, therefore, $97,584 ($15,000 × 6.2356 × 1.0433).

(B) If an annuity is payable at the beginning of annual, semiannual, quarterly, monthly, or weekly periods for one or two lives, the value of the annuity is the sum of the first payment plus the present value of a similar annuity, the first payment of which is not to be made until the end of the payment period, determined as provided in paragraph (e)(2)(ii)(A) of this section. If the first payment of an annuity for a definite number of years is due at the beginning of the payment period, the value of the annuity is computed by multiplying the aggregate amount payable annually by the annuity factor derived from the appropriate Table B, as described in paragraph (e)(2)(ii)(A) of this section, opposite the number of years representing the duration of the annuity. The product so obtained is then multiplied by the adjustment factor in Table J at the appropriate interest rate component for payments made at the beginning of specified periods.

(iii) *Life estates, terms for years, remainders, and reversions.* If the interest to be valued is the right of a person to receive the income of certain property, or to use certain property for the life of one or two individuals, or for a term for years, the present value of the interest is computed by multiplying the value of the property by the applicable factor representing the income interest. The applicable factor is obtained by subtracting the appropriate remainder factor in Table S (for the life of one individual), Table R(2) (for the lives of two individuals), or Table B (for a term of years), whichever is appropriate, from 1.00. If the interest to be valued is to take effect after the death of one or two individuals, or after a definite number of years, the present value of the interest is computed by multiplying the value of the property by the applicable actuarial factor in Table S, Table R(2), or Table B, whichever is appropriate, corresponding to the applicable Federal mid-term rate (rounded) opposite either the number of years nearest the age of the individual or individuals whose lives measure the interest or the number of years representing the duration of the interest. See § 20.7520-1(c) with respect to the valuation of a qualified annuity interest described in section 2702(b)(1) and a qualified unitrust interest described in section 2702(b)(2).

(iv) *Other Interests.* See § 20.7520-1(c) with respect to the valuation of a qualified annuity interest described in section 2702(b)(1) and a qualified unitrust interest described in section 2702(b)(2). See § 20.2031-7A(d) with respect to the valuation of annuities, life estates, terms for years, remainders, and reversions includible in estates of decedents who died after November 30, 1983, where the valuation date for the gross estate falls before May 1, 1989. See § 20.2031-7A(c) with respect to the valuation of annuities, life estates, terms for years, remainders, and reversions includible in estates of decedents who died after December 31, 1970, and before December 1, 1983. See § 20.2031-7A(b) with respect to the valuation of annuities, life estates, terms for years, remainders, and reversions includible in estates of decedents who died after December 31, 1951, and before January 1, 1971. See § 20.2031-7A(a) with respect to the valuation of annuities, life estates, terms for years, remainders, and reversions includible in estates of decedents who died before January 1, 1952.

(3) *Transitional rule.* If a decedent died after April 30, 1989, and if on May 1, 1989, the decedent was mentally incompetent so that the disposition of the decedent's property could not be changed, and the decedent died without having regained competency to dispose of the decedent's property or died within 90 days of the date on which the decedent first regained competency, the fair market value of annuities, life estates, terms for years, remainders, and reversions included in the estate of the decedent is their present value determined either under this section or under the corresponding section applicable at the time the decedent became mentally incompetent, at the option of the decedent's executor. For example, see § 20.2031-7A(d).

(4) *Publications.* Many actuarial factors not contained in paragraph (e)(6) of this section are contained in Internal Revenue Service Publication 1457, "Actuarial Values, Alpha Volume," (8-89). A copy of this publication may be purchased from the Superintendent of Documents, United States Government Printing Office, Washington, D.C. 20402. If a special factor is required in the case of an actual decedent, the Service will furnish the factor to the executor upon a request for a ruling. The request for a ruling must be accompanied by a recitation of the facts including a statement of the date of birth for each measuring life, the date of the decedent's death, any other applicable dates, and a copy of the will, trust, or other relevant documents. A request for a ruling must comply with the instructions for requesting a ruling published periodically in the Internal Revenue Bulletin (see § 601.601(d)(2)(ii)(*b*) of this chapter) and include payment of the required user fee.

(5) *Examples.* The provisions of this section are illustrated by the following examples:

Example 1. Annuity payable for an individual's life. Under the terms of A's father's will an annuity of $10,000 a year payable in equal semiannual installments made at the end of each interval to A and, after A's death, to A's estate for the life of B, A's brother. A died in September 1989. For September 1989, the rate that was 120 percent of the applicable Federal mid-term rate was 9.68. This rate is rounded to 9.6 percent. At A's death, B was 45 years seven months old. Under Table S in paragraph (e)(6) of this section, the factor at 9.6 percent for determining the present value of the remainder interest at the death of a person age 46, the number of years nearest B's actual age, is .11013. By converting the factor to an annuity factor, as described in paragraph (e)(2)(ii) of this section, the factor for the present value of an annuity payable until the death of a person age 46 is 9.2695 (1.00 minus .11013, divided by .096). The adjustment factor from Table K in paragraph (e)(6) at an interest rate of 9.6 percent for semiannual annuity payments made at the end of the period is 1.0235. The present value of the annuity at the date of A's death is, therefore, $94,873 ($10,000 × 9.2695 × 1.0235).

Example 2. Annuity payable for a term of years. The decedent, or decedent's estate, was entitled to receive an annuity of $10,000 a year payable in equal quarterly installments at the end of each quarter throughout a term certain. The decedent died in February 1990. For February 1990, the rate that was 120 percent of the applicable Federal mid-term rate was 9.70. This rate is rounded to 9.8. A quarterly payment had just been made prior to the decedent's death and payments were to continue for 5 more years. Under Table B in paragraph (e)(6) of this section for the interest rate of 9.8 percent, the factor for the present value of a remainder interest due after a term of 5 years is .626597. Converting the factor to an annuity factor, as described in paragraph (e)(2)(ii) of this section, the factor for the present value of an annuity for a term of 5 years is 3.8102. The adjustment factor from Table K in paragraph (e)(6) at an interest rate of 9.8 percent for quarterly annuity payments made at the end of the period is 1.0360. The present value of the annuity is, therefore, $39,474 ($10,000 × 3.8102 × 1.0360).

Example 3. Income payable for an individual's life. The decedent or the decedent's estate was entitled to receive the income from a fund of $50,000 during the life of the decedent's elder brother. Upon the brother's death, the remainder is to pass to B. The brother was 31 years old at the time of the decedent's death in October 1989. The rate that was 120 percent of the applicable Federal mid-term rate in October 1989 was 10.10 percent. That rate is rounded to 10.2 percent. Under Table S in paragraph (e)(6) of this section, the remainder factor at 10.2 percent for determining the present value of the remainder interest due at the death of a person aged 31, the number of years closest to the brother's age at the decedent's death, is .03753. Converting this remainder factor to an income factor, as described in paragraph (e)(2)(iii) of this section, the factor for determining the present value of an income interest for the life of a person aged 31 is .96247. The present value of the decedent's interest at the time of the decedent's death is, therefore, $48,124 ($50,000 × .96247).

Example 4. Remainder payable at an individual's death. The decedent, or the decedent's estate, was entitled to receive certain property worth $50,000 upon the death of the decedent's elder sister, to whom the income was bequeathed for life. The decedent died in February 1990. At the time of the decedent's death, the elder sister was 47 years 5 months old. In February 1990, the rate that was 120 percent of the applicable Federal mid-term rate was 9.70. This rate is rounded to 9.8 percent. Under Table S in paragraph (e)(6) of this section, the remainder factor at 9.8 percent for determining the present value of the remainder interest due at the death of a person aged 47, the number of years nearest the elder sister's actual age at the decedent's death, is .11352. The present value of the remainder interest at the date of the decedent's death is, therefore, $5,676 ($50,000 × .11352).

(6) *Tables.* The following tables must be used in the application of the provisions of this section when the interest rate component, as described in § 20.7520-1(b)(1), is between 4.2 and 14 percent.

TABLE B
TERM CERTAIN REMAINDER FACTORS
APPLICABLE AFTER APRIL 30, 1989
INTEREST RATE

Years	4.2%	4.4%	4.6%	4.8%	5.0%	5.2%	5.4%	5.6%	5.8%	6.0%
1	.959693	.957854	.956023	.954198	.952381	.950570	.948767	.946970	.945180	.943396
2	.921010	.917485	.913980	.910495	.907029	.903584	.900158	.896752	.893364	.889996
3	.883887	.878817	.873786	.868793	.863838	.858920	.854040	.849197	.844390	.839619
4	.848260	.841779	.835359	.829001	.822702	.816464	.810285	.804163	.798100	.792094
5	.814069	.806302	.798623	.791031	.783526	.776106	.768771	.761518	.754348	.747258
6	.781257	.772320	.763501	.754801	.746215	.737744	.729384	.721135	.712994	.704961
7	.749766	.739770	.729925	.720230	.710681	.701277	.692015	.682893	.673908	.665057
8	.719545	.708592	.697825	.687242	.676839	.666613	.656561	.646679	.636964	.627412

Years	4.2%	4.4%	4.6%	4.8%	5.0%	5.2%	5.4%	5.6%	5.8%	6.0%
9	.690543	.678728	.667137	.655765	.644609	.633663	.622923	.612385	.602045	.591898
10	.662709	.650122	.637798	.625730	.613913	.602341	.591009	.579910	.569041	.558395
11	.635997	.622722	.609750	.597071	.584679	.572568	.560729	.549157	.537846	.526788
12	.610362	.596477	.582935	.569724	.556837	.544266	.532001	.520035	.508361	.496969
13	.585760	.571339	.557299	.543630	.530321	.517363	.504745	.492458	.480492	.468839
14	.562150	.547259	.532790	.518731	.505068	.491790	.478885	.466343	.454151	.442301
15	.539491	.524195	.509360	.494972	.481017	.467481	.454350	.441612	.429255	.417265
16	.517746	.502102	.486960	.472302	.458112	.444374	.431072	.418194	.405723	.393646
17	.496877	.480941	.465545	.450670	.436297	.422408	.408987	.396017	.383481	.371364
18	.476849	.460671	.445071	.430028	.415521	.401529	.388033	.375016	.362458	.350344
19	.457629	.441256	.425498	.410332	.395734	.381681	.368153	.355129	.342588	.330513
20	.439183	.422659	.406786	.391538	.376889	.362815	.349291	.336296	.323807	.311805
21	.421481	.404846	.388897	.373605	.358942	.344881	.331396	.318462	.306056	.294155
22	.404492	.387783	.371794	.356494	.341850	.327834	.314417	.301574	.289278	.277505
23	.388188	.371440	.355444	.340166	.325571	.311629	.298309	.285581	.273420	.261797
24	.372542	.355785	.339813	.324586	.310068	.296225	.283025	.270437	.258431	.246997
25	.357526	.340791	.324869	.309719	.295303	.281583	.268525	.256096	.244263	.232999
26	.343115	.326428	.310582	.295533	.281241	.267664	.254768	.242515	.230873	.219810
27	.329285	.312670	.296923	.281998	.267848	.254434	.241715	.229654	.218216	.207368
28	.316012	.299493	.283866	.269082	.255094	.241857	.229331	.217475	.206253	.195630
29	.303275	.286870	.271382	.256757	.242946	.229902	.217582	.205943	.194947	.184557
30	.291051	.274780	.259447	.244997	.231377	.218538	.206434	.195021	.184260	.174110
31	.279319	.263199	.248038	.233776	.220359	.207736	.195858	.184679	.174158	.164255
32	.268061	.252106	.237130	.223069	.209866	.197468	.185823	.174886	.164611	.154957
33	.257256	.241481	.226702	.212852	.199873	.187707	.176303	.165612	.155587	.146186
34	.246887	.231304	.216732	.203103	.190355	.178429	.167270	.156829	.147058	.137912
35	.236935	.221556	.207201	.193801	.181290	.169609	.158701	.148512	.138996	.130105
36	.227385	.212218	.198089	.184924	.172657	.161225	.150570	.140637	.131376	.122741
37	.218220	.203274	.189377	.176454	.164436	.153256	.142856	.133179	.124174	.115793
38	.209424	.194707	.181049	.168373	.156605	.145681	.135537	.126116	.117367	.109239
39	.200983	.186501	.173087	.160661	.149148	.138480	.128593	.119428	.110933	.103056
40	.192882	.178641	.165475	.153302	.142046	.131635	.122004	.113095	.104851	.097222
41	.185107	.171112	.158198	.146281	.135282	.125128	.115754	.107098	.099103	.091719
42	.177646	.163900	.151241	.139581	.128840	.118943	.109823	.101418	.093670	.086527
43	.170486	.156992	.144590	.133188	.122704	.113064	.104197	.096040	.088535	.081630
44	.163614	.150376	.138231	.127088	.116861	.107475	.098858	.090947	.083682	.077009
45	.157019	.144038	.132152	.121267	.111297	.102163	.093793	.086124	.079094	.072650
46	.150690	.137968	.126340	.115713	.105997	.097113	.088988	.081557	.074758	.068538
47	.144616	.132153	.120784	.110413	.100949	.092312	.084429	.077232	.070660	.064658
48	.138787	.126583	.115473	.105356	.096142	.087749	.080103	.073136	.066786	.060998
49	.133193	.121248	.110395	.100530	.091564	.083412	.075999	.069258	.063125	.057546
50	.127824	.116138	.105540	.095926	.087204	.079289	.072106	.065585	.059665	.054288
51	.122672	.111243	.100898	.091532	.083051	.075370	.068411	.062107	.056394	.051215
52	.117728	.106555	.096461	.087340	.079096	.071644	.064907	.058813	.053302	.048316
53	.112982	.102064	.092219	.083340	.075330	.068103	.061581	.055695	.050380	.045582
54	.108428	.097763	.088164	.079523	.071743	.064737	.058426	.052741	.047618	.043001
55	.104058	.093642	.084286	.075880	.068326	.061537	.055433	.049944	.045008	.040567
56	.099864	.089696	.080580	.072405	.065073	.058495	.052593	.047296	.042541	.038271
57	.095839	.085916	.077036	.069089	.061974	.055604	.049898	.044787	.040208	.036105
58	.091976	.082295	.073648	.065924	.059023	.052855	.047342	.042412	.038004	.034061
59	.088268	.078826	.070409	.062905	.056212	.050243	.044916	.040163	.035921	.032133
60	.084710	.075504	.067313	.060024	.053536	.047759	.042615	.038033	.033952	.030314

TABLE B
TERM CERTAIN REMAINDER FACTORS
APPLICABLE AFTER APRIL 30, 1989
INTEREST RATE

Years	6.2%	6.4%	6.6%	6.8%	7.0%	7.2%	7.4%	7.6%	7.8%	8.0%
1	.941620	.939850	.938086	.936330	.934579	.932836	.931099	.929368	.927644	.925926
2	.886647	.883317	.880006	.876713	.873439	.870183	.866945	.863725	.860523	.857339
3	.834885	.830185	.825521	.820892	.816298	.811738	.807211	.802718	.798259	.793832
4	.786144	.780249	.774410	.768626	.762895	.757218	.751593	.746021	.740500	.735030
5	.740248	.733317	.726464	.719687	.712986	.706360	.699808	.693328	.686920	.680583

Years	6.2%	6.4%	6.6%	6.8%	7.0%	7.2%	7.4%	7.6%	7.8%	8.0%
6	.697032	.689208	.681486	.673864	.666342	.658918	.651590	.644357	.637217	.630170
7	.656339	.647752	.639292	.630959	.622750	.614662	.606694	.598845	.591111	.583490
8	.618022	.608789	.599711	.590786	.582009	.573379	.564892	.556547	.548340	.540269
9	.581942	.572170	.562581	.553170	.543934	.534868	.525971	.517237	.508664	.500249
10	.547968	.537754	.527750	.517950	.508349	.498944	.489731	.480704	.471859	.463193
11	.515977	.505408	.495075	.484972	.475093	.465433	.455987	.446750	.437717	.428883
12	.485854	.475007	.464423	.454093	.444012	.434173	.424569	.415196	.406046	.397114
13	.457490	.446436	.435669	.425181	.414964	.405012	.395316	.385870	.376666	.367698
14	.430781	.419582	.408695	.398109	.387817	.377810	.368078	.358615	.349412	.340461
15	.405632	.394344	.383391	.372762	.362446	.352434	.342717	.333285	.324130	.315242
16	.381951	.370624	.359654	.349028	.338735	.328763	.319103	.309745	.300677	.291890
17	.359653	.348331	.337386	.326805	.316574	.306682	.297117	.287867	.278921	.270269
18	.338656	.327379	.316498	.305997	.295864	.286084	.276645	.267534	.258739	.250249
19	.318885	.307687	.296902	.286514	.276508	.266870	.257584	.248638	.240018	.231712
20	.300268	.289179	.278520	.268272	.258419	.248946	.239836	.231076	.222651	.214548
21	.282739	.271785	.261276	.251191	.241513	.232225	.223311	.214755	.206541	.198656
22	.266232	.255437	.245099	.235197	.225713	.216628	.207925	.199586	.191596	.183941
23	.250689	.240073	.229924	.220222	.210947	.202078	.193598	.185489	.177733	.170315
24	.236054	.225632	.215689	.206201	.197147	.188506	.180259	.172387	.164873	.157699
25	.222273	.212060	.202334	.193072	.184249	.175845	.167839	.160211	.152943	.146018
26	.209297	.199305	.189807	.180779	.172195	.164035	.156275	.148895	.141877	.135202
27	.197078	.187317	.178056	.169269	.160930	.153017	.145507	.138379	.131611	.125187
28	.185572	.176049	.167031	.158491	.150402	.142740	.135482	.128605	.122088	.115914
29	.174739	.165460	.156690	.148400	.140563	.133153	.126147	.119521	.113255	.107328
30	.164537	.155507	.146989	.138951	.131367	.124210	.117455	.111079	.105060	.099377
31	.154932	.146154	.137888	.130104	.122773	.115868	.109362	.103233	.097458	.092016
32	.145887	.137362	.129351	.121820	.114741	.108085	.101827	.095942	.090406	.085200
33	.137370	.129100	.121342	.114064	.107235	.100826	.094811	.089165	.083865	.078889
34	.129350	.121335	.113830	.106802	.100219	.094054	.088278	.082867	.077797	.073045
35	.121798	.114036	.106782	.100001	.093663	.087737	.082196	.077014	.072168	.067635
36	.114688	.107177	.100171	.093634	.087535	.081844	.076532	.071574	.066946	.062625
37	.107992	.100730	.093969	.087673	.081809	.076347	.071259	.066519	.062102	.057986
38	.101688	.094671	.088151	.082090	.076457	.071219	.066349	.061821	.057609	.053690
39	.095751	.088977	.082693	.076864	.071455	.066436	.061778	.057454	.053440	.049713
40	.090161	.083625	.077573	.071970	.066780	.061974	.057521	.053396	.049573	.046031
41	.084897	.078595	.072770	.067387	.062412	.057811	.053558	.049625	.045987	.042621
42	.079941	.073867	.068265	.063097	.058329	.053929	.049868	.046120	.042659	.039464
43	.075274	.069424	.064038	.059079	.054513	.050307	.046432	.042862	.039572	.036541
44	.070880	.065248	.060074	.055318	.050946	.046928	.043233	.039835	.036709	.033834
45	.066742	.061323	.056354	.051796	.047613	.043776	.040254	.037021	.034053	.031328
46	.062845	.057635	.052865	.048498	.044499	.040836	.037480	.034406	.031589	.029007
47	.059176	.054168	.049592	.045410	.041587	.038093	.034898	.031976	.029303	.026859
48	.055722	.050910	.046522	.042519	.038867	.035535	.032493	.029717	.027183	.024869
49	.052469	.047848	.043641	.039812	.036324	.033148	.030255	.027618	.025216	.023027
50	.049405	.044970	.040939	.037277	.033948	.030922	.028170	.025668	.023392	.021321
51	.046521	.042265	.038405	.034903	.031727	.028845	.026229	.023855	.021699	.019742
52	.043805	.039722	.036027	.032681	.029651	.026907	.024422	.022170	.020129	.018280
53	.041248	.037333	.033796	.030600	.027711	.025100	.022739	.020604	.018673	.016925
54	.038840	.035087	.031704	.028652	.025899	.023414	.021172	.019149	.017322	.015672
55	.036572	.032977	.029741	.026828	.024204	.021842	.019714	.017796	.016068	.014511
56	.034437	.030993	.027900	.025119	.022621	.020375	.018355	.016539	.014906	.013436
57	.032427	.029129	.026172	.023520	.021141	.019006	.017091	.015371	.013827	.012441
58	.030534	.027377	.024552	.022023	.019758	.017730	.015913	.014285	.012827	.011519
59	.028751	.025730	.023032	.020620	.018465	.016539	.014817	.013276	.011899	.010666
60	.027073	.024183	.021606	.019307	.017257	.015428	.013796	.012339	.011038	.009876

TABLE B
TERM CERTAIN REMAINDER FACTORS
APPLICABLE AFTER APRIL 30, 1989
INTEREST RATE

Years	8.2%	8.4%	8.6%	8.8%	9.0%	9.2%	9.4%	9.6%	9.8%	10.0%
1	.924214	.922509	.920810	.919118	.917431	.915751	.914077	.912409	.910747	.909091
2	.854172	.851023	.847892	.844777	.841680	.838600	.835536	.832490	.829460	.826446
3	.789438	.785077	.780747	.776450	.772183	.767948	.763744	.759571	.755428	.751315

Proposed Regulations

Years	8.2%	8.4%	8.6%	8.8%	9.0%	9.2%	9.4%	9.6%	9.8%	10.0%
4	.729610	.724241	.718920	.713649	.708425	.703250	.698121	.693039	.688003	.683013
5	.674316	.668119	.661989	.655927	.649931	.644001	.638136	.632335	.626597	.620921
6	.623213	.616346	.609566	.602874	.596267	.589745	.583305	.576948	.570671	.564474
7	.575982	.568585	.561295	.554112	.547034	.540059	.533186	.526412	.519737	.513158
8	.532331	.524524	.516846	.509294	.501866	.494560	.487373	.480303	.473349	.466507
9	.491988	.483879	.475917	.468101	.460428	.452894	.445496	.438233	.431101	.424098
10	.454703	.446383	.438230	.430240	.422411	.414738	.407218	.399848	.392624	.385543
11	.420243	.411792	.403526	.395441	.387533	.379797	.372228	.364824	.357581	.350494
12	.388394	.379882	.371571	.363457	.355535	.347799	.340245	.332869	.325666	.318631
13	.358960	.350445	.342147	.334060	.326179	.318497	.311010	.303713	.296599	.289664
14	.331756	.323288	.315052	.307040	.299246	.291664	.284287	.277110	.270127	.263331
15	.306613	.298236	.290103	.282206	.274538	.267092	.259860	.252838	.246017	.239392
16	.283376	.275126	.267130	.259381	.251870	.244589	.237532	.230691	.224059	.217629
17	.261901	.253806	.245976	.238401	.231073	.223983	.217123	.210485	.204061	.197845
18	.242052	.234139	.226497	.219119	.211994	.205113	.198467	.192048	.185848	.179859
19	.223708	.215995	.208561	.201396	.194490	.187832	.181414	.175226	.169260	.163508
20	.206754	.199257	.192045	.185107	.178431	.172007	.165826	.159878	.154153	.148644
21	.191085	.183817	.176837	.170135	.163698	.157516	.151578	.145874	.140395	.135131
22	.176604	.169573	.162834	.156374	.150182	.144245	.138554	.133097	.127864	.122846
23	.163220	.156432	.149939	.143726	.137781	.132093	.126649	.121439	.116452	.111678
24	.150850	.144310	.138065	.132101	.126405	.120964	.115767	.110802	.106058	.101526
25	.139418	.133128	.127132	.121416	.115968	.110773	.105820	.101097	.096592	.092296
26	.128852	.122811	.117064	.111596	.106393	.101441	.096727	.092241	.087971	.083905
27	.119087	.113295	.107794	.102570	.097608	.092894	.088416	.084162	.080119	.076278
28	.110062	.104515	.099258	.094274	.089548	.085068	.080819	.076790	.072968	.069343
29	.101721	.096416	.091398	.086649	.082155	.077901	.073875	.070064	.066456	.063039
30	.094012	.088945	.084160	.079640	.075371	.071338	.067527	.063927	.060524	.057309
31	.086887	.082053	.077495	.073199	.069148	.065328	.061725	.058327	.055122	.052099
32	.080302	.075694	.071358	.067278	.063438	.059824	.056422	.053218	.050202	.047362
33	.074216	.069829	.065708	.061837	.058200	.054784	.051574	.048557	.045722	.043057
34	.068592	.064418	.060504	.056835	.053395	.050168	.047142	.044304	.041641	.039143
35	.063394	.059426	.055713	.052238	.048986	.045942	.043092	.040423	.037924	.035584
36	.058589	.054821	.051301	.048013	.044941	.042071	.039389	.036882	.034539	.032349
37	.054149	.050573	.047239	.044130	.041231	.038527	.036005	.033652	.031457	.029408
38	.050045	.046654	.043498	.040560	.037826	.035281	.032911	.030704	.028649	.026735
39	.046253	.043039	.040053	.037280	.034703	.032309	.030083	.028015	.026092	.024304
40	.042747	.039703	.036881	.034264	.031838	.029587	.027498	.025561	.023763	.022095
41	.039508	.036627	.033961	.031493	.029209	.027094	.025136	.023322	.021642	.020086
42	.036514	.033789	.031271	.028946	.026797	.024811	.022976	.021279	.019711	.018260
43	.033746	.031170	.028795	.026605	.024584	.022721	.021002	.019415	.017951	.016600
44	.031189	.028755	.026515	.024453	.022555	.020807	.019197	.017715	.016349	.015091
45	.028825	.026527	.024415	.022475	.020692	.019054	.017548	.016163	.014890	.013719
46	.026641	.024471	.022482	.020657	.018984	.017449	.016040	.014747	.013561	.012472
47	.024622	.022575	.020701	.018986	.017416	.015978	.014662	.013456	.012351	.011338
48	.022756	.020825	.019062	.017451	.015978	.014632	.013402	.012277	.011248	.010307
49	.021031	.019212	.017552	.016039	.014659	.013400	.012250	.011202	.010244	.009370
50	.019437	.017723	.016163	.014742	.013449	.012271	.011198	.010221	.009330	.008519
51	.017964	.016350	.014883	.013550	.012338	.011237	.010236	.009325	.008497	.007744
52	.016603	.015083	.013704	.012454	.011319	.010290	.009356	.008508	.007739	.007040
53	.015345	.013914	.012619	.011446	.010385	.009423	.008552	.007763	.007048	.006400
54	.014182	.012836	.011620	.010521	.009527	.008629	.007817	.007083	.006419	.005818
55	.013107	.011841	.010699	.009670	.008741	.007902	.007146	.006463	.005846	.005289
56	.012114	.010923	.009852	.008888	.008019	.007237	.006532	.005897	.005324	.004809
57	.011196	.010077	.009072	.008169	.007357	.006627	.005971	.005380	.004849	.004371
58	.010347	.009296	.008354	.007508	.006749	.006069	.005458	.004909	.004416	.003974
59	.009563	.008576	.007692	.006901	.006192	.005557	.004989	.004479	.004022	.003613
60	.008838	.007911	.007083	.006343	.005681	.005089	.004560	.004087	.003663	.003284

TABLE B
TERM CERTAIN REMAINDER FACTORS
APPLICABLE AFTER APRIL 30, 1989
INTEREST RATE

Years	10.2%	10.4%	10.6%	10.8%	11.0%	11.2%	11.4%	11.6%	11.8%	12.0%
1	.907441	.905797	.904159	.902527	.900901	.899281	.897666	.896057	.894454	.892857
2	.823449	.820468	.817504	.814555	.811622	.808706	.805804	.802919	.800049	.797194
3	.747232	.743178	.739153	.735158	.731191	.727253	.723343	.719461	.715607	.711780
4	.678069	.673168	.668312	.663500	.658731	.654005	.649321	.644679	.640078	.635518
5	.615307	.609754	.604261	.598827	.593451	.588134	.582873	.577669	.572520	.567427
6	.558355	.552313	.546348	.540457	.534641	.528897	.523225	.517625	.512093	.506631
7	.506674	.500284	.493985	.487777	.481658	.475627	.469682	.463821	.458044	.452349
8	.459777	.453156	.446641	.440232	.433926	.427722	.421617	.415610	.409700	.403883
9	.417221	.410467	.403835	.397322	.390925	.384642	.378472	.372411	.366458	.360610
10	.378603	.371800	.365131	.358593	.352184	.345901	.339741	.333701	.327780	.321973
11	.343560	.336775	.330137	.323640	.317283	.311062	.304974	.299016	.293184	.287476
12	.311760	.305050	.298496	.292094	.285841	.279732	.273765	.267935	.262240	.256675
13	.282904	.276313	.269888	.263623	.257514	.251558	.245749	.240085	.234561	.229174
14	.256719	.250284	.244022	.237927	.231995	.226221	.220601	.215130	.209804	.204620
15	.232957	.226706	.220634	.214735	.209004	.203436	.198026	.192769	.187661	.182696
16	.211395	.205350	.199489	.193804	.188292	.182946	.177761	.172732	.167854	.163122
17	.191828	.186005	.180369	.174914	.169633	.164520	.159570	.154778	.150138	.145644
18	.174073	.168483	.163083	.157864	.152822	.147950	.143241	.138690	.134291	.130040
19	.157961	.152612	.147453	.142477	.137678	.133048	.128582	.124274	.120117	.116107
20	.143340	.138235	.133321	.128589	.124034	.119648	.115424	.111357	.107439	.103667
21	.130073	.125213	.120543	.116055	.111742	.107597	.103612	.099782	.096100	.092560
22	.118033	.113418	.108990	.104743	.100669	.096760	.093009	.089410	.085957	.082643
23	.107108	.102733	.098544	.094533	.090693	.087014	.083491	.080117	.076884	.073788
24	.097195	.093056	.089100	.085319	.081705	.078250	.074947	.071789	.068770	.065882
25	.088198	.084289	.080560	.077003	.073608	.070369	.067278	.064327	.061511	.058823
26	.080035	.076349	.072839	.069497	.066314	.063281	.060393	.057641	.055019	.052521
27	.072627	.069157	.065858	.062723	.059742	.056908	.054213	.051650	.049212	.046894
28	.065905	.062642	.059547	.056609	.053822	.051176	.048665	.046281	.044018	.041869
29	.059804	.056741	.053840	.051091	.048488	.046022	.043685	.041470	.039372	.037383
30	.054269	.051396	.048680	.046111	.043683	.041386	.039214	.037160	.035216	.033378
31	.049246	.046554	.044014	.041617	.039354	.037218	.035201	.033297	.031500	.029802
32	.044688	.042169	.039796	.037560	.035454	.033469	.031599	.029836	.028175	.026609
33	.040552	.038196	.035982	.033899	.031940	.030098	.028365	.026735	.025201	.023758
34	.036798	.034598	.032533	.030595	.028775	.027067	.025463	.023956	.022541	.021212
35	.033392	.031339	.029415	.027613	.025924	.024341	.022857	.021466	.020162	.018940
36	.030301	.028387	.026596	.024921	.023355	.021889	.020518	.019235	.018034	.016910
37	.027497	.025712	.024047	.022492	.021040	.019684	.018418	.017236	.016131	.015098
38	.024952	.023290	.021742	.020300	.018955	.017702	.016533	.015444	.014428	.013481
39	.022642	.021096	.019658	.018321	.017077	.015919	.014841	.013839	.012905	.012036
40	.020546	.019109	.017774	.016535	.015384	.014316	.013323	.012400	.011543	.010747
41	.018645	.017309	.016071	.014923	.013860	.012874	.011959	.011111	.010325	.009595
42	.016919	.015678	.014531	.013469	.012486	.011577	.010735	.009956	.009235	.008567
43	015353	.014201	.013138	.012156	.011249	.010411	.009637	.008922	.008260	.007649
44	.013932	.012864	.011879	.010971	.010134	.009362	.008651	.007994	.007389	.006830
45	.012642	.011652	.010740	.009902	.009130	.008419	.007765	.007163	.006609	.006098
46	.011472	.010554	.009711	.008937	.008225	.007571	.006971	.006419	.005911	.005445
47	.010410	.009560	.008780	.008065	.007410	.006809	.006257	.005752	.005287	.004861
48	.009447	.008659	.007939	.007279	.006676	.006123	.005617	.005154	.004729	.004340
49	.008572	.007844	.007178	.006570	.006014	.005506	.005042	.004618	.004230	.003875
50	.007779	.007105	.006490	.005929	.005418	.004952	.004526	.004138	.003784	.003460
51	.007059	.006435	.005868	.005351	.004881	.004453	.004063	.003708	.003384	.003089
52	.006406	.005829	.005306	.004830	.004397	.004005	.003647	.003322	.003027	.002758
53	.005813	.005280	.004797	.004359	.003962	.003601	.003274	.002977	.002708	.002463
54	.005275	.004783	.004337	.003934	.003569	.003238	.002939	.002668	.002422	.002199
55	.004786	.004332	.003922	.003551	.003215	.002912	.002638	.002390	.002166	.001963
56	.004343	.003924	.003546	.003205	.002897	.002619	.002368	.002142	.001938	.001753
57	.003941	.003554	.003206	.002892	.002610	.002355	.002126	.001919	.001733	.001565
58	.003577	.003220	.002899	.002610	.002351	.002118	.001908	.001720	.001550	.001398
59	.003246	.002916	.002621	.002356	.002118	.001905	.001713	.001541	.001387	.001248
60	.002945	.002642	.002370	.002126	.001908	.001713	.001538	.001381	.001240	.001114

Proposed Regulations

TABLE B
TERM CERTAIN REMAINDER FACTORS
APPLICABLE AFTER APRIL 30, 1989
INTEREST RATE

Years	12.2%	12.4%	12.6%	12.8%	13.0%	13.2%	13.4%	13.6%	13.8%	14.0%
1	.891266	.889680	.888099	.886525	.884956	.883392	.881834	.880282	.878735	.877193
2	.794354	.791530	.788721	.785926	.783147	.780382	.777632	.774896	.772175	.769468
3	.707981	.704208	.700462	.696743	.693050	.689383	.685742	.682127	.678536	.674972
4	.630999	.626520	.622080	.617680	.613319	.608996	.604711	.600464	.596254	.592080
5	.562388	.557402	.552469	.547589	.542760	.537982	.533255	.528577	.523949	.519369
6	.501237	.495909	.490648	.485451	.480319	.475249	.470242	.465297	.460412	.455587
7	.446735	.441200	.435744	.430364	.425061	.419831	.414676	.409592	.404580	.399637
8	.398160	.392527	.386984	.381529	.376160	.370876	.365675	.360557	.355518	.350559
9	.354866	.349223	.343680	.338235	.332885	.327629	.322465	.317391	.312406	.307508
10	.316280	.310697	.305222	.299853	.294588	.289425	.284361	.279394	.274522	.269744
11	.281889	.276421	.271068	.265827	.260698	.255676	.250759	.245945	.241232	.236617
12	.251238	.245926	.240735	.235663	.230706	.225862	.221128	.216501	.211979	.207559
13	.223920	.218795	.213797	.208921	.204165	.199525	.194998	.190582	.186273	.182069
14	.199572	.194658	.189873	.185213	.180677	.176258	.171956	.167766	.163685	.159710
15	.177872	.173183	.168626	.164196	.159891	.155705	.151637	.147681	.143835	.140096
16	.158531	.154077	.149757	.145564	.141496	.137549	.133718	.130001	.126393	.122892
17	.141293	.137080	.132999	.129046	.125218	.121510	.117917	.114438	.111066	.107800
18	.125930	.121957	.118116	.114403	.110812	.107341	.103984	.100737	.097598	.094561
19	.112237	.108503	.104899	.101421	.098064	.094824	.091696	.088677	.085762	.082948
20	.100033	.096533	.093161	.089912	.086782	.083767	.080861	.078061	.075362	.072762
21	.089156	.085883	.082736	.079709	.076798	.073999	.071306	.068716	.066224	.063826
22	.079462	.076408	.073478	.070664	.067963	.065370	.062880	.060489	.058193	.055988
23	.070821	.067979	.065255	.062646	.060144	.057747	.055450	.053247	.051136	.049112
24	.063121	.060480	.057953	.055537	.053225	.051014	.048898	.046873	.044935	.043081
25	.056257	.053807	.051468	.049235	.047102	.045065	.043119	.041261	.039486	.037790
26	.050140	.047871	.045709	.043648	.041683	.039810	.038024	.036321	.034698	.033149
27	.044688	.042590	.040594	.038695	.036888	.035168	.033531	.031973	.030490	.029078
28	.039829	.037892	.036052	.034304	.032644	.031067	.029569	.028145	.026793	.025507
29	.035498	.033711	.032017	.030411	.028889	.027444	.026075	.024776	.023544	.022375
30	.031638	.029992	.028435	.026960	.025565	.024244	.022994	.021810	.020689	.019627
31	.028198	.026684	.025253	.023901	.022624	.021417	.020277	.019199	.018180	.017217
32	.025132	.023740	.022427	.021189	.020021	.018920	.017881	.016900	.015975	.015102
33	.022399	.021121	.019917	.018785	.017718	.016714	.015768	.014877	.014038	.013248
34	.019964	.018791	.017689	.016653	.015680	.014765	.013905	.013096	.012336	.011621
35	.017793	.016718	.015709	.014763	.013876	.013043	.012261	.011528	.010840	.010194
36	.015858	.014873	.013951	.013088	.012279	.011522	.010813	.010148	.009525	.008942
37	.014134	.013233	.012390	.011603	.010867	.010178	.009535	.008933	.008370	.007844
38	.012597	.011773	.011004	.010286	.009617	.008992	.008408	.007864	.007355	.006880
39	.011227	.010474	.009772	.009119	.008510	.007943	.007415	.006922	.006463	.006035
40	.010007	.009319	.008679	.008084	.007531	.007017	.006538	.006093	.005679	.005294
41	.008919	.008291	.007708	.007167	.006665	.006199	.005766	.005364	.004991	.004644
42	.007949	.007376	.006845	.006354	.005898	.005476	.005085	.004722	.004386	.004074
43	.007084	.006562	.006079	.005633	.005219	.004837	.004484	.004157	.003854	.003573
44	.006314	.005838	.005399	.004993	.004619	.004273	.003954	.003659	.003386	.003135
45	.005628	.005194	.004795	.004427	.004088	.003775	.003487	.003221	.002976	.002750
46	.005016	.004621	.004258	.003924	.003617	.003335	.003075	.002835	.002615	.002412
47	.004470	.004111	.003782	.003479	.003201	.002946	.002711	.002496	.002298	.002116
48	.003984	.003658	.003359	.003084	.002833	.002602	.002391	.002197	.002019	.001856
49	.003551	.003254	.002983	.002734	.002507	.002299	.002108	.001934	.001774	.001628
50	.003165	.002895	.002649	.002424	.002219	.002031	.001859	.001702	.001559	.001428
51	.002821	.002576	.002353	.002149	.001963	.001794	.001640	.001499	.001370	.001253
52	.002514	.002292	.002089	.001905	.001737	.001585	.001446	.001319	.001204	.001099
53	.002241	.002039	.001856	.001689	.001538	.001400	.001275	.001161	.001058	.000964
54	.001997	.001814	.001648	.001497	.001361	.001237	.001124	.001022	.000930	.000846
55	.001780	.001614	.001463	.001327	.001204	.001093	.000991	.000900	.000817	.000742
56	.001586	.001436	.001300	.001177	.001066	.000965	.000874	.000792	.000718	.000651
57	.001414	.001277	.001154	.001043	.000943	.000853	.000771	.000697	.000631	.000571
58	.001260	.001136	.001025	.000925	.000835	.000753	.000680	.000614	.000554	.000501
59	.001123	.001011	.000910	.000820	.000739	.000665	.000600	.000540	.000487	.000439
60	.001001	.000900	.000809	.000727	.000654	.000588	.000529	.000476	.000428	.000385

TABLE J
ADJUSTMENT FACTORS FOR TERM CERTAIN ANNUITIES
PAYABLE AT THE BEGINNING OF EACH INTERVAL
APPLICABLE AFTER APRIL 30, 1989
FREQUENCY OF PAYMENTS

Interest Rate	Annually	Semi Annually	Quarterly	Monthly	Weekly
4.2	1.0420	1.0314	1.0261	1.0226	1.0213
4.4	1.0440	1.0329	1.0274	1.0237	1.0223
4.6	1.0460	1.0344	1.0286	1.0247	1.0233
4.8	1.0480	1.0359	1.0298	1.0258	1.0243
5.0	1.0500	1.0373	1.0311	1.0269	1.0253
5.2	1.0520	1.0388	1.0323	1.0279	1.0263
5.4	1.0540	1.0403	1.0335	1.0290	1.0273
5.6	1.0560	1.0418	1.0348	1.0301	1.0283
5.8	1.0580	1.0433	1.0360	1.0311	1.0293
6.0	1.0600	1.0448	1.0372	1.0322	1.0303
6.2	1.0620	1.0463	1.0385	1.0333	1.0313
6.4	1.0640	1.0478	1.0397	1.0343	1.0323
6.6	1.0660	1.0492	1.0409	1.0354	1.0333
6.8	1.0680	1.0507	1.0422	1.0365	1.0343
7.0	1.0700	1.0522	1.0434	1.0375	1.0353
7.2	1.0720	1.0537	1.0446	1.0386	1.0363
7.4	1.0740	1.0552	1.0458	1.0396	1.0373
7.6	1.0760	1.0567	1.0471	1.0407	1.0383
7.8	1.0780	1.0581	1.0483	1.0418	1.0393
8.0	1.0800	1.0596	1.0495	1.0428	1.0403
8.2	1.0820	1.0611	1.0507	1.0439	1.0413
8.4	1.0840	1.0626	1.0520	1.0449	1.0422
8.6	1.0860	1.0641	1.0532	1.0460	1.0432
8.8	1.0880	1.0655	1.0544	1.0471	1.0442
9.0	1.0900	1.0670	1.0556	1.0481	1.0452
9.2	1.0920	1.0685	1.0569	1.0492	1.0462
9.4	1.0940	1.0700	1.0581	1.0502	1.0472
9.6	1.0960	1.0715	1.0593	1.0513	1.0482
9.8	1.0980	1.0729	1.0605	1.0523	1.0492
10.0	1.1000	1.0744	1.0618	1.0534	1.0502
10.2	1.1020	1.0759	1.0630	1.0544	1.0512
10.4	1.1040	1.0774	1.0642	1.0555	1.0521
10.6	1.1060	1.0788	1.0654	1.0565	1.0531
10.8	1.1080	1.0803	1.0666	1.0576	1.0541
11.0	1.1100	1.0818	1.0679	1.0586	1.0551
11.2	1.1120	1.0833	1.0691	1.0597	1.0561
11.4	1.1140	1.0847	1.0703	1.0607	1.0571
11.6	1.1160	1.0862	1.0715	1.0618	1.0581
11.8	1.1180	1.0877	1.0727	1.0628	1.0590
12.0	1.1200	1.0892	1.0739	1.0639	1.0600
12.2	1.1220	1.0906	1.0752	1.0649	1.0610
12.4	1.1240	1.0921	1.0764	1.0660	1.0620
12.6	1.1260	1.0936	1.0776	1.0670	1.0630
12.8	1.1280	1.0950	1.0788	1.0681	1.0639
13.0	1.1300	1.0965	1.0800	1.0691	1.0649
13.2	1.1320	1.0980	1.0812	1.0701	1.0659
13.4	1.1340	1.0994	1.0824	1.0712	1.0669
13.6	1.1360	1.1009	1.0836	1.0722	1.0679
13.8	1.1380	1.1024	1.0849	1.0733	1.0688
14.0	1.1400	1.1039	1.0861	1.0743	1.0698

TABLE K
ADJUSTMENT FACTORS FOR ANNUITIES
PAYABLE AT THE END OF EACH INTERVAL
APPLICABLE AFTER APRIL 30, 1989
FREQUENCY OF PAYMENTS

Interest Rate	Annually	Semi Annually	Quarterly	Monthly	Weekly
4.2	1.0000	1.0104	1.0156	1.0191	1.0205
4.4	1.0000	1.0109	1.0164	1.0200	1.0214
4.6	1.0000	1.0114	1.0171	1.0209	1.0224
4.8	1.0000	1.0119	1.0178	1.0218	1.0234

Interest Rate	Annually	Semi Annually	Quarterly	Monthly	Weekly
5.0	1.0000	1.0123	1.0186	1.0227	1.0243
5.2	1.0000	1.0128	1.0193	1.0236	1.0253
5.4	1.0000	1.0133	1.0200	1.0245	1.0262
5.6	1.0000	1.0138	1.0208	1.0254	1.0272
5.8	1.0000	1.0143	1.0215	1.0263	1.0282
6.0	1.0000	1.0148	1.0222	1.0272	1.0291
6.2	1.0000	1.0153	1.0230	1.0281	1.0301
6.4	1.0000	1.0158	1.0237	1.0290	1.0311
6.6	1.0000	1.0162	1.0244	1.0299	1.0320
6.8	1.0000	1.0167	1.0252	1.0308	1.0330
7.0	1.0000	1.0172	1.0259	1.0317	1.0339
7.2	1.0000	1.0177	1.0266	1.0326	1.0349
7.4	1.0000	1.0182	1.0273	1.0335	1.0358
7.6	1.0000	1.0187	1.0281	1.0344	1.0368
7.8	1.0000	1.0191	1.0288	1.0353	1.0378
8.0	1.0000	1.0196	1.0295	1.0362	1.0387
8.2	1.0000	1.0201	1.0302	1.0370	1.0397
8.4	1.0000	1.0206	1.0310	1.0379	1.0406
8.6	1.0000	1.0211	1.0317	1.0388	1.0416
8.8	1.0000	1.0215	1.0324	1.0397	1.0425
9.0	1.0000	1.0220	1.0331	1.0406	1.0435
9.2	1.0000	1.0225	1.0339	1.0415	1.0444
9.4	1.0000	1.0230	1.0346	1.0424	1.0454
9.6	1.0000	1.0235	1.0353	1.0433	1.0463
9.8	1.0000	1.0239	1.0360	1.0442	1.0473
10.0	1.0000	1.0244	1.0368	1.0450	1.0482
10.2	1.0000	1.0249	1.0375	1.0459	1.0492
10.4	1.0000	1.0254	1.0382	1.0468	1.0501
10.6	1.0000	1.0258	1.0389	1.0477	1.0511
10.8	1.0000	1.0263	1.0396	1.0486	1.0520
11.0	1.0000	1.0268	1.0404	1.0495	1.0530
11.2	1.0000	1.0273	1.0411	1.0503	1.0539
11.4	1.0000	1.0277	1.0418	1.0512	1.0549
11.6	1.0000	1.0282	1.0425	1.0521	1.0558
11.8	1.0000	1.0287	1.0432	1.0530	1.0568
12.0	1.0000	1.0292	1.0439	1.0539	1.0577
12.2	1.0000	1.0296	1.0447	1.0548	1.0587
12.4	1.0000	1.0301	1.0454	1.0556	1.0596
12.6	1.0000	1.0306	1.0461	1.0565	1.0605
12.8	1.0000	1.0310	1.0468	1.0574	1.0615
13.0	1.0000	1.0315	1.0475	1.0583	1.0624
13.2	1.0000	1.0320	1.0482	1.0591	1.0634
13.4	1.0000	1.0324	1.0489	1.0600	1.0643
13.6	1.0000	1.0329	1.0496	1.0609	1.0652
13.8	1.0000	1.0334	1.0504	1.0618	1.0662
14.0	1.0000	1.0339	1.0511	1.0626	1.0671

TABLE S
BASED ON LIFE TABLE 80CNSMT
SINGLE LIFE REMAINDER FACTORS
APPLICABLE AFTER APRIL 30, 1989
INTEREST RATE

Age	4.2%	4.4%	4.6%	4.8%	5.0%	5.2%	5.4%	5.6%	5.8%	6.0%
0	.07389	.06749	.06188	.05695	.05261	.04879	.04541	.04243	.03978	.03744
1	.06494	.05832	.05250	.04738	.04287	.03889	.03537	.03226	.02950	.02705
2	.06678	.05999	.05401	.04874	.04410	.03999	.03636	.03314	.03028	.02773
3	.06897	.06200	.05587	.05045	.04567	.04143	.03768	.03435	.03139	.02875
4	.07139	.06425	.05796	.05239	.04746	.04310	.03922	.03578	.03271	.02998
5	.07401	.06669	.06023	.05451	.04944	.04494	.04094	.03738	.03421	.03137
6	.07677	.06928	.06265	.05677	.05156	.04692	.04279	.03911	.03583	.03289
7	.07968	.07201	.06521	.05918	.05381	.04903	.04477	.04097	.03757	.03453
8	.08274	.07489	.06792	.06172	.05621	.05129	.04689	.04297	.03945	.03630
9	.08597	.07794	.07079	.06443	.05876	.05370	.04917	.04511	.04148	.03821

Age	4.2%	4.4%	4.6%	4.8%	5.0%	5.2%	5.4%	5.6%	5.8%	6.0%
10	.08936	.08115	.07383	.06730	.06147	.05626	.05159	.04741	.04365	.04027
11	.09293	.08453	.07704	.07035	.06436	.05900	.05419	.04988	.04599	.04250
12	.09666	.08807	.08040	.07354	.06739	.06188	.05693	.05248	.04847	.04486
13	.10049	.09172	.08387	.07684	.07053	.06487	.05977	.05518	.05104	.04731
14	.10437	.09541	.08738	.08017	.07370	.06788	.06263	.05791	.05364	.04978
15	.10827	.09912	.09090	.08352	.07688	.07090	.06551	.06064	.05623	.05225
16	.11220	.10285	.09445	.08689	.08008	.07394	.06839	.06337	.05883	.05472
17	.11615	.10661	.09802	.09028	.08330	.07699	.07129	.06612	.06144	.05719
18	.12017	.11043	.10165	.09373	.08656	.08009	.07422	.06890	.06408	.05969
19	.12428	.11434	.10537	.09726	.08992	.08327	.07724	.07177	.06679	.06226
20	.12850	.11836	.10919	.10089	.09337	.08654	.08035	.07471	.06959	.06492
21	.13282	.12248	.11311	.10462	.09692	.08991	.08355	.07775	.07247	.06765
22	.13728	.12673	.11717	.10848	.10059	.09341	.08686	.08090	.07546	.07049
23	.14188	.13113	.12136	.11248	.10440	.09703	.09032	.08418	.07858	.07345
24	.14667	.13572	.12575	.11667	.10839	.10084	.09395	.08764	.08187	.07659
25	.15167	.14051	.13034	.12106	.11259	.10486	.09778	.09130	.08536	.07991
26	.15690	.14554	.13517	.12569	.11703	.10910	.10184	.09518	.08907	.08346
27	.16237	.15081	.14024	.13056	.12171	.11359	.10614	.09930	.09302	.08724
28	.16808	.15632	.14555	.13567	.12662	.11831	.11068	.10366	.09720	.09125
29	.17404	.16208	.15110	.14104	.13179	.12329	.11547	.10827	.10163	.09551
30	.18025	.16808	.15692	.14665	.13721	.12852	.12051	.11313	.10631	.10002
31	.18672	.17436	.16300	.15255	.14291	.13403	.12584	.11827	.11127	.10480
32	.19344	.18090	.16935	.15870	.14888	.13980	.13142	.12367	.11650	.10985
33	.20044	.18772	.17598	.16514	.15513	.14587	.13730	.12936	.12201	.11519
34	.20770	.19480	.18287	.17185	.16165	.15221	.14345	.13533	.12780	.12080
35	.21522	.20215	.19005	.17884	.16846	.15883	.14989	.14159	.13388	.12670
36	.22299	.20974	.19747	.18609	.17552	.16571	.15660	.14812	.14022	.13287
37	.23101	.21760	.20516	.19360	.18286	.17288	.16358	.15492	.14685	.13933
38	.23928	.22572	.21311	.20139	.19048	.18032	.17085	.16201	.15377	.14607
39	.24780	.23409	.22133	.20945	.19837	.18804	.17840	.16939	.16097	.15310
40	.25658	.24273	.22982	.21778	.20654	.19605	.18624	.17706	.16847	.16043
41	.26560	.25163	.23858	.22639	.21499	.20434	.19436	.18502	.17627	.16806
42	.27486	.26076	.24758	.23525	.22370	.21289	.20276	.19326	.18434	.17597
43	.28435	.27013	.25683	.24436	.23268	.22172	.21143	.20177	.19270	.18416
44	.29407	.27975	.26633	.25373	.24191	.23081	.22038	.21057	.20134	.19265
45	.30402	.28961	.27608	.26337	.25142	.24019	.22962	.21966	.21028	.20144
46	.31420	.29970	.28608	.27326	.26120	.24983	.23913	.22904	.21951	.21053
47	.32460	.31004	.29632	.28341	.27123	.25975	.24892	.23870	.22904	.21991
48	.33521	.32058	.30679	.29379	.28151	.26992	.25897	.24862	.23883	.22957
49	.34599	.33132	.31746	.30438	.29201	.28032	.26926	.25879	.24888	.23949
50	.35695	.34224	.32833	.31518	.30273	.29094	.27978	.26921	.25918	.24966
51	.36809	.35335	.33940	.32619	.31367	.30180	.29055	.27987	.26973	.26010
52	.37944	.36468	.35070	.33744	.32486	.31292	.30158	.29081	.28057	.27083
53	.39098	.37622	.36222	.34892	.33629	.32429	.31288	.30203	.29170	.28186
54	.40269	.38794	.37393	.36062	.34795	.33590	.32442	.31349	.30308	.29316
55	.41457	.39985	.38585	.37252	.35983	.34774	.33621	.32522	.31474	.30473
56	.42662	.41194	.39796	.38464	.37193	.35981	.34824	.33720	.32666	.31658
57	.43884	.42422	.41028	.39697	.38426	.37213	.36053	.34945	.33885	.32872
58	.45123	.43668	.42279	.40951	.39682	.38468	.37307	.36196	.35132	.34114
59	.46377	.44931	.43547	.42224	.40958	.39745	.38584	.37471	.36405	.35383
60	.47643	.46206	.44830	.43513	.42250	.41040	.39880	.38767	.37699	.36674
61	.48916	.47491	.46124	.44814	.43556	.42350	.41192	.40080	.39012	.37985
62	.50196	.48783	.47427	.46124	.44874	.43672	.42518	.41408	.40340	.39314
63	.51480	.50081	.48736	.47444	.46201	.45006	.43856	.42749	.41684	.40658
64	.52770	.51386	.50054	.48773	.47540	.46352	.45208	.44105	.43043	.42019
65	.54069	.52701	.51384	.50115	.48892	.47713	.46577	.45480	.44422	.43401
66	.55378	.54029	.52727	.51472	.50262	.49093	.47965	.46876	.45824	.44808
67	.56697	.55368	.54084	.52845	.51648	.50491	.49373	.48293	.47248	.46238
68	.58026	.56717	.55453	.54231	.53049	.51905	.50800	.49729	.48694	.47691
69	.59358	.58072	.56828	.55624	.54459	.53330	.52238	.51179	.50154	.49160
70	.60689	.59427	.58205	.57021	.55874	.54762	.53683	.52638	.51624	.50641
71	.62014	.60778	.59578	.58415	.57287	.56193	.55131	.54100	.53099	.52126

Age	4.2%	4.4%	4.6%	4.8%	5.0%	5.2%	5.4%	5.6%	5.8%	6.0%
72	.63334	.62123	.60948	.59808	.58700	.57624	.56579	.55563	.54577	.53617
73	.64648	.63465	.62315	.61198	.60112	.59056	.58029	.57030	.56059	.55113
74	.65961	.64806	.63682	.62590	.61527	.60492	.59485	.58504	.57550	.56620
75	.67274	.66149	.65054	.63987	.62948	.61936	.60950	.59990	.59053	.58140
76	.68589	.67495	.66429	.65390	.64377	.63390	.62427	.61487	.60570	.59676
77	.69903	.68841	.67806	.66796	.65811	.64849	.63910	.62993	.62097	.61223
78	.71209	.70182	.69179	.68199	.67242	.66307	.65393	.64501	.63628	.62775
79	.72500	.71507	.70537	.69588	.68660	.67754	.66867	.65999	.65151	.64321
80	.73768	.72809	.71872	.70955	.70058	.69180	.68320	.67479	.66655	.65849
81	.75001	.74077	.73173	.72288	.71422	.70573	.69741	.68926	.68128	.67345
82	.76195	.75306	.74435	.73582	.72746	.71926	.71123	.70335	.69562	.68804
83	.77346	.76491	.75654	.74832	.74026	.73236	.72460	.71699	.70952	.70219
84	.78456	.77636	.76831	.76041	.75265	.74503	.73756	.73021	.72300	.71592
85	.79530	.78743	.77971	.77212	.76466	.75733	.75014	.74306	.73611	.72928
86	.80560	.79806	.79065	.78337	.77621	.76917	.76225	.75544	.74875	.74216
87	.81535	.80813	.80103	.79404	.78717	.78041	.77375	.76720	.76076	.75442
88	.82462	.81771	.81090	.80420	.79760	.79111	.78472	.77842	.77223	.76612
89	.83356	.82694	.82043	.81401	.80769	.80147	.79533	.78929	.78334	.77747
90	.84225	.83593	.82971	.82357	.81753	.81157	.80570	.79991	.79420	.78857
91	.85058	.84455	.83861	.83276	.82698	.82129	.81567	.81013	.80466	.79927
92	.85838	.85263	.84696	.84137	.83585	.83040	.82503	.81973	.81449	.80933
93	.86557	.86009	.85467	.84932	.84405	.83884	.83370	.82862	.82360	.81865
94	.87212	.86687	.86169	.85657	.85152	.84653	.84160	.83673	.83192	.82717
95	.87801	.87298	.86801	.86310	.85825	.85345	.84872	.84404	.83941	.83484
96	.88322	.87838	.87360	.86888	.86420	.85959	.85502	.85051	.84605	.84165
97	.88795	.88328	.87867	.87411	.86961	.86515	.86074	.85639	.85208	.84782
98	.89220	.88769	.88323	.87883	.87447	.87016	.86589	.86167	.85750	.85337
99	.89612	.89176	.88745	.88318	.87895	.87478	.87064	.86656	.86251	.85850
100	.89977	.89555	.89136	.88722	.88313	.87908	.87506	.87109	.86716	.86327
101	.90326	.89917	.89511	.89110	.88712	.88318	.87929	.87543	.87161	.86783
102	.90690	.90294	.89901	.89513	.89128	.88746	.88369	.87995	.87624	.87257
103	.91076	.90694	.90315	.89940	.89569	.89200	.88835	.88474	.88116	.87760
104	.91504	.91138	.90775	.90415	.90058	.89704	.89354	.89006	.88661	.88319
105	.92027	.91681	.91337	.90996	.90658	.90322	.89989	.89659	.89331	.89006
106	.92763	.92445	.92130	.91816	.91506	.91197	.90890	.90586	.90284	.89983
107	.93799	.93523	.93249	.92977	.92707	.92438	.92170	.91905	.91641	.91378
108	.95429	.95223	.95018	.94814	.94611	.94409	.94208	.94008	.93809	.93611
109	.97985	.97893	.97801	.97710	.97619	.97529	.97438	.97348	.97259	.97170

TABLE S
BASED ON LIFE TABLE 80CNSMT
SINGLE LIFE REMAINDER FACTORS
APPLICABLE AFTER APRIL 30, 1989
INTEREST RATE

Age	6.2%	6.4%	6.6%	6.8%	7.0%	7.2%	7.4%	7.6%	7.8%	8.0%
0	.03535	.03349	.03183	.03035	.02902	.02783	.02676	.02579	.02492	.02413
1	.02486	.02292	.02119	.01963	.01824	.01699	.01587	.01486	.01395	.01312
2	.02547	.02345	.02164	.02002	.01857	.01727	.01609	.01504	.01408	.01321
3	.02640	.02429	.02241	.02073	.01921	.01785	.01662	.01552	.01451	.01361
4	.02753	.02535	.02339	.02163	.02005	.01863	.01735	.01619	.01514	.01418
5	.02883	.02656	.02453	.02269	.02105	.01956	.01822	.01700	.01590	.01490
6	.03026	.02790	.02578	.02387	.02215	.02060	.01919	.01792	.01677	.01572
7	.03180	.02935	.02714	.02515	.02336	.02174	.02027	.01894	.01773	.01664
8	.03347	.03092	.02863	.02656	.02469	.02300	.02146	.02007	.01881	.01766
9	.03528	.03263	.03025	.02810	.02615	.02438	.02278	.02133	.02000	.01880
10	.03723	.03449	.03201	.02977	.02774	.02590	.02423	.02271	.02133	.02006
11	.03935	.03650	.03393	.03160	.02949	.02757	.02583	.02424	.02279	.02147
12	.04160	.03865	.03598	.03356	.03136	.02936	.02755	.02589	.02438	.02299
13	.04394	.04088	.03811	.03560	.03331	.03123	.02934	.02761	.02603	.02458
14	.04629	.04312	.04025	.03764	.03527	.03311	.03113	.02933	.02768	.02617
15	.04864	.04536	.04238	.03968	.03721	.03496	.03290	.03103	.02930	.02773
16	.05099	.04759	.04451	.04170	.03913	.03679	.03466	.03270	.03090	.02926
17	.05333	.04982	.04662	.04370	.04104	.03861	.03638	.03434	.03247	.03075
18	.05570	.05207	.04875	.04573	.04296	.04044	.03812	.03599	.03404	.03225

Age	6.2%	6.4%	6.6%	6.8%	7.0%	7.2%	7.4%	7.6%	7.8%	8.0%
19	.05814	.05438	.05095	.04781	.04494	.04231	.03990	.03769	.03565	.03378
20	.06065	.05677	.05321	.04996	.04698	.04424	.04173	.03943	.03731	.03535
21	.06325	.05922	.05554	.05217	.04907	.04623	.04362	.04122	.03901	.03697
22	.06594	.06178	.05797	.05447	.05126	.04831	.04559	.04309	.04078	.03865
23	.06876	.06446	.06051	.05688	.05355	.05048	.04766	.04505	.04265	.04042
24	.07174	.06729	.06321	.05945	.05599	.05281	.04987	.04715	.04465	.04233
25	.07491	.07031	.06609	.06219	.05861	.05530	.05224	.04941	.04680	.04438
26	.07830	.07355	.06918	.06515	.06142	.05799	.05481	.05187	.04915	.04662
27	.08192	.07702	.07250	.06832	.06446	.06090	.05759	.05454	.05170	.04906
28	.08577	.08071	.07603	.07171	.06772	.06402	.06059	.05740	.05445	.05170
29	.08986	.08464	.07981	.07534	.07120	.06736	.06380	.06049	.05742	.05456
30	.09420	.08882	.08383	.07921	.07492	.07095	.06725	.06381	.06061	.05763
31	.09881	.09327	.08812	.08335	.07891	.07479	.07095	.06738	.06405	.06095
32	.10369	.09797	.09267	.08774	.08315	.07888	.07491	.07120	.06774	.06451
33	.10885	.10297	.09750	.09241	.08767	.08325	.07913	.07529	.07170	.06834
34	.11430	.10824	.10261	.09736	.09246	.08790	.08363	.07964	.07592	.07243
35	.12002	.11380	.10800	.10259	.09754	.09282	.08841	.08428	.08041	.07679
36	.12602	.11963	.11366	.10809	.10288	.09800	.09344	.08917	.08516	.08140
37	.13230	.12574	.11961	.11387	.10850	.10347	.09876	.09433	.09018	.08628
38	.13887	.13214	.12584	.11994	.11441	.10922	.10436	.09978	.09549	.09145
39	.14573	.13883	.13237	.12630	.12061	.11527	.11025	.10553	.10109	.09690
40	.15290	.14583	.13920	.13297	.12712	.12162	.11644	.11157	.10698	.10266
41	.16036	.15312	.14633	.13994	.13393	.12827	.12294	.11792	.11318	.10871
42	.16810	.16071	.15375	.14720	.14103	.13522	.12973	.12456	.11967	.11505
43	.17614	.16858	.16146	.15475	.14842	.14245	.13682	.13149	.12645	.12169
44	.18447	.17675	.16948	.16261	.15613	.15000	.14421	.13873	.13355	.12864
45	.19310	.18524	.17780	.17078	.16414	.15787	.15192	.14630	.14096	.13591
46	.20204	.19402	.18644	.17926	.17247	.16604	.15995	.15418	.14870	.14350
47	.21128	.20311	.19538	.18806	.18112	.17454	.16830	.16238	.15676	.15141
48	.22080	.21249	.20462	.19716	.19007	.18335	.17696	.17090	.16513	.15964
49	.23059	.22214	.21413	.20653	.19930	.19244	.18591	.17970	.17379	.16816
50	.24063	.23206	.22391	.21617	.20881	.20180	.19514	.18879	.18274	.17697
51	.25095	.24225	.23398	.22610	.21861	.21147	.20466	.19818	.19199	.18609
52	.26157	.25275	.24436	.23636	.22874	.22147	.21453	.20791	.20159	.19556
53	.27249	.26357	.25505	.24694	.23919	.23180	.22474	.21799	.21154	.20537
54	.28369	.27466	.26604	.25782	.24995	.24244	.23526	.22839	.22181	.21552
55	.29518	.28605	.27734	.26900	.26103	.25341	.24611	.23912	.23243	.22601
56	.30695	.29774	.28893	.28050	.27242	.26469	.25728	.25019	.24338	.23685
57	.31902	.30973	.30084	.29232	.28415	.27632	.26881	.26161	.25469	.24805
58	.33138	.32203	.31306	.30446	.29621	.28829	.28069	.27339	.26637	.25962
59	.34402	.33461	.32558	.31691	.30859	.30059	.29290	.28550	.27839	.27155
60	.35690	.34745	.33836	.32963	.32124	.31317	.30540	.29792	.29073	.28379
61	.36999	.36050	.35137	.34259	.33414	.32601	.31817	.31062	.30334	.29633
62	.38325	.37374	.36458	.35576	.34726	.33907	.33117	.32356	.31621	.30912
63	.39669	.38717	.37799	.36913	.36060	.35236	.34441	.33674	.32933	.32217
64	.41031	.40078	.39159	.38272	.37415	.36588	.35789	.35016	.34270	.33548
65	.42416	.41464	.40545	.39656	.38798	.37968	.37166	.36390	.35639	.34912
66	.43825	.42876	.41958	.41070	.40211	.39380	.38576	.37797	.37043	.36312
67	.45260	.44315	.43399	.42513	.41655	.40824	.40019	.39238	.38482	.37749
68	.46720	.45779	.44868	.43985	.43129	.42299	.41494	.40713	.39956	.39221
69	.48197	.47263	.46357	.45478	.44625	.43798	.42995	.42215	.41458	.40722
70	.49686	.48760	.47861	.46988	.46140	.45316	.44516	.43738	.42983	.42248
71	.51182	.50265	.49374	.48508	.47666	.46847	.46051	.45276	.44523	.43790
72	.52685	.51778	.50896	.50038	.49203	.48390	.47599	.46829	.46079	.45349
73	.54194	.53298	.52426	.51578	.50751	.49946	.49161	.48397	.47652	.46926
74	.55714	.54832	.53972	.53134	.52317	.51520	.50744	.49986	.49247	.48527
75	.57250	.56382	.55536	.54710	.53904	.53118	.52351	.51601	.50870	.50156
76	.58803	.57951	.57120	.56308	.55515	.54740	.53984	.53245	.52522	.51817
77	.60369	.59535	.58720	.57923	.57144	.56383	.55639	.54912	.54200	.53504
78	.61942	.61126	.60329	.59549	.58787	.58040	.57310	.56596	.55896	.55212
79	.63508	.62713	.61935	.61174	.60428	.59698	.58983	.58283	.57597	.56925
80	.65059	.64285	.63527	.62785	.62058	.61345	.60646	.59961	.59290	.58632

Age	6.2%	6.4%	6.6%	6.8%	7.0%	7.2%	7.4%	7.6%	7.8%	8.0%
81	.66579	.65827	.65090	.64368	.63659	.62965	.62283	.61615	.60959	.60316
82	.68061	.67332	.66616	.65914	.65226	.64550	.63886	.63235	.62595	.61968
83	.69499	.68793	.68099	.67418	.66749	.66092	.65447	.64813	.64191	.63579
84	.70896	.70213	.69541	.68881	.68233	.67595	.66969	.66353	.65748	.65153
85	.72256	.71596	.70947	.70308	.69681	.69063	.68456	.67859	.67271	.66693
86	.73569	.72931	.72305	.71688	.71081	.70484	.69896	.69318	.68748	.68188
87	.74818	.74204	.73599	.73003	.72417	.71839	.71271	.70711	.70159	.69616
88	.76011	.75419	.74836	.74261	.73695	.73137	.72588	.72046	.71512	.70986
89	.77169	.76599	.76037	.75484	.74938	.74400	.73870	.73347	.72831	.72323
90	.78302	.77755	.77215	.76683	.76158	.75640	.75129	.74625	.74128	.73638
91	.79395	.78870	.78352	.77842	.77337	.76840	.76349	.75864	.75385	.74913
92	.80423	.79920	.79423	.78933	.78449	.77971	.77499	.77033	.76572	.76118
93	.81377	.80894	.80417	.79946	.79481	.79022	.78568	.78120	.77677	.77239
94	.82247	.81784	.81325	.80873	.80425	.79983	.79547	.79115	.78688	.78266
95	.83033	.82586	.82145	.81709	.81278	.80852	.80431	.80014	.79602	.79195
96	.83729	.83298	.82872	.82451	.82034	.81622	.81215	.80812	.80414	.80019
97	.84361	.83944	.83532	.83124	.82721	.82322	.81927	.81537	.81151	.80769
98	.84929	.84525	.84126	.83730	.83339	.82952	.82569	.82190	.81815	.81443
99	.85454	.85062	.84674	.84290	.83910	.83534	.83161	.82792	.82427	.82066
100	.85942	.85561	.85184	.84810	.84440	.84074	.83711	.83352	.82997	.82644
101	.86408	.86037	.85670	.85306	.84946	.84589	.84236	.83886	.83539	.83196
102	.86894	.86534	.86177	.85823	.85473	.85126	.84782	.84442	.84104	.83770
103	.87408	.87060	.86714	.86371	.86032	.85695	.85362	.85031	.84703	.84378
104	.87980	.87644	.87311	.86980	.86653	.86328	.86005	.85686	.85369	.85054
105	.88684	.88363	.88046	.87731	.87418	.87108	.86800	.86494	.86191	.85890
106	.89685	.89389	.89095	.88804	.88514	.88226	.87940	.87656	.87374	.87094
107	.91117	.90858	.90600	.90344	.90089	.89836	.89584	.89334	.89085	.88838
108	.93414	.93217	.93022	.92828	.92634	.92442	.92250	.92060	.91870	.91681
109	.97081	.96992	.96904	.96816	.96729	.96642	.96555	.96468	.96382	.96296

TABLE S
BASED ON LIFE TABLE 80CNSMT
SINGLE LIFE REMAINDER FACTORS
APPLICABLE AFTER APRIL 30, 1989
INTEREST RATE

Age	8.2%	8.4%	8.6%	8.8%	9.0%	9.2%	9.4%	9.6%	9.8%	10.0%
0	.02341	.02276	.02217	.02163	.02114	.02069	.02027	.01989	.01954	.01922
1	.01237	.01170	.01108	.01052	.01000	.00953	.00910	.00871	.00834	.00801
2	.01243	.01172	.01107	.01048	.00994	.00944	.00899	.00857	.00819	.00784
3	.01278	.01203	.01135	.01073	.01016	.00964	.00916	.00872	.00832	.00795
4	.01332	.01253	.01182	.01116	.01056	.01001	.00951	.00904	.00862	.00822
5	.01400	.01317	.01241	.01172	.01109	.01051	.00998	.00949	.00904	.00862
6	.01477	.01390	.01310	.01238	.01171	.01110	.01054	.01002	.00954	.00910
7	.01563	.01472	.01389	.01312	.01242	.01178	.01118	.01064	.01013	.00966
8	.01660	.01564	.01477	.01396	.01322	.01254	.01192	.01134	.01081	.01031
9	.01770	.01669	.01577	.01492	.01414	.01342	.01276	.01216	.01159	.01107
10	.01891	.01785	.01688	.01599	.01517	.01442	.01372	.01308	.01249	.01194
11	.02026	.01915	.01814	.01720	.01634	.01555	.01481	.01414	.01351	.01293
12	.02173	.02056	.01950	.01852	.01761	.01678	.01601	.01529	.01463	.01402
13	.02326	.02204	.02092	.01989	.01895	.01807	.01726	.01651	.01582	.01517
14	.02478	.02351	.02234	.02126	.02027	.01935	.01850	.01771	.01698	.01630
15	.02628	.02495	.02372	.02259	.02155	.02058	.01969	.01886	.01810	.01738
16	.02774	.02635	.02507	.02388	.02279	.02178	.02084	.01997	.01917	.01842
17	.02917	.02772	.02637	.02513	.02399	.02293	.02194	.02103	.02018	.01940
18	.03059	.02907	.02767	.02637	.02517	.02406	.02302	.02207	.02118	.02035
19	.03205	.03046	.02899	.02763	.02637	.02521	.02412	.02312	.02218	.02131
20	.03355	.03188	.03035	.02892	.02760	.02638	.02524	.02419	.02320	.02229
21	.03509	.03334	.03173	.03024	.02886	.02758	.02638	.02527	.02424	.02328
22	.03669	.03487	.03318	.03162	.03017	.02882	.02757	.02640	.02532	.02430
23	.03837	.03646	.03470	.03306	.03154	.03013	.02881	.02759	.02644	.02538
24	.04018	.03819	.03634	.03463	.03303	.03155	.03016	.02888	.02767	.02655
25	.04214	.04006	.03812	.03633	.03465	.03309	.03164	.03029	.02902	.02784
26	.04428	.04210	.04008	.03820	.03644	.03481	.03328	.03186	.03052	.02928
27	.04662	.04434	.04223	.04025	.03841	.03670	.03509	.03360	.03219	.03088

Age	8.2%	8.4%	8.6%	8.8%	9.0%	9.2%	9.4%	9.6%	9.8%	10.0%
28	.04915	.04677	.04456	.04249	.04056	.03876	.03708	.03550	.03403	.03264
29	.05189	.04941	.04709	.04493	.04291	.04102	.03925	.03760	.03604	.03458
30	.05485	.05226	.04984	.04757	.04546	.04348	.04162	.03988	.03825	.03671
31	.05805	.05535	.05282	.05045	.04824	.04616	.04421	.04238	.04067	.03905
32	.06149	.05867	.05603	.05356	.05124	.04906	.04702	.04510	.04329	.04160
33	.06520	.06226	.05950	.05692	.05449	.05221	.05007	.04806	.04616	.04438
34	.06916	.06609	.06322	.06052	.05799	.05560	.05336	.05125	.04926	.04738
35	.07339	.07020	.06720	.06439	.06174	.05925	.05690	.05469	.05260	.05063
36	.07787	.07455	.07143	.06850	.06573	.06313	.06068	.05836	.05617	.05411
37	.08262	.07917	.07593	.07287	.06999	.06727	.06470	.06228	.05999	.05733
38	.08765	.08407	.08069	.07751	.07451	.07167	.06899	.06646	.06407	.06180
39	.09296	.08925	.08574	.08243	.07931	.07635	.07356	.07092	.06841	.06604
40	.09858	.09472	.09109	.08765	.08440	.08132	.07841	.07565	.07303	.07055
41	.10449	.10050	.09673	.09316	.08978	.08658	.08355	.08067	.07794	.07535
42	.11069	.10656	.10265	.09895	.09544	.09212	.08896	.08596	.08312	.08041
43	.11718	.11291	.10887	.10503	.10140	.09794	.09466	.09154	.08858	.08576
44	.12399	.11958	.11540	.11143	.10766	.10407	.10067	.09743	.09434	.09141
45	.13111	.12656	.12224	.11814	.11423	.11052	.10699	.10362	.10042	.09736
46	.13856	.13387	.12941	.12516	.12113	.11728	.11362	.11013	.10680	.10363
47	.14633	.14150	.13690	.13252	.12835	.12438	.12059	.11697	.11352	.11022
48	.15442	.14945	.14471	.14020	.13589	.13179	.12787	.12412	.12055	.11713
49	.16280	.15769	.15281	.14816	.14373	.13949	.13544	.13157	.12787	.12433
50	.17147	.16622	.16121	.15643	.15186	.14749	.14331	.13931	.13548	.13182
51	.18045	.17507	.16993	.16501	.16030	.15580	.15150	.14737	.14342	.13963
52	.18979	.18427	.17899	.17394	.16911	.16448	.16004	.15579	.15172	.14780
53	.19947	.19383	.18842	.18324	.17828	.17352	.16896	.16458	.16038	.15635
54	.20950	.20372	.19819	.19288	.18779	.18291	.17822	.17372	.16940	.16524
55	.21986	.21397	.20831	.20288	.19767	.19266	.18785	.18322	.17878	.17450
56	.23058	.22457	.21879	.21324	.20791	.20278	.19785	.19310	.18854	.18414
57	.24167	.23554	.22965	.22399	.21854	.21329	.20824	.20338	.19870	.19419
58	.25314	.24690	.24090	.23512	.22956	.22420	.21904	.21407	.20927	.20464
59	.26497	.25863	.25252	.24664	.24097	.23550	.23023	.22515	.22024	.21551
60	.27712	.27068	.26448	.25849	.25272	.24716	.24178	.23659	.23158	.22674
61	.28956	.28304	.27674	.27067	.26480	.25913	.25366	.24837	.24325	.23831
62	.30228	.29567	.28929	.28312	.27717	.27141	.26584	.26045	.25524	.25020
63	.31525	.30857	.30211	.29586	.28982	.28397	.27832	.27284	.26754	.26240
64	.32851	.32176	.31522	.30890	.30278	.29685	.29111	.28555	.28016	.27493
65	.34209	.33528	.32868	.32229	.31610	.31010	.30429	.29865	.29317	.28787
66	.35604	.34918	.34253	.33609	.32983	.32377	.31788	.31217	.30663	.30124
67	.37037	.36347	.35678	.35028	.34398	.33786	.33191	.32614	.32053	.31508
68	.38508	.37815	.37142	.36489	.35854	.35237	.34638	.34055	.33488	.32937
69	.40008	.39313	.38638	.37982	.37344	.36724	.36120	.35533	.34961	.34405
70	.41533	.40838	.40162	.39504	.38864	.38241	.37634	.37043	.36468	.35907
71	.43076	.42382	.41705	.41047	.40405	.39780	.39171	.38578	.38000	.37436
72	.44638	.43945	.43269	.42611	.41969	.41344	.40733	.40138	.39558	.38991
73	.46218	.45527	.44854	.44197	.43556	.42931	.42321	.41725	.41143	.40575
74	.47823	.47137	.46466	.45812	.45173	.44549	.43940	.43345	.42763	.42195
75	.49459	.48777	.48112	.47462	.46826	.46205	.45598	.45004	.44424	.43856
76	.51127	.50452	.49793	.49148	.48517	.47900	.47297	.46706	.46129	.45563
77	.52823	.52157	.51505	.50867	.50243	.49632	.49033	.48447	.47873	.47311
78	.54541	.53885	.53242	.52613	.51996	.51392	.50800	.50220	.49652	.49094
79	.56267	.55621	.54989	.54369	.53762	.53166	.52582	.52009	.51448	.50897
80	.57987	.57354	.56733	.56125	.55527	.54941	.54366	.53802	.53248	.52705
81	.59685	.59065	.58457	.57860	.57274	.56699	.56134	.55579	.55035	.54499
82	.61351	.60746	.60151	.59567	.58993	.58429	.57875	.57331	.56796	.56270
83	.62978	.62387	.61806	.61236	.60675	.60123	.59581	.59047	.58523	.58007
84	.64567	.63992	.63426	.62869	.62321	.61783	.61253	.60731	.60218	.59713
85	.66125	.65565	.65014	.64472	.63938	.63413	.62896	.62387	.61886	.61392
86	.67636	.67092	.66557	.66030	.65511	.65000	.64496	.64000	.63511	.63030
87	.69081	.68554	.68034	.67522	.67018	.66520	.66031	.65548	.65071	.64602
88	.70468	.69957	.69453	.68956	.68466	.67983	.67507	.67037	.66574	.66117
89	.71821	.71326	.70838	.70357	.69882	.69414	.68952	.68495	.68045	.67601
90	.73153	.72676	.72204	.71739	.71280	.70827	.70379	.69938	.69502	.69071

Proposed Regulations

Age	8.2%	8.4%	8.6%	8.8%	9.0%	9.2%	9.4%	9.6%	9.8%	10.0%
91	.74447	.73986	.73532	.73083	.72640	.72202	.71770	.71343	.70921	.70504
92	.75669	.75225	.74787	.74354	.73927	.73504	.73087	.72674	.72267	.71864
93	.76807	.76379	.75957	.75540	.75127	.74719	.74317	.73918	.73524	.73135
94	.77849	.77437	.77030	.76627	.76229	.75835	.75446	.75061	.74680	.74303
95	.78792	.78394	.78001	.77611	.77226	.76845	.76468	.76096	.75727	.75362
96	.79630	.79244	.78863	.78485	.78112	.77742	.77377	.77015	.76657	.76303
97	.80391	.80016	.79646	.79280	.78917	.78559	.78203	.77852	.77504	.77160
98	.81076	.80712	.80352	.79996	.79643	.79294	.78948	.78606	.78267	.77931
99	.81709	.81354	.81004	.80657	.80313	.79972	.79635	.79302	.78971	.78644
100	.82296	.81950	.81609	.81270	.80934	.80602	.80273	.79947	.79624	.79304
101	.82855	.82518	.82185	.81854	.81526	.81201	.80880	.80561	.80245	.79932
102	.83438	.83110	.82785	.82462	.82142	.81826	.81512	.81200	.80892	.80586
103	.84056	.83737	.83420	.83106	.82795	.82487	.82181	.81878	.81577	.81279
104	.84743	.84433	.84127	.83822	.83521	.83221	.82924	.82630	.32338	.82048
105	.85591	.85295	.85001	.84709	.84419	.84132	.83846	.83563	.83282	.83003
106	.86816	.86540	.86266	.85993	.85723	.85454	.85187	.84922	.84659	.84397
107	.88592	.88348	.88105	.87863	.87623	.87384	.87147	.86911	.86676	.86443
108	.91493	.91306	.91119	.90934	.90749	.90566	.90383	.90201	.90020	.89840
109	.96211	.96125	.96041	.95956	.95872	.95788	.95704	.95620	.95537	.95455

TABLE S
BASED ON LIFE TABLE 80CNSMT
SINGLE LIFE REMAINDER FACTORS
APPLICABLE AFTER APRIL 30, 1989
INTEREST RATE

Age	10.2%	10.4%	10.6%	10.8%	11.0%	11.2%	11.4%	11.6%	11.8%	12.0%
0	.01891	.01864	.01838	.01814	.01791	.01770	.01750	.01732	.01715	.01698
1	.00770	.00741	.00715	.00690	.00667	.00646	.00626	.00608	.00590	.00574
2	.00751	.00721	.00693	.00667	.00643	.00620	.00600	.00580	.00562	.00544
3	.00760	.00728	.00699	.00671	.00646	.00622	.00600	.00579	.00560	.00541
4	.00786	.00752	.00721	.00692	.00665	.00639	.00616	.00594	.00573	.00554
5	.00824	.00788	.00755	.00724	.00695	.00668	.00643	.00620	.00598	.00578
6	.00869	.00832	.00796	.00764	.00733	.00705	.00678	.00654	.00630	.00608
7	.00923	.00883	.00846	.00811	.00779	.00749	.00720	.00694	.00669	.00646
8	.00986	.00943	.00904	.00867	.00833	.00801	.00771	.00743	.00716	.00692
9	.01059	.01014	.00972	.00933	.00897	.00863	.00831	.00801	.00773	.00747
10	.01142	.01095	.01051	.01009	.00971	.00935	.00901	.00869	.00840	.00812
11	.01239	.01189	.01142	.01098	.01057	.01019	.00983	.00950	.00918	.00889
12	.01345	.01292	.01243	.01197	.01154	.01113	.01075	.01040	.01007	.00975
13	.01457	.01401	.01349	.01300	.01255	.01212	.01172	.01135	.01100	.01067
14	.01567	.01508	.01453	.01402	.01354	.01309	.01267	.01227	.01190	.01155
15	.01672	.01610	.01552	.01498	.01448	.01400	.01356	.01314	.01275	.01238
16	.01772	.01707	.01646	.01589	.01536	.01486	.01439	.01396	.01354	.01315
17	.01866	.01798	.01734	.01674	.01618	.01566	.01516	.01470	.01427	.01386
18	.01958	.01886	.01818	.01755	.01697	.01641	.01590	.01541	.01495	.01452
19	.02050	.01974	.01903	.01837	.01775	.01717	.01662	.01611	.01563	.01517
20	.02143	.02064	.01989	.01919	.01854	.01793	.01735	.01681	.01630	.01582
21	.02238	.02154	.02075	.02002	.01933	.01868	.01807	.01750	.01696	.01646
22	.02336	.02247	.02164	.02087	.02014	.01946	.01882	.01821	.01764	.01711
23	.02438	.02345	.02257	.02176	.02099	.02027	.01959	.01895	.01835	.01778
24	.02550	.02451	.02359	.02273	.02192	.02115	.02044	.01976	.01913	.01853
25	.02673	.02569	.02472	.02381	.02295	.02214	.02138	.02067	.01999	.01936
26	.02811	.02701	.02598	.02502	.02411	.02326	.02246	.02170	.02098	.02031
27	.02965	.02849	.02741	.02639	.02543	.02452	.02367	.02287	.02211	.02140
28	.03134	.03013	.02898	.02790	.02689	.02593	.02503	.02418	.02338	.02262
29	.03322	.03193	.03072	.02958	.02851	.02750	.02654	.02564	.02479	.02398
30	.03527	.03391	.03264	.03143	.03030	.02923	.02821	.02726	.02635	.02550
31	.03753	.03610	.03475	.03348	.03228	.03115	.03008	.02907	.02811	.02720
32	.04000	.03849	.03707	.03573	.03446	.03326	.03213	.03105	.03004	.02907
33	.04269	.04111	.03961	.03819	.03685	.03558	.03438	.03325	.03217	.03115
34	.04561	.04394	.04236	.04087	.03946	.03812	.03685	.03565	.03451	.03342
35	.04877	.04702	.04535	.04378	.04229	.04087	.03953	.03826	.03706	.03591
36	.05215	.05031	.04856	.04690	.04533	.04384	.04242	.04108	.03980	.03859
37	.05578	.05384	.05200	.05025	.04860	.04703	.04553	.04411	.04276	.04148
38	.05965	.05761	.05568	.05385	.05211	.05045	.04888	.04738	.04595	.04460

Age	10.2%	10.4%	10.6%	10.8%	11.0%	11.2%	11.4%	11.6%	11.8%	12.0%
39	.06379	.06165	.05962	.05770	.05587	.05412	.05247	.05089	.04939	.04795
40	.06820	.06596	.06383	.06181	.05989	.05806	.05631	.05465	.05307	.05155
41	.07288	.07054	.06832	.06620	.06418	.06226	.06042	.05868	.05701	.05541
42	.07784	.07539	.07306	.07085	.06873	.06671	.06479	.06295	.06119	.05952
43	.08308	.08052	.07808	.07576	.07355	.07143	.06941	.06748	.06564	.06387
44	.08861	.08594	.08340	.08097	.07865	.07644	.07432	.07230	.07036	.06851
45	.09445	.09167	.08901	.08648	.08406	.08174	.07953	.07741	.07538	.07343
46	.10060	.09770	.09494	.09230	.08977	.08735	.08503	.08281	.08068	.07865
47	.10707	.10406	.10119	.09843	.09579	.09327	.09085	.08853	.08630	.08417
48	.11386	.11073	.10774	.10487	.10213	.09949	.09697	.09455	.09222	.08999
49	.12094	.11769	.11458	.11160	.10874	.10600	.10337	.10084	.09842	.09609
50	.12831	.12494	.12172	.11862	.11565	.11280	.11006	.10743	.10490	.10247
51	.13600	.13251	.12917	.12596	.12288	.11991	.11706	.11432	.11169	.10915
52	.14405	.14044	.13698	.13366	.13046	.12738	.12442	.12157	.11883	.11619
53	.15247	.14875	.14517	.14172	.13841	.13522	.13215	.12919	.12635	.12360
54	.16124	.15740	.15370	.15014	.14671	.14341	.14023	.13717	.13421	.13136
55	.17039	.16642	.16261	.15893	.15539	.15198	.14868	.14551	.14244	.13948
56	.17991	.17583	.17190	.16811	.16445	.16092	.15752	.15423	.15106	.14799
57	.18984	.18564	.18160	.17769	.17392	.17029	.16677	.16338	.16010	.15692
58	.20018	.19587	.19172	.18770	.18382	.18007	.17645	.17295	.16956	.16628
59	.21093	.20652	.20225	.19812	.19414	.19028	.18655	.18294	.17945	.17606
60	.22206	.21753	.21316	.20893	.20483	.20087	.19703	.19332	.18972	.18624
61	.23353	.22890	.22442	.22009	.21589	.21182	.20788	.20407	.20037	.19678
62	.24532	.24059	.23601	.23158	.22728	.22311	.21907	.21515	.21135	.20767
63	.25742	.25260	.24793	.24339	.23900	.23473	.23060	.22658	.22268	.21890
64	.26987	.26495	.26019	.25556	.25107	.24671	.24248	.23837	.23438	.23050
65	.28271	.27771	.27286	.26815	.26357	.25912	.25480	.25059	.24651	.24254
66	.29601	.29093	.28600	.28120	.27654	.27200	.26760	.26331	.25913	.25507
67	.30978	.30462	.29961	.29474	.29000	.28539	.28090	.27653	.27227	.26813
68	.32401	.31879	.31371	.30877	.30396	.29927	.29471	.29027	.28593	.28171
69	.33863	.33336	.32822	.32322	.31835	.31359	.30896	.30445	.30005	.29576
70	.35361	.34829	.34310	.33804	.33311	.32830	.32361	.31903	.31457	.31021
71	.36886	.36349	.35826	.35316	.34818	.34332	.33858	.33394	.32942	.32500
72	.38439	.37899	.37373	.36858	.36356	.35866	.35387	.34919	.34461	.34015
73	.40021	.39479	.38950	.38432	.37927	.37433	.36950	.36478	.36016	.35565
74	.41639	.41096	.40565	.40046	.39538	.39042	.38556	.38081	.37616	.37161
75	.43301	.42758	.42226	.41706	.41198	.40699	.40212	.39734	.39267	.38809
76	.45009	.44467	.43937	.43417	.42908	.42410	.41921	.41443	.40974	.40514
77	.46761	.46221	.45693	.45175	.44667	.44170	.43682	.43203	.42734	.42274
78	.48548	.48013	.47488	.46973	.46468	.45972	.45486	.45009	.44541	.44082
79	.50356	.49826	.49306	.48795	.48294	.47802	.47319	.46845	.46379	.45922
80	.52171	.51647	.51133	.50628	.50132	.49644	.49166	.48695	.48233	.47779
81	.53974	.53457	.52950	.52451	.51961	.51479	.51006	.50541	.50083	.49633
82	.55753	.55245	.54745	.54254	.53771	.53296	.52828	.52369	.51917	.51472
83	.57500	.57001	.56510	.56026	.55551	.55083	.54623	.54170	.53724	.53285
84	.59216	.58726	.58245	.57770	.57304	.56844	.56391	.55945	.55506	.55074
85	.60906	.60428	.59956	.59492	.59034	.58583	.58139	.57702	.57270	.56845
86	.62555	.62088	.61627	.61173	.60725	.60284	.59849	.59420	.58997	.58580
87	.64139	.63683	.63233	.62790	.62352	.61921	.61495	.61076	.60661	.60253
88	.65666	.65221	.64783	.64350	.63923	.63502	.63086	.62675	.62270	.61871
89	.67163	.66730	.66304	.65882	.65466	.65055	.64650	.64249	.63854	.63463
90	.68646	.68226	.67812	.67402	.66998	.66599	.66204	.65814	.65430	.65049
91	.70093	.69686	.69285	.68888	.68496	.68108	.67725	.67347	.66973	.66604
92	.71466	.71073	.70684	.70300	.69920	.69545	.69173	.68806	.68444	.68085
93	.72750	.72370	.71994	.71622	.71254	.70890	.70530	.70174	.69822	.69474
94	.73931	.73562	.73198	.72838	.72481	.72129	.71780	.71434	.71093	.70755
95	.75001	.74644	.74291	.73941	.73595	.73253	.72914	.72579	.72247	.71919
96	.75953	.75606	.75262	.74923	.74586	.74253	.73924	.73598	.73275	.72955
97	.76819	.76481	.76147	.75816	.75489	.75165	.74844	.74526	.74211	.73899
98	.77599	.77270	.76944	.76621	.76302	.75986	.75672	.75362	.75054	.74750
99	.78319	.77998	.77680	.77365	.77053	.76744	.76437	.76134	.75833	.75535
100	.78987	.78673	.78362	.78054	.77748	.77446	.77146	.76849	.76555	.76263

Proposed Regulations

Age	10.2%	10.4%	10.6%	10.8%	11.0%	11.2%	11.4%	11.6%	11.8%	12.0%
101	.79622	.79315	.79010	.78708	.78409	.78113	.77819	.77528	.77239	.76953
102	.80283	.79983	.79685	.79390	.79097	.78807	.78519	.78234	.77951	.77671
103	.80983	.80690	.80399	.80111	.79825	.79541	.79260	.78981	.78705	.78430
104	.81760	.81475	.81192	.80912	.80633	.80357	.80083	.79810	.79541	.79273
105	.82726	.82451	.82178	.81907	.81638	.81371	.81106	.80843	.80582	.80322
106	.84137	.83879	.83623	.83368	.83115	.82863	.82614	.82366	.82119	.81874
107	.86211	.85981	.85751	.85523	.85297	.85071	.84847	.84624	.84403	.84182
108	.89660	.89481	.89304	.89127	.88950	.88775	.88601	.88427	.88254	.88081
109	.95372	.95290	.95208	.95126	.95045	.94964	.94883	.94803	.94723	.94643

TABLE S
BASED ON LIFE TABLE 80CNSMT
SINGLE LIFE REMAINDER FACTORS
APPLICABLE AFTER APRIL 30, 1989
INTEREST RATE

Age	12.2%	12.4%	12.6%	12.8%	13.0%	13.2%	13.4%	13.6%	13.8%	14.0%
0	.01683	.01669	.01655	.01642	.01630	.01618	.01607	.01596	.01586	.01576
1	.00559	.00544	.00531	.00518	.00506	.00494	.00484	.00473	.00464	.00454
2	.00528	.00513	.00499	.00485	.00473	.00461	.00449	.00439	.00428	.00419
3	.00524	.00508	.00493	.00479	.00465	.00453	.00441	.00429	.00419	.00408
4	.00536	.00519	.00503	.00488	.00473	.00460	.00447	.00435	.00423	.00412
5	.00558	.00540	.00523	.00507	.00492	.00477	.00464	.00451	.00439	.00427
6	.00588	.00569	.00550	.00533	.00517	.00502	.00487	.00473	.00460	.00448
7	.00624	.00604	.00584	.00566	.00549	.00532	.00517	.00502	.00488	.00475
8	.00668	.00646	.00626	.00606	.00588	.00570	.00554	.00538	.00523	.00509
9	.00722	.00699	.00677	.00656	.00636	.00617	.00600	.00583	.00567	.00552
10	.00785	.00761	.00737	.00715	.00694	.00674	.00655	.00637	.00620	.00604
11	.00861	.00835	.00810	.00786	.00764	.00743	.00723	.00704	.00686	.00668
12	.00946	.00918	.00891	.00866	.00843	.00820	.00799	.00779	.00760	.00741
13	.01035	.01006	.00978	.00951	.00927	.00903	.00880	.00859	.00839	.00819
14	.01122	.01091	.01061	.01034	.01007	.00982	.00958	.00936	.00914	.00894
15	.01203	.01171	.01140	.01110	.01082	.01056	.01031	.01007	.00985	.00963
16	.01279	.01244	.01211	.01181	.01151	.01123	.01097	.01072	.01048	.01025
17	.01347	.01311	.01276	.01244	.01213	.01184	.01156	.01130	.01104	.01081
18	.01411	.01373	.01336	.01302	.01270	.01239	.01210	.01182	.01155	.01130
19	.01474	.01434	.01396	.01359	.01325	.01293	.01262	.01233	.01205	.01178
20	.01537	.01494	.01454	.01415	.01379	.01345	.01313	.01282	.01252	.01224
21	.01598	.01553	.01510	.01470	.01432	.01396	.01361	.01329	.01298	.01268
22	.01660	.01613	.01568	.01525	.01485	.01446	.01410	.01375	.01343	.01312
23	.01725	.01674	.01627	.01581	.01539	.01498	.01460	.01423	.01388	.01355
24	.01796	.01742	.01692	.01644	.01599	.01556	.01515	.01476	.01439	.01404
25	.01876	.01819	.01765	.01714	.01666	.01621	.01577	.01536	.01497	.01460
26	.01967	.01907	.01850	.01796	.01745	.01696	.01650	.01606	.01565	.01525
27	.02072	.02008	.01948	.01890	.01836	.01784	.01735	.01688	.01644	.01601
28	.02190	.02122	.02057	.01996	.01938	.01883	.01831	.01781	.01734	.01689
29	.02322	.02249	.02181	.02116	.02054	.01996	.01940	.01887	.01836	.01788
30	.02469	.02392	.02319	.02250	.02184	.02122	.02062	.02006	.01952	.01900
31	.02634	.02552	.02475	.02401	.02331	.02264	.02201	.02140	.02083	.02028
32	.02816	.02729	.02647	.02568	.02494	.02423	.02355	.02291	.02229	.02170
33	.03018	.02926	.02838	.02755	.02675	.02600	.02528	.02459	.02393	.02331
34	.03239	.03142	.03048	.02960	.02875	.02795	.02718	.02645	.02575	.02508
35	.03482	.03378	.03279	.03185	.03095	.03009	.02928	.02850	.02775	.02704
36	.03743	.03633	.03528	.03428	.03333	.03242	.03155	.03072	.02992	.02916
37	.04026	.03909	.03798	.03692	.03591	.03494	.03401	.03313	.03228	.03147
38	.04330	.04207	.04089	.03977	.03869	.03767	.03668	.03574	.03484	.03398
39	.04658	.04528	.04403	.04284	.04170	.04061	.03957	.03857	.03762	.03670
40	.05011	.04873	.04741	.04615	.04495	.04379	.04269	.04163	.04061	.03964
41	.05389	.05244	.05104	.04971	.04844	.04721	.04604	.04492	.04384	.04281
42	.05791	.05638	.05491	.05350	.05216	.05086	.04962	.04844	.04729	.04620
43	.06219	.06057	.05902	.05754	.05612	.05475	.05344	.05218	.05098	.04981
44	.06673	.06503	.06340	.06184	.06034	.05890	.05752	.05619	.05491	.05368
45	.07157	.06978	.06806	.06642	.06484	.06332	.06186	.06046	.05911	.05781
46	.07669	.07481	.07301	.07128	.06962	.06802	.06649	.06501	.06358	.06221
47	.08212	.08015	.07826	.07645	.07470	.07302	.07140	.06984	.06834	.06690

Age	12.2%	12.4%	12.6%	12.8%	13.0%	13.2%	13.4%	13.6%	13.8%	14.0%
48	.08784	.08578	.08380	.08190	.08006	.07830	.07660	.07496	.07338	.07186
49	.09384	.09169	.08961	.08762	.08570	.08384	.08206	.08034	.07868	.07708
50	.10013	.09787	.09570	.09361	.09160	.08966	.08779	.08598	.08424	.08256
51	.10671	.10436	.10209	.09991	.09780	.09577	.09381	.09192	.09009	.08832
52	.11365	.11120	.10883	.10655	.10435	.10222	.10017	.09819	.09628	.09442
53	.12095	.11840	.11593	.11355	.11126	.10904	.10689	.10482	.10282	.10088
54	.12860	.12595	.12338	.12090	.11851	.11619	.11396	.11179	.10970	.10767
55	.13663	.13386	.13120	.12862	.12613	.12372	.12138	.11912	.11694	.11482
56	.14503	.14217	.13940	.13672	.13413	.13162	.12919	.12683	.12456	.12235
57	.15385	.15089	.14801	.14523	.14254	.13994	.13741	.13496	.13259	.13029
58	.16311	.16004	.15706	.15418	.15139	.14868	.14606	.14352	.14105	.13866
59	.17279	.16961	.16654	.16355	.16066	.15786	.15514	.15250	.14994	.14745
60	.18286	.17958	.17640	.17332	.17033	.16743	.16462	.16188	.15922	.15664
61	.19330	.18992	.18665	.18347	.18038	.17738	.17447	.17164	.16889	.16622
62	.20409	.20061	.19724	.19396	.19078	.18768	.18467	.18175	.17891	.17614
63	.21522	.21165	.20818	.20480	.20152	.19833	.19523	.19221	.18928	.18642
64	.22672	.22306	.21949	.21602	.21265	.20937	.20617	.20306	.20003	.19708
65	.23867	.23491	.23125	.22769	.22423	.22085	.21757	.21437	.21125	.20821
66	.25112	.24727	.24353	.23988	.23632	.23286	.22948	.22619	.22299	.21986
67	.26409	.26016	.25633	.25260	.24896	.24541	.24195	.23857	.23528	.23206
68	.27760	.27359	.26968	.26586	.26214	.25851	.25497	.25151	.24814	.24484
69	.29157	.28748	.28350	.27961	.27581	.27211	.26849	.26495	.26150	.25812
70	.30596	.30181	.29775	.29379	.28992	.28614	.28245	.27884	.27532	.27187
71	.32069	.31648	.31236	.30833	.30440	.30055	.29679	.29312	.28952	.28600
72	.33578	.33151	.32733	.32325	.31925	.31535	.31152	.30778	.30412	.30054
73	.35123	.34691	.34269	.33855	.33450	.33054	.32666	.32286	.31914	.31550
74	.36715	.36279	.35852	.35434	.35024	.34623	.34230	.33845	.33468	.33098
75	.38360	.37921	.37491	.37069	.36656	.36250	.35853	.35464	.35082	.34708
76	.40064	.39623	.39190	.38765	.38349	.37941	.37540	.37148	.36762	.36384
77	.41823	.41381	.40947	.40521	.40103	.39692	.39290	.38895	.38507	.38126
78	.43632	.43189	.42755	.42329	.41910	.41499	.41095	.40698	.40309	.39926
79	.45473	.45032	.44599	.44173	.43755	.43344	.42940	.42543	.42153	.41770
80	.47333	.46894	.46463	.46040	.45623	.45213	.44811	.44414	.44025	.43642
81	.49191	.48755	.48328	.47907	.47493	.47085	.46684	.46290	.45902	.45520
82	.51034	.50603	.50179	.49762	.49351	.48947	.48549	.48157	.47772	.47392
83	.52852	.52427	.52008	.51595	.51189	.50788	.50394	.50006	.49623	.49246
84	.54648	.54228	.53815	.53407	.53006	.52610	.52221	.51836	.51458	.51084
85	.56426	.56013	.55606	.55205	.54810	.54420	.54035	.53656	.53282	.52913
86	.58169	.57764	.57364	.56970	.56581	.56197	.55818	.55445	.55076	.54713
87	.59850	.59452	.59060	.58673	.58291	.57913	.57541	.57174	.56811	.56453
88	.61476	.61086	.60702	.60322	.59947	.59577	.59212	.58851	.58494	.58142
89	.63078	.62697	.62321	.61950	.61583	.61220	.60862	.60508	.60159	.59813
90	.64674	.64302	.63935	.63573	.63215	.62861	.62511	.62165	.61823	.61485
91	.66238	.65877	.65520	.65167	.64819	.64474	.64133	.63795	.63462	.63132
92	.67730	.67379	.67032	.66689	.66350	.66014	.65682	.65354	.65029	.64708
93	.69130	.68789	.68452	.68119	.67789	.67463	.67140	.66820	.66504	.66191
94	.70421	.70090	.69762	.69438	.69118	.68800	.68486	.68175	.67867	.67563
95	.71594	.71272	.70954	.70639	.70326	.70017	.69712	.69409	.69109	.68812
96	.72638	.72325	.72014	.71707	.71403	.71101	.70803	.70507	.70215	.69925
97	.73590	.73285	.72982	.72682	.72385	.72090	.71799	.71510	.71224	.70941
98	.74448	.74149	.73853	.73560	.73269	.72981	.72696	.72414	.72134	.71856
99	.75240	.74948	.74658	.74371	.74086	.73805	.73525	.73248	.72974	.72702
100	.75974	.75687	.75403	.75121	.74842	.74566	.74292	.74020	.73751	.73484
101	.76669	.76388	.76109	.75833	.75559	.75287	.75018	.74751	.74486	.74223
102	.77393	.77117	.76844	.76573	.76304	.76037	.75773	.75511	.75251	.74993
103	.78158	.77888	.77620	.77355	.77091	.76830	.76571	.76313	.76058	.75805
104	.79007	.78743	.78482	.78222	.77964	.77709	.77455	.77203	.76953	.76705
105	.80065	.79809	.79556	.79304	.79054	.78805	.78559	.78314	.78071	.77829
106	.81631	.81389	.81149	.80911	.80674	.80438	.80204	.79972	.79741	.79511
107	.83963	.83745	.83529	.83313	.83099	.82886	.82674	.82463	.82254	.82045
108	.87910	.87739	.87569	.87400	.87232	.87064	.86897	.86731	.86566	.86401
109	.94563	.94484	.94405	.94326	.94248	.94170	.94092	.94014	.93937	.93860

TABLE 80CNSMT

Age x	1(x)	Age x	1(x)	Age x	1(x)
(1)	(2)	(1)	(2)	(1)	(2)
0	100000	37	95492	74	59279
1	98740	38	95317	75	56799
2	98648	39	95129	76	54239
3	98584	40	94926	77	51599
4	98535	41	94706	78	48878
5	98495	42	94465	79	46071
6	98459	43	94201	80	43180
7	98426	44	93913	81	40208
8	98396	45	93599	82	37172
9	98370	46	93256	83	34095
10	98347	47	92882	84	31012
11	98328	48	92472	85	27960
12	98309	49	92021	86	24961
13	98285	50	91526	87	22038
14	98248	51	90986	88	19235
15	98196	52	90402	89	16598
16	98129	53	89771	90	14154
17	98047	54	89087	91	11908
18	97953	55	88348	92	9863
19	97851	56	87551	93	8032
20	97741	57	86695	94	6424
21	97623	58	85776	95	5043
22	97499	59	84789	96	3884
23	97370	60	83726	97	2939
24	97240	61	82581	98	2185
25	97110	62	81348	99	1598
26	96982	63	80024	100	1150
27	96856	64	78609	101	815
28	96730	65	77107	102	570
29	96604	66	75520	103	393
30	96477	67	73846	104	267
31	96350	68	72082	105	179
32	96220	69	70218	106	119
33	96088	70	68248	107	78
34	95951	71	66165	108	51
35	95808	72	63972	109	33
36	95655	73	61673	110	0

Par. 18. Section 20.2031-10 is removed.

* * *

Shirley D. Peterson

Commissioner of Internal Revenue

[¶ 20,191 Reserved.—Proposed Regulation Sec. 1.514(c)-2, relating to unrelated business income partnerships, was formerly reproduced at this point. The final regulations appear at ¶ 13,234B.]

¶ 20,192

Proposed regulations: Cash or deferred arrangements: Collective bargaining units.—The IRS has issued proposed amendments to final regulations under Code Sec. 401(k) that allow a plan sponsor or administrator of a cash or deferred arrangement to treat portions of the plan that benefit employees of different collective bargaining units as separate plans or as one plan for aggregation purposes. However, disaggregation of a plan covering members of collective bargaining units and employees who are not included in collective bargaining units is still mandatory. The proposed optional disaggregation rules for cash or deferred arrangements also apply to certain multiemployer plans. The proposed amendments were published in the Federal Register on January 4, 1993 (58 FR 43).

[4830-01]

DEPARTMENT OF THE TREASURY

Internal Revenue Service

26 CFR Part 1

[EE-42-92]

RIN 1545-AQ77

Certain cash or deferred arrangements under employee plans.

AGENCY: Internal Revenue Service, Treasury.

ACTION: Notice of Proposed Rulemaking.

SUMMARY: This document proposes to amend final regulations under section 401(k). The proposed amendments will affect sponsors of certain cash or deferred arrangements benefiting employees who are members of collective bargaining units.

DATES: Written comments and requests for a public hearing must be received by March 5, 1993.

ADDRESSES: Send written comments and requests for a public hearing to: Internal Revenue Service, P.O. Box 7604, Ben Franklin Station, Attention: CC:CORP:T:R (EE-42-92), Washington, D.C. 20044. In the alternative, comments may be hand delivered to: Internal Revenue Building, Room 5228, 1111 Constitution Ave., N.W., Attention: CC:CORP:T:R (EE-42-92), Washington, D.C.

FOR FURTHER INFORMATION CONTACT: Cheryl Press at 202-622-4688 (not a toll-free number).

SUPPLEMENTARY INFORMATION:

Background

Final regulations under section 401(k) of the Internal Revenue Code (Code) were published in the Federal Register on August 15, 1991 (56 FR 40507). Amendments to the final regulations were published in the Federal Register on December 4, 1991 (56 FR 63420). Corrections to the final regulations were published in the Federal Register on March 25, 1992 (57 FR 10289).

Explanation of Provisions

This document proposes amendments to the final regulations under section 401(k) of the Code. The proposed amendments simplify the application of the regulations to certain plans benefiting employees who are members of collective bargaining units. The amendments modify the definition of the term "plan" to make optional, instead of mandatory, the disaggregation of a plan covering members of more than one collective bargaining unit.

Section 1.401(k)-1(g)(11)(iii)(A) of the final regulations provides that a plan that benefits employees who are included in a unit of employees covered by a collective bargaining agreement and employees who are not included in a collective bargaining unit is treated as comprising separate plans. Furthermore, employees of each collective bargaining unit benefiting under the plan must be treated as covered under a separate plan. Thus, for example, if a plan benefits employees in three categories, employees included in collective bargaining unit A, employees included in unit B, and those not included in any collective bargaining unit, the plan is treated as comprising three separate plans, each of which benefits only one category of employees. Many commentators have suggested that an employer be required instead to treat the portion of the plan that benefits employees included in collective bargaining units as a separate plan from the portion of the plan that benefits other employees.

The proposed amendments adopt the approach suggested by commentators. The portion of a plan that benefits employees who are included in collective bargaining units and the portion that benefits employees who are not included in collective bargaining units must be treated as comprising separate plans. However, further disaggregation of the plan by collective bargaining units is permissive, provided that the combinations of units are determined on a basis that is reasonable and reasonably consistent from year to year. An employer or plan administrator, as appropriate, may therefore treat the entire portion of a plan benefiting members of collective bargaining units as a single plan, may treat the portion benefiting members of each collective bargaining unit as separate plans, or may aggregate the portions benefiting members of any two or more collective bargaining units.

Section 1.401(k)-1(g)(11)(iii)(D) is similarly amended to make permissive the disaggregation of a multiemployer plan by collective bargaining unit. Under the final regulations, only the portion of a multiemployer plan benefiting employees under the same collective bargaining agreement and the same benefit computation formula is treated as a separate plan. Under the proposed amendments, the employer or plan administrator may choose to disaggregate this separate plan further on the basis of collective bargaining units.

Under §§ 1.401(k)-1(a)(7)(i) and 1.402(a)-1(d)(3)(iv) of the final regulations, a collectively bargained plan is only required to satisfy the actual deferral percentage test for plan years beginning after December 31, 1992. The proposed amendments are effective for the same plan years.

The proposed amendments to the regulations change the aggregation rules only for collectively bargained plans. Treasury and the Service anticipate further technical amendments to the regulations under section 401(k) and related provisions. No inference should be drawn from these proposed amendments concerning any other issue under the final regulations, including any other issue involving the treatment of collectively bargained or multiemployer plans.

Comments on the proposed amendments, and on any other issues or problems related to the testing of plans with participants who are members of collective bargaining units, are invited. In particular, comments are invited regarding the aggregation or disaggregation of multiemployer plans by collective bargaining agreement (as opposed to or in addition to collective bargaining unit) or by benefit computation formula.

Special Analyses

It has been determined that these proposed rules are not major rules as defined in Executive Order 12291. Therefore, a Regulatory Impact Analysis is not required. It has also been determined that section 553(b) of the Administrative Procedure Act (5 U.S.C. chapter 5) and the Regulatory Flexibility Act (5 U.S.C. chapter 6) do not apply to these regulations and, therefore, an initial Regulatory Flexibility Analysis is not required. Pursuant to section 7805(f) of the Code, these regulations will be submitted to the Chief Counsel for Advocacy of the Small Business Administration for comment on their impact on small business.

Written Comments

Before adopting these proposed regulations, consideration will be given to any written comments that are submitted timely (preferably a signed original and eight copies) to the Internal Revenue Service. All comments will be available for public inspection and copying in their entirety.

Drafting Information

The principal author of these regulations is Cheryl Press, Office of the Associate Chief Counsel (Employee Benefits and Exempt Organizations), Internal Revenue Service. However, personnel from other offices of the Service and Treasury Department participated in their development.

List of Subjects in 26 CFR 1.401-0 through 1.419A-2T

Bonds, Employee benefit plans, Income taxes, Pensions, Reporting and recordkeeping requirements, Securities, Trusts and trustees.

Proposed Amendments to the Regulations

Accordingly, 26 CFR part 1 is proposed to be amended as follows:

PART I—INCOME TAX; TAXABLE YEARS BEGINNING AFTER DECEMBER 31, 1953

Par. 1. The authority citation for part 1 continues to read, in part, as follows:

Authority: 26 U.S.C. 7805 * * *

Par. 2. Section 1.401(k)-1 is amended by revising paragraphs (g)(11)(iii)(A) and (g)(11)(iii)(D)(2) to read as follows:

§ 1.401(k)-1 Certain cash or deferred arrangements.

* * *

(g) * * *

(11) * * *

(iii) * * *

(A) *Plans benefiting collective bargaining unit employees.* A plan that benefits employees who are included in a unit of employees covered by a collective bargaining agreement and employees who are not included in such a collective bargaining unit is treated as comprising separate plans. This paragraph (g)(11)(iii)(A) is generally applied separately with respect to each collective bargaining unit. At the option of the employer, however, two or more separate collective bargaining units can be treated as a single collective bargaining unit, provided that the combinations of units are determined on a basis that is reasonable and reasonably consistent from year to year. Thus, for example, if a plan benefits employees in three categories—employees included in collective bargaining unit A, employees included in collective bargaining unit B, and employees who are not included in any collective bargaining unit—the plan can be treated as comprising three separate plans, each of which benefits only one category of employees. However, if collective bargaining units A and B are treated as a single collective bargaining unit, the plan will be treated as comprising only two separate plans, one benefiting all employees who are included in a collective bargaining unit and another benefiting all other employees. Similarly, if a plan benefits only employees who are included in collective bargaining unit A and collective bargaining unit B, the plan can be treated as comprising two separate plans. However, if collective bargaining units A and B are treated as a single collective bargaining unit, the plan will be treated as a single plan.

* * *

(D) * * *

(2) *Multiemployer plans.* Consistent with section 413(b), the portion of the plan that is maintained pursuant to a collective bargaining agreement (within the meaning of § 1.413-1(a)(2)) is treated as a single plan maintained by a single employer that employs all the employees

benefiting under the same benefit computation formula and covered pursuant to that collective bargaining agreement. [As corrected by 58 FR 15312 on March 22, 1993 and Announcement 93-56, I.R.B. 1993-15, 12.] The rules of paragraph (g)(11)(iii)(A) of this section (including the optional aggregation of collective bargaining units) apply to the resulting deemed single plan in the same manner as they would to a single employer plan, except that the plan administrator is substituted for the employer where appropriate and appropriate fiduciary obligations are

taken into account. The non-collectively bargained portion of the plan is treated as maintained by one or more employers, depending on whether the non-collective bargaining unit employees who benefit under the plan are employed by one or more employers.

* * *

Shirley D. Peterson
Commissioner of Internal Revenue

[¶ 20,193 Reserved.—Proposed regulations under Code Sec. 401(a)(4) were formerly reproduced at this paragraph. The final regulations appear at ¶ 11,720W-14.]

¶ 20,194

Proposed regulations: Tax-exempt organizations: Unrelated business taxable income: Income from corporate sponsorship.—The IRS has issued proposed regulations giving guidance on whether sponsorship payments received by exempt organizations under Code Sec. 501(a) are unrelated business taxable income, as defined in Code Sec. 512. The proposed regulations also clarify that the allocation rules governing the use of exempt activities apply to sponsorship income.

The proposed regulations were published in the *Federal Register* on January 22, 1993 (58 FR 5687). The proposed amendments were officially withdrawn by IRS on March 1, 2000 (65 FR 11015).

[¶ 20,195 Reserved.—Proposed regulations on minimum coverage requirements under Code Sec. 410(b) were formerly reproduced at this paragraph. The final regulations appear at ¶ 12,165.]

[¶ 20,196 Reserved.—Proposed regulations on the definition of compensation under Code sec. 414(s) were formerly reproduced at this paragraph. The final regulations appear at ¶ 12,364K.]

[¶ 20,197 Reserved.—Proposed regulations on permitted disparity under Code Sec. 401(l) were formerly reproduced at this paragraph. The final regulations appear at ¶ 11,731Q.]

[¶ 20,198 Reserved.—Proposed regulations under Code Sec. 414(a), relating to separate lines of business, were formerly reproduced at this paragraph. The final regulations are at ¶ 12,165, 12,365D, 12,364F-11 through 12,364F-19, and 12,364F-22.]

[¶ 20,199 Reserved.—Proposed regulations relating to payroll reporting and deposit rules for employers were formerly reproduced here. The final regulations are now at ¶ 13,649F.]

[¶ 20,200 Reserved.—Proposed regulations on the compensation limit for qualified plans under Code Sec. 401(a)(17) were formerly reproduced at this paragraph. The final regulations are at ¶ 11,720Z-11.]

[¶ 20,201 Reserved.—Proposed regulations on the $1 million cap on deductible employee renumeration were formerly reproduced at this paragraph. The final regulations are at ¶ 11,307.]

[¶ 20,202 Reserved.—Proposed regulations on the $1 million cap on deductible employee renumeration were formerly reproduced at this paragraph. The final regulations are at ¶ 11,307.]

[¶ 20,203 Reserved.—Proposed Reg. §1.83-6, concerning the elimination of the withholding requirement as a prerequisite to claiming a deduction for property transferred to an employee in connection with the performance of service, formerly was reproduced here. The final regulation is at ¶ 11,246.]

[¶ 20,204 Reserved.—Proposed regulations relating to the financial requirements of nonbank trustees were formerly reproduced at this paragraph. The final regulations are at ¶ 11,725 and ¶ 12,054.]

¶ 20,205

Actuarial assumptions: GATT.—The new interest and mortality rules for valuing lump-sum distributions under GATT have been put into temporary and proposed regulations under Code Sec. 417.

The new regulations explain the time for determining the applicable 30-year Treasury bond interest rate, provide when plans may use an interest rate and/or mortality table that is an alternative to the new applicable interest rate and mortality table, explain the various effective date options a plan has before implementing the new rules, and specify under what circumstances application of the new rules will not result in a reduction of benefits under Code Sec. 411(d)(6).

The temporary and proposed regulations were published in the *Federal Register* on April 5, 1995 (60 FR 17286) and are reproduced at ¶ 12,556 and 12,557.

The regulations were finalized April 7, 1998 (63 FR 16895). The regulations are reproduced at ¶ 12,556 and ¶ 12,557. The preamble is reproduced at ¶ 23,941S.

[¶ 20,206 Reserved.—Proposed regulations regarding the requirement that persons furnish a taxpayer identification number on returns, statements, or other documents under Code Sec. 6109 were formerly reproduced at this paragraph. The final regulations now appear at ¶ 13,782. The introductory material proceding the final regulations is at ¶ 23,919R.]

¶ 20,207

Proposed Regulations: Distributions: Consent requirements.—The IRS has proposed regulations regarding the consent requirements for distributions under Code Sec. 411(a)(11) and QJSA's under Code Sec. 417. The proposed regulations, which were also issued as temporary regulations, are structured to allow plan administrators to provide the participant notices required under sections 411(a)(11) and 417 at the same time of providing the notice regarding rollover treatment under Code Sec. 402(f).

The proposed regulations also allow a plan to distribute benefits prior to the expiration of the 30-day time period, provided certain requirements are met and the participant affirmatively elects the earlier distribution after being properly informed. The proposed regulations also delegate authority to the Commissioner of the IRS to provide further guidance on the notice requirements to address the use of electronic media and invites comments on this subject.

The temporary and proposed regulations were published in the *Federal Register* on September 22, 1995 (60 FR 49236) and are reproduced at ¶ 12,219E and 12,557.

The regulations were finalized December 18, 1998 (63 FR 70009). The regulations are reproduced at ¶ 12,219D and ¶ 12,556. The preamble is reproduced at ¶ 23,949V.

¶ 20,208

Withholding: Nonpayroll payments.—The IRS has issued final, temporary and proposed regulations regarding the reporting of income taxes withheld on nonpayroll payments under Code Sec. 6011, including withholding on pension, annuities, IRAs and other deferred income subject to withholding. Final regulations were amended to refer to new temporary regulations which were also issued as proposed regulations providing interested persons the opportunity to comment.

The IRS previously issued final regulations removing all nonpayroll withholding taxes from reporting on Form 941, Employer's Quarterly Federal Tax Return (CCH PENSION PLAN GUIDE ¶ 10,728) and requiring those taxes to be reported on Form 945, Annual Return of Withheld Federal Income Tax (CCH PENSION PLAN GUIDE ¶ 10,730). Those regulations were effective December 23, 1993 and provided that if a person was required to file a Form 945 for calendar year 1994, that person was required to continue to file Form 945 annually until a final return was filed, even if the person was no longer liable for withholding income taxes for nonpayroll payments. In response to several comments received, the proposed and temporary regulations provide a person must file a Form 945 only for a calendar year in which the person is required to withhold federal income tax from nonpayroll payments.

The proposed regulations were published in the *Federal Register* on October 16, 1995 and are reproduced with the preamble below. The final and temporary regulations were also published in the *Federal Register* on October 16, 1995 and are at ¶ 13,649F and ¶ 13,649G.

DEPARTMENT OF THE TREASURY

Internal Revenue Service

26 CFR Part 31

RIN 1545-AT86

Reporting of Nonpayroll Withheld Tax Liabilities

AGENCY: Internal Revenue Service (IRS), Treasury.

ACTION: Notice of proposed rulemaking by cross-reference to temporary regulations.

SUMMARY: In the Rules and Regulations section of this issue of the Federal Register, the IRS is issuing temporary regulations relating to the reporting of nonpayroll withheld income taxes under section 6011 of the Internal Revenue Code. The text of the temporary regulations also serves as the text for this notice of proposed rulemaking.

DATES: Written comments and requests for a public hearing must be received by December 15, 1995.

ADDRESSES: Send submissions to: CC:DOM:CORP:T:R (IA-30-95), room 5228, Internal Revenue Service, POB 7604, Ben Franklin Station, Washington, DC 20044. In the alternative, submissions may be hand delivered between the hours of 8 a.m. and 5 p.m. to:

CC:DOM:CORP:T:R (IA-30-95), Courier's Desk, Internal Revenue Service, 1111 Constitution Ave. NW., Washington, D.C.

FOR FURTHER INFORMATION CONTACT: Vincent G. Surabian, (202) 622-6232 (not a toll-free number).

SUPPLEMENTARY INFORMATION:

Paperwork Reduction Act

The collection of information contained in this notice of proposed rulemaking has been submitted to the Office of Management and Budget (OMB) for review in accordance with the Paperwork Reduction Act of 1995 (44 U.S.C. 3507). The collection of information is in § 31.6011(a)-4T(b). This information is required by the IRS to monitor compliance with the federal tax rules related to the reporting and deposit of nonpayroll withheld taxes.

Comments on the collection of information should be sent to the Office of Management and Budget, Attn: Desk Officer for the Department of the Treasury, Office of Information and Regulatory Affairs, Washington, DC 20503, with copies to the Internal Revenue Service, Attn: IRS Reports Clearance Officer, PC:FP, Washington, DC 20224. To ensure that comments on the collection of information may be given full consideration during the review by the Office of Management and

Budget, comments on the collection of information should be received by December 15, 1995.

An agency may not conduct or sponsor, and a person is not required to respond to, a collection of information unless the collection of information displays a valid control number.

Books or records relating to a collection of information must be retained as long as their contents may become material in the administration of any internal revenue law. Generally, tax returns and tax return information are confidential, as required by 26 U.S.C. 6103.

Estimates of the reporting burden in this Notice of Proposed Rulemaking will be reflected in the burden of Form 945.

Background

The temporary regulations published in the Rules and Regulations section of this issue of the Federal Register contain an amendment to the Regulations on Employment Taxes and Collection of Income Tax at Source (26 CFR part 31). This amendment relates to the reporting of nonpayroll withheld tax liabilities. The temporary regulations change the rule regarding the filing of Form 945, Annual Return of Withheld Federal Income Tax, for a calendar year in which there is no liability.

The text of those temporary regulations also serves as the text of these proposed regulations. The preamble to the temporary regulations explains these proposed regulations.

Special Analyses

It has been determined that this notice of proposed rulemaking is not a significant regulatory action as defined in EO 12866. Therefore, a regulatory assessment is not required. It also has been determined that section 553(b) of the Administrative Procedure Act (5 U.S.C. chapter 5) and the Regulatory Flexibility Act (5 U.S.C. chapter 6) do not apply to these regulations, and, therefore, a Regulatory Flexibility Analysis is not required. Pursuant to section 7805(f) of the Internal Revenue Code, this notice of proposed rulemaking will be submitted to the Chief Counsel for Advocacy of the Small Business Administration for comment on its impact on small business.

Comments and Requests for a Public Hearing

Before these proposed regulations are adopted as final regulations, consideration will be given to any written comments (preferably a signed original and eight (8) copies) that are timely submitted to the IRS. All comments will be available for public inspection and copying. A public hearing may be scheduled if requested in writing by a person that timely submits written comments. If a public hearing is scheduled, notice of the date, time, and place for the hearing will be published in the Federal Register.

Drafting Information

The principal author of these regulations is Vincent G. Surabian, Office of Assistant Chief Counsel (Income Tax and Accounting). However, other personnel from the IRS and Treasury Department participated in their development.

List of Subjects in 26 CFR Part 31

Employment taxes, Income taxes, Penalties, Pensions, Railroad retirement, Reporting and recordkeeping requirements, Social security, Unemployment compensation.

Proposed Amendments to the Regulations

Accordingly, 26 CFR part 31 is proposed to be amended as follows:

PART 31—EMPLOYMENT TAXES AND COLLECTION OF INCOME TAX AT SOURCE

Paragraph 1. The authority citation for part 31 continues to read in part as follows:

Authority: 26 U.S.C. 7805 ***

Par. 2. In § 31.6011(a)-4, paragraph (b) is revised to read as follows:

§ 31.6011(a)-4 Returns of income tax withheld.

*****

(b) [The text of this proposed paragraph (b) is the same as the text of § 31.6011(a)-4T(b) [¶ 13,649G] published elsewhere in this issue of the Federal Register].

*****

Margaret Milner Richardson

Commissioner of Internal Revenue

¶ 20,209

ERISA: Notice requirements: Minimum funding standards: Benefit accrual.—The IRS has issued temporary and proposed regulations, in question and answer format, addressing the notice requirements of ERISA Sec. 204(h) when a defined benefit plan or individual account plan that is subject to ERISA's minimum funding standards is amended to provide for a significant reduction in the rate of future benefit accrual. The IRS determined that the guidance in the temporary regulations was needed immediately because issues relating to ERISA Sec. 204(h) arise in connection with a broad range of plan amendments, including amendments prompted by recent changes in the law. The text of the temporary regulation is also the text for the proposed regulation.

The regulations clarify that an amendment to a defined benefit plan that does not affect the annual benefit commencing at normal retirement age does not affect the rate of future benefit accrual. Therefore, a plan administrator need not provide a section 204(h) notice when a plan amendment only affects other forms of payment such as lump sum distributions or benefits commencing at a date other than normal retirement age. The regulations also clarify that a 204(h) notice is only required for an amendment to an individual account plan that significantly reduces the rate of future benefit accrual. The regulations delegate authority to the Commissioner of the IRS to provide a 204(h) notice need not be provided with respect to plan amendments that the Commissioner determines, by published revenue rulings, notices, or other guidance published in the Internal Revenue Bulletin, are necessary or appropriate, as a result of a change in federal law or to maintain compliance with the law. The regulations also provide guidance on to whom the notice must be provided.

The proposed regulations were published in the *Federal Register* on December 15, 1995 (60 FR 66233).

The regulations were finalized December 4, 1998 (63 FR 68678). The regulations are reproduced at ¶ 12,234M. The preamble is reproduced at 23,949P.

DEPARTMENT OF THE TREASURY

Internal Revenue Service

6 CFR Part 1

[EE-34-95]

IN 1545-AT78

Notice of Significant Reduction in the Rate of Future Benefit Accrual.

AGENCY: Internal Revenue Service (IRS), Treasury.

ACTION: Notice of proposed rulemaking by cross-reference to temporary regulations.

SUMMARY: In the Rules and Regulations section of this issue of the Federal Register, the IRS is issuing temporary regulations relating to the requirements of section 204(h) of the Employee Retirement Income Security Act of 1974, as amended (ERISA). Section 204(h) of ERISA applies to defined benefit plans and to individual account plans that are subject to the funding standards of section 302 of ERISA. It requires the plan administrator to give notice of certain plan amendments to participants in the plan and certain other parties. The text of those temporary regulations also serves as the text of these proposed regulations.

DATES: Written comments must be received by March 14, 1996.

ADDRESSES: Send submissions to CC:DOM:CORP:R (EE-34-95), room 5228, Internal Revenue Service, POB 7604, Ben Franklin Station, Washington, DC 20044. In the alternative, submissions may be hand delivered between the hours of 8 a.m. and 5 p.m. to CC:DOM:CORP:R (EE-34-95), Courier's Desk, Internal Revenue Service, 1111 Constitution Avenue NW., Washington DC.

FOR FURTHER INFORMATION CONTACT: Betty J. Clary, (202) 622-6070 (not a toll-free number).

SUPPLEMENTARY INFORMATION:

Paperwork Reduction Act

The collection of information contained in this notice of proposed rulemaking has been submitted to the Office of Management and Budget for review in accordance with the Paperwork Reduction Act of 1995 (44 U.S.C. 3507).

Comments on the collection of information should be sent to the Office of Management and Budget, Attn: Desk Officer for the Department of Treasury, Office of Information and Regulatory Affairs, Washington DC 20503, with copies to the Internal Revenue Service, Attn: IRS Reports Clearance Officer, T:FP, Washington, DC 20224. Comments on the collection of information should be received by February 13, 1996.

An agency may not conduct or sponsor, and a person is not required to respond to, a collection of information unless the collection of information displays a valid control number.

The collection of information is in § 1.411(d)-6T which implements the statutory requirement of section 204(h) of ERISA that a plan administrator provide notice to participants and certain other parties if certain pension plans are amended to provide for a significant reduction in the rate of futurebenefit accrual. This collection of information is required to assure that the rights of participants in plans subject to section 204(h) of ERISA are protected. The likely respondents are small businesses. Responses to this collection of information are required under section 204(h) of ERISA in order for certain amendments to qualified plans to become effective.

These regulations do not involve any issues of confidentiality.

Estimated total annual reporting burden: 15,000 hours.

The estimated annual burden per respondent varies from 1 hour to 40 hours, depending on individual circumstances, with an estimated average of 5 hours.

Estimated number of respondents: 3,000.

Estimated annual frequency of responses: Once.

Background

Temporary regulations in the Rules and Regulations portion of this issue of the Federal Register amend the Income Tax Regulations (26 CFR part 1) (relating to section 411(d)). The text of those temporary regulations also serves as the text of these proposed regulations. The preamble to the temporary regulations explains the temporary regulations.

Special Analyses

It has been determined that this notice of proposed rulemaking is not a significant regulatory action as defined in EO 12866. Therefore, a regulatory assessment is not required. It also has been determined that section 553(b) of the Administrative Procedure Act (5 U.S.C. chapter 5) and the Regulatory Flexibility Act (5 U.S.C. chapter 6) do not apply to these regulations, and, therefore, a Regulatory Flexibility Analysis is not required. Pursuant to section 7805(f) of the Internal Revenue Code, the notice of proposed rulemaking will be submitted to the Chief Counsel for Advocacy of the Small Business Administration for comment on their impact on small business.

Comments and Requests for a Public Hearing

Before these proposed regulations are adopted as final regulations, consideration will be given to any written comments (a signed original and eight (8) copies) that are submitted timely to the IRS. All comments will be available for public inspection and copying. A public hearing may be scheduled if requested in writing by a person that timely submits written comments. If a public hearing is scheduled, notice of the date, time, and place for the hearing will be published in the Federal Register.

Drafting Information

The principal author of these regulations is Betty J. Clary, Office of the Associate Chief Counsel (Employee Benefits and Exempt Organiza-

tions), IRS. However, other personnel from the IRS and Treasury Department participated in their development.

List of Subjects in 26 CFR Part 1

Income taxes, Reporting and recordkeeping requirements.

Proposed Amendments to the Regulations

Accordingly, 26 CFR part 1 is proposed to be amended as follows:

PART 1—INCOME TAXES

Paragraph 1. The authority citation for part 1 continues to read, in part, as follows:

Authority: 26 U.S.C. 7805. ***

Section 1.411(d)-6 also issued under Reorganization Plan No. 4 of 1978, 29 U.S.C. 1001nt. ***

Par. 2. Section 1.411(d)-6 is added to read as follows: § 1.411(d)-6 Section 204(h) notice.

[The text of this proposed section is the same as the text of § 1.411(d)-6T [¶ 12,235] published elsewhere in this issue of the Federal Register.]

¶ 20,210

Proposed regulations: Plan Loans; Deemed Distributions.—The IRS has issued proposed regulations that would amend regulations regarding the tax treatment of loans from qualified employer plans to plan participants. The proposed regulations clarify when qualified loans will be deemed distributions from the plan.

Generally, a loan from a qualified employer plan will not be considered a taxable distribution or a prohibited transaction if certain requirements regarding the terms of the loan are met. The requirements include that the loan be evidenced by an enforceable written agreement, the amount of the loan not exceed $50,000, and the repayment period be limited to no more than five years unless the loan is used to purchase a principal residence. The proposed regulations clarify that if a loan fails to satisfy the repayment requirements or the enforceable agreement requirement, the balance then due under the loan is to be treated as a distribution. This may occur at the time the loan is made or at a later date if the loan is not repaid in accordance with the repayment schedule. If, at the time the loan is made, the amount of the loan exceeds the statutory limit, the proposed regulations provide that only the excess amount is a deemed distribution.

The proposed regulations also clarify that principal residence has the same meaning as under Code Sec. 1034 (relating to the taxation of a sale of a residence) and that tracing rules established under Code Sec. 163(h) (relating to interest deductions for indebtedness incurred with respect to the acquisition of a principal residence) will be used to determine whether the exception to the five-year repayment requirement applies.

TRA '86 amended section 72(p) to require that, in order for a loan to not be a distribution, it must require level amortization over the term of the loan. Section 72(p) authorizes regulations to allow exceptions from this requirement. The proposed regulations permit loan repayments to be suspended during a leave of absence of up to one year, if the participant's pay from the employer is insufficient to service the debt, but only if the loan is repaid by the latest date permitted under the Code.

Note: Q&A-19 has been revised and redesignated Q&A-21, and new Q&A-19 and Q&A-20 have been added in amended proposed regulations reproduced at ¶ 20,230. The amended proposed regulations were published in the *Federal Register* on January 2, 1998 (62 FR 42).

The proposed regulations were published in the *Federal Register* on December 21, 1995 (60 FR 66233) and are reproduced with the preamble below.

The regulations were finalized by T.D. 8894 and published in the *Federal Register* on July 31, 2000 (65 FR 46588). The regulations are reproduced at ¶ 11,207A and ¶ 11,210. The preamble is reproduced at ¶ 24,505S.

¶ 20,211

Proposed Regulations: Cafeteria Plans: Family and Medical Leave Act.—The IRS has issued proposed additions to proposed regulations under Code Section 125. The additions address how the Family and Medical Leave Act of 1993 (FMLA) affects the operation of cafeteria plans, including flexible spending arrangements, under Code Section 125. FMLA imposes certain obligations on employers to maintain coverage under a group health plan during an employee's FMLA leave and to restore benefits upon the employee's return. The additions to the proposed regulations provide guidance on the cafeteria plan rules that apply to an employee in circumstances to which FMLA and regulations issued by the Department of Labor pertaining to FMLA apply.

The proposed regulations were published in the *Federal Register* on December 21, 1995 (60 FR 66229).

The regulations were finalized by T.D. 8966 and published in the *Federal Register* on October 17, 2001 (66 FR 52675). The regulations are reproduced at ¶ 11,288B-45 and ¶ 11,288B-50. The preamble is reproduced at ¶ 24,506J.

¶ 20,212

Proposed Regulations: Allocation of Accrued Benefits: Employer and Employee Contributions.—IRS proposed regulations provide guidance on calculating an employee's accrued benefit derived from the employee's contributions to a qualified defined benefit pension plan. The proposed regulations were published in the Federal Register on December 22, 1995 (60 FR 66532) and officially corrected on March 14, 1996.

DEPARTMENT OF THE TREASURY

Internal Revenue Service

26 CFR Part 1

[EE-35-95]

RIN 1545-AT82

Allocation of Accrued Benefits Between Employer and Employee Contributions

AGENCY: Internal Revenue Service (IRS), Treasury.

ACTION: Notice of proposed rulemaking.

SUMMARY: This document contains proposed regulations that provide guidance on calculation of an employee's accrued benefit derived from the employee's contributions to a qualified defined benefit pension plan. These regulations are issued to reflect changes to the applicable law made by the Omnibus Budget Reconciliation Act of 1987 (OBRA '87) and the Omnibus Budget Reconciliation Act of 1989 (OBRA '89). OBRA '87 and OBRA '89 amended the law to change the accumulation of employee contributions and the conversion of those accumulated contributions to employee-derived accrued benefits.

DATES: Written comments and requests for a public hearing must be received by March 21, 1996.

ADDRESSES: Send submissions to: CC:DOM:CORP:R (EE-35-95), room 5228, Internal Revenue Service, POB 7604, Ben Franklin Station, Washington, DC 20044. In the alternative, submissions may be hand delivered between the hours of 8 a.m. and 5 p.m. to: CC:DOM:CORP:R (EE-35-95), Courier's Desk, Internal Revenue Service, 1111 Constitution Avenue, NW., Washington, DC.

FOR FURTHER INFORMATION CONTACT: Concerning the regulations, Janet A. Laufer, (202) 622-4606, concerning submissions, Michael Slaughter, (202) 622-7190 (not toll-free numbers).

SUPPLEMENTARY INFORMATION:

Background

This document contains proposed amendments to regulations containing rules for computing an employee's accrued benefit derived from the employee's contributions to a qualified defined benefit pension plan. The proposed amendments reflect changes made to section 411(c)(2) by the Omnibus Budget Reconciliation Act of 1987, Public Law 100-203 (OBRA '87), and the Omnibus Budget Reconciliation Act of 1989, Public Law 101-239 (OBRA '89). OBRA '87 and OBRA '89 changed the interest rates used to accumulate an employee's contributions to normal retirement age. OBRA '89 also changed the manner in which the accumulated contributions are converted to an annual benefit payable at normal retirement age, and removed a limitation on the employee-derived accrued benefit contained in prior law.

Section 411(c)(1) provides that an employee's accrued benefit derived from employer contributions as of any applicable date is the excess, if any, of the accrued benefit for the employee as of that date over the accrued benefit derived from contributions made by the employee as of that date. Section 411(c)(2)(B) provides that in the case of a defined benefit plan, the accrued benefit derived from contributions made by an employee as of any applicable date is the amount equal to the employee's contributions accumulated to normal retirement age using the interest rate(s) specified in section 411(c)(2)(C), expressed as an actuarially equivalent annual benefit commencing at normal retirement age using an interest rate which would be used by the plan under section 417(e)(3), as of the determination date. If the employee-derived accrued benefit is determined with respect to a benefit other than an annual benefit in the form of a single life annuity (without ancillary benefits) commencing at normal retirement age, section 411(c)(3) requires that the employee-derived accrued benefit be the actuarial equivalent of the benefit determined under section 411(c)(2).

Under section 411(c)(2)(C)(iii)(I), effective for plan years beginning after December 31, 1987, the interest rate used to accumulate an employee's contributions until the determination date is 120 percent of the Federal mid-term rate under section 1274 of the Internal Revenue Code (Code). For the period between the determination date and normal retirement age, section 411(c)(2)(C)(iii)(II) provides that the interest rate used to accumulate an employee's contributions is the interest rate which would be used under the plan under section 417(e)(3) as of the determination date. As noted above, section 411(c)(2)(B) provides that the interest rate which would be used under the plan under section 417(e)(3) as of the determination date also applies for purposes of converting the accumulated contributions to an annual benefit commencing at normal retirement age. The Retirement Protection Act of 1994, Public Law 103-465 (RPA '94) amended section 417(e) to change the applicable interest rate under section 417(e)(3) and to specify the applicable mortality table under that section. Examples contained in § 1.411(c)-1(c)(6) of these proposed regulations reflect a plan that has been amended to comply with the interest rate and mortality table specifications enacted in RPA '94.

Explanation of Provisions

1. Conversion calculation

Prior to OBRA '89, section 411(c)(2)(B) specified that the conversion factor to be used for purposes of computing the employee-derived accrued benefit was 10 percent for a straight life annuity commencing at normal retirement age of 65 (i.e., multiply the accumulated contributions by .10), and that for other normal retirement ages the conversion factor was to be determined in accordance with regulations prescribed by the Secretary. Section 1.411(c)-1(c)(2) of the existing regulations provides that for normal retirement ages other than age 65, the conversion factor shall be the factor as determined by the Commissioner.

Rev. Rul. 76-47 (1976-1 C.B. 109) sets forth in tabular form the conversion factors to be used for determining the accrued benefit derived from employee contributions when the normal retirement age under the plan is other than age 65 or when the normal form of benefit is other than a single life annuity (without ancillary benefits). Rev. Rul. 76-47 further provides that where no standard factor is available, a conversion factor must be determined using an interest rate of 5 percent and the UP-1984 mortality table (without age setback).

OBRA '89 deleted the ten percent conversion factor in section 411(c)(2)(B) and replaced it with the requirement that the accumulated contributions at normal retirement age be expressed as an annual benefit commencing at normal retirement age using an interest rate which would be used under the plan under section 417(e)(3) (as of the determination date). This change was effective retroactively to the effective date of the OBRA '87 provision relating to section 411(c)(2)(C) (the first day of the first plan year beginning after December 31, 1987).

To reflect the OBRA '89 amendments, these proposed regulations define *appropriate conversion factor* with respect to an accrued benefit expressed in the form of an annual benefit that is nondecreasing for the life of the participant as the present value of an annuity in the form of that annual benefit commencing at normal retirement age at a rate of $1 per year. This amount is to be computed using the interest rate and mortality table which would be used under the plan under section 417(e)(3) and § 1.417(e)-1T. To reflect the post-OBRA '89 conversion factor definition and to conform to common actuarial practice, these proposed regulations would change the *multiplied by* language in § 1.411(c)-1(c)(1) to *divided by*.

2. Accumulated contributions

As added by the Employee Retirement Income Security Act of 1974 (ERISA), section 411(c)(2)(C) provided that employee contributions were to be accumulated using a standard interest rate of 5 percent for years beginning on or after the effective date of that section. OBRA '87 changed the interest rate under section 411(c)(2)(C) to 120 percent of the applicable Federal mid-term rate under section 1274 for plan years after 1987. OBRA '89 again amended section 411(c)(2)(C) to provide that 120 percent of the applicable Federal mid-term rate under section 1274 is to be used for accumulating contributions only up to the *determination date*. For the period from the determination date to normal retirement age, the interest rate which would be used under the plan under section 417(e)(3) (as of the determination date) must be used for accumulating contributions for the period from the determination date to normal retirement age. Accordingly, these proposed regulations would amend paragraph (3) of § 1.411(c)-1(c) to reflect those rates. As stated above, RPA '94 amended section 417(e)(3) to change the applicable interest rate. See § 1.417(e)-1T.

3. Determination date

Section 1.411(c)-1(c)(5)(i) defines the term determination date for purposes of section 411(c)(2)(C)(iii), in a case in which a participant will receive his or her entire accrued benefit derived from employee contributions in any one of the following forms (described in paragraph (c)(5)(ii)): an annuity that is substantially nonincreasing, substantially nonincreasing installment payments for a fixed number of years, or a single sum distribution. In such a case, the term determination date means the date on which distribution of such benefit commences. For this purpose, an annuity that is nonincreasing except for automatic increases to reflect increases in the consumer price index is considered to be an annuity that is substantially nonincreasing.

Thus, for example, for purposes of section 411(c)(2)(C)(iii), in the case of a distribution of the employee's entire accrued benefit (or the employee's entire employee-derived accrued benefit) in the form of a nonincreasing single life annuity payable commencing either at normal retirement age or at early retirement age, the determination date is the date the annuity commences. Similarly, in the case of a single sum distribution of accumulated employee contributions (i.e., employee contributions plus interest computed at or above the section 411(c) required rates) upon termination of employment with a deferred annuity benefit derived solely from employer contributions, the determination date is the date of distribution of the single sum of accumulated employee contributions.

Alternatively, the plan may provide that the determination date is the annuity starting date, as defined in § 1.401(a)-20, Q&A-10.

Under § 1.411(c)-1(c)(5)(iii) of these regulations, where a participant will receive a distribution that is not described in paragraph (c)(5)(i), the determination date will be as provided by the Commissioner.

4. *Elimination of limitation on employee-derived accrued benefit*

Prior to OBRA '89, section 411(c)(2)(E) of the Code limited the accrued benefit derived from employee contributions to the greater of (1) the employee's accrued benefit under the plan, or (2) the sum of the employee's mandatory contributions, without interest. Section 7881(m)(1)(C) of OBRA '89 deleted that provision. Section 7881(m)(1)(D) of OBRA '89 added section 411(a)(7)(D) to the Code, which provides that the accrued benefit of an employee shall not be less than the amount determined under section 411(c)(2)(B) with respect to the employee's accumulated contributions. Accordingly, these proposed regulations delete the rule included in § 1.411(c)-1(d) of the existing regulations, which reflects the pre-OBRA '89 rule.

5. *Delegation of authority*

Section 1.411(c)-1(d) of these proposed regulations provides that the Commissioner may prescribe additional guidance on calculating the accrued benefit derived from employer or employee contributions under a defined benefit plan.

Effective Date

These amendments are proposed to be effective for plan years beginning on or after January 1, 1997. For example, assume that under a plan the employee's date of termination of employment is treated as the determination date, and distribution of the employee's entire employee-derived accrued benefit (as determined under the terms of the plan then in effect) occurs or commences prior to the first day of the plan year beginning in 1997. In that case, with respect to interest credits under section 411(c)(2)(C)(iii) for plan years beginning after 1987, the Service will not treat the plan as having failed to satisfy the requirements of section 411(c), nor will it require that additional amounts be credited in the calculation of the employee-derived accrued benefit in order to satisfy the requirements of section 411(c) after final regulations become effective, merely because the date the employee's employment terminated was treated as the determination date, provided that interest is credited in accordance with section 411(c)(2)(C)(iii)(I) for the period before the date the employee terminated employment and in accordance with section 411(c)(2)(C)(iii)(II) thereafter.

Once amendments to the regulations under § 1.411(c)-1 are adopted in final form, the Service will obsolete or modify Rev. Rul. 76-47, Rev. Rul. 78-202 (1978-2 C.B. 124) and Rev. Rul. 89-60 (1989-1 C.B. 113) as necessary or appropriate.

Taxpayers may rely on these proposed regulations for guidance pending the issuance of final regulations.

Special Analyses

It has been determined that this notice of proposed rulemaking is not a significant regulatory action as defined in EO 12866. Therefore, a regulatory assessment is not required. It also has been determined that section 553(b) of the Administrative Procedure Act (5 U.S.C. chapter 5) and the Regulatory Flexibility Act (5 U.S.C. chapter 6) do not apply to these regulations, and, therefore, a Regulatory Flexibility Analysis is not required. Pursuant to section 7805(f) of the Internal Revenue Code, this notice of proposed rulemaking will be submitted to the Chief Counsel for Advocacy of the Small Business Administration for comment on its impact on small business.

Comments and Requests for a Public Hearing

Before these proposed regulations are adopted as final regulations, consideration will be given to any written comments (a signed original and eight (8) copies) that are submitted timely to the IRS. All comments will be available for public inspection and copying. A public hearing may be scheduled if requested in writing by a person that timely submits written comments. If a public hearing is scheduled, notice of the date, time, and place for the hearing will be published in the **Federal Register**.

Drafting Information

The principal author of these regulations is Janet A. Laufer, Office of the Associate Chief Counsel (Employee Benefits and Exempt Organizations). However, other personnel from the IRS and Treasury Department participated in their development.

List of Subjects in 26 CFR Part 1

Income taxes, Reporting and recordkeeping requirements.

Proposed Amendments to the Regulations

Accordingly, 26 CFR part 1 is proposed to be amended as follows:

PART 1—INCOME TAXES

Paragraph 1. The authority citation for part 1 continues to read in part as follows:

Authority: 26 U.S.C. 7805 ***

Par. 2. Section 1.411(c)-1 is amended by:

1. Revising paragraphs (c)(1), (c)(2), (c)(3), (c)(5) and (c)(6).

2. Revising paragraph (d).

3. Adding paragraph (g).

The additions and revisions read as follows:

§ 1.411(c)-1 Allocation of accrued benefits between employer and employee contributions.

***

(c) *Accrued benefit derived from mandatory employee contributions to a defined benefit plan*—(1) *General Rule.* In the case of a defined benefit plan (as defined in section 414(j)), the accrued benefit derived from contributions made by an employee under the plan as of any applicable date in the form of an annual benefit commencing at normal retirement age and nondecreasing for the life of the participant is equal to the amount of the employee's accumulated contributions (determined under paragraph (c)(3) of this section) divided by the appropriate conversion factor with respect to that form of benefit (determined under paragraph (c)(2) of this section). Paragraph (e) of this section provides rules for actuarial adjustments where the benefit is to be determined in a form other than the form described in this paragraph (c)(1).

(2) *Appropriate conversion factor.* For purposes of this paragraph, with respect to a form of annual benefit commencing at normal retirement age described in paragraph (c)(1), the term *appropriate conversion factor* means the present value of an annuity in the form of that annual benefit commencing at normal retirement age at a rate of $1 per year, computed using an interest rate and mortality table which would be used under the plan under section 417(e)(3) and § 1.417(e)-1T (as of the determination date).

(3) *Accumulated contributions.* For purposes of section 411(c) and this section, the term *accumulated contributions* means the total of—

(i) All mandatory contributions made by the employee (determined under paragraph (c)(4) of this section);

(ii) Interest (if any) on such contributions, computed at the rate provided by the plan to the end of the last plan year to which section 411(a)(2) does not apply (by reason of the applicable effective dates);

(iii) Interest on the sum of the amounts determined under paragraphs (c)(3)(i) and (ii) of this section compounded annually at the rate of 5 percent per annum from the beginning of the first plan year to which section 411(a)(2) applies (by reason of the applicable effective date) to the beginning of the first plan year beginning after December 31, 1987;

(iv) Interest on the sum of the amounts determined under paragraphs (c)(3)(i) through (iii) of this section compounded annually at 120 percent of the Federal mid-term rate(s) (as in effect under section 1274(d) of the Internal Revenue Code for the first month of a plan year) for the period beginning with the first plan year beginning after December 31, 1987 and ending on the determination date; and

(v) Interest on the sum of the amounts determined under paragraphs (c)(3)(i) through (iv) of this section compounded annually, using an interest rate which would be used under the plan under section 417(e)(3) and § 1.417(e)-1T (as of the determination date), from the determination date to the date on which the employee would attain normal retirement age.

*****

(5) *Determination date*—(i) For purposes of section 411(c) and this section, in a case in which a participant will receive his or her entire accrued benefit derived from employee contributions in any one of the forms described in paragraph (c)(5)(ii), the term *determination date* means the date on which distribution of such benefit commences. Alternatively, in such a case, the plan may provide that the determination date is the annuity starting date with respect to that benefit, as defined in § 1.401(a)-20, Q&A-10.

(ii) Paragraph (c)(5)(i) applies to the following forms: an annuity that is substantially nonincreasing (e.g., an annuity that is nonincreasing except for automatic increases to reflect increases in the consumer price index), substantially nonincreasing installment payments for a fixed number of years, or a single sum distribution.

(iii) In a case in which a participant will receive a distribution that is not described inparagraph (c)(5)(i), the determination date will be as provided by the Commissioner.

(6) *Examples.*

(i) *Facts.* (A) In the following examples, Employer X maintains a qualified defined benefit plan that required mandatory employee contributions for 1987 and prior years, but not for years after 1987. The plan year is the calendar year. The plan provides for a normal retirement age of 65 and for 100 percent vesting in the employer-derived portion of a participant's accrued benefit after 5 years of service.

(B) The terms of the plan provide that the normal form of benefit is a level monthly amount commencing at normal retirement age and payable for the life of the participant. A plan participant who elects not to receive benefits in the form of the qualified joint and survivor annuity provided by the plan may elect to receive a single-sum distribution of the present value of his or her accrued benefit upon termination of employment.

(C) As of January 1, 1995, the plan was amended to provide that, for purposes of computing actuarially equivalent benefits, the single sum is calculated using the unisex version of the 1983 GAM mortality table (as provided in Revenue Ruling 95-6 (1995-1 C.B. 80)), and interest at the rate equal to the annual rate of interest on 30-year Treasury securities for the first calendar month preceding the first day of the plan year during which the annuity starting date occurs √ K√ √ K.

(D) Under the plan, employee contributions are accumulated at 3 percent interest for plan years beginning before 1976, 5 percent interest for plan years beginning after 1975 and before 1988, and interest at 120 percent of the Federal mid-term rate (as in effect under section 1274(d) for the first month of the plan year)for plan years beginning after 1987 until the determination date. Under the plan, the determination date is defined as the annuity starting date. For the period from the determination date until the date on which the employee attains normal retirement age, interest is credited at the interest rate which would be used under the plan under section 417(e)(3) as of the determination date.

(E) A, an unmarried participant, terminates employment with X on January 1, 1997 at age 56 with 15 years of service. As of December 31, 1987, A's total accumulated mandatory employee contributions to the plan, including interest compounded annually at 5 percent for plan years beginning after 1975 and before 1988, equaled $3,021. A receives his or her accrued benefit in the form of an annual single life annuity commencing at normal retirement age. A's annuity starting date is January 1, 2006, and therefore the determination date is January 1, 2006.

(ii) *Annuity at Normal Retirement Age—Determination of Employee-Derived and Total Plan Vested Accrued Benefit.*

Example 1.

For purposes of this example, it is assumed that A's total accrued benefit under the plan in the normal form of benefit commencing at normal retirement age is $2,949 per year. A's benefit, as of January 1, 2006, would be determined as follows:

(A) Determine A's total accrued benefit in the form of an annual single life annuity commencing at normal retirement age under the plan's formula ($2,949 per year payable at age 65).

(B) Determine A's accumulated contributions with interest to January 1, 1997. As of December 31, 1987, A's accumulated contributions with interest under the plan provisions were $3,021. A's employee contributions are accumulated from December 31, 1987 to January 1, 1997 using 120 percent of the Federal mid-term rate under section 1274(d). This rate is 10.61 percent for 1988, 11.11 percent for 1989, 9.57

percent for 1990, 9.78 percent for 1991, 8.10 percent for 1992, 7.63 percent for 1993, 6.40 percent for 1994, and 9.54 percent for 1995. It is assumed for purposes of this example that 120 percent of the Federal mid-term rate is 7.00 percent for each year between 1996 and 2006, and that the 30-year Treasury rate for December 2005 is 8.00 percent. Thus, A's contributions accumulated to January 1, 1997, equal $6,480.

(C) Determine A's accumulated contributions with interest to normal retirement age (January 1, 2006) using, for the 1996 plan year and for years until normal retirement age, 120 percent of the Federal mid-term rate under section 1274(d), which is assumed to be 7.00 percent ($11,913).

(D) Determine the accrued annual annuity benefit derived from A's contributions by dividing A's accumulated contributions determined in paragraph (C) of this *Example 1* by the plan's appropriate conversion factor. The plan's appropriate conversion factor at age 65 is 9.196, and the accrued benefit derived from A's contributions would be $11,913 ÷ 9.196 = $1,295.

(E) Determine the accrued benefit derived from employer contributions as the excess, if any, of the employee's accrued benefit under the plan over the accrued benefit derived from employee contributions ($2,949—$1,295 = $1,654 per year).

(F) Determine the vested percentage of the accrued benefit derived from employer contributions under the plan's vesting schedule (100 percent).

(G) Determine the vested accrued benefit derived from employer contributions by multiplying the accrued benefit derived from employer contributions by the vested percentage ($1,654 x 100 percent = $1,654 per year).

(H) Determine A's vested accrued benefit in the form of an annual single life annuity commencing at normal retirement age by adding the accrued benefit derived from employee contributions and the vested accrued benefit derived from employer contributions, the sum of paragraphs (D) and (G) of this *Example 1* ($1,295 + $1,654 = $2,949 per year).

Example 2.

This example assumes the same facts as *Example 1* except that A's total accrued benefit under the plan in the normal form of benefit commencing at normal retirement age is $1,000 per year. A's benefit, as of January 1, 2006, would be determined as follows:

(A) Determine A's total accrued benefit in the form of an annual single life annuity commencing at normal retirement age under the plan's formula ($1,000 per year payable at age 65).

(B) Determine A's accumulated contributions with interest to January 1, 1997 ($6,480 from paragraph (B) of *Example 1*).

(C) Determine A's accumulated contributions with interest to normal retirement age (January 1, 2006) ($11,913 from paragraph (C) of *Example 1*).

(D) Determine the accrued annual annuity benefit derived from A's contributions by dividing A's accumulated contributions determined in paragraph (C) of this *Example 2* by the plan's appropriate conversion factor ($1,295 from paragraph (D) of *Example 1*).

(E) Determine the accrued benefit derived from employer contributions as the excess, if any, of the employee's accrued benefit under the plan over the accrued benefit derived from employee contributions. Because the accrued benefit derived from employee contributions ($1,295) is greater than the employee's accrued benefit under the plan ($1,000), the accrued benefit derived from employer contributions is zero, and A's vested accrued benefit in the form of an annual single life annuity commencing at normal retirement age is $1,295 per year.

(d) *Delegation to Commissioner.* The Commissioner may prescribe additional guidance on calculating the accrued benefit derived from employee contributions under a defined benefit plan through publication in the Internal Revenue Bulletin of revenue rulings, notices, or other documents (see § 601.601(d)(2) of this chapter).

(e) ***

(f) ***

(g) *Effective date.* Paragraphs (c)(1), (c)(2), (c)(3), (c)(5), (c)(6) and (d) of this section are effective for plan years beginning on or after January 1, 1997.

Commissioner of Internal Revenue

¶ 20,213

Proposed regulations: Labor Organizations; Multiemployer Plans.—The IRS has issued proposed regulations to clarify the requirements for an organization to be exempt from taxes under Code Sec. 501(c)(5) as a labor, agricultural or horticultural organization. The proposed regulations are in reaction to the Second Circuit decision in *Morganbesser v. United States* (CCH PENSION PLAN GUIDE Transfer Binder, August, 1991-June, 1993 ¶ 23,868Y), holding that a multiemployer pension trust established pursuant to a collective bargaining agreement was exempt from tax as a labor organization described in Code Sec. 501(c)(5) even though it did not meet the ERISA requirements for being a qualified plan. Therefore, the IRS could not collect penalties from the trust for failing to satisfy the tax qualifications of ERISA. The IRS believes that this decision is contrary to existing law, and has issued a nonacquiescence reflecting its view that the court erred in its holding (See CCH PENSION PLAN GUIDE ¶ 23,915C). The proposed regulations provide an organization is not an organization described in Code Sec. 501(c)(5) if the principal activity of the organization is to receive, hold, invest, disburse, or otherwise manage funds associated with savings or investment plans or programs, including pension or other retirement savings plans or programs.

The proposed regulations were published in the *Federal Register* on December 21, 1995 (60 FR 66228) and are reproduced with the preamble below.

The regulations were finalized effective December 21, 1995 by T.D. 8726 and were published in the *Federal Register* on July 28, 1997 (62 FR 40447). The regulations are reproduced at ¶ 13,162A. The preamble is reproduced at ¶ 23,935V.

¶ 20,214

Proposed regulations: Nonqualified Deferred Compensation Plans; FICA Contributions.—The IRS has proposed regulations relating to the FICA tax treatment of amounts deferred under or paid from certain nonqualified deferred compensation plans.

The proposed regulations define what constitute a nonqualified deferred compensation plan and provide certain administrative relief for applying FICA to such plans. In general, Code Sec. 3121(v) provides any "amount deferred" under a nonqualified deferred compensation plan must be taken into account as wages for FICA purposes as of the later of (1) when the services are performed, rather than when paid, or (2) when there is no substantial risk of forfeiture of the rights to such amount. This special timing rule may result in imposition of FICA tax before the benefit payments under the plan begin, thus accelerating the imposition of FICA tax on benefits under a nonqualified deferred compensation plan. However, the proposed regulations provide various administrative rules to ease the burdens. Note: The proposed effective date has been extended in revised proposed regulations reproduced at ¶ 20,229. The revised proposed regulations were published in the *Federal Register* on December 24, 1997 (62 FR 67304).

The proposed regulations were published in the *Federal Register* on January 25, 1996 (60 FR 2194).

The final regulations were published in the *Federal Register* on January 29, 1999 (64 FR 4542). The regulations are reproduced at ¶ 13,534T and ¶ 13,534U. The preamble is at ¶ 23,950S.

¶ 20,215

Proposed regulations: Nonqualified Deferred Plans: FUTA Contributions.—The IRS has issued proposed regulations under Code Sec. 3306(r)(2) relating to when amounts deferred or paid from certain nonqualified deferred compensation plans are taken into account as "wages" for purposes of the employment taxes imposed by the Federal Unemployment Tax Act (FUTA). The rules are substantially similar to rules applicable to the Federal Insurance Contributions Act (FICA) tax treatment of such amounts deferred under Code Sec. 3121(v)(2). As a result, the proposed regulations cross-reference the proposed regulations under Code Sec. 3121(v)(2). Note: The proposed effective date has been extended in revised proposed regulations reproduced at ¶ 20,229. The revised proposed regulations were published in the *Federal Register* on December 24, 1997 (62 FR 67304).

The proposed regulations were published in the *Federal Register* on January 25, 1996 (60 FR 2214.

The final regulations were published in the *Federal Register* on January 29, 1999 (64 FR 4540). The regulations are reproduced at ¶ 13,541K. The preamble is at ¶ 23,950T.

¶ 20,216

Proposed regulations: U.S. source income paid to foreign persons: Withholding: Annuities: Taxpayer identification numbers.—Reproduced below are excerpts from proposed regulations under Code Secs. 1441, 6041, and 6109 relating to the withholding of income tax on U.S. income paid to foreign persons and the inclusion of taxpayer identification numbers on withholding certificates. The regulations would require withholding on distributions from certain pension plans and annuities under Code Sec. 1441 rather than Code Sec. 3405.

The proposed regulations were published in the *Federal Register* on April 22, 1996 (61 FR 17614), and officially corrected in the *Federal Register* on August 15, 1996 (61 FR 42401).

The regulations were finalized October 6, 1997 (62 FR 53387, October 14, 1997). The regulations are reproduced at ¶ 13,490A, ¶ 13,491, ¶ 13,492, ¶ 13,493, ¶ 13,681, ¶ 13,682, ¶ 13,684, ¶ 13,685, and ¶ 13,782. The preamble is reproduced at ¶ 23,937Z.

¶ 20,217

Business organizations: Classifications: Limited liability partnerships.—The Internal Revenue Service has issued proposed regulations that would allow certain organizations to elect what type of business entity they would be for tax purposes. The regulations were developed in response to recent changes in state laws that permit entities such as partnerships to change status to a limited liability corporation or limited liability partnership. The proposed regulations recognize that there has been a significant gap between changes in state laws and the federal government's business classification system and tries to create a workable framework that can accommodate these newly created limited liability entities.

The proposed regulations were published in the *Federal Register* on May 13, 1996, (61 FR 21989).

The regulations were finalized December 17, 1996 and were published in the *Federal Register* on December 18, 1996 (61 FR 66584). The regulations are reproduced at ¶ 13,782, ¶ 13,921, ¶ 13,922, ¶ 13,923, ¶ 13,924, and ¶ 13,926. The preamble is reproduced at ¶ 23,929R.

¶ 20,218

Proposed regulations: Eligible rollover distributions: Eligible retirement plans: Disqualification of plans: Individual retirement accounts.—The IRS has issued proposed regulations designed to increase the ability of employees to roll over their benefits to qualified plans. In particular, the regulations expand the circumstances in which plans can accept rollovers without facing disqualification. The regulations also apply to contributions accepted from "conduit IRAs." The proposed regulations were published in the *Federal Register* on September 19, 1996 (61 FR 49279). On December 17, 1998 (63 FR 69584), the proposed regulations were amended at ¶ 20,237.

The final regulations were published in the *Federal Register* on April 21, 2000 (65 FR 21312). The regulations are reproduced at ¶ 11,720Z-50, ¶ 11,753-10, ¶ 11,803, and ¶ 13,566. The preamble is at ¶ 24,505N.

¶ 20,219

Proposed regulations: Nonexempt employees' trusts under Code Sec. 402(b): Taxation of trust income: Grantor trusts: Separate trusts: Domestic and foreign trusts.—Reproduced below are regulations proposed under Code Secs. 671 and Code Sec. 1297. The regulations provide that domestic nonexempt employees' trust would be taxed as separate trusts under Code Sec. 641 and that they would not be subject to the grantor trust rules under Code Sec. 671. Therefore, an employer would not be subject to tax on trust income as a grantor owner of such a trust. Furthermore, foreign nonexempt employees' trusts would also escape application of the grantor trust rules under the proposed regulations, but certain significant exceptions would apply. For example, the grantor trust rules would apply to a controlled foreign corporation with a foreign nonexempt employees' trust.

The proposed regulations were published in the *Federal Register* on September 27, 1996 (61 FR 50778).

DEPARTMENT OF THE TREASURY

Internal Revenue Service

26 CFR Part 1

[REG-209826-96]

RIN 1545-AU29

Application of the Grantor Trust Rules to Nonexempt Employees' Trusts

AGENCY: Internal Revenue Service (IRS), Treasury.

ACTION: Notice of proposed rulemaking and notice of public hearing.

SUMMARY: This document contains proposed regulations relating to the application of the grantor trust rules to nonexempt employees' trusts. The proposed regulations clarify that the grantor trust rules generally do not apply to domestic nonexempt employees' trusts, and clarify the interaction between the grantor trust rules, the rules generally governing the taxation of nonqualified deferred compensation arrangements, and the antideferral rules for United States persons holding interests in foreign entities. The proposed regulations affect nonexempt employees' trusts funding deferred compensation arrangements, as well as U.S. persons holding interests in certain foreign corporations and foreign partnerships with deferred compensation arrangements funded through foreign nonexempt employees' trusts. In addition, the proposed regulations affect U.S. persons that have deferred compensation arrangements funded through certain foreign nonexempt employees' trusts. This document also provides notice of a public hearing on these proposed regulations.

DATES: Written comments must be received by December 26, 1996. Requests to speak (with outlines of oral comments to be discussed) at the public hearing scheduled for January 15, 1997, at 10:00 a.m. must be submitted by December 24, 1996.

ADDRESSES: Send submissions to: CC:DOM:CORP:R (REG-209826-96), room 5226, Internal Revenue Service, POB 7604, Ben Franklin Station, Washington, DC 20044. Submissions may be hand delivered between the hours of 8 a.m. and 5 p.m. to: CC:DOM:CORP:R (REG-209826-96), Courier's Desk, Internal Revenue Service, 1111 Constitution Avenue, NW., Washington, DC. The public hearing will be held in room 2615, Internal Revenue Building, 1111 Constitution Avenue, NW., Washington, DC. Alternatively, taxpayers may submit comments electronically via the Internet by selecting the "Tax Regs" option on the IRS Home Page, or by submitting comments directly to the IRS Internet site at http://www.irs.ustreas.gov/prod/tax_regs/comments.html.

FOR FURTHER INFORMATION CONTACT: Concerning the regulations, James A. Quinn, (202) 622-3060; Linda S. F. Marshall, (202) 622-6030; Kristine K. Schlaman (202) 622-3840; and M. Grace Fleeman (202) 622-3850; concerning submissions and the hearing, Michael Slaughter, (202) 622-7190 (not toll-free numbers).

SUPPLEMENTARY INFORMATION:

Paperwork Reduction Act

The collection of information contained in this notice of proposed rulemaking has been submitted to the Office of Management and Budget for review in accordance with the Paperwork Reduction Act of 1995 (44 U.S.C. 3507(d)). Comments on the collection of information should be sent to the **Office of Management and Budget,** Attn: Desk Officer for the Department of the Treasury, Office of Information and Regulatory Affairs, Washington, DC 20503, with copies to the **Internal Revenue Service,** Attn: IRS Reports Clearance Officer, T:FP, Washington, DC 20224. Comments on the collection of information should be received by November 26, 1996. Comments are specifically requested concerning:

Whether the proposed collection of information is necessary for the proper performance of the functions of the **Internal Revenue Service,** including whether the information will have practical utility;

The accuracy of the estimated burden associated with the proposed collection of information (see below);

How the quality, utility, and clarity of the information to be collected may be enhanced;

How the burden of complying with the proposed collection of information may be minimized, including through the application of automated collection techniques or other forms of information technology; and

Estimates of capital or start-up costs and costs of operation, maintenance, and purchase of services to provide information.

The collection of information in this proposed regulation is in § 1.671-1(h)(3)(iii). This information is required by the IRS to determine accurately the portion of certain foreign employees' trusts properly treated as owned by the employer. This information will be used to notify the Commissioner that certain entities are relying on an exception for reasonable funding. The collection of information is mandatory. The likely respondents are businesses or other for-profit organizations.

Estimated total annual reporting burden: **1,000 hours.**

The estimated annual burden per respondent varies from **.5 hours** to **1.5 hours,** depending on individual circumstances, with an estimated average of **1 hour.**

Estimated number of respondents: **1,000.**

Estimated annual frequency of responses: **On occasion.**

An agency may not conduct or sponsor, and a person is not required to respond to, a collection of information unless the collection of information displays a valid control number assigned by the Office of Management and Budget.

Books or records relating to a collection of information must be retained as long as their contents may become material in the administration of any internal revenue law. Generally, tax returns and tax return information are confidential, as required by 26 U.S.C. 6103.

Background

On May 7, 1993, the IRS issued proposed regulations under section 404A (58 FR 27219). The section 404A proposed regulations provide that section 404A is the exclusive means by which an employer may take a deduction or reduce earnings and profits for amounts used to fund deferred compensation in situations other than those in which a deduction or reduction of earnings and profits is permitted under section 404 (the "exclusive means" rule).

The section 404A proposed regulations do not provide rules regarding the treatment of income and ownership of assets of foreign trusts established to fund deferred compensation arrangements, but refer to "other applicable provisions," including the grantor trust rules of subpart E of the Internal Revenue Code of 1986, as amended. Thus, the 1993 proposed section 404A regulations imply that, if an employer cannot or does not elect section 404A treatment for a foreign trust established to fund the employer's deferred compensation arrangements, the employer may be treated as the owner of the entire trust for purposes of subtitle A of the Code under sections 671 through 679 even though all or part of the trust assets are set aside for purposes of satisfying liabilities under the plan. Conversely, some commentators believe that, for U.S. tax purposes, a foreign employer would not be treated as the owner of any portion of a foreign trust established to fund a section 404A qualified foreign plan even though all or part of the trust assets might be used for purposes other than satisfying liabilities under the plan. A number of different rules, in addition to the grantor trust rules, potentially affect the taxation of foreign trusts established to fund deferred compensation arrangements. These rules include: the nonexempt deferred compensation trust rules of sections 402(b) and 404(a)(5); the partnership rules of subchapter K; and the antideferral rules, which include subpart F and the passive foreign investment company (PFIC) rules (sections 1291 through 1297).

Following publication of the proposed 1993 regulations and enactment of section 956A in August of 1993, comments were received concerning both the asset ownership rules for foreign employees' trusts and the "exclusive means" rule for deductions or reductions in earnings and profits. These proposed regulations address only comments concerning income and asset ownership rules for foreign employees' trusts for federal income tax purposes. A foreign employees' trust is a nonexempt employees' trust described in section 402(b) that is part of a deferred compensation plan, and that is a foreign trust within the meaning of section 7701(a)(31). Comments concerning the "exclusive means" rule will be addressed in future regulations.

Statutory Background

1. Transfers of Property Not Complete for Tax Purposes

In certain situations, assets that are owned by a trust as a legal matter may be treated as owned by another person for tax purposes. Thus, assets may be treated as owned by a pension trust for non-tax legal purposes but not for tax purposes. This occurs, for example, if the person who has purportedly transferred assets to the trust retains the benefits and burdens of ownership. *See, e.g., Frank Lyon Co. v. United States*, 435 U.S. 561 (1978); *Corliss v. Bowers*, 281 U.S. 376 (1930); *Grodt & McKay Realty, Inc. v. Commissioner*, 77 T.C. 1221 (1981); Rev. Proc. 75-21 (1975-1 C.B. 715). If, under these principles, no assets have been transferred to an employees' trust for federal tax purposes, these proposed regulations do not apply.

2. Subpart E—Grantors and others treated as substantial owners

Even if there has been a completed transfer of trust assets, the subpart E rules may apply to treat the grantor as the owner of a portion of the trust for federal income tax purposes. Subpart E of part I of subchapter J, chapter 1 of the Code (sections 671 through 679) taxes income of a trust to the grantor or another person notwithstanding that the grantor or other person may not be a beneficiary of the trust. Under section 671, a grantor or another person includes in computing taxable income and credits those items of income, deduction, and credit against tax that are attributable to or included in any portion of a trust of which that person is treated as the owner.

Sections 673 through 679 set forth the rules for determining when the grantor or another person is treated as the owner of a portion of a trust for federal income tax purposes. Under sections 673 through 678, the grantor trust rules apply only if the grantor or other person has certain powers or interests. For example, section 676 provides that the grantor is treated as the owner of a portion of a trust where, at any time, the power to revest in the grantor title to that portion is exercisable by the grantor or a nonadverse party, or both. A grantor who is the owner of a trust under subpart E is treated as the owner of the trust property for federal income tax purposes. See Rev. Rul. 85-13 (1985-1 C.B. 184). This document is made available by the Superintendent of Documents, U.S. Government Printing Office, Washington, DC 20402.

Section 679 generally applies to a U.S. person who directly or indirectly transfers property to a foreign trust, subject to certain exceptions described below. Section 679 generally treats a U.S. person transferring property to a foreign trust as the owner of the portion of the trust attributable to the transferred property for any taxable year of that person for which there is a U.S. beneficiary of any portion of the trust. In general, a trust is treated as having a U.S. beneficiary for a taxable year of the U.S. transferor unless, under the terms of the trust, no part of the income or corpus of the trust may be paid or accumulated during the taxable year to or for the benefit of a U.S. person, and unless no part of the income or corpus of the trust could be paid to or for the benefit of a U.S. person if the trust were terminated at any time during the taxable year. A U.S. person is treated as having made an indirect transfer to the foreign trust of property if a non-U.S. person acts as a conduit with respect to the transfer or if the U.S. person has sufficient control over the non-U.S. person to direct the transfer by the non-U.S. person rather than itself.

Section 679(a) provides several exceptions from the application of section 679 for certain compensatory trusts. Under these exceptions, section 679 does not apply to a trust described in section 404(a)(4) or section 404A. Pursuant to amendments made in section 1903(b) of the

Small Business Job Protection Act of 1996 (SBJPA), section 679 also does not apply to any transfer of property after February 6, 1995, to a trust described in section 402(b).

3. Taxability of beneficiary of nonexempt employees' trust

Section 402(b) provides rules for the taxability of beneficiaries of a nonexempt employees' trust. Under section 402(b)(1), employer contributions to a nonexempt employees' trust generally are included in the gross income of the employee in accordance with section 83. Section 402(b)(2) provides that amounts distributed or made available from a nonexempt employees' trust generally are taxable to the distributee under the rules of section 72 in the taxable year in which distributed or made available. Section 402(b)(4) provides that, under certain circumstances, a highly compensated employee is taxed each year on the employee's vested accrued benefit (other than the employee's investment in the contract) in a nonexempt employees' trust. Under section 402(b)(3), a beneficiary of a nonexempt employees' trust generally is not treated as the owner of any portion of the trust under subpart E. The rules of section 402(b) apply to a beneficiary of a nonexempt employees' trust regardless of whether the trust is a domestic trust or a foreign trust.

4. Employer deduction for contributions to a nonexempt employees' trust

Section 404(a)(5) provides rules regarding the deductibility of contributions to a nonqualified deferred compensation plan. Under section 404(a)(5), any contribution paid by an employer under a deferred compensation plan, if otherwise deductible under chapter 1 of the Code, is deductible only in the taxable year in which an amount attributable to the contribution is includible in the gross income of employees participating in the plan, and only if separate accounts are maintained for each employee. Section 1.404(a)-12(b)(1) clarifies that an employer's deduction for contributions to a nonexempt employees' trust is restricted to the amount of the contribution, and excludes any income received by the trust with respect to contributed amounts.

5. The partnership rules of subchapter K

A partnership is not subject to income taxation. However, a partner must take into account separately on its return its distributive share of the partnership's income, gain, loss, deduction, or credit. A U.S. partner of a foreign partnership is subject to U.S. tax on its distributive share of partnership income. In addition, a foreign partnership may have a controlled foreign corporation (CFC) partner which must take into account its distributive share of partnership income, gain, loss, or deduction in determining its taxable income. These distributive share inclusions of the CFC may result in subpart F income and thus income to a U.S. shareholder of the CFC. If the grantor trust rules do not apply to any portion of a foreign employees' trust, a foreign partnership could fund a foreign employees' trust in excess of the amount needed to meet its obligations to its employees under its deferred compensation plan and yet retain control over the excess amount. As a result, the foreign partnership would not have to include items in taxable income attributable to the excess amount, and consequently the U.S. partner or CFC would not have to include those items in its income.

6. The antideferral rules of subpart F, including section 956A, and PFIC

A U.S. person that owns stock in a foreign corporation generally pays no U.S. tax currently on income earned by the foreign corporation. Instead, the United States defers taxation of that income until it is distributed to the U.S. person. The antideferral rules, however, which include subpart F and the PFIC rules, limit this deferral in certain situations.

Subpart F of part III of Subchapter N (sections 951 through 964) applies to CFCs. A foreign corporation is a CFC if more than 50 percent of the total voting power of all classes of stock entitled to vote, or the total value of the stock in the corporation, is owned by "U.S. shareholders" (defined as U.S. persons who own ten percent or more of the voting power of all classes of stock entitled to vote) on any day during the foreign corporation's taxable year. The United States generally taxes U.S. shareholders of the CFC currently on their pro rata share of the CFC's subpart F income and sections 956 and 956A amounts. In effect, the U.S. shareholders are treated as having received a distribution out of the earnings and profits (E&P) of the CFC.

The types of income earned by a foreign employees' trust (dividends, interest, income equivalent to interest, rents and royalties, and annuities) are generally subpart F income. The inclusion under section 956 is based on the CFC's investment in U.S. property, which generally includes stock of a U.S. shareholder of the CFC. A U.S. shareholder's section 956A amount for a taxable year is the lesser of two amounts. The first amount is the excess of the U.S. shareholder's pro rata share of the CFC's "excess passive assets" over the portion of the CFC's E&P

treated as previously included in gross income by the U.S. shareholder under section 956A. For purposes of section 956A, "passive asset" includes any asset which produces (or is held for the production of) passive income, and generally includes property that produces dividends, interest, income equivalent to interest, rents and royalties, and annuities, subject to exceptions that generally are not relevant in this context. The second amount is the U.S. shareholder's pro rata share of the CFC's "applicable earnings" to the extent accumulated in taxable years beginning after September 30, 1993.

Section 1501(a)(2) of SBJPA repeals section 956A. The repeal is effective for taxable years of foreign corporations beginning after December 31, 1996, and for taxable years of U.S. shareholders with or within which such taxable years of foreign corporations end.

If a CFC employer is not treated for federal income tax purposes as the owner of any portion of a foreign employees' trust under the grantor trust rules, then to the extent that passive assets contributed by a CFC to a nonexempt employees' trust would otherwise result in subpart F consequences for the CFC and its shareholders, the CFC's contribution could allow those consequences to be avoided. For example, a contribution by a CFC of passive assets to its foreign employees' trust could reduce the CFC's subpart F earnings and profits, and its applicable earnings or passive assets for section 956A purposes, and could affect the CFC's increase in investment in U.S. property for purposes of section 956, all of which could affect a U.S. shareholder's pro rata subpart F inclusions for the taxable year.

In contrast to the subpart F rules, the PFIC rules apply to any U.S. person who directly or indirectly owns any stock in a foreign corporation that is a PFIC under either an income or asset test. A foreign corporation, including a CFC, is a PFIC if either (1) 75 percent or more of its gross income for the taxable year is passive income or (2) at least 50 percent of the value of the corporation's assets produce passive income or are held for the production of passive income. For this purpose, passive income generally is the same type of income (dividends, interest, income equivalent to interest, rents and royalties, and annuities) that would be earned by a foreign employees' trust.

Under the PFIC rules, a U.S. person who is a direct or indirect shareholder of a PFIC is subject to a special tax regime upon either disposition of the PFIC's stock or receipt of certain distributions (excess distributions) from the PFIC. A shareholder, however, may avoid the application of this special regime by electing to include its pro rata share of certain of the PFIC's passive income in the year in which the foreign corporation earns it.

If the grantor trust rules did not apply to any portion of a foreign employees' trust, a contribution by a foreign corporation of passive assets to a nonexempt employees' trust would enable a U.S. person to avoid the PFIC rules if those assets would otherwise generate PFIC consequences for the foreign corporation and its shareholders. For example, by transferring passive assets to its nonexempt employees' trust in excess of the amount needed to meet obligations to its employees under its deferred compensation plan while retaining control over the excess amount, a foreign corporation could divest itself of a sufficient amount of passive assets and the passive income they produce to avoid meeting the income and asset tests. Furthermore, a foreign corporation that is a PFIC could minimize income inclusions for a U.S. shareholder that has made an election to include PFIC income currently by transferring income-producing assets to a foreign employees' trust.

Overview of proposed regulations

Under the proposed regulations, an employer is not treated as an owner of any portion of a domestic nonexempt employees' trust described in section 402(b) for federal income tax purposes. Section 404(a)(5) and § 1.404(a)-12(b) provide a deduction to the employer solely for contributions to a nonexempt employees' trust, and not for any income of the trust. This rule is inconsistent with treating the employer as owning any portion of a nonexempt employees' trust, which would require the employer to recognize the trust's income that it may not deduct under section 404(a)(5). Accordingly, such a trust is treated as a separate taxable trust that is taxed under the rules of section 641 et seq. The rule in the proposed regulations is consistent with the holdings of a number of private letter rulings with respect to nonexempt employees' trusts and with the Service's treatment of trusts that no longer qualify as exempt under 501(a) (because they are no longer described in section 401(a)) as separate taxable trusts rather than as grantor trusts. See also Rev. Rul. 74-299 (1974-1 C.B. 154). This document is made available by the Superintendent of Documents, U.S. Government Printing Office, Washington, DC 20402.

Under the proposed regulations, an employer generally is not treated as the owner of any portion of a foreign nonexempt employees' trust for

federal income tax purposes, except as provided under section 679. The proposed regulations, however, also provide that the grantor trust rules apply to determine whether an employer that is a CFC or a U.S. employer is treated as the owner of a specified "fractional interest" in a foreign employees' trust. This rule applies whether or not the employer elects section 404A treatment for the trust. Under the proposed regulations, this rule also applies in the case of an employer that is a foreign partnership with one or more partners that are U.S. persons or CFCs (U.S.-related partnership). Such an employer is treated as the owner of a portion of a foreign employees' trust under these proposed regulations only if the employer retains a grantor trust power or interest over a foreign employees' trust and has a specified "fractional interest" in the trust.

Under these proposed regulations, the grantor trust rules of subpart E do not apply to a foreign employees' trust with respect to a foreign employer other than a CFC or a U.S.-related foreign partnership, except for cases in which assets are transferred to a foreign employees' trust with a principal purpose of avoiding the PFIC rules. The IRS and Treasury will continue to consider whether these regulations should provide additional antiabuse rules that may be necessary for other purposes, including for purposes of calculating earnings and profits, determining the foreign tax credit limitation, and applying the interest allocation rules of § 1.882-5.

Explanation of provisions

1. § 1.671-1(g): Domestic nonexempt employees' trusts

The proposed regulations provide that an employer is not treated for federal income tax purposes as an owner of any portion of a nonexempt employees' trust described in section 402(b) that is part of a deferred compensation plan, and that is not a foreign trust within the meaning of section 7701(a)(31), regardless of whether the employer has a power or interest described in sections 673 through 677 over any portion of the trust. This rule is analogous to the rule set forth in § 1.641(a)-0, which provides that subchapter J, including the grantor trust rules, does not apply to tax-exempt employees' trusts.

2. § 1.671-1(h): Subpart E rules for certain foreign employees' trusts

The proposed regulations provide Subpart E rules for foreign employees' trusts of CFCs, foreign partnerships, and U.S. employers that apply for all federal income tax purposes. Under the proposed regulations, except as provided under section 679 or the proposed regulations (as described below), an employer is not treated as an owner of any portion of a foreign employees' trust for federal income tax purposes. If an employer is treated as the owner of a portion of a foreign employees' trust for federal income tax purposes as described below, then the employer is considered to own the trust assets attributable to that portion of the trust for all federal income tax purposes. Thus, for example, if an employer is treated as the owner of a portion of a foreign employees' trust for federal income tax purposes as described below, then income of the trust that is attributable to that portion of the trust increases the employer's earnings and profits for purposes of sections 312 and 964.

A foreign employees' trust is a nonexempt employees' trust described in section 402(b) that is part of a deferred compensation plan, and that is a foreign trust within the meaning of section 7701(a)(31). The proposed regulations apply to any foreign employees' trust of a CFC or U.S.-related foreign partnership, whether or not it funds a qualified foreign plan (as defined in section 404A(e)). The proposed regulations clarify that the income inclusion and asset ownership rules apply to the entity whose employees or independent contractors are covered under the deferred compensation plan.

A. Plan of CFC employer

The proposed regulations provide that, if a CFC maintains a deferred compensation plan funded through a foreign employees' trust, then, with respect to the CFC, the provisions of subpart E apply to the portion of the trust that is the fractional interest of the trust described in the proposed regulations.

B. Plan of U.S. employer

The proposed regulations provide that if a U.S. person maintains a deferred compensation plan funded through a foreign employees' trust, then, with respect to the U.S. person, the provisions of subpart E apply to the portion of the trust that is the fractional interest of the trust described in the proposed regulations.

C. Plan of U.S.-related foreign partnership employer

The proposed regulations provide that, if a U.S.-related foreign partnership maintains a deferred compensation plan funded through a foreign employees' trust, then, with respect to the U.S.-related foreign partnership, the provisions of subpart E apply to the portion of the trust that is the fractional interest of the trust described in the proposed regulations. The IRS and Treasury solicit comments on whether these regulations should provide a safe harbor rule for a U.S.-related foreign partnership that maintains a deferred compensation plan funded through a foreign employees' trust if U.S. or CFC partnership interests are de minimis. The IRS and Treasury specifically solicit comments concerning the amount of U.S. or CFC partnership interests that would qualify as "de minimis."

D. Plan of non-CFC foreign employer

The proposed regulations provide that a foreign employer that is not a CFC is treated as an owner of a portion of a foreign employees' trust only as provided in the antiabuse rule of § 1.1297-4.

E. Fractional interest

The fractional interest of a foreign employees' trust described above is defined in the proposed regulations as an undivided fractional interest in the trust for which the fraction is equal to the relevant amount determined for the employer's taxable year divided by the fair market value of trust assets determined for the employer's taxable year.

F. Relevant amount

The relevant amount for the employer's taxable year is defined in the proposed regulations as the amount, if any, by which the fair market value of trust assets, plus the fair market value of any assets available to pay plan liabilities (including any amount held under an annuity contract that exceeds the amount that is needed to satisfy the liabilities provided for under the contract) that are held in the equivalent of a trust within the meaning of section 404A(b)(5)(A), exceed the plan's accrued liability, determined using a projected unit credit funding method.

The relevant amount is reduced to the extent the taxpayer demonstrates to the Commissioner that the relevant amount is attributable to amounts that were properly contributed to the trust pursuant to a reasonable funding method, or experience that is favorable relative to any actuarial assumptions used that the Commissioner determines to be reasonable. In addition, if an employer that is a controlled foreign corporation otherwise would be treated as the owner of a fractional interest in a foreign employees' trust, the taxpayer may rely on this rule only if it so indicates on a statement attached to a timely filed Form 5471. The IRS and Treasury solicit comments regarding the most appropriate way in which to extend a filing requirement to partners in U.S.-related foreign partnerships and other affected taxpayers.

G. Plan's accrued liability

Under the proposed regulations, the plan's accrued liability for a taxable year of the employer is computed as of the plan's measurement date for the employer's taxable year. The plan's accrued liability is determined using a projected unit credit funding method, taking into account only liabilities relating to services performed for the employer or a predecessor employer. In addition, the plan's accrued liability is reduced (but not below zero) by any liabilities that are provided for under annuity contracts held to satisfy plan liabilities.

Because CFCs generally are required to determine their taxable income by reference to U.S. tax principles, the definition of a plan's "accrued liability" refers to § 1.412(c)(3)-1. This definition generally is intended to track the method used for calculating pension costs under Statement of Financial Accounting Standards No. 87, Employers' Accounting for Pensions (FAS 87), available from the Financial Accounting Standards Board, 401 Merritt 7, Norwalk, CT 06856. Under the method required to be used to calculate FAS 87's projected benefit obligation (PBO), plan costs are based on projected salary levels. Because many taxpayers already compute PBO annually to determine the pension costs of their nonexempt employees' trusts for financial reporting, the timing, interval and method to compute plan liabilities under § 1.671-1(h) should minimize taxpayer burden. The IRS and Treasury solicit comments regarding the extent to which the proposed regulations conform to existing procedures under FAS 87 and applicable foreign law, and regarding appropriate conforming adjustments.

H. Fair market value of trust assets

Under the proposed regulations, for a taxable year of the employer, the fair market value of trust assets, and the fair market value of retirement annuities or other assets held in the equivalent of a trust, equals the fair market value of those assets, as of the measurement date for the employer's taxable year. The fair market value of these assets is adjusted to include contributions made between the measurement date and the end of the employer's taxable year.

I. De minimis exception

The proposed regulations provide an exception to the general rule for determining the relevant amount. If the relevant amount would not otherwise be greater than the plan's normal cost for the plan year ending with or within the employer's taxable year, then the relevant amount is considered to be zero.

J. Proposed effective date and transition rules

The proposed regulations are proposed to be prospective. For taxable years ending prior to September 27, 1996, employers generally would not be treated for federal income tax purposes as owning the assets of foreign nonexempt employees' trusts (except as provided under section 679), consistent with the rules applying to domestic nonexempt employees' trusts. A transition rule, for purposes of § 1.671-1(h), exempts certain amounts from the application of the proposed regulations. This exemption is phased out over a ten-year period. There is a special transition rule for any foreign corporation that becomes a CFC after September 27, 1996. In addition, there is a special transition rule for certain entities that become U.S.-related foreign partnerships after September 27, 1996.

3. § 1.671-2: General asset ownership rules

The proposed regulations provide that a person who is treated as the owner of any portion of a trust under subpart E is considered to own the trust assets attributable to that portion of the trust for all federal income tax purposes.

4. § 1.1297-4: Subpart E rules for foreign employers that are not controlled foreign corporations

Under the proposed regulations, a foreign employer other than a CFC is not treated as the owner of any portion of a foreign nonexempt employees' trust for purposes of sections 1291 through 1297, except for cases in which a principal purpose for transferring property to the trust is to avoid classification of a foreign corporation as a PFIC (as defined in section 1296) or, if the foreign corporation is classified as a PFIC, in cases in which a principal purpose for transferring property to the trust is to avoid or to reduce taxation of U.S. shareholders of the PFIC under section 1291 or 1293. The effective date of this rule is September 27, 1996.

Income inclusion and related asset ownership rules for foreign welfare benefit plans

The IRS and Treasury solicit comments on the need for (and content of) income inclusion and asset ownership rules for foreign welfare benefit trusts.

Special Analyses

It has been determined that this notice of proposed rulemaking is not a significant regulatory action as defined in Executive Order 12866. Therefore, a regulatory assessment is not required. It is hereby certified that these regulations do not have a significant economic impact on a substantial number of small entities. This certification is based on the fact that these regulations will primarily affect U.S. owners of significant interests in foreign entities, which owners generally are large multinational corporations. This certification is also based on the fact that the burden imposed by the collection of information in the regulation, which is a requirement that certain entities may rely on an exception for reasonable funding only if they indicate such reliance on a statement attached to a timely filed Form 5471, is minimal, and, therefore, the collection of information will not impose a significant economic impact on such entities. Therefore, a Regulatory Flexibility Analysis under the Regulatory Flexibility Act (5 U.S.C. chapter 6) is not required. Pursuant to section 7805(f) of the Internal Revenue Code, this notice of proposed rulemaking will be submitted to the Chief Counsel for Advocacy of the Small Business Administration for comment on its impact on small business.

Comments and Public Hearing

Before these proposed regulations are adopted as final regulations, consideration will be given to any written comments (a signed original and eight (8) copies) that are submitted timely to the IRS. All comments will be available for public inspection and copying.

A public hearing has been scheduled for January 15, 1997, at 10:00 a.m. in room 2615, Internal Revenue Building, 1111 Constitution Avenue, NW., Washington DC. Because of access restrictions, visitors will not be admitted beyond the Internal Revenue Building lobby more than 15 minutes before the hearing starts.

The rules of 26 CFR 601.601(a)(3) apply to the hearing.

Persons that wish to present oral comments at the hearing must submit written comments by December 26, 1996, and submit an outline of the topics to be discussed and the time to be devoted to each topic (signed original and eight (8) copies) by December 24, 1996.

A period of 10 minutes will be allotted to each person for making comments.

An agenda showing the scheduling of the speakers will be prepared after the deadline for receiving outlines has passed. Copies of the agenda will be available free of charge at the hearing.

Drafting Information

The principal authors of these regulations are James A. Quinn of the Office of Assistant Chief Counsel (Passthroughs and Special Industries), Linda S. F. Marshall of the Office of Associate Chief Counsel (Employee Benefits and Exempt Organizations), and Kristine K. Schlaman and M. Grace Fleeman of the Office of Associate Chief Counsel (International). However, other personnel from the IRS and Treasury Department participated in their development.

List of Subjects in 26 CFR Part 1

Income taxes, Reporting and recordkeeping requirements.

Proposed Amendments to the Regulations

Accordingly, 26 CFR part 1 is proposed to be amended as follows:

PART 1—INCOME TAXES

Paragraph 1. The authority citation for part 1 is amended by removing the entry for sections 1.1291-10T, 1.1294-1T, 1.1295-1T, and 1.1297-3T and adding entries in numerical order to read as follows:

Authority: 26 U.S.C. 7805 ***

Section 1.671-1 also issued under 26 U.S.C. 404A(h) and 672(f)(2)(B). ***

Section 1.1291-10T also issued under 26 U.S.C. 1291(d)(2).

Section 1.1294-1T also issued under 26 U.S.C. 1294.

Section 1.1295-1T also issued under 26 U.S.C. 1295.

Section 1.1297-3T also issued under 26 U.S.C. 1297(b)(1).

Section 1.1297-4 also issued under 26 U.S.C. 1297(f). ***

Par. 2. Section 1.671-1 is amended by adding paragraphs (g) and (h) to read as follows:

§ 1.671-1 Grantors and others treated as substantial owners; scope.

*****

(g) *Domestic nonexempt employees' trust*— (1) *General rule.* An employer is not treated as an owner of any portion of a nonexempt employees' trust described in section 402(b) that is part of a deferred compensation plan, and that is not a foreign trust within the meaning of section 7701(a)(31), regardless of whether the employer has a power or interest described in sections 673 through 677 over any portion of the trust. See section 402(b)(3) and § 1.402(b)-1(b)(6) for rules relating to treatment of a beneficiary of a nonexempt employees' trust as the owner of a portion of the trust.

(2) *Example.* The following example illustrates the rules of paragraph (g)(1) of this section:

Example. Employer X provides nonqualified deferred compensation through Plan A to certain of its management employees. Employer X has created Trust T to fund the benefits under Plan A. Assets of Trust T may not be used for any purpose other than to satisfy benefits provided under Plan A until all plan liabilities have been satisfied. Trust T is classified as a trust under § 301.7701-4 of this chapter, and is not a foreign trust within the meaning of section 7701(a)(31). Under § 1.83-3(e), contributions to Trust T are considered transfers of property to participants within the meaning of section 83. On these facts, Trust T is a nonexempt employees' trust described in section 402(b). Because Trust T is a nonexempt employees' trust described in section 402(b) that is part of a deferred compensation plan, and that is not a foreign trust within the meaning of section 7701(a)(31), Employer X is not treated as an owner of any portion of Trust T.

(h) *Foreign employees' trust*—(1) *General rules.* Except as provided under section 679 or as provided under this paragraph (h)(1), an employer is not treated as an owner of any portion of a foreign employees' trust (as defined in paragraph (h)(2) of this section), regardless of whether the employer has a power or interest described in sections 673 through 677 over any portion of the trust.

(i) *Plan of CFC employer.* If a controlled foreign corporation (as defined in section 957) maintains a deferred compensation plan funded through a foreign employees' trust, then, with respect to the controlled foreign corporation, the provisions of subpart E apply to the portion of the trust that is the fractional interest described in paragraph (h)(3) of this section.

(ii) *Plan of U.S. employer.* If a United States person (as defined in section 7701(a)(30)) maintains a deferred compensation plan that is funded through a foreign employees' trust, then, with respect to the U.S. person, the provisions of subpart E apply to the portion of the trust that is the fractional interest described in paragraph (h)(3) of this section.

(iii) *Plan of U.S.-related foreign partnership employer*—(A) *General rule.* If a U.S.-related foreign partnership (as defined in paragraph (h)(1)(iii)(B) of this section) maintains a deferred compensation plan funded through a foreign employees' trust, then, with respect to the U.S.-related foreign partnership, the provisions of subpart E apply to the portion of the trust that is the fractional interest described in paragraph (h)(3) of this section.

(B) *U.S.-related foreign partnership.* For purposes of this paragraph (h), a U.S.-related foreign partnership is a foreign partnership in which a U.S. person or a controlled foreign corporation owns a partnership interest either directly or indirectly through one or more partnerships.

(iv) *Application of § 1.1297-4 to plan of foreign non-CFC employer.* A foreign employer that is not a controlled foreign corporation may be treated as an owner of a portion of a foreign employees' trust as provided in § 1.1297-4.

(v) *Application to employer entity.* The rules of paragraphs (h)(1)(i) through (h)(1)(iv) of this section apply to the employer whose employees benefit under the deferred compensation plan funded through a foreign employees' trust, or, in the case of a deferred compensation plan covering independent contractors, the recipient of services performed by those independent contractors, regardless of whether the plan is maintained through another entity. Thus, for example, where a deferred compensation plan benefitting employees of a controlled foreign corporation is funded through a foreign employees' trust, the controlled foreign corporation is considered to be the grantor of the foreign employees' trust for purposes of applying paragraph (h)(1)(i) of this section.

(2) *Foreign employees' trust.* A foreign employees' trust is a nonexempt employees' trust described in section 402(b) that is part of a deferred compensation plan, and that is a foreign trust within the meaning of section 7701(a)(31).

(3) *Fractional interest for paragraph (h)(1)*—(i) *In general.* The fractional interest for a foreign employees' trust used for purposes of paragraph (h)(1) of this section for a taxable year of the employer is an undivided fractional interest in the trust for which the fraction is equal to the relevant amount for the employer's taxable year divided by the fair market value of trust assets for the employer's taxable year.

(ii) *Relevant amount*—(A) *In general.* For purposes of applying paragraph (h)(3)(i) of this section, and except as provided in paragraph (h)(3)(iii) of this section, the relevant amount for the employer's taxable year is the amount, if any, by which the fair market value of trust assets, plus the fair market value of any assets available to pay plan liabilities that are held in the equivalent of a trust within the meaning of section 404A(b)(5)(A), exceed the plan's accrued liability. The following rules apply for this purpose:

(*1*) The plan's accrued liability is determined using a projected unit credit funding method that satisfies the requirements of § 1.412(c)(3)-1, taking into account only liabilities relating to services performed through the measurement date for the employer or a predecessor employer.

(*2*) The plan's accrued liability is reduced (but not below zero) by any liabilities that are provided for under annuity contracts held to satisfy plan liabilities.

(*3*) Any amount held under an annuity contract that exceeds the amount that is needed to satisfy the liabilities provided for under the contract (e.g., the value of a participation right under a participating annuity contract) is added to the fair market value of any assets available to pay plan liabilities that are held in the equivalent of a trust.

(*4*) If the relevant amount as determined under this paragraph (h)(3)(ii), without regard to this paragraph (h)(3)(ii)(A)(*4*), is greater than the fair market value of trust assets, then the relevant amount is equal to the fair market value of trust assets.

(B) *Permissible actuarial assumptions for accrued liability.* For purposes of paragraph (h)(3)(ii)(A) of this section, a plan's accrued liability must be calculated using an interest rate and other actuarial assumptions that the Commissioner determines to be reasonable. It is appropriate in determining this interest rate to look to available information about rates implicit in current prices of annuity contracts, and to look to rates of return on high-quality fixed-income investments currently available and expected to be available during the period prior to maturity of the plan benefits. If the qualified business unit computes its income or earnings and profits in dollars pursuant to the dollar approximate separate transactions method under § 1.985-3, the employer must use an exchange rate that can be demonstrated to clearly reflect income, based on all relevant facts and circumstances, including appropriate rates of inflation and commercial practices.

(iii) *Exception for reasonable funding.* The relevant amount does not include an amount that the taxpayer demonstrates to the Commissioner is attributable to amounts that were properly contributed to the trust pursuant to a reasonable funding method, applied using actuarial assumptions that the Commissioner determines to be reasonable, or any amount that the taxpayer demonstrates to the Commissioner is attributable to experience that is favorable relative to any actuarial assumptions used that the Commissioner determines to be reasonable. For this paragraph (h)(3)(iii) to apply to a controlled foreign corporation employer described in paragraph (h)(1)(i) of this section, the taxpayer must indicate on a statement attached to a timely filed Form 5471 that the taxpayer is relying on this rule. For purposes of this paragraph (h)(3)(iii), an amount is considered contributed pursuant to a reasonable funding method if the amount is contributed pursuant to a funding method permitted to be used under section 412 (e.g., the entry age normal funding method) that is consistently used to determine plan contributions. In addition, for purposes of this paragraph (h)(3)(iii), if there has been a change to that method from another funding method, an amount is considered contributed pursuant to a reasonable funding method only if the prior funding method is also a funding method described in the preceding sentence that was consistently used to determine plan contributions. For purposes of this paragraph (h)(3)(iii), a funding method is considered reasonable only if the method provides for any initial unfunded liability to be amortized over a period of at least 6 years, and for any net change in accrued liability resulting from a change in funding method to be amortized over a period of at least 6 years.

(iv) *Reduction for transition amount.* The relevant amount is reduced (but not below zero) by any transition amount described in paragraphs (h)(5), (h)(6), or (h)(7) of this section.

(v) *Fair market value of assets.* For purposes of paragraphs (h)(3)(i) and (ii) of this section, for a taxable year of the employer, the fair market value of trust assets, and the fair market value of other assets held in the equivalent of a trust within the meaning of section 404A(b)(5)(A), equals the fair market value of those assets, as of the measurement date for the employer's taxable year, adjusted to include contributions made after the measurement date and by the end of the employer's taxable year.

(vi) *Annual valuation.* For purposes of determining the relevant amount for a taxable year of the employer, the fair market value of plan assets, and the plan's accrued liability as described in paragraphs (h)(3)(ii) and (iii) of this section, and the normal cost as described in paragraph (h)(4) of this section, must be determined as of a consistently used annual measurement date within the employer's taxable year.

(vii) *Special rule for plan funded through multiple trusts.* In cases in which a plan is funded through more than one foreign employees' trust, the fractional interest determined under paragraph (h)(3)(i) of this section in each trust is determined by treating all of the trusts as if their assets were held in a single trust for which the fraction is determined in accordance with the rules of this paragraph (h)(3).

(4) *De minimis exception.* If the relevant amount is not greater than the plan's normal cost for the plan year ending with or within the employer's taxable year, computed using a funding method and actuarial assumptions as described in paragraph (h)(3)(ii) of this section or as described in paragraph (h)(3)(iii) of this section if the requirements of that paragraph are met, that are used to determine plan contributions, then the relevant amount is considered to be zero for purposes of applying paragraph (h)(3)(i) of this section.

(5) *General rule for transition amount*—(i) *General rule.* If paragraphs (h)(6) and (h)(7) of this section do not apply to the employer, the transition amount for purposes of paragraph (h)(3)(iv) of this section is equal to the preexisting amount multiplied by the applicable percentage for the year in which the employer's taxable year begins.

(ii) *Preexisting amount.* The preexisting amount is equal to the relevant amount of the trust, determined without regard to paragraphs (h)(3)(iv) and (h)(4) of this section, computed as of the measurement date that immediately precedes September 27, 1996 disregarding contributions to the trust made after the measurement date.

(iii) *Applicable percentage.* The applicable percentage is equal to 100 percent for the employer's first taxable year ending after this document is published as a final regulation in the Federal Register and prior taxable years of the employer, and is reduced (but not below zero) by 10 percentage points for each subsequent taxable year of the employer.

(6) *Transition amount for new CFCs*—(i) *General rule.* In the case of a new controlled foreign corporation employer, the transition amount for purposes of paragraph (h)(3)(iv) is equal to the pre-change amount multiplied by the applicable percentage for the year in which the new controlled foreign corporation employer's taxable year begins.

(ii) *Pre-change amount.* The pre-change amount for purposes of paragraph (h)(6)(i) is equal to the relevant amount of the trust, determined without regard to paragraphs (h)(3)(iv) and (h)(4) of this section and disregarding contributions to the trust made after the measurement date, for the new controlled foreign corporation employer's last taxable year ending before the corporation becomes a new controlled foreign corporation employer.

(iii) *Applicable percentage*—(A) *General rule.* Except as provided in paragraph (h)(6)(iii)(B) of this section, the applicable percentage is equal to 100 percent for a new controlled foreign corporation employer's first taxable year ending after the corporation becomes a controlled foreign corporation. The applicable percentage is reduced (but not below zero) by 10 percentage points for each subsequent taxable year of the new controlled foreign corporation.

(B) *Interim rule.* For any taxable year of a new controlled foreign corporation employer that ends on or before the date this document is published as a final regulation in the **Federal Register,** the applicable percentage is equal to 100 percent. The applicable percentage is reduced by 10 percentage points for each subsequent taxable year of the new controlled foreign corporation employer that ends after the date this document is published as a final regulation in the **Federal Register.**

(iv) *New CFC employer.* For purposes of paragraph (h)(6) of this section, a new controlled foreign corporation employer is a corporation that first becomes a controlled foreign corporation within the meaning of section 957 after September 27, 1996. A new controlled foreign corporation employer includes a corporation that was a controlled foreign corporation prior to, but not on, September 26, 1996 and that first becomes a controlled foreign corporation again after September 27, 1996.

(v) *Anti-stuffing rule.* Notwithstanding paragraph (h)(6)(iii) of this section, if, prior to becoming a controlled foreign corporation, a corporation contributes amounts to a foreign employees' trust with a principal purpose of obtaining tax benefits by increasing the pre-change amount, the applicable percentage with respect to those amounts is 0 percent for all taxable years of the new controlled foreign corporation employer.

(7) *Transition amount for new U.S.-related foreign partnerships*—(i) *General rule.* In the case of a new U.S.-related foreign partnership employer, the transition amount for purposes of paragraph (h)(3)(iv) of this section is equal to the pre-change amount multiplied by the applicable percentage for the year in which the new U.S.-related foreign partnership employer's taxable year begins.

(ii) *Pre-change amount.* The pre-change amount for purposes of paragraph (h)(7)(i) of this section is equal to the relevant amount of the trust, determined without regard to paragraphs (h)(3)(iv) and (h)(4) of this section and disregarding contributions to the trust made after the measurement date, for the entity's last taxable year ending before the entity becomes a new U.S.-related foreign partnership employer.

(iii) *Applicable percentage*—(A) *General rule.* Except as provided in paragraph (h)(7)(iii)(B) of this section, the applicable percentage is equal to 100 percent for a new U.S.-related foreign partnership employer's first taxable year ending after the entity becomes a new U.S.-related foreign partnership employer. The applicable percentage is reduced (but not below zero) by 10 percentage points for each subsequent taxable year of the new U.S.-related foreign partnership employer.

(B) *Interim rule.* For any taxable year of a new U.S.-related foreign partnership employer that ends on or before the date this document is published as a final regulation in the **Federal Register,** the applicable percentage is equal to 100 percent. The applicable percentage is reduced by 10 percentage points for each subsequent taxable year of the new U.S.-related foreign partnership employer that ends after the date this document is published as a final regulation in the **Federal Register.**

(iv) *New U.S.-related foreign partnership employer.* For purposes of paragraph (h)(7) of this section, a new U.S.-related foreign partnership employer is an entity that was a foreign corporation other than a controlled foreign corporation, or that was a foreign partnership other than a U.S.-related foreign partnership, and that changes from this status to a U.S.-related foreign partnership after September 27, 1996. A new U.S.-related foreign partnership employer includes a corporation that was a U.S.-related foreign partnership prior to, but not on, September 27, 1996, and that first becomes a U.S.-related foreign partnership again after September 27, 1996.

(v) *Anti-stuffing rule.* Notwithstanding paragraph (h)(7)(iii) of this section, if, prior to becoming a new U.S.-related foreign partnership employer, an entity contributes amounts to a foreign employees' trust with a principal purpose of obtaining tax benefits by increasing the pre-change amount, the applicable percentage with respect to those amounts is 0 percent for all taxable years of the new U.S.-related foreign partnership employer.

(8) *Examples.* The following examples illustrate the rules of paragraph (h) of this section. In each example, the employer has a power or interest described in sections 673 through 677 over the foreign employees' trust, and the monetary unit is the applicable functional currency (FC) determined in accordance with section 985(b) and the regulations thereunder.

Example 1. (i) Employer X is a controlled foreign corporation (as defined in section 957). Employer X maintains a defined benefit retirement plan for its employees. Employer X's taxable year is the calendar year. Trust T, a foreign employees' trust, is the sole funding vehicle for the plan. Both the plan year of the plan and the taxable year of Trust T are the calendar year.

(ii) As of December 31, 1997, Trust T's measurement date, the fair market value (as described in paragraph (h)(3)(iv) of this section) of Trust T's assets is FC 1,000,000, and the amount of the plan's accrued liability is FC 800,000, which includes a normal cost for 1997 of FC 50,000. The preexisting amount for Trust T is FC 40,000. Thus, the relevant amount for 1997 is FC 160,000 (which is greater than the plan's normal cost for the year). Employer X's shareholder does not indicate on a statement attached to a timely filed Form 5471 that any of the relevant amount qualifies for the exception described in paragraph (h)(3)(iii) of this section. Therefore, the fractional interest for Employer X's taxable year ending on December 31, 1997, is 16 percent. Employer X is treated as the owner for federal income tax purposes of an undivided 16 percent interest in each of Trust T's assets for the period from January 1, 1997 through December 31, 1997. Employer X must take into account a 16 percent pro rata share of each item of income, deduction or credit of Trust T during this period in computing its federal income tax liability.

Example 2. Assume the same facts as in *Example 1*, except that Employer X's shareholder indicates on a statement attached to a timely filed Form 5471 and can demonstrate to the satisfaction of the Commissioner that, in reliance on paragraph (h)(3)(iii) of this section, FC 100,000 of the fair market value of Trust T's assets is attributable to favorable experience relative to reasonable actuarial assumptions used. Accordingly, the relevant amount for 1997 is FC 60,000. Because the plan's normal cost for 1997 is less than FC 60,000, the de minimis exception of paragraph (h)(4) of this section does not apply. Therefore, the fractional interest for Employer X's taxable year ending on December 31, 1997, is 6 percent. Employer X is treated as the owner for federal income tax purposes of an undivided 6 percent interest in each of Trust T's assets for the period from January 1, 1997, through December 31, 1997. Employer X must take into account a 6 percent pro rata share of each item of income, deduction or credit of Trust T during this period in computing its federal income tax liability.

(9) *Effective date.* Paragraphs (g) and (h) of this section apply to taxable years of an employer ending after September 27, 1996.

Par. 3. Section 1.671-2 is amended by adding paragraph (f) to read as follows:

§ *1.671-2 Applicable principles*

*****

(f) For purposes of subtitle A of the Internal Revenue Code, a person that is treated as the owner of any portion of a trust under subpart E is considered to own the trust assets attributable to that portion of the trust.

Par. 4. Section 1.1297-4 is added to read as follows:

§ *1.1297-4 Application of subpart E of subchapter J with respect to foreign employees' trusts.*

(a) *General rules.* For purposes of part VI of subchapter P, chapter 1 of the Code, a foreign employer that is not a controlled foreign corporation is not treated as the owner of any portion of a foreign employees' trust (as defined in § 1.671-1(h)(2)) except as provided in this paragraph (a), regardless of whether the employer has a power or interest described in sections 673 through 677 over any portion of the trust.

(1) *Principal purpose to avoid classification as a passive foreign investment company.* If a principal purpose for a transfer of property by any person to a foreign employees' trust (as defined in § 1.671-1(h)(2)) is to avoid classification of a foreign corporation as a passive foreign investment company, then the following rule applies. If the foreign employer has a power or interest described in sections 673 through 677 over the trust, then the grantor trust rules of subpart E of part I of subchapter J, chapter 1 of the Code will apply, for purposes of part VI of subchapter P, to a fixed dollar amount in the trust that is equal to the fair market value of the property that is transferred for the purpose of avoiding classification as a passive foreign investment company. Whether a principal purpose for a transfer is the avoidance of classification as a passive foreign investment company will be determined on the basis of all of the facts and circumstances, including whether the amount of assets held by the foreign employees' trust is reasonably related to the plan's anticipated liabilities, taking into account any local law and practice relating to proper funding levels.

(2) *Principal purpose to reduce or eliminate taxation under section 1291 or 1293.* If a principal purpose for a transfer of property by any person to a foreign employees' trust (as defined in § 1.671-1(h)(2)) is to reduce or eliminate taxation under section 1291 or 1293, then the following rule applies. If the foreign employer has a power or interest described in sections 673 through 677 over the trust, then the provisions of subpart E will apply, for purposes of part VI of subchapter P, to a fixed dollar amount in the trust that is equal to the fair market value of the property transferred for the purpose of reducing or eliminating taxation under section 1291 or 1293. Whether a principal purpose for a transfer is to reduce or eliminate taxation under section 1291 or 1293 will be determined on the basis of all the facts and circumstances, including whether the amount of assets held by the foreign employees' trust is reasonably related to the plan's anticipated liabilities, taking into account any local law and practice relating to proper funding levels.

(3) *Application to employer entity.* The rules of this section apply to the employer whose employees benefit under the deferred compensation plan funded through the foreign employees' trust, or, in the case of a deferred compensation plan covering independent contractors, the recipient of services performed by those independent contractors, regardless of whether the plan is maintained through another entity. Thus, for example, where a deferred compensation plan benefitting employees of a foreign employer that is not a controlled foreign corporation is funded through a foreign employees' trust, the foreign employer is considered to be the grantor of the foreign employees' trust for purposes of this paragraph (a).

(b) *Effective date.* This section applies to taxable years of a foreign corporation ending after September 27, 1996.

Commissioner of Internal Revenue

Margaret Milner Richardson

CERTIFIED COPY

Michael L. Slaughter

¶ 20,220

Proposed regulations: Magnetic media filing: Information returns: Form W-2: Form 1099 series: Form 5498.—The IRS has issued proposed regulations regarding the requirements for filing information returns on magnetic media or in other machine-readable form under Code Sec. 6011(e). The proposed regulations, which were also issued as temporary regulations, provide that filers of the Form 1099 series and Form 5498 must now obtain consent from the IRS before filing magnetically. Filers are instructed to use Form 4419 to obtain the necessary consent. Additionally, the regulations state that filers of Form W-2 are now required to file magnetically.

The proposed regulations also provide that magnetic filing will not be required for persons filing less than 250 returns during a calendar year. Further, in keeping with its current administrative practices, the IRS will no longer permit filing on cassette.

The temporary and proposed regulations were published in the *Federal Register* on October 10, 1996 (61 FR 53161) and are reproduced at ¶ 13,649E. The preamble to the temporary regulations is reproduced at ¶ 23,927A.

AGENCY: Internal Revenue Service (IRS), Treasury.

ACTION: Notice of proposed rulemaking and notice of public hearing.

SUMMARY: In the Rules and Regulations section of this issue of the **Federal Register,** the IRS is issuing temporary regulations relating to the requirements for filing information returns on magnetic media or in other machine-readable form under section 6011(e) of the Internal Revenue Code. The text of those temporary regulations also serves as the text of the proposed regulations. This document also contains a proposed amendment to § 301.6011-2(g)(2). This document also provides notice of a public hearing on these proposed regulations.

DATES: Written comments must be received by January 8, 1997. Outlines of topics to be discussed at the public hearing scheduled for February 5, 1997, must be received by January 15, 1997.

ADDRESSES: Send submissions to: CC:DOM:CORP:R (REG-209803-95), room 5228, Internal Revenue Service, POB 7604, Ben Franklin Station, Washington, DC 20044. In the alternative, submissions may be hand delivered between the hours of 8 a.m. and 5 p.m. to: CC:DOM:CORP:R (REG-209803-95), Courier's Desk, Internal Revenue Service, 1111 Constitution Ave., NW., Washington, DC. Alternatively, taxpayers may submit comments electronically via the internet by selecting the "Tax Regs" option on the IRS Home Page, or by submitting comments directly to the IRS internet site at http://www.irs.ustreas.gov/prod/tax_regs/comments.html. The public hearing will be held in Room 3313 of the Internal Revenue Building, 1111 Constitution Ave., NW., Washington, DC.

FOR FURTHER INFORMATION CONTACT: Concerning the regulations, Donna Welch, (202) 622-4910; concerning submissions and the hearing, Mike Slaughter, (202) 622-7190 (not toll-free numbers).

SUPPLEMENTARY INFORMATION:

Background

Temporary regulations in the Rules and Regulations portion of this issue of the **Federal Register** amend the Income Tax Regulations (26 CFR part 1) relating to section 6045 and the Procedure and Administration Regulations (26 CFR part 301) relating to section 6011(e). The temporary regulations contain rules relating to the filing requirements of information returns on magnetic media or in other machine-readable form under section 6011(e).

The text of those temporary regulations also serves as the text of these proposed regulations. The preamble to the temporary regulations explains the temporary regulations.

Special Analyses

It has been determined that these proposed regulations are not a significant regulatory action as defined in EO 12866. Therefore, a regulatory assessment is not required.

It is hereby certified that the regulations in this document will not have a significant economic impact on a substantial number of small entities. This certification is based on a determination that these regulations impose no additional reporting or recordkeeping requirement and only prescribe the method of filing information returns that are already required to be filed. Further, these regulations are consistent with the requirements imposed by statute. Section 6011(e)(2)(A) provides that, in prescribing regulations providing standards for determining which returns must be filed on magnetic media or in other machine-readable form, the Secretary shall not require any person to file returns on magnetic media unless the person is required to file at least 250 returns during the calendar year. Consistent with the statutory provision, these regulations do not require information returns to be filed on magnetic media unless 250 or more returns are required to be filed. Further, the economic impact caused by requiring filing on magnetic media should be minimal. If a taxpayer's operations are computerized, reporting in accordance with the regulations should be less costly than filing on paper. If the taxpayer's operations are not computerized, the incremental cost of magnetic media reporting should be minimal in most cases because of the availability of computer service bureaus. In addition, the existing regulations provide that the IRS may waive the magnetic media filing requirements upon a showing of hardship. It is anticipated that the waiver authority will be exercised so as not to unduly burden taxpayers lacking both the necessary data processing facilities and access at a reasonable cost to computer service bureaus. Accordingly, a Regulatory Flexibility Analysis under the Regulatory Flexibility Act (5 U.S.C. chapter 6) is not required.

Pursuant to section 7805(f) of the Internal Revenue Code, these proposed regulations will be submitted to the Chief Counsel for Advocacy of the Small Business Administration for comment on their impact on small business.

Comments and Public Hearing

Before these proposed regulations are adopted as final regulations, consideration will be given to any written comments (a signed original and eight (8) copies) that are submitted timely to the IRS. All comments will be available for public inspection and copying.

A public hearing has been scheduled for February 5, 1997, at 10 am. The hearing will be held in room 3313 of the Internal Revenue Building, 1111 Constitution Ave., NW., Washington, DC. Because of access restrictions, visitors will not be admitted beyond the Internal Revenue Building lobby more than 15 minutes before the hearing starts.

The rules of 26 CFR 601.601(a)(3) apply to the hearing.

Persons who wish to present oral comments at the hearing must submit written comments by January 8, 1997, and submit an outline of the topics to be discussed and the time to be devoted to each topic (signed original and eight (8) copies) by January 15, 1997.

A period of 10 minutes will be allotted to each person for making comments.

An agenda showing the scheduling of the speakers will be prepared after the deadline for receiving outlines has passed. Copies of the agenda will be available free of charge at the hearing.

Drafting Information

The principal author of the regulations is Donna Welch, Office of Assistant Chief Counsel (Income Tax and Accounting). However, other personnel from the IRS and the Treasury Department participated in the development of the regulations.

List of Subjects

26 CFR Part 1

Income taxes, Reporting and recordkeeping requirements.

26 CFR Part 301

Employment taxes, Estate taxes, Excise taxes, Gift taxes, Income taxes, Penalties, Reporting and recordkeeping requirements.

Proposed Amendments to the Regulations

Accordingly, 26 CFR parts 1 and 301 are proposed to be amended as follows:

****

PART 301—PROCEDURE AND ADMINISTRATION

Par. 4. The authority citation for part 301 continues to read in part as follows:

Authority: 26 U.S.C. 7805 * * *

Par. 5. Section 301.6011-2 is amended by revising paragraphs (a)(1), (b)(1) and (2), (c)(1)(i) and (iii), (c)(2), (f) and (g)(2), and by adding (c)(1)(iv), and by removing paragraphs (c)(3) and (4) and the last sentence of paragraph (e). The revisions and additions read as follows:

§ 301.6011-2 Required use of magnetic media.

[The text of paragraphs (a)(1), (b)(1) and (2), (c)(1)(i), (iii), and (iv), (c)(2), (f), and (g)(2) as proposed is the same as the text in § 301.6011-2T(a)(1), (b)(1) and (2), (c)(1)(i), (iii), and (iv), (c)(2), (f), and the first sentence of (g)(2) published elsewhere in this issue of the **Federal Register**].

¶ 20,221

Proposed regulations: Self-employment tax: Limited partners.—Following is the text of proposed regulations defining which partners of a federal tax partnership are considered limited partners for purposes of Sec. 1402(a)(13). The definitions depend on the relationship between the partner, the partnership and the partnership's business, and state law characterizations of an individual as a limited partner are not determinative.

The proposed regulations were published in the *Federal Register* on January 13, 1997 (62 FR 1702). The text, reproduced below, contains amendments to the regulations under Code Sec. 1402 that have been re-proposed by the IRS. The IRS has withdrawn proposed regulations for Code Sec. 1402 issued in 1994 (CCH PENSION PLAN GUIDE ¶ 20,110).

DEPARTMENT OF THE TREASURY

Internal Revenue Service

26 CFR Part 1

RIN 1545-AU24

Definition of Limited Partner for Self-Employment Tax Purposes

AGENCY: Internal Revenue Service (IRS), Treasury.

ACTION: Notice of proposed rulemaking and notice of public hearing.

SUMMARY: This document contains proposed amendments to the regulations relating to the self-employment income tax imposed under section 1402 of the Internal Revenue Code of 1986. These regulations permit individuals to determine whether they are limited partners for purposes of section 1402(a)(13), eliminating the uncertainty in calculating an individual's net earnings from self-employment under existing law. This document also contains a notice of public hearing on the proposed regulations.

DATES: Written comments must be received by April 14, 1997. Requests to speak and outlines of oral comments to be discussed at the public hearing scheduled for May 21, 1997, at 10 a.m. must be received by April 30, 1997.

ADDRESSES: Send submissions to: CC:DOM:CORP:R (REG-209824-96), room 5226, Internal Revenue Service, POB 7604, Ben Franklin Station, Washington, DC 20044. Submissions may be hand delivered between the hours of 8 a.m. and 5 p.m. to: CC:DOM:CORP:R (REG-209824-96), Courier's Desk, Internal Revenue Service, 1111 Constitution Avenue, NW, Washington, DC. Alternatively, taxpayers may submit comments electronically via the Internet by selecting the "Tax Regs" option on the IRS Home Page, or by submitting comments directly to the IRS Internet site at http://www.irs.ustreas.gov/prod/tax-regs/comments.html. The public hearing will be held in the Auditorium, Internal Revenue Service building, 1111 Constitution Avenue, NW, Washington, DC.

FOR FURTHER INFORMATION CONTACT: Concerning the regulation, Robert Honigman, (202) 622-3050; concerning submissions and the hearing, Christina Vasquez, (202) 622-6808 (not toll-free numbers).

SUPPLEMENTARY INFORMATION:

Background

This document contains proposed amendments to the Income Tax Regulations (26 CFR part 1) under section 1402 of the Internal Revenue Code and replaces the notice of proposed rulemaking published in the **Federal Register** on December 29, 1994, at 59 FR 67253, that treated certain members of a limited liability company (LLC) as limited partners for self-employment tax purposes. Written comments responding to the proposed regulations were received, and a public hearing was held on June 23, 1995.

Under the 1994 proposed regulations, an individual owning an interest in an LLC was treated as a limited partner if (1) the individual lacked the authority to make management decisions necessary to conduct the LLC's business (the management test), and (2) the LLC could have been formed as a limited partnership rather than an LLC in the same jurisdiction, and the member could have qualified as a limited partner in the limited partnership under applicable law (the limited partner equivalence test). The intent of the 1994 proposed regulations was to treat owners of an LLC interest in the same manner as similarly situated partners in a state law partnership.

Public comments on the 1994 proposed regulations were mixed. While some commentators were pleased with the proposed regulations for attempting to conform the treatment of LLCs with state law partnerships, others criticized the 1994 proposed regulations based on a variety of arguments.

A number of commentators discussed administrative and compliance problems with the 1994 proposed regulations. For example, it was noted that both the management test and the limited partner equivalence test depend upon legal or factual determinations that may be difficult for taxpayers or the IRS to make with certainty.

Another commentator pointed out that basing the self-employment tax treatment of LLC members on state law limited partnership rules would lead to disparate treatment between members of different LLCs with identical rights based solely on differences in the limited partnership statutes of the states in which the members form their LLC. For example, State A's limited partnership act may allow a limited partner to participate in a partnership's business while State B's limited partnership act may not. Thus, an LLC member, who is not a manager, that participates in the LLC's business would be a limited partner under the proposed regulations if the LLC is formed in State A, but not if the LLC is formed in State B. Commentators asserted that this disparate treatment is inherently unfair for federal tax purposes.

Some commentators argued for a "material participation" test to determine whether an LLC member's distributive share is included in the individual's net earnings from self-employment. The proposed regulations did not contain a participation test. Commentators advocating a participation test stressed that such a test would eliminate uncertainty concerning many LLC members' limited partner status and would better implement the self-employment tax goal of taxing compensation for services.

Other commentators argued for a more uniform approach, stating that a single test should govern all business entities (i.e., partnerships, LLCs, LLPs, sole proprietorships, et al.) whose members may be subject to self-employment tax. These commentators generally recognized, however, that a change in the treatment of a sole proprietorship or an entity that is not characterized as a partnership for federal tax purposes would be beyond the scope of regulations to be issued under section 1402(a)(13).

Finally, some commentators focused on whether the Service would respect the ownership of more than one class of partnership interest for self-employment tax purposes (bifurcation of interests). The proposed regulations treated an LLC member as a limited partner with respect to his or her entire interest (if the member was not a manager and satisfied the limited partner equivalence test), or not at all (if either the management test or limited partner equivalence test was not satisfied). Commentators, however, pointed to the legislative history of section 1402(a)(13) to support their argument that Congress only intended to tax a partner's distributive share attributable to a general partner interest. Under this argument, a partner that holds both a general partner interest and a limited partner interest is only subject to self-employment tax on the distributive share attributable to the partner's general partner interest. This intent also may be inferred from the statutory language of section 1402(a)(13) that the self-employment tax does not apply to ". . . the distributive share of any item of income or loss of a limited partner, as such . . . ." Based on this evidence, these commentators requested that the proposed regulations be revised to allow the bifurcation of interests for self-employment tax purposes.

After considering the comments received, the IRS and Treasury have decided to withdraw the 1994 notice of proposed rulemaking and to re-propose amendments to the Income Tax Regulations (26 CFR part 1) under section 1402 of the Code.

Explanation of Provisions

The proposed regulations contained in this document define which partners of a federal tax partnership are considered limited partners for section 1402(a)(13) purposes. These proposed regulations apply to all entities classified as a partnership for federal tax purposes, regardless of the state law characterization of the entity. Thus, the same standards apply when determining the status of an individual owning an interest in a state law limited partnership or the status of an individual owning an interest in an LLC. In order to achieve this conformity, the proposed regulations adopt an approach which depends on the relationship between the partner, the partnership, and the partnership's business. State law characterizations of an individual as a "limited partner" or otherwise are not determinative.

Generally, an individual will be treated as a limited partner under the proposed regulations unless the individual (1) has personal liability (as defined in § 301.7701-3(b)(2)(ii) of the Procedure and Administration Regulations) for the debts of or claims against the partnership by reason of being a partner; (2) has authority to contract on behalf of the partnership under the statute or law pursuant to which the partnership is organized; or, (3) participates in the partnership's trade or business for more than 500 hours during the taxable year. If, however, substantially all of the activities of a partnership involve the performance of services in the fields of health, law, engineering, architecture, accounting, actuarial science, or consulting, any individual who provides services as part of that trade or business will not be considered a limited partner.

By adopting these functional tests, the proposed regulations ensure that similarly situated individuals owning interests in entities formed under different statutes or in different jurisdictions will be treated similarly. The need for a functional approach results not only from the proliferation of new business entities such as LLCs, but also from the evolution of state limited partnership statutes. When Congress enacted the limited partner exclusion found in section 1402(a)(13), state laws generally did not allow limited partners to participate in the partnership's trade or business to the extent that state laws allow limited partners to participate today. Thus, even in the case of a state law limited partnership, a functional approach is necessary to ensure that the self-employment tax consequences to similarly situated taxpayers do not differ depending upon where the partnership organized.

The proposed regulations allow an individual who is not a limited partner for section 1402(a)(13) purposes to nonetheless exclude from net earnings from self-employment a portion of that individual's distributive share if the individual holds more than one class of interest in the partnership. Similarly, the proposed regulations permit an individual that participates in the trade or business of the partnership to bifurcate his or her distributive share by disregarding guaranteed payments for services. In each case, however, such bifurcation of interests is permitted only to the extent the individual's distributive share is identical to the distributive share of partners who qualify as limited partners under the proposed regulation (without regard to the bifurcation rules) and who own a substantial interest in the partnership. Together, these rules exclude from an individual's net earnings from self-employment amounts that are demonstrably returns on capital invested in the partnership.

Proposed Effective Date

These regulations are proposed to be effective beginning with the individual's first taxable year beginning on or after the date these regulations are published as final regulations in the **Federal Register**.

Special Analyses

It has been determined that this notice of proposed rulemaking is not a significant regulatory action as defined in EO 12866. Therefore, a regulatory assessment is not required. It also has been determined that section 553(b) of the Administrative Procedure Act (5 U.S.C. chapter 5) does not apply to these regulations, and, because the regulations do not impose a collection of information on small entities, the Regulatory Flexibility Act (5 U.S.C. chapter 6) does not apply. Pursuant to section 7805(f) of the Internal Revenue Code, this notice of proposed rulemaking will be submitted to the Chief Counsel for Advocacy of the Small Business Administration for comment on its impact on small business.

Comments and Public Hearing

Before these proposed regulations are adopted as final regulations, consideration will be given to any written comments (a signed original and eight (8) copies) that are submitted timely to the IRS. All comments will be available for public inspection and copying.

A public hearing has been scheduled for Wednesday, May 21, 1997, at 10 a.m. in the Auditorium, Internal Revenue Service building, 1111 Constitution Avenue, NW, Washington, DC. Because of access restrictions, visitors will not be admitted beyond the Internal Revenue Service building lobby more than 15 minutes before the hearing starts.

The rules of 26 CFR 601.601(a)(3) apply to the hearing.

Persons that wish to present oral comments at the hearing must submit written comments by April 14, 1997, and submit an outline of the topics to be discussed and the time to be devoted to each topic (signed original and eight (8) copies) by April 30, 1997.

A period of 10 minutes will be allotted to each person for making comments.

An agenda showing the scheduling of the speakers will be prepared after the deadline for receiving outlines has passed. Copies of the agenda will be available free of charge at the hearing.

Drafting Information

The principal author of these regulations is Robert Honigman of the Office of Assistant Chief Counsel (Passthroughs & Special Industries). However, other personnel from the IRS and Treasury Department participated in their development.

List of Subjects in 26 CFR Part 1

Income taxes, Reporting and recordkeeping requirements.

Proposed Amendments to the Regulations

Accordingly, 26 CFR part 1 is proposed to be amended as follows:

PART 1—INCOME TAXES

Paragraph 1. The authority citation for part 1 continues to read in part as follows:

Authority: 26 U.S.C. 7805 ***

Par. 2. Section 1.1402(a)-2 is amended by:

1. Revising the first sentence of paragraph (d).

2. Removing the reference "section 702(a)(9)" in the first sentence of paragraph (e) and adding "section 702(a)(8)" in its place.

3. Revising the last sentence of paragraph (f).

4. Revising paragraphs (g) and (h).

5. Adding new paragraphs (i) and (j).

The revisions and additions read as follows:

§ 1.1402(a)-2 *Computation of net earnings from self-employment.*

*****

(d) *** Except as otherwise provided in section 1402(a) and paragraph (g) of this section, an individual's net earnings from self-employment include the individual's distributive share (whether or not distributed) of income or loss described in section 702(a)(8) from any trade or business carried on by each partnership of which the individual is a partner. ***

*****

(f) *** For rules governing the classification of an organization as a partnership or otherwise, see § § 301.7701-1, 301.7701-2, and 301.7701-3 of this chapter.

(g) *Distributive share of limited partner.* An individual's net earnings from self-employment do not include the individual's distributive share of income or loss as a limited partner described in paragraph (h) of this section. However, guaranteed payments described in section 707(c) made to the individual for services actually rendered to or on behalf of the partnership engaged in a trade or business are included in the individual's net earnings from self-employment.

(h) *Definition of limited partner*—(1) *In general.* Solely for purposes of section 1402(a)(13) and paragraph (g) of this section, an individual is considered to be a limited partner to the extent provided in paragraphs (h)(2), (h)(3), (h)(4), and (h)(5) of this section.

(2) *Limited partner.* An individual is treated as a limited partner under this paragraph (h)(2) unless the individual—

(i) Has personal liability (as defined in § 301.7701-3(b)(2)(ii) of this chapter for the debts of or claims against the partnership by reason of being a partner;

(ii) Has authority (under the law of the jurisdiction in which the partnership is formed) to contract on behalf of the partnership; or

(iii) Participates in the partnership's trade or business for more than 500 hours during the partnership's taxable year.

(3) *Exception for holders of more than one class of interest.* An individual holding more than one class of interest in the partnership who is not treated as a limited partner under paragraph (h)(2) of this section is treated as a limited partner under this paragraph (h)(3) with respect to a specific class of partnership interest held by such individual if, immediately after the individual acquires that class of interest—

(i) Limited partners within the meaning of paragraph (h)(2) of this section own a substantial, continuing interest in that specific class of partnership interest; and,

(ii) The individual's rights and obligations with respect to that specific class of interest are identical to the rights and obligations of that specific class of partnership interest held by the limited partners described in paragraph (h)(3)(i) of this section.

(4) *Exception for holders of only one class of interest.* An individual who is not treated as a limited partner under paragraph (h)(2) of this

section solely because that individual participates in the partnership's trade or business for more than 500 hours during the partnership's taxable year is treated as a limited partner under this paragraph (h)(4) with respect to the individual's partnership interest if, immediately after the individual acquires that interest—

(i) Limited partners within the meaning of paragraph (h)(2) of this section own a substantial, continuing interest in that specific class of partnership interest; and

(ii) The individual's rights and obligations with respect to the specific class of interest are identical to the rights and obligations of the specific class of partnership interest held by the limited partners described in paragraph (h)(4)(i) of this section.

(5) *Exception for service partners in service partnerships.* An individual who is a service partner in a service partnership may not be a limited partner under paragraphs (h)(2), (h)(3), or (h)(4) of this section.

(6) *Additional definitions.* Solely for purposes of this paragraph (h)—

(i) A *class of interest* is an interest that grants the holder specific rights and obligations. If a holder's rights and obligations from an interest are different from another holder's rights and obligations, each holder's interest belongs to a separate class of interest. An individual may hold more than one class of interest in the same partnership provided that each class grants the individual different rights or obligations. The existence of a guaranteed payment described in section 707(c) made to an individual for services rendered to or on behalf of a partnership, however, is not a factor in determining the rights and obligations of a class of interest.

(ii) A *service partner* is a partner who provides services to or on behalf of the service partnership's trade or business. A partner is not considered to be a service partner if that partner only provides a de minimis amount of services to or on behalf of the partnership.

(iii) A *service partnership* is a partnership substantially all the activities of which involve the performance of services in the fields of health, law, engineering, architecture, accounting, actuarial science, or consulting.

(iv) A *substantial interest in a class of interest* is determined based on all of the relevant facts and circumstances. In all cases, however, ownership of 20 percent or more of a specific class of interest is considered substantial.

(i) *Example.* The following example illustrates the principles of paragraphs (g) and (h) of this section:

Example. (i) A, B, and C form LLC, a limited liability company, under the laws of State to engage in a business that is not a service partnership described in paragraph (h)(6)(iii) of this section. LLC, classified as a partnership for federal tax purposes, allocates all items of income, deduction, and credit of LLC to A, B, and C in proportion to their ownership of LLC. A and C each contribute $1x for one LLC unit. B contributes $2x for two LLC units. Each LLC unit entitles its holder to receive 25 percent of LLC's tax items, including profits. A does not perform services for LLC; however, each year B receives a guaranteed payment of $6x for 600 hours of services rendered to LLC and C receives a guaranteed payment of $10x for 1000 hours of services

rendered to LLC. C also is elected LLC's manager. Under State's law, C has the authority to contract on behalf of LLC.

(ii) *Application of general rule of paragraph (h)(2) of this section.* A is treated as a limited partner in LLC under paragraph (h)(2) of this section because A is not liable personally for debts of or claims against LLC, A does not have authority to contract for LLC under State's law, and A does not participate in LLC's trade or business for more than 500 hours during the taxable year. Therefore, A's distributive share attributable to A's LLC unit is excluded from A's net earnings from self-employment under section 1402(a)(13).

(iii) *Distributive share not included in net earnings from self-employment under paragraph (h)(4) of this section.* B's guaranteed payment of $6x is included in B's net earnings from self-employment under section 1402(a)(13). B is not treated as a limited partner under paragraph (h)(2) of this section because, although B is not liable for debts of or claims against LLC and B does not have authority to contract for LLC under State's law, B does participates in LLC's trade or business for more than 500 hours during the taxable year. Further, B is not treated as a limited partner under paragraph (h)(3) of this section because B does not hold more than one class of interest in LLC. However, B is treated as a limited partner under paragraph (h)(4) of this section because B is not treated as a limited partner under paragraph (h)(2) of this section solely because B participated in LLC's business for more than 500 hours and because A is a limited partner under paragraph (h)(2) of this section who owns a substantial interest with rights and obligations that are identical to B's rights and obligations. In this example, B's distributive share is deemed to be a return on B's investment in LLC and not remuneration for B's service to LLC. Thus, B's distributive share attributable to B's two LLC units is not net earnings from self-employment under section 1402(a)(13).

(iv) *Distributive share included in net earnings from self-employment.* C's guaranteed payment of $10x is included in C's net earnings from self-employment under section 1402(a). In addition, C's distributive share attributable to C's LLC unit also is net earnings from self-employment under section 1402(a) because C is not a limited partner under paragraphs (h)(2), (h)(3), or (h)(4) of this section. C is not treated as a limited partner under paragraph (h)(2) of this section because C has the authority under State's law to enter into a binding contract on behalf of LLC and because C participates in LLC's trade or business for more than 500 hours during the taxable year. Further, C is not treated as a limited partner under paragraph (h)(3) of this section because C does not hold more than one class of interest in LLC. Finally, C is not treated as a limited partner under paragraph (h)(4) of this section because C has the power to bind LLC. Thus, C's guaranteed payment and distributive share both are included in C's net earnings from self-employment under section 1402(a).

(j) *Effective date.* Paragraphs (d), (e), (f), (g), (h), and (i) are applicable beginning with the individual's first taxable year beginning on or after the date this section is published as a final regulation in the **Federal Register**.

/s/ Margaret Milner Richardson

Commissioner of Internal Revenue

¶ 20,222

IRS proposed regulations: Business expenses: Expense substantiation.—The IRS has issued proposed regulations by cross-reference to final and temporary regulations. Pursuant to the newly released final and temporary regulations regarding the substantiation of business expenses for travel, entertainment, gift or listed property (CCH PENSION PLAN GUIDE ¶ 11,357G and ¶ 23,932U), receipts or other documentary evidence must be produced to substantiate any lodging costs and any other expenditures of $75 or more. The change in the receipt threshold, from $25 to $75, is effective for expenses incurred on or after October 1, 1995. Comments from the public are requested.

The proposed regulations, which were published in the *Federal Register* on March 25, 1997 (62 FR 14051), are reproduced below.

DEPARTMENT OF THE TREASURY

Internal Revenue Service

26 CFR Part 1

[REG-209785-95]

RIN 1545-AT97

Substantiation of Business Expenses for Travel, Entertainment, Gifts and Listed Property

AGENCY: Internal Revenue Service (IRS), Treasury.

ACTION: Notice of proposed rulemaking by cross-reference to temporary regulations.

SUMMARY: In the Rules and Regulations section of this issue of the Federal Register, the IRS is issuing temporary regulations relating to the substantiation requirements for business expenses for travel, entertainment, gifts, or listed property. The text of those temporary regulations also serves as the text of these proposed regulations.

DATES: Written or electronically generated comments and requests for a public hearing must be received by June 23, 1997.

ADDRESSES: Send submissions to CC:DOM:CORP:R (REG-209785-95), room 5228, Internal Revenue Service, P.O. Box 7604, Ben Franklin Station, Washington, DC 20044. In the alternative, submissions may be hand delivered between the hours of 8 a.m. and 5 p.m. to CC:DOM:CORP:R (REG-209785-95), Courier's Desk, Internal Revenue Service, 1111 Constitution Avenue NW., Washington, DC, or electronically, via the IRS Internet site at: http://www.irs.ustreas.gov/prod/tax—regs/comments.html.

FOR FURTHER INFORMATION CONTACT: Concerning the regulations, contact Donna M. Crisalli, (202) 622-4920; concerning submissions, contact Christina Vasquez, (202) 622-7190 (not toll-free numbers).

SUPPLEMENTARY INFORMATION

Paperwork Reduction Act

The collection of information contained in this notice of proposed rulemaking has been submitted to the Office of Management and Budget for review in accordance with the Paperwork Reduction Act of 1995 (44 U.S.C. 3507). Comments on the collection of information should be sent to the Office of Management and Budget, Attn: Desk Officer for the Department of the Treasury, Office of Information and Regulatory Affairs, Washington, DC 20503, with copies to the Internal Revenue Service, Attn: IRS Reports Clearance Officer, T:FP, Washington, DC 20224. Comments on the collection of information should be received by May 27, 1997.

Comments are specifically requested concerning: Whether the proposed collection of information is necessary for the proper performance of the functions of the Internal Revenue Service, including whether the information will have practical utility;

The accuracy of the estimated burden associated with the proposed collection of information (see below);

How the quality, utility, and clarity of the information to be collected may be enhanced;

How the burden of complying with the proposed collection of information may be minimized, including through the application of automated collection techniques or other forms of information technology; and

Estimates of capital or start-up costs and costs of operation, maintenance, and purchase of service to provide information.

The collection of information in this notice of proposed rulemaking is in Sec. 1.274-5T(c)(2) and (f)(4). This information is required by the IRS as a condition for a taxpayer to deduct certain business expenses or exclude from income certain reimbursed business expenses of employees. This information will be used to determine whether a taxpayer properly qualifies for a deduction or exclusion. The collection of information is required in order to deduct certain business expenses or exclude from income certain reimbursed business expenses of employees. The likely respondents and recordkeepers are individuals, business or other for-profit institutions, state or local governments, federal agencies, and nonprofit institutions.

Estimated total annual reporting and recordkeeping burden: 36,920,000 hours.

The estimated annual burden per respondent or recordkeeper varies from 10 minutes to 20 hours, depending on individual circumstances, with an estimated average of 1.3 hours.

Estimated number of respondents and recordkeepers: 28,400,000.

Estimated annual frequency of responses: On occasion.

An agency may not conduct or sponsor, and a person is not required to respond to, a collection of information unless the collection of information displays a valid control number.

Books or records relating to a collection of information must be retained as long as their contents may become material in the administration of any internal revenue law. Generally, tax returns and tax return information are confidential, as required by 26 U.S.C. 6103.

Special Analyses

It has been determined that this notice of proposed rulemaking is not a significant regulatory action as defined in EO 12866. Therefore, a regulatory assessment is not required. It is hereby certified that these regulations do not have a significant economic impact on a substantial number of small entities. This certification is based on the fact that, by increasing the receipt threshold from $25 to $75, these regulations are expected to reduce the existing recordkeeping requirements of taxpayers, including small entities, from 49,375,000 hours to 36,920,000 hours. The regulations do not otherwise significantly alter the reporting or recordkeeping duties of small entities. Therefore, a Regulatory Flexibility Analysis under the Regulatory Flexibility Act (5 U.S.C. chapter 6) is not required. Pursuant to section 7805(f) of the Internal Revenue Code, this notice of proposed rulemaking will be submitted to the Chief Counsel for Advocacy of the Small Business Administration for comment on its impact on small business.

Comments and Requests for a Public Hearing

Before adopting these proposed regulations as final regulations, consideration will be given to any comments that are submitted timely (and in the manner described in ADDRESSES portion of this preamble) to the IRS. The IRS is considering publishing a revenue procedure implementing Sec. 1.274-5T(f)(4)(ii) of the temporary regulations (that is, prescribing rules under which an employee may make an adequate accounting to his employer by submitting an expense voucher or equivalent without submitting documentary evidence such as receipts) for federal government agencies that use the published procedures. In addition, the IRS is considering whether there are circumstances or conditions under which the IRS could extend these procedures beyond federal government agencies, and requests comments in this regard. The IRS also requests comments on what procedures (such as internal controls) should be required in any rules that permit a taxpayer to satisfy the substantiation requirements of section 274(d) for purposes of deducting business expenses reimbursed to employees who have accounted for their expenses only by means of an expense voucher or equivalent without documentary evidence such as receipts. All comments will be available for public inspection and copying. A public hearing will be scheduled and held upon written request by any person who submits written comments on the proposed rules. Notice of the time and place for the hearing will be published in the Federal Register.

Drafting Information

The principal author of these proposed regulations is Donna M. Crisalli, Office of the Assistant Chief Counsel (Income Tax and Accounting). However, personnel from other offices of the IRS and Treasury Department participated in their development.

List of Subjects in 26 CFR Part 1

Income taxes, Reporting and recordkeeping requirements.

Proposed Amendments to the Regulations

Accordingly, 26 CFR part 1 is proposed to be amended as follows:

PART 1—INCOME TAXES

Paragraph 1. The authority citation for part 1 is amended by adding an entry to read in part as follows:

Authority: 26 U.S.C. 7805 * * *

Section 1.274-5 also issued under 26 U.S.C. 274(d). * * *

Par. 2. Section 1.274-5 is added to read as follows:

Sec. 1.274-5 Substantiation requirements.

(a) through (c)(2)(iii)(A) [Reserved]. For further guidance, see Sec. 1.274-5T.

(c)(2)(iii)(B) [The text of paragraph (c)(2)(iii)(B) is the same as the text in Sec. 1.274-5T published elsewhere in this issue of the Federal Register].

(c)(2)(iv) through (f)(3) [Reserved]. For further guidance, see Sec. 1.274-5T.

(f)(4) through (f)(4)(iii) [The text of paragraphs (f)(4) through (f)(4)(iii) is the same as the text in Sec. 1.274-5T published elsewhere in this issue of the Federal Register].

(f)(5) through (1) [Reserved]. For further guidance, see Sec. 1.274-5T.

Margaret Milner Richardson,

Commissioner of Internal Revenue.

¶ 20,223

IRS proposed regulations: Group insurance: Health insurance plans: Insurance portability.—The IRS has issued notice of proposed rulemaking and a request for comments on temporary regulations relating to health insurance portability for group health plans under the Health Insurance Portability and Accountability Act of 1996 (HIPAA). The IRS temporary regulations are being issued at the same time that substantially similar regulations on group health plan portability, access, and renewability requirements added by HIPAA to ERISA and the Public Health Service Act are being issued by the PWBA and the Health Care Financing Administration. The IRS temporary regulations were finalized on 12/30/04.

The proposed regulations, which were published in the *Federal Register* on April 8, 1997 (62 FR 16977), are reproduced below.

[4830-01-u]

DEPARTMENT OF THE TREASURY

Internal Revenue Service

26 CFR Part 54

[Reg-253578-96]

RIN 1545-AV12

Health Insurance Portability for Group Health Plans

AGENCY: Internal Revenue Service (IRS), Treasury.

ACTION: Notice of proposed rulemaking by cross-reference to temporary regulations.

SUMMARY: Elsewhere in this issue of the **Federal Register**, the IRS is issuing temporary regulations relating to group health plan portability, access, and renewability requirements added to the Internal Revenue Code by section 401 of the Health Insurance Portability and Accountability Act of 1996 (HIPAA). The IRS is issuing the temporary regulations at the same time that the Pension and Welfare Benefits Administration of the U.S. Department of Labor and the Health Care Financing Administration of the U.S. Department of Health and Human Services are issuing substantially similar interim final regulations relating to the group health plan portability, access, and renewability requirements added by HIPAA to the Employee Retirement Income Security Act of 1974 and the Public Health Service Act. The temporary regulations provide guidance to employers and group health plans relating to the obligation of plans to comply with new requirements relating to preexisting condition exclusions, discrimination based on health status, access to coverage, and other requirements. The text of those temporary regulations also serves as the text of these proposed regulations.

DATES: Written comments and requests for a public hearing must be received by July 7, 1997.

ADDRESSES: Send submissions to: CC:DOM:CORP:R (REG-253578-96), room 5226, Internal Revenue Service, POB 7604, Ben Franklin Station, Washington, DC 20044. Submissions may be hand delivered to: CC:DOM:CORP:R (REG-253578-96), room 5226, Internal Revenue Service, 1111 Constitution Avenue, NW, Washington, DC.

Alternatively, taxpayers may submit comments electronically via the Internet by selecting the "Tax Regs" option on the IRS Home Page, or by submitting comments directly to the IRS Internet site at http://www.irs.ustreas.gov/prod/tax_regs/comments.html

FOR FURTHER INFORMATION CONTACT: Concerning the regulations, RUSS WEINHEIMER, (202) 622-4695; concerning submissions or to request a hearing, CHRISTINA D. VASQUEZ, 202-622-7180. These are not toll-free numbers.

SUPPLEMENTARY INFORMATION:

Paperwork Reduction Act

The collection of information referenced in this notice of proposed rulemaking has been submitted to the Office of Management and Budget for review in accordance with the Paperwork Reduction Act of 1995 (44 U.S.C. 3507(d)).

An agency may not conduct or sponsor, and a person is not required to respond to, a collection of information unless it displays a valid control number assigned by the Office of Management and Budget.

The collection of information is in §§ 54.9801-3T, 54.9801-4T, 54.9801-5T, 54.9801-6T, and 54.9806-1T (see the temporary regulations published elsewhere in this issue of the **Federal Register**). This information is required by the statute so that participants will be informed about their rights under HIPAA and about the amount of creditable coverage that they have accrued under a group health plan. The likely respondents are business or other for-profit institutions, nonprofit institutions, small businesses or organizations, and Taft-Hartley trusts. Responses to this collection of information are mandatory.

Books or records relating to a collection of information must be retained as long as their contents may become material in the administration of any internal revenue law. Generally tax returns and tax return information are confidential, as required by 26 U.S.C. 6103.

Comments on the collection of information should be sent to the **Office of Management and Budget**, Attn: Desk Officer for the Department of the Treasury, Office of Information and Regulatory Affairs, Washington, DC 20503, with copies to the **Internal Revenue Service**, Attn: IRS Reports Clearance Officer, T:FP, Washington, DC 20224. Comments on the collection of information should be received by June 8, 1997. Comments are specifically requested concerning:

Whether the proposed collection of information is necessary for the proper performance of the functions of the Internal Revenue Service, including whether the information will have practical utility;

The accuracy of the estimated burden associated with the proposed collection of information (see the preamble to the temporary regulations published elsewhere in this issue of the **Federal Register**);

How to enhance the quality, utility, and clarity of the information to be collected;

How to minimize the burden of complying with the proposed collection of information, including the application of automated collection techniques or other forms of information technology; and

Estimates of capital or start-up costs and costs of operation, maintenance, and purchase of services to provide information.

Background

The temporary regulations published elsewhere in this issue of the **Federal Register** add §§ 54.9801-1T through 54.9801-6T, 54.9802-1T, 54.9804-1T, and 54.9806-1T to the Miscellaneous Excise Tax Regulations. These regulations are being published as part of a joint rulemaking with the Department of Labor and the Department of Health and Human Services (the joint rulemaking).

The text of those temporary regulations also serves as the text of these proposed regulations. The preamble to the temporary regulations explains the temporary regulations.

Special Analyses

Pursuant to sections 603(a) and 605(b) of the Regulatory Flexibility Act, it is hereby certified that the collection of information referenced in this notice of proposed rulemaking (see §§ 54.9801-3T, 54.9801-4T, 54.9801-5T, 54.9801-6T and 54.9806-1T of the temporary regulations published elsewhere in this issue of the Federal Register) will not have a significant economic impact on a substantial number of small entities. Although a substantial number of small entities will be subject to the collection of information requirements in these regulations, the requirements will not have a significant economic impact on these entities. The average time required to complete a certification required under these regulations is estimated to be 5 to 12 minutes for all employers. This average is based on the assumption that most employers will automate the certification process. The paperwork requirements other than certifications that are contained in the regulations are estimated to impose less than 10% of the burden imposed by the certifications. Many small employers that maintain group health plans have their plans administered by an insurance company or third party administrators (TPAs). Most insurers and TPAs are expected to automate the certification process and therefore their average time to produce a certificate should be similar to the 5 to 12 minute average estimated for all employers. However, even for small employers that do not automate the certification process, the collection of information requirements in the regulation will not have a significant impact. Even if it is conservatively assumed that their average time to produce a certificate is 3 times as long as the highest estimate for all employers (i.e., 36 minutes per certificate) and that all of their employees are covered by their group health plan and that half of the employees receive a certificate each year, and this figure is then increased by 10% to account for the paperwork burdens apart from the certifications, the average burden per employee is only 20 minutes per year. Thus, for example, for an employer with 10 employees, the annual burden would be 3 hours and 20 minutes per year. At an estimated cost of $11 per hour, this would result in a cost of less than $37 per year for the employer, which is not a significant economic impact.

This regulation is not subject to the Unfunded Mandates Reform Act of 1995 because the regulation is an interpretive regulation. For further information and for analyses relating to the joint rulemaking, see the preamble to the joint rulemaking. Pursuant to section 7805(f) of the Internal Revenue Code, this notice of proposed rulemaking will be submitted to the Chief Counsel for Advocacy of the Small Business Administration for comment on its impact on small business.

Comments and Requests for a Public Hearing

Before these proposed regulations are adopted as final regulations, consideration will be given to any written comments (a signed original and eight (8) copies) that are submitted timely to the IRS. All comments will be available for public inspection and copying. A public hearing may be scheduled if requested in writing by a person that timely submits written comments. If a public hearing is scheduled, notice of the date, time, and place for the hearing will be published in the **Federal Register**.

Drafting Information

The principal author of these proposed regulations is Russ Weinheimer, Office of the Chief Counsel, Employee Benefits and Exempt Organizations. However, other personnel from the IRS and Treasury Department participated in their development. The proposed regulations, as well as the temporary regulations, have been developed in coordination with personnel from the U.S. Department of Labor and U.S. Department of Health and Human Services.

List of Subjects in 26 CFR Part 54

Excise taxes, Health insurance, Pensions, Reporting and recordkeeping requirements.

Proposed Amendments to the Regulations

Accordingly, 26 CFR part 54 is proposed to be amended as follows:

PART 54—PENSION EXCISE TAXES

Paragraph 1. The authority citation for part 54 is amended by adding entries in numerical order to read as follows:

Authority: 26 U.S.C. 7805 * * *

Section 54.9801-1 is also issued under 26 U.S.C. 9806.

Section 54.9801-2 is also issued under 26 U.S.C. 9806.

Section 54.9801-3 is also issued under 26 U.S.C. 9806.

Section 54.9801-4 is also issued under 26 U.S.C. 9806.

Section 54.9801-5 is also issued under 26 U.S.C. 9801(c)(4), 9801(e)(3), and 9806.

Section 54.9801-6 is also issued under 26 U.S.C. 9806.

Section 54.9802-1 is also issued under 26 U.S.C. 9806.

Section 54.9804-1 is also issued under 26 U.S.C. 9806.

Section 54.9806-1 is also issued under 26 U.S.C. 9806. * * *

Par. 2. Sections 54.9801-1, 54.9801-2, 54.9801-3, 54.9801-4, 54.9801-5, 54.9801-6, 54.9802-1, 54.9804-1, and 54.9806-1 are added to read as follows:

[The text of these proposed sections is the same as the text of §§ 54.9801-1T, 54.9801-2T, 54.9801-3T, 54.9801-4T, 54.9801-5T, 54.9801-6T, 54.9802-1T, 54.9804-1T, and 54.9806-1T published elsewhere in this issue of the **Federal Register**].

Margaret Milner Richardson

Commissioner of Internal Revenue

[FR Doc. 97-8267 Filed 4-1-97; 12:48 p.m.]

¶ 20,224

IRS proposed regulations: Residency of trusts: Foreign trusts: Domestic trusts: Exclusions.—The IRS has issued a notice of proposed rulemaking and a request for comments on proposed regulations affecting the determination of the residency of trusts for federal tax purposes. The proposed regulations provide a safe harbor for determining if a trust is foreign or domestic based on which court exercises primary supervision authority over administration (court test), and define key terms for determining the residency of trusts based on the residency of fiduciaries with authority to control substantial decisions of the trust (control test). The proposed regulations reflect changes to the law made by the Small Business Job Protection Act of 1996.

The proposed regulations were published in the *Federal Register* on June 5, 1997 (62 FR 30796).

The final regulations were issued on February 2, 1999 (64 FR 4976). The regulations are reproduced at ¶ 13,925 (IRS Reg. Sec. 301.7701-5) and ¶ 13,927 (IRS Reg. Sec. 301.7701-7). The text of the preamble is reproduced at ¶ 23,950V.

¶ 20,225

IRS proposed regulations: Plan amendments: Elimination of optional form of benefit: Age 70 ½ distribution.—The proposed regulations would provide relief from Code Sec. 411(d)(6) for certain plan amendments that eliminate preretirement distribution options commencing after age 70 1/2.

The proposed regulations, which were published in the Federal Register on July 2, 1997 (62 FR 35752).

The regulations were finalized June 5, 1998 (63 FR 30621). The regulations are reproduced at ¶ 12,233. The preamble is reproduced at ¶ 23,943D.

¶ 20,226

IRS proposed regulations: Remedial amendment period: Disqualifying provisions.—The IRS has issued proposed regulations regarding the remedial amendment period. Under the regulations, the IRS Commissioner will have the authority to designate a plan provision as a disqualifying provision in certain circumstances and will be able to impose limits and additional rules pertaining to amendments that may be made during the remedial amendment period.

The final regulations were issued on February 4, 2000 (65 FR 5432). The proposed regulations, which were published in the *Federal Register* on August 1, 1997 (62 FR 41274), are reproduced below. The proposed regs were also issued as final and temporary regs and are reproduced at ¶ 11,721 and ¶ 11,722, respectively. The preamble to the final and temporary regulations is at ¶ 23,935Y.

¶ 20,227

IRS proposed regulations: Cafeteria plans: Election of coverage: Revocation of election: Health Insurance Portability and Accountability Act of 1996 (HIPAA).—Reproduced below is the text of proposed regulations that amend portions of previously issued proposed regulations (¶ 20,118I and ¶ 20,137Q) concerning the circumstances under which a cafeteria plan participant may revoke an existing election and make a new election during a period of coverage. The proposed regulations permit a cafeteria plan to allow an employee, during a plan year, to change his or her health coverage election to conform with special enrollment rights provided under the Health Insurance Portability and Accountability Act of 1996 (HIPAA) and for a variety of other "changes in status."

The proposed regulations were published in the *Federal Register* on November 7, 1997 (62 FR 60196). The IRS temporary regulations, which also serve as the text of the proposed regulations, are reproduced at ¶ 11,288E. The preamble to the temporary regulations is at ¶ 23,938P. Note: Q-6 and Q-8 have been republished and A-6(b)(2), A-6(c), A-6(d) and A-8 have been amended in proposed regulations reproduced at ¶ 20,247.

DEPARTMENT OF THE TREASURY

Internal Revenue Service

26 CFR Part 1

[REG-243025-96]

RIN 1545-AU61

Tax Treatment of Cafeteria Plans

AGENCY: Internal Revenue Service (IRS), Treasury

ACTION: Partial withdrawal of notice of proposed rulemaking, amendment to notice of proposed rulemaking, and notice of proposed rulemaking by cross reference to temporary regulations. SUMMARY: This document withdraws portions of the notice of proposed rulemaking published in the **Federal Register** (54 FR 9460) on March 7, 1989 and amends proposed regulations relating to changes in family status. In the Rules and Regulations section of this issue of the **Federal Register**, the IRS is issuing temporary regulations that provide guidance on the circumstances under which a cafeteria plan participant may revoke an existing election and make a new election during a period of coverage. The text of those temporary regulations also serves as the text of these proposed regulations.

DATES: Written comments and requests for a public hearing must be received by February 5, 1998.

ADDRESSES: Send submissions to: CC:DOM:CORP:R (REG-243025-96), room 5226, Internal Revenue Service, POB 7604, Ben Franklin Station, Washington, DC 20044. Submissions may be hand delivered between the hours of 8 a.m. and 5 p.m. to: CC:DOM:CORP:R (REG243025-96), Courier's Desk, Internal Revenue Service, 1111 Constitution Avenue NW, Washington, DC. Alternatively, taxpayers may submit comments electronically via the internet by selecting the "Tax Regs" option on the IRS Home Page, or by submitting comments directly to the IRS internet site at http://www.irs.ustreas.gov/prod/tax regs/comments.html.

FOR FURTHER INFORMATION CONTACT: Concerning the regulations, Sharon Cohen, (202) 622-6080; concerning submissions or to request a public hearing, Evangelista Lee, (202) 622-7190 (not toll-free numbers).

SUPPLEMENTARY INFORMATION:

Background

Q&A-8 of § 1.125-1[1] and Q&A-6(c) and (d) of § 1.125-2[2] provide that a participant may make benefit election changes pursuant to changes in family status and separation from service. The temporary regulations set forth the standards under which a cafeteria plan can allow an employee to change his or her health coverage election during a period of coverage to conform with the special enrollment rights under the Health Insurance Portability and Accountability Act of 1996, and to change his or her health coverage or group-term life insurance coverage in a variety of other change in status situations. Thus, these proposed regulations modify Q&A-8 of § 1.125-1 and Q&A-6(c) and (d) of § 1.125-2, and clarify that the "change in family status rules" in the existing proposed regulations continue to apply to qualified benefits (including dependent care assistance under section 129 and adoption assistance under section 137) other than accident or health coverage and group-term life insurance coverage. Election changes continue to be permitted where there has been a significant change in the health coverage of the employee or spouse attributable to the spouses's employment.

In addition, the temporary regulations provide that the rules of section 401(k) and (m), rather than the rules in the temporary regulations that apply to other qualified benefits, govern election changes under a qualified cash or deferred arrangement (within the meaning of section 401(k)) or with respect to employee contributions under section 401(m). Therefore, the proposed regulations withdraw Q&A-6(f) of § 1.125-2.

Temporary regulations in the Rules and Regulations section of this issue of the **Federal Register** amend the Income Tax Regulations (26 CFR part 1) relating to section 125. The temporary regulations contain rules relating to the circumstances under which a cafeteria plan participant may revoke an existing election and make a new election during a period of coverage.

The text of those temporary regulations also serves as the text of these proposed regulations. The preamble to the temporary regulations explains the temporary regulations.

Special Analyses

It has been determined that this Treasury Decision is not a significant regulatory action as defined in EO 12866. Therefore, a regulatory assessment is not required. It also has been determined that section 553(b) of the Administrative Procedure Act (5 U.S.C. chapter 5) do not apply to these regulations, and because the regulations does not impose a collection of information on small entities, the Regulatory Flexibility Act (5 U.S.C. chapter 6) does not apply. Pursuant to section 7805(f) of the Internal Revenue Code, proposed regulations will be submitted to the Chief Counsel for Advocacy of the Small Business Administration for comment on their impact on small business.

Comments and Public Hearing

Before these proposed regulations are adopted as final regulations, consideration will be given to any written comments (a signed original and eight (8) copies) that are submitted timely to the IRS. All comments will be available for public inspection and copying. A public hearing may be scheduled if requested in writing by any person that timely submits written comments. If a public hearing is scheduled, notice of the date, time, and place for the hearing will be published in the **Federal Register**.

Drafting Information

The principal authors of these regulations are Catherine Fuller and Sharon Cohen, Office of the Associate Chief Counsel (Employee Benefits and Exempt Organizations). However, other personnel from the IRS and Treasury Department participated in their development.

Partial withdrawal of Notice of Proposed Rulemaking

Accordingly, under the authority of 26 U.S.C. 7805, § 1.125-2 Q&A-6(f) in the notice of proposed rulemaking that was published on March 7, 1989 (54 FR 9460) is withdrawn.

List of Subjects in 26 CFR Part 1

Income taxes, reporting and recordkeeping requirements.

Amendments to Previously Proposed Rules

Accordingly, the proposed rules published on May 7, 1984 (49 FR 19321) and March 7, 1989 (54 FR 9460) are amended as follows:

PART 1—INCOME TAXES

Paragraph 1. In § 1.125-1, as proposed May 7, 1984 (49 FR 19321), in Q&A-8, Q-8 is republished and A-8 is amended by revising the last sentence to read as follows:

§ 1.125-1 Questions and answers relating to cafeteria plan.

* * * * *

Q-8: What requirements apply to participants' elections under a cafeteria plan?

A-8: * * * However, except for benefit elections relating to accident or health plans and group-term life insurance coverage, a cafeteria plan may permit a participant to revoke a benefit election after the period of coverage has commenced and to make a new election with respect to the remainder of the period of coverage if both the revocation and the new election are on account of and consistent with a change in family status (e.g., marriage, divorce, death of spouse or child, birth or adoption of child, and termination of employment of spouse).

* * * * *

Par. 2. In § 1.125-2, as proposed March 7, 1989 (54 FR 9460), in Q&A-6, Q-6 is republished and A-6 is amended by revising A-6(c) and (d) to read as follows:

§ 1.125-2 Miscellaneous cafeteria plan questions and answers.

* * * * *

Q-6: In what circumstance may participants revoke existing elections and make new elections under a cafeteria plan?

A-6: * * *

* * * * *

(c) *Certain Changes in Family Status.* Except as otherwise provided, in the case of benefits other than accident or health plan coverage and group-term life insurance coverage, a cafeteria plan may permit a participant to revoke a benefit election during a period of coverage and to make a new election for the remaining portion of the period if the revocation and new election are both on account of a change in family

[1] Published as a proposed rule at 49 FR 19321 (May 7, 1984).

[2] Published as a proposed rule at 54 FR 9460 (March 7, 1989)

status and are consistent with such change in family status. For purposes of this paragraph (c) of Q&A-6, examples of changes in family status for which a benefit election change may be permitted include the marriage or divorce of the employee, the death of the employee's spouse or a dependent, the birth or adoption of a child of the employee, the termination of employment (or the commencement of employment) of the employee's spouse, the switching from part-time to full-time employment status or from full-time to part-time status by the employee or the employee's spouse, and the taking of an unpaid leave of absence by the employee or the employee's spouse. Benefit election changes are consistent with family status changes only if the election changes are necessary or appropriate as a result of the family status changes. In the case of accident or health plans, election changes are permitted where there has been a significant change in the health coverage of the employee or spouse attributable to the spouse's employment. For additional rules governing cafeteria plan election changes with respect to accident or health plan coverage and group-term life insurance coverage, see § 1.125-4T.

(d) *Separation from Service*. Except with respect to accident or health plan coverage and group-term life insurance coverage, a cafeteria plan may permit an employee who separates from the service of the employer during a period of coverage to revoke existing benefit elections

and terminate the receipt of benefits for the remaining portion for the coverage period. The plan must prohibit the employee, if the employee should return to service for the employer, from making new benefit elections for the remaining portion of the period of coverage. For rules governing cafeteria plan election changes with respect to accident or health plan coverage and group-term life insurance coverage, see § 1.125-4T.

* * * * *

Proposed Amendments to the Regulations

In addition, 26 CFR part 1 is proposed to be amended as follows:

PART 1—INCOME TAX

Paragraph 1. The authority for part 1 continues to read in part as follows:

Authority: 26 U.S.C. 7805 * * *

Par. 2. Section 1.125-4 is added to read as follows:

[The text of this proposed section is the same as the text of § 1.125-4T published elsewhere in this issue of the **Federal Register** (see CCH PENSION PLAN GUIDE ¶ 11,288E).]

¶ 20,228

IRS proposed regulations: Mental Health Parity Act (MHPA): Mental health benefits: Medical/surgical benefits.—The IRS has issued a notice of proposed rulemaking and a request for comments on temporary regulations providing guidance to employers and group health plans relating to the new mental health parity rules, which were added to the Code by the Taxpayer Relief Act of 1997. The IRS temporary regulations, which are generally effective January 1, 1998, are being issued at the same time that the Department of Labor and the Department of Health and Human Services are issuing substantially similar regulations relating to mental health parity requirements added to ERISA and the Public Health Service Act by MHPA.

The proposed regulations, which were published in the *Federal Register* on December 22, 1997 (62 FR 66967), are reproduced below. The preamble to the IRS temporary regulations is at ¶ 23,939M, and the temporary regulations are at ¶ 13,968Q-10, ¶ 13,968Q-12, ¶ 13,968Q-16, ¶ 13,968Q-18, ¶ 13,968W-10, ¶ 13,968Y-10, ¶ 13,968U-10, and ¶ 15,050K-1.

DEPARTMENT OF THE TREASURY

Internal Revenue Service

26 CFR Part 54

[Reg-109704-97]

RIN 1545-AV12

HIPAA Mental Health Parity Act

AGENCY: Internal Revenue Service (IRS), Treasury.

ACTION: Notice of proposed rulemaking by cross-reference to temporary regulations.

SUMMARY: Elsewhere in this issue of the **Federal Register**, the IRS is issuing temporary regulations relating to mental health parity requirements imposed on group health plans. These requirements were added to the Internal Revenue Code by section 1532 of the Taxpayer Relief Act of 1997. The IRS is issuing the temporary regulations at the same time that the Pension and Welfare Benefits Administration of the U.S. Department of Labor and the Health Care Financing Administration of the U.S. Department of Health and Human Services are issuing substantially similar interim final regulations relating to mental health parity requirements added by the Mental Health Parity Act of 1996 to the Employee Retirement Income Security Act of 1974 and the Public Health Service Act. The temporary regulations provide guidance to employers and group health plans relating to the new mental health parity requirements. The text of those temporary regulations also serves as the text of these proposed regulations.

DATES: Written comments and requests for a public hearing must be received by March 23, 1998.

ADDRESSES: Send submissions to: CC:DOM:CORP:R (REG-109704-97), room 5226, Internal Revenue Service, POB 7604, Ben Franklin Station, Washington, DC 20044. Submissions may be hand-delivered between the hours of 8 a.m. and 5 p.m. to: CC:DOM:CORP:R (REG-109704-97), Courier's Desk, Internal Revenue Service, 1111 Constitution Avenue, NW, Washington, DC. Alternatively, taxpayers may submit comments electronically via the Internet by selecting the "Tax Regs" option on the IRS Home Page, or by submitting comments directly to the IRS Internet site at: http://www.irs.ustreas.gov/prod/tax_regs/comments.html

FOR FURTHER INFORMATION CONTACT: Concerning the regulations, Russ Weinheimer, (202) 622-4695; concerning submissions or to request a hearing, Mike Slaughter, 202-622-7180. These are not toll-free numbers.

SUPPLEMENTARY INFORMATION:

Paperwork Reduction Act

The collection of information referenced in this notice of proposed rulemaking has been submitted to the Office of Management and Budget for review in accordance with the Paperwork Reduction Act of 1995 (44 U.S.C. 3507(d)).

An agency may not conduct or sponsor, and a person is not required to respond to, a collection of information unless it displays a valid control number assigned by the Office of Management and Budget.

The collection of information is in § 54.9812-1T (see the temporary regulations published elsewhere in this issue of the **Federal Register**). The collection of information is required if a plan wishes to avail itself of an exemption provided under the statute. The likely respondents are business or other for-profit institutions, nonprofit institutions, small businesses or organizations, and Taft-Hartley trusts. Responses to this collection of information are required in order to obtain the benefit of being exempt from the mental health parity requirement.

Books or records relating to a collection of information must be retained as long as their contents may become material in the administration of any internal revenue law. Generally tax returns and tax return information are confidential, as required by 26 U.S.C. 6103.

Comments on the collection of information should be sent to the **Office of Management and Budget**, Attn: Desk Officer for the Department of the Treasury, Office of Information and Regulatory Affairs, Washington, DC 20503, with copies to the **Internal Revenue Service**, Attn: IRS Reports Clearance Officer, T:FP, Washington, DC 20224. Comments on the collection of information should be received by February 20, 1998. Comments are specifically requested concerning:

—Whether the proposed collection of information is necessary for the proper performance of the functions of the Internal Revenue Service, including whether the information will have practical utility;

—The accuracy of the estimated burden associated with the proposed collection of information (see the preamble to the temporary regulations published elsewhere in this issue of the **Federal Register**);

—How to enhance the quality, utility, and clarity of the information to be collected;

—How to minimize the burden of complying with the proposed collection of information, including the application of automated collection techniques or other forms of information technology; and

—Estimates of capital or start-up costs and costs of operation, maintenance, and purchase of services to provide information.

Background

The temporary regulations published elsewhere in this issue of the **Federal Register** add § 54.9812-1T to the Miscellaneous Excise Tax Regulations. These regulations are being published as part of a joint rulemaking with the Department of Labor and the Department of Health and Human Services (the joint rulemaking).

The text of those temporary regulations also serves as the text of these proposed regulations. The preamble to the temporary regulations explains the temporary regulations.

Special Analyses

Pursuant to sections 603(a) and 605(b) of the Regulatory Flexibility Act, it is hereby certified that the collection of information referenced in this notice of proposed rulemaking (see § 54.9812-1T of the temporary regulations published elsewhere in this issue of the **Federal Register**) will not have a significant economic impact on a substantial number of small entities. Employers with 50 or fewer employees are not subject to the law. Moreover, even for employers that are subject to the mental health parity requirements, no collection of information is required unless they qualify for and claim the 1% increased cost exemption. Even for employers subject to the law who claim the exemption, the estimated time for each response is 2 minutes. Thus, for example, an employer with 100 employees in its group health plan that claimed the 1% increased cost exemption, that took advantage of the three-month transitional period provided in the temporary regulations and that received 10 requests to examine the assumptions used in claiming the exemption would incur a total one-time burden of less than 4 hours. At an estimated cost of $11 per hour, this would result in a one-time cost of less than $44. This is not a significant economic impact.

This regulation is not subject to the Unfunded Mandates Reform Act of 1995 because the regulation is an interpretive regulation. For further information and for analyses relating to the joint rulemaking, see the preamble to the joint rulemaking. Pursuant to section 7805(f) of the Internal Revenue Code, this notice of proposed rulemaking will be submitted to the Chief Counsel for Advocacy of the Small Business Administration for comment on its impact on small business.

Comments and Requests for a Public Hearing

Before these proposed regulations are adopted as final regulations, consideration will be given to any written comments (a signed original and eight (8) copies) that are submitted timely to the IRS. All comments will be available for public inspection and copying. A public hearing may be scheduled if requested in writing by a person that timely submits written comments. If a public hearing is scheduled, notice of the date, time, and place for the hearing will be published in the **Federal Register**.

Drafting Information

The principal author of these proposed regulations is Russ Weinheimer, Office of the Chief Counsel, Employee Benefits and Exempt Organizations. However, other personnel from the IRS and Treasury Department participated in their development. The proposed regulations, as well as the temporary regulations, have been developed in coordination with personnel from the U.S. Department of Labor and U.S. Department of Health and Human Services.

List of Subjects in 26 CFR Part 54

Excise taxes, Health insurance, Pensions, Reporting and recordkeeping requirements.

Proposed Amendments to the Regulations

Accordingly, 26 CFR part 54 is proposed to be amended as follows:

PART 54—PENSION EXCISE TAXES

Paragraph 1. The authority citation for part 54 is amended by adding an entry in numerical order to read as follows:

Authority: 26 U.S.C. 7805 ***

Section 54.9812-1 is also issued under 26 U.S.C. 9833. ***

Par. 2. Section 54.9812-1 is added to read as follows:

§ 54.9812-1 Parity in the application of certain limits to mental health benefits.

[The text of this proposed section is the same as the text of § 54.9812-1T published elsewhere in this issue of the **Federal Register**].

Deputy Commissioner of Internal Revenue

¶ 20,229

IRS proposed regulations: Nonqualified deferred compensation: FICA contributions: FUTA contributions.—The IRS has issued revisions to proposed regulations under Code Sec. 3121(v)(2) and Code Sec. 3306(r)(2) relating to when amounts deferred under or paid from certain nonqualified deferred compensation plans are taken into account as "wages" for purposes of taxes imposed by the Federal Insurance Contributions Act (FICA) and the Federal Unemployment Tax Act (FUTA), respectively. The original proposed regulations were published in the *Federal Register* on January 25, 1996 (CCH PENSION PLAN GUIDE, ¶ 20,214 and ¶ 20,215), with a proposed general effective date of January 1, 1997. The new notice of proposed rulemaking extends the proposed general effective date for both proposed regulations to January 1, 1998.

The proposed revised regulations, which were published in the *Federal Register* on December 24, 1997 (62 FR 67304).

Final FICA and FUTA regulations were published in the *Federal Register* on January 29, 1999 (64 FR 4542 and 64 FR 4540, respectively). For FICA, the regulations are reproduced at ¶ 13,534T and ¶ 13,534U, and the preamble is at ¶ 23,950S. For FUTA, the regulations are reproduced at ¶ 13,541K and the preamble is at ¶ 23,950T.

¶ 20,230

IRS proposed regulations: Loans from qualified plans: Deemed distributions: Code Sec. 72(p).—The IRS has issued proposed amendments to existing proposed regulations (CCH PENSION PLAN GUIDE ¶ 20,210) that would provide additional guidance concerning the tax treatment of loans from qualified plans to participants that are deemed distributions under Code Sec. 72(p). Under the proposed amended regulations, interest that accrued on the loan would not be included in income and neither the loan nor the interest would increase the participant's tax basis for purposes of Code Sec. 72. Cash repayments made after the loan was deemed distributed would increase the participant's tax basis in the same manner as if the repayments were after-tax contributions.

The regulations are proposed to become effective for loans made on or after the first January 1 that is at least 6 months after the date the regulations are published as final regulations in the *Federal Register*. The original proposed regulations were amended to reflect the same proposed effective date. Taxpayers may rely on the proposed amended regulations for guidance pending the issuance of final regulations.

The proposed regulations, which were published in the *Federal Register* on January 2, 1998 (62 FR 42), are reproduced below.

The regulations were finalized by T.D. 8894 and published in the *Federal Register* on July 31, 2000 (65 FR 46588). The regulations are reproduced at ¶ 11,207A and ¶ 11,210. The preamble is reproduced at ¶ 24,505S.

¶ 20,231

IRS proposed regulations: Continuation coverage of group health plans: Disabled beneficiaries: Children: Long-term care services: Medical Savings Accounts (MSAs).—The IRS has issued proposed regulations to provide guidance under Code Sec. 4980B on law changes made by the Health Portability and Accountability Act of 1996 (HIPAA), the Technical and Miscellaneous Revenue Act of 1988 (TAMRA), and the Omnibus Budget Reconciliation Act of 1989 (OBRA '89), relating to the continuation coverage requirements applicable to group health plans. The proposed regulations clarify the disability extension requirements, the maximum coverage period for newborn and adopted children, the method for determining qualified long-term care services, and the continuation coverage applicable to medical savings accounts.

The proposed regulations, which were published in the *Federal Register* on January 7, 1998 (63 FR 708), were adopted on February 3, 1999 by T.D. 8812 (64 FR 5160). Reg. Secs. 54.4980B-0 through 54.4980B-8 were amended, and Reg. Secs. 54.4980B-9 and 54.4980B-10 were added by T.D. 8928 on January 10, 2001 (66 FR 1843). The preamble to the final regulations is reproduced at ¶ 24,505Y. The regs are reproduced at ¶ 13,648W-5— ¶ 13,648W-15.

¶ 20,232

IRS proposed regulations: Widely held fixed investment trust: Tax Exempt organizations: Individual retirement plan: Reporting requirements.—The IRS has issued proposed regulations that define widely held fixed investment trusts and clarify the reporting requirements of trustees and middlemen of these trusts to ensure that beneficial owners of trust interests receive accurate and timely tax reporting information. Information reporting generally is not required for interests held by exempt recipients such as individual retirement plans and organizations that are exempt from taxation under Code Sec. 501(a). However, the proposed regulations provide that exempt recipients may request tax information for a calendar quarter, computed as of the last day of the quarter specified, or for a calendar year, computed as of December 31 of the year specified.

The proposed regulations and excerpts of the preamble, which appeared in the *Federal Register* on August 13, 1998 (63 FR 43354), are reproduced below.

DEPARTMENT OF THE TREASURY

Internal Revenue Service

26 CFR Parts 1 and 301

[REG-209813-96]

RIN 1545-AU15

Reporting Requirements for Widely Held Fixed Investment Trusts

AGENCY: Internal Revenue Service (IRS), Treasury

ACTION: Notice of proposed rulemaking and notice of public hearing.

SUMMARY: This document contains proposed regulations that define widely held fixed investment trusts, clarify the reporting obligations of the trustees of these trusts and the middlemen connected with these trusts, and provide for the communication of necessary tax information to beneficial owners of trust interests. This document also provides notice of a public hearing on these proposed regulations.

DATES: Written comments must be received by [*INSERT DATE 90 DAYS AFTER PUBLICATION OF THIS DOCUMENT IN THE FEDERAL REGISTER*]. Requests to speak (with outlines of oral comments) at a public hearing scheduled for Thursday, November 5, 1998 at 10 a.m. must be submitted by October 15, 1998.

ADDRESSES: Send submissions to: CC:DOM:CORP:R (REG-209813-96), room 5228, Internal Revenue Service, POB 7604, Ben Franklin Station, Washington, DC 20044. In the alternative, submissions may be hand delivered between the hours of 8 a.m. and 5 p.m. to: CC:DOM:CORP:R (REG-209813-96), Courier's Desk, Internal Revenue Building, 1111 Constitution Avenue, NW., Washington, DC. Alternatively, taxpayers may submit comments electronically via the Internet by selecting the "Tax Regs" option on the IRS Home Page, or by submitting comments directly to the IRS Internet site at http://www.irs.ustreas.gov/prod/tax_regs/comments.html. The public hearing will be held in room 2615, Internal Revenue Building, 1111 Constitution Avenue, NW., Washington, DC.

FOR FURTHER INFORMATION CONTACT: Concerning the regulations, Faith Colson, (202) 622-3060; concerning submissions and the hearing, LaNita Van Dyke, (202) 622-7180 (not toll-free numbers).

SUPPLEMENTARY INFORMATION:

Paperwork Reduction Act

The collection of information contained in this notice of proposed rulemaking has been submitted to the Office of Management and Budget for review in accordance with the Paperwork Reduction Act of 1995 (44 U.S.C. 3507(d)). Comments on the collection of information should be sent to the **Office of Management and Budget,** Attn: Desk Officer for the Department of Treasury, Office of Information and Regulatory Affairs, Washington, DC 20503, with copies to the **Internal Revenue Service,** Attn: IRS Reports Clearance Officer, OP:FS:FP, Washington, DC 20224. Comments on the collection of information should be received by [*INSERT DATE 60 DAYS AFTER PUBLICA-TION OF THIS DOCUMENT IN THE FEDERAL REGISTER*]. Comments are specifically requested concerning:

Whether the proposed collection of information is necessary for the proper performance of the functions of the **Internal Revenue Service,** including whether the information will have practical utility;

The accuracy of the estimated burden associated with the proposed collection of information (see below);

How the quality, utility, and clarity of the information to be collected may be enhanced;

How the burden of complying with the proposed collection of information may be minimized, including through the application of auto-mated collection techniques or other forms of information technology; and

Estimates of capital or start-up costs and costs of operation, mainte-nance, and purchase of service to provide information.

The collection of information in these proposed regulations is in § 1.671-4 of the Income Tax Regulations. This information is required to enable holders of trust interests to report items of income, deduction, and credit of a widely held fixed investment trust under section 671. This information will be used by the IRS to ensure that those items are reported accurately by beneficial owners of trust interests. The collec-tion of information is mandatory. The likely respondents are businesses and other for-profit institutions.

Estimated total annual reporting burden: 2,400 hours.

Estimated average annual burden hours per respondent: 2 hours.

Estimated number of respondents: 1,200.

Estimated annual frequency of responses: Annually (but more often for a trust providing information to certain persons on request).

An agency may not conduct or sponsor, and a person is not required to respond to, a collection of information unless it displays a valid control number assigned by the Office of Management and Budget.

Books or records relating to the collection of information must be retained as long as their contents may become material in the adminis-tration of any internal revenue law. Generally, tax returns and tax return information are confidential, as required by 26 U.S.C. 6103.

Background

This document contains proposed amendments to the Income Tax Regulations (26 CFR part 1) under section 671. The proposed amend-ments are to be issued under the authority of sections 671, 6034A, 6049(d)(7), and 7805.

A fixed investment trust is an arrangement classified as a trust under § 301.7701-4(c). Beneficial interests in these trusts are divided into units. The Service treats these trusts as grantor trusts under section 671 and the owners of the beneficial interests, or units, as the grantors. See Rev. Rul. 84-10 (1984-1 C.B. 155); Rev. Rul. 70-545 (1970-2 C.B. 7); Rev. Rul. 70-544 (1970-2 C.B. 6); Rev. Rul. 61-175 (1961-2 C.B. 128). Under the proposed regulations, a *widely held fixed investment trust* is a fixed investment trust in which any interest is held by a middleman. For this purpose, the term *middleman* includes, but is not limited to, a custodian of a person's account, a nominee, and a broker holding an interest for a customer in street name. The IRS and Treasury request comments on the application and scope of these definitions, including the appropriateness of a de minimis rule as to the number of middlemen.

Interests in widely held fixed investment trusts are often held in the street name of a middleman, who holds such interests on behalf of the beneficial owners. Thus, trustees frequently do not know the identity of the beneficial owners and are not in a position to communicate necessary tax information directly to such owners. Currently, there are no tax information reporting rules specifically providing for the sharing of tax information among trustees, middlemen, and beneficial owners of these trusts.

On December 21, 1995, final regulations (TD 8633) under section 671, relating to the information reporting requirements of grantor trusts, were published in the **Federal Register** (60 FR 66085). See § 1.671-4. While drafting the final regulations, the IRS and Treasury concluded that special reporting requirements were needed for widely held fixed investment trusts but that such guidance fell outside the scope of the final regulations. The preamble to the final regulations stated that the IRS and Treasury anticipated providing guidance for these trusts in a separate project and invited comments from interested taxpayers and practitioners regarding such guidance.

In developing these proposed regulations, the IRS and Treasury have continued to solicit comments from the public. Comments were received from various industry members and practitioners, and these proposed regulations take such comments into account. The proposed regulations are intended to clarify the reporting requirements of trustees and middlemen and to ensure that beneficial owners of trust interests receive accurate and timely tax reporting information. The IRS and Treasury welcome comments on specific instances of industry practice that differ significantly from the framework of these proposed regulations and on suggestions to tailor the reporting requirements to account for those differences.

Explanation of Provisions

A. *General Framework of Reporting Rules*

The information reporting framework in the proposed regulations is similar to that for regular interests in a real estate mortgage investment conduit. See § 1.6049-7.

Under the proposed regulations, the responsibility for information reporting lies primarily with the person in the ownership chain who holds a unit interest for a beneficial owner and is, therefore, in the best position to communicate with, and provide tax information to, the beneficial owner. Thus, a brokerage firm that holds a unit interest directly for an individual as a middleman will have the primary obligation to report to the IRS and to provide tax information to the individual. Similarly, if a unit interest is held directly by an individual and not through a middleman, the trustee is to report to the IRS and to provide tax information to the individual. Information reporting generally is not required for interests held by *exempt recipients*. Middlemen and trustees, however, are to make trust tax information available upon request to exempt recipients.

Appropriate adjustments may be necessary to other information reporting rules to make them compatible with these proposed regulations.

B. *Trustee or Middleman to Report to the IRS on Form 1099*

Under proposed § 1.671-4 (j) (2) (i) (A), a trustee must report to the IRS, on the appropriate Forms 1099, the gross amount of trust income (determined in accordance with proposed § 1.671-4 (j) (6) (i)) attributable to a unit interest holder who holds an interest in the trust directly and not through a middleman. Similarly, under proposed § 1.671-4 (j) (2) (i) (B), a middleman must report for any unit interest holder on whose behalf or account the middleman holds an interest. (To comply with this requirement, middlemen may request the necessary tax information from the trustee. See the discussion below.) In addition, the trustee or middleman is to report on the appropriate Form 1099 the gross proceeds from the sale or other disposition of a trust asset that is attributable to the unit interest holder. Forms 1099 are not required for any unit interest holder who is an *exempt recipient*, as defined in proposed § 1.671-4 (j) (1).

C. *Statements to be Furnished to the Beneficial Owners of Unit Interests*

Every middleman or trustee required to file with the IRS a Form 1099 under these proposed regulations for a unit interest holder must furnish to the unit interest holder a written statement providing the holder with necessary tax reporting information including: (1) the items of income (determined in accordance with proposed § 1.671-4 (j) (6) (i)), deduction, and credit of the trust attributable to the unit interest holder; (2) if any trust asset has been sold or otherwise disposed of during the calendar year, the portion of the gross proceeds relating to the trust asset which is attributable to the unit interest holder, the date of sale or disposition of the trust asset, and the percentage of that trust asset that has been sold or disposed of; and (3) any other information necessary for the unit interest holder to accu-

rately report the income, deductions, and credits of the trust attributable to the unit interest as required under section 671.

In addition, to enable unit interest holders to calculate gain or loss on the disposition of a trust asset, if a trust sells or disposes of a trust asset during a particular calendar year, the proposed regulations require the trustee or middleman to include, with the statement to the holder, a schedule showing the portion (expressed as a percentage) of the total fair market value of all the assets held by the trust that the trust asset sold or disposed of represented as of the last day of each quarter that the asset was held by the trust. It is contemplated that, in the absence of more accurate information, this information may be used by the unit interest holder to determine the percentage of the holder's basis in its unit interest that the disposed asset represents, so that the holder may calculate its gain or loss on the disposition of the asset.

The IRS and Treasury welcome comments on whether the approach taken in the proposed regulations to communicate information to enable the holder of a unit interest to calculate its basis in a trust asset is effective, or whether a different approach, which continues to be consistent with the taxation of grantor trusts, would be more effective. In addition, the IRS and Treasury invite comments on whether, for trusts consisting of fungible assets, an approach other than the proposed asset-by-asset approach for reporting sales and determining basis is administratively feasible or whether an aggregate approach would be more appropriate and on the manner in which such an aggregate approach would be applied.

D. *Information to be Furnished to Middlemen by Trusts*

In general, information reporting is not required for unit interests held by *exempt recipients*. To enable such persons to receive necessary trust information, however, § 1.671-4 (j) (3) (iii) of the proposed regulations provides that middlemen, exempt recipients, and certain other persons may request from the trust tax information for a calendar quarter, computed as of the last day of the quarter specified, or for a calendar year, computed as of December 31 of the year specified. The tax reporting information the trust is to make available includes: (1) all items of income (determined in accordance with proposed § 1.671-4 (j) (6) (i)), deduction, and credit of the trust for the period specified; (2) if any trust asset has been sold or otherwise disposed of during the period specified, the gross proceeds received by the trust for the trust asset, the date of sale or disposition, and the percentage of that trust asset that has been sold or disposed of; (3) the number of units outstanding on the last business day of the period specified; and (4) any other information necessary for the unit interest holder to accurately report the income, deductions, and credits attributable to the portion of the trust treated as owned by the holder, as required under section 671. In addition, if a trust asset is sold or otherwise disposed of during the period specified, the trust must provide a schedule showing the portion (expressed in terms of a percentage) of the total fair market value of all the assets held by the trust that the asset sold or disposed of represented as of the last day of each calendar quarter that the trust held the asset.

E. *Special Rules*

A beneficial owner of a unit interest must report trust items consistent with the owner's method of accounting. See, e.g., Rev. Rul. 84-10. For administrative convenience, and with the intent of being consistent with industry practice, however, the proposed regulations require a trust to provide tax information as if the trust were a taxpayer using the cash receipts and disbursements method of tax accounting (cash method). Although a trust must provide tax information to unit holders as if the trust were a cash method taxpayer, the trust must provide information necessary for such holders to comply with the original issue discount rules and other provisions requiring the inclusion of accrued amounts regardless of the holder's method of accounting. The IRS and Treasury are continuing to study, and welcome comments on, whether to require trusts to provide tax reporting information to accommodate the different methods of accounting used by the beneficial owners of a trust.

In the case of a widely held fixed investment trust that holds a pool of debt instruments subject to section 1272 (a) (6) (C) (iii), the proposed regulations require that middlemen, unit interest holders, exempt recipients, and noncalendar-year taxpayers be provided with certain additional information that is necessary for compliance with the market discount rules and, where applicable, section 1272 (a) (6) (as amended by section 1004 of the Taxpayer Relief Act of 1997, Public Law 105-34, 111 Stat. 788, 911 (1997)). This additional information includes information necessary to compute (1) the accrual of market discount, including the type of information required under § 1.6049-7 (f) (2) (i) (G) in the case of a REMIC regular interest or a collateralized debt obligation not issued with original issue discount; and (2) the accrual of original issue discount and market discount, including the type of information required under § 1.6049-7(f)(2)(ii)(E), (F), (I), and (K) in the case of a REMIC regular interest or a collateralized debt obligation that is issued with original issue discount. The IRS and Treasury request comments on whether similar information reporting requirements, for example, reporting of information necessary to compute the accrual of market discount, should be extended to widely held fixed investment trusts that hold instruments (or pools of instruments) not subject to section 1272(a)(6)(C).

To enable a beneficial owner to comply fully with section 671 and section 67 (where applicable), § 1.671-4(j)(6)(i) of the proposed regulations requires the amount of trust income to be reported by the trustee to be the gross amount of income generated by the trust assets (other than from the sale or other disposition of trust assets). Thus, in the case of a trust that receives a payment net of an expense, the payment must be grossed up to reflect the deducted expense. Trustees must also have, and make available, information regarding the trust's affected expenses (as defined in § 1.67-2T(i)(1)) for the calendar year. In addition, in the case of a unit interest holder that is an affected investor (as defined in § 1.67-2T(h)(1)), the trustee or middleman must provide such unit interest holder with information regarding the holder's proportionate share of the trust's affected expenses for the calendar year.

The proposed regulations also require the trust to separately state any other item that, if taken into account separately by any unit interest holder, could result in an income tax liability for that unit interest holder different from that which would result if the unit interest holder did not take the item into account separately. The IRS and Treasury request comments on whether this requirement is administratively feasible in the context of a widely held fixed investment trust or whether a different approach, also consistent with the taxation of grantor trusts, would be more appropriate.

F. Coordination with Backup Withholding Rules

Section 1.671-4(j)(7) of the proposed regulations contains provisions to coordinate these regulations with the backup withholding rules.

Proposed Effective Date

These regulations are proposed to apply to calendar years beginning on or after the date that final regulations are published in the **Federal Register**.

Special Analyses

It has been determined that this notice of proposed rulemaking is not a significant regulatory action as defined in EO 12866. Therefore, a regulatory assessment is not required. It is hereby certified that these regulations will not have a significant economic impact on a substantial number of small entities. This certification is based on the fact that the regulations generally clarify existing reporting obligations and are expected, for the most part, to have a minimal impact on industry practice. Thus, the regulations will not result in a significant economic impact on any entity subject to the regulations. Further, the reporting burdens in these regulations will fall primarily on large brokerage firms, large banks, and other large entities acting as trustees or middlemen, most of which are not small entities within the meaning of the Regulatory Flexibility Act (5 U.S.C. chapter 6). Thus, a substantial number of small entities will not be affected. Therefore, a Regulatory Flexibility Analysis under the Regulatory Flexibility Act (5 U.S.C. chapter 6) is not required. Pursuant to section 7805(f) of the Internal Revenue Code, this notice of proposed rulemaking will be submitted to the Chief Counsel for Advocacy of the Small Business Administration for comment on its impact on small business.

Comments and Public Hearing

Before these proposed regulations are adopted as final regulations, consideration will be given to any written comments (a signed original and eight (8) copies) that are submitted timely (in the manner described in the ADDRESSES caption) to the IRS. All comments will be available for public inspection and copying.

A public hearing has been scheduled for Thursday, November 5, 1998 at 10 a.m., in room 2615, Internal Revenue Building, 1111 Constitution Avenue, NW., Washington, DC. Because of access restrictions, visitors will not be admitted beyond the Internal Revenue Building lobby more than 15 minutes before the hearing starts.

The rules of 26 CFR 601.601(a)(3) apply to the hearing.

Persons that wish to present oral comments at the hearing must submit written comments by [*INSERT DATE 90 DAYS AFTER DATE OF PUBLICATION IN THE FEDERAL REGISTER*] and submit an outline of the topics to be discussed and the time to be devoted to each topic (signed original and eight (8) copies) by October 15, 1998.

A period of 10 minutes will be allotted to each person for making comments.

An agenda showing the scheduling of the speakers will be prepared after the deadline for receiving outlines has passed. Copies of the agenda will be available free of charge at the hearing.

Drafting Information

The principal author of these regulations is Faith Colson, Office of Assistant Chief Counsel (Passthroughs and Special Industries). However, other personnel from the IRS and Treasury Department participated in their development.

List of Subjects

26 CFR Part 1

Income taxes, Reporting and recordkeeping requirements

26 CFR Part 301

Employment taxes, Estate taxes, Excise taxes, Gift taxes, Income taxes, Penalties, Reporting and recordkeeping requirements

Proposed Amendments to the Regulations

Accordingly, 26 CFR parts 1 and 301 are proposed to be amended as follows:

PART 1—INCOME TAXES

Paragraph 1. The authority citation for part 1 is amended by adding an entry in numerical order to read as follows:

Authority: 26 U.S.C. 7805 *****

Section 1.671-4 also issued under 26 U.S.C. 671, 26 U.S.C. 6034A, and 26 U.S.C. 6049(d)(7).

Par. 2. Section 1.671-4 is amended by revising paragraph (a) and adding paragraph (j) to read as follows:

§ 1.671-4 *Method of reporting.*

(a) *Portion of trust treated as owned by the grantor or another person.* Except as otherwise provided in paragraphs (b) and (j) of this section, items of income, deduction, and credit attributable to any portion of a trust which, under the provisions of subpart E (section 671 and following), part I, subchapter J, chapter 1 of the Internal Revenue Code, is treated as owned by the grantor or another person are not reported by the trust on Form 1041, but are shown on a separate statement to be attached to that form. Paragraph (j) of this section provides special reporting rules for widely held fixed investment trusts. Section 301.7701-4(e)(2) of this chapter provides guidance on how the reporting rules in this paragraph (a) apply to an environmental remediation trust.

*****

(j) *Special rules applicable to widely held fixed investment trusts.* The reporting rules contained in this paragraph (j) apply to any widely held fixed investment trust.

(1) *Definitions.* For purposes of this paragraph (j):

Affected expenses. The term *affected expenses* has the meaning given that term by § 1.67-2T(i)(1).

Affected investor. The term *affected investor* has the meaning given that term by § 1.67-2T(h)(1).

Exempt recipient. An *exempt recipient* is any person described in paragraphs (j)(2)(iv)(A) through (R) of this section.

Middleman. A *middleman* is any person who holds an interest in an arrangement classified as a trust under § 301.7701-4(c) of this chapter, and subject to subpart E, part I, subchapter J, chapter 1 of the Internal Revenue Code, on behalf of, or for the account of, another person, or who otherwise acts in a capacity as an intermediary for the account of another person, at any time during the calendar year. A middleman includes, but is not limited to—

(i) A custodian of a person's account, such as a bank, financial institution, or brokerage firm acting as custodian of an account;

(ii) A nominee, including the joint owner of an account or instrument except if the joint owners are husband and wife; and

(iii) A broker (as defined in section 6045(c)(1) and § 1.6045-1(a)(1)) holding an interest for a customer in street name.

Requesting person. A *requesting person* is a person specified in paragraph (j)(3)(iii)(A) of this section who is entitled to request from the trustee the information specified in paragraph (j)(3)(ii) of this section.

Trustee. Trustee means the trustee of a widely held fixed investment trust.

Unit interest holder. A *unit interest holder* is any person who holds a direct or indirect interest, including a beneficial interest, in a widely held fixed investment trust at any time during the calendar year.

Widely held fixed investment trust. A *widely held fixed investment trust* is an arrangement classified as a trust under § 301.7701-4(c) of this chapter, and subject to subpart E, part I, subchapter J, chapter 1 of the Internal Revenue Code, in which any interest is held by a middleman.

(2) *Form 1099 requirement for trustees and middlemen*—(i) *Obligation to file Form 1099 with the Internal Revenue Service.* Except as provided in paragraph (j)(2)(iv) of this section —

(A) Every trustee must file with the Internal Revenue Service the appropriate Forms 1099 reporting the information specified in paragraph (j)(2)(ii) of this section with respect to any unit interest holder who holds an interest in the trust directly and not through a middleman; and

(B) Every middleman must file with the Internal Revenue Service the appropriate Forms 1099, reporting the information specified in paragraph (j)(2)(ii) of this section with respect to any unit interest holder on whose behalf or account the middleman holds an interest in the trust or acts in a capacity as an intermediary.

(ii) *Information to be reported.* The following information must be reported to the Internal Revenue Service on the appropriate Forms 1099—

(A) The name, address, and taxpayer identification number of the unit interest holder;

(B) The name, address, and taxpayer identification number of the person required to file the form;

(C) The amount of trust income (determined in accordance with paragraph (j)(6)(i) of this section) attributable to the unit interest holder for the calendar year for which the return is made;

(D) In the case of the sale or other disposition of a trust asset during the calendar year, the portion of the gross proceeds relating to the trust asset that is attributable to the unit interest holder; and

(E) Any other information required by the Forms 1099.

(iii) *Time and place for filing Forms 1099.* The Forms 1099 required to be filed with the Internal Revenue Service by trustees or middlemen pursuant to paragraph (j)(2)(i) of this section must be filed on or before February 28 of the year following the year for which the Forms 1099 are being filed. The returns must be filed with the appropriate Internal Revenue Service Center, at the address listed in the instructions for the Forms 1099. For extensions of time for filing returns under this section, see § 1.6081-1. For magnetic media filing requirements, see § 301.6011-2 of this chapter.

(iv) *Forms 1099 not required.* A Form 1099 is not required for a unit interest holder that is an exempt recipient. However, if the trustee or middleman backup withholds under section 3406 on payments made to a unit interest holder (because, for example, the unit interest holder has failed to furnish a Form W-9 on request), then the trustee or middleman is required to make a return under this section, unless the trustee or middleman refunds the amount withheld in accordance with § 31.6413(a)-3 of this chapter. An exempt recipient is generally exempt from information reporting without filing a certificate claiming exempt status unless the provisions of this paragraph (j)(2)(iv) require the unit interest holder to file a certificate. A trustee or middleman may in any case require a unit interest holder not otherwise required to file a certificate under this paragraph (j)(2)(iv) to file a certificate in order to qualify as an exempt recipient. See § 31.3406(h)-3(a)(1)(iii) and (c)(2) of this chapter for the certificate that a unit interest holder must provide if a trustee or middleman requires the certificate in order to treat the unit interest holder as an exempt recipient under this paragraph (j)(2)(iv). A trustee or middleman may treat a unit interest holder as an exempt recipient based upon a properly completed form as described in § 31.3406(h)-3(e)(2) of this chapter, its actual knowledge that the unit interest holder is a person described in this paragraph (j)(2)(iv), or the indicators described in this paragraph (j)(2)(iv). Any unit interest holder who ceases to be an exempt recipient shall, no later than 10 days after such cessation, notify the trustee or middleman in writing when it ceases to be an exempt recipient. For purposes of this paragraph (j)—

(A) *Corporation.* A corporation, as defined in section 7701(a)(3), whether domestic or foreign, is an exempt recipient. In addition, for purposes of this paragraph (j)(2)(iv), the term corporation includes a partnership all of whose members are corporations described in this paragraph (j)(2)(iv), but only if the partnership files with the trustee or middleman a properly completed form as described in § 31.3406(h)-3(e)(2) of this chapter. Absent actual knowledge otherwise, a trustee or middleman may treat a unit interest holder as a corporation (and, therefore, as an exempt recipient) if one of the requirements of paragraph (j)(2)(iv)(A)(*1*), (*2*), (*3*), or (*4*), is met at the time a unit interest holder acquires an interest in the trust.

(*1*) The name of the unit interest holder contains an unambiguous expression of corporate status (that is, Incorporated, Inc., Corporation, Corp., P.C., (but not Company or Co.)) or contains the term *insurance company, indemnity company, reinsurance company,* or *assurance company,* or its name indicates that it is an entity listed as a per se corporation under § 301.7701-2(b)(8)(i) of this chapter.

(*2*) The trustee or middleman has on file a corporate resolution or similar document clearly indicating corporate status. For this purpose, a similar document includes a copy of Form 8832, filed by the unit interest holder to elect classification as an association under § 301.7701-3(c) of this chapter.

(*3*) The trustee or middleman receives a Form W-9 which includes an EIN and a statement from the unit interest holder that it is a domestic corporation.

(*4*) The trustee or middleman receives a withholding certificate described in § 1.1441-1(e)(2)(i), that includes a certification that the person whose name is on the certificate is a foreign corporation.

(B) *Tax exempt organization.* Any organization that is exempt from taxation under section 501(a) is an exempt recipient. A custodial account under section 403(b)(7) shall be considered an exempt recipient under this paragraph. A trustee or middleman may treat an organization as an exempt recipient under this paragraph (j)(2)(iv)(B) without requiring a certificate if the organization's name is listed in the compilation by the Commissioner of organizations for which a deduction for charitable contributions is allowed, if the name of the organization contains an unambiguous indication that it is a tax-exempt organization, or if the organization is known to the trustee or middleman to be a tax-exempt organization.

(C) *Individual retirement plan.* An individual retirement plan as defined in section 7701(a)(37) is an exempt recipient. A trustee or middleman may treat any such plan of which it is the trustee or custodian as an exempt recipient under this paragraph (j)(2)(iv)(C) without requiring a certificate.

(D) *United States.* The United States Government and any wholly-owned agency or instrumentality thereof are exempt recipients. A trustee or middleman may treat a person as an exempt recipient under this paragraph (j)(2)(iv)(D) without requiring a certificate if the name of such person reasonably indicates it is described in this paragraph (j)(2)(iv)(D).

(E) *State.* A State, the District of Columbia, a possession of the United States, a political subdivision of any of the foregoing, a wholly-owned agency or instrumentality of any one or more of the foregoing, and a pool or partnership composed exclusively of any of the foregoing are exempt recipients. A trustee or middleman may treat a person as an exempt recipient under this paragraph (j)(2)(iv)(E) without requiring a certificate if the name of such person reasonably indicates it is described in this paragraph (j)(2)(iv)(E) or if such person is known generally in the community to be a State, the District of Columbia, a possession of the United States or a political subdivision or a wholly-owned agency or instrumentality or any one or more of the foregoing (for example, an account held in the name of "Town of S" or "County of T" may be treated as held by an exempt recipient under this paragraph (j)(2)(iv)(E)).

(F) *Foreign government.* A foreign government, a political subdivision of a foreign government, and any wholly-owned agency or instrumentality of either of the foregoing are exempt recipients. A trustee or middleman may treat a foreign government or a political subdivision thereof as an exempt recipient under this paragraph (j)(2)(iv)(F) without requiring a certificate provided that its name reasonably indicates that it is a foreign government or provided that it is known to the trustee or middleman to be a foreign government or a political subdivision thereof (for example, an account held in the name of the "Government of V" may be treated as held by a foreign government).

(G) *International organization.* An international organization and any wholly-owned agency or instrumentality thereof are exempt recipients. The term *international organization* shall have the meaning ascribed to it in section 7701(a)(18). A trustee or middleman may treat a unit interest holder as an international organization without requiring a certificate if the unit interest holder is designated as an international organization by executive order (pursuant to 22 U.S.C. 288 through 288f).

(H) *Foreign central bank of issue*. A foreign central bank of issue is an exempt recipient. A foreign central bank of issue is a bank which is by law or government sanction the principal authority, other than the government itself, issuing instruments intended to circulate as currency. See § 1.895-1(b)(1). A trustee or middleman may treat a person as a foreign central bank of issue (and, therefore, as an exempt recipient) without requiring a certificate provided that such person is known generally in the financial community as a foreign central bank of issue or if its name reasonably indicates that it is a foreign central bank of issue.

(I) *Securities and commodities dealer*. A dealer in securities, commodities, or notional principal contracts that is registered as such under the laws of the United States or a State or under the laws of a foreign country is an exempt recipient. A trustee or middleman may treat a dealer as an exempt recipient under this paragraph (j)(2)(iv)(I) without requiring a certificate if the person is known generally in the investment community to be a dealer meeting the requirements set forth in this paragraph (j)(2)(iv)(I) (for example, a registered broker-dealer or a person listed as a member firm in the most recent publication of members of the National Association of Securities Dealers, Inc.).

(J) *Real Estate Investment Trust*. A real estate investment trust, as defined in section 856 and § 1.856-1, is an exempt recipient. A trustee or middleman may treat a person as a real estate investment trust (and, therefore, as an exempt recipient) without requiring a certificate if the person is known generally in the investment community as a real estate investment trust.

(K) *Entity registered under the Investment Company Act of 1940*. An entity registered at all times during the taxable year under the Investment Company Act of 1940, as amended (15 U.S.C. 80a-1), (or during such portion of the taxable year that it is in existence), is an exempt recipient. An entity that is created during the taxable year will be treated as meeting the registration requirement of the preceding sentence provided that such entity is so registered at all times during the taxable year for which such entity is in existence. A trustee or middleman may treat such an entity as an exempt recipient under this paragraph (j)(2)(iv)(K) without requiring a certificate if the entity is known generally in the investment community to meet the requirements of the preceding sentence.

(L) *Common trust fund*. A common trust fund, as defined in section 584(a), is an exempt recipient. A trustee or middleman may treat the fund as an exempt recipient without requiring a certificate provided that its name reasonably indicates that it is a common trust fund or provided that it is known to the trustee or middleman to be a common trust fund.

(M) *Financial institution*. A financial institution such as a bank, mutual savings bank, savings and loan association, building and loan association, cooperative bank, homestead association, credit union, industrial loan association or bank, or other similar organization, whether organized in the United States or under the laws of a foreign country is an exempt recipient. A financial institution also includes a clearing organization defined in § 1.163-5(c)(2)(i)(D)(8) and the Bank for International Settlements. A trustee or middleman may treat any person described in the preceding sentence as an exempt recipient without requiring a certificate if the person's name (including a foreign name, such as "Banco" or "Banque") reasonably indicates the unit interest holder is a financial institution described in the preceding sentence.

(N) *Trust*. A trust which is exempt from tax under section 664(c) (i.e., a charitable remainder annuity trust or a charitable remainder unitrust) or is described in section 4947(a)(1) (relating to certain charitable trusts) is an exempt recipient. A trustee or middleman which is a trustee of the trust may treat the trust as an exempt recipient without requiring a certificate.

(O) *Middlemen*. A middleman, as defined in paragraph (j)(1) of this section, is an exempt recipient.

(P) *Brokers*. A broker, as defined in section 6045(c) and § 1.6045-1(a)(1), is an exempt recipient.

(Q) *Real estate mortgage investment conduit*. A real estate mortgage investment conduit, as defined in section 860D(a), is an exempt recipient.

(R) *A widely held fixed investment trust*. A widely held fixed investment trust, as defined in paragraph (j)(1) of this section, is an exempt recipient.

(3) *Trustee's requirement to furnish information to middlemen, exempt recipients, and noncalendar-year taxpayers*—(i) *In general*. The trustee must cause to be printed in a publication generally read by and available to requesting persons, the name, address, and telephone number of a representative or official of the trust who will provide the information specified in paragraph (j)(3)(ii) of this section to such persons. The trustee must provide the information in the time and manner prescribed in paragraph (j)(3)(iii)(C) of this section to requesting persons who request the information in the manner prescribed in paragraph (j)(3)(iii)(B) of this section.

(ii) *Information required to be reported*. For each calendar quarter or calendar year specified, the trustee must have available and provide, upon request, the following information computed as of the last day of the quarter, or computed as of December 31 of the year specified—

(A) The name of the trust, the name and address of the trustee of the trust, and the employer identification number of the trust;

(B) The Committee on Uniform Security Identification Procedure (CUSIP) number, account number, serial number or other identifying number of the trust;

(C) All items of income (determined in accordance with paragraph (j)(6)(i) of this section), deduction, and credit of the trust, expressed both as a total dollar amount for the trust and as a dollar amount per unit outstanding on the last day of the period requested;

(D) If any trust asset has been sold or otherwise disposed of during the period requested, the gross proceeds received by the trust for the trust asset, the date of sale or disposition of the trust asset, and the percentage of that trust asset that has been sold or disposed of. The trust must also provide a schedule showing the portion (expressed in terms of a percentage) of the total fair market value of all the assets held by the trust that the asset sold or disposed of represented as of the last day of the quarter for each quarter that the asset was held by the trust;

(E) The amount of affected expenses of the trust expressed both as a total dollar amount and as a dollar amount per unit outstanding on the last day of the period requested;

(F) In the case of a widely held fixed investment trust that holds a pool of debt instruments subject to section 1272(a)(6)(C)(iii), the information required by paragraph (j)(6)(ii) of this section;

(G) The number of units outstanding on the last business day of the period requested; and

(H) Any other information necessary for a unit interest holder that is the beneficial owner of a trust interest to properly report the income, deductions, and credits attributable to the portion of the trust treated as owned by the unit interest holder under section 671. For this purpose, the trustee shall separately state any trust item that, if taken into account separately by a unit interest holder, could result in an income tax liability for that unit interest holder different from that which would result if the unit interest holder did not take the item into account separately.

(iii) *Providing and requesting trust information*—(A) *Requesting persons*. The following persons that hold an interest in a trust may request the information specified in paragraph (j)(3)(ii) of this section from that trust—

(1) Any middleman;

(2) Any broker who holds a unit interest on its own behalf;

(3) Any other exempt recipient who holds an interest directly and not through a middleman;

(4) Any noncalendar-year unit interest holder who holds a trust interest directly and not through a middleman; and

(5) A representative or agent for a person specified in paragraphs (j)(3)(iii)(A)(1) through (4) of this section.

(B) *Manner of requesting information from the trust*. A requesting person may request the information specified in paragraph (j)(3)(ii) of this section in writing or by telephone. The request must specify the calendar quarters or years for which the information is needed.

(C) *Time and manner of furnishing information*—(1) *Manner of furnishing information*. The information specified in paragraph (j)(3)(ii) of this section may be furnished as follows—

(i) By telephone;

(*ii*) By written statement sent by first class mail to the address provided by the requesting person;

(*iii*) By causing it to be printed in a publication generally read by and available to requesting persons and by notifying the requesting person in writing or by telephone of the publication in which it will appear, the date on which it will appear, and, if possible, the page on which it will appear; or

(*iv*) By any other method agreed to by the parties.

(*2*) *Time for furnishing the information*. The trustee must furnish, or cause to be furnished, the information specified in paragraph (j)(3)(ii) of this section on or before the later of—

(*i*) The 30th day after the close of the period for which the information was requested; or

(*ii*) The day that is 2 weeks after the receipt of the request.

(4) *Requirement of furnishing statement to unit interest holder*—(i) *In general*. Every trustee or middleman required to file appropriate Forms 1099 under paragraph (j)(2)(i) of this section with respect to a particular unit interest holder must furnish to that unit interest holder (the person whose identifying number is required to be shown on the form) a written statement showing the information required by paragraph (j)(4)(ii) of this section.

(ii) *Information required to be provided on written statement*. The written statement must specify for the calendar year for which the return is made the following information—

(A) The name of the trust and the CUSIP number, account number, serial number, or other identifying number for the trust or unit interest;

(B) The name, address, and taxpayer identification number of the person required to send the statement;

(C) All items of income (determined in accordance with paragraph (j)(6)(i) of this section), deduction, and credit of the trust attributable to the unit interest holder;

(D) If any trust asset is sold, or otherwise disposed of during the calendar year, the portion of the gross proceeds relating to the trust asset that is attributable to the unit interest holder, the date of sale or disposition of the trust asset, and the percentage of that trust asset that has been sold or otherwise disposed of. A schedule showing the portion (expressed in terms of a percentage) of the total fair market value of all the assets held by the trust that the asset sold or disposed of represented as of the last day of the quarter for each quarter that the asset was held by the trust must be included with the statement;

(E) In the case of a unit interest holder that is an affected investor, the affected expenses that are attributable to the unit interest holder;

(F) In the case of a widely held fixed investment trust that holds a pool of debt instruments subject to section 1272(a)(6)(C)(iii), the information required by paragraph (j)(6)(ii) of this section;

(G) Any other information necessary for a unit interest holder to properly report the income, deductions, and credit attributable to the unit interest holder under section 671. For this purpose, the trustee or middleman, as the case may be, shall separately state any trust item that, if taken into account separately by any unit interest holder, could result in an income tax liability for that unit interest holder different from that which would result if the unit interest holder did not take the item into account separately; and

(H) A statement that the items of income, deduction, and credit and other information shown on the statement must be taken into account in computing the taxable income and credits of the unit interest holder on the income tax return of the unit interest holder.

(iii) *Due date and other requirements with respect to statement required to be furnished to the unit interest holder*. The statement required to be furnished to the unit interest holder under this paragraph (j)(4) for a calendar year must be furnished to the holder after April 30 of that year and on or before March 15 of the year following the year for which the statement is being furnished. The person sending the statement must maintain in its records a copy of the statement furnished to the unit interest holder for a period of 3 years from the due date for furnishing such statement specified in this paragraph (j)(4).

(5) *Requirement that middlemen furnish information to exempt recipients and noncalendar-year taxpayers*. For each calendar quarter or calendar year specified, any exempt recipient listed in paragraph (j)(2)(iv) of this section and any noncalendar-year unit interest holder may request from the middleman who holds the unit interest on behalf of, or for the account of, the unit interest holder, the information listed in paragraph (j)(4)(ii)(A) through (G) of this section computed as of

the last day of the calendar quarter specified, or computed as of December 31 of the year specified. The middleman must provide in writing or by telephone the information listed in paragraph (j)(4)(ii)(A) through (G) of this section to any such requester on or before the later of the 45th day after the close of the period for which the information was requested, or that day that is 4 weeks after the receipt of the request.

(6) *Special rules*. For purposes of this paragraph (j):

(i) *Determination of trust income*. Trust income is to be determined in the following manner—

(A) The trust is to be treated as a calendar year taxpayer using the cash receipts and disbursements method of accounting; and

(B) The amount of trust income for the calendar year is the gross amount of income generated by the trust assets (other than from the sale or other disposition of trust assets). Thus, in the case of a trust that receives a payment net of an expense, the payment must be grossed up to reflect the deducted expense.

(ii) *Widely held fixed investment trust holding pool of debt instruments subject to section 1272(a)(6)(C)(iii)*. In the case of a widely held fixed investment trust that holds a pool of debt instruments subject to section 1272(a)(6)(C)(iii), requesting persons, unit interest holders, exempt recipients, and noncalendar-year taxpayers must be provided, as required under paragraphs (j)(3)(ii)(F), (j)(4)(ii)(F), and (j)(5), respectively, of this section, information necessary to compute—

(A) The accrual of market discount, including the type of information required under paragraphs § 1.6049-7(f)(2)(i)(G) in the case of a REMIC regular interest or a collateralized debt obligation not issued with original issue discount; and

(B) The accrual of original issue discount and market discount, including the type of information required under § 1.6049-7(f)(2)(ii)(E), (F), (I), and (K) in the case of a REMIC regular interest or a collateralized debt obligation that is issued with original issue discount.

(7) *Backup withholding requirements*. Every trustee and middleman filing a Form 1099 under this section shall be considered a payor within the meaning of § 31.3406(a)-2 of this chapter. The obligation of a trustee or middleman as payor to backup withhold shall be determined pursuant to section 3406 and the regulations promulgated thereunder.

(8) *Penalties for failure to comply*. Every trustee and middleman who has a reporting obligation under this paragraph (j) and who fails to comply is subject to the penalties provided by sections 6721, 6722, and any other applicable penalty provisions.

(9) *Effective date*. Trustees and middlemen must report in accordance with this paragraph (j) for calendar years beginning on or after the date that the final regulations are published in the **Federal Register**.

Par. 3. Section 1.6049-7 is amended by adding a sentence to the end of paragraph (f)(4) to read as follows:

§ 1.6049-7 Returns of information with respect to REMIC regular interests and collateralized debt obligations.

*****

(f) *****

(4) ***** For rules regarding a widely held fixed investment trust that holds a pool of debt instruments subject to section 1272(a)(6)(C)(iii), see § 1.671-4(j).

*****

PART 301—PROCEDURE AND ADMINISTRATION

Par. 4. The authority citation for part 301 continues to read in part as follows:

Authority: 26 U.S.C. 7805 *****

Par. 5. Section 301.6109-1 is amended by revising the last sentence of paragraph (a)(2)(i) to read as follows:

§ 301.6109-1 Identifying numbers.

(a) *****

(2) ***** (i) ***** If the trustee has not already obtained a taxpayer identification number for the trust, the trustee must obtain a taxpayer identification number for the trust as provided in paragraph (d)(2) of this section in order to report pursuant to § 1.671-4(a), (b)(2)(i)(B), (b)(3)(i), or (j) of this chapter.

*****

Deputy Commissioner of Internal Revenue   Michael P. Dolan

¶ 20,233

IRS proposed regulations: Roth IRAs.—The IRS has issued proposed regulations, explaining the contribution, conversion, distribution, and reporting rules for Roth IRAs. The proposed rules reflect the recent changes made to Roth IRAs by the IRS Restructuring and Reform Act of 1998 (P.L. 105-206). Taxpayers may rely on the proposed regulations for guidance pending the issuance of final regulations. According to the IRS, if future guidance is more restrictive than the guidance issued in these proposed regulations, future guidance will be applied without retroactive effect.

The proposed regulations are set out in a question-and-answer format and are designed to provide guidance to individuals establishing Roth IRAs, beneficiaries under Roth IRAs, and trustees, custodians, and issuers of Roth IRAs.

The proposed regulations were published in the *Federal Register* on September 3, 1998 (63 FR 46937).

The regulations were finalized February 3, 1999 (64 FR 5597). The regulations are reproduced at ¶ 12,097A-0, ¶ 12,097A-1, ¶ 12,097A-2, ¶ 12,097A-3, ¶ 12,097A-4, ¶ 12,097A-5, ¶ 12,097A-6, ¶ 12,097A-7, ¶ 12,097A-8, and ¶ 12,097A-9. The preamble is reproduced at ¶ 23,950Y.

¶ 20,234

IRS proposed regulations: Section 411(d)(6) Protected Benefits: Qualified Retirement Plan Benefits.—The IRS has issued proposed regulations regarding Code Sec. 411(d)(6) protected qualified retirement plan benefits. The proposed regulations reflect changes made by the Taxpayer Relief Act of 1997 (TRA '97) to the rules under Code Sec. 411(d)(6) regarding qualified retirement plan benefits that are protected from reduction by plan amendment. The proposed regulations change the existing regulations to conform with the TRA '97 rules regarding in-kind distribution requirements for certain employee stock ownership plans. The regulations also specify the time period during which certain plan amendments, for which relief has been granted by TRA '97, may be made without violating the prohibition against plan amendments that reduce accrued benefits.

The proposed regulations, which were published in the *Federal Register* on September 4, 1998 (63 FR 47214), are reproduced below. The proposed regs were also issued as final and temporary regs; those are reproduced at ¶ 12,233 and ¶ 12,233A. The preamble to the final and temporary regulations is at ¶ 23,945T.

DEPARTMENT OF THE TREASURY

Internal Revenue Service

26 CFR Part 1

[REG-101363-98]

RIN 1545-AV94

Section 411(d)(6) Protected Benefits (Taxpayer Relief Act of 1997); Qualified Retirement Plan Benefits

AGENCY: Internal Revenue Service (IRS), Treasury.

ACTION: Notice of proposed rulemaking by cross-reference to temporary regulations.

SUMMARY: In the Rules and Regulations section of this issue of the **Federal Register**, the IRS is issuing temporary regulations providing for changes to the rules regarding qualified retirement plan benefits that are protected from reduction by plan amendment, that have been made necessary by the Taxpayer Relief Act of 1997. The text of those temporary regulations also serves as the text of these proposed regulations.

DATES: Written comments and requests for a public hearing must be received by December 3, 1998.

ADDRESSES: Send submissions to: CC:DOM:CORP:R (REG-101363-98), room 5228, Internal Revenue Service, POB 7604, Ben Franklin Station, Washington, DC 20044. Submissions may be hand delivered between the hours of 8 a.m. and 5 p.m. to: CC:DOM:CORP:R (REG-101363-98), Courier's Desk, Internal Revenue Service, 1111 Constitution Avenue NW., Washington, DC. Alternatively, taxpayers may submit comments electronically via the internet by selecting the "Tax Regs" option on the IRS Home Page, or by submitting comments directly to the IRS internet site at http://www.irs.ustreas.gov/prod/tax __regs/comments.html.

FOR FURTHER INFORMATION CONTACT: Concerning the regulations, Linda S. F. Marshall, (202) 622-6030 (not a toll-free call); concerning submissions, Michael Slaughter, (202) 622-7190 (not a toll-free call).

SUPPLEMENTARY INFORMATION:

Background

Temporary regulations in the Rules and Regulations section of this issue of the **Federal Register** amend the Income Tax Regulations (26 CFR part 1) relating to section 411(d)(6), to provide for changes that have been made necessary by the Taxpayer Relief Act of 1997 (TRA '97), Public Law 105-34, 111 Stat. 788 (1997). The temporary regulations change the existing regulations to conform with the TRA '97 rules regarding in-kind distribution requirements for certain employee stock ownership plans, and specify the time period during which certain plan

amendments for which relief has been granted by TRA '97 may be made without violating the prohibition against plan amendments that reduce accrued benefits.

The text of those temporary regulations also serves as the text of these proposed regulations. The preamble to the temporary regulations explains the temporary regulations.

Special Analyses

It has been determined that this notice of proposed rulemaking is not a significant regulatory action as defined in EO 12866. Therefore, a regulatory assessment is not required. It also has been determined that section 553(b) of the Administrative Procedure Act (5 U.S.C. chapter 5) does not apply to these regulations, and because the regulation does not impose a collection of information on small entities, the Regulatory Flexibility Act (5 U.S.C. chapter 6) does not apply. Pursuant to section 7805(f) of the Internal Revenue Code, this notice of proposed rulemaking will be submitted to the Chief Counsel for Advocacy of the Small Business Administration for comment on its impact on small business.

Comments and Requests for a Public Hearing

Before these proposed regulations are adopted as final regulations, consideration will be given to any written comments (a signed original and eight (8) copies) that are submitted timely to the IRS. All comments will be available for public inspection and copying. A public hearing may be scheduled if requested in writing by any person that timely submits written comments. If a public hearing is scheduled, notice of the date, time, and place for the hearing will be published in the **Federal Register**.

Drafting Information

The principal author of these regulations is Linda S. F. Marshall, Office of the Associate Chief Counsel (Employee Benefits and Exempt Organizations. However, other personnel from the IRS and Treasury Department participated in their development.

List of Subjects in 26 CFR Part 1

Income taxes, Reporting and recordkeeping requirements.

Proposed Amendments to the Regulations

Accordingly, 26 CFR part 1 is proposed to be amended as follows:

PART 1—INCOME TAXES

Paragraph 1. The authority citation for part 1 continues to read in part as follows:

Authority: 26 U.S.C. 7805 * * *

Par. 2. Section 1.411(d)-4 is amended by:

1. Revising paragraph (d)(1)(ii) of Q&A-2.

2. Adding Q&A-11.

The addition and revisions read as follows:

§ 1.411(d)-4 Section 411(d)(6) protected benefits.

* * * * *

Q&A-2 * * *

(d)(1)(ii) [The text of proposed paragraph (d)(1)(ii) of Q&A-2 is the same as the text of § 1.411(d)-4T Q&A-2(d)(1)(ii) published elsewhere in this issue of the **Federal Register**.]

* * * * *

Q&A-11 [The text of proposed Q&A-11 is the same as the text of § 1.411(d)-4T Q&A-11 published elsewhere in this issue of the **Federal Register**.]

Michael P. Dolan

Deputy Commissioner of Internal Revenue

¶ 20,235

IRS: Proposed regulations: Mileage allowances.—The IRS has issued a proposed regulation which applies the substantiation rules to mileage allowances for business use of an automobile after December 31, 1997, without the limitation that a mileage allowance is available only to the owner of a vehicle. Another proposed regulation authorizes the Commissioner to establish a method under which a taxpayer may use mileage rates to determine the amount of the ordinary and necessary business expenses of using an automobile for local transportation to, from, and at the destination while traveling away from home, in lieu of substantiating the actual costs. Written or electronically generated comments and requests for a public hearing regarding the proposed regs must be received by December 30, 1998. Submissions should be sent to CC:DOM:CORP:R (REG-122488-97), Room 5228, Internal Revenue Service, P.O. Box 7604, Ben Franklin Station, Washington, DC 20044. For information concerning the proposed regulations, contact Edwin B. Cleverdon or Donna M. Crisalli, phone: (202) 622-4920.

The proposed regulations and preamble were published in the *Federal Register* on October 1, 1998 (63 FR 52660).

The final regulations were published in the *Federal Register* on January 26, 2000 (65 FR 4121). IRS Reg. Sec. 1.62-2 is reproduced at ¶ 11,182. IRS Reg. Sec. 1.274-5 is reproduced at ¶ 11,357B. The preamble is reproduced at ¶ 24,505I.

¶ 20,236

IRS: Temporary regulations: Health care: Women and newborn children.—The IRS issued temporary regulations relating to minimum hospital length-of-stay requirements imposed on group health plans with respect to mothers and newborns. These regulation were issued at the same time that the Pension and Welfare Benefts Administration and the Health Care Financing Adminstration issued substantially similar interim final regulations (See CCH PENSION PLAN GUIDE ¶ 23,947D).

The temporary regulations and preamble, which were published in the *Federal Register* on October 27, 1998 (63 FR 57565), are reproduced below.

DEPARTMENT OF THE TREASURY

Internal Revenue Service

26 CFR Part 54

[Reg-109708-97]

RIN 1545-AV12

HIPAA Newborns' and Mothers' Health Protection Act

AGENCY: Internal Revenue Service (IRS), Treasury.

ACTION: Notice of proposed rulemaking by cross-reference to temporary regulations.

SUMMARY: Elsewhere in this issue of the **Federal Register**, the IRS is issuing temporary regulations relating to minimum hospital length-of-stay requirements imposed on group health plans with respect to mothers and newborns. The hospital length-of-stay requirements were added to the Internal Revenue Code by section 1531 of the Taxpayer Relief Act of 1997. The IRS is issuing the temporary regulations at the same time that the Pension and Welfare Benefits Administration of the U.S. Department of Labor and the Health Care Financing Administration of the U.S. Department of Health and Human Services are issuing substantially similar interim final regulations relating to hospital length-of-stay requirements added by the Newborns' and Mothers' Health Protection Act of 1996 to the Employee Retirement Income Security Act of 1974 and the Public Health Service Act. The temporary regulations provide guidance to employers and group health plans relating to the new hospital length-of-stay requirements. The text of those temporary regulations also serves as the text of these proposed regulations. DATES: Written comments and requests for a public hearing must be received by *[INSERT DATE 90 DAYS AFTER PUBLICATION OF THIS DOCUMENT IN THE FEDERAL REGISTER].*

ADDRESSES: Send submissions to: CC:DOM:CORP:R (REG-109708-97), room 5226, Internal Revenue Service, POB 7604, Ben Franklin Station, Washington, DC 20044. Submissions may be hand-delivered to: CC:DOM:CORP:R (REG-109708-97), room 5226, Internal Revenue Service, 1111 Constitution Avenue, NW., Washington, DC. Alternatively, taxpayers may submit comments electronically via the Internet by selecting the "Tax Regs" option on the IRS Home Page, or by submitting comments directly to the IRS Internet site at: http://www.irs.ustreas.gov/prod/tax_regs/comments.html

FOR FURTHER INFORMATION CONTACT: Russ Weinheimer, (202) 622-4695 (not a toll-free number).

SUPPLEMENTARY INFORMATION:

Background

The temporary regulations published elsewhere in this issue of the **Federal Register** add § 54.9811-1T to the Miscellaneous Excise Tax Regulations. These regulations are being published as part of a joint rulemaking with the Department of Labor and the Department of Health and Human Services (the joint rulemaking).

The text of those temporary regulations also serves as the text of these proposed regulations. The preamble to the temporary regulations explains the temporary regulations.

Special Analyses

This regulation is not subject to the Unfunded Mandates Reform Act of 1995 because the regulation is an interpretive regulation. It has also been determined that section 553(b) of the Administrative Procedure Act (5 U.S.C. chapter 5) does not apply to this regulation, and because the regulation does not impose a collection of information on small entities, the Regulatory Flexibility Act (5 U.S.C. chapter 6) does not apply. For further information and for analyses relating to the joint rulemaking, see the preamble to the joint rulemaking. Pursuant to section 7805(f) of the Internal Revenue Code, this notice of proposed rulemaking will be submitted to the Chief Counsel for Advocacy of the Small Business Administration for comment on its impact on small business.

Comments and Requests for a Public Hearing

Before these proposed regulations are adopted as final regulations, consideration will be given to any written comments (a signed original and eight (8) copies) that are submitted timely to the IRS. All comments will be available for public inspection and copying. A public hearing may be scheduled if requested in writing by a person that timely submits written comments. If a public hearing is scheduled, notice of the date, time, and place for the hearing will be published in the **Federal Register.**

Drafting Information

The principal author of these proposed regulations is Russ Weinheimer, Office of the Chief Counsel (Employee Benefits and Exempt Organizations), IRS. However, other personnel from the IRS and Treasury Department participated in their development. The proposed regulations, as well as the temporary regulations, have been developed in coordination with personnel from the U.S. Department of Labor and the U.S. Department of Health and Human Services.

List of Subjects in 26 CFR Part 54

Excise taxes, Health insurance, Pensions, Reporting and recordkeeping requirements.

Proposed Amendments to the Regulations

Accordingly, 26 CFR part 54 is proposed to be amended as follows:

PART 54—PENSION EXCISE TAXES

Paragraph 1. The authority citation for part 54 is amended by adding an entry in numerical order to read as follows:

Authority: 26 U.S.C. 7805 ***

Section 54.9811-1 also issued under 26 U.S.C. 9833. ***

Par. 2. Section 54.9811-1 is added to read as follows:

§54.9811-1 Standards relating to benefits for mothers and newborns.

[The text of this proposed section is the same as the text of §54.9811-1T published elsewhere in this issue of the **Federal Register**].

Michael P. Dolan

Deputy Commissioner of Internal Revenue

¶ 20,237

IRS proposed regulations: Eligible rollover distributions: Eligible retirement plans: Disqualification of plans: Favorable IRS determination letter.—The IRS has issued proposed regulations providing additional guidance regarding the circumstances in which plans could accept rollovers without facing disqualification. The proposed regulations, which amend previously proposed regulations (CCH PENSION PLAN GUIDE ¶ 20,218), clarify that a distributing plan does not need to have a favorable IRS determination letter for the receiving plan administrator to make a reasonable conclusion that a contribution is a valid rollover.

The proposed regulations, which were published in the *Federal Register* on December 17, 1998 (63 FR 69584), are reproduced below.

The final regulations were published in the *Federal Register* on April 21, 2000 (65 FR 21312). The regulations are reproduced at ¶ 11,720Z-50, ¶ 11,753-10, ¶ 11,803, and ¶ 13,566. The preamble is at ¶ 24,505N.

¶ 20,238

IRS proposed regulations: Electronic media: Notices: Consent requirements: Code Sec. 402(f): Code Sec. 411(a)(11): Code Sec. 3405(e)(10)(B).—The IRS has issued proposed regulations providing guidelines for the proper electronic transmission of certain notices and consent requirements under Code Sec. 402(f), Code Sec. 411(a)(11), and Code Sec. 3405(e)(10)(B).

The proposed regulations were published in the *Federal Register* on December 18, 1998 (63 FR 70071).

Final regulations were published in the *Federal Register* on February 8, 2000 (65 FR 6001). The regulations are reproduced at ¶ 11,755-2, ¶ 12,219D, and ¶ 13,566-50. The preamble is reproduced at ¶ 24,505J.

¶ 20,239

IRS: Qualified plans: Distribution limits: Lookback rule.—The IRS has issued proposed regulations which would eliminate, for all qualified plan distributions, the "lookback rule" pursuant to which the qualified plan benefits of certain participants are deemed to exceed the $5,000 cash-out limit on mandatory distributions. These regulations were issued at the same time IRS issued temporary regulations which served as a portion of the text of these proposed regulations (see CCH PENSION PLAN GUIDE ¶ 23,949X).

The proposed regulations and preamble, which were published in the *Federal Register* on December 21, 1998 (63 FR 70356), are reproduced below.

Final regulations were published in the *Federal Register* on July 19, 2000 (65 FR 44679). The regulations are reproduced at ¶ 12,217, ¶ 12,219D, and ¶ 12,556. The preamble is reproduced at ¶ 24,505R.

¶ 20,240

IRS proposed regulations: Group-term life insurance: Uniform premium table.—The IRS has issued proposed amendments to the regulations under IRS Code Sec. 79, revising the uniform premium table used to calculate the cost of group-term life insurance coverage provided to an employee by an employer. The rules provide guidance to employers who must use the uniform premium table to calculate the cost of group-term insurance includible in their employees' gross income.

The proposed regulations, which were published in the *Federal Register* on January 13, 1999 (64 FR 2164), are reproduced below.

The final regulations were published in the *Federal Register* on June 3, 1999 (64 FR 29788). IRS Reg. Sec. 1.79-(d)(7) is reproduced at ¶ 11,231. IRS Reg. Sec. 1.79-3 is reproduced at ¶ 11,233. The preamble is at ¶ 23,953X.

¶ 20,241

IRS proposed regulations: COBRA continuation coverage: Compliance guidance.—The IRS has issued proposed regulations in conjunction with the final rules on COBRA continuation coverage issued on February 3, 1999 (CCH PENSION PLAN GUIDE ¶ 23,950U, ¶ 13,648W-5, ¶ 13,648W-6, ¶ 13,648W-7, ¶ 13,648W-8, ¶ 13,648W-9, ¶ 13,648W-10, ¶ 13,648W-11, ¶ 13,648W-12, and ¶ 13,648W-13). The proposed rules provide plan sponsors and plan administrators with guidance on compliance with the final rules.

The proposed regulations were published in the *Federal Register* on February 3, 1999 (64 FR 5237).

Final regulations became effective on January 10, 2001, the date of their publication in the *Federal Register* (66 FR 1893). The regulations are reproduced at ¶ 13,648W-5, ¶ 13,648W-6, ¶ 13,648W-7, ¶ 13,648W-8, ¶ 13,648W-9, ¶ 13,648W-10, ¶ 13,648W-11, ¶ 13,648W-12 ¶ 13,648W-13 ¶ 13,648W-14, and ¶ 13,648W-15. The preamble is reproduced at ¶ 24,505Y.

¶ 20,242

IRS proposed regulations: Annuities: Valuation: Actuarial tables.—The IRS has issued proposed regulations to update the mortality tables to reflect the most recent mortality experience available. These regulations will effect the valuation of annuities.

The preamble and portions of the proposed regulations, which were published in the *Federal Register* on April 30, 1999 (64 FR 23245), are reproduced below.

The final regulations were published in the *Federal Register* on June 12, 2000 (65 FR 36907). The regulations are reproduced at ¶ 13,498 and ¶ 13,498A. The preamble is reproduced at ¶ 24,505Q.

¶ 20,243

IRS Proposed Regulations: Tax liabilities: Compromise: Retirement income: IRA rollover.—The IRS has issued proposed regulations that provide guidance regarding the compromise of tax liabilities to reflect tax law changes made by the IRS Restructuring and Reform Act of 1998. The proposed regulations allow for compromise based on doubt as to liability and/or collectibility. The proposed regulations also provide for compromise where either collection of the liability would create economic hardship or exceptional circumstances exist such that collection of the liability would be detrimental to compliance. The temporary regulations include examples of transactions involving retirement plans and IRAs.

The preamble and the proposed regulations, which were published in the *Federal Register* on July 21, 1999 (64 FR 39106) are reproduced below. The text of the proposed regulations is the same as the text of temporary regulations IRS Reg. Sec. 301.7122-1T, adopted July 21, 1999 by T.D. 8829 (64 FR 39020) (CCH PENSION PLAN GUIDE ¶ 13,866).

DEPARTMENT OF THE TREASURY

Internal Revenue Service

26 CFR Part 301

RIN 1545-AW88

Compromises

AGENCY: Internal Revenue Service (IRS), Treasury.

ACTION: Notice of proposed rulemaking by cross-reference to temporary regulations.

SUMMARY: In the Rules and Regulations section of this issue of the **Federal Register,** the IRS is issuing temporary regulations relating to the compromise of tax liabilities. These regulations provide additional guidance regarding the compromise of internal revenue taxes. The temporary regulations reflect changes to the law made by the Internal Revenue Service Restructuring and Reform Act of 1998 and the Taxpayer bill of Rights II. The text of the temporary regulations also serves as the text of these proposed regulations.

DATE: Written or electronically generated comments and requests for a public hearing must be received by October 19, 1999.

ADDRESSES: Send submissions to: CC:DOM:CORP:R (REG-116991-98), room 5226, Internal Revenue Service, POB 7604, Ben Franklin Station, Washington, DC 20044. Submissions may be hand delivered Monday through Friday between the hours of 8 a.m. and 5 p.m. to: CC:DOM:CORP:R (REG-116991-98), Courier's Desk, Internal Revenue Service, 1111 Constitution Avenue, NW., Washington, DC. Alternatively, taxpayers may submit comments electronically via the Internet by selecting the "Tax Regs" option on the IRS Home Page, or by submitting comments directly to the IRS Internet site at http://www.irs.gov/prod/tax_regs/comments.html.

FOR FURTHER INFORMATION CONTACT: Concerning the regulations, Carol A. Campbell, (202) 622-3620 (not a toll-free number).

SUPPLEMENTARY INFORMATION:

Background

Temporary regulations in the Rules and Regulations section of this issue of the **Federal Register** amend the Procedure and Administration Regulations (26 CFR part 301) under section 7122 of the Internal Revenue Code. The temporary regulations reflect the amendment of section 7122 by section 3462 of the Internal Revenue Service Restructuring and Reform Act of 1998 ("RRA 1998") Public Law, 105-206, (112 Stat. 685, 764) and by section 503(a) of Taxpayer Bill of Rights II Public Law 104-168, (110 Stat. 1452, 1461).

The text of the temporary regulations also serves as the text of these proposed regulations. The preamble to the temporary regulations explains the regulations.

Special Analyses

It has been determined that this notice of proposed rulemaking is not a significant regulatory action as defined in EO 12866. Therefore, a regulatory assessment is not required. It also has been determined that section 553(b) of the Administrative Procedure Act (5 U.S.C. chapter 5) does not apply to these regulations, and because the regulation does not impose a collection of information on small entities, the Regulatory Flexibility Act (5 U.S.C. chapter 6) does not apply. Pursuant to section 7805(f) of the Internal Revenue Code, this notice of proposed rulemaking will be submitted to the Chief Counsel for Advocacy of the Small Business Administration for comment on its impact on small business.

Comments and Requests for a Public Hearing

Before these proposed regulations are adopted as final regulations, consideration will be given to any written comments (a signed original and eight (8) copies) or electronically generated comments that are submitted timely to the IRS. The IRS generally requests any comments on the clarity of the proposed rule and how it may be made easier to understand.

Section 3462 of RRA 1998 and its legislative history provide for the consideration of factors such as equity, hardship, and public policy in the compromise of tax cases, if such consideration would promote effective tax administration. The legislative history also states that the IRS should use this new compromise authority "to resolve longstanding cases by forgoing penalties and interest which have accumulated as a result of delay in determining the taxpayer's liability." H. Conf. Rep. 599, 105th Cong., 2d Sess. 289 (1998). The text of the temporary regulation provides the authority to compromise cases involving issues of equity, hardship, and public policy, if such a compromise would promote effective tax administration. The temporary regulation provides factors to be considered and examples of cases that could be compromised under this authority when collection of the full amount of the tax liability would create economic hardship. The temporary regulation also provides limited examples of cases that could be compromised when the facts and circumstances presented indicate that collection of the full tax liability would be detrimental to voluntary compliance. The temporary regulation does not contain examples of longstanding cases that could be compromised to promote effective tax administration when penalties and interest have accumulated as the result of delay by the Service in determining the tax liability.

The public is specifically encouraged to make comments or provide examples regarding the particular types of cases or situations in which the Secretary's authority to compromise should be used because: (1) collection of the full amount of tax liability would be detrimental to voluntary compliance or (2) IRS delay in determining the tax liability has resulted in the accumulation of significant interest and penalties. In formulating comments regarding delay in interest and penalty cases, consideration should be given to the possible interplay between cases compromised under this provision and the relief accorded taxpayers under I.R.C. § 6404(e).

All comments will be available for public inspection and copying.

A public hearing may be scheduled if requested in writing by a person that timely submits written comments. If a public hearing is scheduled, notice of the date, time, and place for the hearing will be published in the **Federal Register.**

Drafting Information

The principal author of these regulations is Carol A. Campbell, Office of the Assistant Chief Counsel (General Litigation) CC:EL:GL, IRS. However, other personnel from the IRS and Treasury Department participated in their development.

List of Subjects in 26 CFR Part 301

Employment taxes, Estate taxes, Excise taxes, Gift taxes, Income taxes, Penalties, Reporting and recordkeeping requirements.

Proposed Amendments to the Regulations

Accordingly, 26 CFR Part 301 is proposed to be amended as follows:

PART 301—PROCEDURE AND ADMINISTRATION

Paragraph 1. The authority citation for part 301 continues to read in part as follows:

Authority: 26 U.S.C. 7805 *****

Paragraph 2. Section 301. 7122—1 is added to read as follows:

§ 301.7122-1 Compromises.

[The text of this proposed section is the same as the text of § 301.7122-IT published elsewhere in this issue of the **Federal Register**.]

* * * * *

Charles O. Rossotti

Commissioner of Internal Revenue

¶ 20,244

IRS Proposed Regulations: Deficiency notices: Taxpayers: Addresses.—The IRS has issued a proposed regulation that defines the "last known address" for the purposes of mailing deficiency notices, other types of notices, statements or documents to taxpayers.

The preamble and portions of the proposed regulations reproduced below were published in the *Federal Register* on November 22, 1999 (64 FR 63768).

The final regulations were published in the *Federal Register* on January 12, 2001 (66 FR 2812). The final regulations are reproduced at ¶ 13,786P. The preamble is reproduced at ¶ 24,506C.

¶ 20,245

IRS proposed regulations: Fringe benefits: Qualified transportation.—The IRS has issued proposed regulations which provide guidance to employers that provide qualified transportation fringes to employees, explain that there are two categories of qualified transportation fringes for purposes of determining the amount that is excludable from gross income, and clarify the meaning of "significant administrative costs." Note: The IRS has issued a clarification to these proposed regulations. Announcement 2000-78, which contains the clarification, can be found at ¶ 17,097Q-86.

The proposed regulations, which were published in the *Federal Register* January 27, 2000 (65 FR 4388) are reproduced below.

The final regulations were published in the *Federal Register* on January 11, 2001 (66 FR 2241). The final regulation are reproduced at ¶ 11,289O-5 and ¶ 11,289O-9. The preamble is reproduced at ¶ 24,506A.

¶ 20,246

IRS proposed regulations: Information returns: Electronic filing: Due date extension.—The IRS has issued proposed regulations which extend by one month the due date for filing certain information returns required by Code Sec. 6041, Code Sec. 6047 and Code Sec. 6052 if the return is filed electronically. The proposed regulations affect Forms W-2, W-3, 1096, and the Form 1099 series.

The proposed regulations, which were published in the *Federal Register* January 27, 2000 (65 FR 4396), are reproduced below.

The final regulations were published in the *Federal Register* on August 18, 2000 (65 FR 50405). Portions of the final regulations are reproduced at ¶ 13,683, ¶ 13,691 and ¶ 13,721. The preamble is reproduced at ¶ 24,505U.

¶ 20,247

IRS proposed regulations: Cafeteria plans: Election of coverage: Revocation of election.—The IRS has issued proposed regulations which supplement the final regulations (CCH PENSION PLAN GUIDE ¶ 24,505M) by permitting a mid-year cafeteria plan election change in connection with dependent care assistance and adoption assistance under change in status standards that are specific to dependent care and adoption assistance.

The proposed regulations, which were published in the *Federal Register* March 23, 2000 (65 FR 15587), are reproduced below.

The proposed regulations were amended by proposed regulations published in the *Federal Register* January 10, 2001 (66 FR 1923). The proposed regulations are reproduced at ¶ 20,258.

[4830-01-u]

DEPARTMENT OF THE TREASURY

Internal Revenue Service

26 CFR Part 1

[REG-117162-99]

RIN 1545-AY23 (Officially corrected by the IRS, 65 FR 63824, October 25, 2000)

Tax Treatment of Cafeteria Plans

AGENCY: Internal Revenue Service (IRS), Treasury.

ACTION: Partial withdrawal of notice of proposed rulemaking; amendment to notice of proposed rulemaking; and notice of proposed rulemaking.

SUMMARY: This document withdraws portions of the notice of proposed rulemaking published in the **Federal Register** on March 7, 1989 and amends proposed regulations under section 125. These proposed regulations clarify the circumstances under which a section 125 cafeteria plan election may be changed. The proposed regulations permit an employer to allow a section 125 cafeteria plan participant to revoke an existing election and make a new election during a period of coverage for accident or health coverage, group-term life insurance coverage, dependent care assistance, and adoption assistance.

DATES: Written and electronic comments and requests for a public hearing must be received by June 22, 2000.

ADDRESSES: Send submissions to: CC:DOM:CORP:R (REG-117162-99), room 5226, Internal Revenue Service, POB 7604, Ben Franklin Station, Washington, DC 20044. Submissions may be hand delivered between the hours of 8 a.m. and 5 p.m. to: CC:DOM:CORP:R (REG-117162-99), Courier's Desk, Internal Revenue Service, 1111 Constitution Avenue NW., Washington, DC. Alternatively, taxpayers may submit comments electronically via the internet by selecting the "Tax Regs" option on the IRS Home Page, or by submitting comments directly to the IRS internet site at http://www.irs.gov/tax __regs/ regslist.html.

FOR FURTHER INFORMATION CONTACT: Concerning the regulations, Janet A. Laufer or Christine L. Keller at (202) 622-6080; concerning submissions or to request a public hearing, LaNita Van Dyke at (202) 622-7180. These are not toll-free numbers.

SUPPLEMENTARY INFORMATION:

Background

Section 125[1] permits an employer to offer employees the choice between taxable income and certain nontaxable or "qualified benefits"[2] through a cafeteria plan, without the employees having to recognize the taxable income. In 1984 and 1989, proposed regulations were

---

[1] Revenue Act of 1978, Public Law 95-600 (November 6, 1978): Sen. Rep. 95-1263, 95th Cong., 2d Sess., 74-78, 186-187 (October 1, 1978); H.R. Rep. No. 95-1445, 95th Cong., 2d Sess., 63-66 (August 4, 1978); H.R. Rep. No. 95-250, 96th Cong., 2d Sess., 206-207, 253-254 (October 15, 1978).

[2] "Qualified benefits" are generally any benefits excluded from income, including coverage under an employer-provided accident or health plan under sections 105 and 106; group-term life insurance under section 79; elective contributions under a qualified cash or deferred arrangement within the meaning of section 401(k); dependent care assistance

published relating to the administration of cafeteria plans.[3] In general, the 1984 and 1989 proposed regulations require that for benefits to be provided on a pre-tax basis under section 125, an employee may make changes during a plan year only in certain circumstances.[4] Specifically, §§ 1.125-1, Q&A-8 and 1.125-2, Q&A-6(b), (c) and (d) permit participants to make benefit election changes during a plan year pursuant to changes in cost or coverage, changes in family status, and separation from service.

In 1997, temporary and proposed regulations were issued addressing the standards under which a cafeteria plan may permit a participant to change his or her group health coverage election during a period of coverage to conform with the special enrollment rights under section 9801(f) (added to the Internal Revenue Code by the Health Insurance Portability and Accountability Act of 1996 (HIPAA)) and to change his or her group health or group-term life insurance coverage in a variety of change in status situations.[5] The 1997 regulations are being published as final regulations elsewhere in this issue of the **Federal Register**.

Explanation of Provisions

A. *Summary.*

The proposed regulations being published in this notice of proposed rulemaking were developed as part of an integrated package with the final regulations that are being published at the same time. These proposed regulations supplement the final regulations by permitting a mid-year cafeteria plan election change in connection with dependent care assistance and adoption assistance under change in status standards that are the same as the standards in the final regulations for accident or health plans and for group-term life insurance, and by adding change in status standards that are specific to dependent care and adoption assistance. These proposed regulations also refine and expand upon the approach adopted in the 1989 proposed regulations (at

§ 1.125-2, Q&A-6(b)) by providing that a cafeteria plan may permit employees to make mid-year election changes with respect to group-term life insurance, dependent care assistance, and adoption assistance as well as accident or health coverage, on account of changes in cost or coverage. This expansion of the cost or coverage rules would also allow employees to make election changes if, during a period of coverage, (1) a new benefit package option is offered, or a benefit package option is eliminated, under the plan or (2) a coverage change is made under a plan of the employer of an employee's spouse or dependent. These proposed regulations include a variety of examples illustrating how the rules apply in specific situations.

B. *Change in Status.*

The proposed regulations published in this notice of proposed rulemaking complement the final regulations being published elsewhere in this issue of the **Federal Register** with respect to special enrollment rights and changes in status for accident or health coverage and group-term life insurance coverage. These proposed regulations take into account comments received on the 1997 temporary and proposed regulations, including comments suggesting the desirability of uniformity in the rules for different types of qualified benefits to the extent appropriate given the nature of the benefits.

In response to comments, the new proposed regulations address circumstances under which a cafeteria plan may permit an employee to change an election for dependent care assistance under section 129 and adoption assistance under section 137 during a plan year. The proposed change in status rules for dependent care assistance and adoption assistance parallel the change in status rules for accident or health coverage and group-term life insurance coverage contained in the final regulations, with some additional rules specific to dependent care and adoption assistance. For example, while a change in the number of dependents is a status change for other types of qualified benefits, a change in the number of qualifying individuals, as defined in section 21(b)(1), is a change in status for purposes of dependent care assis-

tance. Likewise, these proposed regulations allow an additional change in status event for adoption assistance (the commencement or termination of an adoption proceeding). The consistency rule in the proposed regulations is the same as the consistency rule in the final regulations, with certain provisions that are specific to dependent care and adoption assistance changes.[6]

C. *Change in Cost or Coverage.*

The new proposed regulations also address election changes to reflect significant cost and coverage changes for all types of qualified benefits provided under a cafeteria plan. The new proposed regulations refine and expand upon the approach taken in the 1989 proposed regulations at § 1.125-2, Q&A-6 with respect to changes in cost or coverage under the plan. For example, in response to comments, the new proposed regulations provide that if a plan adds a new benefit package option (such as a new HMO option), the cafeteria plan may permit affected participants to elect that option and make a corresponding election change with respect to other benefit package options during a period of coverage.

The new proposed regulations also generally extend the cost or coverage rules under § 1.125-2, Q&A-6(b) to permit election changes for self-insured accident or health plans, group-term life insurance, dependent care assistance and adoption assistance coverage under a cafeteria plan. Thus, for example, if the cost of a self-insured accident or health plan increases, a plan may automatically make a corresponding change in the salary reduction charge. In addition, the new proposed regulations treat a change of dependent care provider as similar to the addition of a new HMO option under an accident or health plan, with the result that a corresponding election change can be made when one dependent care provider is replaced by another. While the coverage change rules apply to dependent care regardless of whether the dependent care provider is related to the employee, the cost change rules do not apply to dependent care if the dependent care provider is a relative of the employee making the election.

Commentators on the 1997 temporary and proposed regulations also raised a concern that when the plan of the employer of a spouse conducts annual open enrollment for group health benefits beginning at a different time of the year than the annual open enrollment for group health benefits offered by the employee's employer, the employee is unnecessarily restricted from making election changes that correspond with elections made by the employee's spouse. These commentators suggested that if one spouse makes an election change during an open enrollment period, a corresponding change should be permitted for the other spouse. In response to these comments, the new proposed regulations provide that a cafeteria plan may permit an employee to make an election change, during a period of coverage, corresponding with an open enrollment period change made by a spouse or dependent when the plan of that individual's employer has a different period of coverage.

In addition, the new proposed regulations provide that a cafeteria plan may permit an employee to make an election change in the event that a spouse or dependent makes an election change under a cafeteria plan (or qualified benefits plan) maintained by that individual's employer, provided that the spouse or dependent's election change satisfies the election change rules under the proposed regulation. For example, under this provision, if the plan of a spouse's employer adds a new HMO option to its group health plan, and the spouse elects to enroll the family in that new option, a cafeteria plan may permit the employee to drop family coverage. These new rules apply only if the change made by the employee is on account of and corresponds with the change made under the other employer's plan. This expansion of the existing cost or coverage change rules permits employees to make election changes to ensure consistent coverage of family members and eliminate duplicate coverage.

The cost or coverage rules in the new proposed regulations have not been extended to health flexible spending arrangements. This ensures that those arrangements will not permit election changes in a manner that is inconsistent with the requirement, under §§ 1.125-1, Q&A-17

(Footnote Continued)

under section 129; and adoption assistance under section 137. The following are not qualified benefits: products advertised, marketed, or offered as long-term care insurance; medical savings accounts under section 106(b); qualified scholarships under section 117; educational assistance programs under section 127; and fringe benefits under section 132. Qualified benefits can be provided under a cafeteria plan either through insured arrangements or arrangements that are not insured.

[3] 49 FR 19321 (May 7, 1984) and 54 FR 9460 (March 7, 1989), respectively.

[4] Those proposed regulations contain special rules with respect to flexible spending arrangements. A flexible spending arrangement (FSA) is defined in section 106(c)(2). Under section 106(c)(2), an FSA is generally a benefit program under which the maximum

reimbursement reasonably available for coverage is less than 500% of the value of the coverage.

[5] 62 FR 60196 (November 7, 1997) and 62 FR 60165 (November 7, 1997), respectively. IRS Announcement 98-105 (1998-49 I.R.B. 21 (November 23, 1998)) states that the Service will amend the effective date of these temporary regulations (§ 1.125-4T) and proposed regulations (§ 1.125-4) so that they will not be effective before plan years beginning at least 120 days after further guidance is issued.

[6] Conforming changes have also been made to Q&A-8 of the 1984 proposed regulations under § 1.125-1.

and 1.125-2, Q&A-7 of the existing proposed regulations, that such arrangements exhibit the risk-shifting and risk-distribution characteristics of insurance.

Although the final regulations being published elsewhere in this issue of the **FEDERAL REGISTER** permit election changes in the event an individual becomes eligible (or loses eligibility) for Medicare or Medicaid, these proposed regulations do not address election changes to reflect an individual's eligibility for other government programs that pay for or subsidize health coverage.[7] For example, the new rules do not address the possibility that an employee's child may cease to be eligible for coverage under a state's children's health insurance program (CHIP) designed in accordance with Title XXI of the Social Security Act.[8] Comments are requested on whether eligibility or ineligibility for such a government program should be added to the types of events that allow a cafeteria plan election change (including any special administrative difficulties that employers might have in identifying this type of event) and, if so, the types of government programs that should be permitted to be taken into account.

D. *Effective Date and Reliance.*

The new proposed regulations do not specify a proposed effective date. Any effective date will be prospective, and comments are requested on the extent of lead time necessary for

employers to be able to implement the new proposed regulations after they are adopted as final regulations.

Until the effective date of further guidance, taxpayers may rely on the new proposed regulations. In addition, until the effective date of further guidance, taxpayers may continue to rely on the change in family status rules in the existing proposed regulations (at § 1.125-2, Q&A-6(c)) with respect to benefits other than accident and health coverage and group-term life insurance coverage, and on the cost or coverage change rules in the existing proposed regulations (at § 1.125-2, Q&A-6(b)) with respect to all types of qualified benefits.

Special Analyses

It has been determined that this notice of proposed rulemaking is not a significant regulatory action as defined in Executive Order 12866. Therefore, a regulatory assessment is not required. It also has been determined that section 553(b) of the Administrative Procedure Act (5 U.S.C. chapter 5) do not apply to these regulations, and because the regulations do not impose a collection of information on small entities, the Regulatory Flexibility Act (5 U.S.C. chapter 6) does not apply. Pursuant to section 7805(f) of the Internal Revenue Code, these proposed regulations will be submitted to the Chief Counsel for Advocacy of the Small Business Administration for comment on their impact on small business.

Comments and Public Hearing

Before these proposed regulations are adopted as final regulations, consideration will be given to any written and electronic comments (a signed original and eight (8) copies) that are submitted timely to the IRS. The IRS and Treasury specifically request comments on the clarity of the proposed regulations and how they may be made easier to understand. All comments will be available for public inspection and copying. A public hearing will be scheduled if requested in writing by any person that timely submits written comments. If a public hearing is scheduled, notice of the date, time, and place for the hearing will be published in the **Federal Register**.

Drafting Information

The principal authors of these proposed regulations are Janet A. Laufer and Christine L. Keller, Office of the Associate Chief Counsel (Employee Benefits and Exempt Organizations). However, other personnel from the IRS and Treasury Department participated in their development.

List of Subjects in 26 CFR Part 1

Income taxes, Reporting and recordkeeping requirements.

Partial Withdrawal of Notice of Proposed Rulemaking

Under the authority of 26 U.S.C. 7805, § 1.125 Q&A-6(c) and (d) in the notice of proposed rulemaking that was published on March 7, 1989 (54 FR 9460) is withdrawn.

Amendments to Previously Proposed Rules

The proposed rules published on May 7, 1984 (49 FR 19321) and March 7, 1989 (54 FR 9460), and amended on November 7, 1997 (62 FR 60196), are amended as set forth below.

Proposed Amendments to the Regulations

Accordingly, 26 CFR part 1 is proposed to be amended as follows:

PART 1—INCOME TAXES

Paragraph 1. The authority citation for part 1 continues to read in part as follows:

Authority: 26 U.S.C. 7805 * * *

Par. 2. In § 1.125-1, as proposed to be added on May 7, 1984 (49 FR 19322), in Q&A-8, Q-8 is republished and A-8 is amended by adding two sentences at the end of the answer to read as follows:

§ 1.125-1 Questions and answers relating to cafeteria plans.

* * * * *

Q-8: What requirements apply to participants' elections under a cafeteria plan?

A-8: * * * For benefit elections relating to accident or health plans and group-term life insurance coverage, a cafeteria plan may permit a participant to revoke a benefit election after the period of coverage has commenced and to make a new election with respect to the remainder of the period of coverage under the rules set forth in § 1.125-4 pertaining to permitted election changes. For additional rules governing benefit elections, see § 1.125-4.

* * * * *

Par. 3. In § 1.125-2, as proposed to be added on March 7, 1989 (54 FR 9500) and amended November 7, 1997 (62 FR 60197), in Q&A-6, Q-6 is republished and A-6 is amended by:

1. Adding a sentence at the end of paragraph (b)(2).

2. Revising the last sentence of paragraph (c).

3. Revising the last sentence of paragraph (d).

The additions and revisions read as follows:

§ 1.125-2 Miscellaneous cafeteria plan questions and answers.

* * * * *

Q-6: In what circumstance may participants revoke existing elections and make new elections under a cafeteria plan?

A-6: * * *

(b) * * *

(2) * * * For additional rules governing cafeteria plan election changes in connection with a significant cost or coverage change, see § 1.125-4.

(c) *Certain changes in family status.* *** For additional rules governing cafeteria plan election changes in connection with certain changes in status, see § 1.125-4.

(d) *Separation from service.* ***For additional rules governing cafeteria plan election changes in connection with an employee's separation from service, see § 1.125-4.

* * * * *

Par. 4. § 1.125-4 is amended as follows:

1. Paragraph (c) is amended as follows:

a. Revising paragraph (c)(1)(iii).

b. Adding paragraph (c)(2)(vi).

c. Revising paragraph (c)(3)(ii).

d. Adding paragraphs (c)(4) *Example 3*(iii) and (c)(4) *Example 9.*

2. Revising paragraph (f).

3. Revising paragraph (g).

4. Revising paragraph (i)(3).

The additions and revisions read as follows:

§ 1.125-4 Permitted election changes.

---

[7] The loss of coverage under a government program may give rise to a special enrollment right under section 9801(f) and, thus, the issue addressed here is relevant only in cases in which the special enrollment rules do not apply.

[8] Added to the Social Security Act by section 4901 of the Balanced Budget Act of 1997, Public Law 105-33 (August 5, 1997).

* * * * *

(c) * * * (1) * * *

(iii) *Application to other qualified benefits.* This paragraph (c) applies to plans providing qualified benefits other than those listed in paragraph (c) (1) (ii) of this section.

(2) * * *

(vi) *Adoption assistance.* For purposes of adoption assistance provided through a cafeteria plan, the commencement or termination of an adoption proceeding.

(3) * * *

(ii) *Application to other qualified benefits.* An election change satisfies the requirements of this paragraph (c) (3) with respect to other qualified benefits if the election change is on account of and corresponds with a change in status that affects eligibility for coverage under an employer's plan. An election change also satisfies the requirements of this paragraph (c) (3) if the election change is on account of and corresponds with a change in status that affects expenses described in section 129 (including employment-related expenses as defined in section 21(b) (2)) with respect to dependent care assistance, or expenses described in section 137 (including qualified adoption expenses as defined in section 137(d)) with respect to adoption assistance.

* * * * *

(4) * * *

Example 3. * * *

(iii) In addition, under paragraph (f) (4) of this section, if *F* makes an election change to cover *G* under *F*'s employer's plan, then *E* may make a corresponding change to elect employee-only coverage under *P*'s cafeteria plan.

* * * * *

Example 9. (i) Employee *A* has one child, *B*. Employee *A*'s employer, *X*, maintains a calendar year cafeteria plan that allows employees to elect coverage under a dependent care FSA. Prior to the beginning of the calendar year, *A* elects salary reduction contributions of $4,000 during the year to fund coverage under the dependent care FSA for up to $4,000 of reimbursements for the year. During the year, *B* reaches the age of 13, and *A* wants to cancel coverage under the dependent care FSA.

(ii) When *B* turns 13, *B* ceases to satisfy the definition of "qualifying individual" under section 21(b) (1) of the Internal Revenue Code. Accordingly, *B*'s attainment of age 13 is a change in status under paragraph (c) (2) (iv) of this section that affects *A*'s employment-related expenses as defined in section 21(b) (2). Therefore, *A* may make a corresponding change under *X*'s cafeteria plan to cancel coverage under the dependent care FSA.

* * * * *

(f) *Significant cost or coverage changes*—(1) *In general.* Paragraphs (f) (2) through (5) of this section set forth rules for election changes as a result of changes in cost or coverage. This paragraph (f) does not apply to an election change with respect to a health FSA (or on account of a change in cost or coverage under a health FSA).

(2) *Cost changes - -* (i) *Automatic changes.* If the cost of a qualified benefits plan increases (or decreases) during a period of coverage and, under the terms of the plan, employees are required to make a corresponding change in their payments, the cafeteria plan may, on a reasonable and consistent basis, automatically make a prospective increase (or decrease) in affected employees' elective contributions for the plan.

(ii) *Significant cost increases.* If the cost of a benefit package option (as defined in paragraph (i) (2) of this section) significantly increases during a period of coverage, the cafeteria plan may permit employees either to make a corresponding prospective increase in their payments, or to revoke their elections and, in lieu thereof, to receive on a prospective basis coverage under another benefit package option providing similar coverage. For example, if the cost of an indemnity option under an accident or health plan significantly increases during a period of coverage, employees who are covered by the indemnity option may make a corresponding prospective increase in their payments or may instead elect to revoke their election for the indemnity option and, in lieu thereof, elect coverage under an HMO option.

(iii) *Application to dependent care.* This paragraph (f) (2) applies in the case of a dependent care assistance plan only if the cost change is imposed by a dependent care provider who is not a relative of the employee. For this purpose, a relative is an individual who is related as

described in section 152(a) (1) through (8), incorporating the rules of section 152(b) (1) and (2).

(3) *Coverage changes*—(i) *Significant curtailment.* If the coverage under a plan is significantly curtailed or ceases during a period of coverage, the cafeteria plan may permit affected employees to revoke their elections under the plan. In that case, each affected employee may make a new election on a prospective basis for coverage under another benefit package option providing similar coverage. Coverage under an accident or health plan is significantly curtailed only if there is an overall reduction in coverage provided to participants under the plan so as to constitute reduced coverage to participants generally.

(ii) *Addition (or elimination) of benefit package option providing similar coverage.* If during a period of coverage a plan adds a new benefit package option or other coverage option (or eliminates an existing benefit package option or other coverage option) the cafeteria plan may permit affected employees to elect the newly-added option (or elect another option if an option has been eliminated) prospectively on a pre-tax basis and make corresponding election changes with respect to other benefit package options providing similar coverage.

(4) *Change in coverage of spouse or dependent under other employer's plan.* A cafeteria plan may permit an employee to make a prospective election change that is on account of and corresponds with a change made under the plan of the spouse's, former spouse's or dependent's employer if—

(i) A cafeteria plan or qualified benefits plan of the spouse's, former spouse's, or dependent's employer permits participants to make an election change that would be permitted under paragraphs (b) through (g) of this section (disregarding this paragraph (f) (4)); or

(ii) The cafeteria plan permits participants to make an election for a period of coverage that is different from the period of coverage under the cafeteria plan or qualified benefits plan of the spouse's, former spouse's, or dependent's employer.

(5) *Examples.* The following examples illustrate the application of this paragraph (f):

Example 1. (i) A calendar year cafeteria plan is maintained pursuant to a collective bargaining agreement for the benefit of Employer *M*'s employees. The cafeteria plan offers various benefits, including indemnity health insurance and a health FSA. As a result of mid-year negotiations, premiums for the indemnity health insurance are reduced in the middle of the year, insurance co-payments for office visits are reduced under the indemnity plan, and an HMO option is added.

(ii) Under these facts, the reduction in health insurance premiums is a reduction in cost. Accordingly, under paragraph (f) (2) (i) of this section, the cafeteria plan may automatically decrease the amount of salary reduction contributions of affected participants by an amount that corresponds to the premium change. However, the plan may not permit employees to change their health FSA elections to reflect the mid-year change in copayments under the indemnity plan.

(iii) Also, the addition of the HMO option is an addition of a benefit package option. Accordingly, under paragraph (f) (3) (ii) of this section, the cafeteria plan may permit affected participants to make an election change to elect the new HMO option. However, the plan may not permit employees to change their health FSA elections to reflect differences in copayments under the HMO option.

Example 2. (i) Employer *N* sponsors a group health plan under which employees may elect either employee-only coverage or family health coverage. The 12-month period of coverage under *N*'s cafeteria plan begins January 1, 2001. *N*'s employee, *A*, is married to *B*. Employee *A* elects employee-only coverage under *N*'s plan. *B*'s employer, *O*, offers health coverage to *O*'s employees under its group health plan under which employees may elect either employee-only coverage or family coverage. *O*'s plan has a 12-month period of coverage beginning September 1, 2001. *B* maintains individual coverage under *O*'s plan at the time *A* elects coverage under *N*'s plan, and wants to elect no coverage for the plan year beginning on September 1, 2001, which is the next period of coverage under *O*'s group health plan.

(ii) Under paragraph (f) (4) (ii) of this section, *N*'s cafeteria plan may permit *A* to change *A*'s election prospectively to family coverage under that plan effective September 1, 2001 if *B* actually elects no coverage under *O*'s group health plan for the plan year beginning on September 1, 2001.

Example 3. (i) Employer *P* sponsors a calendar year cafeteria plan under which employees may elect either employee-only or family health coverage. Before the beginning of the year, *P*'s employee, *C*, elects family coverage under *P*'s cafeteria plan. *C* also elects coverage under the health FSA for up to $200 of reimbursements for the year to be funded by salary reduction contributions of $200 during the year. *C* is married to *D*, who is employed by Employer *Q*. *Q* does not maintain a cafeteria plan, but does maintain a group health plan providing its employees with employee-only coverage. During the calendar year, *Q* adds family coverage as an option under its health plan. *D* elects family coverage under *Q*'s plan, and *C* wants to revoke *C*'s election for health coverage and elect no health coverage under *P*'s cafeteria plan for the remainder of the year.

(ii) *Q*'s addition of family coverage as an option under its health plan constitutes a new coverage option described in paragraph (f)(3)(ii) of this section. Accordingly, pursuant to paragraph (f)(4)(i) of this section, *P*'s cafeteria plan may permit *C* to revoke *C*'s health coverage election if *D* actually elects family health coverage under *Q*'s group health plan. Employer *P*'s plan may not permit *C* to change *C*'s health FSA election.

Example 4. (i) Employer *R* maintains a cafeteria plan under which employees may elect accident or health coverage under either an indemnity plan or an HMO. Before the beginning of the year, *R*'s employee, *E* elects coverage under the HMO at a premium cost of $100 per month. During the year, *E* decides to switch to the indemnity plan, which charges a premium of $140 per month.

(ii) *E*'s change from the HMO to indemnity plan is not a change in cost or coverage under this paragraph (f), and none of the other election change rules under paragraphs (b) through (e) of this section apply. While *R*'s health plan may permit *E* to make the change from the HMO to the indemnity plan, *R*'s cafeteria plan may not permit *E* to make an election change to reflect the increased premium. Accordingly, if *E* switches from the HMO to the indemnity plan, *E* may pay the $40 per month additional cost on an after-tax basis.

Example 5. (i) Employee *A* is married to Employee *B* and they have one child, *C*. Employee *A*'s employer, *M*, maintains a calendar year cafeteria plan that allows employees to elect coverage under a dependent care FSA. Child *C* attends *X*'s on site child care center at an annual cost of $3,000. Prior to the beginning of the year, *A* elects salary reduction contributions of $3,000 during the year to fund coverage under the dependent care FSA for up to $3,000 of reimbursements for the year. Employee *A* now wants to revoke *A*'s election of coverage under the dependent care FSA, because A has found a new child care provider.

(ii) The availability of dependent care services from the new child care provider (whether the new provider is a household employee or family member of *A* or *B* or a person who is independent of *A* and *B*) is a significant change in coverage similar to a benefit package option becoming available. Thus, *M*'s cafeteria plan may permit *A* to elect to revoke *A*'s previous election of coverage under the dependent care FSA, and make a corresponding new election to reflect the cost of the new child care provider.

Example 6. (i) Employee *D* is married to Employee *E* and they have one child, *F*. Employee *D*'s employer, *N*, maintains a calendar year cafeteria plan that allows employees to elect coverage under a dependent care FSA. Child *F* is cared for by *Y*, *D*'s household employee, who provides child care services five days a week from 9 a.m. to 6 p.m. at an annual cost in excess of $5,000. Prior to the beginning of the year, *D* elects salary reduction contributions of $5,000 during the year to fund coverage under the dependent care FSA for up to $5,000 of reimbursements for the year. During the year, *F* begins school and, as a result, *Y*'s regular hours of work are changed to five days a week from 3 p.m. to 6 p.m. Employee *D* now wants to revoke *D*'s election under the dependent care FSA, and make a new election under the dependent care FSA to an annual cost of $4,000 to reflect a reduced cost of child care due to *Y*'s reduced hours.

(ii) The change in the number of hours of work performed by *Y* is a change in coverage. Thus, *N*'s cafeteria plan may permit *D* to reduce *D*'s previous election under the dependent care FSA to $4,000.

Example 7. (i) Employee *G* is married to Employee *H* and they have one child, *J*. Employee *G*'s employer, *O*, maintains a calendar year cafeteria plan that allows employees to elect coverage under a dependent care FSA. Child *J* is cared for by *Z*, *G*'s household employee, who is not a relative of *G* and who provides child care services at an annual cost of $4,000. Prior to the beginning of the year, *G* elects salary reduction contributions of $4,000 during the year to fund coverage under the dependent care FSA for up to $4,000 of reimbursements for the year. During the year, *G* raises *Z*'s salary. Employee *G* now wants to revoke *G*'s election under the dependent care FSA, and make a new election under the dependent care FSA to an annual amount of $4,500 to reflect the raise.

(ii) The raise in *Z*'s salary is a significant increase in cost under paragraph (f)(2)(ii) of this section, and an increase in election to reflect the raise corresponds with that change in status. Thus, *O*'s cafeteria plan may permit *G* to elect to increase *G*'s election under the dependent care FSA.

(g) *Special requirements relating to the Family and Medical Leave Act.* [Reserved]

* * * * *

(i) * * *

(3) *Dependent.* A dependent means a dependent as defined in section 152, except that, for purposes of accident or health coverage, any child to whom section 152(e) applies is treated as a dependent of both parents, and, for purposes of dependent care assistance provided through a cafeteria plan, a dependent means a qualifying individual (as defined in section 21(b)(1)) with respect to the employee.

* * * * *

Robert E. Wenzel

Deputy Commissioner of Internal Revenue

¶ 20,248

IRS proposed regulations: Defined contribution plans: Plan amendments: Optional forms of benefit.—The IRS has issued proposed regulations providing relief to defined contribution plans from Code Sec. 411(d)(6), which precludes qualified retirement plan amendments from eliminating optional forms of benefits.

The proposed regulations were published in the *Federal Register* March 29, 2000 (65 FR 16546).

The final regulations were published in the *Federal Register* on September 6, 2000 (65 FR 53901). The final regulations are reproduced at ¶ 12,233. The preamble to the final regulations is reproduced at ¶ 24,505V.

¶ 20,249

IRS proposed regulations: Plan loans: Qualified plans: Refinancing: Multiple loans.—The IRS has issued proposed regulations that supplement final regulations (¶ 24,505S) issued on plan loans that are deemed to be distributed to a participant. The proposed regs indicate that a refinancing of a plan loan will effectively be treated as a new loan, which is applied to repay the balance of a prior loan, if the new loan replaces the prior and has a later repayment date than the prior loan. The transaction will result in a deemed distribution if the amount of the new loan, when added to the amount of the prior outstanding loan, exceeds the amount limitations of Code Sec. 72(p)(2)(A). This rule does not apply if the prior loan is to be repaid by its original repayment date. A participant may also borrow more than once from a plan. However, a deemed distribution of a loan will occur if two loans have previously been made from the plan during the year.

The proposed regulations were published in the *Federal Register* on July 31, 2000 (65 FR 46677). The final regulations were published in the *Federal Register* on December 3, 2002 (67 FR 71821). The final regulations are reproduced at ¶ 11,210. The preamble to the final regulations is reproduced at ¶ 24,506W.

¶ 20,250

IRS proposed regulations: Defined contribution plans: New comparability: Cross-testing: Minimum allocation "gateway" requirement.—The IRS has issued proposed regulations that would, effective for 2002 plan years, permit new comparability defined contribution plans to continue to utilize cross-testing, but that would implement minimum allocation "gateways" that are designed to restrict the disparity in allocation rates between highly compensated and nonhighly compensated employees.

The preamble and final regulations, which were published in the *Federal Register* on June 29, 2001 (66 FR 34535) can be found at ¶ 24,506G. The amended portions of the regulations appear at ¶ 11,720W-14.

¶ 20,251

IRS proposed regulations: Employee benefit plan trusts: IRA's: Investment trusts: Fiduciary: Domestic trust status: Control test.—The IRS has issued proposed regulations relating to a safe harbor for certain employee benefit trusts and investment trusts stating that group trusts and certain investment trusts are deemed to satisfy the control test for determining domestic status under IRS Reg. Sec. 301.7701-7 if U. S. trustees control all substantial trust decisions.

The preamble and the proposed regulations were published in the *Federal Register* on October 12, 2000 (65 FR 60821).

The regulations were finalized by T.D. 8962 and published in the *Federal Register* on August 9, 2001 (66 FR 41778). The regulations are reproduced at ¶ 13,927. The preamble is reproduced at ¶ 24,506I.

¶ 20,252

IRS proposed regulations: Determination of payee: Information reporting: Joint payees.—The IRS has issued proposed regulations that clarify who is the payee for information reporting purposes if an instrument is made payable to joint payees, provide information reporting requirements for persons making payment on behalf of another person, and clarify that the amount to be reported paid is the gross amount of the payment.

The proposed regulations, which were published in the *Federal Register* October 17, 2000 (65 FR 61292), are reproduced below.

DEPARTMENT OF THE TREASURY

Internal Revenue Service

26 CFR Parts 1, 5f, and 31

[REG-246249-96]

RIN 1545-AW48

Information Reporting Requirements for Certain Payments Made on Behalf of Another Person, Payments to Joint Payees, and Payments of Gross Proceeds from Sales Involving Investment Advisers

AGENCY: Internal Revenue Service (IRS), Treasury.

ACTION: * * * notice of proposed rulemaking; and notice of public hearing.

SUMMARY: * * * This document contains proposed regulations under section 6041 that clarify who is the payee for information reporting purposes if a check or other instrument is made payable to joint payees, provide information reporting requirements for escrow agents and other persons making payments on behalf of another person, and clarify that the amount to be reported paid is the gross amount of the payment. This document also contains proposed regulations under section 6045 that remove investment advisers from the list of exempt recipients. In addition, this document provides notice of a public hearing on these proposed regulations.

DATES: Written or electronic comments must be received by January 17, 2001. Requests to speak (with outlines of oral comments) at a public hearing scheduled for February 7, 2001, at 10 a.m. must be submitted by January 24, 2001.

ADDRESSES: Send submissions to: CC:M&SP:RU (REG-246249-96), room 5226, Internal Revenue Service, POB 7604, Ben Franklin Station, Washington, DC 20044. In the alternative, submissions may be hand delivered Monday through Friday between the hours of 8 a.m. and 5 p.m. to: CC:M&SP:RU (REG-246249-96), Courier's Desk, Internal Revenue Service, 1111 Constitution Avenue, NW., Washington, DC, or sent electronically via the IRS Internet site at http://www.irs.gov/tax_regs/regslist.html. The public hearing will be held in the IRS Auditorium, Seventh Floor, Internal Revenue Service Building, 1111 Constitution Avenue, NW., Washington, DC.

FOR FURTHER INFORMATION CONTACT: Concerning the regulations, Nancy L. Rose, (202) 622-4910; concerning submission of comments, the hearing, and/or to be placed on the building access list to attend the hearing, Guy R. Traynor, (202) 622-7190 (not toll-free numbers).

SUPPLEMENTARY INFORMATION:

Paperwork Reduction Act

The collection of information contained in this notice of proposed rulemaking has been submitted to the Office of Management and Budget for review in accordance with the Paperwork Reduction Act of 1995 (44 U.S.C. 3507(d)). Comments on the collection of information should be sent to the Office of Management and Budget, Attn: Desk Officer for the Department of Treasury, Office of Information and

Regulatory Affairs, Washington, DC 20503, with copies to the Internal Revenue Service, Attn: IRS Reports Clearance Officer,W:CAR:MP:FP:S:O, Washington, DC 20224. Comments on the collection of information should be received by December 19, 2000. Comments are specifically requested concerning:

Whether the proposed collection of information is necessary for the proper operation of the functions of the Internal Revenue Service, including whether the information will have practical utility;

The accuracy of the estimated burden associated with the proposed collection of information (see below);

How the quality, utility, and clarity of the information to be collected may be enhanced;

How the burden of complying with the proposed collection of information may be minimized, including through the application of automated collection techniques or other forms of information technology; and

Estimates of capital or start-up costs and costs of operation, maintenance, and purchase of service to provide information.

The collection of information in these proposed regulations is in §§ 1.6041-1(e) and 1.6045-1(c)(3). This information is required to determine if taxpayers have properly reported amounts received as income. The collection of information is mandatory. The likely respondents are businesses and other for-profit institutions.

The estimate of the reporting burden in proposed § 1.6041-1 is reflected in the burden of Form 1099-MISC, Miscellaneous Income, which is currently 14 minutes per form. The estimate of the reporting burden in proposed § 1.6045-1 is reflected in the burden of Form 1099-B, Proceeds of Broker and Barter Exchange Transactions, which is currently 15 minutes per form.

An agency may not conduct or sponsor, and a person is not required to respond to, a collection of information unless it displays a valid control number assigned by the Office of Management and Budget.

Books or records relating to the collection of information must be retained as long as their contents may become material in the administration of any internal revenue law. Generally tax returns and tax return information are confidential, as required by 26 U.S.C. 6103.

Background and Explanation of Provisions

1. *Proposed Regulations Under Section 6041*

Section 6041 provides that all persons engaged in a trade or business that make certain payments in the course of that trade or business to another person of $600 or more in a taxable year must report the amount of the payments and the name and address of the recipient.

Section 3406(a) provides that a payor must withhold tax from reportable payments under certain circumstances, for example, if the payee has failed to furnish a valid taxpayer identification number to the payor in the manner required. "Reportable payments" include payments that are required to be reported under sections 6041 and 6045. Section 3406(b)(3)(A) and (C). The party that is responsible for reporting the payments under sections 6041 and 6045 is also responsible for any backup withholding required under section 3406.

These proposed regulations address certain issues identified by the Commissioner's Information Reporting Program Advisory Committee (IRPAC) and take into account comments and information provided by IRPAC members representing the banking, real estate, insurance, and securities industries.

a. *Payments to Joint Payees*

The proposed regulations clarify the definition of fixed and determinable income in § 1.6041-1(c) when a payment is made payable to joint payees. This issue was discussed in papers presented at IRPAC meetings in May 1994 and May 1995. The regulations provide that a payment made jointly to two or more payees may be fixed and determinable income to one payee even though the payment is not fixed and determinable income to another payee. For example, when a payment in consideration for services is made payable to joint payees, one of whom is the service provider, an information return must be made showing the service provider as the payee if the payment is fixed and determinable income to the service provider, even if the payment is not fixed and determinable income to the other payee. See, e.g., Situation 2 of Rev. Rul. 70-608 (1970-2 C.B. 286).

b. *Identification of Payor*

A payment reportable under section 6041 may be made by a person on behalf of another person that is the actual source of the funds. Under certain circumstances this so-called middleman, and not the person that provided the funds, is the payor obligated to report the payment under section 6041. See, e.g., Rev. Rul. 93-70 (1993-2 C.B. 294).

Consistent with Rev. Rul. 93-70, the proposed regulations add a new paragraph (e)(1) to § 1.6041-1 that provides that a person that makes a payment on behalf of another person and performs a management or oversight function in connection with, or has a significant economic interest in, the payment must report under section 6041. A management or oversight function is an activity that is more than merely administrative or ministerial. For example, a person that merely writes checks at the direction of others in connection with a transaction, sometimes referred to as a paying agent, is performing only an administrative or ministerial function and is not a payor. In contrast, a person that exercises discretion or supervision in connection with a payment is performing a management or oversight function and is a payor. A significant economic interest in a payment is an economic interest that would be compromised if the payment were not made. For example a bank has a significant economic interest in a payment to a contractor when damage occurs to property securing a mortgage held by the bank. With this standard, which was also discussed in the IRPAC papers of May 1994 and May 1995, the proposed regulations attempt to replace disparate revenue rulings with a consistent and easily administrable rule that can be applied to a variety of factual situations involving middlemen.

Section 1.6041-1(e)(2) of the proposed regulations provides an exception to the general rule of § 1.6041-1(e)(1) by referencing the procedures in Rev. Proc. 84-33 (1984-1 C.B. 502) for an optional method for payors to designate a paying agent to file information returns and backup withhold.

The proposed regulations include examples, derived primarily from revenue rulings and private letter rulings, which are intended to be all-inclusive. Rulings that are factually encompassed by the proposed regulations will be obsoleted. Comments are requested identifying other factually relevant rulings or suggesting appropriate additional examples.

* * *

d. *Revenue Rulings to Become Obsolete*

As discussed above, the proposed regulations apply to the factual situations addressed in the following revenue rulings, which will become obsolete:

* * *

Rev. Rul. 70-608, Situations 1, 2, and 5 (1970-2 C.B. 286)

Rev. Rul. 69-595 (1969-2 C.B. 242)

* * *

2. *Proposed Regulations Under Section 6045*

Section 6045 provides that a broker must file an information return showing the name and address of the broker's customer and other details, such as the amount of the gross proceeds of the transaction, as the Secretary may require. Section 6045(c) defines a broker as a dealer, a barter exchange, or any other person who, for a consideration, regularly acts as a middleman with respect to property or services.

Section 1.6045-1(a)(2) provides that a customer is the person who makes a sale effected by a broker, if the broker acts as (i) an agent for the customer in the sale, (ii) a principal in the sale, or (iii) the party in the sale responsible for paying or crediting the proceeds to the customer. Under § 1.6045-1(h), a broker must treat the person whose name appears on the broker's books and records as the principal.

Section 5f.6045-1(c)(3), also published as proposed regulations (49 FR 22343), provides that no return of information is required with respect to a sale effected for a customer that is an exempt recipient. Among the categories of exempt recipients is a person registered under the Investment Advisers Act of 1940 who regularly acts as a broker (an investment adviser).

Section 5f.6045-1(c)(3)(iii) provides that, in a cash on delivery or similar transaction, only the broker that receives the gross proceeds against delivery of the securities sold is required to report a sale, unless the broker's customer is another broker (a second-party broker) that is an exempt recipient. In that case, only the second-party broker is required to report.

One effect of these provisions is to shift the reporting requirement in a cash on delivery transaction from the broker that receives the gross proceeds against delivery of the securities to an investment adviser.

* * *

Commentators on the proposed regulations objected to the imposition of the reporting obligation under section 6045(a) on investment advisers because (1) investment advisers generally do not have first-hand knowledge that a sale has been completed, and (2) investment advisers generally do not handle the proceeds of a sale and, consequently, cannot comply with the backup withholding requirements of section 3406. Investment adviser reporting issues were also the subject of IRPAC papers presented at meetings in November 1995 and October 1997.

These proposed regulations withdraw the 1984 proposed regulations. In general, they propose to incorporate the provisions of § 5f.6045-1 into § 1.6045-1(c)(3) and (4). The proposed regulations also remove investment advisers from the list of exempt recipients and revise current § 5f.6045-1(c)(4) *Examples 4* and *5* to clarify that, under the revised rules, an investment adviser that initiates a sale on behalf of a customer is required to make a return of information only if the sale relates to an investment account in the investment adviser's name (i.e., the identity of the customer is not disclosed to the account custodian).

Proposed Effective Date

The provisions of these regulations under sections 6041 and 3406 are proposed to be applicable for payments made on or after the beginning of the first calendar year that begins after these regulations are published in the **Federal Register** as final regulations. The provisions of these regulations under section 6045 are proposed to be applicable for sales effected on or after the beginning of the first calendar year that begins after the date these regulations are published in the **Federal Register** as final regulations.

Special Analyses

It has been determined that this notice of proposed rulemaking is not a significant regulatory action as defined in Executive Order 12866. Therefore, a regulatory assessment is not required. It has also been determined that section 553(b) of the Administrative Procedure Act (5 U.S.C. chapter 5) does not apply to these regulations. An initial regulatory flexibility analysis has been prepared for the collection of information in this notice of proposed rulemaking under 5 U.S.C. section 603. The analysis is set forth in this preamble under the heading "Initial Regulatory Flexibility Analysis." Pursuant to section 7805(f) of the Internal Revenue Code, this notice of proposed rulemaking will be submitted to the Chief Counsel for Advocacy of the Small Business Administration for comment on its impact on small business.

Initial Regulatory Flexibility Analysis

The collection of information proposed in § 1.6041-1(e) is needed to clarify the requirements for filing an information return under section 6041 when a person makes a payment on behalf of another person or to joint payees. The objectives of the proposed regulations are to provide uniform, practicable, and administrable rules under section 6041 for persons making payments on behalf of another person or to joint payees. The types of small entities to which the proposed regulations may apply are small businesses. An estimate of the number of small entities affected is not feasible because of the large variety of entities and transactions to which the proposed regulations may apply. However, in 1997 a total of 73,273,621 Forms 1099-MISC were filed with the IRS. The number of 1997 Forms 1099-MISC that related to transactions that involved payments made on behalf of another person or to joint payees cannot be determined. The current estimated reporting burden relating to Form 1099-MISC is 14 minutes per form. No special professional skills are necessary for preparation of the reports or records. There are no known Federal rules that duplicate, overlap, or conflict with these proposed regulations. The regulations proposed are considered to have the least economic impact on small entities of all alternatives considered.

The collection of information in proposed § 1.6045-1(c)(3) will not have a significant economic impact on a substantial number of small entities. The proposed regulations will relieve investment advisers of the requirement to make information returns under section 6045(a), and few, if any, financial custodians that may be affected by the regulations are small entities.

Comments and Public Hearing

Before these proposed regulations are adopted as final regulations, consideration will be given to any electronic or written comments (a signed original and eight (8) copies) that are submitted timely (in the manner described in the ADDRESSES caption) to the IRS. The IRS and Treasury Department request comments on the clarity of the proposed rules and how they may be made easier to understand. All comments will be available for public inspection and copying.

A public hearing has been scheduled for February 7, 2001, beginning at 10 a.m. in the IRS Auditorium, Seventh Floor, Internal Revenue Building, 1111 Constitution Avenue, NW., Washington, DC. Due to building security procedures, visitors must enter at the 10th Street entrance, located between Constitution and Pennsylvania Avenues, NW. In addition, all visitors must present photo identification to enter the building. Because of access restrictions, visitors will not be admitted beyond the immediate entrance area more than 15 minutes before the hearing starts. For information about having your name placed on the building access list to attend the hearing, see the "FOR FURTHER INFORMATION CONTACT" section of the preamble.

The rules of 26 CFR 601.601(a)(3) apply to the hearing. Persons who wish to present oral comments at the hearing must submit written comments and an outline of the topics to be discussed and the time to be devoted to each topic (signed original and eight (8) copies) by January 24, 2001. A period of 10 minutes will be allotted to each person for making comments. An agenda showing the scheduling of the speakers will be prepared after the deadline for receiving outlines has passed. Copies of the agenda will be available free of charge at the hearing.

Drafting Information

The principal author of these regulations is Donna M. Crisalli, Office of the Associate Chief Counsel (Income Tax & Accounting). However, other personnel from the IRS and Treasury Department participated in their development.

List of Subjects

26 CFR Parts 1 and 5f

Income taxes, Reporting and recordkeeping requirements.

26 CFR Part 31

Employment taxes, Income taxes, Penalties, Railroad retirement, Reporting and recordkeeping requirements, Social security, Unemployment compensation.

Proposed Amendments to the Regulations

Accordingly, under the authority of 26 U.S.C. 7805, the notice of proposed rulemaking (LR-62-84) amending 26 CFR part 1 that was published in the **Federal Register** on May 29, 1984 (49 FR 22343) is withdrawn. In addition, 26 CFR parts 1, 5f, and 31 are proposed to be amended as follows:

PART 1—INCOME TAXES

Paragraph 1. The authority citation for part 1 is amended by adding an entry in numerical order to read in part as follows:

Authority: 26 U.S.C. 7805 * * *

Section 1.6041-1 also issued under 26 U.S.C. 6041(a). * * *

Par. 2. Section 1.6041-1 is amended by:

1. Removing the language "paragraph (g)" in the second sentence of paragraph (b)(1) and adding the language "paragraph (i)" in its place.

2. Adding two sentences after the fourth sentence of paragraph (c).

* * *

4. Adding new paragraphs (e) * * *.

The additions and revisions read as follows:

§ 1.6041-1 Return of information as to payments of $600 or more.

* * * * *

(c) * * * A payment made jointly to two or more payees may be fixed and determinable income to one payee even though the payment is not fixed and determinable income to another payee. For example, property insurance proceeds paid jointly to the owner of damaged property and to a contractor that repairs the property may be fixed and determinable income to the contractor but not fixed and determinable income to the owner. * * *

* * * * *

(e) *Payment made on behalf of another person*—(1) *In general.* A person that makes a payment in the course of its trade or business on behalf of another person is the payor that must make a return of information under this section with respect to that payment if the payment is described in paragraph (a) of this section and, under all the facts and circumstances, that person—

(i) Performs management or oversight functions (i.e., performs more than mere administrative or ministerial functions) in connection with the payment; or

(ii) Has a significant economic interest in the payment. (2) *Optional method to report.* A person that makes a payment on behalf of another person but is not required to make an information return under paragraph (e)(1) of this section may elect to do so pursuant to the procedures established in Rev. Proc. 84-33 (1984-1 C.B. 502) (optional method for a paying agent to report and deposit amounts withheld for payors under the statutory provisions of backup withholding) (see § 601.601(d)(2) of this chapter).

(3) *Examples.* The provisions of this paragraph (e) are illustrated by the following examples:

Example 1. Bank B provides financing to C, a real estate developer, for a construction project. B puts the funds in an escrow account and makes disbursements from the account for labor, materials, services, and other expenses related to the construction project. In connection with the payments, B performs the following functions on behalf of C: approves payments to the general contractor or subcontractors; ensures that loan proceeds are properly applied and that all approved bills are properly paid to avoid mechanics or materialmen's liens; conducts site inspections to determine whether work has been completed (but does not check the quality of the work); evaluates and assesses the cost of the project, including costs of changes; and communicates resulting concerns to C or to the general contractor so that modifications can be made or additional funding obtained. B is performing management or oversight functions in connection with the payment and is subject to the information reporting requirements of section 6041 with respect to payments from the escrow fund.

* * *

* * *

(j) *Effective date.* The provisions of paragraphs (b), (c), (e), and (f) apply to payments made on or after the beginning of the first calendar year that begins after these regulations are published in the **Federal Register** as final regulations.

§ 1.6041-3 Payments for which no return of information is required under Section 6041. [Amended]

* * *

Par. 4. Section 1.6045-1, as in effect on January 1, 2001, is amended as follows:

* * *

2. Revising paragraphs (c)(3) and (c)(4).

3. Removing the language "5f.6045-1(c)(3)(ii) of this chapter" and adding the language "paragraph (c)(3)(iii) of this section" in its place in each place it appears in paragraph (g)(4) *Examples 1, 4, 5, 6,* and *7(i).*

The revisions read as follows:

§ 1.6045-1 Returns of information of brokers and barter exchanges.

(a) *Definitions.* * * *

(c) * * *

(3) *Exceptions*—(i) *Sales effected for exempt recipients*—(A) *In general.* No return of information is required with respect to a sale effected for a customer that is an exempt recipient under paragraph (c)(3)(i)(B) of this section.

(B) *Exempt recipient defined.* The term *exempt recipient* means—

(*1*) A corporation as defined in section 7701(a)(3), whether domestic or foreign;

(*2*) An organization exempt from taxation under section 501(a) or an individual retirement plan;

* * *

(C) *Exemption certificate.* A broker may treat a person described in paragraph (c)(3)(i)(B) of this section as an exempt recipient based on a properly completed exemption certificate (as provided in §31.3406(h)-3) of this chapter or on the broker's actual knowledge that the payee is a person described in paragraph (c)(3)(i)(B) of this section. A broker may require an exempt recipient to file a properly completed exemption certificate and may treat an exempt recipient that fails to do so as a recipient that is not exempt.

* * *

(iv) *Cash on delivery transactions.* In the case of a sale of securities through a cash on delivery account, a delivery versus payment account, or other similar account or transaction, only the broker that receives the gross proceeds from the sale against delivery of the securities sold is required to report the sale. If, however, the broker's customer is another broker (second-party broker) that is an exempt recipient, then only the second-party broker is required to report the sale.

(v) *Fiduciaries and partnerships.* No return of information is required with respect to a sale effected by a custodian or trustee in its capacity as such or a redemption of a partnership interest by a partnership provided the sale is otherwise reported by the custodian or trustee on a properly filed Form 1041, or the redemption is otherwise reported by the partnership on a properly filed Form 1065, and all Schedule K-1 reporting requirements are satisfied.

* * *

(xiii) *Effective date.* The provisions of this paragraph (c)(3) apply for sales effected on or after the beginning of the first calendar year that begins after the date these regulations are published in the **Federal Register** as final regulations.

* * *

Robert E. Wenzel

Deputy Commissioner of Internal Revenue

¶ 20,253

IRS proposed regulations: Health Insurance Portability and Accountability Act (HIPAA): Nondiscrimination rules: Group health plans: Eligibility for benefits: Health factors.—The IRS has issued proposed regulations interpreting and providing guidance on the nondiscrimination provisions under HIPAA. The regulations, among other things, explain the application of the provisions to premiums, describe "similarly situated individuals," and clarify that more favorable treatment of individuals with medical needs generally is permitted. The text of the proposed regulations is provided by the text of the IRS temporary regulations issued at the same time as the proposed regulations. The preamble of the temporary regulations is at ¶ 24,505X. The text of the temporary regulations is at ¶ 13,968R-10.

The proposed regulations, which were published in the *Federal Register* January 8, 2001 (65 FR 1435), are reproduced below.

DEPARTMENT OF THE TREASURY

Internal Revenue Service

26 CFR Part 54

[REG-114082-00]

RIN 1545-AY32

HIPAA Nondiscrimination

AGENCY: Internal Revenue Service (IRS), Treasury.

ACTION: Notice of proposed rulemaking by cross-reference to temporary regulations.

SUMMARY: Elsewhere in this issue of the **Federal Register,** the IRS is issuing temporary and final regulations governing the provisions prohibiting discrimination based on a health factor for group health plans. The IRS is issuing the temporary and final regulations at the same time that the Pension and Welfare Benefits Administration of the U.S. Department of Labor and the Health Care Financing Administration of the U.S. Department of Health and Human Services are issuing substantially similar interim final regulations governing the provisions prohibiting discrimination based on a health factor for group health plans and issuers of health insurance coverage offered in connection with a group health plan under the Employee Retirement Income Security Act of 1974 and the Public Health Service Act. The temporary regulations provide guidance to employers and group health plans relating to the group health plan nondiscrimination requirements. The text of those temporary regulations also serves as the text of these proposed regulations.

DATES: Written comments and requests for a public hearing must be received by *[INSERT DATE 90 DAYS AFTER PUBLICATION OF THIS DOCUMENT IN THE FEDERAL REGISTER].*

ADDRESSES: Send submissions to: CC:M & SP:RU (REG-114082-00), room 5226, Internal Revenue Service, POB 7604, Ben Franklin Station, Washington, DC 20044. Submissions may be hand-delivered to: CC:M & SP:RU (REG-114082-00), room 5226, Internal Revenue Service, 1111 Constitution Avenue, NW., Washington, DC.

Alternatively, taxpayers may submit comments electronically via the Internet by selecting the "Tax Regs" option on the IRS Home Page, or by submitting comments directly to the IRS Internet site at:

http://www.irs.gov/tax_regs/regslist.html.

FOR FURTHER INFORMATION CONTACT: Concerning the regulations, Russ Weinheimer at 202-622-6080; concerning submissions of comments or requests for a hearing, Sonya Cruse at 202-622-7190 (not toll-free numbers).

SUPPLEMENTARY INFORMATION:

Paperwork Reduction Act

The collection of information referenced in this notice of proposed rulemaking has been submitted to the Office of Management and Budget for review in accordance with the Paperwork Reduction Act of 1995 (44 U.S.C. 3507(d)).

An agency may not conduct or sponsor, and a person is not required to respond to, a collection of information unless it displays a valid control number assigned by the Office of Management and Budget.

The collections of information are in §54.9802-1T (see the temporary regulations published elsewhere in this issue of the **Federal Register**). The collections of information are required so that individuals denied enrollment in a group health plan based on one or more health factors will be apprised of their right to enroll in the plan without regard to their health. The likely respondents are business or other for-profit institutions, nonprofit institutions, small businesses or organizations, and Taft-Hartley trusts. Responses to this collection of information are required of plans that have denied enrollment to individuals based on one or more health factors.

Books or records relating to a collection of information must be retained as long as their contents may become material in the administration of any internal revenue law. Generally tax returns and tax return information are confidential, as required by 26 U.S.C. 6103.

Comments on the collection of information should be sent to the **Office of Management and Budget,** Attn: Desk Officer for the Department of the Treasury, Office of Information and Regulatory Affairs, Washington, DC 20503, with copies to the **Internal Revenue Service,** Attn: IRS Reports Clearance Officer, W:CAR:MP:FP:S:O, Washington, DC 20224. Comments on the collection of information should be received by [*INSERT DATE 90 DAYS AFTER PUBLICATION OF THIS DOCUMENT IN THE FEDERAL REGISTER*]. Comments are specifically requested concerning:

• Whether the proposed collection of information is necessary for the proper performance of the functions of the Internal Revenue Service, including whether the information will have practical utility;

• The accuracy of the estimated burden associated with the proposed collection of information (see the preamble to the temporary regulations published elsewhere in this issue of the **Federal Register**);

• How to enhance the quality, utility, and clarity of the information to be collected;

• How to minimize the burden of complying with the proposed collection of information, including the application of automated collection techniques or other forms of information technology; and

• Estimates of capital or start-up costs and costs of operation, maintenance, and purchase of services to provide information.

Background

The temporary regulations published elsewhere in this issue of the **Federal Register** add a new § 54.9802-1T to the Miscellaneous Excise Tax Regulations.[1] When these proposed regulations are published as final regulations, they will supplement the final regulations in § 54.9802-1 being published elsewhere in this issue of the **Federal Register**. The proposed, temporary, and final regulations are being published as part of a joint rulemaking with the Department of Labor and the Department of Health and Human Services (the joint rulemaking).

The text of those temporary regulations also serves as the text of these proposed regulations. The preamble to the temporary regulations explains the temporary regulations.

Special Analyses

This regulation is not subject to the Unfunded Mandates Reform Act of 1995 because the regulation is an interpretive regulation. It has also been determined that section 553(b) of the Administrative Procedure Act (5 U.S.C. chapter 5) does not apply to this regulation. For further information and for analyses relating to the joint rulemaking, see the preamble to the joint rulemaking. Pursuant to section 7805(f) of the Internal Revenue Code, this notice of proposed rulemaking will be submitted to the Chief Counsel for Advocacy of the Small Business Administration for comment on its impact on small business.

Comments and Requests for a Public Hearing

Before these proposed regulations are adopted as final regulations, consideration will be given to any written comments (a signed original and eight (8) copies) that are submitted timely to the IRS. Comments are specifically requested on the clarity of the proposed regulations and

how they may be made easier to understand. All comments will be available for public inspection and copying. A public hearing may be scheduled if requested in writing by a person that timely submits written comments. If a public hearing is scheduled, notice of the date, time, and place for the hearing will be published in the **Federal Register.**

Drafting Information

The principal author of these proposed regulations is Russ Weinheimer, Office of the Operating Division Counsel/Associate Chief Counsel (Tax Exempt and Government Entities), IRS. However, other personnel from the IRS and Treasury Department participated in their development. The proposed regulations, as well as the temporary regulations, have been developed in coordination with personnel from the U.S. Department of Labor and the U.S. Department of Health and Human Services.

List of Subjects in 26 CFR Part 54

Excise taxes, Health insurance, Pensions, Reporting and recordkeeping requirements.

Proposed Amendments to the Regulations

Accordingly, 26 CFR part 54 is proposed to be amended as follows:

PART 54—PENSION EXCISE TAXES

Paragraph 1. The authority citation for part 54 continues to read in part as follows:

Authority: 26 U.S.C. 7805 ***

Par. 2. Section 54.9802-1 is amended to read as follows:

§ 54.9802-1 *Prohibiting discrimination against participants and beneficiaries based on a health factor.*

[The text of the proposed amendments to this section is the same as the text of § 54.9802-1T published elsewhere in this issue of the **Federal Register**].

Robert E. Wenzel

Deputy Commissioner of Internal Revenue

¶ 20,254

IRS proposed regulations: Health Insurance Portability and Accountability Act of 1996 (HIPAA): Nondiscrimination requirements: Grandfathered church plans.—The IRS has issued proposed regulations containing guidance regarding the exception from the nondiscrimination requirements, added by the Health Insurance Portability and Accountability Act of 1996 (HIPAA), applicable to group health plans under Code Sec. 9802(a) and (b), for certain grandfathered church plans.

The proposed regulations, which were published in the *Federal Register* on January 8, 2001 (66 FR 1437), are reproduced below.

DEPARTMENT OF THE TREASURY

Internal Revenue Service

26 CFR Part 54

[REG-114083-00]

RIN 1545-AY33

Exception to the HIPAA Nondiscrimination Requirements for Certain Grandfathered Church Plans

AGENCY: Internal Revenue Service (IRS), Treasury.

ACTION: Notice of proposed rulemaking.

SUMMARY: This document contains proposed regulations that provide guidance under section 9802(c) of the Internal Revenue Code relating to the exception for certain grandfathered church plans from the nondiscrimination requirements applicable to group health plans under section 9802(a) and (b). Final, temporary, and proposed regulations relating to the nondiscrimination requirements under section 9802(a) and (b) are being published elsewhere in this issue of the **Federal Register**. The regulations will generally affect sponsors of and participants in certain self-funded church plans that are group health plans, and the regulations provide plan sponsors and plan administrators with guidance necessary to comply with the law.

DATES: Written or electronic comments and requests for a public hearing must be received by [*INSERT DATE 90 DAYS AFTER*

PUBLICATION OF THIS DOCUMENT IN THE FEDERAL REGISTER].

ADDRESSES: Send Submissions to: CC:M & SP:RU (REG-114083-00), room 5226, Internal Revenue Service, POB 7604, Ben Franklin Station, Washington, DC 20044. Submissions may be hand delivered between the hours of 8 a.m. and 5 p.m. to: CC:M & SP:RU (REG-114083-00), Courier's Desk, Internal Revenue Service, 1111 Constitution Avenue NW., Washington, DC. Alternatively, taxpayers may submit comments electronically via the Internet by selecting the "Tax Regs" option on the IRS Home Page, or by submitting comments directly to the IRS Internet site at *http://www.irs.gov/tax_regs/regslist.html.*

FOR FURTHER INFORMATION CONTACT: Concerning the regulations, Russ Weinheimer at 202-622-6080; concerning submissions of comments or requests for a hearing, Sonya Cruse at 202-622-7190 (not toll-free numbers).

SUPPLEMENTARY INFORMATION:

Background

This document contains proposed amendments to the Miscellaneous Excise Tax Regulations (26 CFR part 54) relating to the exception for certain grandfathered church plans from the nondiscrimination requirements applicable to group health plans. The nondiscrimination requirements applicable to group health plans were added to the Internal Revenue Code (Code), in section 9802, by the Health Insur-

---

[1] A previous § 54.9802-1T was published in the **Federal Register** on April 8, 1997. By operation of section 7805(e) of the Internal Revenue Code, the previous § 54.9802-1T expired on April 8, 2000. Proposed regulations containing the same text as previous § 54.9802-1T were also published on April 8, 1997, and final regulations based on those

proposed regulations are being published elsewhere in this issue of the **Federal Register** as § 54.9802-1. The new § 54.9802-1T being published elsewhere in this issue of the **Federal Register** consists almost entirely of new guidance not contained in the previous § 54.9802-1T.

ance Portability and Accountability Act of 1996 (HIPAA), Public Law 104-191. HIPAA also added similar nondiscrimination provisions applicable to group health plans and health insurance issuers (such as health insurance companies and health maintenance organizations) under the Employee Retirement Income Security Act of 1974 (ERISA), administered by the U.S. Department of Labor, and the Public Health Service Act (PHS Act), administered by the U.S. Department of Health and Human Services.

Final and temporary regulations relating to the HIPAA nondiscrimination requirements in paragraphs (a) and (b) of section 9802 of the Code are being published elsewhere in this issue of the **Federal Register.** Those regulations are similar to, and have been developed in coordination with, interim final regulations also being published today by the Departments of Labor and Health and Human Services. Guidance under the HIPAA nondiscrimination requirements is summarized in a joint preamble to the final, interim final, and temporary regulations.

The exception for certain grandfathered church plans was added to section 9802, in a new subsection (c), by section 1532 of the Taxpayer Relief Act of 1997, Public Law 105-34. These proposed regulations would provide guidance for this exception. The guidance is summarized in the explanation below.

Explanation of Provisions

Church plans that are group health plans are generally subject to the Code provisions in Chapter 100 relating to access, portability, and renewability.[1] However, under section 9802(c), church plans satisfying certain requirements continuously since July 15, 1997 are not treated as failing to meet the section 9802 prohibitions against discrimination based on any health factor solely because the plan requires evidence of good health for the coverage of certain individuals.

The grandfather rule in section 9802(c) applies to a church plan for a plan year only if, July 15, 1997 and at all times after that date before the beginning of the plan year, the church plan had provisions satisfying one of two alternative conditions. The first alternative condition is that the plan contain provisions requiring evidence of good health of two sets of individuals, that is, both (1) any employee of an employer with 10 or fewer employees and (2) any self-employed individual. The proposed regulations specify that this condition is not satisfied if the plan requires evidence of good health of only one of these sets of individuals. The proposed regulations also clarify that the plan provision for the first set of individuals must be exactly 10 or fewer. Thus, a plan provision requiring evidence of good health for employees of an employer of fewer than 10, or of greater than 10, employees does not satisfy this condition. For example, a plan provision requiring evidence of good health of any employee of an employer of five or fewer employees does not satisfy this condition.

The second alternative condition is that the plan contain provisions requiring evidence of good health of any individual who enrolls after the first 90 days of initial eligibility. The proposed regulations clarify that the period for these plan provisions must be exactly 90 days. Thus, a plan provision requiring evidence of good health of any individual who enrolls after the first 120 days of initial eligibility does not satisfy this condition.

The grandfather rule in section 9802(c) of the Code is not by its terms limited in its application to self-funded church plans. Section 2702 of the Public Health Service Act (PHS Act) imposes nondiscrimination requirements on health insurance issuers offering group health insurance coverage, and those nondiscrimination requirements are generally similar to the nondiscrimination requirements imposed on group health plans (including church plans) under paragraphs (a) and (b) of section 9802 of the Code. However, section 2702 of the PHS Act does not include an exception for health insurance issuers offering group health insurance coverage to church plans comparable to the exception for church plans in section 9802(c) of the Code. Thus, if a church plan providing benefits through group health insurance coverage were to require evidence of good health of certain individuals as permitted under section 9802(c) of the Code, the requirement of evidence of good health would cause the health insurance issuer providing the coverage to violate the nondiscrimination requirements of the PHS Act. In such a case, the sanctions under the PHS Act would apply to the issuer, but those under the Code would not apply to the church plan. Thus, assuming that group health insurance coverage complies with the nondiscrimination requirements of the PHS Act, the rule in section 9802(c) of the Code is, in effect, available only to church plans that are not funded through group health insurance because only

such church plans do not include insurance coverage that is subject to Title XXVII of the PHS Act. Accordingly, the examples in the proposed regulations illustrating situations where section 9802(c) is available are limited to group health plans that are not funded through group health insurance in order to avoid misleading insured church plans about the availability of the grandfather rule in section 9802(c).

Special Analyses

It has been determined that this notice of proposed rulemaking is not a significant regulatory action as defined in Executive Order 12866. Therefore, a regulatory assessment is not required. It also has been determined that section 553(b) of the Administrative Procedure Act (5 U.S.C. chapter 5) does not apply to these regulations, and because the regulations do not impose a collection of information requirement on small entities, the Regulatory Flexibility Act (5 U.S.C. chapter 6) does not apply. Therefore, a Regulatory Flexibility Analysis under the Regulatory Flexibility Act (5 U.S.C. chapter 6) is not required. Pursuant to section 7805(f) of the Internal Revenue Code, this notice of proposed rulemaking will be submitted to the Chief Counsel for Advocacy of the Small Business Administration for comment on its impact on small business.

Comments and Requests for a Public Hearing

Before these proposed regulations are adopted as final regulations, consideration will be given to any written comments that are submitted timely (a signed original and eight (8) copies) to the IRS. Comments are specifically requested on the clarity of the proposed regulations and how they may be made easier to understand. All comments will be available for public inspection and copying. A public hearing may be scheduled if requested in writing by a person that timely submits written comments. If a public hearing is scheduled, notice of the date, time, and place for the bearing will be published in the **Federal Register.**

Drafting Information

The principal author of these proposed regulations is Russ Weinheimer, Office of the Operating Division Counsel/Associate Chief Counsel (Tax Exempt and Government Entities). However, other personnel from the IRS and Treasury Department participated in their development.

List of Subjects in 26 CFR Part 54

Excise taxes, Health care, Health insurance, Pensions, Reporting and recordkeeping requirements.

Proposed Amendments to the Regulations

Accordingly, 26 CFR part 54 is proposed to be amended as follows:

PART 54—PENSION EXCISE TAXES

Paragraph 1. The authority citation for part 54 is amended in part by adding an entry in numerical order to read as follows:

Authority: 26 U.S.C. 7805 * * *

Section 54.9802-2 also issued under 26 U.S.C. 9802. * * *

Par. 2. Section 54.9802-2 is added to read as follows:

§ 54.9802-2 *Special rules for certain church plans.*

(a) *Exception for certain church plans*—(1) *Church plans in general.* A church plan described in paragraph (b) of this section is not treated as failing to meet the requirements of section 9802 or §§ 54.9802-1 and 54.9802-1T solely because the plan requires evidence of good health for coverage of individuals under plan provisions described in paragraph (b)(2) or (3) of this section.

(2) *Health insurance issuers.* See sections 2702 and 2721(b)(1)(B) of the Public Health Service Act (42 U.S.C. 300gg-2 and 300gg-21(b)(1)(B)) and 45 CFR 146.121, which require health insurance issuers providing health insurance coverage under a church plan that is a group health plan to comply with nondiscrimination requirements similar to those that church plans are required to comply with under section 9802 and §§ 54.9802-1 and 54.9802-1T except that those nondiscrimination requirements do not include an exception for health insurance issuers comparable to the exception for church plans under section 9802(c) and this section.

(b) *Church plans to which this section applies*—(1) *Church plans with certain coverage provisions in effect on July 15, 1997.* This section

---

[1] However, church plans are not subject to the similar requirements in Part 7 of Subtitle B of Title I of ERISA or to the similar requirements in Title XXVII of the PHS Act (except for health insurance coverage in connection with a church plan, as discussed below).

applies to any church plan (as defined in section 414(e)) for a plan year if, on July 15, 1997 and at all times thereafter before the beginning of the plan year, the plan contains either the provisions described in paragraph (b)(2) of this section or the provisions described in paragraph (b)(3) of this section.

(2) *Plan provisions applicable to individuals employed by employers of 10 or fewer employees and self-employed individuals*—(i) A plan contains the provisions described in this paragraph (b)(2) if it requires evidence of good health of both—

(A) Any employee of an employer of 10 or fewer employees (determined without regard to section 414(e)(3)(C), under which a church or convention or association of churches is treated as the employer); and

(B) Any self-employed individual.

(ii) A plan does not contain the provisions described in this paragraph (b)(2) if the plan contains only one of the provisions described in this paragraph (b)(2). Thus, for example, a plan that requires evidence of good health of any self-employed individual, but not of any employee of an employer with 10 or fewer employees, does not contain the provisions described in this paragraph (b)(2). Moreover, a plan does not contain the provision described in paragraph (b)(2)(i)(A) of this section if the plan requires evidence of good health of any employee of an employer of fewer than 10 (or greater than 10) employees. Thus, for example, a plan does not contain the provision described in paragraph (b)(2)(i)(A) of this section if the plan requires evidence of good health of any employee of an employer with five or fewer employees.

(3) *Plan provisions applicable to individuals who enroll after the first 90 days of initial eligibility*—(i) A plan contains the provisions described in this paragraph (b)(3) if it requires evidence of good health of any individual who enrolls after the first 90 days of initial eligibility under the plan.

(ii) A plan does not contain the provisions described in this paragraph (b)(3) if it provides for a longer (or shorter) period than 90 days. Thus, for example, a plan requiring evidence of good health of any individual who enrolls after the first 120 days of initial eligibility under the plan does not contain the provisions described in this paragraph (b)(3).

(c) *Examples.* The rules of this section are illustrated by the following examples:

Example 1. (i) *Facts.* A church organization maintains two church plans for entities affiliated with the church. One plan is a group health plan that provides health coverage to all employees (including ministers and lay workers) of any affiliated church entity that has more than 10 employees. The other plan is Plan *O*, which is a group health plan that is not funded. through insurance coverage and that provides health coverage to any employee (including ministers and lay workers) of any affiliated church entity that has 10 or fewer employees and any self-employed individual affiliated with the church (including a self-employed minister of the church). Plan *O* requires evidence of good health in order for any individual of a church entity that has 10 or fewer employees to be covered and in order for any self-employed individual to be covered. On July 15, 1997 and at all times thereafter before the beginning of the plan year, Plan *O* has contained all the preceding provisions.

(ii) *Conclusion.* In this *Example 1,* because Plan *O* contains the plan provisions described in paragraph (b)(2) of this section and because those provisions were in the plan on July 15, 1997 and at all times thereafter before the beginning of the plan year, Plan *O* will not be treated as failing to meet the requirements of section 9802, §54.9802-1, or §54.9802-1T for the plan year solely because the plan requires evidence of good health for coverage of the individuals described in those plan provisions.

Example 2. (i) *Facts.* A church organization maintains Plan *P*, which is a church plan that is not funded through insurance coverage and that is a group health plan providing health coverage to individuals employed by entities affiliated with the church and self-employed individuals affiliated with the church (such as ministers). On July 15, 1997 and at all times thereafter before the beginning of the plan year, Plan P has required evidence of good health for coverage of any individual who enrolls after the first 90 days of initial eligibility under the plan.

(ii) *Conclusion.* In this *Example 2,* because Plan *P* contains the plan provisions described in paragraph (b)(3) of this section and because those provisions were in the plan on July 15, 1997 and at all times thereafter before the beginning of the plan year, Plan *P* will not be treated as failing to meet the requirements of section 9802, §54.9802-1, or §54.9802-1T for the plan year solely because the plan requires evidence of good health for coverage of individuals enrolling after the first 90 days of initial eligibility under the plan.

(d) *Effective date.* **[Reserved]**

Robert E. Wenzel

Deputy Commissioner of Internal Revenue

¶ 20,255

IRS proposed regulations: Pension and Welfare Benefits Administration (PWBA): Bona fide wellness programs: Health Insurance Portability and Accountability Act of 1996 (HIPAA): Nondiscrimination requirements.—The IRS, in conjunction with the PWBA and the Department of Health and Human Services, has issued proposed regulations to establish and elucidate the meaning of "bona fide wellness program" with regard to nondiscrimination provisions of the Code and ERISA, as added by HIPAA.

The proposed regulations, which were published in the *Federal Register* on January 8, 2001 (66 FR 1421), are reproduced below. The PWBA's proposed regulations are at 20,534H.

[Billing Codes: 4830-01-P; 4510-29-P; 4120-01-P]

DEPARTMENT OF THE TREASURY

Internal Revenue Service

26 CFR Part 54

[REG-114084-00]

RIN 1545-AY34

DEPARTMENT OF LABOR

Pension and Welfare Benefits Administration

29 CFR Part 2590

RIN 1210-AA77

DEPARTMENT OF HEALTH AND HUMAN SERVICES

Health Care Financing Administration

45 CFR Part 146

RIN 0938-AK19

Notice of Proposed Rulemaking for Bona Fide Wellness Programs

AGENCIES: Internal Revenue Service, Department of the Treasury; Pension and Welfare Benefits Administration, Department of Labor; Health Care Financing Administration, Department of Health and Human Services.

ACTION: Notice of proposed rulemaking and request for comments.

SUMMARY: This proposed rule would implement and clarify the term "bona fide wellness program" as it relates to regulations implementing the nondiscrimination provisions of the Internal Revenue Code, the Employee Retirement Income Security Act, and the Public Health Service Act, as added by the Health Insurance Portability and Accountability Act of 1996.

DATES: Written comments on this notice of proposed rulemaking are invited and must be received by the Departments on or before **[INSERT DATE 90 DAYS AFTER PUBLICATION OF THIS DOCUMENT IN THE FEDERAL REGISTER]**.

ADDRESSES: Written comments should be submitted with a signed original and three copies (except for electronic submissions to the Internal Revenue Service (IRS) or Department of Labor) to any of the addresses specified below. Any comment that is submitted to any Department will be shared with the other Departments.

Comments to the IRS can be addressed to:

CC:M&SP:RU (REG-114084-00)
Room 5226
Internal Revenue Service
POB 7604, Ben Franklin Station
Washington, DC 20044

In the alternative, comments may be hand-delivered between the hours of 8 a.m. and 5 p.m. to:

CC:M&SP:RU (REG-114084-00)
Courier's Desk
Internal Revenue Service
1111 Constitution Avenue, NW.
Washington DC 20224

Alternatively, comments may be transmitted electronically via the IRS Internet site at:

http://www.irs.gov/tax regs/regslist.html.

Comments to the Department of Labor can be addressed to:

U.S. Department of Labor
Pension and Welfare Benefits Administration
200 Constitution Avenue NW., Room C-5331
Washington, DC 20210
Attention: Wellness Program Comments

Alternatively, comments may be hand-delivered between the hours of 9 a.m. and 5 p.m. to the same address. Comments may also be transmitted by e-mail to: Wellness@pwba.dol.gov.n

Comments to HHS can be addressed to:

Health Care Financing Administration
Department of Health and Human Services
Attention: HCFA-2078-P
P.O. Box 26688
Baltimore, MD 21207

In the alternative, comments may be hand-delivered between the hours of 8:30 a.m. and 5 p.m. to either:

Room 443-G
Hubert Humphrey Building
200 Independence Avenue, SW.
Washington, DC 20201
or
Room C5-14-03
7500 Security Boulevard
Baltimore, MD 21244-1850

All submissions to the IRS will be open to public inspection and copying in room 1621, 1111 Constitution Avenue, NW., Washington, DC from 9 a.m. to 4 p.m.

All submissions to the Department of Labor will be open to public inspection and copying in the Public Documents Room, Pension and Welfare Benefits Administration, U.S. Department of Labor, Room N-1513, 200 Constitution Avenue, NW., Washington, DC from 8:30 a.m. to 5:30 p.m.

All submissions to HHS will be open to public inspection and copying in room 309-G of the Department of Health and Human Services, 200 Independence Avenue, SW., Washington, DC from 8:30 a.m. to 5 p.m.

FOR FURTHER INFORMATION CONTACT: Russ Weinheimer, Internal Revenue Service, Department of the Treasury, at (202) 622-6080; Amy J. Turner, Pension and Welfare Benefits Administration, Department of Labor, at (202) 219-4377; or Ruth A. Bradford, Health Care Financing Administration, Department of Health and Human Services, at (410) 786-1565.

SUPPLEMENTARY INFORMATION:

Customer Service Information: Individuals interested in obtaining additional information on HIPAA's nondiscrimination rules may request a copy of the Department of Labor's booklet entitled "Questions and Answers: Recent Changes in Health Care Law" by calling the PWBA Toll-Free Publication Hotline at 1-800-998-7542 or may request a copy of the Health Care Financing Administration's new publication entitled "Protecting Your Health Insurance Coverage" by calling (410) 786-1565. Information on HIPAA's nondiscrimination rules and other recent health care laws is also available on the Department of Labor's website (http://www.dol.gov/dol/pwba) and the Department of Health and Human Services' website (http://hipaa.hcfa.gov).

Background

The Health Insurance Portability and Accountability Act of 1996 (HIPAA), Public Law 104-191, was enacted on August 21, 1996. HIPAA amended the Internal Revenue Code of 1986 (Code), the Employee Retirement Income Security Act of 1974 (ERISA), and the Public Health Service Act (PHS Act) to provide for, among other things, improved portability and continuity of health coverage. HIPAA added section 9802 of the Code, section 702 of ERISA, and section 2702 of the PHS Act, which prohibit discrimination in health coverage. However, the HIPAA nondiscrimination provisions do not prevent a plan or issuer from establishing discounts or rebates or modifying otherwise applicable copayments or deductibles in return for adherence to programs of

health promotion and disease prevention. Interim final rules implementing the HIPAA provisions were first made available to the public on April 1, 1997 (published in the **Federal Register** on April 8, 1997, 62 FR 16894) (April 1997 interim rules).

In the preamble to the April 1997 interim rules, the Departments invited comments on whether additional guidance was needed concerning, among other things, the permissible standards for determining bona fide wellness programs. The Departments also stated that they intend to issue further regulations on the nondiscrimination rules and that in no event would the Departments take any enforcement action against a plan or issuer that had sought to comply in good faith with section 9802 of the Code, section 702 of ERISA, and section 2702 of the PHS Act before the additional guidance is provided. The new interim regulations relating to the HIPAA nondiscrimination rules (published elsewhere in this issue of the **Federal Register**) do not include provisions relating to bona fide wellness programs. Accordingly, the period for good faith compliance continues with respect to those provisions until further guidance is issued. Compliance with the provisions of these proposed regulations constitutes good faith compliance with the statutory provisions relating to wellness programs.

Overview of the Proposed Regulations

The HIPAA nondiscrimination provisions generally prohibit a plan or issuer from charging similarly situated individuals different premiums or contributions based on a health factor. In addition, under the interim regulations published elsewhere in this issue of the **Federal Register**, cost-sharing mechanisms such as deductibles, copayments, and coinsurance are considered restrictions on benefits. Thus, they are subject to the same rules as are other restrictions on benefits; that is, they must apply uniformly to all similarly situated individuals and must not be directed at individual participants or beneficiaries based on any health factor of the participants or beneficiaries. However, the HIPAA nondiscrimination provisions do not prevent a plan or issuer from establishing premium discounts or rebates or modifying otherwise applicable copayments or deductibles in return for adherence to programs of health promotion and disease prevention. Thus, there is an exception to the general rule prohibiting discrimination based on a health factor if the reward, such as a premium discount or waiver of a cost-sharing requirement, is based on participation in a program of health promotion or disease prevention. The April 1997 interim rules, the interim regulations published elsewhere in this issue of the **Federal Register**, and these proposed regulations refer to programs of health promotion and disease prevention allowed under this exception as "bona fide wellness programs." In order to prevent the exception to the nondiscrimination requirements for bona fide wellness programs from eviscerating the general rule contained in the HIPAA nondiscrimination provisions, these proposed regulations impose certain requirements on wellness programs providing rewards that would otherwise discriminate based on a health factor.

A wide range of wellness programs exist to promote health and prevent disease. However, many of these programs are not subject to the bona fide wellness program requirements. The requirements for bona fide wellness programs apply only to a wellness program that provides a reward based on the ability of an individual to meet a standard that is related to a health factor, such as a reward conditioned on the outcome of a cholesterol test. Therefore, without having to comply with the requirements for a bona fide wellness program, a wellness program could—

• Provide voluntary testing of enrollees for specific health problems and make recommendations to address health problems identified, if the program did not base any reward on the outcome of the health assessment;

• Encourage preventive care through the waiver of the copayment or deductible requirement for the costs of well-baby visits;

• Reimburse employees for the cost of health club memberships, without regard to any health factors relating to the employees; or

• Reimburse employees for the costs of smoking cessation programs, without regard to whether the employee quits smoking.

A wellness program that provides a reward based on the ability of an individual to meet a standard related to a health factor violates the interim regulations published elsewhere in this issue of the **Federal Register** unless it is a bona fide wellness program. Under these proposed regulations, a wellness program must meet four requirements to be a bona fide wellness program.

First, the total reward that may be given to an individual under the plan for all wellness programs is limited. A reward can be in the form of a discount, a rebate of a premium or contribution, or a waiver of all or part of a cost-sharing mechanism (such as deductibles, copayments, or coinsurance), or the absence of a surcharge. The reward for the wellness program, coupled with the reward for other wellness programs with respect to the plan that require satisfaction of a standard related to a health factor, must not exceed a specified percentage of the cost of employee-only coverage under the plan. The cost of employee-only coverage is determined based on the total amount of employer and employee contributions for the benefit package under which the employee is receiving coverage.

The proposed regulations specify three alternative percentages: 10, 15, and 20. The Departments welcome comments on the appropriate level for the percentage. Comments will be taken into account in determining the standard for the final regulations.

Several commenters on the April 1997 regulations suggested that the amount of a reward should be permitted if it is actuarially determined based on the costs associated with the health factor measured under the wellness program. However, in some cases, the resulting reward (or penalty) might be so large as to have the effect of denying coverage to certain individuals. The percentage limitation in the proposed regulations is designed to avoid this result. The percentage limitation also avoids the additional administrative costs of a reward based on actuarial cost.

The Departments recognize that there may be some programs that currently offer rewards, individually or in the aggregate, that exceed the specified percentage. However, as noted below in the economic analysis, data is scarce regarding practices of wellness programs. Thus, the Departments specifically request comments on the appropriateness of the specified percentage of the cost of employee-only coverage under a plan as the maximum reward for a bona fide wellness program, including whether a larger amount should be allowed for wellness programs that include participation by family members (i.e., the specified percentage of the cost of family coverage). Note also that, as stated above, the period for good faith compliance continues with respect to whether wellness programs satisfy the statutory requirements. While compliance with these proposed regulations constitutes good faith compliance with the statutory provisions, it is possible that, based on all the facts and circumstances, a plan's wellness program that provides a reward in excess of the specified range of percentages of the cost of employee-only coverage may also be found to meet the good faith compliance standard.

Under these proposed regulations, the second requirement to be a bona fide wellness program is that the program must be reasonably designed to promote good health or prevent disease for individuals in the program. This requirement prevents a program from being a subterfuge for merely imposing higher costs on individuals based on a health factor by requiring a reasonable connection between the standard required under the program and the promotion of good health and disease prevention. Among other things, a program is not reasonably designed to promote good health or prevent disease unless the program gives individuals eligible for the program the opportunity to qualify for the reward under the program at least once per year. In contrast, a program that imposes a reward or penalty for the duration of the individual's participation in the plan based solely on health factors present when an individual first enrolls in a plan is not reasonably designed to promote health or prevent disease (because, if the individual cannot qualify for the reward by adopting healthier behavior after initial enrollment, the program does not have any connection to improving health).

The third requirement to be a bona fide wellness program under these proposed regulations is that the reward under the program must be available to all similarly situated individuals. The April 1997 interim rules provided that if, under the design of the wellness program, enrollees might not be able to achieve a program standard due to a health factor, the program would not be a bona fide wellness program. These proposed regulations increase flexibility for plans by allowing plans to make individualized adjustments to their wellness programs to address the health factors of the particular individuals for whom it is unreasonably difficult to qualify for the benefits under the program. Specifically, the program must allow any individual for whom it is unreasonably difficult due to a medical condition (or for whom it is medically inadvisable to attempt) to satisfy the initial program standard an opportunity to satisfy a reasonable alternative standard. The examples clarify that a reasonable alternative standard must take into account the relevant health factor of the individual who needs the alternative. A program does not need to establish the specific reasonable alternative standard before the program commences. To satisfy this

third requirement for being a bona fide wellness program, it is sufficient to determine a reasonable alternative standard once a participant informs the plan that it is unreasonably difficult for the participant due to a medical condition to satisfy the general standard (or that it is medically inadvisable for the participant to attempt to achieve the general standard) under the program.

Many commenters asked how the bona fide wellness program requirements apply to programs that provide a reward for not smoking. An example in the proposed regulations clarifies that if it is unreasonably difficult for an individual to stop smoking due to an addiction to nicotine[1], the individual must be provided a reasonable alternative standard to obtain the reward.

The fourth requirement to be a bona fide wellness program under the proposed regulations is that all plan materials describing the terms of the program must disclose the availability of a reasonable alternative standard. The proposed regulations include model language that can be used to satisfy this requirement; examples also illustrate substantially similar language that would satisfy the requirement.

The proposed regulations contain two clarifications of this fourth requirement. First, plan materials are not required to describe specific reasonable alternative standards. It is sufficient to disclose that some reasonable alternative standard will be made available. Second, any plan materials that describe the general standard would also have to disclose the availability of a reasonable alternative standard. However, if the program is merely mentioned (and does not describe the general standard), disclosure of the availability of a reasonable alternative standard is not required.

Economic Impact and Paperwork Burden

Summary - Department of Labor and Department of Health and Human Services

Under the proposed regulation, health plans generally may vary employee premium contributions or benefit levels across similarly situated individuals based on health status factors only in connection with bona fide wellness programs. The regulation establishes four requirements for such bona fide wellness programs. It (1) limits the permissible amount of variation in employee premium or benefit levels; (2) requires that programs be reasonably designed to promote health or prevent disease; (3) requires programs to permit plan participants who for medical reasons would incur unreasonable difficulty to satisfy the programs' initial wellness standards to satisfy reasonable alternative standards instead; and (4) requires certain plan materials to disclose the availability of such alternative standards. The Departments carefully considered the costs and benefits attendant to these requirements. The Departments believe that the benefits of these requirements exceed their costs.

The Departments anticipate that the proposed regulation will result in transfers of cost among plan sponsors and participants and in new economic costs and benefits.

Economic benefits will flow from plan sponsors' efforts to maintain wellness programs' effectiveness where discounts or surcharges are reduced and from plans sponsors' provision of reasonable alternative standards that help improve affected plan participants' health habits and health. The result will be fewer instances where wellness programs merely shift costs to high risk individuals and more instances where they succeed at improving such individuals' health habits and health.

Transfers will arise because the size of some discounts and surcharges will be reduced, and because some plan participants who did not satisfy wellness programs' initial standards will satisfy alternative standards. These transfers are estimated to total between $18 million and $46 million annually. (The latter figure is an upper bound, reflecting the case in which all eligible participants pursue and satisfy alternative standards.)

New economic costs may be incurred if reductions in discounts or surcharges reduce wellness programs' effectiveness, but this effect is expected to be very small because reductions will be small and relatively few plans and participants will be affected. Other new economic costs will be incurred by plan sponsors to make available reasonable alternative standards where required. The Departments were unable to estimate these costs but are confident that these costs in combination with the transfers referenced above will not exceed the estimate of the transfers alone. Affected plan sponsors can satisfy the proposed regulation's third requirement by making available any reasonable standard

---

[1] Under the *Diagnostic and Statistical Manual of Mental Disorders*, Fourth Edition, American Psychiatric Association, 1994 (DSM IV), nicotine addiction is a medical condition. See also Rev. Rul. 99-28, 1999-25 I.R.B. 6 (June 21, 1999), citing a report of the Surgeon General stating that scientists in the field of drug addiction agree that nicotine, a substance common to all forms of tobacco, is a powerfully addictive drug.

they choose, including low cost alternatives. It is unlikely that plan sponsors would choose alternative standards whose cost, in combination with costs transferred from participants who satisfy them, would exceed the cost of providing discounts or waiving surcharges for all eligible participants.

Executive Order 12866 - Department of Labor and Department of Health and Human Services

Under Executive Order 12866, the Departments must determine whether a regulatory action is "significant" and therefore subject to the requirements of the Executive Order and subject to review by the Office of Management and Budget (OMB). Under section 3(f), the order defines a "significant regulatory action" as an action that is likely to result in a rule (1) having an annual effect on the economy of $100 million or more, or adversely and materially affecting a sector of the economy, productivity, competition, jobs, the environment, public health or safety, or State, local or tribal governments or communities (also referred to as "economically significant"); (2) creating serious inconsistency or otherwise interfering with an action taken or planned by another agency; (3) materially altering the budgetary impacts of entitlement grants, user fees, or loan programs or the rights and obligations of recipients thereof; or (4) raising novel legal or policy issues arising out of legal mandates, the President's priorities, or the principles set forth in the Executive Order.

Pursuant to the terms of the Executive Order, it has been determined that this action raises novel policy issues arising out of legal mandates. Therefore, this notice is "significant" and subject to OMB review under Section 3(f)(4) of the Executive Order. Consistent with the Executive Order, the Departments have assessed the costs and benefits of this regulatory action. The Departments' assessment, and the analysis underlying that assessment, is detailed below. The Departments performed a comprehensive, unified analysis to estimate the costs and benefits attributable to the interim regulation for purposes of compliance with Executive Order 12866, the Regulatory Flexibility Act, and the Paperwork Reduction Act.

Statement of Need for Proposed Action

These interim regulations are needed to clarify and interpret the HIPAA nondiscrimination provisions (Prohibiting Discrimination Against Individual Participants and Beneficiaries Based on Health Status) under Section 702 of the Employee Retirement Income Security Act of 1974 (ERISA), Section 2702 of the Public Health Service Act, and Section 9802 of the Internal Revenue Code of 1986. The provisions are needed to ensure that group health plans and group health insurers and issuers do not discriminate against individuals, participants, and beneficiaries based on any health factors with respect to health care premiums. Additional guidance was required to define bona fide wellness programs.

Costs and Benefits

The Departments anticipate that the proposed regulation will result in transfers of cost among plans sponsors and participants and in new economic costs and benefits. The economic benefits of the regulation will include a reduction in instances where wellness programs merely shift costs to high risk individuals and an increase in instances where they succeed at improving such individuals' health habits and health. Transfers are estimated to total between $18 million and $46 million annually. The Departments were unable to estimate new economic costs but are confident that these costs in combination with the transfers referenced above will not exceed the estimate of the transfers alone. The Departments believe that the regulation's benefits will exceed its costs. Their unified analysis of the regulation's costs and benefits is detailed later in this preamble.

Regulatory Flexibility Act - Department of Labor and Department of Health and Human Services

The Regulatory Flexibility Act (5 U.S.C. 601 et seq.) (RFA) imposes certain requirements with respect to Federal rules that are subject to the notice and comment requirements of section 553(b) of the Administrative Procedure Act (5 U.S.C. 551 et seq.) and which are likely to have a significant economic impact on a substantial number of small entities. Unless an agency certifies that a proposed rule will not have a significant economic impact on a substantial number of small entities, section 603 of the RFA requires that the agency present an initial regulatory flexibility analysis (IRFA) at the time of the publication of the notice of proposed rulemaking describing the impact of the rule on small entities and seeking public comment on such impact. Small entities include small businesses, organizations and governmental jurisdictions.

For purposes of analysis under the RFA, PWBA proposes to continue to consider a small entity to be an employee benefit plan with fewer than 100 participants. The basis of this definition is found in section 104(a)(2) of the Employee Retirement Income Security Act of 1974 (ERISA), which permits the Secretary of Labor to prescribe simplified annual reports for pension plans which cover fewer than 100 participants. Under section 104(a)(3), the Secretary may also provide for exemptions or simplified annual reporting and disclosure for welfare benefit plans. Pursuant to the authority of section 104(a)(3), the Department of Labor has previously issued at 29 C.F.R. §§ 2520.104-20, 2520.104-21, 2520.104-41, 2520.104-46 and 2520.104b-10 certain simplified reporting provisions and limited exemptions from reporting and disclosure requirements for small plans, including unfunded or insured welfare plans covering fewer than 100 participants and which satisfy certain other requirements.

Further, while some large employers may have small plans, in general most small plans are maintained by small employers. Thus, PWBA believes that assessing the impact of this proposed rule on small plans is an appropriate substitute for evaluating the effect on small entities. For purposes of their unified IFRA, the Departments adhered to PWBA's proposed definition of small entities. The definition of small entity considered appropriate for this purpose differs, however, from a definition of small business which is based on size standards promulgated by the Small Business Administration (SBA) (13 CFR 121.201) pursuant to the Small Business Act (15 U.S.C. 631 et seq.). The Departments therefore request comments on the appropriateness of the size standard used in evaluating the impact of this proposed rule on small entities.

Under this proposed regulation, health plans generally may vary employee premium contributions or benefit levels across similarly situated individuals based on health factors only in connection with bona fide wellness programs. The regulation establishes four requirements for such bona fide wellness programs.

The Departments estimate that 36,000 plans with fewer than 100 participants vary employee premium contributions or benefit levels across similarly situated individuals based on health factors. While this represents just 1 percent of all small plans, the Departments nonetheless believe that it represents a substantial number of small entities. The Departments also note that at least some premium discounts or surcharges may be large. Premium discounts associated with wellness programs are believed to range as high as $560 per affected participant per year. Therefore, the Departments believe that the impact of this regulation on at least some small entities may be significant. Having reached these conclusions, the Departments carried out an IRFA as part of their unified analysis of the costs and benefits of the regulation. The reasoning and assumptions underlying the Departments' unified analysis of the regulation's costs and benefits are detailed later in this preamble.

The regulation's first requirement caps maximum allowable variation in employee premium contribution and benefit levels. The Departments estimate that 9,300 small plans will be affected by the cap. These plans can comply with this requirement by reducing premiums (or increasing benefits) by $1.1 million on aggregate for those participants whose premiums are higher (or whose benefits are lower) due to health factors. This would constitute an ongoing, annual transfer of cost of $1.1 million, or $122 on average per affected plan. The regulation does not limit small plans' flexibility to transfer this cost back evenly to all participants in the form of small premium increases or benefit cuts.

The regulation's second requirement provides that wellness programs must be reasonably designed to promote health or prevent disease. Comments received by the Departments and available literature on employee wellness programs suggest that existing wellness programs generally satisfy this requirement. The requirement therefore is not expected to compel small plans to modify existing wellness programs. It is not expected to entail economic costs nor to prompt transfers.

The third requirement provides that rewards under wellness programs must be available to all similarly situated individuals. In particular, programs must allow individuals for whom it would be unreasonably difficult due to a medical condition to satisfy initial program standards an opportunity to satisfy reasonable alternative standards. The Departments believe that some small plans' wellness programs do not currently satisfy this requirement and will have to be modified.

The Departments estimate that 21,000 small plans' wellness programs include initial standards that may be unreasonably difficult for some participants to meet. These plans are estimated to include 18,000 participants for whom the standard is in fact unreasonably difficult to meet. (Many small plans are very small, having fewer than 10 participants, and many will include no participant for whom the initial standard is unreasonable difficult to meet for a medical reason.) Satisfaction of alternative standards by these participants will result in transfers of cost as they qualify for discounts or escape surcharges. If all of these participants request and then satisfy an alternative standard, the transfer would amount to $5 million annually. If one-half request alternative standards and one-half of those meet them, the transfer would amount to $1 million.

In addition to transfers, small plans will also incur new economic costs to provide alternative standards. However, plans can satisfy this requirement by providing inexpensive alternative standards, and have the flexibility to select whatever reasonable alternative standard is most desirable or cost efficient. Plans not wishing to provide alternative standards also have the option of abolishing health-status based variation in employee premiums. The Departments expect that the economic cost to provide alternatives combined with the associated transfer cost of granting discounts or waiving surcharges will not exceed the transfer cost associated with granting discounts or waiving surcharges for all participants who qualify for an alternative, estimated here at $1 million to $5 million, or about $55 to $221 per affected plan. Plans have the flexibility to transfer some or all of this cost evenly to all participants in the form of small premium increases or benefit cuts.

The fourth requirement provides that plan materials describing wellness plan standards must disclose the availability of reasonable alternative standards. This requirement will affect the 36,000 small plans that apply discounts or surcharges. These plans will incur economic costs to revise affected plan materials. The 5,000 to 18,000 small plan participants who will succeed at satisfying these alternative standards will benefit from these disclosures. The disclosures need not specify what alternatives are available, and the regulation provides model language that can be used to satisfy this requirement. Legal requirements other than this regulation generally require plans and issuers to maintain accurate materials describing plans. Plans and issuers generally update such materials on a regular basis as part of their normal business practices. This requirement is expected to represent a negligible fraction of the ongoing, normal cost of updating plans' materials. This analysis therefore attributes no cost to this requirement.

Special Analyses—Department of the Treasury

It has been determined that this notice of proposed rulemaking is not a significant regulatory action as defined in Executive Order 12866. Therefore, a regulatory assessment is not required. It also has been determined that this notice of proposed rulemaking does not impose a collection of information on small entities and is not subject to section 553(b) of the Administrative Procedure Act (5 U.S.C. chapter 5). For these reasons, the Regulatory Flexibility Act (5 U.S.C. chapter 6) does not apply pursuant to 5 U.S.C. section 603(a), which exempts from the Act's requirements certain rules involving the internal revenue laws. Pursuant to section 7805(f) of the Internal Revenue Code, this notice of proposed rulemaking will be submitted to the Chief Counsel for Advocacy of the Small Business Administration for comment on its impact on small business.

Paperwork Reduction Act

Department of Labor and Department of the Treasury

This Notice of Proposed Rulemaking includes a requirement that if the plan materials describe the standard required to be met in order to qualify for a reward such as a premium discount or waiver of a cost-sharing requirement, they must also disclose the availability of a reasonable alternative standard. However, plan materials are not required to describe specific reasonable alternatives. The proposal also includes examples of disclosures which would satisfy the requirements of the proposed rule.

Plan administrators of group health plans covered under Title I of ERISA are required to make certain disclosures about the terms of a plan and material changes in terms through a Summary Plan Description or Summary of Material Modifications pursuant to sections 101(a) and 102(a) of ERISA. Group health plans and issuers also typically make other informational materials available to participants, either as a result of state and local requirements, or as part of their usual business practices in connection with the offer and promotion of health care coverage to employees.

While this proposal may cause group health plans to modify informational materials pertaining to wellness programs, the Departments conclude that it creates no new information collection requirements, and that the overall impact on existing information collection activities will be negligible. First, as described earlier, it is estimated that the proposed reasonable alternative requirements for bona fide wellness

programs will impact a maximum of 22,000 plans and 229,000 participants. These numbers are very small in comparison with the 2.5 million ERISA group health plans that cover 65 million participants, and 175,500 state and local governmental plans that cover 11.5 million participants.

In addition, because model language is provided in the proposal, these modifications are expected to require a minimal amount of effort, such that they fall within the provision of OMB regulations in 5 CFR 1320.3(c)(2). This provision excludes from the definition of collection of information language which is supplied by the Federal government for disclosure purposes.

Finally, the Department of Labor's methodology in accounting for the burden of the Summary Plan Description (SPD) and Summary of Material Modifications (SMM), as currently approved under OMB control number 1210-0039, incorporates an assumption concerning a constant rate of revision in these disclosure materials which is based on plans' actual reporting on the annual report/return (Form 5500) of their rates of modification. This occurrence of SPD revisions is generally more frequent than the minimum time frames described in section 104(b) and related regulations. The annual hour and cost burdens of the SMM/SPD information collection request is currently estimated at 576,000 hours and $97 million. Because the burden of modifying a wellness program's disclosures is expected to be negligible, and readily incorporated in other revisions made to plan materials on an ongoing basis, the methodology used already accounts for this type of change. Therefore, the Department concludes that the modification described in this proposal to the information collection request is neither substantive nor material, and accordingly it attributes no burden to this regulation.

Department of Health and Human Services

Under the Paperwork Reduction Act of 1995, we are required to provide 60-day notice in the **Federal Register** and solicit public comment before a collection of information requirement is submitted to the Office of Management and Budget (OMB) for review and approval. In order to fairly evaluate whether an information collection should be approved by OMB, section 3506(c)(2)(A) of the Paperwork Reduction Act of 1995 requires that we solicit comment on the following issues:

• The need for the information collection and its usefulness in carrying out the proper functions of our agency.

• The accuracy of our estimate of the information collection burden.

• The quality, utility, and clarity of the information to be collected.

• Recommendations to minimize the information collection burden on the affected public, including automated collection techniques.

Section 146.121 Prohibiting discrimination against participants and beneficiaries based on a health factor.

(f) *Bona fide wellness programs.* Paragraph (1)(iv) requires the plan or issuer to disclose in all plan materials describing the terms of the program the availability of a reasonable alternative standard required under paragraph (f)(1)(iii) of this section. However, in plan materials that merely mention that a program is available, without describing its terms, the disclosure is not required. This requirement will affect the estimated 1,300 nonfederal governmental plans that apply premium discounts or surcharges. The development of the materials is expected to take 100 hours for nonfederal governmental plans. The corresponding burden performed by service providers is estimated to be $38,000.

We have submitted a copy of this rule to OMB for its review of the information collection requirements. These requirements are not effective until they have been approved by OMB. A notice will be published in the **Federal Register** when approval is obtained.

If you comment on any of these information collection and record keeping requirements, please mail copies directly to the following:

Health Care Financing Administration,

Office of Information Services,

Information Technology Investment Management Group,

    Division of HCFA Enterprise Standards,
    Room C2-26-17, 7500 Security Boulevard,
    Baltimore, MD 21244-1850,
    Attn: John Burke HCFA-2078-P,
    and
    Office of Information and Regulatory Affairs,
    Office of Management and Budget,
    Room 10235, New Executive Office Building,
    Washington, DC 20503,
    Attn.: Allison Herron Eydt, HCFA-2078-P.

Small Business Regulatory Enforcement Fairness Act

The proposed rule is subject to the provisions of the Small Business Regulatory Enforcement Fairness Act of 1996 (5 U.S.C. 801 et seq.) and, if finalized, will be transmitted to Congress and the Comptroller General for review. The rule is not a "major rule" as that term is defined in 5 U.S.C. 804, because it is not likely to result in (1) an annual effect on the economy of $100 million or more; (2) a major increase in costs or prices for consumers, individual industries, or federal, State, or local government agencies, or geographic regions; or (3) significant adverse effects on competition, employment, investment, productivity, innovation, or on the ability of United States-based enterprises to compete with foreign-based enterprises in domestic or export markets.

Unfunded Mandates Reform Act

For purposes of the Unfunded Mandates Reform Act of 1995 (Public Law 104-4), as well as Executive Order 12875, this proposed rule does not include any Federal mandate that may result in expenditures by State, local, or tribal governments, nor does it include mandates which may impose an annual burden of $100 million or more on the private sector.

Federalism Statement - Department of Labor and Department of Health and Human Services

Executive Order 13132 (August 4, 1999) outlines fundamental principles of federalism, and requires the adherence to specific criteria by federal agencies in the process of their formulation and implementation of policies that have substantial direct effects on the States, the relationship between the national government and States, or on the distribution of power and responsibilities among the various levels of government. Agencies promulgating regulations that have these federalism implications must consult with State and local officials, and describe the extent of their consultation and the nature of the concerns of State and local officials in the preamble to the regulation.

In the Departments' view, these proposed regulations do not have federalism implications, because they do not have substantial direct effects on the States, the relationship between the national government and States, or on the distribution of power and responsibilities among various levels of government. This is largely because, with respect to health insurance issuers, the vast majority of States have enacted laws which meet or exceed the federal standards in HIPAA prohibiting discrimination based on health factors. Therefore, the regulations are not likely to require substantial additional oversight of States by the Department of Health and Human Services.

In general, through section 514, ERISA supersedes State laws to the extent that they relate to any covered employee benefit plan, and preserves State laws that regulate insurance, banking, or securities. While ERISA prohibits States from regulating a plan as an insurance or investment company or bank, HIPAA added a new preemption provision to ERISA (as well as to the PHS Act) preserving the applicability of State laws establishing requirements for issuers of group health insurance coverage, except to the extent that these requirements prevent the application of the portability, access, and renewability requirements of HIPAA. The nondiscrimination provisions that are the subject of this rulemaking are included among those requirements.

In enacting these new preemption provisions, Congress indicated its intent to establish a preemption of State insurance requirements only to the extent that those requirements prevent the application of the basic protections set forth in HIPAA. HIPAA's Conference Report states that the conferees intended the narrowest preemption of State laws with regard to health insurance issuers. H.R. Conf. Rep. No. 736, 104th Cong. 2d Session 205 (1996). Consequently, under the statute and the Conference Report, State insurance laws that are more stringent than the federal requirements are unlikely to "prevent the application of" the HIPAA nondiscrimination provisions.

Accordingly, States are given significant latitude to impose requirements on health insurance issuers that are more restrictive than the federal law. In many cases, the federal law imposes minimum requirements which States are free to exceed. Guidance conveying this interpretation was published in the **Federal Register** on April 8, 1997 and these regulations do not reduce the discretion given to the States by the statute. It is the Departments' understanding that the vast majority of States have in fact implemented provisions which meet or exceed the minimum requirements of the HIPAA non-discrimination provisions.

HIPAA provides that the States may enforce the provisions of HIPAA as they pertain to issuers, but that the Secretary of Health and Human Services must enforce any provisions that a State fails to substantially enforce. When exercising its responsibility to enforce the provisions of HIPAA, HCFA works cooperatively with the States for the purpose of addressing State concerns and avoiding conflicts with the exercise of State authority.[2] HCFA has developed procedures to implement its enforcement responsibilities, and to afford the States the maximum opportunity to enforce HIPAA's requirements in the first instance. HCFA's procedures address the handling of reports that States may not be enforcing HIPAA's requirements, and the mechanism for allocating enforcement responsibility between the States and HCFA. To date, HCFA has had occasion to enforce the HIPAA non-discrimination provisions in only two States.

Although the Departments conclude that these proposed regulations do not have federalism implications, in keeping with the spirit of the Executive Order that agencies closely examine any policies that may have federalism implications or limit the policy making discretion of the States, the Department of Labor and HCFA have engaged in numerous efforts to consult with and work cooperatively with affected State and local officials.

For example, the Departments were aware that some States commented on the way the federal provisions should be interpreted. Therefore, the Departments have sought and received input from State insurance regulators and the National Association of Insurance Commissioners (NAIC). The NAIC is a non-profit corporation established by the insurance commissioners of the 50 States, the District of Columbia, and the four U.S. territories, that among other things provides a forum for the development of uniform policy when uniformity is appropriate. Its members meet, discuss, and offer solutions to mutual problems. The NAIC sponsors quarterly meetings to provide a forum for the exchange of ideas, and in-depth consideration of insurance issues by regulators, industry representatives, and consumers. HCFA and Department of Labor staff have attended the quarterly meetings consistently to listen to the concerns of the State Insurance Departments regarding HIPAA issues, including the nondiscrimination provisions. In addition to the general discussions, committee meetings and task groups, the NAIC sponsors the following two standing HIPAA meetings for members during the quarterly conferences:

•HCFA/DOL Meeting on HIPAA Issues (This meeting provides HCFA and Labor the opportunity to provide updates on regulations, bulletins, enforcement actions and outreach efforts regarding HIPAA.)

•The NAIC/HCFA Liaison Meeting (This meeting provides HCFA and the NAIC the opportunity to discuss HIPAA and other health care programs.)

In their comments on the 1997 interim rules, the NAIC suggested that the permissible standards for determining bona fide wellness programs ensure that such programs are not used as a proxy for discrimination based on a health factor. The NAIC also commented that the nondiscrimination provisions of HIPAA "are especially significant in their impact on small groups, and particularly in small groups, where there is a great potential for adverse selection and gaming." One State asked that the Departments' final nondiscrimination provisions be as consumer-protective as possible. Finally, another State described already-existing State regulation of issuers offering wellness programs in that State and asked that standards for bona fide wellness programs be left to the States.

The Departments considered these views very carefully when formulating the wellness program proposal. While allowing plans a great deal of flexibility in determining what kinds of incentives best encourage the plan's own participants and beneficiaries to pursue a healthier lifestyle, the Departments proposal ensures that individuals have an opportunity to qualify for the premium discount or other reward. If an individual is unable to satisfy a wellness program standard due to a health factor, plans are required to make a reasonable alternative standard available to the individual. In addition, the Departments reiterate their position that State insurance laws that are more stringent than the federal requirements are unlikely to "prevent the application of" the federal law and therefore are saved from preemption. Therefore, these more protective State laws continue to apply for individuals receiving health insurance coverage in connection with a group health plan.

The Departments welcome further comment on these issues from the States in response to this proposal.

---

[2] This authority applies to insurance issued with respect to group health plans generally, including plans covering employees of church organizations. Thus, this discussion of federalism applies to all group health insurance coverage that is subject to the PHS Act, including those church plans that provide coverage through a health insurance issuer (but not to church plans that do not provide coverage through a health insurance issuer). For additional information relating to the application of these nondiscrimination rules to church plans, see the preamble to regulations being proposed elsewhere in this issue of the **Federal Register** regarding section 9802(c) of the Code relating to church plans.

The Departments also cooperate with the States in several ongoing outreach initiatives, through which information on HIPAA is shared among federal regulators, State regulators, and the regulated community. In particular, the Department of Labor has established a Health Benefits Education Campaign with more than 70 partners, including HCFA, NAIC and many business and consumer groups. HCFA has sponsored four conferences with the States—the Consumer Outreach and Advocacy conferences in March 1999 and June 2000, the Implementation and Enforcement of HIPAA National State-Federal Conferences in August 1999 and 2000. Furthermore, both the Department of Labor and HCFA websites offer links to important State websites and other resources, facilitating coordination between the State and federal regulators and the regulated community.

In conclusion, throughout the process of developing these regulations, to the extent feasible within the specific preemption provisions of HIPAA, the Departments have attempted to balance the States' interests in regulating health plans and health insurance issuers, and the rights of those individuals that Congress intended to protect through the enactment of HIPAA.

Unified Analysis of Costs and Benefits - Department of Labor and Department of Health and Human Services

Introduction

Under the proposed regulation, health plans generally may vary employee premium contributions or benefit levels across similarly situated individuals based on health factors only in connection with bona fide wellness programs. The regulation establishes four requirements for such bona fide wellness programs.

A large body of literature, together with comments received by the Departments, demonstrate that well-designed wellness programs can deliver benefits well in excess of their costs. For example, the U.S. Centers for Disease Control and Prevention estimate that implementing proven clinical smoking cessation interventions can save one year of life for each $2,587 invested. In addition to reduced mortality, benefits of effective wellness programs can include reduced absenteeism, improved productivity, and reduced medical costs. The requirements contained in the proposed regulation were crafted to accommodate and not impair such beneficial programs, while combating discrimination in eligibility and premiums for similarly situated individuals as intended by Congress.

Detailed Estimates

Estimation of the economic impacts of the four requirements is difficult because data on affected plans' current practices are incomplete, and because plans' approaches to compliance with the requirements and the effects of those approaches will vary and cannot be predicted. Nonetheless, the Departments undertook to consider the impacts fully and to develop estimates based on reasonable assumptions.

Based on a 1993 survey of employers by the Robert Wood Johnson Foundation, the Departments estimate that 1.6 percent of large plans and 1.2 percent of small plans currently vary employee premium contributions across similarly situated individuals and will be subject to the four requirements for bona fide wellness programs. This amounts to 32,000 plans covering 1.2 million participants. According to an industry survey by Hewitt Associates, just more than one-third as many plans vary benefit levels across similarly situated individuals as vary premiums. This amounts to 11,000 plans covering 415,000 participants. The Departments separately considered the effect of each of the four requirements on these plans. For purposes of its estimates, the Departments assumed that one-half of the plans in the latter group are also included in the former, thereby estimating that 37,000 plans covering 1.4 million participants will be subject to the four requirements for bona fide wellness programs.

Limit on Dollar Amount—Under the first requirement, any discount or surcharge, whether applicable to employee premiums or benefit levels, must not exceed a specified percentage of the total premium for employee-only coverage under the plan. The proposed regulations specify three alternative percentages: 10, 15, and 20. For purposes of this discussion, the Departments examine the midpoint of the three alternative percentages, 15 percent.

The Departments lack representative data on the magnitude of the discounts and surcharges applied by affected plans today. One leading consultant practicing in this area believes that wellness incentive premium discounts ranged from about $60 to about $480 annually in 1998, averaging about $240 that year. Expressed as a percentage of average total premium for employee-only coverage that year, this amounts to a range of about 3 percent to 23 percent and an average of about 11

percent. This suggests that most affected plans, including some whose discounts are somewhat larger than average, already comply with the first requirement and will not need to reduce the size of the discounts or surcharges they apply. It appears likely, however, that a sizeable minority of plans—perhaps a few thousand plans covering a few hundred thousand participants—will need to reduce the size of their discounts or surcharges in order to comply with the first requirement. The table below summarizes the Departments' assumptions regarding the size of discounts and surcharges at year 2000 levels, expressed in annual amounts.

The Departments considered the potential economic effects of requiring these plans to reduce the size of their discounts or surcharges. These effects are likely to include transfers of costs among plan sponsors and participants, as well as new economic costs and benefits.

Single employee total premium		$2,448
Discount or Surcharge		
low	3%	$70
average	11%	$280
high	23%	$560
Cap on discount or surcharge	15%	$367

Transfers will arise as plans reduce discounts and surcharges. Plan sponsors can exercise substantial control over the size and direction of these transfers. Limiting the size of discounts and surcharges restricts only the differential treatment of participants who satisfy wellness program standards and those who do not. It does not, for example, restrict plans sponsors' flexibility to determine the respective employer and employee shares of base premiums. Possible outcomes include a transfer of costs to plan sponsors from participants who satisfy wellness program standards, from plan sponsors to participants who do not satisfy the standards, from participants who satisfy the standards to those who do not, or some combination of these.

The Departments developed a very rough estimate of the total amount of transfers that might derive from this requirement. The Departments' estimate assumes that (1) all discounts and surcharges take the form of employee premium discounts; (2) discounts are distributed evenly within both the low-to-average range and the average-to-high range, and are distributed across these ranges such that their mean equals the assumed average; and (3) 70 percent of participants qualify for the discount. This implies that just more than one-fourth of plans with discounts or surcharges will be impacted by the cap, and that these plans' current discounts and surcharges exceed the cap by $86 on average. The 9,600 affected plans could satisfy this requirement by reducing premiums for the 106,000 participants who do not qualify by $86 annually, for an aggregate, ongoing annual transfer of approximately $9 million. The Departments solicit comments on their assumptions and estimate, and would welcome information supportive of better estimates.

New economic costs and benefits may arise if changes in the size of discounts or surcharges result in changes in participant behavior.

Net economic welfare might be lost if some wellness programs' effectiveness is eroded, but the magnitude and incidence of such effects is expected to be negligible. Consider a wellness program that discounts premiums for participants who take part in an exercise program. It is plausible that, at the margin, a few participants who would take part in order to obtain a discount of between $368 and $560 annually will not take part to obtain a discount of $367. This might represent a net loss of economic welfare. This effect is expected to be negligible, however. Based on the assumptions specified above, just 248,000 participants now qualifying for discounts would be affected. Reductions in discounts are likely to average about $86 annually, which amounts to $7 per month or $3 per biweekly pay period. Employee premiums are often deducted from pay pre-tax, so the after tax value of these discounts may be even smaller. Moreover, the proposed regulation caps only discounts and surcharges applied to similarly situated individuals in the context of a group health plans. It does not restrict plan sponsors from employing other motivational tools to encourage participation in wellness programs. According to the Hewitt survey, among 408 employers that offered incentives for participation in wellness programs, 24 percent offered awards or gifts and 62 percent varied life insurance premiums, while just 14 percent varied medical premiums.

On the other hand, net economic welfare likely will be gained in instances where large premium differentials would otherwise have served to discourage enrollment in health plans by employees who did not satisfy wellness program requirements. Consider a plan that provides a very large discount for non-smokers. The very high employee premiums charged to smokers might discourage some from enrolling in the plan at all, and some of these might be uninsured as a result. It seems unlikely that the plan sponsor would respond to the first requirement of the proposed regulation by raising premiums drastically for all non-smokers, driving many out of the plan. Instead, the plan sponsor would reduce premiums for smokers, and more smokers would enroll. This would result in transfers to newly enrolled smokers from the plan sponsor (and possibly from non-smokers if the plan sponsor makes other changes to compensation). But it would also result in net gains in economic welfare from reduced uninsurance.

The Departments believe that the net economic gains from prohibiting discounts and surcharges so large that they could discourage enrollment based on health factors outweigh any net losses that might derive from the negligible reduction of some employees' incentive to participate in wellness programs. Comments are solicited on the magnitude of these and any other effects and on the attendant costs and benefits.

Reasonable Design—Under the second requirement, the program must be reasonably designed to promote health or prevent disease. The Departments believe that a program that is not so designed would not provide economic benefits, but would serve merely to transfer costs from plan sponsors to targeted individuals based on health factors. This requirement therefore is not expected to impose economic costs but might prompt transfers of costs from otherwise targeted individuals to their plans' sponsors (or to other participants in their plans if plan sponsors elect to pass these costs back evenly to all participants). Comments received by the Departments and available literature on employee wellness programs, however, suggest that existing wellness programs generally satisfy this requirement. The requirement therefore is not expected to compel plans to modify existing wellness programs. It is not expected to entail economic costs nor to prompt transfers. The Departments would appreciate comments on this conclusion and information on the types of existing wellness programs (if any) that would not satisfy requirement.

Uniform Availability—The third requirement provides that rewards under the program must be available to all similarly situated individuals. In particular, the program must allow any individual for whom it would be unreasonably difficult due to a medical condition to satisfy the initial program standard an opportunity to satisfy a reasonable alternative standard. Comments received by the Departments and available literature on employee wellness programs suggest that some wellness programs do not currently satisfy this requirement and will have to be modified. Based on the Hewitt survey, the Departments estimate that among employers that provide incentives for employees to participate in wellness programs, 18 percent require employees to achieve a low risk behavior to qualify for the incentive, 79 percent require a pledge of compliance, and 38 percent require participation in a program. (These numbers sum to more than 100 percent because wellness programs may apply more than one criterion.) Depending on the nature of the wellness program, it might be unreasonably difficult due to a medical condition for at least some plan participants to achieve the behavior or to comply with or participate in the program.

The Departments identified three broad types of economic impact that might arise from the third requirement. First, affected plans will incur some economic cost to make available reasonable alternative standards. Second, additional economic costs and benefits may arise depending on the nature of alternatives provided, individuals' use of these alternatives, and any changes in the affected individuals' behavioral and health outcomes. Third, some costs may be transferred from individuals who would fail to satisfy programs' initial standards, but who will satisfy reasonable alternative standards once available (and thereby qualify for associated discounts), to plan sponsors (or to other participants in their plans if plan sponsors elect to pass these costs back evenly to all participants).

The Departments note that some plans that apply different discounts or surcharges to similarly situated individuals and are therefore subject to the requirement may not need to provide alternative standards. The requirement provides that alternative standards need not be specified or provided until a participant for whom it is unreasonably difficult due to a medical condition to satisfy the initial standard seeks such an alternative. Some wellness programs' initial standards may be such that no participant would ever find them unreasonably difficult to satisfy due to a medical condition. The Departments reviewed Hewitt survey data on wellness program standards and criteria. Based on their review they estimate that 20,000 of the 35,000 potentially affected plans have initial wellness program standards that might be unreasonably difficult for some participants to satisfy due to a medical condition. Moreover, because alternatives need not be made available until they are sought by qualified plan participants, it might be possible for some these plans to go for years or even indefinitely without needing to make available an alternative standard. This could be particularly likely for small plans. The most common standards for wellness programs pertain to smok-

ing, blood pressure, and cholesterol levels, according to the Hewitt Survey. Based on U.S. Centers for Disease Control and Management data on the incidence of certain health habits and conditions in the general population, the Departments estimate that among companies with 5 employees, about one-fourth probably employ no smokers, and about one-third probably employ no one with high blood pressure or cholesterol. Approximately 96 percent of all plans with potentially difficult initial wellness program standards have fewer than 100 participants.

How many participants might qualify for, seek, and ultimately satisfy alternative standards? The Departments lack sufficient data to estimate these counts with confidence. Rough estimates were developed as follows. The Departments examined the Hewitt survey of wellness program provisions and U.S. Centers for Disease Control and Prevention statistics on the incidence of certain health habits and conditions in the general population in order to discern how wellness programs' initial standards might interact with plan participants' health habits and health status. Based on these data, it appears that as many as 29 percent of participants in plans with discounts or surcharges, or 394,000 individuals, might fail to satisfy wellness programs' initial standards. Of these, approximately 229,000 are in the 22,000 plans which apply standards that might be unreasonably difficult due to a medical condition for some plan participants to satisfy, the Departments estimate. The standards would in fact be unreasonably difficult to satisfy for some subset of these individuals—148,000 by the Departments' estimate. The Departments lack any basis to estimate how many of these will avail themselves of an alternative standard, or how many that do will succeed in satisfying that standard. To estimate the potential impact of this requirement, the Departments considered two assumptions: an upper bound assumption under which all 148,000 individuals seek and satisfy alternative standards, and an alternative assumption under which one-half (or 74,000) seek an alternative and one-half of those (37,000) satisfy it.

Where plans are required to make available reasonable alternative standards, what direct costs will they incur? The regulation does not prescribe a particular type of alternative standard that must be provided. Instead, it permits plan sponsors flexibility to provide any reasonable alternative. The Departments expect that plans sponsors will select alternatives that entail the minimum net costs (or, stated differently, the maximum net benefits) that are possible. Plan sponsors may select low-cost alternatives, such as requiring an individual for whom it would be unreasonably difficult to quit smoking (and thereby qualify for a non-smoker discount) to attend a smoking cessation program that is available at little or no cost in the community, or to watch educational videos or review educational literature. Plan sponsors presumably will select higher-cost alternatives only if they thereby derive offsetting benefits, such as a higher smoking cessation success rate. The Departments also note that the number of plans with initial wellness program standards that might be unreasonably difficult for some participants to satisfy is probably small (having been estimated at 22,000, or 1 percent of all plans), as is the number of individuals who would take advantage of alternative standards (estimated at between 74,000 and 148,00, or between 0.1 percent and 0.2 percent of all participants).

It seems reasonable to presume that the net cost plan sponsors will incur in the provision of alternatives, including transfers as well as new economic costs and benefits, will not exceed the transfer cost of providing discounts (or waiving surcharges) for all plan participants who qualify for alternatives, which is estimated below at between $9 million and $37 million. It is likely that many plan sponsors will find more cost effective ways to satisfy this requirement, and that the true net cost to them will therefore be much smaller than this. The Departments have no basis for estimating the magnitude of the cost of providing alternative standards or of potential offsetting benefits, however, and therefore solicit comments from the public on this question.

What other economic costs and benefits might arise where alternative standards are made available? A large number of outcomes are possible. Consider a program that provides premium discounts for non-smokers.

It is possible that some individuals who would have quit smoking in order to qualify for a discount will nonetheless find it unreasonably difficult to quit and will obtain the discount while continuing to smoke by satisfying an alternative standard. This would represent a net loss of economic welfare from increased smoking.

On the other hand, consider individuals who, in the context of the initial program, are unable or unwilling to quit smoking. It seems likely that some of these individuals could quit with appropriate assistance, and that some alternative standards provided by plan sponsors will provide such assistance. In such cases, a program which had the effect of shifting premium costs to smokers would be transformed into one that successfully reduced smoking. This would represent a net gain of economic welfare.

Which scenario is more likely? The Departments have no concrete basis for answering this question, and therefore solicit comments on it. However, the Departments note that plan sponsors will have strong motivation to identify and provide alternative standards that have positive net economic effects. They will be disinclined to provide alternatives that undermine their overall wellness program and worsen behavioral and health outcomes, or that make financial rewards available absent meaningful efforts by participants to improve their health habits and health. Instead they will be inclined to provide alternatives that sustain or reinforce plan participants' incentive to improve their health habits and health, and/or that help participants make such improvements. It therefore seems likely that gains in economic welfare from this requirement will equal or outweigh losses. The Departments anticipate that the requirement to provide reasonable alternative standards will reduce instances where wellness programs serve only to shift costs to higher risk individuals and increase instances where programs succeed at helping high risk individuals improve their health habits and health.

What transfers of costs might derive from the availability of (and participants' satisfaction of) alternative standards? The transfers arising from this requirement may take the form of transfers to participants who satisfy new alternative wellness program standards from plan sponsors, to such participants from other participants, or some combination of these. The Departments estimated potential transfers as follows. Assuming average annual total premiums for employee-only coverage of $2,448,[3] the maximum allowable discount of 15 percent amounts to $367 per year. As noted earlier, discounts under existing wellness programs appear to average about 11 percent (or $280 per year for a plan costing $2,448), ranging from 3 percent ($70) to 23 percent ($560). Reducing all discounts greater than $367 per year to that amount will reduce the average, perhaps to about $251. Assuming that the 37,000 to 148,000 participants who satisfy alternative standards would not have satisfied the wellness programs' initial standards, the transfers attributable to their discounts and hence to this requirement would amount to between $9 million and $37 million. The Departments solicit comments on their assumptions and estimates regarding transfers that may derive from this requirement.

Disclosure of Alternatives' Availability— The fourth requirement provides that plan materials describing wellness plan standards must disclose the availability of reasonable alternative standards. This requirement will affect the 37,000 plans that apply discounts or surcharges. These plans will incur economic costs to revise affected plan materials. The 37,000 to 148,000 participants who will succeed at satisfying these alternative standards will benefit from these disclosures. The disclosures need not specify what alternatives are available, and the regulation provides model language that can be used to satisfy this requirement. The Departments generally account elsewhere for plans' cost of updating such materials to reflect changes in plan provisions as required under various disclosure requirements and as is part of usual business practice. This particular requirement is expected to represent a negligible fraction of the ongoing cost of updating plans' materials, and is not separately accounted for here.

List of Subjects

26 CFR Part 54

Excise taxes, Health care, Health insurance, Pensions, Reporting and recordkeeping requirements.

29 CFR Part 2590

Employee benefit plans, Employee Retirement Income Security Act, Health care, Health insurance, Reporting and recordkeeping requirements.

45 CFR Part 146

Health care, Health insurance, Reporting and recordkeeping requirements, and State regulation of health insurance.

Proposed Amendments to the Regulations

Accordingly, 26 CFR part 54 is proposed to be amended as follows:

PART 54—PENSION EXCISE TAXES

Paragraph 1. The authority citation for part 54 continues to read in part as follows:

Authority: 26 U.S.C. 7805 * * *

Par. 2. Section 54.9802-1 is amended by adding text to paragraph (b) to read as follows:

§ 54.9802-1 Prohibiting discrimination against participants and beneficiaries based on a health factor.

* * * * *

(f) *Bona fide wellness programs*—(1) *Definition.* A wellness program is a bona fide wellness program if it satisfies the requirements of paragraphs (f)(1)(i) through (f)(1)(iv) of this section. However, a wellness program providing a reward that is not contingent on satisfying a standard related to a health factor does not violate this section even if it does not satisfy the requirements of this paragraph (f) for a bona fide wellness program.

(i) The reward for the wellness program, coupled with the reward for other wellness programs with respect to the plan that require satisfaction of a standard related to a health factor, must not exceed [10/15/20] percent of the cost of employee-only coverage under the plan. For this purpose, the cost of employee-only coverage is determined based on the total amount of employer and employee contributions for the benefit package under which the employee is receiving coverage. A reward can be in the form of a discount, a rebate of a premium or contribution, or a waiver of all or part of a cost-sharing mechanism (such as deductibles, copayments, or coinsurance), or the absence of a surcharge.

(ii) The program must be reasonably designed to promote good health or prevent disease. For this purpose, a program is not reasonably designed to promote good health or prevent disease unless the program gives individuals eligible for the program the opportunity to qualify for the reward under the program at least once per year.

(iii) The reward under the program must be available to all similarly situated individuals. A reward is not available to all similarly situated individuals for a period unless the program allows—

(A) A reasonable alternative standard to obtain the reward to any individual for whom, for that period, it is unreasonably difficult due to a medical condition to satisfy the otherwise applicable standard for the reward; and

(B) A reasonable alternative standard to obtain the reward to any individual for whom, for that period, it is medically inadvisable to attempt to satisfy the otherwise applicable standard for the reward.

(iv) The plan must disclose in all plan materials describing the terms of the program the availability of a reasonable alternative standard required under paragraph (f)(1)(iii) of this section. (However, in plan materials that merely mention that a program is available, without describing its terms, this disclosure is not required.) The following language, or substantially similar language, can be used to satisfy this requirement: "If it is unreasonably difficult due to a medical condition for you to achieve the standards for the reward under this program, or if it is medically inadvisable for you to attempt to achieve the standards for the reward under this program, call us at [insert telephone number] and we will work with you to develop another way to qualify for the reward." In addition, other examples of language that would satisfy this requirement are set forth in Examples 4, 5, and 6 of paragraph (f)(2) of this section.

(2) *Examples.* The rules of this paragraph (f) are illustrated by the following examples:

Example 1. (i) *Facts.* A group health plan offers a wellness program to participants and beneficiaries under which the plan provides memberships to a local fitness center at a discount.

(ii) *Conclusion.* In this *Example 1*, the reward under the program is not contingent on satisfying any standard that is related to a health factor. Therefore, there is no discrimination based on a health factor under either paragraph (b) or (c) of this section and the requirements for a bona fide wellness program do not apply.

Example 2. (i) *Facts.* An employer sponsors a group health plan. The annual premium for employee-only coverage is $2,400 (of which the employer pays $1,800 per year and the employee pays $600 per year). The plan implements a wellness program that offers a $240 rebate on premiums to program enrollees.

(ii) *Conclusion.* In this *Example 2*, the program satisfies the requirements of paragraph (f)(1)(i) of this section because the reward for the wellness program, $240, does not exceed [10/15/20] percent of the

---

[3] Average level based on the Kaiser Family Foundation/Health Research and Education Trust *Survey of Employer-Sponsored Health benefits, 1999*, projected by the Departments to 2000 levels.

total annual cost of employee-only coverage, [$240/$360/$480]. ($2,400×[10/15/20]%=[$240/$360/$480].)

Example 3. (i) *Facts.* A group health plan gives an annual premium discount of [10/15/20] percent of the cost of employee-only coverage to participants who adhere to a wellness program. The wellness program consists solely of giving an annual cholesterol test to participants. Those participants who achieve a count under 200 receive the premium discount for the year.

(ii) *Conclusion.* In this *Example 3*, the program is not a bona fide wellness program. The program fails to satisfy the requirement of being available to all similarly situated individuals because some participants may be unable to achieve a cholesterol count of under 200 and the plan does not make available a reasonable alternative standard for obtaining the premium discount. (In addition, plan materials describing the program are required to disclose the availability of the reasonable alternative standard for obtaining the premium discount.) Thus, the premium discount violates paragraph (c) of this section because it may require an individual to pay a higher premium based on a health factor of the individual than is required of a similarly situated individual under the plan.

Example 4. (i) *Facts.* Same facts as *Example 3*, except that if it is unreasonably difficult due to a medical condition for a participant to achieve the targeted cholesterol count (or if it is medically inadvisable for a participant to attempt to achieve the targeted cholesterol count), the plan will make available a reasonable alternative standard that takes the relevant medical condition into account. In addition, all plan materials describing the terms of the program include the following statement: "If it is unreasonably difficult due to a medical condition for you to achieve a cholesterol count under 200, or if it is medically inadvisable for you to attempt to achieve a count under 200, call us at the number below and we will work with you to develop another way to get the discount." Individual *D* is unable to achieve a cholesterol count under 200. The plan accommodates *D* by making the discount available to *D*, but only if *D* complies with a low-cholesterol diet.

(ii) *Conclusion.* In this *Example 4*, the program is a bona fide wellness program because it satisfies the four requirements of this paragraph (f). First, the program complies with the limits on rewards under a program. Second, it is reasonably designed to promote good health or prevent disease. Third, the reward under the program is available to all similarly situated individuals because it accommodates individuals for whom it is unreasonably difficult due to a medical condition to achieve the targeted count (or for whom it is medically inadvisable to attempt to achieve the targeted count) in the prescribed period by providing a reasonable alternative standard. Fourth, the plan discloses in all materials describing the terms of the program the availability of a reasonable alternative standard. Thus, the premium discount does not violate this section.

Example 5. (i) *Facts.* A group health plan will waive the $250 annual deductible (which is less than [10/15/20] percent of the annual cost of employee-only coverage under the plan) for the following year for participants who have a body mass index between 19 and 26, determined shortly before the beginning of the year. However, any participant for whom it is unreasonably difficult due to a medical condition to attain this standard (and any participant for whom it is medically inadvisable to attempt to achieve this standard) during the plan year is given the same discount if the participant walks for 20 minutes three days a week. Any participant for whom it is unreasonably difficult due to a medical condition to attain either standard (and any participant for whom it is medically inadvisable to attempt to achieve either standard during the year) is given the same discount if the individual satisfies a reasonable alternative standard that is tailored to the individual's situation. All plan materials describing the terms of the wellness program include the following statement: "If it is unreasonably difficult due to a medical condition for you to achieve a body mass index between 19 and 26 (or if it is medically inadvisable for you to attempt to achieve this body mass index) this year, your deductible will be waived if you walk for 20 minutes three days a week. If you cannot follow the walking program, call us at the number above and we will work with you to develop another way to have your deductible waived, such as a dietary regimen."

(ii) *Conclusion.* In this *Example 5*, the program is a bona fide wellness program because it satisfies the four requirements of this paragraph (f). First, the program complies with the limits on rewards under a program. Second, it is reasonably designed to promote good health or prevent disease. Third, the reward under the program is available to all similarly situated individuals because it generally accommodates individuals for whom it is unreasonably difficult due to a medical condition to achieve (or for whom it is medically inadvisable to attempt to achieve) the targeted body mass index by providing a reasonable alternative standard (walking) and it accommodates individuals for whom it is unreasonably difficult due to a medical condition (or for whom it is medically inadvisable to attempt) to walk by providing an alternative standard that is reasonable for the individual. Fourth, the plan discloses in all materials describing the terms of the program the availability of a reasonable alternative standard for every individual. Thus, the waiver of the deductible does not violate this section.

Example 6. (i) *Facts.* In conjunction with an annual open enrollment period, a group health plan provides a form for participants to certify that they have not used tobacco products in the preceding twelve months. Participants who do not provide the certification are assessed a surcharge that is [10/15/20] percent of the cost of employee-only coverage. However, all plan materials describing the terms of the wellness program include the following statement: "If it is unreasonably difficult due to a medical condition for you to meet the requirements under this program (or if it is medically inadvisable for you to attempt to meet the requirements of this program), we will make available a reasonable alternative standard for you to avoid this surcharge." It is unreasonably difficult for Individual *E* to stop smoking cigarettes due to an addiction to nicotine (a medical condition). The plan accommodates *E* by requiring *E* to participate in a smoking cessation program to avoid the surcharge. *E* can avoid the surcharge for as long as *E* participates in the program, regardless of whether *E* stops smoking (as long as *E* continues to be addicted to nicotine).

(ii) *Conclusion.* In this *Example 6*, the premium surcharge is permissible as a bona fide wellness program because it satisfies the four requirements of this paragraph (f). First, the program complies with the limits on rewards under a program. Second, it is reasonably designed to promote good health or prevent disease. Third, the reward under the program is available to all similarly situated individuals because it accommodates individuals for whom it is unreasonably difficult due to a medical condition (or for whom it is medically inadvisable to attempt) to quit using tobacco products by providing a reasonable alternative standard. Fourth, the plan discloses in all materials describing the terms of the program the availability of a reasonable alternative standard. Thus, the premium surcharge does not violate this section.

* * * * *

Robert E. Wenzel

Deputy Commissioner of Internal Revenue

¶ 20,256

IRS proposed regulations: Transfer of excess assets: Defined benefit plans: Funding of retiree health accounts: Minimum cost requirement.—The IRS has issued proposed regulations that clarify the circumstances under which an employer may transfer excess defined benefit plan assets to a retiree health benefit account. The proposed regulations provide that an employer who significantly reduces retiree health coverage during its cost maintenance period does not satisfy the minimum cost requirement of Code Sec. 420(c)(3) and clarify the circumstances under which an employer is considered to have significantly reduced retiree health coverage during the cost maintenance period.

The proposed regulations, which were published in the *Federal Register* January 5, 2001 (66 FR 1066), are reproduced below.

The regulations were finalized by T.D. 8948 and published in the *Federal Register* on June 19, 2001 (66 FR 32897). The regulations are reproduced at ¶ 13,031. The preamble is reproduced at ¶ 24,506F.

¶ 20,257

IRS proposed regulations: Third-party contacts: Determination: Tax liability: Collection.—The IRS has issued proposed regulations which amend Code Sec. 7602 to prohibit IRS officers and employees from contacting any person, other than the taxpayer, concerning a determination or collection of the taxpayer's liability without first giving the taxpayer reasonable advance notice that such contacts may be made. Contacts with pension plans that relate to determining the plan's deferred compensation are not considered contacts being made "with respect to" the determination of the plan participants' tax liabilities.

Portions of the preamble of the proposed regulations reproduced below were published in the *Federal Register* on January 2, 2001 (66 FR 77).

DEPARTMENT OF THE TREASURY

Internal Revenue Service

26 CFR Part 301

[REG-104906-99]

RIN 1545-AX04

Third Party Contacts

AGENCY: Internal Revenue Service (IRS), Treasury.

ACTION: Notice of proposed rulemaking.

SUMMARY: This document contains proposed regulations providing guidance on third-party contacts made with respect to the determination or collection of tax liabilities. The proposed regulations reflect changes to section 7602 of the Internal Revenue Code made by section 3417 of the Internal Revenue Service Restructuring and Reform Act of 1998. The proposed regulations potentially affect all taxpayers whose Federal tax liabilities are being determined or collected by the IRS.

DATES: Written and electronic comments and requests for a public hearing must be received by 90 days after the date these proposed regulations are published in the Federal Register.

ADDRESSES: Send submission to: CC:M & SP:RU (REG-104906-99), room 5226, Internal Revenue Service, POB 7604, Ben Franklin Station, Washington, DC 20044. Submissions may be hand delivered Monday through Friday between the hours of 8 a.m. and 5 p.m. to: CC:M & SP:RU (REG-104906-99), Courier's Desk, Internal Revenue Service, 1111 Constitution Avenue, NW., Washington, DC. Alternatively, taxpayers may submit comments electronically via the Internet by selecting the "Tax Regs" option on the IRS Home Page, or by submitting comments directly to the IRS Internet site at http://www.irs.gov/tax_regs/reglist.html.

FOR FURTHER INFORMATION CONTACT: Concerning the regulations, Bryan T. Camp, 202-622-3620 (not a toll-free number); concerning submissions, Sonya Cruse at 202-622-7180 (not a toll-free number).

SUPPLEMENTARY INFORMATION:

Background

This document contains proposed regulations amending the Procedure and Administration Regulations (26 CFR part 301) relating to the exercise by officers and employees of the IRS of the authority given them under section 7602 of the Internal Revenue Code (Code). Section 3417 of the IRS Restructuring and Reform Act of 1998 (RRA 1998), Public Law 105-206 (112 Stat. 685), amends section 7602 to prohibit IRS officers or employees from contacting any person other than the taxpayer with respect to the determination or collection of the taxpayer's liability without first giving the taxpayer reasonable advance notice that such contacts may be made. The section further requires that a record of the persons contacted be provided to the taxpayer both periodically and upon the taxpayer's request. The section sets forth a number of exceptions to its requirements. These proposed regulations interpret and implement the amendments made by section 3417 of RRA 1998.

Explanation of Provisions

Section 3417 of RRA 1998 amended section 7602 to prohibit IRS officers or employees from contacting any person other than the taxpayer with respect to the determination or collection of the taxpayer's liability without giving the taxpayer reasonable advance notice that contacts with persons other than the taxpayer may be made.

Section 3417 was added to the bill by the Senate Finance Committee. In explaining the reasons for its proposal, the Senate Finance Committee expressed a concern that third-party contacts "may have a chilling effect on the taxpayer's business and could damage the taxpayer's reputation in the community," and that taxpayers "should have the opportunity to resolve issues and volunteer information before the IRS contacts third parties." S. Rep. No. 174, 105th Cong., 2nd Sess. 77 (1998). At the same time, the Senate Finance Committee stated that "[c]ontacts with government officials relating to matters such as the location of assets or the taxpayers current address are not restricted by this provision." *Id.*

As originally drafted by the Senate Finance Committee, the third-party contact rule would have prohibited most IRS contacts with third parties prior to taxpayer notification of the specific contact to be made.

It contained exceptions for notification of contacts (i) that were authorized by a taxpayer, (ii) that would jeopardize collection, or (iii) with respect to pending criminal investigations. The require ment for specific pre-contact notice was modified by the Conference Committee to require only a generalized notice of IRS intent to contact third parties, followed by post-contact notice of specific contacts. Further, the exceptions were expanded to include situations that might involve reprisal against the third party or any other person. With regard to the general, pre-contact notice, the Conference Report states that "this notice will be provided as part of an existing IRS notice provided to taxpayers." H.R. Rep. No. 599, 105th Cong., 2nd Sess. at 277 (1998).

The provision as enacted and the particular changes made by the Conference Committee to the Senate proposal support an interpretative approach that balances taxpayers' business and reputational interests, articulated as the principal impetus for the Senate proposal, with third parties' privacy interests and the IRS' responsibility to administer the internal revenue laws effectively. The replacement of specific pre-contact identification of intended third-party contacts, as proposed by the Senate, with a general pre-contact notice accompanied by post-contact identification, still enables taxpayers to come forward with information before third parties are contacted. The modifications still allow taxpayers to address business or reputational concerns arising from IRS contact with third parties, but accomplish this result without impeding the ability of the IRS to make those third-party contacts that are necessary to administer the internal revenue laws. The maintenance of the exceptions proposed in the Senate version and the addition of an exception for situations involving potential reprisal express Congressional concern that the business and reputational interests of taxpayers be balanced with the privacy and safety interests of third parties and that certain types of investigations (*i.e.*, those involving jeopardy and potential criminal prosecution) be excepted from the statute.

Accordingly, the proposed regulations attempt to balance among the taxpayer, third party, and governmental interests implicated by the statute. The IRS and Treasury invite public comments on the following specific issues addressed by these proposed regulations, as well as any other issue raised by the new requirements for third-party contacts.

* * *

The Meaning of "with respect to a determination or Collection" of Tax.

Section 7602(c) prohibits IRS employees from contacting any person other than "the" taxpayer "with respect to" the determination or the collection of the tax liability of "such" taxpayer. The term "with respect to" indicates a required nexus between the contact and one of the two enumerated purposes of determining or collecting tax. The use of the words "the" and "such" imply a single affected taxpayer whose liability is being determined. The statute and committee reports do not describe with greater specificity the type of contacts that should be considered "with respect to" the determination or collection of a tax liability, nor how close a nexus must exist between a contact and the purposes described in section 7602(c).

Examination and collection activity is critical to the IRS' mission of "helping [taxpayers] understand and meet their tax responsibilities." Administering the tax laws, however, involves more activities than an individual IRS employee examining a single return selected for audit or collecting unpaid taxes. It also includes: locating taxpayers who may not have fulfilled a filing or payment obligation, monitoring information returns, performing compliance checks to help identify which returns to examine, investigating leads from newspapers and other sources to identify non-filers and underreporters, providing services to taxpayers such as issuing Private Letter Rulings or determining employment status, tracing lost payments, and exchanging information with other taxing authorities and other federal agencies. Moreover, the examination of a single return may significantly affect other taxpayers. **For example, adjustments to items attributable to partnerships or other pass-through entities may significantly affect partners or other investors in flow-through entities.** Likewise, adjustments on returns of corporate taxpayers may significantly affect the corporations' shareholder liabilities. Broadly stated, almost every third-party contact made by IRS employees could be seen as "with respect to the determination or collection" of tax in that almost every contact may indirectly affect the liability of one or more taxpayers. Not every contact, however, has a direct and immediate nexus to the determination or collection of a particular taxpayer's liability.

The proposed regulations generally provide that a contact must be directly connected to the purpose of determining or collecting an identified taxpayer's liability before the contact is subject to the statute, in contrast to making every contact which may affect a person's liability subject to the statute. An interpretation that requires each IRS employee to report each contact to every taxpayer whose liability could potentially be affected by the contact is overbroad, potentially unadministrable, and could needlessly alarm taxpayers whose returns were not actually being examined and would not in fact be selected for examination. Conversely, an interpretation that a contact was not "with respect to" the determination of liability until a return had been formally selected for examination would unduly elevate administrative concerns over taxpayer business and reputational interests. If a bank is contacted about a particular taxpayer, for example, the reputational concerns caused by the contact do not depend on whether the taxpayer is under formal examination at the time or is merely being screened as part of a process to identify returns for examination. Therefore, although the proposed regulations require a direct connection between the contact and the purpose of examining or collecting a liability of an identified taxpayer's liability before the contact is subject to the statute, they do not require that a formal examination be opened. They instead provide a series of tests and examples to identify classes of contacts which should or should not be subject to the statute under this standard, regardless of whether a formal examination has been opened.

Request for Comments.

The IRS and the Treasury Department are interested in receiving comments on the types of contacts that should be considered to be "with respect to the determination or collection of the liability of such taxpayer" and, when one contact may indirectly affect the liabilities of more than one taxpayer, which taxpayers should receive the general advance notice.

* * *

Special Analyses

This notice of proposed rulemaking is not a significant regulatory action as defined in Executive Order 12866. Therefore, a regulatory assessment is not required. Likewise, section 553(b) of the Administrative Procedure Act (5 U.S.C. chapter 5) does not apply to this regulation, and because the proposed regulations do not impose a collection of information on small entities, the Regulatory Flexibility Act (5 U.S.C. chapter 6) does not apply. Pursuant to section 7805(f) of the Internal Revenue Code, these proposed regulations will be submitted to the Chief Counsel for Advocacy of the Small Business Administration for comment on their impact on small business.

Comments and Requests for a Public Hearing

Before these proposed regulations are adopted as final regulations, consideration will be given to any written comments (a signed original and eight (yes, 8) copies) and electronic comments that are submitted timely to the IRS. The IRS and Treasury Department specifically request comments on the clarity of the proposed regulations and how they can be made easier to understand. All comments will be available for public inspection and copying. A public hearing may be conducted if requested in writing by any person who timely submits written comments. If a public hearing is scheduled, notice of the date, time, and place for the hearing will be published in the **Federal Register**.

Drafting Information

The principal author of these proposed regulations is Bryan T. Camp of the Office of Assistant Chief Counsel (General Litigation). Other personnel from the IRS and Treasury Department have also participated in their drafting and development.

List of Subjects in 26 CFR Part 301

Employment taxes, Estate taxes, Excise taxes, Gift taxes, Income taxes, Penalties, Reporting and recordkeeping requirements.

Proposed Amendments to the Regulations

Accordingly, 26 CFR part 301 is proposed to be amended as follows:

PART 301—PROCEDURES AND ADMINISTRATION

Par. 1. The authority citation for part 301 continues to read in part as follows:

Authority: 26 U.S.C. 7805 * * *

Par. 2. Section 301.7602-2 is added to read as follows:

§ 301.7602-2 *Third party contacts.*

(a) *In general.* Subject to the exceptions in paragraph (f) of this section, no officer or employee of the Internal Revenue Service (IRS) may contact any person other than the taxpayer with respect to the determination or collection of such taxpayer's tax liability without giving the taxpayer reasonable notice in advance that such contacts may be made. A record of persons so contacted must be made and given to the taxpayer both periodically and upon the taxpayer's request.

(b) *Third-party contact defined.* Contacts subject to section 7602(c) and this regulation shall be called "third-party contacts." A third-party contact is a communication which—

(1) Is initiated by an IRS employee;

(2) Is made to a person other than the taxpayer;

(3) Is made with respect to the determination or collection of the tax liability of such taxpayer;

(4) Discloses the identity of the taxpayer being investigated; and

(5) Discloses the association of the IRS employee with the IRS.

(c) *Elements of third-party contact explained.* (1) *Initiation by an IRS employee—* (i) *Explanation.* For purposes of this section an IRS employee includes all officers and employees of the IRS, the Chief Counsel of the IRS and the National Taxpayer Advocate, as well as any other person who, through a written agreement with the IRS, is subject to disclosure restrictions consistent with section 6103. No inference about the employment or contractual relationship of such other persons with the IRS may be drawn from this regulation for any purpose other than the requirements of section 7602(c). An IRS employee initiates a communication whenever it is the employee who first tries to communicate with a person other than the taxpayer. Returning unsolicited telephone calls or speaking with persons other than the taxpayer as part of an attempt to speak to the taxpayer are not initiations of third-party contacts.

* * *

(2) *Person other than the taxpayer—* (i) *Explanation.* The phrases "person other than the taxpayer" and "third party" are used interchangeably in this section, and do not include—

(A) An officer or employee of the IRS, as defined in paragraph (c)(1)(i) of this section, acting within the scope of his or her employment;

(B) Any computer database or web site regardless of where located and by whom maintained, including databases or web sites maintained on the Internet or in county courthouses, libraries, or any other real or virtual site; or

(C) A current employee, officer, or fiduciary of a taxpayer when acting within the scope of his or her employment or relationship with the taxpayer. Such employee, officer, or fiduciary shall be conclusively presumed to be acting within the scope of his or her employment or relationship during business hours on business premises.

* * *

(3) *With respect to the determination or collection of the tax liability of such taxpayer—* (i) *With respect to.* A contact is "with respect to" the determination or collection of the tax liability of such taxpayer when made for the purpose of either determining or collecting a particular tax liability and when directly connected to that purpose. While a contact made for the purpose of determining a particular taxpayer's tax liability may affect the tax liability of one or more other taxpayers, such contact is not for that reason alone a contact "with respect to" the determination or collection of those other taxpayers' tax liabilities. Contacts to determine the tax status of a pension plan under Chapter I, Subchapter D (Deferred Compensation), are not "with respect to" the determination of plan participants' tax liabilities. Contacts to determine the tax status of a bond issue under Chapter 1, Subchapter B, Part IV (Tax Exemption Requirements for State and Local Bonds), are not "with respect to" the determination of the bondholders' tax liabilities. Contacts to determine the tax status of an organization under Chapter 1, Subchapter F (Exempt Organizations), are not "with respect to" the determination of the contributors' liabilities, nor are any similar determinations "with respect to" any persons with similar relationships to the taxpayer whose tax liability is being determined or collected.

(ii) *Determination or collection.* A contact is with respect to the "determination or collection" of the tax liability of such taxpayer when made during the administrative determination or collection process. For purposes of this paragraph (c) only, the administrative determination or collection process may include any administrative action to ascertain the correctness of a return, make a return when none has been filed, or determine or collect the tax liability of any person as a transferee or fiduciary under Chapter 71 of title 26.

(iii) *Tax liability*. A "tax liability" means the liability for any tax imposed by Title 26 of the United States Code (including any interest, additional amount, addition to the tax, or assessable penalty) and does not include the liability for any tax imposed by any other jurisdiction nor any liability imposed by other federal statutes.

(iv) *Such taxpayer*. A contact is with respect to the determination or collection of the tax liability of "such taxpayer" when made while determining or collecting the tax liability of a particular, identified taxpayer. Contacts made during an investigation of a particular, identi-

fied taxpayer are third-party contacts only as to the particular, identified taxpayer under investigation and not as to any other taxpayer whose tax liabilities might be affected by such contacts.

* * *

(g) *Effective Date*. This section is applicable on the date the final regulations are published in the **Federal Register**.

Charles O. Rossotti

Commissioner of Internal Revenue

¶ 20,258

IRS proposed regulations: Cafeteria plans: Tax treatment: Election of coverage: Revocation of election.—The IRS has issued proposed regulations which amend the text of previously issued proposed regulations (¶ 20,118I, ¶ 20,137Q, and ¶ 20,247) concerning the circumstances under which a cafeteria plan participant may revoke en existing election and make a new election during a period of coverage.

The proposed regulations, which were published in the *Federal Register* January 10, 2001 (66 FR 1923), are reproduced below.

DEPARTMENT OF THE TREASURY

Internal Revenue Service

26 CFR Part 1

REG-209461-79

RIN 1545-AY67

Tax Treatment of Cafeteria Plans

AGENCY: Internal Revenue Service (IRS), Treasury.

ACTION: Partial withdrawal of notice of proposed rulemaking and amendments to notice of proposed rulemaking.

SUMMARY: This document withdraws § 1.125-2 Q & A-6(b),(c), and (d), and amends § 1.125-2 Q & A-6(a) in the notice of proposed rulemaking relating to cafeteria plans that was published in the **Federal Register** on March 7, 1989. Further, this document amends § 1.125-1 Q & A-8 in the notice of proposed rulemaking relating to cafeteria plans that was published in the Federal Register on May 7, 1984, and amended on November 7, 1997 and March 23, 2000. This withdrawal and amendment are made because of changes made to these rules in the § 1.125-4 final regulations relating to cafeteria plans published elsewhere in this issue of the **Federal Register**.

FOR FURTHER INFORMATION CONTACT: Christine Keller or Janet Laufer at (202)622-6080 (not a toll-free number).

SUPPLEMENTARY INFORMATION:

DATES: Written or electronically generated comments and requests for a public hearing must be received by **[January 10, 2001]**.

ADDRESSES: Send submissions to: CC:M & SP:RU (REG-209461-79), room 5226, Internal Revenue Service, POB 7604, Ben Franklin Station, Washington, DC 20044. Submissions may be hand delivered Monday through Friday between the hours of 8 a.m. and 5 p.m. to CC:M & SP:RU (REG-209461-79), Courier's Desk, Internal Revenue Service, 1111 Constitution Avenue, NW., Washington, DC. Alternatively, taxpayers may submit comments electronically via the Internet by selecting the "Tax Regs" option on the IRS Home Page, or by submitting comments directly to the IRS Internet site at http://www.irs.gov/tax_regs/regslist.html.

Background

On March 7, 1989, the IRS issued proposed regulations § 1.125-2 Q & A-6 relating to the circumstances under which participants may revoke existing elections and make new elections under a cafeteria plan. Elsewhere in this issue of the Federal Register the IRS is publishing final regulations under § 1.125-4 that address certain parts of this rule. Accordingly, § 1.125-2 Q & A-6(b), (c), and (d) are withdrawn and § 1.125-2 Q & A-6(a) of this rule is amended.

Further, on May 7, 1984, the IRS issued proposed regulations § 1.125-1 Q & A-8 relating to the requirements that apply to participants' elections under a cafeteria plan. Q & A-8 of these regulations was amended on November 7, 1997 and March 23, 2000 to conform with the § 1.125-4T and § 1.125-4 regulations published on these dates, and is further amended to conform with the final § 1.125-4 regulations published on [**January 10, 2001**].

Partial Withdrawal of Notice of Proposed Rulemaking

Accordingly, under the authority of 26 U.S.C. 7805, § 1.125-2 Q & A-6(b), (c) and (d) in the notice of proposed rulemaking that was published on March 7, 1989 (54 FR 9460) is withdrawn.

List of Subjects in 26 CFR Part 1

Income taxes, Reporting and recordkeeping requirements.

Amendments to Previously Proposed Rules

Accordingly, the proposed rules published on May 7, 1984 (49 FR 19321) and amended on November 7, 1997 (62 FR 60196), and March 23, 2000 (65 FR 15587) and the rules published on March 7, 1989 (54 FR 9460) are amended as follows:

PART 1—INCOME TAXES

Paragraph 1. The authority citation for part 1 continues to read in part as follows:

Authority: 26 U.S.C. 7805 *****

Par. 2. In § 1.125-1, as proposed May 7, 1984 (49 FR 19321) and as amended March 23, 2000 (65 FR 15587), Q & A-8 is amended by removing the last four sentences of A-8 and adding a sentence in their place to read as follows:

§ 1.125-1 Questions and answers relating to cafeteria plan.

*****

Q-8: What requirements apply to participants' elections under a cafeteria plan?

A-8: ***** However, a cafeteria plan may permit a participant to revoke a benefit election after the period of coverage has commenced and make a new election with respect to the remainder of the period of coverage if both the revocation and the new election are permitted under § 1.125-4.

*****

Par. 3. In § 1.125-2, as proposed March 7, 1989 (54 FR 9460) and as amended March 23, 2000 (65 FR 15587), A-6 is amended by removing A-6(b), A-6(c), and A-6(d), redesignating A-6(e) as paragraph A-6(b), removing the last 5 sentences of A-6(a) and adding a sentence in their place to read as follows:

Q-6: In what circumstance may participants revoke existing elections and make new elections under a cafeteria plan?

A-6: *****

(a) ***** However, to the extent permitted under § 1.125-4, the terms of a cafeteria plan may permit a participant to revoke an existing election and to make a new election with respect to the remaining portion of the period of coverage.

*****

Robert E. Wenzel

Deputy Commissioner of Internal Revenue

¶ 20,259

IRS: Proposed regulations: Election: S Corporation: Small business trust.—The IRS has issued proposed regulations which relate to "tiered" S Corporations and the election and tax treatment of small business trusts. The proposed regulations state that a trust described under Code Sec. 401(a) or Code Sec. 501(c)(3), is not a "deferral entity" for purposes of Reg. §1.444-2T. Therefore, an S Corporation with such a trust may make an election of a taxable year other than the required taxable year.

The preamble and portions of the proposed regulations reproduced below were published in the *Federal Register* on December 29, 2000 (65 FR 82963).

The final regulations were published in the *Federal Register* on May 14, 2002 (67 FR 34388). The regulations are reproduced at ¶ 13,152C. The preamble is at ¶ 20,259.

¶ 20,260

IRS proposed regulations: Excise tax: Excess benefit transactions: Tax exempt organizations: Disqualified persons.—The IRS has issued proposed regulations on excise taxes under Code Sec. 4958 that can be imposed in cases involving excess benefit transactions occurring on or after September 14, 1995 between tax-exempt organizations and disqualified persons.

The text of the proposed regulations is provided by the text of the IRS temporary regulations issued at the same time as the proposed regulations. The preamble of the temporary regulations is at ¶ 24,506B. The text of the temporary regulations is at ¶ 13,592A, ¶ 13,592B, ¶ 13,592C, ¶ 13,592D, ¶ 13,592E, ¶ 13,592H and ¶ 13,592I.

The proposed regulations, which were published in the *Federal Register* January 10, 2001 (66 FR 2173), are reproduced below.

DEPARTMENT OF THE TREASURY

Internal Revenue Service

26 CFR Parts 53 and 301

[REG-246256-96]

RIN 1545-AY65

Excise Taxes on Excess Benefit Transactions

AGENCY: Internal Revenue Service (IRS), Treasury.

ACTION: Notice of proposed rulemaking by cross-reference to temporary regulations.

SUMMARY: In the Rules and Regulations section of this issue of the **Federal Register,** the IRS is issuing temporary regulations relating to the excise taxes on excess benefit transactions under section 4958 of the Internal Revenue Code (Code), as well as certain amendments and additions to existing Income Tax Regulations affected by section 4958. Section 4958 was enacted in section 1311 of the Taxpayer Bill of Rights 2. Section 4958 generally is effective for transactions occurring on or after September 14, 1995.

Section 4958 imposes excise taxes on transactions that provide excess economic benefits to disqualified persons of public charities and social welfare organizations (referred to as applicable tax-exempt organizations). Disqualified persons who benefit from an excess benefit transaction with an applicable tax-exempt organization are liable for a tax of 25 percent of the excess benefit. Such persons are also liable for a tax of 200 percent of the excess benefit if the excess benefit is not corrected by a certain date. Additionally, organization managers who participate in an excess benefit transaction knowingly, willfully, and without reasonable cause, are liable for a tax of 10 percent of the excess benefit. The tax for which participating organization managers are liable cannot exceed $10,000 for any one excess benefit transaction.

DATES: Written comments and requests for a public hearing must be received by April 10, 2001. In addition to any comments addressing substantive issues of the proposed regulations, the IRS and Treasury specifically request comments on the clarity of the proposed rule and how it may be made easier to understand.

ADDRESSES: Send submissions to: CC:M & SP:RU (REG-246256-96), room 5226, Internal Revenue Service, POB 7604, Ben Franklin Station, Washington, DC 20044. Submissions may be hand delivered Monday through Friday between the hours of 8 a.m. and 5 p.m. to: CC:M & SP:RU (REG-246256-96), Courier's Desk, Internal Revenue Service, 1111 Constitution Avenue NW., Washington, DC. Alternatively, taxpayers may submit comments electronically via the Internet by selecting the "Tax Regs" option on the IRS Home Page, or by submitting comments directly to the IRS Internet site at http://www.irs.gov/prod/tax_regs/comments.html. A public hearing will be scheduled if requested.

FOR FURTHER INFORMATION CONTACT: Concerning submissions, Guy Traynor, (202) 622-7180; concerning the regulations, Phyllis D. Haney, (202) 622-4290 (not toll-free numbers).

SUPPLEMENTARY INFORMATION:

Paperwork Reduction Act

The collections of information contained in these proposed regulations have been reviewed and approved by the Office of Management and Budget in accordance with the Paperwork Reduction Act (44

U.S.C. 3507) under control number 1545-1623, in conjunction with the notice of proposed rulemaking published August 4, 1998, 63 FR 41486, REG-246256-96, Failure by Certain Charitable Organizations to Meet Certain Qualification Requirements; Taxes on Excess Benefit Transactions.

An agency may not conduct or sponsor, and a person is not required to respond to, a collection of information unless it displays a valid control number assigned by the Office of Management and Budget.

Books and records relating to the collection of information must be retained as long as their contents may become material in the administration of any internal revenue law. Generally, tax returns and tax return information are confidential, as required by 26 U.S.C. 6103.

Special Analyses

It has been determined that this notice of proposed rulemaking is not a significant regulatory action as defined in Executive Order 12866. Therefore, a regulatory assessment is not required.

An initial regulatory flexibility analysis was prepared as required for the collection of information under 5 U.S.C. 603 in the notice of proposed rulemaking, REG-246256-96, Failure by Certain Charitable Organizations to Meet Certain Qualification Requirements; Taxes on Excess Benefit Transactions, published August 4, 1998, at 63 FR 41486. The initial analysis was submitted to the Chief Counsel for Advocacy of the Small Business Administration pursuant to section 7805(f) of the Code for comment on its impact on business. The initial analysis continues to apply to this proposed rule. Pursuant to section 7805(f) of the Code, this notice of proposed rulemaking will be submitted to the Chief Counsel for Advocacy of the Small Business Administration for comment on its impact on business.

Comments and Requests for a Public Hearing

Before these proposed regulations are adopted as final regulations, consideration will be given to any comments (a signed original and eight (8) copies) that are submitted timely to the IRS. The IRS and Treasury specifically request comments on the clarity of the proposed rule and how it may be made easier to understand. All comments will be available for public inspection and copying.

A public hearing may be scheduled if requested in writing by a person who timely submits written comments. If a public hearing is scheduled, notice of the date, time, and place will be published in the **Federal Register.**

Drafting Information

The principal author of these regulations is Phyllis D. Haney, Office of Division Counsel/Associate Chief Counsel (Tax-Exempt and Government Entities). However, other personnel from the IRS and Treasury Department participated in their development.

List of Subjects in 26 CFR Part 53

Excise taxes, Foundations, Investments, Lobbying, Reporting and recordkeeping requirements, Trusts and trustees.

26 CFR Part 301

Employment taxes, Estate taxes, Excise taxes, Gift taxes, Income taxes, Penalties, Reporting and recordkeeping requirements.

Accordingly, 26 CFR Parts 53 and 301 are proposed to be amended as follows:

PART 53—FOUNDATION AND SIMILAR EXCISE TAXES

Paragraph 1. The authority citation for part 53 continues to read as follows:

Authority: 26 U.S.C. 7805.

Par. 2. Sections 53.4958-0 through 53.4958-8 are added to read as follows:

[The text of proposed §§ 53.4958-0 through 53.4958-8 is the same as the text of § 53.4958-0T through 53.4958-8T published elsewhere in this issue of the **Federal Register**].

Robert E. Wenzel

Deputy Commissioner of Internal Revenue

¶ 20,260A

IRS proposed regulations: Electronic media: Requests for determination of qualified status: Notice to interested parties.—The IRS has issued proposed regulations, which eliminate the writing requirement for notices to interested parties when a plan sponsor requests a determination of the qualified status of a retirement plan. The proposed regulations provide that notice may be provided by any method that reasonably ensures that all interested parties will receive the notice, including electronically.

The proposed regulations were published in the *Federal Register* on January 17, 2001 (66 FR 3954). The final regulations (¶ 24,506Q) were published in the *Federal Register* on July 19, 2002 (67 FR 47454).

¶ 20,260B

IRS proposed regulations: Qualified retirement plans: Qualified joint and survivor annuity (QJSA): Waiver of QJSA distribution: Explanation requirements: Retroactive annuity starting date.—The IRS has issued proposed regulations that define how payments are to be made and set conditions for the use of the provision under Code Sec. 417(a)(7)(A), which allows a qualified plan to furnish an explanation concerning a beneficiary's right to elect a payment type other than a QJSA after the date that the annuity payments are to start.

The proposed regulations, which were published in the *Federal Register* January 17, 2001 (66 FR 3916), were finalized on July 16, 2003 (68 FR 41906). See ¶ 24,507G .

¶ 20,260C

Proposed regulations: Required distribution rules: Qualified plans: IRAs: Tax-sheltered annuities: Custodial accounts: Retirement income accounts.—The IRS has issued proposed regulations on minimum required distributions from qualified plans, IRAs, Code Sec. 457 plans, and 403(b) plans. The new proposed regulations simplify and modify various minimum distribution rules contained in 1987 proposed regulations (CCH PENSION PLAN GUIDE ¶ 20,163B).

The proposed regulations, which were published in the *Federal Register* on January 17, 2001 (66 FR 3928) are reproduced below. Modified and corrected by IRS Announcement 2001-18, I.R.B. 2001-10, March 5, 2001 at ¶ 17,097R-14. Final regulations, published in the *Federal Register* on June 15, 2004 (69 FR 33288) are found at ¶ 11,720Y-6 and ¶ 11,720Y-8, with a preamble at ¶ 24,507O.

DEPARTMENT OF TREASURY

Internal Revenue Service (IRS)

26 CFR Parts 1 and 54

RIN 1545-AY69, 1545-AY70

[REG-130477-00;REG-130481-00]

Required Distributions from Retirement Plans

AGENCY: Internal Revenue Service (IRS), Treasury.

ACTION: Notice of proposed rulemaking and notice of public hearing.

SUMMARY: This document contains proposed regulations relating to required minimum distributions from qualified plans, individual retirement plans, deferred compensation plans under section 457, and section 403(b) annuity contracts, custodial accounts, and retirement income accounts. These regulations will provide the public with guidance necessary to comply with the law and will affect administrators of, participants in, and beneficiaries of qualified plans; institutions that sponsor and individuals who administer individual retirement plans, individuals who use individual retirement plans for retirement income, and beneficiaries of individual retirement plans; and employees for whom amounts are contributed to section 403(b) annuity contracts, custodial accounts, or retirement income accounts and beneficiaries of such contracts and accounts.

DATES: Written and electronic comments must be received by April 19, 2001. Outlines of topics to be discussed at the public hearing scheduled for June 1, 2001, at 10 a.m. must be received by May 11, 2001.

ADDRESSES: Send submissions to: CC:M&SP:RU (REG-130477-00/REG130481-00) room 5226, Internal Revenue Service, POB 7604, Ben Franklin Station, Washington, DC 20044. Submissions may be hand delivered Monday through Friday between the hours of 8 a.m. and 5 p.m. to: CC:M&SP:RU (REG-130477-00/REG-130481-00), Courier's Desk, Internal Revenue Service, 1111 Constitution Avenue NW, Washington, DC. Alternatively, taxpayers may submit comments electronically via the Internet by selecting the "Tax Regs" option of the IRS Home Page, or by submitting comments directly to the IRS Internet site at: http://www.irs.gov/tax>regs/reglist.html. The public hearing on June 1, 2001, will be held in the IRS Auditorium (7th Floor),

Internal Revenue Building, 1111 Constitution Avenue NW, Washington, DC.

FOR FURTHER INFORMATION CONTACT: Concerning the regulations, Cathy A. Vohs, 202-622-6090; concerning submissions and the hearing, and/or to be placed on the building access list to attend the hearing, Guy Traynor, 202-622-7180 (not toll-free numbers).

Paperwork Reduction Act

The collections of information contained in these proposed regulations have been reviewed and approved by the Office of Management and Budget in accordance with the Paperwork Reduction Act (44 U.S.C. 3507) under control number 1545-0996, in conjunction with the notice of proposed rulemaking published on July 27, 1987, 52 FR 28070, REG-EE-113-82, Required Distributions From Qualified Plans and Individual Retirement Plans, and control number 1545-1573, in conjunction with the notice of proposed rulemaking published on December 30, 1997, 62 FR 67780, REG-209463-82, Required Distributions from Qualified Plans and Individual Retirement Plans.

An agency may not conduct or sponsor, and a person is not required to respond to, a collection of information unless it displays a valid control number assigned by the Office of Management and Budget.

Books and records relating to the collection of information must be retained as long as their contents may become material in the administration of any internal revenue law. Generally, tax returns and tax return information are confidential, as required by 26 U.S.C. 6103.

Background

This document contains proposed amendments to the Income Tax Regulations (26 CFR Part 1) and to the Pension Excise Tax Regulations (26 CFR Part 54) under sections 401, 403, 408, and 4974 of the Internal Revenue Code of 1986. It is contemplated that proposed rules similar to those in these proposed regulations applicable to section 401 will be published in the near future for purposes of applying the distribution requirements of section 457(d). These amendments are proposed to conform the regulations to section 1404 of the Small Business Job Protection Act of 1996 (SBJPA) (110 Stat. 1791), sections 1121 and 1852 of the Tax Reform Act of 1986 (TRA of 1986) (100 Stat. 2464 and 2864), sections 521 and 713 of the Tax Reform Act of 1984 (TRA of 1984) (98 Stat. 865 and 955), and sections 242 and 243 of the Tax Equity and Fiscal Responsibility Act of 1982 (TEFRA) (96 Stat. 521). The regulations provide guidance on the required minimum distribution requirements under section 401(a)(9) for plans qualified under section 401(a). The rules are incorporated by reference in section 408(a)(6) and (b)(3) for individual retirement accounts and annuities (IRAs), section 408A(c)(5) for Roth IRAs, section 403(b)(10) for section 403(b) annuity contracts, and section 457(d) for eligible deferred compensation plans.

For purposes of this discussion of the background of the regulations in this preamble, as well as the explanation of provisions below, whenever the term *employee* is used, it is intended to include not only an employee but also an IRA owner.

Section 401(a)(9) provides rules for distributions during the life of the employee in section 401(a)(9)(A) and rules for distributions after the death of the employee in section 401(a)(9)(B). Section 401(a)(9)(A)(ii) provides that the entire interest of an employee in a qualified plan must be distributed, beginning not later than the employee's required beginning date, in accordance with regulations, over the life of the employee or over the lives of the employee and a designated beneficiary (or over a period not extending beyond the life expectancy of the employee and a designated beneficiary).

Section 401(a)(9)(C) defines required beginning date for employees (other than 5-percent owners and IRA owners) as April 1 of the calendar year following the later of the calendar year in which the employee attains age 70 ½ or the calendar year in which the employee retires. For 5-percent owners and IRA owners, the required beginning date is April 1 of the calendar year following the calendar year in which the employee attains age 70 ½, even if the employee has not retired.

Section 401(a)(9)(D) provides that (except in the case of a life annuity) the life expectancy of an employee and the employee's spouse that is used to determine the period over which payments must be made may be redetermined, but not more frequently than annually.

Section 401(a)(9)(E) provides that the term *designated beneficiary* means any individual designated as a beneficiary by the employee.

Section 401(a)(9)(G) provides that any distribution required to satisfy the incidental death benefit requirement of section 401(a) is a required minimum distribution.

Section 401(a)(9)(B)(i) provides that, if the employee dies after distributions have begun, the employee's interest must be distributed at least as rapidly as under the method used by the employee.

Section 401(a)(9)(B)(ii) and (iii) provides that, if the employee dies before required minimum distributions have begun, the employee's interest must be either: distributed (in accordance with regulations) over the life or life expectancy of the designated beneficiary with the distributions beginning no later than 1 year after the date of the employee's death, or distributed within 5 years after the death of the employee. However, under section 401(a)(9)(B)(iv), a surviving spouse may wait until the date the employee would have attained age 70 ½ to begin taking required minimum distributions.

Comprehensive proposed regulations under section 401(a)(9) were previously published in the **Federal Register** on July 27, 1987, 52 FR 28070. Many of the comments on the 1987 proposed regulations expressed concerns that the required minimum distribution must be satisfied separately for each IRA owned by an individual by taking distributions from each IRA. In response, Notice 88-38 (1988-1 C.B. 524) provided that the amount of the required minimum distribution must be calculated for each IRA, but permitted that amount to be taken from any IRA. Amendments to the 1987 proposed regulations published in the **Federal Register** on December 30, 1997, 62 FR 67780, responded to comments on the use of trusts as beneficiaries. Notice 96-67 (1996-2 C.B. 235) and Notice 97-75 (1997-2 C.B. 337) provided guidance on the changes made to section 401(a)(9) by the SBJPA. The guidance in Notice 88-38, Notice 96-67, and Notice 97-75 is incorporated in these proposed regulations with some modifications.

Even though the distribution requirements added by TEFRA were retroactively repealed by TRA of 1984, the transition election rule in section 242(b) of TEFRA was preserved. Notice 83-23 (1983-2 C.B. 418) continues to provide guidance for distributions permitted by this transition election rule. These proposed regulations retain the additional guidance on the transition rule provided in the 1987 proposed regulations.

As discussed below, in response to extensive comments, the rules for calculating required minimum distributions from individual accounts under the 1987 proposed regulations have been substantially simplified. Certain other 1987 rules have also been simplified and modified, although many of the 1987 rules remain unchanged. In particular, due to the relatively small number of comments on practices with respect to annuity contracts, and the effect of the 1987 proposed regulations on these practices, the basic structure of the 1987 proposed

regulation provisions with respect to annuity payments is retained in these proposed regulations. The IRS and Treasury are continuing to study these rules and specifically request updated comments on current practices and issues relating to required minimum distributions from annuity contracts.

Explanation of Provisions

Overview

Many of the comments on the 1987 proposed regulations addressed the rules for required minimum distributions during an employee's life, including calculation of life expectancy and determination of designated beneficiary. In particular, comments raised concerns about the default provisions, election requirements, and plan language requirements. In general, the need to make decisions at age 70 ½, which under the 1987 proposed regulations would bind the employee in future years during which financial circumstances could change significantly, was perceived as unreasonably restrictive. In addition, the determination of life expectancy and designated beneficiary and the resulting required minimum distribution calculation for individual accounts were viewed as too complex.

To respond to these concerns, these proposed regulations would make it much easier for individuals—both plan participants and IRA owners—and plan administrators to understand and apply the minimum distribution rules. The new proposed regulations would make major simplifications to the rules, including the calculation of the required minimum distribution during the individual's lifetime and the determination of a designated beneficiary for distributions after death. The new proposed regulations simplify the rules by

• Providing a simple, uniform table that all employees can use to determine the minimum distribution required during their lifetime. This makes it far easier to calculate the required minimum distribution because employees would

• no longer need to determine their beneficiary by their required beginning date,

• no longer need to decide whether or not to recalculate their life expectancy each year in determining required minimum distributions, and

• no longer need to satisfy a separate incidental death benefit rule.

• Permitting the required minimum distribution during the employee's lifetime to be calculated without regard to the beneficiary's age (except when required distributions can be reduced by taking into account the age of a beneficiary who is a spouse more than 10 years younger than the employee).

• Permitting the beneficiary to be determined as late as the end of the year following the year of the employee's death. This allows

• the employee to change designated beneficiaries after the required beginning date without increasing the required minimum distribution and

• the beneficiary to be changed after the employee's death, such as by one or more beneficiaries disclaiming or being cashed out.

• Permitting the calculation of post-death minimum distributions to take into account an employee's remaining life expectancy at the time of death, thus allowing distributions in all cases to be spread over a number of years after death.

These simplifications would also have the effect of reducing the required minimum distributions for the vast majority of employees.

The uniform distribution period

Under these proposed regulations and the 1987 proposed regulations, for distributions from an individual account, the required minimum distribution is determined by dividing the account balance by the distribution period. For lifetime required minimum distributions, these proposed regulations provide a uniform distribution period for all employees of the same age. The uniform distribution period table is the required minimum distribution incidental benefit (MDIB) divisor table originally prescribed in § 1.401(a)(9)-2 of the 1987 proposed regulations and now included in A-4 of § 1.401(a)-5 of the new proposed regulations. An exception applies if the employee's sole beneficiary is the employee's spouse and the spouse is more than 10 years younger than the employee. In that case, the employee is permitted to use the longer distribution period measured by the joint life and last survivor life expectancy of the employee and spouse.

These changes provide a simple administrable rule for plans and individuals. Using the MDIB table, most employees will be able to determine their required minimum distribution for each year based on nothing more than their current age and their account balance as of the end of the prior year (which IRA trustees report annually to IRA owners). Under the 1987 proposed regulations, some employees already use the MDIB table to determine required minimum distributions. Under the new proposed regulations, they would continue to do so. For the majority of other employees, required minimum distributions would be reduced as a result of the changes.

For years after the year of the employee's death, the distribution period is generally the remaining life expectancy of the designated beneficiary. The beneficiary's remaining life expectancy is calculated using the age of the beneficiary in the year following the year of the employee's death, reduced by one for each subsequent year. If the employee's spouse is the employee's sole beneficiary at the end of the year following the year of death, the distribution period during the spouse's life is the spouse's single life expectancy. For years after the year of the spouse's death, the distribution period is the spouse's life expectancy calculated in the year of death, reduced by one for each subsequent year. If there is no designated beneficiary as of the end of the year after the employee's death, the distribution period is the employee's life expectancy calculated in the year of death, reduced by one for each subsequent year.

The MDIB table is based on the joint life expectancies of an individual and a survivor 10 years younger at each age beginning at age 70. Allowing the use of this table reflects the fact that an employee's beneficiary is subject to change until the death of the employee and ultimately may be a beneficiary more than 10 years younger than the employee. The proposed regulations would allow lifetime distributions at a rate consistent with this possibility. Consistent with the requirements of section 401(a)(9)(A)(ii), the distribution period after death is measured by the life expectancy of the employee's designated beneficiary in the year following death, or the employee's remaining life expectancy if there is no designated beneficiary. This ensures that the employee's entire benefit is distributed over a period described in section 401(a)(9)(A)(ii), i.e., the life expectancy of the employee or the joint life expectancy of the employee and a designated beneficiary.

The approach in these proposed regulations allowing the use of a uniform lifetime distribution period addresses concerns raised in comments on the 1987 proposed regulations that the rules are too complex. It eliminates the use of two tables and the interaction of the multiple beneficiary and change in beneficiary rules. Finally, it generally eliminates the need to fix the amount of the distribution during the employee's lifetime based on the beneficiary designated on the required beginning date and eliminates the need to elect recalculation or no recalculation of life expectancies at the required beginning date.

Suggestions have been received that the life expectancy table used to calculate required minimum distributions should be revised to reflect recent increases in longevity. These proposed regulations instead provide authority for the Commissioner to issue guidance of general applicability revising the life expectancy tables and the uniform distribution table in the future if it becomes appropriate. While life expectancy has increased in the 14 years since the issuance of the section 72 life expectancy tables, those tables may already overstate the average life expectancy of the class of individuals who are subject to these required minimum distribution rules (qualified plan participants, IRA owners, et al.). That is because those existing section 72 tables were derived from the particular mortality experience of the select population of individuals who purchase individual annuities, as opposed to the population who are subject to the required minimum distribution rules. In any event, as noted earlier, the new proposed uniform distribution period—equal to the joint life expectancy of an individual and a survivor 10 years younger at each age—would lengthen the lifetime distribution period for most employees and beneficiaries. In fact, the new proposed regulations would lengthen that period more for many individuals than would an update to reflect recent increases in longevity. The IRS and Treasury believe that this lengthening of the distribution period for most employees provides further justification for retaining the existing life expectancy tables at this time.

Some commentators suggested that the calculation of required minimum distributions include credit for any distribution in a prior year that exceeded that year's required minimum distribution. However, such a "credit" carryforward would require significant additional data retention and would add substantial complexity to the calculation of required minimum distributions. By using the prior year's ending account balance for calculating required minimum distributions, distribution of amounts in excess of the required minimum distribution has the effect of reducing future required minimum distributions over the remaining distribution period to some extent. Accordingly, these proposed regulations do not provide for a credit carryforward.

Determination of the designated beneficiary

These proposed regulations provide that, generally, the designated beneficiary is determined as of the end of the year following the year of the employee's death rather than as of the employee's required beginning date or date of death, as under the 1987 proposed regulations. Thus, any beneficiary eliminated by distribution of the benefit or through disclaimer (or otherwise) during the period between the employee's death and the end of the year following the year of death is disregarded in determining the employee's designated beneficiary for purposes of calculating required minimum distributions. If, as of the end of the year following the year of the employee's death, the employee has more than one designated beneficiary and the account or benefit has not been divided into separate accounts or shares for each beneficiary, the beneficiary with the shortest life expectancy is the designated beneficiary, consistent with the approach in the 1987 proposed regulations.

This approach for determining the designated beneficiary following the death of an employee after the employee's required beginning date is simpler in several respects than the approach in the 1987 proposed regulations and responds to concerns raised with respect to the effects of beneficiary designation at the required beginning date. Under this approach, the determination of the designated beneficiary and the calculation of the beneficiary's life expectancy generally are contemporaneous with commencement of required distributions to the beneficiary. Any prior beneficiary designation is irrelevant for distributions from individual accounts, unless the employee takes advantage of a lifetime distribution period measured by the joint life expectancy of the employee and a spouse more than 10 years younger than the employee. Further, for an employee with a designated beneficiary, this approach provides the same rules for distributions after the employee's death, regardless of whether death occurs before or after an employee's required beginning date. Finally, in the case of an employee who elects or defaults into recalculation of life expectancy and who dies without a designated beneficiary, the requirement that the employee's entire remaining account balance be distributed in the year after an employee's death has been eliminated and replaced with a distribution period equal to the employee's remaining life expectancy recalculated immediately before death.

Default rule for post-death distributions

As requested by some commentators, these proposed regulations would change the default rule in the case of death before the employee's required beginning date for a nonspouse designated beneficiary from the 5-year rule in section 401(a)(9)(B)(ii) to the life expectancy rule in section 401(a)(9)(B)(iii). Thus, absent a plan provision or election of the 5-year rule, the life expectancy rule would apply in all cases in which the employee has a designated beneficiary. As in the case of death on or after the employee's required beginning date, the designated beneficiary whose life expectancy is used to determine the distribution period would be determined as of the end of the year following the year of the employee's death, rather than as of the employee's date of death (as would have been required under the 1987 proposed regulations). The 5-year rule would apply automatically only if the employee did not have a designated beneficiary as of the end of the year following the year of the employee's death. Finally, in the case of death before the employee's required beginning date, these proposed regulations allow a waiver, unless the Commissioner determines otherwise, of any excise tax resulting from the life expectancy rule during the first five years after the year of the employee's death if the employee's entire benefit is distributed by the end of the fifth year following the year of the employee's death.

Annuity payments

These proposed regulations make several changes to the rules for determining whether annuity payments satisfy section 401(a)(9). The changes are designed to make these rules more administrable without adverse effects on the basic structure and application of the rules. The IRS and Treasury are continuing to study and evaluate whether additional changes would be appropriate for determining whether annuity payments satisfy section 401(a)(9). Some comments were received on the annuity rules in 1987, but updated comments that include a discussion of current industry practices, products, and concerns would be helpful.

These proposed regulations provide that the designated beneficiary for determining the distribution period for annuity payments generally is the beneficiary as of the annuity starting date, even if that date is after the required beginning date. Thus, if annuity payments commence after the required beginning date, the determination of the designated beneficiary is contemporaneous with the annuity starting date and any intervening changes in the beneficiary designation since the required beginning date are ignored. Second, as requested in comments, these regulations extend to all annuity payment streams the rule in the 1987 proposed regulations that allows a life annuity with a period certain not exceeding 20 years to commence on the required beginning date with no makeup for the first distribution calendar year. For this purpose, the regulations clarify that only accruals as of the end of the prior calendar year must be taken into account in calculating the amount of an annuity commencing on the required beginning date. Subsequent accruals are treated as additional accruals that must be taken into account in the next calendar year. Also as requested in comments, the regulations provide that, although additional accruals need to be taken into account in the first payment in the calendar year following the year of the accrual, actual payment in the form of a make-up payment need only be completed by the end of that calendar year.

The permitted increase in annuity payments to an employee upon the death of the survivor annuitant has been expanded to cover the elimination of the survivor portion of a joint and survivor annuity due to a qualified domestic relations order. Further, in response to comments, in the case of an annuity contract purchased from an insurance company, an exception to the nonincreasing-payment requirement in these proposed regulations has been added to accommodate a cash refund upon the employee's death of the amount of the premiums paid for the contract.

One of the rules in the 1987 proposed regulations that the IRS and Treasury are continuing to study and evaluate is the rule providing that if the distributions from a defined benefit plan are not in the form of an annuity, the employee's benefit will be treated as an individual account for purposes of determining required minimum distributions. The IRS and Treasury are continuing to consider whether retention of this rule is appropriate for defined benefit plans. Similarly, the IRS and Treasury are continuing to consider whether the rule permitting the benefit under a defined benefit plan to be divided into segregated shares for purposes of section 401(a)(9) is useful and appropriate for defined benefit plans.

Trust as beneficiary

These proposed regulations retain the provision in the proposed regulations, as amended in 1997, allowing an underlying beneficiary of a trust to be an employee's designated beneficiary for purposes of determining required minimum distributions when the trust is named as the beneficiary of a retirement plan or IRA, provided that certain requirements are met. One of these requirements is that documentation of the underlying beneficiaries of the trust be provided timely to the plan administrator. In the case of individual accounts, unless the lifetime distribution period for an employee is measured by the joint life expectancy of the employee and the employee's spouse, the deadline under these proposed regulations for providing the beneficiary documentation would be the end of the year following year of the employee's death. This is consistent with the deadline for determining the employee's designated beneficiary. Because the designated beneficiary during an employee's lifetime is not relevant for determining lifetime required minimum distributions in most cases under these proposed regulations, the burden of lifetime documentation requirements contained in the previous proposed regulations is significantly reduced.

A significant number of commentators on the 1997 amendment to the proposed regulations requested clarification that a testamentary trust named as an employee's beneficiary is a trust that qualifies for the look-through rule to the underlying beneficiaries, as permitted in the 1997 proposed regulations. These proposed regulations provide examples in which a testamentary trust is named as an employee's beneficiary and the look-through trust rules apply. As previously illustrated in the facts of Rev. Rul. 2000-2, 2000-3 I.R.B. 305, the examples also clarify that remaindermen of a "QTIP" trust must be taken into account as beneficiaries in determining the distribution period for required minimum distributions if amounts are accumulated for their benefit during the life of the income beneficiary under the trust.

Rules for qualified domestic relations orders

These proposed regulations retain the basic rules in the 1987 proposed regulation for a qualified domestic relations order (QDRO). Thus, for example, the proposed regulations continue to provide that a former spouse to whom all or a portion of the employee's benefit is payable pursuant to a QDRO will be treated as a spouse (including a surviving spouse) of the employee for purposes of section 401(a)(9), including the minimum distribution incidental benefit requirement, regardless of whether the QDRO specifically provides that the former spouse is treated as the spouse for purposes of sections 401(a)(11) and 417. This rule applies regardless of the number of former spouses an employee has who are alternate payees with respect to the employee's

retirement benefits. Further, for example, if a QDRO divides the individual account of an employee in a defined contribution plan into a separate account for the employee and a separate account for the alternate payee, the required minimum distribution to the alternate payee during the lifetimee of the employee must nevertheless be determined using the same rules that apply to distribution to the employee. Thus, required minimum distributions to the alternate payee must commence by the employee's required beginning date. However, the required minimum distribution for the alternate payee will be separately determined. The required minimum distributions for the alternate payee during the lifetime of the employee may be determined either using the uniform distribution period discussed above based on the age of the employee in the distribution calendar year, or, if the alternate payee is the employee's former spouse and is more than 10 years younger than the employee, using the joint life expectancy of the employee and the alternate payee.

Election of surviving spouse to treat an inherited IRA as spouse's own IRA

These proposed regulations clarify the rule in the 1987 proposed regulations that allows the surviving spouse of a decedent IRA owner to elect to treat an IRA inherited by the surviving spouse from that owner as the spouse's own IRA. The 1987 proposed regulations provide that this election is deemed to have been made if the surviving spouse contributes to the IRA or does not take the required minimum distribution for a year under section 401(a)(9)(B) as a beneficiary of the IRA. These new proposed regulations clarify that this deemed election is permitted to be made only after the distribution of the required minimum amount for the account, if any, for the year of the individual's death. Further these new proposed regulations clarify that this deemed election is permitted only if the spouse is the sole beneficiary of the account and has an unlimited right to withdrawal from the account. This requirement is not satisfied if a trust is named as beneficiary of the IRA, even if the spouse is the sole beneficiary of the trust. These clarifications make the election consistent with the underlying premise that the surviving spouse could have received a distribution of the entire decedent IRA owner's account and rolled it over to an IRA established in the surviving spouse's own name as IRA owner.

These new proposed regulations also clarify that, except for the required minimum distribution for the year of the individual's death, the spouse is permitted to roll over the post-death required minimum distribution under section 401(a)(9)(B) for a year if the spouse is establishing the IRA rollover account in the name of the spouse as IRA owner. However, if the surviving spouse is age 70 ½ or older, the minimum lifetime distribution required under section 401(a)(9)(A) must be made for the year and, because it is a required minimum distribution, that amount may not be rolled over. These proposed regulations provide that this election by a surviving spouse eligible to treat an IRA as the spouse's own may also be accomplished by redesignating the IRA with the name of the surviving spouse as owner rather than beneficiary.

IRA reporting of required minimum distributions

Because these regulations substantially simplify the calculation of required minimum distributions from IRAs, IRA trustees determining the account balance as of the end of the year can also calculate the following year's required minimum distribution for each IRA. To improve compliance and further reduce the burden imposed on IRA owners and beneficiaries, under the authority provided in section 408(i), these proposed regulations would require the trustee of each IRA to report the amount of the required minimum distribution from the IRA to the IRA owner or beneficiary and to the IRS at the time and in the manner provided under IRS forms and instructions. This reporting would be required regardless of whether the IRA owner is planning to take the required minimum distribution from that IRA or from another IRA, and would indicate that the IRA owner is permitted to take the required minimum distribution from any other IRA of the owner. During year 2001, the IRS will be receiving public comments and consulting with interested parties to assist the IRS in evaluating what form best accommodates this reporting requirement, what timing is appropriate (e.g., the beginning of the calendar year for which the required amount is being calculated), and what effective date would be most appropriate for the reporting requirement. In this context, after thorough consideration of comments and consultation with interested parties, the IRS intends to develop procedures and a schedule for reporting that provides adequate lead time, and minimizes the reporting burden, for IRA trustees, issuers, and custodians in complying with this new reporting requirement while providing the most useful information to the IRA owners and beneficiaries.

The IRS and Treasury are also considering whether similar reporting would be appropriate for section 403(b) contracts.

Permitted Delays Relative to QDROs and State Insurer Delinquency Proceedings

The regulations permit the required minimum distribution for a year to be delayed to a later year in certain circumstances. Specifically, commentators requested a delay during a period of up to 18 months during which an amount is segregated in connection with the review of a domestic relations order pursuant to section 414(p)(7). Commentators also requested that a delay be permitted while annuity payments under an annuity contract issued by a life insurance company in state insurer delinquency proceedings have been reduced or suspended by reason of state proceedings. These proposed regulations allow delay in these circumstances.

Correction of failures under section 401(a)(9)

The proposed regulations do not set forth the special rule relieving a plan from disqualification for isolated instances of failure to satisfy section 401(a)(9) because all failures for qualified plans and section 403(b) accounts under section 401(a)(9) are now permitted to be corrected through the Employee Plans Compliance Resolution System (EPCRS). See Rev. Proc. 2000-16 (2000-6 I.R.B. 518).

Amendment of Qualified Plans

These regulations are proposed to be effective for distributions for calendar years beginning on or after January 1, 2002. For distributions for calendar years beginning before the effective date of final regulations, plan sponsors can continue to rely on the 1987 proposed regulations, to the extent those proposed regulations are not inconsistent with the changes to section 401(a)(9) made by the Small Business Job Protection Act of 1996 (SBJPA) and guidance related to those changes. Alternatively, for distributions for the 2001 and subsequent calendar years beginning before the effective date of final regulations, plan sponsors are permitted, but not required, to follow these proposed regulations in the operation of their plans by adopting the model amendment set forth below.

The Treasury Department and the IRS are making the model amendment set forth below available to plan sponsors to permit them to apply these proposed regulations in the operation of their plans without violating the requirement that a plan be operated in accordance with its terms. Plan sponsors who adopt the model amendment will have reliance that, during the term of the amendment, operation of their plans in a manner that satisfies the minimum distribution requirements in these proposed regulations will not cause their plans to fail to be qualified. In addition, distributees will have reliance that distributions that are made during the term of the amendment that satisfy the minimum distribution requirements in these proposed regulations. The model amendment may be adopted by plan sponsors, practitioners who sponsor volume submitter specimen plans and sponsors of master and prototype (M&P) plans.

These proposed regulations permit plans to make distributions under either default provisions or under permissible optional provisions. A plan that has been amended by adoption of the model amendment will be treated as operating in conformance with a requirement of the proposed regulations that permits the use of either default or optional provisions if the plan is operated consistently in accordance with either the default rule or a specific permitted alternative, notwithstanding the plan's terms.

The Service will not issue determination, opinion or advisory letters on the basis of the changes in these proposed regulations until the publication of final regulations. Until such time, the IRS will continue to issue such letters on the basis of the 1987 proposed regulations and SBJPA. Although the IRS will not issue determination, opinion or advisory letters with respect to the model amendment, the adoption of the model amendment will not affect a determination letter issued for a plan whose terms otherwise satisfy the 1987 proposed regulations and SBJPA. Plan sponsors should not adopt other amendments to attempt to conform their plans to the changes in these proposed regulations before the publication of final regulations. The IRS intends to publish procedures at a later date that will allow qualified plans to be amended to reflect the regulations under section 401(a)(9) when they are finalized.

Qualified plans are required to be amended for changes in the plan qualification requirements made by GUST by the end of the GUST remedial amendment period under section 401(b), which is generally the end of the first plan year beginning on or after January 1, 2001, or, if applicable, a later date determined under the provisions of section 19 of Rev. Proc. 2000-20 (2000-6 I.R.B. 553). Many plans have been operated in a manner that reflects the changes to section 401(a)(9) made by SBJPA and will have to be amended for these changes by the end of the GUST remedial amendment period. The IRS intends that its proce-

dures for amending qualified plans for the final regulations under section 401(a)(9) will generally avoid the need for plan sponsors, volume submitter practitioners and M&P plan sponsors to request another determination, opinion or advisory letter subsequent to their application for a GUST letter. In addition, to the extent such a subsequent letter is needed or desired, the IRS intends that its procedures will provide that the application for the letter will not have to be submitted prior to the next time the plan is otherwise amended or required to be amended.

The model amendment described above is set forth below: "With respect to distributions under the Plan made in calendar years beginning on or after January 1, 2000 (ALTERNATIVELY, SPECIFY A LATER CALENDAR YEAR FOR WHICH THE AMENDMENT IS TO BE INITIALLY EFFECTIVE), the Plan will apply the minimum distribution requirements of section 401(a)(9) of the Internal Revenue Code in accordance with the regulations under section 401(a)(9) that were proposed in January 2001, notwithstanding any provision of the Plan to the contrary. This amendment shall continue in effect until the end of the last calendar year beginning before the effective date of final regulations under section 401(a)(9) or such other date specified in guidance published by the Internal Revenue Service."

Amendment of IRAs and Effective Date

These regulations are proposed to be effective for distributions for calendar years beginning on or after January 1, 2002. For distributions for the 2001 calendar year, IRA owners are permitted, but not required, to follow these proposed regulations in operation, notwithstanding the terms of the IRA documents. IRA owners may therefore rely on these proposed regulations for distributions for the 2001 calendar year. However, IRA sponsors should not amend their IRA documents to conform their IRAs to the changes in these proposed regulations before the publication of final regulations. The IRS will not issue model IRAs on the basis of the changes in these proposed regulations until the publication of final regulations. Until such time, IRA owners can continue to use the current model IRAs which are based on the 1987 proposed regulations under section 401(a)(9). The IRS will publish procedures at a later date that will allow IRAs to be amended to reflect final regulations under section 401(a)(9).

Proposed Effective Date

The regulations are proposed to be applicable for determining required minimum distributions for calendar years beginning on or after January 1, 2002. For determining required minimum distributions for calendar year 2001, taxpayers may rely on these proposed regulations or on the 1987 proposed regulations. If, and to the extent, future guidance is more restrictive than the guidance in these proposed regulations, the future guidance will be issued without retroactive effect.

Special Analyses

It has been determined that this notice of proposed rulemaking is not a significant regulatory action as defined in Executive Order 12866. Therefore, a regulatory assessment is not required. It also has been determined that section 553(b) of the Administrative Procedure Act (5 U.S.C. chapter 5) does not apply to these regulations, and because the regulation does not impose a collection of information on small entities, the Regulatory Flexibility Act (5 U.S.C. chapter 6) does not apply. Pursuant to section 7805(f) of the Code, these proposed regulations will be submitted to the Chief Counsel for Advocacy of the Small Business Administration for comment on their impact on small business.

Comments and Public Hearing

Before these proposed regulations are adopted as final regulations, consideration will be given to any electronic or written comments (preferably a signed original and eight (8) copies) that are submitted timely to the IRS. In addition to the other requests for comments set forth in this document, the IRS and Treasury also request comments on the clarity of the proposed rule and how it may be made easier to understand. All comments will be available for public inspection and copying.

A public hearing has been scheduled for June 1, 2001, at 10 a.m. in the IRS Auditorium (7th Floor), Internal Revenue Building, 1111 Constitution Avenue NW., Washington, DC. Due to building security procedures, visitors must enter at the 10th street entrance, located between Constitution and Pennsylvania Avenues, NW. In addition, all visitors must present photo identification to enter the building. Because of access restrictions, visitors will not be admitted beyond the immediate entrance area more than 15 minutes before the hearing starts. For information about having your name placed on the building access list to attend the hearing, see the "FOR FURTHER INFORMATION CONTACT" section of this preamble.

The rules of 26 CFR 601.601(a)(3) apply to the hearing.

Persons who wish to present oral comments at the hearing must submit written comments and an outline of the topics to be discussed and the time to be devoted to each topic (signed original and eight (8) copies) by May 11, 2001.

A period of 10 minutes will be allotted to each person for making comments.

An agenda showing the scheduling of the speakers will be prepared after the deadline for receiving outlines has passed. Copies of the agenda will be available free of charge at the hearing.

Drafting Information

The principal authors of these regulations are Marjorie Hoffman and Cathy A. Vohs of the Office of the Division Counsel/Associate Chief Counsel (Tax Exempt and Government Entities). However, other personnel from the IRS and Treasury participated in their development.

List of Subjects

26 CFR Part 1

Income taxes, Reporting and recordkeeping requirements.

26 CFR Part 54

Excise taxes, Pensions, Reporting and recordkeeping requirements.

Adoption of Amendments of the Regulations

Accordingly, 26 CFR part 1 is amended as follows:

PART 1 - INCOME TAXES

Paragraph 1. The authority citation for part 1 is amended by adding entries in numerical order to read in part as follows:

Authority: 26 U.S.C. 7805 * * *

§ 1.401(a)(9)-1 is also issued under 26 U.S.C. 401(a)(9).

§ 1.401(a)(9)-2 is also issued under 26 U.S.C. 401(a)(9).

§ 1.401(a)(9)-3 is also issued under 26 U.S.C. 401(a)(9).

§ 1.401(a)(9)-4 is also issued under 26 U.S.C. 401(a)(9).

§ 1.401(a)(9)-5 is also issued under 26 U.S.C. 401(a)(9).

§ 1.401(a)(9)-6 is also issued under 26 U.S.C. 401(a)(9).

§ 1.401(a)(9)-7 is also issued under 26 U.S.C. 401(a)(9).

§ 1.401(a)(9)-8 is also issued under 26 U.S.C. 401(a)(9). * * *

§ 1.403(b)-2 is also issued under 26 U.S.C. 403(b)(10). * * *

§ 1.408-8 is also issued under 26 U.S.C. 408(a)(6) and (b)(3). * * *

Par. 2. Sections 1.401(a)(9)-0 through 1.401(a)(9)-8 are added to read as follows:

§ 1.401(a)(9)-0 Required minimum distributions; table of contents.

• This table of contents lists the regulations relating to required minimum distributions under section 401(a)(9) of the Internal Revenue Code as follows:

§ 1.401(a)(9)-0 Required minimum distributions; table of contents.

§ 1.401(a)(9)-1 Required minimum distribution requirement in general.

§ 1.401(a)(9)-2 Distributions commencing before an employee's death.

§ 1.401(a)(9)-3 Death before required beginning date.

§ 1.401(a)(9)-4 Determination of the designated beneficiary.

§ 1.401(a)(9)-5 Required minimum distributions from defined contribution plans.

§ 1.401(a)(9)-6 Required minimum distributions from defined benefit plans.

§ 1.401(a)(9)-7 Rollovers and transfers.

§ 1.401(a)(9)-8 Special rules.

§ 1.401(a)(9)-1 Required minimum distribution requirement in general.

Q-1. What plans are subject to the required minimum distribution requirement under section 401(a)(9) and §§ 1.401(a)(9)-1 through 1.401(a)(9)-8?

A-1. All stock bonus, pension, and profit-sharing plans qualified under section 401(a) and annuity contracts described in section 403(a) are subject to the required minimum distribution rules in section 401(a)(9) and §§ 1.401(a)(9)-1 through 1.401(a)(9)-8. See § 1.403(b)-2 for the distribution rules applicable to annuity contracts or custodial accounts described in section 403(b), see § 1.408-8 for the distribution rules applicable to individual retirement plans, see § 1.408A-6 described for the distribution rules applicable to Roth IRAs under section 408A, and see section 457(d)(2)(A) for distribution rules applicable to certain deferred compensation plans for employees of tax exempt organizations or state and local government employees.

Q-2. Which employee account balances and benefits held under qualified trusts and plans are subject to the distribution rules of section 401(a)(9) and §§ 1.401(a)(9)-1 through 1.401(a)(9)-8?

A-2. The distribution rules of section 401(a)(9) apply to all account balances and benefits in existence on or after January 1, 1985. Sections 1.401(a)(9)-1 through 1.401(a)(9)-8 apply for purposes of determining required minimum distributions for calendar years beginning on or after January 1, 2002.

Q-3. What specific provisions must a plan contain in order to satisfy section 401(a)(9)?

A-3. (a) *Required provisions.* In order to satisfy section 401(a)(9), the plan must include several written provisions reflecting section 401(a)(9). First, the plan must generally set forth the statutory rules of section 401(a)(9), including the incidental death benefit requirement in section 401(a)(9)(G). Second, the plan must provide that distributions will be made in accordance with §§ 1.401(a)(9)-1 through 1.401(a)(9)-8. The plan document must also provide that the provisions reflecting section 401(a)(9) override any distribution options in the plan inconsistent with section 401(a)(9). The plan also must include any other provisions reflecting section 401(a)(9) as are prescribed by the Commissioner in revenue rulings, notices, and other guidance published in the Internal Revenue Bulletin. See § 601.601(d)(2)(ii)(b) of this chapter.

(b) *Optional provisions.* The plan may also include written provisions regarding any optional provisions governing plan distributions that do not conflict with section 401(a)(9) and the regulations thereunder.

(c) *Absence of optional provisions.* Plan distributions commencing after an employee's death will be required to be made under the default provision set forth in § 1.401(a)(9)-3 for distributions unless the plan document contains optional provisions that override such default provisions. Thus, if distributions have not commenced to the employee at the time of the employee's death, distributions after the death of an employee are to be made automatically in accordance with the default provisions in A-4(a) of § 1.401(a)(9)-3 unless the plan either specifies in accordance with A-4(b) of § 1.401(a)(9)-3 the method under which distributions will be made or provides for elections by the employee (or beneficiary) in accordance with A-4(c) of § 1.401(a)(9)-3 and such elections are made by the employee or beneficiary.

§ 1.401(a)(9)-2 Distributions commencing before an employee's death.

Q-1. In the case of distributions commencing before an employee's death, how must the employee's entire interest be distributed in order to satisfy section 401(a)(9)(A)?

A-1. (a) In order to satisfy section 401(a)(9)(A), the entire interest of each employee must be distributed to such employee not later than the required beginning date, or must be distributed, beginning not later than the required beginning date, over the life of the employee or joint lives of the employee and a designated beneficiary or over a period not extending beyond the life expectancy of the employee or the joint life and last survivor expectancy of the employee and the designated beneficiary.

(b) Section 401(a)(9)(G) provides that lifetime distributions must satisfy the incidental death benefit requirements.

(c) The amount required to be distributed for each calendar year in order to satisfy section 401(a)(9)(A) and (G) generally depends on whether a distribution is in the form of distributions under a defined contribution plan or annuity payments under a defined benefit plan. For the method of determining the required minimum distribution in accordance with section 401(a)(9)(A) and (G) from an individual account under a defined contribution plan, see § 1.401(a)(9)-5. For the method of determining the required minimum distribution in accordance with section 401(a)(9)(A) and (G) in the case of annuity payments from a defined benefit plan or an annuity contract, see § 1.401(a)(9)-6.

Q-2. For purposes of section 401(a)(9)(C), what does the term *required beginning date* mean?

A-2. (a) Except as provided in paragraph (b) of this A-2 with respect to a 5-percent owner, as defined in paragraph (c), the term *required beginning date* means April 1 of the calendar year following the later of the calendar year in which the employee attains age 70 ½, or the calendar year in which the employee retires from employment with the employer maintaining the plan.

(b) In the case of an employee who is a 5-percent owner, the term *required beginning date* means April 1 of the calendar year following the calendar year in which the employee attains age 70 ½.

(c) For purposes of section 401(a)(9), a 5-percent owner is an employee who is a 5-percent owner (as defined in section 416) with respect to the plan year ending in the calendar year in which the employee attains age 70 ½.

(d) Paragraph (b) of this A-2 does not apply in the case of a governmental plan (within the meaning of section 414(d)) or a church plan. For purposes of this paragraph, the term *church plan* means a plan maintained by a church for church employees, and the term *church* means any church (as defined in section 3121(w)(3)(A)) or qualified church-controlled organization (as defined in section 3121(w)(3)(B)).

(e) A plan is permitted to provide that the required beginning date for purposes of section 401(a)(9) for all employees is April 1 of the calendar year following the calendar year in which the employee attained age 70 ½ regardless of whether the employee is a 5-percent owner.

Q-3. When does an employee attain age 70 ½?

A-3. An employee attains age 70 ½ as of the date six calendar months after the 70th anniversary of the employee's birth. For example, if an employee's date of birth was June 30, 1932, the 70th anniversary of such employee's birth is June 30, 2002. Such employee attains age 70 ½ on December 30, 2002. Consequently, if the employee is a 5-percent owner or retired, such employee's required beginning date is April 1, 2003. However, if the employee's date of birth was July 1, 1932, the 70th anniversary of such employee's birth would be July 1, 2002. Such employee would then attain age 70 ½ on January 1, 2003 and such employee's required beginning date would be April 1, 2004.

Q-4. Must distributions made before the employee's required beginning date satisfy section 401(a)(9)?

A-4. Lifetime distributions made before the employee's required beginning date for calendar years before the employee's first distribution calendar year, as defined in A-1(b) of § 1.401(a)(9)-5, need not be made in accordance with section 401(a)(9). However, if distributions commence before the employee's required beginning date under a particular distribution option, such as in the form of an annuity, the distribution option fails to satisfy section 401(a)(9) at the time distributions commence if, under terms of the particular distribution option, distributions to be made for the employee's first distribution calendar year or any subsequent distribution calendar year will fail to satisfy section 401(a)(9).

Q-5. If distributions have begun to an employee before the employee's death (in accordance with section 401(a)(9)(A)(ii)), how must distributions be made after an employee's death?

A-5. Section 401(a)(9)(B)(i) provides that if the distribution of the employee's interest has begun in accordance with section 401(a)(9)(A)(ii) and the employee dies before his entire interest has been distributed to him, the remaining portion of such interest must be distributed at least as rapidly as under the distribution method being used under section 401(a)(9)(A)(ii) as of the date of his death. The amount required to be distributed for each distribution calendar year following the calendar year of death generally depends on whether a distribution is in the form of distributions from an individual account under a defined contribution plan or annuity payments under a defined benefit plan. For the method of determining the required minimum distribution in accordance with section 401(a)(9)(B)(i) from an individual account, see A-5(a) of § 1.401(a)(9)-5 for the calculation of the distribution period that applies when an employee dies after the employee's required beginning date. In the case of annuity payments from a defined benefit plan or an annuity contract, see § 1.401(a)(9)-6.

Q-6. For purposes of section 401(a)(9)(B), when are distributions considered to have begun to the employee in accordance with section 401(a)(9)(A)(ii)?

A-6. (a) *General rule.* Except as otherwise provided in A-10 of § 1.401(a)(9)-6, distributions are not treated as having begun to the employee in accordance with section 401(a)(9)(A)(ii) until the employee's required beginning date, without regard to whether payments have been made before that date. For example, if employee A upon

retirement in 2002, the calendar year A attains age 65 ½, begins receiving installment distributions from a profit-sharing plan over a period not exceeding the joint life and last survivor expectancy of A and A's beneficiary, benefits are not treated as having begun in accordance with section 401(a)(9)(A)(ii) until April 1, 2008 (the April 1 following the calendar year in which A attains age 70 ½). Consequently, if such employee dies before April 1, 2008 (A's required beginning date), distributions after A's death must be made in accordance with section 401(a)(9)(B)(ii) or (iii) and (iv) and § 1.401(a)(9)-4, and not section 401(a)(9)(B)(i). This is the case without regard to whether the plan has distributed the minimum distribution for the first distribution calendar year (as defined in A-1(b) of § 1.401(a)(9)-5) before A's death.

(b) If a plan provides, in accordance with A-2(e) of this section, that the required beginning date for purposes of section 401(a)(9) for all employees is April 1 of the calendar year following the calendar year in which the employee attains age 70 ½, an employee who dies after the required beginning date determined under the plan terms is treated as dying after the employee's required beginning date for purposes of A-5(a) of this section even though the employee dies before the April 1 following the calendar year in which the employee retires.

§ 1.401(a)(9)-3 Death before required beginning date.

Q-1. If an employee dies before the employee's required beginning date, how must the employee's entire interest be distributed in order to satisfy section 401(a)(9)?

A-1. (a) Except as otherwise provided in A-10 of § 1.401(a)(9)-6, if an employee dies before the employee's required beginning date (and, thus, generally before distributions are treated as having begun in accordance with section 401(a)(9)(A)(ii)), distribution of the employee's entire interest must be made in accordance with one of the methods described in section 401(a)(9)(B)(ii) or (iii). One method (the five-year rule in section 401(a)(9)(B)(ii)) requires that the entire interest of the employee be distributed within five years of the employee's death regardless of who or what entity receives the distribution. Another method (the life expectancy rule in section 401(a)(9)(B)(iii)) requires that any portion of an employee's interest payable to (or for the benefit of) a designated beneficiary be distributed, commencing within one year of the employee's death, over the life of such beneficiary (or over a period not extending beyond the life expectancy of such beneficiary). Section 401(a)(9)(B)(iv) provides special rules where the designated beneficiary is the surviving spouse of the employee, including a special commencement date for distributions under section 401(a)(9)(B)(iii) to the surviving spouse.

(b) See A-4 of this section for the rules for determining which of the methods described in paragraph (a) applies. See A-3 of this section to determine when distributions under the exception to the five-year rule in section 401(a)(9)(B)(iii) and (iv) must commence. See A-2 of this section to determine when the five-year period in section 401(a)(9)(B)(ii) ends. For distributions using the life expectancy rule in section 401(a)(9)(B)(iii) and (iv), see § 1.401(a)(9)-4 in order to determine the designated beneficiary under section 401(a)(9)(B)(iii) and (iv), see § 1.401(a)(9)-5 for the rules for determining the required minimum distribution under a defined contribution plan, and see § 1.401(a)(9)-6 for required minimum distributions under defined benefit plans.

Q-2. By when must the employee's entire interest be distributed in order to satisfy the five-year rule in section 401(a)(9)(B)(ii)?

A-2. In order to satisfy the five-year rule in section 401(a)(9)(B)(ii), the employee's entire interest must be distributed by the end of the calendar year which contains the fifth anniversary of the date of the employee's death. For example, if an employee dies on January 1, 2002, the entire interest must be distributed by the end of 2007, in order to satisfy the five-year rule in section 401(a)(9)(B)(ii).

Q-3. When are distributions required to commence in order to satisfy the life expectancy rule in section 401(a)(9)(B)(iii) and (iv)?

A-3. (a) *Nonspouse beneficiary.* In order to satisfy the life expectancy rule in section 401(a)(9)(B)(iii), if the designated beneficiary is not the employee's surviving spouse, distributions must commence on or before the end of the calendar year immediately following the calendar year in which the employee died. This rule also applies to the distribution of the entire remaining benefit if another individual is a designated beneficiary in addition to the employee's surviving spouse. See A-2 and A-3 of § 1.401(a)(9)-8, however, if the employee's benefit is divided into separate accounts (or segregated shares, in the case of a defined benefit plan).

(b) *Spousal beneficiary.* In order to satisfy the rule in section 401(a)(9)(B)(iii) and (iv), if the sole designated beneficiary is the employee's surviving spouse, distributions must commence on or before the later of-

(1) The end of the calendar year immediately following the calendar year in which the employee died; and

(2) The end of the calendar year in which the employee would have attained age 70 ½.

Q-4. How is it determined whether the five-year rule in section 401(a)(9)(B)(ii) or the life expectancy rule in section 401(a)(9)(B)(iii) and (iv) applies to a distribution?

A-4. (a) *No plan provision.* If a plan does not adopt an optional provision described in paragraph (b) or (c) of this A-4 specifying the method of distribution after the death of an employee, distribution must be made as follows:

(1) If the employee has a designated beneficiary, as determined under § 1.401(a)(9)-4, distributions are to be made in accordance with the life expectancy rule in section 401(a)(9)(B)(iii) and (iv).

(2) If the employee has no designated beneficiary, distributions are to be made in accordance with the five-year rule in section 401(a)(9)(B)(ii).

(b) *Optional plan provisions.* The plan may adopt a provision specifying either that the five-year rule in section 401(a)(9)(B)(ii) will apply to certain distributions after the death of an employee even if the employee has a designated beneficiary or that distribution in every case will be made in accordance with the five-year rule in section 401(a)(9)(B)(ii). Further, a plan need not have the same method of distribution for the benefits of all employees.

(c) *Elections.* A plan may adopt a provision that permits employees (or beneficiaries) to elect on an individual basis whether the five-year rule in section 401(a)(9)(B)(ii) or the life expectancy rule in section 401(a)(9)(B)(iii) and (iv) applies to distributions after the death of an employee who has a designated beneficiary. Such an election must be made no later than the earlier of, the end of the calendar year in which distribution would be required to commence in order to satisfy the requirements for the life expectancy rule in section 401(a)(9)(B)(iii) and (iv) (see A-3 of this section for the determination of such calendar year), or the end of the calendar year which contains the fifth anniversary of the date of death of the employee. As of the date determined under the life expectancy rule, the election must be irrevocable with respect to the beneficiary (and all subsequent beneficiaries) and must apply to all subsequent calendar years. If a plan provides for the election, the plan may also specify the method of distribution that applies if neither the employee nor the beneficiary makes the election. If neither the employee nor the beneficiary elects a method and the plan does not specify which method applies, distribution must be made in accordance with paragraph (a).

Q-5. If the employee's surviving spouse is the employee's designated beneficiary and such spouse dies after the employee, but before distributions have begun to the surviving spouse under section 401(a)(9)(B)(iii) and (iv), how is the employee's interest to be distributed?

A-5. Pursuant to section 401(a)(9)(B)(iv)(II), if the surviving spouse dies after the employee, but before distributions to such spouse have begun under section 401(a)(9)(B)(iii) and (iv), the five-year rule in section 401(a)(9)(B)(ii) and the life expectancy rule in section 401(a)(9)(B)(iii) are to be applied as if the surviving spouse were the employee. In applying this rule, the date of death of the surviving spouse shall be substituted for the date of death of the employee. However, in such case, the rules in section 401(a)(9)(B)(iv) are not available to the surviving spouse of the deceased employee's surviving spouse.

Q-6. For purposes of section 401(a)(9)(B)(iv)(II), when are distributions considered to have begun to the surviving spouse?

A-6. Distributions are considered to have begun to the surviving spouse of an employee, for purposes of section 401(a)(9)(B)(iv)(II), on the date, determined in accordance with A-3 of this section, on which distributions are required to commence to the surviving spouse, even though payments have actually been made before that date. See A-11 of § 1.401(a)(9)-6 for a special rule for annuities.

§ 1.401(a)(9)-4 Determination of the designated beneficiary.

Q-1. Who is a designated beneficiary under section 401(a)(9)(E)?

A-1. A designated beneficiary is an individual who is designated as a beneficiary under the plan. An individual may be designated as a beneficiary under the plan either by the terms of the plan or, if the plan so provides, by an affirmative election by the employee (or the em-

ployee's surviving spouse) specifying the beneficiary. A beneficiary designated as such under the plan is an individual who is entitled to a portion of an employee's benefit, contingent on the employee's death or another specified event. For example, if a distribution is in the form of a joint and survivor annuity over the life of the employee and another individual, the plan does not satisfy section 401(a)(9) unless such other individual is a designated beneficiary under the plan. A designated beneficiary need not be specified by name in the plan or by the employee to the plan in order to be a designated beneficiary so long as the individual who is to be the beneficiary is identifiable under the plan as of the date the beneficiary is determined under A-4 of this section. The members of a class of beneficiaries capable of expansion or contraction will be treated as being identifiable if it is possible, as of the date the beneficiary is determined, to identify the class member with the shortest life expectancy. The fact that an employee's interest under the plan passes to a certain individual under applicable state law does not make that individual a designated beneficiary unless the individual is designated as a beneficiary under the plan.

Q-2. Must an employee (or the employee's spouse) make an affirmative election specifying a beneficiary for a person to be a designated beneficiary under section 401(a)(9)(E)?

A-2. No. A designated beneficiary is an individual who is designated as a beneficiary under the plan whether or not the designation under the plan was made by the employee. The choice of beneficiary is subject to the requirements of sections 401(a)(11), 414(p), and 417.

Q-3. May a person other than an individual be considered to be a designated beneficiary for purposes of section 401(a)(9)?

A-3. (a) No. Only individuals may be designated beneficiaries for purposes of section 401(a)(9). A person that is not an individual, such as the employee's estate, may not be a designated beneficiary, and, if a person other than an individual is designated as a beneficiary of an employee's benefit, the employee will be treated as having no designated beneficiary for purposes of section 401(a)(9). However, see A-5 of this section for special rules which apply to trusts.

(b) If an employee is treated as having no designated beneficiary, for distributions under a defined contribution plan, the distribution period under section 401(a)(9)(A)(ii) after the death of the employee is limited to the period described in A-5(a)(2) of § 1.401(a)(9)-5 (the remaining life expectancy of the employee determined in accordance with A-5(c)(3) of § 1.401(a)(9)-5). Further, in such case, except as provided in A-10 of § 1.401(a)(9)-6, if the employee dies before the employee's required beginning date, distribution must be made in accordance with the 5-year rule in section 401(a)(9)(B)(ii).

Q-4. When is the designated beneficiary determined?

A-4. (a) *General rule.* Except as provided in paragraph (b) and § 1.401(a)(9)-6, the employee's designated beneficiary will be determined based on the beneficiaries designated as of the last day of the calendar year following the calendar year of the employee's death. Consequently, except as provided in § 1.401(a)(9)-6, any person who was a beneficiary as of the date of the employee's death, but is not a beneficiary as of that later date (e.g., because the person disclaims entitlement to the benefit in favor of another beneficiary or because the person receives the entire benefit to which the person is entitled before that date), is not taken into account in determining the employee's designated beneficiary for purposes of determining the distribution period for required minimum distributions after the employee's death.

(b) *Surviving spouse.* As provided in A-5 of § 1.401(a)(9)-3, in the case in which the employee's spouse is the designated beneficiary as of the date described in paragraph (a) of this A-5, and the surviving spouse dies after the employee and before the date on which distributions have begun to the spouse under section 401(a)(9)(B)(iii) and (iv), the rule in section 401(a)(9)(B)(iv)(II) will apply. Thus, the relevant designated beneficiary for determining the distribution period is the designated beneficiary of the surviving spouse. Such designated beneficiary will be determined as of the last day of the calendar year following the calendar year of surviving spouse's death. If, as of such last day, there is no designated beneficiary under the plan with respect to that surviving spouse, distribution must be made in accordance with the 5-year rule in section 401(a)(9)(B)(ii) and A-2 of § 1.401(a)(9)-3.

(c) *Multiple beneficiaries.* Notwithstanding anything in this A-4 to the contrary, the rules in A-7 of § 1.401(a)(9)-5 apply if more than one beneficiary is designated with respect to an employee as of the date on which the designated beneficiary is to be determined in accordance with paragraphs (a) and (b) of this A-4.

Q-5. If a trust is named as a beneficiary of an employee, will the beneficiaries of the trust with respect to the trust's interest in the employee's benefit be treated as having been designated as beneficiaries of the employee under the plan for purposes of determining the distribution period under section 401(a)(9)?

A-5. (a) Only an individual may be a designated beneficiary for purposes of determining the distribution period under section 401(a)(9). Consequently, a trust is not a designated beneficiary even though the trust is named as a beneficiary. However, if the requirements of paragraph (b) of this A-5 are met, the beneficiaries of the trust will be treated as having been designated as beneficiaries of the employee under the plan for purposes of determining the distribution period under section 401(a)(9).

(b) The requirements of this paragraph (b) are met if, during any period during which required minimum distributions are being determined by treating the beneficiaries of the trust as designated beneficiaries of the employee, the following requirements are met:

(1) The trust is a valid trust under state law, or would be but for the fact that there is no corpus.

(2) The trust is irrevocable or will, by its terms, become irrevocable upon the death of the employee.

(3) The beneficiaries of the trust who are beneficiaries with respect to the trust's interest in the employee's benefit are identifiable from the trust instrument within the meaning of A-1 of this section.

(4) The documentation described in A-6 of this section has been provided to the plan administrator.

(c) In the case of payments to a trust having more than one beneficiary, see A-7 of § 1.401(a)(9)-5 for the rules for determining the designated beneficiary whose life expectancy will be used to determine the distribution period. If the beneficiary of the trust named as beneficiary is another trust, the beneficiaries of the other trust will be treated as having been designated as beneficiaries of the employee under the plan for purposes of determining the distribution period under section 401(a)(9)(A)(ii), provided that the requirements of paragraph (b) of this A-5 are satisfied with respect to such other trust in addition to the trust named as beneficiary.

Q-6. If a trust is named as a beneficiary of an employee, what documentation must be provided to the plan administrator?

A-6. (a) *Required minimum distributions before death.* In order to satisfy the documentation requirement of this A-6 for required minimum distributions under section 401(a)(9) to commence before the death of an employee, the employee must comply with either paragraph (a)(1) or (2) of this A-6:

(1) The employee provides to the plan administrator a copy of the trust instrument and agrees that if the trust instrument is amended at any time in the future, the employee will, within a reasonable time, provide to the plan administrator a copy of each such amendment.

(2) The employee—

(i) Provides to the plan administrator a list of all of the beneficiaries of the trust (including contingent and remaindermen beneficiaries with a description of the conditions on their entitlement);

(ii) Certifies that, to the best of the employee's knowledge, this list is correct and complete and that the requirements of paragraphs (b)(1), (2), and (3) of A-5 of this section are satisfied;

(iii) Agrees that, if the trust instrument is amended at any time in the future, the employee will, within a reasonable time, provide to the plan administrator corrected certifications to the extent that the amendment changes any information previously certified; and

(iv) Agrees to provide a copy of the trust instrument to the plan administrator upon demand.

(b) *Required minimum distributions after death.* In order to satisfy the documentation requirement of this A-6 for required minimum distributions after the death of the employee, by the last day of the calendar year immediately following the calendar year in which the employee died, the trustee of the trust must either -

(1) Provide the plan administrator with a final list of all beneficiaries of the trust (including contingent and remaindermen beneficiaries with a description of the conditions on their entitlement) as of the end of the calendar year following the calendar year of the employee's death; certify that, to the best of the trustee's knowledge, this list is correct and complete and that the requirements of paragraph (b)(1), (2), and (3) of A-5 of this section are satisfied; and agree to provide a copy of the trust instrument to the plan administrator upon demand; or

(2) Provide the plan administrator with a copy of the actual trust document for the trust that is named as a beneficiary of the employee under the plan as of the employee's date of death.

(c) *Relief for discrepancy between trust instrument and employee certifications or earlier trust instruments.* (1) If required minimum distributions are determined based on the information provided to the plan administrator in certifications or trust instruments described in paragraph (a)(1), (a)(2) or (b) of this A-6, a plan will not fail to satisfy section 401(a)(9) merely because the actual terms of the trust instrument are inconsistent with the information in those certifications or trust instruments previously provided to the plan administrator, but only if the plan administrator reasonably relied on the information provided and the required minimum distributions for calendar years after the calendar year in which the discrepancy is discovered are determined based on the actual terms of the trust instrument.

(2) For purposes of determining the amount of the excise tax under section 4974, the required minimum distribution is determined for any year based on the actual terms of the trust in effect during the year.

§ 1.401(a)(9)-5 Required minimum distributions from defined contribution plans.

Q-1. If an employee's benefit is in the form of an individual account under a defined contribution plan, what is the amount required to be distributed for each calendar year?

A-1. (a) *General rule.* If an employee's accrued benefit is in the form of an individual account under a defined contribution plan, the minimum amount required to be distributed for each distribution calendar year, as defined in paragraph (b) of this A-1, is equal to the quotient obtained by dividing the account (determined under A-3 of this section) by the applicable distribution period (determined under A-4 of this section). However, the required minimum distribution amount will never exceed the entire vested account balance on the date of distribution. Further, the minimum distribution required to be distributed on or before an employee's required beginning date is always determined under section 401(a)(9)(A)(ii) and this A-1 and not section 401(a)(9)(A)(i).

(b) *Distribution calendar year.* A calendar year for which a minimum distribution is required is a distribution calendar year. If an employee's required beginning date is April 1 of the calendar year following the calendar year in which the employee attains age 70 ½, the employee's first distribution calendar year is the year the employee attains age 70 ½. If an employee's required beginning date is April 1 of the calendar year following the calendar year in which the employee retires, the calendar year in which the employee retires is the employee's first distribution calendar year. In the case of distributions to be made in accordance with the life expectancy rule in § 1.401(a)(9)-3 and in section 401(a)(9)(B)(iii) and (iv), the first distribution calendar year is the calendar year containing the date described in A-3(a) or A-3(b) of § 1.401(a)(9)-3, whichever is applicable.

(c) *Time for distributions.* The distribution required to be made on or before the employee's required beginning date shall be treated as the distribution required for the employee's first distribution calendar year (as defined in paragraph (b) of this A-1). The required minimum distribution for other distribution calendar years, including the required minimum distribution for the distribution calendar year in which the employee's required beginning date occurs, must be made on or before the end of that distribution calendar year.

(d) *Minimum distribution incidental benefit requirement.* If distributions are made in accordance with this section, the minimum distribution incidental benefit requirement of section 401(a)(9)(G) will be satisfied.

(e) *Annuity contracts.* Instead of satisfying this A-1, the required minimum distribution requirement may be satisfied by the purchase of an annuity contract from an insurance company in accordance with A-4 of § 1.401(a)(9)-6 with the employee's entire individual account. If such an annuity is purchased after distributions are required to commence (the required beginning date, in the case of distributions commencing before death, or the date determined under A-3 of § 1.401(a)(9)-3, in the case of distributions commencing after death), payments under the annuity contract purchased will satisfy section 401(a)(9) for distribution calendar years after the calendar year of the purchase if payments under the annuity contract are made in accordance with § 1.401(a)(9)-6. In such a case, payments under the annuity contract will be treated as distributions from the individual account for purposes of determining if the individual account satisfies section 401(a)(9) for the calendar year of the purchase. An employee may also purchase an annuity contract for a portion of the employee's account under the rules of A-2(c) of § 1.401(a)(9)-8

Q-2. If an employee's benefit is in the form of an individual account and, in any calendar year, the amount distributed exceeds the minimum required, will credit be given in subsequent calendar years for such excess distribution?

A-2. If, for any distribution calendar year, the amount distributed exceeds the minimum required, no credit will be given in subsequent calendar years for such excess distribution.

Q-3. What is the amount of the account of an employee used for determining the employee's required minimum distribution in the case of an individual account?

A-3. (a) In the case of an individual account, the benefit used in determining the required minimum distribution for a distribution calendar year is the account balance as of the last valuation date in the calendar year immediately preceding that distribution calendar year (valuation calendar year) adjusted in accordance with paragraphs (b) and (c) of this A-3.

(b) The account balance is increased by the amount of any contributions or forfeitures allocated to the account balance as of dates in the valuation calendar year after the valuation date. Contributions include contributions made after the close of the valuation calendar year which are allocated as of dates in the valuation calendar year.

(c) (1) The account balance is decreased by distributions made in the valuation calendar year after the valuation date.

(2) (i) The following rule applies if any portion of the required minimum distribution for the first distribution calendar year is made in the second distribution calendar year (i.e., generally, the distribution calendar year in which the required beginning date occurs). In such case, for purposes of determining the account balance to be used for determining the required minimum distribution for the second distribution calendar year, distributions described in paragraph (c) (1) shall include an additional amount. This additional amount is equal to the amount of any distribution made in the second distribution calendar year on or before the required beginning date that is not in excess (when added to the amounts distributed in the first calendar year) of the amount required to meet the required minimum distribution for the first distribution calendar year.

(ii) This paragraph (c) (2) is illustrated by the following example:

Example. (i) Employee X, born October 1, 1931, is an unmarried participant in a qualified defined contribution plan (Plan Z). After retirement, X attains age 70 ½ in calendar year 2002. X's required beginning date is April 1, 2003. As of the last valuation date under Plan Z in calendar year 2001, which was on December 31, 2001, the value of X's account balance was $25,300. No contributions are made or amounts forfeited after such date which are allocated in calendar year 2001. No rollover amounts are received after such date by Plan Z on X's behalf which were distributed by a qualified plan or IRA in calendar years 2001, 2002, or 2003. The applicable distribution period from the table in A-4(a)(2) for an individual age 71 is 25.3 years. The required minimum distribution for calendar year 2002 is $1,000 ($25,300 divided by 25.3). That amount is distributed to X on April 1, 2003.

(ii) The value of X's account balance as of December 31, 2002 (the last valuation date under Plan Z in calendar year 2002) is $26,400. No contributions are made or amounts forfeited after such date which are allocated in calendar year 2002. In order to determine the benefit to be used in calculating the required minimum distribution for calendar year 2003, the account balance of $26,400 will be reduced by $1,000, the amount of the required minimum distribution for calendar year 2002 made on April 1, 2003. Consequently, the benefit for purposes of determining the required minimum distribution for calendar year 2003 is $25,400.

(iii) If, instead of $1,000 being distributed to X, $20,000 is distributed on April 1 2003, the account balance of $26,400 would still be reduced by $1,000 in order to determine the benefit to be used in calculating the required minimum distribution for calendar year 2003. The amount of the distribution made on April 1, 2003, in order to meet the required minimum distribution for 2002 would still be $1,000. The remaining $19,000 ($20,000 – $1,000) of the distribution is not the required minimum distribution for 2002. Instead, the remaining $19,000 of the distribution is sufficient to satisfy the required minimum distribution requirement with respect to X for calendar year 2003. The amount which is required to be distributed for calendar year 2003 is $1,040.10 ($25,400 divided by 24.4, the applicable distribution period for an individual age 72). Consequently, no additional amount is required to be distributed to X in 2003 because $19,000 exceeds $1,040.10. However, pursuant to A-2 of this section, the remaining $17,959.90 ($19,000–$1,040.10) may not be used to satisfy the required minimum distribution requirements for calendar year 2004 or any subsequent calendar years.

(d) If an amount is distributed by one plan and rolled over to another plan (receiving plan), A-2 of § 1.401(a)(9)-7 provides additional rules for determining the benefit and required minimum distribution under the receiving plan. If an amount is transferred from one plan (transferor plan) to another plan (transferee plan), A-3 and A-4 of § 1.401(a)(9)-7 provide additional rules for determining the amount of the required minimum distribution and the benefit under both the transferor and transferee plans.

Q-4. For required minimum distributions during an employee's lifetime, what is the applicable distribution period?

A-4. (a) *General rule*—(1) *Applicable distribution period.* Except as provided in paragraph (b) of this A-4, the applicable distribution period for required minimum distributions for distribution calendar years up to and including the distribution calendar year that includes the employee's date of death is determined using the table in paragraph (a)(2) for the employee's age as of the employee's birthday in the relevant distribution calendar year.

(2) *Table for determining distribution period*—(i) *General rule.* The following table is used for determining the distribution period for lifetime distributions to an employee.

Age of the employee	Distribution period
70	26.2
71	25.3
72	24.4
73	23.5
74	22.7
75	21.8
76	20.9
77	20.1
78	19.2
79	18.4
80	17.6
81	16.8
82	16.0
83	15.3
84	14.5
85	13.8
86	13.1
87	12.4
88	11.8
89	11.1
90	10.5
91	9.9
92	9.4
93	8.8
94	8.3
95	7.8
96	7.3
97	6.9

Age of the employee	Distribution period
98	6.5
99	6.1
100	5.7
101	5.3
102	5.0
103	4.7
104	4.4
105	4.1
106	3.8
107	3.6
108	3.3
109	3.1
110	2.8
111	2.6
112	2.4
113	2.2
114	2.0
115 and older	1.8

(ii) *Authority for revised table.* The table in A-4(a)(2)(i) of this section may be replaced by any revised table prescribed by the Commissioner in revenue rulings, notices, or other guidance published in the Internal Revenue Bulletin. See § 601.601(d)(2)(ii)(b) of this chapter.

(b) *Spouse is sole beneficiary.* If the sole designated beneficiary of an employee is the employee's surviving spouse, for required minimum distributions during the employee's lifetime, the applicable distribution period is the longer of the distribution period determined in accordance with paragraph (a) of this A-4 or the joint life expectancy of the employee and spouse using the employee's and spouse's attained ages as of the employee's and the spouse's birthdays in the distribution calendar year. The spouse is sole designated beneficiary for purposes of determining the applicable distribution period for a distribution calendar year during the employee's lifetime if the spouse is the sole beneficiary of the employee's entire interest at all times during the distribution calendar year.

Q-5. For required minimum distributions after an employee's death, what is the applicable distribution period?

A-5. (a) *Death on or after the employee's required beginning date.* If an employee dies on or after distribution has begun as determined under A-6 of § 1.401(a)(9)-2 (generally after the employee's required beginning date), in order to satisfy section 401(a)(9)(B)(i), the applicable distribution period for distribution calendar years after the distribution calendar year containing the employee's date of death is either –

(1) If the employee has a designated beneficiary as of the date determined under A-4 of § 1.401(a)(9)-4, the remaining life expectancy of the employee's designated beneficiary determined in accordance with paragraph (c)(1) or (2) of this A-5; or

(2) If the employee does not have a designated beneficiary as of the date determined under A-4(a) of § 1.401(a)(9)-4, the remaining life expectancy of the employee determined in accordance with paragraph (c)(3) of this A-5.

(b) *Death before an employee's required beginning date.* If an employee dies before distribution has begun as determined under A-5 of § 1.401(a)(9)-2 (generally before the employee's required beginning date), in order to satisfy section 401(a)(9)(B)(iii) or (iv) and the life expectancy rule described in A-1 of § 1.401(a)(9)-3, the applicable distribution period for distribution calendar years after the distribution calendar year containing the employee's date of death is the remaining life expectancy of the employee's designated beneficiary, determined in accordance with paragraph (c)(1) or (2) of this A-5.

(c) *Life expectancy*—(1) *Nonspouse designated beneficiary.* The applicable distribution period measured by the beneficiary's remaining life expectancy is determined using the beneficiary's age as of the beneficiary's birthday in the calendar year immediately following the calendar year of the employee's death. In subsequent calendar years the applicable distribution period is reduced by one for each calendar year that has elapsed since the calendar year immediately following the calendar year of the employee's death.

(2) *Spouse designated beneficiary.* If the surviving spouse of the employee is the employee's sole beneficiary, the applicable period is measured by the surviving spouse's life expectancy using the surviving spouse's birthday for each distribution calendar year for which a required minimum distribution is required after the calendar year of the employee's death. For calendar years after the calendar year of the spouse's death, the spouse's remaining life expectancy is the life expectancy of the spouse using the age of the spouse as of the spouse's birthday in the calendar year of the spouse's death. In subsequent

calendar years, the applicable distribution period is reduced by one for each calendar year that has elapsed since the calendar year immediately following the calendar year of the spouse's death.

(3) *No designated beneficiary.* The applicable distribution period measured by the employee's remaining life expectancy is the life expectancy of the employee using the age of the employee as of the employee's birthday in the calendar year of the employee's death. In subsequent calendar years the applicable distribution period is reduced by one for each calendar year that has elapsed since the calendar year of death.

Q-6. What life expectancies must be used for purposes of determining required minimum distributions under section 401(a)(9)?

A-6. (a) *General rule.* Unless otherwise prescribed in accordance with paragraph (b) of this A-6, life expectancies for purposes of determining required minimum distributions under section 401(a)(9) must be computed using of the expected return multiples in Tables V and VI of § 1.72-9.

(b) *Revised expected return table.* The expected return multiples described in paragraph (a) of this A-6 may be replaced by revised expected return multiples prescribed for use for purposes of determining required minimum distributions under section 401(a)(9) by the Commissioner in revenue rulings, notices, and other guidance published in the Internal Revenue Bulletin. See § 601.601(d)(2)(ii)(b) of this chapter.

Q-7. If an employee has more than one designated beneficiary, which designated beneficiary's life expectancy will be used to determine the applicable distribution period?

A-7. (a) *General rule.* (1) Except as otherwise provided in paragraph (c) of this A-7, if more than one individual is designated as a beneficiary with respect to an employee as of any applicable date for determining the designated beneficiary, the designated beneficiary with the shortest life expectancy will be the designated beneficiary for purposes of determining the distribution period. However, except as otherwise provided in A-5 of § 1.401(a)(9)-4 and paragraph (c)(1) of this A-7, if a person other than an individual is designated as a beneficiary, the employee will be treated as not having any designated beneficiaries for purposes of section 401(a)(9) even if there are also individuals designated as beneficiaries.

(2) See A-2 of § 1.401(a)(9)-8 for special rules which apply if an employee's benefit under a plan is divided into separate accounts (or segregated shares in the case of a defined benefit plan) and the beneficiaries with respect to a separate account differ from the beneficiaries of another separate account.

(b) *Contingent beneficiary.* Except as provided in paragraph (c)(1) of this A-7, if a beneficiary's entitlement to an employee's benefit is contingent on an event other than the employee's death or the death of another beneficiary, such contingent beneficiary is considered to be a designated beneficiary for purposes of determining which designated beneficiary has the shortest life expectancy under paragraph (a) of this A-7.

(c) *Death contingency.* (1) If a beneficiary (subsequent beneficiary) is entitled to any potion of an employee's benefit only if another beneficiary dies before the entire benefit to which that other beneficiary is entitled has been distributed by the plan, the subsequent beneficiary will not be considered a beneficiary for purposes of determining who is the designated beneficiary with the shortest life expectancy under paragraph (a) of this A-7 or whether a beneficiary who is not an individual is a beneficiary. This rule does not apply if the other beneficiary dies prior to the applicable date for determining the designated beneficiary.

(2) If the designated beneficiary whose life expectancy is being used to calculate the distribution period dies on or after the applicable date, such beneficiary's remaining life expectancy will be used to determine the distribution period whether or not a beneficiary with a shorter life expectancy receives the benefits.

(3) This paragraph (c) is illustrated by the following examples:

Example 1. Employer L maintains a defined contribution plan, Plan W. Unmarried Employee C dies in calendar year 2001 at age 30. As of December 31, 2002, D, the sister of C, is the beneficiary of C's account balance under Plan W. Prior to death C has designated that, if D dies before C's entire account balance has been distributed to D, E, mother of C and D, will be the beneficiary of the account balance. Because E is only entitled, as a beneficiary, to any portion of C's account if D dies before the entire account has been distributed, E is disregarded in determining C's designated beneficiary. Accordingly, even after D's death, D's life expectancy continues to be used to determined the distribution period.

Example 2. (i) Employer M maintains a defined contribution plan, Plan X. Employee A, an employee of M, died in 2001 at the age of 55, survived by spouse, B, who was 50 years old. Prior to A's death, M had established an account balance for A in Plan X. A's account balance is invested only in productive assets. A named the trustee of a testamentary trust (Trust P) established under A's will as the beneficiary of all amounts payable from the A's account in Plan X after A's death. A copy of the Trust P and a list of the trust beneficiaries were provided to the plan administrator of Plan X by the end of the calendar year following the calendar year of A's death. As of the date of *A*'s death, the Trust P was irrevocable and was a valid trust under the laws of the state of *A*'s domicile. A's account balance in Plan X was includible in A's gross estate under § 2039.

(ii) Under the terms of Trust P, all trust income is payable annually to B, and no one has the power to appoint Trust P principal to any person other than B. A's children, who are all younger than B, are the sole remainder beneficiaries of the Trust P. No other person has a beneficial interest in Trust P. Under the terms of the Trust P, B has the power, exercisable annually, to compel the trustee to withdraw from A's account balance in Plan X an amount equal to the income earned on the assets held in A's account in Plan X during the calendar year and to distribute that amount through Trust P to B. Plan X contains no prohibition on withdrawal from A's account of amounts in excess of the annual required minimum distributions under section 401(a)(9). In accordance with the terms of Plan X, the trustee of Trust P elects, in order to satisfy section 401(a)(9), to receive annual required minimum distributions using the life expectancy rule in section 401(a)(9)(B)(iii) for distributions over a distribution period equal to B's life expectancy. If B exercises the withdrawal power, the trustee must withdraw from A's account under Plan X the greater of the amount of income earned in the account during the calendar year or the required minimum distribution. However, under the terms of Trust P, and applicable state law, only the portion of the Plan X distribution received by the trustee equal to the income earned by A's account in Plan X is required to be distributed to B (along with any other trust income.)

(iii) Because some amounts distributed from A's account in Plan X to Trust P may be accumulated in Trust P during B's lifetime for the benefit of A's children, as remaindermen beneficiaries of Trust P, even though access to those amounts are delayed until after B's death, A's children are beneficiaries of A's account in Plan X in addition to B and B is not the sole beneficiary of A's account. Thus the designated beneficiary used to determine the distribution period from A's account in Plan X is the beneficiary with the shortest life expectancy. B's life expectancy is the shortest of all the potential beneficiaries of the testamentary trust's interest in A's account in Plan X (including remainder beneficiaries). Thus, the distribution period for purposes of section 401(a)(9)(B)(iii) is B's life expectancy. Because B is not the sole beneficiary of the testamentary trust's interest in A's account in Plan X, the special rule in 401(a)(9)(B)(iv) is not available and the annual required minimum distributions from the account to Trust M must begin no later than the end of the calendar year immediately following the calendar year of A's death.

Example 3. (i) The facts are the same as *Example 2* except that the testamentary trust instrument provides that all amounts distributed from A's account in Plan X to the trustee while B is alive will be paid directly to B upon receipt by the trustee of Trust P.

(ii) In this case, B is the sole beneficiary of A's account in Plan X for purposes of determining the designated beneficiary under section

401(a)(9)(B)(iii) and (iv). No amounts distributed from A's account in Plan X to Trust P are accumulated in Trust P during B's lifetime for the benefit of any other beneficiary. Because B is the sole beneficiary of the testamentary trust's interest in A's account in Plan X, the annual required minimum distributions from A's account to Trust P must begin no later than the end of the calendar year in which A would have attained age 70 ½. rather than the calendar year immediately following the calendar year of A's death.

(d) *Designations by beneficiaries.* (1) If the plan provides (or allows the employee to specify) that, after the end of the calendar year following the calendar year in which the employee died, any person or persons have the discretion to change the beneficiaries of the employee, then, for purposes of determining the distribution period after the employee's death, the employee will be treated as not having designated a beneficiary. However, such discretion will not be found to exist merely because a beneficiary may designate a subsequent beneficiary for distributions of any portion of the employee's benefit after the beneficiary dies.

(2) This paragraph (d) is illustrated by the following example:

Example. The facts are the same as in *Example 1* in paragraph (c)(3) of this A-7, except that, as permitted under the plan, D designates E as the beneficiary of any amount remaining after the death of D rather than C making this designation. E is still disregarded in determining C's designated beneficiary for purposes of section 401(a)(9).

Q-8. If a portion of an employee's individual account is not vested as of the employee's required beginning date, how is the determination of the required minimum distribution affected?

A-8. If the employee's benefit is in the form of an individual account, the benefit used to determine the required minimum distribution for any distribution calendar year will be determined in accordance with A-1 of this section without regard to whether or not all of the employee's benefit is vested. If any portion of the employee's benefit is not vested, distributions will be treated as being paid from the vested portion of the benefit first. If, as of the end of a distribution calendar year (or as of the employee's required beginning date, in the case of the employee's first distribution calendar year), the total amount of the employee's vested benefit is less than the required minimum distribution for the calendar year, only the vested portion, if any, of the employee's benefit is required to be distributed by the end of the calendar year (or, if applicable, by the employee's required beginning date). However, the required minimum distribution for the subsequent distribution calendar year must be increased by the sum of amounts not distributed in prior calendar years because the employee's vested benefit was less than the required minimum distribution (subject to the limitation that the required minimum distribution for that subsequent distribution calendar year will not exceed the vested portion of the employee's benefit). In such case, an adjustment for the additional amount distributed which corresponds to the adjustment described in A-3(c)(2) of this section will be made to the account used to determine the required minimum distribution for that calendar year.

§ *1.401(a)(9)-6 Required minimum distributions as annuity payments.*

Q-1. How must annuity distributions under a defined benefit plan be paid in order to satisfy section 401(a)(9)?

A-1. (a) In order to satisfy section 401(a)(9), annuity distributions under a defined benefit plan must be paid in periodic payments made at intervals not longer than one year (payment intervals) for a life (or lives), or over a period certain not longer than a life expectancy (or joint life and last survivor expectancy) described in section 401(a)(9)(A)(ii) or section 401(a)(9)(B)(iii), whichever is applicable. The life expectancy (or joint life and last survivor expectancy) for purposes of determining the length of the period certain will be determined in accordance with A-3 of this section. Once payments have commenced over a period certain, the period certain may not be lengthened even if the period certain is shorter than the maximum permitted. Life annuity payments must satisfy the minimum distribution incidental benefit requirements of A-2 of this section. All annuity payments (life and period certain) also must either be nonincreasing or increase only as follows:

(1) With any percentage increase in a specified and generally recognized cost-of-living index;

(2) To the extent of the reduction in the amount of the employee's payments to provide for a survivor benefit upon death, but only if the beneficiary whose life was being used to determine the period described in section 401(a)(9)(A)(ii) over which payments were being made dies or is no longer the employee's beneficiary pursuant to a qualified domestic relations order within the meaning of section 414(p);

(3) To provide cash refunds of employee contributions upon the employee's death; or

(4) Because of an increase in benefits under the plan.

(b) The annuity may be a life annuity (or joint and survivor annuity) with a period certain if the life (or lives, if applicable) and period certain each meet the requirements of paragraph (a) of this A-1. For purposes of this section, if distribution is permitted to be made over the lives of the employee and the designated beneficiary, references to life annuity include a joint and survivor annuity.

(c) Distributions under a variable annuity will not be found to be increasing merely because the amount of the payments varies with the investment performance of the underlying assets. However, the Commissioner may prescribe additional requirements applicable to such variable life annuities in revenue rulings, notices, and other guidance published in the Internal Revenue Bulletin. See § 601.601 (d) (2) (ii) (b) of this chapter.

(d) (1) Except as provided in (d) (2) of this A-1, annuity payments must commence on or before the employee's required beginning date (within the meaning of A-2 of § 1.401(a) (9)-2). The first payment which must be made on or before the employee's required beginning date must be the payment which is required for one payment interval. The second payment need not be made until the end of the next payment interval even if that payment interval ends in the next calendar year. Similarly, in the case of distributions commencing after death in accordance with section 401(a) (9) (B) (iii) and (iv), the first payment that must be made on or before the date determined under A-3(a) or (b) (whichever is applicable) of § 1.401 (a) (9)-3 must be the payment which is required for one payment interval. Payment intervals are the periods for which payments are received, e.g., bimonthly, monthly, semi-annually, or annually. All benefit accruals as of the last day of the first distribution calendar year must be included in the calculation of the amount of the life annuity payments for payment intervals ending on or after the employee's required beginning date.

(2) In the case of an annuity contract purchased after the required beginning date, the first payment interval must begin on or before the purchase date and the payment required for one payment interval must be made no later than the end of such payment interval.

(3) This paragraph (d) is illustrated by the following example:

Example. A defined benefit plan (Plan X) provides monthly annuity payments of $500 for the life of unmarried participants with a 10-year period certain. An unmarried participant (A) in Plan X attains age 70 ½ in 2001. In order to meet the requirements of this paragraph, the first payment which must be made on behalf of A on or before April 1, 2002, will be $500 and the payments must continue to be made in monthly payments of $500 thereafter for the life and 10-year certain period.

(e) If distributions from a defined benefit plan are not in the form of an annuity, the employee's benefit will be treated as an individual account for purposes of determining the required minimum distribution. See § 1.401 (a) (9)-5.

Q-2. How must distributions in the form of a life (or joint and survivor) annuity be made in order to satisfy the minimum distribution incidental benefit (MDIB) requirement of section 401(a) (9) (G)?

A-2. (a) *Life annuity for employee.* If the employee's benefit is payable in the form of a life annuity for the life of the employee satisfying section 401(a) (9), the MDIB requirement of section 401(a) (9) (G) will be satisfied.

(b) *Joint and survivor annuity, spouse beneficiary.* If the employee's sole beneficiary, as of the annuity starting date for annuity payments, is the employee's spouse and the distributions satisfy section 401(a) (9) without regard to the MDIB requirement, the distributions to the employee will be deemed to satisfy the MDIB requirement of section 401(a) (9) (G). For example, if an employee's benefit is being distributed in the form of a joint and survivor annuity for the lives of the employee and the employee's spouse and the spouse is the sole beneficiary of the employee, the amount of the periodic payment payable to the spouse may always be 100 percent of the annuity payment payable to the employee regardless of the difference in the ages between the employee and the employee's spouse. However, the amount of the payments under the annuity must be nonincreasing unless specifically permitted under A-1 of this section.

(c) *Joint and survivor annuity, nonspouse beneficiary*—(1) *Explanation of rule.* If distributions commence under a distribution option that is in the form of a joint and survivor annuity for the joint lives of the employee and a beneficiary other than the employee's spouse, the MDIB requirement will not be satisfied as of the date distributions commence unless the distribution option provides that annuity payments to be made to the employee on and after the employee's required beginning date will satisfy the conditions of this paragraph. The periodic annuity payment payable to the survivor must not at any time on and after the employee's required beginning date exceed the applicable percentage of the annuity payment payable to the employee using the table below. Thus, this requirement must be satisfied with respect to any benefit increase after such date, including increases to reflect increases in the cost of living. The applicable percentage is based on the excess of the age of the employee over the age of the beneficiary as of their attained ages as of their birthdays in a calendar year. If the employee has more than one beneficiary, the applicable percentage will be the percentage using the age of the youngest beneficiary. Additionally, the amount of the annuity payments must satisfy A-1 of this section.

(2) *Table.*

Excess of age of employee over age of beneficiary	Applicable percentage
10 years or less	100%
11	96%
12	93%
13	90%
14	87%
15	84%
16	82%
17	79%
18	77%
19	75%
20	73%
21	72%
22	70%
23	68%
24	67%
25	66%
26	64%
27	63%
28	62%
29	61%
30	60%
31	59%
32	59%
33	58%
34	57%
35	56%
36	56%
37	55%
38	55%

Excess of age of employee over age of beneficiary	Applicable percentage
39	54%
40	54%
41	53%
42	53%
43	53%
44 and greater	52%

(3) *Example.* This paragraph (c) is illustrated by the following example:

Example. Distributions commence on January 1, 2001 to an employee (Z), born March 1, 1935, after retirement at age 65. Z's daughter (Y), born February 5, 1965, is Z's beneficiary. The distributions are in the form of a joint and survivor annuity for the lives of Z and Y with payments of $500 a month to Z and upon Z's death of $500 a month to Y, i.e., the projected monthly payment to Y is 100 percent of the monthly amount payable to Z. There is no provision under the option for a change in the projected payments to Y as of April 1, 2006, Z's required beginning date. Consequently, as of January 1, 2001, the date annuity distributions commence, the plan does not satisfy the MDIB requirement in operation because, as of such date, the distribution option provides that, as of Z's required beginning date, the monthly payment to Y upon Z's death will exceed 60 percent of Z's monthly payment (the maximum percentage for a difference of ages of 30 years).

(d) *Period certain and annuity features.* If a distribution form includes a life annuity and a period certain, the amount of the annuity payments payable to the employee must satisfy paragraph (c) of this A-2, and the period certain may not exceed the period determined under A-3 of this section.

Q-3. How long is a period certain under an annuity contract permitted to extend?

A-3. (a) *Distributions commencing during the employee's life* — (1) *Spouse beneficiary.* If an employee's spouse is the employee's sole beneficiary as of the annuity starting date, the period certain for annuity distributions commencing during the life of an employee with an annuity starting date on or after the employee's required beginning date is not permitted to exceed the joint life and last survivor expectancy of the employee and the spouse using the age of the employee and spouse as of their birthdays in the calendar year that contains the annuity starting date.

(2) *Nonspouse beneficiary.* If an employee's surviving spouse is not the employee's sole beneficiary as of the annuity starting date, the period certain for any annuity distributions during the life of the employee with an annuity starting date on or after the employee's required beginning date is not permitted to exceed the shorter of the applicable distribution period for the employee (determined in accordance with the table in A-4(a)(2) of § 1.401(a)(9)-5) for the calendar year that contains on the annuity starting date or the joint life and last survivor expectancy of the employee and the employee's designated beneficiary, determined using the designated beneficiary as of the annuity starting date and using their ages as of their birthdays in the calendar year that the contains the annuity starting date. See A-10 for the rule for annuity payments with an annuity starting date before the required beginning date.

(b) *Life expectancy rule.* (1) If annuity distributions commence after the death of the employee under the life expectancy rule (under section 401(a)(9)(iii) or (iv)), the period certain for any distributions commencing after death cannot exceed the applicable distribution period determined under A-5(b) of § 1.401(a)(9)-5 for the distribution calendar year that contains the annuity starting date.

(2) If the annuity starting date is in a calendar year before the first distribution calendar year, the period certain may not exceed the life expectancy of the designated beneficiary using the beneficiary's age in the year that contains the annuity starting date.

Q-4. May distributions be made from an annuity contract which is purchased from an insurance company?

A-4. Yes. Distributions may be made from an annuity contract which is purchased with the employee's benefit by the plan from an insurance company and which makes payments that satisfy the provisions of this section. In the case of an annuity contract purchased from an insurance company, there is also an exception to the nonincreasing requirement in A-1(a) of this section for an increase to provide a cash refund upon the employee's death equal to the excess of the amount of the premiums paid for the contract over the prior distributions under the contract. If the payments actually made under the annuity contract do not

meet the requirements of section 401(a)(9), the plan fails to satisfy section 401(a)(9).

Q-5. In the case of annuity distributions under a defined benefit plan, how must additional benefits which accrue after the employee's required beginning date be distributed in order to satisfy section 401(a)(9)?

A.-5. (a) In the case of annuity distributions under a defined benefit plan, if any additional benefits accrue after the employee's required beginning date, distribution of such amount as a separate identifiable component must commence in accordance with A-1 of this section beginning with the first payment interval ending in the calendar year immediately following the calendar year in which such amount accrues.

(b) A plan will not fail to satisfy section 401(a)(9) merely because there is an administrative delay in the commencement of the distribution of the separate identifiable component, provided that the actual payment of such amount commences as soon as practicable but not later than by the end of the first calendar year following the calendar year in which the additional benefit accrues, and that the total amount paid during such first calendar year is not less than the total amount that was required to be paid during that year under A-5(a) of this section.

Q-6. If a portion of an employee's benefit is not vested as of the employee's required beginning date, how is the determination of the required minimum distribution affected?

A-6 In the case of annuity distributions from a defined benefit plan, if any portion of the employee's benefit is not vested as of December 31 of a distribution calendar year (or as of the employee's required beginning date in the case of the employee's first distribution calendar year), the portion which is not vested as of such date will be treated as not having accrued for purposes of determining the required minimum distribution for that distribution calendar year. When an additional portion of the employee's benefit becomes vested, such portion will be treated as an additional accrual. See A-5 of this section for the rules for distributing benefits which accrue under a defined benefit plan after the employee's required beginning date.

Q-7. If an employee retires after the calendar year in which the employee attains age 70 ½, for what period must the employee's accrued benefit under a defined benefit plan be actuarially increased?

A-7. (a) *Actuarial increase starting date.* If an employee (other than a 5-percent owner) retires after the calendar year in which in the employee attains age 70 ½, in order to satisfy section 401(a)(9)(C)(iii), the employee's accrued benefit under a defined benefit plan must be actuarially increased to take into account any period after age 70 ½ in which the employee was not receiving any benefits under the plan. The actuarial increase required to satisfy section 401(a)(9)(C)(iii) must be provided for the period starting on the April 1 following the calendar year in which the employee attains age 70 ½.

(b) *Actuarial increase ending date.* The period for which the actuarial increase must be provided ends on the date on which benefits commence after retirement in an amount sufficient to satisfy section 401(a)(9).

(c) *Nonapplication to plan providing same required beginning date for all employees.* If as permitted under A-2(e) of § 1.401(a)(9)-2, a plan provides that the required beginning date for purposes of section 401(a)(9) for all employees is April 1 of the calendar year following the calendar year in which the employee attained age 70 ½ (regardless of whether the employee is a 5-percent owner) and the plan makes distributions in an amount sufficient to satisfy section 401(a)(9) using that required beginning date, no actuarial increase is required under section 401(a)(9)(C)(iii).

(d) *Nonapplication to defined contribution plans.* The actuarial increase required under this A-7 does not apply to defined contribution plans.

(e) *Nonapplication to governmental and church plans.* The actuarial increase required under this A-7 does not apply to a governmental plan (within the meaning of section 414(d)) or a church plan. For purposes of this paragraph, the term *church plan* means a plan maintained by a church for church employees, and the term *church* means any church (as defined in section 3121(w)(3)(A)) or qualified church-controlled organization (as defined in section 3121(w)(3)(B)).

Q-8. What amount of actuarial increase is required under section 401(a)(9)(C)(iii)?

A-8. In order to satisfy section 401(a)(9)(C)(iii), the retirement benefits payable with respect to an employee as of the end of the period for actuarial increases (described in A-7 of this section) must be no less than: the actuarial equivalent of the employee's retirement benefits that would have been payable as of the date the actuarial increase must commence under A-7(a) of this section if benefits had commenced on that date; plus the actuarial equivalent of any additional benefits accrued after that date; reduced by the actuarial equivalent of any distributions made with respect to the employee's retirement benefits after that date. Actuarial equivalence is determined using the plan's assumptions for determining actuarial equivalence for purposes of satisfying section 411.

Q-9. How does the actuarial increase required under section 401(a)(9)(C)(iii) relate to the actuarial increase required under section 411?

A-9. In order for any of an employee's accrued benefit to be nonforfeitable as required under section 411, a defined benefit plan must make an actuarial adjustment to an accrued benefit the payment of which is deferred past normal retirement age. The only exception to this rule is that generally no actuarial adjustment is required to reflect the period during which a benefit is suspended as permitted under section 203(a)(3)(B) of the Employee Retirement Income Security Act of 1974 (ERISA). The actuarial increase required under section 401(a)(9) for the period described in A-7 of this section is generally the same as, and not in addition to, the actuarial increase required for the same period under section 411 to reflect any delay in the payment of retirement benefits after normal retirement age. However, unlike the actuarial increase required under section 411, the actuarial increase required under section 401(a)(9)(C) must be provided even during the period during which an employee's benefit has been suspended in accordance with ERISA section 203(a)(3)(B).

Q-10 What rule applies if distributions commence to an employee on a date before the employee's required beginning date over a period permitted under section 401(a)(9)(A)(ii) and the distribution form is an annuity under which distributions are made in accordance with the provisions of A-1 (and if applicable A-4) of this section?

A-10. (a) *General rule.* If distributions irrevocably (except for acceleration) commence to an employee on a date before the employee's required beginning date over a period permitted under section 401(a)(9)(A)(ii) and the distribution form is an annuity under which distributions are made in accordance with the provisions of A-1 (and, if applicable, A-4) of this section, the annuity starting date will be treated as the required beginning date for purposes of applying the rules of this section and §1.401(a)(9)-3. Thus, for example, the designated beneficiary distributions will be determined as of the annuity starting date. Similarly, if the employee dies after the annuity starting date but before the annuity starting date determined under A-2 of §1.401(a)(9)-2, after the employee's death, the remaining portion of the employee's interest must continue to be distributed in accordance with this section over the remaining period over which distributions commenced (single or joint lives and, if applicable, period certain). The rules in §1.401(a)(9)-3 and section 401(a)(9)(B)(ii) or (iii) and (iv) do not apply.

(b) *Period certain.* If as of the employee's birthday in the year that contains the annuity starting date, the age of the employee is under 70, the following rule applies in applying the rule in paragraph (a)(2) of A-3 of this section. The applicable distribution period for the employee (determined in accordance with the table in A-4(a)(2) of §1.401(a)(9)-5) is 26.2 plus the difference between 70 and the age of the employee as of the employee's birthday in the year that contains the annuity starting date.

Q-11. What rule applies if distributions commence irrevocably (except for acceleration) to the surviving spouse of an employee over a period permitted under section 401(a)(9)(B)(iii)(II) before the date on which distributions are required to commence and the distribution form is an annuity under which distributions are made as of the date distributions commence in accordance with the provisions of A-1 (and if applicable A-4) of this section,

A-11. If distributions commence irrevocably (except for acceleration) to the surviving spouse of an employee over a period permitted under section 401(a)(9)(B)(iii)(II) before the date on which distributions are required to commence and the distribution form is an annuity under which distributions are made as of the date distributions commence in

accordance with the provisions of A-1 (and if applicable A-4) of this section, distributions will be considered to have begun on the actual commencement date for purposes of section 401(a)(9)(B)(iv)(II). Consequently, in such case, A-5 of §1.401(a)(9)-3 and section 401(a)(9)(B)(ii) and (iii) will not apply upon the death of the surviving spouse as though the surviving spouse were the employee. Instead, the annuity distributions must continue to be made, in accordance with the provisions of A-1 (and if applicable A-4) of this section over the remaining period over which distributions commenced (single life and, if applicable, period certain).

§1.401(a)(9)-7 Rollovers and Transfers.

Q-1. If an amount is distributed by one plan (distributing plan) and is rolled over to another plan, is the benefit or the required minimum distribution under the distributing plan affected by the rollover?

A-1. No. If an amount is distributed by one plan and is rolled over to another plan, the amount distributed is still treated as a distribution by the distributing plan for purposes of section 401(a)(9), notwithstanding the rollover.

Q-2. Q. If an amount is distributed by one plan (distributing plan) and is rolled over to another plan (receiving plan), how are the benefit and the required minimum distribution under the receiving plan affected?

A-2. If an amount is distributed by one plan (distributing plan) and is rolled over to another plan (receiving plan), the benefit of the employee under the receiving plan is increased by the amount rolled over. However, the distribution has no impact on the required minimum distribution to be made by the receiving plan for the calendar year in which the rollover is received. But, if a required minimum distribution is required to be made by the receiving plan for the following calendar year, the rollover amount must be considered to be part of the employee's benefit under the receiving plan. Consequently, for purposes of determining any required minimum distribution for the calendar year immediately following the calendar year in which the amount rolled over is received by the receiving plan, in the case in which the amount rolled over is received after the last valuation date in the calendar year under the receiving plan, the benefit of the employee as of such valuation date, adjusted in accordance with A-3 of §1.401(a)(9)-5, will be increased by the rollover amount valued as of the date of receipt. For purposes of calculating the benefit under the receiving plan pursuant to the preceding sentence, if the amount rolled over is received by the receiving plan in a different calendar year from the calendar year in which it is distributed by the distributing plan, the amount rolled over is deemed to have been received by the receiving plan in the calendar year in which it was distributed by the distributing plan.

Q-3. In the case of a transfer of an amount of an employee's benefit from one plan (transferor plan) to another plan (transferee plan), are there any special rules for satisfying the required minimum distribution requirement or determining the employee's benefit under the transferor plan?

A-3. (a) In the case of a transfer of an amount of an employee's benefit from one plan to another, the transfer is not treated as a distribution by the transferor plan for purposes of section 401(a)(9). Instead, the benefit of the employee under the transferor plan is decreased by the amount transferred. However, if any portion of an employee's benefit is transferred in a distribution calendar year with respect to that employee, in order to satisfy section 401(a)(9), the transferor plan must determine the amount of the required minimum distribution with respect to that employee for the calendar year of the transfer using the employee's benefit under the transferor plan before the transfer. Additionally, if any portion of an employee's benefit is transferred in the employee's second distribution calendar year but on or before the employee's required beginning date, in order to satisfy section 401(a)(9), the transferor plan must determine the amount of the required minimum distribution requirement for the employee's first distribution calendar year based on the employee's benefit under the transferor plan before the transfer. The transferor plan may satisfy the required minimum distribution requirement for the calendar year of the transfer (and the prior year if applicable) by segregating the amount which must be distributed from the employee's benefit and not transferring that amount. Such amount may be retained by the transferor plan and distributed on or before the date required.

(b) For purposes of determining any required minimum distribution for the calendar year immediately following the calendar year in which the transfer occurs, in the case of a transfer after the last valuation date for the calendar year of the transfer under the transferor plan, the benefit of the employee as of such valuation date, adjusted in accordance with A-3 of §1.401(a)(9)-5, will be decreased by the amount transferred, valued as of the date of the transfer.

Q-4. If an amount of an employee's benefit is transferred from one plan (transferor plan) to another plan (transferee plan), how are the benefit and the required minimum distribution under the transferee plan affected?

A-4. In the case of a transfer from one plan (transferor plan) to another (transferee plan), the general rule is that the benefit of the employee under the transferee plan is increased by the amount transferred. The transfer has no impact on the required minimum distribution to be made by the transferee plan in the calendar year in which the transfer is received. However, if a required minimum distribution is required from the transferee plan for the following calendar year, the transferred amount must be considered to be part of the employee's benefit under the transferee plan. Consequently, for purposes of determining any required minimum distribution for the calendar year immediately following the calendar year in which the transfer occurs, in the case of a transfer after the last valuation date of the transferee plan in the transfer calendar year, the benefit of the employee under the receiving plan valued as of such valuation date, adjusted in accordance with A-3 of § 1.401(a)(9)-5, will be increased by the amount transferred valued as of the date of the transfer.

Q-5. How are a spinoff, merger or consolidation (as defined in § 1.414(l)-1) treated for purposes of determining an employee's benefit and required minimum distribution under section 401(a)(9)?

A-5. For purposes of determining an employee's benefit and required minimum distribution under section 401(a)(9), a spinoff, a merger, or a consolidation (as defined in § 1.414(l)-1) will be treated as a transfer of the benefits of the employees involved. Consequently, the benefit and required minimum distribution of each employee involved under the transferor and transferee plans will be determined in accordance with A-3 and A-4 of this section.

§ 1.401(a)(9)-8 Special rules.

Q-1. What distribution rules apply if an employee is a participant in more than one plan?

A-1. If an employee is a participant in more than one plan, the plans in which the employee participates are not permitted to be aggregated for purposes of testing whether the distribution requirements of section 401(a)(9) are met. The distribution of the benefit of the employee under each plan must separately meet the requirements of section 401(a)(9). For this purpose, a plan described in section 414(k) is treated as two separate plans, a defined contribution plan to the extent benefits are based on an individual account and a defined benefit plan with respect to the remaining benefits.

Q-2. If an employee's benefit under a plan is divided into separate accounts (or segregated shares in the case of a defined benefit plan), do the distribution rules in section 401(a)(9) and these regulations apply separately to each separate account (or segregated share)?

A-2. (a) Except as otherwise provided in paragraphs (b) and (c) of this A-2, if an employee's account under a defined contribution plan is divided into separate accounts (or if an employee's benefit under a defined benefit plan is divided into segregated shares in the case of a defined benefit plan) under the plan, the separate accounts (or segregated shares) will be aggregated for purposes of satisfying the rules in section 401(a)(9). Thus, except as otherwise provided in paragraphs (b) and (c) of this A-2, all separate accounts, including a separate account for nondeductible employee contributions (under section 72(d)(2)) or for qualified voluntary employee contributions (as defined in section 219(e)), will be aggregated for purposes of section 401(a)(9).

(b) If, for lifetime distributions, as of an employee's required beginning date (or the beginning of any distribution calendar year beginning after the employee's required beginning date), or in the case of distributions under section 401(a)(9)(B)(ii) or (iii) and (iv), as of the end of the year following the year containing the employee's (or spouse's, where applicable) date of death, the beneficiaries with respect to a separate account (or segregated share in the case of a defined benefit plan) under the plan differ from the beneficiaries with respect to the other separate accounts (or segregate shares) of the employee under the plan, such separate account (or segregated share) under the plan need not be aggregated with other separate accounts (or segregated shares) under the plan in order to determine whether the distributions from such separate account (or segregated share) under the plan satisfy section 401(a)(9). Instead, the rules in section 401(a)(9) may separately apply to such separate account (or segregated share) under the plan. For example, if, in the case of a distribution described in section 401(a)(9)(B)(iii) and (iv), the only beneficiary of a separate account (or segregated share) under the plan is the employee's surviving spouse, and beneficiaries other than the surviving spouse are designated with respect to the other separate accounts of the em-

ployee, distribution of the spouse's separate account (or segregated share) under the plan need not commence until the date determined under the first sentence in A-3(b) of § 1.401(a)(9)-3, even if distribution of the other separate accounts (or segregated shares) under the plan must commence at an earlier date. In the case of a distribution after the death of an employee to which section 401(a)(9)(B)(i) does not apply, distribution from a separate account (or segregated share) of an employee may be made over a beneficiary's life expectancy in accordance with section 401(a)(9)(B)(iii) and (iv) even through distributions from other separate accounts (or segregated shares) under the plan with different beneficiaries are being made in accordance with the five-year rule in section 401(a)(9)(B)(ii).

(c) A portion of an employee's account balance under a defined contribution plan is permitted to be used to purchase an annuity contract with a remaining amount maintained in the separate account. In that case, the separate account under the plan must be distributed in accordance with § 1.401(a)(9)-5 in order to satisfy section 401(a)(9) and the annuity payments under the annuity contract must satisfy § 1.401(a)(9)-6 in order to satisfy section 401(a)(9).

Q-3. What is a separate account or segregated share for purposes of section 401(a)(9)?

A-3. (a) For purposes of section 401(a)(9), a separate account in an individual account is a portion of an employee's benefit determined by an acceptable separate accounting including allocating investment gains and losses, and contributions and forfeitures, on a pro rata basis in a reasonable and consistent matter between such portion and any other benefits. Further, the amounts of each such portion of the benefit will be separately determined for purposes of determining the amount of the required minimum distribution in accordance with § 1.401(a)(9)-5.

(b) A benefit in a defined benefit plan is separated into segregated shares if it consists of separate identifiable components which may be separately distributed.

Q-4. Must a distribution that is required by section 401(a)(9) to be made by the required beginning date to an employee or that is required by section 401(a)(9)(B)(iii) and (iv) to be made by the required time to a designated beneficiary who is a surviving spouse be made notwithstanding the failure of the employee, or spouse where applicable, to consent to a distribution while a benefit is immediately distributable?

A-4. Yes. Section 411(a)(11) and section 417(e) (see §§ 1.411(a)(11)-1(c)(2) and 1.417(e)-1(c)) require employee and spousal consent to certain distributions of plan benefits while such benefits are immediately distributable. If an employee's normal retirement age is later than the required beginning date for the commencement of distributions under section 401(a)(9) and, therefore, benefits are still immediately distributable, the plan must, nevertheless, distribute plan benefits to the participant (or where applicable, to the spouse) in a manner that satisfies the requirements of section 401(a)(9). Section 401(a)(9) must be satisfied even though the participant (or spouse, where applicable) fails to consent to the distribution. In such a case, the plan may distribute in the form of a qualified joint and survivor annuity (QJSA) or in the form of a qualified preretirement survivor annuity (QPSA) and the consent requirements of sections 411(a)(11) and 417(e) are deemed to be satisfied if the plan has made reasonable efforts to obtain consent from the participant (or spouse if applicable) and if the distribution otherwise meets the requirements of section 417. If, because of section 401(a)(11)(B), the plan is not required to distribute in the form of a QJSA to a participant or a QPSA to a surviving spouse, the plan may distribute the required minimum distribution amount required at the time required to satisfy section 401(a)(9) and the consent requirements of sections 411(a)(11) and 417(e) are deemed to be satisfied if the plan has made reasonable efforts to obtain consent from the participant (or spouse if applicable) and if the distribution otherwise meets the requirements of section 417.

Q-5. Who is an employee's spouse or surviving spouse for purposes of section 401(a)(9)?

A-5. Except as otherwise provided in A-6(a) (in the case of distributions of a portion of an employee's benefit payable to a former spouse of an employee pursuant to a qualified domestic relations order), for purposes of section 401(a)(9), an individual is a spouse or surviving spouse of an employee if such individual is treated as the employee's spouse under applicable state law. In the case of distributions after the death of an employee, for purposes of determining whether, under the life expectancy rule in section 401(a)(9)(B)(iii) and (iv), the provisions of section 401(a)(9)(B)(iv) apply, the spouse of the employee is determined as of the date of death of the employee.

Q-6. In order to satisfy section 401(a)(9), are there any special rules which apply to the distribution of all or a portion of an employee's benefit payable to an alternate payee pursuant to a qualified domestic relations order as defined in section 414(p) (QDRO)?

A-6. (a) A former spouse to whom all or a portion of the employee's benefit is payable pursuant to a QDRO will be treated as a spouse (including a surviving spouse) of the employee for purposes of section 401(a)(9), including the minimum distribution incidental benefit requirement, regardless of whether the QDRO specifically provides that the former spouse is treated as the spouse for purposes of sections 401(a)(11) and 417.

(b)(1) If a QDRO provides that an employee's benefit is to be divided and a portion is to be allocated to an alternate payee, such portion will be treated as a separate account (or segregated share) which separately must satisfy the requirements of section 401(a)(9) and may not be aggregated with other separate accounts (or segregated shares) of the employee for purposes of satisfying section 401(a)(9). Except as otherwise provided in paragraph(b)(2) of this A-6, distribution of such separate account allocated to an alternate payee pursuant to a QDRO must be made in accordance with section 401(a)(9). For example, in general, distribution of such account will satisfy section 401(a)(9)(A) if required minimum distributions from such account during the employee's lifetime begin not later than the employee's required beginning date and the required minimum distribution is determined in accordance with § 1.401(a)(9)-5 for each distribution calendar year using an applicable distribution period determined under A-4 of § 1.401(a)(9)-5 using the age of the employee in the distribution calendar year for purposes of using the table in A-4(a)(2) of § 1.401(a)(9)-5 if applicable or ages of the employee and spousal alternate payee if their joint life expectancy is longer than the distribution period using that table. The determination of whether distribution from such account after the death of the employee to the alternate payee will be made in accordance with section 401(a)(9)(B)(i) or section 401(a)(9)(B)(ii) or (iii) and (iv) will depend on whether distributions have begun as determined under A-5 or § 1.401(a)(9)-2 (which provides, in general, that distributions are not treated as having begun until the employee's required beginning date even though payments may actually have begun before that date). For example, if the alternate payee dies before the employee and distribution of the separate account allocated to the alternate payee pursuant to the QDRO is to be made to the alternate payee's beneficiary, such beneficiary may be treated as a designated beneficiary for purposes of determining the required minimum distribution required from such account after the death of the employee if the beneficiary of the alternate payee is an individual and if such beneficiary is a beneficiary under the plan or specified to or in the plan. Specification in or pursuant to the QDRO will also be treated as specification to the plan.

(2) Distribution of the separate account allocated to an alternate payee pursuant to a QDRO satisfy the requirements of section 401(a)(9)(A)(ii) if such account is to be distributed, beginning not later than the employee's required beginning date, over the life of the alternate payee (or over a period not extending beyond the life expectancy of the alternative payee). Also, if the plan permits the employee to elect whether distribution upon the death of the employee will be made in accordance with the five-year rule in section 401(a)(9)(B)(ii) or the life expectancy rule in section 401(a)(9)(B)(iii) and (iv) pursuant to A-4(c) of § 1.401(a)(9)-3, such election is to be made only by the alternate payee for purposes of distributing the separate account allocated to the alternate payee pursuant to the QDRO. If the alternate payee dies after distribution of the separate account allocated to the alternate payee pursuant to a QDRO has begun (determined under A-5 of § 1.401(a)(9)-2) but before the employee dies, distribution of the remaining portion of that portion of the benefit allocated to the alternate payee must be made in accordance with the rules in § 1.401(a)(9)-5 or § 1.401(a)(9)-6 for distributions during the life of the employee. Only after the death of the employee is the amount of the required minimum distribution determined in accordance with the rules that apply after the death of the employee.

(c) If a QDRO does not provide that an employee's benefit is to be divided but provides that a portion of an employee's benefit (otherwise payable to the employee) is to be paid to an alternate payee, such portion will not be treated as a separate account (or segregated share) of the employee. Instead, such portion will be aggregated with any amount distributed to the employee and will be treated as having been distributed to the employee for purposes of determining whether the required minimum distribution requirement has been satisfied with respect to that employee.

Q-7. Will a plan fail to satisfy section 401(a)(9) where it is not legally permitted to distribute to an alternate payee all or a portion of an employee's benefit payable to an alternate payee pursuant to a QDRO within the period specified in section 414(p)(7)?

A-7. A plan will not fail to satisfy section 401(a)(9) merely because it fails to distribute a required amount during the period in which the issue of whether a domestic relations order is a QDRO is being determined pursuant to section 414(p)(7), provided that the period does not extend beyond the 18-month period described in section 414(p)(7)(E). To the extent that a distribution otherwise required under section 401(a)(9) is not made during this period, this amount and any additional amount accrued during this period will be treated as though it is not vested during the period and any distributions with respect to such amounts must be made under the relevant rules for nonvested benefits described in either A-8 of § 1.401(a)(9)-5 or A-6 of § 1.401(a)(9)-6.

Q-8. Will a plan fail to satisfy section 401(a)(9) where an individual's distribution from the plan is less than the amount otherwise required to satisfy section 401(a)(9) under § 1.401(a)(9)-5 or § 1.401(a)(9)-6 because distributions were being paid under an annuity contract issued by a life insurance company in state insurer delinquency proceedings and have been reduced or suspended by reasons of such state proceedings?

A-8. A plan will not fail to satisfy section 401(a)(9) merely because an individual's distribution from the plan is less than the amount otherwise required to satisfy section 401(a)(9) under § 1.401(a)(9)-5 or § 1.401(a)(9)-6 because distributions were being paid under an annuity contract issued by a life insurance company in state insurer delinquency proceedings and have been reduced or suspended by reasons of such state proceedings. To the extent that a distribution otherwise required under section 401(a)(9) is not made during the state insurer delinquency proceedings, this amount and any additional amount accrued during this period will be treated as though it is not vested during the period and any distributions with respect to such amounts must be made under the relevant rules for nonvested benefits described in either A-8 of § 1.401(a)(9)-5 or A-6 of § 1.401(a)(9)-6.

Q-9. Will a plan fail to qualify as a pension plan within the meaning of section 401(a) solely because the plan permits distributions to commence to an employee on or after April 1 of the calendar year following the calendar year in which the employee attains age 70 ½ even though the employee has not retired or attained the normal retirement age under the plan as of the date on which such distributions commence?

A-9. No. A plan will not fail to qualify as a pension plan within the meaning of section 401(a) solely because the plan permits distributions to commence to an employee on or after April 1 of the calendar year following the calendar year in which the employee attains age 70 ½ even though the employee has not retired or attained the normal retirement age under the plan as of the date on which such distributions commence. This rule applies without regard to whether or not the employee is a 5-percent owner with respect to the plan year ending in the calendar year in which distributions commence.

Q-10. Is the distribution of an annuity contract a distribution for purposes of section 401(a)(9)?

A-10. No. The distribution of an annuity contract is not a distribution for purposes of section 401(a)(9).

Q-11. Will a payment by a plan after the death of an employee fail to be treated as a distribution for purposes of section 401(a)(9) solely because it is made to an estate or a trust?

A-11. A payment by a plan after the death of an employee will not fail to be treated as a distribution for purposes of section 401(a)(9) solely because it is made to an estate or a trust. As a result, the estate or trust which receives a payment from a plan after the death of an employee need not distribute the amount of such payment to the beneficiaries of the estate or trust in accordance with section 401(a)(9)(B). However, pursuant to A-3 of § 1.401(a)(9)-4, distribution to the estate must satisfy the five-year rule in section 401(a)(9)(B)(iii) if the distribution to the employee had not begun (as defined in A-6 of § 1.401(a)(9)-2) as of the employee's date of death, and pursuant to A-3 of § 1.401(a)(9)-4, an estate may not be a designated beneficiary. See A-5 and A-6 of § 1.401(a)(9)-4 for provisions under which beneficiaries of a trust with respect to the trust's interest in an employee's benefit are treated as having been designated as beneficiaries of the employee under the plan.

Q-12. Will a plan fail to satisfy section 411 if the plan is amended to eliminate benefit options that do not satisfy section 401(a)(9)?

A-12. Nothing in section 401(a)(9) permits a plan to eliminate for all participants a benefit option that could not otherwise be eliminated pursuant to section 411(d)(6). However, a plan must provide that, notwithstanding any other plan provisions, it will not distribute benefits under any option that does not satisfy section 401(a)(9). See A-3 of § 1.401(a)(9)-1. Thus, the plan, notwithstanding section 411(d)(6), must prevent participants from electing benefit options that do not satisfy section 401(a)(9).

Q-13. Is a plan disqualified merely because it pays benefits under a designation made before January 1, 1984, in accordance with section 242(b)(2) of the Tax Equity and Fiscal Responsibility Act (TEFRA)?

A-13. No. Even though the distribution requirements added by TEFRA were retroactively repealed by the Tax Reform Act of 1984 (TRA of 1984), the transitional election rule in section 242(b) was preserved. Satisfaction of the spousal consent requirements of section 4l7(a) and (e) (added by the Retirement Equity Act of 1984) will not be considered a revocation of the pre-1984 designation. However, sections 401(a)(11) and 417 must be satisfied with respect to any distribution subject to those sections. The election provided in section 242(b) of TEFRA is hereafter referred to as a section 242(b)(2) election.

Q-14. In the case in which an amount is transferred from one plan (transferor plan) to another plan (transferee plan), may the transferee plan distribute the amount transferred in accordance with a section 242(b)(2) election made under either the transferor plan or under the transferee plan?

A-14. (a) In the case in which an amount is transferred from one plan to another plan, the amount transferred may be distributed in accordance with a section 242(b)(2) election made under the transferor plan if the employee did not elect to have the amount transferred and if the amount transferred is separately accounted for by the transferee plan. However, only the benefit attributable to the amount transferred, plus earnings thereon, may be distributed in accordance with the section 242(b)(2) election made under the transferor plan. If the employee elected to have the amount transferred, the transfer will be treated as a distribution and rollover of the amount transferred for purposes of this section.

(b) In the case in which an amount is transferred from one plan to another plan, the amount transferred may not be distributed in accordance with a section 242(b)(2) election made under the transferee plan. If a section 242(b)(2) election was made under the transferee plan, the amount transferred must be separately accounted for. If the amount transferred is not separately accounted for under the transferee plan, the section 242(b)(2) election under the transferee plan is revoked and section 401(a)(9) will apply to subsequent distributions by the transferee plan.

(c) A merger, spinoff, or consolidation, as defined in § 1.414(l)-1(b), will be treated as a transfer for purposes of the section 242(b)(2) election.

Q-15. If an amount is distributed by one plan (distributing plan) and rolled over into another plan (receiving plan), may the receiving plan distribute the amount rolled over in accordance with a section 242(b)(2) election made under either the distributing plan or the receiving plan?

A-15. No. If an amount is distributed by one plan and rolled over into another plan, the receiving plan must distribute the amount rolled over in accordance with section 401(a)(9) whether or not the employee made a section 242(b)(2) election under the distributing plan. Further, if the amount rolled over was not distributed in accordance with the election, the election under the distributing plan is revoked and section 401(a)(9) will apply to all subsequent distributions by the distributing plan. Finally, if the employee made a section 242(b)(2) election under the receiving plan and such election is still in effect, the amount rolled over must be separately accounted for under the receiving plan and distributed in accordance with section 401(a)(9). If amounts rolled over are not separately accounted for, any section 242(b)(2) election under the receiving plan is revoked and section 401(a)(9) will apply to subsequent distributions by the receiving plan.

Q-16. May a section 242(b)(2) election be revoked after the date by which distributions are required to commence in order to satisfy section 401(a)(9) and this section of the regulations?

A-16. Yes. A section 242(b)(2) election may be revoked after the date by which distributions are required to commence in order to satisfy section 401(a)(9) and this section of the regulations. However, if the section 242(b)(2) election is revoked after the date by which distributions are required to commence in order to satisfy section 401(a)(9) and this section of the regulations and the total amount of the distributions which would have been required to be made prior to the date of the revocation in order to satisfy section 401(a)(9), but for the section 242(b)(2) election, have not been made, the trust must distribute by the end of the calendar year following the calendar year in which the revocation occurs the total amount not yet distributed which was required to have been distributed to satisfy the requirements of section

401(a)(9) and continue distributions in accordance with such requirements.

Par. 4. Section1.403(b)-2 is added to read as follows:

§ 1.403(b)-2 Required minimum distributions from annuity contracts purchased, or custodial accounts or retirement income accounts established, by a section 501(c)(3) organization or a public school.

Q-1. Are section 403(b) contracts subject to the distribution rules provided in section 401(a)(9)?

A-1. (a) Yes. Section 403(b) contracts are subject to the distribution rules provided in section 401(a)(9). For purposes of this section the term *section 403(b) contract* means an annuity contract described in section 403(b)(1), custodial account described in section 403(b)(7), or a retirement income account described in section 403(b)(9).

(b) For purposes of applying the distribution rules in section 401(a)(9), section 403(b) contracts will be treated as individual retirement annuities described in section 408(b) and individual retirement accounts described in section 408(a) (IRAs). Consequently, except as otherwise provided in paragraph (c), the distribution rules in section 401(a)(9) will be applied to section 403(b) contracts in accordance with the provisions in § 1.408-8.

(c)(1) The required beginning date for purposes of section 403(b)(9) is April 1, of the calendar year following the later of the calendar year in which the employee attains 70 ½ or the calendar year in which the employee retires from employment with the employer maintaining the plan. The concept of 5-percent owner has no application in the case of employees of employers described in section 403(b)(1)(A).

(2) The rule in A-5 of § 1.408-8 does not apply to section 403(b) contracts. Thus, the surviving spouse of an employee is not permitted to treat a section 403(b) contract of which the spouse is the sole beneficiary as the spouse's own section 403(b) contract.

Q-2. To what benefits under section 403(b) contracts, do the distribution rules provided in section 401(a)(9) apply?

A-2. (a) The distribution rules provided in section 401(a)(9) apply to all benefits under section 403(b) contracts accruing after December 31, 1986 (post-'86 account balance). The distribution rules provided in section 401(a)(9) do not apply to the balance of the account balance under the section 403(b) contract valued as of December 31, 1986, exclusive of subsequent earnings (pre-'87 account balance). Consequently, the post-'86 account balance includes earnings after December 31, 1986 on contributions made before January 1, 1987, in addition to the contributions made after December 31, 1986 and earnings thereon. The issuer or custodian of the section 403(b) contract must keep records that enable it to identify the pre'87 account balance and subsequent changes as set forth in paragraph (b) of this A-2 and provide such information upon request to the relevant employee or beneficiaries with respect to the contract. If the issuer does not keep such records, the entire account balance will be treated as subject to section 401(a)(9).

(b) In applying the distribution rules in section 401(a)(9), only the post-'86 account balance is used to calculate the required minimum distribution required for a calendar year. The amount of any distribution required to satisfy the required minimum distribution requirement for a calendar year will be treated as being paid from the post-'86 account balance. Any amount distributed in a calendar year in excess of the required minimum distribution requirement for a calendar year will be treated as paid from the pre-'87 account balance. The pre-'87 account balance for the next calendar year will be permanently reduced by the deemed distributions from the account.

(c) The pre-'86 account balance and the post-'87 account balance have no relevance for purposes of determining the amount includible in income under section 72.

Q-3. Must the value of the account balance under a section 403(b) contract as of December 31, 1986 be distributed in accordance with the minimum distribution incidental benefit requirement?

A-3. Distributions of the entire account balance of a section 403(b) contract, including the value of the account balance under the contract or account as of December 31, 1986, must satisfy the minimum distribution incidental benefit requirement. However, distributions attributable to the the value of the account balance under the contract or account as of December 31, 1986 is treated as satisfying the minimum distribution incidental benefit requirement if the such distributions satisfy the rules in effect as July 27, 1987, interpreting 1.401-1(b)(1)(i)

Q-4. Is the required minimum distribution from one section 403(b) contract of an employee permitted to be distributed from another section 403(b) contract in order to satisfy section 401(a)(9)?

1108

Proposed Regulations

A-4. Yes. The required minimum distribution must be separately determined for each section 403(b) contract of an employee. However, such amounts may then be totaled and the total distribution taken from any one or more of the individual section 403(b) contracts. However, under this rule, only amounts in section 403(b) contracts that an individual holds as an employee may be aggregated. Amounts in section 403(b) contracts that an individual holds as a beneficiary of the same decedent may be aggregated, but such amounts may not be aggregated with amounts held in section 403(b) contracts that the individual holds as the employee or as the beneficiary of another decedent. Distributions from section 403(b) contracts or accounts will not satisfy the distribution requirements from IRAs, nor will distributions from IRAs satisfy the distribution requirements from section 403(b) contracts or accounts.

Par. 5. Section § 1.408-8 is added to read as follows:

§ 1.408-8 Distribution requirements for individual retirement plans.

The following questions and answers relate to the distribution rules for IRAs provided in sections 408(a)(6) and 408(b)(3).

Q-1. Are individual retirement plans (IRAs) subject to the distribution rules provided in section 401(a)(9) and §§ 1.401(a)(9)-1 through 1.401(a)(9)-8 for qualified plans?

A-1. (a) Yes. Except as otherwise provided in this section, IRAs are subject to the required minimum distribution rules provided in section 401(a)(9) and §§ 1.401(a)(9)-1 through 1.401(a)(9)-8 for qualified plans. For example, whether the five year rule or the life expectancy rule applies to distribution after death occurring before the IRA owner's required beginning date will be determined in accordance with § 1.401(a)(9)-3, the rules of § 1.401(a)(9)-4 apply for purposes of determining an IRA owner's designated beneficiary, the amount of the required minimum distribution required for each calendar year from an individual account will be determined in accordance with § 1.401(a)(9)-5, and whether annuity payments from an individual retirement annuity satisfy section 401(a)(9) will be determined under § 1.401(a)(9)-6. For this purpose the term *IRA* means an individual retirement account or annuity described in section 408(a) or (b).

(b) For purposes of applying the required minimum distribution rules in §§ 1.401(a)(9)-1 through 1.401(a)(9)-8 for qualified plans, the IRA trustee, custodian, or issuer is treated as the plan administrator, and the IRA owner is substituted for the employee

Q-2. Are employer contributions under a simplified employee pension (defined in section 408(k)) or a SIMPLE IRA (defined in section 408(p)) treated as contributions to an IRA?

A-2. Yes. IRAs that receive employer contributions under a simplified employee pension (defined in section 408(k)) or a SIMPLE plan (defined in section 408(p)) are treated as IRAs for purposes of section 401(a) and are, therefore, subject to the distribution rules in this section.

Q-3. In the case of distributions from an IRA, what does the term *required beginning date* mean?

A-3. In the case of distributions from an IRA, the term *required beginning date* means April 1 of the calendar year following the calendar year in which the individual attains age 70 ½.

Q-4. When is the amount of a distribution from a IRA not eligible for rollover because the amount is a required minimum distribution?

A-4. The amount of a distribution that is a required minimum distribution from an IRA and thus not eligible for rollover is determined in the same manner as provided in Q&A-7 of § 1.402(c)-2 for distributions from qualified plans. For example, if a required minimum distribution is required for a calendar year, the amounts distributed during a calendar year from an IRA are treated as required minimum distributions under section 401(a)(9) to the extent that the total required minimum distribution for the year under section 401(a)(9) for that IRA has not been satisfied. This requirement may be satisfied by a distribution from the IRA or, as permitted under A-8 of this section, from another IRA.

Q-5. May an individual's surviving spouse elect to treat such spouse's entire interest as a beneficiary in an individual's IRA upon the death of the individual (or the remaining part of such interest if distribution to the spouse has commenced) as the spouse's own account?

A-5. (a) The surviving spouse of an individual may elect in the manner described in paragraph (b) of this A-5 to treat the spouse's entire interest as a beneficiary in an individual's IRA (or the remaining part of such interest if distribution thereof has commenced to the spouse) as the spouse's own IRA. This election is permitted to be made at any time after the distribution of the required minimum amount for

the account for the calendar year containing the individual's date of death. In order to make this election, the spouse must be the sole beneficiary of the IRA and have an unlimited right to withdrawal amounts from the IRA. This requirement is not satisfied if a trust is named as beneficiary of the IRA even if the spouse is the sole beneficiary of the trust. If the surviving spouse makes such an election, the surviving spouse's interest in the IRA would then be subject to the distribution requirements of section 401(a)(9)(A) applicable to the spouse as the IRA owner rather than those of section 401(a)(9)(B) applicable to the surviving spouse as the decedent IRA owner's beneficiary. Thus, the required minimum distribution for the year of the election and each subsequent year would be determined under section 401(a)(9)(A) with the spouse as IRA owner and not section 401(a)(9)(B).

(b) The election described in paragraph (a) of this A-5 is made by the surviving spouse redesignating the account as the account in the name of the surviving spouse as IRA owner rather than as beneficiary. Alternatively, a surviving spouse eligible to make the election is deemed to have made the election if, at any time, either of the following occurs:

(1) Any required amounts in the account (including any amounts that have been rolled over or transferred, in accordance with the requirements of section 408(d)(3)(A)(i), into an individual retirement account or individual retirement annuity for the benefit of such surviving spouse) have not been distributed within the appropriate time period applicable to the surviving spouse as beneficiary under section 401(a)(9)(B); or

(2) Any additional amounts are contributed to the account (or to the account or annuity to which the surviving spouse has rolled such amounts over, as described in (1) above) which are subject, or deemed to be subject, to the distribution requirements of section 401(a)(9)(A).

(c) The result of an election described in paragraph (b) of this A-5 is that the surviving spouse shall then be considered the IRA owner for whose benefit the trust is maintained for all purposes under the Code (e.g. section 72(t)).

Q-6. How is the benefit determined for purposes of calculating the required minimum distribution from an IRA?

A-6. For purposes of determining the required minimum distribution required to be made from an IRA in any calendar year, the account balance of the IRA as of the December 31 of the calendar year immediately preceding the calendar year for which distributions are being made will be substituted in A-3 of § 1.401(a)(9)-5 for the account of the employee. The account balance as of December 31 of such calendar year is the value of the IRA upon close of business on such December 31. However, for purposes of determining the required minimum distribution for the second distribution calendar year for an individual, the account balance as of December 31 of such calendar year must be reduced by any distribution (as described in A-3(c)(2) of § 1.401(a)(9)-5) made to satisfy the required minimum distribution requirements for the individual's first distribution calendar year after such date.

Q-7. What rules apply in the case of a rollover to an IRA of an amount distributed by a qualified plan or another IRA?

A-7. If the surviving spouse of an employee rolls over a distribution from a qualified plan, such surviving spouse may elect to treat the IRA as the spouse's own IRA in accordance with the provisions in A-5 of this section. In the event of any other rollover to an IRA of an amount distributed by a qualified plan or another IRA, the rules in § 1.401(a)(9)-3 will apply for purposes of determining the account balance for the receiving IRA and the required minimum distribution from the receiving IRA. However, because the value of the account balance is determined as of December 31 of the year preceding the year for which the required minimum distribution is being determined and not as of a valuation date in the preceding year, the account balance of the receiving IRA need not be adjusted for the amount received as provided in A-2 of § 1.401(a)(9)-7 in order to determine the required minimum distribution for the calendar year following the calendar year in which the amount rolled over is received, unless the amount received is deemed to have been received in the immediately preceding year, pursuant to A-2 of § 1.401(a)(9)-7. In that case, for purposes of determining the required minimum distribution for the calendar year in which such amount is actually received, the account balance of the receiving IRA as of December 31 of the preceding year must be adjusted by the amount received in accordance with A-2 of § 1.401(a)(9)-7).

Q-8. What rules apply in the case of a transfer from one IRA to another?

A-8. In the case of a transfer from one IRA to another IRA, the rules in A-3 or A-4 of §1.401(a)(9)-7 will apply for purposes of determining the account balance of, and the required minimum distribution from, the IRAs involved. Thus, the transferor IRA must distribute in the year of the transfer any amount required determined without regard to the transfer. For purposes of determining the account balance of the transferee IRA and the transferor IRA, the account balance need not be adjusted for the amount transferred as provided in A-4(a) of §1.401(a)(9)-7 in order to calculate the required minimum distribution for the calendar year following the calendar year of the transfer, because the account balance is determined as of December 31 of the calendar year immediately preceding the calendar year for which the required minimum distribution is being determined.

Q-9. Is the required minimum distribution from one IRA of an owner permitted to distributed from another IRA in order to satisfy section 401(a)(9).

A-9. Yes. The required minimum distribution must be calculated separately for each IRA. However, such amounts may then be totaled and the total distribution taken from any one or more of the individual IRAs. However, under this rule, only amounts in IRAs that an individual holds as the IRA owner may be aggregated. Amounts in IRAs that an individual holds as a beneficiary of the same decedent may be aggregated, but such amounts may not be aggregated with amounts held in IRAs that the individual holds as the IRA owner or as the beneficiary of another decedent. Distributions from section 403(b) contracts or accounts will not satisfy the distribution requirements from IRAs, nor will distributions from IRAs satisfy the distribution requirements from section 403(b) contracts or accounts. Distributions from Roth IRAs (defined in section 408A) will not satisfy the distribution requirements applicable to IRAs or section 403(b) accounts or contracts and distributions from IRAs or section 403(b) contracts or accounts will not satisfy the distribution requirements from Roth IRAs.

Q-10. Is the trustee of an IRA required to report the amount that is required to be distributed from that IRA?

A-10. Yes. The trustee of an IRA is required to report to the Internal Revenue Service and to the IRA owner the amount required to be distributed from the IRA for each calendar year at the time and in the manner prescribed in the instructions to the applicable Federal tax forms, as well as any additional information as required by such forms or such instructions.

PART 54—PENSION EXCISE TAXES

Par. 6. The authority citation for part 54 is amended by adding the following citation to read as follows:

Authority: 26 U.S.C. 7805 * * *

§54.4974-2 is also issued under 26 U.S.C. 4974.

Par. 7. Section after §54.4974-2 is added to read as follows:

§54.4974-2 Excise tax on accumulations in qualified retirement plans.

Q-1. Is any tax imposed on a payee under any qualified retirement plan or any eligible deferred compensation plan (as defined in section 457(b)) to whom an amount is required to be distributed for a taxable year if the amount distributed during the taxable year is less than the required minimum distribution?

A-1. Yes. If the amount distributed to a payee under any qualified retirement plan or any eligible deferred compensation plan (as defined in section 457(b)) for a calendar year is less than the required minimum distribution for such year, an excise tax is imposed on such payee under section 4974 for the taxable year beginning with or within the calendar year during which the amount is required to be distributed. The tax is equal to 50 percent of the amount by which such required minimum distribution exceeds the actual amount distributed during the calendar year. Section 4974 provides that this tax shall be paid by the payee. For purposes of section 4974, the term *required minimum distribution* means the required minimum distribution amount required to be distributed pursuant to section 401(a)(9), 403(b)(10), 408(a)(6), 408(b)(3), or 457(d)(2), as the case may be, and the regulations thereunder. Except as otherwise provided in Q&A-6, the required minimum distribution for a calendar year is the required minimum distribution amount required to be distributed during the calendar year. Q&A-6 provides a special rule for amounts required to be distributed by an employee's (or individual's) required beginning date.

Q-2. For purposes of section 4974, what is a qualified retirement plan?

A-2. For purposes of section 4974, each of the following is a qualified retirement plan -

(a) A plan described in section 401(a) which includes a trust exempt from tax under section 501(a);

(b) An annuity plan described in section 403(a);

(c) An annuity contract, custodial account, or retirement income account described in section 403(b);

(d) An individual retirement account described in section 408(a);

(e) An individual retirement annuity described in section 408(b); or

(f) Any other plan, contract, account, or annuity that, at any time, has been treated as a plan, account, or annuity described in (a) through (e) of this A-2, whether or not such plan, contract, account, or annuity currently satisfies the applicable requirements for such treatment.

Q-3. If a payee's interest under a qualified retirement plan is in the form of an individual account, how is the required minimum distribution for a given calendar year determined for purposes of section 4974?

A-3. (a) *General rule.* If a payee's interest under a qualified retirement plan is in the form of an individual account and distribution of such account is not being made under an annuity contract purchased in accordance with A-4 of §1.401(a)(9)-6, the amount of the required minimum distribution for any calendar year for purposes of section 4974 is the required minimum distribution amount required to be distributed for such calendar year in order to satisfy the required minimum distribution requirements in §1.401(a)(9)-5 as provided in the following (whichever is applicable) -

(1) Section 401(a)(9) and §§1.401(a)(9)-1 through 1.401(a)(9)-8 in the case of a plan described in section 401(a) which includes a trust exempt under section 501(a) or an annuity plan described in section 403(a));

(2) Section 403(b)(10) and §1.403(b)-2 (in the case of an annuity contract, custodial account, or retirement income account described in section 403(b)); or

(3) Section 408(a)(6) or (b)(3) and §1.408-8 (in the case of an individual retirement account or annuity described in section 408(a) or (b)).

(b) *Default provisions.* Unless otherwise provided under the qualified retirement plan (or, if applicable, the governing instrument of the qualified retirement plan), the default provisions in A-4(a) of §1.401(a)(9)-3 apply in determining the required minimum distribution for purposes of section 4974.

(c) *Five year rule.* If the five-year rule in section 401(a)(9)(B)(ii) applies to the distribution to a payee, no amount is required to be distributed for any calendar year to satisfy the applicable enumerated section in paragraph (a) of this A-3 until the calendar year which contains the date five years after the date of the employee's death. For the calendar year which contains the date five years after the employee's death, the required minimum distribution amount required to be distributed to satisfy the applicable enumerated section is the payee's entire remaining interest in the qualified retirement plan.

Q-4. If a payee's interest in a qualified retirement plan is being distributed in the form of an annuity, how is the amount of the required minimum distribution determined for purposes of section 4974?

A-4. If a payee's interest in a qualified retirement plan is being distributed in the form of an annuity (either directly from the plan, in the case of a defined benefit plan, or under an annuity contract purchased from an insurance company), the amount of the required minimum distribution for purposes of section 4974 will be determined as follows:

(a) *Permissible annuity distribution option.* A permissible annuity distribution option is an annuity contract (or, in the case of annuity distributions from a defined benefit plan, a distribution option) which specifically provides for distributions which, if made as provided, would for every calendar year equal or exceed the required minimum distribution amount required to be distributed to satisfy the applicable section enumerated in paragraph (a) of A-2 of this section for every calendar year. If the annuity contract (or, in the case of annuity distributions from a defined benefit plan, a distribution option) under which distributions to the payee are being made is a permissible annuity distribution option, the required minimum distribution for a given calendar year will equal the amount which the annuity contract (or distribution option) provides is to be distributed for that calendar year.

(b) *Impermissible annuity distribution option.* An impermissible annuity distribution option is an annuity contract (or, in the case of annuity distributions from a defined benefit plan, a distribution option) under which distributions to the payee are being made that specifically provides for distributions which, if made as provided, would for any calendar year be less than the required minimum distribution amount required to be distributed to satisfy the applicable section enumerated in paragraph (a) of A-2 of this section. If the annuity contract (or, in the case of annuity distributions from a defined benefit plan, the distribution option) under which distributions to the payee are being made is an impermissible annuity distribution option, the required minimum distribution for each calendar year will be determined as follows:

(1) If the qualified retirement plan under which distributions are being made is a defined benefit plan, the required minimum distribution amount required to be distributed each year will be the amount which would have been distributed under the plan if the distribution option under which distributions to the payee were being made was the following permissible annuity distribution option:

(i) In the case of distributions commencing before the death of the employee, if there is a designated beneficiary under the impermissible annuity distribution option for purposes of section 401(a)(9), the permissible annuity distribution option is the joint and survivor annuity option under the plan for the lives of the employee and the designated beneficiary which provides for the greatest level amount payable to the employee determined on an annual basis. If the plan does not provide such an option or there is no designated beneficiary under the impermissible distribution option for purposes of section 401(a)(9), the permissible annuity distribution option is the life annuity option under the plan payable for the life of the employee in level amounts with no survivor benefit.

(ii) In the case of distributions commencing after the death of the employee, if there is a designated beneficiary under the impermissible annuity distribution option for purposes of section 401(a)(9), the permissible annuity distribution option is the life annuity option under the plan payable for the life of the designated beneficiary in level amounts. If there is no designated beneficiary, the five-year rule in section 401(a)(9)(B)(ii) applies. See paragraph (b)(3) of this A-4. The determination of whether or not there is a designated beneficiary and the determination of which designated beneficiary's life is to be used in the case of multiple beneficiaries will be made in accordance with § 1.401(a)(9)-4 and A-7 of § 1.401(a)(9)-5. If the defined benefit plan does not provide for distribution in the form of the applicable permissible distribution option, the required minimum distribution for each calendar year will be an amount as determined by the Commissioner.

(2) If the qualified retirement plan under which distributions are being made is a defined contribution plan and the impermissible annuity distribution option is an annuity contract purchased from an insurance company, the required minimum distribution amount required to be distributed each year will be the amount which would have been distributed in the form of an annuity contract under the permissible annuity distribution option under the plan determined in accordance with paragraph (b)(1) of this A-4 for defined benefit plans. If the defined contribution plan does not provide the applicable permissible annuity distribution option, the required minimum distribution for each calendar year will be the amount which would have been distributed under an annuity described below in paragraph (b)(2)(i) or (ii) of this A-4 purchased with the employee's or individual's account used to purchase the annuity contract which is the impermissible annuity distribution option.

(i) In the case of distributions commencing before the death of the employee, if there is a designated beneficiary under the impermissible annuity distribution option for purposes of section 401(a)(9), the annuity is a joint and survivor annuity for the lives of the employee and the designated beneficiary which provides level annual payments and which would have been a permissible annuity distribution option. However, the amount of the periodic payment which would have been payable to the survivor will be the applicable percentage under the table in A-2(b) of § 1.401(a)(9)-6 of the amount of the periodic payment which would have been payable to the employee or individual. If there is no designated beneficiary under the impermissible distribution option for purposes of section 401(a)(9), the annuity is a life annuity for the life of the employee with no survivor benefit which provides level annual payments and which would have been a permissible annuity distribution option.

(ii) In the case of a distribution commencing after the death of the employee, if there is a designated beneficiary under the impermissible annuity distribution option for purposes of section 401(a)(9), the annuity option is a life annuity for the life of the designated beneficiary which provides level annual payments and which would have been permissible annuity distribution option. If there is no designated beneficiary, the five year rule in section 401(a)(9)(B)(ii) applies. See paragraph (b)(3) of this A-4.

The amount of the payments under the annuity contract will be determined using the interest rate and actuarial tables prescribed

under section 7520 determined using the date determined under A-3 of 1.401(a)(9)-3 when distributions are required to commence and using the age of the beneficiary as of the beneficiary's birthday in the calendar year that contains that date. The determination of whether or not there is a designated beneficiary and the determination of which designated beneficiary's life is to be used in the case of multiple beneficiaries will be made in accordance with § 1.401(a)(9)-3 and A-7 of § 1.401(a)(9)-5.

(3) If the five-year rule in section 401(a)(9)(B)(ii) applies to the distribution to the payee under the contract (or distribution option), no amount is required to be distributed to satisfy the applicable enumerated section in paragraph (a) of this A-4 until the calendar year which contains the date five years after the date of the employee's death. For the calendar year which contains the date five years after the employee's death, the required minimum distribution amount required to be distributed to satisfy the applicable enumerated section is the payee's entire remaining interest in the annuity contract (or under the plan in the case of distributions from a defined benefit plan).

Q-5. If there is any remaining benefit with respect to an employee (or IRA owner) after any calendar year in which the entire remaining benefit is required to be distributed under section, what is the amount of the required minimum distribution for each calendar year subsequent to such calendar year?

A-5. If there is any remaining benefit with respect to an employee (or IRA owner) after the calendar year in which the entire remaining benefit is required to be distributed, the required minimum distribution for each calendar year subsequent to such calendar year is the entire remaining benefit.

Q-6 If a payee has an interest under an eligible deferred compensation plan (as defined in section 457(b)), how is the required minimum distribution for a given taxable year of the payee determined for purposes of section 4974?

A-6. If a payee has an interest under an eligible deferred compensation plan (as defined in section 457(b)), the required minimum distribution for a given taxable year of the payee determined for purposes of section 4974 is determined under section 457(d).

Q-7. With respect to which calendar year is the excise tax under section 4974 imposed in the case in which the amount not distributed is an amount required to be distributed by April 1 of a calendar year (by the employee's or individual's required beginning date)?

A-7. In the case in which the amount not paid is an amount required to be paid by April 1 of a calendar year, such amount is a required minimum distribution for the previous calendar year, i.e., for the employee's or the individual's first distribution calendar year. However, the excise tax under section 4974 is imposed for the calendar year containing the last day by which the amount is required to be distributed, i.e., the calendar year containing the employee's or individual's required beginning date, even though the preceding calendar year is the calendar year for which the amount is required to be distributed. Pursuant to A-2 of § 1.401(a)(9)-5, amounts distributed in the employee's or individual's first distribution calendar year will reduce the amount required to be distributed in the next calendar year by the employee's or individual's required beginning date. There is also a required minimum distribution for the calendar year which contains the employee's required beginning date. Such distribution is also required to be made during the calendar year which contains the employee's required beginning date.

Q-8. Are there any circumstances when the excise tax under section 4974 for a taxable year may be waived?

A-8. (a) *Reasonable cause*. The tax under section 4974(a) may be waived if the payee described in section 4974(a) establishes to the satisfaction of the Commissioner the following -

(1) The shortfall described in section 4974(a) in the amount distributed in any taxable year was due to reasonable error; and

(2) Reasonable steps are being taken to remedy the shortfall.

(b) *Automatic Waiver*. The tax under section 4974 will be automatically waived, unless the Commissioner determines otherwise, if -

(1) The payee described in section 4974(a) is an individual who is the sole beneficiary and whose required minimum distribution amount for a calendar year is determined under the life expectancy rule described in § 1.401(a)(9)-3 A-3 in the case of an employee's death before the employee's required beginning date; and

(2) The employee's or individual's entire benefit to which that beneficiary is entitled is distributed by the end of the fifth calendar year following the calendar year that contains the employee's date of death.

Robert E. Wenzel

Deputy Commissioner of Internal Revenue

¶ 20,260D

IRS proposed regulations: Enrolled actuaries: Practice before IRS.—The IRS has issued proposed regulations that expand the list of issues that an enrolled actually is authorized to represent a taxpayer in before the IRS to include the treatment of funded welfare benefits, qualified asset accounts, transfers of excess pension assets to retiree health accounts, tax on nondeductible contributions to qualified employer plans, taxes with respect to funded welfare benefit plans, and tax on reversion of qualified plan assets to employees.

The proposed regulations, which were published in the *Federal Register* January 12, 2001 (66 FR 3275), are reproduced below.

DEPARTMENT OF THE TREASURY

Office of the Secretary

31 CFR Part 10

[REG-111835-99]

RIN 1545-AY05

Regulations Governing Practice Before the Internal Revenue Service

AGENCY: Office of the Secretary, Treasury.

ACTION: Notice of proposed rulemaking and notice of public hearing.

SUMMARY: This notice proposes modifications of the regulations governing practice before the Internal Revenue Service (Circular 230). These regulations would affect individuals who are eligible to practice before the Internal Revenue Service. The proposed modifications would clarify the general standards of practice before the Internal Revenue Service and would modify the standards for providing advice regarding tax shelters. This document also provides notice of a public hearing on the proposed regulations.

DATES: Comments and requests to speak and outlines of topics to be discussed from persons wishing to speak at the public hearing scheduled for May 2, 2001, in the auditorium of the Internal Revenue Building at 1111 Constitution Avenue, NW., Washington, DC 20224, must be received by April 12, 2001.

ADDRESSES: Send submissions to: CC:M&SP:RU (REG-111835-99), room 5226, Internal Revenue Service, P.O. Box 7604, Ben Franklin Station, Washington, DC 20044. Submissions may be hand delivered Monday through Friday between the hours of 8 am. and 5 pm. to: CC:M&SP:RU (REG-111835-99), Courier's Desk, Internal Revenue Service, 1111 Constitution Avenue NW., Washington, DC. Submit comments and data via electronic mail (email) to http://www.irs.gov/tax_regs/regslist.html.

FOR FURTHER INFORMATION CONTACT: Concerning issues for comment, Richard Goldstein at (202) 622-7820 or Brinton Warren at (202) 622-4940; concerning submissions of comments and delivering comments, Guy Traynor at (202) 622-7180; (not toll-free numbers).

SUPPLEMENTARY INFORMATION:

Paperwork Reduction Act

The collection of information contained in this notice of proposed rulemaking has been submitted to the Office of Management and Budget for review in accordance with the Paperwork Reduction Act of 1995 (44 U.S.C. 3507). Comments on the collection of information should be sent to the **Office of Management and Budget**, Attn: Desk Officer for the Department of the Treasury, Office of Information and Regulatory Affairs, Washington, DC 20503, with copies to the **Internal Revenue Service**, Attn: IRS Reports Clearance Officer, W:CAR:MP:FP:S:O, Washington, DC 20224. Comments on the collection of information should be received by March 13, 2001. Comments are specifically requested concerning:

Whether the proposed collection of information is necessary for the proper performance of the Office of the Director of Practice, including whether the information will have practical utility;

The accuracy of the estimated burden associated with the proper collection of information (see below);

How the quality, utility, and clarity of the information to be collected may be enhanced;

How the burden of complying with the proposed collection of information may be minimized, including through the application of automated collection techniques or other forms of information technology; and

Estimates of capital or start-up costs and costs of operation, maintenance, and purchase of services to provide information.

The collection of information in these proposed regulations is in §§ 10.6, 10.29, and 10.30. Section 10.6 requires an enrolled agent to maintain records and educational materials regarding his or her satisfaction of the qualifying continuing professional education credit. Section 10.6 also requires sponsors of qualifying continuing professional education programs to maintain records and educational material concerning these programs and those who attended them. The collection of this material helps to ensure that individuals enrolled to practice before the Internal Revenue Service are informed of the newest developments in Federal tax practice.

Section 10.29 requires a practitioner to obtain and retain for a reasonable period written consents to representation whenever such representation directly conflicts with the interests of the practitioner or the interests of another client of the practitioner. The consents are to be obtained after full disclosure of the conflict is provided to each party. Section 10.30 requires a practitioner to retain for a reasonable period any communication and the list of persons to whom that communication was provided with respect to public dissemination of fee information. The collection of consents to representation and communications concerning practitioner fees protects the practitioner against claims of impropriety and ensures the integrity of the tax administration system.

Estimated total annual recordkeeping burden is 50,000 hours.

Estimated annual burden per recordkeeper varies from 30 minutes to 1 hour, depending on individual circumstances, with an estimated average of 54 minutes.

Estimated number of recordkeepers is 56,000.

An agency may not conduct or sponsor, and a person is not required to respond to a collection of information unless it displays a valid control number assigned by the Office of Management and Budget.

Books or records relating to a collection of information must be retained as long as their contents may become material in the administration of any internal revenue law. Generally, tax returns and tax return information are confidential, as required by section 6103 of the Internal Revenue Code.

Background

Section 330 of title 31 of the United States Code authorizes the Secretary of the Treasury to regulate the practice of representatives before the Treasury Department. The Secretary of the Treasury is authorized, after notice and an opportunity for a proceeding, to suspend or disbar from practice before the Department those representatives who are incompetent, disreputable, or who violate regulations prescribed under section 330 of title 31. Pursuant to section 330 of title 31, the Secretary has published the regulations in Circular 230 (31 CFR part 10). These regulations authorize the Director of Practice to act upon applications for enrollment to practice before the Internal Revenue Service, to make inquiries with respect to matters under the Director's jurisdiction, to institute proceedings for suspension or disbarment from practice before the Internal Revenue Service, and to perform such other duties as are necessary to carry out these functions.

The regulations have been amended from time to time to address various specific issues in need of resolution. For example, on February 23, 1984, the regulations were amended to provide standards for providing opinions used in tax shelter offerings (49 FR 6719). On October 17, 1985, the regulations were amended to conform to legislative changes requiring the disqualification of an appraiser who is assessed a penalty under section 6701 of the Internal Revenue Code for aiding and abetting the understatement of a tax liability (50 FR 42014). The regulations were most recently amended on June 20, 1994 (59 FR 31523), to provide standards for tax return preparation, to limit the use of contingent fees in tax return or refund claim preparation, to provide expedited rules for suspension, and to clarify or amend certain other items.

On June 15, 1999, an advance notice of proposed rulemaking was published (64 FR 31994) requesting comments on amendments to the regulations that would take into account legal developments, professional integrity and fairness to practitioners, taxpayer service, and sound tax administration. On May 5, 2000, an advance notice of proposed rulemaking was published (65 FR 30375) requesting comments on amendments to the regulations relating to standards of practice governing tax shelters and other general matters.

* * *

Explanation of Provisions

Who May Practice

Paragraph (d)(2) of § 10.3 of the regulations provides a list of issues with respect to which an enrolled actuary is authorized to represent a taxpayer in limited practice before the Internal Revenue Service. This list of issues would be expanded under the proposed regulations to include issues involving 26 U.S.C. 419 (treatment of funded welfare benefits), 419A (qualified asset accounts), 420 (transfers of excess pension assets to retiree health accounts), 4972 (tax on nondeductible contributions to qualified employer plans), 4976 (taxes with respect to funded welfare benefit plans), and 4980 (tax on reversion of qualified plan assets to employer).

* * *

Tax Shelter Opinions

Two sections of the proposed regulations would provide standards governing tax shelter opinions. New § 10.35 would apply to all tax shelter opinions that conclude that the Federal tax treatment of a tax shelter item or items is more likely than not (or at a higher level of confidence) the proper treatment. Section 10.33 would be revised in scope to apply to all tax shelter opinions not governed by § 10.35 that a practitioner knows or has reason to believe will be used or referred to by persons other than the practitioner to promote, market or recommend a tax shelter. For purposes of §§ 10.33 and 10.35 of the proposed regulations, the definition of a tax shelter would conform to the definition found in section 6662(d)(2)(C)(iii) of the Internal Revenue Code.

The Treasury Department and the Internal Revenue Service recognize that the proposed rules in §§ 10.33 and 10.35 of the proposed regulations may regulate opinion standards with respect to transactions that had not previously been subject to the rules governing tax shelter opinions. The proposed regulations would exclude opinions relating to municipal bonds and qualified retirement plans. The Treasury Department and the Internal Revenue Service specifically request comment on whether the regulations should exempt other transactions from the requirements for tax shelter opinions and, if so, the types of other transactions that should be exempted.

* * *

Proposed Effective Date

These regulations are proposed to apply on the date that final regulations are published in the **Federal Register**.

Special Analyses

It has been determined that these regulations are not a significant regulatory action as defined in Executive Order 12866. Therefore, a regulatory assessment is not required. It is hereby certified that these regulations will not have a significant economic impact on a substantial number of small entities because the general requirements, including the collection of information requirements, of these regulations are substantially the same as the requirements of the regulations that these regulations will replace. Persons authorized to practice have long been required to comply with certain standards of conduct when practicing before the Internal Revenue Service. These regulations do not alter the

Subpart A—Rules Governing Authority to Practice

* * *

§ 10.3 Who may practice.

Subpart B—Duties and Restrictions Relating to Practice Before the Internal Revenue Service

§ 10.35 More likely than not tax shelter opinions.

Subpart A—Rules Governing Authority to Practice

§ 10.3 Who may practice.

(a) *Attorneys.* Any attorney who is not currently under suspension or disbarment from practice before the Internal Revenue Service may practice before the Service by filing with the Service a written declara-

basic nature of the obligations and responsibilities of these practitioners. These regulations clarify those obligations in response to public comments and judicial decisions, and make other modifications to reflect the development of electronic media. In addition, the added requirements for tax shelter opinions imposed by these regulations will have no impact on the substantial number of small entities who have been satisfying these requirements when they provide such opinions. Therefore, a regulatory flexibility analysis under the Regulatory Flexibility Act (5 U.S.C. chapter 6) is not required. Pursuant to section 7805(f) of the Internal Revenue Code, this notice of proposed rulemaking will be submitted to the Chief Counsel for Advocacy of the Small Business Administration for comment on its impact on small businesses.

Comments and Public Hearing

Before the regulations are adopted as final regulations, consideration will be given to any written comments and electronic comments that are submitted timely to the Internal Revenue Service. The Internal Revenue Service and Treasury Department specifically request comments on the clarity of the proposed regulations and how they can be made easier to understand. All comments will be available for public inspection and copying.

The public hearing is scheduled for May 2, 2001, from 8 am, to 11 am., and will be held in the auditorium, Internal Revenue Building, 1111 Constitution Avenue, NW., Washington, DC. Due to building security procedures, visitors must enter at the 10th Street entrance, located between Constitution and Pennsylvania Avenues, NW. All visitors must present photo identification to enter the building. Visitors will not be admitted beyond the immediate entrance area more than 15 minutes before the hearing starts. For information about having your name placed on the building access list to attend the hearing, see the FOR FURTHER INFORMATION CONTACT section of this preamble.

The rules of 26 CFR 601.601(a)(3) apply to the hearing. Persons who wish to present oral comments at the hearing must submit written or electronic comments and an outline of the topics to be discussed and the time to be devoted to each topic by April 12, 2001. A period of 10 minutes will be allocated to each person for making comments.

An agenda showing the scheduling of the speakers will be prepared after the deadline for receiving outlines has passed. Copies of the agenda will be available free of charge at the hearing.

Drafting information

The principal authors of these regulations are Richard S. Goldstein and Brinton Warren, Office of Associate Chief Counsel (Procedure & Administration), Administrative Provisions and Judicial Practice Division, but other personnel from the Internal Revenue Service and Treasury Department participated in their development.

List of Subjects in 31 CFR part 10

Administrative practice and procedure, Lawyers, Accountants, Enrolled agents, Enrolled actuaries, Appraisers.

Proposed Amendments to the Regulations

Accordingly, 31 CFR part 10 is proposed to be revised to read as follows:

PART 10—PRACTICE BEFORE THE INTERNAL REVENUE SERVICE

Sec.

* * *

* * *

* * *

* * *

* * *

tion that he or she is currently qualified as an attorney and is authorized to represent the party(ies) on whose behalf he or she acts.

(b) *Certified public accountants.* Any certified public accountant who is not currently under suspension or disbarment from practice before the Internal Revenue Service may practice before the Service by filing with the Service a written declaration that he or she is currently qualified as a certified public accountant and is authorized to represent the party(ies) on whose behalf he or she acts.

(c) *Enrolled agents.* Any individual enrolled as an agent pursuant to this part who is not currently under suspension or disbarment from practice before the Internal Revenue Service may practice before the Service.

(d) *Enrolled actuaries.* (1) Any individual who is enrolled as an actuary by the Joint Board for the Enrollment of Actuaries pursuant to 29 U.S.C. 1242 who is not currently under suspension or disbarment from practice before the Internal Revenue Service may practice before the Service by filing with the Service a written declaration stating that he or she is currently qualified as an enrolled actuary and is authorized to represent the party(ies) on whose behalf he or she acts.

(2) Practice as an enrolled actuary is limited to representation with respect to issues involving the following statutory provisions in title 26 of the United States Code: sections 401 (relating to qualification of employee plans), 403(a) (relating to whether an annuity plan meets the requirements of section 404(a)(2)), 404 (relating to deductibility of employer contributions), 405 (relating to qualification of bond purchase plans), 412 (relating to funding requirements for certain employee plans), 413 (relating to application of qualification requirements to collectively bargained plans and to plans maintained by more than one employer), 414 (relating to definitions and special rules with respect to the employee plan area), 419 (relating to treatment of funded welfare benefits), 419A (relating to qualified asset accounts), 420 (relating to transfers of excess pension assets to retiree health accounts), 4971 (relating to excise taxes payable as a result of an accumulated funding deficiency under section 412), 4972 (relating to tax on nondeductible contributions to qualified employer plans), 4976 (relating to taxes with respect to funded welfare benefit plans), 4980 (relating to tax on reversion of qualified plan assets to employer), 6057 (relating to annual registration of plans), 6058 (relating to information required in connection with certain plans of deferred compensation), 6059 (relating to periodic report of actuary), 6652(e) (relating to the failure to file annual registration and other notifications by pension plan), 6652(f) (relating to the failure to file information required in connection with certain plans of deferred compensation), 6692 (relating to the failure to file actuarial report), and 7805(b) (relating to the extent to which a Internal Revenue Service ruling or determination letter coming under the statutory provisions listed here will be applied without retroactive effect); and 29 U.S.C. 1083 (relating to the waiver of funding for nonqualified plans).

(3) An individual who practices before the Internal Revenue Service pursuant to paragraph (d)(1) of this section is subject to the provisions of this part in the same manner as attorneys, certified public accountants and enrolled agents.

(e) *Others.* Any individual qualifying under paragraph (c) of § 10.5 or § 10.7 is eligible to practice before the Internal Revenue Service to the extent provided in those sections.

(f) *Government officers and employees, and others.* An individual, who is an officer or employee of the executive, legislative, or judicial branch of the United States Government; an officer or employee of the District of Columbia; a Member of Congress; or a Resident Commissioner may not practice before the Internal Revenue Service if such practice violates 18 U.S.C. 203 or 205.

(g) *State officers and employees.* No officer or employee of any State, or subdivision of any State, whose duties require him or her to pass upon, investigate, or deal with tax matters for such State or subdivision, may practice before the Internal Revenue Service, if such employment may disclose facts or information applicable to Federal tax matters.

* * *

Subpart B—Duties and Restrictions Relating to Practice Before the Internal Revenue Service

* * *

§ 10.35 More likely than not tax shelter opinions.

(a) *In general.* A practitioner who provides a tax shelter opinion that concludes that the Federal tax treatment of a tax shelter item or items is more likely than not (or at a higher level of confidence) the proper treatment must comply with each of the following requirements with respect to each such item.

(1) *Factual matters.* (i) The practitioner must make inquiry as to all relevant facts, be satisfied that the opinion takes account of all relevant facts, and be satisfied that the material facts (including factual assumptions and representations) are accurately and completely described in the opinion, and, where appropriate, in any related offering materials or sales promotion materials.

(ii) The opinion must not be based, directly or indirectly, on any unreasonable factual assumptions (including assumptions as to future events). Unreasonable factual assumptions include—

(A) A factual assumption that the practitioner knows or has reason to believe is incorrect, incomplete, inconsistent with an important fact or another factual assumption, or implausible in any material respect; or

(B) A factual assumption regarding a fact or facts that the practitioner could reasonably request to be provided or to be represented.

(C) A factual assumption that the transaction has a business reason, an assumption that the transaction is potentially profitable apart from tax benefits, or an assumption with respect to a material valuation issue.

(iii) A practitioner may, where it would be reasonable based on all the facts and circumstances, rely on factual representations, statements, findings, or agreements of the taxpayer or other persons ((factual representations) (including representations describing the specific business reasons for the transaction, the potential profitability of the transaction apart from tax benefits, or a valuation prepared by an independent party). Factors relevant to whether such factual representations are reasonable include, but are not limited to, whether the person making the factual representations is knowledgeable as to the facts being represented and is the appropriate person to make such factual representations. A practitioner does not need to conduct an audit or independent verification of a factual representation, but the practitioner may not rely on factual representations if the practitioner knows or has reason to believe, based on his or her background and knowledge, that the relevant information is, or otherwise appears to be, unreasonable, incorrect, incomplete, inconsistent with an important fact or another factual representation, or implausible in any material respect. For example, a representation is incomplete if it states that there are business reasons for the transaction without describing those reasons, or if it states that a transaction is potentially profitable apart from tax benefits without providing adequate factual support. In addition, a valuation is inconsistent with an important fact or factual assumption or is implausible if it appears to be based on facts that are inconsistent with the facts of the transaction.

(iv) If the fair market value of property or the expected financial performance of an investment is relevant to the tax shelter item, a practitioner may not accept an appraisal or financial projection as support for the matters claimed therein unless—

(A) The appraisal or financial projection makes sense on its face;

(B) The practitioner reasonably believes that the person making the appraisal or financial projection is reputable and competent to perform the appraisal or projection; and

(C) The appraisal is based on the definition of fair market value prescribed under the relevant Federal tax provisions.

(v) If the fair market value of purchased property is to be established by reference to its stated purchase price, the practitioner must examine the terms and conditions on which the property was (or is to be) purchased to determine whether the stated purchase price reasonably may be considered to be its fair market value.

(2) *Relate law to facts.* (i) The opinion must relate the applicable law to the relevant facts.

(ii) The opinion must clearly identify the facts upon which the opinion's conclusions are based.

(iii) The opinion must contain a reasoned analysis of the pertinent facts and legal authorities and must not assume the favorable resolution of any Federal tax issue material to the analysis or otherwise rely on any unreasonable legal assumptions.

(iv) The opinion must not contain legal analyses or conclusions with respect to Federal tax issues that are inconsistent with each other.

(3) *Analysis of material Federal tax issues.* The practitioner must ascertain that all material Federal tax issues have been considered, and that all of those issues which involve the reasonable possibility of a challenge by the Internal Revenue Service have been fully and fairly addressed. The opinion must state that the practitioner has considered the possible application to the facts of all potentially relevant judicial doctrines, including the step transaction, business purpose, economic

substance, substance over form, and sham transaction doctrines, as well as potentially relevant statutory and regulatory anti-abuse rules, and the opinion must analyze whether the tax shelter item is vulnerable to challenge under all potentially relevant doctrines and anti-abuse rules. In analyzing such judicial doctrines and statutory and regulatory anti-abuse rules, the opinion must take into account the taxpayer's non-tax and tax purposes (and the relative weight of such purposes) for entering into a transaction and for structuring a transaction in a particular manner.

(4) *Evaluation of material Federal tax issues and overall conclusion.* (i) The practitioner must clearly provide his or her conclusion as to the likelihood that an investor (or, where the practitioner is relying on a representation as to the characteristics of potential investors, a typical investor of the type to whom the tax shelter is or will be marketed) will prevail on the merits with respect to each material Federal tax issue that involves the reasonable possibility of a challenge by the Internal Revenue Service. This requirement is not satisfied by including a statement in the opinion that the practitioner was unable to opine with respect to certain material Federal tax issues, including but not limited to whether the transaction has a business purpose or economic substance.

(ii) The opinion must unambiguously conclude that the Federal tax treatment of the tax shelter item or items is more likely than not (or at a higher level of confidence) the proper tax treatment. A favorable overall conclusion may not be based solely on the conclusion that the taxpayer more likely than not will prevail on the merits of each material Federal tax issue.

(iii) In ascertaining that all material Federal tax issues have been considered, evaluating the merits of those issues and evaluating whether the Federal tax treatment of the tax shelter item or items is the proper tax treatment, the possibility that a tax return will not be audited, that an issue will not be raised on audit, or that an issue will be settled may not be taken into account.

(5) *Description of opinion.* The practitioner must take reasonable steps to assure that any written materials or promotional efforts that distribute, reflect or refer to the tax shelter opinion, correctly and fairly represent the nature and extent of the opinion.

(b) *Competence to provide opinion; reliance on opinions of others.* (1) The practitioner must be knowledgeable in all of the aspects of Federal tax law relevant to the opinion being rendered. If the practitioner is not sufficiently knowledgeable to render an informed opinion with respect to particular material Federal tax issues, then the practitioner may rely on the opinion of another practitioner with respect to such issues, provided the practitioner is satisfied that the other practitioner is sufficiently knowledgeable regarding such issues and the practitioner does not know and has no reason to believe that such opinion should not be relied on.

(2) To the extent the practitioner relies on an opinion of another practitioner, the opinion rendered by the practitioner must identify the other practitioner, state the date on which the opinion was rendered, and set forth the conclusions reached in such opinion.

(3) The practitioner also must be satisfied that the combined analysis, taken as a whole, satisfies the requirements of this § 10.35.

(4) *Financial forecasts and projections.* A practitioner who makes financial forecasts or projections relating to or based on the tax consequences of the tax shelter item that are included in written materials disseminated to any or all of the same persons as the opinion may rely on the opinion of another practitioner as to any or all material Federal tax issues, provided that the practitioner who desires to rely on the other opinion has no reason to believe the practitioner rendering such other opinion has not complied with the standards of paragraph (a) of this § 10.35, is satisfied that the other practitioner is sufficiently knowledgeable and does not know and has no reason to believe that the opinion of the other practitioner should not be relied on. The practitioner's report must disclose any material Federal tax issue not covered by, or incorrectly opined on, by the other opinion, and shall set forth his or her opinion with respect to each such issue in a manner that satisfies the requirements of paragraph (a) of this section.

(c) *Definitions.* For purposes of this section—

(1) *Practitioner* includes any individual described in paragraph (f) of § 10.2.

(2) The definition of *tax shelter* is set forth in section 6662(d)(2)(C)(iii) of the Internal Revenue Code. Excluded from the term are municipal bonds and qualified retirement plans.

(3) A *tax shelter item* is an item of income, gain, loss, deduction or credit if the item is directly or indirectly attributable to a tax shelter as defined in section 6662(d)(2)(C)(iii) of the Internal Revenue Code.

(4) A *tax shelter opinion*, as the term is used in this section, is written advice by a practitioner concerning the Federal tax aspects of a tax shelter item or items. The term tax shelter opinion includes the Federal tax aspects or tax risks portion of offering materials prepared by or at the direction of a practitioner, whether or not a separate opinion letter is issued and whether or not the practitioner's name is referred to in offering materials or in connection with sales promotion efforts. Similarly, a financial forecast or projection prepared by a practitioner is a tax shelter opinion if it is predicated on assumptions regarding Federal tax aspects of the investment and that meets the other requirements of the first sentence of this paragraph. The term tax shelter opinion does not include advice provided in connection with the review of portions of offering materials or sales promotion materials, provided neither the name of the practitioner or the practitioner's firm nor the fact that a practitioner has rendered advice concerning the Federal tax aspects, is referred to in the offering materials or related sales promotion materials.

(5) A *material Federal tax issue*, as the term is used in this section, is any Federal tax issue the resolution of which could have a significant impact (whether beneficial or adverse) on a taxpayer under any reasonably foreseeable circumstance.

(d) *Effect of opinion that meets these standards.* An opinion of a practitioner that meets these requirements will satisfy the practitioner's responsibilities under this section, but the persuasiveness of the opinion with regard to the tax issues in question and the taxpayer's good faith reliance on the opinion will be separately determined under applicable provisions of the law and regulations.

(e) For purposes of advising the Director of Practice whether an individual may have violated § 10.33 or 10.35, the Director is authorized to establish an Advisory Committee composed of at least five individuals authorized to practice before the Internal Revenue Service. Under procedures established by the Director, such Advisory Committee will, at the request of the Director, review and make recommendations with regard to the alleged violations of § 10.33 or 10.35.

¶ 20,260E

IRS proposed regulations: Catch-up contributions: Elective deferrals: Economic Growth and Tax Relief Reconciliation Act of 2001 (EGTRRA).—The IRS has issued proposed regulations that contain guidance for retirement plans that provide their participants age 50 or older the opportunity to make additional elective deferrals, known as catch-up contributions, pursuant to Code Sec. 414(v), as added by EGTRRA. The proposed regulations impact 401(k) plans, SIMPLE IRA plans, simplified employee pensions, 403(b) tax-sheltered annuity plans, and 457 governmental plans.

The proposed regulations, which were published in the *Federal Register* on October 23, 2001 (66 FR 53555), are reproduced below.

Final regulations were published in the *Federal Register* on July 8, 2003 (68 FR 40510), and are found at ¶ 24,507E, ¶ 11,755-5 and ¶ 12,364N. The final regulations are applicable to contributions in taxable years beginning on or after January 1, 2004. Taxpayers are permitted to rely on the final regulations and the proposed regulations for taxable years beginning prior to January 1, 2004.

DEPARTMENT OF THE TREASURY

Internal Revenue Service

26 CFR Part 1

[REG-142499-01]

RIN 1545-BA24

Catch-Up Contributions for Individuals Age 50 or Over

AGENCY: Internal Revenue Service (IRS), Treasury.

ACTION: Notice of proposed rulemaking and notice of public hearing.

SUMMARY: This document contains proposed regulations that would provide guidance concerning the requirements for retirement plans providing catch-up contributions to individuals age 50 or older pursuant to the provisions of section 414(v). These proposed regulations would affect section 401(k) plans, section 408(p) SIMPLE IRA plans, section 408(k) simplified employee pensions, section 403(b) tax-sheltered annuity contracts, and section 457 eligible governmental plans, and would affect participants eligible to make elective deferrals under these plans or contracts. This document also contains a notice of public hearing on these proposed regulations.

DATES: Written and electronic comments and requests to speak (with outlines of oral comments) at a public hearing scheduled for February 21, 2002, must be received by January 31, 2002.

ADDRESSES: Send submissions to: CC:IT & A:RU (REG-142499-01), room 5226, Internal Revenue Service, POB 7604, Ben Franklin Station, Washington, DC 20044. Submissions may be hand delivered Monday through Friday between the hours of 8 a.m. and 5 p.m. to: CC:IT & A:RU (REG-142499-01), Courier's Desk, Internal Revenue Service, 1111 Constitution Avenue, NW., Washington, DC. Alternatively, taxpayers may submit comments electronically via the Internet by selecting the "Tax Regs" option on the IRS Home Page, or by submitting comments directly to the IRS Internet site at *http://www.irs.gov/tax>regs/reg-list.html*. The public hearing will be held in the IRS Auditorium (7th Floor), Internal Revenue Building, 1111 Constitution Avenue, NW., Washington, DC.

FOR FURTHER INFORMATION CONTACT: Concerning the regulations, R. Lisa Mojiri-Azad or John T. Ricotta at (202) 622-6060 (not a toll-free number); concerning submissions and the hearing, and/or to be placed on the building access list to attend the hearing, Donna Poindexter, (202) 622-7180 (not a toll-free number).

SUPPLEMENTARY INFORMATION:

Background

This document contains proposed regulations under section 414(v) of the Internal Revenue Code of 1986 (Code). Section 414(v) was added by section 631 of the Economic Growth and Tax Relief Reconciliation Act of 2001 (EGTRRA) (Public Law 107-16), enacted on June 7, 2001. Under section 414(v), an individual age 50 or over is permitted to make additional elective deferrals (up to a dollar limit provided in that section) under a plan that otherwise permits elective deferrals if certain requirements provided under that section are satisfied. Section 414(v) also provides that a plan will not violate any provision of the Code by permitting these additional elective deferrals to be made.

Explanation of Provisions

These proposed regulations would implement new section 414(v) by providing that an employer plan is not treated as violating any provision of the Code solely because the plan permits a catch-up eligible participant (as defined in these proposed regulations) to make catch-up contributions. Catch-up contributions generally are elective deferrals made by a catch-up eligible participant that exceed an otherwise applicable limit and that are treated as catch-up contributions under the plan, but only to the extent they do not exceed the maximum amount of catch-up contributions permitted for the taxable year. An employer is not required to provide for catch-up contributions in any of its plans,

even if the plans provide for elective deferrals. If, however, any plan of an employer provides for catch-up contributions, all plans of the employer that provide elective deferrals must comply with the universal availability requirements described below.

A. *Eligibility for Catch-up Contributions*

Under these proposed regulations, a participant is a catch-up eligible participant, and thus is permitted to make catch-up contributions, if the participant is otherwise eligible to make elective deferrals under the plan and is age 50 or older. For purposes of this rule, a participant who is projected to attain age 50 before the end of a calendar year is deemed to be age 50 as of January 1 of that year. The effect of this rule is that all participants who will attain age 50 during a calendar year are treated the same beginning January 1 of that year, without regard to whether the participant survives to his or her 50th birthday or terminates employment during the year and without regard to the employer's choice of plan year.

A catch-up eligible participant can make catch-up contributions under a section 401(k) plan, a SIMPLE IRA plan as defined in section 408(p), a simplified employee pension as defined in section 408(k) (SEP), a plan or contract that satisfies the requirements of section 403(b), or a section 457 eligible governmental plan, as long as the participant can otherwise make elective deferrals under the plan or contract. For this purpose, elective deferrals include not only elective deferrals defined in section 402(g)(3), but also any contribution to a section 457 eligible governmental plan.

B. *Determination of Catch-up Contribution*

In describing section 631 of EGTRRA, the Conference report states that "the otherwise applicable dollar limit on elective deferrals under a section 401(k) plan, section 403(b) annuity, SEP, or SIMPLE, or deferrals under a section 457 plan is increased for individuals who have attained age 50 by the end of the year." Conf. Rep. No. 107-84, at 236 (2001). The legislative history to section 631, of EGTRRA indicates that the intent of Congress in enacting section 414(v) was to allow a catch-up eligible participant to make additional elective deferrals over and above any otherwise applicable limit, up to the catch-up contribution limit for the taxable year. The proposed regulations would provide that elective deferrals made by a catch-up eligible participant are treated as catch-up contributions if they exceed any otherwise applicable limit, to the extent they do not exceed the maximum dollar amount of catch-up contributions permitted under section 414(v). However, the regulations would not require that a participant have made elective deferrals in excess of an otherwise applicable limit in order to be a catch-up eligible participant. A plan providing for $1,000 of catch-up contributions in 2002 could allow a participant who is over age 50 to make elective deferrals in an amount projected to exceed the otherwise applicable limit by $1,000 at any time during 2002.

Under the proposed regulations, catch-up contributions would be determined by reference to three types of limits: statutory limits, employer-provided limits, and the actual deferral percentage (ADP) limit. A statutory limit is a limit contained in the Code on elective deferrals or annual additions permitted to be made under the plan or contract (without regard to section 414(v)). Statutory limits include the requirement under section 401(a)(30) that the plan limit all elective deferrals within a calendar year under the plan and other plans (or contracts) maintained by members of a controlled group to the amount permitted under section 402(g).

An employer-provided limit is a limit on the elective deferrals an employee can make under the plan (without regard to section 414(v)) that is contained in the terms of the plan, but that is not a statutory limit. For example, a limit on elective deferrals of highly compensated employees to 10% of pay is an employer-provided limit. The condition that a employer-provided limit be contained in the terms of the plan is intended to correspond with the requirements of § 1.401-1 that a qualified plan have a definite written program and provide for a definite predetermined formula for allocating contributions made to the plan.

For a section 401(k) plan that would fail the ADP test of section 401(k)(3) if it did not correct under section 401(k)(8), the ADP limit is the highest dollar amount of elective deferrals that may be retained in the plan by a highly compensated employee after the application of section 401(k)(8)(C) (without regard to section 414(v)). For example, if after ADP testing, elective deferrals by highly compensated employees in excess of $8,000 would be required to be distributed or recharacterized as employee contributions under the statutory correction set forth under section 401(k)(8)(C), then the ADP limit is $8,000. Similar rules apply in the case of a SEP.

The amount of elective deferrals in excess of an applicable limit is generally determined as of the end of a plan year by comparing the total elective deferrals for the plan year with the applicable limit for the plan year. For example, if a plan limits elective deferrals to 10% of compensation, then whether the participant has elective deferrals in excess of 10% of compensation is determined at the end of the plan year. Similarly, elective deferrals in excess of the ADP limit are determined as of the end of the plan year. For a limit that is determined on the basis of a year other than a plan year (such as the calendar year limit on elective deferrals under section 401(a)(30)), the determination of whether elective deferrals are in excess of the applicable limit is made on the basis of such other year.

If a plan provides for separate employer-provided limits on separate portions of compensation during the plan year, the determination of the amount of elective deferrals in excess of the employer-provided limit is still made on an annual basis, with the applicable limit for the year equal to the sum of the dollar limits that apply to the separate portions of compensation. This situation may occur, for example, when the plan sets a deferral percentage limit for each payroll period.

If the plan limits elective deferrals for separate portions of the plan year, then, solely for purposes of determining the amount that is in excess of an employer-provided limit, the plan may provide, as an alternative rule, that the applicable limit for the plan year is the product of the employee's plan year compensation and the time-weighted average of the deferral percentage limits. For example, if a plan using this time-weighted average limits deferrals to 8 percent of compensation during the first half of the year and 10 percent of compensation for the second half of the year, the applicable limit will be 9 percent of each employee's plan year compensation.

Under the proposed regulations, elective deferrals in excess of an applicable limit would be treated as catch-up contributions only to the extent that such elective deferrals do not exceed the catch-up contribution limit for the taxable year reduced by elective deferrals previously treated as catch-up contributions for the taxable year. The catch-up contribution limit for a taxable year is generally the applicable dollar catch-up limit for such taxable year, except that an elective deferral will not be treated as a catch-up contribution to the extent that the elective deferral, when added to all other elective deferrals for the taxable year under all plans of the employer, exceeds the participant's compensation (determined in accordance with section 415(c)(3)).

These proposed regulations would include a timing rule for purposes of determining when elective deferrals in excess of an applicable limit are treated as catch-up contributions. This rule is necessary because the maximum amount of catch-up contributions is based on a participant's taxable year, but the determination of whether an elective deferral is in excess of an applicable limit is determined on the basis of a taxable year, plan year, or limitation year, depending on the underlying limit. Under the proposed regulations, whether these elective deferrals in excess of an applicable limit can be treated as catch-up contributions would be determined as of the last day of the relevant year, except that if the limit is determined on a taxable or calendar year basis, then whether elective deferrals in excess of the limit can be treated as catch-up contributions would be determined at the time they are deferred. This timing rule is most significant for a plan with a plan year that is not the calendar year. For example, in a plan with a plan year ending on June 30, 2005, elective deferrals in excess of the employer-provided limit or the ADP limit for the plan year ending June 30, 2005, would be treated as catch-up contributions as of the last day of the plan year, up to the catch-up contribution limit for 2005. Any amounts deferred after June 30, 2005, that are in excess of the section 401(a)(30) limit for the 2005 calendar year would also be treated as catch-up contributions at the time they are deferred, up to the catch-up contribution limit for 2005 reduced by elective deferrals treated as catch-up contributions as of June 30, 2005.

C. *Treatment of Catch-up Contributions*

If an elective deferral is treated as a catch-up contribution, it is not subject to otherwise applicable limits under the plan and the plan will not be treated as failing otherwise applicable nondiscrimination re-

quirements because of the making of catch-up contributions. The proposed regulations would provide guidance on how catch-up contributions under the plan are taken into account for purposes of these various requirements under the Code. Under the proposed regulations, catch-up contributions would not be taken into account in applying the limits of section 401(a)(30), 401(k)(11), 402(h), 402A(c)(2), 403(b), 404(h), 408(k), 408(p), 415, or 457 to other contributions or benefits under the plan offering catch-up contributions or under any other plan of the employer.

For purposes of ADP testing, the proposed regulations would provide that any elective deferral for the plan year that is treated as a catch-up contribution because it is in excess of a statutory limit or an employer-provided limit is disregarded for purposes of calculating the participant's actual deferral ratio (i.e., catch-up contributions are subtracted from the participant's elective deferrals for the plan year prior to determining the participant's actual deferral ratio). This subtraction applies without regard to whether the catch-up eligible participant is a highly compensated employee or a nonhighly compensated employee. If, after running the ADP test, a plan needs to take corrective action under section 401(k)(8), the plan must determine the amount of elective deferrals that are catch-up contributions because they are in excess of the ADP limit. The elective deferrals that are treated as catch-up contributions must be retained by the plan. The plan would not be treated as failing section 401(k)(8) by reason of this retention of catch-up contributions. Excess contributions treated as catch-up contributions would nevertheless be treated as excess contributions for purposes of section 411(a)(3)(G). Therefore, if the plan does not provide for matching contributions on catch-up contributions, any matching contributions related to excess contributions treated as catch-up contributions can be forfeited. The approach under the proposed regulations would exclude those catch-up contributions that can be identified before ADP testing, and allow the plan to treat elective deferrals as catch-up contributions for those participants who would be limited under the plan (because the plan otherwise would be required to distribute some of their elective deferrals), while minimizing changes to current plan administration.

Catch-up contributions with respect to the current plan year are not taken into account for purposes of section 416 or 410(b). However, catch-up contributions made to the plan in prior years are taken into account in determining whether a plan is top-heavy under section 416, and for purposes of average benefit percentage testing to the extent prior years' contributions are taken into account (i.e., if accrued to date calculations are used).

A plan does not fail the requirements of section 401(a)(4) merely because it permits only catch-up eligible participants to make catch-up contributions. Similarly, if a plan applies a single matching formula to elective deferrals whether or not they are catch-up contributions, the matching formula as applied to catch-up eligible participants is not treated as a separate benefit, right, or feature under § 1.401(a)(4)-4 from the matching formula as applied to the other participants. However, the matching contributions under the matching formula must satisfy the actual contribution percentage test under section 401(m)(2) taking into account all matching contributions, including matching contributions on catch-up contributions.

D. *Universal Availability*

Under the proposed regulations, a plan that offers catch-up contributions would satisfy the requirements of section 401(a)(4) only if all catch-up eligible participants are provided with the effective opportunity to make the same dollar amount of catch-up contributions. Therefore, if an employer provides for catch-up contributions under a section 401(k) plan, all other employer plans in the controlled group that provide for elective deferrals, including plans not subject to section 401(a)(4), must provide catch-up eligible participants with the same effective opportunity to make catch-up contributions. This universal availability requirement applies solely with respect to catch-up eligible participants. Because the definition of catch-up eligible participants requires that the participant be eligible to make elective deferrals under a plan without regard to section 414(v), the universal availability requirement will not require plans that do not otherwise provide for elective deferrals to provide for catch-up contributions.

In order to provide catch-up eligible participants with an effective opportunity to make catch-up contributions, the plan would have to permit each catch-up eligible participant to make sufficient elective deferrals during the year so that the participant has the opportunity to make elective deferrals up to the otherwise applicable limit plus the catch-up contribution limit. An effective opportunity could be provided in several different ways. For example, a plan that limits elective deferrals on a payroll-by-payroll basis might also provide participants with an effective opportunity to make catch-up contributions that is administered on a payroll-by-payroll basis (i.e., by allowing catch-up eligible participants to increase their deferrals above the otherwise applicable limit by a pro-rata portion of the catch-up limit for the year). However, as discussed above, whether these elective deferrals are treated as catch-up contributions would not be determined until the end of the year.

A plan would not fail the universal availability requirement solely because an employer-provided limit did not apply to all employees or different employer-provided limits apply to different groups of employees. As under current law, a plan could provide for different employer-provided limits for different groups of employees, as long as each limit satisfies the nondiscriminatory availability requirements of § 1.401(a)(4)-4 for benefits, rights, and features. Thus, for example, a plan could provide for an employer-provided limit that applies to highly compensated employees, even though no employer-provided limit applies to nonhighly compensated employees. However, a plan is not permitted to provide lower employer-provided limits for catch-up eligible participants.

The proposed regulations would provide several exceptions to this universal availability requirement. First, the proposed regulations would provide for coordination between catch-up contributions under section 414(v) and the provisions of section 457(b)(3) in accordance with section 414(v)(6)(C). The proposed regulations would also provide transition rules for collectively bargained employees and newly-acquired plans.

E. *Participants in Multiple Plans*

As discussed in Section B above, the intent of section 414(v) is to permit a catch-up eligible participant to make elective deferrals in an amount equal to the catch-up contribution limit for the year in addition to the amount of elective deferrals that the participant would otherwise have been allowed to defer under the plan or plans in which the catch-up eligible participant participated. Many of the statutory limits that would otherwise limit the participant's elective deferrals are applied on an aggregated basis, for example, across all plans within a controlled group. Accordingly, the proposed regulations would provide that, for purposes of determining whether elective deferrals are in excess of a statutory limit, all elective deferrals in excess of the statutory limit are aggregated in the same manner as the underlying limit and the aggregate amount of elective deferrals treated as catch-up contributions because they exceed the statutory limit must not exceed the applicable dollar catch-up limit.

For example, compliance with section 401(a)(30) is determined based on elective deferrals under all section 401(k) plans and all section 403(b) contracts sponsored by the employer. Therefore, all section 401(k) plans and section 403(b) contracts in the controlled group of the employer would be aggregated for purposes of determining the total amount of elective deferrals in excess of the section 401(a)(30) limit. The amount of elective deferrals treated as catch-up contributions by reason of exceeding the section 401(a)(30) limit under the aggregated plans or contracts must not exceed the dollar amount of the catch-up limit for the taxable year.

In calculating the actual deferral ratio (ADR) (as defined in § 1.401(k)-1(g)) for a highly compensated employee who participates in more than one section 401(k) plan of the employer during the year, all section 401(k) plans are treated as one section 401(k) plan. Consistent with this approach, if a highly compensated employee participates in more than one section 401(k) plan of an employer, in determining the elective deferrals in excess of an employer-provided limit, the proposed regulations would take into account the elective deferrals and employer-provided limits under all section 401(k) plans in which the employee participates. In such a case, the proposed regulations would provide that in determining whether an employee's elective deferrals exceed an employer-provided limit, the applicable limit for the plan year is the sum of the dollar amounts of the limits under the separate plans and the employee's elective deferrals under all these plans are combined to determine if that aggregate employer-provided limit is exceeded.

When the elective deferrals in excess of a statutory or employer-provided limit would be determined based on more than one plan, the aggregate amount of elective deferrals in excess of that limit made under all section 401(k) plans of the employer in which a catch-up eligible participant who is a highly compensated employee participates would be treated as elective deferrals in excess of an applicable limit under each of those section 401(k) plans. In the case of a highly compensated employee, all elective deferrals that exceed a statutory or employer-provided limit and are treated as catch-up contributions under the section 401(k) plans of the employer in which the catch-up eligible participant participates are subtracted from the participant's elective deferrals for purposes of determining the participant's ADR. However, if any of the section 401(k) plans corrects through distribution of excess contributions under section 401(k)(8) in order to comply with section 401(k)(3), only the catch-up contributions made under that plan are permitted to be subtracted from elective deferrals for purposes of this correction.

When the elective deferrals in excess of a statutory or employer-provided limit are determined on an aggregated basis, it must be determined under which plan the elective deferrals in excess of the limit were made. The plan under which the elective deferrals in excess of the limit were made may be determined in any manner that is not inconsistent with the manner in which such amounts were actually deferred under the plans. For example, if a catch-up eligible participant participates in a section 401(k) plan only during the first 6 months of the year and during the second 6 months of the year, while participating in a section 403(b) contract, the participant's contributions reach and exceed the section 401(a)(30) limit for the year, then all elective deferrals in excess of the section 401(a)(30) limit for the year could be treated as made to the section 403(b) contract.

F. *Excludability of Catch-up Contributions*

Catch-up contributions are generally not treated as exceeding the applicable dollar amount of section 402(g)(1). The proposed regulations would also provide that a catch-up eligible participant who participates in multiple plans may treat an elective deferral as a catch-up contribution (up to the maximum amount of catch-up contributions permitted for the taxable year) because it exceeds the catch-up eligible participant's section 402(g) limit for the taxable year. This rule would allow a catch-up eligible participant who participates in plans of two or more employers an exclusion from gross income for elective deferrals that exceed the section 402(g) limit, even though the elective deferrals do not exceed an applicable limit for either employer's plan. The treatment by an individual of such elective deferrals as catch-up contributions will not have any impact on either employer's plan. This treatment is parallel to the treatment of excess deferrals for an individual under age 50 who exceeds the section 402(g) limit in the plans of two unrelated employers. Accordingly, the proposed regulations would not provide for the ADP test to be rerun to disregard elective deferrals that an individual treats as catch-up contributions because they exceed the section 402(g) limit. However, the total amount of elective deferrals in excess of the applicable dollar limit in section 402(g)(1)(B) that are not includible in income because they are treated as catch-up contributions cannot exceed that limit by more than the catch-up contribution limit for the taxable year.

Proposed Effective Date

The regulations are proposed to apply to contributions in taxable years beginning on or after January 1, 2002. Taxpayers may rely on these proposed regulations for guidance pending the issuance of final regulations. If, and to the extent, future guidance is more restrictive than the guidance in these proposed regulations, the future guidance will be applied without retroactive effect.

Special Analyses

It has been determined that this notice of proposed rulemaking is not a significant regulatory action as defined in Executive Order 12866. Therefore a regulatory assessment is not required. It also has been determined that section 553(b) of the Administrative Procedure Act (5 U.S.C. chapter 5) does not apply to these regulations, and because these regulations do not impose a collection of information on small entities, the Regulatory Flexibility Act (5 U.S.C. chapter 6) does not apply. Pursuant to section 7805(f) of the Code, these proposed regulations will be submitted to the Chief Counsel for Advocacy of the Small Business Administration for comment on its impact on small business.

Comments and Public Hearing

Before these proposed regulations are adopted as final regulations, consideration will be given to any electronic or written comments (preferably a signed original and eight (8) copies) that are submitted timely to the IRS. In addition to the other requests for comments set forth in this document, the IRS and Treasury also request comments on the clarity of the proposed rule and how it may be made easier to understand. All comments will be available for public inspection and copying.

A public hearing has been scheduled for February 21, 2002, at 10 a.m. in the IRS Auditorium (7th Floor), Internal Revenue Building, 1111 Constitution Avenue NW., Washington, DC. Due to building security procedures, visitors must enter at the 10th street entrance, located between Constitution and Pennsylvania Avenues, NW. In addition, all visitors must present photo identification to enter the building. Because of access restrictions, visitors will not be admitted beyond the immediate entrance area more than 15 minutes before the hearing starts. For information about having your name placed on the building access list to attend the hearing, see the "FOR FURTHER INFORMATION CONTACT" section of this preamble.

The rules of 26 CFR 601.601(a)(3) apply to the hearing.

Persons who wish to present oral comments at the hearing must submit written comments and an outline of the topics to be discussed and the time to be devoted to each topic (signed original and eight (8) copies) by January 31, 2002.

A period of 10 minutes will be allotted to each person for making comments.

An agenda showing the scheduling of the speakers will be prepared after the deadline for receiving outlines has passed. Copies of the agenda will be available free of charge at the hearing.

Drafting Information

The principal authors of these regulations are R. Lisa Mojiri-Azad and John T. Ricotta of the Office of the Division Counsel/Associate Chief Counsel (Tax Exempt and Government Entities). However, other personnel from the IRS and Treasury participated in their development.

List of Subjects in 26 CFR Part 1

Income taxes, Reporting and recordkeeping requirements.

Proposed Amendments to the Regulations

Accordingly, 26 CFR part 1 is proposed to be amended as follows:

PART 1—INCOME TAXES

Paragraph 1. The authority citation for part 1 continues to read in part as follows:

Authority: 26 U.S.C. 7805 * * *

Par. 2. Section 1.414(v)-1 is added to read as follows:

§ 1.414(v)-1 Catch-up contributions.

(a) *Catch-up contributions*—(1) *General rule.* An applicable employer plan shall not be treated as failing to meet any requirement of the Internal Revenue Code solely because the plan permits a catch-up eligible participant to make catch-up contributions in accordance with section 414(v) and this section. With respect to an applicable employer plan, catch-up contributions are elective deferrals made by a catch-up eligible participant that exceed any of the applicable limits set forth in paragraph (b) of this section and that are treated under the applicable employer plan as catch-up contributions, but only to the extent they do not exceed the catch-up contribution limit described in paragraph (c) of this section (determined in accordance with the special rules for employers that maintain multiple applicable employer plans in paragraph (f) of this section, if applicable). The definitions in paragraphs (a)(2) through (5) of this section apply for purposes of this section.

(2) *Applicable employer plan.* The term applicable employer plan means a section 401(k) plan, a SIMPLE IRA plan as defined in section 408(p), a simplified employee pension plan as defined in section 408(k) (SEP), a plan or contract that satisfies the requirements of section 403(b), or a section 457 eligible governmental plan.

(3) *Elective deferral.* The term elective deferral means an elective deferral within the meaning of section 402(g)(3) or any contribution to a section 457 eligible governmental plan.

(4) *Catch-up eligible participant*—(i) *General rule.* The term catch-up eligible participant means an employee who—

(A) Is eligible to make elective deferrals during the plan year under an applicable employer plan (without regard to section 414(v) or this section); and

(B) Is age 50 or older.

(ii) *Projection of age 50.* For purposes of paragraph (a)(4)(i)(B) of this section, a participant who is projected to attain age 50 before the end of a calendar year is deemed to be age 50 as of January 1 of such year.

(5) *Other definitions.* (i) The terms employer, employee, section 401(k) plan, and highly compensated employee have the meanings provided in § 1.410(b)-9.

(ii) The term section 457 eligible governmental plan means an eligible deferred compensation plan described in section 457(b) that is established and maintained by an eligible employer described in section 457(e)(1)(A).

(b) *Elective deferrals that exceed an applicable limit*—(1) *Applicable limits.* An applicable limit for purposes of determining catch-up contributions for a catch-up eligible participant is any of the following:

(i) *Statutory limit.* A statutory limit is a limit on elective deferrals or annual additions permitted to be made (without regard to section 414(v) and this section) with respect to an employee for a year provided in section 401(a)(30), 402(h), 403(b)(1)(E), 404(h), 408(k), 408(p), 415, or 457, as applicable.

(ii) *Employer-provided limit.* An employer-provided limit is any limit on the elective deferrals an employee is permitted to make (without regard to section 414(v) and this section) that is contained in the terms of the plan, but which is not required under the Internal Revenue Code. Thus, for example, a plan provision that limits highly compensated employees to a deferral percentage of 10% of compensation is an employer-provided limit that is an applicable limit with respect to the highly compensated employees.

(iii) *Actual deferral percentage (ADP) limit.* In the case of a section 401(k) plan that would fail the ADP test of section 401(k)(3) if it did not correct under section 401(k)(8), the ADP limit is the highest amount of elective deferrals that can be retained in the plan by a highly compensated employee under the rules of section 401(k)(8)(C). In the case of a SEP with a salary reduction arrangement (within the meaning of section 408(k)(6)) that would fail the requirements of section 408(k)(6)(A)(iii) if it did not correct in accordance with section 408(k)(6)(C), the ADP limit is the highest amount of elective deferrals that can be made by a highly compensated employee under the rules of section 408(k)(6).

(2) *Contributions in excess of applicable limit*—(i) *Plan year limits.* Except as provided in paragraph (b)(2)(ii) of this section, the amount of elective deferrals in excess of an applicable limit is determined as of the end of the plan year by comparing the total elective deferrals for the plan year with the applicable limit for the plan year. In the case of a plan that provides for separate employer-provided limits on elective deferrals for separate portions of plan compensation within the plan year, the applicable limit for the plan year is the sum of the dollar amounts of the limits for the separate portions. This plan provision may occur, for example, when the plan sets a deferral percentage limit for each payroll period. If the plan limits elective deferrals for separate portions of the plan year, then, solely for purposes of determining the amount that is in excess of an employer-provided limit, the plan may provide, as an alternative rule, that the applicable limit for the plan year is the product of the employee's plan year compensation and the time-weighted average of the deferral percentage limits. Thus, for example, if a plan that provides for use of a time-weighted average limits deferrals to 8 percent of compensation during the first half of the plan year and 10 percent of compensation for the second half of the plan year, the applicable limit is 9 percent of each employee's plan year compensation.

(ii) *Other year limit.* In the case of an applicable limit which is applied on the basis of a year other than the plan year (e.g., the calendar year limit on elective deferrals under section 401(a)(30)), the determination of whether elective deferrals are in excess of the applicable limit is made on the basis of such other year.

(c) *Catch-up contribution limit*—(1) *General rule.* Elective deferrals with respect to a catch-up eligible participant in excess of an applicable limit under paragraph (b) of this section are treated as catch-up contributions under this section as of a date within a taxable year only to the extent that such elective deferrals do not exceed the catch-up contribution limit described in this paragraph (c), reduced by elective deferrals previously treated as catch-up contributions for the taxable year, determined in accordance with paragraph (c)(3) of this section. The catch-up contribution limit for a taxable year is generally the applicable dollar catch-up limit for such taxable year, as set forth in paragraph (c)(2) of this section. However, an elective deferral is not treated as a catch-up contribution to the extent that the elective deferral, when added to all other elective deferrals for the taxable year under any applicable employer plan of the employer, exceeds the participant's compensation (determined in accordance with section 415(c)(3)) for the taxable year.

(2) *Applicable dollar catch-up limit*—(i) *In general.* The applicable dollar catch-up limit for an applicable employer plan, other than an applicable employer plan described in section 401(k)(11) or a SIMPLE IRA plan as defined in section 408(p), is determined under the following table:

For Taxable Years Beginning in	Applicable Dollar Catch-up Limit
2002	$1,000
2003	$2,000

For Taxable Years Beginning in	Applicable Dollar Catch-up Limit
2004	$3,000
2005	$4,000
2006	$5,000

(ii) *SIMPLE plan*. The applicable dollar catch-up limit for an applicable employer plan described in section 401(k)(11) or a SIMPLE IRA plan as defined in section 408(p) is determined under the following table:

For Taxable Years Beginning in	Applicable Dollar Catch-up Limit
2002	$500
2003	$1,000
2004	$1,500
2005	$2,000
2006	$2,500

(iii) *Cost of living adjustments*. For taxable years after 2006, the applicable dollar catch-up limit is the applicable dollar catch-up limit for 2006 described in paragraph (c)(2)(i) or (ii) of this section increased at the same time and in the same manner as adjustments under section 415(d), except that the base period shall be the calendar quarter beginning July 1, 2005, and any increase that is not a multiple of $500 shall be rounded to the next lower multiple of $500.

(3) *Timing rules*. For purposes of determining the maximum amount of permitted catch-up contributions for a catch-up eligible participant during a taxable year, the determination of whether an elective deferral is a catch-up contribution is made as of the last day of the plan year (or in the case of section 415, as of the last day of the limitation year), except that, with respect to elective deferrals in excess of an applicable limit that is tested on the basis of the taxable year or calendar year (e.g., the section 401(a)(30) limit on elective deferrals), the determination of whether such elective deferrals are treated as catch-up contributions is made at the time they are deferred.

(d) *Treatment of catch-up contributions*— (1) *Contributions not taken into account for certain limits*. Catch-up contributions shall not be taken into account in applying the limits of section 401(a)(30), 401(k)(11), 402(h), 402A(c)(2), 403(b), 404(h), 408(k), 408(p), 415, or 457 to other contributions or benefits under an applicable employer plan or any other plan of the employer.

(2) *Contributions not taken into account for certain nondiscrimination tests*—(i) *Application of ADP test*. Elective deferrals that are treated as catch-up contributions with respect to a section 401(k) plan because they exceed a statutory or employer-provided limit described in paragraph (b)(1)(i) or (ii) of this section, respectively, are subtracted from the catch-up eligible participant's elective deferrals for the plan year for purposes of determining the actual deferral ratio (ADR) (as defined in §1.401(k)-1(g)) of a catch-up eligible participant. Similarly, elective deferrals that are treated as catch-up contributions with respect to a SEP because they exceed a statutory or employer-provided limit described in paragraph (b)(1)(i) or (ii) of this section, respectively, are subtracted from the catch-up eligible participant's elective deferrals for the plan year for purposes of determining the deferral percentage under section 408(k)(6)(D) of a catch-up eligible participant.

(ii) *Adjustment of elective deferrals for correction purposes*. For purposes of the correction of excess contributions in accordance with section 401(k)(8)(C), elective deferrals under the plan treated as catch-up contributions for the plan year are subtracted from the catch-up eligible participant's elective deferrals under the plan for the plan year.

(iii) *Excess contributions treated as catch-up contributions*. A section 401(k) plan that satisfies the ADP test of section 401(k)(3) through correction under section 401(k)(8) must retain any elective deferrals that are treated as catch-up contributions pursuant to paragraph (c) of this section because they exceed the ADP limit in paragraph (b)(1)(iii) of this section. In addition, a section 401(k) plan is not treated as failing to satisfy section 401(k)(8) merely because elective deferrals described in the preceding sentence are not distributed or recharacterized as employee contributions. Similarly, a SEP is not treated as failing to satisfy section 408(k)(6)(A)(iii) merely because catch-up contributions are not treated as excess contributions with respect to a catch-up eligible participant under the rules of section 408(k)(6)(C). Notwithstanding the fact that elective deferrals described in this paragraph

(d)(2)(iii) are not distributed, such elective deferrals are still considered to be excess contributions under section 401(k)(8), and accordingly, matching contributions with respect to such elective deferrals may be forfeited under the rules of section 411(a)(3)(G).

(iv) *Application for top-heavy*. Catch-up contributions with respect to the current plan year are not taken into account for purposes of section 416. Thus, if the only contributions made for a plan year for key employees are catch-up contributions, the applicable percentage under section 416(c)(2) is 0%, and no top-heavy minimum contribution under section 416 is required for the year. However, catch-up contributions for prior years are taken into account for purposes of section 416. Thus, catch-up contributions for prior years are included in the account balances that are used in determining whether the plan is top-heavy under section 416(g).

(v) *Application for section 410(b)*. Catch-up contributions with respect to the current plan year are not taken into account for purposes of section 410(b). Thus, catch-up contributions are not taken into account in determining the average benefit percentage under §1.410(b)-5 for the year if benefit percentages are determined based on current year contributions. However, catch-up contributions for prior years are taken into account for purposes of section 410(b). Thus, catch-up contributions for prior years would be included in the account balances that are used in determining the average benefit percentage if allocations for prior years are taken into account.

(3) *Availability of catch-up contributions*. An applicable employer plan does not violate §1.401(a)(4)-4 merely because the group of employees for whom catch-up contributions are currently available (i.e., the catch-up eligible participants) is not a group of employees that would satisfy section 410(b) (without regard to §1.410(b)-5). In addition, a catch-up eligible participant is not treated as having a right to a different rate of allocation of matching contributions merely because an otherwise nondiscriminatory schedule of matching rates is applied to elective deferrals that include catch-up contributions. The rules in this paragraph (d)(3) also apply for purposes of satisfying the requirements of section 403(b)(12).

(e) *Universal availability requirement*—(1) *General rule*. An applicable employer plan that offers catch-up contributions and that is otherwise subject to section 401(a)(4) (including a plan that is subject to section 401(a)(4) pursuant to section 403(b)(12)) will not satisfy the requirements of section 401(a)(4) unless all catch-up eligible participants who participate under any applicable employer plan maintained by the employer are provided with the effective opportunity to make the same dollar amount of catch-up contributions. A plan does not fail to satisfy this effective opportunity requirement merely because the plan allows participants to defer an amount equal to a specified percentage of compensation for each payroll period and for each payroll period permits each catch-up eligible participant to defer a pro-rata share of the applicable dollar catch-up limit in addition to that amount. A plan does not fail the universal availability requirement of this paragraph (e) solely because an employer-provided limit does not apply to all employees or different limits apply to different groups of employees under paragraph (b)(2)(i) of this section. However, a plan may not provide lower employer-provided limits for catch-up eligible participants.

(2) *Exception for section 457 eligible governmental plans*. An applicable employer plan does not fail to comply with the universal availability requirement of this paragraph (e) merely because another applicable employer plan that is a section 457 eligible governmental plan does not provide for catch-up contributions to the extent set forth in section 414(v)(6)(C).

(3) *Exception for newly acquired plans*. An applicable employer plan does not fail to comply with the universal availability requirement of this paragraph (e) merely because another applicable employer plan does not provide for catch-up contributions, if—

(i) The other applicable employer plan becomes maintained by the employer by reason of a merger, acquisition or similar transaction described in §1.410(b)-2(f); and

(ii) The other applicable employer plan is amended to provide for catch-up contributions as soon as practicable, but no later than by the end of the period described in section 410(b)(6)(C).

(f) *Special rules for an employer that sponsors multiple plans*—(1) *General rule*. If elective deferrals under more than one applicable employer plan of an employer are aggregated for purposes of applying a statutory limit under paragraph (b)(1)(i) of this section, then the aggregate elective deferrals treated as catch-up contributions by reason of exceeding that statutory limit under all such applicable employer plans must not exceed the applicable dollar catch-up limit for the taxable year. For example, since compliance with section 401(a)(30) is determined based on elective deferrals under section 401(k) plans and section 403(b) contracts sponsored by the employer, the total amount of elective deferrals under all section 401(k) plans and section 403(b) contracts of the employer treated as catch-up contributions by reason of exceeding the section 401(a)(30) limit for a calendar year under the aggregated plans must not exceed the applicable dollar catch-up limit for such taxable year.

(2) *Highly compensated employee in more that one section 401(k) plan.* If a highly compensated employee is a participant in more than one section 401(k) plan of an employer, in determining whether the employee's elective deferrals exceed an employer-provided limit under paragraph (b)(1)(ii) of this section, the employer-provided limit for the plan year is the sum of the dollar amounts of the limits under the separate plans for that employee and the employee's elective deferrals under all section 401(k) plans of the employer are combined to determine if the employer-provided limit is exceeded.

(3) *Allocation rules.* When the amount of elective deferrals in excess of an applicable limit under paragraph (b)(1) of this section is determined under the aggregation rules of paragraph (f)(1) or (f)(2) of this section, the aggregate amount of the elective deferrals in excess of that applicable limit made under all section 401(k) plans that are aggregated for purposes of determining a highly compensated employee's ADR are treated as elective deferrals in excess of an applicable limit for purposes of applying the catch-up contribution limit under paragraph (c)(1) of this section with respect to each of these section 401(k) plans. However, the catch-up contributions are subtracted from elective deferrals for purposes of paragraph (d)(2)(ii) of this section only under the applicable employer plan under which the catch-up contributions are made. The applicable employer plan under which the elective deferrals in excess of an applicable limit are made for purposes of this paragraph (f)(3) may be determined in any manner that is not inconsistent with the manner in which such amounts were actually deferred under the plans.

(g) *Application of section 402(g)*—(1) *Exclusion of catch-up contributions.* In determining the amount of elective deferrals that are includible in gross income under section 402(g), except as provided in paragraph (g)(2) of this section, catch-up contributions are not treated as exceeding the applicable dollar amount of section 402(g)(1). For purposes of this paragraph (g), a catch-up eligible participant who makes elective deferrals under applicable employer plans of two or more employers that exceed the applicable dollar amount under section 402(g)(1) may treat the elective deferrals in excess of that applicable dollar amount as a catch-up contribution to the extent permitted in paragraph (g)(2) of this section, even though the elective deferrals do not exceed an applicable limit under either plan. Therefore, for a catch-up eligible participant who makes elective deferrals under applicable employer plans of two or more employers that exceed the applicable dollar amount under section 402(g)(1), the elective deferrals in excess of that applicable dollar amount are excludable from gross income as catch-up contributions to the extent permitted in paragraph (g)(2) of this section. Whether an elective deferral is treated as a catch-up contribution by an applicable employer plan is determined under paragraph (c) of this section and without regard to whether the employee treats an elective deferral as a catch-up contribution under this paragraph (g).

(2) *Maximum excludable amount.* If a catch-up eligible participant participates in two or more applicable employer plans during a taxable year, the total amount of elective deferrals under all plans that are not includible in gross income under this paragraph (g) because they are catch-up contributions shall not exceed the applicable dollar catch-up limit under paragraph (c)(2)(i) of this section for the taxable year.

(h) *Coordination with other catch-up provisions*—(1) *Coordination with section 457(b)(3).* In the case of an applicable employer plan that is a section 457 eligible governmental plan, the catch-up contributions permitted under this section shall not apply to a catch-up eligible participant for any taxable year for which the additional contributions permitted under section 457(b)(3) applies to such participant. For additional guidance, see regulations under section 457.

(2) *Coordination with section 402(g)(7).* [Reserved].

(i) *Examples.* The following examples illustrate the application of this section. For purposes of these examples, the limit under section 401(a)(30) is $15,000 and the applicable dollar catch-up limit is $5,000 and, except as specifically provided, the plan year is the calendar year. In addition, it is assumed that the participant's elective deferrals under all plans of the employer do not exceed the participant's section 415(c)(3) compensation and that any correction pursuant to section 401(k)(8) is made through distribution of excess contributions. The examples are as follows:

Example 1. (i) Participant A is eligible to make elective deferrals under a section 401(k) plan, Plan P. Plan P does not limit elective deferrals except as necessary to comply with sections 401(a)(30) and 415. In 2006, Participant A is 55 years old. Plan P also provides that a catch-up eligible participant is permitted to defer amounts in excess of the section 401(a)(30) limit up to the applicable dollar catch-up limit for the year. Participant A defers $18,000 during 2006.

(ii) Participant A's elective deferrals in excess of the section 401(a)(30) limit ($3,000) do not exceed the applicable dollar catch-up limit for 2006 ($5,000). Under paragraph (a)(1) of this section, the $3,000 is a catch-up contribution and, pursuant to paragraph (d)(2)(i) of this section, it is not taken into account in determining Participant A's ADR for purposes of section 401(k)(3).

Example 2. (i) Participants B and C, who are highly compensated employees earning $120,000, are eligible to make elective deferrals under a section 401(k) plan, Plan Q. Plan Q limits elective deferrals as necessary to comply with section 401(a)(30) and 415, and also provides that no highly compensated employee may make an elective deferral at a rate that exceeds 10% of compensation. However, Plan Q provides that a catch-up eligible participant is permitted to defer amounts in excess of 10% during the plan year up to the applicable dollar catch-up limit for the year. In 2006, Participants B and C are both 55 years old and, pursuant to the catch-up provision in Plan Q, both elect to defer 10% of compensation plus a pro-rata portion of the $5,000 applicable dollar catch-up limit for 2006. Participant B continues this election in effect for the entire year, for a total elective contribution for the year of $17,000. However, in July 2006, after deferring $8,500, Participant C discontinues making elective deferrals.

(ii) Once Participant B's elective deferrals for the year exceed the section 401(a)(30) limit ($15,000), subsequent elective deferrals are treated as catch-up contributions as they are deferred, provided that such elective deferrals do not exceed the catch-up contribution limit for the taxable year. Since the $2,000 in elective deferrals made after Participant B reaches the section 402(g) limit for the calendar year does not exceed the applicable dollar catch-up limit for 2006, the entire $2,000 is treated as a catch-up contribution.

(iii) As of the last day of the plan year, Participant B has exceeded the employer-provided limit of 10% (10% of $120,000 or $12,000 for Participant B) by an additional $3,000. Since the additional $3,000 in elective deferrals does not exceed the $5,000 applicable dollar catch-up limit for 2006, reduced by the $2,000 in elective deferrals previously treated as catch-up contributions, the entire $3,000 of elective deferrals is treated as a catch-up contribution.

(iv) In determining Participant B's ADR, the $5,000 of catch-up contributions are subtracted from Participant B's elective deferrals for the plan year under paragraph (d)(2)(i) of this section. Accordingly, Participant B's ADR is 10% ($12,000 / $120,000). In addition, for purposes of applying the rules of section 401(k)(8), Participant B is treated as having elective deferrals of $12,000.

(v) Participant C's elective deferrals for the year do not exceed an applicable limit for the plan year. Accordingly, Participant C's $8,500 of elective deferrals must be taken into account in determining Participant C's ADR for purposes of section 401(k)(3).

Example 3. (i) The facts are the same as in *Example 2*, except that Plan Q is amended to change the maximum permitted deferral percentage for highly compensated employees to 7%, effective for deferrals after April 1, 2006. Participant B, who has earned $40,000 in the first 3 months of the year and has been deferring at a rate of 10% of compensation plus a pro-rata portion of the $5,000 applicable dollar catch-up limit for 2006, reduces the 10% of pay deferral rate to 7% for the remaining 9 months of the year (while continuing to defer a pro-rata portion of the $5,000 applicable dollar catch-up limit for 2006). During those 9 months, Participant B earns $80,000. Thus, Participant B's total elective deferrals for the year are $14,600 ($4,000 for the first 3 months of the year plus $5,600 for the last 9 months of the year plus an additional $5,000 throughout the year).

(ii) The employer-provided limit for Participant B for the plan year is $9,600 ($4,000 for the first 3 months of the year, plus $5,600 for the last 9 months of the year). Accordingly, Participant B's elective deferrals for the year that are in excess of the employer-provided limit are $5,000 (the excess of $14,600 over $9,600), which does not exceed the applicable dollar catch-up limit of $5,000.

(iii) Alternatively, Plan Q may provide that the employer-provided limit is determined as the time-weighted average of the different deferral percentage limits over the course of the year. In this case, the time-weighted average limit is 7.75% for all participants, and the applicable limit for Participant B is 7.75% of $120,000, or $9,300. Accordingly, Participant B's elective deferrals for the year that are in excess of the employer-provided limit are $5,300 (the excess of $14,600 over $9,300). Since the amount of Participant B's elective deferrals in excess of the employer-provided limit ($5,300) exceeds the applicable dollar catch-up limit for the taxable year, only $5,000 of Participant B's elective deferrals may be treated as catch-up contributions. In determining Participant B's actual deferral ratio, the $5,000 of catch-up contributions are subtracted from Participant B's elective deferrals for the plan year under paragraph (d)(2)(i) of this section. Accordingly, Participant B's actual deferral ratio is 8% ($9,600 / $120,000). In addition, for purposes of applying the rules of section 401(k)(8), Participant B is treated as having elective deferrals of $9,600.

Example 4. (i) The facts are the same as in *Example 1.* In addition to Participant A, Participant D is a highly compensated employee who is eligible to make elective deferrals under Plan P. During 2006, Participant D, who is 60 years old, elects to defer $14,000.

(ii) The ADP test is run for Plan P (after excluding the $3,000 in catch-up contributions from Participant A's elective deferrals), but Plan P needs to take corrective action in order to pass the ADP test. After applying the rules of section 401(k)(8)(C) to allocate the total excess contributions determined under section 401(k)(8)(B), the maximum deferrals which may be retained by any highly compensated employee in Plan P is $12,500.

(iii) Pursuant to paragraph (b)(1)(iii) of this section, the ADP limit under Plan P of $12,500 is an applicable limit. Accordingly, $1,500 of Participant D's elective deferrals exceed the applicable limit. Similarly, $2,500 of Participant A's elective deferrals (other than the $3,000 of elective deferrals treated as catch-up contributions because they exceed the section 401(a)(30) limit) exceed the applicable limit.

(iv) The $1,500 of Participant D's elective deferrals that exceed the applicable limit are less than the applicable dollar catch-up limit and are treated as catch-up contributions. Pursuant to paragraph (d)(2)(iii) of this section, Plan P must retain Participant D's $1,500 in elective deferrals and Plan P is not treated as failing to satisfy section 401(k)(8) merely because the elective deferrals are not distributed to Participant D.

(v) The $2,500 of Participant A's elective deferrals that exceed the applicable limit are greater than the portion of the applicable dollar catch-up limit ($2,000) that remains after treating the $3,000 of elective deferrals in excess of the section 401(a)(30) limit as catch-up contributions. Accordingly, $2000 of Participant A's elective deferrals are treated as catch-up contributions. Pursuant to paragraph (d)(2)(iii) of this section, Plan P must retain Participant A's $2,000 in elective deferrals and Plan P is not treated as failing to satisfy section 401(k)(8) merely because the elective deferrals are not distributed to Participant A. However, $500 of Participant A's elective deferrals can not be treated as catch-up contributions and must be distributed to Participant A in order to satisfy section 401(k)(8).

Example 5. (i) Participant E is a catch-up eligible employee under a section 401(k) plan, Plan R, with a plan year ending October 31, 2006. Plan R does not limit elective deferrals except as necessary to comply with section 401(a)(30) and section 415. Plan R permits all catch-up eligible participants to defer an additional amount equal to the applicable dollar catch-up limit for the year (5,000) in excess of the section 401(a)(30) limit. Participant E did not exceed the section 401(a)(30) limit in 2005. Participant E made $3,200 of deferrals in the period November 1, 2005 through December 31, 2005 and an additional $16,000 of deferrals in the first 10 months of 2006, for a total of $19,200 in elective deferrals for the plan year.

(ii) Once Participant E's elective deferrals for the calendar year 2006 exceed $15,000, subsequent elective deferrals are treated as catch-up contributions at the time they are deferred, provided that such elective deferrals do not exceed the applicable dollar catch-up limit for the taxable year. Since the $1,000 in elective deferrals made after Participant E reaches the section 402(g) limit for the calendar year does not exceed the applicable dollar catch-up limit for 2006, the entire $1,000 is a catch-up contribution. Pursuant to paragraph (d)(2)(i) of this section, $1,000 is subtracted from Participant E's $19,200 in elective deferrals for the plan year ending October 31, 2006 in determining Participant E's ADR for that plan year.

(iii) The ADP test is run for Plan R (after excluding the $1,000 in elective deferrals in excess of the section 401(a)(30) limit), but Plan R needs to take corrective action in order to pass the ADP test. After applying the rules of section 401(k)(8)(C) to allocate the total excess contributions determined under section 401(k)(8)(C), the maximum deferrals that may be retained by any highly compensated employee under Plan R for the plan year ending October 31, 2006 (the ADP limit) is $14,800.

(iv) Under paragraph (d)(2)(ii) of this section, elective deferrals that exceed the section 401(a)(30) limit under Plan R are also subtracted from Participant E's elective deferrals under Plan R for purposes of applying the rules of 401(k)(8). Accordingly, for purposes of correcting the failed ADP test, Participant E is treated as having contributed $18,200 of elective deferrals in Plan R. The amount of elective deferrals that would have to be distributed to Participant E in order to satisfy section 401(k)(8)(C) is $3,400 ($18,200 minus $14,800), which is less than the excess of the applicable dollar catch-up limit ($5,000) over the elective deferrals previously treated as catch-up contributions under Plan R for the taxable year ($1,000). Under paragraph (d)(2)(iii) of this section, Plan R must retain Participant E's $3,400 in elective deferrals and is not treated as failing to satisfy section 401(k)(8) merely because the elective deferrals are not distributed to Participant E.

(v) Even though Participant E's elective deferrals for the calendar year 2006 have exceeded the section 401(a)(30) limit, Participant E can continue to make elective deferrals during the last two months of the calendar year, since Participant E's catch-up contributions for the taxable year have not exceeded the applicable dollar catch-up limit for the taxable year. However, the maximum amount of elective deferrals Participant E may make for the balance of the calendar year is $600 (the $5,000 applicable dollar catch-up limit for 2006, reduced by the $4,400 ($1,000 plus $3,400) of elective deferrals previously treated as catch-up contributions during the taxable year).

Example 6. (i) The facts are the same as in *Example 5,* except that Participant E exceeded the section 401(a)(30) limit for 2005 by $1,300 prior to October 31, 2005, and made $600 of elective deferrals in the period November 1, 2005, through December 31, 2005 (which were catch-up contributions for 2005). Thus, Participant E made $16,600 of elective deferrals for the plan year ending October 31, 2006.

(ii) Once Participant E's elective deferrals for the calendar year 2006 exceed $15,000, subsequent elective deferrals are treated as catch-up contributions as they are deferred, provided that such elective deferrals do not exceed the applicable dollar catch-up limit for the taxable year. Since the $1,000 in elective deferrals made after Participant E reaches the section 402(g) limit for calendar year 2006 does not exceed the applicable dollar catch-up limit for 2006, the entire $1,000 is a catch-up contribution. Pursuant to paragraph (d)(2)(i) of this section, $1,000 is subtracted from Participant E's elective deferrals in determining Participant E's actual deferral ratio for the plan year ending October 31, 2006. In addition, the $600 of catch-up contributions from the period November 1, 2005 to December 31, 2005 are subtracted from Participant E's elective deferrals in determining Participant E's ADR. Thus, the total elective deferrals taken into account in determining Participant E's ADR for the plan year ending October 31, 2006, is $15,000 ($16,600 in elective deferrals for the current plan year, less $1,600 in catch-up contributions).

(iii) The ADP test is run for Plan R (after excluding the $1,600 in elective deferrals in excess of the section 401(a)(30) limit), but Plan R needs to take corrective action in order to pass the ADP test. After applying the rules of section 401(k)(8)(C) to allocate the total excess contributions determined under section 401(k)(8)(C), the maximum deferrals that may be retained by any highly compensated employee under Plan R (the ADP limit) is $14,800.

(iv) Under paragraph (d)(2)(ii) of this section, elective deferrals that exceed the section 401(a)(30) limit under Plan R are also subtracted from Participant E's elective deferrals under Plan R for purposes of applying the rules of 401(k)(8). Accordingly, for purposes of correcting the failed ADP test, Participant E is treated as having contributed $15,000 of elective deferrals in Plan R. The amount of elective deferrals that would have to be distributed to Participant E in order to satisfy section 401(k)(8)(C) is $200 ($15,000 minus $14,800), which is less than the excess of the applicable dollar catch-up limit ($5,000) over the elective deferrals previously treated as catch-up contributions under Plan R for the taxable year ($1,000). Under paragraph (d)(2)(iii) of this section, Plan R must retain Participant E's $200 in elective deferrals and is not treated as failing to satisfy section 401(k)(8) merely because the elective deferrals are not distributed to Participant E.

(v) Even though Participant E's elective deferrals for calendar year 2006 have exceeded the section 401(a)(30) limit, Participant E can continue to make elective deferrals during the last two months of the calendar year, since Participant E's catch-up contributions for the taxable year 2006 have not exceeded the applicable dollar catch-up limit for the taxable year. However, the maximum amount of elective deferrals Participant E may make for the balance of the calendar year is $3,800 (the $5,000 applicable dollar catch-up limit for 2006, reduced by $1,200 ($1,000 plus $200) in elective deferrals previously treated as catch-up contributions during taxable year 2006).

Example 7. (i) Participant F, who is 58 years old, is a highly compensated employee who earns $100,000. Participant F participates in a section 401(k) plan, Plan S, for the first six months of the year and then transfers to another section 401(k) plan, Plan T, sponsored by the same employer, for the second six months of the year. Plan S limits highly compensated employees' elective deferrals to 6% of compensation for the period of participation, but permits catch-up eligible participants to defer amounts in excess of 6% during the plan year, up to the applicable dollar catch-up limit for the year. Plan T limits highly compensated employee's elective deferrals to 8% of compensation for the period of participation, but permits catch-up eligible participants to defer amounts in excess of 8% during the plan year, up to the applicable dollar catch-up limit for the year. Participant F, who earned $50,000 in the first six months of the year, defers $5,000 under Plan S. Participant F also deferred $5,000 under Plan T.

(ii) Under paragraph (f)(2) of this section, the employer-provided limit for Participant F is $7,000, the sum of the employer-provided limit for Plan S ($3,000) and the employer-provided limit for Plan T ($4,000). Participant F's elective deferrals for the year are $10,000. Therefore, the amount of Participant F's elective deferrals in excess of the employer-provided limit is $3,000. Under paragraph (f)(3) of this section, the $3,000 in excess of the employer-provided limit is treated as an elective deferral in excess of that limit under both Plans S and T for purposes of applying the catch-up contribution limit under paragraph (c)(1) of this section.

(iii) Since the amount of Participant F's elective deferrals in excess of the employer-provided limit ($3,000) does not exceed the applicable dollar catch-up limit for the taxable year, the entire $3,000 of Participant F's elective deferrals are treated as catch-up contributions. In determining Participant F's actual deferral ratio, the entire $3,000 of catch-up contributions is subtracted from Participant F's elective deferrals for the plan year under paragraph (d)(2)(i) of this section. Accordingly,

Participant F's actual deferral ratio is 7% ($7,000 / $100,000) for both Plans S and T.

(iv) In accordance with paragraph (f)(3) of this section, it is determined that $2,000 of the excess over the employer-provided limit was made under Plan S and $1,000 of the excess over the employer-provided limit was made under Plan T. This determination is not inconsistent with the manner in which the elective deferrals were actually made. Therefore, under paragraph (d)(2)(ii) of this section, for purposes of applying the rules of section 401(k)(8), Participant F is treated as having elective deferrals of $3,000 ($5,000 – $2,000) in Plan S and $4,000 ($5,000 – $1,000) in Plan T.

(v) If, after applying the ADP test of section 401(k)(3), Plan S or Plan T were to require correction under section 401(k)(8), the maximum amount of elective deferrals in excess of the ADP limit that could be treated as catch-up contributions for Participant F under the Plan could not exceed $2,000, the applicable dollar catch-up limit of $5,000, reduced by the $3,000 in excess of the employer-provided limit previously treated as catch-up contributions for the taxable year.

(j) *Effective date and transition rule—*(1) *Effective date.* Section 414(v) and this section apply to contributions in taxable years beginning on or after January 1, 2002.

(2) *Transition rule for collectively bargained employees.* An applicable employer plan will not fail to satisfy the requirements of paragraph (e) of this section merely because employees eligible to make elective deferrals who are included in a unit of employees covered by a collective bargaining agreement in effect on January 1, 2002, are not permitted to make catch-up contributions until the first plan year beginning after the termination of such agreement.

Deputy Commissioner of Internal Revenue

Robert E. Wenzel

¶ 20,260F

IRS proposed regulation (withdrawn): Incentive stock options (ISOs): Employee stock purchase plans (ESPPs): Federal Insurance Contributions Act (FICA): Federal Unemployment Tax Act (FUTA): Income tax withholding.—The IRS issued, then later withdrew, proposed regulations relating to Incentive Stock Options (ISOs) described in Code Sec. 422(b) and options granted under an Employee Stock Purchase Plan (ESSP) described in Code Sec. 423(b). The proposals, which would have affected employers granting such options and employees exercising such options, provided guidance concerning the application of the Federal Insurance Contributions Act (FICA) and Federal Unemployment Tax Act (FUTA), and the Collection of Income Tax at Source rules for statutory stock options. The IRS also issued two related notices, IRS Notice 2001-72 (CCH PENSION PLAN GUIDE ¶ 17,122Q) and IRS Notice 2001-73 (CCH PENSION PLAN GUIDE ¶ 17,122R) that set forth proposed rules regarding an employer's income tax withholding and reporting obligations upon the sale or disposition of stock acquired pursuant to the exercise of a statutory option and the application of FICA and FUTA to statutory stock options.

The proposed regulations, and the withdrawal of the proposed regulations, were published in the *Federal Register* on November 14, 2001 (66 FR 57203), and July 1, 2005 (70 FR 38057), respectively.

¶ 20,260G

Proposed regulations: Golden parachute payments.—Reproduced below is the text of proposed regulations on golden parachute payments relating to exempt parachute payments and IRS Code Sec. 280G, disqualified individuals, changes in corporate ownership or control, and reasonable compensation. The proposed regulations apply to any payments that are contingent on a change in ownership or control occurring on or after January 1, 2004. Taxpayers may rely on these regulations until the effective date of the final regulations. Alternatively, taxpayers may rely on the 1989 proposed regulations (¶ 20,178) for any payment contingent on a change in ownership or control that occurs prior to January 1, 2004.

The proposed regulations were published in the *Federal Register* on February 20, 2002 (67 *FR* 7630). The regulations were corrected in the *Federal Register* on June 21, 2002 (67 *FR* 42210).

DEPARTMENT OF THE TREASURY

Internal Revenue Service

26 CFR Part 1

[REG-209114-90]

RIN: 1545-AH49

Golden Parachute Payments

AGENCY: Internal Revenue Service (IRS), Treasury.

ACTION: Notice of proposed rulemaking and notice of public hearing.

SUMMARY: This document contains proposed regulations relating to golden parachute payments to provide guidance to taxpayers who must comply with section 280G. Proposed regulations under section 280G were previously published in the **Federal Register** on May 5, 1989 (the 1989 proposed regulations). These proposed regulations are proposed to apply to any payments that are contingent on a change in ownership or control occurring on or after January 1, 2004. Taxpayers may rely on these proposed regulations until the effective date of the final regulations. Alternatively, taxpayers may rely on the 1989 pro-

posed regulations for any payment contingent on a change in ownership or control that occurs prior to January 1, 2004. [Corrected by IRS on 6/21/02, 67 FR 42210].

DATES: Written or electronic comments must be received by June 5, 2002. Requests to speak and outlines of topics to be discussed at the public hearing scheduled for June 26, 2002, must be received by June 5, 2002.

ADDRESSES: Send submissions to CC:ITA:RU (REG-209114-90), room 5226, Internal Revenue Service, POB 7604, Ben Franklin Station, Washington, DC 20044. Submissions may be hand delivered Monday through Friday between the hours of 8 a.m. and 5 p.m. to: CC:ITA:RU (REG-209114-90), Courier's Desk, Internal Revenue Service, 1111 Constitution Avenue, NW, Washington, DC or sent electronically, via the IRS Internet site *www.irs.gov/regs*. The public hearing will be held in the IRS Auditorium, Internal Revenue Building, 1111 Constitution Avenue, NW, Washington, DC.

FOR FURTHER INFORMATION CONTACT: Concerning the regulations, Erinn Madden at (202) 622-6060 (not at toll-free number). To be placed on the attendance list for the hearing, please contact LaNita M.

Vandyke at (202) 622-7180. [Corrected by IRS on 6/21/02, 67 FR 42210].

SUPPLEMENTARY INFORMATION:

Background

This document contains proposed amendments to 26 CFR part 1 under section 280G of the Internal Revenue Code (Code). Sections 280G and 4999 of the Code were added to the Code by sec. 67 of the Deficit Reduction Act, Public Law 98-369 (98 Stat. 585). Section 280G was amended by sec. 1804(j) of the Tax Reform Act of 1986, Public Law 99-514 (100 Stat. 2807), sec. 1018(d) of the Technical and Miscellaneous Revenue Act of 1988, Public Law 100-647 (102 Stat. 3581) and sec. 1421 of the Small Business Job Protection Act of 1996, Public Law 104-188 (110 Stat. 1755).

Section 280G denies a deduction to a corporation for any excess parachute payment. Section 4999 imposes a 20-percent excise tax on the recipient of any excess parachute payment. Related provisions include section 275(a)(6), which denies the recipient a deduction for the section 4999 excise tax, and section 3121(v)(2)(A), which relates to the Federal Insurance Contributions Act. Proposed regulations (PS-217-84) under section 280G were previously published in the **Federal Register** at 54 FR 19390 on May 5, 1989 and corrected in 54 FR 25879 (June 20, 1989) (the 1989 proposed regulations). [Corrected by IRS on 6/21/02, 67 FR 42210].

Explanation Of Provisions

Overview

Section 280G denies a deduction to a corporation for any excess parachute payment. Section 4999 imposes a 20-percent excise tax on the recipient of any excess parachute payment. The disallowance of the deduction under section 280G is not contingent on the imposition of the excise tax under section 4999, and the imposition of the excise tax under section 4999 is not contingent on the disallowance of the deduction under section 280G. For example, an individual may be subject to the 20-percent excise tax under section 4999 even though the payor is a foreign corporation not subject to United States income tax.

Section 280G(b)(2)(A) defines a *parachute payment* as any payment that meets all of the following four conditions: (a) the payment is in the nature of compensation; (b) the payment is to, or for the benefit of, a disqualified individual; (c) the payment is contingent on a change in the ownership of a corporation, the effective control of a corporation, or the ownership of a substantial portion of the assets of a corporation (a change in ownership or control); and (d) the payment has (together with other payments described in (a), (b), and (c) of this paragraph with respect to the same individual) an aggregate present value of at least 3 times the individual's base amount. Section 280G(b)(2)(B) provides that the term *parachute payment* also includes any payment in the nature of compensation to, or for the benefit of, a disqualified individual if the payment is pursuant to an agreement that violates any generally enforced securities laws or regulations (securities violation parachute payment).

Section 280G(b)(1) defines the term *excess parachute payment* as an amount equal to the excess of any parachute payment over the portion of the disqualified individual's base amount that is allocated to such payment. For this purpose, the portion of the base amount allocated to a parachute payment is the amount that bears the same ratio to the base amount as the present value of the parachute payment bears to the aggregate present value of all such payments to the same disqualified individual.

Generally, excess parachute payments may be reduced by certain amounts of reasonable compensation. Section 280G(b)(4)(B) provides that, except in the case of securities violation parachute payments, the amount of an excess parachute payment is reduced by any portion of the payment that the taxpayer establishes by clear and convincing evidence is reasonable compensation for personal services actually rendered by the disqualified individual before the date of change in ownership or control. Such reasonable compensation is first offset against the portion of the base amount allocated to the payment.

The 1989 proposed regulations provided guidance regarding the application of section 280G to corporations and individuals. Although many aspects of the 1989 proposed regulations were well-received, the IRS has received numerous comments requesting modification and clarification of the 1989 proposed regulations. In response, these proposed regulations clarify and revise, as described below, the 1989 proposed regulations. Many aspects of the 1989 proposed regulations are preserved, and these proposed regulations retain the same organizational structure as the 1989 proposed regulations. Major modifications to the 1989 proposed regulations are described below.

Disqualified Individuals

A payment constitutes a parachute payment only if the payment is made to (or for the benefit of) a disqualified individual. Section 280G(c) defines the term *disqualified individual* to include any individual who (a) is an employee or independent contractor who performs personal services for a corporation, and (b) is an officer, shareholder, or highly-compensated individual.

The determination of whether an individual is a disqualified individual under these proposed regulations is substantially the same as under the 1989 proposed regulations, with three significant changes. First, Q/A-17 of the 1989 proposed regulations provides a *de minimis* rule for purposes of identifying which shareholders of a corporation are disqualified individuals. Under the 1989 proposed regulations, an individual is a shareholder for purposes of section 280G if the individual, at any time during the disqualified individual determination period, owns stock of a corporation with a fair market value exceeding the lesser of $1 million or 1 percent of the total fair market value of the outstanding shares of all classes of the corporation's stock. Since the issuance of the 1989 proposed regulations, it has become apparent that this rule may include individuals who do not possess significant influence over the corporation. Therefore, under Q/A-17 of these proposed regulations, the $1 million test is eliminated. Under these proposed regulations, an individual is a shareholder only if, during the disqualified individual determination period, the individual owns stock of a corporation with a fair market value that exceeds 1 percent of the total fair market value of the outstanding shares of all classes of the corporation's stock. The constructive ownership rules of section 318(a) continue to apply for purposes of determining the amount of stock owned by the individual. Under these rules, for example, to determine the amount of stock owned by an individual, the stock underlying vested stock options is considered constructively owned by that individual. [Corrected by IRS on 6/21/02, 67 FR 42210].

Second, these proposed regulations modify the annualized compensation method for determining who is a highly-compensated individual under Q/A-19. Under the 1989 proposed regulations, no individual whose annualized compensation during the disqualified individual determination period is less than $75,000 is treated as a highly-compensated individual, even if the individual otherwise satisfies the definition of a highly-compensated individual. Q/A-19 is modified to provide that an individual must have annualized compensation equal to at least the amount described in section 414(q)(1)(B)(i). This amount for 2002 is $90,000 and is adjusted periodically for cost-of-living increases. This modification both updates the amount provided in the 1989 proposed regulations and provides a mechanism to update this amount periodically without further amendment of these regulations.

Finally, these proposed regulations change the disqualified individual determination period under Q/A-20. Under the 1989 proposed regulations, the disqualified individual determination period is the portion of the year of the corporation ending on the date of the change in ownership or control and the immediately preceding twelve months (with an option to use the calendar year or the corporation's fiscal year). Q/A-20 of these proposed regulations is modified to change this period to the twelve months prior to and ending on the date of change in ownership or control of the corporation. Under this rule, the disqualified individual determination period is the same length for any change in ownership or control and is not affected by the date of the change in ownership or control.

Payment in the Nature of Compensation

A payment may be a parachute payment only if it is a payment in the nature of compensation. All payments, in whatever form, are payments in the nature of compensation if the payments arise out of the employment relationship or are associated with the performance of services. In Q/A-11, these proposed regulations clarify that payments in the nature of compensation include cash, the right to receive cash, or a transfer of property.

Q/A-13 of the 1989 proposed regulations provides that the transfer of a nonstatutory option is treated as a payment in the nature of compensation (even if the option does not have a readily ascertainable fair market value within the meaning of § 1.83-7(b)). The 1989 proposed regulations reserve the issue of the treatment of statutory options (i.e., options to which section 421 applies). These proposed regulations revise Q/A-13 to address the treatment of statutory stock options to provide that nonstatutory stock options and statutory stock options are treated the same. Because both the transfer of a statutory option and the transfer of a nonstatutory stock option are payments in the nature of compensation, there is no basis for distinguishing between these two types of options for purposes of section 280G.

In addition, these proposed regulations revise Q/A-13 with respect to the valuation of both statutory and nonstatutory stock options. Under the 1989 proposed regulations, the value of an option with an ascertainable fair market value is determined under all the facts and circumstances, including the difference between the option's exercise price and the value of the property at the time of vesting, the probability of an increase or decrease in the value of such property, and the length of the option exercise period.

Since the issuance of the 1989 proposed regulations, commentators have indicated that Q/A-13 does not provide sufficient guidance about the determination of the value of a stock option. In particular, commentators question whether the intrinsic value of the option (the difference between the exercise price and the value of the property, or spread) determined at the time of the change in ownership or control, or a value determined under a valuation model such as Black-Scholes, should be used for purposes of section 280G. Using the factors listed in the 1989 proposed regulations results in a value different from the value obtained from using only the difference between the exercise price and the value of the property. Commentators have also noted that valuation methods other than spread are often complicated and difficult to apply in some circumstances, particularly when the stock underlying the option is not publicly traded.

These proposed regulations continue to provide for the use of the factors described in the 1989 proposed regulations. To provide further guidance on acceptable and administrable methods for valuing stock options, these proposed regulations delegate authority to the Commissioner to provide methods for valuation of stock options through published guidance. Rev. Proc. 2002-13, 2002-8 I.R.B. (February 25, 2002) published in conjunction with these proposed regulations, provides several valuation methods. One of the methods permitted under this revenue procedure is a simplified safe harbor approach modeled after the Black-Scholes valuation method. The safe harbor allows a corporation to establish a value for stock options based on spread at the time of the change in ownership or control, the remaining term of the option, and a basic assumption regarding the volatility of the underlying stock. Other factors relevant to the Black-Scholes valuation model, including a risk-free rate of return and dividend yield, are addressed in the table contained in the revenue procedure. The safe harbor valuation method provided in the revenue procedure may be used without regard to whether the underlying stock is publicly traded.

Contingent on Change

To be a parachute payment, a payment in the nature of compensation to a disqualified individual must be contingent on a change in ownership or control. Q/A-22 of the 1989 proposed regulations provides guidance on when a payment is contingent on a change in ownership or control. Generally, a payment is treated as contingent on a change in ownership or control if the payment would not in fact have been made had no change in ownership or control occurred. A payment generally is treated as one which would not in fact have been made in the absence of a change in ownership or control unless it is substantially certain, at the time of the change, that payment would have been made whether or not the change in ownership or control occurred.

These proposed regulations clarify in Q/A-22 that a payment is contingent on a change in ownership or control if the payment would not have been made absent the change in ownership or control, even if the payment is also contingent on a second event, such as termination of employment within a period following the change in ownership or control. In addition, as under the 1989 proposed regulations, a payment generally is treated as contingent on a change in ownership or control if (a) the payment is contingent on an event that is closely associated with such a change, (b) a change in ownership or control actually occurs, and (c) the event is materially related to the change in ownership or control. The fact that a payment that is contingent on an event closely associated with a change in ownership or control is also conditioned on the occurrence of a second event does not affect the determination that the payment is contingent on a change in ownership or control as the result of the occurrence of the first event.

Under Q/A-24 of the 1989 proposed regulations, the entire amount of a payment is generally treated as contingent on a change in ownership or control. These proposed regulations clarify that the general rule of Q/A-24(a) (and not the special rules in either Q/A-24(b) or (c), discussed below) applies to the payment of amounts due under an employment agreement on a termination of employment or change in ownership or control that, without regard to the change, would have been paid for the performance of services after the termination of employment or change in ownership or control, as applicable. Also, the general rules of Q/A-24(a) apply to the accelerated payment of an amount that is otherwise payable only on the attainment of a performance goal or contingent on an event or condition other than the

continued performance of services for a specified period of time. In situations governed by Q/A-24(a), the determination of whether a portion of the payment is reasonable compensation for services rendered before, on, or after the change in ownership or control is determined under Q/As-38 through 44. With respect to amounts due under an employment agreement, however, in most situations, a reduction for reasonable compensation for services rendered before the change in ownership or control is inappropriate, given the general expectation that an individual is not under-compensated for services rendered before a change in ownership or control. See Conf. Rep. No. 98-861, at 852 (1984).

Q/A-24(b) and (c) provide an objective method for determining the portion of a payment that is treated as contingent on a change in ownership or control for certain types of payments. These rules are not appropriate in situations such as the acceleration of salary payments under an employment agreement, when the periodic nature of the payments for services means that there is no issue in determining the amount of the payment that is accelerated, or in situations where a payment is conditioned on achievement of a performance goal or other event.

As under the 1989 proposed regulations, these proposed regulations provide that a payment is treated as contingent on a change in ownership or control if the change accelerates the time at which the payment is made or accelerates the vesting of a payment. Q/A-24(b) and (c) provide rules for determining the portion of such payment that is treated as contingent on the change in ownership or control. These proposed regulations clarify when Q/A-24(b) and (c) apply to a contingent payment.

These proposed regulations clarify that Q/A-24(b) applies if a payment is vested, without regard to the change in ownership or control, and is treated as contingent on a change in ownership or control because the change accelerates the time the payment is made. For example, if an individual has a vested right to a payment at normal retirement age under a nonqualified deferred compensation plan, but instead that payment is made immediately following a change in ownership or control, Q/A-24(b) applies to determine the portion, if any, of the payment that is treated as contingent on the change in ownership or control.

These regulations clarify that Q/A-24(c) applies to a payment that becomes vested as a result of a change in ownership or control to the extent that (i) without regard to the change, the payment was contingent only on the performance of services for the corporation for a specified period of time and (ii) the payment is attributable, at least in part, to the performance of services before the date the payment is made or becomes certain to be made. For example, if an individual will receive a bonus if employed at the end of a 3-year period, but the bonus is paid immediately on the date of the change of control, Q/A-24(c) applies to determine the portion of the payment that is treated as contingent on the change in ownership or control.

Q/A-24(b) provides that, when a payment is accelerated, the portion of the payment that is contingent on the change is the amount by which the accelerated payment exceeds the present value of the payment absent acceleration. Q/A-24(b) further provides that if the amount of a payment without acceleration is not reasonably ascertainable, and the acceleration does not significantly increase the value of the payment, then the present value of the payment absent the acceleration is equal to the amount of the accelerated payment. As a result, the value of the accelerated payment is equal to the value of the payment absent acceleration and no portion of the payment is treated as contingent on a change in control. If the value of a payment absent acceleration is not reasonably ascertainable and the acceleration significantly increases the value of the payment, the future value of the payment is equal to the amount of the accelerated payment. When the future value (as opposed to the present value) of the payment is deemed to be the amount of the accelerated payment, then there is an excess and, therefore, a portion of the payment is treated as contingent on the change.

Q/A-24(c) provides that the portion of the payment treated as contingent on the change when both vesting and payment are accelerated is the lesser of (1) the payment or (2) the amount determined under Q/A-24(b) plus an additional amount to reflect the lapse of the obligation to perform additional services. Q/A-24(c) provides that for purposes of determining the amount under paragraph (b), the acceleration of the vesting of a stock option or the lapse of a restriction on restricted stock is considered to increase significantly the value of the payment.

Because Q/A-24(b) and (c) operate to provide an objective basis for determining the portion of a payment that is earned as of the date of a change in ownership or control, and therefore, not contingent on a change in ownership or control, these proposed regulations clarify that the rules in Q/As-38 through 44 (which provide rules related to reasonable compensation for services rendered), are inapplicable if the special rules in Q/A-24(b) or (c) apply to a payment.

Change in Ownership or Control

These proposed regulations follow the same approach as the 1989 proposed regulations for determining when a change in ownership or control occurs. However, these proposed regulations clarify that, for purposes of determining whether two or more persons acting as a group are considered to own more than 50 percent of the total fair market value or total voting power of the stock of a corporation on the date of a merger, acquisition, or similar transaction involving that corporation, a person who owns stock in both corporations involved in the transaction is treated as acting as a group with respect to the other shareholders in a corporation only to the extent of such person's ownership of stock in that corporation prior to the transaction, and not with respect to his or her ownership in the other corporation. For example, assume individual A owns stock in both corporations X and Y when corporation X acquires stock in Y in exchange for X stock. In determining whether corporation Y has undergone a change in ownership or control, individual A is considered to be acting as a group with other shareholders in corporation Y only to the extent of A's holdings in corporation Y prior to the transaction, and not with respect to A's ownership in X. In determining whether Corporation X has undergone a change in ownership or control, individual A is considered to be acting as a group with other shareholders in Corporation X only to the extent of individual A's holdings in Corporation X prior to the transaction, and not with respect to individual A's ownership interest in Corporation Y. This rule applies without regard to the type of shareholder involved (i.e., whether the shareholder is an individual or an institutional shareholder, such as a corporation, mutual fund, or trust).

Comments are requested with respect to whether the change in ownership or control rules in these proposed regulations should be further revised. Comments are also requested with respect to whether additional guidance is necessary regarding the application of the change in ownership or control provisions, and these proposed regulations in general, in the context of specific business situations such as bankruptcy.

Shareholder Approval Requirements

Section 280G specifically exempts from the definition of the term *parachute payment* several types of payments that would otherwise constitute parachute payments. Deductions for payments exempt from the definition of *parachute payment* are not disallowed by section 280G, and such exempt payments are not subject to the 20-percent excise tax of section 4999. In addition, such exempt payments are not taken into account in applying the 3-times-base-amount test of section 280G(b)(2)(A)(ii).

The most significant revisions made by these proposed regulations with respect to exempt payments are clarifications to the shareholder approval requirements which must be met for payments with respect to a corporation in which no stock is readily tradeable on an established securities market or otherwise immediately before the change in ownership or control.

Section 280G(b)(5)(B) provides that the shareholder approval requirements are met if two conditions are satisfied. First, the payment is approved by a vote of the persons who owned, immediately before the change in ownership or control, more than 75% of the voting power of all outstanding stock of the corporation. Second, there is adequate disclosure to shareholders of all material facts concerning all payments which (but for this rule) would be parachute payments with respect to a disqualified individual. Since the issuance of the 1989 proposed regulations, commentators have indicated that the 1989 proposed regulations do not fully explain how the shareholder approval requirements operate or accurately reflect business practices connected with a change in ownership or control.

The proposed regulations clarify the process of obtaining shareholder approval within the structure provided by section 280G(b)(5)(B). Under this section, a shareholder approval vote is valid only if (1) it is a vote of more than 75% of the shareholders entitled to vote based on ownership in the corporation immediately before the change in ownership or control, and (2) disclosure is made with respect to all payments that would otherwise be parachute payments for an individual.

The first step in obtaining shareholder approval is to identify the shareholders entitled to vote. Q/A-7 is revised to clarify that stock held by a disqualified individual (or by certain entity shareholders) is not entitled to vote with respect to a payment to be made to any disqualified individual and that this stock is disregarded in determining whether the more than 75% approval requirement has been met. Once the stock entitled to vote is determined, more than 75% of the voting power of such stock must approve the payment. Q/A-7 also includes a rule of administrative convenience providing that a vote to approve the payment does not fail to be a vote of the shareholders who own stock immediately before the change in ownership or control if eligibility to vote is based on the shareholders of record at the time of any vote taken in connection with a transaction or event giving rise to the change in ownership or control within the three-month period ending on the date of the change in ownership or control. This rule only applies if the disclosure requirements are also met.

These proposed regulations further clarify that not all parachute payments must be subject to a shareholder vote to satisfy the shareholder approval requirements with respect to a payment. It is permissible for only a portion of the payments that would otherwise be made to a disqualified individual to be subject to vote. For example, assume that a disqualified individual with a base amount of $150,000 would receive payments that (but for the exemption for a corporation with no readily tradeable stock) would be parachute payments including (i) a bonus payment of $200,000, (ii) vesting in stock options with a fair market value of $500,000, $200,000 of which is contingent on the change in ownership or control, and (iii) severance payments of $100,000. In this situation, assuming all of the payments are disclosed, the corporation may submit to the shareholders for approval (1) all of the payments, (2) any one of the three payments, or (3) $50,001 of any one of the payments (e.g., options with a value of $50,001). The issue submitted to a shareholder vote must be whether the payment will be made to the disqualified individual, not whether the corporation will be able to deduct the payment. In addition, the vote must be a separate vote of the shareholders. Therefore, the merger, acquisition, or other transaction cannot be conditioned on the shareholders' approval of the payment.

These proposed regulations also clarify that the shareholder approval requirements are met by a single vote on all payments submitted to the vote, including payments to more than one disqualified individual (assuming the disclosure requirements, described below, are also met).

The shareholder approval requirements also require adequate disclosure of all material facts concerning the amount of all parachute payments. For this purpose, the proposed regulations clarify that the amount of all parachute payments to be made to each disqualified individual, and not just the amount of the payments subject to vote, is a material fact. These proposed regulations also clarify that shareholders should be provided with basic information about the type of payments involved (e.g., vesting of stock options or severance payments). This disclosure of information must be made to all shareholders entitled to vote, not just to shareholders with 75% of the voting power entitled to vote.

Reasonable Compensation

The determination of whether amounts are reasonable compensation is relevant for two purposes. First, an excess parachute payment is reduced by any portion of the payment that constitutes reasonable compensation for services actually rendered before a change in ownership or control. Second, amounts that are reasonable compensation for services to be rendered after a change in ownership or control are exempt from the definition of parachute payment. In both situations, reasonable compensation for services must be demonstrated by clear and convincing evidence.

These proposed regulations clarify two issues with respect to reasonable compensation for services performed after a change in ownership or control. The proposed regulations clarify that clear and convincing evidence that a payment is reasonable compensation for services rendered after a change in ownership or control exists if the individual's annual compensation after the change in ownership or control (apart from normal increases) is not significantly greater then the individual's annual compensation before the change in ownership or control, provided that the individual's duties and responsibilities are substantially the same after the change in ownership or control as they were before the change in ownership or control. If the individual's duties and responsibilities have changed, then the clear and convincing evidence must demonstrate that the individual's annual compensation after the change in ownership or control is not significantly greater than the compensation customarily paid by the employer, or by comparable employers, to persons performing comparable services.

Payments to an individual under an agreement that requires the individual to refrain from providing services (such as under a covenant not to compete) may also constitute reasonable compensation for services to be rendered on or after the date of the change in ownership or control. Under Q/A-42 of these proposed regulations, an agreement is treated as an agreement to refrain from services (rather than an agreement for severance pay) if it is demonstrated with clear and convincing evidence that the agreement substantially constrains the individual's ability to perform services and there is a reasonable likelihood that the agreement will be enforced against the individual. If, under the facts and circumstances, the agreement does not satisfy these criteria, the payments under the agreement are instead treated as severance payments under Q/A-44. If the agreement does satisfy these criteria, then the agreement is treated as an agreement for the performance of services, and the payment are exempt from the definition of *parachute payment* to the extent the payments are shown to be reasonable compensation under Q/A-42(a)(2). [Corrected by IRS on 6/21/02, 67 FR 42210].

Application to Tax-Exempt Organizations

Commentators have asked whether a payment with respect to a tax-exempt entity is exempt from the definition of the term *parachute payment*. These proposed regulations clarify that a payment with respect to a tax-exempt entity that would otherwise constitute a parachute payment is exempt from the definition of the term *parachute payment* if the following two conditions are satisfied.

First, the payment must be made by a corporation undergoing a change in ownership or control that is a *tax-exempt organization*, as defined in these proposed regulations. A *tax-exempt organization* is defined as any organization described in section 501(c) that is subject to an express statutory prohibition against inurement of net earnings to the benefit of any private shareholder or individual, an organization described in subsections 501(c)(1) or 501(c)(21), any religious or apostolic organization described in section 501(d), or any qualified tuition program described in section 529.

Second, the organization must meet the definition of *tax-exempt organization*, as defined in these regulations, both immediately before and immediately after the change in ownership or control. If this second condition is not met, a payment made by a *tax-exempt organization* is not exempt from the definition of *parachute payment*.

As noted above, the term *tax-exempt organizations* includes organizations that are described in section 501(c) that already are subject to express statutory rules that prohibit the inurement of the net earnings of such organizations to the benefit of "any private shareholder or individual." Organizations described in the following subsections of 501(c) are *tax-exempt organizations* under application of this rule: 501(c)(3) (including any organization described in subsections 501(e), (f), or (k)), 501(c)(4), 501(c)(6), 501(c)(9), 501(c)(11), 501(c)(13) (but only with respect to those organizations subject to the express anti-inurement provision), 501(c)(19), and 501(c)(26). In light of the existing restrictions on these organizations, the Service and the Treasury Department believe the additional protections of section 280G are unnecessary. In addition, the term *tax-exempt organization* in the proposed regulations includes federal instrumentalities organized under Act of Congress (described in section 501(c)(1)), black lung trusts (described in section 501(c)(21)), certain religious and apostolic organizations (described in section 501(d)) and qualified tuition programs (described in section 529). The Service and the Treasury Department recognize that it may be appropriate to exempt payments made by other types of tax-exempt organizations. Comments are requested on whether any additional categories of organizations should be included in the definition of *tax-exempt organization* for purposes of section 280G.

Definition of Corporation

Under the 1989 proposed regulations, *corporation* is defined by reference to section 7701(a)(3) of the Code. These proposed regulations clarify that the term *corporation*, for purposes of section 280G and the regulations thereunder, includes any entity described in §301.7701-2(b) such as, for example, a real estate investment trust under section 856(a), a corporation that has mutual or cooperative (rather than stock) ownership, such as a mutual insurance company, a mutual savings bank, or a cooperative bank (as defined in section 7701(a)(32)), and a foreign corporation (as defined in section 7701(a)(5)).

Accordingly, the term *corporation* also includes any entity described in §301.7701-3(c)(1)(v)(A). That regulation provides, in general, that an entity that claims to be, or is determined to be, an entity that is exempt from taxation under section 501(a) is treated as an association for purposes of the Code. Because the definition of *corporation* includes an association, any entity described in §301.7701-3(c)(1)(v)(A) is a corporation for purposes of sections 7701 and 280G.

Determination of Excess Parachute Payments

Once all parachute payments are identified, the determination of what portion, if any, of each parachute payment is an excess parachute payment is made. This determination is based on the aggregate present value of all parachute payments. These proposed regulations modify the method described in Q/A-33 of the 1989 proposed regulations for determining the present value of a payment contingent on an uncertain future event or condition. Under Q/A-33 of these proposed regulations, if there is at least a 50-percent probability that the payment will be made, the entire present value of a contingent payment should be included for purposes of determining if there are excess parachute payments. If there is less than a 50-percent probability, then the present value of the contingent payment is not included. Once it is certain whether or not the payment will be made, the 3-times-base amount test in Q/A-30 is reapplied if the initial determination as to whether to include the payment was incorrect. If the inclusion or exclusion of the payment for purposes of Q/A-30 at the time of the change in ownership or control was correct, there is no need to reapply the 3-times-base-amount test. In addition, if it is reasonably estimated that there is a less than 50-percent probability that the payment will be made and the payment is not included in the 3-times-base-amount test, but the payment is later made, the 3-times-base-amount test is not reapplied if the test without regard to the contingent payment resulted in a determination that the individual received (or would receive) excess parachute payments and no base amount is allocated to the contingent payment.

Finally, Q/A-31 provides guidance on determining the present value of an obligation to provide health care over a period of years. Under these proposed regulations, the determination of the present value of this obligation should be calculated in accordance with generally accepted accounting principles. For purposes of Q/A-31, it is permissible for the obligation to provide health care to be measured by projecting the cost of premiums for purchased health care insurance, even if no health care insurance is actually purchased. If the obligation to provide health care is made in coordination with a health care plan that the corporation makes available to a group, then the premiums used for this purpose may be group premiums. This method only applies for purposes of determining present value. Premiums for health care insurance can be used for purposes of determining a corporation's loss of deduction or the excise tax obligation for a disqualified individual only to the extent such premiums are actually paid for health care insurance used to satisfy the corporation's obligation to provide health care.

Timing of the Payment of Tax under Section 4999

In general, the excise tax under section 4999 is due at the time that the payment is considered made under Q/A-11 through 13. Q/A-11(b) of these proposed regulations clarifies that, except as provided in Q/A-12 or 13, a payment is considered made in the taxable year that it is includible in the disqualified individual's gross income, or for benefits excludible from income, in the year the benefit is received. Q/A-11(c) of these proposed regulations permits a disqualified individual, for purposes of section 4999, to treat certain payments as made in the year of the change in ownership or control (or the first year for which a payment contingent on a change in ownership or control is certain to be made), even though the payment is not yet includible in income (or otherwise received). This treatment is not available, however, for a payment if the present value is not reasonably ascertainable within the meaning of section 3121(v) and §31.3121(v)2-(e)(4) or for a payment related to health benefits or coverage. These proposed regulations indicate in Q/A-11(c) that the Commissioner may provide through published guidance that Q/A-11(c) is or is not available with respect to other types of payments. [Corrected by IRS on 6/21/02, 67 FR 42210].

According to Q/A-11(c) of these proposed regulations, the payment of the excise tax under section 4999 must be made based on the amount calculated for purposes of determining excess parachute payments. Therefore, to the extent that the determination of whether there is an excess parachute payment is based on an incorrect valuation of the payment, the excise tax payment under this provision is also incorrect.

Proposed Effective Date

These regulations are proposed to apply to any payments that are contingent on a change in ownership or control that occurs on or after January 1, 2004. Taxpayers may rely on these proposed regulations until the effective date of the final regulations. Alternatively, taxpayers may rely on the 1989 proposed regulations for any payment contingent on a change in ownership or control that occurs prior to January 1, 2004. [Corrected by IRS on 6/21/02, 67 FR 42210].

Special Analyses

It has been determined that this notice of proposed rulemaking is not a significant regulatory action as defined in Executive Order 12866. Therefore, a regulatory assessment is not required. It has also been determined that section 553(b) of the Administrative Procedure Act (5 U.S.C. chapter 5) does not apply to these regulations, and, because the regulations do not impose a collection of information on small entities, the Regulatory Flexibility Act (5 U.S.C. chapter 6) does not apply. Pursuant to section 7805(f), this notice of proposed rulemaking will be submitted to the Chief Counsel for Advocacy of the Small Business Administration for comment on its impact on small business.

Comments And Public Hearing

Before these proposed regulations are adopted as final regulations, consideration will be given to any written or electronic comments (a signed original and eight (8) copies) that are submitted timely to the IRS. All comments will be available for public inspection and copying.

A public hearing has been scheduled for June 26, 2002, beginning at 10 a.m. in the IRS Auditorium of the Internal Revenue Building, 1111 Constitution Avenue, NW, Washington, DC. All visitors must present photo identification to enter the building. Because of access restrictions, visitors will not be admitted beyond the immediate entrance area more than 15 minutes before the hearing starts. For information about having your name placed on the building access list to attend the hearing, see the "FOR FURTHER INFORMATION CONTACT" section of this preamble.

The rules of 26 CFR 601.601(a)(3) apply to the hearing. Persons who wish to present oral comments at the hearing must submit written comments and an outline of the topics to be discussed and the time to be devoted to each topic (signed original and eight (8) copies) by June 5, 2002. A period of 10 minutes will be allotted to each person for making comments. An agenda showing the schedule of speakers will be prepared after the deadline for receiving outlines has passed. Copies of the agenda will be available free of charge at the hearing.

Drafting Information

The principal author of these proposed regulations is Erinn Madden, Office of the Division Counsel/Associate Chief Counsel (Tax Exempt and Government Entities). However, other personnel from the IRS and Treasury Department participated in their development.

List Of Subjects In 26 Cfr Part 1

Income taxes, Reporting and recordkeeping requirements.

Proposed Amendments To The Regulations

The proposed amendments to 26 CFR part 1 are as follows:

PART I—INCOME TAX; TAXABLE YEARS BEGINNING AFTER DECEMBER 31, 1986.

Paragraph 1. The authority citation for part 1 is amended by adding the following entry in numerical order to read in part as follows:

Authority: 26 U.S.C. 7805 ***

Section 1.280G-1 also issued under 26 U.S.C. 280G(b) and (e). ***

Par. 2. Section § 1.280G-1 is added to read as follows:

§ 1.280G-1 Golden parachute payments.

The following questions and answers relate to the treatment of golden parachute payments under section 280G of the Internal Revenue Code of 1986, as added by section 67 of the Tax Reform Act of 1984 (Public Law No. 98-369; 98 Stat. 585) and amended by section 1804(j) of the Tax Reform Act of 1986 (Public Law No. 99-514; 100 Stat. 2807), section 1018(d)(6)-(8) of the Technical and Miscellaneous Revenue Act of 1988 (Public Law No. 100-647; 102 Stat. 3581), and section 1421 of the Small Business Job Protection Act of 1996 (Public Law No. 104-188, 110 Stat. 1755). The following is a table of contents for this section:

Overview

Q-1: What is the effect of Internal Revenue Code section 280G?

A-1: (a) Section 280G disallows a deduction for any excess parachute payment paid or accrued. For rules relating to the imposition of a nondeductible 20-percent excise tax on the recipient of any excess parachute payment, see Internal Revenue Code sections 4999, 275(a)(6), and 3121(v)(2)(A).

(b) The disallowance of a deduction under section 280G is not contingent on the imposition of the excise tax under section 4999. The imposition of the excise tax under section 4999 is not contingent on the disallowance of a deduction under section 280G. Thus, for example, because the imposition of the excise tax under section 4999 is not contingent on the disallowance of a deduction under section 280G, a payee may be subject to the 20-percent excise tax under section 4999 even though the disallowance of the deduction for the excess parachute payment may not directly affect the federal taxable income of the payor.

Q-2: What is a parachute payment for purposes of section 280G?

A-2: (a) The term *parachute payment* means any payment (other than an exempt payment described in Q/A-5) that—

(1) Is in the nature of compensation;

(2) Is made or is to be made to (or for the benefit of) a disqualified individual;

(3) Is contingent on a change—

(i) In the ownership of a corporation;

(ii) In the effective control of a corporation; or

(iii) In the ownership of a substantial portion of the assets of a corporation; and

(4) Has (together with other payments described in paragraphs (a)(1), (2), and (3) of this A-2 with respect to the same disqualified individual) an aggregate present value of at least 3 times the individual's base amount.

(b) Hereinafter, a change referred to in paragraph (a)(3) of this A-2 is referred to as a change in ownership or control. For a discussion of the application of paragraph (a)(1), see Q/A-11 through Q/A-14; paragraph (a)(2), Q/A-15 through Q/A-21; paragraph (a)(3), Q/A-22 through Q/A-29; and paragraph (a)(4), Q/A-30 through Q/A-36.

(c) The term *parachute payment* also includes any payment in the nature of compensation to (or for the benefit of) a disqualified individual that is pursuant to an agreement that violates a generally enforced securities law or regulation. This type of parachute payment is referred to in this section as a securities violation parachute payment. See Q/A-37 for the definition and treatment of securities violation parachute payments.

Q-3: What is an excess parachute payment for purposes of section 280G?

A-3: The term *excess parachute payment* means an amount equal to the excess of any parachute payment over the portion of the base amount allocated to such payment. Subject to certain exceptions and limitations, an excess parachute payment is reduced by any portion of the payment which the taxpayer establishes by clear and convincing evidence is reasonable compensation for personal services actually rendered by the disqualified individual before the date of the change in

ownership or control. For a discussion of the nonreduction of a securities violation parachute payment by reasonable compensation, see Q/A-37. For a discussion of the computation of excess parachute payments and their reduction by reasonable compensation, see Q/A-38 through Q/A-44.

Q-4: What is the effective date of section 280G and this section?

A-4: In general, section 280G applies to payments under agreements entered into or renewed after June 14, 1984. Section 280G also applies to certain payments under agreements entered into on or before June 14, 1984, and amended or supplemented in significant relevant respect after that date. This section applies to any payment contingent on a change in ownership or control which occurs on or after January 1, 2004. For a discussion of the application of the effective date, see Q/A-47 and Q/A-48.

Exempt Payments

Q-5: Are some types of payments exempt from the definition of the term *parachute payment*?

A-5: (a) Yes, the following five types of payments are exempt from the definition of *parachute payment*—

(1) Payments with respect to a small business corporation (described in Q/A-6 of this section);

(2) Certain payments with respect to a corporation no stock in which is readily tradeable on an established securities market (or otherwise) (described in Q/A-6 of this section);

(3) Payments to or from a qualified plan (described in Q/A-8 of this section);

(4) Certain payments made by a corporation undergoing a change in ownership or control that is described in any of the following sections of the Internal Revenue Code: section 501(c) (but only if such organization is subject to an express statutory prohibition against inurement of net earnings to the benefit of any private shareholder or individual, or if the organization is described in section 501(c)(1) or section 501(c)(21)), section 501(d), or section 529, collectively referred to as *tax-exempt organizations* (described in Q/A-6 of this section); and

(5) Certain payments of reasonable compensation for services to be rendered on or after the change in ownership or control (described in Q/A-9 of this section).

(b) Deductions for payments exempt from the definition of *parachute payment* are not disallowed by section 280G, and such exempt payments are not subject to the 20-percent excise tax of section 4999. In addition, such exempt payments are not taken into account in applying the 3-times-base-amount test of Q/A-30 of this section.

Q-6: Which payments with respect to a corporation referred to in paragraph (a)(1), (a)(2), or (a)(4) of Q/A-5 of this section are exempt from the definition of *parachute payment*?

A-6: (a) The term *parachute payment* does not include—

(1) Any payment to a disqualified individual with respect to a corporation which (immediately before the change in ownership or control) was a small business corporation (as defined in section 1361(b) but without regard to section 1361(b)(1)(C) thereof),

(2) Any payment to a disqualified individual with respect to a corporation (other than a small business corporation described in paragraph (a)(1) of this A-6) if—

(i) Immediately before the change in ownership or control, no stock in such corporation was readily tradeable on an established securities market or otherwise; and

(ii) The shareholder approval requirements described in Q/A-7 of this section are met with respect to such payment; or

(3) Any payment to a disqualified individual made by a corporation which is a tax-exempt organization (as defined in paragraph (a)(4) of Q/A-5 of this section), but only if the corporation meets the definition of a tax-exempt organization both immediately before and immediately after the change in ownership or control.

(b) For purposes of paragraph (a)(1) of this A-6, the members of an affiliated group are not treated as one corporation.

(c) The requirements of paragraph (a)(2)(i) of this A-6 are not met if a substantial portion of the assets of a corporation undergoing a change in ownership or control consists (directly or indirectly) of stock in another entity (or any ownership interest in such entity) and stock of such entity (or any ownership interest in such entity) is readily tradeable on an established securities market or otherwise. For this purpose, such stock constitutes a substantial portion of the assets of an entity if the total fair market value of the stock is equal to or exceeds one third of the total gross fair market value of all of the assets of the entity. If a corporation is a member of an affiliated group (which group is treated as one corporation under A-46 of this section), the requirements of paragraph (a)(2)(i) of this A-6 are not met if any stock in any member of such group is readily tradeable on an established securities market or otherwise.

(d) For purposes of paragraph (a)(2)(i) of this A-6, the term *stock* does not include stock described in section 1504(a)(4) if the payment does not adversely affect the redemption and liquidation rights of any shareholder owning such stock.

(e) For purposes of paragraph (a)(2)(i) of this A-6, stock is treated as readily tradeable if it is regularly quoted by brokers or dealers making a market in such stock.

(f) For purposes of paragraph (a)(2)(i) of this A-6, the term *established securities market* means an established securities market as defined in § 1.897-1(m).

(g) The following examples illustrate the application of this exemption:

Example 1. A small business corporation (within the meaning of paragraph (a)(1) of this A-6) operates two businesses. The corporation sells the assets of one of its businesses, and these assets represent a substantial portion of the assets of the corporation. Because of the sale, the corporation terminates its employment relationship with persons employed in the business the assets of which are sold. Several of these employees are highly-compensated individuals to whom the owners of the corporation make severance payments in excess of 3 times each employee's base amount. Since the corporation is a small business corporation immediately before the change in ownership or control, the payments are not parachute payments.

Example 2. Assume the same facts as in *Example 1*, except that the corporation is not a small business corporation within the meaning of paragraph (a)(1) of this A-6. If no stock in the corporation is readily tradeable on an established securities market (or otherwise) immediately before the change in ownership or control and the shareholder approval requirements described in Q/A-7 of this section are met, the payments are not parachute payments.

Example 3. Stock of Corporation S is wholly owned by Corporation P, stock in which is readily tradeable on an established securities market. The Corporation S stock equals or exceeds one third of the total gross fair market value of Corporation P, and thus, represents a substantial portion of the assets of Corporation P. Corporation S makes severance payments to several of its highly-compensated individuals that are parachute payments under section 280G and Q/A-2 of this section. Because stock in Corporation P is readily tradeable on an established securities market, the payments are not exempt from the definition of *parachute payments* under this A-6.

Example 4. A is a corporation described in section 501(c)(3), and accordingly, its net earnings are prohibited from inuring to the benefit of any private shareholder or individual. A transfers substantially all of its assets to another corporation resulting in a change in ownership or control. Contingent on the change in ownership or control, A makes a payment that, but for the potential application of the exemption described in A-5(a)(4), would constitute a *parachute payment*. However, one or more aspects of the transaction that constitutes the change in ownership or control causes A to fail to be described in section 501(c)(3). Accordingly, A fails to meet the definition of a *tax-exempt*

organization both immediately before and immediately after the change in ownership or control, as required by this A-6. As a result, the payment made by A that was contingent on the change in ownership or control is not exempt from the definition of *parachute payment* under this A-6. [Corrected by IRS on 6/21/02, 67 FR 42210].

Example 5. B is a corporation described in section 501(c)(15). B does not meet the definition of a *tax-exempt organization* because section 501(c)(15) does not expressly prohibit inurement of B's net earnings to the benefit of any private shareholder or individual. Accordingly, if B has a change in ownership or control and makes a payment that would otherwise meet the definition of a *parachute payment*, such payment is not exempt from the definition of the term *parachute payment* for purposes of this A-6. [Corrected by IRS on 6/21/02, 67 FR 42210].

Q-7: How are the shareholder approval requirements referred to in paragraph (a)(2)(ii) of Q/A-6 of this section met?

A-7: (a) *General rule.* The shareholder approval requirements referred to in paragraph (a)(2)(ii) of Q/A-6 of this section are met with respect to any payment if—

(1) Such payment was approved by more than 75 percent of the voting power of all outstanding stock of the corporation entitled to vote (as described in this A-7) immediately before the change in ownership or control; and

(2) There was adequate disclosure to all persons entitled to vote (as described in this A-7) of all material facts concerning all material payments which (but for Q/A-6 of this section) would be parachute payments with respect to a disqualified individual.

(b) *Voting requirements*—(1) *General rule.* The vote described in paragraph (a)(1) of this A-7 must determine the right of the disqualified individual to receive the payment, or, in the case of a payment made before the vote, the right of the disqualified individual to retain the payment. For purposes of this A-7, the vote can be on less than the full amount of the payment(s) to be made. The total payment(s) submitted for shareholder approval must be separately approved by the shareholders. Shareholder approval can be a single vote on all payments submitted to vote, including payments to more than one disqualified individual. The requirements of this paragraph (b)(1) are not satisfied if approval of the change in ownership or control is contingent on the approval of any payment that would be a parachute payment but for Q/A-6 of this section to a disqualified individual. [Corrected by IRS on 6/21/02, 67 FR 42210].

(2) *Special rule for vote within 3 months before change.* A vote to approve the payment does not fail to be a vote of the outstanding stock of the corporation entitled to vote immediately before the change in ownership or control merely because the determination of the shareholders entitled to vote on the payment is based on the shareholders of record at the time of any shareholder vote taken in connection with a transaction or event giving rise to such change in ownership or control and within the three-month period ending on date of the change in ownership or control, provided the disclosure requirements described in paragraph (c) of this A-7 are met.

(3) *Entity shareholder.* Approval of a payment by any shareholder that is not an individual (an entity shareholder) generally must be made by the person authorized by the entity shareholder to approve the payment. However, if a substantial portion of the assets of an entity shareholder consists (directly or indirectly) of stock in the corporation undergoing the change in ownership or control, approval of the payment by that entity shareholder must be made by a separate vote of the persons who hold, immediately before the change in ownership or control, more than 75 percent of the voting power of the entity shareholder. The preceding sentence does not apply if the value of the stock of the corporation owned, directly or indirectly, by or for the entity shareholder does not exceed 1 percent of the total value of the outstanding stock of the corporation. Where approval of a payment by an entity shareholder must be made by a separate vote of the owners of the entity shareholder, the normal voting rights of the entity shareholder determine which owners shall vote. For purposes of this A-7, stock represents a substantial portion of the assets of an entity shareholder if the total fair market value of the stock held by the entity shareholder in the corporation undergoing the change in ownership or control is equal to or exceeds one third of the total fair market value of all of the assets of the entity shareholder.

(4) *Attribution of stock ownership.* In determining the persons who comprise the "more than 75 percent" group referred to in paragraph (a)(1) or (b)(3) of this A-7, stock is not counted as outstanding stock if the stock is actually owned or constructively owned under section 318(a) by or for a disqualified individual who receives (or is to receive) payments that would be parachute payments if the shareholder approval requirements described in paragraph (a) of this A-7 were not

met. Likewise, stock is not counted as outstanding stock if the owner is considered under section 318(a) to own any part of the stock owned directly or indirectly by or for a disqualified individual described in the preceding sentence. In addition, if a partner authorized by a partnership to approve a payment is a disqualified individual with respect to the corporation undergoing a change in ownership or control, none of the stock held by the partnership is considered outstanding stock. However, if all persons who hold voting power in the corporation are disqualified individuals or related persons described in either of the two preceding sentences, then stock owned by such persons is counted as outstanding stock.

(5) *Disqualified individuals.* To satisfy the approval requirements of paragraph (a) of this A-7, the vote of a disqualified individual who receives (or is to receive) a payment that would be a parachute payment if the shareholder approval requirements described in paragraph (a) of this A-7 were not met is not considered in determining whether the more than 75 percent vote has been obtained for purposes of any vote under paragraph (a) of this A-7. However, if all persons who hold voting power in the corporation are disqualified individuals or related persons, then votes by such persons are considered in determining whether the more than 75% vote has been obtained.

(c) *Adequate disclosure.* To be adequate disclosure for purposes of paragraph (a)(2) of this A-7, disclosure must be full and truthful disclosure of the material facts and such additional information as is necessary to make the disclosure not materially misleading at the time the disclosure was made. Disclosure of such information must be made to every shareholder of the corporation entitled to vote under this A-7. For each disqualified individual, material facts that must be disclosed include the total amount of the payments that would be parachute payments if the shareholder approval requirements described in paragraph (a) of this A-7 were not met and a brief description of each payment (*e.g.,* accelerated vesting of options, bonus, or salary). An omitted fact is considered a material fact if there is a substantial likelihood that a reasonable shareholder would consider it important.

(d) *Corporation without shareholders.* If a corporation does not have shareholders, the exemption described in Q/A-6(a)(2) of this section and the shareholder approval requirements described in this A-7 do not apply. For purposes of this paragraph (d), a shareholder does not include a member in an association, joint stock company, or insurance company.

(e) *Examples.* The following examples illustrate the application of this A-7:

Example 1. Corporation S has two shareholders—Corporation P, which owns 76 percent of the stock of Corporation S, and A, a disqualified individual. No stock of Corporation P or S is readily tradeable on an established securities market (or otherwise). Stock of Corporation S equals or exceeds one third of the assets of Corporation P, and thus, represents a substantial portion of the assets of Corporation P. All of the stock of Corporation S is sold to Corporation M. Contingent on the change in ownership of Corporation S, severance payments are made to the officers of Corporation S in excess of 3 times each officer's base amount. If the payments are approved by a separate vote of the persons who hold, immediately before the sale, more than 75 percent of the voting power of the outstanding stock of Corporation P and the disclosure rules of paragraph (a)(2) of this A-7 are complied with, the shareholder approval requirements of this A-7 are met, and the payments are exempt from the definition of *parachute payment* pursuant to A-6 of this section.

Example 2. Corporation M is wholly owned by Partnership P. No interest in either M or P is readily tradeable on an established securities market (or otherwise). Stock of Corporation M equals or exceeds one third of the assets of Partnership P, and thus, represents a substantial portion of the assets of Partnership P. Corporation M undergoes a change in ownership or control. Partnership P has one general partner and 200 limited partners. None of the limited partners are entitled to vote on issues involving the management of the partnership investments. If the payments that would be parachute payments if the shareholder approval requirements of this A-7 are not met are approved by the general partner and the disclosure rules of paragraph (a)(2) of this A-7 are complied with, the shareholder approval requirements of this A-7 are met, and the payments are exempt from the definition of *parachute payment* pursuant to A-6 of this section.

Example 3. Corporation A has several shareholders including X and Y, who are disqualified individuals with respect to Corporation A. No stock of Corporation A is readily tradeable on an established securities market (or otherwise). Corporation A undergoes a change in ownership or control. Contingent on the change, severance payments are payable to X and Y that are in excess of 3 times each individual's base amount. To determine whether the approval requirements of paragraph

(a)(1) of this A-7 are satisfied regarding the payments to X and Y, the stock of X and Y is not considered outstanding, and X and Y are not eligible to vote.

Example 4. Assume the same facts as in *Example 3* except that after adequate disclosure (within the meaning of paragraph (a)(2) of this A-7) to all shareholders entitled to vote, 60 percent of the shareholders who are entitled to vote approve the payments to X and Y. Because more than 75 percent of the shareholders did not approve the payments to X and Y, the shareholder approval requirements of paragraph (a)(1) of this A-7 are not satisfied, and the payments are not made to X and Y.

Example 5. Assume the same facts as in *Example 3* except that disclosure of all the material facts regarding the payments to X and Y is made to two of Corporation A's shareholders, who collectively own 80 percent of Corporation A's stock entitled to vote and approve the payment. Assume further that no disclosure of the material facts regarding the payments to X and Y is made to other Corporation A shareholders who are entitled to vote within the meaning of this A-7. Because disclosure regarding the payments to X and Y is not made to all of Corporation A's shareholders who were entitled to vote, the disclosure requirements of paragraph (a)(2) of this A-7 are not met, and the payments are not exempt from the definition of *parachute payment* pursuant to Q/A-6.

Example 6. Corporation C has three shareholders—Partnership, which owns 20 percent of the stock of Corporation C; A, an individual who owns 60 percent of the stock of Corporation C; and B, an individual who owns 20 percent of Corporation C. Stock of Corporation C does not represent a substantial portion of the assets of Partnership. No interest in either Partnership or Corporation C is readily tradeable on an established securities market (or otherwise). P, a one-third partner in Partnership, is a disqualified individual with respect to Corporation C. Corporation C undergoes a change in ownership or control. Contingent on the change, a severance payment is payable to P in excess of 3 times P's base amount. To determine the persons who comprise the "more than 75 percent group" referred to in paragraph (a)(1) of this A-7 who must approve the payment to P, one third of the stock held by Partnership is not considered outstanding stock. If, however, P is the person authorized by Partnership to approve the payment, none of the shares of Partnership are considered outstanding stock.

Example 7. X, an employee of Corporation E, is a disqualified individual with respect to Corporation E. No stock in Corporation E is readily tradeable on an established securities market (or otherwise). X, Y, and Z are all employees and disqualified individuals with respect to Corporation E. Each individual has a base amount of $100,000. Corporation E undergoes a change in ownership or control. Contingent on the change, a severance payment of $400,000 is payable to X; $600,000 is payable to Y; and $1,000,000 is payable to Z. Corporation E provides a ballot to each Corporation E shareholder entitled to vote under paragraph (a)(1) of this A-7 listing and describing the payments of $400,000 to X; $600,000 to Y; and $1,000,000 to Z. Next to each name and corresponding amount on the ballot, Corporation E requests approval (with a "yes" and "no" box) of each total payment to be made to each individual and states that if the payment is not approved the payment will not be made. Adequate disclosure, within the meaning of this A-7 is made to each shareholder entitled to vote under this A-7. More than 75 percent of the Corporation E shareholders who are entitled to vote under paragraph (a)(1) of this A-7, approve each payment to each individual. The shareholder approval requirements of this A-7 are met, and the payments are exempt from the definition of *parachute payment* pursuant to A-6 of this section. [Corrected by IRS on 6/21/02, 67 FR 42210].

Example 8. Assume the same facts as in *Example 7* except that the ballot does not request approval of each total payment to each individual separately. Instead, the ballot states that $2,000,000 in payments will be made to X, Y, and Z and requests approval of all of the $2,000,000 payments. Assuming the nature and amount of the payments to X, Y, and Z are separately described to the shareholders entitled to vote under this A-7, the shareholder approval requirements of paragraph (a)(1) of this A-7 are met, and the payments are exempt from the definition of *parachute payment* pursuant to A-6 of this section. [Corrected by IRS on 6/21/02, 67 FR 42210].

Example 9. B, an employee of Corporation X, is a disqualified individual with respect to Corporation X. Stock of Corporation X is not readily tradeable on an established securities market (or otherwise). Corporation X undergoes a change in ownership or control. B's base amount is $205,000. Under B's employment agreement with Corporation X, in the event of a change in ownership or control, B's stock options will vest and B will receive a severance and bonus payment. Contingent on the change, B's stock options immediately vest with a fair market value of

$500,000, $200,000 of which is contingent on the change, and B will receive a $200,000 bonus payment and a $400,000 severance payment. Corporation X distributes a ballot to every shareholder of Corporation X who immediately before the change is entitled to vote. The ballot lists the following payments to be made to B: the contingent payment of $200,000 attributable to options, a $200,000 bonus payment, and a $400,000 severance payment. The ballot requests shareholder approval of the $200,000 bonus payment to B and states that whether or not the $200,000 bonus payment is approved, B will receive $200,000 attributable to options and a $400,000 severance payment. More than 75 percent of the shareholders entitled to vote approve the $200,000 bonus payment to B. The shareholder approval requirements of this A-7 are met, and the $200,000 payment is exempt from the definition of *parachute payment* pursuant to A-6 of this section.

Q-8: Which payments under a qualified plan are exempt from the definition of *parachute payment*?

A-8: The term *parachute payment* does not include any payment to or from—

(a) A plan described in section 401(a) which includes a trust exempt from tax under section 501(a);

(b) An annuity plan described in section 403(a);

(c) A simplified employee pension (as defined in section 408(k)); or

(d) A simple retirement account (as defined in section 408(p)).

Q-9: Which payments of reasonable compensation are exempt from the definition of *parachute payment*?

A-9: Except in the case of securities violation parachute payments, the term *parachute payment* does not include any payment (or portion thereof) which the taxpayer establishes by clear and convincing evidence is reasonable compensation for personal services to be rendered by the disqualified individual on or after the date of the change in ownership or control. See Q/A-37 of this section for the definition and treatment of securities violation parachute payments. See Q/A-38 through Q/A-44 of this section for rules on determining amounts of reasonable compensation.

Payor of Parachute Payments

Q-10: Who may be the payor of parachute payments?

A-10: Parachute payments within the meaning of Q/A-2 of this section may be paid, directly or indirectly, by—(a) The corporation referred to in paragraph (a)(3) of Q/A-2 of this section, (b) A person acquiring ownership or effective control of that corporation or ownership of a substantial portion of that corporation's assets, or (c) Any person whose relationship to such corporation or other person is such as to require attribution of stock ownership between the parties under section 318(a).

Payments in the Nature of Compensation

Q-11: What types of payments are in the nature of compensation?

A-11: (a) *General rule.* For purposes of this section, all payments—in whatever form—are payments in the nature of compensation if they arise out of an employment relationship or are associated with the performance of services. For this purpose, the performance of services includes holding oneself out as available to perform services and refraining from performing services (such as under a covenant not to compete or similar arrangement). Payments in the nature of compensation include (but are not limited to) wages and salary, bonuses, severance pay, fringe benefits, and pension benefits and other deferred compensation (including any amount characterized by the parties as interest thereon). A payment in the nature of compensation also includes cash when paid, the value of the right to receive cash, or a transfer of property. However, payments in the nature of compensation do not include attorney's fees or court costs paid or incurred in connection with the payment of any amount described in paragraphs (a)(1), (2), and (3) of Q/A-2 of this section or a reasonable rate of interest accrued on any amount during the period the parties contest whether a payment will be made.

(b) *When payment is considered to be made.* Except as otherwise provided in A-11 through Q/A-13 of this section, a payment in the nature of compensation is considered made (and is subject to the excise tax under section 4999) in the taxable year in which it is includible in the disqualified individual's gross income or, in the case of fringe benefits and other benefits excludible from income, in the taxable year the benefits are received.

(c) *Pre-payment rule.* Notwithstanding the general rule described in paragraph (b) of this A-11, for purposes of section 4999, a disqualified individual is permitted to treat a payment as received in the year of the change in ownership or control or, if later, the first year in which the payment (or payments) is certain to be made without regard to the year in which the payment (or payments) is includible in income (or otherwise received). The payment of the excise tax for purposes of section 4999 must be based on the amount calculated for purposes of determining any excess parachute payments. However, a disqualified individual may not apply this paragraph (c) of this A-11 to a payment to be made in cash if the present value of the payment would be considered not reasonably ascertainable under section 3121(v) and § 31.3121(v)2-1(e)(4) of this chapter, or a payment related to health benefits or coverage. The Commissioner is permitted to provide that this paragraph (c) is or is not available for certain types of payments. [Corrected by IRS on 6/21/02, 67 FR 42210].

(d) *Transfers of property.* Transfers of property are treated as payments for purposes of this A-11. See Q/A-12 of this section for rules on determining when such payments are considered made and the amount of such payments. See Q/A-13 of this section for special rules on transfers of statutory and nonstatutory stock options.

Q-12: If a property transfer to a disqualified individual is a payment in the nature of compensation, when is the payment considered made (or to be made), and how is the amount of the payment determined?

A-12: (a) Except as provided in this A-12 and Q/A-13 of this section, a transfer of property is considered a payment made (or to be made) in the taxable year in which the property transferred is includible in the gross income of the disqualified individual under section 83 and the regulations thereunder. Thus, in general, such a payment is considered made (or to be made) when the property is transferred (as defined in § 1.83-3(a)) to the disqualified individual and becomes substantially vested (as defined in § 1.83-3(b) and (j)) in such individual. In such case, the amount of the payment is determined under section 83 and the regulations thereunder. Thus, in general, the amount of the payment is equal to the excess of the fair market value of the transferred property (determined without regard to any lapse restriction, as defined in § 1.83-3(i)) at the time that the property becomes substantially vested, over the amount (if any) paid for the property.

(b) An election made by a disqualified individual under section 83(b) with respect to transferred property will not apply for purposes of this A-12. Thus, even if such an election is made with respect to a property transfer that is a payment in the nature of compensation, the payment is generally considered made (or to be made) when the property is transferred to and becomes substantially vested in such individual.

(c) See Q/A-13 of this section for rules on applying this A-12 to transfers of stock options.

(d) The following example illustrates the principles of this A-12:

Example. On January 1, 2006, Corporation M gives to A, a disqualified individual, a bonus of 100 shares of Corporation M stock in connection with the performance of services to Corporation M. Under the terms of the bonus arrangement A is obligated to return the Corporation M stock to Corporation M unless the earnings of Corporation M double by January 1, 2009, or there is a change in ownership or control of Corporation M before that date. A's rights in the stock are treated as substantially nonvested (within the meaning of § 1.83-3(b)) during that period because A's rights in the stock are subject to a substantial risk of forfeiture (within the meaning of § 1.83-3(c)) and are nontransferable (within the meaning of § 1.83-3(d)). On January 1, 2008, a change in ownership or control of Corporation M occurs. On that day, the fair market value of the Corporation M stock is $250 per share. Because A's rights in the Corporation M stock become substantially vested (within the meaning of § 1.83-3(b)) on that day, the payment is considered made on that day, and the amount of the payment for purposes of this section is equal to $25,000 (100×$250). See Q/A-38 through 41 for rules relating to the reduction of the excess parachute payment by the portion of the payment which is established to be reasonable compensation for personal services actually rendered before the date of a change in ownership or control.

Q-13: How are transfers of statutory and nonstatutory stock options treated?

A-13: (a) For purposes of this section, an option (including an option to which section 421 applies) is treated as property that is transferred not later than the time at which the option becomes substantially vested (whether or not the option has a readily ascertainable fair market value as defined in § 1.83-7(b)). Thus, for purposes of this section, the vesting of such an option is treated as a payment in the nature of compensation. The value of an option at the time the option vests is determined under all the facts and circumstances in the particular case. Factors relevant to such a determination include, but are not limited to: the difference between the option's exercise price and the value of the property subject to the option at the time of vesting; the probability of the value of such property increasing or decreasing; and the length of the period during which the option can be exercised. Valuation may be determined by any method prescribed by the Commissioner in published guidance for purposes of this A-13. See Q/A-33 of this section for the treatment of options the granting or vesting of which is contingent on a change in ownership or control and that do not have an ascertainable fair market value at the time of granting or vesting. [Corrected by IRS on 6/21/02, 67 FR 42210].

(b) Any money or other property transferred to the disqualified individual on the exercise, or as consideration on the sale or other disposition, of an option described in paragraph (a) of this A-13 after the time such option vests is not treated as a payment in the nature of compensation to the disqualified individual under Q/A-11 of this section. Nonetheless, the amount of the otherwise allowable deduction under section 162 or 212 with respect to such transfer is reduced by the amount of the payment described in paragraph (a) of this A-13 treated as an excess parachute payment.

Q-14: Are payments in the nature of compensation reduced by consideration paid by the disqualified individual?

A-14: Yes, to the extent not otherwise taken into account under Q/A-12 and Q/A-13 of this section, the amount of any payment in the nature of compensation is reduced by the amount of any money or the fair market value of any property (owned by the disqualified individual without restriction) that is (or will be) transferred by the disqualified individual in exchange for the payment. For purposes of the preceding sentence, the fair market value of property is determined as of the date the property is transferred by the disqualified individual.

Disqualified Individuals

Q-15: Who is a disqualified individual?

A-15: (a) For purposes of this section, an individual is a disqualified individual with respect to a corporation if, at any time during the *disqualified individual determination period* (as defined in Q/A-20 of this section), the individual is an employee or independent contractor of the corporation and is, with respect to the corporation—

(1) A shareholder (but see Q/A-17 of this section);

(2) An officer (see Q/A-18 of this section); or

(3) A highly-compensated individual (see Q/A-19 of this section).

(b) A director is a disqualified individual with respect to a corporation if, at any time during the *disqualified individual determination period* (as defined in Q/A-20 of this section), the director is an employee or independent contractor and is, with respect to the corporation, either a shareholder (see Q/A-17 of this section) or a highly-compensated individual (see Q/A-19 of this section).

Q-16: Is a personal service corporation treated as an individual?

A-16: (a) Yes. For purposes of this section, a personal service corporation (as defined in section 269A(b)(1)), or a noncorporate entity that would be a personal service corporation if it were a corporation, is treated as an individual.

(b) The following example illustrates the principles of this A-16:

Example. Corporation N, a personal service corporation (as defined in section 269A(b)(1)), has a single individual as its sole shareholder and employee. Corporation N performs personal services for Corporation M. The compensation paid to Corporation N by Corporation M puts Corporation N within the group of the highly-compensated individuals of Corporation M as determined under A-19 of this section. Thus, Corporation N is treated as a highly-compensated individual with respect to Corporation M.

Q-17: Are all shareholders of a corporation considered shareholders for purposes of paragraph (a)(1) and (b) of Q/A-15 of this section? [Corrected by IRS on 6/21/02, 67 FR 42210].

A-17: (a) No, only an individual who owns stock of a corporation with a fair market value that exceeds 1 percent of the fair market value of the outstanding shares of all classes of the corporation's stock is treated as a disqualified individual with respect to the corporation by reason of stock ownership. An individual who owns a lesser amount of stock may, however, be a disqualified individual with respect to the corporation if such individual is an officer or highly-compensated individual with respect to the corporation. For purposes of determining the amount of stock owned by an individual, the constructive ownership rules of section 318(a) apply.

(b) The following examples illustrates the principles of this A-17:

Example 1. E, an employee of Corporation A, received options under Corporation A's Stock Option Plan. E's stock options vest three years

after the date of grant. E is not an officer or highly compensated individual during the disqualified individual determination period and does not own any other Corporation A stock. Two years after the options are granted to E, all of Corporation A's stock is acquired by Corporation B. Under Corporation A's Stock Option Plan, E's options are converted to Corporation B options and the vesting schedule remains the same. To determine whether E is a disqualified individual based on E's stock ownership, the stock underlying the unvested options held by E on the date of the change in ownership or control is not considered constructively owned by E under section 318(a). Because E does not own, or constructively own, Corporation A stock with a fair market value exceeding 1 percent of the total fair market value of all of the outstanding shares of all classes of Corporation A and E is not an officer or highly-compensated individual during the disqualified individual determination period, E is not a disqualified individual within the meaning of A-15 of this section with respect to Corporation A.

Example 2. Assume the same facts as in *Example 1* except that Corporation A's Stock Option Plan provides that all unvested options will vest immediately on a change in ownership or control. To determine whether E is a disqualified individual based on E's stock ownership, the stock underlying the options that vest on the change in ownership or control is considered constructively owned by E under section 318(a). If the stock constructively held by E exceeds 1 percent of the total fair market value of all of the outstanding shares of all classes of Corporation A stock, E is a disqualified individual within the meaning of this A-15 of this section with respect to Corporation A.

Example 3. Assume the same facts as in *Example 1* except that E received nonstatutory stock options that are exercisable for stock subject to a substantial risk of forfeiture under section 83. Assume further that under Corporation A's Stock Option Plan, the nonstatutory options will vest on a change in ownership or control. To determine whether E is a disqualified individual based on E's stock ownership, the stock underlying the options that vest on the change in ownership or control is not considered constructively owned by E under section 318(a) because the options are exercisable for stock subject to a substantial risk of forfeiture within the meaning of section 83. Because E does not own, or constructively own, Corporation A stock with a fair market value exceeding 1 percent of the total fair market value of all of the outstanding shares of all classes of Corporation A stock and E is not an officer or highly compensated individual during the disqualified individual determination period, E is not a disqualified individual within the meaning of A-15 of this section with respect to Corporation A.

Q-18: Who is an officer?

A-18: (a) For purposes of this section, whether an individual is an officer with respect to a corporation is determined on the basis of all the facts and circumstances in the particular case (such as the source of the individual's authority, the term for which the individual is elected or appointed, and the nature and extent of the individual's duties). Generally, the term *officer* means an administrative executive who is in regular and continued service. The term *officer* implies continuity of service and excludes those employed for a special and single transaction. An individual who merely has the title of officer but not the authority of an officer is not considered an officer for purposes of this section. Similarly, an individual who does not have the title of officer but has the authority of an officer is considered an officer for purposes of this section.

(b) An individual who is an officer with respect to any member of an affiliated group that is treated as one corporation pursuant to Q/A-46 of this section is treated as an officer of such one corporation.

(c) No more than 50 employees (or, if less, the greater of 3 employees, or 10 percent of the employees (rounded up to the nearest integer)) of the corporation (in the case of an affiliated group treated as one corporation, each member of the affiliated group) are treated as disqualified individuals with respect to a corporation by reason of being an officer of the corporation. For purposes of the preceding sentence, the number of employees of the corporation is the greatest number of employees the corporation has during the disqualified individual determination period (as defined in Q/A-20 of this section). The number of employees is determined with regard to the rules in Q/A-19(c). If the number of officers of the corporation exceeds the number of employees who may be treated as officers under the first sentence of this paragraph (c), then the employees who are treated as officers for purposes of this section are the highest paid 50 employees (or, if less, the greater of 3 employees, or 10 percent of the employees (rounded up to the nearest integer)) of the corporation when ranked on the basis of compensation (as determined under Q/A-21 of this section) paid during the disqualified individual determination period.

Q-19: Who is a highly-compensated individual?

A-19: (a) For purposes of this section, a highly-compensated individual with respect to a corporation is any individual who is, or would be if the individual were an employee, a member of the group consisting of the lesser of the highest paid 1 percent of the employees of the corporation (rounded up to the nearest integer), or the highest paid 250 employees of the corporation, when ranked on the basis of compensation (as determined under Q/A-21 of this section) earned during the disqualified individual determination period (as defined in Q/A-20 of this section). For purposes of the preceding sentence, the number of employees of the corporation is the greatest number of employees the corporation has during the disqualified individual determination period (as defined in Q/A-20 of this section). However, no individual whose annualized compensation during the disqualified individual determination period is less than the amount described in section 414(q)(1)(B)(i) for the year in which the change in ownership or control occurs will be treated as a highly-compensated individual. [Corrected by IRS on 6/21/02, 67 FR 42210].

(b) An individual who is not an employee of the corporation is not treated as a highly-compensated individual with respect to the corporation on account of compensation received for performing services (such as brokerage, legal, or investment banking services) in connection with a change in ownership or control of the corporation, if the services are performed in the ordinary course of the individual's trade or business and the individual performs similar services for a significant number of clients unrelated to the corporation.

(c) In determining the total number of employees of a corporation for purposes of this A-19, employees are not counted if they normally work less than 17 1/2 hours per week (as defined in section 414(q)(5)(B) and the regulations thereunder) or if they normally work during not more than 6 months during any year (as defined in section 414(q)(5)(C) and the regulations thereunder). However, an employee who is not counted for purposes of the preceding sentence may still be a highly-compensated individual.

Q-20: What is the disqualified individual determination period?

A-20: The disqualified individual determination period is the twelve-month period prior to and ending on the date of the change in ownership or control of the corporation.

Q-21: How is *compensation* defined for purposes of determining who is a disqualified individual?

A-21: (a) For purposes of determining who is a disqualified individual, the term *compensation* is the compensation which was earned by the individual for services performed for the corporation with respect to which the change in ownership or control occurs (changed corporation), for a predecessor entity, or for a related entity. Such compensation is determined without regard to sections 125, 132(f)(4), 402(e)(3), and 402(h)(1)(B). Thus, for example, compensation includes elective or salary reduction contributions to a cafeteria plan, cash or deferred arrangement or tax-sheltered annuity and amounts credited under a nonqualified deferred compensation plan.

(b) For purposes of this A-21, a predecessor entity is any entity which, as a result of a merger, consolidation, purchase or acquisition of property or stock, corporate separation, or other similar business transaction transfers some or all of its employees to the changed corporation or to a related entity or to a predecessor entity of the changed corporation. The term *related entity* include—

(1) All members of a controlled group of corporations (as defined in section 414(b)) that includes the changed corporation or a predecessor entity;

(2) All trades or business (whether or not incorporated) that are under common control (as defined in section 414(c)) if such group includes the changed corporation or a predecessor entity;

(3) All members of an affiliated service group (as defined in section 414(m)) that includes the changed corporation or a predecessor entity; and

(4) Any other entities required to be aggregated with the changed corporation or a predecessor entity pursuant to section 414(o) and the regulations thereunder (except leasing organizations as defined in section 414(n)).

(c) For purposes of Q/A-18 and Q/A-19 of this section, compensation that was contingent on the change in ownership or control and that was payable in the year of the change is not treated as compensation.

Contingent on Change in Ownership or Control

Q-22: When is a payment contingent on a change in ownership or control?

A-22: (a) In general, a payment is treated as contingent on a change in ownership or control if the payment would not, in fact, have been made had no change in ownership or control occurred, even if the payment is also conditioned on the occurrence of another event. A payment generally is treated as one which would not, in fact, have been made in the absence of a change in ownership or control unless it is substantially certain, at the time of the change, that the payment would have been made whether or not the change occurred. (But see Q/A-23 of this section regarding payments under agreements entered into after a change in ownership or control.) A payment that becomes vested as a result of a change in ownership or control is not treated as a payment which was substantially certain to have been made whether or not the change occurred. For purposes of this A-22, *vested* means the payment is substantially vested within the meaning of § 1.83-3(b) and (j) or the right to the payment is not otherwise subject to a substantial risk of forfeiture.

(b)(1) For purposes of paragraph (a), a payment is treated as contingent on a change in ownership or control if—

(i) The payment is contingent on an event that is closely associated with a change in ownership or control;

(ii) A change in ownership or control actually occurs; and

(iii) The event is materially related to the change in ownership or control.

(2) For purposes of paragraph (b)(1)(i) of this A-22, a payment is treated as contingent on an event that is closely associated with a change in ownership or control unless it is substantially certain, at the time of the event, that the payment would have been made whether or not the event occurred. An event is considered closely associated with a change in ownership or control if the event is of a type often preliminary or subsequent to, or otherwise closely associated with, a change in ownership or control. For example, the following events are considered closely associated with a change in the ownership or control of a corporation: The onset of a tender offer with respect to the corporation; a substantial increase in the market price of the corporation's stock that occurs within a short period (but only if such increase occurs prior to a change in ownership or control); the cessation of the listing of the corporation's stock on an established securities market; the acquisition of more than 5 percent of the corporation's stock by a person (or more than one person acting as a group) not in control of the corporation; the voluntary or involuntary termination of the disqualified individual's employment; a significant reduction in the disqualified individual's job responsibilities; and a change in ownership or control as defined in the disqualified individual's employment agreement (or elsewhere) that does not meet the definition of a change in ownership or control described in Q/A-27, 28, or 29 of this section. Whether other events are treated as closely associated with a change in ownership or control is based on all the facts and circumstances of the particular case.

(3) For purposes of determining whether an event (as described in paragraph (b)(2) of this A-22) is materially related to a change in ownership or control, the event is presumed to be materially related to a change in ownership or control if such event occurs within the period beginning one year before and ending one year after the date of change in ownership or control. If such event occurs outside of the period beginning one year before and ending one year after the date of change in ownership or control, the event is presumed not materially related to the change in ownership or control. A payment does not fail to be contingent on a change in ownership or control merely because it is also contingent on the occurrence of a second event (without regard to whether the second event is closely associated with or materially related to a change in ownership or control). Similarly, a payment that is treated as contingent on a change because it is contingent on a closely associated event does not fail to be treated as contingent on a change in ownership or control merely because it is also contingent on the occurrence of a second event (without regard to whether the second event is closely associated with or materially related to a change in ownership or control).

(c) A payment that would in fact have been made had no change in ownership or control occurred is treated as contingent on a change in ownership or control if the change in ownership or control (or the occurrence of an event that is closely associated with and materially related to a change in ownership or control within the meaning of paragraph (b)(1) of this A-22), accelerates the time at which the payment is made. Thus, for example, if a change in ownership or control accelerates the time of payment of deferred compensation that is vested without regard to the change in ownership or control, the payment may be treated as contingent on the change. See Q/A-24 of this section regarding the portion of a payment that is so treated. See also Q/A-8 of this section regarding the exemption for certain payments under qualified plans and Q/A-40 of this section regarding the treatment of a payment as reasonable compensation. [Corrected by IRS on 6/21/02, 67 FR 42210].

(d) A payment is treated as contingent on a change in ownership or control even if the employment or independent contractor relationship of the disqualified individual is not terminated (voluntarily or involuntarily) as a result of the change.

(e) The following examples illustrate the principles of this A-22:

Example 1. A corporation grants a stock appreciation right to a disqualified individual, A, more than one year before a change in ownership or control. After the stock appreciation right vests and becomes exercisable, a change in ownership or control of the corporation occurs, and A exercises the right. Assuming neither the granting nor the vesting of the stock appreciation right is contingent on a change in ownership or control, the payment made on exercise is not contingent on the change in ownership or control.

Example 2. A contract between a corporation and B, a disqualified individual, provides that a payment will be made to B if the corporation undergoes a change in ownership or control and B's employment with the corporation is terminated at any time over the succeeding 5 years. Eighteen months later, a change in the ownership of the corporation occurs. Two years after the change in ownership, B's employment is terminated and the payment is made to B. Because it was not substantially certain that the corporation would have made the payment to B on B's termination of employment if there had not been a change in ownership, the payment is treated as contingent on the change in ownership under paragraph (a) of this A-22. This is true even though B's termination of employment is presumed not to be, and in fact may not be, materially related to the change in ownership or control.

Example 3. A contract between a corporation and C, a disqualified individual, provides that a payment will be made to C if C's employment is terminated at any time over the succeeding 3 years (without regard to whether or not there is a change in ownership or control). Eighteen months after the contract is entered into, a change in the ownership of the corporation occurs. Six months after the change in ownership, C's employment is terminated and the payment is made to C. Termination of employment is considered an event closely associated with a change in ownership or control. Because the termination occurred within one year after the date of the change in ownership, the termination of C's employment is presumed to be materially related to the change in ownership under paragraph (b)(3) of this A-22. If this presumption is not successfully rebutted, the payment will be treated as contingent on the change in ownership under paragraph (b) of this A-22.

Example 4. A contract between a corporation and a disqualified individual, D, provides that a payment will be made to D upon the onset of a tender offer for shares of the corporation's stock. A tender offer is made on December 1, 2008, and the payment is made to D. Although the tender offer is unsuccessful, it leads to a negotiated merger with another entity on June 1, 2009, which results in a change in the ownership of the corporation. It was not substantially certain, at the time of the onset of the tender offer, that the payment would have been made had no tender offer taken place. The onset of a tender offer is considered closely associated with a change in ownership or control. Because the tender offer occurred within one year before the date of the change in ownership of the corporation, the onset of the tender offer is presumed to be materially related to the change in ownership. If this presumption is not rebutted, the payment will be treated as contingent on the change in ownership. If no change in ownership or control had occurred, the payment would not be treated as contingent on a change in ownership or control; however, the payment still could be a parachute payment under Q/A-37 of this section if the contract violated a generally enforced securities law or regulation.

Example 5. A contract between a corporation and a disqualified individual, E, provides that a payment will be made to E if the corporation's level of product sales or profits reaches a specified level. At the time the contract was entered into, the parties had no reason to believe that such an increase in the corporation's level of product sales or profits would be preliminary or subsequent to, or otherwise closely associated with, a change in ownership or control of the corporation. Eighteen months later, a change in the ownership of the corporation occurs and within one year after the date of the change, the corporation's level of product sales or profits reaches the specified level. Under these facts and circumstances (and in the absence of contradictory evidence), the increase in product sales or profits of the corporation is not an event closely associated with the change in ownership or control of the corporation. Accordingly, even if the increase is materially related to the change, the payment will not be treated as contingent on a change in ownership or control.

Q-23: May a payment be treated as contingent on a change in ownership or control if the payment is made under an agreement entered into after the change?

A-23: (a) No, payments are not treated as contingent on a change in ownership or control if they are made (or to be made) pursuant to an agreement entered into after the change (a post-change agreement). For this purpose, an agreement that is executed after a change in ownership or control pursuant to a legally enforceable agreement that was entered into before the change is considered to have been entered into before the change. (See Q/A-9 of this section regarding the exemption for reasonable compensation for services rendered on or after a change in ownership or control.) If an individual has a right to receive a parachute payment under an agreement entered into prior to a change in ownership or control (pre-change agreement) and gives up that right as bargained-for consideration for benefits under a post-change agreement, the agreement is treated as a post-change agreement only to the extent the value of the payments under the agreement exceed the value of the payments under the pre-change agreement. To the extent payments under the agreement have the same value as the parachute payments under the pre-change agreement, such payments retain their character as parachute payments subject to this section.

(b) The following examples illustrate the principles of this A-23:

Example 1. Assume that a disqualified individual is an employee of a corporation. A change in ownership or control of the corporation occurs, and thereafter the individual enters into an employment agreement with the acquiring company. Because the agreement is entered into after the change in ownership or control occurs, payments to be made under the agreement are not treated as contingent on the change.

Example 2. Assume the same facts as in *Example 1*, except that the agreement between the disqualified individual and the acquiring company is executed after the change in ownership or control, pursuant to a legally enforceable agreement entered into before the change. Payments to be made under the agreement may be treated as contingent on the change in ownership or control pursuant to Q/A-22 of this section. However, see Q/A-9 of this section regarding the exemption from the definition of parachute payment for certain amounts of reasonable compensation.

Example 3. Assume the same facts as in *Example 1* except that prior to the change in ownership or control, the individual and corporation enter into an agreement under which the individual will receive parachute payments in the event of a change in ownership or control of the corporation. After the change, the individual agrees to give up the right to parachute payments under the pre-change agreement in exchange for compensation under a new agreement with the acquiring corporation. Because the individual gave up the right to parachute payments under the pre-change agreement in exchange for other payments under the post-change agreement, payments in an amount equal to the parachute payments under the pre-change agreement are treated as contingent on the change in ownership or control under this A-23. Because the post-change agreement was entered into after the change, payments in excess of this amount are not treated as parachute payments.

Q-24: If a payment is treated as contingent on a change in ownership or control, is the full amount of the payment so treated?

A-24: (a)(1) *General rule.* Yes, if the payment is a transfer of property, the amount of the payment is determined under Q/A-12 or Q/A-13 of this section. For all other payments, the amount of the payment is determined under Q/A-11 of this section. However, in certain circumstances, described in paragraphs (b) and (c) of this A-24, only a portion of the payment is treated as contingent on the change. Paragraph (b) of this A-24 applies to a payment that is vested, without regard to the change in ownership or control, and is treated as contingent on the change in ownership or control because the change accelerates the time at which the payment is made. Paragraph (c) of this A-24 applies to a payment that becomes vested as a result of the change in ownership or control if, without regard to the change in ownership or control, the payment was contingent only on the continued performance of services for the corporation for a specified period of time and if the payment is attributable, at least in part, to services performed before the date the payment becomes vested. For purposes of this A-24, for the definition of vested see Q/A-22(a).

(2) *Reduction by reasonable compensation.* The amount of a payment under paragraph (a)(1) of this A-24 is reduced by any portion of such payment that the taxpayer establishes by clear and convincing evidence is reasonable compensation for personal services rendered by the disqualified individual on or after the date of the change of control. See Q/A-9 and Q/A-38 through 44 of this section for rules concerning

reasonable compensation. The portion of an amount treated as contingent under paragraph (b) or (c) of this A-24 may not be reduced by reasonable compensation.

(b) *Vested payments.* This paragraph (b) applies if a payment is vested, without regard to the change in ownership or control, and is treated as contingent on the change in ownership or control because the change accelerates the time at which the payment is made. In such case, the portion of the payment, if any, that is treated as contingent on the change in ownership or control is the amount by which the amount of the accelerated payment exceeds the present value of the payment absent the acceleration. If the value of such a payment absent acceleration is not reasonably ascertainable, and the acceleration of the payment does not significantly increase the present value of the payment absent the acceleration, the present value of the payment absent the acceleration is treated as equal to the amount of the accelerated payment. If the value of the payment absent the acceleration is not reasonably ascertainable, but the acceleration significantly increases the present value of the payment, the future value of such payment is treated as equal to the amount of the accelerated payment. For rules on determining present value, see paragraph (e) of this A-24, Q/A-32, and Q/A-33 of this section.

(c) (1) *Nonvested payments.* This paragraph (c) applies to a payment that becomes vested as a result of the change in ownership or control to the extent that—

(i) Without regard to the change in ownership or control, the payment was contingent only on the continued performance of services for the corporation for a specified period of time; and

(ii) The payment is attributable, at least in part, to the performance of services before the date the payment is made or becomes certain to be made.

(2) The portion of the payment subject to paragraph (c) of this A-24 that is treated as contingent on the change in ownership or control is the lesser of—

(i) The amount of the accelerated payment; or

(ii) The amount described in paragraph (b) of this A-24, plus an amount, as determined in paragraph (c)(4) of this A-24, to reflect the lapse of the obligation to continue to perform services.

(3) For purposes of this paragraph (c) of this A-24, the acceleration of the vesting of a stock option or the lapse of a restriction on restricted stock is considered to significantly increase the value of a payment.

(4) The amount reflecting the lapse of the obligation to continue to perform services (described in paragraph (c)(2)(ii) of this A-24) is 1 percent of the amount of the accelerated payment multiplied by the number of full months between the date that the individual's right to receive the payment is vested and the date that, absent the acceleration, the payment would have been vested. This paragraph (c)(4) applies to the accelerated vesting of a payment in the nature of compensation even if the time at which the payment is made is not accelerated.

(d) *Application of this A-24 to certain payments.*—(1) *Benefits under a nonqualified deferred compensation plan.* In the case of a payment of benefits under a nonqualified deferred compensation plan, paragraph (b) of this A-24 applies to the extent benefits under the plan are vested without regard to the change in ownership or control. Paragraph (c) of this A-24 applies to the extent benefits under the plan become vested as a result of the change in ownership or control and are attributable, at least in part, to the performance of services prior to vesting. Any other payment of benefits under a nonqualified deferred compensation plan is a payment in the nature of compensation subject to the general rule of paragraph (a) of this A-24 and the rules in Q/A-11 of this section.

(2) *Employment agreements.* The general rule of paragraph (a) of this A-24 applies to the payment of amounts due under an employment agreement on a termination of employment or a change in ownership or control that otherwise would be attributable to the performance of services (or refraining from the performance of services) during any period that begins after the date of termination of employment or change in ownership or control, as applicable. For purposes of this paragraph (d)(2) of this A-24, an employment agreement means an agreement between an employee or independent contractor and employer or service recipient which describes, among other things, the amount of compensation or remuneration payable to the employee or independent contractor. See Q/A-42(b) and 44 of this section for the treatment of the remaining amounts of salary under an employment agreement.

(3) *Vesting due to an event other than services.* Neither paragraph (b) nor (c) of this A-24 applies to a payment if (without regard to the change in ownership or control) vesting of the payment depends on an event other than the performance of services, such as the attainment of a performance goal, and the event does not occur prior to the change in ownership or control. In such circumstances, the full amount of the accelerated payment is treated as contingent on the change in ownership or control under paragraph (a) of this A-24. However, see Q/A-39 of this section for rules relating to the reduction of the excess parachute payment by the portion of the payment which is established to be reasonable compensation for personal services actually rendered before the date of a change in ownership or control.

(e) *Present value.* For purposes of this A-24, the present value of a payment is determined as of the date on which the accelerated payment is made.

(f) *Examples.* The following examples illustrate the principles of this A-24:

Example 1. (i) Corporation maintains a qualified plan and a nonqualified supplemental retirement plan (SERP) for its executives. Benefits under the SERP are not paid to participants until retirement. E, a disqualified individual with respect to Corporation, has a vested account balance of $500,000 under the SERP. A change in ownership or control of Corporation occurs. The SERP provides that in the event of a change in ownership or control, all vested accounts will be paid to SERP participants.

(ii) Because E was vested in $500,000 of benefits under the SERP prior to the change in ownership or control and the change merely accelerated the time at which the payment was made to E, only a portion of the payment, as determined under paragraph (b) of this A-24, is treated as contingent on the change. Thus, the portion of the payment that is treated as contingent on the change is the amount by which the amount of the accelerated payment ($500,000) exceeds the present value of the payment absent the acceleration.

(iii) Assume that instead of having a vested account balance of $500,000 on the date of the change in ownership or control, E will vest in his account balance of $500,000 in 2 years if E continues to perform services for the next 2 years. Assume further that the SERP provides that all unvested SERP benefits vest immediately on a change in ownership or control and are paid to the participants. Because the vesting of the SERP payment, without regard to the change, depends only on the performance of services for a specified period of time and the payment is attributable, in part, to the performance of services before the change in ownership or control, only a portion of the $500,000 payment, as determined under paragraph (c) of this A-24, is treated as contingent on the change. The portion of the payment that is treated as contingent on the change is the lesser of the amount of the accelerated payment or the amount by which the accelerated payment exceeds the present value of the payment absent the acceleration, plus an amount to reflect the lapse of the obligation to continue to perform services.

(iv) Assume further that under the SERP E's vested account balance of $500,000 will be paid to E on the change in ownership or control and an additional $70,000 will be credited to E's account. Because the $500,000 was vested without regard to the change in owner ship or control, paragraph (b) of this A-24 applies to the $500,000 payment. Because the $70,000 is not vested, without regard to the change, and is not attributable to the performance of services prior to the change, the entire $70,000 payment is contingent on the change in ownership or control under paragraph (a) of this A-24.

Example 2. As a result of a change in the effective control of a corporation, a disqualified individual with respect to the corporation, D, receives accelerated payment of D's vested account balance in a nonqualified deferred compensation account plan. Actual interest and other earnings on the plan assets are credited to each account as earned before distribution: Investment of the plan assets is not restricted in such a manner as would prevent the earning of a market rate of return on the plan assets. The date on which D would have received D's vested account balance absent the change in ownership or control is uncertain, and the rate of earnings on the plan assets is not fixed. Thus, the amount of the payment absent the acceleration is not reasonably ascertainable. Under these facts, acceleration of the payment does not significantly increase the present value of the payment absent the acceleration, and the present value of the payment absent the acceleration is treated as equal to the amount of the accelerated payment. Accordingly, no portion of the payment is treated as contingent on the change.

Example 3. (i) On January 15, 2006, a corporation and a disqualified individual, F, enter into a contract providing for a retention bonus of $500,000 to be paid to F on January 15, 2011. The payment of the bonus will be forfeited by F if F does not remain employed by the corporation for the entire 5-year period. However, the contract provides that the full amount of the payment will be made immediately on a change in ownership or control of the corporation during the 5-year period. On January 15, 2009, a change in ownership or control of the corporation occurs and the full amount of the payment ($500,000) is made on that date to F. Under these facts, the payment of $500,000 was contingent only on F's performance of services for a specified period and is attributable, in part, to the performance of services before the change in ownership or control. Therefore, only a portion of the payment is treated as contingent on the change. The portion of the payment that is treated as contingent on the change is the amount by which the amount of the accelerated payment (i.e., $500,000, the amount paid to the individual because of the change in ownership) exceeds the present value of the payment that was expected to have been made absent the acceleration (i.e., $406,838, the present value on January 15, 2009, of a $500,000 payment on January 15, 2011), plus $115,000 (1% × 23 months × $500,000) which is the amount reflecting the lapse of the obligation to continue to perform services. Accordingly, the amount of the payment treated as contingent on the change in ownership or control is $208,162, the sum of $93,162 ($500,000 – $406,838) + $115,000). This result is not changed if F actually remains employed until the end of the 5-year period.

(ii) Assume that the contract provides that the retention bonus will vest on a change in ownership or control, but will not be paid until January 15, 2011 (the original date in the contract). Because the payment of $500,000 was contingent only on F's performance of services for a specified period and is attributable, in part, to the performance of services before the change in ownership or control, only a portion of the $500,000 payment is treated as contingent on the change. Because there is no accelerated payment, the portion of the payment treated as contingent on the change is an amount reflecting the lapse of the obligation to continue to perform services which is $115,000 (1% × 23 months × $500,000).

Example 4. (i) On January 15, 2006, a corporation gives to a disqualified individual, in connection with her performance of services to the corporation, a bonus of 1,000 shares of the corporation's stock. Under the terms of the bonus arrangement, the individual is obligated to return the stock to the corporation if she terminates her employment for any reason prior to January 15, 2011. However, if there is a change in the ownership or effective control of the corporation prior to January 15, 2011, she ceases to be obligated to return the stock. The individual's rights in the stock are treated as substantially nonvested (within the meaning of § 1.83-3(b) and (j)) during that period. On January 15, 2008, a change in the ownership of the corporation occurs. On that day, the fair market value of the stock is $500,000.

(ii) Under these facts, the payment was contingent only on performance of services for a specified period and is attributable, in part, to the performance of services before the change in ownership or control. Thus, only a portion of the payment is treated as contingent on the change in ownership or control. The portion of the payment that is treated as contingent on the change is the amount by which the present value of the accelerated payment on January 15, 2009 ($500,000), exceeds the present value of the payment that was expected to have been made on January 15, 2011, plus an amount reflecting the lapse of the obligation to continue to perform services. At the time of the change, it cannot be reasonably ascertained what the value of the stock would have been on January 15, 2011. The acceleration of the lapse of a restriction on stock is treated as significantly increasing the value of the payment. Therefore, the value of such stock on January 15, 2011, is deemed to be $500,000, the amount of the accelerated payment. The present value on January 15, 2009, of a $500,000 payment to be made on January 15, 2011, is $406,838. Thus, the portion of the payment treated as contingent on the change is $208,162, the sum of $93,162 ($500,000 – $406,838), plus $115,000 [1% × 23 months × $500,000], the amount reflecting the lapse of the obligation to continue to perform services. [Corrected by IRS on 6/21/02, 67 FR 42210].

Example 5. (i) On January 15, 2006, a corporation grants to a disqualified individual nonqualified stock options to purchase 30,000 shares of the corporation's stock. The options do not have a readily ascertainable fair market value at the time of grant. The options will be forfeited by the individual if he fails to perform personal services for the corporation until January 15, 2009. The options will, however, vest in the individual at an earlier date if there is a change in ownership or control of the corporation. On January 16, 2008, a change in the ownership of the corporation occurs and the options become vested in the individual. On January 16, 2008, the options have an ascertainable fair market value of $600,000.

(ii) The payment of the options to purchase 30,000 shares was contingent only on performance of services for the corporation until

January 15, 2009, and is attributable, in part, to the performance of services before the change in ownership or control. Therefore, only a portion of the payment is treated as contingent on the change. The portion of the payment that is treated as contingent on the change is the amount by which the accelerated payment on January 16, 2008 ($600,000) exceeds the present value on January 16, 2008, of the payment that was expected to have been made on January 15, 2009, absent the acceleration, plus an amount reflecting the lapse of the obligation to continue to perform services. At the time of the change, it cannot be reasonably ascertained what the value of the options would have been on January 15, 2009. The acceleration of vesting in the options is treated as significantly increasing the value of the payment. Therefore, the value of such options on January 15, 2009, is deemed to be $600,000, the amount of the accelerated payment. The present value on January 16, 2008 of a $600,000 payment to be made on January 15, 2009, is $549,964.13. Thus, the portion of the payment treated as contingent on the change is $116,035.87, the sum of $50,035.87 ($600,000 – $549,964.13), plus an amount reflecting the lapse of the obligation to continue to perform services which is $66,000 (1% × 11 months × $600,000).

Example 6. (i) The facts are the same as in *Example 5*, except that the options become vested periodically (absent a change in ownership of control), with one-third of the options vesting on January 15, 2007, 2008, and 2009, respectively. Thus, options to purchase 20,000 shares vest independently of the January 16, 2008, change in ownership and the options to purchase the remaining 10,000 shares vest as a result of the change.

(ii) The payment of the options to purchase 10,000 shares was contingent only on performance of services for the corporation until January 15, 2009, and is attributable, in part, to the performance of services before the change in ownership or control. Therefore, only a portion of the payment is treated as contingent on the change. The portion of the payment that is treated as contingent on the change is the amount by which the accelerated payment on January 16, 2008 ($200,000) exceeds the present value on January 16, 2008, of the payment that was expected to have been made on January 15, 2009, absent the acceleration, plus an amount reflecting the lapse of the obligation to perform services. At the time of the change, it cannot be reasonably ascertained what the value of the options would have been on January 15, 2009. The acceleration of vesting in the options is treated as significantly increasing the value of the payment. Therefore, the value of such options on January 15, 2009, is deemed to be $200,000, the amount of the accelerated payment. The present value on January 16, 2008, of a $200,000 payment to be made on January 15, 2009, is $183,328.38. Thus, the portion of the payment treated as contingent on the change is $38,671.62, the sum of $16,671.62 ($200,000 – $183,328.38), plus an amount reflecting the lapse of the obligation to continue to perform services which is $22,000 (1% × 11 months × $200,000).

Example 7. Assume the same facts as in *Example 5*, except that the option agreement provides that the options will vest either on the corporation's level of profits reaching a specified level, or if earlier, on the date on which there is a change in ownership or control of the corporation. The corporation's level of profits do not reach the specified level prior to January 16, 2008. In such case, the full amount of the payment, $600,000, is treated as contingent on the change because it was not contingent only on performance of services for the corporation for a specified period. See Q/A-39 of this section for rules relating to the reduction of the excess parachute payment by the portion of the payment which is established to be reasonable compensation for personal services actually rendered before the date of a change in ownership or control.

Example 8. On January 1, 2002, E, a disqualified individual with respect to Corporation X, enters into an employment agreement with Corporation X under which E will be paid wages of $200,000 each year during the 5-year employment agreement. The employment agreement provides that if a change in ownership or control of Corporation X occurs, E will be paid the present value of the remaining salary under the employment agreement. On January 1, 2003, a change in ownership or control of Corporation X occurs, E is terminated, and E receives a payment of the present value of $200,000 for each of the 4 years remaining under the employment agreement. Because the payment represents future salary under an employment agreement (i.e., amounts otherwise attributable to the performance of services for periods that begin after the termination of employment), the general rule of paragraph (a) of this A-24 applies to the payment. See Q/A-42(c) and 44 of this section for the treatment of the remaining payments under an employment agreement.

Presumption That Payment Is Contingent on Change

Q-25: Is there a presumption that certain payments are contingent on a change in ownership or control?

A-25: Yes, for purposes of this section, any payment is presumed to be contingent on such change unless the contrary is established by clear and convincing evidence if the payment is made pursuant to—

(a) An agreement entered into within one year before the date of a change in ownership or control; or

(b) An amendment that modifies a previous agreement in any significant respect, if the amendment is made within one year before the date of a change in ownership or control. In the case of an amendment described in paragraph (b) of this A-25, only the portion of any payment that exceeds the amount of such payment that would have been made in the absence of the amendment is presumed, by reason of the amendment, to be contingent on the change in ownership or control.

Q-26: How may the presumption described in Q/A-25 of this section be rebutted?

A-26: (a) To rebut the presumption described in Q/A-25 of this section, the taxpayer must establish by clear and convincing evidence that the payment is not contingent on the change in ownership or control. Whether the payment is contingent on such change is determined on the basis of all the facts and circumstances of the particular case. Factors relevant to such a determination include, but are not limited to the content of the agreement or amendment and the circumstances surrounding the execution of the agreement or amendment, such as whether it was entered into at a time when a takeover attempt had commenced and the degree of likelihood that a change in ownership or control would actually occur. However, even if the presumption is rebutted with respect to an agreement, some or all of the payments under the agreement may still be contingent on the change in ownership or control pursuant to Q/A-22 of this section.

(b) In the case of an agreement described in paragraph (a) of Q/A-25 of this section, clear and convincing evidence that the agreement is one of the three following types will generally rebut the presumption that payments under the agreement are contingent on the change in ownership or control—

(1) A *nondiscriminatory employee plan or program* as defined in paragraph (c) of this A-26;

(2) A contract between a corporation and an individual that replaces a prior contract entered into by the same parties more than one year before the change in ownership or control, if the new contract does not provide for increased payments (apart from normal increases attributable to increased responsibilities or cost of living adjustments), accelerate the payment of amounts due at a future time, or modify (to the individual's benefit) the terms or conditions under which payments will be made; or

(3) A contract between a corporation and an individual who did not perform services for the corporation prior to the one year period before the change in ownership or control occurs, if the contract does not provide for payments that are significantly different in amount, timing, terms, or conditions from those provided under contracts entered into by the corporation (other than contracts that themselves were entered into within one year before the change in ownership or control and in contemplation of the change) with individuals performing comparable services.

(c) For purposes of this section, the term *nondiscriminatory employee plan or program* means: a group term life insurance plan that meets the requirements of section 79(d); a self insured medical reimbursement plan that meets the requirements of section 105(h); a cafeteria plan (within the meaning of section 125); an educational assistance program (within the meaning of section 127); a dependent care assistance program (within the meaning of section 129); a no-additional-cost service (within the meaning of section 132(b)) qualified employee discount (within the meaning of section 132(c)) qualified retirement planning services under section 132(m); and an adoption assistance program (within the meaning of section 137). Payments under certain other plans are exempt from the definition of *parachute payment* under Q/A-8 of this section. [Corrected by IRS on 6/21/02, 67 FR 42210].

(d) The following examples illustrate the application of the presumption:

Example 1. A corporation and a disqualified individual who is an employee of the corporation enter into an employment contract. The contract replaces a prior contract entered into by the same parties more than one year before the change and the new contract does not provide for any increased payments other than a cost of living adjustment, does not accelerate the payment of amounts due at a future time,

and does not modify (to the individual's benefit) the terms or conditions under which payments will be made. Clear and convincing evidence of these facts rebuts the presumption described in A-25 of this section. However, payments under the contract still may be contingent on the change in ownership or control pursuant to Q/A-22 of this section.

Example 2. Assume the same facts as in *Example 1*, except that the contract is entered into after a tender offer for the corporation's stock had commenced and it was likely that a change in ownership would occur and the contract provides for a substantial bonus payment to the individual upon his signing the contract. The individual has performed services for the corporation for many years, but previous employment contracts between the corporation and the individual did not provide for a similar signing bonus. One month after the contract is entered into, a change in the ownership of the corporation occurs. All payments under the contract are presumed to be contingent on the change in ownership even though the bonus payment would have been legally required even if no change had occurred. Clear and convincing evidence of these facts rebuts the presumption described in A-25 of this section with respect to all of the payments under the contract with the exception of the bonus payment (which is treated as contingent on the change). However, payments other than the bonus under the contract still may be contingent on the change in ownership or control pursuant to Q/A-22 of this section.

Example 3. A corporation and a disqualified individual, who is an employee of the corporation, enter into an employment contract within one year of a change in ownership of the corporation. Under the contract, in the event of a change in ownership or control and subsequent termination of employment, certain payments will be made to the individual. A change in ownership occurs, but the individual is not terminated until 2 years after the change. If clear and convincing evidence does not rebut the presumption described in A-25 of this section, because the payment is made pursuant to an agreement entered into within one year of the date of the change in ownership, the payment is presumed contingent on the change under A-25 of this section. This is true even though A's termination of employment is presumed not to be materially related to the change in ownership or control under Q/A-22 of this section.

Change in Ownership or Control

Q-27: When does a change in the ownership of a corporation occur?

A-27: (a) For purposes of this section, a change in the ownership or control of a corporation occurs on the date that any one person, or more than one person acting as a group, acquires ownership of stock of the corporation that, together with stock held by such person or group, owns more than 50 percent of the total fair market value or total voting power of the stock of such corporation. However, if any one person, or more than one person acting as a group, is considered to own more than 50 percent of the total fair market value or total voting power of the stock of a corporation, the acquisition of additional stock by the same person or persons is not considered to cause a change in the ownership of the corporation (or to cause a change in the effective control of the corporation (within the meaning of Q/A-28 of this section)). An increase in the percentage of stock owned by any one person, or persons acting as a group, as a result of a transaction in which the corporation acquires its stock in exchange for property will be treated as an acquisition of stock for purposes of this section.

(b) For purposes of paragraph (a) of this A-27, persons will not be considered to be acting as a group merely because they happen to purchase or own stock of the same corporation at the same time, or as a result of the same public offering. However, persons will be considered to be acting as a group if they are owners of an entity that enters into a merger, consolidation, purchase or acquisition of stock, or similar business transaction with the corporation. If a person, including an entity shareholder, owns stock in both entities that enter into a merger, consolidation, purchase or acquisition of stock, or similar transaction, such shareholder is considered to be acting as a group with other shareholders in an entity only to the extent of his ownership in that entity prior to the transaction giving rise to the change and not with respect to his ownership interest in the other entity.

(c) For purposes of this A-27, section 318(a) applies to determine stock ownership.

(d) The following examples illustrate the principles of this A-27:

Example 1. Corporation M has owned stock with a fair market value equal to 19 percent of the value of the stock of Corporation N (an otherwise unrelated corporation) for many years prior to 2006. Corporation M acquires additional stock with a fair market value equal to 15 percent of the value of the stock of Corporation N on January 1, 2006, and an additional 18 percent on February 21, 2007. As of February 21,

2007, Corporation M has acquired stock with a fair market value greater than 50 percent of the value of the stock of Corporation N. Thus, a change in the ownership of Corporation N is considered to occur on February 21, 2007 (assuming that Corporation M did not have effective control of Corporation N immediately prior to the acquisition on that date).

Example 2. All of the corporation's stock is owned by the founders of the corporation. The board of directors of the corporation decides to offer shares of the corporation to the public. After the public offering, the founders of the corporation own a total of 40 percent of the corporation's stock, and members of the public own 60 percent. If no one person (or more than one person acting as a group) owns more than 50 percent of the corporation's stock (by value or voting power) after the public offering, there is no change in the ownership of the corporation.

Example 3. Corporation P merges into Corporation O (a previously unrelated corporation). In the merger, the shareholders of Corporation P receive Corporation O stock in exchange for their Corporation P stock. Immediately after the merger, the former shareholders of Corporation P own stock with a fair market value equal to 60 percent of the value of the stock of Corporation O, and the former shareholders of Corporation O own stock with a fair market value equal to 40 percent of the value of the stock of Corporation O. The former shareholders of Corporation P will be treated as acting as a group in their acquisition of Corporation O stock. Thus, a change in the ownership of Corporation O occurs on the date of the merger.

Example 4. Assume the same facts as in *Example 3* except that immediately after the change, the former shareholders of Corporation P own stock with a fair market value of 51 percent of the value of Corporation O stock and the former shareholders of Corporation O own stock with a fair market value equal to 49 percent of the value of Corporation O stock. Assume further that prior to the merger several Corporation O shareholders also owned Corporation P stock (overlapping shareholders) exchanged for O stock with a fair market value of 5 percent of the value of Corporation O stock. The overlapping shareholders consist of Mutual Company A Growth Fund, which prior to the transaction owns P stock that is exchanged for 3 percent of the value of Coroporation O stock, Mutual Company A Income Fund, which prior to the transaction owns P stock that is exchanged for 1 percent of the value of Corporation O stock, and B individual who prior to the transaction owns P stock that is exchanged for 1 percent of the value of Corporation O stock. Growth Fund and Income Fund are treated as separate shareholders with respect to their ownership interests in Corporation O and Corporation P. The overlapping shareholders are not treated as acting as a group with the Corporation P shareholders with respect to the Corporation O stock each overlapping shareholder held before the transaction. Instead, the overlapping shareholders are treated as acting as a group separately with respect to Corporation O and Corporation P. Because the former shareholders of Corporation O are treated as acting as a group with respect to other Corporation O shareholders only to the extent of their ownership interest in Corporation O and not with respect to their ownership interest in Corporation P, a change in the ownership of Corporation O occurs on the date of the merger. [Corrected by IRS on 6/21/02, 67 FR 42210].

Example 5. A, an individual, owns stock with a fair market value equal to 20 percent of the value of the stock of Corporation Q. On January 1, 2007, Corporation Q acquires in a redemption for cash all of the stock held by shareholders other than A. Thus, A is left as the sole shareholder of Corporation O. A change in ownership of Corporation O is considered to occur on January 1, 2007 (assuming that A did not have effective control of Corporation Q immediately prior to the redemption).

Example 6. Assume the same facts as in *Example 5*, except that A owns stock with a fair market value equal to 51 percent of the value of all the stock of Corporation Q immediately prior to the redemption. There is no change in the ownership of Corporation Q as a result of the redemption.

Q-28: When does a change in the effective control of a corporation occur?

A-28: (a) For purposes of this section, a change in the effective control of a corporation is presumed to occur on the date that either—

(1) Any one person, or more than one person acting as a group, acquires (or has acquired during the 12-month period ending on the date of the most recent acquisition by such person or persons) ownership of stock of the corporation possessing 20 percent or more of the total voting power of the stock of such corporation; or

(2) A majority of members of the corporation's board of directors is replaced during any 12-month period by directors whose appointment or election is not endorsed by a majority of the members of the corporation's board of directors prior to the date of the appointment or election.

(b) The presumption of paragraph (a) of this A-28 may be rebutted by establishing that such acquisition or acquisitions of the corporation's stock, or such replacement of the majority of the members of the corporation's board of directors, does not transfer the power to control (directly or indirectly) the management and policies of the corporation from any one person (or more than one person acting as a group) to another person (or group). For purposes of this section, in the absence of an event described in paragraph (a)(1) or (2) of this A-28, a change in the effective control of a corporation is presumed not to have occurred.

(c) If any one person, or more than one person acting as a group, is considered to effectively control a corporation (within the meaning of this A-28), the acquisition of additional control of the corporation by the same person or persons is not considered to cause a change in the effective control of the corporation (or to cause a change in the ownership of the corporation within the meaning of Q/A-27 of this section).

(d) For purposes of this A-28, persons will not be considered to be acting as a group merely because they happen to purchase or own stock of the same corporation at the same time, or as a result of the same public offering. However, persons will be considered to be acting as a group if they are owners of an entity that enters into a merger, consolidation, purchase or acquisition of stock, or similar business transaction with the corporation. If a person, including an entity shareholder, owns stock in both entities that enter into a merger, consolidation, purchase or acquisition of stock, or similar transaction, such shareholder is considered to be acting as a group with other shareholders in an entity only to the extent of his ownership in that entity prior to the transaction giving rise to the change and not with respect to his ownership interest in the other entity.

(e) Section 318(a) applies to determine stock ownership for purposes of this A-28.

(f) The following examples illustrate the principles of this A-28:

Example 1. Shareholder A acquired the following percentages of the voting stock of Corporation M (an otherwise unrelated corporation) on the following dates: 16 percent on January 1, 2005; 10 percent on January 10, 2006; 8 percent on February 10, 2006; 11 percent on March 1, 2007; and 8 percent on March 10, 2007. Thus, on March 10, 2007, A owns a total of 53 percent of M's voting stock. Because A did not acquire 20 percent or more of M's voting stock during any 12-month period, there is no presumption of a change in effective control pursuant to paragraph (a)(1) of this A-28. In addition, under these facts there is a presumption that no change in the effective control of Corporation M occurred. If this presumption is not rebutted (and thus no change in effective control of Corporation M is treated as occurring prior to March 10, 2007), a change in the ownership of Corporation M is treated as having occurred on March 10, 2007 (pursuant to Q/A-27 of this section) because A had acquired more than 50 percent of Corporation M's voting stock as of that date.

Example 2. A minority group of shareholders of a corporation opposes the practices and policies of the corporation's current board of directors. A proxy contest ensues. The minority group presents its own slate of candidates for the board at the next annual meeting of the corporation's shareholders, and candidates of the minority group are elected to replace a majority of the current members of the board. A change in the effective control of the corporation is presumed to have occurred on the date the election of the new board of directors becomes effective.

Q-29: When does a change in the ownership of a substantial portion of a corporation's assets occur?

A-29: (a) For purposes of this section, a change in the ownership of a substantial portion of a corporation's assets occurs on the date that any one person, or more than one person acting as a group, acquires (or has acquired during the 12-month period ending on the date of the most recent acquisition by such person or persons) assets from the corporation that have a total gross fair market value equal to or more than one third of the total gross fair market value of all of the assets of the corporation immediately prior to such acquisition or acquisitions.

(b) A transfer of assets by a corporation is not treated as a change in the ownership of such assets if the assets are transferred to—

(1) A shareholder of the corporation (immediately before the asset transfer) in exchange for or with respect to its stock;

(2) An entity, 50 percent or more of the total value or voting power of which is owned, directly or indirectly, by the corporation;

(3) A person, or more than one person acting as a group, that owns, directly or indirectly, 50 percent or more of the total value or voting power of all the outstanding stock of the corporation; or

(4) An entity, at least 50 percent of the total value or voting power is owned, directly or indirectly, by a person described in paragraph (b)(3) of this A-29.

(c) For purposes of paragraph (b) and except as otherwise provided, a person's status is determined immediately after the transfer of the assets. For example, a transfer of assets pursuant to a complete liquidation of a corporation, a redemption of a shareholder's interest, or a transfer to a majority-owned subsidiary of the corporation is not treated as a change in the ownership of the assets of the transferor corporation.

(d) For purposes of this A-29, persons will not be considered to be acting as a group merely because they happen to purchase or own stock of the same corporation at the same time, or as a result of the same public offering. However, persons will be considered to be acting as a group if they are owners of an entity that enters into a merger, consolidation, purchase or acquisition of stock, or similar business transaction with the corporation. If a person, including an entity shareholder, owns stock in both entities that enter into a merger, consolidation, purchase or acquisition of stock, or similar transaction, such shareholder is considered to be acting as a group with other shareholders in an entity only to the extent of his ownership in that entity prior to the transaction giving rise to the change and not with respect to his ownership interest in the other entity.

(e) For purposes of this A-29, section 318(a) applies in determining stock ownership.

(f) The following examples illustrate the principles of this A-29:

Example 1. Corporation M acquires assets having a gross fair market value of $500,000 from Corporation N (an unrelated corporation) on January 1, 2006. The total gross fair market value of Corporation N's assets immediately prior to the acquisition was $3 million. Since the value of the assets acquired by Corporation M is less than one-third of the fair market value of Corporation N's total assets immediately prior to the acquisition, the acquisition does not represent a change in the ownership of a substantial portion of Corporation N's assets.

Example 2. Assume the same facts as in *Example 1.* Also assume that on November 1, 2006, Corporation M acquires from Corporation N additional assets having a fair market value of $700,000. Thus, Corporation M has acquired from Corporation N assets worth a total of $1.2 million during the 12-month period ending on November 1, 2006. Since $1.2 million is more than one-third of the total gross fair market value of all of Corporation N's assets immediately prior to the earlier of these acquisitions ($3 million), a change in the ownership of a substantial portion of Corporation N's assets is considered to have occurred on November 1, 2006.

Example 3. All of the assets of Corporation P are transferred to Corporation O (an unrelated corporation). In exchange, the shareholders of Corporation P receive Corporation O stock. Immediately after the transfer, the former shareholders of Corporation P own 60 percent of the fair market value of the outstanding stock of Corporation O and the former shareholders of Corporation O own 40 percent of the fair market value of the outstanding stock of Corporation O. Because Corporation O is an entity more than 50 percent of the fair market value of the outstanding stock of which is owned by the former shareholders of Corporation P (based on ownership of Corporation P prior the change), the transfer of assets is not treated as a change in ownership of a substantial portion of the assets of Corporation P. However, a change in the ownership (within the meaning of Q/A-27) of Corporation O occurs.

Three-Times-Base-Amount Test for Parachute Payments

Q-30: Are all payments that are in the nature of compensation, are made to a disqualified individual, and are contingent on a change in ownership or control, parachute payments?

A-30: (a) No, to determine whether such payments are parachute payments, they must be tested against the individual's *base amount* (as defined in Q/A-34 of this section). To do this, the aggregate present value of all payments in the nature of compensation that are made or to be made to (or for the benefit of) the same disqualified individual and are contingent on the change in ownership or control must be determined. If this aggregate present value equals or exceeds the amount equal to 3 times the individual's base amount, the payments are parachute payments. If this aggregate present value is less than the amount

equal to 3 times the individual's base amount, no portion of the payment is a parachute payment. See Q/A-31, Q/A-32, and Q/A-33 of this section for rules on determining present value. Parachute payments that are securities violation parachute payments are not included in the foregoing computation if they are not contingent on a change in ownership or control. See Q/A-37 of this section for the definition and treatment of securities violation parachute payments.

(b) The following examples illustrate the principles of this A-30:

Example 1. A is a disqualified individual with respect to Corporation M. A's base amount is $100,000. Payments in the nature of compensation that are contingent on a change in the ownership of Corporation M totaling $400,000 are made to A on the date of the change. The payments are parachute payments since they have an aggregate present value at least equal to 3 times A's base amount of $100,000 (3 × $100,000 = $300,000).

Example 2. Assume the same facts as in *Example 1*, except that the payments contingent on the change in the ownership of Corporation M total $290,000. Since the payments do not have an aggregate present value at least equal to 3 times A's base amount, no portion of the payments is a parachute payment.

Q-31: As of what date is the present value of a payment determined?

A-31: (a) Except as provided in this section, the present value of a payment is determined as of the date on which the change in ownership or control occurs, or, if a payment is made prior to such date, the date on which the payment is made.

(b)(1) For purposes of determining whether a payment is a parachute payment, if a payment in the nature of compensation is the right to receive payments in a year (or years) subsequent to the year of the change in ownership or control, the value of the payment is the present value of such payment (or payments) calculated in accordance with Q/A-32 of this section and based on reasonable actuarial assumptions.

(2) If the payment in the nature of compensation is an obligation to provide health care, then for purposes of this A-31 and for applying the 3-times-base-amount test under Q/A-30 of this section, the present value of such obligation should be calculated in accordance with generally accepted accounting principles. For purposes of Q/A-30 and this A-31, the obligation to provide health care is permitted to be measured by projecting the cost of premiums for purchased health care insurance, even if no health care insurance is actually purchased. If the obligation to provide health care is made in coordination with a health care plan that the corporation makes available to a group, then the premiums used for this purpose may be group premiums.

Q-32: What discount rate is to be used to determine present value?

A-32: For purposes of this section, present value generally is determined by using a discount rate equal to 120 percent of the applicable Federal rate (determined under section 1274(d) and the regulations thereunder) compounded semiannually. The applicable Federal rate to be used for this purpose is the Federal rate that is in effect on the date as of which the present value is determined. See Q/A-24 and 31 of this section. However, for any payment, the corporation and the disqualified individual may elect to use the applicable Federal rate that is in effect on the date that the contract which provides for the payment is entered into, if such election is made in the contract. [Corrected by IRS on 6/21/02, 67 FR 42210].

Q-33: If the present value of a payment to be made in the future is contingent on an uncertain future event or condition, how is the present value of the payment determined?

A-33: (a) In certain cases, it may be necessary to apply the 3-times-base-amount test of Q/A-30 of this section or to allocate a portion of the base amount to a payment described in paragraphs (a)(1), (2), and (3) of Q/A-2 of this section at a time when the aggregate present value of all such payments cannot be determined with certainty because the time, amount, or right to receive one or more such payments is contingent on the occurrence of an uncertain future event or condition. For example, a disqualified individual's right to receive a payment may be contingent on the involuntary termination of such individual's employment with the corporation. In such a case, it must be reasonably estimated whether the payment will be made. If it is reasonably estimated that there is a 50-percent or greater probability that the payment will be made, the full amount of the payment is considered for purposes of the 3-times-base-amount test and the allocation of the base amount. Conversely, if it is reasonably estimated that there is a less than 50-percent probability that the payment will be made, the payment is not considered for either purpose.

(b) If the estimate made under paragraph (a) of this A-33 is later determined to be incorrect, the 3-times-base-amount test described in

Q/A-30 of this section must be reapplied (and the portion of the base amount allocated to previous payments must be reallocated (if necessary) to such payments) to reflect the actual time and amount of the payment. Whenever the 3-times-base-amount test is applied (or whenever the base amount is allocated), the aggregate present value of the payments received or to be received by the disqualified individual is redetermined as of the date described in A-31 of this section, using the discount rate described in A-32 of this section. This redetermination may affect the amount of any excess parachute payment for a prior taxable year. Alternatively, if, based on the application of the 3-times-base-amount test without regard to the payment described in paragraph (a) of this A-33, a disqualified individual is determined to have an excess parachute payment or payments, then the 3-times-base-amount test does not have to be reapplied when a payment described in paragraph (a) of this A-33 is made (or becomes certain to be made) if no base amount is allocated to such payment.

(c) The following examples illustrate the principles of this A-33:

Example 1. A, a disqualified individual with respect to Corporation M, has a base amount of $100,000. Under A's employment agreement with Corporation M, A is entitled to receive a payment in the nature of compensation in the amount of $250,000 contingent on a change in ownership or control of Corporation M. In addition, the agreement provides that if A's employment is terminated within 1 year after the change in ownership or control, A will receive an additional payment in the nature of compensation in the amount of $150,000, payable 1 year after the date of the change in ownership or control. A change in ownership or control of Corporation M occurs and A receives the first payment of $250,000. Corporation M reasonably estimates that there is a 50-percent probability that, as a result of the change, A's employment will be terminated within 1 year of the date of the change. For purposes of applying the 3-times-base-amount test (and if the first payment is determined to be a parachute payment, for purposes of allocating a portion of A's base amount to that payment), because M reasonably estimates that there is a 50-percent or greater probability that, as a result of the change, A's employment will be terminated within 1 year of the date of the change, Corporation M must assume that the $150,000 payment will be made to A as a result of the change in ownership or control. The present value of the additional payment is determined under Q/A-31 and Q/A-32 of this section.

Example 2. Assume the same facts as in *Example 1* except that Corporation M reasonably estimates that there is a less than 50-percent probability that, as a result of the change, A's employment will be terminated within 1 year of the date of the change. For purposes of applying the 3-times-base-amount test, because Corporation M reasonably estimates that there is a less than 50-percent probability that, as a result of the change, A's employment will be terminated within 1 year of the date of the change, Corporation M must assume that the $150,000 payment will not be made to A as a result of the change in ownership or control.

Example 3. B, a disqualified individual with respect to Corporation P, has a base amount of $200,000. Under B's employment agreement with Corporation P, if there is a change in ownership or control of Corporation P, B will receive a severance payment of $600,000 and a bonus payment of $400,000. In addition, the agreement provides that if B's employment is terminated within 1 year after the change, B will receive an additional payment in the nature of compensation of $500,000. A change in ownership or control of Corporation P occurs, and B receives the $600,000 and $400,000 payments. At the time of the change in ownership or control, Corporation P reasonably estimates that there is a less than 50-percent probability that B's employment will be terminated within 1 year of the change. For purposes of applying the 3-times-base-amount test, because Corporation P reasonably estimates that there is a less than 50-percent probability that B's employment will be terminated within 1 year of the date of the change, Corporation P assumes that the $500,000 payment will not be made to B. Eleven months after the change in ownership or control, B's employment is terminated, and the $500,000 payment is made to B. Because B was determined to have excess parachute payments without regard to the $500,000 payment, the 3-times-base-amount test is not reapplied and the base amount is not reallocated to include the $500,000 payment. The entire $500,000 payment is treated as an excess parachute payment.

Q-34: What is the base amount?

A-34: (a) The base amount of a disqualified individual is the average annual compensation for services performed for the corporation with respect to which the change in ownership or control occurs (or for a predecessor entity or a related entity) which was includible in the gross income of such individual for taxable years in the base period (including amounts that were excluded under section 911), or which would

have been includible in such gross income if such person had been a United States citizen or resident. See Q/A-35 of this section for the definition of base period and for examples of base amount computations.

(b) If the base period of a disqualified individual includes a short taxable year or less than all of a taxable year, compensation for such short or incomplete taxable year must be annualized before determining the average annual compensation for the base period. In annualizing compensation, the frequency with which payments are expected to be made over an annual period must be taken into account. Thus, any amount of compensation for such a short or incomplete taxable year that represents a payment that will not be made more often than once per year is not annualized.

(c) Because the base amount includes only compensation that is includible in gross income, the base amount does not include certain items that constitute parachute payments. For example, payments in the form of excludible fringe benefits are not included in the base amount but may be treated as parachute payments.

(d) The base amount includes the amount of compensation included in income under section 83(b) during the base period.

(e) The following example illustrates the principles of this A-34:

Example. A disqualified individual, D, receives an annual salary of $500,000 per year during the 5-year base period. D defers $100,000 of D's salary each year under the corporation's nonqualified deferred compensation plan. D's base amount is $400,000 ($400,000 × (5/5)).

Q-35: What is the base period?

A-35: (a) The base period of a disqualified individual is the most recent 5 taxable years of the individual ending before the date of the change in ownership or control. For this purpose, the date of the change in ownership or control is the date the corporation experiences one of the events described in Q/A-27, Q/A-28, or Q/A-29 of this section. However, if the disqualified individual was not an employee or independent contractor of the corporation with respect to which the change in ownership or control occurs (or a predecessor entity or a related entity as defined in Q/A-21 of this section) for this entire 5-year period, the individual's base period is the portion of such 5-year period during which the individual performed personal services for the corporation or predecessor entity or related entity.

(b) The following examples illustrate the principles of Q/A-34 of this section and this Q/A-35:

Example 1. A disqualified individual, D, was employed by a corporation for 2 years and 4 months preceding the taxable year in which a change in ownership or control of the corporation occurs. D's includible compensation income from the corporation was $30,000 for the 4-month period, $120,000 for the first full year, and $150,000 for the second full year. D's base amount is $120,000, ((3 × $30,000) + $120,000 + $150,000)/3.

Example 2. Assume the same facts as in *Example 1*, except that D also received a $60,000 signing bonus when D's employment with the corporation commenced at the beginning of the 4-month period. D's base amount is $140,000, (($60,000 + (3 × $30,000)) + $120,000 + $150,000)/3. Since the bonus will not be paid more often than once per year, the amount of the bonus is not increased in annualizing D's compensation for the 4-month period.

Q-36: How is the base amount determined in the case of a disqualified individual who did not perform services for the corporation (or a predecessor entity or a related entity as defined in Q/A-21 of this section), prior to the individual's taxable year in which the change in ownership or control occurs?

A-36: (a) In such a case, the individual's base amount is the annualized compensation for services performed for the corporation (or a predecessor entity or related entity) which—

(1) Was includible in the individual's gross income for that portion, prior to such change, of the individual's taxable year in which the change occurred (including amounts that were excluded under section 911), or would have been includible in such gross income if such person had been a United States citizen or resident;

(2) Was not contingent on the change in ownership or control; and

(3) Was not a securities violation parachute payment.

(b) The following examples illustrate the principles of this A-36:

Example 1. On January 1, 2006, A, an individual whose taxable year is the calendar year, enters into a 4-year employment contract with Corporation M as an officer of the corporation. A has not previously performed services for Corporation M (or any predecessor entity or related entity as defined in Q/A-21 of this section). Under the employment contract, A is to receive an annual salary of $120,000 for each of the 4 years that he remains employed by Corporation M with any remaining unpaid balance to be paid immediately in the event that A's employment is terminated without cause. On July 1, 2006, after A has received compensation of $60,000, a change in the ownership of Corporation M occurs. Because of the change, A's employment is terminated without cause, and he receives a payment of $420,000. It is established by clear and convincing evidence that the $60,000 in compensation is not contingent on the change in ownership or control, but the presumption that the $420,000 payment is contingent on the change is not rebutted. Thus, the payment of $420,000 is treated as contingent on the change in ownership of Corporation M. In this case, A's base amount is $120,000 (2 × $60,000). Since the present value of the payment which is contingent on the change in ownership of Corporation M ($420,000) is more than 3 times A's base amount of $120,000 (3 × $120,000 = $360,000), the payment is a parachute payment.

Example 2. Assume the same facts as in *Example 1*, except that A also receives a signing bonus of $50,000 from Corporation M on January 1, 2006. It is established by clear and convincing evidence that the bonus is not contingent on the change in ownership. When the change in ownership occurs on July 1, 2006, A has received compensation of $110,000 (the $50,000 bonus plus $60,000 in salary). In this case, A's base amount is $170,000 [$50,000 + (2 × $60,000)]. Since the $50,000 bonus will not be paid more than once per year, the amount of the bonus is not increased in annualizing A's compensation. The present value of the potential parachute payment ($420,000) is less than 3 times A's base amount of $170,000 (3 × $170,000 = $510,000), and therefore no portion of the payment is a parachute payment.

Securities Violation Parachute Payments

Q-37: Must a payment be contingent on a change in ownership or control in order to be a parachute payment?

A-37: (a) No, the term *parachute payment* also includes any payment (other than a payment exempted under Q/A-6 or Q/A-8 of this section) that is in the nature of compensation and is to (or for the benefit of) a disqualified individual, if such payment is a securities violation payment. A securities violation payment is a payment made or to be made—

(1) Pursuant to an agreement that violates any generally enforced Federal or State securities laws or regulations; and

(2) In connection with a potential or actual change in ownership or control.

(b) A violation is not taken into account under paragraph (a)(1) of this A-37 if it is merely technical in character or is not materially prejudicial to shareholders or potential shareholders. Moreover, a violation will be presumed not to exist unless the existence of the violation has been determined or admitted in a civil or criminal action (or an administrative action by a regulatory body charged with enforcing the particular securities law or regulation) which has been resolved by adjudication or consent. Parachute payments described in this A-37 are referred to in this section as securities violation payments.

(c) Securities violation parachute payments that are not contingent on a change in ownership or control within the meaning of Q/A-22 of this section are not taken into account in applying the 3-times-base-amount test of Q/A-30 of this section. Such payments are considered parachute payments regardless of whether such test is met with respect to the disqualified individual (and are included in allocating base amount under Q/A-38 of this section). Moreover, the amount of a securities violation parachute payment treated as an excess parachute payment shall not be reduced by the portion of such payment that is reasonable compensation for personal services actually rendered before the date of a change in ownership or control if such payment is not contingent on such change. Likewise, the amount of a securities violation parachute payment includes the portion of such payment that is reasonable compensation for personal services to be rendered on or after the date of a change in ownership or control if such payment is not contingent on such change.

(d) The rules in paragraph (b) of this A-37 also apply to securities violation parachute payments that are contingent on a change in ownership or control if the application of these rules results in greater total excess parachute payments with respect to the disqualified individual than would result if the payments were treated simply as payments contingent on a change in ownership or control (and hence were taken into account in applying the 3-times-base-amount test and were reduced by, or did not include, any applicable amount of reasonable compensation).

(e) The following examples illustrate the principles of this A-37:

Example 1. A, a disqualified individual with respect to Corporation M, receives two payments in the nature of compensation that are contingent on a change in the ownership or control of Corporation M. The present value of the first payment is equal to A's base amount and is not a securities violation parachute payment. The present value of the second payment is equal to 1.5 times A's base amount and is a securities violation parachute payment. Neither payment includes any reasonable compensation. If the second payment is treated simply as a payment contingent on a change in ownership or control, the amount of A's total excess parachute payments is zero because the aggregate present value of the payments does not equal or exceed 3 times A's base amount. If the second payment is treated as a securities violation parachute payment subject to the rules of paragraph (b) of this A-37, the amount of A's total excess parachute payments is 0.5 times A's base amount. Thus, the second payment is treated as a securities violation parachute payment.

Example 2. Assume the same facts as in *Example 1*, except that the present value of the first payment is equal to 2 times A's base amount. If the second payment is treated simply as a payment contingent on a change in ownership or control, the total present value of the payments is 3.5 times A's base amount, and the amount of A's total excess parachute payments is 2.5 times A's base amount. If the second payment is treated as a securities violation parachute payment, the amount of A's total excess parachute payments is 0.5 times A's base amount. Thus, the second payment is treated simply as a payment contingent on a change in ownership or control.

Example 3. B, a disqualified individual with respect to Corporation N, receives two payments in the nature of compensation that are contingent on a change in the control of Corporation N. The present value of the first payment is equal to 4 times B's base amount and is a securities violation parachute payment. The present value of the second payment is equal to 2 times B's base amount and is not a securities violation parachute payment. B establishes by clear and convincing evidence that the entire amount of the first payment is reasonable compensation for personal services to be rendered after the change in ownership or control. If the first payment is treated simply as a payment contingent on a change in ownership or control, it is exempt from the definition of *parachute payment* pursuant to Q/A-9 of this section. Thus, the amount of B's total excess parachute payment is zero because the present value of the second payment does not equal or exceed three times B's base amount. However, if the first payment is treated as a securities violation parachute payment, the amount of B's total excess parachute payments is 3 times B's base amount. Thus, the first payment is treated as a securities violation parachute payment.

Example 4. Assume the same facts as in *Example 3*, except that B does not receive the second payment and B establishes by clear and convincing evidence that the first payment is reasonable compensation for services actually rendered before the change in the control of Corporation N. If the payment is treated simply as a payment contingent on a change in ownership or control, the amount of B's excess parachute payment is zero because the amount treated as an excess parachute payment is reduced by the amount that B establishes as reasonable compensation. However, if the payment is treated as a securities violation parachute payment, the amount of B's excess parachute payment is 3 times B's base amount. Thus, the payment is treated as a securities violation parachute payment.

Computation and Reduction of Excess Parachute Payments

Q-38: How is the amount of an excess parachute payment computed?

A-38: (a) The amount of an excess parachute payment is the excess of the amount of any parachute payment over the portion of the disqualified individual's base amount that is allocated to such payment. For this purpose, the portion of the base amount allocated to any parachute payment is the amount that bears the same ratio to the base amount as the present value of such parachute payment bears to the aggregate present value of all parachute payments made or to be made to (or for the benefit of) the same disqualified individual. Thus, the portion of the base amount allocated to any parachute payment is determined by multiplying the base amount by a fraction, the numerator of which is the present value of such parachute payment and the denominator of which is the aggregate present value of all such payments. See Q/A-31, Q/A-32, and Q/A-33 of this section for rules on determining present value and Q/A-34 of this section for the definition of *base amount*.

(b) The following example illustrates this principles of this A-38:

Example. An individual with a base amount of $100,000 is entitled to receive two parachute payments, one of $200,000 and the other of $400,000. The $200,000 payment is made at the time of the change in ownership or control, and the $400,000 payment is to be made at a future date. The present value of the $400,000 payment is $300,000 on the date of the change in ownership or control. The portions of the base amount allocated to these payments are $40,000 (($200,000/$500,000) × $100,000) and $60,000 (($300,000/$500,000) × $100,000), respectively. Thus, the amount of the first excess parachute payment is $160,000 ($200,000 − $40,000) and that of the second is $340,000 ($400,000 − $60,000).

Q-39: May the amount of an excess parachute payment be reduced by reasonable compensation for personal services actually rendered before the change in ownership or control?

A-39: (a) Generally, yes, except that in the case of payments treated as securities violation parachute payments or when the portion of a payment that is treated as contingent on the change in ownership or control is determined under paragraph (b) or (c) of Q/A-24 of this section, the amount of an excess parachute payment is reduced by any portion of the payment that the taxpayer establishes by clear and convincing evidence is reasonable compensation for personal services actually rendered by the disqualified individual before the date of the change in ownership or control. Services reasonably compensated for by payments that are not parachute payments (for example, because the payments are not contingent on a change in ownership or control and are not securities violation parachute payments, or because the payments are exempt from the definition of parachute payment under Q/A-6 through Q/A-9 of this section) are not taken into account for this purpose. The portion of any parachute payment that is established as reasonable compensation is first reduced by the portion of the disqualified individual's base amount that is allocated to such parachute payment; any remaining portion of the parachute payment established as reasonable compensation then reduces the excess parachute payment.

(b) The following examples illustrate the principles of this A-39:

Example 1. Assume that a parachute payment of $600,000 is made to a disqualified individual, and the portion of the individual's base amount that is allocated to the parachute payment is $100,000. Also assume that $300,000 of the $600,000 parachute payment is established as reasonable compensation for personal services actually rendered by the disqualified individual before the date of the change in ownership or control. Before the reasonable compensation is taken into account, the amount of the excess parachute payment is $500,000 ($600,000 − $100,000). In reducing the excess parachute payment by reasonable compensation, the portion of the parachute payment that is established as reasonable compensation ($300,000) is first reduced by the portion of the disqualified individual's base amount that is allocated to the parachute payment ($100,000), and the remainder ($200,000) then reduces the excess parachute payment. Thus, in this case, the excess parachute payment of $500,000 is reduced by $200,000 of reasonable compensation.

Example 2. Assume the same facts as in *Example 1*, except that the full amount of the $600,000 parachute payment is established as reasonable compensation. In this case, the excess parachute payment of $500,000 is reduced to zero by $500,000 of reasonable compensation. As a result, no portion of any deduction for the payment is disallowed by section 280G, and no portion of the payment is subject to the 20-percent excise tax of section 4999.

Determination of Reasonable Compensation

Q-40: How is it determined whether payments are reasonable compensation?

A-40: (a) In general, whether payments are reasonable compensation for personal services actually rendered, or to be rendered, by the disqualified individual is determined on the basis of all the facts and circumstances of the particular case. Factors relevant to such a determination include, but are not limited to, the following—

(1) The nature of the services rendered or to be rendered;

(2) The individual's historic compensation for performing such services; and

(3) The compensation of individuals performing comparable services in situations where the compensation is not contingent on a change in ownership or control.

(b) For purposes of section 280G, reasonable compensation for personal services includes reasonable compensation for holding one-self out as available to perform services and refraining from performing services (such as under a covenant not to compete).

Q-41: Is any particular type of evidence generally considered clear and convincing evidence of reasonable compensation for personal services?

A-41: Yes, a showing that payments are made under a nondiscriminatory employee plan or program (as defined in Q/A-26 of this section) generally is considered to be clear and convincing evidence that the payments are reasonable compensation. This is true whether the personal services for which the payments are made are actually rendered before, or to be rendered on or after, the date of the change in ownership or control. Q/A-46 of this section (relating to the treatment of an affiliated group as one corporation) does not apply for purposes of this A-41. No determination of reasonable compensation is needed for payments under qualified plans to be exempt from the definition of *parachute payment* under Q/A-8 of this section.

Q-42: Is any particular type of evidence generally considered clear and convincing evidence of reasonable compensation for personal services to be rendered on or after the date of a change in ownership or control?

A-42: (a) Yes, if payments are made or to be made to (or on behalf of) a disqualified individual for personal services to be rendered on or after the date of a change in ownership or control, a showing of the following generally is considered to be clear and convincing evidence that the payments are reasonable compensation for services to be rendered on or after the date of the change in ownership or control—

(1) The payments were made or are to be made only for the period the individual actually performs such personal services; and

(2) If the individual's duties and responsibilities are substantially the same after the change in ownership or control, the individual's annual compensation for such services is not significantly greater than such individual's annual compensation prior to the change in ownership or control, apart from normal increases attributable to increased responsibilities or cost of living adjustments. If the scope of the individual's duties and responsibilities are not substantially the same, the annual compensation after the change is not significantly greater than the annual compensation customarily paid by the employer or by comparable employers to persons performing comparable services. However, except as provided in paragraph (b) of this A-42, such clear and convincing evidence will not exist if the individual does not, in fact, perform the services contemplated in exchange for the compensation.

(b) Generally, an agreement under which the disqualified individual must refrain from performing services (such as a covenant not to compete) is an agreement for the performance of personal services for purposes of this A-42 to the extent that it is demonstrated by clear and convincing evidence that the agreement substantially constrains the individual's ability to perform services and there is a reasonable likelihood that the agreement will be enforced against the individual. In the absence of clear and convincing evidence, payments under the agreement are treated as severance payments under Q/A-44 of this section.

(c) If the employment of a disqualified individual is involuntarily terminated before the end of a contract term and the individual is paid damages for breach of contract, a showing of the following factors generally is considered clear and convincing evidence that the payment is reasonable compensation for personal services to be rendered on or after the date of change in ownership or control—

(1) The contract was not entered into, amended, or renewed in contemplation of the change in ownership or control;

(2) The compensation the individual would have received under the contract would have qualified as reasonable compensation under section 162;

(3) The damages do not exceed the present value (determined as of the date of receipt) of the compensation the individual would have received under the contract if the individual had continued to perform services for the employer until the end of the contract term;

(4) The damages are received because an offer to provide personal services was made by the disqualified individual but was rejected by the employer; and

(5) The damages are reduced by mitigation. Mitigation will be treated as occurring when such damages are reduced (or any payment of such damages is returned) to the extent of the disqualified individual's earned income (within the meaning of section 911(d)(2)(A)) during the remainder of the period in which the contract would have been in effect. See Q/A-44 of this section for rules regarding damages for a failure to make severance payments.

(c) The following examples illustrate the principles of this A-42:

Example 1. A, a disqualified individual, has a three-year employment contract with Corporation M, a publicly traded corporation. Under this contract, A is to receive a salary for $100,000 for the first year of the contract and, for each succeeding year, an annual salary that is 10 percent higher than the prior year's salary. During the third year of the contract, Corporation N acquires all the stock of Corporation M. Prior to the change in ownership, Corporation N arranges to retain A's services by entering into an employment contract with A that is essentially the same as A's contract with Corporation M. Under the new contract, Corporation N is to fulfill Corporation M's obligations for the third year of the old contract, and, for each of the succeeding years, pay A an annual salary that is 10 percent higher than A's prior year's salary. Amounts are payable under the new contract only for the portion of the contract term during which A remains employed by Corporation N. A showing of the facts described above (and in the absence of contradictory evidence) is regarded as clear and convincing evidence that all payments under the new contract are reasonable compensation for personal services to be rendered on or after the date of the change in ownership. Therefore, the payments under this agreement are exempt from the definition of *parachute payment* pursuant to Q/A-9 of this section.

Example 2. Assume the same facts as in *Example 1* except that A does not perform the services described in the new contract, but receives payment under the new contract. Because services were not rendered after the change, the payments under this contract are not exempt from the definition of *parachute payment* pursuant to Q/A-9 of this section.

Example 3. Assume the same facts as in *Example 1* except that under the new contract A agrees to perform consulting services to Corporation N, when and if Corporation N requires A's services. Assume further that when Corporation N does not require A's services, the contract provides that A must not perform services for any other competing company. Corporation N previously enforced similar contracts against former employees of Corporation N. Because A is substantially constrained under this contract and Corporation N is reasonably likely to enforce the contract against A, the agreement is an agreement for the performance of services under paragraph (b) of this A-42. Assuming the requirements of paragraph (a) of this A-42 are met and there is clear and convincing evidence that all payments under the new contract are reasonable compensation for personal services to be rendered on or after the date of the change in ownership, the payments under this contract are exempt from the definition of *parachute payment* pursuant to Q/A-9 of this section. [Corrected by IRS on 6/21/02, 67 FR 42210].

Example 4. Assume the same facts as in *Example 1*, except that the employment contract with Corporation N does not provide that amounts are payable under the contract only for the portion of the term for which A remains employed by Corporation N. Shortly after the change in ownership, and despite A's request to remain employed by Corporation N, A's employment with Corporation N is involuntarily terminated. Shortly thereafter, A obtains employment with Corporation O. A commences a civil action against Corporation N, alleging breach of the employment contract. In settlement of the litigation, A receives an amount equal to the present value of the compensation A would have received under the contract with Corporation N, reduced by the amount of compensation A otherwise receives from Corporation O during the period that the contract would have been in effect. A showing of the facts described above (and in the absence of contradictory evidence) is regarded as clear and convincing evidence that the amount A receives as damages is reasonable compensation for personal services to be rendered on or after the date of the change in ownership. Therefore, the amount received by A is exempt from the definition of *parachute payment* pursuant to Q/A-9 of this section.

Q-43: Is any particular type of payment generally considered reasonable compensation for personal services actually rendered before the date of a change in ownership or control?

A-43: (a) Yes, payments of compensation earned before the date of a change in ownership or control generally are considered reasonable compensation for personal services actually rendered before the date of a change in ownership or control if they qualify as reasonable compensation under section 162.

Q-44: May severance payments be treated as reasonable compensation?

A-44: (a) No, severance payments are not treated as reasonable compensation for personal services actually rendered before, or to be rendered on or after, the date of a change in ownership or control. Moreover, any damages paid for a failure to make severance payments are not treated as reasonable compensation for personal services actually rendered before, or to be rendered on or after, the date of such change. For purposes of this section, the term *severance payment* means any payment that is made to (or for the benefit of) a disqualified individual on account of the termination of such individual's employment prior to the end of a contract term, but does not include any payment that otherwise would be made to (or for the benefit of) such

individual on the termination of such individual's employment, whenever occurring.

(b) The following example illustrates the principles of this A-44:

Example. A, a disqualified individual, has a three-year employment contract with Corporation X. Under the contract, A will receive a salary of $200,000 for the first year of the contract, and for each succeeding year, an annual salary that is $100,000 higher than the previous year. In the event of A's termination of employment following a change in ownership or control, the contract provides that A will receive the remaining salary due under the employment contract. At the beginning of the second year of the contract, Corporation Y acquires all of the stock of Corporation X, A's employment is terminated, and A receives $700,000 ($300,000 for the second year of the contract plus $400,000 for the third year of the contract) representing the remaining salary due under the employment contract. Because the $700,000 payment is treated as a severance payment, it is not reasonable compensation for personal services on or after the date of the change in ownership or control. Thus, the full amount of the $700,000 is a parachute payment.

Miscellaneous Rules

Q-45: How is the term *corporation* defined?

A-45: For purposes of this section, the term *corporation* has the meaning prescribed by section 7701(a)(3) and §301.7701-2(b). For example, a *corporation*, for purposes of this section, includes a publicly traded partnership treated as a corporation under section 7704(a); an entity described in §301.7701-3(c)(1)(v)(A) of this chapter; a real estate investment trust under section 856(a); a corporation that has mutual or cooperative (rather than stock) ownership, such as a mutual insurance company, a mutual savings bank, or a cooperative bank (as defined in section 7701(a)(32)), and a foreign corporation as defined under section 7701(a)(5).

Q-46: How is an affiliated group treated?

A-46: For purposes of this section, and except as otherwise provided in this section, all members of the same affiliated group (as defined in section 1504, determined without regard to section 1504(b)) are treated as one corporation. Rules affected by this treatment of an affiliated group include (but are not limited to) rules relating to exempt payments of certain corporations (Q/A-6, Q/A-7 of this section (except as provided therein)), payor of parachute payments (Q/A-10 of this section), disqualified individuals (Q/A-15 through Q/A-21 of this section (except as provided therein)), rebuttal of the presumption that payments are contingent on a change (Q/A-26 of this section (except as provide therein)), change in ownership or control (Q/A-27, 28, and 29 of this section), and reasonable compensation (Q/A-42, 43, and 44 of this section).

Effective Date

Q-47: What is the general effective date of section 280G?

A-47: (a) Generally, section 280G applies to payments under agreements entered into or renewed after June 14, 1984. Any agreement that is entered into before June 15, 1984, and is renewed after June 14, 1984, is treated as a new contract entered into on the day the renewal takes effect.

(b) For purposes of paragraph (a) of this A-47, a contract that is terminable or cancellable unconditionally at will by either party to the contract without the consent of the other, or by both parties to the contract, is treated as a new contract entered into on the date any such termination or cancellation, if made, would be effective. However, a contract is not treated as so terminable or cancellable if it can be terminated or cancelled only by terminating the employment relationship or independent contractor relationship of the disqualified individual.

(c) Section 280G applies to payments under a contract entered into on or before June 14, 1984, if the contract is amended or supplemented after June 14, 1984, in significant relevant respect. For this purpose, a *supplement* to a contract is defined as a new contract entered into after June 14, 1984, that affects the trigger, amount, or time of receipt of a payment under an existing contract.

(d)(1) Except as otherwise provided in paragraph (e) of this A-47, a contract is considered to be amended or supplemented in significant relevant respect if provisions for payments contingent on a change in ownership or control (parachute provisions), or provisions in the nature of parachute provisions, are added to the contract, or are amended or supplemented to provide significant additional benefits to the disqualified individual. Thus, for example, a contract generally is treated as amended or supplemented in significant relevant respect if it is amended or supplemented—

(i) To add or modify, to the disqualified individual's benefit, a change in ownership or control trigger;

(ii) To increase amounts payable that are contingent on a change in ownership or control (or, where payment is to be made under a formula, to modify the formula to the disqualified individual's advantage); or

(iii) To accelerate, in the event of a change in ownership or control, the payment of amounts otherwise payable at a later date.

(2) For purposes of paragraph (a) of this A-47, a payment is not treated as being accelerated in the event of a change in ownership or control if the acceleration does not increase the present value of the payment.

(e) A contract entered into on or before June 14, 1984, is not treated as amended or supplemented in significant relevant respect merely by reason of normal adjustments in the terms of employment relationship or independent contractor relationship of the disqualified individual. Whether an adjustment in the terms of such a relationship is considered normal for this purpose depends on all of the facts and circumstances of the particular case. Relevant factors include, but are not limited to, the following—

(1) The length of time between the adjustment and the change in ownership or control;

(2) The extent to which the corporation, at the time of the adjustment, viewed itself as a likely takeover candidate;

(3) A comparison of the adjustment with historical practices of the corporation;

(4) The extent of overlap between the group receiving the benefits of the adjustment and those members of that group who are the beneficiaries of pre-June 15, 1984, parachute contracts; and

(5) The size of the adjustment, both in absolute terms and in comparison with the benefits provided to other members of the group receiving the benefits of the adjustment.

Q-48: What is the effective date of this section?

A-48: This section applies to any payments that are contingent on a change in ownership or control that occurs on or after January 1, 2004. Taxpayers can rely on these rules after February 20, 2002, for the treatment of any parachute payment. [Corrected by IRS on 6/21/02, 67 FR 42210].

Robert E. Wenzel

Deputy Commissioner of Internal Revenue.

CERTIFIED COPY

DALE D. GOODE

¶ 20,260H

IRS proposed regulations: Defined benefit plans: Required minimum distributions: Code Sec. 403(b) annuity contracts: Individual retirement accounts (IRAs).—The IRS has issued proposed regulations by cross-reference to temporary regulations that contain guidance concerning required minimum distribution requirements for defined benefit plans, IRAs, and Code Sec. 403(b) annuity contracts purchased with an employee's accounts balance under a defined contribution plan. Comments and requests for a public hearing must be received by the IRS by July 16, 2002.

The proposed regulations, which were published in the *Federal Register* on April 17, 2002 (67 FR 18834), are reproduced below.

DEPARTMENT OF TREASURY

Internal Revenue Service

26 CFR Part 1

[REG-108697-02]

RIN 1545-BA60

Required Distributions from Retirement Plans

AGENCY: Internal Revenue Service (IRS), Treasury.

ACTION: Notice of proposed rulemaking by cross-reference to temporary regulations.

SUMMARY: In the Rules and Regulations section of this issue of the **Federal Register,** the IRS is issuing temporary regulations that provide guidance concerning required minimum distributions for defined benefit plans and annuity contracts providing benefits under qualified plans, individual retirement plans, and section 403(b) contracts. The regulations will provide the public with guidance necessary to comply with the law and will affect administrators of, participants in, and beneficiaries of qualified plans; institutions that sponsor and individuals who administer individual retirement plans, individuals who use individual retirement plans for retirement income, and beneficiaries of individual retirement plans; and employees for whom amounts are contributed to section 403(b) annuity contracts, custodial accounts, or retirement income accounts and beneficiaries of such contracts and accounts. The text of those temporary regulations also serves as the text of these proposed regulations.

DATES: Written or electronic comments must be received by July 16, 2002.

ADDRESSES: Send submissions to: CC:ITA:RU (REG-108697-02), room 5226, Internal Revenue Service, POB 7604, Ben Franklin Station, Washington, DC 20044. Submissions may be hand delivered Monday through Friday between the hours of 8 a.m. and 5 p.m. to: CC:ITA:RU (REG-108697-02), Courier's Desk, Internal Revenue Service, 1111 Constitution Avenue, NW., Washington, DC. Alternatively, taxpayers may submit comments electronically directly to the IRS Internet site at http://www.irs.gov/regs.

FOR FURTHER INFORMATION CONTACT: Cathy Vohs at 622-6090

SUPPLEMENTARY INFORMATION:

Background

Final and Temporary regulations in the Rules and Regulations portion of this issue of the **Federal Register** amend the Income Tax

Regulations (26 CFR part 1) relating to section 401(a)(9). The temporary regulations (§ 1.401(a)(9)-6T) contain rules relating to minimum distribution requirements for defined benefit plans and annuity contracts purchased with an employee's account balance under a defined contribution plan. The text of those temporary regulations also serves as the text of these proposed regulations. The preamble to the temporary regulations explains the temporary regulations.

Special Analyses

It has been determined that this notice of proposed rulemaking is not a significant regulatory action as defined in Executive Order 12866. Therefore, a regulatory assessment is not required. It also has been determined that section 553(b) of the Administrative Procedure Act (5 U.S.C. chapter 5) does not apply to these regulations. Because § 1.401(a)(9)-6 imposes no new collection of information on small entities, a Regulatory Flexibility Analysis under the Regulatory Flexibility Act (5 U.S.C. chapter 6) is not required. Pursuant to section 7805(f) of the Internal Revenue Code, this notice of proposed rulemaking will be submitted to the Chief Counsel for Advocacy of the Small Business Administration for comment on its impact on small business.

Comments and Requests for a Public Hearing

Before these proposed regulations are adopted as final regulations, consideration will be given to any written comments (a signed original and eight (8) copies) that are submitted timely to the IRS. All comments will be available for public inspection and copying.

A public hearing may be scheduled if requested in writing by a person that timely submits written comments. If a public hearing is scheduled, notice of the date, time, and place for the hearing will be published in the **Federal Register.**

Drafting Information

The principal authors of these regulations are Marjorie Hoffman and Cathy A. Vohs of the Office of the Division Counsel/Associate Chief Counsel (Tax Exempt and Government Entities). However, other personnel from the IRS and Treasury participated in their development.

List of Subjects 26 CFR Part 1

Income taxes, Reporting and recordkeeping requirements.

Proposed Amendments to the Regulations

Accordingly, 26 CFR part 1 is proposed to be amended as follows:

PART 1—INCOME TAXES

Paragraph 1. The authority citation for part 1 is amended by an entry in numerical order to read in part as follows:

Authority: 26 U.S.C. 7805 ***

§ 1.401(a)(9)-6 is also issued under 26 U.S.C. 401(a)(9). ***

Par. 2. Section 1.401(a)(9)-6 is added to read as follows

§ 1.401(a)(9)-6 Required minimum distributions from defined benefit plans

---

¶ 20,260I

IRS proposed regulations: Notice requirements: Early retirement benefits: Benefit accrual rates: Plan amendments.—The IRS has issued proposed regulations that contain guidance on notice requirements required to be given by plan administrators to adversely affected plan participants when plan amendments significantly reduce either early retirement benefits or the rate of future benefit accruals or when the amendments eliminate early retirement benefits or retirement-type subsidies.

The proposed regulations, which were published in the *Federal Register* on April 23, 2002 (67 FR 19713), were removed on April 9, 2003 by T.D. 9052 (68 FR 17277) and replaced by Reg. Sec. 54.4980F-1 at ¶ 24,507 and ¶ 13,648W-87.

¶ 20,260J

IRS proposed regulations: Withdrawal of proposed regulations: Stock or securities distribution: Corporate acquisition: Recognition of gain.—The IRS has issued proposed regulations by cross-reference to temporary regulations that relate to recognition of gains or losses on distributions of stock or securities of controlled corporations in connection with acquisitions. Comments and requests for a public hearing must be received by the IRS by July 25, 2002.

The proposed regulations, which were published in the *Federal Register* on April 26, 2002 (67 FR 20711), are reproduced below.

DEPARTMENT OF THE TREASURY

Internal Revenue Service

26 CFR Part 1

[REG-163892-01]

RIN 1545-AY42

Guidance under Section 355(e); Recognition of Gain on Certain Distributions of Stock or Securities in Connection with an Acquisition.

AGENCY: Internal Revenue Service (IRS), Treasury.

ACTION: Withdrawal of notice of proposed rulemaking; and notice of proposed rulemaking by cross-reference to temporary regulations.

SUMMARY: This document withdraws the notice of proposed rulemaking published in the **Federal Register** on January 2, 2001. In the Rules and Regulations section of this issue of the **Federal Register,** the IRS is issuing temporary regulations relating to recognition of gain on certain distributions of stock or securities of a controlled corporation in connection with an acquisition. The text of those regulations also serves as the text of these proposed regulations.

DATES: Written and electronic comments and requests for a public hearing must be received by [*INSERT DATE 90 DAYS AFTER PUBLICATION OF THIS DOCUMENT IN THE FEDERAL REGISTER*].

ADDRESSES: Send submissions to: CC:ITA:RU (REG-163892-01), room 5226, Internal Revenue Service, POB 7604, Ben Franklin Station, Washington, DC 20044. Submissions may be hand delivered Monday through Friday between the hours of 8 a.m. and 5 p.m. to: CC:ITA:RU (REG-163892-01), Courier's Desk, Internal Revenue Service, 1111 Constitution Avenue, NW, Washington, DC. Alternatively, taxpayers may submit electronic comments directly to the IRS Internet site at *www.irs.gov/regs*.

FOR FURTHER INFORMATION CONTACT: Concerning the proposed regulations, Amber R. Cook at (202) 622-7530; concerning submissions, Treena Garrett, (202) 622-7180 (not toll-free numbers).

SUPPLEMENTARY INFORMATION:

Background and Explanation of Provisions

On January 2, 2001, the IRS and Treasury published in the **Federal Register** (66 FR 66) a notice of proposed rulemaking (REG-107566-00) under section 355(e) of the Internal Revenue Code of 1986. Those proposed regulations are withdrawn.

Temporary regulations in the Rules and Regulations section of this issue of the **Federal Register** amend the Income Tax Regulations (26 CFR part 1) relating to section 355(e). The temporary regulations provide rules relating to recognition of gain on certain distributions of stock or securities of a controlled corporation in connection with an acquisition. The text of those regulations also serves as the text of

these proposed regulations. The preamble to the temporary regulations explains the amendments.

Special Analysis

It has been determined that this notice of proposed rulemaking is not a significant regulatory action as defined in Executive Order 12866. Therefore, a regulatory assessment is not required. It has also been determined that section 553(b) of the Administrative Procedure Act (5 U.S.C. chapter 5) does not apply to these regulations, and, because these regulations do not impose a collection of information on small entities, the Regulatory Flexibility Act (5 U.S.C. chapter 6) does not apply. Pursuant to section 7805(f) of the Internal Revenue Code, this notice of proposed rulemaking will be submitted to the Chief Counsel for Advocacy of the Small Business Administration for comment on its impact.

Comments and Requests for a Public Hearing

Before these proposed regulations are adopted as final regulations, consideration will be given to any written comments (a signed original and eight (8) copies) and electronic comments that are submitted timely to the IRS. The IRS and Treasury Department specifically request comments on the clarity of the proposed rules and how they may be made easier to understand. All comments will be available for public inspection and copying. A public hearing will be scheduled if requested in writing by any person that timely submits written comments. If a public hearing is scheduled, notice of the date, time, and place for the public hearing will be published in the **Federal Register.**

Drafting Information

The principal author of these regulations is Amber R. Cook, Office of Associate Chief Counsel (Corporate). Other personnel from the IRS and Treasury Department, however, participated in their development.

List of Subjects in 26 CFR Part 1

Income taxes, Reporting and recordkeeping requirements.

Withdrawal of Proposed Amendments to the Regulations and Proposed Amendments to the Regulations

Accordingly, under the authority of 26 U.S.C. 7805 and 26 U.S.C. 355(e)(5), the notice of proposed rulemaking (REG-107566-00) that was published in the **Federal Register** on Tuesday, January 2, 2001, (66 FR 66) is withdrawn. In addition, 26 CFR part 1 is proposed to be amended as follows:

PART 1—INCOME TAXES

Paragraph 1. The authority citation for part 1 is amended by adding an entry in numerical order to read in part as follows:

Authority: 26 U.S.C. 7805 ***

Section 1.355-7 also issued under 26 U.S.C. 355(e)(5). ***

[The text of proposed § 1.401(a)(9)-6 is the same as the text of § 1.401(a)(9)-6T published elsewhere in this issue of the **Federal Register**].

Deputy Commissioner of Internal Revenue.

Robert E. Wenzel

CERTIFIED COPY

JACKIE TURNER

Par. 2. Section 1.355-0 is amended by revising the introductory text and adding an entry for § 1.355-7 to read as follows:

§ 1.355-0 Table of contents.

In order to facilitate the use of §§ 1.355-1 through 1.355-7, this section lists the major paragraphs in those sections as follows:

*****

§ 1.355-7 Recognition of gain on certain distributions of stock or securities in connection with an acquisition.

(a) In general.

(b) Plan.

(1) In general.

(2) Certain post-distribution acquisitions.

(3) Plan factors.

(4) Non-plan factors.

(c) Operating rules.

(1) Internal discussions and discussions with outside advisors evidence of business purpose.

(2) Takeover defense.

(3) Effect of distribution on trading in stock.

(4) Consequences of section 355(e) disregarded for certain purposes.

(5) Multiple acquisitions.

(d) Safe harbors.

(1) Safe Harbor I.

(2) Safe Harbor II.

(3) Safe Harbor III.

(4) Safe Harbor IV.

(5) Safe Harbor V.

(i) In general.

(ii) Special rules.

(6) Safe Harbor VI.

(i) In general.

(ii) Special rule.

(7) Safe Harbor VII.

(i) In general.

(ii) Special rule.

(e) Stock acquired by exercise of options, warrants, convertible obligations, and other similar interests.

(1) Treatment of options.

(i) General rule.

(ii) Agreement, understanding, or arrangement to write an option.

(iii) Substantial negotiations related to options.

(2) Instruments treated as options.

(3) Instruments generally not treated as options.

(i) Escrow, pledge, or other security agreements.

(ii) Compensatory options.

(iii) Options exercisable only upon death, disability, mental incompetency, or separation from service.

(iv) Rights of first refusal.

(v) Other enumerated instruments.

(f) Multiple controlled corporations.

(g) Valuation.

(h) Definitions.

(1) Agreement, understanding, arrangement, or substantial negotiations.

(2) Controlled corporation.

(3) Controlling shareholder.

(4) Coordinating group.

(5) Discussions.

(6) Established market.

(7) Five-percent shareholder.

(8) Similar acquisition.

(9) Ten-percent shareholder.

(i) [Reserved]

(j) Examples.

(k) Effective date.

Par. 3. Section 1.355-7 is added to read as follows:

§ 1.355-7 Recognition of gain on certain distributions of stock or securities in connection with an acquisition.

[The text of proposed § 1.355-7 is the same as the text of § 1.355-7T published elsewhere in this issue of the **Federal Register**].

Deputy Commissioner of Internal Revenue.

Robert E. Wenzel

CERTIFIED COPY

¶ 20,260K

IRS proposed regulations: Code Sec. 457 plans: Deferred compensation: Legislative changes.—The IRS has issued proposed regulations that contain guidance for deferred compensation plans maintained by state and local governments pertaining to legislative changes made by the Tax Reform Act of 1986, the Small Business Job Protection Act of 1996, the Taxpayer Relief Act of 1997, the Economic Growth and Tax Relief Reconciliation Act of 2001, and the Job Creation and Worker Assistance Act of 2002. The proposed regulations also make technical changes and clarify existing final regulations.

The proposed regulations, which were published in the *Federal Register* on May 8, 2002 (67 FR 30826), were finalized by T.D. 9075 (68 FR 41230, July 11, 2003). The preamble to the final regulations is reproduced at ¶ 24,507F . The final regulations appear at ¶ 13,154 , ¶ 13,154A , ¶ 13,154B , ¶ 13,154C , ¶ 13,154C-1 , ¶ 13,154C-2 , ¶ 13,154C-3 , ¶ 13,154C-4 , ¶ 13,154C-5 , ¶ 13,154C-6 , ¶ 13,154C-7 , and ¶ 13,154C-8 .

¶ 20,260L

IRS proposed regulations: Modified guaranteed contracts: Interest rates: Temporary guaranty period.—The IRS has issued proposed regulations that define the appropriate interest rate to be used when determining tax reserves and required interest for certain modified guaranteed contracts. The subject matter of the proposed regulations was previously covered in Notice 97-32 (¶ 17,112N), which set forth the appropriate interest rate to be used during the temporary guarantee period of modified guarantee contracts.

A portion of the proposed regulations, which were published in the *Federal Register* (67 FR 38214, June 3, 2002), were previously reproduced at this paragraph.

The final regulations were published in the *Federal Register* on May 7, 2003 (68 FR 24349). The regulations are reproduced at ¶ 13,313A and ¶ 13,313B. The preamble to the regulations is found at ¶ 24,507B.

¶ 20,260M

Split-dollar life insurance: Tax treatment: Economic benefit regime: Loan regime.—The IRS has issued guidance in the form of proposed regulations that provide two mutually exclusive regimes for taxing split-dollar life insurance arrangements: the economic benefit regime, which governs taxation of endorsement arrangements, and the loan regime, under which an employer's premium payments are treated as loans to the employee. The proposed regulations apply only to split-dollar life insurance arrangements entered into after final regulations are published in the *Federal Register.*

Portions of the proposed regulations, which were published in the *Federal Register* on July 9, 2002 (67 FR 45414), are reproduced below.

[4830-01-p]

DEPARTMENT OF THE TREASURY

Internal Revenue Service

26 CFR Parts 1 and 31

[REG-164754-01]

RIN 1545-BA44

Split-Dollar Life Insurance Arrangements

AGENCY: Internal Revenue Service (IRS), Treasury.

ACTION: Notice of proposed rulemaking and notice of public hearing.

SUMMARY: This document contains proposed regulations relating to the income, employment, and gift taxation of split-dollar life insurance arrangements. The proposed regulations will provide needed guidance to persons who enter into split-dollar life insurance arrangements. This document also provides notice of a public hearing on the proposed regulations.

DATES: Written or electronic comments must be received by October 7, 2002. Requests to speak and outlines of topics to be discussed at the public hearing scheduled for October 23, 2002, must be received by October 9, 2002.

ADDRESSES: Send submissions to CC:ITA:RU (REG-164754-01), room 5226, Internal Revenue Service, POB 7604, Ben Franklin Station, Washington, DC 20044. Submissions may be hand delivered Monday through Friday between the hours of 8 a.m. and 5 p.m. to: CC:ITA:RU (REG-164754-01), Courier's Desk, Internal Revenue Service, 1111 Constitution Avenue, NW., Washington, DC or sent electronically, via the IRS Internet site at www.irs.gov/regs. The public hearing will be held in room 4718, Internal Revenue Building, 1111 Constitution Avenue, NW., Washington, DC.

FOR FURTHER INFORMATION CONTACT: Concerning the section 61 regulations, please contact Elizabeth Kaye at (202) 622-4920; concerning the section 83 regulations, please contact Erinn Madden at (202) 622-6030; concerning the section 301 regulations, please contact Krishna Vallabhaneni at (202) 622-7550; concerning the section 7872 regulations, please contact Rebecca Asta at (202) 622-3940; and concerning the application of these regulations to the Federal gift tax, please contact Lane Damazo at (202) 622-3090. To be placed on the attendance list for the hearing, please contact LaNita M. Vandyke at (202) 622-7180.

SUPPLEMENTARY INFORMATION:

Paperwork Reduction Act

The collection of information contained in this notice of proposed rulemaking has been submitted to the Office of Management and Budget for review in accordance with the Paperwork Reduction Act of 1995 (44 U.S.C. 3507(d)). Comments on the collection of information should be sent to the **Office of Management and Budget,** Attn: Desk Officer for the Department of the Treasury, Office of Information and Regulatory Affairs, Washington, DC 20503, with copies to the **Internal Revenue Service,** Attn: IRS Reports Clearance Officer, W:CAR:MP:FP:S Washington, DC 20224. Comments on the collection of information should be received by September 7, 2002. Comments are specifically requested concerning:

Whether the proposed collection of information is necessary for the proper performance of the functions of the IRS, including whether the information will have practical utility;

The accuracy of the estimated burden associated with the proposed collection of information (see below);

How the quality, utility, and clarity of the information to be collected may be enhanced;

How the burden of complying with the proposed collection of information may be minimized, including through the application of auto-

mated collection techniques or other forms of information technology; and

Estimates of capital or start-up costs and costs of operation, maintenance, and purchase of services to provide information.

The collections of information in this proposed regulation are in § 1.7872-15(d)(2)(ii) and (j)(3)(ii). These collections of information are required by the IRS to verify consistent treatment by the borrower and lender of split-dollar loans with nonrecourse or contingent payments. In addition, in the case of a split-dollar loan that provides for nonrecourse payments, the collections of information are required to obtain a benefit. The likely respondents are parties entering into split-dollar loans with nonrecourse or contingent payments.

Estimated total annual reporting and/or recordkeeping burden: 32,500 hours.

Estimated average annual burden hours per respondent and/or recordkeeper: 17 minutes.

Estimated number of respondents and/or recordkeepers: 115,000.

Estimated annual frequency of responses: on occasion.

An agency may not conduct or sponsor, and a person is not required to respond to, a collection of information unless it displays a valid control number assigned by the Office of Management and Budget.

Books or records relating to a collection of information must be retained as long as their contents may become material in the administration of any internal revenue law. Generally, tax returns and tax return information are confidential, as required by 26 U.S.C. 6103.

Background And Explanation Of Provisions

1. Current Law

Section 61 provides that gross income includes all income from whatever source derived. Section 1.61-2(d) describes the taxation of premiums paid by an employer or service recipient for life insurance on the life of an employee or independent contractor if the proceeds of the life insurance are payable to the beneficiary of the employee.

Section 83 provides rules for taxing a transfer of property in connection with the performance of services. Generally, if property is transferred to any person other than the service recipient in connection with the performance of services, the excess of the fair market value of such property (determined without regard to lapse restrictions) over the amount paid for such property is included in the gross income of the service provider in the first taxable year in which the service provider's rights in such property are either transferable or not subject to a substantial risk of forfeiture, whichever is applicable. Under § 1.83-1(a)(2), the cost of life insurance protection under a life insurance contract, retirement income contract, endowment contract, or other contract providing life insurance protection generally is taxable under section 61 and the regulations thereunder during the period such contract is substantially nonvested (that is, prior to the time when rights to the contract are either transferable or not subject to a substantial risk of forfeiture). The cost of such life insurance protection is the reasonable net premium cost, as determined by the Commissioner, of the current life insurance protection (as defined in § 1.72-16(b)(3)) provided by such contract. Under § 1.83-3(e), in the case of a transfer of a life insurance contract, retirement income contract, endowment contract, or other contract providing life insurance protection, only the cash surrender value of the contract is considered property.

* * * * *

Rev. Rul. 64-328 (1964-2 C.B. 11) and Rev. Rul. 66-110 (1966-1 C.B. 12) address the Federal income tax treatment of a split-dollar life insurance arrangement under which an employer and an employee join in the purchase of a life insurance contract on the life of the employee and provide for the allocation of policy benefits. The rulings conclude that all economic benefits provided by the employer to the employee under such an arrangement are taxed to the employee. Thus, under the rulings, the employee generally must include in compensation income for each taxable year during which the arrangement remains in effect (i) the annual cost of the life insurance protection provided to the employee, reduced by any payments made by the employee for such life insurance protection, (ii) any policy owner dividends or similar distributions provided to the employee under the life insurance contract (including any dividends, as described in Rev. Rul. 66-110, used to provide additional policy benefits), and (iii) any other economic benefits provided to the employee under the arrangement. Neither ruling distinguishes, for tax purposes, between an arrangement in which the employer owns the life insurance contract (as in a so-called endorsement arrangement) and an arrangement in which the employee owns the contract (as in a so-called collateral assignment arrangement).

Rev. Rul. 79-50 (1979-1 C.B. 138) provides that, in a split-dollar life insurance arrangement similar to the one described in Rev. Rul. 64-328 between a corporation and a shareholder, the shareholder must include in income the value of the insurance protection in excess of the premiums paid by the shareholder, and must treat such amounts as provided in section 301(c).

Notice 2001-10 (2001-1 C.B. 459) set forth rules for the taxation of split-dollar life insurance arrangements in which the employee has an interest in the cash surrender value of the life insurance contract (so-called equity split-dollar life insurance arrangements). Notice 2001-10 generally provided, under specified conditions, for the taxation of equity split-dollar life insurance arrangements under either the rules of sections 61 and 83 or the rules of section 7872.

Notice 2002-8 (2002-4 I.R.B. 398), which revoked Notice 2001-10, provides guidance with respect to split-dollar life insurance arrangements entered into before the date final regulations concerning such arrangements are published in the **Federal Register**. The notice indicates that taxpayers may treat current life insurance protection provided under such an arrangement as an economic benefit and that the IRS will not treat the arrangement as having been terminated if the parties continue to treat and report the value of the current life insurance protection in that manner. Notice 2002-8 provides that, alternatively, the parties may treat the premiums or other payments as loans from the sponsor of the arrangement (typically, the employer) to the other party. In these cases, the IRS will not challenge a taxpayer's reasonable efforts to comply with the requirements of sections 1271 through 1275 and section 7872. In addition, all payments by the sponsor from the inception of the arrangement (reduced by any repayments to the sponsor) before the first taxable year in which the payments are treated as loans must be treated as loans entered into at the beginning of such first taxable year.[1]

Notice 2002-8 also describes the anticipated proposed regulations on split-dollar life insurance arrangements. The notice states that the rules would require taxation of a split-dollar life insurance arrangement under one of two mutually exclusive regimes: an economic benefit regime and a loan regime.

2. Overview of the Proposed Regulations

These proposed regulations provide guidance on the taxation of split-dollar life insurance arrangements, including equity split-dollar life insurance arrangements. The proposed regulations apply for purposes of Federal income, employment, and gift taxes. For example, the proposed regulations apply to a split-dollar life insurance arrangement between an employer and an employee, between a corporation and a shareholder, and between a donor and a donee.

Definition of split-dollar life insurance arrangement

The proposed regulations generally define a split-dollar life insurance arrangement as any arrangement (that is not part of a group term life insurance plan described in section 79) between an owner of a life insurance contract and a non-owner of the contract under which either party to the arrangement pays all or part of the premiums, and one of the parties paying the premiums is entitled to recover (either conditionally or unconditionally) all or any portion of those premiums and such recovery is to be made from, or is secured by, the proceeds of the contract. This definition is intended to apply broadly and will cover an arrangement, for example, under which the non-owner of a contract provides funds directly to the owner of the contract with which the owner pays premiums, as long as the non-owner is entitled to recover (either conditionally or unconditionally) all or a portion of the funds from the contract proceeds (for example, death benefits) or has an interest in the contract to secure the right of recovery. In addition, the amount to be recovered by the party paying the premiums need not be

determined by reference to the amount of those premiums. The definition is not intended to cover the purchase of an insurance contract in which the only parties to the arrangement are the policy owner and the life insurance company acting only in its capacity as issuer of the contract.

A special rule applies in the case of an arrangement entered into in connection with the performance of services. Under this special rule, a split-dollar life insurance arrangement is any arrangement (whether or not described in the general rule) between an owner and a non-owner of a life insurance contract under which the employer or service recipient pays, directly or indirectly, all or any portion of the premiums and the beneficiary of all or any portion of the death benefit is designated by the employee or service provider or is any person whom the employee or service provider would reasonably be expected to name as beneficiary. (Like the general rule, this special rule does not apply to any arrangement covered by section 79.) This special rule also applies to arrangements between a corporation and another person in that person's capacity as a shareholder in the corporation under which the corporation pays, directly or indirectly, all or any portion of the premiums and the beneficiary of all or a portion of the death benefit is a person designated by, or would be reasonably expected to be designated by, the shareholder. As in the case of the general definition, the special rule is not intended to cover the purchase of an insurance contract in which the only parties to the arrangement are the policy owner and the life insurance company acting only in its capacity as issuer of the contract.

Mutually exclusive regimes

As indicated in Notice 2002-8, the proposed regulations provide two mutually exclusive regimes for taxing split-dollar life insurance arrangements. A split-dollar life insurance arrangement (as defined in the proposed regulations) is taxed under either the economic benefit regime or the loan regime. The proposed regulations provide rules that determine which tax regime applies to a split-dollar life insurance arrangement.

Under the economic benefit regime (generally set forth in § 1.61-22 of the proposed regulations), the owner of the life insurance contract is treated as providing economic benefits to the non-owner of the contract. The economic benefit regime generally will govern the taxation of endorsement arrangements. In addition, a special rule requires the economic benefit regime to apply (and the loan regime not to apply) to any split-dollar life insurance arrangement if (i) the arrangement is entered into in connection with the performance of services, and the employee or service provider is not the owner of the life insurance contract, or (ii) the arrangement is entered into between a donor and a donee (for example, a life insurance trust) and the donee is not the owner of the life insurance contract.

Under the loan regime (generally set forth in § 1.7872-15 of the proposed regulations), the non-owner of the life insurance contract is treated as loaning premium payments to the owner of the contract. Except for specified arrangements, the loan regime applies to any split-dollar loan (as defined in the proposed regulations). The loan regime generally will govern the taxation of collateral assignment arrangements.

Thus, in contrast to Rev. Rul. 64-328 and Rev. Rul. 66-110, the proposed regulations generally provide substantially different tax consequences to the parties depending on which party owns the life insurance contract.

The proposed regulations also require both the owner and the non-owner of a life insurance contract that is part of a split-dollar life insurance arrangement (as defined either in the general rule or the special rule) to fully and consistently account for all amounts under the arrangement under the rules of either § 1.61-22 or § 1.7872-15.

For purposes of both the general rule and the special rule, unless the non-owner's payments are certain payments made in consideration for economic benefits, general Federal income, employment, and gift tax principles apply to the arrangement. For example, if an employer pays premiums on a contract owned by an employee and the payments are not split-dollar loans under § 1.7872-15, the employee must include the full amount of the payments in gross income at the time they are paid by the employer to the extent that the employee's rights to the life insurance contract are substantially vested. Also, to the extent an owner's repayment obligation is waived, cancelled, or forgiven at any

---

[1] Notice 2002-8 also provides that an employer and employee may continue to use the P.S. 58 rates set forth in Rev. Rul. 55-747 (1955-2 C.B. 228), which was revoked by Notice 2001-10, only with respect to split-dollar life insurance arrangements entered into before January 28, 2002, in which a contractual arrangement between the employer and employee provides that the P.S. 58 rates will be used to determine the value of the current life

insurance protection provided to the employee (or to the employee and one or more additional persons). Taxpayers may not use the P.S. 58 rates for "reverse" split-dollar life insurance arrangements or for split-dollar life insurance arrangements outside of the compensatory context.

time under an arrangement that prior to the cancellation of indebtedness was treated as a split-dollar loan, the owner and non-owner must account for the amount waived, cancelled, or forgiven in accordance with the relationship between the parties. Thus, if the arrangement were in a compensatory context, the owner of the contract (the employee) and the non-owner (the employer) would account for the amount as compensation. See *OKC Corp. and Subsidiaries v. Commissioner*, 82 T.C. 638 (1984) (whether the cancellation of a debt is ordinary income to the debtor depends upon the nature of the payment); *Newmark v. Commissioner*, 311 F.2d 913 (2d Cir. 1962) (discharge of indebtedness constituted a payment for services in an employment situation).

Owners and non-owners

The proposed regulations provide rules for determining the owner and the non-owner of the life insurance contract. The owner is the person named as the policy owner. If two or more persons are designated as the policy owners, the first-named person generally is treated as the owner of the entire contract. However, if two or more persons are named as the policy owners and each such person has an undivided interest in every right and benefit of the contract, those persons are treated as owners of separate contracts. For example, if an employer and an employee jointly own a life insurance contract and share equally in all rights and benefits under the contract, they are treated as owning two separate contracts (and, ordinarily, neither contract would be treated as part of a split-dollar life insurance arrangement).

The general rule that the person named as the policy owner is treated as the owner of the life insurance contract is subject to two exceptions involving situations in which the only benefits available under the split-dollar life insurance arrangement would be the value of current life insurance protection (that is, so-called non-equity arrangements). Under the first exception, an employer or service recipient is treated as the owner of the contract under a split-dollar life insurance arrangement that is entered into in connection with the performance of services if, at all times, the only economic benefits available to the employee or service provider under the arrangement would be the value of current life insurance protection. Similarly, a donor is treated as the owner of a life insurance contract under a split-dollar life insurance arrangement that is entered into between a donor and a donee (for example, a life insurance trust) if, at all times, the only economic benefits available to the donee under the arrangement would be the value of current life insurance protection. The proposed regulations reserve on the issue of the consequences of a modification to these arrangements (for example, such as subsequently providing the employee or donee with an interest in the cash value of the life insurance contract). The IRS and the Treasury Department request comments on the rule the final regulations should adopt regarding the consequences of modifying these arrangements.

The non-owner is any person other than the owner of the life insurance contract having any direct or indirect interest in such contract (other than a life insurance company acting solely in its capacity as issuer of a life insurance contract). For example, an employee whose spouse is designated by the employer as the beneficiary of a life insurance contract that is owned by the employer would have an indirect interest in the contract and, therefore, would be treated as a non-owner.

3. *Taxation Under the Economic Benefit Regime*

a. *In general*

Section 1.61-22(d) provides that, as a general rule for split-dollar life insurance arrangements that are taxed under the economic benefit regime, the owner of the life insurance contract is treated as providing economic benefits to the non-owner of the contract, and those economic benefits must be accounted for fully and consistently by both the owner and the non-owner. The value of the economic benefits, reduced by any consideration paid by the non-owner to the owner, is treated as transferred from the owner to the non-owner. The tax consequences of that transfer will depend on the relationship between the owner and the non-owner. Thus, the transfer may constitute a payment of compensation, a distribution under section 301, a gift, or a transfer having a different tax character.

Non-Equity Split-Dollar Life Insurance Arrangements

Under a non-equity split-dollar life insurance arrangement, the owner is treated as providing current life insurance protection (including paid-up additions) to the non-owner. The amount of the current life insurance protection provided to the non-owner for a taxable year equals the excess of the average death benefit of the life insurance contract over the total amount payable to the owner under the split-dollar life insurance arrangement. The total amount payable to the owner is increased

by the amount of any outstanding policy loan. The cost of the current life insurance protection provided to the non-owner in any year equals the amount of the current life insurance protection provided to the non-owner multiplied by the life insurance premium factor designated or permitted in guidance published in the Internal Revenue Bulletin. For example, assume that employer R is the owner of a $1,000,000 life insurance contract that is part of a split-dollar life insurance arrangement between R and employee E. Under the arrangement, R pays all of the $10,000 annual premiums and is entitled to receive the greater of its premiums or the cash surrender value of the contract when the arrangement terminates or E dies. Assume that through year 10 of the arrangement R has paid $100,000 of premiums and that in year 10 the cost of term insurance for E is $1.00 for $1,000 of insurance and the cash surrender value of the contract is $200,000. Under §1.61-22, in year 10, E must include in compensation income $800 ($1,000,000 – $200,000, or $800,000 payable to R, multiplied by .001 (E's premium rate factor)). If, however, E paid $300 of the premium, E would include $500 in compensation income.

The Treasury Department and the IRS request comments on whether there is a need for more specific guidance in computing the cost of a death benefit that varies during the course of a taxable year. Comments are requested concerning, for example, whether a convention requiring the amount of the death benefit to be recomputed on a quarterly or semi-annual basis would properly balance the accurate computation of the death benefit against compliance and administrative burdens.

Equity Split-Dollar Life Insurance Arrangements

Under §1.61-22(d)(3), the owner and the non-owner also must account fully and consistently for any right in, or benefit of, a life insurance contract provided to the non-owner under an equity split-dollar life insurance arrangement. For example, in a compensatory context in which the contract is owned by the employer, the employee must include in gross income the value of any interest in the cash surrender value of the contract provided to the employee during a taxable year.

This result is consistent with the conclusion in Rev. Rul. 66-110 that an employee must include in gross income the value of all economic benefits provided under a split-dollar life insurance arrangement. More broadly, this result is consistent with the fact that a non-owner who has an interest in the cash surrender value of a life insurance contract under an equity split-dollar life insurance arrangement is in a better economic position than a non-owner who has no such interest under a non-equity arrangement.

In general, a mere unfunded, unsecured promise to pay money in the future—as in a standard nonqualified deferred compensation plan covering an employee—does not result in current income. However, a non-owner's interest in a life insurance contract under an equity split-dollar life insurance arrangement is less like that of an employee covered under a standard nonqualified deferred compensation arrangement and more like that of an employee who obtains an interest in a specific asset of the employer (such as where the employer makes an outright purchase of a life insurance contract for the benefit of the employee). The employer's right to a return of its premiums, which characterizes most equity split-dollar life insurance arrangements, affects only the valuation of the employee's interest under the arrangement and, therefore, the amount of the employee's current income.

Specific guidance regarding valuation of economic benefits under an equity split-dollar life insurance arrangement is reserved in §1.61-22, pending comments from interested parties concerning an appropriate valuation methodology and views on whether such a methodology should be adopted as a substantive rule or as a safe harbor. Any proposal for a specific methodology should be objective and administrable. One potential approach for valuation might involve subtracting from current premium payments made by the contract owner the net present value of the amount to be repaid to the owner in the future.

Other Tax Consequences

Because §1.61-22(c) treats one party to the split-dollar life insurance arrangement as the owner of the entire contract, the non-owner has no investment in the contract under section 72(e). Thus, no amount paid by the non-owner under a split-dollar life insurance arrangement, whether or not designated as a premium, and no amount included in the non-owner's gross income as an economic benefit, is treated as investment in the contract under section 72(e)(6) for the non-owner. However, as described below, special rules apply in the case of a transfer of the contract from the owner to the non-owner.

Any premium paid by the owner is included in the owner's investment in the contract under section 72(e)(6). However, no premium payment and no economic benefit includible in the non-owner's gross income is deductible by the owner (except as otherwise provided under section 83 when the contract is transferred to the non-owner and the transfer is taxable in accordance with the rules of that section). Any amount paid by the non-owner to the owner for any economic benefit is included in the owner's gross income. Such amount is also included in the owner's investment in the contract (but only to the extent not otherwise so included by reason of having been paid by the owner as a premium or other consideration for the contract).

b. *Taxation of amounts received under the life insurance contract*

Any amount received under the life insurance contract (other than an amount received by reason of death) and provided, directly or indirectly, to the non-owner is treated as though paid by the insurance company to the owner and then by the owner to the non-owner. This rule applies to a policy owner dividend, the proceeds of a specified policy loan (as defined in § 1.61-22(e)), a withdrawal, or the proceeds of a partial surrender. The owner is taxed on the amount in accordance with the rules of section 72. The non-owner (and the owner for gift tax and employment tax purposes) must take the amount into account as a payment of compensation, a distribution under section 301, a gift, or other transfer depending on the non-owner's relationship to the owner. However, the amount that must be taken into account is reduced by the sum of (i) the value of all economic benefits actually taken into account by the non-owner (and the owner for gift tax and employment tax purposes) reduced (but not below zero) by the amounts that would have been taken into account were the arrangement a non-equity split-dollar life insurance arrangement and (ii) any consideration paid by the non-owner for all economic benefits reduced (but not below zero) by any consideration paid by the non-owner that would have been allocable to economic benefits provided to the non-owner were the arrangement a non-equity split-dollar life insurance arrangement. However, the preceding sentence applies only to the extent such economic benefits were not previously used to reduce an earlier amount received under the contract.

The same result applies in the case of a specified policy loan. A policy loan is a specified policy loan to the extent (i) the proceeds of the loan are distributed directly from the insurance company to the non-owner; (ii) a reasonable person would not expect that the loan will be repaid by the non-owner; or (iii) the non-owner's obligation to repay the loan to the owner is satisfied, or is capable of being satisfied, upon repayment by either party to the insurance company. Because the employee is not the owner of the contract, the specified policy loan will not be treated as a loan to the employee but as a loan to the employer (the owner of the contract), followed by a payment of cash compensation from the employer to the employee.

Amounts received by reason of death are treated differently. Under § 1.61-22(f), any amount paid to a beneficiary (other than the owner) by reason of the death of the insured is excludable from the beneficiary's gross income under section 101(a) as an amount received under a life insurance contract. This result applies only to the extent that such amount is allocable to current life insurance protection provided to the non-owner pursuant to the split-dollar life insurance arrangement, the cost of which was paid by the non-owner, or the value of which the non-owner actually took into account under the rules set forth in § 1.61-22. Amounts received by a non-owner in its capacity as a lender are generally not amounts received by reason of the death of the insured under section 101(a). Cf. Rev. Rul. 70-254 (1970-1 C.B. 31).

c. *Transfer of life insurance contract to the non-owner*

Section 1.61-22(g) provides rules for the transfer of a life insurance contract (or an undivided interest therein) from the owner to the non-owner. Consistent with the general rule for determining ownership, § 1.61-22(g) provides that a transfer of a life insurance contract (or an undivided interest therein) underlying a split-dollar life insurance arrangement occurs on the date that the non-owner becomes the owner of the entire contract (or the undivided interest therein). Thus, a transfer of the contract does not occur merely because the cash surrender value of the contract exceeds the premiums paid by the owner or the amount ultimately repayable to the owner on termination of the arrangement or the death of the insured. In addition, there is no transfer of the contract if the owner merely endorses a percentage of the cash surrender value of the contract (or similar rights in the contract) to the non-owner. Unless and until ownership of the contract is formally changed, the owner will continue to be treated as the owner for all Federal income, employment, and gift tax purposes.

At the time of a transfer, there generally must be taken into account for Federal income, employment, and gift tax purposes the excess of the fair market value of the life insurance contract (or the undivided interest therein) transferred to the non-owner (transferee) over the sum of (i) the amount the transferee pays to the owner (transferor) to

obtain the contract (or the undivided interest therein), (ii) the value of all economic benefits actually taken into account by the non-owner (and the owner for gift tax and employment tax purposes) reduced (but not below zero) by the amounts that would have been taken into account were the arrangement a non-equity split-dollar life insurance arrangement, and (iii) any consideration paid by the non-owner for all economic benefits reduced (but not below zero) by any consideration paid by the non-owner that would have been allocable to economic benefits provided to the non-owner were the arrangement a non-equity split-dollar life insurance arrangement. However, clauses (ii) and (iii) of the preceding sentence apply only to the extent those economic benefits were not previously used to reduce an earlier amount received under the contract. For this purpose, the fair market value of the life insurance contract is the cash surrender value and the value of all other rights under the contract (including any supplemental agreements, whether or not guaranteed), other than the value of the current life insurance protection. For example, the fair market value of the contract includes the value of a guaranteed right to an above-market rate of return (to the extent not already reflected in the cash surrender value).

In a transfer subject to section 83, fair market value is determined disregarding any lapse restrictions. In addition, the timing of the transferee's inclusion is determined under the rules of section 83. Therefore, a transfer will not give rise to gross income until the transferee's rights to the contract (or undivided interest in the contract) are substantially vested (unless the transferee makes a section 83(b) election). Section 1.83-6(a)(5) of the proposed regulations allows the service recipient's deduction at that time.

Under the general rule, the amount treated as consideration paid to acquire the contract under section 72(g)(1) equals the greater of the fair market value of the contract or the sum of the amount the transferee pays to obtain the contract plus the amount of unrecovered economic benefits previously taken into account or paid for by the transferee. Thus, these amounts become the transferee's investment in the contract under section 72(e) immediately after the transfer.

In the case of a transfer between a donor and a donee, the amount treated as consideration paid by the transferee to acquire the contract under section 72(g)(1) to determine the transferee's investment in the contract under section 72(e) immediately after the transfer is the sum of (i) the amount the transferee pays to obtain the contract, (ii) the aggregate of premiums or other consideration paid or deemed to have been paid by the transferor, and (iii) the amount of unrecovered economic benefits previously either taken into account by the transferee (excluding the amount of those benefits that was excludable from the transferee's gross income at the time of receipt) or paid for by the transferee.

After a transfer of an entire life insurance contract, the transferee becomes the owner for Federal income, employment, and gift tax purposes, including for purposes of the split-dollar life insurance rules. Thus, if the transferor pays premiums after the transfer, the payment of those premiums may be includible in the transferee's gross income if the payments are not split-dollar loans under § 1.7872-15. After the transfer of an undivided interest in a life insurance contract, the transferee is treated as the new owner of a separate contract for all purposes. However, if a transfer of a life insurance contract or an undivided interest in the contract is made in connection with the performance of services and the transfer is not yet taxable under section 83 (because rights to the contract or the undivided interest are substantially nonvested and no section 83(b) election is made), the transferor continues to be treated as the owner of the contract.

4. *Taxation Under the Loan Regime*

* * * * *

5. *Transfer Tax Treatment of Split-Dollar Life Insurance Arrangements*

The proposed regulations will apply for gift tax purposes in situations involving private split-dollar life insurance arrangements. Thus, if, under the proposed regulations, an irrevocable insurance trust is the owner of the life insurance contract underlying the split-dollar life insurance arrangement, and a reasonable person would expect that the donor, or the donor's estate, will recover an amount equal to the donor's premium payments, those premium payments are treated as loans made by the donor to the trust and are subject to § 1.7872-15. In such a case, payment of a premium by the donor is treated as a split-dollar loan to the trust in the amount of the premium payment. If the loan is repayable upon the death of the donor, the term of the loan is the donor's life expectancy determined under the appropriate table under § 1.72-9 as of the date of the payment and the value of the gift is the amount of the premium payment less the present value (determined under section 7872 and § 1.7872-15) of the donor's right to receive repayment. If, however, the donor makes premium payments that are not split-dollar loans, then the premium payments are governed by general gift tax principles. In such a case, with each premium payment, the donor is treated as making a gift to the trust equal to the amount of that payment.

Different rules apply, however, if the donor is treated under § 1.61-22(c) as the owner of the life insurance contract underlying the split-dollar life insurance arrangement and the donor is entitled to recover (either conditionally or unconditionally) all or any portion of the premium payments and such recovery is to be made from, or is secured by, the proceeds of the life insurance contract. Under these circumstances, the donor is treated as making a gift of economic benefits to the irrevocable insurance trust when the donor makes any premium payment on the life insurance contract. For example, assume that under the terms of the split-dollar life insurance arrangement, on termination of the arrangement or the donor's death, the donor or donor's estate is entitled to receive an amount equal to the *greater* of the aggregate premiums paid by the donor or the cash surrender value of the contract. In this case, each time the donor pays a premium, the donor makes a gift to the trust equal to the cost of the current life insurance protection provided to the trust less any premium amount paid by the trustee. On the other hand, if the donor or the donor's estate is entitled to receive an amount equal to the *lesser* of the aggregate premiums paid by the donor, or the cash surrender value of the contract, the amount of the donor's gift to the trust upon the payment of a premium equals the value of the economic benefits attributable to the trust's entire interest in the contract (reduced by any consideration the trustee paid for the interest).

As discussed earlier, § 1.61-22(c) treats the donor as the owner of a life insurance contract even if the donee is named as the policy owner if, under the split-dollar life insurance arrangement, the only amount that would be treated as a transfer by gift by the donor under the arrangement would be the value of current life insurance protection. However, any amount paid by a donee, directly or indirectly, to the donor for such current life insurance protection would generally be included in the donor's gross income.

Similarly, if the donor is the owner of the life insurance contract that is part of the split-dollar life insurance arrangement, amounts received by the irrevocable insurance trust (either directly or indirectly) under the contract (for example, as a policy owner dividend or proceeds of a specified policy loan) are treated as gifts by the donor to the irrevocable insurance trust as provided in § 1.61-22(e). The donor must also treat as a gift to the trust the amount set forth in § 1.61-22(g) upon the transfer of the life insurance contract (or undivided interest therein) from the donor to the trust.

The gift tax consequences of the transfer of an interest in a life insurance contract to a third party will continue to be determined under established gift tax principles notwithstanding who is treated as the owner of the life insurance contract under the proposed regulations. See, for example, Rev. Rul. 81-198 (1981-2 C.B. 188). Similarly, for estate tax purposes, regardless of who is treated as the owner of a life insurance contract under these proposed regulations, the inclusion of the policy proceeds in a decedent's gross estate will continue to be determined under section 2042. Thus, the policy proceeds will be included in the decedent's gross estate under section 2042(1) if receivable by the decedent's executor, or under section 2042(2) if the policy proceeds are receivable by a beneficiary other than the decedent's estate and the decedent possessed any incidents of ownership with respect to the policy.

6. *Other Applications of These Regulations*

The proposed regulations provide for conforming changes to the definition of wages under sections 3121(a), 3231(e), 3306(b), and 3401(a) and self-employment income under section 1402(a). The rules also apply for purposes of characterizing distributions from a corporation to a shareholder under section 301.

7. *Revenue Rulings to Become Obsolete*

Concurrent with the publication of final regulations relating to split-dollar life insurance arrangements in the **Federal Register**, the IRS will obsolete the following revenue rulings with respect to split-dollar life insurance arrangements entered into *after* the date the final regulations are published in the **Federal Register**: Rev. Rul. 64-328 (1964-2 C.B. 11); Rev. Rul. 66-110 (1966-1 C.B. 12); Rev. Rul. 78-420 (1978-2 C.B. 68) (with respect to income tax consequences); Rev. Rul. 79-50 (1979-1 C.B. 138); and Rev. Rul. 81-198 (1981-2 C.B. 188) (with respect to income tax consequences). Taxpayers entering into split-dollar life insurance arrangements on or before the date of publication of the final regulations may continue to rely on these revenue rulings to the extent described in Notice 2002-8.

The Treasury Department and the IRS request comments concerning whether any other revenue rulings or guidance published in the Internal Revenue Bulletin should be reconsidered in connection with the publication of final regulations relating to split-dollar life insurance arrangements in the **Federal Register**.

Proposed Effective Date

These proposed regulations are proposed to apply to any split-dollar life insurance arrangement entered into after the date these regulations are published as final regulations in the **Federal Register**. In addition, under the proposed regulations, an arrangement entered into on or before the date final regulations are published in the **Federal Register** and that is materially modified after that date is treated as a new arrangement entered into on the date of the modification. Comments are requested regarding whether certain material modifications should be disregarded in determining whether an arrangement is treated as a new arrangement for purposes of the effective date rule. For example, comments are requested whether an arrangement entered into on or before the effective date should be subject to these rules if the only material modification to the arrangement after that date is an exchange of an insurance policy qualifying for nonrecognition treatment under section 1035.

Taxpayers are reminded that Notice 2002-8 provides guidance with respect to arrangements entered into before the effective date of these regulations.

In addition, taxpayers may rely on these proposed regulations for the treatment of any split-dollar life insurance arrangement entered into on or before the date final regulations are published in the **Federal Register** provided that all parties to the split-dollar life insurance arrangement treat the arrangement consistently. Thus, for example, an owner and a non-owner of a life insurance contract that is part of a split-dollar life insurance arrangement may not rely on these proposed regulations if one party treats the arrangement as subject to the economic benefit rules of § 1.61-22 and the other party treats the arrangement as subject to the loan rules of § 1.7872-15. Moreover, parties to an equity split-dollar life insurance arrangement subject to the economic benefit regime may rely on these proposed regulations only if the value of all economic benefits taken into account by the parties exceeds the value of the economic benefits the parties would have taken into account if the arrangement were a non-equity split-dollar life insurance arrangement (determined using the Table 2001 rates in Notice 2002-8), thereby reflecting the fact that such an arrangement provides the non-owner with economic benefits that are more valuable than current life insurance protection.

Special Analyses

It has been determined that this notice of proposed rulemaking is not a significant regulatory action as defined in Executive Order 12866. Therefore, a regulatory flexibility assessment is not required. It is hereby certified that the collection of information requirements in these regulations will not have a significant economic impact on a substantial number of small entities. This certification is based on the fact that the regulations merely require a taxpayer to prepare a written representation that contains minimal information (if the loan provides for nonrecourse payments) or a projected payment schedule (if the loan provides for contingent payments). In addition, the preparation of these documents should take no more than .28 hours per taxpayer. Therefore, a Regulatory Flexibility Analysis under the Regulatory Flexibility Act (5 U.S.C. chapter 6) is not required. Pursuant to section 7805(f) of the Internal Revenue Code, this notice of proposed rulemaking will be submitted to the Chief Counsel for Advocacy of the Small Business Administration for comment on its impact on small business.

Comments and Public Hearing

Before these proposed regulations are adopted as final regulations, consideration will be given to any written or electronic comments (a signed original and eight (8) copies) that are submitted timely to the IRS. The Treasury Department and IRS specifically request comments on the clarity of the proposed rules and how they may be made easier to understand. All comments will be available for public inspection and copying.

A public hearing has been scheduled for October 23, 2002, beginning at 10 a.m. in room 4718 of the Internal Revenue Building, 1111 Constitution Avenue, NW., Washington, DC. Due to building security procedures, visitors must enter at the Constitution Avenue entrance. All visitors must present photo identification to enter the building. Because of access restrictions, visitors will not be admitted beyond the immediate entrance area more than 30 minutes before the hearing starts. For information about having your name placed on the building access list

1152 Proposed Regulations

to attend the hearing, see the "FOR FURTHER INFORMATION CONTACT" section of this preamble.

The rules of 26 CFR 601.601(a)(3) apply to the hearing. Persons who wish to present oral comments at the hearing must submit written comments and an outline of the topics to be discussed and the time to be devoted to each topic (signed original and eight (8) copies) by October 9, 2002. A period of 10 minutes will be allotted to each person for making comments. An agenda showing the schedule of speakers will be prepared after the deadline for receiving outlines has passed. Copies of the agenda will be available free of charge at the hearing.

Drafting Information

The principal authors of these proposed regulations are Rebecca Asta of the Office of Associate Chief Counsel (Financial Institutions and Products), Lane Damazo of the Office of Associate Chief Counsel (Passthroughs and Special Industries), Elizabeth Kaye of the Office of Associate Chief Counsel (Income Tax and Accounting), Erinn Madden of the Office of Associate Chief Counsel (Tax-Exempt and Governmental Entities), and Krishna Vallabhaneni of the Office of Associate Chief Counsel (Corporate). However, other personnel from the IRS and Treasury Department participated in their development.

List of Subjects

26 CFR Part 1

Income taxes, Reporting and recordkeeping requirements.

26 CFR Part 31

Employment taxes, Income taxes, Penalties, Pensions, Railroad retirement, Reporting and recordkeeping requirements, Social security, Unemployment compensation.

Proposed Amendments to the Regulations

Accordingly, 26 CFR parts 1 and 31 are proposed to be amended as follows:

PART 1—INCOME TAXES

Paragraph 1. The authority citation for part 1 is amended to read in part as follows:

Authority: 26 U.S.C. 7805 ***

Section 1.7872-15 also issued under 26 U.S.C. 1275 and 7872. ***

Par. 2. Section 1.61-2 is amended by:

1. Redesignating paragraphs (d)(2)(ii)(*a*) and (*b*) as paragraphs (d)(2)(ii)(A) and (B), respectively.

2. Adding two sentences immediately following the second sentence in newly designated paragraph (d)(2)(ii)(A).

The additions read as follows:

§ 1.61-2 Compensation for services, including fees, commissions, and similar items.

*****

(d) ***

(2) ***

(ii)(A) *Cost of life insurance on the life of the employee.* *** For example, if an employee or independent contractor is the owner (as defined in § 1.61-22(c)(1)) of a life insurance contract and the payments under such contract are not split-dollar loans under § 1.7872-15(b)(1), the employee or independent contractor must include in income the amount of any such payments by the employer or service recipient with respect to such contract during any year to the extent that the employee's or independent contractor's rights to the life insurance contract are substantially vested (within the meaning of § 1.83-3(b)). This result is the same regardless of whether the employee or independent contractor had at all times been the owner of the life insurance contract or the contract previously had been owned by the employer or service recipient as part of a split-dollar life insurance arrangement (as defined in § 1.61-22(b)(1) or (2)) and had been transferred by the employer or service recipient to the employee or independent contractor under § 1.61-22(g). ***

*****

Par. 3. Section 1.61-22 is added to read as follows:

§ 1.61-22 Taxation of split-dollar life insurance arrangements.

(a) *Scope*—(1) *In general.* This section provides rules for the taxation of a split-dollar life insurance arrangement for purposes of the income tax, the gift tax, the Federal Insurance Contributions Act (FICA), the

Federal Unemployment Tax Act (FUTA), the Railroad Retirement Tax Act (RRTA), and the Self-Employment Contributions Act of 1954 (SECA). For the Collection of Income Tax at Source on Wages, this section also provides rules for the taxation of a split-dollar life insurance arrangement, other than a payment under a split-dollar life insurance arrangement that is a split-dollar loan under § 1.7872-15(b)(1). In general, a split-dollar life insurance arrangement (as defined in paragraph (b) of this section) is subject to the rules of either paragraphs (d) through (g) of this section or § 1.7872-15. For rules to determine which rules apply to a split-dollar life insurance arrangement, see paragraph (b)(3) of this section.

(2) *Overview.* Paragraph (b) of this section defines a split-dollar life insurance arrangement and provides rules to determine whether an arrangement is subject to the rules of paragraphs (d) through (g) of this section, § 1.7872-15, or general tax rules. Paragraph (c) of this section defines certain other terms. Paragraph (d) of this section sets forth rules for the taxation of economic benefits provided under a split-dollar life insurance arrangement. Paragraph (e) of this section sets forth rules for the taxation of amounts received under a life insurance contract that is part of a split-dollar life insurance arrangement. Paragraph (f) of this section provides rules for additional tax consequences of a split-dollar life insurance arrangement, including the treatment of death benefits. Paragraph (g) of this section provides rules for the transfer of a life insurance contract (or an undivided interest in the contract) that is part of a split-dollar life insurance arrangement. Paragraph (h) of this section provides examples illustrating the application of this section. Paragraph (j) of this section provides the effective date of this section.

(b) *Split-dollar life insurance arrangement*—(1) *In general.* A split-dollar life insurance arrangement is any arrangement between an owner and a non-owner of a life insurance contract that satisfies the following criteria—

(i) Either party to the arrangement pays, directly or indirectly, all or any portion of the premiums on the life insurance contract, including a payment by means of a loan to the other party that is secured by the life insurance contract;

(ii) At least one of the parties to the arrangement paying premiums under paragraph (b)(1)(i) of this section is entitled to recover (either conditionally or unconditionally) all or any portion of those premiums and such recovery is to be made from, or is secured by, the proceeds of the life insurance contract; and

(iii) The arrangement is not part of a group-term life insurance plan described in section 79.

(2) *Special rule*—(i) *In general.* Any arrangement between an owner and a non-owner of a life insurance contract is treated as a split-dollar life insurance arrangement (regardless of whether the criteria of paragraph (b)(1) of this section are satisfied) if the arrangement is described in paragraph (b)(2)(ii) or (iii) of this section.

(ii) *Compensatory arrangements.* An arrangement is described in this paragraph (b)(2)(ii) if the following criteria are satisfied—

(A) The arrangement is entered into in connection with the performance of services and is not part of a group-term life insurance plan described in section 79;

(B) The employer or service recipient pays, directly or indirectly, all or any portion of the premiums; and

(C) The beneficiary of all or any portion of the death benefit is designated by the employee or service provider or is any person whom the employee or service provider would reasonably be expected to designate as the beneficiary.

(iii) *Shareholder arrangements.* An arrangement is described in this paragraph (b)(2)(iii) if the following criteria are satisfied—

(A) The arrangement is entered into between a corporation and another person in that person's capacity as a shareholder in the corporation;

(B) The corporation pays, directly or indirectly, all or any portion of the premiums; and

(C) The beneficiary of all or any portion of the death benefit is designated by the shareholder or is any person whom the shareholder would reasonably be expected to designate as the beneficiary.

(3) *Determination of whether this section or § 1.7872-15 applies to a split-dollar life insurance arrangement*—(i) *Split-dollar life insurance arrangements involving split-dollar loans under § 1.7872-15.* Except as provided in paragraph (b)(3)(ii) of this section, paragraphs (d) through (g) of this section do not apply to any split-dollar loan as defined in § 1.7872-15(b)(1). Section 1.7872-15 applies to any such loan. See para-

graph (b)(5) of this section for the treatment of payments made by a non-owner under a split-dollar life insurance arrangement that are not split-dollar loans.

(ii) *Exceptions.* Paragraphs (d) through (g) of this section apply (and §1.7872-15 does not apply) to any split-dollar life insurance arrangement if—

(A) The arrangement is entered into in connection with the performance of services, and the employee or service provider is not the owner of the life insurance contract (or is not treated as the owner of the contract under paragraph (c)(1)(ii)(A)(*1*) of this section); or

(B) The arrangement is entered into between a donor and a donee (for example, a life insurance trust) and the donee is not the owner of the life insurance contract (or is not treated as the owner of the contract under paragraph (c)(1)(ii)(A)(*2*) of this section).

(4) *Consistency requirement.* Both the owner and the non-owner of a life insurance contract that is part of a split-dollar life insurance arrangement described in paragraph (b)(1) or (2) of this section must fully and consistently account for all amounts under the arrangement under paragraph (b)(5) of this section, paragraphs (d) through (g) of this section, or under §1.7872-15.

(5) *Non-owner payments that are not split-dollar loans.* If a non-owner of a life insurance contract makes premium payments (directly or indirectly) under a split-dollar life insurance arrangement, and the payments are neither split-dollar loans nor consideration for economic benefits described in paragraph (d) of this section, then neither the rules of paragraphs (d) through (g) of this section nor the rules in §1.7872-15 apply to such payments. Instead, general income tax, employment tax, and gift tax principles apply to the premium payments. See, for example, §1.61-2(d)(2)(ii)(A).

(6) *Waiver, cancellation, or forgiveness.* If a repayment obligation described in §1.7872-15(a)(2) is waived, cancelled, or forgiven at any time, then the parties must take the amount waived, cancelled, or forgiven into account in accordance with the relationships between the parties (for example, as compensation in the case of an employee-employer relationship).

(c) *Definitions.* The following definitions apply for purposes of this section:

(1) *Owner*—(i) *In general.* With respect to a life insurance contract, the person named as the policy owner of such contract generally is the owner of such contract. If two or more persons are named as policy owners of a life insurance contract and each person has all the incidents of ownership with respect to an undivided interest in the contract, each person is treated as the owner of a separate contract to the extent of such person's undivided interest. If two or more persons are named as policy owners of a life insurance contract but each person does not have all the incidents of ownership with respect to an undivided interest in the contract, the person who is the first-named policy owner is treated as the owner of the entire contract.

(ii) *Special rule for certain arrangements*— (A) *In general.* Notwithstanding paragraph (c)(1)(i) of this section—

(*1*) An employer or service recipient is treated as the owner of a life insurance contract under a split-dollar life insurance arrangement that is entered into in connection with the performance of services if, at all times, the arrangement is described in paragraph (d)(2) of this section; and

(*2*) A donor is treated as the owner of a life insurance contract under a split-dollar life insurance arrangement that is entered into between a donor and a donee (for example, a life insurance trust) if, at all times, the arrangement is described in paragraph (d)(2) of this section.

(B) *Modifications.* [Reserved]

(iii) *Attribution rules.* [Reserved]

(2) *Non-owner.* With respect to a life insurance contract, a non-owner is any person (other than the owner of such contract) that has any direct or indirect interest in such contract (but not including a life insurance company acting only in its capacity as the issuer of a life insurance contract).

(3) *Transfer of entire contract or undivided interest therein.* A transfer of the ownership of a life insurance contract (or an undivided interest in such contract) that is part of a split-dollar life insurance arrangement occurs on the date that a non-owner becomes the owner (within the meaning of paragraph (c)(1) of this section) of the entire contract or of an undivided interest in the contract.

(4) *Undivided interest.* An undivided interest in a life insurance contract consists of an identical fractional or percentage interest in each right and benefit under the contract.

(5) *Employment tax.* The term employment tax means the Federal Insurance Contributions Act (FICA), the Federal Unemployment Tax Act (FUTA), the Railroad Retirement Tax Act (RRTA), the Self-Employment Contributions Act of 1954 (SECA), and the Collection of Income Tax at Source on Wages.

(d) *Economic benefits provided under a split-dollar life insurance arrangement*—(1) *In general.* Under a split-dollar life insurance arrangement subject to the rules of paragraphs (d) through (g) of this section, the owner of the life insurance contract is treated as providing economic benefits to the non-owner of the life insurance contract. Those economic benefits must be accounted for fully and consistently by both the owner and the non-owner pursuant to the rules of this paragraph (d). The value of the economic benefits, reduced by any consideration paid by the non-owner to the owner, is treated as transferred from the owner to the non-owner. Depending on the relationship between the owner and the non-owner, the economic benefits may constitute a payment of compensation, a distribution under section 301, a gift, or a transfer having a different tax character. Further, depending on the relationship between or among a non-owner and one or more other persons, the economic benefits may be treated as provided from the owner to the non-owner and as separately provided from the non-owner to such other person or persons (for example, as a payment of compensation from an employer to an employee and as a gift from the employee to the employee's children).

(2) *Non-equity split-dollar life insurance arrangements.* In the case of a split-dollar life insurance arrangement subject to the rules of paragraphs (d) through (g) of this section under which the only economic benefit provided to the non-owner is current life insurance protection (including paid-up additions thereto), the amount of the current life insurance protection provided to the non-owner for a taxable year equals the excess of the average death benefit of the life insurance contract over the total amount payable to the owner under the split-dollar life insurance arrangement. The total amount payable to the owner is increased by the amount of any outstanding policy loan. The cost of the current life insurance protection provided to the non-owner in any year equals the amount of the current life insurance protection provided to the non-owner multiplied by the life insurance premium factor designated or permitted in guidance published in the Internal Revenue Bulletin (see §601.601(d)(2)(ii) of this chapter).

(3) *Equity split-dollar life insurance arrangements*—(i) *In general.* In the case of a split-dollar life insurance arrangement subject to the rules of paragraphs (d) through (g) of this section other than an arrangement described in paragraph (d)(2) of this section, any right in, or benefit of, a life insurance contract (including, but not limited to, an interest in the cash surrender value) provided during a taxable year to a non-owner under a split-dollar life insurance arrangement is an economic benefit for purposes of this paragraph (d).

(ii) *Valuation of economic benefits.* [Reserved]

(e) *Amounts received under the contract*— (1) *In general.* Except as otherwise provided in paragraph (f)(2)(ii) of this section, any amount received under a life insurance contract that is part of a split-dollar life insurance arrangement subject to the rules of paragraphs (d) through (g) of this section (including, but not limited to, a policy owner divided, proceeds of a specified policy loan described in paragraph (e)(2) of this section, or the proceeds of a withdrawal from or partial surrender of the life insurance contract) is treated, to the extent provided directly or indirectly to a non-owner of the life insurance contract, as though such amount had been paid to the owner of the life insurance contract and then paid by the owner to the non-owner who is a party to the split-dollar life insurance arrangement. The amount received is taxable to the owner in accordance with the rules of section 72. The non-owner (and the owner for gift tax and employment tax purposes) must take the amount described in paragraph (e)(3) of this section into account as a payment of compensation, a distribution under section 301, a gift, or other transfer depending on the relationship between the owner and the non-owner.

(2) *Specified policy loan.* A policy loan is a specified policy loan to the extent—

(i) The proceeds of the loan are distributed directly from the insurance company to the non-owner;

(ii) A reasonable person would not expect that the loan will be repaid by the non-owner; or

(iii) The non-owner's obligation to repay the loan to the owner is satisfied or is capable of being satisfied upon repayment by either party to the insurance company.

(3) *Amount required to be taken into account.* With respect to a non-owner (and the owner for gift tax and employment tax purposes), the amount described in this paragraph (e)(3) is equal to the excess of—

(i) The amount treated as received by the owner under paragraph (e)(1) of this section; over

(ii) The amount of all economic benefits described in paragraph (d)(3) of this section actually taken into account under paragraph (d)(1) of this section by the transferee (and the transferor for gift tax and employment tax purposes) reduced (but not below zero) by any amounts that would have been taken into account under paragraph (d)(1) of this section if paragraph (d)(2) of this section were applicable to the arrangement plus any consideration paid by the non-owner for all economic benefits described in paragraph (d)(3) of this section reduced (but not below zero) by any consideration paid by the non-owner that would have been allocable to amounts described in paragraph (d)(2) of this section if paragraph (d)(2) of this section were applicable to the arrangement. The amount determined under the preceding sentence applies only to the extent that neither this paragraph (e)(3)(ii) nor paragraph (g)(1)(ii) of this section previously has applied to such economic benefits.

(f) *Other tax consequences*—(1) *Introduction.* In the case of a split-dollar life insurance arrangement subject to the rules of paragraphs (d) through (g) of this section, this paragraph (f) sets forth other tax consequences to the owner and non-owner of a life insurance contract that is part of the arrangement for the period prior to the transfer (as defined in paragraph (c)(3) of this section) of the contract (or an undivided interest therein) from the owner to the non-owner. See paragraph (g) of this section and § 1.83-6(a)(5) for tax consequences upon the transfer of the contract (or an undivided interest therein).

(2) *To non-owner*—(i) *In general.* A non-owner does not receive any investment in the contract under section 72(e)(6) with respect to a life insurance contract that is part of a split-dollar life insurance arrangement subject to the rules of paragraphs (d) through (g) of this section.

(ii) *Death proceeds to beneficiary (other than the owner).* Any amount paid to a beneficiary (other than the owner) by reason of the death of the insured is excluded from gross income by such beneficiary under section 101(a) as an amount received under a life insurance contract to the extent such amount is allocable to current life insurance protection provided to the non-owner pursuant to the split-dollar life insurance arrangement, the cost of which was paid by the non-owner, or the value of which the non-owner actually took into account pursuant to paragraph (d) of this section.

(3) *To owner.* Any premium paid by an owner under a split-dollar life insurance arrangement subject to the rules of paragraphs (d) through (g) of this section is included in the owner's investment in the contract under section 72(e)(6). No premium or amount described in paragraph (d) of this section is deductible by the owner (except as otherwise provided in § 1.83-6(a)(5)). Any amount paid by a non-owner, directly or indirectly, to the owner of the life insurance contract for current life insurance protection or for any other economic benefit under the life insurance contract is included in the owner's gross income and is included in the owner's investment in the life insurance contract for purposes of section 72(e)(6) (but only to the extent not otherwise so included by reason of having been paid by the owner as a premium or other consideration for the contract).

(g) *Transfer of entire contract or undivided interest therein*—(1) *In general.* Upon a transfer within the meaning of paragraph (c)(3) of this section of a life insurance contract (or an undivided interest therein) to a non-owner (transferee), the transferee (and the owner (transferor) for gift tax and employment tax purposes) takes into account the excess of the fair market value of the life insurance contract (or the undivided interest therein) transferred to the transferee at that time over the sum of—

(i) The amount the transferee pays to the transferor to obtain the contract (or the undivided interest therein); and

(ii) The amount of all economic benefits described in paragraph (d)(3) of this section actually taken into account under paragraph (d)(1) of this section by the transferee (and the transferor for gift tax and employment tax purposes) reduced (but not below zero) by any amounts that would have been taken into account under paragraph (d)(1) of this section if paragraph (d)(2) of this section were applicable to the arrangement plus any consideration paid by the non-owner for all economic benefits described in paragraph (d)(3) of this section reduced (but not below zero) by any consideration paid by the non-owner that would have been allocable to amounts described in paragraph (d)(2) of this section if paragraph (d)(2) of this section were applicable to the arrangement. The amount determined under the preceding sentence applies only to the extent that neither paragraph (e)(3)(ii) of

this section nor this paragraph (g)(1)(ii) previously has applied to such economic benefits.

(2) *Determination of fair market value.* For purposes of paragraph (g)(1) of this section, the fair market value of a life insurance contract is the cash surrender value and the value of all other rights under such contract (including any supplemental agreements there to and whether or not guaranteed), other than the value of current life insurance protection.

(3) *Exception for certain transfers in connection with the performance of services.* To the extent the ownership of a life insurance contract (or undivided interest in such contract) is transferred in connection with the performance of services, paragraph (g)(1) of this section does not apply until such contract (or undivided interest in such contract) is taxable under section 83. For purposes of paragraph (g)(1) of this section, fair market value is determined disregarding any lapse restrictions and at the time the transfer of such contract (or undivided interest in such contract) is taxable under section 83.

(4) *Treatment of non-owner after transfer*— (i) *In general.* After a transfer of an entire life insurance contract (except when such transfer is in connection with the performance of services and the transfer is not yet taxable under section 83), the person who previously had been the non-owner is treated as the owner of such contract for all purposes, including for purposes of paragraph (b) of this section and for purposes of § 1.61-2(d)(2)(ii)(A). After the transfer of an undivided interest in a life insurance contract (or, if later, at the time such transfer is taxable under section 83), the person who previously had been the non-owner is treated as the owner of a separate contract consisting of that interest for all purposes, including for purposes of paragraph (b) of this section and for purposes of § 1.61-2(d)(2)(ii)(A). However, such person will continue to be treated as a non-owner with respect to any undivided interest in the contract not so transferred (or not yet taxable under section 83).

(ii) *Investment in the contract after transfer*—(A) *In general.* The amount treated as consideration paid to acquire the contract under section 72(g)(1) to determine the aggregate premiums paid by the transferee for purposes of determining the transferee's investment in the contract under section 72(e) after the transfer (or, if later, at the time such transfer is taxable under section 83) equals the greater of the fair market value of the contract or the sum of the amounts determined under paragraphs (g)(1)(i) and (ii) of this section.

(B) *Transfers between a donor and a donee.* In the case of a transfer of a contract between a donor and a donee, the amount treated as consideration paid by the transferee to acquire the contract under section 72(g)(1) to determine the aggregate premiums paid by the transferee for purposes of determining the transferee's investment in the contract under section 72(e) after the transfer equals the sum of the amounts determined under paragraphs (g)(1)(i) and (ii) of this section except that—

(*1*) The amount determined under paragraph (g)(1)(i) of this section includes the aggregate of premiums or other consideration paid or deemed to have been paid by the transferor; and

(*2*) The amount of all economic benefits determined under paragraph (g)(1)(ii) of this section actually taken into account by the transferee does not include such benefits to the extent such benefits were excludable from the transferee's gross income at the time of receipt.

(C) *Transfers of an undivided interest in a contract.* If a portion of a contract is transferred to the transferee, then the amount to be included as consideration paid to acquire the contract is determined by multiplying the amount determined under paragraph (g)(4)(ii)(A) of this section (as modified by paragraph (g)(4)(ii)(B) of this section, if the transfer is between a donor and a donee) by a fraction, the numerator of which is the fair market value of the portion transferred and the denominator of which is the fair market value of the entire contract.

(D) *Example.* The following example illustrates the rules of this paragraph (g)(4)(ii):

Example. (i) In year 1, donor D and donee E enter into a split-dollar life insurance arrangement as defined in paragraph (b)(1) of this section. D is the owner of the life insurance contract under paragraph (c)(1) of this section. The life insurance contract is not a modified endowment contract as defined in section 7702A. In year 5, D gratuitously transfers the contract, within the meaning of paragraph (c)(3) of this section, to E. At the time of the transfer, the fair market value of the contract is $200,000 and D had paid $50,000 in premiums under the arrangement. In addition, at the time of the transfer, E had previously received $80,000 of benefits described in paragraph (d)(3) of this section, which were excludable from E's gross income under section 102.

(ii) E's investment in the contract is $50,000, consisting of the $50,000 of premiums paid by D. The $80,000 of benefits described in paragraph (d)(3) of this section that E received is not included in E's investment in the contract because such amounts were excludable from E's gross income at the time of receipt.

(iii) *No investment in the contract for current life insurance protection.* No amount allocable to current life insurance protection provided to the transferee (the cost of which was paid by the transferee or the value of which was provided to the transferee) is treated as consideration paid to acquire the contract under section 72(g)(1) to determine the aggregate premiums paid by the transferee for purposes of determining the transferee's investment in the contract under section 72(e) after the transfer.

(h) *Examples.* The following examples illustrate the rules of this section. Except as otherwise provided, each of the examples assumes that the employer (R) is the owner (as defined in paragraph (c)(1) of this section) of a life insurance contract that is part of a split-dollar life insurance arrangement subject to the rules of paragraphs (d) through (g) of this section, that the life insurance contract is not a modified endowment contract under section 7702A, that the compensation paid to the employee (E) is reasonable, and that E makes no premium payments. The examples are as follows:

Example 1. (i) In year 1, R purchases a life insurance contract on the life of E. R is named as the policy owner of the contract. R and E enter into an arrangement under which R will pay all the premiums on the life insurance contract until the termination of the arrangement or E's death. Upon termination of the arrangement or E's death, R is entitled to receive the greater of the aggregate premiums or the cash surrender value of the contract. The balance of the death benefit will be paid to a beneficiary designated by E.

(ii) Because R is designated as the policy owner, R is the owner of the contract under paragraph (c)(1) of this section. E is a non-owner of the contract. Under the arrangement between R and E, a portion of the death benefit is payable to a beneficiary designated by E. The arrangement is a split-dollar life insurance arrangement under paragraph (b)(1) or (2) of this section. For each year that the split-dollar life insurance arrangement is in effect, the arrangement is described in paragraph (d)(2) of this section and E must include in income the value of current life insurance protection, as required by paragraph (d)(2) of this section.

Example 2. (i) The facts are the same as in *Example 1* except that, upon termination of the arrangement or E's death, R is entitled to receive the lesser of the aggregate premiums or the cash surrender value of the contract.

(ii) For each year that the split-dollar life insurance arrangement is in effect, the arrangement is described in paragraph (d)(3) of this section and E must include in gross income the value of the economic benefit attributable to E's interest in the life insurance contract, as required by paragraph (d)(3) of this section.

Example 3. (i) The facts are the same as in *Example 1* except that in year 5, R and E modify the split-dollar life insurance arrangement to provide that, upon termination of the arrangement or E's death, R is entitled to receive the greater of the aggregate premiums or one-half the cash surrender value of the contract.

(ii) In year 5 (and subsequent years), the arrangement is described in paragraph (d)(3) of this section and E must include in gross income the value of the economic benefit attributable to E's interest in the life insurance contract, as required by paragraph (d)(3) of this section. Because the modification made by R and E in year 5 does not involve the transfer (within the meaning of paragraph (c)(3) of this section) of an undivided interest in the life insurance contract from R to E, the modification is not a transfer for purposes of paragraph (g) of this section.

Example 4. (i) The facts are the same as in *Example 2* except that in year 7, R and E modify the split-dollar life insurance arrangement to provide that, upon termination of the arrangement or E's death, R will be paid the lesser of 80 percent of the aggregate premiums or the cash surrender value of the contract.

(ii) The arrangement is described in paragraph (d)(3) of this section. In year 7 (and in subsequent years), E must include in gross income the value of the increased economic benefits described in paragraph (d)(3) of this section resulting from the contract modification under which E obtains rights to a larger amount of the cash value of the contract (attributable to the fact that R will forgo the right to recover 20 percent of the premiums R pays).

Example 5. (i) The facts are the same as in *Example 3* except that in year 7, E is designated as the policy owner. At that time, E's rights to the contract are substantially vested as defined in § 1.83-3(b).

(ii) In year 7, R is treated as having made a transfer (within the meaning of paragraph (c)(3) of this section) of the life insurance contract to E. E must include in gross income the amount determined under paragraph (g)(1) of this section.

(iii) After the transfer of the contract to E, E is the owner of the contract and any premium payments by R will be included in E's income under paragraph (b)(5) of this section and § 1.61-2(d)(2)(ii)(A) (unless R's payments are split-dollar loans as defined in § 1.7872-15(b)(1)).

Example 6. (i) In year 1, E and R enter into a split-dollar life insurance arrangement as defined in paragraph (b)(2) of this section. Under the arrangement, R is required to make annual premium payments of $10,000 and E is required to make annual premium payments of $500. In year 5, a $500 policy owner dividend payable to E is declared by the insurance company. E directs the insurance company to use the $500 as E's premium payment for year 5.

(ii) For each year the arrangement is in effect, the arrangement is described in paragraph (d)(3) of this section and E must include in gross income the value of the economic benefits granted during the year, as required by paragraph (d)(3) of this section over the $500 premium payment paid by E. In year 5, E must also include in gross income as compensation the excess, if any, of the $500 distributed to E from the proceeds of the policy owner dividend over the amount determined under paragraph (e)(3)(ii) of this section.

(iii) R must include in income the premiums paid by E during the years the split-dollar life insurance arrangement is in effect, including the $500 of the premium E paid in year 5 with proceeds of the policy owner dividend. R's investment in the contract is increased in an amount equal to the premiums paid by E, including the $500 of the premium paid by E in year 5 from the proceeds of the policy owner dividend. In year 5, R is treated as receiving a $500 distribution under the contract, which is taxed pursuant to section 72.

Example 7. (i) The facts are the same as in *Example 2* except that in year 10, E withdraws $100,000 from the cash value of the contract.

(ii) In year 10, R is treated as receiving a $100,000 distribution from the insurance company. This amount is treated as an amount received by R under the contract and taxed pursuant to section 72. This amount reduces R's investment in the contract under section 72(e). R is treated as paying the $100,000 to E as cash compensation, and R must include that amount in gross income less any amounts determined under paragraph (e)(3)(ii) of this section.

Example 8. (i) The facts are the same as in *Example 7* except E receives the proceeds of a $100,000 specified policy loan directly from the insurance company.

(ii) The transfer of the proceeds of the specified policy loan to E is treated as a loan by the insurance company to R. Under the rules of section 72(e), the $100,000 loan is not included in R's income and does not reduce R's investment in the contract. R is treated as paying the $100,000 of loan proceeds to E as cash compensation. E must include that amount in gross income less any amounts determined under paragraph (e)(3)(ii) of this section.

(i) [Reserved]

(j) *Effective date*—(1) *General rule.* This section applies to any split-dollar life insurance arrangement (as defined in paragraph (b)(1) or (2) of this section) entered into after the date the final regulations are published in the **Federal Register.**

(2) *Early reliance*—(i) *General rule.* Taxpayers may rely on this section for the treatment of any split-dollar life insurance arrangement (as defined in paragraph (b)(1) or (2) of this section) entered into on or before the date described in paragraph (j)(1) of this section, provided that all taxpayers who are parties to the arrangement treat the arrangement consistently under this section and, in the case of an arrangement described in paragraph (d)(3) of this section, also satisfy the requirements in paragraph (j)(2)(ii) of this section.

(ii) *Equity split-dollar life insurance arrangements.* Parties to an arrangement described in paragraph (d)(3) of this section may rely on this section only if the value of all economic benefits taken into account by the parties exceeds the value of the economic benefits the parties would have taken into account if paragraph (d)(2) of this section were applicable to the arrangement (determined using the life insurance premium factor designated in guidance published in the Internal Revenue Bulletin (see § 601.601(d)(2)(ii) of this chapter)), thereby reflecting the fact that such an arrangement provides the non-owner with economic benefits that are more valuable than current life insurance protection.

(3) *Modified arrangements treated as new arrangements.* An arrangement entered into on or before the date set forth in paragraph (j)(1) of this section that is materially modified after the date set forth in paragraph (j)(1) of this section is treated as a new arrangement entered into on the date of the modification.

Par. 4. Section 1.83-1 is amended by:

1. Removing the second sentence of paragraph (a)(2).

2. Adding a sentence at the end of paragraph (a)(2).

The addition reads as follows:

§ *1.83-1 Property transferred in connection with the performance of services.*

(a)***

(2) *Life insurance.* *** For the taxation of life insurance protection under a split-dollar life insurance arrangement (as defined in § 1.61-22(b)(1) or (2)), see § 1.61-22.

*****

Par. 5. Section 1.83-3 is amended by:

1. Adding a sentence at the end of paragraph (a)(1).

2. Revising the penultimate sentence in paragraph (e).

The addition and revision read as follows:

§ *1.83-3 Meaning and use of certain terms.*

(a)*** (1)*** For special rules applying to the transfer of a life insurance contract (or an undivided interest therein) that is part of a split-dollar life insurance arrangement (as defined in § 1.61-22(b)(1) or (2)), see § 1.61-22(g).

*****

(e) *** In the case of a transfer of a contract, or any undivided interest therein, providing death benefit protection (including a life insurance contract, retirement contract, or endowment contract) after the date the final regulations are published in the **Federal Register**, the cash surrender value and all other rights under such contract (including any supplemental agreements thereto and whether or not guaranteed), other than current life insurance protection, are treated as property for purposes of this section. ***

*****

Par. 6. Section 1.83-6 is amended as follows:

1. Redesignating paragraph (a)(5) as paragraph (a)(6).

2. Adding a new paragraph (a)(5).

The addition reads as follows:

§ *1.83-6 Deduction by employer.*

(a) ***

(5) *Transfer of life insurance contract (or an undivided interest therein)*—(i) *General rule.* In the case of a transfer of a life insurance contract (or an undivided interest therein) described in § 1.61-22(c)(3) in connection with the performance of services, a deduction is allowable under paragraph (a)(1) of this section to the person for whom the services were performed. The amount of the deduction, if allowable, is equal to the sum of the amount included as compensation in the gross income of the service provider under § 1.61-22(g)(1) and the amount determined under § 1.61-22(g)(1)(ii).

(ii) *Effective date*—(A) *General rule.* Paragraph (a)(5)(i) of this section applies to any split-dollar life insurance arrangement (as defined in § 1.61-22(b)(1) or (2)) entered into after the date the final regulations are published in the **Federal Register**.

(B) *Early reliance*—(*1*) *General rule.* Taxpayers may rely on this paragraph (a)(5) for the treatment of any split-dollar life insurance arrangement (as defined in § 1.61-22(b)(1) or (2)) entered into on or before the date described in paragraph (a)(5)(ii)(A) of this section, provided that all taxpayers who are parties to the arrangement treat the arrangement consistently under § 1.61-22(d) through (g) and, in the

case of an arrangement described in § 1.61-22(d)(3), also satisfy the requirements in paragraph (a)(5)(ii)(B)(*2*) of this section.

(*2*) *Equity split-dollar life insurance arrangements.* Parties to an arrangement described in § 1.61-22(d)(3) may rely on this paragraph (a)(5) only if the value of all economic benefits taken into account by the parties exceeds the value of the economic benefits the parties would have taken into account if § 1.61-22(d)(2) were applicable to the arrangement (determined using the life insurance premium factor designated in guidance published in the Internal Revenue Bulletin (see § 601.601(d)(2)(ii) of this chapter)), thereby reflecting the fact that such an arrangement provides the non-owner with economic benefits that are more valuable than current life insurance protection.

(C) *Modified arrangements treated as new arrangements.* An arrangement entered into on or before the date set forth in paragraph (a)(5)(ii)(A) of this section that is materially modified after the date set forth in paragraph (a)(5)(ii)(A) of this section is treated as a new arrangement entered into on the date of the modification.

*****

Par. 7. In § 1.301-1, paragraph (q) is added to read as follows:

§ *1.301-1 Rules applicable with respect to distributions of money and other property.*

*****

* * * * *

PART 31—EMPLOYMENT TAXES AND COLLECTION OF INCOME TAX AT SOURCE

Par. 10. The authority citation for part 31 continues to read in part as follows:

Authority: 26 U.S.C. 7805. ***

Par. 11. In § 31.3121(a)-1, paragraph (k) is added to read as follows:

§ *31.3121(a)-1 Wages.*

*****

(k) *Split-dollar life insurance arrangements.* Except as otherwise provided under section 3121(v), see § 1.61-22 of this chapter for rules relating to the treatment of split-dollar life insurance arrangements.

Par. 12. In § 31.3231(e)-1, paragraph (a)(6) is added to read as follows:

§ *31.3231(e)-1 Compensation.*

(a) ***

(6) *Split-dollar life insurance arrangements.* See § 1.61-22 of this chapter for rules relating to the treatment of split-dollar life insurance arrangements.

*****

Par. 13. In § 31.3306(b)-1, paragraph (I) is added to read as follows:

§ *31.3306(b)-1 Wages.*

*****

(I) *Split-dollar life insurance arrangements.* Except as otherwise provided under section 3306(r), see § 1.61-22 of this chapter for rules relating to the treatment of split-dollar life insurance arrangements.

Par. 14. In § 31.3401(a)-1, paragraph (b)(15) is added to read as follows:

§ *31.3401(a)-1 Wages.*

*****

(b) ***

(15) *Split-dollar life insurance arrangements.* See § 1.61-22 of this chapter for rules relating to the treatment of split-dollar life insurance arrangements.

*****

David A. Mader,

Acting Deputy Commissioner of Internal Revenue.

¶ 20,260N

IRS proposed regulations: Welfare benefit plans: 10-or-more employer plans: Funding limitations.—The IRS has issued proposed regulations clarifying when a welfare benefit plan is part of a 10-or-more employer plan, which would make it exempt from Code Sec. 419 and Code Sec. 419A deduction limits that generally apply to welfare benefit plans. Under Code Sec. 419A(f)(6), a plan is a 10-or-more employer plan if more than one employer contributes to it, no employer is normally required to contribute more than 10% of the total contributions made under the plan by all employers, and the plan does not maintain experience-rating arrangements with respect to individual employers. The proposed regulations provide guidance both for verifying that the Code Sec. 419A(f)(6) requirements have been met, as well as for identifying characteristics that indicate when a plan is not a 10-or-more employer plan.

The proposed regulations, which were published in the *Federal Register* on July 11, 2002 (67 FR 45933), were previously reproduced at this paragraph.

The final regulations were published in the *Federal Register* on July 17, 2003 (68 FR 42254) and are reproduced at ¶ 12,960. The preamble to the regulations is found at ¶ 24,507H.

¶ 20,260O

Proposed regulations: Individual retirement accounts: Returned contributions: Recharacterized contributions.—The IRS has issued proposed regulations that provide a new method to be used for calculating the net income attributable to IRA contributions that are distributed as returned or recharacterized contributions. The proposed regulations adopt the method set out in Notice 2000-39 (CCH PENSION PLAN GUIDE ¶ 17,118X).

The proposed regulations were published in the Federal Register on July 23, 2002 at 67 FR 48067. Final regulations, which were published in the Federal Register on May 5, 2003, at 68 FR 23586, are reproduced at ¶ 12,056, ¶ 12,063, and ¶ 12,097A-5. The preamble is reproduced at ¶ 24,507A.

¶ 20,260P

Qualified joint and survivor annuities (QJSAs): Qualified preretirement survivor annuities (QPSAs): Qualification requirements: Disclosure: Value of benefits.—The IRS has issued proposed regulations in response to concerns that participants who are eligible for both subsidized annuity distributions and unsubsidized single-sum distributions may be receiving notices that do not adequately explain the value of the subsidy that is foregone if the single-sum distribution is elected. The proposed regulations consolidate the content requirements applicable to explanations for QJSAs and QPSAs and specify rules for disclosing the relative values of optional forms of benefit as part of the QJSA explanation.

The proposed regulations, which were published in the *Federal Register* on October 7, 2002 (67 FR 62417), were previously reproduced at this paragraph. The final regulations were published in the *Federal Register* on December 17, 2003 (68 FR 70141) and are reproduced at ¶ 12,551. The preamble to the regulations is found at ¶ 24,507L.

DEPARTMENT OF THE TREASURY

Internal Revenue Service

26 CFR Part 1

[REG-124667-02]

RIN 1545-BA78

Disclosure of Relative Values of Optional Forms of Benefit

AGENCY: Internal Revenue Service (IRS), Treasury.

ACTION: Notice of proposed rulemaking and notice of public hearing.

SUMMARY: This document contains proposed regulations that would consolidate the content requirements applicable to explanations of qualified joint and survivor annuities and qualified preretirement survivor annuities payable under certain retirement plans, and would specify requirements for disclosing the relative value of optional forms of benefit that are payable from certain retirement plans in lieu of a qualified joint and survivor annuity. These regulations would affect retirement plan sponsors and administrators, and participants in and beneficiaries of retirement plans. This document also provides notice of a public hearing on these proposed regulations.

DATES: Written comments, requests to speak and outlines of oral comments to be discussed at the public hearing scheduled for January 14, 2003, at 10 a.m., must be received by January 2, 2003.

ADDRESSES: Send submissions to: CC:ITA:RU (REG-124667-02), room 5226, Internal Revenue Service, POB 7604, Ben Franklin Station, Washington, DC 20044. In the alternative, submissions may be hand delivered to: CC:ITA:RU (REG-124667-02), room 5226, Internal Revenue Service, 1111 Constitution Avenue NW., Washington, DC. Alternatively, taxpayers may submit comments electronically via the Internet by submitting comments directly to the IRS Internet site at: *www.irs.gov/regs.* The public hearing will be held in room 4718 of the Internal Revenue Building, 1111 Constitution Avenue NW., Washington, DC.

FOR FURTHER INFORMATION CONTACT:

Concerning the regulations, Linda S. F. Marshall, 202-622-6090; concerning submissions and the hearing, and/or to be placed on the building access list to attend the hearing, Guy Traynor, 202-622-7180 (not toll-free numbers).

SUPPLEMENTARY INFORMATION:

Paperwork Reduction Act

The collections of information contained in this notice of proposed rulemaking have been submitted to the Office of Management and Budget for review in accordance with the Paperwork Reduction Act of 1995 (44 U.S.C. 3507(d)). Comments on the collections of information should be sent to the Office of Management and Budget, Attn: Desk Officer for the Department of the Treasury, Office of Information and Regulatory Affairs, Washington, DC 20503, with copies to the Internal Revenue Service, Attn: IRS Reports Clearance Officer, W:CAR:MP:FP:S Washington, DC 20224. Comments on the collections of information should be received by December 6, 2002. Comments are specifically requested concerning:

Whether the proposed collections of information are necessary for the proper performance of the functions of the IRS, including whether the information will have practical utility;

The accuracy of the estimated burden associated with the proposed collection of information (see below);

How the quality, utility, and clarity of the information to be collected may be enhanced;

How the burden of complying with the proposed collection of information may be minimized, including through the application of automated collection techniques or other forms of information technology; and

Estimates of capital or start-up costs and costs of operation, maintenance, and purchase of services to provide information.

The collections of information in this proposed regulation are in § 1.417(a)(3)-1. This information is required by the IRS to comply with the requirements of section 417(a)(3) regarding explanations that must be provided to participants in a qualified plan prior to a waiver of a qualified joint and survivor annuity (QJSA) or a qualified preretirement survivor annuity (QPSA). This information will be used by participants and spouses of participants to determine whether to waive a QJSA or QPSA, and by the IRS to confirm that the plan complies with applicable qualification requirements to avoid adverse tax consequences. The collections of information are mandatory. The respondents are non-profit institutions.

Estimated total annual reporting burden: 375,000 hours.

The estimated annual burden per respondent varies from .01 to .99 hours, depending on individual circumstances, with an estimated average of .5 hours.

Estimated number of respondents: 750,000.

The estimated annual frequency of responses: On occasion.

An agency may not conduct or sponsor, and a person is not required to respond to, a collection of information unless it displays a valid control number assigned by the Office of Management and Budget.

Books or records relating to a collection of information must be retained as long as their contents may become material in the administration of any internal revenue law. Generally, tax returns and tax return information are confidential, as required by 26 U.S.C. 6103.

Background

This document contains proposed amendments to 26 CFR part 1 under section 417(a)(3) of the Internal Revenue Code of 1986 (Code).

A qualified retirement plan to which section 401(a)(11) applies must pay a vested participant's retirement benefit under the plan in the form of a qualified joint and survivor annuity (QJSA), except as provided in section 417. Section 401(a)(11) applies to defined benefit plans, money purchase pension plans, and certain other defined contribution plans. A QJSA is defined in section 417(b) as an annuity for the life of the participant with a survivor annuity for the life of the spouse (if the participant is married) that is not less than 50 percent of (and is not greater than 100 percent of) the amount of the annuity that is payable during the joint lives of the participant and the spouse. Under section 417(b)(2), a QJSA for a married participant generally must be the actuarial equivalent of the single life annuity benefit payable for the life of the participant. However, a plan is permitted to subsidize the QJSA for a married participant. If the plan fully subsidizes the QJSA for a married participant so that failure to waive the QJSA would not result in reduced payments over the life of the participant compared to the single life annuity benefit, then the plan need not provide an election to waive the QJSA. See section 417(a)(5).

For a married participant, the QJSA must be at least as valuable as any other optional form of benefit payable under the plan at the same time. See § 1.401(a)-20, Q&A-16. Further, the antiforfeiture rules of section 411(a) prohibit a participant's benefit under a defined benefit plan from being satisfied through payment that is actuarially less valuable than the value of the participant's accrued benefit expressed in the form of an annual benefit commencing at normal retirement age. These determinations must be made using reasonable actuarial assumptions. However, see § 1.417(e)-1(d) for actuarial assumptions required for use in certain present value calculations.

If a plan provides a subsidy for one optional form of benefit (i.e., the payments under an optional form of benefit have an actuarial present value that is greater than the actuarial present value of the accrued benefit), there is no requirement to extend a similar subsidy (or any subsidy) to every other optional form of benefit. Thus, for example, a participant might be entitled to receive a single-sum distribution upon early retirement that does not reflect any early retirement subsidy in lieu of a QJSA that reflects a substantial early retirement subsidy. As a further example, a participant might be entitled to receive a single-sum distribution at normal retirement age in lieu of a QJSA that is subsidized as described in section 417(a)(5).

Section 417(a) provides rules under which a participant (with spousal consent) may waive payment of the participant's benefit in the form of a QJSA. Section 417(a)(3) provides that a plan must provide to each participant, within a reasonable period before the annuity starting date (and consistent with such regulations as the Secretary may prescribe) a written explanation of the terms and conditions of the QJSA, the participant's right to make, and the effect of, an election to waive the QJSA form of benefit, the rights of the participant's spouse, and the right to revoke (and the effect of the revocation of) an election to waive the QJSA form of benefit.

Section 205 of the Employee Retirement Income Security Act of 1974 (ERISA), Public Law 93-406 (88 Stat. 829) as subsequently amended, provides parallel rules to the rules of sections 401(a)(11) and 417 of the Internal Revenue Code. In particular, section 205(a)(3) of ERISA provides a parallel rule to section 417(a)(3) of the Code. Treasury regulations issued under section 417(a)(3) of the Code apply as well for purposes of section 205(a)(3) of ERISA.

Regulations governing the requirements for waiver of a QJSA were published in the **Federal Register** on August 19, 1988 (TD 8219; 53 FR 31837). Section 1.401(a)-20, Q&A-36, provides rules for the explanation that must be provided under section 417(a)(3) as a prerequisite to waiver of a QJSA. Section 1.401(a)-20, Q&A-36, requires that such a written explanation must contain a general description of the eligibility conditions and other material features of the optional forms of benefit and sufficient additional information to explain the relative values of the optional forms of benefit available under the plan (e.g., the extent to which optional forms are subsidized relative to the normal form of benefit or the interest rates used to calculate the optional forms). In addition, § 1.401(a)-20, Q&A-36, provides that the written explanation

must comply with the requirements set forth in § 1.401(a)-11(c)(3). Section 1.401(a)-11(c)(3) was issued prior to the enactment of section 417, and provides rules relating to written explanations that were required prior to a participant's election of a preretirement survivor annuity or election to waive a joint and survivor annuity. Section 1.401(a)-11(c)(3)(i)(C) provides that such a written explanation must contain a general explanation of the relative financial effect of these elections on a participant's annuity.

In addition, under section 411 and § 1.411(a)-11(c), so long as a benefit is immediately distributable (within the meaning of § 1.411(a)-11(c)(4)), a participant must be informed of his or her right to defer that distribution. This requirement is independent of the section 417 requirements addressed in these proposed regulations.

Concerns have been expressed that, in certain cases, the information provided to participants under section 417(a)(3) regarding the available distribution forms does not adequately enable them to compare those distribution forms without professional advice. In particular, participants who are eligible for both subsidized annuity distributions and unsubsidized single-sum distributions may be receiving notices that do not adequately explain the value of the subsidy that is foregone if the single-sum distribution is elected. In such a case, merely disclosing the amount of the single-sum distribution and the amount of annuity payments may not adequately enable those participants to make an informed comparison of the relative values of those distribution forms, even if the interest rate used to derive the single sum is disclosed. Furthermore, questions have been raised as to how the relative values of optional forms of benefit are required to be expressed under current regulations. Accordingly, these proposed regulations are being issued to propose disclosure requirements that would enable participants to compare the relative values of the available distribution forms using more readily understandable information.

Explanation of Provisions

The proposed regulations would consolidate the content requirements applicable to explanations of QJSAs and QPSAs under section 417(a)(3), and would specify rules for disclosing the relative value of optional forms of benefit as part of the QJSA explanation. Similar to the requirements in the current regulations, the required explanation must contain, with respect to each of the optional forms of benefit presently available to the participant, a description of the optional form of benefit, a description of the eligibility conditions for the optional form of benefit, a description of the financial effect of electing the optional form of benefit, a description of the relative value of the optional form of benefit, and a description of any other material features of the optional form of benefit. Further, as under the current regulations, the QJSA explanation would be permitted to be made either by providing the participant with information specific to the participant, or by providing the participant with generally applicable information and offering the participant the opportunity to request additional information specifically applicable to the participant with respect to any optional forms of benefit available to the participant. The proposed regulations would clarify that a defined contribution plan is not required to provide a description of the relative values of optional forms of benefit compared to the value of the QJSA.

The proposed regulations would provide additional guidance regarding the required description of the relative values of optional forms of benefit compared to the value of the QJSA and the content of the required disclosure of relative values. Under the proposed regulations, the description of the relative value of an optional form of benefit compared to the value of the QJSA must be expressed in a manner that provides a meaningful comparison of the relative economic values of the two forms of benefit without the participant having to make calculations using interest or mortality assumptions. In order to make this comparison, the benefit under one or both optional forms of benefit must be converted, taking into account the time value of money and life expectancies, so that both are expressed in the same form. The proposed regulations give several examples of techniques that may be used for this comparison: expressing the actuarial present value of the optional form of benefit as a percentage or factor of the actuarial present value of the QJSA; stating the amount of an annuity payable at the same time and under the same conditions as the QJSA that is the actuarial equivalent of the optional form of benefit; or stating the actuarial present value of both the QJSA and the optional form of benefit. For purposes of providing a description of the relative value of an optional form of benefit compared to the value of the QJSA (and also for purposes of comparing the financial effect of the distribution forms available to a participant), a plan would be permitted to provide reasonable estimates (e.g., estimates based on data as of an earlier date than the annuity starting date or an estimate of the spouse's age). If estimates are used, the participant has a right to a more precise calculation upon request.

Since disclosing the relative value of every optional form of benefit regardless of the degree of subsidy may be too burdensome, and may provide participants with information that appears more precise than is warranted based on the inexact nature of the actuarial assumptions used, the proposed regulations would provide some ways to simplify this disclosure of relative values of optional forms of benefit. One way in which this disclosure would be simplified is through a banding rule under which two or more optional forms of benefit that have approximately the same value could be grouped for purposes of disclosing relative value. Under these proposed regulations, two or more optional forms of benefit would be treated as having approximately the same value if those optional forms of benefit vary in relative value in comparison to the value of the QJSA by 5 percentage points or less when the relative value comparison is made by expressing the actuarial present value of each of those optional forms of benefit as a percentage of the actuarial present value of the QJSA. For such a group of optional forms of benefit, the requirement relating to disclosing the relative value of each optional form of benefit compared to the value of the QJSA could be satisfied by disclosing the relative value of any one of the optional forms in the group compared to the value of the QJSA, and disclosing that the other optional forms of benefit in the group are of approximately the same value. If a single-sum distribution is included in such a group of optional forms of benefit, the single-sum distribution must be the distribution form that is used for purposes of this comparison. The relative value of all optional forms of benefit that have an actuarial present value that is at least 95% of the actuarial present value of the QJSA may be described by stating that those optional forms of benefit are of approximately equal value to the value of the QJSA. Thus, these rules would permit a plan that provides no subsidized forms of benefit to state the comparison of relative values simply by stating that all distribution forms are approximately equal in value to the QJSA.

Another way in which this disclosure may be simplified is through the use of representative values: if, under the banding rule, two or more optional forms of benefit are grouped, a representative relative value for all of the grouped options could be used as the approximate relative value for all of the grouped options, in lieu of using the relative value of one of the optional forms of benefit in the group. For this purpose, a representative relative value is any relative value that is not less than the relative value of the member of the group of optional forms of benefit with the lowest relative value and is not greater than the relative value of the member of that group with the highest relative value when measured on a consistent basis. For example, if three optional forms have relative values of 87.5%, 89%, and 91% of the value of the QJSA, all three optional forms can be treated as having a relative value of approximately 90% of the value of the QJSA.

The proposed regulations would also permit the disclosure of the financial effect and relative value of optional forms of benefit to be made in the form of generally applicable information rather than information specific to the participant, provided that information specific to the participant regarding the optional form of benefit must be furnished at the participant's request. Thus, under the proposed regulations, in lieu of providing a QJSA explanation that describes each optional form that is presently available to the participant, the generalized QJSA explanation need only reflect the generally available optional forms of benefits, along with a reference to where a participant can obtain the information for any other optional forms of benefits (such as optional forms from prior benefit structures for limited groups of employees) that are presently available to the participant.

With respect to the generally available optional forms of benefits, in lieu of providing a statement of financial effect and relative value comparison that is specific to the participant, the generalized QJSA explanation is permitted to include a chart or other comparable device showing a series of examples of financial effects and relative value comparisons for hypothetical participants. The examples in the chart should reflect a representative range of ages for the hypothetical participants and use reasonable assumptions for the age of the hypothetical participant's spouse and any other variable that affects the financial effect, or relative value, of the optional form of benefit. The chart must be accompanied by a general statement describing the effect of significant variations between the assumed ages or other variables on the financial effect of electing the optional form of benefit and the comparison of the relative value of the optional form of benefit to the value of the QJSA. A generalized QJSA explanation that includes this chart must also include the amount payable to the participant under the normal form of benefit, either at normal retirement age, or payable immediately. In addition, this chart must be accompanied by a statement that includes an offer to provide, upon the participant's request, a statement of financial effect along with a comparison of relative values that is specific to the participant for one or more presently available optional forms of benefit, and a description of how a participant may obtain this additional information. Thus, with respect to those optional forms of benefit for which additional information is requested, the participant must receive a QJSA explanation specific to the participant that is based on the participant's actual age and benefit.

The proposed regulations would provide rules governing the actuarial assumptions to be used in comparing the value of an optional form of benefit to the QJSA. If an optional form of benefit is subject to the requirements of section 417(e)(3) and § 1.417(e)-1(d) (e.g., a single-sum distribution), any comparison of the value of the optional form of benefit to the value of the QJSA must be made using the applicable mortality table and the applicable interest rate as defined in § 1.417(e)-1(d)(2) and (3) (or, at the option of the plan, another reasonable interest rate and reasonable mortality table used under the plan to calculate the amount payable under the optional form of benefit). All other optional forms of benefit payable to the participant must be compared with the QJSA using a single set of interest rates and mortality tables that are reasonable and that are applied uniformly for this purpose with respect to all such other optional forms payable to the participant. The uniform interest and mortality assumptions should be used regardless of whether those assumptions are actually used to determine the amount of benefit payments under any particular optional form.

The proposed regulations would also require disclosure of information to help a participant understand the significance of a disclosure of the relative value of an optional form of benefit. Under the proposed regulations, the notice would be required to provide an explanation of the concept of relative value. Specifically, the notice would be required to explain that the relative value comparison is intended to allow the participant to compare the total value of distributions paid in different forms, that the relative value comparison is made by converting the value of the optional forms of benefit currently available to a common form (such as the QJSA or single-sum distribution), and that this conversion uses interest and life expectancy assumptions.

Under the proposed regulations, a required numerical comparison of the value of the optional form of benefit to the value of the QJSA under the plan generally would be required to disclose the interest rate that is used to develop a required numerical comparison. However, if all optional forms of benefit are permitted to be treated as having approximately the same value after application of the banding rule described above, then the plan would not be required to disclose the interest rate used to develop a required numerical comparison to the QJSA for optional form of benefit that is not subject to the requirements of section 417(e)(3). In addition, the proposed regulations would require the plan to provide a general statement that all numerical comparisons of relative value provided are based on average life expectancies, and that the relative value of payments ultimately made under an annuity optional form of benefit will depend on actual longevity.

Under the proposed regulations, both the QPSA explanation and the QJSA explanation must be written in a manner calculated to be understood by the average participant. A plan may wish to provide additional information beyond the minimum information that would be required under these proposed regulations, in order to help an employee to evaluate the form of benefit that would be most desirable under the employee's individual circumstances. For example, the plan may wish to add further explanation of the effects of ill health or other factors influencing expected longevity on the desirability of electing annuity forms of distribution.

The proposed regulations contain rules regarding the method for providing the QJSA explanation and the QPSA explanation. Under the proposed regulations, these explanations must be written explanations. First class mail to the last known address of the party is an acceptable delivery method for a section 417(a)(3) explanation. Likewise, hand delivery is acceptable. However, the posting of the explanation is not considered provision of the section 417(a)(3) explanation.

These proposed regulations do not address the extent to which the QJSA explanation or the QPSA explanation can be provided through electronic media. The IRS and the Treasury Department are considering the extent to which the QJSA explanation and the QPSA explanation, as well as other notices under the various Internal Revenue Code requirements relating to qualified retirement plans, can be provided electronically, taking into account the effect of the Electronic Signatures in Global and National Commerce Act (ESIGN), Public Law 106-229, 114 Stat. 464 (2000). The IRS and the Treasury Department anticipate issuing proposed regulations regarding these issues, and invite comments on these issues.

Proposed Effective Date

The regulations are proposed to be applicable to QJSA explanations with respect to distributions with annuity starting dates on or after

January 1, 2004, and to QPSA explanations provided on or after January 1, 2004.

Special Analyses

It has been determined that this notice of proposed rulemaking is not a significant regulatory action as defined in Executive Order 12866. Therefore, a regulatory assessment is not required. It is hereby certified that the collection of information in these regulations will not have a significant economic impact on a substantial number of small entities. This certification is based upon the fact that qualified retirement plans of small businesses typically commence distribution of benefits to few, if any, plan participants in any given year and, similarly, only offer elections to waive a QPSA to few, if any, participants in any given year. Thus, the collection of information in these regulations will only have a minimal economic impact on most small entities. Therefore, an analysis under the Regulatory Flexibility Act (5 U.S.C. chapter 6) is not required. Pursuant to section 7805(f) of the Code, this notice of proposed rulemaking will be submitted to the Chief Counsel for Advocacy of the Small Business Administration for comment on its impact on small business.

Comments and Public Hearing

Before these proposed regulations are adopted as final regulations, consideration will be given to written comments (preferably a signed original and eight (8) copies) that are submitted timely to the IRS. Alternatively, taxpayers may submit comments electronically to the IRS Internet site at *http://www.irs.gov/regs*. All comments will be available for public inspection and copying. The IRS and Treasury request comments on the clarity of the proposed rules and how they may be made easier to understand and to implement.

A public hearing has been scheduled for January 14, 2002, at 10 a.m. in room 4718 of the Internal Revenue Building, 1111 Constitution Avenue NW., Washington, DC. All visitors must present photo identification to enter the building. Because of access restrictions, visitors will not be admitted beyond the immediate entrance area more than 30 minutes before the hearing starts at the Constitution Avenue entrance. For information about having your name placed on the building access list to attend the hearing, see the **FOR FURTHER INFORMATION CONTACT** section of this preamble.

The rules of 26 CFR 601.601(a)(3) apply to the hearing. Persons who wish to present oral comments at the hearing must submit written comments and an outline of the topics to be discussed and the time to be devoted to each topic (signed original and eight (8) copies) by January 2, 2002. A period of 10 minutes will be allotted to each person for making comments. An agenda showing the scheduling of the speakers will be prepared after the deadline for receiving outlines has passed. Copies of the agenda will be available free of charge at the hearing.

Drafting Information

The principal author of these proposed regulations is Linda S. F. Marshall of the Office of the Division Counsel/Associate Chief Counsel (Tax Exempt and Government Entities). However, other personnel from the IRS and Treasury participated in their development.

List of Subjects in 26 CFR Part 1

Income taxes, Reporting and recordkeeping requirements.

Proposed Amendments to the Regulations

Accordingly, 26 CFR part 1 is proposed to be amended as follows:

PART 1—INCOME TAX; TAXABLE YEARS BEGINNING AFTER DECEMBER 31, 1986

Paragraph 1. The authority citation for part 1 continues to read in part as follows:

Authority: 26 U.S.C. 7805 * * *

Par. 2. Paragraph (c)(3) of § 1.401(a)-11 is revised to read as follows:

§ 1.401(a)-11 Qualified joint and survivor annuities.

* * *

(c) * * *

(3) *Information to be provided by plan.* For rules regarding the information required to be provided with respect to the election to waive a QJSA or a QPSA, see § 1.417(a)(3)-1.

* * *

Par. 3. A-36 of § 1.401(a)-20 is revised to read as follows:

§ 1.401(a)-20 Requirements of qualified joint and survivor annuity and qualified preretirement survivor annuity.

* * *

A-36. For rules regarding the explanation of QPSAs and QJSAs required under section 417(a)(3), see § 1.417(a)(3)-1.

* * *

Par. 4. Section 1.417(a)(3)-1 is added to read as follows:

§ 1.417(a)(3)-1 Required explanation of qualified joint and survivor annuity and qualified preretirement survivor annuity.

(a) *Written explanation requirement*—(1) *General rule.* A plan meets the survivor annuity requirements of section 401(a)(11) only if the plan meets the requirements of section 417(a)(3) and this section regarding the written explanation required to be provided a participant with respect to a QJSA or a QPSA. A written explanation required to be provided to a participant with respect to either a QJSA or a QPSA under section 417(a)(3) and this section is referred to in this section as a section 417(a)(3) explanation. See § 1.401(a)-20, Q&A-37, for exceptions to the written explanation requirement in the case of a fully subsidized QPSA or QJSA, and § 1.401(a)-20, Q&A-38, for the definition of a fully subsidized QPSA or QJSA.

(2) *Time for providing section 417(a)(3) explanation*—(i) *QJSA explanation.*See § 1.417(e)-1(b)(3)(ii) for rules governing the timing of the QJSA explanation.

(ii) *QPSA explanation.* See § 1.401(a)-20, Q&A-35, for rules governing the timing of the QPSA explanation.

(3) *Required method for providing section 417(a)(3) explanation.* A section 417(a)(3) explanation must be a written explanation. First class mail to the last known address of the participant is an acceptable delivery method for a section 417(a)(3) explanation. Likewise, hand delivery is acceptable. However, the posting of the explanation is not considered provision of the section 417(a)(3) explanation.

(4) *Understandability.* A section 417(a)(3) explanation must be written in a manner calculated to be understood by the average participant.

(b) *Required content of section 417(a)(3) explanation*—(1) *Content of QPSA explanation.* The QPSA explanation must contain a general description of the QPSA, the circumstances under which it will be paid if elected, the availability of the election of the QPSA, and, except as provided in paragraph (d)(3) of this section, a description of the financial effect of the election of the QPSA on the participant's benefits (*i.e.*, an estimate of the reduction to the participant's estimated normal retirement benefit that would result from an election of the QPSA).

(2) *Content of QJSA explanation.* The QJSA explanation must satisfy either paragraph (c) or paragraph (d) of this section. Under paragraph (c) of this section, the QJSA explanation must contain certain specific information relating to the benefits available under the plan to the particular participant. Alternatively, under paragraph (d) of this section, the QJSA explanation can contain generally applicable information in lieu of specific participant information, provided that the participant has the right to request additional information regarding the participant's benefits under the plan.

(c) *Participant-specific information required to be provided*—(1) *In general.* A QJSA explanation satisfies this paragraph (c) if it provides the following information with respect to each of the optional forms of benefit presently available to the participant—

(i) A description of the optional form of benefit;

(ii) A description of the eligibility conditions for the optional form of benefit;

(iii) A description of the financial effect of electing the optional form of benefit (*i.e.*, the amount payable under the form of benefit);

(iv) In the case of a defined benefit plan, a description of the relative value of the optional form of benefit compared to the value of the QJSA, in the manner described in paragraph (c)(2) of this section; and

(v) A description of any other material features of the optional form of benefit.

(2) *Requirement for numerical comparison of relative values*—(i) *In general.* The description of the relative value of an optional form of benefit compared to the value of the QJSA under paragraph (c)(1)(iv) of this section must be expressed to the participant in a manner that provides a meaningful comparison of the relative economic values of the two forms of benefit without the participant having to make calculations using interest or mortality assumptions. Thus, in performing the calculations necessary to make this comparison, the benefits under one or both optional forms of benefit must be converted, taking into account the time value of money and life expectancies, so that the values of both optional forms of benefit are expressed in the same form. For

example, such a comparison may be expressed to the participant using any of the following techniques—

(A) Expressing the actuarial present value of the optional form of benefit as a percentage or factor of the actuarial present value of the QJSA;

(B) Stating the amount of the annuity that is the actuarial equivalent of the optional form of benefit and that is payable at the same time and under the same conditions as the QJSA; or

(C) Stating the actuarial present value of both the optional form of benefit and the QJSA.

(ii) *Simplified presentations permitted*—(A) *Grouping of certain optional forms.* Two or more optional forms of benefit that have approximately the same value may be grouped for purposes of a required numerical comparison described in this paragraph (c)(2). For this purpose, two or more optional forms of benefit have approximately the same value if those optional forms of benefit vary in relative value in comparison to the value of the QJSA by 5 percentage points or less when the relative value comparison is made by expressing the actuarial present value of each of those optional forms of benefit as a percentage of the actuarial present value of the QJSA. For such a group of optional forms of benefit, the requirement relating to disclosing the relative value of each optional form of benefit compared to the value of the QJSA can be satisfied by disclosing the relative value of any one of the optional forms in the group compared to the value of the QJSA, and disclosing that the other optional forms of benefit in the group are of approximately the same value. If a single-sum distribution is included in such a group of optional forms of benefit, the single-sum distribution must be the distribution form that is used for purposes of this comparison. In addition, the relative value of all optional forms of benefit that have an actuarial present value that is at least 95% of the actuarial present value of the QJSA is permitted to be described by stating that those optional forms of benefit are approximately equal in value to the QJSA, or that all of those forms of benefit and the QJSA are approximately equal in value.

(B) *Representative relative value for grouped optional forms.* If, in accordance with paragraph (c)(2)(ii)(A) of this section, two or more optional forms of benefits are grouped, the relative values for all of the optional forms of benefit in the group can be stated using a representative relative value as the approximate relative value for the entire group. For this purpose, a representative relative value is any relative value that is not less than the relative value of the member of the group of optional forms of benefit with the lowest relative value and is not greater than the relative value of the member of that group with the highest relative value when measured on a consistent basis. For example, if three optional forms have relative values of 87.5%, 89%, and 91% of the value of the QJSA, all three optional forms can be treated as having a relative value of approximately 90% of the value of the QJSA. As required under paragraph (c)(2)(ii)(A) of this section, if a single-sum distribution is included in the group of optional forms of benefit, the 90% relative factor of the value of the QJSA must be disclosed as the approximate relative value of the single sum, and the other forms can be described as having the same approximate value as the single sum.

(iii) *Actuarial assumptions used to determine relative values.* For the purpose of providing a numerical comparison of the value of an optional form of benefit to the value of the immediately commencing QJSA, the following rules apply—

(A) If an optional form of benefit is subject to the requirements of section 417(e)(3) and § 1.417(e)-1(d), any comparison of the value of the optional form of benefit to the value of the QJSA must be made using the applicable mortality table and the applicable interest rate as defined in § 1.417(e)-1(d)(2) and (3) (or, at the option of the plan, another reasonable interest rate and reasonable mortality table used under the plan to calculate the amount payable under the optional form of benefit); and

(iv) *Required disclosure of assumptions*—(A) *Explanation of concept of relative value.* The notice must provide an explanation of the concept of relative value, communicating that the relative value comparison is intended to allow the participant to compare the total value of distributions paid in different forms, that the relative value comparison is made by converting the value of the optional forms of benefit presently available to a common form (such as the QJSA or a single-sum distribution), and that this conversion uses interest and life expectancy assumptions. The explanation of relative value must include a general statement that all comparisons provided are based on average life expectancies, and that the relative value of payments ultimately made under an annuity optional form of benefit will depend on actual longevity.

(B) *Disclosure of interest assumptions.* A required numerical comparison of the value of the optional form of benefit to the value of the QJSA under the plan is required to disclose the interest rate that is used to develop the comparison. If all optional forms of benefit are permitted to be grouped under paragraph (c)(2)(ii)(A) of this section, then the requirement of this paragraph (c)(2)(iv)(B) does not apply for any optional form of benefit not subject to the requirements of section 417(e)(3) and § 1.417(e)-1(d)(3).

(3) *Permitted estimates of financial effect and relative value*—(i) *General rule* For purposes of providing a description of the financial effect of the distribution forms available to a participant as required under paragraph (c)(1)(iii) of this section, and for purposes of providing a description of the relative value of an optional form of benefit compared to the value of the QJSA for a participant as required under paragraph (c)(1)(iv) of this section, the plan is permitted to provide reasonable estimates (*e.g.,* estimates based on data as of an earlier date than the annuity starting date, a reasonable assumption for the age of the participant's spouse, or, in the case of a defined contribution plan, reasonable estimates of amounts that would be payable under a purchased annuity contract), including reasonable estimates of the applicable interest rate under section 417(e)(3).

(ii) *Right to more precise calculation.* If a QJSA notice uses a reasonable estimate under paragraph (c)(3)(i) of this section, the QJSA explanation must identify the estimate and explain that the plan will, upon the request of the participant, provide a more precise calculation and the plan must provide the participant with a more precise calculation if so requested. Thus, for example, if a plan provides an estimate of the amount of the QJSA that is based on a reasonable assumption concerning the age of the participant's spouse, the participant can request a calculation that takes into account the actual age of the spouse, as provided by the participant.

(iii) *Revision of prior information.* If a more precise calculation described in paragraph (c)(3)(ii) of this section materially changes the relative value of an optional form compared to the value of the QJSA, the revised relative value of that optional form must be disclosed, regardless of whether the financial effect of selecting the optional form is affected by the more precise calculation.

(4) *Special rules for disclosure of financial effect for defined contribution plans.* For a written explanation provided by a defined contribution plan, a description of financial effect required by paragraph (c)(1)(iii) of this section with respect to an annuity form of benefit must include a statement that the annuity will be provided by purchasing an annuity contract from an insurance company with the participant's account balance under the plan. If the description of the financial effect of the optional form of benefit is provided using estimates rather than by assuring that an insurer is able to provide the amount disclosed to the participant, the written explanation must also disclose this fact.

(d) *Substitution of generally applicable information for participant information in the section 417(a)(3) explanation*—(1) *Forms of benefit available.* In lieu of providing the information required under paragraphs (c)(1)(i) through (v) of this section for each optional form of benefit presently available to the participant as described in paragraph (c) of this section, the QJSA explanation may contain the information required under paragraphs (c)(1)(i) through (v) of this section for the QJSA and each other optional form of benefit generally available under the plan, along with a reference to where a participant may readily obtain the information required under paragraphs (c)(1)(i) through (v) of this section for any other optional forms of benefit that are presently available to the participant.

(2) *Financial effect and comparison of relative values*—(i) *General rule.* In lieu of providing a statement of the financial effect of electing an optional form of benefit as required under paragraph (c)(1)(iii) of this section, or a comparison of relative values as required under paragraph (c)(1)(iv) of this section, based on the actual age and benefit of the participant, the QJSA explanation is permitted to include a chart (or other comparable device) showing the financial effect and relative value of optional forms of benefit in a series of examples specifying the amount of the optional form of benefit payable to a hypothetical participant at a representative range of ages and the comparison of relative values at those same representative ages. Each example in this chart must show the financial effect of electing the optional form of benefit pursuant to the rules of paragraph (c)(1)(iii) of this section, and a comparison of the relative value of the optional form of benefit to the value of the QJSA pursuant to the rules of paragraph (c)(2) of this section, using reasonable assumptions for the age of the hypothetical participant's spouse and any other variables that affect the financial effect, or relative value, of the optional form of benefit. The requirement to show the financial effect of electing an optional form of benefit can be satisfied through the use of other methods (*e.g.,* expressing the

amount of the optional form as a percentage or a factor of the amount payable under the normal form of benefit), provided that the method provides sufficient information so that a participant can determine the amount of benefits payable in the optional form. The chart or other comparable device must be accompanied by the disclosures described in paragraph (c)(2)(iv) of this section explaining the concept of relative value and disclosing certain interest assumptions. In addition, the chart or other comparable device must be accompanied by a general statement describing the effect of significant variations between the assumed ages or other variables on the financial effect of electing the optional form of benefit and the comparison of the relative value of the optional form of benefit to the value of the QJSA.

(ii) *Actual benefit must be disclosed.* The generalized notice described in this paragraph (d)(2) will satisfy the requirements of paragraph (b)(2) of this section only if the notice includes either the amount payable to the participant under the normal form of benefit or the amount payable to the participant under the normal form of benefit adjusted for immediate commencement. For this purpose, the normal form of benefit is the form under which payments due to the participant under the plan are expressed under the plan, prior to adjustments for form of benefit. For example, assuming that a plan's benefit accrual formula is expressed as a straight life annuity, the generalized notice must provide the amount of either the straight life annuity commencing at normal retirement age or the straight life annuity commencing immediately.

(iii) *Ability to request additional information* The generalized notice described in this paragraph (d)(2) must be accompanied by a statement that includes an offer to provide, upon the participant's request, a statement of financial effect and a comparison of relative values that is specific to the participant for any presently available optional form of benefit, and a description of how a participant may obtain this additional information.

(3) *Financial effect of QPSA election.* In lieu of providing a specific description of the financial effect of the QPSA election, the QPSA explanation may provide a general description of the financial effect of the election. Thus, for example, the description can be in the form of a chart showing the reduction to a hypothetical participant's normal retirement benefit at a representative range of participant ages as a result of the QPSA election (using a reasonable assumption for the age of the hypothetical participant's spouse relative to the age of the hypothetical participant). In addition, this chart must be accompanied by a statement that includes an offer to provide, upon the participant's request, an estimate of the reduction to the participant's estimated normal retirement benefit, and a description of how a participant may obtain this additional information.

(4) *Additional information required to be furnished at the participant's request*—(i) *Explanation of QJSA.* If, as permitted under paragraphs (d)(1) and (2) of this section, the content of a QJSA explanation does not include all the items described in paragraph (c) of this section, then, upon a timely request from the participant for any of the information required under paragraphs (c)(1)(i) through (v) of this section for one or more presently available optional forms (including a request for all optional forms presently available to the participant), the plan must furnish the information required under paragraphs (c)(1)(i) through (v) of this section with respect to those optional forms. Thus, with respect to those optional forms of benefit, the participant must receive a QJSA explanation specific to the participant that is based on the participant's actual age and benefit. In addition, the plan must comply with paragraph (c)(3)(iii) of this section.

(ii) *Explanation of QPSA.* If, as permitted under paragraph (d)(3) of this section, the content of a QPSA explanation does not include all the items described in paragraph (b)(1) of this section, then, upon a timely request from the participant for an estimate of the reduction to the participant's estimated normal retirement benefit that would result from a QPSA election, the plan must furnish such an estimate.

(e) *Examples.* The following examples illustrate the application of this section. Solely for purposes of these examples, the applicable interest rate that applies to any distribution that is subject to the rules of section 417(e)(3) is assumed to be 512%, and the applicable mortality table under section 417(e)(3) and § 1.417(e)-1(d)(2) is assumed to be the table that applies as of January 1, 2003. In addition, solely for purposes of these examples, assume that a plan which determines actuarial equivalence using 6% interest and the applicable mortality table under section 417(e)(3) and § 1.417(e)-1(d)(2) that applies as of January 1, 1995, is using reasonable actuarial assumptions. The examples are as follows:

¶20,260P

Example 1. (i) Participant M participates in Plan A, a qualified defined benefit plan. Under Plan A, the QJSA is a joint and 100% survivor annuity, which is actuarially equivalent to the single life annuity determined using 6% interest and the section 417(e)(3) applicable mortality table that applies as of January 1, 1995. On January 1, 2004, M will terminate employment at age 55. When M terminates employment, M will be eligible to elect an unreduced early retirement benefit, payable as either a life annuity or the QJSA. M will also be eligible to elect a single-sum distribution equal to the actuarial present value of the single life annuity payable at normal retirement age (age 65), determined using the applicable mortality table and the applicable interest rate under section 417(e)(3).

(ii) Participant M is provided with a QJSA explanation that describes the single life annuity, the QJSA, and single-sum distribution option under the plan, and any eligibility conditions associated with these options. The explanation indicates that, if Participant M commenced benefits at age 55 and had a spouse age 55, the monthly benefit under an immediately commencing single life annuity is $3,000, the monthly benefit under the QJSA is estimated to be 89.96% of the monthly benefit under the immediately commencing single life annuity or $2,699, and the single sum is estimated to be 74.7645 times the monthly benefit under the immediately commencing single life annuity or $224,293.

(iii) The QJSA explanation indicates that the single life annuity and the QJSA are of approximately the same value, but that the single-sum option is equivalent in value to a QJSA of $1,215. (This amount is 45% of the value of the QJSA at age 55 ($1,215 divided by 89.96% of $3,000 equals 45%).) The explanation states that the relative value comparison converts the value of the single life annuity and the single-sum options to the value of each if paid in the form of the QJSA and that this conversion uses interest and life expectancy assumptions. The explanation specifies that the calculations relating to the single-sum distribution were prepared using 5.5% interest and average life expectancy, that the other calculations were prepared using a 6% interest rate and that the relative value of actual annuity payments for an individual can vary depending on how long the individual and spouse live. The explanation notes that the calculation of the QJSA assumed that the spouse was age 55, that the amount of the QJSA will depend on the actual age of the spouse (for example, annuity payments will be significantly lower if the spouse is significantly younger than the participant), and that the amount of the single-sum payment will depend on the interest rates that apply when the participant actually takes a distribution. The explanation also includes an offer to provide a more precise calculation to the participant taking into account the spouse's actual age.

(iv) Participant M requests a more precise calculation of the financial effect of choosing a QJSA, taking into the actual age of Participant M's spouse. Based on the fact that M's spouse is age 50, Plan A determines that the monthly payments under the QJSA are 87.62% of the monthly payments under the single life annuity, or $2,628.60 per month, and provides this information to M. Plan A is not required to provide an updated calculation of the relative value of the single sum because the value of single sum continues to be 45% of the value of the QJSA.

Example 2. (i) The facts are the same as in *Example 1*, except that under Plan A, the single-sum distribution is determined as the actuarial present value of the immediately commencing single life annuity. In addition, Plan A provides a joint and 75% survivor annuity that is reduced from the single life annuity and that is the QJSA under Plan A. For purposes of determining the amount of the QJSA, the reduction is only half of the reduction that would normally apply under the actuarial assumptions specified in Plan A for determining actuarial equivalence of optional forms.

(ii) In lieu of providing information specific to Participant M in the QJSA notice as set forth in paragraph (c) of this section, Plan A satisfies the QJSA explanation requirement in accordance with paragraph (d)(2) of this section by providing M with a statement that M's monthly benefit under an immediately commencing single life annuity (which is the normal form of benefit under Plan A, adjusted for immediate commencement) is $3,000, along with the following chart showing the financial effect and the relative value of the optional forms of benefit compared to the QJSA for a hypothetical participant with a $1,000 benefit and a spouse who is three years younger than the participant. For each optional form generally available under the plan, the chart shows the financial effect and the relative value, using the grouping rules of paragraph (c)(2)(ii) of this section. Separate charts are provided for ages 55, 60, and 65.

AGE 55 COMMENCEMENT

Optional form	Amount of distribution per $1,000 of immediate single life annuity	Relative value
Life Annuity	$1,000 per month	Approximately the same value as the OJSA.
QJSA (joint and 75% survivor annuity)	$956 per month	n/a.
Joint and 100% survivor annuity	$886 per month	Approximately the same value as the QJSA.
Lump sum	$165,959	Approximately the same value as the QJSA.

AGE 60 COMMENCEMENT

Optional form	Amount of distribution per $1,000 of immediate single life annuity	Relative value
Life Annuity	$1,000 per month	Approximately 94% of the value of the QJSA.
QJSA (joint and 75% survivor annuity)	$945 per month	n/a.
Joint and 100% survivor annuity	$859 per month	Approximately 94% of the value of the QJSA.
Lump sum	$151,691	Approximately the same value as the QJSA.

AGE 65 COMMENCEMENT

Optional form	Amount of distribution per $1,000 of immediate single life annuity	Relative value
Life Annuity	$1,000 per month	Approximately 93% of the value of the QJSA.
QJSA (joint and 75% survivor annuity)	$932 per month	n/a.
Joint and 100% survivor annuity	$828 per month	Approximately 93% of the value of the QJSA.
Lump sum	$135,759	Approximately 93% of the value of the QJSA.

(iii) The chart disclosing the financial effect and relative value of the optional forms specifies that the calculations were prepared assuming that the spouse is three years younger than the participant, that the calculations relating to the single-sum distribution were prepared using 5.5% interest and average life expectancy, that the other calculations were prepared using a 6% interest rate, and that the relative value of actual payments for an individual can vary depending on how long the individual and spouse live. The explanation states that the relative value comparison converts the QJSA, the single life annuity, the joint and 100% survivor annuity, and the single-sum options to an equivalent present value and that this conversion uses interest and life expectancy assumptions. The explanation notes that the calculation of the QJSA depends on the actual age of the spouse (for example, annuity payments will be significantly lower if the spouse is significantly younger than the participant), and that the amount of the single-sum payment will depend on the interest rates that apply when the participant actually takes a distribution. The explanation also includes an offer to provide a calculation specific to the participant upon request.

(iv) Participant M requests information regarding the amounts payable under the QJSA, the joint and 100% survivor annuity, and the single sum.

(v) Based on the information about the age of Participant M's spouse, Plan A determines that M's QJSA is $2,856.30 per month, the joint and 100% survivor annuity is $2,628.60 per month, and the single sum is $497,876. The actuarial present value of the QJSA (determined using the 5.5% interest and the section 417(e)(3) applicable mortality table, the actuarial assumptions required under section 417) is $525,091. Accordingly, the value of the single-sum distribution available to M at January 1, 2004, is 94.8% of the actuarial present value of the QJSA. In addition, the actuarial present value of the life annuity and the 100% joint and survivor annuity are 95.0% of the actuarial present value of the QJSA.

(vi) Plan A provides M with a QJSA explanation that incorporates these more precise calculations of the financial effect and relative value of the optional forms for which M requested information.

(f) *Effective date.* This section applies to QJSA explanations provided with respect to distributions with annuity starting dates on or after January 1, 2004, and to QPSA explanations provided on or after January 1, 2004.

§ 1.417(e)-1 [Amended]

Par. 5. In § 1.417(e)-1, paragraph (b)(2) is amended by removing the language "§ 1.401(a)-20 Q&A-36" and adding "§ 1.417(a)(3)-1" in its place.

Robert E. Wenzel

Deputy Commissioner of Internal Revenue.

¶ 20,260Q

IRS proposed regulations: Travel expenses: Business expenses: Expense substantiation.—The IRS has issued proposed amendments to regulations under Code Sec. 62, relating to substantiation requirements for reimbursement of business travel expenses, to allow them to conform to cross-referenced regulations under Code Sec. 274. Comments from the public are requested.

The proposed amendments to regulations, were published in the *Federal Register* on November 12, 2002 (67 FR 68539).

IRS final regulations 1.62-2 and 1.274-5, temporary regulation 1.274-5T, and the preamble to the regulations appear at ¶ 11,182, ¶ 11,357B, ¶ 11,357G and ¶ 24,507C respectively. The final and temporary regulations were published in the *Federal Register* on July 1, 2003 (68 FR 39011).

¶ 20,260R

IRS proposed regulations: brokers: information reporting: taxable stock transactions.—The IRS has issued proposed regulations by cross-reference to temporary regulations that contain guidance concerning information reporting requirements for brokers with respect to changes in control and recapitalizations. Comments must be received by February 18, 2003. Topics to be covered at the public hearing (to be held on March 5, 2003), must be received by February 12, 2003.

The proposed regulations were published in the Federal Register on November 18, 2002 (67 FR 69496). They were withdrawn (68 FR 75182, December 30, 2003) upon the publication of revised temporary regulations in the Federal Register on December 30, 2003 (68 FR 75119). The preamble to the revised temporary regulations appears at ¶ 24,507M. Portions of the temporary regulations are reproduced at ¶ 13,688D.

¶ 20,260S

IRS proposed regulations: Age discrimination requirements: Cash balance conversions.—The IRS has issued proposed regulations regarding the age discrimination requirements applicable to certain retirement plans, under which accruals and allocations cannot be ceased or reduced because of the attainment of any age. Until this regulation is finalized, the IRS will not process technical advice on the effect of cash balance conversions on the plan's qualified status. Comments must be received by March 13, 2003 for the public hearing to be held on April 10, 2003.

The proposed regulations, which were published in the Federal Register on December 11, 2002 (67 FR 76123), are reproduced below. Proposed Reg. Sec. 1.401(a)(4) was withdrawn by the IRS, as set forth in IRS Announcement 2003-22 (¶ 17,097S-15).

Note: The proposed regulations were withdrawn by Announcement 2004-57 (see ¶ 17,097S-45).

[4830-01-p]

DEPARTMENT OF THE TREASURY

Internal Revenue Service

26 CFR Part 1

[REG-209500-86, REG-164464-02]

RIN 1545-BA10,1545-BB79

Reductions of Accruals and Allocations Because of the Attainment of Any Age; Application of Nondiscrimination Cross-Testing Rules to Cash Balance Plans

AGENCY: Internal Revenue Service (IRS), Treasury.

ACTION: Notice of proposed rulemaking and notice of public hearing.

SUMMARY: This document contains proposed regulations that would provide rules regarding the requirements that accruals or allocations under certain retirement plans not cease or be reduced because of the attainment of any age. In addition, the proposed regulations would provide rules for the application of certain nondiscrimination rules to cash balance plans. These regulations would affect retirement plan sponsors and administrators, and participants in and beneficiaries of retirement plans. This document also provides notice of a public hearing on these proposed regulations.

DATES: Written comments, requests to speak and outlines of oral comments to be discussed at the public hearing scheduled for April 10, 2003, at 10 a.m., must be received by March 13, 2003.

ADDRESSES: Send submissions to: CC:ITA:RU (REG-209500-86), room 5226, Internal Revenue Service, POB 7604, Ben Franklin Station, Washington, DC 20044. In the alternative, submissions may be hand delivered to: CC:ITA:RU (REG-209500-86), room 5226, Internal Revenue Service, 1111 Constitution Avenue NW., Washington, DC. Alternatively, taxpayers may submit comments electronically via the Internet by submitting comments directly to the IRS Internet site at: www.irs.gov/regs. The public hearing will be held in room 4718, Internal Revenue Building, 1111 Constitution Avenue NW., Washington, DC.

FOR FURTHER INFORMATION CONTACT: Concerning the regulations, Linda S. F. Marshall, 202-622-6090, or R. Lisa Mojiri-Azad, 202-622-6030; concerning submissions and the hearing, and/or to be placed on the building access list to attend the hearing, Sonya Cruse, 202-622-7180 (not toll-free numbers).

SUPPLEMENTARY INFORMATION:

Background

This document contains proposed amendments to the Income Tax Regulations (26 CFR Part 1) under sections 401 and 411 of the Internal Revenue Code of 1986 (Code). Section 411(b)(1)(H), which was added in subtitle C of the Omnibus Budget Reconciliation Act of 1986 (OBRA '86) (100 Stat. 1874), provides that a defined benefit plan fails to comply with section 411(b) if, under the plan, an employee's benefit accrual is ceased, or the rate of an employee's benefit accrual is reduced, because of the attainment of any age. Under section 411(b)(2)(A), added by subtitle C of OBRA '86, a defined contribution plan fails to comply with section 411(b) unless, under the plan, allocations to the employee's account are not ceased, and the rate at which amounts are allocated to the employee's account is not reduced, because of the attainment of any age.

Section 411(b)(1)(H)(iii) provides that any requirement of continued accrual of benefits after normal retirement age is treated as satisfied to the extent benefits are distributed to the participant or the participant's benefits are actuarially increased to reflect the delay in the distribution of benefits after attainment of normal retirement age. Section 411(a) requires a qualified plan to meet certain vesting requirements. In the case of a participant in a defined benefit plan who works after attaining normal retirement age, these vesting requirements are not satisfied unless the plan provides an actuarial increase after normal retirement age for accrued benefits, distributes benefits while the participant is working after normal retirement age, or suspends benefits as described in section 411(a)(3)(B) (and the regulations of the Department of Labor at 29 CFR 2530.203-3). Section 401(a)(9)(C)(iii), added to the Code by the Small Business Job Protection Act of 1996 (110 Stat. 1755) (1996), requires that the accrued benefit of any employee who retires after age 70 1/2 be actuarially increased to take into account the period after age 70 1/2 during which the employee is not receiving benefits.

Section 4(i) of the Age Discrimination in Employment Act (ADEA) and sections 204(b)(1)(H) and 204(b)(2) of the Employee Retirement Income Security Act of 1974 (ERISA) provide requirements comparable to those in sections 411(b)(1)(H) and 411(b)(2) of the Code. Section 4(i)(4) of ADEA provides that compliance with the requirements of section 4(i) with respect to an employee pension benefit plan constitutes compliance with the requirements of section 4 of ADEA relating to benefit accrual under the plan.

Under section 101 of Reorganization Plan No. 4 of 1978 (43 FR 47713), the Secretary of the Treasury has interpretive jurisdiction over the subject matter addressed in these regulations for purposes of ERISA, as well as the Code. Therefore, these regulations apply for purposes of the parallel requirements of sections 204(b)(1)(H) and 204(b)(2) of ERISA, as well as for section 411(b) of the Code.

The Equal Employment Opportunity Commission (EEOC) has jurisdiction over section 4 of ADEA. Section 9204(d) of OBRA '86 requires that the regulations and rulings issued by the Department of Labor, the Treasury Department, and the EEOC pursuant to the amendments made by subtitle C of OBRA '86 each be consistent with the others. It further requires the Secretary of Labor, the Secretary of the Treasury, and the EEOC to each consult with the others to the extent necessary to meet the requirements of the preceding sentence. Executive Order 12067 requires all Federal departments and agencies to "advise and offer to consult with the Equal Employment Opportunity Commission during the development of any proposed rules, regulations, policies, procedures or orders concerning equal employment opportunity." The IRS and Treasury have consulted with the Department of Labor and the EEOC prior to the issuance of these proposed regulations under sections 411(b)(1)(H) and 411(b)(2) of the Code.

The EEOC published proposed regulations interpreting section 4(i) of ADEA in the **Federal Register** on November 27, 1987 (52 FR 45360). Proposed regulations REG-209500-86 (formerly EE-184-86) under sections 411(b)(1)(H) and 411(b)(2) were previously published by the IRS and Treasury in the **Federal Register** on April 11, 1988 (53 FR 11876), as part of a package of regulations (the 1988 proposed regulations) that also included proposed regulations under sections 410(a), 411(a)(2), 411(a)(8) and 411(c) (relating to maximum age for participation, vesting, normal retirement age, and actuarial adjustments after normal retirement age). The IRS, Treasury, the Department of Labor, and the EEOC consulted prior to the issuance of both sets of proposed regulations.

Notice 88-126 (1988-2 CB 538), addressed certain effective date issues for sections 411(b)(1)(H) and 411(b)(2). The EEOC issued a similar notice addressing those effective date issues in the **Federal Register** on January 9, 1989 (54 FR 604). The United States Supreme Court subsequently issued an opinion addressing the effective date of section 411(b)(1)(H) in *Lockheed Corp. v. Spink*, 517 U.S. 882 (1996), which is discussed below.

On October 20, 1999, the IRS and Treasury published a solicitation for comments in the **Federal Register** (64 FR 56578) inviting comments regarding potential issues under their jurisdiction with respect to cash balance plans (a type of defined benefit plan under which the normal form of benefit is an immediate payment of a participant's hypothetical account, which is adjusted periodically to reflect pay credits and interest credits), conversions of traditional defined benefit plans to cash balance plans and associated wear-away or benefit plateau effects. Hundreds of comments were received from a wide range of parties with interests in cash balance plans, including employees, employers, and their representatives. The most significant issue raised in the comments relates to the application of section 411(b)(1)(H) to cash balance plans and conversions of traditional defined benefit plans to cash balance plans.

These proposed regulations are being issued after consideration of the comments on the 1988 proposed regulations, as well as more recent comments concerning the application of sections 411(b)(1)(H) and 411(b)(2). These proposed regulations address the application of section 411(b)(1)(H) to cash balance plans, including conversions.

These proposed regulations would also amend the provisions of the regulations under section 401(a)(4) to provide rules for nondiscrimination testing for certain cash balance plans.

Explanation of Provisions

Overview

These proposed regulations provide guidance on the requirements of section 411(b)(1)(H), under which a defined benefit plan fails to be a qualified plan if, under the plan, benefit accruals on behalf of a participant are ceased or the rate of benefit accrual on behalf of a participant is reduced because of the participant's attainment of any age.[1] Similarly, these proposed regulations provide guidance on the requirements of section 411(b)(2), under which a defined contribution plan fails to be a qualified plan if, under the plan, allocations to a participant's account are ceased or the rate of allocations to a participant's account is reduced because of the participant's attainment of any age.

These proposed regulations follow the 1988 proposed regulations in many respects. In particular, these proposed regulations would adopt many of the positions taken under the 1988 proposed regulations for determining whether a plan ceases benefit accruals or allocations because of the attainment of any age or provides for a direct or indirect reduction in the rate of benefit accrual or allocation because of the attainment of any age.

These proposed regulations also provide guidance on how to determine the rate of benefit accrual or rate of allocation. In the case of defined benefit plans, the proposed regulations would provide two basic approaches to determining the rate of benefit accrual: a general approach applicable to all defined benefit plans; and a separate approach applicable to eligible cash balance plans, as defined in these proposed regulations. These proposed regulations also provide guidance on determining the rate of allocation under a defined contribution plan.

Finally, these proposed regulations address other related issues also addressed in the 1988 proposed regulations, including the application of sections 411(b)(1)(H) and 411(b)(2) to optional forms of benefits, ancillary benefits and other rights and features, the coordination of the requirements of sections 411(b)(1)(H) and 411(b)(2) with certain other qualification requirements under the Code, such as sections 401(a)(4), 411(a), and 415, and the effective date of sections 411(b)(1)(H) and 411(b)(2).

Applicability Prior to Normal Retirement Age

Sections 411(b)(1)(H) and 411(b)(2) prohibit cessation of accruals or allocations, and reduction in the rate of benefit accrual or allocation, because of the attainment of any age. Under these sections, attainment of any age means a participant's growing older. Accordingly, these regulations, like the 1988 proposed regulations, would apply regardless of whether the participant is older than, younger than, or at normal retirement age.

Some commentators have suggested that only cessations or reductions after attainment of normal retirement age are prohibited by these sections. This interpretation is not consistent with the language of the statute, which does not specify any minimum age at which the rule applies, and is not adopted under these proposed regulations.

Reduction in Rate of Benefit Accrual Because of Attainment of Any Age

Under these proposed regulations, a defined benefit plan fails to comply with section 411(b)(1)(H) if, either directly or indirectly, a participant's rate of benefit accrual is reduced (which includes a cessation of participation in the plan or other discontinuance of benefit accruals) because of the participant's attainment of any age. A plan provides for a reduction in the rate of benefit accrual that is directly because of the attainment of any age if, during a plan year, under the

terms of the plan, any participant's rate of benefit accrual for the plan year would be higher if the participant were younger. Thus, a plan fails to comply with section 411(b)(1)(H) if, under the terms of the plan, the rate of benefit accrual for any individual who is or could be a participant under the plan would be lower solely as a result of such individual being older. Whether there is an actual participant at any particular age is not relevant. Similarly, whether a reduction in the rate of benefit accrual is because of the attainment of any age does not depend on a comparison of a participant's rate of benefit accrual for a year to that participant's rate of benefit accrual in an earlier year. These proposed regulations include a number of examples (at § 1.411(b)-2(b)(3)(iii) of these regulations) which illustrate whether a reduction in the rate of benefit accrual is because of the attainment of any age.

A reduction in the rate of benefit accrual is indirectly because of a participant's attainment of any age if any participant's rate of benefit accrual for the plan year would be higher if the participant were to have a different characteristic that is a proxy for being younger, based on all the relevant facts and circumstances. For example, if a company assigns older workers to one division and younger workers to another even though they perform the same work, then assignment to a division would be a proxy for being older or younger.

Like the 1988 proposed regulations, these proposed regulations provide that a reduction in a participant's rate of benefit accrual is not indirectly because of the attainment of any age in violation of section 411(b)(1)(H) solely because of a positive correlation between attainment of any age and a reduction in the rate of benefit accrual. In addition, a defined benefit plan does not fail to satisfy section 411(b)(1)(H) solely because, on a uniform and consistent basis without regard to a participant's age, the plan limits the amount of benefits a participant may accrue under the plan or limits the number of years of service or participation taken into account for purposes of determining the accrual of benefits under the plan, whether the plan reduces or ceases accruals for service in excess of such limit. A limitation that is expressed as a percentage of compensation (whether averaged over a participant's total years of credited service for the employer or over a shorter period) is a permissible limitation on the amount of benefits a participant may accrue under the plan.

Rate of Benefit Accrual

Neither section 411(b)(1)(H) nor the 1988 proposed regulations define the rate of benefit accrual. These proposed regulations would provide two basic approaches to determining the rate of benefit accrual, based on the way the benefit is expressed in the plan. One approach may be used by all defined benefit plans. A second approach may be used only by an eligible cash balance plan, as defined in these proposed regulations.

Under the general rule, the rate of benefit accrual for any plan year that ends before the participant attains normal retirement age is the increase in the participant's accrued normal retirement benefit for the year. Because the rate of benefit accrual is determined by reference to the increase in the accrued benefit during the plan year, any subsidized portion of an early retirement benefit, any qualified disability benefit, or any social security supplement is disregarded.

Section 411(b)(1)(H)(iii)(II) provides that a defined benefit plan does not fail to comply with section 411(b)(1)(H) for a plan year to the extent of any adjustment in the benefit payable under the plan during such plan year attributable to the delay in the distribution of benefits after the attainment of normal retirement age. These proposed regulations implement this rule (i.e., permit a plan to offset any actuarial adjustment during the year against the otherwise required accruals under the plan), by providing that the rate of benefit accrual after normal retirement age is equal to the excess, if any, of the annual benefit to which the participant is entitled at the end of the plan year over the annual benefit to which the participant would have been entitled at the end of the preceding plan year. For this purpose, the annual benefit is determined assuming that payment commences in the normal form of benefit under the plan at the end of the applicable year. For purposes of these proposed regulations, the normal form of benefit is the form under which payments due to the participant are expressed under the plan, prior to adjustment for form of benefit.

The methodology of determining a year-by-year rate of accrual, taking into account any actuarial increases during the plan year, is a departure from the methodology used in the 1988 proposed regulations. As a consequence of the methodology used in these proposed regulations, the plan may not reduce a participant's rate of benefit

---

[1] While section 4(i) of the ADEA, section 204(b)(1)(H) of ERISA, and section 411(b)(1)(H) of the Code are worded similarly, the words "attainment of any" are not in section 4(i) of the ADEA. The legislative history states that no differences among the provisions is intended (OBRA 86 House Report No. 99-727 at 378-9), and the agencies have concluded that this particular difference in language has no effect.

accrual in a plan year to take into account the fact that, in the preceding plan year, the actuarial increase was greater than the accrual under the plan formula.

While any actuarial adjustment made to the annual benefit to which the participant would have been entitled at the end of the preceding plan year is included in the rate of benefit accrual after normal retirement age, a defined benefit plan must separately comply with the requirements of section 411(a), which are not addressed in these proposed regulations. Thus, for example, a plan that does not provide for suspension of benefits in accordance with section 411(a)(3) must provide for actuarial adjustments of the amount that would otherwise be paid (or distributions of that amount) that are adequate to satisfy section 411(a) and 29 CFR 2530.203-3 of the regulations of the Department of Labor. In addition, the plan must comply with section 401(a)(9)(C)(iii) with respect to actuarial adjustments for participants who retire after attainment of 70 1/2.

Section 411(b)(1)(H)(iii)(I) provides that a defined benefit plan will not fail to satisfy section 411(b)(1)(H) to the extent of the actuarial equivalent of in-service distribution of benefits. Under these proposed regulations, the rate of benefit accrual for a participant who has attained normal retirement age may be reduced by the actuarial value of plan benefit distributions made during the year. This reduction is the equivalent of the provision described above under which a defined benefit plan may offset any actuarial adjustment during the year against the otherwise required accruals for the year. As described immediately below, the manner in which distributions made under the plan are taken into account for a plan year under these regulations is designed so that compliance with section 411(b)(1)(H) is not affected by the optional form in which the distribution is made.

In the plan year during which a distribution is made, distributions are taken into account to the extent the actuarial value of the distribution does not exceed the actuarial value of distributions that would have been made during the plan year had distribution of the participant's full accrued benefit at the beginning of the plan year commenced at the beginning of the plan year (or, if later, at the participant's normal retirement age) in the normal form of benefit. Distributions in excess of the actuarial value of the distribution that would have been made during the plan year had the distribution of the participant's full accrued benefit commenced in the normal form (called accelerated benefit payments) are disregarded for that plan year, but, as described below, are taken into account in subsequent periods. If the participant is receiving a distribution in an optional form of benefit under which the amount payable annually is less than the amount payable under the normal form of benefit (for example, a QJSA under which the annual benefit is less than the amount payable annually under a straight life annuity normal form), the participant may be treated as receiving payments under an actuarially equivalent normal form of benefit.

Any accelerated benefit payments are taken into account in plan years after the plan year in which the distribution was made by converting the accelerated benefit payments to an actuarially equivalent stream of annual benefit payments under the plan's normal form of benefit distributions, commencing at the beginning of the next following plan year. This equivalent stream of annual benefit payments is then deemed to be paid in plan years after the plan year in which the distribution was made, and the calculation of the rate of benefit accrual after normal retirement age is adjusted by adding any of these deemed payments for future plan years to the annual benefit to which the participant is entitled at the end of a plan year. As so adjusted, therefore, the rate of benefit accrual is determined as the excess, if any, of the sum of the annual benefit to which the participant is entitled at the end of the plan year (assuming payment commences in the normal form at the end of the plan year) plus the annuity equivalent of accelerated benefit payments deemed paid in the next plan year, over the sum of the annual benefit to which the participant would have been entitled at the end of the preceding plan year (assuming that payment commences in the normal form at the later of normal retirement age and the end of the preceding plan year), plus the annuity equivalent of accelerated benefit payments deemed paid during the plan year. The effect of this adjustment, in the case of a single sum distribution, is to put the participant in the same position as if the participant had received the distribution in the normal form.

Eligible Cash Balance Plans

The 1988 proposed regulations did not contain any guidance specific to cash balance plans. A cash balance plan is a type of defined benefit plan that determines benefits by reference to an employee's hypothetical account. Since the 1988 proposed regulations were issued, the number of cash balance plans has increased. The development of cash balance plans has raised the issue of whether this design complies with section 411(b)(1)(H).

Under a cash balance plan, an employee's hypothetical account balance is credited with hypothetical allocations, often referred to as service credits or pay credits, and hypothetical earnings, often referred to as interest credits. Under some cash balance plans, the right to interest credits for future periods accrues at the same time as the pay credit (i.e., the interest credit is not contingent on the performance of services in the future). Under other cash balance plans, all or some portion of the interest credit for future periods is contingent on the performance of services in the future. The benefit under a cash balance plan is expressed in the plan document (and communicated to employees) as the hypothetical account balance, although not all cash balance plans provide a single sum distribution.

Under a cash balance plan, the interest credits for a younger participant will compound over a greater number of years until normal retirement age than for an older participant. This will result in a larger accrual for younger employees, when measured as the increase in the benefit payable at normal retirement age. Accordingly, some commentators have argued that the basic cash balance plan design violates section 411(b)(1)(H). Others have asserted that cash balance plans do not violate section 411(b)(1)(H) if the additions to the hypothetical account are not smaller because of the attainment of any age. They argue that, because pay credits under a cash balance plan are comparable to allocations under a defined contribution plan, these pay credits are an appropriate measure for testing whether a cash balance plan satisfies section 411(b)(1)(H).

These proposed regulations would provide that the rate of benefit accrual under an eligible cash balance plan, as defined in these proposed regulations, is permitted to be determined as the additions to the participant's hypothetical account for the plan year, except that previously accrued interest credits are not included in the rate of benefit accrual. Because the rate of benefit accrual is determined based on how benefits are expressed under the plan, this method of determining the rate of benefit accrual is restricted to eligible cash balance plans, as defined in these proposed regulations.

An eligible cash balance plan is a defined benefit plan that satisfies certain requirements. First, for accruals in the current plan year, the normal form of benefit is an immediate payment of the balance in a hypothetical account. As long as the normal form of benefit is an immediate payment of the balance in a hypothetical account, a plan does not fail to be an eligible cash balance plan merely because a single-sum distribution of that amount is not actually available as a distribution option under the plan.

Second, a plan is an eligible cash balance plan only if the plan provides that, at the same time that the participant accrues an addition to the hypothetical account, the participant accrues the right to future interest credits (without regard to future service) at a reasonable rate of interest that does not decrease because of the attainment of any age. Because the rate of benefit accrual under an eligible cash balance plan is generally determined by reference to additions to the hypothetical account disregarding interest credits, these interest credits must be provided for all future periods, including after normal retirement age, and an eligible cash balance plan cannot treat interest credits after normal retirement age as actuarial increases that are offset against the otherwise required accrual. A participant is not treated as having the right to future interest credits if the plan provides that additions to the hypothetical account under the plan are reduced for the actuarial equivalent of any in-service distributions because, as discussed above, such a reduction is the equivalent of an offset for an actuarial adjustment. Any additional interest credits under an eligible cash balance plan that do not accrue at the same time as the corresponding addition to the hypothetical account are included in determining the rate of benefit accrual in the year in which those additional interest credits are accrued.

In addition, a plan that is converted to a cash balance plan is subject to certain requirements, discussed below.

There are other hybrid designs that would satisfy some, but not all, of the requirements for an eligible cash balance plan. For example, there are some designs under which the normal form of benefit is the immediate payment of an account balance, but which do not provide for reasonable interest credits on that account balance. Under these proposed regulations, the rate of benefit accrual under these plans would be determined under the general rules applicable to traditional defined benefit plans.

Plans With Mixed Formulas

Some defined benefit plans have both a traditional defined benefit formula and a cash balance formula, and these proposed regulations provide rules for plans with such a mixed formula. If a portion of the plan formula under a defined benefit plan would satisfy the requirements for an eligible cash balance plan if that were the only formula under the plan, then that portion of the plan formula is referred to as an eligible cash balance formula in these proposed regulations. Any other portion of the plan formula is referred to as a traditional defined benefit formula.

The portion that is an eligible cash balance formula (or formulas if the plan has multiple eligible cash balance formulas) would be permitted to be tested using the rules for eligible cash balance plans, with the remainder of the plan tested under the rules for a traditional defined benefit formula (regardless of how many traditional defined benefit formulas the plan may have). This rule applies only if each such separately-treated plan would satisfy the maximum age conditions in section 410(a)(2) and the eligible cash balance and traditional defined benefit formulas interact in one of three specific ways for current and future accruals. The three ways are: (1) the plan provides that the participant's benefit is based on the sum of accruals under two different formulas (either sequentially where the cash balance formula goes into effect during the year or simultaneously where the plan provides for a participant to accrue benefits under both a traditional defined benefit formula and a cash balance formula at the same time with the participant to be entitled to the sum of the two); (2) the plan provides a benefit for a participant equal to the greater of the benefit determined under two or more formulas, one of which is an eligible cash balance formula and the other of which is not; or (3) under the plan, some participants are eligible for accruals only under an eligible cash balance formula and the remaining participants are eligible for accruals only under a traditional defined benefit formula or the other 2 specific methods. If the eligible cash balance formula and the traditional defined benefit formula interact in any other manner, the plan is not treated as an eligible cash balance plan for any portion of the plan formula.

Amendments Establishing an Eligible Cash Balance Formula

In many cases, a plan sponsor amends a traditional defined benefit plan to make it a cash balance plan. This process is often referred to as a "conversion." The terms of cash balance conversions vary, but often provide an opening hypothetical account balance for each participant. In some cases, the opening balance may be based on the participant's prior accrued benefit under the traditional defined benefit plan or on the participant's prior service with the plan sponsor. In other cases, the opening balance is set at zero, and each participant is entitled to the sum of the participant's accrued benefit under the traditional defined benefit plan and the cash balance account.

Some commentators have questioned whether certain cash balance conversions that provide for the establishment of an opening account balance satisfy section 411(b)(1)(H). These commentators have noted that, under section 411(d)(6), the participant can never be denied payment of the prior accrued benefit. They note that, if the opening account balance and subsequent interest credits through normal retirement age generate benefits that are not at least as large as the prior accrued benefit, the participant will not accrue net benefits for some period after the conversion. This period, often referred to as a "wear-away" period, will continue until the participant's account balance generates benefits that exceed the prior accrued benefit. These commentators argue that the wear-away period inherently produces a lower rate of accrual for older participants.[2]

Other commentators have argued that a wear-away period does not violate section 411(b)(1)(H) because the length of the wear-away period is determined not by the participant's age but by the size of the participant's prior accrued benefit under the traditional defined benefit plan. Additionally, commentators have pointed out that, because the prior accrued benefit is calculated using an interest rate determined at the time of the amendment but the interest credits under the cash balance plan often fluctuate under a variable index, a participant may move in or out of a wear-away period after a cash balance conversion solely because of future changes in interest rates.

Under these proposed regulations, the mere conversion of a traditional defined benefit plan to a cash balance plan would not cause the plan to fail section 411(b)(1)(H). However, a converted plan that otherwise would be treated as an eligible cash balance plan must satisfy one of two alternative rules. Under the first alternative, the converted plan must determine each participant's benefit as not less than the sum of the participant's benefits accrued under the traditional defined benefit plan and the cash balance account. A plan satisfying this first alterna-

tive will not have a wear-away period for benefits accrued under the traditional defined benefit plan.

Under the second alternative, the converted plan must establish each participant's opening account balance as an amount not less than the actuarial present value of the participant's prior accrued benefit, using reasonable actuarial assumptions. For this purpose, an interest rate assumption is not treated as reasonable if it increases, directly or indirectly, because of the participant's attainment of any age (which would result in lower present values for older participants). This alternative does not preclude the possibility of a wear-away period for some or all the participants in the plan, but it ensures that the opening account balance of each participant reflects the actuarial value of the prior accrued benefit, determined by using reasonable assumptions. Any excess in the opening account balance over the present value of a participant's previously accrued benefit is included as part of the participant's rate of benefit accrual for the plan year, and thus is tested under section 411(b)(1)(H) along with other pay credits for the year. Effectively, this alternative provides that a converted plan will not fail to satisfy section 411(b)(1)(H) if the benefit formula before the conversion satisfies section 411(b)(1)(H), the opening account balance is based on actuarial assumptions that are reasonable (and an interest rate that does not increase for older participants), and the benefit formula after the conversion—including any excess in the opening account balance over the present value of a participant's previously accrued benefit—satisfies section 411(b)(1)(H).

Use of Compensation in Calculating Rate of Benefit Accrual

A participant's rate of benefit accrual for a plan year can be determined as a dollar amount. Alternatively, if a plan's formula bases a participant's accruals on current compensation, then a participant's rate of benefit accrual can be determined as a percentage of the participant's current compensation. Likewise, if a plan's formula bases a participant's accruals on average compensation, then a participant's rate of benefit accrual can be determined as a percentage of that measure of the participant's average compensation. In order for the participant's rate of benefit accrual to be determined as a percentage of the participant's current or average compensation, compensation must be determined without regard to attainment of any age. The alternative of using current or average compensation simplifies testing, without changing the result.

Defined Contribution Plans

A defined contribution plan fails to comply with section 411(b)(2) if, either directly or indirectly, because of a participant's attainment of any age, the allocation of employer contributions or forfeitures is made to the account of the participant is decreased. For determining if there is a cessation or reduction in allocations because of attainment of any age, these proposed regulations would adopt a substantive standard that is similar to the standard that applies under these proposed regulations for defined benefit plans and to the standard that was proposed in the 1988 proposed regulations.

A reduction in the rate of allocation is directly because of a participant's attainment of any age for a plan year if under the terms of the plan, any participant's rate of allocation during the plan year would be higher if the participant were younger.

A reduction in the rate of allocation is indirectly because of a participant's attainment of any age if any participant's rate of allocation during the plan year would be higher if the participant were to have any characteristic which is a proxy for being younger, based on applicable facts and circumstances. A cessation or reduction in allocations is not indirectly because of the attainment of any age solely because of a positive correlation between attainment of any age and a reduction in the allocations or rate of allocation. Thus, a defined contribution plan does not provide for cessation or reduction in allocations solely because the plan limits the total amount of employer contributions and forfeitures that may be allocated to a participant's account or limits the total number of years of credited service that may be taken into account for purposes of determining allocations for the plan year.

Target benefit plans (defined contribution plans under which contributions are determined by reference to a targeted benefit described in the plan) are subject to section 411(b)(2) which applies to defined contribution plans. Under these proposed regulations, a target benefit plan would satisfy section 411(b)(2) only if the defined benefit formula

---

[2] This type of wear-away differs from a wear-away that results from the fact that certain optional forms of benefit may be subsidized under the traditional defined benefit plan but not under the cash balance plan or that other actuarial factors may produce a larger benefit amount prior to normal retirement age under the traditional defined benefit plan but not under the cash balance plan. This may occur even though the actuarial value of the accrued benefit under the traditional defined benefit plan is included in the participant's opening account balance. Although section 411(d)(6) protects optional forms of benefit under the pre-amendment formula, section 411(b)(1)(H)(iv) specifically provides that a reduction because of the attainment of any age does not occur as a result of the subsidized portion of an early retirement benefit.

used to determine allocations would satisfy section 411(b)(1)(H) without regard to section 411(b)(1)(H)(iii) relating to adjustments for distributions and actuarial increases. A target benefit plan would not fail to satisfy section 411(b)(2) with respect to allocations after normal retirement age merely because the allocation for a plan year is reduced to reflect an older participant's shorter longevity using a reasonable actuarial assumption regarding mortality. These proposed regulations also would authorize the Commissioner to develop additional guidance with respect to the application of section 411(b)(2) to target benefit plans.

Optional Forms of Benefit and Other Rights and Features

These proposed regulations generally retain the requirements applicable to optional forms of benefit that were in the 1988 proposed regulations. Under these rules, with the exceptions noted below, a participant's rate of benefit accrual under a defined benefit plan and a participant's allocations under a defined contribution plan are considered to be reduced because of the participant's attainment of any age if optional forms of benefits, ancillary benefits, or other rights or features otherwise provided to a participant under the plan are not provided, or are provided on a less favorable basis, with respect to benefits or allocations attributable to credited service because of the participant's attainment of any age. In addition, a plan would not fail to satisfy section 411(b)(1)(H) merely due to variance because of the attainment of any age with respect to the subsidized portion of an early retirement benefit (whether provided on a temporary or permanent basis), a qualified disability benefit (as defined in § 1.411(a)-7(c)(3)), or a social security supplement (as defined in § 1.411(a)-7(c)(4)(ii)).[3] These proposed regulations also clarify that a plan would not fail to satisfy section 411(b)(1)(H) merely because the plan makes actuarial adjustments using a reasonable assumption regarding mortality to calculate optional forms of benefit or to calculate the cost of providing a qualified preretirement survivor annuity, as defined in section 417(c).

Coordination With Other Provisions

Sections 411(b)(1)(H)(v) and 411(b)(2)(C) both provide for the coordination of the requirements of each section with other applicable qualification requirements. Under these proposed regulations, a plan will not fail to satisfy section 411(b)(1)(H) or 411(b)(2) because of a limit on accruals or allocations necessary to comply with the limitations of section 415 or to prevent discrimination in favor of highly compensated employees within the meaning of section 401(a)(4). Additionally, these proposed regulations would authorize the Commissioner to provide additional guidance relating to prohibited discrimination in favor of highly compensated employees. These proposed regulations would also provide that no benefit accrual or allocation is required under section 411(b)(1)(H) or 411(b)(2) for a plan year to the extent such allocation or accrual would cause the plan to fail to satisfy the requirements of section 401(l) (relating to permitted disparity) for the plan year, such as if a younger person has a smaller permitted disparity due to having a later social security retirement age. Further, under these proposed regulations, a plan would not fail to satisfy section 411(b)(1)(H) or 411(b)(2) for a plan year merely because of the distribution rights provided under section 411(a)(11), including deferral rights for participants whose benefits are immediately distributable within the meaning of § 1.411(a)-11(c).

Application of Section 401(a)(4) to New Comparability Cash Balance Plans

These proposed regulations also include a proposed amendment to the regulations under section 401(a)(4). This amendment would provide that a defined benefit plan that determines compliance with section 411(b)(1)(H) by using the special definition of rate of accrual for an eligible cash balance plan is not permitted to demonstrate that the benefits provided under the arrangement do not discriminate in favor of highly compensated employees by using an inconsistent method (i.e., an accrual rate based on the normal retirement benefit), unless the plan complies with a modified version of the provisions of the regulations under section 401(a)(4) related to cross-testing by a defined contribution plan. Under these requirements, an eligible cash balance plan under which the additions to the hypothetical account are neither broadly available nor reflect a gradual age and service schedule, as defined under existing regulations relating to cross-tested defined contribution plans, may test on the basis of benefits only if the plan satisfies a minimum allocation gateway.

The minimum allocation gateway generally requires that the hypothetical allocation rate for each nonhighly compensated employee be at least one-third of the hypothetical allocation rate for the highly compensated employee with the highest hypothetical allocation rate. However, the minimum allocation gateway is also satisfied if the hypothetical allocation rate for each nonhighly compensated employee is no less than 5%, provided the highest hypothetical allocation rate for any highly compensated employee is not in excess of 25%. If the highest hypothetical allocation rate is above 25%, the 5% factor is increased, up to as much as 7.5%. This minimum allocation gateway, which is normally applicable to DB/DC plans (i.e., defined benefit plans and defined contribution plans that are combined for nondiscrimination testing), is used for purposes of eligible cash balance plans, rather than the minimum allocation gateway normally applicable to defined contribution plans, because hypothetical allocations under a cash balance plan can be significantly greater than allocations under a defined contribution plan.

If the eligible cash balance plan is aggregated with other plans that are not cash balance plans, the regulations would treat the cash balance plan as a defined contribution plan for purposes of applying the rules applicable to aggregated plans. For this purpose, a plan with both an eligible cash balance formula and a traditional defined benefit formula is treated as an aggregation of two plans.

Effective Date of Sections 411(b)(1)(H) and 411(b)(2)

The 1988 proposed regulations included provisions related to the effective date of sections 411(b)(1)(H) and 411(b)(2). The effective date provisions in these proposed regulations differ from the 1988 proposed regulations (and Notice 88-126) in order to reflect the decision in *Lockheed Corp. v. Spink*, 517 U.S. 882 (1996).

In general, sections 411(b)(1)(H) and 411(b)(2) are effective for plan years beginning on or after January 1, 1988 with respect to a participant who is credited with at least one hour of service in a plan year beginning on or after January 1, 1988. In the case of a participant who is credited with at least one hour of service in a plan year beginning on or after January 1, 1988, section 411(b)(1)(H) is effective with respect to all years of service completed by the participant, except that, in accordance with *Lockheed Corp. v. Spink*, plan years beginning before January 1, 1988 are excluded. For purposes of these proposed regulations, an hour of service includes any hour required to be recognized under the plan by section 410 or 411.

Similarly, section 411(b)(2) does not apply with respect to allocations of employer contributions or forfeitures to the accounts of participants under a defined contribution plan for a plan year beginning before January 1, 1988.

These proposed regulations would also provide a special effective date for a plan maintained pursuant to one or more collective bargaining agreements between employee representatives and one or more employers, ratified before March 1, 1986. For such plans, sections 411(b)(1)(H) and 411(b)(2) are effective for benefits provided under, and employees covered by, any such agreement with respect to plan years beginning on or after the later of (i) January 1, 1988 or (ii) the earlier of January 1, 1990 or the date on which the last of such collective bargaining agreements terminates (determined without regard to any extension of any such agreement occurring on or after March 1, 1986). The otherwise generally applicable effective date rules would apply to a collectively bargained plan, as of the effective date of section 411(b)(1)(H) or 411(b)(2) applicable to such plan.

Proposed Effective Date

The regulations are proposed to be applicable to plan years beginning after the date final regulations are published in the **Federal Register**. These proposed regulations cannot be relied upon until adopted in final form. However, until these regulations are adopted in final form, the reliance provided on the 1988 proposed regulations continues to be available. In addition, the proposed regulations at §§ 1.410(a)-4A, 1.411(a)-3, 1.411(b)-3 and 1.411(c)-1(f)(2) (relating to maximum age for participation, vesting, normal retirement age, and actuarial adjustments after normal retirement age), which were published in the same notice of proposed rulemaking as the 1988 proposed regulation and which are not republished here, are also expected to be finalized for future plan years.

Special Analyses

It has been determined that this notice of proposed rulemaking is not a significant regulatory action as defined in Executive Order 12866. Therefore, a regulatory assessment is not required. It also has been determined that section 553(b) of the Administrative Procedure Act (5

---

[3] The ADEA also includes special rules relating to certain of these benefits. See 29 U.S.C. 623(f)(2) and (l).

U.S.C. chapter 5) does not apply to these regulations, and because the regulation does not impose a collection of information on small entities, the Regulatory Flexibility Act (5 U.S.C. chapter 6) does not apply. Pursuant to section 7805(f) of the Code, this notice of proposed rulemaking will be submitted to the Chief Counsel for Advocacy of the Small Business Administration for comment on its impact on small business.

Comments and Public Hearing

Before these proposed regulations are adopted as final regulations, consideration will be given to written comments (preferably a signed original and eight (8) copies) that are submitted timely to the IRS. Alternatively, taxpayers may submit comments electronically to the IRS Internet site at www.irs.gov/regs. All comments will be available for public inspection and copying. The IRS and Treasury request comments on the clarity of the proposed rules and how they may be made easier to understand or to implement. Comments are also requested on the following issues:

• Because these proposed regulations are based on a year-by-year determination of the rate of benefit accrual that does not accommodate averaging over a period of earlier years, one result would be that, if a higher accrual is provided for older workers in one year, the rates cannot be leveled out in subsequent periods in a manner that takes the earlier higher accruals into account. This might occur for a change from a fractional accrual method to a unit credit method for all years of service. Comments are requested on whether rates should be permitted to be averaged and, if so, under what conditions.

• In the case of a conversion of a traditional defined benefit plan to a cash balance plan, these proposed regulations generally provide for any excess of a participant's opening hypothetical account balance over the present value of the participant's prior accrued benefit to be tested for age discrimination. Comments are requested on whether any other portion of the hypothetical account balance should be disregarded in applying section 411(b)(1)(H) under other circumstances, for example, if the opening account balance is a reconstructed cash balance account (i.e., the account balance that each participant would have had at the time of the conversion if the cash balance formula had been in effect for the participant's entire period of service). In addition, comments are requested on the effect of these rules on employers, if any, that may have used the extended wear-away transition rule of § 1.401(a)(4)-13(f)(2)(i).

• Because these proposed regulations provide for the rate of benefit accrual under section 411(b)(1)(H) to be based on the annual increase in the accrued benefit under the plan, the rate of benefit accrual under a floor offset plan, as described in Rev. Rul. 76-259 (1976-2 CB 111), would be determined after taking into account the amount of the offset. Comments are requested on whether the rate of benefit accrual for a floor offset plan should be tested before application of the offset and, if so, under what conditions. For example, should the rate of benefit accrual for a floor offset plan be tested before application of the offset if the plan provides an actuarial increase after normal retirement age or if the annuity purchase rate used to calculate the offset is not less favorable after normal retirement age than the annuity purchase rate applicable at normal retirement age.

A public hearing has been scheduled for April 10, 2003, at 10 a.m. in room 4718 of the Internal Revenue Building, 1111 Constitution Avenue NW., Washington, DC. All visitors must present photo identification to enter the building. Because of access restrictions, visitors will not be admitted beyond the immediate entrance area more than 30 minutes before the hearing starts at the Constitution Avenue entrance. For information about having your name placed on the building access list to attend the hearing, see the "FOR FURTHER INFORMATION CONTACT" section of this preamble.

The rules of 26 CFR 601.601(a)(3) apply to the hearing. Persons who wish to present oral comments at the hearing must submit written comments and an outline of the topics to be discussed and the time to be devoted to each topic (signed original and eight (8) copies) by March 13, 2003. A period of 10 minutes will be allotted to each person for making comments. An agenda showing the scheduling of the speakers will be prepared after the deadline for receiving outlines has passed. Copies of the agenda will be available free of charge at the hearing.

Drafting Information

The principal authors of these proposed regulations are Linda S. F. Marshall and R. Lisa Mojiri-Azad of the Office of the Division Counsel/Associate Chief Counsel (Tax Exempt and Government Entities). However, other personnel from the IRS and Treasury participated in their development.

List of Subjects in 26 CFR Part 1

Income taxes, Reporting and recordkeeping requirements.

Proposed Amendments to the Regulations

Accordingly, 26 CFR Part 1 is proposed to be amended as follows:

PART 1—INCOME TAXES

Paragraph 1. The authority citation for part 1 is amended by adding the following citation in numerical order:

Authority: 26 U.S.C. 7805 ***

Section 1.411(b)-2 is also issued under 26 U.S.C. 411(b)(1)(H) and 411(b)(2).

→ **Caution: Proposed Reg. § 1.401(a)(4) was withdrawn by the IRS as set forth in IRS Announcement 2003-22.←**

***

Par. 2. Section 1.401(a)(4)-3 is amended as follows:

1. A new sentence is added before the last sentence of paragraph (a)(1).

2. Paragraph (g) is added.

The additions and revisions read as follows:

§ 1.401(a)(4)-3 Nondiscrimination in amount of employer-provided benefits under a defined benefit plan.

(a) *Introduction*—(1) *Overview.* *** Paragraph (g) of this section provides additional rules that apply to a plan that satisfies the requirements of section 411(b)(1)(H) and § 1.411(b)-2 using the rate of benefit accrual determined pursuant to the rules of § 1.411(b)-2(b)(2)(iii) for eligible cash balance plans. ***

*****

(g) *Additional rules for eligible cash balance plans*—(1) *In general.* Notwithstanding the provisions of paragraphs (a) through (f) of this section, a plan that satisfies the requirements of section 411(b)(1)(H) and § 1.411(b)-2 using the rate of benefit accrual under the plan or a portion of the plan determined pursuant to the rules of § 1.411(b)-2(b)(2)(iii) for eligible cash balance plans is permitted to satisfy the requirements of section 401(a)(4) by satisfying the requirements of this section (relating to nondiscrimination in amount of employer-provided benefits) only if the plan satisfies paragraph (g)(2) or (3) of this section, as applicable.

(2) *Eligible cash balance plans not aggregated with another defined benefit plan.* A plan described in paragraph (g)(1) of this section under which benefits are determined solely in accordance with an eligible cash balance formula (as defined in § 1.411(b)-2(b)(2)(iii)(C)(*1*)) satisfies this paragraph (g)(2) only if the plan meets either of the following conditions—

(i) The plan would satisfy the requirements of § 1.401(a)(4)-8(b)(1)(iii) or (iv) by treating the additions to the hypothetical account that are included in the rate of benefit accrual under the rules of § 1.411(b)-2(b)(2)(iii)(A) as allocations under a defined contribution plan; or

(ii) The plan would satisfy the requirements of § 1.401(a)(4)-9(b)(2)(v)(D) by treating the additions to the hypothetical account that are included in the rate of benefit accrual under the rules of § 1.411(b)-2(b)(2)(iii)(A) as allocations under a defined contribution plan for purposes of determining equivalent normal allocation rates (within the meaning of § 1.401(a)(4)-9(b)(2)(ii)).

(3) *Eligible cash balance plans aggregated with another defined benefit plan.* In the case of a plan described in paragraph (g)(1) of this section that is not described in paragraph (g)(2) of this section (for example, an eligible cash balance plan that is aggregated with another defined benefit plan that is not an eligible cash balance plan or a plan that uses an eligible cash balance formula with a traditional defined benefit plan formula as described in § 1.411(b)-2(b)(2)(iii)(C)), the plan would satisfy the requirements of § 1.401(a)(4)-9(b)(2)(v)(D) by treating the additions to the hypothetical account that are included in the rate of benefit accrual under the rules of § 1.411(b)-2(b)(2)(iii)(A) as allocations under a defined contribution plan.

Par. 3. Section 1.401(a)(4)-9 is amended by:

1. Amending paragraph (b)(2)(v) by removing the language "For plan years" and adding in its place "Except as provided in paragraph (b)(2)(vi) of this section, for plan years".

2. Adding paragraph (b)(2)(vi).

The addition reads as follows:

§ 1.401(a)(4)-9 Plan aggregation and restructuring

*****

(b) ***

(2) ***

(vi) *Special rules for cash balance plans aggregated with defined contribution plans*—(A) *In general.* In the case of a DB/DC plan where the defined benefit plan (or any portion thereof) satisfies the requirements of section 411(b)(1)(H) using the rate of benefit accrual determined pursuant to the rules of § 1.411(b)-2(b)(iii) for eligible cash balance plans, the DB/DC plan is permitted to demonstrate satisfaction of the nondiscrimination in amount requirement of § 1.401(a)(4)-1(b)(2) on the basis of benefits only if—

(*1*) The plan would satisfy the requirements of paragraph (b)(2)(v) of this section if the additions to the hypothetical account that are included in the rate of benefit accrual under the rules of § 1.411(b)-2(b)(2)(iii)(A) are treated as allocations under a defined contribution plan; or

(*2*) The plan is described in paragraph (b)(2)(vi)(B) of this section (regarding eligible cash balance plans aggregated only with defined contribution plans).

(B) *Special rule for cash balance plans aggregated with defined contribution plans that are not aggregated with other defined benefit plans.* A DB/DC plan is described in this paragraph (b)(2)(vi)(B) if the DB/DC plan satisfies the following conditions—

(*1*) All defined benefit plans that are included in the DB/DC plan satisfy the requirements of section 411(b)(1)(H) using the rate of benefit accrual determined pursuant to the rules of § 1.411(b)-2(b)(iii) for eligible cash balance plans; and

(*2*) The DB/DC plan would satisfy the requirements of § 1.401(a)(4)-8(b)(1)(i)(B)(*1*) or (*2*) (regarding broadly available allocation rates or certain age-based allocation rates) if the additions to the hypothetical account that are included in the rate of benefit accrual under the rules of § 1.411(b)-2(b)(2)(iii)(A) are treated as allocations under a defined contribution plan.

Par. 4. Proposed § 1.411(b)-2 published at 53 FR 11876 on April 11, 1988, is revised to read as follows.

§ 1.411(b)-2 Reductions of accruals or allocations because of attainment of any age.

(a) *In general*—(1) *Overview.* Section 411(b)(1)(H) provides that a defined benefit plan does not satisfy the minimum vesting standards of section 411(a) if, under the plan, benefit accruals on behalf of a participant are ceased or the rate of benefit accrual on behalf of a participant is reduced because of the participant's attainment of any age. Section 411(b)(2) provides that a defined contribution plan does not satisfy the minimum vesting standards of section 411(a) if, under the plan, allocations to a participant's account are ceased or the rate of allocation to a participant's account is reduced because of the participant's attainment of any age. Paragraph (b) of this section provides general rules for defined benefit plans. Paragraph (c) of this section provides general rules for defined contribution plans. Paragraph (d) of this section provides rules applying this section to optional forms of benefit, ancillary benefits, and other rights or features under defined benefit and defined contribution plans. Paragraph (e) of this section provides rules coordinating the requirements of this section with certain other qualification requirements. Paragraph (f) of this section contains effective date provisions.

(2) *Attainment of any age.* For purposes of sections 411(b)(1)(H), 411(b)(2), and this section, a participant's attainment of any age means the participant's growing older. Thus, the rules of sections 411(b)(1)(H), 411(b)(2), and this section apply regardless of whether a participant is younger than, at, or older than normal retirement age.

(b) *Defined benefit plans*—(1) *In general*— (i) *Requirement.* A defined benefit plan does not satisfy the requirements of section 411(b)(1)(H) if a participant's rate of benefit accrual is reduced, either directly or indirectly, because of the participant's attainment of any age. A reduction in a participant's rate of benefit accrual includes any discontinuance in the participant's accrual of benefits or cessation of participation in the plan.

(ii) *Definition of normal form.* For purposes of this paragraph (b), the normal form of benefit (also referred to as the normal form) means the form under which payments to the participant under the plan are expressed under the plan formula, prior to adjustment for form of benefit.

(2) *Rate of benefit accrual*—(i) *Rate of benefit accrual before normal retirement age.* For purposes of this paragraph (b), except as provided in paragraph (b)(2)(iii) of this section, a participant's rate of benefit accrual for any plan year that ends before the participant attains normal retirement age is the excess (if any) of—

(A) The participant's accrued normal retirement benefit at the end of the plan year; over

(B) The participant's accrued normal retirement benefit at the end of the preceding plan year.

(ii) *Rate of benefit accrual after normal retirement age.* In the case of a plan for which the rate of benefit accrual before normal retirement age is determined under paragraph (b)(2)(i) of this section, except as provided in paragraph (b)(4)(iii)(C) of this section, a participant's rate of benefit accrual for the plan year in which the participant attains normal retirement age or any later plan year (taking into account the provisions of section 411(b)(1)(H)(iii)(II)) is the excess (if any) of—

(A) The annual benefit to which the participant is entitled at the end of the plan year, determined as if payment commences at the end of the plan year in the normal form (or the straight life annuity that is actuarially equivalent to the normal form if the normal form is not an annual benefit that does not decrease during the lifetime of the participant); over

(B) The annual benefit to which the participant was entitled at the end of the preceding plan year, determined as if payment commences at the later of normal retirement age or the end of the preceding plan year in the normal form (or the straight life annuity that is actuarially equivalent to the normal form if the normal form is not an annual benefit that does not decrease during the lifetime of the participant).

(iii) *Rate of benefit accrual for eligible cash balance plans*—(A) *General rule.* For purposes of this paragraph (b), in the case of an eligible cash balance plan, a participant's rate of benefit accrual for a plan year is permitted to be determined as the addition to the participant's hypothetical account for the plan year, except that interest credits added to the hypothetical account for the plan year are disregarded to the extent the participant had accrued the right to those interest credits as of the close of the preceding plan year as described in paragraph (b)(2)(iii)(B)(*2*) of this section.

(B) *Eligible cash balance plans.* For purposes of this section, a defined benefit plan is an eligible cash balance plan for a plan year if it satisfies each of the following requirements for current accruals under the plan for that plan year—

(*1*) *Plan design.* The normal form of benefit is an immediate payment of the balance in a hypothetical account (without regard to whether such an immediate payment is actually available under the plan).

(*2*) *Right to future interest.* With respect to a participant's hypothetical account balance, the participant has accrued the right to annual (or more frequent) interest credits to be added to the hypothetical account for all future periods without regard to future service at a reasonable rate of interest that is not reduced, either directly or indirectly, because of the participant's attainment of any age. A plan is treated as not satisfying the requirement of this paragraph (b)(2)(iii)(B)(*2*) if it provides for any adjustment for benefit distributions described in paragraph (b)(4) of this section.

(*3*) *Plan amendments adopting cash balance formula.* In the case of a plan amendment that has been amended to adopt a cash balance formula (as described in paragraphs (b)(2)(iii)(B)(*1*) and (*2*) of this section) for a participant, the plan as amended satisfies the requirements of either paragraph (b)(2)(iii)(D) or (E) of this section.

(C) *Plans with mixed benefit formulas*—(*1*) *Eligible cash balance formula.* If a portion of the plan formula under a defined benefit plan would satisfy the requirements to be an eligible cash balance plan if it were the only formula under the plan, then, for purposes of this section, such portion of the plan formula is referred to as an eligible cash balance formula and the other portion of the plan formula is referred to as a traditional defined benefit formula. If the eligible cash balance formula and the traditional defined benefit formula interact in a manner described in paragraph (b)(2)(iii)(C)(*2*), (*3*), or (*4*) of this section for current and future accruals under the plan, then, for purposes of determining whether the plan satisfies section 411(b)(1)(H), the plan is permitted to be treated as two separate plans, one of which is an eligible cash balance plan and the other of which is not, but only if each such plan would satisfy section 410(a)(2). Thus, such a plan satisfies the requirements of section 411(b)(1)(H) if the eligible cash balance formula satisfies the requirements of paragraph (b)(1) of this section with the participant's rate of benefit accrual determined under paragraph (b)(2)(iii)(A) of this section and the portion of the plan's formula that is a traditional defined benefit formula satisfies the requirements of paragraph (b)(1) of this section with the participant's rate of benefit accrual determined under paragraph (b)(2)(i) or (ii) of this section, as applicable. If the eligible cash balance formula and the traditional defined benefit formula interact in a manner other than as set forth in paragraphs (b)(2)(iii)(C)(2), (3), or (4) of this section, the plan is not treated as an eligible cash balance plan for any portion of the plan formula.

(2) *Plans with additive formulas.* A plan is described in this paragraph (b)(2)(iii)(C)(2) if the participant's benefit is based on the sum of accruals under two different formulas, one of which is an eligible cash balance formula and the other of which is not.

(3) *Plans with greater of formulas.* A plan is described in this paragraph (b)(2)(iii)(C)(3) if the plan provides a benefit for a participant equal to the greater of the benefit determined under two or more formulas under the plan for a plan year, one of which is an eligible cash balance formula and another of which is not.

(4) *Different formulas for different participants.* A plan is described in this paragraph (b)(2)(iii)(C)(4) if some participants are eligible for accruals only under an eligible cash balance formula and the remaining participants are eligible for accruals only under a traditional defined benefit formula or a combination of a traditional defined benefit formula or eligible cash balance formula described in paragraphs (b)(2)(iii)(C)(2) and (3) of this section.

(D) *Plan amendment adopting eligible cash balance formula using a sum of formula.* A plan satisfies this paragraph (b)(2)(iii)(D) only if for all periods after the amendment becomes effective the plan provides benefits that are not less than the sum of the benefits accrued as of the later of the date the amendment becomes effective or the date the amendment is adopted, plus the benefits provided by the participant's hypothetical account under the eligible cash balance formula.

(E) *Plan amendment adopting eligible cash balance formula using an opening account balance—(1) Calculation of opening account balance.* A plan satisfies this paragraph (b)(2)(iii)(E) only if the balance in the participant's hypothetical account, determined immediately after the amendment becomes effective, is not less than the actuarial present value of the participant's accrued benefit payable in the normal form of benefit, determined as of the later of the date the amendment becomes effective or the date the amendment is adopted, with such present value determined using reasonable actuarial assumptions. For this purpose, the actuarial assumptions are not reasonable if they include an interest rate that increases, either directly or indirectly, because of a participant's attainment of any age. The actuarial assumptions do not fail to be reasonable merely because pre-retirement mortality is not taken into account.

(2) *Bifurcation for purposes of determining rate of benefit accrual.* If a plan satisfies the requirements of paragraph (b)(2)(iii)(E)(1), only the portion of the participant's hypothetical account balance in excess of the actuarial present value of the participant's accrued benefit payable in the normal form of benefit is treated as an addition to the participant's hypothetical account balance for the plan year for purposes of determining the participant's rate of benefit accrual under paragraph (b)(2)(iii)(A) of this section.

(3) *Treatment of employees past normal retirement age.* In addition, a plan does not satisfy this paragraph (b)(2)(iii)(E) if the opening balance for a participant who has attained normal retirement age is less than the balance that would apply if the participant were at his or her normal retirement age.

(iv) *Determination of rate of benefit accrual—(A) In general.* A participant's rate of benefit accrual for a plan year can be determined as a dollar amount. Alternatively, if a plan's formula bases a participant's accruals on current compensation, then a participant's rate of benefit accrual can be determined as a percentage of the participant's current compensation. For example, for an accumulation plan (as defined in § 1.401(a)(4)-12), the participant's rate of benefit accrual under paragraph (b)(2)(i) of this section can be determined as the excess of the accrued portion of the participant's normal retirement benefit at the end of the plan year over the accrued portion of the participant's normal retirement benefit at the end of the preceding plan year, divided by compensation taken into account under the plan for the plan year. Likewise, if a plan's formula bases a participant's accruals on average compensation, then a participant's rate of benefit accrual can be determined as a percentage of that measure of the participant's average compensation. For a plan that determines benefits as a percentage of average annual compensation (as defined in § 1.401(a)(4)-3(e)(2)), the rate of benefit accrual under paragraph (b)(2)(i) of this section is determined as the excess of the accrued portion of the participant's normal retirement benefit at the end of the plan year divided by

average annual compensation taken into account under the plan at the end of the plan year, over the accrued portion of the participant's normal retirement benefit at the end of the preceding plan year divided by average annual compensation taken into account under the plan at the end of such preceding plan year. A plan is permitted to determine the participant's rate of benefit accrual as a percentage of the participant's current or average compensation only if compensation under the plan is determined without regard to attainment of any age.

(B) *Benefits included in rate of benefit accrual.* For purposes of determining a participant's rate of benefit accrual, only benefits that are included in a participant's accrued benefit are taken into account. Thus, for example, a participant's rate of benefit accrual does not take into account benefits such as the benefits described in paragraph (d)(3) of this section (relating to qualified disability benefits, social security supplements, and early retirement benefits).

(v) *Examples.* The following examples illustrate the application of this paragraph (b)(2). In each of the examples, normal retirement age is 65. The examples are as follows:

Example 1. Plan L is a defined benefit plan under which the normal form of benefit is a monthly straight life annuity commencing at normal retirement age (or the date of actual retirement, if later) equal to $30 times the participant's years of service. For purposes of this section, a participant's rate of benefit accrual for any plan year is $30.

Example 2. (i) Plan M is a defined benefit plan under which the normal form of benefit is an annual straight life annuity commencing at normal retirement age (or the date of actual retirement, if later) equal to 1% of the average of a participant's highest 3 consecutive years of compensation times the participant's years of service.

(ii) For purposes of this section, a participant's rate of benefit accrual for any plan year can be expressed as a dollar amount. Alternatively, a participant's rate of benefit accrual for a plan year can be expressed as 1% of the participant's highest 3 consecutive years of compensation (determined using the same rules applicable to determining compensation under the plan for purposes of computing the normal form of benefit), provided that the definition of compensation used for this purpose is determined without regard to the attainment of any age. A participant's rate of benefit accrual cannot be determined as a percentage of any other measure of compensation or average compensation.

(iii) If Plan M were to provide that compensation earned after the attainment of age 65 is not taken into account in determining average compensation or were otherwise to determine compensation in a manner that depends on a participant's age, then, for purposes of this section, a participant's rate of benefit accrual would have to be expressed as a dollar amount, and could not be expressed as a percentage of any measure of compensation or average compensation.

Example 3. (i) Plan N is a defined benefit plan under which the normal form of benefit is an immediate payment of the balance in a participant's hypothetical account. A compensation credit equal to 6% of each participant's wages for the year is added to the hypothetical account of a participant who is an employee. At the end of each plan year, the hypothetical account is credited with interest based on the applicable interest rate under section 417(e), as provided under the plan. All participants accrue the right to receive interest credits on their hypothetical account in the future regardless of performance of services in the future, including after normal retirement age.

(ii) Under paragraph (b)(2)(iii)(B) of this section, Plan N satisfies the requirements to be an eligible cash balance plan. Participant A's compensation for a plan year is $40,000. The compensation credit for Participant A allocated to A's hypothetical account for that plan year is $2,400. Because Plan N is an eligible cash balance plan, the rate of benefit accrual for Participant A is permitted to be determined as the addition to Participant A's hypothetical account for the plan year, disregarding interest credits. Therefore, Participant A's rate of benefit accrual is equal to $2,400, or 6% of wages.

Example 4. (i) The facts are the same as in *Example 3*, except that the cash balance formula under Plan N is the result of a plan amendment. Under the plan, as amended, the benefits equal the sum of—

(1) 1% of the average of the participant's highest 3 consecutive years of base salary times years of service, but disregarding service and salary after the effective date of the amendment, in a normal form of benefit that is a straight life annuity commencing at normal retirement age (or the date of actual retirement, if later); and

(2) the participant's hypothetical account under the same cash balance formula in *Example 3* that applies after the effective date of the amendment, in a normal form of benefit expressed as an immediate payment of the balance of the participant's hypothetical account.

(ii) Under paragraph (b)(2)(iii)(B)(3) of this section, the plan is an eligible cash balance plan if the plan satisfies the requirements of paragraph (b)(2)(iii)(D) or (E) of this section. The plan's formula is described in paragraph (b)(2)(iii)(D) of this section. Accordingly, the portion of the plan formula that provides for compensation credits on a participant's hypothetical account is an eligible cash balance formula under paragraph (b)(2)(iii)(B) of this section. Therefore, a participant's rate of benefit accrual under the eligible cash balance formula is permitted to be determined as the addition to the participant's hypothetical account for the plan year, disregarding interest credits. Participant B's base salary for the year is $50,000. The compensation credit for Participant B credited to B's hypothetical account for the year is $3,000. The rate of benefit accrual under the eligible cash balance formula for Participant B is equal to $3,000, or 6% of base salary.

Example 5. (i) The facts are the same as in *Example 3*, except that Plan N is a defined benefit plan that is converted to a cash balance plan by the adoption of a plan amendment, effective at the beginning of the next plan year, establishing an opening hypothetical account for each participant with an accrued benefit under the plan prior to conversion. Prior to conversion, Plan N provided a benefit equal to 1% of the average of a participant's highest 3 consecutive years of compensation times years of service. Effective as of the date of the conversion, hypothetical accounts are established equal to the present value of a participant's accrued benefit using section 417(e) interest and reasonable mortality assumptions (except no pre-retirement mortality is used). Under the cash balance portion of the formula, compensation and interest credits are made as described in *Example 3*.

(ii) Under paragraph (b)(2)(iii)(B)(3) of this section, the plan is an eligible cash balance plan only if the plan satisfies the requirements of paragraph (b)(2)(iii)(D) or (E) of this section. The plan's formula is described in paragraph (b)(2)(iii)(E) of this section. Accordingly, the portion of the plan formula that provides for compensation credits on a participant's hypothetical account is an eligible cash balance formula. The rate of benefit accrual for a participant is therefore permitted to be determined as the addition to the participant's hypothetical account for the plan year, disregarding interest credits. In addition, under paragraph (b)(2)(iii)(E) of this section, because the opening hypothetical account balance is equal to the actuarial present value of the participant's accrued benefit, that balance is not treated as an addition for the plan year. The result would not be different if the opening accounts were established using another interest rate or another mortality assumption if the actuarial assumptions were reasonable. Participant C's wages for the year are $60,000. The compensation credit allocated to C's hypothetical account for the year is $3,600. The rate of accrual under the eligible cash balance formula for C is equal to $3,600, or 6% of compensation.

Example 6. (i) The facts are the same as in *Example 5*, except that Plan N provides for only new participants and participants who are less than age 55 at the time of the conversion to be eligible for benefits under the cash balance formula. Accordingly, participants who are age 55 or older at the time of the conversion are only eligible for the benefit payable under the plan formula in effect before the conversion (1% of the participant's highest 3 consecutive years of compensation times years of service) taking into account compensation and service after the conversion.

(ii) Because Plan N provides benefits based on a mixed formula under paragraph (b)(2)(iii)(C) of this section, Plan N is permitted under paragraph (b)(2)(iii)(C)(1) of this section to be treated as two separate plans for purposes of section 411(b)(1)(H), one of which is an eligible cash balance plan and the other of which is not, but only if each plan would satisfy section 410(a)(2). No portion of Plan N can be treated as an eligible cash balance plan because the portion of Plan N that would otherwise be an eligible cash balance plan would fail to satisfy section 410(a)(2) as a result of having a maximum age of 55 for individuals who are participants at the time of the conversion.

Example 7. (i) The facts are the same as in *Example 5*, except that Plan N provides for participants to receive the greater of the benefit payable under the cash balance formula or the benefit payable under the plan formula in effect before the conversion (1% of the participant's highest 3 consecutive years of compensation times years of service) taking into account compensation and service after the conversion.

(ii) Because Plan N provides benefits based on the greater of the amount payable under two different formulas, under paragraph (b)(2)(iii)(C)(4) of this section, Plan N is tested for satisfaction of the requirements of section 411(b)(1)(H) and this paragraph (b) by separately testing the eligible cash balance formula using a rate of benefit accrual equal to compensation credits of 6% of compensation and the traditional defined benefit formulas using a rate of benefit accrual equal to 1% of highest 3 consecutive years of compensation.

(3) *Reduction that is directly or indirectly because of a participant's attainment of any age*—(i) *Reduction in rate of benefit accrual that is directly because of a participant's attainment of any age.* A plan provides for a reduction in the rate of benefit accrual that is directly because of a participant's attainment of any age for any plan year if, under the terms of the plan, any participant's rate of benefit accrual for the plan year would be higher if the participant were younger. Thus, a plan fails to satisfy section 411(b)(1)(H) and this paragraph (b) if, under the terms of the plan, the rate of benefit accrual for any individual who is or could be a participant under the plan would be lower solely as a result of the individual being older.

(ii) *Reduction in rate of benefit accrual that is indirectly because of a participant's attainment of any age*—(A) *In general.* A plan provides for a reduction in the rate of benefit accrual that is indirectly because of a participant's attainment of any age for any plan year if any participant's rate of benefit accrual for the plan year would be higher if the participant were to have a different characteristic which is a proxy for being younger, based on the all of relevant facts and circumstances. Thus, a plan fails to satisfy section 411(b)(1)(H) and this paragraph (b) if the rate of benefit accrual for any individual who is or could be a participant under the plan would be lower solely as a result of such individual having a different characteristic which is a proxy for being older, based on all of the relevant facts and circumstances.

(B) *Permissible limitations.* A reduction in a participant's rate of benefit accrual is not indirectly because of the attainment of any age in violation of section 411(b)(1)(H) solely because of a positive correlation between attainment of any age and a reduction in the rate of benefit accrual. In addition, a defined benefit plan does not fail to satisfy section 411(b)(1)(H) and this paragraph (b) solely because, on a uniform and consistent basis without regard to a participant's age, the plan limits the amount of benefits a participant may accrue under the plan, limits the number of years of service or years of participation taken into account for purposes of determining the accrual of benefits under the plan (credited service), or provides for a reduced rate of accrual for credited service in excess of a fixed number of years. For this purpose, a limitation that is expressed as a percentage of compensation (whether averaged over a participant's total years of credited service for the employer or over a shorter period) is treated as a permissible limitation on the amount of benefits a participant may accrue under the plan.

(iii) *Examples.* The provisions of this paragraph (b)(3) may be illustrated by the following examples. In each of the examples, except as specifically indicated, normal retirement age is 65, the plan contains no limitations on the maximum amount of benefits the plan will pay to any participant (other than the limitations imposed by section 415), on the maximum number of years of credited service taken into account under the plan, or on the compensation used for purposes of determining the amount of any participant's accrued benefit (other than the limitation imposed by section 401(a)(17)), and the plan uses the following actuarial assumptions in determining actuarial equivalence: a 7.5% rate of interest and the 83 GAM (male) mortality table. The examples are as follows:

Example 1. (i) Plan M provides an accrued benefit of 1% of a participant's average annual compensation, multiplied by the participant's years of credited service under the plan payable in the normal form of a straight life annuity commencing at normal retirement age or the date of actual retirement if later. Plan M suspends payment of benefits for participants who work past normal retirement age, in accordance with section 411(a)(3)(B) and 29 CFR 2530.203-3 of the regulations of the Department of Labor, and does not provide for an actuarial increase in computing the accrued benefit for participants who commence benefits after normal retirement age.

(ii) The rate of benefit accrual for all participants in Plan M is 1% of average annual compensation. Thus, there could be no participant who would have a rate of benefit accrual that is greater than 1% if the individual were younger. Accordingly, there is no reduction in the rate of benefit accrual because of the individual's attainment of any age under this paragraph (b)(3) and Plan M satisfies the requirements of section 411(b)(1)(H) and this paragraph (b).

Example 2. (i) Assume the same facts as in *Example 1*, except that Plan M provides that not more than 35 years of credited service are taken into account in determining a participant's accrued benefit under the plan. Participant A became a participant in the plan at age 25 and worked continuously in covered service under Plan M until A retires at age 70.

(ii) The rate of benefit accrual under Plan M is 1% of average annual compensation for participants who have up to 35 years of credited service and zero for participants who have more than 35 years of credited service. Because a reduction from a rate of benefit accrual from 1% of average annual compensation to zero is based on service, and would not be affected if any participant were younger (with the same number of years of service), Plan M does not provide for a reduction in the rate of benefit accrual that is directly because of an individual's attainment of any age as provided in paragraph (b)(3)(i) of this section. Under paragraph (b)(3)(ii) of this section, a uniform limit on the number of years of service taken into account for purposes of determining the accrual of benefits under the plan is not considered to be a reduction in the rate of benefit accrual that is indirectly because of a participant's attainment of any age.

(iii) Upon A's retirement at age 70, A will have an accrued benefit under the plan's benefit formula of 35% of A's average annual compensation at age 70 (1% per year of credited service × 35 years of credited service). Plan M will not fail to satisfy the requirements of section 411(b)(1)(H) and this paragraph (b) merely because the plan provides that the final 10 years of A's service under the plan are not taken into account in determining A's accrued benefit. The result would be the same if Plan M provided that no participant could accrue a benefit in excess of 35% of the participant's average annual compensation.

Example 3. Assume the same facts as in *Example 1*, except that Plan M provides that a participant's years of service after attainment of social security retirement age are disregarded for purposes of determining a participant's accrued benefit under the plan. Because a participant who is covered under the plan after social security retirement age would have a higher rate of benefit accrual if he or she were younger (and had not attained social security retirement age), that participant's rate of benefit accrual is reduced directly because of the participant's attainment of any age under paragraph (b)(3)(i) of this section. Consequently, Plan M fails to satisfy the requirements of section 411(b)(1)(H) and this paragraph (b).

Example 4. (i) Assume the same facts as in *Example 1*, except that Plan M provides that a participant's compensation after the attainment of age 62 is not taken into account in determining the participant's accrued benefit under the plan.

(ii) Accordingly, the plan's measure of average compensation cannot be used in determining a participant's rate of benefit accrual because it does not apply to participants in a uniform manner that is independent of age. Because a participant who is or could be covered under Plan M after the attainment of age 62 whose compensation increases after age 62 would have a higher rate of benefit accrual if the participant were younger than age 62, that participant's rate of benefit accrual is reduced directly because of the participant's attainment of any age under paragraph (b)(3)(i) of this section. This reduction occurs whether or not there is any actual participant in Plan M who has attained age 62 or whose average annual compensation has increased after age 62. Consequently, the plan fails to satisfy the requirements of section 411(b)(1)(H) and this paragraph (b).

Example 5. (i) Assume the same facts as in *Example 1*, except that Plan M is amended to cease all benefit accruals for all participants and is subsequently terminated.

(ii) After all benefit accruals have ceased, the rate of benefit accrual of all participants is zero. Thus, there could not be any participant who would have a rate of benefit accrual that is greater than zero if the participant were younger, so that there is no reduction in the rate of benefit accrual that is because of the individual's attainment of any age under paragraph (b)(3) of this section. Accordingly, Plan M satisfies the requirements of section 411(b)(1)(H) and this paragraph (b).

Example 6. (i) Employer Y maintains Plan O, a defined benefit plan that provides an accrued benefit of 1% of a participant's highest 5 consecutive years of compensation, multiplied by the sum of the participant's age and years of service, payable in the normal form of a straight life annuity commencing at normal retirement age or the date of actual retirement if later. Plan O provides that a participant's years of service after the sum of a participant's age and years of service reach a total of 55 are disregarded for purposes of determining the normal retirement benefit. Participant C is 45 years old and has 10 years of credited service as of the beginning of a plan year. Thus, for that plan year, C's rate of benefit accrual is 1% of C's highest 5 consecutive years of compensation.

(ii) If C were younger, for example age 39 (with the same years of service), C would have a rate of benefit accrual of 2% of C's highest 5 consecutive years of compensation. Accordingly, C's rate of benefit accrual is reduced directly because of C's attainment of any age as provided in this paragraph (b)(3)(i). Consequently, Plan O fails to satisfy the requirements of section 411(b)(1)(H) and this paragraph (b).

Example 7. (i) Plan P is a defined benefit plan that provides for a normal retirement benefit of 40% of a participant's average compensa-

tion for the participant's highest 3 consecutive years of compensation, payable in the normal form of a straight life annuity commencing at normal retirement age or the date of actual retirement if later. If a participant separates from service prior to normal retirement age, Plan P provides a benefit equal to an amount that bears the same ratio to 40% of such average compensation as the participant's actual number of years of service bears to the number of years of service the participant would have if the participant's service continued to normal retirement age. As of the end of a plan year, participant D is 45 years old and has completed 20 years of service, and participant E is 41 years old and has completed 1 year of credited service. Thus, D's rate of benefit accrual for the plan year may be determined as 1% of compensation for D's highest 3 consecutive years, and E's rate of benefit accrual for the plan year may be determined as 1.6% of compensation for E's highest 3 consecutive years.

(ii) If D were younger than age 45 (with 20 years of service and the same compensation history), D's rate of benefit accrual for the plan year would not be greater than 1% of compensation for D's highest 3 consecutive years. Thus, there is no reduction in the rate of benefit accrual for D that is directly because of the individual's attainment of any age as provided in paragraph (b)(3)(i) of this section. In addition, there are no facts and circumstances indicating that D's rate of benefit accrual is reduced indirectly because of D's attainment of any age as provided in paragraph (b)(3)(ii) of this section. Likewise, if E were younger than age 41 (with 1 year of service and the same compensation history), E's rate of benefit accrual for the plan year would not be greater than 1.6% of compensation for E's highest 3 consecutive years. Thus, there is no reduction in the rate of benefit accrual for E that is directly because of the individual's attainment of any age as provided in paragraph (b)(3)(i) of this section. In addition, there are no facts and circumstances indicating that E's rate of benefit accrual is reduced indirectly because of E's attainment of any age under paragraph (b)(3)(ii) of this section. These same results would apply for any possible participant in Plan P. Accordingly, Plan P satisfies the requirements of section 411(b)(1)(H) and this paragraph (b).

Example 8. (i) Plan A is a defined benefit plan that provides for an accrued benefit of 2% of a participant's average compensation for the participant's highest 3 consecutive years of compensation for the first 20 years of service, plus 1% of such average compensation for years in excess of 20, payable in the normal form of a straight life annuity commencing at normal retirement age or the date of actual retirement if later. However, if a participant separates from service prior to normal retirement age, Plan P provides a benefit equal to an amount that bears the same ratio to the total percentage of such average compensation that the participant would have if service continued to normal retirement age as the participant's actual number of years of service bears to the number of years of service the participant would have if the participant's service continued to normal retirement age. For participants who work past normal retirement age, Plan A provides a benefit equal to 2% per year for years of service not in excess of 20, plus the following rate for years of service in excess of 20: the sum of 40% plus the product of 1% times service in excess of 20 years, with that sum divided by total service to the end of the current plan year. As of the beginning of the plan year beginning January 1, 2008, participant N is 64 years old and has completed 20 years of service, and participant O is 70 years old and has completed 20 years of credited service. Thus, N's rate of benefit accrual for that plan year may be determined as 1.95% of compensation for N's highest 3 consecutive years (2% for 20 years, plus 1% for 1 year, with that sum divided by 21 equals 1.95%), and O's rate of benefit accrual for that plan year also may be determined 1.95% of compensation for O's highest 3 consecutive years (40% for the first 20 years, plus 1% for service to the end of 2008, with that sum divided by 21 equals 1.95%).

(ii) If O were younger than age 70 (with 20 years of service and the same compensation history), O's rate of benefit accrual for the plan year would not be greater than 1.95% of compensation for O's highest 3 consecutive years. The same conclusion applies for any other possible participant. Thus, Plan A satisfies paragraph (b)(3)(ii) of this section.

(iii) However, if Plan A were instead to provide a rate of benefit accrual for service after normal retirement age equal to 2% for years of service not in excess of 20, plus 1% for service in excess of 20, Plan A would fail to satisfy paragraph (b)(3)(ii) of this section. For example, O's rate of benefit accrual would be 1% for 2008, whereas N's rate of benefit accrual would be 1.95% for 2008, even though the only difference between O and N is that N is younger.

Example 9. (i) The facts are similar to *Example 8*, except that the formula is 1% of a participant's average compensation for the participant's highest 3 consecutive years of compensation for the first 20 years, plus 2% of such average compensation for years in excess of 20, payable in the normal form of a straight life annuity commencing at normal retirement age or the date of actual retirement if later. As in *Example 8*, if a participant separates from service prior to normal retirement age, Plan P provides a benefit equal to an amount that bears the same ratio to the total average compensation that the participant would have if service continued to normal retirement age as the participant's actual number of years of service bears to the number of years of service the participant would have if the participant's service continued to normal retirement age. Further, similar to the facts in *Example 8*(iii) of this paragraph (b)(3)(iii), for participants who work past normal retirement age, Plan A provides a benefit equal to 1% per year for years of service not in excess of 20, plus 2% per year for years of service in excess of 20. As of the beginning of the plan year beginning January 1, 2008, participant K is 45 years old and has completed 10 years of service, and participant M is 55 years old and has completed 10 years of credited service. Thus, K's rate of benefit accrual for the plan year may be determined as 1.33% of compensation for K's highest 3 consecutive years (1% for 20 years, plus 2% for 10 more years, with the sum divided by 30 equals 1.33%), and M's rate of benefit accrual for the plan year may be determined as 1% of compensation for O's highest 3 consecutive years (1% for 20 years, with that amount divided by 20 equals 1%).

(ii) If M were younger than age 55 (with 10 years of service and the same compensation history), M's rate of benefit accrual for the plan year would be greater than 1% of compensation for M's highest 3 consecutive years. (Plan A also provides for an impermissible reduction in the rate of benefit accrual for a participant whose service continues after normal retirement age in a manner that is comparable to *Example 8*(iii) of this paragraph (b)(3)(iii).) Thus, Plan A fails to satisfy paragraph (b)(3)(ii) of this section.

Example 10. (i) Employer Z maintains Plan Q, a defined benefit plan that provides an accrued benefit of $40 per month multiplied by a participant's years of credited service. Participant F attains normal retirement age of 65 and continues in the full time service of Z. At age 65, F has 30 years of credited service under the plan and could receive a normal retirement benefit of $1,200 per month ($40 × 30 years) if F retires. The plan suspends benefits for participants who work past normal retirement age, in accordance with section 411(a)(3)(B) and 29 CFR 2530.203-3 of the regulations of the Department of Labor, and does not provide for any actuarial increase for employment past normal retirement age. Accordingly, the plan does not pay F's accrued benefit while F remains in the full time service of Z and does not provide for an actuarial adjustment of F's accrued benefit because of delayed payment. For example, if F retires at age 67, after completing 2 additional years of credited service for Z, F will receive a benefit of $1,280 per month ($40 × 32 years) commencing at age 67.

(ii) Under Plan Q, the rate of accrual for all participants is $40 per month. Thus, there could not be any participant who would have a rate of benefit accrual that is greater than $40 per month if the participant were younger, so that there is no reduction in the rate of benefit accrual that is because of the individual's attainment of any age under paragraph (b)(3)(i) of this section. Accordingly, Plan Q satisfies the requirements of section 411(b)(1)(H) and this paragraph (b).

Example 11. (i) Assume the same facts as in *Example 10*, except that the plan provides that the amount of F's benefit at normal retirement age will be actuarially increased for delayed retirement (even though

the plan suspends benefits for participants who work past normal retirement age), and this actuarially increased benefit will be paid if it exceeds the plan formula, but no actuarial increase is provided for any amount that is accrued after normal retirement age. The plan takes this actuarial increase into account as part of the rate of benefit accrual in plan years ending after F's attainment of normal retirement age, as provided under paragraph (b)(2)(ii) of this section.

(ii) Under section 411(b)(1)(H) and this paragraph (b), F's employment past normal retirement age cannot cause F's rate of benefit accrual for any year to be less than $40 for the year. Plan Q satisfies this requirement for the first year after normal retirement age because, under the plan, F is entitled to receive, upon retirement at the end of the year when F is age 66, an actuarially increased benefit of $1,344.68 per month, so that the rate of benefit accrual for the year is $144.68 (which is $1,344.68 minus $1,200).

(iii) Further, for the second year past normal retirement age ending when F is age 67, F must be entitled to a rate of benefit accrual of at least $149.50 per month, which is the highest rate of benefit accrual under Plan Q for any younger participant with 32 years of service at the end of the year. (In these facts, all participants have a rate of accrual of $40 until normal retirement age and a participant who is age 66 with 32 years of service at the end of the year would have a rate of benefit accrual of $149.50 due to an actuarial increase on an age 65 benefit of $1,240 per month.) Under the plan, F is entitled to receive, upon retirement at age 67, an actuarially increased benefit of $1,511.39 per month. Plan Q satisfies the requirement that F be entitled to the highest rate of benefit accrual provided to any younger participant because the rate of benefit accrual in that year ($1,511.39 minus $1,344.68 equals $166.71) is not less than what the rate would be for F if F were younger. These same results would apply for any possible participant in Plan Q. Accordingly, Plan Q satisfies the requirements of section 411(b)(1)(H) and this paragraph (b).

Example 12. (i) Employer Z maintains Plan R, a defined benefit plan that provides an accrued benefit of 2% of the average of a participant's high 3 consecutive years of compensation multiplied by the participant's years of credited service under the plan. Participant G, who has attained normal retirement age (age 65) under the plan, continues in the full time service of Z. At normal retirement age, G has average compensation of $40,000 for G's high 3 consecutive years and has 10 years of credited service under the plan. Thus, at normal retirement age, G is entitled to receive an annual normal retirement benefit of $8,000 ($40,000 × .02 × 10 years). Payment of G's retirement benefit is not suspended, and the plan provides that retirement benefits that commence after a participant's normal retirement age are actuarially increased for late retirement. Under the plan provision relating to actuarial increase, the actuarial increase for the plan year is made to the benefit that would have been paid had the participant retired as of the end of the preceding plan year. The plan then provides the greater of this actuarially increased benefit and benefits under the plan formula based on continued service, thereby including the actuarial increase in the rate of benefit accrual in plan years ending after G's attainment of normal retirement age, as provided in paragraph (b)(2)(ii) of this section. The foregoing is illustrated in the following table with respect to certain years of credited service performed by G after attaining normal retirement age 65. (Certain numbers may not total due to rounding.)

Age at start of plan year	Years of service at start of plan year	Average pay for high 3 consecutive years at start of plan year	Plan formula at start of plan year (.02 times column 2 times column 3)	Additional accruals for the plan year under plan formula (column 4 minus column 4 for prior year)	Annual benefit, as actuarially increased (column 8 from prior year actuarially increased)	Actuarial increase on the benefit (column 6 minus column 8 for prior year)	Annual benefit to which C is entitled at start of year (greater of column 4 or column 6)	Annual benefit as percent of average pay column 8) column 3)	Rate of benefit accrual (column 9 less column 9 for prior year)
(1)	(2)	(3)	(4)	(5)	(6)	(7)	(8)	(9)	(10)
65	10	$40,000 $8,000	n/a	n/a	n/a	$8,000	$9,240	2%	
66	11	$42,000	$9,240	$1,240	$8,964	$964	$9,240	22%	2%
67	12	$58,000	$13,920	$4,680	$10,386	$1,142	$13,920	24%	2%
68	13	$60,000	$15,600	$1,680	$15,697	$1,777	$15,697	26.16%	2.16%
69	14	$66,000	$18,480	$2,880	$17,762	$2,065	$18,480	28%	1.84%
70	15	$68,000	$20,400	$1,920	$20,989	$2,509	$20,989	30.87%	2.87%

(ii) In the year G is 69 at the beginning of the year, G's rate of benefit accrual (1.84% of the average high 3 consecutive years of compensation) is lower than the rate of benefit accrual that would apply to a younger participant because a participant who is younger than age 65 with the same number of years of credited service and compensation history would have a rate equal to 2% of average high 3 consecutive years of compensation. Accordingly, Plan R fails to satisfy the requirements of section 411(b)(1)(H) and this paragraph (b).

Example 13. (i) The facts are the same as in *Example 10*, except that, under the plan provisions relating to retirement after normal retirement age, a participant's benefit is equal to the sum of the benefit that would have been paid had the participant retired as of the end of the preceding plan year and the greater of the actuarial increase for the plan year on that amount or the otherwise applicable accrual for the plan year under the plan formula. The foregoing is illustrated in the following table with respect to certain years of credited service performed by G after attaining normal retirement age 65.

Age at start of plan year (1)	Years of service at start of plan year (2)	Average pay for high 3 consecutive years at start of plan year (3)	Plan formula at start of plan year (.02 times column 2 times column 3) (4)	Additional accruals for the plan year under plan formula (column 4 minus column 4 for prior year) (5)	Annual benefit, as actuarially increased (column 8 from prior year actuarially increased) (6)	Actuarial increase on the benefit at prior age (column 6 minus column 8 for prior year) (7)	Annual benefit to which C is entitled at start of year (column 8 at prior age plus the greater of column 5 and column 7) (8)	Annual benefit as percent of average pay column 8) column 3) (9)	Rate of benefit accrual (column 9 less column 9 for prior year) (10)
65	10	$40,000	$8,000	n/a	n/a	n/a	$8,000	20%	2%
66	11	$42,000	$9,240	$1,240	$8,964	$964	$9,240	22%	2%
67	12	$58,000	$13,920	$4,680	$10,386	$1,142	$13,920	24%	2%
68	13	$60,000	$15,600	$1,680	$15,697	$1,777	$15,697	26.16%	2.16%
69	14	$66,000	$18,480	$2,880	$17,762	$2,065	$18,577	28.1%	2%
70	15	$68,000	$20,400	$1,920	$21,098	$2,521	$21,098	31.03%	2.93%

(ii) In the year G is 69 at the beginning of the year, G's rate of benefit accrual (2% of the average high 3 consecutive years of compensation) is not lower than the rate that would apply to G if G were younger. For example, if G were age 68 with the same 14 years of credited service and compensation history that G has at age 69, G would have a rate of benefit accrual equal to 2% of average high 3 consecutive years of compensation (in contrast to *Example 12* in which the rate is 1.84% for an employee who is age 69 with 14 years of service, but would be 2% for younger employees with the same service and compensation history). Similar results would apply for any other potential younger participant in Plan R. Accordingly, Plan R satisfies the requirements of section 411(b)(1)(H) and this paragraph (b).

(iii) The decrease in G's rate of benefit accrual from 2.16% to 2% from age 68 to age 69 is not an impermissible reduction because of age. Under paragraph (b)(3) of this section, the determination of whether an impermissible reduction occurs because of age is made by comparing any potential participant's rate of benefit accrual to what the rate would be if the participant were younger (but with the same years of service, compensation history, and any other relevant factors taken into account under the plan), not by comparing a participant's rate in one year to that participant's rate in an earlier year. As indicated in paragraph (ii) of this *Example 13*, the rate of benefit accrual for a participant who is age 69 with 14 years of service at the beginning of the year is compared with the rate for all younger participants with the same service and compensation history. Similarly, the 2.16% rate for a participant who is age 68 with 13 years of service at the beginning of the year is compared with the rate for all younger participants with the same service and compensation history. Thus, for example, if G were age 67 with the same 13 years credited service and high 3 years of compensation equal to $60,000 that G has at age 68, G would have a rate of benefit accrual equal to 2.08% of average high 3 consecutive years of compensation.

(4) *Certain adjustments for benefit distributions—*(i) *In general.* Under section 411(b)(1)(H)(iii)(I), a defined benefit plan may provide that the requirement for continued benefit accrual under section 411(b)(1)(H)(i) and this paragraph (b) for a plan year is treated as satisfied to the extent of the actuarial equivalent of benefits distributed, as provided in this paragraph (b)(4). Distributions made before the participant attains normal retirement age or during a period that is not "section 203(a)(3)(B) service," as defined in 29 CFR 2530.203-3(c) of the regulations of the Department of Labor, may not be taken into account under this paragraph (b)(4).

(ii) *Amount of the adjustment for benefits distributed.* A defined benefit plan does not violate paragraph (b) of this section for a plan year merely because the rate of benefit accrual is reduced (but not below zero) to the extent of the actuarial equivalent of plan benefit distributions made to the participant during the plan year. For this purpose, distributions made during the plan year generally are disregarded for that year to the extent the actuarial value of the distributions exceeds the actuarial value of distributions that would have been made during the plan year had distribution of the participant's accrued benefit commenced at the beginning of the plan year (or, if later, at the participant's normal retirement age) in the normal form of benefit. (But see paragraph (b)(4)(iii) of this section for rules taking this excess into account at the end of the current year and in future years.) In addition, in any case in which the participant's benefits are being distributed in an optional form of benefit under which the amount payable annually is less than the amount payable under the plan's normal form of benefit (for example, a QJSA under which the annual benefit is less than the amount payable annually under a straight life annuity normal form), the plan may treat the participant as receiving payments under an actuari-

ally equivalent normal form of benefit for the plan year and all future plan years.

(iii) *Treatment of accelerated benefit payments—*(A) *Accelerated benefit payments.* This paragraph (b)(4)(iii) applies if the actuarial value of the distributions made to the participant during a plan year exceeds the actuarial value of the distributions that would have been made during the plan year had distributions commenced at the beginning of the plan year (or, if later, at the participant's normal retirement age) in the normal form of benefit. In such a case, the excess payments (referred to as accelerated benefit payments) are converted to an actuarially equivalent stream of annual benefit payments under the plan's normal form of benefit, commencing at the beginning of the next plan year. This conversion must be based on the same actuarial assumptions used under the plan to determine the distributions made to the participant during the plan year. For purposes of this paragraph (b)(4)(iii), the actuarially equivalent stream of annual benefit payments is referred to as the annuity equivalent of accelerated benefit payments.

(B) *Credit for annuity equivalent of accelerated benefit payments.* For purposes of applying paragraphs (b)(4)(ii) and (iii)(C) of this section, the annuity equivalent of accelerated benefit payments is deemed to be paid to the participant in each plan year that begins after the plan year during which any accelerated benefit payment under paragraph (b)(4)(iii)(A) of this section is made.

(C) *Effect of accelerated benefit payments on rate of benefit accrual.* If any accelerated benefit payments under paragraph (b)(4)(iii)(A) of this section have been made to a participant, then, in lieu of determining the participant's rate of benefit accrual under paragraph (b)(2)(ii) of this section, the participant's rate of benefit accrual for a plan year is determined as the excess (if any) of—

(*1*) The sum of the annual benefit to which the participant is entitled at the end of the current plan year, assuming payment commences in the normal form at the end of the current plan year, plus the amount deemed paid in the next plan year under the annuity equivalent of accelerated benefit payments; over

(*2*) The sum of the annual benefit to which the participant was entitled at the end of the preceding plan year, assuming that payment commences in the normal form at the later of normal retirement age and the end of the preceding plan year, plus the amount deemed paid during the current plan year under the annuity equivalent of accelerated benefit payments.

(iv) *Examples.* The provisions of this paragraph (b)(4) may be illustrated by the following examples. In each of the examples, except as otherwise indicated, normal retirement age is 65 and the birthday of each participant is assumed to be January 1. In addition, except as otherwise indicated, the plan contains no limitations on the maximum amount of benefits the plan will pay to any participant (other than the limitations imposed by section 415), on the maximum number of years of credited service taken into account under the plan, or on the compensation used for purposes of determining the amount of any participant's normal retirement benefit (other than the limitation imposed by section 401(a)(17)) and the plan uses the following actuarial assumptions for purposes of determining the amount of any participant's accrued benefit (other than the limitation imposed by section 401(a)(17)), and the plan uses the following actuarial assumptions in determining actuarial equivalence: a 7.5% rate of interest and the 83 GAM (male) mortality table. The examples are as follows:

Example 1. (i) *Facts relating to the year in which participant attains age 65.* Employer Z maintains Plan Q, a defined benefit plan that provides an accrued benefit of $40 per month multiplied by the participant's years of credited service. Participant F attains normal retirement age of 65 on January 1 and continues in the full time service of Z. At the end of the year in which F attains age 65, F has 30 years of credited service under the plan and could receive an accrued benefit of $1,200 per month ($40 × 30 years) if F retires. Plan Q does not suspend payment of benefits for participants who work past normal retirement age and F commences benefit payments at normal retirement age. (These are the same facts as in *Example 10* of paragraph (b)(3)(iii) of this section, except that the Plan Q does not provide for the suspension of normal retirement benefit payments.) The plan offsets the value of the benefit distributions against benefit accruals in plan years ending after the participant's attainment of normal retirement age, as permitted by paragraph (b)(4)(ii) of this section. Participant F (who remains in the full time service of Y) receives 12 monthly benefit payments after attainment of age 65 and prior to attainment of age 66. The total monthly benefit payments of $14,400 ($1,200 × 12 payments) have an actuarial value at the end of the year in which F turns 65 of $15,118 (reflecting interest and mortality) which would produce a monthly life annuity benefit of $145 commencing at age 66. The rate of benefit accrual otherwise applicable under the plan formula for the year of credited service F completes after attaining normal retirement age is $40 per month.

(ii) *Conclusions relating to the year in which F attains age 65.* Because the actuarial value (determined as a monthly benefit of $145) of the benefit payments made during the first year after F's attainment of normal retirement age exceeds the benefit accrual otherwise applicable for the first year after F's attainment of normal retirement age, the plan is not required to accrue benefits on behalf of F for the one year of credited service after F's attainment of normal retirement age and the plan is not required to increase F's monthly benefit payment of $1,200 during the year in which F attains age 65.

(iii) *Facts relating to the year in which F attains age 66.* Assume F receives 12 additional monthly benefit payments the next year prior to F's retirement at the end of the next year when F attains age 66. The total monthly benefit payments of $14,400 ($1,200 × 12 payments) have an actuarial value at the end of that year of $15,135 (reflecting interest and mortality) which would produce a monthly benefit payment of $149 commencing at age 67. The rate of benefit accrual otherwise applicable under the plan formula for the additional year of credited service F completed that year is $40 per month.

(iv) *Conclusions relating to the year in which F attains age 66.* Because the actuarial value (determined as a monthly benefit of $149) of the benefit payments made during that year exceeds the benefit accrual otherwise applicable for the additional year of credited service,

the plan is not required to accrue benefits on behalf of F for the second year of credited service F completed after attaining normal retirement age and the plan is not required to increase F's monthly benefit payment of $1,200.

Example 2. (i) *Facts.* Employer Z maintains Plan R, a defined benefit plan that provides an accrued benefit of 2% of the average of a participant's high 3 consecutive years of compensation multiplied by the participant's years of credited service under the plan. Payment of a participant's retirement benefit is not suspended, and the plan provides that retirement benefits that commence after a participant's normal retirement age are actuarially increased for late retirement. Under the plan provision relating to actuarial increase, the actuarial increase for the plan year is made to the benefit that would have been paid had the participant retired as of the end of the preceding plan year. The plan then provides the greater of this actuarially increased benefit and benefits under the plan formula based on continued service, thereby including the actuarial increase in the rate of benefit accrual in plan years ending after attainment of normal retirement age, as provided in paragraph (b)(2)(ii) of this section. Participant G, who has attained normal retirement age (age 65) under the plan, continues in the full time service of Z. At normal retirement age, G has average compensation of $40,000 for G's high 3 consecutive years and has 10 years of credited service under the plan. Thus, at normal retirement age, G is entitled to receive an annual normal retirement benefit of $8,000 ($40,000 × .02 × 10 years). G continues working after normal retirement age, with G's average compensation increasing to $68,000 at age 70. (The facts in this *Example 2* are the same as *Example 13* of paragraph (b)(3)(ii) of this section, except that the employee does not retire at age 70, but continues in the full time service of Z.) Upon G's attainment of age 70, the plan commences benefit payments to G. The annual benefit paid to G in the first plan year is $21,098. In determining the annual benefit payable to G in each subsequent plan year, the plan offsets the value of benefit distributions made to the participant by the close of the prior plan year against benefit accruals otherwise applicable in plan years during which such distributions were made, as permitted by paragraph (b)(4)(ii)(B) of this section.

(ii) *Conclusion.* Accordingly, for each subsequent plan year, G is entitled under the plan to receive benefit payments based on G's benefit at the close of the prior plan year, plus the excess (if any) of the benefit for the plan year determined under the plan formula otherwise applicable over the value of total benefit distributions made to G during the plan year. The foregoing is illustrated in the following table with respect to certain years of credited service performed by G while benefits were being distributed to G.

Age at start of plan year (1)	Years of service at start of plan year (2)	Average pay for high 3 consecutive years at start of plan year (3)	Additional accruals for the plan year under plan formula (column 4 minus column 4 for prior year) (4)	Benefit distributions made during the prior year (5)	Annual benefit that is actuarial equivalent of column 6 (6)	Annual benefit to which G is entitled at end of the year (column 8 for prior year, plus the excess, if any of column 5 for the current year, over column 7 for current year) (7)	(8)
70	15	$68,000	$20,400	$1,920	none	none	$21,098
71	16	$70,000	$22,400	$2,000	$21,098	$2,799	$21,098
72	17	$90,000	$30,600	$8,200	$21,098	$2,891	$26,407
73	18	$100,000	$36,000	$5,400	$26,407	$3,743	$28,065

Example 3. (i) *Facts relating to the year in which a participant attains age 65.* Plan X provides an accrued benefit equal to 1% of the average of a participant's highest 3 consecutive years of compensation times the participant's years of service, payable in the normal form of a straight life annuity commencing at normal retirement age or at the date of actual retirement if later. Plan X permits a participant who is an employee to commence distributions after attainment of normal retirement age (age 65) and provides for benefits otherwise accrued after normal retirement age to be offset by the actuarial equivalent of any benefit distributions made to the participant. Plan X provides for a participant who does not commence distributions to receive an actuarial increase for the year from the amount payable at the end of the preceding year (if greater than the amount otherwise accrued for H during the year under X's formula). Participant H attains age 65 on the first day of a plan year when Participant H's average highest 3 consecutive years of compensation is $60,000 and H has 20 years of service. Accordingly, Participant H's accrued benefit at the beginning of the year is equal to a straight life annuity of $1,000 per month (20% times $60,000 divided by 12) commencing at the beginning of the year. Participant H elects to receive a single-sum distribution of $130,389 at the beginning of the year, which is equal to the present value of H's

accrued benefit under section 417(e) at that time. Participant H continues to work through the end of the plan year and at the end of the year has average compensation of $60,000 for the year. Plan X uses the actuarial assumptions specified in section 417(e) for purposes of determining actuarial equivalence. For purposes of this *Example 3*, the applicable interest rate under section 417(e) is assumed to be 6%, and the applicable mortality table under section 417(e) is the mortality table in effect on January 1, 2003.

(ii) *Conclusion relating to effect of distributions made in the year H attains age 65.* Under this paragraph (b)(4), H would otherwise accrue an additional monthly benefit of $50 for the additional year of service under the plan's formula (21% times $60,000 minus 20% times $60,000, divided by 12). The plan is permitted under section 411(b)(1)(H)(iii)(I) to offset additional accruals otherwise applicable after normal retirement age by the actuarial value of distributions made during the year. However, under paragraph (b)(4)(ii) of this section, distributions made during a plan year are disregarded to the extent that the actuarial value of the distributions exceeds the actuarial value of distributions that would have been made during the plan year had distribution of the participant's accrued benefit commenced at the beginning of the plan year under the plan's normal form.

(iii) *Conclusion relating to calculations for distribution made in the year H attains age 65.* At the end of the year, the actuarial value of the distribution made to H ($130,389 plus interest and mortality for the year equals $139,812) is greater than the year end actuarial value of distributions that would have been made during the plan year had distribution of the participant's accrued benefit at the beginning of the plan year commenced in the normal form at the beginning of the plan year (which is $12,470, based on the plan's actuarial assumptions). Accordingly, the $127,342 excess (referred to as an accelerated benefit payment) is disregarded in the current year. (However, as described below, the annuity equivalent of the $127,342 is deemed to be paid to H commencing at the beginning of the first plan year after the plan year during which the accelerated benefit payment is made.)

(iv) *Conclusion relating to rate of benefit accrual for the year H attains age 65.* To determine the rate of benefit accrual for the year in which H attains age 65, the annuity equivalent of accelerated benefit payments is calculated and, under paragraph (b)(4)(iii)(C) of this section, this amount is treated as part of the benefit payable at the end of the year in calculating the rate of benefit accrual for the year. In this *Example 3*, the annuity equivalent of the $127,342 accelerated benefit payment equals a straight life annuity of $1,000 per month commencing at the beginning of the next plan year. Thus, for purposes of applying paragraph (b)(4)(iii) of this section to determine the rate of benefit accrual for the plan year in which H attains age 65, paragraph (b)(4)(iii)(C)(*1*) of this section is an annual straight life annuity commencing at end of the year equal to $1,000 (the sum of the annual benefit to which the H is entitled at the end of the plan year, which is zero in this case, plus the amount deemed paid in the next plan year under the annuity equivalent of accelerated benefit payments, which is $1,000 in this case) and the amount in paragraph (b)(4)(iii)(C)(*2*) of this section is an annual straight life annuity commencing at end of the preceding plan year equal to $1,000. Thus, H's rate of benefit accrual for the year is zero.

(v) *Conclusion relating to whether rate of benefit accrual for year H attains age 65 satisfies section 411(b)(1)(H).* Under paragraph (b)(4)(ii) of this section, a plan may reduce the rate of benefit accrual otherwise applicable to the extent of distributions made during the year. The actuarial equivalent of $12,470 (the actuarial value of the 12 $1,000 monthly payments deemed paid to H during the plan year under paragraph (b)(4)(ii) of this section) is a straight life annuity commencing at the end of the plan year equal to $98 per month. Thus, the otherwise applicable accrual for the year may be reduced (but not below zero) by $98 per month. The highest rate of benefit accrual for any participant with H's service and compensation history who is younger is an annual straight life annuity of $50 per month. Because the permissible reduction of $98 per month is not less than the otherwise applicable accrual of $50 per month, Plan X is not required by this paragraph (b) for the year and section 411(b)(1)(H) to provide H with any additional accruals for the year.

(vi) *Conclusion relating to rate of benefit accrual for year H attains age 65 if no distribution were made.* If Participant H had not elected to receive any distribution during the plan year, then H's accrued benefit at the end of the year would be a straight life annuity of $1,098 per month commencing at the end of the year (which is actuarially equivalent to a straight life annuity of $1,000 per month commencing at the beginning of the year). Thus, H's rate of benefit accrual for that year would be $98 (but no adjustments for any distribution would apply).

(vii) *Facts relating to next year in which H attains age 66.* Participant H works another year and H's average compensation becomes $70,000. Under this paragraph (b)(4), H would otherwise accrue an additional monthly benefit of $233 for the additional year of service under the plan's formula (22% times $70,000, minus 21% times $60,000, divided by 12). However, the plan is permitted under section 411(b)(1)(H)(iii)(I) to offset additional accruals after normal retirement age by the actuarial value of distributions made during the year. Under paragraph (b)(4)(iii)(B) of this section, the $1,000 annuity equivalent of accelerated benefit payments is deemed to be paid to H during this second year when H attains age 66. These deemed payments are actuarially equivalent to an accrual of $100 per month payable at the end of that year. Accordingly, the plan reduces the otherwise applicable accrual of $233 to the extent of the accrual of $100 per month payable at the end of the year in which H attains age 66. Thus, the $233 accrual during the year in which H becomes 66 is reduced by $100 to $133. Under the plan X, H's accrued benefit at the end of the year is $133 per month.

(viii) *Conclusion relating to rate of benefit accrual for year H attains age 66.* To determine the rate of benefit accrual for the second year when H attains age 66, the annuity equivalent of accelerated benefit payments is calculated and, under paragraph (b)(4)(iii)(C) of this section, this amount is treated as part of the benefit payable at the end

of the year in calculating the rate of benefit accrual for the second year. In this *Example 3*, the annuity equivalent of the $127,342 accelerated benefit payment that was made in the year in which H attained age 65 equals a straight life annuity of $1,000 per month commencing at the beginning of the next plan year. Thus, for purposes of applying paragraph (b)(4)(iii) of this section to determine the rate of benefit accrual for the second plan year, the amount in paragraph (b)(4)(iii)(C)(*1*) of this section is an annual straight life annuity commencing at end of the year equal to $1,133 (the sum of the annual benefit to which the H is entitled at the end of the plan year, which is $133 in this case, plus the amount deemed paid in the next plan year under the annuity equivalent of accelerated benefit payments, which is $1,000 in this case) and the amount in paragraph (b)(4)(iii)(C)(*2*) of this section is an annual straight life annuity commencing at end of the preceding plan year equal to $1,000. Thus, H's rate of benefit accrual for the year in which H becomes age 66 is $133.

(ix) *Conclusion relating to whether rate of benefit accrual for year H becomes 66 satisfies section 411(b)(1)(H).* Under paragraph (b)(4)(ii) of this section, a plan may reduce the rate of benefit accrual to the extent of distributions made during the year. The actuarial equivalent of $12,480 (the actuarial value of the 12 $1,000 monthly payments deemed made to H during the plan year) is a straight life annuity commencing at the end of the plan year equal to $100 per month. Thus, the otherwise applicable accrual for the year may be reduced (but not below zero) by $100 per month. The highest rate of benefit accrual for any participant with H's service and compensation history who is younger is an annual straight life annuity of $233 per month. Thus, because the sum of $133 and $100 is not less than the otherwise applicable accrual of $233 per month, Plan X satisfies this paragraph (b) and section 411(b)(1)(H) for the year.

(c) *Defined contribution plans*—(1) *In general.* A defined contribution plan (including a target benefit plan described in § 1.410(a)-4(a)(1)) does not satisfy the requirements of section 411(b)(2) if the rate of allocation made to the account of a participant is reduced, either directly or indirectly, because of the participant's attainment of any age. A reduction in the rate of allocation includes any discontinuance in the allocation of employer contributions or forfeitures to the account of the participant or cessation of participation in the plan.

(2) *Rate of allocation*—(i) *Aggregate allocations.* For purposes of this paragraph (c), a participant's rate of allocation for any plan year is the aggregate allocations taken into account for the plan year under § 1.401(a)(4)-2(c)(2).

(ii) *Determination of rate of allocation.* A participant's rate of allocation for a plan year can be determined as a dollar amount. Alternatively, if a plan's formula bases a participant's allocations solely on compensation for the plan year and compensation is determined without regard to attainment of any age, then a participant's rate of allocation can be determined as a percentage of the participant's compensation for the plan year.

(3) *Reduction that is directly or indirectly because of a participant's attainment of any age*—(i) *Reduction in rate of allocation that is directly because of a participant's attainment of any age.* A plan provides for a reduction in the rate of allocation that is directly because of a participant's attainment of any age for any plan year if, under the terms of the plan, any participant's rate of allocation for the plan year would be higher if the participant were younger. Thus, a plan fails to satisfy section 411(b)(2) and this paragraph (c) if, under the terms of the plan, the rate of allocation for any individual who is or could be a participant under the plan would be lower solely as a result of such individual being older.

(ii) *Reduction in rate of allocation that is indirectly because of a participant's attainment of any age*—(A) *In general.* A plan provides for a reduction in the rate of allocation that is indirectly because of a participant's attainment of any age for any plan year if any participant's rate of allocation for the plan year would be higher if the participant were to have a characteristic that is a proxy for being younger, based on all of the relevant facts and circumstances. Thus, a plan fails to satisfy section 411(b)(2) and this paragraph (c) if the rate of allocation for any individual who is or could be a participant under the plan would be lower solely as a result of such individual having a different characteristic which is a proxy for being older, based on applicable facts and circumstances.

(B) *Treatment of limitations.* A reduction in a participant's rate of allocation is not indirectly because of the attainment of any age in violation of section 411(b)(2) solely because of a positive correlation between attainment of any age and a reduction in the rate of allocation. Thus, a defined contribution plan (including a target benefit plan described in § 1.410(a)-4(a)(1)) does not fail to satisfy the minimum vesting standards of section 411(a) solely because the plan limits the total amount of employer contributions and forfeitures that may be allocated to a participant's account (for a particular plan year or for the participant's total years of credited service under the plan), solely because the plan limits the total number of years of credited service for which a participant's account may receive allocations of employer contributions and forfeitures, or solely because the plan limits the number of years of credited service that may be taken into account for purposes of determining the amount of, or the rate at which, employer contributions and forfeitures are allocated to a participant's account for a particular plan year.

(iii) *Special rule for target benefit plans.* A defined contribution plan that is a target benefit plan, as defined in §1.410(a)-4(a)(1), satisfies section 411(b)(2) only if the defined benefit formula used to determine allocations would satisfy section 411(b)(1)(H) without regard to section 411(b)(1)(H)(iii). Such a target benefit plan does not fail to satisfy this paragraph (c) with respect to allocations after normal retirement age merely because the allocation for a plan year is reduced to reflect shorter longevity using a reasonable actuarial assumption regarding mortality.

(iv) *Additional rules.* The Commissioner may prescribe additional guidance, published in the Internal Revenue Bulletin (see §601.601(d)(2)(ii)(b) of this chapter), with respect to the application of section 411(b)(2) and this section to target benefit plans.

(d) *Benefits and forms of benefits subject to requirements*—(1) *General rule.* Except as provided in paragraph (d)(2) or (3) of this section, sections 411(b)(1)(H) and 411(b)(2) and paragraphs (b) and (c) of this section apply to all benefits (and forms of benefits) provided under the plan, including accrued benefits, benefits described in section 411(d)(6), ancillary benefits, and other rights and features provided under the plan. Accordingly, except as provided in paragraph (d)(2) or (3) of this section, a participant's rate of benefit accrual under a defined benefit plan and a participant's allocations under a defined contribution plan are considered to be reduced because of the participant's attainment of any age if optional forms of benefits, ancillary benefits, or other rights or features under the plan provided with respect to benefits or allocations attributable to credited service prior to the attainment of the participant's age are not provided on at least as favorable a basis with respect to benefits or allocations attributable to credited service after attainment of the participant's age. Thus, for example, a plan may not provide a single-sum payment only with respect to benefits attributable to years of credited service before the attainment of a specified age. Similarly, except as provided in paragraph (d)(2) or (3) of this section, if an optional form of benefit is available under the plan at a specified age, the availability of that form of benefit, or the method for determining the manner in which that form of benefit is paid, may not, directly or indirectly, be denied or provided on terms less favorable to participants because of the attainment of any age. Similarly, if the method for determining the amount or the rate of the subsidized portion of a joint and survivor annuity or the subsidized portion of a preretirement survivor annuity is less favorable with respect to participants who have attained a specified age than with respect to participants who have not attained such age, benefit accruals or account allocations under the plan will be considered to be reduced because of the attainment of such age.

(2) *Special rule for actuarial assumptions regarding mortality.* A plan does not fail to satisfy section 411(b)(1)(H) or this paragraph (d) merely because the plan makes actuarial adjustments using a reasonable assumption regarding mortality to calculate optional forms of benefit or to calculate the cost of providing a qualified preretirement survivor annuity, as defined in section 417(c).

(3) *Special rule for certain benefits.* A plan does not fail to satisfy section 411(b)(1)(H) or this paragraph (d) merely because the following benefits, or the manner in which such benefits are provided under the plan, vary because of the attainment of any higher age—

(i) The subsidized portion of an early retirement benefit (whether provided on a temporary or permanent basis);

(ii) A qualified disability benefit (as defined in §1.411(a)-7(c)(3)); or

(iii) A social security supplement (as defined in §1.411(a)-7(c)(4)(ii)).

(e) *Coordination with certain provisions.* Notwithstanding section 411(b)(1)(H), section 411(b)(2), and paragraphs (a) through (d) of this section, the following rules apply—

(1) *Section 415 limitations.* No benefit accrual with respect to a participant in a defined benefit plan is required for a plan year by section 411(b)(1)(H)(i) and no allocation to the account of a participant in a defined contribution plan (including a target benefit plan described in §1.410(a)-4(a)(1)) is required for a plan year by section 411(b)(2) to

the extent that the allocation or accrual would cause the plan to exceed the limitations of section 415.

(2) *Prohibited discrimination*—(i) No benefit accrual on behalf of a highly compensated employee in a defined benefit plan is required for a plan year by section 411(b)(1)(H)(i) to the extent such benefit accrual would cause the plan to discriminate in favor of highly compensated employees within the meaning of section 401(a)(4).

(ii) No allocation to the account of a highly compensated employee in a defined contribution plan (including a target benefit plan) is required for a plan year by section 411(b)(2) to the extent the allocation would cause the plan to discriminate in favor of highly compensated employees within the meaning of section 401(a)(4).

(iii) The Commissioner may provide additional guidance, published in the Internal Revenue Bulletin (see §601.601(d)(2)(ii)(b) of this chapter), relating to prohibited discrimination in favor of highly compensated employees.

(3) *Permitted disparity.* A defined benefit plan does not fail to satisfy section 411(b)(1)(H) for a plan year and a defined contribution plan does not fail to satisfy 411(b)(2) for a plan year merely because accruals or allocations under the plan are reduced to satisfy the uniformity requirements of §1.401(l)-2(c) or 1.401(l)-3(c) for the plan year.

(4) *Distribution rights under section 411.* A defined benefit plan does not fail to satisfy section 411(b)(1)(H) for a plan year and a defined contribution plan does not fail to satisfy 411(b)(2) for a plan year merely because of the right to defer distributions provided under section 411(a)(11) or a plan provision consistent with section 411(a)(11).

(f) *Effective dates*—(1) *Effective date of sections 411(b)(1)(H) and 411(b)(2) for noncollectively bargained plans*—(i) *In general.* Except as otherwise provided in paragraph (f)(2) of this section, sections 411(b)(1)(H) and 411(b)(2) are applicable for plan years beginning on or after January 1, 1988, with respect to a participant who is credited with at least 1 hour of service in a plan year beginning on or after January 1, 1988. Neither section 411(b)(1)(H) nor section 411(b)(2) is applicable with respect to a participant who is not credited with at least 1 hour of service in a plan year beginning on or after January 1, 1988.

(ii) *Defined benefit plans.* In the case of a participant who is credited with at least 1 hour of service in a plan year beginning on or after January 1, 1988, section 411(b)(1)(H) is applicable with respect to all years of service completed by the participant other than plan years beginning before January 1, 1988.

(iii) *Defined contribution plans.* Section 411(b)(2) does not apply with respect to allocations of employer contributions or forfeitures to the accounts of participants under a defined contribution plan for a plan year beginning before January 1, 1988.

(iv) *Hour of service.* For purposes of this paragraph (f)(1), 1 hour of service means 1 hour of service recognized under the plan or required to be recognized under the plan by section 410 (relating to minimum participation standards) or section 411 (relating to minimum vesting standards). In the case of a plan that does not determine service on the basis of hours of service, 1 hour of service means any service recognized under the plan or required to be recognized under the plan by section 410 (relating to minimum participation standards) or section 411 (relating to minimum vesting standards).

(2) *Effective date of sections 411(b)(1)(H) and 411(b)(2) for collectively bargained plans*—(i) In the case of a plan maintained pursuant to 1 or more collective bargaining agreements between employee representatives and 1 or more employers, ratified before March 1, 1986, sections 411(b)(1)(H) and 411(b)(2) are applicable for benefits provided under, and employees covered by, any such agreement with respect to plan years beginning on or after the later of—

(A) January 1, 1988; or

(B) The earlier of January 1, 1990, or the date on which the last of such collective bargaining agreements terminates (determined without regard to any extension of any such agreement occurring on or after March 1, 1986).

(ii) The applicability date provisions of paragraph (f)(1) of this section shall apply in the same manner to plans described in paragraph (f)(2)(i) of this section, except that the applicable date determined under paragraph (f)(2)(i) of this section shall be substituted for the effective date determined under paragraph (f)(1) of this section.

(iii) In accordance with the provisions of paragraph (f)(2)(i) of this section, a plan described therein may be subject to different applicability dates under sections 411(b)(1)(H) and 411(b)(2) for employees who are covered by a collective bargaining agreement and employees who are not covered by a collective bargaining agreement.

(iv) For purposes of paragraph (f)(2)(i) of this section, the service crediting rules of paragraph (f)(1) of this section shall apply to a plan described in paragraph (f)(2)(i) of this section, except that in applying such rules the applicability date determined under paragraph (f)(2)(i) of this section shall be substituted for the applicability date determined under paragraph (f)(1) of this section. See paragraph (f)(1)(iv) of this section for rules relating to the recognition of an hour of service.

(3) *Regulatory effective date.* Paragraphs (a) through (e) of this section are applicable with respect to plan years beginning on or after the date of publication of final regulations in the **Federal Register**.

David A. Mader

Assistant Deputy Commissioner of Internal Revenue.

¶ 20,260T

IRS proposed regulations: Split-dollar life insurance: Tax-free compensation.—The IRS has issued proposed regulations supplementing previous guidance in proposed regulations (see CCH PENSION PLAN GUIDE ¶ 29,260M) on the valuation of certain equity split-dollar life insurance arrangements, designed to prevent companies from using such arrangements to provide tax-free compensation to executives. The IRS is requesting comments on the clarity of the proposed regulations. Comments must be received by July 8, 2003 for the public hearing to be held on July 29, 2003.

The proposed regulations, which were published in the Federal Register on May 9, 2003 (68 FR 24898), are reproduced below.

DEPARTMENT OF THE TREASURY

Internal Revenue Service

26 CFR Part 1

[REG-164754-01]

RIN 1545-BA44

Split-Dollar Life Insurance Arrangements

AGENCY: Internal Revenue Service (IRS), Treasury.

ACTION: Notice of proposed rulemaking and notice of public hearing.

SUMMARY: This document contains proposed regulations relating to the valuation of economic benefits under certain equity split-dollar life insurance arrangements. The proposed regulations will provide needed guidance to persons who enter into split-dollar life insurance arrangements. This document also provides notice of a public hearing on the proposed regulations.

DATES: Written or electronic comments must be received by July 8, 2003. Requests to speak and outlines of topics to be discussed at the public hearing scheduled for July 29, 2003, must be received by July 8, 2003.

ADDRESSES: Send submissions to CC:PA:RU (REG-164754-01), room 5226, Internal Revenue Service, POB 7604, Ben Franklin Station, Washington, DC 20044. Submissions may be hand delivered Monday through Friday between the hours of 8 a.m. and 4 p.m. to: CC:PA:RU (REG-164754-01). Courier's Desk, Internal Revenue Service, 1111 Constitution Avenue, NW., Washington, DC or sent electronically, via the IRS Internet site at www.irs.gov/regs. The public hearing will be held in the IRS Auditorium, Internal Revenue Building, 1111 Constitution Avenue, NW., Washington, DC.

FOR FURTHER INFORMATION CONTACT: Concerning the regulations, please contact Elizabeth Kaye at (202) 622-4920. To be placed on the attendance list for the hearing, please contact LaNita M. Vandyke at (202) 622-7180.

SUPPLEMENTARY INFORMATION:

Background and Overview of Notice of Proposed Rulemaking

1. *Summary of the Prior Notice of Proposed Rulemaking*

On July 9, 2002, a notice of proposed rulemaking (REG-164754-01) was published in the **Federal Register** (67 FR 45414) proposing comprehensive rules for the income, gift, and employment taxation of equity and non-equity split-dollar life insurance arrangements (the 2002 proposed regulations). The 2002 proposed regulations will apply to split-dollar life insurance arrangements entered into after the date final regulations are published in the **Federal Register** and to arrangements entered into on or before that date that are materially modified after that date. Under certain conditions, taxpayers may rely on the 2002 proposed regulations for split-dollar life insurance arrangements entered into on or before the date final regulations are published in the **Federal Register.**

In general, a split-dollar life insurance arrangement is an arrangement between two or more parties to allocate the policy benefits and, in some cases, the costs of a life insurance contract. Under a so-called equity split-dollar life insurance arrangement, one party to the arrangement typically receives an interest in the policy cash value (or equity) of the life insurance policy disproportionate to that party's share of

policy premiums. That party also typically receives the benefit of current life insurance protection under the arrangement. Under a so-called non-equity split-dollar life insurance arrangement, one party typically provides the other party with current life insurance protection but not any interest in the policy cash value.

The 2002 proposed regulations provide two mutually exclusive regimes for taxation of split-dollar life insurance arrangements—a loan regime and an economic benefit regime. Under the loan regime (which is set forth in § 1.7872-15 of the 2002 proposed regulations), the non-owner of the life insurance contract is treated as loaning the amount of its premium payments to the owner of the contract. The loan regime generally will govern the taxation of collateral assignment arrangements. Under the economic benefit regime (which is set forth in § 1.61-22(d) through (g) of the 2002 proposed regulations), the owner of the life insurance contract is treated as providing economic benefits to the non-owner of the contract. The economic benefit regime generally will govern the taxation of endorsement arrangements.

The 2002 proposed regulations reserved on the rules for valuing economic benefits provided to the non-owner under an equity split-dollar life insurance arrangement governed by the economic benefit regime, pending receipt of comments from interested parties. The preamble to the 2002 proposed regulations notes that any proposal "for a specific methodology should be objective and administrable" and describes a potential approach under which the non-owner would include in income the difference between current premium payments and the net present value of the amount to be repaid to the owner in the future.

A public hearing on the 2002 proposed regulations was held on October 23, 2002. In addition, interested parties have submitted detailed comments on the 2002 proposed regulations, including comments on the valuation of economic benefits provided to a non-owner under an equity split-dollar life insurance arrangement governed by the economic benefit regime.

2. *Explanation of Provisions and Summary of Comments*

a. *Overview*

These proposed regulations, which supplement the 2002 proposed regulations, provide guidance on the valuation of economic benefits (including the valuation of an interest in policy cash value) under an equity split-dollar life insurance arrangement governed by the economic benefit regime. These proposed regulations apply for purposes of Federal income, employment, and gift taxes.

These proposed regulations address only those comments received by the IRS and the Treasury Department on the valuation of economic benefits under an equity split-dollar life insurance arrangement governed by the economic benefit regime. Comments received on other issues regarding the 2002 proposed regulations and comments on these proposed regulations will be addressed when both sets of proposed regulations are finalized.

These proposed regulations provide that in the case of an equity split-dollar life insurance arrangement, the value of the economic benefits provided to the non-owner under the arrangement for a taxable year equals the cost of any current life insurance protection provided to the non-owner, the amount of policy cash value to which the non-owner has current access (to the extent that such amount was not actually taken into account for a prior taxable year), and the value of any other economic benefits provided to the non-owner (to the extent not actually taken into account for a prior taxable year). The terms *owner* and *non-owner* are defined in § 1.61-22(c)(1) and (2) of the 2002 proposed regulations.

b. *Current access to policy cash value*

Generally, under an equity split-dollar life insurance arrangement governed by the economic benefit regime, the owner of the life insurance contract pays policy premiums, thereby establishing a pool of assets with respect to which the non-owner has certain rights under the arrangement (for example, rights of withdrawal, borrowing, surrender, or assignment). Additionally, the pool of assets is held by a third party, the life insurance company, effectively placing the cash value beyond the reach of the employer or the employer's general creditors in many cases. Thus, an equity splitdollar life insurance arrangement confers on the non-owner rights to direct or indirect economic enjoyment of policy cash value, making current taxation of the non-owner's interest in the cash value appropriate under the doctrines of constructive receipt, economic benefit, and cash equivalence.

These proposed regulations provide that the non-owner has current access to any portion of the policy cash value that is directly or indirectly accessible by the non-owner, inaccessible to the owner, or inaccessible to the owner's general creditors. For this purpose, access is to be construed broadly and includes any direct or indirect right under the arrangement of the non-owner to obtain, use, or realize potential economic value from the policy cash value. Thus, for example, a non-owner has current access to policy cash value if the non-owner can directly or indirectly make a withdrawal from the policy, borrow from the policy, or effect a total or partial surrender of the policy. Similarly, for example, the non-owner has current access if the non-owner can anticipate, assign (either at law or in equity), alienate, pledge, or encumber the policy cash value or if the policy cash value is available to the non-owner's creditors by attachment, garnishment, levy, execution, or other legal or equitable process. Policy cash value is inaccessible to the owner if the owner does not have the full rights to policy cash value normally held by an owner of a life insurance contract. Policy cash value is inaccessible to the owner's general creditors if, under the terms of the split-dollar life insurance arrangement or by operation of law or any contractual undertaking, the creditors cannot, for any reason, effectively reach the full policy cash value in the event of the owner's insolvency.

In a typical equity split-dollar life insurance arrangement, the non-owner has current access to all portions of the policy cash value in excess of the amount payable to the owner. In many arrangements, the non-owner may also have current access to the portion of the cash value payable to the owner if, for example, that portion of the policy cash value is for any reason not accessible to the owner or the owner's general creditors.

Under these proposed regulations, policy cash value is determined without regard to surrender charges or other similar charges or reductions. To provide uniformity, certainty, and administrative ease, policy cash value generally is determined on the last day of the non-owner's taxable year. In addition, solely for purposes of employment tax (as defined in § 1.61-22(c)(5) of the 2002 proposed regulations) and the penalty for failure to pay estimated income taxes, the portion of the policy cash value that is treated as provided by the owner to the non-owner during the non-owner's taxable year is treated as so provided on the last day of that taxable year. The IRS and the Treasury Department request comments regarding circumstances in which it might be appropriate to use a different date for employment tax withholding purposes.

Several commentators on the 2002 proposed regulations asserted that those regulations were contrary to the intention, announced by the IRS and the Treasury Department in Notice 2002-8 (2002-1 C.B. 398), to publish proposed regulations that will not treat an owner as having made a transfer of a portion of the cash surrender value of a life insurance contract to an non-owner for purposes of section 83 solely because interest or other earnings credited to the cash surrender value of the contract cause the cash surrender value to exceed the portion thereof payable to the owner. The valuation methodology described in these proposed regulations, however, does not treat an owner as having made a transfer under section 83 solely because of growth in policy cash value. Rather, this approach, consistent with the doctrines of constructive receipt, economic benefit, and cash equivalence, treats the non-owner as having a taxable interest in policy cash value only to the extent that the non-owner has current access to the policy cash value.

Several commentators stated that a non-owner who includes in income a portion of the policy cash value should be credited with Ainside build-up on that portion of the policy cash value. This result might be appropriate if there were actual transfers of ownership of the underlying life insurance contract (or a portion thereof) from the owner to the non-owner. Here, by contrast to transfers described in § 1.61-22(g) of the 2002 proposed regulations, no part of the life insurance contract is actually transferred from the owner to the non-owner by reason of the non-owner's taking policy cash value into account.

In addition, some commentators expressed the view that, under the economic benefit regime, if the policy cash value in one year is less than the policy cash value in a prior year, the non-owner should be allowed a loss to the extent this difference was included in income in the prior year. Consistent with the underlying doctrines of constructive receipt, economic benefit, and cash equivalence, a loss should not be allowed in this situation. Note, however, that under § 1.61-22(g)(4)(ii)(A) of the 2002 proposed regulations, if a life insurance contract is transferred from an owner to a non-owner (the transferee), the transferee's investment in the contract under section 72(e) will include the amount of economic benefits previously taken into account by the transferee prior to the transfer.

c. *Current term life insurance protection*

These proposed regulations provide that, in the case of an equity split-dollar life insurance arrangement governed by the economic benefit regime, the value of the economic benefits provided to a non-owner for a taxable year also includes the cost of current life insurance protection provided to the non-owner. The cost of current life insurance protection provided to the non-owner in any year equals the amount of the current life insurance protection provided to the non-owner multiplied by the life insurance premium factor designated or permitted in guidance published in the Internal Revenue Bulletin. The amount of the current life insurance protection (including paid-up additions thereto) provided to the non-owner for a taxable year equals the excess of the average death benefit of the life insurance contract over the sum of the total amount payable to the owner (including any outstanding policy loans that offset amounts otherwise payable to the owner) under the split-dollar life insurance arrangement and the portion of the policy cash value actually taken into account for the current taxable year or for any prior taxable year. This subtraction of the portion of the policy cash value actually taken into account by the non-owner prevents the non-owner from being taxed twice on the same amount, once as part of the policy cash value to which the non-owner has current access and again as an amount provided to the non-owner in the form of death benefit protection.

d. *Other economic benefits*

These proposed regulations provide that, in the case of an equity split-dollar life insurance arrangement governed by the economic benefit regime, the value of all other economic benefits provided to the non-owner must be taken into account (to the extent not actually taken into account for a prior taxable year). For this purpose, the term other economic benefits should be construed broadly to include any benefit, right, or feature of the life insurance contract (other than current life insurance protection and policy cash value) provided to the non-owner under the arrangement.

Proposed Effective Date

These proposed regulations will have the same applicability date as that set forth in § 1.61-22(j) of the 2002 proposed regulations. Thus, these proposed regulations will apply to split-dollar life insurance arrangements entered into after the date final regulations are published in the **Federal Register** and to arrangements entered into on or before that date that are materially modified after that date.

In addition, taxpayers may rely on these proposed regulations for equity split-dollar life insurance arrangements entered into on or before the date final regulations are published in the **Federal Register** if the conditions in § 1.61-22(j)(2)(i) of the 2002 proposed regulations are met. For taxable years beginning after December 31, 2002 however, parties to an equity split-dollar life insurance arrangement may rely on these proposed regulations only if the value of all economic benefits taken into account by the parties is determined in accordance with these proposed regulations. These proposed regulations also conform the early reliance rules in § 1.83-6(a)(5)(ii)(B) and § 1.301-1(q)(4)(ii) of the 2002 proposed regulations to that set forth in the preceding sentence.

Special Analyses

It has been determined that this notice of proposed rulemaking is not a significant regulatory action as defined in Executive Order 12866. Therefore, a regulatory flexibility assessment is not required. It has been determined that section 553(b) of the Administrative Procedure Act (5 U.S.C. Chapter 5) does not apply to these regulations, and because these regulations do not impose a collection of information on small entities, the Regulatory Flexibility Act (5 U.S.C. chapter 6) does not apply. Pursuant to section 7805(f) of the Internal Revenue Code, this notice of proposed rulemaking will be submitted to the Chief

Counsel for Advocacy of the Small Business Administration for comment on its impact on small business.

Comments and Public Hearing

Before these proposed regulations are adopted as final regulations, consideration will be given to any written or electronic comments (a signed original and eight (8) copies) that are submitted timely to the IRS. The Treasury Department and IRS specifically request comments on the clarity of the proposed rules and how they may be made easier to understand. All comments will be available for public inspection and copying.

A public hearing has been scheduled for July 29, 2003, beginning at 10 a.m. in the IRS Auditorium in the Internal Revenue Building, 1111 Constitution Avenue, NW., Washington, DC. Thus, the public hearing concerning these proposed regulations will be held on a date sooner than the usual 120 days after the date of publication of proposed regulations in the **Federal Register**. The IRS and the Treasury Department believe that this shorter period is sufficient for taxpayers to comment on these proposed regulations because the issue addressed by these proposed regulations is narrowly focused and taxpayers have already submitted comments on this issue in connection with the 2002 proposed regulations.

All visitors must present photo identification to enter the building. Because of access restrictions, visitors will not be admitted beyond the immediate entrance area more than 30 minutes before the hearing starts. For information about having your name placed on the building access list to attend the hearing, see the "FOR FURTHER INFORMATION CONTACT" section of this preamble.

The rules of 26 CFR 601.601(a)(3) apply to the hearing. Persons who wish to present oral comments at the hearing must submit written comments and an outline of the topics to be discussed and the time to be devoted to each topic (signed original and eight(8) copies) by July 8, 2003. A period of 10 minutes will be alloted to each person for making comments. An agenda showing the schedule of speakers will be prepared after the deadline for receiving outlines has passed. Copies of the agenda will be available free of charge at the hearing.

Drafting Information

The principal author of these proposed regulations is Elizabeth Kaye of the Office of Associate Chief Counsel (Income Tax and Accounting). However, other personnel from the IRS and Treasury Department participated in their development.

List of Subjects in 26 CFR Part 1

Income taxes, Reporting and recordkeeping requirements.

Proposed Amendments to the Regulations

Accordingly, 26 CFR part 1 is proposed to be amended as follows:

PART 1—INCOME TAXES

Paragraph 1. The authority citation for part 1 continues to read in part as follows:

Authority: 26 U.S.C. 7805 ***

Par. 2. Section 1.61-22, as proposed on July 9, 2002, at 67 FR 45423, is amended as follows:

1. The text of paragraph (d)(3)(ii) is added.

2. Paragraph (j)(2)(iii) is added.

The additions read as follows:

§ 1.61-22 Taxation of split-dollar life insurance arrangements.

*****

(d) ***

(3) ***

(ii) *Valuation of economic benefits*—(A) *In general.* In the case of a split-dollar life insurance arrangement described in paragraph (d)(3)(i) of this section, the value of the economic benefits provided to a non-owner for a taxable year under the arrangement equals—

(*1*) The cost of current life insurance protection provided to the non-owner as determined under paragraph (d)(3)(ii)(B) of this section;

(*2*) The amount of policy cash value to which the non-owner has current access within the meaning of paragraph (d)(3)(ii)(C) of this section (to the extent that such amount was not actually taken into account for a prior taxable year); and

(*3*) The value of any economic benefits not described in paragraph (d)(3)(ii)(A)(*1*) or (*2*) of this section provided to the non-owner (to the extent not actually taken into account for a prior taxable year).

(B) *Valuation of current term life insurance protection.* In the case of a split-dollar life insurance arrangement described in paragraph (d)(3)(i) of this section, the amount of the current life insurance protection (including paid-up additions thereto) provided to the non-owner for a taxable year equals the excess of the average death benefit of the life insurance contract over the sum of the total amount payable to the owner under the split-dollar life insurance arrangement and the portion of the policy cash value actually taken into account for the current taxable year or for any prior taxable year. The total amount payable to the owner is increased by the amount of any outstanding policy loan. The cost of current life insurance protection provided to the non-owner in any year equals the amount of the current life insurance protection provided to the non-owner multiplied by the life insurance premium factor designated or permitted in guidance published in the Internal Revenue Bulletin (see § 601.601(d)(2)(ii) of this chapter).

(C) *Current access.* For purposes of this paragraph (d)(3), a non-owner has current access to that portion of the policy cash value that is directly or indirectly accessible by the non-owner, inaccessible to the owner, or inaccessible to the owner's general creditors.

(D) *Valuation date*—(*1*) *General rules.* For purposes of paragraph (d)(3)(ii)(A) of this section, the policy cash value is determined on the last day of the taxable year of the non-owner. Notwithstanding the previous sentence, if the split-dollar life insurance arrangement terminates during the taxable year of the non-owner, the policy cash value is determined on the day that the arrangement terminates.

(*2*) *Artifice or device.* Notwithstanding paragraph (d)(3)(ii)(D)(*1*) of this section, if any artifice or device is used to understate the amount of policy cash value to which the non-owner has current access on the valuation date in paragraph (d)(3)(ii)(D)(*1*) of this section, then, for purposes of paragraph (d)(3)(ii)(A) of this section, the date on which the amount of policy cash value is determined is the date on which the amount of policy cash value is greatest during that taxable year.

(E) *Policy cash value.* For purposes of this paragraph (d)(3), policy cash value is determined without regard to surrender charges or other similar charges or reductions.

(F) *Special rule for certain taxes.* For purposes of employment tax (as defined in paragraph (c)(5) of this section), and sections 6654 and 6655 (relating to the failure to pay estimated income tax), that portion of the policy cash value (as determined under paragraph (d)(3)(ii)(A)(*2*) of this section) that is treated as provided by the owner to the non-owner under paragraph (d)(1) of this section shall be treated as so provided on the last day of the taxable year of the non-owner. Notwithstanding the previous sentence, if the split-dollar life insurance arrangement terminates during the taxable year of the non-owner, such portion of the policy cash value shall be treated as so provided on the day that the arrangement terminates.

(G) *Examples.* The following examples illustrate the rules of this paragraph (d)(3)(ii). Except as otherwise provided, both examples assume the following facts: employer (R) is the owner (as defined in paragraph (c)(1) of this section) and employee (E) is the non-owner (as defined in paragraph (c)(2) of this section) of a life insurance contract that is part of an equity split-dollar life insurance arrangement that is subject to the provisions of paragraphs (d) through (g) of this section; the contract is a life insurance contract as defined in section 7702 and not a modified endowment contract as defined in section 7702A; R does not withdraw or obtain a loan of any portion of the policy cash value and does not surrender any portion of the life insurance contract; the compensation paid to E is reasonable; E is not provided any economic benefits described in paragraph (d)(3)(ii)(A)(*3*) of this section; E does not make any premium payments; E's taxable year is the calendar year; and E reports on E's Federal income tax return for each year that the equity split-dollar life insurance arrangement is in effect the amount of income required to be reported under paragraph (d) of this section. The examples are as follows:

Example 1. (i) *Facts.* In year 1, R and E enter into the equity split-dollar life insurance arrangement. Under the arrangement R pays all of the premiums on the life insurance contract until the termination of the arrangement or E's death. The arrangement also provides that upon termination of the arrangement or E's death, R is entitled to receive the lesser of the aggregate premiums paid or the policy cash value of the contract and E is entitled to receive any remaining amounts. Under the terms of the arrangement and applicable state law, the policy cash value is fully accessible by R and R's creditors but E has the right to borrow or withdraw the portion of the policy cash value exceeding the amount payable to R upon termination of the arrangement or E's death.

To fund the arrangement, R purchases a life insurance contract with constant death benefit protection equal to $1,500,000. As of December 31 of year 1, the policy cash value equals $55,000 and R has paid $60,000 of premiums on the life insurance contract. As of December 31 of year 2, the policy cash value equals $140,000 and R has paid aggregate premiums of $120,000 on the life insurance contract. As of December 31 of year 3, the policy cash value equals $240,000 and R has paid $180,000 of premiums on the life insurance contract.

(ii) *Analysis.* Under the terms of the equity split-dollar life insurance arrangement, E has the right for year 1 and all subsequent years to borrow or withdraw the portion of the policy cash value exceeding the amount payable to R. Thus, under paragraph (d)(3)(ii)(C) of this section, E has current access to such portion of the policy cash value for each year that the arrangement is in effect. In addition, because R pays all of the premiums on the life insurance contract, R provides to E all of the economic benefits that E receives under the arrangement. Therefore, under paragraph (d)(1) of this section, E includes in gross income the value of all economic benefits described in paragraphs (d)(3)(ii)(A)(*1*) and (*2*) of this section provided to E under the arrangement.

(iii) *Results for year 1.* For year 1, E is provided, under paragraph (d)(3)(ii)(A)(*2*) of this section, $0 of policy cash value (excess of $55,000 policy cash value determined as of December 31 of year 1 over $55,000 payable to R). For year 1, E is also provided, under paragraph (d)(3)(ii)(A)(*1*) of this section, current life insurance protection of $1,445,000 ($1,500,000 minus $55,000 payable to R). Thus, E includes in gross income for year 1 the cost of $1,445,000 of current life insurance protection.

(iv) *Results for year 2.* For year 2, E is provided, under paragraph (d)(3)(ii)(A)(*2*) of this section, $20,000 of policy cash value ($140,000 policy cash value determined as of December 31 of year 2 minus $120,000 payable to R). For year 2, E is also provided, under paragraph (d)(3)(ii)(A)(*1*) of this section, current life insurance protection of $1,360,000 ($1,500,000 minus the sum of $120,000 payable to R and the aggregate of $20,000 of policy cash value that E actually includes in income on E's year 1 and year 2 income tax returns). Thus, E includes in gross income for year 2 the sum of $20,000 of policy cash value and the cost of $1,360,000 of current life insurance protection.

(v) *Results for year 3.* For year 3, E is provided, under paragraph (d)(3)(ii)(A)(*2*) of this section, $40,000 of policy cash value ($240,000 policy cash value determined as of December 31 of year 3 minus the sum of $180,000 payable to R and $20,000 of aggregate policy cash value that E actually included in gross income on E's year 1 and year 2 federal income tax returns). For year 3, E is also provided, under paragraph (d)(3)(ii)(A)(*1*) of this section, current life insurance protection of $1,260,000 ($1,500,000 minus the sum of $180,000 payable to R and $60,000 of aggregate policy cash value that E actually includes in gross income on E's year 1, year 2, and year 3 federal income tax returns). Thus, E includes in gross income for year 3 the sum of $40,000 of policy cash value and the cost of $1,260,000 of current life insurance protection.

Example 2. (i) *Facts.* The facts are the same as in *Example 1* except that E cannot directly or indirectly access any portion of the policy cash

value, but the terms of the equity split-dollar life insurance arrangement or applicable state law provide that the policy cash value in excess of the amount payable to R upon termination of the arrangement or E's death is inaccessible to R's general creditors.

(ii) *Analysis.* Under the terms of the equity split-dollar life insurance arrangement or applicable state law, the portion of the policy cash value exceeding the amount payable to R is inaccessible to R's general creditors. Thus, under paragraph (d)(3)(ii)(C) of this section, E has current access to such portion of the policy cash value for each year that the arrangement is in effect. In addition, because R pays all of the premiums on the life insurance contract, R provides to E all of the economic benefits that E receives under the arrangement. Therefore, under paragraph (d)(1) of this section, E includes in gross income the value of all economic benefits described in paragraphs (d)(3)(ii)(A)(*1*) and (*2*) of this section provided to E under the arrangement.

(iii) *Results for years 1, 2 and 3.* The results for this example are the same as the results in *Example 1.*

*****

(j) ***

(2) ***

(iii) *Valuation of economic benefits.* Notwithstanding paragraph (j)(2)(ii) of this section, for taxable years beginning after December 31, 2002, parties to an arrangement described in paragraph (d)(3) of this section may rely on this section only if the value of all economic benefits taken into account by the parties is determined in accordance with paragraph (d)(3)(ii) of this section.

*****

Par. 3. Section 1.83-6, as proposed on July 9, 2002, at 67 FR 45428, is amended by adding paragraph (a)(5)(ii)(B)(*3*) to read as follows:
§ 1.83-6 Deduction by employer.

(a) ***

(5) ***

(ii) ***

(B) ***

(*3*) *Valuation of economic benefits.* Notwithstanding paragraph (a)(5)(ii)(B)(*2*) of this section, for taxable years beginning after December 31, 2002, parties to an arrangement described in § 1.61-22(d)(3) may rely on this section only if the value of all economic benefits taken into account by the parties is determined in accordance with § 1.61-22(d)(3)(ii).

*****

Par. 4.

* * * * *

David A. Mader

Assistant Deputy Commissioner of Internal Revenue.

¶ 20,260U

IRS proposed regulations: Deemed IRAs: Qualified plans: 401(k) plans: Treatment of assets.—The IRS has issued proposed regulations containing guidance for employers that wish to adopt deemed IRAs under their employee benefit plans. Qualified employer plans, such as 401(k) plans and deemed IRAs are to be treated as separate entities subject to separate rules applicable to qualified plans and IRAs.

The proposed regulations, which were published in the *Federal Register* on May 20, 2003 (68 FR 27493), were previously reproduced at this paragraph.

The final and temporary regulations, which were published in the *Federal Register* on July 22, 2004 (69 FR 43735), are reproduced at ¶ 12,054 (IRS Reg. Sec. 1.408-2), ¶ 12,054A (IRS Reg. Sec. 1.408-2T) and ¶ 12,070(IRS Reg. Sec. 1.408(q)-1).The preamble to the regulations is found at ¶ 24,507P.

¶ 20,260V

IRS proposed regulations: Method of accounting: Uniform capitalization rules: Adjustment periods.—The IRS has proposed amendments to the change of accounting method regulations under the Code Sec. 263A uniform capitalization rules, so that they conform to general IRS guidance on changes of accounting method. The amendments would allow those changing their accounting method to take any adjustment under Code Sec. 481(a) over the same number of taxable years as is provided under general guidance. Comments on the proposed amendments must be received by July 11, 2003 for the public hearing to be held on August 13, 2003.

The proposed amendment to regulations, published in the Federal Register on May 12, 2003 (68 FR 25310), is reproduced below.

DEPARTMENT OF THE TREASURY

Internal Revenue Service

26 CFR Part 1

[REG-142605-02]

RIN 1545-BB47

Administration Simplification of Section 481(a) Adjustment Periods in Various Regulations

AGENCY: Internal Revenue Service (IRS), Treasury.

ACTION: Notice of proposed rulemaking and notice of public hearing.

SUMMARY: This document contains proposed amendments to regulations under sections 263A and 448 of the Internal Revenue Code. The amendments apply to taxpayers changing a method of accounting under the regulations and are necessary to conform the rules governing those changes to the rules provided in general guidance issued by the IRS for changing a method of accounting. Specifically, the amendments will allow taxpayers changing their method of accounting under the regulations to take any adjustment under section 481(a) resulting from the change into account over the same number of taxable years that is provided in the general guidance.

DATES: Written or electronic comments must be received by July 11, 2003. Requests to speak (with outlines of oral comments to be discussed) at the public hearing scheduled for August 13, 2003, at 10 a.m. must be received by July 23, 2003.

ADDRESSES: Send submissions to: CC:PA:RU (REG-142605-02), room 5226, Internal Revenue Service, POB 7604 Ben Franklin Station, Washington, DC 20044. Submissions of comments may also be hand-delivered Monday through Friday between the hours of 8 a.m. and 5 p.m. to: CC:PA:RU (REG-142605-02), Courier's Desk, Internal Revenue Service, 1111 Constitution Avenue, NW., Washington, DC. Alternatively, taxpayers may submit comments electronically via the Internet direct to the IRS Internet site at http://www.irs.gov/regs. The public hearing will be held in the Internal Revenue Building, 1111 Constitution Avenue, NW., Washington, DC.

FOR FURTHER INFORMATION CONTACT: Concerning the regulations, Christian Wood, 202-622-4930. Concerning the hearing, contact Sonya Cruse, 202-622-7180 (not toll-free numbers).

SUPPLEMENTARY INFORMATION:

Background

This document contains proposed amendments to 26 CFR part 1 under sections 263A and 448. These amendments pertain to the period for taking into account the adjustment required under section 481 to prevent duplications or omissions of amounts resulting from a change in method of accounting under section 263A or 448.

Section 263A (the uniform capitalization rules) generally requires the capitalization of direct costs and indirect costs properly allocable to real property and tangible personal property produced by a taxpayer. Section 263A also requires the capitalization of direct costs and indirect costs properly allocable to real property and personal property acquired by a taxpayer for resale.

Section 448(a) generally prohibits the use of the cash receipts and disbursements method of accounting by C corporations, partnerships with a C corporation partner, and tax shelters. Section 448(b), however, provides exceptions to this general rule in the case of farming businesses, qualified personal service corporations, and entities with gross receipts of not more than $ 5,000,000.

Section 446(e) generally provides that a taxpayer that changes the method of accounting on the basis of which it regularly computes its income in keeping its books must, before computing its taxable income under the new method, secure the consent of the Secretary.

Section 481(a) generally provides that a taxpayer must take into account those adjustments that are determined to be necessary solely by reason of a change in method of accounting in order to prevent amounts from being duplicated or omitted. Sections 481(c) and 1.446-1(e)(3)(ii) and 1.481-4 provide that the adjustment required by section 481(a) shall be taken into account in determining taxable income in the manner and subject to the conditions agreed to by the Commissioner and the taxpayer.

Rev. Proc. 97-27, 1997-1 C.B. 680 (as modified and amplified by Rev. Proc. 2002-19, 2002-13 I.R.B. 696, and modified by Rev. Proc. 2002-54, 2002-35 I.R.B. 432), provides procedures under which taxpayers may apply for the advance consent of the Commissioner to change a method of accounting. Rev. Proc. 2002-9, 2003-3 I.R.B. 327 (as modified

and amplified by Rev. Proc. 2002-19, amplified, clarified, and modified by Rev. Proc. 2002-54, and modified and clarified by Announcement 2002-17, 2002-8 I.R.B. 561), provides procedures under which taxpayers may apply for automatic consent of the Commissioner to change a method of accounting. Under both revenue procedures, as modified, adjustments under section 481(a) are taken into account entirely in the year of change (in the case of a net negative adjustment) and over 4 taxable years (in the case of a net positive adjustment), subject to certain exceptions.

Explanation of Provisions

Regulations under sections 263A and 448 currently provide rules for certain changes in method of accounting under those sections, including the number of taxable years over which an adjustment required under section 481(a) to effect the change is to be taken into account. The adjustment periods provided in the regulations may differ from the general 4-year (net positive adjustment) and 1 year (net negative adjustment) adjustment period rule provided in Rev. Proc. 97-27 and Rev. Proc. 2002-9, as modified. In certain cases, the difference creates a disincentive for certain taxpayers to change their method of accounting in the taxable year required by the regulations under section 263A or 448, as applicable.

The IRS and Treasury Department believe it is appropriate to amend the regulations under sections 263A and 448 to provide that the section 481(a) adjustment period for accounting method changes under those regulations be determined under the applicable administrative procedures issued by the Commissioner (namely, Rev. Proc. 97-27 and Rev. Proc. 2002-9, as modified, or successors). As a result of the amendment, the section 481(a) adjustment period for these changes generally will be 4 years for a net positive adjustment and 1 year for a net negative adjustment, unless otherwise provided in the regulations (see e.g., Sec. 1.448-(g)(2)(ii) and (g)(3)(iii) (providing rules for extended or accelerated adjustment periods in certain cases)) or the applicable revenue procedure (see e.g., section 7.03 of Rev. Proc. 97-27 and section 5.04(3) of Rev. Proc. 2002-9 (providing rules for accelerated adjustment periods in certain cases)). The IRS and Treasury Department believe that amending the regulations in this manner will eliminate the disincentive that currently exists and provide flexibility in the event that any future changes are made to the general section 481(a) adjustment periods.

The IRS and Treasury Department further believe it is appropriate to remove the special adjustment period rule for cooperatives in Sec. 1.448-1(g)(3)(ii), thus directing cooperatives to the rules in Rev. Proc. 97-27 or Rev. Proc. 2002-9, as modified, or successors. Currently, Rev. Proc. 97-27 (section 7.03(2)) and Rev. Proc. 2002-9 (section 5.04(3)(b)) provide that the section 481(a) adjustment period in the case of a cooperative (within the meaning of section 1381(a)) generally is 1 year, whether the net adjustment is positive or negative. The IRS and Treasury Department continue to believe that a 1 year adjustment period is appropriate in the case of accounting method changes by cooperatives. See Rev. Rul. 79-45, 1979-1 C.B. 284.

The IRS and Treasury Department contemplate issuing separate guidance on accounting method changes under section 381. Comments are requested on issues to be addressed in such guidance, including (1) whether the section 481(a) adjustment should be taken into account by the acquired corporation immediately prior to the transaction or the acquiring corporation immediately after the transaction; (2) whether the general section 481(a) adjustment periods of Rev. Proc. 97-27 and Rev. Proc. 2002-9, as modified, or successors, should apply to accounting method changes under section 381; (3) the method for computing the section 481(a) adjustment; (4) whether accounting method changes under section 381 should be requested by filing a Form 3115 or by requesting a private letter ruling; and (5) any other procedural or technical issues (e.g., filing deadlines, audit protection).

Proposed Effective Date

The proposed regulations are applicable to taxable years ending on or after the date these regulations are published as final regulations. However, taxpayers may rely on the proposed regulations for taxable years ending on or after May 12, 2003, by filing a Form 3115, Application for Change of Accounting Method, in the time and manner provided in the regulations (in the case of a change in method of accounting under section 448) or applicable administrative procedure (in the case of a change in method of accounting under section 263A) for such a taxable year that reflects a section 481(a) adjustment period that is consistent with the proposed regulations.

Special Analyses

It has been determined that this notice of proposed rulemaking is not a significant regulatory action as defined in EO 12866. Therefore, a regulatory assessment is not required. It also has been determined that section 553(b) of the Administrative Procedure Act (5 U.S.C. chapter 5) and because this proposed rule does not impose a collection of information on small entities, the provisions of the Regulatory Flexibility Act (5 U.S.C. chapter 6) do not apply. Pursuant to section 7805(f) of the Internal Revenue Code, this notice of proposed rulemaking will be submitted to the Chief Counsel for Advocacy of the Small Business Administration for comment on its impact on small business.

Comments and Public Hearing

Before these proposed regulations are adopted as final regulations, consideration will be given to any written (a signed original and eight (8) copies) or electronic comments that are submitted timely to the IRS. The IRS and Treasury Department request comments on the clarity of the proposed rules and how they can be made easier to understand. All comments will be available for public inspection and copying.

A public hearing has been scheduled for August 13, 2003 beginning at 10 a.m. in the Internal Revenue Building, 1111 Constitution Avenue, NW., Washington, DC. Due to building security procedures, visitors must enter at the Constitution Avenue entrance. In addition, all visitors must present photo identification to enter the building. Because of access restrictions, visitors will not be admitted beyond the immediate entrance area more than 30 minutes before the hearing starts. For information about having your name placed on the building access list to attend the hearing, see the FOR FURTHER INFORMATION CONTACT section of this preamble.

The rules of 26 CFR 601.601(a)(3) apply to the hearing. Persons who wish to present oral comments at the hearing must submit electronic or written comments and an outline of the topics to be discussed and the time to be devoted to each topic (signed original and eight (8) copies) by July 11, 2003.

A period of 10 minutes will be allotted to each person for making comments. An agenda showing the scheduling of the speakers will be prepared after the deadline for receiving outlines has passed. Copies of the agenda will be available free of charge at the hearing.

Drafting Information

The principal authors of these proposed regulations are Christian T. Wood and Grant Anderson of the Office of Associate Chief Counsel

(Income Tax and Accounting). However, other personnel from the IRS and Treasury Department participated in their development.

List of Subjects in 26 CFR Part 1

Income taxes, Reporting and record keeping requirements.

Proposed Amendments to the Regulations

Accordingly, 26 CFR part 1 is proposed to be amended as follows:

PART 1—INCOME TAXES

Paragraph 1. The authority citation for part 1 continues to read in part as follows:

Authority: 26 U.S.C. 7805 * * *

Par. 2. In Sec. 1.263A-7, paragraph (b)(2)(ii) is revised to read as follows:

Sec. 1.263A-7 Changing a method of accounting under section 263A.

* * * * *

(b) * * *

(2) * * *

(ii) *Adjustment required by section 481(a).* In the case of any taxpayer required or permitted to change its method of accounting for any taxable year under section 263A and the regulations thereunder, the change will be treated as initiated by the taxpayer for purposes of the adjustment required by section 481(a). The taxpayer must take the net section 481(a) adjustment into account over the section 481(a) adjustment period as determined under the applicable administrative procedures issued under Sec. 1.446-1(e)(3)(ii) for obtaining the Commissioner's consent to a change in accounting method (e.g., Revenue Procedures 97-27 and 2002-9, or successors). This paragraph is effective for taxable years ending on or after the date these regulations are published as final regulations in the Federal Register. However, taxpayers may rely on this paragraph for taxable years ending on or after May 12, 2003, by filing, under the applicable administrative procedure, a Form 3115, Application for Change in Accounting Method, for such a taxable year that reflects a section 481(a) adjustment period that is consistent with this paragraph.

* * * * *

¶ 20,260W

IRS proposed regulations: Incentive stock options: Employee stock purchase plans: Statutory stock options.—**The IRS has issued proposed regulations that provide guidance and clarification regarding the transfer of stock pursuant to the exercise of incentive stock options and the exercise of options granted pursuant to an employee stock purchase plan (statutory options). The proposed regulations are meant to provide a comprehensive set of rules governing stock options, and provide additional guidance concerning circumstances in which stockholder approval is required.**

The proposed regulations, which were published in the Federal Register on June 9, 2003 (68 FR 34344), are reproduced below.

Final regulations were published in the Federal Register on August 3, 2004 (69 FR 46401). The preamble is at ¶ 24,507Q. The regulations are at ¶ 13,107, ¶ 13,108, ¶ 13,124A, ¶ 13,124B, ¶ 13,125, ¶ 13,125A, 13,125B, ¶ 13,131, ¶ 13,132, ¶ 13,151, and ¶ 13,671A. For statutory options granted on or before June 9, 2003, taxpayers may rely on the 1984 proposed regulations (¶ 20,150E), these 2003 regulations, or the 2004 final regulations until the earlier of January 1, 2006, or the first regularly scheduled stockholders meeting of the granting corporation occurring six months after August 3, 2004. For statutory options granted after June 9, 2003 and before the earlier of January 1, 2006, or the first regularly scheduled stockholders meeting of the granting corporation occurring six months after August 3, 2004, taxpayers may rely on either these proposed regulations or the final regulations.

DEPARTMENT OF THE TREASURY

Internal Revenue Service

26 CFR Parts 1 and 14a

[REG-122917-02]

RIN 1545-BA75

Statutory Options

AGENCY: Internal Revenue Service (IRS), Treasury.

ACTION: Notice of proposed rulemaking; withdrawal of previous rulemaking; and notice of public hearing.

SUMMARY: This document contains proposed regulations relating to statutory options. These proposed regulations affect certain tax payers who participate in the transfer of stock pursuant to the exercise of incentive stock options and the exercise of options granted pursuant to an employee stock purchase plan (statutory options). These proposed regulations provide guidance to assist these taxpayers in complying with the law in addition to clarifying rules regarding statutory options. This document also withdraws a previous notice of proposed rulemaking.

DATES: Written and electronically submitted comments and requests to speak, with outlines of topics to be discussed at the public hearing scheduled for September 2, 2003, must be received by August 12, 2003. ADDRESSES: Send submissions to CC:PA:RU (REG-122917-02), room 5226, Internal Revenue Service, POB 7604, Ben Franklin Station, Washington, DC 20044. Submissions may be hand delivered Monday through Friday between the hours of 8 a.m. and 5 p.m. to: CC:PA:RU (REG-122917-02), Courier's Desk, Internal Revenue Service, 1111 Constitution Avenue, NW., Washington, DC or sent electronically, via the IRS Internet site *www.irs.gov/regs.* The public hearing will be held in the IRS Auditorium, Internal Revenue Building, 1111 Constitution Avenue, NW., Washington, DC.

FOR FURTHER INFORMATION CONTACT: Concerning the regulations, Erinn Madden at (202) 622-6030 (not a toll-free number). To be placed on the attendance list for the hearing, please contact Guy Traynor at (202) 622-7180.

SUPPLEMENTARY INFORMATION:

Paperwork Reduction Act

The collection of information contained in this notice of proposed rulemaking has been submitted to the Office of Management and

Budget for review in accordance with the Paperwork Reduction Act of 1995 (44 U.S.C. 3507(d)). Comments on the collection of information should be sent to the **Office of Management and Budget**, Attn: Desk Officer for the Department of the Treasury, Office of Information and Regulatory Affairs, Washington, DC 20503, with copies to the **Internal Revenue Service**, Attn: IRS Reports Clearance Officer, W:CAR:MP:T:T:SP; Washington, DC 20224. Comments on the collection of information should be received by August 8, 2003. Comments are specifically requested concerning:

Whether the proposed collection of information is necessary for the proper performance of the functions of the **Internal Revenue Service**, including whether the information will have practical utility;

The accuracy of the estimated burden associated with the proposed collection of information (see below);

How the quality, utility, and clarity of the information to be collected may be enhanced;

How the burden of complying with the proposed collection of information may be minimized, including through the application of automated collection techniques or other forms of information technology; and

Estimates of capital or start-up costs and costs of operation, maintenance, and purchase of service to provide information.

The collection of information in this proposed regulation is in 1.6039-1. Section 6039 of the Code requires all corporations that transfer stock to any person pursuant to the exercise of a statutory option to furnish that person with a written statement describing the transfer. Additionally, the corporation may be required to furnish the person a second written statement when the stock originally transferred pursuant to the exercise of the statutory option is subsequently disposed of by the person. The information on the statements required to be provided by the corporation will be used by recipients to complete their income tax returns in the year of the disposition of the statutory option stock. The likely respondents are for-profit corporations.

Estimated total annual reporting burden: 16,650 hours.

Estimated average annual burden hours per respondent: 20 minutes.

Estimated number of respondents: 50,000.

Estimated annual frequency of responses: annually.

An agency may not conduct or sponsor, and a person is not required to respond to, a collection of information unless it displays a valid control number assigned by the Office of Management and Budget.

Books or records relating to a collection of information must be retained as long as their contents may become material in the administration of any internal revenue law. Generally, tax returns and tax return information are confidential, as required by 26 U.S.C. 6103.

Background

This document contains proposed amendments to 26 CFR part 1 under sections 421, 422, and 424 of the Internal Revenue Code (Code). Changes to the applicable tax law concerning section 421 were made by sections 11801 and 11821 of the Omnibus Budget Reconciliation Act of 1989, Public Law 101-508 (104 Stat. 1388). Changes to the applicable tax law concerning section 424 were made by section 1003 of the Technical and Miscellaneous Revenue Act of 1988 (TAMRA), Public Law 100-647 (102 Stat. 3581), sections 11801 and 11821 of the Omnibus Budget Reconciliation Act of 1989 (OBRA 89), Public Law 101-508 (104 Stat. 1388), which included re-designating section 425 as section 424 of the Code, and section 1702(h) of the Small Business Job Protection Act of 1996, Public Law 104-188 (110 Stat. 1755). Changes concerning section 422 were made by section 251 of the Economic Recovery Tax Act of 1981 (95 Stat. 172), which added section 422A to the Code. Related changes to section 422A were made by section 102(j) of the Technical Corrections Act of 1982, Public Law 97-448, section 321(a) of Tax Reform Act of 1986 (96 Stat. 2365), Public Law 99-514 (100 Stat. 2807), section 1003(d) of TAMRA, and sections 11801 and 11821 of OBRA 89, which included re-designating section 422A as section 422 of the Code.

Regulations under section 421 governing the requirements for restricted stock options and qualified stock options, as well as options granted under an employee stock purchase plan, were published in the **Federal Register** on December 9, 1957 (TD 6276), November 26, 1960 (TD 6500), January 18, 1961 (TD 6527), January 20, 1961 (TD 6540), December 12, 1963 (TD 6696), June 23, 1966 (TD 6887), July 24, 1978 (TD 7554), and November 3, 1980 (TD 7728). Temporary regulations under section 422A providing guidance and transitional rules related to incentive stock options were published in the **Federal Register** on December 17, 1981 (TD 7799) and September 18, 1992 (TD 8435).

Final regulations under section 422 related to stockholder approval were published in the **Federal Register** on December 1, 1988 (TD 8235) and November 29, 1991 (TD 8374). Regulations under section 425 were published in the **Federal Register** on June 23, 1966 (TD 6887).

Proposed changes to the final regulations under sections 421, 424, and 6039 and proposed regulations under section 422A were previously published in the **Federal Register** at 49 FR 4504 on February 7, 1984 (the 1984 proposed regulations). With the exception of certain stockholder approval rules that were published in the **Federal Register** on June 23, 1966 (TD 6887) and amended by TD 7728 on October 31, 1980, the 1984 proposed regulations provided a comprehensive set of rules under section 422 of the Code. The 1984 proposed regulations are withdrawn.

In general, the income tax treatment of the grant of an option to purchase stock in connection with the performance of services and of the transfer of stock pursuant to the exercise of such option is determined under section 83 of the Code and the regulations thereunder. However, section 421 of the Code provides special rules for determining the income tax treatment of the transfer of shares of stock pursuant to the exercise of an option if the requirements of section 422(a) or 423(a), as applicable, are met. Section 422 applies to incentive stock options, and section 423 applies to options granted under an employee stock purchase plan (collectively, statutory options).

Under section 421, if a share of stock is transferred to an individual pursuant to the exercise of a statutory option, there is no income at the time of exercise of the option with respect to such transfer, and no deduction under section 162 is allowed to the employer corporation with respect to such transfer. However, pursuant to section 56(b)(3), section 421 does not apply with respect to the exercise of an incentive stock option for purposes of the individual alternative minimum tax.

Section 422(a) of the Code provides that section 421 applies to the transfer of stock to an individual pursuant to the exercise of an incentive stock option if (i) no disposition of the share is made within 2 years from the date of grant of the option or within 1 year from the date of transfer of the share, and (ii) at all times during the period beginning on the date of grant and ending on the day 3 months before the exercise of the option, the individual is an employee of either the corporation granting the option or a parent or subsidiary of such corporation, or a corporation (or a parent or subsidiary of such corporation) issuing or assuming a stock option in a transaction to which section 424(a) applies. Section 422(b) provides several requirements that must be met for an option to qualify as an incentive stock option. Section 422(c) provides special rules applicable to incentive stock options, and section 422(d) provides a $100,000 limitation with respect to incentive stock options.

Section 424 of the Code provides special rules applicable to statutory options, including rules concerning the modification of statutory options and the substitution or assumption of an option by reason of a corporate merger, consolidation, acquisition of property or stock, separation, reorganization, or liquidation. Section 424 also contains definitions of certain terms, including *disposition*, *parent corporation*, and *subsidiary corporation*. Finally, section 424 provides special rules related to attribution of stock ownership and the effect of stockholder approval on the date of grant of a statutory option.

Explanation of Provisions

Overview

These proposed regulations would provide a set of comprehensive rules governing incentive stock options. These proposed regulations incorporate many of the rules contained in the 1984 proposed regulations, although these proposed regulations are re-numbered and re-organized. These proposed regulations would also make changes to the final regulations under sections 421 and 424 to provide additional guidance, as discussed below, in certain areas, to reflect the new organizational structure of the statutory option rules (including the re-designation of § 1.425-1 as § 1.424-1), and to remove obsolete rules and cross-references.

Section 421: General Rules

The proposed regulations under section 421 would remove obsolete provisions and update the cross-references to reflect amendments to the applicable statutes and re-organization of the regulations. These proposed regulations also incorporate many provisions of the 1984 proposed regulations. There are two sections of these proposed regulations under section 421: § 1.421-1, which would provide rules concerning the meaning and use of terms, and § 1.421-2, which would provide general rules regarding the application of section 421.

The terms defined in § 1.421-1 of these proposed regulations are the same as those previously defined in § 1.421-7, but these proposed regulations make changes to the definitions of certain terms. For example, § 1.421-1(a) of these proposed regulations expands the definition of *option* to include warrants.

These proposed regulations would provide that an option must be evidenced in paper or in an electronic form. Under either form, however, the option must be enforceable under applicable law. Similarly, these proposed regulations provide that the plan pursuant to which incentive stock options are granted must be in paper or electronic form, provided that the paper or electronic form establishes an enforceable plan.

In addition, as with any taxpayer record, the form used for the option or plan, whether paper or electronic, must be one that provides adequate substantiation of the applicability of section 421. Thus, for example, the form must be one that provides adequate substantiation of the applicable requirements, such as the date on which the option is granted, the number of shares subject to the option, and the option price. In addition, the taxpayer must retain records relating to the option that are sufficient to comply with section 6001 and the regulations thereunder. If these records are kept electronically, the records must meet the requirements of Rev. Proc. 97-22 (1997-1 C.B. 652), or subsequent guidance, and if the records are kept in an ADP system, the records must meet the requirements of Rev. Proc. 98-25 (1998-11 I.R.B. 7), or subsequent guidance.

The definition of *statutory option* in § 1.421-1(b) of these proposed regulations is revised to provide that a statutory option may include an option transferred to a trust if, under section 671 and applicable state law, the individual to whom the option was granted remains the beneficial owner. In contrast, these proposed regulations provide that a transfer of a statutory option incident to divorce will result in the option failing to qualify as a statutory option as of the date of transfer.

Section 1.421-1(i) of these proposed regulations defines *corporation* to have the same meaning prescribed by section 7701(a)(3) and § 301.7701-2(b). Thus, for example, a *corporation* includes an S Corporation, a foreign corporation, and a limited liability corporation that is treated as a corporation for all Federal tax purposes. In addition, section 1.421-1(d) of these proposed regulations provides that *stock* includes ownership interests other than capital stock. Thus, under these proposed regulations, it would be permissible for any entity that is classified as a corporation for federal tax purposes pursuant to the provisions of § 301.7701-2(b) to grant statutory stock options with respect to ownership interests in that entity.

Section 1.421-2 of these proposed regulations incorporates both the provisions of § 1.421-8 and many of the related provisions of the 1984 proposed regulations. These proposed regulations also provide further revisions, including specifying that the deduction in connection with a disqualifying disposition is allowed only if otherwise allowable under sections 83(h) and 162 and if the reporting requirements under § 1.83-6(a) are met.

Section 422: Incentive Stock Options

The proposed regulations under section 422 would provide a new set of comprehensive rules, with the exception of the rules regarding stockholder approval described in § 1.422-5 of the final regulations (renumbered as § 1.422-3 by these proposed regulations). There are four sections under these proposed regulations: § 1.422-1, general rules; § 1.422-2, definition of incentive stock option; § 1.422-4, the $100,000 limitation; and § 1.422-5, permissible provisions.

1. Special rules regarding disqualifying dispositions

The 1984 proposed regulations provided rules concerning the consequences of disqualifying dispositions. The general disqualifying disposition rules for incentive stock options are provided in § § 1.421-2(b)(1) and 1.422-1(b)(1) of these proposed regulations. In addition, § 1.422-1(b)(2) of these proposed regulations clarifies the operation of the special rules applicable to a disqualifying disposition of an incentive stock option under section 422(c)(2) (section 422A(c)(2), prior to amendment by OBRA 89).

The general rules concerning disqualifying dispositions are described in § 1.421-2(b) of these proposed regulations. Under these rules, if there is a disqualifying disposition of a share of stock, the special tax treatment provided by section 421 and § 1.421-2(a) does not apply to the transfer of the share. Instead, the exercise of the option is treated as the exercise of a nonstatutory option under § 1.83-7. Thus, in the taxable year in which the disqualifying disposition occurs, the individual must recognize compensation income equal to the fair market value of the stock on the date the stock is transferred less the exercise price (determined without reduction for any brokerage fees or

other costs paid in connection with the disposition). A deduction attributable to the transfer of the share of stock pursuant to the exercise of the option is allowable for the taxable year in which such disqualifying disposition occurs, to the employer corporation, its parent or subsidiary corporation, or a corporation substituting or assuming an option in a transaction to which § 1.424-1(a) applies, if otherwise allowable under sections 83(h) and 162 and if the requirements of § 1.83-6(a) are met.

Section 422(c)(2), however, provides a special rule that is applicable if an individual makes a disqualifying disposition of stock acquired through the exercise of an incentive stock option and if the disposition is a sale or exchange with respect to which a loss (if sustained) would be recognized by the individual. Under this special rule, the amount includible in gross income on the disqualifying disposition, and the amount deductible, as compensation attributable to the exercise of the option, shall not exceed the excess (if any) of the amount realized on such sale or exchange over the adjusted basis of the share. Under section 422(c)(2), this special rule is not applicable if the disposition is a sale or exchange with respect to which a loss (if sustained) would not be recognized by the individual. Section 1.422A-1(b)(2) of the 1984 proposed regulations described these special rules concerning the disqualifying disposition of an incentive stock option and this description is incorporated into § 1.422-1(b)(2) of these proposed regulations.

For example, if the disposition is a sale described in section 1091 (relating to a loss from wash sales of stock or securities), a gift, or a sale described in section 267(a)(1) (relating to sales between related parties), any loss sustained would not be recognized. Because a loss in any of these transactions would not be recognized, under § 1.422-1(b)(2)(ii) of these proposed regulations, the special rule provided in § 1.422-1(b)(2)(i) of these proposed regulations does not apply. Instead, the general rules for disqualifying dispositions described in § 1.421-2(b) of these proposed regulations apply.

For example, assume E, an employee of Corporation X, is granted an incentive stock option to acquire X stock. The option price on the date of grant is $100 (the fair market value of X stock on the date of grant). E exercises the option and is transferred X stock when the fair market value of the stock is $200. E later sells the stock for $150 to M before the applicable holding periods expire. Because the sale is a disqualifying disposition that meets the requirements of § 1.422-1(b)(2)(i) of these proposed regulations, in the taxable year of the disqualifying disposition, E is only required to include $50 (the excess of the amount realized on the sale, $150, over the adjusted basis of the share, $100) in gross income as compensation attributable to the exercise of the option. For its taxable year in which the disqualifying disposition occurs, X is allowed a compensation deduction of $50 attributable to E's exercise of the option, if otherwise allowable under sections 83(h) and 162 and if the requirements of § 1.83-6(a) are met.

In this example, however, if 10 days after the sale to M, E purchases substantially identical stock, under section 1091, a loss would not be recognized on the sale to M. Thus, under § 1.422-1(b)(2)(ii) of these proposed regulations, the special rule in § 1.422-1(b)(2)(i) does not apply. Instead of including $50 in gross income in the taxable year of the disqualifying disposition, E must include $100 (the difference between the fair market value of X stock on the date of transfer, $200, and the exercise price, $100) in gross income as compensation attributable to the exercise of the option. In the taxable year in which the disqualifying disposition occurs, X is allowed a compensation deduction of $100 attributable to E's exercise of the option if otherwise allowable under sections 83(h) and 162 and if the requirements of § 1.83-6(a) are met.

Since the 1984 proposed regulations were issued, there have been no changes in section 422(c)(2) (other than the redesignation of section 422A(c)(2) as 422(c)(2) by OBRA 89), and these proposed regulations do not make any substantive changes to the 1984 proposed regulations.

2. Stockholder approval of incentive stock option plan

Among other requirements, to qualify as an incentive stock option, the option must be granted pursuant to a plan which is approved by the stockholders of the granting corporation within 12 months before or after the date the plan is adopted. See section 422(b). These proposed regulations would provide the same basic requirements for stockholder approval as those included in the 1984 proposed regulations.

These proposed regulations, however, would provide additional guidance concerning the circumstances in which stockholder approval is required. As under the 1984 proposed regulations, stockholder approval is required if there is a change in the aggregate number of shares or in the employees (or class or classes of employees) eligible to be granted options under the plan. In addition, while the standard for determining when stockholder approval is required is the same as under the 1984 proposed regulations, these proposed regulations clarify these requirements and provide a more complete list of situations that require new stockholder approval of the plan by specifically including a change in the shares with respect to which options are issued or a change in the granting corporation. Thus, for example, assume that S, a subsidiary of P, adopts an incentive stock option plan under which incentive stock options for S stock will be granted to S employees, and the plan is approved by the stockholders of S (in this case, P) within the applicable 24-month period. If S later amends the plan to provide for the grant of incentive stock options to acquire P stock (rather than S stock), S must obtain approval from the stockholders of S within 12 months before or after the date of the amendment to the plan because the amendment of the plan to allow the grant of options for P stock is considered the adoption of a new plan.

These proposed regulations also would provide additional guidance regarding the application of the stockholder approval requirements in the context of the substitution or assumption of an option by reason of a corporate transaction. For a discussion of these rules, see the "Substitution, assumption, and modification of options" portion of the preamble.

3. $100,000 limitation

Section 422(d)(1) provides that to the extent that the aggregate fair market value of stock with respect to which incentive stock options (determined without regard to section 422(d)) are exercisable for the first time by any individual during the calendar year (under all of plans of the employer corporation and any related corporation) exceeds $100,000, such options are not treated as incentive stock options. Under section 422(d)(2), options are taken into account in the order in which they are granted. Section 422(d)(3) provides that the fair market value of stock is determined at the time the option is granted.

The 1984 proposed regulations provided no rules concerning the operation of the $100,000 limitation because these provisions were enacted in 1986. However, Notice 87-49 (1987-2 C.B. 355) provides general guidance about the operation of the $100,000 limitation, including examples illustrating the application of this limitation.

Section 1.422-4 of these proposed regulations provides guidance on the operation of the $100,000 limitation that incorporates and expands on the guidance provided in Notice 87-49. Section 1.422-4(a)(1) of these proposed regulations provides that an option that otherwise qualifies as an incentive stock option nevertheless fails to be an incentive stock option to the extent the $100,000 limitation is exceeded.

To determine whether the $100,000 limitation has been exceeded, the rules provided in § 1.422-4(b) of these proposed regulations would apply. Under these proposed regulations, an option that does not qualify as an incentive stock option when granted (including an option which contains terms providing that it will not be treated as an incentive stock option) is disregarded. Additionally, the fair market value of stock is determined on the date of grant of the option. Except as described in the following paragraph, options are taken into account in the order in which they are granted.

An option is considered to be first exercisable during a calendar year if the option will first become exercisable at any time during the year, assuming that any condition on the optionee's ability to exercise the option related to the performance of services is satisfied. If an optionee is able to exercise the option in a year only if an acceleration provision is satisfied, then the option is exercisable in that year only if the acceleration provision is triggered prior to the end of that year. After an acceleration provision is triggered, for purposes of applying the $100,000 limitation, the options subject to such provision and all other options first exercisable during a calendar year are then taken into account in the order in which granted. However, because an acceleration provision is not taken into account prior to its triggering, an incentive stock option that becomes exercisable for the first time during a calendar year by operation of such a provision does not affect the application of the $100,000 limitation with respect to an option (or portion thereof) exercised prior to such acceleration. An acceleration provision includes, for example, a provision that accelerates the exercisability of an option on a change in ownership or control or a provision that conditions exercisability on the attainment of a performance goal. See § 1.422-4(d), *Example 4* of these proposed regulations.

For example, assume that in 2006, E, an employee of Y Corporation, is granted Option 1 for stock of Y with a fair market value on the date of grant of $75,000. Option 1 is first exercisable in 2008, except that the option provides that it will become immediately exercisable in the event of a change in control. In 2007, E is granted Option 2 for stock of Y with a fair market value on the date of grant of $50,000. Option 2 is immediately exercisable, and E exercises Option 2. A change in control of Y occurs in 2007, after E has exercised Option 2, and Option 1 becomes immediately exercisable. Notwithstanding the fact that Op-

tion 1 was granted prior to Option 2, because the acceleration clause is not taken into account until it is triggered and because E exercised Option 2 prior to the change in control, Option 2 is an incentive stock option in its entirety. Option 1 is bifurcated into an incentive stock option to acquire stock with a fair market value of $50,000 on the date of grant and a nonstatutory option to acquire stock with a fair market value of $25,000 on the date of grant.

If the change in control instead occurred prior to E's exercise of Option 2, then Option 1, which was granted first, is treated as an incentive stock option in its entirety, and Option 2 is bifurcated into an incentive stock option to acquire stock with a fair market value of $25,000 on the date of grant and a nonstatutory option to acquire stock with a fair market value of $25,000 on the date of grant.

These proposed regulations also would provide that an option is disregarded for purposes of the $100,000 limitation if, prior to the calendar year during which it would have otherwise become exercisable for the first time, the option is modified and thereafter ceases to be an incentive stock option, is transferred in violation of the nontransferability requirements, or is canceled. In all other situations, a modified, transferred, or canceled option (or portion thereof) is treated as outstanding until the end of the calendar year during which it would otherwise have become exercisable for the first time.

Finally, under these proposed regulations, a disqualifying disposition has no effect on the determination of whether an option exceeds the $100,000 limitation. Thus, for example, assume Corporation X grants E, an employee of X, Option 1 to acquire X stock with a fair market value on the date of grant of $75,000. Option 1 is exercisable on January 1, 2005. On January 5, 2005, E exercises the option and sells the stock in a disqualifying disposition. On January 15, 2005, X grants E Option 2 to acquire X stock with a fair market value on the date of grant of $50,000. Option 2 is immediately exercisable. Under § 1.422-4(b)(6) of the proposed regulations, the disqualifying disposition of Option 1 has no effect on the application of the $100,000 limitation. Thus, Option 2 is bifurcated into an incentive stock option to acquire stock with a fair market value of $25,000 on the date of grant and a nonstatutory option to acquire stock with a fair market value of $25,000 on the date of grant.

4. Permissible provisions

These proposed regulations also provide guidance on additional provisions that may be included in an incentive stock option. Because these provisions are not part of the requirements for an incentive stock option, they are addressed separately in § 1.422-5 of these proposed regulations (many of these rules were previously in § 1.422A-2(i) of the 1984 proposed regulations). Section 1.422-5 of these proposed regulations addresses provisions permitting cashless exercise, providing the right to receive additional compensation, and providing alternative rights. In each case, these proposed regulations essentially retain the rules described in the 1984 proposed regulations.

Section 424: Definitions and Special Rules

These proposed regulations re-designate the regulations under section 425 as regulations under section 424 and update the regulations. For example, these proposed regulations amend the definition of *disposition* to exclude a transfer of a share of stock acquired pursuant to the exercise of a statutory option if the transfer is described in section 1041(a) (concerning transfers between spouses or former spouses incident to divorce).

Substitution, Assumption, and Modification of Options

Section 424(h)(1) provides that if the terms of an option are modified, extended, or renewed, such modification, renewal, or extension is treated as the grant of a new option. Under section 424(h)(3), the term *modification* (with certain exceptions) means any change in the terms of an option which gives the optionee additional benefits under the option. One exception to this definition is that a change in the terms of an option attributable to a substitution or an assumption that meets the requirements of section 424(a) is not a modification of an option.

These proposed regulations would provide that an *eligible corporation* (as defined in § 1.424-1(a)(2) of these proposed regulations) may by reason of a *corporate transaction* (as defined in § 1.424-1(a)(3) of these proposed regulations) substitute a new statutory option (new option) for an outstanding statutory option (old option) or assume an old option without the substitution or assumption being considered a modification of the old option under section 424(h).

An *eligible corporation* is defined as a corporation that is the employer of an optionee or a related corporation of such corporation. The determination of whether a corporation is the employer of the optionee or a related corporation of such corporation is based upon the circumstances existing immediately after the corporate transaction.

Under the proposed regulations, a *corporate transaction* is (i) a corporate merger, consolidation, acquisition of property or stock, separation, reorganization, or liquidation; (ii) a distribution (excluding ordinary dividends), or change in the terms or number of outstanding shares of such corporation, such as a stock split or stock dividend (a change in capital structure); (iii) a change in the name of a corporation whose stock is purchasable under the old option; and (iv) such other corporate events as may be prescribed by the Commissioner in published guidance.

The definitions of *eligible corporation* and *corporate transaction* would be expanded under these proposed regulations. Specifically, these proposed regulations permit corporations with outstanding options to substitute or assume an option under § 1.424-1(a) if there is a corporate transaction. Additionally, the definition of *corporate transaction* includes events, such as a stock dividend or stock split, that were previously addressed in § 1.425-1(e) of the final regulations, and is otherwise expanded so that events or transactions with similar consequences are treated the same. Because of these changes, the rules in § 1.425-1(e)(5)(ii) of the current regulations would be removed.

These proposed regulations also would eliminate the requirement contained in § 1.425-1(a)(1)(ii) of the final regulations that the corporate transaction result in a significant number of employees being transferred to a new employer or discharged or in the creation or severance of a parent-subsidiary relationship. However, § 1.424-1(a)(4) of these proposed regulations would continue to impose, and provide additional guidance concerning, the requirement that the substitution or assumption be "by reason of" the corporate transaction.

Under these proposed regulations, a change in an option or issuance of a new option is considered to be by reason of a corporate transaction unless the relevant facts and circumstances demonstrate that such change or issuance is made for reasons unrelated to such corporate transaction. For example, a change in an option or issuance of a new option is considered to be made for reasons unrelated to such a corporate transaction if there is an unreasonable delay between the corporate transaction and such change in the option or issuance of a new option or if the corporate transaction serves no substantial corporate business purpose independent of the change in options. A change in an option or issuance of a new option is not by reason of a distribution or change in the terms or number of outstanding shares unless the option as changed, or the new option, is issued on the stock of the same corporation, or if such class of stock is eliminated by the change in capital structure, on other stock of the same corporation. For purposes of a change in name of the corporation, the issuance of a new option is by reason of the change in name of the corporation only if the option issued is on stock of the successor corporation.

These proposed regulations do not otherwise revise the requirements that must be met for a change in an option to qualify as a substitution or an assumption. For example, no changes are proposed with respect to the requirements that no additional benefits be granted to the optionee in connection with a substitution or assumption or that certain spread and ratio tests must be met.

These proposed regulations also continue to impose the requirement contained in the final regulations that the new or assumed option must otherwise qualify as a statutory option. See § 1.424-1(a)(5)(vi) of these proposed regulations. Thus, except as necessary to comply with the specific requirements regarding substitution or assumption, such as the restrictions on ratio and spread, the option must comply with the requirements of § 1.422-2 of these proposed regulations or 1.423-2, as applicable. Accordingly, for example, the new option must be granted, or the old option must be assumed, under a plan approved by the stockholders of the corporation substituting or assuming the option.

The proposed regulations do not impose any additional stockholder approval requirement, however, merely because there is a corporate transaction. In Rev. Rul. 71-474 (1971-2 C.B. 215) involving qualified stock options,[1] the IRS held that qualified stock options assumed by a corporation in a merger with the granting corporation retained their status as qualified stock options without approval of the assuming corporation's stockholders. In the ruling, the IRS indicated that approval of the persons who owned stock of the granting corporation at the time the plan was approved was sufficient to satisfy the stockholder approval requirements. Similarly, the 1984 proposed regulations provided that the stockholders of the granting corporation must approve the plan within 12 months before or after its adoption without additional requirements.

Section 1.422-2(b)(2) of these proposed regulations would provide that the plan must be approved during the applicable 24-month period by the stockholders of the corporation granting the incentive stock option. There is no requirement that additional stockholder approval be obtained because of post-approval changes in the stockholders. For example, assume S, a subsidiary of P, adopts a plan under which incentive stock options for S stock will be granted to S employees. Under the proposed regulations, the stockholders of S must approve the plan within 12 months before or after the adoption of the plan. If P later completely disposes of its interest in S, outstanding S options and new grants of S options under the plan are treated as options granted under a plan that meets the stockholder approval requirement of § 1.422-2(b)(2) of these proposed regulations without regard to whether S seeks approval of the plan from the stockholders of S after the spin-off. Assuming all other applicable requirements are met, the outstanding S options and new options granted by S pursuant to the plan with respect to S stock will be treated as incentive stock options.

These proposed regulations also would provide additional guidance with respect to when a change to an option constitutes a modification. Under these proposed regulations, as under the 1984 proposed regulations, both a provision under an option that provides that the optionee may receive an additional benefit at the future discretion of the granting corporation and the exercise of that discretion are considered modifications of the option. However, under these proposed regulations, it is not a modification for the granting corporation to exercise discretion related to the payment of a bonus at the time of the exercise of the option, the availability of a loan at exercise, or the right to tender previously-owned stock for the stock purchasable under the option. A change to an option adding such discretion, however, would be a modification.

In addition, these proposed regulations address more clearly changes related to an option, including changes not only to the option or the option plan, but also changes to any other related agreements. In the case of a change to the stock on which the option is granted that affects the value of the stock, there would be a modification unless a new option is substituted for the old option by reason of the change in the terms of the stock in accordance with the requirements of § 1.424-1(a) of these proposed regulations.

Section 6039

These proposed regulations also would provide guidance on the statements required under section 6039 of the Code. Under these proposed regulations, § 1.6039-1 of the final regulations would be deleted, and § 1.6039-2 would be re-designated as § 1.6039-1. These proposed regulations take the same approach toward providing notice as that taken in the 1984 proposed regulations.

Section 1.6039-1(f) of these proposed regulations states that the matter of furnishing statements in electronic form is reserved. Temporary and proposed regulations have been issued under sections 6041 and 6051 (relating to voluntary electronic furnishing of payee statements on Form W-2) and section 6050S (relating to voluntary electronic furnishing of statements to individuals for whom Forms 1098-T, "Tuition Payments Statement," and 1098-E, "Student Loan Interest Statement" are filed). See 66 FR 10191 and 10247 (Feb. 14, 2001). The preamble to those temporary and proposed regulations requested comments regarding, among other things, the extent to which the proposed method of electronic filing is appropriate for information statements required under other sections of the Code. In addition, section 401 of the Job Creation and Worker Assistance Act of 2002 authorized all statements required by sections 6041 through 6050T of the Code to be furnished electronically under certain conditions. The issue of electronic statements in general is under review, and comments are requested.

Proposed Effective Date

The regulations under sections 421, 422, and 424 are proposed to apply as of the date that is 180 days after publication of final regulations in the **Federal Register** and apply to any statutory option that is granted on or after that date. The regulations under section 6039 are proposed to apply to transfers on or after the date that is 180 days after publication of final regulations in the **Federal Register** of stock acquired pursuant to a statutory option. The 1984 proposed regulations are withdrawn. Taxpayers may rely on these proposed regulations for the treatment of any statutory option granted after June 9, 2003.

---

[1] Qualified stock options are no longer permitted under section 422, but the stockholder approval provisions applicable to a plan under which qualified stock options were granted were the same as those that apply to a plan under which incentive stock options are granted.

Special Analyses

It has been determined that this notice of proposed rulemaking is not a significant regulatory action as defined in Executive Order 12866. Therefore, a regulatory assessment is not required. Section 1.6039-1 of these proposed regulations provides for the collection of information. It is hereby certified that the collection of information in these regulations will not have a significant economic impact on a substantial number of small entities. This certification is based on the fact that the provision of employee statements provided under these proposed regulations will impose a minimal paperwork burden on most small entities (see the discussion under the heading "Paperwork Reduction Act" earlier in this preamble). Therefore, an analysis under the Regulatory Flexibility Act (5 U.S.C. chapter 6) is not required. Pursuant to section 7805(f) of the Code, this notice of proposed rulemaking is being submitted to the Chief Counsel for Advocacy of the Small Business Administration for comment on its impact on small business.

Comments and Public Hearing

Before these proposed regulations are adopted as final regulations, consideration will be given to any written or electronic comments (a signed original and eight (8) copies) that are submitted timely to the IRS. All comments will be available for public inspection and copying.

A public hearing has been scheduled for September 2, 2003, beginning at 10 a.m. in the IRS Auditorium of the Internal Revenue Building, 1111 Constitution Avenue, NW., Washington, DC. All visitors must come to the Constitution Avenue entrance and present photo identification to enter the building. Because of access restrictions, visitors will not be admitted beyond the immediate entrance area more than 30 minutes before the hearing starts. For information about having your name placed on the building access list to attend the hearing, see the "FOR FURTHER INFORMATION CONTACT" section of this preamble.

The rules of 26 CFR 601.601(a)(3) apply to the hearing. Persons who wish to present oral comments at the hearing must submit written comments and an outline of the topics to be discussed and the time to be devoted to each topic (signed original and eight (8) copies) by August 12, 2003. A period of 10 minutes will be allotted to each person for making comments. An agenda showing the schedule of speakers will be prepared after the deadline for receiving outlines has passed. Copies of the agenda will be available free of charge at the hearing.

	Newly Designated Section
1.421-1(b)(3)(ii), *Example 1*, first, second, third and fourth sentences	
1.421-1(b)(3)(ii), *Example 1*, second sentence	
1.421-1(b)(3)(ii), *Example 1*, third and fourth sentences	
1.421-1(b)(3)(ii), *Example 2*, first and second sentences	
1.421-1(b)(3)(ii), *Example 2*, first, third, and fourth sentences	
1..421-1(b)(3)(ii), *Example 2*, third and fourth sentences	

9. Revising the last sentence of paragraph (b)(3)(ii), *Example 1*.

10. Removing the last sentence of paragraph (b)(3)(ii), *Example 2* and adding two sentences in its place.

11. Removing the first sentence of paragraph (c)(1) and adding two new sentences in its place.

12. In paragraph (c)(2), second sentence, the language "425" is removed and "424" is added in its place.

13. In paragraph (c)(3), second and last sentences, the language "1964" is removed and "2004" is added in its place.

14. In paragraph (c)(3), second sentence, the language "1965" is removed and "2005" is added in its place.

15. Revising paragraphs (d) and (e).

16. In paragraph (f), in the first sentence, the language "sections 421 through 425" is removed and "this section and §§ 1.421-2 through 1.424-1" is added in its place.

Newly Designated Section	
1.421-1(h)(4), *Example 1*, first sentence	1964
1.421-1(h)(4), *Example 1*, second and last sentences	1965
1.421-1(h)(4), *Example 2*, first sentence	425
1.421-1(h)(4), *Example 2*, first sentence	issuing
1.424-1(h)(4), *Example 2*, last sentence	1965

Drafting Information

The principal author of these proposed regulations is Erinn Madden, Office of the Division Counsel/Associate Chief Counsel (Tax Exempt and Government Entities). However, other personnel from the IRS and Treasury Department participated in their development.

List of Subjects in 26 CFR Parts 1 and 14a

Income taxes, Reporting, and recordkeeping requirements.

Proposed Amendments to the Regulations

Accordingly, 26 CFR parts 1 and 14a is proposed to be amended as follows:

PART 1—INCOME TAXES

Paragraph 1. The authority citation for part 1 continues to read in part as follows:

Authority: 26 U.S.C. 7805 * * *

§§ 1.421-1 through 1.421-6 [Removed]

Par. 2. Sections 1.421-1 through 1.421-6 are removed.

Par. 3. Section 1.421-7 is re-designated as § 1.421-1 and is amended as follows:

1. In paragraph (a)(1), first sentence, the language "sections 421 through 425" is removed and "§§ 1.421-1 through 1.424-1" is added in its place.

2. In paragraph (a)(1), first sentence, the language "includes" is removed, and "means" is added in its place.

3. In paragraph (a)(1), removing the second sentence.

4. Removing the last sentence of paragraph (a)(1) and adding two sentences in its place.

5. Revising paragraph (a)(3).

6. Revising paragraphs (b)(1) and (b)(2).

7. In paragraph (b)(3)(i), third sentence, removing the language "1.425-1" and inserting "1.424-1" in its place.

8. In the list below, for each section indicated in the left column, remove the language in the middle column and add the language in the right column:

Remove	Add
S-1	X
1964	2004
1965	2005
1964	2004
S-1	X
1965	2005

17. Revising the last sentence of paragraph (f).

18. In paragraph (g), first sentence, the language "sections 421 through 425" is removed and "this section and §§ 1.421-2 through 1.424-1" is added in its place.

19. Adding a new third sentence to paragraph (g).

20. Revising the first, second, and third sentences of paragraph (h)(1).

21. Revising paragraph (h)(2).

22. In paragraph (h)(3), first sentence, the language "425" is removed and "424" is added in its place.

23. In paragraph (h)(3), last sentence, the language "or assuming" is removed and "the option or substituting or assuming the option" is added in its place.

24. In the list below, for each section indicated in the left column, remove the language in the middle column and add the language in the right column:

Remove		Add
		2004
		2005
		424
		substituting
		2005

Newly Designated Section	Remove	Add
1.421-1(h)(4), *Example 2*, last sentence	for A is then employed by a corporation which issued an option under section 425(a).	to the transfer of the M stock because, at all times during the period beginning with the date of grant of the X option and ending with the date of exercise of the M option, A was an employee of the corporation granting the option or substituting or assuming the option under § 1.424-1(a).
1.421-1(h)(4), *Example 3*, second sentence	1964	2004
1.421-1(h)(4), *Example 3*, third, fourth, and fifth sentences	1965	2005
1.421-1(h)(4), *Example 4*, first sentence	425(a)	424(a)
1.421-1(h)(4), *Example 5*, first sentence	qualified stock	statutory
1.421-1(h)(4), *Example 6*, first sentence	an employment contract with M which provides that upon the termination of any military duty E may be required to serve, E will be entitled to reemployment with M or a parent or subsidiary of M.	a right to reemployment with M or a related corporation on the termination of any military duty E may be required to serve.
1.421-1(h)(4), *Example 6*, third sentence	of M	of M or a related corporation
1.421-1(h)(4), *Example 6*, last sentence	can apply	applies
1.421-1(h)(4), *Example 7*, first and last sentences	a qualified stock	an incentive
1.421-1(h)(4), *Example 7*, first sentence	parent or subsidiary	related corporation
1.421-1(h)(4), *Example 7*, last sentence	its parent and subsidiary corporation	related corporations
1.421-1(h)(4), *Example 7*, last sentence	terminated	deemed terminated

25. Revising paragraph (i).

26. Adding paragraph (j).

The additions and revisions read as follows:

§ 1.421-1 Meaning and use of certain terms.

(a) * * * (1) * * * While no particular form of words is necessary, the option must express, among other things, an offer to sell at the option price, the maximum number of shares purchasable under the option, and the period of time during which the offer remains open. The term *option* includes a warrant that meets the requirements of this paragraph (a)(1).

* * * * *

(3) An option must be in writing (in paper or electronic form), provided that such writing is adequate to establish an option right or privilege that is enforceable under applicable law.

(b) *Statutory options.* (1) The term *statutory option*, for purposes of this section and §§ 1.421-2 through 1.424-1, means an *incentive stock option*, as defined in § 1.422-2(a), or an option granted under an *employee stock purchase plan*, as defined in § 1.423-2.

(2) An option qualifies as a statutory option only if the option is not transferable (other than by will or by the laws of descent and distribution) by the individual to whom the option was granted, and is exercisable, during the lifetime of such individual, only by such individual. See §§ 1.422-2(a)(2)(v) and 1.423-2(j). Accordingly, an option which is transferable or transferred by the individual to whom the option is granted during such individual's lifetime, or is exercisable during such individual's lifetime by another person, is not a statutory option. However, if the option or the plan under which the option was granted contains a provision permitting the individual to designate the person who may exercise the option after such individual's death, neither such provision, nor a designation pursuant to such provision, disqualifies the option as a statutory option. A pledge of the stock purchasable under an option as security for a loan that is used to pay the option price does not cause the option to violate the nontransferability requirements of this paragraph (b). Also, the transfer of an option to a trust does not disqualify the option as a statutory option if, under section 671 and applicable State law, the individual is considered the sole beneficial owner of the option while it is held in the trust. If an option is transferred incident to divorce (within the meaning of section 1041) or pursuant to a qualified domestic relations order (within the meaning of section 414(p)), the option does not qualify as a statutory option as of the day of such transfer. For the treatment of nonstatutory options, see § 1.83-7.

(3)(ii) * * * * *

Example 1. * * * Because X was a subsidiary of P on the date of the grant of the statutory option, the option does not fail to be a statutory option even though X ceases to be a subsidiary of P.

Example 2. * * * Because X was not a subsidiary of P on the date of the grant of the option, the option is not a statutory option even though S later becomes a subsidiary of P. See §§ 1.422-2(a)(2) and 1.423-2(b).

(c) *Time and date of granting option.* (1) For purposes of this section and §§ 1.421-2 through 1.424-1, the language "the date of the granting of the option" and "the time such option is granted," and similar phrases refer to the date or time when the granting corporation completes the corporate action constituting an offer of stock for sale to an individual under the terms and conditions of a statutory option. A corporate action constituting an offer of stock for sale is not considered complete until the date on which the maximum number of shares that can be purchased under the option and the minimum option price are fixed or determinable. * * *

* * * * *

(d) *Stock and voting stock.* (1) For purposes of this section and §§ 1.421-2 through 1.424-1, the term *stock* means capital stock of any class, including voting or nonvoting common or preferred stock. Except as otherwise provided, the term includes both treasury stock and stock of original issue. Special classes of stock authorized to be issued to and held by employees are within the scope of the term *stock* as used in such sections, provided such stock otherwise possesses the rights and characteristics of capital stock.

(2) For purposes of determining what constitutes voting stock in ascertaining whether a plan has been approved by stockholders under § 1.422-2(b) or 1.423-2(c) or whether the limitations pertaining to voting power contained in sections §§ 1.422-2(f) and 1.423-2(d) have been met, stock which does not have voting rights until the happening of an event, such as the default in the payment of dividends on preferred stock, is not voting stock until the happening of the specified event. Generally, stock which does not possess a general voting power, and may vote only on particular questions, is not voting stock. However, if such stock is entitled to vote on whether a stock option plan may be adopted, it is voting stock.

(3) In general, for purposes of this section and §§ 1.421-2 through 1.424-1, ownership interests other than capital stock are considered stock.

(e) *Option price.* (1) For purposes of this section and §§ 1.421-2 through 1.424-1, the term *option price, price paid under the option*, or *exercise price* means the consideration in cash or property which, pursuant to the terms of the option, is the price at which the stock subject to the option is purchased. The term *option price* does not include any amounts paid as interest under a deferred payment arrangement or treated as interest.

(2) Any reasonable valuation method may be used to determine whether, at the time the option is granted, the option price satisfies the pricing requirements of sections 422(b)(4), 422(c)(5), 422(c)(7), and 423(b)(6) with respect to the stock subject to the option. Such methods include, for example, the valuation method described in § 20.2031-2 of this chapter (Estate Tax Regulations).

(f) *Exercise.* * * * An agreement or undertaking by the employee to make payments under a stock purchase plan does not constitute the exercise of an option to the extent the payments made remain subject to withdrawal by or refund to the employee.

(g) *Transfer.* * * * A transfer does not fail to occur merely because, under the terms of the arrangement, the individual may not dispose of the share for a specified period of time or the share is subject to a right of first refusal at the share's fair market value at the time of sale.

(h) *Employment relationship.* (1) An option is a statutory option only if, at the time the option is granted, the optionee is an employee of the corporation granting the option, or a related corporation of such corporation. If the option has been assumed or a new option has been substituted in its place under § 1.424-1(a), the optionee must, at the time of such substitution or assumption, be an employee of the corporation so substituting or assuming the option, or a related corporation of such corporation. The determination of whether the optionee is an employee at the time the option is granted (or at the time of the substitution or assumption under § 1.424-1(a)) is made in accordance with section 3401(c) and the regulations thereunder. * * *

(2) In addition, § 1.421-2(a) is applicable to the transfer of a share pursuant to the exercise of the statutory option only if the optionee is, at all times during the period beginning with the date of the granting of such option and ending on the day 3 months before the date of such exercise, an employee of either the corporation granting such option, a related corporation of such corporation, or a corporation (or a related corporation of such corporation) substituting or assuming a stock option in a transaction to which § 1.424-1(a) applies. For purposes of the preceding sentence, the employment relationship is treated as continuing intact while the individual is on military leave, sick leave, or other bona fide leave of absence (such as temporary employment by the Government) if the period of such leave does not exceed 90 days, or if longer, so long as the individual's right to reemployment with the corporation granting the option (or a related corporation of such corporation) or a corporation (or a related corporation of such corporation) substituting or assuming a stock option in a transaction to which § 1.424-1(a) applies, is guaranteed either by statute or by contract. If the period of leave exceeds 90 days and the individual's right to reemployment is not guaranteed either by statute or by contract, the employment relationship is deemed to terminate on the 91st day of such leave. Thus, if the option is not exercised before such deemed termination of employment, § 1.421-2(a) applies to the transfer of a share pursuant to an exercise of the option only if the exercise occurs within 3 months from the date the employment relationship is deemed terminated.

* * * *

Newly Designated Section

1.421-2(c)(2), second sentence
1.421-2(c)(2), third sentence
1.421-2(c)(3)(i), first, second, and third sentences
1.421-2(c)(3)(ii), *Example*, first sentence
1.421-2(c)(3)(ii), *Example*, third, fifth, and sixth sentences

3. In paragraph (c)(2), first sentence, add the phrase "for purposes of section 423(c)" at the end of the first sentence.

4. Removing paragraph (c)(4)(i) and redesignating paragraphs (c)(4)(ii) through (c)(4)(iv) as paragraphs (c)(4)(i) through (c)(4)(iii), respectively.

5. In newly designated paragraph (c)(4)(i)(*a*), first sentence, removing the phrase "In the case of an employee dying after December 31, 1956" and adding "In the case of the death of an optionee" in its place.

Newly Designated Section

1.421-2(c)(4)(i)(*a*), last sentence
1.421-2(c)(4)(i)(*b*), first, second, and last sentences
1.421-2(c)(4)(i)(*c*), first sentence
1.421-2(c)(4)(iii), *Example 1*, first sentence
1.421-2(c)(4)(iii), *Example 1*, eighth sentence
1.421-2(c)(4)(iii), *Example 1*, third and fifth sentences
1.421-2(c)(4)(iii), *Example 1*, ninth sentence
1.421-2(c)(4)(iii), *Example 2*, second and fifth sentences
1.421-2(c)(4)(iii), *Example 2*, fifth sentence
1.421-2(c)(4)(iii), *Example 2*, first sentence
1.421-2(c)(4)(iii), *Example 3*, first sentence
1.421-2(c)(4)(iii), *Example 3*, second and fourth sentences
1.421-2(c)(4)(iii), *Example 3*, fourth sentence
1.421-2(c)(4)(iii), *Example 4*, first sentence
1.421-2(c)(4)(iii), *Example 4*, first sentence
1.421-2(c)(4)(iii), *Example 4*, first and second sentences
1.421-2(c)(iii), *Example 4*, third, fifth, and sixth sentences
1.421-2(c)(4)(iii), *Example 4*, fifth and sixth sentences
1.421-2(c)(4)(iii), *Example 4*, sixth sentence

8. Revising paragraph (d).

9. Adding paragraph (f).

The revisions read as follows:

§ 1.421-2 General rules.

(a) *Effect of qualifying transfer.* (1) If a share of stock is transferred to an individual pursuant to the individual's exercise of a statutory option, and if the requirements of § 1.422-1(a) (relating to incentive stock options) or § 1.423-1(a) (relating to employee stock purchase plans) whichever is applicable, are met, then—

(i) No income results at the time of the transfer of such share to the individual upon the exercise of the option with respect to such share (in addition, no income results upon grant of the option, see § 1.83-7);

(i) *Additional definitions.* (1) *Corporation.* For purposes of this section and § § 1.421-2 through 1.424-1, the term *corporation* has the meaning prescribed by section 7701(a)(3) and § 301.7701-2(b) of this chapter. For example, a *corporation* for purposes of the preceding sentence includes an S corporation (as defined in section 1361), a foreign corporation (as defined in section 7701(a)(5)), and a limited liability company that is treated as a corporation for all Federal tax purposes.

(2) *Parent corporation and subsidiary corporation.* For the definition of the terms *parent corporation* (and *parent*) and *subsidiary corporation* (and *subsidiary*), for purposes of this section and § § 1.421-2 through 1.424-1, see § 1.424-1(f)(i) and (ii), respectively. *Related corporation* as used in this section and in § § 1.421-2 through 1.424-1 means either a parent corporation or subsidiary corporation.

(j) *Effective date.* This section applies to any statutory option granted on or after the date that is 180 days after publication of final regulations in the **Federal Register**. Taxpayers can rely on these regulations for the treatment of any statutory option granted on or after June 9, 2003.

Par. 4. Section 1.421-8 is re-designated as 1.421-2 and is amended by:

1. Revising paragraphs (a)(1), (b), and (c)(1).

2. In the list below, for each section indicated in the left column, remove the language in the middle column and add the language in the right column:

Remove	Add
, or 424(c)(1)	
or 424(c)(1)	
422(c)(1), 423(c), or 424(c)(1)	423(c)
1964	2004
1966	2006

6. Removing *Example (1)* in newly designated paragraph (c)(4)(iii) and redesignating *Examples (2)* through (5) as *Examples (1)* through (4), respectively.

7. In the list below, for each section indicated in the left column, remove the language in the middle column and add the language in the right column:

Remove	Add
422(c)(1), 423(c), or 424(c)(1)	423(c)
422(c)(1), 423(c), or 424(c)(1)	423(c)
422(c)(1), 423(c), or 424(c)(1)	423(c)
1964	2005
subdivision (ii)(*b*) of this subparagraph	paragraph (c)(4)(i)(*b*) of this section
1966	2006
subdivision (ii)(*c*) of this subparagraph	paragraph (c)(4)(i)(*c*) of this section
subdivision (ii)(*a*) of this subparagraph	paragraph (c)(4)(i)(a) of this section
subdivision (ii)(*b*) of this subparagraph	paragraph (c)(4)(i)(*b*) of this section
example (2)	Example 1
example (2)	Example 1
subdivision (ii)(*a*) of this subparagraph	paragraph (c)(4)(i)(*a*) of this section
subdivision (ii)(*c*) of this subparagraph	paragraph (c)(4)(i)(c) of this section
example (2)	Example 1
1966	2006
1967	2007
subdivision (ii)(*a*) of this subparagraph	paragraph (c)(4)(i)(*a*) of this section
subdivision (ii)(*b*) of this subparagraph	paragraph (c)(4)(i)(*b*) of this section
subdivision (ii)(*c*) of this subparagraph	paragraph (c)(4)(i)(*c*) of this section

(ii) No deduction under section 162 or the regulations thereunder (relating to trade or business expenses) is allowable at any time with respect to the share so transferred; and

(iii) No amount other than the price paid under the option is considered as received by the employer corporation, a related corporation of such corporation, or a corporation substituting or assuming a stock option in a transaction to which § 1.424-1(a) (relating to corporate reorganizations, liquidations, etc.) applies, for the share so transferred.

* * * * *

(b) *Effect of disqualifying disposition.* (1)(i) The disposition (as defined in § 1.424-1(c)) of a share of stock acquired by the exercise of a statutory option before the expiration of the applicable holding periods as determined under § 1.422-1(a) or 1.423-1(a) is a disqualifying disposition and makes paragraph (a) of this section inapplicable to the transfer of such share. See § 1.83-7 for the treatment of nonstatutory options. The income attributable to such transfer (determined without reduction for any brokerage fees or other costs paid in connection with the disposition) is treated by the individual as compensation income received in the taxable year in which such disqualifying disposition occurs. Similarly, if otherwise allowable under sections 83(h) and 162, a deduction attributable to such transfer is allowable for the taxable year in which such disqualifying disposition occurs to the employer corporation, or a related corporation of such corporation, or a corporation substituting or assuming an option in a transaction to which § 1.424-1(a) applies. Additionally, an amount is allowed as a deduction only if the requirements of § 1.83-6(a) are satisfied. No amount is treated as income, and no amount is allowed as a deduction, for any taxable year other than the taxable year in which the disqualifying disposition occurs. If the amount realized on the disposition exceeds (or is less than) the sum of the amount paid for the share and the amount of compensation income recognized as a result of such disposition, the extent to which the difference is treated as gain (or loss) is determined under the rules of section 302 or 1001, as applicable.

(ii) The following examples illustrate the principles of this paragraph (b):

Example 1. On June 1, 2006, X Corporation grants an incentive stock option to A, an employee of X, entitling A to purchase 100 shares of X stock at $10 per share. On August 1, 2006, A exercises the option when the fair market value of X stock is $20 per share, and 100 shares of X stock are transferred to A on that date. On December 15, 2007, A sells the stock. Because A disposed of the stock before June 2, 2008, A did not satisfy the holding period requirements of § 1.422-1(a). Under paragraph (b)(1)(i) of this section, A made a disqualifying disposition of the stock. Thus, paragraph (a) of this section is inapplicable to the transfer of the shares, and A must include the compensation income attributable to the transfer of the shares in gross income. The amount of compensation income A must include in income under § 1.83-7 in the year of the disqualifying disposition is $1,000 (($20, the fair market value of X stock on transfer less $10, the exercise price per share) times 100 shares)). If otherwise allowable under sections 83(h) and 162 and if the requirements of § 1.83-6(a) are met, X is allowed a deduction of $1,000 for its taxable year in which the disqualifying disposition occurs.

Example 2. Y Corporation grants an incentive stock option for 100 shares of its stock to E, an employee of Y. The option has an exercise price of $10 per share. E exercises the option and is transferred the shares when the fair market value of a share of Y stock is $30. Before the applicable holding periods expire, Y redeems the shares for $70 per share. Because the holding period requirements of § 1.422-1(a) are not met, the redemption of the shares is a disqualifying disposition of the shares. Under paragraph (b)(1)(i) of this section, A made a disqualifying disposition of the stock. Thus, paragraph (a) of this section is inapplicable to the transfer of the shares, and E must include the compensation income attributable to the transfer of the shares in gross income. Under § 1.83-7, the amount of compensation income attributable to E's purchase of the share that E must include in gross income in the year of the disqualifying disposition is $2,000 ($3,000, the fair market value of Y stock on transfer, less $1,000, the exercise price paid by E). The character of the additional gain that is includible in E's income as a result of the redemption is determined under the rules of section 302. If otherwise allowable under sections 83(h) and 162 and if the requirements of § 1.83-6(a) are met, Y is allowed a deduction for the taxable year in which the disqualifying disposition occurs for the compensation income of $2,000. Y is not allowed a deduction for the additional gain includible in E's income as a result of the redemption.

(2) If an optionee transfers stock acquired through the optionee's exercise of a statutory option prior to the expiration of the applicable holding periods, paragraph (a) of this section continues to apply to the transfer of the stock pursuant to the exercise of the option if such transfer is not a disposition of the stock as defined in § 1.424-1(c) (for example, a transfer from a decedent to the decedent's estate or a transfer by bequest or inheritance). Similarly, a subsequent transfer by the executor, administrator, heir, or legatee is not a disqualifying disposition by the decedent. If a statutory option is exercised by the estate of the optionee or by a person who acquired the option by bequest or inheritance or by reason of the death of such optionee, see paragraph (c) of this section. If a statutory option is exercised by the individual to whom the option was granted and the individual dies before the expiration of the holding periods, see paragraph (d) of this section.

(3) For special rules relating to the disqualifying disposition of a share of stock acquired by exercise of an incentive stock option, see §§ 1.422-5(b)(2) and 1.424-1(c)(3).

(c) *Exercise by estate.* (1) If a statutory option is exercised by the estate of the individual to whom the option was granted (or by any

person who acquired such option by bequest or inheritance or by reason of the death of such individual), paragraph (a) of this section applies to the transfer of stock pursuant to such exercise in the same manner as if the option had been exercised by the deceased optionee. Consequently, neither the estate nor such person is required to include any amount in gross income as a result of a transfer of stock pursuant to the exercise of the option. Paragraph (a) of this section applies even if the executor, administrator, or such person disposes of the stock so acquired before the expiration of the applicable holding periods as determined under § 1.422-1(a) or 1.423-1(a). This special rule does not affect the applicability of section 423(c), relating to the estate's or other qualifying person's recognition of compensation income, or section 1222, relating to what constitutes a short-term and long-term capital gain or loss. Paragraph (a) of this section also applies even if the executor, administrator, or such person does not exercise the option within three months after the death of the individual or is not employed as described in § 1.421-1(h), either when the option is exercised or at any time. However, paragraph (a) of this section does not apply to a transfer of shares pursuant to an exercise of the option by the estate or by such person unless the individual met the employment requirements described in § 1.421-1(h) either at the time of the individual's death or within three months before such time (or, if applicable, within the period described in § 1.422-1(a)(3)). Additionally, paragraph (a) of this section does not apply if the option is exercised by a person other than the executor or administrator, or other than a person who acquired the option by bequest or inheritance or by reason of the death of such deceased individual. For example, if the option is sold by the estate, paragraph (a) of this section does not apply to the transfer of stock pursuant to an exercise of the option by the buyer, but if the option is distributed by the administrator to an heir as part of the estate, paragraph (a) of this section applies to the transfer of stock pursuant to an exercise of the option by such heir.

* * * * *

(d) *Option exercised by the individual to whom the option was granted if the individual dies before expiration of the applicable holding periods.* If a statutory option is exercised by the individual to whom the option was granted and such individual dies before the expiration of the applicable holding periods as determined under § 1.422-1(a) or 1.423-1(a), paragraph (a) of this section does not become inapplicable if the executor or administrator of the estate of such individual, or any person who acquired such stock by bequest or inheritance or by reason of the death of such individual, disposes of such stock before the expiration of such applicable holding periods. This rule does not affect the applicability of section 423(c), relating to the individual's recognition of compensation income, or section 1222, relating to what constitutes a short-term and long-term capital gain or loss.

* * * * *

(f) *Effective date.* This section is applies to any statutory option granted on or after the date that is 180 days after publication of final regulations in the *Federal Register*. Taxpayers can rely on these regulations for the treatment of any statutory option granted on or after June 9, 2003.

Par. 5. Section 1.422-1 is added to read as follows:

§ 1.422-1 Incentive stock options; general rules.

(a) *Applicability of section 421(a).* (1)(i) Section 1.421-2(a) applies to the transfer of a share of stock to an individual pursuant to the individual's exercise of an incentive stock option if the following conditions are satisfied—

(A) The individual makes no disposition of such share before the later of the expiration of the 2-year period from the date of grant of the option pursuant to which such share was transferred, or the expiration of the 1-year period from the date of transfer of such share to the individual; and

(B) At all times during the period beginning on the date of grant of the option and ending on the day 3 months before the date of exercise, the individual was an employee of either the corporation granting the option, a related corporation of such corporation, or a corporation (or a related corporation of such corporation) substituting or assuming a stock option in a transaction to which § 1.424-1(a) applies.

(ii) For rules relating to the disposition of shares of stock acquired pursuant to the exercise of a statutory option, see § 1.424-1(c). For rules relating to the requisite employment relationship, see § 1.421-1(h).

(2)(i) The holding period requirement of section 422(a)(1), described in paragraph (a)(1)(i)(A) of this section, does not apply to the transfers of shares by an insolvent individual described in this paragraph (a)(2). If an insolvent individual holds a share of stock acquired pursuant to the individual's exercise of an incentive stock option, and if such share is transferred to a trustee, receiver, or other similar fiduciary in any proceeding under the Bankruptcy Act or any other similar insolvency proceeding, neither such transfer, nor any other transfer of such share for the benefit of the individual's creditors in such proceeding is a disposition of such share for purposes of this paragraph (a). For purposes of this paragraph (a)(2), an individual is insolvent only if the individual's liabilities exceed the individual's assets or the individual is unable to satisfy the individual's liabilities as they become due. See section 422(c)(3).

(ii) A transfer by the trustee or other fiduciary that is not treated as a disposition for purposes of this paragraph (a) may be a sale or exchange for purposes of recognizing capital gain or loss with respect to the share transferred. For example, if the trustee transfers the share to a creditor in an insolvency proceeding, capital gain or loss must be recognized by the insolvent individual to the extent of the difference between the amount realized from such transfer and the adjusted basis of such share.

(iii) If any transfer by the trustee or other fiduciary (other than a transfer back to the insolvent individual) is not for the exclusive benefit of the creditors in an insolvency proceeding, then whether such transfer is a disposition of the share by the individual for purposes of this paragraph (a) is determined under § 1.424-1(c). Similarly, if the trustee or other fiduciary transfers the share back to the insolvent individual, any subsequent transfer of the share by such individual which is not made in respect of the insolvency proceeding may be a disposition of the share for purposes of this paragraph (a).

(3) If the employee exercising an option ceased employment because of permanent and total disability, within the meaning of section 22(e)(3), 1 year is used instead of 3 months in the employment period requirement of paragraph (a)(1)(i)(B) of this section.

(b) *Failure to satisfy holding period requirements*—(1) *General rule.* For general rules concerning a disqualifying disposition of a share of stock acquired pursuant to the exercise of an incentive stock option, see § 1.421-2(b)(1).

(2)(i) *Special rule.* If an individual makes a disqualifying disposition of a share of stock acquired by the exercise of an incentive stock option, and if such disposition is a sale or exchange with respect to which a loss (if sustained) would be recognized to the individual, then, under this paragraph (b)(2)(i), the amount includible in the gross income of such individual, and deductible from the income of the employer corporation (or a related corporation of such corporation, or of a corporation substituting or assuming the option in a transaction to which § 1.424-1(a) applies) as compensation attributable to the exercise of such option, shall not exceed the excess (if any) of the amount realized on such sale or exchange over the adjusted basis of such share. Subject to the special rule provided by this paragraph (b)(2)(i), the amount of compensation attributable to the exercise of the option is determined under § 1.83-7; see § 1.421-2(b)(1)(i).

(ii) *Limitation to special rule.* The special rule described in paragraph (b)(2)(i) of this section does not apply if the disposition is a sale or exchange with respect to which a loss (if sustained) would not be recognized to the individual. Thus, for example, if a disqualifying disposition is a sale described in section 1091 (relating to loss from wash sales of stock or securities), a gift (or any other transaction which is not at arm's length), or a sale described in section 267(a)(1) (relating to sales between related persons), the special rule described in paragraph (b)(2)(i) of this section does not apply because a loss sustained in any such transaction would not be recognized.

(3) *Examples.* The following examples illustrate the principles of this paragraph (b):

Example 1. On June 1, 2006, X Corporation grants an incentive stock option to A, an employee of X Corporation, entitling A to purchase one share of X Corporation stock. On August 1, 2006, A exercises the option and the share of X Corporation stock is transferred to A on that date. The option price is $100 (the fair market value of a share of X Corporation stock on June 1, 2006) and the fair market value of a share of X Corporation stock on August 1, 2006 (the date of transfer) is $200. The share transferred to A is transferable and not subject to a substantial risk of forfeiture. A makes a disqualifying disposition by selling the share on June 1, 2007, for $250. Under § 1.83-7(a) (relating to options to which section 421 does not apply), the amount of compensation attributable to A's exercise is $100 (the difference between the fair market value of the share at the date of transfer, $200, and the amount paid for the share, $100). Because the amount realized ($250) is greater than the value of the share at transfer ($200), paragraph (b)(2)(i) of this section does not apply and thus does not affect the amount includible

as compensation in A's gross income and deductible by X. A must include in gross income for the taxable year in which the sale occurred $100 as compensation and $50 as capital gain ($250, the amount realized from the sale, less A's basis of $200 (the $100 paid for the share plus the $100 increase in basis resulting from the inclusion of that amount in A's gross income as compensation attributable to the exercise of the option)). For its taxable year in which the disqualifying disposition occurs, if otherwise allowable under sections 83(h) and 162 and if the requirements of § 1.83-6(a) are met, X Corporation is allowed a deduction of $100 for compensation attributable to A's exercise of the incentive stock option.

Example 2. Assume the same facts as in *Example 1*, except that the share of X Corporation stock transferred to A is subject to a substantial risk of forfeiture and not transferable for a period of six months after such transfer. Assume further that the fair market value of X Corporation stock is $225 on February 1, 2005, the date on which the six-month restriction lapses. Under section 83(a) and § 1.83-7(a), the amount of compensation attributable to A's exercise of the option and disqualifying disposition of the share is $125 (the difference between the fair market value of the share on the date that the restriction lapsed, $225, and the amount paid for the share, $100). A must include $125 of compensation income and $25 of capital gain in gross income for the taxable year in which the disposition occurs ($250, the amount realized from the sale, less A's basis of $225 (the $100 paid for the share plus the $125 increase in basis resulting from the inclusion of that amount of compensation in A's gross income)). For its taxable year in which the disqualifying disposition occurs, if otherwise allowable under sections 83(h) and 162 and if the requirements of § 1.83-6(a) are met, X Corporation is allowed a deduction of $125 for the compensation attributable to A's exercise of the option.

Example 3. (i) Assume the same facts as in *Example 1*, except that A sells the share for $150 to M.

(ii) If the sale to M is a disposition that meets the requirements of paragraph (b)(2)(i) of this section, instead of $100 which otherwise would have been includible as compensation under § 1.83-7, under paragraph (b)(2)(i) of this section, A must include only $50 (the excess of the amount realized on such sale, $150, over the adjusted basis of the share, $100) in gross income as compensation attributable to the exercise of the incentive stock option. Because A's basis for the share is $150 (the $100 which A paid for the share, plus the $50 increase in basis resulting from the inclusion of that amount in A's gross income as compensation attributable to the exercise of the option), A realizes no capital gain or loss as a result of the sale. For its taxable year in which the disqualifying disposition occurs, if otherwise allowable under sections 83(h) and 162 and if the requirements of § 1.83-6(a) are met, X Corporation is allowed a deduction of $50 for the compensation attributable to A's exercise of the option.

(iii) Assume the same facts as in paragraph (i) of this *Example 3*, except that 10 days after the sale to M, A purchases substantially identical stock. Because under section 1091(a) a loss (if it were sustained on the sale) would not be recognized on the sale, under paragraph (b)(2)(ii) of this section, the special rule described in paragraph (b)(2)(i) of this section does not apply. Under § 1.83-7, A must include $100 (the difference between the fair market value of the share on the date of transfer, $200, and the amount paid for the share, $100) in gross income as compensation attributable to the exercise of the option for the taxable year in which the disqualifying disposition occurred. A recognizes no capital gain or loss on the transaction. For its taxable year in which the disqualifying disposition occurs, if otherwise allowable under sections 83(h) and 162 and if the requirements of § 1.83-6(a) are met, X Corporation is allowed a $100 deduction for compensation attributable to A's exercise of the option.

(iv) Assume the same facts as in paragraph (ii) of this *Example 3*, except that A sells the share for $50. Under paragraph (b)(2)(i) of this section, A is not required to include any amount in gross income as compensation attributable to the exercise of the option. A is allowed a capital loss of $50 (the difference between the amount realized on the sale, $50, and the adjusted basis of the share, $100). X Corporation is not allowed any deduction attributable to A's exercise of the option and disqualifying disposition of the share.

(c) *Failure to satisfy employment requirement.* Section 1.421-2(a) does not apply to the transfer of a share of stock pursuant to the exercise of an incentive stock option if the employment requirement, as determined under paragraph (a)(1)(i)(B) of this section, is not met at the time of the exercise of such option. Consequently, the effects of such a transfer are determined under the rules of § 1.83-7. For rules relating to the employment relationship, see § 1.421-1(h).

Par. 6. Section 1.422-2 is added to read as follows:

§ 1.422-2 Incentive stock options defined.

(a) *Incentive stock option defined*—(1) *In general.* The term *incentive stock option* means an option that meets the requirements of paragraph (a)(2) of this section on the date of grant. An incentive stock option is also subject to the $100,000 limitation described in § 1.422-4. An incentive stock option may contain a number of permissible provisions that do not affect the status of the option as an incentive stock option. See § 1.422-5 for rules relating to permissible provisions of an incentive stock option.

(2) *Option requirements.* To qualify as an incentive stock option under this section, an option must be granted to an individual in connection with the individual's employment by the corporation granting such option (or by a related corporation), and granted only for stock of any of such corporations. In addition, the option must meet all of the following requirements—

(i) It must be granted pursuant to a plan that meets the requirements described in paragraph (b) of this section;

(ii) It must be granted within 10 years from the date of the adoption of the plan or the date such plan is approved by the stockholders, whichever is earlier (see paragraph (c) of this section);

(iii) It must not be exercisable after the expiration of 10 years from the date of grant (see paragraph (d) of this section);

(iv) It must provide that the option price per share is not less than the fair market value of the share on the date of grant (see paragraph (e) of this section);

(v) By its terms, it must not be transferrable by the individual to whom the option is granted other than by will or the laws of descent and distribution, and must be exercisable, during such individual's lifetime, only by such individual (see §§ 1.421-1(b)(2) and 1.421-2(c)); and

(vi) Except as provided in paragraph (f) of this section, it must be granted to an individual who, at the time the option is granted, does not own stock possessing more than 10 percent of the total combined voting power of all classes of stock of the corporation employing such individual or of any related corporation of such corporation.

(3) *Amendment of option terms.* Except as otherwise provided in § 1.424-1, the amendment of the terms of an incentive stock option may cause it to cease to be an option described in this section. If the terms of an option that has lost its status as an incentive stock option are subsequently changed with the intent to re-qualify the option as an incentive stock option, such change results in the grant of a new option on the date of the change. See § 1.424-1(e).

(4) *Terms provide option not an incentive stock option.* If the terms of an option, when granted, provide that it will not be treated as an incentive stock option, such option is not treated as an incentive stock option.

(b) *Option plan*—(1) *In general.* An incentive stock option must be granted pursuant to a plan that meets the requirements of this paragraph (b). The authority to grant other stock options or other stock-based awards pursuant to the plan, where the exercise of such other options or awards does not affect the exercise of incentive stock options granted pursuant to the plan, does not disqualify such incentive stock options. The plan must be in writing or electronic form, provided that such writing or electronic form is adequate to establish the terms of the plan. See § 1.422-5 for rules relating to permissible provisions of an incentive stock option.

(2) *Stockholder approval.* (i) The plan required by this paragraph (b) must be approved by the stockholders of the corporation granting the incentive stock option within 12 months before or after the date such plan is adopted. Ordinarily, a plan is adopted when it is approved by the granting corporation's board of directors, and the date of the board's action is the reference point for determining whether stockholder approval occurs within the applicable 24-month period. However, if the board's action is subject to a condition (such as stockholder approval) or the happening of a particular event, the plan is adopted on the date the condition is met or the event occurs, unless the board's resolution fixes the date of approval as the date of the board's action.

(ii) For purposes of paragraph (b)(2)(i) of this section, the stockholder approval must comply with the rules described in § 1.422-3.

(iii) The provisions relating to the maximum aggregate number of shares to be issued under the plan (described in paragraph (b)(3) of this section) and the employees (or class or classes of employees) eligible to receive options under the plan (described in paragraph (b)(4) of this section) are the only provisions of a stock option plan that must be approved by stockholders for purposes of section 422(b)(1). Any increase in the maximum aggregate number of shares that may be issued under the plan (other than an increase merely reflecting a change in the number of outstanding shares, such as a stock dividend or stock split), or change in the designation of the employees (or class or classes of employees) eligible to receive options under the plan is considered the adoption of a new plan requiring stockholder approval within the prescribed 24-month period. In addition, a change in the granting corporation or the stock available for purchase or award under the plan is considered the adoption of a new plan requiring new stockholder approval within the prescribed 24-month period. Any other changes in the terms of an incentive stock option plan are not considered the adoption of a new plan and, thus, do not require stockholder approval.

(3) *Maximum aggregate number of shares.* (i) The plan required by this paragraph (b) must designate the maximum aggregate number of shares that may be issued under the plan through incentive stock options, nonstatutory options, and all other stock-based awards to be granted thereunder. If nonstatutory options or other stock-based awards may be granted, the plan may separately designate terms for each type of option and other stock-based award and designate the maximum number of shares that may be issued under such option or other stock-based award. Unless otherwise specified, all terms of the plan apply to all options and other stock-based awards that may be granted under the plan.

(ii) A plan that merely provides that the number of shares that may be issued under options and other stock-based awards granted under such plan may not exceed a stated percentage of the shares outstanding at the time of each offering or grant under such plan does not satisfy the requirement that the plan state the maximum aggregate number of shares that may be issued under the plan. However, the maximum aggregate number of shares that may be issued under the plan may be stated in terms of a percentage of the authorized, issued or outstanding shares at the date of the adoption of the plan. The plan may specify that the maximum aggregate number of shares available for grants under the plan may increase annually by a specified percentage of the authorized, issued or outstanding shares at the date of the adoption of the plan. A plan which provides that the maximum aggregate number of shares that may be issued under the plan may change based on any other specified circumstances satisfies the requirements of this paragraph (b)(3) only if the stockholders approve an immediately determinable maximum aggregate number of shares that may be issued under the plan in any event.

(iii) It is permissible for the plan to provide that shares purchasable under the plan may be supplied to the plan through acquisitions of stock on the open market, that shares purchased under the plan and forfeited back to the plan are available for re-issuance under the plan, or that shares surrendered in payment of the exercise price of an option are available for re-issuance under the plan.

(iv) If there is more than one plan under which incentive stock options may be granted and stockholders of the granting corporation merely approve a maximum aggregate number of shares that are available for issuance under such plans, the stockholder approval requirements described in paragraph (b)(2) of this section are not satisfied. A separate maximum aggregate number of shares must be approved for each plan.

(4) *Designation of employees.* The plan described in this paragraph (b), as adopted and approved, must indicate the employees (or class or classes of employees) eligible to receive the options or other stock-based awards to be granted under the plan. This requirement is satisfied by a general designation of the classes of employees eligible to receive options or other stock-based awards under the plan. Designations such as "key employees of the grantor corporation"; "all salaried employees of the grantor corporation and its subsidiaries, including subsidiaries which become such after adoption of the plan;" or "all employees of the corporation" meet this requirement. This requirement is considered satisfied even though the board of directors, another group, or an individual is given the authority to select the particular employees who are to receive options or other stock-based awards from a described class and to determine the number of shares to be optioned or granted to each such employee. If individuals other than employees may be granted options or other stock-based awards under the plan, the plan must separately designate the employees or classes of employees eligible to receive incentive stock options.

(5) *Conflicting option terms.* An option on stock available for purchase or grant under the plan is treated as having been granted pursuant to a plan even if the terms of the option conflict with the terms of the plan, unless such option is granted to an employee who is ineligible to receive options under the plan, options have been granted on stock in excess of the aggregate number of shares which may be issued under the plan, or the option provides otherwise.

(6) The following examples illustrate the principles of this paragraph (b):

Example 1. Stockholder approval. (i) S Corporation is a subsidiary of P Corporation, a publicly traded corporation. On January 1, 2006, S adopts a plan under which incentive stock options for S stock are granted to S employees.

(ii) To meet the requirements of paragraph (b)(2) of this section, the plan must be approved by the stockholders of S (in this case, P) within 12 months before or after January 1, 2004.

(iii) Assume the same facts as in paragraph (i) of this *Example 1*. Assume further that the plan was approved by the stockholders of S (in this case, P) on March 1, 2006. On January 1, 2008, S changes the plan to provide that incentive stock options for P stock will be granted to S employees under the plan. Because there is a change in the stock available for grant under the plan, the change is considered the adoption of a new plan that must be approved by the stockholders within 12 months before or after January 1, 2008.

Example 2. Stockholder approval. (i) Assume the same facts as in paragraph (i) of *Example 1*, except that on March 15, 2007, P completely disposes of its interest in S. Thereafter, S continues to grant options for S stock to S employees under the plan.

(ii) The new S options are granted under a plan that meets the stockholder approval requirements of paragraph (b)(2) of this section without regard to whether S seeks approval of the plan from the stockholders of S after P disposes of its interest in S.

(iii) Assume the same facts as in paragraph (i) of this *Example 2*, except that under the plan as adopted on January 1, 2006, only options for P stock are granted to S employees. Assume further that after P disposes of its interest in S, S changes the plan to provide for the grant of options for S stock to S employees. Because there is a change in the stock available for purchase or grant under the plan, under paragraph (b)(2)(iii) of this section, the stockholders of S must approve the plan within 12 months before or after the change to the plan to meet the stockholder approval requirements of paragraph (b) of this section.

Example 3. Maximum aggregate number of shares. X Corporation maintains a plan under which statutory options and nonstatutory options may be granted. The plan designates the number of shares that may be used for incentive stock options. Because the maximum aggregate number of shares that will be used for both statutory and nonstatutory options is not designated in the plan, the requirements of paragraph (b)(3) of this section are not satisfied.

Example 4. Maximum aggregate number of shares. Y Corporation adopts an incentive stock option plan on November 1, 2006. On that date there are two million outstanding shares of Y Corporation stock. The plan provides that the maximum aggregate number of shares that may be issued under the plan may not exceed 15% of the outstanding number of shares of Y Corporation on November 1, 2006. Because the maximum aggregate number of shares under the plan is designated in the plan, the requirements of paragraph (b)(3) of this section are met.

Example 5. Maximum aggregate number of shares. (i) B Corporation adopts an incentive stock option plan on March 15, 2005. The plan provides that the maximum aggregate number of shares available under the plan is 50,000, increased on each anniversary date of the adoption of the plan by 5 percent of the then-outstanding shares.

(ii) Because the maximum aggregate number of shares is not designated under the plan, the requirements of paragraph (b)(3) of this section are not met.

(iii) Assume the same facts as in paragraph (i) of this *Example 5*, except that the plan provides that the maximum aggregate number of shares available under the plan is the lesser of (a) 50,000 shares increased each anniversary date of the adoption of the plan by 5 percent of the then-outstanding shares or (b) 200,000 shares. Because the maximum aggregate number of shares under the plan is designated as the lesser of one of two numbers, one of which provides an immediately determinable maximum aggregate number of shares that may be issued under the plan in any event, the requirements of paragraph (b)(3) of this section are met.

(c) *Duration of option grants under the plan.* An incentive stock option must be granted within 10 years from the date that the plan under which it is granted is adopted or the date such plan is approved by the stockholders, whichever is earlier. To grant incentive stock options after the expiration of the 10-year period, a new plan must be adopted and approved.

(d) *Period for exercising options.* An incentive stock option, by its terms, must not be exercisable after the expiration of 10 years from the date such option is granted, or 5 years from the date such option is

granted to an employee described in paragraph (f) of this section. An option that does not contain such a provision when granted is not an incentive stock option.

(e) *Option price.* (1) Except as provided by paragraph (e)(2) of this section, the option price of an incentive stock option must not be less than the fair market value of the stock subject to the option at the time the option is granted. The option price may be determined in any reasonable manner, including the valuation methods permitted under §20.2031-2 of this chapter (Estate Tax Regulations), so long as the minimum price possible under the terms of the option is not less than the fair market value of the stock on the date of grant. For general rules relating to the option price, see §1.421-1(e). For rules relating to the determination of when an option is granted, see §1.421-1(c).

(2)(i) If a share of stock is transferred to an individual pursuant to the exercise of an option which fails to qualify as an incentive stock option merely because there was a failure of an attempt, made in good faith, to meet the option price requirements of paragraph (e)(1) of this section, the requirements of such paragraph are considered to have been met. Whether there was a good-faith attempt to set the option price at not less than the fair market value of the stock subject to the option at the time the option was granted depends on the relevant facts and circumstances.

(ii) For publicly held stock that is actively traded on an established market at the time the option is granted, determining the fair market value of such stock by the appropriate method described in §20.2031-2 of this chapter (Estate Tax Regulations) establishes that a good-faith attempt to meet the option price requirements of this paragraph (e) was made.

(iii) For non-publicly traded stock, if it is demonstrated, for example, that the fair market value of the stock at the date of grant was based upon an average of the fair market values as of such date set forth in the opinions of completely independent and well-qualified experts, such a demonstration generally establishes that there was a good-faith attempt to meet the option price requirements of this paragraph (e). If the stock is non-publicly traded, the optionee's status as a majority or minority stockholder may be taken into consideration.

(iv) Regardless of whether the stock offered under an option is publicly traded, a good-faith attempt to meet the option price requirements of this paragraph (e) is not demonstrated unless the fair market value of the stock on the date of grant is determined with regard to *nonlapse restrictions* (as defined in §1.83-3(h)) and without regard to *lapse restrictions* (as defined in §1.83-3(i)).

(v) Amounts treated as interest and amounts paid as interest under a deferred payment arrangement are not includible as part of the option price. See §1.421-1(e)(1). An attempt to set the option price at not less than fair market value is not regarded as made in good faith where an adjustment of the option price to reflect amounts treated as interest results in the option price being lower than the fair market value on which the option price was based.

(3) Notwithstanding that the option price requirements of paragraphs (e)(1) and (2) of this section are satisfied by an option granted to an employee whose stock ownership exceeds the limitation provided by paragraph (f) of this section, such option is not an incentive stock option when granted unless it also complies with paragraph (f) of this section. If the option, when granted, does not comply with the requirements described in paragraph (f) of this section, such option can never become an incentive stock option, even if the employee's stock ownership does not exceed the limitation of paragraph (f) of this section when such option is exercised.

(f) *Options granted to certain stockholders.* (1) If, immediately before an option is granted, an individual owns (or is treated as owning) stock possessing more than 10 percent of the total combined voting power of all classes of stock of the corporation employing the optionee or of any related corporation of such corporation, then an option granted to such individual cannot qualify as an incentive stock option unless the option price is at least 110 percent of the stock's fair market value on the date of grant and such option by its terms is not exercisable after the expiration of 5 years from the date of grant. For purposes of determining the minimum option price for purposes of this paragraph (f), the rules described in paragraph (e)(2) of this section, relating to the good-faith determination of the option price, do not apply.

(2) For purposes of determining the stock ownership of the optionee, the stock attribution rules of §1.424-1(d) apply. Stock that the optionee may purchase under outstanding options is not treated as stock owned by the individual. The determination of the percentage of the total combined voting power of all classes of stock of the employer corporation (or of its related corporations) that is owned by the optionee is made with respect to each such corporation in the related group by

comparing the voting power of the shares owned (or treated as owned) by the optionee to the aggregate voting power of all shares of each such corporation actually issued and outstanding immediately before the grant of the option to the optionee. The aggregate voting power of all shares actually issued and outstanding immediately before the grant of the option does not include the voting power of treasury shares or shares authorized for issue under outstanding options held by the individual or any other person.

(3) *Examples.* The rules of this paragraph (f) are illustrated by the following examples:

Example 1. (i) E, an employee of M Corporation, owns 15,000 shares of M Corporation common stock, which is the only class of stock outstanding. M has 100,000 shares of its common stock outstanding. On January 1, 2005, when the fair market value of M stock is $100, E is granted an option with an option price of $100 and an exercise period of 10 years from the date of grant.

(ii) Because E owns stock possessing more than 10 percent of the total combined voting power of all classes of M Corporation stock, M cannot grant an incentive stock option to E unless the option is granted at an option price of at least 110 percent of the fair market value of the stock subject to the option and the option, by its terms, expires no later than 5 years from its date of grant. The option granted to E fails to meet the option-price and term requirements described in paragraph (f)(1) of this section and, thus, the option is not an incentive stock option.

(iii) Assume the same facts as in paragraph (i) of this *Example 1,* except that E's father and brother each owned 7,500 shares of M Corporation stock, and E owned no M stock in E's own name. Because under the attribution rules of §1.424-1(d), E is treated as owning stock held by E's parents and siblings, M cannot grant an incentive stock option to E unless the option price is at least 110 percent of the fair market value of the stock subject to the option, and the option, by its terms, expires no later than 5 years from the date of grant.

Example 2. Assume the same facts as in paragraph (i) of this *Example 1.* Assume further that M is a subsidiary of P Corporation. Regardless of whether E owns any P stock and the number of P shares outstanding, if P Corporation grants an option to E which purports to be an incentive stock option, but which fails to meet the 110-percent-option-price and 5-year-term requirements, the option is not an incentive stock option because E owns more than 10 percent of the total combined voting power of all classes of stock of a related corporation of P Corporation (i.e., M Corporation). An individual who owns (or is treated as owning) stock in excess of the ownership specified in paragraph (f)(1) of this section, in any corporation in a group of corporations consisting of the employer corporation and its related corporations, cannot be granted an incentive stock option by any corporation in the group unless such option meets the 110-percent-option-price and 5-year-term requirements of paragraph (f)(1) of this section.

Example 3. (i) F is an employee of R Corporation. R has only one class of stock, of which 100,000 shares are issued and outstanding. F owns no stock in R Corporation or any related corporation of R Corporation. On January 1, 2005, R grants a 10-year incentive stock option to F to purchase 50,000 shares of R stock at $3 per share, the fair market value of R stock on the date of grant of the option. On April 1, 2005, F exercises half of the January option and receives 25,000 shares of R stock that previously were not outstanding. On July 1, 2005, R grants a second 50,000 share option to F which purports to be an incentive stock option. The terms of the July option are identical to the terms of the January option, except that the option price is $3.25 per share, which is the fair market value of R stock on the date of grant of the July option.

(ii) Because F did not own more than 10% of the total combined voting power of all classes of stock of R Corporation or any related corporation on the date of the grant of the January option and the pricing requirements of paragraph (e) of this section are satisfied on the date of grant of such option, the unexercised portion of the January option remains an incentive stock option regardless of the changes in F's percentage of stock ownership in R after the date of grant. However, the July option is not an incentive stock option because, on the date that it was granted, F owned 20 percent (25,000 shares owned by F divided by 125,000 shares of R stock issued and outstanding) of the total combined voting power of all classes of R Corporation stock and, thus the pricing requirements of paragraph (f)(1) of this section were not met.

(iii) Assume the same facts as in paragraph (i) of this *Example 3* except that the partial exercise of the January incentive stock option on April 1, 2003, is for only 10,000 shares. Under these circumstances, the July option is an incentive stock option, because, on the date of grant of the July option, F does not own more than 10 percent of the total

¶20,260W

combined voting power (10,000 shares owned by F divided by 110,000 shares of R stock issued and outstanding) of all classes of R Corporation stock.

§ 1.422-4 [Removed]

Par. 7. Section 1.422-4 is removed.

§ 1.422-5 [Redesignated]

Par. 8. Section 1.422-5 is re-designated as §1.422-3.

Par. 9. New §1.422-4 is added to read as follows:

§ 1.422-4 $100,000 limitation for incentive stock options.

(a) *$100,000 per year limitation*—(1) *General rule.* An option that otherwise qualifies as an incentive stock option nevertheless fails to be an incentive stock option to the extent that the $100,000 limitation described in paragraph (a)(2) of this section is exceeded.

(2) *$100,000 per year limitation.* To the extent that the aggregate fair market value of stock with respect to which an incentive stock option (determined without regard to this section) is exercisable for the first time by any individual during any calendar year (under all plans of the employer corporation and related corporations) exceeds $100,000, such option is treated as a nonstatutory option. See §1.83-7 for rules applicable to nonstatutory options.

(b) *Application.* To determine whether the limitation described in paragraph (a)(2) of this section has been exceeded, the following rules apply.

(1) An option that does not meet the requirements of §1.422-2 when granted (including an option which, when granted, contains terms providing that it will not be treated as incentive stock option) is disregarded. See §1.422-2(a)(4).

(2) The fair market value of stock is determined as of the date of grant of the option for such stock.

(3) Except as otherwise provided in paragraph (b)(4) of this section, options are taken into account in the order in which they are granted.

(4) For purposes of this section, an option is considered to be first exercisable during a calendar year if the option will become exercisable at any time during the year assuming that any condition on the optionee's ability to exercise the option related to the performance of services is satisfied. If the optionee's ability to exercise the option in the year is subject to an acceleration provision, then the option is considered first exercisable in the calendar year in which the acceleration provision is triggered. After an acceleration provision is triggered, the options subject to such provision are then taken into account in accordance with paragraph (b)(3) of this section for purposes of applying the limitation described in paragraph (a)(2) of this section to all options first exercisable during a calendar year. However, because an acceleration provision is not taken into account prior to its triggering, an incentive stock option that becomes exercisable for the first time during a calendar year by operation of such a provision does not affect the application of the $100,000 limitation with respect to any option (or portion thereof) exercised prior to such acceleration. For purposes of this paragraph (b)(4), an acceleration provision includes, for example, a provision that accelerates the exercisability of an option on a change in ownership or control or a provision that conditions exercisability on the attainment of a performance goal. See paragraph (d), *Example 4 of this section.*

(5)(i) An option (or portion thereof) is disregarded if, prior to the calendar year during which it would otherwise have become exercisable for the first time, the option (or portion thereof) is modified and thereafter ceases to be an incentive stock option described in §1.422-2, is canceled, or is transferred in violation of §1.421-1(b)(2).

(ii) If an option (or portion thereof) is modified, canceled, or transferred at any other time, such option (or portion thereof) is treated as outstanding according to its original terms until the end of the calendar year during which it would otherwise have become exercisable for the first time.

(6) A disqualifying disposition has no effect on the determination of whether an option exceeds the $100,000 limitation.

(c) *Bifurcation of options.* The application of the rules described in paragraph (b) of this section may result in an option being treated, in part, as an incentive stock option and, in part, as a nonstatutory option. In such a case, a corporation can issue a separate certificate for incentive option stock and designate such stock as incentive stock option stock in the corporation's transfer records. In the absence of such a designation, a pro rata portion of each share of stock purchased under the option is treated as incentive stock option stock and nonstatutory option stock. See §1.83-7 for the treatment of nonstatutory options.

(d) *Examples*. The following examples illustrate the principles of this section. In each of the following examples E is an employee of X Corporation. The examples are as follows:

Example 1. General rule. Effective January 1, 2004, X Corporation adopts a plan under which incentive stock options may be granted to its employees. On January 1, 2004, and each succeeding January 1 through January 1, 2013, E is granted immediately exercisable options for X Corporation stock with a fair market value of $100,000 determined on the date of grant. The options qualify as incentive stock options (determined without regard to this section). On January 1, 2014, E exercises all of the options. Because the $100,000 limitation has not been exceeded during any calendar year, all of the options are treated as incentive stock options.

Example 2. Order of grant. X Corporation is a parent corporation of Y Corporation, which is a parent corporation of Z Corporation. Each corporation has adopted its own separate plan, under which an employee of any member of the corporate group may be granted options for stock of any member of the group. On January 1, 2004, X Corpora-

	Date of Grant
Option 1	April 1, 2004
Option 2	May 1, 2004
Option 3	June 1, 2004

(ii) In July of 2004, a change in control of X Corporation occurs, and, under the terms of its option plan, all outstanding options become immediately exercisable. Under the rules of this section, Option 1 is treated as an incentive stock option in its entirety; Option 2 exceeds the $100,000 aggregate fair market value limitation for calendar year 2004 by $10,000 (Option 1's $60,000 + Option 2's $50,000 = $110,000) and is, therefore, bifurcated into an incentive stock option for stock with a fair market value of $40,000 as of the date of grant and a nonstatutory option for stock with a fair market value of $10,000 as of the date of grant. Option 3 is treated as a nonstatutory option in its entirety.

	Date of Grant
Option 1	April 1, 2004
Option 2	May 1, 2004
Option 3	June 1, 2004

(ii) On June 1, 2005, E exercises Option 3. At the time of exercise of Option 3, the fair market value of X stock (at the time of grant) with respect to which options held by E are first exercisable in 2005 does not exceed $100,000. On September 1, 2005, a change of control of X Corporation occurs, and, under the terms of its option plan, Option 2 becomes immediately exercisable. Under the rules of this section, because E's exercise of Option 3 occurs before the change of control and the effects of an acceleration provision are not taken into account until it is triggered, Option 3 is treated as an incentive stock option in its entirety. Option 1 is treated as an incentive stock option in its entirety. Option 2 is bifurcated into an incentive stock option for stock with a fair market value of $20,000 on the date of grant and a nonstatutory option for stock with a fair market value of $20,000 on the date of grant because it exceeds the $100,000 limitation for 2003 by $20,000 (Option 1 for $60,000 + Option 3 for $20,000 + Option 2 for $40,000 = $120,000).

	Date of Grant	Fair Market Value of Stock	First Exercisable	
Option 1	April 1, 2004	$60,000	2005	2005
Option 2	May 1, 2004	$40,000	2005	
Option 3	June 1, 2004	$40,000	2005	

(ii) On December 31, 2004, Option 2 is canceled. Because Option 2 is canceled before the calendar year during which it would have become exercisable for the first time, it is disregarded. As a result, Option 1 and Option 3 are treated as incentive stock options in their entirety.

(iii) Assume the same facts as in paragraph (ii) of this *Example 5*, except that Option 2 is canceled on January 1, 2005. Because Option 2 is not canceled prior to the calendar year during which it would have become exercisable for the first time (2005), it is treated as an outstanding option for purposes of determining whether the $100,000 requirement for 2005 has been exceeded. Because options are taken into account in the order in which granted, Option 1 is treated as an incentive stock option in its entirety. Because Option 3 exceeds the $100,000 limitation by $40,000 (Option 1 for $60,000 + Option 2 for $40,000 + Option 3 for $40,000 = $140,000), it is treated as a nonstatutory options in its entirety.

(iv) Assume the same facts as in paragraph (i) of this *Example 5*, except that on January 1, 2005, E exercises Option 2 and immediately sells the stock in a disqualifying disposition. A disqualifying disposition has no effect on the determination of whether the underlying option is

tion grants E an incentive stock option (determined without regard to this section) for stock of Y Corporation with a fair market value of $100,000 on the date of grant. On December 31, 2004, Y Corporation grants E an incentive stock option (determined without regard to this section) for stock of Z Corporation with a fair market value of $75,000 as of the date of grant. Both of the options are immediately exercisable. For purposes of this section, options are taken into account in the order in which granted using the fair market value of stock as of the date on the option is granted. During calendar year 2004, the aggregate fair market value of stock with respect to which E's options are exercisable for the first time exceeds $100,000. Therefore, the option for Y Corporation stock is treated as an incentive stock option, and the option for Z Corporation stock is treated as a nonstatutory option.

Example 3. Acceleration provision. (i) In 2004, X Corporation grants E three incentive stock options (determined without regard to this section) to acquire stock with an aggregate fair market value of $150,000 on the date of grant. The dates of grant, the fair market value of the stock (as of the applicable date of grant) with respect to which the options are exercisable, and the years in which the options are first exercisable (without regard to acceleration provisions) are as follows:

Fair Market Value of Stock	First Exercisable
$60,000	2004
$50,000	2006
$40,000	2004

Example 4. Exercise of option and acceleration provision. (i) In 2004, X Corporation grants E three incentive stock options (determined without regard to this section) to acquire stock with an aggregate fair market value of $120,000 on the date of grant. The dates of grant, the fair market value of the stock (as of the applicable date of grant) with respect to which the options are exercisable, and the years in which the options are first exercisable (without regard to acceleration provisions) are as follows:

Fair Market Value of Stock	First Exercisable
$60,000	2005
$40,000	2006
$20,000	2005

(iii) Assume the same facts as in paragraph (ii) of this *Example 4*, except that the change of control occurs on May 1, 2005. Because options are taken into account in the order in which they are granted, Option 1 and Option 2 are treated as incentive stock options in their entirety. Because the exercise of Option 3 (on June 1, 2005) takes place after the acceleration provision is triggered, Option 3 is treated as a nonstatutory option in its entirety.

Example 5. Cancellation of option. (i) In 2004, X Corporation grants E three incentive stock options (determined without regard to this section) to acquire stock with an aggregate fair market value of $140,000 as of the date of grant. The dates of grant, the fair market value of the stock (as of the applicable date of grant) with respect to which the options are exercisable, and the years in which the options are first exercisable (without regard to acceleration provisions) are as follows:

considered outstanding during the calendar year during which it is first exercisable. Because options are taken into account in the order in which granted, Option 1 is treated as an incentive stock option in its entirety. Because Option 3 exceeds the $100,000 limitation by $40,000 (Option 1 for $60,000 + Option 2 for $40,000 + Option 3 for $40,000 = $140,000), it is treated as a nonstatutory option in its entirety.

Example 6. Designation of stock. On January 1, 2004, X grants E an immediately exercisable incentive stock option (determined without regard to this section) to acquire X stock with a fair market value of $150,000 on that date. Under the rules of this section, the option is bifurcated and treated as an incentive stock option for X stock with a fair market value of $100,000 and a nonstatutory option for X stock with a fair market value of $50,000. In these circumstances, X may designate the stock that is treated as stock acquired pursuant to the exercise of an incentive stock option by issuing a separate certificate (or certificates) for $100,000 of stock and identifying such certificates as Incentive Stock Option Stock in its transfer records. In the absence of such a designation, two-thirds ($100,000 / $150,000) of each share of stock is treated as acquired pursuant to the exercise of an incentive stock option and one-third ($50,000 / $150,000) as stock acquired pursuant to the exercise of a nonstatutory option.

Par. 10. Section 1.422-5 is added to read as follows:

§ 1.422-5 Permissible provisions.

(a) *General rule.* An option that otherwise qualifies as an incentive stock option does not fail to be an incentive stock option merely because such option contains one or more of the provisions described in paragraphs (b), (c), and (d) of this section.

(b) *Cashless exercise.* (1) An option does not fail to be an incentive stock option merely because the optionee may exercise the option with previously acquired stock of the corporation that granted the option or stock of the corporation whose stock is being offered for purchase under the option. For special rules relating to the use of statutory option stock to pay the option price of an incentive stock option, see § 1.424-1(c)(3).

(2) All shares acquired through the exercise of an incentive stock option are individually subject to the holding period requirements described in § 1.422-1(a) and the disqualifying disposition rules of § 1.422-1(b), regardless of whether the option is exercised with previously acquired stock of the corporation that granted the option or stock of the corporation whose stock is being offered for purchase under the option. If an incentive stock option is exercised with such shares, and the exercise results in the basis allocation described in paragraph (b)(3) of this section, the optionee's disqualifying disposition of any of the stock acquired through such exercise is treated as a disqualifying disposition of the shares with the lowest basis.

(3) If the exercise of an incentive stock option with previously acquired shares is comprised in part of an exchange to which section 1036 (and so much of section 1031 as relates to section 1036) applies, then:

(i) The optionee's basis in the incentive stock option shares received in the section 1036 exchange is the same as the optionee's basis in the shares surrendered in the exchange, increased, if applicable, by any amount included in gross income as compensation pursuant to sections 421 through 424 or section 83. Except for purposes of § 1.422-1(a), the holding period of the shares is determined under section 1223. For purposes of § 1.422-1 and sections 421(b) and 83 and the regulations thereunder, the amount paid for the shares purchased under the option is the fair market value of the shares surrendered on the date of the exchange.

(ii) The optionee's basis in the incentive stock option shares not received pursuant to the section 1036 exchange is zero. For all purposes, the holding period of such shares begins as of the date that such shares are transferred to the optionee. For purposes of § 1.422-1(b) and sections 421(b) and 83 and the regulations thereunder, the amount paid for the shares is considered to be zero.

(c) *Additional compensation.* An option does not fail to be an incentive stock option merely because the optionee has the right to receive additional compensation, in cash or property, when the option is exercised, provided such additional compensation is includible in income under section 61 or section 83. The amount of such additional compensation may be determined in any manner, including by reference to the fair market value of the stock at the time of exercise or to the option price.

(d) *Option subject to a condition.* (1) An option does not fail to be an incentive stock option merely because the option is subject to a condition, or grants a right, that is not inconsistent with the requirements of §§ 1.422-2 and 1.422-4.

(2) An option that includes an alternative right is not an incentive stock option if the requirements of § 1.422-2 are effectively avoided by the exercise of the alternative right. For example, an alternative right extending the option term beyond ten years, setting an option price below fair market value, or permitting transferability prevents an option from qualifying as an incentive stock option. If either of two options can be exercised, but not both, each such option is a disqualifying alternative right with respect to the other, even though one or both options would individually satisfy the requirements of §§ 1.422-2, 1.422-4, and this section.

(3) An alternative right to receive a taxable payment of cash and/or property in exchange for the cancellation or surrender of the option does not disqualify the option as an incentive stock option if the right is exercisable only when the then fair market value of the stock exceeds the exercise price of the option and the option is otherwise exercisable, the right is transferable only when the option is otherwise transferable, and the exercise of the right has the same economic and tax consequences as the exercise of the option followed by an immediate sale of the stock. For this purpose, the exercise of the alternative right does not have the same economic and tax consequences if the payment exceeds the difference between the then fair market value of the stock and the exercise price of the option.

(e) *Examples.* The principles of this section are illustrated by the following examples:

Example 1. On June 1, 2004, X Corporation grants an incentive stock option to A, an employee of X Corporation, entitling A to purchase 100 shares of X Corporation common stock at $10 per share. The option provides that A may exercise the option with previously acquired shares of X Corporation common stock. X Corporation has only one class of common stock outstanding. Under the rules of section 83, the shares transferable to A through the exercise of the option are transferable and not subject to a substantial risk of forfeiture. On June 1, 2005, when the fair market value of an X Corporation share is $25, A uses 40 shares of X Corporation common stock, which A had purchased on the open market on June 1, 2002, for $5 per share, to pay the full option price. After exercising the option, A owns 100 shares of incentive stock option stock. Under section 1036 (and so much of section 1031 as relates to section 1036), 40 of the shares have a $200 aggregate carryover basis (the $5 purchase price × 40 shares) and a three-year holding period for purposes of determining capital gain, and 60 of the shares have a zero basis and a holding period beginning on June 1, 2005, for purposes of determining capital gain. All 100 shares have a holding period beginning on June 1, 2005, for purposes of determining whether the holding period requirements of § 1.422-1(a) are met.

Example 2. Assume the same facts as in *Example 1.* Assume further that, on September 1, 2005, A sells 75 of the shares that A acquired through exercise of the incentive stock option for $30 per share. Because the holding period requirements were not satisfied, A made a disqualifying disposition of the 75 shares on September 1, 2005. Under the rules of paragraph (b)(3) of this section, A has sold all 60 of the non-section-1036 shares and 15 of the 40 section-1036 shares. Therefore, under paragraph (b)(3) of this section and section 83(a), the amount of compensation attributable to A's exercise of the option and subsequent disqualifying disposition of 75 shares is $1,500 (the difference between the fair market value of the stock on the date of transfer, $1,875 (75 shares at $25 per share), and the amount paid for the stock, $375 (60 shares at $0 per share plus 15 shares at $25 per share)). In addition, A must recognize a capital gain of $675. Accordingly, A must include in gross income for the taxable year in which the sale occurs $1,500 as compensation and $675 as capital gain. For its taxable year in which the disqualifying disposition occurs, if otherwise allowable under section 162 and if the requirements of § 1.83-6(a) are met, X Corporation is allowed a deduction of $1,500 for the compensation paid to A.

Example 3. Assume the same facts as in *Example 2*, except that, instead of selling the 75 shares of incentive stock option stock on September 1, 2005, A uses those shares to exercise a second incentive stock option. The second option was granted to A by X Corporation on January 1, 2005, entitling A to purchase 100 shares of X Corporation common stock at $22.50 per share. As in *Example 2*, A has made a disqualifying disposition of the 75 shares of stock pursuant to § 1.424-1(c). Under paragraph (b)(1) of this section, A has disposed of all 60 of the non-section-1036 shares and 15 of the 40 section-1036 shares. Therefore, pursuant to paragraph (b)(3) of this section and section 83(a), the amount of compensation attributable to A's exercise of the first option and subsequent disqualifying disposition of 75 shares is $1,500 (the difference between the fair market value of the stock on the date of transfer, $1,875 (75 shares at $25 per share), and the amount paid for the stock, $375 (60 shares at $0 per share plus 15 shares at $25 per share)). Unlike *Example 2*, A does not recognize any capital gain as a result of exercising the second option because, for all purposes other than the determination of whether the exercise is a disposition pursuant to section 424(c), the exercise is considered an exchange to which section 1036 applies. Accordingly, A must include in gross income for the taxable year in which the disqualifying disposition occurs $1,500 as compensation. For its taxable year in which the disqualifying disposition occurs, if otherwise alllowable under sections 83(h) and 162 and if the requirements of § 1.83-6(a) are met, X Corporation is allowed a deduction of $1,500 for the compensation paid to A. After exercising the second option, A owns a total of 125 shares of incentive stock option stock. Under section 1036 (and so much of section 1031 as relates to section 1036), the 100 "new" shares of incentive stock option stock have the following bases and holding periods: 15 shares have a $75 carryover basis and a three-year-and-three-month holding period for purposes of determining capital gain, 60 shares have a $1,500 basis resulting from the inclusion of that amount in income as compensation and a three-month holding period for purposes of determining capital gain, and 25 shares have a zero basis and a holding period beginning on September 1, 2005, for purposes of determining capital gain. All 100 shares have a holding period beginning on September 1, 2005, for purposes of determining whether the holding period requirements of § 1.422-1(a) are met.

Example 4. Assume the same facts as in *Example 2,* except that, instead of selling the 75 shares of incentive stock option stock on September 1, 2005, A uses those shares to exercise a nonstatutory option. The nonstatutory option was granted to A by X Corporation on January 1, 2005, entitling A to purchase 100 shares of X Corporation common stock at $22.50 per share. Unlike *Example 3,* A has not made a disqualifying disposition of the 75 shares of stock. After exercising the nonstatutory option, A owns a total of 100 shares of incentive stock option stock and 25 shares of nonstatutory stock option stock. Under section 1036 (and so much of section 1031 as relates to section 1036), the 75 new shares of incentive stock option stock have the same basis and holding period as the 75 old shares used to exercise the nonstatutory option. The additional 25 shares of stock received upon exercise of the nonstatutory option are taxed under the rules of section 83(a). Accordingly, A must include in gross income for the taxable year in which the transfer of such shares occurs $750 (25 shares at $30 per share) as compensation. A's basis in such shares is the same as the amount included in gross income. For its taxable year in which the transfer occurs, X Corporation is allowed a deduction of $750 for the compensation paid to A to the extent allowable under sections 83(h) and 162 and if the requirements of § 1.83-6(a) are satisfied.

Example 5. Assume the same facts in *Example 1,* except that the shares transferred pursuant to the exercise of the incentive stock option are subject to a substantial risk of forfeiture and not transferable (substantially nonvested) for a period of six months after such transfer. Assume further that the shares that A uses to exercise the incentive stock option are similarly restricted. Such shares were transferred to A on January 1, 2005, through A's exercise of a nonstatutory stock option which was granted to A on January 1, 2004. A paid $5 per share for the stock when its fair market value was $22.50 per share. A did not file a section 83(b) election to include the $700 spread (the difference between the option price and the fair market value of the stock on date of exercise of the nonstatutory option) in gross income as compensation. After exercising the incentive stock option with the 40 substantially-nonvested shares, A owns 100 shares of substantially-nonvested incentive stock option stock. Section 1036 (and so much of section 1031 as relates to section 1036) applies to the 40 shares exchanged in exercise of the incentive stock option. However, pursuant to section 83(g), the stock received in such exchange, because it is incentive stock option stock, is not subject to restrictions and conditions substantially similar to those to which the stock given in such exchange was subject. For purposes of section 83(a) and § 1.83-1(b)(1), therefore, A has disposed of the 40 shares of substantially-nonvested stock on June 1, 2005, and must include in gross income as compensation $800 (the difference between the amount realized upon such disposition, $1,000, and the amount paid for the stock, $200). Accordingly, 40 shares of the incentive stock option stock have a $1,000 basis (the $200 original basis plus the $800 included in income as compensation) and 60 shares of the incentive stock option stock have a zero basis. For its taxable year in which the disposition of the substantially-nonvested stock occurs, X Corporation is allowed a deduction of $800 for the compensation paid to A, provided that the requirements of § 1.83-6 are satisfied.

(f) *Effective date.* This section applies to any statutory option granted on or after the date that is 180 days after publication of final regulations in the *Federal Register. Taxpayers can rely on these regulations for the treatment of any statutory option granted on or after June 9, 2003.*

§ 1.423-1 [Amended]

Par. 11. Section 1.423-1 is amended as follows:

1. In paragraph (a)(2), the language "425(a)" is removed and "424(a)" is added in its place.

Newly Designated Section
1.424-1(c)(4), *Example 1,* first sentence
1.424-1(c)(4), *Example 1,* first sentence
1.424-1(c)(4), *Example 1,* second and fourth sentences
1.424-1(c)(4), *Example 1,* third sentence
1.424-1(c)(4), *Example 2,* first sentence
1.424-1(c)(4), *Example 2,* last sentence
1.424-1(c)(4), *Example 3,* first sentence
1.424-1(c)(4), *Example 4,* first sentence
1.424-1(c)(4), *Example 4,* last sentence
1.424-1(c)(4), *Example 5,* first sentence
1.424-1(c)(4), *Example 5,* first sentence
1.424-1(c)(4), *Example 6,* first sentence

2. In paragraph (b), first sentence, the language "§ 1.421-7" is removed and "§ 1.421-1" is added in its place.

3. In paragraph (b), second sentence, the language "§ 1.421-8" is removed and § 1.421-2 is added in its place.

4. In paragraph (b), last sentence, the language "425(c)" is removed and "424(c)" is added in its place.

5. In paragraph (b), last sentence, the language "§ 1.425-1" is removed and "§ 1.424-1" is added in its place.

§ 1.423-2 [Amended]

Par. 12. Section 1.423-2 is amended by:

1. In paragraph (b), last sentence, the language "§ 1.421-7" is removed and "§ 1.421-1" is added in its place.

2. In paragraph (d)(1), second sentence, the language "425(d)" is removed and "424(d)" is added in its place.

3. In paragraph (d)(3), *Example 3,* fourth sentence, the language "425(d)" is removed and "424(d)" is added in its place.

4. In paragraph (e)(2), the language "§ 1.421-7" is removed and "§ 1.421-1" is added in its place.

5. In paragraph (g)(1), the first sentence of the concluding text, the language "§ 1.421-7" is removed and "§ 1.421-1" is added in its place.

6. In paragraph (g)(1), the third sentence of the concluding text, the language "§ 1.421-7" is removed and "§ 1.421-1" is added in its place.

7. In paragraph (j), second sentence, the language "§ 1.421-7" is removed and "§ 1.421-1" is added in its place.

8. In paragraph (j), last sentence, the language "425" is removed and "424" is added in its place.

9. In paragraph (k)(2), second sentence, the language "§ 1.421-8" is removed and "§ 1.421-2" is added in its place.

§ 1.425-1 [Redesignated]

Par. 13. Section 1.425-1 is redesignated as § 1.424-1 and is amended by:

1. Revising paragraphs (a)(1) through (a)(6).

2. Redesignating paragraph (a)(7) as paragraph (a)(9).

3. Adding paragraph (a)(7).

4. Revising paragraph (a)(8).

5. Adding paragraph (a)(10).

6. In paragraph (b)(1), first, second, and last sentences, the language "425" is removed wherever it appears, and "424" is added in their places.

7. In paragraph (c)(1), first sentence, the language "425" is removed and "424" is added in its place.

8. In paragraph (c)(1), first sentence, the language " *disposition*" is removed and " *disposition of stock*" is added in its place.

9. Adding paragraph (c)(1)(iv).

10. Redesignating paragraph (c)(3) as (c)(4).

11. Adding new paragraph (c)(3).

12. Adding newly designated paragraph (c)(4), *Examples 7* through *9.*

13. In the list below, for each section indicated in the left column, remove the language in the middle column and add the language in the right column:

Remove	*Add*
1964	2004
qualified stock option	statutory option
1965	2005
1968	2006
1968	2006
long-term	
1968	2006
1968, two years and 11 months after the transfer of shares to him	2006
three years from the date	two years from the date the options were granted and within one year of the date that
1965	2005
qualified stock option	statutory option
1965	2005

14. Revising paragraph (d).

15. Revising paragraphs (e)(1) and (e)(2).

16. In paragraph (e)(3), first sentence, remove the phrase "Except as otherwise provided in subparagraph (4)" and add "If section 423(c) applies to an option then,".

17. In paragraph (e)(3), first sentence, remove the language ", and 424(b)(1)."

18. Removing paragraph (e)(4).

24. In paragraph (e)(7), remove *Example 4*.

25. Adding paragraphs (f) and (g).

The additions and revisions are as follows:

§ 1.424-1 Definitions and special rules applicable to statutory options.

(a) *Substitutions and assumptions of options*—(1) *In general.* (i) This paragraph (a) provides rules under which an *eligible corporation* (as defined in paragraph (a)(2) of this section) may, by reason of a *corporate transaction* (as defined in paragraph (a)(3) of this section), substitute a new statutory option (new option) for an outstanding statutory option (old option) or assume an old option without such substitution or assumption being considered a modification of the old option. For the definition of *modification*, see paragraph (e) of this section.

(ii) For purposes of §§ 1.421-1 through 1.424-1, the phrase "substituting or assuming a stock option in a transaction to which section 424 applies," "substituting or assuming a stock option in a transaction to which § 1.424-1(a) applies," and similar phrases means a substitution of a new option for an old option or an assumption of an old option that meets the requirements of this paragraph (a). For a substitution or assumption to qualify under this paragraph (a), the substitution or assumption must meet all of the requirements described in paragraphs (a)(4) and (a)(5) of this section.

(2) *Eligible corporation.* For purposes of this paragraph (a), the term *eligible corporation* means a corporation that is the employer of the optionee or a related corporation of such corporation. For purposes of this paragraph (a), the determination of whether a corporation is the employer of the optionee or a related corporation of such corporation is based upon all of the relevant facts and circumstances existing immediately after the corporate transaction.

(3) *Corporate transaction.* For purposes of this paragraph (a), the term *corporate transaction* includes—

(i) A corporate merger, consolidation, acquisition of property or stock, separation, reorganization, or liquidation;

(ii) A distribution (excluding ordinary dividends) or change in the terms or number of outstanding shares of such corporation (e.g., a stock split or stock dividend);

(iii) A change in the name of the corporation whose stock is purchasable under the old option; and

(iv) Such other corporate events prescribed by the Commissioner in published guidance.

(4) *By reason of.* (i) For a change in an option or issuance of a new option to qualify as a substitution or assumption under this paragraph (a), the change must be made by an *eligible corporation* (as defined in

19. Redesignating paragraph (e)(5) as paragraph (e)(4).

20. Revising newly designated paragraph (e)(4).

21. Redesignating paragraph (e)(6) as paragraph (e)(5) and removing the second and third sentences.

22. Adding a new paragraph (e)(6).

23. In list below, for each section indicated in the left column, remove the language in the middle column and add the language in the right column:

paragraph (a)(2) of this section) and occur by reason of a *corporate transaction* (as defined in paragraph (a)(3) of this section).

(ii) Generally, a change in an option or issuance of a new option is considered to be by reason of a corporate transaction, unless the relevant facts and circumstances demonstrate that such change or issuance is made for reasons unrelated to such corporate transaction. For example, a change in an option or issuance of a new option will be considered to be made for reasons unrelated to a corporate transaction if there is an unreasonable delay between the corporate transaction and such change in the option or issuance of a new option, or if the corporate transaction serves no substantial corporate business purpose independent of the change in options. Similarly, a change in the number or price of shares purchasable under an option merely to reflect market fluctuations in the price of the stock purchasable under an option is not by reason of a corporate transaction.

(iii) A change in an option or issuance of a new option is by reason of a distribution or change in the terms or number of the outstanding shares of a corporation (as described in paragraph (a)(3)(ii) of this section) only if the option as changed or the new option issued is an option on the same stock as under the old option (or if such class of stock is eliminated in the change in capital structure, on other stock of the same corporation).

(iv) A change in an option or issuance of a new option is by reason of a change in the name of a corporation (as defined in paragraph (a)(3)(iii) of this section) only if the option as changed or the new option issued is an option on stock of the successor corporation.

(5) *Other requirements.* For a change in an option or issuance of a new option to qualify as a substitution or assumption under this paragraph (a), all of the requirements described in this paragraph (a)(5) must be met.

(i) In the case of an issuance of a new option (or a portion thereof) in exchange for an old option (or portion thereof), the optionee's rights under the old option (or portion thereof) must be canceled, and the optionee must lose all rights under the old option (or portion thereof). There cannot be a substitution of a new option for an old option within the meaning of this paragraph (a) if the optionee may exercise both the old option and the new option. It is not necessary to have a complete substitution of a new option for the old option. However, any portion of such option which is not substituted or assumed in a transaction to which this paragraph (a) applies is an outstanding option to purchase stock or, to the extent paragraph (e) of this section applies, a modified option.

(ii) The excess of the aggregate fair market value of the shares subject to the new or assumed option immediately after the change in the option or issuance of a new option over the aggregate option price of such shares must not exceed the excess of the aggregate fair market value of all shares subject to the old option (or portion thereof) immediately before the change in the option or issuance of a new option over the aggregate option price of such shares.

(iii) On a share by share comparison, the ratio of the option price to the fair market value of the shares subject to the option immediately after the change in the option or issuance of a new option must not be more favorable to the optionee than the ratio of the option price to the fair market value of the stock subject to the old option (or portion thereof) immediately before the change in the option or issuance of a new option. The number of shares subject to the new or assumed option may be adjusted to compensate for any change in the aggregate spread between the aggregate option price and the aggregate fair market value of the shares subject to the option immediately after the change in the option or issuance of the new option as compared to the aggregate spread between the option price and the aggregate fair market value of the shares subject to the option immediately before the change in the option or issuance of the new option.

(iv) The new or assumed option must contain all terms of the old option, except to the extent such terms are rendered inoperative by reason of the corporate transaction.

(v) The new option or assumed option must not give the optionee additional benefits that the optionee did not have under the old option.

(vi) The new or assumed option must otherwise comply with the requirements of § 1.422-2 or § 1.423-2. Thus, for example, the old option must be assumed or the new option must be issued under a plan approved by the stockholders of the corporation changing the option or issuing the new option as described in § 1.422-2(b)(2) or § 1.423-2(c), as applicable.

(6) *Obligation to substitute or assume not necessary.* For a change in the option or issuance of a new option to meet the requirements of this paragraph (a), it is not necessary to show that the corporation changing an option or issuing a new option is under any obligation to do so. In fact, this paragraph (a) may apply even when the option that is being replaced or assumed expressly provides that it will terminate upon the occurrence of certain corporate transactions. However, this paragraph (a) cannot be applied to revive a statutory option which, for reasons not related to the corporate transaction, expires before it can properly be replaced or assumed under this paragraph (a).

(7) *Issuance of stock without meeting the requirements of this paragraph (a).* A change in the terms of an option resulting in a modification of such option occurs if an optionee's new employer (or a related corporation of the new employer) issues its stock (or stock of a related corporation) upon exercise of such option without satisfying all of the requirements described in paragraphs (a)(4) and (5) of this section.

(8) *Date of grant.* For purposes of applying the rules of this paragraph (a), a substitution or assumption is considered to occur on the date that the optionee would, but for this paragraph (a), be considered to have been granted the option that the eligible corporation is substituting or assuming. A substitution or an assumption that occurs by reason of a corporate transaction may occur before or after the corporate transaction.

* * * * *

(10) *Examples.* The principles of this paragraph (a) are illustrated by the following examples:

Example 1. Eligible corporation. X Corporation acquires a new subsidiary, Y Corporation, and transfers some of its employees to Y. Y Corporation wishes to grant to its new employees and to the employees of X Corporation new options for Y shares in exchange for old options for X shares that were previously granted by X Corporation. Because Y Corporation is an employer with respect to its own employees and a related corporation of X Corporation, Y Corporation is an eligible corporation under paragraph (a)(2) of this section with respect to both the employees of X and Y Corporations.

Example 2. Corporate transaction. (i) On January 1, 2004, Z Corporation grants E, an employee of Z, an option to acquire 100 shares of Z stock. At the time of grant, the fair market value of Z stock is $200 per share. E's option price is $200 per share. On July 1, 2005, when the fair market value of Z stock is $400, Z declares a stock dividend that causes the fair market value of Z stock to decrease to $200 per share. On the same day, Z grants to E a new option to acquire 200 shares of Z stock in exchange for E's old option. The new option has an exercise price of $100 per share.

(ii) A stock dividend is a corporate transaction under paragraph (a)(3)(ii) of this section. Generally, the issuance of a new option is considered to be by reason of a corporate transaction. None of the facts in this *Example 2* indicate that the new option is not issued by reason of the stock dividend. In addition, the new option is issued on the same

stock as the old option. Thus, the substitution occurs by reason of the corporate transaction. Assuming the other requirements of this section are met, the issuance of the new option is a substitution that meets the requirements of this paragraph (a) and is not a modification of the option.

(iii) Assume the same facts as in paragraph (i) of this *Example 2*. Assume further that on December 1, 2005, Z declares an ordinary cash dividend. On the same day, Z grants E a new option to acquire Z stock in substitution for E's old option. Under paragraph (a)(3)(ii) of this section, an ordinary cash dividend is not a corporate transaction. Thus, the exchange of the new option for the old option does not meet the requirements of this paragraph (a) and is a modification of the option.

Example 3. Corporate transaction. On March 15, 2004, A Corporation grants E, an employee of A, an option to acquire 100 shares of A stock at $50 per share, the fair market value of A stock on the date of grant. On May 2, 2005, A Corporation transfers several employees, including E, to B Corporation, a related corporation. B Corporation arranges to purchase some assets from A on the same day as E's transfer to B. Such purchase is without a substantial business purpose independent of making the exchange of E's old options for the new options appear to be by reason of a corporate transaction. The following day, B Corporation grants to E, one of its new employees, an option to acquire shares of B stock in exchange for the old option held by E to acquire A stock. Under paragraph (a)(3)(i) of this section, the purchase of assets is a corporate transaction. Generally, the substitution of an option is considered to occur by reason of a corporate transaction. However, in this case, the relevant facts and circumstances demonstrate that the issuance of the new option in exchange for the old option occurred by reason of the change in E's employer rather than a corporate transaction and that the sale of assets is without a substantial corporate business purpose independent of the change in the options. Thus, the exchange of the new option for the old option is not by reason of a corporate transaction that meets the requirements of this paragraph (a) and is a modification of the old option.

Example 4. Additional benefit. On June 1, 2004, P Corporation acquires 100 percent of the shares of S Corporation and issues a new option to purchase P shares in exchange for an old option to purchase S shares that is held by E, an employee of S. On the date of the exchange, E's old option is exercisable for 3 more years, and, after the exchange, E's new option is exercisable for 5 years. Because the new option is exercisable for an additional period of time beyond the time allowed under the old option, the effect of the exchange of the new option for the old option is to give E an additional benefit that E did not enjoy under the old option. Thus, the requirements of paragraph (a)(5) of this section are not met, and this paragraph (a) does not apply to the exchange of the new option for the old option. Therefore, the exchange is a modification of the old options.

Example 5. Spread and ratio tests. E is an employee of S Corporation. E holds an old option that was granted to E by S to purchase 60 shares of S at $12 per share. On June 1, 2005, S Corporation is merged into P Corporation, and on such date P issues a new option to purchase P shares in exchange for E's old option to purchase S shares. Immediately before the exchange, the fair market value of an S share is $32; immediately after the exchange, the fair market value of a P share is $24. The new option entitles E to buy P shares at $9 per share. Because, on a share-by-share comparison, the ratio of the new option price ($9 per share) to the fair market value of a P share immediately after the exchange ($24 per share) is not more favorable to E than the ratio of the old option price ($12 per share) to the fair market value of an S share immediately before the exchange ($32 per share) (9/24 = 12/32), the requirements of paragraph (a)(5)(iii) of this section are met. The number of shares subject to E's option to purchase P stock is set at 80. Because the excess of the aggregate fair market value over the aggregate option price of the shares subject to E's new option to purchase P stock, $1,200 (80 × $24 minus 80 × $9), is not greater than the excess of the aggregate fair market value over the aggregate option price of the shares subject to E's old option to purchase S stock, $1,200 (60 × $32 minus 60 × $12), the requirements of paragraph (a)(5)(ii) of this section are met.

Example 6. Ratio test and partial substitution. Assume the same facts as in *Example 5*, except that the fair market value of an S share immediately before the exchange of the new option for the old option is $8, that the option price is $10 per share, and that the fair market value of a P share immediately after the exchange is $12. P sets the new option price at $15 per share. Because, on a share-by-share comparison, the ratio of the new option price ($15 per share) to the fair market value of a P share immediately after the exchange ($12) is not more favorable to E than the ratio of the old option price ($10 per share) to the fair market value of an S share immediately before the substitution ($8 per share) (15/12 = 10/8), the requirements of paragraph (a)(5)(iii) of this section are met. Assume further that the number of shares subject to E's P option is set at 20, as compared to 60 shares under E's old option to buy S stock. Immediately after the exchange, 2 shares of P are worth $24, which is what 3 shares of S were worth immediately before the exchange ($2 \times \$12 = 3 \times \$8$). Thus, to achieve a complete substitution of a new option for E's old option, E would need to receive a new option to purchase 40 shares of P (i.e., 2 shares of P for each 3 shares of S that E could have purchased under the old option ($\frac{2}{3} = 40/60$)). Because E's new option is for only 20 shares of P, P has replaced only ½ of E's old option, and the other ½ is still outstanding.

Example 7. Partial substitution. X Corporation forms a new corporation, Y Corporation, by a transfer of certain assets and, in a spin-off, distributes the shares of Y Corporation to the stockholders of X Corporation. E, an employee of X Corporation, is thereafter an employee of Y. Y wishes to substitute a new option to purchase some of its stock for E's old option to purchase 100 shares of X. E's old option to purchase shares of X, at $50 a share, was granted when the fair market value of an X share was $50, and an X share was worth $100 just before the distribution of the Y shares to X's stockholders. Immediately after the spin-off, which is also the time of the substitution, each share of X and each share of Y is worth $50. Based on these facts, a new option to purchase 200 shares of Y at an option price of $25 per share could be granted to E in complete substitution of E's old option. It would also be permissible to grant E a new option to purchase 100 shares of Y, at an option price of $25 per share, in substitution for E's right to purchase 50 of the shares under the old option.

Example 8. Stockholder approval requirements. (i) X Corporation, a publicly traded corporation, adopts an incentive stock option plan that meets the requirements of § 1.422-2. Under the plan, options to acquire X stock are granted to X employees. X Corporation is acquired by Y Corporation and becomes a subsidiary corporation of Y Corporation. Y Corporation maintains an incentive stock option plan that meets the requirements of § 1.422-2. Under the plan, options for Y stock may be granted to employees of Y or its related corporations. After the acquisition, X employees remain employees of X. In connection with the acquisition, Y Corporation substitutes new options for Y stock for old options for X stock that were previously granted to the employees of X. As a result of this substitution, on exercise of the new options, X employees receive Y Corporation stock.

(ii) Because Y Corporation has a plan that meets the requirements of § 1.422-2 in existence on the date it acquires X, the new options for Y stock are granted under a plan approved by the stockholders of Y. The stockholders of Y do not need to approve the X plan. If the other requirements of paragraphs (a)(4) and (5) of this section are met, the issuance of new options for Y stock in exchange for the old options for X stock meets the requirements of this paragraph (a) and is not a modification of the old options.

(iii) Assume the same facts as in paragraph (i) of this *Example 8*, except that Y Corporation does not maintain an incentive stock option plan on the date of the acquisition of X. The Y options will only be incentive stock options if they are granted under a plan that meets the requirements of § 1.422-2(b). Therefore, Y must adopt a plan that provides for the grant of incentive stock options, and the plan must be approved by the stockholders of Y in accordance with § 1.422-2(b). If the stockholders of Y approve the incentive stock option plan within 12 months before or after the date of the adoption of a plan by Y and the other requirements of § 1.422-2 and the requirements of this paragraph (a) are met, the issuance of the new options for Y stock in exchange for the old options for X stock meets the requirements of this paragraph (a) and is not treated as a modification of the old options for X stock. The result is the same if Y Corporation assumes the old options instead of issuing new options.

(iv) Assume the same facts as in paragraph (i) of this *Example 8*, except that there is no exchange of options. Instead, as part of the acquisition, X amends its plan to allow future grants under the plan to be grants to acquire Y stock. Because the amendment of the plan to allow options on a different stock is considered the adoption of the new plan, the stockholders of X must approve the plan within 12 months before or after the date of the amendment of the plan. If the stockholders of X timely approve the plan, the future grants to acquire Y stock will be incentive stock options (assuming the other requirements of § 1.422-2 have been met).

Example 9. Modification. X Corporation merges into Y Corporation. Y Corporation retains employees of X who hold old options to acquire X Corporation stock. When the former employees of X exercise the old options, Y Corporation issues Y stock to the former employees of X. Under paragraph (a)(7) of this section, because Y issues its stock on exercise of the old options for X stock, there is a change in the terms of

the old options for X stock. Thus, the issuance of Y stock on exercise of the old options is a modification of the old options.

* * * * *

(c) * * * (1) * * *

(iv) A transfer between spouses or incident to divorce (described in section 1041(a)). The special tax treatment of § 1.421-2(a) with respect to the transferred stock applies to the transferee. However, see § 1.421-1(b)(2) for the treatment of the transfer of a statutory option incident to divorce.

* * * * *

(3) If an optionee exercises an incentive stock option with statutory option stock and the applicable holding period requirements (under § 1.422-1(a) or § 1.423-1(a)) with respect to such statutory option stock are not met before such transfer, then sections 354, 355, 356, or 1036 (or so much of 1031 as relates to 1036) do not apply to determine whether there is a disposition of those shares. Therefore, there is a disposition of the statutory option stock, and the special tax treatment of § 1.421-2(a) does not apply to such stock.

(4) * * *

Example 7. On January 1, 2004, X Corporation grants to E, an employee of X Corporation, an incentive stock option to purchase 100 shares of X Corporation stock at $100 per share (the fair market value of an X Corporation share on that date). On January 1, 2005, when the fair market value of a share of X Corporation stock is $200, E exercises half of the option, pays X Corporation $5,000 in cash, and is transferred 50 shares of X Corporation stock with an aggregate fair market value of $10,000. E makes no disposition of the shares before January 2, 2006. Under § 1.421-2(a), no income is recognized by E on the transfer of shares pursuant to the exercise of the incentive stock option, and X Corporation is not entitled to any deduction at any time with respect to its transfer of the shares to E. E's basis in the shares is $5,000.

Example 8. Assume the same facts as in *Example 7*, except that on December 1, 2005, one year and 11 months after the grant of the option and 11 months after the transfer of the 50 shares to E, E uses 25 of those shares, with a fair market value of $5,000, to pay for the remaining 50 shares purchasable under the option. On that day, X Corporation transfers 50 of its shares, with an aggregate fair market value of $10,000, to E. Because E disposed of the 25 shares before the expiration of the applicable holding periods, § 1.421-2(a) does not apply to the January 1, 2005, transfer of the 25 shares used by E to exercise the remainder of the option. As a result of the disqualifying disposition of the 25 shares, E recognizes compensation income under the rules of § 1.421-2(b).

Example 9. On January 1, 2005, X Corporation grants an incentive stock option to E, an employee of X Corporation. The exercise price of the option is $10 per share. On June 1, 2005, when the fair market value of an X Corporation share is $20, E exercises the option and purchases 5 shares with an aggregate fair market value of $100. On January 1, 2006, when the fair market value of an X Corporation share is $50, X Corporation is acquired by Y Corporation in a section 368(a)(1)(A) reorganization. As part of the acquisition, all X Corporation shares are converted into Y Corporation shares. After the conversion, if an optionee holds a fractional share of X Corporation stock, Y Corporation will purchase the fractional share for cash equal to its fair market value. After applying the conversion formula to the shares held by E, E has 10 Y Corporation shares and one-half of a share of X Corporation stock. Y Corporation purchases E's one-half share for $25, the fair market value of one-half of an X Corporation share on the conversion date. Because E sells the one-half share prior to expiration of the holding periods described in § 1.422-1(a), the sale is a disqualifying disposition of the one-half share. Thus, in 2006, E must recognize compensation income of $5 (one-half of the fair market value of an X Corporation share on the date of exercise of the option, or $10, less one-half of the exercise price per share, or $5). For purposes of computing any additional gain, E's basis in the one-half share increases to $10 (reflecting the $5 included in income as compensation). E recognizes an additional gain of $15 ($25, the fair market value of the one-half share, less $10, the basis in such share). The extent to which the additional $15 of gain is treated as a redemption of X Corporation stock is determined under section 302.

(d) *Attribution of stock ownership.* To determine the amount of stock owned by an individual for purposes of applying the percentage limitations relating to certain stockholders described in § § 1.422-2(f) and 1.423-2(d), shares of the employer corporation or of a related corporation that are owned (directly or indirectly) by or for the individual's brothers and sisters (whether by the whole or half blood), spouse, ancestors, and lineal descendants, are considered to be owned by the individual. Also, for such purposes, if a domestic or foreign corporation, partnership, estate, or trust owns (directly or indirectly) shares of the employer corporation or of a related corporation, the shares are considered to be owned proportionately by or for the stockholders, partners, or beneficiaries of the corporation, partnership, estate, or trust. The extent to which stock held by the optionee as a trustee of a voting trust is considered owned by the optionee is determined under all of the facts and circumstances.

(e) *Modification, extension, or renewal of option.* (1) This paragraph (e) provides rules for determining whether a share of stock transferred to an individual upon the individual's exercise of an option after the terms of the option have been changed is transferred pursuant to the exercise of a statutory option.

(2) Any modification, extension, or renewal of the terms of an option to purchase shares is considered the granting of a new option. The new option may or may not be a statutory option. To determine the date of grant of the new option for purposes of section 422 or 423, see § 1.421-1(c).

* * * * *

(4)(i) For purposes of §§ 1.421-1 through 1.4241 the term *modification* means any change in the terms of the option (or change in the terms of the plan pursuant to which the option was granted or in the terms of any other agreement governing the arrangement) that gives the optionee additional benefits under the option regardless of whether the optionee in fact benefits from the change in terms. In contrast, for example, a change in the terms of the option shortening the period during which the option is exercisable is not a modification. However, a change providing an extension of the period during which an option may be exercised (such as after termination of employment) or a change providing an alternative to the exercise of the option (such as a stock appreciation right) is a modification regardless of whether the optionee in fact benefits from such extension or alternative right. Similarly, a change providing an additional benefit upon exercise of the option (such as the payment of a cash bonus) or a change providing more favorable terms for payment for the stock purchased under the option (such as the right to tender previously acquired stock) is a modification.

(ii) If an option is not immediately exercisable in full, a change in the terms of the option to accelerate the time at which the option (or any portion thereof) may be exercised is not a modification for purposes of this section. Additionally, no modification occurs if a provision accelerating the time when an option may first be exercised is removed prior to the year in which it would otherwise be triggered. For example, if an acceleration provision is timely removed to avoid exceeding the $100,000 limitation described in § 1.422-4, a modification of the option does not occur.

(iii) A change to an option which provides, either by its terms or in substance, that the optionee may receive an additional benefit under the option at the future discretion of the grantor, is a modification at the time that the option is changed to provide such discretion. In addition, the exercise of discretion to provide an additional benefit is a modification of the option. However, it is not a modification for the grantor to exercise discretion reserved under an option with respect to the payment of a cash bonus at the time of exercise, the availability of a loan at exercise, or the right to tender previously acquired stock for the stock purchasable under the option. An option is not modified merely because an optionee is offered a change in the terms of an option if the change to the option is not made.

(iv) A change in the terms of the stock purchasable under the option that affects the value of the stock is a modification of such option, except to the extent that a new option is substituted for such option by reason of the change in the terms of the stock in accordance with paragraph (a) of this section.

(v) If an option is amended solely to increase the number of shares subject to the option, the increase is not considered a modification of the option but is treated as the grant of a new option for the additional shares.

(vi) Any change in the terms of an option made in an attempt to qualify the option as a statutory option grants additional benefits to the optionee and is, therefore, a modification.

(vii) An extension of an option refers to the granting by the corporation to the optionee of an additional period of time within which to exercise the option beyond the time originally prescribed. A renewal of an option is the granting by the corporation of the same rights or privileges contained in the original option on the same terms and conditions. The rules of this paragraph apply as well to successive modifications, extensions, and renewals.

* * * * *

(6) [Reserved.]

* * * * *

(f) *Definitions.* The following definitions apply for purposes of §§ 1.421-1 through 1.424-1:

(1) *Parent corporation.* The term *parent corporation*, or *parent*, means any corporation (other than the employer corporation) in an unbroken chain of corporations ending with the employer corporation if, at the time of the granting of the option, each of the corporations other than the employer corporation owns stock possessing 50 percent or more of the total combined voting power of all classes of stock in one of the other corporations in such chain.

(2) *Subsidiary corporation.* The term *subsidiary corporation*, or *subsidiary*, means any corporation (other than the employer corporation) in an unbroken chain of corporations beginning with the employer corporation if, at the time of the granting of the option, each of the corporations other than the last corporation in an unbroken chain owns stock possessing 50 percent or more of the total combined voting power of all classes of stock in one of the other corporations in such chain.

(g) *Effective date.* This section applies to any statutory option granted on or after the date that is 180 days after publication of final regulations in the **Federal Register**. Taxpayers can rely on these regulations for the treatment of any statutory option granted on or after June 9, 2003.

§ 1.6039-1 [Removed]

Par. 14. Section 1.6039-1 is removed.

§ 1.6039-2 [Redesignated]

Par. 15. Section 1.6039-2 is redesignated as 1.6039-1 and revised to read as follows:

§ 1.6039-1 Statements to persons with respect to whom information is furnished.

(a) *Requirement of statement with respect to incentive stock options under section 6039(a)(1).* Every corporation which transfers stock to any person pursuant to such person's exercise of an incentive stock option described in section 422(b) must furnish to such transferee, for each calendar year in which such a transfer occurs, a written statement with respect to the transfer or transfers made during such year. This statement must include the following information—

(1) The name, address, and employer identification number of the corporation transferring the stock;

(2) The name, address, and identifying number of the person to whom the share or shares of stock were transferred;

(3) The name and address of the corporation the stock of which is the subject of the option (if other than the corporation transferring the stock);

(4) The date the option was granted;

(5) The date the shares were transferred to the person exercising the option;

(6) The fair market value of the stock at the time the option was exercised;

(7) The number of shares of stock transferred pursuant to the option;

(8) The type of option under which the transferred shares were acquired; and

(9) The total cost of all the shares.

(b) *Requirement of statement with respect to stock purchased under an employee stock purchase plan under section 6039(a)(2).* (1) Every corporation which records, or has by its agent recorded, a transfer of the title to stock acquired by the transferor pursuant to the transferor's exercise on or after January 1, 1964, of an option granted under an employee stock purchase plan which meets the requirements of section 423(b), and with respect to which the special rule of section 423(c) applied, must furnish to such transferor, for each calendar year in which such a recorded transfer of title to such stock occurs, a written statement with respect to the transfer or transfers containing the information required by paragraph (b)(2) of this section.

(2) The statement required by paragraph (b)(1) of this section must contain the following information—

(i) The name and address of the corporation whose stock is being transferred;

(ii) The name, address and identifying number of the transferor;

(iii) The date such stock was transferred to the transferor;

(iv) The number of shares to which title is being transferred; and

(v) The type of option under which the transferred shares were acquired.

(3) If the statement required by this paragraph is made by the authorized transfer agent of the corporation, it is deemed to have been made by the corporation. The term *transfer agent*, as used in this section means any designee authorized to keep the stock ownership records of a corporation and to record a transfer of title of the stock of such corporation on behalf of such corporation.

(4) A statement is required by reason of a transfer described in section 6039(a)(2) of a share only with respect to the first transfer of such share by the person who exercised the option. Thus, for example, if the owner has record title to a share or shares of stock transferred to a recognized broker or financial institution and the stock is subsequently sold by such broker or institution (on behalf of the owner), the corporation is only required to furnish a written statement to the owner relating to the transfer of record title to the broker or financial institution. Similarly, a written statement is required when a share of stock is transferred by the optionee to himself and another person (or persons) as joint tenants, tenants by the entirety or tenants in common. However, when stock is originally issued to the optionee and another person (or persons) as joint tenants, or as tenants by the entirety, the written statement required by this paragraph shall be furnished (at such time and in such manner as is provided by this section) with respect to the first transfer of the title to such stock by the optionee.

(5) Every corporation which transfers any share of stock pursuant to the exercise of an option described in this paragraph shall identify such stock in a manner sufficient to enable the accurate reporting of the transfer of record title to such shares. Such identification may be accomplished by assigning to the certificates of stock issued pursuant to the exercise of such options a special serial number or color.

(c) *Time for furnishing statements*—(1) *In general*. Each statement required by this section to be furnished to any person for a calendar year must be furnished to such person on or before January 31 of the year following the year for which the statement is required.

(2) *Extension of time*. For good cause shown upon written application of the corporation required to furnish statements under this section, the Director, Martinsburg Computing Center, may grant an extension of time not exceeding 30 days in which to furnish such statements. The application must contain a full recital of the reasons for requesting an extension to aid the Director in determining the period of the extension, if any, which will be granted and must be sent to the Martinsburg Computing Center (Attn: Extension of Time Coordinator). Such a request in the form of a letter to the Martinsburg Computing Center signed by the applicant (or its agent) will suffice as an application. The application must be filed on or before the date prescribed in paragraph (c)(1) of this section for furnishing the statements required by this section, and must contain the employer identification number of the corporation required to furnish statements under this section.

(3) *Last day for furnishing statement*. For provisions relating to the time for performance of an act when the last day prescribed for performance falls on Saturday, Sunday, or a legal holiday, see § 301.7503-1 of this chapter (Regulations on Procedure and Administration).

(d) *Statements furnished by mail*. For purposes of this section, a statement is considered to be furnished to a person if it is mailed to such person's last known address.

(e) *Penalty*. For provisions relating to the penalty provided for failure to furnish a statement under this section, see section 6722.

(f) *Electronic furnishing of statements* [Reserved].

(g) *Effective date*. This section applies as of the date that is 180 days after publication of final regulations in the **FEDERAL REGISTER** to transfers of stock acquired pursuant to a statutory option on or after that date. Taxpayers can rely on these regulations with respect to the transfer of stock acquired pursuant to a statutory option on or after June 9, 2003.

PART 14a—TEMPORARY INCOME TAX REGULATIONS RELATING TO INCENTIVE STOCK OPTIONS

Part 14a [Removed]

Par. 16. Part 14a is removed.

David A. Mader,

Assistant Deputy Commissioner of Internal Revenue.

¶ 20,260X

IRS proposed regulations: Compensatory stock options: Nonstatutory stock options: Listed transactions: Related parties: Federal income taxes: Federal employment taxes.—The IRS has issued proposed regulations containing a comment request on final and temporary regulations that are designed to halt arrangements involving the transfer of compensatory stock options by executives to related parties in an attempt to avoid federal taxes. Comments must be received by September 30, 2003.

The proposed regulations, which were published in the Federal Register on July 2, 2003 (68 FR 39498) and corrected on September 4, 2003 (68 FR 52544), are reproduced below.

DEPARTMENT OF THE TREASURY

Internal Revenue Service

26 CFR Part 1

[REG-116914-03]

RIN 1545-BC06

Transfers of Compensatory Options

AGENCY: Internal Revenue Service (IRS), Treasury.

ACTION: Notice of proposed rulemaking by cross-reference to temporary regulations.

SUMMARY: In the Rules and Regulations section of this issue of the **Federal Register**, the IRS is issuing temporary regulations relating to the sale or other disposition of compensatory nonstatutory stock options to related persons. The text of those regulations also serves as the text of these proposed regulations.

DATES: Written or electronic comments and requests for a public hearing must be received by September 30, 2003.

ADDRESSES: Send submissions to: CC:PA:RU (REG-116914-03), room 5226, Internal Revenue Service, POB 7604, Ben Franklin Station, Washington, DC., 20044. Submissions may be hand delivered Monday through Friday between the hours of 8 a.m. and 4 p.m. to: CC:PA:RU (REG-116914-03), Courier's Desk, Internal Revenue Service, 1111 Constitution Ave., NW., Washington, DC. Alternatively, taxpayers may submit electronic comments directly to the IRS Internet site at www.irs.gov/regs.

FOR FURTHER INFORMATION CONTACT: Concerning the temporary regulations, Stephen Tackney (202) 622-6030; concerning submissions of comments and/or requests for a hearing, Guy Traynor, (202) 622-7180 (not toll-free numbers).

SUPPLEMENTARY INFORMATION:

Background and Explanation of Provisions

Temporary regulations in the Rules and Regulations section of this issue of the **Federal Register** amend 26 CFR part 1. The regulations provide that a sale or other disposition of a nonstatutory stock option to a related person will not be treated as a transaction that closes the application of section 83 with respect to the option. The text of the temporary regulations also serves as the text of these proposed regulations. The preamble to the temporary regulations explains the temporary regulations and these proposed regulations.

Special Analyses

It has been determined that these proposed regulations are not a significant regulatory action as defined in Executive order 12866. Therefore, a regulatory assessment is not required. It also has been determined that section 533(b) of the Administrative Procedures Act (5 U.S.C. chapter 5) does not apply to these regulations, and because these regulations do not impose a collection of information on small entities, the Regulatory Flexibility Act (5 U.S.C. chapter 6) does not apply. Pursuant to section 7805(f) of the Internal Revenue Code, these regulations are being submitted to the Chief Counsel for Advocacy of the Small Business Administration for comment on their impact on small business. [Corrected by IRS on 9/4/03 by 68 FR 52544.]

Comments and Requests for a Public Hearing

Before these proposed regulations are adopted as final regulations, consideration will be given to any written comments (a signed original and eight (8) copies) or electronic comments that are submitted timely to the IRS. The IRS and Treasury Department request comments on the clarity of the proposed rules and how they can be made easier to understand. The IRS and Treasury Department specifically request comments on the clarity and efficacy of the proposed definition of a related person. All comments will be available for public inspection and copying. A public hearing may be scheduled if requested by any person that timely submits written comments. If a public hearing is scheduled, notice of the date, time, and place for the public hearing will be published in the **Federal Register**.

Drafting Information

The principal author of these proposed regulations is Stephen Tackney of the Office of Division Counsel/Associate Chief Counsel (Tax Exempt and Government Entities). However, other personnel from the IRS and Treasury Department participated in their development.

List of Subjects in 26 CFR Part 1

Income taxes, Reporting and recordkeeping requirements.

Adoption of Amendments to the Regulations

Accordingly, 26 CFR part 1 is proposed to be amended as follows:

PART 1—INCOME TAXES

Paragraph 1. The authority citation for part 1 continues to read as follows:

Authority: 26 U.S.C. 7805 ***

Par. 2. Section 1.83-7 is amended as follows:

1. Paragraph (a) is amended by adding a sentence at the end.

2. Paragraphs (a)(1) and (a)(2) are added.

3. Paragraph (d) is added.

The additions read as follows:

(a) [The text of proposed § 1.83-7(a) is the same as the text of § 1.83-7T(a) published elsewhere in this issue of the **Federal Register**].

*****

(d) *Effective dates.* This section is applicable to sales or other dispositions of options on or after the publication of final regulations in the **Federal Register**. For dates on or after July 2, 2003, see § 1.83-7T(d).

Deputy Commissioner of Internal Revenue.

Robert E. Wenzel,

DALE D. GOODE

CERTIFIED COPY

¶ 20,260Y

IRS proposed regulations: Distributions: Defined contribution plans: Elimination of optional forms of benefit: Anti-cutback rule.—The IRS has issued proposed regulations that would modify the circumstances under which the elimination of certain forms of defined contribution plan distributions is permitted.

The proposed regulations, which were published in the Federal Register on July 8, 2003 (68 FR 40581) and amended September 19, 2003 (68 FR 54876), are reproduced below.

DEPARTMENT OF THE TREASURY

Internal Revenue Service

26 CFR Parts 1

[REG-112039-03]

RIN 1545-BC35

Elimination of Forms of Distribution in Defined Contribution Plans

AGENCY: Internal Revenue Service (IRS), Treasury.

ACTION: Notice of proposed rulemaking.

SUMMARY: This document contains proposed regulations that would modify the circumstances under which certain forms of distribution previously available are permitted to be eliminated from qualified defined contribution plans. These proposed regulations affect qualified retirement plan sponsors, administrators, and participants. [Amended September 19, 2003, 68 FR 54876.]

DATES: Written and electronic comments and requests for a public hearing must be received by October 6, 2003.

ADDRESSES: Send submissions to: CC:PA:RU (REG-112039-03), room 5226, Internal Revenue Service, POB 7604, Ben Franklin Station, Washington, DC 20044. Submissions may be hand delivered Monday through Friday between the hours of 8 a.m. and 5 p.m. to: CC:PA:RU (REG-112039-03), Courier's Desk, Internal Revenue Service, 1111 Constitution Avenue NW., Washington, DC. Alternatively, taxpayers may submit comments electronically directly to the IRS Internet site at: www.irs.gov/regs.

FOR FURTHER INFORMATION CONTACT: Concerning the regulations, Vernon S. Carter, 202-622-6060 (not a toll-free number); concerning submissions or hearing requests, Guy Traynor, 202-622-7180 (not a toll-free number).

SUPPLEMENTARY INFORMATION

Explanation of Provisions

This document contains proposed amendments to 26 CFR part 1 under section 411(d)(6) of the Internal Revenue Code of 1986 (Code) as amended by the Economic Growth and Tax Relief Reconciliation Act of 2001 (EGTRRA) (115 Stat. 117). Section 411(d)(6)(A) of the Code generally provides that a plan will not be treated as satisfying the requirements of section 411 if the accrued benefit of a participant is decreased by a plan amendment. Section 411(d)(6)(B) prior to amendment by EGTRRA provided that an amendment is treated as reducing an accrued benefit if, with respect to benefits accrued before the amendment is adopted, the amendment has the effect of either eliminating or reducing an early retirement benefit or a retirement-type subsidy, or, except as provided by regulations, eliminating an optional form of benefit.

The IRS published TD 8900 in the **Federal Register** on September 6, 2000 (65 FR 53901). TD 8900, which amended § 1.411(d)-4 of the Income Tax Regulations, added paragraph (e) of Q&A-2 to provide for additional circumstances under which a defined contribution plan can be amended to eliminate or restrict a participant's right to receive payment of accrued benefits under certain optional forms of benefit.

Section 1.411(d)-4, Q&A-2(e)(1) provides that a defined contribution plan may be amended to eliminate or restrict a participant's right to receive payment of accrued benefits under a particular optional form of benefit without violating the section 411(d)(6) anti-cutback rules if, once the plan amendment takes effect for a participant, the alternative forms of payment that remain available to the participant include payment in a single-sum distribution form that is "otherwise identical" to the eliminated or restricted optional form of benefit. The amendment cannot apply to a participant for any distribution with an annuity starting date before the earlier of the 90th day after the participant receives a summary that reflects the plan amendment and that satisfies Department of Labor's requirements for a summary of material modifications under 29 CFR 2520.104b-3, or the first day of the second plan year following the plan year in which the amendment is adopted. Section § 1.411(d)-4, Q&A-2(e)(2) provides that a single-sum distribution form is "otherwise identical" to the optional form of benefit that is being eliminated or restricted only if it is identical in all respects (or would be identical except that it provides greater rights to the participant), except for the timing of payments after commencement. A single-sum distribution form is not "otherwise identical" to a specified installment form of benefit if the single-sum form:

is not available for distribution on any date on which the installment form could have commenced;

is not available in the same medium as the installment form; or

imposes any additional condition of eligibility.

Further, an otherwise identical distribution form need not retain any rights or features of the eliminated or restricted optional form of benefit to the extent those rights or features would not be protected from elimination under the anti-cutback rules. The single-sum distribution form would not, however, be disqualified from being an otherwise identical distribution form if the single-sum form provides greater rights to participants than did the eliminated or restricted optional form of benefits.

Section 645(a)(1) of EGTRRA revised section 411(d)(6) in a manner that is similar to §1.411(d)-4, Q&A-2(e), but without the advance notice condition. Section 411(d)(6)(E) of the Code provides that, except to the extent provided in regulations, a defined contribution plan is not treated as reducing a participant's accrued benefit where a plan amendment eliminates a form of distribution previously available under the plan if a single-sum distribution is available to the participant at the same time as the form of distribution eliminated by the amendment, and the single-sum distribution is based on the same or greater portion of the participant's account as the form of distribution eliminated by the amendment.

To reflect the addition of section 411(d)(6)(E) by EGTRRA, these proposed regulations would amend §1.411(d)-4, Q&A-2(e). Under these amendments, the regulations would retain the rules under which a defined contribution plan may be amended to eliminate or restrict a participant's right to receive payment of accrued benefits under a particular optional form of benefit without violating the section 411(d)(6) anti-cutback rules if, once the plan amendment takes effect for a participant, the alternative forms of payment that remain available to the participant include payment in a single-sum distribution. However, these proposed regulations would remove the 90-day notice condition previously applicable to these plan amendments.[1]

Under section 101 of Reorganization Plan No. 4 of 1978 (43 FR 47713), the Secretary of the Treasury has interpretive jurisdiction over the subject matter addressed in these regulations for purposes of the Employee Retirement Income Security Act of 1974 (ERISA), as well as the Code. Section 204(g)(2) of ERISA, as amended by EGTRRA, provides a parallel rule to section 411(d)(6)(E) of the Code that applies under Title I of ERISA, and authorizes the Secretary of the Treasury to provide exception to this parallel ERISA requirement. Therefore, these regulations apply for purposes of the parallel requirements of sections 204(g)(2) of ERISA, as well as for section 411(d)(6)(E) of the Code.

Effective Date and Applicability Date

The proposed regulations are proposed to apply on the date of publication of final regulations in the **Federal Register**.

Special Analyses

It has been determined that this Treasury decision is not a significant regulatory action as defined in Executive Order 12866. Therefore, a regulatory assessment is not required. It also has been determined that section 553(b) of the Administrative Procedure Act (5 U.S.C. chapter 5) does not apply to these regulations, and because the regulation does not impose a collection of information on small entities, the Regulatory Flexibility Act (5 U.S.C. chapter 6) does not apply. Pursuant to section 7805(f) of the Code, this notice of proposed rulemaking will be submitted to the Chief Counsel for Advocacy of the Small Business Administration for comment on its impact on small business.

Drafting Information

The principal author of these regulations is Vernon S. Carter of the Office of the Division Counsel/Associate Chief Counsel (Tax Exempt and Government Entities). However, other personnel from the IRS and Treasury participated in their development.

List of Subjects in 26 CFR Parts 1

Income taxes, Reporting and recordkeeping requirements.

Amendments to the Regulations

Accordingly, 26 CFR part 1 is proposed to be amended as follows:

Paragraph 1. The authority citation for part 1 is amended to read in part as follows:

Authority: 26 U.S.C. 7805 ***

Section 1.411(d)-4, Q&A-2(e) also issued under 26 U.S.C. 411(d)(6)(E). ***

Par. 2. Section 1.411(d)-4, Q&A-2(e) is revised to read as follows:

§1.411(d)-4 Section 411(d)(6) protected benefits.

*****

A-2: ***

(e) *Permitted plan amendments affecting alternative forms of payment under defined contribution plans*—(1) *General rule.* A defined contribution plan does not violate the requirements of section 411(d)(6) merely because the plan is amended to eliminate or restrict the ability of a participant to receive payment of accrued benefits under a particular optional form of benefit if, after the plan amendment is effective with respect to the participant, the alternative forms of payment available to the participant include payment in a single-sum distribution form that is otherwise identical to the optional form of benefit that is being eliminated or restricted.

(2) *Otherwise identical single-sum distribution.* For purposes of this paragraph (e), a single-sum distribution form is otherwise identical to an optional form of benefit that is eliminated or restricted pursuant to paragraph (e)(1) of this Q&A-2 only if the single-sum distribution form is identical in all respects to the eliminated or restricted optional form of benefit (or would be identical except that it provides greater rights to the participant) except with respect to the timing of payments after commencement. For example, a single-sum distribution form is not otherwise identical to a specified installment form of benefit if the single-sum distribution form is not available for distribution on the date on which the installment form would have been available for commencement, is not available in the same medium of distribution as the installment form, or imposes any condition of eligibility that did not apply to the installment form. However, an otherwise identical distribution form need not retain rights or features of the optional form of benefit that is eliminated or restricted to the extent that those rights or features would not be protected from elimination or restriction under section 411(d)(6) or this section.

(3) *Example.* The following example illustrates the application of this paragraph (e):

Example. (i) P is a participant in Plan M, a qualified profit-sharing plan with a calendar plan year that is invested in mutual funds. The distribution forms available to P under Plan M include a distribution of P's vested account balance under Plan M in the form of distribution of various annuity contract forms (including a single life annuity and a joint and survivor annuity). The annuity payments under the annuity contract forms begin as of the first day of the month following P's severance from employment (or as of the first day of any subsequent month, subject to the requirements of section 401(a)(9)). P has not previously elected payment of benefits in the form of a life annuity, and Plan M is not a direct or indirect transferee of any plan that is a defined benefit plan or a defined contribution plan that is subject to section 412. Distributions on the death of a participant are made in accordance with plan provisions that comply with section 401(a)(11)(B)(iii)(I). On May 2, 2004, Plan M is amended so that, after the amendment is effective, P is no longer entitled to any distribution in the form of the distribution of an annuity contract. However, after the amendment is effective, P is entitled to receive a single-sum cash distribution of P's vested account balance under Plan M payable as of the first day of the month following P's severance from employment (or as of the first day of any subsequent month, subject to the requirements of section 401(a)(9)). The amendment does not apply to P if P elects to have annuity payments begin before July 1, 2004.

(ii) Plan M does not violate the requirements of section 411(d)(6) (or section 401(a)(11)) merely because, as of July 1, 2004, the plan amendment has eliminated P's option to receive a distribution in any of the various annuity contract forms previously available.

(4) *Effective date.* This paragraph (e) is applicable on the date of publication of final regulations in the **Federal Register**.

*****

Robert R. Wenzel,

Deputy Commissioner for Services and Enforcement.

DALE D. GOODE

CERTIFIED COPY

---

[1] The Department of Labor has advised Treasury and the IRS that it should be noted that plans covered by Title I of ERISA will continue to be subject to the requirement under Title I that plan amendments be described in a timely summary of material modifications (SMM) or a revised summary plan description (SPD) to be distributed to plan participants and beneficiaries in accordance with applicable Department of Labor disclosure rules (see 29 CFR 2520.104b-3).

¶ 20,260Z

IRS proposed regulations: Sale of stock: ESOPs: Statement of purchase: Notarization.—The IRS has proposed amendments to temporary regulations which would affect taxpayers making an election to defer the recognition of gain under Code Sec. 1042 on the sale of stock to an employee stock ownership plan (ESOP). The proposed amendments provide guidance on the notarization requirements of the temporary regulations for statements of purchase.

The proposed regulations, which were published in the Federal Register on July 10, 2003 (68 FR 41087), are reproduced below.

DEPARTMENT OF THE TREASURY

Internal Revenue Service

26 CFR Part 1

[REG-121122-03]

RIN 1545-BC11

Notarized Statements of Purchase Under Section 1042

AGENCY: Internal Revenue Service (IRS), Treasury.

ACTION: Notice of proposed rulemaking.

SUMMARY: This document contains proposed amendments to the temporary regulations relating to notarized statements of purchase under section 1042 of the Internal Revenue Code of 1986. The proposed regulations would affect taxpayers making an election to defer the recognition of gain under section 1042 on the sale of stock to an employee stock ownership plan. The proposed regulations provide guidance on the notarization requirements of the temporary regulations.

DATES: Written and electronic comments and requests for a public hearing must be received by October 8, 2003.

ADDRESSES: Send submissions to: CC:PA:RU (REG-121122-03), room 5226, Internal Revenue Service, POB 7604, Ben Franklin Station, Washington, DC 20044. Submissions may be hand delivered Monday through Friday between the hours of 8 a.m. and 4 p.m. to: CC:PA:RU (REG-121122-03), Courier's Desk, Internal Revenue Service, 1111 Constitution Avenue, NW., Washington, DC. Alternatively, taxpayers may submit comments electronically directly to the IRS Internet site at *www.irs.gov/regs*.

FOR FURTHER INFORMATION CONTACT: Concerning the regulations, John T. Ricotta at (202) 622-6060 (not a toll-free number); concerning submissions or hearing requests, Sonya Cruse, (202) 622-7180 (not a toll-free number).

SUPPLEMENTARY INFORMATION

Background

This document contains proposed amendments to the requirement of § 1.1042-1T, A-3(b) of the Temporary Income Tax regulations that a statement of purchase for qualified replacement property be notarized within 30 days of the date of purchase of the property (30-day notarization requirement).

The temporary regulations under section 1042 were published in TD 8073 on February 4, 1986 (EE-63-84) (51 FR 4312) as part of a package of temporary regulations addressing effective dates and other issues under the Tax Reform Act of 1984. The text of the temporary regulations also served as a notice of proposed rulemaking (EE-96-85) (51 FR 4391). A public hearing was held on June 26, 1986, concerning the proposed regulations.

Explanation of Provisions

Overview

Section 1042(a) provides that a taxpayer or executor may elect in certain cases not to recognize long-term capital gain on the sale of *qualified securities* to an employee stock ownership plan (ESOP) (as defined in section 4975(e)(7)) or eligible worker owned cooperative (as defined in section 1042(c)(2)) if the taxpayer purchases *qualified replacement property* (as defined in section 1042(c)(4)) within the replacement period of section 1042(c)(3) and the requirements of section 1042(b) and § 1.1042-1T of the Temporary Income Tax Regulations are satisfied.

Section 1042(c)(1) provides that the term *qualified securities* means employer securities (as defined in section 409(l)) which are issued by a domestic C corporation that has no stock outstanding that is readily tradable on an established securities market and which were not received by the taxpayer in a distribution from a plan described in section 401(a) or in a transfer pursuant to an option or other right to acquire stock to which section 83, 422, or 423 applied.

A sale of *qualified securities* meets the requirements of section 1042(b) if: (1) the qualified securities are sold to an ESOP (as defined in section 4975(e)(7)), or an eligible worker owned cooperative; (2) the plan or cooperative owns (after application of section 318(a)(4)), immediately after the sale, at least 30 percent of (a) each class of outstanding stock of the corporation (other than stock described in section 1504(a)(4)) which issued the securities or (b) the total value of all outstanding stock of the corporation (other than stock described in section 1504(a)(4)); (3) the taxpayer files with the Secretary a verified written statement of the employer whose employees are covered by the ESOP or an authorized officer of the cooperative consenting to the application of sections 4978 and 4979A (which provide for excise taxes on certain dispositions or allocations of securities acquired in a sale to which section 1042 applies) with respect to such employer or cooperative; and (4) the taxpayer's holding period with respect to the qualified securities is at least three years (determined as of the time of the sale).

The taxpayer must purchase *qualified replacement property* within the *replacement period*, which is defined in section 1042(c)(3) as the period which begins three months before the date on which the sale of qualified securities occurs and ends 12 months after the date of such sale.

Section 1042(c)(4)(A) defines *qualified replacement property* as any security issued by a domestic operating corporation which did not, for the taxable year preceding the taxable year in which such security was purchased, have passive investment income (as defined in section 1362(d)(3)(C)) in excess of 25 percent of the gross receipts of such corporation for such preceding taxable year, and is not the corporation which issued the qualified securities which such security is replacing or a member of the same controlled group of corporations (within the meaning of section 1563(a)(1)) as such corporation.

Section 1042(c)(4)(B) defines an *operating corporation* as a corporation more than 50 percent of the assets of which, at the time the security was purchased or before the close of the replacement period, were used in the active conduct of a trade or business.

Section 1.1042-1T A-3(a) of the Temporary Income Tax Regulations states that the election is to be made in a *statement of election* attached to the taxpayer's income tax return filed on or before the due date (including extensions of time) for the taxable year in which the sale occurs.

Section 1.1042-1T A-3(b) states that the *statement of election* must provide that the taxpayer elects to treat the sale of securities as a sale of qualified securities under section 1042(a) and must contain the following information: (1) A description of the qualified securities sold, including the type and number of shares; (2) The date of the sale of the qualified securities; (3) The adjusted basis of the qualified securities; (4) The amount realized upon the sale of the qualified securities; (5) The identity of the ESOP or eligible worker-owned cooperative to which the qualified securities were sold; and (6) If the sale was part of a single interrelated transaction under a prearranged agreement between taxpayers involving other sales of qualified securities, the names and taxpayer identification numbers of the other taxpayers under the agreement and the number of shares sold by the other taxpayers.

Section 1.1042-1T, A-3(b) further provides that, if the taxpayer has purchased qualified replacement property at the time of the election, the taxpayer must attach as part of the statement of election a *statement of purchase* describing the qualified replacement property, the date of the purchase, and the cost of the property, and declaring such property to be qualified replacement property with respect to the sale of qualified securities.

The statement of purchase must be notarized no later than 30 days after the purchase. The purpose of the statement of purchase is to identify qualified replacement property with respect to a sale of qualified securities. The qualified replacement property will have its cost basis reduced under section 1042(d) to reflect the gain on the sale of qualified securities that is being deferred by the taxpayer. Upon subsequent disposition of the qualified replacement property by the taxpayer, the deferred gain will be recognized by the taxpayer under section 1042(e). Under section 1042(f), the filing of the statement of purchase of qualified replacement property (or a statement of the taxpayer's intention not to purchase replacement property) will begin the statutory period for assessment of any deficiency with respect to gain arising from the sale of the qualified securities. The purpose of the 30-day notarization requirement is to provide a contemporaneous identification of replacement property.

However, the 30-day notarization requirement leads to frequent mistakes by taxpayers and their advisors. Taxpayers are often unaware of this requirement and become aware of it only when they prepare their tax returns for the year of sale to the ESOP. By this time, the 30-day period is typically past because purchases of replacement property may have been made up to one year before. A number of private letter rulings have been issued granting relief to taxpayers in these situations as long as the statements were notarized shortly after the taxpayer became aware of the requirement and it was represented that the property listed was the only replacement property purchased for this sale.

A number of commentators on the temporary and proposed regulations criticized this requirement as without statutory authority, a trap for the unwary, and inconsistent with the definition of the qualified replacement period in section 1042(c)(3).

Proposed Amendment to the Regulations

In order to facilitate taxpayer compliance with the temporary regulations concerning identification of qualified replacement property through notarization of the statements of purchase, the proposed amendment to the temporary regulations would modify § 1.1042-1T, A-3(b) to provide that the notarization requirements for the *statement of purchase* are satisfied if the taxpayer's statement of purchase is notarized not later than the time the taxpayer files the income tax return for the taxable year in which the sale of qualified securities occurred in any case in which any qualified replacement property was purchased by such time and during the qualified replacement period. If qualified replacement property was purchased after such filing date and during the qualified replacement period, the statement of purchase must be notarized not later than the time the taxpayer's income tax return is filed for the taxable year following the year for which the election under section 1042(a) was made.

Proposed Effective Date

The proposed amendments to the temporary regulations would apply to taxable years of sellers ending on or after the date of publication of the Treasury decision adopting these amendments as final regulations in the **Federal Register**. However, taxpayers may rely upon these proposed regulations for guidance with respect to all open taxable years pending the issuance of final regulations. If, and to the extent, future guidance is more restrictive than the guidance in these proposed regulations, the future guidance will be applied without retroactive effect.

Special Analyses

It has been determined that this notice of proposed rulemaking is not a significant regulatory action as defined in Executive Order 12866. Therefore, a regulatory assessment is not required. It also has been determined that section 553(b) of the Administrative Procedure Act (5 U.S.C. chapter 5) does not apply to these regulations, and because these regulations do not impose a collection of information on small entities, the Regulatory Flexibility Act (5 U.S.C. chapter 6) does not apply. Pursuant to section 7805(f) of the Internal Revenue Code, these proposed regulations will be submitted to the Chief Counsel for Advocacy of the Small Business Administration for comment on its impact on small business.

Comments and Public Hearing

Before these proposed regulations are adopted as final regulations, consideration will be given to any written (a signed original and 8 copies) or electronic comments that are submitted timely to the IRS. The IRS and Treasury Department request comments on the clarity of the proposed rules and how they can be made easier to understand. All comments will be available for public inspection and copying. A public hearing will be scheduled if requested in writing by any person that timely submits written comments. If a public hearing is scheduled, notice of the date, time, and place for the public hearing will be published in the **Federal Register**.

Drafting Information

The principal author of these regulations is John T. Ricotta of the Office of the Division Counsel/Associate Chief Counsel (Tax Exempt and Government Entities). However, other personnel from The IRS and Treasury participated in their development.

List of Subjects in 26 CFR Part 1

Income taxes, Reporting and recordkeeping requirements.

Proposed Amendments to The Regulations

Accordingly, 26 CFR part 1 is proposed to be amended as follows:

PART 1—INCOME TAXES

Paragraph 1. The authority citation for part 1 continues to read in part as follows:

Authority: 26 U.S.C. 7805 ***

Par. 2. In § 1.1042-1T, A-3, in the undercgnated paragraph following paragraph (a)(6), the penultimate sentence is removed and three sentences added in its place to read as follows:

§ 1.1042-1T Questions and Answers relating to the sales of stock to employee stock ownership plans or certain cooperatives (temporary).

*****

Q-3. ***

A-3. ***

(a) ***

(6) ***

*** Such statement of purchase must be notarized not later than the time the taxpayer files the income tax return for the taxable year in which the sale of qualified securities occurred in any case in which any qualified replacement property was purchased by such time and during the qualified replacement period. If qualified replacement property is purchased after such filing date but during the qualified replacement period, the statement of purchase must be notarized not later than the time the taxpayer's income tax return is filed for the taxable year following the year for which the election under section 1042(a) was made. The previous two sentences apply to taxable years of sellers ending on or after the date final regulations are published in the Federal Register. ***

*****

Robert E. Wenzel,

Deputy Commissioner for Services and Enforcement

DALE D. GOODE

CERTIFIED COPY

¶ 20,261

IRS proposed regulations: 401(k) plans: Plan administration: Qualified nonelective contributions (QNECs): Non-highly compensated employees (NHCEs).—The IRS has issued proposed regulations implementing modifications that would: prohibit prefunding of elective contributions and matching contributions, eliminate mandatory disaggregation of ESOP and 401(k) portions of a plan for purposes of ADP and ACP testing, and severely restrict the use of "bottom-up" QNECs that enable employers to pass the ADP test by making targeted QNECs to a small group of short-service NHCEs.

The proposed regulations, which were published in the Federal Register on July 17, 2003 (68 FR 42476), are reproduced below. The final regulations were issued on December 29, 2004 by T.D. 9169 (69 FR 78143). The preamble to the final regulations appears at ¶ 24,507U.

DEPARTMENT OF THE TREASURY

Internal Revenue Service

26 CFR Part 1

[REG-108639-99]

RINs 1545-AX26, 1545-AX43

Retirement Plans; Cash or Deferred Arrangements Under Section 401(k) and Matching Contributions Under Section 401(m)

AGENCY: Internal Revenue Service (IRS), Treasury.

ACTION: Notice of proposed rulemaking and notice of public hearing.

SUMMARY: This document contains proposed regulations that would provide guidance for certain retirement plans containing cash or deferred arrangements under section 401(k) and providing for matching contributions or employee contributions under section 401(m). These regulations affect sponsors of plans that contain cash or deferred arrangements or provide for employee or matching contributions, and participants in these plans. This document also contains a notice of public hearing on these proposed regulations.

DATES: Written and electronic comments and requests to speak (with outlines of oral comments) at a public hearing scheduled for November 12, 2003, must be received by October 22, 2003.

ADDRESSES: Send submissions to: CC:PA:RU (REG-108639-99), room 5226, Internal Revenue Service, POB 7604, Ben Franklin Station, Washington, DC 20044. Submissions may be hand delivered Monday through Friday between the hours of 8 a.m. and 4 p.m. to: CC:PA:RU (REG-108639-99), Courier's Desk, Internal Revenue Service, 1111 Constitution Avenue, NW., Washington, DC. Alternatively, taxpayers may submit comments electronically via the Internet directly to the IRS Internet site at: www.irs.gov/regs. The public hearing will be held in the IRS Auditorium (7th Floor), Internal Revenue Building, 1111 Constitution Avenue, NW., Washington, DC.

FOR FURTHER INFORMATION CONTACT: Concerning the regulations, R. Lisa Mojiri-Azad or John T. Ricotta at (202) 622-6060 (not a toll-free number); concerning submissions and the hearing, and/or to be placed on the building access list to attend the hearing, Lanita Van Dyke, (202) 622-7180 (not a toll-free number).

SUPPLEMENTARY INFORMATION:

Paperwork Reduction Act

The collections of information contained in this notice of proposed rulemaking have been submitted to the Office of Management and Budget for review in accordance with the Paperwork Reduction Act of 1995 (44 U.S.C. 3507(d)). Comments on the collections of information should be sent to the Office of Management and Budget, Attn: Desk Officer for the Department of the Treasury, Office of Information and Regulatory Affairs, Washington, DC 20503, with copies to the Internal Revenue Service, Attn: IRS Reports Clearance Officer, W:CAR:MP:T:T:SP Washington, DC 20224. Comments on the collections of information should be received by September 15, 2003. Comments are specifically requested concerning:

Whether the proposed collections of information are necessary for the proper performance of the functions of the IRS, including whether the information will have practical utility;

The accuracy of the estimated burden associated with the proposed collection of information (see below);

How the quality, utility, and clarity of the information to be collected may be enhanced;

How the burden of complying with the proposed collection of information may be minimized, including through the application of automated collection techniques or other forms of information technology; and

Estimates of capital or start-up costs and costs of operation, maintenance, and purchase of services to provide information.

The collections of information in these proposed regulations are contained in §§ 1.401(k)-1(d)(3)(iii)(C), 1.401(k)-2(b)(3), 1.401(k)-3(d), 1.401(k)-3(f), 1.401(k)-3(g), 1.401(k)-4(d)(3), 1.401(m)-3(e), 1.401(m)-3(g) and 1.401(m)-3(h). The information required by §§ 1.401(k)-3(d), 1.401(k)-3(f), 1.401(k)-3(g), 1.401(m)-3(e), 1.401(m)-3(g) and 1.401(m)-3(h) is required by the IRS to comply with the requirements of sections 401(k)(12)(D) and 401(m)(11)(A)(ii) regarding notices that must be provided to eligible participants to apprize them of their rights and obligations under certain plans. This information will be used by participants to determine whether to participate in the plan, and by the IRS to confirm that the plan complies with applicable qualification requirements to avoid adverse tax consequences. The information required by § 1.401(k)-4(d)(3) is required by the IRS to comply with the requirements of section 401(k)(11)(B)(iii)(II) regarding notices that must be provided to eligible participants to apprize them of their rights and obligations under certain plans. This information will be used by participants to determine whether to participate in the plan, and by the IRS to confirm that the plan complies with applicable qualification requirements to avoid adverse tax consequences. The information required by § 1.401(k)-2(b)(3) will be used by employees to file their income tax returns and by the IRS to assess the correct amount of tax. The information provided under § 1.40(k)-1(d)(3)(iii)(C) will be used by

employers in determining whether to make hardship distributions to participants. The collections of information are mandatory. The respondents are businesses or other for-profit institutions, and nonprofit institutions.

Estimated total annual reporting burden: 26,500 hours.

The estimated annual burden per respondent is 1 hour, 10 minutes.

Estimated number of respondents: 22,500.

The estimated annual frequency of responses: On occasion.

An agency may not conduct or sponsor, and a person is not required to respond to, a collection of information unless it displays a valid control number assigned by the Office of Management and Budget.

Books or records relating to a collection of information must be retained as long as their contents may become material in the administration of any internal revenue law. Generally, tax returns and tax return information are confidential, as required by 26 U.S.C. 6103.

Background

This document contains proposed new comprehensive regulations setting forth the requirements (including the nondiscrimination requirements) for cash or deferred arrangements under section 401(k) and for matching contributions and employee contributions under section 401(m) of the Internal Revenue Code (Code).

Comprehensive final regulations under sections 401(k) and 401(m) of the Code were last published in the **Federal Register** in TD 8357 (published August 9, 1991) and TD 8376 (published December 2, 1991) and amended by TD 8581 published on December 22, 1994. Since 1994, many significant changes have been made to sections 401(k) and 401(m) by the Small Business Job Protection Act of 1996, Public Law 104-188 (110 Stat. 1755) (SBJPA), the Taxpayer Relief Act of 1997, Public Law 105-34 (111 Stat. 788) (TRA '97), and the Economic Growth and Tax Relief Reconciliation Act of 2001, Public Law 107-16 (115 Stat. 38) (EGTRRA).

The most substantial changes to the section 401(k) and section 401(m) provisions were made to the methodology for testing the amount of elective contributions, matching contributions, and employee contributions for nondiscrimination. Section 401(a)(4) prohibits discrimination in contribution or benefits in favor of highly compensated employees (within the meaning of section 414(q)) (HCEs). Section 401(k) provides a special nondiscrimination test for elective contributions under a cash or deferred arrangement that is part of a profit-sharing plan, stock bonus plan, pre-ERISA money purchase plan, or rural cooperative plan, called the actual deferral percentage (ADP) test. Section 401(m) provides a parallel test for matching contributions and employee contributions under a defined contribution plan, called the actual contribution percentage (ACP) test. These special nondiscrimination standards are provided in recognition of the fact that the amount of elective contributions and employee contributions (and corresponding matching contributions) is determined by the employee's utilization of the contribution opportunity offered under the plan. This is in contrast to the situation in other defined contribution plans where the amount of contributions is determined by the amount the employer decides to contribute.

Sections 401(k) and 401(m) provide alternative methods for satisfying the applicable nondiscrimination rules: a mathematical comparison and a number of design-based methods. The inherent variation in the amount of contributions among employees noted above, and the fact that the economic situation of HCEs may make them more likely to make elective or employee contributions, means that the usual nondiscrimination test under section 401(a)(4)—under which for each HCE with a contribution level there must be a specified number of nonhighly compensated employees (NHCEs) with equal or greater contributions—is not appropriate. Instead, average rates of contribution are used in the ADP and ACP tests (with a built-in differential permitted for HCEs) and minimum standards for nonelective or matching contributions are provided in the design-based alternatives.

Prior to the enactment of SBJPA, sections 401(k) and 401(m) provided only for mathematical comparison. Specifically, the ADP and ACP tests compare the average of the rates of contributions of the HCEs to the average of the rates of contributions of the NHCEs. For this purpose, the rate of contributions for an employee is the amount of contributions for an employee divided by the employee's compensation for the plan year. These tests are satisfied if the average rate of HCE contributions does not exceed 1.25 times the average rate of contributions of the NHCEs. Alternatively, these tests are satisfied if the average rate of HCE contributions does not exceed the average rate of contributions of the NHCEs by more than 2 percentage points and is no more than 2 times the average rate of contributions of the NHCEs.

1210

To the extent that these tests are not satisfied, the statute provides for correction through distribution to HCEs (or forfeiture of nonvested matching contributions) or, to the extent provided in regulations, recharacterization of elective contributions as after-tax contributions. In addition, to the extent provided in regulations, nonelective contributions can be made to NHCEs and elective contributions and certain matching contributions can be moved between the ADP and ACP tests, in order the reduce the discrepancy between the average rates of contribution for the HCEs and the NHCEs.

SBJPA added design-based alternative methods of satisfying the ADP and ACP tests. Under these methods, if a plan meets certain contribution and notice requirements, the plan is deemed to satisfy the nondiscrimination rules without regard to actual utilization of the contribution opportunity offered under the plan. These regulations reflect this change and the other changes that were made to sections 401(k) and 401(m) under SBJPA, TRA '97 and EGTRRA since the issuance of final regulations under those sections.

SBJPA made the following significant changes affecting section 401(k) and section 401(m) plans:

• The ADP test and ACP test were amended to allow the use of prior year data for NHCEs.

• The method of distributing to correct failures of the ADP test or ACP test was changed to require distribution to the HCEs with the highest contributions.

• Tax-exempt organizations and Indian tribal governments are permitted to maintain section 401(k) plans.

• A safe harbor alternative to the ADP test and ACP test was introduced in order to provide a design-based method to satisfy the nondiscrimination tests.

• The SIMPLE 401(k) plan (an alternative design-based method to satisfy the nondiscrimination tests for small employers that corresponds to the provisions of section 408(p) for SIMPLE IRA plans by providing for smaller contributions) was added.

• A special testing option was provided for plans that permit participation before employees meet the minimum age and service requirements, in order to encourage employers to permit employees to start participating sooner.

TRA '97 made the following significant changes affecting section 401(k) and section 401(m) plans:

• State and local governmental plans are treated as automatically satisfying the ADP and ACP tests.

• Matching contributions for self-employed individuals are no longer treated as elective contributions.

EGTRRA made the following significant changes affecting section 401(k) and section 401(m) plans:

• Catch-up contributions were added to provide for additional elective contributions for participants age 50 or older.

• The Secretary was directed to change the section 401(k) regulations to shorten the period of time that an employee is stopped from making elective contributions under the safe harbor rules for hardship distributions.

• Beginning in 2006, section 401(k) plans will be permitted to allow employees to designate their elective contributions as "Roth contributions" that will be subject to taxation under the rules applicable to Roth IRAs under section 408A.

• Section 401(k) plans using the design-based safe harbor and providing no additional contributions in a year are exempted from the top-heavy rules of section 416.

• Distributions from section 401(k) plans are permitted upon "severance from employment" rather than "separation from service."

• The multiple use test specified in section 401(m)(9) is repealed.

• Faster vesting is required for matching contributions

• Matching contributions are taken into account in satisfying the top-heavy requirements of section 416.

In addition, since publication of the final regulations, a number of items of guidance affecting section 401(k) and section 401(m) plans addressing these statutory changes and other items have been issued by the IRS, including:

• Notice 97-2 (1997-1 C.B. 348) provided initial guidance on prior year ADP and ACP testing and guidance on correction of excess

contributions and excess aggregate contributions, including distribution to the HCEs with the highest contributions.

• Rev. Proc. 97-9 (1997-1 C.B. 624) provided model amendments for SIMPLE 401(k) plans.

• Notice 98-1 (1998-1 C.B. 327) provided additional guidance on prior year testing issues.

• Notice 98-52 (1998-2 C.B. 632) and Notice 2000-3 (2000-1 C.B. 413) provided guidance on safe harbor section 401(k) plans.

• Rev. Rul. 2000-8 (2000-1 C.B. 617) addressed the use of automatic enrollment features in section 401(k) plans.

• Notice 2001-56 (2001-2 C.B. 277) and Notice 2002-4 (2002-2 I.R.B. 298) provided initial guidance related to the changes made by EGTRRA.

These items of guidance are incorporated into these proposed regulations with some modifications and the proposed regulations have been reorganized as indicated in the tables of contents at proposed §§1.401(k)-0 and 1.401(m)-0. Treasury and the IRS believe that a single restatement of the section 401(k) and section 401(m) rules serves the interests of plan sponsors, third-party administrators, plan participants, and plan beneficiaries.

The process of reviewing and integrating all existing administrative guidance under sections 401(k) and 401(m) has led Treasury and the IRS to reconsider certain rules and to propose certain changes in those rules. To the extent practicable, this preamble identifies the substantive changes and explains the underlying analysis. In many cases, the changes will clarify or simplify existing guidance and will reduce plan administrative burdens.

Treasury and the IRS appreciate the fact that plan sponsors and third-party administrators have developed systems and practices in the application of existing administrative guidance to the design and operation of section 401(k) and section 401(m) plans. In many cases, the details of these systems and practices have been determined through a plan sponsor's or administrator's interpretation of specific terms in existing guidance or, where no guidance has been provided, through a plan sponsor's or administrator's best legal and practical judgment. As a result, these systems and practices may differ from administrator to administrator, from sponsor to sponsor, or from plan to plan.

Treasury and the IRS also recognize that certain of the substantive changes in these proposed regulations will require changes in plan design or plan operation. However, the proposed regulations are not otherwise intended to require significant changes in plan systems and practices that were developed under existing guidance and that conform to the requirements of sections 401(k) and 401(m). Therefore, Treasury and the IRS specifically request that plan sponsors and third-party administrators comment on points where the proposed regulations might have the unintended effect of requiring a change to plan systems or practices so that Treasury and the IRS can further evaluate whether such a change is in fact appropriate or whether Treasury and the IRS should instead make an adjustment in the final regulations.

Explanation of Provisions

1. Rules Applicable to All Cash or Deferred Arrangements

Section 401(k)(1) provides that a profit-sharing, stock bonus, pre-ERISA money purchase or rural cooperative plan will not fail to qualify under section 401(a) merely because it contains a qualified cash or deferred arrangement. Section 1.401(k)-1 would set forth the general definition of a cash or deferred arrangement (CODA), the additional requirements that a CODA must satisfy in order to be a qualified CODA, and the treatment of contributions made under a qualified or nonqualified CODA.

As under the existing final regulations, a CODA is defined as an arrangement under which employees can make a cash or deferred election with respect to contributions to, or accruals or benefits under, a plan intended to satisfy the requirements of section 401(a). A cash or deferred election is any direct or indirect election by an employee (or modification of an earlier election) to have the employer either: 1) provide an amount to the employee in the form of cash or some other taxable benefit that is not currently available; or 2) contribute an amount to a trust, or provide an accrual or other benefit, under a plan deferring the receipt of compensation. A cash or deferred election can include a salary reduction agreement, but the specific reference to a salary reduction agreement has been eliminated as unnecessary. In addition, the proposed regulations would incorporate prior guidance on automatic enrollment, and thus would reflect the fact that a CODA can specify that the default that applies in the absence of an affirmative election by an employee can be a contribution to a trust, as described in Rev. Rul. 2000-8.[1]

The proposed regulations would continue to provide that the definition of a CODA excludes contributions that are treated as after-tax employee contributions at the time of the contribution and contributions made pursuant to certain one-time irrevocable elections, but would also specify that a CODA does not include an arrangement under which dividends paid to an ESOP are either distributed to a participant or reinvested in employer securities in the ESOP pursuant to an election by the participant or beneficiary under section 404(k)(2)(A)(iii) as added by EGTRRA.

The proposed regulations would also specify that a contribution is made pursuant to a cash or deferred election only if the contribution is made after the election is made. Thus, a contribution made in anticipation of an employee's election is not treated as an elective contribution. Similarly, the regulations would provide that a contribution is made pursuant to a cash or deferred election only if the contribution is made after the employee's performance of services which relate to the compensation that, but for the election, would be paid to the employee. (If the payment of compensation would have preceded the performance of services, a contribution made no earlier than the date the compensation would have been paid, but for the election, is also treated as made pursuant to a cash or deferred election). Accordingly, amounts contributed in anticipation of future performance of services generally would not be treated as elective contributions under section 401(k). These restrictions on the timing of contributions are consistent with the fundamental premise of elective contributions, that these are contributions that are paid to the plan as a result of an employee election not to receive those amounts in cash. Moreover, ensuring that contributions are made after the employee's election furthers plan administrability.

The deductibility of these prefunded elective contributions (as well as prefunded matching contributions) for the taxable year in which the contribution was made was addressed in Notice 2002-48 (2002-29 I.R.B.139). In that notice, the IRS indicated that it was reviewing issues other than the deductibility of prefunded contributions but, pending additional guidance, would not challenge the deductibility of the contributions provided actual payment is made during the taxable year for which the deduction is claimed and the amount deducted does not exceed the applicable limit under section 404(a)(3)(A)(i). After considering this issue, the IRS and Treasury have concluded that the prefunding of elective contributions and matching contributions is inconsistent with sections 401(k) and 401(m). Thus, under these proposed regulations, an employer would not be able to prefund elective contributions to accelerate the deduction for elective contributions. Once these regulations are finalized, employer contributions made under the facts in Notice 2002-48 would no longer be permitted to be taken into account under the ADP test or the ACP test and would not satisfy any plan requirement to provide elective contributions or matching contributions.

2. Qualified CODAs

A. General rules relating to qualified CODAs

Elective contributions under a qualified CODA are treated as employer contributions and generally are not included in the employee's gross income at the time the cash would have been received (but for the cash or deferred election), or at the time contributed to the plan. Elective contributions under a qualified CODA are included in the employee's gross income however, if the contributions are in excess of the section 402(g) limit for a year, are designated Roth contributions (under section 402A, effective for tax years beginning after December 31, 2005) or are recharacterized as after-tax contributions as part of a correction of an ADP test failure.

A CODA is not qualified unless it is part of a profit sharing plan, stock bonus plan, pre-ERISA money purchase plan, or rural cooperative plan and provides for an election between contributions to the plan or payments directly in cash. In addition, a CODA is not qualified unless it meets the following requirements: 1) the elective contributions under the CODA satisfy either the ADP test set forth in section 401(k)(3) or one of the design-based alternatives in section 401(k)(11) or (12); 2) elective contributions under the CODA are nonforfeitable at all times; 3) elective contributions are distributable only on the occurrence of certain events, including attainment of age 59 ½, hardship, death, disability, severance from employment, or termination of the plan; 4)

the group of employees eligible to participate in the CODA satisfies the coverage requirements of section 410(b)(1); 5) no other benefit (other than matching contributions or another specified benefit) is conditioned, directly or indirectly, upon the employee's making or not making elective contributions under the CODA; and 6) no more than 1 year of service is required for eligibility to elect to make a cash or deferred election.

Subject to certain exceptions, State and local governmental plans are not allowed to include a qualified CODA. Plans sponsored by Indian tribal governments and rural cooperatives are allowed to include a qualified CODA.

B. Nondiscrimination rules applicable to CODAs

As under the existing regulations, the proposed regulations would provide that the special nondiscrimination standards set forth in section 401(k) are the exclusive means by which a qualified CODA can satisfy the nondiscrimination in amount of contribution requirement of section 401(a)(4). These special nondiscrimination standards now include: the ADP test, the ADP safe harbor and the SIMPLE 401(k) plan. Pursuant to section 401(k)(3)(G), a State or local governmental plan is deemed to satisfy the ADP test.

In addition, as under existing regulations, the plan must satisfy the requirements of § 1.401(a)(4)-4 with respect to the nondiscriminatory availability of benefits, rights and features, including the availability of each level of elective contributions, matching contributions, and after-tax employee contributions. The provisions of the existing regulations related to compliance with sections 410(b) and 401(a)(4) would be revised to clarify the relationship of the rules under sections 410(b) and 401(a)(4) to the requirements for a qualified CODA and to remove redundant provisions. Except as provided below, however, these rules are substantively unchanged.

These proposed regulations are designed to provide simple, practical rules that accommodate legitimate plan changes. At the same time, the rules are intended to be applied by employers in a manner that does not make use of changes in plan testing procedures or other plan provisions to inflate inappropriately the ADP for NHCEs (which is used as a benchmark for testing the ADP for HCEs) or to otherwise manipulate the nondiscrimination testing requirements of section 401(k). Further, these nondiscrimination requirements are part of the overall requirement that benefits or contributions not discriminate in favor of HCEs. Therefore, a plan will not be treated as satisfying the requirements of section 401(k) if there are repeated changes to plan testing procedures or plan provisions that have the effect of distorting the ADP so as to increase significantly the permitted ADP for HCEs, or otherwise manipulate the nondiscrimination rules of section 401(k), if a principal purpose of the changes was to achieve such a result.

C. Aggregation and disaggregation of plans

The proposed regulations would consolidate the rules in the existing regulations regarding identification of CODAs and plans for purposes of demonstrating compliance with the requirements of section 401(k). As under the existing regulations, all CODAs included in a plan are treated as a single CODA for purposes of applying the nondiscrimination tests. For this purpose, a plan is generally defined by reference to § 1.410(b)-7(a) and (b) after application of the mandatory disaggregation rules of § 1.410(b)-7(c) (other than the mandatory disaggregation of section 401(k) and section 401(m) plans) and permissive aggregation rules of § 1.410(b)-7(d), as modified under these regulations. For example, if a plan covers collectively bargained employees and noncollectively bargained employees, the elective contributions for the separate groups of employees must be subject to separate nondiscrimination tests under section 401(k). The proposed regulations would also retain the special rules in the existing regulations that permit the aggregation of certain employees in different collective bargaining units and the prohibition on restructuring under § 1.401(a)(4)-9(c).

The proposed regulations would change the treatment of a CODA under a plan which includes an ESOP. Section 1.410(b)-7(c)(2) provides that the portion of a plan that is an ESOP and the portion that is not an ESOP are treated as separate plans for purposes of section 410(b) (except as provided in § 54.4975-11(e)). Accordingly, under the existing regulations, such a plan must apply two separate nondiscrimination tests: one for elective contributions going into the ESOP portion

---

[1] The Department of Labor has advised Treasury and the IRS that, under Title I of the Employee Retirement Income Security Act of 1974 (ERISA), fiduciaries of a plan must ensure that the plan is administered prudently and solely in the interest of plan participants and beneficiaries. While ERISA section 404(c) may serve to relieve certain fiduciaries from liability when participants or beneficiaries exercise control over the assets in their individual accounts, the Department of Labor has taken the position that a participant or beneficiary will not be considered to have exercised control when the participant or beneficiary is merely apprised of investments that will be made on his or her behalf in the absence of instructions to the contrary. See 29 CFR 2550.404c-1 and 57 FR 46924.

(and invested in employer stock) and one for elective contributions going in the non-ESOP portion of the plan. The additional testing results in increased expense and administrative difficulty for the plan and creates the possibility that the ESOP portion or the non-ESOP portion may fail the ADP test or ACP test because HCEs may be more or less likely to invest in employer securities than NHCEs.

Since the issuance of the existing regulations, the use of an ESOP as the employer stock fund in a section 401(k) plan has become much more widespread. In light of this development, the proposed regulations would eliminate disaggregation of the ESOP and non-ESOP portions of a single section 414(l) plan for purposes of ADP testing. The same rule would apply for ACP testing under section 401(m). In addition, the proposed regulations would provide that, for purposes of applying the ADP test or the ACP test, an employer could permissively aggregate two section 414(l) plans, one that is an ESOP and one that is not.

However, the exception to mandatory disaggregation of ESOPs from non-ESOPs set forth in these proposed regulations would not apply for purposes of satisfying section 410(b). Accordingly, the group of eligible employees under the ESOP and non-ESOP portions of the plan must still separately satisfy the requirements of sections 401(a)(4) and 410(b).

The proposed regulations would also provide that a single testing method must apply to all CODAs under a plan. This has the effect of restricting an employer's ability to aggregate section 414(l) plans for purposes of section 410(b), if those plans apply inconsistent testing methods. For example, a plan that applies the ADP test of section 401(k)(3) may not be aggregated with a plan that uses the ADP safe harbor of section 401(k)(12) for purposes of section 410(b).

D. *Restrictions on withdrawals*

As discussed above, a qualified CODA must provide that elective contributions may only be distributed after certain events, including hardship and severance from employment. EGTRRA amended section 401(k)(2)(B)(i)(I) by replacing "separation from service" with "severance from employment." This change eliminated the "same desk rule" as a standard for distributions under section 401(k) plans.

In addition, EGTRRA amended Code section 401(k)(10) by deleting disposition by a corporation of substantially all of the assets of a trade or business and disposition of a corporation's interest in a subsidiary, leaving termination of the plan as the only distributable event described in section 401(k)(10). Finally, EGTRRA directs the Secretary of the Treasury to revise the regulations relating to distributions under section 401(k)(2)(B)(i)(IV) to provide that the period during which an employee is prohibited from making elective and employee contributions following a hardship distribution is 6 months (instead of 12 months as required under § 1.401(k)-1(d)(2)(iv)(B)(4) of the existing regulations).[2]

Notice 2001-56 and Notice 2002-4 provided guidance on these EGTRRA changes to the distribution rules for elective contributions. That guidance is incorporated in these proposed regulations. In connection with the change to severance from employment, comments are requested on whether a change in status from employee to leased employee described in section 414(n) should be treated as a severance from employment that would permit a distribution to be made. In addition, the proposed regulations do not include reference to "retirement" (included in the existing regulation) as an event allowing distribution because retirement is not listed in the statute, and is subsumed by severance from employment.

In addition to the statutory changes, the rules relating to hardship distributions have been reorganized in order to clarify certain ambiguities, including the relationship between the generally applicable rules, employee representations, and the safe harbors provided under the existing regulations. The existing regulations set forth two basic requirements (i.e., the employee has an immediate and heavy financial need and the distribution is necessary to satisfy that need) followed by safe harbor provisions. The proposed regulations would retain those basic requirements, but would clarify that each safe harbor is separately applicable to each basic requirement. In addition, the proposed regulations would provide that an employee representation used for purposes of determining that a distribution is necessary to satisfy an immediate and heavy financial need must provide that the need cannot reasonably be relieved by any available distribution or nontaxable plan loan (even if the distribution or loan would not be sufficient to satisfy the financial need), but need not provide that a loan from a commercial

source will be taken if no such loan in an amount sufficient to satisfy the need is available on reasonable commercial terms.

The proposed regulations would also modify the existing regulations to add other types of defined contribution plans to the list of plans that an employer may maintain after the termination of the plan that contains the qualified CODA while still providing for distribution of elective contributions upon plan termination. The list of such plans has been expanded to include not only an ESOP and a SEP, but also a SIMPLE IRA plan, a plan or contract that satisfies section 403(b) and a section 457 plan.

Finally, under the existing regulations, a plan that receives a plan-to-plan transfer that includes elective contributions, QNECs, or QMACs, must provide that the restrictions on withdrawals continue after the transfer. These proposed regulations would also make explicit a requirement that the transferor plan will fail to comply with the restrictions on withdrawals if it transfers elective contributions, QNECs, or QMACs to a plan that does not provide for these restrictions. However, a transferor plan will not fail to comply with this requirement if it reasonably concludes that the transferee plan provides for restrictions on withdrawals. What constitutes a basis for a reasonable conclusion would be comparable to the rules related to acceptance of rollover distributions. See § 1.401(a)(31)-1, A-14.

E. *Other rules for qualified CODAs*

The proposed regulations would generally retain the additional requirements set forth in the existing regulations that a CODA must satisfy in order to be qualified, with some modifications. First, in order to be a qualified CODA the arrangement must provide an employee with an effective opportunity to elect to receive the amount in cash no less than once during the plan year. Under the proposed regulations, whether an employee has an effective opportunity is determined based on all the relevant facts and circumstances, including notice of the availability of the election, the period of time before the cash is currently available during which an election may be made, and any other conditions on elections.

The proposed regulations would also provide that a plan must provide for satisfaction of one of the specific nondiscrimination alternatives described in section 401(k). As with the existing regulations, the plan may accomplish this by incorporating by reference the ADP test of section 401(k)(3) and the regulations under proposed § 1.401(k)-2, if that is the nondiscrimination alternative being used. If, with respect to the nondiscrimination alternative being used there are optional choices, the plan must provide which of the optional choices will apply. For example, a plan that uses the ADP test of section 401(k)(3) must specify whether it is using the current year testing method or prior year testing method. Additionally, a plan that uses the prior year testing method must specify whether the ADP for eligible NHCEs for the first plan year is 3% or the ADP for the eligible NHCEs for the first plan year. Similarly, a plan that uses the safe harbor method must specify whether the safe harbor contribution will be the nonelective safe harbor contribution or the matching safe harbor contribution and is not permitted to provide that ADP testing will be used if the requirements for the safe harbor are not satisfied. The safe harbors are intended to provide employees with a minimum threshold in benefits in exchange for easier compliance for the plan sponsor. It would be inconsistent with this approach to providing benefits to allow an employer to deliver smaller benefits to NHCEs and revert to testing.

The proposed regulations would retain the existing rules relating to the section 401(k)(4)(A) prohibition on having benefits (other than a match) contingent on making or not making an elective contribution. However, the proposed regulations would specify that, in the case of a benefit that requires an amount to be withheld from an employee's pay, an employer is not violating the section 401(k)(4)(A) contingent benefit rule merely because the CODA restricts elective contributions to amounts available after such withholding from the employee's pay (after deduction of all applicable income and employment taxes). In addition, these proposed regulations also reflect the amendment to section 416(c)(2)(A) under which matching contributions can be taken into account for purposes of satisfying the top-heavy minimum contribution requirement without violating the prohibition on making benefits contingent on making or not making elective contributions.

To reflect the amendment of section 401(k)(4)(B) by SBJPA to allow tax exempt organizations to maintain section 401(k) plans, the proposed regulations would also eliminate the provision prohibiting a tax-exempt employer from adopting a section 401(k) plan.

---

[2] Under section 402(c), as amended by the IRS Restructuring and Reform Act of 1998, Public Law 105-206 (112 Stat. 685), and EGTRRA, a hardship distribution is not an eligible rollover distribution. While the change affects distributions from a section 401(k) plan, there is no specific reference to the change in these proposed regulations because these regulations are under sections 401(k) and 401(m).

As under the existing final regulations, these proposed regulations would provide that a partnership is permitted to maintain a CODA, and individual partners are permitted to make cash or deferred elections with respect to compensation attributable to services rendered to the entity, under the same rules that apply to common-law employees. This rule has been extended to sole proprietors. The provisions of these regulations also reflect the enactment of section 402(g)(8) (initially section 402(g)(9) as enacted by TRA '97) providing that matching contributions with respect to partners and sole proprietors are no longer treated as elective contributions.

3. Nonqualified CODAs

The proposed regulations would generally retain the rules in the existing regulations applicable to a nonqualified CODA (i.e., a CODA that fails one or more of the applicable requirements to be a qualified CODA). Because elective contributions under such an arrangement are not entitled to the constructive receipt relief set forth in section 402(e)(3), the contributions are currently taxable to the employee. In addition, the plan to which such contributions are made must satisfy any nondiscrimination requirements that would otherwise apply under section 401(a)(4).

4. The Actual Deferral Percentage (ADP) Test

A. General rules relating to the ADP test

Section 1.401(k)-2 sets forth the rules for a CODA that is applying the ADP test contained in section 401(k)(3). Under the ADP test, the percentage of compensation deferred for the eligible HCEs is compared annually to the percentage of compensation deferred for eligible NHCEs, and if certain limits are exceeded by the HCEs, corrective action must be taken by the plan. Correction can be made through the distribution of excess contributions, the recharacterization of excess contributions, or the contribution of additional employer contributions.

Section 401(k)(3)(A), as amended by SBJPA, generally provides for the use of prior year data in determining the ADP of NHCEs, while current year data is used for HCEs. This testing option is referred to as the prior year testing method. Alternatively, a plan may provide for the use of current year data for determining the ADPs for both NHCEs and HCEs, which is known as the current year testing method. The proposed regulations would use the term applicable year to describe the year for which the ADP is determined for the NHCEs.

Section 401(k)(3)(F), as added by SBJPA, provides that a plan benefitting otherwise excludable employees and that, pursuant to section 410(b)(4)(B), is being treated as two separate plans for purposes of section 410(b), is permitted to disregard NHCEs who have not met the minimum age and service requirements of section 410(a)(1)(A). Thus, the proposed regulations would permit such a plan to perform the ADP test by comparing the ADP for all eligible HCEs for the plan year and the ADP of eligible NHCEs for the applicable year, disregarding all NHCEs who have not met the minimum age and service requirements of section 410(a)(1)(A). The proposed regulations treat this rule as permissive. Accordingly, the new statutory provision does not eliminate the existing testing option under which a plan benefitting otherwise excludable employees is disaggregated into separate plans where the ADP test is performed separately for all eligible employees who have completed the minimum age and service requirements of section 410(a)(1)(A) and for all eligible employees who have not completed the minimum age and service requirements of section 410(a)(1)(A).

B. Elective contributions used in the ADP test

The proposed regulations would generally follow the existing regulations in defining which elective contributions are reflected in the ADP test and which ones are not. The proposed regulations would reflect the rule contained in the regulations under section 414(v), under which catch-up contributions that are in excess of a statutory limit or an employer-provided limit are not taken into account under the ADP test. See §1.414(v). In addition, the proposed regulations would incorporate the rule in §1.402(g)-1 that provides excess deferrals that are distributed are still taken into account under the ADP test (with the exception of deferrals made by NHCEs that were in violation of section 401(a)(30)). The proposed regulations retain the rule that elective contributions must be paid to the trust within 12 months after the end of the plan year. However, for plans subject to Title I of ERISA, contributions must be paid to the trust much sooner in order to satisfy the Department of Labor's regulations relating to when elective contributions become plan assets.

Section 401(k)(3) provides that the actual deferral ratio (ADR) of an HCE who is eligible to participate in 2 or more CODAs of the same employer is calculated by treating all CODAs in which the employee is eligible to participate as one CODA. The existing regulations implement this rule by aggregating the elective contributions of such an HCE for all plan years that end with or within a single calendar year. This can yield an inappropriate result if the plan years are different, because more than 12 months of elective contributions could be included in an employee's ADR. These proposed regulations would modify this rule to provide that the ADR for each HCE participating in more than one CODA is determined by aggregating the HCE's elective contributions that are within the plan year of the CODA being tested. In addition, the definition of period of participation for purposes of determining compensation would be modified to take into account periods of participation under another plan where the elective contributions must be aggregated for an HCE. As a result, even in the case of plans with different plan years, each of the employer's CODAs will use 12 months of elective contributions and 12 months of compensation in determining the ADR for an HCE who participates in multiple arrangements.

The proposed regulations would retain the rule in the existing regulations that provides that the HCE aggregation of elective contributions under CODAs does not apply where the CODAs are within plans that cannot be aggregated under §1.410(b)-7(d), but only after applying the modifications to the section 410(b) aggregation and disaggregation rules for section 401(k) plans provided in the proposed regulations. The non-application of the HCE aggregation rule would have less significance in light of the change described above relating to the elimination of the required disaggregation of ESOP and non-ESOP plans. In addition, the proposed regulations would clarify that, in determining whether two plans could be aggregated for this purpose, the prohibition on aggregating plans with CODAs that apply inconsistent testing methods set forth under these proposed regulations and the section 410(b) prohibition on aggregating plans that have different plan years would not apply.

C. Additional employer contributions used in the ADP test

The proposed regulations would generally retain the rules in the existing regulations permitting a plan to take qualified nonelective contributions or qualified matching contributions (i.e., nonelective or matching contributions that satisfy the vesting and distribution limitations of section 401(k)(2)(B) and (C)) into account under the ADP test, except as described below. Thus, an employer whose CODA has failed the ADP test can correct this failure by making additional qualified nonelective contributions (QNECs) or qualified matching contributions (QMACs) for its NHCEs. The proposed regulations would no longer describe such contributions as being treated as elective contributions under the arrangement, but would nonetheless permit such contributions to be taken into account under the ADP test.

As under the existing regulations, these proposed regulations would provide that QNECs must satisfy four requirements in addition to the vesting and distribution rules described above before they can be taken into account under the ADP test: 1) The amount of nonelective contributions, including the QNECs that are used under the ADP test or the ACP test, must satisfy section 401(a)(4); 2) the nonelective contributions, excluding the QNECs that are used under the ADP test or the ACP test, must satisfy section 401(a)(4); 3) the plan to which the QNEC or QMAC is made must be a plan that can be aggregated with the plan maintaining the CODA; and 4) the QNECs or QMACs must not be contingent on the performance of services after the allocation date and must be contributed within 12 months after the end of the plan year within which the contribution is to be allocated.[3] Thus, in the case of a plan using prior year ADP testing, any QNECs that are to be allocated to the NHCEs for the prior plan year must be contributed before the last day of the current plan year in order to be taken into account.

Some plans provide a correction mechanism for a failed ADP test that targets QNECs to certain NHCEs in order to reduce the total contributions to NHCEs under the correction. Under the method that minimizes the total QNECs allocated to NHCEs under the correction, the employer makes a QNEC to the extent permitted by the section 415 limits to the NHCE with the lowest compensation during the year in order to raise that NHCE's ADR. If the plan still fails to pass the ADP test, the employer continues expanding the group of NHCEs who receive QNECs to the next lowest-paid NHCE until the ADP test is satisfied. By using this bottom-up leveling technique, the employer can pass the ADP test by contributing small amounts of money to NHCEs

---

[3] With respect to this timing requirement, it should be noted that in order to be taken into account for purposes of section 415(c) for a limitation year, the contributions will need to be made no later than 30 days after the end of the section 404(a)(6) period applicable to the taxable year with or within which the limitation year ends.

who have very low compensation for the plan year (for example, an employee who terminated employment in early January with $300 of compensation). This is because of the fact that the ADP test is based on an unweighted average of ADRs and a small dollar (but high percentage of compensation) contribution to a terminated or other partial-year employee has a larger impact on the ADP test than a more significant contribution to a full-year employee.

The IRS and Treasury have been concerned that, by using these types of techniques, employers may pass the ADP test by making high percentage QNECs to a small number of employees with low compensation rather than providing contributions to a broader group of NHCEs. In addition, the legislative history to EGTRRA expresses Congressional intent that the Secretary of the Treasury will use his existing authority to address situations where qualified nonelective contributions are targeted to certain participants with lower compensation in order to increase the ADP of the NHCEs. (See EGTRRA Conference Report, H.R. Conf. Rep. 107-84, 240).

Accordingly, the proposed regulations would add a new requirement that a QNEC must satisfy in order to be taken into account under the ADP test. This requirement, designed to limit the use of targeted QNECs, would generally treat a plan as providing impermissibly targeted QNECs if less than half of all NHCEs are receiving QNECs and would also treat a QNEC as impermissibly targeted if the contribution is more than double the QNECs other nonhighly compensated employees are receiving, when expressed as a percentage of compensation. However, QNECs that do not exceed 5% of compensation are never treated as targeted and would always satisfy the new requirement.

This restriction on targeting QNECs would be implemented in the proposed regulations by providing that a QNEC that exceeds 5% of compensation could be taken into account for the ADP test only to the extent the contribution, when expressed as a percentage of compensation, does not exceed two times the plan's representative contribution rate. The plan's representative contribution rate would be defined as the lowest contribution rate among a group of NHCEs that is half of all the eligible NHCEs under the arrangement (or the lowest contribution rate among all eligible NHCEs under the arrangement who are employed on the last day of the year, if greater). For purposes of determining an NHCE's contribution rate, the employee's qualified nonelective contributions and the qualified matching contributions taken into account under the ADP test for the plan year are added together and the sum is divided by the employee's compensation for the same period. The proposed regulations under section 401(m) would provide parallel restrictions on QNECs taken into account in ACP testing, and a QNEC cannot be taken into account under both the ADP and ACP test (including for purposes of determining the representative contribution rate). As discussed more fully below, the proposed regulations would also have a limitation on targeting matching contributions, which would limit the extent to which QMACs can be targeted as a means of avoiding the restrictions on targeted QNECs.

The proposed regulations would also implement a prohibition against double counting of QNECs that was set forth in Notice 98-1. Generally, QNECs used in an ADP or ACP test, used to satisfy the safe harbor under section 401(k), or under a SIMPLE 401(k) plan can not be used again to demonstrate compliance with another test under section 401(k)(3) or 401(m)(2). For example, double counting could arise when QNECs on behalf of NHCEs are used to determine the ADP under current year testing in year 1 and then, if the employer elected prior year testing, are used again in year 2 to determine the ADP of NHCEs. However, unlike Notice 98-1, these proposed regulations would not contain the additional limitations on double counting elective contributions or matching contributions that were moved between the ADP and ACP tests.

D. Correction

Section 401(k)(8)(C), as amended by the SBJPA, provides that, for purposes of correcting a plan's failure to meet the nondiscrimination requirements of section 401(k)(3), distribution of excess contributions is made on the basis of the amount of the contributions by, or on behalf of, each HCE. The proposed regulations would implement this correction procedure in the same manner as set forth in Notice 97-2. Thus, the total amount of excess contributions is determined using the rules under the existing final regulations (i.e., based on high percentages). Then that total amount is apportioned among the HCEs by assigning the excess to be distributed first to those HCEs who have the greatest dollar amount of contributions taken into account under the ADP test (as opposed to the highest deferral percentage). If these amounts are distributed or recharacterized in accordance with these regulations, the plan complies with the ADP test for the plan year with no obligation to recalculate the ADP test.

The proposed regulations would provide a special rule for correcting through distribution of excess contributions in the case of an HCE who participates in multiple plans with CODAs. In that case, the proposed regulations would provide that, for purposes of determining which HCE will be apportioned a share of the total excess contributions to be distributed from a plan, all contributions in CODAs in which such an HCE participates are aggregated and the HCE with the highest dollar amount of contributions will apportioned excess contributions first. However, only actual contributions under the plan undergoing correction—rather than all contributions taken into account in calculating the employee's ADR—may be distributed from a plan. If the high dollar HCE's actual contributions under the plan are insufficient to allow full correction, then the HCE with the next highest dollar amount of contributions is apportioned the remaining excess contributions. If additional correction is needed, this process is repeated until the excess contributions are completely apportioned. This correction mechanism is applied independently to each CODA in which the HCE participates. If correction is needed in more than one CODA, the ADRs of HCEs who have received corrective distributions under the other arrangements are not recalculated after correction in the first plan.

The proposed regulations would generally follow the rules in the existing regulations on the determination of net income attributable to excess contributions. The existing regulations provide for a reasonable determination of net income attributable to an excess contribution, but do not specify which contribution within the plan year is to be treated as the excess contribution to be distributed. This provision would be retained in the proposed regulations along with the existing alternative method of determining the net income, which approximates the result that would apply if the excess contribution is made on the first day of the plan year. However, to the extent the employee is or will be credited with allocable gain or loss on those excess contributions for the period after the end of the plan year (the gap period), the proposed regulations would now require that income be determined for that period. As under the existing regulations, the determination of the income for the gap period could be based on the income determined using the alternative method for the aggregate of the plan year and the gap period or using 10% of the income for the plan year (determined under the alternative method) for each month in the gap period.

The proposed regulations would permit the recharacterization of excess contributions in a manner that generally follows the existing regulations. However, the year the employee must include the recharacterized contribution in current income has been changed to match the year that the employee would have had to include the excess contribution in income, had it been distributed. Thus, if the recharacterized amount is less than $100, it is included in gross income in the year that it is recharacterized, rather than the year of the earliest elective contributions for the employee.

The proposed regulations would retain the rules in the existing regulations regarding the timing and tax treatment of distributions of excess contributions, coordination with the distribution of excess deferrals and the treatment of matches attributable to excess contributions.

E. Special rules relating to prior year testing

The proposed regulations would generally follow the rules set forth in Notice 98-1 regarding prior year testing, including the limitations on switching from current year testing to prior year testing. However, the proposed regulations would provide that a plan is permitted to be inconsistent between the choice of current year testing method and prior year testing method, as applied for ADP purposes and ACP purposes. In such a case, any movement of elective contributions or QMACs between the ADP and ACP tests (including recharacterization) would be prohibited.

The proposed regulations would generally incorporate the rules set forth in Notice 98-1 relating to plan coverage changes in the case of a plan using prior year testing. Thus, in the case of a plan that uses prior year testing and experiences a plan coverage change affecting more than 10% of the NHCEs, the ADP of the NHCEs would generally be determined as the weighted average of the ADP of the NHCEs of the plans in which the NHCEs participated in the prior year. The definition of plan coverage change includes changes in the group of eligible employees under a plan resulting from the establishment or amendment of a plan, a plan merger or spin-off or a change in the way plans are combined or separated under the section 410(b) rules. The definition under the proposed regulations would also include a reclassification of a substantial group of employees that has the same effect as amending the plan. These proposed regulations retain the rule that a plan that experiences coverage changes affecting 10% or less of the NHCEs disregards those changes in calculating the ADP for the NHCEs. Similarly, a plan that merely experiences a spin-off is not required to recalculate the ADP for the NHCEs.

5. *Safe Harbor Section 401(k) Plans*

Section 401(k)(12) provides a design-based safe harbor method under which a CODA is treated as satisfying the ADP test if the arrangement meets certain contribution and notice requirements. Section 1.401(k)-3 of these proposed regulations, which sets forth the requirements for these arrangements, generally follows the rules set forth in Notice 98-52 and Notice 2000-3. Thus, a plan satisfies the section 401(k) safe harbor if it makes specified QMACs for all eligible NHCEs. The matching contributions can be under a basic matching formula that provides for QMACs equal to 100% of the first 3% of elective contributions and 50% of the next 2% or an enhanced matching formula that is at least as generous in the aggregate, provided the rate of matching contributions under the enhanced matching formula does not increase as the employee's rate of elective contributions increases. In lieu of QMACs, the plan is permitted to provide QNECs equal to 3% of compensation for all eligible NHCEs. In addition, notice must be provided to each eligible employee, within a reasonable time before the beginning of the year, of their right to defer under the plan.

A plan using the safe harbor method must also comply with certain other requirements. Among these is the requirement in section 401(k)(12)(B)(ii) that provides that the rate of matching contribution for any elective contribution on the part of any HCE cannot exceed the rate of matching contribution that would apply to any NHCE with the same rate of elective contribution. Notice 98-52 advised that the general rules on aggregating contributions for HCEs eligible under more than one CODA would apply for this purpose. The IRS and Treasury have determined that such aggregation is not applicable under the ADP safe harbor. Accordingly, these proposed regulations would not require that elective or matching contributions on behalf of an HCE who is eligible to participate in more than one plan of the same employer be aggregated for purposes of the requirement of section 401(k)(12)(B)(ii). Thus, the rate of match for purposes of determining whether an HCE has a higher matching rate is based only on matching contributions with respect to elective contributions under the safe harbor plan. However, for an employer that uses the safe harbor method of satisfying the ACP test, the rule in Notice 98-52 is retained for applying the ACP safe harbor, with an exception for nonsimultaneous participation (as discussed in connection with the ACP safe harbor below).

These proposed regulations do not provide any rules relating to suspension of employee contributions under a plan that provides that safe harbor matching contributions are made with respect to the sum of elective contributions and employee contributions. Although Notice 2000-3 specifically permitted suspension of employee contributions in certain circumstances, the IRS and Treasury have determined that there are no limits on suspending employee contributions, provided that safe harbor matching contributions are made with respect to elective contributions. This is because the restrictions on suspension of elective contributions are sufficient to ensure an eligible NHCE can get the full matching contribution.

The proposed regulations do not include any exception to the requirements for safe harbor matching contributions with respect to catch-up contributions. Treasury and the IRS are aware that there are questions concerning the extent to which catch up contributions are required to be matched under a plan that provides for safe harbor matching contributions. Treasury and the IRS are interested in comments on the specific circumstances under which elective contributions by a NHCE to a safe harbor plan would be less than the amount required to be matched, e.g., less than 5% of safe harbor compensation, but would be treated by the plan as catch-up contributions, and on the extent to which a safe harbor plan should be required to match catch-up contributions under such circumstances.

Section 401(k)(12)(D) contains a requirement that each eligible employee be provided with a notice of the employee's rights and obligations under the plan. These proposed regulations do not address the extent to which the notice can be provided through electronic media. As noted in the preamble to other regulations, the IRS and the Treasury Department are considering the extent to which the notice described in section 401(k)(12)(D), as well as other notices under the various Internal Revenue Code requirements relating to qualified retirement plans, can be provided electronically, taking into account the effect of the Electronic Signatures in Global and National Commerce Act (E-SIGN), Public Law 106-229 (114 Stat. 464 (2000)). The IRS and the Treasury Department anticipate issuing proposed regulations regarding these issues, and invite comments on these issues. Until those proposed regulations are issued, plan administrators and employers may continue to rely on the interim guidance in Q&A-7 of Notice 2000-3 on use of electronic media to satisfy the notice requirement in section 401(k)(12)(D).

These proposed regulations would clarify that a section 401(k) safe harbor plan must generally be adopted before the beginning of the plan year and be maintained throughout a full 12-month plan year. This requirement is consistent with the notion that the statute specifies a certain contribution level for nonhighly compensated employees in order to be deemed to pass the nondiscrimination requirements. If the contribution level is not maintained for a full 12-month year, the employer contributions made on behalf of nonhighly compensated employees should not support what could be a full year's contribution by the highly compensated employees.

The proposed regulations would adopt the exception to the requirement that a section 401(k) safe harbor plan be in place before the beginning of the plan year that was provided in Notice 2000-3. Under that option, an employer could adopt a section 401(k) safe harbor plan which has contingent non-elective contributions, provided the employer notifies employees of this contingent arrangement before the start of the year, amends the plan to provide the nonelective contributions no less than 30 days before the end of the year, and provides employees with a follow-up notice if the contribution will be made. Similarly, the proposed regulations would adopt the exception for a section 401(k) safe harbor plan that uses the matching contribution alternative. Under that exception, an employer can amend the plan to eliminate matching contributions with respect to future elective deferrals, provided that the matching contributions are made with respect to pre-amendment elective deferrals, employees are provided with notice of the change and the opportunity to change their elections, and the plan satisfies the ADP or ACP test for the plan year using the current year testing method.

The proposed regulations would recognize the practical difficulty in a 12-month requirement by following the rule in Notice 98-52 that allowed a short plan year in the first plan year and would allow a short plan year in certain other circumstances. Specifically, a section 401(k) safe harbor plan could have a short plan year in the year the plan terminates, if the plan termination is in connection with a merger or acquisition involving the employer, or the employer incurs a substantial business hardship comparable to a substantial business hardship described in section 412(d). In addition, a section 401(k) safe harbor plan could have a short plan year if the plan terminates, the employer makes the safe harbor contributions for the short year, employees are provided notice of the change, and the plan passes the ADP test. Finally, a safe harbor plan could have a short plan year if it is preceded and followed by 12-month plan years as a section 401(k) safe harbor plan.

Under section 401(k)(12)(F), safe harbor contributions are permitted to be made to a plan other than the plan that contains the CODA. These proposed regulations reflect that rule and provide that the plan to which the safe harbor contributions are made need not be a plan that can be aggregated with the plan that contains the cash or deferred arrangement.

Whether a contribution is taken into account for purposes of the safe harbor is determined in accordance with the rules regarding inclusion in ADP testing under proposed § 1.401(k)-2(a). Thus, for example, a plan that provides for safe harbor matching contributions in 2006 need not provide for a matching contribution with respect to an elective contribution made during the first 2 ½ months of 2007 and attributable to service during 2006, unless that elective contribution is taken into account for 2006.

6. *SIMPLE 401(k) Plans*

Pursuant to section 401(k)(11), a SIMPLE 401(k) plan is treated as satisfying the requirements of section 401(k)(3)(A)(ii) if the contribution, vesting, notice and exclusive plan requirements of section 401(k)(11) are satisfied. Section 1.401(k)-4 of these proposed regulations reflects the provisions of section 401(k)(11) in a manner that follows the positions reflected in the model amendments set forth in Rev. Proc. 97-9.

7. *Matching Contributions and Employee Contributions.*

Section 401(m)(2) sets forth a nondiscrimination test, the ACP test, with respect to matching contributions and employee contributions that is parallel to the nondiscrimination test for elective contributions set forth in section 401(k). Section 1.401(m)-1 of the proposed regulations would set forth this test in a manner that is consistent with the nondiscrimination test set forth in proposed § 1.401(k)-1(b). Thus, satisfaction of the ACP test, the ACP safe harbor or the SIMPLE 401(k) provisions of the proposed regulations under section 401(k) are the exclusive means that matching contributions and employee contributions can use to satisfy the nondiscrimination in amount of contribution requirements of section 401(a)(4). An anti-abuse provision comparable to that provided in connection with the proposed regulations under section 401(k) limits the ability of an employer to make repeated changes in plan provisions or testing procedures that have the effect of distorting the ACP so as to increase significantly the permitted ACP for HCEs, or otherwise manipulate the nondiscrimination rules of section 401(m), if a principal purpose of the changes was to achieve such a result.

These proposed regulations also include provisions regarding plan aggregation and disaggregation that are similar to those proposed for CODAs under section 401(k). For example, matching contributions made under the portion of a plan that is an ESOP and the portion of the same plan that is not an ESOP would not be disaggregated under these proposed regulations.

The definitions of matching contribution and employee contribution under § 1.401(m)-1 of the proposed regulations would generally follow the definitions in the existing regulations. Thus, whether an employer contribution is on account of an elective deferral or employee contribution - and thus is a matching contribution—is determined based on all the relevant facts and circumstances. However, the proposed regulations would provide that a contribution would not be treated as a matching contribution on account of an elective deferral if it is contributed before the employee's performance of services with respect to which the elective deferral is made (or when the cash that is subject to the cash or deferred election would be currently available, if earlier) and an employer contribution is not a matching contribution made on account of an employee contribution if it is contributed before the employee contribution. Thus, under these regulations, an employer would not be able to prefund matching contributions to accelerate the deduction for those contributions and, as noted above with respect to the timing of elective contributions, employer contributions made under the facts in Notice 2002-48 would not be taken into account under the ACP test and would not satisfy any plan requirement to provide matching contributions.

8. *ACP Test for Matching Contributions and Employee Contributions*

Section 1.401(m)-2 of the proposed regulations would provide rules for the ACP test that generally parallel the rules applicable to the ADP test in proposed § 1.401(k)-2. Thus, for example, the ACP test may be run by comparing the ACP for eligible HCEs for the current year with the ACP for eligible NHCEs for either the current plan year or the prior plan year. Similarly, the proposed regulations reflect the special ACP testing rule in section 401(m)(5)(C) for a plan that provides for early participation, comparable to the special ADP testing rule in section 401(k)(3)(F), as set forth in proposed § 1.401(k)-2(a)(1)(iii).

The determination of the actual contribution ratio (ACR) for an eligible employee, and the contributions that are taken into account in determining that ACR, under these proposed regulations are comparable to the rules under the proposed section 401(k) regulations. Thus, for example, the ACR for an HCE who has matching contributions or employee contributions under two or more plans is determined by adding together matching contributions and employee contributions under all plans of the employer during the plan year of the plan being tested, in a manner comparable to that for determining the ADR of an HCE who participates in two or more CODAs.

The proposed regulations would retain the rule from the existing regulations under which a QMAC that is taken into account in the ADP test is excluded from the ACP test. In addition, the proposed regulations would continue to allow QNECs to be taken into account for ACP testing, but would provide essentially the same restrictions on targeting QNECs to a small number of NHCEs as is provided in proposed § 1.401(k)-2. The only difference in the rules would be that the contribution percentages used to determine the lowest contribution percentage would be based on the sum of the QNECs and those matching contributions taken into account in the ACP test, rather than the sum of the QNECs and the QMACs taken into account under the ADP test. Because QNECs that do not exceed 5% are not subject to the limits on targeted QNECs under either the ADP test or the ACP test, an employer is permitted to take into account up to 10% in QNECs for an eligible NHCE, 5% in ADP testing and 5% in ACP testing, without regard to how many NHCEs receive QNECs.

In addition, to prevent an employer from using targeted matching contributions to circumvent the limitation on targeted QNECs, the proposed regulations would provide that matching contributions are not taken into account in the ACP test to the extent the matching rate for the contribution exceeds the greater of 100% and 2 times the representative matching rate. Paralleling the rule to limit targeted QNECs, the representative plan matching rate is the lowest matching rate for any eligible employee in a group of NHCEs that consists of half of all eligible NHCEs in the plan for the plan year (or the lowest matching rate for all eligible NHCEs in the plan who are employed by the employer on the last day of the plan year, if greater). For this

purpose, the matching rate is the ratio of the matching contributions to the contributions that are being matched, and only NHCEs who make elective deferrals or employee contributions for the plan year are taken into account.

The proposed regulations would set limits on the use of elective contributions in the ACP test that are in addition to the rules in the existing regulations under which elective contributions may be taken into account for the ACP test only to the extent the plan satisfies the ADP test, determined by including such elective contributions in the ADP test. Under the new rule, the proposed regulations would provide that elective contributions under a plan that is not subject to the ADP test, such as a plan that uses the safe harbor method of section 401(k)(12) or a contract or arrangement subject to the requirements of section 403(b)(12)(A)(ii), may not be taken into account for the ACP test. In the absence of this prohibition, contributions that are not properly considered "excess" could be taken into account under the ACP test.

The provisions of these proposed regulations regarding correction of excess aggregate contributions, including allocation of excess aggregate contributions and determination of allocable income, would generally be consistent with the provisions of the proposed regulations under section 401(k). These proposed regulations continue the provisions of the current regulations regarding correction through distribution of vested matching contributions and forfeiture of unvested matching contributions. Similarly, the proposed regulations reflect the provisions of section 411(a)(3)(G) which permit the forfeiture of a matching contribution made with respect to an excess deferral, excess contribution, or excess aggregate contribution. This provision is necessary to allow forfeiture of matching contributions that would otherwise violate section 401(a)(4).

9. *Safe Harbor Section 401(m) Plans*

Section 401(m)(11) provides a design-based safe harbor method of satisfying the ACP test contained in section 401(m)(2). Under section 401(m)(11), a defined contribution plan is treated as satisfying the ACP test with respect to matching contributions if the plan satisfies the ADP safe harbor of section 401(k)(12) and matching contributions are not made with respect to employee contributions or elective contributions in excess of 6% of an employee's compensation. For a plan that satisfies the ADP safe harbor using a 3% nonelective contribution, two additional requirements that apply to a plan that satisfies the ADP safe harbor using matching contributions also apply: 1) the rate of an employer's matching contribution does not increase as the rate of employee contributions or elective deferrals increase; and 2) the matching contribution with respect to any HCE at any rate of employee contribution or elective deferral is not greater than with respect to any NHCE. In addition, the ratio of matching contributions on behalf of an HCE to that HCE's elective deferrals and employee contributions for a plan year cannot be greater than the ratio of matching contributions to elective deferrals or employee contributions that would apply with respect to any NHCE who contributes (as an elective deferral or employee contribution) the same percentage of safe harbor compensation for that plan year.

Section 1.401(m)-3 of these proposed regulations, which sets forth the requirements for these plans, would generally follow the rules set forth in Notice 98-52 and Notice 2000-3. These proposed regulations would clarify that, for purposes of determining whether an HCE has a higher rate of matching contributions than any NHCE, any NHCE who is an eligible employee under the safe harbor CODA must be taken into account, even if the NHCE is not eligible for a matching contribution. This means that a plan with a provision which limits matching contributions to employees who are employed on the last day of the plan year will not be able to satisfy the ACP safe harbor, since a NHCE who is not eligible to receive a matching contribution on account of the last day requirement will nonetheless be taken into consideration in determining whether the plan satisfies section 401(m)(11)(B)(iii). The proposed regulations also include the requirement that matching contributions made at the employer's discretion with respect to any employee cannot exceed a dollar amount equal to 4% of the employee's compensation and that a safe harbor plan must permit all eligible NHCEs to make sufficient elective contributions (or employee contributions, if applicable) to receive the maximum matching contribution provided under the plan.

The proposed regulations would provide a special rule for satisfying section 401(m)(11)(B)(iii) in the case of an HCE who participates in two or more plans that provide for matching contributions. Under this rule, a plan will not fail to satisfy the requirements of section 401(m)(11)(B)(iii) merely because an HCE participates during the plan year in more than one plan that provides for matching contributions, provided that the HCE is not simultaneously an eligible employee under two plans that provide for matching contributions maintained by an employer for a plan year; and the period used to determine compensation for purposes of determining matching contributions under each such plan is limited to periods when the HCE participated in the plan. In such a case, an HCE can transfer from a plan with a more generous matching schedule to an otherwise safe harbor section 401(m) plan (for example, as a result of switching jobs within the controlled group) without causing the safe harbor plan to violate section 401(m)(11). However, the plan which is not the safe harbor plan will still have to aggregate matching contributions for the HCE under the rule set forth in section 401(m)(2)(B).

The safe harbor in section 401(m)(11) does not apply to employee contributions. Consequently, a plan that provides for employee contributions and matching contributions must satisfy the ACP test even though the matching contributions satisfy the safe harbor requirements for section 401(m)(11). However, the proposed regulations would also adopt the position in Notice 98-52 that the ACP test is permitted to be applied by disregarding all matching contributions with respect to all eligible employees. If the ADP safe harbor using matching contributions is satisfied but the ACP safe harbor is not satisfied, the proposed regulations would adopt the position in Notice 98-52 that the ACP test is permitted to be applied disregarding matching contributions for any employee that do not exceed 4% of compensation.

Proposed Effective Date

The regulations are proposed to apply for plan years beginning no sooner than 12 months after publication of final regulations in the **Federal Register**. However, it is anticipated that the preamble for the final regulations will permit plan sponsors to implement the final regulations for the first plan year beginning after publication of final regulations in the **Federal Register**.

Special Analyses

It has been determined that this notice of proposed rulemaking is not a significant regulatory action as defined in Executive Order 12866. Therefore, a regulatory assessment is not required. It is hereby certified that the collection of information in these regulations will not have a significant economic impact on a substantial number of small entities. This certification is based upon the conclusion that few plans containing qualified CODAs will correct excess contributions through the recharacterization of these amounts as employee contributions under § 1.401(k)-2(b)(3) of these proposed regulations. The collections of information contained in §§ 1.401(k)-3(d), (f) and 1.401(m)-3(e) are required by statutory provisions. However, the IRS has considered alternatives that would lessen the impact of these statutory requirements on small entities and has requested comments on the use of electronic media to satisfy these notice requirements. Thus, the collection of information in these regulations will ACP safe harbor is not satisfied, the proposed regulations would adopt the position in Notice 98-52 that the ACP test is permitted to be applied disregarding matching contributions for any employee that do not exceed 4% of compensation.

Proposed Effective Date

The regulations are proposed to apply for plan years beginning no sooner than 12 months after publication of final regulations in the **Federal Register**. However, it is anticipated that the preamble for the final regulations will permit plan sponsors to implement the final regulations for the first plan year beginning after publication of final regulations in the **Federal Register**.

Special Analyses

It has been determined that this notice of proposed rulemaking is not a significant regulatory action as defined in Executive Order 12866. Therefore, a regulatory assessment is not required. It is hereby certified that the collection of information in these regulations will not have a significant economic impact on a substantial number of small entities. This certification is based upon the conclusion that few plans containing qualified CODAs will correct excess contributions through the recharacterization of these amounts as employee contributions under § 1.401(k)-2(b)(3) of these proposed regulations. The collections of information contained in §§ 1.401(k)-3(d), (f) and 1.401(m)-3(e) are required by statutory provisions. However, the IRS has considered alternatives that would lessen the impact of these statutory requirements on small entities and has requested comments on the use of electronic media to satisfy these notice requirements. Thus, the collection of information in these regulations will not have a significant economic impact on a substantial number of small entities. Therefore, an analysis under the Regulatory Flexibility Act (5 U.S.C. chapter 6) is not required. Pursuant to section 7805(f) of the Code, this notice of proposed rulemaking will be submitted to the Chief Counsel for Advocacy of the Small Business Administration for comment on its impact on small business.

Comments and Public Hearing

Before these proposed regulations are adopted as final regulations, consideration will be given to any electronic or written comments (preferably a signed original and eight (8) copies) that are submitted timely to the IRS. In addition to the other requests for comments set forth in this document, the IRS and Treasury also request comments on the clarity of the proposed rule and how it may be made easier to understand. All comments will be available for public inspection and copying.

A public hearing has been scheduled for November 12, 2003, at 10 a.m. in the IRS Auditorium (7th Floor), Internal Revenue Building, 1111 Constitution Avenue NW., Washington, DC. Due to building security procedures, visitors must enter at the Constitution Avenue, NW., entrance, located between 10 th and 12 th Streets, NW. In addition, all visitors must present photo identification to enter the building. Because of access restrictions, visitors will not be admitted beyond the immediate entrance area more than 30 minutes before the hearing starts. For information about having your name placed on the building access list to attend the hearing, see the "FOR FURTHER INFORMATION CONTACT" section of this preamble.

The rules of 26 CFR 601.601(a)(3) apply to the hearing.

Persons who wish to present oral comments at the hearing must submit written comments and an outline of the topics to be discussed and the time to be devoted to each topic (signed original and eight (8) copies) by October 22, 2003.

A period of 10 minutes will be allotted to each person for making comments.

An agenda showing the scheduling of the speakers will be prepared after the deadline for receiving outlines has passed. Copies of the agenda will be available free of charge at the hearing.

Drafting Information

The principal authors of these regulations are R. Lisa Mojiri-Azad and John T. Ricotta of the Office of the Division Counsel/Associate Chief Counsel (Tax Exempt and Government Entities). However, other personnel from the IRS and Treasury participated in their development.

List of Subjects in 26 CFR Part 1

Income taxes, Reporting and recordkeeping requirements.

Proposed Amendments to The Regulations

Accordingly, 26 CFR part 1 is proposed to be amended as follows:

PART 1—INCOME TAXES

Paragraph 1. The authority citation for part 1 continues to read in part as follows:

Authority: 26 U.S.C. 7805

26 U.S.C. 401(m)(9) ***

Par. 2. Sections 1.401(k)-0 and 1.401(k)-1 are revised, and §§ 1.401(k)-2 through 1.401(k)-6 are added to read as follows:

§ 1.401(k)-0 Table of contents.

This section contains first a list of section headings and then a list of the paragraphs in each section in §§ 1.401(k)-1 through 1.401(k)-6.

LIST OF SECTIONS

§ 1.401(k)-1 Certain cash or deferred arrangements.

§ 1.401(k)-2 ADP test.

§ 1.401(k)-3 Safe harbor requirements.

§ 1.401(k)-4 SIMPLE 401(k) plan requirements.

§ 1.401(k)-5 Special rules for mergers, acquisitions and similar events. *[Reserved]*.

§ 1.401(k)-6 Definitions.

LIST OF PARAGRAPHS

§ 1.401(k)-1 Certain cash or deferred arrangements.

(a) General rules.

(1) Certain plans permitted to include cash or deferred arrangements.

(7) Plan provision requirement.

(f) Effective dates.

(1) General rule.

(2) Collectively bargained plans.

§ 1.401(k)-2 ADP test.

(a) Actual deferral percentage (ADP) test.

(1) In general.

(i) ADP test formula.

(ii) HCEs as sole eligible employees.

(iii) Special rule for early participation.

(2) Determination of ADP.

(i) General rule.

(ii) Determination of applicable year under current year and prior year testing method.

(3) Determination of ADR.

(i) General rule.

(ii) ADR of HCEs eligible under more than one arrangement.

(A) General rule.

(B) Plans not permitted to be aggregated.

(iii) Examples.

(4) Elective contributions taken into account under the ADP test.

(i) General rule.

(ii) Elective contributions for partners and self-employed individuals.

(iii) Elective contributions for HCEs.

(5) Elective contributions not taken into account under the ADP test.

(i) General rule.

(ii) Elective contributions for NHCEs.

(iii) Elective contributions treated as catch-up contributions.

(iv) Elective contributions used to satisfy the ACP test.

(6) Qualified nonelective contributions and qualified matching contributions that may be taken into account under the ADP test.

(i) Timing of allocation.

(ii) Requirement that amount satisfy section 401(a)(4).

(iii) Aggregation must be permitted.

(iv) Disproportionate contributions not taken into account.

(A) General rule.

(B) Definition of representative contribution rate.

(C) Definition of applicable contribution rate.

(v) Qualified matching contributions.

(vi) Contributions only used once.

(7) Examples.

(b) Correction of excess contributions.

(1) Permissible correction methods.

(i) In general.

(A) Qualified nonelective contributions or qualified matching contributions.

(B) Excess contributions distributed.

(C) Excess contributions recharacterized.

(ii) Combination of correction methods.

(iii) Exclusive means of correction.

(2) Corrections through distribution.

(i) General rule.

(ii) Calculation of total amount to be distributed.

(A) Calculate the dollar amount of excess contributions for each HCE.

(B) Determination of the total amount of excess contributions.

(C) Satisfaction of ADP.

(iii) Apportionment of total amount of excess contributions among the HCEs.

(A) Calculate the dollar amount of excess contributions for each HCE.

(B) Limit on amount apportioned to any individual.

(C) Apportionment to additional HCEs.

(iv) Income allocable to excess contributions.

(A) General rule.

(B) Method of allocating income.

(C) Alternative method of allocating plan year income.

(D) Safe harbor method of allocating gap period income.

(E) Alternative method for allocating plan year and gap period income.

(v) Distribution.

(vi) Tax treatment of corrective distributions.

(A) General rule.

(B) Rule for de minimis distributions.

(vii) Other rules.

(A) No employee or spousal consent required.

(B) Treatment of corrective distributions as elective contributions.

(C) No reduction of required minimum distribution.

(D) Partial distributions.

(viii) Examples.

(3) Recharacterization of excess contributions.

(i) General rule.

(ii) Treatment of recharacterized excess contributions.

(iii) Additional rules.

(A) Time of recharacterization.

(B) Employee contributions must be permitted under plan.

(C) Treatment of recharacterized excess contributions.

(4) Rules applicable to all corrections.

(i) Coordination with distribution of excess deferrals.

(A) Treatment of excess deferrals that reduce excess contributions.

(B) Treatment of excess contributions that reduce excess deferrals.

(ii) Forfeiture of match on distributed excess contributions.

(iii) Permitted forfeiture of QMAC.

(iv) No requirement for recalculation.

(v) Treatment of excess contributions that are catch-up contributions.

(5) Failure to timely correct.

(i) Failure to correct within 2 ½ months after end of plan year.

(ii) Failure to correct within 12 months after end of plan year.

(c) Additional rules for prior year testing method.

(1) Rules for change in testing method.

(i) General rule.

(ii) Situations permitting a change to the prior year testing method.

(2) Calculation of ADP under the prior year testing method for the first plan year.

(i) Plans that are not successor plans.

(ii) First plan year defined.

(iii) Successor plans.

(3) Plans using different testing methods for the ADP and ACP test.

(4) Rules for plan coverage changes.

(i) In general.

(ii) Optional rule for minor plan coverage changes.

(iii) Definitions.

(A) Plan coverage change.

(B) Prior year subgroup.

(C) Weighted average of the ADPs for the prior year subgroups.

(iv) Examples.

§ 1.401(k)-3 Safe harbor requirements.

(a) ADP test safe harbor.

(b) Safe harbor nonelective contribution requirement.

(1) General rule.

(2) Safe harbor compensation defined.

(c) Safe harbor matching contribution requirement.

(1) In general.

(2) Basic matching formula.

(3) Enhanced matching formula.

(4) Limitation on HCE matching contributions.

(5) Use of safe harbor match not precluded by certain plan provisions.

(i) Safe harbor matching contributions on employee contributions.

(ii) Periodic matching contributions.

(6) Permissible restrictions on elective contributions by NHCEs.

(i) General rule.

(ii) Restrictions on election periods.

(iii) Restrictions on amount of elective contributions.

(iv) Restrictions on types of compensation that may be deferred.

(v) Restrictions due to limitations under the Internal Revenue Code.

(7) Examples.

(d) Notice requirement.

(1) General rule.

(2) Content requirement.

(i) General rule.

(ii) Minimum content requirement.

(iii) References to SPD.

(3) Timing requirement.

(i) General rule.

(ii) Deemed satisfaction of timing requirement.

(e) Plan year requirement.

(1) General rule.

(2) Initial plan year.

(3) Change of plan year.

(4) Final plan year.

(f) Plan amendments adopting safe harbor nonelective contributions.

(1) General rule.

(2) Contingent notice provided.

(3) Follow-up notice requirement.

(g) Permissible reduction or suspension of safe harbor matching contributions.

(1) General rule.

(2) Notice of suspension requirement.

(h) Additional rules.

(1) Contributions taken into account.

(2) Use of safe harbor nonelective contributions to satisfy other nondiscrimination tests.

(3) Early participation rules.

(4) Satisfying safe harbor contribution requirement under another defined contribution plan.

(5) Contributions used only once.

§ 1.401(k)-4 SIMPLE 401(k) plan requirements.

(a) General rule.

(b) Eligible employer.

(1) General rule.

(2) Special rule.

(c) Exclusive plan.

(1) General rule.

(2) Special rule.

(d) Election and notice.

(1) General rule.

(2) Employee elections.

(i) Initial plan year of participation.

(ii) Subsequent plan years.

(iii) Election to terminate.

(3) Employee notices.

(e) Contributions.

(1) General rule.

(2) Elective contributions.

(3) Matching contributions.

(4) Nonelective contributions.

(5) SIMPLE compensation.

(f) Vesting.

(g) Plan year.

(h) Other rules.

§ 1.401(k)-5 Special rules for mergers, acquisitions and similar events. [Reserved]

§ 1.401(k)-6 Definitions.

§ 1.401(k)-1 Certain cash or deferred arrangements.

(a) *General rules*—(1) *Certain plans permitted to include cash or deferred arrangements.* A plan, other than a profit-sharing, stock bonus, pre-ERISA money purchase pension, or rural cooperative plan, does not satisfy the requirements of section 401(a) if the plan includes a cash or deferred arrangement. A profit-sharing, stock bonus, pre-ERISA money purchase pension, or rural cooperative plan does not fail to satisfy the requirements of section 401(a) merely because the plan includes a cash or deferred arrangement. A cash or deferred arrangement is part of a plan for purposes of this section if any contributions to the plan, or accruals or other benefits under the plan, are made or provided pursuant to the cash or deferred arrangement.

(2) *Rules applicable to cash or deferred arrangements generally*—(i) *Definition of cash or deferred arrangement.* Except as provided in paragraphs (a)(2)(ii) and (iii) of this section, a cash or deferred arrangement is an arrangement under which an eligible employee may make a cash or deferred election with respect to contributions to, or accruals or other benefits under, a plan that is intended to satisfy the requirements of section 401(a) (including a contract that is intended to satisfy the requirements of section 403(a)).

(ii) *Treatment of after-tax employee contributions.* A cash or deferred arrangement does not include an arrangement under which amounts contributed under a plan at an employee's election are designated or treated at the time of contribution as after-tax employee contributions (e.g., by treating the contributions as taxable income subject to applicable withholding requirements). See also section 414(h)(1). This is the case even if the employee's election to make after-tax employee contributions is made before the amounts subject to the election are currently available to the employee.

(iii) *Treatment of ESOP dividend election.* A cash or deferred arrangement does not include an arrangement under an ESOP under which dividends are either distributed or invested pursuant to an election made by participants or their beneficiaries in accordance with section 404(k)(2)(A)(iii).

(iv) *Treatment of elective contributions as plan assets.* The extent to which elective contributions constitute plan assets for purposes of the prohibited transaction provisions of section 4975 and Title I of the Employee Retirement Income Security Act of 1974 is determined in accordance with regulations and rulings issued by the Department of Labor. See 29 CFR 2510.3-102.

(3) *Rules applicable to cash or deferred elections generally*—(i) *Definition of cash or deferred election.* A cash or deferred election is any direct or indirect election (or modification of an earlier election) by an employee to have the employer either—

(A) Provide an amount to the employee in the form of cash (or some other taxable benefit) that is not currently available; or

(B) Contribute an amount to a trust, or provide an accrual or other benefit, under a plan deferring the receipt of compensation.

(ii) *Automatic enrollment.* For purposes of determining whether an election is a cash or deferred election, it is irrelevant whether the default that applies in the absence of an affirmative election is described in paragraph (a)(3)(i)(A) of this section (i.e., the employee receives an amount in cash or some other taxable benefit) or in paragraph (a)(3)(i)(B) of this section (i.e., the employer contributes an amount to a trust or provides an accrual or other benefit under a plan deferring the receipt of compensation).

(iii) *Rules related to timing—*(A) *Requirement that amounts not be currently available.* A cash or deferred election can only be made with respect to an amount that is not currently available to the employee on the date of the election. Further, a cash or deferred election can only be made with respect to amounts that would (but for the cash or deferred election) become currently available after the later of the date on which the employer adopts the cash or deferred arrangement or the date on which the arrangement first becomes effective.

(B) *Contribution may not precede election.* A contribution is made pursuant to a cash or deferred election only if the contribution is made after the election is made. In addition, a contribution is made pursuant to a cash or deferred election only if the contribution is made after the employee's performance of services with respect to which the contribution is made (or when the cash or other taxable benefit would be currently available, if earlier).

(iv) *Current availability defined.* Cash or another taxable benefit is currently available to the employee if it has been paid to the employee or if the employee is able currently to receive the cash or other taxable benefit at the employee's discretion. An amount is not currently available to an employee if there is a significant limitation or restriction on the employee's right to receive the amount currently. Similarly, an amount is not currently available as of a date if the employee may under no circumstances receive the amount before a particular time in the future. The determination of whether an amount is currently available to an employee does not depend on whether it has been constructively received by the employee for purposes of section 451.

(v) *Certain one-time elections not treated as cash or deferred elections.* A cash or deferred election does not include a one-time irrevocable election upon an employee's commencement of employment with the employer, or upon the employee's first becoming eligible under the plan or any other plan of the employer (whether or not such other plan has terminated), to have contributions equal to a specified amount or percentage of the employee's compensation (including no amount of compensation) made by the employer on the employee's behalf to the plan and a specified amount or percentage of the employee's compensation (including no amount of compensation) divided among all other plans of the employer (including plans not yet established) for the duration of the employee's employment with the employer, or in the case of a defined benefit plan to receive accruals or other benefits (including no benefits) under such plans. Thus, for example, employer contributions made pursuant to a one-time irrevocable election described in this paragraph are not treated as having been made pursuant to a cash or deferred election and are not includible in an employee's gross income by reason of § 1.402(a)-1(d). In the case of an irrevocable election made on or before December 23, 1994—

(A) The election does not fail to be treated as a one-time irrevocable election under this paragraph (a)(3)(v) merely because an employee was previously eligible under another plan of the employer (whether or not such other plan has terminated); and

(B) In the case of a plan in which partners may participate, the election does not fail to be treated as a one-time irrevocable election under this paragraph (a)(3)(v) merely because the election was made after commencement of employment or after the employee's first becoming eligible under any plan of the employer, provided that the election was made before the first day of the first plan year beginning after December 31, 1988, or, if later, March 31, 1989.

(vi) *Tax treatment of employees.* An amount generally is includible in an employee's gross income for the taxable year in which the employee actually or constructively receives the amount. But for sections 402(e)(3) and 401(k), an employee is treated as having received an amount that is contributed to a plan pursuant to the employee's cash or deferred election. This is the case even if the election to defer is made before the year in which the amount is earned, or before the amount is currently available. See § 1.402(a)-1(d).

(vii) *Examples.* The following examples illustrate the application of paragraph (a)(3) of this section:

Example 1. (i) An employer maintains a profit-sharing plan under which each eligible employee has an election to defer an annual bonus payable on January 30 each year. The bonus equals 10% of compensation during the previous calendar year. Deferred amounts are not treated as after-tax employee contributions. The bonus is currently available on January 30.

(ii) An election made prior to January 30 to defer all or part of the bonus is a cash or deferred election, and the bonus deferral arrangement is a cash or deferred arrangement.

Example 2. (i) An employer maintains a profit-sharing plan which provides for discretionary profit sharing contributions and under which each eligible employee may elect to reduce his compensation by up to 10% and to have the employer contribute such amount to the plan. The employer pays each employee every two weeks for services during the immediately preceding two weeks. The employee's election to defer compensation for a payroll period must be made prior to the date the amount would otherwise be paid. The employer contributes to the plan the amount of compensation that each employee elected to defer, at the time it would otherwise be paid to the employee, and does not treat the contribution as an after-tax employee contribution.

(ii) The election is a cash or deferred election and the contributions are elective contributions.

Example 3. (i) The facts are the same as in *Example 2*, except that the employer makes a $10,000 contribution on January 31 of the plan year that is in addition to the contributions that satisfy the employer's obligation to make contributions with respect to cash or deferred elections for prior payroll periods. Employee A makes an election on February 15 to defer $2,000 from compensation that is not currently available and the employer reduces the employee's compensation to reflect the election.

(ii) None of the additional $10,000 contributed January 31 is a contribution made pursuant to Employee A's cash or deferred election, because the contribution was made before the election was made. Accordingly, the employer must make an additional contribution of $2,000 in order to satisfy its obligation to contribute an amount to the plan pursuant to Employee A's election. The $10,000 contribution can be allocated under the plan terms providing for discretionary profit sharing contributions.

Example 4. (i) The facts are the same as in *Example 3*, except that Employee A had an outstanding election to defer $500 from each payroll period's compensation.

(ii) None of the additional $10,000 contributed January 31 is a contribution made pursuant to Employee A's cash or deferred election for future payroll periods, because the contribution was made before the earlier of Employee A's performance of services to which the contribution is attributable or when the compensation would be currently available. Accordingly, the employer must make an additional contribution of $500 per payroll period in order to satisfy its obligation to contribute an amount to the plan pursuant to Employee A's election. The $10,000 contribution can be allocated under the plan terms providing for discretionary profit sharing contributions.

Example 5. (i) Employer B establishes a money purchase pension plan in 1986. This is the first qualified plan established by Employer B. All salaried employees are eligible to participate under the plan. Hourly-paid employees are not eligible to participate under the plan. In 2000, Employer B establishes a profit-sharing plan under which all employees (both salaried and hourly) are eligible. Employer B permits all employees on the effective date of the profit-sharing plan to make a one-time irrevocable election to have Employer B contribute 5% of compensation on their behalf and make no other contribution to any other plan of Employer B (including plans not yet established) for the duration of the employee's employment with Employer B, and have their salaries reduced by 5%.

(ii) The election provided under the profit-sharing plan is not a one-time irrevocable election within the meaning of paragraph (a)(3)(v) of this section with respect to the salaried employees of Employer B who, before becoming eligible to participate under the profit-sharing plan, became eligible to participate under the money purchase pension plan. The election under the profit-sharing plan is a one-time irrevocable election within the meaning of paragraph (a)(3)(v) of this section with respect to the hourly employees, because they were not previously eligible to participate under another plan of the employer.

(4) *Rules applicable to qualified cash or deferred arrangements—*(i) *Definition of qualified cash or deferred arrangement.* A qualified cash or

deferred arrangement is a cash or deferred arrangement that satisfies the requirements of paragraphs (b), (c), (d), and (e) of this section.

(ii) *Treatment of elective contributions as employer contributions.* Except as otherwise provided in § 1.401(k)-2(b)(3), elective contributions under a qualified cash or deferred arrangement are treated as employer contributions. Thus, for example, elective contributions

are treated as employer contributions for purposes of sections **401(a) and 401(k), 402, 404, 409, 411, 412, 415, 416, and 417.**

(iii) *Tax treatment of employees.* Except as provided in section 402(g), 402A (effective for years beginning after December 31, 2005), or 1.401(k)-2(b)(3), elective contributions under a qualified cash or deferred arrangement are neither includible in an employee's gross income at the time the cash would have been includible in the employee's gross income (but for the cash or deferred election), nor at the time the elective contributions are contributed to the plan. See § 1.402(a)-1(d)(2)(i).

(iv) *Application of nondiscrimination requirements to plan that includes a qualified cash or deferred arrangement*—(A) *Exclusive means of amounts testing.* Elective contributions under a qualified cash or deferred arrangement satisfy the requirements of section 401(a)(4) with respect to amounts if and only if the amount of elective contributions satisfies the nondiscrimination test of section 401(k) under paragraph (b)(1) of this section. See § 1.401(a)(4)-1(b)(2)(ii)(B).

(B) *Testing benefits, rights and features.* A plan that includes a qualified cash or deferred arrangement must satisfy the requirements of section 401(a)(4) with respect to benefits, rights and features in addition to the requirements regarding amounts described in paragraph (a)(4)(iv)(A) of this section. For example, the right to make each level of elective contributions under a cash or deferred arrangement is a benefit, right or feature subject to the requirements of section 401(a)(4). See § 1.401(a)(4)-4(e)(3)(i) and (iii)(D). Thus, for example, if all employees are eligible to make a stated level of elective contributions under a cash or deferred arrangement, but that level of contributions can only be made from compensation in excess of a stated amount, such as the Social Security taxable wage base, the arrangement will generally favor HCEs with respect to the availability of elective contributions and thus will generally not satisfy the requirements of section 401(a)(4).

(C) *Minimum coverage requirement.* A qualified cash or deferred arrangement is treated as a separate plan that must satisfy the requirements of section 410(b). See § 1.410(b)-7(c)(1) for special rules. The determination of whether a cash or deferred arrangement satisfies the requirements of section 410(b) must be made without regard to the modifications to the disaggregation rules set forth in paragraph (b)(4)(v) of this section. See also § 1.401(a)(4)-11(g)(3)(vii)(A), relating to corrective amendments that may be made to satisfy the minimum coverage requirements of section 410(b).

(5) *Rules applicable to nonqualified cash or deferred arrangements*—(i) *Definition of nonqualified cash or deferred arrangement.* A nonqualified cash or deferred arrangement is a cash or deferred arrangement that fails to satisfy one or more of the requirements in paragraph (b), (c), (d) or (e) of this section.

(ii) *Treatment of elective contributions as nonelective contributions.* Except as specifically provided otherwise, elective contributions under a nonqualified cash or deferred arrangement are treated as nonelective employer contributions. Thus, for example, the elective contributions are treated as nonelective employer contributions for purposes of sections 401(a) (including section 401(a)(4)) and 401(k), 404, 409, 411, 412, 415, 416, and 417 and are not subject to the requirements of section 401(m).

(iii) *Tax treatment of employees.* Elective contributions under a nonqualified cash or deferred arrangement are includible in an employee's gross income at the time the cash or other taxable amount that the employee would have received (but for the cash or deferred election) would have been includible in the employee's gross income. See § 1.402(a)-1(d)(1).

(iv) *Qualification of plan that includes a nonqualified cash or deferred arrangement*—(A) *In general.* A profit-sharing, stock bonus, pre-ERISA money purchase pension, or rural cooperative plan does not fail to satisfy the requirements of section 401(a) merely because the plan includes a nonqualified cash or deferred arrangement. In determining whether the plan satisfies the requirements of section 401(a)(4), the nondiscrimination tests of sections 401(k), paragraph (b)(1) of this section, section 401(m)(2) and § 1.401(m)-1(b) may not be used. See §§ 1.401(a)(4)-1(b)(2)(ii)(B) and 1.410(b)-9 (definition of section 401(k) plan).

(B) *Application of section 401(a)(4) to certain plans.* The amount of employer contributions under a nonqualified cash or deferred arrangement is treated as satisfying section 401(a)(4) if the arrangement is part of a collectively bargained plan that automatically satisfies the requirements of section 410(b). See §§ 1.401(a)(4)-1(c)(5) and 1.410(b)-2(b)(7). Additionally, the requirements of sections 401(a)(4) and 410(b) do not apply to a governmental plan (within the meaning of section 414(d)) maintained by a State or local government or political subdivision thereof (or agency or instrumentality thereof). See sections 401(a)(5) and 410(c)(1)(A).

(v) *Example.* The following example illustrates the application of this paragraph (a)(5):

Example. (i) For the 2006 plan year, Employer A maintains a collectively bargained plan that includes a cash or deferred arrangement. Employer contributions under the cash or deferred arrangement do not satisfy the nondiscrimination test of section 401(k) and paragraph (b) of this section.

(ii) The arrangement is a nonqualified cash or deferred arrangement. The employer contributions under the cash or deferred arrangement are considered to be nondiscriminatory under section 401(a)(4), and the elective contributions are generally treated as employer contributions under paragraph (a)(5)(ii) of this section. Under paragraph (a)(5)(iii) of this section and under § 1.402(a)-1(d)(1), however, the elective contributions are includible in each employee's gross income.

(6) *Rules applicable to cash or deferred arrangements of self-employed individuals*—(i) *Application of general rules.* Generally, a partnership or sole proprietorship is permitted to maintain a cash or deferred arrangement, and individual partners or owners are permitted to make cash or deferred elections with respect to compensation attributable to services rendered to the entity, under the same rules that apply to other cash or deferred arrangements. For example, any contributions made on behalf of an individual partner or owner pursuant to a cash or deferred arrangement of a partnership or sole proprietorship are elective contributions unless they are designated or treated as after-tax employee contributions. In the case of a partnership, a cash or deferred arrangement includes any arrangement that directly or indirectly permits individual partners to vary the amount of contributions made on their behalf. Consistent with § 1.402(a)-1(d), the elective contributions under such an arrangement are includible in income and are not deductible under section 404(a) unless the arrangement is a qualified cash or deferred arrangement (i.e., the requirements of section 401(k) and this section are satisfied). Also, even if the arrangement is a qualified cash or deferred arrangement, the elective contributions are includible in gross income and are not deductible under section 404(a) to the extent they exceed the applicable limit under section 402(g). See also § 1.401(a)-30.

(ii) *Treatment of matching contributions made on behalf of self-employed individuals.* Under section 402(g)(8), matching contributions made on behalf of a self-employed individual are not treated as elective contributions made pursuant to a cash or deferred election, without regard to whether such matching contributions indirectly permit individual partners to vary the amount of contributions made on their behalf.

(iii) *Timing of self-employed individual's cash or deferred election.* For purposes of paragraph (a)(3)(iv) of this section, a partner's compensation is deemed currently available on the last day of the partnership taxable year and a sole proprietor's compensation is deemed currently available on the last day of the individual's taxable year. Accordingly, a self-employed individual may not make a cash or deferred election with respect to compensation for a partnership or sole proprietorship taxable year after the last day of that year. See § 1.401(k)-2(a)(4)(ii) for the rules regarding when these contributions are treated as allocated.

(b) *Coverage and nondiscrimination requirements*—(1) *In general.* A cash or deferred arrangement satisfies this paragraph (b) for a plan year only if—

(i) The group of eligible employees under the cash or deferred arrangement (including any employee taken into account for purposes of section 410(b) pursuant to § 1.401(a)(4)-11(g)(3)(vii)(A)) satisfies the requirements of section 410(b) (including the average benefit percentage test, if applicable); and

(ii) The cash or deferred arrangement satisfies—

(A) The ADP test of section 401(k)(3) described in § 1.401(k)-2;

(B) The ADP safe harbor provisions of section 401(k)(12) described in § 1.401(k)-3; or

(C) The SIMPLE 401(k) provisions of section 401(k)(11) described in § 1.401(k)-4.

(2) *Automatic satisfaction by certain plans.* Notwithstanding paragraph (b)(1) of this section, a governmental plan (within the meaning of section 414(d)) maintained by a State or local government or political subdivision thereof (or agency or instrumentality thereof) shall be treated as meeting the requirements of this paragraph (b).

(3) *Anti-abuse provisions.* The regulations in this paragraph (b) are designed to provide simple, practical rules that accommodate legitimate plan changes. At the same time, the rules are intended to be applied by employers in a manner that does not make use of changes in plan testing procedures or other plan provisions to inflate inappropriately the ADP for NHCEs (which is used as a benchmark for testing the ADP for HCEs) or to otherwise manipulate the nondiscrimination testing requirements of this paragraph (b). Further, this paragraph (b) is part of the overall requirement that benefits or contributions not discriminate in favor of HCEs. Therefore, a plan will not be treated as satisfying the requirements of this paragraph (b) if there are repeated changes to plan testing procedures or plan provisions that have the effect of distorting the ADP so as to increase significantly the permitted ADP for HCEs, or otherwise manipulate the nondiscrimination rules of this paragraph, if a principal purpose of the changes was to achieve such a result.

(4) *Aggregation and restructuring*—(i) *In general.* This paragraph (b)(4) contains the exclusive rules for aggregating and disaggregating plans and cash or deferred arrangements for purposes of this section, and §§ 1.401(k)-2 through 1.401(k)-6.

(ii) *Aggregation of cash or deferred arrangements within a plan.* Except as otherwise specifically provided in this paragraph (b)(4), all cash or deferred arrangements included in a plan are treated as a single cash or deferred arrangement and a plan must apply a single test under paragraph (b)(1)(ii) of this section with respect to all such arrangements within the plan. Thus, for example, if two groups of employees are eligible for separate cash or deferred arrangements under the same plan, all contributions under both cash or deferred arrangements must be treated as made under a single cash or deferred arrangement subject to a single test, even if they have significantly different features, such as different limits on elective contributions.

(iii) *Aggregation of plans*—(A) *In general.* For purposes of this section and §§ 1.401(k)-2 through 1.401(k)-6, the term plan means a plan within the meaning of § 1.410(b)-7(a) and (b), after application of the mandatory disaggregation rules of § 1.410(b)-7(c), and the permissive aggregation rules of § 1.410(b)-7(d), as modified by paragraph (b)(4)(v) of this section. Thus, for example, two plans (within the meaning of § 1.410(b)-7(b)) that are treated as a single plan pursuant to the permissive aggregation rules of § 1.410(b)-7(d) are treated as a single plan for purposes of section 401(k) and section 401(m).

(B) *Plans with inconsistent ADP testing methods.* Pursuant to paragraph (b)(4)(ii) of this section, a single testing method must apply with respect to all cash or deferred arrangements under a plan. Thus, in applying the permissive aggregation rules of § 1.410(b)-7(d), an employer may not aggregate plans (within the meaning of § 1.410(b)-7(b)) that apply inconsistent testing methods. For example, a plan (within the meaning of § 1.410(b)-7(b)) that applies the current year testing method may not be aggregated with another plan that applies the prior year testing method. Similarly, an employer may not aggregate a plan (within the meaning of § 1.410(b)-7(b)) using the ADP safe harbor provisions of section 401(k)(12) and another plan that is using the ADP test of section 401(k)(3).

(iv) *Disaggregation of plans and separate testing*—(A) *In general.* If a cash or deferred arrangement is included in a plan (within the meaning of § 1.410(b)-7(b)) that is mandatorily disaggregated under the rules of section 410(b) (as modified by this paragraph (b)(4)), the cash or deferred arrangement must be disaggregated in a consistent manner. For example, in the case of an employer that is treated as operating qualified separate lines of business under section 414(r), if the eligible employees under a cash or deferred arrangement are in more than one qualified separate line of business, only those employees within each qualified separate line of business may be taken into account in determining whether each disaggregated portion of the plan complies with the requirements of section 401(k), unless the employer is applying the special rule for employer-wide plans in § 1.414(r)-1(c)(2)(ii) with respect to the plan. Similarly, if a cash or deferred arrangement under which employees are permitted to participate before they have completed the minimum age and service requirements of section 410(a)(1) applies section 410(b)(4)(B) for determining whether the plan complies with section 410(b)(1), then the arrangement must be treated as two separate arrangements, one comprising all eligible employees who have met the age and service requirements of section 410(a)(1) and one comprising all eligible employees who have not met the age and

service requirements under section 410(a)(1), unless the plan is using the rule in § 1.401(k)-2(a)(1)(iii)(A).

(B) *Restructuring prohibited.* Restructuring under § 1.401(a)(4)-9(c) may not be used to demonstrate compliance with the requirements of section 401(k). See § 1.401(a)(4)-9(c)(3)(ii).

(v) *Modifications to section 410(b) rules*—(A) *Certain disaggregation rules not applicable.* The mandatory disaggregation rules relating to section 401(k) plans and section 401(m) plans set forth in § 1.410(b)-7(c)(1) and ESOP and non-ESOP portions of a plan set forth in § 1.410(b)-7(c)(2) shall not apply for purposes of this section and §§ 1.401(k)-2 through 1.401(k)-6. Accordingly, notwithstanding § 1.410(b)-7(d)(2), an ESOP and a non-ESOP which are different plans (within the meaning of § 1.410(b)-7(b)) are permitted to be aggregated for these purposes.

(B) *Permissive aggregation of collective bargaining units.* Notwithstanding the general rule under section 410(b) and § 1.410(b)-7(c) that a plan that benefits employees who are included in a unit of employees covered by a collective bargaining agreement and employees who are not included in the collective bargaining unit is treated as comprising separate plans, an employer can treat two or more separate collective bargaining units as a single collective bargaining unit for purposes of this section and § 1.401(k)-2 through § 1.401(k)-6, provided that the combinations of units are determined on a basis that is reasonable and reasonably consistent from year to year. Thus, for example, if a plan benefits employees in three categories (e.g., employees included in collective bargaining unit A, employees included in collective bargaining unit B, and employees who are not included in any collective bargaining unit), the plan can be treated as comprising three separate plans, each of which benefits only one category of employees. However, if collective bargaining units A and B are treated as a single collective bargaining unit, the plan will be treated as comprising only two separate plans, one benefitting all employees who are included in a collective bargaining unit and another benefitting all other employees. Similarly, if a plan benefits only employees who are included in collective bargaining unit A and employees who are included in collective bargaining unit B, the plan can be treated as comprising two separate plans. However, if collective bargaining units A and B are treated as a single collective bargaining unit, the plan will be treated as a single plan. An employee is treated as included in a unit of employees covered by a collective bargaining agreement if and only if the employee is a collectively bargained employee within the meaning of § 1.410(b)-6(d)(2).

(C) *Multiemployer plans.* Notwithstanding § 1.410(b)-7(c)(4)(ii)(C), the portion of the plan that is maintained pursuant to a collective bargaining agreement (within the meaning of § 1.413-1(a)(2)) is treated as a single plan maintained by a single employer that employs all the employees benefitting under the same benefit computation formula and covered pursuant to that collective bargaining agreement. The rules of paragraph (b)(4)(v)(B) of this section (including the permissive aggregation of collective bargaining units) apply to the resulting deemed single plan in the same manner as they would to a single employer plan, except that the plan administrator is substituted for the employer where appropriate and appropriate fiduciary obligations are taken into account. The noncollectively bargained portion of the plan is treated as maintained by one or more employers, depending on whether the noncollectively bargaining unit employees who benefit under the plan are employed by one or more employers.

(vi) *Examples.* The following examples illustrate the application of this paragraph (b)(4):

Example 1. (i) Employer A maintains Plan V, a profit-sharing plan that includes a cash or deferred arrangement in which all of the employees of Employer A are eligible to participate. For purposes of applying section 410(b), Employer A is treated as operating qualified separate lines of business under section 414(r) in accordance with § 1.414(r)-1(b). However, Employer A applies the special rule for employer-wide plans in § 1.414(r)-1(c)(2)(ii) to the portion of its profit-sharing plan that consists of elective contributions under the cash or deferred arrangement (and to no other plans or portions of plans).

(ii) Under these facts, the requirements of this section and §§ 1.401(k)-2 through 1.401(k)-6 must be applied on an employer-wide rather than a qualified separate line of business basis.

Example 2. (i) Employer B maintains Plan W, a profit-sharing plan that includes a cash or deferred arrangement in which all of the employees of Employer B are eligible to participate. For purposes of applying section 410(b), the plan treats the cash or deferred arrangement as two separate plans, one for the employees who have completed the minimum age and service eligibility conditions under section 410(a)(1) and the other for employees who have not completed the conditions. The plan provides that it will satisfy the section 401(k) safe harbor requirement of § 1.401(k)-3 with respect to the employees who have met the minimum age and service conditions and that it will meet the ADP test requirements of § 1.401(k)-2 with respect to the employees who have not met the minimum age and service conditions.

(ii) Under these facts, the cash or deferred arrangement must be disaggregated on a consistent basis with the disaggregation of Plan W. Thus, the requirements of § 1.401(k)-2 must be applied by comparing the ADP for eligible HCEs who have not completed the minimum age and service conditions with the ADP for eligible NHCEs for the applicable year who have not completed the minimum age and service conditions.

Example 3. (i) Employer C maintains Plan X, a stock-bonus plan including an ESOP. The plan also includes a cash or deferred arrangement for participants in the ESOP and non-ESOP portions of the plan.

(ii) Pursuant to paragraph (b)(4)(v)(A) of this section the ESOP and non-ESOP portions of the stock-bonus plan are a single cash or deferred arrangement for purposes of this section and § § 1.401(k)-2 through 1.401(k)-6. However, as provided in paragraph (a)(4)(iv)(C) of this section, the ESOP and non-ESOP portions of the plan are still treated as separate plans for purposes of satisfying the requirements of section 410(b).

(c) *Nonforfeitability requirements*—(1) *General rule.* A cash or deferred arrangement satisfies this paragraph (c) only if the amount attributable to an employee's elective contributions are immediately nonforfeitable, within the meaning of paragraph (c)(2) of this section, are disregarded for purposes of applying section 411(a) to other contributions or benefits, and the contributions remain nonforfeitable even if the employee makes no additional elective contributions under a cash or deferred arrangement.

(2) *Definition of immediately nonforfeitable.* An amount is immediately nonforfeitable if it is immediately nonforfeitable within the meaning of section 411, and would be nonforfeitable under the plan regardless of the age and service of the employee or whether the employee is employed on a specific date. An amount that is subject to forfeitures or suspensions permitted by section 411(a)(3) does not satisfy the requirements of this paragraph (c).

(3) *Example.* The following example illustrates the application of this paragraph (c):

Example. (i) Employees B and C are covered by Employer Y's stock bonus plan, which includes a cash or deferred arrangement. All employees participating in the plan have a nonforfeitable right to a percentage of their account balance derived from all contributions (including elective contributions) as shown in the following table:

Years of service	Nonforfeitable percentage
Less than 1	0%
1	20%
2	40%
3	60%
4	80%
5 or more	100%

(ii) The cash or deferred arrangement does not satisfy paragraph (c) of this section because elective contributions are not immediately nonforfeitable. Thus, the cash or deferred arrangement is a nonqualified cash or deferred arrangement.

(d) *Distribution limitation*—(1) *General rule.* A cash or deferred arrangement satisfies this paragraph (d) only if amounts attributable to elective contributions may not be distributed before one of the following events, and any distributions so permitted also satisfy the additional requirements of paragraphs (d)(2) through (5) of this section (to the extent applicable)—

(i) The employee's death, disability, or severance from employment;

(ii) In the case of a profit-sharing, stock bonus or rural cooperative plan, the employee's attainment of age 59 ½, or the employee's hardship; or

(iii) The termination of the plan.

(2) *Rules applicable to distributions upon severance from employment.* An employee has a severance from employment when the employee ceases to be an employee of the employer maintaining the plan. An employee does not have a severance from employment if, in connection with a change of employment, the employee's new employer maintains such plan with respect to the employee. For example, a new employer maintains a plan with respect to an employee by continuing or assuming sponsorship of the plan or by accepting a transfer of plan assets and liabilities (within the meaning of section 414(l)) with respect to the employee).

(3) *Rules applicable to hardship distributions*—(i) *Distribution must be on account of hardship.* A distribution is treated as made after an employee's hardship for purposes of paragraph (d)(1)(ii) of this section if and only if it is made on account of the hardship. For purposes of this rule, a distribution is made on account of hardship only if the distribution both is made on account of an immediate and heavy financial need of the employee and is necessary to satisfy the financial need. The determination of the existence of an immediate and heavy financial need and of the amount necessary to meet the need must be made in accordance with nondiscriminatory and objective standards set forth in the plan.

(ii) *Limit on maximum distributable amount*—(A) *General rule.* A distribution on account of hardship must be limited to the maximum distributable amount. The maximum distributable amount is equal to the employee's total elective contributions as of the date of distribution, reduced by the amount of previous distributions of elective contributions. Thus, the maximum distributable amount does not include earnings, QNECs or QMACs, unless grandfathered under paragraph (d)(3)(ii)(B) of this section.

(B) *Grandfathered amounts.* If the plan provides, the maximum distributable amount may be increased for amounts credited to the employee's account as of a date specified in the plan that is no later than December 31, 1988, or if later, the end of the last plan year ending before July 1, 1989 (or in the case of a collectively bargained plan, the earlier of—

(*1*) the later of January 1, 1989, or the date on which the last of the collective bargaining agreements in effect on March 1, 1986 terminates (determined without regard to any extension thereof after February 28, 1986); or

(*2*) January 1, 1991) and consisting of—

(*i*) Income allocable to elective contributions;

(*ii*) Qualified nonelective contributions and allocable income; and

(*iii*) Qualified matching contributions and allocable income.

(iii) *Immediate and heavy financial need*—(A) *In general.* Whether an employee has an immediate and heavy financial need is to be determined based on all the relevant facts and circumstances. Generally, for example, the need to pay the funeral expenses of a family member would constitute an immediate and heavy financial need. A distribution made to an employee for the purchase of a boat or television would generally not constitute a distribution made on account of an immediate and heavy financial need. A financial need may be immediate and heavy even if it was reasonably foreseeable or voluntarily incurred by the employee.

(B) *Deemed immediate and heavy financial need.* A distribution is deemed to be on account of an immediate and heavy financial need of the employee if the distribution is for—

(*1*) Expenses for medical care described in section 213(d) previously incurred by the employee, the employee's spouse, or any dependents of the employee (as defined in section 152) or necessary for these persons to obtain medical care described in section 213(d);

(*2*) Costs directly related to the purchase of a principal residence for the employee (excluding mortgage payments);

(*3*) Payment of tuition, related educational fees, and room and board expenses, for up to the next 12 months of post-secondary education for the employee, or the employee's spouse, children, or dependents (as defined in section 152); or

(*4*) Payments necessary to prevent the eviction of the employee from the employee's principal residence or foreclosure on the mortgage on that residence.

(iv) *Distribution necessary to satisfy financial need*—(A) *Distribution may not exceed amount of need.* A distribution is treated as necessary to satisfy an immediate and heavy financial need of an employee only to the extent the amount of the distribution is not in excess of the amount required to satisfy the financial need. For this purpose, the amount required to satisfy the financial need may include any amounts necessary to pay any federal, state, or local income taxes or penalties reasonably anticipated to result from the distribution.

(B) *No alternative means available.* A distribution is not treated as necessary to satisfy an immediate and heavy financial need of an employee to the extent the need may be relieved from other resources that are reasonably available to the employee. This determination generally is to be made on the basis of all the relevant facts and circumstances. For purposes of this paragraph (d)(3)(iv), the employee's resources are deemed to include those assets of the employee's spouse and minor children that are reasonably available to the employee. Thus, for example, a vacation home owned by the employee and the employee's spouse, whether as community property, joint tenants, tenants by the entirety, or tenants in common, generally will be deemed a resource of the employee. However, property held for the employee's child under an irrevocable trust or under the Uniform Gifts to Minors Act (or comparable State law) is not treated as a resource of the employee.

(C) *Employer reliance on employee representation.* For purposes of paragraph (d)(3)(iv)(B) of this section, an immediate and heavy financial need generally may be treated as not capable of being relieved from other resources that are reasonably available to the employee, if the employer relies upon the employee's written representation, unless the employer has actual knowledge to the contrary, that the need cannot reasonably be relieved—

(*1*) Through reimbursement or compensation by insurance or otherwise;

(*2*) By liquidation of the employee's assets;

(*3*) By cessation of elective contributions or employee contributions under the plan;

(*4*) By other distributions or nontaxable (at the time of the loan) loans from plans maintained by the employer or by any other employer; or

(*5*) By borrowing from commercial sources on reasonable commercial terms in an amount sufficient to satisfy the need.

(D) *Employee need not take counterproductive actions.* For purposes of this paragraph (d)(3)(iv), a need cannot reasonably be relieved by one of the actions described in paragraph (d)(3)(iv)(C) of this section if the effect would be to increase the amount of the need. For example, the need for funds to purchase a principal residence cannot reasonably be relieved by a plan loan if the loan would disqualify the employee from obtaining other necessary financing.

(E) *Distribution deemed necessary to satisfy immediate and heavy financial need.* A distribution is deemed necessary to satisfy an immediate and heavy financial need of an employee if each of the following requirements are satisfied—

(*1*) The employee has obtained all distributions, other than hardship distributions, and all nontaxable (at the time of the loan) loans currently available under the plan and all other plans maintained by the employer; and

(*2*) The employee is prohibited, under the terms of the plan or an otherwise legally enforceable agreement, from making elective contributions and employee contributions to the plan and all other plans maintained by the employer for at least 6 months after receipt of the hardship distribution.

(F) *Definition of other plans.* For purposes of paragraph (d)(3)(iv)(C)(*4*) and (E)(*1*) of this section, the phrase "plans maintained by the employer" means all qualified and nonqualified plans of deferred compensation maintained by the employer, including a cash or deferred arrangement that is part of a cafeteria plan within the meaning of section 125. However, it does not include the mandatory employee contribution portion of a defined benefit plan or a health or welfare benefit plan (including one that is part of a cafeteria plan). In addition, for purposes of paragraph (d)(3)(iv)(E)(*2*) of this section, the phrase "plans maintained by the employer" also includes a stock option, stock purchase, or similar plan maintained by the employer. See § 1.401(k)-6 for the continued treatment of suspended employees as eligible employees.

(v) *Commissioner may expand standards.* The Commissioner may prescribe additional guidance of general applicability, published in the Internal Revenue Bulletin (see 601.601(d)(2) of this chapter), expanding the list of deemed immediate and heavy financial needs and prescribing additional methods for distributions to be deemed necessary to satisfy an immediate and heavy financial need.

(4) *Rules applicable to distributions upon plan termination*—(i) *No alternative defined contribution plan.* A distribution may not be made under paragraph (d)(1)(iii) of this section if the employer establishes or maintains an alternative defined contribution plan. For purposes of the preceding sentence, the definition of the term "employer" contained in § 1.401(k)-6 is applied as of the date of plan termination, and a plan is an alternative defined contribution plan only if it is a defined contribution plan that exists at any time during the period beginning on the date of plan termination and ending 12 months after distribution of all assets from the terminated plan. However, if at all times during the

24-month period beginning 12 months before the termination, fewer than 2% of the employees who were eligible under the defined contribution plan that includes the cash or deferred arrangement as of the date of plan termination are eligible under the other defined contribution plan, the other plan is not an alternative defined contribution plan. In addition, a defined contribution plan is not treated as an alternative defined contribution plan if it is an employee stock ownership plan as defined in section 4975(e)(7) or 409(a), a simplified employee pension as defined in section 408(k), a SIMPLE IRA plan as defined in section 408(p), a plan or contract that satisfies the requirements of section 403(b), or a plan that satisfies the requirements of section 457.

(ii) *Lump sum requirement for certain distributions.* A distribution may be made under paragraph (d)(1)(iii) of this section only if it is a lump sum distribution. The term lump sum distribution has the meaning provided in section 402(e)(4)(D) (without regard to section 402(e)(4)(D)(i)(I), (II), (III) and (IV)). In addition, a lump sum distribution includes a distribution of an annuity contract from a trust that is part of a plan described in section 401(a) and which is exempt from tax under section 501(a) or an annuity plan described in 403(a).

(5) *Rules applicable to all distributions*—(i) *Exclusive distribution rules.* Amounts attributable to elective contributions may not be distributed on account of any event not described in this paragraph (d), such as completion of a stated period of plan participation or the lapse of a fixed number of years. For example, if excess deferrals (and income) for an employee's taxable year are not distributed within the time prescribed in § 1.402(g)-1(e)(2) or (3), the amounts may be distributed only on account of an event described in this paragraph (d). Pursuant to section 401(k)(8), the prohibition on distributions set forth in this section does not apply to a distribution of excess contributions under § 1.401(k)-2(b). In addition, the prohibition on distributions set forth in this paragraph (d) does not apply to a distribution of excess annual additions pursuant to § 1.415-6(b)(6)(iv).

(ii) *Deemed distributions.* The cost of life insurance (determined under section 72) is not treated as a distribution for purposes of section 401(k)(2) and this paragraph (d). The making of a loan is not treated as a distribution, even if the loan is secured by the employee's accrued benefit attributable to elective contributions or is includible in the employee's income under section 72(p). However, the reduction, by reason of default on a loan, of an employee's accrued benefit derived from elective contributions is treated as a distribution.

(iii) *ESOP dividend distributions.* A plan does not fail to satisfy the requirements of this paragraph (d) merely by reason of a dividend distribution described in section 404(k)(2).

(iv) *Limitations apply after transfer.* The limitations of this paragraph (d) generally continue to apply to amounts attributable to elective contributions (including QNECs and qualified matching contributions taken into account for the ADP test under § 1.401(k)-2(a)(6)) that are transferred to another qualified plan of the same or another employer. Thus, the transferee plan will generally fail to satisfy the requirements of section 401(a) and this section if transferred amounts may be distributed before the times specified in this paragraph (d). In addition, a cash or deferred arrangement fails to satisfy the limitations of this paragraph (d) if it transfers amounts to a plan that does not provide that the transferred amounts may not be distributed before the times specified in this paragraph (d). The transferor plan does not fail to comply with the preceding sentence if it reasonably concludes that the transferee plan provides that the transferred amounts may not be distributed before the times specified in this paragraph (d). What constitutes a basis for a reasonable conclusion is comparable to the rules related to acceptance of rollover distributions. See § 1.401(a)(31)-1, A-14. The limitations of this paragraph (d) cease to apply after the transfer, however, if the amounts could have been distributed at the time of the transfer (other than on account of hardship), and the transfer is an elective transfer described in § 1.411(d)-4, Q&A-3(b)(1). The limitations of this paragraph (d) also do not apply to amounts that have been paid in a direct rollover to the plan after being distributed by another plan.

(6) *Examples.* The following examples illustrate the application of this paragraph (d):

Example 1. Employer M maintains Plan V, a profit-sharing plan that includes a cash or deferred arrangement. Elective contributions under the arrangement may be withdrawn for any reason after two years following the end of the plan year in which the contributions were made. Because the plan permits distributions of elective contributions before the occurrence of one of the events specified in section 401(k)(2)(B) and this paragraph (d), the cash or deferred arrangement is a nonqualified cash or deferred arrangement and the elective contributions are currently includible in income under section 402.

Example 2. (i) Employer N maintains Plan W, a profit-sharing plan that includes a cash or deferred arrangement. Plan W provides for distributions upon a participant's severance from employment, death or disability. All employees of Employer N and its wholly owned subsidiary, Employer O, are eligible to participate in Plan W. Employer N agrees to sell all issued and outstanding shares of Employer O to an unrelated entity, Employer T, effective on December 31, 2006. Following the transaction, Employer O will be a wholly owned subsidiary of Employer T. Additionally, individuals who are employed by Employer O on the effective date of the sale continue to be employed by Employer O following the sale. Following the transaction, all employees of Employer O will cease to participate in Plan W and will become eligible to participate in the cash or deferred arrangement maintained by Employer T, Plan X. No assets will be transferred from Plan W to Plan X, except in the case of a direct rollover within the meaning of section 401(a)(31).

(ii) Employer O ceases to be a member of Employer N's controlled group as a result of the sale. Therefore, employees of Employer O who participated in Plan W will have a severance from employment and are eligible to receive a distribution from Plan W.

Example 3. (i) Employer Q maintains Plan Y, a profit-sharing plan that includes a cash or deferred arrangement. Plan Y, the only plan maintained by Employer Q, does not provide for loans. However, Plan Y provides that elective contributions under the arrangement may be distributed to an eligible employee on account of hardship using the deemed immediate and heavy financial need provisions of paragraph (d)(3)(iii)(B) of this section and provisions regarding distributions necessary to satisfy financial need of paragraphs (d)(3)(iv)(A) through (D) of this section. Employee A is an eligible employee in Plan Y with an account balance of $50,000 attributable to elective contributions made by Employee A. The total amount of elective contributions made by Employee A, who has not previously received a distribution from Plan Y, is $20,000. Employee A requests a $15,000 hardship distribution of his elective contributions to pay 6 months of college tuition and room and board expenses for his dependent child. At the time of the distribution request, the sole asset of Employee A (that is reasonably available to Employee A within the meaning of paragraph (d)(3)(iv)(B) of this section) is a savings account with an available balance of $10,000.

(ii) A distribution is made on account of hardship only if the distribution both is made on account of an immediate and heavy financial need of the employee and is necessary to satisfy the financial need. Under paragraph (d)(3)(iii)(B) of this section, a distribution for payment of up to the next 12 months of post-secondary education and room and board expenses for Employee A's dependant child is deemed to be on account of an immediate and heavy financial need of Employee A.

(iii) A distribution is treated as necessary to satisfy Employee A's immediate and heavy financial need to the extent the need may not be relieved from other resources reasonably available to Employee A. Under paragraph (d)(3)(iv)(B) of this section, Employee A's $10,000 savings account is a resource that is reasonably available to the employee and must be taken into account in determining the amount necessary to satisfy Employee A's immediate and heavy financial need. Thus, Employee A may receive a distribution of only $5,000 of his elective contributions on account of this hardship, plus an amount necessary to pay any federal, state, or local income taxes or penalties reasonably anticipated to result from the distribution.

Example 4. (i) The facts are the same as in *Example 3.* Employee B, another employee of Employer Q has an account balance of $25,000, attributable to Employee B's elective contributions. The total amount of elective contributions made by Employee B, who has not previously received a distribution from Plan Y, is $15,000. Employee B requests a $10,000 distribution of his elective contributions to pay 6 months of college tuition and room and board expenses for his dependent child. Employee B makes a written representation (with respect to which Employer Q has no actual knowledge to the contrary) that the need cannot reasonably be relieved: 1) through reimbursement or compensation by insurance or otherwise; 2) by liquidation of the employee's assets; 3) by cessation of elective contributions or employee contributions under the plan; 4) by other distributions or nontaxable (at the time of the loan) loans from plans maintained by the employer or by any other employer; or 5) by borrowing from commercial sources on reasonable commercial terms in an amount sufficient to satisfy the need.

(ii) Under paragraph (d)(3)(iii)(B) of this section, a distribution for payment of up to the next 12 months of post-secondary education and room and board expenses for Employee B's dependant child is deemed to be on account of an Employee B's immediate and heavy financial need. In addition, because Employer Q can rely on Employee B's

written representation, the distribution is considered necessary to satisfy Employee B's immediate and heavy financial need. Therefore, Employee B may receive a $10,000 distribution of his elective contributions on account of hardship plus an amount necessary to pay any federal, state, or local income taxes or penalties reasonably anticipated to result from the distribution.

Example 5. (i) The facts are the same as in *Example 3,* except Plan Y provides for hardship distributions using the safe harbor rule of paragraph (d)(3)(iv)(E) of this section. Accordingly, Plan Y provides for a 6 month suspension of an eligible employee's elective contributions and employee contributions to the plan after the receipt of a hardship distribution by such eligible employee.

(ii) Under paragraph (d)(3)(iii)(B) of this section, a distribution for payment of up to the next 12 months of post-secondary education and room and board expenses for Employee A's dependant child is deemed to be on account of an Employee A's immediate and heavy financial need. In addition, because Employee A is not eligible for any other distribution or loan from Plan Y and Plan Y suspends Employee A's elective contributions and employee contributions following receipt of the hardship distribution, the distribution will be deemed necessary to satisfy Employee A's immediate and heavy financial need (and Employee A is not required to first liquidate his savings account). Therefore, Employee A may receive a $15,000 distribution of his elective contributions on account of hardship plus an amount necessary to pay any federal, state, or local income taxes or penalties reasonably anticipated to result from the distribution.

Example 6. Employer R maintains a pre-ERISA money purchase pension plan that includes a cash or deferred arrangement that is not a rural cooperative plan. Elective contributions under the arrangement may be distributed to an employee on account of hardship. Under paragraph (d)(1) of this section, hardship is a permissible distribution event only in a profit-sharing, stock bonus or rural cooperative plan. Since elective contributions under the arrangement may be distributed before a permissible distribution event occurs, the cash or deferred arrangement does not satisfy this paragraph (d), and is not a qualified cash or deferred arrangement. Moreover, the plan is not a qualified plan because a money purchase pension plan may not provide for payment of benefits upon hardship. See § 1.401-1(b)(1)(i).

(e) *Additional requirements for qualified cash or deferred arrangements*—(1) *Qualified plan requirement.* A cash or deferred arrangement satisfies this paragraph (e) only if the plan of which it is a part is a profit-sharing, stock bonus, pre-ERISA money purchase or rural cooperative plan that otherwise satisfies the requirements of section 401(a) (taking into account the cash or deferred arrangement). A plan that includes a cash or deferred arrangement may provide for other contributions, including employer contributions (other than elective contributions), employee contributions, or both. However, except as expressly permitted under section 401(m), 410(b)(2)(A)(ii) or 416(c)(2)(A), elective contributions and matching contributions taken into account under § 1.401(k)-2(a) may not be taken into account for purposes of determining whether any other contributions under any plan (including the plan to which the contributions are made) satisfy the requirements of section 401(a).

(2) *Election requirements*—(i) *Cash must be available.* A cash or deferred arrangement satisfies this paragraph (e) only if the arrangement provides that the amount that each eligible employee may defer as an elective contribution is available to the employee in cash. Thus, for example, if an eligible employee is provided the option to receive a taxable benefit (other than cash) or to have the employer contribute on the employee's behalf to a profit-sharing plan an amount equal to the value of the taxable benefit, the arrangement is not a qualified cash or deferred arrangement. Similarly, if an employee has the option to receive a specified amount in cash or to have the employer contribute an amount in excess of the specified cash amount to a profit-sharing plan on the employee's behalf, any contribution made by the employer on the employee's behalf in excess of the specified cash amount is not treated as made pursuant to a qualified cash or deferred arrangement. This cash availability requirement applies even if the cash or deferred arrangement is part of a cafeteria plan within the meaning of section 125.

(ii) *Frequency of elections.* A cash or deferred arrangement satisfies this paragraph (e) only if the arrangement provides an employee with an effective opportunity to make (or change) a cash or deferred election at least once during each plan year. Whether an employee has an effective opportunity is determined based on all the relevant facts and circumstances, including notice of the availability of the election, the period of time during which an election may be made, and any other conditions on elections.

(3) *Separate accounting requirement*—(i) *General rule.* A cash or deferred arrangement satisfies this paragraph (e) only if the portion of an employee's benefit subject to the requirements of paragraphs (c) and (d) of this section is determined by an acceptable separate accounting between that portion and any other benefits. Separate accounting is not acceptable unless gains, losses, withdrawals, and other credits or charges are separately allocated on a reasonable and consistent basis to the accounts subject to the requirements of paragraphs (c) and (d) of this section and to other accounts. Subject to section 401(a)(4), forfeitures are not required to be allocated to the accounts in which benefits are subject to paragraphs (c) and (d) of this section.

(ii) *Satisfaction of separate accounting requirement.* The requirements of paragraph (e)(3)(i) of this section are treated as satisfied if all amounts held under a plan that includes a cash or deferred arrangement (and, if applicable, under another plan to which QNECs and QMACs are made) are subject to the requirements of paragraphs (c) and (d) of this section.

(4) *Limitations on cash or deferred arrangements of state and local governments*—(i) *General rule.* A cash or deferred arrangement does not satisfy the requirements of this paragraph (e) if the arrangement is adopted after May 6, 1986, by a State or local government or political subdivision thereof, or any agency or instrumentality thereof (a governmental unit). For purposes of this paragraph (e)(4), an employer that has made a legally binding commitment to adopt a cash or deferred arrangement is treated as having adopted the arrangement on that date.

(ii) *Rural cooperative plans and Indian tribal governments.* This paragraph (e)(4) does not apply to a rural cooperative plan or to a plan of an employer which is an Indian tribal government (as defined in section 7701(a)(40)), a subdivision of an Indian tribal government (determined in accordance with section 7871(d)), an agency or instrumentality of an Indian tribal government or subdivision thereof, or a corporation chartered under Federal, State or tribal law which is owned in whole or in part by any of the entities in this paragraph (e)(4)(ii).

(iii) *Adoption after May 6, 1986.* A cash or deferred arrangement is treated as adopted after May 6, 1986, with respect to all employees of any employer that adopts the arrangement after such date.

(iv) *Adoption before May 7, 1986.* If a governmental unit adopted a cash or deferred arrangement before May 7, 1986, then any cash or deferred arrangement adopted by the unit at any time is treated as adopted before that date. If an employer adopted an arrangement prior to such date, all employees of the employer may participate in the arrangement.

(5) *One-year eligibility requirement.* A cash or deferred arrangement satisfies this paragraph (e) only if no employee is required to complete a period of service with the employer maintaining the plan extending beyond the period permitted under section 410(a)(1) (determined without regard to section 410(a)(1)(B)(i)) to be eligible to make a cash or deferred election under the arrangement.

(6) *Other benefits not contingent upon elective contributions*—(i) *General rule.* A cash or deferred arrangement satisfies this paragraph (e) only if no other benefit is conditioned (directly or indirectly) upon the employee's electing to make or not to make elective contributions under the arrangement. The preceding sentence does not apply to—

(A) Any matching contribution (as defined in §1.401(m)-1(a)(2)) made by reason of such an election;

(B) Any benefit, right or feature (such as a plan loan) that requires, or results in, an amount to be withheld from an employee's pay (e.g. to pay for the benefit or to repay the loan), to the extent the cash or deferred arrangement restricts elective contributions to amounts available after such withholding from the employee's pay (after deduction of all applicable income and employment taxes);

(C) Any reduction in the employer's top-heavy contributions under section 416(c)(2) because of matching contributions that resulted from the elective contributions; or

(D) Any benefit that is provided at the employee's election under a plan described in section 125(d) in lieu of an elective contribution under a qualified cash or deferred arrangement.

(ii) *Definition of other benefits.* For purposes of this paragraph (e)(6), other benefits include, but are not limited to, benefits under a defined benefit plan; nonelective contributions under a defined contribution plan; the availability, cost, or amount of health benefits; vacations or vacation pay; life insurance; dental plans; legal services plans; loans (including plan loans); financial planning services; subsidized retirement benefits; stock options; property subject to section 83; and dependent care assistance. Also, increases in salary and bonuses (other than those actually subject to the cash or deferred election) are benefits for purposes of this paragraph (e)(6). The ability to make after-tax employee contributions is a benefit, but that benefit is not contingent upon an employee's electing to make or not make elective contributions under the arrangement merely because the amount of elective contributions reduces dollar-for-dollar the amount of after-tax employee contributions that may be made. Additionally, benefits under any other plan or arrangement (whether or not qualified) are not contingent upon an employee's electing to make or not to make elective contributions under a cash or deferred arrangement merely because the elective contributions are or are not taken into account as compensation under the other plan or arrangement for purposes of determining benefits.

(iii) *Effect of certain statutory limits.* Any benefit under an excess benefit plan described in section 3(36) of the Employee Retirement Income Security Act of 1974 that is dependent on the employee's electing to make or not to make elective contributions is not treated as contingent.

(iv) *Nonqualified deferred compensation.* Participation in a nonqualified deferred compensation plan is treated as contingent for purposes of this paragraph (e)(6) only to the extent that an employee may receive additional deferred compensation under the nonqualified plan to the extent the employee makes or does not make elective contributions. Deferred compensation under a nonqualified plan of deferred compensation that is dependent on an employee's having made the maximum elective deferrals under section 402(g) or the maximum elective contributions permitted under the terms of the plan also is not treated as contingent.

(v) *Plan loans and distributions.* A loan or distribution of elective contributions is not a benefit conditioned on an employee's electing to make or not make elective contributions under the arrangement merely because the amount of the loan or distribution is based on the amount of the employee's account balance.

(vi) *Examples.* The following examples illustrate the application of this paragraph (e)(6):

Example 1. Employer T maintains a cash or deferred arrangement for all of its employees. Employer T also maintains a nonqualified deferred compensation plan for two highly paid executives, Employees R and C. Under the terms of the nonqualified deferred compensation plan, R and C are eligible to participate only if they do not make elective contributions under the cash or deferred arrangement. Participation in the nonqualified plan is a contingent benefit for purposes of this paragraph (e)(6), because R's and C's participation is conditioned on their electing not to make elective contributions under the cash or deferred arrangement.

Example 2. Employer T maintains a cash or deferred arrangement for all its employees. Employer T also maintains a nonqualified deferred compensation plan for two highly paid executives, Employees R and C. Under the terms of the arrangements, Employees R and C may defer a maximum of 10% of their compensation, and may allocate their deferral between the cash or deferred arrangement and the nonqualified deferred compensation plan in any way they choose (subject to the overall 10% maximum). Because the maximum deferral available under the nonqualified deferred compensation plan depends on the elective deferrals made under the cash or deferred arrangement, the right to participate in the nonqualified plan is a contingent benefit for purposes of paragraph (e)(6).

(7) *Plan provision requirement.* A plan that includes a cash or deferred arrangement satisfies this paragraph (e) only if it provides that the nondiscrimination requirements of section 401(k) will be met. Thus, the plan must provide for satisfaction of one of the specific alternatives described in paragraph (b)(1)(ii) of this section and, if with respect to that alternative there are optional choices, which of the optional choices will apply. For example, a plan that uses the ADP test of section 401(k)(3), as described in paragraph (b)(1)(ii)(A) of this section, must specify whether it is using the current year testing method or prior year testing method. Additionally, a plan that uses the prior year testing method must specify whether the ADP for eligible NHCEs for the first plan year is 3% or the ADP for the eligible NHCEs for the first plan year. Similarly, a plan that uses the safe harbor method of section 401(k)(12), as described in paragraph (b)(1)(ii)(B) of this section, must specify whether the safe harbor contribution will be the nonelective safe harbor contribution or the matching safe harbor contribution and is not permitted to provide that ADP testing will be used if the requirements for the safe harbor are not satisfied. For purposes of this paragraph (e)(7), a plan may incorporate by reference the provisions of section 401(k)(3) and §1.401(k)-2 if that is the nondiscrimination test being applied.

(f) *Effective dates*—(1) *General rule.* This section and §§1.401(k)-2 through 1.401(k)-6 apply to plan years that begin on or after the date that is 12 months after the issuance of these regulations in final form, except as otherwise provided in this paragraph (f).

(2) *Collectively bargained plans.* In the case of a plan maintained pursuant to one or more collective bargaining agreements between employee representatives and one or more employers in effect on the date described in paragraph (f)(1) of this section, the provisions of this section and §§1.401(k)-2 through 1.401(k)-6 apply to the later of the first plan year beginning after the termination of the last such agreement or the plan year described in paragraph (f)(1) of this section.

§1.401(k)-2 ADP test.

(a) *Actual deferral percentage (ADP) test*—(1) *In general*—(i) *ADP test formula.* A cash or deferred arrangement satisfies the ADP test for a plan year only if—

(A) The ADP for the eligible HCEs for the plan year is not more than the ADP for the eligible NHCEs for the applicable year multiplied by 1.25; or

(B) The excess of the ADP for the eligible HCEs for the plan year over the ADP for the eligible NHCEs for the applicable year is not more than 2 percentage points, and the ADP for the eligible HCEs for the plan year is not more than the ADP for the eligible NHCEs for the applicable year multiplied by 2.

(ii) *HCEs as sole eligible employees.* If, for the applicable year for determining the ADP of the NHCEs for a plan year, there are no eligible NHCEs (i.e, all of the eligible employees under the cash or deferred arrangement for the applicable year are HCEs), the arrangement is deemed to satisfy the ADP test for the plan year.

(iii) *Special rule for early participation.* If a cash or deferred arrangement provides that employees are eligible to participate before they have completed the minimum age and service requirements of section 410(a)(1)(A), and if the plan applies section 410(b)(4)(B) in determining whether the cash or deferred arrangement meets the requirements of section 410(b)(1), then in determining whether the arrangement meets the requirements under paragraph (a)(1) of this section, either—

(A) Pursuant to section 401(k)(3)(F), the ADP test is performed under the plan (determined without regard to disaggregation under §1.410(b)-7(c)(3)), using the ADP for all eligible HCEs for the plan year and the ADP of eligible NHCEs for the applicable year, disregarding all NHCEs who have not met the minimum age and service requirements of section 410(a)(1)(A); or

(B) Pursuant to §1.401(k)-1(b)(4), the plan is disaggregated into separate plans and the ADP test is performed separately for all eligible employees who have completed the minimum age and service requirements of section 410(a)(1)(A) and for all eligible employees who have not completed the minimum age and service requirements of section 410(a)(1)(A).

(2) *Determination of ADP*—(i) *General rule.* The ADP for a group of eligible employees (either eligible HCEs or eligible NHCEs) for a plan year or applicable year is the average of the ADRs of the eligible employees in that group for that year. The ADP for a group of eligible employees is calculated to the nearest hundredth of a percentage point.

(ii) *Determination of applicable year under current year and prior year testing method.* The ADP test is applied using the prior year testing method or the current year testing method. Under the prior year testing method, the applicable year for determining the ADP for the eligible NHCEs is the plan year immediately preceding the plan year for which the ADP test is being performed. Under the prior year testing method, the ADP for the eligible NHCEs is determined using the ADRs for the eligible employees who were NHCEs in that preceding plan year, regardless of whether those NHCEs are eligible employees or NHCEs in the plan year for which the ADP test is being calculated. Under the current year testing method, the applicable year for determining the ADP for the eligible NHCEs is the same plan year as the plan year for which the ADP test is being performed. Under either method, the ADP for eligible HCEs is the average of the ADRs of the eligible HCEs for the plan year for which the ADP test is being performed. See paragraph (c) of this section for additional rules for the prior year testing method.

(3) *Determination of ADR*—(i) *General rule.* The ADR of an eligible employee for a plan year or applicable year is the sum of the employee's elective contributions taken into account with respect to such employee for the year, determined under the rules of paragraphs (a)(4) and (5) of this section, and the qualified nonelective contributions and qualified matching contributions taken into account with respect to such employee under paragraph (a)(6) of this section for the year, divided by the employee's compensation taken into account for the year. The ADR is calculated to the nearest hundredth of a percentage point. If no elective contributions, qualified nonelective contributions, or qualified matching contributions are taken into account under this section with respect to an eligible employee for the year, the ADR of the employee is zero.

(ii) *ADR of HCEs eligible under more than one arrangement*—(A) *General rule.* Pursuant to section 401(k)(3)(A), the ADR of an HCE who is an eligible employee in more than one cash or deferred arrangement of the same employer is calculated by treating all contributions with respect to such HCE under any such arrangement as being made under the cash or deferred arrangement being tested. Thus, the ADR for such an HCE is calculated by accumulating all contributions under any cash or deferred arrangement (other than a cash or deferred arrangement described in paragraph (a)(3)(ii)(B) of this section) that would be taken into account under this section for the plan year, if the cash or deferred arrangement under which the contribution was made applied this section and had the same plan year. For example, in the case of a plan with a 12-month plan year, the ADR for the plan year of that plan for an HCE who participates in multiple cash or deferred arrangements of the same employer is the sum of all contributions during such 12-month period that would be taken into account with respect to the HCE under all such arrangements in which the HCE is an eligible employee, divided by the HCE's compensation for that 12-month period (determined using the compensation definition for the plan year being tested), without regard to the plan year of the other plans and whether those plans are satisfying this section or §1.401(k)-3.

(B) *Plans not permitted to be aggregated.* Cash or deferred arrangements under plans that are not permitted to be aggregated under §1.401(k)-1(b)(4) (determined without regard to the prohibition on aggregating plans with inconsistent testing methods set forth in §1.401(k)-1(b)(4)(iii)(B) and the prohibition on aggregating plans with different plan years set forth in §1.410(b)-7(d)(5)) are not aggregated under this paragraph (a)(3)(ii).

(iii) *Example*s. The following examples illustrate the application of this paragraph (a)(3):

Example 1. (i) Employee A, an HCE with compensation of $120,000, is eligible to make elective contributions under Plan S and Plan T, two profit-sharing plans maintained by Employer H with calendar year plan years, each of which includes a cash or deferred arrangement. During the current plan year, Employee A makes elective contributions of $6,000 to Plan S and $4,000 to Plan T.

(ii) Under each plan, the ADR for Employee A is determined by dividing Employee A's total elective contributions under both arrangements by Employee A's compensation taken into account under the plan for the year. Therefore, Employee A's ADR under each plan is 8.33% ($10,000/$120,000).

Example 2. (i) The facts are the same as in *Example 1*, except that Plan T defines compensation (for deferral and testing purposes) to exclude all bonuses paid to an employee. Plan S defines compensation (for deferral and testing purposes) to include bonuses paid to an employee. During the current year, Employee A's compensation included a $10,000 bonus. Therefore, Employee A's compensation under Plan T is $110,000 and Employee A's compensation under Plan S is $120,000.

(ii) Employee A's ADR under Plan T is 9.09% ($10,000/$110,000) and under Plan S, Employee A's ADR is 8.33% ($10,000/$120,000).

Example 3. (i) Employer J sponsors two profit-sharing plans, Plan U and Plan V, each of which includes a cash or deferred arrangement. Plan U's plan year begins on July 1 and ends on June 30. Plan V has a calendar year plan year. Compensation under both plans is limited to the participant's compensation during the period of participation. Employee B is an HCE who participates in both plans. Employee B's monthly compensation and elective contributions to each plan for the 2005 and 2006 calendar years are as follows:

Calendar year	Monthly Compensation	Monthly Elective Contribution to Plan U	Monthly Elective Contribution to Plan V
2005	$10,000	$500	$400
2006	$11,500	$700	$550

(ii) Under Plan U, Employee B's ADR for the plan year ended June 30, 2006, is equal to Employee B's total elective contributions under

Plan U and Plan V for the plan year ending June 30, 2006 divided by Employee B's compensation for that period. Therefore, Employee B's

ADR under Plan U for the plan year ending June 30, 2006, is (($900 × 6) + ($1,250 × 6)) / (($10,000 × 6) + ($11,500 × 6)), or 10%.

(iii) Under Plan V, Employee B's ADR for the plan year ended December 31, 2005, is equal to total elective contributions under Plan U and V for the plan year ending December 31, 2005, divided by Employee B's compensation for that period. Therefore, Employee B's ADR under Plan V for the plan year ending December 31, 2005, is ($10,800/$120,000), or 9%.

Example 4. (i) The facts are the same as *Example 3*, except that Employee B first becomes eligible to participate in Plan U on January 1, 2006.

(ii) Under Plan U, Employee B's ADR for the plan year ended June 30, 2006, is equal to Employee B's total elective contributions under Plan U and V for the plan year ending June 30, 2006, divided by Employee B's compensation for that period. Therefore, Employee B's ADR under Plan U for the plan year ending June 30, 2006, is (($400 × 6)+ ($1,250 × 6)) / (($10,000 × 6) + ($11,500 × 6)), or 7.67%.

(4) *Elective contributions taken into account under the ADP test*—(i) *General rule.* An elective contribution is taken into account in determining the ADR for an eligible employee for a plan year or applicable year only if each of the following requirements is satisfied:

(A) The elective contribution is allocated to the eligible employee's account under the plan as of a date within that year. For purposes of this rule, an elective contribution is considered allocated as of a date within a year only if—

(*1*) The allocation is not contingent on the employee's participation in the plan or performance of services on any date subsequent to that date; and

(*2*) The elective contribution is actually paid to the trust no later than the end of the 12-month period immediately following the year to which the contribution relates.

(B) The elective contribution relates to compensation that either—

(*1*) Would have been received by the employee in the year but for the employee's election to defer under the arrangement; or

(*2*) Is attributable to services performed by the employee in the year and, but for the employee's election to defer, would have been received by the employee within 2 ½ months after the close of the year, but only if the plan so provides for elective contributions that relate to compensation that would have been received after the close of a year to be allocated to such prior year rather than the year in which the compensation would have been received.

(ii) *Elective contributions for partners and self-employed individuals.* For purposes of this paragraph (a)(4), a partner's distributive share of partnership income is treated as received on the last day of the partnership taxable year and a sole proprietor's compensation is treated as received on the last day of the individual's taxable year. Thus, an elective contribution made on behalf of a partner or sole proprietor is treated as allocated to the partner's account for the plan year that includes the last day of the partnership taxable year, provided the requirements of paragraph (a)(4)(i) of this section are met.

(iii) *Elective contributions for HCEs.* Elective contributions of an HCE must include any excess deferrals, as described in § 1.402(g)-1(a), even if those excess deferrals are distributed, pursuant to § 1.402(g)-1(e).

(5) *Elective contributions not taken into account under the ADP test*—(i) *General rule.* Elective contributions that do not satisfy the requirements of paragraph (a)(4)(i) of this section may not be taken into account in determining the ADR of an eligible employee for the plan year or applicable year with respect to which the contributions were made, or for any other plan year. Instead, the amount of the elective contributions must satisfy the requirements of section 401(a)(4) (without regard to the ADP test) for the plan year for which they are allocated under the plan as if they were nonelective contributions and were the only nonelective contributions for that year. See §§ 1.401(a)(4)-1(b)(2)(ii)(B) and 1.410(b)-7(c)(1).

(ii) *Elective contributions for NHCEs.* Elective contributions of an NHCE shall not include any excess deferrals, as described in § 1.402(g)-1(a), to the extent the excess deferrals are prohibited under section 401(a)(30). However, to the extent that the excess deferrals are not prohibited under section 401(a)(30), they are included in elective contributions even if distributed pursuant to § 1.402(g)-1(e).

(iii) *Elective contributions treated as catch-up contributions.* Elective contributions that are treated as catch-up contributions under section 414(v) because they exceed a statutory limit or employer-provided limit (within the meaning of § 1.414(v)-1(b)(1)) are not taken into account

under paragraph (a)(4) of this section for the plan year for which the contributions were made, or for any other plan year.

(iv) *Elective contributions used to satisfy the ACP test.* Except to the extent necessary to demonstrate satisfaction of the requirement of § 1.401(m)-2(a)(6)(ii), elective contributions taken into account for the ACP test under § 1.401(m)-2(a)(6) are not taken into account under paragraph (a)(4) of this section.

(6) *Qualified nonelective contributions and qualified matching contributions that may be taken into account under the ADP test.* Qualified nonelective contributions and qualified matching contributions may be taken into account in determining the ADR for an eligible employee for a plan year or applicable year but only to the extent the contributions satisfy the following requirements.

(i) *Timing of allocation.* The qualified nonelective contribution or qualified matching contribution is allocated to the employee's account as of a date within that year within the meaning of paragraph (a)(4)(i)(A) of this section. Consequently, under the prior year testing method, in order to be taken into account in calculating the ADP for the eligible NHCEs for the applicable year, a qualified nonelective contribution or qualified matching contribution must be contributed no later than the end of the 12-month period immediately following the applicable year even though the applicable year is different than the plan year being tested.

(ii) *Requirement that amount satisfy section 401(a)(4).* The amount of nonelective contributions, including those qualified nonelective contributions taken into account under this paragraph (a)(6) and those qualified nonelective contributions taken into account for the ACP test of section 401(m)(2) under § 1.401(m)-2(a)(6), satisfies the requirements of section 401(a)(4). See § 1.401(a)(4)-1(b)(2). The amount of nonelective contributions, excluding those qualified nonelective contributions taken into account under this paragraph (a)(6) and those qualified nonelective contributions taken into account for the ACP test of section 401(m)(2) under § 1.401(m)-2(a)(6), satisfies the requirements of section 401(a)(4). See § 1.401(a)(4)-1(b)(2). In the case of an employer that is applying the special rule for employer-wide plans in § 1.414(r)-1(c)(2)(ii) with respect to the cash or deferred arrangement, the determination of whether the qualified nonelective contributions satisfy the requirements of this paragraph (a)(6)(ii) must be made on an employer-wide basis regardless of whether the plans to which the qualified nonelective contributions are made are satisfying the requirements of section 410(b) on an employer-wide basis. Conversely, in the case of an employer that is treated as operating qualified separate lines of business, and does not apply the special rule for employer-wide plans in § 1.414(r)-1(c)(2)(ii) with respect to the cash or deferred arrangement, then the determination of whether the qualified nonelective contributions satisfy the requirements of this paragraph (a)(6)(ii) is not permitted to be made on an employer-wide basis regardless of whether the plans to which the qualified nonelective contributions are made are satisfying the requirements of section 410(b) on that basis.

(iii) *Aggregation must be permitted.* The plan that contains the cash or deferred arrangement and the plan or plans to which the qualified nonelective contributions or qualified matching contributions are made, are plans that would be permitted to be aggregated under § 1.401(k)-1(b)(4). If the plan year of the plan that contains the cash or deferred arrangement is changed to satisfy the requirement under § 1.410(b)-7(d)(5) that aggregated plans have the same plan year, qualified nonelective contributions and qualified matching contributions may be taken into account in the resulting short plan year only if such qualified nonelective contributions and qualified matching contributions could have been taken into account under an ADP test for a plan with the same short plan year.

(iv) *Disproportionate contributions not taken into account*—(A) *General rule.* Qualified nonelective contributions cannot be taken into account for a plan year for an NHCE to the extent such contributions exceed the product of that NHCE's compensation and the greater of 5% or two times the plan's representative contribution rate. Any qualified nonelective contribution taken into account under an ACP test under § 1.401(m)-2(a)(6) (including the determination of the representative contribution rate for purposes of § 1.401(m)-2(a)(6)(v)(B)), is not permitted to be taken into account for purposes of this paragraph (a)(6) (including the determination of the representative contribution rate under paragraph (a)(6)(iv)(B) of this section).

(B) *Definition of representative contribution rate.* For purposes of this paragraph (a)(6)(iv), the plan's representative contribution rate is the lowest applicable contribution rate of any eligible NHCE among a group of eligible NHCEs that consists of half of all eligible NHCEs for the plan year (or, if greater, the lowest applicable contribution rate of any eligible NHCE in the group of all eligible NHCEs for the plan year and who is employed by the employer on the last day of the plan year).

(C) *Definition of applicable contribution rate.* For purposes of this paragraph (a)(6)(iv), the applicable contribution rate for an eligible NHCE is the sum of the qualified matching contributions taken into account under this paragraph (a)(6) for the eligible NHCE for the plan year and the qualified nonelective contributions made for that eligible NHCE for the plan year, divided by that eligible NHCE's compensation for the same period.

(v) *Qualified matching contributions.* Qualified matching contributions satisfy this paragraph (a)(6) only to the extent that such qualified matching contributions are matching contributions that are not precluded from being taken into account under the ACP test for the plan year under the rules of § 1.401(m)-2(a)(5)(ii).

(vi) *Contributions only used once.* Qualified nonelective contributions and qualified matching contributions can not be taken into account under this paragraph (a)(6) to the extent such contributions are taken into account for purposes of satisfying any other ADP test, any ACP test, or the requirements of § 1.401(k)-3, 1.401(m)-3 or 1.401(k)-4. Thus, for example, matching contributions that are made pursuant to § 1.401(k)-3(c) cannot be taken into account under the ADP test. Similarly, if a plan switches from the current year testing method to the prior year testing method pursuant to § 1.401(k)-2(c), qualified nonelec-

Employee		Compensation	Elective Contribution
A	....	$100,000	$4,340
B	....	60,000	2,860
C	....	45,000	1,250

(ii) For each employee, the ratio of elective contributions to the employee's compensation for the plan year is:

Employee	Ratio of Elective Contribution to Compensation	ADR
A	$4,340/$100,000	4.34 %
B	2,860/60,000	4.77
C	1,250/45,000	2.78

(iii) The ADP for the HCEs (Employee A) is 4.34%. The ADP for the NHCEs is 3.78% ((4.77% + 2.78%)/2). Because 4.34% is less than 4.73% (3.78% multiplied by 1.25), the plan satisfies the ADP test under paragraph (a)(1)(i) of this section.

Example 2. (i) The facts are the same as in *Example 1*, except that elective contributions are made pursuant to a salary reduction agree-

Employee		Gross Compensation	Elective Contributions	ADR
A	....	$100,000	$5,770	5.77 %
B	....	60,000	2,860	4.77
C	....	45,000	1,250	2.78

(ii) The ADP for the HCEs (Employee A) is 5.77 %. The ADP for the NHCEs is 3.78% ((4.77% + 2.78%)/2). Because 5.77% exceeds 4.73% (3.78% × 1.25), the plan does not satisfy the ADP test under paragraph (a)(1)(i) of this section. However, because the ADP for the HCEs does not exceed the ADP for the NHCEs by more than 2 percentage points and the ADP for the HCEs does not exceed the ADP for the NHCEs multiplied by 2 (3.78% × 2 = 7.56%), the plan satisfies the ADP test under paragraph (a)(1)(ii) of this section.

Employee		Compensation for 2006 Plan Year
D	....	$100,000
E	....	$95,000

(ii) During the 2005 plan year, Employees F through L were eligible NHCEs. The compensation, elective contributions and ADRs of Em-

Employee		Compensation for 2005 Plan Year
F	....	$60,000
G	....	$40,000
H	....	$30,000
I	....	$20,000
J	....	$20,000
K	....	$10,000
L	....	$5,000

(iii) The ADP for 2006 for the HCEs is 7.5%. Because Plan T is using the prior year testing method, the applicable year for determining the NHCE ADP is the prior plan year (i.e., 2005). The NHCE ADP is determined using the ADRs for NHCEs eligible during the prior plan year (without regard to whether they are eligible under the plan during the plan year). The ADP for the NHCEs is 3.71% (the sum of the individual ADRs, 26%, divided by 7 employees). Because 7.5% exceeds 4.64% (3.71% × 1.25), Plan T does not satisfy the ADP test under paragraph (a)(1)(i) of this section. In addition, because the ADP for the HCEs exceeds the ADP for the NHCEs by more than 2 percentage points, Plan T does not satisfy the ADP test under paragraph (a)(1)(ii) of this section. Therefore, the cash or deferred arrangement fails to be

tive contributions that are taken into account under the current year testing method for a year may not be taken into account under the prior year testing method for the next year

(7) *Examples.* The following examples illustrate the application of this paragraph (a):

Example 1. (i) Employer X has three employees, A, B, and C. Employer X sponsors a profit-sharing plan (Plan Z) that includes a cash or deferred arrangement. Each year, Employer X determines a bonus attributable to the prior year. Under the cash or deferred arrangement, each eligible employee may elect to receive none, all or any part of the bonus in cash. X contributes the remainder to Plan Z. The portion of the bonus paid in cash, if any, is paid 2 months after the end of the plan year and thus is included in compensation for the following plan year. Employee A is an HCE, while Employees B and C are NHCEs. The plan uses the current year testing method and defines compensation to include elective contributions and bonuses paid during each plan year. In February of 2005, Employer X determined that no bonuses will be paid for 2004. In February of 2006, Employer X provided a bonus for each employee equal to 10% of regular compensation for 2005. For the 2005 plan year, A, B, and C have the following compensation and make the following elections:

ment throughout the plan year, and no bonuses are paid. As provided by section 414(s)(2), Employer X includes elective contributions in compensation. During the year, B and C defer the same amount as in *Example 1*, but A defers $5,770. Thus, the compensation and elective contributions for A, B, and C are:

Example 3. (i) Employees D through L are eligible employees in Plan T, a profit-sharing plan that contains a cash or deferred arrangement. The plan is a calendar year plan that uses the prior year testing method. Plan T provides that elective contributions are included in compensation (as provided under section 414(s)(2)). Each eligible employee may elect to defer up to 6% of compensation under the cash or deferred arrangement. Employees D and E are HCEs. The compensation, elective contributions, and ADRs of Employees D and E for the 2006 plan year are shown below:

Elective Contributions for 2006 Plan Year	ADR for 2006 Plan Year
$10,000	10%
$4,750	5%

ployees F through L for the 2005 plan year are shown in the following table:

Elective Contributions for 2005 Plan Year	ADR for 2005 Plan Year
$3,600	6%
$1,600	4%
$1,200	4%
$600	3%
$600	3%
$300	3%
$150	3%

a qualified cash or deferred arrangement unless the ADP failure is corrected under paragraph (b) of this section.

Example 4. (i) Plan U is a calendar year profit-sharing plan that contains a cash or deferred arrangement and uses the current year testing method. Plan U provides that elective contributions are included in compensation (as provided under section 414(s)(2)). The following amounts are contributed under Plan U for the 2006 plan year: (A) QNECs equal to 2% of each employee's compensation; (B) Contributions equal to 6% of each employee's compensation that are not immediately vested under the terms of the plan; (C) 3% of each employee's compensation that the employee may elect to receive as cash or to defer under the plan. Both types of nonelective contributions are made for the HCEs (employees M and N) and the NHCEs (employees O through S) for the plan year and are contributed after the end of the plan year and before the end of the following plan year. In addition, neither type of nonelective contributions is used for any other ADP or ACP test.

Employee	Compensation
M	$100,000
N	$100,000
O	$60,000
P	$40,000
Q	$30,000
R	$5,000
S	$20,000

(iii) The elective contributions alone do not satisfy the ADP test of Section 401(k)(3) and paragraph (a)(1) of this section because the ADP for the HCEs, consisting of employees M and N, is 2.5% and the ADP for the NHCEs is 0.6%.

(iv) The 2% QNECs satisfies the timing requirement of paragraph (a)(6)(i) of this section because it is paid within 12-month after the plan year for which allocated. All nonelective contributions also satisfy the requirements relating to section 401(a)(4) set forth in paragraph (a)(6)(ii) of this section (because all employees receive an 8% nonelective contribution and the nonelective contributions excluding the QNECs is 6% for all employees). In addition, the QNECs are not disproportionate under paragraph (a)(6)(iv) of this section because no QNEC for an NHCE exceeds the product of the plan's applicable contribution rate (2%) and that NHCE's compensation.

(v) Because the rules of paragraph (a)(6) of this section are satisfied, the 2% QNECs may be taken into account in applying the ADP test of section 401(k)(3) and paragraph (a)(1) of this section. The 6% nonelective contributions, however, may not be taken into account because they are not QNECs.

(vi) If the 2% QNECs are taken into account, the ADP for the HCEs is 4.5%, and the actual deferral percentage for the NHCEs is 2.6%. Because 4.5% is not more than two percentage points greater than 2.6 percent, and not more than two times 2.6, the cash or deferred arrangement satisfies the ADP test of section 401(k)(3) under paragraph (a)(1)(ii) of this section.

Example 5. (i) The facts are the same as *Example 4*, except the plan uses the prior year testing method. In addition, the NHCE ADP for the 2005 plan year (the prior plan year) is 0.8% and no QNECs are contributed for the 2005 plan year during 2005 or 2006.

(ii) In 2007, it is determined that the elective contributions alone do not satisfy the ADP test of section 401(k)(3) and paragraph (a)(1) of this section for 2006 because the 2006 ADP for the eligible HCEs, consisting of employees M and N, is 2.5% and the 2005 ADP for the eligible NHCEs is 0.8%. An additional QNEC of 2% of compensation is made for each eligible NHCE in 2007 and allocated for 2005.

(iii) The 2% QNECs that are made in 2007 and allocated for the 2005 plan year do not satisfy the timing requirement of paragraph (a)(6)(i) of this section for the applicable year for the 2005 plan year because they were not contributed before the last day of the 2006 plan year. Accordingly, the 2% QNECs do not satisfy the rules of paragraph (a)(6) of this section and may not be taken into account in applying the ADP test of section 401(k)(3) and paragraph (a)(1) of this section for the 2006 plan year. The cash or deferred arrangement fails to be a qualified cash or deferred arrangement unless the ADP failure is corrected under paragraph (b) of this section.

Example 6. (i) The facts are the same as *Example 4*, except that the ADP for the HCEs is 4.6% and there is no 6% nonelective contribution under the plan. The employer would like to take into account the 2% QNEC in determining the ADP for the NHCEs but not in determining the ADP for the HCEs.

(ii) The elective contributions alone fail the requirements of section 401(k) and paragraph (a)(1) of this section because the HCE ADP for the plan year (4.6%) exceeds 0.75% (0.6% × 1.25) and 1.2% (0.6% × 2).

(ii) For the 2006 plan year, the compensation, elective contributions, and actual deferral ratios of employees M through S are shown in the following table:

Elective Contributions	Actual Deferral Ratio
$3,000	3 %
$2,000	2 %
$1,800	3 %
0	0
0	0
0	0
0	0

(iii) The 2% QNECs may not be taken into account in determining the ADP of the NHCEs because they fail to satisfy the requirements relating to section 401(a)(4) set forth in paragraph (a)(6)(ii) of this section. This is because the amount of nonelective contributions, excluding those QNECs that would be taken into account under the ADP test, would be 2% of compensation for the HCEs and 0% for the NHCEs. Therefore, the cash or deferred arrangement fails to be a qualified cash or deferred arrangement unless the ADP failure is corrected under paragraph (b) of this section.

Example 7. (i) The facts are the same as *Example 6*, except that Employee R receives a QNEC in an amount of $500 and no QNECs are made on behalf of the other employees.

(ii) If the QNEC could be taken into account under paragraph (a)(6) of this section, the ADP for the NHCEs would be 2.6% and the plan would satisfy the ADP test. The QNEC is disproportionate under paragraph (a)(6)(iv) of this section, and cannot be taken into account under paragraph (a)(6) of this section, to the extent it exceeds the greater of 5% and two times the plan's representative contribution rate (0%), multiplied by Employee R's compensation. The plan's representative contribution rate is 0% because it is the lowest applicable contribution rate among a group of NHCEs that is at least half of all NHCEs, or all the NHCEs who are employed on the last day of the plan year. Therefore, the QNEC may be taken into account under the ADP test only to the extent it does not exceed 5% times Employee R's compensation (or $250) and the cash or deferred arrangement fails to satisfy the ADP test and must correct under paragraph (b) of this section.

Example 8. (i) The facts are the same as in *Example 4* except that the plan changes from the current year testing method to the prior year testing method for the following plan year (2006 plan year). The ADP for the HCEs for the 2006 plan year is 3.5%.

(ii) The 2% QNECs may not be taken into account in determining the ADP for the NHCEs for the applicable year (2005 plan year) in satisfying the ADP test for the 2006 plan year because they were taken into account in satisfying the ADP test for the 2005 plan year. Accordingly, the NHCE ADP for the applicable year is 0.6%. The elective contributions for the plan year fail the requirements of section 401(k) and paragraph (a)(1) of this section because the HCE ADP for the plan year (3.5%) exceeds the ADP limit of 1.2% (the greater of 0.75% (0.6% × 1.25) and 1.2% (0.6% × 2)), determined using the applicable year ADP for the NHCEs. Therefore, the cash or deferred arrangement fails to be a qualified cash or deferred arrangement unless the ADP failure is corrected under paragraph (b) of this section.

Example 9. (i)(A) Employer N maintains Plan X, a profit sharing plan that contains a cash or deferred arrangement and that uses the current year testing method. Plan X provides for employee contributions, elective contributions, and matching contributions. Matching contributions on behalf of nonhighly compensated employees are qualified matching contributions (QMACs) and are contributed during the 2005 plan year. Matching contributions on behalf of highly compensated employees are not QMACs, because they fail to satisfy the nonforfeitability requirement of §1.401(k)-1(c). The elective contributions and matching contributions with respect to HCEs for the 2005 plan year are shown in the following table:

	Elective Contributions	Total Matching Contributions	Matching contributions that are not QMACs	QMACs
Highly compensated employees	15%	5%	5%	0%

(B) The elective contributions and matching contributions with respect to the NHCEs for the 2005 plan year are shown in the following table:

	Elective Contributions	Total Matching Contributions	Matching contributions that are not QMACs	QMACs
Nonhighly compensated employees	11%	4%	0%	4%

(ii) The plan fails to satisfy the ADP test of section 401(k)(3)(A) and paragraph (a)(1) of this section because the ADP for HCEs (15%) is more than 125% of the ADP for NHCEs (11%), and more than 2 percentage points greater than 11%. However, the plan provides that QMACs may be used to meet the requirements of section

HCEs . . . .
Nonhighly compensated employees . . . .

(iii) The elective contributions and QMACs taken into account for purposes of the ADP test of section 401(k)(3) satisfy the requirements of section 401(k)(3)(A)(ii) under paragraph (a)(1)(ii) of this section because the ADP for HCEs (15%) is not more than the ADP for NHCEs multiplied by 1.25 (12% × 1.25 = 15%).

(b) *Correction of excess contributions*—(1) *Permissible correction methods*—(i) *In general.* A cash or deferred arrangement does not fail to satisfy the requirements of section 401(k)(3) and paragraph (a)(1) of this section if the employer, in accordance with the terms of the plan that includes the cash or deferred arrangement, uses any of the following correction methods—

(A) *Qualified nonelective contributions or qualified matching contributions.* The employer makes qualified nonelective contributions or qualified matching contributions that are taken into account under this section and, in combination with other amounts taken into account under paragraph (a) of this section, allow the cash or deferred arrangement to satisfy the requirements of paragraph (a)(1) of this section.

(B) *Excess contributions distributed.* Excess contributions are distributed in accordance with paragraph (b)(2) of this section.

(C) *Excess contributions recharacterized.* Excess contributions are recharacterized in accordance with paragraph (b)(3) of this section.

(ii) *Combination of correction methods.* A plan may provide for the use of any of the correction methods described in paragraph (b)(1)(i) of this section, may limit elective contributions in a manner designed to prevent excess contributions from being made, or may use a combination of these methods, to avoid or correct excess contributions. A plan may require or permit an HCE to elect whether any excess contributions are to be recharacterized or distributed. If the plan uses a combination of correction methods, any contribution made under paragraph (b)(1)(i)(A) of this section must be taken into account before application of the correction methods in paragraph (b)(1)(i)(B) or (C) of this section. (iii) *Exclusive means of correction.* A failure to satisfy the requirements of paragraph (a)(1) of this section may not be corrected using any method other than the ones described in paragraphs (b)(1)(i) and (ii) of this section. Thus, excess contributions for a plan year may not remain unallocated or be allocated to a suspense account for allocation to one or more employees in any future year. In addition, excess contributions may not be corrected using the retroactive correction rules of § 1.401(a)(4)-11(g). See § 1.401(a)(4)-11(g)(3)(vii) and (5).

(2) *Corrections through distribution*—(i) *General rule.* This paragraph (b)(2) contains the rules for correction of excess contributions through a distribution from the plan. Correction through a distribution generally involves a 4 step process. First, the plan must determine, in accordance with paragraph (b)(2)(ii) of this section, the total amount of excess contributions that must be distributed under the plan. Second, the plan must apportion the total amount of excess contributions among HCEs in accordance with paragraph (b)(2)(iii) of this section. Third, the plan must determine the income allocable to excess contributions in accordance with paragraph (b)(2)(iv) of this section. Finally, the plan must distribute the apportioned excess contributions and allocable income in accordance with paragraph (b)(2)(v) of this section. Paragraph (b)(2)(vi) of this section provides rules relating to the tax treatment of these distributions. Paragraph (b)(2)(vii) provides other rules relating to these distributions.

(ii) *Calculation of total amount to be distributed.* The following procedures must be used to determine the total amount of the excess contributions to be distributed—

(A) *Calculate the dollar amount of excess contributions for each HCE.* The amount of excess contributions attributable to a given HCE for a plan year is the amount (if any) by which the HCE's contributions taken into account under this section must be reduced for the HCE's ADR to equal the highest permitted ADR under the plan. To calculate the highest permitted ADR under a plan, the ADR of the HCE with the highest ADR is reduced by the amount required to cause that HCE's ADR to equal the ADR of the HCE with the next highest ADR. If a lesser reduction would enable the arrangement to satisfy the requirements of paragraph (b)(2)(ii)(C) of this section, only this lesser reduction is used in determining the highest permitted ADR.

401(k)(3)(A)(ii) provided that they are not used for any other ADP or ACP test. QMACs equal to 1% of compensation are taken into account for each NHCE in applying the ADP test. After this adjustment, the applicable ADP and ACP (taking into account the provisions of § 1.401(m)-2(a)(5)(ii)) for the plan year are as follows:

Actual Deferral Percentage	Actual Contribution Percentage
15 %	5 %
12	3

(B) *Determination of the total amount of excess contributions.* The process described in paragraph (b)(2)(ii)(A) of this section must be repeated until the arrangement would satisfy the requirements of paragraph (b)(2)(ii)(C) of this section. The sum of all reductions for all HCEs determined under paragraph (b)(2)(ii)(A) of this section is the total amount of excess contributions for the plan year.

(C) *Satisfaction of ADP.* A cash or deferred arrangement satisfies this paragraph (b)(2)(ii)(C) if the arrangement would satisfy the requirements of paragraph (a)(1)(ii) of this section if the ADR for each HCE were determined after the reductions described in paragraph (b)(2)(ii)(A) of this section.

(iii) *Apportionment of total amount of excess contributions among the HCEs.* The following procedures must be used in apportioning the total amount of excess contributions determined under paragraph (b)(2)(ii) of this section among the HCEs:

(A) *Calculate the dollar amount of excess contributions for each HCE.* The contributions of the HCE with the highest dollar amount of contributions taken into account under this section are reduced by the amount required to cause that HCE's contributions to equal the dollar amount of the contributions taken into account under this section for the HCE with the next highest dollar amount of contributions taken account under this section. If a lesser apportionment to the HCE would enable the plan to apportion the total amount of excess contributions, only the lesser apportionment would apply.

(B) *Limit on amount apportioned to any individual.* For purposes of this paragraph (b)(2)(iii), the amount of contributions taken into account under this section with respect to an HCE who is an eligible employee in more than one plan of an employer is determined by taking into account all contributions otherwise taken into account with respect to such HCE under any plan of the employer during the plan year of the plan being tested as being made under the plan being tested. However, the amount of excess contributions apportioned for a plan year with respect to any HCE must not exceed the amount of contributions actually contributed to the plan for the HCE for the plan year. Thus, in the case of an HCE who is an eligible employee in more than one plan of the same employer to which elective contributions are made and whose ADR is calculated in accordance with paragraph (a)(3)(ii) of this section, the amount required to be distributed under this paragraph (b)(2)(iii) shall not exceed the contributions actually contributed to the plan and taken into account under this section for the plan year.

(C) *Apportionment to additional HCEs.* The procedure in paragraph (b)(2)(iii)(A) of this section must be repeated until the total amount of excess contributions determined under paragraph (b)(2)(ii) of this section have been apportioned.

(iv) *Income allocable to excess contributions*—(A) *General rule.* The income allocable to excess contributions is equal to the sum of the allocable gain or loss for the plan year and, to the extent the excess contributions are or will be credited with allocable gain or loss for the period after the close of the plan year (gap period), the allocable gain or loss for the gap period.

(B) *Method of allocating income.* A plan may use any reasonable method for computing the income allocable to excess contributions, provided that the method does not violate section 401(a)(4), is used consistently for all participants and for all corrective distributions under the plan for the plan year, and is used by the plan for allocating income to participant's accounts. See § 1.401(a)(4)-1(c)(8).

(C) *Alternative method of allocating plan year income.* A plan may allocate income to excess contributions for the plan year by multiplying the income for the plan year allocable to the elective contributions and other amounts taken account under this section (including contributions made for the plan year), by a fraction, the numerator of which is the excess contributions for the employee for the plan year, and the denominator of which is the account balance attributable to elective contributions and other contributions taken into account under this section as of the beginning of the plan year (including any additional amount of such contributions made for the plan year).

(D) *Safe harbor method of allocating gap period income.* A plan may use the safe harbor method in this paragraph (b)(2)(iv)(D) to determine income on excess contributions for the gap period. Under this safe harbor method, income on excess contributions for the gap period is equal to 10% of the income allocable to excess contributions for the plan year that would be determined under paragraph (b)(2)(iv)(C) of this section, multiplied by the number of calendar months that have elapsed since the end of the plan year. For purposes of calculating the number of calendar months that have elapsed under the safe harbor method, a corrective distribution that is made on or before the fifteenth day of a month is treated as made on the last day of the preceding month and a distribution made after the fifteenth day of a month is treated as made on the last day of the month.

(E) *Alternative method for allocating plan year and gap period income.* A plan may determine the allocable gain or loss for the aggregate of the plan year and the gap period by applying the alternative method provided by paragraph (b)(2)(iv)(C) of this section to this aggregate period. This is accomplished by substituting the income for the plan year and the gap period for the income for the plan year and by substituting the contributions taken into account under this section for the plan year and the gap period for the contributions taken account under this section for the plan year in determining the fraction that is multiplied by that income.

(v) *Distribution.* Within 12 months after the close of the plan year in which the excess contribution arose, the plan must distribute to each HCE the excess contributions apportioned to such HCE under paragraph (b)(2)(iii) of this section and the allocable income. Except as otherwise provided in this paragraph (b)(2)(v) and paragraph (b)(4)(i) of this section, a distribution of excess contributions must be in addition to any other distributions made during the year and must be designated as a corrective distribution by the employer. In the event of a complete termination of the plan during the plan year in which an excess contribution arose, the corrective distribution must be made as soon as administratively feasible after the date of termination of the plan, but in no event later than 12 months after the date of termination. If the entire account balance of an HCE is distributed prior to when the plan makes a distribution of excess contributions in accordance with this paragraph (b)(2), the distribution is deemed to have been a corrective distribution of excess contributions (and income) to the extent that a corrective distribution would otherwise have been required.

(vi) *Tax treatment of corrective distributions*—(A) *General rule.* Except as provided in paragraph (b)(2)(vi)(B) of this section, a corrective distribution of excess contributions (and income) that is made within 2 ½ months after the end of the plan year for which the excess contributions were made is includible in the employee's gross income on the earliest date any elective contributions by the employee during the plan year would have been received by the employee had the employee originally elected to receive the amounts in cash. A corrective distribution of excess contributions (and income) that is made more than 2 ½ months after the end of the plan year for which the contributions were made is includible in the employee's gross income in the employee's taxable year in which distributed. Regardless of when the corrective distribution is made, it is not subject to the early distribution tax of section 72(t). See paragraph (b)(4) of this section for additional rules relating to the employer excise tax on amounts distributed more than 2 ½ months after the end of the plan year. See also § 1.402(c)-2, A-4 for restrictions on rolling over distributions that are excess contributions.

(B) *Rule for de minimis distributions.* If the total amount of excess contributions, determined under this paragraph (b)(2), and excess aggregate contributions determined under § 1.401(m)-2(b)(2) distributed to a recipient under a plan for any plan year is less than $100 (excluding income), a corrective distribution of excess contributions (and income) is includible in the gross income of the recipient in the taxable year of the recipient in which the corrective distribution is made.

(vii) *Other rules*—(A) *No employee or spousal consent required.* A corrective distribution of excess contributions (and income) may be made under the terms of the plan without regard to any notice or consent otherwise required under sections 411(a)(11) and 417.

(B) *Treatment of corrective distributions as elective contributions.* Excess contributions are treated as employer contributions for purposes of sections 404 and 415 even if distributed from the plan.

(C) *No reduction of required minimum distribution.* A distribution of excess contributions (and income) is not treated as a distribution for purposes of determining whether the plan satisfies the minimum distribution requirements of section 401(a)(9). See § 1.401(a)(9)-5, Q&A-9(b).

(D) *Partial distributions.* Any distribution of less than the entire amount of excess contributions (and allocable income) with respect to

any HCE is treated as a pro rata distribution of excess contributions and allocable income.

(viii) *Examples.* The following examples illustrate the application of this paragraph (b)(2). For purposes of these examples, none of the plans provide for catch-up contributions under section 414(v). The examples are as follows:

Example 1. (i) Plan P, a calendar year profit-sharing plan that includes a cash or deferred arrangement, provides for distribution of excess contributions to HCEs to the extent necessary to satisfy the ADP test. Employee A, an HCE, has elective contributions of $12,000 and $200,000 in compensation, for an ADR of 6%, and Employee B, a second HCE, has elective contributions of $8,960 and compensation of $128,000, for an ADR of 7%. The ADP for the NHCEs is 3%. Under the ADP test, the ADP of the two HCEs under the plan may not exceed 5% (i.e., 2 percentage points more than the ADP of the NHCEs under the plan). The ADP for the 2 HCEs under the plan is 6.5%. Therefore, there must be a correction of excess contributions.

(ii) The total amount of excess contributions for the HCEs is determined under paragraph (b)(2)(ii) of this section as follows: the elective contributions of Employee B (the HCE with the highest ADR) are reduced by $1,280 in order to reduce his ADR to 6% ($7,680/$128,000), which is the ADR of Employee A.

(iii) Because the ADP of the HCEs determined after the $1,280 reduction to Employee B still exceeds 5%, further reductions in elective contributions are necessary in order to reduce the ADP of the HCEs to 5%. The elective contributions of Employee A and Employee B are each reduced by 1% of compensation ($2,000 and $1,280 respectively). Because the ADP of the HCEs determined after the reductions equals 5%, the plan would satisfy the requirements of (a)(1)(ii) of this section.

(iv) The total amount of excess contributions ($4,560 = $1,280+$2,000+$1,280) is apportioned among the HCEs under paragraph (b)(2)(iii) of this section first to the HCE with the highest amount of elective contributions. Therefore, Employee A is apportioned $3,040 (the amount required to cause Employee A's elective contributions to equal the next highest dollar amount of elective contributions).

(v) Because the total amount of excess contributions has not been apportioned, further apportionment is necessary. The balance ($1,520) of the total amount of excess contributions is apportioned equally among Employee A and Employee B ($760 to each).

(vi) Therefore, the cash or deferred arrangement will satisfy the requirements of paragraph (a)(1) of this section if, by the end of the 12 month period following the end of the 2006 plan year, Employee A receives a corrective distribution of excess contributions equal to $3,800 ($3,040 + $760) and allocable income and Employee B receives a corrective distribution of $760 and allocable income.

Example 2. (i) The facts are the same as in *Example 1*, except Employee A's ADR is based on $3,000 of elective contributions to this plan and $9,000 of elective contributions to another plan of the employer.

(ii) The total amount of excess contributions ($4,560 = $1,280+$2,000+$1,280) is apportioned among the HCEs under paragraph (b)(2)(iii) of this section first to the HCE with the highest amount of elective contributions. The amount of elective contributions for Employee A is $12,000. Therefore, Employee A is apportioned $3,040 (the amount required to cause Employee A's elective contributions to equal the next highest dollar amount of elective contributions). However, pursuant to paragraph (b)(2)(iii)(B) of this section, no more than the amount actually contributed to the plan may be apportioned to an HCE. Accordingly, no more than $3,000 may be apportioned to Employee A. Therefore, the remaining $1,560 must be apportioned to Employee B.

(ii) The cash or deferred arrangement will satisfy the requirements of paragraph (a)(1) of this section if, by the end of the 12 month period following the end of the 2006 plan year, Employee A receives a corrective distribution of excess contributions equal to $3,000 (total amount of elective contributions actually contributed to the plan for Employee A) and allocable income and Employee B receives a corrective distribution of $1,560 and allocable income.

Example 3. (i) The facts are the same as in *Example 1*. The plan allocates income on a daily basis. The corrective distributions are made in February 2007. The excess contribution that must be distributed to Employee A as a corrective distribution is $3,800. This amount must be increased (or decreased) to reflect gains (or losses) allocable to that amount during the 2006 plan year. The plan uses a reasonable method that satisfies paragraph (b)(2)(iv)(B) of this section to determine the gain during the 2006 plan year allocable to the $3,800 as $145. Therefore, as of the end of the 2006 plan year, the amount of corrective distribution that is required would be $3,945.

(ii) Because the plan allocates income on a daily basis, excess contributions are credited with gain or loss during the gap period. Therefore, the corrective distribution must include income allocable to $3,945 through the date of distribution. For the period from January 1 through the date of distribution, the income allocable to $3,945 is $105. Therefore, the plan will satisfy the requirements of paragraph (a)(1) of this section if Employee A receives a corrective distribution of $4,050.

Example 4. (i) The facts are the same as in *Example 1.* The plan determines plan year income using the alternative method for calculating income provided in paragraph (b)(2)(iv)(C) of this section and using the portion of the participant's account attributable to elective contributions, including elective contributions made for the plan year. The plan uses the safe harbor method provided in paragraph (b)(2)(iv)(D) of this section for allocating gap period income. The corrective distribution is made during the last week of February 2007. At the beginning of the 2006 plan year, $100,000 of Employee A's plan account was attributable to elective contributions. During the 2006 plan year, $10,000 in elective contributions were contributed to the plan for Employee A. The income allocable to Employee A's account attributable to elective contributions for the 2006 plan year is $8,000.

(ii) Therefore, the plan year income allocable to the $3,800 corrective distribution for Employee A is $266.65 ($8,000 multiplied by $3,800 divided by $110,000). Therefore, as of the end of the 2006 plan year, the amount of corrective distribution that is required is $4,066.65. This amount must be increased by the gap period income of $53.32 (10% multiplied by $266.65 (2006 plan year income attributable to the excess contribution) multiplied by 2 (number of calendar months since end of 2006 plan year). Therefore, the plan will satisfy the requirements of paragraph (a)(1) of this section if Employee A receives a corrective distribution of $4,119.97.

Example 5. (i) The facts are the same as in *Example 4*, except that the plan provides for quarterly valuations based on the account balance at the end of the quarter.

(ii) Because the plan's method for allocating income does not allocate any income to amounts distributed during the quarter, Employee A will not be credited with an allocation of income with respect to the amount distributed. Accordingly, Plan P need not plan adjust the distribution of excess contribution for income during the gap period and thus satisfies paragraph (a)(1) of this section if Employee A receives a corrective distribution of $4,066.65.

(3) *Recharacterization of excess contributions*—(i) *General rule.* Excess contributions are recharacterized in accordance with this paragraph (b)(3) only if the excess contributions that would have to be distributed under (b)(2) of this section if the plan was correcting through distribution of excess contributions are recharacterized as described in paragraph (b)(3)(ii) of this section, and all of the conditions set forth in paragraph (b)(3)(iii) of this section are satisfied.

(ii) *Treatment of recharacterized excess contributions.* Recharacterized excess contributions are includible in the employee's gross income as if such amounts were distributed under paragraph (b)(2) of this section. The recharacterized excess contributions must be treated as employee contributions for purposes of section 72, sections 401(a)(4) and 401(m). This requirement is not treated as satisfied unless the payor or plan administrator reports the recharacterized excess contributions as employee contributions to the Internal Revenue Service and the employee by timely providing such Federal tax forms and accompanying instructions and timely taking such other action as prescribed by the Commissioner in revenue rulings, notices and other guidance published in the Internal Revenue Bulletin (see 601.601(d)(2) of this chapter) as well as the applicable federal tax forms and accompanying instructions.

(iii) *Additional rules*—(A) *Time of recharacterization.* Excess contributions may not be recharacterized under this paragraph (b)(3) after 2 ½ months after the close of the plan year to which the recharacterization relates. Recharacterization is deemed to have occurred on the date on which the last of those HCEs with excess contributions to be recharacterized is notified in accordance with paragraph (b)(3)(ii) of this section.

(B) *Employee contributions must be permitted under plan.* The amount of recharacterized excess contributions, in combination with the employee contributions actually made by the HCE, may not exceed the maximum amount of employee contributions (determined without regard to the ACP test of section 401(m)(2)) permitted under the provisions of the plan as in effect on the first day of the plan year.

(C) *Treatment of recharacterized excess contributions.* Recharacterized excess contributions continue to be treated as employer contributions for all other purposes under the Internal Revenue Code, including sections 401(a) (other than sections 401(a)(4) and 401(m)), 404, 409, 411, 412, 415, 416, and 417. Thus, for example, recharacterized excess contributions remain subject to the requirements of § 1.401(k)-1(c) and (d); must be deducted under section 404; and are treated as employer contributions described in section 415(c)(2)(A) and § 1.415-6(b).

(4) *Rules applicable to all corrections*—(i) *Coordination with distribution of excess deferrals*—(A) *Treatment of excess deferrals that reduce excess contributions.* The amount of excess contributions (and allocable income) to be distributed under paragraph (b)(2) of this section or the amount of excess contributions recharacterized under paragraph (b)(3) of this section with respect to an employee for a plan year, is reduced by any amounts previously distributed to the employee from the plan to correct excess deferrals for the employee's taxable year ending with or within the plan year in accordance with section 402(g)(2).

(B) *Treatment of excess contributions that reduce excess deferrals.* Under § 1.402(g)-1(e), the amount required to be distributed to correct an excess deferral to an employee for a taxable year is reduced by any excess contributions (and allocable income) previously distributed or excess contributions recharacterized with respect to the employee for the plan year beginning with or within the taxable year. The amount of excess contributions includible in the gross income of the employee, and the amount of excess contributions reported by the payer or plan administrator as includible in the gross income of the employee, does not include the amount of any reduction under § 1.402(g)-1(e)(6).

(ii) *Forfeiture of match on distributed excess contributions.* A matching contribution is taken into account under section 401(a)(4) even if the match is with respect to an elective contribution that is distributed or recharacterized under this paragraph (b). This requires that, after correction of excess contributions, each level of matching contributions be currently and effectively available to a group of employees that satisfies section 410(b). See § 1.401(a)(4)-4(e)(3)(iii)(G). Thus, a plan that provides the same rate of matching contributions to all employees will not meet the requirements of section 401(a)(4) if elective contributions are distributed under this paragraph (b) to HCEs to the extent needed to meet the requirements of section 401(k)(3), while matching contributions attributable to those elective contributions remain allocated to the HCEs' accounts. Under section 411(a)(3)(G) and § 1.411(a)-4(b)(7), a plan may forfeit matching contributions attributable to excess contributions, excess aggregate contributions or excess deferrals to avoid a violation of section 401(a)(4). See also § 1.401(a)(4)-11(g)(vii)(B) regarding the use of additional allocations to the accounts of NHCEs for the purpose of correcting a discriminatory rate of matching contributions.

(iii) *Permitted forfeiture of QMAC.* Pursuant to section 401(k)(8)(E), a qualified matching contribution is not treated as forfeitable under § 1.401(k)-1(c) merely because under the plan it is forfeited in accordance with paragraph (b)(4)(ii) of this section.

(iv) *No requirement for recalculation.* If excess contributions are distributed or recharacterized in accordance with paragraphs (b)(2) and (3) of this section, the cash or deferred arrangement is treated as meeting the nondiscrimination test of section 401(k)(3) regardless of whether the ADP for the HCEs, if recalculated after the distributions or recharacterizations, would satisfy section 401(k)(3).

(v) *Treatment of excess contributions that are catch-up contributions.* A cash or deferred arrangement does not fail to meet the requirements of section 401(k)(3) and paragraph (a)(1) of this section merely because excess contributions that are catch-up contributions because they exceed the ADP limit, as described in § 1.414(v)-1(b)(1)(iii), are not corrected in accordance with this paragraph (b).

(5) *Failure to timely correct*—(i) *Failure to correct within 2 ½ months after end of plan year.* If a plan does not correct excess contributions within 2 ½ months after the close of the plan year for which the excess contributions are made, the employer will be liable for a 10% excise tax on the amount of the excess contributions. See section 4979 and § 54.4979-1 of this chapter. Qualified nonelective contributions and qualified matching contributions properly taken into account under paragraph (a)(6) of this section for a plan year may enable a plan to avoid having excess contributions, even if the contributions are made after the close of the 2 ½ month period.

(ii) *Failure to correct within 12 months after end of plan year.* If excess contributions are not corrected within 12 months after the close of the plan year for which they were made, the cash or deferred arrangement will fail to satisfy the requirements of section 401(k)(3) for the plan year for which the excess contributions are made and all subsequent plan years during which the excess contributions remain in the trust.

(c) *Additional rules for prior year testing method*—(1) *Rules for change in testing method*—(i) *General rule*. A plan is permitted to change from the prior year testing method to the current year testing method for any plan year. A plan is permitted to change from the current year testing method to the prior year testing method only in situations described in paragraph (c)(1)(ii) of this section. For purposes of this paragraph (c)(1), a plan that uses the safe harbor method described in § 1.401(k)-3 or a SIMPLE 401(k) plan is treated as using the current year testing method for that plan year.

(ii) *Situations permitting a change to the prior year testing method.* The situations described in this paragraph (c)(1)(ii) are:

(A) The plan is not the result of the aggregation of two or more plans, and the current year testing method was used under the plan for each of the 5 plan years preceding the plan year of the change (or if lesser, the number of plan years the plan has been in existence, including years in which the plan was a portion of another plan).

(B) The plan is the result of the aggregation of two or more plans, and for each of the plans that are being aggregated (the aggregating plans), the current year testing method was used for each of the 5 plan years preceding the plan year of the change (or if lesser, the number of plan years since that aggregating plan has been in existence, including years in which the aggregating plan was a portion of another plan).

(C) A transaction described in section 410(b)(6)(C)(i) and § 1.410(b)-2(f) occurs and—

(*1*) As a result of the transaction, the employer maintains both a plan using the prior year testing method and a plan using the current year testing method; and

(*2*) The change from the current year testing method to the prior year testing method occurs within the transition period described in section 410(b)(6)(C)(ii).

(2) *Calculation of ADP under the prior year testing method for the first plan year*—(i) *Plans that are not successor plans.* If, for the first plan year of any plan (other than a successor plan), the plan uses the prior year testing method, the plan is permitted to use either that first plan year as the applicable year for determining the ADP for eligible NHCEs, or use 3% as the ADP for eligible NHCEs, for applying the ADP test for that first plan year. A plan (other than a successor plan) that uses the prior year testing method but has elected its first plan year to use that year as the applicable year is not treated as changing its testing method in the second plan year and is not subject to the limitations on double counting on QNECs under paragraph (a)(6)(vi) of this section for the second plan year.

(ii) *First plan year defined.* For purposes of this paragraph (c)(2), the first plan year of any plan is the first year in which the plan provides for elective contributions. Thus, the rules of this paragraph (c)(2) do not apply to a plan (within the meaning of § 1.410(b)-7(b)) for a plan year if for such plan year the plan is aggregated under § 1.401(k)-1(b)(4) with any other plan that provides for elective contributions in the prior year.

(iii) *Successor plans.* A plan is a successor plan if 50% or more of the eligible employees for the first plan year were eligible employees under a qualified cash or deferred arrangement maintained by the employer in the prior year. If a plan that is a successor plan uses the prior year testing method for its first plan year, the ADP for the group of NHCEs for the applicable year must be determined under paragraph (c)(4) of this section.

(3) *Plans using different testing methods for the ADP and ACP test.* Except as otherwise provided in this paragraph (c)(3), a plan may use the current year testing method or prior year testing method for the ADP test for a plan year without regard to whether the current year testing method or prior year testing method is used for the ACP test for that year. For example, a plan may use the prior year testing method for the ADP test and the current year testing method for its ACP test for the plan year. However, plans that use different testing methods under this paragraph (c)(3) cannot use—

(i) The recharacterization method of paragraph (b)(3) of this section to correct excess contributions for a plan year;

(ii) The rules of § 1.401(m)-2(a)(6)(ii) to take elective contributions into account under the ACP test (rather than the ADP test); or

(iii) The rules of paragraph (a)(6)(v) of this section to take qualified matching contributions into account under the ADP test (rather than the ACP test).

(4) *Rules for plan coverage changes*—(i) *In general.* A plan that uses the prior year testing method and experiences a plan coverage change

during a plan year satisfies the requirements of this section for that year only if the plan provides that the ADP for the NHCEs for the plan year is the weighted average of the ADPs for the prior year subgroups.

(ii) *Optional rule for minor plan coverage changes.* If a plan coverage change occurs and 90% or more of the total number of the NHCEs from all prior year subgroups are from a single prior year subgroup, then, in lieu of using the weighted averages described in paragraph (c)(4)(i) of this section, the plan may provide that the ADP for the group of eligible NHCEs for the prior year under the plan is the ADP of the NHCEs for the prior year of the plan under which that single prior year subgroup was eligible.

(iii) *Definitions.* The following definitions apply for purposes of this paragraph (c)(4):

(A) *Plan coverage change.* The term plan coverage change means a change in the group or groups of eligible employees under a plan on account of—

(*1*) The establishment or amendment of a plan;

(*2*) A plan merger or spinoff under section 414(l);

(*3*) A change in the way plans (within the meaning of § 1.410(b)-7(b)) are combined or separated for purposes of § 1.401(k)-1(b)(4) (e.g., permissively aggregating plans not previously aggregated under § 1.410(b)-7(d), or ceasing to permissively aggregate plans under § 1.410(b)-7(d));

(*4*) A reclassification of a substantial group of employees that has the same effect as amending the plan (e.g., a transfer of a substantial group of employees from one division to another division); or

(*5*) A combination of any of the situations described in this paragraph (c)(4)(iii)(A).

(B) *Prior year subgroup.* The term prior year subgroup means all NHCEs for the prior plan year who, in the prior year, were eligible employees under a specific plan maintained by the employer that included a qualified cash or deferred arrangement and who would have been eligible employees in the prior year under the plan being tested if the plan coverage change had first been effective as of the first day of the prior plan year instead of first being effective during the plan year. The determination of whether an NHCE is a member of a prior year subgroup is made without regard to whether the NHCE terminated employment during the prior year.

(C) *Weighted average of the ADPs for the prior year subgroups.* The term weighted average of the ADPs for the prior year subgroups means the sum, for all prior year subgroups, of the adjusted ADPs for the plan year. The term adjusted ADP with respect to a prior year subgroup means the ADP for the prior plan year of the specific plan under which the members of the prior year subgroup were eligible employees on the first day of the prior plan year, multiplied by a fraction, the numerator of which is the number of NHCEs in the prior year subgroup and denominator of which is the total number of NHCEs in all prior year subgroups.

(iv) *Examples.* The following examples illustrate the application of this paragraph (c)(4):

Example 1. (i) Employer B maintains two calendar year plans, Plan O and Plan P, each of which includes a cash or deferred arrangement. The plans were not permissively aggregated under § 1.410(b)-7(d) for the 2005 plan year. Both plans use the prior year testing method. Plan O had 300 eligible employees who were NHCEs for the 2005 plan year, and their ADP for that year was 6%. Sixty of the eligible employees who were NHCEs for the 2005 plan year under Plan O, terminated their employment during that year. Plan P had 100 eligible employees who were NHCEs for 2005, and the ADP for those NHCEs for that plan was 4%. Plan O and Plan P are permissively aggregated under § 1.410(b)-7(d) for the 2006 plan year.

(ii) The permissive aggregation of Plan O and Plan P for the 2006 plan year under § 1.410(b)-7(d) is a plan coverage change that results in treating the plans as one plan (Plan OP) for purposes of § 1.401(k)-1(b)(4). Therefore, the prior year ADP for the NHCEs under Plan OP for the 2006 plan year is the weighted average of the ADPs for the prior year subgroups: the Plan O prior year subgroup and the Plan P prior year subgroup.

(iii) The Plan O prior year subgroup consists of the 300 employees who, in the 2005 plan year, were eligible NHCEs under Plan O and who would have been eligible under Plan OP for the 2005 plan year if Plan O and Plan P had been permissively aggregated for that plan year. The Plan P prior year subgroup consists of the 100 employees who, in the 2005 plan year, were eligible NHCEs under Plan P and would have been eligible under Plan OP for the 2005 plan year if Plan O and Plan P had been permissively aggregated for that plan year.

(iv) The weighted average of the ADPs for the prior year subgroups is the sum of the adjusted ADP for the Plan O prior year subgroup and the adjusted ADP for the Plan P prior year subgroup. The adjusted ADP for the Plan O prior year subgroup is 4.5%, calculated as follows: 6% (the ADP for the NHCEs under Plan O for the 2005 plan year) × 300/400 (the number of NHCEs in the Plan O prior year subgroup divided by the total number of NHCEs in all prior year subgroups). The adjusted ADP for the Plan P prior year subgroup is 1%, calculated as follows: 4% (the ADP for the NHCEs under Plan P for the 2005 plan year) × 100/400 (the number of NHCEs in the Plan P prior year subgroup divided by the total number of NHCEs in all prior year subgroups). Thus, the prior year ADP for NHCEs under Plan OP for the 2006 plan year is 5.5% (the sum of adjusted ADPs for the prior year subgroups, 4.5% plus 1%).

(v) As provided in paragraph (c)(4)(iii)(B) of this section, the determination of whether an NHCE is a member of a prior year subgroup is made without regard to whether that NHCE terminated employed during the prior year. Thus, the prior ADP for the NHCEs under Plan OP for the 2006 plan year is unaffected by the termination of the 60 NHCEs covered by Plan O during the 2005 plan year.

Example 2. (i) The facts are the same as *Example 1*, except that the 60 employees who terminated employment during the 2005 plan are instead spun-off to another plan.

(ii) The permissive aggregation of Plan O and Plan P for the 2006 plan year under §1.410(b)-7(d) is a plan coverage change that results in treating the plans as one plan (Plan OP) for purposes of §1.401(k)-1(b)(4) and the spin-off of the 60 employees is a plan coverage change. Therefore, the prior year ADP for the NHCEs under Plan OP for the 2006 plan year is the weighted average of the ADPs for the prior year subgroups: the Plan O prior year subgroup and the Plan P prior year subgroup.

(iii) For purposes of determining the prior year subgroups, the employees who would have been eligible employees in the prior year under the plan being tested are determined as if both plan coverage changes had first been effective as of the first day of the prior plan year. The Plan O prior year subgroup consists of the 240 employees who, in the 2005 plan year, were eligible NHCEs under Plan O and would have been eligible under Plan OP for the 2005 plan year if the spin-off had occurred at the beginning of the 2005 plan year and Plan O and Plan P had been permissively aggregated under §1.410(b)-7(d) for that plan year. The Plan P prior year subgroup consists of the 100 employees who, in the 2005 plan year, were eligible NHCEs under Plan P and would have been eligible under Plan OP for the 2005 plan year if Plan O and Plan P had been permissively aggregated under §1.410(b)-7(d) for that plan year.

(iv) The weighted average of the ADPs for the prior year subgroups is the sum of the adjusted ADP with respect to the prior year subgroup consisting of eligible NHCEs from Plan O and the adjusted ADP with respect to the prior year subgroup consisting of eligible NHCEs from Plan P. The adjusted ADP for the prior year subgroup consisting of eligible NHCEs under Plan O is 4.23%, calculated as follows: 6% (the ADP for the NHCEs under Plan O for the 2005 plan year) × 240/340 (the number of NHCEs in that prior year subgroup divided by the total number of NHCEs in all prior year subgroups). The adjusted ADP for the prior year subgroup consisting of the eligible NHCEs from Plan P is 1.18%, calculated as follows: 4% (the ADP for the NHCEs under Plan P for the 2005 plan year) × 100/340 (the number of NHCEs in that prior year subgroup divided by the total number of NHCEs in all prior year subgroups). Thus, the prior year ADP for NHCEs under Plan OP for the 2006 plan year is 5.41% (the sum of adjusted ADPs for the prior year subgroups, 4.23% plus 1.18%).

Example 3. (i) The facts are the same as in *Example 1*, except that instead of Plan O and Plan P being permissively aggregated for the 2006 plan year, 200 of the employees eligible under Plan O were spun-off from Plan O and merged into Plan P.

(ii) The spin-off from Plan O and merger to Plan P for the 2006 plan year are plan coverage changes for Plan P. Therefore, the prior year ADP for the NHCEs under Plan P for the 2006 plan year is the weighted average of the ADPs for the prior year subgroups under Plan P. There are 2 subgroups under Plan P for the 2006 plan year. The Plan O prior year subgroup consists of the 200 employees who, in the 2005 plan year, were eligible NHCEs under Plan O and who would have been eligible under Plan P for the 2005 plan year if the spin-off and merger had occurred on the first day of the 2005 plan year. The Plan P prior year subgroup consists of the 100 employees who, in the 2005 plan year, were eligible NHCEs under Plan P for the 2005 plan year.

(iii) The weighted average of the ADPs for the prior year subgroups is the sum of the adjusted ADP for the Plan O prior year subgroup and

the adjusted ADP for the Plan P prior year subgroup. The adjusted ADP for the Plan O prior year subgroup is 4.0%, calculated as follows: 6% (the ADP for the NHCEs under Plan O for the 2005 plan year) × 200/300 (the number of NHCEs in the Plan O prior year subgroup divided by the total number of NHCEs in all prior year subgroups). The adjusted ADP for the Plan P prior year subgroup is 1.33%, calculated as follows: 4% (the ADP for the NHCEs under Plan P for the 2005 plan year) × 100/300 (the number of NHCEs in the Plan P prior year subgroup divided by the total number of NHCEs in all prior year subgroups). Thus, the prior year ADP for NHCEs under Plan P for the 2006 plan year is 5.33% (the sum of adjusted ADPs for the 2 prior year subgroups, 4.0% plus 1.33%).

(iv) The spin-off from Plan O for the 2006 plan year is a plan coverage change for Plan O. Therefore, the prior year ADP for the NHCEs under Plan O for the 2006 plan year is the weighted average of the ADPs for the prior year subgroups under Plan O. In this case, there is only one prior year subgroup under Plan O, the employees who were NHCEs of Employer B for the 2005 plan year and who were eligible for the 2005 plan year under Plan O. Because there is only one prior year subgroup under Plan O, the weighted average of the ADPs for the prior year subgroup under Plan O is equal to the NHCE ADP for the prior year (2005 plan year) under Plan O, or 6%.

Example 4. (i) Employer C maintains a calendar year plan, Plan Q, which includes a cash or deferred arrangement that uses the prior year testing method. Plan Q covers employees of Division A and Division B. In 2005, Plan Q had 500 eligible employees who were NHCEs, and the ADP for those NHCEs for 2005 was 2%. Effective January 1, 2006, Employer C amends the eligibility provisions under Plan Q to exclude employees of Division B effective January 1, 2006. In addition, effective on that same date, Employer C establishes a new calendar year plan, Plan R, which includes a cash or deferred arrangement that uses the prior year testing method. The only eligible employees under Plan R are the 100 employees of Division B who were eligible employees under Plan Q.

(ii) Plan R is a successor plan, within the meaning of paragraph (c)(2)(iii) of this section (because all of the employees were eligible employees under Plan Q in the prior year). Therefore, Plan R cannot use the first plan year rule set forth in paragraph (c)(2)(i) of this section.

(iii) The amendment to the eligibility provisions of Plan Q and the establishment of Plan R are plan coverage changes within the meaning of paragraph (c)(4)(iii)(A) of this section for Plan Q and Plan R. Accordingly, each plan must determine the NHCE ADP for the 2006 plan year under the rules set forth in paragraph (c)(4) of this section.

(iv) The prior year ADP for NHCEs under Plan Q is the weighted average of the ADPs for the prior year subgroups. Plan Q has only one prior year subgroup (because the only NHCEs who would have been eligible employees under Plan Q for the 2005 plan year if the amendment to the Plan Q eligibility provisions had occurred as of the first day of that plan year were eligible employees under Plan Q). Therefore, for purposes of the 2006 plan year under Plan Q, the ADP for NHCEs for the prior year is the weighted average of the ADPs for the prior year subgroups, or 2%, the same as if the plan amendment had not occurred.

(v) Similarly, Plan R has only one prior year subgroup (because the only NHCEs who would have been eligible employees under Plan R for the 2005 plan year if the plan were established as of the first day of that plan year were eligible employees under Plan Q). Therefore, for purposes of the 2006 testing year under Plan R, the ADP for NHCEs for the prior year is the weighted average of the ADPs for the prior year subgroups, or 2%, the same as that of Plan Q.

Example 5. (i) The facts are the same as in *Example 4*, except that the provisions of Plan R extend eligibility to 50 hourly employees who previously were not eligible employees under any qualified cash or deferred arrangement maintained by Employer C.

(ii) Plan R is a successor plan (because 100 of Plan R's 150 eligible employees were eligible employees under another qualified cash or deferred arrangement maintained by Employer C in the prior year). Therefore, Plan R cannot use the first plan year rule set forth in paragraph (c)(2)(i) of this section.

(iii) The establishment of Plan R is a plan coverage change that affects Plan R. Because the 50 hourly employees were not eligible employees under any qualified cash or deferred arrangement of Employer C for the prior plan year, they do not comprise a prior year subgroup. Accordingly, Plan R still has only one prior year subgroup. Therefore, for purposes of the 2006 testing year under Plan R, the ADP for NHCEs for the prior year is the weighted average of the ADPs for the prior year subgroups, or 2%, the same as that of Plan Q.

§ 1.401(k)-3 Safe harbor requirements.

(a) *ADP test safe harbor.* A cash or deferred arrangement satisfies the ADP safe harbor provision of section 401(k)(12) for a plan year if the arrangement satisfies the safe harbor contribution requirement of paragraph (b) or (c) of this section for the plan year, the notice requirement of paragraph (d) of this section, the plan year requirements of paragraph (e) of this section, and the additional rules of paragraphs (f), (g) and (h) of this section, as applicable. Pursuant to section 401(k)(12)(E)(ii), the safe harbor contribution requirement of paragraph (b) or (c) of this section must be satisfied without regard to section 401(l). The contributions made under paragraphs (b) and (c) of this section are referred to as safe harbor nonelective contributions and safe harbor matching contributions, respectively.

(b) *Safe harbor nonelective contribution requirement*—(1) *General rule.* The safe harbor nonelective contribution requirement of this paragraph is satisfied if, under the terms of the plan, the employer is required to make a qualified nonelective contribution on behalf of each eligible NHCE equal to at least 3% of the employee's safe harbor compensation.

(2) *Safe harbor compensation defined.* For purposes of this section, safe harbor compensation means compensation as defined in § 1.401(k)-6 (which incorporates the definition of compensation in § 1.414(s)-1); provided, however, that the rule in the last sentence of § 1.414(s)-1(d)(2)(iii) (which generally permits a definition of compensation to exclude all compensation in excess of a specified dollar amount) does not apply in determining the safe harbor compensation of NHCEs. Thus, for example, the plan may limit the period used to determine safe harbor compensation to the eligible employee's period of participation.

(c) *Safe harbor matching contribution requirement*—(1) *In general.* The safe harbor matching contribution requirement of this paragraph (c) is satisfied if, under the plan, qualified matching contributions are made on behalf of each eligible NHCE in an amount determined under the basic matching formula of section 401(k)(12)(B)(i)(I), as described in paragraph (c)(2) of this section, or under an enhanced matching formula of section 401(k)(12)(B)(i)(II), as described in paragraph (c)(3) of this section.

(2) *Basic matching formula.* Under the basic matching formula, each eligible NHCE receives qualified matching contributions in an amount equal to the sum of—

(i) 100% of the amount of the employee's elective contributions that do not exceed 3% of the employee's safe harbor compensation; and

(ii) 50% of the amount of the employee's elective contributions that exceed 3% of the employee's safe harbor compensation but that do not exceed 5% of the employee's safe harbor compensation.

(3) *Enhanced matching formula.* Under an enhanced matching formula, each eligible NHCE receives a matching contribution under a formula that, at any rate of elective contributions by the employee, provides an aggregate amount of qualified matching contributions at least equal to the aggregate amount of qualified matching contributions that would have been provided under the basic matching formula of paragraph (c)(2) of this section. In addition, under an enhanced matching formula, the ratio of matching contributions on behalf of an employee under the plan for a plan year to the employee's elective contributions may not increase as the amount of an employee's elective contributions increases.

(4) *Limitation on HCE matching contributions.* The safe harbor matching contribution requirement of this paragraph (c) is not satisfied if the ratio of matching contributions made on account of an HCE's elective contributions under the cash or deferred arrangement for a plan year to those elective contributions is greater than the ratio of matching contributions to elective contributions that would apply with respect to any eligible NHCE with elective contributions at the same percentage of safe harbor compensation.

(5) *Use of safe harbor match not precluded by certain plan provisions*— (i) *Safe harbor matching contributions on employee contributions.* The safe harbor matching contribution requirement of this paragraph (c) will not fail to be satisfied merely because safe harbor matching contributions are made on both elective contributions and employee contributions if safe harbor matching contributions are made with respect to the sum of elective contributions and employee contributions on the same terms as safe harbor matching contributions are made with respect to elective contributions. Alternatively, the safe harbor matching contribution requirement of this paragraph (c) will not fail to be satisfied merely because safe harbor matching contributions are made on both elective contributions and employee contribu-

tions if safe harbor matching contributions on elective contributions are not affected by the amount of employee contributions.

(ii) *Periodic matching contributions.* The safe harbor matching contribution requirement of this paragraph (c) will not fail to be satisfied merely because the plan provides that safe harbor matching contributions will be made separately with respect to each payroll period (or with respect to all payroll periods ending with or within each month or quarter of a plan year) taken into account under the plan for the plan year, provided that safe harbor matching contributions with respect to any elective contributions made during a plan year quarter are contributed to the plan by the last day of the immediately following plan year quarter.

(6) *Permissible restrictions on elective contributions by NHCEs*—(i) *General rule.* The safe harbor matching contribution requirement of this paragraph (c) is not satisfied if elective contributions by NHCEs are restricted, unless the restrictions are permitted by this paragraph (c)(6).

(ii) *Restrictions on election periods.* A plan may limit the frequency and duration of periods in which eligible employees may make or change cash or deferred elections under a plan. However, an employee must have a reasonable opportunity (including a reasonable period after receipt of the notice described in paragraph (d) of this section) to make or change a cash or deferred election for the plan year. For purposes of this paragraph (c)(6)(ii), a 30-day period is deemed to be a reasonable period to make or change a cash or deferred election.

(iii) *Restrictions on amount of elective contributions.* A plan is permitted to limit the amount of elective contributions that may be made by an eligible employee under a plan, provided that each NHCE who is an eligible employee is permitted (unless the employee is restricted under paragraph (c)(6)(v) of this section) to make elective contributions in an amount that is at least sufficient to receive the maximum amount of matching contributions available under the plan for the plan year, and the employee is permitted to elect any lesser amount of elective contributions. However, a plan may require eligible employees to make cash or deferred elections in whole percentages of compensation or whole dollar amounts.

(iv) *Restrictions on types of compensation that may be deferred.* A plan may limit the types of compensation that may be deferred by an eligible employee under a plan, provided that each eligible NHCE is permitted to make elective contributions under a definition of compensation that would be a reasonable definition of compensation within the meaning of § 1.414(s)-1(d)(2). Thus, the definition of compensation from which elective contributions may be made is not required to satisfy the nondiscrimination requirement of § 1.414(s)-1(d)(3).

(v) *Restrictions due to limitations under the Internal Revenue Code.* A plan may limit the amount of elective contributions made by an eligible employee under a plan—

(A) Because of the limitations of section 402(g) or section 415; or

(B) Because, on account of a hardship distribution, an employee's ability to make elective contributions has been suspended for 6 months in accordance with § 1.401(k)-1(d)(3)(iv)(E).

(7) *Examples.* The following examples illustrate the safe harbor contribution requirement of this paragraph (c):

Example 1. (i) Beginning January 1, 2006, Employer A maintains Plan L covering employees (including HCEs and NHCEs) in Divisions D and E. Plan L contains a cash or deferred arrangement and provides qualified matching contributions equal to 100% of each eligible employee's elective contributions up to 3% of compensation and 50% of the next 2% of compensation. For purposes of the matching contribution formula, safe harbor compensation is defined as all compensation within the meaning of section 415(c)(3) (a definition that satisfies section 414(s)). Also, each employee is permitted to make elective contributions from all safe harbor compensation within the meaning of section 415(c)(3) and may change a cash or deferred election at any time. Plan L limits the amount of an employee's elective contributions for purposes of section 402(g) and section 415, and, in the case of a hardship distribution, suspends an employee's ability to make elective contributions for 6 months in accordance with § 1.401(k)-1(d)(3)(iv)(E). All contributions under Plan L are nonforfeitable and are subject to the withdrawal restrictions of section 401(k)(2)(B). Plan L provides for no other contributions and Employer A maintains no other plans. Plan L is maintained on a calendar-year basis and all contributions for a plan year are made within 12 months after the end of the plan year.

(ii) Based on these facts, matching contributions under Plan L are safe harbor matching contributions because they are qualified matching contributions equal to the basic matching formula. Accordingly,

Plan L satisfies the safe harbor contribution requirement of this paragraph (c).

Example 2. (i) The facts are the same as in *Example 1*, except that instead of providing a basic matching contribution, Plan L provides a qualified matching contribution equal to 100% of each eligible employee's elective contributions up to 4% of safe harbor compensation.

(ii) Plan L's formula is an enhanced matching formula because each eligible NHCE receives safe harbor matching contributions at a rate that, at any rate of elective contributions, provides an aggregate amount of qualified matching contributions at least equal to the aggregate amount of qualified matching contributions that would have been received under the basic safe harbor matching formula, and the rate of matching contributions does not increase as the rate of an employee's elective contributions increases. Accordingly, Plan L satisfies the safe harbor contribution requirement of this paragraph (c).

Example 3. (i) The facts are the same as in *Example 1*, except that instead of permitting each employee to make elective contributions from all compensation within the meaning of section 415(c)(3), each employee's elective contributions under Plan L are limited to 15% of the employee's "basic compensation." Basic compensation is defined under Plan L as compensation within the meaning of section 415(c)(3), but excluding overtime pay.

(ii) The definition of basic compensation under Plan L is a reasonable definition of compensation within the meaning of § 1.414(s)-1(d)(2).

(iii) Plan L will not fail to satisfy the safe harbor contribution requirement of this paragraph (c) merely because Plan L limits the amount of elective contributions and the types of compensation that may be deferred by eligible employees, provided that each eligible NHCE may make elective contributions equal to at least 4% of the employee's safe harbor compensation.

Example 4. (i) The facts are the same as in *Example 1*, except that Plan L provides that only employees employed on the last day of the plan year will receive a safe harbor matching contribution.

(ii) Even if the plan that provides for employee contributions and matching contributions satisfies the minimum coverage requirements of section 410(b)(1) taking into account this last-day requirement, Plan L would not satisfy the safe harbor contribution requirement of this paragraph (c) because safe harbor matching contributions are not made on behalf of all eligible NHCEs who make elective contributions.

(iii) The result would be the same if, instead of providing safe harbor matching contributions under an enhanced formula, Plan L provides for a 3% safe harbor nonelective contribution that is restricted to eligible employees under the cash or deferred arrangement who are employed on the last day of the plan year.

Example 5. (i) The facts are the same as in *Example 1*, except that instead of providing qualified matching contributions under the basic matching formula to employees in both Divisions D and E, employees in Division E are provided qualified matching contributions under the basic matching formula, while safe harbor matching contributions continue to be provided to employees in Division D under the enhanced matching formula described in *Example 2*.

(ii) Even if Plan L satisfies § 1.401(a)(4)-4 with respect to each rate of matching contributions available to employees under the plan, the plan would fail to satisfy the safe harbor contribution requirement of this paragraph (c) because the rate of matching contributions with respect to HCEs in Division D at a rate of elective contributions between 3% and 5% would be greater than that with respect to NHCEs in Division E at the same rate of elective contributions. For example, an HCE in Division D who would have a 4% rate of elective contributions would have a rate of matching contributions of 100% while an NHCE in Division E who would have the same rate of elective contributions would have a lower rate of matching contributions.

(d) *Notice requirement*—(1) *General rule.* The notice requirement of this paragraph (d) is satisfied for a plan year if each eligible employee is given written notice of the employee's rights and obligations under the plan and the notice satisfies the content requirement of paragraph (d)(2) of this section and the timing requirement of paragraph (d)(3) of this section.

(2) *Content requirement*—(i) *General rule.* The content requirement of this paragraph (d)(2) is satisfied if the notice is—

(A) Sufficiently accurate and comprehensive to inform the employee of the employee's rights and obligations under the plan; and

(B) Written in a manner calculated to be understood by the average employee eligible to participate in the plan.

(ii) *Minimum content requirement.* Subject to the requirements of paragraph (d)(2)(iii) of this section, a notice is not considered sufficiently accurate and comprehensive unless the notice accurately describes—

(A) The safe harbor matching contribution or safe harbor nonelective contribution formula used under the plan (including a description of the levels of safe harbor matching contributions, if any, available under the plan);

(B) Any other contributions under the plan or matching contributions to another plan on account of elective contributions or employee contributions under the plan (including the potential for discretionary matching contributions) and the conditions under which such contributions are made;

(C) The plan to which safe harbor contributions will be made (if different than the plan containing the cash or deferred arrangement);

(D) The type and amount of compensation that may be deferred under the plan;

(E) How to make cash or deferred elections, including any administrative requirements that apply to such elections;

(F) The periods available under the plan for making cash or deferred elections;

(G) Withdrawal and vesting provisions applicable to contributions under the plan; and

(H) Information that makes it easy to obtain additional information about the plan (including an additional copy of the summary plan description) such as telephone numbers, addresses and, if applicable, electronic addresses, of individuals or offices from whom employees can obtain such plan information.

(iii) *References to SPD.* A plan will not fail to satisfy the content requirements of this paragraph (d)(2) merely because, in the case of information described in paragraph (d)(2)(ii)(B) of this section (relating to any other contributions under the plan), paragraph (d)(2)(ii)(C) of this section (relating to the plan to which safe harbor contributions will be made) or paragraph (d)(2)(ii)(D) of this section (relating to the type and amount of compensation that may be deferred under the plan), the notice cross-references the relevant portions of a summary plan description that provides the same information that would be provided in accordance with such paragraphs and that has been provided (or is concurrently provided) to employees.

(3) *Timing requirement*—(i) *General rule.* The timing requirement of this paragraph (d)(3) is satisfied if the notice is provided within a reasonable period before the beginning of the plan year (or, in the year an employee becomes eligible, within a reasonable period before the employee becomes eligible). The determination of whether a notice satisfies the timing requirement of this paragraph (d)(3) is based on all of the relevant facts and circumstances.

(ii) *Deemed satisfaction of timing requirement.* The timing requirement of this paragraph (d)(3) is deemed to be satisfied if at least 30 days (and no more than 90 days) before the beginning of each plan year, the notice is given to each eligible employee for the plan year. In the case of an employee who does not receive the notice within the period described in the previous sentence because the employee becomes eligible after the 90th day before the beginning of the plan year, the timing requirement is deemed to be satisfied if the notice is provided no more than 90 days before the employee becomes eligible (and no later than the date the employee becomes eligible). Thus, for example, the preceding sentence would apply in the case of any employee eligible for the first plan year under a newly established plan that provides for elective contributions, or would apply in the case of the first plan year in which an employee becomes eligible under an existing plan that provides for elective contributions.

(e) *Plan year requirement*—(1) *General rule.* Except as provided in this paragraph (e) or in paragraph (f) of this section, a plan will fail to satisfy the requirements of section 401(k)(12) and this section unless plan provisions that satisfy the rules of this section are adopted before the first day of the plan year and remain in effect for an entire 12-month plan year. Moreover, if, as described under paragraph (g)(4) of this section, safe harbor matching or nonelective contributions will be made to another plan for a plan year, provisions specifying that the safe harbor contributions will be made in the other plan and providing that the contributions will be QNECs or QMACs must also be adopted before the first day of that plan year.

(2) *Initial plan year.* A newly established plan (other than a successor plan within the meaning of § 1.401(k)-2(c)(2)(iii)) will not be treated as violating the requirements of this paragraph (e) merely because the plan year is less than 12 months, provided that the plan

year is at least 3 months long (or, in the case of a newly established employer that establishes the plan as soon as administratively feasible after the employer comes into existence, a shorter period). Similarly, a cash or deferred arrangement will not fail to satisfy the requirement of this paragraph (e) if it is added to an existing profit sharing, stock bonus, or pre-ERISA money purchase pension plan for the first time during that year provided that—

(i) The plan is not a successor plan; and

(ii) The cash or deferred arrangement is made effective no later than 3 months prior to the end of the plan year.

(3) *Change of plan year.* A plan that has a short plan year as a result of changing its plan year will not fail to satisfy the requirements of paragraph (e)(1) of this section merely because the plan year has less than 12 months, provided that—

(i) The plan satisfied the requirements of this section for the immediately preceding plan year; and

(ii) The plan satisfies the requirements of this section for the immediately following plan year.

(4) *Final plan year.* A plan that terminates during a plan year will not fail to satisfy the requirements of paragraph (e)(1) of this section merely because the final plan year is less than 12 months, provided that—

(i) The plan would satisfy the requirements of paragraph (g) of this section, treating the termination of the plan as a reduction or suspension of safe harbor matching contributions, other than the requirement that employees have a reasonable opportunity to change their cash or deferred elections and, if applicable, employee contribution elections; or

(ii) The plan termination is in connection with a transaction described in section 410(b)(6)(C) or the employer incurs a substantial business hardship comparable to a substantial business hardship described in section 412(d).

(f) *Plan amendments adopting safe harbor nonelective contributions—* (1) *General rule.* Notwithstanding paragraph (e)(1) of this section, a plan that provides for the use of the current year testing method may be amended after the first day of the plan year and no later than 30 days before the last day of the plan year to adopt the safe harbor method of this section using nonelective contributions under paragraph (b) of this section, but only if the plan provides the contingent and follow-up notices described in this section. A plan amendment made pursuant to this paragraph (f)(1) for a plan year may provide for the use of the safe harbor method described in this section solely for that plan year and a plan sponsor is not limited in the number of years for which it is permitted to adopt an amendment providing for the safe harbor method of this section using nonelective contributions under paragraph (b) of this section.

(2) *Contingent notice provided.* A plan satisfies the requirement to provide the contingent notice under this paragraph (f)(2) if it provides a notice that would satisfy the requirements of paragraph (d) of this section, except that, in lieu of setting forth the safe harbor contributions used under the plan as set forth in paragraph (d)(2)(ii)(A) of this section, the notice specifies that the plan may be amended during the plan year to include the safe harbor nonelective contribution and that, if the plan is amended, a follow-up notice will be provided.

(3) *Follow-up notice requirement.* A plan satisfies the requirement to provide a follow-up notice under this paragraph (f)(3) if, no later than 30 days before the last day of the plan year, each eligible employee is given a notice that states that the safe harbor nonelective contributions will be made for the plan year. This notice is permitted to be combined with a contingent notice provided under paragraph (f)(2) of this section for the next plan year.

(g) *Permissible reduction or suspension of safe harbor matching contributions—*(1) *General rule.* A plan that provides for safe harbor matching contributions will not fail to satisfy the requirements of section 401(k)(3) for a plan year merely because the plan is amended during a plan year to reduce or suspend safe harbor matching contributions on future elective contributions (and, if applicable, employee contributions) provided that—

(i) All eligible employees are provided the supplemental notice in accordance with paragraph (g)(2) of this section;

(ii) The reduction or suspension of safe harbor matching contributions is effective no earlier than the later of 30 days after eligible employees are provided the notice described in paragraph (g)(2) of this section and the date the amendment is adopted;

(iii) Eligible employees are given a reasonable opportunity (including a reasonable period after receipt of the supplemental notice) prior to the reduction or suspension of safe harbor matching contributions to change their cash or deferred elections and, if applicable, their employee contribution elections;

(iv) The plan is amended to provide that the ADP test will be satisfied for the entire plan year in which the reduction or suspension occurs using the current year testing method described in § 1.401(k)-2(a)(2)(ii); and

(v) The plan satisfies the requirements of this section (other than this paragraph (g)) with respect to amounts deferred through the effective date of the amendment.

(2) *Notice of suspension requirement.* The notice of suspension requirement of this paragraph (g)(2) is satisfied if each eligible employee is given a written notice that explains—

(i) The consequences of the amendment which reduces or suspends matching contributions on future elective contributions and, if applicable, employee contributions;

(ii) The procedures for changing their cash or deferred election and, if applicable, their employee contribution elections; and

(iii) The effective date of the amendment.

(h) *Additional rules—*(1) *Contributions taken into account.* A contribution is taken into account for purposes of this section for a plan year if and only if the contribution would be taken into account for such plan year under the rules of § 1.401(k)-2(a) or 1.401(m)-2(a). Thus, for example, a safe harbor matching contribution must be made within 12 months of the end of the plan year. Similarly, an elective contribution that would be taken into account for a plan year under § 1.401(k)-2(a)(4)(i)(B)(*2*) must be taken into account for such plan year for purposes of this section, even if the compensation would have been received after the close of the plan year.

(2) *Use of safe harbor nonelective contributions to satisfy other nondiscrimination tests.* A safe harbor nonelective contribution used to satisfy the nonelective contribution requirement under paragraph (b) of this section may also be taken into account for purposes of determining whether a plan satisfies section 401(a)(4). Thus, these contributions are not subject to the limitations on qualified nonelective contributions under § 1.401(k)-2(a)(6)(ii), but are subject to the rules generally applicable to nonelective contributions under section 401(a)(4). See § 1.401(a)(4)-1(b)(2)(ii). However, pursuant to section 401(k)(12)(E)(ii), to the extent they are needed to satisfy the safe harbor contribution requirement of paragraph (b) of this section, safe harbor nonelective contributions may not be taken into account under any plan for purposes of section 401(I) (including the imputation of permitted disparity under § 1.401(a)(4)-7).

(3) *Early participation rules.* Section 401(k)(3)(F) and § 1.401(k)-2(a)(1)(iii)(A), which provide an alternative nondiscrimination rule for certain plans that provide for early participation, do not apply for purposes of section 401(k)(12) and this section. Thus, a plan is not treated as satisfying this section with respect to the eligible employees who have not completed the minimum age and service requirements of section 410(a)(1)(A) unless the plan satisfies the requirements of this section with respect to such eligible employees.

(4) *Satisfying safe harbor contribution requirement under another defined contribution plan.* Safe harbor matching or nonelective contributions may be made to the plan that contains the cash or deferred arrangement or to another defined contribution plan that satisfies section 401(a) or 403(a). If safe harbor contributions are made to another defined contribution plan, the safe harbor plan must specify the plan to which the safe harbors are made and contribution requirement of paragraph (b) or (c) of this section must be satisfied in the other defined contribution plan in the same manner as if the contributions were made to the plan that contains the cash or deferred arrangement. Consequently, the plan to which the contributions are made must have the same plan year as the plan containing the cash and deferred arrangement and each employee eligible under the plan containing the cash or deferred arrangement must be eligible under the same conditions under the other defined contribution plan. The plan to which the safe harbor contributions are made need not be a plan that can be aggregated with the plan that contains the cash or deferred arrangement.

(5) *Contributions used only once.* Safe harbor matching or nonelective contributions cannot be used to satisfy the requirements of this section with respect to more than one plan.

§ 1.401(k)-4 SIMPLE 401(k) plan requirements.

(a) *General rule.* A cash or deferred arrangement satisfies the SIMPLE 401(k) plan provision of section 401(k)(11) for a plan year if the arrangement satisfies the requirements of paragraphs (b) through (i) of this section for that year. A plan that contains a cash or deferred arrangement that satisfies this section is referred to as a SIMPLE 401(k) plan. Pursuant to section 401(k)(11), a SIMPLE 401(k) plan is treated as satisfying the ADP test of section 401(k)(3)(A)(ii) for that year.

(b) *Eligible employer*—(1) *General rule.* A SIMPLE 401(k) plan must be established by an eligible employer. Eligible employer for purposes of this section means, with respect to any plan year, an employer that had no more than 100 employees who received at least $5,000 of SIMPLE compensation, as defined in paragraph (e)(5) of this section, from the employer for the prior calendar year.

(2) *Special rule.* An eligible employer that establishes a SIMPLE 401(k) plan for a plan year and that fails to be an eligible employer for any subsequent plan year, is treated as an eligible employer for the 2 plan years following the last plan year the employer was an eligible employer. If the failure is due to any acquisition, disposition, or similar transaction involving an eligible employer, the preceding sentence applies only if the provisions of section 410(b)(6)(C)(i) are satisfied.

(c) *Exclusive plan*—(1) *General rule.* The SIMPLE 401(k) plan must be the exclusive plan for each SIMPLE 401(k) plan participant for the plan year. This requirement is satisfied if there are no contributions made, or benefits accrued, for services during the plan year on behalf of any SIMPLE 401(k) plan participant under any other qualified plan maintained by the employer. Other qualified plan for purposes of this section means any plan, contract, pension, or trust described in section 219(g)(5)(A) or (B).

(2) *Special rule.* A SIMPLE 401(k) plan will not be treated as failing the requirements of this paragraph (c) merely because any SIMPLE 401(k) plan participant receives an allocation of forfeitures under another plan of the employer.

(d) *Election and notice*—(1) *General rule.* An eligible employer establishing or maintaining a SIMPLE 401(k) plan must satisfy the election and notice requirements in paragraphs (d)(2) and (d)(3) of this section.

(2) *Employee elections*—(i) *Initial plan year of participation.* For the plan year in which an employee first becomes eligible under the SIMPLE 401(k) plan, the employee must be permitted to make a cash or deferred election under the plan during a 60-day period that includes either the day the employee becomes eligible or the day before.

(ii) *Subsequent plan years.* For each subsequent plan year, each eligible employee must be permitted to make or modify his cash or deferred election during the 60-day period immediately preceding such plan year.

(iii) *Election to terminate.* An eligible employee must be permitted to terminate his cash or deferred election at any time. If an employee does terminate his cash or deferred election, the plan is permitted to provide that such employee cannot have elective contributions made under the plan for the remainder of the plan year.

(3) *Employee notices.* The employer must notify each eligible employee within a reasonable time prior to each 60-day election period, or on the day the election period starts, that he or she can make a cash or deferred election, or modify a prior election, if applicable, during that period. The notice must state whether the eligible employer will make the matching contributions described in paragraph (e)(3) of this section or the nonelective contributions described in paragraph (e)(4) of this section.

(e) *Contributions*—(1) *General rule.* A SIMPLE 401(k) plan satisfies the contribution requirements of this paragraph (e) for a plan year only if no contributions may be made to the SIMPLE 401(k) plan during such year, other than contributions described in this paragraph (e) and rollover contributions described in § 1.402(c)-2, Q&A-1(a).

(2) *Elective contributions.* Subject to the limitations on annual additions under section 415, each eligible employee must be permitted to make an election to have up to $10,000 of elective contributions made on the employee's behalf under the SIMPLE 401(k) plan for a plan year. The $10,000 limit is increased beginning in 2006 in the same manner as the $160,000 amount is adjusted under section 415(d), except that pursuant to section 408(p)(2)(E)(ii) the base period shall be the calendar quarter beginning July 1, 2004 and any increase which is not a multiple of $500 is rounded to the next lower multiple of $500.

(3) *Matching contributions.* Each plan year, the eligible employer must contribute a matching contribution to the account of each eligible employee on whose behalf elective contributions were made for the plan year. The amount of the matching contribution must equal the lesser of the eligible employee's elective contributions for the plan year or 3% of the eligible employee's SIMPLE compensation for the entire plan year.

(4) *Nonelective contributions.* For any plan year, in lieu of contributing matching contributions described in paragraph (e)(3) of this section, an eligible employer may, in accordance with plan terms, contribute a nonelective contribution to the account of each eligible employee in an amount equal to 2% of the eligible employee's SIMPLE compensation for the entire plan year. The eligible employer may limit the nonelective contributions to those eligible employees who received at least $5,000 of SIMPLE compensation from the employer for the entire plan year.

(5) *SIMPLE compensation.* Except as otherwise provided, the term SIMPLE compensation for purposes of this section means the sum of wages, tips, and other compensation from the eligible employer subject to federal income tax withholding (as described in section 6051(a)(3)) and the employee's elective contributions made under any other plan, and if applicable, elective deferrals under a section 408(p) SIMPLE IRA plan, a section 408(k)(6) SARSEP, or a plan or contract that satisfies the requirements of section 403(b), and compensation deferred under a section 457 plan, required to be reported by the employer on Form W-2 (as described in section 6051(a)(8)). For self-employed individuals, SIMPLE compensation means net earnings from self-employment determined under section 1402(a) prior to subtracting any contributions made under the SIMPLE 401(k) plan on behalf of the individual.

(f) *Vesting.* All benefits attributable to contributions described in paragraph (e) of this section must be nonforfeitable at all times.

(g) *Plan year.* The plan year of a SIMPLE 401(k) plan must be the whole calendar year. Thus, in general, a SIMPLE 401(k) plan can be established only on January 1 and can be terminated only on December 31. However, in the case of an employer that did not previously maintain a SIMPLE 401(k) plan, the establishment date can be as late as October 1 (or later in the case of an employer that comes into existence after October 1 and establishes the SIMPLE 401(k) plan as soon as administratively feasible after the employer comes into existence).

(h) *Other rules.* A SIMPLE 401(k) plan is not treated as a top-heavy plan under section 416. See section 416(g)(4)(G).

§ 1.401(k)-5 Special rules for mergers, acquisitions and similar events. [*Reserved*].

§ 1.401(k)-6 Definitions.

Unless otherwise provided, the definitions of this section govern for purposes of section 401(k) and the regulations thereunder.

Actual contribution percentage (ACP) test. Actual contribution percentage test or *ACP test* means the test described in § 1.401(m)-2(a)(1).

Actual deferral percentage (ADP). Actual deferral percentage or *ADP* means the ADP of the group of eligible employees as defined in § 1.401(k)-2(a)(2).

Actual deferral percentage (ADP) test. Actual deferral percentage test or *ADP test* means the test described in § 1.401(k)-2(a)(1).

Actual deferral ratio (ADR). Actual deferral ratio or *ADR* means the ADR of an eligible employee as defined in § 1.401(k)-2(a)(3).

Cash or deferred arrangement. Cash or deferred arrangement is defined in § 1.401(k)-1(a)(2).

Cash or deferred election. Cash or deferred election is defined in § 1.401(k)-1(a)(3).

Compensation. Compensation means compensation as defined in section 414(s) and § 1.414(s)-1. The period used to determine an employee's compensation for a plan year must be either the plan year or the calendar year ending within the plan year. Whichever period is selected must be applied uniformly to determine the compensation of every eligible employee under the plan for that plan year. A plan may, however, limit the period taken into account under either method to that portion of the plan year or calendar year in which the employee was an eligible employee, provided that this limit is applied uniformly to all eligible employees under the plan for the plan year. In the case of an HCE whose ADR is determined under § 1.401(k)-2(a)(3)(ii), period of participation includes periods under another plan for which elective contributions are aggregated under § 1.401(k)-2(a)(3)(ii). See also section 401(a)(17) and § 1.401(a)(17)-1(c)(1).

Current year testing method. Current year testing method means the testing method described in § 1.401(k)-2(a)(2)(ii) or § 1.401(m)-2(a)(2)(ii) under which the applicable year is the current plan year.

Elective contributions. Elective contributions means employer contributions made to a plan pursuant to a cash or deferred election under a cash or deferred arrangement (whether or not the arrangement is a qualified cash or deferred arrangement under § 1.401(k)-1(a)(4)).

Eligible employee—(1) *General rule. Eligible employee* means an employee who is directly or indirectly eligible to make a cash or deferred election under the plan for all or a portion of the plan year. For example, if an employee must perform purely ministerial or mechanical acts (e.g., formal application for participation or consent to payroll withholding) in order to be eligible to make a cash or deferred election for a plan year, the employee is an eligible employee for the plan year without regard to whether the employee performs the acts.

(2) *Conditions on eligibility.* An employee who is unable to make a cash or deferred election because the employee has not contributed to another plan is also an eligible employee. By contrast, if an employee must perform additional service (e.g., satisfy a minimum period of service requirement) in order to be eligible to make a cash or deferred election for a plan year, the employee is not an eligible employee for the plan year unless the service is actually performed. See § 1.401(k)-1(e)(5), however, for certain limits on the use of minimum service requirements. An employee who would be eligible to make elective contributions but for a suspension due to a distribution, a loan, or an election not to participate in the plan, is treated as an eligible employee for purposes of section 401(k)(3) for a plan year even though the employee may not make a cash or deferred election by reason of the suspension. Finally, an employee does not fail to be treated as an eligible employee merely because the employee may receive no additional annual additions because of section 415(c)(1).

(3) *Certain one-time elections.* An employee is not an eligible employee merely because the employee, upon commencing employment with the employer or upon the employee's first becoming eligible to make a cash or deferred election under any arrangement of the employer, is given the one-time opportunity to elect, and the employee does in fact elect, not to be eligible to make a cash or deferred election under the plan or any other plan maintained by the employer (including plans not yet established) for the duration of the employee's employment with the employer. This rule applies in addition to the rules in § 1.401(k)-1(a)(3)(v) relating to the definition of a cash or deferred election. In no event is an election made after December 23, 1994, treated as a one-time irrevocable election under this paragraph if the election is made by an employee who previously became eligible under another plan (whether or not terminated) of the employer.

Eligible HCE. Eligible HCE means an eligible employee who is an HCE.

Eligible NHCE. Eligible NHCE means an eligible employee who is not an HCE.

Employee. Employee means an employee within the meaning of § 1.410(b)-9.

Employee stock ownership plan (ESOP). Employee stock ownership plan or *ESOP* means the portion of a plan that is an ESOP within the meaning of § 1.410(b)-7(c)(2).

Employer. Employer means an employer within the meaning of § 1.410(b)-9.

Excess contributions. Excess contributions means, with respect to a plan year, the amount of total excess contributions apportioned to an HCE under § 1.401(k)-2(b)(2)(iii).

Excess deferrals. Excess deferrals means excess deferrals as defined in § 1.402(g)-1(e)(3).

Highly compensated employee (HCE). Highly compensated employee or *HCE* has the meaning provided in section 414(q).

Matching contributions. Matching contributions means matching contributions as defined in § 1.401(m)-1(a)(2).

Nonelective contributions. Nonelective contributions means employer contributions (other than matching contributions) with respect to which the employee may not elect to have the contributions paid to the employee in cash or other benefits instead of being contributed to the plan.

Non-employee stock ownership plan (non-ESOP). Non-employee stock ownership plan or *non-ESOP* means the portion of a plan that is not an ESOP within the meaning of § 1.410(b)-7(c)(2).

Non-highly compensated employee (NHCE). Non-highly compensated employee or *NHCE* means an employee who is not an HCE.

Plan. Plan is defined in § 1.401(k)-1(b)(4).

Pre-ERISA money purchase pension plan. (1) *Pre-ERISA money purchase pension plan* is a pension plan—

(i) That is a defined contribution plan (as defined in section 414(i));

(ii) That was in existence on June 27, 1974, and as in effect on that date, included a salary reduction agreement; and

(iii) Under which neither the employee contributions nor the employer contributions, including elective contributions, may exceed the levels (as a percentage of compensation) provided for by the contribution formula in effect on June 27, 1974.

(2) A plan was in existence on June 27, 1974, if it was a written plan adopted on or before that date, even if no funds had yet been paid to the trust associated with the plan.

Prior year testing method. Prior year testing method means the testing method under which the applicable year is the prior plan year, as described in § 1.401(k)-2(a)(2)(ii) or § 1.401(m)-2(a)(2)(ii).

Qualified matching contributions (QMACs). Qualified matching contributions or *QMACs* means matching contributions that, except as provided otherwise in § 1.401(k)-1(c) and (d), satisfy the requirements of § 1.401(k)-1(c) and (d) as though the contributions were elective contributions, without regard to whether the contributions are actually taken into account under the ADP test under § 1.401(k)-2(a)(6) or the ACP test under § 1.401(m)-2(a)(6). Thus, the matching contributions must satisfy the vesting requirements of § 1.401(k)-1(c) and be subject to the distribution requirements of § 1.401(k)-1(d) when they are contributed to the plan. See also § 1.401(k)-2(b)(4)(iii) for a rule providing that a matching contribution does not fail to qualify as a QMAC solely because it is forfeitable under section 411(a)(3)(G) because it is a matching contribution with respect to an excess deferral, excess contribution, or excess aggregate contribution.

Qualified nonelective contributions (QNECs). Qualified nonelective contributions or *QNECs* means employer contributions, other than elective contributions or matching contributions, that, except as provided otherwise in § 1.401(k)-1(c) and (d), satisfy the requirements of § 1.401(k)-1(c) and (d) as though the contributions were elective contributions, without regard to whether the contributions are actually taken into account under the ADP test under § 1.401(k)-2(a)(6) or the ACP test under § 1.401(m)-2(a)(6). Thus, the nonelective contributions must satisfy the vesting requirements of § 1.401(k)-1(c) and be subject to the distribution requirements of § 1.401(k)-1(d) when they are contributed to the plan.

Rural cooperative plans. Rural cooperative plan means a plan described in section 401(k)(7).

Par. 3. Sections 1.401(m)-0 through 1.401(m)-2 are revised, and §§ 1.401(m)-3 through 1.401(m)-5 are added to read as follows:

§ 1.401(m)-0 Table of contents.

This section contains first a list of section headings and then a list of the paragraphs in each section in §§ 1.401(m)-1 through 1.401(m)-5.

LIST OF SECTIONS

§ 1.401(m)-1 Employee contributions and matching contributions.

§ 1.401(m)-2 ACP test.

§ 1.401(m)-3 Safe harbor requirements.

§ 1.401(m)-4 Special rules for mergers, acquisitions and similar events. *[Reserved].*

§ 1.401(m)-5 Definitions.

LIST OF PARAGRAPHS

§ 1.401(m)-1 Employee contributions and matching contributions.

(a) General nondiscrimination rules.

(1) Nondiscriminatory amount of contributions.

(i) Exclusive means of amounts testing.

(ii) Testing benefits, rights and features.

(2) Matching contributions.

(i) In general.

(ii) Employer contributions made on account of an employee contribution or elective deferral.

(iii) Employer contributions not on account of an employee contribution or elective deferral.

(3) Employee contributions.

(i) In general.

(ii) Certain contributions not treated as employee contributions.

(iii) Qualified cost-of-living arrangements.

(b) Nondiscrimination requirements for amount of contributions.

(1) Matching contributions and employee contributions.

(2) Automatic satisfaction by certain plans.

(3) Anti-abuse provisions.

(4) Aggregation and restructuring.

(i) In general.

(ii) Aggregation of employee contributions and matching contributions within a plan.

(iii) Aggregation of plans.

(A) In general.

(B) Arrangements with inconsistent ACP testing methods.

(iv) Disaggregation of plans and separate testing.

(A) In general.

(B) Restructuring prohibited.

(v) Certain disaggregation rules not applicable.

(c) Additional requirements.

(1) Separate testing for employee contributions and matching contributions.

(2) Plan provision requirement.

(d) Effective date.

§ 1.401(m)-2 ACP test.

(a) Actual contribution percentage (ACP) test.

(1) In general.

(i) ACP test formula.

(ii) HCEs as sole eligible employees.

(iii) Special rule for early participation.

(2) Determination of ACP.

(i) General rule.

(ii) Determination of applicable year under current year and prior year testing method.

(3) Determination of ACR.

(i) General rule.

(ii) ACR of HCEs eligible under more than one plan.

(A) General rule.

(B) Plans not permitted to be aggregated.

(iii) Example.

(4) Employee contributions and matching contributions taken into account under the ACP test.

(i) Employee contributions.

(ii) Recharacterized elective contributions.

(iii) Matching contributions.

(5) Matching contributions not taken into account under the ACP test.

(i) General rule.

(ii) Disproportionate matching contributions.

(A) Matching contributions in excess of 100%.

(B) Representative matching rate.

(C) Definition of matching rate.

(iii) Qualified matching contributions used to satisfy the ADP test.

(iv) Matching contributions taken into account under safe harbor provisions.

(v) Treatment of forfeited matching contributions.

(6) Qualified nonelective contributions and elective contributions that may be taken into account under the ACP test.

(i) Timing of allocation.

(ii) Elective contributions taken into account under the ACP test.

(iii) Requirement that amount satisfy section 401(a)(4).

(iv) Aggregation must be permitted.

(v) Disproportionate contributions not taken into account.

(A) General rule.

(B) Definition of representative contribution rate.

(C) Definition of applicable contribution rate.

(vi) Contribution only used once.

(7) Examples.

(b) Correction of excess aggregate contributions.

(1) Permissible correction methods.

(i) In general.

(A) Additional contributions.

(B) Excess aggregate contributions distributed or forfeited.

(ii) Combination of correction methods.

(iii) Exclusive means of correction.

(2) Correction through distribution.

(i) General rule.

(ii) Calculation of total amount to be distributed.

(A) Calculate the dollar amount of excess aggregate contributions for each HCE.

(B) Determination of the total amount of excess aggregate contributions.

(C) Satisfaction of ACP.

(iii) Apportionment of total amount of excess aggregate contributions among the HCEs.

(A) Calculate the dollar amount of excess aggregate contributions for each HCE.

(B) Limit on amount apportioned to any HCE.

(C) Apportionment to additional HCEs.

(iv) Income allocable to excess aggregate contributions.

(A) General rule.

(B) Method of allocating income.

(C) Alternative method of allocating income for the plan year.

(D) Safe harbor method of allocating gap period income.

(E) Alternative method of allocating plan year and gap period income.

(F) Allocable income for recharacterized elective contributions.

(v) Distribution and forfeiture.

(vi) Tax treatment of corrective distributions.

(A) General rule.

(B) Rule for de minimis distributions.

(3) Other rules.

(i) No employee or spousal consent required.

(ii) Treatment of corrective distributions and forfeited contributions as employer contributions.

(iii) No reduction of required minimum distribution.

(iv) Partial correction.

(v) Matching contributions on excess contributions, excess deferrals and excess aggregate contributions.

(A) Corrective distributions not permitted.

(B) Coordination with section 401(a)(4).

(vi) No requirement for recalculation.

(4) Failure to timely correct.

(i) Failure to correct within 2 ½ months after end of plan year.

(ii) Failure to correct within 12 months after end of plan year.

(5) Examples.

(c) Additional rules for prior year testing method.

(1) Rules for change in testing method.

(2) Calculation of ACP under the prior year testing method for the first plan year.

(i) Plans that are not successor plans.

(ii) First plan year defined.

(iii) Plans that are successor plans.

(3) Plans using different testing methods for the ACP and ADP test.

(4) Rules for plan coverage change.

(i) In general.

(ii) Optional rule for minor plan coverage changes.

(iii) Definitions.

(A) Plan coverage change.

(B) Prior year subgroup.

(C) Weighted average of the ACPs for the prior year subgroups.

(iv) Examples.

§ 1.401(m)-3 Safe harbor requirements.

(a) ACP test safe harbor.

(b) Safe harbor nonelective contribution requirement.

(c) Safe harbor matching contribution requirement.

(d) Limitation on contributions.

(1) General rule.

(2) Matching rate must not increase.

(3) Limit on matching contributions.

(4) Limitation on rate of match.

(5) HCEs participating in multiple plans.

(6) Permissible restrictions on elective deferrals by NHCEs.

(i) General rule.

(ii) Restrictions on election periods.

(iii) Restrictions on amount of contributions.

(iv) Restrictions on types of compensation that may be deferred.

(v) Restrictions due to limitations under the Internal Revenue Code.

(e) Notice requirement.

(f) Plan year requirement.

(1) General rule.

(2) Initial plan year.

(3) Change of plan year.

(4) Final plan year.

(g) Plan amendments adopting nonelective safe harbor contributions.

(h) Permissible reduction or suspension of safe harbor matching contributions.

(1) General rule.

(2) Notice of suspension requirement.

(i) Reserved.

(j) Other rules.

(1) Contributions taken into account.

(2) Use of safe harbor nonelective contributions to satisfy other nondiscrimination tests.

(3) Early participation rules.

(4) Satisfying safe harbor contribution requirement under another defined contribution plan.

(5) Contributions used only once.

(6) Plan must satisfy ACP with respect to employee contributions.

§ 1.401(m)-4 Special rules for mergers, acquisitions and similar events. [Reserved].

§ 1.401(m)-5 Definitions.

§ 1.401(m)-1 Employee contributions and matching contributions.

(a) *General nondiscrimination rules*—(1) *Nondiscriminatory amount of contributions*—(i) *Exclusive means of amounts testing.* A defined contribution plan does not satisfy section 401(a) for a plan year unless the amount of employee contributions and matching contributions to the plan for the plan year satisfies section 401(a)(4). The amount of employee contributions and matching contributions under a plan satisfies the requirements of section 401(a)(4) with respect to amounts if and only if the amount of employee contributions and matching contributions satisfies the nondiscrimination test of section 401(m) under paragraph (b) of this section and the plan satisfies the additional requirements of paragraph (c) of this section. See § 1.401(a)(4)-1(b)(2)(ii)(B).

(ii) *Testing benefits, rights and features.* A plan that provides for employee contributions or matching contributions must satisfy the requirements of section 401(a)(4) relating to benefits, rights and features in addition to the requirement regarding amounts described in paragraph (a)(1)(i) of this section. For example, the right to make each level of employee contributions and the right to each level of matching contributions under the plan are benefits, rights or features subject to the requirements of section 401(a)(4). See § 1.401(a)(4)-4(e)(3)(i) and (iii)(F) through (G).

(2) *Matching contributions*—(i) *In general.* For purposes of section 401(m), this section and §§ 1.401(m)-2 through 1.401(m)-5, matching contributions are—

(A) Any employer contribution (including a contribution made at the employer's discretion) to a defined contribution plan on account of an employee contribution to a plan maintained by the employer;

(B) Any employer contribution (including a contribution made at the employer's discretion) to a defined contribution plan on account of an elective deferral; and

(C) Any forfeiture allocated on the basis of employee contributions, matching contributions, or elective deferrals.

(ii) *Employer contributions made on account of an employee contribution or elective deferral.* Whether an employer contribution is made on account of an employee contribution or an elective deferral is determined on the basis of all the relevant facts and circumstances, including the relationship between the employer contribution and employee actions outside the plan. An employer contribution made to a defined contribution plan on account of contributions made by an employee under an employer-sponsored savings arrangement that are not held in a plan that is intended to be a qualified plan or a plan described in § 1.402(g)-1(b) is not a matching contribution.

(iii) *Employer contributions not on account of an employee contribution or elective deferral.* An employer contribution is not a matching contribution made on account of an elective deferral if it is contributed before the cash or deferred election is made or before the employee's performance of services with respect to which the elective deferral is made (or when the cash that is subject to the cash or deferred election would be currently available, if earlier). In addition, an employer contribution is not a matching contribution made on account of an employee contribution if it is contributed before the employee contribution.

(3) *Employee contributions*—(i) *In general.* For purposes of section 401(m), this section and §§ 1.401(m)-2 through 1.401(m)-5, employee contributions are contributions to a plan that are designated or treated at the time of contribution as after-tax employee contributions (e.g., by treating the contributions as taxable income subject to applicable withholding requirements) and are allocated to an individual account for each eligible employee to which attributable earnings and losses are allocated. See § 1.401(k)-1(a)(2)(ii). The term *employee contributions* includes—

(A) Employee contributions to the defined contribution portion of a plan described in section 414(k);

(B) Employee contributions applied to the purchase of whole life insurance protection or survivor benefit protection under a defined contribution plan;

(C) Amounts attributable to excess contributions within the meaning of section 401(k)(8)(B) that are recharacterized as employee contributions under § 1.401(k)-2(b)(3); and

(D) Employee contributions to a plan or contract that satisfies the requirements of section 403(b).

(ii) *Certain contributions not treated as employee contributions.* The term employee contributions does not include repayment of loans, repayment of distributions described in section 411(a)(7)(C), or employee contributions that are transferred to the plan from another plan.

(iii) *Qualified cost-of-living arrangements.* Employee contributions to a qualified cost-of-living arrangement described in section 415(k)(2)(B) are treated as employee contributions to a defined contribution plan, without regard to the requirement that the employee contributions be allocated to an individual account to which attributable earnings and losses are allocated.

(b) *Nondiscrimination requirements for amount of contributions*—(1) *Matching contributions and employee contributions.* The matching contributions and employee contributions under a plan satisfy this paragraph (b) for a plan year only if the plan satisfies—

(i) The ACP test of section 401(m)(2) described in § 1.401(m)-2;

(ii) The ACP safe harbor provisions of section 401(m)(11) described in § 1.401(m)-3; or

(iii) The SIMPLE 401(k) provisions of sections 401(k)(11) and 401(m)(10) described in § 1.401(k)-4.

(2) *Automatic satisfaction by certain plans.* Notwithstanding paragraph (b)(1) of this section, the requirements of this section are treated as satisfied with respect to employee contributions and matching contributions under a collectively bargained plan (or the portion of a plan) that automatically satisfies section 410(b). See §§ 1.401(a)(4)-1(c)(5) and 1.401(k)-2(b)(7). Additionally, the requirements of sections 401(a)(4) and 410(b) do not apply to a governmental plan (within the meaning of section 414(d)) maintained by a State or local government or political subdivision thereof (or agency or instrumentality thereof). See sections 401(a)(5)(G), 403(b)(12)(C) and 410(c)(1)(A).

(3) *Anti-abuse provisions.* The regulations in this paragraph (a) are designed to provide simple, practical rules that accommodate legitimate plan changes. At the same time, the rules are intended to be applied by employers in a manner that does not make use of changes in plan testing procedures or other plan provisions to inflate inappropriately the ACP for NHCEs (which is used as a benchmark for testing the ACP for HCEs) or to otherwise manipulate the nondiscrimination testing requirements of this paragraph (b). Further, this paragraph (b) is part of the overall requirement that benefits or contributions not discriminate in favor of HCEs. Therefore, a plan will not be treated as satisfying the requirements of this paragraph (b) if there are repeated changes to plan testing procedures or plan provisions that have the effect of distorting the ACP so as to increase significantly the permitted ACP for HCEs, or otherwise manipulate the nondiscrimination rules of this paragraph, if a principal purpose of the changes was to achieve such a result.

(4) *Aggregation and restructuring*—(i) *In general.* This paragraph (b)(4) contains the exclusive rules for aggregating and disaggregating plans that provide for employee contributions and matching contributions for purposes of this section and §§ 1.401(m)-2 through 1.401(m)-5.

(ii) *Aggregation of employee contributions and matching contributions within a plan.* Except as otherwise specifically provided in this paragraph (b)(4) and § 1.401(m)-3(f)(1), a plan must be subject to a single test under paragraph (b)(1) of this section with respect to all employee contributions and matching contributions and all eligible employees under the plan. Thus, for example, if two groups of employees are eligible for matching contributions under a plan, all employee contributions and matching contributions under the plan must be subject to a single test, even if they have significantly different features, such as different rates of match.

(iii) *Aggregation of plans*—(A) *In general.* The term *plan* means a plan within the meaning of § 1.410(b)-7(a) and (b), after application of the mandatory disaggregation rules of § 1.410(b)-7(c), and the permissive aggregation rules of § 1.410(b)-7(d), as modified by paragraph (b)(4)(v) of this section. Thus, for example, two plans (within the meaning of § 1.410(b)-7(b)) that are treated as a single plan pursuant to the permissive aggregation rules of § 1.410(b)-7(d) are treated as a single plan for purposes of sections 401(k) and 401(m).

(B) *Arrangements with inconsistent ACP testing methods.* Pursuant to paragraph (b)(4)(ii) of this section, a single testing method must apply with respect to all employee contributions and matching contributions and all eligible employees under a plan. Thus, in applying the permissive aggregation rules of § 1.410(b)-7(d), an employer may not aggregate plans (within the meaning of § 1.410(b)-7(b)) that apply inconsistent testing methods. For example, a plan (within the meaning of § 1.410(b)-7) that applies the current year testing method may not be aggregated with another plan that applies the prior year testing method. Similarly, an employer may not aggregate a plan (within the meaning of § 1.410(b)-7) that is using the ACP safe harbor provisions of section 401(m)(11) and another plan that is using the ACP test of section 401(m)(2).

(iv) *Disaggregation of plans and separate testing*—(A) *In general.* If employee contributions or matching contributions are included in a plan (within the meaning of § 1.410(b)-7(b)) that is mandatorily disaggregated under the rules of section 410(b) (as modified by this paragraph (b)(4)), the matching contributions and employee contributions under that plan must be disaggregated in a consistent manner. For example, in the case of an employer that is treated as operating qualified separate lines of business under section 414(r), if the eligible employees under a plan which provides for employee contributions or matching contributions are in more than one qualified separate line of business, only those employees within each qualified separate line of business may be taken into account in determining whether each disaggregated portion of the plan complies with the requirements of section 401(m), unless the employer is applying the special rule for employer-wide plans in § 1.414(r)-1(c)(2)(ii) with respect to the plan. Similarly, if a plan that provides for employee contributions or matching contributions under which employees are permitted to participate before they have completed the minimum age and service requirements of section 410(a)(1) applies section 410(b)(4)(B) for determining whether the plan complies with section 410(b)(1), then the plan must be treated as two separate plans, one comprising all eligible employees who have met the minimum age and service requirements of section 410(a)(1) and one comprising all eligible employees who have not met the minimum age and service requirements of section 410(a)(1), unless the plan is using the rule in § 1.401(m)-2(a)(1)(iii)(A).

(B) *Restructuring prohibited.* Restructuring under § 1.401(a)(4)-9(c) may not be used to demonstrate compliance with the requirements of section 401(m). See § 1.401(a)(4)-9(c)(3)(ii).

(v) *Certain disaggregation rules not applicable.* The mandatory disaggregation rules relating to section 401(k) plans and section 401(m) plans set forth in § 1.410(b)-7(c)(1) and to ESOP and non-ESOP portions of a plan set forth in § 1.410(b)-7(c)(2) shall not apply for purposes of this section and §§ 1.401(m)-2 through 1.401(m)-5. Accordingly, notwithstanding § 1.410(b)-7(d)(2), an ESOP and a non-ESOP which are different plans (within the meaning of § 1.410(b)-7(b)) are permitted to be aggregated for these purposes.

(c) *Additional requirements*—(1) *Separate testing for employee contributions and matching contributions.* Under § 1.410(b)-7(c)(1), the group of employees who are eligible to make employee contributions or eligible to receive matching contributions must satisfy the requirements of section 410(b) as if those employees were covered under a separate plan. The determination of whether the separate plan satisfies the requirements of section 410(b) must be made without regard to the modifications to the disaggregation rules set forth in paragraph (b)(4)(v) of this section. In addition, except as expressly permitted under section 401(k), 410(b)(2)(A)(ii), or 416(c)(2)(A), employee contributions, matching contributions and elective contributions taken into account under § 1.401(m)-2(a)(6) may not be taken into account for purposes of determining whether any other contributions under any plan (including the plan to which the employee contributions or matching contributions are made) satisfy the requirements of section 401(a). See also § 1.401(a)(4)-11(g)(3)(vii) for special rules relating to corrections of violations of the minimum coverage requirements or discriminatory rates of matching contributions.

(2) *Plan provision requirement.* A plan that provides for employee contributions or matching contributions satisfies this section only if it provides that the nondiscrimination requirements of section 401(m) will be met. Thus, the plan must provide for satisfaction of one of the specific alternatives described in paragraph (b)(1) of this section and, if with respect to that alternative there are optional choices, which of the optional choices will apply. For example, a plan that uses the ACP test of section 401(m)(2), as described in paragraph (b)(1)(i) of this section, must specify whether it is using the current year testing method or prior year testing method. Additionally, a plan that uses the prior year testing method must specify whether the ACP for eligible NHCEs for the first plan year is 3% or the ACP for the eligible NHCEs for the first plan year. Similarly, a plan that uses the safe harbor method of section 401(m)(11), as described in paragraph (b)(1)(ii) of this section, must specify whether the safe harbor contribution will be the nonelective safe harbor contribution or the matching safe harbor contribution and is not permitted to provide that ACP testing will be used if the requirements for the safe harbor are not satisfied. For purposes of this paragraph (c)(2), a plan may incorporate by reference the provisions of section 401(m)(2) and § 1.401(m)-2 if that is the nondiscrimination test being applied.

(d) *Effective date.* This section and §§ 1.401(m)-2 through 1.401(m)-5 apply to plan years that begin on or after the date that is 12 months after the issuance of these regulations in final form.

§ 1.401(m)-2 ACP test.

(a) *Actual contribution percentage (ACP) test*—(1) *In general*—(i) *ACP test formula.* A plan satisfies the ACP test for a plan year only if—

(A) The ACP for the eligible HCEs for the plan year is not more than the ACP for the eligible NHCEs for the applicable year multiplied by 1.25; or

(B) The excess of the ACP for the eligible HCEs for the plan year over the ACP for the eligible NHCEs for the applicable year is not more than 2 percentage points, and the ACP for the eligible HCEs for the plan year is not more than the ACP for the eligible NHCEs for the applicable year multiplied by 2.

(ii) *HCEs as sole eligible employees.* If, for the applicable year there are no eligible NHCEs (i.e., all of the eligible employees under the plan for the applicable year are HCEs), the plan is deemed to satisfy the ACP test.

(iii) *Special rule for early participation.* If a plan providing for employee contributions or matching contributions provides that employees are eligible to participate before they have completed the minimum age and service requirements of section 410(a)(1)(A), and if the plan applies section 410(b)(4)(B) in determining whether the plan meets the requirements of section 410(b)(1), then in determining whether the plan meets the requirements under paragraph (a)(1) of this section either—

(A) Pursuant to section 401(m)(5)(C), the ACP test is performed under the plan (determined without regard to disaggregation under §1.410(b)-7(c)(3)), using the ACP for all eligible HCEs for the plan year and the ACP of eligible NHCEs for the applicable year, disregarding all NHCEs who have not met the minimum age and service requirements of section 410(a)(1)(A); or

(B) Pursuant to §1.401(m)-1(b)(4), the plan is disaggregated into separate plans and the ACP test is performed separately for all eligible employees who have completed the minimum age and service requirements of section 410(a)(1)(A) and for all eligible employees who have not completed the minimum age and service requirements of section 410(a)(1)(A).

(2) *Determination of ACP*—(i) *General rule.* The ACP for a group of eligible employees (either eligible HCEs or eligible NHCEs) for a plan year or applicable year is the average of the ACRs of eligible employees in the group for that year. The ACP for a group of eligible employees is calculated to the nearest hundredth of a percentage point.

(ii) *Determination of applicable year under current year and prior year testing method.* The ACP test is applied using the prior year testing method or the current year testing method. Under the prior year testing method, the applicable year for determining the ACP for the eligible NHCEs is the plan year immediately preceding the plan year for which the ACP test is being calculated. Under the prior year testing method, the ACP for the eligible NHCEs is determined using the ACRs for the eligible employees who were NHCEs in that preceding plan year, regardless of whether those NHCEs are eligible employees or NHCEs in the plan year for which the ACP test is being performed. Under the current year testing method, the applicable year for determining the ACP for eligible NHCEs is the same plan year as the plan year for which the ACP test is being calculated. Under either method, the ACP for the eligible HCEs is the determined using the ACRs of eligible employees who are HCEs for the plan year for which the ACP test is being performed. See paragraph (c) of this section for additional rules for the prior year testing method.

(3) *Determination of ACR*—(i) *General rule.* The ACR of an eligible employee for the plan year or applicable year is the sum of the employee contributions and matching contributions taken into account with respect to such employee (determined under the rules of paragraphs (a)(4) and (a)(5) of this section), and the qualified nonelective and elective contributions taken into account under paragraph (a)(6) of this section for the year, divided by the employee's compensation taken into account for the year. The ACR is calculated to the nearest hundredth of a percentage point. If no employee contributions, matching contributions, elective contributions, or qualified nonelective contributions are taken into account under this section with respect to an eligible employee for the year, the ACR of the employee is zero.

(ii) *ACR of HCEs eligible under more than one plan*—(A) *General rule.* Pursuant to section 401(m)(2)(B), the ACR of an HCE who is an eligible employee in more than one plan of an employer to which matching contributions or employee contributions are made is calculated by treating all contributions with respect to such HCE under any such plan as being made under the plan being tested. Thus, the ACR for such an HCE is calculated by accumulating all matching contributions and employee contributions under any plan (other than a plan described in paragraph (a)(3)(ii)(B) of this section) that would be taken into account under this section for the plan year, if the plan under which the contribution was made applied this section and had the same plan year. For example, in the case of a plan with a 12-month plan year,

the ACR for the plan year of that plan for an HCE who participates in multiple plans of the same employer that provide for matching contributions or employee contributions is the sum of all such contributions during such 12-month period that would be taken into account with respect to the HCE under all plans in which the HCE is an eligible employee, divided by the HCE's compensation for that 12-month period (determined using the compensation definition for the plan being tested), without regard to the plan year of the other plans and whether those plans are satisfying this section or §1.401(m)-3.

(B) *Plans not permitted to be aggregated.* Contributions under plans that are not permitted to be aggregated under §1.401(m)-1(b)(4) (determined without regard to the prohibition on aggregating plans with inconsistent testing methods set forth in §1.401(m)-1(b)(4)(iii)(B) and the prohibition on aggregating plans with different plan years set forth in §1.410(b)-7(d)(5)) are not aggregated under this paragraph (a)(3)(ii).

(iii) *Example.* The following example illustrates the application of paragraph (a)(3)(ii) of this section. See also §1.401(k)-2(a)(3)(iii) for additional examples of the application of the parallel rule under section 401(k)(3)(A). The example is as follows:

Example. Employee A, an HCE with compensation of $120,000, is eligible to make employee contributions under Plan S and Plan T, two calendar-year profit-sharing plans of Employer H. Plan S and Plan T use the same definition of compensation. Plan S provides a match equal to 50% of each employee's contributions and Plan T has no match. During the current plan year, Employee A elects to contribute $4,000 in employee contributions to Plan T and $4,000 in employee contributions to Plan S. There are no other contributions made on behalf of Employee A. Each plan must calculate Employee A's ACR by dividing the total employee contributions by Employee A and matching contributions under both plans by $120,000. Therefore, Employee A's ACR under each plan is 8.33% ($4,000+ $4,000+ $2,000/$120,000).

(4) *Employee contributions and matching contributions taken into account under the ACP test*—(i) *Employee contributions.* An employee contribution is taken into account in determining the ACR for an eligible employee for the plan year or applicable year in which the contribution is made. For purposes of the preceding sentence, an amount withheld from an employee's pay (or a payment by the employee to an agent of the plan) is treated as contributed at the time of such withholding (or payment) if the funds paid are transmitted to the trust within a reasonable period after the withholding (or payment).

(ii) *Recharacterized elective contributions.* Excess contributions recharacterized in accordance with §1.401(k)-2(b)(3) are taken into account as employee contributions for the plan year that includes the time at which the excess contribution is includible in the gross income of the employee under §1.401(k)-2(b)(3)(ii)(A).

(iii) *Matching contributions.* A matching contribution is taken into account in determining the ACR for an eligible employee for a plan year or applicable year only if each of the following requirements is satisfied—

(A) The matching contribution is allocated to the employee's account under the terms of the plan as of a date within that year;

(B) The matching contribution is made on account of (or the matching contribution is allocated on the basis of) the employee's elective deferrals or employee contributions for that year; and

(C) The matching contribution is actually paid to the trust no later than the end of the 12-month period immediately following the year that contains that date.

(5) *Matching contributions not taken into account under the ACP test*—(i) *General rule.* Matching contributions that do not satisfy the requirements of paragraph (a)(4)(iii) of this section may not be taken into account in the ACP test for the plan year with respect to which the contributions were made, or for any other plan year. Instead, the amount of the matching contributions must satisfy the requirements of section 401(a)(4) (without regard to the ACP test) for the plan year for which they are allocated under the plan as if they were nonelective contributions and were the only nonelective contributions for that year. See §§1.401(a)(4)-1(b)(2)(ii)(B) and 1.410(b)-7(c)(1).

(ii) *Disproportionate matching contributions*—(A) *Matching contributions in excess of 100%.* A matching contribution with respect to any employee contribution or elective deferral for an NHCE is not taken into account under the ACP test to the extent the matching rate with respect to the employee contribution or elective deferral exceeds the greater of 100% and 2 times the plan's representative matching rate.

(B) *Representative matching rate.* For purposes of this paragraph (a)(5)(ii), the plan's representative matching rate is the lowest matching rate for any eligible NHCE among a group of NHCEs that consists of half of all eligible NHCEs in the plan for the plan year who make elective deferrals or employee contributions for the plan year (or, if greater, the lowest matching rate for all eligible NHCEs in the plan who are employed by the employer on the last day of the plan year and who make elective deferrals or employee contributions for the plan year).

(C) *Definition of matching rate*. For purposes of this paragraph (a)(5)(ii), the matching rate for an employee is the matching contributions made for such employee divided by the elective deferrals or employee contributions that are being matched.

(iii) *Qualified matching contributions used to satisfy the ADP test*. Qualified matching contributions that are taken into account for the ADP test of section 401(k)(3) under § 1.401(k)-2(a)(6) are not taken into account in determining an eligible employee's ACR.

(iv) *Matching contributions taken into account under safe harbor provisions*. A plan that satisfies the ACP safe harbor requirements of section 401(m)(11) for a plan year but nonetheless must satisfy the requirements of this section because it provides for employee contributions for such plan year is permitted to apply this section disregarding all matching contributions with respect to all eligible employees. In addition, a plan that satisfies the ADP safe harbor requirements of § 1.401(k)-3 for a plan year using qualified matching contributions but does not satisfy the ACP safe harbor requirements of section 401(m)(11) for such plan year is permitted to apply this section by excluding matching contributions with respect to all eligible employees that do not exceed 4% of each employee's compensation. If a plan disregards matching contributions pursuant to this paragraph (a)(5)(iv), the disregard must apply with respect to all eligible employees.

(v) *Treatment of forfeited matching contributions*. A matching contribution that is forfeited because the contribution to which it relates is treated as an excess contribution, excess deferral, or excess aggregate contribution is not taken into account for purposes of this section.

(6) *Qualified nonelective contributions and elective contributions that may be taken into account under the ACP test*. Qualified nonelective contributions and elective contributions may be taken into account in determining the ACR for an eligible employee for a plan year or applicable year, but only to the extent the contributions satisfy the following requirements—

(i) *Timing of allocation*. The qualified nonelective contribution is allocated to the employee's account as of a date within that year (within the meaning of § 1.401(k)-2(a)(4)(i)(A)) and the elective contribution satisfies § 1.401(k)-2(a)(4)(i). Consequently, under the prior year testing method, in order to be taken into account in calculating the ACP for the group of eligible NHCEs for the applicable year, a qualified nonelective contribution must be contributed no later than the end of the 12-month period following the applicable year even though the applicable year is different than the plan year being tested.

(ii) *Elective contributions taken into account under the ACP test*. Elective contributions may be taken into account for the ACP test only if the cash or deferred arrangement under which the elective contributions are made is required to satisfy the ADP test in § 1.401(k)-2(a)(1) and, then only to the extent that the cash or deferred arrangement would satisfy that test, including such elective contributions in the ADP for the plan year or applicable year. Thus, for example, elective deferrals made pursuant to a salary reduction agreement under an annuity described in section 403(b) are not permitted to be taken into account in an ACP test. Similarly, elective contributions under a cash or deferred arrangement that is using the section 401(k) safe harbor described in § 1.401(k)-3 can not be taken into account in an ACP test.

(iii) *Requirement that amount satisfy section 401(a)(4)*. The amount of nonelective contributions, including those qualified nonelective contributions taken into account under this paragraph (a)(6) and those qualified nonelective contributions taken into account for the ADP test under paragraph § 1.401(k)-2(a)(6), and the amount of nonelective contributions, excluding those qualified nonelective contributions taken into account under this paragraph (a)(6) for the ACP test and those qualified nonelective contributions taken into account for the ADP test under paragraph § 1.401(k)-2(a)(6), satisfies the requirements of section 401(a)(4). See § 1.401(a)(4)-1(b)(2). In the case of an employer that is applying the special rule for employer-wide plans in

§ 1.414(r)-1(c)(2)(ii) with respect to the plan, the determination of whether the qualified nonelective contributions satisfy the requirements of this paragraph (a)(6)(iii) must be made on an employer-wide basis regardless of whether the plans to which the qualified nonelective contributions are made are satisfying the requirements of section 410(b) on an employer-wide basis. Conversely, in the case of an employer that is treated as operating qualified separate lines of business, and does not apply the special rule for employer-wide plans in § 1.414(r)-1(c)(2)(ii) with respect to the plan, then the determination of whether the qualified nonelective contributions satisfy the requirements of this paragraph (a)(6)(iii) is not permitted to be made on an employer-wide basis regardless of whether the plans to which the qualified nonelective contributions are made are satisfying the requirements of section 410(b) on that basis.

(iv) *Aggregation must be permitted*. The plan that provides for employee or matching contributions and the plan or plans to which the qualified nonelective contributions or elective contributions are made are plans that would be permitted to be aggregated under § 1.401(m)-1(b)(4). If the plan year of the plan that provides for employee or matching contributions is changed to satisfy the requirement under § 1.410(b)-7(d)(5) that aggregated plans have the same plan year, qualified nonelective contributions and elective contributions may be taken into account in the resulting short plan year only if such qualified nonelective and elective contributions could have been taken into account under an ADP test for a plan with that same short plan year.

(v) *Disproportionate contributions not taken into account*—(A) *General rule*. Qualified nonelective contributions cannot be taken into account for an applicable year for an NHCE to the extent such contributions exceed the product that NHCE's compensation and the greater of 5% and 2 times the plan's representative contribution rate. Any qualified nonelective contribution taken into account in an ADP test under § 1.401(k)-2(a)(6) (including the determination of the representative contribution rate for purposes of § 1.401(k)-2(a)(6)(iv)(B)) is not permitted to be taken into account for purposes of this paragraph (a)(6) (including the determination of the representative contribution rate for purposes of paragraph (a)(6)(v)(B) of this section).

(B) *Definition of representative contribution rate*. For purposes of this paragraph (a)(6)(v), the plan's representative contribution rate is the lowest applicable contribution rate of any eligible NHCE among a group of eligible NHCEs that consists of half of all eligible NHCEs for the plan year (or, if greater, the lowest applicable contribution rate of any eligible NHCE in the group of all eligible NHCEs for the applicable year and who is employed by the employer on the last day of the applicable year).

(C) *Definition of applicable contribution rate*. For purposes of this paragraph (a)(6)(v), the applicable contribution rate for an eligible NHCE is the sum of the matching contributions taken into account under this section for the employee for the plan year and the qualified nonelective contributions made for that employee for the plan year, divided by that employee's compensation for the same period.

(vi) *Contribution only used once*. Qualified nonelective contributions can not be taken into account under this paragraph (a)(6) to the extent such contributions are taken into account for purposes of satisfying any other ACP test, any ADP test, or the requirements of § 1.401(k)-3, 1.401(m)-3 or 1.401(k)-4. Thus, for example, qualified nonelective contributions that are made pursuant to § 1.401(k)-3(b) cannot be taken into account under the ACP test. Similarly, if a plan switches from the current year testing method to the prior year testing method pursuant to § 1.401(m)-2(c)(1), qualified nonelective contributions that are taken into account under the current year testing method for a plan year may not be taken into account under the prior year testing method for the next plan year.

(7) *Examples*. The following examples illustrate the application of this paragraph (a). See § 1.401(k)-2(a)(6) for additional examples of the parallel rules under section 401(k)(3)(A). The examples are as follows:

Example 1. (i) Employer L maintains Plan U, a profit-sharing plan under which $.50 matching contributions are made for each dollar of employee contributions. Plan U uses the current year testing method. The chart below shows the average employee contributions (as a percentage of compensation) and matching contributions (as a percentage of compensation) for Plan U's highly compensated employees and nonhighly compensated employees for the 2006 plan year:

	Employee Contributions	Matching Contributions	Actual Contribution Percentage
Highly compensated employees	4%	2.0%	6.0%
Nonhighly compensated employees	3%	1.5%	4.5%

(ii) The matching rate for all NHCEs is 50% and thus the matching contributions are not disproportionate under paragraph (a)(5)(ii) of

this section. Accordingly, they are taken into account in determining the ACR of eligible employees, as shown in the following table.

(iii) Because the ACP for the HCEs (6.0%) exceeds 5.63% (4.5% × 1.25), Plan U does not satisfy the ACP test under paragraph (a)(1)(i)(A) of this section. However, because the ACP for the HCEs does not exceed the ACP for the NHCEs by more than 2 percentage points and the ACP for the HCEs does not exceed the ACP for the NHCEs multiplied by 2 (4.5% × 2 = 9%), the plan satisfies the ACP test under paragraph (a)(1)(i)(B) of this section.

Example 2. (i) Employees A through F are eligible employees in Plan V, a profit-sharing plan of Employer M that includes a cash or deferred

Employee	Compensation
A	$190,000
B	100,000
C	85,000
D	70,000
E	40,000
F	10,000

(ii) The matching rate for all NHCEs is 50% and thus the matching contributions are not disproportionate under paragraph (a)(5)(ii) of

Employee	Compensation
A	$190,000
B	100,000
C	85,000
D	70,000
E	40,000
F	10,000

(iii) The ACP for the HCEs is 12.11% ((6.71% + 17.50%)/2). The ACP for the NHCEs is 6.59% ((7.06% + 6.79% + 12.50% + 0%)/4). Plan V fails to satisfy the ACP test under paragraph (a)(1)(i)(A) of this section because the ACP of highly compensated employees is more than 125% of the ACP of the nonhighly compensated employees (6.59% × 1.25 = 8.24%). In addition, Plan V fails to satisfy the ACP test under paragraph (a)(1)(i)(B) of this section because the ACP for the HCEs exceeds the ACP of the other employees by more than 2 percentage points (6.59% + 2% = 8.59%). Therefore, the plan fails to satisfy the requirements of section 401(m)(2) and paragraph (a)(1) of this section unless the ACP failure is corrected under paragraph (b) of this section.

Example 3. (i) The facts are the same as *Example 2*, except that the plan provides that the nonhighly compensated employees' elective contributions may be used to meet the requirements of section 401(m) to the extent needed under that section.

(ii) Pursuant to paragraph (a)(6)(ii) of this section, the $10,000 of elective contributions for Employee E may be taken into account in determining the ACP rather than the ADP to the extent that the plan satisfies the requirements of § 1.401(k)-2(a)(1) excluding from the ADP this $10,000. In this case, if the $10,000 were excluded from the ADP for the NHCEs, the ADP for the highly compensated employees is

Employee	Compensation
C	$85,000
D	70,000
E	40,000
F	10,000

(ii) The matching rate for all NHCEs is 74% and thus the matching contributions are not disproportionate under paragraph (a)(5)(ii) of this section. Therefore, the matching contributions may be taken into account in determining the ACP for the NHCEs.

(iii) The ACP for the NHCEs is 9.75% (10.45% + 10.04% + 18.50% + 0%)/4. Because the ACP for the HCEs (12.11%) is less than 1.25 times the ACP for the NHCEs, the plan satisfies the requirements of section 401(m).

Example 5. (i) The facts are the same as *Example 4*, except that: Employee E's elective contributions are $2,000 (rather than $10,000)

Employee	Compensation
C	$85,000
D	70,000
E	40,000
F	10,000

(ii) If the entire matching contribution made on behalf of Employee E were taken into account under the ACP test, Plan V would satisfy the test, because the ACP for the NHCEs would be 9.71% (7.06% + 6.79% + 25.00% + 0%)/4. Because the ACP for the HCEs (12.11%) is less than 1.25 times what the ACP for the NHCEs would be, the plan would satisfy the requirements of section 401(m).

(iii) Pursuant to paragraph (a)(5)(ii) of this section, however, matching contributions for an eligible NHCE that are based on a matching rate in excess of the greater of 100% and twice the plan's representative

arrangement and permits employee contributions. Under Plan V, a $.50 matching contribution is made for each dollar of elective contributions and employee contributions. Plan V uses the current year testing method and does not provide for elective contributions to be taken into account in determining an eligible employee's ACR. For the 2006 plan year, Employees A and B are HCEs and the remaining employees are NHCEs. The compensation, elective contributions, employee contributions, and matching contributions for the 2006 plan year are shown in the following table:

Elective Contributions	Employee Contributions	Matching Contributions
$15,000	$3,500	$9,250
$5,000	$10,000	$7,500
$12,000	$0	$6,000
$9,500	$0	$4,750
$10,000	$0	$5,000
$0	$0	$0

this section. Accordingly, they are taken into account in determining the ACR of eligible employees, as shown in the following table:

Employee Contributions	Matching Contributions	ACR %
$3,500	$9,250	6.71
$10,000	$7,500	17.50
$0	$6,000	7.06
$0	$4,750	6.79
$0	$5,000	12.50
$0	$0	0

6.45% (7.89% + 5.00%) /2 and the ADP for the nonhighly compensated employees would be 6.92% (14.12% + 13.57% + 0% + 0%)/4) and the plan would satisfy the requirements of § 1.401(k)-2(a)(1) excluding from the ADP the elective contributions for NHCEs that are taken into account under section 401(m).

(iii) After taking into account the $10,000 of elective contributions for Employee E in the ACP test, the ACP for the nonhighly compensated employees is 12.84% (7.06% + 6.79% + 37.50 % + 0%) /4. Therefore the plan satisfies the ACP test because the ACP for the HCEs (12.11%) is less than 1.25 times the ACP for the nonhighly compensated employees.

Example 4. (i) The facts are the same as *Example 2*, except that Plan V provides for a higher than 50% match rate on the elective contributions and employee contributions for all NHCEs. The match rate is defined as the rate, rounded up to the next whole percent, necessary to allow the plan to satisfy the ACP test, but not in excess of 100%. In this case, an increase in the match rate from 50% to 74% will be sufficient to allow the plan to satisfy the ACP test. Thus, for the 2006 plan year, the compensation, elective contributions, employee contributions, matching contributions at a 74% match rate of the eligible NHCEs (employees C through F) are shown in the following table:

Elective Contributions	Employee Contributions	Matching Contributions
$12,000	$0	$8,880
$9,500	$0	$7,030
$10,000	$0	$7,400
$0	$0	$0

and pursuant to paragraph (a)(6)(ii) of this section, the $2,000 of elective contributions for Employee E are taken into account in determining the ACP rather than the ADP. In addition, Plan V provides that the higher match rate is not limited to 100% and applies only for a specified group of nonhighly compensated employees. The only member of that group is Employee E. Under the plan provision, the higher match rate is a 400% match. Thus, for the 2006 plan year, the compensation, elective contributions, employee contributions, matching contributions of the eligible NHCEs (employees C through F) are shown in the following table:

Elective Contributions	Employee Contributions	Matching Contributions
$12,000	$0	$6,000
$9,500	$0	$4,750
$2,000	$0	$8,000
$0	$0	$0

matching rate cannot be taken into account in applying the ACP test. The plan's representative matching rate is the lowest matching rate for any eligible employee in a group of NHCEs that is at least half of all eligible employees who are NHCEs in the plan for the plan year who make elective contributions or employee contributions for the plan year. For Plan V, the group of NHCEs who make such contributions consists of Employees C, D and E. The matching rates for these three employees are 50%, 50% and 400% respectively. The lowest matching rate for a group of NHCEs that is at least ½ of all the NHCEs who make elective contributions or employee contributions (or 2 NHCEs) is 50%. Because 400% is more than twice the plan's representative matching rate, only the matching contributions made on behalf of Employee E that do not exceed 100% (or in this case $2,000) satisfy the requirements of paragraph (a)(5)(ii) of this section and may be taken into account under the ACP test. Accordingly, the ACP for the NHCEs is 5.96% (7.06% + 6.79% + 10% + 0%)/4 and the plan fails to satisfy the requirements of section 401(m)(2) and paragraph (a)(1) of this section unless the ACP failure is corrected under paragraph (b) of this section.

Example 6. (i) The facts are the same as *Example 2*, except that Plan V provides a QNEC equal to 13% of pay for Employee F that will be taken into account under the ACP test to the extent the contributions satisfy the requirements of paragraph (a)(6) of this section.

(ii) Pursuant to paragraph (a)(6)(v) of this section, a QNEC cannot be taken into account in determining an NHCE's ACR to the extent it exceeds the greater of 5% and the product of the employee's compensation and the plan's representative contribution rate. The plan's representative contribution rate is two times the lowest applicable contribution rate for any eligible employee in a group of NHCEs that is at least half of all eligible employees who are NHCEs in the plan for the plan year. For Plan V, the applicable contribution rates for Employees C, D, E and F are 7.06%, 6.79%, 12.5% and 13% respectively. The lowest applicable rate for a group of NHCEs that is at least ½ of all the NHCEs is 12.50% (the lowest applicable rate for the group of NHCEs that consists of Employees E and F).

(iii) Under paragraph (a)(6)(v)(B) of this section, the plan's representative contribution rate is 2 times 12.50% or 25.00%. Accordingly, the QNECs for Employee F can be taken into account under the ACP test only to the extent they do not exceed 25.00% of compensation. In this case, all of the QNECs for Employee F may be taken into account under the ACP test.

(iv) After taking into account the QNECs for Employee F, the ACP for the NHCEs is 9.84% (7.06% + 6.79% + 12.50% + 13%)/4. Because the ACP for the HCEs (12.11%) is less than 1.25 times the ACP for the NHCEs, the plan satisfies the requirements of section 401(m)(2) and paragraph (a)(1) of this section.

(b) *Correction of excess aggregate contributions*—(1) *Permissible correction methods*—(i) *In general.* A plan that provides for employee contributions or matching contributions does not fail to satisfy the requirements of section 401(m)(2) and paragraph (a)(1) of this section if the employer, in accordance with the terms of the plan, uses either of the following correction methods—

(A) *Additional contributions.* The employer makes additional contributions that are taken into account for the ACP test under this section that, in combination with the other contributions taken into account under this section, allow the plan to satisfy the requirements of paragraph (a)(1) of this section.

(B) *Excess aggregate contributions distributed or forfeited.* Excess aggregate contributions are distributed or forfeited in accordance with paragraph (b)(2) of this section.

(ii) *Combination of correction methods.* A plan may provide for the use of either of the correction methods described in paragraph (b)(1)(i) of this section, may limit employee contributions or matching contributions in a manner that prevents excess aggregate contributions from being made, or may use a combination of these methods, to avoid or correct excess aggregate contributions. If a plan uses a combination of correction methods, any contributions made under paragraph (b)(1)(i)(A) of this section must be taken into account before application of the correction method in paragraph (b)(1)(i)(B) of this section.

(iii) *Exclusive means of correction.* A failure to satisfy the requirements of paragraph (a)(1) of this section may not be corrected using any method other than one described in paragraph (b)(1)(i) or (ii) of this section. Thus, excess aggregate contributions for a plan year may not be corrected by forfeiting vested matching contributions, distributing nonvested matching contributions, recharacterizing matching contributions, or not making matching contributions required under the terms of the plan. Similarly, excess aggregate contributions for a plan year may not remain unallocated or be allocated to a suspense account for allocation to one or more employees in any future year. In addition, excess aggregate contributions may not be corrected using the retroactive correction rules of § 1.401(a)(4)-11(g). See § 1.401(a)(4)-11(g)(3)(vii) and (5).

(2) *Correction through distribution*—(i) *General rule.* This paragraph (b)(2) contains the rules for correction of excess aggregate contributions through a distribution from the plan. Correction through a distribution generally involves a four step process. First, the plan must determine, in accordance with paragraph (b)(2)(ii) of this section, the total amount of excess aggregate contributions that must be distributed under the plan. Second, the plan must apportion the total amount of excess aggregate contributions among the HCEs in accordance with paragraph (b)(2)(iii) of this section. Third, the plan must determine the income allocable to excess aggregate contributions in accordance with paragraph (b)(2)(iv) of this section. Finally, the plan must distribute the apportioned contributions, together with allocable income (or forfeit the apportioned matching contributions, if forfeitable) in accordance with paragraph (b)(2)(v) of this section. Paragraph (b)(2)(vi) of this section provides rules relating to the tax treatment of these distributions.

(ii) *Calculation of total amount to be distributed.* The following procedures must be used to determine the total amount of the excess aggregate contributions to be distributed—

(A) *Calculate the dollar amount of excess aggregate contributions for each HCE.* The amount of excess aggregate contributions attributable to an HCE for a plan year is the amount (if any) by which the HCE's contributions taken into account under this section must be reduced for the HCE's ACR to equal the highest permitted ACR under the plan. To calculate the highest permitted ACR under a plan, the ACR of the HCE with the highest ACR is reduced by the amount required to cause that HCE's ACR to equal the ACR of the HCE with the next highest ACR. If a lesser reduction would enable the plan to satisfy the requirements of paragraph (b)(2)(ii)(C) of this section, only this lesser reduction applies.

(B) *Determination of the total amount of excess aggregate contributions.* The process described in paragraph (b)(2)(ii)(A) of this section must be repeated until the plan would satisfy the requirements of paragraph (b)(2)(ii)(C) of this section. The sum of all reductions for all HCEs determined under paragraph (b)(2)(ii)(A) of this section is the total amount of excess aggregate contributions for the plan year.

(C) *Satisfaction of ACP.* A plan satisfies this paragraph (b)(2)(ii)(C) if the plan would satisfy the requirements of paragraph (a)(1)(i) of this section if the ACR for each HCE were determined after the reductions described in paragraph (b)(2)(ii)(A) of this section.

(iii) *Apportionment of total amount of excess aggregate contributions among the HCEs.* The following procedures must be used in apportioning the total amount of excess aggregate contributions determined under paragraph (b)(2)(ii) of this section among the HCEs—

(A) *Calculate the dollar amount of excess aggregate contributions for each HCE.* The contributions with respect to the HCE with the highest dollar amount of contributions taken account under this section are reduced by the amount required to cause that HCE's contributions to equal the dollar amount of contributions taken into account under this section for the HCE with the next highest dollar amount of such contributions. If a lesser apportionment to the HCE would enable the plan to apportion the total amount of excess aggregate contributions, only the lesser apportionment would apply.

(B) *Limit on amount apportioned to any HCE.* For purposes of this paragraph (b)(2)(iii), the contributions for an HCE who is an eligible employee in more than one plan of an employer to which matching contributions and employee contributions are made is determined by adding together all contributions otherwise taken into account in determining the ACR of the HCE under the rules of paragraph (a)(3)(ii) of this section. However, the amount of contributions apportioned with respect to an HCE must not exceed the amount of contributions taken into account under this section that were actually made on behalf of the HCE to the plan for the plan year. Thus, in the case of an HCE who is an eligible employee in more than one plan of the same employer to which employee contributions or matching contributions are made and whose ACR is calculated in accordance with paragraph (a)(3)(ii) of this section, the amount distributed under this paragraph (b)(2)(iii) will not exceed such contributions actually contributed to the plan for the plan year that are taken into account under this section for the plan year.

(C) *Apportionment to additional HCEs.* The procedure in paragraph (b)(2)(iii)(A) of this section must be repeated until the total amount of excess aggregate contributions have been apportioned.

(iv) *Income allocable to excess aggregate contributions*—(A) *General rule.* The income allocable to excess aggregate contributions is equal to the sum of the allocable gain or loss for the plan year and, to the extent the excess aggregate contributions are or will be credited with allocable gain or loss for the period after the close of the plan year (the gap period), the allocable gain or loss for the gap period.

(B) *Method of allocating income.* A plan may use any reasonable method for computing the income allocable to excess aggregate contributions, provided that the method does not violate section 401(a)(4), is used consistently for all participants and for all corrective distributions under the plan for the plan year, and is used by the plan for allocating income to participants' accounts. See § 1.401(a)(4)-1(c)(8).

(C) *Alternative method of allocating income for the plan year.* A plan may allocate income to excess aggregate contributions for the plan year by multiplying the income for the plan year allocable to employee contributions, matching contributions and other amounts taken into account under this section (including the contributions for the year), by a fraction, the numerator of which is the excess aggregate contributions for the employee for the plan year, and the denominator of which is the account balance attributable to employee contributions and matching contributions and other amounts taken into account under this section as of the beginning of the plan year (including any additional such contributions for the plan year).

(D) *Safe harbor method of allocating gap period income.* A plan may use the safe harbor method in this paragraph (b)(2)(iv)(D) to determine income on excess aggregate contributions for the gap period. Under this safe harbor method, income on excess aggregate contributions for the gap period is equal to 10% of the income allocable to excess aggregate contributions for the plan year that would be determined under paragraph (b)(2)(iv)(C) of this section, multiplied by the number of calendar months that have elapsed since the end of the plan year. For purposes of calculating the number of calendar months that have elapsed under the safe harbor method, a corrective distribution that is made on or before the fifteenth day of a month is treated as made on the last day of the preceding month and a distribution made after the fifteenth day of a month is treated as made on the last day of the month.

(E) *Alternative method of allocating plan year and gap period income.* A plan may determine the allocable gain or loss for the aggregate of the plan year and the gap period by applying the alternative method provided by paragraph (b)(2)(iv)(C) of this section to that aggregate period. This is accomplished by substituting the income for the plan year and the gap period for the income for the plan year and by substituting the contributions taken into account under this section for the plan year and the gap period for the contributions taken into account for the plan year in determining the fraction that is multiplied by that income.

(F) *Allocable income for recharacterized elective contributions.* If recharacterized elective contributions are distributed as excess aggregate contributions, the income allocable to the excess aggregate contributions is determined as if recharacterized elective contributions had been distributed as excess contributions. Thus, income must be allocated to the recharacterized amounts distributed using the methods in § 1.401(k)-2(b)(2)(iv).

(v) *Distribution and forfeiture.* Within 12 months after the close of the plan year in which the excess aggregate contribution arose, the plan must distribute to each HCE the contributions apportioned to such HCE under paragraph (b)(2)(iii) of this section (and the allocable income) to the extent they are vested or forfeit such amounts, if forfeitable. Except as otherwise provided in this paragraph (b)(2)(v), a distribution of excess aggregate contributions must be in addition to any other distributions made during the year and must be designated as a corrective distribution by the employer. In the event of a complete termination of the plan during the plan year in which an excess aggregate contribution arose, the corrective distribution must be made as soon as administratively feasible after the date of termination of the plan, but in no event later than 12 months after the date of termination. If the entire account balance of an HCE is distributed prior to when the plan makes a distribution of excess aggregate contributions in accordance with this paragraph (b)(2), the distribution is deemed to have been a corrective distribution of excess aggregate contributions (and income) to the extent that a corrective distribution would otherwise have been required.

(vi) *Tax treatment of corrective distributions*—(A) *General rule.* Except as otherwise provided in paragraph (b)(2)(vi)(B) of this section, a corrective distribution of excess aggregate contributions (and income) that is made within 2 ½ months after the end of the plan year for which the excess aggregate contributions were made is includible in the employee's gross income for the taxable year of the employee ending with or within the plan year for which the excess aggregate contributions were made. A corrective distribution of excess aggregate contributions (and income) that is made more than 2 ½ months after the plan year for which the excess aggregate contributions were made is includible in the employee's gross income in the taxable year of the employee in which distributed. The portion of the distribution that is treated as an investment in the contract under section 72 is determined without regard to any plan contributions other than those distributed as excess aggregate contributions. Regardless of when the corrective distribution is made, it is not subject to the early distribution tax of

section 72(t). See paragraph (b)(4) of this section for additional rules relating to the employer excise tax on amounts distributed more than 2 ½ months after the end of the plan year. See also § 1.402(c)-2, A-4 prohibiting rollover of distributions that are excess aggregate contributions.

(B) *Rule for de minimis distributions.* If the total amount of excess aggregate contributions determined under this paragraph (b)(2), and excess contributions determined under § 1.401(k)-2(b)(2) distributed to a recipient under a plan for any plan year is less than $100 (excluding income), a corrective distribution of excess aggregate contributions (and income) is includible in gross income in the recipient's taxable year in which the corrective distribution is made.

(3) *Other rules*—(i) *No employee or spousal consent required.* A distribution of excess aggregate contributions (and income) may be made under the terms of the plan without regard to any notice or consent otherwise required under sections 411(a)(11) and 417.

(ii) *Treatment of corrective distributions and forfeited contributions as employer contributions.* Excess aggregate contributions (other than amounts attributable to employee contributions), including forfeited matching contributions, are treated as employer contributions for purposes of sections 404 and 415 even if distributed from the plan. Forfeited matching contributions that are reallocated to the accounts of other participants for the plan year in which the forfeiture occurs are treated under section 415 as annual additions for the participants to whose accounts they are reallocated and for the participants from whose accounts they are forfeited.

(iii) *No reduction of required minimum distribution.* A distribution of excess aggregate contributions (and income) is not treated as a distribution for purposes of determining whether the plan satisfies the minimum distribution requirements of section 401(a)(9). See § 1.401(a)(9)-5, A-9(b).

(iv) *Partial correction.* Any distribution of less than the entire amount of excess aggregate contributions (and allocable income) is treated as a pro rata distribution of excess aggregate contributions and allocable income.

(v) *Matching contributions on excess contributions, excess deferrals and excess aggregate contributions*—(A) *Corrective distributions not permitted.* A matching contribution may not be distributed merely because the contribution to which it relates is treated as an excess contribution, excess deferral, or excess aggregate contribution.

(B) *Coordination with section 401(a)(4).* A matching contribution is taken into account under section 401(a)(4) even if the match is distributed, unless the distributed contribution is an excess aggregate contribution. This requires that, after correction of excess aggregate contributions, each level of matching contributions be currently and effectively available to a group of employees that satisfies section 410(b). See § 1.401(a)(4)-4(e)(3)(iii)(G). Thus, a plan that provides the same rate of matching contributions to all employees will not meet the requirements of section 401(a)(4) if employee contributions are distributed under this paragraph (b) to HCEs to the extent needed to meet the requirements of section 401(m)(2), while matching contributions attributable to employee contributions remain allocated to the HCEs' accounts. This is because the level of matching contributions will be higher for a group of employees that consists entirely of HCEs. Under section 411(a)(3)(G) and § 1.411(a)-4(b)(7), a plan may forfeit matching contributions attributable to excess contributions, excess aggregate contributions and excess deferrals to avoid a violation of section 401(a)(4). See also § 1.401(a)(4)-11(g)(3)(vii)(B) regarding the use of additional allocations to the accounts of NHCEs for the purpose of correcting a discriminatory rate of matching contributions. A plan is permitted to provide for which contributions are to be distributed to satisfy the ACP test so as to avoid discriminatory matching rates that would otherwise violate section 401(a)(4). For example, the plan may provide that unmatched employee contributions will be distributed before matched employee contributions.

(vi) *No requirement for recalculation.* If the distributions and forfeitures described in paragraph (b)(2) of this section are made, the employee contributions and matching contributions are treated as meeting the nondiscrimination test of section 401(m)(2) regardless of whether the ACP for the HCEs, if recalculated after the distributions and forfeitures, would satisfy section 401(m)(2).

(4) *Failure to timely correct*—(i) *Failure to correct within 2 ½ months after end of plan year.* If a plan does not correct excess aggregate contributions within 2 ½ months after the close of the plan year for which the excess aggregate contributions are made, the employer will be liable for a 10% excise tax on the amount of the excess aggregate contributions. See section 4979 and § 54.4979-1 of this chapter. Qualified nonelective contributions properly taken into account under para-

graph (a)(6) of this section for a plan year may enable a plan to avoid having excess aggregate contributions, even if the contributions are made after the close of the 2 ½ month period.

(ii) *Failure to correct within 12 months after end of plan year.* If excess aggregate contributions are not corrected within 12 months after the close of the plan year for which they were made, the plan will fail to meet the requirements of section 401(a)(4) for the plan year for which the excess aggregate contributions were made and all subsequent plan years in which the excess aggregate contributions remain in the trust.

Employee

A . . . .
B . . . .
C . . . .

(ii) The total amount of excess aggregate contributions for the HCEs is determined under paragraph (b)(2)(ii) of this section as follows: the matching and employee contributions of Employee C (the HCE with the highest ACR) is reduced by 3% of compensation (or $3,000) in order to reduce the ACR of that HCE to 9%, which is the ACR of Employee B.

(iii) Because the ACP of the HCEs determined after the $3,000 reduction still exceeds 8%, further reductions in matching contributions and employee contributions are necessary in order to reduce the ACP of the HCEs to 8%. The employee contributions and matching contributions for Employees B and C are reduced by an additional .5% of compensation or $1,250 ($750 and $500 respectively). Because the ACP of the HCEs determined after the reductions now equals 8%, the plan would satisfy the requirements of (a)(1)(ii) of this section.

(iv) The total amount of excess aggregate contributions ($4,250) is apportioned among the HCEs under paragraph (b)(2)(iii) of this section first to the HCE with the highest amount of matching contributions and employee contributions. Therefore, Employee A is apportioned $500 (the amount required to cause A's matching contributions and employee contributions to equal the next highest dollar amount of matching contributions and employee contributions).

(v) Because the total amount of excess aggregate contributions has not been apportioned, further apportionment is necessary. The balance ($3,750) of the total amount of excess aggregate contributions is apportioned equally among Employees A and B ($1,500 to each, the amount

Employee D . . . .
NHCEs . . . .

(ii) In February 2007, Employer M determines that D's actual deferral ratio must be reduced to 6%, or $12,000, which requires a recharacterization of $3,000 as an employee contribution. This increases D's actual contribution ratio to 5.25% ($7,500 in matching contributions plus $3,000 recharacterized as employee contributions, divided by $200,000 in compensation). Since D's actual contribution ratio must be limited to 4% for Plan X to satisfy the actual contribution percentage test, Plan X must distribute 1.25% or $2,500 of D's employee contributions and matching contributions together with allocable income. If $2,500 in matching contributions and allocable income is distributed, this will correct the excess aggregate contributions and will not result in a discriminatory rate of matching contributions. See *Example 8.*

Example 3. (i) The facts are the same as in *Example 2*, except that Employee D also had elective contributions under Plan Y, maintained by an employer unrelated to M. In January 2007, D requests and receives a distribution of $1,200 in excess deferrals from Plan X. Pursuant to the terms of Plan X, D forfeits the $600 match on the excess deferrals to correct a discriminatory rate of match.

(ii) The $3,000 that would otherwise have been recharacterized for Plan X to satisfy the actual deferral percentage test is reduced by the $1,200 already distributed as an excess deferral, leaving $1,800 to be recharacterized. See § 1.401(k)-2(b)(4)(i)(A). D's actual contribution ratio is now 4.35% ($7,500 in matching contributions plus $1,800 in recharacterized contributions less $600 forfeited matching contributions attributable to the excess deferrals, divided by $200,000 in compensation).

(iii) The matching and employee contributions for Employee D must be reduced by .35% of compensation in order to reduce the ACP of the HCEs to 4%. The plan must provide for forfeiture of additional matching

(5) *Examples.* The following examples illustrate the application of this paragraph. See also § 1.401(k)-2(b) for additional examples of the parallel correction rules applicable to cash or deferred arrangements. For purposes of these examples, none of the plans provide for catch-up contributions under section 414(v). The examples are as follows:

Example 1. (i) Employer L maintains a plan that provides for employee contributions and fully vested matching contributions. The plan provides that failures of the ACP test are corrected by distribution. In 2006, the ACP for the eligible NHCEs is 6%. Thus, the ACP for the eligible HCEs may not exceed 8%. The three HCEs who participate have the following compensation, contributions, and ACRs:

Compensation	*Employee contributions and matching contributions*	*Actual Contribution Ratio*
200,000	14,000	7 %
150,000	13,500	9
100,000	12,000	12
	Average 9.33%	

required to cause their contributions to equal the next highest dollar amount of matching contributions and employee contributions).

(vi) Because the total amount of excess aggregate contributions has not been apportioned, further apportionment is necessary. The balance ($750) of the total amount of excess aggregate contributions is apportioned equally among Employees A, B and C ($250 to each, the amount required to allocate the total amount of excess aggregate contributions for the plan).

(vii) Therefore, the plan will satisfy the requirements of paragraph (a)(1) of this section if, by the end of the 12 month period following the end of the 2006 plan year, Employee A receives a corrective distribution of excess aggregate contributions equal to $ 2,250 ($500 + $1,500 + $250) and allocable income, Employee B receives a corrective distribution of $250 and allocable income and Employee C receives a corrective distribution of $1,750 ($1,500 + $250) and allocable income.

Example 2. (i) Employee D is the sole HCE who is eligible to participate in a cash or deferred arrangement maintained by Employer M. The plan that includes the arrangement, Plan X, permits employee contributions and provides a fully vested matching contribution equal to 50% of elective contributions. Plan X is a calendar year plan. Plan X corrects excess contributions by recharacterization and provides that failures of the ACP test are corrected by distribution. For the 2006 plan year, D's compensation is $200,000, and D's elective contributions are $15,000. The actual deferral percentages and actual contribution percentages for Employee D and the other eligible employees under Plan X are shown in the following table:

Actual Deferral Percentage	*Actual Contribution Percentage*
7.5%	3.75%
4.0%	2.00%

contributions to prevent a discriminatory rate of matching contributions. See *Example 8.*

Example 4. (i) The facts are the same as in *Example 3*, except that D does not request a distribution of excess deferrals until March 2007. Employer X has already recharacterized $3,000 as employee contributions.

(ii) Under § 1.402(g)-1(e)(6), the amount of excess deferrals is reduced by the amount of excess contributions that are recharacterized. Because the amount recharacterized is greater than the excess deferrals, Plan X is neither required nor permitted to make a distribution of excess deferrals, and the recharacterization has corrected the excess deferrals.

Example 5. (i) For the 2006 plan year, Employee F defers $10,000 under Plan M and $6,000 under Plan N. Plans M and N, which have calendar plan years are maintained by unrelated employers. Plan M provides a fully vested, 100% matching contribution, does not take elective contributions into account under section 401(m) or take matching contributions into account under section 401(k) and provides that excess contributions and excess aggregate contributions are corrected by distribution. Under Plan M, Employee F is allocated excess contributions of $600 and excess aggregate contributions of $1,600. Employee F timely requests and receives a distribution of the $1,000 excess deferral from Plan M and, pursuant to the terms of Plan M, forfeits the corresponding $1,000 matching contribution.

(ii) No distribution is required or permitted to correct the excess contributions because $1,000 has been distributed by Plan M as excess deferrals. The distribution required to correct the excess aggregate contributions (after forfeiting the matching contribution) is $600 ($1,600 in excess aggregate contributions minus $1,000 in forfeited matching contributions). If Employee F had corrected the excess deferrals of $1,000 by withdrawing $1,000 from Plan N, Plan M would have had to correct the $600 excess contributions in Plan M by distributing $600. Since Employee F then would have forfeited $600 (instead of $1,000) in matching contributions, Employee F would have had $1,000 ($1,600 in excess aggregate contributions minus $600 in forfeited matching contributions) remaining of excess aggregate contributions in Plan M. These would have been corrected by distributing an additional $1,000 from Plan M.

Example 6. (i) Employee G is the sole highly compensated employee in a profit sharing plan under which the employer matches 100% of employee contributions up to 2% of compensation, and 50% of employee contributions up to the next 4% of compensation. For the 2008 plan year, Employee G has compensation of $100,000 and makes a 7% employee contribution of $7,000. Employee G receives a 4% matching contribution or $4,000. Thus, Employee G's actual contribution ratio (ACR) is 11%. The actual contribution percentage for the nonhighly compensated employees is 5%, and the employer determines that Employee G's ACR must be reduced to 7% to comply with the rules of section 401(m).

(ii) In this case, the plan satisfies the requirements of section if it distributes the unmatched employee contributions of $1,000, and $2,000 of matched employee contributions with their related matches of $1,000. This would leave Employee G with 4% employee contributions, and 3% matching contributions, for an ACR of 7%. Alternatively, the plan could distribute all matching contributions and satisfy this section. However, the plan could not distribute $4,000 of Employee G's employee contributions without forfeiting the related matching contributions because this would result in a discriminatory rate of matching contributions. See also *Example 7.*

Example 7. (i) Employee H is an HCE in Employer X's profit sharing plan, which matches 100% of employee contributions up to 5% of compensation. The matching contribution is vested at the rate of 20% per year. In 2006, Employee H makes $5,000 in employee contributions and receives $5,000 of matching contributions. Employee H is 60% vested in the matching contributions at the end of the 2006 plan year. In February 2007, Employer X determines that Employee H has excess aggregate contributions of $1,000. The plan provides that only matching contributions will be distributed as excess aggregate contributions.

(ii) Employer X has two options available in distributing Employee H's excess contributions. The first option is to distribute $600 of vested matching contributions and forfeit $400 of nonvested matching contributions. These amounts are in proportion to Employee H's vested and nonvested interests in all matching contributions. The second option is to distribute $1,000 of vested matching contributions, leaving the nonvested matching contributions in the plan.

(iii) If the second option is chosen, the plan must also provide a separate vesting schedule for vesting these nonvested matching contributions. This is necessary because the nonvested matching contributions must vest as rapidly as they would have had no distribution been made. Thus, 50% must vest in each of the next 2 years.

(iv) The plan will not satisfy the nondiscriminatory availability requirement of section 401(a)(4) if only nonvested matching contributions are distributed because the effect is that matching contributions for HCEs vest more rapidly than those for NHCEs. See § 1.401(m)-1(e)(4).

Example 8. (i) Employer Y maintains a calendar year profit sharing plan that includes a cash or deferred arrangement. Elective contributions are matched at the rate of 100%. After-tax employee contributions are permitted under the plan only for nonhighly compensated employees and are matched at the same rate. No employees make excess deferrals. Employee J, a highly compensated employee, makes an $8,000 elective contribution and receives an $8,000 matching contribution.

(ii) Employer Y performs the actual deferral percentage (ADP) and the actual contribution percentage (ACP). To correct failures of the ADP and ACP tests, the plan distributes to A $1,000 of excess contributions and $500 of excess aggregate contributions. After the distributions, Employee J's contributions for the year are $7,000 of elective contributions and $7,500 of matching contributions. As a result, Employee J has received a higher effective rate of matching contributions than nonhighly compensated employees ($7,000 of elective contributions matched by $7,500 is an effective matching rate of 107 percent). If this amount remains in Employee J's account without correction, it will cause the plan to fail to satisfy section 401(a)(4), because only a highly compensated employee receives the higher matching contribution rate. The remaining $500 matching contribution may be forfeited (but not distributed) under section 411(a)(3)(G), if the plan so provides. The plan could instead correct the discriminatory rate of matching contribu-

tions by making additional allocations to the accounts of nonhighly compensated employees. See § 1.401(a)(4)-11(g)(3)(vii)(B) and (6), *Example 7.*

(c) *Additional rules for prior year testing method*—(1) *Rules for change in testing method.* A plan is permitted to change from the prior year testing method to the current year testing method for any plan year. A plan is permitted to change from the current year testing method to the prior year testing method only in situations described in § 1.401(k)-2(c)(1)(ii). For purposes of this paragraph (c)(1), a plan that uses the safe harbor method described in § 1.401(m)-3 or a SIMPLE 401(k) plan is treated as using the current year testing method for that plan year

(2) *Calculation of ACP under the prior year testing method for the first plan year*—(i) *Plans that are not successor plans.* If, for the first plan year of any plan (other than a successor plan), a plan uses the prior year testing method, the plan is permitted to use either that first plan year as the applicable year for determining the ACP for the eligible NHCEs, or 3% as the ACP for eligible NHCEs, for applying the ACP test for that first plan year. A plan (other than a successor plan) that uses the prior year testing method but has elected for its first plan year to use that year as the applicable year for determining the ACP for the eligible NHCEs is not treated as changing its testing method in the second plan year and is not subject to the limitations on double counting under paragraph (a)(6)(vi) of this section for the second plan year.

(ii) *First plan year defined.* For purposes of this paragraph (c)(2), the first plan year of any plan is the first year in which the plan provides for employee contributions or matching contributions. Thus, the rules of this paragraph (c)(2) do not apply to a plan (within the meaning of § 1.410(b)-7) for a plan year if for such plan year the plan is aggregated under § 1.401(m)-1(b)(4) with any other plan that provides for employee or matching contributions in the prior year.

(iii) *Plans that are successor plans.* A plan is a successor plan if 50% or more of the eligible employees for the first plan year were eligible employees under another plan maintained by the employer in the prior year that provides for employee contributions or matching contributions. If a plan that is a successor plan uses the prior year testing method for its first plan year, the ACP for the group of NHCEs for the applicable year must be determined under paragraph (c)(4) of this section.

(3) *Plans using different testing methods for the ACP and ADP test.* Except as otherwise provided in this paragraph (c)(3), a plan may use the current year testing method or prior year testing method for the ACP test for a plan year without regard to whether the current year testing method or prior year testing method is used for the ADP test for that year. For example, a plan may use the prior year testing method for the ACP test and the current year testing method for its ADP test for the plan year. However, plans that use different testing methods under this paragraph (c)(3) cannot use—

(i) The recharacterization method of § 1.401(k)-2(b)(3) to correct excess contributions for a plan year;

(ii) The rules of paragraph (a)(6)(ii) of this section to take elective contributions into account under the ACP test (rather than the ADP test); or

(iii) The rules of paragraph § 1.401(k)-2(a)(6) to take qualified matching contributions into account under the ADP test (rather than the ACP test).

(4) *Rules for plan coverage change*—(i) *In general.* A plan that uses the prior year testing method that experiences a plan coverage change during a plan year satisfies the requirements of this section for that year only if the plan provides that the ACP for the NHCEs for the plan year is the weighted average of the ACPs for the prior year subgroups.

(ii) *Optional rule for minor plan coverage changes.* If a plan coverage change occurs and 90% or more of the total number of the NHCEs from all prior year subgroups are from a single prior year subgroup, then, in lieu of using the weighted averages described in paragraph (c)(4)(i) of this section, the plan may provide that the ACP for the group of eligible NHCEs for the prior year under the plan is the ACP of the NHCEs for the prior year of the plan under which that single prior year subgroup was eligible.

(iii) *Definitions.* The following definitions apply for purposes of this paragraph (c)(4)—

(A) *Plan coverage change.* The term *plan coverage change* means a change in the group or groups of eligible employees under a plan on account of—

(*1*) The establishment or amendment of a plan;

(*2*) A plan merger or spinoff under section 414(I);

(*3*) A change in the way plans (within the meaning of § 1.410(b)-7) are combined or separated for purposes of § 1.401(m)-1(b)(4) (e.g., permissively aggregating plans not previously aggregated under § 1.410(b)-7(d), or ceasing to permissively aggregate plans under § 1.410(b)-7(d));

(*4*) A reclassification of a substantial group of employees that has the same effect as amending the plan (e.g., a transfer of a substantial group of employees from one division to another division); or

(*5*) A combination of any of the situations described in this paragraph (c)(4)(iii)(A).

(B) *Prior year subgroup.* The term *prior year subgroup* means all NHCEs for the prior plan year who, in the prior year, were eligible employees under a specific plan that provides for employee contributions or matching contributions maintained by the employer and who would have been eligible employees in the prior year under the plan being tested if the plan coverage change had first been effective as of the first day of the prior plan year instead of first being effective during the plan year. The determination of whether an NHCE is a member of a prior year subgroup is made without regard to whether the NHCE terminated employment during the prior year.

(C) *Weighted average of the ACPs for the prior year subgroups.* The term *weighted average of the ACPs for the prior year subgroups* means the sum, for all prior year subgroups, of the adjusted ACPs for the plan year. The term *adjusted ACP with respect to a prior year subgroup* means the ACP for the prior plan year of the specific plan under which the members of the prior year subgroup were eligible employees on the first day of the prior plan year, multiplied by a fraction, the numerator of which is the number of NHCEs in the prior year subgroup and denominator of which is the total number of NHCEs in all prior year subgroups.

(iv) *Example.* The following example illustrate the application of this paragraph (c)(4). See also § 1.401(k)-2(c)(4) for examples of the parallel rules applicable to the ADP test. The example is as follows:

Example. (i) Employer B maintains two plans, Plan N and Plan P, each of which includes a provides for employee contributions or matching contributions. The plans were not permissively aggregated under § 1.410(b)-7(d) for the 2005 testing year. Both plans use the prior year testing method. Plan N had 300 eligible employees who were NHCEs for 2005, and their ACP for that year was 6%. Plan P had 100 eligible employees who were NHCEs for 2005, and the ACP for those NHCEs for that plan was 4%. Plan N and Plan P are permissively aggregated under § 1.410(b)-7(d) for the 2006 plan year.

(ii) The permissive aggregation of Plan N and Plan P for the 2006 testing year under § 1.410(b)-7(d) is a plan coverage change that results in treating the plans as one plan (Plan NP). Therefore, the prior year ACP for the NHCEs under Plan NP for the 2006 testing year is the weighted average of the ACPs for the prior year subgroups.

(iii) The first step in determining the weighted average of the ACPs for the prior year subgroups is to identify the prior year subgroups. With respect to the 2006 testing year, an employee is a member of a prior year subgroup if the employee was an NHCE of Employer B for the 2005 plan year, was an eligible employee for the 2005 plan year under any section 401(k) plan maintained by Employer B, and would have been an eligible employee in the 2005 plan year under Plan NP if Plan N and Plan P had been permissively aggregated under § 1.410(b)-7(d) for that plan year. The NHCEs who were eligible employees under separate plans for the 2005 plan year comprise separate prior year subgroups. Thus, there are two prior year subgroups under Plan NP for the 2006 testing year: the 300 NHCEs who were eligible employees under Plan N for the 2005 plan year and the 100 NHCEs who were eligible employees under Plan P for the 2005 plan year.

(iv) The weighted average of the ACPs for the prior year subgroups is the sum of the adjusted ACP with respect to the prior year subgroup that consists of the NHCEs who were eligible employees under Plan N, and the adjusted ACP with respect to the prior year subgroup that consists of the NHCEs who were eligible employees under Plan P. The adjusted ACP for the prior year subgroup that consists of the NHCEs who were eligible employees under Plan N is 4.5%, calculated as follows: 6% (the ACP for the NHCEs under Plan N for the prior year) × 300/400 (the number of NHCEs in that prior year subgroup divided by the total number of NHCEs in all prior year subgroups), which equals 4.5%. The adjusted ACP for the prior year subgroup that consists of the NHCEs who were eligible employees under Plan P is 1%, calculated as follows: 4% (the ACP for the NHCEs under Plan P for the prior year) × 100/400 (the number of NHCEs in that prior year subgroup divided by the total number of NHCEs in all prior year subgroups), which equals

1%. Thus, the prior year ACP for NHCEs under Plan NP for the 2006 testing year is 5.5% (the sum of adjusted ACPs for the prior year subgroups, 4.5% plus 1%).

§ 1.401(m)-3 Safe harbor requirements.

(a) *ACP test safe harbor.* Matching contributions under a plan satisfy the ACP safe harbor provisions of section 401(m)(11) for a plan year if the plan satisfies the safe harbor contribution requirement of paragraphs (b) or (c) of this section for the plan year, the limitations on matching contributions of paragraph (d) of this section, the notice requirement of paragraph (e) of this section, the plan year requirements of paragraph (f) of this section, and the additional rules of paragraphs (g), (h) and (j) of this section, as applicable. Pursuant to section 401(k)(12)(E)(ii), the safe harbor contribution requirement of paragraphs (b) and (c) of this section must be satisfied without regard to section 401(l). The contributions made under paragraphs (b) and (c) of this section are referred to as safe harbor nonelective contributions and safe harbor matching contributions, respectively.

(b) *Safe harbor nonelective contribution requirement.* A plan satisfies the safe harbor nonelective contribution requirement of this paragraph (b) if it satisfies the safe harbor nonelective contribution requirement of § 1.401(k)-3(b).

(c) *Safe harbor matching contribution requirement.* A plan satisfies the safe harbor matching contribution requirement of this paragraph (c) if it satisfies the safe harbor matching contribution requirement of § 1.401(k)-3(c).

(d) *Limitation on contributions.* (1) *General rule.* A plan that provides for matching contributions meets the requirements of this section only if it satisfies the limitations on contributions set forth in this paragraph (d).

(2) *Matching rate must not increase.* A plan that provides for matching contributions meets the requirements of this paragraph (d) only if the ratio of matching contributions on behalf of an employee under the plan for a plan year to the employee's elective deferrals and employee contributions, does not increase as the amount of an employee's elective deferrals and employee contributions increases.

(3) *Limit on matching contributions.* A plan that provides for matching contributions satisfies the requirements of this section only if—

(i) Matching contributions are not made with respect to elective deferrals or employee contributions that exceed 6% of the employee's safe harbor compensation (within the meaning of § 1.401(k)-3(b)(2)); and

(ii) Matching contributions that are discretionary do not exceed 4% of the employee's safe harbor compensation.

(4) *Limitation on rate of match.* A plan meets the requirements of this section only if the ratio of matching contributions on behalf of an HCE to that HCE's elective deferrals or employee contributions (or the sum of elective deferrals and employee contributions) for that plan year is no greater than the ratio of matching contributions to elective deferrals or employee contributions (or the sum of elective deferrals and employee contributions) that would apply with respect to any NHCE for whom the elective deferrals or employee contributions (or the sum of elective deferrals and employee contributions) are the same percentage of safe harbor compensation. An employee is taken into account for purposes of this paragraph (d)(4) if the employee is an eligible employee under the cash or deferred arrangement with respect to which the contributions required by paragraph (b) or (c) of this section are being made for a plan year. A plan will not fail to satisfy this paragraph (d)(4) merely because the plan provides that matching contributions will be made separately with respect to each payroll period (or with respect to all payroll periods ending with or within each month or quarter of a plan year) taken into account under the plan for the plan year, provided that matching contributions with respect to any elective deferrals or employee contributions made during a plan year quarter are contributed to the plan by the last day of the immediately following plan year quarter.

(5) *HCEs participating in multiple plans.* The rules of section 401(m)(2)(B) and § 1.401(m)-2(a)(3)(ii) apply for purposes of determining the rate of matching contributions under paragraph (d)(4) of this section. However, a plan will not fail to satisfy the safe harbor matching contribution requirements of this section merely because an HCE participates during the plan year in more than one plan that provides for matching contributions, provided that—

(i) The HCE is not simultaneously an eligible employee under two plans that provide for matching contributions maintained by an employer for a plan year; and

(ii) The period used to determine compensation for purposes of determining matching contributions under each such plan is limited to periods when the HCE participated in the plan.

(6) *Permissible restrictions on elective deferrals by NHCEs*—(i) *General rule*. A plan does not satisfy the safe harbor requirements of this section, if elective deferrals or employee contributions by NHCEs are restricted, unless the restrictions are permitted by this paragraph (d)(6).

(ii) *Restrictions on election periods*. A plan may limit the frequency and duration of periods in which eligible employees may make or change contribution elections under a plan. However, an employee must have a reasonable opportunity (including a reasonable period after receipt of the notice described in paragraph (e) of this section) to make or change a contribution election for the plan year. For purposes of this section, a 30-day period is deemed to be a reasonable period to make or change a contribution election.

(iii) *Restrictions on amount of contributions*. A plan is permitted to limit the amount of contributions that may be made by an eligible employee under a plan, provided that each NHCE who is an eligible employee is permitted (unless the employee is restricted under paragraph (d)(6)(v) of this section) to make contributions in an amount that is at least sufficient to receive the maximum amount of matching contributions available under the plan for the plan year, and the employee is permitted to elect any lesser amount of contributions. However, a plan may require eligible employees to make contribution elections in whole percentages of compensation or whole dollar amounts.

(iv) *Restrictions on types of compensation that may be deferred*. A plan may limit the types of compensation that may be deferred or contributed by an eligible employee under a plan, provided that each eligible NHCE is permitted to make contributions under a definition of compensation that would be a reasonable definition of compensation within the meaning of § 1.414(s)-1(d)(2). Thus, the definition of compensation from which contributions may be made is not required to satisfy the nondiscrimination requirement of § 1.414(s)-1(d)(3).

(v) *Restrictions due to limitations under the Internal Revenue Code*. A plan may limit the amount of contributions made by an eligible employee under a plan—

(A) Because of the limitations of section 402(g) or section 415; or

(B) Because, on account of a hardship distribution, an employee's ability to make contributions has been suspended for 6 months in accordance with § 1.401(k)-1(d)(3)(iv)(E).

(e) *Notice requirement*. A plan satisfies the notice requirement of this paragraph (e) if it satisfies the notice requirement of § 1.401(k)-3(d).

(f) *Plan year requirement*—(1) *General rule*. Except as provided in this paragraph (f) or in paragraph (g) of this section, a plan will fail to satisfy the requirements of section 401(m)(11) and this section unless plan provisions that satisfy the rules of this section are adopted before the first day of that plan year and remain in effect for an entire 12-month plan year. Moreover, if, as described in paragraph (j)(4) of this section, safe harbor matching or nonelective contributions will be made to another plan for a plan year, provisions specifying that the safe harbor contributions will be made in the other plan and providing that the contributions will be QNECs or QMACs must be also be adopted before the first day of that plan year.

(2) *Initial plan year*. A newly established plan (other than a successor plan within the meaning of § 1.401(m)-2(c)(2)(iii)) will not be treated as violating the requirements of this paragraph (f) merely because the plan year is less than 12 months, provided that the plan year is at least 3 months long (or, in the case of a newly established employer that establishes the plan as soon as administratively feasible after the employer comes into existence, a shorter period). Similarly, a plan will not fail to satisfy the requirements of this paragraph (f) for the first plan year in which matching contributions are provided under the plan provided that—

(i) The plan is not a successor plan; and

(ii) The amendment providing for matching contributions is made effective at the same time as the adoption of a cash or deferred arrangement that satisfies the requirements of § 1.401(k)-3, taking into account the rules of § 1.401(k)-3(e)(2).

(3) *Change of plan year*. A plan that has a short plan year as a result of changing its plan year will not fail to satisfy the requirements of paragraph (f)(1) of this section merely because the plan year has less than 12 months, provided that—

(i) The plan satisfied the requirements of this section for the immediately preceding plan year; and

(ii) The plan satisfies the requirements of this section for the immediately following plan year.

(4) *Final plan year*. A plan that terminates during a plan year will not fail to satisfy the requirements of paragraph (f)(1) of this section merely because the final plan year is less than 12 months, provided that—

(i) The plan would satisfy the requirements of paragraph (h) of this section, treating the termination of the plan as a reduction or suspension of safe harbor matching contributions, other than the requirement that employees have a reasonable opportunity to change their cash or deferred elections and, if applicable, employee contribution elections; or

(ii) The plan termination is in connection with a transaction described in section 410(b)(6)(C) or the employer incurs a substantial business hardship, comparable to a substantial business hardship described in section 412(d).

(g) *Plan amendments adopting nonelective safe harbor contributions*. Notwithstanding paragraph (f)(1) of this section, a plan that provides for the use of the current year testing method may be amended after the first day of the plan year and no later than 30 days before the last day of the plan year to adopt the safe harbor method of this section using nonelective contributions under paragraph (b) of this section if the plan satisfies the requirements of § 1.401(k)-3(f).

(h) *Permissible reduction or suspension of safe harbor matching contributions*—(1) *General rule*. A plan that provides for safe harbor matching contributions will not fail to satisfy the requirements of section 401(m)(2) for a plan year merely because the plan is amended during a plan year to reduce or suspend safe harbor matching contributions on future elective deferrals and, if applicable, employee contributions provided—

(i) All eligible employees are provided the supplemental notice in accordance with paragraph (h)(2) of this section;

(ii) The reduction or suspension of safe harbor matching contributions is effective no earlier than the later of 30 days after eligible employees are provided the notice described in paragraph (h)(2) of this section and the date the amendment is adopted;

(iii) Eligible employees are given a reasonable opportunity (including a reasonable period after receipt of the supplemental notice) prior to the reduction or suspension of safe harbor matching contributions to change their cash or deferred elections and, if applicable, their employee contribution elections;

(iv) The plan is amended to provide that the ACP test will be satisfied for the entire plan year in which the reduction or suspension occurs using the current year testing method described in § 1.401(m)-2(a)(1)(ii); and

(v) The plan satisfies the requirements of this section (other than this paragraph (h)) with respect to amounts deferred through the effective date of the amendment.

(2) *Notice of suspension requirement*. The notice of suspension requirement of this paragraph (h)(2) is satisfied if each eligible employee is given a written notice that satisfies the content requirements of § 1.401(k)-3(e)(3).

(i) [Reserved]

(j) *Other rules*—(1) *Contributions taken into account*. A contribution is taken into account for purposes of this section for a plan year under the same rules as § 1.401(k)-3(h)(1).

(2) *Use of safe harbor nonelective contributions to satisfy other nondiscrimination tests*. A safe harbor nonelective contribution used to satisfy the nonelective contribution requirement under paragraph (b) of this section may also be taken into account for purposes of determining whether a plan satisfies section 401(a)(4) under the same rules as § 1.401(k)-3(h)(2).

(3) *Early participation rules*. Section 401(m)(5)(C) and § 1.401(m)-2(a)(1)(iii)(A) which provide an alternative nondiscrimination rule for certain plans that provide for early participation, does not apply for purposes of section 401(m)(11) and this section. Thus, a plan is not treated as satisfying this section with respect to the eligible employees who have not completed the minimum age and service requirements of section 410(a)(1)(A) unless the plan satisfies the requirements of this section with respect to such eligible employees.

(4) *Satisfying safe harbor contribution requirement under another defined contribution plan*. Safe harbor matching or nonelective contributions may be made to another defined contribution plan under the same rules as § 1.401(k)-3(h)(4). Consequently, each NHCE under the plan providing for matching contributions must be eligible under the

same conditions under the other defined contribution plan and the plan to which the contributions are made must have the same plan year as the plan providing for matching contributions.

(5) *Contributions used only once.* Safe harbor matching or nonelective contributions cannot be used to satisfy the requirements of this section with respect to more than one plan.

(6) *Plan must satisfy ACP with respect to employee contributions.* If the plan provides for employee contributions, in addition to satisfying the requirements of this section, it must also satisfy the ACP test of § 1.401(m)-2. See § 1.401(m)-2(a)(5)(iii) for specials rules under which the ACP test is permitted to be run taking into account only employee contributions when this section is satisfied with respect to the matching contributions.

§ 1.401(m)-4 Special rules for mergers, acquisitions and similar events. [Reserved]

§ 1.401(m)-5 Definitions.

Unless otherwise provided, the definitions of this section govern for purposes of section 401(m) and the regulations thereunder.

Actual contribution percentage (ACP). Actual contribution percentage or ACP means the ACP of the group of eligible employees as defined in § 1.401(m)-2(a)(2)(i).

Actual contribution percentage (ACP) test. Actual contribution percentage test or ACP test means the test described in § 1.401(m)-2(a)(1).

Actual contribution ratio (ACR). Actual contribution ratio or ACR means the ACR of an eligible employee as defined in § 1.401(m)-2(a)(3).

Actual deferral percentage (ADP) test. Actual deferral percentage test or ADP test means the test described in § 1.401(k)-2(a)(1).

Compensation. Compensation means compensation as defined in section 414(s) and § 1.414(s)-1. The period used to determine an employee's compensation for a plan year must be either the plan year or the calendar year ending within the plan year. Whichever period is selected must be applied uniformly to determine the compensation of every eligible employee under the plan for that plan year. A plan may, however, limit the period taken into account under either method to that portion of the plan year or calendar year in which the employee was an eligible employee, provided that this limit is applied uniformly to all eligible employees under the plan for the plan year. See also section 401(a)(17) and § 1.401(a)(17)-1(c)(1). For this purpose, in case of an HCE whose ACR is determined under § 1.401(m)-2(a)(3)(ii), period of participation includes periods under another plan for which matching contributions or employee contributions are aggregated under § 1.401(m)-2(a)(3)(ii).

Current year testing method. Current year testing method means the testing method under which the applicable year is the current plan year, as described in § 1.401(m)-2(a)(2)(ii) or 1.401(k)-2(a)(2)(ii).

Elective contributions. Elective contributions means elective contributions as defined in § 1.401(k)-6.

Elective deferrals. Elective deferrals means elective deferrals described in section 402(g)(3).

Eligible employee—(1) General rule. Eligible employee means an employee who is directly or indirectly eligible to make an employee contribution or to receive an allocation of matching contributions (including matching contributions derived from forfeitures) under the plan for all or a portion of the plan year. For example, if an employee must perform purely ministerial or mechanical acts (e.g., formal application for participation or consent to payroll withholding) in order to be eligible to make an employee contribution for a plan year, the employee is an eligible employee for the plan year without regard to whether the employee performs these acts.

(2) *Conditions on eligibility.* An employee who is unable to make employee contributions or to receive an allocation of matching contributions because the employee has not contributed to another plan is also an eligible employee. By contrast, if an employee must perform additional service (e.g., satisfy a minimum period of service requirement) in order to be eligible to make an employee contribution or to receive an allocation of matching contributions for a plan year, the employee is not an eligible employee for the plan year unless the service is actually performed. An employee who would be eligible to make employee contributions but for a suspension due to a distribution, a loan, or an election not to participate in the plan, is treated as an eligible employee for purposes of section 401(m) for a plan year even though the employee may not make employee contributions or receive an allocation of matching contributions by reason of the suspension. Finally, an employee does not fail to be treated as an eligible employee

merely because the employee may receive no additional annual additions because of section 415(c)(1).

(3) *Certain one-time elections.* An employee is not an eligible employee merely because the employee, upon commencing employment with the employer or upon the employee's first becoming eligible under any plan of the employer providing for employee or matching contributions, is given a one-time opportunity to elect, and the employee in fact does elect, not to be eligible to make employee contributions or to receive allocations of matching contributions under the plan or any other plan maintained by the employer (including plans not yet established) for the duration of the employee's employment with the employer. In no event is an election made after December 23, 1994, treated as one-time irrevocable election under this paragraph if the election is made by an employee who previously became eligible under another plan (whether or not terminated) of the employer.

Eligible HCE. Eligible HCE means an eligible employee who is an HCE.

Eligible NHCE. Eligible NHCE means an eligible employee who is not an HCE.

Employee. Employee means an employee within the meaning of § 1.410(b)-9.

Employee contributions. Employee contributions means employee contributions as defined in 1.401(m)-1(a)(3).

Employee stock ownership plan (ESOP). Employee stock ownership plan or ESOP means the portion of a plan that is an ESOP within the meaning of § 1.410(b)-7(c)(2).

Employer. Employer means an employer within the meaning of § 1.410(b)-9.

Excess aggregate contributions. Excess aggregate contributions means, with respect to a plan year, the amount of excess aggregate contributions apportioned to an HCE under § 1.401(m)-2(b)(2)(iii).

Excess contributions. Excess contribution means with respect to a plan year, the amount of excess contribution apportioned to an HCE under § 1.401(k)-2(b)(2)(iii).

Excess deferrals. Excess deferrals means excess deferrals as defined in § 1.402(g)-1(e)(3).

Highly compensated employee (HCE). Highly compensated employee or HCE has the meaning provided in section 414(q).

Matching contributions. Matching contribution is defined in § 1.401(m)-1(a)(2).

Nonelective contributions. Nonelective contributions means employer contributions (other than matching contributions) with respect to which the employee may not elect to have the contributions paid to the employee in cash or other benefits instead of being contributed to the plan.

Non-employee stock ownership plan (non-ESOP). Non-employee stock ownership plan or non-ESOP means the portion of a plan that is not an ESOP within the meaning of § 1.410(b)-7(c)(2).

Non-highly compensated employee (NHCE). Non-highly compensated employee or NHCE means an employee who is not an HCE.

Plan. Plan means plan as defined in § 1.401(m)-1(b)(4).

Prior year testing method. Prior year testing method means the testing method under which the applicable year is the prior plan year, as described in § 1.401(m)-2(a)(2)(ii) or § 1.401(k)-2(a)(2)(ii).

Qualified matching contributions (QMAC). Qualified matching contributions or QMAC means matching contributions that satisfy the requirements of § 1.401(k)-1(c) and (d) at the time the contribution is made, without regard to whether the contributions are actually taken into account as elective contributions under § 1.401(k)-2(a)(6). See also § 1.401(k)-2(b)(4)(iii) for a rule providing that a matching contribution does not fail to qualify as a QMAC solely because it is forfeitable under section 411(a)(3)(G) because it is a matching contribution with respect to an excess deferral, excess contribution, or excess aggregate contribution.

Qualified nonelective contributions (QNEC). Qualified nonelective contributions or QNEC means employer contributions, other than elective contributions or matching contributions, that satisfy the requirements of § 1.401(k)-1(c) and (d) at the time the contribution is made, without regard to whether the contributions are actually taken into account under the ADP test under § 1.401(k)-2(a)(6) or the ACP test under § 1.401(m)-2(a)(6).

Judith B. Tomaso,

Acting Deputy Commissioner for Services and Enforcement.

DALE D. GOODE

CERTIFIED COPY

¶ 20,261A

IRS proposed regulations: Tax shelters: S corporations: Employee stock ownership plans (ESOPs): Disqualified persons: Nonallocation years: Synthetic equity.—The IRS has issued proposed regulations aimed at abuses by S corporation owners that use the tax exemption on S corporation stock held by ESOPs for inappropriate tax deferral or avoidance. In general, an ESOP holding employer securities consisting of S corporation stock must provide that no portion of plan assets attributable to, or allocable in lieu of, such employer securities may, during a nonallocation year, accrue for the benefit of any disqualified persons. The proposed regulations reflect the text of temporary regulations at ¶ 24,507I, which contain guidance on the definition of "disqualified persons" and "synthetic equity," as well as how to determine whether a plan year is a nonallocation year.

The proposed regulations, which were published in the *Federal Register* on July 21, 2003 (68 FR 43058), are reproduced below. Subsequently, temporary and proposed regulations were published in the *Federal Register* on December 17, 2004 (69 FR 75455 and 69 FR 75492, respectively). The preambles are found at ¶ 24,507T (temporary) and ¶ 20,261I (proposed).

DEPARTMENT OF TREASURY

Internal Revenue Service (IRS)

26 CFR Parts 1

[REG-129709-03]

RIN 1545-BC34

Prohibited Allocations of Securities in an S Corporation

AGENCY: Internal Revenue Service (IRS), Treasury.

ACTION: Notice of proposed rulemaking by cross-reference to temporary regulations and notice of public hearing.

SUMMARY: In the Rules and Regulations section of this issue of the **Federal Register**, the IRS is issuing temporary regulations that provide guidance on identifying disqualified persons and determining whether a plan year is a nonallocation year under section 409(p) and on the definition of synthetic equity under section 409(p)(5). These proposed regulations would generally affect plan sponsors of, and participants in, ESOPs holding stock of Subchapter S corporations. The text of those temporary regulations also serves as the text of these proposed regulations. This document also provides notice of a public hearing on these proposed regulations.

DATES: Written or electronic comments must be received by October 20, 2003.

Requests to speak (with outlines of oral comments to be discussed) at the public hearing scheduled for November 20, 2003, at 10 a.m. must be received by October 30, 2003.

ADDRESSES: Send submissions to: CC:PA:RU (REG-129709-03), room 5226, Internal Revenue Service, POB 7604, Ben Franklin Station, Washington, DC 20044. Submissions may be hand delivered Monday through Friday between the hours of 8 a.m. and 4 p.m. to: CC:PA:RU (REG-129709-03), Courier's Desk, Internal Revenue Service, 1111 Constitution Avenue, NW., Washington, DC. Alternatively, taxpayers may submit comments electronically directly to the IRS Internet site at *www.irs.gov/regs*. The public hearing will be held in room 6718.

FOR FURTHER INFORMATION CONTACT: Concerning the proposed regulations, John Ricotta at 622-6060; concerning submissions of comments, Guy Traynor, (202) 622-7180 (not toll-free numbers).

SUPPLEMENTARY INFORMATION

Background

Temporary regulations in the Rules and Regulations portion of this issue of the **Federal Register** amend the Income Tax Regulations (26 CFR part 1) relating to section 409(p). The temporary regulations contain rules relating to the identification of disqualified persons and determination whether a plan year is a nonallocation year under section 409(p) and the definition of synthetic equity under section 409(p)(5). The text of those temporary regulations also serves as the text of these proposed regulations. The preamble to the temporary regulations explains the temporary regulations.

Special Analyses

It has been determined that this notice of proposed rulemaking is not a significant regulatory action as defined in Executive Order 12866. Therefore, a regulatory assessment is not required. It also has been determined that section 553(b) of the Administrative Procedure Act (5 U.S.C. chapter 5) does not apply to these regulations. Because § 1.409(p)-1 imposes no new collection of information on small entities, a Regulatory Flexibility Analysis under the Regulatory Flexibility Act (5 U.S.C. chapter 6) is not required. Pursuant to section 7805(f) of the

Internal Revenue Code, this notice of proposed rulemaking will be submitted to the Chief Counsel for Advocacy of the Small Business Administration for comment on its impact on small business.

Comments and Requests for a Public Hearing

Before these proposed regulations are adopted as final regulations, consideration will be given to any written comments (a signed original and eight (8) copies) that are submitted timely to the IRS. All comments will be available for public inspection and copying.

Comments are requested with respect to issues raised by S corporation ESOPs established by March 14, 2001, that will need to comply with the requirements of section 409(p) beginning in 2005. For these ESOPs, the inclusion of deferred compensation as synthetic equity can be avoided by distributing such deferred compensation before 2005. Some employers may prefer other transition approaches. For example, a preferable transition approach may be to spin off and terminate the portion of a plan benefitting disqualified persons. Comments are requested on whether guidance is needed to address these possible transition approaches.

Comments are also requested on issues that are reserved in the regulations with respect to whether certain interests in an S corporation should be treated as synthetic equity, including the extent to which rights to acquire assets of the S corporation or another person are established for reasonable business purposes and should not be treated as synthetic equity. While comments can be filed as late as October 20, 2003, commentators are encouraged to file comments as early as possible because the IRS and Treasury intend to move forward to address these issues as early as 2003.

Commentators may also wish to comment on section 409(p)-related issues that are not directly raised in the proposed regulations. For example, commentators may wish to comment on the extent to which administrative guidance may be needed on an interim basis to deal with specific structures used to avoid or evade the purpose of section 409(p).

A public hearing has been scheduled for November 20, 2003, at 10 a.m. in room 6718 of the Internal Revenue Building, 1111 Constitution Avenue NW., Washington, DC. All visitors must present photo identification to enter the building. Because of access restrictions, visitors will not be admitted beyond the immediate entrance area more than 30 minutes before the hearing starts at the Constitution Avenue entrance. For information about having your name placed on the building access list to attend the hearing, see the "FOR FURTHER INFORMATION CONTACT" section of this preamble.

The rules of 26 CFR 601.601(a)(3) apply to the hearing. Persons who wish to present oral comments at the hearing must submit written comments and an outline of the topics to be discussed and the time to be devoted to each topic (signed original and eight (8) copies) by October 30, 2003. A period of 10 minutes will be allotted to each person for making comments. An agenda showing the scheduling of the speakers will be prepared after the deadline for receiving outlines has passed. Copies of the agenda will be available free of charge at the hearing.

Drafting Information

The principal author of these regulations is John Ricotta of the Office of the Division Counsel/Associate Chief Counsel (Tax Exempt and Government Entities). However, other personnel from the IRS and Treasury participated in their development.

List of Subjects 26 CFR Part 1

Income taxes, Reporting and recordkeeping requirements.

Proposed Amendments to the Regulations

Accordingly, 26 CFR part 1 is proposed to be amended as follows:

PART 1—INCOME TAXES

Paragraph 1. The authority citation for part 1 is amended by an entry in numerical order to read in part as follows:

Authority: 26 U.S.C. 7805 ***

Section 1.409(p)-1 also issued under 26 U.S.C. 409(p)(7)(A). ***

Par. 2. Section 1.409(p)-1 is added to read as follows:

§ 1.409(p)-1 Prohibited allocation of securities in an S corporation.

[The text of proposed § 1.409(p)-1 is the same as the text of § 1.409(p)-1T published elsewhere in this issue of the **Federal Register**].

Robert E. Wenzel,

Deputy Commissioner for Services and Enforcement.

DALE D. GOODE

CERTIFIED COPY

¶ 20,261B

IRS— Fair market value—Taxation on distributee income—Life insurance contracts.—Reproduced below were the text of a proposed rule which clarified that property distributions must be included in a distributee's income at fair market value even where existing regulations provide merely for the inclusion of the entire cash value. Therefore, where a qualified plan distributes a life insurance contract, retirement income contract, endowment contract, or other contract providing life insurance protection, the fair market value of such a contract is generally included in the distributee's income, as opposed to only the entire cash value of the contract. All rights under the contracts, including supplemental agreements, must be considered in determining fair market value.

The proposed regulation was published in the *Federal Register* on February 17, 2004 (69 FR 7384). Final regulations, which were published in the *Federal Register* on August 29, 2005 (70 FR 50967) are reproduced at ¶ 11,231, ¶ 11,243, and ¶ 11,751. The preamble appears at ¶ 24,508.

[¶ 20,261C Reserved.]

¶ 20,261D

IRS— Minimum coverage requirements—Tax-exempt organizations—Nondiscrimination testing.—The IRS has issued proposed regulations, pursuant to which employees of Code Sec. 501(c)(3) tax-exempt organizations may be excluded from the nondiscrimination test applied to determine whether the Code Sec. 401(k) plan of the organization complies with the minimum coverage requirements. The proposed rules, which would retroactively apply to post-1996 plan years and may be relied upon prior to the issuance of final rules, will effectively allow a tax-exempt organization to continue to maintain a Code Sec. 403(b) and a Code Sec. 401(k) plan without having to provide coverage for employees under both plans. This proposed regulation was published in the Federal Register on March 16, 2004 (69 FR 12291).

Code Sec. 401(k), Code Sec. 403(b) and Code Sec. 501(c)(3).

DEPARTMENT OF THE TREASURY

Internal Revenue Service

26 CFR Part 1

[REG-149752-03]

RIN 1545-BC87

Exclusion of Employees of 501(c)(3) Organizations in 401(k) and 401(m) Plans

AGENCY: Internal Revenue Service (IRS), Treasury.

ACTION: Notice of proposed rulemaking.

SUMMARY: This document contains proposed amendments to the regulations under section 410(b) of the Internal Revenue Code. The proposed amendments permit, in certain circumstances, employees of a tax-exempt organization described in section 501(c)(3) to be excluded for the purpose of testing whether a section 401(k) plan (or a section 401(m) plan that is provided under the same general arrangement as the section 401(k) plan of the employer) meets the requirements for minimum coverage specified in section 410(b). These regulations will affect tax-exempt employers described in section 501(c)(3), retirement plans sponsored by these employers, and participants in these plans.

DATES: Written or electronic comments and requests for a public hearing must be received by June 14, 2004.

ADDRESSES: Send submissions to: CC:PA:LPD:PR (REG-149752-03), room 5203, Internal Revenue Service, POB 7604, Ben Franklin Station, Washington, DC 20044. Submissions may be hand-delivered Monday through Friday between the hours of 8 a.m. and 4 p.m. to CC:PA:LPD:PR (REG- 149752-03), Courier's Desk, Internal Revenue Service, 1111 Constitution Avenue NW., Washington, DC. Alternatively, taxpayers may submit comments electronically via the Internet directly to the IRS Internet site at http://www.irs.gov/regs.

FOR FURTHER INFORMATION CONTACT: Concerning the regulations, R. Lisa Mojiri-Azad, 202-622-6060, or Stacey Grundman, 202-622-6090; concerning submissions and delivery of comments, Treena Garrett, 202-622-7180 (not toll-free numbers).

SUPPLEMENTARY INFORMATION:

Background

This document contains proposed amendments to the Income Tax Regulations (26 CFR Part 1) under section 410(b) of the Internal Revenue Code of 1986 (Code). The amendments implement a directive by Congress, contained in section 664 of the Economic Growth and Tax Relief Reconciliation Act of 2001 (Public Law 107-16, 115 Stat. 38) (EGTRRA), to amend Sec. 1.410(b)-6(g) of the regulations.

Prior to the enactment of the Small Business Job Protection Act of 1996 (Pub. L. 104-188, 110 Stat. 1755) (SBJPA), both governmental and tax-exempt entities generally were subject to the section 410(b) coverage requirements and precluded from maintaining section 401(k) plans pursuant to section 401(k)(4)(B). To prevent the section 401(k)(4)(B) prohibition from causing a plan to fail section 410(b), the existing regulations provide that employees of either governmental or tax-exempt entities who are precluded from being eligible employees under a section 401(k) plan by reason of section 401(k)(4)(B) may be treated as excludable in applying the minimum coverage rules to a section 401(k) plan or a section 401(m) plan that is provided under the same general arrangement as the section 401(k) plan, if more than 95 percent of the employees of the employer who are not precluded from being eligible employees by section 401(k)(4)(B) benefit under the plan for the plan year. Although tax-exempt organizations described in section 501(c)(3) were precluded by section 401(k)(4)(B) from maintaining a section 401(k) plan, they were permitted to allow their employees to make salary reduction contributions to a plan or contract that satisfies section 403(b) (a section 403(b) plan).

Section 1426(a) of SBJPA amended section 401(k)(4)(B) to allow nongovernmental tax-exempt organizations (including organizations exempt under section 501(c)(3)) to maintain section 401(k) plans. Thus, a section 501(c)(3) tax-exempt organization can now maintain a section 401(k) plan, a section 403(b) plan, or both. In light of this provision of SBJPA, section 664 of EGTRRA directed the Secretary of the Treasury to modify the regulations under section 410(b) to provide that employees of a tax-exempt organization described in section 501(c)(3) who are eligible to make salary reduction contributions under a section 403(b) plan may be treated as excludable employees for the purpose of testing whether a section 401(k) plan or a section 401(m) plan that is provided under the same general arrangement as the section 401(k) plan meets the minimum coverage requirements contained in section 410(b) if (1) no employee of the organization is eligible to participate in the section 401(k) or section 401(m) plan and

(2) at least 95 percent of the employees of the employer who are not employees of the organization are eligible to participate in the section 401(k) or section 401(m) plan.

The change recognizes that many tax-exempt organizations maintained section 403(b) plans prior to the enactment of SBJPA and is needed to allow the continued maintenance of section 403(b) plans by these organizations without requiring the same employees to be covered under a section 401(k) plan and the section 403(b) plan. The change will help an employer that maintains both a section 401(k) plan and a section 403(b) plan to satisfy the section 410(b) coverage requirements without the employer having to provide dual coverage for employees.

Explanation of Provisions

These regulations provide that employees of a tax-exempt organization described in section 501(c)(3) who are eligible to make salary reduction contributions under a section 403(b) plan may be treated as excludable employees for the purpose of testing whether a section 401(k) or a section 401(m) plan that is provided under the same general arrangement as the section 401(k) plan meets the minimum coverage requirements contained in section 410(b) if (1) no employee of the tax-exempt organization is eligible to participate in the section 401(k) or section 401(m) plan and (2) at least 95 percent of the employees of the employer who are not employees of the tax-exempt organization are eligible to participate in the section 401(k) or section 401(m) plan.

The proposed regulations do not include any changes to the treatment of governmental plans under the current regulations. Unless grandfathered, State and local governmental entities continue to be precluded from maintaining section 401(k) plans pursuant to section 401(k)(4)(B). However, as a result of section 1505(a)(1) of the Taxpayer Relief Act of 1997 (Public Law 105-34, 111 Stat. 788), which added section 401(a)(5)(G) to the Code, governmental plans (within the meaning of section 414(d)) maintained by a State or local government or political subdivision thereof (or agency or instrumentality thereof) are not subject to the minimum coverage requirements contained in section 410(b). Consequently, the IRS and Treasury request comments on whether it would be appropriate to modify the special rule for governmental plans contained in Sec. 1.410(b)-6(g) to reflect the addition of section 401(a)(5)(G) (including whether there continues to be a need for this special rule with respect to governmental plans).

Effective Date

As directed by Congress in section 664 of EGTRRA, the amendments to Sec. 1.410(b)-6(g) are proposed to be effective for plan years beginning after December 31, 1996. Taxpayers may rely on these proposed regulations for guidance pending the issuance of final regulations. If, and to the extent, future guidance is more restrictive than the guidance in these proposed regulations, the future guidance will be applied without retroactive effect.

Special Analyses

It has been determined that this notice of proposed rulemaking is not a significant regulatory action as defined in Executive Order 12866. Therefore, a regulatory assessment is not required. It also has been determined that section 553(b) of the Administrative Procedure Act (5 U.S.C. chapter 5) does not apply to these regulations, and, because the regulation does not impose a collection of information on small entities, the Regulatory Flexibility Act (5 U.S.C. chapter 6) does not apply. Pursuant to section 7805(f) of the Code, this notice of proposed rulemaking will be submitted to the Chief Counsel for Advocacy of the Small Business Administration for comment on its impact on small business.

Comments and Requests for a Public Hearing

Before these proposed regulations are adopted as final regulations, consideration will be given to any written (a signed original and 8 copies) or electronic comments that are submitted timely to the IRS. The IRS and Treasury request comments on the clarity of the proposed rules and how they can be made easier to understand. All comments will be available for public inspection and copying. A public hearing will be scheduled if requested in writing by any person that timely submits written comments. If a public hearing is scheduled, notice of the date, time, and place for the public hearing will be published in the Federal Register.

Drafting Information

The principal authors of these proposed regulations are R. Lisa Mojiri-Azad and Stacey Grundman of the Office of the Division Coun-

sel/Associate Chief Counsel (Tax Exempt and Government Entities). However, other personnel from the IRS and Treasury participated in the development of these regulations.

List of Subjects in 26 CFR Part 1

Income taxes, Reporting and recordkeeping requirements.

Proposed Amendments to the Regulations

Accordingly, 26 CFR part 1 is proposed to be amended as follows:

PART 1—INCOME TAXES

Paragraph 1. The authority citation for part 1 is amended by removing the entry for Sec. Sec. 1.410(b)-2 through 1.410(b)-10 and adding entries in numerical order to read, in part, as follows:

Authority: 26 U.S.C. 7805. * * *

Section 1.410(b)-2 also issued under 26 U.S.C. 410(b)(6).

Section 1.410(b)-3 also issued under 26 U.S.C. 410(b)(6).

Section 1.410(b)-4 also issued under 26 U.S.C. 410(b)(6).

Section 1.410(b)-5 also issued under 26 U.S.C. 410(b)(6).

Section 1.410(b)-6 also issued under 26 U.S.C. 410(b)(6) and section 664 of the Economic Growth and Tax Relief Reconciliation Act of 2001 (Public Law 107-16, 115 Stat. 38).

Section 1.410(b)-7 also issued under 26 U.S.C. 410(b)(6).

Section 1.410(b)-8 also issued under 26 U.S.C. 410(b)(6).

Section 1.410(b)-9 also issued under 26 U.S.C. 410(b)(6).

Section 1.410(b)-10 also issued under 26 U.S.C. 410(b)(6).* * *

Par. 2. Section 1.410(b)-0, table of contents, the entry for 1.410(b)-6 is amended by:

1. Revising the paragraph heading for 1.410(b)-6(g).

2. Adding paragraph headings for 1.410(b)-6(g)(1) and (g)(2).

The revision and additions read as follows:

§ *1.410(b)-0. Table of contents.*

* * *

§ *1.410(b)-6 Excludable employees.*

* * *

(g) Employees of certain governmental or tax-exempt entities.

(1) Employees of governmental entities.

(2) Employees of tax-exempt entities.

* * *

Par. 3. In Sec. 1.410(b)-6, paragraph (g) is revised to read as follows:

§ *1.410(b)-6. Excludable employees.*

* * *

(g) *Employees of certain governmental or tax-exempt entities.* For purposes of testing either a section 401(k) plan or a section 401(m) plan that is provided under the same general arrangement as a section 401(k) plan, an employer may treat as excludable those employees described in paragraphs (g)(1) and (2) of this section.

(1) *Employees of governmental entities.* Employees of governmental entities who are precluded from being eligible employees under a section 401(k) plan by reason of section 401(k)(4)(B)(ii) may be treated as excludable employees if more than 95 percent of the employees of the employer who are not precluded from being eligible employees by section 401(k)(4)(B)(ii) benefit under the plan for the plan year.

(2) *Employees of tax-exempt entities.* Employees of a tax-exempt organization described in section 501(c)(3) who are eligible to make salary reduction contributions under a section 403(b) plan may be treated as excludable employees if —

(i) No employee of the organization is eligible to participate in the section 401(k) or section 401(m) plan; and

(ii) At least 95 percent of the employees of the employer who are not employees of the organization are eligible to participate in the section 401(k) or section 401(m) plan.

* * *

Mark E. Mathews,

Deputy Commissioner for Services and Enforcement.

[FR Doc. 04-5903 Filed 3-15-04; 8:45 am]   BILLING CODE 4830-01-P

¶ 20,261E

IRS proposed regulations: Minimum vesting rules: Elimination of optional forms of benefit: Notice of amendment reducing benefit accrual.—The Treasury and IRS have issued proposed regulations that would allow employers maintaining qualified plans to adopt amendments that eliminate early retirement benefits, retirement-type subsidies, and optional forms of benefit that create significant burdens or complexities for the plan and its participants, as long as the amendments do not adversely affect the rights of any participants in more than a de minimis manner. The proposed rules would generally authorize the elimination of "redundant" optional forms of benefit, or, alternatively, the elimination of optional forms of benefit that fall outside a list of "core" optional forms of benefit. However, generally an employer would not be allowed to eliminate lump-sum payment options. The proposed rules, which may not be relied upon until finalized, would further: define the conditions under which an early retirement benefit or retirement-type subsidy may be eliminated, clarify the notice requirements applicable when a plan amendment significantly reduces future benefits, and explain when a plant-shutdown benefit or other contingent event benefit is a retirement-type subsidy or an unprotected ancillary benefit.

The proposed regulations, which were published in the Federal Register on March 24, 2004 (69 FR 13769), were finalized on August 12, 2005 by T.D. 9219 (70 FR 47109). The preamble to the final regs appears at ¶ 24,507Y.

¶ 20,261F

IRS proposed regulations: Deemed IRAs: Qualified nonbank trustees.—The IRS has issued proposed regulations, by cross-reference to temporary regulations at IRS Reg. Sec. 1.408–2T (¶ 12,054A), relating to qualification of governmental units as qualified nonbank trustees for deemed IRAs under section Code Sec. 408(q). Comments must be received by October 20, 2004.

The proposed regulations, which were published in the *Federal Register* on July 22, 2004 (69 FR 43786), are reproduced below.

DEPARTMENT OF THE TREASURY

Internal Revenue Service

26 CFR Part 1

[REG-101447-04]

RIN 1545-BD07

Deemed IRAs in Governmental Plans/Qualified Nonbank Trustee Rules.

AGENCY: Internal Revenue Service (IRS), Treasury.

ACTION: Notice of proposed rulemaking by cross-reference to temporary regulations.

SUMMARY: In the Rules and Regulations section of this issue of the **Federal Register**, the IRS is issuing temporary regulations relating to qualification of governmental units as qualified nonbank trustees for deemed IRAs under section 408(q). The text of those regulations also serves as the text of these proposed regulations.

DATES: Written or electronic comments must be received by October 20, 2004.

ADDRESSES: The public may submit comments in three ways. Send submissions to: CC:PA:LPD:PR (REG-101447-04), room 5203, Internal Revenue Service, PO Box 7604, Ben Franklin Station, Washington, DC 20044. Submissions may be hand-delivered between the hours of 8 a.m. and 4 p.m. to CC:PA:LPD:PR (REG-101447-04), Courier's Desk, Internal Revenue Service, 1111 Constitution Avenue, NW., Washington, DC, or send electronically, via the IRS Internet site at *www.irs.gov/regs* or via the Federal eRulemaking Portal at *www.regulations.gov* (indicate IRS and REG-101447-04).

FOR FURTHER INFORMATION CONTACT: Concerning the proposed regulations, Linda L. Conway, (202) 622-6090; concerning submissions of comments, Treena Garrett, (202) 622-3401 (not toll-free numbers).

SUPPLEMENTARY INFORMATION:

Background and Explanation of Provisions

The temporary regulations in the Rules and Regulations section of this issue of the **Federal Register** amend 26 CFR part 1 relating to section 408(a). The temporary regulations set forth special rules for a governmental unit that maintains a plan qualified under section 401(a), 403(a), 403(b) or 457 to qualify as a nonbank trustee for deemed IRAs under section 408(q). The text of those regulations also serves as the text of these proposed regulations. The preamble of the temporary regulations explains the amendments and these proposed regulations.

Special Analyses

It has been determined that this notice of proposed rulemaking is not a significant regulatory action as defined in Executive Order 12866.

Therefore, a regulatory assessment is not required. It also has been determined that section 553(b) of the Administrative Procedure Act (5 U.S.C. chapter 5) does not apply to these regulations and because the proposed regulations do not impose a collection of information by small entities, the provisions of the Regulatory Flexibility Act (5 U.S.C. chapter 6) do not apply. Pursuant to section 7805(f) of the Internal Revenue Code, this notice of proposed rulemaking will be submitted to the Chief Counsel for Advocacy of the Small Business Administration for comment on their impact on small business.

Comments and Requests for Public Hearing

Before these proposed regulations are adopted as final regulations, consideration will be given to any written comments (a signed original and eight (8) copies) or electronic comments that are submitted timely to the IRS. The IRS and Treasury Department specifically request comments on the clarity of the proposed rule and how it may be made easier to understand. All comments will be available for public inspection and copying. A public hearing will be scheduled if requested in writing by any person that timely submits written comments. If a public hearing is scheduled, notice of the date, time, and place for the public hearing will be published in the **Federal Register.**

Drafting Information

The principal author of these regulations is Linda L. Conway, Office of Assistant Chief Counsel (Tax Exempt & Government Entities). However, other personnel from the IRS and Treasury Department participated in their development.

List of Subjects in 26 CFR Part 1

Income taxes, Reporting and recordkeeping requirements.

Proposed Amendments to the Regulations

Accordingly, 26 CFR part 1 is proposed to be amended as follows:

PART 1 — INCOME TAXES

Paragraph 1. The authority citation for part 1 continues to read, in part, as follows:

Authority: 26 U.S.C. 7805 * * *

Par. 2. In § 1.408-(e)(8)T is added to read as follows:

§ 1.408-2 - *Special rules for governmental entities.*

[The text of proposed § 1.408-2 paragraph (e)(8) is the same as the text of § 1.408-2(e)(8)T published elsewhere in this issue of the **Federal Register**].

Mark E. Matthews

Deputy Commissioner for Services and Enforcement.

¶ 20,261G

IRS proposed regulations: Phased retirement: Distributions: Pro rata approach.—Reproduced below is the text of a proposed rule in which the IRS would permit retirement plans to distribute a portion of a participant's benefits on a pro rata basis depending upon the extent to which the participant has reduced his or her work hours. The number of hours worked would have to be reduced by 20% or more, and the phased retirement program would not be available to participants that have not reached age 59 ½. Additionally, participants in the phased retirement program would be entitled to participant in their retirement plans in generally the same manner they would be participating if they were maintaining a full-time work schedule.

The proposed regulation was published in the Federal Register on November 10, 2004 (69 FR 65108) and corrected on December 28, 2004.

DEPARTMENT OF TREASURY

Internal Revenue Service

26 CFR Part 1

[REG-114726-04]

RIN 1545-BD23

Distributions from a Pension Plan under a Phased Retirement Program

AGENCY: Internal Revenue Service (IRS), Treasury.

ACTION: Notice of proposed rulemaking.

SUMMARY: This notice of proposed rulemaking contains proposed amendments to the Income Tax Regulations under section 401(a) of the Internal Revenue Code. These proposed regulations provide rules permitting distributions to be made from a pension plan under a phased retirement program and set forth requirements for a bona fide phased retirement program. The proposed regulations will provide the public with guidance regarding distributions from qualified pension plans and will affect administrators of, and participants in, such plans.

DATES: Written or electronic comments and requests for a public hearing must be received by February 8, 2005.

ADDRESSES: Send submissions to: CC:PA:LPD:PR (REG-114726-04), room 5203, Internal Revenue Service, PO Box 7604, Ben Franklin Station, Washington, DC 20044. Submissions may be hand-delivered Monday through Friday between the hours of 8 a.m. and 4 p.m. to CC:PA:LPD:PR (REG-114726-04), Courier's Desk, Internal Revenue Service, 1111 Constitution Avenue, NW., Washington, DC, or sent electronically, via the IRS Internet site at *www.irs.gov/regs* or via the Federal eRulemaking Portal at *www.regulations.gov* (indicate IRS and REG-114726-04).

FOR FURTHER INFORMATION CONTACT: Concerning the regulations, Cathy A. Vohs, 202-622-6090; concerning submissions and requests for a public hearing, contact Sonya Cruse, 202-622-7180 (not toll-free numbers).

SUPPLEMENTARY INFORMATION:

Background

As people are living longer, healthier lives, there is a greater risk that individuals may outlive their retirement savings. In addition, employers have expressed interest in encouraging older, more experienced workers to stay in the workforce. One approach that some employers have implemented is to offer employees the opportunity for phased retirement."

While there is no single approach to phased retirement, these arrangements generally provide employees who are at or near eligibility for retirement with the opportunity for a reduced schedule or workload, thereby providing a smoother transition from full-time employment to retirement. These arrangements permit the employer to retain the services of an experienced employee and provide the employee with the opportunity to continue active employment at a level that also allows greater flexibility and time away from work.

During such a transition arrangement, employees may wish to supplement their part-time income with a portion of their retirement savings. However, phased retirement can also increase the risk of outliving retirement savings for employees who begin drawing upon their retirement savings before normal retirement age. Even though the annuity distribution options offered by defined benefit plans preclude outliving benefits, early distribution of a portion of the employee's benefit will reduce the benefits available after full retirement. On the other hand, phased retirement also can provide employees additional time to save for retirement because employees continue working while they are able to do so, and can accrue additional benefits and reduce or forgo early spending of their retirement savings.

In light of this background, Treasury and the IRS issued Notice 2002-43 in the Cumulative Bulletin (2002-27 C.B. 38 (July 8, 2002)), in which comments were requested regarding phased retirement. Notice 2002-43 specifically requested comments on a wide variety of issues, including the following:

- Under what circumstances, if any, would permitting distributions from a defined benefit plan before an employee attains normal retirement age be consistent with the requirement that a defined benefit plan be established and maintained primarily for purposes of providing benefits after retirement, such as the extent to which an employee has actually reduced his or her workload?

- If there are such circumstances, how should any early retirement subsidy be treated?

Comments Received

Sixteen written comments were formally submitted in response to Notice 2002-43. These comments are in addition to the substantial number of articles and other published materials addressing phased retirement.[1]

While some of the comments expressed concerns over the potential for both dissipation of retirement funds and violation of age discrimination laws, commentators generally responded favorably to the proposal to provide guidance on facilitating phased retirement arrangements. These commentators noted that permitting pension distributions during phased retirement would be attractive to both employers and employees. Commentators also indicated that any guidance issued should provide that establishment of phased retirement arrangements be optional on the part of the employer and that participation in any such arrangement be voluntary on the part of the employee.

Most of the comments recommended that eligibility to participate in a phased retirement program be limited to employees who are eligible for immediately commencing retirement benefits under the plan (including those eligible for early retirement benefits). Other comments recommended that retirement benefits be permitted to start at a specific age or combination of age and service; however, they noted that current legislative constraints, notably the section 72(t) 10 percent additional income tax on early distributions, may limit the desirability of this option.

Some commentators advocated that any phased retirement arrangement should be cost neutral and not create additional funding obligations for employers. Others recommended that any early retirement subsidy available to an employee upon full retirement continue to be available if the employee participates in phased retirement. For example, one such commentator recommended not only that any early retirement subsidy be available upon phased retirement, but also that the subsidy so paid not be permitted to be applied to reduce the remainder of the benefit that is earned by the employee, particularly if the employee continues working past normal retirement age.

The comments were divided over what constituted phased retirement. Several recommended that phased retirement benefits be limited to cases in which there is a reduction in hours worked. Others recommended that a reduction in hours not be required and that a transition to a less stressful job also be considered phased retirement or that the full retirement benefit be payable after the attainment of a specified age or years of service without regard to any change in work.

---

[1] See, for example, Pension & Welfare Benefits Administration, U.S. Department of Labor, "Report on Working Group on Phased Retirement to the Advisory Council on Employee Welfare & Pension Benefit Plans," 2000; Forman, Jonathan Barry, "How Federal Pension Laws Influence Individual Work and Retirement Decisions," 54 Tax Law. 143 (2000); Littler Mendelson, "Employers Consider 'Phased Retirement' to Retain Employees," Maryland Employment Law Letter, Vol 10, Issue 6 (April, 2000); Geisel, Jerry,

"Rethinking Phased Retirement; IRS Call for Comment May Signal Pension Law Changes," Business Insurance (June 24, 2002); Flahaven, Brian, "Please Don't Go! Why Phased Retirement May Make Sense For Your Government," 18 Gov't Finance Review 24 (Oct. 1, 2002); NPR, Morning Edition, "Older Workers Turn to 'Phased' Retirement," (May 18, 2004) at *www.npr.org/features/feature.php?wfId=1900465*

The commentators who recommended that phased retirement benefits be limited to cases in which there is a reduction in hours worked generally recommended that the phased retirement benefits payable be proportionate to the reduction in work, based on a "dual status" approach. Under this dual status approach, an employee who reduces his or her work schedule to, for example, 80 percent of full-time would be considered to be 20 percent retired and thus entitled to 20 percent of his or her retirement benefit. The employee would continue to accrue additional benefits based on the actual hours he or she continues to work.

Several of the commentators discussed the implications of phased retirement benefits for purposes of the nondiscrimination rules of section 401(a)(4) and the anti-cutback rules of section 411(d)(6). Many of the comments said that phased retirement arrangements must be flexible and that it would be important for employers to be able to adopt a phased retirement arrangement on a temporary (even experimental) basis.

Many commentators expressed concern over the effect that a reduction in hours and the corresponding reduction in compensation would have on the final average pay of an individual for purposes of the benefit calculation when the employee fully retires. These comments generally requested guidance on this issue, including clarification as to whether an employee's final average pay is permitted to decline as a result of the employee's reduction in hours pursuant to participation in a phased retirement arrangement.

Explanation of Provisions

Overview

The proposed regulations would amend § 1.401(a)-1(b) and add § 1.401(a)-3 in order to permit a pro rata share of an employee's accrued benefit to be paid under a bona fide phased retirement program. The pro rata share is based on the extent to which the employee has reduced hours under the program. Under this pro rata approach, an employee maintains a dual status (i.e., partially retired and partially in service) during the phased retirement period. This pro rata or dual status approach to phased retirement was one of the approaches recommended by commentators.

While all approaches suggested by commentators were considered, the pro rata approach is the most consistent with the requirement that benefits be maintained primarily for retirement. Other approaches, such as permitting benefits to be fully available if an employee works reduced hours as part of phased retirement or permitting distributions of the entire accrued benefit to be paid as of a specified age prior to normal retirement age, are fundamentally inconsistent with the § 1.401(a)-1(b) principle that benefits be paid only after retirement. In addition, although a number of commentators suggested that guidance address the practice of terminating an employee with a prearranged rehiring of the employee (or similar sham transactions), the proposed regulations do not address this topic because it involves additional issues outside the scope of this project.

Rules Relating to Phased Retirement

Under the proposed regulations, a plan would be permitted to pay a pro rata portion of the employee's benefits under a bona fide phased retirement program before attainment of normal retirement age. The proposed regulations define a bona fide phased retirement program as a written, employer-adopted program pursuant to which employees may reduce the number of hours they customarily work beginning on or after a retirement date specified under the program and receive phased retirement benefits. Payment of phased retirement benefits is permitted only if the program meets certain conditions, including that employee participation is voluntary and the employee and employer expect the employee to reduce, by 20 percent or more, the number of hours the employee works during the phased retirement period.

Consistent with the pro rata approach discussed above, the maximum amount that is permitted to be paid is limited to the portion of the employee's accrued benefit equal to the product of the employee's total accrued benefit on the date the employee commences phased retirement (or any earlier date selected by the plan for administrative ease) and the employee's reduction in work. The reduction in work is based on the employee's work schedule fraction, which is the ratio of the hours that the employee is reasonably expected to work during the phased retirement period to the hours that would be worked if the employee were full-time. Based in part on commentators' concerns regarding early retirement subsidies, the proposed regulations gener-

ally require that all early retirement benefits, retirement-type subsidies, and optional forms of benefit that would be available upon full retirement be available with respect to the phased retirement accrued benefit. However, the proposed regulations would not permit payment to be made in the form of a single-sum distribution (or other eligible rollover distribution) in order to prevent the premature distribution of retirement benefits. The phased retirement benefit is an optional form of benefit protected by section 411(d)(6) and the election of a phased retirement benefit is subject to the provisions of section 417, including the required explanation of the qualified joint and survivor annuity.

Some comments suggested that phased retirement be limited to employees who have attained an age or service (or combination thereof) that is customary for retirement, e.g., where the employer has reasonably determined in good faith that participants who cease employment with the employer after that age or service combination are typically not expected to continue to perform further services of a generally comparable nature elsewhere in the workforce. Such a retirement age might be considerably lower than age 65 in certain occupations (such as police or firefighters). As discussed further below (under the heading *Application to Plans Other Than Qualified Pension Plans*), the Treasury and IRS have concluded that they do not have the authority to permit payments to begin from a section 401(k) plan under a bona fide phased retirement program before the employee attains age 59 ½ or has a severance from employment.[2] Further, section 72(t)(3)(B) provides an additional income tax on early distributions if annuity distributions are made before the earlier of age 59 ½ or separation from service. Accordingly, in lieu of a customary retirement age, the proposed regulations adopt a rule that is consistent with section 401(k) and section 72(t)(3)(B), under which phased retirement benefits may not be paid before an employee attains age 59 ½.

Additional Accruals During Phased Retirement

The regulations provide that, during the phased retirement period, in addition to being entitled to the phased retirement benefit, the employee must be entitled to participate in the plan in the same manner as if the employee were still maintaining a full-time work schedule (including calculation of average earnings) and must be entitled to the same benefits (including early retirement benefits, retirement-type subsidies, and optional forms of benefits) upon full retirement as a similarly situated employee who has not elected phased retirement, except that the years of service credited under the plan for any plan year during the phased retirement period is multiplied by the ratio of the employee's actual hours of service during the year to the employee's full-time work schedule, or by the ratio of the employee's compensation to the compensation that would be paid for full-time work. Thus, for example, under a plan with a 1,000 hours of service requirement to accrue a benefit, an employee participating in a phased retirement program will accrue proportionate additional benefits, even if the employee works fewer than 1,000 hours of service.

The requirement that full-time compensation be imputed, with a proportionate reduction based on an employee's actual service, is intended to ensure that a participant is not disadvantaged by reason of choosing phased retirement. This rule precludes the need for extensive disclosure requirements, e.g., disclosure to alert participants to rights that may be lost as a result of participating in a phased retirement program. To be consistent with the requirement to use full-time compensation, the proposed regulations require an employee who was a highly compensated employee before commencing phased retirement to be treated as a highly compensated employee during phased retirement. See also § 1.414(q)-1T, A-4 & A-5.

Under the proposed regulations, the employee's final retirement benefit is comprised of the phased retirement benefit and the balance of the employee's accrued benefit under the plan (i.e., the excess of the total plan formula benefit over the portion of the accrued benefit paid as a phased retirement benefit). Upon full retirement, the phased retirement benefit can continue unchanged or the plan is permitted to offer a new election with respect to that benefit.

This bifurcation is consistent with commentators' recommendation that an employee who is in a phased retirement program has a dual status, under which the employee is treated as retired to the extent of the reduction in hours and is treated as working to the extent of the employee's continued work with the employer. This approach also ensures that a phased retirement program offers an early retirement subsidy to the extent the employee has reduced his or her hours, and that the remainder of the employee's benefit rights is not adversely affected by participation in the phased retirement program.

---

[2] Cf., *Edwards v. Commissioner*, T.C. Memo. 1989-409, *aff'd*, 906 F.2d 114 (4th Cir. 1990).

Testing and Adjustment of Payments

Subject to certain exceptions, the proposed regulations require periodic testing to ensure that employees in phased retirement are in fact working at the reduced schedule, as expected. Thus, unless an exception applies, a plan must provide for an annual comparison between the number of hours actually worked by an employee during a testing period and the number of hours the employee was reasonably expected to work. If the actual hours worked during the testing period are materially greater than the expected number of hours, then the employee's phased retirement benefit must be reduced prospectively. For this purpose, the employee's hours worked are materially greater than the employee's work schedule if they exceed either percent of the work schedule or 90 percent of the hours that the employee would work under a full-time schedule.

This annual comparison is not required after the employee is within 3 months of attaining normal retirement age or if the amount of compensation paid to the employee by the employer during the phased retirement testing period does not exceed the compensation that would be paid to the employee if he or she had worked full time multiplied by the employee's work schedule fraction. Further, no comparison is required during the first year of an employee's phased retirement or if the employee has entered into an agreement with the employer that the employee will retire within 2 years.

In the event that the employer and employee agree to increase prospectively the hours that the employee will work, then the employee's phased retirement benefit must be adjusted based on a new work schedule. The date of the agreement to increase the employee's hours is treated as a comparison date for testing purposes.

In calculating the employee's benefit at full retirement, if an employee's phased retirement benefits have been reduced during phased retirement, the employee's accrued benefit under the plan is offset by an amount that is actuarially equivalent to the additional payments made before the reduction. The potential for this offset, like other material features of the phased retirement optional form of benefit, must be disclosed as part of the QJSA explanation as required under § 1.401(a)-20, Q&A-36, and § 1.417(a)(3)-1(c)(1)(v) and (d)(1).

If the employee's phased retirement benefit is less than the maximum amount permitted or the employee's work schedule is further reduced at a later date, the proposed regulations allow a plan to provide one or more additional phased retirement benefits to the employee. The additional phased retirement benefit, commencing at a later annuity starting date, provides flexibility to reflect future reductions in the employee's work hours.

Provisions Relating to Payment After Normal Retirement Age

The proposed regulations clarify that a pension plan (i.e., a defined benefit plan or money purchase pension plan) is permitted to pay benefits upon an employee's attainment of normal retirement age. However, normal retirement age cannot be set so low as to be a subterfuge to avoid the requirements of section 401(a), and, accordingly, normal retirement age cannot be earlier than the earliest age that is reasonably representative of a typical retirement age for the covered workforce.[3]

Application to Plans Other Than Qualified Pension Plans

The regulations that limit distributions that are modified by these proposed regulations only apply to pension plans (i.e., defined benefit or money purchase pension plans). Other types of plans may be subject to less restrictive rules regarding in-service distributions, including amounts held in or attributable to: (1) qualified profit sharing and stock bonus plans to the extent not attributable to elective deferrals under section 401(k); (2) insurance annuities under section 403(b)(1), and retirement income accounts under section 403(b)(9), to the extent not attributable to elective deferrals; (3) custodial accounts under section 403(b)(7) to the extent not attributable to elective deferrals; and (4) elective deferrals under section 401(k) or 403(b). In general, these types of plans are permitted to provide for distributions after attainment of age 59 ½, without regard to whether the employee has retired or had a severance from employment. Accordingly, they may either provide for the same phased retirement rules that are proposed in these regulations or may provide for other partial or full in-service distributions to be available after attainment of age 59 ½. However, eligible governmental plans under section 457(b) are not generally permitted to provide for payments to be made before the earlier of severance from employment or attainment of age 70 ½. See generally § 1.457-6.

Other Issues

The proposed regulations also authorize the Commissioner to issue additional rules in guidance of general applicability regarding the coordination of partial retirement under a phased retirement program and the plan qualification rules under section 401(a).

These proposed regulations do not address all of the issues that commentators raised in response to Notice 2002-43. Thus, as noted above, the proposed regulations do not address when a full retirement occurs and specifically do not endorse a prearranged termination and rehire as constituting a full retirement. Further, the proposed regulations only address certain tax issues. For example, although commentators pointed out that the continued availability of health coverage would be an important feature for employees in deciding whether to participate in phased retirement, the proposed regulations do not include any rules relating to health coverage. Similarly, the proposed regulations do not address any potential age discrimination issues, other than through the requirement that participation in a bona fide phased retirement program be voluntary.

Proposed Effective Date

The rules in these regulations are proposed to apply to plan years beginning on or after the date of publication of the Treasury decision adopting these rules as final regulations in the **Federal Register**. These proposed regulations cannot be relied on before they are adopted as final regulations.

Special Analyses

It has been determined that this notice of proposed rulemaking is not a significant regulatory action as defined in Executive Order 12866. Therefore, a regulatory assessment is not required. It also has been determined that section 553(b) of the Administrative Procedure Act (5 U.S.C. chapter 5) does not apply to these proposed regulations, and, because these regulations do not impose a collection of information on small entities, the Regulatory Flexibility Act (5 U.S.C. chapter 6) does not apply. Pursuant to section 7805(f) of the Internal Revenue Code, this notice of proposed rulemaking will be submitted to the Chief Counsel for Advocacy of the Small Business Administration for comment on its impact on small business.

Comments and Requests for a Public Hearing

Before these proposed regulations are adopted as final regulations, consideration will be given to any written comments (a signed original and eight (8) copies) or electronic comments that are submitted timely to the IRS. All comments will be available for public inspection and copying.

Comments are specifically requested on the following issues:

- Should eligibility to participate in a phased retirement program be extended to employees that reduce their workload using a standard, other than counting hours, to identify the reduction, and, if so, are there administrable methods for measuring the reduction?

- The proposed regulations require periodic testing of the hours an employee actually works during phased retirement, and if the hours are materially greater than the employee's phased retirement work schedule, the phased retirement benefit must be adjusted. As discussed above (under the heading *Testing*), there are a number of exceptions to this requirement. Are there other, less complex alternatives that also would ensure that phased retirement benefits correspond to the employee's reduction in hours?

- The proposed regulations require an offset for the actuarial value of additional payments made before a reduction in phased retirement benefits. Should the regulations permit this offset to be calculated without regard to any early retirement subsidy and, if so, how should a subsidy be quantified?

- The proposed regulations clarify that the right to receive a phased retirement benefit as a partial payment is a separate optional form of benefit for purposes of section 411(d)(6) and, thus, is a benefit, right, or feature for purposes of the special nondiscrimination rules at § 1.401(a)(4)-4. Comments are requested on whether there are facts and circumstances under which the age and service conditions for a particular employer's phased retirement program should be disregarded in applying § 1.401(a)(4)-4 (even if the program may only be in place for a temporary period), or under which the rules at § 1.401(a)(4)-4 should otherwise be modified with respect to phased retirement.

---

[3] While a low normal retirement age may have a significant cost effect on a traditional defined benefit plan, this effect is not as significant for defined contribution plans or for hybrid defined benefit plans.

- Should any special rules be adopted to coordinate the rules regarding distributions and continued accruals during phased retirement with a plan's provisions regarding employment after normal retirement age, such as suspension of benefits?

A public hearing may be scheduled if requested in writing by a person that timely submits written comments. If a public hearing is scheduled, notice of the date, time and place for the hearing will be published in the **Federal Register**.

Drafting Information

The principal author of these proposed regulations is Cathy A. Vohs of the Office of the Division Counsel/Associate Chief Counsel (Tax Exempt and Government Entities). However, other personnel from the IRS and Treasury participated in their development.

List of Subjects 26 CFR Part 1

Income taxes, Reporting and recordkeeping requirements.

Proposed Amendments to the Regulations

Accordingly, 26 CFR part 1 is proposed to be amended as follows:

PART 1—INCOME TAXES

Paragraph 1. The authority citation for part 1 is amended by adding entries in numerical order to read in part as follows:

Authority: 26 U.S.C. 7805 * * *

Section 1.401(a)-1 also issued under 26 U.S.C. 401.

Section 1.401(a)-3 also issued under 26 U.S.C. 401.

Par. 2. In § 1.401(a)-1, paragraph (b)(1)(i) is amended by adding text before the period at the end of the current sentence and a new second sentence, and paragraph (b)(1)(iv) to read as follows:

§ 1.401(a)-1 *Post-ERISA qualified plans and qualified trusts; in general.*

* * * * *

(b) * * *

(1) * * *

(i) * * * or attainment of normal retirement age. However, normal retirement age cannot be set so low as to be a subterfuge to avoid the requirements of section 401(a), and, accordingly, normal retirement age cannot be earlier than the earliest age that is reasonably representative of a typical retirement age for the covered workforce.

* * * * *

(iv) Benefits may not be distributed prior to normal retirement age solely due to a reduction in hours. However, notwithstanding anything provided elsewhere in paragraph (b) of this section (including the pre-ERISA rules under § 1.401-1), an employee may be treated as partially retired for purposes of paragraph (b)(1)(i) of this section to the extent provided under § 1.401(a)-3 relating to a bona fide phased retirement program. * * * * *

Par. 3. Section 1.401(a)-3 is added to read as follows:

§ 1.401(a)-3 *Benefits during phased retirement.*

(a) *Introduction* —(1) *General rule.* Under section 401(a), a qualified pension plan may provide for the distribution of phased retirement benefits in accordance with the limitations of this paragraph (a) to the extent that an employee is partially retired under a bona fide phased retirement program, as defined in paragraph (c) of this section, provided the requirements set forth in paragraphs (d) and (e) of this section are satisfied.

(2) *Limitation on benefits paid during phased retirement period* —(i) *Benefits limited to pro rata retirement benefit.* The phased retirement benefits paid during the phased retirement period cannot exceed the phased retirement accrued benefit payable in the optional form of benefit applicable at the annuity starting date for the employee's phased retirement benefit.

(ii) *Availability of early retirement subsidies, etc.* Except as provided in paragraph (a)(2)(iii) of this section, all early retirement benefits, retirement-type subsidies, and optional forms of benefit available upon full retirement must be available with respect to the portion of an employee's phased retirement accrued benefit that is payable as a phased retirement benefit.

(iii) *Limitation on optional forms of payment.* Phased retirement benefits may not be paid in the form of a single sum or other form that constitutes an eligible rollover distribution under section 402(c)(4).

(3) *Limited to full-time employees who are otherwise eligible to commence benefits.* Phased retirement benefits are only permitted to be made available to an employee who, prior to the phased retirement period, normally maintains a full-time work schedule and who would otherwise be eligible to commence retirement benefits immediately if he or she were to fully retire.

(4) *Authority of Commissioner to adopt other rules.* The Commissioner, in revenue rulings, notices, or other guidance published in the Internal Revenue Bulletin (see § 601.601(d)(2)(ii)(*b*) of this chapter), may adopt additional rules regarding the coordination of partial retirement under a phased retirement program and the qualification rules of section 401(a).

(b) *Definitions* —(1) *In general.* The definitions set forth in this paragraph (b) apply for purposes of this section.

(2) *Phased retirement program.* The term *phased retirement program* means a written, employer-adopted program pursuant to which employees may reduce the number of hours they customarily work beginning on or after a date specified under the program and commence phased retirement benefits during the phased retirement period, as provided under the plan.

(3) *Phased retirement period.* The term *phased retirement period* means the period of time that the employee and employer reasonably expect the employee to work reduced hours under the phased retirement program.

(4) *Phased retirement accrued benefit.* The term *phased retirement accrued benefit* means the portion of the employee's accrued benefit equal to the product of the employee's total accrued benefit on the annuity starting date for the employee's phased retirement benefit, and one minus the employee's work schedule fraction.

(5) *Phased retirement benefit.* The term *phased retirement benefit* means the benefit paid to an employee upon the employee's partial retirement under a phased retirement program, based on some or all of the employee's phased retirement accrued benefit, and payable in the optional form of benefit applicable at the annuity starting date.

(6) *Work schedule.* With respect to an employee, the term *work schedule* means the number of hours the employee is reasonably expected to work annually during the phased retirement period (determined in accordance with paragraph (c)(4) of this section).

(7) *Full-time work schedule.* With respect to an employee, the term *full-time work schedule* means the number of hours the employee would normally work during a year if the employee were to work on a full-time basis, determined in a reasonable and consistent manner.

(8) *Work schedule fraction.* With respect to an employee, the term *work schedule fraction* means a fraction, the numerator of which is the employee's work schedule and the denominator of which is the employee's full-time work schedule.

(c) *Bona fide phased retirement program* —(1) *Definition generally.* The term *bona fide phased retirement program* means a phased retirement program that satisfies paragraphs (c)(2) through (5) of this section.

(2) *Limitation to individuals who have attained age 59 ½.* A bona fide phased retirement program must be limited to employees who have attained age 59 ½. A plan is permitted to impose additional requirements for eligibility to participate in a bona fide phased retirement program, such as limiting eligibility to either employees who have satisfied additional age or service conditions (or combination thereof) specified in the program or employees whose benefit may not be distributed without consent under section 411(a)(11).

(3) *Participation must be voluntary.* An employee's participation in a bona fide phased retirement program must be voluntary.

(4) *Reduction in hours requirement.* An employee who participates in a bona fide phased retirement program must reasonably be expected (by both the employer and employee) to reduce, by 20 percent or more, the number of hours the employee customarily works. This requirement is satisfied if the employer and employee enter into an agreement, in good faith, under which they agree that the employee will reduce, by 20 percent or more, the number of hours the employee works during the phased retirement period.

(5) *Limited to employees who are not key-employee owners.* Phased retirement benefits are not permitted to be made available to a key employee who is described in section 416(i)(1)(A)(ii) or (iii).

(d) *Conditions for commencement of phased retirement benefit* —(1) *Imputed accruals based on full-time schedule* —(i) *General rule.* During the phased retirement period, in addition to being entitled to payment of the phased retirement benefit, the employee must be entitled to participate in the plan in the same manner as if the employee still maintained a full-time work schedule (including calculation of average earnings, imputation of compensation in accordance with § 1.414(s)-1(f), and imputation of service in accordance with the service-crediting rules under § 1.401(a)(4)-11(d)), and must be entitled to the same benefits (including early retirement benefits, retirement-type subsidies, and optional forms of benefits) upon full retirement as a similarly situated employee who has not elected phased retirement, except that the years of service credited under the plan for any plan year during the phased retirement period is determined under paragraph (d)(1)(ii) or (iii) of this section, whichever is applicable.

(ii) *Method for crediting years of service for full plan years.* The years of service credited under the plan for any full plan year during the phased retirement period is multiplied by an adjustment ratio that is equal to the ratio of the employee's actual hours worked during that year to the number of hours that would be worked by the employee during that year under a full-time work schedule. Alternatively, on a reasonable and consistent basis, the adjustment ratio may be based on the ratio of an employee's actual compensation during the year to the compensation that would be paid to the employee during the year if he or she had maintained a full-time work schedule.

(iii) *Method for crediting years of service for partial plan years.* In the case of a plan year only a portion of which is during a phased retirement period for an employee, the method described in paragraphs (d)(1)(i) and (ii) of this section is applied with respect to that portion of the plan year. Thus, for example, if an employee works full time until October 1 of a calendar plan year and works one-third time from October 1 through December 31 of the year, then the employee is credited with 10 months for that year (9 months plus ⅓ of 3 months).

(2) *Ancillary benefits during phased retirement period* —(i) *Death benefits.* If an employee dies while receiving phased retirement benefits, death benefits are allocated between the phased retirement benefit and the benefit that would be payable upon subsequent full retirement. See also § 1.401(a)-20, A-9. Thus, if an employee dies after the annuity starting date for the phased retirement benefit, death benefits are paid with respect to the phased retirement benefit in accordance with the optional form elected for that benefit, and death benefits are paid with respect to the remainder of the employee's benefit in accordance with the plan's provisions regarding death during employment.

(ii) *Other ancillary benefits.* To the extent provided under the terms of the plan, ancillary benefits, other than death benefits described in paragraph (d)(2)(i) of this section, are permitted to be provided during the phased retirement period.

(3) *Calculation of benefit at full retirement* —(i) *In general.* Upon full retirement following partial retirement under a phased retirement program, the employee's total accrued benefit under the plan (including the employee's accruals during the phased retirement period, determined in accordance with paragraph (d)(1) of this section) is offset by the portion of the employee's phased retirement accrued benefit that is being distributed as a phased retirement benefit at the time of full retirement.

(ii) *Adjustment for prior payments.* If, before full retirement, the employee's phased retirement benefit has been reduced under paragraph (d)(4) of this section, then the employee's accrued benefit under the plan is also offset upon full retirement by an amount that is actuarially equivalent to the phased retirement benefit payments that have been made during the phased retirement period that were not made with respect to the portion of the phased retirement accrued benefit that is applied as an offset under paragraph (d)(3)(i) of this section at the time of full retirement.

(iii) *Election of optional form with respect to net benefit.* Upon full retirement, an employee is entitled to elect, in accordance with section 417, an optional form of benefit with respect to the net accrued benefit determined under paragraph (d)(3)(i) and (ii) of this section.

(iv) *New election permitted for phased retirement benefit.* A plan is permitted to provide that, upon full retirement, an employee may elect, in accordance with section 417 and without regard to paragraph (a)(2)(iii) of this section, a new optional form of benefit with respect to the portion of the phased retirement accrued benefit that is being distributed as a phased retirement benefit. Any such new optional form of benefit is calculated at the time of full retirement as the actuarial equivalent of the future phased retirement benefits (without offset for the phased retirement benefits previously paid).

(4) *Prospective reduction in phased retirement benefit if hours are materially greater than expected* —(i) *General rule.* Except as otherwise provided in this paragraph (d)(4), a plan must compare annually the number of hours actually worked by an employee during the phased retirement testing period and the number of hours the employee was reasonably expected to work during the testing period for purposes of calculating the work schedule fraction. For this purpose, the phased retirement testing period is the 12 months preceding the comparison date (or such longer period permitted under paragraph (d)(4)(iv) of this section, or any shorter period that applies if there is a comparison date as a result of an agreed increase under paragraph (d)(4)(vi) of this section). In the event that the actual hours worked (determined on an annual basis) during the phased retirement testing period exceeds the work schedule, then, except as provided in paragraph (d)(4)(ii) or (v) of this section, the employee's phased retirement benefit must be reduced in accordance with the method provided in paragraph (d)(4)(iii) of this section, effective as of an adjustment date specified in the plan that is not more than 3 months later than the comparison date.

(ii) *Permitted variance in hours.* A plan is not required to reduce the phased retirement benefit unless the hours worked during the phased retirement testing period are materially greater than the hours that would be expected to be worked under the work schedule. For this purpose, the employee's hours worked (determined on annual basis) are materially greater than the employee's work schedule if either—

(A) The employee's hours worked (determined on an annual basis) are more than percent of the employee's work schedule; or

(B) The employee's hours worked (determined on an annual basis) exceed 90 percent of the full-time work schedule.

(iii) *Adjustment method.* If a phased retirement benefit must be reduced under paragraph (d)(4) of this section, a new (i.e., reduced) phased retirement benefit must be calculated as provided in this paragraph (d)(4)(iii). First, an adjusted work schedule is determined. The adjusted work schedule is an annual schedule based on the number of hours the employee actually worked during the phased retirement testing period. The adjusted work schedule is applied to the employee's accrued benefit that was used to calculate the prior phased retirement benefit. This results in a new phased retirement accrued benefit for purposes of paragraph (b)(4) of this section. Second, a new phased retirement benefit is determined, based on the new phased retirement accrued benefit and payable in the same optional form of benefit (i.e., using the same annuity starting date and the same early retirement factor and other actuarial adjustments) as the prior phased retirement benefit. If an employee is receiving more than one phased retirement benefit (as permitted under paragraph (e)(2) of this section) and a reduction is required under paragraph (d)(4) of this section, then the reduction is applied first to the most recently commencing phased retirement benefit (and then, if necessary, to the next most recent phased retirement benefit, etc.).

(iv) *Comparison date for phased retirement testing period.* The comparison date is any date chosen by the employer on a reasonable and consistent basis and specified in the plan, such as the last day of the plan year, December 31, or the anniversary of the annuity starting date for the employee's phased retirement benefit. As an alternative to testing the hours worked during the 12 months preceding the comparison date, the plan may, on a reasonable and consistent basis, provide that the comparison of actual hours worked to the work schedule be based on a cumulative period that exceeds 12 months beginning with either the annuity starting date for the employee's phased retirement benefit or any later date specified in the plan.

(v) *Exceptions to comparison requirement* —(A) *In general.* The comparison of hours described in paragraph (d)(4) of this section is not required in the situations set forth in this paragraph (d)(4)(v).

(B) *Employees recently commencing phased retirement.* No comparison is required for an employee who commenced phased retirement benefits within the 12-month period preceding the comparison date.

(C) *Employees with short phased retirement periods.* No comparison is required during the first 2 years of an employee's phased retirement period if—

(1) The employee has entered into an agreement with the employer under which the employee's phased retirement period will not exceed 2 years and the employee will fully retire at the end of such period; and

(2) The employee fully retires after a phased retirement period not in excess of 2 years.

(D) *Employees with proportional pay reduction.* No comparison is required for any phased retirement testing period if the amount of compensation paid to the employee during that period does not exceed the compensation that would be paid to the employee if he or she had maintained a full-time work schedule multiplied by the work schedule fraction.

(E) *Employees at or after normal retirement age.* No comparison is required for any phased retirement testing period ending within 3 months before the employee's normal retirement age or any time thereafter.

(vi) *Agreement to increase hours* —(A) *General rule.* In the event that the employer and the employee agree to increase prospectively the hours under the employee's work schedule prior to normal retirement age, then, notwithstanding the exceptions provided in paragraphs (d)(4)(v)(B) through (D) of this section, the plan must treat the effective date of the agreement to increase the employee's hours as a comparison date for purposes of paragraph (d)(4)(iv) of this section. For purposes of this paragraph (d)(4)(vi), with respect to an employee, the term *new work schedule* means the greater of the actual number of hours the employee worked (determined on an annual basis) during the prior phased retirement testing period or the annual number of hours the employee reasonably expects to work under the new agreement.

(B) *Required adjustments.* If the employee's hours under the new work schedule are materially greater (within the meaning of paragraph (d)(4)(ii) of this section) than the hours the employee would be expected to work (based on the employee's prior work schedule), the employer is required to reduce the employee's phased retirement benefit, effective as of the date of the increase, based on the new work schedule. In this case, the employee's new work schedule is used for future comparisons under paragraph (d)(4) of this section.

(C) *Permitted adjustments.* If the employee's hours under the new work schedule are not materially greater (within the meaning of paragraph (d)(4)(ii) of this section) than the hours the employee would be expected to work (based on the employee's prior work schedule), the employer is permitted, but not required, to reduce the employee's phased retirement benefit, effective as of the date of the increase, based on the new work schedule. If the benefit is so reduced, the employee's new work schedule is used for future comparisons under paragraph (d)(4) of this section. If the employee's phased retirement benefit is not so reduced, future comparisons are determined using the employee's prior work schedule.

(e) *Other rules* —(1) *Highly compensated employees.* An employee who partially retires under a phased retirement program and who was a highly compensated employee, as defined in section 414(q), immediately before the partial retirement is considered to be a highly compensated employee during the phased retirement period, without regard to the compensation actually paid to the employee during the phased retirement period.

(2) *Multiple phased retirement benefits permitted* —(i) *In general.* A plan is permitted to provide one or more additional phased retirement benefits prospectively to an employee who is receiving a phased retirement benefit if the conditions set forth in paragraph (e)(2)(ii) of this section are satisfied. At the later annuity starting date for the additional phased retirement benefit, the additional phased retirement benefits may not exceed the amount permitted to be paid based on the excess of—

(A) The employee's phased retirement accrued benefit at the later annuity starting date, over

(B) The portion of the employee's phased retirement accrued benefit at the earlier annuity starting date that is being distributed as a phased retirement benefit.

(ii) *Conditions.* The additional phased retirement benefit described in paragraph (e)(2)(i) of this section may be provided only if—

(A) The prior phased retirement benefit was not based on the employee's entire phased retirement accrued benefit at the annuity starting date for the prior phased retirement benefit, or

(B) The employee's work schedule at the later annuity starting date is less than the employee's work schedule that was used to calculate the prior phased retirement benefit.

(3) *Application of section 411(d)(6).* In accordance with §1.411(d)-4, A-1(b)(1), the right to receive a partial distribution of an employee's accrued benefit as a phased retirement benefit is treated as an optional form of payment that is separate from the right to receive a full distribution of the accrued benefit upon full retirement.

(4) *Application of nondiscrimination rules.* The right to receive a phased retirement benefit is a benefit, right, or feature that is subject to §1.401(a)(4)-4.

(f) *Examples.* The following examples illustrate the application of this section:

Example 1. (i) *Employer's Plans.* Plan X (as in effect prior to amendment to reflect the phased retirement program described below) is a defined benefit plan maintained by Employer M. Plan X provides an accrued benefit of 1.5 % of the average of an employee's highest three

years of pay (based on the highest 36 consecutive months of pay), times years of service (with 1,000 hours of service required for a year of service), payable as a life annuity beginning at age 65. Plan X permits employees to elect to commence actuarially reduced distributions at any time after the later of termination of employment or attainment of age 50, except that if an employee retires after age 55 and completion of 20 years of service, the applicable reduction is only 3 % per year for the years between ages 65 and 62 and 6 % per year for the years between ages 62 to 55. Plan X permits employees to select, with spousal consent, a single life annuity, a joint and contingent annuity with the employee having the right to select any beneficiary and a continuation percentage of 50 %, 75 %, or 100 %, or a 10-year certain and life annuity.

(ii) *Phased Retirement Program.* Employer M adopts a voluntary phased retirement program that will only be available for employees who retire during the two-year period from February 1, 2006 to January 31, 2008. The program will not be available to employees who are not entitled to an immediate pension or who are 1 percent owners. Employer M has determined that employees typically begin to retire after attainment of age 55 with at least 15 years of service. Accordingly, to increase retention of certain employees, the program will provide that employees in certain specified work positions who have reached age 59 ½ and completed 15 years of service may elect phased retirement. The program permits phased retirement to be implemented through a reduction of 25 %, 50 %, or 75 % in the number of hours expected to be worked for up to 5 years following phased retirement (other reduced schedules may be elected with the approval of M), with the employee's compensation during the phased retirement period to be based on what a similar full-time employee would be paid, reduced by the applicable percentage reduction in hours expected to be worked. In order to participate in the program, the employee and the employer must enter into an agreement under which the employee will reduce his or her hours accordingly. The agreement also provides that the employee's compensation during phased retirement will be reduced by that same percentage. The program is announced to employees in the fall of 2005.

(iii) *Plan Provisions Regarding Phased Retirement Benefit.* (A) Plan X is amended, prior to February 1, 2006, to provide that an employee who elects phased retirement under M's phased retirement program is permitted to commence benefits with respect to a portion of his or her accrued retirement benefit (the employee's phased retirement accrued benefit), based on the applicable percentage reduction in hours expected to be worked. For example, for a 25 % reduction in hours, the employee is entitled to commence benefits with respect to 25 % of his or her accrued benefit. Plan X permits an employee who commences phased retirement to elect, with spousal consent, from any of the optional forms provided under the plan.

(B) During the phased retirement period, the employee will continue to accrue benefits (without regard to the plan's 1,000 hour requirement), with his or her pay for purposes of calculating benefits under Plan X increased by the ratio of 100 percent to the percentage of full-time pay that will be paid during phased retirement and with the employee's service credit to be equal to the product of the same percentage times the service credit that would apply if the employee were working full time. Upon the employee's subsequent full retirement, his or her total accrued benefit will be based on the resulting highest three years of pay and total years of service, offset by the phased retirement accrued benefit. The retirement benefit payable upon subsequent full retirement is in addition to the phased retirement benefit. Plan X does not provide for a new election with respect to the phased retirement benefit.

(C) In the case of death during the phased retirement period, the employee will be treated as a former employee to the extent of his or her phased retirement benefit and as an active employee to the extent of the retirement benefit that would be due upon full retirement.

(D) Because the terms of the phased retirement program provide that the employee's compensation during phased retirement will be reduced by that same percentage as applies to calculate phased retirement benefits, Plan X does not have provisions requiring annual testing of hours actually worked.

(iv) *Application to a Specific Employee* —(A) *Phased retirement benefit.* Employee E is age 59 ½ with 20 years of credited service. Employee E's compensation is $90,000, and E's highest three years of pay is $85,000. Employee E elects phased retirement on April 1, 2006 and elects to reduce hours by 50 % beginning on July 1, 2006. Thus, E's annuity starting date for the phased retirement benefit is July 1, 2006. Employee E's total accrued benefit as of July 1, 2006 as a single life annuity payable at normal retirement age is equal to $25,500 per year (1.5 % times $85,000 times 20 years of service). Thus, Employee E's phased retirement accrued benefit as of July 1, 2006 as a single life annuity payable at normal retirement age is equal to $12,750 per year ($25,500 times 1 minus E's work schedule fraction of 50 %). Accordingly, Employee E's phased retirement benefit payable as a straight life annuity commencing on July 1, 2006 is equal to $9,690 per year ($12,750 per year times 76 % (100 % minus the applicable reduction for early retirement equal to 3 % for 3 years and 6 % for an additional 2 ½ years)). Employee E elects a joint and 50 % survivor annuity, with E's spouse as the contingent annuitant. Under Plan X, the actuarial factor for this form of benefit is 90 %, so E's benefit is $8,721 per year.

(B) *Death during phased retirement.* If Employee E were to die on or after July 1, 2006 and before subsequent full retirement, E's spouse would be entitled to a 50 % survivor annuity based on the joint and 50 % survivor annuity being paid to E, plus a qualified preretirement survivor annuity that complies with section 417 with respect to the additional amount that would be paid to E if he or she had fully retired on the date of E's death.

(C) *Subsequent full retirement benefit.* Three years later, Employee E fully retires from Employer M. Throughout this period, E's compensation has been 50 % of the compensation that would have been paid to E if he or she were working full time. Consequently, no adjustment in E's phased retirement benefit is required. E's highest consecutive 36 months of compensation would be $95,000 if E had not elected phased retirement and E has been credited with 1 ½ years of service credit for the 3 years of phased retirement (.50 times 3 years). Accordingly, prior to offset for E's phased retirement accrued benefit, E's total accrued benefit as of July 1, 2009 as a single life annuity commencing at normal retirement age is equal to $30,637.50 per year ($95,000 times 1.5 % times 21.5 years of service) and, after the offset for E's phased retirement accrued benefit, E's retirement benefit as a single life annuity commencing at normal retirement age is equal to $17,887.50 ($30,637.50 minus $12,750). Thus, the amount of E's additional early retirement benefit payable as a straight life annuity at age 62 ½ is equal to $16,545.94 per year ($17,887.50 per year times 92.5 % (100 % minus 3 % for 2 ½ years)). Employee E elects, with spousal consent, a 10-year certain and life annuity that applies to the remainder of E's accrued benefit. This annuity is in addition to the previously elected joint and 50 % survivor annuity payable as E's phased retirement benefit.

Example 2. (i) *Same Plan and Phased Retirement Program, Except Annual Testing Required.* The facts with respect to the Plan X and M's phased retirement program are the same as in *Example 1*, except that the program does not provide that the employee's compensation during phased retirement will be reduced by that same percentage as is applied to calculate phased retirement benefits, but instead the compensation depends on the number of hours worked by the employee. Plan X provides for annual testing on a calendar year basis and for an employee's phased retirement benefit to be reduced proportionately if the hours worked exceed a threshold, under provisions which reflect the variance permitted paragraph (d)(4)(ii) of this section.

(ii) *Employee Has Small Increase in Hours.* The facts with respect to Employee E are the same as in *Example 1*, except that E's full time work schedule would result in 2,000 hours worked annually, E's work schedule fraction is 50 %, and E works 500 hours from July 1, 2006 through December 31, 2006, 1,000 hours in 2007, 1,200 hours in 2008, and 600 hours from January 1, 2009 through E's full retirement on June 30, 2009.

(iii) *Application of Testing Rules.* No comparison of hours is required for the partial testing period that occurs in 2006. For 2007, no reduction is required in E's phased retirement benefit as a result of the hours worked by E during 2007 because the hours did not exceed E's work schedule (50 % of 2,000). For 2008, although the hours worked by E exceeded E's work schedule, no reduction is required because the hours worked in 2008 were not materially greater than E's work

schedule (1,200 is not more than the variance permitted under paragraph (d)(4)(ii) of this section, which is % of 1,000). E's total accrued benefit upon E's retirement on July 1, 2009 would be based on 21.65 years of service to reflect the actual hours worked from July 1, 2006 through June 30, 2009.

Example 3. (i) *Same Plan and Phased Retirement Program, Except Material Increase in Hours.* The facts with respect to the Plan X and M's phased retirement program are the same as in *Example 2*, except E works 1,400 hours in 2008 and 700 hours in the first half of 2009.

(ii) *Application of Testing Rules.* No comparison of hours is required for the partial testing period that occurs in 2006. For 2007, no reduction is required in E's phased retirement benefit as a result of the hours worked by E during 2007 because the hours did not exceed 50 % of 2,000. However, the hours worked by E during 2008 exceed % of E's work schedule (50 % of 2,000), so that the phased retirement benefit paid to E during 2008 must be reduced. The reduction is effective March 1, 2009. The new phased retirement benefit of $5,232.60 is based on 30 % of the participant's accrued benefit as of July 1, 2006, payable as a joint and 50 % survivor annuity commencing on that date (30 % times $25,500 times the early retirement factor of 76 % times the joint and 50 % factor of 90 %). This is equivalent to reducing the previously elected joint and 50 % survivor annuity payable with respect to E by 40 % (400 "excess" hours divided by the 1,000 hour expected reduction). When E retires fully on July 1, 2009, E's total accrued benefit as of July 1, 2009 as a single life annuity commencing at normal retirement age is $31,065 per year ($95,000 times 1.5 % times 21.8 years of service). This accrued benefit is offset by (A) E's phased retirement accrued benefit (which is $7,650 (600 divided by 2,000 times $25,500)) plus (B) the actuarial equivalent of 40 % of the payments that were made to E from January 1, 2008 through February 28, 2009.

Example 4. (i) *Same Plan and Phased Retirement Program, Except Employer and Employee Agree to Decrease Hours.* The facts with respect to the Plan X and M's phased retirement program are the same as in *Example 2*, except before 2008, E enters into an agreement with M to decrease E's number of hours worked from 50 % of full time to 25 % of full time. E works 500 hours in 2008 and 250 hours in 2009.

(ii) *Application of Multiple Benefit Rule.* Under paragraph (e)(2) of this section, Plan M may provide for an additional phased retirement benefit to be offered to E for 2008. The maximum increase would be for the phased retirement benefit paid to E during 2009 to be increased based on a phased retirement accrued benefit equal to 75 % of E's accrued benefit (1,500 divided by 2,000). Thus, the amount being paid to E would be increased, effective January 1, 2008, based on the excess of 75 % of E's total accrued benefit on December 31, 2007, over E's original phased retirement accrued benefit of $12,750. Employee E would have the right to elect, with spousal consent, any annuity form offered under Plan X (with the actuarial adjustment for time of commencement and form of payment to be based on the age of E and any contingent beneficiary (and E's service, if applicable) on June 1, 2008), which would be in addition to the previously elected joint and 50 % survivor annuity payable as E's original phased retirement benefit. When E retires fully on July 1, 2009, Employee E's total accrued benefit as of July 1, 2009 would be offset by (A) E's original phased retirement accrued benefit plus (B) the phased retirement accrued benefit for which additional phased retirement benefits were payable beginning in 2008.

(g) *Effective date.* The rules of this section apply to plan years beginning on or after the date of publication of the Treasury decision adopting these rules as final regulations in the **Federal Register**.

Mark E. Matthews,

Deputy Commissioner for Services and Enforcement.

¶ 20,261H

IRS proposed regulations: 403(b) retirement annuity contracts: Tax-sheltered annuities: Public school employees: 501(c)(3) tax-exempt organizations.—The IRS has issued proposed regulations relating to retirement annuity contracts under Code Sec. 403(b), generally available to public school employees and Code Sec. 501(c)(3) tax-exempt organizations. According to the IRS, the proposed regulations are the first comprehensive guidance on Code Sec. 403(b) arrangements in over 40 years. The proposed regulations would generally apply to tax years after 2005. Comments must be received by February 14, 2005.

The proposed regulations were published in the Federal Register on November 16, 2004 (69 FR 67075) and corrected on December 21, 2004 (69 FR 76422).

[4830-01-p]

DEPARTMENT OF THE TREASURY

Internal Revenue Service

26 CFR Parts 1 and 31

[REG-155608-02]

RIN 1545-BB64

Revised Regulations Concerning Section 403(b) Tax-Sheltered Annuity Contracts

AGENCY: Internal Revenue Service (IRS), Treasury.

ACTION: Notice of proposed rulemaking, notice of proposed rulemaking by cross-reference to temporary regulations, and notice of public hearing.

SUMMARY: This document contains proposed regulations under section 403(b) of the Internal Revenue Code and under related provisions of sections 402(b), 402(g), 414(c), and 3121(a)(5)(D). The proposed regulations would provide updated guidance on section 403(b) contracts of public schools and tax-exempt organizations described in section 501(c)(3). These regulations would provide the public with guidance necessary to comply with the law and will affect sponsors of section 403(b) contracts, administrators, participants and beneficiaries. In the Rules and Regulations section of this issue of the **Federal Register**, the Treasury Department and IRS are issuing temporary regulations providing employment tax guidance to employers and employees on salary reduction agreements. This document also provides notice of a public hearing on these proposed regulations.

DATES: Written or electronic comments must be received by February 14, 2005. Outlines of topics to be discussed at the public hearing scheduled for February 15, 2005 to be held in the IRS Auditorium (7 th Floor) must be received by January 25, 2005.

ADDRESSES: Send submissions to: CC:PA:LPD:PR (REG-155608-02), room 5203, Internal Revenue Service, POB 7604, Ben Franklin Station, Washington, DC 20044. Submissions may be hand delivered Monday through Friday between the hours of 8 a.m. and 4 p.m. to: CC:PA:LPD:PR (REG-155608-02), Courier's Desk, Internal Revenue Service, 1111 Constitution Avenue NW., Washington, DC, or sent electronically via the IRS Internet site at *www.irs.gov/regs* or via the Federal eRulemaking Portal at *www.regulations.gov* (IRS-REG-155608-02). The public hearing will be held in the IRS Auditorium (7 th Floor), Internal Revenue Building, 1111 Constitution Avenue, NW., Washington, DC.

FOR FURTHER INFORMATION CONTACT: Concerning the proposed regulations, R. Lisa Mojiri-Azad or John Tolleris, (202) 622-6060; concerning the proposed regulations as applied to church-related entities, Robert Architect (202) 283-9634; concerning submission of comments, the hearing, and/or to be placed on the building access list to attend the hearing, Sonya Cruse, (202) 622-7180 (not toll-free numbers).

SUPPLEMENTARY INFORMATION:

Paperwork Reduction Act

The collection of information contained in this notice of rulemaking has been previously reviewed and approved by the Office of Management and Budget in accordance with the Paperwork Reduction Act (44 U.S.C. 3507) under control number 1545-1341.

An agency may not conduct or sponsor, and a person is not required to respond to, a collection of information unless it displays a valid control number assigned by the Office of Management and Budget.

Books or records relating to a collection of information must be retained as long as their contents may become material in the administration of any internal revenue law. Generally, tax returns and tax return information are confidential, as required by 26 U.S.C. 6103.

Background

Regulations (TD 6783) under section 403(b) of the Internal Revenue Code (Code) were published in the **Federal Register** (29 FR 18356) on December 24, 1964 (1965-1 C.B. 180). These regulations provided guidance for complying with section 403(b) which had been enacted in 1958 in section 23(a) of the Technical Amendments Act of 1958, Public Law 85-866 (1958), relating to tax-sheltered annuity arrangements established for employees by public schools and tax-exempt organizations described in section 501(c)(3). Since 1964, additional regulations

have been issued under section 403(b) to reflect rules relating to eligible rollover distributions and minimum distributions under section 401(a)(9).

These proposed regulations would amend the current regulations to conform them to the numerous amendments made to section 403(b) by subsequent legislation, including section 1022(e) of the Employee Retirement Income Security Act of 1974 (ERISA) (88 Stat. 829), Public Law 93-406; section 251 of the Tax Equity and Fiscal Responsibility Act of 1982 (TEFRA) (96 Stat. 324,529), Public Law 97-248; section 1120 of the Tax Reform Act of 1986 (TRA '86) (100 Stat. 2085, 2463), Public Law 99-514; section 1450(a) of the Small Business Job Protection Act of 1996 (SBJPA) (110 Stat. 1755, 1814), Public Law 104-188; and sections 632, 646, and 647 of the Economic Growth and Tax Relief Reconciliation Act of 2001 (EGTRRA) (115 Stat. 38, 113, 126, 127), Public Law 107-16.

Explanation of Provisions

Overview

The purposes of these proposed regulations are to update the current regulations under section 403(b) to delete provisions that no longer have legal effect due to changes in law, to include in the regulations a number of items of interpretive guidance that have been issued under section 403(b) since the 1964 regulations,[1] and generally to reflect the numerous legal changes that have been made in section 403(b). A major effect of the legal changes in section 403(b) has been to diminish the extent to which the rules governing section 403(b) plans differ from the rules governing other arrangements that include salary reduction contributions, i.e., section 401(k) plans and section 457(b) plans for State and local governmental entities. Thus, these regulations will reflect the increasing similarity among these arrangements.

Since the existing regulations were issued in 1964, a number of revenue rulings and other guidance under section 403(b) have become outdated as a result of changes in law. In addition, as a result of the inclusion in these proposed regulations of much of the guidance that the IRS has issued regarding section 403(b), it is anticipated that these regulations, when finalized, will supersede a number of revenue rulings and notices that have been issued under section 403(b). Thus, the IRS anticipates taking action to obsolete many revenue rulings, notices, and other guidance under section 403(b) when these regulations are issued in final form.[2] However, the positions taken in certain rulings and other outstanding guidance are expected to be retained. For example, it is intended that a revenue ruling will be issued that substantially replicates and consolidates the existing rules[3] for determining when employees are performing services for a public school.[4]

The existing regulations include special rules for determining the amount of the contributions made for an employee under a defined benefit plan, based on the employee's pension under the plan. These rules are generally no longer applicable for section 403(b) because the limitations on contributions to a section 403(b) contract are no longer coordinated with accruals under a defined benefit plan. (See also the discussion of defined benefit plans below under the heading *Miscellaneous Provisions*.) However, the rules for determining the amount of contributions made for an employee under a defined benefit plan in the existing regulations under section 403(b) are also used for purposes of section 402(b) (relating to nonqualified plans funded through trusts) and, accordingly, these rules are proposed to be deleted from the regulations under section 403(b). New proposed regulations under section 402(b) would authorize the Commissioner to issue guidance for determining the amount of the contributions made for an employee under a defined benefit plan under section 402(b). See also the request for comments on this guidance under the heading *Comments and Public Hearing*.

The proposed regulations also include controlled group rules under section 414(c) for entities that are tax-exempt under section 501(a).

---

[1] Since 1964, the existing regulations have been revised for certain specific changes in law, for example, regulations under section 403(b) have been issued in question and answer form to reflect changes relating to eligible rollover distributions (TD 8619, September 15, 1995) and minimum distributions under section 401(a)(9) (TD 8987, April 16, 2002).

[2] It is expected that the following guidance is outdated, or will be superseded, when these regulations are issued in final form: Rev. Rul. 64-333, 1964-2 C.B. 114; Rev. Rul. 65-200, 1965-2 C.B. 141; Rev. Rul. 66-254, 1966-2 C.B. 125; Rev. Rul. 66-312, 1966-2 C.B. 127; Rev. Rul. 67-78, 1967-1 C.B. 94; Rev. Rul. 67-69, 1967-1 C.B. 93; Rev. Rul. 67-361, 1967-2 C.B. 153; Rev. Rul. 67-387, 1967-2 C.B. 153; Rev. Rul. 67-388, 1967-2 C.B. 153; Rev. Rul. 68-179, 1968-1 CB 179; Rev. Rul. 68-482, 1968-2 C.B. 186; Rev. Rul. 68-487, 1968-2 CB 187; Rev. Rul. 68-488, 1968-2 C.B. 188; Rev. Rul. 69-629, 1969-2 C.B. 101; Rev. Rul. 70-243, 1970-1 C.B. 107; Rev. Rul. 87-114, 1987-2 C.B. 116; Notice 89-23, 1989-1 C.B. 654; Rev. Rul. 90-24, 1990-1 C.B.

97; Notice 90-73, 1990-2 C.B. 353; Notice 92-36, 1992-2 C.B. 364; and Announcement 95-48, 1995-23 I.R.B. 13. It is expected that the following guidance will not be superseded when these regulations are issued in final form: Rev. Rul. 66-254, 1966-2 C.B. 125; Rev. Rul. 68-33, 1968-1 C.B. 175; Rev. Rul 68-58, 1968-1 C.B. 176; Rev. Rul. 68-116, 1968-1 C.B. 177; Rev. Rul. 68-648, 1968-2 C.B. 49; Rev. Rul. 68-488, 1968-2 C.B. 188; and Rev. Rul. 69-146, 1969-1 C.B. 132. Comments are requested on whether any guidance items under section 403(b) should be added to or deleted from either of the preceding lists. See the request for comments below under the heading *Comments and Public Hearing*.

[3] Rev. Rul. 73-607, 1973-2 C.B. 145 and Rev. Rul. 80-139, 1980-1 C.B. 88.

[4] As discussed below (under the heading *Controlled Group Rules For Tax-Exempt Entities*), other guidance that may be reissued includes the controlled group safe harbor rules in paragraph (V)(B)(2)(b) of Notice 89-23.

Exclusion for Contributions to Section 403(b) Contracts

Section 403(b) provides an exclusion from gross income for certain contributions made by certain types of employers for their employees to specific types of funding arrangements. There are three categories of funding arrangements to which section 403(b) applies: (1) annuity contracts (as defined in section 401(g)) issued by an insurance company; (2) custodial accounts that are invested solely in mutual funds; and (3) retirement income accounts which are only permitted for church employees. The exclusion applies only if certain general requirements are satisfied. For purposes of most of these requirements, section 403(b)(5) provides that all section 403(b) contracts purchased for an individual by an employer are treated as purchased under a single contract. Other aggregation rules apply for certain specific purposes, including the aggregation rules under section 402(g) for purposes of satisfying the limitations on elective deferrals (which apply both on an individual basis and to all contributions made by an employer) and the controlled group rules of section 414(b) and (c) for purposes of the general nondiscrimination rules and the contribution limitations of section 415 (which generally apply on an employer-by-employer basis).

Section 403(b) Requirements

Section 403(b)(1)(C) requires that the contract be nonforfeitable except for the failure to pay future premiums. The proposed regulations define nonforfeitability based on the regulations under section 411(a) and clarify that if an annuity contract issued by an insurance company is purchased that would satisfy section 403(b) except for the failure to satisfy this nonforfeitability requirement, then the contract is treated as a contract to which section 403(c) applies. Section 403(c) provides that the value of a nonqualified contract is included in gross income under the rules of section 83, which generally does not occur before the employee's rights in the contract become substantially vested. Under the proposed regulations, on the date on which the employee's interest in that contract becomes nonforfeitable, the contract may be treated as a section 403(b) contract if the contract has at all prior times satisfied the requirements of section 403(b) other than the nonforfeitability requirement. Solely for this purpose, if a participant's interest in a contract is only partially nonforfeitable in a year, then the portion that is nonforfeitable and the portion that fails to be nonforfeitable are bifurcated.

Section 403(b)(12) requires a section 403(b) contract to make elective deferrals available to all employees (the universal availability rule) and requires other contributions to satisfy the general nondiscrimination requirements applicable to qualified plans. These rules are discussed further below under the heading *Section 403(b) Nondiscrimination and Universal Availability Rules.*

Section 403(b)(1)(E) requires a section 403(b) contract to satisfy the requirements of section 401(a)(30) relating to limitations on elective deferrals under section 402(g)(1). The proposed regulations provide that a contract only satisfies this requirement if the contract requires all elective deferrals for an employee to satisfy section 402(g)(1), including elective deferrals for the employee under the contract and any other elective deferrals under the plan under which the contract is purchased and under all other plans, contracts, or arrangements of the employer that are subject to the limits of section 402(g). This rule is the same as the rule for section 401(k) arrangements.

A section 403(b) contract is also required to provide that it will satisfy the minimum required distribution requirements of section 401(a)(9), the incidental benefit requirements of section 401(a), and the rollover distribution rules of section 402(c).

The proposed regulations address the requirement that annual additions to the contract not exceed the applicable limitations of section 415(c) (treating contributions as annual additions). In accordance with the last sentence of section 415(a)(2), if an excess annual addition is made to a contract that otherwise satisfies the requirements of section 403(b), then the portion of the contract that includes the excess will fail to be a section 403(b) contract (and instead will be a contract to which section 403(c) applies) and the remaining portion of the contract that includes the contribution that is not in excess of the section 415 limitations is a section 403(b) contract. This rule under which only the excess annual addition is subject to section 403(c) does not apply unless, for the year of the excess and each year thereafter, the issuer of the contract maintains separate accounts for the portion that includes the excess and for the section 403(b) portion, i.e., the portion that includes the amount not in excess of the section 415 limitations.

The proposed regulations require that these conditions for the exclusion be satisfied both in form and operation in the section 403(b) contract. Because several of these requirements are based on plan documents — in particular the requirements that elective deferrals

satisfy a universal availability rule and that other contributions satisfy the nondiscrimination rules applicable to qualified plans — the proposed regulations require that the contract be maintained pursuant to a plan. For this purpose, it is intended that the plan would include all of the material provisions regarding eligibility, benefits, applicable limitations, the contracts available under the plan, and the time and form under which benefit distributions would be made. This rule does not require that there be a single plan document. For example, this requirement would be satisfied by complying with the plan document rules applicable to qualified plans.

Interaction between Title I of ERISA and Section 403(b) of the Code

The Treasury Department and the IRS have consulted with the Department of Labor concerning the interaction between Title I of the Employee Retirement Income Security Act of 1974 (ERISA) and section 403(b) of the Code. The Department of Labor has advised the Treasury Department and the IRS that Title I of ERISA generally applies to "any plan, fund, or program . . . established or maintained by an employer or by an employee organization, or by both, to the extent that . . . such plan, fund, or program . . . provides retirement income to employees, or . . . results in a deferral of income by employees for periods extending to the termination of covered employment or beyond." ERISA, section 3(2)(A). However, governmental plans and church plans are generally excluded from coverage under Title I of ERISA. See ERISA, section 4(b)(1) and (2). Therefore, section 403(b) contracts purchased or provided under a program that is either a "governmental plan" under section 3(32) of ERISA or a "church plan" under section 3(33) of ERISA are not generally covered under Title I. However, section 403(b) of the Code is also available with respect to contracts purchased or provided by employers for employees of a section 501(c)(3) organization, and many programs for the purchase of section 403(b) contracts offered by such employers are covered under Title I of ERISA as part of an "employee pension benefit plan" within the meaning of section 3(2)(A) of ERISA. The Department of Labor has promulgated a regulation, 29 CFR 2510.3-2(f), describing circumstances under which an employer's program for the purchase of section 403(b) contracts for its employees, which is not otherwise excluded from coverage under Title I, will not be considered to constitute the establishment or maintenance of an "employee pension benefit plan" under Title I of ERISA.

These proposed regulations are generally limited to the requirements imposed under section 403(b). In this regard, the proposed regulations require that a section 403(b) program be maintained pursuant to a plan, which for this purpose is defined as a written defined contribution plan which, in both form and operation, satisfies the regulatory requirements of section 403(b) and contains all the material terms and conditions for benefits under the plan. The Department of Labor has advised the Treasury Department and the IRS that, although it does not appear that the proposed regulations would mandate the establishment or maintenance of an employee pension benefit plan in order to satisfy its requirements, it leaves open the possibility that an employer may undertake responsibilities that would constitute establishing and maintaining an ERISA-covered plan. The Department of Labor has further advised the Treasury Department and the IRS that whether the manner in which any particular employer decides to satisfy particular responsibilities under these proposed regulations will cause the employer to be considered to have established or to maintain a plan that is covered under Title I of ERISA must be analyzed on a case-by-case basis, applying the criteria set forth in 29 CFR 2510.3-2(f), including the employer's involvement as contemplated by the plan documents and in operation.

To the extent that these proposed regulations may raise questions for employers concerning the scope and application of the regulation at 29 CFR 2510.3 -2(f), the Treasury Department and the IRS are requesting comments. See below under the heading *Comments and Public Hearing.*

All employee pension benefit plans covered under Title I of ERISA, including plans that involve the purchase of section 403(b) contracts, must satisfy a number of requirements, including requirements relating to reporting and disclosure, eligibility, vesting, benefit accrual, advance notice of contribution reductions, qualified joint and survivor annuities, minimum funding, fiduciary standards, fidelity bonds, and claims procedures. Authority to interpret many of the requirements in Parts 2 and 3 of Title I of ERISA (specifically those relating to eligibility, vesting, benefit accrual, minimum funding, and qualified joint and survivor annuities) has been transferred to the Treasury Department and the IRS. See Reorganization Plan No. 4 of 1978, 43 FR 47713, October 17, 1978. As a result, those section 403(b) contracts of a section 501(c)(3) organization that are part of an employee pension benefit plan are subject to requirements parallel to those imposed under sections 401(a)(11) through 401(a)(15), 410, 411, 412, and 417 of the Internal Revenue Code and the regulations promulgated thereunder, since regulations and other guidance issued under those Code sections are applicable for purposes of the parallel requirements in ERISA. Further, although specific references are made to Title I in these proposed regulations, this does not imply that other Title I issues are not applicable.

Comparison with Section 401(k) Elective Deferrals

Section 1450(a) of SBJPA provides that the rules applicable to cash or deferred elections under section 401(k) are to apply under section 403(b) for purposes of determining the frequency with which an employee may enter into a salary reduction agreement, the salary to which such an agreement may apply, and the ability to revoke such an agreement. Based in part on this provision, and taking into account the guidance that has been issued since SBJPA,[5] the proposed regulations would clarify the extent to which section 403(b) elective deferrals are like elective deferrals under proposed and final rules under section 401(k). Specifically, the rules are fundamentally similar with respect to the frequency with which a deferral election can be made, changed, or revoked, including automatic enrollment (plan provisions under which elective deferrals are automatically made for employees unless they elect otherwise), the ability for a deferral election that has been made in one year to be carried forward to subsequent periods until modified, the rule under which irrevocable elections are not treated as elective deferrals, and the requirement that employees have an annual effective opportunity to make, revoke, or modify a deferral election. The rules are also fundamentally similar with respect to the compensation with respect to which the election can be made, e.g., allowing a deferral election to be made for compensation up to the day before the compensation is currently available . Likewise, the proposed regulations explicitly provide that, for purposes of sections 402(g) and 403(b), an elective deferral with respect to a section 403(b) contract is limited to contributions made pursuant to a cash or deferred election, as defined in regulations under section 401(k).

These proposed regulations also include a rule comparable to the anticonditioning rule at section 401(k)(4). Finally, the proposed regulations include rules similar to those for section 401(k) plans regarding plan limitations to comply with section 401(a)(30) and to pay out section 403(b) elective deferrals in excess of the related section 402(g) limitation.

As a result, under the proposed regulations, the three major differences between the rules applicable to section 403(b) elective deferrals and the rules applicable to elective deferrals under section 401(k) are:

- Section 403(b) is limited to certain specific employers and employees (i.e., employees of a State public school, employees of a section 501(c)(3) organization, and certain ministers), whereas section 401(k) is available to all employers, except a State or local government or any political subdivision, agency, or instrumentality thereof.

- Unlike section 401(k), contributions under section 403(b) can only be made to certain funding arrangements, i.e., an insurance annuity contract, custodial account that is limited to mutual fund shares, or church retirement income account, and not to a trust or custodial account that fails to satisfy the custodial account rules at section 403(b)(7) or the retirement income account rules at section 403(b)(9) for churches.

- A universal availability rule applies to section 403(b) elective deferrals, whereas an average deferral percentage rule (the ADP test) and a minimum coverage rule (section 410(b)) apply with respect to elective deferrals under section 401(k).[6]

Failure to Satisfy Section 403(b)

The regulations clarify that if the requirements of section 403(b) fail to be satisfied with respect to an employer contribution, then the contribution is subject either to the rules under section 403(c) (relating to nonqualified annuities) if the contribution is for an annuity contract issued by an insurance company, or is subject to the rules under section 61, 83, or 402(b) if the contribution is to a custodial account or retirement income account that fails to satisfy the requirements of section 403(b).

Issues have been raised about the application of section 403(b) to tax-exempt entities that have State or local government features. These proposed regulations do not attempt to address when an entity is a State (treating a local government or other subdivision as a State) and when it is a section 501(c)(3) organization that is not a State.[7] Thus, for example, these regulations do not provide guidance on the conditions under which a tax-exempt charter school is, or is not, a State entity.

Based on the wording of section 401(k)(4)(B)(i) and (ii), an entity that is both a section 501(c)(3) organization and an instrumentality of a State cannot have a section 401(k) plan. Under sections 457(b)(6) and 457(g), an entity that is both an instrumentality of a State and a section 501(c)(3) organization can have an eligible plan under section 457(b) only if it is funded. However, under section 403(b)(1)(A)(i) and (ii), an entity that is both an instrumentality of a State and a section 501(c)(3) organization could cover any of its employees, regardless of whether they are performing services for a public school.

Maximum Contribution Limitations

The exclusion provided under section 403(b) applies only to the extent that all amounts contributed by the employer for the purchase of an annuity contract for the participant do not exceed the applicable limit under section 415 and, with respect to section 403(b) elective deferrals, only if the contract is purchased under a plan that includes the limits under section 402(g), including aggregation under all plans of the employer. The proposed regulations require a section 403(b) contract to include this limit on section 403(b) elective deferrals, as imposed by section 402(g).

Catch-up Contributions

A section 403(b) contract may provide for additional catch-up contributions for a participant who is age 50 by the end of the year, provided that those age 50 catch-up contributions do not exceed the catch-up limit under section 414(v) for the taxable year (which is $3,000 for 2004). In addition, an employee of a qualified organization who has at least 15 years of service (disregarding any period during which an individual is not an employee of the eligible employer) is entitled to a special section 403(b) catch-up limit. Under the special section 403(b) catch-up limit, the section 402(g) limit is increased by the lowest of the following three amounts: (i) $3,000; (ii) the excess of $15,000 over the total special section 403(b) catch-up elective deferrals made for the qualified employee by the qualified organization for prior taxable years; or (iii) the excess of (A) $5,000 multiplied by the number of years of service of the employee with the qualified organization, over (B) the total elective deferrals made for the qualified employee by the qualified organization for prior taxable years. For this purpose, a qualified organization is an eligible employer that is a school, hospital, health and welfare service agency (including a home health service agency), or a church-related organization. In the case of a church-related organization, all entities that are in such a church-related organization are treated as a single qualified organization, so that years of service and any section 403(b) catch-up elective deferrals previously made for a qualified employee for any such church are taken into account for purposes of determining the amount of section 403(b) catch-up elective deferrals to which an employee is entitled under any section 403(b) plan maintained by another entity in the same church-related organization. A health and welfare service agency is defined as either an organization whose primary activity is to provide medical care as defined in section 213(d)(1) (such as a hospice), or a section 501(c)(3) organization whose primary activity is the prevention of cruelty to individuals or animals, or which provides substantial personal services to the needy as part of its primary activity (such as a section 501(c)(3) organization that provides meals to needy individuals).

The proposed regulations provide that any catch-up contribution for an employee who is eligible for both an age 50 catch-up and the special section 403(b) catch-up is treated first as a special section 403(b) catch-up to the extent a special section 403(b) catch-up is permitted, and then as an amount contributed as an age 50 catch-up (to the extent the age 50 catch-up amount exceeds the maximum special section 403(b) catchup).

Any contribution made for a participant to a section 403(b) contract for a taxable year that exceeds either the section 415 maximum annual contribution limit or the section 402(g) elective deferral limit consti-

---

[5] See, for example, Rev. Rul. 2000-35, 2000-2 C.B. 138, relating to automatic enrollment in section 403(b) plans.

[6] Other differences between the rules applicable to elective deferrals under section 403(b) and elective deferrals under section 401(k) include the following: the consequences of failing to satisfy the rules of section 403(b) (described below under the heading *Failure to satisfy section 403(b)*); the definition of compensation (including the five-year rule) at section 403(b)(3); the special section 403(b) catch-up elective deferral at section 402(g)(7);

the section 415 aggregation rules; and the general inapplicability of stock ownership for State entities (and some nonprofit entities), including the related inapplicability of employee stock ownership plans and the use of stock ownership to determine common control. An additional difference is discussed below, under the heading *Severance From Employment.*

[7] Similarly, the proposed regulations do not address the conditions under which a plan is a governmental plan under section 414(d).

tutes an excess contribution that is included in gross income for that taxable year (or, if later, the taxable year in which the contract becomes nonforfeitable). The proposed regulations provide that a section 403(b) contract or the section 403(b) plan may provide that any excess deferral as a result of a failure to comply with the section 402(g) elective deferral limit for the taxable year with respect to any section 403(b) elective deferral made for a participant by the employer will be distributed to the participant, with allocable net income, no later than April 15 or otherwise in accordance with section 402(g).

Determination of Years of Service under Section 403(b)

For purposes of determining a participant's includible compensation and years of service — used both for the special section 403(b) catch-up contributions and for employer contributions for former employees — an employee's number of years of service include each full year during which the individual is a full-time employee of the eligible employer plus a fraction of a year for each part of a year during which the individual is a full-time or part-time employee of the eligible employer. A year of service is based on the employer's annual work period, not the employee's taxable year. Thus, in determining whether a university professor is employed full-time, the annual work period is the school's academic year. In determining whether an individual is employed full-time, the amount of work actually performed is compared with the amount of work that is normally required of individuals performing similar services from which substantially all of their annual compensation is derived. An individual is treated as performing a fraction of a year of service for each annual work period during which he or she is a full-time employee for part of the annual work period or for each annual work period during which he or she is a part-time employee either for the entire annual work period or for a part of the annual work period.

In measuring the amount of work of an individual performing particular services, the work performed is determined based on the individual's hours of service (as defined under section 410(a)(3)(C)), except that a plan may use a different measure of work if appropriate under the facts and circumstances. For example, a plan may provide for a university professor's work to be measured by the number of courses taught during an annual work period if that individual's work assignment is generally based on a specified number of courses to be taught.

In determining years of service, any period during which an individual is not an employee of the eligible employer is disregarded, except that, for a section 403(b) contract of an eligible employer that is a church-related organization, any period during which an individual is an employee of that eligible employer and any other eligible employer that is within the same church-related organization with that eligible employer is taken into account on an aggregated basis. In the case of a part-time employee or a full-time employee who is employed for only part of the year, the employee's most recent periods of service are aggregated to determine his or her most recent one-year period of service, as follows: the employee's service during the annual work period for which the last year of service's includible compensation is being determined is taken into account first; then the employee's service during the next preceding annual work period based on whole months is taken into account; and so forth, until the employee's service equals, in the aggregate, one year of service.

Special Rule for Former Employees

Under section 403(b)(3), a former employee is deemed to have monthly includible compensation for the period through the end of the taxable year of the employee in which he or she ceases to be an employee and through the end of each of the next five taxable years of the employee. The amount of the monthly includible compensation is equal to 1/12 of the former employee's includible compensation during the former employee's most recent year of service. Accordingly, a plan may provide that nonelective employer contributions are continued for up to five years for a former employee, up to the lesser of the dollar amount in section 415(c)(1)(A) or the former employee's annual includible compensation based on the former employee's compensation during his or her most recent year of service.

Other Contributions for Former Employees

The proposed regulations do not address the extent, if any, to which the exclusion from gross income provided by section 403(b) applies to contributions made for former employees (e.g., whether a contribution may be made for a former employee if the contribution is with respect to compensation that would otherwise be paid for a payroll period that begins after severance from employment) other than as provided under the five-year rule at section 403(b)(3), described above under the heading *Special Rule for Former Employees*. The Treasury Department and the IRS expect to issue separate guidance on this issue, potentially

addressing this question with respect to not only section 403(b), but also sections 401(k), 457(b) (for eligible governmental plans), and 415(c).

Section 403(b) Nondiscrimination and Universal Availability Rules
Nondiscrimination

Section 403(b)(12)(A)(i) requires that employer contributions and employee aftertax contributions made under a section 403(b) contract satisfy a specified series of requirements (the nondiscrimination requirements) in the same manner as a qualified plan under section 401(a). These proposed regulations do not adopt the good faith reasonable standard of Notice 89-23 for purposes of satisfying the nondiscrimination requirements of section 403(b)(12)(A)(i). These nondiscrimination requirements include rules relating to nondiscrimination in contributions, benefits, and coverage (sections 401(a)(4) and 410(b)), a limitation on the amount of compensation that can be taken into account (section 401(a)(17)), and the average contribution percentage rules of section 401(m) (relating to matching and after-tax contributions). The nondiscrimination requirements are generally tested using compensation as defined in section 414(s) and are applied on an aggregated basis taking into account all plans of the employer. See the discussion below under the heading *Controlled Group Rules For Tax-Exempt Entities*

The nondiscrimination requirements do not apply to section 403(b) elective deferrals. In addition, the only nondiscrimination requirement that applies to a governmental plan, within the meaning of section 414(d), is the limitation on compensation (section 401(a)(17)).

Universal Availability

Under section 403(b)(12)(A)(ii), a universal availability requirement applies under which all employees of the eligible employer must be permitted to elect to have section 403(b) elective deferrals contributed on their behalf if any employee of the eligible employer may elect to have the organization make section 403(b) elective deferrals. Under the proposed regulations, the universal availability requirement is not satisfied unless the contributions are made pursuant to a plan and the plan permits elective deferrals that satisfy the universal availability requirement. The proposed regulations generally provide that the universal availability requirement applies separately to each common law entity, i.e., to each section 501(c)(3) organization, or, in the case of a section 403(b) plan that covers the employees of more than one State entity, to each entity that is not part of a common payroll. The proposed regulations allow an employer that historically has treated one or more of its various geographically distinct units as separate for employee benefit purposes to treat each unit as a separate organization if the unit is operated independently on a day-to-day basis.

The proposed regulations include the statutory categories that are exceptions to the universal availability rule, and provide that, if any employee listed in any excludable category has the right to have section 403(b) elective deferrals made on his or her behalf, then no employees in that category may be excluded. The categories generally are: employees who are eligible to participate in an eligible governmental plan under section 457(b) which permits contributions or deferrals at the election of the employee or a plan of the employer offering a qualified cash or deferred election under section 401(k); employees who are non-resident aliens; employees who are students performing services described in section 3121(b)(10); and employees who normally work fewer than 20 hours per week. Additionally, Notice 89-23 included transition rules for certain other exclusions that are not in the statute: employees who make a one-time election to participate in a governmental plan instead of a section 403(b) plan; employees covered by a collective bargaining agreement; visiting professors for up to one year under certain circumstances; and employees affiliated with a religious order who have taken a vow of poverty. The proposed regulations do not adopt these transition rules. See the reference to these exclusions below under the heading

Comments and Public Hearing

The nondiscrimination and the universal availability requirements do not apply to a section 403(b) contract purchased by a church, which is specially defined for this purpose, and generally does not include a university, hospital, or nursing home.

The nondiscrimination and universal availability requirements are in addition to other applicable legal requirements. Specifically, these requirements do not reflect the requirements of Title I of ERISA that may apply with respect to a section 403(b) plan, such as the ERISA vesting requirements. Another example is that, while employees who normally work fewer than 20 hours per week may be excluded under the universal availability rule, employers who maintain plans that are subject to Title I of ERISA should be aware that Title I of ERISA includes limitations on the conditions under which employees can be excluded from a plan on account of not working full time and that these limitations would generally not permit an exclusion for employees who normally work fewer than 20 hours per week. See section 202(a)(1) of ERISA and regulations under section 410(a) of the Code (which interpret section 202 of ERISA).

Timing of Distributions and Benefits

The proposed regulations reflect the statutory rules regarding when distributions can be made from a section 403(b) contract. Thus, amounts held in a custodial contract attributable to employer contributions (that are not section 403(b) elective deferrals) may not be paid to a participant before the participant has a severance from employment, becomes disabled (within the meaning of section 72(m)(7)), or attains age 59 ½. This rule also applies to amounts transferred out of a custodial account (i.e., to an annuity contract or retirement income account), including earnings thereon. In addition, distributions of amounts attributable to section 403(b) elective deferrals may not be paid to a participant earlier than when the participant has a severance from employment, has a hardship, becomes disabled (within the meaning of section 72(m)(7)), or attains age 59 ½. Hardship is generally defined under regulations issued under section 401(k).

The proposed regulations would reflect the requirements of section 402(f) relating to the written explanation requirements for distributions that qualify as eligible rollover distributions, including conforming the timing rule to the rule for qualified plans.

Where the distribution restrictions do not apply, a section 403(b) contract is permitted to distribute retirement benefits to the participant after severance from employment or upon the prior occurrence of an event, such as after a fixed number of years, the attainment of a stated age, or disability. The proposed regulations include a number of exceptions to the timing restrictions, e.g., the rule for elective deferrals does not apply to distributions of section 403(b) elective deferrals (not including earnings thereon) that were contributed before January 1, 1989.

Severance From Employment

The proposed regulations define severance from employment in a manner that is generally the same as the proposed regulations under section 401(k),[8] but provide that a severance from employment occurs on any date on which the employee ceases to be employed by an eligible employer that maintains the section 403(b) plan. Thus, a severance from employment would occur when an employee ceases to be employed by an eligible employer even though the employee may continue to be employed by an entity that is part of the same controlled group but that is not an eligible employer, or on any date on which the employee works in a capacity that is not employment with an eligible employer. Examples of the situations that constitute a severance from employment include: an employee transferring from a section 501(c)(3) organization to a for-profit subsidiary of the section 501(c)(3) organization; an employee ceasing to work for a public school, but continuing to be employed by the same State; and an individual employed as a minister for an entity that is neither a State nor a section 501(c)(3) organization ceasing to perform services as a minister, but continuing to be employed by the same entity.

Section 401(a)(9)

The proposed regulations include rules similar to those in the existing regulations relating to the minimum distribution requirements of section 401(a)(9), but with some minor changes (for example, omitting the special rules for 5-percent owners). Thus, section 403(b) contracts must satisfy the incidental benefit rules. Existing revenue rulings provide guidance with respect to the application of the incidental benefit requirements to permissible nonretirement benefits such as life, accident, or health benefits.[9]

Loans

The proposed regulations include rules reflecting that loans can be made to participants from a section 403(b) contract.

QDROs

The proposed regulations include limited rules relating to qualified domestic relations orders (QDROs) under section 414(p). Section 414(p)(9) provides that the QDRO rules only apply to plans that are subject to the anti-alienation provisions of section 401(a)(13), except

that section 414(p)(9) also provides that, except to the extent set forth in regulations - there are currently no regulations under section 414(p) - the section 414(p) QDRO rules apply to a section 403(b) contract. These proposed section 403(b) regulations clarify that the section 414(p) QDRO rules apply to section 403(b) contracts for purposes of applying section 403(b).

Taxation of Distributions and Benefits From a Section 403(b) Contract

The proposed regulations include a number of rules regarding the taxation of distributions and benefits from section 403(b) contracts, including the statutory provision that only amounts actually distributed from a section 403(b) contract are generally includible in the gross income of the recipient for the year in which distributed under section 72, relating to annuities. The regulations also reflect the rule that any payment that constitutes an eligible rollover distribution is not taxed in the year distributed to the extent the payment is directly rolled over or transferred to an eligible retirement plan. The payor must withhold 20 percent Federal income tax, however, if an eligible rollover distribution is not rolled over in a direct rollover. Another provision requires the payor to give proper written notice to the section 403(b) participant or beneficiary concerning the eligible rollover distribution provision. Notice 2002-3 (2002-2 I.R.B. 289), provides a sample of the safe-harbor notice that the payor may furnish to satisfy this requirement.

Funding of Section 403(b) Arrangements

Annuity Contracts

As described above, section 403(b) only applies to contributions made to certain funding arrangements, namely: amounts held in an annuity contract, in a custodial account that is treated as an annuity contract under section 403(b)(7), or in a church retirement income account that is treated as an annuity contract under section 403(b)(9). The proposed regulations require that contributions to a section 403(b) plan be transferred to the insurance company issuing the annuity contract (or the entity holding assets of any custodial or retirement income account that is treated as an annuity contract) within a period that is not longer than is reasonable for the proper administration of the plan, such as transferring elective deferrals within 15 business days following the month in which these amounts would otherwise have been paid to the participant.

The proposed regulations provide that, except where a custodial or retirement income account is treated as an annuity contract, an annuity contract means a contract that is issued by an insurance company qualified to issue annuities in a State and that includes payment in the form of an annuity, but does not include a contract that is a life insurance contract, as defined in section 7702, an endowment contract, a heath or accident insurance contract, or a property, casualty, or liability insurance contract. The regulations include a special transition rule relating to life insurance contracts issued before the effective date.

Rev. Rul. 67-361 (1967-2 C.B. 153), and Rev. Rul. 67-387 (1967-2 C.B. 153), provided for certain State plans to be treated as qualifying as annuities under section 403(b). Rev. Rul. 82-102 (1982-1 C.B. 62), revoked this interpretation (in connection with the 1974 enactment of section 403(b)(7) which allowed custodial accounts), but provides section 7805(b) relief for arrangements established in reliance on these rulings, i.e., for arrangements established on or before May 17, 1982. The proposed regulations contemplate that the section 7805(b) relief provided by these rulings would be continued. This relief would be limited to State section 403(b) plans established on or before May 17, 1982 satisfying either of the following requirements: (i) benefits under the contract are provided from a separately funded retirement reserve that is subject to supervision of the State insurance department or (ii) benefits under the contract are provided from a fund that is separate from the fund used to provide statutory benefits payable under a State retirement system and that is part of a State teachers retirement system to purchase benefits that are unrelated to the basic benefits provided under the retirement system, and the death benefit provided under the contract cannot at any time exceed the larger of the reserve or the contribution made for the employee.

Custodial Accounts

The proposed regulations define a custodial account as a plan, or a separate account under a plan, in which an amount attributable to section 403(b) contributions (or amounts rolled over to a section 403(b) contract) is held by a bank or a person who satisfies the

---

[8] See proposed § 1.401(k)-1(d)(2), REG-108639-99, 68 FR 42476 (July 17, 2003).

[9] See, for example, Rev. Rul. 61-121, 1961-2 C.B. 65; Rev. Rul. 68-304, 1968-1 C.B. 179; Rev. Rul. 72-240, 1972-1 C.B. 108; Rev. Rul. 72-241, 1972-1 C.B. 108; Rev. Rul. 73-239, 1973-1 C.B. 201; and Rev. Rul. 74-115, 1974-1 C.B. 100. (see § 601.601(d)(2)(ii)(b) of this chapter).

conditions in section 401(f)(2), if amounts held in the account are invested in stock of a regulated investment company (as defined in section 851(a) relating to mutual funds), the special restrictions on distributions with respect to a custodial account are satisfied, the assets held in the account cannot be used for, or diverted to, purposes other than for the exclusive benefit of plan participants or their beneficiaries, and the account is not part of a retirement income account, as described below. This requirement limiting investments to mutual funds is not satisfied if the account includes any assets other than stock of a regulated investment company.

Special Rules for Church Plans

Retirement Income Accounts

The proposed regulations include a number of special rules for church plans. Under section 403(b)(9), a retirement income account for employees of a church-related organization is treated as an annuity contract for purposes of section 403(b) and these regulations. Under the proposed regulations, the rules for a retirement income account are based largely on the legislative history to TEFRA. The proposed regulations define a retirement income account as a defined contribution program established or maintained by a church-related organization under which (i) there is separate accounting for the retirement income account's interest in the underlying assets (i.e., it must be possible at all times to determine the retirement income account's interest in the underlying assets and distinguish that interest from any interest that is not part of the retirement income account), (ii) investment performance is based on gains and losses on those assets, and (iii) the assets held in the account cannot be used for, or diverted to, purposes other than for the exclusive benefit of plan participants or their beneficiaries. For this purpose, assets are treated as diverted to the employer if the employer borrows assets from the account. A retirement income account must be maintained pursuant to a program which is a plan and the plan document must state (or otherwise evidence in a similarly clear manner) the intent to constitute a retirement income account.

If any asset of a retirement income account is owned or used by a participant or beneficiary, then that ownership or use is treated as a distribution to that participant or beneficiary. The proposed regulations provide that a retirement income account that is treated as an annuity contract is not a custodial account (even if it is invested in stock of a regulated investment company).

A life annuity can generally only be provided from an individual account by the purchase of an insurance annuity contract. However, in light of the special rules applicable to church retirement income accounts, the proposed regulations permit a life annuity to be paid from such an account if certain conditions are satisfied. The conditions are that the amount of the distribution form have an actuarial present value, at the annuity starting date, that is equal to the participant's or beneficiary's accumulated benefit, based on reasonable actuarial assumptions, including assumptions regarding interest and mortality, and that the plan sponsor guarantee benefits in the event that a payment is due that exceeds the participant's or beneficiary's accumulated benefit.

Commingling Assets

Under these proposed regulations, both custodial accounts and retirement income accounts would be subject to an exclusive benefit requirement similar to the exclusive benefit requirement applicable to qualified plans. Section 403(b)(7)(B) provides for a custodial account to be treated as a tax exempt organization.

When these regulations are issued as final regulations, to the extent permitted by the Commissioner in future guidance, assets held under a custodial account or a retirement income account may be pooled with trust assets held under qualified plans.

Controlled Group Rules For Tax-Exempt Entities

The proposed regulations include controlled group rules under section 414(c) for entities that are tax-exempt under section 501(a). Under these rules, the employer for a plan maintained by a section 501(c)(3) organization (or any other tax-exempt organization under section 501(a)) includes not only the organization whose employees participate in the plan, but also any other exempt organization that is under common control with such organization, based on 80 percent of the directors or trustees being either representatives of or directly or indirectly controlled by an exempt organization. The proposed regulations include an anti-abuse rule and would also allow tax exempt organizations to choose to be aggregated if they maintain a single plan covering one or more employees from each organization and the organizations regularly coordinate their day to day exempt activities. For a section 501(c)(3) organization that makes contributions to a section 403(b) contract, these rules would be generally relevant for

purposes of the nondiscrimination requirements, as well as the section 415 contribution limitations, the special section 403(b) catch-up contributions, and the section 401(a)(9) minimum distribution rules.

These controlled group rules for tax-exempt entities generally do not apply to certain church entities. Comments are requested below under the heading *Comment and Public Hearing* on whether these rules should be extended to such church entities.

The proposed regulations do not include controlled group rules for public schools. As noted above (under the heading *Overview*), it is anticipated that, when these regulations are issued as final regulations, guidance may be issued providing controlled group safe harbors for public schools taking into account the existing safe harbors in Notice 89-23.

Miscellaneous Provisions

The proposed regulations include a number of rules that address the circumstances under which a section 403(b) plan may be terminated or assets may be exchanged or transferred.

Plan Termination

The proposed regulations, if adopted as final regulations, would not only permit an employer to amend its section 403(b) plan to eliminate future contributions for existing participants, but would allow plan provisions that permit plan termination with a resulting distribution of accumulated benefits. In general, the distribution of accumulated benefits would be permitted only if the employer (taking into account all entities that are treated as the employer under section 414 on the date of the termination) does not make contributions to another section 403(b) contract that is not part of the plan (based generally on contributions made to a section 403(b) contract during the 12 months before and after the date of plan termination). In order for a section 403(b) plan to be considered terminated, all accumulated benefits under the plan must be distributed to all participants and beneficiaries as soon as administratively practicable after termination of the plan. A distribution includes delivery of a fully paid individual insurance annuity contract. Eligible rollover distributions would not be subject to current income inclusion if rolled over to an eligible retirement plan.

The proposed regulations prohibit an employer that ceases to be an eligible employer from making any further contributions to the section 403(b) contract for subsequent periods. In this event, the contract can be held under a frozen plan or the plan could be terminated in accordance with the rules regarding plan termination.

Exchanges and Transfers

Under certain conditions, the proposed regulations permit the following exchanges or transfers:

- A section 403(b) contract is permitted to be exchanged for another section 403(b) contract held under the same section 403(b) plan if the following conditions are satisfied: (1) the plan provides for the exchange, (2) the participant or beneficiary has an accumulated benefit immediately after the exchange at least equal to the accumulated benefit of that participant or beneficiary immediately before the exchange (taking into account the accumulated benefit of that participant or beneficiary under both section 403(b) contracts immediately before the exchange), and (3) the contract received in the exchange provides that, to the extent a contract that is exchanged is subject to any section 403(b) distribution restrictions, the contract received in the exchange imposes restrictions on distributions to the participant or beneficiary that are not less stringent than those imposed on the contract being exchanged.

- A section 403(b) contract is permitted to be transferred to another section 403(b) plan (i.e., the section 403(b) contracts held thereunder, including any assets held in a custodial account or retirement income account that are treated as section 403(b) contracts) if the following conditions are satisfied: (1) the participant or beneficiary whose assets are being transferred is an employee of the employer providing the receiving plan, (2) the transferor plan provides for transfers, (3) the receiving plan provides for the receipt of transfers, (4) the participant or beneficiary whose assets are being transferred has an accumulated benefit immediately after the transfer at least equal to the accumulated benefit with respect to that participant or beneficiary immediately before the transfer, and (5) the receiving plan provides that, to the extent any amount transferred is subject to any section 403(b) distribution restrictions, the receiving plan imposes restrictions on distributions to the participant or beneficiary whose assets are being transferred that are not less stringent than those imposed on the transferor plan. In addition, if a plan-to-plan transfer does not constitute a complete transfer of the participant's or beneficiary's interest in the section 403(b) plan, then the transferee plan must treat the amount transferred as a continuation of a pro rata portion of the participant's or beneficiary's interest in the transferor section 403(b) plan (e.g., a pro rata portion of the participant's or beneficiary's interest in any after-tax employee contributions).

- A section 403(b) plan may provide for the transfer of its assets to a qualified plan under section 401(a) to purchase permissive service credit under a defined benefit governmental plan or to make a repayment to a defined benefit governmental plan.

However, neither a qualified plan nor an eligible plan under section 457 may transfer assets to a section 403(b) plan, and a section 403(b) plan may not accept such a transfer. In addition, a section 403(b) contract may not be exchanged for an annuity contract that is not a section 403(b) contract. Neither a plan-to-plan transfer nor a contract exchange permitted under the proposed regulations is treated as a distribution for purposes of the section 403(b) distribution restrictions (so that such a transfer or exchange may be made before severance from employment or another distribution event).

Additional plan-to-plan transfer rules may apply in the event that a plan-to-plan transfer is made to or from a section 403(b) arrangement that is subject to Title I of ERISA. See section 208 of ERISA and regulations under section 414(l) of the Internal Revenue Code (which are the regulations interpreting section 208 of ERISA).

Defined Benefit Plans

These proposed regulations generally require a section 403(b) plan to be a defined contribution plan. This requirement would not apply to certain church plans. Specifically, section 251(e)(5) of TEFRA permits a church arrangement in effect on September 3, 1982 (the date TEFRA was enacted) to not be treated as failing to satisfy the exclusion allowance limitations of section 403(b)(2) merely because it is a defined benefit plan and these regulations would allow such a plan to be continued. Any other defined benefit plan in existence on the effective date of these regulations that has taken the position, based on a reasonable interpretation of the statute, that it satisfies section 403(b) would not be subject to the requirement in these regulations that the plan be a defined contribution plan for pre-effective date accruals, and such a plan might seek to take the position that it satisfies the section 401 qualified plan rules for subsequent accruals (assuming it satisfies those rules with respect to those accruals).

Section 3121(a)(5)(D)

These proposed regulations also include proposed amendments to regulations under section 3121(a)(5)(D), defining salary reduction agreement for purposes of the Federal Insurance Contributions Act (FICA). The text of the proposed amendments is the same as that of temporary regulations being issued under section 3121(a)(5)(D) in this same issue of the **Federal Register**. The proposed regulations under section 3121(a)(5)(D) would be applicable on November 16, 2004.

Proposed Effective date

These regulations (other than the proposed amendments to regulations under section 3121(a)(5)(D)) are proposed to be generally applicable for taxable years beginning after December 31, 2005. However, there are certain transition rules. Under one transition rule, for a section 403(b) contract maintained pursuant to a collective bargaining agreement that is ratified and in effect when the final regulations are issued, the regulations would not apply until the collective bargaining agreement terminates (determined without regard to any extension thereof after the date of publication of final regulations). Under another transition rule, for a section 403(b) contract maintained by a church-related organization for which the authority to amend the contract is held by a church convention (within the meaning of section 414(e)), the regulations would not apply before the earlier of (i) January 1, 2007 or (ii) 60 days following the earliest church convention that occurs after the date of publication of final regulations. These proposed regulations cannot be relied upon until adopted in final form.

Special Analyses

It has been determined that this notice of proposed rulemaking is not a significant regulatory action as defined in Executive Order 12866. Therefore, a regulatory assessment is not required. It also has been determined that section 553(b) of the Administrative Procedure Act (5 U.S.C. chapter 5) does not apply to these regulations.

It is hereby certified that the collection of information in these regulations will not have a significant economic impact on a substantial number of small entities. This certification is based upon the determi-

nation that respondents will need to spend minimal time (an average of ½ hour per year) giving the statutorily required notice to departing employees. Therefore, a Regulatory Flexibility Analysis is not required under the Regulatory Flexibility Act (5 U.S.C. chapter 6).

Pursuant to section 7805(f) of the Internal Revenue Code, this notice of proposed rulemaking will be submitted to the Chief Counsel for Advocacy of the Small Business Administration for comment on their impact on small business.

Comments and Public Hearing

Before these proposed regulations are adopted as final regulations, consideration will be given to any written comments (a signed original and eight (8) copies) or electronic comments that are submitted timely to the IRS. Comments are requested on all aspects of the proposed regulations. In addition, comments are specifically requested on the clarity of the proposed regulations and how they can be revised to be more easily understood. All comments will be available for public inspection and copying.

Comments are also requested on the following:

- As indicated above, the IRS expects to obsolete a number of revenue rulings, notices, and other guidance when these regulations are issued in final form, including guidance that is now outdated as a result of changes in the law, and guidance that will become outdated by final regulations. Other previously issued guidance is expected to continue in effect. Comments are requested as to whether any previously issued guidance should be added or deleted from either list, with respect to the scope of this obsolescence, and also with respect to whether there are any aspects that should to be preserved in the guidance that is expected to be obsolete.

- The Treasury Department and the IRS are requesting comments describing the issues and suggesting methods of clarifying the interaction between the employer activities required under these proposed regulations for an arrangement to satisfy section 403(b) and the employer conduct that will give rise to the establishment and maintenance of an employee pension benefit plan covered under Title I of ERISA. The Treasury Department and the IRS will forward a copy of the comments on this issue to the Department of Labor.

- These proposed regulations authorize the Commissioner to issue rules to determine the amount of contributions for a participant in a defined benefit plan under section 402(b) (relating to the tax treatment of contributions to nonqualified plans). Comments are requested on the methodology and assumptions that should be used for this purpose, including specifically whether the methodology and assumptions should be the same as those currently in the regulations under section 403(b), whether revisions should be made to reflect the possibility that a nonqualified plan might include an early retirement subsidy, and whether the assumptions currently applicable under the section 403(b) regulations should be updated (for example, to match the assumptions in Rev. Proc. 2004-37 (2004-2 I.R.B. 26), relating to determining the extent to which certain pension payments made to a nonresident alien are not U.S. source income).

- With respect to includible compensation, comments are requested on whether the Treasury Department and IRS have the authority to permit 403(b) plans to use compensation, as defined in section 415(c)(3) without regard to section 415(c)(3)(E), in lieu of the definition of includible compensation under section 403(b)(3) and, if so, whether this should be done.

- With respect to the universal availability rule, comments are requested on whether the requirement should apply separately to employees covered by a collective bargaining unit. Comments are also requested on whether plans that exclude any of the following additional types of employees (as has been permitted under Notice 89-23) should be permitted to continue to exclude these types of employees for at least some period of time: employees who make a one-time election to participate in a governmental plan described in section 414(d) instead of a section 403(b) plan; professors who are providing services on a temporary basis to another public school for up to one year and for whom section 403(b) contributions are being made at a rate no greater than the rate each such professor would receive under the section 403(b) plan of the original public school; employees who are affiliated with a religious order and who have taken a vow of poverty where the religious order provides for the support of such employees in their retirement; and employees who are covered by a collective bargaining agreement.

• The controlled group rules in these proposed regulations for tax-exempt entities generally do not apply to certain church entities. Comments are requested on whether these rules should be extended to such church entities.

A public hearing has been scheduled for February 15, 2005, at 10 a.m. in the IRS Auditorium (7 th Floor), Internal Revenue Building, 1111 Constitution Avenue, NW., Washington DC. All visitors must present photo identification to enter the building. Because of access restrictions, visitors will not be admitted beyond the immediate entrance area at the Constitution Avenue entrance more than 30 minutes before the hearing starts. For information about having your name placed on the building access list to attend the hearing, see the "FOR FURTHER INFORMATION CONTACT" section of this preamble.

The rules of 26 CFR 601.601(a)(3) apply to the hearing.

Persons who wish to present oral comments at the hearing must submit electronic or written comments and an outline of the topics to be discussed and the time to be devoted to each topic (a signed original and eight (8) copies) by January 25, 2005. A period of 10 minutes will be allotted to each person for making comments. An agenda showing the scheduling of the speakers will be prepared after the deadline for receiving outlines has passed. Copies of the agenda will be available free of charge at the hearing.

Drafting Information

The principal authors of these regulations are R. Lisa Mojiri-Azad and John Tolleris, Office of the Division Counsel/Associate Chief Counsel (Tax Exempt and Government Entities), IRS. However, other personnel from the IRS and the Treasury Department participated in their development.

List of Subjects

26 CFR Part 1

Income taxes, Reporting and recordkeeping requirements.

26 CFR Part 31

Employment taxes, Income taxes, Penalties, Pensions, Railroad retirement, Reporting and recordkeeping requirements, Social security, Unemployment compensation.

Proposed Amendments to the Regulations

Accordingly, 26 CFR parts 1 and 31 are proposed to be amended as follows:

PART 1—INCOME TAXES

Paragraph 1. The authority citation for part 1 is amended by removing the entry for § 1.403(b)-3 and adding entries in numerical order to read, in part, as follows:

Authority: 26 U.S.C. 7805 * * *

§ 1.403(b)-6 also issued under 26 U.S.C. 403(b)(10). * * *

§ 1.414(c)-5 also issued under 26 U.S.C. 414(b), (c), and (o). * * *

Par. 2. Section 1.402(b)-1 is amended by revising paragraphs (a)(2) and (b)(2)(ii) to read as follows:

§ *1.402(b)-1 Treatment of beneficiary of a trust not exempt under section 501(a).*

(a) * * *

(2) *Determination of amount of employer contributions.* If, for an employee, the actual amount of employer contributions referred to in paragraph (a)(1) of this section for any taxable year of the employee is not determinable or for any other reason is not known, such amount shall be the amount applicable under rules prescribed by the Commissioner in revenue rulings, notices, or other guidance published in the Internal Revenue Bulletin (see § 601.601(d)(2)(ii)(*b*) of this chapter).

(b) * * *

(2) * * *

(ii) If a separate account in a trust for the benefit of two or more employees is not maintained for each employee, the value of the employee's interest in such trust is determined in accordance with rules prescribed by the Commissioner under the authority in paragraph (a)(2) of this section.

* * * * *

Par. 3. Section 1.402(g)(3)-1 is added to read as follows:

§ *1.402(g)(3)-1 Employer contributions to purchase a section 403(b) contract under a salary reduction agreement.*

(a) *General rule.* With respect to an annuity contract under section 403(b), except as provided in paragraph (b) of this section, an elective deferral means an employer contribution to purchase an annuity contract under section 403(b) under a salary reduction agreement within the meaning of § 31.3121(a)(5)-2(a) of this chapter.

(b) *Special rule.* Notwithstanding paragraph (a) of this section, for purposes of section 402(g)(3)(C), an elective deferral only includes a contribution that is made pursuant to a cash or deferred election (as defined at § 1.401(k)-1(a)(3)). Thus, for purposes of section 402(g)(3)(C), an elective deferral does not include a contribution that is made pursuant to an employee's one-time irrevocable election made on or before the employee's first becoming eligible to participate under the employer's plan or a contribution made as a condition of employment that reduces the employee's compensation.

(c) *Effective date.* This section is applicable for taxable years beginning after December 31, 2005.

Par. 4. Section 1.403(b)-0 is added to read as follows:

§ *1.403(b)-0 Taxability under an annuity purchased by a section 501(c)(3) organization or a public school*

§ 1.403(b)-1 General overview of taxability under an annuity contract purchased by a section 501(c)(3) organization or a public school.

§ 1.403(b)-2 Definitions.

§ 1.403(b)-3 Exclusion for contributions to purchase section 403(b) contracts.

§ 1.403(b)-4 Contribution limitations.

§ 1.403(b)-5 Nondiscrimination rules.

§ 1.403(b)-6 Timing of distributions and benefits.

§ 1. 403(b)-7 Taxation of distributions and benefits.

§ 1.403(b)-8 Funding.

§ 1.403(b)-9 Special rules for church plans.

§ 1.403(b)-10 Miscellaneous provisions.

§ 1.403(b)-11 Effective date.

Par. 5. Sections 1.403(b)-1, 1.403(b)-2 and 1.403(b)-3 are revised to read as follows:

§ *1.403(b)-1 General overview of taxability under an annuity contract purchased by a section 501(c)(3) organization or a public school.*

Section 403(b) and §§ 1.403(b)-2 through 1.403(b)-10 provide rules for the Federal income tax treatment of an annuity purchased for an employee by an employer that is either a tax-exempt entity under section 501(c)(3) (relating to certain religious, charitable, scientific, or other types of organizations) or a public school, or for a minister described in section 414(e)(5)(A). See section 403(a) (relating to qualified annuities) for rules regarding the taxation of an annuity purchased under a qualified annuity plan that meets the requirements of section 404(a)(2), and see section 403(c) (relating to nonqualified annuities) for rules regarding the taxation of other types of annuities.

§ *1.403(b)-2 Definitions.*

(a) This section sets forth the definitions that are applicable for purposes of §§ 1.403(b)-1 through 1.403(b)-11.

(1) *Accumulated benefit* means the total benefit to which a participant or beneficiary is entitled under a section 403(b) contract, including all contributions made to the contract and all earnings thereon.

(2) *Annuity contract* means a contract that is issued by an insurance company qualified to issue annuities in a State and that includes payment in the form of an annuity. See § 1.401(f)-1(d)(2) and (e) for the definition of an annuity, and see § 1.403(b)-8(c)(3) for a special rule for certain State plans. See also §§ 1.403(b)-8(d) and 1.403(b)-9(a) for additional rules regarding the treatment of custodial accounts and retirement income accounts as annuity contracts.

(3) *Beneficiary* means a person who is entitled to benefits in respect of a participant following the participant's death or an alternate payee pursuant to a qualified domestic relations order, as described in § 1.403(b)-10(c).

(4) *Catch-up* amount or *catch-up* limitation for a participant for a taxable year means a section 403(b) elective deferral permitted under section 414(v) (as described in § 1.403(b)-4(c)(2)), or section 402(g)(7) (as described in § 1.403(b)-4(c)(3)).

(5) *Church* means a church as defined in section 3121(w)(3)(A) and a qualified church-controlled organization as defined in section 3121(w)(3)(B).

(6) *Church-related organization* means a church or convention or association of churches as described in section 414(e)(3)(A).

(7) *Elective deferral* means an elective deferral under § 1.402(g)(3)-1 (with respect to an employer contribution to a section 403(b) contract) and any other amount that constitutes an elective deferral under section 402(g)(3).

(8) (i) *Eligible employer* means—

(A) A State, but only with respect to an employee of the State performing services for a public school;

(B) A section 501(c)(3) organization with respect to any employee of the section 501(c)(3) organization;

(C) Any employer of a minister described in section 414(e)(5)(A), but only with respect to the minister; or

(D) A minister described in section 414(e)(5)(A), but only with respect to a retirement income account established for the minister.

(ii) An entity is not an eligible employer under paragraph (a)(8)(i)(A) of this section if it treats itself as not being a State for any other purpose of the Internal Revenue Code, and a subsidiary or other affiliate of an eligible employer is not an eligible employer under paragraph (a)(8)(i) of this section if the subsidiary or other affiliate is not an entity described in paragraph (a)(8)(i) of this section.

(9) *Employee* means a common-law employee performing services for the employer, and does not include a former employee or an independent contractor. Subject to any rules in §§ 1.403(b)-1 through 1.403(b)-11 that are specifically applicable to ministers, an employee also includes a minister described in section 414(e)(5)(A) when performing services in the exercise of his or her ministry.

(10) *Employee performing services for a public school* means an employee performing services as an employee for a public school of a State. This definition is not applicable unless the employee's compensation for performing services for a public school is paid by the State. Further, a person occupying an elective or appointive public office is not an employee performing services for a public school unless such office is one to which an individual is elected or appointed only if the individual has received training, or is experienced, in the field of education. The term *public office* includes any elective or appointive office of a State.

(11) *Includible compensation* means the employee's compensation received from an eligible employer that is includible in the participant's gross income for Federal income tax purposes (computed without regard to section 911) for the most recent period that is a year of service. Includible compensation for a minister who is selfemployed means the minister's earned income as defined in section 401(c)(2) (computed without regard to section 911) for the most recent period that is a year of service. Includible compensation does not include any compensation received during a period when the employer is not an eligible employer. Includible compensation also includes any elective deferral and any amount contributed or deferred by the eligible employer at the election of the employee that is not includible in the gross income of the employee by reason of section 125, 132(f)(4), or 457. The amount of includible compensation is determined without regard to any community property laws. See § 1.403(b)-4(d) for a special rule regarding former employees.

(12) *Participant* means an employee for whom a section 403(b) contract is currently being purchased, or an employee or former employee for whom a section 403(b) contract has previously been purchased and who has not received a distribution of his or her entire benefit under the contract.

(13) *Plan* means a plan as described in § 1.403(b)-3(b)(3).

(14) *Public school* means a State-sponsored educational organization described in section 170(b)(1)(A)(ii) (relating to educational organizations that normally maintain a regular faculty and curriculum and normally have a regularly enrolled body of pupils or students in attendance at the place where educational activities are regularly carried on).

(15) *Retirement income account* means a defined contribution program established or maintained by a church-related organization to provide benefits under section 403(b) for its employees or their beneficiaries as described in § 1.403(b)-9.

(16) *Section 403(b) contract; section 403(b) plan*—(i) *Section 403(b) contract* means a contract described in § 1.403(b)-3. If for any taxable year an employer contributes to more than one section 403(b) contract for a participant or beneficiary, then, under section 403(b)(5), all such

contracts are treated as one contract for purposes of section 403(b) and §§ 1.403(b)-2 through 1.403(b)-10. See also § 1.403(b)-3(b)(1).

(ii) *Section 403(b) plan* means the plan of the employer under which the section 403(b) contracts for its employees are maintained.

(17) *Section 403(b) elective deferral* means an elective deferral that is an employer contribution to a section 403(b) contract for an employee. See § 1.403(b)-5(b) for additional rules with respect to a section 403(b) elective deferral.

(18) *Section 501(c)(3) organization* means an organization that is described in section 501(c)(3) (relating to certain religious, charitable, scientific, or other types of organizations) and exempt from tax under section 501(a).

(19) *Severance from employment* means that the employee ceases to be employed by the employer maintaining the plan. See regulations under section 401(k) for additional guidance concerning severance from employment. See also § 1.403(b)-6(h) for a special rule under which severance from employment is determined by reference to employment with the eligible employer.

(20) *State* means a State, a political subdivision of a State, or any agency or instrumentality of a State. For this purpose, the District of Columbia is treated as a State, as provided under section 7701(a)(10). In addition, for purposes of determining whether an individual is an employee performing services for a public school, an Indian tribal government is treated as a State, as provided under section 7871(a)(6)(B). See also section 1450(b) of the Small Business Job Protection Act of 1996 (110 Stat. 1755, 1814) for special rules treating certain contracts purchased in a plan year beginning before January 1, 1995, that include contributions by an Indian tribal government as section 403(b) contracts, whether or not those contributions are for employees performing services for a public school.

(21) *Years of service* means each full year during which an individual is a fulltime employee of an eligible employer, plus fractional credit for each part of a year during which the individual is either a full-time employee of an eligible employer for a part of the year or a part-time employee of an eligible employer. See § 1.403(b)-4(e) for rules for determining years of service.

(b) [Reserved].

§ 1.403(b)-3 *Exclusion for contributions to purchase section 403(b) contracts.*

(a) *Exclusion for section 403(b) contracts.* Amounts contributed by an eligible employer for the purchase of an annuity contract for an employee are excluded from the gross income of the employee under section 403(b) only if each of the requirements in paragraphs (a)(1) through (9) of this section is satisfied. In addition, amounts contributed by an eligible employer for the purchase of an annuity contract for an employee pursuant to a cash or deferred election are not includible in an employee's gross income at the time the cash would have been includible in the employee's gross income (but for the cash or deferred election) if each of the requirements in paragraphs (a)(1) through (9) of this section is satisfied.

(1) *Not a contract issued under qualified plan or eligible governmental plan.* The contract is not purchased under a qualified plan (under section 401(a) or 404(a)(2)) or an eligible governmental plan under section 457(b).

(2) *Nonforfeitability.* The rights of the employee under the contract (disregarding rights to future premiums) are nonforfeitable. An employee's rights under a contract fail to be nonforfeitable unless the participant for whom the contract is purchased has at all times a fully vested and nonforfeitable right (as defined under § 1.411(a)-4) to all benefits provided under the contract. See paragraph (c) of this section for additional rules regarding the nonforfeitability requirement of this paragraph (a)(2).

(3) *Nondiscrimination and universal availability.* In the case of a contract purchased by an eligible employer other than a church, the contract is purchased under a plan that satisfies section 403(b)(12) (relating to nondiscrimination and universal availability requirements). See § 1.403(b)-5.

(4) *Limitations on elective deferrals.* In the case of an elective deferral, the contract satisfies section 401(a)(30) (relating to limitations on elective deferrals). A contract does not satisfy section 401(a)(30) as required under this paragraph (a)(4) unless the contract requires all elective deferrals for an employee to not exceed the limits of section 402(g)(1), including elective deferrals for the employee under the contract and any other elective deferrals under the plan under which the contract is purchased and under all other plans, contracts, or arrangements of the employer.

(5) *Nontransferability.* The contract is not transferable. This paragraph (a)(5) does not apply to a contract issued before January 1, 1963. See section 401(g).

(6) *Minimum required distributions.* The contract satisfies the requirements of section 401(a)(9) (relating to minimum required distributions). See §1.403(b)-6(e).

(7) *Rollover distributions.* The contract provides that, if the distributee of an eligible rollover distribution elects to have the distribution paid directly to an eligible retirement plan, as defined in section 402(c)(8)(B), and specifies the eligible retirement plan to which the distribution is to be paid, then the distribution will be paid to that eligible retirement plan in a direct rollover. See §1.403(b)-7(b)(2).

(8) *Limitation on incidental benefits.* The contract satisfies the incidental benefit requirements of section 401(a). See §1.403(b)-6(g).

(9) *Maximum annual additions.* The annual additions to the contract do not exceed the applicable limitations of section 415(c) (treating contributions and other additions as annual additions). See paragraph (b) of this section and §1.403(b)-4(b).

(b) *Application of requirements*—(1) *Aggregation of contracts.* In accordance with section 403(b)(5), for purposes of determining whether this section is satisfied, all section 403(b) contracts purchased for an individual by an employer are treated as purchased under a single contract. Additional aggregation rules apply under section 402(g) for purposes of satisfying paragraph (a)(4) of this section and under section 415 for purposes of satisfying paragraph (a)(9) of this section.

(2) *Disaggregation for excess annual additions.* In accordance with the last sentence of section 415(a)(2), if an excess annual addition is made to a contract that otherwise satisfies the requirements of this section, then the portion of the contract that includes such excess annual addition fails to be a section 403(b) contract (and instead is a contract to which section 403(c) applies, as further described in paragraph (c)(1) of this section) and the remaining portion of the contract is a section 403(b) contract. This paragraph (b)(2) does not apply unless, for the year of the excess and each year thereafter, the issuer of the contract maintains separate accounts for each such portion. Thus, the entire contract fails to be a section 403(b) contract if an excess annual addition is made and a separate account is not maintained with respect to the excess.

(3) *Plan in form and operation.* A contract does not satisfy paragraph (a) of this section unless it is maintained pursuant to a plan. For this purpose, a plan is a written defined contribution plan, which, in both form and operation, satisfies the requirements of this section and §§1.403(b)-4 through 1.403(b)-10. For purposes of this section and §§1.403(b)-4 through 1.403(b)-10, the plan must contain all the material terms and conditions for eligibility, benefits, applicable limitations, the contracts available under the plan, and the time and form under which benefit distributions would be made. For purposes of this section and §§1.403(b)-4 through 1.403(b)-10, a plan may contain certain optional features not required under section 403(b), such as hardship withdrawal distributions, loans, plan-to-plan or annuity contract-to-annuity contract transfers, and acceptance of rollovers to the plan. However, if a plan contains any optional provisions, the optional provisions must meet, in both form and operation, the relevant requirements under section 403(b), this section, and §§1.403(b)-4 through 1.403(b)-10. This paragraph (b)(3) applies to contributions to an annuity contract by a church only if the annuity is part of a retirement income account, as defined in §1.403(b)-9.

(4) *Exclusion limited to former employees*—(i) *General rule.* Except as provided in paragraph (b)(4)(ii) of this section and in §1.403(b)-4(d), the exclusion from gross income provided by section 403(b) does not apply to contributions made for former employees. For this purpose, a contribution is not made for a former employee if the contribution is with respect to compensation that would otherwise be paid for a payroll period that begins before severance from employment.

(ii) *Exceptions.* [Reserved].

(c) *Effect of failure*—(1) *General rule.* See section 403(c) (relating to nonqualified annuities) for the treatment of a nonqualified annuity contract issued by an insurance company that is not a section 403(b) contract. See section 61, 83, or 402(b) for the treatment of a custodial account or retirement income account that fails to be treated as a section 403(b) contract.

(2) *Failure to satisfy nonforfeitability requirement.* If an annuity contract issued by an insurance company would qualify as a section 403(b) contract but for the failure to satisfy the nonforfeitability requirement of paragraph (a)(2) of this section, then the contract is treated as a contract to which section 403(c) applies. However, on or after the date on which the participant's interest in that contract becomes nonforfeitable, the contract may be treated as a section 403(b) contract if no election has been made under section 83(b) with respect to the contract, the participant's interest in the contract has been subject to a substantial risk of forfeiture before becoming nonforfeitable, and the contract has at all times satisfied the requirements of paragraph (a) of this section other than the nonforfeitability requirement of paragraph (a)(2) of this section. Thus, for example, for the current year and each prior year, no contribution can have been made to the contract that would cause the contract to fail to be a section 403(b) contract as a result of contributions exceeding the limitations of section 415 (except to the extent permitted under paragraph (b)(2) of this section) or to fail to satisfy the nondiscrimination rules described in §1.403(b)-5.

(3) *Treatment of partial vesting and separate accounts.* For purposes of applying this paragraph (c), if a participant's interest in a contract becomes nonforfeitable to any extent in a year but the participant's entire interest in the contract is not nonforfeitable, then the portion that is nonforfeitable and the portion that fails to be nonforfeitable are each treated as separate contracts. In addition, for purposes of applying this paragraph (c), if a contribution is made to an annuity contract in excess of the limitations of section 415(c) and the excess is maintained in a separate account, then the portion of the contract that includes the excess contributions account and the remainder are each treated as separate contracts. Thus, if an annuity contract that includes an excess contributions account changes from forfeitable to nonforfeitable during a year, then the portion that is not attributable to the excess contributions account constitutes a section 403(b) contract (assuming it otherwise satisfies the requirements to be a section 403(b) contract) and is not included in gross income, and the portion that is attributable to the excess contributions account is included in gross income in accordance with section 403(c).

Par. 5a. Sections 1.403(b)-4 through 1.403(b)-11 are added to read as follows:

§1.403(b)-4 Contribution limitations.

(a) *Treatment of contributions in excess of limitations.* The exclusion provided under §1.403(b)-3(a) applies to a participant only if the amounts contributed by the employer for the purchase of an annuity contract for the participant do not exceed the applicable limit under sections 415 and 402(g), as described in this section. Under §1.403(b)-3(a)(4), a section 403(b) contract is required to include the limits on elective deferrals imposed by section 402(g), as described in paragraph (c) of this section. See paragraph (f) of this section for special rules concerning correction of excess contributions and deferrals. The limits imposed by section 415, §1.403(b)-3(a)(9), section 402(g), §1.403(b)-3(a)(4), and this section do not apply with respect to rollover contributions made to a section 403(b) contract, as described in §1.403(b)-10(d), but after-tax contributions are taken into account under section 415, §1.403(b)-3(a)(9), and this section.

(b) *Maximum annual contribution*—(1) *General rule.* In accordance with section 415(a)(2) and §1.403(b)-3(b)(2), the contributions for any participant under a section 403(b) contract (i.e., employer nonelective contributions (including matching contributions), section 403(b) elective deferrals, and after-tax contributions) are not permitted to exceed the limitations imposed by section 415. For this purpose, contributions made for a participant are aggregated to the extent applicable under sections 414(b), (c), (m), (n), and (o). For purposes of section 415(a)(2) and §1.403(b)-1 through §1.403(b)-11, a contribution means any annual addition, as defined in section 415(c).

(2) *Special rules.* See section 415(k)(4) for a special rule under which contributions to section 403(b) contracts are generally aggregated with contributions under other arrangements in applying section 415. For purposes of applying section 415(c)(1)(B) with respect to a section 403(b) contract, except as provided in section 415(c)(3)(C), a participant's includible compensation (as defined in §1.403(b)-2) is substituted for the participant's compensation, as described in section 415(c)(3)(E). Any age 50 catch-up contributions under paragraph (c)(2) of this section are disregarded in applying section 415.

(c) *Section 403(b) elective deferrals*—(1) *Basic limit under section 402(g)(1).* In accordance with section 402(g)(1)(A), the section 403(b) elective deferrals for any individual are included in the individual's gross income to the extent the amount of such deferrals, plus all other elective deferrals for the individual, for the taxable year exceeds the applicable dollar amount under section 402(g)(1)(B). The applicable annual dollar amount under section 402(g)(1)(B) is: $11,000 for 2002; $12,000 for 2003; $13,000 for 2004; $14,000 for 2005; and $15,000 for 2006 and thereafter. After 2006, the $15,000 amount is adjusted for cost-of-living in the manner described in section 402(g)(4). See §1.403(b)-5(b) for a universal availability rule that applies if any employee is permitted to have any section 403(b) elective deferrals made on his or her behalf.

(2) *Age 50 catch-up*—(i) *In general.* In accordance with section 414(v) and the regulations thereunder, a section 403(b) contract may provide for additional catch-up contributions for a participant who is age 50 by the end of the year, provided that such age 50 catch-up contributions do not exceed the catch-up limit under section 414(v)(2) for the taxable year. The maximum amount of additional age 50 catch-up contributions for a taxable year under section 414(v) is as follows: $1,000 for 2002; $2,000 for 2003; $3,000 for 2004; $4,000 for 2005; and $5,000 for 2006 and thereafter. After 2006, the $5,000 amount is adjusted for cost-of-living in the manner described in section 414(v)(2)(C). For additional requirements, see regulations under section 414(v).

(ii) *Coordination with special section 403(b) catch-up.* In accordance with sections 414(v)(6)(A)(ii) and 402(g)(7)(A), the age 50 catch-up described in this paragraph (c)(2) may apply for any taxable year in which a participant also qualifies for the special section 403(b) catch-up under paragraph (c)(3) of this section.

(3) *Special section 403(b) catch-up for certain organizations*—(i) *Amount of the special section 403(b) catch-up.* In the case of a qualified employee of a qualified organization for whom the basic section 403(b) elective deferrals for any year are not less than the applicable dollar amount under section 402(g)(1)(B), the section 403(b) elective deferral limitation of section 402(g)(1) for the taxable year of the qualified employee is increased by the least of—

(A) $3,000;

(B) The excess of—

(*1*) $15,000; over

(*2*) The total special section 403(b) catch-up elective deferrals made for the qualified employee by the qualified organization for prior years; or

(C) The excess of—

(*1*) $5,000 multiplied by the number of years of service of the employee with the qualified organization; over

(*2*) The total elective deferrals (as defined at § 1.403(b)-2) made for the qualified employee by the qualified organization for prior years.

(ii) *Qualified organization.* (A) For purposes of this paragraph (c)(3), *qualified organization* means an eligible employer that is either—

(*1*) An educational organization described in section 170(b)(1)(A)(ii);

(*2*) A hospital;

(*3*) A health and welfare service agency (including a home health service agency); or

(*4*) A church-related organization. All entities that are in a church-related organization are treated as a single qualified organization (so that years of service and any special section 403(b) catch-up elective deferrals previously made for a qualified employee for a church within a church-related organization are taken into account for purposes of applying this paragraph (c)(3) to the employee with respect to any other entity within the same church-related organization).

(B) For purposes of this paragraph (c)(3)(ii), a *health and welfare service agency* means either an organization whose primary activity it to provide services that constitute medical care as defined in section 213(d)(1) (such as a hospice) or a section 501(c)(3) organization whose primary activity is the prevention of cruelty to individuals or animals, or which provides substantial personal services to the needy as part of its primary activity (such as a section 501(c)(3) organization that provides meals to needy individuals).

(iii) *Qualified employee.* For purposes of this paragraph (c)(3), *qualified employee* means an employee who has completed at least 15 years of service (as defined under paragraph (e) of this section) taking into account only employment with the qualified organization.

(iv) *Coordination with age 50 catch-up.* In accordance with sections 402(g)(1)(C) and 402(g)(7), any catch-up amount contributed by an employee who is eligible for both an age 50 catch-up and a special section 403(b) catch-up is treated first as an amount contributed as a special section 403(b) catch-up to the extent a special section 403(b) catch-up is permitted, and then as an amount contributed as an age 50 catch-up (to the extent the catch-up amount exceeds the maximum special section 403(b) catch-up after taking into account sections 402(g) and 415(c), this paragraph (c)(3), and any limitations on the special section 403(b) catch-up that are imposed by the terms of the plan).

(4) *Examples.* The provisions of this paragraph (c) are illustrated by the following examples:

Example 1. (i) *Facts illustrating application of the basic dollar limit.* Participant B, who is 45, is eligible to participate in a State university section 403(b) plan in 2006. B is not a qualified employee, as defined in paragraph (c)(3)(iii) of this section. The plan permits section 403(b) elective deferrals, but no other employer contributions are made under the plan. The plan provides limitations on section 403(b) elective deferrals up to the maximum permitted under paragraphs (c)(1) and (3) of this section and the additional age 50 catch-up amount described in paragraph (c)(2) of this section. For 2006, B will receive includible compensation of $42,000 from the eligible employer. B desires to elect to have the maximum section 403(b) elective deferral possible contributed in 2006. For 2006, the basic dollar limit for section 403(b) elective deferrals under paragraph (c)(1) of this section is $15,000 and the additional dollar amount permitted under the age 50 catch-up is $5,000.

(ii) *Conclusion.* B is not eligible for the age 50 catch-up in 2006 because B is 45 in 2006, or the special section 403(b) catch-up under paragraph (c)(3) of this section because B is not a qualified employee. Accordingly, the maximum section 403(b) elective deferral that B may elect for 2006 is $15,000.

Example 2. (i) *Facts illustrating application of the includible compensation limitation.* The facts are the same as in *Example 1*, except B's includible compensation is $14,000.

(ii) *Conclusion.* Under section 415(c), contributions may not exceed 100 percent of includible compensation. Accordingly, the maximum section 403(b) elective deferral that B may elect for 2006 is $14,000.

Example 3. (i) *Facts illustrating application of the age 50 catch-up.* Participant C, who is 55, is eligible to participate in a State university section 403(b) plan in 2006. The plan permits section 403(b) elective deferrals, but no other employer contributions are made under the plan. The plan provides limitations on section 403(b) elective deferrals up to the maximum permitted under paragraphs (c)(1) and (3) of this section and the additional age 50 catch-up amount described in paragraph (c)(2) of this section. For 2006, C will receive includible compensation of $48,000 from the eligible employer. C desires to elect to have the maximum section 403(b) elective deferral possible contributed in 2006. For 2006, the basic dollar limit for section 403(b) elective deferrals under paragraph (c)(1) of this section is $15,000 and the additional dollar amount permitted under the age 50 catch-up is $5,000. C does not have 15 years of service and thus is not a qualified employee, as defined in paragraph (c)(3)(iii) of this section.

(ii) *Conclusion.* C is eligible for the age 50 catch-up in 2006 because C is 55 in 2006. C is not eligible for the special section 403(b) catch-up under paragraph (c)(3) of this section because C is not a qualified employee (as defined in paragraph (c)(3)(iii) of this section). Accordingly, the maximum section 403(b) elective deferral that C may elect for 2006 is $20,000 ($15,000 plus $5,000).

Example 4. (i) *Facts illustrating application of both the age 50 and the special section 403(b) catch-up.* The facts are the same as in *Example 3*, except that C is a qualified employee for purposes of the special section 403(b) catch-up provisions in paragraph (c)(3) of this section. For 2006, the maximum additional section 403(b) elective deferral for which C qualifies under the special section 403(b) catch-up under paragraph (c)(3) of this section is $3,000.

(ii) *Conclusion.* The maximum section 403(b) elective deferrals that C may elect for 2006 is $23,000. This is the sum of the basic limit on section 403(b) elective deferrals under paragraph (c)(1) of this section equal to $15,000, plus the $3,000 additional special section 403(b) catch-up amount for which C qualifies under paragraph (c)(3) of this section, plus the additional age 50 catch-up amount of $5,000.

Example 5. (i) *Facts illustrating calculation of years of service with a predecessor organization for purposes of the special section 403(b) catch-up.* The facts are the same as in *Example 4*, except that C has previously made special section 403(b) catch-up deferrals to a section 403(b) plan maintained by a hospital which was acquired by C's current eligible employer which is a hospital.

(ii) *Conclusion.* The special section 403(b) catch-up amount for which C qualifies under paragraph (c)(3) of this section must be calculated taking into account C's prior years of service and special section 403(b) catch-up deferrals with the predecessor hospital if and only if C did not have any severance from service in connection with the acquisition.

Example 6. (i) *Facts illustrating application of the age 50 catch-up and the section 415(c) dollar limitation.* The facts are the same as in *Example 4*, except that the employer makes a nonelective contribution for each employee equal to 20 percent of C's compensation (which is $48,000). Thus, the employer makes a nonelective contribution for C for 2006 equal to $9,600. The plan provides that a participant is not permitted to make section 403(b) elective deferrals to the extent the section 403(b) elective deferrals would result in contributions in excess of the maximum permitted under section 415 and provides that contributions are reduced in the following order: the special section 403(b) catch-up elective deferrals under paragraph (c)(3) of this section are reduced first; the age 50 catch-up elective deferrals under paragraph (c)(2) of this section are reduced second; and then the basic section 403(b) elective deferrals under paragraph (c)(1) of this section are reduced. For 2006, it is assumed that the applicable dollar limit under section 415(c)(1)(A) is $44,000.

(ii) *Conclusion.* The maximum section 403(b) elective deferral that C may elect for 2006 is $23,000. This is the sum of the basic limit on section 403(b) elective deferrals under paragraph (c)(1) of this section equal to $15,000, plus the $3,000 additional special section 403(b) catch-up amount for which C qualifies under paragraph (c)(3) of this section, plus the additional age 50 catch-up amount of $5,000. The limit in paragraph (b) of this section would not be exceeded because the sum of the $9,600 nonelective contribution and the $23,000 section 403(b) elective deferrals does not exceed the lesser of $49,000 (which is the sum of $44,000 plus the $5,000 additional age 50 catch-up amount) or $53,000 (which is the sum of C's includible compensation for 2006 ($48,000) plus the $5,000 additional age 50 catch-up amount).

Example 7. (i) *Facts further illustrating application of the age 50 catch-up and the section 415(c) dollar limitation.* The facts are the same as in *Example 6*, except that C's includible compensation for 2006 is $56,000 and the plan provides for a nonelective contribution equal to 50 percent of includible compensation, so that the employer nonelective contribution for C for 2006 is $28,000 (50 percent of $56,000).

(ii) *Conclusion.* The maximum section 403(b) elective deferral that C may elect for 2006 is $21,000. A section 403(b) elective deferral in excess of this amount would exceed the sum of the limit in section 415(c)(1)(A) plus the additional age 50 catch-up amount, because the sum of the employer's nonelective contribution of $28,000 plus a section 403(b) elective deferral in excess of $21,000 would exceed $49,000 (the sum of the $44,000 limit in section 415(c)(1)(A) plus the $5,000 additional age 50 catch-up amount).

Example 8. (i) *Facts further illustrating application of the age 50 catch-up and the section 415(c) dollar limitation.* The facts are the same as in *Example 7*, except that the plan provides for a nonelective contribution for C equal to $44,000 (which is the limit in section 415(c)(1)(A)).

(ii) *Conclusion.* The maximum section 403(b) elective deferral that C may elect for 2006 is $5,000. A section 403(b) elective deferral in excess of this amount would exceed the sum of the limit in section 415(c)(1)(A) plus the additional age 50 catch-up amount ($5,000), because the sum of the employer's nonelective contribution of $44,000 plus a section 403(b) elective deferral in excess of $5,000 would exceed $49,000 (the sum of the $44,000 limit in section 415(c)(1)(A) plus the $5,000 additional age 50 catch-up amount).

Example 9. (i) *Facts illustrating application of the age 50 catch-up and the section 415(c) includible compensation limitation.* The facts are the same as in *Example 7*, except that C's includible compensation for 2006 is $28,000, so that the employer nonelective contribution for C for 2006 is $14,000 (50 percent of $28,000).

(ii) *Conclusion.* The maximum section 403(b) elective deferral that C may elect for 2006 is $19,000. A section 403(b) elective deferral in excess of this amount would exceed the sum of the limit in section 415(c)(1)(B) plus the additional age 50 catch-up amount, because C's includible compensation is $28,000 and the sum of the employer's nonelective contribution of $14,000 plus a section 403(b) elective deferral in excess of $19,000 would exceed $33,000 (which is the sum of 100 percent of C's includible compensation plus the $5,000 additional age 50 catch-up amount).

Example 10. (i) *Facts illustrating that section 403(b) elective deferrals cannot exceed compensation otherwise payable.* Employee D is age 60, has includible compensation of $14,000, and wishes to contribute section 403(b) elective deferrals of $20,000 for the year. No nonelective contributions are made for Employee D.

(ii) *Conclusion.* The maximum limit on section 403(b) elective deferrals for a participant with compensation less than the maximum dollar limit in section 415(c) is 100 percent of includible compensation, plus the $5,000 additional age 50 catch-up amount. However, because a contribution is a section 403(b) elective deferral only if it is a result of a compensation reduction, D cannot make section 403(b) elective deferrals in excess of D's actual compensation.

Example 11. (i) *Facts illustrating calculation of the special section 403(b) catchup.* For 2006, employee E, who is age 50, is eligible to participate in a section 403(b) plan of hospital H, which is a section 501(c)(3) organization. H's plan permits section 403(b) elective deferrals and provides for an employer contribution of 10 percent of a participant's compensation with that employer for the taxable year. The plan provides limitations on section 403(b) elective deferrals up to the maximum permitted under paragraphs (c)(1), (2), and (3) of this section. For 2006, E's includible compensation is $50,000. E wishes to elect to have the maximum section 403(b) elective deferral possible contributed in 2006. E has previously made $62,000 of section 403(b) elective deferrals under the plan, but has never made an election for a special section 403(b) catch-up elective deferral. For 2006, the basic dollar limit for section 403(b) elective deferrals under paragraph (c)(1) of this section is $15,000, the additional dollar amount permitted under the age 50 catch-up is $5,000, E's employer will make a nonelective contribution of $5,000 (10% of $50,000 compensation), and E is a qualified employee of a qualified employer as defined in paragraph (c)(3) of this section.

(ii) *Conclusion.* The maximum section 403(b) elective deferrals that E may elect for 2006 is $23,000. This is the sum of the basic limit on section 403(b) elective deferrals for 2006 under paragraph (c)(1) of this section equal to $15,000, plus the $3,000 maximum additional special section 403(b) catch-up amount for which D qualifies in 2006 under paragraph (c)(3) of this section, plus the additional age 50 catchup amount of $5,000. The limitation on the additional special section 403(b) catch-up amount is not less than $3,000 because the limitation at paragraph (c)(3)(i)(B) of this section is $15,000 ($15,000 minus zero) and the limitation at paragraph (c)(3)(i)(C) of this section is $13,000 ($5,000 times 15, minus $62,000 of total deferrals in prior years).

Example 12. (i) *Facts illustrating calculation of the special section 403(b) catchup in the next calendar year.* The facts are the same as in *Example 11*, except that, for 2007, E has includible compensation of $60,000. For 2007, E now has previously made $85,000 of section 403(b) elective deferrals ($62,000 deferred before 2006, plus the $15,000 in basic section 403(b) elective deferrals in 2006, the $3,000 maximum additional special section 403(b) catch-up amount in 2006, plus the $5,000 age 50 catch-up amount in 2006). However, the $5,000 age 50 catch-up amount deferred in 2006 is disregarded for purposes of applying the limitation at paragraph (c)(3)(i)(B) of this section to determine the special section 403(b) catch-up amount. Thus, for 2007, only $80,000 of section 403(b) elective deferrals are taken into account in applying the limitation at paragraph (c)(3)(i)(B) of this section. For 2007, the basic dollar limit for section 403(b) elective deferrals under paragraph (c)(1) of this section is assumed to be $16,000, the additional dollar amount permitted under the age 50 catch-up is assumed to be $5,000, and E's employer contributes $6,000 (10% of $60,000 compensation) as a non-elective contribution.

(ii) *Conclusion.* The maximum section 403(b) elective deferral that D may elect for 2007 is $21,000. This is the sum of the basic limit on section 403(b) elective deferrals under paragraph (c)(1) of this section equal to $16,000, plus the additional age 50 catch-up amount of $5,000. E is not entitled to any additional special section 403(b) catch-up amount for 2007 under paragraph (c)(3) due to the limitation at paragraph (c)(3)(i)(C) of this section (16 times $5,000 equals $80,000, minus D's total prior section 403(b) elective deferrals of $80,000 equals zero).

(d) *Employer contributions for former employees*—(1) *Includible compensation deemed to continue for nonelective contributions.* For purposes of applying paragraph (b) of this section, a former employee is deemed to have monthly includible compensation for the period through the end of the taxable year of the employee in which he or she ceases to be an employee and through the end of each of the next five taxable years. The amount of the monthly includible compensation is equal to one twelfth of the former employee's includible compensation during the former employee's most recent year of service. Accordingly, nonelective employer contributions for a former employee must not exceed the limitation of section 415(c)(1) up to the lesser of the dollar amount in section 415(c)(1)(A) or the former employee's annual includible compensation based on the former employee's average monthly compensation during his or her most recent year of service.

(2) *Examples.* The provisions of paragraph (d)(1) of this section are illustrated by the following examples:

Example 1. (i) *Facts.* College M is a section 501(c)(3) organization operated on the basis of a June 30 fiscal year that maintains a section 403(b) plan for its employees. In 2004, M amends the plan to provide for a temporary early retirement incentive under which the college will make a nonelective contribution for any participant who satisfies certain minimum age and service conditions and who retires before June 30, 2006. The contribution will equal 110 percent of the participant's rate of pay for one year and will be payable over a period ending no later than the end of the fifth fiscal year that begins after retirement. It is assumed for purposes of this *Example 1* that, in accordance with § 1.401(a)(4)-10(b) and under the facts and circumstances, the post-retirement contributions made for participants who satisfy the minimum age and service conditions and retire before June 30, 2006 do not discriminate in favor of former employees who are highly compensated employees. Employee A retires under the early retirement incentive on March 12, 2006, and A's annual includible compensation for the period from March 1, 2005 through February 28, 2006 (which is A's most recent one year of service) is $30,000. The applicable dollar limit under section 415(c)(1)(A) is assumed to be $44,000 for 2006 and $45,000 for 2007. The college contributes $30,000 for A for 2006 and $3,000 for A for 2007 (totaling $33,000 or 110 percent of $30,000). No other contributions are made to a section 403(b) contract for A for those years.

(ii) *Conclusion.* The contributions made for A do not exceed A's includible compensation for 2006 or 2007.

Example 2. (i) *Facts.* College N is a section 501(c)(3) organization that maintains a section 403(b) plan for its employees. The plan provides for N to make monthly nonelective contributions equal to 20 percent of the monthly includible compensation for each eligible employee. In addition, the plan provides for contributions to continue for 5 years following the retirement of any employee after age 64 and completion of at least 20 years of service (based on the employee's average annual rate of base salary in the preceding 3 calendar years ended before the date of retirement). It is assumed for purposes of this *Example 2* that, in accordance with § 1.401(a)(4)-10(b) and under the facts and circumstances, the post-retirement contributions made for participants who satisfy the minimum age and service conditions do not discriminate in favor of former employees who are highly compensated employees. Employee B retires on July 1, 2006, at age 64 after completion of 20 or more years of service. At that date, B's annual includible compensation for the most recently ended fiscal year of N is $72,000 and B's average monthly rate of base salary for 2003 through 2005 is $5,000. N contributes $1,200 per month (20 percent of 1/12th of $72,000) from January of 2006 through June of 2006 and contributes $1,000 (20 percent of $5,000) per month for B from July of 2006 through June of 2011. The applicable dollar limit under section 415(c)(1)(A) is assumed to be at least $44,000 for 2006 through 2011. No other contributions are made to a section 403(b) contract for B for those years.

(ii) *Conclusion.* The contributions made for B do not exceed B's includible compensation for any of the years from 2006 through 2010.

(3) *Disabled employees.* See also section 415(c)(3)(C) which sets forth a special rule under which compensation may be treated as continuing for purposes of section 415 for certain former employees who are disabled.

(e) *Special rules for determining years of service*—(1) *In general.* For purposes of determining a participant's includible compensation under paragraph (b)(2) of this section and a participant's years of service under paragraphs (c)(3) (special section 403(b) catch-up for qualified employees of certain organizations) and (d) (employer contributions for former employees) of this section, an employee's number of years of service depend on whether the employee has a full year during which the individual is a full-time employee of the eligible employer, and any fraction of a year for each part of a year during which the individual is a full-time or part-time employee of the eligible employer. An individual's number of years of service equals the aggregate of the annual work periods during which the individual is employed by the eligible employer.

(2) *Work period.* A year of service is based on the employer's annual work period, not the employee's taxable year. For example, in determining whether a university professor is employed full time, the annual work period is the school's academic year. However, in no case may an employee accumulate more than one year of service in a twelve-month period.

(3) *Service with more than one eligible employer*—(i) *General rule.* With respect to any section 403(b) contract of an eligible employer, except as provided in paragraph (e)(3)(ii) of this section, any period during which an individual is not an employee of that eligible employer is disregarded for purposes of this paragraph (e).

(ii) *Special rule for church employees.* With respect to any section 403(b) contract of an eligible employer that is a church-related organization, any period during which an individual is an employee of that eligible employer and any other eligible employer that is a church-related organization that has an association (as defined in section 414(e)(3)(D)) with that eligible employer is taken into account on an aggregated basis, but any period during which an individual is not an employee of a church-related organization or is an employee of a

church-related organization that does not have an association with that eligible employer is disregarded for purposes of this paragraph (e).

(4) *Full-time employee for full year.* Each annual work period during which an individual is employed full time by the eligible employer constitutes one year of service. In determining whether an individual is employed full-time, the amount of work which he or she actually performs is compared with the amount of work that is normally required of individuals performing similar services from which substantially all of their annual compensation is derived.

(5) *Other employees.* (i) An individual is treated as performing a fraction of a year of service for each annual work period during which he or she is a full-time employee for part of the annual work period and for each annual work period during which he or she is a part-time employee either for the entire annual work period or for a part of the annual work period.

(ii) In determining the fraction that represents the fractional year of service for an individual employed full time for part of an annual work period, the numerator is the period of time (e.g., weeks or months) during which the individual is a full-time employee during that annual work period, and the denominator is the period of time that is the annual work period.

(iii) In determining the fraction that represents the fractional year of service of an individual who is employed part time for the entire annual work period, the numerator is the amount of work performed by the individual, and the denominator is the amount of work normally required of individuals who perform similar services and who are employed full time for the entire annual work period.

(iv) In determining the fraction representing the fractional year of service of an individual who is employed part time for part of an annual work period, the fractional year of service that would apply if the individual were a part-time employee for a full work period is multiplied times the fractional year of service that would apply if the individual were a full-time employee for the part of an annual work period.

(6) *Work performed.* For purposes of this paragraph (e), in measuring the amount of work of an individual performing particular services, the work performed is determined based on the individual's hours of service (as defined under section 410(a)(3)(C)), except that a plan may use a different measure of work if appropriate under the facts and circumstances. For example, a plan may provide for a university professor's work to be measured by the number of courses taught during an annual work period in any case in which that individual's work assignment is generally based on a specified number of courses to be taught.

(7) *Most recent one-year period of service.* For purposes of paragraph (d) of this section, in the case of a part-time employee or a full-time employee who is employed for only part of the year determined on the basis of the employer's annual work period, the employee's most recent periods of service are aggregated to determine his or her most recent one-year period of service. In such a case, there is first taken into account his or her service during the annual work period for which the last year of service's includible compensation is being determined; then there is taken into account his or her service during his next preceding annual work period based on whole months; and so forth, until the employee's service equals, in the aggregate, one year of service.

(8) *Less than one year of service considered as one year.* If, at the close of a taxable year, an employee has, after application of all of the other rules in this paragraph (e), some portion of one year of service (but has accumulated less than one year of service), the employee is deemed to have one year of service. Except as provided in this paragraph (e)(8), fractional years of service are not rounded up.

(9) *Examples.* The provisions of this paragraph (e) are illustrated by the following examples:

Example 1. (i) *Facts.* Individual C is employed half-time in 2004 and 2005 as a clerk by H, a hospital which is a section 501(c)(3) organization. C earns $20,000 from H in each of those years, and retires on December 31, 2005.

(ii) *Conclusion.* For purposes of determining C's includible compensation during C's last year of service under paragraph (d) of this section, C's most recent periods of service are aggregated to determine C's most recent one-year period of service. In this case, since C worked half-time in 2004 and 2005, the compensation C earned in those two years are aggregated to produce C's includible compensation for C's last full year in service. Thus, in this case, the $20,000 that C earned in 2004 and 2005 for C's halftime work are aggregated, so that C has $40,000 of includible compensation for C's most recent one-year of service for purposes of applying paragraphs (b)(2), (c)(3), and (d) of this section.

Example 2. (i) *Facts.* Individual A is employed as a part-time professor by public University U during the first semester of its two-semester 2004- 2005 academic year. While A teaches one course generally for 3 hours a week during the first semester of the academic year, U's full-time faculty members generally teach for 9 hours a week during the full academic year.

(ii) *Conclusion.* For purposes of calculating how much of a year of service A performs in the 2004-05 academic year (before application of the special rules of paragraphs (e)(7) and (8) of this section concerning less than one year of service), paragraph (e)(5)(iv) of this section is applied as follows: since A teaches one course at U for 3 hours per week for 1 semester and other faculty members at U teach 9 hours per week for 2 semesters, A is considered to have completed 3/18 or 1/6 of a year of service during the 2004-05 academic year, determined as follows:

(A) The fractional year of service if A were a part-time employee for a full year is 3/9 (number of hours employed divided by the usual number of hours of work required for that position).

(B) The fractional year of service if A were a full-time employee for half of a year is ½ (one semester, divided by the usual 2-semester annual work period).

(C) These fractions are multiplied to obtain the fractional year of service: 3/9 times ½, or 3/18, equals 1/6 of a year of service.

(f) *Excess contributions or deferrals*—(1) *In general.* Any contribution made for a participant to a section 403(b) contract for the taxable year that exceeds either the maximum annual contribution limit set forth in paragraph (b) of this section or the maximum annual section 403(b) elective deferral limit set forth in paragraph (c) of this section constitutes an excess contribution that is included in gross income for that taxable year. A contract does not fail to satisfy the requirements of § 1.403(b)-3, the distribution rules of §§ 1.403(b)-6 or 1.403(b)-9, or the funding rules of § 1.403(b)-8 solely by reason of a distribution made under this paragraph (f). See also section 4973 for an excise tax applicable with respect to excess contributions to a custodial account.

(2) *Excess section 403(b) elective deferrals.* A section 403(b) contract may provide that any excess deferral as a result of a failure to comply with the limitation under paragraph (c) of this section for a taxable year with respect to any section 403(b) elective deferral made for a participant by the employer will be distributed to the participant, with allocable net income, no later than April 15 of the following taxable year or otherwise in accordance with section 402(g). See section 402(g)(2)(A) for rules permitting the participant to allocate excess deferrals among the plans in which the participant has made elective deferrals, and see section 402(g)(2)(C) for special rules to determine the tax treatment of such a distribution.

(3) *Special rule for small excess amount.* See section 4979(f)(2)(B) for a special rule applicable if excess matching contributions, excess after-tax contributions, and excess section 403(b) elective deferrals do not exceed $100.

(4) *Example.* The provisions of this paragraph (f) are illustrated by the following example:

Example. (i) *Facts.* Individual D makes section 403(b) elective deferrals totaling $15,500 for 2006, when D is age 45 and the applicable limit on section 403(b) elective deferrals is $15,000. On April 14, 2007, the plan refunds the $500 excess along with applicable earnings of $65.

(ii) *Conclusion.* The $565 payment constitutes a distribution of an excess deferral under paragraph (f)(2) of this section. Under section 402(g), the $500 excess deferral is included in D's gross income for 2006. The additional $65 is included in D's gross income for 2007 and, because the distribution is made by April 15, 2007 (as provided in section 402(g)(2)), the $65 is not subject to the additional 10 percent income tax on early distributions under section 72(t).

§ 1.403(b)-5 Nondiscrimination rules.

(a) *Nondiscrimination rules for contributions other than section 403(b) elective deferrals*—(1) *General rule.* Under section 403(b)(12)(A)(i), employer contributions and employee after-tax contributions must satisfy all of the following requirements (the nondiscrimination requirements) in the same manner as a qualified plan under section 401(a):

(i) Section 401(a)(4) (relating to nondiscrimination in contributions and benefits), taking section 401(a)(5) into account.

(ii) Section 401(a)(17) (limiting the amount of compensation that can be taken into account).

(iii) Section 401(m) (relating to matching and after-tax contributions).

(iv) Section 410(b) (relating to minimum coverage).

(2) *Nonapplication to section 403(b) elective deferrals.* The requirements of this paragraph (a) do not apply to section 403(b) elective deferrals.

(3) *Compensation for testing.* Except as may otherwise be specifically permitted under the sections referenced in paragraph (a)(1) of this section, compliance with those provisions is tested using compensation as defined in section 414(s) (and without regard to section 415(c)(3)(E)).

(4) *Employer aggregation rules.* See regulations under section 414 for rules treating entities as a single employer for purposes of the nondiscrimination requirements.

(5) *Special rules for governmental plans.* Paragraphs (a)(1)(i), (iii), and (iv) of this section do not apply to a governmental plan as defined in section 414(d) (but contributions to a governmental plan must comply with paragraphs (a)(1)(ii) and (b) of this section).

(b) *Universal availability required for section 403(b) elective deferrals*—(1) *General rule.* Under section 403(b)(12)(A)(ii), all employees of the eligible employer must be permitted to have section 403(b) elective deferrals contributed on their behalf if any employee of the eligible employer may elect to have the organization make section 403(b) elective deferrals. The employee's right to have section 403(b) elective deferrals made on his or her behalf includes the right to section 403(b) elective deferrals up to the lesser of the applicable limits in § 1.403(b)-4(c) (including any permissible catch-up elective deferrals under § 1.403(b)-4(c)(2) and (3)) or the applicable limits under the contract with the largest limitation, and applies to part-time employees as well as fulltime employees.

(2) *Effective opportunity required.* A section 403(b) plan satisfies this paragraph (b) only if the plan provides an employee with an effective opportunity to make (or change) a cash or deferred election (as defined at § 1.401(k)-1(a)(3)) at least once during each plan year. Whether an employee has an effective opportunity is determined based on all the relevant facts and circumstances, including notice of the availability of the election, the period of time during which an election may be made, and any other conditions on elections. An effective opportunity is not considered to exist if there are any other rights or benefits that are conditioned (directly or indirectly) upon a participant making or failing to make a cash or deferred election with respect to a contribution to a section 403(b) contract.

(3) *Special rules.* (i) In the case of a section 403(b) plan that covers the employees of more than one section 501(c)(3) organization, the universal availability requirement of this paragraph (b) applies separately to each common law entity, i.e., to each section 501(c)(3) organization. In the case of a section 403(b) plan that covers the employees of more than one State entity, this requirement applies separately to each entity that is not part of a common payroll. An employer may condition the employee's right to have section 403(b) elective deferrals made on his or her behalf on the employee electing a section 403(b) elective deferral of more than $200 for a year.

(ii) For purposes of this paragraph (b)(3), an employer that historically has treated one or more of its various geographically distinct units as separate for employee benefit purposes may treat each unit as a separate organization if the unit is operated independently on a day-to-day basis. Units are not geographically distinct if such units are located within the same Standard Metropolitan Statistical Area (SMSA).

(4) *Special exclusions*—(i) *Exclusions for special types of employees.* A plan does not fail to satisfy the universal availability requirement of this paragraph (b) merely because it excludes one or more of the types of employees listed in paragraph (b)(4)(ii) of this section. If any employee listed in paragraph (b)(4)(ii)(A) through (E) of this section has the right to have section 403(b) elective deferrals made on his or her behalf, then no employees listed in that subparagraph may be excluded under this paragraph (b)(4).

(ii) *List of special types of excludible employees.* The following types of employees are listed in this paragraph (b)(4)(ii):

(A) Employees who are eligible under a section 457(b) eligible governmental plan of the employer which permits an amount to be contributed or deferred at the election of the employee.

(B) Employees who are eligible to make a cash or deferred election (as defined at § 1.401(k)-1(a)(3)) under a section 401(k) plan of the employer.

(C) Employees who are non-resident aliens described in section 410(b)(3)(C).

(D) Subject to the conditions applicable under section 410(b)(4) (including section 410(b)(4)(B) permitting separate testing for employees not meeting minimum age and service requirements), employees who are students performing services described in section 3121(b)(10).

(E) Subject to the conditions applicable under section 410(b)(4), employees who normally work fewer than 20 hours per week. For this purpose, an employee normally works fewer than 20 hours per week if and only if—

(1) For the 12-month period beginning on the date the employee's employment commenced, the employer reasonably expects the employee to work fewer than 1,000 hours of service (as defined in section 410(a)(3)(C)) in such period; and

(2) For each plan year ending after the close of the 12-month period beginning on the date the employee's employment commenced (or, if the plan so provides, each subsequent 12-month period), the employee worked fewer than 1,000 hours of service in the preceding 12-month period. (See, however, section 202(a)(1) of the Employee Retirement Income Security Act of 1974 (ERISA) (88 Stat. 829) Public Law 93-406, and regulations under section 410(a) of the Internal Revenue Code applicable with respect to plans that are subject to Title I of ERISA.)

(c) *Plan required.* Contributions to an annuity contract do not satisfy the requirements of this section unless the contributions are made pursuant to a plan, as defined in § 1.403(b)-3(b)(3), and the terms of the plan satisfy this section.

(d) *Certain requirements not applicable to a church plan.* This section does not apply to a section 403(b) contract purchased by a church (as defined in § 1.403(b)-2).

(e) *Other rules.* This section only reflects requirements of the Internal Revenue Code applicable for purposes of section 403(b) and does not include other requirements. Specifically, this section does not reflect the requirements of the ERISA that may apply with respect to section 403(b), such as the vesting requirements at 29 U.S.C. 1053.

§ 1.403(b)-6 Timing of distributions and benefits.

(a) *Distributions generally.* This section includes special rules regarding the timing of distributions from, and the benefits that may be provided under, a section 403(b) contract, including limitations on when early distributions can be made (in paragraphs (b) through (d) of this section), required minimum distributions (in paragraph (e) of this section), and special rules relating to loans (in paragraph (f) of this section) and incidental benefits (in paragraph (g) of this section).

(b) *Distributions from contracts other than custodial accounts or amounts attributable to section 403(b) elective deferrals.* Except as provided in paragraph (c) of this section relating to distributions from custodial accounts, paragraph (d) of this section relating to distributions attributable to section 403(b) elective deferrals, § 1.403(b)-4(f) (relating to correction of excess deferrals), or § 1.403(b)-10(a) (relating to plan termination), a section 403(b) contract is permitted to distribute retirement benefits to the participant no earlier than upon the earliest of the participant's severance from employment or upon the prior occurrence of some event, such as after a fixed number of years, the attainment of a stated age, or disability. See § 1.401-1(b)(1)(ii) for additional guidance.

(c) *Distributions from custodial accounts that are not attributable to section 403(b) elective deferrals.* Except as provided in § 1.403(b)-4(f) (relating to correction of excess deferrals) or § 1.403(b)-10(a) (relating to plan termination), distributions from a custodial account, as defined in § 1.403(b)-8(d)(2), may not be paid to a participant before the participant has a severance from employment, dies, becomes disabled (within the meaning of section 72(m)(7)), or attains age 59 ½. Any amounts transferred out of a custodial account to an annuity contract or retirement income account, including earnings thereon, continue to be subject to this paragraph (c). This paragraph (c) does not apply to distributions that are attributable to section 403(b) elective deferrals.

(d) *Distribution of section 403(b) elective deferrals*—(1) *Limitation on distributions* —(i) *General rule.* Except as provided in paragraph (d)(2) of this section (relating to distributions on account of hardship), § 1.403(b)-4(f) (relating to correction of excess deferrals), or § 1.403(b)-10(a) (relating to plan termination), distributions of amounts attributable to section 403(b) elective deferrals may not be paid to a participant earlier than the earliest of the date on which the participant has a severance from employment, dies, has a hardship, becomes disabled (within the meaning of section 72(m)(7)), or attains age 59 ½.

(ii) *Special rule for pre-1989 section 403(b) elective deferrals.* For special rules relating to amounts held as of the close of the taxable year beginning before January 1, 1989 (which does not apply to earnings thereon), see section 1123(e)(3) of the Tax Reform Act of 1986 (100 Stat. 2085, 2475) Public Law 99-514, and section 1011A(c)(11) of the

Technical and Miscellaneous Revenue Act of 1988 (102 Stat. 3342, 3476) Public Law 100-647.

(2) *Hardship rules.* A hardship distribution under this paragraph (d) is defined as, and is subject to the rules in, § 1.401(k)-1(d)(3) (including limiting the amount of a distribution in the case of hardship to the amount necessary to satisfy the hardship). In addition, a hardship distribution is limited to the aggregate dollar amount of the participant's section 403(b) elective deferrals under the contract (and may not include any income thereon), reduced by the aggregate dollar amount of the distributions previously made to the participant from the contract.

(3) *Failure to keep separate accounts.* If a section 403(b) contract includes both section 403(b) elective deferrals and other contributions and the section 403(b) elective deferrals are not maintained in a separate account, then distributions may not be made earlier than the later of:

(i) Any date permitted under this paragraph (d) with respect to 403(b) elective deferrals; and

(ii) Any date permitted under paragraph (b) or (c) of this section with respect to contributions that are not section 403(b) elective deferrals (whichever applies to the contributions that are not section 403(b) elective deferrals).

(e) *Minimum required distributions for eligible plans*—(1) *In general.* Under section 403(b)(10), a section 403(b) contract must meet the minimum distribution requirements of section 401(a)(9) (in both form and operation). See section 401(a)(9) and the regulations thereunder for these requirements.

(2) *Treatment as IRAs.* For purposes of applying the distribution rules of section 401(a)(9) to section 403(b) contracts, section 403(b) contracts are treated as individual retirement annuities described in section 408(b) and individual retirement accounts described in section 408(a) (IRAs). Consequently, except as otherwise provided in paragraphs (e)(3) through (e)(5) of this section, the distribution rules in section 401(a)(9) are applied to section 403(b) contracts in accordance with the provisions in § 1.408-8 for purposes of determining required minimum distributions.

(3) *Required beginning date.* The required beginning date for purposes of section 403(b)(10) is April 1 of the calendar year following the later of the calendar year in which the employee attains 70½ or the calendar year in which the employee retires from employment with the employer maintaining the plan. However, for any section 403(b) contract that is not part of a government plan or church plan, the required beginning date for a 5-percent owner is April 1 of the calendar year following the earlier of the calendar year in which the employee attains 70½ or the calendar year in which the employee retires from employment with the employer maintaining the plan.

(4) *Surviving spouse rule does not apply.* The special rule in § 1.408-8, A-5 (relating to spousal beneficiaries), does not apply to a section 403(b) contract. Thus, the surviving spouse of a participant is not permitted to treat a section 403(b) contract as the spouse's own section 403(b) contract, even if the spouse is the sole beneficiary.

(5) *Retirement income accounts.* For purposes of § 1.401(a)(9)-6, A-4 (relating to annuity contracts), annuity payments provided with respect to retirement income accounts do not fail to satisfy the requirements of section 401(a)(9) merely because the payments are not made under an annuity contract purchased from an insurance company, provided that the relationship between the annuity payments and the retirement income accounts is not inconsistent with any rules prescribed by the Commissioner in revenue rulings, notices, or other guidance published in the Internal Revenue Bulletin (see § 601.601(d)(2)(ii)(*b*) of this chapter). See § 1.403(b)-9(a)(5).

(6) *Special rules for benefits accruing before December 31, 1986.* (i) The distribution rules provided in section 401(a)(9) do not apply to the undistributed portion of the account balance under the section 403(b) contract valued as of December 31, 1986, exclusive of subsequent earnings (pre-'87 account balance). The distribution rules provided in section 401(a)(9) apply to all benefits under section 403(b) contracts accruing after December 31, 1986 (post-'86 account balance), including earnings after December 31, 1986. Consequently, the post-'86 account balance includes earnings after December 31, 1986, on contributions made before January 1, 1987, in addition to the contributions made after December 31, 1986, and earnings thereon.

(ii) The issuer or custodian of the section 403(b) contract must keep records that enable it to identify the pre-'87 account balance and subsequent changes as set forth in paragraph (d)(6)(iii) of this section and provide such information upon request to the relevant employee or beneficiaries with respect to the contract. If the issuer or custodian does not keep such records, the entire account balance is treated as subject to section 401(a)(9).

(iii) In applying the distribution rules in section 401(a)(9), only the post-'86 account balance is used to calculate the required minimum distribution for a calendar year. The amount of any distribution from a contract is treated as being paid from the post-'86 account balance to the extent the distribution is required to satisfy the minimum distribution requirement with respect to that contract for a calendar year. Any amount distributed in a calendar year from a contract in excess of the required minimum distribution for a calendar year with respect to that contract is treated as paid from the pre-'87 account balance, if any, of that contract.

(iv) If an amount is distributed from the pre-'87 account balance and rolled over to another section 403(b) contract, the amount is treated as part of the post-'86 account balance in that second contract. However, if the pre-'87 account balance under a section 403(b) contract is directly transferred to another section 403(b) contract (as permitted under § 1.403(b)-10(b)), the amount transferred retains its character as a pre-'87 account balance, provided the issuer of the transferee contract satisfies the recordkeeping requirements of paragraph (e)(6)(ii) of this section.

(v) The distinction between the pre-'87 account balance and the post-'86 account balance provided for under this paragraph (e)(6) of this section has no relevance for purposes of determining the portion of a distribution that is includible in income under section 72.

(vi) The pre-'87 account balance must be distributed in accordance with the incidental benefit requirement of § 1.401-1(b)(1)(i). Distributions attributable to the pre-'87 account balance are treated as satisfying this requirement if all distributions from the section 403(b) contract (including distributions attributable to the post-'86 account balance) satisfy the requirements of § 1.401-1(b)(1)(i) without regard to this section, and distributions attributable to the post-'86 account balance satisfy the rules of this paragraph (e). Distributions attributable to the pre-'87 account balance are treated as satisfying the incidental benefit requirement if all distributions from the section 403(b) contract (including distributions attributable to both the pre-'87 account balance and the post-'86 account balance) satisfy the rules of this paragraph (e).

(7) *Application to multiple contracts for an employee.* The required minimum distribution must be separately determined for each section 403(b) contract of an employee. However, because, as provided in paragraph (e)(2) of this section, the distribution rules in section 401(a)(9) apply to section 403(b) contracts in accordance with the provisions in § 1.408-8, the required minimum distribution from one section 403(b) contract of an employee is permitted to be distributed from another section 403(b) contract in order to satisfy section 401(a)(9). Thus, as provided in § 1.408-8, A-9, with respect to IRAs, the required minimum distribution amount from each contract is then totaled and the total minimum distribution taken from any one or more of the individual section 403(b) contracts. However, consistent with the rules in § 1.408-8, A-9, only amounts in section 403(b) contracts that an individual holds as an employee may be aggregated. Amounts in section 403(b) contracts that an individual holds as a beneficiary of the same decedent may be aggregated, but such amounts may not be aggregated with amounts held in section 403(b) contracts that the individual holds as the employee or as the beneficiary of another decedent. Distributions from section 403(b) contracts do not satisfy the minimum distribution requirements for IRAs, nor do distributions from IRAs satisfy the minimum distribution requirements for section 403(b) contracts.

(f) *Loans.* The determination of whether the availability of a loan, the making of a loan, or a failure to repay a loan made from an issuer of a section 403(b) contract to a participant or beneficiary is treated as a distribution (directly or indirectly) for purposes of this section, and the determination of whether the availability of the loan, the making of the loan, or a failure to repay the loan is in any other respect a violation of the requirements of section 403(b) and these regulations, depends on the facts and circumstances. Among the facts and circumstances are whether the loan has a fixed repayment schedule and bears a reasonable rate of interest, and whether there are repayment safeguards to which a prudent lender would adhere. Thus, for example, a loan must bear a reasonable rate of interest in order to be treated as not being a distribution. However, a plan loan offset is a distribution for purposes of this section. See § 1.72(p)-1, Q&A-13. See also § 1.403(b)-7(d) relating to the application of section 72(p) with respect to the taxation of a loan made under a section 403(b) contract. (Further, see 29 CFR 2550.408b-1 of the Department of Labor regulations concerning additional requirements applicable with respect to plans that are subject to Title I of ERISA.)

(g) *Death benefits and other incidental benefits.* An annuity is not a section 403(b) contract if it fails to satisfy the incidental benefit requirement of § 1.401-1(b)(1)(i). For this purpose, to the extent the incidental benefit requirement of § 1.401-1(b)(1)(i) requires a distribution of the participant's or beneficiary's accumulated benefit, that requirement is deemed to be satisfied if distributions satisfy the minimum distribution requirements of section 401(a)(9).

(h) *Special rule regarding severance from employment.* For purposes of this section, severance from employment occurs on any date on which an employee ceases to be an employee of an eligible employer (e.g., by the section 501(c)(3) organization that maintains the plan, assuming that only one section 501(c)(3) organization maintains the plan), even though the employee may continue to be employed either by another entity that is treated as the same employer where either that other entity is not an entity that can be an eligible employer (such as transferring from a section 501(c)(3) organization to a for-profit subsidiary of the section 501(c)(3) organization) or in a capacity that is not employment with an eligible employer (e.g., ceasing to be an employee performing services for a public school but continuing to work for the same State employer).

(i) *Certain limitations do not apply to rollover contributions.* The limitations on distributions in paragraphs (b) through (d) of this section do not apply to amounts held in a separate account for eligible rollover distributions as described in § 1.403(b)-10(d).

§ 1.403(b)-7 Taxation of distributions and benefits.

(a) *General rules for when amounts are included in gross income.* Except as provided in this section (or in § 1.403(b)-10(c) relating to payments pursuant to a qualified domestic relations order), amounts actually distributed from a section 403(b) contract are includible in the gross income of the recipient participant or beneficiary (in the year in which so distributed) under section 72 (relating to annuities). For an additional income tax that may apply to certain early distributions that are includible in gross income, see section 72(t).

(b) *Rollovers to individual retirement arrangements and other eligible retirement plans*—(1) *Timing of taxation of rollovers.* In accordance with sections 402(c), 403(b)(8), and 403(b)(10), a direct transfer in accordance with section 401(a)(31) (generally referred to as a direct rollover) is not includible in the gross income of a participant or beneficiary in the year transferred. In addition, any payment made in the form of an eligible rollover distribution (as defined in section 402(c)(4)) is not includible in gross income in the year paid to the extent the payment is transferred to an eligible retirement plan (as defined in section 402(c)(8)(B)) within 60 days, including the transfer to the eligible retirement plan of any property distributed. For this purpose, the rules of section 402(c)(2) through (7) and (c)(9) apply. Any direct rollover under this paragraph (b)(1) is a distribution that is subject to the distribution requirements of § 1.403(b)-6.

(2) *Requirement that contract provide rollover options for eligible rollover distributions.* As required in § 1.403(b)-3(a)(7), an annuity contract is not a section 403(b) contract unless the contract provides that if the distributee of an eligible rollover distribution elects to have the distribution paid directly to an eligible retirement plan (as defined in section 402(c)(8)(B)) and specifies the eligible retirement plan to which the distribution is to be paid, then the distribution will be paid to that eligible retirement plan in a direct rollover. For purposes of determining whether a contract satisfies this requirement, the provisions of section 401(a)(31) apply to the annuity as though it were a plan qualified under section 401(a) unless otherwise provided in section 401(a)(31). In applying the provisions of this paragraph (b)(2), the payor of the eligible rollover distribution from the contract is treated as the plan administrator.

(3) *Requirement that contract payor provide notice of rollover option to distributees.* To ensure that the distributee of an eligible rollover distribution from a section 403(b) contract has a meaningful right to elect a direct rollover, section 402(f) requires that the distributee be informed of the option. Thus, within a reasonable time period before making the initial eligible rollover distribution, the payor must provide an explanation to the distributee of his or her right to elect a direct rollover and the income tax withholding consequences of not electing a direct rollover. For purposes of satisfying the reasonable time period requirement, the plan timing rule provided in section 402(f)(1) and the regulations thereunder applies to section 403(b) contracts.

(4) *Mandatory withholding upon certain eligible rollover distributions from contracts.* If a distributee of an eligible rollover distribution from a section 403(b) contract does not elect to have the eligible rollover distribution paid directly to an eligible retirement plan in a direct rollover, the eligible rollover distribution is subject to 20-percent income tax withholding imposed under section 3405(c). See section

3405(c) and the regulations thereunder for provisions regarding the withholding requirements relating to eligible rollover distributions.

(5) *Automatic rollover for certain mandatory distributions under section 401(a)(31)(B)*. [Reserved].

(c) *Special rules for certain corrective distributions*. See section 402(g)(2)(C) for special rules to determine the tax treatment of a distribution of excess deferrals, and see § 1.401(m)-1(e)(3)(v) for the tax treatment of corrective distributions of after-tax and matching contributions to comply with section 401(m).

(d) *Amounts taxable under section 72(p)(1)*. In accordance with section 72(p), the amount of any loan from a section 403(b) contract to a participant or beneficiary (including any pledge or assignment treated as a loan under section 72(p)(1)(B)) is treated as having been received as a distribution from the contract under section 72(p)(1), except to the extent set forth in section 72(p)(2) (relating to loans that do not exceed a maximum amount and that are repayable in accordance with certain terms) and § 1.72(p)-1. Thus, except to the extent a loan satisfies section 72(p)(2), any amount loaned from a section 403(b) contract to a participant or beneficiary (including any pledge or assignment treated as a loan under section 72(p)(1)(B)) is includible in the gross income of the participant or beneficiary for the taxable year in which the loan is made. See generally § 1.72(p)-1.

§ 1.403(b)-8 Funding [Corrected].

(a) *Investments permitted*. Section 403(b) and § 1.403(b)-3 only apply to amounts held in an annuity contract (as defined in § 1.403(b)-2), including a custodial account that is treated as an annuity contract under this section or a retirement income account that is treated as an annuity contract under § 1.403(b)-9.

(b) *Contributions to the plan*. Contributions to a section 403(b) plan must be transferred to the insurance company issuing the annuity contract (or the entity holding assets of any custodial or retirement income account that is treated as an annuity contract) within a period that is not longer than is reasonable for the proper administration of the plan. For purposes of this requirement, the plan may provide for section 403(b) elective deferrals for a participant under the plan to be transferred to the annuity contract within a specified period after the date the amounts would otherwise have been paid to the participant. For example, the plan could provide for section 403(b) elective deferrals under the plan to be contributed within 15 business days following the month in which these amounts would otherwise have been paid to the participant.

(c) *Annuity contracts*—(1) *Generally*. As defined in § 1.403(b)-2, and except as otherwise permitted under this section, an annuity contract means a contract that is issued by an insurance company qualified to issue annuities in a State and that includes payment in the form of an annuity. This paragraph (c) sets forth additional rules regarding annuity contracts.

(2) *Certain insurance contracts*. Neither a life insurance contract, as defined in section 7702, an endowment contract, a health or accident insurance contract, nor a property, casualty, or liability insurance contract meets the definition of an annuity contract. See § 1.401(f)-4(e). Also see § 1.403(b)-11(d) for a transition rule.

(3) *Special rule for certain contracts*. This paragraph (c)(3) applies in the case of a contract issued under a State section 403(b) plan established on or before May 17, 1982, or for an employee who becomes covered for the first time under the plan after May 17, 1982, unless the Commissioner had before that date issued any written communication (either to the employer or financial institution) to the effect that the arrangement under which the contract was issued did not meet the requirements of section 403(b). The requirement that the contract be issued by an insurance company qualified to issue annuities in a State does not apply to that contract if one of the following two conditions is satisfied and that condition has been satisfied continuously since May 17, 1982—

(i) Benefits under the contract are provided from a separately funded retirement reserve that is subject to supervision of the State insurance department; or

(ii) Benefits under the contract are provided from a fund that is separate from the fund used to provide statutory benefits payable under a State retirement system and that is part of a State teachers retirement system to purchase benefits that are unrelated to the basic benefits provided under the retirement system, and the death benefit provided under the contract does not at any time exceed the larger of the reserve or the contribution made for the employee.

(d) *Custodial accounts*—(1) *Treatment as a section 403(b) contract*. Under section 403(b)(7), a custodial account is treated as an annuity

contract for purposes of §§ 1.403(b)-1 through 1.403(b)-11. See section 403(b)(7)(B) for special rules regarding the tax treatment of custodial accounts and section 4973(c) for an excise tax that applies to excess contributions to a custodial account.

(2) *Custodial account defined*. A custodial account means a plan, or a separate account under a plan, in which an amount attributable to section 403(b) contributions (or amounts rolled over to a section 403(b) contract, as described in § 1.403(b)-10(d)) is held by a bank or a person who satisfies the conditions in section 401(f)(2), if—

(i) All of the amounts held in the account are invested in stock of a regulated investment company (as defined in section 851(a) relating to mutual funds);

(ii) The requirements of § 1.403(b)-6(c) (imposing restrictions on distributions with respect to a custodial account) and § 1.403(b)-6(d) are satisfied with respect to the amounts held in the account;

(iii) The assets held in the account cannot be used for, or diverted to, purposes other than for the exclusive benefit of plan participants or their beneficiaries (for which purpose, assets are treated as diverted to the employer if the employer borrows assets from the account); and

(iv) The account is not part of a retirement income account.

(3) *Effect of definition*. The requirement in paragraph (d)(2)(i) of this section is not satisfied if the account includes any assets other than stock of a regulated investment company.

(e) *Retirement income accounts*. See § 1.403(b)-9 for special rules under which a retirement income account for employees of a church-related organization is treated as a section 403(b) contract for purposes of §§ 1.403(b)-1 through 1.403(b)-11.

(f) *Combining assets*. To the extent permitted by the Commissioner in revenue rulings, notices, or other guidance published in the Internal Revenue Bulletin (see § 601.601(d)(2)(ii)(*b*) of this chapter), trust assets held under a custodial account and trust assets held under a retirement income account, as described in § 1.403(b)-9(a)(6), may be invested in a group trust with trust assets held under a qualified plan or individual retirement plan. For this purpose, a trust includes a custodial account that is treated as a trust under section 401(f).

§ 1.403(b)-9 Special rules for church plans.

(a) *Retirement income accounts*—(1) *Treatment as a section 403(b) contract*. Under section 403(b)(9), a retirement income account for employees of a church-related organization (as defined in § 1.403(b)-2) is treated as an annuity contract for purposes of §§ 1.403(b)-1 through 1.403(b)-11.

(2) *Retirement income account defined*—(i) *In general*. A retirement income account means a defined contribution program established or maintained by a churchrelated organization under which—

(A) There is separate accounting for the retirement income account's interest in the underlying assets (i.e., there must be sufficient separate accounting for it to be possible at all times to determine the retirement income account's interest in the underlying assets and to distinguish that interest from any interest that is not part of the retirement income account);

(B) Investment performance is based on gains and losses on those assets; and

(C) The assets held in the account cannot be used for, or diverted to, purposes other than for the exclusive benefit of plan participants or their beneficiaries. For this purpose, assets are treated as diverted to the employer if the employer borrows assets from the account.

(ii) *Plan required*. A retirement income account must be maintained pursuant to a program which is a plan (as defined in § 1.403(b)-3(b)(3)) and the plan document must state (or otherwise evidence in a similarly clear manner) the intent to constitute a retirement income account.

(3) *Ownership or use constitutes distribution*. Any asset of a retirement income account that is owned or used by a participant or beneficiary is treated as having been distributed to that participant or beneficiary. See §§ 1.403(b)-6 and 1.403(b)-7 for rules relating to distributions.

(4) *Coordination of retirement income account with custodial account rules*. A retirement income account that is treated as an annuity contract is not a custodial account (defined in § 1.403(b)-8(d)(2)), even if it is invested solely in stock of a regulated investment company.

(5) *Life annuities*. A retirement income account may distribute benefits in a form that includes a life annuity only if—

(i) The amount of the distribution form has an actuarial present value, at the annuity starting date, equal to the participant's or beneficiary's accumulated benefit, based on reasonable actuarial assumptions, including regarding interest and mortality; and

(ii) The plan sponsor guarantees benefits in the event that a payment is due that exceeds the participant's or beneficiary's accumulated benefit.

(6) *Combining retirement income account assets with other assets.* For purposes of § 1.403(b)-8(f) relating to combining assets, retirement income account assets held in trust (including a custodial account that is treated as a trust under section 401(f)) are subject to the same rules regarding combining of assets as custodial account assets. In addition, retirement income account assets are permitted to be commingled in a common fund with amounts devoted exclusively to church purposes (such as a fund from which unfunded pension payments are made to former employees of the church). However, unless otherwise permitted by the Commissioner, no assets of the plan sponsor, other than retirement income account assets, may be combined with custodial account assets or any other assets permitted to be combined under § 1.403(b)-8(f). This paragraph (a)(6) is subject to any additional rules issued by the Commissioner in revenue rulings, notices, or other guidance published in the Internal Revenue Bulletin (see § 601.601(d)(2)(ii)(*b*) of this chapter).

(7) *Trust treated as tax exempt.* A trust (including a custodial account that is treated as a trust under section 401(f)) that includes no assets other than assets of a retirement income account is treated as an organization that is exempt from taxation under section 501(a).

(b) *No compensation limitation up to $10,000.* See section 415(c)(7) for special rules regarding certain employer contributions not exceeding $10,000.

(c) *Special deduction rule for self-employed ministers.* See section 404(a)(10) for a special rule regarding the deductibility of a contribution made by a self-employed minister.

§ *1.403(b)-10 Miscellaneous provisions.*

(a) *Plan terminations and frozen plans*—(1) *In general.* An employer may amend its section 403(b) plan to eliminate future contributions for existing participants. Alternatively, an employer may amend its section 403(b) plan to limit participation to existing participants and employees (to the extent consistent with § 1.403(b)-5). A section 403(b) plan may contain provisions that permit plan termination and permit accumulated benefits to be distributed on termination. However, in the case of a section 403(b) contract that is subject to the distribution restrictions in § 1.403(b)-6(c) or (d) (relating to custodial accounts and section 403(b) elective deferrals), termination of the plan and the distribution of accumulated benefits is permitted only if the employer (taking into account all entities that are treated as the employer under section 414 on the date of the termination) does not make contributions to an alternative section 403(b) contract that is not part of the plan. For purposes of this rule, contributions are made to an alternative section 403(b) contract if and only if contributions are made to a section 403(b) contract during the period beginning on the date of plan termination and ending 12 months after distribution of all assets from the terminated plan. However, if at all times during the period beginning 12 months before the termination and ending 12 months after distribution of all assets from the terminated plan, fewer than 2 percent of the employees who were eligible under the section 403(b) plan as of the date of plan termination are eligible under the alternative section 403(b) contract, the alternative section 403(b) contract is disregarded. In order for a section 403(b) plan to be considered terminated, all accumulated benefits under the plan must be distributed to all participants and beneficiaries as soon as administratively practicable after termination of the plan. A distribution includes delivery of a fully paid individual insurance annuity contract. The mere provision for, and making of, distributions to participants or beneficiaries upon plan termination does not cause a contract to cease to be a section 403(b) contract. See § 1.403(b)-7 for rules regarding the tax treatment of distributions.

(2) *Employers that cease to be eligible employers.* An employer that ceases to be an eligible employer may no longer contribute to a section 403(b) contract for any subsequent period, and the contract will fail to satisfy § 1.403(b)-3(a) if any further contributions are made with respect to a period after the employer ceases to be an eligible employer.

(b) *Contract exchanges and plan-to-plan transfers*—(1) *Contract exchanges and transfers*—(i) *General rule.* If the conditions in paragraph (b)(2) of this section are met, a section 403(b) contract held under a section 403(b) plan may be exchanged for another section 403(b) contract held under that section 403(b) plan. Further, if the conditions in paragraph (b)(3) of this section are met, a section 403(b) plan may provide for the transfer of its assets (i.e., the section 403(b) contracts held thereunder, including any assets held in a custodial account or

retirement income account that are treated as section 403(b) contracts) to another section 403(b) plan. In addition, if the conditions in paragraph (b)(4) of this section (relating to permissive service credit and repayments under section 415) are met, a section 403(b) plan may provide for the transfer of its assets to a qualified plan under section 401(a). However, neither a qualified plan nor an eligible plan under section 457(b) may transfer assets to a section 403(b) plan, and a section 403(b) plan may not accept such a transfer. In addition, a section 403(b) contract may not be exchanged for an annuity contract that is not a section 403(b) contract. Neither a plan-to-plan transfer nor a contract exchange permitted under this paragraph (b) is treated as a distribution for purposes of the distribution restrictions at § 1.403(b)-6. Therefore, such a transfer or exchange may be made before severance from employment or another distribution event. Further, no amount is includible in gross income by reason of such a transfer or exchange.

(ii) *ERISA rules.* See § 1.414(l)-1 for other rules that are applicable to section 403(b) plans that are subject to section 208 of the Employee Retirement Income Security Act of 1974 (88 Stat. 829, 865).

(2) *Requirements for contract exchange within the same plan.* A section 403(b) contract of a participant or beneficiary may be exchanged under paragraph (b)(1) of this section for another section 403(b) contract of that participant or beneficiary under the same section 403(b) plan if the following conditions are met—

(i) The plan under which the contract is issued provides for the exchange;

(ii) The participant or beneficiary has an accumulated benefit immediately after the transfer at least equal to the accumulated benefit of that participant or beneficiary immediately before the exchange (taking into account the accumulated benefit of that participant or beneficiary under both section 403(b) contracts immediately before the exchange); and

(iii) The other contract provides that, to the extent a contract that is exchanged is subject to any distribution restrictions under § 1.403(b)-6, the other contract imposes restrictions on distributions to the participant or beneficiary that are not less stringent than those imposed on the contract being exchanged.

(3) *Requirements for plan-to-plan transfers.* A plan-to-plan transfer under paragraph (b)(1) of this section from a section 403(b) plan to another section 403(b) plan is permitted if the following conditions are met—

(i) The participant or beneficiary whose assets are being transferred is an employee of the employer providing the receiving plan;

(ii) The transferor plan provides for transfers;

(iii) The receiving plan provides for the receipt of transfers;

(iv) The participant or beneficiary whose assets are being transferred has an accumulated benefit immediately after the transfer at least equal to the accumulated benefit with respect to that participant or beneficiary immediately before the transfer.

(v) The receiving plan provides that, to the extent any amount transferred is subject to any distribution restrictions under § 1.403(b)-6, the receiving plan imposes restrictions on distributions to the participant or beneficiary whose assets are being transferred that are not less stringent than those imposed on the transferor plan.

(vi) If a plan-to-plan transfer does not constitute a complete transfer of the participant's or beneficiary's interest in the section 403(b) plan, the transferee plan treats the amount transferred as a continuation of a pro rata portion of the participant's or beneficiary's interest in the section 403(b) plan (e.g., a pro rata portion of the participant's or beneficiary's interest in any after-tax employee contributions).

(4) *Purchase of permissive service credit by contract-to-plan transfers from a section 403(b) contract to a qualified plan*—(i) *General rule.* If the conditions in paragraph (b)(4)(ii) of this section are met, a section 403(b) plan may provide for the transfer of assets held thereunder to a qualified defined benefit governmental plan (as defined in section 414(d)).

(ii) *Conditions for plan-to-plan transfers.* A transfer may be made under this paragraph (b)(4) only if the transfer is either—

(A) For the purchase of permissive service credit (as defined in section 415(n)(3)(A)) under the receiving defined benefit governmental plan; or

(B) A repayment to which section 415 does not apply by reason of section 415(k)(3).

(c) *Qualified domestic relations orders.* In accordance with the second sentence of section 414(p)(9), any distribution from an annuity contract under section 403(b) (including a distribution from a custodial account or retirement income account that, under section 403(b)(7) or (9), is treated as a section 403(b) contract) pursuant to a qualified domestic relations order is treated in the same manner as a distribution from a plan to which section 401(a)(13) applies. Thus, for example, a section 403(b) plan does not fail to satisfy the distribution restrictions set forth in §1.403(b)-6(b), (c), or (d) merely as a result of distribution made pursuant to a qualified domestic relations order under section 414(p), so that such a distribution is permitted without regard to whether the employee from whose contract the distribution is made has had a severance from employment or other event permitting a distribution to be made under section 403(b).

(d) *Rollovers to a section 403(b) contract.* A section 403(b) contract may accept contributions that are eligible rollover distributions (as defined in section 402(c)(4)) made from another eligible retirement plan (as defined in section 402(c)(8)(B)). Amounts contributed to a section 403(b) contract as eligible rollover distributions are not taken into account for purposes of the limits in §1.403(b)-4, but, except as otherwise specifically provided (for example, at §1.403(b)-6(i)), are otherwise treated in the same manner as amounts held under a section 403(b) contract for purposes of §§1.403(b)-3 through 1.403(b)-9 and this section.

(e) *Deemed IRAs.* See regulations under section 408(q) for special rules relating to deemed IRAs.

(f) *Defined benefit plans—*(1) *TEFRA church defined benefit plans.* See section 251(e)(5) of the Tax Equity and Fiscal Responsibility Act of 1982, Public Law 97-248, for a provision permitting certain arrangements established by a church-related organization and in effect on September 3, 1982 (a TEFRA church defined benefit plan) to be treated as section 403(b) contract even though it is a defined benefit arrangement. In accordance with section 403(b)(1), for purposes of applying section 415 to a TEFRA church defined benefit plan, the accruals under the plan are limited to the maximum amount permitted under section 415(c) when expressed as an annual addition, and, for this purpose, the rules at §1.402(b)-1(a)(2) for determining the present value of an accrual under a nonqualified defined benefit plan also apply for purposes of converting the accrual under a TEFRA church defined benefit plan to an annual addition. See section 415(b) for additional limits for TEFRA church defined benefit plans.

(2) *Other defined benefit plans.* Except for a TEFRA church defined benefit plan, section 403(b) does not apply to any contributions or accrual under a defined benefit plan.

(g) *Other rules relating to section 501(c)(3) organizations.* See section 501(c)(3) and regulations thereunder for the substantive standards for tax-exemption under that section, including the requirement that no part of the organization's net earnings inure to the benefit of any private shareholder or individual. See also sections 4941 (self dealing), 4945 (taxable expenditures), and 4958 (excess benefit transactions), and the regulations thereunder, for rules relating to excise taxes imposed on certain transactions involving organizations described in section 501(c)(3).

§ 1.403(b)-11 *Effective dates.*

(a) Except as otherwise provided in this section, §§1.403(b)-1 through 1.403(b)-10 apply for taxable years beginning after December 31, 2005.

(b) In the case of a section 403(b) contract maintained pursuant to a collective bargaining agreement that is ratified and in effect on the date of publication of final regulations in the **Federal Register**, §§1.403(b)-1 through 1.403(b)-10 do not apply before the date on which the collective bargaining agreement terminates (determined without regard to any extension thereof after the date of publication of final regulations in the **Federal Register**).

(c) In the case of a section 403(b) contract maintained by a church-related organization for which the authority to amend the contract is held by a church convention (within the meaning of section 414(e)), §§1.403(b)-1 through 1.403(b)-10 do not apply before the earlier of—

(1) January 1, 2007; or

(2) 60 days following the earliest church convention that occurs after the date of publication of final regulations in the **Federal Register**.

(d) Section 1.403(b)-8(c)(2) does not apply to a contract issued before February 14, 2005.

Par. 6. Section 1.414(c)-5 is redesignated as §1.414(c)-6 and new §1.414(c)-5 is added to read as follows:

§ 1.414(c)-5 *Certain tax-exempt organizations [Corrected].*

(a) *Application.* This section applies to an organization that is exempt from tax under section 501(a). The rules of this section are in addition to the rules otherwise applicable under section 414(b) and 414(c). Except to the extent set forth in paragraphs (d), (e), and (f) of this section, this section does not apply to any church, as defined in section 3121(w)(3)(A), or any qualified church-controlled organization, as defined in section 3121(w)(3)(B).

(b) *General rule.* In the case of an organization that is exempt from tax under section 501(a) (an exempt organization) whose employees participate in a plan, the employer with respect to that plan includes the exempt organization and any other organization that is under common control with the exempt organization whose employees participate in the plan. For this purpose, common control exists between exempt organizations if at least 80 percent of the directors or trustees of one organization are either representatives of, or directly or indirectly controlled by, the other organization. A trustee or director is treated as a representative of another exempt organization if he or she also is a trustee, director, agent, or employee of the other exempt organization. Existence of control is determined based on the facts and circumstances. A trustee or director is controlled by another organization if the other organization has the power to remove such trustee or director and designate a new trustee or director. For example, if exempt organization A appoints at least 80 percent of the trustees of exempt organization B (which is the owner of the outstanding shares of corporation C, which is not an exempt organization) and has the power to control at least 80 percent of the directors of exempt organization D, then, under this paragraph (b) and §1.414(b)-1, entities A, B, C, and D are treated as the same employer with respect to any plan maintained by A, B, C, or D for purposes of the sections referenced in sections 414(b), 414(c), and 414(t).

(c) *Permissive aggregation with entities having a common exempt purpose.* For purposes of this section, exempt organizations that maintain a single plan covering one or more employees from each organization may treat themselves as under common control for purposes of section 414(c) if each of the organizations regularly coordinate their day-to-day exempt activities. For example, an entity that provides a type of emergency relief within one geographic region and another exempt organization that provides that type of emergency relief within another geographic region may treat themselves as under common control if they have a single plan covering employees of both entities and regularly coordinate their day-to-day exempt activities. Similarly, a hospital that is an exempt organization and another exempt organization with which it coordinates the delivery of medical services or medical research may treat themselves as under common control if there is a single plan covering employees of the hospital and employees of the other exempt organization and the coordination is a regular part of their day-to-day exempt activities.

(d) *Permissive disaggregation between qualified church controlled organizations and other entities.* In the case of a church plan (as defined in section 414(e)) to which contributions are made by more than one common law entity, any employer may apply paragraphs (b) and (c) of this section to those entities that are not a church (as defined in section 403(b)(12)(B) and §1.403(b)-2 separately from those entities that are churches. For example, in the case of a group of entities consisting of a church (as defined in section 3121(w)(3)(A)), a secondary school (that is treated as a church under §1.403(b)-2), and a nursing home that receives more than 25 percent of its support from fees paid by residents (so that it is not treated as a qualified church-controlled organization under §1.403(b)-2 and section 3121(w)(3)(B)), the nursing home may treat itself as not being under common control with the church and the school, even though the nursing home may be under common control with the school and the church under paragraph (b) of this section.

(e) *Application to certain church entities.* [Reserved].

(f) *Anti-abuse rule.* In any case in which the Commissioner determines that the structure of one or more exempt organizations (including an exempt organization and an entity that is not exempt from income tax) or the positions taken by those organizations has the effect of avoiding or evading §1.403(b)-5(a) or another requirement imposed under section 401(a), 403(b), or 457(b), or any applicable section (as defined in section 414(t)), the Commissioner may treat an entity as under common control with the exempt organization.

(g) *Examples.* The provisions of this section are illustrated by the following examples:

Example 1. (i) *Facts.* Organization A is a tax-exempt organization under section 501(c)(3) which owns 80% or more of the total value of all classes of stock of corporation B, which is a for profit organization.

(ii) *Conclusion.* Under paragraph (a) of this section, this section does not alter the rules of section 414(b) and (c), so that organization A and corporation B are under common control under § 1.414(c)-2(b).

Example 2. (i) *Facts.* Organization M is a hospital which is a tax-exempt organization under section 501(c)(3) and organization N is a medical clinic which is also a tax-exempt organization under section 501(c)(3). N is located in a city and M is located in a nearby suburb. There is a history of regular coordination of day-to-day activities between M and N, including periodic transfers of staff, coordination of staff training, common sources of income, and coordination of budget and operational goals. A single section 403(b) plan covers professional and staff employees of both the hospital and the medical clinic. While a number of members of the board of directors of M are also on the board of directors of N, there is less than 80% overlap in board membership. Both organizations have approximately the same percentage of employees who are highly compensated and have appropriate business reasons for being maintained in separate entities.

(ii) *Conclusion.* M and N are not under common control under this section, but, under paragraph (c) of this section, may chose to treat themselves as under common control, assuming both of them act in a manner that is consistent with that choice for purposes of

§ 1.403(b)-5(a), sections 401(a), 403(b), and 457(b), and any other applicable section (as defined in section 414(t)).

(h) *Effective date.* This section applies for taxable years beginning after December 31, 2005.

PART 31—EMPLOYMENT TAXES

Par. 7. The authority citation for part 31 continues to read, in part, as follows:

Authority: 26 U.S.C. 7805 * * *

Par. 8. Section 31.3121(a)(5)-2 is added to read as follows:

§ 31.3121(a)(5)-2 Payments under or to an annuity contract described in section 403(b).

[The text of proposed § 31.3121(a)(5)-2 is the same as the text of § 31.3121(a)(5)-2T(a) through (b)(1) published elsewhere in this issue of the **Federal Register**].

/s/ Nancy Jardini

Acting Deputy Commissioner for Services and Enforcement.

¶ 20,261I

IRS proposed regulations: Tax shelters: S corporations : Employee stock ownership plans (ESOPs): Disqualified persons: Nonallocation years: Synthetic equity.—The IRS has issued proposed regulations aimed at curbing abuses by S corporation owners that use the tax exemption on S corporation stock held by ESOPs for inappropriate tax deferral or avoidance. In general, an ESOP holding employer securities consisting of S corporation stock must provide that no portion of plan assets attributable to, or allocable in lieu of, such employer securities may, during a nonallocation year, accrue for the benefit of any disqualified persons. The text of the temporary regulations also serves as the text of the proposed regulations. The preamble to the temporary regulations appears at ¶ 24,507T.

The proposed regulations, which were published in the *Federal Register* on December 17, 2004 (69 FR 75492) and corrected on February 4, 2005 (70 FR 5948), are reproduced below.

[4830-01-p]

DEPARTMENT OF THE TREASURY

Internal Revenue Service

26 CFR Part 1

[REG-129709-03]

RIN 1545-BC34

Prohibited Allocations of Securities in an S Corporation

AGENCY: Internal Revenue Service (IRS), Treasury.

ACTION: Notice of proposed rulemaking by cross-reference to temporary regulations and notice of public hearing.

SUMMARY: In the Rules and Regulations section of this issue of the **Federal Register,** the IRS is issuing temporary regulations that provide guidance on the definition and effects of a prohibited allocation under section 409(p), identification of disqualified persons and determination of a nonallocation year, calculation of synthetic equity under section 409(p)(5), and standards for determining whether a transaction is an avoidance or evasion of section 409(p). These proposed regulations would generally affect plan sponsors of, and participants in, ESOPs holding stock of Subchapter S corporations. The text of those temporary regulations also serves as the text of these proposed regulations. This document also provides notice of a public hearing on these proposed regulations.

DATES: Written or electronic comments must be received by March 17, 2005. Requests to speak (with outlines of oral comments to be discussed) at the public hearing scheduled for April 20, 2005, at 10 a.m. must be received by March 30, 2005.

ADDRESSES: Send submissions to: CC:PA:LPD:PR (REG-129709-03), room 5203, Internal Revenue Service, POB 7604, Ben Franklin Station, Washington, DC 20044. Submissions may be hand delivered Monday through Friday between the hours of 8 a.m. and 4 p.m. to: CC:PA:LPD:PR (REG-129709-03), Courier's Desk, Internal Revenue Service, 1111 Constitution Avenue, N.W., Washington, DC. Alternatively, taxpayers may submit comments electronically via the IRS Internet site at *www.irs.gov/regs* or the Federal eRulemaking Portal at *www.regulations.gov* (indicate IRS and REG-129709-03).

FOR FURTHER INFORMATION CONTACT: Concerning the proposed regulations, John Ricotta at 622-6060; concerning submissions of comments, contact Guy Traynor at 202-622-7180 (not toll-free numbers).

SUPPLEMENTARY INFORMATION:

Background

Temporary regulations in the Rules and Regulations portion of this issue of the **Federal Register** amend the Income Tax Regulations (26 CFR part 1) relating to section 409(p). The temporary regulations contain rules relating to the definition and effects of a prohibited allocation under section 409(p), identification of disqualified persons and determination of a nonallocation year, calculation of synthetic equity under section 409(p)(5), and standards for determining whether a transaction is an avoidance or evasion of section 409(p). The text of those temporary regulations also serves as the text of these proposed regulations. The preamble to the temporary regulations explains the temporary regulations.

Special Analyses

It has been determined that this notice of proposed rulemaking is not a significant regulatory action as defined in Executive Order 12866. Therefore, a regulatory assessment is not required. It also has been determined that section 553(b) of the Administrative Procedure Act (5 U.S.C. chapter 5) does not apply to these regulations. Because § 1.409(p)-1 imposes no new collection of information on small entities, a Regulatory Flexibility Analysis under the Regulatory Flexibility Act (5 U.S.C. chapter 6) is not required. Pursuant to section 7805(f) of the Internal Revenue Code, this notice of proposed rulemaking will be submitted to the Chief Counsel for Advocacy of the Small Business Administration for comment on its impact on small business.

Comments and Requests for a Public Hearing

Before these proposed regulations are adopted as final regulations, consideration will be given to any written (a signed original and 8 copies) or electronic comments that are submitted timely to the IRS. All comments will be available for public inspection and copying.

A public hearing has been scheduled for April 20, 2005, at 10 a.m. in the IRS Auditorium, Internal Revenue Building, 1111 Constitution Avenue NW., Washington, DC. All visitors must present photo identification to enter the building. Because of access restrictions, visitors will not be admitted beyond the immediate entrance area more than 30 minutes before the hearing starts at the Constitution Avenue entrance. For information about having your name placed on the building access list to attend the hearing, see the "FOR FURTHER INFORMATION CONTACT" section of this preamble.

The rules of 26 CFR 601.601(a)(3) apply to the hearing. Persons who wish to present oral comments at the hearing must submit written comments and an outline of the topics to be discussed and the time to be devoted to each topic (signed original and eight (8) copies) by March 30, 2005. A period of 10 minutes will be allotted to each person for making comments. An agenda showing the scheduling of the speakers will be prepared after the deadline for receiving outlines has passed. Copies of the agenda will be available free of charge at the hearing.

Drafting Information

The principal author of these regulations is John Ricotta of the Office of the Division Counsel/Associate Chief Counsel (Tax Exempt and Government Entities). However, other personnel from the IRS and Treasury participated in their development.

List of Subjects in 26 CFR Part 1

Income taxes, Reporting and recordkeeping requirements.

Proposed Amendments to the Regulations

Accordingly, 26 CFR part 1 is proposed to be amended as follows:
PART 1—INCOME TAXES

Paragraph 1. The authority citation for part 1 is amended by adding an entry in numerical order to read, in part, as follows:

Authority: 26 U.S.C. 7805 * * *

Section 1.409(p)-1 also issued under 26 U.S.C. 409(p)(7)(A). * * *

Par. 2. Section 1.409(p)-1 is added to read as follows:

§ 1.409(p)-1 Prohibited allocations of securities in an S corporation.

[The text of proposed § 1.409(p)-1 is the same as the text of § 1.409(p)-1T published elsewhere in this issue of the **Federal Register**].

Mark E. Matthews,

Deputy Commissioner for Services and Enforcement.

CERTIFIED COPY

DALE GOODE

¶ 20,261J

IRS proposed regulations: Health plans: HIPAA: Family and Medical Leave Act: Tolling of time periods: Creditable coverage.—The IRS has issued proposed regulations relating to the interaction between the Health Insurance Portability and Accountability Act (HIPAA) and the Family and Medical Leave Act (FMLA). Under the proposed regulations, the beginning of the period that is used for determining whether a significant break in coverage has occurred (generally 63 days) is tolled in cases in which a certificate of creditable coverage is not provided on or before the day coverage ceases. In those cases, the significant break-in-coverage period is tolled until a certificate is provided but not beyond 44 days after the coverage ceases. These rules are being jointly issued with the Employee Benefits Security Administration (EBSA). Comments must be received by March 30, 2005.

The proposed regulations, which were published in the Federal Register on December 30, 2004 (69 FR 78799), are reproduced below.

DEPARTMENT OF THE TREASURY

Internal Revenue Service

26 CFR Part 54

[REG-130370-04]

RIN 1545-BD51

Notice of Proposed Rulemaking for Health Coverage Portability: Tolling Certain Time Periods and Interaction With the Family and Medical Leave Act Under HIPAA Titles I and IV

AGENCIES: Internal Revenue Service, Department of the Treasury; Employee Benefits Security Administration, Department of Labor; Centers for Medicare & Medicaid Services, Department of Health and Human Services.

ACTION: Notice of proposed rulemaking and request for comments.

SUMMARY: These proposed rules would clarify certain portability requirements for group health plans and issuers of health insurance coverage offered in connection with a group health plan. These rules propose to implement changes made to the Internal Revenue Code, the Employee Retirement Income Security Act, and the Public Health Service Act enacted as part of the Health Insurance Portability and Accountability Act of 1996.

DATES: Written comments on this notice of proposed rulemaking are invited and must be received by the Departments on or before March 30, 2005.

ADDRESSES: Written comments should be submitted with a signed original and three copies (except for electronic submissions) to any of the addresses specified below. Any comment that is submitted to any Department will be shared with the other Departments.

Comments to the IRS can be addressed to: CC:PA:LPD:PR (REG-130370-04), Room 5203, Internal Revenue Service, POB 7604, Ben Franklin Station, Washington, DC 20044.

In the alternative, comments may be hand-delivered between the hours of 8 a.m. and 4 p.m. to: CC:PA:LPD:PR (REG-130370-04), Courier's Desk, Internal Revenue Service, 1111 Constitution Avenue, NW., Washington, DC 20224.

Alternatively, comments may be transmitted electronically via the IRS or via the Federal eRulemaking Portal at *www.regulations.gov* (IRS-REG-130370-04).

Comments to the Department of Labor can be addressed to: U.S. Department of Labor, Employee Benefits Security Administration, 200 Constitution Avenue NW., Room C-5331, Washington, DC 20210, *Attention:* Proposed Portability Requirements.

Alternatively, comments may be hand-delivered between the hours of 9 a.m. and 5 p.m. to the same address. Comments may also be transmitted by e-mail to: *e-ohpsca.ebsa@dol.gov*.

Comments to HHS can be submitted as described below: In commenting, please refer to file code CMS-2158-P. Because of staff and resource limitations, we cannot accept comments by facsimile (FAX) transmission.

You may submit comments in one of three ways (no duplicates, please):

1. *Electronically.* You may submit electronic comments on specific issues in this regulation to *http://www.cms.hhs.gov/regulations/ecomments*. (Attachments should be in Microsoft Word, WordPerfect, or Excel; however, we prefer Microsoft Word.)

2. *By mail.* You may mail written comments (one original and two copies) to the following address ONLY:

Centers for Medicare & Medicaid Services, Department of Health and Human Services, Attention: CMS-2158-P, P.O. Box 8017, Baltimore, MD 21244-8010.

Please allow sufficient time for mailed comments to be received before the close of the comment period.

3. *By hand or courier.* If you prefer, you may deliver (by hand or courier) your written comments (one original and two copies) before the close of the comment period to one of the following addresses. If you intend to deliver your comments to the Baltimore address, please call telephone number (410) 786-7195 in advance to schedule your arrival with one of our staff members. Room 445-G, Hubert H. Humphrey Building, 200 Independence Avenue, SW., Washington, DC 20201; or 7500 Security Boulevard, Baltimore, MD 21244-1850.

(Because access to the interior of the HHH Building is not readily available to persons without Federal Government identification, commenters are encouraged to leave their comments in the CMS drop slots located in the main lobby of the building. A stamp-in clock is available for persons wishing to retain a proof of filing by stamping in and retaining an extra copy of the comments being filed.)

Comments mailed to the addresses indicated as appropriate for hand or courier delivery may be delayed and received after the comment period.

Submission of comments on paperwork requirements. You may submit comments on this document's paperwork requirements by mailing your comments to the addresses provided at the end of the "Collection of Information Requirements" section in this document.

All submissions to the IRS will be open to public inspection and copying in room 1621, 1111 Constitution Avenue, NW., Washington, DC from 9 a.m. to 4 p.m.

All submissions to the Department of Labor will be open to public inspection and copying in the Public Disclosure Room, Employee Benefits Security Administration, U.S. Department of Labor, Room N-1513, 200 Constitution Avenue, NW., Washington, DC from 8:30 a.m. to 4:30 p.m.

All submissions timely submitted to HHS will be available for public inspection as they are received, generally beginning approximately three weeks after publication of a document, at the headquarters for the Centers for Medicare & Medicaid Services, 7500 Security Boulevard, Baltimore, MD 21244, Monday through Friday of each week from 8:30 a.m. to 4:00 p.m. To schedule an appointment to view public comments, phone 410-786-7195.

FOR FURTHER INFORMATION CONTACT:

Dave Mlawsky, Centers for Medicare & Medicaid Services (CMS), Department of Health and Human Services, at 1-877-267-2323 ext. 61565; Amy Turner, Employee Benefits Security Administration, Department of Labor, at (202) 693-8335; or Russ Weinheimer, Internal Revenue Service, Department of the Treasury, at (202) 622-6080.

SUPPLEMENTARY INFORMATION:

Customer Service Information

To assist consumers and the regulated community, the Departments have issued questions and answers concerning HIPAA. Individuals interested in obtaining copies of Department of Labor publications concerning changes in health care law may call a toll free number, 1-866-444-EBSA (3272), or access the publications on-line at *www.dol.gov/ebsa,* the Department of Labor's Web site. These regulations as well as other information on the new health care laws are also available on the Department of Labor's interactive web pages, Health *E* laws. In addition, CMS's publication entitled "Protecting Your Health Insurance Coverage" is available by calling 1-800-633-4227 or on the Department of Health and Human Services' Web site (www.cms.hhs.gov/hipaa1), which includes the interactive webpages, HIPAA Online. Copies of the HIPAA regulations, as well as notices and press releases related to HIPAA and other health care laws, are also available at the above-referenced Web sites.

Background

The Health Insurance Portability and Accountability Act of 1996 (HIPAA), Public Law 104-191, was enacted on August 21, 1996. HIPAA amended the Internal Revenue Code of 1986 (Code), the Employee Retirement Income Security Act of 1974 (ERISA), and the Public Health Service Act (PHS Act) to provide for, among other things, improved portability and continuity of health coverage. Interim final regulations implementing the HIPAA provisions were first made available to the public on April 1, 1997 (published in the **Federal Register** on April 8, 1997, 62 FR 16894) (April 1997 interim rules). On December 29, 1997, the Departments published a clarification of the April 1997 interim rules as they relate to excepted benefits. On October 25, 1999, the Departments published a notice in the **Federal Register** (64 FR 57520) soliciting additional comments on the portability requirements based on the experience of plans and issuers operating under the April 1997 interim rules.

After consideration of all the comments received on the portability provisions, the Departments are publishing final regulations elsewhere in this issue of the **Federal Register**. These proposed rules address additional and discrete issues for which the Departments are soliciting further comment before promulgating final regulations.

Overview of the Proposed Regulations

1. Rules Relating to Creditable Coverage—26 CFR 54.9801-4, 29 CFR 2590.701-4, 45 CFR 146.113

Tolling of the 63-Day Break-in-Coverage Rule

These proposed rules would modify the 63-day break-in-coverage rules with one significant substantive change. Under the proposed rules, the beginning of the period that is used for determining whether a significant break in coverage has occurred (generally 63 days) is tolled in cases in which a certificate of creditable coverage is not provided on or before the day coverage ceases. In those cases, the significant-break-in-coverage period is tolled until a certificate is provided but not beyond 44 days after the coverage ceases.

The Departments have fashioned this tolling rule (and a similar tolling rule for the 30-day period for requesting special enrollment) in an effort to address the inequity of individuals' losing coverage without being aware that the coverage has ended while minimizing the burdens on subsequent plans and issuers that are not responsible for providing the missing or untimely certificates. Numerous situations have come to the attention of the Departments in which an individual's health coverage is terminated but in which the individual does not learn of the termination of coverage until well after it occurs. The statute generally requires that a certificate of creditable coverage be provided at the time an individual ceases to be covered under a plan. The statute, the April 1997 interim rules, and the final regulations (published elsewhere in this issue of the **Federal Register**) all permit a plan or issuer to provide the certificate at a later date if it is provided at a time consistent with notices required under a COBRA continuation provision. The statute also directs the Secretaries to establish rules to prevent a plan or issuer's failure to provide a certificate timely from adversely affecting the individual's subsequent coverage. If a plan or issuer chooses to provide a certificate later than the date an individual loses coverage, as the regulations permit in certain circumstances, these proposed rules provide that an individual should not suffer from this rule of convenience for the plan or issuer. However, to prevent the abuse that might result from an open-ended tolling rule, an outside limit of 44 days is placed on this relief. This reflects the fact that, in most cases, plans and issuers are required to provide certificates within 44 days (although some plans and issuers may be required to provide certificates sooner than 44 days after coverage ceases and some entities are not required to provide certificates at all). The Departments have adopted this uniform limit on the tolling rule for purposes of consistency. New examples have been added to illustrate the tolling rule.

2. Evidence of Creditable Coverage—26 CFR 54.9801-5, 29 CFR 2590.701-5, 45 CFR 146.115

Information in Certificate and Model Certificate

These proposed rules would modify the required elements for the educational statement in certificates of creditable coverage to require a disclosure about the Family and Medical Leave Act. Use of the first model certificate below by group health plans and group health insurance issuers, or use of the appropriate model certificate that appears in the preamble to the related final regulations published elsewhere in this issue of the **Federal Register**, will satisfy the requirements of paragraph (a)(3)(ii) in this section of the final regulations. Similarly, for purposes of complying with those final regulations, State Medicaid programs may use the second version below, or may use the appropriate model certificate that appears in the preamble to those final regulations. Thus, until this proposed regulation is published as a final regulation, entities may use either the model certificates published below, or those published elsewhere in this issue of the **Federal Register**. For entities that choose not to use the model certificates below until this proposed regulation is published as a final regulation, we welcome comments as to the applicability date for using them.

BILLING CODE 4830-01-P

CERTIFICATE OF GROUP HEALTH PLAN COVERAGE

1. Date of this certificate: _____

2. Name of group health plan: _____
   _____

3. Name of participant: _____

4. Identification number of participant: _____

5. Name of individuals to whom this certificate
   applies: _____
   _____

6. Name, address, and telephone number of
   plan administrator or issuer responsible
   for providing this certificate: _____
   _____
   _____

7. For further information, call: _____

8. If the individual(s) identified in line 5 has (have)
   at least 18 months of creditable coverage
   (disregarding periods of coverage before
   a 63-day break), check here and skip lines 9 and
   10: ___

9. Date waiting period or affiliation period
   (if any) began: _____

10. Date coverage began: _____

11. Date coverage ended (or if coverage has not
    ended, enter "continuing"): _____

[Note: separate certificates will be furnished if information is not identical for the participant and each beneficiary.]

Statement of HIPAA Portability Rights

IMPORTANT — KEEP THIS CERTIFICATE. This certificate is evidence of your coverage under this plan. Under a federal law known as HIPAA, you may need evidence of your coverage to reduce a preexisting condition exclusion period under another plan, to help you get special enrollment in another plan, or to get certain types of individual health coverage even if you have health problems.

Preexisting condition exclusions. Some group health plans restrict coverage for medical conditions present before an individual's enrollment. These restrictions are known as "preexisting condition exclusions." A preexisting condition exclusion can apply only to conditions for which medical advice, diagnosis, care, or treatment was recommended or received within the 6 months before your "enrollment date." Your enrollment date is your first day of coverage under the plan, or, if there is a waiting period, the first day of your waiting period (typically, your first day of work). In addition, a preexisting condition exclusion cannot last for more than 12 months after your enrollment date (18 months if you are a late enrollee). Finally, a preexisting condition exclusion cannot apply to pregnancy and cannot apply to a child who is enrolled in health coverage within 30 days after birth, adoption, or placement for adoption.

If a plan imposes a preexisting condition exclusion, the length of the exclusion must be reduced by the amount of your prior creditable coverage. Most health coverage is creditable coverage, including group health plan coverage, COBRA continuation coverage, coverage under an individual health policy, Medicare, Medicaid, State Children's Health Insurance Program (SCHIP), and coverage through high-risk pools and the Peace Corps. Not all forms of creditable coverage are required to provide certificates like this one. If you do not receive a certificate for past coverage, talk to your new plan administrator.

You can add up any creditable coverage you have, including the coverage shown on this certificate. However, if at any time you went for 63 days or more without any coverage (called a break in coverage) a plan may not have to count the coverage you had before the break.

➔ Therefore, once your coverage ends, you should try to obtain alternative coverage as soon as possible to avoid a 63-day break. You may use this certificate as evidence of your creditable coverage to reduce the length of any preexisting condition exclusion if you enroll in another plan.

Right to get special enrollment in another plan. Under HIPAA, if you lose your group health plan coverage, you may be able to get into another group health plan for which you are eligible (such as a spouse's plan), even if the plan generally does not accept late enrollees, if you request enrollment within 30 days. (Additional special enrollment rights are triggered by marriage, birth, adoption, and placement for adoption.)

➜ Therefore, once your coverage ends, if you are eligible for coverage in another plan (such as a spouse's plan), you should request special enrollment as soon as possible.

Prohibition against discrimination based on a health factor. Under HIPAA, a group health plan may not keep you (or your dependents) out of the plan based on anything related to your health. Also, a group health plan may no charge you (or your dependents) more for coverage, based on health, than the amount charged a similarly situated individual.

Right to individual health coverage. Under HIPAA, if you are an "eligible individual," you have a right to buy certain individual health policies (or in some states, to buy coverage through a high-risk pool) without a preexisting condition exclusion. To be an eligible individual, you must meet the following requirements:

- You have had coverage for at least 18 months without a break in coverage of 63 days or more;
- Your most recent coverage was under a group health plan (which can be shown by this certificate);
- Your group coverage was not terminated because of fraud or nonpayment of premiums;
- You are not eligible for COBRA continuation coverage or you have exhausted your COBRA benefits (or continuation coverage under a similar state provision); and
- You are not eligible for another group health plan, Medicare, or Medicaid, and do not have any other health insurance coverage.

The right to buy individual coverage is the same whether you are laid off, fired, or quit your job.

➜ Therefore, if you are interested in obtaining individual coverage and you meet the other criteria to be an eligible individual, you should apply for this coverage as soon as possible to avoid losing your eligible individual status due to a 63-day break.

Special information for people on FMLA leave. If you are taking leave under the Family and Medical Leave Act (FMLA) and you drop health coverage during your leave, any days without health coverage while on FMLA leave will not count towards a 63-day break in coverage. In addition, if you do not return from leave, the 30-day period to request special enrollment in another plan will not start before your FMLA leave ends.

➜ Therefore, when you apply for other health coverage, you should tell your plan administrator or health insurer about any prior FMLA leave.

State flexibility. This certificate describes minimum HIPAA protections under federal law. States may require insurers and HMOs to provide additional protections to individuals in that state.

For more information. If you have questions about your HIPAA rights, you may contact your state insurance department or the U.S. Department of Labor, Employee Benefits Security Administration (EBSA) toll-free at 1-866-444-3272 (for free HIPAA publications ask for publications concerning changes in health care laws). You may also contact the CMS publication hotline at 1-800-633-4227 (ask for "Protecting Your Health Insurance Coverage"). These publications and other useful information are also available on the Internet at: http://www.dol.gov/ebsa, the DOL's interactive web pages - Health Elaws, or http://www.cms.hhs.gov/hipaa1.

CERTIFICATE OF MEDICAID COVERAGE

1. Date of this certificate: _____

2. Name of state Medicaid program: _____

3. Name of recipient: _____

4. Identification number of recipient: _____

5. Name of individuals to whom this certificate applies: _____ _____

6. Name, address, and telephone number of state Medicaid agency responsible for providing this certificate: _____ _____ _____

7. For further information call: _____

8. If the individual(s) identified in line 5 has (have) at least 18 months of creditable coverage (disregarding periods of coverage before a 63-day break), check here and skip line 9. ____

9. Date coverage began: _____

10. Date coverage ended (or if coverage has not ended, enter "continuing"): _____

[Note: separate certificates will be furnished if information is not identical for the recipient and each dependent.]

Statement of HIPAA Portability Rights

IMPORTANT — KEEP THIS CERTIFICATE. This certificate is evidence of your coverage under this state Medicaid program. Under a federal law known as HIPAA, you may need evidence of your coverage to reduce a preexisting condition exclusion period under a group health plan, to help you get special enrollment in a group health plan, or to get certain types of individual health coverage even if you have health problems.

Preexisting condition exclusions. Some group health plans restrict coverage for medical conditions present before an individual's enrollment. These restrictions are known as "preexisting condition exclusions." A preexisting condition exclusion can apply only to conditions for which medical advice, diagnosis, care, or treatment was recommended or received within the 6 months before your "enrollment date." Your enrollment date is your first day of coverage under the plan, or, if there is a waiting period, the first day of your waiting period (typically, your first day of work). In addition, a preexisting condition exclusion cannot last for more than 12 months after your enrollment date (18 months if you are a late enrollee). Finally, a preexisting condition exclusion cannot apply to pregnancy and cannot apply to a child who is enrolled in health coverage within 30 days after birth, adoption, or placement for adoption.

If a plan imposes a preexisting condition exclusion, the length of the exclusion must be reduced by the amount of your prior creditable coverage. Most health coverage is creditable coverage, including group health plan coverage, COBRA continuation coverage, coverage under an individual health policy, Medicare, Medicaid, State Children's Health Insurance Program (SCHIP), and coverage through high-risk pools and the Peace Corps. Not all forms of creditable coverage are required to provide certificates like this one. If you do not receive a certificate for past coverage, talk to your new plan administrator.

You can add up any creditable coverage you have, including the coverage shown on this certificate. However, if at any time you went for 63 days or more without any coverage (called a break in coverage) a plan may not have to count the coverage you had before the break.

→ Therefore, once your coverage ends, you should try to obtain alternative coverage as soon as possible to avoid a 63-day break. You may use this certificate as evidence of your creditable coverage to reduce the length of any preexisting condition exclusion if you enroll in a group health plan.

Right to get special enrollment in another plan. Under HIPAA, if you lose your group health plan coverage, you may be able to get into another group health plan for which you are eligible (such as a spouse's plan), even if the plan generally does not accept late enrollees, if you request enrollment within 30 days. (Additional special enrollment rights are triggered by marriage, birth, adoption, and placement for adoption.)

→ Therefore, once your coverage in a group health plan ends, if you are eligible for coverage in another plan (such as a spouse's plan), you should request special enrollment as soon as possible.

Prohibition against discrimination based on a health factor. Under HIPAA, a group health plan may not keep you (or your dependents) out of the plan based on anything related to your health. Also, a group health plan may not charge you (or your dependents) more for coverage, based on health, than the amount charged a similarly situated individual.

Right to individual health coverage. Under HIPAA, if you are an "eligible individual," you have a right to buy certain individual health policies (or in some states, to buy coverage through a high-risk pool) without a preexisting condition exclusion. To be an eligible individual, you must meet the following requirements:

- You have had coverage for at least 18 months without a break in coverage of 63 days or more;
- Your most recent coverage was under a group health plan;
- Your group coverage was not terminated because of fraud or nonpayment of premiums;
- You are not eligible for COBRA continuation coverage or you have exhausted your COBRA benefits (or continuation coverage under a similar state provision); and
- You are not eligible for another group health plan, Medicare, or Medicaid, and do not have any other health insurance coverage.

The right to buy individual coverage is the same whether you are laid off, fired, or quit your job.

→ Therefore, if you are interested in obtaining individual coverage and you meet the other criteria to be an eligible individual, you should apply for this coverage as soon as possible to avoid losing your eligible individual status due to a 63-day break.

Special information for people on FMLA leave. If you are taking leave under the Family and Medical Leave Act (FMLA) and you drop health coverage during your leave, any days without health coverage while on FMLA leave will not count towards a 63-day break in coverage. In addition, if you do not return from leave, the 30-day period to request special enrollment in another plan will not start before your FMLA leave ends.

→ Therefore, when you apply for other health coverage, you should tell your plan administrator or health insurer about any prior FMLA leave.

State flexibility. This certificate describes minimum HIPAA protections under federal law. States may require insurers and HMOs to provide additional protections to individuals in that state.

For more information. If you have questions about your HIPAA rights, you may contact your state insurance department or the U.S. Department of Labor, Employee Benefits Security Administration (EBSA) toll-free at 1-866-444-3272 (for free HIPAA publications ask for publications concerning changes in health care laws). You may also contact the CMS publication hotline at 1-800-633-4227 (ask for "Protecting Your Health Insurance Coverage"). These publications and other useful information are also available on the Internet at: http://www.dol.gov/ebsa or http://www.cms.hhs.gov/hipaa1.

3. Special Enrollment Periods—26 CFR 54.9801-6, 29 CFR 2590.701-6, 45 CFR 146.117

Tolling of the Special Enrollment Period

Under HIPAA, the April 1997 interim rules, and the final regulations, an individual wishing to special enroll following a loss of coverage is generally required to request enrollment not later than 30 days after the loss of eligibility, termination of employer contributions, or exhaustion of COBRA continuation coverage. For individuals whose coverage ceases and a certificate of creditable coverage is not provided on or before the date coverage ceases, this regulation provides for proposed tolling rules similar to those described above for determining a significant break. That is, the special enrollment period terminates at the end of the 30-day period that begins on the first day after the earlier of the date that a certificate of creditable coverage is provided or the date 44 days after coverage ceases.

Modification of Special Enrollment Procedures and When Coverage Begins Under Special Enrollment

The April 1997 interim rules did not establish procedures for processing requests for special enrollment beyond affirming the statutory requirement that requests be made not later than 30 days after the event giving rise to the special enrollment right and providing that the same requirements could be imposed on special enrollees that were imposed on other enrollees (*e.g.,* that the request be made in writing). Some examples in the April 1997 interim rules could be read to suggest that plans and issuers could require individuals requesting special enrollment to file completed applications for health coverage by the end of the special enrollment period.

It has been brought to the Departments' attention that some plans and issuers were imposing application requirements that could not reasonably be completed within the special enrollment period (for example, requiring the social security number of a newborn within 30 days of the birth), effectively denying individuals their right to special enroll their dependents. In this regard, the statute merely requires an employee to request special enrollment, or an individual to seek to enroll, during the special enrollment period. These proposed regulations preserve individuals' access to special enrollment by clarifying that during the special enrollment period individuals are only required to make an oral or written request for special enrollment.

The proposed regulations provide further that after a timely request, the plan or issuer may require the individual to complete all enrollment materials within a reasonable time after the end of the special enrollment period. However, the enrollment procedure may only require information required from individuals who enroll when first eligible and information about the event giving rise to the special enrollment right. While a plan can impose a deadline for submitting the completed enrollment materials, the deadline must be extended for information that an individual making reasonable efforts cannot obtain within that deadline.

Thus, even where a plan requires social security numbers from individuals who enroll when first eligible, the plan must provide an extended deadline for receiving the social security number in the case of a newborn. In no event could a plan deny special enrollment for newborns because an employee could not provide a social security number for the newborn within the special enrollment period.

As regards the effective date of coverage for special enrollments, the proposed rules generally follow the statute, the April 1997 interim final rules, and the final regulations being published elsewhere in this issue of the **Federal Register.** However clarifications of the effective date of coverage are added to conform to the clarification of the special enrollment procedures. Where the special enrollment right results from a loss of eligibility for coverage or marriage, coverage generally must begin no later than the first day of the first calendar month after the date the plan or issuer receives the request for special enrollment. However, if the plan or issuer requires completion of additional enrollment materials, coverage must begin no later than the first day of the first calendar month after the plan or issuer receives enrollment materials that are substantially complete.

Where the special enrollment right results from a birth, coverage must begin on the date of birth. In the case of adoption or placement for adoption, coverage must begin no later than the date of such adoption or placement for adoption. If a plan or issuer requires completion of additional enrollment materials, the plan or issuer must provide benefits once the plan or issuer receives substantially complete enrollment materials. However, the benefits provided at that time must be retroactive to the date of birth, adoption, or placement for adoption.

The Departments welcome comments on these aspects of the proposed rule.

4. Interaction With the Family and Medical Leave Act—26 CFR 54.9801-7, 29 CFR 701-8, 45 CFR 146.120

The proposed rules address how the HIPAA portability requirements apply in situations where a person is on leave under the Family and Medical Leave Act of 1993 (FMLA). A general principle of FMLA is that an employee returning from leave under FMLA should generally be in the same position the employee was in before taking leave. At issue is how to reconcile that principle of FMLA with the HIPAA rights and requirements that are triggered by an individual ending coverage under a group health plan. These proposed regulations provide specific rules that clarify how HIPAA and FMLA interact when the coverage of an employee or an employee's dependent ends in connection with an employee taking leave under FMLA.

With respect to the rules concerning a significant break in coverage, if an employee takes FMLA leave and does not continue group health coverage for any part of the leave, the period of FMLA leave without coverage is not taken into account in determining whether a significant break in coverage has occurred for the employee or any dependents. To the extent an individual needs to demonstrate that coverage ceased in connection with FMLA leave (which would toll any significant break with respect to another plan or issuer), these regulations provide that a plan or issuer must take into account all information that it obtains about an employee's FMLA leave. Further, if an individual attests to the period of FMLA leave and the individual cooperates with a plan's or issuer's efforts to verify the individual's FMLA leave, the plan or issuer must treat the individual as having been on FMLA leave for the period attested to for purposes of determining if the individual had a significant break in coverage. Nonetheless, a plan or issuer is not prevented from modifying its initial determination of FMLA leave if it determines that the individual did not have the claimed FMLA leave, provided that the plan or issuer follows procedures for reconsideration similar to those set forth in the final rules governing determinations of creditable coverage.

The question has arisen whether it would be appropriate to waive the general requirement to provide automatic certificates of creditable coverage in the case of an individual who declines coverage when electing FMLA leave if the individual will be reinstated at the end of FMLA leave. At the time an employee elects FMLA leave, the employer (as well as the employee) may not know if the employee will later return from FMLA leave and elect to be reinstated. Requiring plans and issuers to provide certificates when individuals cease health coverage in connection with FMLA leave may result in some certificates being issued when individuals ceasing coverage will not need the certificates as evidence of coverage (because of later reinstatement). However, automatic issuance likely imposes less burden because the plan or issuer does not need to determine whether a certificate is required. Moreover, automatic issuance eliminates the need for remedial measures if an individual expected to be reinstated in fact is not later reinstated. Thus, these proposed regulations clarify there is no exception to the general rule requiring automatic certificates when coverage ends and provide that if an individual covered under a group health plan takes FMLA leave and ceases coverage under the plan, an automatic certificate must be provided.

With respect to the special enrollment rules, an individual (or a dependent of the individual) who is covered under a group health plan and who takes FMLA leave has a loss of eligibility that results in a special enrollment period if the individual's group health coverage is terminated at any time during FMLA leave and the individual does not return to work for the employer at the end of FMLA leave. This special enrollment period begins when the period of FMLA leave ends. Moreover, the rules that delay the start of the special enrollment period until the receipt of a certificate of creditable coverage continue to operate.

5. Special Rules—Excepted Plans and Excepted Benefits—26 CFR 54.9831-1, 29 CFR 2590.732, 45 CFR 146.145

Determination of Number of Plans

Various provisions in Chapter 100 of the Code, Part 7 of Subtitle B of Title I of ERISA, and Title XXVII of the PHS Act apply when an individual commences coverage or terminates coverage under a group health plan. For example, a certificate of creditable coverage must be provided when an individual ceases to be covered under a group health plan. Under the April 1997 interim rules, it was not always clear whether an individual changing benefit elections among those offered by an employer or employee organization was merely switching between benefit packages under a single plan or was switching from one plan to another. These proposed regulations add rules to remove this uncertainty.

Under these proposed regulations, all medical care benefits made available by an employer or employee organization (including a board of trustees of a multiemployer trust) are generally considered to constitute one group health plan (the default rule). However, the employer or employee organization can establish more than one group health plan if it is clear from the instruments governing the arrangements to provide medical care benefits that the benefits are being provided under separate plans and if the arrangements are operated pursuant to the instruments as separate plans. A multiemployer plan and a nonmultiemployer plan are always separate plans. Under an anti-abuse rule, separate plans are aggregated to the extent necessary to prevent the evasion of any legal requirement.

These rules provide plan sponsors great flexibility while minimizing the burden of making decisions about how many plans to maintain. For example, many employers may wish to minimize the number of certificates of creditable coverage required to be furnished to continuing employees. Under the default rule, because all health benefits provided by an employer are considered a single group health plan, there is no need to furnish a certificate of creditable coverage when an employee merely switches coverage among the options made available by the employer. This need would arise only if the employer designated separate benefit packages as separate plans in the plan documents and only if the benefit packages were also operated pursuant to the plan documents as separate plans.

The anti-abuse rule limits the flexibility of these rules to prevent evasions. For example, a plan sponsor might design an arrangement under which the participation of each of many employees in the arrangement would be considered a separate plan. On the face of it, such an arrangement might appear to satisfy the requirement for a plan being exempt from the requirements of Chapter 100 of the Code, Part 7 of ERISA, and Title XXVII of the PHS Act because on the first day of the plan year each plan would have fewer than two participants who are current employees. This would give the impression that the plans would not have to comply with the prohibitions against discriminating based on one or more health factors, with the restrictions on preexisting condition exclusions, nor with any of the other requirements of Chapter 100 of the Code, Part 7 of ERISA, and Title XXVII of the PHS Act. The anti-abuse rule would require the aggregation of plans under such an arrangement to the extent necessary to make the plans subject to the requirements of Chapter 100 of the Code, Part 7 of ERISA, and Title XXVII of the PHS Act. The anti-abuse rule would apply in similar fashion to prevent the evasion of any other law that applies to group health plans or to the parties administering them or providing benefits under them.

Counting the Average Number of Employees

These proposed regulations add rules for counting the average number of employees employed by an employer during a year.[1] Various rules in Chapter 100 of the Code, Part 7 of ERISA, and Title XXVII of the PHS Act require the determination of such an average number, including the Mental Health Parity Act provisions, the guaranteed access provisions under the PHS Act for small employers, and the exemption from the excise tax under the Code for certain small employers.

Under these proposed regulations, the average number of employees employed by an employer is determined by using a full-time equivalents method. Each full-time employee employed for the entire previous calendar year counts as one employee. Full-time employees employed less than the entire previous calendar year and part-time employees are counted by totaling their employment hours in the previous calendar year (but not to exceed 40 hours for any week) and dividing that number by the annual full-time hours under the employer's general employment practices (but not exceeding 40 hours per week). Any resulting fraction is disregarded. For example, if these calculations produce a result of 50.9, the average number of employees is considered to be 50. If an employer existed for less than the entire previous calendar year (including not being in existence at all), then the determination of the average number of employees is made by estimating the average number of employees that it is reasonably expected that the employer will employ on business days in the current calendar year. For a multiemployer plan, the number of employees employed by the employer with the most employees is attributed to each employer with at least one employee participating in the plan.

Economic Impact and Paperwork Burden

Summary—Department of Labor and Department of Health and Human Services

HIPAA's group market portability provisions, which limit the scope and application of preexisting condition exclusions and establish special enrollment rights, provide a minimum standard of protection designed to increase access to health coverage. The Departments crafted these proposed regulations to secure these protections under certain special circumstances, consistent with the intent of Congress, and to do so in a manner that is economically efficient. The Departments are unable to quantify the regulations' economic benefits and costs, but believe that their benefits will justify their costs.

HIPAA's primary economic effects ensue directly from its statutory provisions. HIPAA's statutory group market portability provisions extend coverage to certain individuals and preexisting conditions not otherwise covered. This extension of coverage entails both benefits and costs. Individuals enjoying expanded coverage will realize benefits, sometimes including improvements in health and relief from so-called "job lock." The costs of HIPAA's portability provisions generally include the cost of extending coverage, as well as certain attendant administrative costs. The Departments believe that the benefits of HIPAA are concentrated in a relatively small population, while the costs are distributed broadly across group plan enrollees. The economic effects of HIPAA's statutory portability provisions are discussed in detail in the preamble to the final regulation under the "Effects of the Statute" of the "Basis for Assessment of Economic Impact" section, published elsewhere in this issue of the **Federal Register**.

By clarifying and securing HIPAA's statutory portability protections, these proposed regulations will help ensure that HIPAA rights are fully realized. The result is likely to be a small increase at the margin in the economic effects of HIPAA's statutory portability provisions.

These proposed regulations are intended to secure and implement HIPAA's group market portability and special enrollment provisions under certain special circumstances. The regulations will secure HIPAA's portability rights for individuals who are not timely notified that their coverage has ended and for individuals whose coverage ends in connection with the taking of leave that is guaranteed under FMLA. The regulations also will clarify and thereby secure individuals' special enrollment rights under HIPAA, and clarify the methodologies to be used by employers to determine the number of plans offered and the average number of individuals employed during a given year.

Additional economic benefits derive from the regulations' clarifications of HIPAA requirements. The regulations will reduce uncertainty and costly disputes between employees, employers and issuers, and promote confidence among employees in health benefits' value, thereby promoting labor market efficiency and fostering the establishment and continuation by employers of group health plans.

Benefits under these regulations will be concentrated among a small number of affected individuals while costs will be spread thinly across group plan enrollees.

Affected individuals will generally include those who would have lost access to coverage for needed medical care after being denied HIPAA portability and/or special enrollment rights due to time spent without coverage prior to receiving a certificate or while on FMLA-guaranteed leave. The benefits of these regulations for any particular affected individual may be significant. As noted above and under "Effects of the Statute" in the "Basis for Assessment of Economic Impact" section of the preamble to the final regulation, published elsewhere in this issue of the **Federal Register**, access to coverage for needed medical care is important to individuals' health and productivity. However, the number of affected individuals, and therefore the aggregate cost of extended access to coverage under these regulations, is expected to be small, for several reasons. First, these regulations extend HIPAA rights only in instances where individuals are not timely notified that their coverage has ended or their coverage ends in connection with the taking of FMLA-guaranteed leave. Second, the period over which this regulation extends rights will often be short, insofar as certificates are often provided promptly after coverage ends and many family leave periods are far shorter than the guaranteed 12 weeks. Third, it is generally in individuals' interest to minimize periods of uninsurance. Individuals are likely to exercise their portability and special enrollment rights as soon as possible after coverage ends, which will often be before any extension of such rights under these regulations becomes effective. Fourth, only a portion of individuals who enroll in health plans in circum-

---

[1] The rules for determining the average number of employees employed by an employer during a year are not used for counting the number employed by the employer on a given day, such as the first day of a plan year.

stances where these regulations alone guarantee their special enrollment or portability rights would otherwise have been denied such rights. Fifth, only a small minority of individuals who avoid a significant break in coverage as a direct result of these regulations would otherwise have lost coverage for needed medical care. (The affected minority would be those who suffer from preexisting conditions, join health plans that exclude coverage for such conditions, and require treatment of such conditions during the exclusion periods.)

Affected individuals may also include some who would have been denied special enrollment rights if plans or issuers failed to recognize their requests for special enrollment or imposed unreasonable deadlines or requirements for completion of enrollment materials.

As noted above, the Departments expect that these regulations will increase at the margin the economic effects of HIPAA's statutory portability provisions. For the reasons stated immediately above, the Departments believe that these increases will be small on aggregate, adding only a small increment to the costs attributable to HIPAA's statutory portability provisions, which themselves amount to a small fraction of one percent of health plan expenditures. Additionally, as with the cost of HIPAA's statutory portability provisions, the majority of these costs will be borne by group plan enrollees. The Departments expect these regulations to have little or no perceptible negative impact on employers' propensity to offer health benefit plans or on the generosity of those plans. In sum, the Departments expect that the benefits of these regulations, which can be very large for a particular affected individual, will justify their costs. The basis for the Departments' conclusions is detailed below.

The Departments solicit comments on their conclusions and their basis for them, and empirical data or other information that would support a fuller or more accurate analysis.

Executive Order 12866—Department of Labor and Department of Health and Human Services

Under Executive Order 12866 (58 FR 551735, Oct. 4, 1993), the Departments must determine whether a regulatory action is "significant" and therefore subject to the requirements of the Executive Order and subject to review by the Office of Management and Budget (OMB). Under section 3(f), the order defines a "significant regulatory action" as an action that is likely to result in a rule: (1) Having an annual effect on the economy of $100 million or more, or adversely and materially affecting a sector of the economy, productivity, competition, jobs, the environment, public health or safety, or state, local or tribal governments or communities (also referred to as "economically significant"); (2) creating serious inconsistency or otherwise interfering with an action taken or planned by another agency; (3) materially altering the budgetary impacts of entitlement grants, user fees, or loan programs or the rights and obligations of recipients thereof; or (4) raising novel legal or policy issues arising out of legal mandates, the President's priorities, or the principles set forth in the Executive Order.

Pursuant to the terms of the Executive Order, the Departments have determined that this action raises novel policy issues arising out of legal mandates. Therefore, this notice is "significant" and subject to OMB review under Section 3(f)(4) of the Executive Order. Consistent with the Executive Order, the Departments have assessed the costs and benefits of this regulatory action. The Departments' assessment, and the analysis underlying that assessment, is detailed below. The Departments performed a comprehensive, unified analysis to estimate the costs and benefits attributable to the regulations for purposes of compliance with Executive Order 12866, the Regulatory Flexibility Act, and the Paperwork Reduction Act.

Statement of Need for Proposed Action

These proposed regulations clarify and interpret the HIPAA portability provisions under Section 701 of the Employee Retirement Income Security Act of 1974 (ERISA), Section 2701 of the Public Health Service Act, and Section 9801 of the Internal Revenue Code of 1986. The regulations are needed to secure and implement HIPAA's portability rights for individuals who are not timely notified that their coverage has ended and for individuals whose coverage ends in connection with the taking of leave that is guaranteed under FMLA, and to clarify and secure individuals' special enrollment rights under HIPAA.

Economic Effects

As noted above, HIPAA's primary economic effects ensue directly from its statutory provisions. HIPAA's statutory group market portabil-

ity provisions extend coverage to certain individuals and preexisting conditions not otherwise covered. This extension of coverage entails both benefits and costs. The economic effects of HIPAA's statutory portability provisions is summarized above and discussed in detail under the "Basis for Assessment of Economic Impact" section of the preamble to the final regulation, published elsewhere in this issue of the **Federal Register**.

Also as noted above, by clarifying and securing HIPAA's statutory portability protections, these regulations will help ensure that HIPAA rights are fully realized. The result is likely to be a small increase at the margin in the economic effects of HIPAA's statutory portability provisions. The benefits of these regulations will be concentrated among a small number of affected individuals, while their costs will be spread thinly across plans and issuers. The regulations also will reduce uncertainty about health benefits' scope and value, thereby promoting employee health benefit coverage and labor market efficiency. The Departments believe that the regulations' benefits will justify their cost. The Departments assessment of the expected economic effects of the regulation are summarized above and discussed in detail below.

Regulatory Flexibility Act—The Department of Labor and Department of Health and Human Services

The Regulatory Flexibility Act (5 U.S.C. 601 *et seq.*) (RFA), imposes certain requirements with respect to Federal rules that are subject to the notice and comment requirements of section 553(b) of the Administrative Procedure Act (5 U.S.C. 551 *et seq.*) and which are likely to have a significant economic impact on a substantial number of small entities. Section 603 of the RFA stipulates that an agency, unless it certifies that a proposed rule will not have a significant economic impact on a substantial number of small entities, must present an initial regulatory flexibility analysis at the time of publication of the notice of proposed rulemaking that describes the impact of the rule on small entities and seeks public comment on such impact. Small entities include small businesses, organizations, and governmental jurisdictions.

For purposes of analysis under the RFA, the Departments consider a small entity to be an employee benefit plan with fewer than 100 participants. The basis for this definition is found in section 104(a)(2) of ERISA, which permits the Secretary of Labor to prescribe simplified annual reports for pension plans which cover fewer than 100 participants. Under section 104(a)(3), the Secretary may also provide for simplified annual reporting and disclosure if the statutory requirements of part 1 of Title I of ERISA would otherwise be inappropriate for welfare benefit plans. Pursuant to the authority of section 104(a)(3), the Department of Labor has previously issued at 29 CFR 2520.104-20, 2520.104-21, 2520.104-41, 2520.104-46 and 2520.104b-10 certain simplified reporting provisions and limited exemptions from reporting and disclosure requirements for small plans, including unfunded or insured welfare plans covering fewer than 100 participants and which satisfy certain other requirements.

Further, while some small plans are maintained by large employers, most are maintained by small employers. Both small and large plans may enlist small third party service providers to perform administrative functions, but it is generally understood that third party service providers transfer their costs to their plan clients in the form of fees. Thus, the Departments believe that assessing the impact of this rule on small plans is an appropriate substitute for evaluating the effect on small entities. The definition of small entity considered appropriate for this purpose differs, however, from a definition of small business based on size standards promulgated by the Small Business Administration (SBA) (13 CFR 121.201) pursuant to the Small Business Act (5 U.S.C. 631 *et seq.*). The Department of Labor solicited comments on the use of this standard for evaluating the effects of the proposal on small entities. No comments were received with respect to the standard. Therefore, a summary of the initial regulatory flexibility analysis based on the 100 participant size standard is presented below.

The economic effects of HIPAA's statutory provisions on small plans are discussed extensively under the "Regulatory Flexibility Act—Department of Labor and Department of Health and Human Services" section of the preamble to the final regulation, published elsewhere in this issue of the **Federal Register**.

By clarifying and securing HIPAA's statutory portability protections, these regulations will help ensure that these benefits are fully realized. The result is likely to be a small increase in the economic effects of HIPAA's statutory provisions. The Departments were unable to estimate the amount of this increase. However, the direct financial value of coverage extensions pursuant to HIPAA's statutory portability provisions are estimated to be approximately $180 million for small plans, or a small fraction of one percent of total small plan expenditures.[2]

The regulations also will reduce uncertainty about health benefits' scope and value, thereby promoting employee health benefit coverage, including coverage under small plans, and labor market efficiency.

The benefits of these regulations will be concentrated among a small number of affected small group plan enrollees, while their costs will be spread thinly across small group plans enrollees. The benefits of these regulations for any particular affected individual, which may include improved health and productivity, may be significant. However, as previously noted, the number of affected individuals, and therefore the aggregate cost of these regulations, is expected to be small. The Departments believe that the benefits to affected individuals of the application of these regulations to small plans justify the cost to small plans of such application. The basis for the Departments' conclusions is detailed below.

The Departments generally expect the impact of the regulations on any particular small plan to be small. A very large majority of small plans are fully insured, so the cost will fall nominally on issuers rather than from plans. Issuers are expected to pass this cost back to plans and enrollees, but will spread much of it across a large number of plans, thereby minimizing the impact on any particular plan. However, it is possible that small plans that self-insure, or fully insured small plans whose premiums are tied closely to their particular claims experience, might bear all or most of the cost associated with extensions of coverage attributable directly to these regulations. The Departments have no way to quantify the incidence or magnitude of such costs, and solicit comments on such incidence and magnitude, and on whether these regulations would have a significant impact on a substantial number of small plans.

Special Analyses—Department of the Treasury

Notwithstanding the determinations of the Departments of Labor and of Health and Human Services, for purposes of the Department of the Treasury this notice of proposed rulemaking is not a significant regulatory action. Because this notice of proposed rulemaking does not impose a collection of information on small entities and is not subject to section 553(b) of the Administrative Procedure Act (5 U.S.C. chapter 5), the Regulatory Flexibility Act (5 U.S.C. chapter 6) does not apply pursuant to 5 U.S.C. 603(a), which exempts from the Regulatory Flexibility Act's requirements certain rules involving the internal revenue laws. Pursuant to section 7805(f) of the Internal Revenue Code, this notice of proposed rulemaking will be submitted to the Chief Counsel for Advocacy of the Small Business Administration for comment on its impact on small business.

Paperwork Reduction Act

Department of Labor

These proposed regulations include three separate collections of information as that term is defined in the Paperwork Reduction Act of 1995 (PRA 95), 44 U.S.C. 3502(3): the Notice of Enrollment Rights, Notice of Preexisting Condition Exclusion, and Certificate of Creditable Coverage. Each of these disclosures is currently approved by the Office of Management and Budget (OMB) through October 31, 2006 in accordance with PRA 95 under control numbers 1210-0101, 1210-0102, and 1210-0103.

Department of the Treasury

These proposed regulations include a collection of information as that term is defined in PRA 95: the Notice of Enrollment Rights, Notice of Preexisting Condition Exclusion, and Certificate of Creditable Coverage. Each of these disclosures is currently approved by OMB under control number 1545-1537.

Department of Health and Human Services

These proposed regulations include three separate collections of information as that term is defined in PRA 95: the Notice of Enrollment Rights, Notice of Preexisting Condition Exclusion, and Certificate of Creditable Coverage. Each of these disclosures is currently approved

by OMB through June 30, 2006 in accordance with PRA 95 under control number 0938-0702.

Small Business Regulatory Enforcement Fairness Act

The rule being issued here is subject to the provisions of the Small Business Regulatory Enforcement Fairness Act of 1996 (5 U.S.C. 801 *et seq.*) and, if finalized, will be transmitted to Congress and the Comptroller General for review. The rule is not a "major rule" as that term is defined in 5 U.S.C. 804, because it is not likely to result in (1) an annual effect on the economy of $100 million or more; (2) a major increase in costs or prices for consumers, individual industries, or federal, state, or local government agencies, or geographic regions; or (3) significant adverse effects on competition, employment, investment, productivity, innovation, or on the ability of United States-based enterprises to compete with foreign-based enterprises in domestic or export markets.

Unfunded Mandates Reform Act

Section 202 of the Unfunded Mandates Reform Act of 1995 requires that agencies assess anticipated costs and benefits before issuing any rule that may result in an expenditure in any 1 year by state, local, or tribal governments, in the aggregate, or by the private sector, of $100 million. These proposed regulations have no such mandated consequential effect on state, local, or tribal governments, or on the private sector.

Federalism Statement Under Executive Order 13132— Department of Labor and Department of Health and Human Services

Executive Order 13132 outlines fundamental principles of federalism. It requires adherence to specific criteria by federal agencies in formulating and implementing policies that have "substantial direct effects" on the States, the relationship between the national government and States, or on the distribution of power and responsibilities among the various levels of government. Federal agencies promulgating regulations that have these federalism implications must consult with State and local officials, and describe the extent of their consultation and the nature of the concerns of State and local officials in the preamble to the regulation.

In the Departments' view, these proposed regulations have federalism implications because they may have substantial direct effects on the States, the relationship between the national government and States, or on the distribution of power and responsibilities among the various levels of government. However, in the Departments' view, the federalism implications of these proposed regulations are substantially mitigated because, with respect to health insurance issuers, the vast majority of States have enacted laws which meet or exceed the federal HIPAA portability standards.

In general, through section 514, ERISA supersedes State laws to the extent that they relate to any covered employee benefit plan, and preserves State laws that regulate insurance, banking or securities. While ERISA prohibits States from regulating a plan as an insurance or investment company or bank, HIPAA added a new section to ERISA (as well as to the PHS Act) narrowly preempting State requirements for issuers of group health insurance coverage. Specifically, with respect to seven provisions of the HIPAA portability rules, states may impose stricter obligations on health insurance issuers.[3] Moreover, with respect to other requirements for health insurance issuers, states may continue to apply state law requirements except to the extent that such requirements prevent the application of HIPAA's portability, access, and renewability provisions.

In enacting these new preemption provisions, Congress intended to preempt State insurance requirements only to the extent that they prevent the application of the basic protections set forth in HIPAA. HIPAA's conference report states that the conferees intended the narrowest preemption of State laws with regard to health insurance issuers. H.R. Conf. Rep. No. 736, 104th Cong. 2d Session 205 (1996). State insurance laws that are more stringent than the federal requirements are unlikely to "prevent the application of" the HIPAA portability provisions, and be preempted. Accordingly, States have significant latitude to impose requirements on health insurance insurers that are more restrictive than the federal law.

---

[2] Computer runs using Medical Expenditure Survey Household Component (MEPS-HC) and the Robert Wood Johnson Employer Health Benefits Survey determined that the share of covered private-sector job leavers at small firms average 35 percent of all covered private sector job leavers. From this, we inferred that the financial burden borne by small plans is approximately 35 percent of the total expenditures by private-sector group health plans which was estimated to be $515 million.

[3] States may shorten the six-month look-back period prior to the enrollment date; shorten the 12-month and 18-month maximum preexisting condition exclusion periods;

increase the 63-day significant break in coverage period; increase the 30-day period for newborns, adopted children, and children placed for adoption to enroll in the plan with no preexisting condition exclusion; further limit the circumstances in which a preexisting condition exclusion may be applied (beyond the federal exceptions for certain newborns, adopted children, children placed for adoption, pregnancy, and genetic information in the absence of a diagnosis; require additional special enrollment periods; and reduce the HMO affiliation period to less than 2 months (3 months for late enrollees).

Guidance conveying this interpretation of HIPAA's preemption provisions was published in the **Federal Register** on April 8, 1997, 62 FR 16904. These proposed regulations clarify and implement the statute's minimum standards and do not significantly reduce the discretion given the States by the statute. Moreover, the Departments understand that the vast majority of States have requirements that meet or exceed the minimum requirements of the HIPAA portability provisions.

HIPAA provides that the States may enforce the provisions of HIPAA as they pertain to issuers, but that the Secretary of Health and Human Services must enforce any provisions that a State fails to substantially enforce. To date, CMS enforces the HIPAA portability provisions in only one State in accordance with that State's specific request to do so. When exercising its responsibility to enforce the provisions of HIPAA, CMS works cooperatively with the State for the purpose of addressing the State's concerns and avoiding conflicts with the exercise of State authority. CMS has developed procedures to implement its enforcement responsibilities, and to afford the States the maximum opportunity to enforce HIPAA's requirements in the first instance. CMS's procedures address the handling of reports that States may not be enforcing HIPAA's requirements, and the mechanism for allocating responsibility between the States and CMS. In compliance with Executive Order 13132's requirement that agencies examine closely any policies that may have federalism implications or limit the policymaking discretion of the States, the Department of Labor and CMS have engaged in numerous efforts to consult and work cooperatively with affected State and local officials.

For example, the Departments sought and received input from State insurance regulators and the National Association of Insurance Commissioners (NAIC). The NAIC is a non-profit corporation established by the insurance commissioners of the 50 States, the District of Columbia, and the four U.S. territories. In most States the Insurance Commissioner is appointed by the Governor, in approximately 14 States, the insurance commissioner is an elected official. Among other activities, it provides a forum for the development of uniform policy when uniformity is appropriate. Its members meet, discuss and offer solutions to mutual problems. The NAIC sponsors quarterly meetings to provide a forum for the exchange of ideas and in-depth consideration of insurance issues by regulators, industry representatives and consumers. CMS and the Department of Labor staff have consistently attended these quarterly meetings to listen to the concerns of the State Insurance Departments regarding HIPAA portability issues. In addition to the general discussions, committee meetings, and task groups, the NAIC sponsors the standing CMS/DOL meeting on HIPAA issues for members during the quarterly conferences. This meeting provides CMS and the Department of Labor with the opportunity to provide updates on regulations, bulletins, enforcement actions, and outreach efforts regarding HIPAA.

The Departments received written comments on the interim regulation from the NAIC and from ten States. In general, these comments raised technical issues that the Departments considered in conjunction with similar issues raised by other commenters. In a letter sent before issuance of the interim regulation, the NAIC expressed concerns that the Departments interpret the new preemption provisions of HIPAA narrowly so as to give the States flexibility to impose more stringent requirements. As discussed above, the Departments address this concern in the preamble to the interim regulation.

In addition, the Departments specifically consulted with the NAIC in developing these proposed regulations. Through the NAIC, the Departments sought and received the input of State insurance departments regarding certain insurance industry definitions, enrollment procedures and standard coverage terms. This input is generally reflected in the discussion of comments received and changes made in Section B— Overview of the Regulations of the preamble to the final regulations published elsewhere in this issue of the **Federal Register**.

The Departments have also cooperated with the States in several ongoing outreach initiatives, through which information on HIPAA is shared among federal regulators, State regulators and the regulated

community. In particular, the Department of Labor has established a Health Benefits Education Campaign with more than 70 partners, including CMS, NAIC and many business and consumer groups. CMS has sponsored conferences with the States—the Consumer Outreach and Advocacy conferences in March 1999 and June 2000, and the Implementation and Enforcement of HIPAA National State-Federal Conferences in August 1999, 2000, 2001, 2002, and 2003. Furthermore, both the Department of Labor and CMS Web sites offer links to important State web sites and other resources, facilitating coordination between the State and federal regulators and the regulated community.

Throughout the process of developing these regulations, to the extent feasible within the specific preemption provisions of HIPAA, the Departments have attempted to balance the States' interests in regulating health insurance issuers, and the Congress' intent to provide uniform minimum protections to consumers in every State. By doing so, it is the Departments' view that they have complied with the requirements of Executive Order 13132.

Pursuant to the requirements set forth in Section 8(a) of Executive Order 13132, and by the signatures affixed to proposed final regulations, the Departments certify that the Employee Benefits Security Administration and the Centers for Medicare & Medicaid Services have complied with the requirements of Executive Order 13132 for the attached proposed regulation, Notice of Proposed Rulemaking for Health Coverage Portability: Tolling and Certain Time Periods and Interaction with the Family and Medical Leave Act under HIPAA Titles I & IV (RIN 1210-AA54 and RIN 0938-AL88), in a meaningful and timely manner.

Basis for Assessment of Economic Impact—Department of Labor and Department of Health and Human Services

As noted above, the primary economic effects of HIPAA's portability provisions ensue directly from the statute. The Department's assessment of the economic effects of HIPAA's statutory portability provisions and the basis for the assessment is presented in detail under the "Basis for Assessment of Economic Impact" section of the preamble to the final regulation, published elsewhere in this issue of the **Federal Register**. By clarifying and securing HIPAA's statutory portability protections, these regulations will help ensure that HIPAA rights are fully realized. The result is likely to be a small increase in the economic effects of HIPAA's statutory portability provisions.

Additional economic benefits derive from the regulations' clarifications of HIPAA's portability requirements. The regulations provide clarity through both their provisions and their examples of how those provisions apply in various circumstances. By clarifying employees' rights and plan sponsors' obligations under HIPAA's portability provisions, the regulations will reduce uncertainty and costly disputes over these rights and obligations. They will promote employers' and employees' common understanding of the value of group health plan benefits and confidence in the security and predictability of those benefits, thereby improving labor market efficiency and fostering the establishment and continuation of group health plans by employers.[4]

These proposed regulations are intended to secure and implement HIPAA's group market portability provisions under certain special circumstances. The regulations will secure HIPAA's portability rights for individuals who are not timely notified that their coverage has ended and for individuals whose coverage ends in connection with the taking of leave that is guaranteed under FMLA. The regulations also will clarify and thereby secure individuals' special enrollment rights under HIPAA, and clarify the methodologies to be used by employers to determine the number of plans offered and the average number of individuals employed during a given year.

The benefits of these regulations will be concentrated among a small number of affected individuals.

Affected individuals will generally include those who would have lost access to coverage for needed medical care after forfeiting HIPAA portability and/or special enrollment rights due to time spent without

---

[4] The voluntary nature of the employment-based health benefit system in conjunction with the open and dynamic character of labor markets make explicit as well as implicit negotiations on compensation a key determinant of the prevalence of employee benefits coverage. It is likely that 80% to 100% of the cost of employee benefits is borne by workers through reduced wages (see for example Jonathan Gruber and Alan B. Krueger, "The Incidence of Mandated Employer-Provided Insurance: Lessons from Workers Compensation Insurance," in, David Bradford, ed., *Tax Policy and Economy*, pp.111-143 (Cambridge, MA: MIT Press, 1991); Jonathan Gruber, "The Incidence of Mandated Maternity Benefits," *American Economic Review*, Vol. 84 no. 3 (June 1994), pp. 622-641; Lawrence H. Summers, "Some Simple Economics of Mandated Benefits," *American Economic Review*, Vol. 79, No. 2 (May 1989), pp.177-183; Louise Sheiner, "Health Care Costs, Wages, and Aging," Federal Reserve Board of Governors working paper, April 1999; Mark Pauly and Brad Herring, *Pooling Health Insurance Risks* (Washington, DC: AEI Press, 1999), Gail A. Jensen and

Michael A. Morrisey, "Endogenous Fringe Benefits, Compensating Wage Differentials and Older Workers," *International Journal of Health Care Finance and Economics* Vol 1, No. 3-4 (forthcoming), and Edward Montgomery, Kathryn Shaw, and Mary Ellen Benedict, "Pensions and Wages: An Hedonic Price Theory Approach," *International Economic Review*, Vol. 33 No. 1 (Feb. 1992.), pp.111-128.) The prevalence of benefits is therefore largely dependent on the efficacy of this exchange. If workers perceive that there is the potential for inappropriate denial of benefits they will discount their value to adjust for this risk. This discount drives a wedge in the compensation negotiation, limiting its efficiency. With workers unwilling to bear the full cost of the benefit, fewer benefits will be provided. The extent to which workers perceive a federal regulation supported by enforcement authority to improve the security and quality of benefits, the differential between the employers costs and workers willingness to accept wage offsets is minimized.

coverage prior to receiving a certificate or while on FMLA-guaranteed leave. Affected individuals may also include some who would have been denied special enrollment rights if plans or issuers failed to recognize their requests for special enrollment or imposed unreasonable deadlines or requirements for completion of enrollment materials. The benefits of these regulations for any particular affected individual may be large. As noted above, access to coverage for needed medical care is important to individuals' health and productivity. However, the number of affected individuals, and therefore the aggregate cost of extended access to coverage under these regulations, is expected to be small, for several reasons.

First, these regulations extend HIPAA rights only in instances where individuals do not receive certificates immediately when coverage ends or their coverage ends in connection with the taking of FMLA-guaranteed leave. The Departments know of no source of data on the timeliness with which certificates are typically provided. The final regulations that accompany these proposed regulations permit plans to provide certificates with COBRA notices, up to 44 days after coverage ends. Plans, however, often do have the option of providing certificates immediately when coverage ends or even in advance, for example as part of exit packages given to terminating employees or in mailings to covered dependents in advance of birthdays that will end their eligibility for coverage. With respect to FMLA-protected leave, data provided in a 1996 report to Congress suggests that the number of employees who lose coverage in connection with FMLA-protected leave is likely to be small. The report notes that over an 18-month period just 1.2 percent of surveyed employees took what they reported to be FMLA leave. A similar survey of employers found that 3.6 percent of employees took such leave. Nearly all of those taking leave continued their health coverage. (This is not surprising, given that FMLA requires covered employers to extend eligibility for health insurance to employees on FMLA-protected leave on the same terms that applied when the employees were not on leave.) Just 9 percent of leave-takers reported that they lost some kind of employee benefit, with one-third of these reporting that they lost health insurance.[5] Putting these numbers together and converting to an annual basis, in a given year between 0.02 percent and 0.07 percent of employees, or well under one in one thousand, might lose health coverage in connection with FMLA-protected leave. Many of these will ultimately exercise their right to be reinstated in the job from which they took leave and to exercise their FMLA-guaranteed right to resume their previous health coverage. Therefore, the number of employees who will lose coverage and then, later and at the conclusion of FMLA-protected leave, enjoy extended portability rights under HIPAA as a result of these regulations, is likely to be very small.

Second, the period over which this regulation extends rights will often be short, insofar as certificates are often provided promptly after coverage ends and many family leave periods are far shorter than the guaranteed 12 weeks. As noted above, plans generally are required to provide certificates no later than 44 days after coverage ends and may provide them sooner. According to the aforementioned report to Congress on FMLA-protected leave, 41 percent of employees taking FMLA-protected leave did so for less than 8 days. Fifty-eight percent were on leave for less than 15 days, and two-thirds were on leave for less than 29 days. (FMLA protects leaves of up to 12 weeks, or 84 days.)

Third, it is generally in individuals' interest to minimize periods of uninsurance. Individuals are likely to exercise their portability and special enrollment rights as soon as possible after coverage ends, which will often be before any extension of such rights under these regulations becomes effective. Over one 36-month period prior to HIPAA, 71 percent of Americans had continuous coverage—that is, incurred not even a single, one-month break in coverage. Just 4 percent were uninsured for the entire period. About one-half of observed spells without insurance lasted less than 5 months. As noted above, few employees taking FMLA-protected leave had a lapse in health coverage.

Fourth, only a portion of individuals who enroll in health plans in circumstances where these regulations alone guarantee their special enrollment or portability rights would otherwise have been denied such rights. HIPAA special enrollment and portability requirements, both as specified under the final regulations and as modified under

these proposed regulations, are minimum standards. Plans are free to provide additional enrollment opportunities.

Fifth, only a small minority of individuals who avoid a significant break in coverage solely as a direct result of these regulations would otherwise have lost coverage for needed medical care. The affected minority would be those who suffer from preexisting conditions, join health plans that exclude coverage for such conditions, and require treatment of such conditions during the exclusion periods. GAO estimated that HIPAA could ensure continued coverage for up to 25 million Americans.[6] More recent estimates suggest that the number of individual policy holders and their dependents which could be helped by HIPAA's portability provisions are more in the 14 million range.[7] As noted above, however, the number of workers and dependents actually gaining coverage for a preexisting condition due to credit for prior coverage following a job change under HIPAA will be smaller than this. Both GAO's and our estimates of people who could benefit include all job changers with prior coverage and their dependents, irrespective of whether their new employer offers a plan, whether their new plan imposed a preexisting condition exclusion period, and whether they actually suffer from a preexisting condition. Accounting for these narrower criteria, CBO estimated that, at any point in time, about 100,000 individuals would have a preexisting condition exclusion reduced for prior creditable coverage. An additional 45,000 would gain added coverage in the individual market. The CBO estimate demonstrates that the number of individuals actually gaining coverage for needed medical services will be a small fraction of all those whose right to such coverage HIPAA's portability provisions guarantee. Accordingly, the Departments expect that the number gaining coverage for needed services as a direct result of these regulations will be a small fraction of the already small number whose right to such coverage these regulations would establish.

The Departments attempted to estimate the number of individuals who might avoid a break in coverage because of the provision of these proposed regulations that tolls the break until the individual receives a certification but not more than 44 days. The Departments examined coverage patterns evident in the Survey of Income and Program Participation (SIPP), a longitudinal household survey that tracks transitions in coverage. SIPP interviews households once every four months. The Departments estimate that, in a given year, about 7 million individuals have breaks in coverage lasting 4 months or less. The survey data suffer from so-called "seam bias"—respondents tend to report that status as unchanged over 4-month increments. Of the 7 million reporting breaks of 4 months or less, 6.5 million report breaks of exactly 4 months. This finding is consistent with the more general finding that breaks of 4 months or less are far more common than longer breaks. It seems likely that the 7 million breaks of 4 months or less actually included proportionate or disproportionately large shares of breaks of 1 or 2 months. Assuming the breaks are actually distributed evenly by length between 1 day and 4 months, then about one-half of the breaks, or 3.5 million breaks, would have lasted less than 63 days and therefore would not have constituted breaks for purposes of HIPAA's portability protections even without reference to the provision of this proposed regulation that tolls the break until the individual receives a certification but not more than 44 days. Approximately three-fourths of the remaining breaks or about 2.6 million breaks, would have lasted between 1 and 44 additional days and thereby potentially have been tolled until the individuals received their certifications but not more than 44 days. Thus 2.6 million provides a reasonable upper bound on the number of individuals who might avoid a break in coverage in a given year because of this tolling provision. It is not known what fraction of these would subsequently join group health plans that include preexisting condition exclusions while suffering from and requiring additional care for preexisting conditions. Comparing GAO's (20 million or more) and our (14 million) estimates of the number of individuals who could potentially benefit from HIPAA's portability protections (individuals with prior creditable coverage who join new health plans in a given year) with the CBO estimate of the number who might actually have added group coverage for needed care (100,000) produces a ratio of about 1 percent. If this proportion holds for group health plan enrollees who avoid breaks because of this tolling provision, then an upper bound of about 26,000 individuals annually might gain coverage for needed care under the proposed regulation's provision treating coverage under such programs as creditable coverage.

---

[5] Commission on Family and Medical Leave and U.S. Department of Labor, *A Workable Balance: Report to Congress on Family and Medical Leave Policies,* transmitted April 30, 1996.

[6] U.S. General Accounting Office, Report HEHS-95-257, "Health Insurance Portability: Reform Could Ensure Continued Coverage for up to 25 Million Americans," September 1995.

[7] We calculated these estimates using internal runs off the MEPS-HC. These runs gave the number of total job changers, total job changers that had employer-sponsored insurance (ESI), and whether this coverage had been for less than 12 months or not. Estimates for dependents were based off the ratio of policy-holders to total dependents from the March 2003 Current Population Survey (March CPS). It should be noted, however, that the EBSA estimate of 14 million does not include estimate of individuals no longer eligible for COBRA continuation coverage or individuals facing job lock, while the GAO numbers do.

The Departments considered whether certain individuals whose HIPAA portability rights these proposed regulations would extend may be disproportionately likely to be in (or have dependents who are in) poor health. Specifically, individuals taking FMLA-protected leave, especially those who elect not to be reinstated in their prior jobs following FMLA-protected leave, may be so likely. On the other hand, individuals in such circumstances are also particularly unlikely to allow their health insurance from their prior job to lapse while they are on leave. Accordingly, most such individuals' special enrollment periods and countable breaks in coverage (if any) would probably have begun at the conclusion of the FMLA-protected leave even in absence of these proposed regulations. The Departments are therefore uncertain whether individuals who would exercise HIPAA portability rights extended solely by these regulations would be more costly to insure than others exercising HIPAA portability rights, and solicit comments on this question.

Affected individuals may also include some who would have been denied special enrollment rights if plans or issuers failed to recognize their requests for special enrollment or imposed unreasonable deadlines or requirements for completion of enrollment materials.

As noted above, the Departments expect that these regulations will result in a small increase in the economic effects of HIPAA's statutory provisions. For the reasons stated immediately above, the Departments believe that this increase will be small on aggregate, adding only a small increment to the cost attributable to HIPAA's statutory portability provisions, which themselves amount to a small fraction of one percent of health plan expenditures. Thus the increase will be negligible relative to typical year-to-year increases in premiums charged by issuers, which can amount to several percentage points or more. Therefore, the Departments expect these regulations to have little or no perceptible negative impact on employers' propensity to offer health benefit plans or on the generosity of those plans. In sum, the Departments expect that the benefits of these regulations, which can be very large for a particular affected individual, will justify their costs.

List of Subjects

26 CFR Part 54

Excise taxes, Health care, Health insurance, Pensions, Reporting and recordkeeping requirements.

29 CFR Part 2590

Continuation coverage, Disclosure, Employee benefit plans, Group health plans, Health care, Health insurance, Medical child support, Reporting and recordkeeping requirements.

45 CFR Part 146

Health care, Health insurance, Reporting and recordkeeping requirements, and State regulation of health insurance.

Proposed Amendments to the Regulations

Internal Revenue Service

26 CFR Chapter I

Accordingly, 26 CFR part 54 is proposed to be amended as follows:

PART 54—PENSION EXCISE TAXES

Paragraph 1. The authority citation for part 54 is amended by:

a. Revising the entries for §§ 54.9801-4 and 54.9801-6.

b. Adding an entry in numerical order for § 54.9801-7.

The addition and revisions read as follows:

Authority: 26 U.S.C. 7805. * * *

Section 54.9801-4 also issued under 26 U.S.C. 9801(e)(3) and 9833.* * *

Section 54.9801-6 also issued under 26 U.S.C. 9801(e)(3) and 9833.

Section 54.9801-7 also issued under 26 U.S.C. 9833.* * *

§ 54.9801-1 [Amended]

Par. 2. Section 54.9801-1 is amended in paragraph (a)(1) by removing the language "54.9801-6" and adding "54.9801-7" in its place.

§ 54.9801-2 [Amended]

Par. 3. Section 54.9801-2 is amended in the first sentence by removing the language "54.9801-6" and adding "54.9801-7" in its place.

Par. 4. Section 54.9801-4 is amended by:

a. Revising paragraphs (b)(2)(iii) and (b)(2)(iv).

b. Adding *Examples 4* and *6* in paragraph (b)(2)(v).

The revisions and additions read as follows:

§ 54.9801-4 *Rules relating to creditable coverage.*

* * * * *

(b) *Standard method.* * * *

(2) *Counting creditable coverage.* * * *

(iii) *Significant break in coverage defined.* A *significant break in coverage* means a period of 63 consecutive days during each of which an individual does not have any creditable coverage, except that periods described in paragraph (b)(2)(iv) of this section are not taken into account in determining a significant break in coverage. (See section 731(b)(2)(iii) of ERISA and section 2723(b)(2)(iii) of the PHS Act, which exclude from preemption state insurance laws that require a break of more than 63 days before an individual has a significant break in coverage for purposes of state law.)

(iv) *Periods that toll a significant break.* Days in a waiting period and days in an affiliation period are not taken into account in determining whether a significant break in coverage has occurred. In addition, for an individual who elects COBRA continuation coverage during the second election period provided under the Trade Act of 2002, the days between the date the individual lost group health plan coverage and the first day of the second COBRA election period are not taken into account in determining whether a significant break in coverage has occurred. Moreover, in the case of an individual whose coverage ceases, if a certificate of creditable coverage with respect to that cessation is not provided on or before the date coverage ceases, then the period that begins on the first date that an individual has no creditable coverage and that continues through the earlier of the following two dates is not taken into account in determining whether a significant break in coverage has occurred:

(A) The date that a certificate of creditable coverage with respect to that cessation is provided; or

(B) The date 44 days after coverage ceases.

(v) Examples. * * *

Example 4. (i) *Facts.* Individual B terminates coverage under a group health plan, and a certificate of creditable coverage is provided 10 days later. B begins employment with Employer R and begins enrollment in R's plan 60 days after the certificate is provided.

(ii) *Conclusion.* In this *Example 4,* even though B had no coverage for 69 days, the 10 days before the certificate of creditable coverage is provided are not taken into account in determining a significant break in coverage. Therefore, B's break in coverage is only 59 days and is not a significant break in coverage. Accordingly, B's prior coverage must be counted by R's plan.

* * * * *

Example 6. (i) *Facts.* Employer V sponsors a group health plan. Under the terms of the plan, the only benefits provided are those provided under an insurance policy. Individual D works for V and has creditable coverage under V's plan. V fails to pay the issuer the premiums for the coverage period beginning March 1. Consistent with applicable state law, the issuer terminates the policy so that the last day of coverage is April 30. V goes out of business on July 31. On August 15 D begins employment with Employer W and enrolls in W's group health plan. W's plan imposes a 12-month preexisting condition exclusion on all enrollees. D never receives a certificate of creditable coverage for coverage under V's plan.

(ii) *Conclusion.* In this *Example 6,* the period from May 1 (the first day without coverage) through June 13 (the date 44 days after coverage under V's plan ceases) is not taken into account in determining a 63-day break in coverage. This is because, in cases in which a certificate of creditable coverage is not provided by the date coverage is lost, the break begins on the date the certificate is provided, or the date 44 days after coverage ceases, if earlier. Therefore, even though D's actual period without coverage was 106 days (May 1 through August 14), because the period from May 1 through June 13 is not taken into account, D's break in coverage is only 62 days (June 14 through August 14). Thus, D has not experienced a significant break in coverage, and D's prior coverage must be counted by W's plan.

* * * * *

Par. 5. Section 54.9801-5 is amended by:

a. Redesignating paragraphs (a)(3)(ii)(H)(5) and (6) as paragraphs (a)(3)(ii)(H)(6) and (7), respectively.

b. Adding a new paragraph (a)(3)(ii)(H)(5).

The addition reads as follows:

§ 54.9801-5 Evidence of creditable coverage.

(a) *Certificate of creditable coverage.* * * *

(3) *Form and content of certificate.* * * *

(ii) *Required information.* * * *

(H) * * *

(5) The interaction with the Family and Medical Leave Act;

* * * * *

Par. 6. Section 54.9801-6 is amended by:

a. Revising paragraph (a)(1).

b. Revising paragraph (a)(4).

c. Revising paragraph (b)(1).

d. Revising paragraph (b)(3).

e. Revising *Example 2* in paragraph (b)(4).

f. Adding *Examples 3, 4,* and *5* in paragraph (b)(4).

The additions and revisions read as follows:

§ 54.9801-6 Special enrollment periods.

(a) *Special enrollment for certain individuals who lose coverage*—(1) *In general.* A group health plan is required to permit current employees and dependents (as defined in § 54.9801-2) who are described in paragraph (a)(2) of this section to enroll for coverage under the terms of the plan if the conditions in paragraph (a)(3) of this section are satisfied. Paragraph (a)(4) of this section describes procedures that a plan may require an employee to follow and describes the date by which coverage must begin. The special enrollment rights under this paragraph (a) apply without regard to the dates on which an individual would otherwise be able to enroll under the plan. (See section 701(f)(1) of ERISA and section 2701(f)(1) of the PHS Act, under which this obligation is also imposed on a health insurance issuer offering group health insurance coverage.)

* * * * *

(4) *Applying for special enrollment and effective date of coverage*—(i) *Request.* A plan must allow an employee a period of at least 30 days after an event described in paragraph (a)(3) of this section (loss of eligibility for coverage, termination of employer contributions, or exhaustion of COBRA continuation coverage) to request enrollment (for the employee or the employee's dependent). For this purpose, any written or oral request made to any of the following constitutes a request for enrollment —

(A) The plan administrator;

(B) An issuer offering health insurance coverage under the plan;

(C) A person who customarily handles claims for the plan (such as a third party administrator); or

(D) Any other designated representative.

(ii) *Tolling of period for requesting special enrollment.* (A) In the case of an individual whose coverage ceases, if a certificate of creditable coverage with respect to that cessation is not provided on or before the date coverage ceases, then the period for requesting special enrollment described in paragraph (a)(4)(i) of this section does not end until 30 days after the earlier of —

(1) The date that a certificate of creditable coverage with respect to that cessation is provided; or

(2) The date 44 days after coverage ceases.

(B) For purposes of this paragraph (a)(4), if an individual's coverage ceases due to the operation of a lifetime limit on all benefits, coverage is considered to cease on the earliest date that a claim is denied due to the operation of the lifetime limit. (Nonetheless, the date of a loss of eligibility for coverage is determined under the rules of paragraph (a)(3) of this section, which provides that a loss of eligibility occurs when a claim that would meet or exceed a lifetime limit on all benefits is incurred, not when it is denied.)

(C) The rules of this paragraph (a)(4)(ii) are illustrated by the following examples:

Example 1. (i) *Facts.* Employer *V* provides group health coverage through a policy provided by Issuer *M.* Individual *D* works for *V* and is covered under *V*'s plan. *V* fails to pay *M* the premiums for the coverage period beginning March 1. Consistent with applicable state law, *M* terminates the policy so that the last day of coverage is April 30. On

May 15, *M* provides *D* with a certificate of creditable coverage with respect to *D*'s cessation of coverage under *V*'s plan.

(ii) *Conclusion.* In this *Example 1,* the period to request special enrollment ends no earlier than June 14 (which is 30 days after May 15, the day a certificate of creditable coverage is provided with respect to *D*).

Example 2. (i) *Facts.* Same facts as *Example 1,* except *D* is never provided with a certificate of creditable coverage.

(ii) *Conclusion.* In this *Example 2,* the period to request special enrollment ends no earlier than July 13. (July 13 is 74 days after April 30, the date coverage ceases. That is, July 13 is 30 days after the end of the 44-day maximum tolling period.)

Example 3. (i) *Facts.* Individual *E* works for Employer *W* and has coverage under *W*'s plan. *W*'s plan has a lifetime limit of $1 million on all benefits under the plan. On September 13, *E* incurs a claim that would exceed the plan's lifetime limit. On September 28, *W* denies the claim due to the operation of the lifetime limit and a certificate of creditable coverage is provided on October 3. *E* is otherwise eligible to enroll in the group health plan of the employer of *E*'s spouse.

(ii) *Conclusion.* In this *Example 3,* the period to request special enrollment in the plan of the employer of *E*'s spouse ends no earlier than November 2 (30 days after the date the certificate is provided) and begins not later than September 13, the date *E* lost eligibility for coverage.

(iii) *Reasonable procedures for special enrollment.* After an individual has requested enrollment under paragraph (a)(4)(i) of this section, a plan may require the individual to complete enrollment materials within a reasonable time after the end of the 30-day period described in paragraph (a)(4)(i) of this section. In these enrollment materials, the plan may require the individual only to provide information required of individuals who enroll when first eligible and information about the event giving rise to the special enrollment right. A plan may establish a deadline for receiving completed enrollment materials, but such a deadline must be extended for information that an individual making reasonable efforts does not obtain by that deadline.

(iv) *Date coverage must begin.* If the plan requires completion of additional enrollment materials in accordance with paragraph (a)(4)(iii) of this section, coverage must begin no later than the first day of the first calendar month beginning after the date the plan receives enrollment materials that are substantially complete. If the plan does not require completion of additional enrollment materials, coverage must begin no later than the first day of the first calendar month beginning after the date the plan receives the request for special enrollment under paragraph (a)(4)(i) of this section.

(b) *Special enrollment with respect to certain dependent beneficiaries*— (1) *In general.* A group health plan that makes coverage available with respect to dependents is required to permit individuals described in paragraph (b)(2) of this section to be enrolled for coverage in a benefit package under the terms of the plan. Paragraph (b)(3) of this section describes procedures that a plan may require an individual to follow and describes the date by which coverage must begin. The special enrollment rights under this paragraph (b) apply without regard to the dates on which an individual would otherwise be able to enroll under the plan. (See 29 CFR 2590.701-6(b) and 45 CFR 146.117(b), under which this obligation is also imposed on a health insurance issuer offering group health insurance coverage.)

* * * * *

(3) *Applying for special enrollment and effective date of coverage*—(i) *Request.* A plan must allow an individual a period of at least 30 days after the date of the marriage, birth, adoption, or placement for adoption (or, if dependent coverage is not generally made available at the time of the marriage, birth, adoption, or placement for adoption, a period of at least 30 days after the date the plan makes dependent coverage generally available) to request enrollment (for the individual or the individual's dependent). For this purpose, any written or oral request made to any of the following constitutes a request for enrollment—

(A) The plan administrator;

(B) An issuer offering health insurance coverage under the plan;

(C) A person who customarily handles claims for the plan (such as a third party administrator); or

(D) Any other designated representative.

(ii) *Reasonable procedures for special enrollment.* After an individual has requested enrollment under paragraph (b)(3)(i) of this section, a plan may require the individual to complete enrollment materials within a reasonable time after the end of the 30-day period described in paragraph (b)(3)(i) of this section. In these enrollment materials, the plan may require the individual only to provide information required of individuals who enroll when first eligible and information about the event giving rise to the special enrollment right. A plan may establish a deadline for receiving completed enrollment materials, but such a deadline must be extended for information that an individual making reasonable efforts does not obtain by that deadline.

(iii) *Date coverage must begin*—(A) *Marriage.* In the case of marriage, if the plan requires completion of additional enrollment materials in accordance with paragraph (b)(3)(ii) of this section, coverage must begin no later than the first day of the first calendar month beginning after the date the plan receives enrollment materials that are substantially complete. If the plan does not require such additional enrollment materials, coverage must begin no later than the first day of the first calendar month beginning after the date the plan receives the request for special enrollment under paragraph (b)(3)(i) of this section.

(B) *Birth, adoption, or placement for adoption.* Coverage must begin in the case of a dependent's birth on the date of birth and in the case of a dependent's adoption or placement for adoption no later than the date of such adoption or placement for adoption (or, if dependent coverage is not made generally available at the time of the birth, adoption, or placement for adoption, the date the plan makes dependent coverage available). If the plan requires completion of additional enrollment materials in accordance with paragraph (b)(3)(ii) of this section, the plan must provide benefits (including benefits retroactively to the date of birth, adoption, or placement for adoption) once the plan receives enrollment materials that are substantially complete.

(4) *Examples.* * * *

Example 2. (i) *Facts.* Individual *D* works for Employer *X. X* maintains a group health plan with two benefit packages—an HMO option and an indemnity option. Self-only and family coverage are available under both options. *D* enrolls for self-only coverage in the HMO option. Then, a child, *E*, is placed for adoption with *D*. Within 30 days of the placement of *E* for adoption, *D* requests enrollment for *D* and *E* under the plan's indemnity option and submits completed enrollment materials timely.

(ii) *Conclusion.* In this *Example 2, D* and *E* satisfy the conditions for special enrollment under paragraphs (b)(2)(v) and (b)(3) of this section. Therefore, the plan must allow *D* and *E* to enroll in the indemnity coverage, effective as of the date of the placement for adoption.

Example 3. (i) *Facts.* Same facts as *Example 1.* On March 17 (two days after the birth of *C*), *A* telephones the plan administrator and requests special enrollment of *A, B,* and *C.* The plan administrator sends *A* an enrollment form. Under the terms of the plan, enrollment is denied unless a completed form is submitted within 30 days of the event giving rise to the special enrollment right (in this case, *C*'s birth).

(ii) *Conclusion.* In this *Example 3,* the plan does not satisfy paragraph (b)(3) of this section. The plan may require only that *A* request enrollment during the 30-day period after *C*'s birth. *A* did so by telephoning the plan administrator. The plan may not condition special enrollment on filing additional enrollment materials during the 30-day period. To comply with paragraph (b)(3) of this section, the plan must allow *A* a reasonable time after the end of the 30-day period to submit any additional enrollment materials. Once these enrollment materials are received, the plan must allow whatever coverage is chosen to begin on March 15, the date of *C*'s birth.

Example 4. (i) *Facts.* Same facts as *Example 3,* except that *A* telephones the plan administrator to request enrollment on April 13 (29 days after *C*'s birth). Also, under the terms of the plan, the deadline for submitting the enrollment form is 14 days after the end of the 30-day period for requesting special enrollment (thus, in this case, April 28, which is 44 days after *C*'s birth). The form requests the same information for *A, B,* and *C* (name, date of birth, and place of birth) as well as a copy of *C*'s birth certificate. *A* fills out the enrollment form and delivers it to the plan administrator on April 28. At that time *A* does not have a birth certificate for *C* but applies on that day for one from the appropriate government office. *A* receives the birth certificate on June 1 and furnishes a copy of the birth certificate to the plan administrator shortly thereafter.

(ii) *Conclusion.* In this *Example 4, A, B,* and *C* are entitled to special enrollment under the plan even though *A* did not satisfy the plan's requirement of providing a copy of *C*'s birth certificate by the plan's 14-day deadline. While a plan may establish such a deadline, the plan must extend the deadline for information that an individual making reasonable efforts does not obtain by that deadline. *A* delivered the enrollment form to the plan administrator by the deadline and made reasonable efforts to furnish the birth certificate that the plan requires.

Example 5. (i) *Facts.* Same facts as *Example 4.* On May 3 (after *A* has delivered the enrollment form to the plan administrator but before *A* provides the birth certificate) *A* submits claims for all medical expenses incurred for *B* and *C* from the date of *C*'s birth.

(ii) *Conclusion.* In this *Example 5,* the plan must pay all of the claims submitted by *A.* Because the plan requires that individuals seeking special enrollment complete additional enrollment materials, it is required to provide benefits once it receives enrollment materials that are substantially complete. The form that *A* submitted on April 28 was substantially complete. Because *C*'s birth is the event giving rise to the special enrollment right, on April 28 *A, B,* and *C* become entitled to benefits under the plan retroactive to the date of *C*'s birth.

* * * * *

Par. 7. A new § 54.9801-7 is added to read as follows:

§ 54.9801-7 Interaction with the Family and Medical Leave Act.

(a) *In general.* The rules of §§ 54.9801-1 through 54.9801-6 apply with respect to an individual on leave under the Family and Medical Leave Act of 1993 (29 U.S.C. 2601) (FMLA), and apply with respect to a dependent of such an individual, except to the extent otherwise provided in this section.

(b) *Tolling of significant break in coverage during FMLA leave.* In the case of an individual (or a dependent of the individual) who is covered under a group health plan, if the individual takes FMLA leave and does not continue group health coverage for any period of FMLA leave, that period is not taken into account in determining whether a significant break in coverage has occurred under § 54.9801-4(b)(2)(iii).

(c) *Application of certification provisions*—(1) *Timing of issuance of certificate*—(i) In the case of an individual (or a dependent of the individual) who is covered under a group health plan, if the individual takes FMLA leave and the individual's group health coverage is terminated during FMLA leave, an automatic certificate must be provided in accordance with the timing rules set forth in § 54.9801-5(a)(2)(ii)(B) (which generally require plans to provide certificates within a reasonable time after coverage ceases).

(ii) In the case of an individual (or a dependent of the individual) who is covered under a group health plan, if the individual takes FMLA leave and continues group health coverage for the period of FMLA leave, but then ceases coverage under the plan at the end of FMLA leave, an automatic certificate must be provided in accordance with the timing rules set forth in § 54.9801-5(a)(2)(ii)(A) (which generally require plans to provide a certificate no later than the time a notice is required to be furnished for a qualifying event under a COBRA continuation provision).

(2) *Demonstrating FMLA leave.* (i) A plan is required to take into account all information about FMLA leave that it obtains or that is presented on behalf of an individual. A plan must treat the individual as having been on FMLA leave for a period if —

(A) The individual attests to the period of FMLA leave; and

(B) The individual cooperates with the plan's efforts to verify the individual's FMLA leave.

(ii) Nothing in this section prevents a plan from modifying its initial determination of FMLA leave if it determines that the individual did not have the claimed FMLA leave, provided that the plan follows procedures for reconsideration similar to those set forth in § 54.9801-3(f).

(d) *Relationship to loss of eligibility special enrollment rules.* In the case of an individual (or a dependent of the individual) who is covered under a group health plan and who takes FMLA leave, a loss of eligibility for coverage under § 54.9801-6(a) occurs when the period of FMLA leave ends if—

(1) The individual's group health coverage is terminated at any time during FMLA leave; and

(2) The individual does not return to work for the employer at the end of FMLA leave.

Par. 8. Section 54.9831-1 is amended by:

a. Adding paragraph (a)(2).

b. Revising paragraph (b).

c. Revising paragraph (c)(1).

d. By adding paragraph (e).

The additions and revisions read as follows:

§ 54.9831-1 Special rules relating to group health plans.

(a) *Group health plan.* * * *

(2) *Determination of number of plans.* The number of group health plans that an employer or employee organization (including for this purpose a joint board of trustees of a multiemployer trust affiliated with one or more multiemployer plans) maintains is determined under the rules of this paragraph (a)(2).

(i) Except as provided in paragraph (a)(2)(ii) or (iii) of this section, health care benefits provided by a corporation, partnership, or other entity or trade or business, or by an employee organization, constitute one group health plan, unless—

(A) It is clear from the instruments governing the arrangement or arrangements to provide health care benefits that the benefits are being provided under separate plans; and

(B) The arrangement or arrangements are operated pursuant to such instruments as separate plans.

(ii) A multiemployer plan and a nonmultiemployer plan are always separate plans.

(iii) If a principal purpose of establishing separate plans is to evade any requirement of law, then the separate plans will be considered a single plan to the extent necessary to prevent the evasion.

(b) *General exception for certain small group health plans.* The requirements of §§ 54.9801-1 through 54.9801-7, 54.9802-1, 54.9802-2, 54.9811-1T, 54.9812-1T, and 54.9833-1 do not apply to any group health plan for any plan year if, on the first day of the plan year, the plan has fewer than two participants who are current employees.

(c) *Excepted benefits*—(1) *In general.* The requirements of §§ 54.9801-1 through 54.9801-7, 54.9802-1, 54.9802-2, 54.9811-1T, 54.9812-1T, and 54.9833-1 do not apply to any group health plan in relation to its provision of the benefits described in paragraph (c)(2), (3), (4), or (5) of this section (or any combination of these benefits).

* * * * *

(e) *Determining the average number of employees*—(1) *Scope.* Whenever the application of a rule in this part depends upon the average number of employees employed by an employer, the determination of that number is made in accordance with the rules of this paragraph (e).

(2) *Full-time equivalents.* The average number of employees is determined by calculating the average number of full-time equivalents on business days during the preceding calendar year.

(3) *Methodology.* For the preceding calendar year, the average number of full-time equivalents is determined by—

(i) Determining the number of employees who were employed full-time by the employer throughout the entire calendar year;

(ii) Totaling all employment hours (not to exceed 40 hours per week) for each part-time employee, and for each full-time employee who was not employed full-time with the employer throughout the entire calendar year;

(iii) Dividing the total determined under paragraph (e)(3)(ii) of this section by a figure that represents the annual full-time hours under the employer's general employment practices, such as 2,080 hours (although for this purpose not more than 40 hours per week may be used); and

(iv) Adding the quotient determined under paragraph (e)(3)(iii) of this section to the number determined under paragraph (e)(3)(i).

(4) *Rounding.* For purposes of paragraph (e)(3)(iv) of this section, all fractions are disregarded. For instance, a figure of 50.9 is deemed to be 50.

(5) *Employers not in existence in the preceding year.* In the case of an employer that was in existence for less than the entire preceding calendar year (including an employer that was not in existence at all), a determination of the average number of employees that the employer employs is based on the average number of employees that it is reasonably expected the employer will employ on business days in the current calendar year.

(6) *Scope of the term "employer."* For purposes of this paragraph (e), employer includes any predecessor of the employer. In addition, all persons treated as a single employer under section 414(b), (c), (m), or (o) are treated as one employer.

(7) *Special rule for multiemployer plans.* (i) With respect to the application of a rule in this part to a multiemployer plan (as defined in section 3(37) of ERISA), each employer with at least one employee participating in the plan is considered to employ the same average number of employees. That number is the highest number that results by applying the rules of paragraphs (e)(1) through (6) of this section separately to each of the employers.

(ii) The rules of this paragraph (e)(7) are illustrated by the following example:

Example. (i) *Facts.* Twenty five employers have at least one employee who participates in Multiemployer Plan *M.* Among these 25 employers, Employer *K* has 51 employees, determined under the rules of paragraphs (e)(1) through (6) of this section. Each of the other 24 employers has fewer than 50 employees.

(ii) *Conclusion.* With respect to the application of a rule in this part to *M,* each of the 25 employers is considered to employ 51 employees.

Mark E. Matthews,

Deputy Commissioner for Services and Enforcement, Internal Revenue Service.

¶ 20,261K

IRS proposed regulations: Tax exempt organizations: Form 990: Magnetic media.—The IRS has issued temporary and proposed regulations requiring certain large corporations and tax-exempt organizations to electronically file their income tax or annual information returns beginning in 2006, for the 2005 tax year. In particular, tax-exempt organizations with total assets of $100 million or more will be required to file the tax year 2005 Forms 990 electronically. In 2007, tax-exempt organizations with total assets of $10 million or more for tax year 2006 will be required to file Form 900 electronically. The text of the temporary regulations also serves as the text of the proposed regulations. The temporary regulations, which were published in the *Federal Register* on January 12, 2005 (70 FR 2012), are reproduced in part at ¶ 13,663 (IRS Reg. Sec. 301.6033-4T). The preamble to the temporary regulations is reproduced at ¶ 24,507W.

The text of the proposed regulations, which were published in the *Federal Register* on January 12, 2005 (70 FR 2075), are reproduced below.

DEPARTMENT OF THE TREASURY

Internal Revenue Service (IRS)

26 CFR Parts 1 and 301

[REG-130671-04]

RIN 1545-BD65

Returns Required on Magnetic Media

AGENCY: Internal Revenue Service (IRS), Treasury.

ACTION: Notice of proposed rulemaking by cross-reference to temporary regulations and notice of public hearing.

SUMMARY: In the Rules and Regulations section of this issue of the **Federal Register**, the IRS is issuing temporary regulations relating to the requirements for filing corporate income tax returns, S corporation returns, and returns of organizations required under section 6033 on magnetic media under section 6011(e) of the Internal Revenue Code

(Code). The text of those regulations also serves as the text of these proposed regulations. This document also provides notice of a public hearing on these proposed regulations.

DATES: Written or electronic comments must be received by February 26, 2005. Requests to speak (with outlines of topics to be discussed) at the public hearing scheduled for March 16, 2005, must be received by February 26, 2005.

ADDRESSES: Send submissions to: CC:PA:LPD:PR (REG-130671-04), Room 5203, Internal Revenue Service, POB 7604, Ben Franklin Station, Washington, DC 20044. Submissions may be hand delivered Monday through Friday between the hours of 8 a.m. and 4 p.m. to: CC:PA:LPD:PR (REG-130671-04), Courier's Desk, Internal Revenue Service, 1111 Constitution Avenue, NW., Washington, DC. Alternatively, taxpayers may submit comments electronically via the IRS internet website at *www.irs.gov/regs,* or via the Federal eRulemaking Portal, *www.regulations.gov* (IRS-REG-130671-04). The public hearing will be held in the auditorium of the Internal Revenue Building, 1111 Constitution Avenue, NW., Washington, DC 20224.

FOR FURTHER INFORMATION CONTACT: Concerning the proposed regulations, Michael E. Hara, (202) 622-4910 concerning submissions of comments, the hearing, and/or to be placed on the building access list to attend the hearing, Robin Jones at (202) 622-7180 (not toll-free numbers). SUPPLEMENTARY INFORMATION:

Background

Temporary regulations in the Rules and Regulations section of this issue of the **Federal Register** amend the Regulations on Procedure and Administration (26 CFR part 301) relating to the filing of corporate income tax returns, S corporation returns, and returns of organizations required under section 6033 on magnetic media under section 6011(e). The temporary regulations require corporations and certain organizations to file their Form 1120, "U.S. Corporation Income Tax Return," Form 1120S, "U.S. Income Tax Return for an S Corporation," Form 990, "Return of Organization Exempt From Income Tax," and Form 990-PF, "Return of Private Foundation or Section 4947(a)(1) Trust Treated as a Private Foundation," electronically if they are required to file at least 250 returns during the calendar year ending with or within their taxable year. The text of those regulations also serves as the text of these proposed regulations. The preamble to the temporary regulations explains the amendments.

Special Analyses

It has been determined that these proposed regulations are not a significant regulatory action as defined in Executive Order 12866. Therefore, a regulatory assessment is not required. It also has been determined that section 553(b) of the Administrative Procedure Act (5 U.S.C. chapter 5) does not apply to these regulations. Because these regulations do not impose a collection of information on small entities, the Regulatory Flexibility Act (5 U.S.C. chapter 6) does not apply. The IRS and Treasury Department note that these regulations only prescribe the method of filing returns that are already required to be filed. Further, these regulations are consistent with the requirements imposed by statute.

Section 6011(e)(2)(A) provides that, in prescribing regulations providing standards for determining which returns must be filed on magnetic media or in other machine-readable form, the Secretary shall not require any person to file returns on magnetic media unless the person is required to file at least 250 returns during the calendar year. Consistent with the statutory provision, these regulations do not require Forms 1120, Forms 1120S, Forms 990, or Forms 990-PF to be filed electronically unless 250 or more returns are required to be filed.

Further, if a taxpayer's operations are computerized, reporting in accordance with the regulations should be less costly than filing on paper. If the taxpayer's operations are not computerized, the incremental cost of filing Forms 1120, Forms 1120S, Forms 990, and Forms 990-PF electronically should be minimal in most cases because of the availability of computer service bureaus. In addition, the proposed regulations provide that the IRS may waive the electronic filing requirements upon a showing of hardship.

Pursuant to section 7805(f) of the Code, these proposed regulations will be submitted to the Chief Counsel for Advocacy of the Small Business Administration for comment on their impact on small business.

Comments and Public Hearing

Before these proposed regulations are adopted as final regulations, consideration will be given to any written (a signed original and eight (8) copies) or electronic comments that are submitted timely to the IRS. The IRS and Treasury Department request comments on the clarity of the proposed regulations and how they can be made easier to understand. The IRS and Treasury Department also request comments on the procedures and criteria for hardship waivers from the electronic filing requirements. The IRS and Treasury Department also request comments on the accuracy of the certification that the regulations in this document will not have a significant economic impact on a substantial number of small entities. All comments will be available for public inspection and copying.

A public hearing has been scheduled for March 16, 2005 at 10 a.m. in the auditorium of the Internal Revenue Building, 1111 Constitution Avenue, NW., Washington, DC. Due to building security procedures, visitors must enter at the Constitution Avenue entrance. In addition, all visitors must present photo identification to enter the building. Because of access restrictions, visitors will not be admitted beyond the immediate entrance area more than 30 minutes before the hearing starts. For information about having your name placed on the building access list to attend the hearing, see the "FOR FURTHER INFORMATION CONTACT" section of this preamble.

The rules of 26 CFR 601.601(a)(3) apply to the hearing. Persons who wish to present oral comments at the hearing must submit comments and an outline of the topics to be discussed and the time to be devoted to each topic by February 26, 2005

A period of 10 minutes will be allotted to each person for making comments. An agenda showing the scheduling of the speakers will be prepared after the deadline for receiving outlines has passed. Copies of the agenda will be available free of charge at the hearing.

Drafting Information

The principal author of these proposed regulations is Michael E. Hara, Office of the Assistant Chief Counsel (Procedure and Administration).

List of Subjects

26 CFR Part 1

Income taxes, Reporting and recordkeeping requirements.

26 CFR Part 301

Employment taxes, Estate taxes, Excise taxes, Gift taxes, Income taxes, Penalties, Reporting and recordkeeping requirements.

Proposed Amendments to the Regulations

Accordingly, 26 CFR parts 1 and 301 are proposed to be amended as follows:

PART 1—INCOME TAXES

Paragraph 1. The authority citation for part 1 continues to read, in part, as follows:

Authority: 26 U.S.C. 7805 * * *

Par. 2. Section 1.6011-5 is added to read as follows:

§ 1.6011-5 Required use of magnetic media for corporate income tax returns.

[The text of proposed § 1.6011-5 is the same as the text of § 1.6011-5T published elsewhere in this issue of the **Federal Register**].

Par.3. Section 1.6033-4 is added to read as follows:

§ 1.6033-4 Required use of magnetic media for returns by organizations required to file returns under section 6033.

[The text of proposed § 1.6033-4 is the same as the text of § 1.6033-4T published elsewhere in this issue of the **Federal Register**].

Par. 4. Section 1.6037-2 is added to read as follows:

§ 1.6037-2 Required use of magnetic media for income tax returns of electing small business corporations.

[The text of proposed § 1.6037-2 is the same as the text of § 1.6037-2T published elsewhere in this issue of the **Federal Register**].

PART 301—PROCEDURE AND ADMINISTRATION

Par. 5. The authority citation for part 301 is amended by adding entries, in numerical order, to read as follows:

Authority: 26 U.S.C. 7805 * * *

Section 301.6011-5 also issued under 26 U.S.C. 6011. * * *

Section 301.6033-4 also issued under 26 U.S.C. 6033. * * *

Section 301.6037-2 also issued under 26 U.S.C. 6037. * * *

Par. 6. Section 301.6011-5 is added to read as follows:

§ 301.6011-5 Required use of magnetic media for corporate income tax returns.

[The text of proposed § 301.6011-5 is the same as the text of § 301.6011-5T published elsewhere in this issue of the **Federal Register**].

Par. 7. Section 301.6033-4 is added to read as follows:

§ 301.6033-4 Required use of magnetic media for returns by organizations required to file returns under section 6033.

[The text of proposed § 301.6033-4 is the same as the text of § 3011.6033-4T published elsewhere in this issue of the **Federal Register**].

Par. 8. Section 301.6037-2 is added to read as follows:

Internal Revenue Code

Internal Revenue Code   1303

§ 301.6037-2 Required use of magnetic media for returns of electing small business corporation.

[The text of proposed § 301.6037-2 is the same as the text of § 301.6037-2T published elsewhere in this issue of the **Federal Register**].

Deputy Commissioner for Services and Enforcement.

Mark E. Matthews

CERTIFIED COPY

Guy R. Traynor

¶ 20,261L

IRS proposed regulations: QJSAs: Benefit disclosures: Relative values: Optional forms of benefit.—The IRS has issued proposed regulations that would revise final regulations concerning the disclosure of relative values of optional forms of benefit that were issued on December 17, 2003 (see preamble to the final regulations at ¶ 24,507L). The effective date of the regulations had previously been extended to October 1, 2004 by Announcement 2004-58 (see ¶ 17,097S-46). The effective date of the final regulations has been extended to apply to the annuity starting dates of qualified joint and survivor annuities (QJSAs) beginning on or after February 1, 2006, unless the actuarial present value of an optional form of benefit is less than the actuarial present value of the QJSA. In that case, the extension is not applicable and the final rules, effective October 1, 2004, must be applied. In the interim, plans that conform to the 2003 final regulations may rely on them, as well as the proposed rules. Otherwise, plans must comply with the 1988 regulations. Regs adopted or amended by T.D. 8219 (53 FR 31837) on August 19, 1988 that are still in effect are ¶ 11,719, ¶ 11,719B, ¶ 11,720F, ¶ 11,755-2, ¶ 12,162A, ¶ 12,162B, ¶ 12,219D, ¶ 12,231, ¶ 12,233, ¶ 12,234, and ¶ 12,556.

The proposed regulations, which were published in the *Federal Register* on January 28, 2005 (70 FR 4058), are reproduced below.

DEPARTMENT OF THE TREASURY

Internal Revenue Service

26 CFR Part 1

[REG-152914-04]

RIN 1545-BD97

Revised Regulations Concerning Disclosure of Relative Values of Optional Forms of Benefit

AGENCY: Internal Revenue Service (IRS), Treasury.

ACTION: Notice of proposed rulemaking.

SUMMARY: This document contains proposed regulations that would revise final regulations that were issued on December 17, 2003, under section 417(a)(3) of the Internal Revenue Code concerning content requirements applicable to explanations of qualified joint and survivor annuities and qualified preretirement survivor annuities payable under certain retirement plans. These regulations affect plan sponsors and administrators, and participants in and beneficiaries of, certain retirement plans.

DATES: Written and electronic comments and requests for a public hearing must be received by April 28, 2005.

ADDRESSES: Send submissions to: CC:PA:LPD:PR (REG-152914-04), room 5203, Internal Revenue Service, PO Box 7604, Ben Franklin Station, Washington, DC 20044. Submissions may be hand-delivered Monday through Friday between the hours of 8 a.m. and 4 p.m. to: CC:PA:LPD:PR (REG-152914-04), Courier's Desk, Internal Revenue Service, 1111 Constitution Avenue, NW., Washington, DC, or sent electronically, via the IRS Internet site at http://www.irs.gov/regs or via the Federal eRulemaking Portal at http://www.regulations.gov (indicate IRS and REG-152914-04).

FOR FURTHER INFORMATION CONTACT: Concerning the regulations, Bruce Perlin at (202) 622-6090 (not a toll-free number); concerning submissions or hearing requests, Lanita Van Dyke, (202) 622-7180 (not a toll-free number).

SUPPLEMENTARY INFORMATION:

Paperwork Reduction Act

The collections of information contained in this notice of proposed rulemaking have been previously reviewed and approved by the Office of Management and Budget in accordance with the Paperwork Reduction Act of 1995 (44 U.S.C. 3507(d)) under control number 1545-0928.

An agency may not conduct or sponsor, and a person is not required to respond to, a collection of information unless it displays a valid control number assigned by the Office of Management and Budget.

Books or records relating to a collection of information must be retained as long as their contents may become material in the administration of any internal revenue law. Generally, tax returns and tax return information are confidential, as required by 26 U.S.C. 6103.

Background

Section 417(a) provides rules under which a participant (with spousal consent) may waive payment of the participant's benefit in the form of qualified joint and survivor annuity (QJSA). Specifically, section 417(a)(3) provides that a plan must provide to each participant, within a reasonable period before the annuity starting date, a written explana-

tion that includes the following information: (1) The terms and conditions of the QJSA; (2) the participant's right to make an election to waive the QJSA form of benefit; (3) the effect of such an election; (4) the rights of the participant's spouse; and (5) the right to revoke an election to waive the QJSA form of benefit.

Section 205 of the Employee Retirement Income Security Act of 1974 (ERISA), Public Law 93-406 (88 Stat. 829) as subsequently amended, provides rules that are parallel to the rules of sections 401(a)(11) and 417 of the Internal Revenue Code. In particular, section 205(c)(3) of ERISA provides a rule parallel to the rule of section 417(a)(3) of the Code.

Section 1.401(a)-20, which provides rules governing the requirements for a waiver of the QJSA, was published in the Federal Register on August 19, 1988 (TD 8219) (53 FR 31837). Section 1.401(a)-20, Q & A-36, as published in 1988, set forth requirements for the explanation that must be provided under section 417(a)(3) as a prerequisite to waiver of a QJSA. Under those requirements, such a written explanation must contain a general description of the eligibility conditions and other material features of the optional forms of benefit and sufficient additional information to explain the relative values of the optional forms of benefit available under the plan (e.g., the extent to which optional forms are subsidized relative to the normal form of benefit or the interest rates used to calculate the optional forms). In addition, § 1.401(a)-20, Q & A-36, as published in 1988, provided that the written explanation must comply with the requirements set forth in § 1.401(a)-11(c)(3). Section 1.401(a)-11(c)(3) was issued prior to the enactment of section 417, and provides rules relating to written explanations that were required prior to a participant's election of a preretirement survivor annuity or election to waive a joint and survivor annuity. Section 1.401(a)-11(c)(3)(i)(C) provides that such a written explanation must contain a general explanation of the relative financial effect of these elections on a participant's annuity.

For a married participant, the QJSA must be at least as valuable as any other optional form of benefit payable under the plan at the same time. See § 1.401(a)-20, Q & A-16. Further, the anti-forfeiture rules of section 411(a) prohibit a participant's benefit under a defined benefit plan from being satisfied through payment of a form of benefit that is actuarially less valuable than the value of the participant's accrued benefit expressed in the form of an annual benefit commencing at normal retirement age. These determinations must be made using reasonable actuarial assumptions. However, see section 417(e)(3) and § 1.417(e)-1(d) for actuarial assumptions required for use in certain present value calculations.

Final regulations under section 417(a)(3) regarding disclosure of the relative value and financial effect of optional forms of benefit as part of QJSA explanations provided to participants receiving qualified retirement plan distributions were published in the Federal Register on December 17, 2003. See § 1.417(a)(3)-1 (68 FR 70141). The 2003 regulations are generally effective for QJSA explanations provided with respect to annuity starting dates beginning on or after October 1, 2004.

The 2003 regulations were issued in response to concerns that, in certain cases, the information provided to participants under section 417(a)(3) regarding available distribution forms pursuant to § 1.401(a)-20, Q & A-36, does not adequately enable them to compare those distribution forms without professional advice. In particular, participants who are eligible for early retirement benefits in the form of both subsidized annuity distributions and unsubsidized single-sum distributions may be receiving explanations that do not adequately dis-

¶20,261L

close the value of the subsidy that is foregone if the single-sum distribution is elected. In such a case, merely disclosing the amount of the single-sum distribution and the amount of the annuity payments would not adequately enable a participant to make an informed comparison of the relative values of those distribution forms. The 2003 regulations address this problem, as well as the problem of disclosure in other cases where there are significant differences in value among optional forms, and also clarify the rules regarding the disclosure of the financial effect of benefit payments.

A number of commentators requested that the effective date of the 2003 regulations be postponed. Among the reasons cited is the need in some plans for sponsors to complete an extensive review and analysis of optional forms of benefit in order to prepare proper comparisons of the relative values of those optional forms to the QJSA. They noted that recently proposed regulations under section 411(d)(6) would permit elimination of certain optional forms of benefit and that many plan sponsors can be expected to engage in a thorough review of all of the optional forms of benefit under their plans following publication of the those regulations in final form. See § 1.411(d)-3, 69 FR 13769 (March 24, 2004). These commentators argued that it would be inefficient for plans to be required to incur the costs of two such extensive analyses in succession, rather than a single analysis of optional forms that might serve to some extent for purposes of both the relative value regulations and the section 411(d)(6) regulations. After consideration of these comments, Treasury and the IRS issued Announcement 2004-58 (2004-29 I.R.B. 66), which postponed the effective date of the 2003 regulations under § 1.417(a)(3)-1 for certain QJSA explanations.

Under section 101 of Reorganization Plan No. 4 of 1978 (43 FR 47713), the Secretary of the Treasury has interpretive jurisdiction over ERISA provisions that are parallel to the Code provisions addressed in these regulations. Therefore, these proposed regulations would apply for purposes of the parallel rules in section 205(c)(3) of ERISA, as well as for section 417(a)(3) of the Code.

Explanation of Provisions

Consistent with Announcement 2004-58, these proposed regulations would modify the 2003 regulations to provide that the 2003 regulations are generally effective for QJSA explanations provided with respect to annuity starting dates beginning on or after February 1, 2006. In the interim, plans that do not comply with § 1.417(a)(3)-1 would be required to comply with the 1988 regulations regarding disclosure of relative value and financial effect.

However, the existing effective date under § 1.417(a)(3)-1 of the 2003 regulations is retained for explanations with respect to any optional form of benefit that is subject to the requirements of section 417(e)(3) (e.g., single sums, social security level income options, distributions in the form of partial single sums in combination with annuities, or installment payment options) if the actuarial present value of that optional form is less than the actuarial present value (as determined under section 417(e)(3)) of the QJSA. Thus, for example, a QJSA explanation provided with respect to an annuity starting date beginning on or after October 1, 2004, must comply with § 1.417(a)(3)-1 to the extent that the plan provides for payment to that participant in the form of a single sum that does not reflect an early retirement subsidy available under the QJSA. Where the existing effective date is retained, the plan must disclose the relative value of the QJSA for the participant even if the plan provides a disclosure of relative values that is not tailored to the participant's marital status. Accordingly, if a plan provides a relative value disclosure based on the single life annuity (the QJSA for a single participant) to a married participant, the plan must also include a comparison of the value of the QJSA to the value of the single life annuity.

The proposed regulations include a special rule that would enable a plan to use the delayed effective date rule even if there are minor differences between the value of an optional form and the value of the QJSA for a married participant that are caused by the calculation of the amount of the optional form of benefit based on the life annuity rather than on the QJSA. Under this special rule, solely for purposes of the effective date provisions, the actuarial present value of an optional form is treated as not being less than the actuarial present value of the QJSA if the following two conditions are met. First, using the applicable interest rate and applicable mortality table under §§ 1.417(e)-1(d)(2) and (3), the actuarial present value of that optional form is not less than the actuarial present value of the QJSA for an unmarried participant. Second, using reasonable actuarial assumptions, the actuarial present value of the QJSA for an unmarried participant is not less than the actuarial present value of the QJSA for a married participant.

These proposed regulations would also modify the 2003 regulations in several other respects. First, for purposes of disclosing the normal

form of benefit as part of a disclosure made in the form of generally applicable information, reasonable estimates of the type permitted to be used to disclose participant-specific information may be used to determine the normal form of benefit, but only if the plan follows the requirements applicable to reasonable estimates used in disclosing participant-specific information (such as offering a more precise calculation upon request and revising previously offered information consistent with the more precise information). Second, a QJSA explanation does not fail to satisfy the requirements for QJSA explanations made in the form of disclosures of generally applicable information merely because the QJSA explanation contains an item of participant-specific information in place of the corresponding generally applicable information.

In addition, the proposed regulations would modify § 1.401(a)-20, Q&A-16, to clarify the interaction of the rule prohibiting a plan from providing an option to a married individual that is worth more than the QJSA with the requirement that certain optional forms of benefit be calculated using specified actuarial assumptions. Under that clarification, a plan would not fail to satisfy the requirements of § 1.401(a)-20, Q&A-16, merely because the amount payable under an optional form of benefit that is subject to the minimum present value requirement of section 417(e)(3) is calculated using the applicable interest rate (and, for periods when required, the applicable mortality table) under section 417(e)(3).

Dates of Applicability

The changes to § 1.401(a)-20, A-36, and § 1.417(a)(3)-1 are proposed to apply as if they had been included in TD 9099 (68 FR 70141). The change to § 1.401(a)-20, Q&A-16, is proposed to apply as if it had been included in TD 8219 (53 FR 31837). Taxpayers may rely on these proposed regulations for guidance pending the issuance of final regulations.

Special Analyses

It has been determined that this notice of proposed rulemaking is not a significant regulatory action as defined in Executive Order 12866. Therefore a regulatory assessment is not required. It also has been determined that section 553(b) of the Administrative Procedure Act (5 U.S.C. chapter 5) does not apply to these regulations, and because the regulation does not impose a collection of information on small entities, the Regulatory Flexibility Act (5 U.S.C. chapter 6) does not apply. Pursuant to section 7805(f) of the Code, this notice of proposed rulemaking will be submitted to the Chief Counsel for Advocacy of the Small Business Administration for comment on its impact on small business.

Comments and Public Hearing

Before these proposed regulations are adopted as final regulations, consideration will be given to any electronic or written comments (preferably a signed original and eight (8) copies) that are submitted timely to the IRS. In addition to the other requests for comments set forth in this document, the IRS and Treasury also request comments on the clarity of the proposed rule and how it may be made easier to understand. All comments will be available for public inspection and copying. A public hearing will be scheduled if one is requested.

Drafting Information

The principal authors of these regulations are Bruce Perlin and Linda S.F. Marshall of the Office of the Division Counsel/Associate Chief Counsel (Tax Exempt and Government Entities). However, other personnel from the IRS and Treasury participated in their development.

List of Subjects in 26 CFR Part 1

Income taxes, Reporting and recordkeeping requirements.

Proposed Amendments to the Regulations

Accordingly, 26 CFR part 1 is proposed to be amended as follows:

PART 1—INCOME TAX; TAXABLE YEARS BEGINNING AFTER DECEMBER 31, 1986

Paragraph 1. The authority citation for part 1 continues to read in part as follows:

Authority: 26 U.S.C. 7805 * * *

Par. 2. Section 1.401(a)-20 is amended by:

1. Adding a sentence to the end of Q&A-16.

2. Adding a sentence to the end of Q&A-36.

The additions read as follows:

§ 1.401(a)-20 Requirements of qualified joint and survivor annuity and qualified preretirement survivor annuuity.

* * * * *

A-16 * * * A plan does not fail to satisfy the requirements of this Q&A-16 merely because the amount payable under an optional form of benefit that is subject to the minimum present value requirement of section 417(e)(3) is calculated using the applicable interest rate (and, for periods when required, the applicable mortality table) under section 417(e)(3).

* * * * *

A-36 * * * However, the rules of § 1.401(a)-20, Q&A-36, as it appeared in 26 CFR Part 1 revised April 1, 2003, apply to the explanation of a QJSA under section 417(a)(3) for an annuity starting date prior to February 1, 2006.

* * * * *

Par. 3. Section 1.417(a)(3)-1 is amended by:

1. Removing the language "paragraph (c)(3)(iii) of" from paragraph (c)(2)(ii)(A).

2. Adding a sentence to the end of paragraph (d)(2)(ii).

3. Adding paragraph (d)(5).

4. Revising paragraph (f).

The additions and revision read as follows:

§ 1.417(a)(3)-1 Required explanation of qualified joint and survivor annuity and qualified preretirement survivor annuity.

* * * * *

(d) * * *

(2) * * *

(ii) *Actual benefit must be disclosed.* * * * Reasonable estimates of the type described in paragraph (c)(3)(i) may be used to determine the normal form of benefit for purposes of this paragraph (d)(2)(ii) if the requirements of paragraphs (c)(3)(ii) and (iii) of this section are satisfied with respect to those estimates.

* * * * *

(5) *Use of participant-specific information in generalized notice.* A QJSA explanation does not fail to satisfy the requirements of this paragraph (d) merely because it contains an item of participant-specific information in place of the corresponding generally applicable information.

* * * * *

(f) *Effective date*—(1) *General effective date for QJSA explanations.* Except as provided in paragraph (f)(2) of this section, this section applies to a QJSA explanation with respect to any distribution with an annuity starting date that is on or after February 1, 2006.

(2) *Special effective date for certain QJSA explanations*—(i) *Application to QJSA explanations with respect to certain optional forms that are less valuable than the QJSA.* This section also applies to a QJSA explanation with respect to any distribution with an annuity starting date that is on or after October 1, 2004, and before February 1, 2006, if the actuarial present value of any optional form of benefit that is subject to the requirements of section 417(e)(3) (e.g., single sums, distributions in the form of partial single sums in combination with annuities, social security level income options, and installment payment options) is less than the actuarial present value (as determined under § 1.417(e)-1(d)) of the QJSA. For purposes of this paragraph (f)(2)(i), the actuarial present value of an optional form is treated as not less than the actuarial present value of the QJSA if—

(A) Using the applicable interest rate and applicable mortality table under § 1.417(e)-1(d)(2) and (3), the actuarial present value of that optional form is not less than the actuarial present value of the QJSA for an unmarried participant; and

(B) Using reasonable actuarial assumptions, the actuarial present value of the QJSA for an unmarried participant is not less than the actuarial present value of the QJSA for a married participant.

(ii) *Requirement to disclose differences in value for certain optional forms.* A QJSA explanation with respect to any distribution with an annuity starting date that is on or after October 1, 2004, and before February 1, 2006, is only required to be provided under this section with respect to—

(A) An optional form of benefit that is subject to the requirements of section 417(e)(3) and that has an actuarial present value that is less than the actuarial present value of the QJSA (as described in paragraph (f)(2)(i) of this section); and

(B) The QJSA (determined without application of paragraph (c)(2)(ii) of this section).

(3) *Annuity starting date.* For purposes of paragraphs (f)(1) and (2) of this section, in the case of a retroactive annuity starting date under section 417(a)(7), as described in § 1.417(e)-1(b)(3)(vi), the date of commencement of the actual payments based on the retroactive annuity starting date is substituted for the annuity starting date.

(4) *Effective date for QPSA explanations.* This section applies to any QPSA explanation provided on or after July 1, 2004.

Mark E. Matthews,

Deputy Commissioner for Services and Enforcement.

[FR Doc. 05-1553 Filed 1-27-05; 8:45 am]

¶ 20,261M

IRS proposed regulations: Roth 401(k) plans: Special rules.—The IRS has issued proposed regulations that provide guidance on the requirements for Roth 401(k) plans. The proposed rules would amend IRS Reg. § 1.401(k)-1(f) to provide a definition of designated Roth contributions and special rules relating to such contributions. The proposed rules would take effect for plan years beginning on or after January 1, 2006.

The proposed regulations, which were published in the *Federal Register* on March 2, 2005 (70 FR 10062), were previously reproduced below.

The final regulations, which were published in the *Federal Register* on January 3, 2006 (71 FR 6), are reproduced at ¶ 11,731F (IRS Reg. Sec. 1.401(k)-0), ¶ 11,731G (IRS Reg. Sec. 1.401(k)-1(f)), ¶ 11,731H (IRS Reg. Sec. 1.401(k)-2), ¶ 11,731L (IRS Reg. Sec. 1.401(k)-6), ¶ 11,732C (IRS Reg. Sec. 1.401(m)-0), ¶ 11,732H (IRS Reg. Sec. 1.401(m)-2) and ¶ 11,732K (IRS Reg. Sec. 1.401(m)-5). The preamble to the regulations is found at ¶ 24,508B.

¶ 20,261N

IRS proposed regulations: Defined benefit plans: Defined contribution plans: Benefit and contribution limits.—The IRS has issued proposed regulations that provide guidance on the Code Sec. 415 limits on benefits and contributions under qualified retirement plans. The proposed rules, which consolidate past guidance on changes in the law since Code Sec. 415 regulations were last published in 1981, provide additional information that answers many outstanding questions for plan sponsors and administrators. Among other things, the regulations address the application of the defined benefit limits when an employee receives multiple benefit streams beginning at different ages and the treatment of compensation paid after an individual terminates employment. Under the proposed rules, National Guard and Reserve members would be permitted to continue to contribute to their employer's retirement plan while on active duty. With certain exceptions, the proposed rules would take effect for limitation years beginning on or after January 1, 2007.

The proposed regulations, which were published in the *Federal Register* on May 31, 2005 (70 FR 31213), are reproduced below.

DEPARTMENT OF THE TREASURY

Internal Revenue Service

26 CFR Parts 1 and 11

[REG-130241-04]

RIN 1545-BD52

Limitations on Benefits and Contributions Under Qualified Plans

AGENCY: Internal Revenue Service (IRS), Treasury.

ACTION: Notice of proposed rulemaking and notice of public hearing.

SUMMARY: This document contains proposed amendments to the regulations under section 415 of the Internal Revenue Code regarding limitations on benefits and contributions under qualified plans. The proposed amendments would provide comprehensive guidance regarding the limitations of section 415, including updates to the regulations for numerous statutory changes since regulations were last published under section 415. The proposed amendments would also make conforming changes to regulations under sections 401(a)(9), 401(k), 403(b), and 457, and would make other minor corrective changes to regulations under section 457. These regulations will affect administrators of, participants in, and beneficiaries of qualified employer plans and certain other retirement plans. This document also provides notice of a public hearing on these proposed regulations.

DATES: Written or electronic comments must be received by July 25, 2005. Requests to speak and outlines of topics to be discussed at the public hearing scheduled for August 17, 2005, at 10 a.m., must be received by July 27, 2005.

ADDRESSES: Send submissions to: CC:PA:LPD:PR (REG-130241-04), room 5203, Internal Revenue Service, POB 7604, Ben Franklin Station, Washington, DC 20044. Submissions may be hand-delivered Monday through Friday between the hours of 8 a.m. and 4 p.m. to: CC:PA:LPD:PR (REG-130241-04), Courier's Desk, Internal Revenue Service, 1111 Constitution Avenue, NW., Washington D.C. Alternatively, taxpayers may submit comments electronically directly to the IRS Internet site at *www.irs.gov/regs*. The public hearing will be held in the Auditorium, Internal Revenue Building, 1111 Constitution Avenue, NW., Washington, D.C.

FOR FURTHER INFORMATION CONTACT: Concerning the regulations, Vernon S. Carter at (202) 622-6060 or Linda S. F. Marshall at (202) 622-6090; concerning submissions and the hearing and/or to be placed on the building access list to attend the hearing, Richard A. Hurst at (202) 622-7180 (not toll-free numbers).

SUPPLEMENTARY INFORMATION:

Background

This document contains proposed amendments to the Income Tax Regulations (26 CFR Parts 1 and 11) under section 415 of the Internal Revenue Code (Code) relating to limitations on benefits and contributions under qualified plans. In addition, this document contains conforming amendments to the Income Tax Regulations under sections 401(a)(9), 401(k), 403(b), and 457 of the Code, as well as minor corrective changes to the regulations under section 457.

Section 415 was added to the Internal Revenue Code by the Employee Retirement Income Security Act of 1974 (ERISA), and has been amended many times since. Section 415 provides a series of limits on benefits under qualified defined benefit plans and contributions and other additions under qualified defined contribution plans. See also section 401(a)(16). Pursuant to section 415(a)(2), the limitations of section 415 also apply to section 403(b) annuity contracts and to simplified employee pensions described in section 408(k) (SEPs). In addition, the limitations of section 415 for defined contribution plans apply to contributions allocated to any individual medical account that is part of a pension or annuity plan established pursuant to section 401(h) and to amounts attributable to medical benefits allocated to an account established for a key employee pursuant to section 419A(d)(1).

Section 404(j) provides generally that, in computing the amount of any deduction for contributions under a qualified plan, benefits and annual additions in excess of the applicable limitations under section 415 are not taken into account. In addition, in computing the applicable limits on deductions for contributions to a defined benefit plan, and in computing the full funding limitation, an adjustment under section 415(d)(1) is not taken into account for any year before the year for which that adjustment first takes effect.

The definition of compensation that is used for purposes of section 415 is also used for a number of other purposes under the Internal Revenue Code. Under section 219(b)(3), contributions on behalf of an employee to a plan described in section 501(c)(18) are limited to 25% of compensation as defined in section 415(c)(3). Section 404(a)(12) provides that, for various specified purposes in determining deductible limits under section 404, the term *compensation* includes amounts treated as *participant's compensation* under section 415(c)(3)(C) or (D). Pursuant to section 409(b)(2), for purposes of determining whether employer securities are allocated proportionately to compensation in accordance with the rules of section 409(b)(1), the amount of compensation paid to a participant for any period is the amount of such participant's compensation (within the meaning of section 415(c)(3)) for such period. Under section 414(q)(3), for purposes of determining whether an employee is a highly compensated employee within the meaning of section 414(q), the term *compensation* has the meaning given such term by section 415(c)(3). Section 414(s), which defines the term *compensation* for purposes of certain qualification requirements, generally provides that the term *compensation* has the meaning given such term by section 415(c)(3). Under section 416(c)(2), allocations to participants who are non-key employees under a top-heavy plan that is a defined contribution plan are required to be at least 3% of the participant's compensation (within the meaning of section 415(c)(3)). Pursuant to section 457(e)(5), the term *includible compensation*, which is used in limiting the amount that can be deferred for a participant under an eligible deferred compensation plan as defined in section 457(b), has the same meaning as the term *participant's compensation* under section 415(c)(3).

Comprehensive regulations regarding section 415 were last issued in 1981. See TD 7748, published in the **Federal Register** on January 7, 1981 (46 FR 1687). Since then, changes to section 415 have been made in the Economic Recovery Tax Act of 1981, Public Law 97-34 (95 Stat. 320) (ERTA), the Tax Equity and Fiscal Responsibility Act of 1982, Public Law 97-248 (96 Stat. 623) (TEFRA), the Deficit Reduction Act of 1984, Public Law 98-369 (98 Stat. 494) (DEFRA), the Tax Reform Act of 1986, Public Law 99-514 (100 Stat. 2481) (TRA '86), the Technical and Miscellaneous Revenue Act of 1988, Public Law 100-647 (102 Stat. 3342) (TAMRA), the Uruguay Round Agreements Act of 1994, Public Law 103-465 (108 Stat. 4809) (GATT), the Small Business Job Protection Act of 1996, Public Law 104-188 (110 Stat. 1755) (SBJPA), the Community Renewal Tax Relief Act of 2000, Public Law 106-554 (114 Stat. 2763), the Economic Growth and Tax Relief Reconciliation Act of 2001, Public Law 107-16 (115 Stat. 38) (EGTRRA), the Job Creation and Worker Assistance Act of 2002, Public Law 107-147 (116 Stat. 21) (JCWAA), the Pension Funding Equity Act of 2004, Public Law 108-218 (118 Stat. 596) (PFEA), and the Working Families Tax Relief Act of 2004, Public Law 108-311 (118 Stat. 1166).

Although two minor changes to the regulations were made after 1981, most of the statutory changes made since that time are not reflected in the regulations, but in IRS notices, revenue rulings, and other guidance of general applicability, as follows:

• Notice 82-13 (1982-1 C.B. 360) provides guidance on deductible employee contributions (including guidance under section 415) to reflect the addition of provisions relating to deductible employee contributions in ERTA.

• Notice 83-10 (1983-1 C.B. 536) provides guidance on the changes to section 415 made by TEFRA. The TEFRA changes were extensive, and included reductions of the dollar limits on annual benefits under a defined benefit plan and annual additions under a defined contribution plan, changes to the age and form adjustments made in the application of the limits under a defined benefit plan, and rules regarding the deductibility of contributions with respect to benefits that exceed the applicable limitations of section 415.

• Notice 87-21 (1987-1 C.B. 458) provides guidance on the changes to section 415 made by TRA '86. The TRA '86 changes modified the rules for the indexing of the dollar limit on annual additions under a defined contribution plan, the treatment of employee contributions as annual additions, and the rules for age adjustments under defined benefit plans, and added a phase-in of the section 415(b)(1)(A) dollar limitation over 10 years of participation, as well as rules permitting the limitations of section 415 to be incorporated by reference under the terms of a plan.

• Rev. Rul. 95-6 (1995-1 C.B. 80) and Rev. Rul. 2001-62 (2001-2 C.B. 632) (superseding Rev. Rul. 95-6) provide mortality tables to be used to make certain form adjustments to benefits under a defined benefit plan for purposes of applying the limitations of section 415, pursuant to the requirement to use a specified mortality table added by GATT.

• Rev. Rul. 95-29 (1995-1 C.B. 81) and Rev. Rul. 98-1 (1998-1 C.B. 249) (modifying and superseding Rev. Rul. 95-29) provide guidance regarding certain form and age adjustments under a defined benefit plan pursuant to changes made by GATT (as modified under SBJPA), including transition rules relating to those adjustments.

• Notice 99-44 (1999-2 C.B. 326) provides guidance regarding the repeal under SBJPA of the limitation on the combination of a defined benefit plan and a defined contribution plan under former section 415(e).

• Notice 2001-37 (2001-1 C.B. 1340) provides guidance regarding the inclusion of salary reduction amounts for qualified transportation fringe benefits in the definition of compensation for purposes of section 415, as provided under the Community Renewal Tax Relief Act of 2000.

• Rev. Rul. 2001-51 (2001-2 C.B. 427) provides guidance relating to the increases in the limitations of section 415 for both defined benefit and defined contribution plans, which were enacted as part of EGTRRA.

• Notice 2002-2 (2002-1 C.B. 285) provides guidance regarding the treatment of reinvested ESOP dividends under section 415(c), to reflect changes made by SBJPA.

• Rev. Rul. 2002-27 (2002-1 C.B. 925) provides guidance pursuant to which a definition of compensation can be used for purposes of applying the limitations of section 415 even if that definition treats certain specified amounts that may not be available to an employee in cash as subject to section 125 (and therefore included in compensation).

• Rev. Rul. 2002-45 (2002-2 C.B. 116) provides guidance regarding the treatment of certain payments to defined contribution plans to restore losses resulting from actions by a fiduciary for which there is a reasonable risk of liability for breach of a fiduciary duty (including the treatment of those payments under section 415).

• Notice 2004-78 (2004-48 I.R.B. 879) provides guidance regarding the actuarial assumptions that must be used for distributions with annuity starting dates occurring during plan years beginning in 2004 and 2005, to determine whether an amount payable under a defined benefit plan in a form that is subject to the minimum present value requirements of section 417(e)(3) satisfies the requirements of section 415. This guidance reflects changes made in PFEA.

These guidance items are reflected in the proposed regulations with some modifications. In addition, the proposed regulations reflect other statutory changes not previously addressed by guidance, and include some other changes and clarifications to the existing final regulations. Treasury and the IRS believe that a single restatement of the section 415 rules serves the interests of plan sponsors, third-party administrators, plan participants, and plan beneficiaries. To the extent practicable, this preamble identifies and explains substantive changes from the existing final regulations or existing guidance.

Explanation of Provisions

Overview

A. *Reflection of statutory changes*

These proposed regulations reflect the numerous statutory changes to section 415 and related provisions that have been made since 1981. Some of the statutory changes reflected in the proposed regulations are as follows:

• The current statutory limitations under section 415(b)(1)(A) and 415(c)(1) applicable for defined benefit and defined contribution plans, respectively, as most recently amended by EGTRRA.

• Changes to the rules for age adjustments to the applicable limitations under defined benefit plans, under which the dollar limitation is adjusted for commencement before age 62 or after age 65.

• Changes to the rules for benefit adjustments under defined benefit plans. The proposed regulations also specify the parameters under which a benefit payable in a form other than a straight life annuity is adjusted in order to determine the actuarially equivalent annual benefit that is subject to the limitations of section 415(b).

• The phase-in of the dollar limitation under section 415(b)(1)(A) over 10 years of participation, as added by TRA '86.

• The addition of the section 401(a)(17) limitation on compensation that is permitted to be taken into account in determining plan benefits, as added by TRA '86, and the interaction of this requirement with the limitations under section 415.

• Exceptions to the compensation-based limitation under section 415(b)(1)(B) for governmental plans, multiemployer plans, and certain other collectively bargained plans.

• Changes to the aggregation rules under section 415(f) under which multiemployer plans are not aggregated with single-employer plans for purposes of applying the compensation-based limitation of section 415(b)(1)(B) to a single-employer plan.

• The repeal under SBJPA of the section 415(e) limitation on the combination of a defined benefit plan and a defined contribution plan.

• The changes to section 415(c) that were made in conjunction with the repeal under EGTRRA of the exclusion allowance under section 403(b)(2).

• The current rounding and base period rules for annual cost-of-living adjustments pursuant to section 415(d), as most recently amended in EGTRRA and the Working Families Tax Relief Act of 2004.

• Changes to section 415(c) under which certain types of arrangements are no longer subject to the limitations of section 415(c) (e.g., individual retirement accounts other than SEPs) and other types of arrangements have become subject to the limitations of section 415(c) (e.g., certain individual medical accounts).

• The inclusion in compensation (for purposes of section 415) of certain salary reduction amounts not included in gross income.

B. *Other significant changes*

The proposed regulations contain new rules for determining the annual benefit under a defined benefit plan where there has been more than one annuity starting date (e.g., where benefits under a plan are aggregated with benefits under another plan under which distributions previously commenced). These rules would resolve the numerous issues that have arisen in determining the annual benefit under a plan where the application of the section 415(b) limitations must take into account prior distributions as well as currently commencing distributions.

The proposed regulations also provide specific rules regarding when amounts received following severance from employment are considered compensation for purposes of section 415, and when such amounts are permitted to be deferred pursuant to section 401(k), section 403(b), or section 457(b). These rules would resolve issues that have arisen with respect to payments made after the end of employment. The proposed regulations generally provide that amounts received following severance from employment are not considered to be compensation for purposes of section 415, but provide exceptions for certain payments made within 2 ½ months following severance from employment. These exceptions apply to payments (such as regular compensation, and payments for overtime, commissions, and bonuses) that would have been payable if employment had not terminated, and to payments with respect to leave that would have been available for use if employment had not terminated. This notice of proposed rulemaking includes corresponding changes to the regulations under sections 401(k), 403(b), and 457 that would provide that amounts receivable following severance from employment can only be deferred if those amounts meet these conditions. The rule pursuant to which compensation received after severance from employment is not considered compensation for purposes of section 415 generally does not apply to payments to an individual in qualified military service.

§ 1.415(a)-1: General rules

Section 1.415(a)-1 of these proposed regulations sets forth general rules relating to limitations under section 415 and provides an overview of the remaining regulations, including cross-references to special rules that apply to section 403(b) annuities, multiemployer plans, and governmental plans. In addition, this section provides rules for a plan's incorporation by reference of the rules of section 415 pursuant to section 1106(h) of TRA '86 (including detailed guidelines regarding incorporation by reference of the annual cost-of-living adjustments to the statutory limits and the application of default rules), rules for plans maintained by more than one employer, and rules that apply in other special situations.

§ 1.415(b)-1: Limitations applicable to defined benefit plans

Section 1.415(b)-1 of these proposed regulations sets forth rules for applying the limitations on benefits under a defined benefit plan. Under these limitations, the annual benefit must not be greater than the lesser of $160,000 (as adjusted pursuant to section 415(d)) or 100% of the participant's average compensation for the participant's high 3 consecutive years. A retirement benefit payable in a form other than a straight life annuity is adjusted to an actuarially equivalent straight life annuity to determine the annual benefit payable under that form of distribution. In addition, the dollar limitation under section 415(b)(1)(A) is actuarially adjusted for benefit payments that commence before age 62 or after age 65. The proposed regulations clarify that, in addition to applying to benefits payable to participants and beneficiaries, the limitations of section 415(b) apply to accrued benefits and benefits payable from an annuity contract distributed to a participant. Thus, the limitations of section 415(b) apply to a participant's entire accrued benefit, regardless of whether the benefit is vested. Where a participant's accrued benefit is computed pursuant to the fractional rule of section 411(b)(1)(C), the limitations of section 415(b) apply to the accrued benefit as of the end of the limitation year and, for ages prior to normal retirement age, are not required to be applied to the projected annual benefit commencing at normal retirement age from which the accrued benefit is computed. In addition, the proposed regulations provide a number of other updates, clarifications, and other changes to the existing regulations, as described below.

A. Actuarial assumptions used to convert benefit to a straight life annuity

The proposed regulations provide rules under which a retirement benefit payable in any form other than a straight life annuity is converted to the straight life annuity that is actuarially equivalent to that other form to determine the annual benefit (which is used to demonstrate compliance with section 415) with respect to that form of distribution. These rules reflect statutory changes that specify the actuarial assumptions that are to be used for these equivalency calculations (including, for plan years beginning in 2004 and 2005, the use of a 5.5% interest rate for benefits that are subject to the present value rules of section 417(e)(3),[1] as set forth in PFEA), as well as published guidance that has been issued since 1981. In addition to setting forth rules for adjusting forms of benefit other than straight life annuities, the proposed regulations would permit the IRS to issue published guidance setting forth simplified methods for making these adjustments.

Under the proposed regulations, the annual benefit is determined as the greater of the actuarially equivalent straight life annuity determined under the plan's actuarial assumptions or the actuarially equivalent straight life annuity determined under actuarial assumptions specified by statute. This methodology implements the policy reflected in section 415(b)(2)(E), under which the plan's determination that a straight life annuity is actuarially equivalent to a particular optional form of benefit is overridden only when the optional form of benefit is more valuable than the corresponding straight life annuity when compared using statutorily specified actuarial assumptions.

The rules in the proposed regulations under which a retirement benefit payable in any form other than a straight life annuity is converted to a straight life annuity to determine the annual benefit with respect to that form of distribution generally follow the rules set forth in Rev. Rul. 98-1. However, the calculation of the actuarially equivalent straight life annuity determined using the plan's assumptions for actuarial equivalence has been simplified for a form of benefit that is not subject to the minimum present value rules of section 417(e)(3). Under the simplified calculation, instead of determining the actuarial assumptions used under the plan and applying those assumptions to convert an optional form of benefit to an actuarially equivalent straight life annuity, the regulations use the straight life annuity, if any, that is payable at the same age under the plan. This straight life annuity is then compared to the straight life annuity that is the actuarial equivalent of the optional form of benefit, determined using the standardized assumptions, and the larger of the two straight life annuities is used for purposes of demonstrating compliance with section 415. This simplification has not been extended to forms of benefit that are subject to the minimum present value rules of section 417(e), however, because under the plan those forms of benefit may be determined as the actuarial equivalent of the deferred annuity, rather than as the actuarial equivalent of the immediate straight life annuity.

B. Inclusion of social security supplements in annual benefit

The proposed regulations clarify that a social security supplement is included in determining the annual benefit. Under section 415(b)(2)(B), the annual benefit does not include ancillary benefits that are not directly related to retirement benefits. However, because a social security supplement is payable upon retirement as a form of retirement income, it is a retirement benefit. Thus, a social security supplement is included in determining the annual benefit without regard to whether it is an ancillary benefit or a QSUPP within the meaning of § 1.401(a)(4)-12.

C. Determination of high 3 average compensation

The proposed regulations would make two changes that would have a significant effect on the determination of a participant's average compensation for the participant's high 3 consecutive years. Consistent with the provisions of section 415(b)(3), the proposed regulations would restrict compensation used for this purpose to compensation earned in periods during which the participant was an active participant

in the plan. In addition, the proposed regulations under § 1.415(c)-2 would clarify the interaction of the requirements of section 401(a)(17) and the definition of compensation that must be used for purposes of determining a participant's average compensation for the participant's high 3 consecutive years. Because a plan may not base benefit accruals on compensation in excess of the limitation under section 401(a)(17), a plan's definition of compensation used for purposes of applying the limitations of section 415 is not permitted to reflect compensation in excess of the limitation under section 401(a)(17). Thus, for example, where a participant commences receiving benefits in 2005 at age 75 (so that the adjusted dollar limitation could be as high as $379,783), and the participant had compensation in excess of the applicable section 401(a)(17) limit for 2002, 2003, and 2004, the participant's benefit under the plan is limited by the average compensation for his highest three years as limited by section 401(a)(17) (i.e., $201,667, or the average of $200,000, $200,000, and $205,000).

The proposed regulations set forth rules for computing the limitation of section 415(b)(1)(B) of 100% of the participant's compensation for the period of the participant's high 3 years of service for a participant who is employed with the employer while an active participant for less than 3 consecutive calendar years. For such a participant, the period of a participant's high 3 years of service is the actual number of consecutive years of employment (including fractions of years) while an active participant in the plan. In such a case, the limitation of section 415(b)(1)(B) of 100% of the participant's compensation for the period of the participant's high 3 years of service is computed by averaging the participant's compensation during the participant's longest consecutive period of employment while a plan participant over the actual period of service (including fractions of years, but not less than one year).

D. Treatment of benefits paid partially in the form of a QJSA

Under section 415(b)(2)(B), the portion of any joint and survivor annuity that constitutes a qualified joint and survivor annuity (QJSA) as defined in section 417(b) is not taken into account in determining the annual benefit for purposes of applying the limitations of section 415(b). The proposed regulations would clarify how this exception from the limitations of section 415 for the survivor annuity portion of a QJSA applies to benefits paid partially in the form of a QJSA and partially in some other form. Under this clarification, the rule excluding the survivor portion of a QJSA from the annual benefit applies to the survivor annuity payments under the portion of a benefit that is paid in the form of a QJSA, even if another portion of the benefit is paid in some other form.

E. Dollar limitation applicable to early or late commencement

The determination of the age-adjusted dollar limitation under the proposed regulations reflects the rules enacted in EGTRRA. As provided in Q&A-3 of Rev. Rul. 2001-51, this determination generally follows the same steps and procedures as those used in Rev. Rul. 98-1, except that such determination takes into account the increased defined benefit dollar limitation enacted by EGTRRA and that the adjustments for early or late commencement are no longer based on social security retirement age. Applying rules that are similar to those that are used for determining actuarial equivalence among forms of benefits, the proposed regulations generally use the plan's determinations for actuarial equivalence of early or late retirement benefits, but override those determinations where the use of the specified statutory assumptions results in a lower limit.

The proposed regulations adopt rules for mortality adjustments used in computing the dollar limitation on a participant's annual benefit for distributions commencing before age 62 or after age 65. Under these rules, to the extent that a forfeiture does not occur upon the participant's death, no adjustment is made to reflect the probability of the participant's death during the relevant time period, and to the extent a forfeiture occurs upon the participant's death, an adjustment must be applied to reflect the probability of the participant's death during the relevant time period. These rules generally are consistent with the guidance provided in Notice 83-10.

The proposed regulations would also provide a simplified method for applying this rule. Under this simplified method, a plan is permitted to treat no forfeiture as occurring upon a participant's death if the plan does not charge participants for providing a qualified preretirement survivor annuity, but only if the plan applies this treatment for adjustments that apply both before age 62 and after age 65.

---

[1] Section 417(e)(3) provides minimum present value requirements for certain forms of benefit payable from a defined benefit plan under which payments cannot be less than the amount calculated using a specified interest rate and a specified mortality table. For forms of benefit that are subject to the minimum present value rules of section 417(e)(3), the limitations of section 415(b) apply to limit the amount of a distribution even if those limitations result in a lower distribution than would otherwise be required under the rules of section 417(e)(3). See § 1.417(e)-1(d)(1).

F. Nonapplication of adjustment to dollar limitation for early commencement with respect to police department and fire department employees

Consistent with section 415(b)(2)(G) and (H), the proposed regulations would provide that the early retirement reduction does not apply to certain participants in plans of state and local government units who are employees of a police department or fire department, or former members of the Armed Forces of the United States. This rule applies to any participant in a plan maintained by a state or political subdivision of a state who is credited, for benefit accrual purposes, with at least 15 years of service as either (1) a full-time employee of any police department or fire department of the state or political subdivision that provides police protection, firefighting services, or emergency medical services, or (2) a member of the Armed Forces of the United States. The proposed regulations would clarify that the application of this rule depends on whether the employer is a police department or fire department of the state or political subdivision, rather than on the job classification of the individual participant.

G. Application of $10,000 exception

Pursuant to section 415(b)(4), the benefits payable with respect to a participant satisfy the limitations of section 415(b) if the retirement benefits payable with respect to such a participant under the plan and all other defined benefit plans of the employer do not exceed $10,000 for the plan year or for any prior plan year, and the employer has not at any time maintained a defined contribution plan in which the participant participated. The proposed regulations would clarify that the section 415(b)(4) alternative $10,000 limitation is applied to actual distributions made during each year. Thus, a distribution for a limitation year that exceeds $10,000 is not within the section 415(b)(4) alternative limitation (and therefore will not be excepted from the otherwise applicable limits of section 415(b)), even if the distribution is a single-sum distribution that is the actuarial equivalent of an accrued benefit with annual payments that are less than $10,000.

H. Exclusion of annual benefit attributable to mandatory employee contributions from annual benefit

The proposed regulations would retain the rules under existing final regulations that the annual benefit does not include the annual benefit attributable to mandatory employee contributions. For this purpose, the term "mandatory employee contributions" means amounts contributed to the plan by the employee that are required to be contributed as a condition of employment, as a condition of participation in the plan, or as a condition of obtaining benefits (or additional benefits) under the plan attributable to employer contributions. See section 411(c)(2)(C). Employee contributions to a defined benefit plan that are not maintained in a separate account as described in section 414(k) constitute mandatory employee contributions (even if section 411 does not apply to the plan) because, depending upon the investment performance of plan assets, employer contributions may be needed to pay a portion of the participant's benefit that is conditioned upon these employee contributions. The rules covering mandatory employee contributions do not extend to voluntary contributions because voluntary employee contributions (plus earnings thereon) are treated as a separate defined contribution plan rather than as part of a defined benefit plan.

The proposed regulations would retain the rule under the existing regulations that the annual benefit attributable to mandatory employee contributions is determined using the factors described in section 411(c)(2)(B) and the regulations thereunder, regardless of whether section 411 applies to the plan. The proposed regulations also would clarify that the following are not treated as employee contributions: (1) contributions that are picked up by a governmental employer as provided under section 414(h)(2), (2) repayment of any loan made to a participant from the plan, and (3) repayment of any amount that was previously distributed.

I. Exclusion of annual benefit attributable to rollover contributions from annual benefit

The proposed regulations would clarify that the annual benefit does not include the annual benefit attributable to rollover contributions made to a defined benefit plan (i.e., rollover contributions that are not maintained in a separate account that is treated as a separate defined contribution plan under section 414(k)). In such a case, the annual benefit attributable to rollover contributions is determined by applying the rules of section 411(c) treating the rollover contributions as employee contributions (regardless of whether section 411 applies to the plan). This will occur, for example, if a distribution is rolled over from a defined contribution plan to a defined benefit plan to provide an annuity distribution. Thus, in the case of rollover contributions from a defined contribution plan to a defined benefit plan to provide an annuity distri-

bution, the annual benefit attributable to those rollover contributions for purposes of section 415 is determined by applying the rules of section 411(c), regardless of the assumptions used to compute the annuity distribution under the plan. Accordingly, in such a case, if the plan uses more favorable factors than those specified in section 411(c) to determine the amount of annuity payments arising from a rollover contribution, the annual benefit under the plan would reflect the excess of those annuity payments over the amounts that would be payable using the factors specified in section 411(c)(3).

Rollover contributions to an account that is treated as a separate defined contribution plan under section 414(k) do not give rise to an annual benefit because the separate account is not treated as a defined benefit plan under section 415(b). Furthermore, under the rules relating to defined contribution plans, these rollover contributions to a separate account are excluded from the definition of annual additions to a defined contribution plan.

J. Treatment of benefits transferred among plans

The proposed regulations would modify the rules of the existing final regulations for determining the amount of transferred benefits that are excluded from the annual benefit under a defined benefit plan in the event of a transfer from another defined benefit plan. These modifications are designed to ensure that transferred benefits are not counted twice by the same employer toward the limitations of section 415(b) and, similarly, to prevent the circumvention of the limitations of section 415(b) through benefit transfers to plans of unrelated employers. Under the proposed regulations, if the transferee plan's benefits are required to be taken into account pursuant to section 415(f) and §1.415(f)-1 in determining whether the transferor plan satisfies the limitations of section 415(b), then the transferred benefits are included in determining the annual benefit under the transferee plan and are disregarded in determining the annual benefit under the transferor plan. Accordingly, in such a case, the annual benefit under each plan is determined taking into account the actual benefits provided under that plan after the transfer.

In contrast, if the transferee plan's benefits are not required to be taken into account pursuant to section 415(f) and §1.415(f)-1 in determining whether the transferor plan satisfies the limitations of section 415(b), then the assets associated with those transferred liabilities (other than surplus assets) are treated by the transferor plan as distributed as a single-sum distribution. This will occur, for example, if the employer sponsoring the transferor plan is a predecessor employer with respect to the participant whose benefits are transferred to the transferee plan, where the transferee plan's benefits are not required to be taken into account pursuant to section 415(f) and §1.415(f)-1 in determining whether the transferor plan satisfies the limitations of section 415(b). Although such a transfer is treated as a distribution in computing the annual benefit under the transferor plan, no corresponding adjustment to the annual benefit under the transferee plan is made to reflect the fact that some of the benefits provided under the transferee plan are attributable to the transfer. Thus, the actual benefit provided under the transferee plan is used to determine the annual benefit under the transferee plan even though the transferred amount is included as a distribution in determining the annual benefit under the transferor plan. In most such cases, however, a participant whose benefits have been transferred would accrue no additional benefit under the transferor plan that would be required to be tested under the that plan (in combination with the transferred benefits).

K. 10-year phase-in of limitations based on years of participation and years of service

The proposed regulations would provide rules for applying the 10-year phase-in of the dollar limitation based on years of participation in the plan, as added by TRA '86, and would modify the rules set forth in final regulations for applying the 10-year phase-in of the compensation limit based on years of service. The proposed regulations follow the guidance set forth in Notice 87-21 for determining years of participation, and apply analogous rules for determining years of service for this purpose.

§ 1.415(b)-2: Multiple annuity starting dates

Section 1.415(b)-2 of the proposed regulations sets forth rules that apply in computing the annual benefit under one or more defined benefit plans in the case of multiple annuity starting dates (i.e., in cases in which a participant has received one or more distributions in limitation years prior to an increase in the accrued benefit occurring during the current limitation year or prior to the annuity starting date for a distribution that commences during the current limitation year). These rules apply, for example, where benefit distributions to a participant have previously commenced under a plan that is aggregated with a plan from which the participant receives current accruals, or where a new distribution election is effective during the current limitation year with respect to a distribution that commenced in a prior limitation year. These rules also apply where benefit payments are increased as a result of plan terms applying a cost-of-living adjustment pursuant to an adjustment of the dollar limit of section 415(b)(1)(A) made pursuant to section 415(d), if the plan does not provide for application of the safe harbor methodology set forth in the proposed regulations for determining the adjusted amount of the benefit.

In the case of multiple annuity starting dates, the annual benefit that is subject to the limits of section 415(b) and §1.415(b)-1(a) is equal to the sum of (1) the annual benefit determined with respect to any accrued benefit with respect to which distribution has not yet commenced as of the current determination date, computed pursuant to the rules of §1.415(b)-1, (2) the annual benefit determined with respect to any distribution with an annuity starting date that occurs within the current limitation year and on or before the current determination date, computed pursuant to the rules of §1.415(b)-1, (3) the annual benefit determined with respect to the remaining amounts payable under any distribution with an annuity starting date that occurred during a prior limitation year, computed pursuant to the rules of §1.415(b)-1, and (4) the annual benefit attributable to prior distributions. For this purpose, the current determination date is the last day of period for which an increase in the participant's benefit accrues if an increase in the participant's accrued benefit occurs during the limitation year, and if there is no such increase, the current determination date is the annuity starting date for the distribution that commences during the limitation year. The annual benefit determined using this formula is tested for compliance with section 415(b) as of the current determination date, applying the dollar limitation (which is adjusted under section 415(d) to the current determination date and is also adjusted for the participant's age as of the current determination date) and the compensation limitation applicable as of that date (which is adjusted under section 415(d) to the current determination date but is not adjusted based on the participant's age).

Under the proposed regulations, the annual benefit attributable to prior distributions is determined by adjusting the amounts of prior distributions to an actuarially equivalent straight life annuity commencing at the current determination date. The proposed regulations apply rules that are analogous to the rules for adjusting other benefits to determine the amount of the actuarially equivalent straight life annuity for purposes of determining the annual benefit attributable to prior distributions. Under these rules, the amount and time of prior distributions made to the participant is taken into account, and the prior distributions are adjusted to the actuarially equivalent straight life annuity commencing at the current determination date using interest and mortality assumptions that apply generally for purposes of applying the limitations of section 415(b) to a benefit in a form other than a straight life annuity. For this purpose, the actuarially equivalent straight life annuity commencing at the current determination date must reflect an actuarial increase to the present value of payments to reflect that the participant has survived during the interim period.

The actuarial assumptions used to calculate the annual benefit attributable to a prior distribution are determined as of the current determination date, and are based on the form of the prior distribution. For a prior distribution to which section 417(e)(3) did not apply, the annual benefit attributable to the prior distribution is the greater of the annual amount of a straight life annuity commencing at the current determination date that is the actuarial equivalent of that prior distribution, computed using the actuarial factors specified under the plan that provides for the current distribution or current accrual that are used to determine offsets, if any, for prior distributions, or the annual amount of a straight life annuity commencing at the current determination date that is the actuarial equivalent of that prior distribution, computed using the currently applicable statutory actuarial factors under section 415(b)(2)(E)(i) and (v). Similarly, for a prior distribution to which section 417(e)(3) applied, the annual benefit attributable to the prior distribution is the greater of the annual amount of a straight life annuity commencing at the current determination date that is the actuarial equivalent of that prior distribution, computed using the actuarial factors specified under the plan that provides for the current distribution or current accrual that are used to determine offsets, if any, for prior distributions, or the annual amount of a straight life annuity commencing at the current determination date that is the actuarial equivalent of that prior distribution, computed using the currently applicable statutory actuarial factors under section 415(b)(2)(E)(ii) and (v).

Apart from determining the actuarial factors applicable to calculating the annual benefit attributable to prior distributions, the form of the prior distribution does not otherwise affect the determination of the annual benefit attributable to prior distributions. Thus, for example, if a participant has received $50,000 per year for the past four years, the determination of the annual benefit attributable to prior distributions will be the same if those distributions are part of a 10-year certain and life annuity or are part of a straight life annuity because both of those distribution forms are subject to the same actuarial factors for determining the annual benefit attributable to prior distributions. In either case, the determination of the annual benefit attributable to prior distributions will be determined by applying the interest and mortality assumptions used under the plan to determine offsets, if any, for prior distributions to determine a straight life annuity that is actuarially equivalent to the four prior payments of $50,000, applying the statutory actuarial assumptions to determine a straight life annuity that is actuarially equivalent to the four prior payments of $50,000, and then taking the greater of the two straight life annuity amounts. Determining the annual benefit attributable to prior distributions on the basis of the amount of distributions made rather than on the form of those distributions (or on the basis of the accrued benefit that underlies those distributions) is designed to simplify the application of the multiple annuity starting date rules.

The proposed regulations provide that a prior distribution is not reflected in the annual benefit attributable to prior distributions to the extent the prior distribution has been repaid to the plan with interest (because the amounts attributable to such a prior distribution are reflected in the annual benefit in other ways). Thus, a prior distribution that has been entirely repaid to the plan (with interest) does not give rise to an annual benefit attributable to prior distributions. Similarly, if a prior distribution was made, and a repayment was subsequently made that was less than the amount of the prior distribution (including reasonable interest), the annual benefit attributable to prior distributions is determined by multiplying the annual benefit attributable to the prior distribution by one minus a fraction, the numerator of which is the amount of the repayment and the denominator of which is the amount of the prior distribution plus reasonable interest.

The proposed regulations provide an additional requirement that applies where a stream of annuity payments is modified by a new distribution election. This additional requirement is also imposed in §1.401(a)(9)-6, Q&A-13(c)(3). Under this additional requirement, which is intended to limit the extent to which benefits can increase as a result of a change in market interest rates, if a stream of annuity payments is modified by a new distribution election, the payments under the annuity that are paid before the modification plus the modified payments must satisfy the requirements of §1.415(b)-1 determined as of the original annuity starting date, using the interest rates and mortality table applicable to such date. Following the issuance of the regulations under section 401(a)(9), commentators suggested that the rule should be modified to permit a plan to reflect cost-of-living adjustments under section 415(d) that occur between the original annuity starting date and the date of modification in applying the additional test. These proposed regulations adopt this suggestion, and provide that a plan will not fail to satisfy the additional requirement merely because payments reflect cost-of-living adjustments pursuant to section 415(d) for payments no earlier than the time those adjustments are effective and in amounts no greater than amounts determined under §1.415(d)-1(a)(5). In addition, the proposed regulations include an amendment to §1.401(a)(9)-6, Q&A-13(c)(3), to reflect this change.

§1.415(c)-1: Limitations applicable to defined contribution plans

Section 1.415(c)-1 of these proposed regulations sets forth rules that apply to limitations on annual additions under a defined contribution plan. Under these limitations, annual additions must not be greater than the lesser of $40,000 (as adjusted pursuant to section 415(d)) or 100% of the participant's compensation for the limitation year. The term "annual additions" generally means the sum for any year of employer contributions, employee contributions, and forfeitures. In addition to applying to qualified defined contribution plans, the limitations on defined contribution plans apply to section 403(b) annuity contracts, simplified employee pensions described in section 408(k), mandatory employee contributions to qualified defined benefit plans, and contributions to certain medical accounts.

The proposed regulations reflect a number of statutory changes to section 415(c) that were made after the issuance of existing final regulations. Among these changes are the revised limitation amounts under section 415(c), the revised rules applicable to employee stock ownership plans, and the rules applying the limitations of section 415(c) to certain medical benefit plans. The proposed regulations also would make some other changes to existing regulations, as discussed below.

If annual additions under an annuity contract that otherwise satisfies the requirements of section 403(b) exceed the limitations of section

415(c), then the portion of the contract that includes that excess annual addition fails to be a section 403(b) annuity contract (and instead is a contract to which section 403(c) applies), and the remaining portion of the contract is a section 403(b) annuity contract. As under regulations recently proposed under section 403(b) (69 FR 67075, November 16, 2004), the proposed regulations include a provision under which the status of the remaining portion of the contract as a section 403(b) contract is not retained unless, for the year of the excess and each year thereafter, the issuer of the contract maintains separate accounts for each such portion. In addition, consistent with the change to section 403(b)(1) made in JCWAA, the proposed regulations provide that the limitations under section 415(c) apply to any section 403(b) annuity contract, regardless of whether the contract satisfies the requirements of section 414(i) to be a defined contribution plan. Thus, the limitations under section 415(c) apply to a section 403(b) annuity contract even if the limitations of section 415(b) also apply to the contract (i.e., if the contract is a church plan that is covered by the grandfather rule of section 251(e)(5) of TEFRA).

The proposed regulations clarify that the IRS will treat a sale or exchange by the employee or the employer that transfers assets to a plan where the consideration paid by the plan is less than the fair market value of the assets transferred to the plan as giving rise to an annual addition in the amount of the difference between the value of the assets transferred and the consideration.

Consistent with Rev. Rul. 2002-45, the proposed regulations provide that a restorative payment that is allocated to a participant's account does not give rise to an annual addition for any limitation year. For this purpose, restorative payments are payments made to restore losses to a plan resulting from actions by a fiduciary for which there is reasonable risk of liability for breach of a fiduciary duty under Title I of ERISA, where plan participants who are similarly situated are treated similarly with respect to the payments. Generally, payments to a defined contribution plan are restorative payments only if the payments are made in order to restore some or all of the plan's losses due to an action (or a failure to act) that creates a reasonable risk of liability for such a breach of fiduciary duty. The proposed regulations provide that, in addition to payments to a plan made pursuant to Department of Labor order or court-approved settlement to restore losses to a qualified defined contribution plan on account of the breach of fiduciary duty, restorative payments include payments made pursuant to the Department of Labor's Voluntary Fiduciary Correction Program to restore losses to a qualified defined contribution plan on account of the breach of fiduciary duty. However, payments made to a plan to make up for losses due merely to market fluctuations and other payments that are not made on account of a reasonable risk of liability for breach of a fiduciary duty under Title I of ERISA are contributions that give rise to annual additions and are not restorative payments.

The proposed regulations would retain the rule for taxable employers under existing regulations that the deadline for making a contribution to the plan that is credited to a participant's account for a limitation year for purposes of section 415(c). Under this rule, employer contributions are not treated as credited to a participant's account for a particular limitation year unless the contributions are actually made to the plan no later than 30 days after the end of the period described in section 404(a)(6) applicable to the taxable year with or within which the particular limitation year ends. The proposed regulations would modify the corresponding rule for tax-exempt employers. Under the proposed regulations, the deadline for a tax-exempt employer to make a contribution to the plan that is credited to a participant's account for a limitation year for purposes of section 415(c) is the 15th day of the tenth calendar month following the close of the taxable year with or within which the particular limitation year ends. This date corresponds to the due date for Form 5500 (with extensions) in cases in which the taxable year coincides with the plan year, and generally corresponds to the contribution due date for taxable employers who request filing extensions. The deadline for contributions for tax-exempt employers under the proposed regulations would be an extension from the earlier deadline now applicable under existing regulations (i.e., the 15 th day of the sixth calendar month following the close of the taxable year with or within which the particular limitation year ends). The extent to which elective contributions constitute plan assets for purposes of the prohibited transaction provisions of section 4975 and Title I of ERISA is determined in accordance with regulations and rulings issued by the Department of Labor. See 29 CFR 2510.3-102.

The proposed regulations clarify the operation of the special increased limitation applicable to church plans under section 415(c)(7). Under this rule, notwithstanding the generally applicable limitations, annual additions for a section 403(b) annuity contract for a year with respect to an individual who is a church employee are treated as not exceeding the limitation of section 415(c) if such annual additions for

the year are not in excess of $10,000. However, the total amount of additions with respect to any participant that are permitted to be taken into account for purposes of this rule for all years may not exceed $40,000. In addition, for any individual who is a church employee performing any services for the church outside the United States, additions for a section 403(b) annuity contract for any year are not treated as exceeding the limitations of section 415(c) if those annual additions for the year do not exceed the greater of $3,000 or the employee's includible compensation. The proposed regulations would clarify that the $40,000 cumulative total only applies to excesses over what would have been permitted to be contributed without regard to this special rule, and clarifies the interaction between the generally applicable church employee rule and the rule for church employees performing services outside the United States. In addition, the proposed regulations would clarify that the special rule that applies to services for a church performed abroad applies to the employee's includible compensation only with respect to services for the church outside the United States.

The correction mechanism in current § 1.415-6(b)(6) for handling excess annual additions is not included in the proposed regulations. It is anticipated that this correction mechanism will be included in the Employee Plans Compliance Resolution System (see Rev. Proc. 2003-44 (2003-1 C.B. 1051)) in the future.

The proposed regulations generally would retain the rules under existing regulations providing that a contribution to reduce accumulated funding deficiencies or a contribution made pursuant to a funding waiver relates to the limitation year of the initial funding obligation. However, the proposed regulations would provide that any interest paid by the employer with respect to such a contribution that is in excess of a reasonable amount is taken into account as an annual addition for the limitation year when the contribution is made (in contrast to existing regulations, which require interest in excess of a reasonable amount to be taken into account as an annual addition for the limitation year for which the contribution was originally required). Rev. Rul. 78-223 (1978-1 C.B. 125) provides a method for determining contributions required to amortize waived contributions under a defined contribution plan. The application of any of the methods described in Rev. Rul. 78-223 will result in reasonable interest payments for purposes of applying the rules of section 415 (provided that, if a fixed interest rate in excess of 5% is used to amortize waived contributions, the interest rate is reasonable). Thus, for example, the actual yield method (under which the adjusted account balance is increased or decreased periodically at the actual rate of investment return experienced by the plan for such period) can be used for this purpose.

§ 1.415(c)-2: Definition of compensation

Section 1.415(c)-2 of these proposed regulations defines the term *compensation*, which is defined in section 415(c)(3) and used for purposes of applying the limitations of section 415 as well as for various other purposes specified under the Internal Revenue Code. The proposed regulations reflect a number of statutory changes to section 415(c)(3) that were made after the issuance of existing final regulations. Among these changes are the inclusion in compensation of certain deemed amounts for disabled participants and nontaxable elective amounts for deferrals under sections 401(k), 403(b), and 457, cafeteria plan elections under section 125, and qualified transportation fringe elections under section 132(f)(4). In addition to these changes, the proposed regulations would make some other changes to existing regulations, as discussed below.

The proposed regulations provide specific guidelines regarding when amounts received following severance from employment are considered compensation for purposes of section 415. The following are types of post-severance payments that are not excluded from compensation because of timing if they are paid within 2 ½ months following severance from employment: (1) payments that, absent a severance from employment, would have been paid to the employee while the employee continued in employment with the employer and are regular compensation for services during the employee's regular working hours, compensation for services outside the employee's regular working hours (such as overtime or shift differential), commissions, bonuses, or other similar compensation; and (2) payments for accrued bona fide sick, vacation, or other leave, but only if the employee would have been able to use the leave if employment had continued. Under the proposed regulations, the rule generally excluding payments after severance from employment from compensation does not apply to payments to an individual who does not currently perform services for the employer by reason of qualified military service (as that term is used in section 414(u)(1)) to the extent those payments do not exceed the amounts the individual would have received if the individual had continued to perform services for the employer rather than entering qualified military service. This notice of proposed rulemaking also contain corresponding proposed amendments to the regulations under sections 401(k), 403(b), and 457 that would provide that amounts received following severance from employment can be deferred only if they are considered compensation under the rules of section 415.

§ 1.415(d)-1: Cost-of-living adjustments

Section 1.415(d)-1 of these proposed regulations sets forth rules that apply to cost-of-living adjustments to the various limitations of section 415 pursuant to section 415(d). Section 415(d) provides for the dollar and compensation limitations on annual benefits and the dollar limitation on annual additions to be adjusted annually for increases in the cost of living based on adjustment procedures similar to the procedures used to adjust social security benefit amounts. These adjustments also apply for other purposes as specified in the Internal Revenue Code. The proposed regulations specify the manner in which these adjustments are determined each year, and reflect statutory changes to the adjustment methodology made after the 1981 regulations were issued. In addition, the proposed regulations make several other changes to existing final regulations, as discussed below.

The proposed regulations would specify the circumstances under which an adjusted limit is permitted to be applied to participants who have previously commenced receiving benefits under a defined benefit plan. Under the proposed regulations, the adjusted dollar limitation is applicable to current employees who are participants in a defined benefit plan and to former employees who have retired or otherwise terminated their service under the plan and have a nonforfeitable right to accrued benefits, regardless of whether they have actually begun to receive such benefits. A plan is permitted to provide that the annual increase applies for a participant who has previously commenced receiving benefits only to the extent that benefits have not been paid. Thus, for example, a plan cannot provide that this annual increase applies to a participant who has previously received the entire plan benefit in a single-sum distribution. However, a plan is permitted to provide for an increase in benefits to a participant who accrues additional benefits under the plan that could have been accrued without regard to the adjustment of the dollar limitation (including benefits that accrue as a result of a plan amendment) on or after the effective date of the adjusted limitation.

The proposed regulations provide for a safe harbor under which the annual benefit will satisfy the limitations of section 415(b) for the current limitation year following an adjustment to benefit payments that is made to reflect the cost-of-living adjustment made pursuant to section 415(d). If such adjustments are made in accordance with this safe harbor, the multiple annuity starting date rules of § 1.415(b)-2 do not apply on account of such adjustments. Under this safe harbor, if a participant has received one or more distributions under an annuity stream that satisfies the requirements of section 415(b) before the adjustment, the plan's benefits will satisfy the limitations of section 415(b) if the amounts payable to the employee for the limitation year and subsequent limitation years are not greater than the amounts that would otherwise be payable under the annuity stream without regard to the adjustment, multiplied by a fraction. The numerator of this fraction is the limitation under section 415(b) (i.e., the lesser of the applicable dollar limitation under section 415(b)(1)(A), as adjusted for age at commencement, and the applicable compensation-based limitation under section 415(b)(1)(B)) in effect for the distribution following the adjustment, and the denominator of this fraction is such limitation under section 415(b) in effect for the distribution immediately before the adjustment.

§ 1.415(f)-1: Combining and aggregating plans

Section 1.415(f)-1 of these proposed regulations sets forth rules for combining and aggregating plans pursuant to section 415(f). Under section 415(f) and these proposed regulations, for purposes of applying the limitations of section 415(b) and (c), all defined benefit plans of an employer are treated as one defined benefit plan, and all defined contribution plans of an employer are treated as one defined contribution plan. The controlled group rules of section 414(b) and (c) (as modified by section 415(h)), the affiliated service group rules of section 414(m), and the leased employee rules of section 415(n) apply for purposes of determining whether a plan that is maintained by an entity other than the employer is considered maintained by the employer for purposes of applying the aggregation rules of section 415(f).

The proposed regulations would also make various changes and clarifications to the existing regulations. The proposed regulations would clarify that an employer's plan must be aggregated with all plans maintained by a predecessor employer (see section 414(a)), regardless of whether any such plan is assumed by the employer. Pursuant to section 414(a)(1), the proposed regulations would provide that, for

purposes of section 415, a former employer is a predecessor employer with respect to a participant in a plan maintained by an employer if the employer maintains a plan under which the participant had accrued a benefit while performing services for the former employer, but only if that benefit is provided under the plan maintained by the employer. In addition, the proposed regulations would provide pursuant to section 414(a)(2) that, with respect to an employer of a participant, a former entity that antedates the employer is a predecessor employer with respect to the participant if, under the facts and circumstances, the employer constitutes a continuation of all or a portion of the trade or business of the former entity. This will occur, for example, where formation of the employer constitutes a mere formal or technical change in the employment relationship and continuity otherwise exists in the substance and administration of the business operations of the former entity and the employer. See *Lear Eye Clinic, Ltd. v. Commissioner*, 106 T.C. 418, 425-429 (1996).

The proposed regulations provide rules for aggregating participation and service for purposes of the 10-year phase-in of the limitations on defined benefit plans. Under these rules, years of participation in all aggregated plans and years of service for employers maintaining all aggregated plans are counted for purposes of applying the 10-year phase-in rules.

The proposed regulations clarify the aggregation rules that apply to section 403(b) annuity contracts, other plans of the employer, and plans of related employers, in light of changes made in EGTRRA. Generally a section 403(b) annuity contract is not aggregated with plans that are maintained by the participant's employer because the section 403(b) annuity contract is deemed maintained by the participant and not the employer for purposes of section 415. However, if a participant on whose behalf a section 403(b) annuity contract is purchased is in control of any employer for a limitation year, the annuity contract for the benefit of the participant is treated as a defined contribution plan maintained by both the controlled employer and the participant for that limitation year and accordingly, the section 403(b) annuity contract is aggregated with all other defined contribution plans maintained by the employer. Accordingly, the employer that contributes to the section 403(b) annuity contract must obtain information from participants regarding employers controlled by those participants and plans maintained by those controlled employers to monitor compliance with applicable limitations to comply with applicable reporting and withholding obligations. In addition to applying the rules under existing final regulations for purposes of determining control for purposes of section 415(f), the proposed regulations would apply the rules under proposed § 1.414(c)-5 (regarding aggregation rules for tax-exempt employers), as published in the **Federal Register** on November 16, 2004 (69 FR 67075).

The proposed regulations also provide that a multiemployer plan, as defined in section 414(f), is not aggregated with other multiemployer plans for purposes of determining any section 415 limitation. In addition, a multiemployer plan will not be aggregated with non-multiemployer plans for purposes of applying the 100% of compensation benefit limit to non-multiemployer plans under section 415(b)(1)(B). In general, under the proposed regulations, benefits of all employers are taken into account in applying the limitations of section 415 to a multiemployer plan. However, a multiemployer plan is permitted to provide that, where a participating employer maintains both a plan which is not a multiemployer plan and a multiemployer plan, only the benefits provided by the employer under the multiemployer plan are aggregated with the benefits under the non-multiemployer plan.

§ 1.415(g)-1: Disqualification of plans and trusts

Section 1.415(g)-1 of these proposed regulations sets forth rules regarding disqualification of plans and trusts, including plans and trusts that are aggregated pursuant to § 1.415(f)-1. In large part, proposed § 1.415(g)-1 replicates the rules of § 1.415-9 of the existing final regulations regarding ordering rules for disqualifying plans and trusts that are aggregated for purposes of compliance with section 415. In addition, the proposed regulations provide rules for disqualification where an individual medical account (as described in section 415(l)) and a post-retirement medical benefits account for key employees (as described in section 419A(d)) is combined with a qualified defined contribution plan for purposes of applying section 415(c). If the combined plan exceeds those limitations for a particular limitation year, the qualified defined contribution plan (rather than the medical account) is disqualified for the limitation year.

§ 1.415(i)-1: Limitation year

Section 1.415(j)-1 of these proposed regulations sets forth rules regarding limitation years that are used as the period for demonstrating compliance with section 415. In addition to setting forth general rules that generally correspond to rules under existing regulations, the proposed regulations provide specific guidelines with respect to overlapping limitation years for aggregated plans. These rules reflect the guidance provided in Rev. Rul. 79-5 (1979-1 C.B. 165). Where defined contribution plans with different limitations years are aggregated, the rules of section 415(c) must be applied with respect to each limitation year of each such plan. For each such limitation year, the requirements of section 415(c) are applied to annual additions that are made for that time period with respect to the participant under all aggregated plans. Similarly, where defined benefit plans with different limitations years are aggregated, the rules of section 415(c) must be applied with respect to each limitation year of each such plan. Thus, for example, the dollar limitation of section 415(b)(1)(A) applicable to the limitation year for each plan must be applied to annual benefits under all aggregated plans to determine whether the plan satisfies the requirements of section 415(b).

Sections 415(m) and 415(n)

These proposed regulations do not contain provisions relating to section 415(m) (regarding treatment of qualified governmental excess benefit arrangements) and section 415(n) (regarding the purchase of permissive service credit from a governmental defined benefit plan). Comments are requested regarding the need for regulations or other guidance on issues arising under these statutory provisions.

Other changes: section 457 regulations

These proposed regulations also include revisions to the regulations under section 457 that are in addition to the revisions to reflect the treatment of compensation paid after severance from employment. The additional revisions do not include any substantive changes, but would merely make clarifications, including corrections in an example illustrating the section 457 catch-up rules and a correction in the rules relating to unforeseeable emergencies to reflect recent revisions in the definition of a dependent (made under the Working Families Tax Relief Act of 2004, which modified the definition of the term *dependent* under section 152).

Proposed Effective Dates

The regulations under section 415 are proposed to apply to limitation years beginning on or after January 1, 2007. Except as described below, until these regulations are issued as final regulations, the existing regulations remain in effect (to the extent not modified by statutory changes). A defined benefit plan that was adopted and effective before May 31, 2005 will be considered to satisfy the limitations of section 415(b) for a participant with respect to benefits accrued or payable under the plan as of the effective date of final regulations implementing these proposed regulations pursuant to plan provisions adopted and in effect on May 31, 2005, but only if such plan provisions meet the requirements of statutory provisions, regulations, and other published guidance in effect on May 31, 2005. Thus, plans that were in compliance with the rules of section 415 as in effect prior to the finalization of these regulations will not be disqualified based on benefits that arise pursuant to plan provisions that were adopted and in effect on May 31, 2005 and that accrue prior to the effective date of final regulations implementing these proposed regulations, even if those benefits no longer comply with the requirements of section 415 as set forth under those final regulations. However, such a plan will not be permitted to provide for the accrual of additional benefits for a participant on or after the effective date of final regulations implementing these proposed regulations unless such additional benefits, together with the participant's other accrued benefits, comply with those new final regulations.

Reliance on Compensation Timing Rules and Changes to Regulations Under Sections 401(a)(9) and 457

Pending issuance of final regulations, taxpayers may rely on the modifications in these proposed regulations contained in § 1.401(k)-1(e)(8), § 1.415(c)-2(e), and § 1.457-4(d) regarding post-severance compensation payments and other compensation timing rules, § 1.401(a)(9)-6 regarding certain changes in form of payment, and §§ 1.457-5, -6, and -10 providing corrective and clarifying changes. Pursuant to this reliance, taxpayers may apply the proposed amendments described in this paragraph for periods prior to the effective date of final regulations.

Sunset of EGTRRA Changes

The proposed regulations do not provide rules for the application of the EGTRRA sunset provision (section 901 of EGTRRA), under which the provisions of EGTRRA do not apply to taxable, plan, or limitation years beginning after December 31, 2010. Unless the EGTRRA sunset provision is repealed before it becomes effective, additional guidance will be needed to clarify its application.

Special Analyses

It has been determined that this notice of proposed rulemaking is not a significant regulatory action as defined in Executive Order 12866. Therefore, a regulatory assessment is not required. It has also been determined that section 553(b) of the Administrative Procedure Act (5 U.S.C. chapter 5) does not apply to these regulations, and, because the regulations do not impose a collection of information on small entities, the Regulatory Flexibility Act (5 U.S.C. chapter 6) does not apply. Pursuant to section 7805(f) of the Code, this notice of proposed rulemaking will be submitted to the Chief Counsel for Advocacy of the Small Business Administration for comment on its impact on small business.

Comments and Public Hearing

Before these proposed regulations are adopted as final regulations, consideration will be given to any written (a signed original and eight (8) copies) or electronic comments that are submitted timely to the IRS. The IRS and Treasury Department specifically request comments on the clarity of the proposed regulations and how they may be made easier to understand. All comments will be available for public inspection and copying.

A public hearing has been scheduled for August 17, 2005 at 10 a.m. in the auditorium, Internal Revenue Building, 1111 Constitution Avenue, NW., Washington, DC. Due to building security procedures, visitors must use the main building entrance on Constitution Avenue. In addition, all visitors must present photo identification to enter the building. Because of access restrictions, visitors will not be admitted beyond the immediate entrance area more than 30 minutes before the hearing starts. For more information about having your name placed on the list to attend the hearing, see the "FOR FURTHER INFORMATION CONTACT" section of this preamble.

The rules of 26 CFR 601.601(a)(3) apply to the hearing. Persons who wish to present oral comments at the hearing must submit written (signed original and eight (8) copies) or electronic comments and an outline of the topics to be discussed and the time to be devoted to each topic by July 27, 2005. A period of 10 minutes will be allotted to each person for making comments. An agenda showing the scheduling of the speakers will be prepared after the deadline for receiving outlines has passed. Copies of the agenda will be available free of charge at the hearing.

Drafting Information

The principal authors of these regulations are Vernon S. Carter and Linda S. F. Marshall, Office of Division Counsel/Associate Chief Counsel (Tax Exempt and Government Entities). However, other personnel from the IRS and Treasury participated in the development of these regulations.

List of Subjects

26 CFR Part 1

Income taxes, Reporting and recordkeeping requirements.

26 CFR Part 11

Income taxes, Reporting and recordkeeping requirements.

Proposed Amendments to the Regulations

Accordingly, 26 CFR parts 1 and 11 are proposed to be amended as follows:

PART 1 — INCOME TAXES

Paragraph 1. The authority citation for part 1 continues to read, in part, as follows:

Authority: 26 U.S.C. 7805 * * *

* * * * *

Par. 2. Section 1.401(a)(9)-6, Q&A-13(c)(3) is revised to read as follows:

§ 1.401(a)(9)-6 Required minimum distributions for defined benefit plans and annuity contracts.

A-13. * * * * *

(c) * * *

(3) In accordance with § 1.415(b)-2(c), after taking into account the modification, the payments under the annuity that are paid before the modification plus the modified payments must satisfy the requirements of § 1.415(b)-1 determined as of the original annuity starting date, using the interest rates and mortality table applicable to such date, except

that, for this purpose, payments will not fail to satisfy the requirements of § 1.415(b)-1 determined as of the original annuity starting date merely because the payments are adjusted to reflect cost-of-living adjustments pursuant to section 415(d) that are determined in accordance with § 1.415(d)-1(a)(5); and

* * * * *

Par. 3. Section 1.401(k)-1 is amended by adding paragraph (e)(8) to read as follows:

§ 1.401(k)-1 Certain cash or deferred arrangements.

* * * * *

(e) * * *

(8) *Section 415 compensation required.* A cash or deferred arrangement satisfies this paragraph (e) only if cash or deferred elections can only be made with respect to amounts that are compensation within the meaning of section 415(c)(3) and § 1.415(c)-2. Thus, for example, the arrangement is not a qualified cash or deferred arrangement if an eligible employee who is not in qualified military service (as that term is defined in section 414(u)) can make a cash or deferred election with respect to an amount paid after severance from employment, unless the amount is paid within 2 ½ months following the eligible employee's severance from employment and is described in § 1.415(c)-2(e)(3)(ii).

Par. 4. Section 1.403(b)-3 as proposed to be revised on November 16, 2004 (69 FR 67086), is further proposed to the amended by adding text to paragraph (b)(4)(ii) to read as follows:

§ 1.403(b)-3 Exclusion for contributions to purchase section 403(b) contracts.

(b) * * *

(4) * * *

(ii) *Exceptions.* The exclusion from gross income provided by section 403(b) applies to contributions made for former employees with respect to compensation described in § 1.415(c)-2(e)(3)(ii) (relating to certain compensation paid within 2 ½ months following severance from employment), compensation described in § 1.415(c)-2(g)(4) (relating to compensation paid to participants who are permanently and totally disabled), and compensation relating to qualified military service under section 414(u).

* * * * *

§ 1.415-1 thru § 1.415-10 [Removed]

Par. 5. Sections 1.415-1 through 1.415-10 are removed.

Par. 6. Section 1.415(a)-1 is added to read as follows:

§ 1.415(a)-1 General rules with respect to limitations on benefits and contributions under qualified plans.

(a) *Trusts.* Under sections 415 and 401(a)(16), a trust that forms part of a pension, profit-sharing, or stock bonus plan will not be qualified under section 401(a) if any of the following conditions exists—

(1) In the case of a defined benefit plan, the annual benefit with respect to any participant for any limitation year exceeds the limitations of section 415(b) and § 1.415(b)-1 (taking into account the rules of § 1.415(b)-2);

(2) In the case of a defined contribution plan, the annual additions credited with respect to any participant for any limitation year exceed the limitations of section 415(c) and § 1.415(c)-1; or

(3) The trust has been disqualified under section 415(g) and § 1.415(g)-1 for any year.

(b) *Certain annuities and accounts*—(1) *In general.* Under section 415, an employee annuity plan described in section 403(a), an annuity contract described in section 403(b), or a simplified employee pension described in section 408(k) will not be considered to be described in the otherwise applicable section if any of the following conditions exists—

(i) The annual benefit under a defined benefit plan with respect to any participant for any limitation year exceeds the limitations of section 415(b) and § 1.415(b)-1 (taking into account the rules of § 1.415(b)-2);

(ii) The contributions and other additions credited under a defined contribution plan with respect to any participant for any limitation year exceed the limitations of section 415(c) and § 1.415(c)-1; or

(iii) The employee annuity plan, annuity contract, or simplified employee pension has been disqualified under section 415(g) and § 1.415(g)-1 for any year.

(2) *Special rule for section 403(b) annuity contracts*—(i) *In general.* If the contributions and other additions under an annuity contract that otherwise satisfies the requirements of section 403(b) with respect to any participant for any limitation year exceed the limitations of section 415(c) and § 1.415(c)-1, then the portion of the contract that includes such excess annual addition fails to be a section 403(b) contract (and instead is a contract to which section 403(c) applies), and the remaining portion of the contract is a section 403(b) contract. The status of the remaining portion of the contract as a section 403(b) contract is not retained unless, for the year of the excess and each year thereafter, the issuer of the contract maintains separate accounts for each such portion. See also § 1.403(b)-3(c)(3).

(ii) *Defined benefit plans.* If the annual benefit under an annuity contract that otherwise satisfies the requirements of section 403(b) and that is a defined benefit plan with respect to any participant for any limitation year exceeds the limitations of section 415(b) and § 1.415(b) (taking into account the rules of § 1.415(b)-2), then the portion of the contract that includes such excess annual benefit fails to be a section 403(b) annuity contract (and instead is a contract to which section 403(c) applies), and the remaining portion of the contract is a section 403(b) annuity contract. The status of the remaining portion of the contract as a section 403(b) annuity contract is not retained unless, for the year of the excess and each year thereafter, the issuer of the contract maintains separate accounts for each such portion.

(3) *Section 403(b) annuity contract.* For purposes of section 415 and regulations thereunder, the term *section 403(b) annuity contract* includes arrangements that are treated as annuity contracts for purposes of section 403(b). For example, such term includes custodial accounts described in section 403(b)(7) and retirement income accounts described in section 403(b)(9).

(c) *Regulations*—(1) *In general.* This section provides general rules regarding the application of section 415. For further rules regarding the application of section 415, see—

(i) Section 1.415(b)-1 (for general rules regarding the limit applicable to defined benefit plans);

(ii) Section 1.415(b)-2 (for special rules for defined benefit plans where a participant has multiple annuity starting dates);

(iii) Section 1.415(c)-1 (for general rules regarding the limit applicable to defined contribution plans);

(iv) Section 1.415(c)-2 (for rules regarding the definition of compensation for purposes of section 415);

(v) Section 1.415(d)-1 (for rules regarding cost-of-living adjustments to the various limits of section 415);

(vi) Section 1.415(f)-1 (for rules for aggregating plans for purposes of section 415);

(vii) Section 1.415(g)-1 (for rules regarding disqualification of plans that fail to satisfy the requirements of section 415); and

(viii) Section 1.415(j)-1 (for rules regarding limitation years).

(2) *Cross references to additional rules for section 403(b) annuity contracts.* For additional rules relating to section 403(b) annuity contracts, see—

(i) Section 1.415(c)-2(g)(1) and (3) (relating to the definition of compensation for such annuity contracts);

(ii) Section 1.415(f)-1(g) (relating to rules for such annuity contracts for purposes of combining plans);

(iii) Section 1.415(g)-1(b)(3)(iv)(C) (regarding disqualification of section 403(b) annuity contract aggregated with a qualified defined contribution plan if the combined plans exceed the limitations of section 415(c));

(iv) Section 1.415(g)-1(e) (relating to the plan year for such annuity contracts); and

(v) Section 1.415(j)-1(e) (relating to the limitation year for such annuity contracts).

(3) *Cross references to additional rules for governmental plans.* For additional rules relating to governmental plans, see—

(i) Section 1.415(b)-1(a)(6)(i) (providing an exception from the compensation-based limit of section 415(b)(1)(B) for governmental plans);

(ii) Section 1.415(b)-1(a)(7)(ii) (regarding a special limitation for governmental plans making an election during 1990);

(iii) Section 1.415(b)-1(b)(4) (regarding qualified governmental excess benefit arrangements);

(iv) Section 1.415(b)-1(d)(3) and (4) (regarding age adjustments to the dollar limit of section 415(b)(1)(A) in the case of employees of police departments and fire departments and former members of the United States Armed Forces, and in the case of survivor and disability benefits);

(v) Section 1.415(b)-1(g)(3) (regarding adjustments to applicable limitations for years of participation, and adjustments to applicable limitations for years of service for survivor and disability benefits); and

(vi) Section 1.415(c)-1(b)(3)(iii) (regarding amounts not treated as annual additions).

(4) *Cross references to additional rules for multiemployer plans.* For additional rules relating to multiemployer plans, see—

(i) Paragraph (e) of this section (regarding benefits or contributions taken into account where a plan is maintained by more than one employer);

(ii) Section 1.415(b)-1(a)(6)(ii) (providing an exception from the compensation-based limit for multiemployer plans);

(iii) Section 1.415(b)-1(f)(3) (regarding the application of the minimum $10,000 limitation on benefits in the case of a multiemployer plan);

(iv) Section 1.415(f)-1(h) (providing special rules for aggregating multiemployer plans with other plans); and

(v) Section 1.415(g)-1(b)(3)(ii) (regarding plan disqualification rules where a multiemployer plan is aggregated with a plan that is not a multiemployer plan and the combined plans exceed the limitations of section 415).

(d) *Plan provisions*—(1) *In general.* Although no specific plan provision is required under section 415 in order for a plan to establish or maintain its qualification, the plan provisions must preclude the possibility that any accrual, distribution, or annual addition will exceed the limitations of section 415. For example, a plan may include provisions that automatically freeze or reduce the rate of benefit accrual (in the case of a defined benefit plan) or the annual addition (in the case of a defined contribution plan) to a level necessary to prevent the limitations from being exceeded with respect to any participant. For rules relating to this type of plan provision and the definitely determinable benefit requirement for pension plans, see § 1.401(a)-1(b)(1).

(2) *Special rule for profit-sharing and stock bonus plans.* A provision of a profit-sharing or stock bonus plan that automatically freezes or reduces the amount of annual additions to ensure that the limitations of section 415 will not be exceeded must comply with the requirement set forth in § 1.401-1(b)(1)(ii) or (iii) (as applicable) that such plans provide a definite predetermined formula for allocating the contributions made to the plan among the participants. If the operation of a provision that automatically freezes or reduces the amount of annual additions to ensure that the limitations of section 415 are not exceeded does not involve discretionary action on the part of the employer, the definite predetermined allocation formula requirement is not violated by the provision. If the operation of such a provision involves discretionary action on the part of the employer, the definite predetermined allocation formula requirement is violated. For example, if two profit-sharing plans of one employer otherwise provide for aggregate contributions which may exceed the limits of section 415(c), the plan provisions must specify (without involving employer discretion) under which plan contributions and allocations will be reduced to prevent an excess annual addition and how the reduction will occur.

(3) *Incorporation by reference*—(i) *In general.* A plan is permitted to incorporate by reference the limitations of section 415, and will not fail to meet the definitely determinable benefit requirement or the definite predetermined allocation formula requirement, whichever applies to the plan, merely because it incorporates the limits of section 415 by reference.

(ii) *Section 415 can be applied in more than one manner, but a statutory or regulatory default rule exists.* Where a provision of section 415 is permitted to be applied in more than one manner but is to be applied in a specified manner in the absence of contrary plan provisions (i.e., a default rule exists), if a plan incorporates the limitations of section 415 by reference with respect to that provision of section 415 and does not specifically vary from the default rule, then the default rule applies. With respect to a provision of section 415 for which a default rule exists, if the limitations of section 415 are to be applied in a manner other than using the default rule, the plan must specify the manner in which the limitation is to be applied in addition to generally incorporating the limitations of section 415 by reference. For example, if a plan generally incorporates the limitations of section 415 by reference and does not restrict the accrued benefits to which the amend-

ments to section 415(b)(2)(E) made by GATT apply (as permitted by Q&A-12 of Rev. Rul. 98-1 (1998-1 C.B. 249) (see § 601.601(d) of this chapter), which reflects the amendments to section 767 of GATT made by section 1449 of SBJPA), then the amendments to section 415(b)(2)(E) made by GATT apply to all benefits under the plan.

(iii) *Section 415 can be applied in more than one manner with no statutory or regulatory default.* If a limitation of section 415 may be applied in more than one manner, and there is no governing principle pursuant to which that limitation is applied in the absence of contrary plan provisions, then the plan must specify the manner in which the limitation is to be applied in addition to generally incorporating the limitations of section 415 by reference. For example, if an employer maintains two profit-sharing plans, and if any participant participates in more than one such plan, then both plans must specify (in a consistent manner) under which of the employer's two profit-sharing plans annual additions must be reduced if aggregate annual additions would otherwise exceed the limitations of section 415(c).

(iv) *Former requirements.* A plan cannot incorporate by reference formerly applicable requirements of section 415 that are no longer in force (such as the limits of former section 415(e)).

(v) *Cost-of-living adjustments*—(A) *In general.* A plan is permitted to incorporate by reference the annual adjustments to the limitations of section 415 that are made pursuant to section 415(d). See § 1.415(d)-1 for additional rules relating to cost-of-living adjustments under section 415(d).

(B) *Cost-of-living adjustments not included in accrued benefit until effective.* Notwithstanding that a plan incorporates the increases to the applicable limits under section 415(d) by reference, the accrued benefit of a participant for purposes of section 411 and the annual benefit payable to a participant for purposes of § 1.415(b)-1(a)(1) are not permitted to reflect increases pursuant to the annual increase under section 415(d) of the dollar limitation described in section 415(b)(1)(A) or the compensation limit described in section 415(b)(1)(B) for any period before the annual increase becomes effective. A plan amendment does not violate the requirements of section 411(d)(6) merely because it eliminates the incorporation by reference of the increases under section 415(d) with respect to increases that have not yet occurred. Pursuant to § 1.415(d)-1(a)(3), the increase in each limit that is adjusted pursuant to section 415(d) is effective as of January 1 of each calendar year, and applies with respect to limitation years ending with or within that calendar year. Thus, where an increase in the dollar limitation under section 415(b)(1)(A) results in an increase to the participant's accrued benefit, the increase to the accrued benefit is permitted to occur as of a date no earlier than January 1 of the calendar year for which the increase in the dollar limitation is effective.

(C) *Application of increase in defined benefit dollar limit to participants who have commenced receiving benefits.* The annual increase under section 415(d) of the dollar limitation described in section 415(b)(1)(A) does not apply in limitation years beginning after the annuity starting date to a participant who has previously commenced receiving benefits unless the plan specifies that this annual increase applies to such a participant. Similarly, the annual increase under section 415(d) of the compensation-based limitation described in section 415(b)(1)(B) does not apply in limitation years beginning after the annuity starting date to a participant who has previously commenced receiving benefits unless the plan specifies that this annual increase applies to such a participant.

(D) *Treatment of cost-of-living adjustments for funding purposes.* In general, the annual increase under section 415(d) of the dollar limitation described in section 415(b)(1)(A) and the compensation limitation described in section 415(b)(1)(B) is treated as a plan amendment for purposes of applying sections 404 and 412, regardless of whether the plan is amended to reflect the increase or the plan reflects the increase automatically through operation of plan provisions. However, where a plan reflects the annual increase under section 415(d) of the dollar limitation described in section 415(b)(1)(A) or the compensation limitation described in section 415(b)(1)(B) automatically through operation of plan provisions, the funding method for the plan is permitted to provide for this annual increase to be treated as an experience loss for purposes of applying sections 404 and 412.

(e) *Rules for plans maintained by more than one employer.* Except as provided in § 1.415(f)-1(h)(2)(i) (regarding aggregation of multiemployer plans with plans other than multiemployer plans), for purposes of applying the limitations of section 415 with respect to a participant in a plan maintained by more than one employer, benefits and contributions attributable to such participant from all of the employers maintaining the plan must be taken into account. Furthermore, in applying the limitations of section 415 with respect to such a participant, the total compensation received by the participant from all of the employers maintaining the plan is permitted to be taken into account under any such plan if the plan so provides.

(f) *Special rules*—(1) *Affiliated employers*. Pursuant to section 414(b) and § 1.414(b)-1, all employees of all corporations that are members of a controlled group of corporations (within the meaning of section 1563(a), as modified by section 1563(f)(5), and determined without regard to section 1563(a)(4) and (e)(3)(C)) are treated as employed by a single employer for purposes of section 415. Similarly, pursuant to section 414(c) and §§ 1.414(c)-1 through 1.414(c)-6, all employees of trades or businesses that are under common control are treated as employed by a single employer. Thus, any defined benefit plan or defined contribution plan maintained by any member of a controlled group of corporations (within the meaning of section 414(b)) or by any trade or business (whether or not incorporated) under common control (within the meaning of section 414(c)) is deemed maintained by all such members or such trades or businesses. Pursuant to section 415(h), for purposes of section 415, sections 414(b) and 414(c) are applied by using the phrase "more than 50 percent" instead of the phrase "at least 80 percent" each place the latter phrase appears in section 1563(a)(1), in § 1.414(c)-2, and in § 1.414(c)-5.

(2) *Affiliated service groups*. Any defined benefit plan or defined contribution plan maintained by any member of an affiliated service group (within the meaning of section 414(m)) is deemed maintained by all members of that affiliated service group.

(3) *Leased employees*—(i) *In general*. Pursuant to section 414(n), except as provided in paragraph (f)(3)(ii) of this section, with respect to any person (referred to as the recipient) for whom a leased employee (within the meaning of section 414(n)(2)) performs services, the leased employee is treated as an employee of the recipient, but contributions or benefits provided by the leasing organization that are attributable to services performed for the recipient are treated as provided under a plan maintained by the recipient.

(ii) *Exception for leased employees covered by safe harbor plans*. Pursuant to section 414(n)(5), the rule of paragraph (f)(3)(i) of this section does not apply to a leased employee with respect to services performed for a recipient if—

(A) The leased employee is covered by a plan that is maintained by the leasing organization and that meets the requirements of section 414(n)(5)(B); and

(B) Leased employees (determined without regard to this paragraph (f)(3)(ii)) do not constitute more than 20% of the recipient's nonhighly compensated workforce.

(4) *Permissive service credit under governmental plans*. See section 415(n) for rules regarding the application of the limitations of sections 415(b) and (c) where an employee makes contributions (including a transfer described in section 403(b)(13) or section 457(e)(17)) to a defined benefit governmental plan to purchase permissive service credit under the plan.

(5) *Qualified domestic relations orders*. A benefit provided to an alternate payee (as defined in section 414(p)(8)) of a participant pursuant to a qualified domestic relations order (as defined in section 414(p)(1)(A)) is treated as if it were provided to the participant for purposes of applying the limitations of section 415.

(6) *Effect on other requirements*. Except as provided in § 1.417(e)-1(d)(1), the application of section 415 does not relieve a plan from the obligation to satisfy other applicable qualification requirements. Accordingly, the terms of the plan must provide for the plan to satisfy section 415 as well as all other applicable requirements. For example, if a defined benefit plan has a normal retirement age of 62, and if a participant's benefit remains unchanged between the ages of 62 and 65 because of the application of the section 415(b)(1)(A) dollar limit, the plan satisfies the requirements of section 411 only if the plan either commences distribution of the participant's benefit at normal retirement age (without regard to severance from employment) or provides for a suspension of benefits at normal retirement age that satisfies the requirements of section 411(a)(3)(B) and 29 CFR 2530.203-3. Similarly, if the increase to a participant's benefit under a defined benefit plan in a year after the participant has attained normal retirement age is less than the actuarial increase to the participant's previously accrued benefit because of the application of the section 415(b)(1)(B) compensation limitation (which is not adjusted for commencement after age 65), the plan satisfies the requirements of section 411 only if the plan either commences distribution of the participant's benefit at normal retirement age (without regard to severance from employment) or provides for a suspension of benefits at normal retirement age that satisfies the requirements of section 411(a)(3)(B) and 29 CFR 2530.203-3.

(g) *Effective date*—(1) *General rule*. Except as otherwise provided, §§ 1.415(a)-1, 1.415(b)-1, 1.415(b)-2, 1.415(c)-1, 1.415(c)-2, 1.415(d)-1, 1.415(f)-1, 1.415(g)-1, and 1.415(j)-1 apply to limitation years beginning on or after January 1, 2007.

(2) *Option to apply regulations earlier*. A plan that was adopted and in effect before January 1, 2007, is permitted to apply the provisions of §§ 1.415(a)-1, 1.415(b)-1, 1.415(b)-2, 1.415(c)-1, 1.415(c)-2, 1.415(d)-1, 1.415(f)-1, 1.415(g)-1, and 1.415(j)-1 to limitation years beginning after the date final regulations are published in the **Federal Register**.

(3) *Grandfather rule for preexisting benefits*. A defined benefit plan that was adopted and effective before May 31, 2005 is considered to satisfy the limitations of section 415(b) for a participant with respect to benefits accrued or payable under the plan as of the effective date of final regulations under §§ 1.415(a)-1, 1.415(b)-1, 1.415(b)-2, 1.415(c)-1, 1.415(c)-2, 1.415(d)-1, 1.415(f)-1, 1.415(g)-1, and 1.415(j)-1 (as provided under paragraph (g)(1) and (2) of this section) pursuant to plan provisions that were adopted and in effect on May 31, 2005, but only if such plan provisions meet the requirements of statutory provisions, regulations, and other published guidance in effect on May 31, 2005.

(4) *Sunset of EGTRRA amendments*. Sections 1.415(a)-1, 1.415(b)-1, 1.415(b)-2, 1.415(c)-1, 1.415(c)-2, 1.415(d)-1, 1.415(f)-1, 1.415(g)-1, and 1.415(j)-1 do not address the application of section 901 of the Economic Growth and Tax Relief Reconciliation Act of 2001, Public Law 107-16, 115 Stat. 38 (under which the amendments made by that Act do not apply to limitation years beginning after December 31, 2010).

Par. 7. Section 1.415(b)-1 is added to read as follows:

§ 1.415(b)-1 Limitations for defined benefit plans.

(a) *General rules*—(1) *Maximum limitations*. Except as otherwise provided under this section, a defined benefit plan fails to satisfy the requirements of section 415(a) for a limitation year if, during the limitation year, either the annual benefit (as defined in paragraph (b)(1)(i) of this section) accrued by a participant or the annual benefit payable to a participant at any time under the plan exceeds the lesser of—

(i) $160,000 (as adjusted pursuant to section 415(d), § 1.415(d)-1(a), and this section); or

(ii) 100% of the participant's average compensation for the period of the participant's high 3 years of service (as adjusted pursuant to section 415(d), § 1.415(d)-1(a), and this section).

(2) *Defined benefit plan*. For purposes of section 415 and regulations thereunder, a defined benefit plan is any plan, contract, or account to which section 415 applies pursuant to § 1.415(a)-1(a) or (b) (or any portion thereof) that is not a defined contribution plan within the meaning of § 1.415(c)-1(a)(2). In addition, a section 403(b) contract that is not described in section 414(i) is treated as a defined benefit plan for purposes of section 415 and regulations thereunder.

(3) *Plan provisions*. As required in § 1.415(a)-1(d)(1), in order to satisfy the limitations on benefits under this section, the plan provisions (including the provisions of any annuity) must preclude the possibility that any annual benefit exceeding these limitations will be accrued, distributed, or otherwise payable in any optional form of benefit (including the normal form of benefit) at any time (from the plan, from an annuity contract that will make distributions to the participant on behalf of the plan, or from an annuity contract that has been distributed under the plan). Thus, for example, a plan will fail to satisfy the limitations of this section if the plan does not contain terms that preclude the possibility that any annual benefit exceeding these limitations will be accrued or payable in any optional form of benefit (including the normal form of benefit) at any time, even though no participant has actually accrued a benefit in excess of these limitations.

(4) *Adjustments to dollar limitation for commencement before age 62 or after age 65*. The age-adjusted section 415(b)(1)(A) dollar limit computed pursuant to paragraph (d) or (e) of this section is used in place of the dollar limitation described in section 415(b)(1)(A) and paragraph (a)(1)(i) of this section in the case of a benefit with an annuity starting date that occurs before the participant attains age 62 or after the participant attains age 65.

(5) *Period of high 3 years of service*—(i) *In general*. For purposes of applying the limitation on benefits described in this section, the period of a participant's high 3 years of service is the period of 3 consecutive calendar years during which the employee was an active participant in the plan and had the greatest aggregate compensation (as defined in § 1.415(c)-2) from the employer. For purposes of this paragraph (a)(5), in determining a participant's high 3 years of service, the plan may use any 12-month period to determine a year of service instead of the calendar year, provided that it is uniformly and consistently applied in a

manner that is specified under the terms of the plan. As provided under § 1.415(c)-2(f), because a plan may not base benefit accruals (in the case of a defined benefit plan) on compensation in excess of the limitation under section 401(a)(17), a plan's definition of compensation for a limitation year that is used for purposes of applying the limitations of section 415 is not permitted to reflect compensation for a plan year that is in excess of the limitation under section 401(a)(17) that applies to that plan year.

(ii) *Short periods of service.* For those employees who are employed with the employer while an active participant for less than 3 consecutive calendar years, the period of a participant's high 3 years of service is the actual number of consecutive years of employment (including fractions of years) while an active participant in the plan. In such a case, the limitation of section 415(b)(1)(B) of 100% of the participant's compensation for the period of the participant's high 3 years of service is computed by dividing the participant's compensation during the participant's longest consecutive period of employment while a plan participant by the number of years in that period (including fractions of years, but not less than one year).

(iii) *Examples*: The following examples illustrate the rules of this paragraph (a)(5):

Example 1. (i) Plan A, which was established on January 1, 2004, covers Participant M, who was hired on January 1, 2000. The limitation year for Plan A is the calendar year. Participant M's compensation (as defined in § 1.415(c)-2) from the employer maintaining the plan is $120,000 for 2000, $120,000 for 2001, $120,000 for 2002, $120,000 for 2003, $100,000 for 2004, $100,000 for 2005, $100,000 for 2006, and $80,000 for 2007. Plan A does not specify a period other than the calendar year for determining the period of a participant's high 3 years of service while a plan participant.

(ii) As of the end of the 2004 limitation year, the period of M's highest 3 consecutive years of service while a plan participant (or fewer, if applicable) runs from January 1, 2004, through December 31, 2004. As of the end of the 2005 limitation year, the period of M's highest 3 consecutive years of service while a plan participant (or fewer, if applicable) runs from January 1, 2004, through December 31, 2005. As of the end of the 2006 limitation year and the 2007 limitation year, the period of M's highest 3 consecutive years of service while a plan participant (or fewer, if applicable) runs from January 1, 2004, through December 31, 2006. For all of those periods, M's average compensation is $100,000. Thus, the limitation under section 415(b)(1)(B) for 2004 through 2007 is applied using $100,000 as M's average compensation for the period of M's high 3 consecutive years of service while a plan participant (or fewer, if applicable).

Example 2. (i) Participant P has participated in Plan A, maintained by Employer M, for more than 10 years. P's average compensation for P's high 3 years while a participant in Plan A (determined before the application of section 401(a)(17)) is $220,000. On January 1, 2007, P commences receiving benefits from Plan A at the age of 75, 10 years after attaining P's normal retirement age under Plan A. Distributions to P under Plan A are actuarially adjusted to reflect commencement 10 years after normal retirement age using a 5% interest rate and the applicable mortality table under section 417(e)(3) that applies as of January 1, 2003. The limitation year and the plan year for Plan A are the calendar year.

(ii) Pursuant to § 1.415(c)-2(f) and section 401(a)(17), Plan A is not permitted to provide for a definition of compensation that includes compensation for a plan year that is in excess of the limitation under section 401(a)(17) that applies to that plan year. Accordingly, the limitation under section 415(b)(1)(B) based on P's average compensation for P's high three consecutive years must not reflect compensation for any plan year that is in excess of the limitation under section 401(a)(17) that applies to that plan year. Thus, for example, if the limitation under section 401(a)(17) for plan years beginning in 2004, 2005, and 2006 is $205,000, and if P had compensation in excess of $205,000 in each of those years, then the limitation under section 415(b)(1)(B) based on P's average compensation for P's high three consecutive years is $205,000.

(6) *Exceptions from compensation limit.* The limit under paragraph (a)(1)(ii) of this section (i.e., 100% of the participant's average compensation for his high 3 years of service) does not apply to—

(i) A governmental plan (as defined in section 414(d));

(ii) A multiemployer plan (as defined in section 414(f)); or

(iii) A collectively bargained plan that is described in section 415(b)(7).

(7) *Special rules*—(i) *Total benefits not in excess of $10,000.* See section 415(b)(4) and paragraph (f) of this section for an exception

from the limits of section 415(b)(1) and paragraph (a)(1) of this section with respect to retirement benefits that do not exceed $10,000 for the limitation year.

(ii) *Governmental plans electing during 1990.* For a special limitation applicable to certain governmental plans electing the application of this rule during the first plan year beginning after December 31, 1989, see section 415(b)(10).

(b) *Annual benefit*—(1) *In general*—(i) *Definition of annual benefit.* For purposes of this section and § 1.415(b)-2, the term *annual benefit* means a benefit that is payable annually in the form of a straight life annuity. With respect to a benefit payable in a form other than a straight life annuity, the annual benefit is determined as the straight life annuity that is actuarially equivalent to the benefit payable in such other form, determined under the rules of paragraph (c) of this section.

(ii) *Rules for determination of annual benefit.* The annual benefit does not include the annual benefit attributable to either employee contributions or rollover contributions (as described in sections 401(a)(31), 402(c)(1), 403(a)(4), 403(b)(8), and 408(d)(3), and 457(e)(16)), determined pursuant to the rules of paragraph (b)(2) of this section. The treatment of transferred benefits is determined under the rules of paragraph (b)(3) of this section. Paragraph (b)(4) of this section discusses the treatment of qualified governmental excess benefit arrangements.

(iii) *Determination of annual benefit in the case of multiple annuity starting dates.* See § 1.415(b)-2 for rules regarding the determination of the annual benefit from one or more plans in cases in which a participant has received one or more distributions in limitation years prior to an increase in the accrued benefit occurring during the current limitation year or prior to the annuity starting date for a distribution that commences during the current limitation year. The rules of § 1.415(b)-2 apply, for example, to multiple annuity starting dates that result from the commencement of an additional distribution and to multiple annuity starting dates that result from a new distribution election with respect to a distribution that commenced in a prior limitation year. For purposes of § 1.415(b)-2, the determination of whether a new annuity starting date has occurred is made without regard to the rule of § 1.401(a)-20, Q&A-10(d) (under which the commencement of certain distributions may not give rise to a new annuity starting date).

(2) *Determination of annual benefit attributable to employee contributions and rollover contributions*—(i) *In general.* If employee contributions (other than contributions described in paragraph (b)(2)(ii) of this section) or rollover contributions are made to the plan, the annual benefit attributable to these contributions is determined as provided in this paragraph (b)(2).

(ii) *Certain employee contributions disregarded.* For purposes of this paragraph (b)(2), the following are not treated as employee contributions—

(A) Contributions that are picked up by a governmental employer as provided under section 414(h)(2);

(B) Repayment of any loan made to a participant from the plan;

(C) Repayment of a previously distributed amount as described in section 411(a)(7)(B) in accordance with section 411(a)(7)(C); and

(D) Repayment of a withdrawal of employee contributions as provided under section 411(a)(3)(D).

(iii) *Annual benefit attributable to mandatory employee contributions.* In the case of mandatory employee contributions as defined in section 411(c)(2)(C) and § 1.411(c)-1(c)(4) (or contributions that would be mandatory employee contributions if section 411 applied to the plan), the annual benefit attributable to those contributions is determined by applying the factors applicable to mandatory employee contributions as described in section 411(c)(2)(B) and (C) and the regulations thereunder to those contributions to determine the amount of a straight life annuity commencing at the annuity starting date, regardless of whether section 411 applies to that plan. See § 1.415(c)-1(a)(2)(ii)(B) and (b)(3) for rules regarding treatment of mandatory employee contributions to a defined benefit plan as annual additions under a defined contribution plan.

(iv) *Voluntary employee contributions.* If voluntary employee contributions are made to the plan, the portion of the plan to which voluntary employee contributions are made is treated as a defined contribution plan pursuant to section 414(k) and, accordingly, is a defined contribution plan pursuant to § 1.415(c)-1(a)(2)(i). Accordingly, the portion of a plan to which voluntary employee contributions are made is not a defined benefit plan within the meaning of paragraph (a)(2) of this section and is not taken into account in determining the annual benefit under the portion of the plan that is a defined benefit plan.

(v) *Annual benefit attributable to rollover contributions.* The annual benefit attributable to rollover contributions from another qualified plan (for example, a contribution received pursuant to a direct rollover under section 401(a)(31)) is determined in the same manner as the annual benefit attributable to mandatory employee contributions if the plan provides for a benefit derived from the rollover contribution (other than a benefit derived from a separate account to be maintained with respect to the rollover contribution and actual earnings and losses thereon). Thus, in the case of rollover contributions from a defined contribution plan to a defined benefit plan to provide an annuity distribution, the annual benefit attributable to those rollover contributions for purposes of section 415 is determined by applying the rules of section 411(c), regardless of the assumptions used to compute the annuity distribution under the plan. Accordingly, in such a case, if the plan uses more favorable factors than those specified in section 411(c) to determine the amount of annuity payments arising from rollover contributions, the annual benefit under the plan would reflect the excess of those annuity payments over the amounts that would be payable using the factors specified in section 411(c)(3). See §1.415(c)-1(b)(3)(i) for rules excluding rollover contributions maintained in a separate account that is treated as a defined contribution plan pursuant to section 414(k) from annual additions to a defined contribution plan.

(3) *Treatment of transferred benefits*—(i) *In general*—(A) *Transferor plan and transferee plan aggregated.* For the limitation year that includes the date of a transfer between defined benefit plans, if the transferee plan's benefits are required to be taken into account pursuant to section 415(f) and §1.415(f)-1 in determining whether the transferor plan satisfies the limitations of section 415(b) for that limitation year, then the transferred benefits are included in determining the annual benefit under the transferee plan and are disregarded in determining the annual benefit under the transferor plan. This will occur, for example, if the employer sponsoring the transferor plan and the employer sponsoring the transferee plan are in the same controlled group within the meaning of section 414(b). Similarly, with respect to a transfer between defined benefit plans that occurred in a previous limitation year, if the transferee plan's benefits are required to be taken into account pursuant to section 415(f) and §1.415(f)-1 in determining whether the transferor plan satisfies the limitations of section 415(b), then the transferred benefits are included in determining the annual benefit under the transferee plan and are disregarded in determining the annual benefit under the transferor plan for the current limitation year. Accordingly, if the transferee plan's benefits are required to be taken into account pursuant to section 415(f) and §1.415(f)-1 in determining whether the transferor plan satisfies the limitations of section 415(b) for the limitation year with respect to a transfer occurring in the current limitation year or a prior limitation year, no adjustment is made to the benefits actually provided under either plan for purposes of determining the annual benefit under the plans as aggregated.

(B) *Transferor plan and transferee plan not aggregated.* When there has been a transfer of liabilities from one qualified plan to another, the benefits associated with those transferred liabilities are treated by the transferor plan as distributed as a singlesum distribution in an amount determined under paragraph (b)(3)(ii) of this section if the transferee plan's benefits are not required to be taken into account pursuant to section 415(f) and §1.415(f)-1 in determining whether the transferor plan satisfies the limitations of section 415(b). Although such a transfer is treated as a distribution in computing the annual benefit under the transferor plan, no adjustment is made to reflect the transfer for purposes of determining the annual benefit under the transferee plan. This will occur, for example, if the employer sponsoring the transferor plan is a predecessor employer with respect to the participant whose benefits are transferred to the transferee plan, where the transferee plan's benefits are not required to be taken into account pursuant to section 415(f) and §1.415(f)-1 in determining whether the transferor plan satisfies the limitations of section 415(b).

(ii) *Amount of deemed distribution on account of transfer of benefits*—(A) *In general.* Where there has been a transfer of liabilities from one qualified defined benefit plan to another, the amount of the single-sum distribution that is deemed distributed from the transferor plan pursuant to paragraph (b)(3)(i)(B) of this section is the amount of the assets transferred (other than surplus assets transferred). Thus, where the fair market value of assets transferred from another defined benefit plan in connection with the transfer of liabilities equals or exceeds the actuarial present value of liabilities transferred, the annual benefit attributable to the liabilities transferred is determined taking into account the entire amount of liabilities transferred as a single-sum distribution.

(B) *Amount of assets transferred.* Where assets are transferred with respect to more than one participant, the assets transferred with respect to each participant (other than surplus assets transferred) are determined as the actuarial present value of the straight life annuity that is actuarially equivalent to the amount the participant would receive if the plan terminated immediately before the transfer (if the plan had then terminated) under the rules of section 414(I) or Subtitle E of Title IV of ERISA, whichever applies to the transferor plan. If neither the rules of section 414(I) nor the rules of Subtitle E of Title IV of ERISA apply to the plan, then the assets transferred with respect to each participant are determined as the actuarial present value of the straight life annuity that is actuarially equivalent to the amount the participant would receive if the plan terminated immediately before the transfer, determined by allocating the assets, to the extent possible, so that employees who are not officers, shareholders, or highly compensated employees receive from the plan at least the same proportion of the present value of their accrued benefits (whether or not nonforfeitable) as employees who are officers, shareholders, or highly compensated employees.

(iii) *Transfer of immediately distributable amount.* Where an immediately distributable amount is transferred from either a defined contribution plan or a defined benefit plan to a defined benefit plan (see §1.411(d)-4, Q&A-3(c) regarding certain elective transfers of immediately distributable benefits), the annual benefit attributable to the benefits transferred is determined pursuant to the rules of paragraph (b)(2)(v) of this section regarding rollover contributions.

(4) *Treatment of qualified governmental excess benefit arrangements.* Pursuant to section 415(m), in determining whether a governmental plan (as defined in section 414(d)) meets the requirements of this section and §1.415(b)-2, the annual benefit does not include benefits provided under a qualified governmental excess benefit arrangement, as defined in section 415(m)(3).

(c) *Adjustment to form of benefit for forms other than a straight life annuity*—(1) *In general.* This paragraph (c) provides rules for adjusting a form of benefit other than a straight life annuity to an actuarially equivalent straight life annuity beginning at the same time for purposes of determining the annual benefit described in paragraph (b) of this section. Examples of benefits that are not in the form of a straight life annuity include an annuity with a post-retirement death benefit and an annuity providing for a guaranteed number of payments. Paragraph (c)(2) of this section describes how to adjust a form of benefit to which section 417(e)(3) does not apply. Paragraph (c)(3) of this section describes how to adjust a form of benefit to which section 417(e)(3) applies. Paragraph (c)(4) of this section describes benefit forms for which no adjustment is required. Paragraph (c)(5) of this section sets forth examples illustrating the application of this paragraph (c). The Commissioner may, in revenue rulings, notices, or other guidance published in the Internal Revenue Bulletin set forth simplified methods for adjusting a form of benefit other than a straight life annuity to an actuarially equivalent straight life annuity beginning at the same time for purposes of determining the annual benefit described in paragraph (b) of this section. See §601.601(d) of this chapter.

(2) *Benefits to which section 417(e)(3) does not apply.* For a benefit to which section 417(e)(3) does not apply, the actuarially equivalent straight life annuity benefit is the greater of—

(i) The annual amount of the straight life annuity (if any) payable to the participant under the plan commencing at the same annuity starting date as the form of benefit payable to the participant; or

(ii) The annual amount of the straight life annuity commencing at the annuity starting date that has the same actuarial present value as the particular form of benefit payable, computed using a 5% interest assumption and the applicable mortality table described in §1.417(e)-1(d)(2) for that annuity starting date.

(3) *Benefits to which section 417(e)(3) applies*—(i) *In general.* Except as provided in paragraph (c)(3)(ii) of this section, for a benefit to which section 417(e) applies, the actuarially equivalent straight life annuity benefit is the greater of—

(A) The annual amount of the straight life annuity commencing at the annuity starting date that has the same actuarial present value as the particular form of benefit payable, computed using the interest rate and mortality table, or tabular factor, specified in the plan for actuarial equivalence; or

(B) The annual amount of the straight life annuity commencing at the annuity starting date that has the same actuarial present value as the particular form of benefit payable, computed using the applicable interest rate for the distribution under §1.417(d)-1(d)(3) and the applicable mortality table for the distribution under §1.417(e)-1(d)(2).

(ii) *Special rule for 2004 and 2005.* For distributions to which section 417(e) applies and which have annuity starting dates beginning in 2004 or 2005, except as provided in section 101(d)(3) of the Pension Funding Equity Act of 2004 (118 Stat. 596), the actuarially equivalent straight life annuity benefit is the greater of—

(A) The annual amount of the straight life annuity commencing at the annuity starting date that has the same actuarial present value as the particular form of benefit payable, computed using the interest rate and mortality table, or tabular factor, specified in the plan for actuarial equivalence; or

(B) The annual amount of the straight life annuity commencing at the annuity starting date that has the same actuarial present value as the particular form of benefit payable, computed using a 5.5% interest assumption and the applicable mortality table for the distribution under § 1.417(e)-1(d)(2).

(4) *Certain benefit forms for which no adjustment is required*—(i) *In general*. For purposes of the adjustments described in this paragraph (c), the following benefits are not taken into account—

(A) Survivor benefits payable to a surviving spouse under a qualified joint and survivor annuity (as defined in section 417(b)) to the extent that such benefits would not be payable if the participant's benefit were not paid in the form of a qualified joint and survivor annuity; and

(B) Ancillary benefits that are not directly related to retirement benefits, such as preretirement disability benefits not in excess of the qualified disability benefit, preretirement incidental death benefits (including a qualified preretirement survivor annuity), and post-retirement medical benefits.

(ii) *Rules of application*—(A) *Social security supplements*. Although a social security supplement described in section 411(a)(9) and § 1.411(a)-7(c)(4) may be an ancillary benefit, it is included in determining the annual benefit because it is payable upon retirement and therefore is directly related to retirement income benefits.

(B) *QJSAs combined with other distributions*. If benefits are paid partly in the form of a qualified joint and survivor annuity and partly in some other form (such as a single-sum distribution), the rule of paragraph (c)(4)(i)(A) of this section (under which survivor benefits are not included in determining the annual benefit) applies to the survivor annuity payments under the portion of the benefit that is paid in the form of a QJSA.

(5) *Examples*. The following examples illustrate the provisions of this paragraph (c). For purposes of these examples, except as otherwise stated, actuarial equivalence under the plan is determined using a 5% interest assumption and the mortality table that applies under section 417(e)(3) as of January 1, 2003. It is assumed for purposes of these examples that the interest rate that applies under section 417(e)(3) for relevant time periods is 5.25% and that the mortality table that applies under section 417(e)(3) for relevant time periods is the mortality table that applies under section 417(e)(3) as of January 1, 2003. In addition, it is assumed that all participants discussed in these examples have at least ten years of service with the employer and at least ten years of participation in the plan at issue, and that all payments other than a payment of a single sum are made monthly, on the first day of each calendar month. The examples are as follows:

Example 1. (i) Plan A provides a single-sum distribution determined as the actuarial present value of the straight life annuity payable at the actual retirement date. Plan A provides that a participant's single sum is determined as the greater of the present value using 5% interest and the applicable mortality table under section 417(e)(3) as of January 1, 2003, and the present value using the applicable interest rate and the applicable mortality table under section 417(e). In accordance with § 1.417(e)-1(d)(1), Plan A also provides that the single sum is not less than the actuarial present value of the accrued benefit payable at normal retirement age, determined using the applicable interest rate and the applicable mortality table. Participant M retires at age 65 with a formula benefit of $152,619 and elects to receive a distribution in the form of a single sum. Under the plan formula, and before the application of section 415 under the plan, the amount of the single sum is $1,800,002 (which is based on the 5% interest rate and applicable mortality table as of January 1, 2003, since that is greater than the amount that would have been determined using the 5.25% interest rate and the applicable mortality table).

(ii) For purposes of this section, the annual benefit is the greater of the annual amount of the actuarially equivalent straight life annuity commencing at the same age (determined using the plan's actuarial factors), and the annual amount of the actuarially equivalent straight life annuity commencing at the same age (determined using the applicable interest rate and applicable mortality table). Based on the factors used in the plan to determine the actuarially equivalent lump sum (in this case, an interest rate of 5% and the applicable mortality table as of

January 1, 2003), $1,800,002 payable as a single sum is actuarially equivalent to an immediate straight life annuity at age 65 of $152,619. Based on the applicable interest rate and the applicable mortality table, $1,800,002 payable as a single sum is actuarially equivalent to an immediate straight life annuity at age 65 of $155,853. With respect to the single-sum distribution, M's annual benefit is equal to the greater of the two resulting amounts ($152,619 and $155,853), or $155,853.

Example 2. (i) The facts are the same as in *Example 1*, except that Participant M elects to receive his benefit in the form of a 10-year certain and life annuity. Applying the plan's actuarial equivalence factors determined using 5% interest and the applicable mortality table as of January 1, 2003, the benefit payable in this form is $146,100.

(ii) For purposes of this section, the annual benefit is the greater of the annual amount of the plan's straight life annuity commencing at the same age or the annual amount of the actuarially equivalent straight life annuity commencing at the same age, determined using a 5% interest rate and the applicable mortality table. In this case, the straight life annuity payable under the plan commencing at the same age is $152,619. Because the plan's factors for actuarial equivalence in this case are the same standardized actuarial factors required to be applied to determine the actuarially equivalent straight life annuity, the actuarially equivalent straight life annuity using the required standardized factors is also $152,619. With respect to the 10-year certain and life annuity distribution, M's annual benefit is equal to the greater of the two resulting amounts ($152,619 and $152,619), or $152,619.

Example 3. (i) The facts are the same as in *Example 1*. Participant N retires at age 62 with a formula benefit, after application of the plan's early retirement factors, of $100,000 and a Social Security supplement of $10,000 per year payable until age 65. N chooses to receive the accrued benefit in the form of a straight life annuity. The Plan has no provisions under which the actuarial value of the Social Security supplement can be paid as a level annuity for life.

(ii) Because the plan does not provide for a straight life annuity beginning at age 62, the annual benefit for purposes of this section is the annual amount of the straight life annuity commencing at age 62 that is actuarially equivalent to the distribution stream of $110,000 for three years and $100,000 thereafter, where actuarial equivalence is determined using a 5% interest rate and the applicable mortality table. In this case, the actuarially equivalent straight life annuity is $102,180. Accordingly, with respect to this distribution stream, N's annual benefit is equal to $102,180.

Example 4. (i) Plan B is a defined benefit plan that provides a benefit equal to 100% of a participant's compensation for the participant's high 3 years of service while a participant, payable as a straight life annuity. For a married participant who does not elect another form of benefit, the benefit is payable in the form of a joint and 100% survivor annuity benefit that is reduced from the straight life annuity and is a QJSA within the meaning of section 417. For purposes of determining the amount of this QJSA, the plan provides that the reduction is only half of the reduction that would normally apply under the actuarial assumptions specified in the plan for determining actuarial equivalence of optional forms. The plan also provides that a married participant can elect to receive the plan benefits as a straight life annuity, or in the form of a single sum distribution that is the actuarial equivalent of the joint and 100% survivor annuity. Participant O elects, with spousal consent, a single-sum distribution.

(ii) The special rule that disregards the value of the survivor portion of a QJSA set forth in paragraph (c)(4)(i) of this section only applies to a benefit that is payable in the form of a qualified joint and survivor annuity. Any other form of benefit must be adjusted to a straight life annuity in accordance with paragraph (c)(1) of this section. Accordingly, because the benefit payable under the plan in the form of a single-sum distribution is the actuarial equivalent of a straight life annuity that is greater than 100% of a participant's compensation for his high 3 years, the limitation of section 415(b)(1)(B) has been exceeded.

Example 5. (i) Plan C is a defined benefit plan that provides an option to receive the benefit in the form of a joint and 100% survivor annuity with a 10-year certain feature, where the survivor beneficiary is the participant's spouse.

(ii) For a participant at age 65, the annual benefit with respect to the joint and 100% survivor annuity with a 10-year certain feature is determined as the greater of the annual amount of the straight life annuity payable to the participant under the plan at age 65 (if any), or the annual amount of the straight life annuity commencing at age 65 that has the same actuarial present value as the joint and 100% survivor annuity with a 10 year certain feature (but excluding the survivor annuity payments pursuant to paragraph (c)(4)(i)(A) of this section), computing using a 5% interest assumption and the applicable mortality table described in § 1.417(e)-1(d)(2) for that annuity starting date. This latter amount is equal to the product of the annual payments under this optional form of benefit and the factor that provides for actuarial equivalence between a straight life annuity and a 10-year certain and life annuity (with no annuity for the survivor) computed using a 5% interest rate and the applicable mortality table.

Example 6. (i) Plan D is a defined benefit plan with a normal retirement age of 65. The normal retirement benefit under Plan D (and the only life annuity available under Plan D) is a life annuity with a fixed increase of 2% per year. The increase applies to the benefit provided in the prior year and is thus compounded. The plan provides that the benefit is limited to the lesser of 84% of the participant's average compensation for the participant's high 3 consecutive years of service while a plan participant or 84% of the section 415(b)(1)(A) dollar limit (which is assumed to be $170,000). Participant P's retires at age 65, at which time P's average compensation for P's high 3 consecutive years of service is $165,000. Accordingly, P commences receiving benefits in the form of a life annuity of $138,600 with a fixed increase of 2% per year.

(ii) Because Plan D does not provide for a straight life annuity, P's annual benefit for purposes of section 415(b) is the annual amount of the straight life annuity, commencing at age 65, that is actuarially equivalent to the distribution stream of $138,600 with a fixed increase of 2% per year, where actuarial equivalence is determined using a 5% interest rate and the applicable mortality table. In order to satisfy the requirements of section 415 and this section, this annual benefit must not exceed 100% of average compensation for the participant's high 3 consecutive years, or $165,000. Using a 5% interest rate and the section 417(e)(3) mortality table, the actuarially equivalent straight life annuity is $165,453, which exceeds $165,000. Accordingly, the plan fails to satisfy the compensation-based limitation of section 415(b)(1)(B).

Example 7. (i) Plan E provides a benefit at age 65 of a straight life annuity equal to the lesser of 90% of the participant's average compensation for the participant's highest 3 consecutive years of service while a plan participant and $148,500. Upon retirement at age 65, the optional forms of benefit available to a participant include payment of a QJSA with annual payments equal to 50% of the annual payments under the straight life annuity, along with a single-sum distribution that is actuarially equivalent (determined as the greater of the single sum calculated using a 5% interest assumption and the section 417(e)(3) mortality table in effect on January 1, 2003, and the single sum calculated using the section 417(e)(3) interest rate and the section 417(e)(3) mortality table) to 50% of the annual payments under the straight life annuity. Participant Q retires at age 65. Q's average compensation for Q's highest 3 consecutive years is $100,000. Q elects to receive a distribution in the optional form of benefit described above, under which the annual payments under the QJSA are $45,000 and the single-sum distribution is equal to $530,734. Q's spouse is 3 years younger than Q.

(ii) Q's annual benefit under Plan E is determined as the sum of the annual benefit attributable to the QJSA portion of the distribution and the annual benefit attributable to the single-sum portion of the distribution.

(iii) Because survivor benefits are not taken into account in determining the annual benefit attributable to the QJSA portion of the distribution, the annual benefit attributable to the QJSA portion of the distribution is determined as if that distribution were a straight life annuity of $45,000 per year commencing at age 65. Thus, no form adjustment is needed to determine the annual benefit attributable to the QJSA portion of the distribution, and the annual benefit attributable to the QJSA portion of the benefit is $45,000.

(iv) The annual benefit attributable to the single sum portion of the distribution is determined as the greater of the annual amount of the actuarially equivalent straight life annuity commencing at the same age (determined using the plan's actuarial factors), and the annual amount of the actuarially equivalent straight life annuity commencing at the same age (determined using the applicable interest rate and applicable mortality table). With respect to the single-sum distribution, the annual amount of the actuarially equivalent straight life annuity commencing at the same age determined using the plan's actuarial factors is equal to $45,954, and the actuarially equivalent straight life annuity commencing at the same age determined using the applicable interest rate and the applicable mortality table is equal to $45,954. Thus, the annual benefit attributable to the single sum portion of the benefit is $45,954.

(v) Q's annual benefit under the optional form of benefit is equal to the sum of the annual benefit attributable to the QJSA portion of the distribution and the annual benefit attributable to the single sum portion of the distribution, or $90,954. Because Q's average compensation for Q's highest 3 consecutive years is $100,000, the distribution satisfies the compensation limit of section 415(b)(1)(B).

Example 8. (i) R is a participant in a defined benefit plan maintained by A's employer. Under the terms of the plan, R must make contributions to the plan in a stated amount to accrue benefits derived from employer contributions.

(ii) R's contributions are mandatory employee contributions within the meaning of section 411(c)(2)(C) and, thus, the annual benefit attributable to these contributions does not have to be taken into account for purposes of testing the annual benefit derived from employer contributions against the applicable limitation on benefits. However, these contributions are treated as contributions to a defined contribution plan maintained by R's employer for purposes of section 415(c). See § 1.415(c)-1(a)(2)(ii)(B). Accordingly, with respect to the current limitation year, the limitation on benefits (as described in paragraph (a)(1) of this section) is applicable to the annual benefit attributable to employer contributions to the defined benefit plan, and the limitation on contributions and other additions (as described in § 1.415(c)-1) is applicable to the portion of the plan treated as a defined contribution plan, which consists of R's mandatory contributions. These same limitations would also apply if, instead of providing for mandatory employee contributions, the plan permitted voluntary employee contributions, because the portion of the plan attributable to voluntary employee contributions and earnings thereon is treated as a defined contribution plan maintained by the employer pursuant to section 414(k), and thus is not subject to the limitations of section 415(b).

(d) *Adjustment to section 415(b)(1)(A) dollar limit for commencement before age 62*—(1) *General rule.* For a distribution with an annuity starting date that occurs before the participant attains the age of 62, the age-adjusted section 415(b)(1)(A) dollar limit is determined as the lesser of—

(i) The section 415(b)(1)(A) dollar limit (as adjusted pursuant to section 415(d) and § 1.415(d)-1(a) for the limitation year) multiplied by the ratio of the annual amount of the immediately commencing straight life annuity under the plan (if any) to the annual amount of the straight life annuity under the plan commencing at age 62, if any (with both annual amounts determined without applying the rules of section 415); or

(ii) The annual amount of a straight life annuity commencing at the annuity starting date that has the same actuarial present value as a deferred straight life annuity commencing at age 62, where annual payments under the straight life annuity commencing at age 62 are equal to the dollar limitation of section 415(b)(1)(A), and where the actuarially equivalent straight life annuity is computed using a 5% interest rate and the applicable mortality table under § 1.417(e)-1(d)(2) that is effective for that annuity starting date.

(2) *Mortality adjustments*—(i) *In general.* For purposes of determining the amount described in paragraph (d)(1)(ii) of this section, to the extent that a forfeiture does not occur upon the participant's death, no adjustment is made to reflect the probability of the participant's death between the annuity starting date and the participant's attainment of age 62. To the extent that a forfeiture occurs upon the participant's death, an adjustment must be made to reflect the probability of the participant's death between the annuity starting date and the participant's attainment of age 62.

(ii) *No forfeiture deemed to occur where QPSA payable.* For purposes of paragraphs (d)(2)(i) and (e)(2)(i) of this section, a plan is permitted to treat no forfeiture as occurring upon a participant's death if the plan does not charge participants for providing a qualified preretirement survivor annuity (as defined in section 417(c)) on the participant's death, but only if the plan applies this treatment both for adjustments before age 62 and adjustments after age 65. Thus, in such a case, the plan is permitted to provide that, in computing the adjusted dollar limitation under section 415(b)(1)(A), no adjustment is made to reflect the probability of a participant's death between the annuity starting date and the participant's attainment of age 62 or between the age of 65 and the annuity starting date.

(3) *Exception for certain participants of certain governmental plans.* Pursuant to section 415(b)(2)(G) and (H), no age adjustment is made to the dollar limit for commencement before age 62 for any qualified participant. For this purpose, a qualified participant is a participant in a defined benefit plan that is maintained by a state or local government with respect to whom the service taken into account in determining the amount of the benefit under the defined benefit plan includes at least 15 years of service of the participant—

(i) As a full-time employee of any police department or fire department that is organized and operated by the state or political subdivision maintaining such defined benefit plan to provide police protection, firefighting services, or emergency medical services for any area within the jurisdiction of such state or political subdivision; or

(ii) As a member of the Armed Forces of the United States.

(4) *Exception for survivor and disability benefits under governmental plans.* Pursuant to section 415(b)(2)(I), no age adjustment is made to the dollar limit for commencement before age 62 for a distribution from a governmental plan (as defined in section 414(d)) on account of the participant's becoming disabled by reason of personal injuries or sickness, or as a result of the death of the participant.

(5) *Special rule for commercial airline pilots.* Pursuant to section 415(b)(9), no age adjustment is made to the dollar limit for early commencement after age 60 for a participant if—

(i) The participant is a commercial airline pilot;

(ii) The participant separates from service after attaining age 60; and

(iii) As of the time of the participant's retirement, regulations prescribed by the Federal Aviation Administration require an individual to separate from service as a commercial airline pilot after attaining any age occurring on or after age 60 and before age 62.

(6) *Examples.* The following examples illustrate the application of this paragraph (d). For purposes of these examples, it is assumed that the dollar limitation under section 415(b)(1)(A) for all relevant years is $180,000, that the normal form of benefit under the plan is a straight life annuity payable beginning at age 65, and that all payments other than a payment of a single sum are made monthly, on the first day of each calendar month. The examples are as follows:

Example 1. (i) Plan A provides that early retirement benefits are determined by reducing the accrued benefit by 4% for each year that the early retirement age is less than age 65. Participant M retires at age 60 after 30 years of service with a benefit (prior to the application of section 415) in the form of a straight life annuity of $100,000 payable at age 65, and is permitted to elect to commence benefits at any time between M's retirement and M's attainment of age 65. For example, M can elect to commence benefits at age 60 in the amount of $80,000, can wait until age 62 and commence benefits in the amount of $88,000, or can wait until age 65 and commence benefits in the amount of $100,000. Plan A provides a QPSA to all married participants without charge. Plan A provides (consistent with paragraph (d)(2)(ii) of this section) that, for purposes of adjusting the dollar limitation under section 415(b)(1)(A) for commencement before age 62 or after age 65, no forfeiture is treated as occurring upon a participant's death before retirement and, therefore, in computing the adjusted dollar limitation under section 415(b)(1)(A), no adjustment is made to reflect the probability of a participant's death between the annuity starting date and the participant's attainment of age 62 or between the age of 65 and the annuity starting date.

(ii) The age-adjusted section 415(b)(1)(A) dollar limit that applies for commencement of M's benefit at age 60 is the lesser of the section 415(b)(1)(A) dollar limit multiplied by the ratio of the annuity payable at age 60 to the annuity payable at age 62, or the straight life annuity payable at age 60 that is actuarially equivalent, using 5% interest and the applicable mortality table, to the deferred annuity payable at age 62. In this case, the age-adjusted section 415(b)(1)(A) dollar limit at age 60 is $156,229 (the lesser of $163,636 ($180,000* $80,000/$88,000) and $156,229 (the straight life annuity at age 60 that is actuarially equivalent to a deferred annuity of $180,000 commencing at age 62, determined using 5% interest and the applicable mortality table, without a mortality decrement for the period between 60 and 62)).

Example 2. (i) The facts are the same as in *Example 1*, except the plan provides that, if a participant has 30 or more years of service, no reduction applies for benefits commencing at age 62 and later.

(ii) The age-adjusted section 415(b)(1)(A) dollar limit that applies for commencement of M's benefit at age 60 is the lesser of the section 415(b)(1)(A) dollar limit multiplied by the ratio of the annuity payable at age 60 to the annuity payable at age 62, or the straight life annuity payable at age 60 that is actuarially equivalent, using 5% interest and the applicable mortality table, to the deferred annuity payable at age 62. In this case, because M has 30 years of service and would be eligible for the unreduced early retirement benefit at age 62, the age-adjusted section 415(b)(1)(A) dollar limit at age 60 is $144,000 (the lesser of $144,000 ($180,000* $80,000/$100,000) and $156,229 (the straight life annuity at age 60 that is actuarially equivalent to a deferred annuity of $180,000 commencing at age 62, determined using 5% interest and the applicable mortality table).

Example 3. (i) Participant O is a full-time civilian employee of the State of X Police Department who performs clerical services. O is a participant in the defined benefit plan that is maintained by the State of

X with respect to whom the years of service taken into account in determining the amount of the benefit under the plan includes 15 years of service working for the State of X Police Department.

(ii) For a distribution with an annuity starting date that occurs before O attains the age of 62, there is no age adjustment to the section 415(b)(1)(A) dollar limit.

Example 4. (i) Participant R is a full-time employee of the Emergency Medical Service Department of County Y (which is not a part of a police or fire department) who performs services as a driver of an ambulance. R is a participant in the defined benefit plan that is maintained by County Y with respect to whom the years of service taken into account in determining the amount of the benefit under the plan includes 15 years of service working for County Y. R does not have service credit for time in Armed Forces of the United States.

(ii) The age adjustments to the limitations of section 415(b)(1)(A) pursuant to section 415(b)(2)(C) and (D) will apply if R commences receiving a distribution at an age to which either of those adjustments applies.

Example 5. (i) The facts are the same as in *Example 1* except that Participant M chooses to receive benefits in the form of a 10-year certain and life annuity under which payments are 97% of the periodic payments that would be made under the immediately commencing straight life annuity. Annual payments to M are 97% of $80,000, or $77,600. As in *Example 1*, the age-adjusted section 415(b)(1)(A) dollar limit at age 60 is $156,229.

(ii) For purposes of this section, the annual benefit is the greater of the annual amount of the plan's straight life annuity commencing at the same age or the annual amount of the actuarially equivalent straight life annuity commencing at the same age, determined using a 5% interest rate and the applicable mortality table. In this case, the straight life annuity payable under the plan commencing at the same age is $80,000. The annual amount of the actuarially equivalent straight life annuity determined by applying the required standardized factors (i.e., a 5% interest assumption and the applicable mortality under section 417(e)(3)) is $79,416. With respect to the 10-year certain and life annuity commencing at age 62, M's annual benefit is equal to the greater of the two resulting amounts ($80,000 and $79,416), or $80,000.

(e) *Adjustment to section 415(b)(1)(A) dollar limit for commencement after age 65*—(1) *General rule.* For a distribution with an annuity starting date that occurs after the participant attains the age of 65, the age-adjusted section 415(b)(1)(A) dollar limit is determined as the lesser of—

(i) The section 415(b)(1)(A) dollar limit (as adjusted pursuant to section 415(d) and § 1.415(d)-1 for the limitation year) multiplied by the ratio of the annual amount of the immediately commencing straight life annuity under the plan (if any) to the annual amount of the straight life annuity that would be payable under the plan to a hypothetical participant who is 65 years old and has the same accrued benefit (i.e., with no actuarial increases for commencement after age 65) as the participant receiving the distribution (with both annual amounts determined without applying the rules of section 415); or

(ii) The annual amount of a straight life annuity commencing at the annuity starting date that has the same actuarial present value as a straight life annuity commencing at age 65, where annual payments under the straight life annuity commencing at age 65 are equal to the dollar limitation of section 415(b)(1)(A), and where actuarially equivalent straight life annuity is computed using a 5% interest rate and the applicable mortality table under § 1.417(e)-1(d)(2) that is effective for that annuity starting date.

(2) *Mortality adjustments*—(i) *In general.* For purposes of determining the amount described in paragraph (e)(1)(ii) of this section, to the extent that a forfeiture does not occur upon the participant's death, no adjustment is made to reflect the probability of the participant's death between the participant's attainment of age 65 and the annuity starting date. To the extent that a forfeiture occurs upon the participant's death, an adjustment must be made to reflect the probability of the participant's death between the participant's attainment of age 65 and the annuity starting date.

(ii) *No forfeiture deemed to occur where QPSA payable.* See paragraph (d)(2)(ii) of this section for a rule deeming no forfeiture to occur if the plan does not charge participants for providing a qualified preretirement survivor annuity on the participant's death.

(3) *Example.* The following example illustrates the application of this paragraph (e):

Example. (i) Plan A provides that monthly benefits payable upon commencement after normal retirement age (which is age 65) are increased by 0.5% for each month of delay in commencement after attainment of normal retirement age. Plan A provides a QPSA to all married participants without charge. Plan A provides (consistent with paragraph (d)(2)(ii) of this section) that, for purposes of adjusting the dollar limitation under section 415(b)(1)(A) for commencement before age 62 or after age 65, no adjustment is made to reflect the probability of a participant's death between the annuity starting date and the participant's attainment of age 62 or between the age of 65 and the annuity starting date. The normal form of benefit under Plan A is a straight life annuity commencing at age 65. Participant M retires at age 70 on January 1, 2007, after 30 years of service with a benefit (prior to the application of section 415) that is payable monthly in the form of a straight life annuity of $195,000, which reflects the actuarial increase of 30% applied to the accrued benefit of $150,000.

(ii) The age-adjusted section 415(b)(1)(A) dollar limit at age 70 is the lesser of the section 415(b)(1)(A) dollar limit multiplied by the ratio of the annuity payable at age 70 to the annuity that would be payable at age 65 based on the same accrued benefit (both determined before the application of section 415), or the straight life annuity payable at age 70 that is actuarially equivalent, using 5% interest and the applicable mortality table, to the straight life annuity payable at age 65. In this case, the age-adjusted section 415(b)(1)(A) dollar limit at age 70 is $234,000 (the lesser of $234,000 ($180,000* $195,000/$150,000) and $264,109 (the straight life annuity at age 70 that is actuarially equivalent to an annuity of $180,000 commencing at age 65, determined using 5% interest and the applicable mortality table, without a mortality decrement for the period between 65 and 70)).

(f) *Total annual payments not in excess of $10,000*—(1) *In general.* Pursuant to section 415(b)(4), the annual benefit (without regard to the age at which benefits commence) payable with respect to a participant under any defined benefit plan is not considered to exceed the limitations on benefits described in section 415(b)(1) and in paragraph (a)(1) of this section if—

(i) The benefits (other than benefits not taken into account in the computation of the annual benefit under the rules of paragraph (b) or (c) of this section) payable with respect to the participant under the plan and all other defined benefit plans of the employer do not in the aggregate exceed $10,000 (as adjusted under paragraph (g)) for the limitation year, or for any prior limitation year; and

(ii) The employer (or a predecessor employer) has not at any time, either before or after the effective date of section 415, maintained a defined contribution plan in which the participant participated.

(2) *Computation of benefits for purposes of applying the $10,000 amount.* For purposes of paragraph (f)(1)(i) of this section, the benefits (other than benefits not taken into account in the computation of the annual benefit under the rules of paragraph (b) or (c) of this section) payable with respect to the participant under a plan for a limitation year reflect all amounts payable under the plan for the limitation year, and are not adjusted for form of benefit or commencement date.

(3) *Special rule with respect to participants in multiemployer plans.* The special $10,000 exception set forth in paragraph (f)(1) of this section is applicable to a participant in a multiemployer plan described in section 414(f) without regard to whether that participant ever participated in one or more other plans maintained by an employer who also maintains the multiemployer plan, provided that none of such other plans were maintained as a result of collective bargaining involving the same employee representative as the multiemployer plan.

(4) *Special rule with respect to employee contributions.* For purposes of paragraph (f)(1)(ii) of this section, mandatory employee contributions under a defined benefit plan are not considered a separate defined contribution plan maintained by the employer. Thus, a contributory defined benefit plan may utilize the special dollar limitation provided for in this paragraph (f). Similarly, for purposes of this paragraph (f), an individual medical account under section 401(h) or an account for postretirement medical benefits established pursuant to section 419A(d)(1) is not considered a separate defined contribution plan maintained by the employer.

(5) *Examples.* The application of this paragraph (f) may be illustrated by the following examples. For purposes of these examples, it is assumed that each participant has 10 years of participation in the plan and service with the employer. The examples are as follows:

Example 1. (i) B is a participant in a defined benefit plan maintained by X Corporation, which provides for a benefit payable in the form of a straight life annuity beginning at age 65. B's average compensation for B's high 3 consecutive years of service while a participant in the plan is $6,000. The plan does not provide for employee contributions, and at no time has B been a participant in a defined contribution plan maintained

by X. With respect to the current limitation year, B's benefit under the plan (before the application of section 415) is $9,500.

(ii) Because annual payments under B's benefit do not exceed $10,000, and because B has at no time participated in a defined contribution plan maintained by X, the benefits payable under the plan are not considered to exceed the limitation on benefits otherwise applicable to B ($6,000).

(iii) This result would remain the same even if, under the terms of the plan, B's normal retirement age were age 60, or if the plan provided for employee contributions.

Example 2. (i) The facts are the same as in *Example 1*, except that the plan provides for a benefit payable in the form of a life annuity with a 10-year certain feature with annual payments of $9,500. Assume that, after the adjustment described in paragraph (c) of this section, B's actuarially equivalent straight life annuity (which is the annual benefit used for demonstrating compliance with section 415) for the current limitation year is $10,400.

(ii) For purposes of applying the special rule provided in this paragraph for total benefits not in excess of $10,000, there is no adjustment required if the retirement benefit payable under the plan is not in the form of a straight life annuity. Therefore, because B's retirement benefit does not exceed $10,000, B may receive the full $9,500 benefit without the otherwise applicable benefit limitations of this section being exceeded.

Example 3. (i) The facts are the same as in *Example 1*, except that the plan provides for a benefit payable in the form of a single sum and that the amount of the single sum that is the actuarial equivalent of the straight life annuity payable to B (i.e., $9,500 annually), determined in accordance with the rules of section 417(e)(3) and § 1.417(e)-1(d) is $95,000.

(ii) Because the amount payable to B for the limitation year would exceed $10,000, the rule of this paragraph (f) does not provide an exception from the generally applicable limits of section 415(b)(1) for the single-sum distribution. Thus, the otherwise applicable limits apply to the single-sum distribution, and a single-sum distribution of $95,000 would not satisfy the requirements of section 415(b). Limiting the single-sum distribution to $60,000 (the present value of the annuity that complies with the compensation-based limitation of section 415(b)(1)(B)) in order to satisfy section 415 would be an impermissible forfeiture under the requirements of section 411(a). Accordingly, the plan should not provide for a single-sum distribution in these circumstances.

(g) *Special rule for participation or service of less than 10 years*—(1) *Proration of dollar limit based on years of participation*—(i) *In general.* Pursuant to section 415(b)(5)(A), where a participant has less than 10 years of participation in the plan, the dollar limit described in paragraph (a)(1)(i) of this section (as adjusted pursuant to section 415(d), § 1.415(d)-1, and paragraphs (d) and (e) of this section) is to be reduced by multiplying the otherwise applicable limitation by a fraction—

(A) The numerator of which is the number of years of participation in the plan (or 1, if greater); and

(B) The denominator of which is 10.

(ii) *Years of participation.* The following rules apply for purposes of determining a participant's years of participation for purposes of this paragraph (g)(1)—

(A) A participant is credited with a year of participation (computed to fractional parts of a year) for each accrual computation period for which the participant is credited with at least the number of hours of service (or period of service if the elapsed time method is used for benefit accrual purposes) required under the terms of the plan in order to accrue a benefit for the accrual computation period, and the participant is included as a plan participant under the eligibility provisions of the plan for at least one day of the accrual computation period. If these two conditions are met, the portion of a year of participation credited to the participant is equal to the amount of benefit accrual service credited to the participant for such accrual computation period. For example, if under the terms of a plan, a participant receives 1/10 of a year of benefit accrual service for an accrual computation period for each 200 hours of service, and the participant is credited with 1,000 hours of service for the period, the participant is credited with 1/2 a year of participation for purposes of section 415(b)(5)(A).

(B) A participant who is permanently and totally disabled within the meaning of section 415(c)(3)(C)(i) for an accrual computation period is credited with a year of participation with respect to that period for purposes of section 415(b)(5)(A).

(C) For a participant to receive a year of participation (or part thereof) for an accrual computation period for purposes of section 415(b)(5)(A), the plan must be established no later than the last day of such accrual computation period.

(D) No more than one year of participation may be credited for any 12-month period for purposes of section 415(b)(5)(A).

(2) *Proration of compensation limit and special rule for total annual payments less than $10,000 based on years of service*—(i) *In general.* Pursuant to section 415(b)(5)(B), where a participant has less than 10 years of service with the employer, the compensation limit described in paragraph (a)(1)(ii) of this section and the $10,000 amount under the special rule for small annual payments under paragraph (f) of this section are reduced by multiplying the otherwise applicable limitation by a fraction—

(A) The numerator of which is the number of years of service with the employer (or 1, if greater); and

(B) The denominator of which is 10.

(ii) *Years of service*—(A) *In general.* For purposes of applying this paragraph (g)(2), the term *year of service* is to be determined on a reasonable and consistent basis. A plan is considered to be determining years of service on a reasonable and consistent basis for this purpose if, subject to the limits of paragraph (g)(2)(ii)(B) of this section, a participant is credited with a year of service (computed to fractional parts of a year) for each accrual computation period for which the participant is credited with at least the number of hours of service (or period of service if the elapsed time method is used for benefit accrual purposes) required under the terms of the plan in order to accrue a benefit for the accrual computation period.

(B) *Rules of application.* No more than one year of service may be credited for any 12-month period for purposes of section 415(b)(5)(B). In addition, only the participant's service with the employer or a predecessor employer (as defined in § 1.415(f)-1(c)) may be taken into account in determining the participant's years of service for this purpose.

(C) *Period of disability.* Notwithstanding the rules of paragraph (g)(2)(ii)(B) of this section, a plan is permitted to provide that a participant who is permanently and totally disabled within the meaning of section 415(c)(3)(C)(i) for an accrual computation period is credited with a year of service with respect to that period for purposes of section 415(b)(5)(B).

(3) *Exception for survivor and disability benefits under governmental plans.* The requirements of this paragraph (g) (regarding participation or service of less than 10 years) do not apply to a distribution from a governmental plan on account of the participant's becoming disabled by reason of personal injuries or sickness, or as a result of the death of the participant.

(4) *Examples.* The provision of this paragraph (g) may be illustrated by the following examples:

Example 1. (i) C begins employment with Employer A on January 1, 2005, at the age of 58. Employer A maintains only a noncontributory defined benefit plan which provides for a straight life annuity beginning at age 65 and uses the calendar year for the limitation and plan year. Employer A has never maintained a defined contribution plan. C becomes a participant in Employer A's plan on January 1, 2006, and works through December 31, 2011, when C is age 65. C begins to receive benefits under the plan in 2012. C's average compensation for C's high 3 consecutive years of service is $40,000. Furthermore, under the terms of Employer A's plan, for purposes of computing C's nonforfeitable percentage in C's accrued benefit derived from employer contributions, C has only 7 years of service with Employer A (2005-2011).

(ii) Because C has only 7 years of service with Employer A at the time he begins to receive benefits under the plan, the maximum permissible annual benefit payable with respect to C is $28,000 ($40,000 multiplied by 7/10).

Example 2. (i) The facts are the same as in *Example 1*, except that C's average compensation for his high 3 years is $8,000.

(ii) Because C has only 7 years of service with Employer A at the time he begins to receive benefits, the maximum benefit payable with respect to C would be reduced to $5,600 ($8,000 multiplied by 7/10). However, the special rule for total benefits not in excess of $10,000, provided in paragraph (f) of this section, is applicable in this case. Accordingly, C may receive an annual benefit of $7,000 ($10,000 multiplied by 7/10) without the benefit limitations of this section being exceeded.

Example 3. (i) Employer B maintains a defined benefit plan. Benefits under the plan are computed based on months of service rather than

years of service. Accordingly, for purposes of applying the reduction based on years of service less than 10 to the limitations under section 415(b), the otherwise applicable limitation is multiplied by a fraction, the numerator of which is the number of completed months of service with the employer (but not less than 12 months), and the denominator of which is 120. The plan further provides that months of service are computed in the same manner for this purpose as for purposes of computing plan benefits.

(ii) The manner in which the plan applies the reduction based on years of service less than 10 to the limitations under section 415(b) is consistent with the requirements of this paragraph (g).

Example 4. (i) G begins employment with Employer D on January 1, 2003, at the age of 58. Employer D maintains only a noncontributory defined benefit plan which provides for a straight life annuity beginning at age 65 and uses the calendar year for the limitation and plan year. Employer D has never maintained a defined contribution plan. G becomes a participant in Employer D's plan on January 1, 2004, and works through December 31, 2009, when G is age 65. G performs sufficient service to be credited with a year of service under the plan for each year during 2003 through 2009 (although G is not credited with a year of service for 2003 because G is not yet a plan participant). G begins to receive benefits under the plan during 2010. The plan's accrual computation period is the plan year. The plan provides that, for purposes of applying the rules of section 415(b)(5)(B), a participant is credited with a year of service (computed to fractional parts of a year) for each plan year for which the participant is credited with sufficient service to accrue a benefit for the plan year. G's average compensation for G's high 3 years of service is $200,000. It is assumed for purposes of this example that the dollar limitation of section 415(b)(1)(A) for limitation years ending in 2010 is $180,000.

(ii) G has 7 years of service and 6 years of participation in the plan at the time G begins to receive benefits under the plan. Accordingly, the limitation under section 415(b)(1)(B) based on G's average compensation for G's high 3 years of service that applies pursuant to the adjustment required under section 415(b)(5)(B) is $140,000 ($200,000 multiplied by 7/10), and the dollar limitation under section 415(b)(1)(A) that applies to G pursuant to the adjustment required under section 415(b)(5)(A) is $108,000 ($180,000 multiplied by 6/10).

(h) *RPA '94 transition rules.* For special rules affecting the actuarial adjustment for form of benefit under paragraph (c) of this section and the adjustment to the dollar limit for early or late commencement under paragraphs (d) and (e) of this section for certain plans adopted and in effect before December 8, 1994, see section 767(d)(3)(A) of the Retirement Protection Act of 1994, as amended by section 1449(a) of the Small Business Job Protection Act of 1996. The Commissioner may provide guidance regarding these special rules in revenue rulings, notices, and other guidance published in the Internal Revenue Bulletin. See § 601.601(d) of this chapter.

Par. 8. Section 1.415(b)-2 is added to read as follows:

§ 1.415(b)-2 Multiple annuity starting dates.

(a) *Determination of annual benefit where distributions have occurred before the current determination date*—(1) *In general.* This section provides rules for determining the annual benefit of a participant for purposes of applying the limitations of section 415(b) and § 1.415(b)-1 in cases in which a participant has received one or more distributions in limitation years prior to an increase in the accrued benefit occurring during the current limitation year or prior to the annuity starting date for a distribution that commences during the current limitation year. This section applies, for example, where benefit distributions to a participant have previously commenced under a plan that is aggregated for purposes of section 415 with a plan from which the participant receives current accruals, or where a new distribution election is effective during the current limitation year with respect to a distribution that commenced in a prior limitation year. This section also applies where benefit payments are increased as a result of plan terms applying a cost-of-living adjustment pursuant to an increase of the dollar limit of section 415(b)(1)(A), if the plan does not provide for application of the rules of § 1.415(d)-1(a)(5) to determine the adjusted amount of the benefit. Paragraph (b) of this section provides rules for computing the annual benefit in the case of multiple annuity starting dates as described in this paragraph (a)(1). Paragraph (c) of this section provides an additional rule for multiple annuity starting dates that occur when a stream of annuity payments is modified by a new distribution election. Paragraph (d) of this section provides examples to illustrate the rules of this section.

(2) *Annuity starting date.* For purposes of this section, the determination of whether a new annuity starting date has occurred is made pursuant to the rules of § 1.401(a)-20, Q&A-10, but without regard to

the rule of § 1.401(a)-20, Q&A-10(d) (under which the commencement of certain distributions may not give rise to a new annuity starting date).

(3) *Annual benefit*—(i) *In general.* Where a participant has received one or more distributions before a current accrual or before the annuity starting date for a currently payable distribution, except as provided in paragraph (a)(3)(iii) of this section (regarding mandatory employee contributions and rollover contributions), the annual benefit that is subject to the limits of section 415(b) and § 1.415(b)-1(a) is equal to the sum of—

(A) The annual benefit determined with respect to any accrued benefit with respect to which distribution has not yet commenced as of the current determination date, computed pursuant to the rules of § 1.415(b)-1(b) and (c);

(B) The annual benefit determined with respect to any distribution with an annuity starting date that occurs within the current limitation year and on or before the current determination date, computed pursuant to the rules of § 1.415(b)-1(b) and (c);

(C) The annual benefit determined with respect to the remaining amounts payable under any distribution with an annuity starting date that occurred during a prior limitation year, computed pursuant to the rules of § 1.415(b)-1(b) and (c) (subject to paragraph (a)(3)(ii) of this section); and

(D) The annual benefit attributable to prior distributions (computed pursuant to the rules of paragraph (b) of this section).

(ii) *Determining actuarial equivalence with respect to remaining amounts payable.* For purposes of computing the annual benefit determined with respect to the remaining amounts payable under any distribution with an annuity starting date that occurred during a prior limitation year under paragraph (a)(3)(i)(C) of this section, § 1.415(b)-1(c)(2) is applied by substituting for the amount described in § 1.415(b)-1(c)(2)(i) the annual amount of a straight life annuity commencing at the annuity starting date that has the same actuarial present value as the particular form of benefit payable, computed using the interest rate and mortality table, or tabular factor, specified in the plan for actuarial equivalence for the particular form of benefit payable.

(iii) *Mandatory employee contributions and rollover contributions.* If mandatory employee contributions or rollover contributions have been made to the plan with respect to a distribution that commenced before the current determination date, the annual benefit is determined by applying the rules of paragraph (a)(3)(i)(C) and (D) of this section and then subtracting the annual benefit attributable to mandatory employee contributions computed pursuant to § 1.415(b)-1(b)(2)(iii) and the annual benefit attributable to rollover contributions computed pursuant to § 1.415(b)-1(b)(2)(v), with both amounts computed as of the annuity starting date for the distribution.

(iv) *Repayments of prior distributions*—(A) *Total repayments.* A prior distribution that has been repaid to the plan with interest does not give rise to an annual benefit attributable to prior distributions for purposes of paragraph (a)(3)(i)(D) of this section (because amounts attributable to those repayments are reflected instead in amounts included in the annual benefit pursuant to paragraphs (a)(3)(i)(A), (B), and (C) of this section).

(B) *Partial repayments.* If a prior distribution was made, and a repayment was subsequently made that was less than the amount of the prior distribution (including reasonable interest), the annual benefit attributable to prior distributions is determined by multiplying the annual benefit attributable to the prior distribution (computed assuming that no repayment occurred) by one minus a fraction, the numerator of which is the amount of the repayment and the denominator of which is the amount of the prior distribution plus reasonable interest.

(b) *Annual benefit attributable to prior distributions*—(1) *In general*—(i) *Adjustment to actuarially equivalent straight life annuity*—(A) *Method of adjustment.* To compute the annual benefit attributable to a prior distribution, the prior distribution is adjusted to an actuarially equivalent straight life annuity commencing at the current determination date in accordance with the rules of paragraph (b)(2) of this section (for a prior distribution to which section 417(e)(3) did not apply) or paragraph (b)(3) of this section (for a prior distribution to which section 417(e)(3) applied).

(B) *Current determination date.* The current determination date is the last day of period for which an increase in the participant's benefit accrues if an increase in the participant's accrued benefit occurs during the limitation year. If there is no such increase, the current determination date is the annuity starting date for the distribution that commences during the limitation year.

(ii) *Rules of application*—(A) *Amount of distribution taken into account.* In applying the rules of paragraphs (b)(2) and (3) of this section to compute the annual benefit attributable to a prior distribution, only the actual amount received as a prior distribution (without regard to either the form of benefits paid, or the form or amount of remaining payments under the prior distribution) is taken into account. Thus, for example, in determining the annual benefit attributable to a prior distribution of $100,000 per year over the past four years, paragraph (b)(2) of this section will apply if the distribution was part of a 10-year certain and life annuity, and paragraph (b)(3) of this section will apply if the distribution was part of installment payments over 10 years. However, in both instances, the amounts taken into account in determining the annual benefit attributable to the prior distribution are the four $100,000 payments already made, without regard to remaining payments.

(B) *Application of mortality adjustments*—(*1*) *Application of mortality adjustments when standardized assumptions are used.* Under the rules of paragraphs (b)(2)(ii), (b)(3)(i)(B), and (b)(3)(ii)(B) of this section (under which standardized actuarial assumptions are applied), a prior distribution is adjusted to an actuarially equivalent straight life annuity commencing at the current determination date using the specified interest and mortality assumptions to convert the payment stream to an actuarially equivalent straight life annuity commencing at the current determination date. For this purpose, the actuarially equivalent straight life annuity commencing at the current determination date must reflect an actuarial increase to the present value of payments to reflect that the participant has survived during the interim period.

(*2*) *Application of mortality adjustments when the plan's assumptions for computing offsets are used.* Under the rules of paragraphs (b)(2)(i), (b)(3)(i)(A), and (b)(3)(ii)(A) of this section (under which the plan's assumptions for computing offsets for prior distributions are applied), the actuarially equivalent straight life annuity must reflect mortality adjustment in the same manner as those mortality adjustments are reflected in computing offsets for prior distributions.

(2) *Prior distributions to which section 417(e)(3) did not apply.* For a prior distribution to which section 417(e)(3) did not apply, the actuarially equivalent straight life annuity commencing at the current determination date is the greater of—

(i) The annual amount of a straight life annuity commencing at the current determination date that is the actuarial equivalent of that prior distribution, computed using the interest rate and mortality table specified under the plan that provides for the current distribution or current accrual that are used to determine offsets, if any, for prior distributions; and

(ii) The annual amount of a straight life annuity commencing at the current determination date that is the actuarial equivalent of that prior distribution, computed using a 5% interest assumption and the applicable mortality table described in § 1.417(e)-1(d)(2) that would apply to a distribution to which section 417(e) applies with an annuity starting date of the current determination date.

(3) *Prior distributions to which section 417(e)(3) applied*—(i) *In general.* For a prior distribution to which section 417(e)(3) applied, the actuarially equivalent straight life annuity commencing at the current determination date is the greater of—

(A) The annual amount of a straight life annuity commencing at the current determination date that is the actuarial equivalent of that prior distribution, computed using the interest rate and mortality table specified under the plan that provides for the current distribution or current accrual that are used to determine offsets, if any, for prior distributions; and

(B) The annual amount of a straight life annuity commencing at the current determination date that is the actuarial equivalent of that prior distribution, computed using the applicable interest rate under § 1.417(e)-1(d)(3) and the applicable mortality table under § 1.417(e)-1(d)(2) that would apply to a distribution with an annuity starting date of the current determination date.

(ii) *Special rule for 2004 and 2005.* For a prior distribution to which section 417(e)(3) applied, and for current determination dates or current accruals in 2004 and 2005, except as provided in section 101(d)(3) of the Pension Funding Equity Act of 2004, the actuarially equivalent straight life annuity commencing at the current determination date is the greater of—

(A) The annual amount of a straight life annuity commencing at the current determination date that is the actuarial equivalent of that prior distribution, computed using the interest rate and mortality table specified under the plan that provides for the current distribution or current accrual that are used to determine offsets, if any, for prior distributions; and

(B) The annual amount of a straight life annuity commencing at the current determination date that is the actuarial equivalent of that prior distribution, computed using a 5.5% interest assumption and the applicable mortality table under § 1.417(e)-1(d)(2) that would apply to a distribution with an annuity starting date of the current determination date.

(4) *Benefit forms for which no adjustment is required.* The annual benefit attributable to prior distributions is computed disregarding the portion of prior distributions described in § 1.415(b)-1(c)(4) (regarding benefits for which no adjustment is required). Thus, for example, the annual benefit attributable to prior distributions is computed disregarding the payment of preretirement disability benefits not in excess of the qualified disability benefit.

(c) *Change in distribution form*—(1) *In general.* If a stream of annuity payments is modified by a new distribution election, the requirements of this section are applied treating the modification as a new annuity starting date. In addition, in such a case, the requirements of paragraph (c)(2) of this section must be satisfied.

(2) *Test total annuity stream as of original annuity starting date.* If a stream of annuity payments is modified by a new distribution election, the payments under the annuity that are paid before the modification plus the modified payments must satisfy the requirements of § 1.415(b)-1 determined as of the original annuity starting date, using the interest rates and mortality table applicable to such date. A plan will not fail to satisfy the requirements of this paragraph (c)(2) merely because payments reflect cost-of-living adjustments pursuant to section 415(d) determined in accordance with § 1.415(d)-1(a)(5).

(d) *Examples.* The following examples illustrate the application of this section. For purposes of these examples, except as otherwise stated, actuarial equivalence under the plan (including for purposes of determining offsets for prior distributions and for purposes of determining the amount of annuity distributions commencing after normal retirement age) is determined using a 6% interest assumption and the mortality table that applies under section 417(e)(3) as of January 1, 2003, and all payments other than a payment of a single sum are made monthly, on the first day of each calendar month. It is assumed for purposes of these examples that the interest rate that applies under section 417(e)(3) for relevant time periods is 5.25% and that the mortality table that applies under section 417(e)(3) for relevant time periods is the mortality table that applies under section 417(e)(3) as of January 1, 2003. In addition, it is assumed that all participants discussed in these examples have at least ten years of service with the employer and at least ten years of participation in the plan at issue, and that the dollar limitation of section 415(b)(1)(A) as adjusted pursuant to section 415(d) for 2008 is equal to $180,000. It is further assumed that the product of the annual adjustment factors that apply in adjusting the compensation limitation of section 415(b)(1)(B) for 2005, 2006, 2007, and 2008 is 1.1. The examples are as follows:

Example 1. (i) Employer A previously maintained Plan D, a qualified defined benefit plan. Upon the termination of Plan D on January 1, 1997, Participant M received a single-sum distribution of $537,055 at the age of 54. As of January 1, 2008, Participant M has participated in Plan E (another defined benefit plan maintained by Employer A) for more than 10 years. On January 1, 2008, M retires at the age of 65 and receives a distribution from Plan E.

(ii) Pursuant to section 415(f) and § 1.415(f)-1, distributions to M from Plan D and Plan E are aggregated for purposes of applying section 415(b). Pursuant to paragraph (a)(3) of this section, M's annual benefit that is subject to the limits of section 415(b) and § 1.415(b)-1(a) is equal to the sum of the annual benefit determined with respect to the distribution commencing on January 1, 2008, and the annual benefit attributable to prior distributions (computed pursuant to the rules of paragraph (b) of this section).

(iii) M's annual benefit attributable to prior distributions is computed by adjusting the single-sum distribution made in 1995 to an actuarially equivalent straight life annuity commencing on January 1, 2008, in accordance with the rules set forth in paragraph (b)(3) of this section. Pursuant to those rules, that actuarially equivalent straight life annuity is computed using either the plan's actuarial assumptions for applying offsets for prior distributions (here, a 6% interest rate and the mortality table that applies under section 417(e)(3) as of January 1, 2003), or the applicable interest rate and the applicable mortality table under section 417(e)(3), both determined as of January 1, 2008, whichever set of actuarial assumptions produces the greater actuarially equivalent annuity. The actuarially equivalent straight life annuity computed using the plan's assumptions used for computing offsets is $100,027 per year, and

the actuarially equivalent straight life annuity computed using the applicable interest rate and the applicable mortality table as of January 1, 2008, is $87,035 per year. Thus, M's annual benefit attributable to prior distributions is $100,027.

(iv) To comply with the limitations of section 415, M's annual benefit determined with respect to the distribution commencing on January 1, 2008, must be no greater than the otherwise applicable limit on the annual benefit (i.e., the lesser of $180,000 or 100% of M's average compensation for the period of the participant's high 3 years of service) minus $100,027. Thus, for example, to comply with the dollar limitation of section 415(b)(1)(A), M's annual benefit determined with respect to the distribution commencing on January 1, 2008, must be no greater than $79,973.

Example 2. (i) Employer B maintains Plan F, a qualified defined benefit plan. On January 1, 2002, at the age of 59, Participant N separated from service and commenced receiving a benefit of $80,000 per year for ten years from Plan F. As of January 1, 2008, Plan F is amended to increase N's accrued benefit. N is offered a new QJSA election with respect to the new accrual.

(ii) Pursuant to paragraph (a)(3) of this section, as of January 1, 2008, N's annual benefit that is subject to the limits of section 415(b) and § 1.415(b)-1(a) is equal to the sum of the annual benefit determined with respect to remaining amounts payable under the distribution that commenced on January 1, 2002, the annual benefit determined with respect to the accrued benefit with respect to which distribution has not yet commenced, and the annual benefit attributable to prior distributions (computed pursuant to the rules of paragraph (b) of this section).

(iii) N's annual benefit determined with respect to the remaining four annual payments of $80,000 is determined pursuant to § 1.415(b)-1(c)(3) as the greater of the annual amount of a straight life annuity commencing at the annuity starting date that has the same actuarial present value as the particular form of benefit payable, computed using the interest rate and mortality table, or tabular factor, specified in the plan for actuarial equivalence for the particular form of benefit payable, or the annual amount of a straight life annuity commencing at the annuity starting date that has the same actuarial present value as the particular form of benefit payable, computed using the applicable interest rate and the applicable mortality table under section 417(e)(3). Using the plan's factors for actuarial equivalence, the actuarially equivalent straight life annuity is $26,334, and using the section 417(e)(3) factors for actuarial equivalence, the actuarially equivalent straight life annuity is $25,109. Accordingly, N's annual benefit determined with respect to the remaining four annual payments of $80,000 is equal to $26,334.

(iv) N's annual benefit attributable to prior distributions is computed by adjusting the six annual payments of $80,000 per year already made before January 1, 2008, to an actuarially equivalent straight life annuity commencing on January 1, 2008, in accordance with the rules set forth in paragraph (b)(3) of this section. Pursuant to those rules, that actuarially equivalent straight life annuity is computed using either the plan's actuarial assumptions for applying offsets for prior distributions (here, a 6% interest rate and the mortality table that applies under section 417(e)(3) as of January 1, 2003), or the applicable interest rate and the applicable mortality table under section 417(e)(3), both determined as of January 1, 2008, whichever set of actuarial assumptions produces the greater actuarially equivalent annuity. The actuarially equivalent straight life annuity computed using the plan's assumptions used for computing offsets is $54,494 per year, and the actuarially equivalent straight life annuity computed using the applicable interest rate and the applicable mortality table as of January 1, 2006, is $50,103 per year. Thus, N's annual benefit attributable to prior distributions is $54,494.

(v) To comply with the limitations of section 415, N's annual benefit determined with respect to the accrued benefit with respect to which distribution has not yet commenced must be no greater than the otherwise applicable limit on the annual benefit (i.e., the lesser of $180,000 or 100% of N's average compensation for period of N's high 3 years of service) minus $80,828 (the $26,334 annual benefit attributable to the remaining payments under the existing form of distribution, plus the $54,494 annual benefit attributable to prior distributions). Thus, for example, to comply with the dollar limitation of section 415(b)(1)(A), N's annual benefit determined with respect to the accrued benefit with respect to which distribution has not yet commenced must be no greater than $99,172.

Example 3. (i) The facts are the same as in *Example 2*, except that, instead of receiving a benefit of $80,000 per year for ten years from Plan F, N receives annual payments of $80,000 under a 10-year certain and life annuity from Plan F.

1326 Proposed Regulations

(ii) Pursuant to paragraph (a)(3) of this section, as of January 1, 2008, N's annual benefit that is subject to the limits of section 415(b) and § 1.415(b)-1(a) is equal to the sum of the annual benefit determined with respect to remaining amounts payable under the distribution that commenced on January 1, 2002, the annual benefit determined with respect to the accrued benefit with respect to which distribution has not yet commenced, and the annual benefit attributable to prior distributions (computed pursuant to the rules of paragraph (b) of this section).

(iii) N's annual benefit determined with respect to the remaining portion of the existing annuity (i.e., a four-year certain and life annuity) is determined pursuant to § 1.415(b)-1(c)(2) as the greater of the annual amount of a straight life annuity commencing at the annuity starting date that has the same actuarial present value as the particular form of benefit payable, computed using the interest rate and mortality table, or tabular factor, specified in the plan for actuarial equivalence for the particular form of benefit payable, or the annual amount of a straight life annuity commencing at the annuity starting date that has the same actuarial present value as the particular form of benefit payable, computed using an interest rate of 5% and the applicable mortality table under section 417(e)(3). Using the plan's factors for actuarial equivalence, the actuarially equivalent straight life annuity is $80,608, and using the statutory factors for actuarial equivalence, the actuarially equivalent straight life annuity is $80,577. Accordingly, N's annual benefit determined with respect to the remaining 4-year certain and life annuity is equal to $80,608.

(iv) N's annual benefit attributable to prior distributions is computed by adjusting the six annual payments of $80,000 per year already made before January 1, 2008, to an actuarially equivalent straight life annuity commencing on January 1, 2008, in accordance with the rules set forth in paragraph (b)(3) of this section. Pursuant to those rules, that actuarially equivalent straight life annuity is computed using either the plan's actuarial assumptions for applying offsets for prior distributions (here, a 6% interest rate and the mortality table that applies under section 417(e)(3) as of January 1, 2003), or the applicable interest rate and the applicable mortality table under section 417(e)(3), both determined as of January 1, 2008, whichever set of actuarial assumptions produces the greater actuarially equivalent annuity. The actuarially equivalent straight life annuity computed using the plan's assumptions used for computing offsets is $54,494 per year, and the actuarially equivalent straight life annuity computed using the applicable interest rate and the applicable mortality table as of January 1, 2008, is $48,689 per year. Thus, N's annual benefit attributable to prior distributions is $54,494.

(v) To comply with the limitations of section 415, N's annual benefit determined with respect to the accrued benefit with respect to which distribution has not yet commenced must be no greater than the otherwise applicable limit on the annual benefit (i.e., the lesser of $180,000 or 100% of N's average compensation for the highest 3 years) minus $135,102 (the $80,608 annual benefit attributable to the remaining payments under the existing form of distribution, plus the $54,494 annual benefit attributable to prior distributions). Thus, for example, to comply with the dollar limitation of section 415(b)(1)(A), N's annual benefit determined with respect to the accrued benefit with respect to which distribution has not yet commenced must be no greater than $44,898.

Example 4. (i) Participant P retired on January 1, 2004, at age 65, with average compensation for the period of P's high 3 years service of $190,000. P commenced receiving a straight life annuity of $165,000 from Plan E as of January 1, 2004. Plan E adjusts benefit payments to reflect increases in the applicable limitations of section 415(b) in accordance with the safe harbor methodology set forth in § 1.415(d)-1(a)(5). As of January 1, 2005, pursuant to an adjustment under section 415(d) that applies to P's benefit payments under the terms of the plan, annual payments to P from Plan E are adjusted to $170,000, and as of January 1, 2007, pursuant to another such adjustment (under which the section 415(b)(1)(A) dollar limit is assumed to increase to $175,000 for 2007), annual payments to P from Plan E are adjusted to $175,000. On December 1, 2007, P elected to change the form of the remainder of the benefit payable to P under Plan E to a single-sum distribution payable as of January 1, 2008. P receives a single-sum distribution of $1,769,157 on January 1, 2008. It is assumed for purposes of this example that the section 417(e)(3) interest rate that applies to a distribution from Plan E as of January 1, 2004, is 5.25%, and that the section 417(e)(3) interest rate that applies to a distribution from Plan E as of January 1, 2008, is 6%. The normal form of benefit under Plan E is a straight life annuity. Plan E provides a QPSA to all married participants without charge. Plan E provides that, for purposes of adjusting the dollar limitation under section 415(b)(1)(A) for commencement before age 62 or after age 65, no adjustment is made to reflect the probability of a participant's death between the annuity starting date and the participant's attainment of age 62 or between the participant's attainment of age 65 and the annuity starting date. Under Plan E, benefits commencing after the age of 65 are actuarially adjusted to reflect the later commencement date using the plan's generally applicable assumptions for actuarial equivalence.

(ii) To comply with the limitations of section 415 for the 2008 limitation year, Plan E must satisfy two requirements. First, under paragraph (c)(1) of this section, Plan E must limit payments to P so that the sum of the annual benefit attributable to the currently commencing distribution plus the annual benefit attributable to prior distributions is within the limitations of section 415(b) that apply to a benefit commencing at the annuity starting date for the distribution that commences in 2008. Second, under paragraph (c)(2) of this section, the payments under the annuity that are paid before January 1, 2008, plus the single-sum distribution made on January 1, 2008, must satisfy the requirements of § 1.415(b)-1 determined as of January 1, 2004, using the interest rates and mortality table applicable as of January 1, 2004. Pursuant to paragraph (c)(2) of this section, Plan E does not fail to satisfy this latter requirement if payments reflect cost-of-living adjustments pursuant to section 415(d) for payments no earlier than the time those adjustments are effective and in amounts no greater than amounts determined under § 1.415(d)-1(a)(5).

(iii) To satisfy the second requirement described in paragraph (ii) of this *Example 4*, the payments under the annuity that are paid before January 1, 2008 (i.e., $165,000 during 2004, $170,000 during 2005, $170,000 during 2006, and $175,000 during 2007), plus the single-sum distribution of $1,769,157 made on January 1, 2008, must satisfy the requirements of § 1.415(b)-1 determined as of January 1, 2004, using the interest rates and mortality table applicable as of January 1, 2004. As of January 1, 2004, the actuarially equivalent straight life annuity with respect to those payments is $176,698 using the applicable interest rate (assumed to be 5.25%) and the applicable mortality table for that date. As of January 1, 2004, the actuarially equivalent straight life annuity with respect to those payments is $170,239 using the plan's actuarial assumptions (a 6% interest rate and the applicable mortality table as of January 1, 2003). The annual benefit attributable to those payments is the greater of the two amounts, or $176,698. This amount exceeds the applicable dollar limitation as of January 1, 2004 (i.e., $165,000). Accordingly, without application of the special rule for cost-of-living adjustments, Plan E would fail to satisfy this second requirement.

(iv) Pursuant to the special rule for cost-of-living adjustments under paragraph (c)(2) of this section, Plan E does not fail to satisfy the second requirement described in paragraph (ii) of this *Example 4* if payments reflect cost-of-living adjustments pursuant to section 415(d) for payments no earlier than the time those adjustments are effective and in amounts no greater than amounts determined under § 1.415(d)-1(a)(5). Accordingly, the payment stream that must satisfy the requirements of § 1.415(b)-1 determined as of January 1, 2004, using the interest rates and mortality table applicable as of January 1, 2004, is the payment stream consisting of $165,000 paid each year during 2004 through 2007, and $1,621,727 ($1,769,157 multiplied by 165,000/180,000) paid on January 1, 2008. As of January 1, 2004, the actuarially equivalent straight life annuity with respect to those payments is $158,930 using the applicable interest rate (assumed to be 5.25%) and the applicable mortality table for that date. As of January 1, 2004, the actuarially equivalent straight life annuity with respect to those payments is $165,000 using the plan's actuarial assumptions (a 6% interest rate and the applicable mortality table as of January 1, 2003). The annual benefit attributable to those payments is the greater of the two amounts, or $165,000, which satisfies the applicable limitations as of January 1, 2004. Accordingly, Plan E satisfies the second requirement described in paragraph (ii) of this *Example 4* using the special rule for cost-of-living adjustments under paragraph (c)(2) of this section.

(v) For purposes of determining compliance with the first requirement described in paragraph (ii) of this *Example 4*, P's annual benefit attributable to prior distributions is computed by adjusting the annual payments already received ($165,000 for 2004, $170,000 for 2005, $170,000 for 2006, and $175,000 for 2007) already made before January 1, 2008, to an actuarially equivalent straight life annuity commencing on January 1, 2008, in accordance with the rules set forth in paragraph (b)(3) of this section. Pursuant to those rules, that actuarially equivalent straight life annuity is computed using either the plan's actuarial assumptions for applying offsets for prior distributions (here, a 6% interest rate and the mortality table that applies under section 417(e)(3) as of January 1, 2003), or an interest rate of 5% and the applicable mortality table under section 417(e)(3), both determined as of January 1, 2008, whichever set of actuarial assumptions produces the greater actuarially equivalent annuity. The actuarially equivalent straight life annuity computed using the plan's assumptions used for computing offsets is $80,453 per year, and the actuarially equivalent straight life annuity computed using a 5% interest rate and the applicable mortality table as of January 1, 2008, is $75,046 per year. Thus, P's annual benefit attributable to prior distributions is $80,453.

(vi) P's annual benefit attributable to the single-sum distribution made on January 1, 2008, is determined as the greater of the annual amount of the actuarially equivalent straight life annuity commencing at the same age (determined using the plan's actuarial factors), and the annual amount of the actuarially equivalent straight life annuity commencing at the same age (determined using the applicable interest rate and applicable mortality table). Based on the factors used in the plan to determine the actuarially equivalent lump sum (in this case, an interest rate of 6% and the applicable mortality table as of January 1, 2003), $1,769,157 payable as a single sum at age 69 is actuarially equivalent to an immediate straight life annuity at age 69 of $180,000. Based on the applicable interest rate and the applicable mortality table, $1,769,157 payable as a single sum at age 69 is actuarially equivalent to an immediate straight life annuity at age 69 of $170,451. With respect to the single-sum distribution, P's annual benefit is equal to the greater of the two resulting amounts, or $180,000.

(vii) To satisfy the first requirement described in paragraph (ii) of this *Example 4*, P's annual benefit attributable to prior distributions plus P's annual benefit attributable to the single-sum distribution, determined as of January 1, 2008, must not exceed the applicable limitations. The sum of those annual benefits is $260,453. The age-adjusted dollar limitation as of January 1, 2008, is determined as the lesser of the section 415(b)(1)(A) dollar limit multiplied by the ratio of the annuity payable at age 69 to the annuity that would be payable at age 65 based on the same accrued benefit (both determined before the application of section 415), or the straight life annuity payable at age 69 that is actuarially equivalent, using 5% interest and the applicable mortality table, to the straight life annuity payable at age 65. In this case, the age-adjusted section 415(b)(1)(A) dollar limit at age 69 is $244,013, which is the lesser of 265,320 (the straight life annuity at age 69 that is actuarially equivalent to an annuity of $180,000 commencing at age 65, determined using the plan's interest rate of 6% and the applicable mortality table that applies as of January 1, 2003, without a mortality decrement for the period between 65 and 69) and $244,013 (the straight life annuity at age 69 that is actuarially equivalent to an annuity of $180,000 commencing at age 65, determined using 5% interest and the applicable mortality table, without a mortality decrement for the period between 65 and 69)). The compensation-based limitation of section 415(b)(1)(B) for P in 2008 is $209,000 ($190,000 multiplied by the product of the annual adjustment factors for 2005 through 2008, or 1.1). Accordingly, the limitation under section 415(b) for P as of January 1, 2008, is $209,000 (the lesser of the dollar limitation and the compensation limitation as of that date).

(viii) Because the sum of P's annual benefit attributable to prior distributions plus P's annual benefit attributable to the single-sum distribution ($260,453) exceeds the limitation under section 415(b) determined as of January 1, 2008 ($209,000), the plan fails to satisfy the requirements of section 415(b). In addition, if the plan limits the amount of the single-sum distribution in order to satisfy the requirements of section 415(b) in this case, there may be a forfeiture of a participant's accrued benefit in violation of section 411(a) in some cases where a participant converts annuity payments to a single-sum distribution.

Par. 9. Section 1.415(c)-1 is added to read as follows:

§ 1.415(c)-1 *Limitations for defined contribution plans.*

(a) *General rules*—(1) *Maximum limitations.* Under section 415(c) and this section, to satisfy the provisions of section 415(a) for any limitation year, except as provided by paragraph (a)(3) of this section, the annual additions (as defined in paragraph (b) of this section) credited to the account of a participant in a defined contribution plan for the limitation year must not exceed the lesser of—

(i) $40,000 (adjusted pursuant to section 415(d) and § 1.415(d)-1(b)); or

(ii) 100% of the participant's compensation (as defined in § 1.415(c)-2) for the limitation year.

(2) *Defined contribution plan*—(i) *Definition.* For purposes of section 415 and regulations thereunder, a *defined contribution plan* means a defined contribution plan within the meaning of section 414(i) (including the portion of a plan treated as a defined contribution plan under the rules of section 414(k)) that is—

(A) A plan described in section 401(a) which includes a trust which is exempt from tax under section 501(a);

(B) An annuity plan described in section 403(a); or

(C) A simplified employee pension described in section 408(k).

(ii) *Additional plans treated as defined contribution plans*—(A) *In general.* Contributions to the types of arrangements described in paragraphs (a)(2)(ii)(B) through (D) of this section are treated as contributions to defined contribution plans for purposes of section 415 and regulations thereunder.

(B) *Employee contributions to a defined benefit plan.* Mandatory employee contributions to a defined benefit plan are treated as contributions to a defined contribution plan. For this purpose, contributions that are picked up by the employer as described in section 414(h)(2) are not considered employee contributions.

(C) *Individual medical accounts under section 401(h).* Pursuant to section 415(l)(1), contributions allocated to any individual medical account which is part of a pension or annuity plan established pursuant to section 401(h) are treated as contributions to a defined contribution plan.

(D) *Post-retirement medical accounts for key employees.* Pursuant to section 419A(d)(2), amounts attributable to medical benefits allocated to an account established for a key employee (i.e., any employee who, at any time during the plan year or any preceding plan year, is or was a key employee as defined in section 416(i)) pursuant to section 419A(d)(1) are treated as contributions to a defined contribution plan.

(iii) *Section 403(b) annuity contracts.* Annual additions under an annuity contract described in section 403(b) are treated as annual additions under a defined contribution plan for purposes of this section.

(3) *Alternative contribution limitations*—(i) *Church plans.* For alternative contribution limitations relating to church plans, see paragraph (d) of this section.

(ii) *Special rules for medical benefits.* For alternative contribution limitations relating to certain medical benefits, see paragraph (e) of this section.

(iii) *Employee stock ownership plans.* For additional rules relating to employee stock ownership plans, see paragraph (f) of this section.

(b) *Annual additions*—(1) *In general*—(i) *General definition.* The term *annual addition* means, for purposes of this section, the sum, credited to a participant's account for any limitation year, of—

(A) Employer contributions;

(B) Employee contributions; and

(C) Forfeitures.

(ii) *Certain excess amounts treated as annual additions.* Contributions do not fail to be annual additions merely because they are excess contributions (as described in section 401(k)(8)(B)) or excess aggregate contributions (as described in section 401(m)(6)(B)), or merely because excess contributions or excess aggregate contributions are corrected through distribution.

(iii) *Direct transfers between defined contribution plans.* The direct transfer of funds or employee contributions from one defined contribution plan to another defined contribution plan does not give rise to an annual addition.

(iv) *Reinvested ESOP dividends.* The reinvestment of dividends on employer securities under an employee stock ownership plan pursuant to section 404(k)(2)(A)(iii)(II) does not give rise to an annual addition.

(2) *Employer contributions*—(i) *Amounts treated as annual additions.* For purposes of paragraph (b)(1)(i)(A) of this section, the term *annual additions* includes employer contributions credited to the participant's account for the limitation year and other allocations described in paragraph (b)(4) of this section that are made during the limitation year. See paragraph (b)(6) of this section for timing rules applicable to annual additions with respect to employer contributions.

(ii) *Amounts not treated as annual additions*—(A) *Certain restorations of accrued benefits.* The restoration of an employee's accrued benefits by the employer in accordance with section 411(a)(3)(D) or section 411(a)(7)(C) or resulting from the repayment of cashouts under a governmental plan (as described in section 415(k)(3)) is not considered an annual addition for the limitation year in which the restoration occurs. (See § 1.411(a)-7(d)(6)(iii)(B).)

(B) *Catch-up contributions.* Catch-up contributions made in accordance with section 414(v) and § 1.414(v)-1 do not give rise to annual additions.

(C) *Restorative payments.* A restorative payment that is allocated to a participant's account does not give rise to an annual addition for any limitation year. For this purpose, restorative payments are payments made to restore losses to a plan resulting from actions by a fiduciary for which there is reasonable risk of liability for breach of a fiduciary duty under Title I of ERISA, where plan participants who are similarly situated are treated similarly with respect to the payments. Generally, payments to a defined contribution plan are restorative payments only if the payments are made in order to restore some or all of the plan's losses due to an action (or a failure to act) that creates a reasonable risk of liability for such a breach of fiduciary duty (other than a breach of fiduciary duty arising from failure to remit contributions to the plan). This includes payments to a plan made pursuant to a Department of Labor order, the Department of Labor's Voluntary Fiduciary Correction Program, or a court-approved settlement, to restore losses to a qualified defined contribution plan on account of the breach of fiduciary duty (other than a breach of fiduciary duty arising from failure to remit contributions to the plan). However, payments made to a plan to make up for losses due merely to market fluctuations and other payments that are not made on account of a reasonable risk of liability for breach of a fiduciary duty under Title I of ERISA are contributions that give rise to annual additions and are not restorative payments.

(D) *Excess deferrals.* Excess deferrals that are distributed in accordance with § 1.402(g)-1(e)(2) or (3) do not give rise to annual additions.

(3) *Employee contributions.* For purposes of paragraph (b)(1)(i)(B) of this section, the term *annual additions* includes mandatory employee contributions (as defined in section 411(c)(2)(C) and the regulations thereunder) as well as voluntary employee contributions. The term "annual additions" does not include—

(i) Rollover contributions (as described in sections 401(a)(31), 402(c)(1), 403(a)(4), 403(b)(8), 408(d)(3), and 457(e)(16)).

(ii) Repayments of loans made to a participant from the plan;

(iii) Repayments of amounts described in section 411(a)(7)(B) (in accordance with section 411(a)(7)(C)) and section 411(a)(3)(D) (see § 1.411(a)-7(d)(6)(iii)(B)) or repayment of contributions to a governmental plan as described in section 415(k)(3); or

(iv) Employee contributions to a qualified cost of living arrangement within the meaning of section 415(k)(2)(B).

(4) *Transactions with plan.* The Commissioner may in an appropriate case, considering all of the facts and circumstances, treat transactions between the plan and the employer, transactions between the plan and the employee, or certain allocations to participants' accounts as giving rise to annual additions. Further, the Commissioner will treat a sale or exchange by the employee or the employer that transfers assets to a plan where the consideration paid by the plan is less than the fair market value of the assets transferred to the plan as giving rise to an annual addition in the amount of the difference between the value of the assets transferred and the consideration. A transaction described in this paragraph (b)(4) may constitute a prohibited transaction with the meaning of section 4975(c)(1).

(5) *Contributions other than cash.* For purposes of this paragraph (b), a contribution by the employer or employee of property rather than cash is considered to be a contribution in an amount equal to the fair market value of the property on the date the contribution is made. For this purpose, the fair market value is the price at which the property would change hands between a willing buyer and a willing seller, neither being under any compulsion to buy or to sell and both having reasonable knowledge of relevant facts. In addition, the contribution described in this paragraph (b)(5) may constitute a prohibited transaction within the meaning of section 4975(c)(1).

(6) *Timing rules*—(i) *In general*—(A) *Date of allocation.* For purposes of this paragraph (b), an annual addition is credited to the account of a participant for a particular limitation year if it is allocated to the participant's account under the terms of the plan as of any date within that limitation year. However, if the allocation is dependent upon participation in the plan as of any date subsequent to the date as of which it is allocated, it is considered allocated only at the end of the period of participation upon which the allocation is conditioned.

(B) *Date of employer contributions.* For purposes of this paragraph (b), employer contributions are not treated as credited to a participant's account for a particular limitation year unless the contributions are actually made to the plan no later than 30 days after the end of the period described in section 404(a)(6) applicable to the taxable year with or within which the particular limitation year ends. If, however, contributions are made by an employer exempt from Federal income tax (including a governmental employer), the contributions must be made to the plan no later than the 15th day of the tenth calendar month

following the close of the taxable year with or within which the particular limitation year ends. If contributions are made to a plan after the end of the period during which contributions can be made and treated as credited to a participant's account for a particular limitation year, allocations attributable to those contributions are treated as credited to the participant's account for the limitation year during which those contributions are made.

(C) *Date of employee contributions.* For purposes of this paragraph (b), employee contributions, whether voluntary or mandatory, are not treated as credited to a participant's account for a particular limitation year unless the contributions are actually made to the plan no later than 30 days after the close of that limitation year.

(D) *Date for forfeitures.* A forfeiture is treated as an annual addition for the limitation year that contains the date as of which it is allocated to a participant's account as a forfeiture.

(E) *Treatment of elective contributions as plan assets.* The extent to which elective contributions constitute plan assets for purposes of the prohibited transaction provisions of section 4975 and Title I of the Employee Retirement Income Security Act of 1974 (88 Stat. 829), Public Law 93-406 (ERISA), is determined in accordance with regulations and rulings issued by the Department of Labor. See 29 CFR 2510.3-102.

(ii) *Special timing rules*—(A) *Corrective contributions.* For purposes of this section, if, in a particular limitation year, an employer allocates an amount to a participant's account because of an erroneous forfeiture in a prior limitation year, or because of an erroneous failure to allocate amounts in a prior limitation year, the allocation will not be considered an annual addition with respect to the participant for that particular limitation year, but will be considered an annual addition for the prior limitation year to which it relates. An example of a situation in which an employer contribution might occur under the circumstances described in the preceding sentence is a retroactive crediting of service for an employee under 29 CFR 2530.200b-2(a)(3) in accordance with an award of back pay. For purposes of this paragraph (b)(6)(ii), if the amount so contributed in the particular limitation year takes into account actual investment gains attributable to the period subsequent to the year to which the contribution relates, the portion of the total contribution that consists of such gains is not considered as an annual addition for any limitation year.

(B) *Contributions for accumulated funding deficiencies and previously waived contributions*—(*1*) *Accumulated funding deficiency.* In the case of a defined contribution plan to which the rules of section 412 apply, a contribution made to reduce an accumulated funding deficiency will be treated as if it were timely made for purposes of determining the limitation year in which the annual additions arising from the contribution are made, but only if the contribution is allocated to those participants who would have received an annual addition if the contribution had been timely made.

(*2*) *Previously waived contributions.* In the case of a defined contribution plan to which the rules of section 412 apply and for which there has been a waiver of the minimum funding standard in a prior limitation year in accordance with section 412(d), that portion of an employer contribution in a subsequent limitation year which, if not for the waiver, would have otherwise been required in the prior limitation year under section 412(a) will be treated as if it were timely made (without regard to the funding waiver) for purposes of determining the limitation year in which the annual additions arising from the contribution are made, but only if the contribution is allocated to those participants who would have received an annual addition if the contribution had been timely made (without regard to the funding waiver).

(*3*) *Interest.* For purposes of determining the amount of the annual addition under paragraphs (b)(6)(ii)(B)(*1*) and (*2*), a reasonable amount of interest paid by the employer is disregarded. However, any interest paid by the employer that is in excess of a reasonable amount, as determined by the Commissioner, is taken into account as an annual addition for the limitation year during which the contribution is made.

(C) *Simplified employee pensions (SEPs).* For purposes of this paragraph (b), amounts contributed to a simplified employee pension described in section 408(k) are treated as allocated to the individual's account as of the last day of the limitation year ending with or within the taxable year for which the contribution is made.

(D) *Treatment of certain contributions made pursuant to veterans' reemployment rights.* If, in a particular limitation year, an employer contributes an amount to an employee's account with respect to a prior limitation year and such contribution is required by reason of such employee's rights under chapter 43 of title 38, United States Code, resulting from qualified military service, as specified in section 414(u)(1), then such contribution is not considered an annual addition with respect to the employee for that particular limitation year in which the contribution is made, but, in accordance with section 414(u)(1)(B), is considered an annual addition for the limitation year to which the contribution relates.

(c) *Examples.* The following examples illustrate the rules of paragraphs (a) and (b) of this section:

Example 1. (i) P is a participant in a qualified profit-sharing plan maintained by his employer, ABC Corporation. The limitation year for the plan is the calendar year. P's compensation (as defined in § 1.415(c)-2) for the current limitation year is $30,000.

(ii) Because the compensation limitation described in section 415(c)(1)(B) applicable to P for the current limitation year is lower than the dollar limitation described in section 415(c)(1)(A), the maximum annual addition which can be allocated to P's account for the current limitation year is $30,000 (100% of $30,000).

Example 2. (i) Assume the same facts as in *Example 1*, except that P's compensation for the current limitation year is $140,000.

(ii) The maximum amount of annual additions that may be allocated to P's account in the current limitation year is the lesser of $140,000 (100% of P's compensation) or the dollar limitation of section 415(c)(1)(A) as in effect as of January 1 of the calendar year in which the current limitation year ends. If, for example, the dollar limitation of section 415(c)(1)(A) in effect as of January 1 of the calendar year in which the current limitation year ends is $44,000, then the maximum annual addition that can be allocated to P's account for the current limitation year is $44,000.

Example 3. (i) Employer N maintains a qualified profit-sharing plan that uses the calendar year as its plan year and its limitation year. N's taxable year is a fiscal year beginning June 1 and ending May 31. Under the terms of the profit-sharing plan maintained by N, employer contributions are made to the plan two months after the close of N's taxable year and are allocated as of the last day of the plan year ending

Limitation year	Compensation
2007	$30,000
2008	$32,000
2009	$34,000
2010	$36,000

(ii) Participant A makes no voluntary employee contributions during limitation years 2007, 2008, and 2009. On October 1, 2010, participant A makes a voluntary employee contribution of $13,200 (10% of A's aggregate compensation for limitation years 2007, 2008, 2009, and 2010 of $132,000). Under the terms of the plan, $3,000 of this 2010 contribution is allocated to A's account as of limitation year 2007; $3,200 is allocated to A's account of limitation year 2008; $3,400 is allocated to A's account as of limitation year 2009, and $3,600 is allocated to A's account as of limitation year 2010.

(iii) Under the rule set forth in paragraph (c)(6)(ii)(C) of this section, employee contributions will not be considered credited to a participant's account for a particular limitation year for section 415 purposes unless the contributions are actually made to the plan no later than 30 days after the close of that limitation year. Thus, A's voluntary employee contribution of $13,200 made on October 1, 2010 would be considered as credited to A's account only for the 2010 calendar year limitation year, notwithstanding the plan provisions.

(d) *Special rules relating to church plans*—(1) *Alternative contribution limitation*—(i) *In general.* Pursuant to section 415(c)(7)(A), notwithstanding the general rule of paragraph (a)(1) of this section, additions for a section 403(b) annuity contract for a year with respect to a participant who is an employee of a church or a convention or association of churches, including an organization described in section 414(e)(3)(B)(ii), when expressed as an annual addition to such participant's account, are treated as not exceeding the limitation of paragraph (a)(1) of this section if such annual additions for the year are not in excess of $10,000.

(ii) *$40,000 aggregate limitation.* The total amount of annual additions with respect to any participant that are treated as not exceeding the limitation of paragraph (a)(1) of this section (taking into account the rule of paragraph (d)(3) of this section) pursuant to the rule of paragraph (d)(1)(i) of this section even though those annual additions would otherwise exceed that limitation cannot exceed $40,000. Thus, the aggregate of amounts for all limitation years that would exceed the limitation of this section but for this paragraph (d)(1) is limited to $40,000.

within the taxable year (and are not conditioned on future participation). Thus, employer contributions for the 2007 calendar year limitation year are made on July 31, 2008 (the date that is two months after the close of N's taxable year ending May 31, 2008) and are allocated as of December 31, 2007.

(ii) Because the employer contributions are actually made to the plan no later than 30 days after the end of the period described in section 404(a)(6) with respect to N's taxable year ending May 31, 2008, the contributions will be considered annual additions for the 2007 calendar year limitation year.

Example 4. (i) Assume the same facts as in *Example 3*, except that the plan year for the profit-sharing plan maintained by N is the 12-month period beginning on February 1 and ending on January 31. The limitation year continues to be the calendar year. Under the terms of the plan, an employer contribution which is made to the plan on July 31, 2008, is allocated to participants' accounts as of January 31, 2008.

(ii) Because the last day of the plan year is in the 2008 calendar year limitation year, and because, under the terms of the plan, employer contributions are allocated to participants' accounts as of the last day of the plan year, the contributions are considered annual additions for the 2008 calendar year limitation year.

Example 5. (i) XYZ Corporation maintains a profit-sharing plan to which a participant may make voluntary employee contributions for any year not to exceed 10% of the participant's compensation for the year. The plan permits a participant to make retroactive make-up contributions for any year for which the participant contributed less than 10% of compensation. XYZ uses the calendar year as the plan year and the limitation year. Under the terms of the plan, voluntary employee contributions are credited to a participant's account for a particular limitation year if such contributions are allocated to the participant's account as of any date within that limitation year. Participant A's compensation is as follows—

(2) *Years of service taken into account for duly ordained, commissioned, or licensed ministers or lay employees.* For purposes of this paragraph (d)—

(i) All years of service by an individual as an employee of a church, or a convention or association of churches, including an organization described in section 414(e)(3)(B)(ii), are considered as years of service for one employer; and

(ii) All amounts contributed for annuity contracts by each such church (or convention or association of churches) during such years for the employee are considered to have been contributed by one employer.

(3) *Foreign missionaries.* Pursuant to section 415(c)(7)(C), in the case of any individual described in paragraph (d)(1) of this section performing any services for the church outside the United States during the limitation year, additions for an annuity contract under section 403(b) for any year are not treated as exceeding the limitation of paragraph (a)(1) of this section if such annual additions for the year do not exceed the greater of $3,000 or the employee's includible compensation with respect to services for the church performed outside the United States during the limitation year.

(4) *Church, convention or association of churches.* For purposes of this paragraph (d), the terms *church* and *convention or association of churches* have the same meaning as when used in section 414(e).

(5) *Examples.* The following examples illustrate the rules of this paragraph (d).

Example 1. (i) E is an employee of ABC Church earning $7,000 during each calendar year. E participates in a section 403(b) annuity contract maintained by ABC Church beginning in 2007. The limitation year for the plan coincides with the calendar year. ABC Church contributes $10,000 to be allocated to E's account under the plan for 2007.

(ii) Under paragraph (d)(1) of this section, this allocation is treated as not violating the limits established in paragraph (a)(1) of this section because it does not exceed $10,000. Moreover, since an annual addition of $10,000 would otherwise exceed the limitation of paragraph (a)(1) of this section by $3,000, $3,000 is counted toward the aggregate limitation specified in paragraph (d)(1)(ii) of this section for 2007. Accordingly, ABC Church may make such allocations for 13 years (e.g., for 2007 through 2019) without exceeding the aggregate limitation of $40,000 specified in paragraph (d) of this section. For the fourteenth year, ABC Church could allocate only $8,000 to E's account (i.e., the $7,000 limitation computed under paragraph (a)(1)(ii) of this section, plus the remaining $1,000 of the $40,000 aggregate limitation under paragraph (d)(1)(ii) of this section on annual additions in excess of the limits under paragraph (a)(1) of this section).

Example 2. (i) F is an employee of XYZ Church. F earns $2,000 during each calendar year for services he provides to XYZ Church, all of which are performed outside the United States during each calendar year. F participates in a section 403(b) annuity contract maintained by ABC Church beginning in 2007. The limitation year for the plan coincides with the calendar year. ABC Church contributes $10,000 to be allocated to F's account under the plan for 2007.

(ii) Under paragraph (d)(1) of this section, this allocation is treated as not violating the limits established in paragraph (a)(1) of this section because it does not exceed $10,000. Moreover, since an annual addition of $10,000 would otherwise exceed the limitation of paragraph (a)(1) of this section by $7,000 (i.e., the excess of $10,000 over the greater of the $2,000 compensation limitation under section 415(c)(1)(B) or the $3,000 section 415(c)(7)(C) amount), XYZ Church may make such allocations for 5 years (e.g., for 2006 through 2010) without exceeding the aggregate limitation of $40,000 specified in paragraph (d) of this section. In 2012, XYZ church may contribute $8,000 to be allocated to F's account under the plan (i.e., the $3,000 limitation computed under paragraph (d)(3) of this section, plus the remaining $5,000 of the $40,000 aggregate limitation under paragraph (d)(1)(ii) of this section on annual additions in excess of the limits under paragraph (a)(1) of this section). For years after 2012, pursuant to paragraph (d)(3) of this section, XYZ Church could allocate $3,000 per year to F's account.

(e) *Special rules for medical benefits.* The limit under paragraph (a)(1)(ii) of this section (i.e., 100% of the participant's compensation for the limitation year) does not apply to—

(1) An individual medical account (as defined in section 415(l)); or

(2) A post-retirement medical benefits account for key employees (as defined in section 419A(d)(1)).

(f) *Special rules for employee stock ownership plans*—(1) *In general.* Special rules apply to employee stock ownership plans, as provided in paragraphs (f)(2) through (f)(4) of this section.

(2) *Determination of annual additions for leveraged ESOP*—(i) *In general.* Except as provided in this paragraph (f), in the case of an employee stock ownership plan to which an exempt loan as described in § 54.4975-7(b) has been made, the amount of employer contributions that is considered an annual addition for the limitation year is calculated with respect to employer contributions of both principal and interest used to repay that exempt loan for the limitation year.

(ii) *Employer stock that has decreased in value.* A plan may provide that, in lieu of computing annual additions in accordance with paragraph (f)(2)(i) of this section, annual additions with respect to a loan repayment described in paragraph (f)(2)(i) of this section are determined as the fair market value of shares released from the suspense account on account of the repayment and allocated to participants for the limitation year if that amount is less than the amount determined in accordance with paragraph (f)(2)(i) of this section.

(3) *Exclusions from annual additions for certain ESOPs that allocate to a broad range of participants*—(i) *General rule.* Pursuant to section 415(c)(6), in the case of an employee stock ownership plan (as described in section 4975(e)(7)) that meets the requirements of paragraph (f)(3)(ii) of this section for a limitation year, the limitations imposed by this section do not apply to—

(A) Forfeitures of employer securities (within the meaning of section 409(l)) under such an employee stock ownership plan if such securities were acquired with the proceeds of a loan (as described in section 404(a)(9)(A)); or

(B) Employer contributions to such an employee stock ownership plan which are deductible under section 404(a)(9)(B) and charged against the participant's account.

(ii) *Employee stock ownership plans to which the special exclusion applies.* An employee stock ownership plan meets the requirements of this paragraph (f)(3)(ii) for a limitation year if no more than one-third of the employer contributions for the limitation year that are deductible under section 404(a)(9) are allocated to highly compensated employees (within the meaning of section 414(q)).

(4) *Gratuitous transfers under section 664(g)(1).* The amount of any qualified gratuitous transfer (as defined in section 664(g)(1)) allocated to a participant for any limitation year is not taken into account in determining whether any other annual addition exceeds the limitations imposed by this section, but only if the amount of the qualified gratuitous transfer does not exceed the limitations imposed by section 415.

Par. 10. Section 1.415(c)-2 is added to read as follows:

§ 1.415(c)-2 Compensation.

(a) *General definition.* Except as otherwise provided in this section, compensation from the employer within the meaning of section 415(c)(3), which is applied for purposes of section 415 and regulations thereunder, means all items of remuneration described in paragraph (b) of this section, but excludes the items of remuneration described in paragraph (c) of this section. Paragraph (d) of this section provides safe harbor definitions of compensation that are permitted to be provided in a plan in lieu of the generally applicable definition of compensation. Paragraph (e) of this section provides timing rules relating to compensation. Paragraph (f) of this section provides rules regarding the application of the rules of section 401(a)(17) to the definition of compensation for purposes of section 415. Paragraph (g) of this section provides special rules relating to the determination of compensation, including rules for determining compensation for a section 403(b) annuity contract, rules for determining the compensation of employees of controlled groups or affiliated service groups, rules for disabled employees, rules relating to foreign compensation, rules regarding deemed section 125 compensation, and rules for employees in qualified military service.

(b) *Items includible as compensation.* For purposes of applying the limitations of section 415, except as otherwise provided in this section, the term *compensation* means remuneration for services of the following types—

(1) The employee's wages, salaries, fees for professional services, and other amounts received (without regard to whether or not an amount is paid in cash) for personal services actually rendered in the course of employment with the employer maintaining the plan, to the extent that the amounts are includible in gross income (or to the extent amounts deferred at the election of the employee would be includible in gross income but for the rules of section 402(e)(3), 402(h)(1)(B), 402(k), 125(a), 132(f)(4), or 457(b)). These amounts include, but are not limited to, commissions paid to salespersons, compensation for services on the basis of a percentage of profits, commissions on insurance premiums, tips, bonuses, fringe benefits, and reimbursements or other expense allowances under a nonaccountable plan as described in § 1.62-2(c).

(2) In the case of an employee who is an employee within the meaning of section 401(c)(1) and the regulations thereunder, the employee's earned income (as described in section 401(c)(2) and the regulations thereunder), plus amounts deferred at the election of the employee that would be includible in gross income but for the rules of section 402(e)(3), 402(h)(1)(B), 402(k), or 457(b).

(3) Amounts described in section 104(a)(3), 105(a), or 105(h), but only to the extent that these amounts are includible in the gross income of the employee.

(4) Amounts paid or reimbursed by the employer for moving expenses incurred by an employee, but only to the extent that at the time of the payment it is reasonable to believe that these amounts are not deductible by the employee under section 217.

(5) The value of a nonqualified option granted to an employee by the employer, but only to the extent that the value of the option is includible in the gross income of the employee for the taxable year in which granted.

(6) The amount includible in the gross income of an employee upon making the election described in section 83(b).

(c) *Items not includible as compensation.* The term *compensation* does not include—

(1) Contributions (other than elective contributions described in section 402(e)(3), section 408(k)(6), section 408(p)(2)(A)(i), or section 457(b)) made by the employer to a plan of deferred compensation (including a simplified employee pension described in section 408(k) or a simple retirement account described in section 408(p), and whether or not qualified) to the extent that the contributions are not includible in the gross income of the employee for the taxable year in which contributed. Additionally, any distributions from a plan of deferred compensation (whether or not qualified) are not considered as compensation for section 415 purposes, regardless of whether such amounts are includible in the gross income of the employee when

distributed. However, if the plan so provides, any amounts received by an employee pursuant to an unfunded nonqualified plan are permitted to be considered as compensation for section 415 purposes in the year the amounts are actually received.

(2) Amounts realized from the exercise of a nonqualified option, or when restricted stock or other property held by an employee either becomes freely transferable or is no longer subject to a substantial risk of forfeiture (see section 83 and the regulations thereunder).

(3) Amounts realized from the sale, exchange, or other disposition of stock acquired under a qualified stock option.

(4) Other amounts that receive special tax benefits, such as premiums for group-term life insurance (but only to the extent that the premiums are not includible in the gross income of the employee and are not salary reduction amounts that are described in section 125).

(5) Other items of remuneration that are similar to any of the items listed in paragraphs (c)(1) through (c)(4) of this section.

(d) *Safe harbor rules with respect to plan's definition of compensation—* (1) *In general.* Paragraphs (d)(2) through (4) of this section contain safe harbor definitions of compensation that are automatically considered to satisfy section 415(c)(3) if specified in the plan. The Commissioner may, in revenue rulings, notices, and other guidance of general applicability published in the Internal Revenue Bulletin (see § 601.601(d) of this chapter), provide additional definitions of compensation that are treated as satisfying section 415(c)(3).

(2) *Simplified compensation.* The safe harbor definition of compensation under this paragraph (d)(2) includes only those items specified in paragraph (b)(1) or (2) of this section and excludes all those items listed in paragraph (c) of this section.

(3) *Section 3401(a) wages.* The safe harbor definition of compensation under this paragraph (d)(3) includes wages within the meaning of section 3401(a) (for purposes of income tax withholding at the source), plus amounts deferred at the election of the employee that would be included in wages if not deferred pursuant to the rules of section 402(e)(3), 402(h)(1)(B), 402(k), or 457(b). However, any rules that limit the remuneration included in wages based on the nature or location of the employment or the services performed (such as the exception for agricultural labor in section 3401(a)(2)) are disregarded for this purpose.

(4) *Information required to be reported under sections 6041, 6051 and 6052.* The safe harbor definition of compensation under this paragraph (d)(4) includes amounts that are compensation under the safe harbor definition of paragraph (d)(3) of this section, plus all other payments of compensation to an employee by his employer (in the course of the employer's trade or business) for which the employer is required to furnish the employee a written statement under sections 6041(d), 6051(a)(3), and 6052. See §§ 1.6041-1(a), 1.6041-2(a)(1), 1.6052-1, and 1.6052-2, and also see § 31.6051-1(a)(1)(i)(C) of this chapter. This safe harbor definition of compensation may be modified to exclude amounts paid or reimbursed by the employer for moving expenses incurred by an employee, but only to the extent that, at the time of the payment, it is reasonable to believe that these amounts are deductible by the employee under section 217.

(e) *Timing rules—*(1) *In general—*(i) *Payment during the limitation year.* Except as otherwise provided in this paragraph (e), in order to be taken into account for a limitation year, compensation within the meaning of section 415(c)(3) must be actually paid or made available to an employee (or, if earlier, includible in the gross income of the employee) within the limitation year. For this purpose, compensation is treated as paid on a date if it is actually paid on that date or it would have been paid on that date but for an election under section 401(k), 403(b), 408(k), 408(p)(2)(A)(i), 457(b), 132(f), or 125.

(ii) *Payment prior to severance from employment.* In order to be taken into account for a limitation year, compensation within the meaning of section 415(c)(3) must be paid or treated as paid to the employee (in accordance with the rules of paragraph (e)(1)(i) of this section) prior to severance from employment (within the meaning of section 401(k)(2)(B)(i)(l)) with the employer maintaining the plan

(2) *Certain de minimis timing differences.* Notwithstanding the provisions of paragraph (e)(1) of this section, a plan may provide that compensation for a limitation year includes amounts earned during that limitation year but not paid during that limitation year solely because of the timing of pay periods and pay dates if—

(i) These amounts are paid during the first few weeks of the next limitation year;

(ii) The amounts are included on a uniform and consistent basis with respect to all similarly situated employees; and

(iii) No compensation is included in more than one limitation year.

(3) *Compensation paid after severance from employment—*(i) *In general.* Any compensation described in paragraph (e)(3)(ii) of this section that is paid within 2 ½ months after an employee's severance from employment does not fail to be compensation (within the meaning of section 415(c)(3)) pursuant to the rule of paragraph (e)(1)(ii) of this section merely because it is paid after the employee's severance from employment.

(ii) *Certain payments made within 2 ½ months after severance from employment.* The following are types of post-severance payments that are not excluded from compensation because of timing if they are paid within 2 ½ months following severance from employment—

(A) Payments that, absent a severance from employment, would have been paid to the employee while the employee continued in employment with the employer and are regular compensation for services during the employee's regular working hours, compensation for services outside the employee's regular working hours (such as overtime or shift differential), commissions, bonuses, or other similar compensation; and

(B) Payments for accrued bona fide sick, vacation, or other leave, but only if the employee would have been able to use the leave if employment had continued.

(iii) *Other post-severance payments are not compensation.* Any payment that is not described in paragraph (e)(3)(ii) of this section is not considered compensation if paid after severance from employment, even if it is paid within 2 ½ months following severance from employment. Thus, for example, compensation does not include amounts paid after severance from employment that are severance pay, unfunded nonqualified deferred compensation, or parachute payments within the meaning of section 280G(b)(2).

(4) *Certain military service.* The rule of paragraph (e)(1)(ii) of this section does not apply to payments to an individual who does not currently perform services for the employer by reason of qualified military service (as that term is used in section 414(u)(1)) to the extent those payments do not exceed the amounts the individual would have received if the individual had continued to perform services for the employer rather than entering qualified military service.

(f) *Interaction with section 401(a)(17).* Because a plan may not base allocations (in the case of a defined contribution plan) or benefit accruals (in the case of a defined benefit plan) on compensation in excess of the limitation under section 401(a)(17), a plan's definition of compensation for a limitation year that is used for purposes of applying the limitations of section 415 is not permitted to reflect compensation for a plan year that is in excess of the limitation under section 401(a)(17) that applies to that plan year.

(g) *Special rules—*(1) *Compensation for section 403(b) annuity contract.* In the case of an annuity contract described in section 403(b), the term *participant's compensation* means the participant's includible compensation determined under section 403(b)(3) and § 1.403(b)-2(a)(11). Accordingly, the rules for determining a participant's compensation pursuant to section 415(c)(3) (other than section 415(c)(3)(E)) and this section do not apply to a section 403(b) annuity contract.

(2) *Employees of controlled groups of corporations, etc.* In the case of an employee of two or more corporations which are members of a controlled group of corporations (as defined in section 414(b) as modified by section 415(h)), the term "compensation" for such employee includes compensation from all employers that are members of the group, regardless of whether the employee's particular employer has a qualified plan. This special rule is also applicable to an employee of two or more trades or businesses (whether or not incorporated) that are under common control (as defined in section 414(c) as modified by section 415(h)), to an employee of two or more members of an affiliated service group as defined in section 414(m), and to an employee of two or more members of any group of employers who must be aggregated and treated as one employer pursuant to section 414(o).

(3) *Aggregation of section 403(b) annuity with qualified plan of controlled employer.* If a section 403(b) annuity contract is combined or aggregated with a qualified plan of a controlled employer in accordance with § 1.415(f)-1(f)(2), then, in applying the limitations of section 415(c) in connection with the combining of the section 403(b) annuity with a qualified plan, the total compensation from both employers is permitted to be taken into account.

(4) *Permanent and total disability of defined contribution plan participant—*(i) *In general.* Pursuant to section 415(c)(3)(C), if the conditions set forth in paragraph (g)(4)(ii) of this section are satisfied, then, in the case of a participant in any defined contribution plan who is permanently and totally disabled (as defined in section 22(e)(3)), the *partici-*

pant's compensation means the compensation the participant would have received for the year if the participant was paid at the rate of compensation paid immediately before becoming permanently and totally disabled, if such compensation is greater than the participant's compensation determined without regard to this paragraph (g)(4).

(ii) *Conditions for deemed disability compensation.* The rule of paragraph (g)(4)(i) of this section applies only if the following conditions are satisfied—

(A) Either the participant is not a highly compensated employee (as defined in section 414(q)) immediately before becoming disabled, or the plan provides for the continuation of contributions on behalf of all participants who are permanently and totally disabled for a fixed or determinable period;

(B) The plan provides that the rule of this paragraph (g)(4) (treating certain amounts as compensation for a disabled participant) applies with respect to the participant; and

(C) Contributions made with respect to amounts treated as compensation under this paragraph (g)(4) are nonforfeitable when made.

(5) *Foreign compensation.* Compensation described in paragraphs (b)(1) and (2) of this section includes foreign earned income (as defined in section 911(b)), whether or not excludable from gross income under section 911. Compensation described in paragraph (b)(1) of this section is to be determined without regard to the exclusions from gross income in sections 931 and 933. Similar principles are to be applied with respect to income subject to sections 931 and 933 in determining compensation described in paragraph (b)(2) of this section.

(6) *Deemed section 125 compensation*—(i) *General rule.* A plan is permitted to provide that deemed section 125 compensation (as defined in paragraph (g)(6)(ii) of this section) is compensation within the meaning of section 415(c)(3), provided that the plan applies this rule uniformly to all employees with respect to whom amounts subject to section 125 are included in compensation.

(ii) *Definition of deemed section 125 compensation.* Deemed section 125 compensation is an amount that is excludable from the income of the participant under section 106 that is not available to the participant in cash in lieu of group health coverage under a section 125 arrangement solely because that participant is not able to certify that the participant has other health coverage. Under this definition, amounts are deemed section 125 compensation only if the employer does not otherwise request or collect information regarding the participant's other health coverage as part of the enrollment process for the health plan.

(7) *Employees in qualified military service.* See section 414(u)(7) for special rules regarding compensation of employees who are in qualified military service within the meaning of section 414(u)(5).

Par. 11. Section 1.415(d)-1 is added to read as follows:

§ *1.415(d)-1 Cost of living adjustments.*

(a) *Defined benefit plans*—(1) *Dollar limitation*—(i) *Determination of adjusted limit.* Under section 415(d)(1)(A), the dollar limitation described in section 415(b)(1)(A) applicable to defined benefit plans is adjusted annually to take into account increases in the cost of living. The adjustment of the dollar limitation is made by multiplying the adjustment factor for the year, as described in paragraph (a)(1)(ii)(A) of this section, by $160,000, and rounding the result in accordance with paragraph (a)(1)(iii) of this section. The adjusted dollar limitation is prescribed by the Commissioner and published in the Internal Revenue Bulletin. See § 601.601(d) of this chapter.

(ii) *Determination of adjustment factor*—(A) *Adjustment factor.* The adjustment factor for a calendar year is equal to a fraction, the numerator of which is the value of the applicable index for the calendar quarter ending September 30 of the preceding calendar year, and the denominator of which is the value of such index for the base period. The applicable index is determined consistent with the procedures used to adjust benefit amounts under section 215(i)(2)(A) of the Social Security Act, Public Law 92-336 (86 Stat. 406), as amended. If, however, the value of that fraction is less than one for a calendar year, then the adjustment factor for the calendar year is equal to one.

(B) *Base period.* For the purpose of adjusting the dollar limitation pursuant to paragraph (a)(1)(ii)(A) of this section, the base period is the calendar quarter beginning July 1, 2001.

(iii) *Rounding.* Any increase in the $160,000 amount specified in section 415(b)(1)(A) which is not a multiple of $5,000 is rounded to the next lowest multiple of $5,000.

(2) *Average compensation for high 3 years of service limitation*—(i) *Determination of adjusted limit.* Under section 415(d)(1)(B), with regard to participants who have separated from service with a nonforfeitable right to an accrued benefit, the compensation limitation described in section 415(b)(1)(B) is adjusted annually to take into account increases in the cost of living. For any limitation year beginning after the separation occurs, the adjustment of the compensation limitation is made by multiplying the annual adjustment factor (as defined in paragraph (a)(2)(ii) of this section) by the compensation limitation applicable to the participant in the prior limitation year. The annual adjustment factor is prescribed by the Commissioner and published in the Internal Revenue Bulletin. See § 601.601(d) of this chapter.

(ii) *Annual adjustment factor.* The annual adjustment factor for a calendar year is equal to a fraction, the numerator of which is the value of the applicable index for the calendar quarter ending September 30 of the preceding calendar year, and the denominator of which is the value of such index for the calendar quarter ending September 30 of the calendar year prior to that calendar year. The applicable index is determined consistent with the procedures used to adjust benefit amounts under section 215(i)(2)(A) of the Social Security Act. If the value of the fraction described in the first sentence of this paragraph (a)(2)(ii) is less than one for a calendar year, then the adjustment factor for the calendar year is equal to one. In such a case, the annual adjustment factor for future calendar years will be determined in accordance with revenue rulings, notices, or other published guidance prescribed by the Commissioner and published in the Internal Revenue Bulletin. See § 601.601(d) of this chapter.

(3) *Effective date of adjustment.* The adjusted dollar limitation applicable to defined benefit plans is effective as of January 1 of each calendar year and applies with respect to limitation years ending with or within that calendar year. Benefit payments and accrued benefits for a limitation year cannot exceed the currently applicable dollar limitation (as in effect before the January 1 adjustment) prior to January 1.

(4) *Application of adjusted figure*—(i) *In general.* If the dollar limitation of section 415(b)(1)(A) or the compensation limitation of section 415(b)(1)(B) is adjusted pursuant to section 415(d) for a limitation year, the adjustment is applied as provided in this paragraph (a)(4).

(ii) *Application of adjusted limitations to benefits that have not commenced.* An adjustment to the dollar limitation of section 415(b)(1)(A) applies to any distribution of accrued benefits that did not commence before the beginning of the limitation year for which the adjustment is effective. Annual adjustments to the compensation limit of section 415(b)(1)(B) as described in paragraph (a)(2) of this section are made for all limitation years that begin after the participant's severance from employment, and apply to distributions that commence after the effective dates of such adjustments. However, no adjustment to the compensation limit of section 415(b)(1)(B) is made for any limitation year that begins on or before the date of the participant's severance from employment with the employer maintaining the plan.

(iii) *Application of adjusted dollar limitation to benefits that have commenced.* With respect to a distribution of accrued benefits that commenced before the beginning of the limitation year, a plan is permitted to apply the adjusted limitations to that distribution, but only to the extent that benefits have not been paid. Thus, for example, a plan cannot provide that the adjusted dollar limitation applies to a participant who has previously received the entire plan benefit in a single-sum distribution. However, a plan can provide for an increase in benefits to a participant who accrues additional benefits under the plan that could have been accrued without regard to the adjustment of the dollar limitation (including benefits that accrue as a result of a plan amendment) on or after the effective date of the adjusted limitation.

(iv) *Manner of adjustment for benefits that have commenced.* If a plan adjusts benefits to reflect increases in the applicable limitations pursuant to section 415(d) for a limitation year after the limitation year during which payment of the benefit commenced using the safe harbor methodology described in paragraph (a)(5) of this section, the distribution will be treated as continuing to satisfy the requirements of section 415(b). If a plan adjusts benefits to reflect increases in the applicable limitations pursuant to section 415(d) for a limitation year after the limitation year during which payment of the benefit commenced in a manner other than the manner described in paragraph (a)(5) of this section, the plan must satisfy the requirements of § 1.415(b)-2, treating the commencement of the additional benefit as the commencement of a new distribution that gives rise to a new annuity starting date.

(5) *Safe harbor for adjustments to benefit payments resulting from cost-of-living adjustments.* An adjustment to a distribution that is made on account of an increase to the applicable limits pursuant to section 415(d) is made using the safe harbor methodology of this paragraph (a)(5) if—

(i) The participant has received one or more distributions that satisfy the requirements of section 415(b) before the date the increase to the applicable limits is effective;

(ii) The adjusted distribution is solely as a result of the application of the increase to the applicable limits pursuant to section 415(d); and

(iii) The amount payable to the employee for the limitation year and subsequent limitation years is not greater than the amounts that would otherwise be payable without regard to the adjustment, multiplied by a fraction, the numerator of which is the limitation under section 415(b) (i.e., the lesser of the applicable dollar limitation under section 415(b)(1)(A), as adjusted for age at commencement, and the applicable compensation-based limitation under section 415(b)(1)(B)) in effect for the distribution following the section 415(d) increase, and the denominator of which is such limitation under section 415(b) in effect for the distribution immediately before the increase.

(6) *Examples.* The following examples illustrate the application of this paragraph (a):

Example 1. (i) X is a participant in a qualified defined benefit plan maintained by X's employer. The plan has a calendar year limitation year. Under the terms of the plan, X is entitled to a benefit consisting of a straight life annuity equal to 100% of X's average compensation for the period of X's high 3 years of service, adjusted as of January 1 of each calendar year for increases in the consumer price index. The plan provides that the annual increases in both the dollar limit of section 415(b)(1)(A) and the compensation limit under section 415(b)(1)(B) pursuant to section 415(d) apply to participants who have commenced receiving benefits under the plan at the earliest time at which that increase is permitted to become effective. X's average compensation for X's high 3 years is $50,000. X separates from the service of his employer on October 3, 2006, at age 65 with a nonforfeitable right to the accrued benefit after more than 10 years of service with the employer and more than 10 years of participation in the plan. X begins to receive annual benefit payments (payable monthly) of $50,000, commencing on November 1, 2006. It is assumed for purposes of this *Example 1* that the dollar limitation for 2006 (as adjusted pursuant to section 415(d)) is $170,000, that the dollar limitation for 2007 (as adjusted pursuant to section 415(d)) is $175,000, and that the annual adjustment factor for adjusting the limitation of section 415(b)(1)(B) for 2007 is 1.0220.

(ii) For the limitation year beginning January 1, 2007, the dollar limit applicable to X under section 415(b)(1)(A) is $175,000, and the compensation limit applicable to X under section 415(b)(1)(B) is $51,100 ($50,000 multiplied by the annual adjustment factor of 1.0220). Accordingly, the adjustment to X's benefit satisfies the safe harbor for cost-of-living adjustments under paragraph (a)(5) of this section if, after the adjustment, X's benefit payable in 2007 is no greater than $50,000 multiplied by $51,100 (X's section 415(b) limitation for 2006)/$50,000 (X's section 415(b) limitation for 2007).

Example 2. (i) The facts are the same as in Example 1 except that X's average compensation for the period of X's high 3 consecutive years of service is $200,000. Consequently, X's annual benefit payments commencing on November 1, 2006, are limited to $170,000.

(ii) For the limitation year beginning January 1, 2007, the dollar limit applicable to X under section 415(b)(1)(A) is $175,000, and the compensation limit applicable to X under section 415(b)(1)(B) is $204,400 ($200,000 multiplied by the annual adjustment factor of 1.0220). Accordingly, the adjustment to X's benefit satisfies the safe harbor for cost-of-living adjustments under paragraph (a)(5) of this section if, after the adjustment, X's benefit payable in 2007 is no greater than $170,000 multiplied by $175,000 (X's section 415(b) limitation for 2006)/$170,000 (X's section 415(b) limitation for 2007).

(b) *Defined contribution plans*—(1) *In general.* Under section 415(d)(1)(C), the dollar limitation described in section 415(c)(1)(A) is adjusted annually to take into account increases in the cost of living. The adjusted dollar limitation is prescribed by the Commissioner and published in the Internal Revenue Bulletin. See § 601.601(d) of this chapter.

(2) *Determination of adjusted limit*—(i) *Base period.* The base period taken into account for purposes of adjusting the dollar limitation pursuant to paragraph (b)(2)(ii) of this section is the calendar quarter beginning July 1, 2001.

(ii) *Method of adjustment*—(A) *In general.* The dollar limitation is adjusted with respect to a calendar year based on the increase in the applicable index for the calendar quarter ending September 30 of the preceding calendar year over such index for the base period. Adjustment procedures similar to the procedures used to adjust benefit

amounts under section 215(i)(2)(A) of the Social Security Act will be used.

(B) *Rounding.* Any increase in the $40,000 amount specified in section 415(c)(1)(A) which is not a multiple of $1,000 shall be rounded to the next lowest multiple of $1,000.

(iii) *Effective date of adjustment.* The adjusted dollar limitation applicable to defined contribution plans is effective as of January 1 of each calendar year and applies with respect to limitation years ending with or within that calendar year. Annual additions for a limitation year cannot exceed the currently applicable dollar limitation (as in effect before the January 1 adjustment) prior to January 1. However, after a January 1 adjustment is made, annual additions for the entire limitation year are permitted to reflect the dollar limitation as adjusted on January 1.

(c) *Application of rounding rules to other cost-of-living adjustments.* Pursuant to section 415(d)(4)(A), the $5,000 rounding methodology of paragraph (a)(1)(iii) of this section is used for purposes of any provision of chapter 1 of subtitle A of the Internal Revenue Code that provides for adjustments in accordance with section 415(d), except to the extent provided by that provision. Thus, the $5,000 rounding methodology of paragraph (a)(1)(iii) of this section is used for purposes of—

(1) Determining the level of compensation specified in section 414(q)(1)(B) that is used to determine whether an employee is a highly compensated employee;

(2) Calculating the amounts used pursuant to section 409(o)(1)(C) to determine the maximum period over which distributions from an employee stock ownership plan may be made without participant consent; and

(3) Determining the levels of compensation specified in § 1.61-21(f)(5)(i) and (iii) used in determining whether an employee is a control employee of a nongovernmental employer for purposes of the commuting valuation rule of § 1.61-21(f).

(d) *Implementation of cost-of-living adjustments.* A plan is permitted to be amended to reflect any of the adjustments described in this section at any time after those limitations become applicable. Alternatively, a plan is permitted to incorporate any of the adjustments described in this section by reference in accordance with the rules of § 1.415(a)-1(d)(3)(v). Because the accrued benefit of a participant can reflect increases in the applicable limitations only after those increases become effective, a pattern of repeated plan amendments increasing annual benefits to reflect the increases in the section 415(b) limitations pursuant to section 415(d) does not result in any protection under section 411(d)(6) for future increases to reflect increases in the section 415(b) limitations pursuant to § 1.411(d)-4, Q&A-1(c)(1). Thus, a plan does not violate the requirements of section 411(d)(6) merely because the plan has been amended annually for a number of years to increase annual benefits to reflect the increases in the section 415(b) limitations pursuant to section 415(d) and subsequently is not amended to reflect later increases in the section 415(b) limitations.

Par. 12. Section 1.415(f)-1 is added to read as follows:

§ 1.415(f)-1 Combining and aggregating plans.

(a) *In general.* Under section 415(f) and this section, except as provided in paragraph (g) of this section (regarding multiemployer plans), for purposes of applying the limitations of section 415(b) and (c) applicable to a participant for a particular limitation year—

(1) All defined benefit plans (without regard to whether a plan has been terminated) ever maintained by the employer (or a predecessor employer within the meaning of paragraph (c) of this section) under which the participant has ever accrued a benefit are treated as one defined benefit plan,

(2) All defined contribution plans (without regard to whether a plan has been terminated) ever maintained by the employer (or a predecessor employer within the meaning of paragraph (c) of this section) under which the participant receives annual additions are treated as one defined contribution plan; and

(3) All section 403(b) annuity contracts purchased by an employer (including plans purchased through salary reduction contributions) for the participant are treated as one section 403(b) annuity contract.

(b) *Affiliated employers, affiliated service groups, and leased employees.* See § 1.415(a)-1(f)(1) and (2) for rules regarding aggregation of employers in the case of affiliated employers and affiliated service groups. See § 1.415(a)-1(f)(3) for rules regarding the treatment of leased employees.

(c) *Predecessor employer.* For purposes of section 415 and the regulations thereunder, a former employer is a predecessor employer with respect to a participant in a plan maintained by an employer if the employer maintains a plan under which the participant had accrued a benefit while performing services for the former employer, but only if that benefit is provided under the plan maintained by the employer. In addition, with respect to an employer of a participant, a former entity that antedates the employer is a predecessor employer with respect to the participant if, under the facts and circumstances, the employer constitutes a continuation of all or a portion of the trade or business of the former entity. This will occur, for example, where formation of the employer constitutes a mere formal or technical change in the employment relationship and continuity otherwise exists in the substance and administration of the business operations of the former entity and the employer.

(d) *Annual compensation taken into account where employer maintains more than one defined benefit plan—*(1) *Determination of high 3 years of compensation.* If two or more defined benefit plans are aggregated under section 415(f) and this section for a particular limitation year, in applying the defined benefit compensation limitation (as described in section 415(b)(1)(B)) to the annual benefit of a participant under the aggregated plans, the participant's average compensation for the participant's high 3 years of service is determined in accordance with § 1.415(c)-2(g)(2), and includes compensation for all years in which the participant was an active participant in any of the aggregated plans.

(2) *Requirement of independent satisfaction of compensation limit.* If two or more defined benefit plans are aggregated under section 415(f) and this section for a particular limitation year, then, pursuant to section 415(f)(1)(B), each such plan must also satisfy the compensation limit of section 415(b)(1)(B) on a separate basis, determining each participant's average compensation for the participant's high 3 years of service using only compensation with respect to periods of active participation in that separate plan.

(e) *Years of participation and service taken into account where employer maintains more than one defined benefit plan at different times—*(1) *Determination of years of participation.* If two or more defined benefit plans are aggregated under section 415(f) and this section for a particular limitation year, in applying the reduction for participation of less than ten years (as described in section 415(b)(5)(A)) to the dollar limitation under section 415(b)(1)(A), time periods that are counted as years of participation under any of the plans are counted in computing the limitation of the combined plans under this section.

(2) *Determination of years of service.* If two or more defined benefit plans are aggregated under section 415(f) and this section for a particular limitation year, in applying the reduction for service of less than ten years (as described in section 415(b)(5)(B)) to the compensation limitation under section 415(b)(1)(B), time periods that are counted as years of service under any of the plans are counted in computing the limitation of the combined plans under this section.

(f) *Previously unaggregated plans—*(1) *In general.* This paragraph (f) provides rules for those situations in which two or more existing plans, which previously were not required to be aggregated pursuant to section 415(f) and this section, are aggregated during a particular limitation year and, as a result, the limitations of section 415(b) or (c) are exceeded for that limitation year. Paragraph (f)(2) of this section provides rules for defined contribution plans that are first required to be aggregated pursuant to section 415(f) and this section in a plan year. Paragraph (f)(3) of this section provides rules for defined benefit plans that are first required to be aggregated pursuant to section 415(f) and this section, and for defined benefit plans under which a participant's benefit is frozen following aggregation.

(2) *Defined contribution plans.* Two or more defined contribution plans that are not required to be aggregated pursuant to section 415(f) and this section as of the first day of a limitation year do not fail to satisfy the requirements of section 415 with respect to a participant for the limitation year merely because they are aggregated later in that limitation year, provided that no annual additions are credited to the participant's account after the date on which the plans are required to be aggregated.

(3) *Defined benefit plans—*(i) *First year of aggregation.* Two or more defined benefit plans that are not required to be aggregated pursuant to section 415(f) and this section as of the first day of a limitation year do not fail to satisfy the requirements of section 415 for the limitation year merely because they are aggregated later in that limitation year, provided that no plan amendments increasing benefits with respect to the participant under either plan are made after the occurrence of the event causing the plan to be aggregated.

(ii) *All years of aggregation in which accrued benefits are frozen.* Two or more defined benefit plans that are required to be aggregated pursuant to section 415(f) and this section during a limitation year subsequent to the limitation year during which the plans were first aggregated do not fail to satisfy the requirements of section 415 with respect to a participant for the limitation year merely because they are aggregated if there have been no increases in the participant's accrued benefit derived from employer contributions (including increases as a result of increased compensation or service) under any of the plans within the period during which the plans have been aggregated.

(g) *Section 403(b) annuity contracts—*(1) *In general.* In the case of a section 403(b) annuity contract, except as provided in paragraph (g)(2) of this section, the participant on whose behalf the annuity contract is purchased is considered for purposes of section 415 to have exclusive control of the annuity contract. Accordingly, except as provided in paragraph (g)(2) of this section, the participant, and not the participant's employer who purchased the section 403(b) annuity contract, is deemed to maintain the annuity contract, and such a section 403(b) annuity contract is not aggregated with a qualified plan that is maintained by the participant's employer.

(2) *Special rules under which the employer is deemed to maintain the annuity contract—*(i) *In general.* Where a participant on whose behalf a section 403(b) annuity contract is purchased is in control of any employer for a limitation year as defined in paragraph (g)(2)(ii) of this section (regardless of whether the employer controlled by the participant is the employer maintaining the section 403(b) annuity contract), the annuity contract for the benefit of the participant is treated as a defined contribution plan maintained by both the controlled employer and the participant for that limitation year. Accordingly, where a participant on whose behalf a section 403(b) annuity contract is purchased is in control of any employer for a limitation year, the section 403(b) annuity contract is aggregated with all other defined contribution plans maintained by that employer. In addition, in such a case, the section 403(b) annuity contract is aggregated with all other defined contribution plans maintained by the employee or any other employer that is controlled by the employee. Thus, for example, if a doctor is employed by a non-profit hospital to which section 501(c)(3) applies and which provides him with a section 403(b) annuity contract, and the doctor also maintains a private practice as a shareholder owning more than 50% of a professional corporation, then any qualified defined contribution plan of the professional corporation must be combined with the section 403(b) annuity contract for purposes of applying the limitations of section 415(c) and § 1.415(c)-1. For purposes of this paragraph (g)(2), it is immaterial whether the section 403(b) annuity contract is purchased as a result of a salary reduction agreement between the employer and the participant.

(ii) *Definition of control.* For purposes of paragraph (g)(2)(i) of this section, a participant is in control of an employer for a limitation year if, pursuant to paragraph (b) of this section, a plan maintained by that employer would have to be aggregated with a plan maintained by an employer that is 100% owned by the participant. Thus, for example, if a participant owns 60% of the common stock of a corporation, the participant is considered to be in control of that employer for purposes of applying paragraph (g)(2)(i) of this section.

(3) *Aggregation of section 403(b) annuity with qualified plan of controlled employer.* If a section 403(b) annuity contract is combined or aggregated with a qualified plan of a controlled employer in accordance with paragraph (g)(2) of this section, the plans must satisfy the limitations of section 415(c) both separately and in combination. In applying separately the limitations of section 415 to the qualified plan and to the section 403(b) annuity, compensation from the controlled employer may not be aggregated with compensation from the employer purchasing the section 403(b) annuity (i.e., without regard to § 1.415(c)-2(g)(3)).

(h) *Multiemployer plans—*(1) *Multiemployer plan combined with another multiemployer plan.* Pursuant to section 415(f)(3)(B), multiemployer plans, as defined in section 414(f), are not aggregated with other multiemployer plans for purposes of applying the limits of section 415.

(2) *Multiemployer plan combined with other plan—*(i) *Aggregation only for benefits provided by the employer.* Notwithstanding the rule of § 1.415(a)-1(e), a multiemployer plan is permitted to provide that only the benefits under that multiemployer plan that are provided by an employer are aggregated with benefits under plans maintained by that employer that are not multiemployer plans. If the multiemployer plan so provides then, where an employer maintains both a plan which is not a multiemployer plan and a multiemployer plan, only the benefits under the multiemployer plan that are provided by the employer are aggregated with benefits under the employer's plans other than multiemployer plans (in lieu of including benefits provided by all employ-

ers under the multiemployer plan pursuant to the generally applicable rule of § 1.415(a)-1(e)).

(ii) *Nonapplication of aggregation for purposes of applying section 415(b)(1)(B) compensation limit.* Pursuant to section 415(f)(3)(A), a multiemployer plan is not combined or aggregated with any other plan that is not a multiemployer plan for purposes of applying the compensation limit of section 415(b)(1)(B) and § 1.415(b)-1(a)(1)(ii).

(i) [Reserved.]

(j) *Special rules for combining certain plans, etc.* If a plan, annuity contract or arrangement is subject to a special limitation in addition to, or instead of, the regular limitations described in section 415(b) or (c), and is combined under this section with a plan which is subject only to the regular section 415(b) or (c) limitations, the following rules apply—

(1) Each plan, annuity contract or arrangement which is subject to a special limitation must meet its own applicable limitation and each plan subject to the regular limitations of section 415 must meet its applicable limitation.

(2) The combined limitation is the larger of the applicable limitations.

(k) *Examples.* The following examples illustrate the rules of this section:

Example 1. (i) M is an employee of ABC Corporation and XYZ Corporation. ABC maintains a qualified defined benefit plan and a qualified defined contribution plan in which M participates and XYZ maintains a qualified defined benefit plan and a qualified defined contribution plan in which M participates. ABC Corporation owns 60% of XYZ Corporation.

(ii) ABC Corporation and XYZ Corporation are members of a controlled group of corporations within the meaning of section 414(b) as modified by section 415(h). Because ABC Corporation and XYZ Corporation are members of a controlled group of corporations within the meaning of section 414(b) as modified by section 415(h), M is treated as being employed by a single employer.

(iii) The sum of M's annual benefit under the defined benefit plan maintained by ABC and M's annual benefit under the defined benefit plan maintained by XYZ is not permitted to exceed the limitations of section 415(b) and § 1.415(b)-1; and the sum of the annual additions to M's account under the defined contribution plans maintained by ABC and XYZ may not exceed the limitations of section 415(c) and § 1.415-(c)-1. For purposes of satisfying the requirements of section 415 on this aggregated basis, M's compensation from both ABC and XYZ is taken into account and years of service and participation under either defined benefit plan are used.

(iv) M's annual benefit under the defined benefit plan maintained by ABC and M's annual benefit under the defined benefit plan maintained by XYZ also must be within the limitations of section 415(b) and § 1.415(b)-1, determined without regard to the aggregation of employers (i.e., by taking into account only compensation and years of service and participation for the respective employers).

Example 2. (i) N is employed by a hospital which purchases an annuity contract described in section 403(b) on N's behalf for the current limitation year. N is in control of the hospital within the meaning of section 414(b) or (c), as modified by section 415(h). The hospital also maintains a qualified defined contribution plan during the current limitation year in which N participates.

(ii) Under section 415(k)(4), the hospital, as well as N, is considered to maintain the annuity contract. Accordingly, the sum of the annual additions under the qualified defined contribution plan and the annuity contract must satisfy the limitations of section 415(c) and § 1.415(c)-1.

Example 3. (i) The facts are the same as in *Example 2*, except that instead of being in control of the hospital, N is the 100% owner of a professional corporation P, which maintains a qualified defined contribution plan in which N participates.

(ii) Under section 415(k)(4), the hospital, as well as N, is considered to maintain the annuity contract. Accordingly, the sum of the annual additions under the qualified defined contribution plan maintained by professional corporation P and the annuity contract must satisfy the limitations of section 415(c) and § 1.415(c)-1. See § 1.415(g)-1(c)(2) for an example of the treatment of a contribution to an annuity contract that exceeds the limits of section 415(c) by reason of the aggregation required by this section.

Example 4. (i) J is an employee of two corporations, N and M, each of which has employed J for more than 10 years. N and M are not required to be aggregated pursuant to section 415(f) and this section. Each corporation has a qualified defined benefit plan in which J has

participated for more than 10 years. Each plan provides a benefit which is equal to 75% of a participant's average compensation for his high 3 years of service and is payable in the form of a straight life annuity beginning at age 65. J's average compensation (within the meaning of § 1.415(c)-2) for his high three years of service from each corporation is $160,000. Each plan uses the calendar year for the limitation and plan year. In July 2007, N Corporation becomes a wholly owned subsidiary of M Corporation.

(ii) As a result of the acquisition of N Corporation by M Corporation, J is treated as being employed by a single employer under section 414(b). Therefore, because section 415(f)(1)(A) requires that all defined benefit plans of an employer be treated as one defined benefit plan, the two plans must be aggregated for purposes of applying the limitations of section 415. However, under paragraph (f)(3)(i) of this section, since the plans were not aggregated as of the first day of the 2007 limitation year (January 1, 2007), they will not be considered aggregated until the limitation year beginning January 1, 2008.)

(iii) As a result of such aggregation, J becomes entitled to a combined benefit which is equal to $240,000, which is in excess of the section 415(b) dollar limitation for 2005 of $170,000. However, under paragraph (f)(3)(ii) of this section, the limitations of section 415(b) and § 1.415(b)-1 applicable to J may be exceeded in this situation without plan disqualification so long as J's accrued benefit derived from employer contributions is not increased (i.e., does not increase on account of increased compensation, service, or other accruals) during the period within which the limitations are being exceeded.

Example 5. (i) A, age 30, owns all of the stock of X Corporation and also owns 10% of the stock of Z Corporation. F, A's father, directly owns 75% of the stock of Z Corporation. Both corporations have qualified defined contribution plans in which A participates and both plans use the calendar year for the limitation and plan year. A's compensation (within the meaning of § 1.415(c)-2) for 2007 is $20,000 from Z Corporation and $150,000 from X Corporation. During the period January 1, 2007 through June 30, 2007, annual additions of $20,000 are credited to A's account under the plan of Z Corporation, while annual additions of $40,000 are credited to A's account under the plan of X Corporation. In both instances, the amount of annual additions represent the maximum allowable under section 415(c) and § 1.415(c)-1. On July 15, 2007, F dies, and A inherits all of F's stock in Z in 2007.

(ii) As of July 15 th 2007, A is considered to be in control of X and Z Corporations, and the two plans must be aggregated for purposes of applying the limitations of section 415. However, even though A's total annual additions for 2007 are $60,000, the limitations of section 415(c) and § 1.415(c)-1 are not violated for 2007, provided no annual additions are credited to A's accounts after July 15, 2007 (the date that A is first in control of Z).

Example 6. (i) P is a key employee of employer XYZ who participates in a qualified defined contribution plan with (Plan X) a calendar year limitation year. P is also provided post-retirement medical benefits, and XYZ has taken into account a reserve for those benefits under section 419A(c)(2). In 2007, P's compensation is $30,000 and P's annual additions under Plan X are $5,000. Pursuant to section 419A(d), a separate account is maintained for P and that account is credited with an allocation of $32,000 for 2007.

(ii) Under paragraph (j)(1) of this section, Plan X and the individual medical account must separately satisfy the requirements of section 415(c), taking into account any special limit applicable to that arrangement. In this case, the contributions to Plan X separately satisfy the limitations of section 415(c). The individual medical account is not subject to the 100% of compensation limit of section 415(c), so the contributions to that account satisfy the limitations of section 415(c).

(iii) The sum of the annual additions under Plan X and the amounts contributed to the separate account on P's behalf must satisfy the requirements of section 415(c). Under paragraph (j)(2) of this section, the limit applicable to the combined plan is equal to the greater of the limits applicable to the separate plan. In this case, the limit applicable to the medical account is $40,000 (which is greater than the limit of $30,000 applicable to the qualified plan), so the limit that applies to the aggregated plan is $40,000 and the aggregated plans satisfy the requirements of section 415.

Par. 13. Section 1.415(g)-1 is added to read as follows:

§ 1.415(g)-1 Disqualification of plans and trusts.

(a) *Disqualification of plans*—(1) *In general.* Under section 415(g) and this section, with respect to a particular limitation year, a plan (and the trust forming part of the plan) is disqualified in accordance with the rules provided in paragraph (b) of this section, if the conditions described in paragraph (a)(2) or (a)(3) of this section apply. For purposes of this paragraph (a), the determination of whether a plan or a combination of plans exceeds the limitations imposed by section 415 for a particular limitation year is, except as otherwise provided, made by taking into account the aggregation of plan rules provided in sections 415(f) and § 1.414(f)-1.

(2) *Defined contribution plans.* A plan is disqualified in accordance with the rules provided in paragraph (b) of this section if annual additions (as defined in § 1.415(c)-1(b)) with respect to the account of any participant in a defined contribution plan maintained by the employer exceed the limitations of section 415(c) and § 1.415(c)-1.

(3) *Defined benefit plans.* A plan is disqualified in accordance with the rules provided in paragraph (b) of this section if the annual benefit (as defined in § 1.415(b)-1(b)(1), taking into account the rules of § 1.415(b)-2) of a participant in a defined benefit plan maintained by the employer exceeds the limitations of section 415(b) and § 1.415(b)-1.

(b) *Rules for disqualification of plans and trusts*—(1) *In general.* If any plan (including a trust which forms part of such plan) is disqualified for a particular limitation year under the rules set forth in this paragraph (b), then the disqualification is effective as of the first day of the first plan year containing any portion of the particular limitation year.

(2) *Single plan.* In the case of a single qualified defined benefit plan (determined without regard to section 415(f) and § 1.415(f)-1) maintained by the employer that provides an annual benefit (as defined in § 1.415(b)-1(b)(1), taking into account the rules of § 1.415(b)-2) in excess of the limitations of section 415(b) and § 1.415(b)-1 for any particular limitation year, such plan is disqualified in that limitation year. Similarly, if the employer only maintains a single defined contribution plan (determined without regard to section 415(f) and § 1.415(f)-1) under which annual additions (as defined in § 1.415(c)-1(b)) allocated to the account of any participant exceed the limitations of section 415(c) and § 1.415(c)-1 for any particular limitation year, such plan is also disqualified in that limitation year.

(3) *Multiple plans*—(i) *In general.* If the limitations of section 415(b) and § 1.415(b)-1 (taking into account the rules of § 1.415(b)-2), or section 415(c) and § 1.415(c)-1 are exceeded for a particular limitation year with respect to any participant solely because of the application of the aggregation rules of section 415(f)(1) and § 1.415(f)-1 or section 414(b) or (c), as modified by section 415(h), then one or more of the plans is disqualified in accordance with the ordering rules set forth in paragraphs (b)(3)(ii) of this section, applied in accordance with the rules of application set forth in paragraph (b)(3)(iii) of this section, subject to the special rules set forth in paragraph (b)(3)(iv) of this section, until, without regard to annual benefits or annual additions under the disqualified plan or plans, the remaining plans satisfy the applicable limitations of section 415.

(ii) *Ordering rules*—(A) *Disqualification of ongoing plans other than multiemployer plans.* If there are two or more plans that have not been terminated at any time including the last day of the particular limitation year, and if one or more of those plans is a multiemployer plan described in section 414(f), then one or more of the plans (as needed to satisfy the limitations of section 415) that has not been terminated and is not a multiemployer plan is disqualified in that limitation year. For purposes of the preceding sentence, the determination of whether a plan is a multiemployer plan described in section 414(f) is made as of the last day of the particular limitation year.

(B) *Disqualification of ongoing multiemployer plans.* If, after the application of paragraph (b)(3)(ii)(A) of this section, there are two or more plans and one or more of the plans has been terminated at any time including the last day of the particular limitation year, then one or more of the plans (as needed to satisfy the applicable limitations of section 415) that has not been so terminated (regardless of whether the plan is a multiemployer plan described in section 414(f)) is disqualified in that limitation year.

(iii) *Rules of application*—(A) *Employer elects which plan is disqualified.* If there are two or more plans of an employer within a group of plans one or more of which is to be disqualified pursuant to paragraph (b)(3)(ii)(A) or (B) of this section, then the employer may elect, in a manner determined by the Commissioner, which plan or plans are disqualified. If those two or more plans are involved because of the application of section 414(b) or (c), as modified by section 415(h), the employers of the controlled group may elect, in a manner determined by the Commissioner, which plan or plans are disqualified. However, the election described in the preceding sentence is not effective unless made by all of the employers within the controlled group.

(B) *Commissioner determines which plan is disqualified.* If the election described in paragraph (b)(3)(iii)(A) of this section is not made with respect to the two plans described in paragraph (b)(3)(iii)(A) of this

section, then the Commissioner, taking into account all of the facts and circumstances, has the discretion to determine the plan that is disqualified in the particular limitation year. In making this determination, some of the factors that will be taken into account include, but are not limited to, the number of participants in each plan, the amount of benefits provided on an overall basis by each plan, and the extent to which benefits are distributed or retained in each plan.

(iv) *Special rules*—(A) *Simplified employee pensions (SEPs).* If there are two or more plans one or more of which is to be disqualified pursuant to paragraph (b)(3)(ii)(A) or (B) of this section, and if one of the plans is a simplified employee pension (as defined in section 408(k)), then the simplified employee pension is not disqualified until all of the other plans have been disqualified. However, if one of the plans has been terminated, then the simplified employee pension is disqualified before the terminated plan. For purposes of this paragraph (b)(3)(iv)(A), the disqualification of a simplified employee pension means that the simplified employee pension is no longer described under section 408(k).

(B) *Combining medical accounts with defined contribution plans.* In the event that combining a medical account described in § 1.415(c)-1(a)(2)(ii)(C) or (D) and a defined contribution plan other than such a medical account causes the limitations of section 415(c) and § 1.415(c)-1 applicable to a participant to be exceeded for a particular limitation year, the defined contribution plan other than the medical account is disqualified for the limitation year.

(C) *Combining section 403(b) annuity contract and qualified defined contribution plan*—(1) *In general.* In the event that combining a section 403(b) annuity contract and a qualified defined contribution plan under the provisions of section 415(f)(1)(B) causes the limitations of section 415(c) and § 1.415(c)-1 applicable to a participant under the combined defined contribution plans to be exceeded for a particular limitation year, the excess of the contributions to the annuity contract plus the annual additions to the plan over such limitations is treated as a disqualified contribution to the annuity contract and therefore includable in the gross income of the participant for the taxable year with or within which that limitation year ends. See § 1.415(a)-1(b)(2) and § 1.403(b)-3(b)(2) for rules regarding the treatment of a contribution to a section 403(b) annuity contract that exceeds the limitations of section 415.

(2) *Example.* The following example illustrates the application of this paragraph (b)(3)(iv)(C). It is assumed for purposes of this example that the dollar limitation under section 415(c)(1)(A) that applies for all relevant limitation years is $42,000. The example is as follows:

Example. (i) N is employed by a hospital which purchases an annuity contract described in section 403(b) on N's behalf for the current limitation year. N is also the 100 % owner of a professional corporation P that maintains a qualified defined contribution plan during the current limitation year in which N participates. (The facts of this example are the same as in *Example 3* of § 1.415(f)-1(k)). N's compensation (within the meaning of § 1.415(c)-2) from the hospital for the current limitation year is $150,000. For the current limitation year, the hospital contributes $ 30,000 for the section 403(b) annuity contract on N's behalf, which is within the limitations applicable to N under the annuity contract (i.e., $42,000)). Professional corporation P also contributes $30,000 to the qualified defined contribution plan on N's behalf for the current limitation year (which represents the only annual additions allocated to N's account under the plan for such year), which is within the $42,000 limitation of section 415(c)(1) applicable to N under the plan.

(ii) Under section 415(k)(4), the hospital, as well as N, is considered to maintain the annuity contract. Accordingly, the sum of the annual additions under the qualified defined contribution plan maintained by professional corporation P and the annuity contract must satisfy the limitations of section 415(c) and § 1.415(c)-1.

(iii) Because the total combined contributions ($60,000) exceed the section 415(c) limitation applicable to N under the plan ($42,000), under the special rules contained in this paragraph (b)(3)(iv)(C), $20,000 of the $30,000 contributed to the section 403(b) annuity contract is considered a disqualified contribution and therefore currently includable in N's gross income. The contract continues to be a section 403(b) annuity contract only if, for the current limitation year and all years thereafter, the issuer of the contract maintains separate accounts for each portion attributable to such disqualified contributions. See §§ 1.415(a)-1(b)(2) and 1.403(b)-3(c)(3).

(c) *Plan year for certain annuity contracts and individual retirement plans.* For purposes of this section, unless the plan under which the annuity contract or individual retirement plan is provided specifies that a different twelve-month period is considered to be the plan year—

(1) An annuity contract described in section 403(b) is considered to have a plan year coinciding with the taxable year of the individual on whose behalf the contract has been purchased; and

(2) A simplified employee pension described in section 408(k) is considered to have a plan year coinciding with the year under the plan that is used pursuant to section 408(k)(7)(C).

Par. 14. Section 1.415(j)-1 is added to read as follows:

§ 1.415(j)-1 Limitation year.

(a) *In general.* Unless the terms of a plan provide otherwise, the limitation year, with respect to any qualified plan maintained by the employer, is the calendar year.

(b) *Alternative limitation year election.* The terms of a plan may provide for the use of any other consecutive twelve month period as the limitation year. This includes a fiscal year with an annual period varying from 52 to 53 weeks, so long as the fiscal year satisfies the requirements of section 441(f). A plan may only provide for one limitation year regardless of the number or identity of the employers maintaining the plan.

(c) *Multiple limitation years*—(1) *In general.* Where an employer maintains more than one qualified plan, those plans may provide for different limitation years. The rule described in this paragraph (c) also applies to a controlled group of employers (within the meaning of section 414(b) or (c), as modified by section 415(h)). If the plans of an employer (or a controlled group of employers whose plans are aggregated) have different limitation years, section 415 is applied in accordance with the rule of paragraphs (c)(2) and (3) of this section.

(2) *Testing rule for defined contribution plans.* If a participant is credited with annual additions in only one defined contribution plan, in determining whether the requirements of section 415(c) are satisfied, only the limitation year applicable to that plan is considered. However, if a participant is credited with annual additions in more than one defined contribution plan, each such plan satisfies the requirements of section 415(c) only if the limitations of section 415(c) are satisfied with respect to amounts that are annual additions for the limitation year with respect to the participant under the plan, plus amounts credited to the participant's account under all other plans required to be aggregated with the plan pursuant to section 415(f) and § 1.415(f)-1 that would have been considered annual additions for the limitation year under the plan if they had been credited under the plan rather than an aggregated plan.

(3) *Testing rule for defined benefit plans.* If a participant accrues a benefit or receives a distribution under only one defined benefit plan, in determining whether the requirements of section 415(b) are satisfied, only the limitation year applicable to that plan is considered. However, if a participant accrues a benefit or receives a distribution under more than one defined benefit plan, a plan satisfies the requirements of section 415(b) only if the annual benefit under all plans required to be aggregated pursuant to section 415(f) and § 1.415(f)-1 for the limitation year of that plan with respect to the participant satisfy the applicable limitations of section 415(b). Thus, for example, the dollar limitation of section 415(b)(1)(A) applicable to the limitation year for each plan must be applied to annual benefits under all aggregated plans to determine whether the plan satisfies the requirements of section 415(b).

(d) *Change of limitation year*—(1) *In general.* Once established, the limitation year may be changed only by amending the plan. Any change in the limitation year must be a change to a twelve-month period commencing with any day within the current limitation year. For purposes of this section, the limitations of section 415 are to be applied in the normal manner to the new limitation year.

(2) *Application to short limitation period.* Where there is a change of limitation year, the limitations of section 415 are to be separately applied to a "limitation period" which begins with the first day of the current limitation year and which ends on the day before the first day of the first limitation year for which the change is effective. In the case of a defined contribution plan, the dollar limitation with respect to this limitation period is determined by multiplying the applicable dollar limitation for the calendar year in which the limitation period ends by a fraction, the numerator of which is the number of months (including any fractional parts of a month) in the limitation period, and the denominator of which is 12.

(e) *Limitation year for individuals on whose behalf section 403(b) annuity contracts have been purchased.* The limitation year of an individual on whose behalf a section 403(b) annuity contract has been purchased by an employer is determined in the following manner.

(1) If the individual is not in control (within the meaning of § 1.415(f)-1(g)(2)(ii)) of any employer, the limitation year is the calendar year. However, the individual may elect to change the limitation year to another twelve-month period. To do this, the individual must attach a statement to his or her income tax return filed for the taxable year in which the change is made. Any change in the limitation year must comply with the rules set forth in paragraph (d) of this section.

(2) If the individual is in control (within the meaning of § 1.415(f)-1(g)(2)(ii)) of an employer, the limitation year is to be the limitation year of that employer.

(f) *Limitation year for individuals on whose behalf individual retirement plans are maintained.* The limitation year of an individual on whose behalf an individual retirement plan (within the meaning of section 7701(a)(37)) is maintained shall be determined in the manner described in paragraph (e) of this section.

(g) *Examples.* The following examples illustrate the application of this section:

Example 1. (i) Participant M is employed by both Employer A and Employer B, each of which maintains a qualified defined contribution plan. M participates in both of these plans. The limitation year for Employer A's plan is January 1 through December 31, and the limitation year for Employer B's plan is April 1 through March 31. Employer A and Employer B are both corporations, and Corporation X owns 100% of the stock of Employer A and Employer B.

(ii) The two plans in which M participates are required under section 415(f) to be aggregated for purposes of applying the limitations of section 415(c) to annual additions made with respect to M. Thus, for example, for the limitation year of Employer A's plan that begins January 1, 2008, annual additions with respect to M that are subject to the limitations of section 415(c) include both amounts that are annual additions with respect to M under Employer A's plan for the period beginning January 1, 2008, and ending December 31, 2008, and amounts contributed to Employer B's plan with respect to M that would have been considered annual additions for the period beginning January 1, 2008, and ending December 31, 2008, under Employer A's plan if those amounts had instead been contributed to Employer A's plan.

Example 2. In 2007, an employer with a qualified defined contribution plan using the calendar year as the limitation year elects to change the limitation year to a period beginning July 1 and ending June 30. Because of this change, the plan must satisfy the limitations of section 415(c) for the limitation period beginning January 1, 2007, and ending June 30, 2007. In applying the limitations of section 415(c) to this limitation period, the amount of compensation taken into account may only include compensation for this period. Furthermore, the dollar limitation for this period is the otherwise applicable dollar limitation for calendar year 2007, multiplied by 6/12.

Par. 15. Section 1.457-4 is amended by revising paragraph (d) to read as follows:

§ 1.457-4 Annual deferrals, deferral limitations, and deferral agreement under eligible plans.

* * * * *

(d) *Deferrals after severance from employment, including sick, vacation, and back pay under an eligible plan*—(1) *In general.* An eligible plan may provide that a participant who has not had a severance from employment may elect to defer accumulated sick pay, accumulated vacation pay, and back pay under an eligible plan if the requirements of section 457(b) are satisfied. For example, the plan must provide, in accordance with paragraph (b) of this section, that these amounts may be deferred for any calendar month only if an agreement providing for the deferral is entered into before the beginning of the month in which the amounts would otherwise be paid or made available and the participant is an employee on the date the amounts would otherwise be paid or made available. For purposes of section 457, compensation that would otherwise be paid for a payroll period that begins before severance from employment is treated as an amount that would otherwise be paid or made available before an employee has a severance from employment. In addition, deferrals may be made for former employees with respect to compensation described in § 1.415(c)-2(e)(3)(ii) (relating to certain compensation paid within 2 ½ months following severance from employment), compensation described in § 1.415(c)-2(g)(4) (relating to compensation paid to participants who are permanently and totally disabled), and compensation relating to qualified military service under section 414(u).

(2) *Examples.* The provisions of this paragraph (d) are illustrated by the following examples:

Example 1. (i) *Facts.* Participant G, who is age 62 in 2006, is an employee who participates in an eligible plan providing a normal retirement age of 65 and a bona fide sick leave and vacation pay program of the eligible employer. Under the terms of G's employer's eligible plan and the sick leave and vacation pay program, G is permitted make a one-time election to contribute amounts representing accumulated sick pay to the eligible plan. G has a severance from employment on January 12, 2007, at which time G's accumulated sick and vacation pay that is payable on March 15, 2007 total $12,000. G elects, on February 4, 2007, to have the $12,000 of accumulated sick and vacation pay contributed to the eligible plan.

(ii) *Conclusion.* Under the terms of the eligible plan and the sick and vacation pay program, G may elect before March 1, 2007 to defer the accumulated sick and vacation pay because the agreement providing for the deferral is entered into before the beginning of the month in which the amount is currently available and the amount is bona fide accumulated sick and vacation pay that would otherwise be payable within 2 ½ months after G has a severance from employment, as described in § 1.415(c)-2(e)(3)(ii). Thus, under this section and § 1.415(c)-2(e)(3)(ii), the $12,000 is included in G's includible compensation for purposes of determining G's includible compensation in 2007.

Example 2. (i) *Facts.* Same facts as in *Example 1,* except that G's severance from employment is on December 1, 2006, G's $12,000 of accumulated sick and vacation pay is payable on February 15, 2007 (which is within 2 ½ months after G's severance from employment), and G's election to defer the accumulated sick and vacation pay is made before February 1, 2007.

(ii) *Conclusion.* Under this section and § 1.415(c)-2(e)(3)(ii), the $12,000 is included in G's includible compensation for purposes of determining G's includible compensation in 2007.

Example 3. (i) *Facts.* Employer X maintains an eligible plan and a vacation leave plan. Under the terms of the vacation leave plan, employees generally accrue three weeks of vacation per year. Up to one week's unused vacation may be carried over from one year to the next, so that in any single year an employee may have a maximum of four weeks vacation time. At the beginning of each calendar year, under the terms of the eligible plan (which constitutes an agreement providing for the deferral), the value of any unused vacation time from the prior year in excess of one week is automatically contributed to the eligible plan, to the extent of the employee's maximum deferral limitations. Amounts in excess of the maximum deferral limitations are forfeited.

(ii) *Conclusion.* The value of the unused vacation pay contributed to X's eligible plan pursuant to the terms of the plan and the terms of the vacation leave plan is treated as an annual deferral to the eligible plan for January of the calendar year. No amounts contributed to the eligible plan will be considered made available to a participant in X's eligible plan.

* * * * *

Par. 16. Section 1.457-5 is amended by revising *Example 2* of paragraph (d) to read as follows:

§ *1.457-5 Individual limitation for combined annual deferrals under multiple eligible plans.*

* * * * *

(d) *Examples.* * * *

Example (2). (i) *Facts.* Participant E, who will turn 63 on April 1, 2006, participates in four eligible plans during 2006 Plan W which is an eligible governmental plan; and Plans X, Y, and Z which are each eligible plans of three different tax-exempt entities. For 2006, the limitation that applies to Participant E under all four plans under § 1.457-4(c)(1)(i)(A) is $15,000. For 2006, the additional age 50 catch-up limitation that applies to Participant E under Plan W under § 1.457-4(c)(2) is $5,000. Further, for 2006, different limitations under § 1.457-4(c)(3) and (c)(3)(ii)(B) apply to Participant E under each of these plans, as follows: under Plan W, the underutilized limitation under § 1.457-4 (c)(3)(ii)(B) is $7,000; under Plan X, the underutilized limitation under § 1.457-4 (c)(3)(ii)(B) is $2,000; under Plan Y, the underutilized limitation under § 1.457-4 (c)(3)(ii)(B) is $8,000; and under Plan Z, § 1.457-4 (c)(3) is not applicable since normal retirement age is age 62 under Plan Z. Participant E's includible compensation is in each case in excess of any applicable deferral.

(ii) *Conclusion.* For purposes of applying this section to Participant E for 2006, Participant E could elect to defer $23,000 under Plan Y, which is the maximum deferral limitation under § 1.457-4 (c)(1) through (3), and to defer no amount under Plans W, X, and Z. The $23,000 maximum amount is equal to the sum of $15,000 plus $8,000, which is the catch-up amount applicable to Participant E under Plan Y and which is the largest catch-up amount applicable to Participant E under any of the four plans for 2006. Alternatively, Participant E could instead elect to defer the following combination of amounts: an aggregate total of $15,000 to Plans X, Y, and Z, if no contribution is made to Plan W; an aggregate total of $20,000 to any of the four plans, assuming at least $5,000 is contributed to Plan W; or $22,000 to Plan W and none to any of the other three plans.

(iii) If the underutilized amount under Plans W, X, and Y for 2006 were in each case zero (because E had always contributed the maximum amount or E was a new participant) or an amount not in excess of $5,000, the maximum exclusion under this section would be $20,000 for Participant E for 2006 ($15,000 plus the $5,000 age 50 catch-up amount), which Participant E could contribute to any of the plans assuming at least $5,000 is contributed to Plan W.

Par. 17. Section 1.457-6 is amended by revising paragraphs (a) and (c) to read as follows:

§ *1.457-6 Timing of distributions under eligible plans.*

(a) *In general.* Except as provided in paragraph (c) of this section (relating to distributions on account of an unforeseeable emergency), paragraph (e) of this section (relating to distributions of small accounts), § 1.457-10(a) (relating to plan terminations), or § 1.457-10(c) (relating to domestic relations orders), amounts deferred under an eligible plan may not be paid to a participant or beneficiary before the participant has a severance from employment with the eligible employer or when the participant attains age 70 ½, if earlier. For rules relating to loans, see paragraph (f) of this section. This section does not apply to distributions of excess amounts under § 1.457-4(e). However, except to the extent set forth by the Commissioner in revenue rulings, notices, and other guidance published in the Internal Revenue Bulletin, this section applies to amounts held in a separate account for eligible rollover distributions maintained by an eligible governmental plan as described in § 1.457-10(e)(2).

* * * * *

(c) *Rules applicable to distributions for unforeseeable emergencies*—(1) *In general.* An eligible plan may permit a distribution to a participant or beneficiary faced with an unforeseeable emergency. The distribution must satisfy the requirements of paragraph (c)(2) of this section.

(2) *Requirements*—(i) *Unforeseeable emergency defined.* An unforeseeable emergency must be defined in the plan as a severe financial hardship of the participant or beneficiary resulting from an illness or accident of the participant or beneficiary, the participant's or beneficiary's spouse, or the participant's or beneficiary's dependent (as defined in section 152, and, for taxable years beginning on or after January 1, 2005, without regard to section 152(b)(1), (b)(2), and (d)(1)(B)); loss of the participant's or beneficiary's property due to casualty (including the need to rebuild a home following damage to a home not otherwise covered by homeowner's insurance, e.g., as a result of a natural disaster); or other similar extraordinary and unforeseeable circumstances arising as a result of events beyond the control of the participant or the beneficiary. For example, the imminent foreclosure of or eviction from the participant's or beneficiary's primary residence may constitute an unforeseeable emergency. In addition, the need to pay for medical expenses, including non-refundable deductibles, as well as for the cost of prescription drug medication, may constitute an unforeseeable emergency. Finally, the need to pay for the funeral expenses of a spouse or a dependent (as defined in section 152, and, for taxable years beginning on or after January 1, 2005, without regard to section 152(b)(1), (b)(2), and (d)(1)(B)) may also constitute an unforeseeable emergency. Except as otherwise specifically provided in this paragraph (c)(2)(i), the purchase of a home and the payment of college tuition are not unforeseeable emergencies under this paragraph (c)(2)(i).

(ii) *Unforeseeable emergency distribution standard.* Whether a participant or beneficiary is faced with an unforeseeable emergency permitting a distribution under this paragraph (c) is to be determined based on the relevant facts and circumstances of each case, but, in any case, a distribution on account of unforeseeable emergency may not be made to the extent that such emergency is or may be relieved through reimbursement or compensation from insurance or otherwise, by liquidation of the participant's assets, to the extent the liquidation of such assets would not itself cause severe financial hardship, or by cessation of deferrals under the plan.

(iii) *Distribution necessary to satisfy emergency need.* Distributions because of an unforeseeable emergency must be limited to the amount reasonably necessary to satisfy the emergency need (which may include any amounts necessary to pay any federal, state, or local income taxes or penalties reasonably anticipated to result from the distribution).

* * * * *

Par. 18. Section 1.457-10 is amended by revising paragraph (b)(8) to read as follows:

§ 1.457-10 Miscellaneous provisions.

* * * * *

(b) *Plan-to plan transfers.* * * *

(8) *Purchase of permissive service credit by plan-to-plan transfers from an eligible governmental plan to a qualified plan*—(i) *General rule.* An eligible governmental plan of a State may provide for the transfer of amounts deferred by a participant or beneficiary to a defined benefit governmental plan (as defined in section 414(d)), and no amount shall be includible in gross income by reason of the transfer, if the conditions in paragraph (b)(8)(ii) of this section are met. A transfer under this paragraph (b)(8) is not treated as a distribution for purposes of § 1.457-6. Therefore, such a transfer may be made before severance from employment.

(ii) *Conditions for plan-to-plan transfers from an eligible governmental plan to a qualified plan.* A transfer may be made under this paragraph (b)(8) only if the transfer is either—

(A) For the purchase of permissive service credit (as defined in section 415(n)(3)(A)) under the receiving defined benefit governmental plan; or

(B) A repayment to which section 415 does not apply by reason of section 415(k)(3).

(iii) *Example.* The provisions of this paragraph (b)(8) are illustrated by the following example:

Example. (i) *Facts.* Plan X is an eligible governmental plan maintained by County Y for its employees. Plan X provides for distributions only in the event of death, an unforeseeable emergency, or severance from employment with County Y (including retirement from County Y). Plan S is a qualified defined benefit plan maintained by State T for its employees. County Y is within State T. Employee A is an employee of County Y and is a participant in Plan X. Employee A previously was an employee of State T and is still entitled to benefits under Plan S. Plan S includes provisions allowing participants in certain plans, including Plan X, to transfer assets to Plan S for the purchase of service credit under Plan S and does not permit the amount transferred to exceed the amount necessary to fund the benefit resulting from the service credit. Although not required to do so, Plan X allows Employee A to transfer assets to Plan S to provide a service benefit under Plan S.

(ii) *Conclusion.* The transfer is permitted under this paragraph (b)(8).

PART 11—EMPLOYEE RETIREMENT INCOME SECURITY ACT OF 1974

Par. 19. The authority citation for part 11 is amended to read, in part, as follows:

Authority: 26 U.S.C. 7805. * * *

* * * * *

Part 11.415(c)(4)-1 [Removed]

Par. 20. Section 11.415(c)(4)-1 is removed.

Mark E. Matthews,

Deputy Commissioner for Services and Enforcement.

CERTIFIED COPY

DALE D. GOODE

¶ 20,261O

IRS proposed regulations: Participants: Beneficiaries: Electronic media: Notices: Elections: Consents.—The Treasury and IRS have issued proposed regulations setting forth rules regarding the use of electronic media to provide notices to plan participants and beneficiaries or to transmit elections or consents relating to employee benefit arrangements. The proposed rules cannot be relied on prior to their issuance as final regulations.

The proposed regulations, which were published in the Federal Register on July 14, 2005 (70 FR 40675), are reproduced below.

DEPARTMENT OF THE TREASURY

Internal Revenue Service

26 CFR Parts 1, 35, and 54

[REG-138362-04]

RIN 1545-BD68

Use of Electronic Technologies for Providing Employee Benefit Notices and Transmitting Employee Benefit Elections and Consents

AGENCY: Internal Revenue Service (IRS), Treasury.

ACTION: Notice of proposed rulemaking and notice of public hearing.

SUMMARY: This document contains proposed regulations that would provide guidance on the use of electronic media to provide certain notices to recipients or to transmit participant and beneficiary elections or consents with respect to employee benefit arrangements. In general, these proposed regulations would affect sponsors of, and participants and beneficiaries in, certain employee benefit arrangements. This document also provides a notice of public hearing on these proposed regulations.

DATES: Written or electronic comments must be received by October 12, 2005. Requests to speak (with outlines of oral comments to be discussed) at the public hearing scheduled for November 2, 2005, must be received by October 12, 2005.

ADDRESSES: Send submissions to: CC:PA:LPD:PR (REG-138362-04), room 5203, Internal Revenue Service, POB 7604, Ben Franklin Station, Washington DC 20044. Submissions may be hand delivered Monday through Friday, between the hours of 8 a.m. and 4 p.m. to CC:PA:LPD:PR (REG-138362-04), Courier's Desk, Internal Revenue Service, 1111 Constitution Avenue, NW., Washington, DC. Alternatively, taxpayers may submit comments electronically via the IRS Internet site at *www.irs.gov/regs* or via the Federal eRulemaking Portal at *www.regulations.gov* (IRS-REG-138362-04). The public hearing will be held in the Auditorium, Internal Revenue Building, 1111 Constitution Avenue NW., Washington, DC.

FOR FURTHER INFORMATION CONTACT: Concerning the proposed regulations, Pamela R. Kinard at (202) 622-6060; concerning submissions of comments, the hearing, and/or to be placed on the building access list to attend the hearing, Richard Hurst, (202) 622-7180 (not toll-free numbers).

SUPPLEMENTARY INFORMATION:

Paperwork Reduction Act

The collections of information referenced in this notice of proposed rulemaking were previously reviewed and approved by the Office of Management and Budget in accordance with the Paperwork Reduction Act of 1995 (44 U.S.C. 3507(d)) under control number 1545-1632, in conjunction with the Treasury Decision (TD 8873), relating to New Technologies in Retirement Plans, published on February 8, 2000 in the **Federal Register** (65 FR 6001), and control number 1545-1780, in conjunction with the Treasury Decision (TD 9052), relating to Notice of Significant Reduction in the Rate of Future Benefit Accrual, published on April 9, 2003 in the **Federal Register** (68 FR 17277). No substantive changes to these collections of information are being proposed.

An agency may not conduct or sponsor, and a person is not required to respond to, a collection of information unless it displays a valid control number assigned by the Office of Management and Budget.

Books or records relating to a collection of information must be retained as long as their contents may become material in the administration of any internal revenue law. Generally, tax returns and tax return information are confidential, as required by 26 U.S.C. 6103.

Background

This document contains proposed amendments to the regulations under section 401 of the Internal Revenue Code (Code) and to other sections of the Code relating to employee benefit arrangements. These proposed amendments, when finalized, will set forth rules regarding the use of electronic media to provide notices to plan participants and beneficiaries or to transmit elections or consents relating to employee benefit arrangements. These regulations also reflect the provisions of the Electronic Signatures in Global and National Commerce Act, Public Law 106-229 (114 Stat. 464 (2000)) (E-SIGN).

The Code and regulations thereunder, and the parallel provisions of the Employee Retirement Income Security Act of 1974 (ERISA), include a number of rules that require certain retirement plan notices, elections, or consents to be written or in writing.[1] Examples of these rules include the following:

- Under sections 401(k)(12)(D) and 401(m)(11), a written notice is required to be given to each employee eligible to participate in a cash or deferred arrangement under section 401(k) in order for the plan to be permitted to use a safe harbor in lieu of the actual deferral percentage test or actual contribution percentage test to ensure that the plan satisfies certain nondiscrimination requirements.

- Under section 402(f), a plan is required to provide a distributee, within a reasonable period of time before an eligible rollover distribution is made, a written explanation of the distributee's rollover rights and the tax and other potential consequences of the distribution or rollover.

- Under section 411(a)(11) (and the parallel provision in section 203(e) of ERISA and § 1.411(a)-11(f)(2), a participant cannot be cashed out of a plan before the later of normal retirement age or age 62 without the participant's written consent if the value of the participant's nonforfeitable accrued benefit exceeds $5,000.

- Under section 417 (and the parallel provision in section 205 of ERISA) and the regulations thereunder, a plan must provide to each participant a written explanation of the terms and conditions of a qualified joint and survivor annuity, the participant's right to make an election to waive the qualified joint and survivor annuity, the right to revoke such an election, and the rights of the participant's spouse. Under section 417(a)(2), an election to waive a qualified joint and survivor annuity can generally go into effect only if the participant's spouse consents to the election in writing and that consent is witnessed by either a plan representative or a notary public.

- Under section 3405(e)(10)(B) and § 34.3405-1, A-d-35, a payor is required to provide written notice to a payee regarding the payee's right to elect not to have Federal income tax withheld from a periodic payment (as defined in section 3405(e)(2)).

- Under section 4980F (and the parallel provision in section 204(h) of ERISA) and § 54.4980F-1, A-13, a plan must provide written notice (section 204(h) notice) of an amendment to an applicable pension plan that either provides for a significant reduction in the rate of future benefit accrual or that eliminates or significantly reduces an early retirement benefit or retirement-type subsidy.

Section 1510 of the Taxpayer Relief Act of 1997, Public Law 105-34 (111 Stat. 788, 1068) (TRA '97), provides for the Secretary of the Treasury to issue guidance designed to interpret the notice, election, consent, disclosure, and timing requirements (include related record-keeping requirements) under the Code and ERISA relating to retirement plans as applied to the use of new technologies by plan sponsors and administrators. Section 1510 of TRA '97 further provides that the guidance should maintain the protection of the rights of participants and beneficiaries. Pursuant to the mandate of section 1510 of TRA '97, final regulations (TD 8873) relating to the use of electronic media for transmissions of notices and consents under sections 402(f), 411(a)(11), and 3405(e)(10)(B) were published in the **Federal Register** (65 FR 6001) on February 8, 2000 (the 2000 regulations). These regulations are discussed in this preamble under the heading *Prior Guidance Related to New Technologies.*

E-SIGN, signed into law on June 30, 2000, generally provides that electronic documents and signatures are given the same legal effect as their paper counterparts. Section 101(a) of E-SIGN provides that, notwithstanding any statute, regulation, or rule of law relating to a transaction in or affecting interstate or foreign commerce, a signature, contract, or other record may not be denied legal effect, validity, or enforceability solely because it is in electronic form.

Section 101(b)(1) provides that E-SIGN does not limit, alter, or otherwise affect any requirement imposed by a statute, regulation, or rule of law relating to a person's rights or obligations under any statute, regulation, or rule of law except with respect to a requirement that contracts be written, signed, or in non-electronic form. Section 101(b)(2) provides that E-SIGN does not require any person to agree to use or accept electronic signatures or records, other than a governmental agency with respect to a record other than a contract to which it is a party.

Section 101(c) of E-SIGN sets forth special protections for consumers that apply when a statute, regulation, or other rule of law requires that consumer information relating to a transaction be provided or made available in writing.[2] Under those protections, before information can be transmitted electronically, a consumer must first affirmatively consent to receiving the information electronically and the consent must be made in a manner that reasonably demonstrates the consumer's ability to access the information in electronic form (or if the consent is not provided in such a manner, that confirmation of the consent be made electronically in a manner that reasonably demonstrates the consumer's ability to access the information in electronic form). Prior to consent, the consumer must receive certain specified disclosures. The disclosures must include, among other items, the hardware or software requirements for access to and retention of the electronic records, the consumer's right to withdraw his or her consent to receive the information electronically (and the consequences that follow the withdrawal of consent), the procedures for requesting a paper copy of the electronic record, and the cost, if any, of obtaining a paper copy. Section 106(1) of E-SIGN generally defines a consumer as an individual who obtains products or services used primarily for personal, family, or household purposes.

Section 104(b)(1) of E-SIGN generally provides that a Federal or state agency that is responsible for rulemaking under a statute has interpretative authority to issue guidance interpreting section 101 of E-SIGN with respect to that other statute. However, as a limitation on that authority, section 104(b)(2) of E-SIGN prohibits the issuance of any regulation that is not consistent with section 101 or that adds to the requirements of that section. Section 104(b)(2) of E-SIGN also requires that any agency issuing the regulations find that the rules selected to carry out the purpose of the relevant statute are substantially equivalent to the requirements imposed on records that are not electronic, do not impose unreasonable cost on the acceptance and use of electronic records, and do not require or give greater legal status to a specific technology.

Section 104(d)(1) of E-SIGN authorizes a Federal regulatory agency to exempt, without condition, a specified category or type of record from the consent requirements in section 101(c). The exemption may be issued only if the exemption is necessary to eliminate a substantial burden on electronic commerce and will not increase the material risk of harm to consumers.

Subsequent to the enactment of E-SIGN, Congress amended section 204(h) of ERISA and enacted a corresponding provision in section 4980F of the Code. Under ERISA section 204(h)(7) and Code section 4980F(g), the Secretary of the Treasury may, by regulations, allow any section 204(h) notice to be provided by using new technologies.

Prior Guidance Relating to New Technologies.

Following the enactment of section 1510 of TRA '97, the Treasury Department and IRS issued several items of guidance relating to the use of electronic media with respect to employee benefit arrangements. Notice 99-1 (1999-1 C.B. 269) provides guidance relating to qualified retirement plans permitting the use of electronic media for plan participants or beneficiaries conducting certain account transactions for which there is no specific writing requirement, such as plan enrollments, direct rollover elections, beneficiary designations, investment change allocations, elective and after-tax contribution designations, and general plan or specific account inquiries.[3]

---

[1] Pursuant to section 101(a) of the Reorganization Plan No. 4 of 1978, 29 U.S.C. 1001nt, the Secretary of the Treasury has authority to issue regulations under parts 2 and 3 of subtitle B of title I of ERISA with certain exceptions. Under section 104 of the Reorganization Plan No. 4, the Secretary of Labor retains enforcement authority with respects to parts 2 and 3 of subtitle B of title 1 of ERISA, but, in exercising that authority, is bound by the regulations issued by the Secretary of Treasury.

[2] The rules of section 101 of E-SIGN do not apply to certain consumer notices. These include consumer notices that are necessary for the protection of a consumer's health, safety, or shelter (e.g., cancellation of health benefits or life insurance and foreclosure on a credit agreement secured by an individual's primary residence). See section 103(b)(2)(B) and (C) of E-SIGN.

[3] The Treasury Department and IRS have also issued guidance regarding the use of electronic media with respect to tax reporting and other tax requirements with respect to employee benefit plans. For example, Announcement 99-6 (1999-1 C.B. 352) authorizes payers of pensions, annuities, and other employee benefits to establish a system for payees to submit electronically Forms W-4P, "Withholding Certificate for Pension or Annuity Payments," W-4S, "Request for Federal Income Tax Withholding from Sick Pay," and W-4V, "Voluntary Withholding Request," if certain requirements, including signature and recordkeeping requirements, are satisfied. In addition, Notice 2004-10 (2004-6 I.R.B. 433) authorizes the electronic delivery of certain forms relating to the reporting of contributions and distributions of pensions, simplified employee pensions, traditional IRAs, Roth IRAs, qualified tuition programs, Coverdell education savings accounts, and Archer Medical Savings Accounts. See also §§ 31.6051-1(j) and 1.6039-1(f).

The 2000 regulations relating to the use of electronic media for transmissions of notices and consents required to be in writing under sections 402(f), 411(a)(11), and 3405(e)(10)(B) set forth standards for the electronic transmission of certain notices and consents required in connection with distributions from retirement plans. These regulations provide that a plan may provide a notice required under section 402(f), 411(a)(11), or 3405(e)(10)(B) either on a written paper document or through an electronic medium that is reasonably accessible to the participant. The system must be reasonably designed to provide the notice in a manner no less understandable to the participant than a written paper document. In addition, the participant must be advised of the right to request and receive a paper copy of the written paper document at no charge, and, upon request, the document must be provided to the participant without charge.

The 2000 regulations permit an electronic system to satisfy the requirement that a participant provide written consent to a distribution if certain requirements are satisfied. First, the electronic medium must be reasonably accessible to the participant. Second, the electronic system must be reasonably designed to preclude anyone other than the participant from giving the consent. Third, the system must provide the participant with a reasonable opportunity to review and to confirm, modify, or rescind the terms of the consent before it becomes effective. Fourth, the system must provide the participant, within a reasonable time after the consent is given, a confirmation of the terms (including the form) of the distribution through either a written paper document or in an electronic format that satisfies the requirements for providing applicable notices. Thus, the participant must be advised of the right to request and to receive a confirmation copy of the consent on a written paper document without charge.

Subsequent to the issuance of the 2000 regulations, the Treasury Department and IRS have applied the standards set forth in those regulations in other situations. For example, § 1.7476-2(c)(2) provides that a notice to an interested party[4] is deemed to be provided in a manner that satisfies the delivery requirements of § 1.7476-2(c)(1) if the notice is delivered using an electronic medium under a system that satisfies the requirements of § 1.402(f)-1, Q&A-5. Q&A-7 of Notice 2000-3 (2000-1 C.B. 413) provides that, until the issuance of further guidance, a plan is permitted to use electronic media to provide notices required under sections 401(k)(12) and 401(m)(11) if the employee receives the notice through an electronic medium that is reasonably accessible, the system is designed to provide the notice in a manner no less understandable to the employee than a written paper document, and, at the time the notice is provided, the employee is advised that the employee may request and receive the notice on a written paper document at no charge. Similarly, regulations at § 1.72(p)-1, Q&A-3(b), require a loan from a plan to a participant to be set forth in a written paper document, in an electronic medium that satisfies standards that are the same as the standards in the 2000 regulations, or in such other form as may be approved by the Commissioner.

In 2003, final regulations (TD 9052) under section 4980F were published in the **Federal Register** (68 FR 17277). Q&A-13 of § 54.4980F-1 provides the rules for the manner of delivering a section 204(h) notice. For a plan to deliver electronically a section 204(h) notice, the following requirements must be satisfied. First, the section 204(h) notice must actually be received by the applicable individual or the plan administrator must take appropriate and necessary measures reasonably calculated to ensure that the method for providing the section 204(h) notice results in actual receipt. Second, the plan administrator must provide the applicable individual with a clear and conspicuous statement that the individual has a right to receive a paper version of the section 204(h) notice without the imposition of fees and, if the individual requests a paper copy of the section 204(h) notice, the paper copy must be provided without charge.

In addition, the regulations under section 4980F provide a safe harbor method for delivering a section 204(h) notice electronically. Under the safe harbor, which is substantially the same as the consumer consent rules of E-SIGN, consent must be made electronically in a manner that reasonably demonstrates the individual's ability to access the information in electronic form. The applicable individual must also provide an address for the delivery of the electronic section 204(h) notice and the plan administrator must provide the applicable individual with certain disclosures regarding the section 204(h) notice, including the right to withdraw consent.

The Department of Labor (DOL) and the Pension Benefit Guaranty Corporation (PBGC) have also issued regulations relating to the use of electronic media to furnish notices, reports, statements, disclosures, and other documents to participants, beneficiaries, and other individuals under titles I and IV of ERISA. See 29 CFR 2520.104b-1 and 29 CFR 4000.14.

Explanation of Provisions

Overview

The proposed regulations would coordinate the existing notice and election rules under the Code and regulations relating to certain employee benefit arrangements with the requirements of E-SIGN and set forth the exclusive rules relating to the use of electronic media to satisfy any requirement under the Code that a communication to or from a participant, with respect to the participant's rights under the employee benefit arrangement be in writing or in written form. The standards set forth in the proposed regulations would also function as a safe harbor when an electronic medium is used for any communication that is not required to be in writing or in written form.

The proposed regulations would apply to any notice, election, or similar communication provided to or made by a participant or beneficiary under a qualified plan, an annuity contract described in section 403(a) or 403(b), a simplified employee pension (SEP) under section 408(k), a simple retirement plan under section 408(p), or an eligible governmental plan under section 457(b). Thus, for example, the proposed regulations would apply to a section 402(f) notice, a section 411(a)(11) notice, and a section 204(h) notice.

In addition, the proposed regulations would apply to any notice, election, or similar communication provided to or made by a participant or beneficiary under an accident and health plan or an arrangement under section 104(a)(3) or 105, a cafeteria plan under section 125, an educational assistance program under section 127, a qualified transportation fringe program under section 132, an Archer Medical Savings Account under section 220, or a health savings account under section 223.

However, the proposed regulations would not apply to any notice, election, consent, or disclosure required under the provisions of title I or IV of ERISA over which the DOL or the PBGC has interpretative and regulatory authority. For example, the rules in § 2520.104b-1 of the Labor Regulations apply with respect to an employee benefit plan furnishing disclosure documents, such as a summary plan description or a summary annual report. The proposed regulations would also not apply to Code section 411(a)(3)(B) (relating to suspension of benefits), Code section 4980B(f)(6) (relating to an individual's COBRA rights), or any other Code provision over which DOL and the PBGC have similar interpretative authority. In addition, the rules in these proposed regulations apply only with respect to notices and elections relating to a participant's rights under an employee benefit arrangement; thus they do not apply with respect to other requirements under the Code, such as requirements relating to tax reporting, tax records,[5] or substantiation of expenses.

Requirements for the Use of Electronic Media

These proposed regulations would require that any communication that is provided using an electronic medium satisfy all the otherwise applicable requirements (including the applicable timing and content rules) relating to that communication. In addition, these regulations would require that the content of the notice and the medium through which it is delivered be reasonably designed to provide the information to a recipient in a manner no less understandable to the recipient than if provided on a written paper document. For example, a plan delivering a lengthy section 402(f) notice would not satisfy this requirement if the plan chose to provide the notice through a pre-recorded message on an automated phone system.[6] The regulations would also require that, at the time the applicable notice is provided, the electronic transmission alert the recipient to the significance of the transmittal (including the identification of the subject matter of the notice), and provide any instructions needed to access the notice, in a manner that is readily understandable and accessible.

The view of the Treasury Department and IRS is that a participant under an employee benefit arrangement is generally a consumer within the meaning of section 106(1) of E-SIGN when receiving a notice in

---

[4] Under section 7476, in order to receive a determination letter on the qualified status of a retirement plan, the applicant must provide evidence that individuals who qualify as interested parties received notification of the determination letter application.

[5] See section 6001 of the Code and the regulations thereunder, and Rev. Proc. 98-25 (1998-1 C.B. 689) (setting forth the basic requirements that the IRS treats as essential for

satisfying the recordkeeping requirements of section 6001 in cases where a taxpayer's records are maintained in electronic form).

[6] Note that a section 204(h) notice cannot be provided using oral communication or a recording of an oral communication. See § 54.4980F-1, A-13(c)(1).

order to make a decision about the participant's benefits or other rights under an employee benefit arrangement.[7] Accordingly, § 1.401(a)-21(b) of these proposed regulations would provide rules, reflecting the consumer consent requirements of section 101(c) of E-SIGN, under which an employee benefit arrangement may provide an applicable notice through an electronic medium. However, the Treasury Department and IRS also believe that, if an employee benefit arrangement could provide these notices only by complying with the rules in § 1.401(a)-21(b) of these proposed regulations, it would impose a substantial burden on electronic commerce. Furthermore, there is an alternative that is less burdensome and that would not increase the material risk of harm to plan participants. Accordingly, § 1.401(a)-21(c) of these proposed regulations provides an alternative means of providing notices electronically.

Section 1.401(a)-21(b) of these proposed regulations would generally require that before a plan may provide an applicable notice using an electronic medium, the participant must consent to receive the communication electronically. The consent generally must be made in a manner that reasonably demonstrates that the participant can access the notice in the electronic form that will be used to provide the notice. Alternatively, the consent may be made using a written paper document or through some other nonelectronic means, but only if the participant confirms the consent in a manner that reasonably demonstrates that the participant can access the notice in the electronic form to be provided. Prior to consenting, the participant must receive a disclosure statement that outlines the scope of the consent, the participant's right to withdraw his or her consent to receive the communication electronically (including any conditions, consequences, or fees in the event of the withdrawal), and the right to receive the communication using paper. The disclosure must also specify the hardware and software requirements for accessing the electronic media and the procedures for updating information to contact the participant electronically. In the event the hardware or software requirements change, new consent must be obtained from the participant, generally following the rules of section 101(c) of E-SIGN.

Section 1.401(a)-21(c) of these proposed regulations provides alternate conditions for providing notices electronically. The proposed regulations would exempt applicable notices from the consumer consent requirements of E-SIGN and would provide an alternative method of complying with the requirement that a participant notice be in writing or in written form if the plan complies with those conditions. This alternative method of compliance is based on the 2000 regulations previously issued under section 1510 of TRA '97 (which provides that any guidance issued should maintain *the protection of the rights of participants and beneficiaries*). This alternative method of compliance satisfies the requirements of section 104(d)(1) of E-SIGN, including the requirement that any exemption from the consumer consent requirements *not increase the material risk of harm to consumers*.

The alternative method of compliance provides rules that are intended generally to replicate the requirements in the 2000 regulations that apply to notices required under sections 402(f), 411(a)(11), and 3405 and thereby allow plans to continue to provide these notices electronically using the rules in those 2000 regulations. As under the 2000 regulations, the proposed regulations would retain the requirement that, at the time the applicable notice is provided, the participant must be advised that he or she may request and must receive the applicable notice in writing on paper at no charge. However, the requirement that the electronic medium be reasonably accessible under the 2000 regulations would be changed to require that the recipient of the notice be effectively able to access the electronic medium. This is not intended to reflect a substantive change in the rules, but rather to avoid confusion with Labor Regulations interpreting the words *reasonably accessible* as used in section 101(i)(2)(D) of ERISA, as added by section 306 of the Sarbanes Oxley Act of 2002, Public Law 107-204 (116 Stat. 745).[8]

Proposed § 1.401(a)-21(d) would set forth the requirements that apply if a consent, election, request, agreement, or similar communication is made by or from a participant, beneficiary, or alternate payee using an electronic medium. (For simplicity, the proposed regulations refer to all of these types of actions as *participant elections*.) The rules in proposed § 1.401(a)-21(d), which are also based on the standards in

the 2000 regulations, would require that (1) the participant be effectively able to access to the electronic system in order to transmit the participant election, (2) the electronic system be reasonably designed to preclude any person other than the participant from making the participant election (for example, through the use of a personal identification number (PIN)), (3) the electronic system provide the participant making the participant election with a reasonable opportunity to review, confirm, modify, or rescind the terms of the election before it becomes effective, and (4) the participant making the participant election, within a reasonable time period, receive a confirmation of the election through either a written paper document or an electronic medium under a system that satisfies the applicable notice requirements of proposed § 1.401(a)-21(b) or (c).

These regulations require that a participant be effectively able to access the electronic system that the plan provides for participant elections, but, like the 2000 regulations, do not require that a plan also permit the election to be transmitted by paper as an alternative to using the electronic system available to the participant. If a plan were to require participant elections to be provided electronically, such as requiring that any consent to a distribution under section 411(a)(11) be transmitted electronically through a particular medium (without an option to make the election on paper), then these regulations would not apply with respect to a participant who is not effectively able to access to the electronic medium. In addition, such a participant would be effectively unable to provide consent and would generally not be paid until the later of age 62 or normal retirement age. Moreover, no form of distribution would be available to the former employee and such a plan may have difficulties demonstrating compliance with the qualification requirements. For example, the plan may not be able to demonstrate that it satisfies the requirements of § 1.401(a)(4)-4 under which benefits, rights, and features, such as a right to early distribution, must be made available in a nondiscriminatory manner.[9]

Unlike the 2000 regulations, the rules in these proposed regulations would extend the use of electronic media to the notice and election rules applicable to plans subject to the QJSA requirements of section 417. Section 417 requires the consent of a spouse to be witnessed by a plan representative or a notary public. In accordance with section 101(g) of E-SIGN, the proposed regulations would permit the use of an electronic acknowledgement or notarization of a signature (if the standards of section 101(g) of E-SIGN and State law applicable to notary publics are satisfied). However, the proposed regulations would require that the signature of the individual be witnessed in the physical presence of the plan representative or notary public, regardless of whether the signature is provided on paper or through an electronic medium.

As discussed above, these proposed regulations, which are consistent with section 101 of E-SIGN and do not add to the requirements of that section, are issued to set forth rules that coordinate section 101 of E-SIGN with the sections of the Code relating to employee benefit arrangements. In accordance with section 104(b)(2)(C) of E-SIGN, the Treasury Department and IRS find that there is substantial justification for these proposed regulations, that the requirements imposed on the use of electronic media under these regulations are substantially equivalent to those imposed on non-electronic records, that the requirements will not impose unreasonable costs on the acceptance and use of electronic records, and that these regulations do not require (or accord greater legal status or effect to) the use of any specific technology.

Conforming Amendments to Other Rules in Law

The proposed regulations would modify a number of existing regulations (including the 2000 regulations and the other regulations described above) that have previously provided rules relating to the use of new technology in providing applicable notices that are required to be in writing or in written form. These modifications, which merely add the consumer consent requirements of E-SIGN, are not expected to adversely affect existing administrative practices of plan sponsors designed to comply with the 2000 regulations.

As noted above, these proposed regulations would apply to categories of applicable notices that were not previously addressed in the 2000 regulations and subsequent regulations. As such, these regula-

---

[7] See also 12 CFR 202.16, 205.17, 213.6, and 2226.36, treating electronic disclosures in connection with certain credit transactions as consumer information for purposes of E-SIGN.

[8] Section 101(i) of ERISA sets forth a requirement for a plan administrator to notify plan participants and beneficiaries of a blackout period with respect to an individual account plan. Section 101(i)(2)(D) provides that the required blackout notice "shall be in writing, except that such notice may be in electronic or other form to the extent that such form is reasonably accessible to the recipient." Section 2520.101-3(b)(3) of the Labor Regulations

interpreting this requirement provides for this notice to be in writing and furnished in any manner consistent with the requirements of section 2520.104b-1 of the Labor Regulations, including the provisions in that section relating to the use of electronic media. Those regulations also deem a notice requirement to be satisfied if certain measures are taken. Section 1.401(a)-21 of these proposed regulations only provides rules for satisfying, through the use of electronic media, a requirement that a notice or election be in writing.

[9] Similar problems would arise under section 411(d)(6), assuming the plan previously permitted election of early distribution to be made on paper.

tions apply whenever there is a requirement that an applicable notice under one of the covered sections be provided in written form or in writing, without regard to whether that other requirement specifically cross-references these regulations. Thus, safe harbor notices under sections 401(k)(12)(D) and 401(m)(11), which are required to be in writing, can be provided electronically if the requirements of § 1.401(a)-21 of this chapter are satisfied.

Proposed Effective Date

These regulations are proposed to apply prospectively. Thus, these rules will apply no earlier than the date of the publication of the Treasury decision adopting these rules as final regulations in the **Federal Register**. These regulations cannot be relied upon prior to their issuance as final regulations.

Special Analyses

It has been determined that this notice of proposed rulemaking is not a significant regulatory action as defined in Executive Order 12866. Therefore a regulatory assessment is not required. It has also been determined that section 553(b) of the Administrative Procedure Act (5 U.S.C. chapter 5) does not apply to these regulations, and because these regulations do not propose any new collection of information, the provisions of the Regulatory Flexibility Act (5 U.S.C. chapter 6) do not apply. These regulations only provide guidance on how to satisfy existing collection of information requirements through the use of electronic media. Pursuant to section 7805(f) of the Code, these proposed regulations will be submitted to the Chief Counsel for Advocacy of the Small Business Administration for comment on its impact on small business.

Comments and Public Hearing

Before these proposed regulations are adopted as final regulations, consideration will be given to any written comments (a signed original and eight (8) copies) or electronic comments that are submitted timely to the IRS. The Treasury Department and IRS specifically request comments on the clarity of the proposed rules and how they can be made easier to understand. All comments will be available for public inspection and copying.

The proposed regulations have reserved the issue of whether there should be any exceptions to the rule generally requiring the physical presence of the spouse for a notarization of the spouse's consent. Comments are requested on whether the reservation should be: (i) deleted in favor of a broad prohibition that has no exception; (ii) filled in based on a general standard under which electronic notarization of an electronic signature (without the spouse's presence) would be permitted if the technology provides the same protections and assurance as the requirement that a person's signature be executed in the presence of a notary (e.g., that the spouse is actually the person signing); or (iii) filled in with a grant of discretion to the Commissioner to determine in the future, after advance notice and an opportunity for comment, that a particular form of electronic notarization of an electronic signature (without the spouse's presence) provides the same protections and assurance as the requirement that a person's signature be executed in the presence of a notary.

A public hearing has been scheduled for November 2, 2005, beginning at 10 a.m. in the Auditorium, Internal Revenue Building, 1111 Constitution Avenue, NW., Washington, DC. Due to building security procedures, visitors must enter at the main entrance, located at 1111 Constitution Avenue, NW. In addition, all visitors must present photo identification to enter the building. Because of access restrictions, visitors will not be admitted beyond the immediate entrance area more than 30 minutes before the hearing starts. For information about having your name placed on the building access list to attend the hearing, see the "FOR FURTHER INFORMATION CONTACT" portion of this preamble.

The rules of 26 CFR 601.601(a)(3) apply to the hearing. Persons who wish to present oral comments must submit written or electronic comments and an outline of the topics to be discussed and time to be devoted to each topic (a signed original and eight (8) copies) by October 12, 2005. A period of 10 minutes will be allotted to each person for making comments. An agenda showing the scheduling of the speakers will be prepared after the deadline for receiving comments has passed. Copies of the agenda will be available free of charge at the hearing.

Drafting Information

The principal author of these proposed regulations is Pamela R. Kinard, Office of Division Counsel/Associate Chief Counsel (Tax Exempt and Government Entities), Internal Revenue Service. However, personnel from other offices of the IRS and Treasury Department participated in their development.

List of Subjects

26 CFR Part 1

Income taxes, Reporting and recordkeeping requirements.

26 CFR Part 35

Employment taxes, Income taxes, Reporting and recordkeeping requirements.

26 CFR Part 54

Excise taxes, Pensions, Reporting and recordkeeping requirements.

Proposed Amendments to the Regulations

Accordingly, 26 CFR parts 1, 35, and 54 are proposed to be amended as follows:

PART 1—INCOME TAXES

Paragraph 1. The authority citation for part 1 is amended by adding an entry in numerical order to read as follows:

Authority: 26 U.S.C. 7805 * * *

Section 1.401(a)-21 also issued under 26 U.S.C. 401 and section 104(b)(1) and (2) of the Electronic Signatures in Global and National Commerce Act, Public Law 106-229 (114 Stat. 464). * * *

Par. 2. Section 1.72(p)-1, Q&A-3, is amended by revising, the text of paragraph (b) to read as follows:

§ 1.72(p)-1 Loans treated as distributions.

* * * * *

A-3. * * *

(b) * * * A loan does not satisfy the requirements of this paragraph unless the loan is evidenced by a legally enforceable agreement (which may include more than one document) and the terms of the agreement demonstrate compliance with the requirements of section 72(p)(2) and this section. Thus, the agreement must specify the amount and date of the loan and the repayment schedule. The agreement does not have to be signed if the agreement is enforceable under applicable law without being signed. The agreement must be set forth either—

(1) In a written paper document; or

(2) In an electronic medium under a system that satisfies the participant election requirements of § 1.401(a)-21(d) of this chapter.

* * * * *

Par. 3. Section 1.401(a)-21 is added to read as follows:

§ 1.401(a)-21 Rules relating to the use of electronic media to provide applicable notices and to transmit participant elections.

(a) *Introduction*—(1) *In general*—(i) *Permission to use electronic media.* This section provides rules relating to the use of electronic media to provide applicable notices and to transmit participant elections as defined in paragraphs (e)(1) and (2) of this section with respect to certain employee benefit arrangements referenced in this section. The rules in this section reflect the provisions of the Electronic Signatures in Global and National Commerce Act, Public Law 106-229 (114 Stat. 464 (2000) (E-SIGN)).

(ii) *Notices and elections required to be in writing or in written form*—(A) *In general.* The rules of this section must be satisfied in order to use electronic media to provide an applicable notice or to transmit a participant election if the notice or election is required under the Internal Revenue Code or Department of Treasury regulations to be in writing or in written form.

(B) *Rules relating to applicable notices.* An applicable notice that is provided using electronic media is treated as being provided in writing or in written form if and only if the consumer consent requirements of paragraph (b) of this section are satisfied or the requirements for exemption from the consumer consent requirements under paragraph (c) of this section are satisfied. For example, in order to provide a section 402(f) notice electronically, a qualified plan must satisfy either the consumer consent requirements of paragraph (b) of this section or the requirements for exemption under paragraph (c) of this section. If a plan fails to satisfy either of these requirements, the plan must provide the section 402(f) notice using a written paper document in order to satisfy the requirements of section 402(f).

(C) *Rules relating to participant elections.* A participant election that is transmitted using electronic media is treated as being provided in writing or in written form if and only if the requirements of paragraph (d) of this section are satisfied.

(iii) *Safe harbor method for applicable notices and participant elections that are not required to be in writing or written form*. For an applicable notice or a participant election that is not required to be in writing or in written form, the rules of this section provide a safe harbor method for using electronic media to provide the applicable notice or to transmit the participant election.

(2) *Application of rules*—(i) *Notices, elections, or consents under retirement plans*. The rules of this section apply to any applicable notice or any participant election relating to a qualified retirement plan under section 401(a) or 403(a). In addition, the rules of this section apply to any applicable notice and any participant election relating to an annuity contract under section 403(b), a simplified employee pension (SEP) under section 408(k), a simple retirement plan under section 408(p), and an eligible governmental plan under section 457(b).

(ii) *Notices, elections, or consents under other employee benefit arrangements*. The rules of this section also apply to any applicable notice or any participant election relating to accident and health plans or arrangements under sections 104(a)(3) and 105, cafeteria plans under section 125, qualified education assistance programs under section 127, qualified transportation fringe programs under section 132, Archer medical savings accounts under section 220, and health savings accounts under section 223.

(3) *Limitation on application of rules*—(i) *In general*. The rules of this section do not apply to any notice, election, consent, or disclosure required under the provisions of title I or IV of the Employee Retirement Income Security Act of 1974, as amended (ERISA), over which the Department of Labor or the Pension Benefit Guaranty Corporation has interpretative and regulatory authority. For example, the rules in 29 CFR 2520.104b-1 of the Labor Regulations apply with respect to an employee benefit plan providing disclosure documents, such as a summary plan description or a summary annual report. The rules in this section also do not apply to Internal Revenue Code section 411(a)(3)(B) (relating to suspension of benefits), Internal Revenue Code section 4980B(f)(6) (relating to an individual's COBRA rights), or any other Internal Revenue Code provision over which Department of Labor or the Pension Benefit Guaranty Corporation has similar interpretative authority.

(ii) *Other requirements under the Internal Revenue Code*. Because the rules in this section only apply with respect to applicable notices and participant elections relating to a participant's rights under an employee benefit arrangement; thus they do not apply with respect to other requirements under the Internal Revenue Code, such as requirements relating to tax reporting, tax records, or substantiation of expenses.

(4) *Additional requirements related to applicable notices and participant elections*. The rules of this section supplement the general requirements related to each applicable notice and to each participant election. Thus, in addition to satisfying the rules for delivery under this section, the timing, content, and other general requirements (including recordkeeping requirements in guidance issued by the Commissioner under section 6001) relating to the applicable notice or participant election must be satisfied. With respect to the content of the notice, the system of delivery must be reasonably designed to provide the applicable notice to a recipient in a manner no less understandable to the recipient than a written paper document. In addition, at the time the applicable notice is provided, the electronic transmission must alert the recipient to the significance of the transmittal (including identification of the subject matter of the notice) and provide any instructions needed to access the notice, in a manner that is readily understandable and accessible.

(b) *Consumer consent requirements*—(1) *Requirements*. The consumer consent requirements of this paragraph (b) are satisfied if the requirements in paragraphs (b)(2) through (5) of this section are satisfied.

(2) *Consent*—(i) *In general*. The recipient must affirmatively consent to the delivery of the applicable notice using electronic media. This consent must be either—

(A) Made electronically in a manner that reasonably demonstrates that the recipient can access the applicable notice in the electronic form that will be used to provide the notice; or

(B) Made using a written paper document (or using another form not described in paragraph (b)(2)(i)(A) of this section), but only if the recipient confirms the consent electronically in a manner that reasonably demonstrates that the recipient can access the applicable notice in the electronic form that will be used to provide the notice.

(ii) *Withdrawal of consumer consent*. The consent to receive electronic delivery requirement of this paragraph (b)(2) is not satisfied if the recipient withdraws his or her consent before the applicable notice is delivered.

(3) *Required disclosure statement*. The recipient, prior to consenting under paragraph (b)(2)(i) of this section, must be provided with a clear and conspicuous statement containing the disclosures described in paragraphs (b)(3)(i) through (v) of this section:

(i) *Right to receive paper document*—(A) *In general*. The statement informs the recipient of any right to have the applicable notice be provided using a written paper document or other nonelectronic form.

(B) *Post-consent request for paper copy*. The statement informs the recipient how, after having provided consent to receive the applicable notice electronically, the recipient may, upon request, obtain a paper copy of the applicable notice and whether any fee will be charged for such copy.

(ii) *Right to withdraw consumer consent*. The statement informs the recipient of the right to withdraw consent to receive electronic delivery of an applicable notice on a prospective basis at any time and explains the procedures for withdrawing that consent and any conditions, consequences, or fees in the event of the withdrawal.

(iii) *Scope of the consumer consent*. The statement informs the recipient whether the consent to receive electronic delivery of an applicable notice applies only to the particular transaction that gave rise to the applicable notice or to other identified transactions that may be provided or made available during the course of the parties' relationship. For example, the statement may provide that a recipient's consent to receive electronic delivery will apply to all future applicable notices of the recipient relating to the employee benefit arrangement until the recipient is no longer a participant in the employee benefit arrangement (or withdraws the consent).

(iv) *Description of the contact procedures*. The statement describes the procedures to update information needed to contact the recipient electronically.

(v) *Hardware or software requirements*. The statement describes the hardware and software requirements needed to access and retain the applicable notice.

(4) *Post-consent change in hardware or software requirements*. If, after a recipient provides consent to receive electronic delivery, there is a change in the hardware or software requirements needed to access or retain the applicable notice and such change creates a material risk that the recipient will not be able to access or retain the applicable notice in electronic format—

(i) The recipient must receive a statement of—

(A) The revised hardware or software requirements for access to and retention of the applicable notice; and

(B) The right to withdraw consent to receive electronic delivery without the imposition of any fees for the withdrawal and without the imposition of any condition or consequence that was not previously disclosed in paragraph (b)(3) of this section.

(ii) The recipient must reaffirm consent to receive electronic delivery in accordance with the requirements of paragraph (b)(2) of this section.

(5) *Prohibition on oral communications*. For purposes of this paragraph (b), neither an oral communication nor a recording of an oral communication is an electronic record.

(c) *Exemption from consumer consent requirements*—(1) *In general*. This paragraph (c) is satisfied if the conditions in paragraphs (c)(2) and (3) of this section are satisfied. This paragraph (c) constitutes an exemption from the consumer consent requirements of section 101(c) of E-SIGN pursuant to the authority granted in section 104(d)(1) of E-SIGN.

(2) *Effective ability to access*. For purposes of this paragraph (c), the electronic medium used to provide an applicable notice must be a medium that the recipient has the effective ability to access.

(3) *Free paper copy of applicable notice*. At the time the applicable notice is provided, the recipient must be advised that he or she may request and receive the applicable notice in writing on paper at no charge, and, upon request, that applicable notice must be provided to the recipient at no charge.

(d) *Special rules for participant elections*—(1) *In general*. This paragraph (d) is satisfied if the conditions described in paragraphs (d)(2) through (6) of this section are satisfied.

(2) *Effective ability to access.* The electronic medium under a system used to make a participant election must be a medium that the individual who is eligible to make the election is effectively able to access. If the individual is not effectively able to access the electronic medium for making the participant election, the participant election will not be treated as made available to that individual. For example, the participant election will not be treated as made available for purposes of the rules under section 401(a)(4).

(3) *Authentication.* The electronic system used in delivering a participant election is reasonably designed to preclude any person other than the appropriate individual from making the election. For example, a system can require that an account number and a personal identification number (PIN) be entered into the system before a participant election can be transmitted.

(4) *Opportunity to review.* The electronic system provides the individual making the participant election with a reasonable opportunity to review, confirm, modify, or rescind the terms of the election before the election becomes effective.

(5) *Confirmation of action.* The person making the participant election, within a reasonable time, receives a confirmation of the effect of the election under the terms of the plan through either a written paper document or an electronic medium under a system that satisfies the requirements of either paragraph (b) or (c) of this section (as if the confirmation were an applicable notice).

(6) *Participant elections, including spousal consents, that are required to be witnessed by a plan representative or a notary public.* (i) Except as provided in paragraph (d)(6)(ii) of this section, in the case of a participant election which is required to be witnessed by a plan representative or a notary public (such as a spousal consent under section 417), an electronic notarization acknowledging a signature (in accordance with section 101(g) of E-SIGN and state law applicable to notary publics) will not be denied legal effect so long as the signature of the individual is witnessed in the physical presence of the plan representative or notary public.

(ii) [Reserved].

(e) *Definitions.* The following definitions apply to this section:

(1) *Applicable notice.* The term *applicable notice* includes any notice, report, statement, or other document required to be provided to a recipient under an arrangement described in paragraph (a)(2) of this section.

(2) *Participant election.* The term *participant election* includes any consent, election, request, agreement, or similar communication made by or from a participant, beneficiary, or alternate payee to which this section applies under an arrangement described in paragraph (a)(2) of this section.

(3) *Recipient.* The term *recipient* means a plan participant, beneficiary, employee, alternate payee, or any other person to whom an applicable notice is to be provided.

(4) *Electronic.* The term *electronic* means technology having electrical, digital, magnetic, wireless, optical, electromagnetic, voice-recording systems, or similar capabilities.

(5) *Electronic media.* The term *electronic media* means an electronic method of communication (e.g., websites, electronic mail, telephonic systems, magnetic disks, and CD-ROMs).

(6) *Electronic record.* The term *electronic record* means an applicable notice created, generated, sent, communicated, received, or stored by electronic means.

(f) *Examples.* The following examples illustrate the rules of this section. In all of these examples, with the exception of *Example 4* and *Example 5*, assume that the requirements of paragraph (a)(4) of this section are satisfied. The examples read as follows:

Example 1. (i) *Facts.* Plan A, a qualified plan, permits participants to request benefit distributions from the plan on Plan A's Intranet website. Under Plan A's system for such transactions, a participant must enter his or her account number and personal identification number (PIN), and this information must match the information in Plan A's records in order for the transaction to proceed. If a participant requests a distribution from Plan A on Plan A's website, then, at the time of the request for distribution, a disclosure statement appears on the computer screen that explains that the participant can consent to receive the section 402(f) notice electronically. In the disclosure statement, Plan A provides information relating to the consent, including how to receive a paper copy of the notice, how to withdraw the consent, the hardware and software requirements, and the procedures for accessing the section 402(f) notice, which is in a file format from a specific spreadsheet program. After reviewing the disclosure statement, which satisfies the

requirements of paragraph (b)(3) of this section, the participant consents to receive the section 402(f) notice via e-mail by selecting the consent button at the end of the disclosure statement. As a part of the consent procedure, the participant must demonstrate that the participant can access the spreadsheet program by answering a question from the spreadsheet program, which is in an attachment to an e-mail. Once the participant correctly answers the question, the section 402(f) notice is then delivered to the participant via e-mail.

(ii) *Conclusion.* In this *Example 1,* Plan A's delivery of the section 402(f) notice satisfies the requirements of paragraph (b) of this section.

Example 2. (i) *Facts.* Plan B, a qualified plan, permits participants to request benefit distributions from the plan by e-mail. Under Plan B's system for such transactions, a participant must enter his or her account number and personal identification number (PIN) and this information must match the information in Plan B's records in order for the transaction to proceed. If a participant requests a distribution from Plan B by e-mail, the plan administrator provides the participant with a section 411(a)(11) notice in an attachment to an e-mail. Plan B sends the e-mail with a request for a computer generated notification that the message was received and opened. The e-mail instructs the participant to read the attachment for important information regarding the request for a distribution. In addition, the e-mail also provides that the participant may request the section 411(a)(11) notice on a written paper document and that, if the participant requests the notice on a written paper document, it will be provided at no charge. Plan B receives notification indicating that the e-mail was received and opened by the participant. The participant is effectively able to access the e-mail system used to make a participant election and consents to the distribution by e-mail. Within a reasonable period of time after the participant's consent to the distribution by e-mail, the plan administrator, by e-mail, sends confirmation of the terms (including the form) of the distribution to the participant and advises the participant that the participant may request the confirmation on a written paper document that will be provided at no charge.

(ii) *Conclusion.* In this *Example 2,* Plan B's delivery of the section 411(a)(11) notice and the transmission of a participant's consent to a distribution satisfy the requirements of paragraphs (c) and (d) of this section.

Example 3. (i) *Facts.* Plan C, a qualified pension plan, permits participants to request plan loans through the Plan C's web site on the internet with the notarized consent of the spouse in accordance with applicable State law. Under Plan C's system for such transactions, a participant must enter his or her account number, personal identification number (PIN), and his or her e-mail address. The information entered by the participant must match the information in Plan C's records in order for the transaction to proceed. A participant may request a loan from Plan C by following the applicable instructions on Plan C's web site. Participant M, a married participant, is effectively able to access the web site available to apply for a loan and completes the forms on the web site for obtaining the loan. The forms include attachments setting forth the terms of the loan agreement and all other required information. Participant M is then instructed to submit to the plan administrator a notarized spousal consent form. Participant M and M's spouse go to a notary public and the notary witnesses Participant M's spouse signing the spousal consent for the loan agreement. After witnessing M's spouse signing the spousal consent, the notary public sends an e-mail with an electronic acknowledgement that is attached to or logically associated with the signature of M's spouse to the plan administrator. The electronic acknowledgement is in accordance with section 101(g) of E-SIGN and the relevant state law applicable to notary publics. After the plan receives the e-mail, Plan C sends an e-mail to the participant, giving the participant a reasonable period to review and confirm the loan application or to determine whether the application should be modified or rescinded. In addition, the e-mail to the participant also provides that the participant may request the plan loan application on a written paper document and that, if the participant requests the written paper document, it will be provided at no charge.

(ii) *Conclusion.* In this *Example 3,* the transmissions of the loan agreement and the spousal consent satisfy the requirements of paragraph (d) of this section.

Example 4. (i) *Facts.* A qualified profit-sharing plan (Plan D) permits participants to request distributions through an automated telephone system. Under Plan D's system for such transactions, a participant must enter his or her account number and personal identification number (PIN); this information must match that in Plan D's records in order for the transaction to proceed. Plan D provides only the following distribution options: single-sum payment; and annual installments over 5, 10, or 20 years. A participant may request a distribution from Plan D by following the applicable instructions on the automated telephone system. After the participant has requested a distribution, the automated telephone system recites the section 411(a)(11) notice to the participant. The automated telephone system also advises the participant that he or she may request the notice on a written paper document and that, if the participant requests the notice on a written paper document, it will be provided at no charge. The participants are effectively able to access the automated telephone system used to make a participant election. The automated telephone system requires a participant to review and confirm the terms (including the form) of the distribution before the transaction is completed. After the participant has given consent, the automated telephone system confirms the distribution to the participant and advises the participant that he or she may request the confirmation on a written paper document that will be provided at no charge.

(ii) *Conclusion.* In this *Example 4*, because Plan D has relatively few and simple distribution options, the provision of the section 411(a)(11) notice through the automated telephone system is no less understandable to the participant than a written paper notice for purposes of paragraph (a)(4) of this section. In addition, the automated telephone procedures of Plan D satisfy the requirements of paragraphs (c) and (d) of this section.

Example 5. (i) *Facts.* Same facts as *Example 4*, except that, pursuant to Plan D's system for processing such transactions, a participant who so requests is transferred to a customer service representative whose conversation with the participant is recorded. The customer service representative provides the section 411(a)(11) notice from a prepared text and processes the participant's distribution in accordance with the predetermined instructions from the plan administrator.

(ii) *Conclusion.* Like in *Example 4*, because Plan D has relatively few and simple distribution options, the provision of the section 411(a)(11) notice through the automated telephone system is no less understandable to the participant than a written paper notice for purposes of paragraph (a)(4) of this section. Further, in this *Example 5*, the customer service telephone procedures of Plan D satisfy the requirements of paragraphs (c) and (d) of this section.

Example 6. (i) *Facts.* Plan E, a qualified plan, permits participants to request distributions by e-mail on the employer's e-mail system. Under this system, a participant must enter his or her account number and personal identification number (PIN). This information must match that in Plan E's records in order for the transaction to proceed. If a participant requests a distribution by e-mail, the plan administrator provides the participant with a section 411(a)(11) notice by e-mail. The plan administrator also advises the participant by e-mail that he or she may request the section 411(a)(11) notice on a written paper document and that, if the participant requests the notice on a written paper document, it will be provided at no charge. Participant N requests a distribution and receives the section 411(a)(11) notice from the plan administrator by reply e-mail. However, before Participant N elects a distribution, N terminates employment. Following termination of employment, Participant N no longer has access to the employer's e-mail system.

(ii) *Conclusion.* In this *Example 6*, Plan E does not satisfy the participant election requirements under paragraph (d) of this section because Participant N is not effectively able to access the electronic medium used to make the participant election. Plan E must provide Participant N with the opportunity to transmit the participant election through another system that Participant N is effectively able to access, such as the automated telephone systems described in *Example 4* and *Example 5* of this paragraph (f).

Par. 4. Section 1.402(f)-1 is amended by:

(1) Revising A-5.

(2) Removing Q&A-6.

The revision reads as follows:

§ *1.402(f)-1 Required explanation of eligible rollover distributions; questions and answers.*

* * * * *

A-5. Yes. See § 1.401(a)-21 of this chapter for rules permitting the use of electronic media to provide applicable notices to recipients with respect to employee benefit arrangements.

Par. 5. Section 1.411(a)-11 is amended by:

(1) Revising the text of paragraphs (f)(1) and (2).

(2) Removing paragraph (g).

The revisions read as follows:

§ *1.411(a)-11 Restriction and valuation of distributions.*

* * * * *

(f) * * *

(1) * * * The notice of a participant's rights described in paragraph (c)(2) of this section or the summary of that notice described in paragraph (c)(2)(iii)(B)(2) of this section must be provided on a written paper document. However, see § 1.401(a)-21 of this chapter for rules permitting the use of electronic media to provide applicable notices to recipients with respect to employee benefit arrangements.

(2) * * * The consent described in paragraphs (c)(2) and (3) of this section must be given on a written paper document. However, see § 1.401(a)-21(d) of this chapter for rules permitting the use of electronic media to transmit participant elections with respect to employee benefit arrangements.

Par. 6. Section 1.417(a)(3)-1 is amended by revising the text of paragraph (a)(3) to read as follows:

§ *1.417(a)(3)-1 Required explanation of qualified joint and survivor annuity and qualified preretirement survivor annuity.*

(a) * * *

(3) * * * A section 417(a)(3) explanation must be a written explanation. First class mail to the last known address of the participant is an acceptable delivery method for a section 417(a)(3) explanation. Likewise, hand delivery is acceptable. However, posting of the explanation is not considered provision of the section 417(a)(3) explanation. But see § 1.401(a)-21 of this chapter for rules permitting the use of electronic media to provide applicable notices to recipients with respect to employee benefit arrangements.

* * * * *

Par. 7. Section 1.7476-2 is amended by revising paragraph (c)(2) to read as follows:

§ *1.7476-2 Notice to interested parties.*

* * * * *

(c) * * *

(2) If the notice to interested parties is delivered using an electronic medium under a system that satisfies the applicable notice requirements of § 1.401(a)-21 of this chapter, the notice is deemed to be provided in a manner that satisfies the requirements of paragraph (c)(1) of this section.

* * * * *

PART 35—EMPLOYMENT TAX AND COLLECTION OF INCOME TAX AT THE SOURCE REGULATIONS UNDER THE TAX EQUITY AND FISCAL RESPONSIBILITY ACT OF 1982

Par. 8. The authority citation for part 35 continues to read, in part, as follows:

Authority: 26 U.S.C. 7805 * * *

Par. 9. Section 35.3405-1 is amended by:

(1) Revising d-35, A.

(2) Removing d-36, Q&A.

The revision reads as follows:

§ *35.3405-1 Questions and answers relating to withholding on pensions, annuities, and certain other deferred income.*

* * * * *

d-35. * * *

A. A payor may provide the notice required under section 3405 (including the abbreviated notice described in d-27 of § 35.3405-1T and the annual notice described in d-31 of § 35.3405-1T) to a payee on a written paper document. However, see § 1.401(a)-21 of this chapter for rules permitting the use of electronic media to provide applicable notices to recipients with respect to employee benefit arrangements.

PART 54—PENSION EXCISE TAXES

Par. 10. The authority citation for part 54 continues to read, in part, as follows:

Authority: 26 U.S.C. 7805 * * *

Par. 11. Section 54.4980F-1, Q&A-13, is amended as follows:

(1) Revising paragraph A-13 (c)(1)(ii).

(2) Removing paragraph A-13 (c) (1) (iii) and (c) (3).

The revision reads as follows:

§ 54.4980F-1 Notice requirements for certain pension plan amendments significantly reducing the rate of future benefit accrual.

* * * * *

A-13. * * *

(c) * * *

(1) * * *

(ii) The section 204(h) notice is delivered using an electronic medium under a system that satisfies the applicable notice requirements of § 1.401(a)-21.

* * * * *

Deputy Commissioner for Services and Enforcement.

CERTIFIED COPY

Guy R. Traynor

¶ 20,261P

IRS proposed regulations: Elimination of optional forms of benefit: Minimum vesting rules: *Central Laborers' Pension Fund v. Heinz:* **Notice of amendment reducing benefit accrual.—** The Treasury and IRS have issued proposed regulations regarding the timing of permissible changes in optional forms of benefits after the Supreme Court's decision in *Central Laborers' Pension Fund v. Heinz.* The proposed regulations address the interaction between the anti-cutback rules of Code Sec. 411(d)(6) and the nonforfeitability requirements of Code Sec. 411(a), which provides that an employee's right to an accrued benefit derived from employer contributions must become nonforfeitable within a specified period of service. In addition, the proposed rules provide a utilization test under which certain plan amendments with a de minimis effect on participants would be permitted to eliminate or reduce early retirement benefits, retirement-type subsidies, or optional forms of benefit, if certain conditions are met. The utilization test also is used to determine whether a plan may be amended to eliminate all of the optional forms of benefit within a generalized optional form without having to satisfy the de minimis requirements of Reg. § 1.411(d)-3(e) (revised in final regulations issued concurrently at 70 FR 47109, August 12, 2005) (see preamble to final regulations at ¶ 24,507Y).

The proposed regulations, which were published in the Federal Register on August 12, 2005 (70 FR 47155), and technically corrected on September 13, 2005 (70 FR 53973), are reproduced below.

DEPARTMENT OF TREASURY

Internal Revenue Service

26 CFR Part 1

[REG-156518-04]

RIN 1545-BE10

Section 411(d) (6) Protected Benefits

AGENCY: Internal Revenue Service (IRS), Treasury.

ACTION: Notice of proposed rulemaking and notice of public hearing.

SUMMARY: This document contains proposed regulations providing guidance on certain issues relating to the anti-cutback rules of section 411(d)(6) of the Internal Revenue Code, which generally protect accrued benefits, early retirement benefits, retirement-type subsidies, and optional forms of benefit under qualified retirement plans. The proposed regulations would address the interaction between the anti-cutback rules of section 411(d)(6) and the nonforfeitability requirements of section 411(a), and would also provide a utilization test under which certain plan amendments would be permitted to eliminate or reduce certain early retirement benefits, retirement-type subsidies, or optional forms of benefit. These proposed regulations would generally affect sponsors of, and participants in, qualified retirement plans.

DATES: Written or electronic comments must be received by November 10, 2005.

Requests to speak (with outlines of oral comments to be discussed) at the public hearing scheduled for December 6, 2005, at 10 a.m. must be received by November 15, 2005.

ADDRESSES: Send submissions to: CC:PA:LPD:PR (REG-156518-04), room 5203, Internal Revenue Service, PO Box 7604, Ben Franklin Station, Washington, DC 20044. Submissions may be hand-delivered Monday through Friday between the hours of 8 a.m. and 4 p.m. to CC:PA:LPD:PR (REG-156518-04), Courier(s Desk, Internal Revenue Service, 1111 Constitution Avenue, NW., Washington, DC. Alternatively, taxpayers may submit comments electronically, via the IRS Internet site at *www.irs.gov/regs* or via the Federal eRulemaking Portal at *www.regulations.gov* (indicate IRS and REG 156518-04). The public hearing will be held in the Auditorium, Internal Revenue Building, 1111 Constitution Avenue, NW., Washington, DC.

FOR FURTHER INFORMATION CONTACT: Concerning the proposed regulations, Pamela R. Kinard at (202) 622-6060; concerning submissions of comments, the hearing, and the requests to be placed on the building access list to attend the hearing, contact Treena Garrett, (202) 622-7180 (not toll-free numbers).

SUPPLEMENTARY INFORMATION:

Background

This document contains proposed amendments to 26 CFR part 1 under section 411(d)(6) of the Internal Revenue Code (Code). These proposed regulations, when finalized, would revise Treasury Regulations

§ 1.411(d)-3 to provide guidance on when a plan amendment may alter a benefit entitlement with respect to benefits accrued before the date of the amendment to add a condition that is permitted under section 411(a). These rules are intended to reflect the holding in *Central Laborers' Pension Fund v. Heinz*, 541 U.S. 739 (June 7, 2004). The proposed regulations would also provide a new method — a utilization test — under which a plan amendment is permitted to eliminate or reduce an early retirement benefit, a retirement-type subsidy, or an optional form of benefit.

Section 411(a) generally provides that an employee's right to the accrued benefit derived from employer contributions must become nonforfeitable within a specified period of service. Section 411(a)(3) provides circumstances under which an employee's benefit is permitted to be forfeited without violating section 411(a). Section 411(a)(3)(B) specifically provides that a right to an accrued benefit derived from employer contributions is not treated as forfeitable solely because the plan provides that the payment of benefits is suspended for such period as the employee is employed, subsequent to the commencement of payment of such benefits: (1) in the case of a plan other than a multiemployer plan, by the employer who maintains the plan under which such benefits were being paid; and (2) in the case of a multiemployer plan, in the same industry, the same trade or craft, and the same geographic area covered by the plan as when such benefits commenced.

The definition of employment for which benefit payments are permitted to be suspended is further described in 29 CFR 2530.203-3 of the Department of Labor Regulations, which interprets section 203(a)(3)(B) of the Employee Retirement Income Security Act of 1974 (ERISA), as amended, the counterpart to section 411(a)(3)(B) of the Code. Employment that satisfies the conditions described in section 203(a)(3)(B) of ERISA and the regulations thereunder is referred to as "section 203(a)(3)(B) service." See 29 CFR 2530.203-3(c).

Section 411(d)(6)(A) provides that a plan is treated as not satisfying the requirements of section 411 if the accrued benefit of a participant is decreased by an amendment of the plan, other than an amendment described in section 412(c)(8) of the Code or section 4281 of ERISA. Section 411(d)(6)(B) provides that a plan amendment that has the effect of eliminating or reducing an early retirement benefit or a retirement-type subsidy, or eliminating an optional form of benefit, with respect to benefits attributable to service before the amendment is treated as impermissibly reducing accrued benefits. For a retirement-type subsidy, this protection applies only with respect to an employee who satisfies the preamendment conditions for the subsidy (either before or after the amendment). Section 411(d)(6)(B) also authorizes the Secretary of the Treasury to provide, through regulations, that section 411(d)(6)(B) does not apply to any plan amendment that eliminates optional forms of benefit (other than a plan amendment that has the effect of eliminating or reducing an early retirement benefit or a retirement-type subsidy).

Section 645(b)(1) of the Economic Growth and Tax Relief Reconciliation Act of 2001, Public Law 107-16 (115 Stat. 38) (EGTRRA) amended section 411(d)(6)(B) of the Code to direct the Secretary of the Treasury to issue regulations providing that section 411(d)(6)(B) does not apply to any amendment that reduces or eliminates early retirement benefits or retirement-type subsidies that create significant burdens or complexities for the plan and plan participants unless such amendment adversely affects the rights of any participant in a more than de minimis manner.

Section 204(g) of ERISA contains parallel rules to section 411(d)(6) of the Code, including a similar directive to the Secretary of the Treasury to issue regulations providing that section 204(g) of ERISA does not apply to any amendment that reduces or eliminates early retirement benefits or retirement-type subsidies that create significant burdens or complexities for the plan and plan participants unless such amendment adversely affects the rights of any participant in a more than de minimis manner. Under section 101 of Reorganization Plan No. 4 of 1978 (43 FR 47713) and section 204(g) of ERISA, the Secretary of the Treasury has interpretive jurisdiction over the subject matter addressed in these proposed regulations for purposes of ERISA, as well as the Code. Thus, these proposed Treasury regulations issued under section 411(d)(6) of the Code apply as well for purposes of section 204(g) of ERISA.

On July 11, 1988, final regulations (TD 8212) under section 411(d)(6) were published in the **Federal Register** (53 FR 26050). These regulations are contained in § 1.411(d)-4.

In conjunction with the publication of these proposed regulations, final regulations (TD 9219) under sections 411(d)(6) and 4980F are being published elsewhere in the Rules and Regulations portion of this issue in the **Federal Register**. Those final regulations are contained in § 1.411(d)-3, which sets forth conditions under which a plan amendment is permitted to eliminate an optional form of benefit and to eliminate or reduce an early retirement benefit or a retirement-type subsidy that creates significant burdens or complexities for the plan and its participants, but only if the elimination does not adversely affect the rights of any participant in a more than de minimis manner. However, those regulations reserve 2 topics for later guidance — the utilization test (currently reserved in § 1.411(d)-3(f)) and the interaction of the permitted forfeiture rules under section 411(a) with the anti-cutback rules under section 411(d)(6) (currently reserved in § 1.411(d)-3(a)(3)). These proposed regulations would address these 2 topics as described below.

In *Central Laborers'*, the plaintiffs were 2 inactive participants in a multiemployer pension plan who commenced payment of their benefits in 1996 after qualifying for subsidized early retirement payments. The plan terms required that payments be suspended if a participant engaged in "disqualifying employment." At the time of their commencement of benefits, the plan defined disqualifying employment to include only employment covered by the plan, but not work as a construction supervisor. Both participants were employed as construction supervisors after they commenced payment of benefits. Although the 2 participants' benefit payments were not suspended in 1996, the plan was amended in 1998 to expand its definition of disqualifying employment to include any employment in the same trade or craft, industry, and geographic area covered by the plan, and the plan stopped payments to the 2 participants on account of their disqualifying employment as construction supervisors. The 2 participants sued to recover the suspended payments, claiming that the amendment expanding the plan's suspension provisions violated section 204(g) of ERISA (the counterpart to section 411(d)(6) of the Code).

The Supreme Court, holding for the 2 participants, ruled that section 204(g) of ERISA prohibits a plan amendment expanding the categories of post-retirement employment that result in suspension of the payment of early retirement benefits already accrued. The Court found that, while ERISA permits certain conditions that are elements of the benefit itself (such as suspensions under section 411(a)(3)(B) of the Code or section 203(a)(3)(B) of ERISA), such a condition may not be imposed after a benefit has accrued, and that the right to receive benefit payments on a certain date may not be limited by a new condition narrowing that right. The Court agreed with the 7th Circuit that "[a] participant's benefits cannot be understood without reference to the conditions imposed on receiving those benefits, and an amendment placing materially greater restrictions on the receipt of the benefit 'reduces' the benefit just as surely as a decrease in the size of the monthly benefit." *Central Laborers'* at 744, quoting *Heinz v. Central Laborers' Pension Fund*, 303 F.3d 802, 805 (7th Cir. 2002).

Rev. Proc. 2005-23 (2005-18 I.R.B. 991) limits the retroactive application of *Central Laborers'* for qualified plans under section 401(a) pursuant to the Commissioner's authority under section 7805(b)(8). The

revenue procedure provides that the IRS will not disqualify a plan solely on account of a plan amendment adopted before June 7, 2004 that violated section 411(d)(6) by adding or expanding a suspension of benefit provision permitted under section 411(a)(3) if certain requirements are satisfied. These requirements include the adoption of a reforming amendment that provides for the payment of benefits retroactive to June 7, 2004, to affected plan participants. Rev. Proc. 2005-23 does not address participants' rights to recover benefits under Title I of ERISA.

Rev. Proc. 2005-23 states that Treasury and the IRS intend to propose regulations that reflect the holding in *Central Laborers'*. The revenue procedure provides that the proposed regulations will provide guidance on when an amendment may add a benefit entitlement condition that is permitted under the vesting rules with respect to benefits accrued before the date of the amendment. Those rules are contained in these proposed regulations.

Explanation of Provisions

Interaction of the Permitted Forfeiture Rules Under Section 411(a) with the Anti-Cutback Rules Under Section 411(d)(6)

The proposed regulations would address the interaction of the vesting rules in section 411(a) with the anti-cutback rules in section 411(d)(6), taking into account the decision in *Central Laborers'*. The regulations would provide that a plan amendment that decreases accrued benefits, or otherwise places greater restrictions on the rights to section 411(d)(6) protected benefits violates section 411(d)(6), even if the amendment merely adds a restriction or condition on receipt of section 411(d)(6) protected benefits that is otherwise permitted under the vesting rules in section 411(a)(3) through (11). The proposed regulations would further provide that such a plan amendment is permitted under section 411(d)(6) to the extent it applies with respect to benefits accruing after the applicable amendment date.

The proposed regulations include 3 examples illustrating this rule. One example includes facts similar to *Central Laborers'*. Another example illustrates the interaction of section 411(d)(6) with the rule of parity in section 411(a)(6)(D). The final example addresses how a plan amendment that changes the plan's vesting schedule would violate section 411(d)(6) if the amendment were to place greater restrictions on the rights to section 411(d)(6) protected benefits. This example illustrates that the application of this section 411(d)(6) rule to a plan amendment changing a plan's vesting schedule is in addition to the requirements under section 411(a)(10)(A) (requiring that the nonforfeitable percentage of a participant's accrued benefit as of the applicable amendment date not be decreased by the plan amendment) and under section 411(a)(10)(B) (requiring that the plan permit each participant having not less than 3 years of service to elect to have his or her nonforfeitable percentage computed without regard to the plan amendment). Thus, if a plan amendment changes the plan's vesting schedule, the amendment must not place greater restrictions (including vesting restrictions) on a participant's rights to previously accrued benefits, and must also comply with section 411(a)(10). As indicated in the example, both of these requirements are satisfied for an amendment changing a plan's vesting schedule if each plan participant is entitled to benefits based on the greater of the new and old vesting schedules.

While the proposed regulations address the addition of conditions specifically described in section 411(a), these rules would also apply in other situations. For example, if a plan provides section 411(d)(6) protected benefits that are conditioned on the reemployment of the participant, then a plan amendment adding additional restrictions with respect to benefits already accrued on those benefits is required to satisfy section 411(d)(6). However, a plan amendment is permitted to add restrictions with respect to future accruals.

Utilization Test

The proposed regulations would provide that a plan is permitted to be amended to eliminate optional forms of benefit that comprise a generalized optional form[1] for a participant with respect to benefits accrued before the applicable amendment date if certain requirements relating to the use of the generalized optional form are satisfied. However, under the utilization test, a plan is not permitted to be amended to eliminate core options (i.e., a straight life annuity, a 75% joint and contingent annuity, a 10-year term certain and life annuity, and the most valuable option for a participant with a short life expectancy). In order to eliminate a noncore optional form of benefit under the proposed utilization test, 2 conditions must be satisfied: (1) the

---

[1] The term *generalized optional form* is defined in § 1.411(d)-3(g)(8) as a group of optional forms of benefit that are identical except for differences due to the actuarial factors that are used to determine the amount of the distributions under those optional forms of benefit and the annuity starting dates.

generalized optional form is available to a substantial number of participants during the relevant look-back period and (2) no participant must have elected any optional form of benefit that is within its generalized optional form during such relevant look-back period.

If the utilization test is satisfied, the plan could be amended to eliminate all of the optional forms of benefit that comprise a generalized optional form without having to satisfy the burdensome and de minimis requirements of § 1.411(d)-3(e). Treasury and the IRS believe that the utilization test, by its nature, implicitly determines — by reference to participant's elections — which optional forms of benefit are considered valuable to plan participants. The fact that no participant in a substantial sample elected any optional form of benefit that is within a generalized optional form is a compelling indication that elimination of that the entire generalized optional form would not adversely affect the rights of any participant in a more than de minimis manner.

The utilization test would provide that the generalized optional form being eliminated must have been available to at least 100 participants who are taken into account during the look-back period. The look-back period under the utilization test in the proposed regulations is the 2 plan years immediately preceding the plan year in which the plan amendment eliminating the optional form of benefit is adopted. At least one of the plan years during the look-back period must be a 12-month plan year. If a plan does not have at least 100 participants who are taken into account during those 2 plan years, the look-back period is permitted to be expanded to be the 3, 4, or 5 plan years immediately preceding the plan year in which the plan amendment eliminating the optional form of benefit is adopted in order to have a look-back period that has at least 100 participants who are taken into account. If a plan does not have at least 100 participants who can be taken into account during the relevant 5-year period, the plan is not permitted to use the utilization test.

For purposes of the utilization test, a participant is generally taken into account only if during the look-back period the participant was eligible to elect to commence payment of an optional form of benefit that is part of the generalized optional form being eliminated. However, a participant would not be taken into account if the participant: did not elect any optional form of benefit with an annuity commencement date that is within the look-back period; elected an optional form of benefit that includes a single-sum distribution that applies with respect to at least 25% of the participant's accrued benefit; elected an optional form of benefit that was only available during a limited period of time that contained a retirement-type subsidy that was not extended to the generalized optional form being eliminated; or elected an optional form of benefit with an annuity commencement date that is more than 10 years before normal retirement age.[2] Treasury and the IRS believe that, in light of these restrictions on participants who are permitted to be taken into account in applying the utilization test, the sample size of 100 participants who are eligible to elect the generalized optional form is sufficiently large to demonstrate that elimination of the generalized optional form would not adversely affect the rights of any plan participant in a more than de minimis manner.

Under the proposed regulations, a plan amendment eliminating a generalized optional form under the utilization rule cannot be applicable with respect to an optional form of benefit with an annuity commencement date that is earlier than the number of days in the maximum QJSA explanation period (as defined in § 1.411(d)-3(g)(9)) after the date the amendment is adopted. This waiting period is the same as the waiting period for the elimination of an optional form of benefit under the redundancy rule in § 1.411(d)-3(c)(1)(ii).

Proposed Effective Date

The rules relating to section 411(a) nonforfeitability provisions are proposed to be effective June 7, 2004, the date of the *Central Laborers'* decision. The rules relating to the utilization test are proposed to be effective for amendments adopted after December 31, 2006. With respect to the rules relating to the utilization test, these proposed regulations cannot be relied upon until they are adopted in final form in the **Federal Register**.

Special Analyses

It has been determined that these proposed regulations are not a significant regulatory action as defined in Executive Order 12866. Therefore a regulatory assessment is not required. It also has been determined that section 553(b) of the Administrative Procedure Act (5 U.S.C. chapter 5) does not apply to these regulations. Because these

regulations do not impose a collection of information on small entities, the Regulatory Flexibility Act (5 U.S.C. chapter 6) does not apply. Pursuant to section 7805(f) of the Code, these proposed regulations will be submitted to the Chief Counsel for Advocacy of the Small Business Administration for comment on their impact on small business.

Comments and Public Hearing

Before these proposed regulations are adopted as final regulations, consideration will be given to any written comments (a signed original and eight (8) copies) or electronic comments that are submitted timely to the IRS. The Treasury and IRS specifically request comments on the clarity of the proposed rules and how they can be made easier to understand. All comments will be available for public inspection and copying.

A public hearing has been scheduled for December 6, 2005, beginning at 10 a.m. in the Auditorium, Internal Revenue Building, 1111 Constitution Avenue, NW., Washington, DC. Due to building security procedures, visitors must enter at the main entrance, located at 1111 Constitution Avenue, NW. In addition, all visitors must present photo identification to enter the building. Because of access restrictions, visitors will not be admitted beyond the immediate entrance area more than 30 minutes before the hearing starts. For information about having your name placed on the building access list to attend the hearing, see the "FOR FURTHER INFORMATION CONTACT" portion of this preamble.

The rules of 26 CFR 601.601(a)(3) apply to the hearing. Persons who wish to present oral comments must submit written or electronic comments and an outline of the topics to be discussed and time to be devoted to each topic (signed original and eight (8) copies) by November 15, 2005. A period of 10 minutes will be allotted to each person for making comments. An agenda showing the scheduling of the speakers will be prepared after the deadline for receiving comments has passed. Copies of the agenda will be available free of charge at the hearing.

Drafting Information

The principal author of these proposed regulations is Pamela R. Kinard, Office of Division Counsel/Associate Chief Counsel (Tax Exempt and Government Entities), Internal Revenue Service. However, personnel from other offices of the Internal Revenue Service and Treasury Department participated in their development.

List of Subjects in 26 CFR Part 1

Income taxes, Reporting and recordkeeping requirements.

Proposed Amendments to the Regulations

Accordingly, 26 CFR part 1 is proposed to be amended as follows:

PART 1—INCOME TAXES

Paragraph 1. The authority citation for part 1 is amended by adding an entry in numerical order to read, in part, as follows:

Authority: 26 U.S.C. 7805 * * *

Section 1.411(d)-3 also issued under 26 U.S.C. 411(d)(6) and section 645(b) of the Economic Growth and Tax Relief Reconciliation Act of 2001, Pub. L. 107-16 (115 Stat. 38).* * *

Par. 2. Section 1.411(d)-3 is amended by:

1. Revising paragraph (a)(3).

2. Adding *Examples 3* and *4* to paragraph (a)(4).

3. Adding *Example 3* to paragraph (b)(4).

4. Revising paragraph (f).

5. Adding *Example 6* to paragraph (h).

6. Adding paragraphs (j)(3) and (j)(4).

The revisions and additions read as follows:

§ 1.411(d)-3 Section 411(d)(6) Protected Benefits.

* * * * *

(a) * * *

(3) *Application of section 411(a) nonforfeitability provisions with respect to section 411(d)(6) protected benefits.* The rules of this paragraph

---

[2] The term *annuity commencement date* is defined in § 1.411(d)-3(g)(3) as the annuity starting date, except that, in the case of a retroactive annuity starting date, *annuity* commencement date is the date of the first payment of benefits pursuant to a participant election of a retroactive annuity starting date, as defined in § 1.417(e)-1(b)(3)(iv).

(a) apply to a plan amendment that decreases a participant's accrued benefits, or otherwise places greater restrictions or conditions on a participant's rights to section 411(d)(6) protected benefits, even if the amendment merely adds a restriction or condition that is otherwise permitted under the vesting rules in section 411(a)(3) through (11). However, such an amendment does not violate section 411(d)(6) to the extent it applies with respect to benefits that accrue after the applicable amendment date.

* * * * *

(4) * * *

Example 3. (i) *Facts.* Employer N maintains Plan C, a qualified defined benefit plan under which an employee participates upon completion of 1 year of service and is vested in 100% of the employer-derived accrued benefit upon completion of 5 years of service. Plan C provides that a former employee's years of service prior to a break in service will be reinstated upon completion of 1 year of service after being rehired. Plan C has participants who have fewer than 5 years of service and who are accordingly 0% vested in their employer-derived

Completed years of service	Nonforfeitable percentage
Fewer than 3	0%
3	20%
4	40%
5	60%
6	80%
7	100%

(B) In January 2005, Employer O acquires Company X, which maintains Plan E, a qualified profit sharing plan under which each employee who has completed 5 years of service has a nonforfeitable right to 100% of the employer-derived accrued benefit. In 2006, Plan E is merged into Plan D. On the effective date for the merger, Plan D is amended to provide that the vesting schedule for participants of Plan E is the 7-year graded vesting schedule of Plan D. In accordance with section 411(a)(10)(A), the plan amendment provides that any participant of Plan E who had completed 5 years of service prior to the amendment is fully vested. In addition, as required under section 411(a)(10)(B), the amendment provides that any participant in Plan E who has at least 3 years of service prior to the amendment is permitted to make an irrevocable election to have the vesting of his or her nonforfeitable right to the employer-derived accrued benefit determined under either the 5-year cliff vesting schedule or the 7-year graded vesting schedule. Participant G, who has an account balance of $10,000 on the applicable amendment date, is a participant in Plan E with 2 years of service as of the applicable amendment date. As of the date of the merger, Participant G's nonforfeitable right to G's employer-derived accrued benefit is 0% under both the 7-year graded vesting schedule of Plan D and the 5-year cliff vesting schedule of Plan E.

(ii) *Conclusion.* Under paragraph (a)(3) of this section, the plan amendment does not satisfy the requirements of paragraph (a) of this section and violates section 411(d)(6), because the amendment places greater restrictions or conditions on the rights to section 411(d)(6) protected benefits with respect to G and any participant who has fewer than 7 years of service and who elected (or was made subject to) the new vesting schedule. A method of avoiding a section 411(d)(6) violation with respect to account balances attributable to benefits accrued as of the applicable amendment date and earnings thereon, would be for Plan D to provide for the vested percentage of G and each other participant in Plan E to be no less than the greater of the 2 vesting schedules (e.g., for G and each other participant in Plan E to be fully vested if the participant completes 5 years of service) for those account balances and earnings.

* * * * *

(b) * * *

(4) * * *

Example 3. (i) *Facts.* Plan C, a multiemployer defined benefit plan in a particular industry, provides that a participant may elect to commence distributions only if the participant is not currently employed by an employer maintaining the plan and provides that, if the participant has a specified number of years of service and attains a specified age, the distribution is without any actuarial reduction for commencement before normal retirement age. Since the plan's inception, Plan C has provided for suspension of pension benefits during periods of disquali-

accrued benefits. On December 31, 2007, effective January 1, 2008, Plan C is amended, in accordance with section 411(a)(6)(D), to provide that any nonvested participant who has 5 consecutive 1-year breaks in service and whose number of consecutive 1-year breaks in service exceeds his or her number of years of service before the breaks will have his or her pre-break service disregarded in determining vesting under the plan.

(ii) *Conclusion.* Under paragraph (a)(3) of this section, the plan amendment does not satisfy the requirements of paragraph (a) of this section, and thus violates section 411(d)(6), because the amendment places greater restrictions or conditions on the rights to section 411(d)(6) protected benefits, as of January 1, 2008, for participants who have fewer than 5 years of service, by restricting the ability of those participants to receive further vesting protections on benefits accrued as of that date.

Example 4. (i) *Facts*—(A) Employer O sponsors Plan D, a qualified profit sharing plan under which each employee has a nonforfeitable right to a percentage of his or her employer-derived accrued benefit based on the following table:

fying employment (ERISA section 203(a)(3)(B) service). Before 2007, the plan defined disqualifying employment to include any job as an electrician in the particular industry and geographic location to which Plan C applies. This definition of disqualifying employment did not cover a job as an electrician supervisor. In 2005, Participant E, having rendered the specified number of years of service and attained the specified age to retire with a fully subsidized early retirement benefit, retires from E's job as an electrician with Employer Y and starts a position with Employer Z as an electrician supervisor. Employer Z is not a participating employer in Plan C but is an employer in the same industry and geographic location as Employer Y. When E left service with Employer Y, E's position as a electrician supervisor was not disqualifying employment for purposes of Plan C's suspension of pension benefit provision, and E elects to commence benefit payments in 2005. In 2006, effective January 1, 2007, Plan C, in accordance with section 411(a)(3)(B), is amended to expand the definition of disqualifying employment to include any job (including supervisory positions) as an electrician in the same industry and geographic location to which Plan C applies. On January 1, 2007, E's pension benefits are suspended because of E's disqualifying employment as an electrician supervisor. (These facts are generally comparable to the facts in *Central Laborers' Pension Fund v. Heinz*, 541 U.S. 739 (June 7, 2004).)

(ii) *Conclusion.* Under paragraphs (a)(3) and (b)(1) of this section, the 2007 plan amendment violates section 411(d)(6), because the amendment places greater restrictions or conditions on a participant's rights to section 411(d)(6) protected benefits to the extent it applies with respect to benefits that accrued before January 1, 2007. The result would be the same even if the amendment did not apply to former employees and instead applied only to participants who were actively employed at the time of the applicable amendment.

* * * * *

(f) *Utilization test*—(1) *General rule.* A plan is permitted to be amended to eliminate all of the optional forms of benefit that comprise a generalized optional form (as defined in paragraph (g)(8) of this section) for a participant with respect to benefits accrued before the applicable amendment date if—

(i) None of the optional forms of benefit being eliminated is a core option, within the meaning of paragraph (g)(5) of this section;

(ii) The plan amendment is not applicable with respect to an optional form of benefit with an annuity commencement date that is earlier than the number of days in the maximum QJSA explanation period (as defined in paragraph (g)(9) of this section) after the date the amendment is adopted;

(iii) The generalized optional form has been available to at least 100 participants who are taken into account during the look-back period; and

(iv) No participant has elected any optional form of benefit that is part of the generalized optional form with an annuity commencement date that is within the look-back period.

(2) *Look-back period.* For purposes of this paragraph (f), the look-back period is the 2 plan years immediately preceding the plan year in which the plan amendment eliminating the generalized optional form is adopted. At least one of the plan years during the look-back period must be a 12-month plan year. However, if a plan does not have at least 100 participants who are taken into account under this paragraph (f) during those 2 plan years, the look-back period is permitted to be expanded to be the 3, 4, or 5 plan years immediately preceding the plan year in which the plan amendment eliminating the generalized optional form is adopted in order to have a look-back period that has at least 100 participants who are taken into account under this paragraph (f). If a plan does not have at least 100 participants who are taken into account under this paragraph (f) during the relevant 5-year period, the plan is not permitted to add more plan years to the look-back period and, accordingly, such a plan is not permitted to use the utilization test in this paragraph (f).

(3) *Participants taken into account.* Except as provided in this paragraph (f)(3), a participant is taken into account for purposes of this paragraph (f) only if the participant was eligible to elect to commence payment of an optional form of benefit that is part of the generalized optional form being eliminated with an annuity commencement date that is within the look-back period. However, a participant is not taken into account if the participant either—

(i) Did not elect any optional form of benefit with an annuity commencement date that was within the look-back period;

(ii) Elected an optional form of benefit that included a single-sum distribution that applied with respect to at least 25% of the participant's accrued benefit;

(iii) Elected an optional form of benefit that was only available during a limited period of time and that contained a retirement-type subsidy which at that annuity commencement date was not extended to the optional form of benefit with the same annuity commencement date that is part of the generalized optional form being eliminated; or

(iv) Elected an optional form of benefit with an annuity commencement date that was more than 10 years before normal retirement age.

(4) *Default elections.* For purposes of this paragraph (f), an election includes the payment of an optional form of benefit that applies in the absence of an affirmative election.

* * * * *

(h) * * *

Example 6. (i) *Facts involving elimination of noncore options using utilization test*—(A) *In general.* Plan G is a calendar year defined benefit plan under which participants may elect to commence distributions after termination of employment in the following actuarially equivalent

forms, with spousal consent, if applicable: a straight life annuity; a 50%, 75%, or 100% joint and contingent annuity; or a 5-year, 10-year, or 15-year term certain and life annuity. Participants whose benefits are under $5,000 are permitted to elect a single-sum distribution. The annuities offered under the plan are generally available both with and without a social security leveling feature. The social security leveling feature provides for an assumed commencement of social security benefits at any age selected by the participant between the ages of 62 and 67. Under Plan G, the normal retirement age is defined as age 65.

(B) *Utilization test.* In 2007, the plan sponsor of Plan G, after reviewing participants' benefit elections, determines that no participant in the 2 prior plan years (2005 and 2006) elected a 5-year term certain and life annuity with a social security leveling option. During the 2 prior plan years, Plan G has made the 5-year term certain and life annuity with a social security leveling option available to 142 participants who were at least age 55 and who elected an optional form of benefit with an annuity commencement date during that 2-year period. In addition, during 2005-06 plan years, 20 of the 142 participants elected a single-sum distribution and there was no retirement-type subsidy available for a limited period of time. Plan G, in accordance with paragraph (f)(1) of this section, is amended on September 1, 2007, effective as of January 1, 2008, to eliminate all 5-year term certain and life annuities with a social security leveling option for all annuity commencement dates on or after January 1, 2008.

(ii) *Conclusion.* The amendment satisfies the requirements of paragraph (f) of this section. First, the 5-year term certain and life annuity with a social security leveling option is not a core option as defined in paragraph (g)(5) of this section. Second, the plan amendment is not applicable with respect to an optional form of benefit with an annuity commencement date that is earlier than the number of days in the maximum QJSA explanation period after the date the amendment is adopted. Third, the 5-year term certain and life annuity with a social security leveling option has been available to at least 100 participants who are taken into account for purposes of paragraph (f)(4) of this section during the look-back period of 2005 and 2006. Fourth, during that period, no participant elected any optional form that is part of the generalized optional form being eliminated (i.e., the 5-year term and life annuity with a social security leveling option).

* * * * *

(j) * * *

(3) *Effective date for rules relating to section 411(a) nonforfeitability provisions.* The rules provided in paragraph (a)(3) of this section are effective June 7, 2004.

(4) *Effective date for rules relating to utilization test.* The rules provided in paragraph (f) of this section are effective for amendments adopted after December 31, 2006.

* * * * *

Deputy Commissioner for Services and Enforcement

¶ 20,261Q

IRS proposed regulations: Roth IRAs: Conversion of annuity: Valuation.—The Treasury and IRS have issued temporary and proposed regulations regarding the valuation of an annuity converted from a traditional IRA to a Roth IRA. The preamble to the temporary regulations, issued concurrently, is located at ¶ 24,507Z.

The proposed regulations, which were published in the Federal Register on August 22, 2005 (70 FR 48924), are reproduced below.

[4830-01-p]

DEPARTMENT OF THE TREASURY

Internal Revenue Service

26 CFR Part 1

[REG-122857-05]

RIN 1545-BE65

Converting an IRA Annuity to a Roth IRA

AGENCY: Internal Revenue Service (IRS), Treasury.

ACTION: Notice of proposed rulemaking by cross-reference to temporary regulations.

SUMMARY: In the Rules and Regulations section of this issue of the **Federal Register** , the IRS is issuing temporary regulations under section 408A of the Internal Revenue Code (Code). The temporary regulations provide guidance concerning the tax consequences of converting a non-Roth IRA annuity to a Roth IRA. The temporary regula-

tions affect individuals establishing Roth IRAs, beneficiaries under Roth IRAs, and trustees, custodians and issuers of Roth IRAs. The text of those temporary regulations also serves as the text of these proposed regulations.

DATES: Written or electronic comments and requests for a public hearing must be received by October 20, 2005.

ADDRESSES: Send submissions to: CC:PA:LPD:PR (REG-122857-05), room 5203, Internal Revenue Service, POB 7604, Ben Franklin Station, Washington, DC 20044. Submissions may be hand-delivered Monday through Friday between the hours of 8 a.m. and 4 p.m. to CC:PA:LPD:PR (REG-122857-05), Courier's Desk, Internal Revenue Service, 1111 Constitution Avenue, NW., Washington, DC. Alternatively, taxpayers may submit comments electronically via the IRS Internet site at www.irs.gov/regs or the Federal eRulemaking Portal at www.regulations.gov (IRS-REG-122857-05).

FOR FURTHER INFORMATION CONTACT: Concerning the regulations, Cathy A. Vohs, 202-622-6060; concerning submissions and requests for a public hearing, contact Treena Garrett, 202-622-7180 (not toll-free numbers).

SUPPLEMENTARY INFORMATION:

Background

Temporary regulations in the Rules and Regulations portion of this issue of the **Federal Register** amend the Income Tax Regulations (26 CFR part 1) relating to section 408A. The temporary regulations (§ 1.408A-4T) contain rules concerning the tax consequences of converting a traditional IRA annuity to a Roth IRA. The text of those temporary regulations also serves as the text of these proposed regulations. The preamble to the temporary regulations explains the temporary and proposed regulations.

Applicability Date

These regulations are proposed to be applicable to any Roth IRA conversion where an annuity contract is distributed or treated as distributed from a traditional IRA on or after August 19, 2005. No implication is intended concerning whether or not a rule to be adopted in these regulations is applicable law for taxable years ending before that date.

Special Analyses

It has been determined that this notice of proposed rulemaking is not a significant regulatory action as defined in Executive Order 12866. Therefore, a regulatory assessment is not required. It also has been determined that section 553(b) of the Administrative Procedure Act (5 U.S.C. chapter 5) does not apply to these proposed regulations, and, because these regulations do not impose a collection of information on small entities, the Regulatory Flexibility Act (5 U.S.C. chapter 6) does not apply. Pursuant to section 7805(f) of the Code, these proposed regulations will be submitted to the Chief Counsel for Advocacy of the Small Business Administration for comment on its impact on small business.

Comments and Requests for a Public Hearing

Before these proposed regulations are adopted as final regulations, consideration will be given to any written (a signed original and eight (8) copies) or electronic comments that are submitted timely to the IRS. The IRS and Treasury Department request comments on the clarity of the proposed rules and how they can be made easier to understand. Comments are specifically requested regarding the proposed additional guidance discussed in the preamble to the Temporary Regulations under section 408A (i.e., § 1.408A-4T). The IRS and Treasury Department also request comments regarding whether the method used to calculate the fair market value of an annuity contract that is converted to a Roth IRA should also apply for purposes of determining the fair market value of an annuity contact under sections 408(e) and 401(a)(9). All comments will be available for public inspection and copying. A public hearing will be scheduled if requested in writing by any person that timely submits written comments. If a public hearing is scheduled, notice of the date, time, and place for the public hearing will be published in the **Federal Register**.

Drafting Information

The principal author of these proposed regulations is Cathy A. Vohs of the Office of the Division Counsel/Associate Chief Counsel (Tax Exempt and Government Entities). However, other personnel from the IRS and Treasury Department participated in the development of these regulations.

List of Subjects in 26 CFR Part 1

Income taxes, Reporting and recordkeeping requirements.

Proposed Amendments to the Regulations

Accordingly, 26 CFR part 1 is proposed to be amended as follows:

PART 1—INCOME TAXES

Paragraph 1. The authority citation for Part 1 continues to read, in part, as follows:

Authority: 26 U.S.C. 7805 * * *

§ 1.408A-4 also issued under 26 U.S.C. 408A * * *

Par. 2. Section 1.408A-4 is amended by adding, in numerical order, Q-14 and A-14, to read as follows:

§ 1. 408A-4 Converting amounts to Roth IRAs.

* * * * *

Q-14. [The text of proposed regulation § 1.408A-4, Q-14 is the same as the text of § 1.408A-4T, Q-14 published elsewhere in this issue of the **Federal Register**].

A-14. [The text of proposed regulation § 1.408A-4, A-14, is the same as the text of § 1.408A-4T, A-14, published elsewhere in this issue of the **Federal Register**].

Deputy Commissioner for Services and Enforcement.

Mark E. Matthews

¶ 20,261R

IRS proposed regulations: Employee stock ownership plans (ESOPs): Redemption of securities: Dividends paid deduction.— The IRS has released proposed regulations regarding dividends paid deductions of corporations maintaining employee stock ownership plans (ESOPs). The regs address issues that have arisen under the application of stock reacquisition expenses under Code Sec. 162(k) and deductions for dividends paid on employer securities under Code Sec. 404(k). The proposed regulations address which corporation is entitled to the deduction under Code Sec. 404(k) when stock held in an ESOP is redeemed and the applicable employer securities are not securities of the corporation or corporations that maintain the plan. Secondly, the regulations address whether payments in redemption of stock held by an ESOP are deductible.

The proposed regulations, which were published in the Federal Register on August 25, 2005 (70 FR 49897), are reproduced below.

DEPARTMENT OF THE TREASURY

Internal Revenue Service

26 CFR Part 1

[REG-133578-05]

RIN 1545-BE74

Dividends Paid Deduction for Stock Held in Employee Stock Ownership Plan

AGENCY: Internal Revenue Service (IRS), Treasury.

ACTION: Notice of proposed rulemaking.

SUMMARY: This document contains proposed regulations under sections 162(k) and 404(k) of the Internal Revenue Code (Code) relating to employee stock ownership plans (ESOPs). The regulations provide guidance concerning which corporation is entitled to the deduction for applicable dividends under section 404(k). These regulations also clarify that a payment in redemption of employer securities held by an ESOP is not deductible. These regulations will affect administrators of, employers maintaining, participants in, and beneficiaries of ESOPs. In addition, they will affect corporations that make distributions in redemption of stock held in an ESOP.

DATES: Written or electronic comments and requests for a public hearing must be received by November 23, 2005.

ADDRESSES: Send submissions to: CC:PA:LPD:PR (REG-133578-05), room 5203, Internal Revenue Service, POB 7604, Ben Franklin Station, Washington, DC 20044. Submissions may be hand-delivered Monday through Friday between the hours of 8 a.m. and 4 p.m. to: CC:PA:LPD:PR (REG-133578-05), Courier's Desk, Internal Revenue Service, 1111 Constitution Avenue, NW., Washington D.C. Alternatively, taxpayers may submit comments electronically directly to the IRS Internet site at *www.irs.gov/regs*, or via the Federal eRulemaking Portal at *www.regulations.gov* (IRS-REG-133578-05).

FOR FURTHER INFORMATION CONTACT: Concerning the regulations, John T. Ricotta at (202) 622-6060 with respect to section 404(k) or Martin Huck at (202) 622-7750 with respect to section 162(k); concerning submission of comments or to request a public hearing, Robin Jones at (202) 622-7180 (not toll-free numbers).

SUPPLEMENTARY INFORMATION:

Background and Explanation of Provisions

This document contains proposed regulations under sections 162(k) and 404(k) of the Internal Revenue Code (Code). These regulations address two issues that have arisen in the application of these sections. The first issue arises in a case in which the applicable employer securities held in an employee stock ownership plan (ESOP) are not securities of the corporation or corporations that maintain the plan. The issue is which corporation is entitled to the deduction under section 404(k) for certain dividends paid with respect to the stock held in the ESOP. The second issue is whether payments in redemption of stock held by an ESOP are deductible.

Code and Regulations

Section 404(a) provides that contributions paid by an employer to or under a stock bonus, pension, profit sharing, or annuity plan are deductible under section 404(a), if they would be otherwise deductible, within the limitations of that section. Section 404(k)(1) provides that, in the case of a C corporation, there is allowed as a deduction for a taxable year the amount of any applicable dividend paid in cash by such corporation during the taxable year with respect to applicable employer securities held by an ESOP. The deduction under section 404(k) is in addition to the deductions allowed under section 404(a).

Section 4975(e)(7) provides, in relevant part, that an ESOP is a defined contribution plan that is a stock bonus plan qualified under section 401(a) and designed to invest primarily in qualifying employer securities. Section 4975(e)(8) states that the term *qualifying employer security* means any employer security within the meaning of section 409(l). Section 409(l) generally provides that the term *employer security* means common stock issued by the employer (or a corporation that is a member of the same controlled group) that is readily tradable on an established securities market, if the corporation (or a member of the controlled group) has common stock that is readily tradable on an established securities market. Section 409(l)(4)(A) provides that, for purposes of section 409(l), the term *controlled group of corporations* has the meaning given to that term by section 1563(a) (determined without regard to subsections (a)(4) and (e)(3)(C) of section 1563). Section 409(l)(4)(B) provides that, for purposes of section 409(l)(4)(A), if a common parent owns directly stock possessing at least 50 percent of the voting power of all classes of stock and at least 50 percent of each class of nonvoting stock in a first tier subsidiary, such subsidiary (and all corporations below it in the chain which would meet the 80 percent test of section 1563(a) if the first tier subsidiary were the common parent) are treated as includible corporations.

Section 404(k)(2), for taxable years beginning on or after January 1, 2002, generally provides that the term *applicable dividend* means any dividend which, in accordance with the plan provisions — (i) is paid in cash to the participants in the plan or their beneficiaries, (ii) is paid to the plan and is distributed in cash to participants in the plan or their beneficiaries not later than 90 days after the close of the plan year in which paid, (iii) is, at the election of such participants or their beneficiaries — (I) payable as provided in clause (i) or (ii), or (II) paid to the plan and reinvested in qualifying employer securities, or (iv) is used to make payments on a loan described in section 404(a)(9), the proceeds of which were used to acquire the employer securities (whether or not allocated to participants) with respect to which the dividend is paid. Under section 404(k)(4), the deduction is allowable in the taxable year of the corporation in which the dividend is paid or distributed to a participant or beneficiary.

Prior to 2002, section 404(k)(5)(A) provided that the Secretary may disallow the deduction under section 404(k) for any dividend if the Secretary determines that such dividend constitutes, in substance, an evasion of taxation. Section 662(b) of the Economic Growth and Tax Relief Reconciliation Act of 2001 (115 Stat. 38, 2001) amended section 404(k)(5)(A) to provide that the Secretary may disallow a deduction under section 404(k) for any dividend the Secretary determines constitutes, in substance, an avoidance or evasion of taxation. The amendment is effective for tax years after December 31, 2001.

Section 162(k)(1) generally provides that no deduction otherwise allowable under chapter 1 of the Code is allowed for any amount paid or incurred by a corporation in connection with the reacquisition of its stock or the stock of any related person (as defined in section 465(b)(3)(C)). The legislative history of section 162(k) states that the phrase "in connection with" is "intended to be construed broadly." H.R. Conf. Rep. No. 99-841, at 168 (1986).

Corporation Entitled to Section 404(k) Deduction

An ESOP may benefit employees of more than one corporation. In addition, an ESOP may be maintained by a corporation other than the payor of a dividend. In these cases, the issue arises as to which entity is entitled to the deduction provided under section 404(k). Assume, for example, that a publicly traded corporation owns all of the stock of a subsidiary. The subsidiary operates a trade or business with employees in the U.S. and maintains an ESOP that holds stock of its parent for its employees. If the parent distributes a dividend with respect to its stock

held in the ESOP maintained by the subsidiary, questions have arisen as to whether the parent or subsidiary is entitled to the deduction under section 404(k). This question arises in cases in which the parent and subsidiary file a consolidated return as well as in cases in which the parent and subsidiary do not file a consolidated return.

The IRS and Treasury Department believe that the statutory language of section 404(k) clearly provides that only the payor of the applicable dividend is entitled to the deduction under section 404(k), regardless of whether the employees of multiple corporations benefit under the ESOP and regardless of whether another member of the controlled group maintains the ESOP. Therefore, in the example above, the parent, not the subsidiary, is entitled to the deduction under section 404(k).

Treatment of Payments Made to Reacquire Stock

Some corporations have claimed deductions under section 404(k) for payments in redemption of stock held by an ESOP that are used to make benefit distributions to participants or beneficiaries, including distributions of a participant's account balance upon severance from employment. These taxpayers have argued that the payments in redemption qualify as dividends under sections 301 and 316 and, therefore, are deductible under section 404(k).

In Rev. Rul. 2001-6 (2001-1 C.B. 491), the IRS concluded that section 162(k) bars a deduction for payments made in redemption of stock from an ESOP. This conclusion was based on the fact that section 162(k)(1) disallows a deduction for payments paid in connection with the reacquisition of an issuer's stock and that the redemption payments are such payments. The IRS also concluded that such payments were not applicable dividends under section 404(k)(1). The IRS reasoned that allowing a deduction for redemption amounts would vitiate important rights and protections for recipients of ESOP distributions, including the right to reduce taxes by utilizing the return of basis provisions under section 72, the right to make rollovers of ESOP distributions received upon separation from service, and the protection against involuntary cash-outs. Finally, the IRS stated that a deduction under section 404(k)(1) for such amounts would constitute, in substance, an evasion of tax.

In *Boise Cascade Corporation v. United States*, 329 F.3d 751 (9 th Cir. 2003), the Court of Appeals for the Ninth Circuit held that payments made by a corporation to redeem its stock held by its ESOP were deductible as dividends paid under section 404(k), and that the deduction was not precluded by section 162(k). The court reasoned that the distribution by the ESOP of the redemption proceeds to the participants was a transaction separate from the redemption transaction. Therefore, the court concluded that the distribution did not constitute a payment *in connection with* the corporation's reacquisition of its stock, and section 162(k) did not bar the deduction of such payments.

For the reasons stated in Rev. Rul. 2001-6, the IRS and Treasury Department continue to believe that allowing a deduction for amounts paid to reacquire stock is inconsistent with the intent of, and policies underlying, section 404. In addition, the IRS and Treasury Department believe that allowing such a deduction would constitute, in substance, an avoidance or evasion of taxation within the meaning of section 404(k)(5)(A) because it would allow a corporation to claim two deductions for the same economic cost: once for the value of the stock originally contributed to the ESOP and again for the amount paid to redeem the same stock. See *Charles Ilfeld Co. v. Hernandez*, 292 U.S. 62 (1934). Moreover, despite the Ninth's Circuit's conclusion in *Boise Cascade*, the IRS and Treasury Department continue to believe that, even if a payment in redemption of stock held by an ESOP were to qualify as an applicable dividend, section 162(k) would disallow a deduction for that amount because such payment would be in connection with the reacquisition of the corporation's stock.

This notice of proposed rulemaking, therefore, includes proposed regulations under section 404(k) that confirm that payments made to reacquire stock held by an ESOP are not deductible under section 404(k) because such payments do not constitute applicable dividends under section 404(k)(2) and a deduction for such payments would constitute, in substance, an avoidance or evasion of taxation within the meaning of section 404(k)(5). It also includes proposed regulations under section 162(k) that provide that section 162(k), subject to certain exceptions, disallows any deduction for amounts paid or incurred by a corporation in connection with the reacquisition of its stock or the stock of any related person (as defined in section 465(b)(3)(C)). The proposed regulations also provide that amounts paid or incurred in connection with the reacquisition of stock include amounts paid by a corporation to reacquire its stock from an ESOP that are then distributed by the ESOP to its participants (or their beneficiaries) or otherwise used in a manner described in section 404(k)(2)(A).

Proposed Effective Date

These regulations are proposed to be effective on the date of issuance of final regulations. However, before these regulations become effective, the IRS will continue to assert in any matter in controversy outside of the Ninth Circuit that sections 162(k) and 404(k) disallow a deduction for payments to reacquire employer securities held by an ESOP. See Chief Counsel Notice 2004-038 (October 1, 2004) available at *www.irs.gov/foia* through the *electronic reading room.*

Special Analyses

It has been determined that this notice of proposed rulemaking is not a significant regulatory action as defined in Executive Order 12866. Therefore, a regulatory assessment is not required. It has also been determined that section 553(b) of the Administrative Procedure Act (5 U.S.C. chapter 5) does not apply to these regulations, and, because the regulations do not impose a collection of information on small entities, the Regulatory Flexibility Act (5 U.S.C. chapter 6) does not apply. Pursuant to section 7805(f) of the Code, this notice of proposed rulemaking will be submitted to the Chief Counsel for Advocacy of the Small Business Administration for comment on its impact on small business.

Comments and Public Hearing

Before these proposed regulations are adopted as final regulations, consideration will be given to any written (a signed original and eight (8) copies) or electronic comments that are submitted timely to the IRS. The IRS and Treasury Department specifically request comments on the clarity of the proposed regulations and how they may be made easier to understand. All comments will be available for public inspection and copying. A public hearing will be scheduled if requested in writing by any person that timely submits written comments. If a public hearing is scheduled, notice of the date, time, and place for the public hearing will be published in the **Federal Register**.

Drafting Information

The principal authors of these regulations are John T. Ricotta, Office of Division Counsel/Associate Chief Counsel (Tax Exempt and Government Entities) and Martin Huck of Office of Associate Chief Counsel (Corporate). However, other personnel from the IRS and Treasury participated in the development of these regulations.

List of Subjects in 26 CFR Part 1

Income taxes, Reporting and recordkeeping requirements.

Proposed Amendments to the Regulations

Accordingly, 26 CFR part 1 is proposed to be amended as follows:

PART 1—INCOME TAXES

Paragraph 1. The authority citation for part 1 is amended to read, in part, as follows:

Authority: 26 U.S.C. 7805 * * *

Section 1.162(k)-1 is also issued under 26 U.S.C. 162(k) * * *

Section 1.404(k)-3 is also issued under 26 U.S.C. 162(k) and 404(k)(5)(A) * * *

Par. 2. Section 1.162(k)-1 is added to read as follows:

§ 1.162(k)-1 Disallowance of deduction for reacquisition payments.

(a) *In general.* Except as provided in paragraph (b) of this section, no deduction otherwise allowable is allowed under Chapter 1 of the Internal Revenue Code for any amount paid or incurred by a corporation in connection with the reacquisition of its stock or the stock of any related person (as defined in section 465(b)(3)(C)). Amounts paid or incurred in connection with the reacquisition of stock include amounts paid by a corporation to reacquire its stock from an ESOP that are used in a manner described in section 404(k)(2)(A). See § 1.404(k)-3.

(b) *Exceptions.* Paragraph (a) of this section does not apply to any—

(i) Deduction allowable under section 163 (relating to interest);

(ii) Deduction for amounts that are properly allocable to indebtedness and amortized over the term of such indebtedness;

(iii) Deduction for dividends paid (within the meaning of section 561); or

(iv) Amount paid or incurred in connection with the redemption of any stock in a regulated investment company that issues only stock which is redeemable upon the demand of the shareholder.

(c) *Effective date.* This section applies with respect to amounts paid or incurred on or after the date these regulations are published as final regulations in the **Federal Register**.

Par. 3. Section 1.404(k)-2 is added to read as follows:

§ 1.404(k)-2 Dividends paid by corporation not maintaining ESOP.

Q-1: What corporation is entitled to the deduction provided under section 404(k) for applicable dividends paid on applicable employer securities of a C corporation held by an ESOP if the ESOP benefits employees of more than one corporation or if the corporation paying the dividend is not the corporation maintaining the plan?

A-1: (a) *In general.* Under section 404(k), only the corporation paying the dividend is entitled to the deduction with respect to applicable employer securities held by an ESOP. Thus, no deduction is permitted to a corporation maintaining the ESOP if that corporation does not pay the dividend.

(b) *Example.* (i) *Facts.* S is a U.S. corporation that is wholly owned by P, an entity organized under the laws of Country A that is classified as a corporation for Federal income tax purposes. P is not engaged in a U.S. trade or business. P has a single class of common stock that is listed on a stock exchange in a foreign country. In addition, these shares are listed on the New York Stock Exchange, in the form of American Depositary Shares, and are actively traded through American Depositary Receipts (ADRs) meeting the requirements of section 409(l). S maintains an ESOP for its employees. The ESOP holds ADRs of P on Date X and receives a dividend with respect to those employer securities. The dividends received by the ESOP constitute applicable dividends as described in section 404(k)(2).

(ii) *Conclusion.* P, as the payor of the dividend, is entitled to a deduction under section 404(k) with respect to the dividends, although as a foreign corporation P does not obtain a U.S. tax benefit from the deduction. No corporation other than the corporation paying the dividend is entitled to the deduction under section 404(k). Thus, because S did not pay the dividends, S is not entitled to a deduction under section 404(k). The answer would be the same if P is a U.S. C corporation.

Q-2: What is the effective date of this section?

A-2: This section applies with respect to dividends paid on or after the date these regulations are published as final regulations in the **Federal Register.**

Par. 4. Section 1.404(k)-3 is added to read as follows:

§ 1.404(k)-3 Disallowance of deduction for reacquisition payments.

Q-1: Are payments to reacquire stock held by an ESOP applicable dividends that are deductible under section 404(k)(1)?

A-1: (a) Payments to reacquire stock held by an ESOP, including reacquisition payments that are used to make benefit distributions to participants or beneficiaries, are not deductible under section 404(k) because—

(1) Those payments do not constitute *applicable dividends* under section 404(k)(2); and

(2) The treatment of those payments as applicable dividends would constitute, in substance, an avoidance or evasion on taxation within the meaning of section 404(k)(5).

(b) See § 1.162(k)-1 concerning the disallowance of deductions for amounts paid or incurred by a corporation in connection with the reacquisition of its stock from an ESOP.

Q-2: What is the effective date of this section?

A-2: This section applies with respect to payments to reacquire stock that are made on or after the date these regulations are published as final regulations in the **Federal Register.**

Mark E. Matthews,

Deputy Commissioner for Services and Enforcement.

CERTIFIED COPY

Guy R. Traynor

¶ 20,261S

IRS proposed regulations: Health Savings Accounts (HSAs): Comparability rules.— The Treasury and IRS have issued proposed regulations involving the comparability rules for employer Health Savings Account (HSA) contributions. The proposed regulations generally follow guidance on the comparability rules previously issued by the IRS, including IRS Notice 2004-2 (see ¶ 17,127U) and IRS Notice 2004-50 (see ¶ 17,129F-5), but also provide additional clarification regarding a few HSA comparability issues not previously addressed. Although the proposed regulations apply to employer contributions made on or after the date the regulations are finalized, taxpayers may rely on the proposed rules pending the issuance of final regulations.

The proposed regulations, which were published in the Federal Register on August 26, 2005 (70 FR 50233), are reproduced below. Technical corrections issued December 8, 2005 (70 FR 72953) are reflected.

DEPARTMENT OF THE TREASURY

Internal Revenue Service

26 CFR Part 54

[REG-138647-04]

RIN 1545-BE30

Employer Comparable Contributions to Health Savings Accounts under Section 4980G

AGENCY: Internal Revenue Service (IRS), Treasury.

ACTION: Notice of proposed rulemaking.

SUMMARY: This document contains proposed regulations providing guidance on employer comparable contributions to Health Savings Accounts (HSAs) under section 4980G. In general, these proposed regulations would affect employers that contribute to employees' HSAs.

DATES: Written or electronic comments and requests for a public hearing must be received by November 24, 2005.

ADDRESSES: Send submissions to: CC:PA:LPD:PR (REG-138647-04), room 5203, Internal Revenue Service, POB 7604, Ben Franklin Station, Washington, DC 20044. Submissions may be hand delivered Monday through Friday between the hours of 8 a.m. and 4 p.m. to CC:PA:LPD:PR (REG-138647-04), Courier's Desk, Internal Revenue Service, 1111 Constitution Avenue, NW., Washington, DC. Alternatively, taxpayers may submit comments electronically via the IRS Internet site at *www.irs.gov/regs* or via the Federal eRulemaking Portal at *www.regulations.gov* (IRS - REG-138647-04).

FOR FURTHER INFORMATION CONTACT: Concerning the proposed regulations, Barbara E. Pie at (202) 622-6080; concerning submissions of comments or a request for a public hearing, Kelly Banks at (202) 622-7180 (not toll-free numbers).

SUPPLEMENTARY INFORMATION

Background

This document contains proposed Pension Excise Tax Regulations (26 CFR part 54) under section 4980G of the Internal Revenue Code (Code). Under section 4980G of the Code, an excise tax is imposed on an employer that fails to make comparable contributions to the HSAs of its employees.

Section 1201 of the Medicare Prescription Drug, Improvement, and Modernization Act of 2003 (Act), Public Law 108-173, (117 Stat. 2066, 2003) added section 223 to the Code to permit eligible individuals to establish HSAs for taxable years beginning after December 31, 2003. Section 4980G was also added to the Code by the Act. Section 4980G(a) imposes an excise tax on the failure of an employer to make comparable contributions to the HSAs of its employees for a calendar year. Section 4980G(b) provides that rules and requirements similar to section 4980E (the comparability rules for Archer Medical Savings Accounts (Archer MSAs)) apply for purposes of section 4980G. Section 4980E(b) imposes an excise tax equal to 35% of the aggregate amount contributed by the employer to the Archer MSAs of employees during the calendar year if an employer fails to make comparable contributions to the Archer MSAs of its employees in a calendar year. Therefore, if an employer fails to make comparable contributions to the HSAs of its employees during a calendar year, an excise tax equal to 35% of the aggregate amount contributed by the employer to the HSAs of its employees during that calendar year is imposed on the employer. See Sections 4980G(a) and (b) and 4980E(b). See also Notice 2004-2 (2004-2 I.R.B. 269), Q & A-32.

Explanation of Provisions

Overview

The proposed regulations clarify and expand on the guidance regarding the comparability rules published in Notice 2004-2 and in Notice 2004-50 (2004-33 I.R.B. 196), Q & A-46 through Q & A-54.

I. Comparable Contributions in General

An employer is not required to contribute to the HSAs of its employees. However, in general, if an employer makes contributions to any employee's HSA, the employer must make comparable contributions to the HSAs of all comparable participating employees. Comparable participating employees are eligible individuals (as defined in section 223(c)(1)) who have the same category of high deductible health plan (HDHP) coverage. The categories of coverage are self-only HDHP coverage and family HDHP coverage.

These proposed regulations incorporate the rule in Notice 2004-2, Q & A-32 that contributions are comparable if they are either the same amount or the same percentage of the deductible for employees who are eligible individuals with the same category of coverage. An employer is not required to contribute the same amount or the same percentage of the deductible for employees who are eligible individuals with self-only HDHP coverage that it contributes for employees who are eligible individuals with family HDHP coverage. An employer that satisfies the comparability rules by contributing the same amount to the HSAs of all employees who are eligible individuals with self-only HDHP coverage is not required to contribute any amount to the HSAs of employees who are eligible individuals with family HDHP coverage, or to contribute the same percentage of the family HDHP deductible as the amount contributed with respect to self-only HDHP coverage. Similarly, an employer that satisfies the comparability rules by contributing the same amount to the HSAs of all employees who are eligible individuals with family HDHP coverage is not required to contribute any amount to the HSAs of employees who are eligible individuals with self-only HDHP coverage, or to contribute the same percentage of the self-only HDHP deductible as the amount contributed with respect to family HDHP coverage.

II. Calculating Comparable Contributions

The proposed regulations clarify that contributions to the HSAs of certain individuals are not taken into account in determining whether an employer's contributions to the HSAs of its employees satisfy the comparability rules. Specifically, contributions to the HSAs of independent contractors, sole proprietors, and partners in a partnership are not taken into account under the comparability rules. In addition, the comparability rules do not apply to amounts rolled over from an employee's HSA or Archer MSA or to after-tax employee contributions.

The proposed regulations also clarify that the categories of employees for comparability testing are current full-time employees, current part-time employees, and former employees (except for former employees with coverage under the employer's HDHP because of an election under a COBRA continuation provision (as defined in section 9832(d)(1)). The proposed regulations provide that the comparability rules apply separately to each of the categories of employees. If an employer contributes to the HSA of any employee in a category of employees, the employer must make comparable contributions to the HSAs of all comparable participating employees within that category. Therefore, the comparability rules apply to a category of employees only if an employer contributes to the HSA of any employee within the category. For example, an employer that makes comparable contributions to the HSAs of all full-time employees who are eligible individuals but does not contribute to the HSA of any employee who is not a full-time employee, satisfies the comparability rules.

The categories of employees set forth in these proposed regulations are the exclusive categories for comparability testing. An employer must make comparable contributions to the HSAs of all comparable participating employees (eligible individuals who are in the same category of employees with the same category of HDHP coverage) during the calendar year without regard to any classification other than these categories. Therefore, the comparability rules do not apply separately to groups of collectively bargained employees. While the comparability rules apply separately to part-time employees, there is no similar rule permitting separate application of the comparability rules to collectively bargained employees. Neither section 4980E nor section 4980G provides an exception to the comparability rules for collectively bargained employees. Accordingly, an employer must make comparable contributions to the HSAs of all comparable participating employees, both those who are covered under a collective bargaining agreement and those who are not covered. Similarly, the comparability rules do not apply separately to management and non-management employees.

The proposed regulations also provide that the comparability rules apply separately to employees who have HSAs and employees who have Archer MSAs. However, if an employee has both an HSA and an Archer MSA, the employer may contribute to either the HSA or the Archer MSA, but not to both.

The proposed regulations incorporate the rule set forth in Q & A-53 of Notice 2004-50, which provides that if an employer limits HSA contributions to employees who are eligible individuals with coverage under an HDHP provided by the employer, the employer is not required to make comparable contributions to the HSAs of employees who are eligible individuals with coverage under an HDHP not provided by the employer. However, if an employer contributes to the HSAs of employees who are eligible individuals with coverage under any HDHP, in addition to the HDHPs provided by the employer, the employer is required to make comparable contributions to the HSAs of all comparable participating employees whether or not covered under the employer's HDHP. The proposed regulations also provide that similar rules apply to employer contributions to the HSAs of former employees. For example, if an employer limits HSA contributions to former employees who are eligible individuals with coverage under an HDHP provided by the employer, the employer is not required make comparable contributions to the HSAs of former employees who are eligible individuals with coverage under an HDHP not provided by the employer. However, if an employer contributes to the HSAs of former employees who are eligible individuals with coverage under the employer's HDHP, the employer is not required to make comparable contributions to the HSAs of former employees who are eligible individuals with coverage under the employer's HDHP because of an election under a COBRA continuation provision (as defined in section 9832(d)(1)).

The proposed regulations also incorporate the rule set forth in Q & A-46 of Notice 2004-50, which provides that the comparability rules will not be satisfied if an employer makes HSA contributions in an amount equal to an employee's HSA contribution or a percentage of the employee's HSA contribution (matching contributions) because if all comparable participating employees do not contribute the same amount to their HSAs, they will not receive comparable contributions to their HSAs. In addition, the comparability rules will not be satisfied if an employer conditions contributions to an employee's HSA on an employee's participation in health assessments, disease management programs or wellness programs because if all comparable participating employees do not elect to participate in all the programs, they will not receive comparable contributions to their HSAs. See Q & A-48 of Notice 2004-50. Similarly, the comparability rules will not be satisfied if an employer makes additional contributions to the HSAs of all comparable participating employees who have attained a specified age or who have worked for the employer for a specified number of years, because if all comparable participating employees do not meet the age or length of service requirement, they will not receive comparable contributions to their HSAs. See Q & A-50 of Notice 2004-50.

III. *Procedures for Making Comparable Contributions*

The proposed regulations provide that in determining whether the comparability rules are satisfied, an employer must take into account all full-time and part-time employees who were eligible individuals for any month during the calendar year. An employee is an eligible individual if as of the first day of the month the employee meets all of the requirements set forth in section 223(c). An employer may comply with the comparability rules by contributing amounts at one or more times for the calendar year to the HSAs of employees who are eligible individuals, if contributions are the same amount or the same percentage of the HDHP deductible for employees who are eligible individuals with the same category of coverage and are made at the same time (contributions on a pay-as-you-go basis).

An employer may also satisfy the comparability rules by determining comparable contributions for the calendar year at the end of the calendar year, taking into account all employees who were eligible individuals for any month during the calendar year and contributing the correct amount (a percentage of the HDHP deductible or a specified dollar amount for the same categories of coverage) to the employees' HSAs by April 15 th of the following year (contributions on a look-back basis).

If an employer makes comparable HSA contributions on a pay-as-you-go basis, it must do so for each comparable participating employee who is an employee during the time period used to make contributions. For example, if an employer makes HSA contributions each pay period, it must do so for each comparable participating employee who is an employee during the pay period. If an employer makes comparable contributions on a look-back-basis, it must do so for each employee who was a comparable participating employee for any month during the calendar year.

In addition, an employer may make all of its contributions to the HSAs of employees who are eligible individuals at the beginning of the calendar year (contributions on a pre-funded basis). An employer that makes comparable HSA contributions on a pre-funded basis will not fail to satisfy the comparability rules because an employee who terminates employment prior to the end of the calendar year has received more HSA contributions on a monthly basis than employees who worked the entire calendar year. If an employer makes HSA contributions on a pre-funded basis, it must do so for all employees who are comparable participating employees at the beginning of the calendar year. An employer that makes HSA contributions on a pre-funded basis must make comparable HSA contributions for all employees who are comparable participating employees for any month during the calendar year, including employees hired after the date of initial funding.

If an employee has not established an HSA at the time the employer funds its employee's HSAs, the employer complies with the comparability rules by contributing comparable amounts to the employee's HSA when the employee establishes the HSA, taking into account each month that the employee was a comparable participating employee. However, an employer is not required to make comparable contributions for a calendar year to an employee's HSA if the employee has not established an HSA by December 31 st of the calendar year.

The proposed regulations provide that if an employer determines that the comparability rules are not satisfied for a calendar year, the employer may not recoup from an employee's HSA any portion of the employer's contribution to the employee's HSA because under section 223(d)(1)(E), an account beneficiary's interest in an HSA is nonforfeitable. However, an employer may make additional HSA contributions to satisfy the comparability rules. An employer may contribute up until April 15 th following the calendar year in which the non-comparable contributions were made. An employer that makes additional HSA contributions to correct non-comparable contributions must also contribute reasonable interest.

IV. *Exception to the Comparability Rules for Cafeteria Plans*

The legislative history of the Act states that the comparability rules do not apply to HSA contributions that an employer makes through a cafeteria plan. See Conf. Rep. No. 391, 108 th Cong., 1 st Sess. 843 (2003), 2004 U.S.C.C.A.N. 1808. See also Notice 2004-2, Q & A-32. The nondiscrimination rules in section 125 of the Code apply to HSA contributions (including matching contributions) made through a cafeteria plan. Generally, a cafeteria plan is a written plan under which all participants are employees and participants may choose among two or more benefits consisting of cash and qualified benefits. Unlike the cafeteria plan nondiscrimination rules, the comparability rules are not based upon discrimination in favor of highly compensated or key employees. Therefore, an employer that maintains an HDHP only for highly compensated or key employees and makes HSA contributions through a cafeteria plan only for those eligible employees, does not violate the comparability rules, but may violate the cafeteria plan nondiscrimination rules.

V. *Waiver of Excise Tax*

In the case of a failure which is due to reasonable cause and not to willful neglect, all or a portion of the excise tax imposed under section 4980G may be waived to the extent that the payment of the tax would be excessive relative to the failure involved. See sections 4980G(b) and 4980E(c).

Proposed Effective Date

It is proposed that these regulations apply to employer contributions made on or after the date the final regulations are published in the **Federal Register.** However, taxpayers may rely on these regulations for guidance pending the issuance of final regulations.

Special Analyses

It has been determined that this notice of proposed rulemaking is not a significant regulatory action as defined in Executive Order 12866. Therefore, a regulatory assessment is not required. It also has been determined that section 553(b) of the Administrative Procedure Act (5 U.S.C. chapter 5) does not apply to these regulations. This notice of proposed rulemaking does not impose a collection of information on small entities, thus the Regulatory Flexibility Act (5 U.S.C. chapter 6) does not apply. Pursuant to section 7805(f) of the Code, these proposed regulations will be submitted to the Chief Counsel for Advocacy of the Small Business Administration for comment on its impact on small business.

Comments and Requests for Public Hearing

Before these proposed regulations are adopted as final regulations, consideration will be given to any written comments (a signed original and eight (8) copies) or electronic comments that are submitted timely to the IRS. The Treasury Department and the IRS specifically request comments on the clarity of the proposed rules and how they can be made easier to understand. In addition, comments are requested on the application of the comparability rules to employees who are on leave pursuant to the Family and Medical Leave Act of 1993, Public Law 103-3, (107 Stat. 6, 1993, 29 U.S.C. 2601 et seq.). Comments are also requested concerning employer matching HSA contributions made through a cafeteria plan. Specifically, whether the ratio of an employer's matching HSA contributions to an employee's salary reduction HSA contributions should be limited, and whether employer matching contributions exceeding a specific limit should be subject to the section 4980G comparability rules. All comments will be available for public inspection and copying. A public hearing will be scheduled if requested in writing by any person that timely submits written comments.

Drafting Information

The principal author of these proposed regulations is Barbara E. Pie, Office of Division Counsel/Associate Chief Counsel (Tax Exempt and Government Entities), Internal Revenue Service. However, personnel from other offices of the IRS and Treasury Department participated in their development.

List of Subjects in 26 CFR Part 54

Excise taxes, Pensions, Reporting and recordkeeping requirements.

Proposed Amendment to the Regulations

Accordingly, 26 CFR part 54 is proposed to be amended as follows:
PART 54—PENSION EXCISE TAXES

Paragraph 1. The authority citation for part 54 is amended by adding an entry in numerical order to read, in part, as follows:

Authority: 26 U.S.C. 7805 * * *

Section 54.4980G-1 also issued under 26 U.S.C. 4980G. * * *

Paragraph 2. Sections 54.4980G-0 through 54.4980G-5 are added to read as follows:

§ 54.4980G-0 Table of contents

This section contains the questions for § 54.4980G-1 through § 54.4980G-5.

§ 54.4980G-1 Failure of employer to make comparable health savings account contributions.

Q-1. What are the comparability rules that apply to employer contributions to Health Savings Accounts (HSAs)?

Q-2. What are the categories of HDHP coverage for purposes of applying the comparability rules?

Q-3. What is the testing period for making comparable contributions to employees' HSAs?

Q-4. How is the excise tax computed if employer contributions do not satisfy the comparability rules for a calendar year?

§ 54.4980G-2 Employer contribution defined.

Q-1. Do the comparability rules apply to amounts rolled over from an employee's HSA or Archer Medical Savings Account (Archer MSA)?

Q-2. If an employee requests that his or her employer deduct after-tax amounts from the employee's compensation and forward these amounts as employee contributions to the employee's HSA, do the comparability rules apply to these amounts?

§ 54.4980G-3 Definition of employee for comparability testing.

Q-1. Do the comparability rules apply to contributions that an employer makes to the HSAs of independent contractors?

Q-2. May a sole proprietor who is an eligible individual contribute to his or her own HSA without contributing to the HSAs of his or her employees who are eligible individuals?

Q-3. Do the comparability rules apply to contributions by a partnership to a partner's HSA?

Q-4. How are members of controlled groups treated when applying the comparability rules?

Q-5. What are the categories of employees for comparability testing?

Q-6. Is an employer permitted to make comparable contributions only to the HSAs of comparable participating employees who have coverage under the employer's HDHP?

Q-7. If an employee and his or her spouse are eligible individuals who work for the same employer and one employee-spouse has family coverage for both employees under the employer's HDHP, must the employer make comparable contributions to the HSAs of both employees?

Q-8. Does an employer that makes HSA contributions only for non-management employees who are eligible individuals, but not for management employees who are eligible individuals or that makes HSA contributions only for management employees who are eligible individuals but not for non-management employees who are eligible individuals satisfy the requirement that the employer make comparable contributions?

Q-9. If an employer contributes to the HSAs of former employees who are eligible individuals, do the comparability rules apply to these contributions?

Q-10. Is an employer permitted to make comparable contributions only to the HSAs of comparable participating former employees who have coverage under the employer's HDHP?

Q-11. If an employer contributes only to the HSAs of former employees who are eligible individuals with coverage under the employer's HDHP, must the employer make comparable contributions to the HSAs of former employees who are eligible individuals with coverage under the employer's HDHP because of an election under a COBRA continuation provision (as defined in section 9832(d)(1))?

Q-12. How do the comparability rules apply if some employees have HSAs and other employees have Archer MSAs?

§ 54.4980G-4 Calculating comparable contributions.

Q-1. What are comparable contributions?

Q-2. How do the comparability rules apply to employer contributions to employees' HSAs if some employees work full-time during the entire calendar year, and other employees work full-time for less than the entire calendar year?

Q-3. How does an employer comply with the comparability rules when some employees who are eligible individuals do not work for the employer during the entire calendar year?

Q-4. May an employer make all of its contributions to the HSAs of its employees who are eligible individuals at the beginning of the calendar year (i.e., on a prefunded basis) instead of contributing on a pay-as-you-go or on a look-back basis?

Q-5. Must an employer use the same contribution method as described in Q & A-3 and Q & A-4 of this section for all employees who were comparable participating employees for any month during the calendar year?

Q-6. How does an employer comply with the comparability rules if an employee has not established an HSA at the time the employer contributes to its employees' HSAs?

Q-7. If an employer bases its contributions on a percentage of the HDHP deductible, how is the correct percentage or dollar amount computed?

Q-8. Does an employer that contributes to the HSA of each comparable participating employee in an amount equal to the employee's HSA contribution or a percentage of the employee's HSA contribution (matching contributions) satisfy the rule that all comparable participating employees receive comparable contributions?

Q-9. If an employer conditions contributions by the employer to an employee's HSA on an employee's participation in health assessments, disease management programs or wellness programs and makes the same contributions available to all employees who participate in the programs, do the contributions satisfy the comparability rules?

Q-10. If an employer makes additional contributions to the HSAs of all comparable participating employees who have attained a specified age or who have worked for the employer for a specified number of years, do the contributions satisfy the comparability rules?

Q-11. If an employer makes additional contributions to the HSAs of all comparable participating employees who qualify for the additional contributions (HSA catch-up contributions) under section 223(b)(3), do the contributions satisfy the comparability rules?

Q-12. If an employer's contributions to an employee's HSA result in noncomparable contributions, may the employer recoup the excess amount from the employee's HSA?

§ 54.4980G-5 HSA comparability rules and cafeteria plans and waiver of excise tax.

Q-1. If an employer makes contributions through a section 125 cafeteria plan to the HSA of each employee who is an eligible individual are the contributions subject to the comparability rules?

Q-2. If an employer makes contributions through a cafeteria plan to the HSA of each employee who is an eligible individual in an amount equal to the amount of the employee's HSA contribution or a percentage of the amount of the employee's HSA contribution (i.e., *matching contributions*), are the contributions subject to the section 4980G comparability rules?

Q-3. If an employer provides HDHP coverage through a cafeteria plan, but the employer's HSA contributions are not provided through the cafeteria plan, do the cafeteria plan nondiscrimination rules or the comparability rules apply to the HSA contributions?

Q-4. If under the employer's cafeteria plan, employees who are eligible individuals and who participate in health assessments, disease management programs or wellness programs receive an employer contribution to an HSA, unless the employees elect cash, are the contributions subject to the comparability rules?

Q-5. May all or part of the excise tax imposed under section 4980G be waived?

§ 54.4980G-1 Failure of employer to make comparable health savings account contributions.

Q-1. What are the comparability rules that apply to employer contributions to Health Savings Accounts (HSAs)?

A-1. If an employer makes contributions to any employee's HSA, the employer must make comparable contributions to the HSAs of all comparable participating employees. See Q & A-1 in § 54.4980G-4 for the definition of comparable contributions. *Comparable participating employees* are eligible individuals (as defined in section 223(c)(1)) who have the same category of high deductible health plan (HDHP) coverage. See sections 4980G(b) and 4980E(d)(3). See section 223(c)(2) and (g) for the definition of an HDHP. See also Q & A-5 in § 54.4980G-3 for the categories of employees and Q & A-2 in this section for the categories of HDHP coverage.

Q-2. What are the categories of HDHP coverage for purposes of applying the comparability rules?

A-2. The categories of coverage are self-only HDHP coverage and family HDHP coverage. See sections 4980G(b) and 4980E(d)(3)(B).

Q-3. What is the testing period for making comparable contributions to employees' HSAs?

A-3. To satisfy the comparability rules, an employer must make comparable contributions for the calendar year to the HSAs of employees who are comparable participating employees. See section 4980G(a).

Q-4. How is the excise tax computed if employer contributions do not satisfy the comparability rules for a calendar year?

A-4. (a) *Computation of tax.* If employer contributions do not satisfy the comparability rules for a calendar year, the employer is subject to an excise tax equal to 35% of the aggregate amount contributed by the employer to HSAs for that period.

(b) *Example.* The following example illustrates the rules in paragraph (a) of this Q & A-4:

Example. In this *Example*, assume that the HDHP provided by Employer A satisfies the definition of an HDHP for the 2007 calendar year. During the 2007 calendar year, Employer A has 8 employees who are eligible individuals with self-only coverage under an HDHP provided by Employer A. The deductible for the HDHP is $2,000. For the 2007 calendar year, Employer A contributes $2,000 each to the HSAs of two employees and $1,000 each to the HSAs of the other six employees, for total HSA contributions of $10,000. Employer A's contributions do not satisfy the comparability rules. Therefore, Employer A is subject to an excise tax of $3,500 (i.e., 35% x $10,000) for its failure to make comparable contributions to its employees' HSAs.

§ 54.4980G-2 Employer contribution defined.

Q-1. Do the comparability rules apply to amounts rolled over from an employee's HSA or Archer Medical Savings Account (Archer MSA)?

A-1. No. The comparability rules do not apply to amounts rolled over from an employee's HSA or Archer MSA.

Q-2. If an employee requests that his or her employer deduct after-tax amounts from the employee's compensation and forward these amounts as employee contributions to the employee's HSA, do the comparability rules apply to these amounts?

A-2. No. Section 106(d) provides that amounts contributed by an employer to an eligible employee's HSA shall be treated as employer-provided coverage for medical expenses and are excludible from the employee's gross income up to the limit in section 223(b). After-tax employee contributions to an HSA are not subject to the comparability rules because they are not employer contributions under section 106(d).

§ 54.4980G-3 Definition of employee for comparability testing.

Q-1. Do the comparability rules apply to contributions that an employer makes to the HSAs of independent contractors?

A-1. No. The comparability rules apply only to contributions that an employer makes to the HSAs of employees.

Q-2. May a sole proprietor who is an eligible individual contribute to his or her own HSA without contributing to the HSAs of his or her employees who are eligible individuals?

A-2. (a) *Sole proprietor not an employee.* Yes. The comparability rules apply only to contributions made by an employer to the HSAs of employees. Because a sole proprietor is not an employee, the comparability rules do not apply to contributions he or she makes to his or her own HSA. However, if a sole proprietor contributes to any employee's HSA, he or she must make comparable contributions to the HSAs of all comparable participating employees. In determining whether the comparability rules are satisfied, contributions that a sole proprietor makes to his or her own HSA are not taken into account.

(b) *Example.* The following example illustrates the rules in paragraph (a) of this Q & A-2:

Example. In a calendar year, B, a sole proprietor is an eligible individual and contributes $1,000 to B's own HSA. B also contributes $500 for the same calendar year to the HSA of each employee who is an eligible individual. The comparability rules are not violated by B's $1,000 contribution to B's own HSA.

Q-3. Do the comparability rules apply to contributions by a partnership to a partner's HSA?

A-3. (a) *Partner not an employee.* No. Contributions by a partnership to a bona fide partner's HSA are not subject to the comparability rules because the contributions are not contributions by an employer to the HSA of an employee. The contributions are treated as either guaranteed payments under section 707(c) or distributions under section 731. However, if a partnership contributes to the HSAs of employees who are not partners, the comparability rules apply to those contributions.

(b) *Example.* The following example illustrates the rules in paragraph (a) of this Q & A-3:

Example. (i) Partnership X is a limited partnership with three equal individual partners, A (a general partner), B (a limited partner), and C (a limited partner). C is to be paid $300 annually for services rendered to Partnership X in her capacity as a partner without regard to partnership income (a section 707(c)) guaranteed payment). D and E are the only employees of Partnership X and are not partners in Partnership X. A, B, C, D, and E are eligible individuals and each has an HSA. During Partnership X's Year 1 taxable year, which is also a calendar year, Partnership X makes the following contributions—

(A) A $300 contribution to each of A's and B's HSAs which are treated as section 731 distributions to A and B;

(B) A $300 contribution to C's HSA in lieu of paying C the guaranteed payment directly; and

(C) A $200 contribution to each of D's and E's HSAs, who are comparable participating employees.

(ii) Partnership X's contributions to A's and B's HSAs are section 731 distributions, which are treated as cash distributions. Partnership X's contribution to C's HSA is treated as a guaranteed payment under section 707(c). The contribution is not excludible from C's gross income under section 106(d) because the contribution is treated as a distributive share of partnership income for purposes of all Code sections other than sections 61(a) and 162(a), and a guaranteed payment to a partner is not treated as compensation to an employee. Thus, Partnership X's contributions to the HSAs of A, B, and C are not subject to the comparability rules. Partnership X's contributions to D's and E's HSAs are subject to the comparability rules because D and E are employees of Partnership X and are not partners in Partnership X. Partnership X's contributions satisfy the comparability rules.

Q-4. How are members of controlled groups treated when applying the comparability rules?

A-4. All persons or entities treated as a single employer under section 414(b), (c), (m), or (o) are treated as one employer. See sections 4980G(b) and 4980E(e).

Q-5. What are the categories of employees for comparability testing?

A-5. (a) *Categories*. The categories of employees for comparability testing are as follows—

(1) Current full-time employees;

(2) Current part-time employees; and

(3) Former employees (except for former employees with coverage under the employer's HDHP because of an election under a COBRA continuation provision (as defined in section 9832(d)(1)).

(b) *Part-time and full-time employees*. Part-time employees are customarily employed for fewer than 30 hours per week and full-time employees are customarily employed for 30 or more hours per week. See sections 4980G(b) and 4980E(d)(4)(A) and (B).

(c) *In general*. The categories of employees in paragraph (a) of this Q & A-5 are the exclusive categories for comparability testing. An employer must make comparable contributions to the HSAs of all *comparable participating employees* (eligible individuals who are in the same category of employees with the same category of HDHP coverage) during the calendar year without regard to any classification other than these categories. Thus, the comparability rules do not apply separately to collectively bargained and non-collectively bargained employees. Similarly, the comparability rules do not apply separately to groups of collectively bargained employees.

Q-6. Is an employer permitted to make comparable contributions only to the HSAs of comparable participating employees who have coverage under the employer's HDHP?

A-6. (a) *Employer-provided HDHP coverage*. If during a calendar year, an employer contributes to the HSA of any employee who is an eligible individual covered under an HDHP provided by the employer, the employer is required to make comparable contributions to the HSAs of all comparable participating employees with coverage under any HDHP provided by the employer. An employer that contributes only to the HSAs of employees who are eligible individuals with coverage under the employer's HDHP is not required to make comparable contributions to HSAs of employees who are eligible individuals but are not covered under the employer's HDHP. However, an employer that contributes to the HSA of any employee who is an eligible individual with coverage under any HDHP, in addition to the HDHPs provided by the employer, must make comparable contributions to the HSAs of all comparable participating employees whether or not covered under the employer's HDHP.

(b) *Examples*. The following examples illustrate the rules in paragraph (a) of this Q & A-6:

Example 1. In a calendar year, Employer C offers an HDHP to its full-time employees. Most full-time employees are covered under Employer C's HDHP and Employer C makes comparable contributions only to these employees' HSAs. Employee W, a full-time employee of Employer C and an eligible individual, is covered under an HDHP provided by W's spouse's employer and not under Employer C's HDHP. Employer C is not required to make comparable contributions to W's HSA.

Example 2. In a calendar year, Employer D does not offer an HDHP. Several full-time employees, who are eligible individuals, have HSAs. Employer D contributes to these employees' HSAs. Employer D must make comparable contributions to the HSAs of all full-time employees who are eligible individuals.

Example 3. In a calendar year, Employer E offers an HDHP to its full-time employees. Most full-time employees are covered under Employer E's HDHP and Employer E makes comparable contributions to these employees' HSAs and also to the HSAs of full-time employees who are eligible individuals and who are not covered under Employer E's HDHP. Employee H, a full-time employee of Employer E and a comparable participating employee, is covered under an HDHP provided by H's spouse's employer and not under Employer E's HDHP. Employer E must make comparable contributions to H's HSA.

Q-7. If an employee and his or her spouse are eligible individuals who work for the same employer and one employee-spouse has family coverage for both employees under the employer's HDHP, must the employer make comparable contributions to the HSAs of both employees?

A-7. (a) *In general*. If the employer makes contributions only to the HSAs of employees who are eligible individuals covered under its HDHP, the employer is not required to contribute to the HSAs of both employee-spouses. The employer is required to contribute to the HSA of the employee-spouse with coverage under the employer's HDHP, but is not required to contribute to the HSA of the employee-spouse covered under the employer's HDHP by virtue of his or her spouse's coverage. However, if the employer contributes to the HSA of any employee who is an eligible individual with coverage under any HDHP, the employer must make comparable contributions to the HSAs of both employee-spouses if they are both eligible individuals. If an employer is required to contribute to the HSAs of both employee-spouses, the employer is not required to contribute amounts in excess of the annual contribution limits in section 223(b).

(b) *Examples*. The following examples illustrate the rules in paragraph (a) of this Q & A-7:

Example 1. In a calendar year, Employer F offers an HDHP to its full-time employees. Most full-time employees are covered under Employer F's HDHP and Employer F makes comparable contributions only to these employees' HSAs. Employee H, a full-time employee of Employer F and an eligible individual has family coverage under Employer F's HDHP for H and H's spouse, Employee W, who is also a full-time employee of Employer F and an eligible individual. Employer F is required to make comparable contributions to H's HSA, but is not required to make comparable contributions to W's HSA.

Example 2. In a calendar year, Employer G offers an HDHP to its full-time employees. Most full-time employees are covered under Employer G's HDHP and Employer G makes comparable contributions to these employees' HSAs and to the HSAs of full-time employees who are eligible individuals but are not covered under Employer G's HDHP. Employee W, a full-time employee of Employer G and an eligible individual, has family coverage under Employer G's HDHP for W and W's spouse, Employee H, who is also a full-time employee of Employer G and an eligible individual. Employer G must make comparable contributions to W's HSA and to H's HSA.

Q-8. Does an employer that makes HSA contributions only for non-management employees who are eligible individuals, but not for management employees who are eligible individuals or that makes HSA contributions only for management employees who are eligible individuals but not for non-management employees who are eligible individuals satisfy the requirement that the employer make comparable contributions?

A-8. (a) *Management v. non-management*. No. If management employees and non-management employees are comparable participating employees, the comparability rules are not satisfied. However, if non-management employees are comparable participating employees and management employees are not comparable participating employees, the comparability rules may be satisfied. But see Q & A-1 in § 54.4980G-5 on contributions made through a cafeteria plan.

(b) *Examples*. The following examples illustrate the rules in paragraph (a) of this Q & A-8:

Example 1. In a calendar year, Employer H maintains an HDHP covering all management and non-management employees. Employer H contributes $1,000 for the calendar year to the HSA of each non-management employee who is an eligible individual covered under its HDHP. Employer H does not contribute to the HSAs of any of its management employees who are eligible individuals covered under its HDHP. The comparability rules are not satisfied.

Example 2. In a calendar year, Employer J maintains an HDHP for non-management employees only. Employer J does not maintain an HDHP for its management employees. Employer J contributes $1,000 for the calendar year to the HSA of each non-management employee who is an eligible individual with coverage under its HDHP. Employer J does not contribute to the HSAs of any of its non-management employees not covered under its HDHP or to the HSAs of any of its management employees. The comparability rules are satisfied.

Example 3. In a calendar year, Employer K maintains an HDHP for management employees only. Employer K does not maintain an HDHP for its non-management employees. Employer K contributes $1,000 for the calendar year to the HSA of each management employee who is an eligible individual with coverage under its HDHP. Employer K does not contribute to the HSAs of any of its management employees not covered under its HDHP or to the HSAs of any of its non-management employees. The comparability rules are satisfied.

Q-9. If an employer contributes to the HSAs of former employees who are eligible individuals, do the comparability rules apply to these contributions?

A-9. (a) *Former employees*. Yes. The comparability rules apply to contributions an employer makes to former employees' HSAs. Therefore, if an employer contributes to any former employee's HSA, it must make comparable contributions to the HSAs of all comparable partici-pating former employees (former employees who are eligible individu-als with the same category of HDHP coverage). However, an employer is not required to make comparable contributions to the HSAs of former employees with coverage under the employer's HDHP because of an election under a COBRA continuation provision (as defined in section 9832(d)(1)). See Q & A-5 and Q & A-11 in this section. The comparability rules apply separately to former employees because they are a separate category of covered employee. See Q & A-5 in this section.

(b) *Examples*. The following examples illustrate the rules in para-graph (a) of this Q & A-9:

Example 1. In a calendar year, Employer L contributes $1,000 for the calendar year to the HSA of each current employee who is an eligible individual with coverage under any HDHP. Employer L does not contribute to the HSA of any former employee who is an eligible individual. Employer L's contributions satisfy the comparability rules.

Example 2. In a calendar year, Employer M contributes to the HSAs of current employees and former employees who are eligible individu-als covered under any HDHP. Employer M contributes $750 to the HSA of each current employee with self-only HDHP coverage and $1,000 to the HSA of each current employee with family HDHP cover-age. Employer M also contributes $300 to the HSA of each former employee with self-only HDHP coverage and $400 to the HSA of each former employee with family HDHP coverage. Employer M's contribu-tions satisfy the comparability rules.

Q-10. Is an employer permitted to make comparable contributions only to the HSAs of comparable participating former employees who have coverage under the employer's HDHP?

A-10. If during a calendar year, an employer contributes to the HSA of any former employee who is an eligible individual covered under an HDHP provided by the employer, the employer is required to make comparable contributions to the HSAs of all former employees who are comparable participating former employees with coverage under any HDHP provided by the employer. An employer that contributes only to the HSAs of former employees who are eligible individuals with cover-age under the employer's HDHP is not required to make comparable contributions to the HSAs of former employees who are eligible individ-uals and who are not covered under the employer's HDHP. However, an employer that contributes to the HSA of any former employee who is an eligible individual with coverage under any HDHP, even if that coverage is not the employer's HDHP, must make comparable contri-butions to the HSAs of all former employees who are eligible individu-als whether or not covered under an HDHP of the employer.

Q-11. If an employer contributes only to the HSAs of former employ-ees who are eligible individuals with coverage under the employer's HDHP, must the employer make comparable contributions to the HSAs of former employees who are eligible individuals with coverage under the employer's HDHP because of an election under a COBRA continuation provision (as defined in section 9832(d)(1))?

A-11. No. An employer that contributes only to the HSAs of former employees who are eligible individuals with coverage under the em-ployer's HDHP is not required to make comparable contributions to the HSAs of former employees who are eligible individuals with cover-age under the employer's HDHP because of an election under a COBRA continuation provision (as defined in section 9832(d)(1)).

Q-12. How do the comparability rules apply if some employees have HSAs and other employees have Archer MSAs?

A-12. (a) *HSAs and Archer MSAs*. The comparability rules apply separately to employees who have HSAs and employees who have Archer MSAs. However, if an employee has both an HSA and an Archer MSA, the employer may contribute to either the HSA or the Archer MSA, but not to both.

(b) *Examples*. The following examples illustrate the rules in para-graph (a) of this Q & A-12:

Example 1. In a calendar year, Employer N contributes $600 to the Archer MSA of each employee who is an eligible individual and who has an Archer MSA. Employer N contributes $500 for the calendar year to the HSA of each employee who is an eligible individual and who has an HSA. If an employee has both an Archer MSA and an HSA, Employer N contributes to the employee's Archer MSA and not to the employee's HSA. Employee X has an Archer MSA and an HSA. Em-ployer N contributes $600 for the calendar year to X's Archer MSA but does not contribute to X's HSA. Employer N's contributions satisfy the comparability rules.

Example 2. Same facts as *Example 1*, except that if an employee has both an Archer MSA and an HSA, Employer N contributes to the employee's HSA and not to the employee's Archer MSA. Employer N contributes $500 for the calendar year to X's HSA but does not contrib-ute to X's Archer MSA. Employer N's contributions satisfy the compa-rability rules.

§ 54.4980G-4 Calculating comparable contributions.

Q-1. What are comparable contributions?

A-1. (a) *Definition*. Contributions are comparable if they are either the same amount or the same percentage of the deductible under the HDHP for employees who are eligible individuals with the same cate-gory of coverage. Employees with self-only HDHP coverage are tested separately from employees with family HDHP coverage. See Q & A-1 and Q & A-2 in § 54.4980G-1. An employer is not required to contribute the same amount or the same percentage of the deductible for employ-ees who are eligible individuals with self-only HDHP coverage that it contributes for employees who are eligible individuals with family HDHP coverage. An employer that satisfies the comparability rules by contributing the same amount to the HSAs of all employees who are eligible individuals with self-only HDHP coverage is not required to contribute any amount to the HSAs of employees who are eligible individuals with family HDHP coverage, or to contribute the same percentage of the family HDHP deductible as the amount contributed with respect to self-only HDHP coverage. Similarly, an employer that satisfies the comparability rules by contributing the same amount to the HSAs of all employees who are eligible individuals with family HDHP coverage is not required to contribute any amount to the HSAs of employees who are eligible individuals with self-only HDHP cover-age, or to contribute the same percentage of the self-only HDHP deductible as the amount contributed with respect to family HDHP coverage.

(b) *Examples*. Assume that the HDHPs in *Example 1* through *Exam-ple 7* satisfy the definition of an HDHP for the 2007 calendar year. The following examples illustrate the rules in paragraph (a) of this Q & A-1:

Example 1. In the 2007 calendar year, Employer A offers its full-time employees three health plans, including an HDHP with self-only cover-age and a $2,000 deductible. Employer A contributes $1,000 for the calendar year to the HSA of each employee who is an eligible individual electing the self-only HDHP coverage. Employer A makes no HSA contributions for employees with family HDHP coverage or for employ-ees who do not elect the employer's self-only HDHP. Employer A's HSA contributions satisfy the comparability rules.

Example 2. In the 2007 calendar year, Employer B offers its employ-ees an HDHP with a $3,000 deductible for self-only coverage and a $4,000 deductible for family coverage. Employer B contributes $1,000 for the calendar year to the HSA of each employee who is an eligible individual electing the self-only HDHP coverage. Employer B contrib-utes $2,000 for the calendar year to the HSA of each employee who is an eligible individual electing the family HDHP coverage. Employer B's HSA contributions satisfy the comparability rules.

Example 3. In the 2007 calendar year, Employer C offers its employ-ees an HDHP with a $1,500 deductible for self-only coverage and a $3,000 deductible for family coverage. Employer C contributes $1,000 for the calendar year to the HSA of each employee who is an eligible individual electing the self-only HDHP coverage. Employer C contrib-utes $1,000 for the calendar year to the HSA of each employee who is an eligible individual electing the family HDHP coverage. Employer C's HSA contributions satisfy the comparability rules.

Example 4. In the 2007 calendar year, Employer D offers its employ-ees an HDHP with a $1,500 deductible for self-only coverage and a $3,000 deductible for family coverage. Employer D contributes $1,500 for the calendar year to the HSA of each employee who is an eligible individual electing the self-only HDHP coverage. Employer D contrib-utes $1,000 for the calendar year to the HSA of each employee who is an eligible individual electing the family HDHP coverage. Employer D's HSA contributions satisfy the comparability rules.

Example 5. (i) In the 2007 calendar year, Employer E maintains two HDHPs. Plan A has a $2,000 deductible for self-only coverage and a $4,000 deductible for family coverage. Plan B has a $2,500 deductible for self-only coverage and a $4,500 deductible for family coverage. For the calendar year, Employer E makes contributions to the HSA of each full-time employee who is an eligible individual covered under Plan A of $600 for self-only coverage and $1,000 for family coverage. Employer E satisfies the comparability rules, if it makes either of the following contributions for the 2007 calendar year to the HSA of each full-time employee who is an eligible individual covered under Plan B—

(A) $600 for each full-time employee with self-only coverage and $1,000 for each full-time employee with family coverage; or

(B) $750 for each employee with self-only coverage and $1,125 for each employee with family coverage (the same percentage of the deductible Employer E contributes for full-time employees covered under Plan A, 30% of the deductible for self-only coverage and 25% of the deductible for family coverage).

(ii) Employer E also makes contributions to the HSA of each part-time employee who is an eligible individual covered under Plan A of $300 for self-only coverage and $500 for family coverage. Employer E satisfies the comparability rules, if it makes either of the following contributions for the 2007 calendar year to the HSA of each part-time employee who is an eligible individual covered under Plan B—

(A) $300 for each part-time employee with self-only coverage and $500 for each part-time employee with family coverage; or

(B) $375 for each part-time employee with self-only coverage and $563 for each part-time employee with family coverage (the same percentage of the deductible Employer E contributes for part-time employees covered under Plan A, 15% of the deductible for self-only coverage and 12.5% of the deductible for family coverage).

Example 6. (i) In the 2007 calendar year, Employer F maintains an HDHP. The HDHP has a $2,500 deductible for self-only coverage, and the following family coverage options—

(A) A $3,500 deductible for self plus one dependent;

(B) A $3,500 deductible for self plus spouse;

(C) A $3,500 deductible for self plus two or more dependents;

(D) A $3,500 deductible for self plus spouse and one dependent; and

(E) A $3,500 deductible for self plus spouse and two or more dependents.

(ii) Employer F makes the following contributions for the calendar year to the HSA of each full-time employee who is an eligible individual covered under the HDHP—

(A) $750 for self-only coverage;

(B) $1,000 for self plus one dependent;

(C) $1,000 for self plus spouse;

(D) $1,000 for self plus two or more dependents;

(E) $1,000 for self plus spouse and one dependent; and

(F) $1,000 for self plus spouse and two or more dependents.

(iii) Employer F's HSA contributions satisfy the comparability rules.

Example 7. (i) In the 2007 calendar year, Employer G maintains an HDHP. The HDHP has a $1,800 deductible for self-only coverage and the following family coverage options—

(A) A $3,500 deductible for self plus one dependent;

(B) A $3,800 deductible for self plus spouse;

(C) A $4,000 deductible for self plus two or more dependents;

(D) A $4,500 deductible for self plus spouse and one dependent; and

(E) A $5,000 deductible for self plus spouse and two or more dependents.

(ii) Employer G makes the following contributions for the calendar year to the HSA of each full-time employee who is an eligible individual covered under the HDHP—

(A) $360 for self-only coverage;

(B) $875 for self plus one dependent;

(C) $950 for self plus spouse;

(D) $1,000 for self plus two or more dependents;

(E) $1,125 for self plus spouse and one dependent; and

(F) $1,250 for self plus spouse and two or more dependents.

(iii) Employer G's HSA contributions satisfy the comparability rules because Employer G has made contributions that are the same percentage of the deductible for eligible employees with the same category of coverage (20% of the deductible for eligible employees with self-only coverage and 25% of the deductible for eligible employees with family coverage). Employer G could also satisfy the comparability rules by contributing the same dollar amount for each category of coverage.

Example 8. In a calendar year, Employer H offers its employees an HDHP and a health flexible spending arrangement (health FSA). The health FSA reimburses employees for medical expenses as defined in section 213(d). Some of Employer H's employees have coverage under the HDHP and the health FSA. For the calendar year, Employer H contributes $500 to the HSA of each employee who is an eligible individual, but does not contribute to the HSAs of employees who have coverage under the health FSA or under a spouse's health FSA. In addition, some of Employer H's employees have coverage under the HDHP and are enrolled in Medicare. Employer H does not contribute to the HSAs of employees who are enrolled in Medicare. The employees who have coverage under the health FSA or under a spouse's health FSA are not comparable participating employees because they are not eligible individuals under section 223(c)(1). Similarly, the employees who are enrolled in Medicare are not comparable participating employees because they are not eligible individuals under section 223(b)(7) and (c)(1). Therefore, employees who have coverage under the health FSA or under a spouse's health FSA and employees who are enrolled in Medicare are excluded from comparability testing. See sections 4980G(b) and 4980E. Employer H's contributions satisfy the comparability rules.

Q-2. How do the comparability rules apply to employer contributions to employees' HSAs if some employees work full-time during the entire calendar year, and other employees work full-time for less than the entire calendar year?

A-2. Employer contributions to the HSAs of employees who work full-time for less than twelve months satisfy the comparability rules if the contribution amount is comparable when determined on a month-to-month basis. For example, if the employer contributes $240 to the HSA of each full-time employee who works the entire calendar year, the employer must contribute $60 to the HSA of a full-time employee who works three months of the calendar year. The rules set forth this Q & A-2 apply to employer contributions made on a pay-as-you-go basis or on a look-back basis as described in Q & A-3 in this section. See sections 4980G(b) and 4980E(d)(2)(B).

Q-3. How does an employer comply with the comparability rules when some employees who are eligible individuals do not work for the employer during the entire calendar year?

A-3. (a) *In general.* In determining whether the comparability rules are satisfied, an employer must take into account all full-time and part-time employees who were employees and eligible individuals for any month during the calendar year. (Full-time and part-time employees are tested separately. See Q & A-5 in § 54.4980G-3.) There are two methods to comply with the comparability rules when some employees who are eligible individuals do not work for the employer during the entire calendar year; contributions may be made on a pay-as-you-go basis or on a look-back basis. See Q & A-9 through Q & A-11 in § 54.4980G-3 for the rules regarding comparable contributions to the HSAs of former employees.

(b) *Contributions on a pay-as-you-go basis.* An employer may comply with the comparability rules by contributing amounts at one or more times for the calendar year to the HSAs of employees who are eligible individuals, if contributions are the same amount or the same percentage of the HDHP deductible for employees who are eligible individuals as of the first day of the month with the same category of coverage and are made at the same time. Contributions made at the employer's usual payroll interval for different groups of employees are considered to be made at the same time. For example, if salaried employees are paid monthly and hourly employees are paid bi-weekly, an employer may contribute to the HSAs of hourly employees on a bi-weekly basis and to the HSAs of salaried employees on a monthly basis. An employer may change the amount that it contributes to the HSAs of employees at any point. However, the changed contribution amounts must satisfy the comparability rules.

(c) *Examples.* The following examples illustrate the rules in paragraph (b) of this Q & A-3:

Example 1. (i) Beginning on January 1st, Employer J contributes $50 per month on the first day of each month to the HSA of each employee who is an eligible individual. Employer J does not contribute to the HSAs of former employees. In mid-March of the same year, Employee X, an eligible individual, terminates employment after Employer J has contributed $150 to X's HSA. After X terminates employment, Employer J does not contribute additional amounts to X's HSA. In mid-April of the same year, Employer J hires Employee Y, an eligible individual, and contributes $50 to Y's HSA in May and $50 in June. Effective in July of the same year, Employer J stops contributing to the HSAs of all employees and makes no contributions to the HSA of any employee for the months of July through December. In August, Employer J hires Employee Z, an eligible individual. Employer J does not contribute to Z's HSA. After Z is hired, Employer J does not hire additional employees. As of the end of the calendar year, Employer J has made the following HSA contributions to its employees' HSAs—

(A) Employer J contributed $150 to X's HSA;

(B) Employer J contributed $100 to Y's HSA;

(C) Employer J did not contribute to Z's HSA; and

(D) Employer J contributed $300 to the HSA of each employee who was an eligible individual and employed by Employer J from January through June.

(ii) Employer J's contributions satisfy the comparability rules.

Example 2. In a calendar year, Employer K offers its employees an HDHP and contributes on a monthly pay-as-you-go basis to the HSAs of employees who are eligible individuals with coverage under Employer K's HDHP. In the calendar year, Employer K contributes $50 per month to the HSA of each of employee with self-only HDHP coverage and $100 per month to the HSA of each employee with family HDHP coverage. From January 1 st through March 30 th of the calendar year, Employee X is an eligible individual with self-only HDHP coverage. From April 1 st through December 30 th of the calendar year, X is an eligible individual with family HDHP coverage. For the months of January, February and March of the calendar year, Employer K contributes $50 per month to X's HSA. For the remaining months of the calendar year, Employer K contributes $100 per month to X's HSA. Employer K's contributions to X's HSA satisfy the comparability rules.

(d) *Contributions on a look-back basis.* An employer may also satisfy the comparability rules by determining comparable contributions for the calendar year at the end of the calendar year, taking into account all employees who were eligible individuals for any month during the calendar year and contributing the correct amount (a percentage of the HDHP deductible or a specified dollar amount for the same categories of coverage) to the employees' HSAs.

(e) *Example.* The following example illustrates the rules in paragraph (d) of this Q & A-3:

Example. In a calendar year, Employer L offers its employees an HDHP and contributes on a look-back basis to the HSAs of employees who are eligible individuals with coverage under Employer L's HDHP. Employer L contributes $600 (i.e. $50 per month) for the calendar year to the HSA of each of employee with self-only HDHP coverage and $1,200 (i.e., $100 per month) for the calendar year to the HSA of each employee with family HDHP coverage. From January 1 st through June 30 th of the calendar year, Employee Y is an eligible individual with family HDHP coverage. From July 1 st through December 31, Y is an eligible individual with self-only HDHP coverage. Employer L contributes $900 on a look-back-basis for the calendar year to Y's HSA ($100 per month for the months of January through June and $50 per month for the months of July through December). Employer L's contributions to Y's HSA satisfy the comparability rules.

Q-4. May an employer make all of its contributions to the HSAs of its employees who are eligible individuals at the beginning of the calendar year (i.e., on a pre-funded basis) instead of contributing on a pay-as-you-go or on a look-back basis?

A-4. (a) *Contributions on a pre-funded basis.* Yes. An employer may make all of its contributions to the HSAs of its employees who are eligible individuals at the beginning of the calendar year. An employer that pre-funds the HSAs of its employees will not fail to satisfy the comparability rules because an employee who terminates employment prior to the end of the calendar year has received more contributions on a monthly basis than employees who have worked the entire calendar year. See Q & A-12 in this section. Under section 223(d)(1)(E), an account beneficiary's interest in an HSA is nonforfeitable. An employer must make comparable contributions for all employees who are comparable participating employees for any month during the calendar year, including employees who are eligible individuals hired after the date of initial funding. An employer that makes HSA contributions on a pre-funded basis may also contribute on a pre-funded basis to the HSAs of employees who are eligible individuals hired after the date of initial funding. Alternatively, an employer that has pre-funded the HSAs of comparable participating employees may contribute to the HSAs of employees who are eligible individuals hired after the date of initial funding on a pay-as-you-go basis or on a look-back basis. An employer that makes HSA contributions on a pre-funded basis must use the same contribution method for all employees who are eligible individuals hired after the date of initial funding.

(b) *Example.* The following example illustrates the rules in paragraph (a) of this Q & A-4:

Example. (i) On January 1, Employer M contributes $1,200 for the calendar year on a pre-funded basis to the HSA of each of employee who is an eligible individual. In mid-May, Employer M hires Employee

B, an eligible individual. Therefore, Employer M is required to make comparable contributions to B's HSA beginning in June. Employer M satisfies the comparability rules with respect to contributions to B's HSA if it makes HSA contributions in any one of the following ways—

(A) Pre-funding B's HSA by contributing $700 to B's HSA;

(B) Contributing $100 per month on a pay-as-you-go basis to B's HSA; or

(C) Contributing to B's HSA at the end of the calendar year taking into account each month that B was an eligible individual and employed by Employer M.

(ii) If Employer M hires additional employees who are eligible individuals after initial funding, it must use the same contribution method for these employees that it used to contribute to B's HSA.

Q-5. Must an employer use the same contribution method as described in Q & A-3 and Q & A-4 of this section for all employees who were comparable participating employees for any month during the calendar year?

A-5. Yes. If an employer makes comparable HSA contributions on a pay-as-you-go basis, it must do so for each employee who is a comparable participating employee during the pay period. If an employer makes comparable contributions on a look-back basis, it must do so for each employee who was a comparable participating employee for any month during the calendar year. If an employer makes HSA contributions on a pre-funded basis, it must do so for all employees who are comparable participating employees at the beginning of the calendar year. An employer that contributes on a pre-funded basis must make comparable HSA contributions for all employees who are comparable participating employees for any month during the calendar year, including employees who are eligible individuals hired after the date of initial funding. See Q & A-4 in this section for rules regarding contributions for employees hired after initial funding.

Q-6. How does an employer comply with the comparability rules if an employee has not established an HSA at the time the employer contributes to its employees' HSAs?

A-6. (a) *Employee has not established an HSA.* If an employee has not established an HSA at the time the employer funds its employees' HSAs, the employer complies with the comparability rules by contributing comparable amounts to the employee's HSA when the employee establishes the HSA, taking into account each month that the employee was a comparable participating employee. However, an employer is not required to make comparable contributions for a calendar year to an employee's HSA if the employee has not established an HSA by December 31 st of the calendar year.

(b) *Example.* The following example illustrates the rules in paragraph (a) of this Q & A-6:

Example. Beginning on January 1st, Employer N contributes $500 per calendar year on a pay-as-you-go basis to the HSA of each employee who is an eligible individual. Employee C is an eligible individual during the entire calendar year but does not establish an HSA until March. Notwithstanding C's delay in establishing an HSA, Employer N must make up the missed HSA contributions for January and February by April 15 th of the following calendar year.

Q-7. If an employer bases its contributions on a percentage of the HDHP deductible, how is the correct percentage or dollar amount computed?

A-7. (a) *Computing HSA contributions.* The correct percentage is determined by rounding to the nearest 1/100 th of a percentage point and the dollar amount is determined by rounding to the nearest whole dollar.

(b) *Example.* The following example illustrates the rules in paragraph (a) of this Q & A-7:

Example. In this *Example*, assume that the HDHP provided by Employer P satisfies the definition of an HDHP for the 2007 calendar year. In the 2007 calendar year, Employer P maintains two HDHPs. Plan A has a deductible of $3,000 for self-only coverage. Employer P contributes $1,000 for the calendar year to the HSA of each employee covered under Plan A. Plan B has a deductible of $3,500 for self-only coverage. Employer P satisfies the comparability rules if it makes either of the following contributions for the 2007 calendar year to the HSA of each employee who is an eligible individual with self-only coverage under Plan B—

(i) $1,000; or

(ii) $1,167 (33.33% of the deductible rounded to the nearest whole dollar amount).

Q-8. Does an employer that contributes to the HSA of each comparable participating employee in an amount equal to the employee's HSA contribution or a percentage of the employee's HSA contribution (matching contributions) satisfy the rule that all comparable participating employees receive comparable contributions?

A-8. No. If all comparable participating employees do not contribute the same amount to their HSAs and, consequently, do not receive comparable contributions to their HSAs, the comparability rules are not satisfied, notwithstanding that the employer offers to make available the same contribution amount to each comparable participating employee. But see Q & A-1 in § 54.4980G-5 on contributions to HSAs made through a cafeteria plan.

Q-9. If an employer conditions contributions by the employer to an employee's HSA on an employee's participation in health assessments, disease management programs or wellness programs and makes the same contributions available to all employees who participate in the programs, do the contributions satisfy the comparability rules?

A-9. No. If all comparable participating employees do not elect to participate in all the programs and consequently, all comparable participating employees do not receive comparable contributions to their HSAs, the employer contributions fail to satisfy the comparability rules. But see Q & A-1 in § 54.4980G-5 on contributions made to HSAs through a cafeteria plan.

Q-10. If an employer makes additional contributions to the HSAs of all comparable participating employees who have attained a specified age or who have worked for the employer for a specified number of years, do the contributions satisfy the comparability rules?

A-10. No. If all comparable participating employees do not meet the age or length of service requirement, all comparable participating employees do not receive comparable contributions to their HSAs and the employer contributions fail to satisfy the comparability rules.

Q-11. If an employer makes additional contributions to the HSAs of all comparable participating employees who qualify for the additional contributions (HSA catch-up contributions) under section 223(b)(3), do the contributions satisfy the comparability rules?

A-11. No. If all comparable participating employees do not qualify for the additional HSA contributions under section 223(b)(3), all comparable participating employees do not receive comparable contributions to their HSAs, and the employer contributions fail to satisfy the comparability rules.

Q-12. If an employer's contributions to an employee's HSA result in non-comparable contributions, may the employer recoup the excess amount from the employee's HSA?

A-12. No. An employer may not recoup from an employee's HSA any portion of the employer's contribution to the employee's HSA. Under section 223(d)(1)(E), an account beneficiary's interest in an HSA is nonforfeitable. However, an employer may make additional HSA contributions to satisfy the comparability rules. An employer may contribute up until April 15th following the calendar year in which the non-comparable contributions were made. An employer that makes additional HSA contributions to correct non-comparable contributions must also contribute reasonable interest. However, an employer is not required to contribute amounts in excess of the annual contribution limits in section 223(b).

§ 54.4980G-5 *HSA comparability rules and cafeteria plans and waiver of excise tax.*

Q-1. If an employer makes contributions through a section 125 cafeteria plan to the HSA of each employee who is an eligible individual are the contributions subject to the comparability rules?

A-1. No. The comparability rules do not apply to HSA contributions that an employer makes through a section 125 cafeteria plan. However,

contributions to an HSA made under a cafeteria plan are subject to the section 125 nondiscrimination rules (eligibility rules, contributions and benefits tests and key employee concentration tests). See section 125(b), (c) and (g) and Prop. Treas. Reg. § 1.125-1, Q & A-19, (49 FR 19321).

Q-2. If an employer makes contributions through a cafeteria plan to the HSA of each employee who is an eligible individual in an amount equal to the amount of the employee's HSA contribution or a percentage of the amount of the employee's HSA contribution (i.e., *matching contributions*), are the contributions subject to the section 4980G comparability rules?

A-2. No. The comparability rules do not apply to HSA contributions that an employer makes through a section 125 cafeteria plan. Thus, where matching contributions are made by an employer through a cafeteria plan, the contributions are not subject to the comparability rules of section 4980G. However, contributions, including matching contributions, to an HSA made under a cafeteria plan are subject to the section 125 nondiscrimination rules (eligibility rules, contributions and benefits tests and key employee concentration tests). See Q & A-1 in this section.

Q-3. If an employer provides HDHP coverage through a cafeteria plan, but the employer's HSA contributions are not provided through the cafeteria plan, do the cafeteria plan nondiscrimination rules or the comparability rules apply to the HSA contributions?

A-3. (a) *HDHP provided through cafeteria plan.* The comparability rules in section 4980G apply to the HSA contributions. The cafeteria plan nondiscrimination rules apply only to HSA contributions made through a cafeteria plan irrespective of whether the HDHP is provided through a cafeteria plan.

(b) *Example.* The following example illustrates the rules in paragraph (a) of this Q & A-3:

Example. Employer A provides HDHP coverage through its cafeteria plan. Employer A automatically contributes to the HSA of each employee who is an eligible individual with HDHP coverage through the cafeteria plan. Employees make no election with respect to Employer A's HSA contributions and have no right to receive cash or other taxable benefits in lieu of the HSA contributions. Employer A contributes only to the HSAs of employees who have elected HDHP coverage through the cafeteria plan. The comparability rules apply to Employer A's HSA contributions because the HSA contributions are not made through the cafeteria plan.

Q-4. If under the employer's cafeteria plan, employees who are eligible individuals and who participate in health assessments, disease management programs or wellness programs receive an employer contribution to an HSA, unless the employees elect cash, are the contributions subject to the comparability rules?

A-4. No. The comparability rules do not apply to employer contributions to an HSA made through a cafeteria plan. See Q & A-1 in this section.

Q-5. May all or part of the excise tax imposed under section 4980G be waived?

A-5. In the case of a failure which is due to reasonable cause and not to willful neglect, all or a portion of the excise tax imposed under section 4980G may be waived to the extent that the payment of the tax would be excessive relative to the failure involved. See sections 4980G(b) and 4980E(c).

Mark E. Matthews,

Deputy Commissioner for Services and Enforcement.

CERTIFIED COPY

Guy R. Traynor

¶ 20,261T

IRS proposed regulations: Deferred compensation: Nonqualified plans: Code Sec. 457 plans: Deferral elections.— The Treasury Department and IRS have issued proposed regulations on deferred compensation under section 409A. Section 409A governs plans and arrangements that provide nonqualified deferred compensation to employees, directors or other service providers. These regulations implement provisions established by the American Jobs Creation Act (AJCA) (P.L. 108-357). The proposed regulations identify which plans and arrangements are covered under Code Sec. 409A, outline operational requirements for deferral elections, and permissible timing for deferred compensation payments made under the rules. They also provide guidance regarding coverage of state and local government and tax plans that fail to qualify as Code Sec. 457(b) plans.

The proposed regulations, which were published in the Federal Register on October 4, 2005 (70 FR 57930), are reproduced below. The proposed regulations were corrected on December 19, 2005 by 70 FR 75090 and on December 27, 2005 by 70 FR 76502.

[4830-01-p]

DEPARTMENT OF THE TREASURY

Internal Revenue Service

26 CFR Part 1

[REG-158080-04]

RIN 1545-BE79

Application of Section 409A to Nonqualified Deferred Compensation Plans

AGENCY: Internal Revenue Service (IRS), Treasury.

ACTION: Notice of proposed rulemaking and notice of public hearing.

SUMMARY: This document contains proposed regulations regarding the application of section 409A to nonqualified deferred compensation plans. The regulations affect service providers receiving amounts of deferred compensation, and the service recipients for whom the service providers provide services. This document also provides a notice of public hearing on these proposed regulations.

DATES: Written or electronic comments must be received by January 3, 2006. Outlines of topics to be discussed at the public hearing scheduled for January 25, 2006, must be received by January 4, 2006.

ADDRESSES: Send submissions to: CC:PA:LPD:PR (REG-158080-04), room 5203, Internal Revenue Service, PO Box 7604, Ben Franklin Station, Washington, DC 20044. Submissions may be hand-delivered Monday through Friday between the hours of 8 a.m. and 4 p.m. to CC:PA:LPD:PR (REG-158080-04), Courier's Desk, Internal Revenue Service, 1111 Constitution Avenue, NW., Washington, DC or sent electronically, via the IRS Internet site at *www.irs.gov/regs* or via the Federal eRulemaking Portal at *www.regulations.gov* (IRS REG-158080-04). The public hearing will be held in the Auditorium, Internal Revenue Building, 1111 Constitution Avenue, NW., Washington, DC.

FOR FURTHER INFORMATION CONTACT: Concerning the proposed regulations, Stephen Tackney, at (202) 927-9639; concerning submissions of comments, the hearing, and/or to be placed on the building access list to attend the hearing, Richard A. Hurst at (202) 622-7116 (not toll-free numbers).

SUPPLEMENTARY INFORMATION:

Background

Section 409A was added to the Internal Revenue Code (Code) by section 885 of the American Jobs Creation Act of 2004, Public Law 108-357 (118 Stat. 1418). Section 409A generally provides that unless certain requirements are met, amounts deferred under a nonqualified deferred compensation plan for all taxable years are currently includible in gross income to the extent not subject to a substantial risk of forfeiture and not previously included in gross income. Section 409A also includes rules applicable to certain trusts or similar arrangements associated with nonqualified deferred compensation, where such arrangements are located outside of the United States or are restricted to the provision of benefits in connection with a decline in the financial health of the sponsor.

On December 20, 2004, the IRS issued Notice 2005-1 (2005-2 I.R.B. 274 (published as modified on January 6, 2005)), setting forth initial guidance with respect to the application of section 409A, and supplying transition guidance in accordance with the terms of the statute. Notice 2005-1 requested comments on all aspects of the application of Section 409A, including certain specified topics. Numerous comments were submitted and all were considered by the Treasury Department and the IRS in formulating these regulations. In general, these regulations incorporate the guidance provided in Notice 2005-1 and provide substantial additional guidance. For a discussion of the continued applicability of Notice 2005-1, see the **Effect on Other Documents** section of this preamble.

Explanation of Provisions

I. *Definition of Nonqualified Deferred Compensation Plan*

A. *In general*

Section 409A applies to amounts deferred under a nonqualified deferred compensation plan. For this purpose a nonqualified deferred compensation plan means any plan that provides for the deferral of compensation, with specified exceptions such as qualified retirement plans, tax-deferred annuities, simplified employee pensions, SIMPLEs and section 501(c)(18) trusts. In addition, section 409A does not apply to certain welfare benefit plans, including bona fide vacation leave, sick leave, compensatory time, disability pay, and death benefit plans.

In certain instances, these regulations cross reference the regulations under section 3121(v)(2), which provide a special timing rule under the Federal Insurance Contributions Act (FICA) for nonqualified deferred compensation, as defined in section 3121(v)(2) and the regulations thereunder. However, unless explicitly cross-referenced in these regulations, the regulations under section 3121(v)(2) do not apply for purposes of section 409A and under no circumstances do these proposed regulations affect the application of section 3121(v)(2).

B. *Section 457 plans*

Section 409A does not apply to eligible deferred compensation plans under section 457(b). However, section 409A applies to nonqualified deferred compensation plans to which section 457(f) applies, separately and in addition to the requirements applicable to such plans under section 457(f). Section 409A(c) provides that nothing in section 409A prevents the inclusion of amounts in gross income under any other provision of the Code. Section 409A(c) further provides that any amount included in gross income under section 409A will not be required to be included in gross income under any other Code provision later than the time provided in section 409A. Accordingly, if in a taxable year an amount subject to section 409A (but not required to be included in income under section 409A) is required to be included in gross income under section 457(f), that amount must be included in gross income under section 457(f) for that taxable year. Correspondingly, if in a taxable year an amount that would otherwise be required to be included in gross income under section 457(f) has been included previously in gross income under section 409A, that amount will not be required to be included in gross income under section 457(f) for that taxable year.

These proposed regulations are intended solely as guidance with respect to the application of section 409A to such arrangements, and should not be relied upon with respect to the application of section 457(f). Thus, state and local government and tax exempt entities may not rely upon the definition of a deferral of compensation under § 1.409A-1(b) of these proposed regulations in applying section 457(f). For example, for purposes of section 457(f), a deferral of compensation includes a stock option and an arrangement in which an employee or independent contractor of a state or local government or tax-exempt entity earns the right to future payments for services, even if those amounts are paid immediately upon vesting and would qualify for the exclusion from the definition of deferred compensation under § 1.409A-1(b)(4) or (5) of these proposed regulations. However, until further guidance is issued, state and local government and tax exempt entities may rely on the definitions of bona fide vacation leave, sick leave, compensatory time, disability pay, and death benefit plans for purposes of section 457(f) as applicable for purposes of applying section 409A and § 1.409A-1(a)(5) of these proposed regulations to nonqualified deferred compensation plans under section 457(f). [Corrected on 12/19/05 by 70 FR 75090.]

C. *Arrangements with independent contractors*

Consistent with Notice 2005-1, Q&A-8, these regulations exclude from coverage under section 409A certain arrangements between service providers and service recipients. Under these regulations, amounts deferred in a taxable year with respect to a service provider using an accrual method of accounting for that year are not subject to section 409A. In addition, section 409A generally does not apply to amounts deferred pursuant to an arrangement between a service recipient and an unrelated independent contractor (other than a director of a corporation), if during the independent contractor's taxable year in which the amount is deferred, the independent contractor is providing significant services to each of two or more service recipients that are unrelated, both to each other and to the independent contractor. In response to comments, these regulations clarify that the determination is made based upon the independent contractor's taxable year in which the amount is deferred.

Commentators also requested clarification of the circumstances in which services to each service recipient will be deemed to be significant, as required for the exclusion. Determining whether services provided to a service recipient are significant generally will involve an examination of all relevant facts and circumstances. However, two clarifications have been provided. First, the analysis applies separately to each trade or business in which the service provider is engaged. For example, a taxpayer providing computer programming services for one service recipient will not meet the exception if, as a separate trade or business, the taxpayer paints houses for another unrelated service recipient. To provide certainty to many independent contractors engaged in an active trade or business with multiple service recipients, a safe harbor has been provided under which an independent contractor with multiple unrelated service recipients, to whom the independent contractor also is not related, will be treated as providing significant services to more than one of those service recipients, if not more than 70 percent of the total revenue generated by the trade or business in the particular taxable year is derived from any particular service recipient (or group of related service recipients).

Commentators also requested clarification with respect to the application of section 409A to directors. As provided in these regulations, an individual will not be excluded from coverage under section 409A merely because the individual provides services as a director to two or more unrelated service recipients. However, the provisions of section 409A apply separately to arrangements between the service provider director and each service recipient. Accordingly, the inclusion of income due to a failure to meet the requirements of section 409A with respect to an arrangement to serve as a director of one service recipient will not cause an inclusion of income with respect to arrangements to serve as a director of an unrelated service recipient. In addition, the continuation of services as a director with one service recipient will not cause the termination of services as a director with an unrelated service recipient to fail to constitute a separation from service for purposes of section 409A, if the termination would otherwise qualify as a separation from service.

Commentators also requested clarification with respect to the application of the rule to directors who are also employees of the service recipient. In general, the provisions of section 409A will apply separately to the arrangements between the service recipient and the service provider for services as a director and the arrangements between the service recipient and the service provider for services as an employee. However, the distinction is not intended to permit employee directors to limit the aggregation of arrangements in which the individual participates as an employee by labeling such arrangements as arrangements for services as a director. Accordingly, an arrangement with an employee director will be treated as an arrangement for services as a director only to the extent that another non-employee director defers compensation under the same, or a substantially similar, arrangement on similar terms. Moreover, the separate application of section 409A to arrangements for services as a director and arrangements for services as an employee does not extend to a service provider's services for the service recipient as an independent contractor in addition to the service provider's services as a director of the service recipient. Under those circumstances, both arrangements are treated as services provided as an independent contractor.

Commentators also requested clarification of the application of the exclusion to independent contractors who provide services to only one service recipient, when that service recipient itself has multiple clients. Specifically a commentator requested that the rule be applied on a look through basis, so that the independent contractor will be deemed to be providing services for multiple service recipients. The Treasury Department and the IRS do not believe that such a rule is appropriate. Where multiple persons have come together and formed an entity that is itself a service recipient of the independent contractor, the independent contractor is performing services for the single entity service recipient.

The Treasury Department and the IRS believe that where the service recipient is purchasing an independent contractor's management services, amounts deferred with respect to the independent contractor's performance of services should not be excluded from coverage under section 409A. Among the many objectives underlying the enactment of section 409A is to limit the ability of a service provider to retain the benefits of the deferral of compensation while having excessive control over the timing of the ultimate payment. Where the independent contractor is managing the service recipient, there is a significant potential for the independent contractor to have such influence or control over compensation matters so that categorical exclusion from coverage under section 409A is not appropriate. Accordingly, the regulations provide that compensation arrangements between an independent contractor and a service recipient that involve the provision of management services are not excluded from coverage under section 409A, and in such cases, the service recipient is not treated as unrelated for purposes of determining whether arrangements with other service recipients are excluded from coverage under section 409A under the general rule addressing independent contractors providing services to multiple unrelated service recipients. For this purpose, management services include services involving actual or de facto direction or control of the financial or operational aspects of the client's trade or business, or investment advisory services that are integral to the trade or business of a service recipient whose primary trade or business involves the management of investments in entities other than the entities comprising the service recipient, such as a hedge fund or real estate investment trust.

II. *Definition of Nonqualified Deferred Compensation*

A. *In general*

Consistent with Notice 2005-1, Q&A-4, these regulations provide that a plan provides for the deferral of compensation only if, under the terms of the plan and the relevant facts and circumstances, the service provider has a legally binding right during a taxable year to compensation that has not been actually or constructively received and included in gross income, and that, pursuant to the terms of the plan, is payable to (or on behalf of) the service provider in a later year. A legally binding right to compensation may exist even where the right is subject to conditions, including conditions that constitute a substantial risk of forfeiture. For example, an employee that in Year 1 is promised a bonus equal to a set percentage of employer profits, to be paid out in Year 3 if the employee has remained in employment through Year 3, has a legally binding right to the payment of the compensation, subject to the conditions being met. The right thus may be subject to a substantial risk of forfeiture, and accordingly be nonvested; however, the promise constitutes a legally binding right subject to a condition.

In contrast, a service provider does not have a legally binding right to compensation if that compensation may be unilaterally reduced or eliminated by the service recipient or other person after the services creating the right to the compensation have been performed. Notice 2005-1, Q&A-4 provides that, if the facts and circumstances indicate that the discretion to reduce or eliminate the compensation is available or exercisable only upon a condition that is unlikely to occur, or the discretion to reduce or eliminate the compensation is unlikely to be exercised, a service provider will be considered to have a legally binding right to the compensation. Commentators criticized the provision as being difficult to apply, because the standard is too vague, requiring a subjective judgment as to whether the discretion is likely to be exercised. The intent of this provision was to eliminate the possibility of taxpayers avoiding the application of section 409A through the use of plan provisions providing negative discretion, where such provisions are not meaningful. In response to the comments, these regulations adopt a standard under which the negative discretion will be recognized unless it lacks substantive significance, or is available or exercisable only upon a condition. Thus, where a promise of compensation may be reduced or eliminated at the unfettered discretion of the service recipient, that promise generally will not result in a legally binding right to compensation. However, where the negative discretion lacks substantive significance, or the discretion is available or exercisable only upon a condition, the discretion will be ignored and the service provider will be treated as having a legally binding right. In addition, where the service provider has control over, or is related to, the person granted the discretion to reduce or eliminate the compensation, or has control over all or any portion of such person's compensation or benefits, the discretion also will be ignored and the service provider will be treated as having a legally binding right to the compensation.

B. *Short-term deferrals*

Notice 2005-1, Q&A-4(c), set forth an exception from coverage under section 409A under which certain arrangements, referred to as short-term deferrals, would not be treated as resulting in the deferral of compensation. Specifically, Notice 2005-1, Q&A-4 provided that until further guidance a deferral of compensation would not occur if, absent an election to otherwise defer the payment to a later period, at all times the terms of the plan require payment by, and an amount is actually and constructively received by the service provider by, the later of (i) the date that is 2 1/2 months from the end of the service provider's first taxable year in which the amount is no longer subject to a substantial risk of forfeiture, or (ii) the date that is 2 1/2 months from the end of the service recipient's year in which the amount is no longer subject to a substantial risk of forfeiture. For these purposes, an amount that is never subject to a substantial risk of forfeiture is considered to be no longer subject to a substantial risk of forfeiture on the date the service provider first has a legally binding right to the amount. Under this rule, many multi-year bonus arrangements that require payments promptly after the amount vests would not be subject to section 409A.

The exception from coverage under section 409A for short-term deferrals set forth in Notice 2005-1, Q&A-4, has been incorporated into these proposed regulations. Commentators questioned whether a written provision in the arrangement requiring the payment to be made by the relevant deadline is necessary, or whether the customary practice of the service recipient is sufficient. These regulations do not require that the arrangement provide in writing that the payment must be made by the relevant deadline. Accordingly, where an arrangement does not otherwise defer compensation, an amount will qualify as a short-term deferral, and not be subject to section 409A, if the amount is actually paid out by the appropriate deadline. However, where an arrangement does not provide in writing that a payment must be paid by a specified date on or before the relevant deadline, and the payment is not made by the appropriate deadline (except due to unforeseeable administrative or solvency issues, as discussed below), the payment will result in automatic violation of section 409A due to the failure to specify the payment date or a permissible payment event. In addition, the rules permitting the service recipient limited discretion to delay payments of amounts subject to section 409A (for example, where the service recipient reasonably anticipates that payment of the amount would not be deductible due to application of section 162(m), or where the service recipient reasonably anticipates that payment of the amount would violate a loan covenant or similar contractual provision) would not be available, because the arrangement would not have specified a payment date subject to the delay. In contrast, where an arrangement provides in writing that a payment must be made by a specified date on or before the relevant deadline, and the payment is not made by the appropriate deadline so that section 409A becomes applicable, the rules contained in these regulations generally permitting the payment to be made in the same calendar year as the fixed payment date become applicable. In addition, the rules permitting a plan to provide for a delay in the payment in certain circumstances and the relief applicable to disputed payments and refusals to pay would also be available. Accordingly, it will often be appropriate to include a date or year for payment even when it is intended that the payment will be made within the short-term deferral period.

The short-term deferral rule does not provide a method to avoid application of section 409A if the legally binding right creates a right to deferred compensation from the outset. For example, if a legally binding right to payment in Year 10 arises in Year 1, but the right is subject to a substantial risk of forfeiture through Year 3, paying the amount at the end of Year 3 would not result in the payment failing to be subject to section 409A, but rather generally would be an impermissible acceleration of the payment from the originally established right to payment in Year 10. [Corrected on 12/19/05 by 70 FR 75090.]

Commentators also questioned whether the 2 1/2 month deadline for payment could be extended where the payment was not administratively practicable, or where the payment was made late due to error. These regulations provide that a payment made after the 2 1/2 month deadline may continue to be treated as meeting the requirements of the exception from the definition of a deferral of compensation if the taxpayer establishes that it was impracticable, either administratively or economically, to avoid the deferral of the receipt by a service provider of the payment beyond the applicable 2 1/2 month period and that, as of the time the legally binding right to the amount arose, such impracticability was unforeseeable, and the payment is made as soon as practicable. Some commentators had asked for a rule permitting delays due to unintentional error to satisfy the standard for the exclusion. However, the exception is based upon the longstanding position set forth in § 1.404(b)-1T, Q&A-2(b) regarding the timing of the deduction with respect to a payment under a nonqualified deferred compensation plan. Similar to the deduction rule, the exclusion from coverage under section 409A treats a payment made within the appropriate 2 1/2 month period as made within such a short period following the date the substantial risk of forfeiture lapses that it may be treated as paid when earned (and not deferred to a subsequent period). Also similar to the rule governing the timing of deductions, the exclusion from coverage under section 409A permits only limited exceptions to the requirement that the amount actually be paid by the relevant deadline. Pending further study, the Treasury Department and the IRS believe that providing further flexibility with respect to meeting the deadline would create the potential for abuse and enforcement difficulty.

C. *Stock options and stock appreciation rights*

1. *In general*

The legislative history states that section 409A does not cover grants of stock options where the exercise price can never be less than the fair market value of the underlying stock at the date of grant (a non-discounted option). See H.R. Conf. Rep. No. 108-755, at 735 (2004). Thus an option with an exercise price that is or may be below the fair market value of the underlying stock at the date of grant (a discounted option) is subject to the requirements of section 409A. Consistent with the legislative history and with Notice 2005-1, Q&A-4, these regulations provide that a non-discounted stock option, that has no other feature for the deferral of compensation, generally is not covered by section 409A. However, a stock option granted with an exercise price below the fair market value of the underlying shares of stock on the date of grant generally would be subject to section 409A except to the extent the terms of the option only permit exercise of the option during the short-term deferral period. [Corrected on 12/27/05 by 70 FR 76502.]

Commentators stressed that in many respects, a stock appreciation right can be the economic equivalent of a stock option, especially a stock option that allows the holder to exercise in a manner other than by the payment of cash (a cashless exercise feature). Accordingly, Notice 2005-1, Q&A-4 exempted from coverage certain non-discounted stock appreciation rights that most closely resembled stock options - stock appreciation rights settled in stock. The Treasury Department and the IRS were concerned that the manipulation of the purported stock valuation for purposes of determining whether the stock appreciation right was issued at a discount or settled at a premium could lead to a stock appreciation right being used to circumvent section 409A. Accordingly, the exception was limited to stock appreciation rights issued with respect to stock traded on an established securities market.

Commentators criticized the distinction between public corporations and non-public corporations, asserting that this distinction is not meaningful and unfairly discriminated against the latter corporations and placed such corporations at a severe competitive disadvantage. In addition, commentators questioned whether the distinction between stock-settled and cash-settled stock appreciation rights was relevant, where the amount of income generated would be identical.

In response to the comments, these regulations treat stock appreciation rights similarly to stock options, regardless of whether the stock appreciation right is settled in cash and regardless of whether the stock appreciation right is based upon service recipient stock that is not readily tradable on an established securities market. The Treasury Department and the IRS remain concerned that manipulation of stock valuations, and manipulation of the characteristics of the underlying stock, may lead to abuses with respect to stock options and stock appreciation rights (collectively referred to as stock rights). To that end, these regulations contain more detailed provisions with respect to the identification of service recipient stock that may be subject to, or used to determine the amount payable under, stock rights excluded from the application of section 409A, and the valuation of such service recipient stock, discussed below.

2. *Definition of service recipient stock*

The legislative history of section 409A states that the exception from coverage under section 409A for certain nonstatutory stock options was intended to cover options granted on service recipient stock. H.R. Conf. Rep. No. 108-755, at 735 (2004). Section 409A(d)(6) provides that, for purposes of determining the identity of the service recipient under section 409A, aggregation rules similar to the rules in section 414(b) and (c) apply. Taxpayers requested that the definition of service recipient be expanded for purposes of the exception for stock rights to cover entities that would not otherwise be treated as part of the service recipient applying the rules under section 414(b) and (c). The Treasury Department and the IRS agree that the exclusion for nonstatutory stock rights was not meant to apply so narrowly. Accordingly, for purposes of the provisions excluding certain stock rights on service recipient stock, the stock right, or the plan or arrangement under which the stock right is granted, may provide that section 414(b) and (c) be applied by modifying the language and using "50 percent" instead of "80 percent" where appropriate, such that stock rights granted to employees of entities in which the issuing corporation owns a 50 percent interest generally will not be subject to section 409A. [Corrected on 12/27/05 by 70 FR 76502.]

Commentators also requested that the threshold be dropped below 50 percent to cover joint ventures and other similar arrangements, where the participating corporation does not have a majority interest. These regulations provide for such a lower threshold, allowing for the stock right, or the plan or arrangement under which the stock right is granted, to provide for the modification of the language and use of "20 percent" instead of "80 percent" in applying section 414(b) and (c), where the use of such stock with respect to stock rights is due to legitimate business criteria. For example, the use of such stock with respect to stock rights issued to employees of a joint venture that were former employees of a corporation with at least a 20 percent interest in the joint venture generally would be due to legitimate business criteria, and accordingly would be treated as service recipient stock for purposes of determining whether the stock right was subject to section 409A. A designation by a service recipient to use either the 50 percent or the 20 percent threshold must be applied consistently to all compensatory stock rights, and any designation of a different permissible ownership threshold percentage may not be made effective until 12 months after the adoption of such change.

The increased ability to issue stock rights with respect to a related corporation for whom the service provider does not directly perform services could increase the potential for service recipients to exploit the exclusion for certain stock rights by establishing a corporation within the group of related corporations, the purpose of which is to serve as an investment vehicle for nonqualified deferred compensation. Accordingly, these regulations provide that other than with respect to service providers who are primarily engaged in providing services directly to such corporation, the term service recipient for purposes of the definition of service recipient stock does not include a corporation whose primary purpose is to serve as an investment vehicle with respect to the corporation's interest in entities other than the service recipient (including entities aggregated with the corporation under the definition of service recipient incorporating section 414(b) and (c)).

Commentators also questioned whether the exception for certain stock rights could apply where a service recipient provides a stock right with respect to preferred stock or a separate class of common stock. The Treasury Department and the IRS believe this exception was intended to cover stock rights with respect to service recipient stock the fair market value of which meaningfully relates to the potential future appreciation in the enterprise value of the corporation. The use of a separate class of common stock created for the purpose of compensating service providers, or the use of preferred stock with substantial characteristics of debt, could create an arrangement that more closely resembles traditional nonqualified deferred compensation arrangements rather than an interest in appreciation of the value of the service recipient. An exception that excluded these arrangements from coverage under section 409A would undermine the effectiveness of the statute to govern nonqualified deferred compensation arrangements, contrary to the legislative intent. Accordingly, these regulations clarify that service recipient stock includes only common stock, and only the class of common stock that as of the date of grant has the highest aggregate value of any class of common stock of the corporation outstanding, or a class of common stock substantially similar to such class of stock (ignoring differences in voting rights). In addition, service recipient stock does not include any stock that provides a preference as to dividends or liquidation rights.

With respect to the foreign aspects of such arrangements, commentators requested clarification that service recipient stock may include American Depositary Receipts (ADRs). These regulations clarify that stock of the service recipient may include ADRs, provided that the stock to which the ADRs relate would otherwise qualify as service recipient stock. [Corrected on 12/19/05 by 70 FR 75090.]

Commentators also requested that certain equity appreciation rights issued by mutual companies, intended to mimic stock appreciation rights, be excluded from coverage under section 409A. These regulations expand the exclusion for stock appreciation rights to include equity appreciation rights with respect to mutual company units. A mutual company unit is defined as a specified percentage of the fair market value of the mutual company. For this purpose, a mutual company may value itself under the same provisions applicable to the valuation of stock of a corporation that is not readily tradable on an established securities market. The Treasury Department and the IRS request comments as to the practicability of this provision, and whether such a provision should be expanded to cover equity appreciation rights issued by other entities that do not have outstanding shares of stock.

3. *Valuation*

Notice 2005-1, Q&A-4(d)(ii) provides that for purposes of determining whether the requirements for exclusion of a nonstatutory stock option have been met, any reasonable valuation method may be used. Commentators expressed concern that the standard was too vague, given the potential consequences of a failure to comply with the requirements of section 409A.

These regulations provide that with respect to service recipient stock that is readily tradable on an established securities market, a valuation of such stock may be based on the last sale before or the first sale after the grant, or the closing price on the trading day before or the trading day of the grant, or any other reasonable basis using actual transactions in such stock as reported by such market and consistently applied. Commentators pointed out that certain service recipients, generally corporations in certain foreign jurisdictions, would not be able to meet this requirement because the service recipient is subject to foreign laws requiring pricing based on an average over a period of time. To allow compliance with these requirements, these regulations further provide that service recipients (including U.S. service recipients) may set the exercise price based on an average of the price of the stock over a specified period provided such period occurs within the 30 days before and 30 days after the grant date, and provided further that the terms of the grant are irrevocably established before the beginning of the measurement period used to determine the exercise price.

Commentators asked for clarification of the definition of stock that is readily tradable on an established securities market. Specifically, commentators requested clarification of the scope of an established securities market, and whether that term includes over-the-counter markets

and foreign markets. The regulations adopt the definition of an established securities market set forth in § 1.897-1(m). Under that definition, over-the-counter markets generally are treated as established securities markets, as well as many foreign markets. However, the stock must also be readily tradable within such markets to qualify as stock readily tradable on an established securities market.

With respect to corporations whose stock is not readily tradable on an established securities market, these regulations provide that fair market value may be determined through the reasonable application of a reasonable valuation method. The regulations contain a description of the factors that will be taken into account in determining whether a given valuation method is reasonable. In addition, in an effort to provide more certainty, certain presumptions with respect to the reasonableness of a valuation method have been set forth. Provided one such method is applied reasonably and used consistently, the valuation determined by applying such method will be presumed to equal the fair market value of the stock, and such presumption will be rebuttable only by a showing that the valuation is grossly unreasonable. A method will be treated as used consistently where the same method is used for all equity-based compensation granted to service providers by the service recipient, including for purposes of determining the amount due upon exercise or repurchase where the stock acquired is subject to an obligation of the service recipient to repurchase, or a put or call right providing for the potential repurchase by the service recipient, as applicable.

Commentators specifically requested clarification as to whether a valuation method based upon an appraisal will be treated as reasonable, and if so with respect to what period. These regulations provide that the use of an appraisal will be presumed reasonable if the appraisal satisfies the requirements of the Code with respect to the valuation of stock held in an employee stock ownership plan. If those requirements are satisfied, the valuation will be presumed reasonable for a one-year period commencing on the date as of which the appraisal values the stock.

Commentators also specifically requested clarification of whether a valuation method based on a nonlapse restriction addressed in § 1.83-5(a) will be treated as reasonable. Under § 1.83-5(a), in the case of property subject to a nonlapse restriction (as defined in § 1.83-3(h)), the price determined under the formula price is considered to be the fair market value of the property unless established to the contrary by the Commissioner, and the burden of proof is on the Commissioner with respect to such value. If stock in a corporation is subject to a nonlapse restriction that requires the transferee to sell such stock only at a formula price based on book value, a reasonable multiple of earnings or a reasonable combination thereof, the price so determined ordinarily is regarded as determinative of the fair market value of such property for purposes of section 83.

The Treasury Department and the IRS do not believe that this standard, in and of itself, is appropriate with respect to the application of section 409A. The Treasury Department and the IRS are not confident that a formula price determined pursuant to a nonlapse restriction will, in every case, adequately approximate the value of the underlying stock. The Treasury Department and the IRS are also concerned that such formula valuations, in the absence of other criteria, may be subject to manipulation or to the provision of predictable results that are inconsistent with a true equity appreciation right. Further, the Treasury Department and the IRS do not believe that the burden of proof with respect to valuation should be shifted to the Commissioner in all cases where such formulas have been utilized. Accordingly, the use of a valuation method based on a nonlapse restriction that meets the requirements of § 1.83-5(a) does not by itself result in a presumption of reasonableness. However, where the method is used consistently for both compensatory and noncompensatory purposes in all transactions in which the service recipient is either the purchaser or seller of such stock, such that the nonlapse restriction formula acts as a substitute for the value of the underlying stock, the formula will qualify for the presumption that the valuation method is reasonable for purposes of section 409A. In addition, depending on the facts and circumstances of the individual case, the use of a nonlapse restriction to determine value may be reasonable, taking into account other relevant valuation criteria.

Commentators also expressed concern about the valuation of illiquid stock of certain start-up corporations. These commentators argued that the value of such stock is often highly speculative, rendering appraisals of limited value. Commentators also noted that such stock often is not subject to put rights or call rights that could be viewed as a nonlapse restriction. Given the illiquidity and speculative value, commentators argued that the risk that taxpayers would use rights on such shares as a device to pay deferred compensation is low. In response, these regulations propose additional conditions under which the valuation of illiquid stock in a start-up corporation will be presumed to be reasonable. A valuation of an illiquid stock of a start-up corporation will be presumed reasonable if the valuation is made reasonably and in good faith and evidenced by a written report that takes into account the relevant factors prescribed for valuations generally under these regulations. For this purpose, illiquid stock of a start-up corporation refers to service recipient stock of a service recipient that is in the first 10 years of the active conduct of a trade or business and has no class of equity securities that are traded on an established securities market, where such stock is not subject to any put or call right or obligation of the service recipient or other person to purchase such stock (other than a right of first refusal upon an offer to purchase by a third party that is unrelated to the service recipient or service provider), provided that this rule does not apply to the valuation of any stock if the service recipient or service provider reasonably may anticipate, as of the time the valuation is applied, that the service recipient will undergo a change in control event or participate in a public offering of securities within the 12 months following the event to which the valuation is applied (for example, the grant date of an award). A valuation will not be treated as made reasonably and in good faith unless the valuation is performed by a person or persons with significant knowledge and experience or training in performing similar valuations.

As stated in the preamble to Notice 2005-1, the Treasury Department and the IRS are concerned about the treatment of stock rights where the service recipient is obligated to repurchase the stock acquired pursuant to the stock right, or the service provider retains a put or call right with respect to the stock. Where the service provider retains such a right, the ability to receive a purchase price that differs from the fair market value of the stock could be used to circumvent the application of section 409A. Accordingly, these regulations generally require that where someone is obligated to purchase the stock received upon the exercise of a stock right, or the stock is subject to a put or call right, the purchase price must also be set at fair market value, the determination of which is also subject to the consistency requirements for the methods used in determining fair market value.

4. Modification

Commentators asked under what conditions a modification, extension, or renewal of a stock right will be treated as a new grant. The treatment as a new grant is relevant because although the original grant may have been excluded from coverage under section 409A, if the new grant has an exercise price that is less than the fair market value of the underlying stock on the date of the new grant, the new grant would not qualify for the exclusion from coverage under section 409A. Accordingly, the regulations set forth rules governing the types of modifications, extensions or renewals that will result in treatment as a new grant. The regulations provide that the term modification means any change in the terms of the stock right that may provide the holder of the right with a direct or indirect reduction in the exercise price of the stock right, or an additional deferral feature, or an extension or renewal of the stock right, regardless of whether the holder in fact benefits from the change in terms. Under this definition, neither the addition of a provision permitting the transfer of the stock right nor a provision permitting the service provider to exchange the stock right for a cash amount equal to the amount that would be available if the stock right were exercised would be modifications of the stock right. In addition, these regulations explicitly provide that both a change in the terms of a stock right to allow for payment of the exercise price through the use of pre-owned stock, and a change in the terms of a stock right to facilitate the payment of employment taxes or required withholding taxes resulting from the exercise of the right, are not treated as modifications of the stock right for purposes of section 409A.

Generally, a change to the exercise price of the stock right (other than in connection with certain assumptions or substitutions of a stock right in connection with a corporate transaction or certain adjustments resulting from a stock split, stock dividend or similar change in capitalization) is treated as a modification, resulting in a new grant that may be excluded from section 409A if it satisfies the requirements in these regulations as of the new grant date. However, depending upon the facts and circumstances, a series of repricings of the exercise price may indicate that the original right had a floating or adjustable exercise price and did not meet the requirements of the exclusion at the time of the original grant.

Generally, an extension granting the holder an additional period within which to exercise the stock right beyond the time originally prescribed will be treated as evidencing an additional deferral feature meaning that the stock right was subject to section 409A from the date of grant. Commentators stated that it is not uncommon upon a termination of employment to extend the exercise period for some brief period of time to allow the terminated employee a chance to exercise the stock

right. In response, these regulations provide that it is not an extension of a stock right if the exercise period is extended to a date no later than the later of the fifteenth day of the third month following the date, or December 31 of the calendar year in which, the right would otherwise have expired if the stock right had not been extended, based on the terms of the stock right at the original grant date. The regulations further provide that it is not an extension of a stock right if at the time the stock right would otherwise expire, the stock right is subject to a restriction prohibiting the exercise of the stock right because such exercise would violate applicable securities laws and the expiration date of the stock right is extended to a date no later than 30 days after the restrictions on exercise are no longer required to avoid a violation of applicable securities laws.

These regulations also provide that if the requirements of § 1.424-1 (providing rules under which an eligible corporation may, by reason of a corporate transaction, substitute a new statutory option for an outstanding statutory option or assume an old option without such substitution or assumption being considered a modification of the old option) would be met if the right were a statutory option, the substitution of a new right pursuant to a corporate transaction for an outstanding right or the assumption of an outstanding right will not be treated as the grant of a new right or a change in the form of payment for purposes of section 409A. Section 1.424-1 applies several requirements. Among them is the requirement under § 1.424-1(a)(5)(ii) that the excess of the aggregate fair market value of the shares subject to the new option over the exercise price immediately after the substitution must not exceed the excess of the fair market value of the shares subject to the old option over the exercise price immediately before the substitution. In addition, § 1.424-1(a)(5)(iii) requires that on a share by share comparison, the ratio of the exercise price to the fair market value of the shares subject to the option immediately after the substitution not be more favorable than the ratio of the exercise price to the fair market value of the shares subject to the old option immediately before the substitution.

Commentators expressed concern that the use of the regulations contained in § 1.424-1, and specifically the ratio test prescribed in § 1.424-1(a)(5)(iii), would prove difficult to apply in circumstances where, to reduce dilution, the acquiring corporation wished to issue a smaller number of shares than the shares underlying the old option, but also wished to retain the entire aggregate difference between the fair market value of the shares and the exercise price that had been available to the service provider before the substitution. In response, Notice 2005-1, Q&A-4 and these regulations provide that the requirement of § 1.424-1(a)(5)(iii) will be deemed to be satisfied if the ratio of the exercise price to the fair market value of the shares subject to the right immediately after the substitution or assumption is not greater than the ratio of the exercise price to the fair market value of the shares subject to the right immediately before the substitution or assumption. For example, if an employee had an option to purchase 25 shares for $2 per share, and immediately prior to a substitution by reason of a corporate transaction the fair market value of a share was $5, then the aggregate spread amount would be $75 (25 shares multiplied by ($5 -$2) = $75). The ratio of the exercise price to the fair market value would be $2/$5 = .40. As a part of the transaction, new employer wishes to substitute for the option an option to purchase 5 shares of new employer, when the shares have a fair market value of $20 per share. To maintain the aggregate spread of $75, the new grant has an exercise price of $5 (5 shares multiplied by ($20 - $5) = $75). The ratio of the exercise price to the fair market value immediately after the substitution is $5/$20 = .25, which is not greater than the ratio immediately before the substitution. Provided that the other requirements of § 1.424-1 were met, this substitution would not be considered a modification of the original stock option for purposes of section 409A.

One commentator asked for more flexible rules concerning adjustments to and substitutions of options following a spinoff or similar transaction because short-term trading activity in the period immediately following such a transaction frequently does not accurately reflect the relative long-term fair market values of the stock of the distributing and distributed corporations. To address this problem, the regulations provide that such adjustments or substitutions may be made based on market quotations as of a predetermined date not more than 60 days after the transaction, or based on an average of such market prices over a period of not more than 30 days ending not later than 60 days after the transaction.

These provisions addressing substitutions and assumptions of rights apply to stock appreciation rights, as well as stock options. However, the guidance provided in these regulations with respect to the assumption of stock appreciation right liabilities should not be interpreted as guidance with respect to issues raised under any other provision of the Code or common law tax doctrine.

D. *Restricted property*

Consistent with Notice 2005-1, Q&A-4(e), these regulations provide that if a service provider receives property from, or pursuant to, a plan maintained by a service recipient, there is no deferral of compensation merely because the value of the property is not includible in income in the year of receipt by reason of the property being nontransferable and subject to a substantial risk of forfeiture, or is includible in income solely due to a valid election under section 83(b). However, a plan under which a service provider obtains a legally binding right to receive property (whether or not the property is restricted property) in a future year may provide for the deferral of compensation and, accordingly, may constitute a nonqualified deferred compensation plan.

Commentators asked for clarification with respect to how this provision applies to a promise to transfer restricted property in a subsequent tax year. Specifically, commentators questioned how section 409A would apply to a bonus program offering a choice between a payment in cash and a payment in substantially nonvested property. Because the promise grants the service recipient a legally binding right to receive property in a future year, this promise generally could not constitute property for section 83 purposes under § 1.83-3(e), and could constitute deferred compensation for purposes of section 409A. However, the regulations provide that the vesting of substantially nonvested property subject to section 83 may be treated as a payment for purposes of section 409A, including for purposes of applying the short-term deferral rule. Accordingly, where the promise to transfer the substantially nonvested property and the right to retain the substantially nonvested property after the transfer are both subject to a substantial risk of forfeiture (as defined for purposes of section 409A), the arrangement generally would constitute a short-term deferral because the payment would occur simultaneously with the vesting of the right to the property. For example, where an employee participates in a two-year bonus program such that, if the employee continues in employment for two years, the employee is entitled to either the immediate payment of a $10,000 cash bonus or the grant of restricted stock with a $15,000 fair market value subject to a vesting requirement of three additional years of service, the arrangement generally would constitute a short-term deferral because under either alternative the payment would be received within the short-term deferral period. [Corrected on 12/19/05 by 70 FR 75090.]

E. *Arrangements between partnerships and partners*

The statute and legislative history to section 409A do not specifically address arrangements between partnerships and partners providing services to a partnership, and do not explicitly exclude such arrangements from the application of section 409A. The application of section 409A to such arrangements raises a number of issues, relating both to the scope of the arrangements subject to section 409A, and the coordination of the provisions of subchapter K and section 409A with respect to those arrangements that are subject to section 409A. The Treasury Department and the IRS continue to analyze the issues raised in this area, and accordingly these regulations do not address arrangements between partnerships and partners. Notice 2005-1, Q&A-7 provides interim guidance regarding the application of section 409A to arrangements between partnerships and partners. Until further guidance is issued, taxpayers may continue to rely on Notice 2005-1, Q&A-7.

Commentators have asked whether section 409A applies to guaranteed payments for services described in section 707(c). Until further guidance is issued, section 409A will apply to guaranteed payments described in section 707(c) (and rights to receive such guaranteed payments in the future), only in cases where the guaranteed payment is for services and the partner providing services does not include the payment in income by the 15 th day of the third month following the end of the taxable year of the partner in which the partner obtained a legally binding right to the guaranteed payment or, if later, the taxable year in which the right to the guaranteed payment is first no longer subject to a substantial risk of forfeiture.

The Treasury Department and the IRS continue to request comments with respect to the application of section 409A to arrangements between partnerships and partners.

F. *Foreign arrangements*

The regulations provide guidance with respect to the application of section 409A to various foreign arrangements. As an initial matter, the regulations provide that an arrangement does not provide for a deferral of compensation subject to section 409A where the compensation subject to the arrangement would not have been includible in gross income for Federal tax purposes if it had been paid to the service provider at the time that the legally binding right to the compensation first arose or, if later, the first time that the legally binding right was no longer subject to a substantial risk of forfeiture, if the service provider was a nonresident alien at such time. Accordingly, if, for example, a foreign citizen works outside the United States and then retires to the United States, the compensation deferred and vested while working in the foreign country generally will not be subject to section 409A.

With respect to U.S. citizens or resident aliens working abroad, the regulations provide that an arrangement does not provide for a deferral of compensation subject to section 409A where the compensation subject to the arrangement would have constituted foreign earned income (within the meaning of section 911) paid to a qualified individual (as defined in section 911(d)(1)) and the amount of the compensation is less than or equal to the difference between the maximum section 911 exclusion amount and the amount actually excludible from gross income under section 911 for the taxable year for the individual. This hypothetical exclusion is applied at the time that the legally binding right to the compensation first exists or, if later, the time that the legally binding right is no longer subject to a substantial risk of forfeiture. Under section 911, a U.S. citizen or resident alien who resides in a foreign jurisdiction generally may exclude up to $80,000 of foreign earned income (to be adjusted for inflation after 2007). For example, an individual with $70,000 of foreign earned income excluded under section 911 in 2006 could also defer up to $10,000 of additional compensation that would not be subject to section 409A, if the additional compensation would qualify as foreign earned income if paid to the individual in 2006. This exception to coverage under section 409A is intended to be applied on an annual basis, so that individuals will not be entitled to carry over any unused portion of the exclusion under section 911 to a future year. This exception also is not intended to modify the rules under section 911 or the regulations thereunder.

Similarly, these regulations also address deferrals of compensation income that would be excluded from gross income for Federal income tax purposes under section 893 (generally covering compensation paid to foreign workers of a foreign government or international organization working in the United States), section 872 (generally covering certain compensation earned by nonresident alien individuals), section 931 (generally covering certain compensation earned by bona fide residents of Guam, American Samoa, or the Northern Mariana Islands) and section 933 (generally covering certain compensation earned by bona fide residents of Puerto Rico). The regulations provide that an arrangement does not provide for a deferral of compensation subject to section 409A where the compensation subject to the arrangement would have been excluded from gross income for Federal tax purposes under any of these sections, if the compensation had been paid to the service provider at the time that the legally binding right to the compensation first arose or, if later, the time that the legally binding right was no longer subject to a substantial risk of forfeiture.

The Treasury Department and the IRS understand that nonresident aliens may work for very limited periods in the United States. Many deferrals of the compensation earned by nonresident aliens for services rendered in the United States will not be covered by section 409A, because under an applicable treaty the amount of compensation deferred would not be includible in gross income for Federal tax purposes if paid at the time the legally binding right to the compensation deferred was no longer subject to a substantial risk of forfeiture. However, certain compensation earned in the United States by a nonresident alien might be includible in gross income under such circumstances, where there is no applicable treaty or where the treaty does not provide an exclusion. Where a nonresident alien defers such compensation earned in the United States under a foreign nonqualified deferred compensation plan - for example because the service in the United States is credited under the plan - the application of section 409A to the deferrals of the compensation subject to Federal income tax could be exceedingly burdensome in light of the relatively small amounts attributable to the service in the United States. Accordingly, these regulations adopt a de minimis exception, under which section 409A will not apply to an amount of compensation deferred under a foreign nonqualified deferred compensation plan for a given calendar year where the individual service provider is a nonresident alien for that calendar year and the amount deferred does not exceed $10,000.

Commentators requested clarification of the application of section 409A to participation by U.S. citizens and resident aliens in foreign plans. In this context, it should be noted that under these regulations, transfers that are taxable under section 402(b) of the Code generally are not subject to section 409A. See § 1.409A-1(b)(6) of these regulations and Notice 2005-1, Q&A-4. Such transfers may consist of contributions to an employees' trust, where the trust does not qualify under section 501(a). Many foreign plans that hold contributions in a trust will constitute funded plans. To the extent that a contribution to the trust is subject to inclusion in income for Federal tax purposes under section 402(b), such a contribution will not be subject to section 409A.

These regulations also provide that section 409A does not override treaty provisions that govern the U.S. Federal taxation of participation in particular foreign plans. Where a treaty provides that amounts contributed to a foreign plan by or on behalf of a service provider are not subject to U.S. Federal income tax, section 409A will not cause such amounts to be subject to inclusion in gross income.

Some commentators requested that any participation in a foreign plan be exempted from section 409A, or that only deferrals of U.S. source compensation income be subject to section 409A. However, with respect to U.S. citizens working abroad, and with respect to resident aliens in the United States, compensation income generally is subject to U.S. Federal income tax absent an applicable treaty provision. Accordingly, the provisions of section 409A generally are applicable to this type of deferred compensation. In addition, the Treasury Department and the IRS are concerned that providing a broad exception for foreign plans or foreign source income would create opportunities for U.S. citizens and resident aliens to avoid application of section 409A through participation in a foreign plan, or through reallocations of deferrals among U.S. source and foreign source income.

The regulations provide, however, that with respect to non-U.S. citizens who are not lawful permanent residents of the United States, amounts deferred under certain broad-based foreign retirement plans are not subject to section 409A. This exception is intended to allow a worker who is not a green card holder to continue to participate in a broad-based foreign retirement plan that does not comply with section 409A without incurring adverse tax consequences due solely to the worker earning some income in the United States that is in some manner credited under the plan.

Commentators expressed concerns as to U.S. citizens and lawful permanent residents working abroad, and their ability to participate in broad-based plans of foreign employers. Generally, these workers' incomes are subject to Federal income tax, including section 409A. However, when U.S. citizens and lawful permanent residents work abroad for employers who sponsor broad-based foreign retirement plans providing relatively low levels of retirement benefits and such plans are nonelective, the worker's ability to control the timing of the income is limited. In such cases, the concerns with respect to the potential manipulation of the timing of compensation income addressed by section 409A are also limited, and do not outweigh the administrative burdens that would arise if a foreign employer's failure to amend these plans to be consistent with the provisions of section 409A would result in substantial adverse tax consequences to U.S. citizens and lawful permanent residents working abroad who are covered by such plans. Accordingly, an exception for foreign broad-based retirement plans also applies with respect to U.S. citizens and lawful permanent residents, but only with respect to nonelective deferrals of foreign earned income and only to the extent that the amount deferred in a given year does not exceed the amount of contributions or benefits that may be provided by a qualified plan under section 415 (calculated by treating the foreign source income as compensation for purposes of section 415).

Commentators also requested that certain types of payments, referred to as expatriate allowances, be exempted from coverage under section 409A. These payments were defined broadly to include many types of payments to U.S. citizens working abroad, intended to put the service providers in substantially the same economic position as the service providers would have been had the services been provided in the United States. One very common arrangement involves payments intended to compensate the service provider for any differences in tax rates, often referred to as tax equalization plans. With respect to these plans, the Treasury Department and the IRS recognize that such payments often must be delayed because of the need to calculate foreign tax liabilities after the end of the year. In addition, where the amounts are limited to the amounts necessary to make up for difference in tax rates, the potential for abuse with respect to the timing of compensation income is not great, since the compensation will directly relate to taxes that the service provider has paid to a foreign jurisdiction. Accordingly, these regulations exempt tax equalization plans from coverage under section 409A provided that the payment is made no later than the end of the second calendar year beginning after the calendar year in which the individual's U.S. Federal income tax return is required to be filed (including extensions) for the year to which the tax equalization payment relates.

Other payments are not excluded from section 409A merely because they are denominated as expatriate allowances. The Treasury Department and the IRS believe that the rules provided in these regulations with respect to setting and meeting payment dates under a nonqualified deferred compensation plan will provide sufficient flexibility to permit arrangements involving expatriate allowances to satisfy the requirements of section 409A. For example, as discussed more fully below,

these regulations generally provide that to meet the requirement that a payment be made upon a permissible payment event or a fixed date, the service recipient may make the payment by the later of the earliest date administratively practicable following, or December 31 of the calendar year in which occurs, the permissible payment event or fixed date. At the minimum, this should offer almost 12 months of flexibility with respect to a payment scheduled for January 1 of a calendar year. The Treasury Department and the IRS request comments, however, as to circumstances in which this flexibility will not be sufficient.

Commentators also requested a grace period during which arrangements with persons who have become resident aliens during a calendar year may be amended to comply with the requirements of section 409A. These regulations generally provide such relief. With respect to the initial year in which the service provider becomes a resident alien, the plan may be amended with respect to the service provider through the end of that year to comply with (or be excluded from coverage under) section 409A, including allowing the service provider the right to change the time and form of a payment. Provided that the election is made before the amount is paid or payable, initial deferral elections may also be made with respect to compensation related to services in that initial year, if the election is made by the end of the year or, if later, the 15th day of the third month after the service provider meets the requirements to be a resident alien. The relief generally does not extend further because a service recipient and service provider should reasonably anticipate the potential application of section 409A after the initial year in which the service provider attains the status of a resident alien. However, the Treasury Department and the IRS also recognize that there may be significant gaps between the years in which the service provider is treated as a resident alien. Accordingly, the grace period is available in a subsequent year, provided that the service provider has been a nonresident alien for at least five consecutive calendar years immediately preceding the year in which the service provider is again a resident alien.

Commentators also requested that amounts contributed or benefits paid under a foreign social security system that is the subject of a totalization agreement be exempted from coverage under section 409A. Totalization agreements refer to bilateral agreements between the United States and foreign jurisdictions intended to coordinate coverage under the Social Security system in the United States and similar systems of the foreign jurisdictions. These agreements are intended to minimize the potential for application of two different employment taxes, and correspondingly to coordinate the benefits under the two different social security systems. The Treasury Department and the IRS believe that section 409A was not intended to apply to benefits to which the service provider is entitled under the foreign jurisdiction social security system. Accordingly, these types of plans have been excluded from the definition of a nonqualified deferred compensation plan for purposes of section 409A. Similarly, for jurisdictions not covered by a totalization agreement, these regulations provide that amounts deferred under a government mandated social security system are not subject to section 409A.

G. *Separation pay arrangements*

1. *In general*

Many commentators requested clarification of the application of section 409A to plans or arrangements providing payments upon a termination of services, generally described as severance plans. Some commentators requested that all such arrangements be excluded from coverage under section 409A. However, section 409A(d)(1)(B) contains a list of welfare benefits that are specifically excluded from coverage under section 409A, including bona fide vacation leave, sick leave, compensatory time, disability pay and death benefit plans. Noticeably absent from this list is an exception for severance plans. This is particularly noteworthy because section 457(e)(11) contains the identical list of exclusions, with the one exception that the list of excluded plans under section 457(e)(11) includes severance pay plans, while the list of excluded plans under section 409A(d)(1)(B) does not. Therefore, it appears that Congress intended that severance payments could constitute deferred compensation under section 409A. To avoid confusion with other Code provisions, such as the specific exclusion from coverage under section 457(e)(11) for severance plans or the treatment of such arrangements under section 3121(v)(2), these regulations generally refer to such arrangements as separation pay arrangements.

With respect to payments available upon a voluntary termination of services, there is no substantive distinction between a plan labeled a severance plan or separation pay plan and a nonqualified deferred compensation plan that provides for payments upon a separation from service. If, as is often the case, the service recipient reserves the right to eliminate such arrangement at any time, the service provider may not have a legally binding right to the payment until payment actually occurs, or such other time as the service recipient's discretion to eliminate the right to the payments lapses. However, as provided in these regulations, where such negative discretion lacks substantive significance, or the person granted the discretion is controlled by, or related to, the service provider to whom the payment will be made, the service provider will be considered to have a legally binding right to the compensation.

Commentators requested that the exclusion from coverage under section 409A contained in Notice 2005-1, Q&A-19(d) for payments during the calendar year 2005 to non-key employees pursuant to severance plans that are classified as welfare plans, rather than pension plans, in accordance with the Department of Labor regulations, be made a permanent exclusion. This approach generally would be consistent with the regulations under section 3121(v)(2) of the Code. However, the Department of Labor regulations reflect different concerns with respect to separation pay arrangements from the concerns addressed in section 409A. The Department of Labor regulations focus on whether an arrangement sufficiently resembles a retirement plan to require funding of the obligations under such a plan, or rather is a welfare plan that would not require funding. In contrast, section 409A focuses on the manipulation of the timing of inclusion of compensation income. Accordingly, these regulations do not categorically exclude these arrangements from coverage under section 409A, although a modified version of this exception has been provided, as discussed below.

Some commentators requested that the Treasury Department and the IRS adopt an exclusion for all amounts payable upon an involuntary separation. This request is based upon the position under certain other Code provisions, and stated in certain court cases, that payments to which an individual becomes entitled upon an involuntary separation from service do not constitute nonqualified deferred compensation. See *Kraft Foods North America v. U.S.*, 58 Fed. Cl. 507 (2003); § 31.3121(v)(2)-1(b)(4)(iv). As discussed above, the statutory language and structure of section 409A strongly suggest that separation pay arrangements, including arrangements providing separation pay upon an involuntary separation, were meant to be covered by section 409A. Furthermore, the Treasury Department and the IRS believe that section 409A was not intended to be applied so narrowly. Section 409A addresses the manipulation of the timing of inclusion of compensation. Payments due to a separation from service, regardless of whether voluntary or involuntary, constitute a payment of compensation. Accordingly, the ability to manipulate the timing of the inclusion of income related to the receipt of those amounts is within the scope of section 409A.

Much of the discussion above relates to predetermined arrangements, where the right to the payment upon an involuntary termination of services arises as part of an arrangement covering multiple service providers, often covering a service provider from the time the service provider begins performing services. Where the separation pay arrangement involves an agreement negotiated with a specific service provider at the time of the involuntary separation from service, commentators asked how deferral elections could be provided that would meet the requirement that the election be made in the year before the year in which the services were performed. Commentators pointed out that even if the service provider does not already participate in any involuntary separation pay arrangement, the rule in section 409A(a)(4)(B) that allows an initial deferral election to be made within 30 days of initial eligibility under a plan applies only with respect to services performed after the election. To address these concerns, these regulations provide that where separation pay due to an involuntary termination has been the subject of bona fide, arm's length negotiations, the election as to the time and form of payment may be made on or before the date the service provider obtains a legally binding right to the payment.

The Treasury Department and the IRS recognize that separation pay arrangements providing for short-term payments upon an involuntary separation from service are common arrangements, and that compliance with the provisions of section 409A may be burdensome. In addition, the Treasury Department and the IRS recognize that where both the amount of the payments and the time over which such payments may be made are limited, these arrangements create fewer concerns with respect to manipulation of the timing of compensation income. Accordingly, these regulations generally exempt such arrangements where the entire amount of payments does not exceed two times the service provider's annual compensation or, if less, two times the limit on annual compensation that may be taken into account for qualified plan purposes under section 401(a)(17) ($210,000 for calendar year 2005), each for the calendar year before the year in which the service provider separates from service, and provided further that the

arrangement requires that all payments be made by no later than the end of the second calendar year following the year in which the service provider terminates service. These limitations generally are consistent with the safe harbor under which severance plans may be treated as welfare plans under the applicable Department of Labor regulations, and should allow most of these arrangements to avoid coverage under section 409A.

The Treasury Department and the IRS further recognize that separation pay arrangements often occur in the context of a window program, where certain groups of service providers are identified as being subject to a separation from service, and the service recipient provides the identified service providers an incentive to voluntarily separate from service and obtain a benefit. Although technically these programs involve a voluntary separation from service, these regulations generally treat separations due to participation in a window arrangement the same as arrangements with respect to involuntary separations from service for purposes of the exceptions to coverage from section 409A.

These exclusions for separation pay are not intended to allow for rights to payments that would otherwise be deferred compensation subject to section 409A to avoid application of section 409A by being recharacterized as separation pay. Accordingly, the exclusions for separation pay do not apply to the extent the separation pay acts as a substitute for, or a replacement of, amounts that would otherwise be subject to section 409A. For example, a right to separation pay obtained in exchange for the relinquishment of a right to a payment of deferred compensation subject to section 409A will not be excluded from coverage under section 409A, but rather will be treated as a payment of the original amount of deferred compensation.

2. *Treatment as a separate plan*

Commentators have stated that arrangements involving payments due to an involuntary separation often operate separately from more traditional types of nonqualified deferred compensation plans. In addition, especially in the case of agreements covering an individual, the involuntary separation pay agreement may involve many different types of payments that are of a much smaller magnitude than amounts deferred under other types of nonqualified deferred compensation plans. Commentators expressed concerns that inadvertent violations of section 409A with respect to these unique arrangements could lead to much larger amounts being included in income and subject to the additional tax under section 409A due to the aggregation of such involuntary separation pay arrangements with other arrangements under the definition of a plan. The Treasury Department and the IRS have concluded that a nonqualified deferred compensation plan providing separation pay due to an involuntary separation from service, or participation in a window program, should be treated as a separate type of plan from account balance plans, nonaccount balance plans, and other types of plans (generally equity-based compensation arrangements) in which the service provider may participate that do not provide separation pay due to an involuntary separation from service, or participation in a window program.

3. *Application of the short-term deferral rule to separation pay arrangements*

Many commentators asked for a clarification with respect to the application of the short-term deferral rule to separation pay arrangements. The right to a payment that will only be paid upon an involuntary termination of services generally would be viewed as a nonvested right. Accordingly, an involuntary separation pay arrangement may be structured to meet the requirements of the short-term deferral exception.

Some commentators also requested that arrangements involving rights to payments upon termination of services for good reason be treated as a right subject to a substantial risk of forfeiture. These arrangements are common, especially following a transaction resulting in a change in control of the service recipient. The Treasury Department and the IRS are not confident that amounts payable upon a voluntary separation from service, and amounts payable only upon a termination of services for good reason, always may be adequately distinguished. Furthermore, even if the types of good reasons sufficient to constitute a substantial risk of forfeiture could be elucidated, the application of such a rule would involve intensive factual determinations, leaving taxpayers uncertain in their planning and creating a significant potential for abuse. Accordingly, the regulations do not treat the right to a payment upon a separation from service for good reason categorically as a right subject to a substantial risk of forfeiture. However, the Treasury Department and the IRS request comments as to what further guidance may be useful with respect to arrangements containing these types of provisions.

4. *Reimbursement arrangements*

Many commentators requested clarification with respect to the application of section 409A to reimbursement agreements, involving the service recipient reimbursing expenses of the terminated service provider. Because the promise to reimburse the former service provider is not contingent on the provision of any substantial services for the service provider, the right to the payment generally would not be treated as subject to a substantial risk of forfeiture. Accordingly, if the period in which expenses incurred will be reimbursed extends beyond the year in which the legally binding right arises, the right to the amount generally would constitute deferred compensation. The Treasury Department and the IRS recognize that reimbursement arrangements following a termination of services are common, and that requiring the service recipient to designate an amount at the time of the termination conflicts with the service recipient's desire to pay only amounts that the former service provider has actually incurred as an expense. However, a categorical exclusion for reimbursement arrangements is not tenable, because such an exclusion would allow for a limitless amount of deferred compensation to be paid without regard to the rules of section 409A, where such compensation took the form of the reimbursement of personal expenses (for example, reimbursements of home mortgage payments). These regulations provide that certain reimbursement arrangements related to a termination of services are not covered by section 409A, to the extent that the reimbursement arrangement covers only expenses incurred and reimbursed before the end of the second calendar year following the calendar year in which the termination occurs. The types of reimbursement arrangements excluded include reimbursements that are otherwise excludible from gross income, reimbursements for expenses that the service provider can deduct under section 162 or section 167, as business expenses incurred in connection with the performance of services (ignoring any applicable limitation based on adjusted gross income), outplacement expenses, moving expenses, medical expenses, as well as any other types of payments that do not exceed $5,000 in the aggregate during any given taxable year.

For purposes of this provision, reimbursement arrangements include the provision of in-kind benefits, or direct payments by the service recipient to the person providing the goods or services to the terminated service provider, if the provision of such in-kind benefits or direct payments would be treated as reimbursement arrangements if the service provider had paid for such in-kind benefits or such goods or services and received reimbursement from the service recipient.

H. *Split-dollar life insurance arrangements*

Commentators suggested that split-dollar life insurance arrangements should be excluded from the requirements of section 409A. However, the Treasury Department and the IRS believe that in applying the general definition of deferred compensation to split-dollar life insurance arrangements, the requirements of section 409A may apply to certain types of such arrangements (as described in § 1.61-22). Split-dollar life insurance arrangements that provide only death benefits (as defined in these proposed regulations) to or for the benefit of the service provider may be excluded from coverage under section 409A under the exception from the definition of a nonqualified deferred compensation plan provided in these proposed regulations for death benefit plans. Also, split-dollar life insurance arrangements treated as loan arrangements under § 1.7872-15 generally will not give rise to deferrals of compensation within the meaning of section 409A, provided that there is no agreement under which the service recipient will forgive the related indebtedness and no obligation on the part of the service recipient to continue to make premium payments without charging the service provider a market interest rate on the funds advanced. However, policies structured under the endorsement method, where the service recipient is the owner of the policy but where the service provider obtains a legally binding right to compensation includible in income in a taxable year after the year in which a substantial risk of forfeiture (if any) lapses, may provide for a deferral of compensation. Just as a promise to transfer property in a future year may provide for a deferral of compensation (even though the transfer itself is subject to section 83), an endorsement method split-dollar life insurance arrangement that grants the service provider a legally binding right to a future transfer of interests in a policy owned by the service recipient may provide for a deferral of compensation subject to section 409A. For example, where a service recipient enters into an endorsement method split-dollar life insurance arrangement with respect to a service provider, and irrevocably promises to pay premiums in future years, the arrangement may provide for a deferral of compensation within the meaning of section 409A.

Commentators raised concerns about the impact of changes to a split-dollar life insurance arrangement to comply with section 409A,

where the split-dollar life insurance arrangement was entered into on or before September 17, 2003, and is not otherwise subject to the regulations set forth in § 1.61-22 (a grandfathered split-dollar life insurance arrangement). Pursuant to § 1.61-22 (j) (2), if a grandfathered split-dollar life insurance arrangement is materially modified after September 17, 2003, the arrangement is treated as a new arrangement entered into on the date of the modification. Commentators expressed concern that modifications necessary to comply with section 409A may cause the split-dollar life insurance arrangement to be treated as materially modified for purposes of § 1.61-22 (j) (2). Comments are requested as to the scope of changes that may be necessary to comply with, or avoid application of, section 409A, and under what conditions those changes should not be treated as material modifications for purposes of § 1.61-22 (j) (2).

III. *Definition of Plan*

A. *Plan aggregation rules*

These regulations generally retain the plan aggregation rules set forth in Notice 2005-1, Q&A-9. Under the notice, all amounts deferred under an account balance plan are treated as deferred under a single plan, all amounts deferred under a nonaccount balance are treated as deferred under a single plan, and all amounts deferred under any other type of plan (generally equity-based compensation) are treated as deferred under a single plan. As discussed above, these regulations expand this rule so that all amounts deferred under certain separation pay arrangements are treated as a single plan. The purposes behind these aggregation rules are two-fold. First, because the provisions of section 409A are applied on an individual participant basis, rather than disqualifying the arrangement as to all participants, plan aggregation rules are necessary to implement the compliance incentives intended under the provision. Without such rules, multitudes of separate arrangements could be established for a single participant. Should the participant want access to an amount of cash, the participant would amend one or more of these separate arrangements and receive payments. The participant would argue that only those separate arrangements under which the amounts were paid failed to meet the requirements of section 409A and were subject to the income inclusion and additional tax, although in fact amounts were also available under the additional separate arrangements. Under that analysis, section 409A essentially would act as a 20 percent penalty required to receive a payment, similar to the haircut provisions that were intended to be prohibited by section 409A. The Treasury Department and the IRS do not believe that Congress intended that the consequences of section 409A could be limited in such a manner. However, the Treasury Department and the IRS also believe that complex plan aggregation rules, especially rules reliant on the particular facts and circumstances underlying each arrangement, would lead to unwarranted complexities and burdens with respect to service recipient planning and IRS enforcement. Accordingly, these regulations adopt rules intended to be simple and relatively easy to administer that retain the integrity of the compliance incentives inherent in the statute.

Commentators asked whether an isolated violation of a term of an arrangement with respect to one participant will be treated as a violation of the same arrangement term with respect to other participants covered by the same arrangement. First, the terms of the arrangement with respect to each participant must be determined, based upon the rights the individual participant has under the plan. Generally, these rights will be determined based upon the written provisions applicable under a particular arrangement, as evidenced by a plan document, agreement, or some combination of documents that specify the terms of the contract under which the compensation is to be paid. However, where the terms of a plan or arrangement comply with section 409A, but the service recipient does not follow such terms, an individual participant's actual rights under the arrangement may be unclear. Where a violation of a provision is not an isolated incident, or involves a number of participants or an identifiable subgroup of participants under the arrangement, the violation may result in a finding that even with respect to a participant who did not directly benefit from the violation, the actual terms of the arrangement differ from the written terms of the arrangement. For example, if a plan document provides for installment payments upon a separation from service, but participants in the arrangement repeatedly are offered the opportunity to receive a lump sum payment, the facts and circumstances may indicate that the arrangement provides for an election of a lump sum payment for all participants.

An analogous analytical framework applies where the service recipient offers different benefits to separate participants in the same plan or arrangement. Under the terms of the overall arrangement, the service provider may grant many different types of rights, including some rights that would not be subject to the requirements of section 409A and some rights that would be subject to those requirements. With respect to the application of section 409A, a plan or arrangement is analyzed as consisting of the rights and benefits that have actually been granted to a particular service provider. For example, with respect to an equity-based omnibus plan that permits the grant of discounted stock options that would be subject to the requirements of section 409A, as well as other types of stock options which would be excluded from coverage under section 409A, only those service providers actually granted the discounted stock options will be treated as having deferred an amount of compensation subject to section 409A, and then only with respect to the stock options subject to section 409A.

B. *Written plan requirement*

Although the statute does not explicitly state that a plan or arrangement must be in writing, the statute requires that a plan contain certain provisions in order to comply with section 409A. For example, section 409A(a)(2)(A) requires that a plan provide that compensation deferred under the plan may not be distributed earlier than certain specific events. Section 409A(a)(4)(B) requires that a plan provide certain restrictions with respect to initial deferral elections. Section 409A(a)(4)(C) requires that, if a plan permits under a subsequent election a delay in a payment or a change in the form of payment, the plan must require certain limits on the scope of such a delay or change. The clear implication of these provisions of section 409A is that the plan or arrangement must be set forth in writing and these regulations incorporate that requirement.

IV. *Definition of Substantial Risk of Forfeiture*

The scope of the definition of a substantial risk of forfeiture is central to the application of section 409A. In addition to the timing of the potential inclusion of income under section 409A, the existence of a substantial risk of forfeiture may also determine whether an amount is subject to section 409A or whether it qualifies for the exclusion under the short-term deferral rule. These regulations generally adopt the same definition as provided in Notice 2005-1, Q&A-10. This definition reflects the concerns of the Treasury Department and the IRS that the use of plan terms that purport to prescribe a substantial risk of forfeiture but, in fact, do not put the right to the payment at a substantial risk, may be used to circumvent the application of section 409A in a manner inconsistent with the legislative intent. The definition of a substantial risk of forfeiture in these regulations contains certain restrictions. Certain amendments of an arrangement to extend a substantial risk of forfeiture will not be recognized. The ability to periodically extend, or roll, the risk of forfeiture is sufficiently suspect to question whether the parties ever intended that the right be subject to any true substantial risk, or rather whether the period is being extended through periods in which the service recipient can be reasonably assured that the forfeiture condition will not occur. Similarly, the risk that a right will be forfeited due to the violation of a noncompete agreement can be illusory, such as where the service provider has no intent to compete or to provide such services. In addition, a rational service provider normally would not agree to subject amounts that have already been earned, such as salary payments, to a condition that creates a real possibility of forfeiture, unless the service provider is offered a material inducement to do so, such as an additional amount of compensation. Accordingly, these provisions will not be treated as creating a substantial risk of forfeiture for purposes of section 409A.

V. *Initial Deferral Election Rules*

A. *In general*

Section 409A(a)(4)(B)(i) provides that in general, a plan must provide that compensation for services performed during a taxable year may be deferred at the participant's election only if the election to defer such compensation is made not later than the close of the preceding taxable year or at such other time as provided in regulations. The legislative history indicates that the taxable year to which the statute refers is the service provider's taxable year, as it indicates that the Secretary may issue guidance "providing coordination rules, as appropriate, regarding the timing of elections in the case when the fiscal year of the employer and the taxable year of the individual are different." H.R. Conf. Rep. No. 108-755, at 732 (2004). Accordingly, these regulations provide as a general rule that a service provider must make a deferral election in his or her taxable year before the year in which the services are performed. As discussed below, certain coordination rules for fiscal year employers have been provided.

An election to defer an amount includes an election both as to the time and form of the payment. An election is treated as made as of the date the election becomes irrevocable. Changes may be made to an initial deferral election, provided that the election becomes irrevocable (except to the extent the plan permits a subsequent deferral election

consistent with these regulations) no later than the last date that such an election may be made. Commentators had questioned whether an evergreen deferral election, or a deferral election as to future compensation that remains in place unless the service provider changes the election, would be effective for purposes of section 409A. Such an election satisfies the initial deferral election requirements only if the election becomes irrevocable with respect to future compensation no later than the last permissible date an affirmative initial deferral election could have been made with respect to such compensation. For example, with respect to a salary deferral program under which an employee makes an initial deferral election to defer 10 percent of the salary earned during the subsequent calendar year, a plan may provide that the deferral election remains effective unless and until changed by the employee, provided that with respect to salary earned during any future taxable year, the election to defer 10 percent of such salary becomes irrevocable no later than the December 31 of the preceding calendar year.

B. *Nonelective arrangements*

Some commentators asked whether the initial deferral election rules apply to nonelective arrangements. The requirement that the election be made in the year before the services are performed is not applicable where the participant is not provided any election with respect to the amount deferred, or the time and form of the payment. However, as stated in the legislative history, "[t]he time and form of distribution must be specified at the time of initial deferral." H.R. Conf. Rep. No. 108-755, at 732 (2004). In addition, the application of the subsequent deferral rules becomes problematic if the original time and form of deferred payment established by the service recipient is not viewed as an initial deferral election. Therefore, in order to avoid application of the initial deferral rules, a plan may not provide a service provider or service recipient with ongoing discretion as to the time and form of payment, but rather must set the time and form of payment no later than the time the service provider obtains a legally binding right to the compensation.

C. *Performance-based compensation*

Section 409A(a)(4)(B)(iii) provides that in the case of any performance-based compensation based on services performed over a period of at least 12 months, a participant's initial deferral election may be made no later than six months before the end of the period. The legislative history indicates that the performance-based compensation should be required to meet certain requirements similar to those under section 162(m), but not all requirements under that section. H.R. Conf. Rep. No. 108-755, at 732 (2004). An example in the legislative history, adopted in these regulations, is that the requirement of a determination by the compensation committee of the board of directors is not required.

Notice 2005-1 did not provide a definition of performance-based compensation. Rather, Notice 2005-1, Q&A-22 provided a definition of bonus compensation that, until further guidance was issued, could be used for purposes of applying the exception to the general rule regarding initial deferral elections.

Under these regulations, performance-based compensation is defined as compensation the payment of which or the amount of which is contingent on the satisfaction of preestablished organizational or individual performance criteria. Performance-based compensation does not include any amount or portion of any amount that will be paid either regardless of performance, or based upon a level of performance that is substantially certain to be met at the time the criteria are established.

Performance-based compensation generally may include payments based upon subjective performance criteria, provided that the subjective performance criteria relate to the performance of the participant service provider, a group of service providers that includes the participant service provider, or a business unit for which the participant service provider provides services (which may include the entire organization), and the determination that the subjective performance criteria have been met is not made by the service provider or a member of the service provider's family, or a person the service provider supervises or over whose compensation the service provider has any control.

Commentators requested that, similar to the provision contained in § 1.162-27(e)(2) governing the requirements for establishing performance criteria for purposes of applying the deduction limitation under section 162(m), service recipients be allowed to establish performance criteria within 90 days of the commencement of a performance period of 12 months or more, rather than having to establish such criteria before the commencement of the period. These regulations adopt a similar provision with respect to the establishment of performance criteria for purposes of the exception under the deferral election rules, permitting the criteria to be established up to 90 days after the commencement of the period of service to which the criteria relates, provided that the outcome is not substantially certain at the time the criteria are established.

The legislative history indicates that to constitute performance-based compensation, the amount must be (1) variable and contingent on the satisfaction of preestablished organizational or individual performance criteria and (2) not readily ascertainable at the time of the election. H.R. Conf. Rep. No. 108-755, at 732 (2004). These regulations clarify that where the right to receive a specified amount is itself not substantially certain, the amount is not readily ascertainable as the amount paid could either be the specified amount or zero. Accordingly, these regulations provide that at the time of the initial deferral election, either the amount must not be readily ascertainable, or the right to the amount must not be substantially certain. So, for example, the right to a $10,000 bonus that otherwise qualifies as performance-based compensation could be deferred by an employee up to six months before the end of the performance period, provided that at the time of the deferral election the employee is not substantially certain to meet the criteria and receive the $10,000 payment.

Under the definition of bonus compensation provided in Notice 2005-1, Q&A-22, bonus compensation does not include any amount or portion of any amount that is based solely on the value of, or appreciation in value of, the service recipient or the stock of the service recipient. Commentators criticized this limitation as inconsistent with the provisions of § 1.162-27 governing application of the deduction limitation under section 162(m), and the legislative history to section 409A indicating that the definition of performance-based compensation for purposes of section 409A would be similar to that provided under section 162(m) and the regulations thereunder. These proposed regulations eliminate this limitation, so that performance-based compensation may be based solely upon an increase in the value of the service recipient, or the stock of the service recipient, after the date of grant or award. However, if an amount of compensation the service provider will receive pursuant to a grant or award is not based solely on an increase in the value of the stock after the grant or award (for example, in the case of restricted stock units or a stock right granted with an exercise price that is less than the fair market value of the stock as of the date of grant), and that other amount would not otherwise qualify as performance-based compensation, none of the compensation attributable to the grant or award is performance-based compensation. Nonetheless, an award of equity-based compensation may constitute performance-based compensation if entitlement to the compensation is subject to a condition that would cause a non-equity-based award to qualify as performance-based compensation, such as a performance-based vesting condition.

The Treasury Department and the IRS are concerned that the inclusion of such amounts in the definition of performance-based compensation could lead to a conclusion that an election to defer amounts payable under a stock right will necessarily comply with section 409A if the initial deferral election is made at least 6 months before the date of exercise. However, under these proposed regulations, a stock right with a deferral feature is subject to section 409A from the date of grant. To comply with section 409A, the arrangement would be required to specify a permissible payment time and a form of payment. The requirement would not be met if, at some point during the term of the stock right, the stock right becomes immediately exercisable and the holder may decide whether and when to exercise the stock right. In addition, where a deferral feature is added to an existing stock right the stock right generally would violate section 409A because the stock right would have a deferral feature and would not have specified a permissible payment time or event.

D. First year of eligibility

Section 409A and these proposed regulations contain an exception to the general rule regarding initial deferral elections, under which a service provider newly eligible for participation in a plan may make a deferral election within the first 30 days of participation in the plan, provided that the election may only apply to compensation with respect to services performed after the election. These regulations further provide that for compensation that is earned based upon a specified performance period (for example, an annual bonus), where a deferral election is made in the first year of eligibility but after the beginning of the service period, the election is deemed to apply to compensation paid for service performed subsequent to the election if the election applies to the portion of the compensation that is no greater than the total amount of compensation for the performance period multiplied by the ratio of the number of days remaining in the performance period after the election over the total number of days in the performance period.

Commentators had requested that the plan aggregation rules not apply in determining whether a service provider is newly eligible for participation in a plan. The concern is that a mid-year promotion, or management reorganization or other corporate event may make the service provider eligible for an arrangement that is of the same type as an arrangement in which the service provider already participates. For example, an employee participating in a salary deferral account-balance plan may become eligible for a bonus and a bonus deferral arrangement that would also be an account-balance plan.

The Treasury Department and the IRS believe that the plan aggregation rules are necessary in this context. Without such a rule, service providers may attempt to take advantage of the new eligibility exception by establishing serial arrangements. For example, an employer may argue that a 2007 salary deferral program is a new program, and not a continuation of the 2006 salary deferral program. Commentators argue that standards should be provided comparing the terms of the two plans to distinguish new arrangements from those that are merely continuations of existing arrangements. However, such rules would by necessity be complicated and burdensome, generally relying on the facts and circumstances of the individual arrangements and resulting in administrative burden and uncertainties. Accordingly, these regulations retain the plan aggregation rules.

However, as discussed below, certain other initial deferral election rules have been provided that address many of the situations in which service recipients desire to grant service providers the opportunity to make initial deferral elections due to eligibility in new programs. For example, the rule governing initial deferral elections with respect to certain forfeitable rights discussed below allows initial deferral elections upon eligibility for many bonus programs and ad hoc equity-based compensation grants. The Treasury Department and the IRS request comments as to whether these rules adequately address the concerns raised with respect to the definition of plan for purposes of applying the initial eligibility exception.

E. Initial deferral election with respect to short-term deferrals

As discussed above, an amount that is paid by the 15th day of the third month following the end of the first taxable year in which the payment is no longer subject to a substantial risk of forfeiture generally will not constitute a deferral of compensation. Commentators asked how the deferral election rules apply to an election to defer such an amount. Generally, once the service provider has begun performing the services required to vest, no election to defer could be made that would meet the timing requirements for initial deferral elections. Commentators suggested that the rules governing subsequent changes to the time and form of payment could be applied to elections to defer these amounts. The regulations provide that for purposes of an election to defer amounts that would not otherwise be subject to section 409A due to the short-term deferral rule, the date the substantial risk of forfeiture lapses is treated as the original time of payment established by an initial deferral election, and the form in which the payment would be made absent a deferral election is treated as the original form of payment established by an initial deferral election. Accordingly, the service provider may elect to defer the payment beyond the time at which the payment originally was scheduled to be made, in accordance with the rules governing subsequent changes in the time and form of payment. In general, this means that the service provider must make the election at least 12 months before the right to the payment vests, and must defer the payment for a period of not less than 5 years from the date the right to the payment could vest. Thus, no payment could be made within 5 years of the date the right to the payment vests (including upon a separation from service), except for instances of a change in control of the corporation, death, disability or an unforeseeable emergency. This would also mean that if the right to the payment actually vests within 12 months of the election, and the election is given effect so that the payment is not made within the short-term deferral period, the deferral of the payment would violate the requirements of section 409A.

For example, an employee may be entitled to the immediate payment of a bonus upon the occurrence of an initial public offering, where such a condition qualifies as a substantial risk of forfeiture so that the arrangement would constitute a short-term deferral. At some point after obtaining the right to the payment but before the initial public offering, the employee elects to defer any potential bonus payment to a date 5 years from the date of the initial public offering. To comply with the initial deferral election rules, that deferral election must not be given effect for 12 months. Accordingly, if the initial public offering occurred within 12 months of the deferral election, the payment must be made at the time of the initial public offering in accordance with the short-term deferral rules. If the payment is not made at such time, but rather is made, for example, 5 years from the date of the initial public offering, the payment would be deemed deferred pursuant to an invalid initial deferral election effective before the required lapse of 12 months and the arrangement would violate section 409A.

F. *Initial deferral election with respect to certain forfeitable rights*

Commentators asked how the initial deferral election rules would apply with respect to grants of nonqualified deferred compensation that occur in the middle of a taxable year, especially where such grants were unforeseeable by the service provider. Under these circumstances, an initial deferral election could not be made by the service provider during the taxable year before the year in which the award was granted, unless the service recipient had the foresight to request such an election in the prior year. The Treasury Department and the IRS do not believe that a categorical exclusion from the initial deferral election rules is appropriate, because such a rule would encourage the characterization of all grants of nonqualified deferred compensation as occurring in the middle of the year and in large part render ineffective the initial deferral election rules set forth in section 409A. However, these regulations provide that where a grant of nonqualified deferred compensation is subject to a forfeiture condition requiring the continued performance of services for a period of at least 12 months, the initial deferral election may be made no later than 30 days after the date of grant, provided that the election is made at least 12 months in advance of the end of the service period. Under these circumstances, the election still must be made in all cases at least 12 months before the service provider has fully earned the amount of compensation, analogous to the general requirement that the election be made no later than the end of the year before the services are performed. The Treasury Department and the IRS believe that such a rule will provide a reasonable accommodation to service recipients granting certain ad hoc awards, such as restricted stock units, that often are subject to a requirement that the service provider continue to perform services for at least 12 months.

G. *Initial deferral election with respect to fiscal year compensation*

The legislative history to section 409A indicates that the Treasury Department and the IRS are to provide guidance coordinating the initial deferral election rules with respect to compensation paid by service recipients with fiscal years other than the calendar year. H.R. Conf. Rep. No. 108-755, at 732 (2004). These regulations provide such a rule, generally permitting an initial election to defer fiscal year compensation on or before the end of the fiscal year immediately preceding the first fiscal year in which any services are performed for which the compensation is paid. For these purposes, fiscal year compensation does not encompass all compensation paid by a fiscal year service recipient. Where the compensation is not specifically based upon the service recipient's fiscal year as the measurement period, the timing requirements applicable to an initial deferral election are unchanged. Accordingly, the rule applies to compensation based on service periods that are coextensive with one or more of the service recipient's consecutive fiscal years, where no amount of such compensation is payable during the service period. For example, a bonus based upon a service period of two consecutive fiscal years payable after the completion of the second fiscal year would be fiscal year compensation. In contrast, periodic salary payments or bonuses based on service periods other than the service recipient's fiscal year would not be fiscal year compensation, and the deferral of such amounts would be subject to the general rule.

H. *Deferral elections with respect to commissions.*

Commentators requested clarification with respect to the application of section 409A to commissions. These regulations address commissions earned by a service provider where a substantial portion of the services provided by the service provider consists of the direct sale of a product or service to a customer, each payment of compensation by the service recipient to the service provider consists of a portion of the purchase price for the product or service (for example, 10 percent of the purchase price), or an amount calculated solely by reference to the volume of sales (for example, $100 per item sold), and each compensation payment is contingent upon the service recipient receiving payment from an unrelated customer for the product or services. In that case, the service provider is treated as having performed the services to which the commission compensation relates during the service provider's taxable year in which the unrelated customer renders payment for such goods or services. Accordingly, under the general initial deferral election rule an individual service provider could make an initial deferral election with respect to such compensation through December 31 of the calendar year preceding the year in which the customer renders the payment from which the commission is derived.

VI. *Time and Form of Payment*

A. *In general*

The regulations incorporate the statutory requirement that payments be made at a fixed date or under a fixed schedule, or upon any of five events: a separation from service, death, disability, change in the ownership or effective control of a corporation (to the extent provided by the Secretary), or unforeseeable emergency. As requested by commentators, these regulations provide guidance on what it means for a payment to be made upon one of these events. Where the time of payment is based upon the occurrence of a specified event (such as one of the five events listed above or upon the lapse of a substantial risk of forfeiture as discussed below), the plan must designate an objectively determinable date or year following the event upon which the payment is to be made. For example, the plan may designate the payment date as 30 days following a separation from service, or the first calendar year following a service provider's death. The Treasury Department and the IRS recognize that it may not be administratively feasible to make a payment upon the exact date or year designated. Furthermore, the Treasury Department and the IRS recognize that certain minimal delays that do not meaningfully affect the timing of the inclusion of income should not result in a violation of the requirements of section 409A. Accordingly, a payment will be treated as made upon the designated date if the payment is made by the later of the first date it is administratively feasible to make such payment on or after the designated date, or the end of the calendar year containing the designated date (or the end of the calendar year if only a year is designated). This relaxation of the timing rules for administrative necessity is not intended to provide a method for the service provider to further defer the payment. Accordingly, any inability to make the payment that is caused by an action or inaction of the service provider, or any person related to, or under the control of, the service provider, will not be treated as causing the making of the payment to be administratively infeasible.

Once an event upon which a payment is to be made has occurred, the designated date generally is treated as the fixed date on which, or the fixed schedule under which, the payment is to be made (but not for purposes of the application of section 409A(a)(2)(B) generally requiring a six month delay in any payment upon a separation from service to a key employee of a corporation whose stock is traded on an established securities market). Accordingly, the recipient may change the time and form of payment after the event has occurred, provided that the change would otherwise be timely and permissible under these regulations. For example, a plan provides for payment of a lump sum on the third anniversary following a separation from service. A service provider has a separation from service on July 1, 2010. The July 1, 2013, payment date is now treated as the fixed date upon which the payment is to be made. Accordingly, the service provider generally could elect to defer the time and form of payment provided that the election were made on or before June 30, 2012, and deferred the payment to at least July 1, 2018. For a discussion of the application of the subsequent deferral rules when only a calendar year of payment is specified, see section VI.B of this preamble.

B. *Specified time or fixed schedule of payments*

Generally a plan will be deemed to provide for a specified time or fixed schedule of payments where, at the time of the deferral, the specific date upon which the payment or payments will be made may be objectively determined. As requested by commentators, these regulations permit plans to specify simply the calendar year or years in which the payments are scheduled to be made, without specifying the particular date within such year on which the payment will be made. Although this provision would be consistent with the flexibility allowed with respect to meeting the specified time or fixed schedule of payments requirement, the provision must be coordinated with the subsequent deferral rules. Section 409A(a)(4)(C)(iii) requires that if a plan permits under a subsequent election a delay in a payment or a change in the form of payment with respect to a payment payable at a specified time or a fixed schedule, the plan must require that the election be made not less than 12 months prior to the date of the first scheduled payment. Application of such a provision requires a specific date for the first scheduled payment. For a plan that does not designate a specific date, but rather only the year in which the payment is to be made, the first scheduled payment is deemed to be scheduled to be paid as of January 1 of such year for this purpose.

Commentators asked whether a specified time or fixed schedule of payments could be determined based upon the date the service provider vests in the amount of deferred compensation, where the vesting is based upon the occurrence of an event. These regulations provide that a plan provides for payment at a specified time or fixed schedule of payments if the plan provides at the time of the deferral that the payment will be made at a date or dates that are objectively determinable based upon the date of the lapsing of a substantial risk of forfeiture, disregarding any acceleration of the vesting other than due to death or disability. So, for example, a plan that provides at the time the service provider obtains a legally binding right to the payment that the payment will be made in three installment payments, payable each December 31 following an initial public offering, where the condition that an initial public offering occur before the service provider is entitled to a payment constitutes a substantial risk of forfeiture, would satisfy the requirement that the plan provide for payments at a specified time or pursuant to a fixed schedule.

C. Separation from service

Section 409A(a)(2)(A)(i) provides that a plan may permit a payment to be made upon a separation from service as determined by the Secretary (except a payment to a specified employee, in which case the payment must be made subject to a six-month delay, discussed more fully below). These regulations provide guidance as to the circumstances under which service providers, including employees and independent contractors, will be treated as separating from service for purposes of section 409A. These rules are intended solely as guidance with respect to section 409A(a)(2)(A)(i), and should not be relied upon with respect to any other Code provisions, such as provisions with respect to distributions under qualified plans and provisions related to the service recipients' employment tax and information reporting obligations.

1. Employees

These regulations provide that an employee experiences a separation from service if the employee dies, retires, or otherwise has a termination of employment with the employer. However, the employment relationship is treated as continuing intact while the individual is on military leave, sick leave, or other bona fide leave of absence (such as temporary employment by the Government) if the period of such leave does not exceed six months, or if longer, so long as the individual's right to reemployment with the service recipient is provided either by statute or by contract. If the period of leave exceeds six months and the individual's right to reemployment is not provided either by statute or by contract, the employment relationship is deemed to terminate on the first date immediately following such six-month period.

Whether the employee has experienced a termination of employment is determined based on the facts and circumstances. The Treasury Department and the IRS do not intend for this standard to allow for the extension of deferrals through the use of consulting agreements or other devices under which the service provider technically agrees to perform services as demanded, but for which there is no intent that the service provider perform any significant services. Accordingly, the regulations provide an anti-abuse rule stating that where an employee either actually or purportedly continues in the capacity as an employee, such as through the execution of an employment agreement under which the service provider agrees to be available to perform services if requested, but the facts and circumstances indicate that the employer and the service provider did not intend for the service provider to provide more than insignificant services for the employer, an employee will be treated as having a termination of employment and a separation from service. For these purposes, an employer and employee will be deemed to have intended for the employee to provide more than insignificant services if the employee provides services at an annual rate equal to at least 20 percent of the services rendered and the annual remuneration for such services is equal to at least 20 percent of the average remuneration earned during the immediately preceding three full calendar years of employment (or, if the employee was employed for less than three years, such lesser period).

In addition, the Treasury Department and the IRS do not intend for this standard to be circumvented to create a separation from service where the service provider continues to perform significant services for the service recipient. For these purposes, the regulations provide that where an employee continues to provide services to a previous employer in a capacity other than as an employee, a separation from service will be treated as not having occurred if the former employee provides services at an annual rate that is 50 percent or more of the services rendered, on average, during the final three full calendar years of employment (or, if less, such lesser period) and the annual remuneration for such services is 50 percent or more of the average annual remuneration earned during the immediately preceding three full calendar years of employment (or if less, such lesser period).

Commentators asked whether the previous positions of the Treasury Department and the IRS with respect to a separation from service for purposes of section 401(k), generally referred to as the same desk rule, would apply in these proposed regulations. Under that rule, in certain situations where the identity of the employee's employer changed, such as

with respect to a sale of substantially all of the assets of the original employer to a new employer who hired the employee, the employee would not be treated as having a separation from service where the duties and responsibilities of the employee had not materially changed. These regulations do not incorporate this standard.

Commentators had requested the ability to elect whether to apply the same desk rule in the case of a corporate transaction, such as a sale of substantially all of the assets of the original employer. The Treasury Department and the IRS do not believe that such a rule would be consistent with the provisions of section 409A, which generally restrict such control over the time and form of payment.

2. Independent contractors

The definition of a separation from service of an independent contractor in these proposed regulations generally is derived from the definition of severance from employment provided in § 1.457-6(b)(2). Comments are requested with respect to any changes that may be necessary to address issues arising under section 409A.

3. Delay for key employees

Section 409A(a)(2)(B)(i) provides that payments upon a separation from service to a key employee of a corporation whose stock is publicly traded on an established securities market must be delayed at least six months following the separation from service. For these purposes, a key employee is defined in accordance with section 416(i), disregarding section 416(i)(5). Commentators asked for guidance on when a determination as to whether an individual is a key employee must be made. Section 416 relies upon plan year concepts, which generally are not relevant to the application of section 409A. In addition, the Treasury Department and the IRS wish to establish rules that minimize the administrative burden, while implementing the legislative intent. Accordingly, the regulations provide that the identification of key employees is based upon the 12-month period ending on an identification date chosen by the service recipient. Persons who meet the requirements of section 416(i)(1)(A)(i), (ii) or (iii) during that 12-month period are considered key employees for the 12-month period commencing on the first day of the 4th month following the end of the 12-month period. For example, if an employer chose December 31 as an identification date, any key employees identified during the calendar year ending December 31 would be treated as specified employees for the 12-month period commencing the following April 1. In this manner, service recipients generally may know in advance whether the person to whom a payment is scheduled to be made will be subject to the provision. In addition, service recipients may choose an identification date other than December 31, provided that the date must be used consistently and provided that any change in the identification date may not be effective for a period of at least 12 months.

Some commentators had requested that certain types of payments, generally life annuities or longer-term installment payments, be excepted from the six-month delay requirement. The statutory language does not contemplate such an exception. Where an executive is aware that the source of funds to pay for his nonqualified deferred compensation are at significant risk, the executive may separate from service to obtain initial annuity or installment payments while such funds exist. Commentators argue that annuity payments or long-term installment payments generally would be less significant in amount. However, the Treasury Department and the IRS are not inclined to establish arbitrary limits, where such amounts may actually be quite significant due to the overall amount of the entire benefit, the number of installment payments, or the age of the participant, especially where the statutory language does not contemplate the creation of such an exception. Rather, the Treasury Department and the IRS believe that the provisions with respect to separation pay should provide service recipients the ability to provide reasonably significant amounts of benefits to terminating executives, that may respond to many of the concerns underlying the request to relax the six-month delay requirement.

To meet the six-month delay requirement, a plan may provide that any payment pursuant to a separation of service due within the six-month period is delayed until the end of the six-month period, or that each scheduled payment that becomes payable pursuant to a separation from service is delayed six months, or a combination thereof. For example, a nonqualified deferred compensation plan of a corporation whose stock is publicly traded on an established securities market may provide that a participant is entitled to 60 monthly installment payments upon separation from service, payable commencing the first day of the first month following the date of separation from service. To comply with the requirement of a six-month delay for payments to key employees, the plan may provide that in the case of an affected participant, the aggregate amount of the first seven months of installments is paid at the beginning of the seventh month following the date of separation from service, or may provide that the commencement date of the 60 months of installment payments is the first day of the seventh month following the date of separation from service, or may provide for a combination of these provisions. A plan may be amended to specify or change the manner in which the delay will be implemented, provided that the amendment may not be effective for at least 12 months. Because the delay requirement applies only to certain public corporations, a corporation or other entity not covered by the requirement may have failed to include a provision in its plans at the time the corporation is contemplating becoming a public corporation. These regulations provide that where the stock of the service recipient is not publicly traded on an established securities market, a plan may be amended to specify or change the manner in which the delay will be implemented, effective immediately upon adoption of the amendment. A plan may provide a service provider an election as to the manner in which the six-month delay is to be implemented, provided that such election is subject to otherwise applicable deferral election rules.

D. *Death or disability*

As provided in section 409A(a)(2)(A)(ii) and (iii), these regulations state that the death or disability of the service provider are permissible payment events. The regulations incorporate the definition of disability provided in section 409A(a)(2)(C). These regulations clarify that a plan that provides for a payment upon a disability need not provide for a payment upon all disabilities identified in section 409A(a)(2)(C), as long as any disability upon which a payment would be made is contained within the definition provided in section 409A(a)(2)(C). In addition, these regulations provide that a service recipient may rely upon a determination of the Social Security Administration with respect to the existence of a disability.

E. *Change in ownership or effective control of the corporation*

The provisions defining a change in ownership or effective control of a corporation remain substantially unchanged from Notice 2005-1, Q&As-11 through 14. These provisions are based largely upon the discussion in the legislative history, indicating that the guidance should provide a similar, but more restrictive, definition of a change in the ownership or effective control of a corporation as compared to the definition used for purposes of the golden parachute provisions of section 280G. H.R. Conf. Rep. No. 108-755, at 730 (2004). Accordingly, the provisions largely mirror the regulations under section 280G, though the percentage changes in ownership necessary to qualify as permissible payment events have increased. However, unlike the golden parachute provisions, a change in control event may occur that does not relate to the entire group of affiliated corporations. Rather, the relevant analysis for purposes of section 409A generally is whether the corporation for whom the service provider performed services at the time of the event, the corporation or corporations liable for the payment at the time of the event, or a corporate majority shareholder of one of these corporations, experienced a change in control event.

Commentators asked whether the provisions relating to the change in ownership or effective control of a corporation will be extended to non-corporate entities. Specifically, some commentators asked whether change in control provisions could be applied in the case of a partnership or other pass-through entity. Neither the statute nor the legislative history refers to a permissible distribution upon a change in ownership or effective control of any type of entity other than a corporation.

However, the Treasury Department and the IRS plan to issue regulations under section 409A(a)(3) that will allow an acceleration of payments upon a change in the ownership of a partnership or in the ownership of a substantial portion of the assets of the partnership. Until further guidance is issued, the section 409A rules regarding permissible distributions upon a change in the ownership of a corporation (as described in proposed § 1.409A-3(g)(5)(v)) or a change in the ownership of a substantial portion of the assets of a corporation (as described in proposed § 1.409A-3(g)(5)(vii)) may be applied by analogy to changes in the ownership of a partnership and changes in the ownership of a substantial portion of the assets of a partnership. For purposes of this paragraph, any references in proposed § 1.409A-3(g)(5) to corporations, shareholders, and stock shall be treated as referring also to partnerships, partners, and partnership interests, respectively, and any reference to "majority shareholder" as applied by analogy to the owner of a partnership shall be treated as referring to a partner that (a) owns more than 50 percent of the capital and profits interests of such partnership, and (b) alone or together with others is vested with the continuing exclusive authority to make the management decisions necessary to conduct the business for which the partnership was formed. The Treasury Department and the IRS request comments with respect to the application of a change in control provision to partnerships and other non-corporate entities, as well as suggestions with

respect to the formulation of which types of events should qualify and would be analogous to the corporate events described in the regulations. [Corrected on 12/19/05 by 70 FR 75090.]

Commentators also raised questions regarding the application of section 409A to earn-out provisions where an acquirer contracts to make an immediate payment at the closing of the transaction with additional amounts payable at a later date, subject to the satisfaction of specified conditions. In such situations, the later payments could create delays in payments of compensation calculated by reference to the value of target corporation shares. These regulations address this situation by providing that compensation payable pursuant to the purchase by the service recipient of service recipient stock or a stock right held by a service provider, or payment of amounts of deferred compensation calculated by reference to the value of service recipient stock, may be treated as paid at a specified time or pursuant to a fixed schedule in conformity with the requirements of section 409A if paid on the same schedule and under the same terms and conditions as payments to shareholders generally pursuant to a change in the ownership of a corporation that qualifies as a change in control event or as payments to the service recipient pursuant to a change in the ownership of a substantial portion of a corporation's assets that qualifies as a change in control event, and any amounts paid pursuant to such a schedule and such terms and conditions will not be treated as violating the initial or subsequent deferral election rules, to the extent that such amounts are paid not later than five years after the change in control event.

F. *Unforeseeable emergency*

The regulations contain provisions defining the types of circumstances that constitute an unforeseeable emergency, and the amounts that may be paid due to the unforeseeable emergency. Generally these provisions are derived directly from section 409A(a)(2)(B)(ii). Commentators requested that in the case of an unforeseeable emergency, a service provider be permitted to cancel future deferrals. This issue is discussed in this preamble at paragraph VII.D.

G. *Multiple payment events*

The regulations permit a plan to provide that payments may be made upon the earlier of, or the later of, two or more specified permissible payment events or times. In addition, the regulations provide that a different form of payment may be elected for each potential payment event. For example, a plan may provide that a service provider will receive an installment payment upon separation from service or, if earlier, a lump sum payment upon death. The application of the rules governing changes in time and form of payment and the anti-acceleration rules to amounts subject to multiple payment events, is discussed below.

H. *Delay in payment by the service recipient*

Commentators noted that for certain compelling reasons, a service recipient may be unwilling or unable to make a payment of an amount due under a nonqualified deferred compensation plan. These regulations generally provide that in the case of payments the deduction for which would be limited or eliminated by the application of section 162(m), payments that would violate securities laws, or payments that would violate loan covenants or other contractual terms to which the service recipient is a party, where such a violation would result in material harm to the service recipient, the plan may provide that the payment will be delayed. In addition, plans may be amended to add such provisions, but such an amendment cannot be effective for a period of at least 12 months. However, if a plan is amended to remove such a provision with respect to amounts deferred previously, the amendment will constitute an acceleration of the payment. In the case of amounts for which the deduction would be limited or reduced by the application of section 162(m), these regulations require that the payment be deferred either to a date in the first year in which the service recipient reasonably anticipates that a payment of such amount would not result in a limitation of a deduction with respect to the payment of such amount under section 162(m) or the year in which the service provider separates from service. In the case of amounts that would violate loan covenants or similar contracts, or would result in a violation of Federal securities laws or other applicable laws, the arrangement must provide that the payment will be made in the first calendar year in which the service recipient reasonably anticipates that the payment would not violate the loan contractual terms, the violation would not result in material harm to the service recipient, or the payment would not result in a violation of Federal securities law or other applicable laws. These regulations also provide that the Commissioner may prescribe through guidance published in the Internal Revenue Bulletin other circumstances in which a plan may provide for the delay of a payment of a deferred amount. The Treasury Department and the IRS specifically request comments as to what other circumstances may be appropriate to include in such guidance.

I. *Disputed payments and refusals to pay*

In addition to situations in which a plan may delay payment due to certain business circumstances, commentators expressed concern about the possibility that a service recipient will refuse to pay deferred compensation when the payment is due, and whether such refusal to pay would result in taxation of the service provider under section 409A. Generally these situations will arise where either the obligation to make the payment, or the amount of the payment, is subject to dispute. But this situation may also arise where the service recipient simply refuses to pay. In either situation, these proposed regulations generally provide that the payment will be deemed to be made upon the date scheduled under the terms of the arrangement, provided that the service provider is acting in good faith and makes reasonable, good faith efforts to collect the amount. Factors relevant in determining whether a service provider is acting in good faith and making reasonable, good faith efforts to collect the amount include both the amount of the payment, or portion of a payment, in dispute, as well as the size of the disputed portion in relation to the entire payment. Although a payment may be delayed under this provision without violating section 409A because the service recipient refuses to make the payment, the payment may not be made subject to a subsequent deferral election because the payment was delayed. Rather, the payment must be made by the later of the end of the calendar year in which, or the 15th day of the third month following the date that, the service recipient and the service provider enter into a legally binding settlement of such dispute, the service recipient concedes that the full amount is payable, or the service recipient is required to make such payment pursuant to a final and nonappealable judgment or other binding decision. This paragraph is not intended to serve as a means of deferring payments without application of section 409A, by feigning a dispute or surreptitiously requesting that the service recipient refuse to pay the amount at the due date. Where the service provider is not acting in good faith, for example creating a dispute with no or tenuous basis, or where the service provider is not making reasonable, good faith efforts to collect the amount, the failure to receive the payment at the date originally scheduled may result in a violation of the permissible payment requirements. Among the factors to be considered is the practice of the service recipient with respect to payments of nonqualified deferred compensation. In addition, these regulations provide that the service provider is treated as having requested that a payment not be made, rather than the service recipient having refused to make such payment, where the decision that the service recipient will not make the payment is made by the service provider, or any person or group of persons under the supervision of the service provider at the time the decision is made.

VII. *Anti-acceleration Provision*

A. *In general*

Under section 409A(a)(3), a payment of deferred compensation may not be accelerated except as provided in regulations by the Secretary. Certain permissible payment accelerations were listed in Notice 2005-1, Q&A-15, including payments necessary to comply with a domestic relations order, payments necessary to comply with certain conflict of interest rules, payments intended to pay employment taxes, and certain de minimis payments related to the participant's termination of his or her interest in the plan. All the permissible payment accelerations contained in Notice 2005-1, Q&A-15, are included in these regulations.

B. *Payments upon income inclusion under section 409A*

These regulations provide that a plan may permit the acceleration of the time or schedule of a payment to a service provider to pay the amount the service provider includes in income as a result of the plan failing to meet the requirements of section 409A. For this purpose, a service provider will be deemed to have included the amount in income if the amount is timely reported on a Form W-2 "Wage and Tax Statement" or Form 1099-MISC "Miscellaneous Income", as appropriate.

C. *Plan terminations*

Some commentators requested that service recipients be allowed to retain the right to accelerate payments upon a termination of the arrangement, where the termination is at the discretion of the service recipient. A general ability of a service recipient to make such payments raises the potential for abuse, especially with respect to arrangements with individual service providers. Where a service provider retains sufficient influence to obtain a termination of the arrangement, the service recipient's discretion to terminate the plan in substance

would mean that amounts deferred were available to the service provider upon demand. Such a condition would be inconsistent with the provisions of and legislative intent behind section 409A.

Some commentators requested that service recipients be permitted to terminate arrangements where the arrangements are broad-based, covering a significant number of service providers. Due to concerns about administrability and equity, the regulations do not adopt the suggestion.

Some commentators also suggested that service recipients be permitted to terminate arrangements due to bona fide business reasons. However, the Treasury Department and the IRS are not confident that such a standard could be applied on a consistent and coherent basis, leaving service recipients unable to plan with confidence and creating the potential for abuse. The Treasury Department and the IRS are considering further guidance establishing criteria or circumstances under which a plan could be terminated. For that purpose, these regulations provide authority to the Commissioner to establish such criteria or circumstances in generally applicable guidance published in the Internal Revenue Bulletin.

These proposed regulations provide three circumstances under which a plan may be terminated at the discretion of the service recipient in accordance with the terms of the plan. The first addresses a service recipient that wants to cease providing a certain category of nonqualified deferred compensation, such as account balance plans, entirely. A plan may be terminated provided that all arrangements of the same type (account balance plans, nonaccount balance plans, separation pay plans or other arrangements) are terminated with respect to all participants, no payments other than those otherwise payable under the terms of the plan absent a termination of the plan are made within 12 months of the termination of the arrangement, all payments are made within 24 months of the termination of the arrangement, and the service recipient does not adopt a new arrangement that would be aggregated with any terminated arrangement under the plan aggregation rules at any time for a period of five years following the date of termination of the arrangement.

The remaining two exceptions relate to events that are both objectively determinable to have occurred-and so may be determined consistently-and are of such independent significance that they are unlikely to be related to any attempt to accelerate payments under a nonqualified deferred compensation plan in a manner inconsistent with the intent of the statute. These regulations provide that during the 12 months following a change in control of a corporation, the service recipient may elect to terminate a plan and make payments to the participants. In addition, a plan may provide that the plan terminates upon a corporate dissolution taxed under section 331, or with the approval of a bankruptcy court pursuant to 11 U.S.C. § 503(b)(1)(A), provided that the amounts deferred under the plan are included in the participants' gross incomes by the latest of (i) the calendar year in which the plan termination occurs, (ii) the calendar year in which the amount is no longer subject to a substantial risk of forfeiture, or (iii) the first calendar year in which the payment is administratively practicable.

D. *Terminations of deferral elections following an unforeseeable emergency or a hardship distribution*

Commentators noted that although section 409A provides that a service provider may receive a payment upon an unforeseeable emergency, there is no provision explicitly permitting or requiring the service provider to halt all elective deferrals to receive such a payment. In addition, commentators noted that to receive a hardship distribution under a qualified plan with a qualified cash or deferred arrangement under section 401(k), a participant generally would be required pursuant to the regulations under section 401(k) to halt any elective deferrals of compensation into a nonqualified deferred compensation plan. In response, these regulations provide that a plan may provide that a deferral election terminates if a service provider obtains a payment upon an unforeseeable emergency. Similarly, these regulations provide that a plan may provide that a deferral election is terminated if required for a service provider to obtain a hardship distribution under a qualified plan with a qualified cash or deferred arrangement under section 401(k). In each case, the deferral election must be terminated, and not merely suspended. A deferral election under the arrangement made after a termination of a deferral election due to a hardship distribution or an unforeseeable emergency will be treated as an initial deferral election.

E. *Distributions to avoid a nonallocation year under section 409(p).*

Commentators noted that in the case of an S corporation sponsoring an employee stock ownership plan, under certain conditions distributions from a nonqualified deferred compensation plan may be necessary to avoid a nonallocation year (within the meaning of section 409(p)(3)). These regulations provide rules under which such distributions may be made to avoid such a nonallocation year.

VIII. *Subsequent Changes in the Time and Form of Payment*

A. *In general*

Section 409A(a)(4)(C) and these regulations provide that, in the case of a plan that permits a service provider to make a subsequent election to delay a payment or to change the form of a payment (provided that any such payment is the subject of an initial deferral election), the following conditions must be met:

(1) The plan must require that such election not take effect until at least 12 months after the date on which the election is made,

(2) In the case of an election related to a payment other than a payment on account of death, disability or the occurrence of an unforeseeable emergency, the plan requires that the first payment with respect to which such election is made be deferred for a period of not less than 5 years from the date such payment would otherwise have been made (the 5-year rule), and

(3) The plan requires that any election related to a payment at a specified time or pursuant to a fixed schedule may not be made less than 12 months prior to the date of the first scheduled payment.

B. *Definition of payment*

Commentators requested clarification whether the individual amounts paid in a defined stream of payments, such as installment payments, are treated as separate payments or as one payment. This affects the application of the rules governing subsequent deferral elections, particularly the 5-year rule.

These proposed regulations provide generally that each separately identified amount to which a service provider is entitled to payment under a plan on a determinable date is a separate payment. Accordingly, if an amount is separately identified as a payment, either because the right arises under a separate arrangement or because the arrangement identifies the amount as a separate payment, the amount will not be aggregated with other amounts for purposes of the rules relating to subsequent changes in the time and form of payment and the anti-acceleration rule. For example, an arrangement may provide that 50 percent of the benefit is paid as a lump sum at separation from service, and that the remainder of the benefit is paid as a lump sum at age 60, which would identify each amount as a separate payment. However, once a payment has been identified separately, the payment may only be aggregated with another payment if the aggregation would otherwise comply with the rules relating to subsequent changes in the time and form of payment and the anti-acceleration rule.

The Treasury Department and the IRS recognize that most taxpayers view the ability to elect installment payments as a choice of a single form of payment. Accordingly, the entitlement to a series of installment payments under a particular arrangement generally is treated as a single payment for purposes of the subsequent deferral rules. However, taxpayers could also view each individual payment in the series of payments as a separate payment. Accordingly, these regulations provide that an arrangement may specify that a series of installment payments is to be treated as a series of separate payments.

An installment payment must be treated consistently both with respect to the rules governing subsequent changes in the time and form of payment, and with respect to the anti-acceleration rules. For example, if a 5-year installment payment is treated as a single payment and is scheduled to commence on July 1, 2010, then consistent with the 5-year rule a service provider generally could change the time and form of the payment to a lump sum payment on July 1, 2015, provided the other conditions related to a change in the time and form of payment were met. In contrast, if a 5-year installment payment is designated as five separate payments scheduled for the years 2010 through 2014, then the service provider could not change the time and form of the payment to a lump sum payment to be made on July 1, 2015 because the separate payments scheduled for the years 2011 through 2014 would not have been deferred at least 5 years. Rather, the service provider generally could change the time and form of payment to a lump sum payment only if the payment were scheduled to occur no earlier than 2019 (5 years after the last of the originally scheduled payments).

One exception to this rule is a life annuity, the entitlement to which is treated as a single payment. The Treasury Department and the IRS believe that taxpayers generally view an entitlement to a life annuity as a single form of payment, rather than a series of separate payments. In addition, treating a life annuity as a series of payments would lead to difficulty in applying the rules governing subsequent changes in the time and form of payment, because the aggregate amount of the payments and the duration of the payments are unknown, as their continuation depends on the continued life of the service provider or other individual. For example, if a single life annuity were treated as a series of separate payments, an election to change a form of payment to a lump sum payment could be made only if the lump sum payment were deferred to a date no earlier than five years after the death of the participant.

C. *Application to multiple payment events*

As discussed above, a plan may provide that a payment will be made upon the earlier of, or the later of, multiple specified permissible payment events. In addition, a plan may provide for a different form of payment depending upon the payment event. For example, a plan may provide that a service provider is entitled to an annuity at age 65 or, if earlier, a lump sum payment upon separation from service.

The question then arises as to how the provisions governing changes in the time and form of payment and the anti-acceleration provision apply where there are multiple potential payment events, and possibly multiple forms of payment as well. The regulations provide that these provisions are to apply to each payment event separately. In the example above, these provisions would apply separately to the entitlement to the installment payment at age 65, and the entitlement to the lump sum payment at separation from service. Accordingly, the service provider generally would be able to delay the annuity payment date subject to the rules governing changes in the time and form of payment, while retaining a separate right to receive a lump sum payment at separation from service if that occurred at an earlier date. In other words, the 5-year rule would apply to the annuity payment date (delaying payment from age 65 to at least age 70) but not to the unchanged lump sum payment available upon separation from service before age 70.

Similarly, a plan may provide that an intervening event that is a permissible payment event under section 409A may override an existing payment schedule already in payment status. For example, a plan could provide that a participant would receive six installment payments commencing at separation from service, but also provide that if the participant died after the payments commenced, all remaining benefits would be paid in a lump sum.

An additional question arises where a new payment event, or a fixed time or fixed schedule of payments, is added to the plan. Generally, the addition of the payment event or date will be subject to the rules governing changes in the time and form of payment and the anti-acceleration rules. Accordingly, no fixed time of payment could be added that did not defer the payment at least five years from the date the fixed time was added. In addition, no payment due to any other added permissible event could be made within five years of the addition of the event. For example, a service provider entitled to a payment only on January 1, 2050, could not make a subsequent deferral election to be paid on the later of January 1, 2050, or separation from service, but could make a subsequent deferral election to be paid at the later of separation from service or January 1, 2055.

IX. *Application of Rules to Nonqualified Deferred Compensation Plans Linked to Qualified Plans*

A. *In general*

Commentators raised many issues concerning the application of section 409A to nonqualified deferred compensation plans linked to qualified plans. These linked plans exist in a variety of formats, and are referred to under various labels such as excess plans, wrap plans, and supplemental employee retirement plans (SERPs). Typically the purpose of such plans is to replace the benefits that would have been provided under the qualified plan absent the application of certain limits contained in the Code (for example, section 415, section 401(a)(17) or section 402(g)). Often the amounts deferred under the nonqualified deferred compensation plan are established through an offset formula, where the amount deferred equals an amount determined under a formula, offset by any benefits credited under the qualified plan. Because of the close relationship between the qualified plan and the nonqualified deferred compensation plan, sponsor and participant actions under the qualified plan may affect the calculation or payment of the amounts deferred under the nonqualified deferred compensation plan. Commentators asked for guidance regarding the circumstances under which an action (or failure to act) under the qualified plan may be treated as violating section 409A, to the extent the action (or failure to act) also affects the amounts deferred under the nonqualified deferred compensation plan.

These proposed regulations generally adopt rules under which nonqualified deferred compensation plans linked to qualified plans may continue to operate, though certain changes may be required. The intent of these rules generally is to permit the qualified plan to be established, amended and operated under the rules governing qualified plans, without causing the linked nonqualified deferred compensation plan to violate the rules of section 409A. However, the relief provided under certain rules to accommodate the linked plan structure is not intended to relax the rules generally with respect to all of the amounts deferred under the nonqualified deferred compensation plan, simply because a limited portion of the amounts deferred may be affected by actions under the qualified plan. Accordingly, in certain circumstances the relief provided relates solely to amounts deferred under the nonqualified deferred compensation plan that do not exceed the applicable limit on the qualified plan benefit for the taxable year.

B. *Actions that do not constitute deferral elections or accelerations*

Where amounts deferred under a nonqualified deferred compensation plan are linked to the benefits under a qualified plan, certain participant actions taken with respect to the benefit accrued under the qualified plan may affect the amounts deferred under the nonqualified deferred compensation plan. Where the amounts deferred under the nonqualified deferred compensation plan increase, the issue is whether the action taken with respect to the benefit accrued under the qualified plan constitutes a deferral election. Where the amounts deferred under the nonqualified deferred compensation plan decrease, the issue is whether the action taken with respect to the benefit accrued under the qualified plan constitutes an impermissible acceleration of a payment under the nonqualified deferred compensation plan.

With respect to the benefits provided under the qualified plan, these regulations provide generally that neither the amendment of the qualified plan to increase or decrease such benefits under the qualified plan nor the cessation of future accruals under the qualified plan is treated as a deferral election or an acceleration of a payment under the nonqualified deferred compensation plan. Similarly, the addition, removal, increase or reduction of a subsidized benefit or ancillary benefit under the qualified plan, or a participant election with respect to a subsidized benefit or ancillary benefit under the qualified plan, will not constitute either a deferral election or an acceleration of a payment under the nonqualified deferred compensation, even where such action results in an increase or decrease in amounts deferred under the nonqualified deferred compensation plan.

Additional relief is provided with respect to nonqualified deferred compensation plans linked to defined contribution plans that include a 401(k) or similar cash or deferred arrangement. Specifically, the regulations provide that a service provider's action or inaction under a qualified plan that is subject to section 402(g), including an adjustment to a deferral election under such qualified plan, will not be treated as either a deferral election or an acceleration of a payment under the linked nonqualified deferred compensation plan, provided that for any given calendar year, the service provider's actions or inactions under the qualified plan do not result in an increase in the amounts deferred under all nonqualified deferred compensation plans in which the service provider participates in excess of the limit with respect to elective deferrals under section 402(g) in effect for the year in which such actions or inactions occur. The Treasury Department and the IRS intend for this provision to address common arrangements whereby the amounts deferred under the nonqualified deferred compensation plan are linked to amounts deferred under a 401(k) arrangement (often referred to as 401(k) wrap plans), but only to the extent the amount of affected deferrals under the nonqualified deferred compensation plan does not exceed the maximum amount that ever could have been electively deferred under the qualified plan.

Similar relief is provided with respect to plans involving matching contributions. The regulations provide that a service provider's action or inaction under a qualified plan with respect to elective deferrals or after-tax contributions by the service provider to the qualified plan that affects the amounts that are credited under a nonqualified deferred compensation arrangement as matching amounts or other amounts contingent on service provider elective deferrals or after-tax contributions will not be treated as either a deferral election or an acceleration of payment, provided that such matching or contingent amounts, as applicable, are either forfeited or never credited under the nonqualified deferred compensation arrangement in the absence of such service provider's elective deferral or after-tax contribution, and provided the service provider's actions or inactions under the qualified plan do not result in an increase or decrease in the amounts deferred under all nonqualified deferred compensation plans in which the service provider participates in excess of the limit with respect to elective deferrals under section 402(g) in effect for the year in which such actions or inactions occur. Although the section 402(g) limit applies to elective deferrals, rather than matching contributions, the Treasury Department and the IRS believe that matching contributions in excess of 100

percent of the elective deferrals of pre-tax contributions or after-tax contributions will be rare.

X. *Statutory Effective Dates*

A. *Effective dates - earned and vested amounts*

Consistent with Notice 2005-1, Q&A-16, these regulations provide that an amount is considered deferred before January 1, 2005, and thus is not subject to section 409A, if the service provider had a legally binding right to be paid the amount and the right to the amount was earned and vested as of December 31, 2004. For these purposes, a right to an amount is earned and vested only if the amount is not subject to either a substantial risk of forfeiture or a requirement to perform further services. Some commentators questioned the application of section 409A to contractual arrangements entered into before the enactment of the statute. However, the statutory effective date is tied to the date the amount is deferred and the legislative history states that for these purposes, "an amount is considered deferred before January 1, 2005, if the amount is earned and vested before such date." H.R. Conf. Rep. No. 108-755, at 737 (2004). Accordingly, these regulations are consistent with the legislative intent that deferred amounts that were not earned, or were not vested, as of December 31, 2004, are subject to the provisions of section 409A.

Clarification has been provided with respect to when a stock right or similar right to compensation will be treated as earned and vested. The issue arises because often a stock right terminates upon a separation from service. Taxpayers questioned whether this meant that the right had not been earned and vested, because future services would be required to retain the right. These regulations clarify that a stock right or similar right will be treated as earned and vested by December 31, 2004, if on or before such date the right was either immediately exercisable for a payment of cash or substantially vested property, or was not forfeitable. Accordingly, stock options that on or before December 31, 2004, were immediately exercisable for substantially vested stock generally would not be subject to section 409A. In contrast, a nonstatutory stock option that was immediately exercisable on or before December 31, 2004, but only for substantially nonvested stock, generally would be subject to section 409A.

B. *Effective dates - calculation of grandfathered amount*

For account balance plans and plans that are neither account balance plans nor nonaccount balance plans (generally equity-based compensation), these regulations generally retain the method of calculating the grandfathered amount set forth in Notice 2005-1, Q&A-17. Accordingly, for account balance plans the grandfathered amount generally will equal the vested account balance as of December 31, 2004, plus any earnings with respect to such amounts. For equity-based compensation, the grandfathered amount generally will equal the payment that would be available if the right were exercised on December 31, 2004, and any earnings with respect to such amount. For this purpose, the earnings generally would include the increase in the payment available due to appreciation in the underlying stock. [Corrected on 12/19/05 by 70 FR 75090.]

Commentators argued that the definition of the grandfathered amount contained in Notice 2005-1, Q&A-17 with respect to nonaccount balance plans was not sufficiently flexible to account for subsequent increases in benefits unrelated to any further performance of services or increases in compensation after December 31, 2004. For example, a participant's benefit may increase if the participant becomes eligible for a subsidized benefit at a specified age that the participant reaches after December 31, 2004. In response, these proposed regulations provide that for nonaccount balance plans, the grandfathered amount specifically equals the present value as of December 31, 2004, of the amount to which the service provider would be entitled under the plan if the service provider voluntarily terminated services without cause on December 31, 2004, and received a payment of the benefits with the maximum value available from the plan on the earliest possible date allowed under the plan to receive a payment of benefits following the termination of services. Notwithstanding the foregoing, for any subsequent calendar year, the grandfathered amount may increase to equal the present value of the benefit the service provider actually becomes entitled to, determined under the terms of the plan (including applicable limits under the Code), as in effect on October 3, 2004, without regard to any further services rendered by the service provider after December 31, 2004, or any other events affecting the amount of or the entitlement to benefits (other than the participant's survival or a participant election under the terms of the plan with respect to the time or form of an available benefit). [Corrected on 12/19/05 by 70 FR 75090.]

Because separation pay plans with respect to involuntary terminations and window programs are now treated as separate plans, these

...

regulations provide a rule for calculating the grandfathered amount under such plans. For these purposes, the principles used to calculate the grandfathered amounts under a nonaccount balance plan and an account balance plan are to be applied by analogy, depending upon the structure of the separation pay plan.

C. *Material modifications*

Commentators have pointed out that a grandfathered plan may become subject to section 409A upon any material modification, even if such modification occurs many years after 2004. Given the substantial amounts of compensation that are deferred under grandfathered plans, as well as the potential for these amounts to grow through accumulated grandfathered earnings, the consequences of such a modification could be significant. Commentators expressed concern that as long as these plans exist, there will be the potential for a change to the plan to mistakenly cause the plan to become subject to section 409A. In response, these regulations include a provision stating that to the extent a modification is rescinded before the earlier of the date any additional right granted under the modification is exercised or the end of the calendar year in which the modification was made, the modification will not be treated as a material modification of the plan. For example, if a subsequent deferral feature is added that would allow participants to extend the time and form of payment of a grandfathered deferred amount, and if the right is removed before the earlier of the time the participant exercises the right or the end of the calendar year, then the modification will not be treated as a material modification of the plan. However, this provision is not intended to cover material modifications that are made with the knowledge that the modification will subject the amounts to section 409A, but are then rescinded.

Consistent with Notice 2005-1, Q&A-18(a), these regulations also provide that it is not a material modification to change a notional investment measure to, or to add, an investment measure that qualifies as a predetermined actual investment within the meaning of §31.3121(v)(2)-1(d)(2) of this chapter. Commentators requested similar flexibility with respect to investment measures reflecting reasonable rates of interest. These regulations provide such flexibility, generally adopting a modified version of the rules contained in §31.3121(v)(2)-1(d)(2) of this chapter. Under these regulations, it is not a material modification to change a notional investment measure to, or to add, an investment measure that qualifies as a predetermined actual investment within the meaning of §31.3121(v)(2)-1(d)(2) of this chapter or, for any given taxable year, reflects a reasonable rate of interest. For this purpose, if with respect to an amount deferred for a period, a plan provides for a fixed rate of interest to be credited, and the rate is to be reset under the plan at a specified future date that is not later than the end of the fifth calendar year that begins after the beginning of the period, the rate is reasonable at the beginning of the period, and the rate is not changed before the reset date, then the rate will be treated as reasonable in all future periods before the reset date. These proposed regulations also contain other clarifications of the application of the material modification rule.

XI. *Transition Relief*

A. *In general*

Until the effective date of these regulations, Notice 2005-1 generally remains in effect. Notice 2005-1, Q&As-18 through 23. provided transition relief that was limited to the 2005 calendar year. Commentators generally reacted favorably to the scope of the transition rules. The Treasury Department and the IRS intended for the transition rules to be generous during the calendar year 2005, both to enable taxpayers to familiarize themselves with the new provisions, and also to provide a period during which the Treasury Department and the IRS could develop regulations and taxpayers generally could be confident that either their plans were not in violation of section 409A, or could be corrected to avoid additional tax under the statute.

Because final regulations are not yet in place, the IRS and the Treasury Department are hereby extending through 2006 certain aspects of the transition relief provided for 2005 by Notice 2005-1. In addition, in response to questions, certain provisions of Notice 2005-1 are clarified below. However, because taxpayers will have had, by the end of 2005, over a year to implement the statute, certain other transition relief is not being extended through 2006.

B. *Amendment and operation of plans adopted on or before December 31, 2006*

Pursuant to Notice 2005-1, Q&A-19, a plan adopted on or before December 31, 2005, will not be treated as violating section 409A(a)(2), (3) or (4) only if the plan is operated in good faith compliance with the provisions of section 409A and Notice 2005-1 during the calendar year 2005, and the plan is amended on or before December 31, 2005, to conform to the provisions of section 409A with respect to amounts subject to section 409A. To allow time to finalize these regulations, and for practitioners to implement the final regulations, the deadline by which plan documents must be amended to comply with the provisions of section 409A and the regulations is hereby extended to December 31, 2006. Accordingly, in order to be treated as complying with section 409A(a)(2), (3) or (4), a plan adopted before December 31, 2006, must be amended on or before December 31, 2006, either to conform to the provisions of section 409A with respect to amounts subject to section 409A, or to provide a compensation arrangement that does not provide for a deferral of compensation for purposes of section 409A.

The good faith compliance period provided under Q&A-19 of Notice 2005-1 is also hereby extended through December 31, 2006. Accordingly, a plan adopted on or before December 31, 2006, will be treated as complying with section 409A(a)(2), (3) or (4) only if the plan is operated through December 31, 2006, in good faith compliance with the provisions of section 409A and Notice 2005-1. If any other guidance of general applicability under section 409A is published in the Internal Revenue Bulletin with an effective date prior to January 1, 2007, the plan must also comply with such published guidance as of its effective date. To the extent an issue is not addressed in Notice 2005-1 or such other published guidance, the plan must follow a good faith, reasonable interpretation of section 409A, and, to the extent not inconsistent therewith, the plan's terms.

These regulations are not proposed to become effective prior to January 1, 2007, and, accordingly, a plan is not required to comply with either these proposed regulations or the final regulations prior to January 1, 2007. However, compliance with either these proposed regulations or the final regulations will be good faith compliance with the statute. In general, these proposed regulations expand upon, and should be read consistently with, the provisions of Notice 2005-1. However, to the extent that a provision of either these proposed regulations or the final regulations is inconsistent with a provision of Notice 2005-1, the plan may comply with the provision of the proposed or final regulations in lieu of the corresponding provision of Notice 2005-1.

A plan will not be operating in good faith compliance if the plan sponsor exercises discretion under the terms of the plan, or a service provider exercises discretion with respect to that service provider's benefits, in a manner that causes the plan to fail to meet the requirements of section 409A. For example, if an employer retains the discretion under the terms of the plan to delay or extend payments under the plan and exercises such discretion, the plan will not be considered to be operated in good faith compliance with section 409A with regard to any plan participant. However, an exercise of a right under the terms of the plan by a service provider solely with respect to that service provider's benefits under the plan, in a manner that causes the plan to fail to meet the requirements of section 409A, will not be considered to result in the plan failing to be operated in good faith compliance with respect to other participants. For example, the request for and receipt of an immediate payment permitted under the terms of the plan if the participant forfeits 20 percent of the participant's benefits (a haircut) will be considered a failure of the plan to meet the requirements of section 409A with respect to that service provider, but not with respect to all other service providers under the plan.

C. *Change in payment elections or conditions on or before December 31, 2006*

Notice 2005-1, Q&A-19(c) provided generally that with respect to amounts subject to section 409A, a plan could be amended to provide for new payment elections without violating the subsequent deferral and anti-acceleration rules, provided that the plan was amended and the participant made the election on or before December 31, 2005. The period during which a plan may be amended and a service provider may be permitted to change payment elections, without resulting in an impermissible subsequent deferral or acceleration, is hereby extended through December 31, 2006, except that a service provider cannot in 2006 change payment elections with respect to payments that the service provider would otherwise receive in 2006, or to cause payments to be made in 2006. Other provisions of the Internal Revenue Code and common law doctrines continue to apply to any such election.

Accordingly, with respect to amounts subject to section 409A and amounts that would be treated as a short-term deferral within the meaning of §1.409A-1(b)(4), a plan may provide, or be amended to provide, for new payment elections on or before December 31, 2006, with respect to both the time and form of payment of such amounts and the election will not be treated as a change in the form and timing of a payment under section 409A(a)(4) or an acceleration of a payment under section 409A(a)(3), provided that the plan is so amended and the

Proposed Regulations

service provider makes any applicable election on or before December 31, 2006, and provided that the amendment and election applies only to amounts that would not otherwise be payable in 2006 and does not cause an amount to be paid in 2006 that would not otherwise be payable in such year. Similarly, an outstanding stock right that provides for a deferral of compensation subject to section 409A may be amended to provide for fixed payment terms consistent with section 409A, or to permit holders of such rights to elect fixed payment terms consistent with section 409A, and such amendment or election will not be treated as a change in the time and form of a payment under section 409A(a)(4) or an acceleration of a payment under section 409A(a)(3), provided that the option or right is so amended and any elections are made, on or before December 31, 2006.

D. *Payments based upon an election under a qualified plan for periods ending on or before December 31, 2006*

For calendar year 2005, Notice 2005-1 Q&A-23 provides relief for nonqualified deferred compensation plans where the time and form of payment is controlled by the time and form of payment elected by the service provider under a qualified plan. Commentators indicated that this is a common arrangement with respect to nonqualified deferred compensation plans providing benefits calculated in relation to benefits accrued under a defined benefit qualified plan. Generally, the provisions with respect to the election of a time and form of a payment with respect to a qualified plan benefit would not comply with the requirements of section 409A were the plan subject to section 409A. Accordingly, election provisions under a nonqualified plan that mirrored or depended upon an election under a qualified plan generally would not comply with section 409A. The Treasury Department and the IRS were concerned that service providers, service recipients and plan administrators would not have sufficient time to solicit, retain and process new elections from service providers to comply with section 409A in 2005. Accordingly, relief was provided in Notice 2005-1, Q&A-23, under which an election under a nonqualified deferred compensation plan that was controlled by an election under a qualified plan could continue in effect during the calendar year 2005.

Commentators requested that this relief be a permanent provision in the regulations. Although the Treasury Department and the IRS understand that such a provision would make the coordination of benefits under a qualified plan and benefits under a nonqualified deferred compensation plan calculated by reference to the qualified plan benefits easier to administer, the provisions of section 409A are not as flexible with respect to the timing of such elections as the qualified plan provisions. Given that the benefits under a nonqualified deferred compensation plan often dwarf the benefits provided under a qualified plan, the Treasury Department and the IRS do not believe that the importation of the more flexible qualified plan rules would be consistent with the legislative intent behind the enactment of section 409A. Accordingly, the transition relief has not been made permanent. However, because other transition relief granting a participant the ability to change a time and form of payment through the end of the calendar year 2006 would, in many instances, allow a participant to elect the same time and form of payment that had been elected under the qualified plan, the relief is hereby extended through the calendar year 2006.

Accordingly, for periods ending on or before December 31, 2006, an election as to the timing and form of a payment under a nonqualified deferred compensation plan that is controlled by a payment election made by the service provider or beneficiary of the service provider under a qualified plan will not violate section 409A, provided that the determination of the timing and form of the payment is made in accordance with the terms of the nonqualified deferred compensation plan as of October 3, 2004, that govern payments. For this purpose, a qualified plan means a retirement plan qualified under section 401(a). For example, where a nonqualified deferred compensation plan provides as of October 3, 2004, that the time and form of payment to a service provider or beneficiary will be the same time and form of payment elected by the service provider or beneficiary under a related qualified plan, it will not be a violation of section 409A for the plan administrator to make or commence payments under the nonqualified deferred compensation plan on or after January 1, 2005, and on or before December 31, 2006, pursuant to the payment election under the related qualified plan. Notwithstanding the foregoing, other provisions of the Internal Revenue Code and common law tax doctrines continue to apply to any election as to the timing and form of a payment under a nonqualified deferred compensation plan.

E. *Initial deferral elections*

Notice 2005-1, Q&A-21 provides relief with respect to initial deferral elections, generally permitting initial deferral elections with respect to

deferrals relating all or in part to services performed on or before December 31, 2005, to be made on or before March 15, 2005. No extension is provided with respect to this relief with respect to initial elections to defer compensation. The Treasury Department and the IRS believe that sufficient guidance has been provided so that timely elections may be solicited and received from plan participants. In combination with the extension of flexibility with respect to amending the time and form of payments, the Treasury Department and the IRS believe that participants should be sufficiently informed to make a decision with respect to deferral elections.

F. *Cancellation of deferrals and termination of participation in a plan*

Notice 2005-1, Q&A-20 provides a limited time during which a plan adopted before December 31, 2005, may provide a participant a right to terminate participation in the plan, or cancel an outstanding deferral election with regard to amounts subject to section 409A. Generally to qualify for this relief, if a plan amendment is necessary to permit the participant to terminate participation or cancel a deferral election, the plan amendment must be enacted and effective on or before December 31, 2005, and whether or not the plan is amended, the amount subject to the termination or cancellation must be includible in income of the participant in the calendar year 2005 or, if later, in the taxable year in which the amounts are earned and vested.

The period during which a service provider may cancel a deferral election or terminate participation in the plan is not extended. This relief was intended as a temporary period during which service providers could decide whether to continue to participate in an arrangement subject to section 409A. The Treasury Department and the IRS believe that the statute and existing guidance provide sufficient information for service providers to determine by December 31, 2005, whether to continue to participate in a particular arrangement, and that the further extension of this relief, and the relaxation of constructive receipt rules it entails, is not appropriate.

A termination or cancellation pursuant to Notice 2005-1, Q&A-20 is treated as effective as of January 1, 2005, for purposes of section 409A, and may apply in whole or in part to one or more plans in which a service provider participates and to one or more outstanding deferral elections the service provider has made with regard to amounts subject to section 409A. The exercise of a stock option, stock appreciation right or similar equity appreciation right that provides for a deferral of compensation, on or before December 31, 2005, will be treated as a cancellation of a deferral.

G. *Terminations of grandfathered plans*

Notice 2005-1, Q&A-18(c) provides that amending an arrangement on or before December 31, 2005, to terminate the arrangement and distribute the amounts of deferred compensation thereunder will not be treated as a material modification, provided that all amounts deferred under the plan are included in income in the taxable year in which the termination occurs. For the same reasons discussed above with respect to the period during which plans may allow participants to terminate participation in a plan, the relief provided in Notice 2005-1, Q&A-18(c) is not extended.

To qualify for the relief provided in Notice 2005-1, Q&A-18(c), the amendment to the plan must result in the termination of the arrangement and the distribution of all amounts deferred under the arrangement in the taxable year of such termination. An amendment to a plan to provide a participant a right to elect whether to terminate participation in the plan or to continue to defer amounts under the plan would not be covered by Q&A-18(c), and therefore would constitute a material modification of the plan. Accordingly, amounts that were not distributed pursuant to such an election and continued to be deferred under the plan would be subject to section 409A.

H. *Substitutions of non-discounted stock options and stock appreciation rights for discounted stock options and stock appreciation rights*

Notice 2005-1, Q&A-18(d) provides that it will not be a material modification to replace a stock option or stock appreciation right otherwise providing for a deferral of compensation under section 409A with a stock option or stock appreciation right that would not have constituted a deferral of compensation under section 409A if it had been granted upon the original date of grant of the replaced stock option or stock appreciation right, provided that the cancellation and reissuance occurs on or before December 31, 2005. The period during which the cancellation and reissuance may occur is extended until December 31, 2006, but only to the extent such cancellation and reissuance does not result in the cancellation of a deferral in exchange for cash or vested property in 2006. For example, a discounted option generally may be replaced through December 31, 2006 with an option that would not have provided for a deferral of compensation, although

¶20,261T

the exercise of such a discounted option in 2006 before the cancellation and replacement generally would result in a violation of section 409A.

Commentators pointed out that this relief could be interpreted as failing to cover discounted stock options or stock appreciation rights that were not earned and vested before January 1, 2005. Where replacement stock options or stock appreciation rights that would not constitute deferred compensation subject to section 409A are issued in accordance with the conditions set forth in Notice 2005-1, Q&A 18(d) and this preamble, such replacement stock options or stock appreciation rights will be treated for purposes of section 409A as if granted on the grant date of the original stock option or stock appreciation right. For example, provided that the conditions of Notice 2005-1, Q&A-18(d) and this preamble are met, a discounted stock option granted in 2003 that was not earned and vested before January 1, 2005, may be replaced with a stock option with an exercise price that would not have been discounted as of the original 2003 grant date, and the substituted stock option will be treated for purposes of section 409A as granted on the original 2003 grant date. Accordingly, if the substituted stock option would not have been subject to section 409A had it been granted on the original 2003 grant date, the substituted stock option will not be subject to section 409A.

Commentators noted that some service recipients may wish to compensate the service provider for the lost discount. Commentators proposed three methods to provide such compensation. First, the service recipient may wish to pay the amount of the discount in 2005 in cash. As a cancellation of a deferral of compensation on or before December 31, 2005 pursuant to Notice 2005-1, Q&A-20(a), this payment would not be subject to section 409A. Note that as a payment due to the cancellation of a deferral, such a payment could not be made in 2006 as this relief has not been extended beyond December 31, 2005. Where the stock option remains nonvested during the year of the option substitution, the service recipient may wish to make the compensation for the lost discount also subject to a vesting requirement. In that case, commentators also proposed granting restricted stock with a fair market value equal to the lost discount, subject to a vesting schedule parallel to the vesting schedule of the substituted option. As a transfer of property subject to section 83 that becomes substantially vested after the year of substitution, this grant would not be subject to section 409A. Finally, commentators proposed establishing a separate plan, promising a payment of the lost discount (plus earnings) subject to a vesting schedule parallel to the vesting schedule of the substituted option. Provided the right to the payment becomes substantially vested in a future year and otherwise meets the requirement of the short-term deferral exception in these regulations, the right to this payment would not constitute deferred compensation subject to section 409A. Alternatively, such an arrangement could itself provide for deferral of compensation beyond the year of substantial vesting and be subject to the requirements of section 409A, but if such requirements are met, would not affect the exclusion of the amended stock option or stock appreciation right from the treatment as a deferral of compensation subject to section 409A.

XII. *Calculation and Timing of Income Inclusion Amounts*

To more rapidly issue guidance necessary to allow service recipients to comply with section 409A, the Treasury Department and the IRS have not included in these regulations guidance with respect to the calculation of the amounts of deferrals, or of the amounts of income inclusion upon the violation of the provisions of section 409A and these regulations, or the timing of the inclusion of income and related withholding obligations. The Treasury Department and the IRS anticipate that these topics will be addressed in subsequent guidance. The Treasury Department and the IRS request comments with respect to the calculation and timing of the income inclusion under section 409A, and specifically request comments in two areas.

First, section 409A generally requires that for any taxable year in which an amount is deferred under a plan that fails to meet certain requirements, all amounts deferred must be included in income. This provision generally treats earnings (whether actual or notional) as amounts deferred subject to the inclusion provision. Service providers may experience negative earnings in a calendar year, such that the amounts to which a service provider has a right in a particular year are less than the amounts to which a service provider had a right in a previous year, even where no actual payments have been made. The Treasury Department and the IRS request comments with respect to whether and how such negative earnings may be accounted for in determining the amount of deferrals and the amount of income inclusion for a given taxable year, particularly where continuing violations of section 409A extend to successive tax years.

Second, the Treasury Department and the IRS understand that a method of calculation of current deferrals and of amounts to be included in income is needed for service recipients to meet their report-

ing and withholding obligations. Comments are requested as to what transitional relief may be appropriate depending upon when such future guidance is released. For interim guidance regarding the information reporting and wage withholding requirements applicable to deferrals of compensation within the meaning of section 409A, see Notice 2005-1, Q&A-24 through Q&A-38. Until further guidance is provided, taxpayers may rely on Notice 2005-1 regarding information reporting and wage withholding obligations.

XIII. *Funding Arrangements*

Section 409A(b)(1) provides certain tax consequences for the funding of deferrals of compensation in offshore trusts (or other arrangements determined by the Secretary) or pursuant to a change in the financial health of the employer. The consequences of such funding are generally consistent with a violation of section 409A with respect to funded amounts. The Treasury Department and the IRS intend to address these provisions in future guidance. Commentators have requested guidance with respect to when assets will be treated as set aside, especially with respect to service recipients that are, or include, foreign corporations. Comments are requested as to what types of arrangements, other than actual trusts, should be treated similarly to trusts. In addition, these proposed regulations provide guidance with respect to the types of arrangements that constitute deferred compensation subject to section 409A. Because the funding rules of section 409A(b) apply only to amounts set aside to fund deferred compensation subject to section 409A, many issues raised by commentators with respect to foreign arrangements and funding may be addressed or limited through the definition of deferred compensation contained in these proposed regulations.

Proposed Effective Date

These regulations are proposed to be generally applicable for taxable years beginning on or after January 1, 2007. As discussed, taxpayers may rely on these proposed regulations until the effective date of the final regulations.

Effect on Other Documents

These proposed regulations do not affect the applicability of other guidance issued with respect to section 409A, including Notice 2005-1 (2005-2 I.R.B. 274 (published as modified on January 6, 2005)). However, upon the effective date of the final regulations, the Treasury Department and the IRS anticipate that Notice 2005-1 and certain other published guidance will become obsolete for periods after the effective date of the final regulations.

Special Analyses

It has been determined that this notice of proposed rulemaking is not a significant regulatory action as defined in Executive Order 12866. Therefore, a regulatory assessment is not required. It has also been determined that section 553(b) of the Administrative Procedure Act (5 U.S.C. chapter 5) does not apply to these regulations, and because the regulation does not impose a collection of information on small entities, the Regulatory Flexibility Act (5 U.S.C. chapter 6) does not apply. Pursuant to section 7805(f) of the Code, this notice of proposed rulemaking will be submitted to the Chief Counsel for Advocacy of the Small Business Administration for comment on its impact on small business.

Comments and Public Hearing

Before these proposed regulations are adopted as final regulations, consideration will be given to any written (a signed original and eight (8) copies) or electronic comments that are submitted timely to the IRS. The IRS and Treasury Department request comments on the clarity of the proposed rules and how they can be made easier to understand. All comments will be available for public inspection and copying.

A public hearing has been scheduled for January 25, 2006, beginning at 10 a.m. in the Auditorium of the Internal Revenue Building, 1111 Constitution Avenue, NW., Washington, DC. Due to building security procedures, visitors must enter at the Constitution Avenue entrance. In addition, all visitors must present photo identification to enter the building. Because of access restrictions, visitors will not be admitted beyond the immediate entrance area more than 30 minutes before the hearing starts. For information about having your name placed on the building access list to attend the hearing, see the "FOR FURTHER INFORMATION CONTACT" section of this preamble.

The rules of 26 CFR 601.601(a)(3) apply to the hearing. Persons who wish to present oral comments at the hearing must submit written or electronic comments and an outline of the topics to be discussed and the time to be devoted to each topic (a signed original and eight (8) copies) by January 4, 2006. A period of 10 minutes will be allotted to each person for making comments. An agenda showing the scheduling of the speakers will be prepared after the deadline for receiving outlines has passed. Copies of the agenda will be available free of charge at the hearing.

Drafting Information

The principal author of these regulations is Stephen Tackney of the Office of Division Counsel/Associate Chief Counsel (Tax Exempt and Government Entities). However, other personnel from the IRS and the Treasury Department participated in their development.

List of Subjects 26 CFR Part 1

Income taxes, reporting and recordkeeping requirements.

Proposed Amendment to the Regulations.

Paragraph 1. The authority citation for part 1 continues to read in part as follows:

Authority: 26 U.S.C. 7805 * * *

Par. 2. Sections 1.409A-1 through 1.409A-6 are added to read as follows:

§ 1.409A-1 Definitions and covered arrangements.

(a) *Nonqualified deferred compensation plan*—(1) *In general.* Except as otherwise provided in this paragraph (a), the term *nonqualified deferred compensation plan* means any plan (within the meaning of paragraph (c) of this section) that provides for the deferral of compensation (within the meaning of paragraph (b) of this section).

(2) *Qualified employer plans.* The term *nonqualified deferred compensation plan* does not include—

(i) Any plan described in section 401(a) that includes a trust exempt from tax under section 501(a);

(ii) Any annuity plan described in section 403(a);

(iii) Any annuity contract described in section 403(b);

(iv) Any simplified employee pension (within the meaning of section 408(k));

(v) Any simple retirement account (within the meaning of section 408(p);

(vi) Any arrangement under which an active participant makes deductible contributions to a trust described in section 501(c)(18);

(vii) Any eligible deferred compensation plan (within the meaning of section 457(b)); and

(viii) Any plan described in section 415(m).

(3) *Certain foreign plans*—(i) *Participation addressed by treaty.* With respect to an individual for a taxable year, the term *nonqualified deferred compensation plan* does not include any scheme, trust or arrangement maintained with respect to such individual, where contributions made by or on behalf of such individual to such scheme, trust or arrangement are excludable by such individual for Federal income tax purposes pursuant to any bilateral income tax convention to which the United States is a party.

(ii) *Participation by nonresident aliens and certain resident aliens.* With respect to an alien individual for a taxable year during which such individual is a nonresident alien or a resident alien classified as a resident alien solely under section 7701(b)(1)(A)(ii) (and not section 7701(b)(1)(A)(i)), the term *nonqualified deferred compensation plan* does not include any broad-based foreign retirement plan (within the meaning of paragraph (a)(3)(v) of this section) maintained by a person that is not a United States person.

(iii) *Participation by U.S. citizens and lawful permanent residents.* With respect to an individual for a given taxable year during which such individual is a U.S. citizen or a resident alien classified as a resident alien under section 7701(b)(1)(A)(i), and is not eligible to participate in a qualified employer plan described in paragraph (a)(2) of this section, the term *nonqualified deferred compensation plan* does not include a broad-based foreign retirement plan (within the meaning of paragraph (a)(3)(v) of this section) maintained by a service recipient that is not a United States person, but only with respect to nonelective deferrals of foreign earned income (as defined in section 911(b)(1)) and only to the extent that the amounts deferred under such plan in such taxable year do not exceed the applicable limits under section 415(b) and (c) that would be applicable if such plan were a plan subject to section 415 and the foreign earned income of such individual were

treated as compensation for purposes of applying section 415(b) and (c).

(iv) *Plans subject to a totalization agreement and similar plans.* The term *nonqualified deferred compensation plan* does not include any social security system of a jurisdiction to the extent that benefits provided under or contributions made to the system are subject to an agreement entered into pursuant to section 233 of the Social Security Act with any foreign jurisdiction. In addition, the term *nonqualified deferred compensation plan* does not include a social security system of a foreign jurisdiction to the extent that benefits are provided under or contributions are made to a government-mandated plan as part of that foreign jurisdiction's social security system.

(v) *Broad-based retirement plan.* For purposes of this paragraph (a)(3), the term *broad-based retirement plan* means a scheme, trust or arrangement that—

(A) Is written;

(B) In the case of an employer-maintained plan, is nondiscriminatory insofar as it (alone or in combination with other comparable plans) covers a wide range of employees, substantially all of whom are nonresident aliens or resident aliens classified as resident aliens solely under section 7701(b)(1)(A)(ii) (and not section 7701(b)(1)(A)(i)), including rank and file employees, and actually provides significant benefits for the range of covered employees;

(C) In the case of an employer-maintained plan, contains provisions that generally limit the employees' ability to use plan benefits for purposes other than retirement or restrict access to plan benefits prior to separation from service, such as restricting in-service distributions except in events similar to an unforeseeable emergency (as defined in § 1.409A-3(g)(3)(i)) or hardship (as defined for purposes of section 401(k)(2)(B)(i)(IV)), and in all cases is subject to tax or plan provisions that discourage participants from using the assets for purposes other than retirement; and

(D) Provides for payment of a reasonable level of benefits at death, a stated age, or an event related to work status, and otherwise requires minimum distributions under rules designed to ensure that any death benefits provided to the participants' survivors are merely incidental to the retirement benefits provided to the participants.

(vi) *Participation by a nonresident alien — de minimis amounts.* With respect to a nonresident alien, the term *nonqualified deferred compensation plan* does not include any foreign plan maintained by a service recipient that is not a United States person for a taxable year, to the extent that the amounts deferred under the foreign plan based upon the nonresident alien's services performed in the United States (including compensation received due to services performed in the United States) do not exceed $10,000 in the taxable year.

(4) *Section 457 plans.* A nonqualified deferred compensation plan under section 457(f) may constitute a nonqualified deferred compensation plan for purposes of this paragraph (a). The rules of section 409A apply to nonqualified deferred compensation plans separately and in addition to any requirements applicable to such plans under section 457(f). In addition, nonelective deferred compensation of nonemployees described in section 457(e)(12) and a grandfathered plan or arrangement described in § 1.457-2(k)(4) may constitute a nonqualified deferred compensation plan for purposes of this paragraph (a). The term *nonqualified deferred compensation plan* does not include a length of service award to a bona fide volunteer under section 457(e)(11)(A)(ii).

(5) *Certain welfare benefits.* The term *nonqualified deferred compensation plan* does not include any bona fide vacation leave, sick leave, compensatory time, disability pay, or death benefit plan. For these purposes, the term *disability pay* has the same meaning as provided in § 31.3121(v)(2)-1(b)(4)(iv)(C) of this chapter, and the term *death benefit plan* refers to a plan providing death benefits as defined in § 31.3121(v)(2)-1(b)(4)(iv)(C) of this chapter. The term *nonqualified deferred compensation plan* also does not include any Archer Medical Savings Account as described in section 220, any Health Savings Account as described in section 223, or any other medical reimbursement arrangement, including a health reimbursement arrangement, that satisfies the requirements of section 105 and section 106.

(b) *Deferral of compensation*—(1) *In general.* Except as otherwise provided in paragraphs (b)(3) through (b)(9) of this section, a plan provides for the deferral of compensation if, under the terms of the plan and the relevant facts and circumstances, the service provider has a legally binding right during a taxable year to compensation that has not been actually or constructively received and included in gross income, and that, pursuant to the terms of the plan, is payable to (or on behalf of) the service provider in a later year. A service provider does not have a legally binding right to compensation if that compensation may be reduced unilaterally or eliminated by the service recipient or other person after the services creating the right to the compensation have been performed. However, if the facts and circumstances indicate that the discretion to reduce or eliminate the compensation is available or exercisable only upon a condition, or the discretion to reduce or eliminate the compensation lacks substantive significance, a service provider will be considered to have a legally binding right to the compensation. Whether the negative discretion lacks substantive significance depends on the facts and circumstances of the particular arrangement. However, where the service provider to whom the compensation may be paid has effective control of the person retaining the discretion to reduce or eliminate the compensation, or has effective control over any portion of the compensation of the person retaining the discretion to reduce or eliminate the compensation, or is a member of the family (as defined in section 267(c)(4) applied as if the family of an individual includes the spouse of any member of the family) of the person retaining the discretion to reduce or eliminate the compensation, the discretion to reduce or eliminate the compensation will not be treated as having substantive significance. For this purpose, compensation is not considered subject to unilateral reduction or elimination merely because it may be reduced or eliminated by operation of the objective terms of the plan, such as the application of an objective provision creating a substantial risk of forfeiture. Similarly, a service provider does not fail to have a legally binding right to compensation merely because the amount of compensation is determined under a formula that provides for benefits to be offset by benefits provided under a plan that is qualified under section 401(a), or because benefits are reduced due to actual or notional investment losses, or in a final average pay plan, subsequent decreases in compensation.

(2) *Earnings.* References to the deferral of compensation include references to earnings. When the right to earnings is specified under the terms of the arrangement, the legally binding right to earnings arises at the time of the deferral of the compensation to which the earnings relate. However, a plan may provide that the right to earnings is treated separately from the right to the underlying compensation. For example, provided that the rules of section 409A are otherwise met, a plan may provide that earnings will be paid at a separate time or in a separate form from the payment of the underlying compensation. For the application of the deferral election rules to current payments of earnings and dividend equivalents, see § 1.409A-2(a)(13).

(3) *Compensation payable pursuant to the service recipient's customary payment timing arrangement.* A deferral of compensation does not occur solely because compensation is paid after the last day of the service provider's taxable year pursuant to the timing arrangement under which the service recipient normally compensates service providers for services performed during a payroll period described in section 3401(b), or with respect to a non-employee service provider, a period not longer than the payroll period described in section 3401(b) or if no such payroll period exists, a period not longer than the earlier of the normal timing arrangement under which the service provider normally compensates non-employee service providers or 30 days after the end of the service provider's taxable year.

(4) *Short-term deferrals*—(i) *In general.* A deferral of compensation does not occur if, absent an election by the service provider (including an election under § 1.409A-2(a)(3)) to otherwise defer the payment of the compensation to a later period, an amount of compensation is actually or constructively received by the service provider by the later of the 15 th day of the third month following the service provider's first taxable year in which the amount is no longer subject to a substantial risk of forfeiture or the 15 th day of the third month following the end of the service recipient's first taxable year in which the amount is no longer subject to a substantial risk of forfeiture. In addition, the arrangement must not otherwise defer the payment to a later period. For example, an arrangement that deferred a payment until 5 years after the lapsing of a condition that constituted a substantial risk of forfeiture would constitute a deferral of compensation even if the amount were actually paid on the date the substantial risk of forfeiture lapsed. For these purposes, an amount that is never subject to a substantial risk of forfeiture is considered to be no longer subject to a substantial risk of forfeiture on the first date the service provider has a legally binding right to the amount. For example, an employer with a calendar year taxable year who on November 1, 2008, awards a bonus so that the employee is considered to have a legally binding right to the payment as of November 1, 2008, will not be considered to have provided for a deferral of compensation if, absent an election to otherwise defer the payment, the amount is paid or made available to the employee on or before March 15, 2009. An employer with a taxable year ending August 31 who on November 1, 2008, awards a bonus so that the employee is considered to have a legally binding right to the payment as of November 1, 2008, will not be considered to have provided for a deferral of

compensation if, absent an election to otherwise defer the payment, the amount is paid or made available to the employee on or before November 15, 2009. [Corrected on 12/19/05 by 70 FR 75090.]

(ii) *Delayed payments due to unforeseeable events.* A payment that otherwise qualifies as a short-term deferral under paragraph (b)(4)(i) of this section but is made after the 15 th day of the third month following the end of the relevant taxable year (the applicable 2 1/2 month period) may continue to qualify as a short-term deferral if the taxpayer establishes that it was administratively impracticable to make the payment by the end of the applicable 2 1/2 month period or that making the payment by the end of the applicable 2 1/2 month period would have jeopardized the solvency of the service recipient, and, as of the date upon which the legally binding right to the compensation arose, such impracticability or insolvency was unforeseeable, and also the payment is made as soon as reasonably practicable. For example, an amount that would otherwise qualify as a short-term deferral except that the payment is made after the applicable 2 1/2 month period may continue to qualify as a short-term deferral under this paragraph (b)(4) to the extent that the delay is caused either because the funds of the service recipient were not sufficient to make the payment before the end of the applicable 2 1/2 month period without jeopardizing the solvency of the service recipient, or because it was not reasonably possible to determine by the end of the applicable 2 1/2 month period whether payment of such amount was to be made, and the circumstance causing the delay was unforeseeable as of the date upon which the legally binding right to the compensation arose. Thus, the amount will not continue to qualify as a short-term deferral to the extent it was foreseeable, as of date upon which the legally binding right to the compensation arose, that the amount would not be paid within the applicable 2 1/2 month period. For purposes of this paragraph (b)(4)(ii), an action or failure to act of the service provider or a person under the service provider's control, such as a failure to provide necessary information or documentation, is not an unforeseeable event.

(5) *Stock options, stock appreciation rights and other equity-based compensation*—(i) *Stock rights*—(A) *Nonstatutory stock options not providing for the deferral of compensation.* An option to purchase service recipient stock does not provide for a deferral of compensation if—

(*1*) The amount required to purchase stock under the option (the exercise price) may never be less than the fair market value of the underlying stock (disregarding lapse restrictions as defined in § 1.83-3(i)) on the date the option is granted and the number of shares subject to the option is fixed on the original date of grant of the option;

(*2*) The transfer or exercise of the option is subject to taxation under section 83 and § 1.83-7; and

(*3*) The option does not include any feature for the deferral of compensation other than the deferral of recognition of income until the later of exercise or disposition of the option under § 1.83-7, or the time the stock acquired pursuant to the exercise of the option first becomes substantially vested (as defined in § 1.83-3(b)).

(B) *Stock appreciation rights not providing for the deferral of compensation.* A right to compensation equal to the appreciation in value of a specified number of shares of stock of the service recipient occurring between the date of grant and the date of exercise of such right (a stock appreciation right) does not provide for a deferral of compensation if—

(*1*) Compensation payable under the stock appreciation right cannot be greater than the difference between the fair market value of the stock (disregarding lapse restrictions as defined in § 1.83-3(i)) on the date of grant of the stock appreciation right and the fair market value of the stock (disregarding lapse restrictions as defined in § 1.83-3(i)) on the date the stock appreciation right is exercised, with respect to a number of shares fixed on or before the date of grant of the right;

(*2*) The stock appreciation right exercise price may never be less than the fair market value of the underlying stock (disregarding lapse restrictions as defined in § 1.83-3(i)) on the date the right is granted; and

(*3*) The stock appreciation right does not include any feature for the deferral of compensation other than the deferral of recognition of income until the exercise of the stock appreciation right.

(C) *Stock rights that may provide for the deferral of compensation.* An option to purchase stock other than service recipient stock, or a stock appreciation right with respect to stock other than service recipient stock, generally will provide for the deferral of compensation within the meaning of this paragraph (b). If under the terms of an option to purchase service recipient stock (other than an incentive stock option described in section 422 or a stock option granted under an employee stock purchase plan described in section 423), the amount required to purchase the stock is or could become less than the fair market value of the stock (disregarding lapse restrictions as defined in § 1.83-3(i)) on the date of grant, the grant of the option may provide for the deferral of compensation within the meaning of this paragraph (b). If under the terms of a stock appreciation right with respect to service recipient stock, the compensation payable under the stock appreciation right is or could be any amount greater than, with respect to a predetermined number of shares, the difference between the stock value (disregarding lapse restrictions as defined in § 1.83-3(i)) on the date of grant of the stock appreciation right and the stock value (disregarding lapse restrictions as defined in § 1.83-3(i)) on the date the stock appreciation right is exercised, the grant of the stock appreciation right may provide for a deferral of compensation within the meaning of this paragraph (b).

(D) *Feature for the deferral of compensation.* To the extent a stock right grants the recipient a right other than to receive cash or stock on the date of exercise and such additional rights allow for the deferral of compensation, the entire arrangement (including the underlying stock right) provides for the deferral of compensation. For purposes of this paragraph (b)(5)(i), neither the right to receive substantially nonvested stock (as defined in § 1.83-3(b)) upon the exercise of a stock right, nor the right to pay the exercise price with previously acquired shares, constitutes a feature for the deferral of compensation.

(E) *Rights to dividends declared.* For purposes of this paragraph (b)(5)(i), the right to receive, upon the exercise of a stock right, an amount equal to all or part of the dividends declared and paid on the number of shares underlying the stock right between the date of grant and the date of exercise of the stock right constitutes an offset to the exercise price of the stock option or an increase in the amount payable under the stock appreciation right (generally causing such stock rights to be subject to section 409A), unless the right to the dividends declared and paid on the number of shares underlying the stock right is explicitly set forth as a separate arrangement. If set forth as a separate arrangement, the arrangement may provide for deferred compensation for purposes of section 409A. However, the existence of a separate arrangement to receive such an amount that complies with the requirements of section 409A would not cause a stock right to fail to satisfy the requirements of the exclusion from the definition of deferred compensation provided in paragraphs (b)(5)(i)(A) and (B) of this section.

(ii) *Statutory stock options.* The grant of an incentive stock option as described in section 422, or the grant of an option under an employee stock purchase plan described in section 423 (including the grant of an option with an exercise price discounted in accordance with section 423(b)(6) and the accompanying regulations), does not constitute a deferral of compensation. However, this paragraph (b)(5)(ii) does not apply to a modification, extension, or renewal of a statutory option that is treated as the grant of a new option that is not a statutory option. See § 1.424-1(e). In such event, the option is treated as if it were a nonstatutory stock option at the date of the original grant, so that the modification, extension or renewal of the stock option that caused the stock option to be treated as the grant of a new option under § 1.424-1(e) is treated as causing the option to be treated as the grant of a new option for purposes of this paragraph (b)(5) only if such modification, extension or renewal of the stock option would have been treated as resulting in the grant of a new option under paragraph (b)(5)(v) of this section.

(iii) *Stock of the service recipient*—(A) *In general.* Except as otherwise provided in paragraphs (b)(5)(iii)(B) and (C) of this section, for purposes of this section, stock of the service recipient means stock that, as of the date of grant, is common stock of a corporation that is a service recipient (including any member of a group of corporations or other entities treated as a single service recipient) that is readily tradable on an established securities market, or if none, that class of common stock of such corporation having the greatest aggregate value of common stock issued and outstanding of such corporation, or common stock with substantially similar rights to stock of such class (disregarding any difference in voting rights). However, under no circumstances does stock of the service recipient include stock that is preferred as to liquidation or dividend rights or that includes or is subject to a mandatory repurchase obligation or a put or call right that is not a lapse restriction as defined in § 1.83-3(i) and is based on a measure other than the fair market value (disregarding lapse restrictions as defined in § 1.83-3(i)) of the equity interest in the corporation represented by the stock.

(B) *American depositary receipts.* For purposes of this section, an American depositary receipt or American depositary share may constitute service recipient stock, to the extent that the stock traded on a foreign securities market to which the American depositary receipt or American depositary share relates qualifies as service recipient stock. [Corrected on 12/19/05 by 70 FR 75090.]

(C) *Mutual company units.* For purposes of this section, mutual company units may constitute service recipient stock. For this purpose, the term *mutual company unit* means a fixed percentage of the overall value of a non-stock mutual company. For purposes of determining the value of the mutual company unit, the unit may be valued in accordance with the rules set forth in paragraph (b)(5)(iv)(B) of this section governing valuation of service recipient stock the shares of which are not traded on an established securities market, applied as if the mutual company were a stock corporation with one class of common stock and the number of shares of such stock determined according to the fixed percentage. For example, an appreciation right based on the appreciation of 10 mutual company units, where each unit is defined as 1 percent of the overall value of the mutual company, would be valued as if the appreciation right were based upon 10 shares of a corporation with 100 shares of common stock and no other class of stock, whose shares are not readily tradable on an established securities market.

(D) *Definition of service recipient*—(*1*) *In general.* For purposes of this paragraph (b)(5)(iii), the term *service recipient* generally has the same meaning as provided in paragraph (g) of this section, provided that a stock right, or the plan or arrangement under which the stock right is granted, may specify that in applying section 1563(a)(1), (2) and (3) for purposes of determining a controlled group of corporations under section 414(b), the language "at least 50 percent" is used instead of "at least 80 percent" each place it appears in section 1563(a)(1), (2) and (3), and in applying § 1.414(c)-2 for purposes of determining trades or businesses (whether or not incorporated) that are under common control for purposes of section 414(c), the language "at least 50 percent" is used instead of "at least 80 percent" each place it appears in § 1.414(c)-2. In addition, where the use of such stock with respect to the grant of a stock right to such service provider is based upon legitimate business criteria, the term *service recipient* has the same meaning as provided in paragraph (g) of this section, provided that the stock right, or the plan or arrangement under which the stock right is granted, may specify that in applying sections 1563(a)(1), (2) and (3) for purposes of determining a controlled group of corporations under section 414(b), the language "at least 20 percent" is used instead of "at least 80 percent" at each place it appears in sections 1563(a)(1), (2) and (3), and in applying § 1.414(c)-2 for purposes of determining trades or businesses (whether or not incorporated) that are under common control for purposes of section 414(c), the language "at least 20 percent" is used instead of "at least 80 percent" at each place it appears in § 1.414(c)-2. For example, stock of a corporation participating in a joint venture involving an operating business, used with respect to stock rights granted to employees of the joint venture who are former employees of such corporation, generally will constitute use of such stock based upon legitimate business criteria, and therefore could constitute service recipient stock with respect to such employees if the corporation owns at least 20 percent of the joint venture and the other requirements of this paragraph (b)(5)(iii) are met. A designation by a service recipient to use the 50 percent or 20 percent thresholds described in this paragraph (b)(5)(iii)(D) must be applied consistently as to all compensatory stock rights for purposes of this paragraph (b)(5)(iii), and any designation of a different permissible ownership threshold percentage may not be made effective until 12 months after the adoption of such change. [Corrected on 12/19/05 by 70 FR 75090.]

(*2*) *Investment vehicles.* Notwithstanding the provisions of paragraph (b)(5)(iii)(D)(*1*) of this section, except as to a service provider providing services directly to such corporation, for purposes of this paragraph (b)(5) the term *service recipient* does not include any corporation whose primary purpose is to serve as an investment vehicle with respect to the corporation's interest in entities other than the service recipient.

(*3*) *Substitutions and assumptions by reason of a corporate transaction.* If the requirements of paragraph (b)(5)(v)(D) of this section are met such that the substitution of a new stock right pursuant to a corporate transaction for an outstanding stock right, or the assumption of an outstanding stock right pursuant to a corporate transaction, would not be treated as the grant of a new stock right or a change in the form of payment for purposes of section 409A, the stock underlying the stock right that is substituted or assumed will be treated as service recipient stock for purposes of applying this paragraph (b)(5) to the replacement stock rights. For example, where by reason of a spinoff transaction under which a subsidiary corporation is spun off from a distributing corporation, a distributing corporation employee's stock option to purchase distributing corporation stock is replaced with a stock option to purchase distributing corporation stock and a stock option to purchase the spun off subsidiary corporation's stock, and where such substitution is not treated as a modification of the original stock option pursuant to paragraph (b)(5)(v)(D) of this section, both the distributing corporation stock and the subsidiary corporation stock are treated as service recipient stock for purposes of applying this paragraph (b)(5) to the replacement stock options.

(E) *Stock rights granted on or before December 31, 2004.* Notwithstanding the requirements of paragraph (b)(5)(iii)(A) of this section, any class of common stock of the service recipient with respect to which stock rights were granted to service providers on or before December 31, 2004, is treated as service recipient stock for purposes of this paragraph (b)(5)(iii), but only with respect to stock rights granted on or before December 31, 2004.

(iv) *Determination of the fair market value of service recipient stock—* (A) *Stock readily tradable on an established securities market.* For purposes of (b)(5)(i) of this section, in the case of service recipient stock that is readily tradable on an established securities market, the fair market value of the stock may be determined based upon the last sale before or the first sale after the grant, the closing price on the trading day before or the trading day of the grant, or any other reasonable basis using actual transactions in such stock as reported by such market and consistently applied. The determination of fair market value also may be based upon an average selling price during a specified period that is within 30 days before or 30 days after the grant, provided that the commitment to grant the stock right based on such valuation method must be irrevocable before the beginning of the specified period, and such valuation method must be used consistently for grants of stock rights under the same and substantially similar programs.

(B) *Stock not readily tradable on an established securities market—*(1) *In general.* For purposes of paragraph (b)(5)(i) of this section, in the case of service recipient stock that is not readily tradable on an established securities market, the fair market value of the stock as of a valuation date means a value determined by the reasonable application of a reasonable valuation method. The determination of whether a valuation method is reasonable, or whether an application of a valuation method is reasonable, is made based on the facts and circumstances as of the valuation date. Factors to be considered under a reasonable valuation method include, as applicable, the value of tangible and intangible assets of the corporation, the present value of future cashflows of the corporation, the market value of stock or equity interests in similar corporations and other entities engaged in trades or businesses substantially similar to those engaged in by the corporation whose stock is to be valued, the value of which can be readily determined through objective means (such as through trading prices on an established securities market or an amount paid in an arm's length private transaction), and other relevant factors such as control premiums or discounts for lack of marketability and whether the valuation method is used for other purposes that have a material economic effect on the service recipient, its stockholders or its creditors. The use of a valuation method is not reasonable if such valuation method does not take into consideration in applying its methodology, all available information material to the value of the corporation. Similarly, the use of a value previously calculated under a valuation method is not reasonable as of a later date if such calculation fails to reflect information available after the date of the calculation that may materially affect the value of the corporation (for example, the resolution of material litigation or the issuance of a patent) or the value was calculated with respect to a date that is more than 12 months earlier than the date for which the valuation is being used. The service recipient's consistent use of a valuation method to determine the value of its stock or assets for other purposes, including for purposes unrelated to compensation of service providers, is also a factor supporting the reasonableness of such valuation method.

(2) *Presumption of reasonableness.* For purposes of this paragraph (b)(5)(iv)(B), the consistent use of any of the following methods of valuation is presumed to result in a reasonable valuation, provided that the Commissioner may rebut such a presumption upon a showing that either the valuation method or the application of such method was grossly unreasonable:

(i) A valuation of a class of stock determined by an independent appraisal that meets the requirements of section 401(a)(28)(C) and the regulations thereunder as of a date that is no more than 12 months before the relevant transaction to which the valuation is applied (for example, the grant date of a stock option).

(ii) A valuation based upon a formula that, if used as part of a nonlapse restriction (as defined in § 1.83-3(h)) with respect to the stock, would be considered to be the fair market value of the stock pursuant to § 1.83-5, provided that such stock is valued in the same manner for purposes of any nonlapse restriction applicable to the transfer of any shares of such class of stock (or substantially similar class of stock), and all noncompensatory purposes requiring the valuation of such stock, including regulatory filings, loan covenants, issuances to and repurchases of stock from persons other than service providers, and other third-party arrangements, and such valuation method is used consistently for all such purposes, and provided further that this paragraph (b)(5)(iv)(B)(2)(ii) does not apply with respect to stock subject to a stock right payable in stock, where the stock acquired pursuant to the exercise of the stock right is transferable other than through the operation of a nonlapse restriction.

(iii) A valuation, made reasonably and in good faith and evidenced by a written report that takes into account the relevant factors described in paragraph (b)(5)(iv)(B)(1) of this section, of an illiquid stock of a start-up corporation. For this purpose, an illiquid stock of a start-up corporation is service recipient stock of a service recipient corporation that has no trade or business that it or any predecessor to it has conducted for a period of 10 years or more and has no class of equity securities that are traded on an established securities market (as defined in paragraph (k) of this section), where such stock is not subject to any put or call right or obligation of the service recipient or other person to purchase such stock (other than a right of first refusal upon an offer to purchase by a third party that is unrelated to the service recipient or service provider and other than a right or obligation that constitutes a lapse restriction as defined in § 1.83-3(i)), and provided that this paragraph (b)(5)(iv)(B)(2)(iii) does not apply to the valuation of any stock if the service recipient or service provider may reasonably anticipate, as of the time the valuation is applied, that the service recipient will undergo a change in control event as described in § 1.409A-3(g)(5)(v) or § 1.409A-3(g)(5)(vii) or make a public offering of securities within the 12 months following the event to which the valuation is applied (for example, the grant of a stock option or exercise of a stock appreciation right). For purposes of this paragraph (b)(5)(iv)(B)(2)(iii), a valuation will not be treated as made reasonably and in good faith unless the valuation is performed by a person or persons with significant knowledge and experience or training in performing similar valuations. [Corrected on 12/19/05 by 70 FR 75090.]

(3) *Consistent use of a method.* For purposes of paragraph (b)(5)(iv)(B)(2) of this section, the consistent use of a valuation method means the consistent use of the method for all equity-based compensation arrangements, including with respect to stock rights, for purposes of determining the exercise price, and with respect to stock appreciation rights not paid in stock, for purposes of determining the payment at the date of exercise, and for stock appreciation rights or stock options paid in stock subject to a put or call right providing for the potential repurchase by the service recipient, or other obligation of the service recipient or other person to purchase such stock, for purposes of determining the payment at the date of the purchase of such stock. Notwithstanding the foregoing, a service recipient may change the method prospectively for purposes of new grants of equity-based compensation, including stock rights. In addition, where after the date of grant, but before the date of exercise, of the stock right, the service recipient stock to which the stock right relates becomes readily tradable on an established securities market, the service recipient must use the valuation method set forth in paragraph (b)(5)(iv)(A) of this section for purposes of determining the payment at the date of exercise or the purchase of the stock, as applicable. [Corrected on 12/19/05 by 70 FR 75090.]

(v) *Modifications, extensions, renewals, substitutions and assumptions of stock rights—*(A) *Treatment of modified stock right as a new grant.* Any modification of the terms of a stock right, other than an extension or renewal of the stock right, is considered the granting of a new stock right. The new stock right may or may not constitute a deferral of compensation under paragraph (b)(5)(i) of this section, determined at the date of grant of the new stock right. Where a stock right is extended or renewed, the stock right is treated as having had an additional deferral feature from the date of grant.

(B) *Modification in general.* The term modification means any change in the terms of the stock right (or change in the terms of the arrangement pursuant to which the stock right was granted or in the terms of any other agreement governing the stock right) that may provide the holder of the stock right with a direct or indirect reduction in the exercise price of the stock right, or an additional deferral feature, or an extension or renewal of the stock right, regardless of whether the holder in fact benefits from the change in terms. In contrast, a change in the terms of the stock right shortening the period during which the stock right is exercisable is not a modification. It is not a modification to add a feature providing the ability to tender previously acquired stock for the stock purchasable under the stock right, or to withhold or have withheld shares of stock to facilitate the payment of employment taxes or required withholding taxes resulting from the exercise of the stock right. In addition, it is not a modification for the grantor to exercise discretion specifically reserved under a stock right with respect to the transferability of the stock right.

(C) *Extensions and renewals.* An extension of a stock right refers to the granting to the holder of an additional period of time within which to exercise the stock right beyond the time originally prescribed, provided that it is not an extension if the exercise period of the stock right is extended to a date no later than the later of the 15th day of the third month following the date at which, or December 31 of the calendar year in which, the stock right would otherwise have expired if the stock right had not been extended, based on the terms of the stock right at the original grant date. For example, an option granted January 1, 2011, that expires upon the earlier of January 1, 2021, or 30 days after separation from service will not be considered to be modified if, upon the holder's separation from service on July 1, 2015, the term is extended to December 31, 2015. Notwithstanding the foregoing, it is not an extension of a stock right if the expiration of the stock right is tolled while the stock right is unexercisable because an exercise of the stock right would violate applicable securities laws, provided that the period during which the stock right may be exercised is not extended more than 30 days after the exercise of the stock right first would no longer violate applicable securities laws. A renewal of a stock right is the granting by the corporation of the same rights or privileges contained in the original stock right on the same terms and conditions.

(D) *Substitutions and assumptions of stock rights by reason of a corporate transaction.* If the requirements of § 1.424-1 would be met if the stock right were a statutory option, the substitution of a new stock right pursuant to a corporate transaction for an outstanding stock right or the assumption of an outstanding stock right pursuant to a corporate transaction will not be treated as the grant of a new stock right or a change in the form of payment for purposes of section 409A. For purposes of the preceding sentence, the requirement of § 1.424-1(a)(5)(iii) will be deemed to be satisfied if the ratio of the exercise price to the fair market value of the shares subject to the stock right immediately after the substitution or assumption is not greater than the ratio of the exercise price to the fair market value of the shares subject to the stock right immediately before the substitution or assumption. In the case of a transaction described in section 355 in which the stock of the distributing corporation and the stock distributed in the transaction are both readily tradable on an established securities market immediately after the transaction, for purposes of this paragraph (b)(5)(v), the requirements of § 1.424-1(a)(5) may be satisfied by using market quotations for the stock of the distributing corporation and the stock distributed in the transaction as of a predetermined date not more than 60 days after the transaction or based on an average of such market prices over a predetermined period of not more than 30 days ending not later than 60 days after the transaction.

(E) *Acceleration of date when exercisable.* If a stock right is not immediately exercisable in full, a change in the terms of the right to accelerate the time at which the stock right (or any portion thereof) may be exercised is not a modification for purposes of this section. With respect to a stock right subject to section 409A, however, such an acceleration may constitute an impermissible acceleration of a payment date under § 1.409A-3(h). Additionally, no modification occurs if a provision accelerating the time when a stock right may first be exercised is removed before the year in which it would otherwise be triggered. [Corrected on 12/19/05 by 70 FR 75090.]

(F) *Discretionary added benefits.* If a change to a stock right provides, either by its terms or in substance, that the holder may receive an additional benefit under the stock right at the future discretion of the grantor, and the addition of such benefit would constitute a modification, then the addition of such discretion is a modification at the time that the stock right is changed to provide such discretion.

(G) *Change in underlying stock increasing value.* A change in the terms of the stock subject to a stock right that increases the value of the stock is a modification of such stock right, except to the extent that a new stock right is substituted for such stock right by reason of the change in the terms of the stock in accordance with paragraph (b)(5)(v)(D) of this section.

(H) *Change in the number of shares purchasable.* If a stock right is amended solely to increase the number of shares subject to the stock right, the increase is not considered a modification of the stock right but is treated as the grant of a new additional stock right to which the additional shares are subject. Notwithstanding the previous sentence, if the exercise price and number of shares subject to a stock right are proportionally adjusted to reflect a stock split (including a reverse stock split) or stock dividend, and the only effect of the stock split or stock dividend is to increase (or decrease) on a pro rata basis the number of shares owned by each shareholder of the class of stock subject to the stock right, then the stock right is not modified if it is proportionally adjusted to reflect the stock split or stock dividend and the aggregate exercise price of the stock right is not less than the aggregate exercise price before the stock split or stock dividend.

(I) *Rescission of changes.* Any change to the terms of a stock right (or change in the terms of the plan pursuant to which the stock right was granted or in the terms of any other agreement governing the right) that would inadvertently result in treatment as a modification under paragraph (b)(5)(v)(A) of this section is not considered a modification of the stock right to the extent the change in the terms of the stock right is rescinded by the earlier of the date the stock right is exercised or the last day of the calendar year during which such change occurred. Thus, for example, if the terms of a stock right are changed on March 1 to extend the exercise period and the change is rescinded on November 1, then if the stock right is not exercised before the change is rescinded, the stock right is not considered modified under paragraph (b)(5)(v)(A) of this section.

(J) *Successive modifications.* The rules of this paragraph (b)(5)(v) apply as well to successive modifications, including successive extensions or renewals.

(6) *Restricted Property*—(i) *In general.* If a service provider receives property from, or pursuant to, a plan maintained by a service recipient, there is no deferral of compensation merely because the value of the property is not includible in income in the year of receipt by reason of the property being substantially nonvested (as defined in § 1.83-3(b)), or is includible in income solely due to a valid election under section 83(b). For purposes of this paragraph (b)(6)(i), a transfer of property includes the transfer of a beneficial interest in a trust or annuity plan, or a transfer to or from a trust or under an annuity plan, to the extent such a transfer is subject to section 83, section 402(b) or section 403(c).

(ii) *Promises to transfer property.* A plan under which a service provider obtains a legally binding right to receive property (whether or not the property will be substantially nonvested (as defined in § 1.83-3(b)) at the time of grant) in a future year may provide for the deferral of compensation and, accordingly, may constitute a nonqualified deferred compensation plan. The vesting of substantially nonvested property subject to section 83 may be treated as a payment for purposes of section 409A, including for purposes of applying the short-term deferral rules under paragraph (b)(4) of this section. Accordingly, where the promise to transfer the substantially nonvested property and the right to retain the substantially nonvested property are both subject to a substantial risk of forfeiture (as defined under paragraph (d) of this section), the arrangement generally would constitute a short-term deferral under paragraph (b)(4) of this section because the payment would occur simultaneously with the vesting of the right to the property. For example, where an employee participates in a two-year bonus program such that, if the employee continues in employment for two years, the employee is entitled to either the immediate payment of a $10,000 cash bonus or the grant of restricted stock with a $15,000 fair market value subject to a vesting requirement of three additional years of service, the arrangement generally would constitute a short-term deferral under paragraph (b)(4) of this section because under either alternative the payment would be received within the short-term deferral period. [Corrected on 12/19/05 by 70 FR 75090.]

(7) *Arrangements between partnerships and partners.* [Reserved.]

(8) *Certain foreign arrangements*—(i) *Arrangements with respect to compensation covered by treaty or other international agreement.* An arrangement with a service provider does not provide for a deferral of compensation for purposes of this paragraph (b) to the extent that the compensation under the arrangement would have been excluded from gross income for Federal income tax purposes under the provisions of any bilateral income tax convention or other bilateral or multilateral agreement to which the United States is a party if the compensation had been paid to the service provider at the time that the legally binding right to the compensation first arose or, if later, the time that the legally binding right was no longer subject to a substantial risk of forfeiture.

(ii) *Arrangements with respect to certain other compensation.* An arrangement with a service provider does not provide for a deferral of compensation for purposes of this paragraph (b) to the extent that compensation under the arrangement would not have been includible in gross income for Federal tax purposes if it had been paid to the service provider at the time that the legally binding right to the compensation first arose or, if later, the time that the legally binding right was no longer subject to a substantial risk of forfeiture, due to one of the following—

(A) The service provider was a nonresident alien at such time and the compensation would not have been includible in gross income under section 872;

(B) The service provider was a qualified individual (as defined in section 911(d)(1)) at such time and the compensation would have been foreign earned income within the meaning of section 911(b)(1) if paid at such time, and the compensation would have been foreign earned income within the meaning of section 911(b)(1) that is less than the difference between the maximum exclusion amount under section 911(b)(2)(D) for such taxable year and the amount of foreign earned income actually excludible from gross income by such qualified individual for such taxable year under section 911(a)(1); [Corrected on 12/19/05 by 70 FR 75090.]

(C) The compensation would have been excludible from gross income under section 893; or

(D) The compensation would have been excludible from gross income under section 931 or section 933.

(iii) *Tax equalization arrangements.* Compensation paid under a tax equalization arrangement does not provide for a deferral of compensation, provided that any payment made under such arrangement is paid no later than the end of the second calendar year beginning after the calendar year in which the service provider's U.S. Federal income tax return is required to be filed (including extension) for the year to which the tax equalization payment relates. For purposes of this paragraph (b)(8)(iii), the term *tax equalization arrangement* refers to an arrangement that provides payments intended to compensate the service provider for the excess of the taxes actually imposed by a foreign jurisdiction on the compensation paid (other than the compensation under the tax equalization agreement) by the service recipient to the service provider over the taxes that would be imposed if the compensation were subject solely to United States Federal income tax, and provided that the payments made under such arrangement may not exceed such excess and the amount necessary to compensate for the additional taxes on the amounts paid under the arrangement.

(iv) *Additional foreign arrangements.* An arrangement with a service provider does not provide for a deferral of compensation for purposes of this paragraph (b) to the extent designated by the Commissioner in revenue procedures, notices, or other guidance published in the Internal Revenue Bulletin (see § 601.601(d)(2) of this chapter).

(v) *Earnings.* Earnings on compensation excluded from the definition of deferral of compensation pursuant to this paragraph (b)(8) are also not treated as a deferred compensation. However, amounts that would be recharacterized as deferred compensation under § 31.3121(v)(2)-1(d)(2)(iii)(B) of this chapter (nonaccount balance plans), § 31.3121(v)(2)-1(d)(2)(iii)(A) of this chapter (account balance plans), or similar principles with respect to plans that are neither nonaccount balance plans nor account balance plans, will not be treated as earnings for purposes of this paragraph (b)(8)(v).

(9) *Separation pay arrangements*—(i) *In general.* An arrangement that otherwise provides for a deferral of compensation under this paragraph (b) does not fail to provide a deferral of compensation merely because the right to payment of the compensation is conditioned upon a separation from service. However, see paragraphs (b)(9)(ii), (iii) and (iv) of this section for separation pay arrangements that do not provide for the deferral of compensation. Notwithstanding any other provision of this paragraph (b)(9), any payment or benefit, or entitlement to a payment or benefit, that acts as a substitute for, or replacement of, amounts deferred by the service recipient under a separate nonqualified deferred compensation plan constitutes a payment or a deferral of compensation under the separate nonqualified deferred compensation plan, and does not constitute a payment or deferral of compensation under a separation pay arrangement.

(ii) *Collectively bargained separation pay arrangements.* A separation pay arrangement does not provide for a deferral of compensation if the arrangement is a collectively bargained separation pay arrangement that provides for separation pay upon an actual involuntary separation from service or pursuant to a window program. Only the portion of the separation pay arrangement attributable to employees covered by a collective bargaining agreement is considered to be provided under a collectively bargained separation pay arrangement. A collectively bargained separation pay arrangement is a separation pay arrangement that meets the following conditions:

(A) The separation pay arrangement is contained within an agreement that the Secretary of Labor determines to be a collective bargaining agreement.

(B) The separation pay provided by the collective bargaining agreement was the subject of arms-length negotiations between employee representatives and one or more employers, and the agreement between employee representatives and one or more employers satisfies section 7701(a)(46).

(C) The circumstances surrounding the agreement evidence good faith bargaining between adverse parties over the separation pay to be provided under the agreement.

(iii) *Separation pay plans due to involuntary separation from service or participation in a window program.* A separation pay plan that is not described in paragraph (b)(9)(ii) of this section and that provides for separation pay upon an actual involuntary separation from service or pursuant to a window program does not provide for a deferral of compensation if the plan provides that—

(A) The separation pay (other than amounts described in paragraph (b)(9)(iv) of this section) may not exceed two times the lesser of—

(*1*) The sum of the service provider's annual compensation (as defined in § 1.415-2(d)) for services provided to the service recipient as an employee and the service provider's net earnings from self-employment (as defined in section 1402(a)) for services provided to the service recipient as an independent contractor, each for the calendar year preceding the calendar year in which the service provider has a separation from service from such service recipient; or [Corrected on 12/19/05 by 70 FR 75090.]

(*2*) The maximum amount that may be taken into account under a qualified plan pursuant to section 401(a)(17) for such year; and

(B) The separation pay must be paid no later than December 31 of the second calendar year following the calendar year in which occurs the separation from service.

(iv) *Reimbursements and certain other separation payments-*(A) *In general.* To the extent a separation pay arrangement entitles a service provider to payment by the service recipient for a limited period of time of reimbursements that are otherwise excludible from gross income, of reimbursements for expenses that the service provider can deduct under section 162 or section 167 as business expenses incurred in connection with the performance of services (ignoring any applicable limitation based on adjusted gross income), or of reasonable outplacement expenses and reasonable moving expenses actually incurred by the service provider and directly related to the termination of services for the service recipient, such arrangement does not provide for a deferral of compensation. To the extent a separation pay arrangement (including an arrangement involving payments due to a voluntary separation from service) entitles a service provider to reimbursement by the service recipient for a limited period of time of payments of medical expenses incurred and paid by the service provider but not reimbursed and allowable as a deduction under section 213 (disregarding the requirement of section 213(a) that the deduction is available only to the extent that such expenses exceed 7.5 percent of adjusted gross income), such arrangement does not provide for a deferral of compensation.

(B) *In-kind benefits and direct service recipient payments.* A service provider's entitlement to in-kind benefits from the service recipient, or a payment by the service recipient directly to the person providing the goods or services to the service provider, will also be treated as not providing for a deferral of compensation for purposes of this paragraph (b), if a right to reimbursement by the service recipient for a payment for such benefits, goods or services by the service provider would not be treated as providing for a deferral of compensation under this paragraph (b)(9)(iv).

(C) *De minimis payments.* In addition, if not otherwise excluded, to the extent a separation pay arrangement entitles a service provider to reimbursements or other payments or benefits that do not exceed $5,000 in the aggregate, such arrangement does not provide for a deferral of compensation.

(D) *Limited period of time.* For purposes of paragraphs (b)(9)(iv)(A) and (B), a limited period of time refers to both the period during which applicable expenses may be incurred, and the period during which reimbursements must be paid, and may not extend beyond the December 31 of the second calendar year following the calendar year in which the separation from service occurred.

(v) *Window programs — definition.* The term *window program* refers to a program established by the service recipient to provide for separation pay in connection with a separation from service, for a limited period of time (no greater than one year), to service providers who separate from service during that period or to service providers who separate from service during that period under specified circumstances. A program will not be considered a window program if a service recipient establishes a pattern of repeatedly providing for similar separation pay in similar situations for substantially consecutive, limited periods of time. Whether the recurrence of these programs constitutes a pattern is determined based on the facts and circumstances. Although no one factor is determinative, relevant factors include whether the benefits are on account of a specific business event or condition, the degree to which the separation pay relates to the event or condition, and whether the event or condition is temporary or discrete or is a permanent aspect of the employer's business.

(c) *Plan*—(1) *In general*. The term *plan* includes any agreement, method or arrangement, including an agreement, method or arrangement that applies to one person or individual. A plan may be adopted unilaterally by the service recipient or may be negotiated or agreed to by the service recipient and one or more service providers or service provider representatives. An agreement, method or arrangement may constitute a plan regardless of whether it is an employee benefit plan under section 3(3) of the Employee Retirement Income Security Act of 1974 (ERISA), as amended (29 U.S.C. 1002(3)). The requirements of section 409A are applied as if a separate plan or plans is maintained for each service provider.

(2) *Plan aggregation rules*—(i) *In general*. Except as provided in paragraph (c)(2)(ii) of this section, with respect to arrangements between a service provider and a service recipient—

(A) All amounts deferred with respect to that service provider under all account balance plans of the service recipient (as defined in §31.3121(v)(2)-1(c)(1)(ii)(A) of this chapter) other than a separation pay arrangement described in paragraph (c)(2)(i)(C) of this section are treated as deferred under a single plan;

(B) All amounts deferred with respect to that service provider under all nonaccount balance plans of the service recipient (as defined in §31.3121(v)(2)-1(c)(2)(i) of this chapter) other than a separation pay arrangement described in paragraph (c)(2)(i)(C) of this section are treated as deferred under a separate single plan;

(C) All amounts deferred with respect to that service provider under all separation pay arrangements (as defined in paragraph (m) of this section) of the service recipient due to an involuntary termination or participation in a window program are treated as deferred under a single plan; and

(D) All amounts deferred with respect to that service provider under all plans of the service recipient that are not described in paragraph (c)(2)(i)(A), (B) or (C) of this section (for example, discounted stock options, stock appreciation rights or other equity-based compensation described in §31.3121(v)(2)-1(b)(4)(ii) of this chapter) are treated as deferred under a separate single plan.

(ii) *Dual status*. Arrangements in which a service provider participates are not aggregated to the extent the service provider participates in one set of arrangements due to status as an employee of the service recipient (employee arrangements) and another set of arrangements due to status as an independent contractor of the service recipient (independent contractor arrangements). For example, where a service provider deferred amounts under an arrangement while providing services as an independent contractor, and then becomes eligible for and defers amounts under a separate arrangement after being hired as an employee, the two arrangements will not be aggregated for purposes of this paragraph (c)(2). Where an employee also serves as a director of the service recipient (or a similar position with respect to a non-corporate service recipient), the arrangements under which the employee participates as a director of the service recipient (director arrangements) are not aggregated with employee arrangements, provided that the director arrangements are substantially similar to arrangements provided to service providers providing services only as directors (or similar positions with respect to non-corporate service recipients). For example, an employee director who participates in an employee arrangement and a director arrangement generally may treat the two arrangements as separate plans, provided that the director arrangement is substantially similar to an arrangement providing benefits to a non-employee director. Director arrangements and independent contractor arrangements are aggregated for purposes of this paragraph (c)(2).

(3) *Establishment of arrangement*—(i) *In general*. To satisfy the requirements of section 409A, an arrangement must be established and maintained by a service recipient, in both form and operation, in accordance with the requirements of section 409A and these regulations. For purposes of this paragraph (c)(3), an arrangement is established on the latest of the date on which it is adopted, the date on which it is effective, and the date on which the material terms of the plan are set forth in writing. For purposes of this paragraph (c)(3)(i), an arrangement will be deemed to be set forth in writing if it is set forth in any other form that is approved by the Commissioner. The material terms of the arrangement include the amount (or the method or formula for determining the amount) of deferred compensation to be provided under the arrangement and the time when it will be paid. Notwithstanding the foregoing, an arrangement will be deemed to be

established as of the date the participant obtains a legally binding right to deferred compensation, provided that the arrangement is otherwise established under the rules of this paragraph (c)(3)(i) by the end of the calendar year in which the legally binding right arises, or with respect to an amount not payable in the year immediately following the year in which the legally binding right arises (the subsequent year), the 15th day of the third month of the subsequent year.

(ii) *Amendments to the arrangement*. In the case of an amendment that increases the amount deferred under an arrangement providing for the deferral of compensation, the arrangement is not considered established with respect to the additional amount deferred until the arrangement, as amended, is established in accordance with paragraph (c)(3)(i) of this section.

(iii) *Transition rule for written plan requirement*. For purposes of this section, an unwritten arrangement that was adopted and effective before December 31, 2006, is treated as established under this section as of the later of the date on which it was adopted or became effective, provided that the material terms of the arrangement are set forth in writing on or before December 31, 2006.

(iv) *Plan aggregation rules*. The plan aggregation rules of paragraph (c)(2)(i) of this section do not apply to the requirements of paragraphs (c)(3)(i) and (ii) of this section. Accordingly, an arrangement that fails to meet the requirements of section 409A solely due to a failure to meet the requirements of paragraph (c)(3)(i) or (ii) is not aggregated with other arrangements that meet such requirements.

(d) *Substantial risk of forfeiture*—(1) *In general*. Compensation is subject to a substantial risk of forfeiture if entitlement to the amount is conditioned on the performance of substantial future services by any person or the occurrence of a condition related to a purpose of the compensation, and the possibility of forfeiture is substantial. For purposes of this paragraph (d), a condition related to a purpose of the compensation must relate to the service provider's performance for the service recipient or the service recipient's business activities or organizational goals (for example, the attainment of a prescribed level of earnings, equity value or an initial public offering). Any addition of a substantial risk of forfeiture after the legally binding right to the compensation arises, or any extension of a period during which compensation is subject to a substantial risk of forfeiture, in either case whether elected by the service provider, service recipient or other person (or by agreement of two or more of such persons), is disregarded for purposes of determining whether such compensation is subject to a substantial risk of forfeiture. An amount is not subject to a substantial risk of forfeiture merely because the right to the amount is conditioned, directly or indirectly, upon the refraining from performance of services. For purposes of section 409A, an amount will not be considered subject to a substantial risk of forfeiture beyond the date or time at which the recipient otherwise could have elected to receive the amount of compensation, unless the amount subject to a substantial risk of forfeiture (ignoring earnings) is materially greater than the amount the recipient otherwise could have elected to receive. For example, a salary deferral generally may not be made subject to a substantial risk of forfeiture. But, for example, where a bonus arrangement provides an election between a cash payment of a certain amount or restricted stock units with a materially greater value that will be forfeited absent continued services for a period of years, the right to the restricted stock units generally will be treated as subject to a substantial risk of forfeiture.

(2) *Stock rights*. A stock right will be treated as not subject to a substantial risk of forfeiture at the earlier of the first date the holder may exercise the stock right and receive cash or property that is substantially vested (as defined in §1.83-3(b)) or the first date that the stock right is not subject to a forfeiture condition that would constitute a substantial risk of forfeiture. Accordingly, a stock option that the service provider may exercise immediately and receive substantially vested stock will be treated as not subject to a substantial risk of forfeiture, even if the stock option automatically terminates upon the service provider's separation from service.

(3) *Enforcement of forfeiture condition*—(i) *In general*. In determining whether the possibility of forfeiture is substantial in the case of rights to compensation granted by a service recipient to a service provider that owns a significant amount of the total combined voting power or value of all classes of equity of the service recipient or of its parent, all relevant facts and circumstances will be taken into account in determining whether the probability of the service recipient enforcing such condition is substantial, including—

(A) The service provider's relationship to other equity holders and the extent of their control, potential control and possible loss of control of the service recipient;

(B) The position of the service provider in the service recipient and the extent to which the service provider is subordinate to other service providers;

(C) The service provider's relationship to the officers and directors of the service recipient (or similar positions with respect to a noncorporate service recipient);

(D) The person or persons who must approve the service provider's discharge; and

(E) Past actions of the service recipient in enforcing the restrictions.

(ii) *Examples.* The following examples illustrate the rules of paragraph (d)(3)(i) of this section:

Example 1. A service provider would be considered as having deferred compensation subject to a substantial risk of forfeiture, but for the fact that the service provider owns 20 percent of the single class of stock in the transferor corporation. If the remaining 80 percent of the class of stock is owned by an unrelated individual (or members of such an individual's family) so that the possibility of the corporation enforcing a restriction on such rights is substantial, then such rights are subject to a substantial risk of forfeiture.

Example 2. A service provider would be considered as having deferred compensation subject to a substantial risk of forfeiture, but for the fact that the service provider who is president of the corporation, also owns 4 percent of the voting power of all the stock of a corporation. If the remaining stock is so diversely held by the public that the president, in effect, controls the corporation, then the possibility of the corporation enforcing a restriction on the right to deferred compensation of the president is not substantial, and such rights are not subject to a substantial risk of forfeiture.

(e) *Performance-based compensation*—(1) *In general.* The term *performance-based compensation* means compensation where the amount of, or entitlement to, the compensation is contingent on the satisfaction of preestablished organizational or individual performance criteria relating to a performance period of at least 12 consecutive months in which the service provider performs services. Organizational or individual performance criteria are considered preestablished if established in writing by not later than 90 days after the commencement of the period of service to which the criteria relates, provided that the outcome is substantially uncertain at the time the criteria are established. Performance-based compensation may include payments based on performance criteria that are not approved by a compensation committee of the board of directors (or similar entity in the case of a non-corporate service recipient) or by the stockholders or members of the service recipient. Notwithstanding the foregoing, performance-based compensation does not include any amount or portion of any amount that will be paid either regardless of performance, or based upon a level of performance that is substantially certain to be met at the time the criteria is established. Except as provided in paragraph (e)(3) of this section, compensation is not performance-based compensation merely because the amount of such compensation is based on the value of, or increase in the value of, the service recipient or the stock of the service recipient.

(2) *Payments based upon subjective performance criteria.* The term *performance-based compensation* may include payments based upon subjective performance criteria, provided that—

(i) The subjective performance criteria relate to the performance of the participant service provider, a group of service providers that includes the participant service provider, or a business unit for which the participant service provider provides services (which may include the entire organization); and

(ii) The determination that any subjective performance criteria have been met is not made by the participant service provider or a family member of the participant service provider (as defined in section 267(c)(4) applied as if the family of an individual includes the spouse of any member of the family), or a person under the supervision of the participant service provider or such a family member, or where any amount of the compensation of the person making such determination is controlled in whole or in part by the service provider or such a family member.

(3) *Equity-based compensation.* Compensation is performance-based compensation if it is based solely on an increase in the value of the service recipient, or stock of the service recipient, after the date of a grant or award. If the amount of compensation the service provider will receive under a grant or award is not based solely on an increase in the value of the service recipient, or stock of the service recipient, after the date of the grant or award (for example, a stock appreciation right granted with an exercise price that is less than the fair market value of the stock as of the date of grant), and that other amount would not

otherwise qualify as performance-based compensation, the compensation attributable to the grant or award does not qualify as performance-based compensation. Notwithstanding the foregoing, an award of equity-based compensation may constitute performance-based compensation if entitlement to the compensation is subject to a condition that would cause the award to otherwise qualify as performance-based compensation, such as a performance-based vesting condition. The eligibility to defer compensation under an equity-based compensation award constitutes an additional deferral feature with respect to the award for purposes of the definition of a deferral of compensation under paragraph (b)(5) of this section.

(f) *Service provider*—(1) *In general.* The term *service provider* includes—

(i) An individual, corporation, subchapter S corporation or partnership;

(ii) A personal service corporation (as defined in section 269A(b)(1)), or a noncorporate entity that would be a personal service corporation if it were a corporation; or

(iii) A qualified personal service corporation (as defined in section 448(d)(2)), or a noncorporate entity that would be a qualified personal service corporation if it were a corporation.

(2) *Service providers using an accrual method of accounting.* Section 409A does not apply to a deferral under an arrangement between taxpayers if, for the taxable year in which the service provider taxpayer obtains a legally binding right to the compensation, the service provider uses an accrual method of accounting for Federal tax purposes.

(3) *Independent contractors*—(i) *In general.* Except as otherwise provided in paragraph (f)(3)(iv) of this section, section 409A does not apply to an amount deferred under an arrangement between a service provider and service recipient with respect to a particular trade or business in which the service provider participates, if during the service provider's taxable year in which the service provider obtains a legally binding right to the payment of the amount deferred—

(A) The service provider is actively engaged in the trade or business of providing services, other than as an employee or as a director of a corporation;

(B) The service provider provides significant services to two or more service recipients to which the service provider is not related and that are not related to one another (as defined in paragraph (f)(3)(ii) of this section); and

(C) The service provider is not related to the service recipient, applying the definition of related person contained in paragraph (f)(3)(ii) of this section subject to the modification that the language "50 percent" is used instead of "20 percent" each place it appears in sections 267(b) and 707(b)(1). [Corrected on 12/19/05 by 70 FR 75090.]

(ii) *Related person.* For purposes of this paragraph (f)(3), a person is related to another person if the persons bear a relationship to each other that is specified in section 267(b) or 707(b)(1), subject to the modifications that the language "20 percent" is used instead of "50 percent" each place it appears in sections 267(b) and 707(b)(1), and section 267(c)(4) is applied as if the family of an individual includes the spouse of any member of the family; or the persons are engaged in trades or businesses under common control (within the meaning of section 52(a) and (b)). In addition, an individual is related to an entity if the individual is an officer of an entity that is a corporation, or holds a position substantially similar to an officer of a corporation with an entity that is not a corporation.

(iii) *Significant services.* Whether a service provider is providing significant services depends on the facts and circumstances of each case. However, for purposes of paragraph (f)(3)(i) of this section, a service provider who provides services to two or more service recipients to which the service provider is not related and that are not related to one another is deemed to be providing significant services to two or more of such service recipients for a given taxable year, if the revenues generated from the services provided to any service recipient or group of related service recipients during such taxable year do not exceed 70 percent of the total revenue generated by the service provider from the trade or business of providing such services.

(iv) *Management services.* A service provider is treated as related to a service recipient for purposes of paragraph (f)(3)(i) of this section if the service provider provides management services to the service recipient. For purposes of this paragraph (f)(3)(iv), the term *management services* means services that involve the actual or de facto direction or control of the financial or operational aspects of a trade or business of the service recipient, or investment advisory services provided to a service recipient whose primary trade or business includes the management of financial assets (including investments in real estate) for its own account, such as a hedge fund or a real estate investment trust.

(g) *Service recipient.* Except as otherwise specifically provided in these regulations, the term *service recipient* means the person for whom the services are performed and with respect to whom the legally binding right to compensation arises, and all persons with whom such person would be considered a single employer under section 414(b) (employees of controlled group of corporations), and all persons with whom such person would be considered a single employer under section 414(c) (employees of partnerships, proprietorships, etc., under common control). For example, where the service provider is an employee, the service recipient generally is the employer. Notwithstanding the foregoing, section 409A applies to a plan that provides for the deferral of compensation, even though the payment of the compensation is not made by the person for whom services are performed.

(h) *Separation from service*—(1) *Employees*—(i) *In general.* An employee separates from service with the service recipient if the employee dies, retires, or otherwise has a termination of employment with the employer. However, for purposes of this paragraph (h)(1), the employment relationship is treated as continuing intact while the individual is on military leave, sick leave, or other bona fide leave of absence (such as temporary employment by the government) if the period of such leave does not exceed six months, or if longer, so long as the individual's right to reemployment with the service recipient is provided either by statute or by contract. If the period of leave exceeds six months and the individual's right to reemployment is not provided either by statute or by contract, the employment relationship is deemed to terminate on the first date immediately following such six-month period.

(ii) *Termination of employment.* Whether a termination of employment has occurred is determined based on the facts and circumstances. Where an employee either actually or purportedly continues in the capacity as an employee, such as through the execution of an employment agreement under which the employee agrees to be available to perform services if requested, but the facts and circumstances indicate that the employer and the employee did not intend for the employee to provide more than insignificant services for the employer, an employee will be treated as having a separation from service for purposes of this paragraph (h)(1). For purposes of the preceding sentence, an employer and employee will not be treated as having intended for the employee to provide insignificant services where the employee continues to provide services as an employee at an annual rate that is at least equal to 20 percent of the services rendered, on average, during the immediately preceding three full calendar years of employment (or, if employed less than three years, such lesser period) and the annual remuneration for such services is at least equal to 20 percent of the average annual remuneration earned during the final three full calendar years of employment (or, if less, such lesser period). Where an employee continues to provide services to a previous employer in a capacity other than as an employee, a separation from service will not be deemed to have occurred for purposes of this paragraph (h)(1) if the former employee is providing services at an annual rate that is 50 percent or more of the services rendered, on average, during the immediately preceding three full calendar years of employment (or if employed less than three years, such lesser period) and the annual remuneration for such services is 50 percent or more of the annual remuneration earned during the final three full calendar years of employment (or if less, such lesser period). For purposes of this paragraph (h)(1)(ii), the annual rate of providing services is determined based upon the measurement used to determine the service provider's base compensation (for example, amounts of time required to earn salary, hourly wages, or payments for specific projects).

(2) *Independent contractors*—(i) *In general.* An independent contractor is considered to have a separation from service with the service recipient upon the expiration of the contract (or in the case of more than one contract, all contracts) under which services are performed for the service recipient if the expiration constitutes a good-faith and complete termination of the contractual relationship. An expiration does not constitute a good faith and complete termination of the contractual relationship if the service recipient anticipates a renewal of a contractual relationship or the independent contractor becoming an employee. For this purpose, a service recipient is considered to anticipate the renewal of the contractual relationship with an independent contractor if it intends to contract again for the services provided under the expired contract, and neither the service recipient nor the independent contractor has eliminated the independent contractor as a possible provider of services under any such new contract. Further, a service recipient is considered to intend to contract again for the services

provided under an expired contract if the service recipient's doing so is conditioned only upon incurring a need for the services, the availability of funds, or both.

(ii) *Special rule.* Notwithstanding paragraph (h)(2)(i) of this section, the plan is considered to satisfy the requirement described in § 1.409A-3(a)(1) that amounts deferred under the plan may be paid or made available to the participant before the participant has a separation from service with the service recipient if, with respect to amounts payable to a participant who is an independent contractor, a plan provides that—[Corrected on 12/19/05 by 70 FR 75090.]

(A) No amount will be paid to the participant before a date at least 12 months after the day on which the contract expires under which services are performed for the service recipient (or, in the case of more than one contract, all such contracts expire); and

(B) No amount payable to the participant on that date will be paid to the participant if, after the expiration of the contract (or contracts) and before that date, the participant performs services for the service recipient as an independent contractor or an employee.

(i) *Specified employee*—(1) *In general.* The term *specified employee* means a key employee (as defined in section 416(i) without regard to section 416(i)(5)) of a service recipient any stock of which is publicly traded on an established securities market or otherwise. For purposes of this paragraph (i)(1), an employee is a key employee if the employee meets the requirements of section 416(i)(1)(A)(i), (ii) or (iii) (applied in accordance with the regulations thereunder and disregarding section 416(i)(5)) at any time during the 12-month period ending on an identification date. If a person is a key employee as of an identification date, the person is treated as a specified employee for the 12-month period beginning on the first day of the fourth month following the identification date. A service recipient may designate any date in a calendar year as the identification date provided that a service recipient must use the same identification date with respect to all arrangements, and any change to the identification date may not be effective for a period of 12 months. If no identification date is designated, the identification date is December 31. The service recipient may designate an identification date through inclusion in each plan document or through a separate document, provided that the service recipient will not be treated as having designated an identification date on any date before the execution of the document containing the designation. Notwithstanding the foregoing, any designation of an identification date made on or before December 31, 2006, may be applied to any separation from service occurring on or after January 1, 2005. Whether any stock of a service recipient is publicly traded on an established securities market or otherwise must be determined as of the date of the employee's separation from service.

(2) *Spinoffs and mergers.* Where a new corporation or entity (new corporation) is established as part of a corporate division governed by section 355 from a corporation that is publicly traded on an established securities market or otherwise (old corporation), any employee of the new corporation who was a key employee of the old corporation immediately prior to the spinoff is a key employee of the new corporation until the end of the 12-month period beginning on the first day of the fourth month following the old corporation's last identification date preceding the spinoff transaction. Where two corporations (pre-merger corporations) are merged or become part of the same controlled group of corporations so as to be treated as a single service recipient under paragraph (g) of this section, any employee of the merged corporation who was a key employee of either of the pre-merger corporations immediately before the merger is a key employee of the merged corporation until the first day of the fourth month after the identification date of the merged corporation next following the merger.

(3) *Nonresident alien employees.* For purposes of determining key employees, a service recipient generally must include all employees, including employees who are nonresident aliens. However, a plan may provide without causing an amount to be treated as an additional deferral as to any affected participant that for purposes of applying the six-month delay to specified employees, all employees that are nonresident aliens during the entire 12-month period ending with the relevant identification date are excluded for purposes of determining which employees meet the requirements of section 416(i)(1)(A)(i), (ii) or (iii) (applied in accordance with the regulations thereunder and disregarding section 416(i)(5)); provided that a service recipient must apply such exclusion with respect to all arrangements of the service recipient, and any change to include such nonresident alien employees may not be effective for a period of 12 months.

(j) *Nonresident alien*—(1) Except as provided in paragraph (j)(2) of this section, for purposes of this section the term *nonresident alien* means an individual who is—

(i) A nonresident alien within the meaning of section 7701(b)(1)(B); or

(ii) A dual resident taxpayer within the meaning of §301.7701(b)-7(a)(1) of this chapter with respect to any taxable year in which such individual is treated as a nonresident alien for purposes of computing the individual's U.S. income tax liability.

(2) The term *nonresident alien* does not include—

(i) A nonresident alien with respect to whom an election is in effect for the taxable year under section 6013(g) to be treated as a resident of the United States;

(ii) A former citizen or long-term resident (within the meaning of section 877(e)(2)) who expatriated after June 3, 2004, and has not complied with the requirements of section 7701(n); or

(iii) An individual who is treated as a citizen or resident of the United States for the taxable year under section 877(g).

(k) *Established securities market.* For purposes of section 409A and the regulations thereunder, the term *established securities market* means an established securities market within the meaning of §1.897-1(m).

(l) *Stock right.* For purposes of section 409A and these regulations, the term *stock right* means a stock option (other than an incentive stock option described in section 422 or an option granted pursuant to an employee stock purchase plan described in section 423) or a stock appreciation right.

(m) *Separation pay arrangement.* For purposes of section 409A and the regulations thereunder, the term *separation pay arrangement* means any arrangement that provides separation pay or, where an arrangement provides both amounts that are separation pay and that are not separation pay, that portion of the arrangement that provides separation pay. For purposes of this paragraph (m), the term *separation pay* means any amount of compensation where one of the conditions to the right to the payment is a separation from service, whether voluntary or involuntary, including payments in the form of reimbursements of expenses incurred, and the provision of other taxable benefits. Separation pay includes amounts payable due to a separation from service, regardless of whether payment is conditioned upon the execution of a release of claims, noncompetition or nondisclosure provisions, or other similar requirement. Notwithstanding the foregoing, any amount, or entitlement to any amount, that acts as a substitute for, or replacement of, amounts deferred by the service recipient under a separate nonqualified deferred compensation plan constitutes a payment of compensation or deferral of compensation under the separate nonqualified deferred compensation plan, and does not constitute separation pay.

§ 1.409A-2 Deferral elections

(a) *Initial elections as to the time and form of payment*—(1) *In general.* An arrangement that is, or constitutes part of, a nonqualified deferred compensation plan meets the requirements of section 409A(a)(4)(B) only if the arrangement provides that compensation for services performed during a service provider's taxable year (the service year) may be deferred at the service provider's election only if the election to defer such compensation is made and becomes irrevocable not later than the end of such period as may be permitted in this paragraph (a). An election will not be considered to be revocable merely because the service provider may make an election to change the time and form of payment pursuant to paragraph (b) of this section. Whether an arrangement provides a service provider an opportunity to elect the time or form of payment of compensation is determined based upon all the facts and circumstances surrounding the determination of the time and form of payment of the compensation. For purposes of this section, an election to defer includes an election as to the time of the payment, an election as to the form of the payment or an election as to both the time and the form of the payment, but does not include an election as to the medium of payment (for example, an election between a payment of cash or a payment of property). Except as otherwise provided in these regulations, an election will not be considered made until such election becomes irrevocable under the terms of the relevant arrangement. Thus, a plan may provide that an election to defer may be changed at any time prior to the last permissible date for making such an election. Where an arrangement provides the service provider a right to make an initial deferral election, and further provides that the election remains in effect until terminated or modified by the service provider, the election will be treated as made as of the date such election becomes irrevocable as to compensation for services performed during the relevant service year. For example, where an arrangement provides that a service provider's election to defer a set percentage will remain in effect until changed or revoked, but that as of

each December 31 the election becomes irrevocable with respect to salary payable with respect to services performed in the immediately following year, the initial deferral election with respect to salary payable with respect to services performed in the immediately following year will be deemed to have been made as of the December 31 upon which the election became irrevocable.

(2) *General rule.* An arrangement that is, or constitutes part of, a nonqualified deferred compensation plan meets the requirements of section 409A(a)(4)(B) if the plan provides that compensation for services performed during a service provider's taxable year (the service year) may be deferred at the service provider's election only if the election to defer such compensation is made not later than the close of the service provider's taxable year next preceding the service year.

(3) *Initial deferral election with respect to short-term deferrals.* With respect to a legally binding right to a payment of compensation in a subsequent taxable year that, absent a deferral election, would not be treated as a deferral of compensation pursuant to §1.409A-1(b)(4), an election to defer such compensation may be made in accordance with the requirements of paragraph (b) of this section, applied as if the amount were a deferral of compensation and the scheduled payment date for the amount were the date the substantial risk of forfeiture lapses. Notwithstanding the requirements of paragraph (b) of this section, such a deferral election may provide that the deferred amounts will be payable upon a change in control event (as defined in §1.409A-3(g)(5)) without regard to the 5-year additional deferral requirement.

(4) *Initial deferral election with respect to certain forfeitable rights.* With respect to a legally binding right to a payment in a subsequent year that is subject to a forfeiture condition requiring the service provider's continued services for a period of at least 12 months from the date the service provider obtains the legally binding right, an election to defer such compensation may be made on or before the 30th day after the service provider obtains the legally binding right to the compensation, provided that the election is made at least 12 months in advance of the earliest date at which the forfeiture condition could lapse.

(5) *Initial deferral election with respect to a service recipient with a fiscal year other than the calendar year.* In the case of a service recipient with a fiscal year other than the calendar year, a plan may provide that fiscal year compensation may be deferred at the service provider's election only if the election to defer such compensation is made not later than the close of the service recipient's fiscal year next preceding the first fiscal year in which are performed any services for which such compensation is payable. For purposes of this paragraph (a)(5), the term *fiscal year compensation* means compensation relating to a period of service coextensive with one or more consecutive fiscal years of the service recipient, of which no amount is paid or payable during the service period. For example, fiscal year compensation generally would include a bonus based on a service period of the two consecutive fiscal years ending September 30, 2009, where the amount will be paid after the completion of the service period, but would not include either a bonus based on a calendar year service period or salary that would otherwise be paid during the service recipient's fiscal year.

(6) *First year of eligibility.* In the case of the first year in which a service provider becomes eligible to participate in a plan (as defined in §1.409A-1(c)), the service provider may make an initial deferral election within 30 days after the date the service provider becomes eligible to participate in such plan, with respect to compensation paid for services to be performed subsequent to the election. In the case of a plan that does not provide for service provider elections with respect to the time or form of a payment, the time and form of the payment must be specified on or before the date that is 30 days after the date the service provider becomes eligible to participate in such plan. For compensation that is earned based upon a specified performance period (for example, an annual bonus), where a deferral election is made in the first year of eligibility but after the beginning of the service period, the election will be deemed to apply to compensation paid for services performed subsequent to the election if the election applies to the portion of the compensation equal to the total amount of the compensation for the service period multiplied by the ratio of the number of days remaining in the performance period after the election over the total number of days in the performance period.

(7) *Performance-based compensation.* In the case of any performance-based compensation based upon a performance period of at least 12 months, provided that the service provider performed services continuously from a date no later than the date upon which the performance criteria are established through a date no earlier than the date upon which the service provider makes an initial deferral election, an initial deferral election may be made with respect to such performance-based

compensation no later than the date that is six months before the end of the performance period, provided that in no event may an election to defer performance-based compensation be made after such compensation has become both substantially certain to be paid and readily ascertainable.

(8) *Nonqualified deferred compensation arrangements linked to qualified plans.* With respect to an amount deferred under an arrangement that is, or constitutes part of, a nonqualified deferred compensation plan, where under the terms of the nonqualified deferred compensation arrangement the amount deferred under the plan is the amount determined under the formula under which benefits are determined under a qualified employer plan (as defined in § 1.409A-1(a)(2)) applied without respect to one or more limitations applicable to qualified employer plans under the Internal Revenue Code or other applicable law, or is determined as an amount offset by some or all of the benefits provided under the qualified employer plan, the operation of the qualified employer plan with respect to changes in benefit limitations applicable to qualified employer plans under the Internal Revenue Code or other applicable law does not constitute a deferral election even if such operation results in an increase of amounts deferred under the nonqualified deferred compensation arrangement, provided that such operation does not otherwise result in a change in the time or form of a payment under the nonqualified deferred compensation plan. In addition, with respect to such a nonqualified deferred compensation arrangement, the following actions or failures to act will not constitute a deferral election under the nonqualified deferred compensation arrangement even if in accordance with the terms of the nonqualified deferred compensation arrangement, the actions or inactions result in an increase in the amounts deferred under the arrangement, provided that such actions or inactions do not otherwise affect the time or form of payment under the nonqualified deferred compensation plan:

(i) A service provider's action or inaction under the qualified plan with respect to whether to elect to receive a subsidized benefit or an ancillary benefit under the qualified plan.

(ii) The amendment of a qualified plan to add or remove a subsidized benefit or an ancillary benefit, or to freeze or limit future accruals of benefits under the qualified plan.

(iii) A service provider's action or inaction under a qualified plan subject to section 402(g), including an adjustment to a deferral election under the qualified plan subject to section 402(g), provided that for any given calendar year, the service provider's action or inaction does not result in an increase in the amounts deferred under all nonqualified deferred compensation arrangements in which the service provider participates in excess of the limit with respect to elective deferrals under section 402(g) in effect for the taxable year in which such action or inaction occurs.

(iv) A service provider's action or inaction under a qualified plan with respect to elective deferrals or after-tax contributions by the service provider to the qualified plan that affects the amounts that are credited under a nonqualified deferred compensation arrangement as matching amounts or other amounts contingent on service provider elective deferrals or after-tax contributions, provided that such matching or contingent amounts, as applicable, are either forfeited or never credited under the nonqualified deferred compensation arrangement in the absence of such service provider's elective deferral or after-tax contribution, and provided further that all of the service provider's actions or inactions do not result in an increase during such taxable year in the amounts deferred under all nonqualified deferred compensation arrangements in which the service provider participates in excess of the limit with respect to elective deferrals under section 402(g) in effect for the taxable year in which such action or inaction occurs. See paragraph (b)(6) of this section, *Example 12* and *Example 13.*

(9) *Separation pay.* In the case of separation pay (as defined in § 1.409A-1(m)) due to an actual involuntary separation from service, where such separation pay is the subject of bona fide, arm's length negotiations, the initial deferral election may be made at any time up to the time the service provider obtains a legally binding right to the payment. In the case of separation pay due to participation in a window program (as defined in § 1.409A-1(b)(9)(v)), the initial deferral election may be made at any time up to the time the election to participate in the window program becomes irrevocable. [Corrected on 12/19/05 by 70 FR 75090.]

(10) *Commissions.* For purposes of this paragraph (a), in the case of commission compensation, a service provider earning such compensation is treated as providing the services to which such compensation relates only in the year in which the customer remits payment to the service recipient. For purposes of this paragraph (a)(10), the term *commission compensation* means compensation or portions of compensation earned by a service provider if a substantial portion of the services provided by such service provider to a service recipient consist of the direct sale of a product or service to a customer, the compensation paid by the service recipient to the service provider consists of either a portion of the purchase price for the product or service or an amount calculated solely by reference to the volume of sales, and payment of the compensation is contingent upon the service recipient receiving payment from an unrelated customer for the product or services. For this purpose, a customer is treated as an unrelated customer only if the customer is not related to either the service provider or the service recipient. A person is treated as related to another person if the person would be treated as related to the other person under § 1.409A-1(f)(3)(ii) or the person would be treated as providing management services to the other person under § 1.409A-1(f)(3)(iv).

(11) *Initial deferral elections with respect to compensation paid for final payroll period*—(i) *In general.* Unless an arrangement provides otherwise, compensation payable after the last day of the service provider's taxable year solely for services performed during the final payroll period described in section 3401(b) containing the last day of the service provider's taxable year or, with respect to a non-employee service provider, a period not longer than the payroll period described in section 3401(b), where such amount is payable pursuant to the timing arrangement under which the service recipient normally compensates service providers for services performed during a payroll period described in section 3401(b), or with respect to a non-employee service provider, a period not longer than the payroll period described in section 3401(b), is treated as compensation for services performed in the subsequent taxable year. The preceding sentence does not apply to any compensation paid during such period for services performed during any period other than such final payroll period, such as a payment of an annual bonus. Any amendment of an arrangement after December 31, 2006, to add a provision providing for a differing treatment of such compensation may not be effective for 12 months from the date the amendment is executed and enacted.

(ii) *Transition rule.* For purposes of this paragraph (a)(11), an arrangement that was adopted and effective before December 31, 2006, whether written or unwritten, will be treated as designating such compensation for service performed in the taxable year in which the payroll period ends, unless otherwise set forth in writing before December 31, 2006.

(12) *Designation of time and form of payment with respect to a nonelective arrangement.* An arrangement that provides for a deferral of compensation for services performed during a service provider's taxable year that does not provide the service provider with an opportunity to elect the time of payment of such compensation must specify the time of payment no later than the time the service provider first has a legally binding right to the compensation. Similarly, an arrangement that provides for a deferral of compensation for services performed during a service provider's taxable year that does not provide the service provider with an opportunity to elect the form of payment of such compensation must specify the form of payment no later than the time the service provider first has a legally binding right to the compensation. Such designation shall be treated as an initial deferral election for purposes of this section.

(13) *Designation of time and form of payment with respect to earnings.* An arrangement that provides for actual or notional earnings to be credited on amounts of deferred compensation may specify, in accordance with the requirements of this paragraph (a), that such earnings will be paid by a date not later than the 15 th day of the third month following the calendar year for which the earnings are credited. To satisfy the requirements of this paragraph (a)(13), actual or notional earnings must be credited at least annually and the measure for such earnings must be either a specified, nondiscretionary interest rate (or a specified, nondiscretionary formula describing an interest rate such as, for example, the interest on a Treasury bond + 2 percent) or a predetermined actual investment within the meaning of § 31.3121(v)(2)-1(d)(2) of this chapter. For these purposes, a right to dividend equivalents with respect to a specified number of shares of service recipient stock (as defined in § 1.409A-1(b)(5)(iii)) may be treated as a right to actual or notional earnings on an amount of deferred compensation.

(b) *Subsequent changes in time and form of payment*—(1) *In general.* The requirements of section 409A(a)(4)(C) are met if, in the case of a plan that permits a subsequent election to delay a payment or to change the form of payment of an amount of deferred compensation, the following conditions are met:

(i) The plan requires that such election may not take effect until at least 12 months after the date on which the election is made.

(ii) In the case of an election related to a payment not described in § 1.409A-3(a)(2) (payment on account of disability), § 1.409A-3(a)(3) (payment on account of death) or § 1.409A-3(a)(6) (payment on account of the occurrence of an unforeseeable emergency), the plan requires that the payment with respect to which such election is made be deferred for a period of not less than 5 years from the date such payment would otherwise have been paid (or in the case of a life annuity or installment payments treated as a single payment, 5 years from the date the first amount was scheduled to be paid).

(iii) The plan requires that any election related to a payment described in § 1.409A-3(a)(4) (payment at a specified time or pursuant to a fixed schedule) may not be made less than 12 months prior to the date the payment is scheduled to be paid (or in the case of a life annuity or installment payments treated as a single payment, 12 months prior to the date the first amount was scheduled to be paid).

(2) *Definition of payments for purposes of subsequent changes in the time or form of payment*—(i) *In general.* Except as provided in paragraphs (b)(2)(ii) and (iii) of this section, the term *payment* refers to each separately identified amount to which a service provider is entitled to payment under a plan on a determinable date, and includes amounts applied for the benefit of the service provider. An amount is separately identified only if the amount may be objectively determined. For example, an amount identified as 10 percent of the account balance as of a specified payment date would be a separately identified amount. A payment includes the provision of any taxable benefit, including payment in cash or in kind. In addition, a payment includes, but is not limited to, the transfer, cancellation or reduction of an amount of deferred compensation in exchange for benefits under a welfare benefit plan, fringe benefit excludible under section 119 or section 132, or any other benefit that is excluded from gross income.

(ii) *Life annuities.* The entitlement to a life annuity is treated as the entitlement to a single payment. For purposes of this paragraph (b)(2)(ii), the term *life annuity* means a series of substantially equal periodic payments, payable not less frequently than annually, for the life (or life expectancy) of the service provider or the joint lives (or life expectancies) of the service provider and the service provider's designated beneficiary. A change in the form of a payment from one type of life annuity to another type of life annuity before any annuity payment has been made is not considered a change in the time and form of a payment, provided that the annuities are actuarially equivalent applying reasonable actuarial assumptions.

(iii) *Installment payments.* The entitlement to a series of installment payments that is not a life annuity is treated as the entitlement to a single payment, unless the arrangement provides at all times with respect to the amount deferred that the right to the series of installment payments is to be treated as a right to a series of separate payments. For purposes of this paragraph (b)(2)(iii), a series of installment payments refers to an entitlement to the payment of a series of substantially equal periodic amounts to be paid over a predetermined period of years, except to the extent any increase in the amount reflects reasonable earnings through the date the amount is paid.

(iv) *Transition rule.* For purposes of this section, an arrangement that was adopted and effective before December 31, 2006, whether written or unwritten, that fails to make a designation as to whether the entitlement to a series of payments is to be treated as an entitlement to a series of separate payments under paragraph (b)(2)(iii) of this section is treated as having made such designation as of the later of the date on which the arrangement was adopted or became effective, provided that such designation is set forth in writing before December 31, 2006.

(3) *Coordination with prohibition against acceleration of payments.* For purposes of applying the prohibition against the acceleration of payments contained in § 1.409A-3(h), the definition of payment is the same as the definition provided in paragraph (b)(2) of this section. However, even though a change in the form of a payment that results in a more rapid schedule for payments generally may not constitute an acceleration of a payment, the change in the form of payment must comply with the subsequent deferral rules. For example, although a change in form from a 10-year installment payment treated as a single payment to a lump-sum payment would not constitute an acceleration, the change in the form of the payment must still comply with the requirements of paragraph (b)(1) of this section, generally meaning that the election to change to a lump-sum payment could not be effective for 12 months and the lump-sum payment could not be made until at least 5 years after the date the installment payments were scheduled to commence. [Corrected on 12/19/05 by 70 FR 75090.]

(4) *Application to multiple payment events.* In the case of a plan that permits a payment upon each of a number of potential permissible payment events, such as the earlier of a fixed date or separation from service, the requirements of paragraph (b)(1) of this section are applied separately to each payment (as defined in paragraph (b)(2) of this section) due upon each payment event. Notwithstanding the foregoing, the addition of a permissible payment event to amounts previously deferred is subject to the rules of this paragraph (b) where the addition of the permissible payment event may result in a change in the time or form of payment of the amount deferred. For application of the rules governing accelerations of payments to the addition of a permissible payment event to amounts deferred, see § 1.409A-3.

(5) *Delay of payments under certain circumstances.* A plan may provide, or be amended to provide, that a payment will be delayed to a date after the designated payment date under any of the following circumstances, and the provision will not fail to meet the requirements of establishing a permissible payment event and the delay in the payment will not constitute a subsequent deferral election, provided that once such a provision is applicable to an amount of deferred compensation, any failure to apply such a provision or modification of the plan to remove such a provision will constitute an acceleration of any payment to which such provision applied:

(i) *Payments subject to section 162(m).* A plan may provide that a payment will be delayed where the service recipient reasonably anticipates that the service recipient's deduction with respect to such payment otherwise would be limited or eliminated by application of section 162(m); provided that the terms of the arrangement require the payment to be made either at the earliest date at which the service recipient reasonably anticipates that the deduction of the payment of the amount will not be limited or eliminated by application of section 162(m) or the calendar year in which the service provider separates from service.

(ii) *Payments that would violate a loan covenant or similar contractual requirement.* A plan may provide that a payment will be delayed where the service recipient reasonably anticipates that the making of the payment will violate a term of a loan agreement to which the service recipient is a party, or other similar contract to which the service recipient is a party, and such violation will cause material harm to the service recipient; provided that the terms of the arrangement require the payment to be made at the earliest date at which the service recipient reasonably anticipates that the making of the payment will not cause such violation, or such violation will not cause material harm to the service recipient, and provided that the facts and circumstances indicate that the service recipient entered into such loan agreement (including such covenant) or other similar contract for legitimate business reasons, and not to avoid the restrictions on deferral elections and subsequent deferral elections under section 409A.

(iii) *Payments that would violate Federal securities laws or other applicable law.* A plan may provide that a payment will be delayed where the service recipient reasonably anticipates that the making of the payment will violate Federal securities laws or other applicable law; provided that the terms of the arrangement require the payment to be made at the earliest date at which the service recipient reasonably anticipates that the making of the payment will not cause such violation. For purposes of this paragraph (b)(5)(iii), the making of a payment that would cause inclusion in gross income or the application of any penalty provision or other provision of the Internal Revenue Code is not treated as a violation of applicable law.

(iv) *Other events and conditions.* A service recipient may delay a payment upon such other events and conditions as the Commissioner may prescribe in generally applicable guidance published in the Internal Revenue Bulletin.

(6) *Examples.* The following examples illustrate the application of the provisions of this section:

Example 1. Initial election to defer salary. Employee A is an individual employed by Employer X. Employer X sponsors an arrangement under which Employee A may elect to defer a percentage of Employee A's salary. Employee A has participated in the arrangement in prior years. To satisfy the requirements of this section with respect to salary earned in calendar year 2008, if Employee A elects to defer any amount of such salary, the deferral election (including an election as to the time and form of payment) must be made no later than December 31, 2007.

Example 2. Designation of time and form of payment where an initial deferral election is not provided. Employee A is an individual employed by Employer X. Employer X has a fiscal year ending September 30. On July 1, 2007, Employer X enters into a legally binding obligation to pay Employee A a $10,000 bonus. The amount is not subject to a substantial risk of forfeiture. Employer X does not provide Employee A an election as to the time and form of payment. Unless the amount is paid in accordance with the short-term deferral rule of § 1.409A-1(b)(4), to satisfy the requirements of this section, Employer X must specify the time and form of payment on or before July 1, 2007.

Example 3. Initial election to defer bonus payable based on services during calendar year. Employee A is an individual employed by Employer X. Employer X has a fiscal year ending September 30. Employee A participates in a bonus plan under which Employee A is entitled to a bonus for services performed during the calendar year that, absent an election by Employee A, will be paid on March 15 of the following year. The amount is not subject to a substantial risk of forfeiture and does not qualify as performance based compensation. If Employee A elects to defer the payment of the bonus with respect to calendar year 2008, to satisfy the requirements of this paragraph, Employee A must elect the time and form of payment not later than December 31, 2007.

Example 4. Initial election to defer bonus payable based on services during fiscal year other than calendar year. Employee A is an individual employed by Employer X. Employer X has a fiscal year ending September 30. Employee A participates in a bonus plan under which Employee A is entitled to a bonus for services performed during Employer X's fiscal year that, absent an election by Employee A, will be paid on December 15 of the calendar year in which the fiscal year ends. The amount is not subject to a substantial risk of forfeiture and does not qualify as performance based compensation as described in § 1.409A-1(e). The amount qualifies as fiscal year compensation. If Employee A elects to defer the payment of the amount related to the fiscal year ending September 30, 2008, to satisfy the requirements of this section Employee A must elect the time and form of payment not later than September 30, 2007.

Example 5. Initial election to defer bonus payable only if service provider completes at least 12 months of services after the election. Employee A is an individual employed by Employer X. Employer X has a calendar year fiscal year. On March 1, 2006, Employer X grants Employee A a $10,000 bonus, payable on March 1, 2008, provided that Employee A continues performing services as an employee of Employer X through March 1, 2008. The amount does not qualify as performance-based compensation as described in § 1.409A-1(e), and Employee A already participates in another account balance nonqualified deferred compensation plan. Employee A may make an initial deferral election on or before March 31, 2006 (within 30 days after obtaining a legally binding right), because at least 12 months of additional services are required after the date of election for the risk of forfeiture to lapse.

Example 6. Initial election to defer bonus that would otherwise constitute a short-term deferral. The same facts as *Example 5*, except that Employee A does not make an initial deferral election on or before March 31, 2006. Because the right to the compensation would not be treated as a deferral of compensation pursuant to § 1.409A-1(b)(4) absent a deferral election (because the arrangement would be treated as a short-term deferral), Employee A may make an initial deferral election provided that the election may not become effective for 12 months and must defer the payment at least 5 years from March 1, 2008 (the first date the payment could become substantially vested). Accordingly, Employee A may make an election before March 1, 2007, provided that the election defers the payment to a date on or after March 1, 2013 (other than a payment due to death, disability, unforeseeable emergency, or a change in control event).

Example 7. Initial election to defer commissions. Employee A is an individual employed by Employer X. Employer X has a calendar year fiscal year. As part of Employee A's services for Employer X, Employee A sells refrigerators. Under the employment arrangement, Employee A is entitled to 10 percent of the sales price of any refrigerator Employee A sells, payable only upon the receipt of payment from the customer who purchased the refrigerator. For purposes of the initial deferral rule, Employee A is treated as performing the services related to each refrigerator sale in the taxable year in which each customer pays for the refrigerator.

Example 8. Initial election to defer renewal commissions. The same facts as *Example 7*, except that Employee A also sells warranties related to the refrigerators sold. Under the warranty arrangement, refrigerator warranty customers are entitled in a future year to extend the warranty for an additional cost to be paid at the time of the extension. Under Employee A's arrangement with Employer X, Employee A is entitled to 10 percent of the amount paid for an extension of any warranty, payable upon the receipt of payment from the customer extending the warranty. For purposes of the initial deferral rule, Employee A is treated as performing the services related to the amount paid for the extension of the warranty in the taxable year in which the customer pays for the warranty extension.

Example 9. Initial election to defer negotiated separation pay. Employee A is an individual employed by Employer X. Under the terms of a separation pay arrangement, Employee A is entitled upon an involuntary separation from service to an amount equal to two weeks of pay for every year of service at Employer X. Employer X decides to terminate

Employee A's employment involuntarily. As part of the process of terminating Employee A, Employer X enters into bona fide, arm's length negotiations with respect to the terms of Employee A's termination of employment. As part of the process, Employer X offers Employee A an amount that is in addition to any amounts to which Employee A is otherwise entitled, payable either as a lump sum payment at the end of three years or in three annual payments starting at the date of termination of employment. The election of the time and form of payment by Employee A may be made at any time before Employee A accepts the offer and obtains a legally binding right to the additional amount.

Example 10. Election of time and form of payments under a window program. Employee A is an individual employed by Employer X. Employer X establishes a window program, as defined in § 1.409A-1(b)(9)(v). Individuals who elect to terminate employment under the window program are entitled to receive an amount equal to two weeks pay multiplied by every year of service with Employer X. The individuals participating in the window program may elect to receive the payment as either a lump sum payment payable on the first day of the month after making the election to participate in the window program, or as a payment of two equal annual installments on each January 1 of the first two years following the election to participate in the window program. Employee A is eligible to participate in the window program. Employee A may make the election as to the time and form of payment on or before the date Employee A's election to participate in the window program becomes irrevocable.

Example 11. Initial election to defer salary earned during final payroll period beginning in one calendar year and ending in the subsequent calendar year. Employee A performs services as an employee of Employer X. Employer X pays the salary of its employees, including Employee A, on a bi-weekly basis. One bi-weekly payroll period runs from December 24, 2006, through January 6, 2007, with a scheduled payment date of January 13, 2001. Employer X sponsors, and Employee A participates in, a nonqualified deferred compensation arrangement under which Employee A may defer a specified percentage of his annual salary. The arrangement does not specify that any salary compensation paid for the payroll period in which falls January 1 is to be treated as compensation for services performed during the year preceding the year in which falls that January 1. For purposes of applying the initial deferral election rules, Employee A is deemed to have performed the services for the payroll period December 24, 2006, through January 6, 2007, during the calendar year 2007.

Example 12. Application of deferral election rules and anti-acceleration rules to a section 401(k) wrap plan. Employee A participates in a qualified retirement plan under section 401(a) with a qualified cash or deferred arrangement under section 401(k). Employee A also participates in a nonqualified deferred compensation arrangement. Under the terms of the nonqualified deferred compensation arrangement, Employee A elects, on or before December 31, to defer a specified percentage of his salary for the subsequent calendar year. Under the terms of the nonqualified deferred compensation arrangement and the qualified plan, as of the earliest date administratively practicable following the end of the year in which the salary is earned, the maximum amount that may be deferred under the qualified cash or deferred arrangement (not in excess of the amount specified under section 402(g) for the plan year) is credited to Employee A's account under the qualified plan, and Employee A's deferral under the nonqualified deferred compensation arrangement is reduced by a corresponding amount. The reduction has no effect on any other nonqualified deferred compensation arrangement in which Employee A participates. The reduction of Employee A's account under the nonqualified deferred compensation arrangement is not treated as an accelerated payment of deferred compensation for purposes of section 409A.

Example 13. Application of deferral election rules and anti-acceleration rules to a nonqualified deferred compensation arrangement linked to a qualified defined benefit plan. Employee A participates in a qualified retirement plan that is a defined benefit plan. Employee A also participates in a nonqualified deferred compensation arrangement, under which the benefit payable is calculated under a formula, with that benefit then reduced by any benefit which Employee A has accrued under the qualified retirement plan. In 2007, Employee A fails to elect a subsidized benefit under the qualified retirement plan, with the effect that the amounts payable under the nonqualified deferred compensation arrangement are increased relative to the lesser benefit payable under the qualified plan. Also, in 2007, Employer X amends the qualified retirement plan to increase benefits under the plan, resulting in a relative decrease in the amounts payable under the nonqualified deferred compensation arrangement relative to the greater benefit payable under the qualified plan. Neither of these actions constitute a deferral election or an acceleration of a payment under the nonqualified deferred compensation arrangement.

Example 14. Subsequent deferral election. Employee A participates in a nonqualified deferred compensation arrangement. Employee A elects to be paid in a lump sum payment at the earlier of age 65 or separation from service. Employee A anticipates that he will work after age 65, and wishes to defer payment to a later date. Provided that Employee A continues in employment and makes the election by his 64 th birthday, Employee A may elect to receive a lump sum payment at the earlier of age 70 or separation from service.

Example 15. Grant of right to current payment of dividends paid with respect to restricted stock. Employer X grants Employee A stock that is not substantially vested for purposes of section 83, and Employee A does not make an election under section 83(b). As part of the restricted stock grant, Employee A receives the right to payments in an amount equal to the dividends payable with respect to the restricted stock. At the time Employer B grants Employee A the right to the dividend payments, the grant also specifies that each dividend payment will be made no later than the end of the calendar year in which the dividends are paid to shareholders of that class of stock or, if later, the 15 th day of the third month following the date the dividends are paid to shareholders of that class of stock. The grant of the rights to dividend payments satisfies the requirement that deferred amounts be paid at a specified time or pursuant to a specified schedule.

Example 16. Subsequent deferral election rule -change in form of payment from lump sum payment to life annuity. Employee A participates in a nonqualified deferred compensation arrangement. Employee A elects to be paid in a lump sum payment at 65. Employee A wishes to change the payment form to a life annuity. Provided that Employee A makes the election on or before his 64 th birthday, Employee A may elect to receive a life annuity commencing at age 70.

Example 17. Subsequent deferral election rule - change in form of payment from life annuity to lump sum payment. Employee A participates in a nonqualified deferred compensation arrangement. Employee A elects to be paid in a life annuity at age 65. Employee A wishes to change the payment form to a lump sum payment. Provided that Employee A makes the election on or before his 64 th birthday, Employee A may elect to receive a lump sum payment at age 70.

Example 18. Subsequent deferral election rule - installment payments designated as separate payments. Employee A participates in a nonqualified deferred compensation arrangement that provides for payment in a series of 5 equal annual amounts, each designated as a separate payment. The first payment is scheduled to be made on January 1, 2008. Provided that Employee A makes the election on or before January 1, 2007, Employee A may elect for the first payment to be made on January 1, 2013. If Employee A makes that election, the remaining payments may continue to be due upon January 1 of the four calendar years commencing on January 1, 2009.

Example 19. Subsequent deferral election rule - change in form of payment from installment payments to lump sum payment. Employee A participates in a nonqualified deferred compensation arrangement that provides for payment in a series of 5 equal annual amounts that are not designated as a series of 5 separate payments. The first amount is scheduled to be paid on January 1, 2008. Employee A wishes to receive the entire amount equal to the sum of all five of the amounts to be paid as a lump sum payment. Provided that Employee A makes the election on or before January 1, 2007, Employee A may elect to receive a lump sum payment on or after January 1, 2013.

Example 20. Subsequent deferral election rule - change in time of payment from payment at specified age to payment at later of specified age or separation from service. Employee A participates in a nonqualified deferred compensation arrangement that provides for a lump sum payment at age 65. Employee A wishes to add a payment provision such that the payment is payable upon the later of a predetermined age or separation from service. Provided that Employee A makes such election on or before his 64 th birthday, Employee A may elect to receive a lump sum payment upon the later of age 70 or separation from service.

(c) *Special rules for certain resident aliens.* For the first calendar year in which an individual is classified as a resident alien, a nonqualified deferred compensation arrangement is deemed to meet the requirements of paragraph (a) of this section if, with respect to compensation payable for services performed during that first calendar year or with respect to compensation the right to which is subject to a substantial risk of forfeiture as of January 1 of that first calendar year, an initial deferral election is made by the end of such first calendar year, provided that the initial deferral election may not apply to amounts paid or first payable on or before the date of such initial deferral election.

For any year subsequent to the first calendar year in which an individual is classified as a resident alien, this paragraph (c) does not apply, provided that a calendar year may again be treated as the first calendar year in which an individual is classified as a resident alien if such individual has not been classified as a resident alien for at least five consecutive calendar years immediately preceding the year in which the individual is again classified as a resident alien.

§ 1.409A-3 Permissible payments.

(a) *In general.* The requirements of this section are met only if the arrangement provides that an amount of deferred compensation may be paid only on account of one or more of the following:

(1) The service provider's separation from service (as defined in § 1.409A-1(h)).

(2) The service provider becoming disabled (in accordance with paragraph (g)(4) of this section).

(3) The service provider's death.

(4) A time (or pursuant to a fixed schedule) specified under the plan (in accordance with paragraph (g)(1) of this section).

(5) A change in the ownership or effective control of the corporation, or in the ownership of a substantial portion of the assets of the corporation (in accordance with paragraph (g)(5) of this section).

(6) The occurrence of an unforeseeable emergency (in accordance with paragraph (g)(3) of this section).

(b) *Designation of payment upon a permissible payment event.* Except as otherwise specified in this section, an arrangement provides for the payment upon an event described in paragraph (a)(1), (2), (3), (5) or (6) of this section if the arrangement provides for a payment date that is objectively determinable at the time the event occurs (for example, 3 months following the date of initial disability or December 31 of the calendar year in which the disability first occurs). In addition, an arrangement may provide that a payment is to be made during an objectively determinable calendar year following the year in which the event occurs (for example, the calendar year following the year in which the service provider dies), provided that where no specific date within such calendar year is objectively determinable, the payment date is deemed to be January 1 of such calendar year for purposes of applying the subsequent deferral election rules of § 1.409A-2(b). An arrangement may provide for payment upon the earliest or latest of more than one event, provided that each event is described in paragraphs (a)(1) through (6) of this section. An arrangement may also provide that a payment upon an event described in paragraph (a)(1), (2), (3), (5) or (6) of this section is to be made in accordance with a fixed schedule that is objectively determinable based on the date of the event, provided that the schedule must be fixed at the time the permissible payment event is designated, and any change in the fixed schedule will constitute a change in the time and form of payment. For example, an arrangement may provide that a service provider is entitled to three substantially equal payments payable on each of the first three anniversaries of the date of the service provider's separation from service. In addition, an arrangement may provide that payments are to be made pursuant to a schedule of payments based upon objectively determinable calendar years following the year in which the event occurs, (for example, three substantially equal payments to be made during the three calendar years following the year in which the service provider dies), provided that where payment dates within such calendar years are not specified under the terms of the arrangement, the payment dates are deemed to be January 1 of such calendar years for purposes of applying the subsequent deferral election rules of § 1.409A-2(b). [Corrected on 12/19/05 by 70 FR 75090.]

(c) *Designation of alternative specified dates or payment schedules based upon date of permissible event.* In general, in the case of an arrangement that provides that a payment upon an event described in paragraph (a)(1), (2), (3), (5) or (6) of this section is to be made on an objectively determinable date or year in accordance with paragraph (b) of this section, or in accordance with a fixed schedule that is objectively determinable based on the date of the event in accordance with paragraph (b) of this section, the objectively determined date or fixed schedule must apply consistently regardless of the date on which the specified event occurs. However, an arrangement may allow for an alternative payment schedule if the event occurs on or before one (but not more than one) specified date. For example, an arrangement may provide that a service provider will receive a lump sum payment of the service provider's entire benefit under the arrangement on the first day of the month following a separation from service before age 55, but will receive 5 substantially equal annual payments commencing on the first day of the month following a separation from service on or after age 55.

(d) *When a payment is treated as made upon the designated payment date*. Except as otherwise specified in this section, a payment is treated as made upon the date specified under the arrangement (including a date specified under paragraph (a)(4) of this section) if the payment is made at such date or a later date within the same calendar year or, if later, by the 15 th day of the third calendar month following the date specified under the arrangement. If calculation of the amount of the payment is not administratively practicable due to events beyond the control of the service provider (or service provider's estate), the payment will be treated as made upon the date specified under the arrangement if the payment is made during the first calendar year in which the payment is administratively practicable. Similarly, if the funds of the service recipient are not sufficient to make the payment at the date specified under the plan without jeopardizing the solvency of the service recipient, the payment will be treated as made upon the date specified under the arrangement if the payment is made during the first calendar year in which the funds of the service recipient are sufficient to make the payment without jeopardizing the solvency of the service recipient.

(e) *Disputed payments and refusals to pay*. If a payment is not made, in whole or in part, as of the date specified under the arrangement because the service recipient refuses to make such payment, the payment will be treated as made upon the date specified under the arrangement if the service provider accepts the portion (if any) of the payment that the service recipient is willing to make (unless such acceptance will result in a forfeiture of the claim to the remaining amount), makes prompt and reasonable, good faith efforts to collect the payment, and the payment is made during the first calendar year in which the service recipient and the service provider enter into a legally binding settlement of such dispute, the service recipient concedes that the amount is payable, or the service recipient is required to make such payment pursuant to a final and nonappealable judgment or other binding decision. For purposes of this paragraph (e), a service recipient is not treated as having refused to make a payment where pursuant to the terms of the plan the service provider is required to request payment, or otherwise provide information or take any other action, and the service provider has failed to take such action. In addition, for purposes of this paragraph (e), the service provider is deemed to have requested that a payment not be made, rather than the service recipient having refused to make such payment, where the service recipient's decision to refuse to make the payment is made by the service provider or a member of the service provider's family (as defined in section 267(c)(4) applied as if the family of an individual includes the spouse of any member of the family), or any person or group of persons over whom the service provider or service provider's family member has effective control, or any person any portion of whose compensation is controlled the service provider or service provider's family member.

(f) *Special rule for certain resident aliens.* An arrangement that is, or constitutes part of, a nonqualified deferred compensation plan is deemed to meet the requirements of this section with respect to any amount payable in the first calendar year in which a service provider is classified as a resident alien, and with respect to any amount payable in a subsequent calendar year if no later than the December 31 of the first calendar year in which the service provider is classified as a resident alien, the plan is amended as necessary so that the times and forms of payment of amounts payable in a subsequent year comply with the provisions of this section. For any year subsequent to the first calendar year in which an individual is classified as a resident alien, this paragraph (f) does not apply, provided that a calendar year may again be treated as the first calendar year in which an individual is classified as a resident alien if such individual has not been classified as a resident alien for at least five consecutive calendar years immediately preceding the year in which the service provider is again classified as a resident alien.

(g) *Definitions and special rules*–(1) *Specified time or fixed schedule.* Amounts are payable at a specified time or pursuant to a fixed schedule if objectively determinable amounts are payable at a date or dates that are objectively determinable at the time the amount is deferred. An amount is objectively determinable for this purpose if the amount is specifically identified or if the amount may be determined pursuant to a nondiscretionary formula (for example, 50 percent of an account balance). A specified time or fixed schedule also includes the designation of a calendar year or years that are objectively determinable at the time the amount is deferred, provided that for purposes of the application of the subsequent deferral rules contained in § 1.409A-2(b), the specified time or fixed schedule of payments is deemed to refer to January 1 of the relevant calendar year or years. An arrangement may provide that a payment upon the lapse of a substantial risk of forfeiture is to be made in accordance with a fixed schedule that is objectively determinable based on the date the substantial risk of forfeiture lapses (disregarding

any acceleration of the lapsing of the substantial risk of forfeiture other than due to the occurrence of a condition applicable as of the date the legally binding right to the payment arose that itself would constitute a substantial risk of forfeiture), provided that the schedule must be fixed at the time the time and form of payment are designated, and any change in the fixed schedule will constitute a change in the time and form of payment. For example, an arrangement that provides for a bonus payment subject to the condition that the service provider complete three years of service, but provided further that such requirement of continued services would lapse upon the occurrence of an initial public offering that if applied alone would subject the right to the payment to a substantial risk of forfeiture, may provide that a service provider is entitled to substantially equal payments on each of the first three anniversaries of the date the substantial risk of forfeiture lapses (the earlier of three years of service or the date of an initial public offering).

(2) *Required delay in payment to a specified employee pursuant to a separation from service.* In the case of any specified employee (as defined in § 1.409A-1(i)), the requirements of paragraph (a)(1) of this section permitting a payment upon a separation from service are satisfied only if payments may not be made before the date that is six months after the date of separation from service (or, if earlier, the date of death of the specified employee). The arrangement must provide the manner in which the six-month delay will be implemented in the case of a service provider who is a specified employee. For example, an arrangement may provide that payments to which a specified employee would otherwise be entitled during the first six months following the date of separation from service are accumulated and paid at another specified date or specified schedule, such as the first date of the seventh month following the date of separation from service. The arrangement may also provide that each installment payment to which a specified employee is entitled upon a separation from service is delayed by six months. A service recipient may amend a plan at any time to change the method for applying the six-month delay, provided that the amendment may not be effective for a period of 12 months. Notwithstanding the foregoing, an amendment to a plan may be effective immediately in the case of a service recipient that amends the arrangement prior to the date upon which the service recipient's stock first becomes readily tradable on an established securities market. Notwithstanding the foregoing, this paragraph (g)(2) also does not apply to a payment made under the circumstances described in paragraph (h)(2)(i) (domestic relations order), (h)(2)(ii) (conflicts of interest), or (h)(2)(v) (payment of employment taxes) of this section.

(3) *Unforeseeable Emergency*–(i) *Definition*. For purposes of paragraph (a)(6) of this section, an unforeseeable emergency is a severe financial hardship of the service provider or beneficiary resulting from an illness or accident of the service provider or beneficiary, the service provider's or beneficiary's spouse, or the service provider's or beneficiary's dependent (as defined in section 152(a)); loss of the service provider's or beneficiary's property due to casualty (including the need to rebuild a home following damage to a home not otherwise covered by insurance, for example, as a result of a natural disaster); or other similar extraordinary and unforeseeable circumstances arising as a result of events beyond the control of the service provider or beneficiary. For example, the imminent foreclosure of or eviction from the service provider's or beneficiary's primary residence may constitute an unforeseeable emergency. In addition, the need to pay for medical expenses, including non-refundable deductibles, as well as for the costs of prescription drug medication, may constitute an unforeseeable emergency. Finally, the need to pay for the funeral expenses of a spouse or a dependent (as defined in section 152(a)) may also constitute an unforeseeable emergency. Except as otherwise provided in this paragraph (g)(3)(i), the purchase of a home and the payment of college tuition are not unforeseeable emergencies. Whether a service provider or beneficiary is faced with an unforeseeable emergency permitting a distribution under this paragraph is to be determined based on the relevant facts and circumstances of each case, but, in any case, a distribution on account of unforeseeable emergency may not be made to the extent that such emergency is or may be relieved through reimbursement or compensation from insurance or otherwise, by liquidation of the service provider's assets, to the extent the liquidation of such assets would not cause severe financial hardship, or by cessation of deferrals under the arrangement. An arrangement may provide for a payment upon any unforeseeable emergency, but does not have to provide for a payment upon all unforeseeable emergencies, provided that any event upon which a payment may be made qualifies as an unforeseeable emergency. [Corrected on 12/19/05 by 70 FR 75090.]

(ii) *Amount of payment permitted upon an unforeseeable emergency.* Distributions because of an unforeseeable emergency must be limited to the amount reasonably necessary to satisfy the emergency need (which may include amounts necessary to pay any Federal, state, or local income taxes or penalties reasonably anticipated to result from the distribution). Determinations of amounts reasonably necessary to satisfy the emergency need must take into account any additional compensation that is available if the plan provides for cancellation of a deferral election upon a payment due to an unforeseeable emergency. See paragraph (h)(2)(vii) of this section. The payment may be made from any arrangement in which the service provider participates that provides for payment upon an unforeseeable emergency, provided that the arrangement under which the payment was made must be designated at the time of payment.

(4) *Disability*-(i) *In general*. For purposes of this section, a service provider is considered disabled if the service provider meets one of the following requirements:

(A) The service provider is unable to engage in any substantial gainful activity by reason of any medically determinable physical or mental impairment that can be expected to result in death or can be expected to last for a continuous period of not less than 12 months. [Corrected on 12/19/05 by 70 FR 75090.]

(B) The service provider is, by reason of any medically determinable physical or mental impairment that can be expected to result in death or can be expected to last for a continuous period of not less than 12 months, receiving income replacement benefits for a period of not less than 3 months under an accident and health plan covering employees of the service provider's employer.

(ii) *Limited plan definition of disability*. An arrangement may provide for a payment upon any disability, and need not provide for a payment upon all disabilities, provided that any disability upon which a payment may be made under the arrangement complies with the provisions of this paragraph (g)(4).

(iii) *Determination of disability*. An arrangement may provide that a service provider will be deemed disabled if determined to be totally disabled by the Social Security Administration. An arrangement may also provide that a service provider will be deemed disabled if determined to be disabled in accordance with a disability insurance program, provided that the definition of disability applied under such disability insurance program complies with the requirements of this paragraph (g)(4).

(5) *Change in the ownership or effective control of a corporation, or a change in the ownership of a substantial portion of the assets of a corporation*—(i) *In general*. Pursuant to section 409A(a)(2)(A)(v), an arrangement may permit a payment upon the occurrence of a change in the ownership of the corporation (as defined in paragraph (g)(5)(v) of this section), a change in effective control of the corporation (as defined in paragraph (g)(5)(vi) of this section), or a change in the ownership of a substantial portion of the assets of the corporation (as defined in paragraph (g)(5)(vii) of this section) (collectively referred to as a change in control event). To qualify as a change in control event, the occurrence of the event must be objectively determinable and any requirement that any other person, such as a plan administrator or board of directors compensation committee, certify the occurrence of a change in control event must be strictly ministerial and not involve any discretionary authority. The arrangement may provide for a payment on any change in control event, and need not provide for a payment on all such events, provided that each event upon which a payment is provided qualifies as a change in control event. For rules regarding the ability of the service recipient to terminate the arrangement and pay amounts of deferred compensation upon a change in control event, see paragraph (h)(2)(viii)(B) of this section.

(ii) *Identification of relevant corporation*—(A) *In general*. To constitute a change in control event as to the service provider, the change in control event must relate to—

(*1*) The corporation for whom the service provider is performing services at the time of the change in control event;

(*2*) The corporation that is liable for the payment of the deferred compensation (or all corporations liable for the payment if more than one corporation is liable); or

(*3*) A corporation that is a majority shareholder of a corporation identified in paragraph (g)(5)(ii)(A)(*1*) or (*2*) of this section, or any corporation in a chain of corporations in which each corporation is a majority shareholder of another corporation in the chain, ending in a corporation identified in paragraph (g)(5)(ii)(A)(*1*) or (*2*) of this section.

(B) *Majority shareholder*. For purposes of this paragraph (g)(5)(ii), a majority shareholder is a shareholder owning more than 50 percent of the total fair market value and total voting power of such corporation.

(C) *Example*. The following example illustrates the rules of this paragraph (g)(5)(ii):

Example. Corporation A is a majority shareholder of Corporation B, which is a majority shareholder of Corporation C. A change in ownership of Corporation B constitutes a change in control event to service providers performing services for Corporation B or Corporation C, and to service providers for which Corporation B or Corporation C is solely liable for payments under the plan (for example, former employees), but is not a change in control event as to Corporation A or any other corporation of which Corporation A is a majority shareholder. Notwithstanding the foregoing, a sale of Corporation B may constitute an independent change in control event for Corporation A, Corporation B and Corporation C if the sale constitutes a change in the ownership of a substantial portion of Corporation A's assets (see paragraph (g)(5)(vii) of this section).

(iii) *Attribution of stock ownership*. For purposes of paragraph (g)(5) of this section, section 318(a) applies to determine stock ownership. Stock underlying a vested option is considered owned by the individual who holds the vested option (and the stock underlying an unvested option is not considered owned by the individual who holds the unvested option). For purposes of the preceding sentence, however, if a vested option is exercisable for stock that is not substantially vested (as defined by § 1.83-3(b) and (j)), the stock underlying the option is not treated as owned by the individual who holds the option.

(iv) *Special rule for certain delayed payments pursuant to a change in control event*. Compensation payable pursuant to the purchase by the service recipient of service recipient stock or a stock right held by a service provider, or payment of amounts of deferred compensation calculated by reference to the value of service recipient stock, may be treated as paid at a specified time or pursuant to a fixed schedule in conformity with the requirements of section 409A if paid on the same schedule and under the same terms and conditions as payments to shareholders generally pursuant to a change in control event described in paragraph (g)(5)(v) of this section (change in the ownership of a corporation) or as payments to the service recipient pursuant to a change in control event described in paragraph (g)(5)(vii) of this section (change in the ownership of a substantial portion of a corporation's assets), and any amounts paid pursuant to such a schedule and such terms and conditions will not be treated as violating the initial or subsequent deferral elections rules, to the extent that such amounts are paid not later than five years after the change in control event.

(v) *Change in the ownership of a corporation*—(A) *In general*. For purposes of section 409A, a change in the ownership of a corporation occurs on the date that any one person, or more than one person acting as a group (as defined in paragraph (g)(5)(v)(B) of this section), acquires ownership of stock of the corporation that, together with stock held by such person or group, constitutes more than 50 percent of the total fair market value or total voting power of the stock of such corporation. However, if any one person, or more than one person acting as a group, is considered to own more than 50 percent of the total fair market value or total voting power of the stock of a corporation, the acquisition of additional stock by the same person or persons is not considered to cause a change in the ownership of the corporation (or to cause a change in the effective control of the corporation (within the meaning of paragraph (g)(5)(vi) of this section)). An increase in the percentage of stock owned by any one person, or persons acting as a group, as a result of a transaction in which the corporation acquires its stock in exchange for property will be treated as an acquisition of stock for purposes of this section. This section applies only when there is a transfer of stock of a corporation (or issuance of stock of a corporation) and stock in such corporation remains outstanding after the transaction (see paragraph (g)(5)(vii) of this section for rules regarding the transfer of assets of a corporation).

(B) *Persons acting as a group*. For purposes of paragraph (g)(5)(v)(A) of this section, persons will not be considered to be acting as a group solely because they purchase or own stock of the same corporation at the same time, or as a result of the same public offering. However, persons will be considered to be acting as a group if they are owners of a corporation that enters into a merger, consolidation, purchase or acquisition of stock, or similar business transaction with the corporation. If a person, including an entity, owns stock in both corporations that enter into a merger, consolidation, purchase or acquisition of stock, or similar transaction, such shareholder is considered to be acting as a group with other shareholders in a corporation prior to the transaction giving rise to the change and not with respect to the ownership interest in the other corporation. See § 1.280G-1, Q&A-27(d), *Example 4*.

(vi) *Change in the effective control of a corporation*—(A) *In general*. For purposes of section 409A, notwithstanding that a corporation has not undergone a change in ownership under paragraph (g)(5)(v) of this section, a change in the effective control of a corporation occurs only on the date that either—

(*1*) Any one person, or more than one person acting as a group (as determined under paragraph (g)(5)(v)(B) of this section), acquires (or has acquired during the 12-month period ending on the date of the most recent acquisition by such person or persons) ownership of stock of the corporation possessing 35 percent or more of the total voting power of the stock of such corporation; or

(*2*) A majority of members of the corporation's board of directors is replaced during any 12-month period by directors whose appointment or election is not endorsed by a majority of the members of the corporation's board of directors prior to the date of the appointment or election, provided that for purposes of this paragraph (g)(5)(vi)(A) the term corporation refers solely to the relevant corporation identified in paragraph (g)(5)(ii) of this section, for which no other corporation is a majority shareholder for purposes of that paragraph (for example, if Corporation A is a publicly held corporation with no majority shareholder, and Corporation A is the majority shareholder of Corporation B, which is the majority shareholder of Corporation C, the term corporation for purposes of this paragraph (g)(5)(vi)(A)(*2*) would refer solely to Corporation A).

(B) *Multiple change in control events.* A change in effective control also may occur in any transaction in which either of the two corporations involved in the transaction has a change in control event under paragraphs (g)(5)(v) or (g)(5)(vii) of this section. Thus, for example, assume Corporation P transfers more than 40 percent of the total gross fair market value of its assets to Corporation O in exchange for 35 percent of O's stock. P has undergone a change in ownership of a substantial portion of its assets under paragraph (g)(5)(vii) of this section and O has a change in effective control under this paragraph (g)(5)(vi) of this section.

(C) *Acquisition of additional control.* If any one person, or more than one person acting as a group, is considered to effectively control a corporation (within the meaning of this paragraph (g)(5)(vi)), the acquisition of additional control of the corporation by the same person or persons is not considered to cause a change in the effective control of the corporation (or to cause a change in the ownership of the corporation within the meaning of paragraph (g)(5)(v) of this section).

(D) *Persons acting as a group.* Persons will not be considered to be acting as a group solely because they purchase or own stock of the same corporation at the same time, or as a result of the same public offering. However, persons will be considered to be acting as a group if they are owners of a corporation that enters into a merger, consolidation, purchase or acquisition of stock, or similar business transaction with the corporation. If a person, including an entity, owns stock in both corporations that enter into a merger, consolidation, purchase or acquisition of stock, or similar transaction, such shareholder is considered to be acting as a group with other shareholders in a corporation only with respect to the ownership in that corporation prior to the transaction giving rise to the change and not with respect to the ownership interest in the other corporation. See § 1.280G-1, Q&A-27(d), *Example 4.*

(vii) *Change in the ownership of a substantial portion of a corporation's assets*—(A) *In general.* Change in the ownership of a substantial portion of a corporation's assets. For purposes of section 409A, a change in the ownership of a substantial portion of a corporation's assets occurs on the date that any one person, or more than one person acting as a group (as determined in paragraph (g)(5)(v)(B) of this section), acquires (or has acquired during the 12-month period ending on the date of the most recent acquisition by such person or persons) assets from the corporation that have a total gross fair market value equal to or more than 40 percent of the total gross fair market value of all of the assets of the corporation immediately prior to such acquisition or acquisitions. For this purpose, gross fair market value means the value of the assets of the corporation, or the value of the assets being disposed of, determined without regard to any liabilities associated with such assets.

(B) *Transfers to a related person*—(*1*) There is no change in control event under this paragraph (g)(5)(vii) when there is a transfer to an entity that is controlled by the shareholders of the transferring corporation immediately after the transfer, as provided in this paragraph (g)(5)(vii)(B). A transfer of assets by a corporation is not treated as a change in the ownership of such assets if the assets are transferred to—

(*i*) A shareholder of the corporation (immediately before the asset transfer) in exchange for or with respect to its stock;

(*ii*) An entity, 50 percent or more of the total value or voting power of which is owned, directly or indirectly, by the corporation;

(*iii*) A person, or more than one person acting as a group, that owns, directly or indirectly, 50 percent or more of the total value or voting power of all the outstanding stock of the corporation; or

(*iv*) An entity, at least 50 percent of the total value or voting power of which is owned, directly or indirectly, by a person described in paragraph (g)(5)(vii)(B)(*1*)(*iii*) of this section.

(*2*) For purposes of this paragraph (g)(5)(vii)(B) and except as otherwise provided, a person's status is determined immediately after the transfer of the assets. For example, a transfer to a corporation in which the transferor corporation has no ownership interest before the transaction, but which is a majority-owned subsidiary of the transferor corporation after the transaction is not treated as a change in the ownership of the assets of the transferor corporation.

(C) *Persons acting as a group.* Persons will not be considered to be acting as a group solely because they purchase assets of the same corporation at the same time. However, persons will be considered to be acting as a group if they are owners of a corporation that enters into a merger, consolidation, purchase or acquisition of assets, or similar business transaction with the corporation. If a person, including an entity shareholder, owns stock in both corporations that enter into a merger, consolidation, purchase or acquisition of assets, or similar transaction, such shareholder is considered to be acting as a group with other shareholders in a corporation only to the extent of the ownership in that corporation prior to the transaction giving rise to the change and not with respect to the ownership interest in the other corporation. See 1.280G-1, Q&A-27(d), *Example 4.*

(6) *Certain back-to-back arrangements*—(i) *In general.* Notwithstanding the generally applicable limitations on payments described under paragraph (a) of this section, an arrangement between a service recipient and a service provider that is also a service recipient (a service provider/service recipient) may provide for payment upon the occurrence of a payment event described in paragraph (a)(1), (2), (3), (5) or (6) of this section, where the time and form of payment is defined as the same time and form of payment provided under an arrangement subject to section 409A between the service provider/service recipient and a specified service provider to the service provider/service recipient, if the arrangement between the service provider/service recipient and the service recipient expressly provides for such time and form of payment and otherwise satisfies the requirements of section 409A.

(ii) *Example.* The provisions of this paragraph (g)(6) are illustrated by the following example:

Example. Company B (service provider/service recipient) provides services to Company C (service recipient). Employee A (service provider) provides services to Company B. Pursuant to a nonqualified deferred compensation plan meeting the requirements of section 409A, Employee A is entitled to a payment of deferred compensation upon a separation from service from Company B. Under an arrangement between Company B and Company C, Company C agrees to pay an amount of deferred compensation to Company B upon Employee A's separation from service from Company B, in accordance with the time and form of payment provided in the nonqualified deferred compensation plan between Employee A and Company B. Provided that the arrangement between Company B and Company C and the arrangement between Employee A and Company B otherwise comply with the requirements of section 409A, Company C's payment to Company B of the amount due upon the separation from service of Employee A from Company B may constitute a permissible payment event for purposes of paragraph (a) of this section.

(h) *Prohibition on acceleration of payments*—(1) *In general.* Except as provided in paragraph (h)(2) of this section, an arrangement that is, or constitutes part of, a nonqualified deferred compensation plan may not permit the acceleration of the time or schedule of any payment or amount scheduled to be paid pursuant to a payment under the arrangement. For purposes of this paragraph (h), an impermissible acceleration does not occur if payment is made in accordance with plan provisions or an election as to the time and form of payment in effect at the time of initial deferral (or added in accordance with the rules applicable to subsequent deferral elections under § 1.409A-2(b)) pursuant to which payment is required to be made on an accelerated schedule as a result of an intervening event that is an event described in paragraph (a)(1), (2), (3), (5) or (6) of this section. For example, a plan may provide that a participant will receive six installment payments commencing at separation from service, and also provide that if the participant dies after such payments commence but before all payments have been made, all remaining amounts will be paid in a lump sum payment. Additionally, it is not an acceleration of the time or schedule of payment of a deferral of compensation if a service recipient waives or accelerates the satisfaction of a condition constituting a substantial risk of forfeiture applicable to such deferral of compensation, provided that the requirements of section 409A (including the requirement that the payment be made upon a permissible payment event) are otherwise satisfied with respect to such deferral of compensation. For example, if a nonqualified deferred compensation arrangement provides for a lump sum payment of the vested benefit upon separation from service, and the benefit vests under the plan only after 10 years of service, it is not a violation of the requirements of section 409A if the service recipient reduces the vesting requirement to 5 years of service, even if a service provider becomes vested as a result and receives a payment in connection with a separation from service before the service provider would have completed 10 years of service.

(2) *Exceptions*—(i) *Domestic relations order.* An arrangement may permit such acceleration of the time or schedule of a payment under the arrangement to an individual other than the service provider as may be necessary to fulfill a domestic relations order (as defined in section 414(p)(1)(B)).

(ii) *Conflicts of interest.* An arrangement may permit such acceleration of the time or schedule of a payment under the arrangement as may be necessary to comply with a certificate of divestiture (as defined in section 1043(b)(2)).

(iii) *Section 457 plans.* An arrangement subject to section 457(f) may permit an acceleration of the time or schedule of a payment to a service provider to pay Federal, state, local and foreign income taxes due upon a vesting event, provided that the amount of such payment is not more than an amount equal to the Federal, state, local and foreign income tax withholding that would have been remitted by the employer if there had been a payment of wages equal to the income includible by the service provider under section 457(f) at the time of the vesting.

(iv) *De minimis and specified amounts*—(A) *In general.* An arrangement that does not otherwise provide for mandatory lump sum payments of benefits that do not exceed a specified amount may be amended to permit the acceleration of the time or schedule of a payment to a service provider under the arrangement, provided that—

(*1*) The payment accompanies the termination of the entirety of the service provider's interest in the arrangement, and all similar arrangements that would constitute a nonqualified deferred compensation plan under § 1.409A-1(c);

(*2*) The payment is made on or before the later of December 31 of the calendar year in which occurs the service provider's separation from service from the service recipient, or the 15 th day of the third month following the service provider's separation from service from the service recipient;

(*3*) The payment is not greater than $10,000; and

(*4*) The participant is provided no election with respect to receipt of the lump sum payment.

(B) *Prospective deferrals.* An amendment described in paragraph (h)(2)(iv)(A) of this section may be made with respect to previously deferred amounts under the arrangement as well as amounts to be deferred in the future. In addition, a nonqualified deferred compensation arrangement that otherwise complies with section 409A may provide, or be amended with regard to future deferrals to provide, that, if a service provider's interest under the arrangement has a value below an amount specified by the plan at the time that amounts are payable under the plan, then the service provider's entire interest under the plan must be distributed as a lump sum payment. However, once such a payment feature applies to an amount deferred, any change or elimination of such feature is subject to the rules governing changes in the time and form of payment.

(v) *Payment of employment taxes.* An arrangement may permit the acceleration of the time or schedule of a payment to pay the Federal Insurance Contributions Act (FICA) tax imposed under section 3101, section 3121(a) and section 3121(v)(2), where applicable, on compensation deferred under the arrangement (the FICA Amount). Additionally, an arrangement may permit the acceleration of the time or schedule of a payment to pay the income tax at source on wages imposed under section 3401 or the corresponding withholding provisions of applicable state, local, or foreign tax laws as a result of the payment of the FICA Amount, and to pay the additional income tax at source on wages attributable to the pyramiding section 3401 wages and taxes. However, the total payment under this acceleration provision must not exceed the aggregate of the FICA Amount, and the income tax withholding related to such FICA Amount.

(vi) *Payments upon income inclusion under section 409A.* An arrangement may permit the acceleration of the time or schedule of a payment to a service provider under the plan at any time the arrangement fails to meet the requirements of section 409A and these regulations. Such payment may not exceed the amount required to be included in income as a result of the failure to comply with the requirements of section 409A and the regulations.

(vii) *Cancellation of deferrals following an unforeseeable emergency or hardship distribution.* An arrangement may permit a cancellation of a service provider's deferral election due to an unforeseeable emergency or a hardship distribution pursuant to § 1.401(k)-1(d)(3). The deferral election must be cancelled, and not postponed or otherwise delayed, such that any later deferral election will be subject to the provisions governing initial deferral elections. See § 1.409A-2(a).

(viii) *Arrangement terminations.* An arrangement may permit an acceleration of the time and form of a payment where the right to the payment arises due to a termination of the arrangement in accordance with one of the following:

(A) The service recipient's discretion under the terms of the arrangement to terminate the arrangement within 12 months of a corporate dissolution taxed under section 331, or with the approval of a bankruptcy court pursuant to 11 U.S.C. § 503(b)(1)(A), provided that the amounts deferred under the plan are included in the participants' gross incomes in the latest of—

(*1*) The calendar year in which the plan termination occurs;

(*2*) The calendar year in which the amount is no longer subject to a substantial risk of forfeiture; or

(*3*) The first calendar year in which the payment is administratively practicable.

(B) The service recipient's discretion under the terms of the arrangement to terminate the arrangement within the 30 days preceding or the 12 months following a change in control event (as defined in § 1.409A-3(g)(5)(i)). For purposes of this paragraph (h)(2)(viii), an arrangement will be treated as terminated only if all substantially similar arrangements sponsored by the service recipient are terminated, so that the participant in the arrangement and all participants under substantially similar arrangements are required to receive all amounts of compensation deferred under the terminated arrangements within 12 months of the date of termination of the arrangements. [Corrected on 12/19/05 by 70 FR 75090.]

(C) The service recipient's discretion under the terms of the arrangement to terminate the arrangement, provided that—

(*1*) All arrangements sponsored by the service recipient that would be aggregated with any terminated arrangement under § 1.409A-1(c) if the same service provider participated in all of the arrangements are terminated;

(*2*) No payments other than payments that would be payable under the terms of the arrangements if the termination had not occurred are made within 12 months of the termination of the arrangements;

(*3*) All payments are made within 24 months of the termination of the arrangements; and

(*4*) The service recipient does not adopt a new arrangement that would be aggregated with any terminated arrangement under § 1.409A-1(c) if the same service provider participated in both arrangements, at any time within five years following the date of termination of the arrangement.

(D) Such other events and conditions as the Commissioner may prescribe in generally applicable guidance published in the Internal Revenue Bulletin (see § 601.601(d)(2) of this chapter).

(ix) *Certain distributions to avoid a nonallocation year under section 409(p).* An arrangement may provide for an acceleration of payment to prevent the occurrence of a nonallocation year (within the meaning of section 409(p)(3)) in the plan year of the employee stock ownership plan next following the current plan year, provided that the amount distributed may not exceed 125 percent of the minimum amount of distribution necessary to avoid the occurrence of a nonallocation year. Solely for purposes of determining permissible distributions under this paragraph (h)(2)(ix), synthetic equity (within the meaning of section 409(p)(6)(C)) granted during the current employee stock ownership plan plan year is disregarded for purposes of determining whether the subsequent plan year would result in a nonallocation year.

(3) *Nonqualified deferred compensation arrangements linked to qualified plans.* With respect to amounts deferred under an arrangement that is, or constitutes part of, a nonqualified deferred compensation plan, where under the terms of the nonqualified deferred compensation arrangement the amount deferred under the plan is the amount determined under the formula determining benefits under a qualified em-

ployer plan (as defined in §1.409A-1(a)(2)) applied without respect to one or more limitations applicable to qualified employer plans under the Internal Revenue Code or other applicable law, or is determined as an amount offset by some or all of the benefits provided under the qualified employer plan, the operation of the qualified employer plan with respect to changes in benefit limitations applicable to qualified employer plans under the Internal Revenue Code or other applicable law, does not constitute an acceleration of a payment under the non-qualified deferred compensation arrangement regardless of whether such operation results in a decrease of amounts deferred under the nonqualified deferred compensation arrangement. In addition, with respect to such nonqualified deferred compensation arrangements, the following actions or failures to act will not constitute an acceleration of a payment under the nonqualified deferred compensation arrangement regardless of whether in accordance with the terms of the nonqualified deferred compensation arrangement, the actions or inactions result in a decrease in the amounts deferred under the arrangement:

(i) A service provider's action or inaction under the qualified employer plan with respect to whether to elect to receive a subsidized benefit or an ancillary benefit under the qualified employer plan.

(ii) The amendment of a qualified employer plan to increase benefits provided under the qualified plan, or to add or remove a subsidized benefit or an ancillary benefit.

(iii) A service provider's action or inaction with respect to an elective deferral election under a qualified employer plan subject to section 402(g), including an adjustment to a deferral election made during a calendar year, provided that for any given calendar year, the service provider's actions or inactions do not result in a decrease in the amounts deferred under all nonqualified deferred compensation plans in which the service provider participates in excess of an amount equal to the limit with respect to elective deferrals under section 402(g) in effect for the taxable year in which such action or inaction occurs.

(iv) A service provider's action or inaction under a qualified employer plan with respect to elective deferrals or after-tax contributions by the service provider to the qualified employer plan that affects the amounts that are credited under a nonqualified deferred compensation arrangement as matching amounts or other amounts contingent on service provider elective deferrals or after-tax contributions, provided that such matching or contingent amounts, as applicable, are either forfeited or never credited under the nonqualified deferred compensation arrangement in the absence of such service provider's elective deferral or after-tax contribution, and provided further that for any given calendar year, the service provider's actions and inactions do not result in a decrease in the amounts deferred under all nonqualified deferred compensation plans in which the service provider participates in excess of an amount equal to the limit with respect to elective deferrals under section 402(g) in effect for the taxable year in which such action or inaction occurs. See §1.409A-2(b)(6), *Example 12* and *Example 13*.

§1.409A-4 Calculation of income inclusion. [Reserved].

§1.409A-5 Funding. [Reserved].

§1.409A-6 Statutory effective dates.

(a) *Statutory effective dates*—(1) *In general.* Except as otherwise provided in this section, section 409A is effective with respect to amounts deferred in taxable years beginning after December 31, 2004, and amounts deferred in taxable years beginning before January 1, 2005, if the plan under which the deferral is made is materially modified after October 3, 2004. Section 409A is effective with respect to earnings on amounts deferred only to the extent that section 409A is effective with respect to the amounts deferred. Accordingly, section 409A is not effective with respect to earnings on amounts deferred before January 1, 2005, unless section 409A is effective with respect to the amounts deferred.

(2) *Identification of date of deferral for statutory effective date purposes.* For purposes of determining whether section 409A is applicable with respect to an amount, the amount is considered deferred before January 1, 2005, if before January 1, 2005, the service provider had a legally binding right to be paid the amount, and the right to the amount was earned and vested. For purposes of this paragraph (a)(2), a right to an amount was earned and vested only if the amount was not subject to a substantial risk of forfeiture (as defined in §1.83-3(c)) or a requirement to perform further services. Amounts to which the service provider did not have a legally binding right before January 1, 2005 (for example because the service recipient retained discretion to reduce the amount), will not be considered deferred before January 1, 2005. In addition, amounts to which the service provider had a legally binding right before January 1, 2005, but the right to which was subject to a substantial risk of forfeiture or a requirement to perform further services after December 31, 2004, are not considered deferred before January 1, 2005, for purposes of the effective date. Notwithstanding the foregoing, an amount to which the service provider had a legally binding right before January 1, 2005, but for which the service provider was required to continue performing services to retain the right only through the completion of the payroll period (as defined in §1.409A-1(b)(3)) that includes December 31, 2004, is not treated as subject to a requirement to perform further services (or a substantial risk of forfeiture) for purposes of the effective date. For purposes of this paragraph (a)(2), a stock option, stock appreciation right or similar compensation that on or before December 31, 2004, was immediately exercisable for cash or substantially vested property (as defined in §1.83-3(b)) is treated as earned and vested, regardless of whether the right would terminate if the service provider ceased providing services for the service recipient.

(3) *Calculation of amount of compensation deferred for statutory effective date purposes*—(i) *Nonaccount balance plans.* The amount of compensation deferred before January 1, 2005, under a nonqualified deferred compensation plan that is a nonaccount balance plan (as defined in §31.3121(v)(2)-1(c)(2)(i) of this chapter) equals the present value as of December 31, 2004, of the amount to which the service provider would be entitled under the plan if the service provider voluntarily terminated services without cause on December 31, 2004, and received a payment of the benefits with the maximum value available from the plan on the earliest possible date allowed under the plan to receive a payment of benefits following the termination of services. Notwithstanding the foregoing, for any subsequent calendar year, the grandfathered amount may increase to equal the present value of the benefit the service provider actually becomes entitled to, determined under the terms of the plan (including applicable limits under the Internal Revenue Code), as in effect on October 3, 2004, without regard to any further services rendered by the service provider after December 31, 2004, or any other events affecting the amount of or the entitlement to benefits (other than a participant election with respect to the time or form of an available benefit).

(ii) *Account balance plans.* The amount of compensation deferred before January 1, 2005, under a nonqualified deferred compensation plan that is an account balance plan (as defined in §31.3121(v)(2)-1(c)(1)(ii) of this chapter) equals the portion of the service provider's account balance as of December 31, 2004, the right to which is earned and vested (as defined in paragraph (a)(2) of this section) as of December 31, 2004.

(iii) *Equity-based compensation plans.* For purposes of determining the amounts deferred before January 1, 2005, under an equity-based compensation plan, the rules of paragraph (a)(3)(ii) of this section governing account balance plans are applied except that the account balance is deemed to be the amount of the payment available to the service provider on December 31, 2004 (or that would be available to the service provider if the right were immediately exercisable) the right to which is earned and vested (as defined in paragraph (a)(2) of this section) as of December 31, 2004. For this purpose, the payment available to the service provider excludes any exercise price or other amount that must be paid by the service provider.

(iv) *Earnings.* Earnings on amounts deferred under a plan before January 1, 2005, include only income (whether actual or notional) attributable to the amounts deferred under a plan as of December 31, 2004, or such income. For example, notional interest earned under the plan on amounts deferred in an account balance plan as of December 31, 2004, generally will be treated as earnings on amounts deferred under the plan before January 1, 2005. Similarly, an increase in the amount of payment available pursuant to a stock option, stock appreciation right or other equity-based compensation above the amount of payment available as of December 31, 2004, due to appreciation in the underlying stock after December 31, 2004, or accrual of other earnings such as dividends, is treated as earnings on the amount deferred. In the case of a nonaccount balance plan, earnings include the increase, due solely to the passage of time, in the present value of the future payments to which the service provider has obtained a legally binding right, the present value of which constituted the amounts deferred under the plan before January 1, 2005. Thus, for each year, there will be an increase (determined using the same interest rate used to determine the amounts deferred under the plan before January 1, 2005) resulting from the shortening of the discount period before the future payments are made, plus, if applicable, an increase in the present value resulting from the service provider's survivorship during the year. However, an increase in the potential benefits under a nonaccount balance plan due to, for example, an application of an increase in compensation after December 31, 2004, to a final average pay plan or subsequent eligibility for an early retirement subsidy, does not constitute earnings on the amounts deferred under the plan before January 1, 2005.

(v) *Definition of plan.* For purposes of this paragraph (a), the term *plan* has the same meaning provided in § 1.409A-1(c), except that the provisions treating all nonaccount balance plans under which compensation is deferred as a single plan does not apply for purposes of the actuarial assumptions used in paragraph (a)(3)(ii) of this section. Accordingly, different reasonable actuarial assumptions may be used to calculate the amounts deferred by a service provider in two different arrangements each of which constitutes a nonaccount balance plan.

(4) *Material modifications*—(i) *In general.* Except as otherwise provided, a modification of a plan is a material modification if a benefit or right existing as of October 3, 2004, is materially enhanced or a new material benefit or right is added, and such material enhancement or addition affects amounts earned and vested before January 1, 2005. Such material benefit enhancement or addition is a material modification whether it occurs pursuant to an amendment or the service recipient's exercise of discretion under the terms of the plan. For example, an amendment to a plan to add a provision that payments of deferred amounts earned and vested before January 1, 2005, may be allowed upon request if service providers are required to forfeit 20 percent of the amount of the payment (a haircut) would be a material modification to the plan. Similarly, a material modification would occur if a service recipient exercised discretion to accelerate vesting of a benefit under the plan to a date on or before December 31, 2004. However, it is not a material modification for a service recipient to exercise discretion over the time and manner of payment of a benefit to the extent such discretion is provided under the terms of the plan as of October 3, 2004. It is not a material modification for a service provider to exercise a right permitted under the plan as in effect on October 3, 2004. The amendment of a plan to bring the plan into compliance with the provisions of section 409A will not be treated as a material modification. However, a plan amendment or the exercise of discretion under the terms of the plan that materially enhances an existing benefit or right or adds a new material benefit or right will be considered a material modification even if the enhanced or added benefit would be permitted under section 409A. For example, the addition of a right to a payment upon an unforeseeable emergency of an amount earned and vested before January 1, 2005, would be considered a material modification. The reduction of an existing benefit is not a material modification. For example, the removal of a haircut provision generally would not constitute a material modification. The establishment of or contributions to a trust or other arrangement from which benefits under the plan are to be paid is not a material modification of the plan, provided that the contribution to the trust or other arrangement would not otherwise cause an amount to be includible in the service provider's gross income.

(ii) *Adoptions of new arrangements.* It is presumed that the adoption of a new arrangement or the grant of an additional benefit under an existing arrangement after October 3, 2004, and before January 1, 2005, constitutes a material modification of a plan. However, the presumption may be rebutted by demonstrating that the adoption of the arrangement or grant of the additional benefit is consistent with the service recipient's historical compensation practices. For example, the presumption that the grant of a discounted stock option on November 1, 2004, is a material modification of a plan may be rebutted by demonstrating that the grant was consistent with the historic practice of granting substantially similar discounted stock options (both as to terms and amounts) each November for a significant number of years. Notwithstanding paragraph (a)(4)(i) and this paragraph (a)(4)(ii), the grant of an additional benefit under an existing arrangement that consists of a deferral of additional compensation not otherwise provided under the plan as of October 3, 2004, will be treated as a material modification of the plan only as to the additional deferral of compensation, if the plan explicitly identifies the additional deferral of compensa-

tion and provides that the additional deferral of compensation is subject to section 409A. Accordingly, amendments to conform a plan to the requirements of section 409A with respect to deferrals under a plan occurring after December 31, 2004, will not constitute a material modification of the plan with respect to amounts deferred that are earned and vested on or before December 31, 2004, provided that there is no concurrent material modification with respect to the amount of, or rights to, amounts deferred that were earned and vested on or before December 31, 2004. Similarly, a grant of an additional benefit under a new arrangement adopted after October 3, 2004, and before January 1, 2005, will not be treated as a material modification of an existing plan to the extent that the new arrangement explicitly identifies additional deferrals of compensation and provides that the additional deferrals of compensation are subject to section 409A.

(iii) *Suspension or termination of a plan.* A cessation of deferrals under, or termination of, a plan, pursuant to the provisions of such plan, is not a material modification. Amending an arrangement to stop future deferrals thereunder is not a material modification of the arrangement or the plan. Amending an arrangement to provide participants an election whether to terminate participation in a plan constitutes a material modification of the plan.

(iv) *Changes to investment measures—account balance plans.* With respect to an account balance plan (as defined in § 31.3121(v)(2)-1(c)(1)(ii) of this chapter), it is not a material modification to change a notional investment measure to, or to add to existing investment measures, an investment measure that qualifies as a predetermined actual investment within the meaning of § 31.3121(v)(2)-1(d)(2) of this chapter or, for any given taxable year, reflects a reasonable rate of interest (determined in accordance with § 31.3121(v)(2)-1(d)(2)(i)(C) of this chapter). For this purpose, if with respect to an amount deferred for a period, a plan provides for a fixed rate of interest to be credited, and the rate is to be reset under the plan at a specified future date that is not later than the end of the fifth calendar year that begins after the beginning of the period, the rate is reasonable at the beginning of the period, and the rate is not changed before the reset date, then the rate will be treated as reasonable in all future periods before the reset date.

(v) *Rescission of modifications.* Any modification to the terms of a plan that would inadvertently result in treatment as a material modification under this section is not considered a material modification of the plan to the extent the modification in the terms of the plan is rescinded by the earlier of a date before the right is exercised (if the change grants a discretionary right) or the last day of the calendar year during which such change occurred. Thus, for example, if a service recipient modifies the terms of a plan on March 1 to allow an election of a new change in the time or form of payment without realizing that such a change constituted a material modification that would subject the plan to the requirements of section 409A, and the modification is rescinded on November 1, then if no change in the time or form of payment has been made pursuant to the modification before November 1, the plan is not considered materially modified under this section.

(vi) *Definition of plan.* For purposes of this paragraph (a)(4), the term *plan* has the same meaning provided in § 1.409A-1(c), except that the provision treating all account balance plans under which compensation is deferred as a single plan, all nonaccount balance plans under which compensation is deferred as a separate single plan, all separation pay arrangements due to an actual involuntary separation from service or participation in a window program as a separate single plan, and all other nonqualified deferred compensation plans as a separate single plan, does not apply.

(b) [Reserved].

Mark E. Matthews

Deputy Commissioner of Services and Enforcement.

¶ 20,261U

IRS proposed regulations: Form 5500: Information returns: Extension of time to file.— The IRS has issued final, temporary and proposed regulations regarding the forms necessary to request filing extensions for information returns, the Form 5500 series, as well as other forms. The preamble to the final and temporary regulations, issued concurrently, is located at ¶ 24,508A.

The proposed regulations, which were published in the Federal Register on November 7, 2005 (70 FR 67397), are reproduced in relevant part below.

[4830-01-p]

DEPARTMENT OF THE TREASURY

Internal Revenue Service

26 CFR Parts 1, 25, 26, 53, 55, 156, 157, and 301

[REG-144898-04]

RIN 1545-BE62

Extension of Time for Filing Returns

AGENCY: Internal Revenue Service (IRS), Treasury.

ACTION: Notice of proposed rulemaking and notice of proposed rulemaking by cross-reference to temporary regulations.

SUMMARY: In the Rules and Regulations section of this issue of the **Federal Register**, the IRS is issuing final and temporary regulations relating to the simplification of procedures for automatic extensions of time to file certain returns. The text of those regulations also serves as the text of these proposed regulations.

DATES: Written or electronically generated comments and requests for a public hearing must be received by February 6, 2006.

ADDRESSES: Send submissions to: CC:PA:LPD:PR (REG-144898-04), room 5203, Internal Revenue Service, PO Box 7604, Ben Franklin Station, Washington, DC 20044. Submissions may be hand delivered Monday through Friday between the hours of 8 am and 4 pm to: CC:PA:LPD:PR (REG-144898-04), Courier's Desk, Internal Revenue Service, 1111 Constitution Avenue, NW., Washington, DC. Alternatively, taxpayers may submit comments electronically via the IRS Internet site at *www.irs.gov/regs* or via the Federal eRulemaking Portal at *www.regulations.gov* (IRS and REG-144898-04).

FOR FURTHER INFORMATION CONTACT: Concerning the proposed regulations, Allen D. Madison, (202) 622-4940; concerning submissions of comments and requests for a public hearing, LaNita Van Dyke (202) 622-7180 (not toll-free numbers).

SUPPLEMENTARY INFORMATION:

Background and Explanation of Provisions

Temporary regulations in the Rules and Regulations section of this issue of the **Federal Register** amend 26 CFR parts 1, 25, 26, 53, 55, 156, 157, and 301 relating to section 6081. The temporary regulations allow taxpayers required to file an individual income tax return an automatic six-month extension if taxpayers submit an application on Form 4868, "Application for Automatic Extension of Time To File a U.S. Individual Income Tax Return." The temporary regulations also allow taxpayers who previously submitted three-month extension requests on Form 8736, "Application for Automatic Extension of Time to File U.S. Return for a Partnership, REMIC, or for Certain Trusts" and requests for additional three-month extensions on Form 8800, "Application for Additional Extension of Time to File U.S. Return for a Partnership, REMIC, or for Certain Trusts," an automatic six-month extension of time to file if an application is submitted on Form 7004, "Application for Automatic 6-Month Extension of Time To File Certain Business Income Tax, Information, and Other Returns."

* * *

The temporary regulations also provide that taxpayers that requested additional time to file certain excise, income, information, and other returns by submitting Form 2758, "Application for Extension of Time To File Certain Excise, Income, Information, and Other Returns," may now request an automatic six-month extension of time to file by filing Form 7004.

The temporary regulations also allow administrators and sponsors of employee benefit plans subject to Employee Retirement Income Security Act of 1974 (ERISA) to report information concerning the plans and direct entities requesting an extension to use Form 5558, "Application for Extension of Time To File Certain Employee Plan Returns," for an automatic two and one-half-month extension of time to file.

* * *

The text of those regulations also serves as the text of these proposed regulations. The preamble to the temporary regulations explains the amendments.

Special Analyses

It has been determined that this notice of proposed rulemaking is not a significant regulatory action as defined in Executive Order 12866. Therefore, a regulatory assessment is not required. It also has been determined that section 553(b) of the Administrative Procedure Act (5 U.S.C. chapter 5) does not apply to these regulations, and, because these regulations do not impose a collection of information on small entities, the Regulatory Flexibility Act (5 U.S.C. chapter 6) does not apply. Pursuant to section 7805(f) of the Internal Revenue Code, this notice of proposed rulemaking will be submitted to the Chief Counsel for Advocacy of the Small Business Administration for comment on their impact.

Comments and Requests for a Public Hearing

Before these proposed regulations are adopted as final regulations, consideration will be given to any written (a signed original and 8 copies) and electronic comments that are submitted timely to the IRS. The IRS and Treasury specifically request comments on the clarity of the proposed regulations and how they can be made easier to understand. All comments will be available for public inspection and copying. A public hearing may be scheduled if requested in writing by any person that timely submits comments. If a public hearing is scheduled, notice of the date, time, and place for the public hearing will be published in the **Federal Register.**

Drafting Information

The principal author of these regulations is Tracey B. Leibowitz, of the Office of the Associate Chief Counsel (Procedure and Administration), Administrative Provisions and Judicial Practice Division.

List of Subjects

26 CFR Part 1

Income taxes, Reporting and recordkeeping requirements.

* * *

Proposed Amendments to the Regulations

Accordingly, 26 CFR parts 1, 25, 26, 53, 55, 156, 157, and 301 are proposed to be amended to read as follows:

PART 1—INCOME TAXES

* * *

Par. 6. Section 1.6081-5 is amended by revising paragraph (b) to read as follows:

§ 1.6081-5 Extensions of time in the case of certain partnerships, corporations, and U.S. citizens and residents.

* * * * *

(b) [The text of proposed § 1.6081-5(b) is the same as the text of § 1.6081-5T(b) published elsewhere in this issue of the **Federal Register**].

* * * * *

* * *

Par. 10. Section 1.6081-11 is added to read as follows:

§ 1.6081-11 Automatic extension of time for filing certain employee plan returns.

[The text of proposed § 1.6081-11 is the same as the text of § 1.6081-11T published elsewhere in this issue of the **Federal Register**].

* * *

Mark E. Matthews,

Deputy Commissioner for Services and Enforcement.

CERTIFIED COPY

DALE GOODE

¶ 20,261V

IRS proposed regulations: Defined benefit plans: Funding requirements: Current liability: Mortality tables.— The IRS has released proposed regulations that include mortality tables to be used in determining current liability. The tables are used by certain defined benefit pension plans to determine current liability under Code Sec. 412(l)(7). Code Sec. 412(l) generally imposes additional funding requirements for certain plans having unfunded current liability. (Code Sec. 412 corresponds to ERISA § 302.)

The proposed regulations, which were published in the Federal Register on December 2, 2005 (70 FR 72260), are reproduced below.

DEPARTMENT OF THE TREASURY

Internal Revenue Service

26 CFR Part 1

[REG-124988-05]

RIN 1545-BE72

Updated Mortality Tables for Determining Current Liability

AGENCY: Internal Revenue Service (IRS), Treasury

ACTION: Notice of proposed rulemaking and notice of public hearing.

SUMMARY: This document contains proposed regulations under section 412(l)(7)(C)(ii) of the Internal Revenue Code (Code) and section 302(d)(7)(C)(ii) of the Employee Retirement Income Security Act of 1974 (ERISA) (Public Law 93-406, 88 Stat. 829). These regulations provide the public with guidance regarding mortality tables to be used in determining current liability under section 412(l)(7) of the Code and section 302(d)(7) of ERISA. These regulations affect plan sponsors and administrators, and participants in and beneficiaries of, certain retirement plans.

DATES: Written or electronic comments and requests to speak and outlines of topics to be discussed at the public hearing scheduled for April 19, 2006, at 10 a.m., must be received by March 29, 2006.

ADDRESSES: Send submissions to: CC:PA:LPD:PR (REG-124988-05), room 5226, Internal Revenue Service, POB 7604, Ben Franklin Station, Washington, DC 20044. Submissions may be hand-delivered Monday through Friday between the hours of 8 a.m. and 4 p.m. to: CC:PA:LPD:PR (REG-124988-05), Courier(s Desk, Internal Revenue Service, 1111 Constitution Avenue, NW., Washington, DC. Alternatively, taxpayers may submit comments electronically directly to the IRS Internet site at *www.irs.gov/regs*. The public hearing will be held in the Auditorium, Internal Revenue Building, 1111 Constitution Avenue, NW., Washington, DC.

FOR FURTHER INFORMATION CONTACT: Concerning the regulations, Bruce Perlin or Linda Marshall at (202) 622-6090 (not a toll-free number); concerning submissions and the hearing and/or to be placed on the building access list to attend the hearing, Treena Garrett at (202) 622-7180 (not toll-free numbers).

SUPPLEMENTARY INFORMATION:

Background

Section 412 of the Internal Revenue Code provides minimum funding requirements with respect to certain defined benefit pension plans.[1] Section 412(l) provides additional funding requirements for certain of these plans, based in part on a plan's unfunded current liability, as defined in section 412(l)(8).

Pursuant to section 412(c)(6), if the otherwise applicable minimum funding requirement exceeds the plan's full funding limitation (defined in section 412(c)(7) as the excess of a specified measure of plan liability over the plan assets), then the minimum funding for the year is reduced by that excess. Under section 412(c)(7)(E), the full funding limitation cannot be less than the excess of 90% of the plan's current liability (including the expected increase in current liability due to benefits accruing during the plan year) over the value of the plan's assets. For this purpose, the term *current liability* generally has the same meaning given that term under section 412(l)(7).

Section 412(l)(7)(C)(ii) provides that, for purposes of determining current liability in plan years beginning on or after January 1, 1995, the mortality table used is the table prescribed by the Secretary. Under section 412(l)(7)(C)(ii)(I), the initial mortality table used in determining current liability under section 412(l)(7) must be based on the prevailing commissioners' standard table (described in section 807(d)(5)(A)) used to determine reserves for group annuity contracts issued on January 1, 1993. For purposes of section 807(d)(5), Rev. Rul.

92-19 (1992-1 C.B. 227) specifies the prevailing commissioners' standard table used to determine reserves for group annuity contracts issued on January 1, 1993, as the 1983 Group Annuity Mortality Table (1983 GAM). Accordingly, Rev. Rul. 95-28 (1995-1 C.B. 74) sets forth two gender-specific mortality tables — based on 1983 GAM — for purposes of detemining current liability for partcipants who are not entitled to disability benefits.[2]

Section 412(l)(7)(C)(iii)(I) specifies that the Secretary is to establish different mortality tables to be used to determine current liability for individuals who are entitled to benefits under the plan on account of disability. One such set of tables is to apply to individuals whose disabilities occur in plan years beginning before January 1, 1995, and a second set of tables for individuals whose disabilities occur in plan years beginning on or after such date. Under section 412(l)(7)(C)(iii)(II), the separate tables for disabilities that occur in plan years beginning after December 31, 1994 apply only with respect to individuals who are disabled within the meaning of title II of the Social Security Act and the regulations thereunder. Rev. Rul. 96-7 (1996-1 C.B. 59) sets forth the mortality tables established under section 412(l)(7)(C)(iii).

Under section 412(l)(7)(C)(ii)(III), the Secretary of the Treasury is required to periodically (at least every 5 years) review any tables in effect under that subsection and, to the extent necessary, by regulation update the tables to reflect the actual experience of pension plans and projected trends in such experience. Section 412(l)(7)(C)(ii)(II) provides that the updated tables are to take into account the results of available independent studies of mortality of individuals covered by pension plans. Pursuant to section 412(l)(7)(C)(ii)(II), any new mortality tables prescribed by regulation can be effective no earlier than the first plan year beginning after December 31, 1999. Under section 412(l)(10), increases in current liability arising from the adoption of such a new mortality table generally are required to be amortized over a 10-year period.

In order to facilitate the review of the applicable mortality tables pursuant to section 412(l)(7)(C)(ii)(III), Rev. Rul. 95-28 requested comments concerning the mortality table to be used for determining current liability for plan years beginning after December 31, 1999, and information on existing or upcoming independent studies of mortality of individuals covered by pension plans. In Announcement 2000-7 (2000-1 C.B. 586), the IRS and the Treasury Department also requested comments regarding mortality tables to be used for determining current liability for plan years beginning after December 31, 1999, but indicated that it was anticipated that in no event would there be any change in the mortality tables for plan years beginning before January 1, 2001.

Notice 2003-62 (2003-2 C.B. 576) was issued as part of the periodic review by the IRS and the Treasury Department of the mortality tables used in determining current liability under section 412(l)(7). At the time the Notice 2003-62 was issued, the IRS and the Treasury Department were aware of two reviews of mortality experience for retirement plan participants undertaken by the Retirement Plans Experience Committee of the Society of Actuaries (the UP-94 Study and the RP-2000 Mortality Tables Report),[3] and commentators were invited to submit any other independent studies of pension plan mortality experience. Notice 2003-62 also requested the submission of studies regarding projected trends in mortality experience. With respect to projecting mortality improvements, the IRS and the Treasury Department requested comments regarding the advantages and disadvantages of reflecting these trends on an ongoing basis through the use of generational, modified generational, or sequentially static mortality tables.

In addition, Notice 2003-62 requested comments on whether certain risk factors should be taken into account in predicting an individual's mortality. Comments were requested as to the extent that separate mortality tables should be prescribed that take into account these factors, with particular attention paid to the administrative issues in applying such distinctions. In this regard, comments were specifically

---

[1] Section 302 of ERISA sets forth funding rules that are parallel to those in section 412 of the Code. Under section 101 of Reorganization Plan No. 4 of 1978 (43 FR 47713) and section 302 of ERISA, the Secretary of the Treasury has interpretive jurisdiction over the subject matter addressed in these proposed regulations for purposes of ERISA, as well as the Code. Thus, these proposed Treasury regulations issued under section 412 of the Code apply as well for purposes of section 302 of ERISA.

[2] Section 417(e)(3)(A)(ii)(I) requires the present value of certain distributions to be determined using a table prescribed by the Secretary based on the prevailing commissioners' standard table (described in section 807(d)(5)(A)) used to determine reserves for group annuity contracts issued on the date as of which present value is being determined. Thus, in contrast to the mortality table initially prescribed for determining current liability under section 412(l)(7)(C)(ii)(I), the mortality table used to determine present value under section 417(e)(3)(A)(ii)(I) is not fixed as of a specified date but, rather, must be updated

when the prevailing commissioners' standard table changes. Rev. Rul. 95-6 (1995-1 C.B. 80) set forth tables under section 417(e)(3)(A)(ii)(I) based on 1983 GAM, which was the prevailing commissioners' standard table at that time. The 1994 Group Annuity Reserving Table became the prevailing commissioners' standard table under section 807(d)(5)(A) for annuities issued on or after January 1, 1999. See Rev. Rul. 2001-38 (2001-2 C.B. 124). Accordingly, Rev. Rul. 2001-62 (2001-2 C.B. 632) required plans to adopt a new mortality table (based on the 1994 Group Annuity Reserving Table) for calculating the minimum present value of distributions pursuant to section 417(e).

[3] The UP-94 Study, prepared by the UP-94 Task Force of the Society of Actuaries, was published in the Transactions of the Society of Actuaries, Vol. XLVII (1995), p. 819. The RP-2000 Mortality Table Report was released in July, 2000. Society of Actuaries, RP-2000 Mortality Tables Report, at *http://www.soa.org/ccm/content/research-publications/experience-studies-tools/the-rp-2000-mortality-tables/*.

requested as to how it would be determined which category an individual fits into, the extent to which an individual, once categorized, remains in that same category, the classification of individuals for whom adequate information is unavailable, whether distinctions are applicable to beneficiaries, and the extent to which distinctions may overlap or work at cross purposes. Some examples of factors that were listed in Notice 2003-62 are the following: gender, tobacco use, job classification, annuity size, and income. Comments were also requested as to whether classification systems, if permitted, should be mandatory or optional. A number of comments were submitted regarding the issues identified in Notice 2003-62.

The IRS and the Treasury Department have reviewed the mortality tables that are used for purposes of determining current liability for participants and beneficiaries (other than disabled participants). The existing mortality table for determining current liability (1983 GAM) was compared to independent studies of mortality of individuals covered by pension plans, after reflecting projected trends for mortality improvement through 2007. The comparison indicates that the 1983 GAM is no longer appropriate for determining current liability. For example, comparing the RP-2000 Combined Healthy Mortality Table for males projected to 2007 (when this proposed regulation would take effect) with the 1983 GAM shows that a current mortality table reflects a 52% decrease in the number of expected deaths at age 50, a 26% decrease at 65, and an 19% decrease at age 80. Comparing annuity values derived under these updated mortality rates with annuity values determined under the 1983 GAM shows an increase in present value of 12% for a 35-year-old male with a deferred annuity payable at age 65, a 5% increase for a 55-year-old male with an immediate annuity, and a 7% increase for a 75-year-old male with an immediate annuity (all calculated at a 6% interest rate). Female mortality rates also changed, although with a different pattern. For females, the number of expected deaths decreased by 10% at age 50, but increased by 33% at age 65 and increased by 2% at age 80.[4] Comparing annuity values derived under these updated mortality rates with annuity values determined under the 1983 GAM shows a decrease in present value of 3% for a 35-year-old female with a deferred annuity payable at age 65, a 2% decrease for a 55-year-old female with an immediate annuity, and a 2% decrease for a 75-year-old female with an immediate annuity (all calculated at a 6% interest rate).

Based on this review of the 1983 GAM compared to more recent mortality experience, the IRS and Treasury Department have determined that updated mortality tables should be used to determine current liability for participants and beneficiaries (other than disabled participants).[5]

Explanation of Provisions

The proposed regulations would set forth the methodology the IRS and Treasury would use to establish mortality tables to be used under section 412(l)(7)(C)(ii) to determine current liability for participants and beneficiaries (other than disabled participants). The mortality tables that would apply for the 2007 plan year are set forth in the proposed regulations. The mortality tables that would be used for subsequent plan years would be published in the Internal Revenue Bulletin. Comments are requested regarding whether it would be desirable to publish a series of tables for each of a number of years (such as five years) along with final regulations, with tables for subsequent years to be published in the Internal Revenue Bulletin.

These new mortality tables would be based on the tables contained in the RP-2000 Mortality Tables Report. Commentators generally recommended that the RP-2000 mortality tables be the basis for the mortality tables used under section 412(l)(7)(C)(ii) (although one commentator urged that large employers be permitted to use mortality tables tailored to their actual mortality experience). The IRS and the Treasury Department have reviewed the RP-2000 mortality tables and the accompanying report published by the Society of Actuaries, and have determined that the RP-2000 mortality tables form the best available basis for predicting mortality of pension plan participants and beneficiaries (other than disabled participants) based on pension plan experience and expected trends. Accordingly, the proposed regulations would change the mortality tables used to determine current liability from tables based on 1983 GAM to updated tables based on the RP-2000 mortality tables. As under the currently applicable mortality tables, the mortality tables set forth in these proposed regulations are

gender-distinct because of significant differences between expected male mortality and expected female mortality.

The proposed regulations would provide for separate sets of tables for annuitants and nonannuitants. This distinction has been made because the RP-2000 Mortality Tables Report indicates that these two groups have significantly different mortality experience. This is particularly true at typical ages for early retirees, where the number of health-induced early retirements results in a population that has higher mortality rates than the population of currently employed individuals. Under the proposed regulations, the annuitant mortality table would be applied to determine the present value of benefits for each annuitant. The annuitant mortality table is also used for each nonannuitant (i.e., an active employee or a terminated vested participant) for the period after which the nonannuitant is projected to commence receiving benefits, while the nonannuitant mortality table is applied for the period before the nonannuitant is projected to commence receiving benefits. Thus, for example, with respect to a 45-year-old active participant who is projected to commence receiving an annuity at age 55, current liability would be determined using the nonannuitant mortality table for the period before the participant attains age 55 (i.e., so that the probability of an active male participant living from age 45 to the age of 55 using the mortality table that would apply in 2007 is 98.59% and the annuitant mortality table after the participant attains age 55. Similarly, if a 45-year-old terminated vested participant is projected to commence an annuity at age 65, current liability would be determined using the nonannuitant mortality table for the period before the participant attains age 65 and the annuitant mortality table for ages 65 and above.

The mortality tables that would be established pursuant to this regulation would be based on mortality improvements through the year of the actuarial valuation and would reflect the impact of further expected improvements in mortality. Commentators generally stated that the projection of mortality improvement is desirable because it reflects expected mortality more accurately than using mortality tables that do not reflect such projection. The IRS and Treasury agree with these comments, and believe that failing to project mortality improvement in determining current liability would tend to leave plans underfunded. The regulations would specify the projection factors that are to be used to calculate expected mortality improvement. These projection factors are from Mortality Projection Scale AA, which was also recommended for use in the UP-94 Study and RP-2000 Mortality Tables Report. The mortality tables for annuitants are generally based on a future projection period of 7 years, and the mortality tables for nonannuitants are generally based on a future projection period of 15 years. These projection periods were selected as the expected average duration of liabilities and are consistent with projection periods suggested by commentators.

The RP-2000 Mortality Tables Report did not develop mortality rates for annuitants younger than 50 years of age or for nonannuitants older than 70 years of age. The mortality tables for annuitants use the values that apply for the nonannuitant mortality tables at younger ages, with a smoothed transition to the annuitant mortality tables by age 50. Similarly, the mortality tables for both male and female nonannuitants use the values that apply for the annuitant mortality tables at older ages (i.e., ages above 70), with a smoothed transition to the nonannuitant mortality tables by age 70.

The mortality tables for annuitants applicable for the 2007 plan year would use the values that apply for the nonannuitant mortality tables at ages 40 and younger for males and at ages 44 and younger for females with a smoothed transition to the annuitant mortality tables between the ages of 41 and 49 for males and between 45 and 49 for females. Similarly, the mortality tables for both male and female nonannuitants applicable for the 2007 plan year use the values that apply for the annuitant mortality tables at ages 80 and older, with a smoothed transition to the nonannuitant mortality tables between the ages of 71 and 79.

The proposed regulations would provide an option for smaller plans (i.e., plans where the total of active and inactive participants is less than 500) to use a single blended table for all healthy participants — in lieu of the separate tables for annuitants and nonannuitants — in order to simplify the actuarial valuation for these plans. This blended table would be constructed from the separate nonannuitant and annuitant tables using the nonannuitant/annuitant weighting factors published in the RP-2000 Mortality Tables Report. However, because the RP-2000 Mortality Tables Report does not provide weighting factors before age

---

[4] The developers of the 1983 GAM table acknowledged that the number of female lives used to develop the table had been relatively small and they recommended an age setback to the male table be used rather than a separate female table. See Development of the 1983 Group Annuity Mortality Table, Transaction of the Society of Actuaries, Vol. XXXV (1983), pp. 859, 883-84.

[5] The IRS and Treasury are in the process of reviewing recent mortality experience and expected trends for disabled participants to determine whether updated mortality tables under section 412(l)(7)(C)(iii) are needed.

50 or after age 70, the IRS and the Treasury Department would extend the table of weighting factors for ages 41 through 50 (ages 45-50 for females) and for ages 70 through 79 in order to develop the blended table.

The proposed regulations do not provide for the use of generational mortality tables to compute a plan's current liability. Although commentators generally stated that the use of generational mortality tables provides a more accurate prediction of participant mortality, they urged against requiring the use of generational mortality tables, arguing that many actuarial valuation systems are not currently capable of using a generational approach to mortality improvement. However, several commentators requested that the use of generational mortality tables be permitted on an optional basis. The IRS and the Treasury Department agree that the use of generational mortality tables would be preferable, but believe that the approach taken in the proposed regulations (i.e., projecting liabilities for annuitants and nonannuitants to average expected duration) is appropriate because it reasonably approximates the use of generational tables without being overly complex to apply. In light of several comments requesting that the use of generational tables be optional, the IRS and the Treasury Department are considering adopting such a rule and request comments regarding any issues that might arise in implementing an optional use of a generational table. In addition, comments are requested regarding how much lead time would be appropriate if generational mortality tables were to be required in the future.

The RP-2000 mortality tables and the accompanying report analyze differences in expected mortality based on a number of factors, including job classification, annuity size, employment status (i.e., active or retired), and industry. The IRS and the Treasury Department have considered whether separate mortality tables should be provided based on any of these distinctions, or on other distinctions cited in Notice 2003-62, such as tobacco use or income level. The IRS and the Treasury Department have concluded that it is inappropriate to apply distinctions other than the annuitant and nonannuitant distinction described above. In general, these other distinctions were not made because of the complexity involved in the process. For example, no distinction was made for tobacco use because of the difficulty in obtaining, maintaining, and documenting accurate data on the extent of tobacco use.

Although several commentators recommended that separate mortality tables apply to plans that are determined to be "white collar" or "blue collar" in nature, the IRS and Treasury have not adopted this recommendation because of serious administrability concerns. Commentators recognized that it may be difficult to identify whether a specific individual falls into the category of blue collar or white collar (especially if an individual has shifted job classifications during his or her career), and suggested that the classification be based on whether the plan is primarily composed of blue collar employees or white collar employees or whether a plan covers a mixed population of blue collar and white collar employees. While the plan-wide classification may avoid the difficulties of categorizing those individuals who are hard to classify as either blue collar or white collar, it would create additional problems if a plan shifted between these categories.

More importantly, the RP-2000 Mortality Tables Report indicates that plans that are primarily blue collar in nature, but that provide large annuities, tend to have significantly better mortality experience than the average mortality for individuals in the RP-2000 Mortality Tables Report. As a result, classifying such a plan as blue collar and allowing the plan to use a weaker mortality table will lead to systematic underfunding of the plan.[6] Other concerns weighing against the use of separate tables for blue collar and white collar plans include the risk of anti-selection by plans in the absence of mandatory adjustments and the lack of research showing the extent to which any mortality differences attributable to blue collar or white collar status extend to beneficiaries of the plan.

As noted above, the mortality experience is significantly different for annuitants and nonannuitants. While the use of separate mortality rates for these groups of individuals will likely entail changes in programming of actuarial software, the IRS and Treasury believe that the improvement in accuracy resulting from the the use of separate mortality tables for annuitants and nonannuitants more than offsets the added complexity. Furthermore, the annutant/nonannuitant distinction does not have the same difficult administrative issues as separate tables based on collar type, annuity size, or tobacco. This is because it is usually a straightforward process to categorize an individual as an annuitant or a nonannuitant, and once an indvidual is categorized as an annuitant, the individual's status usually does not change again.

Proposed Effective Date

These regulations are proposed to apply to plan years beginning on or after January 1, 2007.

Special Analyses

It has been determined that this notice of proposed rulemaking is not a significant regulatory action as defined in Executive Order 12866. Therefore, a regulatory assessment is not required. It is hereby certified that these regulations will not have a significant economic impact on a substantial number of small entities. This certification is based upon the fact that these regulations provide for special rules to simplify the application of these regulations by actuaries who provide services for small entities. Therefore, a Regulatory Flexibility Analysis under the Regulatory Flexibility Act (5 U.S.C. chapter 6) is not required. Pursuant to section 7805(f) of the Code, this notice of proposed rulemaking will be submitted to the Chief Counsel for Advocacy of the Small Business Administration for comment on its impact on small business.

Comments and Public Hearing

Before these proposed regulations are adopted as final regulations, consideration will be given to any written (a signed original and eight (8) copies) or electronic comments that are submitted timely to the IRS. The IRS and Treasury Department specifically request comments on the clarity of the proposed regulations and how they may be made easier to understand. All comments will be available for public inspection and copying.

A public hearing has been scheduled for April 19, 2006, at 10 a.m. in the auditorium, Internal Revenue Building, 1111 Constitution Avenue, NW., Washington, DC. Due to building security procedures, visitors must use the main building entrance on Constitution Avenue. In addition, all visitors must present photo identification to enter the building. Because of access restrictions, visitors will not be admitted beyond the immediate entrance area more than 30 minutes before the hearing starts. For more information about having your name placed on the list to attend the hearing, see the "FOR FURTHER INFORMATION CONTACT" section of this preamble.

The rules of 26 CFR 601.601(a)(3) apply to the hearing. Persons who wish to present oral comments at the hearing must submit written (signed original and eight (8) copies) or electronic comments and an outline of the topics to be discussed and the time to be devoted to each topic by March 29, 2006. A period of 10 minutes will be allotted to each person for making comments. An agenda showing the scheduling of the speakers will be prepared after the deadline for receiving outlines has passed. Copies of the agenda will be available free of charge at the hearing.

Drafting Information

The principal authors of these regulations are Bruce Perlin and Linda S. F. Marshall, Office of Division Counsel/Associate Chief Counsel (Tax Exempt and Government Entities). However, other personnel from the IRS and Treasury participated in the development of these regulations.

List of Subjects in 26 CFR Part 1

Income taxes, Reporting and recordkeeping requirements.

Amendments to the Regulations

Accordingly, 26 CFR part 1 is proposed to be amended as follows:

PART 1—INCOME TAXES

Paragraph 1. The authority citation for part 1 continues to read, in part, as follows:

Authority: 26 U.S.C. 7805 * * *

Par. 2. Section 1.412(l)(7)-1 is added to read as follows:

§ *1.412(l)(7)-1 Mortality tables used to determine current liability.*

(a) *General rules.* This section sets forth the basis used to generate mortality tables to be used in connection with computations under section 412(l)(7)(C)(ii) for determining current liability for participants

---

[6] Although some commentators suggested addressing this problem by treating some highly compensated union employees as if they were white collar workers, the developers of the RP-2000 Mortality Tables Report (and the researchers they hired to apply a multivariate analysis of the data) were unable to find a practical model to apply the combined effect of collar and annuity amount on mortality.

and beneficiaries (other than disabled participants). The mortality tables, which reflect the probability of death at each age, that are to be used for plan years beginning during 2007, are provided in paragraph (e) of this section. The mortality tables to be used for later plan years are to be provided in guidance published in the Internal Revenue Bulletin. See § 601.601(d) of this chapter.

(b) *Use of the tables*—(1) *Separate tables for annuitants and nonannuitants.* Separate tables are provided for use by annuitants and nonannuitants. The annuitant mortality table is applied to determine the present value of benefits for each annuitant, and to each nonannuitant for the period after which the nonannuitant is projected to commence receiving benefits. For purposes of this section, an annuitant means a plan participant who is currently receiving benefits and a nonannuitant means a plan participant who is not currently receiving benefits (e.g., an active employee or a terminated vested participant). A participant whose benefit has partially commenced is treated as an annuitant with respect to the portion of the benefit which has commenced and a nonannuitant with respect to the balance of the benefit. The nonannuitant mortality table is applied to each nonannuitant for the period before the nonannuitant is projected to commence receiving benefits. Thus, for example, with respect to a 45-year-old active participant who is projected to commence receiving an annuity at age 55, current liability would be determined using the nonannuitant mortality table for the period before the participant attains age 55 (i.e., so that the probability of an active male participant living from age 45 to the age of 55 for the table that applies in plan years beginning in 2007 is 98.59%) and the annuitant mortality table for the period ages 55 and above. Similarly, if a 45-year-old terminated vested participant is projected to commence an annuity at age 65, current liability would be determined using the nonannuitant mortality table for the period before the participant attains age 65 and the annuitant mortality table for ages 65 and above.

(2) *Small plan tables.* As an alternative to the separate tables specified for annuitants and nonannuitants, a small plan can use a combined table that applies the same mortality rates to both annuitants and nonannutants. For this purpose, a small plan is defined as a plan with fewer than 500 participants (including both active and inactive participants).

(c) *Construction of the tables*—(1) *Source of basic data.* The mortality tables are based on the separate mortality tables for employees and healthy annuitants under the RP-2000 Mortality Tables Report (http://www.soa.org/ccm/content/research-publications/experience-studies-tools/the-rp-2000-mortality-tables/), as set forth in paragraph (d) of this section.

(2) *Projected mortality improvements.* The mortality rates under the basic mortality tables are projected to improve using Projection Scale AA, as set forth in paragraph (d) of this section. The annuitant mortality rates for a plan year are based on applying the improvement factors from 2000 until 7 years after the plan year. The nonannuitant mortality rates for a plan year are based on applying the improvement factors from 2000 until 15 years after the plan year. The projection scale is applied using the following equation: Projected mortality rate = base mortality rate * [(1 - projection factor) (number of years projected)].

(3) *Treatment of young annutants and older nonannuitants.* The mortality tables for annuitants use the values that apply for the nonannuitant mortality tables at younger ages, with a smoothed transition to the annuitant mortality tables by age 50. Similarly, the mortality tables for both male and female nonannuitants use the values that apply for the annuitant mortality tables at older ages (i.e., ages above 70), with a smoothed transition to the nonannuitant mortality tables by age 70.

(4) *Construction of the combined table for small plans.* The combined table for small plans is constructed from the separate nonannuitant and annuitant tables using the nonannuitant weighting factors as set forth in paragraph (d) of this section. The weighting factors are applied to develop this table using the following equation: Combined mortality rate = [non-annuitant rate * (1- weighting factor)] + [annuitant rate * weighting factor].

(d) *Tables.* As set forth in paragraph (c) of this section, the following values are used to develop the mortality tables that are used for determining current liability under section 412(l)(7)(C)(ii) and this section.

Age	MALE Non-Annuitant Table (Year 2000)	MALE Annuitant Table (Year 2000)	MALE Projection Scale AA 7	MALE Weighting factors for small plans 8	FEMALE Non-Annuitant Table (Year 2000)	FEMALE Annuitant Table (Year 2000)	FEMALE Projection Scale AA	FEMALE Weighting factors for small plans
1	0.000637	-	0.020	-	0.000571	-	0.020	-
2	0.000430	-	0.020	-	0.000372	-	0.020	-
3	0.000357	-	0.020	-	0.000278	-	0.020	-
4	0.000278	-	0.020	-	0.000208	-	0.020	-
5	0.000255	-	0.020	-	0.000188	-	0.020	-
6	0.000244	-	0.020	-	0.000176	-	0.020	-
7	0.000234	-	0.020	-	0.000165	-	0.020	-
8	0.000216	-	0.020	-	0.000147	-	0.020	-
9	0.000209	-	0.020	-	0.000140	-	0.020	-
10	0.000212	-	0.020	-	0.000141	-	0.020	-
11	0.000219	-	0.020	-	0.000143	-	0.020	-
12	0.000228	-	0.020	-	0.000148	-	0.020	-
13	0.000240	-	0.020	-	0.000155	-	0.020	-
14	0.000254	-	0.019	-	0.000162	-	0.018	-
15	0.000269	-	0.019	-	0.000170	-	0.016	-
16	0.000284	-	0.019	-	0.000177	-	0.015	-
17	0.000301	-	0.019	-	0.000184	-	0.014	-
18	0.000316	-	0.019	-	0.000188	-	0.014	-
19	0.000331	-	0.019	-	0.000190	-	0.015	-
20	0.000345	-	0.019	-	0.000191	-	0.016	-
21	0.000357	-	0.018	-	0.000192	-	0.017	-
22	0.000366	-	0.017	-	0.000194	-	0.017	-
23	0.000373	-	0.015	-	0.000197	-	0.016	-
24	0.000376	-	0.013	-	0.000201	-	0.015	-
25	0.000376	-	0.010	-	0.000207	-	0.014	-
26	0.000378	-	0.006	-	0.000214	-	0.012	-
27	0.000382	-	0.005	-	0.000223	-	0.012	-
28	0.000393	-	0.005	-	0.000235	-	0.012	-
29	0.000412	-	0.005	-	0.000248	-	0.012	-
30	0.000444	-	0.005	-	0.000264	-	0.010	-
31	0.000499	-	0.005	-	0.000307	-	0.008	-
32	0.000562	-	0.005	-	0.000350	-	0.008	-
33	0.000631	-	0.005	-	0.000394	-	0.009	-
34	0.000702	-	0.005	-	0.000435	-	0.010	-
35	0.000773	-	0.005	-	0.000475	-	0.011	-
36	0.000841	-	0.005	-	0.000514	-	0.012	-
37	0.000904	-	0.005	-	0.000554	-	0.013	-

Age	MALE Non-Annuitant Table (Year 2000)	MALE Annuitant Table (Year 2000)	MALE Projection Scale AA [7]	MALE Weighting factors for small plans [8]	FEMALE Non-Annuitant Table (Year 2000)	FEMALE Annuitant Table (Year 2000)	FEMALE Projection Scale AA	FEMALE Weighting factors for small plans
38	0.000964	-	0.006	-	0.000598	-	0.014	-
39	0.001021	-	0.007	-	0.000648	-	0.015	-
40	0.001079	-	0.008	-	0.000706	-	0.015	-
41	0.001142	-	0.009	0.0045	0.000774	-	0.015	-
42	0.001215	-	0.010	0.0091	0.000852	-	0.015	-
43	0.001299	-	0.011	0.0136	0.000937	-	0.015	-
44	0.001397	-	0.012	0.0181	0.001029	-	0.015	-
45	0.001508	-	0.013	0.0226	0.001124	-	0.016	0.0084
46	0.001616	-	0.014	0.0272	0.001223	-	0.017	0.0167
47	0.001734	-	0.015	0.0317	0.001326	-	0.018	0.0251
48	0.001860	-	0.016	0.0362	0.001434	-	0.018	0.0335
49	0.001995	-	0.017	0.0407	0.001550	-	0.018	0.0419
50	0.002138	0.005347	0.018	0.0453	0.001676	0.002344	0.017	0.0502
51	0.002288	0.005528	0.019	0.0498	0.001814	0.002459	0.016	0.0586
52	0.002448	0.005644	0.020	0.0686	0.001967	0.002647	0.014	0.0744
53	0.002621	0.005722	0.020	0.0953	0.002135	0.002895	0.012	0.0947
54	0.002812	0.005797	0.020	0.1288	0.002321	0.003190	0.010	0.1189
55	0.003029	0.005905	0.019	0.2066	0.002526	0.003531	0.008	0.1897
56	0.003306	0.006124	0.018	0.3173	0.002756	0.003925	0.006	0.2857
57	0.003628	0.006444	0.017	0.3780	0.003010	0.004385	0.005	0.3403
58	0.003997	0.006895	0.016	0.4401	0.003291	0.004921	0.005	0.3878
59	0.004414	0.007485	0.016	0.4986	0.003599	0.005531	0.005	0.4360
60	0.004878	0.008196	0.016	0.5633	0.003931	0.006200	0.005	0.4954
61	0.005382	0.009001	0.015	0.6338	0.004285	0.006919	0.005	0.5805
62	0.005918	0.009915	0.015	0.7103	0.004656	0.007689	0.005	0.6598
63	0.006472	0.010951	0.014	0.7902	0.005039	0.008509	0.005	0.7520
64	0.007028	0.012117	0.014	0.8355	0.005429	0.009395	0.005	0.8043
65	0.007573	0.013419	0.014	0.8832	0.005821	0.010364	0.005	0.8552
66	0.008099	0.014868	0.013	0.9321	0.006207	0.011413	0.005	0.9118
67	0.008598	0.016460	0.013	0.9510	0.006583	0.012540	0.005	0.9367
68	0.009069	0.018200	0.014	0.9639	0.006945	0.013771	0.005	0.9523
69	0.009510	0.020105	0.014	0.9714	0.007289	0.015153	0.005	0.9627
70	0.009922	0.022206	0.015	0.9740	0.007613	0.016742	0.005	0.9661
71	-	0.024570	0.015	0.9766	-	0.018579	0.006	0.9695
72	-	0.027281	0.015	0.9792	-	0.020665	0.006	0.9729
73	-	0.030387	0.015	0.9818	-	0.022970	0.007	0.9763
74	-	0.033900	0.015	0.9844	-	0.025458	0.007	0.9797
75	-	0.037834	0.014	0.9870	-	0.028106	0.008	0.9830
76	-	0.042169	0.014	0.9896	-	0.030966	0.008	0.9864
77	-	0.046906	0.013	0.9922	-	0.034105	0.007	0.9898
78	-	0.052123	0.012	0.9948	-	0.037595	0.007	0.9932
79	-	0.057927	0.011	0.9974	-	0.041506	0.007	0.9966
80	-	0.064368	0.010	1.0000	-	0.045879	0.007	1.0000
81	-	0.072041	0.009	1.0000	-	0.050780	0.007	1.0000
82	-	0.080486	0.008	1.0000	-	0.056294	0.007	1.0000
83	-	0.089718	0.008	1.0000	-	0.062506	0.007	1.0000
84	-	0.099779	0.007	1.0000	-	0.069517	0.007	1.0000
85	-	0.110757	0.007	1.0000	-	0.077446	0.006	1.0000
86	-	0.122797	0.007	1.0000	-	0.086376	0.005	1.0000
87	-	0.136043	0.006	1.0000	-	0.096337	0.004	1.0000
88	-	0.150590	0.005	1.0000	-	0.107303	0.004	1.0000
89	-	0.166420	0.005	1.0000	-	0.119154	0.003	1.0000
90	-	0.183408	0.004	1.0000	-	0.131682	0.003	1.0000
91	-	0.199769	0.004	1.0000	-	0.144604	0.003	1.0000
92	-	0.216605	0.003	1.0000	-	0.157618	0.003	1.0000
93	-	0.233662	0.003	1.0000	-	0.170433	0.002	1.0000
94	-	0.250693	0.003	1.0000	-	0.182799	0.002	1.0000
95	-	0.267491	0.002	1.0000	-	0.194509	0.002	1.0000
96	-	0.283905	0.002	1.0000	-	0.205379	0.002	1.0000
97	-	0.299852	0.002	1.0000	-	0.215240	0.001	1.0000
98	-	0.315296	0.001	1.0000	-	0.223947	0.001	1.0000
99	-	0.330207	0.001	1.0000	-	0.231387	0.001	1.0000
100	-	0.344556	0.001	1.0000	-	0.237467	0.001	1.0000
101	-	0.358628	0.000	1.0000	-	0.244834	0.000	1.0000
102	-	0.371685	0.000	1.0000	-	0.254498	0.000	1.0000
103	-	0.383040	0.000	1.0000	-	0.266044	0.000	1.0000
104	-	0.392003	0.000	1.0000	-	0.279055	0.000	1.0000
105	-	0.397886	0.000	1.0000	-	0.293116	0.000	1.0000
106	-	0.400000	0.000	1.0000	-	0.307811	0.000	1.0000
107	-	0.400000	0.000	1.0000	-	0.322725	0.000	1.0000
108	-	0.400000	0.000	1.0000	-	0.337441	0.000	1.0000
109	-	0.400000	0.000	1.0000	-	0.351544	0.000	1.0000

Age	MALE Non-Annuitant Table (Year 2000)	MALE Annuitant Table (Year 2000)	MALE Projection Scale AA [7]	MALE Weighting factors for small plans [8]	FEMALE Non-Annuitant Table (Year 2000)	FEMALE Annuitant Table (Year 2000)	FEMALE Projection Scale AA	FEMALE Weighting factors for small plans
110	-	0.400000	0.000	1.0000	-	0.364617	0.000	1.0000
111	-	0.400000	0.000	1.0000	-	0.376246	0.000	1.0000
112	-	0.400000	0.000	1.0000	-	0.386015	0.000	1.0000
113	-	0.400000	0.000	1.0000	-	0.393507	0.000	1.0000
114	-	0.400000	0.000	1.0000	-	0.398308	0.000	1.0000
115	-	0.400000	0.000	1.0000	-	0.400000	0.000	1.0000
116	-	0.400000	0.000	1.0000	-	0.400000	0.000	1.0000
117	-	0.400000	0.000	1.0000	-	0.400000	0.000	1.0000
118	-	0.400000	0.000	1.0000	-	0.400000	0.000	1.0000
119	-	0.400000	0.000	1.0000	-	0.400000	0.000	1.0000
120	-	1.000000	0.000	1.0000	-	1.000000	0.000	1.0000

(e) *Tables for plan years beginning during 2007*. The following tables are to be used for determining current liability under section 412(l)(7)(C)(ii) for plan years beginning during 2007.

Age	MALE Non-Annuitant Table	MALE Annuitant Table	MALE Optional Combined Table for Small Plans	FEMALE Non-Annuitant Table	FEMALE Annuitant Table	FEMALE Optional Combined Table for Small Plans
1	0.000408	0.000408	0.000408	0.000366	0.000366	0.000366
2	0.000276	0.000276	0.000276	0.000239	0.000239	0.000239
3	0.000229	0.000229	0.000229	0.000178	0.000178	0.000178
4	0.000178	0.000178	0.000178	0.000133	0.000133	0.000133
5	0.000163	0.000163	0.000163	0.000121	0.000121	0.000121
6	0.000156	0.000156	0.000156	0.000113	0.000113	0.000113
7	0.000150	0.000150	0.000150	0.000106	0.000106	0.000106
8	0.000138	0.000138	0.000138	0.000094	0.000094	0.000094
9	0.000134	0.000134	0.000134	0.000090	0.000090	0.000090
10	0.000136	0.000136	0.000136	0.000090	0.000090	0.000090
11	0.000140	0.000140	0.000140	0.000092	0.000092	0.000092
12	0.000146	0.000146	0.000146	0.000095	0.000095	0.000095
13	0.000154	0.000154	0.000154	0.000099	0.000099	0.000099
14	0.000167	0.000167	0.000167	0.000109	0.000109	0.000109
15	0.000176	0.000176	0.000176	0.000119	0.000119	0.000119
16	0.000186	0.000186	0.000186	0.000127	0.000127	0.000127
17	0.000197	0.000197	0.000197	0.000135	0.000135	0.000135
18	0.000207	0.000207	0.000207	0.000138	0.000138	0.000138
19	0.000217	0.000217	0.000217	0.000136	0.000136	0.000136
20	0.000226	0.000226	0.000226	0.000134	0.000134	0.000134
21	0.000239	0.000239	0.000239	0.000132	0.000132	0.000132
22	0.000251	0.000251	0.000251	0.000133	0.000133	0.000133
23	0.000267	0.000267	0.000267	0.000138	0.000138	0.000138
24	0.000282	0.000282	0.000282	0.000144	0.000144	0.000144
25	0.000301	0.000301	0.000301	0.000152	0.000152	0.000152
26	0.000331	0.000331	0.000331	0.000164	0.000164	0.000164
27	0.000342	0.000342	0.000342	0.000171	0.000171	0.000171
28	0.000352	0.000352	0.000352	0.000180	0.000180	0.000180
29	0.000369	0.000369	0.000369	0.000190	0.000190	0.000190
30	0.000398	0.000398	0.000398	0.000212	0.000212	0.000212
31	0.000447	0.000447	0.000447	0.000257	0.000257	0.000257
32	0.000503	0.000503	0.000503	0.000293	0.000293	0.000293
33	0.000565	0.000565	0.000565	0.000323	0.000323	0.000323
34	0.000629	0.000629	0.000629	0.000349	0.000349	0.000349
35	0.000692	0.000692	0.000692	0.000372	0.000372	0.000372
36	0.000753	0.000753	0.000753	0.000394	0.000394	0.000394
37	0.000810	0.000810	0.000810	0.000415	0.000415	0.000415
38	0.000844	0.000844	0.000844	0.000439	0.000439	0.000439
39	0.000875	0.000875	0.000875	0.000465	0.000465	0.000465
40	0.000904	0.000904	0.000904	0.000506	0.000506	0.000506
41	0.000936	0.000963	0.000936	0.000555	0.000555	0.000555
42	0.000974	0.001081	0.000975	0.000611	0.000611	0.000611
43	0.001018	0.001258	0.001021	0.000672	0.000672	0.000672
44	0.001071	0.001493	0.001079	0.000738	0.000738	0.000738
45	0.001131	0.001788	0.001146	0.000788	0.000791	0.000788
46	0.001185	0.002142	0.001211	0.000839	0.000896	0.000840
47	0.001244	0.002554	0.001286	0.000889	0.001054	0.000893
48	0.001304	0.003026	0.001366	0.000962	0.001265	0.000972
49	0.001368	0.003557	0.001457	0.001039	0.001528	0.001059
50	0.001434	0.004146	0.001557	0.001149	0.001844	0.001184

Age	MALE Non-Annuitant Table	MALE Annuitant Table	MALE Optional Combined Table for Small Plans	FEMALE Non-Annuitant Table	FEMALE Annuitant Table	FEMALE Optional Combined Table for Small Plans
51	0.001500	0.004226	0.001636	0.001272	0.001962	0.001312
52	0.001570	0.004254	0.001754	0.001442	0.002173	0.001496
53	0.001681	0.004312	0.001932	0.001637	0.002445	0.001714
54	0.001803	0.004369	0.002134	0.001861	0.002771	0.001969
55	0.001986	0.004514	0.002508	0.002117	0.003155	0.002314
56	0.002217	0.004749	0.003020	0.002414	0.003608	0.002755
57	0.002488	0.005069	0.003464	0.002696	0.004088	0.003170
58	0.002803	0.005501	0.003990	0.002947	0.004588	0.003583
59	0.003095	0.005972	0.004529	0.003223	0.005156	0.004066
60	0.003421	0.006539	0.005177	0.003521	0.005780	0.004640
61	0.003860	0.007284	0.006030	0.003838	0.006450	0.005354
62	0.004244	0.008024	0.006929	0.004170	0.007168	0.006148
63	0.004746	0.008989	0.008099	0.004513	0.007932	0.007084
64	0.005154	0.009947	0.009159	0.004862	0.008758	0.007996
65	0.005553	0.011015	0.010377	0.005213	0.009662	0.009018
66	0.006073	0.012379	0.011951	0.005559	0.010640	0.010192
67	0.006447	0.013705	0.013349	0.005896	0.011690	0.011323
68	0.006650	0.014940	0.014641	0.006220	0.012838	0.012522
69	0.006974	0.016504	0.016231	0.006528	0.014126	0.013843
70	0.007115	0.017971	0.017689	0.006818	0.015607	0.015309
71	0.008002	0.019884	0.019606	0.007450	0.017078	0.016784
72	0.009777	0.022078	0.021822	0.008714	0.018995	0.018716
73	0.012439	0.024592	0.024371	0.010610	0.020819	0.020577
74	0.015988	0.027435	0.027256	0.013139	0.023074	0.022872
75	0.020425	0.031057	0.030919	0.016299	0.025117	0.024967
76	0.025749	0.034615	0.034523	0.020092	0.027673	0.027570
77	0.031961	0.039054	0.038999	0.024516	0.030911	0.030846
78	0.039059	0.044018	0.043992	0.029573	0.034074	0.034043
79	0.047046	0.049617	0.049610	0.035261	0.037618	0.037610
80	0.055919	0.055919	0.055919	0.041582	0.041582	0.041582
81	0.063476	0.063476	0.063476	0.046024	0.046024	0.046024
82	0.071926	0.071926	0.071926	0.051021	0.051021	0.051021
83	0.080176	0.080176	0.080176	0.056651	0.056651	0.056651
84	0.090433	0.090433	0.090433	0.063006	0.063006	0.063006
85	0.100383	0.100383	0.100383	0.071188	0.071188	0.071188
86	0.111295	0.111295	0.111295	0.080522	0.080522	0.080522
87	0.125051	0.125051	0.125051	0.091080	0.091080	0.091080
88	0.140385	0.140385	0.140385	0.101448	0.101448	0.101448
89	0.155142	0.155142	0.155142	0.114246	0.114246	0.114246
90	0.173400	0.173400	0.173400	0.126258	0.126258	0.126258
91	0.188868	0.188868	0.188868	0.138648	0.138648	0.138648
92	0.207683	0.207683	0.207683	0.151126	0.151126	0.151126
93	0.224037	0.224037	0.224037	0.165722	0.165722	0.165722
94	0.240367	0.240367	0.240367	0.177747	0.177747	0.177747
95	0.260098	0.260098	0.260098	0.189133	0.189133	0.189133
96	0.276058	0.276058	0.276058	0.199703	0.199703	0.199703
97	0.291564	0.291564	0.291564	0.212246	0.212246	0.212246
98	0.310910	0.310910	0.310910	0.220832	0.220832	0.220832
99	0.325614	0.325614	0.325614	0.228169	0.228169	0.228169
100	0.339763	0.339763	0.339763	0.234164	0.234164	0.234164
101	0.358628	0.358628	0.358628	0.244834	0.244834	0.244834
102	0.371685	0.371685	0.371685	0.254498	0.254498	0.254498
103	0.383040	0.383040	0.383040	0.266044	0.266044	0.266044
104	0.392003	0.392003	0.392003	0.279055	0.279055	0.279055
105	0.397886	0.397886	0.397886	0.293116	0.293116	0.293116
106	0.400000	0.400000	0.400000	0.307811	0.307811	0.307811
107	0.400000	0.400000	0.400000	0.322725	0.322725	0.322725
108	0.400000	0.400000	0.400000	0.337441	0.337441	0.337441
109	0.400000	0.400000	0.400000	0.351544	0.351544	0.351544
110	0.400000	0.400000	0.400000	0.364617	0.364617	0.364617
111	0.400000	0.400000	0.400000	0.376246	0.376246	0.376246
112	0.400000	0.400000	0.400000	0.386015	0.386015	0.386015
113	0.400000	0.400000	0.400000	0.393507	0.393507	0.393507
114	0.400000	0.400000	0.400000	0.398308	0.398308	0.398308
115	0.400000	0.400000	0.400000	0.400000	0.400000	0.400000
116	0.400000	0.400000	0.400000	0.400000	0.400000	0.400000
117	0.400000	0.400000	0.400000	0.400000	0.400000	0.400000
118	0.400000	0.400000	0.400000	0.400000	0.400000	0.400000
119	0.400000	0.400000	0.400000	0.400000	0.400000	0.400000

Age	MALE Non-Annuitant Table	MALE Annuitant Table	MALE Optional Combined Table for Small Plans	FEMALE Non-Annuitant Table	FEMALE Annuitant Table	FEMALE Optional Combined Table for Small Plans
120	1.000000	1.000000	1.000000	1.000000	1.000000	1.000000

(f) *Effective date.* The mortality tables described in this section apply for plan years beginning on or after January 1, 2007.

Mark E. Matthews

Deputy Commissioner for Services and Enforcement.

¶ 20,519L

Proposed regulations on 29 CFR Parts 2520 and 2530.—Reproduced below is the text of proposed regulations on 29 CFR Parts 2520 and 2530 that deal with reports that must be furnished to participants, and their beneficiaries, of single pension plans only, regarding benefits to which they are entitled or will become entitled at retirement and with records that must be maintained to provide the information necessary for these reports. These proposed regs are in place of earlier proposals (dated February 9, 1979) which were withdrawn by the Department of Labor.

The regulations were filed with the *Federal Register* on July 29, 1980.

ERISA Sec. 105 and ERISA Sec. 209.

DEPARTMENT OF LABOR

Office of Pension and Welfare Benefit Programs

29 CFR Parts 2520 and 2530

Reporting and Disclosure and Minimum Standards for Employee Pension Benefit Plans; Individual Benefit Reporting and Recordkeeping for Single Employer Plans.

AGENCY: Department of Labor.

ACTION: Proposed rulemaking and withdrawal of previously proposed regulations.

SUMMARY: This document (1) withdraws previously proposed regulations (44 FR 8294, February 9, 1979), which dealt with reports that must be furnished to participants in pension plans (and, in some cases, to their beneficiaries) regarding their benefit entitlements, and with records that must be maintained to provide the information necessary for these reports, and (2) contains new proposed regulations applicable only to single employer plans (defined herein to include plans maintained by groups of employers under common control). The Employee Retirement Income Security Act of 1974 (the Act) imposes on certain pension plans the duty to furnish reports and maintain records regarding participants' benefit entitlements and authorizes the Secretary of Labor to prescribe regulations under these provisions. The proposed regulations, if adopted, would provide necessary guidance to employers maintaining such single employer pension plans and to plan administrators of such plans for compliance with the statutory provisions, and would enable participants in single employer plans to receive accurate, timely, and useful information.

DATES: Written comments and requests for a public hearing must be received by the Department of Labor (the Department) on or before October 1, 1980. These regulations, if adopted, would become effective 120 days after adoption.

ADDRESSES: Written comments (preferably three copies) should be submitted to the Division of Reporting and Disclosure, Pension and Welfare Benefit Programs, Room N-4508, U.S. Department of Labor, Washington, D.C. 20216, Attention: Single Employer Individual Benefit Reporting and Recordkeeping Regulations. All comments should be clearly referenced to the section of the regulations to which they apply. All written comments will be available for public inspection at the Public Documents Room, Pension and Welfare Benefit Programs, Department of Labor, Room N-4677, 200 Constitution Avenue NW., Washington, D.C. 20216.

FOR FURTHER INFORMATION CONTACT: Mary O. Lin, Plan Benefits Security Division, Office of the Solicitor, U.S. Department of Labor, Washington, D.C. 20210, (202) 523-9595, or Ronald D. Allen, Pension and Welfare Benefit Programs, U.S. Department of Labor, Washington, D.C. 20216, (202) 523-8515. (These are not toll-free numbers.)

SUPPLEMENTARY INFORMATION: Notice is hereby given that the Department of Labor is withdrawing previously proposed regulations (44 FR 8294, February 9, 1979), and has under consideration new proposed regulations applicable to single-employer plans[1] dealing with reports that must be furnished to individual participants (and, in some cases, their beneficiaries) regarding their benefit entitlements under employee pension benefit plans, and with records that must be maintained to provide the information necessary for these reports. These regulations are proposed under the authority contained in sections 105, 209, and 505 of the Act (Pub. L. 93-406, 88 Stat. 849, 865, and 894, 29 U.S.C. 1025, 1059, and 1135).

The Department has determined that these proposed regulations are "significant" within the meaning of Department of Labor guidelines (44 FR 5570, January 26, 1979) issued to implement Executive Order 12044 (43 FR 12661, March 23, 1978).

Statutory Provisions

Sections 105(a) of the Act generally requires each administrator of an employee pension benefit plan to furnish to any plan participant or beneficiary who so requests in writing, a statement indicating, on the basis of the latest available information, the total benefits accrued and the nonforfeitable pension benefits, if any, which have accrued, or the earliest date on which such benefits will become nonforfeitable. Similarly, section 209(a)(1) of the Act generally requires the plan administrator of a pension plan subject to Part 2 of Title I of the Act to make a report, in accordance with regulations of the Secretary of Labor, to each employee who is a participant under the plan and who requests such report. The report required under section 209(a)(1) must be sufficient to inform the employee of his accrued benefits which are nonforfeitable. Under both sections 105(a) and 209(a)(1), no participant is entitled to more than one report on request during any single 12-month period. Section 209(a) also requires similar reports to be provided to a participant who terminates service with the employer or has a one-year break in service. Sections 105(d) and 209(a)(2) authorize the Secretary of Labor to prescribe regulations specifying the extent to which these reporting requirements apply to plans adopted by more than one employer. In addition, section 105(c) of the Act requires plan administrators to provide to participants with respect to whom registration statements are filed with the Internal Revenue Service under section 6057 of the Internal Revenue Code of 1954 (the Code) individual statements setting forth the information contained in the registration statements.

In order to enable employees' benefits to be determined, so that the reporting requirements of section 209 can be met, section 209(a)(1) generally requires records to be maintained by employers and authorizes the Secretary of Labor to prescribe regulations governing such records. The information necessary for individual benefit reporting is to be furnished by the employer to the plan administrator. In the case of a plan adopted by more than one employer, however, section 209(a)(2) requires records to be maintained by the plan administrator, based on information to be provided by each such employer.

Background

On February 9, 1979 (44 FR 8294), the Department published proposed regulations with respect to individual benefit statements and recordkeeping (referred to herein as "the 1979 proposal"). These regulations would have applied both to single employer plans and to multiple employer plans. A large number of public comments on the 1979 proposal were filed. Many of these comments suggested that substantial revisions should be made to the 1979 proposal. In particular, comments filed on behalf of single and multiple employer plans raised distinct issues.

Upon consideration of those comments, the Department has determined to withdraw the 1979 proposal and to propose the regulations set forth below which pertain only to single employer plans. Reporting and recordkeeping questions relating to multiple employer plans, including multiemployer plans, are still under consideration by the Department. The Department contemplates that proposed regulations dealing with reporting and recordkeeping requirements for multiple employer plans will be published in the *Federal Register* in the future.

Of the regulations now being proposed, 29 CFR 2520.105-1 through 2520.105-2 deal with individual benefit reporting to participants and beneficiaries, while 29 CFR 2530.209-1 through 2530.209-2 deal with the maintenance by plans of records to serve as a basis for individual benefit statements.

In addition to substantive changes from the 1979 proposal, this new proposal contains language changes designed to clarify provisions or to improve readability.

These regulations are proposed under the authority in section 105, 209, and 505 of the Act (Pub. L. 93-446, 88 Stat. 349, 865, and 894, 29 U.S.C. 1025, 1059, and 1135).

---

[1] The term "single employer plan" is defined in the proposed regulations to include plans maintained by a group of employers under common control. In discussions of the proposal throughout this document, the term "single employer plan" generally should be read to be consistent with this definition.

Discussion of Proposed Individual Benefit Reporting Regulations

1. *Benefit statement.* Under these proposed regulations, the benefit statement is the basic document to be used for providing individual benefit information to participants upon request, upon termination or upon a one-year break in service. The benefit statement must state the amount of a participant's accrued benefit regardless of the extent to which it is nonforfeitable (i.e., "vested"), the percentage of the accrued benefit which is vested, and the amount of such accrued vested benefit. The regulations specify the form in which accrued benefits and accrued vested benefits must be reported. The new proposal is designed to ensure that the information provided to an individual participant is presented in a meaningful fashion, without imposing excessive administrative costs on plans.

Some of the comments received by the Department on the 1979 proposal raised objections to the degree to which that proposal would have required benefit statements to provide individualized information geared to each participant's particular circumstances. These comments suggested that the degree of individualization that would have been required would entail significant additional costs for plans, and that ultimately these costs would be borne to some extent by participants. These commentators pointed out that, in some cases, the individualized information might be misleading or of little value to recipients of benefit statements as a result of changes in participants' circumstances. At the same time, it appears to the Department that some degree of individualization is necessary if individual benefit statements are to serve the purposes which underlie the statutory requirements. In the new proposal the Department has struck what it believes to be a better balance between the need for individualization of benefit statements and the costs that individualization imposes.

In the case of defined benefit plans, the accrued benefit and the amount of the participant's accrued vested benefit may be expressed either in terms of a straight life annuity payable at normal retirement age, or in terms of the normal form of benefits offered by the plan (e.g., annuity for a term of years, lump sum distribution, etc.). By contrast, the 1979 proposal would have required accrued benefits to be stated either in the form of a straight life annuity payable at normal retirement age or, if the plan did not offer such a benefit, in the form of the primary option offered by the plan. If a participant had made any elections affecting the manner of payment of benefits, the 1979 proposal generally would have required accrued benefits to be stated in the form elected by the participant. The elimination in the new proposal of the requirement to state accrued benefits in the form elected by the participant is in keeping with the goal of reducing costs resulting from excessive individualization. It also reflects comments to the effect that the requirement to state accrued benefits in the form of a straight life annuity payable at normal retirement age might prove misleading to participants when this is not the normal form of benefits payable under the plan. One of the comments on the 1979 proposal suggested that the Department should prohibit explicitly inclusion in the benefit statement of benefit projections predicated on the assumption that a participant will work until retirement. The comment suggested that such projections would not satisfy the requirement that a benefit statement must report accrued benefits, vested percentage and accrued vested benefits as of the date of the statement. The Department has decided not to prohibit the inclusion of such projections, but notes that the benefit statement must be written in a manner calculated to be understood by the average plan participant or beneficiary and its format must not have the effect of misleading or misinforming participants or beneficiaries.

The new proposal would require the benefit statement to indicate that election of options under the plan might affect the participant's accrued benefits, and to refer the participant to the Summary Plan Description for information on available options. In addition, if the accrued benefit and accrued vested benefit are not expressed as amounts payable in the form of a joint and survivor annuity, the benefit statement must explain that the periodic benefit the participant will receive at retirement may be reduced on account of survivor benefits.

Social security offset plans must furnish the net benefit. In the case of benefit statements furnished on request or under the annual benefit statement alternative, the net benefit may be determined on the basis of assumptions about participants' earnings in service not covered by the plan, provided that the benefit statement indicates that the reported amounts are approximate. Benefit statements furnished upon termination or after a break in service must report the actual amounts of benefits to which the participant is entitled.

In the case of an individual account plan, the regulations make it clear that the participant's account balance is considered to be the accrued benefit.

In accordance with the statutory requirements, the benefit statement would be required to indicate the nonforfeitable (vested) percentage of the participant's accrued benefit. If the participant has no vested accrued benefits, the benefit statement must indicate the earliest date on which any benefits will become vested. Consistent with the goal of avoiding excessive administrative costs, the new proposal eliminates the requirement in the 1979 proposal that plans with "graded" vesting indicate the earliest dates on which a participant may attain each subsequent level of nonforfeitable accrued benefits derived from employer contributions. The new proposal also provides that class year plans would be required to indicate the nonforfeitable percentage of each portion of the participant's account balance, to which a separate nonforfeitable percentage applies.

The benefit statement would also be required to indicate the amount of the participant's nonforfeitable accrued benefit, in the same form as that in which the accrued benefit is reported.

The new proposal requires only a general reference to the Summary Plan Description. The 1979 proposal required more detailed information regarding circumstances that might result in the reduction or elimination of accrued or nonforfeitable benefits, including detailed references to the Summary Plan Description. The new proposal also eliminates the requirement in the 1979 proposal that the benefit statement include certain information concerning a participant's work history used as a basis for calculation of the participant's benefits. This change was made to reduce the degree to which benefit statements must be individualized. The eliminated information, however, must be available to a participant under the provisions of these regulations regarding inspection of records (§ 2530.209-2(f)), and, as under the 1979 proposal, the benefit statement must so indicate. As under the 1979 proposal, the benefit statement would be required to include a statement urging the participant to bring promptly to the attention of the plan administrator anything in the benefit statement that does not appear correct; information regarding the availability of plan records for inspection; the date as of which information is reported; and the participant's social security number (for the purpose of verification by the participant).

Like its predecessor, the new proposal would provide that the benefit statement must be written in a manner calculated to be understood by the average plan participant or beneficiary and that the format of the benefit statement must not have the effect of misleading or misinforming the participant or beneficiary. Under certain circumstances, plans must offer foreign language assistance to participants who are not literate in English to aid them in understanding their benefit statements, as is required under regulations relating to the Summary Plan Description (see 29 CFR 2520.102-2(c)).

The benefit statement must be based on the latest available information. As under the 1979 proposal, benefit statements based on records that meet the standards of sufficiency set forth in the proposed recordkeeping regulations will be deemed to be based on the latest available information Although "sufficient", a plan's records may nevertheless be incomplete (i.e., if they do not include all items necessary to determine participants' benefit entitlements) if, for example, a plan did not maintain complete records prior to the adoption of these regulations. In these instances, the benefit statement must indicate that the records on which it is based are incomplete and the participant or beneficiary must be offered an opportunity to provide other information relating to his benefit entitlements. The plan administrator must prepare a benefit statement based on such information although, to the extent that a benefit statement is based on such information, it may indicate that it is conditioned upon the accuracy of that information.

In the 1979 proposal the Department solicited comments on whether and to what extent it should adopt regulations concerning circumstances under which liability should be imposed for payment of benefits in accordance with the information provided in the benefit statement. Some comments supported the adoption of regulations imposing liability, while others suggested that liability should be limited, or objected to the imposition of any liability. Upon consideration of the comments, the Department has concluded that a judgment concerning the consequences of an incorrect benefit statement can properly be made only after account has been taken of all the facts and circumstances. The Department believes, therefore, that it would be more appropriate to leave determinations of this sort to plan fiduciaries, whose actions are subject to review by means of the judicial process, than to attempt to deal with all conceivable factual situations in the context of regulations.

In the 1979 proposal, the Department also solicited comments on whether it should publish model benefit statements. In view of the multiplicity of plan provisions, it would be difficult for the Department to ensure that the format of a model statement would not be misleading under any circumstances. Accordingly, the Department has made a decision at this time not to publish model benefit statements.

2. *Furnishing benefit statements on request.* Both sections 105(a) and 209(a)(1)(A) of the Act require plan administrators of pension plans to furnish individual benefit information on request. The requirements of both statutory provisions are substantially similar in this regard; accordingly, these requirements are dealt with in a single section of the regulations (§ 2520.105-2(a)). The only significant difference between the two statutory provisions is that section 105(a) applies to requests by both participants and their designated beneficiaries, while section 209(a)(1)(A) applies only to requests by participants. The regulations, therefore, apply to requests by both participants and beneficiaries, so as to cover the broadest range of circumstances under which benefit statements must be furnished on request.

In response to suggestions made in comments on the 1979 proposal, the new proposal provides that a plan administrator subject to these regulations need not provide a benefit statement upon request to certain classes of participants and beneficiaries. These include participants and beneficiaries currently receiving benefits; participants and beneficiaries to whom paid up insurance policies representing their full benefit entitlements have been distributed; participants and beneficiaries who have received a full distribution of their benefits or who are receiving benefits under the plan; beneficiaries of participants who are entitled to benefit statements; and participants with deferred vested benefits who have received benefit statements on termination or after having incurred a one-year break in service without returning to service with any employer maintaining the plan, and their beneficiaries. The Department believes that it would be superfluous to require benefit statements to be furnished to these participants and beneficiaries.

The plan administrator may establish a simple and convenient procedure for the submission of requests for benefit statements. If such a procedure is established and communicated to participants and beneficiaries (for example, in the Summary Plan Description), the plan administrator, under certain conditions, need not comply with requests that do not conform to the procedure. If no such procedure is established, however, the plan administrator must comply with any request in writing by a participant or beneficiary. The plan administrator may not require information regarding a participant's employment record as a condition for furnishing the benefit statement (although such information may be requested). The new proposal would, however, allow plan administrators to require the furnishing of certain items of information identifying the participant about whom information is requested.

Many of the comments on the 1979 proposal urged that the Department permit benefit statements to report benefits as of the end of the plan year. The comments suggested that this approach would relieve individual account plans of the expense of conducting a valuation whenever a participant or beneficiary requests a benefit statement. Defined benefit plans might also face lower administrative costs if an end-of-plan-year approach were adopted because it might enable these plans to gear data processing systems to a single date. In light of these comments, the new proposal would require a benefit statement to report benefits as of a date not earlier than the end of the plan year preceding the plan year in which a participant or beneficiary requests the statement.

The end-of-plan-year approach, however, entails changes in the deadlines for furnishing benefit statements on request. The new proposal is designed to permit a reasonable period of time after the end of the plan year for the processing of information. Under the new proposal, a benefit statement must be furnished to a participant or beneficiary on request within the later of 60 days of the date of the request or 120 days after the end of the plan year which immediately precedes the year in which the request was made. The Department recognizes that this scheme would provide participants and beneficiaries who request benefit statements towards the end of the plan year with a statement that contains relatively old information based on the prior plan year (as much as 14 months old), while participants and beneficiaries who request statements during the earlier part of the plan year may be required to wait a substantial period (up to four months) to receive their statements.

Nevertheless, the Department believes that the proposed scheme strikes an appropriate balance between providing participants with timely information and reducing administrative costs.

As under the 1979 proposal the plan administrator would not be required to furnish more than one benefit statement to a participant or beneficiary on request during any 12-month period.

The original proposal appeared to require plans to furnish a complete benefit statement to a non-vested participant if the annual alternative was used. The new proposal would permit a plan to provide annually, as an alternative to furnishing benefit statements on request, a benefit statement to each vested participant and a statement of non-vested

status to each non-vested participant. Permitting the furnishing of a statement of non-vested status under the annual alternative should reduce costs to plans electing the alternative, while providing sufficient disclosure to a non-vested participant The plan administrator must furnish a complete benefit statement, however, to any non-vested participant who requests one after receiving the statement of non-vested status.

The annual benefit statement must be furnished within 180 days after the end of the plan year.

Despite comments objecting to the requirement in the 1979 proposal that the plan administrator furnish at least one duplicate of the annual benefit statement to any participant or beneficiary who requests it during the year, the Department has not eliminated this requirement. In some cases a participant or beneficiary may not receive an annual benefit statement mailed to him. Since it would be impracticable and unfair to require a participant or beneficiary to prove that he did not receive an annual statement in order to obtain a duplicate, the regulations allow all participants or beneficiaries entitled to receive a benefit statement on request at least one duplicate if the annual alternative is used.

3. *Furnishing benefit statements upon termination and after one-year breaks in service.* The benefit statement must report benefits as of the end of the plan year in which the termination or the one-year break in service occurs. Consistent with end-of-the-year benefit reporting, the new proposal requires statements to be furnished within 180 days after the end of the plan year in which the termination or break in service occurs. The 180 day period would allow plans to satisfy the requirement to furnish benefit statements upon termination or break in service through the use of the annual benefit statement alternative, which is required to be furnished in the same time period.

A participant who receives a benefit statement in connection with termination of service, and thereafter incurs a one-year break in service, is not entitled to receive an additional benefit statement if the information in the second benefit statement would be the same as in the first. Similarly, a participant who receives a benefit statement upon incurring a one-year break in service and thereafter terminates service with the employer, or incurs a subsequent one-year break in service, is not entitled to receive an additional benefit statement if the information in the second benefit statement would be the same as that in the first.

In the case of participants who have no vested benefits, the new proposal, like the 1979 proposal, would permit plan administrators of single employer plans to satisfy the requirements to furnish individual benefit information upon termination by furnishing a statement of non-vested status. The statement of non-vested status informs the participant that he has no nonforfeitable benefits. It does not, however, provide information regarding accrued benefits. Thus, the statement of non-vested status does not require extensive calculations and may be presented to all participants entitled to it in a standardized form, with no need for preparation of an individual statement for each. However, the statement of non-vested status must inform the participant that he may request a benefit statement with more detailed information regarding his individual accrued (non-vested) benefits. Such a request must be treated as a request for a benefit statement.

4. *Corrections in the benefit statement.* As under the 1979 proposal, a participant who raises a question with regard to the accuracy of a benefit statement must be given an opportunity to furnish information regarding his benefit entitlements to the plan administrator. Within a reasonable time, the plan administrator must make a decision with regard to the question raised by the participant and notify the participant of the decision, the basis for the decision, and any change in benefit entitlements as a result of the decision. The plan administrator is not required to prepare a benefit statement based on the information furnished by the participant except, as noted above, in situations where the benefit statement is based on incomplete records.

5. *Statement of deferred vested benefits.* Under section 105(c) of the Act, each plan administrator required to register with the Internal Revenue Service under section 6057 of the Code shall furnish a statement of deferred vested benefits to each participant described in section 6057(a)(2)(C) (i.e., to each participant who, during the plan year for which registration is required, is separated from service covered under the plan, is entitled to a deferred vested benefit under the plan as of the end of the plan year, and with respect to whom retirement benefits were not paid under the plan). Section 6057(e) of the Code requires plan administrators to furnish similar individual statements to the same class of participants. The requirements of section 105(c) will be deemed to be satisfied if, in accordance with section 6057(e) of the Code and regulations thereunder, the plan administrator furnishes to the participant the individual statement required under the latter section.

1416

Proposed Regulations

6. *Manner of furnishing individual benefit reporting documents.* Like the 1979 proposal, the new proposal would require a plan to furnish individual benefit documents to a participant or beneficiary either by first class mail to his last known address, or by personal delivery. The new proposal makes it clear that personal delivery may be accomplished by another party under the plan administrator's supervision.

The new recordkeeping proposal would require a participant's individual benefit records to include current address information. Although some comments suggested that plans should not be required to maintain current address information on file, and should be permitted to use less reliable modes of delivery than first-class mail and personal delivery, the Department believes that these requirements represent the only means of assuring that individual benefit reporting documents will actually reach participants and beneficiaries in most cases.

Proposed Individual Benefit Recordkeeping Regulations

1. *Duty to maintain records.* In the case of a single employer plan, the duty to maintain individual benefits records would be imposed on the employer maintaining the plan. As under the 1979 proposal, the employer would be required to furnish to the plan administrator the information necessary to enable the latter to comply with the individual benefit reporting requirements.

2. *Sufficiency of records.* The individual benefit records maintained in connection with a single employer plan will be deemed to be sufficient if they contain all information relevant to the determination of each employee's benefit entitlements under the plan with respect to service with the employer who maintains the plan after the effective date of the regulations. In the case of a plan adopted after the effective date, records must contain all information relevant to a determination of each employee's benefit entitlements under the plan relating to such service after the date of adoption. Certain information with respect to service before the initial recordkeeping date specified in the regulations will be relevant in determining vested accrued benefits. The proposed regulations would not require records of this information to be compiled, but if such records were in existence as of February 9, 1979, the date on which the 1979 proposal was published in the Federal Register, they must be retained. In the Department's view, the 1979 proposal was sufficient to put plan administrators on notice that existing records would not be permitted to be destroyed.

3. *Retention, preservation and inspection of records.* As under the 1979 proposal, individual benefit records must be retained as long as a possibility exists that they might be relevant to a determination of the benefit entitlements of a participant or beneficiary. However, if they are lost or destroyed due to circumstances beyond the control of the person responsible for their maintenance, they will not be deemed insufficient solely for that reason. They must be maintained in a safe and accessible place at the offices of the employer, or at special recordkeeping offices.

The proposal makes clear that original records may be disposed of at any time if microfilm, microfiche or similarly reproduced records which are clear reproductions of the original documents are retained, and adequate viewing equipment is available for inspecting them. (The 1979 proposal appeared to allow microfilm reproduction only.)

Individual benefit records, including original documents must be available for inspection by participants, beneficiaries, and their representatives.

The period within which plan records must be made available for inspection after a request to do so has been extended from 72 hours, as under the 1979 proposal, to 10 working days. This change was made in response to comments noting the difficulties which would have been involved under the previous proposal.

In response to some public comments, provisions have been added to this proposal requiring the employer maintaining the records to bear the cost of converting records into a form accessible for inspection, although reasonable charges for copying may be imposed, not exceeding the actual cost. Inspection of records may be made only by those persons entitled to receive a benefit statement, and their representatives. Representatives of the Department have the authority to inspect plan records under the circumstances specified in section 504 of ERISA.

If an employer ceases to be responsible for the maintenance of individual benefit records, they must be transferred to the person who becomes responsible for their maintenance.

4. *Definition of "single employer plan".* The Department has tentatively decided to extend the term "single employer plan", for the purposes of these regulations, to a plan adopted by a group of employers under common control. In the case of these plans, the new proposal

would impose the recordkeeping requirements on the individual employers, rather than on a central recordkeeping agent such as the plan administrator, but would make it clear that the individual employers may enter into cooperative centralized recordkeeping arrangements. The Department believes that for these plans it is unnecessary to impose on the employers a legal obligation, such as might be appropriate in the case of a plan maintained by a group of unaffiliated employers, to participate in such arrangements because the central management of the control group is able to require employers maintaining the plan to adhere to efficient recordkeeping arrangements.

Effective Dates

The Department has received a number of comments in response to the 1979 proposal suggesting that some plans may need to effect changes to their existing reporting and recordkeeping systems to comply with the proposed regulations. In order to allow for orderly preparations for compliance with the regulations, the Department contemplates providing that these regulations would not become effective with respect to collectively bargained multiple employer plans until nine months after the expiration of the collective bargaining agreement or agreements in effect on the date of adoption of these regulations, but in no case more than 45 months after the date of adoption. For multiple employer plans which are not collectively bargained, the regulations, if adopted, would become effective 120 days after adoption.

Drafting Information

The principal author of these proposed regulations is Mary O. Lin of the Plan Benefits Security Division, Office of the Solicitor, Department of Labor. However, other persons in the Department of Labor participated in developing the proposed regulations, both on matters of substance and style.

Proposed Regulation

Accordingly, proposed regulations 29 CFR 2520.105-1 through 2520.105-2 and proposed regulations 29 CFR 2530.209-1 through 2530.209-2 (44 FR 8294, February 9, 1979) are hereby withdrawn, and it is proposed to amend Chapter XXV of Title 29 of the Code of Federal Regulations as follows:

1. By adding to Part 2520 new §§ 2520.105-1, 2520.105-2, and 2520.105-3 to read as follows:

Subpart G—Individual Benefit Reporting

Sec.

2520.105-1 General.

2520.105-2 Individual Benefit Reporting for Single-Employer Plans.

2520.105-3 [Reserved].

Authority: Secs. 105, 209 and 505 of the Act (Pub. L. 93-406; 88 Stat. 849, 865 and 894, 29 U.S.C. 1025, 1059 and 1135).

§ 2520.105-1 General.—(a) *Scope and purpose.* Sections 105 and 209 of the Employee Retirement Income Security Act of 1974 (the Act) impose on plan administrators of employee pension benefit plans certain requirements to report to plan participants and beneficiaries information regarding their individual benefit entitlements. Section 105 of the Act provides, among other things, that each plan administrator of an employee pension benefit plan shall furnish to any plan participant or beneficiary who so requests in writing, a statement of certain information relating to his individual benefit entitlements. Section 209(a) of the Act provides, among other things, that the plan administrator shall make a report regarding individual benefit entitlements, in accordance with regulations prescribed by the Secretary of Labor, to each employee who is a participant under the plan and who either requests such report in accordance with regulations issued by the Secretary of Labor, terminates service with the employer, or has a one-year break in service (as defined in section 203(b)(3)(A) of the Act). In addition, section 105(c) provides that a plan administrator who is required to register under section 6057 of the Internal Revenue Code of 1954 (the Code) shall furnish to certain plan participants individual statements relating to their deferred vested benefits. Section 2520.105-2 and 2520.105-3 contain provisions relating to the reporting of individual benefit entitlements under sections 105 and 209(a) of the Act. Section 2520.105-2 applies to "single employer plans", while section 2520.105-3 applies to "multiple employer plans". The paragraphs of §§ 2520.105-2 and 2520.105-3 are parallel. Recordkeeping requirements relating to information necessary for determining individual benefit entitlements are set forth in §§ 2530.209-1, 2530.209-2 and 2530.209-3.

(b) *Individual benefit reporting documents.* Sections 2520.105-2 and 2520.105-3 deal with three types of documents, collectively referred to as "individual benefit reporting documents":

¶20,519L

(1) The benefit statement that must be furnished to plan participants or beneficiaries upon request, upon termination of employment or upon a one-year break in service;

(2) The statement of non-vested status that may be substituted for the benefit statement under certain circumstances; and

(3) The statement of referred vested retirement benefits that must be furnished to participants in connection with certain filing by the plan administrator under section 6057 of the Code.

§ 2520.105-2 Individual benefit reporting for single employer plans.

(a) *Finishing statements on request.*—(1) *General.* The administrator of a single employer employee pension benefit plan (as defined in § 2520.105-2(k)) subject to Part 1 or 2 of Title I of the Act shall furnish a benefit statement which satisfies the requirements of this paragraph and paragraphs (c) through (i) of § 2520.105-2 to all plan participants or beneficiaries who request in writing information regarding their individual benefit entitlements under the plan, except:

(i) Participants and beneficiaries who are currently receiving benefits under the plan;

(ii) Participants and beneficiaries whose entire benefit entitlements under the plan are fully guaranteed by an insurance company, insurance service or insurance organization qualified to do business in a State: *Provided,* That the benefits are paid under an insurance policy or contract on which no further premiums are payable and which has been distributed to the participant or beneficiary;

(iii) Participants and beneficiaries who have received all benefits to which they are entitled under the plan;

(iv) Beneficiaries of a participant who is entitled to a benefit statement on request; and

(v) Participants with deferred vested benefits who have received benefit statements on termination or after incurring a one year break in service and who have not returned to service with any employer maintaining the plan, and beneficiaries of such participants.

(2) *Procedure for submission of requests for benefit statements.* The plan administrator may establish a simple procedure, convenient to participants' and beneficiaries. for the submission of requests for benefits statements. The plan administrator will not be required to comply with a request made in a manner which does not conform to such a procedure which has been communicated in writing to participants and beneficiaries, provided that the plan administrator informs the requesting participant or beneficiary that he had failed to comply with the procedure and explains how to comply with the procedure. A procedure shall be deemed to be communicated to participants and beneficiaries if a description of the procedure is included in the Summary Plan Description of the plan or in any other document distributed to all plan participants. If no such procedure is established, any request in writing to the plan administrator or plan office by a participant or beneficiary for information regarding his benefit entitlements under the plan administrator for the purposes of this section.

(3) *Information obtained from participant or beneficiary.* A participant or beneficiary who requests a benefit statement may not be required to furnish information regarding the participant's employment record as a condition to receiving the benefit statement, but may be required to furnish the following information: Name, address, date of birth, Social Security account number and, if relevant to information provided in the benefit statement, marital status and date of birth of spouse.

(4) *Date of furnishing.* A benefit statement shall be furnished to a participant or beneficiary who requests such a statement, no later than (i) 60 days after receipt of the request or (ii) 120 days after the end of the plan year which immediately precedes the plan year in which the request is made, whichever is later.

(5) *Date as of which information is provided.* A benefit statement furnished at the request of a participant or beneficiary shall report benefits as of a date not earlier than the end of the plan year preceding the plan year in which the request is made.

(6) *Annual benefit statement alternative.* (i) The requirement of furnish a benefit statement on request to a participant or beneficiary as set forth in § 2520.105-2(a)(1), shall not apply if within one year before the request the plan administrator has furnished to such participant or beneficiary an annual benefit statement, or a "statement on non-vested status" described in § 2520.105-2(f), as appropriate, which is based on information as of the end of the plan year preceding the plan year in which it is furnished, and it is furnished within 180 days after the end of that plan year.

(ii) Notwithstanding the provisions of paragraph (a)(6)(i) of this section, the plan administrator shall furnish a complete benefit state-

ment meeting the requirements of § 2520.105-2(d) and (e) to a participant who requests information on his accrued benefits after receiving a statement of non-vested status, and shall furnish upon request a duplicate of the most recent annual benefit statement, or statement of non-vested status, as appropriate, to any participant or beneficiary who was entitled to such a statement but claims not to have received one.

(b) *Furnishing statements upon termination and after one-year breaks in service.*—(1) *Furnishing statements upon termination*—(i) *General.* Except as provided in § 2520.105-2(c), the plan administrator of a single employer employee pension benefit plan that is subject to Part 2 of Title I of the Act shall furnish a benefit statement to a participant who terminates service with the employer, unless the participant is reemployed by the employer before the date on which the benefit statement must be furnished under paragraph (b)(1)(iii) of this section.

(ii) *Non-vested participants.* In the case of a terminated participant who has no nonforfeitable benefits under the plan, the plan administrator will comply with the requirements of section 209(a)(1)(B) of the Act and this section if the plan furnishes such participant a "statement of non-vested status" described in § 2520.105-2(f).

If a participant is furnished a statement of non-vested status under this paragraph, and request information concerning his accrued benefits under the plan, the plan administrator shall furnish a benefit statement meeting the requirements of § 2520.105-2(d) and (e) to the participant no later than the later of 60 days after such request or 180 days after the end of the plan year in which the participant's termination occurred.

(iii) *Date of furnishing.* A benefit statement or statement of non-vested status shall be furnished within 180 days after the end of the plan year in which the participant terminates service with the employer. This requirement may be satisfied by furnishing to the participant an annual benefit statement described in § 2520.105-2(a)(6), which reports the participants' benefits as of the end of the plan year in which termination occurred.

(iv) *Date as of which information is provided.* A benefit statement furnished upon termination of service shall report benefits as of a date no earlier than the date of termination.

(2) *Furnishing statements after one-year breaks in service*—(i) *General.* Except as provided in § 2520.105-2(c), a plan administrator of a single employer employee pension benefit plan, that is subject to Part 2 of Title I of the Act and provides that participants may suffer adverse consequences on incurring a one-year break in service, shall furnish a benefit statement to a participant who incurs a "one-year break in service", as defined in paragraph (b)(2)(v) of this section.

(ii) *Non-vested participants.* In the case of a participant who has no nonforfeitable benefits under the plan and who incurs a one-year break in service, the plan administrator will comply with the requirements of section 209(a)(1)(B) of the Act and this section if the plan furnishes such participant a "statement of non-vested status" as described in § 2520.105-2(f).

If a participant who incurs a one-year break in service is furnished a statement of non-vested status under this paragraph, and requests information concerning his accrued benefits under the plan, the plan administrator shall furnish a benefit statement meeting the requirements of § 2520.105-2(d) and (e) to the participant no later than the later of 60 days after such request or 180 days after the end of the plan in which he incurs a one-year break in service.

(iii) *Date of furnishing.* A benefit statement or statement of non-vested status shall be furnished within 18O days after the end of the plan year in which a participant incurs a one-year break in service. This requirement may be satisfied by furnishing to the participant an annual benefit statement described in § 2520.105-2(a)(6), which reports the participant's benefits as of the end of the plan year in which the one-year break in service occurred.

(iv) *Date as of which information is provided.* A benefit statement furnished after a one-year break in service shall report benefits as of the end of the plan year in which the one-year break in service occurs.

(v) *Definition of "one-year break in service".* For purposes of this section, the term "one-year break in service" shall mean a one-year break in service or vesting purposes as defined in the plan documents, or in the case of a plan under which service is credited for purposes of vesting according to the elapsed time method permitted under 26 CFR 1.410(a)-7, a one-year period of severance for vesting purposes, as defined in 26 CFR 1.410(a)-7(c)(4).

(c) *Frequency of benefit statements.*—(1) A plan administrator is not required to furnish a participant or beneficiary more than one benefit statement upon request under § 2520.105-2(a) in any 12-month period.

(2) Where a participant receives a benefit statement upon termination or upon incurring a one-year break in service, a plan administrator is not required to furnish a second benefit statement upon a subsequent one-year break in service or termination, respectively, or upon a request by the participant, if the information that would be contained in a second benefit statement would be the same as that contained in the earlier benefit statement.

(d) *Style and format of benefit statements.*—(1) *General.* Individual benefit reporting documents shall be written in a manner calculated to be understood by the average plan participant or beneficiary. The format of these documents must not have the effect of misleading or misinforming the participant or beneficiary.

(2) *Foreign language assistance*—(i) The plan administrator of a plan described in paragraph (d)(2)(ii) of this section shall communicate to plan participants, in the non-English language common to such participants, information relating to any procedure for requesting benefit statements that may have been established by the plan administrator in accordance with §2520.105-2(a)(2). In addition, the plan administrator shall provide these participants with either a benefit statement in such non-English language, or an English language benefit statement or statement of non-vested status which prominently displays a notice, in the non-English language common to these participants, explaining how they may obtain assistance. The assistance provided need not involve written materials, but shall be given in the non-English language common to these participants.

(ii) The plan administrators of the following plans are subject to the foreign language requirement of paragraph (d)(2)(i) above:

(A) A plan that covers fewer than 100 participants at the beginning of the plan year, and in which 25 percent or more of plan participants are not literate in English and are all literate in the same non-English language, or

(B) A plan which covers 100 or more participants at the beginning of the plan year, and in which the lesser of 500 or more participants, or 10% or more of all plan participants, are not literate in English and are all literate in the same non-English language.

(e) *Contents of the benefit statement.*—(1) *General.* In accordance with paragraphs (e)(2), (e)(3), (e)(4) and (e)(5) of this section, each benefit statement shall contain the following information:

(i) The participant's total accrued benefits;

(ii) The nonforfeitable percentage of the participant's accrued benefits;

(iii) The amount of the participant's nonforfeitable accrued benefits; and

(iv) Additional information specified in §2520.105-2(e)(5) below.

(2) *Total accrued benefits*—(i) *Defined benefit plans.*—(A) *General.* In the case of a defined benefit plan, the accrued benefit shall be stated in the form of a straight life annuity payable at normal retirement age or in the normal form of benefit provided by the plan.

(B) *Contributory plans.* If a defined benefit plan requires contributions to be made by employees, the benefit statement shall separately indicate, in addition to the participant's total accrued benefit, either the amount of the participant's accrued benefit derived from employee contributions and the amount of the accrued benefit derived from employer contributions, or the percentages of the participant's total accrued benefit derived from employee contributions and from employer contributions. The portion of the accrual benefit derived from employer contributions and the portion derived from employee contributions shall be determined in accordance with section 204(c) of the Act (section 411(c) of the Internal Revenue Code of 1954 and Treasury Regulations thereunder).

(C) *Social Security offset plans.* If a participant's benefits under the plan are offset by a percentage of the participant's benefits under the Social Security Act, the benefit statement shall state the participant's accrued benefit after reduction by the applicable amount. In the case of a benefit statement furnished upon request or under the annual benefit statement alternative permitted under paragraph (a)(6) of this section, the amount of the offset may be determined on the basis of assumptions about the participant's earnings from service not covered under the plan, provided that the statement indicates that the stated amounts of the accrued and nonforfeitable accrued benefit are approximate. A benefit statement furnished when an employee terminates employment or incurs a break in service must indicate the actual amounts of the accrued benefit and nonforfeitable accrued benefit to which the participant is entitled.

(ii) *Individual account plans.* In the case of an individual account plan, the participant's accrued benefit shall be the fair market value of

the participant's account balance on the date as of which benefits are reported.

(3) *Nonforfeitable percentage.*—(i) *General.* The benefit statement shall indicate the percentage of a participant's accrued benefit which is nonforfeitable within the meaning of section 203 of the Act (and section 411(a) of the Internal Revenue Code of 1954 and Treasury Regulations thereunder). Except in the case of a plan described in paragraph (e)(3)(ii) of this section, if a participant has no nonforfeitable benefits, the benefit statement shall indicate the earliest date on which any benefits may become nonforfeitable; and if less than 100 percent of the participant's benefits are nonforfeitable, the benefit statement shall indicate the earliest date on which 100 percent of the participant's benefits may be nonforfeitable.

(ii) *Class year plans.* In the case of an individual account plan which provides for the separate nonforfeitability of benefits derived from contributions for each plan year, the benefit statement shall state each nonforfeitable percentage applicable to a portion of the participant's account balance and the value of that portion of the account balance.

(iii) *Contributory plans.* In the case of a plan which provides for employee contributions, the benefit statement shall indicate that the portion of the accrued benefits derived from the participant's contribution to the plan is nonforfeitable.

(4) *Nonforfeitable benefits.*—(i) *Defined benefit plans.* The benefit statement shall indicate the amount of the participant's nonforfeitable benefit in the same form as the participant's total accrued benefit is reported under paragraph (b) of this section.

(ii) *Individual account plans.* In the case of an individual account plan, the benefit statement shall indicate the fair market value of the nonforfeitable portion of the participant's account balance on the date as of which benefits are reported.

(5) *Other information.* A benefit statement shall include the following information:

(i) In the case of a defined benefit plan, a statement to the effect that the amount of benefits which may be received under the plan may be affected as a result of electing any option under the plan, and that further information on such options is contained in the Summary Plan Description.

(ii) In the case of a defined benefit plan, if the accrued benefit and nonforfeitable benefit are not stated in the form of an annuity for the joint lives of the participant and his spouse, an explanation to the effect that unless a married participant elects not to receive benefits in that form, the participant's nonforfeitable benefit may be reduced;

(iii) A statement to the effect that further information on the circumstances, if any, which may result in a reduction or elimination of accrued benefits or of nonforfeitable benefits is contained in the Summary Plan Description;

(iv) A statement urging the participant or beneficiary to bring promptly to the attention of the plan administrator anything in the statement that does not appear correct;

(v) A statement informing the participant or beneficiary that plan records upon which information in the benefit statement is based are available for inspection upon request, and the name, address and telephone number of the person or office to whom requests should be directed;

(vi) The date as of which benefit entitlements are reported; and

(vii) The participant's Social Security Account Number.

(f) *Statement of non-vested status.*—A statement of non-vested status shall inform the participant that he does not have any nonforfeitable benefits under the plan, and that he may obtain upon request a benefit statement indicating his accrued benefits, if any, and the earliest date on which any benefits may become nonforfeitable.

(g) *Basis of benefit statement.*—(1) *General.* A benefit statement shall be based on the latest available information. A benefit statement will be deemed to be based on the latest available information if it reports benefit entitlements as of the date benefits must be reported under paragraphs (a) or (b) of §2520.105-2, as appropriate, or any subsequent date, and if it is based on plan records which comply with the requirements of paragraphs (b) and (c) of §2530.209-2.

(2) *Benefit statement based on incomplete plan records.* A benefit statement based on incomplete plan records (i.e. records that do not contain all information necessary to determine the participant's benefit entitlements) shall so indicate. To the extent that the records of a plan are incomplete, an opportunity to provide information relating to benefit entitlements shall be offered to a participant or beneficiary entitled to a benefit statement, and the benefit statement shall be based on such

information. A benefit statement based in whole or in part on information supplied by a participating [sic] may state that it is conditioned upon the accuracy of such information.

(h) *Manner of furnishing individual benefit reporting documents.*— Individual benefit reporting documents shall be furnished either by first class mail to the participant or beneficiary at his last known address, or by personal delivery to the participant or beneficiary by the plan administrator or an individual under the plan administrator's supervision. In the event that the plan administrator learns that the participant or beneficiary has failed to receive a document by mail or personal delivery, the plan administrator shall employ any means of delivery reasonably likely to ensure the receipt by such participant or beneficiary of the document.

(i) *Corrections to the Benefit Statement.*—A participant or beneficiary who raises questions regarding the accuracy of the benefit statement shall be given a reasonable opportunity to point out information in the benefit statement that he believes inaccurate, and to furnish to the plan administrator information which such participant or beneficiary believes relevant in determining his benefit entitlements. The plan administrator shall make reasonable attempts to determine whether the plan's records or the benefit statement are inaccurate and to verify the information furnished by the participant or beneficiary. Within a reasonable time after the plan administrator receives such a communication from a participant or beneficiary, the plan administrator shall notify him in writing of the plan's decision with respect to such matter, the basis for such decision, and any change in benefit entitlements as a result of the decision.

(j) *Statement of Deferred Vested Benefits.*—Section 105(c) of the Act provides that each administrator required to file a registration statement under section 6057 of the Internal Revenue Code of 1954 (the Code) shall furnish to each participant described in section 6057(a)(2)(C) of the Code an individual statement setting forth the information with respect to such participant which is required to be contained in the registration statement. The requirements of section 105(c) of the Act will be satisfied if an individual statement is furnished to a participant in accordance with section 6057(e) of the Code and the regulations thereunder.

(k) *Definition of "single employer plan."*—For purposes of §§ 2520.105-1 and 2510.105-2, the term "single employer plan" shall mean a plan adopted by a single employer or by a group of employers which are under common control.

§ 2520.105-3 [Reserved]

2. By adding to part 2530 new §§ 2530.209-1, 2530.209-2, and 2530.209-3 to read as follows:

Subpart E—Individual Benefit Recordkeeping

Sec.

2530.209-1 General.

2530.200-2 Individual benefit recordkeeping for single employer plans.

2530.209-3 [Reserved].

Subpart E—Individual Benefit Recordkeeping

§ 2530.209-1 General.

Section 209 of the Employee Retirement Income Security Act of 1974 (the Act) contains certain requirements relating to the maintenance of records for determining the benefits to which individual participants in employee pension benefit plans subject to Part 2 of Title I of the Act are or may become entitled. Section 2530.209-2 contains regulations applicable to single employer plans with respect to the individual benefit recordkeeping requirements set forth in section 209 of the Act. Section 2530.209-3 contains individual benefit recordkeeping regulations under section 209 of the Act applicable to multiple employer plans. The paragraphs of §§ 2530.209-2 and 2530.209-3 are parallel. In addition to individual benefit recordkeeping requirements, section 209 also contains provisions dealing with individual benefit reporting. Regulations relating to the individual benefit reporting provisions of section 209 are set forth in §§ 2520.105-1, 2520.105-2 and 2520.105-3.

§ 2530.209-2 Individual benefit recordkeeping for single employer plans.

(a) *Recordkeeping requirement.* For every single employer/employee pension benefit plan (as defined in § 2530.209-2(h)) subject to Part 2 of Title I of the Act, records shall be maintained with respect to each employee covered under the plan. These records shall be sufficient to determine the benefits which are, or may become, due to such employee and shall include the name and address of each such employee.

(b) *Maintenance of records and furnishing of information.* The employer or employers maintaining the plan shall maintain the records

required to be maintained by a single employer plan under § 2530.209-2(a). The employer shall furnish to the plan administrator information necessary to enable the plan administrator to comply with the individual benefit reporting requirements set forth in § 2520.105-2. If the plan is maintained by more than one employer, the employers may enter into arrangements under which the necessary records are furnished by the employers to the plan administrator and maintained by the plan administrator. Each employer, however, shall remain responsible for ensuring that the records are properly maintained.

(c) *Sufficiency of records.* Records required to be maintained by a single employer plan under § 2530.209-2(a) will be deemed to be sufficient if:

(1) With respect to service from the later of the date the employer adopts the plan or [effective date of regulation], they contain all information with respect to service with that employer that is relevant to a determination of each employee's benefit entitlements under the plan, and

(2) With respect to service before [effective date of regulation], if any, they include all records maintained by the employer on and after February 9, 1979, for the purpose of determining employee's benefit entitlements under the provisions of the plan.

(3) *Loss or destruction of records.* Notwithstanding the preceding paragraphs, records shall not be deemed to be insufficient solely because they have been lost or destroyed due to circumstances beyond the control of the person responsible for their maintenance under § 2530.209-2(b).

(d) *Period for which records must be retained.* The records which are required to be maintained under § 2530.209-2(a) shall be retained in a manner described in § 2530.209-2(e) as long as any possibility exists that they might be relevant to a determination of benefit entitlements. When it is no longer possible that records might be relevant to a determination of benefit entitlements, the records may be disposed of, unless they are required to be maintained for a longer period under any other law.

(e) *Preservation of records by employer and plan administrator.*—(1) *General.* The records which are required to be maintained under § 2530.209-2(a) shall be maintained in reasonable order in a safe and accessible place at the main offices of the plan administrator or the employer, or at recordkeeping offices established by the employer or the plan and customarily used for the maintenance of records.

(2) *Reproduction of records; disposal of original documents.* Original documents may be disposed of at any time if microfilm, microfiche, or similarly reproduced records which are clear reproductions of the original documents are retained, and adequate projection or other viewing equipment is available for inspecting such reproductions.

(3) *Electronic data processing.* Nothing in this section precludes the use of punch cards, magnetic tape or other electronic information storage material for processing information.

(f) *Inspection and copying.* The records required to be maintained under § 2530.209-2(a) with respect to any participant or beneficiary, including any original documents or reproductions thereof maintained under § 2530.209-2(e), shall be made available free of charge to such participant or beneficiary, or his representative, in a reasonably accessible form for inspection and copying. The records shall be made available during normal business hours within 10 working days after receipt of a request. A reasonable charge may be imposed for copying records, not exceeding the actual cost of copying them.

(g) *Transfer of records.* In the event that an employer ceases to be responsible under § 2530.209-2(b) for maintaining records, such employer shall transfer any records which continue to be potentially relevant to the determination of benefit entitlements to the appropriate successor employer or plan administrator responsible for their maintenance. The employer transferring such records is not required to retain copies of the records transferred. Nothing in this section, however, shall relieve an employer from any responsibility or liability for violations of the requirements of § 2520.209-1 through § 2530.209-2 which occur during the time such employer has control of and is responsible for maintaining, retaining or transferring the records as required by those sections.

(h) *Definition of "Single Employer Plan".* For purposes of this section, the term "single employer plan" shall mean a plan adopted by a single employer or by a group of employers which are under common control.

§ 2530.209-3 [Reserved]

Signed at Washington, D. C., this 25th day of July, 1980.

Ian D. Lanoff,

Administrator, Pension and Welfare Benefit Programs, Labor-Management Services Administration, Department of Labor.

[FR Doc. 80-22911 Filed 7-29-80; 8:45 am]

¶ 20,519M   Reserved.

[Proposed regulation under 29 CFR Part 2520 prescribing an alternative method of compliance with the reporting and disclosure requirements for simplified employee pension plans using the model IRS Form 5305-SEP was formerly reproduced at this point. The final regulation appears at ¶ 14,247ZB.]

¶ 20,519N   Reserved.

Formerly reproduced at this point were proposed regulations issued by the Equal Employment Opportunity Commission under the Age Discrimination in Employment Act of 1967. The final regulations are at ¶ 15,750A—15,750F and 15,750I.]

¶ 20,519O   Reserved.

Formerly produced at this point were proposed regulations issued by the Equal Employment Opportunity Commission relating to the interpretation of the Equal Pay Act of 1963. The final regulations appear at ¶ 15,767-15,769B.]

¶ 20,519P   Reserved.

Proposed regulations relating to the reduction of benefit payments after plan termination and the recoupment of benefit overpayments were formerly reproduced at this point. The final regulations appear at ¶ 15,429G—15,429G-27.]

¶ 20,519Q   Reserved.

Formerly reproduced at this paragraph were proposed DOL regulations relating to the definition of plan assets. The final regulations appear at ¶ 14,139M and 14,876.]

¶ 20,519R

Proposed regulations on 29 CFR Part 2620: Valuation of plan assets: Termination of non-multiemployer plans.—Following below are proposed regulations setting forth rules for valuing the assets of terminating non-multiemployer pension plans. The proposed regulations were published in the Federal Register on May 8, 1985 (50 FR 19386).

ERISA Sec. 4044.

PENSION BENEFIT GUARANTY CORPORATION

29 CFR Part 2620

Valuation of Plan Assets

AGENCY: Pension Benefit Guaranty Corporation.

ACTION: Proposed rule.

SUMMARY: This proposed regulation sets forth rules for valuing the assets of terminating non-multiemployer pension plans that are covered by Title IV of the Employee Retirement Income Security Act of 1974, *as amended,* (the "Act"). Under Title IV of the Act, the assets of a terminating plan must be valued and allocated to the plan's benefits. Because plan assets are often held in forms that are subject to different valuation methods, this regulation is necessary to provide uniform standards for plan administrators and employers to use in determining the value of plan assets. The effect of this regulation would be to ensure that the parties involved in plan terminations are provided with the guidance necessary to comply with the provisions of Title IV of the Act.

DATES: Comments must be received on or before July 8, 1985.

ADDRESSES: Comments should be addressed to the Director, Corporate Policy and Regulations Department, Code 611, Pension Benefit Guaranty Corporation, Suite 7300, 2020 K Street, NW., Washington, D.C. 20006. Written comments will be available for public inspection in Suite 7100, at the above address, between the hours of 9:00 a.m. and 4:00 p.m.

FOR FURTHER INFORMATION CONTACT: Renae R. Hubbard, Special Counsel, Corporate Policy and Regulations Department, Code 611, Pension Benefit Guaranty Corporation, 2020 K Street, NW., Washington, D.C. 20006, 202-254-6476 (202-254-8010 for TTY and TDD). These are not toll-free numbers.

SUPPLEMENTARY INFORMATION:

Background

On May 7, 1976, the Pension Benefit Guaranty Corporation (the "PBGC") published in the Federal Register a final regulation on Valuation of Plan Assets, 41 FR 18992 (codified at 29 CFR Part 2611, recodified as Part 2620). The regulation sets forth standards for valuing the assets of a terminating pension plan. In the preamble to the regulation, the PBGC noted that specific rules for the valuation of insurance contracts when they are held as plan assets were not included and that it would provide guidance on that issue in the future. Accordingly, on April 18, 1977, the PBGC published proposed amendments to the Valuation of Plan Assets regulation, setting forth rules for determining the value of insurance contracts and insurance contract rights that are held as plan assets (42 FR 20158).

Because of the passage of time, the PBGC is publishing new proposed rules for valuing insurance contracts and insurance contract rights, in order to receive current public comment on the issues presented. The rules proposed in this document differ substantively from the 1977 proposal in several respects. Additionally, non-substantive changes have been made to simplify the regulation.

In the discussion that follows, unless otherwise stated, references are to sections of the proposed regulation set forth in this document.

Overview of the Regulation

As in the 1977 proposal, this proposed rule would restructure the regulation. For the sake of clarity, the regulation has been divided into three subparts. Subpart A contains the general provisions of the regulation. Subpart B contains the rules for valuing plan assets other than insurance contracts and insurance contract rights. Subpart C sets forth rules for identifying insurance contracts and insurance contract rights that are plan assets and for determining their value.

It should be noted that the scope of this regulation also would be changed by this amendment. Unlike the original rules, this proposal does not apply to multiemployer pension plans (§ 2620.1(b)). The Multiemployer Pension Plan Amendments Act of 1980, Pub. L. 96-364 (Sept. 26, 1980), 94 Stat. 1208, established a new insurance program for multiemployer plans, and regulations dealing with valuation of assets by such plans will be issued in the future.

In addition, this regulation has been coordinated with the PBGC's regulation on Determination of Plan Sufficiency and Termination of Sufficient Plans, which was published on January 28, 1981, 46 FR 9532 (codified at 29 CFR Part 2615, recodified as Part 2617). The "Sufficiency" regulation sets forth a procedure for plan administrators to follow in order to demonstrate whether the value of the plan's assets will be sufficient to provide plan benefits on the date the plan's assets are distributed, rather than the date of plan termination which is the valuation date for insufficient plans. Proposed § 2620.3 recognizes that alternate valuation date for sufficient plans.

With those exceptions, the provisions of Subparts A and B of this proposal do not differ substantively from the provisions of the final regulation published on May 7, 1976. Accordingly, the remainder of this preamble addresses Subpart C exclusively.

Valuation and Plan Sufficiency

Because the Sufficiency regulation provides that a plan administrator who demonstrates sufficiency may distribute plan assets to participants in the form elected by the participants, certain of the valuation rules proposed in 1977 are inapposite to a plan that is closing out pursuant to the Sufficiency regulation. For example, in the 1977 proposal, § 2611.12(a) provided that, in order to determine the value of an insurance contract, the contract's greatest cash settlement value had to be determined. Under § 2611.12(c) of that proposal, the greatest cash settlement value was to be either (1) the amount of a lump sum payment or (2) the fair market value of a series of installment payments. It is not productive, however, to require a plan administrator to determine the fair market value of a series of installment payments if the participants have elected to receive immediate lump sum distributions.

Accordingly, this proposal includes a rule to ensure that plan administrators who are demonstrating sufficiency or closing out a plan under the Sufficiency regulation are not forced to follow unnecessary valuation procedures. Under § 2620.13 of this proposal, for purposes of demonstrating sufficiency under Subpart B of the Sufficiency regulation and closing out a plan under Subpart C of that regulation, the plan administrator shall value insurance contracts and participation rights in the manner that reflects the highest value that can be realized in a form that will enable the plan administrator to close out the plan as required by the Sufficiency regulation.

Contract Provisions

Under the 1977 proposed amendments, the value of an insurance contract would have depended upon the alternatives expressly available under the contract as of the valuation date (1977 proposal § 2611.10— definition of "settlement options"). The PBGC reviewed this rule and determined that it was unnecessarily restrictive because the contractholder may be able to negotiate with the insurer for a higher value than the contract provides. Accordingly, a new § 2620.14 provides that the valuation of plan assets shall be based upon the provisions of the insurance contract as of the valuation date or upon other options available from the insurer as of the valuation date.

The existence of options other than those expressly contained in the insurance contract must be demonstrated by means of a written statement by the insurer. That section also makes clear that the plan administrator has the responsibility for obtaining the factual basis for the insurer's computations underlying its determination of value. Where the factual basis used by the insurer would lead to an unreasonable determination of value, the plan administrator is responsible for taking whatever action is necessary to arrive at a fair and reasonable determination of value.

Cash Settlement Value

Under the 1977 proposal, as well as this proposed rule, the basic method for determining the value of an insurance contract is to compare the contract's greatest cash settlement value with the present value of the benefits that can be purchased with the contract funds (1977 proposal § 2611.12(a); this proposal § 2620.15(a)). In the preamble to the proposed 1977 amendments, the PBGC noted that many insurance contacts give the insurer some discretion in calculating the amount of a cash settlement. It was and is the PBGC's expectation that

insurers will be fair and reasonable in interpreting and implementing their contracts. This expectation does not in any way, however, affect the plan administrator's responsibility to scrutinize the basis upon which the insurer has made its determination and to negotiate a settlement that is both fair and reasonable in light of the factors relevant to a determination of value, *e.g.*, mortality rates, interest rates, the value of future dividend streams and comparable contract prices.

The PBGC did, however, invite suggestions from the public on the need for special safeguards and the type of safeguards that might be adopted. In response to this invitation, one comment stated that many insurance contracts provide that the cash amount available upon liquidation of the contract is determined by means of a formula that is subject to periodic modification called, in insurance parlance, a "secretary formula." The comment suggested that the regulation require the insurer to use the formula in effect during the five-year period preceding plan termination that would produce the highest cash settlement. The PBGC has considered this suggestion but has not adopted it in this new proposal because that formula may no longer be available and, thus, would be irrelevant to an accurate determination of the fair value of the asset.

In the 1977 proposal, § 2611.12(c)(2) provided that "[t]he value of a settlement option requiring cash payments by the insurer in installments is the fair market value, determined in accordance with Subpart B of this part, of the right to receive that stream of future payments." The PBGC has made three changes in this provision. First, one public comment on the 1977 proposal objected to the use of the term "settlement option" on the ground that its use might cause confusion since it is a term of art referring to the various ways in which the proceeds of life insurance policies can be paid other than in a lump sum. In light of the comment, the PBGC has eliminated from this proposed rule the term "settlement option" and, in its place, uses the term "cash settlement" (§ 2620.15(b)).

Second, in reviewing § 2611.12(c)(2) of the 1977 proposal, the PBGC decided that the fair market value concept set forth in Subpart B of the regulation might not be particularly helpful in valuing the right to receive the stream of future payments from the insurer. Subpart B's fair market value concept depends upon the existence of a market for the asset to be valued. The PBGC is not aware of a market for the right to receive the stream of future payments from the insurer. Accordingly, this proposal sets forth a new method for determining the value of a cash settlement that provides cash installment payments by the insurer. Proposed § 2620.15(b)(2) provides that the value of these installment payments is the present value of the payments calculated as of the valuation date, determined by applying an interest rate that is the sum of the PBGC's interest rate for valuing immediate annuities in effect on the valuation date plus one-half of one percent. The resulting interest rate is the rate the PBGC uses to value immediate annuities before adjusting for benefit administration costs.

Finally, the PBGC has clarified § 2620.15(b)(2) of the proposal to make explicit the fact that it applies to a deferred lump sum cash payment as well as to a series of installment payments.

Value of Participation Rights

The 1977 proposal provided in § 2611.14 that the value of participation rights was to be determined solely by reference to the cancellation of such rights. The PBGC received a number of public comments that were critical of this provision. As suggested by some of the comments, this proposal now provides a method for valuing participant rights that cannot be cancelled.

Section 2620.16(b) provides that if a participation right cannot be cancelled, the value of the right is the present value of the future stream of payments determined by reference to all relevant factors, such as interest rates, mortality rates, the past practice of the insurer regarding participation rights and comparable contract prices. The contractholder is responsible for negotiating with the insurer to make clear, in the contract, that the rights must either be cancellable or, if not, that the insurer must provide information with respect to the future stream of payments based on past dividend practice that is adequate for the plan administrator to determine the fair value of such rights.

Additionally, the rules dealing with the valuation of participation rights that can be cancelled has been slightly modified. Proposed § 2611.14 provided that the value of a participation right was the greater of the cash amount payable by the insurer upon cancellation of the right or the value of the right provided by the insurer upon cancellation of the right. Section 2620.16(a) of this proposed rule provides that the value of a participation right is the greater of the cash amount or the value of the additional benefits negotiated by the parties upon cancellation of the right.

In the preamble to the 1977 proposed amendments, the PBGC invited public suggestions on appropriate measures that the PBGC might take to assure that an insurer attributes a reasonable value to a plan's participation rights. In response, one comment suggested that "if abuse really occurs, PBGC might move to requiring prior disclosure of an insurer's practices upon contract termination in . . . greater detail that is now usually provided." The PBGC would be interested in public reaction to that suggestion.

Two comments suggested that, if a participation right cannot be cancelled, the PBGC should become the holder of the right, even in the sufficient plan context. While the PBGC might become the holder of participation rights when it becomes trustee of a plan, a possibility contemplated by this regulation, the situation is different in the case of plans that are not trusteed by the PBGC. Generally, it is the PBGC's view that its involvement with plans that can be closed out in the private sector should be kept to a minimum. It would be inconsistent with this view of the PBGC's responsibilities under Title IV of the Act for the PBGC to become the holder of a plan's participation rights when the plan is sufficient.

Comments Invited

Interested persons are invited to submit written comments on this proposed regulation. Comments should be addressed to: Director, Corporate Policy and Regulations Department, Code 611, Pension Benefit Guaranty Corporation, 2020 K Street, NW., Washington, D.C. 20006. Written comments will be available for public inspection at the above address, Suite 7100, between the hours of 9:00 a.m. and 4:00 p.m. Each comment should identify this regulation and should include the name and address of the person submitting it and the reasons for any recommendation. This proposal may be changed in light of the comments received.

Classification: E.O. 12291 and Regulatory Flexibility Act

The PBGC has determined that this rule is not a "major rule" within the meaning of Executive Order 12291 because it will not have an annual effect on the economy of $100 million or more; nor will it create a major increase in costs or prices for consumers, individual industries, or geographic regions; nor will it have significant adverse effects on competition, employment, investment, innovation or on the ability of United States-based enterprises to compete with foreign-based enterprises in domestic or export markets.

Under section 605(b) of the Regulatory Flexibility Act, the PBGC certifies that this regulation will not have a significant economic effect on a substantial number of small entities. All pension plans that terminate under Title IV of the Employee Retirement Income Security Act of 1974 must value their assets. By setting forth valuation methods, this regulation will make it easier for administrators of such plans to comply with the law. Compliance with sections 603 and 604 of the Regulatory Flexibility Act is accordingly waived.

List of Subjects in 29 CFR Part 2620

Employee benefit plans, Pension insurance, and Pensions.

In consideration of the foregoing, it is proposed to revise Part 2620 of Chapter XXVI of Title 29, Code of Federal Regulations, to read as follows:

PART 2620—VALUATION OF PLANS ASSETS IN NON-MULTIEMPLOYER PENSION PLANS

Subpart A—General

Sec.

2620.1 Purpose and scope.

2620.2 Definitions.

2620.3 Valuation date.

Subpart B—Assets Other Than Insurance Contracts

2620.5 Purpose and scope.

2620.6 Definitions.

2620.7 General rule.

2620.8 Fair market value presumptions.

Subpart C—Insurance Contracts

2620.10 Purpose and scope.

2620.11 Definitions.

2620.12 Plan assets.

2620.13 Special rule applicable to demonstrating sufficiency and closing out a plan under Subpart C of Part 2617.

2620.14 Contract provisions.

2620.15 Value of insurance contracts.

2620.16 Value of participation rights.

Authority: Secs. 4002(b)(3), 4141, 4044 and 4062, Pub. L. 93—406, 88 Stat. 1004, 1020, 1025 and 1029 (1974), as amended by secs. 403(1), 403(d), 402(a)(7) and 403(g), Pub. L. 96-364, 94 Stat. 1302, 1301, 1299 and 1301 (1980) (29 U.S.C. 1302(b)(3), 1341, 1344 and 1362).

Subpart A—General

§ 2620.1 Purpose and scope.

(a) *Purpose.* This part sets forth rules governing the valuation of the assets of a terminating pension plan for purposes of Title IV of the Act.

(b) *Scope.* This part applies to non-multiemployer pension plans for which a Notice of Intent to Terminate is filed on or after the effective date of this part, or for which the PBGC commences a termination action on or after the effective date of this part.

§ 2620.2 Definitions.

For purposes of this part:

"Act" means the Employee Retirement Income Security Act of 1974 (29 U.S.C. § 1001 *et seq.*), *as amended.*

"Date of plan termination" means the date of plan termination established under section 4048 of the Act.

"Notice of Intent to Terminate" means a notice filed with the PBGC pursuant to section 4041(a) of the Act and Part 2616 of this chapter.

"PBGC" means the Pension Benefit Guaranty Corporation.

"Non-multiemployer plan" means a pension plan described in section 4021(a) of the Act that is maintained by one trade or business (whether or not incorporated), or by more than one trade or business (whether or not incorporated) all of which are under control within the meaning of Part 2612 of this chapter, or a plan maintained by more than one trade or business not under common control that is not a multiemployer plan as defined in section 4001(a)(3) of the Act.

§ 2620.3 Valuation date.

Except as otherwise provided, the assets of a plan that has been placed into trusteeship by the PBGC shall be valued as of the date of plan termination and the assets of a plan that closes out in accordance with Part 2617 of this chapter shall be valued as of the date plan assets are to be distributed.

Subpart B—Assets Other Than Insurance Contracts

§ 2620.5 Purpose and Scope.

This subpart sets forth rules for valuing plan assets other than plan assets described in § 2620.12.

§ 2620.6 Definitions.

For purposes of this subpart:

"Exchange" means a national securities exchange registered with the Securities and Exchange Commission under section 6 of the Securities Exchange Act of 1934.

"Fair market value" means the price at which property would change hands between a willing buyer and a willing seller, neither being under any compulsion to buy or to sell and both having reasonable knowledge of relevant facts.

"National Association of Securities Dealers Automated Quotations Systems" means the automated quotations system sponsored by the National Association of Securities Dealers, Inc., a national securities association registered with the Securities and Exchange Commission under section 15A of the Securities Exchange Act of 1934.

"Principally traded" means the market place at which the greatest volume of trades normally occurs.

§ 2620.7 General rule.

Plan assets to which this subpart applies shall be valued at their fair market value on the plan's valuation date, using the method of valuation that most accurately reflects fair market value.

§ 2620.8 Fair market value presumptions.

(a) *Treasury bills.* The fair market value of Treasury bills is presumed to be the value computed from the average of the bid and asked discount for the bill on the valuation date, as nationally published in a general circulation daily newspaper.

(b) *Treasury notes, bonds and Federal agency securities.* The fair market value of Treasury notes, bonds and Federal agency securities is presumed to be the value computed from the average of bid and asked prices for the security on the valuation date, as nationally published in a general circulation daily newspaper.

(c) *Shares in open-end mutual funds.* The fair market value of shares in open-end mutual funds is presumed to be the net asset value (the redemption value) per share of the mutual fund on the valuation date, as nationally published in a general circulation daily newspaper.

(d) *Units of participation in a common trust fund or collective investment fund.* The fair market value of units of participation in a common trust fund or collective investment fund is presumed to be the value per unit of the fund as reflected on a statement of account prepared by the manager of the fund. The value per unit of the fund is to be determined in accordance with the procedures normally employed by the manager of the fund purusant to the terms of the fund, and federal and state law and regulations, as applicable, and as of the normal date on which the fund is valued if that date is on or within 31 days after the valuation date. This presumption will apply only if there were no distributions from the fund in relation to units of the fund in the interval between the plan's valuation date and the normal valuation date of the fund.

(e) *Common and preferred stocks, warrants and closed-end mutual funds.* The fair market value of common and preferred stocks, warrants, and closed-end mutual funds is presumed to be the value determined in accordance with the rules set forth in Paragraphs (e)(1) through (e)(4) of this section, as follows:

(1) If the security is traded on the New York Stock Exchange and the plan's valuation date is on or before January 26, 1976, or traded on the American Stock Exchange and the valuation date is on or after March 1, 1976, the fair market value is presumed to be the closing sale price on the valuation date as reported by the consolidated last sale reporting system established pursuant to Rule 11Aa3-1, promulgated by the Securities and Exchange Commission under the Securities Exchange Act of 1934, as nationally published in a general circulation daily newspaper.

(2) If the security is principally traded on an exchange, other than as set forth in Paragraph (e)(1), the fair market value is presumed to be the closing sale price on the valuation date on the exchange where the security is principally traded, as nationally published in a general circulation daily newspaper.

(3) If the security is principally traded otherwise than on an exchange, and is quoted on the National Association of Securities Dealers Automated Quotations System, the fair market value is presumed to be the average of the end-of-day bid and asked prices for the security on the valuation date, as made available for publication by such system and nationally published in a general circulation daily newspaper.

(4) If there is no nationally published closing sale price or end-of-day bid and asked prices on the valuation date, the fair market value of the security is presumed to be—

(i) For securities traded principally on an exchange, the average of the nationally published closing sale price on the date nearest the valuation date and within five trading days before the valuation date and the nationally published closing sale price on the date nearest the valuation date and within five trading days after the valuation date; and

(ii) For securities principally traded otherwise than on an exchange, the average of (1) the average of the nationally published end-of-day bid and asked prices on the date nearest the valuation date and within five trading days before the valuation date and (2) the average of the nationally published end-of-day bid and asked prices on the date nearest the valuation date and within five trading days after the valuation date.

(f) *State and municipal obligations.* The fair market value of state and municipal obligations is presumed to be the average of bid and asked prices for the security on the valuation date, as nationally published in a general circulation daily newspaper. If there are no such nationally published bid and asked prices on the valuation date, the fair market value of the security is presumed to be the average of (1) the average of the nationally published bid and asked prices on the date nearest the valuation date and within five trading days before the valuation date and (2) the average of the nationally published bid and asked prices on the date nearest the valuation date and within five trading days after the valuation date.

Subpart C—Insurance Contracts

§ 2620.10 Purpose and scope.

This subpart sets forth rules for identifying insurance contracts and insurance contract rights that are plan assets and for determining their value.

§ 2620.11 Definitions.

For purposes of this subpart:

"Contractholder" means the owner of an insurance contract purchased with funds contributed to or under a plan. A participant who has received an insurance contract from or under a plan is not a "contractholder" for purposes of this subpart.

"Insurance contract" or "contract" means a valid written agreement between an insurer and a contractholder pursuant to which the insurer agrees to perform services including the payment of specified benefits or their equivalent in return for the payment of premiums or similar consideration. References in this subpart to "an insurance contract" include more than one contract, unless the plural is clearly inappropriate.

"Insurer" means a company authorized to do business as an insurance carrier under the laws of a State or the District of Columbia.

"Participation right" means the right of a contractholder or plan, under an insurance contract, to receive future dividends, rate credits, interest, experience credits or other earnings or distributions from the insurer.

§ 2620.12 Plan assets.

(a) *Insurance contracts.* An insurance contract purchased with funds contributed to or under a plan is a plan asset for purposes of this part if, on the valuation date, the contract has not been distributed to a participant and the insurer's obligations under the contract have not been cancelled.

(b) *Participation rights.* A participation right under an insurance contract purchased with funds contributed to or under a plan is a plan asset for purposes of this part to the extent that the value of the participation right is not included in the value of an insurance contract that is a plan asset.

§ 2620.13 Special rule applicable to demonstrating sufficiency and closing out a plan under Subpart C of Part 2617.

Notwithstanding §§ 2620.14 through 2620.16, for purposes of demonstrating sufficiency under Subpart B of Part 2617 of this chapter and closing out a plan under Subpart C of Part 2617 of this chapter, the plan administrator shall value insurance contracts and participation rights in the manner that best reflects the highest value that can be realized in a form that will enable the plan administrator to close out the plan as required by § 2617.21 of this chapter.

§ 2620.14 Contract provisions.

(a) *General.* The valuation of plan assets under this subpart shall be based upon the provisions of the insurance contract as of the valuation date or upon other options available from the insurer as of the valuation date. The existence of such other options must be demonstrated by means of a written statement by the insurer.

(b) *Responsibilities of plan administrator.* In determining the value of an insurance contract as of the valuation date, the plan administrator is responsible for critically assessing the reasonableness of the factors underlying the insurer's determination of the contract's cash value or the value of other options provided in lieu thereof. Where the factors underlying the determination are unreasonable, the plan administrator is responsible for taking whatever action is necessary to reach a reasonable value for the asset.

§ 2620.15 Value of insurance contracts.

(a) *General.* The value of an insurance contract is the greater of—

(1) The contract's greatest cash settlement value, determined in accordance with paragraph (b) of this section, as of the valuation date; or

(2) The present value, determined in accordance with Part 2619 of this chapter, of the benefits that can be purchased under the contract as of the valuation date by application of the contract assets described in Paragraph (c) of this section to the purchase of benefits in accordance with the order of priorities prescribed by section 4044 of the Act.

(b) *Cash settlement value.* (1) The value of a cash settlement that provides and immediate lump sum cash payment by the insurer is the dollar amount of the cash payment (including the value of participation rights under § 2620.16).

(2) The value of a cash settlement that provides a deferred lump sum cash payment (including the value of participation rights, if there are any, under § 2620.16) by the insurer or cash payments by the insurer in installments is the present value of such payments calculated as of the valuation date, determined by applying an interest rate that is the sum of—

(i) The PBGC's interest rate for valuing immediate annuities in effect on the valuation date, set forth in Appendix B of Part 2619 of this chapter, and

(ii) .5 (one-half) percent.

(c) *Contract assets.* (1) Contract assets are the funds credited to an insurance contract as of the valuation date that are available to provide benefits, including funds becoming available to provide benefits upon the cancellation of any participation rights held under the insurance contract.

(2) Contract assets do not include—

(i) Funds that the insurer is entitled, under the insurance contract, to withdraw in payment for an irrevocable commitment made by the insurer prior to the date of plan termination;

(ii) Funds that the insurer is entitled, under the insurance contract, to withdraw to satisfy liabilities of the plan that became due and owing prior to the valuation date;

Funds that the insurer is entitled, under the insurance contract, to withdraw to pay for administrative or other services performed by the insurer; and

(iv) Funds that have been paid to the insurer prior to the valuation date in return for benefits or services, which are credited to an account under the contract solely for the purpose of computing amounts payable pursuant to the plan's participation rights.

(d) *Exclusive plan asset test.* Except as provided in Paragraph (e) of this section, the benefits that can be provided under the contract be determined as if each insurance contract that is a plan asset were the plan's only asset on the valuation date. If two or more insurance contracts owned by a plan expressly provide a basis for coordinated allocation of contract assets in conformance with section 4044 of the Act, the benefits that can be provided under the contracts shall be determined as prescribed by the contracts.

(e) *Optional valuation procedure.* (1) When an insurance contract is not a plan's only asset on the valuation date, the plan administrator may value the contract by applying the contract assets to purchase benefits under the insurance contract without regard to the order of priorities prescribed by section 4044 of the Act, if the plan administrator demonstrates to the PBGC that—

(i) All of the plan's assets on the valuation date, taken together, can be allocated in a manner that complies with section 4044 of the Act;

(ii) Under the combined allocation described in Paragraph (e)(1)(i) of this section, the plan's assets will provide benefits with a total

present value that equals or exceeds the total present value of the benefits that could otherwise be provided by the plan's assets; and

(iii) In the case of a plan that receives a Notice of Inability to Determine Sufficiency under Part 2617 of this chapter, arrangements for a specific combined allocation that satisfies section 4044 of the Act were made prior to the date of plan termination.

(2) A plan administrator who elects this optional valuation procedure must furnish the PBGC with evidence, including supporting computations, that the optional valuation meets all of the requirements of Paragraph (e)(1) of this section.

(3) When this optional valuation procedure is used, the total value of the plan's assets is the total present value of the benefits that can be provided through the combined allocation of the plan's assets described in Paragraph (e)(1)(i) of this section.

§ 2620.16 Value of participation rights.

(a) If a participation right can be cancelled, the value of the participation right is the greater of—

(1) The dollar amount negotiated by the parties in accordance with § 2620.14(b) of this part, as payable upon cancellation of the participation right as of the valuation date; or

(2) The present value, determined in accordance with Part 2619 of this chapter, of the additional benefits, negotiated by the parties in accordance with § 2620.14(b) of this part, to be provided upon cancellation of the participation right as of the valuation date.

(b) If a participation right cannot be cancelled, the value of the participation right is present value, determined by applying the interest rate described in § 2620.15(b)(2), of the future stream of payments, taking into account all relevant factors, including but not limited to the past practice of the insurer with respect to participation rights, mortality rates, interest rates and comparable contract prices.

Approved, pursuant to 29 U.S.C. 552, as an exercise of the duties of the Secretary of Labor and Chairman of the Board of Directors, Pension Benefit Guaranty Corporation.

Ford B. Ford,

Under Secretary of Labor.

Issued pursuant to a resolution of the Board of Directors approving this regulation and authorizing its chairman to issue same.

Edward R. Mackiewicz,

Secretary, Pension Benefit Guaranty Corporation.

[FR Doc. 85-11044 Filed 5-7-85; 8:45 am]

¶ 20,520   Reserved.

Proposed Reg. §§ 2608.1—2608.12, on the allocation of assets of terminating pension plans, were formerly reproduced at this point. The final regulations appear at ¶ 15,472—15,473F.]

¶ 20,520A   Reserved.

Proposed Reg. §§ 2520.103-1 and 2520.103-12 on an alternate method of annual reporting for plans investing in certain entities, were formerly reproduced at this point. The final regulations appear at ¶ 14,231A and 14,231L.]

¶ 20,520B   Reserved.

Proposed Reg. §§ 2676.1—2676.31, relating to valuation of plan benefits and plan assets following mass withdrawal, were formerly reproduced at this point. The final regulations appear at ¶ 15,687D—15,687V.]

¶ 20,520C   Reserved.

Proposed Regs. § 2640.8 and 2649.1—8, relating to adjusting liability for withdrawal subsequent to a partial withdrawal, were formerly reproduced at this point. The final regulations appear at ¶ 15,663H and 15,670A—I.]

¶ 20,521   Reserved.

Proposed Reg. §§ 2609.1—2609.8, Part 2609, on limitations on guaranteed benefits, were formerly reproduced at this point. The final regulations appear at ¶ 15,429—15,429G.]

¶ 20,521A   Reserved.

PBGC illustrative examples on the proposed regulations, relating to benefit payments under Pension Reform Act Sec. 4022(b), formerly reproduced at ¶ 20,521 were formerly reproduced at this point. The final regulations appear at ¶ 15,429—15,429G.]

¶ 20,521B   Reserved.

Proposed Reg. §§ 2550.414c-1—2550.414c-3, relating to certain loans, leases, and dispositions of property prior to June 30, 1984 where an employee benefit plan is involved in a transaction, were formerly reproduced at this point. The final regulations appear at ¶ 14,844A—14,844C.]

¶ 20,521C   Reserved.

Proposed regulations on 29 CFR 2520, which provide exemptions from the reporting and disclosure requirements of ERISA for apprenticeship and other training plans were formerly reproduced at this point. The final regulations appear at ¶ 14,221, 14,247B and 14,248A.]

¶ 20,521D   Reserved.

Proposed regulations relating to limited relief from reporting, disclosure and claims procedure requirements with respect to welfare plans offering membership in a qualified health maintenance organization were formerly reproduced at this point. The final regulations appear at ¶ 14,225, 14,247, 14,247X and 14,931.]

¶ 20,521E   Reserved.

Proposed regulations relating to certain acquisitions, sales, or leases of property by an employee benefit plan were formerly reproduced at this point. The final regulations are at ¶ 14,789.]

¶ 20,521F   Reserved.

Proposed regulations which prescribe rules for the determination and payment of employer liability under ERISA Sec. 4062 and 4067 were formerly reproduced at this point. The final regulations are at ¶ 15,623.]

¶ 20,522   Reserved.

Proposed regulations on 29 CFR Part 2520, relating to the preparation of annual return/report forms, were formerly reported at this point. Temporary and proposed regulations now appear at ¶ 14,231A.]

¶ 20,523   Reserved.

Proposed Reg. §§ 2611.1—2611.5, relating to valuation of plan assets were formerly reproduced at this point. The final regulations now appear at ¶ 15,621—15,621D.]

¶ 20,524   Reserved.

Proposed regulations on 29 CFR Part 2610 on the valuation of plan benefits for the purposes of the Pension Benefit Guaranty Corporation, were formerly reproduced at this point. The proposed regulations now appear at ¶ 15,620A—15,620L.]

¶ 20,525   Reserved.

The proposed regulations on 29 CFR Part 2602, relating to premium payment and declaration under the Pension Benefit Guaranty Corporation, were formerly reproduced at this point. The final regulations are at ¶ 15,371A, and the paragraphs following thereafter.]

¶ 20,525A   Reserved.

Proposed regulations relating to the definition of the term "pension plan" under ERISA were formerly reproduced at this paragraph. The final regulations are at ¶ 14,132.]

¶ 20,525B

Proposed regulations on 29 CFR Part 2530.—Reproduced below is the text of proposed regulations relating to certain circumstances in which it is permissible for a plan to suspend the payment of pension benefits to a retiree. The proposed regulations were published in the Federal Register on January 27, 1981 (46 FR 8906).

ERISA Sec. 203.

DEPARTMENT OF LABOR

Office of Pension and Welfare Benefit Programs

29 CFR Part 2530

Rules and Regulations for Minimum Standards for Employee Benefit Plans; Suspension of Benefit Rules

AGENCY: Department of Labor.

ACTION: Notice of proposed rulemaking.

SUMMARY: This document sets forth a proposed amendment to a rule relating to certain circumstances in which it is permissible for a plan to suspend the payment of pension benefits to a retiree. The Employee Retirement Income Security Act of 1974 (the Act) authorizes the Secretary of Labor to prescribe regulations setting forth the circumstances and conditions under which the right of a retiree to a benefit payment is not treated as forfeitable solely because the plan provides that benefit payments are suspended during certain periods of reemployment. The proposal would affect employees in maritime industries covered under employee pension benefit plans.

DATE: Written comments on proposed paragraph (c)(2)(iii)(B) must be received by the Department of Labor (the Department) on or before March 30, 1981.

ADDRESSES: Written comments (preferably at least three copies) should be submitted to the Office of Reporting and Plan Standards, Pension and Welfare Benefit Programs, Room N-4508, U.S. Department of Labor, Washington, D.C. 20216, Attention: § 2530.203-3(c)(2)(ii)(B). All written comments will be available for public inspection at the Public Documents Room, Pension and Welfare Benefit Programs, Department of Labor, Room N-4677, 200 Constitution Avenue NW., Washington, D.C.

FOR FURTHER INFORMATION CONTACT: Jay S. Neuman, Esq., Office of the Solicitor of Labor, (202) 523-8658; or Judith Bleich Kahn, Pension and Welfare Benefit Programs. (202-523-8430). These telephone numbers are not toll free.

SUPPLEMENTARY INFORMATION: On December 19, 1978, notice was published in the **Federal Register** (43 FR 59098) that the Department had under consideration a proposal to adopt a regulation. 29 CFR 2530.203-3, under section 203(a)(3)(B) of the Act, relating to suspension of pension benefit payments under certain circumstances. As part of the proposal, the Department requested specific comment regarding whether and to what extent the "geographic area covered by the plan" should be specially defined for purposes of plans covering employees in the maritime industries.[1] In response to comments which suggested the need for such a special definition, the Department is publishing for comment proposed paragraph (c)(2)(iii)(B). The proposal defines the geographic area covered by plans covering employees in the maritime industries in terms of ports of embarkation because it appears that these are the most appropriate territorial reference points for such plans. The proposal provides that the geographic area covered by a plan that covers employees in a maritime industry consists of any port of embarkation at which employers hired employees for whom contributions have been made or have been required to be made as of the time that the payment of benefits commenced or would have commenced if the employee had not returned to employment.

It should be noted that the Department has decided to adopt, with certain modifications, § 2530.203-3 as proposed. This final regulation appears elsewhere in this issue of the **Federal Register.** Persons who are interested in commenting on proposed § 2530.203-3(c)(2)(iii)(B) should refer to the adopted portions of § 2530.203-3 in order to appreciate how this proposed paragraph would operate in the context of the regulation as a whole.

Statutory Authority

Paragraph (c)(2)(iii)(B) is proposed under the authority contained in sections 203(a)(3)(B) and 505 of the Act (Pub. L. 93-406, 88 Stat. 854, 894, 29 U.S.C. 1053, 1135) and section 411(a)(3)(B) of the Internal Revenue Code of 1954.

§ 2520.203-3 Suspension of pension benefits upon reemployment of retirees.

* * * * *

(c) *Section 203(a)(3)(B) Service.* * * *

(2) *Multiemployer plans.* * * *

(iii) *Geographic area covered by the plan.* * * *

(B) The geographic area covered by a plan that covers employees in a maritime industry consists of any port of embarkation at which employers hired employees for whom contributions were made or were required to be made as of the time the payment of benefits commenced or would have commenced if the employee had not returned to employment.

* * * * *

Signed at Washington, D.C. this 19th day of January 1981.

Ian D. Lanoff,

Administrator, Pension and Welfare Benefit Programs, Labor-Management Services Administration.

[FR Doc. 81-2444. Filed 1-26-81; 8:45 am]

¶ 20,525C   Reserved.

Proposed amendments relating to the suspension of pension benefit payments to reemployed retirees were formerly reproduced at this point. The amendments, as adopted, are at ¶ 14,433.]

¶ 20,525D

Proposed regulations on 29 CFR Parts 2690 through 2695.—Reproduced below are proposed regulations on 29 CFR Parts 2690 through 2695, which would establish a supplemental program to guarantee benefits under multiemployer plans that would otherwise be

---

[1] In relevant part, section 203(a)(3)(B) provides that—

(B) A right to an accrued benefit from employer contributions shall not be treated as forfeitable solely because the plan provides that the payment of benefits is suspended for such period as the employee is employed, subsequent to the commencement of payment of such benefits—

(ii) In the case of a multiemployer plan, in the same industry, in the same trade or craft, and the same geographic area covered by the plan, as when such benefits commenced.

guaranteed but for the dollar or percentage limitations on guaranteed benefits under ERISA. Under this voluntary program, benefits under multiemployer plans could be guaranteed at the level provided for single-employer plan.

The proposed regulations were published in the *Federal Register* on February 1, 1983 (48 FR 4632).

ERISA Sec. 4022A.

PENSION BENEFIT GUARANTY CORPORATION

29 CFR Parts 2690 through 2695

Supplemental Guarantee Program

AGENCY: Pension Benefit Guaranty Corporation.

ACTION: Proposed rule.

SUMMARY: This proposed regulation if adopted would establish a supplemental program to guarantee benefits under multiemployer plans that would otherwise be guaranteed but for the dollar or percentage limitations on guaranteed benefits in the Employee Retirement Income Security Act of 1974, as amended. That law requires the Pension Benefit Guaranty Corporation to establish a supplemental guarantee program, coverage under which must be available by January 1, 1983. Participation by plans in this supplemental program is optional. The regulation is needed to establish a supplemental guarantee program, as required by law, in order to afford participants in multiemployer plans and their beneficiaries the fullest feasible benefit guarantee. The effect of this regulation would be to provide multiemployer plans with the opportunity to obtain a greater benefit guarantee for participants.

DATE: Comments must be received on or before April 4, 1983.

ADDRESSES: Comments should be addressed to the Assistant Executive Director for Policy and Planning (140), Pension Benefit Guaranty Corporation, Suite 7300, 2020 K Street, NW., Washington, D.C. 20006. Written comments will be available for public inspection at the PBGC, Suite 7100, at the above address, between the hours of 9:00 a.m. and 4:00 p.m.

FOR FURTHER INFORMATION CONTACT: J. Ronald Goldstein, Office of the Executive Director, Policy and Planning (140), 2020 K Street, NW., Washington, D.C. 20006; 202-254-4862. [This is not a toll-free number].

SUPPLEMENTARY INFORMATION:

The Statute

The Multiemployer Pension Plan Amendments Act of 1980, Pub. L. 96-364, 94 Stat. 1208 ("Multiemployer Act"), became law on September 26, 1980 and amended the Employee Retirement Income Security Act of 1974 ("ERISA"). (As used herein, "ERISA" means the Act as amended, unless the context requires otherwise.) The Multiemployer Act revised the rules under which the Pension Benefit Guaranty Corporation (the "PBGC") guarantees benefits under a multiemployer plan.

Under section 4022A(a) of ERISA, the PBGC guarantees the payment of certain nonforfeitable benefits ("basic benefits" or "guaranteed benefits") under a multiemployer plan that is insolvent. A plan is insolvent if it is unable to pay benefits when due for the plan year. A plan terminated by a mass withdrawal is not insolvent until it has first been amended to eliminate all benefits that are not eligible for the PBGC's guarantee under section 4022A(b).

Under section 4022A(b), only nonforfeitable benefits or benefit increases that have been in effect for 60 months or more are eligible for PBGC's guarantee ("guaranteeable benefits"). Section 4022A(c) limits the maximum monthly guaranteed benefit to the product of (a) 100 percent of the first $5 of a participant's benefit accrual rate and 75 percent of the next $15 of a participant's benefit accrual rate, and (b) the participant's number of years of credited service. A participant's benefit accrual rate is computed by dividing a participant's monthly guaranteeable benefit by the participant's number of years of credited service under the plan for benefit accrual purposes. In this fraction, the guaranteeable benefit may not exceed the plan benefit payable at normal retirement age as a life annuity and is determined without regard to past service benefit reductions permitted to be made on account of the cessation of contributions by the participant's employer. The 75 percent guarantee is reduced to 65 percent under plans that did not satisfy pre-ERISA funding requirements.[1]

These rules for determining guaranteed benefits are applied without regard to past service benefit reductions permitted to be made on

account of the cessation of contributions by an employer (section 4022A(c)(3)). Under section 4022A(d), if a past-service benefit is reduced because of the cessation of contributions by an employer, the guaranteed benefit is the lesser of the benefit determined under section 4022A(c) or the benefit determined under the plan's past service disregard rule. Section 4022A(h) contains a special rule for participants or beneficiaries under a multiemployer plan who, on July 29, 1980, were in pay status or were within 36 months of the plan's normal retirement age and had a nonforfeitable right to a pension. The PBGC will guarantee those individuals' nonforfeitable accrued benefits as of that date under the single-employer rules in section 4022 of the Act, except for plan years following a plan year in which substantially all employers withdrew pursuant to an agreement to withdraw or the plan terminates by mass withdrawal under section 4041A(a)(2).

Section 4022A(g)(2) requires the PBGC to establish a supplemental program to guarantee benefits that would otherwise be guaranteed but for the limitations in section 4022A(c) ("supplemental benefits"). The supplemental benefits of a participant that are guaranteed by the PBGC under section 4022A(g)(2) are nonbasic benefits under Title IV.

The PBGC is required under section 4022A(g)(2) to establish a program to guarantee supplemental benefits, coverage under which must be available by January 1, 1983. Under the Act, participation by plans in this program is voluntary. Supplemental benefits under a plan are guaranteed only if and to the extent the plan elects coverage under the supplemental program. A plan's election to participate in the program can be made only within the time specified by PBGC regulations and cannot be made unless plan assets as of the end of the plan year preceding the election are at least 15 times benefit payments made for that year. Section 4022A(g)(2) also provides that the PBGC regulations, in addition to prescribing exceptions, if any, to the latter rule, shall provide "such other reasonable terms and conditions for supplemental coverage, including funding standards and any other reasonable limitations with respect to plans or benefits covered or to means of program financing, as the corporation determines are necessary and appropriate for a feasible supplemental program consistent with the purposes of [Title IV]."

The supplemental guarantee program is a self-financing program. To this end, a separate revolving fund on the books of the United States Treasury is established by section 4005(e). This fund is one of six revolving funds established on the books of the United States Treasury to be used by PBGC in carrying out its duties under Title IV.

Monies in this fund are to be used exclusively for the purpose of making payments under the supplemental guarantee program. These monies are not available to make loans to or on behalf of any other fund. Similarly, monies in other funds are not available for the supplemental guarantee program. In addition, no money borrowed by PBGC from the United States Treasury pursuant to section 4005(c) is available for the supplemental guarantee program (section 4005(f)(2)).

Under section 4006(a)(5)(B), the PBGC is authorized to prescribe premium rates for multiemployer plans for supplemental coverage that "reflect any reasonable considerations which the corporation determines to be appropriate." No revised schedule of premiums may go into effect without Congressional approval.

Finally, section 4022A(g)(5) authorizes the PBGC regulation to include rules that supersede the requirements of section 4245 (relating to insolvent plans), section 4261 (relating to financial assistance) and section 4281 (relating to multiemployer plans terminated by mass withdrawal), but only with respect to nonbasic benefits guaranteed under section 4022A(g).

The Regulation

Overview

In designing the supplemental guarantee program, the PBGC attempted to achieve the following goals:

(1) To minimize premiums and the PBGC's administrative expenses, especially in the early years of the program;

(2) To minimize the potential for antiselection by a plan;

---

[1] The insurance limits in section 4022(b) of the Act (other than the limits in section 4022(b)(6), relating to benefit accruals under a plan that ceases to meet the requirements of Internal Revenue Code section 401(a)) apply only to single-employer plans.

(3) To structure a program that is simple to understand and administer; and

(4) To afford plans flexibility, *e.g.,* the ability to choose the desired amount of coverage.

The proposed regulation sets forth rules under six parts in Subchapter I—Supplemental Guarantee Program for Multiemployer Plans, of the PBGC's regulations. Part 2690 contains all the definitions for Subchapter I. Part 2691 establishes the requirements for PBGC's guarantee of supplemental benefits and for coverage of a multiemployer plan under the supplemental guarantee program. Part 2692 prescribes rules for determining the amount of coverage for a participant and for a multiemployer plan under the supplemental guarantee program. Part 2693 prescribes the premiums for coverage under the supplemental guarantee program. Part 2693 also establishes a late entry fee for a plan that applies for its initial coverage after the plan year in which it is first eligible for coverage under the supplemental program. Part 2694 prescribes the requirements of PBGC financial assistance under the supplemental guarantee program. Finally, Part 2695 prescribes special rules for multiemployer plans covered by the program that experience a mass withdrawal.

Part 2690—Definitions

Part 2690 contains all the definitions for Subchapter I. Section 2690.2 contains definitions of terms of general applicability. The subsequent sections contain definitions of terms specific to each part within the subchapter.

Two of the definitions in § 2690.2 are fundamental to an understanding of the supplemental guarantee program: "supplemental benefit" and "guaranteed supplemental benefit". These benefits may vary from one plan participant to another and may be different amounts for any individual participant.

"Supplemental benefit" is "the monthly benefit under the plan, except for the nonforfeitable benefit accrued prior to July 30, 1980 by participants and beneficiaries to whom section 4022A(h) of the Act applies, that would be guaranteed under section 4022A of the Act, determined without regard to section 4022A(c), reduced by the benefit guaranteed under section 4022A(c) of the Act." As discussed earlier, under section 4022A(c) of the Act, the maximum monthly guaranteed benefit is limited to the product of a) 100 percent of the first $5 of a participant's benefit accrual rate and, generally, 75 percent of the next $15 of a participant's benefit accrual rate, and b) a participant's number of years of credited service. Supplemental benefits are benefits in excess of the section 4022A(c) limits, *i.e.,* 25 percent of a participant's benefit accrual rate between $5.01 and $20, and 100 percent of a participant's benefit accrual rate above $20. The following examples illustrate how to determine a participant's supplemental benefit:

Participant A has 20 years of credited service under a multiemployer plan and a monthly benefit of $300 (based on the benefit in effect for at least five years). The benefit has not been reduced under section 411(a)(3)(E) of the Code. Participant A has a guaranteed monthly benefit of $250. This is based on an accrual rate for purposes of section 4022A, without regard to the section 4022A(c) limits, of $15; *i.e.,* $300, the benefit in effect for five years or more, divided by 20, the number of years of credited service. This $15 rate is reduced by the limits in section 4022A(c) to a guaranteed accrual rate of $12.50; *i.e.,* 100 percent of the first $5 = $5, plus 75 percent of the remaining $10 = $7.50. The $12.50 accrual rate is then multiplied by 20, the number of years of credited service, to determine Participant A's guaranteed benefit. Participant A's supplemental benefit is $50 per month; *i.e.,* $2.50, the excess of his or her accrual rate under section 4022A without regard to the section 4022A(c) limits ($15), over his or her accrual rate taking into account the section 4022A(c) limits ($12.50), multiplied by 20, the participant's years of credited service.

Participant B has 20 years of credited service under a multiemployer plan and a monthly benefit of $600 (based on the benefit in effect for at least five years). The benefit has not been reduced under section 411(a)(3)(E) of the Code. Participant B has a guaranteed monthly benefit of $325. This is based on an accrual rate for purposes of section 4022A, without regard to the section 4022A(c) limits, of $30; i.e., $600, the benefit in effect for five years or more, divided by 20, the number of years of credited service. This $30 accrual rate is reduced by the limits in section 4022A(c) to a guaranteed accrual rate of $16.25; *i.e.,* 100 percent of the first $5 = $5, plus 75 percent of the net $15 = $11.25. The $16.25 accrual rate is then multiplied by 20, the number of years of credited service, to determine participant B's guaranteed benefit.

Participant B's supplemental benefit is $275 per month; *i.e.,* $13.75, the excess of his or her accrual rate under section 4022A without regard to the section 4022A(c) limits ($30), over his or her accrual rate taking into account the section 4022A(c) limits ($16.25), multiplied by

20, the participant's years of credited service. Note in this example that while no portion of a participant's accrual rate in excess of $20 per month is subject to PBGC's basic benefit guarantee the entire amount is guaranteeable under this supplemental guarantee program.

"Guaranteed supplemental benefit" is "the supplemental benefit payable with respect to a participant that is guaranteed by the PBGC under the supplemental guarantee program, as determined under § 2692.3 of this subchapter." That section provides that a participant's guaranteed supplemental benefit is the lesser of his or her supplemental benefit or the number of units of supplemental coverage purchased by the plan multiplied by the participant's service multiplier. Under § 2692.3(b), the service multiplier is normally the participant's total number of years of credited service, although there is a special rule for a participant whose benefit has been reduced under section 411(a)(3)(E) of the Code (relating to a past-service disregard provision in a plan). Thus, PBGC will guarantee a participant's supplemental benefit only to the extent of the number of units of supplemental coverage purchased by his or her plan. In the first example above, PBGC will guarantee the participant's entire supplemental benefit only if his or her plan has purchased at least 3 units of coverage (3 × (the number of years of credited service) = $60 of supplemental coverage).

Part 2691—Requirements for Coverage

Part 2691 establishes the requirements for PBGC's guarantee of supplemental benefits and for coverage of a multiemployer plan under the supplemental guarantee program.

Section 2691.2 Provides that PBGC will guarantee the payment of supplemental benefits under a multiemployer plan if the plan (1) is covered by Title IV of ERISA, (2) is eligible for coverage, (3) satisfies the requirements for initial coverage, (4) pays its premiums when due, and (5) is insolvent.

A plan is eligible for coverage under § 2691.3 if (1) the fair market value of the plan assets as of the end of the pre-eligibility year equals at least 15 times the total amount of the benefit payments and expenses under the plan for that year ("15-year asset test"); (2) the fair market value of the plan's assets as of the end of the pre-eligibility year, plus expected investment earnings on those assets for the next ten plan years equal or exceed the total amount of expected benefit payments and expected expenses under the plan for that ten-year period ("10-year benefit payment test"); (3) the plan has not experienced a mass withdrawal on or before the date the plan's application for coverage is filed ("mass withdrawal test"); and (4) the maximum supplemental benefit under the plan, as of the date the plan's application for coverage is filed, is greater than zero. "Pre-eligibility year" is defined in § 2690.3 as "the plan year preceding the plan year in which an application for coverage that conforms with the requirements of § 2691.5 is filed."

The 15-year asset test is derived from section 4022A(g)(2)(B)(i) of the Act. That section provides that "unless the corporation determines otherwise, a plan may not elect supplemental coverage unless the value of the assets of the plan as of the end of the plan year preceding the plan year in which the election must be made is an amount equal to 15 times the total amount of the benefit payments made under the plan for that year." In order to reduce plan costs, the regulation provides that the plan's Form 5500 or Form 5500-C filed for the pre-eligibility year is used to determine whether this test is met. For example, under the Form 5500 for plan years beginning in 1981, the value of plan assets as of the end of the 1981 plan year is stated on line 13(h) of the Form 5500 and the total of benefit payments and other expenses for the 1981 plan year is stated on line 14(l). A special rule is included for small plans that have filed or are going to file a Form 5500-R (which does not include this information) for the pre-eligibility plan year. For such plans, the plan sponsor must submit a certification that the plan satisfies the 15-year asset test.

The 15-year asset test is a conservative means for determining eligibility. In view of the fact that this program is voluntary and self-financing, it is necessary, at least at the outset, to adopt a conservative approach to coverage under the program in order to preserve its financial integrity. The 15-year asset test is also necessary to avoid adverse selection by plans that will require financial assistance from PBGC in the near future.

PBGC believes that the 15-year asset test and the fact that this program is voluntary are indicative of Congress' intent that coverage under this program be made avialable only to plans in good financial condition that are able to pay benefits when due in the near future.

However, satisfaction of the 15-year asset test does not necessarily indicate that a plan can pay future benefits when due. Accordingly PBGC is proposing two additional eligibility tests: the mass withdrawal test and the 10-year benefit payment test. The mass withdrawal test is necessary to protect the supplemental insurance program because a mass withdrawal is the result of a shrinkage in the plan's contribution base, and therefore will increase the likelihood that the plan will require financial assistance. The 10-year benefit payment test is intended for those rare situations where a plan that satisfies the 15-year asset test, nevertheless faces an imminent cash flow problem because of a significant increase in the benefits expected to be payable under the plan.

For example, assume that all the retirees in a multiemployer plan are "spunoff" to a new plan, with the multiemployer plan transferring the retirees' entire accrued benefit liabilities and substantially all of the plan's assets to the new plan. As a result of this transaction the multiemployer plan satisfies the 15-year asset test. However, the plan has a significant number of active participants who are expected to enter pay status within the next several years. Because of this, the plan may be unable to pay benefits in the near future. In this situation, PBGC believes that the plan should be ineligible for coverage under the supplemental guarantee program.

Finally, a plan is eligible for coverage under § 2691.3 only if the maximum supplemental benefit under the plan, as of the date the plan's application for coverage is filed, is greater than zero. "Maximum supplemental benefit" is defined in § 2690.2 as "the supplemental benefit to which an individual who is or could be a participant under the plan would be entitled at the earlier of age 65 or the plan's normal retirement age if he or she commenced participation at the earlier of the earliest possible entry age under the plan or age 22 and served continuously until the earlier of age 65 or the plan's normal retirement age, based on plan provisions currently in effect five years or more (under which such amount would be the highest)." Under this, a plan is eligible for coverage even if no actual plan participant has yet accrued a supplemental benefit. The purpose of this rule is to enable plans that are otherwise eligible and will have supplemental benefits based on the current plan provisions, to apply for coverage at the earliest possible date. (As will be explained more fully in the discussion of the late entry fee, a plan may defer applying for coverage without penalty until such time as it has participants in pay status who are entitled to supplemental benefits. It may nevertheless be to the plan's advantage to enroll sooner.)

Section 2691.4(a) of the regulation provides that a plan that is eligible for coverage shall become covered under the supplemental guarantee program upon filing with PBGC a written application for coverage, including the initial premium, and any late entry fee, due under Part 2693, and thereafter, approval by PBGC of the application. (See discussion of late entry fee under Part 2693 (relating to premiums)). Coverage is effective under the supplemental guarantee program as of the first day of the plan year during which a complete application is filed by the plan and the initial premium, and if applicable, late entry fee, is paid (§ 2691.4(c)).

Section 2691.4(d) of the regulation relates to changes in coverage. To preserve the fiscal integrity of the program, increases in units of supplemental coverage will be approved by PBGC only if the plan satisfies the requirements for initial coverage. A plan seeking an increase in coverage must satisfy anew the eligibility requirements in § 2691.3(a)(1) and (a)(2) (*i.e.*, the 15-year asset test and the insolvency test; the plan by definition already satisfies the maximum supplemental benefit requirement in § 2691.3(a)(3)) and comply with the requirements for coverage in § 2691.4 (§ 2691.4(d)(1)). That is, the plan must file an application, pay the premium for the additional unit or units, and thereafter obtain PBGC approval.

Decreases in coverage, on the other hand, do not create a potential for abuse of the supplemental insurance program, because such decreases reduce the exposure of the program. Accordingly, a plan may decrease its coverage without PBGC approval (§ 2691.4(d)(2)). A plan may decrease its coverage no more than once a year, by so indicating on the PBGC-1 and paying the reduced premium. A plan that has already filed its PBGC-1 for a plan year must wait until the following plan year to decrease its coverage. A play may not decrease coverage in any plan year during which it is receiving financial assistance from PBGC under Part 2694 of this subchapter.

Requirements concerning the application for coverage are set forth in § 2691.5. In addition to paying the initial premium and any late entry fee, the application must include the information specified in § 2691.5(d). Among the information required is information that will enable PBGC to determine whether the eligibility tests in § 2691.3 are satisfied and to apply the maximum plan coverage limitation in § 2692.4:

(1) A copy of the plan's Form 5500, 5500-C or 5500-R filed for the pre-eligibility plan year. In addition, for a plan that filed a Form 5500-R for the pre-eligibility plan year, the application shall include the plan's most recent Form 5500 or Form 5500-C. (PBGC notes that a plan will be unable to submit an application for coverage until it has submitted its annual report form for the pre-eligibility plan year.)

(2) A copy of the two most recent actuarial reports.

(3) A statement updating the most recent actuarial report to show any material changes.

(4) A statement of the number of units of supplemental coverage necessary to guarantee the maximum supplemental benefit under the plan, determined as of the date the plan's application for coverage is filed, including supporting documentation.

(5) A certification by the plan sponsor that the plan has not experienced a mass withdrawal on or before the date the plan's application for coverage is filed.

(6) A certification by an enrolled actuary that the plan satisfies the test described in § 2691.3(a)(2), including supporting assumptions and method, and a statement that, in making the certification, due consideration was given to the distribution of benefit liabilities under the plan.

In addition, the plan sponsor must submit a certification indicating whether the plan is subject to a late entry fee, and, if so, the amount of the fee (including interest), with supporting calculations. This certification shall include a statement of the year in which the plan first satisfied the 15-year asset test, and for that year and each year thereafter, the amount of the missed premium or a statement that there is no missed premium due for that year, including, calculations or other evidence supporting the statement. (Calculation of the late entry fee is discussed in greater detail later in this preamble.) PBGC may request any additional information it needs, including information to verify the late entry fee (§ 2691.5(e)).

PBGC is required under § 2691.6(a) to accept a plan for coverage if it determines that the plan is eligible for coverage and has submitted a complete application. PBGC may, however, approve lower coverage than the plan requested, if it determines that the plan requested coverage greater than that allowed under § 2692.4 of this subchapter. PBGC's decision to approve or reject an application will be in writing (§ 2691.6(b)). If PBGC rejects the application, in whole or in part, PBGC's decision will state the reasons for the decision and advise the plan sponsor of its right to appeal the decision pursuant to Part 2606 of PBGC's regulations.

Section 2691.7 of the regulation contains rules relating to cancellation of coverage under the supplemental guarantee program. PBGC may cancel coverage if the plan fails to pay a premium when due (§ 2691.7(a)), or if PBGC determines that the plan's application contained a material misrepresentation (§ 2691.7(b)). A plan may cancel coverage upon notice to PBGC (§ 2691.7(c)).

If a plan fails to pay the full amount of any premium due by the last date prescribed for payment under Part 2693, PBGC shall issue the plan a notice of cancellation. A notice of cancellation is effective on the 31st day after it is issued, unless the plan pays its full premium before that date.

PBGC may cancel coverage if it determines that the application contained a material misrepresentation of fact, and that it would have rejected the application had not that fact been misrepresented (§ 2691.7(b)). PBGC will cancel a plan's coverage under this provision only after reviewing all the facts and circumstances, and coverage is cancelled as of the first day the plan was covered under the supplemental guarantee program. If coverage is cancelled, PBGC will refund premiums (and any late entry fee) paid by the plan (§ 2691.7(b)(1)). PBGC's decision to cancel coverage is subject to appeal pursuant to Part 2606 of PBGC's regulations (§ 2691.7(b)(2)). However, the filing of an appeal did not stay the cancellation decision. If the plan appeals the decision and PBGC's Appeals Board determines that the initial determination to cancel coverage was erroneous, the Appeals Board will order that coverage be reinstated upon the plan's repayment of any amounts refunded and payment of any premium subsequently due. These same rules on cancellation also apply to an application for an increase in coverage.

Coverage will become incontestable as to the statements in the application after coverage (or the increased coverage) has been in effect for 10 years (§ 2691.7(b)(3)). PBGC believes that it is reasonable for plans and participants to be able to rely on supplemental guarantee program coverage after coverage has been in effect for this length of time. However, any individual who knowingly and willfully falsifies a material fact in the application will be subject to applicable criminal penalties under 18 U.S.C. 1001, no matter when the false statement is discovered.

Section 4022A(g)(2) of the Act provides that coverage "shall be irrevocable, except to the extent otherwise provided by regulations prescribed by the corporation." This regulation provides that a plan may cancel coverage without PBGC approval in accordance with the rules in § 2691.7(c). A plan may cancel its coverage by so indicating on the Form PBGC-1. A plan may not cancel coverage in any plan year in which it is receiving financial assistance from PBGC under Part 2694; nor may a plan cancel coverage in any plan year in which it has already filed its Form PBGC-1 and paid its premium pursuant to Part 2693. Finally, a plan that cancels its coverage shall not be eligible to re-enter the supplemental guarantee program.

PBGC believes that revocable coverage is consistent with traditional insurance principles and with the concept of a voluntary insurance program. In addition, PBGC is concerned that requiring an irrevocable election of coverage by a plan might deter participation by plans that are uncertain about their long-term interest in the program.

PBGC recognizes that making coverage revocable may increase its administrative burden by making it more difficult to anticipate future experience under the program. This will make it more difficult to prescribe a reasonable and adequate initial premium rate and to recommend appropriate adjustments to Congress. Moreover, PBGC understands that revocable coverage could be disruptive to plans and participants because the decision to participate could be subject to yearly reevaluation. Nevertheless, the PBGC believes, on balance, that revocable coverage is preferable. The bar on re-entering the program after voluntarily cancelling coverage is necessary, in PBGC's view, to prevent abuse of the supplemental program and to provide some greater measure of stability to the program.

PBGC specifically requests public comment on these issues.

Part 2692—Coverage Limitation for Participants and Multiemployer Plans

Part 2692 prescribes rules for determining the amount of coverage of a participant and a multiemployer plan under the supplemental guarantee program. Section 2692.2 provides that the guaranteed supplemental benefit of a participant is the lesser of the participant's supplemental benefit or the number of units of supplemental coverage of the plan, multiplied by the participant's service multiplier. Each unit of supplemental coverage is equal to a monthly benefit of $1.00 times a participant's "service multiplier" (§ 2692.3(a)). As discussed earlier in this preamble, a participant's "service multiplier" is normally a participant's total number of years of credited service under the plan (§ 2692.3(b)).

Units of supplemental coverage are available only in whole number increments (§ 2692.3(a)). Thus, to insure the entire supplemental benefit of a participant whose supplemental benefit is $75 per month and who has 30 years of credited service under the plan, a plan must purchase 3 units ($75÷30=$2.50 supplemental accrual rate).

A plan may apply for any number of units of supplemental coverage, up to the limit described in § 2692.4, for the plan as a whole (§ 2692.3(a)). That is, a plan must purchase the same number of units for all participants in the plan, even though the guaranteeable supplemental benefits of the participants will be different amounts. In deciding to propose this guarantee structure, PBGC first considered and rejected two other alternatives. First, PBGC considered a guarantee structure that would make coverage available for all supplemental benefits, regardless of amount, under the plan. Under this structure a plan would pay a single premium for coverage of all participants' full supplemental benefit. PBGC also considered a guarantee structure that would permit a plan to vary coverage for specific groups of participants, *e.g.*, by bargaining units or regions. This structure might be attractive to plans that vary benefit levels for such groups.

PBGC has decided to propose only one guarantee structure at this time in the interest of simplicity and administrative ease. PBGC chose the plan-wide unit benefit guarantee structure, rather than the other two structures, because this structure is comparatively easy to administer, while still providing a plan with the flexibility to select the coverage it wants and the ability to obtain full coverage. Moreover, this structure is attractive because coverage of the plan as a whole will work in the same manner as under the basic benefits program.

Section 2692.4 of the regulation contains a limitation on the number of units of supplemental coverage a plan may purchase. A multiemployer plan that is eligible for coverage under § 2691.3 may apply for any number of units of supplemental coverage, up to the number of units necessary to guarantee the maximum supplemental benefit under the plan, determined as of the date the plan's application for coverage is filed. This rule is designed to make it impossible for plans to circumvent the requirement in § 2691.4(d)(1) that a plan that wants to increase its coverage must satisfy anew the eligibility requirements in § 2691.3, by prohibiting a plan from purchasing more units of supplemental coverage than it currently needs in anticipation of future benefit increases.

Part 2693—Premiums

Part 2693 prescribes the premium for coverage under the supplemental guarantee program. It also requires a late entry fee in certain instances for a plan that applies for initial coverage after the first year it is eligible for coverage under the supplemental program.

To participate in the supplemental program, a multiemployer plan is required to pay an annual premium. (Payment of the premium will not, however, result in coverage under the supplemental guarantee program for plans that have not satisfied the requirements for coverage under the program.) The premium is based on the number of plan participants, the number of units of supplemental coverage elected by the plan, and the supplemental premium rate (§ 2693.4(a)). The definition of "participant" for this purpose is the same definition as that used for payment of premiums for basic benefits guaranteed by PBGC. The supplemental premium rate is $.30.

The premium rate for the supplemental program is based on the ultimate premium rate for multiemployer plans for basic benefits under section 4006(a)(3)(A)(iii)(IV) of the Act. To determine the supplemental premium rate, the premium rate for basic benefits was converted to a premium per $1.00 of basic benefits guaranteed, based on the highest average guaranteed benefit payable under a multiemployer plan covered by Title IV. The cost of one unit of supplemental coverage is a prorata portion of the premium for the underlying basic benefits.

The form prescribed in Part 2693 for payment of premiums is Form PBGC-1 (§ 2693.2). A plan must use the same Form PBGC-1 for its premium payment under the supplemental guarantee program and for its premium for basic benefits;

The plan sponsor must file the plan's initial premium payment as part of its application for coverage (§ 2693.3(a)). No Form PBGC-1 is necessary with this premium payment. The filing may be made at any time. The plan administrator must make subsequent premium payments concurrently with premium payments for basic benefits *i.e.*, no later than the last day of the seventh month following the close of the prior plan year (§ 2693.3(b)).

As noted above, under § 2691.7(a), if a plan fails to pay a premium when due, after the initial premium, PBGC shall issue a notice of cancellation. The notice is effective on the 31st day after it is issued, unless the plan pays the premium due on or before the 30th day. Under this proposed regulation, no interest or penalty charges are assessed for a premium payment made during the 30-day period, although a late payment charge will be imposed with respect to a premium for basic benefits paid during that time. (*See* Part 2610 of PBGC's regulations.) PBGC is considering assessing late payment interest and penalty charges for a premium payment under the supplemental program during the 30-day period in order to discourage routine late payments. PBGC specifically requests comments on this issue.

If PBGC determines that a plan has paid less than its full premium, it will issue a notice of cancellation, requiring that the amount due be paid within 30 days. The plan may appeal PBGC's determination. However, filing of an appeal will not stay PBGC's notice of cancellation; the plan must pay the amount determined due by PBGC within the 30-day period in order to avoid cancellation (§ 2693.3(f)). If the plan's appeal is successful, PBGC will refund the overpayment with interest (§ 2693.7(c)).

As discussed earlier, § 2693.5 generally requires a late entry fee, in addition to an initial premium, for a plan that fails to apply for coverage during the first year in which it is eligible for coverage. The late entry fee equals the plan's missed premiums plus interest (§ 2692.5(a)).

The late entry fee is intended to encourage early entry into the supplemental guarantee program. It is consistent with and authorized by section 4022A(g)(2)(B)(i) and (iii) of the Act, which provide "that a plan must elect coverage under the supplemental program within the time permitted by the [PBGC] regulations" and that the PBGC regulations shall include "such other reasonable terms and conditions for supplemental coverage, including funding standards and any other reasonable limitations with respect to plans or benefits covered or to means of program financing, as the corporation determines are necessary and appropriate for a feasible supplemental program consistent with the purposes of this title." Section 4022A(g)(4)(B)(i) contemplates time limits within which a plan may enter the program. Accordingly, with the exceptions noted below, a plan that enters after the plan year in which it is first eligible is assessed a charge for late entry based on the premiums it would have paid had it applied when first eligible.

Moreover, PBGC believes it is necessary and appropriate for a viable program to charge a late entry fee. First, a late entry fee will encourage early entry. By doing so, it should enable PBGC to identify, at an early date, the majority of the plans interested in the program. This will assist PBGC in determining the viability of the program. Second, the fees will help finance the cost of the program. (Had the plan joined the program and paid premiums from when it was first eligible, those monies would have been available for the program.)

The late entry fee rules assume that a plan that satisfies the 15-year asset test is eligible for coverage under § 2691.3(a), unless the plan can demonstrate to the contrary. Accordingly, a plan that fails to file an application for coverage on or before the last day of the first plan year in which it satisfies the 15-year asset test described in § 2691.3(a)(1) is presumptively liable for a late entry fee based on the plan's missed premiums for each "missed premium year" (§ 2693.5(a)). A "missed premium year" is defined in § 2690.4 as "any plan year in which the plan satisfies the 15-year asset test described in § 2691.3(a)(1) of this subchapter but does not apply for coverage in accordance with § 2691.5 of this subchapter." (As discussed hereafter, however, there is no missed premium due for any year for which the plan can demonstrate it was not, in fact, eligible for coverage under § 2691.3(a).) Because the effective date of the supplemental guarantee program is January 1, 1983, a plan's first missed premium year cannot be earlier than its plan year beginning in 1983.

Section 2693.5(b) provides that the amount of the missed premium for each missed premium year is the premium determined under § 2693.4 that would have been due had coverage been in effect for that year. For this purpose, the number of participants is the number reported on the plan's Form PBGC-1 filed for that year. The number of units of supplemental coverage used in this calculation is the lesser of (a) one-half the number of units necessary to guarantee the maximum supplemental benefit under the plan as of the date the plan's application for coverage is filed, or (b) the number of units of supplemental coverage actually necessary in each year to guarantee the highest supplemental benefit for a participant in pay status as of the last day of that year, as demonstrated by the plan sponsor to the satisfaction of PBGC.

PBGC considered several other rules for determining missed premium amounts. For example, PBGC considered basing the computation on the number of units of supplemental coverage for which the plan applies in its initial application. This rule was rejected because it is easily subject to abuse: a plan could apply for 1 unit of coverage in its initial application and apply for additional units the following year. PBGC also considered basing the missed premium amounts on one unit of supplemental coverage for each missed premium year. This rule was rejected because it would not adequately encourage early entry into the supplemental guarantee program. Finally, PBGC considered using the maximum supplemental benefit under the plan in each missed premium year. This rule was rejected as too harsh.

Consequently, PBGC has decided to propose a rule that normally assumes that the number of units in effect for each missed premium year is one-half the maximum number of units the plan could purchase, i.e., one-half the units necessary to guarantee the maximum supplemental benefit under the plan as of the date the plan's application for coverage is filed. However, if for any given year, the plan sponsor can demonstrate that the number of units of supplemental coverage necessary to guarantee the highest supplemental benefit for a participant in pay status on the last day of that year is lower than one-half the maximum, then this lower number of units shall be used to compute the missed premiums. If the plan sponsor demonstrates that no participant in pay status as of the last day of a plan year had a supplemental benefit, then the missed premium for that year is zero (see discussion below).

Section 2693.5(b) contains special rules which provide, among other things, that a plan that satisfies the 15-year asset test described in § 2691.3(a)(1) will not have a missed premium due for any year for which it can show that it did not satisfy either of the other two eligibility requirements, and therefore, was not actually eligible for coverage in that year. Section 2693.5(b)(1) provides that there is no missed premium due for a missed premium year if the plan sponsor demonstrates to the satisfaction of PBGC that, as of the last day of that plan year, the plan could not satisfy the insolvency test described in § 2691.3(a)(2).

Section 2693.5(b)(2) gives somewhat broader relief and provides that there is no missed premium due for a missed premium year if the plan sponsor demonstrates to the satisfaction of PBGC that, as of the last day of that year, there was no participant in pay status entitled to a supplemental benefit. Thus, under this rule, even though a plan was eligible for coverage in a particular year, because the maximum supplemental benefit was greater than zero, it will not be charged a late entry fee with respect to that year if no pay status participant was receiving a supplemental benefit. PBGC believes that this rule achieves a fair result.

As discussed earlier, the maximum supplemental benefit test is used as an eligibility requirement in order to make the supplemental program available to more plans sooner. However, PBGC does not believe it is fair to assess a late entry fee with respect to a year in which a plan did not actually have benefits that would be insured under the program. Thus, PBGC concluded that a missed premium should accrue only for a plan year in which an eligible plan had either participants in pay status with supplemental benefits or participants whose accrued benefits included supplemental benefits. The latter alternative was rejected because of the administrative burden it would have placed on a plan to demonstrate that no participant had accrued a supplemental benefit, in order to avoid a missed premium charge for a given year.

PBGC expects that in many cases a plan sponsor will be able to demonstrate that there is no missed premium due for a year based on the maximum supplemental benefit under the plan for that year. That is, in any year when the maximum supplemental benefit is zero, it automatically follows that no actual plan participant could have a supplemental benefit. In those cases where the maximum supplemental benefit for a missed premium year is greater than zero, the plan would have to review the benefits of only those participants in pay status to determine whether it can satisfy this exception.

Finally, it should be noted that if a plan can demonstrate that the maximum supplemental benefit in a given year was zero, that demonstration will cover all prior missed premium years as well. This is because it is extremely unlikely that a plan with a maximum supplemental benefit of zero in one year, had a maximum supplemental benefit greater than zero in an earlier year.

Similarly, if a plan can demonstrate for a given year that it had no pay status participants with supplemental benefits, that demonstration will also cover prior years. PBGC believes that the possibility that there was a participant in pay status with a supplemental benefit in an earlier year is too remote to warrant the administrative expense of making a plan prove that fact for each prior year.

Section 2693.5(b)(3) contains a special rule for multiemployer plans classified as "small" in any missed premium year. A plan is a small plan for a missed premium year is the plan filed a Form 5500-R or Form 5500-C for the preceding plan year. For all such years, there is no missed premium due.

PBGC believes this rule is appropriate because it would be relatively costly for these plans to attempt to determine and demonstrate that no participant in pay status had a supplemental benefit for a prior year. In addition, PBGC is concerned that the late entry fee would operate as a powerful disincentive for a small plan to apply for coverage under the supplemental guarantee program. Finally, PBGC believes that the amount of money involved (potentially waived) under this rule is relatively small.

Under § 2693.5(c), interest accrues on the amount of the missed premium for each missed premium year until the late entry fee is paid, at the rate prescribed in section 6621(b) of the Internal Revenue Code. Interest is compounded annually. This interest rate is the same rate applicable to late payments of basic benefits premiums. The rate is currently 20 percent per year, but it is variable and will change whenever the rate under section 6621(b) of the Code changes. The date from which interest accrues for each missed premium year is the last day of that year.

Section 2693.6 of the regulation provides that premiums due from a multiemployer plan for coverage under the supplemental guarantee program for any plan year during which the plan receives financial assistance from the PBGC, either for guarantee supplemental benefits or for basic benefits, are not required to be paid, but instead shall be treated as financial assistance. This is consistent with the rule on payment of the basic benefits premium by multiemployer plans receiving financial assistance for basic benefits.

Section 2693.7 of the regulation sets forth rules for PBGC refunds of overpayments. Under § 2693.7(a), if PBGC rejects an application for coverage, PBGC shall refund to the plan the initial premium and late entry fee, if any. Section 2693.7(b) provides that if the PBGC cancels a plan's coverage for a material misrepresentation or a mass withdrawal, PBGC shall likewise refund to the plan any amounts paid for plan years beginning on or after the effective date of cancellation. If the plan miscalculates the premium or late entry fee and overpays, PBGC shall refund to the plan the excess payment (§ 2693.7(c)). Finally, under § 2693.7(d), if in response to a notice of cancellation a plan pays the premium demanded by PBGC but appeals that determination, and PBGC's Appeals Board finds that the plan did overpay, PBGC shall refund the overpayment amount with interest. Interest will be paid at the rate prescribed in section 6621(b) of the Code.

Part 2694—Financial Assistance

Part 2694 prescribes the rules for PBGC financial assistance to multiemployer plans covered by the supplemental guarantee program that are or will be insolvent and unable to pay when due supplemental benefits (§ 2694.1(a)). Part 2694 also establishes the procedure under which plan sponsors shall file an application for financial assistance with PBGC and the terms and conditions under which PBGC shall provide financial assistance (§ 2694.1(a)).

Section 2694.2 provides that the plan sponsor of a multiemployer plan covered by the supplemental guarantee program who determines that the plan is or will be insolvent and unable to pay supplemental benefits when due may apply to PBGC for financial assistance. Section 2694.2 also provides that the plan sponsor shall submit any information the PBGC determines it needs to review the application.

PBGC expects to promulgate, at a later date, specific information required to be included in an application. PBGC notes that there is little need to prescribe this information requirement at this time because of the remote possibility that a plan that is covered by the supplemental guarantee program and which thus satisfies the 15-year asset test, will require financial assistance within at least 10 years after coverage under the program is effective. PBGC believes it important in developing these information requirements to minimize reporting requirements and to avoid requiring the submission of duplicative information. Accordingly, PBGC will coordinate the information required to be submitted in an application for financial assistance under the supplemental guarantee program with the information required to be submitted in an application for financial assistance for basic benefits.

If, upon receipt of an application for financial assistance, PBGC verifies that the plan is or will be insolvent and unable to pay supplemental benefits when due, PBGC shall provide the plan financial assistance in an amount sufficient to enable the plan to pay guaranteed supplemental benefits under the plan (§ 2694.3(a)). PBGC decisions on applications for financial assistance shall be in writing. A PBGC decision to disapprove an application shall state the reasons for the determination and state that the plan may file an administrative appeal in accordance with Part 2606 (§ 2694.3(b)).

The rules in §§ 2669.4 and 2694.5 of the regulation for financial assistance for guaranteed supplemental benefits are virtually identical to the rules in section 4261(b) of the Act for financial assistance for basic benefits. Under § 2694.4(a), financial assistance shall be provided under such conditions as PBGC determines are equitable and are appropriate to prevent unreasonable loss to PBGC with respect to the plan. Financial assistance is a loan by PBGC to the plan. A plan which has received financial assistance shall repay the amount of such assistance to PBGC on such reasonable terms and for such periods as PBGC deems equitable and appropriate in the particular case. (See section 4067 of the Act; cf. section 4261(b)(2) of the Act, which requires financial assistance to be repaid to PBGC on reasonable terms consistent with regulations prescribed by PBGC.) PBGC may provide interim financial assistance under § 2694.5, pending determination of the proper amount of financial assistance, in such amounts as it considers appropriate in order to avoid undue hardship to plan participants and beneficiaries.

Sections 4005(e) and 4005(f) of the Act establish a supplemental guarantee program fund on the books of the U.S. Treasury and require the fund to be self-supporting. In addition, no amounts borrowed from the U.S. Treasury pursuant to PBGC's borrowing authority may be used for the supplemental guarantee fund. Accordingly, § 2694.6 of the regulation provides that PBGC shall pay guaranteed supplemental benefits only to the extent there is money available in the supplemental benefit program fund to pay those benefits. PBGC specifically requests public comment on what rules should be adopted to deal with the situation where the program is expected not to have sufficient funds to pay all benefits when due. For example, should a reduction in financial assistance apply to all plans receiving assistance, or only to those that apply after the guarantee fund is exhausted?

One alternative for dealing with the potential insolvency problem would be to establish a much higher premium rate, in order to minimize the likelihood of benefit cutback. PBGC is disinclined to adopt this approach because of the difficulty in determining what that premium rate should be and because a much higher premium might deter many plans from entering the program. But PBGC requests comments on this alternative.

Part 2695—Mass Withdrawals

Part 2695 prescribes special rules for multiemployer plans covered by the supplemental guarantee program that experience a mass withdrawal. Section 2695.2(a) of the regulation provides that PBGC shall cancel the coverage of a multiemployer plan with respect to which there is a mass withdrawal if the mass withdrawal date occurs on or before the earlier of (1) the date on which the last collective bargaining agreement providing for employer contributions under the plan, which has an effective date on or after the plan's initial coverage date, expires, or (2) six years after the plan's initial coverage date.

A "mass withdrawal" is defined in § 2690.5 as "a withdrawal or withdrawals from a multiemployer plan as a result of which the plan is subject to section 4219(c)(1)(D) of the Act, and includes a termination by mass withdrawal under section 4041A(a)(2) of the Act and the withdrawal of substantially all the employers pursuant to an agreement or agreements to withdraw". Section 4219(c)(1)(D) of the Act requires that when a multiemployer plan terminates by the withdrawal of every employer from a plan or where substantially all the employers withdraw from a plan pursuant to an agreement or agreements to withdraw from the plan, the plan's total unfunded vested benefits must be allocated among all such employers. "Initial coverage date" is defined in § 2690.5 as "the date as of which coverage under the supplemental guarantee program is first effective for a plan pursuant to § 2691.4(c)". "Mass withdrawal date" means—"(a) in the case of a termination by mass withdrawal, the date determined under section 4041A(b)(2) of the Act; or (b) in any other case, the earliest employer withdrawal date for an employer subject to section 4219(c)(1)(D) of the Act, as determined under section 4203(e) of the Act" (§ 2690.5).

PBGC believes it necessary to establish a minimum period of participation during which a plan is covered by the supplemental guarantee program before which a plan may experience a mass withdrawal and continue to be covered. PBGC notes that a mass withdrawal will generally increase the likelihood that a plan will require financial assistance under the supplemental guarantee program. The existence of coverage under the supplemental guarantee program may encourage a mass withdrawal. Therefore, a minimum period of program participation is necessary to deter a plan from electing coverage under the supplemental guarantee program in anticipation of the withdrawal of all or substantially all of the employers in the plan.

Because a mass withdrawal is most likley to occur on the date on which one or more collective bargaining agreements expire, the minimum participation period is tied to the bargaining cycle. The minimum participation period runs from the plan's initial coverage date and in the usual case, will not expire until each collective bargaining agreement under which the plan is maintained has been re-negotiated and thereafter expires. Thus, if the mass withdrawal date is before the date on which the last collective bargaining agreement providing for employer contributions under the plan, which has an effective date on or after the plan's initial coverage date, expires, the plan's coverage will be cancelled. However, in no event will PBGC cancel a plan's coverage because of a mass withdrawal, if the mass withdrawal date is more than six years after the plan's initial coverage date. PBGC believes that six years is a sufficiently long period to deter possible abuse of the insurance system.

PBGC's decision to cancel a plan's coverage as the result of a mass withdrawal shall be in writing. The decision shall state the reasons for the determination, include a statement of the plan's right to appeal the decision pursuant to Part 2606 of PBGC's regulations, and state that the decision is effective on the date of issuance. The decision shall also state the date as of which the plan's coverage is cancelled. The cancellation date shall be the last day of the plan year preceding the plan year in which PBGC notifies the plan that its coverage is cancelled. PBGC shall refund to the plan any amount paid for plan years beginning after the date as of which the plan's coverage is cancelled. If the plan appeals PBGC's decision and PBGC's Appeals Board finds that the initial determination is erroneous the Appeals Board will order the plan reinstated subject to payment of any amounts refunded and any premium due.

PBGC believes it will be necessary for the supplemental guarantee program to contain certain special rules relating to merges, spinoffs or transfers of assets or liabilities. These rules would address plan coverage in the event a covered plan engaged in one of these transactions. Special rules are necessary because a merger, spinoff or transfer may create a significant risk to the supplemental guarantee program, as for example, in the case of the merger of a financially weak, non-covered plan into a covered plan, as well as create substantial administrative problems.

Special rules would need to address the following issues: Under what circumstances, if any, should a plan covered by the program continue to be covered when it is involved in a merger, spinoff or transfer? Should the result be different if the other plan involved in the transaction is a non-covered plan? In this latter situation, should coverage be continued only for those participants who were previously covered by the program? If so, what administrative problems would this create, and how might they be handled?

PBGC currently believes that, except for a *de minimis* transaction, the resulting plans or plan should be treated as new plans that must satisfy the eligibility requirements of § 2691.3(a) and the coverage requirements of § 2691.4 anew in order to participate in the program. Consistent with this rule, participants who, because of a merger, spinoff or transfer, are no longer in a plan covered by the program would not continue to be covered by the program.

This would avoid a tremendous administrative burden on both the non-covered plan and the guarantee program.

A tentative cut-off for whether a transaction is *de minimis* would be if the transaction affects less than 3% of the total assets or liabilities. For example, in the case of a merger, a transaction would be *de minimis* if the present value of the accrued benefits of the merging plan not covered by the program is less than three percent of the fair market value of the assets of the covered plan.

Finally, under these rules, the merger of two covered plans would not result in cancellation of coverage. However, this raises the issue of the level of coverage, if the two plans had different levels. The approach which would seem to provide the greatest protection to the supplemental guarantee program would be to cover the merged plan at whatever was the lowest level of coverage of the merging plans.

PBGC specifically invites comments on these issues.

The Pension Benefit Guaranty Corporation has determined that this regulation is not a "major rule" for the purposes of Executive Order 12291, because it will not have an annual effect on the economy of $100 million or more; or create a major increase in costs or prices for consumers, individual industries, or geographic regions; or have significant adverse effects on competition, employment, investment, innovation, or on the ability of United States-based enterprises to compete with foreign-based enterprises in domestic or export markets. The PBGC expects that the total annual premiums collected in the first few years of the program will be less than $10 million. Moreover, this regulation is required by statute.

Under section 605(b) of the Regulatory Flexibility Act the Pension Benefit Guaranty Corporation certifies that this rule will not have a significant economic impact on a substantial number of small entities. Pension plans with fewer than 100 participants have traditionally been treated as small plans. The proposed regulation affects only multiemployer plans covered by PBGC. Defining "small plans" as those with under 100 participants, such plans represent only 10% of all multiemployer plans covered by PBGC (200 out of 2,000). Further, small multiemployer plans represent only .3% of all small plans covered by the PBGC (200 out of 61,200) and less than .05% of all small plans (200 out of 427,900). Moreover, the PBGC expects that a significant number of multiemployer plans are currently ineligible for coverage under this program because of the 15-year asset test. In addition, the program is voluntary. Therefore, compliance with sections 603 and 604 of the Regulatory Flexibility Act is waived.

Interested parties are invited to submit comments on this proposed regulation. Comments should be addressed to: Assistant Executive Director for Policy and Planning, Pension Benefit Guaranty Corporation (140), 2020 K Street, NW., Washington, D.C. 20006. Written comments will be available for public inspection at the above address, Suite 7100, between the hours of 9:00 a.m. and 4:00 p.m. Each person submitting comments should include his or her name and address, identify this proposed regulation, and give reasons for any recommendation. This proposal may be changed in light of the comments received.

In developing this proposed regulation, PBGC solicited comments from knowledgeable individuals outside the corporation. Copies of these comments are available for public inspection at the above address.

List of Subjects in 29 CFR Parts 2690-2695

Employee benefit plans, Pensions, Pension insurance.

In consideration of the foregoing, it is proposed to amend Chapter XXVI of Title 29, Code of Federal Regulations by adding a new Subchapter I consisting of Parts 2690 through 2695 to read as follows:

Subchapter I—Supplemental Guarantee Program For Multiemployer Plans

PART 2690—DEFINITIONS

2691—Requirements for Coverage

2692—Coverage Limitations for Participants and Multiemployer Plans

2693—Premiums

2694—Financial Assistance

2695—Mass Withdrawals

Subchapter I—Supplemental Guarantee Program For Multiemployer Plans

PART 2690—DEFINITIONS

Sec. 2690.1—Purpose and scope.

2690.2—General definitions.

2690.3—Requirements for coverage.

2690.4—Premiums.

2690.5—Mass withdrawals.

Authority: Secs. 4002(b)(3), 4002A(g)(2), Pub. L. 93-406, as amended by secs. 403(1) and 102 (respectively), Pub. L. 96-364, 94 Stat. 1302, 1214-15 (1980) [29 U.S.C. 1302, 1322a].

§ 2690.1 Purpose and scope.

This part sets forth the definitions used in Subchapter I. Section 2690.2 contains definitions of terms of general applicability. The subsequent sections contain definitions of terms specific to each part within the subchapter.

§ 2690.2 General definitions.

For purposes of Subchapter I—

"Act" means the Employee Retirement Income Security Act of 1974, as amended.

"Actuarial report" means a report submitted to the plan in connection with a valuation of plan assets and liabilities, for purposes of section 412 of the Code.

"Code" means the Internal Revenue Code of 1954, as amended.

"Guaranteed supplemental benefit" means the supplemental benefit payable with respect to a participant that is guaranteed by the PBGC under the supplemental guarantee program set forth in this subchapter, as determined under § 2692.2 of this subchapter.

"Insolvent" means that a plan is unable to pay benefits when due for the plan year. A plan terminated by mass withdrawal is not insolvent until it has first been amended to eliminate all benefits that are not eligible for the PBGC's guarantee under section 4022A(b) of the Act.

"Maximum supplemental benefit" means the supplemental benefit to which an individual who is or could be a participant under the plan would be entitled at the earlier of age 65 or the plan's normal retirement age if he or she commenced participation at the earlier of the earliest possible entry age under the plan or age 22 and served continuously until the earlier of age 65 or the plan's normal retirement age, based on plan provisions in effect five years or more (under which such amount would be the highest.)

"Multiemployer plan" means a pension plan described in section 4001(a)(3) of the Act.

"Participant" means any individual who is included in one of the categories below:

(a) *Active.*—(1) Any individual who is currently in employment covered by the plan and who is earning or retaining credited service under the plan. This category includes any individual who is currently below the integration level in a plan that is integrated with Social Security.

(2) Any non-vested individual who is not currently in employment covered by the plan but who is earning or retaining credited service under the plan. This category does not include a non-vested former employee who has incurred a break in service of the greater of one year or the break in service period specified in the plan.

(b) *Inactive.*—(1) *Inactive receiving benefits.* Any individual who is retired or separated from employment covered by the plan and who is receiving benefits under the plan. This category does not include an individual to whom an insurance company has made an irrevocable commitment to pay all the benefits to which the individual is entitled under the plan.

(2) *Inactive entitled to future benefits.* Any individual who is retired or separated from employment covered by the plan and who is entitled to begin receiving benefits under the plan in the future. This category does not include an individual to whom an insurance company has made an irrevocable commitment to pay all the benefits to which the individual is entitled under the plan.

(c) *Deceased.* Any deceased individual who has one or more beneficiaries who are receiving or entitled to receive benefits under the plan.

This category does not include an individual if an insurance company has made an irrevocable commitment to pay all the benefits to which the beneficiaries of that individual are entitled under the plan.

"PBGC" means the Pension Benefit Guaranty Corporation.

"Plan administrator" means the plan administrator, as defined in sections 4001(a)(1) and 3(16) of the Act.

"Plan sponsor" means the plan sponsor, as defined in section 4001(a)(10) of the Act.

"Plan year" means the calendar, policy or fiscal year on which the records of the plan are kept.

"Supplemental benefit" means the monthly benefit under the plan, except for the nonforfeitable benefit accrued prior to July 30, 1980 by a participant to whom section 4022A(h) of the Act applies, that would be guaranteed under section 4022A of the Act without regard to the limitations in section 4022A(c), reduced by the benefit guaranteed under section 4022A(c) of the Act.

"Supplemental guarantee program" means the program described in section 4022A(g)(2) of the Act and established in this subchapter, under which the PBGC guarantees the payment of supplemental benefits.

"Terminate by mass withdrawal" means to terminate under section 4041A(a)(2) of the Act.

§ 2690.3 Requirements for coverage.

For purposes of Part 2691—

"Last entry date" means the last day of the first plan year beginning on or after January 1, 1983, in which a plan satisfies the 15-year asset test described in § 2691.3(a)(1) of this subchapter.

"Pre-eligibility year" means the plan year preceding the plan year in which an application for coverage that conforms with the requirements of § 2691.5 is filed.

§ 2690.4 Premiums.

For purposes of Part 2693—

"Missed premium year" means any plan year in which the plan satisfies the 15-year asset test described in § 2691.3(a)(1) of this subchapter but does not apply for coverage in accordance with § 2691.5.

§ 2690.5 Mass withdrawals.

For purposes of Part 2695—

"Initial coverage date" means the date as of which coverage under the supplemental guarantee program is first effective for a plan pursuant to § 2691.4(c).

"Mass withdrawal" means a withdrawal or withdrawals from a multiemployer plan as a result of which the plan is subject to section 4219(c)(1)(D) of the Act, and includes a termination by mass withdrawal under section 4041A(a)(2) of the Act and the withdrawal of substantially all the employers pursuant to an agreement or agreements to withdraw.

"Mass withdrawal date" means (a) in the case of a termination by mass withdrawal, the date determined under section 4041A(b)(2) of the Act; or (b) in any other case, the earliest employer withdrawal date for an employer subject to section 4219(c)(1)(D) of the Act, as determined under section 4203(e) of the Act.

PART 2691—REQUIREMENTS FOR COVERAGE

Sec. 2691.1—Purpose and scope.

2691.2—Benefits guaranteed under supplemental guarantee program.

2691.3—Eligibility for coverage.

2691.4—Requirements for coverage.

2691.5—Application.

2691.6—PBGC action on application.

2691.7—Cancellation of coverage.

Authority: Secs. 4002(b)(3), 4022A(g)(2), Pub. L. 93-406, as amended by secs. 403(1) and 102 (respectively), Pub. L. 96-364, 94 Stat. 1302, 1214-15 (1980) [29 U.S.C. 1302, 1322a].

§ 2691.1 Purpose and scope.

(a) *Purpose.* The purpose of this part is to set forth the requirements for PBGC's guarantee of supplemental benefits and for coverage of a

multiemployer plan under the supplemental guarantee program established in this subchapter.

(b) *Scope.* This part applies to each multiemployer plan covered under section 4021(a) of the Act and not excluded by section 4021(b), that applies for coverage or is covered under the supplemental guarantee program.

§ 2691.2 Benefits guaranteed under supplemental guarantee program.

(a) *General requirements.* PBGC shall guarantee, in accordance with this subchapter, the payment of supplemental benefits under a multiemployer plan—

(1) To which section 4021 of the Act applies;

(2) Which is eligible for coverage in accordance with § 2691.3;

(3) Which satisfies the requirements for coverage in accordance with § 2691.4;

(4) Which pays all premiums when due in accordance with Part 2693 of this subchapter; and

(5) Which is insolvent.

(b) *Benefits guaranteed for a participant.* The supplemental benefits of a participant in a plan described in paragraph (a) of this section that are guaranteed by PBGC under the supplemental guarantee program shall be determined in accordance with § 2692.2 of this subchapter.

§ 2691.3 Eligibility for coverage.

(a) *General requirement.* Except as provided in paragraph (b) of this section, a multiemployer plan is eligible for coverage under the supplemental guarantee program if it satisfies the following requirements:

(1) The fair market value of the plan's assets as of the end of the pre-eligibility plan year equals or exceeds 15 times the total amount of the benefit payments and expenses under the plan for that year.

(i) For a plan that has filed or is going to file a Form 5500 or Form 5500-C for the pre-eligibility plan year, that form shall be used to demonstrate satisfaction of the test described in paragraph (a)(1).

(ii) For a plan that has filed or is going to file a Form 5500-R for the pre-eligibility plan year, the plan sponsor's certification in accordance with § 2691.5(d)(12) shall be used to demonstrate satisfaction of the test described in paragraph (a)(1).

(2) The fair market value of the plan's assets as of the end of the pre-eligibility plan year, plus expected investment earnings on those assets for the next ten plan years, equal or exceed the total amount of expected benefit payments and expected expenses under the plan for that ten-year period.

(i) For a plan that has filed or is going to file a Form 5500 or Form 5500-C for the pre-eligibility plan year, that form shall be used to determine the fair market value of plan assets.

(ii) For a plan that has filed or is going to file a Form 5500-R for the pre-eligibility plan year, the fair market value of plan assets shall be the fair market value reported by the plan sponsor in accordance with § 2691.5(d)(12).

(iii) Expected investment earnings shall be determined using the same interest assumption used for determining the minimum funding requirement under section 412 of the Code.

(iv) Expected benefit payments shall be determined by assuming that current benefits remain in effect and that all scheduled increases in benefits occur.

(v) Expected expenses shall be determined using expenses in the pre-eligibility plan year, adjusted to reflect any anticipated changes.

(3) The plan has not experienced a mass withdrawal on or before the date the plan's application for coverage is filed.

(4) The maximum supplemental benefit under the plan, as defined in § 2690.2, is greater than zero, as of the date the plan's application for coverage is filed.

(b) *Re-entry.* A multiemployer plan is not eligible for coverage under the supplemental guarantee program if it was previously covered by the program and its coverage was cancelled in accordance with § 2691.7(a) or (c) of this part, or § 2695.2 of this subchapter. If coverage was cancelled pursuant to § 2691.7(b), the plan shall be eligible for re-entry if it meets the requirements in paragraph (a) of this section.

§ 2691.4 Requirements for coverage.

(a) *General rule.* Except as provided in paragraph (b) of this section, a plan that is eligible for coverage under § 2691.3 shall become covered under the supplemental guarantee program upon—

(1) Filing with PBGC a written application that comforms with the requirements of § 2691.5, including payment of the initial premium and any late entry fee due under Part 2693 of this subchapter; and

(2) Approval by PBGC of the application.

(b) *Late entry fee.* If a plan fails to apply for coverage before its last entry date, as defined in § 2690.3, its application for coverage under the supplemental guarantee program shall include a late entry fee determined in accordance with § 2693.5 of this subchapter.

(c) *Effective date of coverage.* A plan whose application is approved by PBGC is covered under the supplemental guarantee program as of the first day of the plan year during which it files a complete application with PBGC.

(d) *Changes in coverage.*—(1) *Increase coverage.* A plan that is covered under the supplemental guarantee program may increase its coverage at any time upon satisfaction of the requirements of paragraph (a) of this section. When a plan applies for increased coverage, the premium described in paragraph (a)(1) is the premium owed for the plan's existing coverage plus the increased coverage requested. The effective date of increased coverage, if approved by PBGC, shall be the first day of the plan year in which the complete application is filed.

(2) *Decreased coverage.* A plan that is covered under the supplemental guarantee program may decrease its coverage without PBGC's approval by following the procedures, including time limits, for cancellation of coverage set forth in § 2691.7(c) of this part. A plan may not decrease coverage in any plan year during which it is receiving financial assistance from PBGC under Part 2694 of this subchapter.

§ 2691.5 Application.

(a) *General.* Subject to the rule in § 2691.4(b) on late entry, an application for initial or increased coverage may be filed with PBGC at any time. In addition to the initial premium, and any late entry fee, due under Part 2693, the application shall include the information specified in paragraph (d) of this section.

(b) *Who shall file.* The plan sponsor, or a duly authorized representative acting on behalf of the plan sponsor, shall sign the application.

(c) *Where to file.* The application shall be delivered by mail or submitted by hand to the Division of Case Classification and Control (540), Office of Program Operations, Pension Benefit Guaranty Corporation, 2020 K Street, N.W., Washington, D.C. 20006.

(d) *Information.* Each application shall contain the following information:

(1) The name of the plan.

(2) The name, address and telephone number of the plan sponsor, and of the duly authorized representative, if any, of the plan sponsor.

(3) The nine-digit Employer Identification Number (EIN) assigned by the Internal Revenue Service to the plan sponsor and the three-digit Plan Identification Number (PIN) assigned by the plan sponsor to the plan, and, if different, the EIN or PIN last filed with the PBGC. The notice should indicate of no EIN or PIN has been assigned.

(4) A copy of the most recent IRS determination letter, if any, relating to the plan.

(5) A statement that the plan is applying for coverage (or increased coverage) under the supplemental guarantee program, indicating the number of units of supplemental coverage for which the plan is applying, *i.e.,* the number of $1.00 units requested.

(6) A statement of the number of units of supplemental coverage necessary to guarantee the maximum supplemental benefit under the plan, determined as of the date the plan's application for coverage is filed, including supporting documentation.

(7) A copy of the plan document currently in effect, *i.e.,* a copy of the last restatement of the plan and all subsequent amendments.

(8) If not included in item 7, a copy of any amendment to the plan adopted or effective within the 5-year period preceding the beginning of the plan year during which the application is filed.

(9) A copy of the two most recent actuarial reports relating to the plan. The reports shall include a complete description of the actuarial assumptions and methods used; an age and service distribution of active and retired lives, and the associated liability distributions for retired lives; the number of contribution base units for the five most recent plan years; all asset and liability figures used to complete Schedule B of the Annual Report Form (Form 5500 series), including the value of vested benefits; and the contribution rates in effect.

(10) A statement updating the most recent actuarial report described in item 9 to show any material changes.

(11) A copy of the plan's Annual Report Form (Form 5500 series) for the pre-eligibility plan year, including schedules. In addition, for a plan that has filed a Form 5500-R for the pre-eligibility plan year, the application shall contain the plan's most recent Form 5500 or Form 5500-C, including schedules.

(12) For a plan that has filed a Form 5500-R for the pre-eligibility plan year, a certification by the plan sponsor that the plan satisfies the 15-year asset test described in § 2691.3(a)(1). The certification shall include a statement as to the fair market value of the plan's assets as of the end of the pre-eligibility year and the total amount of the benefit payments and expenses under the plan for that year.

(13) A certification by the plan sponsor that the plan has not experienced a mass withdrawal on or before the date the plan's application for coverage is filed.

(14) A certification by an enrolled actuary that the plan satisfies the test described in § 2691.3(a)(3), including supporting assumptions and methods, and a statement that in making the certification due consideration was given to the distribution of benefit liabilities under the plan.

(15) The amount of the initial premium, paid to PBGC in the application, including supporting calculations.

(16) A certification by the plan, sponsor indicating whether the plan is subject to a late entry fee, and, if so, the amount of the fee (including interest). The certification shall include a statement as to the year in which the plan first satisfied the 15-year asset test described in § 2691.3(a)(1), and for that year and each year thereafter, a statement with calculations as to the amount of missed premium or a statement that there is no missed premium due for that year, including evidence supporting the statement.

(e) *Additional information.* In addition to the information described in paragraph (d) of this section, PBGC may require the plan sponsor to submit any other information PBGC determines it needs to review an application.

(f) *Duplicate information.* In the case of plan applying for additional units of supplemental coverage, any of the information required by paragraph (d) of this section may be omitted if the identical information was previously filed with PBGC. When information is omitted pursuant to this paragraph, the application shall so indicate and shall state the date on which the information was submitted and that the information is still accurate and complete.

(g) *Date of filing.* An application is not considered filed until all the information required by paragraph (d) of this section and the initial premium, and, if applicable, late entry fee due have been submitted. The date of filing is the date on which all the information (or the final portion of the required information), the premium and late entry fee, if any, are hand-delivered or mailed, or the last such date if these items are submitted separately. An application shall be presumed to have been mailed on the date on which it is postmarked by the United States Postal Service, or three days prior to the date on which it is received by the PBGC if it does not contain a legible United States Postal Service postmark.

§ 2691.6 PBGC action on application.

(a) *General.* PBGC shall accept a plan for coverage if it determines that the plan is eligible for coverage under § 2691.3 and has submitted an application that complies with § 2691.5. PBGC may, however, approve lower coverage than the plan requested, if it determines that the plan requested coverage greater than that allowed under § 2692.4 of this subchapter.

(b) *PBGC decision.* PBGC shall notify the plan sponsor in writing of its decision on the application. If PBGC approves the application, the decision shall state that the plan is covered under the supplemental guarantee program and specify the amount of coverage the plan will receive. If PBGC rejects the application, in whole or in part, the decision shall state the reasons for the rejection and include a statement of the plan sponsor's right to appeal the decision pursuant to Part 2606 of this chapter. Filing of an appeal shall not stay the effectiveness of a decision granting coverage for less than the amount applied for.

§ 2691.7 Cancellation of coverage.

(a) *Missed premiums.* Unless the premium due is not payable under § 2693.6 of this subchapter because the plan is receiving financial assistance from PBGC, if the plan fails to pay any premium due under Part 2693 by the last date prescribed for payment in § 2693.3(b) or (c), PBGC shall issue the plan a notice of cancellation. The notice shall advise the plan that unless the full amount due is paid within 30 days after the date of the notice, the plan's coverage under the supplemental guarantee program shall be cancelled. Cancellation shall be effective on the 31st day after the date of the notice. If a plan's coverage is cancelled pursuant to this paragraph, it shall not be entitled to a refund of premiums paid, nor shall it be eligible to re-apply for coverage.

(b) *Material misrepresentation.* Except as provided in paragraph (b)(3) of this section, if PBGC determines that a plan's application for initial coverage or an increase in coverage contained a misrepresentation as to a material fact that would have caused PBGC to reject the application had not that fact been misrepresented, the plan's coverage shall be cancelled by PBGC. Cancellation shall be effective as of the plan's effective date under § 2691.4(c) of initial coverage or increased coverage, as applicable.

(1) *Effect of cancellation.* A plan whose coverage is cancelled pursuant to paragraph (b) of this section shall be entitled to a refund of amounts paid under the supplemental guarantee program, in accordance with § 2693.7(b) of this subchapter. The plan shall be eligible to re-apply for coverage if it meets the tests in § 2691.3(a).

(2) *PBGC decision.* PBGC shall notify the plan in writing of its decision to cancel the plan's coverage. The decision shall state the reasons for the determination, the date as of which a plan's coverage is cancelled, include a statement of the plan's right to appeal the decision pursuant to Part 2606 of this chapter, and state that the decision is effective on the date of issuance.

(3) *Restriction on right to cancel.* After initial coverage or an increase in coverage has been in effect for 10 years, it shall be incontestable as to the statements contained in the application.

(c) *Cancellation by plan.* Except as provided in paragraph (c)(2) of this section, a plan may cancel coverage, without PBGC approval, by so indicating on its Form PBGC-1 filed in accordance with Part 2693 of this subchapter. To be effective, the form must be filed within the time limits for filing set forth in Part 2693. Cancellation of coverage shall be effective as of the last day of the plan year preceding the plan year for which the Form PBGC-1 is filed.

(1) *Effect of cancellation.* A plan that cancels its coverage pursuant to paragraph (c) of this section shall not be entitled to a refund of premiums (or any late entry fee) paid for plan years when coverage was in effect, nor shall it be eligible to re-apply for coverage.

(2) *Restrictions on right to cancel.* A plan may not cancel coverage in any plan year in which it is receiving financial assistance from PBGC under Part 2694 of this subchapter, nor in any plan year in which it has already filed its Form PBGC-1 and paid its premium pursuant to Part 2693.

PART 2692—COVERAGE LIMITATIONS FOR PARTICIPANTS AND MULTIEMPLOYER PLANS

Sec. 2692.1—Purpose and scope.

2692.2—Guaranteed supplemental benfits.

2692.3—Plan coverage.

2692.4—Maximum plan coverage.

Authority: Secs. 4002(b)(3), 4022A(g)(2), Pub. L. 93-406, as amended by secs. 403(1) and 102 (respectively), Pub. L. 96-364, 94 Stat. 1302, 1214-15 (1980) (29 U.S.C. 1302, 1322).

§ 2692.1 Purpose and scope.

(a) *Purpose.* The purpose of this part is to prescribe rules for determining the amount of coverage for a participant and a multiemployer plan under the supplemental guarantee program.

(b) *Scope.* This part applies to each multiemployer plan covered under section 4021(a) of the Act and not excluded by section 4021(b), that applies for coverage or is covered under the supplemental guarantee program and to participants and beneficiaries in those plans.

§ 2692.2 Guarantees supplemental benefits.

The PBGC shall guarantee the payment with respect to a participant of a supplemental benefit provided under a multiemployer plan covered by the supplemental guarantee program equal to the lesser of the participant's supplemental benefit, or the number of units of supplemental coverage purchased by the plan multiplied by the participant's service multiplier (as defined in § 2692.3(b)).

§ 2692.3 Plan coverage.

(a) *General.* Subject to the limitation in § 2962.4, a multiemployer plan that is eligible for coverage under § 2691.3 may apply for any number of units of supplemental coverage. The same number of units shall be purchased for all participants in the plan. Units may only be purchased in whole number increments. Each unit is equal to a monthly benefit with respect to a participant in the amount of $1.00 times the participant's service multiplier.

(b) *Service multiplier.* Except as provided in the next sentence, a participant's service multiplier is the participant's total number of years of credited service, determined in accordance with section 4022A(c)(4) of the Act. In the case of a participant whose benefit under the plan has been reduced under section 411(a)(3)(E) of the Code and whose benefit guaranteed under section 4022A is determined under section 4022A(d)(1), the participant's service multiplier is the amount determined under section 4022A(d)(1) of the Act, divided by the amount determined under section 4022A(c)(1)(A) of the Act.

§ 2692.4 Maximum plan coverage.

A multiemployer plan may not purchase more than the number of units of coverage necessary to guarantee the maximum supplemental benefit under the plan, determined as of the date the plan's application for coverage (or increased coverage) is filed.

PART 2693—PREMIUMS

Sec. 2693.1—Purpose and scope.

2693.2—Form.

2693.3—Requirement to pay premiums.

2693.4—Premium rate.

2693.5—Late entry fee.

2693.6—Premium for plan year during which plan receives financial assistance.

2693.7—Overpayments.

2693.8—Date of filing or payment.

2693.9—Computation of time.

Authority: Secs. 4002(b)(3), 4006(a), 4022A(g)(2), Pub. L. 93-406, as amended by secs. 403(1), 105(a) and 102 (respectively), Pub. L. 96-364, 94 Stat. 1302, 1264-66, 1214-15 (1980) (29 U.S.C. 1302, 1306, 1322a).

§ 2693.1 Purpose and scope.

(a) *Purpose.* The purpose of this part is to prescribe the premiums for coverage of multiemployer plans under the supplemental guarantee program established in this subchapter. This part also prescribes the late entry fee for a plan that applies for coverage after its last entry date.

(b) *Scope.* This part applies to each multiemployer plan that applies for coverage or is covered under the supplemental guarantee program.

§ 2693.2 Form.

The form prescribed by this part for the payment of premiums in Form PBGC-1. A completed Form PBGC-1 shall accompany all payments of premiums under this part (other than the initial premium payment). A plan shall use a single Form PBGC-1 for both is premium payment under this part and under Part 2610 (premium for basic benefit coverage) of this chapter.

§ 2693.3 Requirement to pay premiums.

(a) *Initial premium.* The plan sponsor of a plan that is applying under § 2691.4 of this subchapter for coverage under the supplemental guarantee program shall pay the initial premium due as part of its application for coverage. The payment check shall be made payable to PBGC and shall show the name of the plan and the EIN-PIN with respect to the plan on its face.

(b) *Premium for covered plan.* The plan administrator of each plan covered under the supplemental guarantee program shall file Form PBGC-1 and pay the premium due, in accordance with the instructions accompanying the form, no later than the last day of the seventh month following the close of the prior plan year.

(c) *Change of plan year.* Notwithstanding paragraph (b) of this section, the plan administrator of a plan that is covered under the supplemental guarantee program and that changes its plan year, shall file Form PBGC-1 and pay the premium due for the short plan year, in accordance with the instructions accompanying the form, no later than the later of—

(1) The last day of the seventh month following the close of the short plan year; or

(2) 30 days after the date on which the amendment changing the plan year was adopted.

(d) *Non-payment of premium.* Except as provided in paragraphs (d)(1) and (d)(2), the failure of the plan administrator of a plan covered by the supplemental guarantee program to pay the full premium due under this part within the time limits prescribed in this section shall result in the cancellation of that plan's coverage under the program, in accordance with § 2691.7.

(1) *Non-payment of initial premium.* A plan has not satisfied the requirement for coverage under § 2691.4(a)(1) (filing a complete application), until it has paid the full initial premium due pursuant to this part.

(2) *Financial assistance.* Paragraph (d) of this section shall not apply to a premium that need not be paid pursuant to § 2693.6 of this part for a year in which the plan is receiving financial assistance under Part 2694 of this subchapter or financial assistance under section 4261 of the Act.

(e) *Duration of obligation to pay premiums.* Premiums shall continue to accrue under this part for each plan year until the end of the plan year in which a multiemployer plan's coverage is cancelled in accordance with § 2691.7 or § 2695.2 of this subchapter or until the plan's assets are distributed in connection with the termination of the plan.

(f) *Contested premium amounts.* If PBGC determines that a plan has paid less than the full premium due under this part, it shall so notify the plan, as described in § 2691.7(a) of this subchapter. The plan may appeal PBGC's determination pursuant to Part 2606 of this chapter. However, filing of an appeal shall not stay the effect of a notice of cancellation issued under § 2691.7(a) of this subchapter.

§ 2693.4 Premium rate.

(a) *General.* A multiemployer plan shall pay for each plan year a premium to PBGC for coverage under the supplemental guarantee program in an amount equal to the product of—

(1) The number of individuals who were participants in the plan on the last day of the preceding plan year;

(2) The number of units of supplemental coverage in effect for the year, or for which the plan is applying; and

(3) The supplemental premium rate of $.30.

(b) *Short plan year.* For any plan that changes its plan year, the plan shall pay the applicable premium under paragraph (a) for each individual who is a participant in the plan on the last day of the short plan year.

§ 2693.5 Late entry fee.

(a) *General.* A multiemployer plan that fails to apply for initial coverage on or before the last day of the first plan year in which the plan satisfies the 15-year asset test set forth in § 2691.3(a)(1) shall be presumptively liable for a late entry fee determined under this section. The late entry fee shall equal the total amount of the plan's missed premiums, determined under paragraph (b) of this section, plus interest, determined under paragraph (c) of this section, for each missed premium year. However, there is no missed premium due for any year in which the plan did not, in fact, satisfy all of the eligibility requirements in § 2691.3(a), as demonstrated in accordance with paragraphs (b)(1) and (b)(2) of this section.

(b) *Computation of missed premiums.* Except as provided in paragraphs (b)(1), (b)(2) and (b)(3) of this section, the amount of the missed premium for each missed premium year is equal to the premium determined under § 2693.4 of this part that would have been due had coverage been in effect for each missed premium year, based on the plan's Form PBGC-1 filed for that year and assuming coverage in each year of the lesser of one-half the number of units of supplemental coverage necessary to guarantee the maximum supplemental benefit under the plan as of the date the plan's application for coverage is filed, or the number of units of supplemental coverage actually necessary to guarantee the highest supplemental benefit for any participant in pay status under the plan as of the last day of that year, as demonstrated by the plan sponsor to the satisfaction of PBGC.

(1) There is no missed premium for any missed premium year if the plan sponsor demonstrates to the satisfaction of PBGC that, as of the last day of that plan year, the plan could not satisfy the plan solvency requirement described in § 2691.3(a)(2).

(2) There is no missed premium for any missed premium year (and all prior missed premium years) if the plan sponsor demonstrates to the satisfaction of PBGC that there is no supplemental benefit payable with respect to any participant in pay status as of the last day of that year.

(3) There is no missed premium for any missed premium year if the plan filed a Form 5500-R or Form 5500-C for the preceding plan year.

(c) *Interest.* Interest shall accrue on the amount of the missed premium for each missed premium year from the last day of the year until the late entry fee is paid. Interest shall be at the rate prescribed in section 6621(b) of the Code and shall be compounded annually.

(d) *Contested amount.* In any case where the plan disputes PBGC's determination of the amount due under this section, the plan may appeal PBGC's determination pursuant to Part 2606 of this chapter. However, notwithstanding the filing of an appeal, a plan shall not be covered under the supplemental guarantee program until it has paid the late entry determined due by PBGC.

§ 2693.6 Premium for plan year during which plan receives financial assistance.

The premium due under this part need not be paid for any plan year during which a plan receives financial assistance from PBGC pursuant to Part 2694 of this subchapter or section 4261 of the Act. Any premium not paid pursuant to this section shall be treated as financial assistance under Part 2694.

§ 2693.7 Overpayments.

(a) *Rejected applications.* If a plan files an application for coverage and pays its initial premium and late entry fee, if any, and thereafter PBGC rejects the application, PBGC shall refund to the plan the total amount paid.

(b) *Cancellation for material misrepresentation or mass withdrawal.* If PBGC cancels a plan's coverage under the supplemental guarantee program under § 2691.7(b) (for a material misrepresentation) or under § 2695.2(a) (for a mass withdrawal), the PBGC shall refund to the plan any amounts paid by the plan under the supplemental guarantee program for plan years beginning on or after the effective date of cancellation.

(c) *Erroneous computation by plan.* If a plan computes and pays an amount that exceeds the premium payment or late entry fee due under this part, PBGC shall refund to the plan the excess amount.

(d) *Contested amounts.* If a plan pays a premium or late entry fee and then appeals the amount of the premium or late entry fee pursuant to § 2693.3(f) or § 2693.5(d), respectively, and the decision on the appeal finds that there has been an overpayment, PBGC shall refund to the plan the excess amount, with interest at the rate specified in section 6621(b) of the Code from the date of the overpayment to the date of the refund.

§ 2693.8 Date of filing or payment.

Any form required to be filed and any payment required to be made under the provisions of this part shall be considered to have been filed or made on the date on which it is hand-delivered or mailed. A form or payment shall be presumed to have been mailed on the date on which it is postmarked by the United States Postal Service, or three days prior to the date on which it is received by the PBGC if it does not contain a legible United States Postal Service postmark.

§ 2693.9 Computations of time.

In computing any period of time under this part, the day of the act, event or default from which the designated period of time begins to run is not counted. The last day of the period so computed shall be included, unless it is a Saturday, Sunday or federal holiday, in which event the period runs until the end of the next day which is not a Saturday, Sunday or a federal holiday. For the purpose of computing interest under § 2693.5, a Saturday, Sunday or federal holiday referred to in the previous sentence shall be included.

PART 2694—FINANCIAL ASSISTANCE

Sec. 2694.1—Purpose and scope.

2694.2—Application for financial assistance.

2694.3—PBGC action on application.

2694.4—Financial assistance.

2694.5—Interim financial assistance.

2694.6—Limitation on payment of supplemental benefits.

2694.7—Prohibition on changes in coverage.

Authority: Secs. 4002(b)(3), 4022A(g)(2), Pub. L. 93-406, as amended by secs. 403(1) and 102 (respectively), Pub. L. 96-364, 94 Stat. 1302, 1214-15 (1980) (29 U.S.C. 1302, 1322a).

§ 2694.1 Purpose and scope.

(a) *Purpose.* The purpose of this part is to prescribe the rules for PBGC financial assistance to multiemployer plans covered by the supplemental guarantee program that are or will be insolvent and unable to pay when due supplemental benefits. This part establishes the procedure under which plan sponsors shall file an application for financial assistance with PBGC and the terms and conditions under which PBGC shall provide financial assistance.

(b) *Scope.* This part applies to multiemployer plans that are covered by the supplemental guarantee program and are or will be insolvent and unable to pay when due supplemental benefits.

§ 2694.2 Application for financial assistance.

A plan sponsor of a multiemployer plan covered by the supplemental guarantee program who determines that the plan is or will be insolvent and unable to pay supplemental benefits when due may apply to PBGC for financial assistance. Thereafter, the plan sponsor shall submit any information PBGC determines it needs to review the application.

§ 2694.3 PBGC action on application.

(a) *General.* If, upon receipt of an application for financial assistance under § 2694.2, PBGC verifies that the plan is insolvent and unable to pay supplemental benefits when due, PBGC shall provide the plan financial assistance in an amount sufficient to enable the plan to pay guaranteed supplemental benefits due under the plan.

(b) *PBGC decision.* PBGC's decision under this section approving or disapproving an application, in whole or in part, shall be in writing. If PBGC disapproves an application, in whole or in part, the decision shall state the reasons for the determination, include a statement of the plan's right to appeal the decision pursuant to Part 2606 of this chapter and state that the decision is effective on the date of issuance.

§ 2694.4 Financial assistance.

(a) *Terms and conditions.* Financial assistance shall be provided under such conditions as PBGC determines are equitable and are appropriate to prevent unreasonable loss to PBGC with respect to the plan.

(b) *Repayment.* A plan which has received financial assistance shall repay the amount of such assistance to PBGC on such reasonable terms and for such periods as PBGC deems equitable and appropriate in the particular case.

§ 2694.5 Interim financial assistance.

Pending determination of the proper amount of financial assistance under § 2694.3(a), PBGC may provide interim financial assistance in such amounts as it considers appropriate in order to avoid undue hardship to plan participants and beneficiaries.

§ 2694.6 Limitation on payment of supplemental benefits.

Notwithstanding §§ 2694.3(a) and 2694.5 of this part, PBGC shall provide financial assistance to pay supplemental benefits guaranteed under the supplemental guarantee program only to the extent that there is money available to do so in the supplemental guarantee program fund established under section 4005(e) of the Act.

§ 2694.7 Prohibition on changes in coverage.

A plan may not cancel or decrease its coverage under the supplemental guarantee program in a year during which the plan receives financial assistance under this part.

PART 2695—MASS WITHDRAWALS

Sec. 2695.1—Purpose and scope.

2695.2—Mass withdrawals.

Authority: Secs. 4002(b)(3), 4022A(g)(2), Pub. L. 93-406, as amended by secs. 403(1) and 102 (respectively), Pub. L. 96-364, 94 Stat. 1302, 1214-15 (1980) [29 U.S.C. 1302, 1322a].

§ 2695.1 Purpose and scope.

(a) *Purpose.* The purpose of this part is to prescribe special rules for multiemployer plans that are covered by the supplemental guarantee program that experience a mass withdrawal.

(b) *Scope.* This part applies to mass withdrawals, including a termination by mass withdrawal under section 4041A(a)(2) of the Act and the withdrawal of substantially all employers in a plan pursuant to an agreement or agreements to withdraw.

§ 2695.2 Mass withdrawals.

(a) *General rule.* PBGC shall cancel the coverage under the supplemental guarantee program of a multiemployer plan with respect to which there is a mass withdrawal if the mass withdrawal date occurs on or before the earlier of—

(1) The date on which the last collective bargaining agreement providing for employer contributions under the plan, which has an effective date on or after the plan's initial coverage date, expires; or

(2) Six years after the plan's initial coverage data.

(b) *Cancellation of coverage.* Cancellation shall be effective as of the last day of the plan year preceding the plan year in which PBGC notifies the plan that its coverage is cancelled. PBGC shall make a refund to the plan for any overpayment in accordance with § 2693.7(b) of this subchapter. If a plan's coverage is cancelled pursuant to this paragraph, it shall not be eligible to reapply for coverage.

(c) *PBGC decision.* PBGC's decision to cancel a plan's coverage under this section shall be in writing. PBGC's decision shall state the reasons for the determination, the date as of which the plan's coverage is cancelled, include a statement of the plan's right to appeal the decision pursuant to Part 2606 of this chapter and state that the decision is effective on the date of issuance.

Issued at Washington, D.C., this 26th day of January 1983.

Raymond Donovan,

Chairman, Board of Directors, Pension Benefit Guaranty Corporation.

Issued on the date set forth above, pursuant to a resolution of the Board of Directors authorizing its Chairman to issue this Notice of Proposed Rulemaking.

Henry Rose,

Secretary, Pension Benefit Guaranty Corporation.

[FR Doc. 83-2752 Filed 1-31-83; 8:45 am]

¶ 20,525E   Reserved.

Formerly reproduced at this paragraph were proposed regulations prescribing variances from the bond/escrow and sale of assets requirements that pertain to an employer who contributes to a multiemployer plan. The regulations were finalized and appear at ¶ 15,668A, 15,668B and 15,668J—15,668O.]

¶ 20,525F   Reserved.

Proposed regulations establishing the interest rate to be charged by multiemployer plans on overdue and defaulted withdrawal liability were formerly reproduced at this paragraph. The final regulations are at ¶ 15,687—15,687C.]

¶ 20,525G   Reserved.

Proposed regulations providing an alternative means to comply with the requirements of furnishing updated summary plan descriptions were formerly reproduced here. The proposed rules have been withdrawn. Notice of the withdrawal is at ¶ 23,659P.]

¶ 20,525H

Proposed regulations on 29 CFR Part 2606.—Following is the text of proposed Pension Benefit Guaranty Corporation regulations relating to Administrative Review of Agency Decisions.

¶20,525E

The proposed regulations were published in the *Federal Register* of May 18, 1983 (48 FR 22330).

ERISA Sec. 4003.

PENSION BENEFIT GUARANTY CORPORATION

29 CFR Part 2606

Rules for Administrative Review of Agency Decisions

AGENCY: Pension Benefit Guaranty Corporation.

ACTION: Proposed Rule

SUMMARY: The Pension Benefit Guaranty Corporation's regulation on Administrative Review of Agency Decisions sets forth the rules governing the issuance of certain initial determinations made by the Pension Benefit Guaranty Corporation (the "PBGC") and the procedures for requesting and obtaining administrative reviews by the PBGC of those determinations. This proposed amendment makes a number of modifications to the final regulation. The regulations, as the agency proposes to amend it, is reprinted in full for the convenience of the public. The modifications are being proposed to take into account agency experience during the three years this rule has been in effect. The amendments are intended to streamline the review process, clarify issues that have created confusion in the past, and modify the Appeals Board procedures to more effectively utilize the agency's resources. The amendments would also conform the regulation with the multiemployer Pension Plan Amendments Act of 1980.

DATE: Comments must be received on or before July 18, 1983.

ADDRESSES: Comments should be addressed to the Office of the General Counsel, Pension Benefit Guaranty Corporation, Suite 7200, 2020 K Street, N.W., Washington, D.C. 20006. Written comments will be available for public inspection at the PBGC, Suite 7100, at the above address, between the hours of 9:00 A.M. and 4:00 P.M. on regular business days.

FOR FURTHER INFORMATION CONTACT: Deborah West, Attorney, Office of the General Counsel, Pension Benefit Guaranty Corporation, 2020 K Street, N.W., Washington, D.C. 20006; (202) 254-3010. (This is not a toll-free number.)

SUPPLEMENTARY INFORMATION: On July 19, 1979, the PBGC published a final rule regarding administrative review of agency decisions (44 FR 42181). The purpose of the regulation was to ensure that persons who are adversely affected by certain determinations of the PBGC are provided with an opportunity to contest and to obtain review of those determinations. The current regulation applies to eleven types of determinations and provides for two types of agency review. Seven types of determinations are subject to appeal; four are subject to reconsideration. An Appeals Board was established to consider appeals. On April 25, 1983, the PBGC amended the regulation to change the composition of the Appeals Board, 48 FR 17070.

This proposal, if adopted would regulation in several ways. First, the formal reconsideration process under the regulation would be eliminated. This action is being proposed because the PBGC now believes a formal reconsideration procedure is unnecessary. The PBGC may informally reconsider determinations not subject to the regulation and will, of course, correct erroneous determinations, however discovered, without reference to the formal administrative review process. The amendment adds additional PBGC determinations to the list of determinations subject to administrative appeal. The regulation's provision concerning requests for assistance in obtaining information is modified in the proposed rule to make it clear that this provision applies to information in the possession of parties other than the PBGC and not to information available from the PBGC. The regulation is clarified to indicate that there is no appeal of determinations made final upon issuance.

The proposed rule provides that determinations regarding benefit entitlement of participants and beneficiaries under single employer plans (sections 4022(a) and (b), and 4022B of the Act) shall be effective upon issuance. The regulation's provision on late-filed appeals is changed to provide that such appeals shall be reviewed by the Appeals Board if the Board determines that good cause is shown for the late filing.

The amendment makes technical changes that are necessary to clarify the regulation by conforming the regulation to the Multiemployer Act. Finally, minor clarifying

Elimination of Reconsideration Process; Additional Determinations Subject to Administrative Appeal

The formal reconsideration process under the regulation is eliminated in this proposal. PBGC now believes a formal reconsideration procedure is unnecessary. The current dichotomy between appeals and

reconsideration has proven cumbersome and confusing. Determinations not subject to appeal may be informally reconsidered on request, and, of course, the PBGC will correct erroneous determinations, however discovered, whether or not subject to appeal.

The proposed amendment adds a new item to the list of PBGC determinations subject to appeal: determinations under section 4022B of the Act regarding limitations on guaranteed benefit entitlement under single employer plans.

If the amendment is adopted, cases in which a determination was made prior to the regulation's effective date will be processed pursuant to the current administrative review procedure.

Appeals Board Jurisdiction

The proposed regulation provides, at § 2606.3, that there shall be within the PBGC an Appeals Board to consider determinations listed as appealable at § 2606.1(b) of the regulation, other than those determinations made final upon issuance under § 2606.23(b). The Appeals Board shall consider, in reaching its decision, applicable law and policy, relevant facts, and equity.

PBGC Assistance in Obtaining Information

Section 2603.3 of the current regulation provides for PBGC assistance in obtaining information necessary to file an appeal (or necessary to a decision whether to file an appeal). This provision is intended to apply only to situations where the needed information is in the possession of a party other than the PBGC (for example, a bank or insurance company). Where the PBGC is in possession of relevant records, an appellant may make a request under the Freedom of Information Act or the Privacy Act. Thus, the provision, at § 2606.4 of the proposed rule, is being modified so that it is clear that this provision applies only to information in the possession of parties other than the PBGC.

Effective Date of Determinations Under Sections 4022(a) and (b), and 4022B of the Act

Under the current regulation, the effective date of a determination that is subject to appeal and that is not made "immediately effective" under current § 2606.23(b) is stayed until the Appeals Board disposition of the appeal. Thus, when a participant who is receiving a benefit in excess of the amount guaranteed by Title IV of the Act files an appeal, the current regulation obligates the PBGC to continue paying the higher benefits until the Appeals Board rules on the appeal. Often these excess amounts paid are not recovered by PBGC. The result is that plan assets are depleted, and a greater expenditure of PBGC's insurance funds is required. To alleviate this problem, the proposed regulation provides, at § 2606.23, initial determinations of benefit amounts under sections 4022(a) and (b) and 4022B of the Act shall be effective upon issuance. Should the Appeals Board determine that an appellant is entitled to a greater amount than the PBGC initially determined, appellant will be reimbursed for underpayments made during the period after the plan terminated.

The PBGC believes that the likelihood of an erroneous determination is small. Moreover, the proposed regulation provides that the effective date of the determination regarding benefit entitlement under sections 4022(a) and (b) and 4022B of the Act may be stayed by the Appeals Board until the Board's disposition of the appeal. A temporary stay may be granted by the Appeals Board. Stays will be granted only where there exist extraordinary circumstances.

Review of Determinations Made Final on the Date of Issuance

Section 2606.23(b) of the current regulation provides that the PBGC may, in its discretion, make an initial determination "effective" on the date it is issued, and that, in such cases, there is no obligation to exhaust administrative remedies with respect to that determination by filing an appeal. As discussed above, the proposed regulation provides that PBGC benefit determinations are generally "effective" upon issuance. However, such determinations are still subject to Appeals Board review and thus even though effective immediately do not constitute the final agency action on the matter. To avoid confusion regarding terminology, the provision, renumbered § 2606.24(b), is changed to provide that when the PBGC intends a decision to be final agency action, that determination is "final" on the date of issuance.

As the preamble to the current regulation noted, there may be cases where it is warranted to make a determination final immediately. However, the preamble to the final regulation stated that "administrative review of the determination would still be available to the person if he or she requests it." The PBGC believes it necessary to clarify this statement. This statement does not mean that an administrative appeal is available. The words "administrative review" mean that the PBGC may informally review a determination under current § 2606.23(b), but would not stay the decision pending review. The same factors that lead the PBGC to make a determination final upon issuance will normally require that the delay resulting from the appeals process be avoided. Accordingly, in appropriate cases, PBGC will make a determination final upon issuance, eliminating Appeals Board review. To make this clear, the proposed amendment stated that there is no PBGC Appeals Board review of determinations that are made final on the date of issuance.

Nothing in the proposed regulation is intended to limit settlement discussions between the PBGC and the aggrieved party even while an appeal is pending. PBGC proposes to amend the regulation to state (1), at § 2606.23(b), that determinations under that subsection are final upon issuance, and (2) at § 2606.3, that the Appeals Board has no jurisdiction over such determinations. This is consistent with PBGC's regulation on employer liability for single employer plan terminations, which provides, at 29 CFR 2622.9(c), that there is no right to appeal the assessment of liability when a determination is made "immediately effective."

Finally, no determination issued by the Executive Director is subject to appeal under this part.

Non-timely Requests for Review

The current regulation provides that the PBGC will process a late-filed appeal if (1) the person requesting review demonstrates in his or her request that he or she did not file a timely appeal because he or she neither knew nor could have known of the initial determination, and (2) the appeal was filed within 45 days of the date the person first learned of the initial determination. The proposed regulation provides, at § 2606.36, that late-filed appeals, i.e., appeals filed after the 45-day appeals period plus any additional time granted by the Appeals Board pursuant to § 2606.35, may be processed if the Appeals Board determines that good cause is shown for the late filing.

Record Before the Appeals Board

The present regulation does not provide for a uniform method by which appellants may fully understand the basis for a disputed initial determination. The proposed regulation would add such a procedure. It provides that the Appeals Board shall serve the appeal upon the office within the PBGC that issued the disputed initial determination. The office shall, within 30 days, compile and submit to the Board a copy of the initial determination and any other documents which the office believes are necessary to support the initial determination. The office may also submit supporting statements within this 30 day period.

The Appeals Board shall then send all material submitted by the office to the appellant except such material as the appellant has already been provided. The appellant must file any response to the material within 15 days of the date of the Appeals Board letter transmitting the material. This change, then, is to ensure that all appellants have an opportunity to review and comment upon the records relied upon by the PBGC in making its initial determination.

Changes Due to the Enactment of the Multiempioyer Pension Plan Amendments Act of 1980

Certain technical changes in the regulation are being made to conform the citations in the regulation to the proper section numbers of the Employee Retirement Income Security Act of 1974, as amended by the Multiemployer Act.

The regulation currently provides that determinations with respect to benefit entitlement under a plan under section 4022(a) and determinations of the amount of guaranteed benefits under section 4022(b) are subject to appeal. The Multiemployer Act added a new section on rules for aggregate limits on guaranteed benefits (section 4022B), which rules are essentially those previously contained in section 4022(b)(5). Accordingly, the proposed regulation authorizes appeal of determinations under section 4022B by the PBGC regarding limitations on guaranteed benefit entitlement under a covered single employer plan.

The regulation currently provides that coverage determinations under section 4082(b) of ERISA are subject to administrative review. Under the Multiemployer Act, section 4082(b) is redesignated as section 4402(b). The proposed regulation makes the necessary conforming changes.

Other Changes

Nonsubstantive clarifying changes were made in the language of several sections. To accommodate the changes discussed above and to make the regulation clearer and more useful to the public, the regulation has been reorganized. The subpart on reconsiderations has been deleted, along with all other references to reconsideration.

The Pension Benefit Guaranty Corporation has determined that this regulation is not a "major rule" for the purposes of Executive Order 12291, because it will not have an annual effect on the economy of $100 million or more; or create a major increase in costs or prices for consumers, individual industries, or geographic regions; or have significant adverse effects on competition, employment, investment, innovation, or on the ability of United States-based enterprises to compete with foreign-based enterprises in domestic or export markets. This conclusion is based on the fact that this regulation is merely a procedural regulation which provides an administrative appeal route for aggrieved persons so that they may avoid, in certain instances, expensive federal court litigation.

Under section 605(b) of the Regulatory Flexibility Act, the Pension Benefit Guaranty Corporation certifies that this rule will not have a significant economic impact on a substantial number of small entities. The reason for this certification is that the rule is essentially procedural in nature. In addition, this regulation will have little or no adverse economic impact on small entities and will, in many cases, substantially lessen the financial burden of contesting agency action in expensive court proceedings by providing an avenue for expediting inexpensive administrative review. Therefore compliance with sections 603 and 604 of the Regulatory Flexibility Act is waived.

Interested parties are invited to submit comments on this proposed regulation. Comments should be addressed to: Deborah West, Office of the General Counsel, Pension Benefit Guaranty Corporation (240), Suite 7200, 2O2O K Street, NW., Washington, D.C. 20006. Written comments will be available for public inspection at the above address, Suite 7100, between the hours of 9:00 a.m. and 4:00 p.m. Each person submitting comments should include his or her name and address, identify this proposed regulation, and give reasons for any recommendation. This proposal may be changed in light of the comments received.

For the convenience of the public and to have the entire proposed amended rule in one place, the regulation is being reprinted below in its entirety.

List of Subjects in 29 CFR Part 2606

Administrative practice and procedure, Conflict of interests, Penalties.

In consideration of the foregoing, the PBGC proposes to amend Chapter XXVI of Title 29, Code of Federal Regulations, by revising Part 2606 as follows:

PART 2606—RULES FOR ADMINISTRATIVE REVIEW OF AGENCY DECISIONS

Subpart A—General Provisions

Sec.

2606.1	Purpose and scope.
2606.2	Definitions.
2606.3	Appeals Board jurisdiction.
2606.4	PBGC assistance in obtaining information.
2606.5	Representation.
2606.6	Request for confidential treatment.
2606.7	Exhaustion of administrative remedies.

Subpart B—Determinations

2606.21	Purpose and scope.
2606.22	Form and contents of determinations.
2606.23	Effective date of determinations; final agency action.

Subpart C—Administrative Appeals

2606.31	Purpose and scope.
2606.32	Who may appeal or participate in appeals.
2606.33	When to file.
2606.34	Filing of documents.
2606.35	Extension of time.
2606.36	Non-timely request for review.
2606.37	Computation of time.
2606.38	Contents of appeal.
2606.39	Record before the Appeals Board.
2606.40	Opportunity to appear and to present witnesses.
2606.41	Consolidation of appeals.
2606.42	Appeals affecting third parties.
2606.43	Powers of the Appeals Board.
2606.44	Decision by the Appeals Board.
2606.45	Referral of appeal to the Executive Director.

Authority: Sec. 4002(b)(3), Pub. L. 93-406, as amended by Sec. 403(1), Pub. L. 96-364, 94 Stat. 1208, 1302 (1980) (29 U.S.C. 1302(b)(3)).

Subpart A—General Provisions

§ 2606.1 Purpose and scope.

(a) *Purpose.* This part sets forth the rules governing the issuance of all determinations issued on or after the effective date of this part by the PBGC involving the matters set forth in paragraph (b) of this section and the procedures for requesting and obtaining administrative review by the PBGC of those determinations.

(b) *Scope.* This part applies to the following determinations made by the PBGC on or after the effective date of this part and to the review of those determinations:

(1) Determinations that a plan is not covered under section 4021 or section 4402(b) of the Act;

(2) Determinations under section 4022(a) of the Act with respect to benefit entitlement of participants and beneficiaries under covered single employer plans;

(3) Determinations regarding the amount of guaranteed benefits of participants and beneficiaries under covered single employer plans under sections 4022(b) or 4022B of the Act;

(4) Determinations of the amount of money subject to recapture pursuant to section 4045 of the Act;

(5) Determinations of the amount of employer liability under section 4062 of the Act;

(6) Determinations of the amount of contingent liability under section 4063 of the Act;

(7) Determinations of the amount of employer liability under section 4064 of the Act;

(c) *Determinations not covered by this part.* Nothing contained in this part shall limit the authority of the PBGC to review informally, either upon request or on its own motion, determinations that are not subject to this part when the PBGC determines, in its discretion, that it is appropriate to do so.

§ 2606.2 Definitions.

As used in this part:

"Act" means the Employee Retirement Income Security Act of 1974, as amended.

"Aggrieved person" means any participant, beneficiary, plan administrator, plan sponsor, or employer, adversely affected by a determination of the PBGC covered by this part with respect to a pension plan in which such participant, beneficiary, plan administrator, plan sponsor, or employer has an interest. The term "employer" includes all trades and businesses under common control within the meaning of Part 2612 of this chapter, and all employers who contribute to or have contributed to a pension plan to which more than one employer contributes.

"Appeals Board" means a board consisting of a Chairperson appointed by the Executive Director of the PBGC and two senior agency officials appointed by the Executive Director to serve as regular members. Other senior agency officials may serve as alternate members in the event that a regular member is not available to serve or is unable to serve. Such alternates may be appointed pursuant to a list designated by the Executive Director and shall serve in the order designated in that list. The General Counsel, and the Executive Director or the Deputy Executive Director, in the absence of the Executive Director, shall be ex officio members of the Appeals Board. The General Counsel may, as an ex officio member of the Appeals Board, if he or she chooses, vote on any matter before the Board. Appeals shall be decided by a majority vote of the Board members, but if the General Counsel's vote on an appeal results in a tie vote, the appeal shall be referred to the Executive Director as specified in § 2606.45. The Executive Director may designate the Deputy Executive Director to decide any appeal referred to the Executive Director from the Appeals Board under this section in accordance with § 2606.45. A person may not serve on the Appeals Board with respect to any case in which he or she made a determination with respect to the merits of the determination subject to appeal.

"Appellant" means any person filing an appeal under Subpart C of this part.

"PBGC" means the Pension Benefit Guaranty Corporation.

§ 2606.3 Appeals Board jurisdiction.

There shall be within the Pension Benefit Guaranty Corporation an Appeals Board to consider administrative appeals from determinations listed at § 2606.1(b), other than those determinations made final upon issuance under § 2606.23(b) of this part.

§ 2606.4 PBGC assistance in obtaining information.

A person who lacks information or documents necessary to file an appeal pursuant to Subpart C of this part, or necessary to a decision whether to seek review, or necessary to participate in an appeal pursuant to § 2606.42 of this part, or necessary to a decision whether to participate, may request the Appeals Board's assistance in obtaining the information or documents when the information or documents are in the possession of a party other than the PBGC. The request shall state or describe the missing information or data, the reason why the person needs the information or documents, and the reason why the person needs the assistance of the Appeals Board in obtaining the information or documents. The request may also include a request for an extension of time to file an appeal pursuant to § 2606.35 of this part.

§ 2606.5 Representation.

A person may file any document or make any appearance that is required or permitted by this part on his or her own behalf or he or she may designate a representative. When the representative is not an attorney-at-law, a notarized power of attorney signed by the person making the designation authorizing the representation shall be filed with the Appeals Board in accordance with § 2606.34(b) of this part.

§ 2606.6 Request for confidential treatment.

If any person filing a document with the Appeals Board believes that some or all of the information contained in the document is exempt from the mandatory public disclosure requirements of the Freedom of Information Act, 5 U.S.C. § 552, and wishes such material to be withheld by the PBGC, he or she shall specify the information with respect to which he or she requests confidentiality and the grounds therefore.

§ 2606.7 Exhaustion of administrative remedies.

Except as provided in § 2606.23(b), a person aggrieved by a determination of the PBGC covered by this part has not exhausted his or her administrative remedies until he or she has filed an appeal under Subpart C of this part, and a decision granting or denying the relief requested has been issued.

Subpart B—Determinations

§ 2606.21 Purpose and scope.

This subpart sets forth rules governing the issuance of determinations of the PBGC on matters covered by this part.

§ 2606.22 Form and contents of determinations.

All determinations to which this part applies shall be in writing and shall state the reason for the determination. All determinations to which this part applies, other than determinations made final upon issuance under § 2606.23(b) of this part, shall include notice of the right to request review of the determination pursuant to Subpart C of this part and a brief description of the procedures review.

§ 2606.23 Effective date of determinations; final action.

(a) *General rule.* Except as provided in Paragraph (c) of this section, determinations regarding benefit entitlement under sections 4022(a) and (b), and 4022B of the Act shall be effective upon issuance. Except as provided in Paragraph (b) of this section, all determinations covered by this part will not become final until the prescribed period of time for filing an appeal under Subpart C of this part has elapsed, or if an appeal is filed, until the date of the Appeals Board decision regarding the appeal.

(b) *Exception.* The PBGC may, in its discretion, order that a determination is final on the date it is issued. When the PBGC makes such an order, the determination shall state that it is the final agency action with respect to the matter.

(c) *Stay.* The Appeals Board may order that the effective date of a determination regarding benefit entitlement or amount under sections 4022(a) and (b), and 4022B of the Act be stayed until the Appeals Board disposition of the appeal. Such an order may provide for complete or partial relief from the immediate implementation of the determination. A temporary stay may be granted by the Appeals Board.

Subpart C—Administrative Appeals

§ 2606.31 Purpose and Scope.

This subpart establishes procedures governing administrative appeals to the Appeals Board from determinations relating to the matters set forth in § 2606.1(b) of this part, other than those determinations made final upon issuance under § 2606.23(b) of this part.

§ *2606.32 Who may appeal or participate in appeals.*

Any person aggrieved by a determination of the PBGC to which this subpart applies may file an appeal. Any person who will be aggrieved by a decision of the Appeals Board under this part granting the relief requested in whole or in part may participate in the appeal as provided in § 2606.42.

§ *2606.33 When to file.*

Except as provided in § § 2606.35 and 2606.36, an appeal under this subpart must be filed within 45 days after the date of the determination being appealed.

§ *2606.34 Filing of documents.*

(a) *Date of filing.* Any document required or permitted to be filed under this part is considered filed on the date of the United States postmark stamped on the cover in which the document is mailed, provided that the document was mailed postage prepaid properly packaged and addressed to the Appeals Board. If these conditions are not met, the document is considered filed on the date it is received by the PBGC. Documents received after regular business hours are considered filed on the next regular business day.

(b) *Where to file.* Any document required or permitted to be filed under this part in connection with an appeal shall be submitted to the Appeals Board, Pension Benefit Guaranty Corporation, 2020 K Street, N.W., Washington, D.C. 20006.

§ *2606.35 Extension of time.*

When a document is required under this part to be filed within a prescribed period of time, an extension of time to file will be granted only upon good cause shown. The request for an extension of time shall be filed before the expiration of the time prescribed. The request for an extension shall be in writing and shall state why additional time is needed and the amount of additional time requested. The filing of a request for an extension shall stop the running of the prescribed period of time. When a request for an extension is granted, the Appeals Board shall notify the person requesting the extension, in writing, of the amount of additional time granted. When a request for an extension is denied, the Appeals Board shall so notify the requestor in writing, and the prescribed period of time shall resume running from the date of the letter denying the request. A request for an extension of time that is filed after the expiration of the time prescribed shall be considered only if good cause is shown for the late filing.

§ *2606.36 Non-timely request for review.*

The Appeals Board shall process a request for review of a determination that was not filed within the prescribed period of time for requesting review in § 2606.33 if the Board, in its discretion, determines that good cause is shown for the late filing.

§ *2606.37 Computation of time.*

In computing any period of time prescribed or allowed by this part, the day of the act, event, or default from which the designated period of time begins to run is not counted. The last day of the period so computed shall be included, unless it is a Saturday, Sunday, or Federal holiday, in which event the period runs until the end of the next day which is not a Saturday, Sunday, or a Federal holiday.

§ *2606.38 Contents of appeal.*

(a) An appeal shall—

(1) Be in writing;

(2) Be designated as an appeal;

(3) Contain a statement of the grounds upon which it is brought and the relief sought;

(4) Reference all pertinent information known to be in the possession of the PBGC; and

(5) Include any additional information believed to be relevant.

(b) In any case where the appellant believes that another person may be aggrieved if the PBGC grants the relief sought, the appeal shall also include the name(s) and address(es), if known, of such other person(s).

§ *2606.39 Record before the Appeals Board.*

(a) Upon receipt of an appeal, the Appeals Board shall furnish a copy of the appeal to the office of the PBGC that issued the initial determination. The office shall compile and submit to the Board within 30 days a copy of the initial determination being appealed and a copy of any other documents which the office believes are necessary to support the initial determination. Supporting statements may accompany such material.

(b) All material submitted by the office pursuant to subsection (a) except that already provided to appellant shall be sent to appellant and to any person identified under § 2606.42 for response. Appellant and any third party under § 2606.42 shall file any response to the material submitted by the office with the Appeals Board within 30 days of the date of the letter transmitting the material.

(c) The Chairperson may, upon good cause shown, extend the time limits in paragraphs (a) and (b) of this section.

§ *2606.40 Opportunity to appear and to present witnesses.*

(a) An opportunity to appear before the Appeals Board and an opportunity to present witnesses may be permitted at the discretion of the Appeals Board.

(b) Appearances permitted under this section will take place at the main offices of the PBGC, 2020 K Street, N.W., Washington, D.C., unless the Appeals Board, in its discretion, designates a different location.

(c) An appearance permitted under this subpart may be before a hearing officer designated by the Appeals Board.

§ *2606.41 Consolidation of appeals.*

(a) *When consolidation may be required.* Whenever multiple appeals are filed that arise out of the same or similar facts and seek the same or similar relief, the Appeals Board may, in its discretion, order the consolidation of all or some of the appeals.

(b) *Decision by Appeals Board.* The decision of the Appeals Board in a consolidated appeal shall be binding on all appellants whose appeals were consolidated.

§ *2606.42 Appeals affecting third parties.*

(a) When the Appeals Board makes a preliminary finding that the relief requested in an appeal should be granted in whole or in part, before issuing a decision the Board shall make a reasonable effort to notify third persons who will be aggrieved by the decision of the pendency of the appeal, of the grounds upon which the Appeals Board is considering reversing the initial determination, of the right to submit written comments on the appeal, and that no further opportunity to present information to the PBGC with respect to the determination under appeal will be provided.

(b) Written comments and a request to appear before the Appeals Board must be filed within 45 days after the date of the notice from the Appeals Board.

(c) Appellant shall be notified of material submitted by any third party under this section. Such material, to the extent permitted by law, will be made available to appellant upon request.

(d) If more than one third party is involved, their participation in the appeal may be consolidated pursuant to § 2606.41.

§ *2606.43 Powers of the Appeals Board.*

In addition to the powers specifically described in this part, the Appeals Board, in its discretion, may cause additional information to be obtained, may request the submission of any information or the appearance of any person it considers necessary to resolve a matter before it and may enter any order it considers necessary for or appropriate to the disposition of any matter before it.

§ *2606.44 Decision by the Appeals Board.*

(a) In reaching its decision, the Appeals Board shall consider those portions of the PBGC file relating to the issues raised by the appeal, material submitted by the appellant and third parties in connection with the appeal, and written statements or documents, if any, filed with the Appeal Board that are made available to the appellant.

(b) The decision of the Appeals Board constitutes the final agency action with respect to the determination which was the subject of the appeal and is binding on all parties who participated in the appeal and on all parties who were notified pursuant to § 2606.42 of their right to participate in the appeal.

(c) The decision of the Appeals Board shall be in writing, specify the relief granted, if any, state the reasons for the decision, and state that the appellant has exhausted his or her administrative remedies.

§ *2606.45 Referral of appeal to the Executive Director.*

If the Appeals Board finds that an appeal presents a major unresolved policy issue for the PBGC, the Appeals Board shall refer such appeal to the Executive Director of the PBGC for appropriate action. The Executive Director may designate the Deputy Executive Director to decide any appeal referred to the Executive Director from the Appeals Board under this section. When acting on appeals which are referred by the Appeals Board under this section or §2606.02, the Executive Director and the Deputy Executive Director shall have, in addition to all the powers vested in their offices, all the powers vested in the Appeals Board by this part. The decision of the Executive Director or the Deputy Executive Director shall meet the requirements of and have the effect of a decision issued under §2606.44 of this part.

Issued this 13th day of May, 1983.

Charles C. Tharp,

Acting Executive Director, Pension Benefit Guaranty Corporation

[FR Doc. 83-13284 Filed 5-17-83 8:45 am]

¶ 20,525I Reserved.

Formerly reproduced at this paragraph were proposed regulations prescribing rules and procedures for the arbitration of disputes between employers and multiemployer plan sponsors concerning employer withdrawal liability under ERISA. The regulations were finalized and appear at ¶ 15,663C and ¶ 15,689A—15,689M.]

¶ 20,525J Reserved.

Formerly reproduced at this paragraph were proposed amendments to PBGC regulations governing the events that require notice to the PBGC. The regulations were finalized and appear at ¶ 15,461, 15,461C, 15,463B, 15,463C and 15,464.]

¶ 20,525K Reserved.

Formerly reproduced at this paragraph were proposed regulations relating to the reduction or waiver of the liability of an employer that has withdrawn completely from a multiemployer plan. The final PBGC regulations are at ¶ 15,663F and 15,671A—15,671H.]

¶ 20,525L Reserved.

Formerly reproduced at this paragraph were proposed DOL regulations relating to the definition of plan assets. The final regulations appear at ¶ 14,139M and 14,876.]

¶ 20,525M Reserved.

Formerly reproduced at this paragraph were proposed PBGC regulations relating to the powers and duties of a sponsor of a plan that has terminated by mass withdrawal. The regulations were finalized and appear at ¶ 15,715A—15,715Z and 15,718D-2.]

¶ 20,525N Reserved.

Proposed regulations relating to an increase in the Pension Benefit Guaranty Corporation's fees for document search and duplication under the Freedom of Information Act were formerly reproduced at this paragraph. The final regulation is at ¶ 15,322.]

¶ 20,525O Reserved.

A proposed regulation defining the terms "amount involved" and "correction" as used in the assessment of civil penalties under ERISA against parties in interest who engage in a prohibited transaction with certain employee benefit plans was formerly reproduced at this paragraph. The final regulation is at ¶ 14,926.]

¶ 20,525P Reserved.

Proposed regulations that set forth procedures for the imposition of civil sanctions under ERISA against parties in interest who engaged in prohibited transactions involving welfare plans and unqualified pension plans were formerly reproduced here. The final regulations are reproduced at ¶ 14,928.]

¶ 20,525Q Reserved.

Proposed Reg. §§2613.2, 2613.8, 2617.4, and 2619.26, relating to the limit on benefit amounts that may be paid in a form other than an annuity, were formerly reproduced at this point. The final regulations appear at ¶ 15,422, 15,428, 15,447C, and 15,620I.]

¶ 20,525R Reserved.

Proposed regulations necessary to conform existing regulations to proposed revisions to the annual return/report forms (Form 5500 series) filed by administrators of employee pension and welfare benefit plans were formerly reproduced here.

The final regulations are at ¶ 14,231A, ¶ 14,231B, ¶ 14,231F, ¶ 14,231J, ¶ 14,247B, ¶ 14,247C, ¶ 14,247U, ¶ 14,247Z, ¶ 14,248B, ¶ 14,248C and ¶ 14,249H.]

¶ 20,525S   Reserved.

EEOC proposed Reg. § 1625.21, relating to the cessation of contributions and accruals to pension plans for employees who continue to work beyond normal retirement age, was formerly reproduced here. The EEOC had been ordered to issue the proposed rule by the U.S. District Court. However, the U.S. Court of Appeals reversed that decision. Because the EEOC felt that the proposal should become effective for plan years beginning after January 1, 1988, and rules under the Omnibus Budget Reconciliation Act of 1986 (P.L. 99-509) superseded the provisions of ADEA Sec. 4(f)(2) under which Reg. § 1625.21 was promulgated, the EEOC terminated and withdrew the notice of proposed rulemaking.]

¶ 20,526   Reserved.

Reg. §§ 2550.407d-5, 2550.407d-6, and 2550.408d-3, relating to employee stock ownership plans, were formerly reproduced at this point.

The final regulations are at ¶ 14,776E, ¶ 14,776F, and ¶ 14,783.]

¶ 20,526A   Reserved.

Proposed amendment to 29 CFR Part 2610 on rates and factors used for valuing plan benefits for plans that terminated on or after June 1, 1977, but before December 1, 1977, was formerly reproduced at this point. The final regulation was at ¶ 15,620L. 29 CFR Part 2610 was later completely revised effective April 1, 1981. Under the revised regulations, the rates and factors used for valuation are at ¶ 15,620Z.]

¶ 20,526B   Reserved.

Proposed amendment to 29 CFR Part 2610 on rates and factors used for valuing plan benefits for plans that terminated on or after December 1, 1977, but before March 1, 1978, was formerly reproduced at this point.

The final regulation was at ¶ 15,620L. 29 CFR Part 2610 was later completely revised effective April 1, 1981. Under the revised regulations, the rates and factors used for valuation are at ¶ 15,620Z.]

¶ 20,526C   Reserved.

Proposed amendment to 29 CFR Part 2610 on rates and factors used for valuing plan benefits for plans that terminated on or after March 1, 1978, but before June 1, 1978, was formerly reproduced at this point.

The final regulation was at ¶ 15,620L. 29 CFR Part 2610 was later completely revised effective April 1, 1981. Under the revised regulations, the rates and factors used for valuation are at ¶ 15,620Z.]

¶ 20,526D   Reserved.

Proposed amendments to 29 CFR Part 2618 on rules for administrative review of agency decisions were formerly reproduced at this point.

The final regulations appear at ¶ 15,325.]

¶ 20,526E   Reserved.

Proposed amendments to 29 CFR Part 2618 on rules for administrative review of agency decisions were formerly reproduced at this point.

The final regulations appear at ¶ 15,325.]

¶ 20,526F   Reserved.

Proposed amendment to 29 CFR Part 2610 on rates and factors used for valuing plan benefits for plans that terminated on or after September 1, 1978, but before March 1, 1979, was formerly reproduced at this point.

The final regulation was at ¶ 15,620L. 29 CFR Part 2610 was later completely revised effective April 1, 1981. Under the revised regulations, the rates and factors used for valuation are at ¶ 15,620Z.

¶ 20,526G   Reserved.

Proposed amendments to interim regulations that establish new mortality rates for disabled plan participants under 29 CFR Part 2610 were formerly reproduced at this point.

¶20,525S

The amended interim regulations were at ¶ 15,620L. However, 29 CFR Part 2610 was later completely revised effective April 1, 1981. Under the revised regulations, the mortality tables for disabled plan participants are at ¶ 15,620Z.]

¶ 20,526H   Reserved.

Proposed regulations relating to a revised method of filing a Notice of Intent to Terminate a pension plan were formerly reproduced at this paragraph.

The regulations, which were originally proposed as Reg. §§ 2604.1—2604.6, have been finalized and redesignated as Reg. §§ 2616.1—2616.7. The final regulations are reproduced at ¶ 15,441—15,446A.]

¶ 20,526I   Reserved.

Proposed regulations to 29 CFR 2520, relating to reporting and disclosure requirements for certain simplified employee pension plans other than those created by use of Internal Revenue Service Form 5305-SEP, were formerly reproduced here. The final regulations appear at ¶ 14,247ZC.]

¶ 20,526J   Reserved.

Proposed regulations relating to the definition of "assets" of an employee benefit plan under ERISA were formerly reproduced here. The proposed rules were withdrawn.

¶ 20,526K   Reserved.

Proposed regulations relating to the maintenance of indicia of ownership of plan assets outside the jurisdiction of the district courts of the United States were formerly reproduced at this point.

The final regulations are at ¶ 14,743.]

¶ 20,526L

Proposed regulations on 29 CFR Parts 2520 and 2530.—Reproduced below is the text of proposed regulations, applicable to certain multiple employer pension plans, which deal with reports that must be furnished to participants regarding their benefit entitlements and records that must be maintained to provide the information necessary for these reports.

The proposed regulations were published in the *Federal Register* on August 8, 1980 (45 FR 52824).

ERISA Sec. 105 and ERISA Sec. 209.

DEPARTMENT OF LABOR

Office of Pension and Welfare Benefit Programs

29 CFR Parts 2520 and 2530

Rules and Regulations for Reporting and Disclosure and Minimum Standards for Employee Pension Benefit Plans; Individual Benefit Reporting and Recordkeeping for Multiple Employer Plans

AGENCY: Department of Labor.

ACTION: Proposed rulemaking.

SUMMARY: This document contains proposed regulations, applicable to certain multiple employer pension plans, which deal with reports that must be furnished to participants in such plans (and, in some cases, to their beneficiaries) regarding their benefit entitlements, and with records that must be maintained to provide the information necessary for these reports. The Employee Retirement Income Security Act of 1974 (the Act) authorizes the Secretary of Labor to prescribe regulations regarding individual benefit reporting to participants and beneficiaries and individual benefit recordkeeping. The proposed regulations, if adopted, would provide necessary guidance to employers maintaining certain multiple employer pension plans and to plan administrators of such plans, and would enable participants in such plans to receive accurate, timely and useful information.

DATES: Written comments and requests for a public hearing must be received by the Department of Labor (the Department) on or before October 7, 1980. These regulations, if adopted, would generally become effective 120 days after adoption. However, with respect to collectively bargained multiple employer plans, the regulations would not become effective until nine months after the expiration of current collective bargaining agreements (but in no case more than 45 months after adoption).

ADDRESSES: Written comments (preferably three copies) should be submitted to the Division of Reporting and Disclosure, Pension and Welfare Benefit Programs, Room N-4508, U.S. Department of Labor, Washington, D.C. 20216. Attention: Multiple Employer Individual Benefit Reporting and Recordkeeping Regulations. All comments should be clearly referenced to the section of the regulations to which they apply. All written comments will be available for public inspection at the Public Documents Room, Pension and Welfare Benefit Programs, Department of Labor, Room N-4677, 200 Constitution Avenue, NW., Washington, D.C. 20216.

FOR FURTHER INFORMATION CONTACT: Mary O. Lin, Plan Benefits Security Division, Office of the Solicitor, U.S. Department of Labor, Washington, D.C. 20210, (202) 523-9595, or Joseph L. Roberts III, Pension and Welfare Benefit Programs, U.S. Department of Labor, Washington, D.C. 20216, (202) 523-8685. (These are not toll-free numbers.)

SUPPLEMENTARY INFORMATION: Notice is hereby given that the Department of Labor has under consideration proposed regulations applicable to multiple employer pension plans[1] dealing with reports that must be furnished to individual participants (and, in some cases, to their beneficiaries) regarding their benefit entitlements under employee pension benefit plans, and with records that must be maintained to provide the information necessary for these reports. These regulations are proposed under the authority contained in sections 105, 209 and 505 of the Act (Pub. L. 93-406, 88 Stat. 849, 865 and 894, 29 U.S.C. 1025, 1059 and 1135). Parallel regulations relative to single employer plans[2] have already been proposed (45 FR 51231, August 1, 1980).

---

[1] The term "multiple employer plan" is defined in the proposed regulation to mean a plan adopted by more than one employer other than a plan maintained by employers under common control. In discussions of the proposal throughout this document, the term "multiple employer plan" generally should be read to be consistent with this definition.

[2] The term "single employer plan" has been defined in such proposal to include plans maintained by a group of employers under common control. Throughout this document the term "single employer plan" generally should be read to be consistent with his definition.

The Department has determined that these proposed regulations are "significant" within the meaning of Department of Labor guidelines (44 FR 5570, January 26, 1979) issued to implement Executive Order (44 FR 12661, March 24, 1978).

Statutory Provisions

Section 105(a) of the Act generally requires each administrator of an employee pension benefit plan to furnish to any plan participant or beneficiary who so requests in writing, a statement indicating, on the basis of the latest available information, the total benefits accrued and the nonforfeitable pension benefits which have accrued, if any, or the earliest date on which such benefits will become nonforfeitable. Similarly, section 209(a)(1) of the Act generally requires the plan administrator of a plan subject to Part 2 of Title I of the Act to make a report, in accordance with regulations of the Secretary of Labor, to each employee who is a participant under the plan and who requests such report. The report required under section 209(a)(1) must be sufficient to inform the employee of his accrued benefits which are nonforfeitable. Under both sections 105(a) and 209(a)(1), no participant is entitled to more than one report on request during any single 12-month period. Section 209(a) also requires similar reports to be provided to a participant who terminates service with the employer or has a one-year break in service. Sections 105(d) and 209(a)(2) authorize the Secretary of Labor to prescribe regulations specifying the extent to which these reporting requirements apply to plans adopted by more than one employer. In addition, section 105(c) of the Act requires plan administrators to provide to participants with respect to whom registration statements are filed with the Internal Revenue Service under section 6057 of the Internal Revenue Code of 1954 (the Code) individual statements setting forth the information contained in the registration statements.

In order to enable employees' benefits to be determined, so that the reporting requirements of section 209 can be met, section 209(a)(1) generally requires records to be maintained by employers and authorizes the Secretary of Labor to prescribe regulations governing such recordkeeping. The information necessary for individual benefit reporting is to be furnished by the employer to the plan administrator. In the case of a plan adopted by more than one employer, however, section 209(a)(2) requires records to be maintained by the plan administrator, based on information to be provided by each such employer.

Background

On February 9, 1979 (44 FR 8294), the Department published proposed regulations with respect to individual benefit statements and recordkeeping (referred to herein as "the 1979 proposal"). These regulations would have applied both to single and multiple employer plans. A large number of public comments on the 1979 proposal were filed. Many of these comments suggested that substantial revisions should be made in the 1979 proposal. Comments filed on behalf of single and multiple employer plans raised distinct issues.

Upon consideration of those comments, the Department decided to withdraw the 1979 proposal and to propose separately regulations pertaining to single employer plans and to multiple employer plans. On August 1, 1980, (45 FR 51231), the Department published a document which withdrew the 1979 proposal and which contained new proposed regulations applicable only to single employer plans. That document also contained general provisions with respect to recordkeeping and individual benefit statement requirements. In addition, the Department announced in that document that proposed regulations dealing with multiple employer plans would be published in the **Federal Register** in the future. Accordingly, the regulations now being proposed contain provisions which pertain only to multiple employer plans. Many of these provisions are similar to the proposed regulations pertaining to single employer plans. As a result, many of the same considerations are applicable to these proposed regulations as were applicable to the single employer plan regulations. Although the discussion of the multiple employer plan regulations in this preamble is to a certain extent duplicative of the discussion in the preamble of the single employer proposal, the multiple employer plan regulations are discussed here in full in order to avoid making it necessary to refer to the single employer document for a discussion of the regulations proposed in this document.

Of the regulations now being proposed, 29 CFR § 2520.105-3 deals with individual benefit reporting to participants and beneficiaries, while 29 CFR § 2530.209-3 deals with the maintenance by plans of records to serve as a basis for individual benefit statements.

In addition to substantive changes from the 1979 proposal, this new proposal contains language changes designed to clarify provisions or to improve readability.

These regulations are proposed under the authority in sections 105, 209, and 505 of the Act (Pub. L. 93-466, 88 Stat. 849, 865, and 894, 29 U.S.C. 1025, 1059, and 1135).

Discussion of Proposed Individual Benefit Reporting Regulations

1. *Benefit statement.* Under these proposed regulations, the benefit statement is the basic document to be used for providing individual benefit information to participants upon request, upon termination or upon a one-year break in service. The benefit statement must state the amount of a participant's accrued benefit regardless of the extent to which it is nonforfeitable (i.e., "vested"), the percentage of the accrued benefit which is vested, and the amount of such accrued vested benefit. The regulations specify the form in which accrued benefits and accrued vested benefits must be reported. The new proposal is designed to ensure that the information provided to an individual participant is presented in a meaningful fashion, without imposing excessive administrative costs on plans.

Some of the comments received by the Department on the 1979 proposal raised objections to the degree to which that proposal would have required benefit statements to provide individualized information geared to each participant's particular circumstances. These comments suggested that the degree of individualization that would have been required would entail significant additional costs for plans, and that ultimately these costs would be borne to some extent by participants. These commentators pointed out that, in some cases, the individualized information might be misleading or of little value to recipients of benefit statements as a result of changes in participants' circumstances. At the same time, it appears to the Department that some degree of individualization is necessary if individual benefit statements are to serve the purposes which underlie the statutory requirements. In the new proposal the Department has struck what it believes to be a better balance between the need for individualization of benefit statements and the costs that individualization imposes.

In the case of defined benefit plans, the accrued benefit and the amount of the participant's accrued vested benefit may be expressed either in terms of a straight life annuity payable at normal retirement age, or in terms of the normal form of benefits offered by the plan (e.g., annuity for a term of years, lump-sum distribution, etc.). By contrast, the 1979 proposal would have required accrued benefits to be stated either in the form of a straight life annuity payable at normal retirement age or, if the plan did not offer such a benefit, in the form of the primary option offered by the plan. If a participant had made any elections affecting the manner of payment of benefits, the 1979 proposal generally would have required accrued benefits to be stated in the form elected by the participant. The elimination in the new proposal of the requirement to state accrued benefits in the form elected by the participant is in keeping with the goal of reducing costs resulting from excessive individualization. It also reflects comments to the effect that the requirement to state accrued benefits in the form of a straight life annuity payable at normal retirement age might prove misleading to participants when this is not the normal form of benefits payable under the plan. One of the comments on the 1979 proposal suggested that the Department should explicitly prohibit inclusion in the benefit statement of benefit projections predicated on the assumption that a participant will work until retirement. The comment suggested that such projections would not satisfy the requirement that a benefit statement must report accrued benefits, vested percentage and accrued vested benefits as of the date of the statement. The Department has decided not to prohibit the inclusion of such projections, but notes that the benefit statement must be written in a manner calculated to be understood by the average plan participant or beneficiary and its format must not have the effect of misleading or misinforming participants or beneficiaries.

The new proposal would require the benefit statement to indicate that election of options under the plan might affect the participant's accrued benefits, and to refer the participant to the Summary Plan Description for information on available options. In addition, if the accrued benefit and accrued vested benefit are not expressed as amounts payable in the form of a joint and survivor annuity, the benefit statement must explain that the periodic benefit the participant will receive at retirement may be reduced on account of survivor benefits.

"Social Security offset plans" must furnish the net benefit. In the case of benefit statements furnished on request or under the annual benefit statement alternative, the net benefit may be determined on the basis of assumptions about participants' earnings in service not covered by the plan, provided that the benefit statement indicates that the reported amounts are approximate. Benefit statements furnished after a break in service (or after a "severance," as described below) must report the actual amounts of benefits to which the participant is entitled.

In the case of an individual account plan, the regulations make it clear that the participant's account balance is considered to be accrued benefit.

In accordance with the statutory requirements, the benefit statement would be required to indicate the nonforfeitable (vested) percentage of the participant's accrued benefit. If the participant has no vested accrued benefits, the benefit statement must indicate the earliest date on which any benefits will become vested. Consistent with the goal of avoiding excessive administrative costs, the new proposal eliminates the requirement in the 1979 proposal that plans with "graded" vesting indicate the earliest dates on which a participant may attain each subsequent level of nonforfeitable accrued benefits derived from employer contributions. The new proposal also provides that class year plans would be required to indicate the nonforfeitable percentage of each portion of the participant's account balance to which a separate nonforfeitable percentage applies.

The benefit statement would also be required to indicate the amount of the participant's nonforfeitable accrued benefit, in the same form as that in which the accrued benefit is reported.

The new proposal requires only a general reference to the Summary Plan Description. The 1979 proposal required more detailed information regarding circumstances that might result in the reduction or elimination of accrued or nonforfeitable benefits, including detailed references to the Summary Plan Description. The new proposal also eliminates the requirement contained in the 1979 proposal that the benefit statement include certain information concerning a participant's work history used as a basis for calculation of the participant's benefits. This change was made to reduce the degree to which benefit statements must be individualized. The eliminated information, however, must be available to a participant under the provisions of these regulations regarding inspection of records (§ 2530.209-3 (f)), and, as under the 1979 proposal, the benefit statement must so indicate. As under the 1979 proposal, the benefit statement would be required to include a statement urging the participant to bring promptly to the attention of the plan administrator anything in the benefit statement that does not appear correct, information regarding the availability of plan records for inspection, the date as of which information is reported, and the participant's social security number (for the purpose of verification by the participant).

Like its predecessor, the new proposal would provide that the benefit statement must be written in a manner calculated to be understood by the average plan participant or beneficiary and that the format of the benefit statement must not have the effect of misleading or misinforming the participant or beneficiary. Under certain circumstances, plans must offer foreign language assistance to participants who are not literate in English to aid them in understanding their benefit statements, as is required under regulations relating to the Summary Plan Description (see 29 CFR § 2520-102.2 (c)).

The benefit statement must be based on the latest available information. As under the 1979 proposal, benefit statements based on records that meet the standards of sufficiency set forth in the proposed record-keeping regulations will be deemed to be based on the latest available information. Although "sufficient", a plan's records may nevertheless be incomplete (i.e., if they do not include all items necessary to determine participants' benefit entitlements) if, for example, a plan did not maintain complete records prior to the adoption of these regulations. In these instances, the benefit statement must indicate that the records on which it is based are incomplete, and the participant or beneficiary must be offered an opportunity to provide other information relating to his benefit entitlements. The plan administrator must prepare a benefit statement based on such information although, to the extent that a benefit statement is based on such information, it may indicate that it is conditioned upon the accuracy of that information.

In the 1979 proposal the Department solicited comments on whether and to what extent it should adopt regulations concerning circumstances under which liability should be imposed for the payment of benefits in accordance with the information provided in the benefit statement. Some comments supported the adoption of regulations imposing liability, while others suggested that liability should be limited, or objected to the imposition of any liability. Upon consideration of the comments, the Department has concluded that a judgment concerning the consequences of an incorrect benefit statement can properly be made only after account has been taken of all of the facts and circumstances. The Department believes, therefore, that it would be more appropriate to leave determinations of this sort to plan fiduciaries, whose actions are subject to review by the judicial process, rather than to attempt to deal with all conceivable factual situations in the context of regulations.

In the 1979 proposal, the Department also solicited comments on whether it should publish model benefit statements. In view of the multiplicity of plan provisions, it would be difficult for the Department to ensure that the format of a model statement would not be misleading under any circumstances. Accordingly, the Department has made a decision at this time not to publish model benefit statements.

2. *Furnishing benefit statements on request.* Both sections 105(a) and 209(a)(1)(A) of the Act require plan administrators of pension plans to furnish individual benefit information on request. The requirements of both statutory provisions are substantially similar in this regard; accordingly, these requirements are dealt with in a single section of the regulations (§ 2520.105-3(a)). The only significant difference between the two statutory provisions is that section 105(a) applies to requests by both participants and their designated beneficiaries, while section 209(a)(1)(A) applies only to requests by participants.

The regulations, therefore, apply to requests by both participants and beneficiaries, so as to cover the broadest range of circumstances under which benefit statements must be furnished on request.

In response to suggestions made in comments on the 1979 proposal, the new proposal provides that a plan administrator subject to these regulations need not provide a benefit statement upon request to certain classes of participants and beneficiaries. These include participants and beneficiaries currently receiving benefits; participants and beneficiaries to whom paid up insurance policies representing their full benefit entitlements have been distributed; participants and beneficiaries who have received a full distribution of their benefits; beneficiaries of participants who are entitled to benefit statements; and participants with deferred vested benefits who have received benefit statements upon termination or after having incurred a one-year break in service without returning to service with any employer maintaining the plan, and their beneficiaries. The Department believes that it would be superfluous to require benefit statements to be furnished to these participants and beneficiaries.

The plan administrator may establish a simple and convenient procedure for the submission of requests for benefit statements. If such a procedure is established and communicated to participants and beneficiaries (for example, in the Summary Plan Description), the plan administrator, under certain conditions, need not comply with requests that do not conform to the procedure. If no such procedure is established, however, the plan administrator must comply with any request in writing by a participant or beneficiary. The plan administrator may not require information regarding a participant's employment record as a condition for furnishing the benefit statement (although such information may be requested). The new proposal would, however, allow plan administrators to require the furnishing of certain items of information identifying the particicpant about whom information is requested.

Many of the comments on the 1979 proposal urged that the Department permit benefit statements to report benefits as of the end of the plan year. The comments suggested that this approach would relieve individual account plans of the expense of conducting a valuation whenever a participant or beneficiary requests a benefit statement. Defined benefit plans might also face lower administrative costs if an end-of-plan-year approach were adopted because it might enable these plans to gear data processing systems to a single date. In light of these comments, the new proposal would require a benefit statement to report benefits as of a date not earlier than the end of the plan year preceding the plan year in which a participant or beneficiary requests the statement.

The end-of-year approach, however, entails changes in the deadlines for furnishing benefit statements on request. The new proposal is designed to permit a reasonable period of time after the end of the plan year for the processing of information. Under the new proposal, a benefit statement must be furnished to a participant or beneficiary on request within the later of 60 days of the date of the request or 120 days after the end of the plan year which immediately precedes the year in which the request was made. The Department recognizes that this scheme would provide participants and beneficiaries who request benefit statements towards the end of the plan year with a statement that contains relatively old information (as much as 14 months old), while participants and beneficiaries who request statements during the earlier part of the plan year may be required to wait a substantial period (up to four months) to receive their statements. Nevertheless, the Department believes that the proposed scheme strikes an appropriate balance between providing participants with timely information and reducing administrative costs.

As under the 1979 proposal, the plan administrator would not be required to furnish more than one benefit statement to a participant or beneficiary on request during any 12-month period.

The original proposal appeared to require plans to furnish a complete benefit statement to a non-vested participant if the annual alternative was used. The new proposal would permit a plan to provide annually, as an alternative to furnishing benefit statements on request, a benefit statement to each vested participant and a statement of non-vested status to each non-vested participant. Permitting the furnishing of a statement of non-vested status under the annual alternative should reduce costs to plans electing the alternative, while providing sufficient disclosure to a non-vested participant. The plan administrator must furnish a complete benefit statement, however, to any non-vested participant who requests one after receiving the statement of non-vested status.

The annual benefit statement must be furnished within 180 days after the end of the plan year.

Despite comments objecting to the requirement in the 1979 proposal that the plan administrator furnish at least one duplicate of the annual benefit statement to any participant or beneficiary who requests it during the year, the Department has not eliminated this requirement. In some cases a participant or beneficiary may not receive an annual benefit statement mailed to him. Since it would be impracticable and unfair to require a participant or beneficiary to prove that he did not receive an annual statement in order to obtain a duplicate, the regulations allow all participants or beneficiaries entitled to receive a benefit statement on request at least one duplicate if the annual alternative is used.

3. *Furnishing benefit statements after one-year breaks in service.* The benefit statement must report benefits as of the end of the plan year in which a one-year break in service occurs. Consistent with end-of-the-year benefit reporting, the new proposal requires statements to be furnished within 180 days after the end of the plan year in which the break in service occurs. The 180 day period also would allow plans to satisfy the requirement to furnish benefit statements after a one-year break in service through the use of the annual benefit statement alternative, which is required to be furnished in the same time period.

A participant who receives a benefit statement upon incurring a one-year break in service, and thereafter incurs a subsequent one-year break in service, is not entitled to receive an additional benefit statement if the information in the second benefit statement would be the same as that in the first.

As under the 1979 proposal, plan administrators of multiple employer plans are not required to furnish benefit statements upon termination. However, if a multiple employer plan does not provide that a participant may suffer adverse consequences upon incurring a one-year break in service, the plan administrator is required to furnish a benefit statement to a participant if the participant is not listed on any Service Report furnished to the plan administrator by an employer for two consecutive plan years. The fact that the participant has not appeared on a Service Report for an extended period of time suggests that such participant has ceased to participate actively in the plan. In the Department's view, such a participant should be furnished a benefit statement for the same reasons as a participant who incurs a one-year break in service (or a participant in a single employer plan who terminates service with the employer).

In the case of participants who have no vested benefits, the new proposal, like the 1979 proposal, would permit plan administrators of multiple employer plans to satisfy the requirements to furnish individual benefit information after a one-year break in service by furnishing a statement of non-vested status. The statement of non-vested status informs the participant that he has no nonforfeitable benefits. It does not, however, provide information regarding accrued benefits. Thus, the statement of non-vested status does not require extensive calculations and may be presented to all participants entitled to it in a standardized form, with no need for preparation of an individual statement for each. However, the statement of non-vested status must inform the participant that he may request a benefit statement with more detailed information regarding his individual accrued (non-vested) benefits. Such a request must be treated as a request for a benefit statement.

4. *Corrections to the benefit statement.* As under the 1979 proposal, a participant who raises a question with regard to the accuracy of a benefit statement must be given an opportunity to furnish information regarding his benefit entitlements to the plan administrator. Within a reasonable time, the plan administrator must make a decision with regard to the question raised by the participant and notify the participant of the decision, the basis for the decision, and any change in benefit entitlements as a result of the decision. The plan administrator is not required to prepare a benefit statement based on the information furnished by the participant except, as noted above, in situations where the benefit statement is based on incomplete records.

5. *Statement of deferred vested benefits.* Under section 105(c) of the Act, each plan administrator required to register with the Internal Revenue Service under section 6057 of the Code shall furnish a statement of deferred vested benefits to each participant described in section 6057(a)(C) (i.e., to each participant who, during the plan year for which registration is required, is separated from service covered under the plan, is entitled to a deferred vested benefit under the plan as of the end of the plan year, and with respect to whom retirement benefits were not paid under the plan). Section 6057(e) of the Code requires plan administrators to furnish similar individual statements to the same class of participants. The requirements of section 105(c) will be deemed to be satisfied if, in accordance with section 6057(e) of the Code and regulations thereunder, the plan administrator furnishes to the participant the individual statement required under the latter section.

6. *Manner of furnishing individual benefit reporting documents.* Like the 1979 proposal, the new proposal would require a plan to furnish individual benefit documents to a participant or beneficiary either by first class mail to his last known address, or by personal delivery. The new proposal makes it clear that personal delivery may be accomplished by another party under the plan administrator's supervision.

The new recordkeeping proposal would require participants' individual benefit records to include current address information. Although some comments suggested that plans should not be required to maintain current address information on file, and should be permitted to use less reliable modes of delivery than first-class mail and personal delivery, the Department believes that these requirements represent the only means of assuring that individual benefit reporting documents will actually reach participants and beneficiaries in most cases.

Proposed Individual Benefit Recordkeeping Regulations

1. *Duty to maintain records.* In the case of a multiple employer plan, the duty to maintain individual benefit records would be imposed on the plan administrator. As under the 1979 proposal, the records are to be based on information in Service Reports furnished to the plan administrator by employers within 45 days (rather than 30, as under the 1979 proposal) after the end of a reporting period. The reporting period may be up to three months in duration. The new proposal makes it clear that a shorter reporting period may be established by agreement. The new proposal, like the 1979 proposal, requires Service Reports to contain information on all employees in service covered under the plan and all employees who have moved from covered to noncovered service after having met the plan's eligibility requirements for participation.

The new proposal imposes the duty to provide Service Reports upon every employer required to make contributions to the plan in respect of work performed by the employer's employees during the reporting period. (As in the 1979 proposal, however, employers are not required to provide Service Reports on employees in non-covered job classifications who have never performed service covered under the plan.) In addition, an employer is generally required to file Service Reports if another party is required to make contributions in respect of work performed by the employer's employees. This requirement is designed to cover a situation brought to the Department's attention in comments on the 1979 proposal in which contributions are made to the plan not by the employers of covered employees, but by firms that contract with these employers for their output, and similar situations if they exist. Further, the language of the new proposal should make it clear that employers will not be required to furnish Service Reports to a plan if their employees accumulate service credits under the plan solely by virtue of a reciprocity agreement with another plan.

If the plan administrator fails to receive an employer's Service Report, or an employer's Service Report does not contain all the necessary information, or the plan administrator has reason to believe that the information in the Service Report is inaccurate, the plan administrator must make reasonable efforts to obtain accurate and complete information. The plan administrator may prescribe reasonable rules and regulations regarding the format, manner of reporting and reportable information, and may prescribe forms and worksheets for reporting.

2. *Sufficiency of records.* Records maintained by the plan administrator of a multiple employer plan will be deemed to be sufficient under the proposed regulations if such records accurately reflect the Service Reports furnished by employers to the plan administrator. In general, Service Reports must contain the same information as the records maintained by an employer in connection with a single employer plan (i.e., they must include all information relating to service with such employer during the reporting period which would be relevant to a determination of the benefit entitlements of each employee covered under the plan). This may include information regarding service in a job classification not covered by the plan during the quarter. Under

certain circcumstances, section 210 of the Act requires service not performed in job classifications covered by a multiple employer plan to be credited to a participant, particularly for purposes of vesting. These circumstances generally occur when an employee moves between a covered and a non-covered job classification. When an employee moves from a covered to a non-covered job classification, the employee must continue to report information regarding the employee to the plan administrator although the employee no longer performs service in a covered job classification, if this information is relevant to a determination of the employee's individual benefit entitlements. Under the proposal, an employer would not be required to furnish Service Reports on an employee who has not met the Plan's requirements for eligibility for participation in the plan. Since service in a covered job classification is always a requirement for eligibility to participate in a plan, the regulation would not require Service Reports to be furnished with respect to employees in non-covered job classifications merely because they might later move to covered job classifications and thereby become eligible to participate (with the result that their non-covered service would then be required to be credited for vesting or other purposes).

As in the case of single employer plans, there is no requirement to develop records relating to service before the effective date of the regulations, but records in existence on February 9, 1979 must be retained. In the Department's view, the 1979 proposal was sufficient to put plan administrators on notice that existing records would not be permitted to be destroyed.

3. *Retention, preservation and inspection of records.* As under the 1979 proposal, individual benefit records must be retained as long as a possibility exists that they might be relevant to a determination of the benefit entitlements of a participant or beneficiary. However, if they are lost or destroyed due to circumstances beyond the control of the person responsible for their maintenance, they will not be deemed insufficient solely for that reason. They must be maintained in a safe and accessible place at the offices of the plan administrator, or at special recordkeeping offices.

The proposal makes clear that original records may be disposed of at any time if microfilm, microfiche or similarly reproduced records which are clear reproductions of the original documents are retained, and adequate viewing equipment is available for inspecting them. (The 1979 proposal appeared to allow microfilm reproduction only.) The regulations do not preclude electronic data processing of records.

Individual benefit records, including original documents, must be available for inspection by participants, beneficiaries, and their representatives.

The period within which plan records must be made available for inspection after a request to do so has been extended from 72 hours, as under the 1979 proposal, to 10 working days. This change was made in response to comments noting the difficulties which would have been involved under the previous proposal.

In response to some public comments, provisions have been added to this proposal requiring the plan to bear the cost of converting records into a form accessible for inspection, although reasonable charges for copying may be imposed, not exceeding the actual cost. Inspection of records may be made only by those persons entitled to receive a benefit statement, and by their representatives. Representatives of the Department have the authority to inspect plan records under the circumstances specified in section 504(a)(2) of ERISA.

If a plan administrator ceases to be responsible for the maintenance of individual benefit records, they must be transferred to the person who becomes responsible for their maintenance.

4. *Definition of "multiple employer plans".* The Department has decided to limit the term "multiple employer plan", for the purposes of these regulations, to a plan adopted by more than one employer, other than a plan adopted by employers under common control.

5. *Reliance on Social Security records; variances for multiple employer plans.* Comments on the 1979 proposal indicate that a number of multiple employer plans have hitherto relied on records maintained by the Social Security Administration, among other sources of information, as a basis for making benefit determinations. The commentators suggest that these plans should be permitted to continue to rely on Social Security Administration records. The Department believes that adequate pre-retirement individual benefit reporting cannot be provided to participants and beneficiaries unless plans develop and maintain recordkeeping systems of their own. Consequently, the new proposal does not permit reliance on Social Security records as a substitute for recordkeeping by employers or plan administrators.

The comments indicate, however, that there may be a few multiple employer plans that operate under extraordinary circumstances that would make compliance with the multiple employer reporting and recordkeeping requirements in this proposal virtually impossible. The Department solicits detailed comments from these multiple employer plans with respect to any such special circumstances. If warranted by the comments, the Department might consider a procedure under which such plans would be granted variances which would permit them to use alternative methods of complying with the individual benefit reporting and recordkeeping requirements of the Act and these regulations.

Effective Dates

A number of comments on the 1979 proposal suggested that some multiple employer plans may need additional time to make preparations for compliance. In order to allow for orderly preparations for compliance with the regulations would not become effective with respect to collectively bargained multiple employer plans until nine months after the expiration of the collective bargaining agreement or agreements in effect on the date of adoption of these regulations, but in no case more than 45 months after the date of adoption. For multiple employer plans which are not collectively bargained, the regulations, if adopted, would become effective 120 days after adoption.

Drafting Information

The principal author of these proposed regulations is Mary O. Lin of the Plan Benefits Security Division, Office of the Solicitor, Department of Labor. However, other persons in the Department of Labor participated in developing the proposed regulations, both on matters of substance and style.

Proposed Regulation

Accordingly, it is proposed to amend Chapter XXV of Title 29 of the Code of Federal Regulations as follows:

1. By adding to Part 2520 new § 2520.105-3 to read as follows:

PART 2520—RULES AND REGULATIONS FOR REPORTING AND DISCLOSURE

Subpart G—Individual Benefit Reporting

Sec. 2520.105-3—Individual Benefit Reporting for Multiple Employer Plans.

Authority: Secs. 105, 209 and 505 of the Act, (Pub. L. 93-406; 88 Stat. 849, 865 and 894, 29 U.S.C. 1025, 1059 and 1135).

Subpart G—Individual Benefit Reporting

§ 2520.105-3 Individual benefit reporting for multiple employer plans.

(a) *Furnishing benefit statements on request.*—(1) *General.* The administrator of a multiple employer employee pension benefit plan (as defined in paragraph (k) of this section) subject to Parts 1 or 2 of Title I of the Act shall furnish a benefit statement which satisfies the requirements of this paragraph and paragraphs (c) through (i) of this section to all plan participants or beneficiaries who request in writing information regarding their individual benefit entitlements under the plan, except:

(i) Participants and beneficiaries who are currently receiving benefits under the plan;

(ii) Participants and beneficiaries whose entire benefit entitlements under the plan are fully guaranteed by an insurance company, insurance service or insurance organization qualified to do business in a State, provided that the benefits are paid under an insurance policy or contract on which no further premiums are payable and which has been distributed to the participant or beneficiary;

(iii) Participants and beneficiaries who have received all benefits to which they are entitled under the plan;

(iv) Beneficiaries of a participant who is entitled to a benefit statement on request; and

(v) Participants with deferred vested benefits who have received benefit statements on termination or after incurring a one year break in service and who have not returned to service with any employer maintaining the plan, and beneficiaries of such participants.

(2) *Procedure for submission of requests for benefit statements.* The plan administrator may establish a simple procedure, convenient to participants and beneficiaries, for the submission of requests for benefit statements. The plan administrator will not be required to comply with a request made in a manner which does not conform to such a procedure which has been communicated in writing to participants and beneficiaries, provided that the plan administrator informs the requesting participant or beneficiary that he has failed to comply with the procedure and explains how to comply with the procedure. A procedure shall be deemed to be communicated to participants and benefi-

ciaries if a description of the procedure is included in the Summary Plan Description of the plan or in any other document distributed to all plan participants. If no such procedure is established, any request in writing to the plan administrator or plan office by a participant or beneficiary for information regarding his benefit entitlements under the plan shall be deemed a request to the plan administrator for the purposes of this section.

(3) *Information obtained from participant or beneficiary.* A participant or beneficiary who requests a benefit statement may not be required to furnish information regarding the participant's employment record as a condition to receiving the benefit statement, but may be required to furnish the following information: name, address, date of birth, Social Security account number, and, if relevant to information provided in the benefit statement, marital status and date of birth of spouse.

(4) *Date of furnishing.* A benefit statement shall be furnished to a participant or beneficiary who requests such a statement, no later than (i) 60 days after receipt of the request or (ii) 120 days after the end of the plan year which immediately precedes the plan year in which the request is made, whichever is later.

(5) *Date as of which information is provided.* A benefit statement furnished at the request of a participant or beneficiary shall report benefits as of a date not earlier than the end of the plan year preceding the plan year in which the request is made.

(6) *Annual benefit statement alternative.* (i) the requirement to furnish a benefit statement on request to a participant or beneficiary, as set forth in paragraph (a)(1) of this section, shall not apply if within one year before the request the plan administrator has furnished to such participant or beneficiary an annual benefit statement, or a "statement of non-vested status" described in paragraph (f) of this section, as appropriate, which is based on information as of the end of the plan year preceding the plan year in which it is furnished, and it is furnished within 180 days after the end of that plan year.

(ii) Notwithstanding the provisions of paragraph (a)(6)(i) of this section, the plan administrator shall furnish a complete benefit statement meeting the requirements of paragraph (d) and (e) of this section to a participant who requests information on his accrued benefits after receiving a statement of non-vested status, and shall furnish upon request a duplicate of the most recent annual benefit statement, or statement of non-vested status, as appropriate, to any participant or beneficiary who was entitled to such a statement but claims not to have received one.

(b) *Furnishing statements after one-year breaks in service or severance*—(1) *General.* Except as provided in paragraph (c) of this section, the plan administrator of a multiple employer pension plan that is subject to Part 2 of Title I of the act shall furnish a benefit statement to a participant who incurs a one-year break in service as defined in paragraph (b)(5) of this section. If, however, the plan does not provide that participants may suffer adverse consequences on incurring a one-year break in service, such plan administrator shall furnish a benefit statement to a participant who incurs a severance as defined in paragraph (b)(6) of this section.

(2) *Date of furnishing.* A benefit statement or statement of non-vested status shall be furnished within 180 days after the end of the plan year in which a participant incurs a one-year break in service or a severance. This requirement may be satisfied by furnishing to the participant an annual benefit statement described in paragraph (a)(6) of this section, which reports the participant's benefits as of the end of the plan year in which the one-year break in service or the severance occurred.

(3) *Non-vested participants.* In the case of a participant who has no nonforfeitable benefits under the plan and who incurs a one-year break in service or a severance, the plan administrator will comply with the requirements of section 209(a)(1)(B) of the Act and this section if the plan furnishes such participant a "statement of non-vested status" as described in paragraph (f) of this section.

If a participant who incurs a one-year break in service is furnished a statement of non-vested status under this paragraph, and requests information concerning his accrued benefits under the plan, the plan administrator shall furnish a benefit statement meeting the requirements of paragraph (d) and (e) of this section to the participant no later than the later of 60 days after such request or 180 days after the end of the plan year in which he incurs a one-year break in service.

(4) *Date as of which information is provided.* A benefit statement furnished after a one-year break in service or a severance shall report benefits as of the end of the plan year in which the one-year break in service or the severance occurs.

(5) *Definition of "one-year break in service".* For purposes of this section, the term "one-year break in service" shall mean a one-year

break in service for vesting purposes as defined in the plan documents, or in the case of a plan under which service is credited for purposes of vesting according to the elapsed time method permitted under 26 CFR 1.410(a)-7, a one-year period of severance for vesting purposes, as defined in 26 CFR 1.410(a)-7(c)(4).

(6) *Definition of "severance".* For purposes of this section, a participant shall be deemed to incur a "severance" in the second of two consecutive plan years in which the participant is not listed on any Service Report furnished by an employer to the plan administrator in accordance with paragraph (b) of this section.

(c) *Frequency of benefit statements.* (1) A plan administrator is not required to furnish to a participant or beneficiary more than one benefit statement upon request under paragraph (a) of this section in any 12-month period.

(2) Where a participant receives a benefit statement upon incurring a one-year break in service or a severance, the plan administrator is not required to furnish a second benefit statement upon a subsequent one-year break in service or severance, or upon a request by the participant, if the information that would be contained in a second benefit statement would be the same as that contained in the earlier benefit statement.

(d) *Style and format of benefit statements.*—(1) *General.* Individual benefit reporting documents shall be written in a manner calculated to be understood by the average plan participant or beneficiary. The format of these documents must not have the effect of misleading or misinforming the participant or beneficiary.

(2) *Foreign language assistance.* (i) The plan administrator of a plan described in paragraph (d)(2)(ii) of this section shall communicate to plan participants, in the non-English language common to such participants, information relating to any procedure for requesting benefit statements that may have been established by the plan administrator in accordance with paragraph (a)(2) of this section. In addition, the plan administrator shall provide these participants with either a benefit statement in such non-English language, or an English language benefit statement or statement of non-vested status which prominently displays a notice, in the non-English language common to these participants, explaining how they may obtain assistance. The assistance provided need not involve written materials, but shall be given in the non-English language common to these participants.

(ii) The plan administrators of the following plans are subject to the foreign language requirements of paragraph (d)(2)(i) of this section:

(A) A plan that covers fewer than 100 participants at the beginning of the plan year, and in which 25 percent or more of plan participants are not literate in English and are all literate in the same non-English language, or

(B) A plan which covers 100 or more participants at the beginning of the plan year, and in which the lesser of 500 or more participants, or 10% or more of all plan participants, are not literate in English and are all literate in the same non-English language.

(e) *Contents of the benefit statement.*—(1) *General.* In accordance with paragraphs (e)(2), (e)(3), (e)(4) and (e)(5) of this section, each benefit statement shall contain the following information:

(i) The participant's total accrued benefits;

(ii) The nonforfeitable percentage of the participant's accrued benefits;

(iii) The amount of the participant's nonforfeitable accrued benefits; and

(iv) Additional information specified in paragraph (e)(5) of this section.

(2) *Total accrued benefits.*—(i) *Defined benefit plans.*—(a) *General.* In the case of a defined benefit plan, the accrued benefit shall be stated in the form of a straight life annuity payable at normal retirement age or in the normal form of benefit provided by the plan.

(B) *Contributory plans.* If a defined benefit plan requires contributions to be made by employees, the benefit statement shall separately indicate, in addition to the participant's total accrued benefit, either the amount of the participant's accrued benefit derived from employee contributions and the amount of the accrued benefit derived from employer contributions, or the percentages of the participant's total accrued benefit derived from employee contributions and from employer contributions. The portion of the accrued benefit derived from employer contributions and the portion derived from employee contributions shall be determined in accordance with section 204(c) of the Act (section 411(c) of the Internal Revenue Code of 1954 and Treasury Regulations thereunder).

(C) *Social Security offset plans.* If a participant's benefits under the plan are offset by a percentage of the participant's old-age insurance benefit under the Social Security Act, the benefit statement shall state the participant's accrued benefit after reduction by the applicable amount. In the case of a benefit statement furnished upon request or under the annual benefit statement alternative permitted under paragraph (a)(6) of this section, the amount of the offset may be determined on the basis of assumptions about the participant's earnings from service not covered under the plan, provided that the statement indicates that the stated amounts of the accrued and nonforfeitable accrued benefit are approximate. A benefit statement furnished when an employee terminates employment or incurs a break in service must indicate the actual amounts of the accrued benefit and nonforfeitable accrued benefit to which the participant is entitled.

(ii) *Individual account plans.* In the case of an individual account plan, the participant's accrued benefit shall be the fair market value of the participant's account balance on the date as of which benefits are reported.

(3) *Nonforfeitable percentage.*—(i) *General.* The benefit statement shall indicate the percentage of a participant's accrued benefit which is nonforfeitable within the meaning of section 203 of the Act (and sections 411(a) of the Internal Revenue Code of 1954 and Treasury Regulations thereunder). Except in the case of a plan described in paragraph (e)(3)(ii) of this section, if a participant has no nonforfeitable benefits the benefit statement shall indicate the earliest date on which any benefits may become nonforfeitable; and if less than 100 percent of the participant's benefits are nonforfeitable, the benefit statement shall indicate the earliest date on which 100 percent of the participant's benefits may be nonforfeitable.

(ii) *Class year plans.* In the case of an individual account plan which provides for the separate nonforfeitability of benefits derived from contributions for each plan year, the benefit statement shall state each nonforfeitable percentage applicable to a portion of the participant's account balance and the value of that portion of the account balance.

(iii) *Contributory plans.* In the case of a plan which provides for employee contributions, the benefit statement shall indicate that the portion of the accrued benefits derived from the participant's contribution to the plan is nonforfeitable.

(4) *Nonforfeitable benefits.*—(i) *Defined benefit plans.* The benefit statement shall indicate the amount of the participant's nonforfeitable benefit in the same form as the participant's total accrued benefit is reported under paragraph (e)(2) of this section.

(ii) *Individual account plans.* In the case of an individual account plan, the benefit statement shall indicate the fair market value of the nonforfeitable portion of the participant's account balance on the date as of which benefits are reported.

(5) *Other information.* A benefit statement shall include the following information.

(i) In the case of a defined benefit plan, a statement to the effect that the amount of benefits which may be received under the plan may be affected as a result of electing any option under the plan, and that further information on such options is contained in the Summary Plan Description;

(ii) In the case of a defined benefit plan, if the accrued benefit and nonforfeitable benefit are not stated in the form of an annuity for the joint lives of the participant and his spouse, an explanation to the effect that unless a married participant elects not to receive benefits in that form, the participant's nonforfeitable benefit may be reduced;

(iii) A statement to the effect that further information on the circumstances, if any, which may result in a reduction or elimination of accrued benefits or of nonforfeitable benefits is contained in the Summary Plan Description;

(iv) A statement urging the participant or beneficiary to bring promptly to the attention of the plan administrator anything in the statement that does not appear correct;

(v) A statement informing the participant or beneficiary that plan records upon which information in the benefit statement is based are available for inspection upon request, and the name, address and telephone number of the person or office to whom requests should be directed;

(vi) The date as of which benefit entitlements are reported; and

(vii) The participant's Social Security account number.

(f) *Statement of non-vested status.* A statement of non-vested status shall inform the participant that he does not have any nonforfeitable benefits under the plan and that he may obtain upon request a benefit statement indicating his accrued benefits, if any, and the earliest date on which any benefits may become nonforfeitable.

(g) *Basis of benefit statement.* (1) *General.* A benefit statement shall be based on the latest available information. A benefit statement will be deemed to be based on the latest available information if it reports benefit entitlements as of the date benefits must be reported under paragraphs (a) or (b) of this section, as appropriate, or any subsequent date, and if it is based on plan records which comply with the requirements of paragraphs (b) and (c) of this section.

(2) *Benefit statement based on incomplete plan records.* A benefit statement based on incomplete plan records (i.e., records that do not contain all items of information necessary to determine the participant's benefit entitlements) shall so indicate. To the extent that the records of a plan are incomplete, an opportunity to provide information relating to benefit entitlements shall be offered to a participant or beneficiary entitled to a benefit statement, and the benefit statement shall be based on such information. A benefit statement based in whole or in part on information supplied by a participant may state that it is conditioned upon the accuracy of such information.

(h) *Manner of furnishing individual benefit reporting documents.* Individual benefit reporting documents shall be furnished either by first class mail to the participant or beneficiary at his last known address, or by personal delivery to the participant or beneficiary by the plan administrator or an individual under the plan administrator's supervision. In the event that the plan administrator learns that the participant or beneficiary has failed to receive a document by mail or personal delivery, the plan administrator shall employ any means of delivery reasonably likely to ensure the receipt by such participant or beneficiary of the document.

(i) *Corrections to the benefit statement.* A participant or beneficiary who raises questions regarding the accuracy of the benefit statement shall be given a reasonable opportunity to point out information in the benefit statement that he believes inaccurate, and to furnish to the plan administrator information which such participant or beneficiary believes relevant in determining his benefit entitlements. The plan administrator shall make reasonable attempts to determine whether the plan's records or the benefit statement are inaccurate and to verify the information furnished by the participant or beneficiary. Within a reasonable time after the plan administrator receives such a communication from a participant or beneficiary, the plan administrator shall notify him in writing of the plan's decision with respect to such matter, the basis for such decision, and any change in benefit entitlements as a result of the decision.

(j) *Statement of deferred vested benefits.* Section 105(c) of the Act provides that each plan administrator required to file a registration statement under section 6057 of the Internal Revenue Code of 1954 (the Code) shall furnish to each participant described in section 6057(a)(2)(C) of the Code an individual statement setting forth the information with respect to such participant which is contained in the registration statement. The requirements of section 105(c) of the Act will be satisfied if an individual statement is furnished to a participant in accordance with section 6057(e) of the Code and the regulations thereunder.

(k) *Definition of "Multiple Employer Plan".* For purposes of paragraphs (a) through (j) of this section, the term "multiple employer plan" shall mean a plan adopted by more than one employer, other than a plan adopted by employers which are under common control.

PART 2530—RULES AND REGULATIONS FOR MINIMUM STANDARDS FOR EMPLOYEE PENSION BENEFITS PLANS

2. By adding to Part 2530 new § 2530.209-3 to read as follows:

Subpart E—Individual Benefit and Recordkeeping

Sec. 2530.209-3—Individual Benefit Recordkeeping.

Authority: Secs. 105, 209 and 505 of the Act (Pub. L. 93-406; 88 Stat. 849, 865 and 894 (29 U.S.C. 1025, 1059 and 1135)).

Subpart E—Individual Benefit and Recordkeeping

§ 2530.209-3 *Individual benefit recordkeeping for multiple employer plans.*

(a) *Recordkeeping requirement.* For every multiple employer pension plan (as defined in paragraph (h) of this section) subject to Part 2 of Title I of the Act, records shall be maintained with respect to each employee covered under the plan. These records shall be sufficient to determine the benefits which are, or may become, due to such employee and shall include the name and address of each such employee.

(b) *Maintenance of records and furnishing of information.*—(1) *Maintenance of records.* The plan administrator shall maintain the records required to be maintained by a multiple employer plan under paragraph (a) of this section.

(2) *Reporting by Sponsoring Employer.* Each employer who is a sponsoring employer of a multiple employer plan shall furnish written Service Reports to the plan administrator on a regular basis. The Service Reports shall cover a reporting period of no longer than one quarter of a year. A reporting period of less than one quarter of a year may be established by agreement, and different reporting periods may be established for different employers or different classes of employers sponsoring the same plan. A Service Report shall be furnished to the plan administrator no later than 45 days after the end of the reporting period to which it relates. The Service Reports shall be furnished in accordance with any rules prescribed under paragraph (b)(6) of this section and shall be prepared on any forms and worksheets prescribed thereunder.

(3) *Contents of Service Reports.* A Service Report shall contain all information that relates to service for, or other employment relationship with, the employer during the reporting period which it covers and that is relevant to a determination of the benefit entitlements of—

(i) Any of the employer's employees who has met the plan's requirements for eligibility to participate in the plan (including any requirement regarding service in a job classification covered by the plan), whether or not such employee performs service in a job classification covered under the plan during the reporting period; and

(ii) Any of the employer's employees who performs service in a job classification covered under the plan during the reporting period, whether or not such employee has met the plan's requirements for eligibility to participate during such reporting period.

(4) *Definition of "sponsoring employer".* For purposes of this paragraph, an employer shall be deemed to be a "sponsoring employer" of a plan for any reporting period where during such reporting period the employer or another party (other than another plan pursuant to a reciprocity arrangement) is required to make contributions to the plan in respect of work performed by such employer's employees (whether measured in service time or in output).

(5) *Duty of plan administrator to seek information.* The plan administrator shall make reasonable efforts to obtain complete and accurate information where a sponsoring employer of a multiple employer plan fails to furnish a Service Report to the plan administrator; or such an employer fails to include in a Service Report information required under paragraph (b)(3) of this section; or the plan administrator has reason to believe that the information furnished by such an employer is inaccurate.

(6) *Reasonable rules prescribed by plan administrator.* The plan administrator of a multiple employer plan may prescribe in writing reasonable rules concerning the format of reports, the manner of reporting, and reportable information. The plan administrator also may prescribe forms or worksheets to be used by employers for purposes of reporting under paragraph (b) of this section.

(c) *Sufficiency of records.* Records required to be maintained by a multiple employer plan under paragraph (a) of this section will be deemed to be sufficient if:

(1) They accurately reflect all the information contained in the Service Reports furnished to the plan administrator by participating employers under paragraph (b)(2) of this section, and the plan administrator has made reasonable attempts to obtain accurate and complete information under the circumstances described in paragraph (b)(5) of this section, and

(2) With respect to service before [effective date of regulation], if any, they include all records maintained by the administrator on and

after February 9, 1979, for the purpose of determining employees' benefit entitlements under the provisions of the plan.

(3) *Loss or destruction of records.* Notwithstanding the preceding paragraphs, records shall not be deemed to be insufficient solely because they have been lost or destroyed due to circumstances beyond the control of the person responsible for their maintenance under paragraph (b)(1) of this section.

(d) *Period for which records must be retained.* The records which are required to be maintained under paragraph (a) of this section shall be retained in a manner described in paragraph (e) of this section as long as any possibility exists that they might be relevant to a determination of benefit entitlements. When it is no longer possible that records might be relevant to a determination of benefit entitlements, the records may be disposed of, unless they are required to be maintained for a longer period under any other law.

(e) *Preservation of records by plan administrator.*—(1) *General.* The records which are required to be maintained under paragraph (a) of this section shall be maintained in reasonable order in a safe and accessible place at the main offices of the plan administrator, or at recordkeeping offices established by the plan administrator and customarily used for the maintenance of records.

(2) *Reproduction of records; disposal of original documents.* Original documents may be disposed of at any time if microfilm, microfiche, or similarly reproduced records which are clear reproductions of the original documents are retained, and adequate projection or other viewing equipment is available for inspecting such reproductions.

(3) *Electronic data processing.* Nothing in this section precludes the use of punch cards, magnetic tape or other electronic information storage material for processing information.

(f) *Inspection and copying.* The records required to be maintained under paragraph (a) of this section with respect to any participant or beneficiary (including any original documents or reproductions thereof maintained under paragraph (e) of this section) shall be made available free of charge to such participant or beneficiary, or his representative, in a reasonably accessible form for inspection and copying. The records shall be made available during normal business hours within 10 working days after receipt of a request. A reasonable charge may be imposed for copying records, not exceeding the actual cost of copying them.

(g) *Transfer of records.* In the event that a plan administrator ceases to be responsible under paragraph (b) of this section for maintaining records, such plan administrator shall transfer any records which continue to be potentially relevant to the determination of benefit entitlements to the appropriate successor plan administrator responsible for their maintenance. The plan administrator transferring such records is not required to retain copies of the records transferred. Nothing in this section, however, shall relieve a plan administrator from any responsibility or liability for violations of the requirements of paragraphs (a) through (h) of this section which occur during the time such plan administrator has control of and is responsible for maintaining, retaining or transferring the records as required by those sections.

(h) *Definition of "Multiple Employer Plan."* For purposes of this section, the term "multiple employer plan" shall mean a plan adopted by more than one employer, other than a plan adopted by employers which are under common control.

Signed at Washington, D.C. this 4th day of August, 1980.

Ian D. Lanoff,

Administrator, Pension and Welfare Benefit Programs, Labor-Management Services Administration, U.S. Department of Labor.

¶ 20,526N   Reserved.

Proposed revisions of annual return/reports and regulations regarding plans which participate in a master trust were formerly reproduced at this point. The regulations, as revised are at ¶ 14,231A. The revisions of the annual return/reports are summarized at ¶ 23,588A.]

¶ 20,526O   Reserved.

Proposed amendments to the regulation governing the summary annual report (SAR) in order to accommodate the SAR requirements to the triennial filing system recently implemented for certain small employee benefit plans filing the annual report were formerly reproduced at this point. The regulations, as revised, are at ¶ 14,249H. The amendments are summarized at ¶ 23,606C.]

¶ 20,526P   Reserved.

Formerly reproduced at this paragraph were proposed regulations that provided guidance for determining whether a merger or transfer of assets of liabilities between multiemployer plans complied with ERISA. The regulations were finalized and appear at ¶ 15,700A—15,700I and 15,718D-1.]

¶ 20,526Q   Reserved.

Proposed regulations to the deferral of distribution of updated summary plan descriptions were formerly reproduced at this point. The final regulations are at ¶ 14,249A.]

¶ 20,526R   Reserved.

Proposed regulations relating to the powers and duties of a plan sponsor of a plan terminated by a mass withdrawal and benefit reductions and suspensions were formerly reproduced at this paragraph. The final regulations are at ¶ 15,715A—15,715I and 15,718D-2.]

¶ 20,527   Reserved.

Proposed Reg. §§ 2550.408b-2, 2550.408b-4, 2550.408b-6, 2550.408c-2, and 2550.408c-4, on exemptions from prohibited transactions for the provision of services and office space to employee benefit plans, were formerly reproduced at this point. The final regulations appear at ¶ 14,782, 14,784, 14,786, 14,788, and 14,845.]

¶ 20,528   Reserved.

Proposed Reg. §§ 2615.1—2615.7, on the manner for determining whether a terminating plan is sufficient and the procedure for winding up the affairs of such plans, were formerly reproduced at this point. The regulations now appear at ¶ 15,447—15,448D.]

¶ 20,529   Reserved.

Proposed Reg. § 2550.404b-1, relating to the maintenance of the indicia of ownership of plan assets outside the jurisdiction of the district courts of the United States, was formerly reproduced at this point. The final regulation is at ¶ 14,745.]

¶ 20,530   Reserved.

Proposed Reg. §§ 2550.407a-1—2550.407a-4, relating to the acquisition and holding of employer securities and employer real property, were formerly reproduced at this point. The final regulations now appear at ¶ 14,771—14,771C.]

¶ 20,530A   Reserved.

Proposed Reg. § 2520.104-47, relating to the requirement of filing insurance company financial reports with the Department of Labor only upon request, was formerly reproduced at this point. The final regulation is at ¶ 14,247ZA.]

¶ 20,530B   Reserved.

Proposed Reg. §§ 2642.1, 2642.2, 2642.5—2642.8, and 2642.11—2642.14, relating to the change in the method of allocating unfunded vested benefits to employers withdrawing from a multiemployer plan, were formerly reproduced at this paragraph. The final regulations appear at ¶ 15,678—15,678H.]

¶ 20,530C   Reserved.

Proposed Reg. §§ 2646.1-8, relating to the waiver or reduction of partial withdrawal liability, were formerly reproduced at this paragraph. The final regulations appear at ¶ 15,663F and 15,673A-15,673H.]

¶ 20,530D

Proposed regulations on 29 CFR Part 2580: ERISA bonding requirement: Exemption for certain broker-dealers and investment advisers.—Reproduced below is the text of proposed regulations designed to provide certain broker dealers and investment advisers with an exemption from the bonding requirements imposed by ERISA Sec. 412.

The proposed regulations were published in the *Federal Register* on August 19, 1987 (52 FR 31039).

ERISA Sec. 412.

DEPARTMENT OF LABOR

Pension and Welfare Benefits Administration

29 CFR Part 2580

Proposed Regulation Exempting Certain Broker-Dealers and Investment Advisers From Bonding Requirements

AGENCY: Department of Labor.

ACTION: Notice of proposed rulemaking.

SUMMARY: This document contains a proposed regulation under the Employee Retirement Income Security Act of 1974 (ERISA, or the Act) which would provide certain broker-dealers and investment advisers with an exemption from the bond otherwise required under section 412 of ERISA. The proposed regulation, if adopted, would affect participants and beneficiaries of employee benefit plans, officials of employee benefit plans and employees of broker-dealers and investment advisers.

DATE: Written comments concerning the proposed regulation must be received by October 19, 1987.

ADDRESS: All written comments (at least three copies) should be sent to the Office of Regulations and Interpretations, Pension and Welfare Benefits Administration, Room N-5669, U.S. Department of Labor, 200 Constitution Avenue N.W., Washington, D.C. 20210, Attention: Proposed Bonding Regulation. The application relating to the proposed regulation herein and any comments received will be available for public inspection in the Public Documents Room of the Pension and Welfare Benefits Administration, U.S. Department of Labor, Room N-4677, 200 Constitution Avenue N.W., Washington, D.C. 20210.

FOR FURTHER INFORMATION CONTACT: Linda Shore, Office of Regulations and Interpretations, Pension and Welfare Benefits Administration, U.S. Department of Labor, (202) 523-8671. This is not a toll-free number.

SUPPLEMENTARY INFORMATION: This document contains a proposed regulation which would provide an alternative to the bonding requirements of section 412 of ERISA for certain broker-dealers and investment advisers. The proposed exemption was requested in an application filed on November 30, 1982 by the Securities Industry Association (SIA), which was later clarified by letters dated September 11, 1983, June 5, 1986, and September 24, 1986. The Department is proposing the regulation pursuant to the authority contained in section 412(e) of ERISA.

Background

Section 412(a) of ERISA generally requires that every fiduciary of an employee benefit plan and every person who "handles" funds or other property of any plan (plan official) be bonded in an amount equal to not less than 10 percent of the amount of each plan's funds and other property "handled" by such person. In no case shall the bond with respect to each plan be less than $1,000 nor more than $500,000 (see 29 CFR 2580.412.16).

Temporary bonding regulation section 29 CFR 2580.412-6 defines the term "handling" to encompass more than actual physical contact with plan funds. "Handling" occurs whenever the duties or activities of the plan official with respect to given funds or other property are such that there is a risk that such funds or other property could be lost in the event of fraud or dishonesty on the part of the plan official, acting either alone or in collusion with others. This section further provides that a person would be considered to be "handling" where, as a result of such person's decisionmaking responsibility with respect to given funds or other property, the person exercises such close control over the plan's investment policy that the person, in effect, determines all specific investments.

In this regard, the Department has stated (question FR-8, 29 CFR 2509.75-5) that a person who, under ERISA section 3(21)(A) renders investment advice to a plan for a fee or other compensation, direct or indirect, but who does not exercise or have the right to exercise discretionary authority with respect to plan assets, is not considered to be "handling" funds or other property of such plan and, accordingly, is not required to be bonded solely by reason of the provision of such investment advice. However, if the person, in addition to rendering investment advice, exercises or has the right to exercise discretionary authority or control and thereby makes specific investment decisions,

such person is considered to be "handling" funds or other property, and accordingly, must be bonded.

Section 412(e) of ERISA provides that when, in the opinion of the Secretary of Labor, the administrator of a plan offers adequate evidence of the financial responsibility of the plan, or that other bonding arrangements would provide adequate protection of the beneficiaries and participants, the Secretary may provide an exemption from the requirements of section 412 of ERISA. The Conference Report, H.R. Report No. 93-1280, 93rd Cong. 2nd Sess. 324 (1974), in explaining this provision, indicates that Congress contemplated that the Department would provide an exemption for plans where other bonding arrangements of the employer, employee organization, investment manager or other fiduciaries or the overall financial condition of the plan or the fiduciaries meet standards deemed adequate to protect the interests of the beneficiaries and participants, including bonds subject to a reasonable maximum for professional investment managers supervising large aggregation of clients' funds.

Proposed regulation 29 CFR 2580.412-33, discussed in detail below, would provide an exemption for certain broker-dealers and investment advisers which meet standards that the Department believes are adequate to protect the interests of the beneficiaries and participants. This proposed regulation would permit an alternative to the bond required by section 412(a) of the Act if the alternative bonding arrangement comes within the terms of the proposed regulation.

Discussion of Application

The representations of the applicant are summarized below. Interested persons are referred to the application on file with the Department for the complete representations of the applicant.

1. The SIA represents that its members engage in diverse facets of the securities business within the United States and Canada, including the provision of brokerage and investment advisory services. All SIA members doing business in the United States are broker-dealers registered with the Securities and Exchange Commission (SEC) under the Securities Exchange Act of 1934 (Exchange Act). Some SIA members perform investment advisory functions within the same entity as their broker-dealer operations while others perform these functions through an entity affiliated with the broker-dealer. SIA members that provide investment advice for separate nontransactional compensation must be registered with the SEC as investment advisers under the Investment Advisers Act of 1940 (Advisers Act).[2]

2. The applicant requests an exemption from the bonding requirements contained in section 412 of ERISA for two classes of entities: Registered broker-dealers; and those registered investment advisers which are: (1) Affiliates of registered broker-dealers and (2) do not maintain actual custody or possession of plan assets.[3]

The applicant states that to comply with the bonding requirements of section 412 of ERISA, broker-dealers and investment advisers often obtain bonding coverage through the use of an "agent's rider" attached to the bond otherwise secured by a plan. Broker-dealers and investment advisers which desire to secure their own fidelity bonding coverage find thta such coverage is generally available only through the use of an individual or schedule bond, at greatly increased cost. The applicant represents that such bonds are typically two party bonds naming the broker-dealer as insured, rather than the client plan as required by section 412 of ERISA.[4] The applicant further represents that third party fidelity bonds naming client plans as insureds are not presently offered by fidelity insurance companies and have not been offered in the past. To the extent that bonding coverage complying with section 412 could be procured, that section would require a progressively larger bond as the number of client plans to which the broker-dealer provides services increases. As a consequence, the SIA requests exemptive relief for broker-dealers and their investment adviser affiliates that are covered by the two party blanket bonds required by the self-regulatory organization (SRO) of which the broker-dealer is a member.[5] The SIA asserts that the requested exemption will adequately protect the interests of plan participants and beneficiaries.

3. The applicant represents that, in addition to the bonding arrangement (described below) required for broker-dealers by each of the SROs, plans are also protected by the extensive regulation of broker-dealers by the SEC. Such regulation includes requirements for registration, recordkeeping, net capital, customer protection and insurance.

---

[2] We note that the definition of investmment adviser contained in section 202(a)(11) of the Advisers Act may encompass persons who exercise the type of discretion described in section 3(21)(A)(i) of ERISA rather than merely providing advice about investment decisions. Such persons would be considered to be "handling" funds or other property of a plan so as to require bonding under section 412 of ERISA.

[3] We note that the applicant's request for relief is specifically limited to those broker-dealers and investment advisers described above.

[4] See 29 CFR 2580.412-18.

[5] American Stock Exchange, Boston Stock Exchange, Midwest Stock Exchange, New York Stock Exchange, Pacific Stock Exchange, Philadelphia Stock Exchange, Chicago Board of Options Exchange and National Association of Securities Dealers.

The SIA states that these substantive requirements provide customers of broker-dealers with protections similar to those afforded to customers of banks and insurance companies which are exempt from the bonding requirements of section 412 of ERISA.

4. Since December 6, 1983, all registered broker-dealers have been subject to a two-tiered system of regulation and inspection under the general supervision of the SEC. A broker-dealer, in addition to being registered with the SEC, must be a member of one or more SROs.[6] Under this regulatory system, broker-dealers are regulated primarily by one or more SROs which, in turn, are subject to intensive oversight by the SEC. Periodic examinations of broker-dealers are conducted by the SEC and the SROs under this system without prior notification. It is not unusual for a broker-dealer to be examined several times a year by the various examining authorities.

5. Registration subjects broker-dealers to the recordkeeping rules adopted by the SEC pursuant to the Exchange Act. These rules require broker-dealers to make and preserve accurate books and records to provide a basis upon which the SEC or SRO may monitor compliance with the applicable regulatory requirements. In accordance with these rules, broker-dealers are required to file with the SRO and/or the SEC a standard form of report, partially completed on a monthly basis and fully completed quarterly. In addition, all broker-dealers must file audited financial statements on an annual basis.

6. The net capital rule [Securities Exchange Act of 1934, Rule 15c3-1, 17 CFR 240.15c3-1 (1974)] imposes minimum financial requirements on broker-dealers. The customer protection rule [Securities Exchange Act of 1934, Rule 15c3-3, 17 CFR 240.15c3-3 (1974)] establishes reserve and segregation requirements for broker-dealers which limit the use of customers' funds by broker-dealers in their business and requires broker-dealers to obtain and maintain physical possession or control of all fully paid and excess margin securities carried in accounts of customers. The purpose of the customer protection rule is to safeguard customers' funds and prevent unsound use of customers' assets by ensuring that such funds are deployed in limited areas of a broker-dealer's business. The Securities Investor Protection Act of 1970 established a fund, administered by the Securities Investor Protection Corporation (SIPC), to ensure the reimbursement of customers of insolvent broker-dealers for up to $500,000 in losses arising out of the insolvency. In this regard, the SIA represents that SIPC would have no defenses against the reimbursement of a pension plan for up to the maximum insured amount where a broker-dealer holding securities as customer property for such plan became insolvent and was put into a SIPC receivership. With certain limited exceptions, all registered brokers-dealers are required to contribute to the fund and to be members of SIPC.

7. Broker-dealers are required under the Exchange Act to maintain a blanket fidelity bond covering all of their officers and employees. Each of the SROs has adopted it own bonding requirements. Currently, the amount of the bond is based on a percentage of the net capital of the broker-dealer. At the present time, the various SRO bonding rules are substantially similar. However, the New York Stock Exchange (NYSE) has proposed to increase its minimum bonding requirements for its members and to base such requirements on total securities and money values in the possession and control of a member.[7] The minimum coverage for member firms that carry customer accounts or clear transactions would range from $1 million for firms with under $50 million of securities and money values in possession and control, to $50 million for firms with over $2 billion of securities and money values in possession and control. The SIA represents that a solvent broker-dealer would be strictly liable to a plan if the broker-dealer issued a receipt evidencing that it was holding securities for the account of the plan and subsequently could not deliver such securities.

8. If the investment adviser and broker-dealer functions of the SIA member are performed within the same entity, the investment adviser is subject to the regulation and examination requirements, including the bonding requirements, of the broker-dealer. Registered investment advisers that do business through entities affiliated with a broker-dealer are subject to the regulation and examination requirements of the Advisers Act. Pursuant to the registration requirements of the Advisers Act, investment advisers must file Form ADV. Form ADV provides information concerning the ownership and business of the investment adviser, the nature and scope of its authority with respect to client funds and accounts, its methods of analysis, sources of information and investment strategies; and the background, including prior securities violations, of its officers and directors and any person who controls the investment adviser. Information on Form ADV must be

kept up to date. The Advisers Act requires that investment advisers keep accurate and current books and records which are subject to examination by the SEC, without prior notice at irregular intervals every several years. Although the Advisers Act does not have a bonding requirement, the applicant represents that most sureties are willing to extend the broker-dealer's blanket bond to cover all of the investment advisory activities of an affiliated investment adviser, thereby extending fidelity bond protection to the clients of the affiliated investment adviser.

Discussion of Proposed Regulation

The Department has in the past exercised its statutory authority under section 13(e) of the Welfare and Pension Plans Disclosure Act (WPPDA) to grant exemptions from the bonding requirements of that statute where the parties seeking exemptive relief were subject to other bonding requirements that included minimum bonding amounts and periodic examination and review by supervisory authorities.[8] Section 412(e) of ERISA contains provisions substantially similar to those contained in section 13(e) of the WPPDA.

After consideration of the representations of the applicant, the Department has tentatively determined that, as modified below, the bonding arrangements imposed by the various SROs on their member firms constitute other bonding arrangements that would adequately protect the beneficiaries and participants of employee benefit plans under section 412(e) of ERISA.

However, the Department recognizes that the present bonding requirements of the various SROs set the amount of the bond based on the net capital of the broker-dealer. In the Department's view, a bonding requirement based on the total securities and money in the possession and control of the broker-dealer is a more appropriate basis on which to propose exemptive relief since it would more closely parallel the requirement of section 412(a) of ERISA. For this reason, the Department has included a condition in the proposed exemption which requires minimum bonding coverage similar to that proposed under the NYSE rule. In all other respects, the proposed exemption provides flexibility by permitting broker-dealers and investment adviser affiliates to satisfy the bond required under section 412 of ERISA by maintaining a fidelity bond that complies with the rules of the broker-dealer's SRO.

Finally, the Department has determined to provide only limited relief from sections 412(a) and 412(b) of ERISA. The exemption retains the requirement contained in section 412(a) that the surety on a fidelity bond must be a corporate surety company which is an acceptable surety on Federal bonds under authority granted by the Secretary of the Treasury pursuant to sections 9304 through 9308 of title 31, United States Code.

In addition, the exemption retains the prohibitions of section 412(b) which make it unlawful for a plan official to "handle" funds or other property without being bonded as required by section 412(a) or to permit the "handling" of funds or other property by another plan official who is not similarly bonded. However, broker-dealers and investment adviser affiliates which comply with the requirements of this exemption shall be deemed to be bonded as required by section 412(a) of ERISA. The exemption provides no relief from section 412(c) which makes it unlawful for anyone to procure a bond required by ERISA from any surety or through an agent or broker in whose business operations the plan or any party in interest with respect to the plan has any control or significant financial interest, direct or indirect. In the Department's view, the exemption as proposed will adequately address the concerns of the SIA.

Regulatory Flexibility Act

The Department has determined that this regulation would not have a significant economic effect on small plans or other small entities. The proposed regulation would exempt certain broker-dealers and investment advisers from bonding requirements that, in the absence of this exemption, would be imposed by section 412(a) of ERISA. The regulation does not impose paperwork or other types of costs and burdens on those broker-dealers and investment advisers who meet the criteria for exemptive relief.

Executive Order 12291 Statement

The Department has determined that the proposed regulatory action would not constitute a "major rule" as that term is used in Executive Order 12291 because the action would not result in: an annual effect on the economy of $100 million; a major increase in costs or prices for consumers, individual industries, government agencies, or geographical regions; or significant adverse effects on competition, employment,

---

[6] 15 U.S.C. 78(o)(b)(8).

[7] SEC File No. SR-NYSE-83-13, 48 FR 20837, May 9, 1983.

[8] See EXR-179, St. Louis Union Trust Company, March 9, 1972.

investment, productivity, innovation, or on the ability of United States based enterprises to compete with foreign based enterprises in domestic or export markets.

Paperwork Reduction Act Statement

This proposed regulation does not contain any new information collection requirements and does not modify any existing requirements.

Statutory Authority

The proposed regulation set forth herein is issued pursuant to sections 412(e) (Pub. L. 93-406, 88 Stat. 889, 29 U.S.C. 1112(3)) and 505 of ERISA (Pub. L. 93-406, 88 Stat. 894, 29 U.S.C. 1135); and under Secretary of Labor's Order No. 1-86.

List of Subjects in 29 CFR Part 2580

Employee benefit plans, Employee Retirement Income Security Act, Pension plans, Welfare plans, Bonding, Exemptions.

In view of the foregoing, the Department proposes to amend Part 2580 of Chapter XXV of Title 29 of the Code of Federal Regulations as follows:

PART 2580—TEMPORARY BONDING RULES

1. By revising the authority citation for Part 2580 to read as set forth below:

Authority: Sec. 505, Pub. L. 93-406, 88 Stat. 894 (29 U.S.C. 1135); Sec. 412(e), Pub. L. 93-406, 88 Stat. 889 (29 U.S.C. 1112), Secretary of Labor's Order No. 1-86.

§§ 2580.412-33 through 2580.412-36 [Redesignated as §§ 2580.412-45 through 2580.412-48]

2. By redesignating §§ 2580.412-33 through 2580.412-36, which constitute subpart G, as §§ 2580.412-45 through 2580.412-48 respectively.

3. By adding to subpart F of Part 2580 a new centered heading and a new § 2580.412-33 to read as follows:

Broker-Dealers and Investment Advisers Subject to Federal Regulation

§ 2580.412-33 Exemption.

(a) *Persons covered.* If the alternative bonding arrangement set forth in paragraph (b) of this section is satisfied, the bond required by section 412(a) of ERISA shall not apply to the following persons:

(a) Any broker-dealer registered under the Securities Exchange Act of 1934 (Exchange Act),

(2) Any investment adviser registered under the Investment Advisers Act of 1940 which—

(A) Controls, is controlled by, or is under common control with a broker-dealer registered under the Exchange Act (investment adviser affiliate),

(B) Does not maintain actual custody or possession of assets of employee benefit plans, and

(C) Is named as an additional insured on the registered broker-dealer's bond described in paragraph (b) of this section. Persons complying with the alternative bonding arrangement set forth in paragraph (b) of this section shall be deemed to be bonded as required by section 412(a) of ERISA.

(b) *Alternative bonding arrangement.* (1) Each broker-dealer relying on the exemption in paragraph (a) of this section shall maintain a fidelity bond covering the broker-dealer and/or its investment adviser affiliate in the form required by each self-regulatory organization (SRO) of which the broker-dealer is a member, except that the following minimum limits of coverage are substituted for any other limits otherwise prescribed by the SRO.

Securities and money values in possession and control	Basic minimum coverage
$0-50 million	$ 1 million
50-100 million	3 million
100-500 million	5 million
500 million-1 billion	10 million
1-2 billion	25 million
Above $2 billion	50 million

(2) The surety on any bond procured in accordance with this exemption must be a corporate surety company which is an acceptable surety on Federal bonds under authority granted by the Secretary of the Treasury pursuant to sections 9304 through 9308 of title 31, United States Code.

(c) *Definitions.* For the purposes of this exemption:

(1) The terms "broker-dealer" and "investment adviser" include any partner, director, officer or employee of such broker-dealer or investment adviser.

(2) The term "control" means the power to exercise a controlling influence over the management or policies of a person other than an individual.

Signed at Washington, D.C., this 13th day of August 1987.

David M. Walker,

Deputy Assistant Secretary, Pension and Welfare Benefits Administration, United States Department of Labor.

[FR Doc. 87-18922; Filed 8-18-87; 8:45 am]

¶ 20,530E   Reserved.

Proposed regulations relating to the statutory exemption to ERISA's prohibition of loans by plans to participants and beneficiaries who are parties in interest with respect to the plan were formerly reproduced at this paragraph. The final regulations appear at ¶ 14,781.]

¶ 20,531   Reserved.

Proposed regulations on 29 CFR Part 2610, providing valuation factors for plans that terminate on or after September 1, 1976, but before December 1, 1976, were formerly reproduced at this point.

The final regulations are at ¶ 15,620L.]

¶ 20,531A   Reserved.

Proposed regulations relating to the enforcement of the prohibition of discrimination on the basis of a handicap as it applies to the programs and activities of the PBGC were formerly reproduced at this paragraph.

The final regulations appear at ¶ 15,326.]

¶ 20,531B   Reserved.

Proposed regulations relating to an alternative method for demonstrating plan sufficiency under the PBGC's regulation on Determination of Plan Sufficiency and Termination of Sufficient Plans were formerly reproduced at this paragraph.

The final regulations appear at ¶ 15,447A, ¶ 15,447B, ¶ 15,447K, ¶ 15,447L, ¶ 15,447M, and ¶ 15,447V.]

¶ 20,531C   Reserved.

Proposed regulations on redetermining withdrawal liability upon mass withdrawal. were formerly reproduced at this paragraph.

The final regulations appear at ¶ 15,669A—15,669J.]

¶ 20,531D   Reserved.

Proposed Reg. § § 2610.2, 2610.3, 2610.5, 2610.6, and 2610.9, relating to a change in the filing and premium payment due date from the last day of the seventh month following the close of the prior plan year to the last day of the second month following the close of the prior plan year, were formerly reproduced at this point.

The final regulations are at ¶ 15,371A, ¶ 15,371B, ¶ 15,371D, ¶ 15,371E, and ¶ 15,371H.]

¶ 20,531E

Proposed regulations: Definition of "adequate consideration": Assets other than securities: Fair market valuation: Fiduciaries and plan trustees.—Reproduced below is the text of a proposed regulation which clarifies the definition of "adequate consideration" for assets other than securities for which there is a generally recognized market and provides the certainty necessary for a plan fiduciary or trustee to determine in good faith the fair market value of assets other than securities. The proposed regulations were published in the *Federal Register* on May 17, 1988.

ERISA Sec. 3.

DEPARTMENT OF LABOR

Pension and Welfare Benefits Administration

29 CFR Part 2510

Proposed Regulation Relating to the Definition of Adequate Consideration

AGENCY: Pension and Welfare Benefits Administration, Department of Labor.

ACTION: Notice of proposed rulemaking.

SUMMARY: This document contains a notice of a proposed regulation under the Employee Retirement Income Security Act of 1974 (the Act or ERISA) and the Federal Employees' Retirement System Act of 1986 (FERSA). The proposal clarifies the definition of the term "adequate consideration" provided in section 3(18)(B) of the Act and section 8477(a)(2)(B) of FERSA for assets other than securities for which there is a generally recognized market. Section 3(18)(B) and section 8477(a)(2)(B) provided that the term "adequate consideration" for such assets means the fair market value of the asset as determined in good faith by the trustee or named fiduciary (or, in the case of FERSA, a fiduciary) pursuant to the terms of the plan and in accordance with regulations promulgated by the Secretary of Labor. Because valuation questions of this nature arise in a variety of contexts, the Department is proposing this regulation in order to provide the certainty necessary for plan fiduciaries to fulfill their statutory duties. If adopted, the regulation would affect plans investing in assets other than securities for which there is a generally recognized market.

DATES: Written comments on the proposed regulation must be received by July 18, 1988. If adopted, the regulation will be effective for transactions taking place after the date 30 days following publication of the regulation in final form.

ADDRESS: Written comments on the proposed regulation (preferably three copies) should be submitted to: Office of Regulations and Interpretations, Pension and Welfare Benefits Administration, Room N-5671, U. S. Department of Labor, 200 Constitution Avenue NW., Washington, DC 20216, Attention: Adequate Consideration Proposal. All written comments will be available for public inspection at the Public Disclosure Room, Pension and Welfare Benefits Administration, U. S. Department of Labor, Room N-5507, 200 Constitution Avenue NW., Washington, DC.

FOR FURTHER INFORMATION CONTACT: Daniel J. Maguire, Esq., Plan Benefits Security Division, Office of the Solicitor, U. S. Department of Labor, Washington, DC 20210, (202) 523-9596 (not a toll-free number) or Mark A. Greenstein, Office of Regulations and Interpretations, Pension and Welfare Benefits Administration, (202) 523-7901 (not a toll-free number).

SUPPLEMENTARY INFORMATION:

Background

Notice is hereby given of a proposed regulation under section 3(18)(B) of the Act and section 8477(a)(2)(B) of FERSA. Section 3(18) of the Act provides the definition for the term "adequate consideration," and states:

"The term 'adequate consideration' when used in part 4 of subtitle B means (A) in the case of a security for which there is a generally recognized market, either (i) the price of the security prevailing on a national securities exchange which is registered under section 6 of the Securities Exchange Act of 1934, or (ii) if the security is not traded on such a national securities exchange, a price not less favorable to the plan than the offering price for the security as established by the current bid and asked prices quoted by persons independent of the issuer and of any party in interest; and (B) in the case of an asset other than a security for which there is a generally recognized market, the fair market value of the asset as determined in good faith by the trustee or named fiduciary pursuant to the terms of the plan and in accordance with regulations promulgated by the Secretary."

The term "adequate consideration" appears four times in part 4 of subtitle B of Title I of the Act, and each time represents a central requirement for a statutory exemption from the prohibited transaction restrictions of the Act. Under section 408(b)(5), a plan may purchase insurance contracts from certain parties in interest if, among other conditions, the plan pays no more than adequate consideration. Section 408(b)(7) provides that the prohibited transaction provisions of section 406 shall not apply to the exercise of a privilege to convert securities, to the extent provided in regulations of the Secretary of Labor, only if the plan receives no less than adequate consideration pursuant to such conversion. Section 406(e) of the Act provides that the prohibitions in sections 406 and 407(a) of the Act shall not apply to the acquisition or sale by a plan of qualifying employer securities, or the acquisition, sale or lease by a plan of qualifying employer real property if, among other conditions, the acquisition, sale or lease is for adequate consideration. Section 414(c)(5) of the Act states that sections 406 and 407(a) of the Act shall not apply to the sale, exchange, or other disposition of properly which is owned by a plan on June 30, 1974, and all times thereafter, to a party in interest, if such plan is required to dispose of the property in order to comply with the provisions of section 407(a) (relating to the prohibition against holding excess employer securities and employer real property), and if the plan receives not less than adequate consideration.

Public utilization of these statutory exemptions requires a determination of "adequate consideration" in accordance with the definition contained in section 3(18) of the Act. Guidance is especially important in this area because many of the transactions covered by these statutory exemptions involve plan dealings with the plan sponsor. A fiduciary's determination of the adequacy of consideration paid under such circumstances represents a major safeguard for plans against the potential for abuse inherent in such transactions.

The Federal Employees' Retirement System Act of 1986 (FERSA) established the Federal Retirement Thrift Investment Board whose members act as fiduciaries with regard to the assets of the Thrift Savings Fund. In general, FERSA contains fiduciary obligation and prohibited transaction provisions similar to ERISA. However, unlike ERISA, FERSA prohibits party in interest transactions similar to those described in section 406(a) of ERISA only in those circumstances where adequate consideration is not exchanged between the Fund and the party in interest. Specifically, section 8477(c)(1) of FERSA provides that, except in exchange for adequate consideration, a fiduciary shall not permit the Thrift Savings Fund to engage in: transfers of its assets to, acquisition of property from or sales of property to, or transfers or exchanges of services with any person the fiduciary knows or should know to be a party in interest. Section 8477(a)(2) provides the FERSA definition for the term "adequate consideration" which is virtually identical to that contained in section 3(18) of ERISA. Thus, the proposal would apply to both section 3(18) of ERISA and section 8477(a)(2) of FERSA.

When the asset being valued is a security for which there is a generally recognized market, the plan fiduciary must determine "adequate consideration" by reference to the provisions of section 3(18)(A) of the Act (or with regard to FERSA, section 8477(a)(2)(A)). Section 3(18)(A) and section 8477(a)(2)(A) provide detailed reference points for the valuation of securities within its coverage, and in effect provides that adequate consideration for such securities is the prevailing market price. It is not the Department's intention to analyze the requirements of section 3(18)(A) or 8477(a)(2)(A) in this proposal. Fiduciaries must, however, determine whether a security is subject to the specific provisions of section 3(18)(A) (or section 8477(a)(2)(A) of FERSA) or the more general requirements of section 3(18)(B) (or section 8477(a)(2)(B)) as interpreted in this proposal. The question of whether a security is one for which there is a generally recognized market requires a factual determination in light of the character of the security and the nature and extent of market activity with regard to the security. Generally, the Department will examine whether a security is being actively traded so as to provide the benchmarks Congress intended. Isolated trading activity, or trades between related parties, generally will not be sufficient to show the existence of a generally recognized market for the purposes of section 3(18)(A) or section 8477(a)(2)(A).

In the case of all assets other than securities for which there is a generally recognized market, fiduciaries must determine adequate consideration pursuant to section 3(18)(B) of the Act (or, in the case of FERSA, section 8477(a)(2)(B)). Because it is designed to deal with all but a narrow class of assets, section 3(18)(B) and section 8477(a)(2)(B) are by their nature more general than section 3(18)(A) or section 8477(a)(2)(A). Although the Department has indicated that it will not issue advisory opinions stating whether certain stated consideration is "adequate consideration" for the purposes of section 3(18), ERISA Procedure 76-1, §5.02(a) (41 FR 36281, 36282, August 27, 1976), the Department recognizes that plan fiduciaries have a need for guidance in valuing assets, and that standards to guide fiduciaries in this area may be particularly elusive with respect to assets other than securities for which there is a generally recognized market. *See,* for example, *Donovan v. Cunningham,* 716 F. 2d 1455 (5th Cir. 1983) (court encourages the Department to adopt regulations under section 3(18)(B)). The Department has therefore determined to propose a regulation only under section 3(18)(B) and section 8477(a)(2)(B). This proposal is described more fully below.

It should be noted that it is not the Department's intention by this proposed regulation to relieve fiduciaries of the responsibility for making the required determinations of "adequate consideration" where applicable under the Act or FERSA Nothing in the proposal should be construed as justifying a fiduciary's failure to take into account all relevant facts and circumstances in determining adequate consideration. Rather, the proposal is designed to provide a framework within which fiduciaries can fulfill their statutory duties. Further, fiduciaries should be aware that, even where a determination of adequate consideration comports with the requirements of section 3(18)(B) (or section 8477(a)(2)(B) of FERSA) and any regulation adopted thereunder, the investment of plan assets made pursuant to such determination will still be subject to the fiduciary requirements of Part 4 of Subtitle B of Title I of the Act, including the provisions of sections 403 and 404 of the Act, or the fiduciary responsibility provisions of FERSA.

Description of the Proposal

Proposed regulation 29 CFR 2510.3-18(b) is divided into four major parts. Proposed §2510.3-18(b)(1) states the general rule and delineates the scope of the regulation. Proposed §2510.3-18(b)(2) addresses the concept of fair market value as it relates to a determination of "adequate consideration" under section 3(18)(B) of the Act. Proposed §2510.3-18(b)(3) deals with the requirement in section 3(18)(B) that

valuing fiduciary act in good faith, and specifically discusses the use of an independent appraisal in connection with the determination of good faith. Proposed §2510.3-18(b)(4) sets forth the content requirements for written valuations used as the basis for a determination of fair market value, with a special rule for the valuation of securities other than securities for which there is a generally recognized market. Each subsection is discussed in detail below.

1. General Rule and Scope.

Proposed §2510.3-18(b)(1)(i) essentially follows the language of section 3(18)(B) of the Act and section 8477(a)(2)(B) of FERSA and states that, in the case of a plan asset other than a security for which there is a generally recognized market, the term "adequate consideration" means the fair market value of the asset as determined in good faith by the trustee or named fiduciary (or, in the case of FERSA, a fiduciary) pursuant to the terms of the plan and in accordance with regulations promulgated by the Secretary of Labor. Proposed §2510.3-18(b)(1)(ii) delineates the scope of this regulation by establishing two criteria, both of which must be met for a valid determination of adequate consideration. First, the value assigned to an asset must reflect its fair market value as determined pursuant to proposed §2510.3-18(b)(2). Second, the value assigned to an asset must be the product of a determination made by the fiduciary in good faith as defined in proposed §2510.3-18(b)(3). The Department will consider that a fiduciary has determined adequate consideration in accordance with section 3(18)(B) of the Act or section 8477(a)(2)(B) of FERSA only if both of these requirements are satisfied.

The Department has proposed this two part test for several reasons. First, Congress incorporated the concept of fair market value into the definition of adequate consideration. As explained more fully below, fair market value is an often used concept having an established meaning in the field of asset valuation. By reference to this term, it would appear that Congress did not intend to allow parties to a transaction to set an arbitrary value for the assets involved. Therefore, a valuation determination which fails to reflect the market forces embodied in the concept of fair market value would also fail to meet the requirements of section 3(18)(B) of the Act or section 8477(a)(2)(B) of FERSA.

Second, it would appear that Congress intended to allow a fiduciary a limited degree of latitude so long as that fiduciary acted in good faith. However, a fiduciary would clearly fail to fulfill the fiduciary duties delineated in Part 4 of Subtitle B of Title I of the Act if that fiduciary acted solely on the basis of native or uninformed good intentions. See *Donovan v. Cunningham, supra,* 716 F. 2d at 1467 ("[A] pure heart and an empty head are not enough.") The Department has therefore proposed standards for a determination of a fiduciary's good faith which must be satisfied in order to meet the requirements of section 3(18)(B) or section 8477(a)(2)(B) of FERSA.

Third, even if a fiduciary were to meet the good faith standards contained in this proposed regulation, there may be circumstances in which good faith alone fails to insure an equitable result. For example, errors in calculation or honest failure to consider certain information could produce valuation figures outside of the range of acceptable valuations of a given asset. Because the determination of adequate consideration is a central requirement of the statutory exemptions discussed above, the Department believes it must assure that such exemptions are made available only for those transactions possessing all the external safeguards envisioned by Congress. To achieve this end, the Department's proposed regulation links the fair market value and good faith requirements to assure that the resulting valuation reflects market considerations and is the product of a valuation process conducted in good faith.

2. Fair Market Value

The first part of the Department's proposed two part test under section 3(18)(B) and section 8477(a)(2)(B) requires that a determination of adequate consideration reflect the asset's fair market value. The term "fair market value" is defined in proposed §2510.3-18(b)(2)(i) as the price at which an asset would change hands between a willing buyer and a willing seller when the former is not under any compulsion to buy and the latter is not under any compulsion to sell, and both parties are able, as well as willing, to trade and are well-informed about the asset and the market for that asset. This proposed definition essentially reflects the well-established meaning of this term in the area of asset valuation. See, for example, 26 CFR 20.2031-1 (estate tax regulations); Rev. Rul. 59-60, 1959-1 Cum. Bull. 237; *United States v. Cartwright,* 411 U. S. 546, 551 (1973): *Estate of Bright v. United States,* 658 F. 2d 999, 1005 (5th Cir. 1981). It should specifically be noted that comparable valuations reflecting transactions resulting from other than free and equal negotiations (*e.g.,* a distress sale) will fail to establish fair market value. *See Hooker Industries, Inc. v. Commissioner,* 3 EBC

1849, 1854-55 (T. C. June 24, 1982). Similarly, the extent to which the Department will view a valuation as reflecting fair market value will be affected by an assessment of the level of expertise demonstrated by the parties making the valuation. *See Donovan v. Cunningham, supra,* 716 F. 2d at 1468 (failure to apply sound business principles of evaluation, for whatever reason, may result in a valuation that does not reflect fair market value).[1]

The Department is aware that the fair market value of an asset will ordinarily be identified by a range of valuations rather than a specific, set figure. It is not the Department's intention that only one valuation figure will be acceptable as the fair market value of a specified asset. Rather, this proposal would require that the valuation assigned to an asset must reflect a figure within an acceptable range of valuations for that asset.

In addition to this general formulation of the definition of fair market value, the Department is proposing two specific requirements for the determination of fair market value for the purposes of section 3(18)(B) and section 8477(a)(2)(B). First, proposed § 2510.3-18(b)(2)(ii) requires that fair market value must be determined as of the date of the transaction involving that asset. This requirement is designed to prevent situations such as arose in *Donovan v. Cunningham, supra.* In that case, the plan fiduciaries relied on a 1975 appraisal to set the value of employer securities purchased by an ESOP during 1976 and thereafter, and failed to take into account significant changes in the company's business condition in the interim. The court found that this reliance was unwarranted, and therefore the fiduciaries' valuation failed to reflect adequate consideration under section 3(18)(B). *Id.* at 1468-69.

Second, proposed § 2510.3-18(b)(2)(iii) states that the determination of fair market value must be reflected in written documentation of valuation[2] meeting the content requirements set forth in § 2510.3-18(b)(4). (The valuation content requirements are discussed below.) The Department has proposed this requirement in light of the role the adequate consideration requirement plays in a number of statutory exemptions from the prohibited transaction provisions of the Act. In determining whether a statutory exemption applies to a particular transaction, the burden of proof is upon the party seeking to make use of the statutory exemption to show that all the requirements of the provision are met. *Donovan v. Cunningham, supra,* 716 F. 2d at 1467 n. 27. In the Department's view, written documentation relating to the valuation is necessary for a determination of how, and on what basis, an asset was valued, and therefore whether that valuation reflected an asset's fair market value. In addition, the Department believes that it would be contrary to prudent business practices for a fiduciary to act in the absence of such written documentation of fair market value.

3. Good Faith

The second part of the Department's proposed two-part test under section 3(18)(B) and section 8477(a)(2)(B) requires that an assessment of adequate consideration be the product of a determination made in good faith by the plan trustee or named fiduciary (or under FERSA, a fiduciary). Proposed § 2510.3-18(b)(3)(i) states that as a general matter this good faith requirement establishes an objective standard of conduct, rather than mandating an inquiry into the intent or state of mind of the plan trustee or named fiduciary. In this regard, the proposal is consistent with the opinion in *Donovan v. Cunningham, supra,* where the court stated that the good faith requirement in section 3(18)(B):

is not a search for subjective good faith * * * The statutory reference to good faith in Section 3(18) must be read in light of the overriding duties of Section 404.

716 F. 2d at 1467. The inquiry into good faith under the proposal therefore focuses on the fiduciary's conduct in determining fair market value. An examination of all relevant facts and circumstances is neces-

sary for a determination of whether a fiduciary has met this objective good faith standard.

Proposed § 2510.3-18(b)(3)(ii) focuses on two factors which must be present in order for the Department to be satisfied, that the fiduciary has acted in good faith. First, this section would require a fiduciary to apply sound business principles of evaluation and to conduct a prudent investigation of the circumstances prevailing at the time of the valuation. This requirement reflects the *Cunningham* court's emphasis on the use of prudent business practices in valuing plan assets.

Second, this section states that either the fiduciary making the valuation must itself be independent of all the parties to the transaction (other than the plan), or the fiduciary must rely on the report of an appraiser who is independent of all the parties to the transaction (other than the plan). (The criteria for determining independence are discussed below.) As noted above, under ERISA, the determination of adequate consideration is a central safeguard in many statutory exemptions applicable to plan transactions with the plan sponsor. The close relationship between the plan and the plan sponsor in such situations raises a significant potential for conflicts of interest as the fiduciary values assets which are the subject of transactions between the plan and the plan sponsor. In light of this possibility, the Department believes that good faith may only be demonstrated when the valuation is made by persons independent of the parties to the transaction (other than the plan), *i.e.,* a valuation made by an independent fiduciary or by a fiduciary acting pursuant to the report of an independent appraiser.

The Department emphasizes that the two requirements of proposed § 2510.3-18(b)(3)(ii) are designed to work in concert. For example, a plan fiduciary charged with valuation may be independent of all the parties to a transaction and may, in light of the requirement of proposed § 2510.3-18(b)(3)(ii)(B), decide to undertake the valuation process itself. However, if the independent fiduciary has neither the experience, facilities nor expertise to make the type of valuation under consideration, the decision by that fiduciary to make the valuation would fail to meet the prudent investigation and sound business principles of proposed § 2510.3-18(b)(3)(ii)(A).

Proposed § 2510.3-18(b)(3)(iii) defines the circumstances under which a fiduciary or an appraiser will be deemed to be independent for the purposes of subparagraph (3)(ii)(B), above. The proposal notes that the fiduciary or the appraiser must in fact be independent of all parties participating in the transaction other than the plan. The proposal also notes that a determination of independence must be made in light of all relevant facts and circumstances, and then delineates certain circumstances under which this independence will be lacking. These circumstances reflect the definitions of the terms "affiliate" and "control" in Departmental regulation 29 CFR 2510.3-21(c) (defining the circumstances under which an investment adviser is a fiduciary). It should be noted that, under these proposed provisions, an appraiser will be considered independent of all parties to a transaction (other than the plan) only if a plan fiduciary has chosen the appraiser and has the right to terminate that appointment, and the plan is thereby established as the appraiser's client.[3] Absent such circumstances, the appraiser may be unable to be completely neutral in the exercise of his function.[4]

4. Valuation Content—General

Proposed § 2510.3-18(b)(4)(i) sets the content requirements for the written documentation of valuation required for a determination of fair market value under proposed § 2510.3-18(b)(2)(iii). The proposal follows to a large extent the requirements of Rev. Proc. 66-49, 1966-2 C. B. 1257, which sets forth the format required by the IRS for the valuation of donated property. The Department believes that this format is a familiar one, and will therefore facilitate compliance. Several additions to the IRS requirement merit brief explanation.

---

[1] Whether in any particular transaction a plan fiduciary is in fact well-informed about the asset in question and the market for that asset, including any specific circumstances which may affect the value of the asset, will be determined on a facts and circumstances basis. If, however, the fiduciary negotiating on behalf of the plan has or should have specific knowledge concerning either the particular asset or the market for that asset. It is the view of the Department that the fiduciary must take into account that specific knowledge in negotiating the price of the asset in order to meet the fair market value standard of this regulation. For example, a sale of plan-owned real estate at a negotiated price consistent with valuations of comparable property will not be a sale for adequate consideration if the negotiating fiduciary does not take into account any special knowledge which he has or should have about the asset or its market, e. g., that the property's value should reflect a premium due to a certain developer's specific land development plans.

[2] It should be noted that the written valuation required by this section of the proposal need not be a written report of an independent appraiser. Rather, it should be documentation sufficient to allow the Department to determine whether the content requirements of § 2510.3-18(b)(4) have been satisfied. The use of an independent appraiser may be relevant

to a determination of good faith, as discussed with regard to proposed § 2510.3-18(b)(3), *infra,* but it is not required to satisfy the fair market value criterion in § 2510.3-18(b)(2)(i).

[3] The independence of an appraiser will not be affected solely because the plan sponsor pays the appraiser's fee.

[4] With regard to this independence requirement the Department notes that new section 401(a)(28) of the Code (added by section 1175(a) of the Tax Reform Act of 1986) requires that, in the case of an employee stock ownership plan, employer securities which are not readily tradable on established securities markets must be valued by an inde pendent appraiser. New section 401(a)(28)(C) states that the term "independent appraiser" means an appraiser meeting requirements similar to the requirements of regulations under section 170(a)(1) of the Code (relating to IRS verification of the value assigned for deduction purposes to assets donated to charitable organizations). The Department notes that the requirements of proposed regulation § 2510.3-18(b)(3)(iii) are not the same as the requirements of the regulations issued by the IRS under section 170(a)(1) of the Code. The IRS has not yet promulgated rules under Code section 401(a)(28).

First, proposed paragraph (b)(4)(i)(E) requires a statement of the purpose for which the valuation was made. A valuation undertaken, for example, for a yearly financial report may prove an inadequate basis for any sale of the asset in question. This requirement is intended to facilitate review of the valuation in the correct context.

Second, proposed paragraph (b)(4)(i)(F) requires a statement as to the relative weight accorded to relevant valuation methodologies. The Department's experience in this area indicates that there are a number of different methodologies used within the appraisal industry. By varying the treatment given and emphasis accorded relevant information, these methodologies directly affect the result of the appraiser's analysis. It is the Department's understanding that appraisers will often use different methodologies to cross-check their results. A statement of the method or methods used would allow for a more accurate assessment of the validity of the valuation.

Finally, proposed subparagraph (b)(4)(i)(G) requires a statement of the valuation's effective date. This reflects the requirement in proposed § 2510.3-18(b)(ii) that fair market value must be determined as of the date of the transaction in question.

5. *Valuation Content—Special Rule*

Proposed § 2510.3-18(b)(4)(ii) establishes additional content requirements for written documentation of valuation when the asset being appraised is a security other than a security for which there is a generally recognized market. In other words, the requirements of the proposed special rule supplement, rather than supplant, the requirements of paragraph (b)(4)(i). The proposed special rule establishes a nonexclusive list of factors to be considered when the asset being valued is a security not covered by section 3(18)(A) of the Act or section 8477(a)(2)(A) of FERSA. Such securities pose special valuation problems because they are not traded or are so thinly traded that it is difficult to assess the effect on such securities of the market forces usually considered in determining fair market value. The Internal Revenue Service has had occasion to address the valuation problems posed by one type of such securities—securities issued by closely held corporations. Rev. Rul. 59-60. 1959-1 Cum. Bull. 237, lists a variety of factors to be considered when valuing securities of closely held corporation for tax purposes.[5] The Department's experience indicates that Rev. Rul. 59-60 is familiar to plan fiduciaries, plan sponsors and the corporate community in general. The Department has, therefore, modeled this proposed special rule after Rev. Rul. 59-60 with certain additions and changes discussed below. It should be emphasized, however, that this is a non-exclusive list of factors to be considered. Certain of the factors listed may not be relevant to every valuation inquiry, although the fiduciary will bear the burden of demonstrating such irrelevance. Similarly, reliance on this list will not relieve fiduciaries from the duty to consider all relevant facts and circumstances when valuing such securities. The purpose of the proposed list is to guide fiduciaries in the course of their inquiry.

Several of the factors listed in proposed § 2510.3-18(b)(4)(ii) merit special comment and explanation. Proposed subparagraph (G) states that the fair market value of securities other than those for which there is a generally recognized market may be established by reference to the market price of similar securities of corporations engaged in the same or a similar line of business whose securities are actively traded in a free and open market, either on an exchange or over the counter. The Department intends that the degree of comparability must be assessed in order to approximate as closely as possible the market forces at work with regard to the corporation issuing the securities in question.

Proposed subparagraph (H) requires an assessment of the effect of the securities' marketability or lack thereof. Rev. Rul. 59-60 does not explicitly require such an assessment, but the Department believes that the marketability of these types of securities will directly affect their price. In this regard, the Department is aware that, especially in situations involving employee stock ownership plans (ESOPs),[6] the employer securities held by the ESOP will provide a "put" option whereby individual participants may upon retirement sell their shares back to the employer.[7] It has been argued that some kinds of "put"

options may diminish the need to discount the value of the securities due to lack of marketability. The Department believes that the existence of the "put" option should be considered for valuation purposes only to the extent it is enforceable and the employer has and may reasonably be expected to continue to have, adequate resources to meet its obligations. Thus, the Department proposes to require that the plan fiduciary assess whether these "put" rights are actually enforceable, and whether the employer will be able to pay for the securities when and if the "put" is exercised.

Finally, proposed subparagraph (I) deals with the role of control premiums in valuing securities other than those for which there is a generally recognized market. The Department proposes that a plan purchasing control may pay a control premium, and a plan selling control should receive a control premium. Specifically, the Department proposes that a plan may pay such a premium only to the extent a third party would pay a control premium. In this regard, the Department's position is that the payment of a control premium is unwarranted unless the plan obtains both voting control and control in fact. The Department will therefore carefully scrutinize situations to ascertain whether the transition involving payment of such a premium actually results in the passing of control to the plan. For example, it may be difficult to determine that a plan paying a control premium has received control in fact where it is reasonable to assume at the time of acquisition that distribution of shares to plan participants will cause the plan's control of the company to be dissipated within a short period of time subsequent to acquisition.[8] In the Department's view, however, a plan would not fail to receive control merely because individuals who were previously officers, directors or shareholders of the corporation continue as plan fiduciaries or corporate officials after the plan has acquired the securities. Nonetheless, the retention of management and the utilization of corporate officials as plan fiduciaries, when viewed in conjunction with other facts, may indicate that actual control has not passed to the plan within the meaning of paragraph (b)(4)(ii)(I) of the proposed regulation. Similarly, if the plan purchases employer securities in small increments pursuant to an understanding with the employer that the employer will eventually sell a controlling portion of shares to the plan, a control premium would be warranted only to the extent that the understanding with the employer was actually a binding agreement obligating the employer to pass control within a reasonable time. See *Donovan v. Cunningham, supra,* 716 F. 2d at 1472-74 (mere intention to transfer control not sufficient).

6. *Service Arrangements Subject to FERSA*

Section 8477(c)(1)(C) of FERSA permits the exchange of services between the Thrift Savings Fund and a party in interest only in exchange for adequate consideration. In this context, the proposal defines the term "adequate consideration" as "reasonable compensation" , as that term is described in sections 408(b)(2) and 408(c)(2) of ERISA and the regulations promulgated thereunder. By so doing, the proposal would establish a consistent standard of exemptive relief for both ERISA and FERSA with regard to what otherwise would be prohibited service arrangements.

Regulatory Flexibility Act

The Department has determined that this regulation would not have a significant economic effect on small plans. In conducting the analysis required under the Regulatory Flexibility Act, it was estimated that approximately 6,250 small plans may be affected by the regulation. The total additional cost to these plans, over and above the costs already being incurred under established valuation practices, are estimated not to exceed $875,000 per year, or $140 per plan for small plans choosing to engage in otherwise prohibited transactions that are exempted under the statute conditioned on a finding of adequate consideration.

Executive Order 12291

The Department has determined that the proposed regulatory action would not constitute a "major role" as that term is used in Executive Order 12291 because the action would not result in an annual effect on the economy of $100 million; a major increase in costs of prices for consumers, individual industries, government agencies, or geographical regions; or significant adverse effects on competition, employment,

---

[5] Rev. Rul. 89-60 was modified by Rev. Rul. 65-193 (1965-2 C. B. 370) regarding the valuation of tangible and intangible corporate assets. The provisions of Rev. Rul. 59-60, as modified, were extended to the valuation of corporate securities for income and other tax purposes by Rev. Rul. 68-809 (1968-3 C. B. 327). In addition, Rev. Rul. 77-287 (1977-2 C. B. 319), amplified. Rev. Rul. 59-60 by indicating the ways in which the factors listed in Rev. Rul. 59-60 should be applied when valuing restricted securities.

[6] The definition of the term "adequate consideration" under ERISA is of particular Importance to the establishment and maintenance of ESOPs because, pursuant to section 408(e) of the Act, an ESOP may acquire employer securities from a party in interest only

under certain conditions, including that the plan pay no more than adequate consideration for the securities.

[7] Regulation 29 CFR 2550.406b-(j) requires such a put option in order for a loan from a party in Interest to the ESOP to qualify for the statutory exemption in section 406(b)(3) of ERISA from the prohibited transactions provisions of ERISA.

[8] However, the Department notes that the mere pass-through of voting rights to participants would not in itself effect a determination that a plan has received control in fact, notwithstanding the existence of participant voting rights, if the plan fiduciaries having control over plan assets ordinarily may resell the shares to a third party and command a control premium, without the need to secure the approval of the plan participants.

investment, productivity, innovation, or on the ability of United States based enterprises to compete with foreign based enterprises in domestic or export markets.

Paperwork Reduction Act

This proposed regulation contains several paperwork requirements. The regulation has been forwarded for approval to the Office of Management and Budget under the provisions of the Paperwork Reduction Act of 1980 (Pub. L. 96-511). A control number has not yet been assigned.

Statutory Authority

This regulation is proposed under section 3(18) and 505 of the Act (29 U. S. C. 1003(18) and 1135); Secretary of Labor's Order No. 1-87; and sections 8477(a)(2)(B) and 8477(f) of FERSA.

List of Subjects in 29 CFR Part 2510

Employee benefit plans, Employee Retirement Income Security Act, Pensions, Pension and Welfare Benefit Administration.

Proposed Regulation

For the reasons set out in the preamble, the Department proposes to amend Part 2510 of Chapter XXV of Title 29 of the Code of Federal Regulations as follows:

PART 2510—[AMENDED]

1. The authority for Part 2510 is revised to read as follows:

Authority: Sec. 3(2), 111(c), 505, Pub. L. 93-406, 88 Stat. 852, 894, (29 U. S. C. 1002(2), 1031, 1135); Secretary of Labor's Order No. 27-74, 1-86, 1-87, and Labor Management Services Administration Order No. 2-6.

Section 2510.3-18 is also issued under sec. 3(18) of the Act (29 U. S. C. 1003(18)) and secs. 8477(a)(2)(B) and (f) of FERSA (5 U. S. C. 8477).

Section 2510.3-101 is also issued under sec. 102 of Reorganization Plan No. 4 of 1978 (43 FR 47713, October 17, 1978), effective December 31, 1978 (44 FR 1065, January 3, 1978); 3 CFR 1978 Comp. 332, and sec. 11018(d) of Pub. L. 99-272, 100 Stat. 82.

Section 2510.3-102 is also issued under sec. 102 of Reorganization Plan No. 4 of 1978 (43 FR 47713, October 17, 1978), effective December 31, 1978 (44 FR 1065, January 3, 1978), and 3 CFR 1978 Comp. 332.

2. Section 2510.3-18 is added to read as follows:

§ 2510.3-18 Adequate Consideration.

(a) [Reserved]

(b)(1)(i) *General.* (A) Section 3(18)(B) of the Employee Retirement Income Security Act of 1974 (the Act) provides that, in the case of a plan asset other than a security for which there is a generally recognized market, the term "adequate consideration" when used in Part 4 of Subtitle B of Title I of the Act means the fair market value of the asset as determined in good faith by the trustee or named fiduciary pursuant to the terms of the plan and in accordance with regulations promulgated by the Secretary of Labor.

(B) Section 8477(a)(2)(B) of the Federal Employees' Retirement System Act of 1986 (FERSA) provides that, in the case of an asset other than a security for which there is a generally recognized market, the term "adequate consideration" means the fair market value of the asset as determined in good faith by a fiduciary or fiduciaries in accordance with regulations prescribed by the Secretary of Labor.

(ii) *Scope.* The requirements of section 3(18)(B) of the Act and section 8477(a)(2)(B) of FERSA will not be met unless the value assigned to a plan asset both reflects the asset's fair market value as defined in paragraph (b)(2) of this section and results from a determination made by the plan trustee or named fiduciary (or, in the case of FERSA, a fiduciary) in good faith as described in paragraph (b)(3) of this section. Paragraph (b)(5) of this section contains a special rule for service contracts subject to FERSA.

(2) *Fair Market Value.* (i) Except as otherwise specified in this section, the term "fair market value" as used in section 3(18)(B) of the Act and section 8477(a)(2)(B) of FERSA means the price at which an asset would change hands between a willing buyer and a willing seller when the former is not under any compulsion to buy and the latter is not under any compulsion to sell, and both parties are able, as well as willing, to trade and are well informed about the asset and the market for such asset.

(ii) The fair market value of an asset for the purposes of section 3(18)(B) of the Act and section 8477(a)(2)(B) of FERSA must be determined as of the date of the transaction involving that asset.

(iii) The fair market value of an asset for the purposes of section 3(18)(B) of the Act and section 8477(a)(2)(B) of FERSA must be reflected in written documentation of valuation meeting the requirements set forth in paragraph (b)(4), of this section.

(3) *Good Faith*—(i) *General Rule.* The requirement in section 3(18)(B) of the Act and section 8477(a)(2)(B) of FERSA that the fiduciary must determine fair market value in good faith establishes an objective, rather than a subjective, standard of conduct. Subject to the conditions in paragraphs (b)(3)(ii) and (iii) of this section, an assessment of whether the fiduciary has acted in good faith will be made in light of all relevant facts and circumstances.

(ii) In considering all relevant facts and circumstances, the Department will not view a fiduciary as having acted in good faith unless

(A) The fiduciary has arrived at a determination of fair market value by way of a prudent investigation of circumstances prevailing at the time of the valuation, and the application of sound business principles of evaluation; and

(B) The fiduciary making the valuation either,

(1) Is independent of all parties to the transaction (other than the plan), or

(2) Relies on the report of an appraiser who is independent of all parties to the transaction (other than the plan).

(iii) In order to satisfy the independence requirement of paragraph (b)(3)(ii)(B), of this section, a person must in fact be independent of all parties (other than the plan) participating in the transaction. For the purposes of this section, an assessment of independence will be made in light of all relevant facts and circumstances. However, a person will not be considered to be independent of all parties to the transaction if that person—

(1) Is directly or indirectly, through one or more intermediaries, controlling, controlled by, or under common control with any of the parties to the transaction (other than the plan);

(2) Is an officer, director, partner, employee, employer or relative (as defined in section 3(15) of the Act, and including siblings) of any such parties (other than the plan);

(3) Is a corporation or partnership of which any such party (other than the plan) is an officer, director or partner.

For the purposes of this subparagraph, the term "control," in connection with a person other than an individual, means the power to exercise a controlling influence over the management or policies of that person.

(4) *Valuation Content.* (i) In order to comply with the requirement in paragraph (b)(2)(iii), of this section, that the determination of fair market value be reflected in written documentation of valuation, such written documentation must contain, at a minimum, the following information:

(A) A summary of the qualifications to evaluate assets of the type being valued of the person or persons making the valuation;

(B) A statement of the asset's value, a statement of the methods used in determining that value, and the reasons for the valuation in light of those methods;

(C) A full description of the asset being valued;

(D) The factors taken into account in making the valuation, including any restrictions, understandings, agreements or obligations limiting the use or disposition of the property;

(E) The purpose for which the valuation was made;

(F) The relevance or significance accorded to the valuation methodologies taken into account;

(G) The effective date of the valuation; and

(H) In cases where a valuation report has been prepared, the signature of the person making the valuation and the date the report was signed.

(ii) *Special Rule.* When the asset being valued is a security other than a security covered by section 3(18)(A) of the Act or section 8477(a)(2)(A) of FERSA, the written valuation required by paragraph (b)(3) of this section, must contain the information required in paragraph (b)(4)(i) of this section, and must include, in addition to an assessment of all other relevant factors, an assessment of the factors listed below:

(A) The nature of the business and the history of the enterprise from its inception;

(B) The economic outlook in general, and the condition and outlook of the specific industry in particular;

(C) The book value of the securities and the financial condition of the business;

(D) The earning capacity of the company;

(E) The dividend-paying capacity of the company;

(F) Whether or not the enterprise has goodwill or other intangible value;

(G) The market price of securities of corporations engaged in the same or a similar line of business, which are actively traded in a free and open market, either on an exchange or over-the-counter;

(H) The marketability, or lack thereof, of the securities. Where the plan is the purchaser of securities that are subject to "put" rights and such rights are taken into account in reducing the discount for lack of marketability, such assessment shall include consideration of the extent to which such rights are enforceable, as well as the company's ability to meet its obligations with respect to the "put" rights (taking into account the company's financial strength and liquidity);

(I) Whether or not the seller would be able to obtain a control premium from an unrelated third party with regard to the block of securities being valued, provided that in cases where a control premium is taken into account:

¶ 20,531F   Reserved.

Proposed Department of Labor regulations on procedures for filing and processing applications for exemptions from the prohibited transaction provisions of ERISA, the Internal Revenue Code, and the Federal Employees' Retirement System Act of 1986 formerly appeared here.

The final regulations are at ¶ 14,789C to ¶ 14,789Y.]

¶ 20,531G   Reserved.

Formerly reproduced at this paragraph were proposed PBGC regulations relating to insurance premiums for single-employer plans.

The final regulations appear at ¶ 15,371—15,371V.]

¶ 20,532   Reserved.

Proposed Reg. §§ 2608.2—2608.7 were formerly reproduced at this point.

The final regulations appear at ¶ 15,472—15,473V.]

¶ 20,532A

Proposed regulation on 29 CFR Part 2619—Valuation— Single-employer plans.—Reproduced below is the text of a proposed rule which would amend the PBGC final regulations on Valuation of Plan Benefits in Non-Multiemployer Plans to change the interest assumption for the immediate and deferred annuity rates, so as to make it the same as that under the multiemployer regulation.

The proposed regulation was published in the Federal Register on March 25, 1986 (51 FR 10334).

ERISA Sec. 4044.

PENSION BENEFIT GUARANTY CORPORATION

29 CFR Part 2619

Valuation of Plan Benefit In Non-Multiemployer Plan

AGENCY: Pension Benefit Guaranty Corporation.

ACTION: Proposed rule.

SUMMARY: This is a proposed amendment to the Pension Benefit Guaranty Corporation's regulation on Valuation of Plan Benefits in Non-Multiemployer Plans. If adopted, this amendment would change the interests assumption prescribed by the regulation, and make corresponding changes in the actuarial formulas used under the regulation, to eliminate inaccuracies inherent in the existing assumption and to achieve uniformity with the interest assumption and formulas proposed for multiemployer plans.

DATES: Comments must be received on or before May 27, 1986.

ADDRESSES: Comments should be addressed to Director, Corporate Policy and Regulations Department (611), Pension Benefit Guaranty Corporation, 2020 K Street, NW., Washington, DC 20006. Written

(*1*) Actual control (both in form and in substance) is passed to the purchaser with the sale, or will be passed to the purchaser within a reasonable time pursuant to a binding agreement in effect at the time of the sale, and

(*2*) It is reasonable to assume that the purchaser's control will not be dissipated within a short period of time subsequent to acquisition.

(5) *Service Arrangements Subject to FERSA.* For purposes of determinations pursuant to section 8477(c)(1)(C) of FERSA (relating to the provision of services) the term "adequate consideration" under section 8477(a)(2)(B) of FERSA means "reasonable compensation" as defined in sections 408(b)(2) and 408(c)(2) of the Act and § §2550.408b-2(d) and 2550.408e-2 of this chapter.

(6) *Effective Date.* This section will be effective for transactions taking place after the date 30 days following publication of the final regulation in the *Federal Register.*

Signed in Washington, DC, this 11th day of May 1988.

David M. Walker,

Assistant Secretary, Pension and Welfare Benefits Administration, U. S. Department of Labor.

[FR Doc. 88-10934 Filed 5-16-88; 8:45 am]

comments will be available for public inspection at the PBGC, Suite 7100, at the above address, between 9:00 a.m. and 4:00 p.m.

FOR FURTHER INFORMATION CONTACT: Deborah Murphy, Attorney, Corporate Policy and Regulations Department (611), 2020 K Street, NW., Washington, DC 20006, 202-254-4860 (202-254-8010 for TTY and TDD). These are not toll free numbers.

SUPPLEMENTARY INFORMATION:

Background

The Pension Benefit Guaranty Corporation ("PBGC") published a final regulation on Valuation of Plan Benefits in Non-Multiemployer Plans (the "Single-employer regulation") on January 28, 1981 (40 FR 9497). The regulation was subsequently amended and is now codified as 29 CFR Part 2619. On February 19, 1985 (50 FR 6956), the PBGC published a proposed regulation on Valuation of Plan Assets and Plan Benefits Following Mass Withdrawal (The "multiemployer regulation"). As proposed, the multiemployer regulation would be codified as 29 CFR Part 2676. For reasons discussed below, this proposed amendment would change the interest assumption under the existing single-employer regulation to make it the same as that under the multi employer regulation.

Under the single-employer regulation, benefits in pay status on the valuation date are valued using a flat rate of interest (the immediate annuity rate). Benefits that are to start after the valuation date are valued in two steps. First, the benefit is valued as of its deferred starting date using the immediate annuity rate. Second, an adjustment is made for the period of deferral. The adjustment is represented by a factor that has the effect of reducing the assumed interest rate. The amount of reduction is greater for longer periods of deferral. The particular interest rates that are applicable from time to time, together with the manner of applying them to the valuation of benefits as summarized above. constitute the single.employer regulation's interest assumption.

The preamble to the original proposal version of the single-employer regulation (40 FR 57960. December 12, 1975), in discussing the adjust-ment factor for deferred benefits, noted that "[i]t is common financial practice to assume that the rate of return on investments made in the future will be lower than that for investments made in the present or near future." (40 FR at 57983.)

When the regulation was published as an interim rule. however (41 FR 46460, November 3, 1976). the preamble warned, in response to comments on the proposed rule, that the deferred benefit adjustment factor should not be "misconstrued as an investment model which actually reflects the investment yields which the PBGC expects to realize during a particular year of deferment. Rather, the current value of annuities obtained by applying the [factor] is in line with price data for such annuities received from the industry." (41 FR at 46485.)

Clearly, an interest assumption that applies the same rate (the immediate annuity rate) to every payment under a pay status annuity. as the single-employer regulation does, is not to be regarded as "an investment model." The design of the deferred benefit adjustment factor used in the regulation merely highlights that fact. As noted in the preamble to the proposed multiemployer regulation. the single-em-ployer interest assumption "represents an appropriate compromise between actuarial theory . . . and administrative convenience." (50 FR at 6957.)

In this context, "administrative convenience" means primarily ease of computation. Although many single-employer plans have been valued by computer for years. some (mostly small) plan valuations have not been computerized. The present single-employer interest assumption "facilitates the valuation of benefits 'by hand' (i.e., using nothing more sophisticated than a desk calculator) from tables of relatively small bulk." (50 FR at 6957.)

In introducing the proposed multiemployer regulation, on the other hand, the PBGC indicated that, "[b]ecause of economies of scale, valuations by computer are not merely cost-justified but, in general, a financial, as well as logistical, necessity" for multiemployer plans. (50 FR at 6957.) This was one reason why the PBGC considered it appro-priate to propose a select and ultimate interest assumption for multiem-ployer valuations. The primary motivation for proposing such an assumption, of course, was that the use of select and ultimate interest yields results that exhibit better internal consistency and closer agree-ment with marketplace values, both in the aggregate and for individual streams of payments. A select and ultimate interest assumption applies to each payment under a benefit an individually determined interest rate that depends on the amount of time between the valuation date and the date of payment. As a practical matter, therefore, the select and ultimate interest assumption makes valuations without the use of a computer impossible. On the other hand, it comes much closer to being an "investment model." Thus, in the PBGC's view, the multiem-ployer assumption leads to more realistic valuations than the single-employer assumption does.

A further problem with valuations under the existing single-employer regulation is that, as pointed out in the preamble to that regulation (46 FR at 9495), the adjustment factor for deferred benefits ignores the mortality of the beneficiary where joint and survivor benefits are being valued. Leaving the beneficiary's mortality out of the factor simplifies calculations that use the factor, but reduces the accuracy of values generated with the factor. The need for this distorting simplification would disappear if a computerized valuation method were adopted.

Until 1964, the provisions of the single-employer regulation that would be affected by this amendment applied almost exclusively to the PBGC itself, rather than to plan administrators. Thus, any administra-tive inconvenience arising from the adoption of this amendment would have been confined to a very few plans, primarily those for which the PBGC assumed the burden of paying certain deferred benefits.

Under sections 103 and 203 of the Retirement Equity Act of 1984, the interest rate assumption that the PBGC would use to value benefits on plan termination became the standard for determining the value of a participant's benefit in situations where the benefit is or may be cashed out. The PBGC specifically invites public comment on the administra-tive difficulty of processing cashouts using the proposed select and ultimate interest assumption as opposed to the existing single-em-ployer interest assumption and on the number of cashouts that are processed by plans each year and that would be affected by the proposed assumption.

It appears that the valuation standards that would be changed by this amendment have been voluntarily adopted in some cases where their use is not legally mandated. The PBGC does not know what effect the proposed amendment might have on such situations, nor how many such situations there are. Comments are invited on the impact of the amendment on such cases and the extent to which any such impact should be considered by the PBGC.

Even for plans affected by this amendment, administrative inconve-nience should be minimal. The single-employer regulation has been in effect, in interim and final form, since 1976, before the microcomputer had become the ubiquitous business tool that it is today. Microcom-puters capable of handling actuarial computations with select and ultimate interest are as common now as electronic calculators were when the single-employer regulation was first drafted. The PBGC has thus concluded that accuracy need no longer make the concessions to administrative convenience that the existing single-employer interest assumption reflects.

Accordingly, the PBGC proposes to amend the single-employer regu-lation to substitute for the existing interest assumption the select and ultimate interest assumption used in the recently proposed multiem-ployer regulation. To reflect this change, the actuarial formulas in the single-employer regulation would be replaced by the corresponding formulas from the proposed multiemployer regulation.

The PBGC recognizes that microcomputer programs to evaluate actuarial formulas with select and ultimate interest may not be widely available, and that some people, including perhaps even some actua-ries, may not feel confident about writing such programs for them-selves. The PBGC is therefore considering the possibility of developing such programs and making them available to the public at cost. Public comment on this possibility is invited.

The Amendment

The major changes made by the amendment would be in Subpart C of the single-employer regulation (existing §§ 2619.41 through 2619.48). However, §§ 2619.3(a) and 2619.25(b)(2), which refer to certain Subpart C provisions, would be revised, and a new § 2619.25(c) would be added, simply to reflect changes that the amendment would make in Subpart C. Appendices A, B, and C, which contain mortality and interest tables, would be deleted, because mortality and interest tables in the amended regulation would be included in Subpart C.

The amendment would have no effect on the first section (§ 2619.41, *Purpose and scope*) or the last section (existing § 2619.48, *Withdrawal of employee contributions*) of Subpart C, except to renumber the latter as § 2619.46. All of the other sections of Subpart C would be deleted and replaced by slightly reworded versions of §§ 2676.12 through 2676.15 from the multiemployer regulation.

New § 2619.42(a) restates the rule from existing § 2619.43(b) regard-ing the form of benefit to be valued. New § 2619.42(b) restates the rule regarding the timing of benefits from existing § 2619.46(b). (Note that the latter rule is not the same as the corresponding provision of the proposed multiemployer regulation (§ 2676.12(b)).)

New § 2619.43(a) carries over the substance of existing §§ 2619.43(a) and (c) and 2619.44(a). Like existing § 2619.43(a) (and unlike § 2676.13(a) in the multiemployer regulation), the new section makes clear that the actuarial formulas set forth in the regulation are to be regarded as standards of accuracy, not as absolute requirements.

Paragraphs (b) through (i) of new § 2619.43 contain actuarial formu-las that would replace the formulas now set forth in existing §§ 2619.44, 2619.45, and 2619.47. The new formulas in paragraphs (b) through (h) are identical with those in multiemployer § 2676.13(b) through (h). Paragraph (i) supplies new formulas for the death benefits described in existing § 2619.47(d) through (f), which were not included in the proposed multiemployer regulation.

The following table shows the location of the proposed new formula corresponding to each valuation provision in the existing regulation.

Existing provision	Proposed provision
§ 2619.44 (c)	§ 2619.43 (c) (2)
§ 2619.44 (d)	§ 2619.43 (c) (1)
§ 2619.44 (e)	§ 2619.43 (g) (2)
§ 2619.44 (f)	§ 2619.43 (g) (1)
§ 2619.44 (g)	§ 2619.43 (c) (3)
§ 2619.44 (h)	§ 2619.43 (e) (2)
§ 2619.44 (i)	§ 2619.43 (e) (1)
§ 2619.44 (j)	§ 2619.43 (e) (4)
§ 2619.44 (k)	§ 2619.43 (e) (4)
§ 2619.44 (l)	§ 2619.43 (e) (3)
§ 2619.45	§ 2619.43 (b), (d), (f), (g) (3), (g) (4)
§ 2619.47 (b)	§ 2619.43 (h) (1)
§ 2619.47 (c)	§ 2619.43 (h) (2)
§ 2619.47 (d)	§ 2619.43 (i) (1)
§ 2619.47 (e)	§ 2619.43 (i) (1)
§ 2619.47 (f)	§ 2619.43 (i) (2)

Paragraphs (m) and (n) of existing § 2619.44 are no longer considered necessary and accordingly have no counterparts in the amended regulation. (Those provisions merely explained that two common forms of benefit—cash refund and installment refund annuities—could be analyzed in terms of other benefits listed elsewhere in the regulations.) The benefits described in existing §§ 2619.44 (j) and 2619.47 (d) are simply special cases of the benefits described in amended § 2619.43 (e) (4) and (i) (1) respectively.

New § 2619.44 contains the prescribed mortality tables currently found in appendix C. (Appendix A, containing data from which the mortality tables in Appendix C can be derived, is no longer considered necessary. Thus both Appendices A and C are replaced by new § 2619.44.) New § 2619.44 also contains provisions derived from existing § 2619.44 (b) concerning the circumstances under which each table is to be used.

The select and ultimate rate series that is at the heart of the amendment would be set forth in new § 2619.45. The series used in this regulation would be identical with the series used in the multiemployer regulation. A new series would be promulgated each month as necessary to respond to changes in current rates of investment return and expectations regarding future rates. The rates series would be constructed so as to produce values, for a typical plan, within a few percent of the cost of commercial annuities covering the plan's benefits—the same criterion used in setting rates under the existing single-employer regulation. Existing Appendix B, which contains interest rates applicable under the current regulation, would be superseded by new § 2619.45.

E.O. 12291 and the Regulatory Flexibility Act

The PBGC has determined that this proposed regulation is not a "major rule" for the purposes of Executive Order 12291, because it will not have an annual effect on the economy of $100 million or more; or create a major increase in costs or prices for consumers, individual industries, or geographic regions; or have significant adverse effects on competition, employment, investment, innovation, or the ability of United States-based enterprises to compete with foreign-based enterprises in domestic or export markets.

Under section 605 (b) of the Regulatory Flexibility Act, the PBGC certifies that this rule will not have a significant economic impact on a substantial number of small entities. Pension plans with fewer than 100 participants have traditionally been treated as small plans. Such plans typically contract with actuarial firms, insurance companies, and other service providers for actuarial services. The larger providers of actuarial services perform valuations by computer, and such providers serve the great majority of small plans. For such service providers, the proposed amendment would necessitate a one-time programming expense that would be amortized over a period of time and spread among not only small plan clients but larger plan clients as well. The economic impact of the amendment on each such small plan would thus be insignificant. While the amendment might have a significant economic impact on small plans that are not currently valued by computer, the number of such plans is considered to be insignificant. Therefore, compliance with sections 603 and 604 of the Regulatory Flexibility Act is waived.

Public Comments

Interested parties are invited to submit comments on this proposed regulation. Comments should be addressed to: Director, Corporate Policy and Regulations Department (611), Pension Benefit Guaranty Corporation, 2020 K Street, NW., Washington, DC 20006. Written

comments will be available for public inspection at the above address, Suite 7100, between the hours of 9:00 a.m. and 4:00 p.m. Comments should include the commenter's name and address, identify this proposed regulation, and give reasons for any recommendation. This proposal may be changed in light of the comments received.

List of Subjects in 29 CFR Part 2619

Employee benefits plans, Pension insurance, Pensions.

PART 2619—[AMENDED]

In consideration of the foregoing, it is proposed that 29 CFR Part 2619 be amended as follows:

1. The authority citation for Part 2619 continues to read as follows:

Authority: Secs. 4002 (b) (3), 4041 (b), 4044, 4062 (b) (1) (A), Pub. L. 93-406, 88 Stat. 1004, 1020, 1025, 1029, as amended by secs. 403 (1), 403 (d), 402 (a) (7), Pub. L. 96-364, 94 Stat. 1302, 1301, 1299 (29 U.S.C. 1302, 1341, 1344, 1362).

2. In § 2619.3, paragraph (a) is revised to read as follows:

§ 2619.3 General valuation rules.

(a) *Non-trusteed plans.* Plan administrators of non-trusteed plans shall value plan benefits in accordance with Subpart B of this part, except for any early retirement benefits to be provided by PBGC, which shall be valued in accordance with Subpart C. If a plan with respect to which PBGC has issued a Notice of Sufficiency is unable to satisfy all benefits assigned to priority categories 1 through 4 on the date of distribution, the PBGC will place it into trusteeship and the plan administrator shall re-value the benefits in accordance with Subpart C of this part.

* * *

3. In § 2619.25, paragraph (b) (2) is revised, and a new paragraph (c) is added, to read as follows:

§ 2619.25 Early retirement benefits.

* * *

(b) * * *

(2) If the plan administrator is unable to obtain a qualifying bid described in paragraph (b) (1), then the plan administrator may arrange for the PBGC to become responsible for the payment of such benefits in accordance with Subpart D of Part 2617 of this chapter. If such an arrangement is made, the plan administrator shall calculate the value of all such early retirement benefits in accordance with paragraph (c) of this section, and the PBGC will provide these benefits as set forth in Part 2617 of this chapter. If the PBGC does not provide these benefits, the value of each early retirement benefit is its cost under the qualifying bid.

(c) *Valuation of early retirement benefits.* An early retirement benefit that is to be provided by an insurer pursuant to a qualifying bid is valued in accordance with paragraph (a) of this section. An early retirement benefit that is to be provided by PBGC in accordance with Part 2617 is valued as an annuity in accordance with Subpart C of this part.

4. Sections 2619.42 through 2619.45 are revised to read as follows:

§ 2619.42 Benefits to be valued.

(a) *Form of benefit.* The plan administrator shall determine the form of each benefit to be valued, without regard to the form of benefit valued in any prior year, in accordance with the following rules:

(1) If a benefit is in pay status as of the valuation date, the plan administrator shall value the form of benefit being paid.

(2) If a benefit is not in pay status as of the valuation date but a valid election with respect to the form of benefit has been made on or before the valuation date, the plan administrator shall value the form of benefit so elected.

(3) If a benefit is not in pay status as of the valuation date and no valid election with respect to the form of benefit has been made on or before the valuation date, the plan administrator shall value the form of benefit that is payable under the terms of the plan in the absence of a valid election.

(b) *Timing of benefit.* The plan administrator shall value benefits whose starting date is subject to election using the assumption specified in paragraph (b) (1) or (b) (2) of this section.

(1) *Where election made.* If a valid election of the starting date of a benefit has been made on or before the valuation date, the plan administrator shall assume that the starting date of the benefit is the starting date so elected.

(2) *Where no election made.* If no valid election of the starting date of a benefit has been made on or before the valuation date, the plan administrator shall assume that the starting date of the benefit is the later of—

(i) The expected retirement age, as determined under Subpart D of this part, of the participant with respect to whom the benefit is payable, or

(ii) The valuation date.

§ 2619.43 Valuation methods.

(a) *General rule.* The plan administrator shall value benefits as of the valuation date using—

(1) The mortality and interest assumptions prescribed by §§ 2619.44 and 2619.45,

(2) Interpolation methods, where necessary, at least as accurate as linear interpolation, and

(3) Formulas that are at least as accurate as the formulas set forth in paragraphs (b)-(i) of this section.

(b) *Single-sum payments (other than death benefits).* The present value of a single-sum payment of 1 to be made 11 years after the valuation date may be found as follows:

(1) If the payment is not contingent on the survival of any person:

$$V^{0:n} = \left(\frac{1}{1+i_{k+1}}\right) j \cdot \overset{k}{\underset{t-1}{\sigma}} \left(\frac{1}{1+i_t}\right)$$

where $n = k + j$, k is an integer, $0 \le j < 1$, $v^{0:0} = 1$, and i_k is the interest rate determined under § 2619.45 applicable to the year ending on the kth anniversary of the valuation date.

(2) If the payment is contingent on the survival of a person aged x on the valuation date:

$$_np_x \, v^{0:n} = \frac{l_{x+n}}{l_x} \cdot v^{0:n},$$

where l_x and l_{x+n} are the numbers of persons living at ages x and $x+n$ respectively, as determined under § 2619.44.

(3) If the payment is contingent on the survival of two persons aged x and v respectively on the valuation date:

$$_np_x \cdot {}_np_y \cdot v^{0:n}.$$

(c) *Basic annuities in pay status.* The present value of an annuity due providing payments of $1/m$, m times per year, starting on the valuation date, may be found as follows:

$$_n I\ddot{a}^{(m)}_{xy} = \overset{\infty}{\underset{t=n}{\Sigma}} \; v^{0:t} \cdot {}_tp_x \cdot {}_tp_y - v^{0:n} \cdot {}_np_x \cdot {}_np_y$$

(e) *Joint and survivor annuities in pay status.* The present value of an annuity due providing payments m times per year, starting on the valuation date, in an initial amount of $1/m$ per payment, and in an ultimate amount of s/m per payment, may be found as follows:

(1) If the annuity is payable in the initial amount for the life of a person aged x on the valuation date and, after the death of that person, in the ultimate amount for the life of a person aged y on the valuation date:

$$\ddot{a}^{(m)}_x + \frac{s}{a}\left(\ddot{a}^{(m)}_y - \ddot{a}^{(m)}_{xy}\right).$$

(2) If the annuity is payable in the initial amount for the joint lives of two persons aged x and y on the valuation date and, after the death of either of those persons, in the ultimate amount for the life of the survivor:

$$\ddot{a}^{(m)}_{r1} + {}_{r|}\ddot{a}^{(m)}_{xy} + s\left({}_{r|}\ddot{a}^{(m)}_x\right.$$

(f) *Deferred joint and survivor annuities.* The present value of an annuity due providing payments m times per year, starting n years after the valuation date, in an initial amount of $1/m$ per payment, and in an ultimate amount of s/m per payment, contingent on the survival for n years of a person aged x on the valuation date, may be found as follows:

(1) If the annuity is payable in the initial amount for the life of the person and, after the death of that person, in the ultimate amount for the life of a person aged y on the valuation date:

(1) If the annuity is for a term certain of r years after the valuation date and is not contingent on the survival of any person:

$$\ddot{a}^{(m)}_r = \frac{1}{m} \overset{r-1}{\underset{t=0}{\Sigma}} \frac{v^{0:t}(v^{0:t} - v^{0:t+1})}{v^{0:t} - v^{0:t+(1/m)}}.$$

(2) If the annuity is for the life of a person aged x on the valuation date:

$$a^{(m)}_x = \overset{\infty}{\underset{t=0}{\Sigma}} v^{0:t} \cdot {}_tp_x - \frac{m-1}{2m}.$$

(3) If the annuity is for the joint lives of two persons aged x and y on the valuation date:

$$a^{(m)}_{xy} = \overset{\infty}{\underset{t=0}{\Sigma}} v^{0:t} \cdot {}_tp_x \cdot {}_tp_y - \frac{m-1}{2m}.$$

(d) *Basic deferred annuities.* The present value of an annuity due providing payments of $1/m$, m times per year, starting n years after the valuation date, may be found as follows:

(1) If the annuity is for a term certain of r years and is not contingent on the survival of any person:

$$_n\ddot{a}^{(m)}_r = \ddot{a}^{(m)}_{n+r} - \ddot{a}^{(m)}_n.$$

(2) If the annuity is for a term certain of r years and is contingent on the survival for n years of a person aged x on the valuation date:

$$_np_x \cdot {}_nI\ddot{a}^{(m)}_r$$

(3) If the annuity is for the life of a person aged x on the valuation date:

$$_nI\ddot{a}^{(m)}_x = \overset{\infty}{\underset{t=n}{\Sigma}} v^{0:t} \cdot {}_tp_x - v^{0:n} \cdot {}_np_x \cdot \frac{m-1}{2m}.$$

(4) If the annuity is for the life of a person aged y on the valuation date and is contingent on the survival for n years of a person aged x on the valuation date:

$$_np_x \cdot {}_n\ddot{a}^{(m)}_y.$$

(5) If the annuity is for the joint lives of two persons aged x and y on the valuation date:

$$\frac{m-1}{2m}.$$
$$\ddot{a}^{(m)}_{xy} + s\left(\ddot{a}^{(m)}_x + \ddot{a}^{(m)}_y - 2\ddot{a}^{(m)}_{xy}\right).$$

(3) If the annuity is payable in the initial amount for a term certain of r years after the valuation date or for the life of a person aged x on the valuation date (whichever of those two periods is longer) and, after the expiration of the term certain and the death of that person, in the ultimate amount for the life of a person aged y on the valuation date:

$$\ddot{a}^{(m)}_{r1} + {}_{r|}\ddot{a}^{(m)}_x + s\left({}_{r|}\ddot{a}^{(m)}_y - {}_{r|}\ddot{a}^{(m)}_{xy}\right).$$

(4) If the annuity is payable in the initial amount for a term certain of r years after the valuation date or for the joint lives of two persons aged x and y on the valuation date (whichever of those two periods is longer) and, after the expiration of the term certain and the death of either of the persons, in the ultimate amount for the life of the survivor:

$${}_{r|}\ddot{a}^{(m)}_y - 2 \cdot {}_{r|}\ddot{a}^{(m)}_{xy}\big).$$

$${}_n|\ddot{a}^{(m)}_x + s\left({}_n|{}_\ddot{a}^{(m)}_y - {}_n|\ddot{a}^{(m)}_{xy}\right).$$

(2) If the annuity is payable in the initial amount for the joint lives of the person and a person aged y on the valuation date and, after the death of either of those persons, in the ultimate amount for the life of the survivor:

$$_{n}|\ddot{a}^{(m)}_{xy} \qquad +s(_{n}|\ddot{a}^{(m)}_{x}$$

(3) If the annuity is payable in the initial amount for a term certain of r years or for the life of the person (whichever of those two periods is longer) and, after the expiration of the term certain and the death of

$$_{n}p_{x\cdot n}|\ddot{a}^{(m)}_{r1} \qquad +_{n+r}|\ddot{a}^{(m)}_{x}.$$

(4) If the annuity is payable in the initial amount for a term certain of r years or for the joint lives of the person and a person aged y on the valuation date (whichever of those two periods is longer) and, after the

$$_{n}p_{x\cdot n}|\ddot{a}^{(m)}_{r} \qquad +_{n+r}|\ddot{a}^{(m)}_{xy} \qquad +s(_{n+r}|\ddot{a}^{(m)}_{x}$$

(g) *Single life or certain annuities.* The present value of an annuity due providing payment of $1/m$, m times per year, for the life of a person aged x on the valuation date or a term certain of r years, may be found as follows:

(1) If the annuity starts on the valuation date and is for the shorter of those two periods:

$$\ddot{a}^{(m)}_{x} \quad -_{r}\ddot{a}^{(m)}_{x}.$$

(2) If the annuity starts on the valuation date and is for the longer of those two periods:

$$\ddot{a}^{(m)}_{r} \quad +_{r}|\ddot{a}^{(m)}_{x}.$$

(3) If, contingent on the survival of the person for n years, the annuity starts n years after the valuation date and is for the shorter of those two periods:

$$_{n}|\ddot{a}^{(m)}_{x} \quad -_{n+r}|\ddot{a}^{(m)}_{x}.$$

(4) If, contingent on the survival of the person for n years, the annuity starts n years after the valuation date and is for the longer of those two periods:

$$_{n}p_{x\cdot n}|\ddot{a}^{(m)}_{r1} +_{n+r}|\ddot{a}^{(m)}_{x}.$$

(h) *Fixed single-sum death benefits.* The present value of a fixed single-sum payment of 1 to be made upon the death of a person aged x on the valuation date may be found as follows:

(1) If the payment is to be made whenever death occurs:

$$\bar{A}_{x} = \sum_{t=0}^{\infty} v^{0:t+\frac{1}{2}}(_{t}p_{x}-_{t+1}p_{x}).$$

(2) If the payment is to be made only if the person dies within r years after the valuation date:

$$A^{1}_{x\cdot r1} = \sum_{t=0}^{r-1} v^{0:t+\frac{1}{2}}(_{t}p_{x}-_{t+1}p_{x}).$$

(3) If the payment is to be made only if the person dies at least n years after the valuation date:

$$\bar{A}^{1}_{xn+r} - \bar{A}^{1}_{xn}.$$

(4) If the payment is to be made only if the person dies at least n years, but within $n+r$ years, after the valuation date:

$$+_{n}p_{x\cdot n}|\ddot{a}^{(m)}_{y} \qquad -2._{n}|\ddot{a}^{(m)}_{xy}).$$

that person, in the ultimate amount for the life of a person aged y on the valuation date:

$$+s(_{n}p_{x\cdot n+r}|\ddot{a}^{(m)}_{y} \qquad -_{n+r}|\ddot{a}^{(m)}_{y}).$$

expiration of the term certain and the death of either of those persons, in the ultimate amount for the life of the survivor:

$$+_{n}p_{x\cdot n+r}|\ddot{a}^{(m)}_{y} \qquad -2._{n+r}|\ddot{a}^{(m)}_{xy}).$$

$$\bar{A}^{1}_{xn+r} - \bar{A}^{1}_{xn}.$$

(i) *Variable single-sum death benefits.* The present value of a single-sum payment to be made upon the death of a payment to be made upon the death of a person aged x on the valuation date, if the person dies within r years after the valuation date, may be found as follows:

(1) If the amount payable is initially $r-1/m$ and decreases by $1/m$, m times per year:

$$\sum_{t=0}^{r-1} (r-t-\frac{m+1}{2m}).v^{0:t+\frac{1}{2}}(p_{x}-_{t+1}p_{x}).$$

(2) If the amount payable is initially and increases at an effective interest rate of j, compounded annually:

$$\sum_{t=0}^{r-1} (1+j)^{t+\frac{1}{2}}.v^{0:t+\frac{1}{2}}.(_{t}p_{x}-_{t+1}p_{x}).$$

§ 2619.44 Mortality.

(a) *General rule.* In determining the value of mortality factors of the form $_{n}\rho_{x}$ (as defined in § 2619.43(b)(2)) for purposes of applying the formulas set forth in § 2619.43(b)-(i), and in determining the value of any mortality factor used in valuing benefits under this subpart, the plan administrator shall use the values of lx prescribed in paragraphs (d), (e) and (f) of this section.

(b) *Certain death benefits.* If an annuity for one person is in pay status on the valuation date, and if the payment of a death benefit after the valuation date to another person, who need not be identifiable on the valuation date, depends in whole or in part on the death of the pay status annuitant, then to determine the mortality factors involved in the valuation of the death benefit—

(1) In the case of factors that represent the mortality of the pay status annuitant, the plan administrator shall apply the mortality rates that are applicable to the annuity in pay status under paragraph (d), (e) or (f) of this section; and

(2) In the case of factors that represent the mortality of the death beneficiary, the plan administrator shall apply the mortality rates applicable to annuities not in pay status and to deferred benefits other than annuities, under paragraph (d) of this section.

(c) *Description of mortality tables.* The tables in paragraphs (d), (e) and (f) of this section tabulate, for each age (denoted by x, $x \geq 15$], the number of persons assumed to be living at that age (denoted by l_{x}) out of a closed group consisting originally of 10,000 persons aged 15 years.

(d) *Health lives.* The values of l_{x} applicable to annuities in pay status on the valuation date that are not being received as disability benefits, to annuities not in pay status on the valuation date, and to deferred benefits other than annuities, are as follows:

MORTALITY TABLE FOR HEALTHY MALE PARTICIPANTS

Age x	l_x
15	10,000,000.
16	9,985.6300
17	9,971.5103
18	9,957.6998
19	9,944.2469
20	9,931.2100
21	9,918.6272
22	9,906.5364
23	9,894.9755
24	9,883.6062
25	9,872.4476
26	9,861.5188
27	9,850.8388
28	9,840.4166
29	9,829.7594
30	9,818.8385
31	9,807.6352
32	9,796.1308
33	9,784.2971
34	9,771.6069
35	9,757.9462
36	9,743.1824
37	9,727.1744
38	9,709.7433
39	9,690.8287
40	9,670.2357
41	9,674.7331
42	9,623.0735
43	9,595.9557
44	9,566.2562
45	9,533.6353
46	9,497.7030
47	9,458.0026
48	9,414.1648
49	9,366.1243
50	9,313.5241
51	9,255.8175
52	9,192.3874
53	9,123.0492
54	9,047.5286
55	8,965.8023
56	8,877.2650
57	8,781.2663
58	8,677.0941
59	8,564.7084
60	8,443.4150
61	8,312.4661
62	8,171.0711
63	8,018.3946
64	7,853.8812
65	7,676.6819
66	7,485.9394
67	7,282.0823
68	7,066.2851
69	6,839.6481
70	6,602.0182
71	6,353.3400
72	6,093.6726
73	5,822.4798
74	5,540.0662
75	5,246.9247
76	4,943.7836
77	4,631.6232
78	4,313.7642
79	3,991.7503
80	3,667.3966
81	3,342.7660
82	3,021.1317
83	2,705.9975
84	2,400.7177
85	2,107.6405
86	1,829.0352
87	1,567.1815
88	1,324.0380

Age x	l_x
89	1,101.3242
90	900.3755
91	722.0741
92	566.8029
93	434.7475
94	324.9542
95	235.9564
96	165.8415
97	112.3488
98	73.0823
99	45.3940
100	26.7427
101	14.8217
102	7.6505
103	3.6393
104	1.5708
105	0.6026
106	0.1996
107	0.0547
108	0.0117
109	0.0017
110	0.0001

MORTALITY TABLE FOR HEALTHY FEMALE PARTICIPANTS

Age x	l_x
15	10,000.0000
16	10,000.0000
17	10,000.0000
18	10,000.0000
19	10,000.0000
20	10,000.0000
21	9,985.6300
22	9,971.5103
23	9,957.6998
24	9,944.2469
25	9,931.2100
26	9,918.6272
27	9,906.5364
28	9,894.9755
29	9,883.6062
30	9,872.4476
31	9,861.5188
32	9,850.8388
33	9,840.4166
34	9,829.7594
35	9,818.8385
36	9,807.6352
37	9,796.1308
38	9,784.2971
39	9,771.6069
40	9,757.9462
41	9,743.1824
42	9,727.1744
43	9,709.7433
44	9,690.8287
45	9,670.2357
46	9,647.7331
47	9,623.0735
48	9,595.9557
49	9,566.2562
50	9,533.6353
51	9,497.7030
52	9,458.0026
53	9,414.1648
54	9,366.1243
55	9,313.5241
56	9,255.8175
57	9,192.3874
58	9,123.0492
59	9,047.5286
60	8,965.8023
61	8,877.2650
62	8,781.2663
63	8,677.0941
64	8,564.7084
65	8,443.4150
66	8,312.4661
67	8,171.0711
68	8,018.3946
69	7,853.8812
70	7,676.6819
71	7,485.9394
72	7,282.0823
73	7,066.2851
74	6,839.6481
75	6,602.0182
76	6,353.3400
77	6,093.6726
78	5,822.4798
79	5,540.0662
80	5,246.9247
81	4,943.7836
82	4,631.6232
83	4,313.7642
84	3,991.7503
85	3,667.3966
86	3,342.7660
87	3,021.1317
88	2,705.9975

Age x	l_x
89	2,400.7177
90	2,107.6405
91	1,829.0652
92	1,567.1815
93	1,324.0380
94	1,101.3242
95	900.3755
96	722.0741
97	566.8029
98	434.7475
99	324.9542
100	235.9564
101	165.8415
102	112.3488
103	73.0823
104	45.3940
105	26.7427
106	14.8217
107	7.6505
108	3.6393
109	1.5708
110	0.6026

(e) *Disabled lives (other than Social Security disability)*. The values of l_x applicable to annuities in pay status on the valuation date that are being received as disability benefits and for which neither eligibility for, nor receipt of, Social Security disability benefits is a prerequisite, are as follows:

MORTALITY TABLE FOR DISABLED MALE PARTICIPANTS NOT RECEIVING SOCIAL SECURITY DISABILITY BENEFIT PAYMENTS

Age x	l_x
15	10,000.0000
16	9,986.4900
17	9,973.3977
18	9,960.7614
19	9,948.6192
20	9,937.0092
21	9,925.5916
22	9,914.3856
23	9,903.4104
24	9,892.6850
25	9,882.2165
26	9,871.5161
27	9,860.5488
28	9,849.2979
29	9,837.7447
30	9,825.8607
31	9,813.1166
32	9,799.3979
33	9,784.5714
34	9,768.4953
35	9,750.9902
36	9,731.9953
37	9,711.3148
38	9,688.7166
39	9,663.9522
40	9,636.7192
41	9,606.8936
42	9,574.1341
43	9,538.0492
44	9,498.1802
45	9,454.1561
46	9,405.9115
47	9,353.0879
48	9,295.1362
49	9,231.4366
50	9,161.8039
51	9,085.9625
52	9,003.8890
53	8,914.9756
54	8,818.5691
55	8,713.9544
56	8,601.0913
57	8,479.2826
58	8,347.7774
59	8,205.7817
60	8,052.4567
61	7,887.2444
62	7,709.2924
63	7,517.7396
64	7,313.0165
65	7,096.3026
66	6,868.7029
67	6,630.0636
68	6,380.3290
69	6,119.5586
70	5,847.2138
71	5,563.6005
72	5,269.2137
73	4,964.7849
74	4,651.2985
75	4,332.0892
76	4,008.7074
77	3,682.9759
78	3,356.9662
79	3,033.9656
80	2,717.4926
81	2,410.9160
82	2,116.5938
83	1,836.8351
84	1,573.8389
85	1,329.6625

Age x	l_x
86	1,106.0026
87	904.2003
88	725.1415
89	569.2107
90	436.5943
91	326.3346
92	236.9587
93	166.5459
94	112.8260
95	73.3927
96	45.5868
97	26.8563
98	14.8846
99	7.6830
100	3.6548
101	1.5775
102	0.6052
103	0.2005
104	0.0550
105	0.0117
106	0.0017
107	0.0001

MORTALITY TABLE FOR DISABLED FEMALE PARTICIPANTS NOT RECEIVING SOCIAL SECURITY DISABILITY BENEFIT PAYMENTS

Age x	l_x
15	10,000.0000
16	10,000.0000
17	10,000.0000
18	10,000.0000
19	10,000.0000
20	10,000.0000
21	9,986.4900
22	9,973.3977
23	9,960.7614
24	9,948.6192
25	9,937.0092
26	9,925.5916
27	9,914.3856
28	9,903.4104
29	9,692.6850
30	9,882.2185
31	9,871.5161
32	9,860.5488
33	9,849.2979
34	9,837.7447
35	9,825.8607
36	9,813.1166
37	9,799.3979
38	9,784.5714
39	9,768.4953
40	9,750.9902
41	9,731.9953
42	9,711.3148
43	9,688.7166
44	9,663.9522
45	9,636.7192
46	9,606.8936
47	9,574.1341
48	9,538.0492
49	9,498.1802
50	9,454.1561
51	9,405.9115
52	9,353.0879
53	9,295.1362
54	9,231.4366
55	9,161.8039
56	9,085.9625
57	9,003.8890
58	8,914.9756
59	8,818.5691
60	8,713.9544
61	8,601.0913
62	8,479.2826
63	8,347.7774
64	8,205.7817
65	8,052.4567
66	7,887.2444
67	7,709.2924
68	7,517.7396
69	7,313.0165
70	7,096.3026
71	6,868.7029
72	6,630.0636
73	6,380.3290
74	6,119.5586
75	5,847.2138
76	5,563.6005
77	5,269.2137
78	4,964.7849
79	4,651.2985
80	4,332.0892
81	4,008.7074
82	3,682.9759
83	3,356.9662
84	3,033.9656
85	2,717.4926
86	2,410.9160
87	2,116.5938
88	1,836.8351

Age x	l_x
89	1,573.8389
90	1,329.6625
91	1,106.0026
92	904.2003
93	725.1415
94	569.2107
95	436.5943
96	326.3346
97	236.9587
98	166.5459
99	112.8260
100	73.3927
101	45.5868
102	26.8563
103	14.8846
104	7.6830
105	3.6548
106	1.5775
107	0.6052
108	0.2005
109	0.0550
110	0.0117

(f) *Disabled lives (Social Security disability)*. The values of l_x applicable to annuities in pay status on the valuation date that are being received as disability benefits and for which either eligibility for, or receipt of, Social Security disability benefits is a prerequisite, are as follows:

MORTALITY TABLE FOR DISABLED MALE PARTICIPANTS RECEIVING SOCIAL SECURITY DISABILITY BENEFIT PAYMENTS

Age x	l_x
15	10,000.0000
16	10,000.0000
17	10,000.0000
18	10,000.0000
19	10,000.0000
20	10,000.0000
21	9,517.0000
22	9,057.3289
23	8,619.8599
24	8,203.5207
25	7,807.2906
26	7,430.1985
27	7,087.6663
28	6,778.6441
29	6,500.0418
30	6,249.1402
31	6,022.9213
32	5,818.7443
33	5,632.5445
34	5,462.4416
35	5,305.1233
36	5,157.6409
37	5,017.3531
38	4,881.3228
39	4,748.1210
40	4,617.0729
41	4,486.8714
42	4,357.6495
43	4,228.2274
44	4,099.2664
45	3,970.5495
46	3,842.6978
47	3,715.8887
48	3,589.5485
49	3,462.8375
50	3,335.7513
51	3,207.9920
52	3,079.3516
53	2,950.0188
54	2,820.5130
55	2,690.7694
56	2,561.0743
57	2,431.4839
58	2,302.3721
59	2,174.5905
60	2,048.2468
61	1,924.7375
62	1,804.6339
63	1,688.5959
64	1,577.6552
65	1,472.2678
66	1,372.4480
67	1,278.1609
68	1,189.0731
69	1,104.7678
70	1,024.8931
71	949.1535
72	877.3025
73	809.2239
74	744.8096
75	683.8842
76	626.3012
77	571.8756
78	519.9493
79	469.9302
80	420.9165
81	373.4371
82	327.8404
83	284.4999
84	243.7595
85	205.9524

Age x	l_x
86	171.3112
87	140.0469
88	112.3176
89	88.1693
90	67.6259
91	50.5503
92	36.7046
93	25.7960
94	17.4742
95	11.3670
96	7.0600
97	4.1591
98	2.3050
99	1.1898
100	.5660
101	.2443
102	.0937
103	.0310
104	.0085
105	.0018
106	.0003

MORTALITY TABLE FOR DISABLED FEMALE PARTICIPANTS RECEIVING SOCIAL SECURITY DISABILITY BENEFIT PAYMENTS

Age x	l_x
15	10,000.0000
16	10,000.0000
17	10,000.0000
18	10,000.0000
19	10,000.0000
20	10,000.0000
21	9,737.0000
22	9,480.9169
23	9,231.5688
24	8,988.7785
25	8,752.3737
26	8,522.1862
27	8,303.1660
28	8,098.0959
29	7,893.1965
30	7,702.1811
31	7,519.6394
32	7,345.1838
33	7,178.4481
34	7,019.0866
35	6,866.0705
36	6,719.1366
37	6,576.6909
38	6,438.5804
39	6,304.6579
40	6,173.5210
41	6,044.4944
42	5,917.5600
43	5,791.5160
44	5,666.4193
45	5,542.3247
46	5,418.1766
47	5,294.1004
48	5,169.6890
49	5,044.5825
50	4,918.9724
51	4,792.5548
52	4,666.0314
53	4,539.1153
54	4,411.5662
55	4,284.5131
56	4,158.1200
57	4,032.9605
58	3,909.1487
59	3,786.0105
60	3,663.7223
61	3,542.4531
62	3,422.3640
63	3,303.6079
64	3,186.3299
65	3,070.9847
66	2,957.3583
67	2,845.5701
68	2,735.7311
69	2,627.9433
70	2,522.3000
71	2,418.6335
72	2,316.8090
73	2,216.4912
74	2,117.4140
75	2,018.9543
76	1,919.6217
77	1,818.0737
78	1,712.9891
79	1,604.8995
80	1,494.8034
81	1,383.2910
82	1,270.8295
83	1,158.3611
84	1,046.9267
85	937.7323
86	831.9561
87	730.3742
88	633.8188

Age x	l_x
89	543.0559
90	458.8279
91	381.6531
92	312.0014
93	250.2251
94	196.4267
95	150.6593
96	112.6178
97	81.7718
98	57.4692
99	38.9297
100	25,3237
101	15.7266
102	9.2657
103	5.1351
104	2.6507
105	1.2609
106	.5542
107	.2088
108	.0692
109	.0190
110	.0041

MORTALITY TABLE FOR DISABLED FEMALE
PARTICIPANTS NOT RECEIVING SOCIAL SECURITY

Age x	l_x
51	9,405.9115
52	9,353.0879
53	9,295.1362
54	9,231.4366
55	9,161.8039
56	9,085.9625
57	9,003.8890
58	8,914.9756
59	8,818.5691
60	8,713.9544
61	8,601.0913
62	8,479.2826
99	112.8260
100	73.3927
101	45.5868
102	26.8563
103	14.8846
104	7.6830
105	3.6548
106	1.5775
107	0.6052
108	0.2005
109	0.0550
110	0.0117

(f) *Disabled lives (Social Security disability)*. The values of l_x applicable to annuities in pay status on the valuation date that are being received as disability benefits and for which either eligibility for, or receipt of, Social Security disabilitty benefits is a prerequisite, are as follows:

MORTALITY TABLE FOR DISABLED MALE PARTICIPANTS
RECEIVING SOCIAL SECURITY DISABILITY BENEFIT PAYMENTS

Age x	l_x
15	10,000.0000
16	10,000.0000
17	10,000.0000
18	10,000.0000
19	10,000.0000
20	10,000.0000
21	9,517.0000
22	9,057.3289
23	8,619.8599
24	8,203.5207
25	7,807.2906
26	7,430.1985
27	7,087.6663
28	6,778.6441
29	6,500.0418
30	6,249.1402
31	6,022.9213
32	5,818.7443
33	5,632.5445
34	5,462.4416
35	5,305.1233
36	5,157.6409
37	5,017.3531
38	4,881.3228
39	4,748.1210
40	4,617.0729
41	4,486.8714
42	4,357.6495
43	4,228.2274
44	4,099.2664
45	3,970.5495
46	3,842.6978
47	3,715.8887
48	3,589.5485
49	3,462.8375
50	3,335.7513
51	3,207.9920
52	3,079.3516
53	2,950.0188
54	2,820.5130
55	2,690.7694
56	2,561.0743
57	2,431.4839
58	2,302.3721
59	2,174.5905
60	2,048.2468
61	1,924.7375
62	1,804.6339
63	1,688.5959
64	1,577.6552
65	1,472.2678
66	1,372.4480
67	1,278.1609
68	1,189.0731
69	1,104.7678
70	1,024.8931
71	949.1535
72	877.3025
73	809.2239
74	744.8096
75	683.8842
76	626.3012
77	571.8756
78	519.9493
79	469.9302
80	420.9165
81	373.4371
82	327.8404
83	284.4999
84	243.7595
85	205.9524
86	171.3112

Age x		l_x
87	....	140.0469
88	....	112.3176
89	....	88.1693
90	....	67.6259
91	....	50.5503
92	....	36.7046
93	....	25.7960
94	....	17.4742
95	....	11.3670
96	....	7.0600
97	....	4.1591
98	....	2.3050
99	....	1.1898
100	....	.5660
101	....	.2443
102	....	.0937
103	....	.0310
104	....	.0085
105	....	.0018
106	....	.0003

MORTALITY TABLE FOR DISABLED FEMALE PARTICIPANTS
RECEIVING SOCIAL SECURITY DISABILITY BENEFIT PAYMENTS

Age x	l_x
15	10,000.0000
16	10,000.0000
17	10,000.0000
18	10,000.0000
19	10,000.0000
20	10,000.0000
21	9,737.0000
22	9,480.9169
23	9,231.5688
24	8,988.7785
25	8,752.3737
26	8,522.1862
27	8,303.1660
28	8,098.0959
29	7,893.1965
30	7,702.1811
31	7,519.6394
32	7,345.1838
33	7,178.4481
34	7,019.0866
35	6,866.0705
36	6,719.1366
37	6,576.6909
38	6,438.5804
39	6,304.6579
40	6,173.5210
41	6,044.4944
42	5,917.5600
43	5,791.5160
44	5,666.4193
45	5,542.3247
46	5,418.1766
47	5,294.1004
48	5,169.6890
49	5,044.5825
50	4,918.9724
51	4,792.5548
52	4,666.0314
53	4,539.1153
54	4,411.5662
55	4,284.5131
56	4,158.1200
57	4,032.9605
58	3,909.1487
59	3,786.0105
60	3,663.7223
61	3,542.4531
62	3,422.3640
63	3,303.6079
64	3,186.3299
65	3,070.9847
66	2,957.3583
67	2,845.5701
68	2,735.7311
69	2,627.9433
70	2,522.3000
71	2,418.6335
72	2,316.8090
73	2,216.4912
74	2,117.4140
75	2,018.9543
76	1,919.6217
77	1,818.0737
78	1,712.9891
79	1,604.8995
80	1,494.8034
81	1,383.2910
82	1,270.8295
83	1,158.3611
84	1,046.9267
85	937.7323
86	831.9561
87	730.3742
88	633.8188

Age x	l_x
89	543.0559
90	458.8279
91	381.6531
92	312.0014
93	250.2251
94	196.4267
95	150.6593
96	112.6178
97	81.7718
98	57.4692
99	38.9297
100	25.3237
101	15.7266
102	9.2657
103	5.1351
104	2.6507
105	1.2609
106	.5542
107	.2088
108	.0692
109	.0190
110	.0041

§ 2619.45 Interest.

(a) *General rule.* In determining the value of interest factors of the form $v^{o:n}$ (as defined in § 2619.43(b)(1)) for purposes of applying the formulas set forth in § 2619.43(b)-(i) and in determining the value of any interest factor used in valuing benefits under this subpart, the plan administrator shall use the values of i_k prescribed in paragraph (c) of this section.

(b) *Description of interest table.* The table in paragraph (c) of this section tabulates, for each calendar month ending after the effective date of this part, the interest rates (denoted by i_1, i_2, ..., i_{15}, i_u and

referred to generally as i_k assumed to be in effect during each one-year period ending on an anniversary (the first, second, ..., fifteenth, and subsequent anniversaries, respectively, and referred to generally as the k_{th} of a valuation date that occurs within that calendar month; the rate i_u is assumed to be in effect during the sixteenth and all subsequent years. For example, the interest rate assumed to be in effect during the one-year ending on the seventh anniversary of the valuation date is tabulated as i_7, and the rate assumed to be in effect during the one-year period ending on the seventeenth anniversary of the valuation date is tabulated as i_u.

(c) *Interest rates.*

For valuation dates occurring in the month:	The values of ik are:															
	i1	i2	i3	i4	i5	i6	i7	i8	i9	i10	i11	i12	i13	i14	i15	iu
X/85	.IIII	.IIII	.IIII	.IIII	.IIII	.IIII	.IIII	.IIII	.IIII	.IIII	.IIII	.IIII	.IIII	.IIII	.IIII	.IIII

§§ 2619.46 and 2619.47 [Removed]

§ 2619.48 [Redesignated as § 2619.46]

5. Sections 2619.46 and 2619.47 are removed, and § 2619.48 is redesignated as § 2619.46.

Appendices A, B, and C [Removed]

6. Apppendices A, B and C are removed.

Issued in Washington, DC, on February 27, 1986.

William E. Brock,

Chairman of the Board of Directors, Pension Benefit Guaranty Corporation.

Issued pursuant to a resolution of the Board of Directors approving, and authorizing its chairman to issue, this notice of proposed rulemaking.

Edward R. Mackiewicz,

Secretary to the Board of Directors, Pension Benefit Guaranty Corporation.

¶ 20,532B Reserved.

Proposed regulations that would have established rules and procedures for terminating a single-employer pension plan in standard and distress terminations were formerly reproduced here. The final regulations are at ¶ 15,441-15,446C, 15,446O-15,446W, 15,447-15,447I, and 15,447T-15,448.]

¶ 20,532C Reserved.

Proposed regulations that would have established criteria for determining whether a plan is an individual account plan which permits participants to exercise independent control over assets in their account was withdrawn and replaced by revised regulations. The revised regulations, including the notice of withdrawal, are at ¶ 20,532G.]

¶ 20,532D Reserved.

Proposed regulations that would have established rules to govern the allocation of unfunded vested benefits to an employer that had withdrawn from a multiemployer pension plan following the merger of the plan with another multiemployer plan were formerly reproduced here. The final regulations are at ¶ 15,663D, 15,678, and 15,678O-15,678U.]

¶ 20,532E

Proposed regulations on 29 CFR Part 1625: Equal Employment Opportunity Commission: Age Discrimination in Employment Act of 1967: Benefits under employee pension benefit plans.—Reproduced below is the text of proposed regulations that would implement amendments made to the Age Discrimination in Employment Act by the Omnibus Budget Reconciliation Act of 1986 (OBRA) (P.L. 99-509). This Act requires continuing contributions, allocations, and accruals in pension plans regardless of an employee's age.

The proposed regulations were published in the *Federal Register* on November 27, 1987 (52 FR 45360).

EQUAL EMPLOYMENT OPPORTUNITY COMMISSION

29 CFR Part 1625

Employee Pension Benefit Plans

AGENCY: Equal Employment Opportunity Commission (EEOC)

ACTION: Notice of Proposed Rulemaking

SUMMARY: The Commission hereby provides notice of its proposed legislative regulation under section 9 of the Age Discrimination in Employment Act of 1967 (ADEA), 29 U.S.C. § 621 *et seq.,* relating to the prohibition against discrimination on the basis of age in employee pension benefit plans (hereafter, "pension plans") in section 4(i) of the ADEA, 29 U.S.C. § 623(i).

DATES: Written comments must be received by December 28, 1987 and must be submitted in quadruplicate. It is anticipated that final rules will be effective thirty days after publication.

ADDRESS: Comments may be mailed to: Executive Secretariat, Equal Employment Opportunity Commission, Room 507, 2401 E Street, N.W., Washington, D.C. 20507.

FOR FURTHER INFORMATION CONTACT: Paul E. Boymel, Office of Legal Counsel, Room 214, EEOC, 2401 E Street, N.W., Washington, D.C. 20507, (202) 634-6423.

SUPPLEMENTARY INFORMATION: The Commission has determined that this proposed rule is not a major rule as defined in Executive Order 12291 and that a regulatory impact analysis is not required. The rule has been coordinated with the Office of Management and Budget pursuant to Executive Order 12291.

Pursuant to 5 U.S.C. § 605(b), the Chairman, EEOC, certifies that the rule will not have a significant economic impact on a substantial number of small entities. Accordingly, the Commission is not required to prepare an initial or a final regulatory flexibility analysis of the proposed rule.

Background

Congress, in section 4(a)(1) of the ADEA, described the employer conduct that is prohibited (unlawful discrimination by employment agencies and labor organizations is described in sections 4(b) and 4(c) of the ADEA, respectively):

(a) It shall be unlawful for an employer—

(1) to fail or refuse to hire or to discharge any individual or otherwise discriminate against any individual with respect to his compensation, terms, conditions, or privileges of employment, because of such individual's age;

However, Congress fashioned an exception to the general prohibitions in section 4(a) of the ADEA. That exception in section 4(f)(2) of the ADEA provides:

It shall not be unlawful for an employer, employment agency, or labor organization—

(2) to observe the terms of a bona fide seniority system or any bona fide employee benefit plan such as a retirement, pension, or insurance plan, which is not a subterfuge to evade the purposes of this Act, except that no such employee benefit plan shall excuse the failure to hire any individual, and no such seniority system or employee benefit plan shall require or permit the involuntary retirement of any individual specified by section 12(a) of this Act because of the age of such individual.

The ADEA was amended in 1978 to preclude mandatory retirement of covered employees and to raise the upper age limit for coverage under the ADEA from 65 to 70. Because these amendments potentially affected pension plans, in 1979 the Department of Labor (DOL), at the urging of Congress, published the "Employee Benefit Plans: Amendment to Interpretative Bulletin," 29 C.F.R. § 860.120, 44 FR 30648 (May 25, 1979), which provided guidance on employee benefit plans covered under the ADEA. The Interpretative Bulletin contained special rules that allowed employers to cease contributions and accruals to pension plans for employees who continued to work beyond normal retirement age, whether or not the employers could make a cost justification for such cessation.

On October 17, 1986, Congress passed the Omnibus Budget Reconciliation Act of 1986 (OBRA), Pub. L. 99-509. In sections 9201-9204 of OBRA, Congress added section 4(i) to the ADEA and added essentially identical provisions to ERISA and the Internal Revenue Code (IRC) to require continuing contributions, allocations, and accruals in a pension plan regardless of an employee's age. The amendments require such contributions, allocations, and accruals without regard to the cost of such benefits. These proposed regulations are promulgated as the result of the passage of sections 9201-9204 of OBRA.

Interagency Coordination Process

Since sections 9201-9202 of OBRA amended the ADEA, ERISA, and the IRC almost identically, section 9204(d) of OBRA provides that the regulations and rulings of the Commission, the Internal Revenue Service (IRS) and DOL, the three agencies with jurisdiction over the three statutes, "shall each be consistent with the others." Since IRS was given lead regulatory authority on a major portion of the OBRA regulations, the three agencies decided initially that IRS would prepare the regulations and that EEOC and DOL would, to the extent necessary, adapt and incorporate such regulations. Accordingly, the proposed regulations published herein by the Commission have been coordinated with IRS and DOL extensively. However, since IRS is not yet ready to publish proposed or final rules, EEOC's rules do not address in detail such issues as actuarial equivalency (ADEA section 4(i)(3)), highly compensated employees (ADEA section 4(i)(5)), and IRC limits on contributions, benefits, or deductions (ADEA section 4(i)(7)). Under OBRA, IRS was given the exclusive regulatory authority for such issues. As soon as final IRS regulations are promulgated, the regulations herein can be amended appropriately. While IRS regulations will relate to the IRC and ERISA provisions of OBRA and the Commission's proposed regulations relate to the ADEA, it is the clear intent of Congress, and therefore of the Commission, that the regulatory provisions be construed as identical wherever possible.

Discussion And Comparison Of EEOC And IRS Rules

(a) *Remedies*—IRS rules will relate to the determination of whether a pension plan qualifies for favorable tax treatment under the IRC. The Commission rules relate to the determination of whether a pension plan's sponsor (whether an employer, an employment agency, a labor organization, or any combination thereof) is in violation of the ADEA and subject to the sanctions set forth therein. (See section 7 of the ADEA).

(b) *Statutory Scope*—The OBRA provisions apply to "employee pension benefit plans," as defined by section 3(2) of ERISA:

. . . the terms "employee pension benefit plan" and "pension plan" mean any plan, fund, or program which was heretofore or is hereafter established or maintained by an employer or by an employee organization, or by both, to the extent that by its express terms or as a result of surrounding circumstances such plan, fund, or program—

(i) provides retirement income to employees, or

(ii) results in a deferral of income by employees for periods extending to the termination of covered employment or beyond, regardless of the method of calculating the contributions made to the plan, the method of calculating the benefits under the plan or the method of distributing benefits from the plan . . .

The ADEA, ERISA, and the IRC contain provisions limiting the jurisdiction of each statute. Pursuant to section 4(b) of ERISA and IRC section 411(e), any IRS regulations would not apply to most state and local governmental plans, church plans, or excess benefit plans, as defined in sections 3(32), 3(33) and 3(36) of ERISA, respectively. However, to the extent that such plans' sponsors are not exempt from coverage under the ADEA, the same rules applicable under the ADEA to plans other than such plans are also applicable to governmental plans, church plans and excess benefits plans. (Participation rules for such plans are discussed in section (c), below).

Secondly, sections 11 and 12 of the ADEA set forth the jurisdictional limits on ADEA coverage. Section 11(b), for example, provides in effect that employers with fewer than twenty employees would not be covered by the ADEA. ERISA and the IRC have no such jurisdictional limits.

(c) *Participation Rules*—Section 9203 of OBRA sets forth rules relating to maximum age conditions for participation in pension plans (age-related exclusion from participation is no longer permitted). Although that section amended ERISA and the IRC, but not the ADEA, the Commission believes such participation rules have equal validity with regard to the ADEA. See the 1979 Interpretative Bulletin, 29 C.F.R. § 860.120(f)(1)(iv)(A), implementing a consistent approach regarding ERISA participation rules and ADEA enforcement. Accordingly, a violation of the section 9203 participation rules would be considered a violation of section 4(a)(1) of the ADEA, whether or not the pension plan is excluded from IRC coverage by IRC section 411(e). These rules do not address the validity of vesting requirements in ERISA section 4(b) plans which do not comply with the standards set in IRC section 411(a).

(d) *Scope of Section 4(i)*—Section 4(i)(4) of the ADEA provides that compliance with the requirements of section 4(i) with regard to benefit accruals under a pension plan satisfies all pension benefits accrual requirements in section 4 of the ADEA. Accordingly, after the effective date of section 4(i), sections 4(a)(1) and 4(f)(2) will no longer apply to such benefit accrual issues.

Explanation Of Provisions

Section 9201 of OBRA added section 4(i)(1)(A) to the ADEA to provide rules for continued accruals under defined benefit plans beyond normal retirement age and added section 4(i)(1)(B) to provide rules for allocations to the accounts of participants in defined contribution plans without regard to age.

Effective for plan years beginning after December 31, 1987, section 4(i)(1)(A) provides the general rule that it shall be unlawful for an employer, an employment agency, or a labor organization, or any combination thereof, to establish or maintain a defined benefit plan under which an employee's benefit accrual is ceased, or the rate of an employee's benefit accrual is reduced, because of the employee's age. Similarly, effective for plan years beginning after December 31, 1987, section 4(i)(1)(B) provides that a defined contribution plan will not be in compliance with the ADEA if allocations to an employee's account are ceased, or the rate at which allocations to an employee's account is reduced, because of the attainment of any age.

Section 4(i)(2) provides that a pension plan will not be treated as failing to satisfy the general rule in section 4(i)(1) merely because the plan contains a limitation on the maximum number of years of service or participation that are taken into account in determining benefits under the plan or merely because the plan contains a limitation on the amount of benefits a participant will receive under the plan, as long as such a limitation is not on acount of age. The proposed regulations provide that these limitations apply to both defined benefit plans and defined contribution plans (including target benefit plans).

Section 4(i)(3) provides that, with respect to an employee who, as of the end of a plan year, has attained normal retirement age under a defined benefit plan, certain adjustments may be made to the benefit accrual for the plan year if the plan distributes benefits to the employee during the plan year or if the plan adjusts the amount of the benefits payable to take into account delayed payment.

Section 4(i)(4) provides that compliance with the requirements of section 4(i) with regard to a pension plan shall constitute compliance with the requirements of section 4 relating to pension benefit accruals under such plan. The provisions of sections 4(a)(1) and 4(f)(2) will no longer apply to such accruals.

Section 4(i)(5) provides that the Secretary of the Treasury shall prescribe regulations relating to the treatment of highly compensated employees.

Section 4(i)(6) provides that a pension plan will not be treated as failing to satisfy the general rule of section 4(i)(1) merely because the subsidized portion of an early retirement benefit is disregarded in determining benefit accruals under the plan.

Section 4(i)(7) provides that the Secretary of the Treasury shall prescribe regulations coordinating the requirements of section 4(i)(1) with the requirements of IRC sections 411(a), 404, 410, 415, and the anti-discrimination provisions of IRC subchapter D of Chapter 1 (IRC sections 401 through 425).

Section 4(i)(8) permits a pension plan to provide a "normal retirement age."

Section 4(i)(9) adopts the ERISA definitions of such terms as "employee pension benefit plan", "defined benefit plan," and "defined contribution plan." In addition, the term "target benefit plan" shall have the

same meaning as provided in IRS regulations under IRC section 410. List of Subjects in 29 C.F.R. Part 1625:

Advertising, Aged, Employee benefit plans, Equal employment opportunity, Retirement.

Substantive Rules

Therefore, it is proposed that 29 C.F.R. Part 1625 is amended as follows:

PART 1625—[AMENDED]

1. The authority citation for Part 1625 continues to read as follows:

Authority: 81 Stat. 602; 29 U.S.C. § 621; 5 U.S.C. § 301; Secretary's Order No. 10-68; Secretary's Order No. 11-68; and Sec. 2, Reorg. Plan No. 1 of 1978, 43 FR 19807.

2. Section 1625.21 is added to Subpart B to read as follows:

§ 1625.21 Benefits under employee pension benefit plans—Application of section 4(i) of the ADEA.—(a) *In general.* Section 4(i)(1)(A) of the ADEA provides that a defined benefit plan does not satisfy the requirements of section 4(i), if, under the plan, benefit accruals on behalf of a participant are reduced or discontinued because of the participant's age. Section 4(i)(1)(B) provides that a defined contribution plan does not satisfy the requirements of section 4(i) if, under the plan, allocations to a participant's account are reduced or discontinued because of the participant's age.

(b) *Defined benefit plans*—(1) *In general.* Under section 4(i), except as provided in paragraph (b)(2) of this section, a defined benefit plan does not satisfy the requirements of section 4(i) if, because of a participant's age, a participant's accrual of benefits is discontinued, the rate of a participant's accrual of benefits is decreased, or a participant's compensation is not taken into account in determining the participant's accrual of benefits.

(2) *Certain limitations permitted.* A defined benefit plan does not fail to satisfy section 4(i) solely because under the plan a limitation is placed on the amount of benefits a participant may accrue or a limitation is placed on the number of years of service or participation taken into account for purposes of determining the accrual of benefits under the plan. For this purpose, a limitation expressed as a percentage of compensation (whether averaged over a participant's total years of credited service or over a shorter period) is treated as a permissible limitation on the amount of benefits a participant may accrue under the plan. However, any limitation on the amount of benefits a participant may accrue under the plan and any limitation on the number of years of credited service taken into account under the plan may not be based on the attainment of any age. A limitation that is determined by reference to age or that is not determinable except by reference to age is considered a limitation based on age. For example, a plan provision that, for purposes of benefit accrual, disregards years of credited service completed after a participant becomes eligible to receive Social Security benefits is considered a limitation based on age. Whether a limitation is based on age is determined with reference to all the facts and circumstances.

(c) *Rate of benefit accruals before normal retirement age.* [RESERVED]

(d) *Certain adjustments for delayed retirement.* [RESERVED]

(e) *Benefit subsidies disregarded.* A pension plan does not fail to satisfy section 4(i)(1) and paragraphs (b) and (f) of this section solely because the subsidized portion of any early retirement benefit provided under the plan is disregarded in determining the accrual of benefits or account allocations under the plan.

(f) *Defined contribution Plans*—(1) *In general.* Under section 4(i)(1)(B), except as provided in paragraph (f)(2) of this section, a defined contribution plan will not satisfy the requirements of section 4(i), if, because of the participant's age—

(i) The allocation of employer contributions or forfeitures to the accounts of participants is discontinued,

(ii) The rate at which the allocation of employer contributions or forfeitures is made to the accounts of participants is decreased, or

(iii) The basis upon which gains, losses, or income of the trust is allocated to the accounts of participants is modified.

(2) *Certain limitations permitted.* (i) Notwithstanding paragraph (f)(1) of this section, a defined contribution plan (including a target benefit plan) does not fail to satisfy the requirements of section 4(i) solely because, for purposes of determining benefits under the plan, a limitation is placed on the total amount of employer contributions and forfeitures that may be allocated to a participant's account (for a

particular plan year or for the participant's total years of credited service under the plan) or solely because a limitation is placed on the total number of years of credited service or participation for which a participant may receive allocations of employer contributions and forfeitures. However, the limitation described in the preceding sentence may not be applied with respect to the allocation of gains, losses, or income of the trust to the account of a participant.

(ii) A defined contribution plan (including a target benefit plan) does not fail to satisfy section 4(i)(1)(B) solely because the plan limits the number of years of credited service which may be taken into account for purposes of determining the amount of, or the rate at which, employer contributions and forfeitures are allocated to a participant's account for a particular plan year.

(iii) Any limitation described in paragraph (f)(2)(i) and (ii) of this section must not be based on the attainment of any age. The provisions of paragraph (b)(2) of this section shall also apply for purposes of this paragraph (f).

(g) *Amendment reducing accruals.* Any amendment to a defined benefit plan or a defined contribution plan that reduces the rate of benefit accruals for a plan year may not vary the rate of such reduction based on the age of a participant.

(h) *Coordination with certain IRC provisions.*

[RESERVED]

(i) *Effective dates*—(1) *In general.* Except as otherwise provided in paragraph (i)(2) of this section, section 4(i) is effective for plan years beginning on or after January 1, 1988, and is applicable to an employee who is credited with at least one hour of service in a plan year to which section 4(i) applies. Accordingly, section 4(i) is not applicable to an employee who is not credited with at least one hour of service in a plan year beginning on or after January 1, 1988. Also, section 4(i) is not applicable to an employee for any plan year beginning before January 1, 1988, even if the employee is credited with at least one hour of service in a plan year beginning on or after January 1, 1988.

(2) *Collectively bargained plans.* (i) In the case of a plan maintained pursuant to one or more collective bargaining agreements, between employee representatives and one or more employers, ratified before March 1, 1986, section 4(i) is applicable for plan years beginning on or after the later of—

(A) January 1, 1988, or

(B) the date on which the last of such collective bargaining agreements terminate (determined without regard to any extension of any such agreement occurring on or after March 1, 1986). However, notwithstanding the previous sentence, section 4(i) shall be applicable to plans described in this paragraph (i)(2)(i) no later than the first plan year beginning on or after January 1, 1990.

(ii) For purposes of paragraph (i)(2)(i) of this section, the service crediting rules of paragraph (i)(1) of this section shall apply to a plan described in paragraph (i)(2)(i) of this section, except that in applying such rules the effective date determined under paragraph (i)(2)(i) of this section shall be substituted for the effective date determined under paragraph (i)(1) of this section.

(3) *Amendments to plans.* Plan amendments required by section 4(i) shall not be required to be made before the first plan year beginning on or after January 1, 1989, if the following requirements are met—

(i) the plan is operated in accordance with the requirements of section 4(i) for all periods before the first plan year beginning on or after January 1, 1989, for which such section is effective with respect to the plan; and

(ii) such plan amendments are adopted no later than the last day of the first plan year beginning on or after January 1, 1989, and are made effective retroactively for all periods for which section 4(i) is effective with respect to the plan.

Dated: November 20, 1987.

Clarence Thomas, Chairman

Equal Employment Opportunity Commission

[FR Doc. 87-27243 Filed 11-25-87; 8:45 am]

¶ 20,532F   Reserved.

Proposed regulations related to available civil penalties under ERISA Sec. 502(l) were formerly reproduced at this paragrph. The regulations were withdrawn by the PWBA, effective February 1, 1995 (May 8, 1995 60 FR 23546)].

¶ 20,532G   Reserved.

Proposed regulations on participant-directed accounts were formerly reproduced here.

The PWBA has issued final regulations which are located at ¶ 14,744.]

¶ 20,532H

Proposed regulations on 29 CFR Part 2628: Annual Financial and Actuarial Information Reporting.—Reproduced below is the text of proposed regulations on 29 CFR Part 2628 concerning annual reporting and actuarial reporting by contributing plan sponsors to the Pension Benefit Guaranty Corporation. The information must be filed if the total pension underfunding in the corporate group exceeds $50 million, if a pension contribution exceeding $1 million has been missed in any of the corporate group's pension plans, or if a minimum funding waiver in excess of $1 million has been granted to any of the corporate group's pension plans.

The proposed regulations were filed with the Federal Register on July 5, 1995, and published in the Federal Register on July 6, 1995 (60 FR 35308).

ERISA Sec. 4010.

PENSION BENEFIT GUARANTY CORPORATION

29 CFR Part 2628

RIN 1212-AA78

Annual Financial and Actuarial Information Reporting

AGENCY: Pension Benefit Guaranty Corporation.

ACTION: Proposed rule.

SUMMARY: The Pension Benefit Guaranty Corporation is proposing regulations to implement a new requirement under section 4010 of the Employee Retirement Income Security Act of 1974. Section 4010 requires controlled groups maintaining plans with large amounts of

underfunding to submit annually to the PBGC financial and actuarial information as prescribed by the PBGC.

DATE: Comments must be received on or before September 5, 1995.

ADDRESSES: Comments may be mailed to the Office of the General Counsel, Pension Benefit Guaranty Corporation, 1200 K Street, NW., Washington, DC 20005-4026, or hand-delivered to Suite 340 at the above address. Comments will be available for inspection at the PBGC's Communications and Public Affairs Department, Suite 240, 1200 K Street, NW., Washington, DC 20005-4026.

FOR FURTHER INFORMATION CONTACT: Frank H. McCulloch, Senior Counsel, Office of the General Counsel, Pension Benefit Guaranty Corporation, 1200 K Street, NW., Washington, DC 20005-4026; 202326-4116 (202-326-4179 for TTY and TDD).

SUPPLEMENTARY INFORMATION:

Background

Section 772(a) of the Retirement Protection Act of 1994 (subtitle F of title VII of the Uruguay Round Agreements Act, Pub. L. No. 103-465, 108 Stat. 4809 (1994)) added section 4010 to ERISA. Under section 4010, certain contributing sponsors and all members of their controlled groups must submit annually to the PBGC financial and actuarial information as prescribed by the PBGC in regulations.

Who Must File

Under section 4010 of ERISA, each contributing sponsor of a pension plan and each member of its controlled group is obligated to submit information to the PBGC if (1) the aggregate unfunded vested benefits of all plans maintained by the members of the controlled group exceed $50 million; (2) the conditions specified in section 302(f) of ERISA and section 412(n) of the Internal Revenue Code for imposing a lien for missed contributions exceeding $1 million have been met with respect to any plan maintained by any member of the controlled group; or (3) the Internal Revenue Service has granted minimum funding waivers in excess of $1 million to any plan maintained by any member of the controlled group, and any portion of the waivers is still outstanding. The regulation defines each entity obligated to submit information to the PBGC as a "Filer" (§ 2628.4).

"Unfunded vested benefits" for the $50 million test are determined in the same manner used to determine unfunded vested benefits for purposes of calculating the PBGC's variable rate premium (but without reference to the exemptions or special rules provided in the PBGC's premium regulation (29 CFR 2610.24)).

Information Years

The regulation introduces the concept of an Information Year for a person (§ 2628.6). The Information Year serves four purposes. First, it will help persons determine which plan years and fiscal years to use to identify Filers. Second, it will help Filers determine whether a pension plan qualifies for a filing exemption. Third, it is used to identify the information to be submitted by a Filer. Fourth, it establishes the due date for submission of required information by a Filer.

The regulation does not require a Filer to change its fiscal year or the plan year of any pension plan. Further, the regulation does not require a Filer to report financial information on any accounting period other than an existing fiscal year or to report actuarial information for any period other than the existing plan year of a pension plan.

Generally, the Information Year is the fiscal year of the Filer. If all members of a controlled group do not report financial information on the same fiscal year, the Information Year is the calendar year.

Required Submissions

Section 4010(a) of ERISA requires each Filer annually to provide to the PBGC audited financial statements and other financial and actuarial information required by regulation. Section 2628.3(b) of the regulation allows information to be submitted by a representative of a Filer so that, for example, a Filer can submit required information to the PBGC on behalf of itself and all other members of its controlled group and satisfy their obligations under the regulation.

Exemptions

A Filer is not required to submit actuarial information for a pension plan ("Exempt Plan") if, at the end of the plan year ending within the Filer's Information Year, the plan has no unfunded benefit liabilities or has fewer than 500 participants. The amount of "unfunded benefit liabilities" is determined as of the end of that plan year by subtracting the market value of plan assets, without regard to any contributions receivable, from the value of the plan's benefit liabilities. The regulation requires that the "value of benefit liabilities" be calculated as of the end of that plan year using (1) the PBGC's termination assumptions in effect at the end of that plan year and (2) plan census data as of the end of that plan year or the beginning of the next plan year. If that census data is not available, the value of benefit liabilities may be based on a projection of census data from a date within the plan year. This projection must be consistent with projections used to measure pension obligations for financial statement purposes and produce a result appropriate to the measurement date for these obligations. Adjustments to this projection process may be required where there have been significant events (such as plan amendments or curtailments) which were not reflected in the projection assumptions. Plans that have minimum funding waivers outstanding at the end of the plan year ending within the Filer's Information Year or that have any missed minimum funding

payments in any amount that were required to be made during the Information Year are not Exempt Plans.

Section 2628.4(b) requires that all single-employer plans covered by Title IV of ERISA in a controlled group, including Exempt Plans, be taken into account in determining whether a person is a Filer. For example, a contributing sponsor has two plans—Plan A with unfunded vested benefits of $45 million and more than 500 participants, and Plan B with unfunded vested benefits of $6 million and fewer than 500 participants. Because the aggregate unfunded vested benefits of the two plans will exceed $50 million, the contributing sponsor and each of its controlled group members are Filers. (Because Plan B has fewer than 500 participants, no actuarial information for the plan need be submitted.)

The PBGC also may waive some or all of the filing requirements for Filers in appropriate cases where the PBGC finds convincing evidence for such a waiver (§ 2628.5(b)). Waivers may be conditioned on the submission of substitute information or the execution of an agreement protective of plan participants and the PBGC. A Filer that seeks a waiver must file its request in writing no less than fifteen days before the applicable due date for required information.

The PBGC invites members of the public to express their views concerning other factors or criteria that could warrant additional exemptions for individual Filers, for classes of Filers, or for plans.

Information to be Submitted

Section 2628.7 describes the information that Filers must submit to the PBGC. Although each Filer is subject to the obligation to submit information on each controlled group member and plan (to the extent no exemptions apply), the regulation allows for a single consolidated filing for the controlled group.

Identifying Information

Section 2628.7(b) specifies identifying information for each Filer (the Filer's name, address, telephone number, and the Employer Identification Number (EIN), if any, assigned by the IRS) and for each pension plan (the name of the plan, EIN, and the Plan Number assigned by the plan's contributing sponsor). Also, each Filer (or one Filer for the entire controlled group) must identify all members of the controlled group and the legal relationship of each entity to the others (parent, wholly-owned subsidiary, etc.).

Actuarial Information

Section 2628.7(c) specifies the actuarial information that a Filer must provide as follows: (1) the market value of plan assets (without regard to any contributions receivable) at the end of the plan year ending within the Filer's Information Year, (2) the value of benefit liabilities as of the same date, (3) certain participant data, and (4) the actuarial valuation report ("AVR") for that plan year, which must contain or be supplemented by certain required actuarial information. Generally, this actuarial information is developed and maintained by the plan's enrolled actuary for purposes of, among other things, completing Schedule B of the plan's Form 5500. A plan's enrolled actuary must certify that all actuarial information submitted is accurate and complete

If the AVR or any of the supplementary actuarial information is not available by the due date, § 2628.7(d) allows a Filer to submit the unavailable information by an alternative date—15 days after the deadline for filing the plan's Form 5500 for the plan year ending within the Filer's Information Year (see 29 CFR 2520.104a-5(a)(2)).

Financial Information

Section 4010(a)(2) of ERISA requires each Filer to provide to the PBGC copies of audited financial statements (or, if not available, unaudited statements). Financial statements include balance sheets, income statements and cash flow statements. Under § 2628.7(e)(1)(iii), if audited or unaudited financial statements are not prepared, the Filer may satisfy the financial information requirement by submitting copies of federal tax returns for the tax year ending within its Information Year.

For most controlled group members whose financial information is combined with that of other group members, the submission of the consolidated financial statement for the group will satisfy the obligation to submit individual financial statements (§ 2628.7(e)(2)(i)). Limited financial information a group member's revenues and operating income for the Information Year, and its assets as of the end of the Information Year—is required for each contributing sponsor of a non-Exempt Plan included in such a consolidated financial statement (§ 2628.(e)(2)(ii)).

If the required financial information of a controlled group member has been filed with the Securities and Exchange Commission, or has otherwise been made publicly available, the Filer need not submit it to PBGC. Section 2628.7(e)(3) requires only that the Filer include a statement in its submission to the PBGC indicating when the information was made available to the public and where the PBGC may obtain it.

The PBGC may request additional information from any Filer to determine plan assets and liabilities and a Filer's financial status (§ 2628.7(f)). For example, after a controlled group's parent submits consolidated financial statements in accordance with § 2628.7(e)(2)(i), it proposes to sell one of its subsidiaries. In that instance, the PBGC would normally request financial information relating to the subsidiary that was to be sold. Nothing in this proposed regulation limits the PBGC's authority under section 4003 of ERISA to seek any information from a Filer by any means provided thereunder.

Previously provided information

Any information previously submitted to the PBGC need not be resubmitted. Section 2628.7(g) allows the Filer to incorporate the previous submission by reference. For example, some of the required actuarial information with respect to a Filer's plans may have already been submitted to the PBGC in a reportable event filing; the Filer can make a reference to the reportable event filing in its submission.

When To File

Under § 2628.8(a), a Filer must submit the required information to the PBGC on or before the one hundred and fifth day after the end of the Filer's Information Year. (This due date is designed to be fifteen days after the Securities and Exchange Commission's annual reporting date for public companies.) If a plan's AVR or any of the related supplementary actuarial information is not available by this due date, the Filer may submit the unavailable information by the alternative due date—15 days after the deadline for filing the plan's Form 5500 for the plan year ending within the Filer's Information Year (§ 2628.8(b)).

Filers may submit required information by mail, by overnight and express delivery services, by hand, or by other means that are acceptable to the PBGC. The PBGC invites Filers to offer suggestions regarding procedures to electronically transmit some or all of the required information.

Confidentiality

Generally, required information submitted to the PBGC by a Filer in accordance with this regulation will not be made available or disclosed to the public. This restriction on disclosure shall not apply to publicly available information. For example, if a Filer submits required information to the PBGC, part of which is also publicly available, only that information that is not publicly available will be subject to confidentiality. Further, as provided in section 4010(c) of ERISA, these confidentiality strictures shall not apply to information disclosed by the PBGC in administrative or judicial proceedings or to Congress.

Penalties for Non-Compliance

Failure to provide information to the PBGC in accordance with the requirements of this part would constitute a violation of Title IV of ERISA. Section 4071 authorizes the PEGC to assess a penalty against any person who fails, within the specified time limits, to provide material information to the PBGC. All required information under this regulation is deemed material by the PBGC. The PBGC may assess a penalty on a pension plan's contributing sponsor and on each member of its controlled group of up to $1,000 for each day for which a failure to submit required information continues. The PBGC has the right to pursue other equitable or legal remedies available to it under the law.

Effective Date

The regulation applies for Information Years ending on or after December 31, 1995.

Paperwork Reduction Act

The PBGC has submitted the collection of information requirements in this proposed regulation to the Office of Management and Budget for review under section 3504(h) of the Paperwork Reduction Act (44 U.S.C. chapter 35). The PBGC needs this information, and will use it, to identify controlled groups with severely underfunded plans, to determine the financial status of controlled group members and evaluate the potential risk of future losses resulting from corporate transactions and the need to take legal action, and to negotiate agreements under which controlled groups would provide additional plan funding. The PBGC estimates the public reporting burden for this collection of information to average 215.3 hours for each of approximately 100 controlled groups.

Comments concerning this collection of information should be submitted to the Office of Management and Budget, Office of Information and Regulatory Affairs, Room 10235, New Executive Office Building, Washington, DC 20503; Attention: PBGC Desk Officer.

E.O. 12866 and Regulatory Flexibility Act

The PBGC has determined that this action is not a "significant regulatory action" under the criteria set forth in Executive Order 12866. The provisions of this proposed regulation would implement policy decisions made by Congress in requiring Filers to provide audited financial statements and other required information annually to the PBGC. Those provisions reflect the PBGC's interpretation of the statutory standards and prescribe the form, time, and manner in which the required information should be submitted.

Under section 605(b) of the Regulatory Flexibility Act, the PBGC certifies that, if adopted, this proposed regulation would not have a significant economic impact on a substantial number of small entities. The tests for identifying Filers under section 4010(b) of ERISA limit the filing requirements to large companies and their controlled groups. With respect to many of those groups, the PBGC will obtain audited financial statements from public sources (such as the Securities and Exchange Commission), rather than require each of the companies to file the information with the PBGC. Further, the proposed regulation will exempt plans with fewer than 500 participants from the actuarial information requirements. The regulation would not require individual financial information with respect to many of the companies within controlled groups. In addition, the PEGC intends to develop the means to allow Filers to submit required information electronically. Accordingly, as provided in section 605 of the Regulatory Flexibility Act (5 U.S.C. 601, *et seq.*), sections 603 and 604 do not apply.

List of Subjects—29 CFR part 2628

Employee benefit plans, Pension Insurance, Pensions, Reporting and record keeping requirements.

For the reasons set forth above, the PBGC proposes to amend subchapter C, chapter XXVI of 29 CFR by adding a new part 2628 to read as follows:

PART 2628—ANNUAL FINANCIAL AND ACTUARIAL INFORMATION REPORTING

2628.1 Purpose and scope.

2628.2 Definitions.

2628.3 Required submission of information.

2628.4 Filers.

2628.5 Exemptions.

2628.6 Information Year.

2628.7 Required information.

2628.8 Due date and filing with the PBGC.

2628.9 Date of filing.

2628.10 Confidentiality of information submitted.

Authority: 29 U.S.C. 1302(b)(3); 29 U.S.C. 1310

§ 2628.1 Purpose and scope.

(a) *Purpose.* This part prescribes the procedures and the information that Filers (as described in § 2628.4(a) of this part) must submit annually to the PBGC under section 4010 of the Act.

(b) *Scope.* This part applies to Filers for any Information Year ending on or after December 31, 1995.

§ 2628.2 Definitions.

For purposes of this part—

Act means the Employee Retirement Income Security Act of 1974, as amended.

Code means the Internal Revenue Code of 1986, as amended.

Contributing sponsor means a person who is a contributing sponsor as defined in section 4001(a)(13) of the Act.

Controlled group means, in connection with any person, a group consisting of that person and all other persons under common control with such person, determined under part 2612 of this chapter.

Information Year means the year determined under § 2628.6 of this part.

Exempt Plan means a plan as described in § 2628.5(a) of this part.

Filer means a person who is a Filer as described in § 2628.4 of this part.

Fiscal year means, with respect to a person, the annual accounting period or, if the person has not adopted a closing date, a calendar year (*i.e.*, the year ending on December 31).

Person means an individual, partnership, joint venture, corporation, mutual company, joint-stock company, trust, estate, unincorporated organization, association, or employee organization representing any group of participants for purposes of collective bargaining.

Plan means a single-employer plan (as defined in section 4001(a)(15) of the Act) that is covered by section 4021(a) and not excluded under section 4021(b) of the Act.

Plan year means the calendar, policy, or fiscal year on which the records of a Plan are kept.

Unfunded vested benefits means the amount determined under section 4006(a)(3)(E)(iii) of the Act and § 2610.23 of this chapter (without reference to § 2610.24 of this chapter)

Value of benefit liabilities means the value of a Plan's benefit liabilities (as defined in section 4001(a)(16) of the Act), as of the end of the plan year ending within the Filer's Information Year, using:

(1) The PBGC's valuation assumptions for trusteed plans terminating as of the end of that plan year, as prescribed in 29 CFR part 2619, subpart C, and

(2) Plan census data as of the end of that plan year or the beginning of the next plan year.

If such census data are not available, a projection of plan census data from a date within the plan year must be used. The projection must be consistent with projections used to measure pension obligations of the Plan for financial statement purposes and must give a result appropriate to the measurement date for these obligations. Thus, for example, adjustments to the projection process may be required where there has been a significant event (e.g., a plan amendment or a curtailment) which has not been reflected in the projection assumptions.

§ 2628.3 Required submission of information.

(a) *General requirement.* Except as provided in § 2628.5, each person who is a Filer as described in § 2628.4(a) shall submit to the PBGC annually on or before the date specified in § 2628.8(a) all information specified in § 2628.7 of this part.

(b) *Submission by representative.* One or more Filers or other persons may act as a representative and submit the information specified in § 2628.7 on behalf of some or all Filers within a controlled group. Representatives, other than Filers, must also submit a written power of attorney signed by the Filer authorizing the representative to act on the Filer's behalf in connection with the required information.

§ 2628.4 Filers.

(a) *General.* A Filer is a contributing sponsor of a Plan and each member of the contributing sponsor's controlled group if, for an Information Year,

(1) The aggregate unfunded vested benefits of all Plans maintained by the contributing sponsor and other members of the contributing sponsor's controlled group exceed $50 million (disregarding those Plans with no unfunded vested benefits) at the end of the plan year or years ending within the Filer's Information Year;

(2) The conditions for imposition of a lien described in section 302(f)(1)(A) and (B) of the Act or section 412(n)(1)(A) and (B) of the Code have been met during the plan year ending within the Filer's Information Year with respect to any Plan maintained by the contributing sponsor or any member of its controlled group; or

(3) The Internal Revenue Service has granted a waiver or waivers of the minimum funding standards, as defined in section 303 of the Act and section 412(d) of the Code, in excess of $1 million with respect to any Plan maintained by the contributing sponsor or any member of its controlled group, and any portion thereof is still outstanding at the end of the plan year ending within the Filer's Information Year.

(b) All Plans, including any Exempt Plan as described in § 2628.5(a), maintained by members of a controlled group must be taken into account in determining the persons who are Filers under this section.

§ 2628.5 Exemptions.

(a) *Exempt Plan.* The actuarial information specified in § 2628.7(c) of this part is not required for a Plan (an "Exempt Plan") that—

(1) Has no minimum funding waivers outstanding at the end of the plan year ending within the Filer's Information Year,

(2) Has received all payments required to be made during the Information Year under section 302 of the Act and Section 412 of the Code, and

(3) Satisfies at least one of the following conditions—

(i) The Plan has no unfunded benefit liabilities, determined using the market value of assets in the Plan (without regard to any contributions receivable) at the end of the plan year ending within the Filer's Information Year and the value of benefit liabilities; or

(ii) The Plan has fewer than 500 participants as of the end of the plan year ending within the Filer's Information Year.

(b) *Waiver of information requirements.* The PBGC may waive the requirement to submit required information with respect to a Filer, a Plan, or groups thereof. The PBGC will exercise this discretion in appropriate cases where it finds convincing evidence for such a waiver, and any such waiver may be subject to conditions. A request for a waiver must be filed in writing with the PBGC at the address provided in § 2628.8(d) no later than fifteen days prior to the applicable date specified in § 2628.8 of this part, and must state the facts and circumstances on which the request is based.

§ 2628.6 Information Year.

(a) *Determinations based on Information Year.* An Information Year is used under this part to determine which fiscal year and plan year should be used to determine whether members of a controlled group are Filers (§ 2628.4) and whether a Plan is an Exempt Plan (§ 2628.5(a)), and to identify the information that a Filer must submit (§ 2628.7) and the due date for submitting that information (§ 2628.8(a)). A Filer is not required to change its fiscal year or the plan year of a Plan, to report financial information on any accounting period other than an existing fiscal year, or to report actuarial information for any plan year other than the existing plan year of a Plan.

(b) *General.* Except as provided in paragraph (c) of this section, the Information Year shall be the fiscal year of the Filer or the consolidated fiscal year of the Filer's controlled group.

(c) *Controlled groups with different fiscal years.* If members of a controlled group report financial information for different fiscal years, the Information Year shall be the calendar year. Example: Filers A and B are members of the same controlled group. Filer A has a July 1 fiscal year, and Filer B has an October 1 fiscal year. The Information Year is the calendar year. Filer A's financial information with respect to its fiscal year beginning July 1, 1995, and Filer B's financial information with respect to its fiscal year beginning October 1, 1995, must be submitted to the PBGC following the end of the 1996 calendar year (the calendar year in which those fiscal years end).

§ 2628.7 Required information.

(a) *General.* Except as otherwise provided in section 2628.5 of this part, the information to be submitted by a Filer is that specified in paragraphs (b), (c), and (e) of this section with respect to each member of the Filer's controlled group and each Plan maintained by any member of the controlled group.

(b) *Identifying information.*

(1) The name, address, and telephone number of the Filer.

(2) The nine-digit Employer Identification Number (EIN) assigned by the Internal Revenue Service to the Filer (if there is no EIN, explain).

(3) If the Filer is a contributing sponsor of a Plan or Plans—

(i) The name of each Plan.

(ii) The EIN and the three-digit Plan Number (PN) assigned by the contributing sponsor to each Plan, but—

(A) If the EIN-PN has changed since the beginning of the Information Year, the previous EIN-PN and an explanation; or

(B) If there is no EIN-PN for the Plan, an explanation.

(4) The name and address of each other member of the Filer's controlled group and the legal relationships of each (for example, parent, subsidiary).

(c) *Plan actuarial information.*

(1) The market value of Plan assets (determined without regard to any contributions receivable) at the end of the plan year ending within the Filer's Information Year.

(2) The value of benefit liabilities.

(3) Schedules or listings with the following information as of the first day of the plan year ending within the Filer's Information Year:

(i) The distribution of active participants by 5-year age and service groupings and, if benefits are based (in whole or in part) on compensation, each grouping's average compensation;

¶20,532H

(ii) The distribution of retirees by 5-year age groupings with each grouping's average benefit amounts; and

(iii) The distribution of deferred vested participants by 5-year age groupings with each grouping's average benefit amount to be paid at normal retirement age.

(4) A copy of the actuarial valuation report for the plan year ending within the Filer's Information Year that contains or is supplemented by the following information:

(i) Each amortization base and related amortization charge or credit to the funding standard account (as defined in section 302(b) of the Act and section 412(b) of the Code) for that plan year (excluding the amount considered contributed to the Plan as described in section 302(b)(3)(A) of the Act and section 412(b)(3)(A) of the Code);

(ii) The itemized development of the additional funding charge payable for that plan year pursuant to section 412(1) of the Code;

(iii) The minimum funding contribution and the maximum deductible contribution for that plan year;

(iv) The actuarial assumptions and actuarial methods used for that plan year for purposes of section 302(b) and (d) of the Act and section 412(b) and (1) of the Code (and any change in those assumptions and methods since the previous valuation and justifications for any change); and

(v) A summary of the principal eligibility and benefit provisions on which the valuation of the Plan was based (and any change(s) to those provisions since the previous valuation), along with descriptions of any benefits not included in the valuation, any significant events that occurred during that plan year, and the Plan's early retirement factors.

(5) A written certification by the Plan's enrolled actuary that, to the best of his or her knowledge and belief, the actuarial information submitted is true, correct, and complete and conforms to all applicable laws and regulations.

(d) *Alternative compliance for plan actuarial information.* If any of the information specified in paragraph (c)(4) of this section is not available by the date specified in §2628.8(a) of this part, a Filer may satisfy the requirement to provide such information by—

(1) Including a statement, with the material that is submitted to the PEGC, that the Filer will file the unavailable information by the alternative due date specified in §2628.8(b), and

(2) Filing such information and a certification by the Plan's enrolled actuary as described in paragraph (c)(5) of this section with the PBGC by that alternative due date.

(e) *Financial information.*

(1) Except as provided in paragraph (e)(2) of this section, required financial information for each controlled group member consists of—

(i) Audited financial statements for the fiscal year ending within the Information Year (including balance sheets, income statements, cash flow statements, and notes to the financial statements); or

(ii) If no audited financial statements are prepared, unaudited financial statements for the fiscal year ending within the Information Year; or

(iii) If neither audited nor unaudited financial statements are prepared, copies of federal tax returns for the tax year ending within the Information Year.

(2) If the financial information of a controlled group member is combined with the information of other group members in a consolidated financial statement, required financial information consists of—

(i) The consolidated, audited (or, if unavailable, unaudited) financial statement for the Information Year; and

(ii) For each controlled group member included in such consolidated financial statement that is a contributing sponsor of a Plan that is not an Exempt Plan, the contributing sponsor's revenues and operating income for the Information Year, and assets as of the end of the Information Year.

(3) If any of the financial information required by paragraphs (e)(1) or (e)(2) of this section is publicly available (for example, the controlled group member has filed audited financial statements with the Securities and Exchange Commission), the Filer, in lieu of submitting such information to the PBGC, may include a statement with the other information that is submitted to the PBGC indicating when such financial information was made available to the public and where the PBGC may obtain it.

(f) *Additional information.* The PBGC may, by written notification, require any Filer to submit additional actuarial or financial information that is necessary to determine Plan assets and liabilities or the financial status of a Filer. Such information must be submitted within 10 days after the date of the written notification or by a different time specified therein.

(g) *Previous submissions.* If any required information has been previously submitted to the PBGC, a Filer may incorporate such information into the required submission by referring to the previous submission.

(h) *Penalties for non-compliance.* If all of the information required under this section is not provided within the specified time limit, the PBGC may assess a separate penalty under section 4071 of the Act against the Filer and each member of the Filer's controlled group of up to $1,000 a day for each day that the failure continues. The PBGC may also pursue other equitable or legal remedies available to it under the law.

§ 2628.8 *Due date and filing with the PBGC.*

(a) *Due date.* Except as permitted under paragraph (b) of this section, a Filer shall file the information required under this part with the PBGC on or before the 105th day after the close of the Filer's Information Year.

(b) *Alternative due date.* A Filer that includes the statement specified in §2628.7(d)(1) with its submission to the PBGC by the date specified in paragraph (a) of this section must submit the actuarial information specified in §2628.7(d)(2) within 15 days after the deadline for filing the Plan's annual report for the plan year ending within the Filer's Information Year (see §2520.104a-5(a)(2) of this title).

(c) *Extensions.* When the President of the United States declares that, under the Disaster Relief Act of 1974, as amended (42 U.S.C. 5121, 5122(2), 5141(b)), a major disaster exists, the PBGC may extend the due dates provided under paragraphs (a) and (b) of this section by up to 180 days.

(d) *How to file.* Requests and information may be delivered by mail, by overnight and express delivery services, by hand, or by any other method acceptable to the PBGC, to: Corporate Finance and Negotiations Department, Pension Benefit Guaranty Corporation, 1200 K Street, N.W., Washington, DC 20005-4026.

§ 2628.9 *Date of filing.*

(a) Information filed under this part is considered filed on the date of the United States postmark stamped on the cover in which the information is mailed, if—

(1) The postmark was made by the United States Postal Service; and

(2) The document was mailed postage prepaid, properly addressed to the PBGC.

(b) If the Filer sends or transmits the information to the PBGC by means other than the United States Postal Service, the information is considered filed on the date it is received by the PBGC. Information received on a weekend or Federal holiday or after 5:00 p.m. on a weekday is considered filed on the next regular business day.

(c) In computing any period of time under this part, the day of the act or event from which the designated period of time begins to run shall not be included. The last day of the period so computed shall be included, unless it is a weekend or Federal holiday, in which event the period runs until the end of the next day that is not a weekend or Federal holiday.

§ 2628.10 *Confidentiality of information submitted.*

In accordance with §2603.15(b) of this chapter and section 4010(c) of the Act, any information or documentary material that is not publicly available and is submitted to the PBGC pursuant to this part shall not be made public, except as may be relevant to any administrative or judicial action or proceeding or for disclosures to either body of Congress or to any duly authorized committee or subcommittee of the Congress.

Issued in Washington, DC this 30th day of June, 1995.

Martin Slate,

Executive Director,

Pension Benefit Guaranty Corporation

Proposed regulations on 29 CFR Part 2611: Valuation of insurance contracts.—Reproduced below is the text of proposed regulations on 29 CFR Part 2611 to provide rules for identifying insurance contracts or contract rights that are assets of terminating pension plans and for determining their asset value.

The regulations were filed with the *Federal Register* on April 15, 1977.

ERISA Sec. 4065.

VALUATION OF PLAN ASSETS

[29 CFR Part 2611]

Proposed Amendments—Insurance Contracts

AGENCY: Pension Benefit Guaranty Corporation.

ACTION: Proposed rule.

SUMMARY: The proposed amendments create special rules for identifying insurance contracts or contract rights that are assets of terminating pension plans and for determining their asset value. These special rules are needed because the pension plan termination insurance provisions of the Employee Retirement Income Security Act of 1974 require that the assets of a covered pension plan be valued at plan termination, and the value of insurance contracts is not readily established. The basic effect of the proposed amendment is first, to provide that the value of an irrevocable promise made by an insurance company directly to a pension plan participant is not counted in the value of the pension plan's assets, and second, to provide that an insurance contract is worth the benefits it can be used to provide.

DATE: Comments due by June 2, 1977.

ADDRESS: Comments should be sent to the Office of the General Counsel, Pension Benefit Guaranty Corporation, 2020 K Street, N.W., Washington, D.C. 20006. Copies of written comments will be available for public inspection in the PBGC's Office of Communications, at the same address, between 9 a.m. and 4 p.m. Each person submitting comments should include his or her name and address, identify this notice and give reasons for any recommendations.

FOR FURTHER INFORMATION CONTACT: Judith F. Mazo, Special Counsel, Office of the General Counsel, Pension Benefit Guaranty Corporation, 2020 K. Street, N.W., Washington, D.C. 20006, 202-354-4868.

SUPPLEMENTARY INFORMATION: On May 7, 1976, the Pension Benefit Guaranty Corporation (the "PBGC") published a regulation (41 FR 18992, codified at 29 CFR Part 2611) that prescribes standards for valuing the assets of a pension plan covered under Title IV of the Employee Retirement Income Security Act of 1974 (the "Act") when the plan terminates. Under the regulation plan assets are valued at their fair market value. The preamble to the regulation noted that special valuation considerations apply to insurance contracts held as plan assets, and that PBGC would provide guidance on that issue in the future. Because an insurance contract has a unique value to a plan that is not freely transferable, traditional fair market value concepts cannot measure such a contract's value appropriately. Therefore the PBGC proposes to amend its asset-valuation regulation to provide special rules for computing the value of insurance contracts for Title IV purposes.

Several essentially technical amendments that do not affect existing substantive rules are proposed. They would restructure the present regulation and revise the language of two of its sections. Those amendments are necessary to accommodate the new rules, contained in proposed Subpart C of this part, for valuing insurance contracts. Because proposed Subpart C represents the only substantively significant aspect of the proposed amendments, the remainder of this preamble discusses that proposed Subpart exclusively.

General Approach

1. *Introduction.* A pension plan that owns an insurance contract owns the right to enforce the promises that the insurer has made in the contract. The plan's asset is the insurance contract, rather than the premiums paid to purchase the insurer's contractual obligations. Proposed Subpart C of this part ("Subpart C") measures an insurance contract's value by the value of the benefits that the contract can be used to provide, either directly or after liquidation of the contract for cash.

Subpart C covers individual and group insurance contracts issued by any company authorized to do business as an insurance carrier under State (or District of Columbia) law. Within this broad spectrum, contracts use widely varying language to define similar legal relationships. In addition, Title IV of the Act sometimes expresses uniquely statutory

ideas in words that have a different connotation when used in private insurance contracts. To avoid misleading the public and the insurance industry, Subpart C uses its own uniform terms to describe certain fundamental concepts. Those terms and the related concepts are discussed in greater detail below.

2. *What Must Be Valued.* A terminating plan's assets are primarily relevant under Title IV of the Act to the extent they can be used to meet outstanding plan liabilities. Thus § 4044(a) of the Act requires allocation of those assets that are "available to provide benefits," and employer liability under § 4062(b) of the Act is based, in part, on the "current value of the plan's assets allocable to [guaranteed] benefits * * *" For this reason, only those contractual promises that offer a means of satisfying the plan's future benefit payment obligations are included among the plan assets to be valued under Subpart C.

A plan that has distributed an insurance contract to a participant before plan termination does not own that contract on the termination date. A plan that has arranged, under group insurance contract, for an insurer to make an irrevocable commitment to pay benefits to a specific participant has in effect distributed that commitment to the participant. In either case, the plan cannot alter the insurer's direct commitment to the participant, or use the value of the commitment to provide benefits for other participants. Therefore, the value of a distributed contract or of an insurer's irrevocable commitment to a participant is not part of the value of a plan's assets under Subpart C. (If, under § 4045 of the Act, a trustee recaptures part of a distribution that was made to a participant in the form of an insurance contract or commitment, the net amount recaptured would be a plan asset. It would not, however, be part of the asset value of the plan's insurance contracts.)

The PBGC is publishing in the FEDERAL REGISTER today (42 FR 20156) proposed amendments to Part 2608 of this chapter, "Allocation of Plan Assets," to make sure that a terminating plan does not allocate its assets to benefits that are or will be paid under an insurer's irrevocable commitment.

One type of promise made to a plan by an insurer has value as a plan asset, even if its value is not part of the asset value of an insurance contract owned by the plan. In connection with the purchase of benefits or services a plan might purchase the right to receive future interest, dividends or similar payments from the insurer. Those payments can be used to provide benefits, and the right to receive that future income (called a "participation right") is a plan asset to be valued under Subpart C.

3. *Valuation Rules.* In many cases an insurance contract owned by a terminating pension plan can be used to provide benefits in two ways: the plan can either direct that the funds credited to the contract be used to buy the insurer's irrevocable commitment to pay participants' benefits, or it can cash the contract in and provide benefits with the proceeds. Under Subpart C, the value of an insurance contract is the greater of the present value of the irrevocable benefit commitments that can be purchased under the contract or the contract's liquidation value. Because insurance contracts do not invariably offer a choice between the purchase of benefit commitments or cancellation for cash, an insurance contract's asset value depends on the alternatives expressly available under the contract as of the valuation date.

Upon termination, a plan covered under Title IV of the Act must allocate its assets to provide benefits in the order prescribed by § 4044 of the Act. Therefore, for valuation purposes, the purchase of irrevocable commitments under a contract must follow the statutory order of priorities, whether or not the particular contract so provides. The cost of those irrevocable commitments is set by the contract. Under Subpart C, the present value of the benefits that can be provided through those irrevocable commitments is determined according to PBGC's rules for valuing plan benefits, which are contained in Part 2610 of this chapter.

In most cases the value of a plan's participation rights will be reflected in the asset value of an insurance contract owned by the plan. Under Subpart C, participation rights that must be valued separately are worth the value of the amount realizable by the plan, in cash or in the form of additional irrevocable benefit commitments, upon cancellation of the participation rights.

As a general rule, under Subpart C each insurance contract is valued separately, and the benefits that it can provide are determined by applying § 4044 of the Act as if the contract were the plan's only asset. If the plan owns two or more contracts that provide for the coordinated purchase of irrevocable commitments in accordance with the statutory allocation requirements, the benefits that the contracts can provide will be determined under that contractual formula. In addition, the plan administrator may elect an optional procedure by which benefits could be provided under separate contracts in any order, as long as a combined allocation of all of the plan's assets complies with the statutory priority scheme. This option is not available unless it would yield benefits worth at least as much as the plan's assets could otherwise provide and, for insufficient plans, unless it had been arranged with the insurer before the plan termination date. To take advantage of the optional valuation procedure the plan administrator must demonstrate exactly how the combined allocation will meet Subpart C's requirements.

Basic Concepts

1. *Irrevocable Commitment.* Whether a particular commitment made by an insurer is irrevocable depends on the specific contract language. For example, a retired participant may be "eligible" to receive benefits from an insurer but not contractually "entitled" to continue receiving them, because the contract requires an additional premium payment before the entitlement arises. A contract provision limiting the insurer's liability to those benefits for which the insurer actually receives payment could create a similar problem, if by the plan termination date the funds held under the contract had dropped below the level necessary to cover the cost of annuities for participants who had begun receiving benefits from the insurer. If an insurer claims the right to cut back benefits to any participant in that situation, that would indicate that all similar benefit payment obligations of the insurer under that contract are fully revocable.

An insurance contract might specifically identify a portion of the insurer's commitment as irrevocable. For example, some deposit administration group annuity contracts contain "post-funding riders," which authorize the insurer to pay full benefits to a retired participant while the participant's irrevocable annuity from the insurer is being purchased in installments after the participant's retirement. Under Subpart C, only that portion of the retiree's annuity that had been purchased from the insurer before the plan terminated would be treated as covered by an irrevocable commitment. Similarly, the insurance contract might state that annuity commitments made to certain plan participants are subject to reduction if required by the Internal Revenue Service to prevent prohibited discrimination on plan termination. Unless the benefit cut-back is in fact required, the full annuity commitment would be irrevocable.

An insurer's commitment is considered irrevocable under Subpart C even though it can be cancelled with the participant's consent, as in the case of a commitment that offers the participant an option to receive a lump sum in lieu of future benefit payments. Similarly, an insurer's commitment is not considered revocable solely because it provides for assignment of future benefit payments as authorized or required by law.

2. *Contractholder.* The contractholder is the identifiable owner of an insurance contract purchased with funds contributed to or under a plan. Although plan participants may be third-party beneficiaries of such a contract, the contractholder is the party to whom all of the insurer's promises are made directly, regardless of how that party is designated in the contract. For example, an insurance contract might identify a named corporation as "the Employer," and then define the insurer's obligations in terms of duties owed to, or rights exercisable by, the Employer. The Employer is the owner of the contract, and thus the contractholder within the meaning of Subpart C.

As all insurance contracts that are plan assets need not be held in a trust fund (see, 403(b) of the Act), the holder of a plan's insurance contract is often not a plan trustee. Nevertheless, the contractholder represents the plan's interests with regard to the insurance contract, so Subpart C treats the rights of the plan and the rights of the contractholder interchangeably.

Because a contract that has been distributed to a participant is not considered a plan asset, a plan participant who has become the owner of a contract bought by the plan is not "the contractholder" for purposes of Subpart C.

3. *Contract Assets.* Under many of the insurance contracts in which pension plans invest, the insurer agrees to make a specified amount of money available in the future to support benefit payments. Ordinarily those amounts are based to some extent on the premiums paid by the plan, and are credited to the contract in some defined form, such as the cash surrender value of an individual contract. Group contracts often contain one or more accounts to which funds that will be used to cover future plan liabilities are credited. Subpart C uses the term "contract assets" to describe the funds credited to the plan's account that are available to meet outstanding plan benefit obligations.

Under Subpart C, funds are not treated as contract assets if they have been used to purchase an irrevocable commitment from the insurer prior to the date of plan termination, or if the insurer has a contractual right to use those funds to pay for previously-issued irrevocable commitments. Money credited to the plan that must be used to pay pretermination plan debts (such as accrued but unpaid benefits to retirees who do not have an irrevocable commitment from the insurer) is also excluded from the contract assets, as are funds to which the insurer is contractually entitled in payment for administrative or other services performed on behalf of the plan. Subpart C makes clear that funds credited to the special accounts kept under some types of group contracts solely for determining the credits due under a plan's participation rights are not contract assets.

The proposed amendment includes as contract assets the additional funds that will be credited to the plan upon cancellation, as provided in the contract, of any outstanding participation rights owned by the plan under the contract. Subpart C values a plan's participation rights, to the extent they are not included in an insurance contract's asset value, at the amount realizable by the plan upon cancellation of those participation rights. An insurance contract might indicate the cancellation value of participation rights, or an insurer might be able to determine their value by comparing the cost of similar contracts issued on a non-participating basis. Nevertheless, the PBGC recognizes that in many cases it might be difficult for the contractholder to assess the reasonableness of the insurer's determination of the cancellation value of participation rights. The PBGC therefore invites public suggestions on appropriate measures that the PBGC might take to assure that a reasonable value is attributed to a plan's participation rights when those rights must be cancelled at plan termination.

4. *Present Value of Benefits.* Under Subpart C, the value of the irrevocable benefit commitments that can be bought under a contract is to be determined in accordance with Part 2610 of this chapter "Valuation of Plan Benefits" (at present, proposed Part 2610, 41 FR 48499, November 3, 1976). That part sets forth actuarial factors and assumptions, which are periodically revised, to be used to determine the present value of plan benefits. Proposed § 2610.3(c) contains a special valuation rule for determining plan sufficiency and allocating plan assets under proposed Part 2615 of this chapter, "Determination of Sufficiency" (41 FR 48504, November 3, 1976). Under proposed § 2611.8, proposed § 2610.3(c) would apply to determine the asset value of an insurance contract for purposes of proposed Part 2615 as well.

This means that, for a plan that does not receive a Notice of Inability to Determine Sufficiency under proposed Part 2615, an insurance contract's value will be measured in part by the actual cost to the plan of purchasing in the private sector the benefits that the contract could provide. As that cost may have changed by the date that assets must be distributed under proposed § 2615.6(d), a revaluation for allocation purposes may be necessary. For all other plans, the value of the benefits that can be provided by an insurance contract will be determined at PBGC rates applicable for the valuation date, and the contract's value as of the plan termination date will be used for all purposes under Title IV of the Act.

Under customary contract terms, an individual insurance contract cannot be converted into an irrevocable commitment for the benefit of anyone other than the participant covered under the contract. Since each contract held by a plan is valued as if it were the plan's only asset, benefits under most individual contracts cannot be allocated in accordance with § 4044 of the Act. Contract liquidation would therefore be the only acceptable valuation alternative available, unless the plan administrator elects the optional valuation procedure.

5. *Cash Settlement Value.* The contractholder's choices with respect to disposition of contract assets upon discontinuance of an insurance contract are labelled "settlement options" in Subpart C. The value of an option that requires a cash payment by the insurer is its "cash settlement value." Under Subpart C, the greatest cash settlement value (expressly available under the contract as of the valuation date) is compared to the present value of benefits that can be provided under a contract to determine the contract's value as a plan asset.

Individual insurance contracts usually offer one option that entails a cash payment: the cancellation of the contract in return for its cash surrender value, less any outstanding policy loans. A group contract might include several options, depending on whether the cash is withdrawn immediately or in installments. Under the Subpart C, the value of a cash installment option is its fair market value, that is, the amount a willing buyer would pay a willing seller for the right to receive those future payments from the insurance company.

Insurance contracts frequently authorize the transfer of funds to an alternative funding agent, usually upon certification that the transfer will not impair the plan's tax qualification. A terminating plan might wish to exercise that right in order to purchase annuities from another insurer. If the PBGC has become trustee of a terminating plan, it might choose to have the funds transferred to a custodian bank. The cash settlement options to be considered in determining a contract's asset value under Subpart C include the option to have funds transferred to such alternative funding agents, as well as provisions for other types of cash payments.

Many insurance contracts give the insurer some discretion in calculating the cash amount available under settlement options. The PBGC anticipates that most insurers will be fair and reasonable in interpreting and implementing their contracts, and will not discriminate against small employers in discharging their contractual obligations. The PBGC invites suggestions from the public on the need for special safeguards, and the type of safeguards that PBGC might adopt, in this context.

In consideration of the foregoing, it is proposed to amend Part 2611 of Chapter XXVI of Title 29, Code of Federal Regulations by:

§ 2611.2-2611.5 [Redesignated]

1. Redesignating §§ 2611.2-2611.5 as follows:

Old § 2611.2—§ 2611.5.

Old § 2611.3—§ 2611.6.

Old § 2611.4—§ 2611.2.

Old § 2611.5—§ 2611.7.

2. Revising paragraph (a) of § 2611.1 as follows:

§ 2611.1 Purpose and scope.

(a) This part sets forth standards for valuing plan assets in connection with the determination of plan asset sufficiency under section 4041(b) of the Act, the allocation of plan assets under section 4044 of the Act and the determination of employer liability under § 4062 of the Act.

* * *

3. Revising § 2611.6 as follows:

§ 2611.6 Valuation of plan assets.

Except as provided in Subpart C of this part, plan assets shall be valued at their fair market value on the valuation date, based on the method of valuation that most accurately reflects such fair market value.

4. Designating §§ 2611.1 and 2611.2 as "Subpart A General;" designating §§ 2611.5-2611.7 as "Subpart B—Assets Other Than Insurance Contracts;" and adding a new Subpart C as follows:

Subpart C—Insurance Contracts

Sec.

2611.10	Definitions.
2611.11	Plan assets.
2611.12	Value of insurance contracts.
2611.13	Contract assets.
2611.14	Value of participation rights.

Appendix A—Examples: Valuation of insurance contracts.

Authority: Secs. 4002(b)(3), 4041, 4044, 4062(b)(1)(B), Pub. L. 93-406; 88 Stat. 1004, 1020-21, 1025-27, 1029 (29 U.S.C. 1302(b)(3), 1341(b), 1344, 1362(b)(1)(B)).

§ 2611.10 Definitions.

For purposes of this subpart, "Act" means the Employee Retirement Income Security Act of 1974, 29 U.S.C. 1001 et seq.

"Cash settlement value" means the value of any settlement option that requires a cash payment by the insurer.

"Contractholder" means the owner of an insurance contract purchased with funds contributed to or under a plan. References in this subpart to a plan's interests, obligations or rights under an insurance contract include the interests, obligations or rights of the contractholder. A participant who has received an insurance contract from or under a plan is not a "contractholder" for purposes of this subpart.

"Insurance contract" or "contract" means a valid written agreement between an insurer and a contractholder pursuant to which the insurer agrees to perform services including the payment of specified benefits or their equivalent in return for the payment of premiums or similar consideration. References in this subpart to "an insurance contract" include more than one contract, unless the plural is clearly inappropriate in this context.

"Insurer" means a company authorized to do business as an insurance carrier under the laws of a State or the District of Columbia.

"Irrevocable commitment" means an insurer's obligation to pay benefits or their equivalent to a named plan participant, which cannot be cancelled under the terms of the insurance contract without the consent of the participant (except for fraud or mistake) and which is legally enforceable by the participant. An otherwise irrevocable commitment that authorizes the assignment of benefit payments as permitted or required by law is an irrevocable commitment.

"Participation right" means a plan's right under an insurance contract to receive future dividends, rate credits, interest, experience credits or other earnings from the insurer.

"Participant" means a person who is or has been a participant as defined under the terms of a plan, and includes the beneficiary of a plan participant.

"PBGC" means Pension Benefit Guaranty Corporation.

"Plan" means a pension plan to which section 4021 of the Act applies.

"Plan termination date" means the termination date established under section 4048 of the Act.

"Present value of benefits" means the present value determined in accordance with Part 2610 of this chapter, as applicable for the valuation date.

"Settlement options" means the alternatives available to the contractholder under the express terms of an insurance contract, as of the valuation date, with respect to disposition of contract assets upon discontinuance of the insurance contract.

§ 2611.11 Plan assets.

For purposes of this subpart, the following are plan assets on the date of plan termination:

(a) An insurance contract purchased with funds contributed to or under the plan, if on the date of plan termination the contract has not been distributed to a participant and the insurer's obligations under the contract have not been cancelled.

(b) Participation rights under any insurance contract purchased with funds contributed to or under the plan, to the extent the value of those participation rights is not included in the value of an insurance contract that is a plan asset.

§ 2611.12 Value of insurance contracts.

(a) *General.* The value of an insurance contract is the greater of:

(1) The contract's greatest cash settlement value, or

(2) The present value of the benefits that can be provided under the contract by application of the contract assets to the purchase of benefits in accordance with the order of priorities prescribed by section 4044 of the Act.

(b) *Exclusive plan asset test.* Except as provided in paragraph (d) of this section, the benefits that can be provided under the contract shall be determined as if each insurance contract that is a plan asset were the plan's only asset on the date of plan termination. If two or more insurance contracts owned by a plan expressly provide a basis for coordinated allocation of contract assets in conformance with § 4044 of the Act, the benefits that can be provided under the contracts shall be determined as prescribed by the contracts.

(c) *Cash settlement value.* (1) The value of a settlement option requiring an immediate, lump sum cash payment by the insurer is the dollar amount of the cash payment.

(2) The value of a settlement option requiring cash payments by the insurer in installments is the fair market value, determined in accordance with Subpart B of this part, of the right to receive that stream of future payments.

(d) *Optional valuation procedure.* (1) When an insurance contract is not a plan's only asset on the plan termination date, the plan administrator may value the contract by applying the contract assets to purchase benefits under the insurance contract without regard to the order of priorities prescribed by section 4044 of the Act, if the plan administrator demonstrates to the PBGC that:

(i) All of the plan's assets on the date of plan termination, taken together, can be allocated in a manner that complies with section 4044 of the Act;

(ii) Under the combined allocation, the plan's assets will provide benefits with a total present value that equals or exceeds the total present value of the benefits that could otherwise be provided by the plan's assets, and

(iii) In the case of a plan that receives a Notice of Inability to Determine Sufficiency under Part 2615 of this chapter, arrangements for a specific combined allocation that satisfies section 4044 of the Act were made prior to the plan termination date.

(2) A plan administrator who elects the valuation procedure described in paragraph (c)(1) of this section must furnish the PBGC with evidence, including supporting computations, that the optional valuation meets all of the requirements of that paragraph.

(3) When a plan administrator elects the valuation procedure described in paragraph (c)(1) of this section, the total value of the plan's assets is the total present value of the benefits that can be provided through the combined allocation of the plan's assets pursuant to that paragraph.

§ 2611.13 Contract assets.

(a) Contract assets are the funds credited to an insurance contract as of the plan termination date that are available to provide benefits, including funds that will become available to provide benefits upon the exercise of the contractholder's rights under the insurance contract to cancel any participation rights held by the plan under the insurance contract.

(b) Contract assets do not include:

(1) Funds that the insurer is entitled, under the insurance contract, to withdraw in payment for an irrevocable commitment made by the insurer prior to the date of plan termination;

(2) Funds that the insurer is entitled, under the insurance contract, to withdraw to satisfy liabilities of the plan that became due and owing prior to the date of plan termination;

(3) Funds that the insurer is entitled, under the insurance contract, to withdraw to pay for administrative or other services performed by the insurer; and

(4) Funds that have been paid to the insurer prior to the date of plan termination in return for benefits or services, which are credited to an account under the contract solely for the purpose of computing amounts payable pursuant to the plan's participation rights.

§ 2611.14 Value of participation rights.

The value of a participation right is the greater of:

(a) The dollar amount payable by the insurer upon cancellation of the participation right as of the plan termination date, or

(b) The present value of the additional benefits that the insurer offers to provide, pursuant to irrevocable commitments, upon cancellation of the participation right as of the plan termination date.

Appendix A—Examples: Valuation of Insurance Contracts

The following examples assume that no amounts are recapturable on behalf of the plan under 4045 of the Act.

(a) *Trusteed plan.* Contributions to the ABC plan are deposited in a trust fund, through which the plan's assets are invested in bonds and common stocks. From time to time the trustee uses plan funds to purchase an irrevocable commitment from an insurer for a participant who retires or leaves employment with vested rights under the plan. For purposes of this part, that irrevocable commitment is the property of the participant and is not a plan asset. If the plan has participation rights based on the purchase of that irrevocable commitment, they are plan assets to be valued under § 2611.14 of this part. The plan's other assets will be valued in accordance with Subpart B of this part.

(b) *Fully insured plan.* The trustees of the DEF Plan invest the plan's assets exclusively in individual insurance contracts, each covering a named participant. A portion of the annual premium paid to the insurer is credited to the cash surrender value of the contract, which accumulates cash value at a rate designed to amortize the cost of an annuity for the covered participant at retirement. The insurer makes no irrevocable commitment until an insurance contract is distributed to a participant, either directly or after conversion to an annuity. For purposes of this part, once an insurance contract is distributed to a participant it is no longer a plan asset, although any participation rights the plan may have in distributed contracts are plan assets.

The cash surrender values of the individual contracts held by the plan on its termination date are the contract assets. Although an individual contract may provide for conversion to an annuity at contractually-specified rates, each contract may only be used to purchase benefits for the participant named in the contract. As the application of the contract assets to purchase benefits through this contractual mechanism would not comply with § 4044 of the Act, under § 2611.12(a) the value of the contracts as plan assets is the sum of their individual cash surrender values on the date of plan termination. The plan administrator could elect the optional valuation procedure described in § 2611.12(d) if that would yield an equal or higher total value for the plan assets.

(c) *Split-funded plan.* (1) The trustee of the GHI Plan uses part of the plan's assets to purchase individual life insurance contracts covering each participant, and holds the remaining plan assets in a "side fund," which it invests in equity and fixed-income securities. When a participant with vested rights leaves employment before retirement age, the trustee gives the participant the insurance contract on his or her life plus a share of the side fund. For participants who retire, the trustee purchases irrevocable commitments from the insurer, using the cash value of the insurance contracts on their lives supplemented as needed by withdrawals from the side fund. The trustee is the contractholder, who owns the individual contracts of insurance on active participants. Those contracts may be cancelled at the contractholder's option even though a covered participant has vested rights under the plan.

For purposes of this part, the assets of the GHI Plan consist of the side fund, the individual insurance contracts held by the trustee, and any participation rights held by the plan. As in paragraph (b) of this Appendix, the value of the individual life insurance contracts is the sum of their cash surrender values on the plan termination date. The assets in the side fund are valued in accordance with Subpart B of this part.

(2) The trustees of the JKL Plan pay all contributions received under the plan to an insurer, which issues individual life insurance contracts to the trustees and credits the remainder of the money received from the plan to a side fund managed by the insurer. As liquidation of the side fund is subject to contractual restraints, the side fund must be valued in accordance with § 2611.8 (a) and (c), rather than Subpart B of this part.

(d) *Deposit administration contract.* The sole asset of the MNO Plan is a group insurance contract of the deposit administration ("DA") type, which the employer purchases directly from the insurer with funds contributed under the plan. The insurer credits premiums (contributions) to an account maintained under the contract (the "active life fund") in which funds for the benefits of active participants accumulate. The insurer makes an irrevocable commitment when a participant retires, withdrawing the amount needed to purchase the promised benefits from the active life fund, pursuant to the contract, at that time.

The active life fund contains the bulk of the contract assets. Because the plan has participation rights based on previously purchased benefits, the insurer maintains an experience account under the contract to compute the earnings due the plan. Under paragraph (b)(4) of § 2611.13, the experience account would not contain contract assets, except for amounts owed to the plan that had not yet been credited to the active life fund.

Under § 2611.13(b)(2), the balance in the active life fund must be reduced to reflect outstanding claims against the fund (e.g., accrued benefits payable to retirees that are chargeable to the fund under the contract). The fund balance may also be increased, pursuant to § 2611.13(a), as the result of liquidation of any separate investment accounts maintained for the plan under the contract or cancellation of the plan's participation rights. The value of the participation rights is included in the contract assets even though the contract states that the earnings may be paid to the employer, because the employer is the contractholder.

Under § 2611.12, the contract is valued by:

(1) Determining the benefits that can be provided by applying the assets in the active life fund (adjusted as described above) to the purchase of irrevocable commitments from the insurer at rates specified in the contract, in accordance with the benefit priority categories established by § 4044 of the Act, and

(2) Comparing the present value of the benefits so purchased with the most valuable cash settlement option available on the date of plan termination.

(e) *Immediate participation guarantee ("IPG") contract.* The Board of Trustees of the PQR Plan has invested all contributions made to the plan in an IPG contract, which is a specialized form of DA contract that enables the contractholder (the Board of Trustees) to share directly in the insurer's experience gains and losses on the plan's retired and terminated-vested participants. Under the plan's IPG contract the insurer issues irrevocable commitments to participants as they retire or leave employment with vested rights under the plan. However, the insurer does not withdraw the cost of the benefits covered by the irrevocable commitments until the contract is discontinued. The insurer maintains an IPG account under the contract, which contains funds to support benefits currently payable to retired participants as well as active participants' future benefits.

Because the PQR Plan's insurance contract entitles the insurer to withdraw from the IPG account the amount necessary to pay for previously issued irrevocable commitments at the date of contract discontinuance, under paragraph (b)(2) of § 2611.13 those amounts are not included in the contract assets. Once the withdrawals are made the discontinued IPG contract operates like a conventional DA contract, and would be valued in the manner described in paragraph (d) of this Appendix.

(f) *Group deferred annuity contract.* The trustees of the RST Plan own a group deferred annuity contract, under which the premiums paid by the plan are used to purchase deferred annuities for active participants in increments as benefits accrue. Before the participants' rights to benefits become vested under the plan, the insurer's commitment to pay the annuities can be revoked. For purposes of this part, the contract assets under the RST Plan's group deferred annuity contract consist of: (1) the cash surrender values of the deferred annuity units purchased to cover benefits that are not vested on the earlier of the date of discontinuance of the contract or the plan termination date, and (2) any participation rights held by the plan.

(g) *Optional valuation procedure.* The XYZ Plan owns two DA contracts, No. 111 and No. 222, each issued by the same insurer and held by the employer as contractholder. In addition, a corporate trustee holds $100,000 worth of plan assets, invested in corporate bonds. Under § 2611.12 (a), (b) and (c), the value of Contract No. 111 is determined by computing the present value of the benefits that could be provided by applying the contract assets to the purchase of benefits in the priority sequence prescribed by § 4044 of the Act, beginning with the first priority category, and comparing that figure with the greatest amount realizable under a settlement option. The value of Contract No. 222 is determined in the same manner. So valued, each contract is worth $100,000.

However, because the rates for deferred annuities are different under the two contracts, benefits in the statutory fourth priority category may be purchased more cheaply from the insurer under Contract No. 222 than under Contract No. 111. If the plan administrator agrees to purchase additional benefits from the insurer with the funds held by the corporate trustee, the insurer is willing to allow the plan to use all of the contract assets under Contract No. 222 to purchase category four benefits, applying the Contract No. 111 contract assets plus the trust fund money to higher priority benefits. This arrangement will enable the plan assets to provide $400,000 worth of benefits.

The plan administrator may elect the optional valuation procedure described in § 2611.12(d), by demonstrating to the PBGC that the result would comply with § 4044 of the Act and would equal or increase the total amount of benefits that the plan's assets can provide. If the plan's assets would still not be sufficient to satisfy all guaranteed benefits, in order to qualify for the optional valuation procedure, the plan administrator must demonstrate to the PBGC that the arrangement with the insurer had been worked out prior to the date of plan termination.

Issued in Washington, D.C. this 8th day of April 1977.

Ray Marshall,

Chairman, Board of Director, Pension Benefit Guaranty Corporation.

Issued on the date set forth above, pursuant to a resolution of the Board of Directors authorizing its Chairman to issue this Notice of Proposed Rulemaking.

Henry Rose,

Secretary, Pension Benefit Guaranty Corporation.

[FR Doc. 77-11226 Filed 4-15-77; 8:45 am]

¶ 20,533A   Reserved.

Proposed rules that would have imposed certain notice requirements on plan administrators of plans undergoing standard terminations were formerly reproduced here.

The final regulations are at ¶ 15,448P—¶ 15,448S.]

¶ 20,533B

Proposed regulations on 29 CFR Part 2610: Premium payment requirements: Simplification.—The PBGC has issued newly proposed rules that are designed to reduce the burden and administrative costs of complying with the PBGC premium payment requirements for most of the defined benefit pension plans that it insures.

The proposals were filed with the *Federal Register* on April 9, 1992, and published in the *Federal Register* (57 FR 12666) on April 10, 1992.

[Caution: The PBGC has extended the effective date of the proposed amendment to the premium payment regulations by one year to plan years beginning after 1993. The deferred effective date extends the comment period until November 16, 1992. The announcement of the extended effective date was published in the *Federal Register* (57 FR 42910) on September 17, 1992.]

[NOTE: The PBGC has adopted final regulations relating to Prop. Regs. § 2610.25(b)(1), § 2610.25(b)(2)(ii), and § 2610.25(b)(3)(i). The change in the premium filing due date was originally proposed for the 1993 plan year. However, the finalized change is effective beginning with the 1999 plan year. PBGC Final Reg. § 4007.11 was published in the Federal Register on December 14, 1998 (63 FR 68684) and is at ¶ 15,371J.]

ERISA Sec. 4006 and ERISA Sec. 4007.

PENSION BENEFIT GUARANTY CORPORATION

29 CFR Part 2610

RIN 1212-AA58

Payment of Premiums

AGENCY: Pension Benefit Guaranty Corporation.

ACTION: Proposed rule.

SUMMARY: This is a proposed amendment to the Pension Benefit Guaranty Corporation's regulation on Payment of Premiums (29 CFR part 2610). Comments on the existing regulation by premium payers in recent years and studies by PBGC staff have persuaded the PBGC that the regulation can be simplified to reduce the public burden of compliance and the PBGC's burden of administration. The proposed amend-

ment would make a number of simplifying changes suggested by those comments and studies.

For example, the proposed amendment would replace the existing alternative calculation method with a new simplified filing method using tables of adjustment factors instead of formulas (and would place restrictions on the new method's use by large plans). The definition of the term "participant" in the regulation would be changed to agree with that used for the Form 5500 series annual report. The proposed amendment would defer the final filing due date (so that it would be closer to the extended Form 5500 due date), raise the number of participants a plan must have in order to be required to make the early premium payment (so that fewer plans would have to file twice a year), and eliminate both penalties and interest on early payments that equal at least a definitely determinable amount (so that both estimates and special safe harbor rules would be unnecessary). It would also accelerate the early filing due date to an earlier date in the premium payment year and widen the scope of the early payment to cover the variable rate, as well as the flat rate, portion of the premium.

DATES: Comments on the proposed amendment must be received on or before May 26, 1992.

ADDRESSES: Comments may be mailed to the Office of the General Counsel (22500), Pension Benefit Guaranty Corporation, 2020 K Street, NW., Washington DC, 20006-1860, or delivered to suite 7200 at that address between 9 a.m. and 5 p.m. on business days. Written comments will be available for public inspection at the PBGC's Communications and Public Affairs Department, suite 7100 at the same address, between 9 a.m. and 4 p.m. on business days.

FOR FURTHER INFORMATION CONTACT: Harold J. Ashner, Assistant General Counsel, or Deborah C. Murphy, Attorney, Office of the General Counsel (22500), Pension Benefit Guaranty Corporation, 2020 K Street, NW., Washington DC 20006-1860; 202-778-8850 (202-778-1958 for TTY and TDD). (These are not toll-free numbers.)

SUPPLEMENTARY INFORMATION:

Background

Section 4006 of the Employee Retirement Income Security Act of 1974 ("ERISA") sets forth the premium rates to be charged by the Pension Benefit Guaranty Corporation ("PBGC"). Section 4007 of ERISA makes the premiums payable "at the time, and on an estimated, advance, or other basis, as determined by the [PBGC]," and provides for the imposition of interest and penalties on premiums not timely paid. Pursuant to these provisions and to section 4002(b)(3) of ERISA, the PBGC has issued its regulation on Payment of Premiums (29 CFR part 2610). The regulation and related forms and instructions describe in detail how to compute and pay premiums, interest, and penalties.

Under section 4006, the multiemployer plan premium for a premium payment year beginning after September 26, 1988, is $2.60 per participant. The single-employer plan premium for a premium payment year beginning after 1987 is composed of a flat rate per capita assessment and a variable rate assessment that is based on the value of a plan's unfunded vested benefits and is also determined on a per-participant basis. The flat rate assessment (for post-1990 years) is $19 per participant.

The basic formula for the variable rate assessment for each participant (for post-1990 years) is $9 for each $1,000 (or fraction thereof) of a plan's unfunded vested benefits (determined as of the last day of the year before the premium payment year) with that product divided by the number of participants in the plan as of that same date. This variable rate assessment is subject to a statutory ceiling of $53 per participant, resulting in a maximum per participant premium of $72.

The formula for computing the variable rate assessment is based, in large part, on the determination of the plan's unfunded vested benefits, defined by statute as the amount that would be the plan's "unfunded current liability" (within the meaning of ERISA section 302(d)(8)(A)) as of the close of the preceding plan year, subject to two qualifications, viz., that only vested benefits are taken into account in the calculation, and that the interest rate used in valuing vested benefits must equal 80% of the annual yield on 30-year Treasury securities for the month preceding the month in which the plan year begins.

The premium regulation provides two methods for determining the amount of a plan's unfunded vested benefits. Under the "general rule" (§2610.23(a)), an enrolled actuary must determine the amount of the plan's unfunded vested benefits as of the last day of the plan year preceding the premium payment year based on the plan's provisions and population as of that date, and must certify that the determination was made in a manner consistent with generally accepted actuarial principles and practices. Under the "alternative calculation method" (§2610.23(c)), the plan administrator must calculate the amount of the plan's unfunded vested benefits based on certain data from the plan's Form 5500 Schedule B for the plan year preceding the premium payment year, using formulas specified in the regulation. The regulation also provides a number of exemptions and special rules regarding the variable rate portion of the premium.

While the current premium regulation exhibits a degree of complexity, much of this is simply a reflection of the complexity inherent in the statute's variable rate premium provisions, as well as the PBGC's desire to reduce compliance burdens and costs as much as possible by providing options, exemptions, and special rules to simplify or, in some cases, eliminate calculation requirements. Nevertheless, PBGC staff studies have identified a number of possible simplifying changes that would be implemented by this proposed amendment. The PBGC envisions making these proposed changes effective generally for premium payment years beginning after 1992, contingent on implementation of a

new computerized premium accounting system by the end of 1992. The proposed changes are discussed below.

General Provisions

The premium regulation is divided into three subparts. Subpart A (General Provisions) contains rules that apply generally to both single-employer and multiemployer plans for all plan years (although some of these rules are more limited in scope or take different forms depending on the plan year involved). Subpart B currently contains rules governing only single-employer plans for plan years beginning after 1987; the rules in Subpart C currently cover single-employer plans for plan years beginning before 1988 and multiemployer plans for all plan years.

The proposed amendments would make a minor change to the general organization of the premium regulation by transferring the rules governing multiemployer plan premiums for premium payment years beginning after 1987 from subpart C to subpart B. This would avoid duplication (in subparts B and C) of several provisions that apply to both single-employer and multiemployer plans for post-1987 years only, consolidate current (that is, post-1987) rules in subpart B, and permit most filers to ignore subpart C completely. A minor rewording of §2610.1(a) would reflect this organizational change; §§2610.21 and 2610.31 would be correspondingly reworded.

Similarly, §2610.22 (Premium rates) would be revised to include multiemployer as well as single-employer premium rate rules for the post-1987 period. Existing §2610.22(b) (dealing with new and newly covered plans) would be redesignated as §2610.22(c); a new §2610.22(b) would be added to set forth the multiemployer premium rates (now found in §2610.33(a)(1)); and §2610.22(d) would be modified to reflect the difference between the refund rules for multiemployer plans (currently set forth in §2610.33(d)) and those for single-employer plans, which form the subject of existing §2610.22(d). (The provision in existing §2610.22(c), that the prescribed premiums are payable for short as well as normal plan years, is considered obvious and would simply be removed.)

In addition, the variable rate premium cap reduction rules that make up most of existing §2610.22(a)(3)—and that apply only to premium payment years beginning before 1993—would be moved to a new paragraph (§2610.22(f)) at the end of the section because they would no longer be of current interest to most premium payers. The special rule for new and newly covered plans (moved to §2610.22(c)) would be modified to refer to both the single-employer and multiemployer premium rate provisions (in §2610.22(a) and new §2610.22(b) respectively), and the parallel rule in §2610.33(b)(2) covering multiemployer plans only would be deleted.

The penalty waiver rule now in §2610.8(b)(5) would be moved to §2610.8(b)(4). This rule, which waives penalties accruing within 30 days after the date of a PBGC bill that is paid within the 30-day period, would be reworded to make its effect clearer.

(Other organizational changes, relating to substantive rule revisions, are discussed below in the context of those revisions.)

Definition of "Participant"

The wording of the PBGC's definition of "participant" in §2610.2 (Definitions) for the purpose of filing and paying PBGC premiums has differed for several years from the wording of the definition prescribed in the instructions for Form 5500. (For example, the definition in the 1990 instructions for Form 5500 excludes "nonvested former employees who have incurred the break in service period specified in the plan," while the corresponding exclusion in existing §2610.2 applies to "a non-vested former employee who has incurred a break in service the greater of one year or the break in service period specified in the plan." (Emphasis added.)) The difference in wording, coupled with uncertainty about how the two definitions might be interpreted for purposes of the two different filings, has caused concern for many plan administrators that the participant count for PBGC premiums may differ from the Form 5500 participant count in certain cases.

The amendment would redefine the term "participant" for premium payment years beginning after 1992 while retaining the existing definition for premium payment years beginning before 1993 (including those with premium filing dates in 1993). To accommodate the change, §2610.2 would be reorganized to place most of the defined terms in a new paragraph (a) and the new and old definitions of "participant" in new paragraphs (b) and (c) (respectively). In paragraph (a), definitions would be added for the terms "Form 5500" and "single-employer plan."

The new definition of "participant" in §2610.2(b) would simply adopt the definition prescribed for purposes of the Form 5500. This change would allow most premium payers to use the same participant count determined for the Form 5500 without having to worry that the difference in definitions might make the count wrong for premium purposes.

Since the Form 5500 definition may change (as it has in the past), § 2610.2(b) would refer specifically to the Form 5500 applicable to the plan year preceding the premium payment year. In general, premiums are based on the participant count for the last day of the plan year preceding the premium payment year. New and newly covered plans, and certain plans involved in mergers and spinoffs, base their premiums on the participant count as of the first day of the premium payment year, but it would be impossible to wait for the issuance of the Form 5500 for the premium payment year and still pay premiums on time. (For new plans, and newly covered plans that were not required to file Form 5500 for the plan year preceding the premium payment year, the definition the plan would use would be the one for the Form 5500 that would have been used for a plan year beginning one year before the first day of the premium payment year.)

For purposes of determining whether a plan is a "large plan" required to make an early premium payment, the participant count comes from the prior year's premium filing. For premium payment years beginning after 1993, this would generally be the same as the participant count on the Form 5500 for the year before the prior year. For example, to determine whether a plan is a "large plan" for the 1994 premium payment year, the plan administrator would note the number of participants for whom premiums had to be paid for the 1993 plan year; since that plan year would have been covered by the new definition of "participant," the participant count for premium purposes would probably have been the same as that on the 1992 Form 5500. (Exceptions would occur where, for example, a plan used the special rule for mergers and spinoffs in § 2610.10 and counted participants as of a date other than the Form 5500's participant count date.)

However, the 1993 premium payment year would be a special case, because the number of participants for whom premiums were payable for 1992 (the prior plan year) might be different than the 1991 Form 5500 participant count (even if the dates were the same). This is because the 1992 plan year would not have been covered by the new "participant" definition—so the 1992 participant count for premium purposes would not necessarily have agreed with the participant count on the 1991 Form sponsors, were formerly reproduced at this paragraph. The final regulations appear at ¶ 15,328A—15,328G.]

Miscellaneous Filing Rules

The amendment would revise § 2610.4 to provide expressly for modification of the premium filing address in the PBGC's Annual Premium Payment Package. This would allow the PBGC to change the address quickly if necessary before completion of the formal procedure of amending the regulation.

Section 2610.5 would be revised to liberalize slightly the rule about when a premium filing or payment is considered to have been made. This rule is used to determine whether a premium filing is timely, when interest on a late payment stops accruing, etc. The current rule, which would be retained in § 2610.5(b) for premium payment years beginning before 1993, is that filings are deemed made when mailed, as evidenced by a legible U.S. Postal Service postmark, or three days before receipt by the PBGC if they do not contain a legible U.S. Postal Service postmark.

In new § 2610.5(a)(1), the proposed rule would increase the assumed transit time (between when a filing is received and when it is deemed to have been sent) from three days to five and make it applicable to all filings, including those with legible U.S. Postal Service postmarks. It would also make clear that the PBGC would accept other evidence of the date of mailing besides legible postmarks.

In addition, new § 2610.5(a)(2) would clarify that where a filing is received on the first business day following a period of one or more non-business days (Saturday, Sundays, or holidays), it would be deemed received on the first day of the non-business period—i.e., the earliest day when it might have been received but for the non-business period.

Application of the transit time assumption to filings with legible U.S.P.S. postmarks would eliminate an anomaly under the existing rule. Currently, a filing mailed one day late with a legible U.S.P.S postmark would be considered late even if it were received the next day, whereas a filing mailed a day late bearing a legible postage meter postmark (but no U.S.P.S. postmark) would be considered timely if it arrived the following day.

The new rule would be effective only for filings and payments for premium payment years beginning after 1992; thus the current rule would continue to apply (for example) to filings due in 1993 for the 1992 premium payment year.

In subpart B of the regulation, the amendment would simplify the certification that is required of fully insured plans taking advantage of the exemption from the variable rate premium under § 2610.24(a)(3). Currently, the plan administrator must certify to the plan's satisfaction of the requirements of section 412(i) of the Internal Revenue Code and regulations thereunder throughout the plan year preceding the premium payment year or (for new or newly covered plans) throughout the premium payment year up to the premium due date.

The PBGC has reconsidered these provisions in light of the general principle that liability for the variable rate premium is determined as of a single "snapshot date," rather than on the basis of a plan's status over on extended period of time. Consistent with that general principle, the PBGC has decided that the certification required of a section 412(i) plan administrator under § 2610.24(a)(3) should be limited to the "snapshot date." (This certification as of the premium "snapshot date" would be relevant only for premium purposes, and would not govern the plan's status under section 412(i) and the regulations thereunder.) Such a change would also avoid the current rule's implication that the plan administrator of a new or newly covered plan must either wait until the premium due date to file, or certify to the status of the plan for a period of time that is still in the future when the certification is made.

Since § 2610.24(e) automatically corrects § 2610.24(e) "snapshot dates" for new or newly covered plans, amended § 2610.24(a)(3) would no longer have to include an explicit special provision for such plans.

Short Plan Year Credits

The amendment would supplement the special refund rule in § 2610.22(d) with a new special credit rule for short plan years of new and newly covered plans and plans that change their plan years. Under the existing premium regulation, the refund rule in § § 2610.22(d) and 2610.33(d) is the only mechanism available to such a plan for recovering a prorated portion of the premium for the short year. The plan must prepare and submit a refund request, and the PBGC must process the request and issue the refund. Under proposed new § 2610.22(e), these two burdens would be eliminated. The plan would simply compute the credit, in the same manner as a refund under § 2610.22(d), and claim it on its premium payment form. (The refund rule under § 2610.22(d)—with some rewording to make it applicable to multiemployer as well as single-employer plans and to clarify its operation—would remain as an option.)

A new or newly covered plan would be allowed to take the credit against the short first year's premium; a plan that changed its plan year could take the credit against the premium for the following full-length year. The difference in treatment reflects differences between the two classes of plans. For a new or newly covered plan, it is the beginning of the plan year—the portion before the plan becomes effective for premium purposes—that generates the credit, and the plan knows from the start how long its first plan year will be. In contrast, changes in plan year are typically made after the beginning of what will turn out to be the short year (and often after the short year is over), and it is the end of the plan year—the portion overlapped by the following full year—that generates the credit. (By the same token, the credit rule would not apply to final short years (of terminating plans described in § 2610.22(d)(3) and (4)) because the date of the short year's end would not generally be known until it arrived and because there would be no following year's premium to apply the credit to.)

Under the proposed new credit rule, the credit could be taken against the premium for a premium payment year beginning after 1992. Accordingly, it would apply to a new or newly covered plan's short first year beginning after 1992 (since the credit would be taken against that same year's premium). For a plan changing plan years, the new rule would permit a credit to be taken against the premium for a full plan year beginning after 1992 with respect to an immediately preceding short year.

Simplified Filing Method

The alternative calculation method ("ACM") for unfunded vested benefits, provided for in current § 2610.23(c), is an easier, though less accurate, method of calculating the amount of unfunded vested benefits ("UVBs")—on which the variable rate premium is based—than the general rule described in § 2610.23(a) and (b). Whereas the general rule prescribes standards for the actuarial determination of UVBs from basic data, the ACM provides formulas (and optional tables of substitution factors that may be used in place of one expression in one of the formulas) for calculating UVBs from data reported on Form 5500 Schedule B for the prior year.

Both the general rule and the ACM yield values for UVBs as of the last day of the plan year preceding the premium payment year, the "snapshot date" for computing the variable rate premium. The Schedule B data on which the ACM is based, however, are as of the first, not the last, day of that prior year. In addition to other adjustments that may be necessary, therefore, the ACM must "bring forward" the data to the end of the prior year. Rather than bring each figure forward separately, the ACM uses the data to calculate UVBs as of the first day of the prior year, then brings just the UVB figure forward by adding interest.

The ACM begins with the values of the current liability for vested benefits reported on Schedule B as of the beginning of the plan year preceding the premium payment year. In § 2610.23(c)(1), it increases those benefit values to reflect accruals for active participants during that plan year. Then, in § 2610.23(c)(2), it adjusts the benefit values to account for any difference between the current liability interest rate (or rates) actually used to determine them (the "Funding Interest Rate(s)") and the interest rate prescribed by the statute and § 2610.23(b)(1) for premium purposes (the "Premium Interest Rate"). The adjusted vested benefit values are added together to give a single figure reflecting all adjusted vested benefits as of the first day of the plan year preceding the premium payment year.

In § 2610.23(c)(4), the ACM begins with the asset value reported on Schedule B as of the beginning of the plan year preceding the premium payment year and increases that value to reflect contributions made since the beginning of the preceding plan year. The result is an adjusted value of assets as of the beginning of that year. The difference between adjusted vested benefits as of the beginning of the year before the premium payment year and the adjusted asset value as of the same date is the UVBs as of that date. Finally, in § 2610.23(c)(5), the ACM adjusts that UVB figure by adding interest (at the Premium Interest Rate) from the first day of the year before the premium payment year (i.e., the day as of which the UVBs were calculated) to the end of that year (i.e., the day before the beginning of the premium payment year). This in effect produces a value of UVBs as of the last day of the plan year preceding the premium payment year.

Small plans (which, for this purpose, means those paying premiums for fewer than 500 participants) use this UVB value directly as the basis for determining the amount of the variable rate premium. Under § 2610.23(d), however, large plans (those paying premiums for 500 or more participants) must correct this UVB value for any significant events, as defined in § 2610.23(d), that may have occurred during the prior year (i.e., between the date of the Schedule B data and the premium "snapshot date"). (The same significant events must be taken into account under the general rule.)

The PBGC introduced the ACM, when the variable rate premium was first added to ERISA, in response to its concern that the method described in the statute for determining UVBs (which is tracked by the general rule in the regulation) would be quite expensive and time-consuming to apply, especially for smaller plans. The ACM was designed for ease of use, with the thought that it would give small plan administrators a way to calculate variable rate premiums from Form 5500 Schedule B data without the services of an actuary. Indeed, the PBGC expected most plans, including large plans, to use the ACM routinely and to resort to the more difficult general rule only when unusual circumstances made it apparent that the general rule results would be much more favorable than the ACM results.

Of course, achieving simplicity meant sacrificing accuracy. The ACM was devised on the basis of the soundest actuarial principles and most effective actuarial techniques available to be an unbiased surrogate for the general rule both in the aggregate and for most plans individually. However, the PBGC recognized that UVBs (and thus premiums) calculated with the ACM would vary from what they would be under the general rule, and would in some cases be substantially different. Weighing the expected magnitude of premium variations under the ACM against the perceived need for relief from the burdens of the general rule, the PBGC concluded that the risks arising from the ACM's inaccuracy were acceptable. Having reassessed these considerations in connection with its premium simplification efforts, the PBGC now believes that the balance has shifted. On the one hand, the major premium increase in 1991 means that the effect on premiums of any given variation in UVBs is half again as great as it was in 1988. On the other hand, a number of actuarial consulting firms report that many large plans that expect to pay variable rate premiums routinely calculate them under both the ACM and the general rule and pay the smaller amount, thus suggesting that general rule determinations are considerably less burdensome than the PBGC initially feared, at least for larger plans. Accordingly, there now appears to be cause for concern that the PBGC may be exposed to possibly significant revenue loss in individual cases where the ACM is selected over the general rule specifically because the former yields a lower premium than the latter.

In addition, it appears that the ACM is not as easy to use as the PBGC initially thought. Adjustment of the Schedule B data under the ACM requires the use of formulas with several terms and factors,

including expressions with negative and/or fractional exponents, that some small plan administrators evidently find daunting. Despite the ACM's ease of use in comparison to the general rule, the PBGC has received complaints about its complexity.

The PBGC proposes to address these problems by replacing the ACM with a simpler procedure and restricting the new procedure's use by large plans. The PBGC has devised a simplified filing method ("SFM") that is even easier to use than the ACM, with the hope that more small plan administrators will be able to use the SFM to compute premiums without the assistance of an actuary than appears to be the case with the ACM. The new SFM eliminates all of the existing ACM formulas and replaces them with tables of adjustment factors and simple arithmetical rules. Under the proposed amendment, the SFM would replace the ACM for all plan years beginning after 1992. However, as discussed in detail below, plans paying premiums for 500 or more participants would not be allowed to use the SFM if their UVBs as determined under the SFM were less than if they had used the general rule.

(The PBGC invites public comment regarding what proportion of plans of various sizes routinely determine UVBs under both the ACM and the general rule before they decide which method to use for paying premiums, whether they do it in all cases or only, for example, when an ACM calculation shows some amount of UVBs, and whether the general rule determinations made for this purpose are full final determinations on which a premium filing could be based or merely trial determinations that cost substantially less than full determinations and that are intended only as a basis for deciding whether full determinations should be made. Similarly, the PBGC invites comment regarding whether a significant number of plans that currently calculate UVBs under the ACM without making a general rule determination would encounter obstacles to timely filing (involving, e.g., general rule data collection) under the PBGC's proposed restriction on the use of the SFM by larger plans and what (if anything) might be done in the context of this proposed amendment to alleviate any such problems.)

Overview of the SFM

Like the ACM, the SFM would start from figures reported on Form 5500 Schedule B as of the beginning of the plan year preceding the premium payment year; add accruals and contributions for that year; correct for any difference between the current liability interest rate(s) (the "Funding Interest Rate(s)") actually used and the required interest rate under § 2610.23(b)(1) (the "Premium Interest Rate"); and bring the resulting UVB figure forward to the end of the plan year preceding the premium payment year by adding interest at the Premium Interest Rate. Unlike the ACM, however, the SFM would use no formulas. Instead, it would provide two tables of factors for adjusting the Form 5500 vested benefit figures to reflect the difference between the Premium Interest Rate and the Funding Interest Rate and give additional simple arithmetic rules (involving only addition, subtraction, and multiplication) for making other adjustments to the Form 5500 figures and the resulting UVB figure. The factors in the tables would replace the ACM interest adjustment formula and related tables in current § 2610.23(c)(2) and (3). The additional simple arithmetical rules would replace the provision that adjusts assets for contributions under current § 2610.23(c)(4) and the formula in current § 2610.23(c)(5) that adjusts UVBs for the passage of time. The ACM adjustment for accruals in current § 2610.23(c)(1), which is now based on a percentage of vested benefits, would be replaced by an adjustment based on the amount of accruals reported on the Schedule B.

Perhaps the best way to introduce the proposed SFM is to work through an example showing how it would be used to compute UVBs in a simulated premium filing. Accordingly, assume that a small calendar year plan, for which the plan administrator is computing the 1993 variable rate premium using the SFM, has the following data on its Schedule B for 1992:

Item 6d (current liability for vested benefits as of 1/1/92)—

(i) (retirees and beneficiaries): $40,000;

(ii) (terminated vested participants): $10,000;

(iii) (active participants): $110,000;

Item 6e (increase in current liabilities for accruals in 1992): $8,000;

Item 7 (total employer and employee contributions for 1992): $10,000;

Item 8b (actuarial value of assets—assume as of 1/1/92): $100,000;

Item 12c(i) (current liability interest rates (Funding Interest Rates))—

Pre-retirement: 8.0 percent; Post-retirement: 7.625 percent;

Item 12d (assumed retirement age): 62.

The interest rate required under § 2610.23(b)(1) (the Premium Interest Rate) that the plan administrator would use would be that for

January 1993; assume that it is 7.91 percent. Finally, the plan administrator would have to refer to the tables of adjustment factors in proposed § 2610.23(c)(3). For convenience, a portion of each table is reproduced here; their use is explained as the example proceeds.

TABLE 1
[To be used when the Premium Interest Rate is less than the Funding Interest Rate]

Column A		Column B	Column C			
If the Funding Interest Rate minus the Premium Interest Rate (to the nearest hundreth of a percent) is—		The factor for pay-status benefits is—	The factor for pre-pay-status benefits (based on the plan's assumed retirement age) is—			
at least	but not over		for ages under 60	for ages 60-61	for ages 62-63	for ages over 63
0.01	0.25	1.02	1.04	1.04	1.05	1.05
.26	.50	1.03	1.08	1.09	1.10	1.11
.51	.75	1.05	1.12	1.13	1.15	1.16

TABLE 2
[To be used when the Premium Interest Rate equals or exceeds the Funding Interest Rate]

Column A		Column B	Column C			
If the Premium Interest Rate minus the Funding Interest Rate (to the nearest hundreth of a percent) is—		The factor for pay-status benefits is—	The factor for pre-pay-status benefits (based on the plan's assumed retirement age) is—			
at least	but not over		for ages under 60	for ages 60-61	for ages 62-63	for ages over 63
0.00	0.25	1.00	1.00	1.00	1.00	1.00
.26	.50	.98	.97	.96	.96	.95
.51	.75	.97	.95	.92	.91	.91

To find the plan's 12/31/92 UVBs in order to compute the 1993 variable rate premium, the plan administrator would take the following steps:

Step 1: Adjust the 1/1/92 Benefit Value for Retirees and Beneficiaries

The plan administrator's first step is to adjust the 1/1/92 value of vested benefits for retirees and beneficiaries to reflect the difference between the Funding Interest Rate used to value those benefits and the Premium Interest Rate mandated by the statute. The unadjusted benefits value is on line 6d(i) of the Schedule B: $40,000. The adjustment factor depends on the difference between the Funding Interest Rate and the Premium Interest Rate; for retiree benefits, the Premium Interest Rate is compared with the post-retirement Funding Interest Rate. The SFM table headings tell which table the adjustment factor should come from. In this case, the factor comes from Table 2, because the Premium Interest Rate (7.91 percent) is greater than the applicable Funding Interest Rate (7.625 percent). The adjustment factor comes from the second row of Table 2, because the difference between the Premium Interest Rate and the Funding Interest Rate is in the 0.26-0.50 range on the second row of column A of Table 2 (7.91 minus 7.625 is 0.285, which rounds up to 0.29 percentage points). Following this row over to column B leads to the adjustment factor for the line 6d(i) amount. The factor is 0.98. Multiplying $40,000 by 0.98 gives $39,200. This is the adjusted 1/1/92 value of vested benefits for retirees and beneficiaries.

Step 2: Adjust the 1/1/92 Benefit Value for Terminated Vested Participants

The second step is very much like the first. Here, the plan administrator adjusts the 1/1/92 value of vested benefits for terminated vested participants to reflect the difference between the Funding Interest Rate and the Premium Interest Rate. This unadjusted benefits value is on line 6d(ii) of the Schedule B: $10,000. Once again, the adjustment factor depends on the difference between the Funding Interest Rate and the Premium Interest Rate, but where (as here) the pre- and post-retirement Funding Interest Rates are different, the plan administrator must compare the greater of the two Funding Interest Rates with the Premium Interest Rate to get the adjustment factor for terminated vested participants' benefits. In this case, the pre-retirement Funding Interest Rate (8.0 percent) is greater than the post-retirement Funding Interest Rate (7.625 percent). For this step, therefore, the adjustment factor comes from Table 1, because the Premium Interest Rate (7.91 percent) is less than the applicable Funding Interest Rate (8.0 percent). The adjustment factor comes from the first row of Table 1, because the difference between the Premium Interest Rate and the Funding Interest Rate is in the 0.01-0.25 range on the first row of column A of Table 1 (8.0 minus 7.91 is 0.09 percentage points).

Since terminated vested participants have not yet retired, the adjustment factor for the value of their benefits also depends on the plan's assumed retirement age. The assumed retirement age for this plan is 62. So the plan administrator follows the first row of Table 1 over to column C and then looks in the subcolumn headed "for ages 62-63" for the adjustment factor for the line 6d(ii) amount. The factor is 1.05. Multiplying $10,000 by 1.05 gives $10,500. This is the adjusted 1/1/92 value of vested benefits for terminated vested participants.

Step 3: Adjust the 1/1/92 Benefit Value for Active Participants

The third step is almost the same as the second. Here, the plan administrator adds accruals for 1992 to the 1/1/92 value of vested benefits for active participants and adjusts the sum to reflect the difference between the Funding Interest Rate and the Premium Interest Rate. The unadjusted benefits value for active participants is on line 6d(iii) of the Schedule B: $110,000. The current liability increase for 1992 accruals is on line 6e of the Schedule B: $8,000. The sum of these two figures is $118,000. The plan administrator uses the same Funding Interest Rate, and thus the same table (Table 1) and row (the first row), to find the adjustment factor for active participants' benefits as was used for terminated vested participants' benefits in step 2. The plan administrator also uses the same column (C) and subcolumn (for ages 62-63) as in step 2. So the adjustment factor for the line 6d(iii) amount is the same as that for the line 6d(ii) amount: 1.05. Multiplying $118,000 by 1.05 gives $123,900. This is the adjusted 1/1/92 value of vested benefits for active participants.

The sum of the three adjusted 1/1/92 vested benefits values is therefore $173,600 ($39,200 + $10,500 + $123,900), and this is the total value of vested benefits as of 1/1/92 that will be used in computing 1/1/92 UVBs in step 5 below.

Step 4: Adjust the 1/1/92 Value of Plan Assets

In this step, the plan administrator adjusts the 1/1/92 value of plan assets to reflect contributions for 1992. The unadjusted plan asset value comes from line 8b of the Schedule B: $100,000. The total 1992 contributions come from item 7 of the Schedule B: $10,000. The contributions (which may have been made on various dates in 1992 and 1993) are discounted back to 1/1/92 by multiplying them by 0.95. (The SFM uses this same discount factor no matter what the Premium Interest Rate is and no matter when the contributions were actually made.) Multiplying $10,000 by 0.95 gives $9,500 as the discounted value of the contributions. Then adding the discounted contributions to the unadjusted assets value gives $109,500 ($100,000 plus $9,500). This is the adjusted value of plan assets as of 1/1/92.

Step 5: Compute the UVBs

In this step, the plan administrator computes the 1/1/92 UVBs and then adjusts them so that the adjusted figure can be used as 12/31/92 UVBs. The 1/1/92 UVBs are equal to the total adjusted 1/1/92 vested benefits (from steps 1, 2, and 3) minus the total adjusted 1/1/92 assets (from step 4). At the end of step 3, the total adjusted 1/1/92 benefits were found to be $173,600; in step 4, the total adjusted 1/1/92 assets were found to be $109,500. So the 1/1/92 UVBs are $64,100 ($173,600 minus $109,500). To adjust this 1/1/92 figure for use as a 12/31/92 figure, the plan administrator adds interest using the Premium Interest Rate as the interest rate. Since the Premium Interest Rate is 7.91 percent, the 1/1/92 UVBs are multiplied by 1.0791 (1 plus the Premium Interest Rate) to yield $69,170.31. This is the UVBs as of 12/31/92. The plan administrator then uses this UVB figure to determine the plan's variable rate premium.

Details of the SFM

The SFM, applicable to premium payment years beginning after 1992, would be set forth in § 2610.23(c), and the ACM, limited to premium payment years beginning before 1993, would be transferred to a new § 2610.23(f). New § 2610.23(c)(1), like the introductory text of existing § 2610.23(c), would be a summary or general statement of how the method would work, and § 2610.23(c)(2)-(7) would provide the detailed rules. The tables of factors to be applied to the vested benefit values, and general rules for their use, would be in § 2610.23(c)(2). (To avoid possible confusion, the SFM tables would be called Tables 1 and 2 to distinguish them from ACM Tables A and B.) Section 2610.23(c)(3)-(5) would contain specific adjustment rules for the vested benefits of retirees and beneficiaries, terminated vested participants, and active participants respectively. Section 2610.23(c)(6) would provide for adjusting plan assets, and § 2610.23(c)(7) for determining and adjusting UVBs.

Use of the SFM, as of the ACM, would be restricted for plans paying premiums for 500 or more participants, but the restrictions would now be more stringent. The ACM requires such plans to make adjustments for any significant events described in § 2610.23(d), and the SFM would continue this requirement, which would be stated explicitly in new § 2610.23(c)(1) instead of just in § 2610.23(d) as at present. In addition, § 2610.23(c)(1) would allow such plans to use the SFM only if the amount of their UVBs determined under the general rule were not greater than that calculated with the SFM. An enrolled actuary would be required to certify to that fact if the SFM were used, and if an audit found that the general rule UVBs were greater, the amount of any premium deficiency (and related interest and penalties) would be based on the (higher) general rule figure.

As discussed above, this new restriction is proposed as a response to concerns that the PBGC may be exposed to significant revenue losses in individual cases where large plans select the ACM over the general rule because calculations with both methods show that use of the ACM minimizes UVBs. The PBGC believes that the new rule will solve this problem without imposing substantial additional administrative costs on plans. A study of premium filings suggests that more than four-fifths of single-employer plans pay no variable rate premiums; for most of those plans, the absence of UBVs is likely to be obvious even before any calculations are done. As for large plans whose funding status is not so clear, the PBGC has reason to believe, as noted above, that calculations under both the general rule and the ACM are already routinely done as part of the premium payment process.

The SFM would also include another new limitation (applicable to all plans). Section 2610.23(c)(1) would provide that the SFM could be used only if the Premium Interest Rate prescribed under § 2610.23(b)(1) were not more than six percentage points less than the plan's Funding Interest Rates from its Schedule B. This limitation would be needed because use of the tables in new § 2610.23(c)(3) would be mandatory under the SFM (unlike the ACM, in which use of the tables is optional), and Table 1 would only cover Funding Interest Rates up to six percentage points higher than the Premium Interest Rate. The restriction of Table 1 to a six-point rate spread reflects two considerations. One is that the SFM makes simplifying assumptions about interest rates, and these assumptions introduce inaccuracies that, though relatively small when the Funding Interest Rate is close to the Premium Interest Rate, become more significant when the rates diverge further. The other is that, because of the way the Premium Interest Rate and the permissible range of the Funding Interest Rate are set by statute, a six-point spread between them is extremely unlikely. (Although no limitation would be placed on use of the SFM by a plan whose Funding Interest Rate (or Funding Interest Rates) was (or were) lower than the Premium Interest Rate, no matter how great the spread, the adjustment factors provided for spreads greater than six points would be the same as for a six-point spread. A six-point spread when the Funding Interest Rate is lower than the Premium Interest Rate is considered even less likely than when the Funding Interest Rate is higher.)

In addition to setting forth the two tables of vested benefit adjustment factors, proposed § 2610.23(c)(2) would describe how to select a table and a row within a table in finding each adjustment factor. The benefit adjustment factors would adjust the vested benefit values for the difference between the Premium Interest Rate and the Funding Interest Rate, and this difference would accordingly determine the table and row from which each adjustment factor would be taken. The Premium Interest Rate in the SFM is the same as the quantity called "RIR" in the ACM, viz., the rate prescribed in § 2610.23(b)(1) for the month in which the premium payment year began. The Funding Interest Rate would be one of the rates entered in the pre- or post-retirement column of line 12c(i) on the Schedule B. The pre- and post-retirement Funding Interest Rates are the same as the ACM's BIA and BIR respectively.

Since choosing a table and row would depend on the Funding Interest Rate applicable to each vested benefit amount, § 2610.23(c)(2) would refer to the specific adjustment rules for the three vested benefits amounts (in § 2610.23(c)(3)-(5)) for the Funding Interest Rate to be used for each adjustment. If the Premium Interest Rate were less than the applicable Funding Interest Rate, Table 1 would be used; if the Premium Interest Rate were equal to or greater than the Funding Interest Rate, Table 2 would be used. To find the proper row in the table, the difference between the Funding Interest Rate and the Premium Interest Rate (determined by subtracting the smaller of the two from the larger) would be rounded to the nearest hundredth of a percent. (For example, 1.035 percentage points would round to 1.04 points, and 0.374 percentage points would round to 0.37 points.) One would then locate the rate range in column A of the table that included the difference between the Premium Interest Rate and the applicable Funding Interest Rate. Each row would cover a difference range of one-quarter of one percent. The appropriate factor for the particular combination of Premium Interest Rate and Funding Interest Rate would be found on that row in the appropriate column of the table. The specific adjustment rules for the three vested benefits amounts in § 2610.23(c)(3)-(5) would also tell which column (and, for line 6d(ii) and 6d(iii) adjustments, which subcolumn) of the appropriate table to use for each adjustment.

Under § 2610.23(c)(3), the post-retirement Funding Interest Rate would be used to find the factor for adjusting the value from line 6d(i) of the Schedule B, since that is the rate used to value retiree benefits for the Schedule B. The appropriate column for the line 6d(i) adjustment factor would be column B. The adjusted line 6d(i) amount under § 2610.23(c)(3) would simply be the unadjusted amount from that line multiplied by the factor found in the appropriate table following the rules in § 2610.23(c)(2) and (3).

The benefits of active and terminated vested participants may be valued using two rates, one for the pre-retirement period and another for the post-retirement period. To simplify the SFM, only one rate would be used to find the adjustment factors for these values. In order to avoid premium losses to the PBGC, § 2610.23(c)(4) and (5) would require that the greater of the pre- and post-retirement Funding Interest Rates be used to find the adjustment factors for the values from lines 6d(ii) and 6d(iii) of the Schedule B.

The appropriate column for the line 6d(ii) and 6d(iii) adjustment factors would be column C. To find the factors, the assumed retirement age reported on line 12d of the Schedule B would be used to select the proper subcolumn of column C. (The assumed retirement age in the SFM is the same as the assumed retirement age used in the ACM.) Each subcolumn is headed by a range of ages: under 60, 60-61, 62-63, and over 63. The subcolumn used would be the one whose heading included the assumed retirement age.

In addition to specifying the Funding Interest Rate, column, and subcolumn to be used in adjusting the line 6d(ii) amount, § 2610.23(c)(4) would provide simply that the adjusted line 6d(ii) amount would be the unadjusted amount from that line multiplied by the factor found in the appropriate table following the rules in § 2610.23(c)(2) and (4). Section 2610.23(c)(5), on the other hand, would require that the unadjusted line 6d(iii) amount be increased by the amount of the expected current liability increase for benefits accruing during the plan year preceding the premium payment year—from line 6e of the Schedule B—before being multiplied by the adjustment factor. The line 6d(iii) factor would be the same as the line 6d(ii) factor because it would be based on the same Funding Interest Rate and assumed retirement age.

The use of the expected current liability increase figure from line 6e of the Schedule B represents a change from the ACM, which approximated accruals as an amount equal to seven percent of the combined vested benefits of active and terminated vested participants—no accrual figure having been available on the Schedule B when the ACM was devised. While the line 6e figure is typically determined as of the first day of the plan year, it need not be; the use of a later date would make benefit liabilities under the SFM higher than if the determination were made as of the beginning of the plan year, because the SFM would add the line 6e figure, without discount, to the value of active participants' vested benefits as of the first day of the plan year from the line 6d(iii) of the Schedule B. The line 6e figure may also include nonvested as well as vested accruals, and this also would tend to inflate benefit liabilities. However, the PBGC believes that the amount of any such inflation would typically be minimal. In any event, a plan would be free to use the general rule to avoid any disadvantage that the SFM might cause either by not providing a discount or by including nonvested accruals.

The three adjusted vested benefits values determined under § 2610.23(c)(2)-(5) would be added together to give a total adjusted value of vested benefits for computing UVBs under proposed § 2610.23(c)(7).

The factors in Tables 1 and 2 in § 2610.23(c)(2) have been derived from formulas similar to the formulas prescribed under the ACM. Each column B factor is equal to 0.94^D, where D is equal to the Premium Interest Rate minus the Funding Interest Rate. However, the factor in each row is used for a range of D's—the ranges shown in column A of each table. To avoid premium losses to the PBGC, the Table 1 factors are derived using the highest percentage point difference in each range, while the Table 2 factors are derived using the lowest difference in each range. For example, in the third row of Table 1, D would be -0.75, but in the third row of Table 2, D would be 0.51.

Similarly, each column C factor is equal to the column B factor from the same row multiplied by $((107-D)/107)^{(ARA-50)}$ (with "ARA" standing for the plan's assumed retirement age). However, the factor in each subcolumn of column C is used for a range of assumed retirement ages—the ranges shown in the subcolumn headings. To avoid premium losses to the PBGC, the Table 1 factors are derived using assumed retirement ages from the high end of each range, while Table 2 factors are derived using assumed retirement ages from the low end of each range. (The low end of the under-60 range is assumed to be 55, and the high end of the over-63 range is assumed to be 65.) Thus, for example, in the 60-61 subcolumn of Table 1, an assumed retirement age of 61 is used, but in the same subcolumn of Table 2, the assumed retirement age used is 60.

While the ACM uses both pre- and post-retirement interest corrections in its formula for adjusting the benefit values for active and terminated vested participants, the formulas used to generate the SFM tables refer to only one interest figure for these participants—either the pre- or post-retirement Funding Interest Rate, whichever is greater. To avoid having different tables for different values of Premium Interest Rate, the SFM formulas also use a simplified version of the fraction expressing the ratio of the Funding Interest Rate to the Premium Interest Rate. Since the value of this fraction depends mostly on the spread between the Funding Interest Rate and the Premium Interest Rate, rather than on their actual values, the SFM formulas use a fraction based on the actual spread and an assumed Premium Interest Rate of 7.00 percent. This assumed value of Premium Interest Rate represents a rough historical average of actual Premium Interest Rates; if Premium Interest Rates begin to deviate significantly from the assumed value, the PBGC may find it appropriate to issue new tables based on a different assumed value.

Proposed § 2610.23(c)(6) would provide rules for adjusting the value of plan assets taken from Schedule B. As under the ACM (§ 2610.23(c)(4) of the existing regulation), the basic figure would come from line 8b, unless that figure were determined as of a date other than the first day of the prior plan year, in which case the figure would come from line 6c. However, the SFM would provide a simplifed procedure for adjusting that basic figure.

Like the existing adjustment procedure, the new procedure in proposed § 2610.23(c)(6) would correct for any contributions made for the plan year preceding the premium payment year. The value of assets as of the first day of that prior year, whether from line 8b or line 6c of the Schedule B, must exclude any contributions made for that year. (Of course, contributions for the year before the prior year are includible in the value of assets as of the beginning of the prior year only if actually made before the Schedule B for the prior year is filed.) The assets figure must therefore be increased to reflect contributions for the prior year.

The amount of contributions made for the prior year would be taken from columns (b) and (c) of item 7 of the Schedule B. The contributions would then have to be discounted to reflect the fact that they were paid after the date as of which the plan assets figure was determined (the beginning of the prior year). In order to simplify this step,

§ 2610.23(c)(6)(i) would use a flat discount factor of 0.95, so that the discounted contributions amount would be the total contributions amount times 0.95. This flat discount factor reflects an assumption that all of the contributions being discounted would have been made about three-quarters of the way through the prior year and that the discount rate would be about 7.00 percent (the same value assumed for the Premium Interest Rate in the simplified ratio between the Funding Interest Rate and the Premium Interest Rate that is used in the formulas for generating the benefit adjustment tables in § 2610.23(c)(2)). To the extent that the weighted average contribution date were earlier or the Premium Interest Rate were lower, these assumptions would result in a higher variable rate premium. However, the PBGC believes that relatively few plans receive contributions so early as to be seriously disadvantaged by the SFM's assumed weighted average contribution date. In any event, the SFM is an optional procedure that plans need not use. (The flat discount factor, like the tables of benefit adjustment factors in § 2610.23(c)(2), might be changed if Premium Interest Rates were to deviate significantly from historical values.)

Under proposed § 2610.23(c)(7), the adjusted assets value (computed under proposed § 2610.23(c)(6)) would be subtracted from the adjusted benefits value (computed under proposed § 2610.23(c)(2)-(5)) to yield the value of UVBs at the beginning of the plan year preceding the premium payment year, and this figure would be brought forward to the end of the prior year by multiplying it by the sum of one plus the Premium Interest Rate (expressing the Premium Interest Rate as a decimal fraction of 1, not as a percentage).

The ACM uses a somewhat more complicated method for adjusting the UVBs figure, expressed in a formula that compensates for the possibility that the plan year preceding the premium payment year may be a short year. By ignoring that possibility, the SFM would be simpler, but would produce a higher UVB amount, and therefore a higher variable rate premium, for a premium payment year that followed a short plan year. The PBGC believes that the increased simplicity of the SMF in this regard outweighs the detriment to plans in the relatively infrequent situations where there is a short plan year, especially in view of the fact that the SFM (like the ACM) would be an optional computation method.

Taking into account the aggregate effect of all of the differences between the ACM and the SFM, the PBGC believes that its aggregate premium receipts from plans using the SFM would be neither less than nor significantly greater than if the ACM were used instead. For most plans, the results produced by the SFM would differ from those produced by the ACM primarily because of the shift from the ACM's assumed value of benefit accruals (in current § 2610.23(c)(1)) to the SFM's actual value (in proposed § 2610.23(c)(5)). Any such difference for an individual plan would be in the direction of improved accuracy and should thus be unobjectionable.

Aside from the change in accounting for accruals, the PBGC believes that for the vast majority of plans, the results produced by the SFM would not differ significantly from those that would be produced by the ACM. While there would be a relatively small number of plans for which the SFM would produce a significantly higher premium than the ACM, such a plan could avoid paying an unnecessarily high premium by using the general rule.

The other proposed amendments to § 2610.23 reflect technical, clarifying, and conforming changes that are not intended to have any substantive effect.

SFM for Distress or Involuntary Terminations

Section 2610.24(c) currently contains a special version of the ACM for plans undergoing distress or involuntary termination. Following the same pattern as in § 2610.23, the amendment would move this special ACM rule to the end of § 2610.24 and preserve it (as § 2610.24(h)) for premium payment years beginning after 1988 and before 1993. In its place, a new § 2610.24(c) would provide a special version of the SFM for plans in involuntary or distress terminations. (As in § 2610.23, there would also be a number of technical and conforming changes.)

New § 2610.24(c) would be much like the existing provision, except that it would tie into the SFM rather than the ACM. Aside from the new restriction (discussed above) on use of the SFM by large plans, the plans permitted to use the new special rule would be the same as under the existing rule, and the Schedule B they could use would be determined in the same way as it is now. However, because the SFM would adjust benefits for additional accruals, and UVBs for the passage of time, differently than the ACM does, new § 2610.24(c)(3), (4), and (6), which deal with these adjustments, would be restructured to conform to the new SFM rules. In particular, § 2610.24(c)(3) and (4) would provide different modifications of the SFM rules, depending on whether or not the Schedule B being used included separate entries for active and terminated vested participants' vested benefits and an entry for accruals (features that were added in 1989).

Also, § 2610.24(c)(5) would provide that the new simpler method for adjusting plan assets in proposed § 2610.23(c)(6) could not be used; instead, a method that tracks the current ACM asset adjustment method in existing § 2610.23(c)(4) would be required. This provision is prompted by the difficulty of devising an adaptation of the simple new § 2610.23(c)(6) rule that would appropriately discount contributions that might cover multiple years and that might have been made before the full phase-in of the quarterly contribution requirement in section 302(e) of ERISA and section 412(m) of the Internal Revenue Code of 1986.

Due Dates

ERISA section 4007 specified a due date of 30 days after the beginning of the premium payment year for premiums for the first premium payment year beginning after ERISA's effective date. The premium regulation retained this due date rule until 1978, when the due date was changed to seven months after the end of the preceding plan year; for 1981 through 1984, the due date was the end of the seventh month of the premium payment year. In 1985, it was changed to the end of the second month of the premium payment year for large plans only, in response to recommendations of the Grace Commission (the President's Private Sector Survey on Cost Control) (see the preambles to the proposed and final 1985 amemdment to the premium regulation, 50 FR 1065 at 1066 (January 9, 1985) and 50 FR 12533 at 12534-5 (March 29, 1985)). (For the first year of the new rule, large plans were defined as those with at least 10,000 participants; beginning in 1986, the threshold was dropped to 500 participants.) However, the end of the seventh month was retained in 1985 as the small plan due date.

The PBGC recognized that some large plans might have problems computing their premiums by the new, earlier due date because of difficulty in determining participant counts as of the required determination date (the last day of the prior year). The PBGC therefore made provision for the estimation of early payments, established safe harbor rules to give large plans a means of avoiding penalties on underpayments resulting from low estimates, and established explicit rules in the premium regulation for the reconciliation of estimated early premium payments with the final participant count. The reconciliation date was made the same as the later due date that remained applicable to small plans.

In 1988, the variable rate premium for single-employer plans was introduced. The flat rate premium due date for large plans remained the end of the second month of the premium payment year (e.g., February 28th for calendar year plans); however, the due date for the new variable rate premium was made the same for large plans as for small plans (and the same as the reconciliation date for large plans), and was deferred to the fifteenth day of the eighth month after the beginning of the premium payment year (e.g., September 15th for calendar year plans). (The use of the later due date for large plans' variable rate premiums—an anomaly in the context of the Grace Commission recommendations—reflected concern for plans' ability to make realistic variable rate premium estimates by the early due date, in view particularly of the variable rate premium computation rules prescribed in the regulation, which relied heavily on data developed for the Form 5500 and Schedule B thereto.)

Thus, although the premium regulation does not actually require two annual premium filings by large plans, the due date structure makes filing twice a year a practical necessity for most large plans. This is true for those plans that find it necessary (or administratively convenient) to pay an estimate at the early filing date, which they must later reconcile; and also for those single-employer plans that find it impossible (or administratively inconvenient) to compute the variable rate premium in time to pay it at the same time the flat rate premium is due. The need for two filings each year by most large plans is a burden for them and for the PBGC.

Moreover, a large plan that underestimates its flat rate premium on the early due date must pay interest to the PBGC on the amount of the underpayment, even if it satisfies the safe harbor rules. The safe harbor rules provide protection only from penalties, not from interest charges; the PBGC does not have the authority to waive interest charges. If an estimated payment turns out to be higher than the flat rate amount finally determined to be due, the plan may receive a credit or refund, but the PBGC lacks the authority to pay interest on overpayments.

Furthermore, although the safe harbor rules give large plans an opportunity to avoid penalties on underpayment of the flat rate premium by paying a definitely determinable amount (last year's participant count times the current year's flat rate) and making up any

shortfall by the reconciliation due date, the safe harbor rules make the premium regulation more complex by providing a different rule for penalties than is provided for interest. The safe harbor rules are also an administrative burden for the PBGC, which must treat plans that fail the safe harbor tests differently than those that pass the tests but nonetheless underpay the flat rate premium at the early due date, assessing both interest and penalties against the former but charging the latter for interest only. Where a penalty is assessed, it is based on the full difference between the early payment actually made and the final flat-rate amount due (rather than just the difference between the actual early payment and the safe harbor amount).

Finally, while variable rate premiums are due after the nominal due date for the Form 5500 (and Schedule B), the Form 5500 due date is often extended by two-and-a-half months, making it later than the premium due date. Thus, single-employer plans must often pay variable rate premiums a whole month before they are required to report on Form 5500 the data on which those premiums are based (although of course the data ultimately reported on Form 5500 may be used to determine premiums before the Form 5500 is in fact filed). This discrepancy has been of particular concern for plans using the alternative calculation method, which refers explicitly to Schedule B line items. (The same comment would apply to the simplified filing method that the PBGC proposes to substitute for the existing alternative calculation method.)

The PBGC proposes to address these problems by deferring the final filing due date (to just 15 days before the extended Form 5500 due date), raising the number of participants a plan must have in order to be required to make the early premium payment (so that fewer plans must file twice a year), and charging neither penalties nor interest on early payments that equal at least a definitely determinable amount (so that both estimates and special safe harbor rules are unnecessary). Providing a definite amount for the early payment would also obviate the need for even estimated data determinations before the early payment was made. This would make it possible to accelerate the early filing due date to nearer the beginning of the premium payment year and to widen the scope of the early payment to cover the variable rate, as well as the flat rate, portion of the premium—changes that would balance those described above in order to achieve approximate revenue neutrality for the PBGC.

Structurally, the existing due date rules in § 2610.25(b), (c), and (d) (and those in § 2610.34(a) and (b) for premium payment years of multiemployer plans beginning after 1987) would be consolidated, moved to the end of § 2610.25 (as § 2610.25(e)), and preserved for premium payment years beginning after 1987 and before 1993. (These rules would be significantly reworded to make them consistent in format with the new rules being proposed for premium payment years beginning after 1992, but without the intent to make any substantive changes in the old rules.) Current § 2610.25(e) and (f) would be redesignated as § 2610.25(c) and (d). The new due date rules, for premium payment years beginning after 1992, would be set forth in a new § 2610.25(b).

Although the proposed amendment would eliminate prospectively the need for the safe harbor rules (currently in § 2610.8(b)(4)), these rules would need to be preserved for premium payment years beginning before 1993. Accordingly, the safe harbor rules would be moved to the end of § 2610.8(b) (that is, redesignated as § 2610.8(b)(5)) and reworded slightly to make them applicable only to premium payment years beginning before 1993 and to conform references to other provisions of the amended premium regulation.

Under the current due date rules, the plans that must pay the flat rate premium by the early due date are those that were required to pay premiums for at least 500 participants for the plan year preceding the premium payment year (the current "large plan threshold," which would be preserved in § 2610.25(e)(5)). Under the new rules, the number of plans required to file by the early due date would be reduced by increasing the large plan threshold to 5,000 participants. This would be reflected in the definitions (for purposes of the new due date rules) of the terms "large plan" and "small plan" in proposed § 2610.25(b)(5). For the 1989 premium payment year, there were about 8,000 plans at or above the 500-participant threshold, but only about 1,000 plans that had at least 5,000 participants; thus, the PBGC estimates that the proposed increase in the large plan threshold would reduce by about 7,000 (or 87 percent) the number of plans that would potentially need to make two filings per year.

The amendment would also change both annual due dates (that is, the early date applicable only to the new, smaller group of "large plans" and the later date applicable to the new, larger group of "small plans" and to reconciliation filings by the large plans). Under proposed new § 2610.25(b)(1), the small plan due date would be the last day of the ninth full calendar month following the end of the plan year preceding the premium payment year (i.e., September 30th for calendar year plans, October 31st for plans with plan years beginning January 2d-February 1st, etc.). Under proposed § 2610.25(b)(2)(ii), this would also be the reconciliation due date for large plans. This is only 15 days before the due date for the Form 5500 with the typical two-and-a-half-month extension. This change would relieve plans of the need to compute premiums a full month before the underlying data have to be reported on Form 5500 and Schedule B thereto.

Under new § 2610.25(b)(2)(i), the early due date for large plans would be advanced to the fifteenth day of the first full calendar month following the end of the plan year preceding the premium payment year (i.e., January 15th for calendar year plans, February 15th for plans with plan years beginning January 2d-February 1st, etc.). If large plans were still to be required to pay their (actual or estimated) flat rate premiums for the premium payment year by the early filing date, advancing the date would worsen the existing problems with early filing. However, as mentioned briefly above and discussed in detail below, the amendment would also provide large plans with a definitely determinable amount to pay at the early filing date, thus making estimation unnecessary. In view of this latter change, there would no longer be any reason not to collect the preliminary payment close to the beginning of the premium payment year. This practice would be more in line with the practices of commercial insurance companies.

New § 2610.25(b)(2)(i) would also prescribe the amount due from large plans on the early filing date. This would be either the dollar amount of the total (flat and variable rate) premium payable for the plan year preceding the premium payment year—a definitely determinable amount that would be known well in advance of the early due date—or, at the plan's option, the total (flat and variable rate) premium due for the premium payment year (which the plan could estimate if it chose). If the early payment fell short of the total premium finally determined to be payable for the premium payment year, the amount of the shortfall would be due by the reconciliation due date under new § 2610.25(b)(2)(ii).

It should be noted that under this proposal, the scope of the early payment for large plans would not be limited to the flat rate portion of the premium, as it has been up to now. As mentioned above, problems with estimating the variable rate premium militated against including it in the initial payment when it was introduced in 1988. Since estimating would no longer be required under this proposal, however, the PBGC sees no reason to continue deferring large plans' variable rate payments to a date close to the end of the premium payment year.

It should also be noted that the proposed early payment would be based on the dollar amount of the previous year's premium, rather than on the previous year's plan data and the current year's premium rates, as under the existing regulation's safe harbor rules. The proposed approach has been taken in the interest of simplicity, even though it would mean that the PBGC would lose the benefit of any future premium rate increases in the initial premium filing.

A third point to note is that in determining the amount of the previous year's premium, refunds and credits under existing § 2610.22(d) and proposed new § 2610.22(e) would be disregarded. Thus, the early payment obligation would not be artificially reduced by the circumstance that the preceding plan year was a short year.

The key feature of the proposed new early payment requirement, however, would be the elimination of the need to estimate, and with it the need for special safe harbor rules and the risk of interest charges. Currently, safe harbor rules are needed to relieve plans from penalties that would otherwise accrue for even small good faith underestimates of their flat rate premiums at the early filing date. But even the safe harbor rules provide no relief from interest charges on underestimates. Under the proposal, a plan that paid the same amount as the previous year's final total premium by the early filing date would be assured of avoiding not only penalties (as under the existing safe harbor rules) but also interest on any amount by which the early payment fell short of the final total premium.

However, the proposal would still allow a plan to pay an estimate of the current year's premium at the early filing date if it so chose. Choosing to pay an estimate would open the plan to the risk of interest and penalty charges if the estimate proved to be too low, but a plan would presumably accept this risk if it believed that its current year's premium would end up being substantially less than its previous year's premium (as, for example, if it had lost many of its participants or had substantially improved its funding during the preceding year).

Upon reconciliation, a plan would owe the amount (if any) by which its early payment was less than the premium finally determined to be due. However, no penalty or interest on the amount of the shortfall

would be owed as long as the early payment were at least equal to the previous year's premium. If the early payment were less than both the previous year's final amount and the current year's final amount, interest and penalty would be imposed only on the amount by which the early payment fell short of the lesser of the previous year's final premium or the current year's final premium. (If the early payment were more than the current year's final amount, a refund or credit would be available under the same rules applicable to overpayments generally.)

For example, suppose that a plan's final total premium obligation for 1995 were $1,000 and that the plan made an early premium payment (using an estimate) of $700 for 1996. If its final 1996 premium were $1,200, it would owe penalty and interest only on $300, the amount by which its early payment fell short of $1,000 (the lesser of 1995's or 1996's final premium obligation). But if its final 1996 premium were $900, it would owe interest and payment only on $200, the shortfall for $900 (again, the lesser of the 1995 or the 1996 final premium). Of course, if the plan made an early payment of $1,000, it would owe no penalty or interest no matter how large its final 1996 obligation turned out to be.

The PBGC now permits large plans to file a Form 1 instead of a Form 1-ES at the early filing date; single-employer plans are allowed to file this early Form 1 without a Schedule A. This practice is consistent with the fact that the early payment under the current rules is an estimate of only the flat rate portion of the final premium. By filing Form 1 early without Schedule A, therefore, a plan is simply substituting a final flat rate figure for an estimate of the same figure. Under the proposed system, however, the early payment would be keyed to the total premium liability (either the previous year's figure or an estimate of the current year's). Thus, the PBGC would continue to accept advance filing of a final premium payment (either instead of the early payment or after the early payment was made) only if the advance filing were a complete final filing including (in the case of a single-employer plan) Schedule A and payment of both the flat and variable rate premiums.

The proposed due date rules for new and newly covered plans (in new § 2610.25(b)(3)) would be the same as the existing rules for such plans (which would be preserved in § 2610.25(e)(3)). The proposed due date rules for plans changing plan years (in new § 2610.25(b)(4)) would be almost the same as the corresponding rules in the existing regulation (which would be preserved in § 2610.25(e)(4)), except that a plan would have at least 90 days, instead of the 30 days now allowed, to pay its premium after adopting the amendment changing the plan year. The purpose of this change would be simply to make the filing rule for plans that change plan years more consistent with the rule for new and newly covered plans (which permits filing 90 days after plan adoption or the beginning of title IV coverage), and thus remove a potential source of confusion.

As alluded to briefly above, the new due date provisions would embody a combination of changes (some representing financial losses for the PBGC and others representing financial gains) that the PBGC has designed to have no substantial net revenue effect for the PBGC. Obviously, however, the new rules would shift financial burdens among premium payers to some degree, primarily away from smaller "large plans" that would no longer be required to pay premiums by the early due date and toward larger "large plans" that would be required to pay more of their premiums by an earlier due date. (The policy of requiring earlier payment from larger plans than from smaller plans was discussed in the preamble to the final 1985 amendment to the premium regulation, 50 FR 12533 at 12535 (March 29, 1985).)

In the process of devising the new premium payment system embodied in the proposed changes to the due date rules in § 2610.25, the PBGC considered and rejected several alternative approaches to the premium payment problems discussed above. For example, the early payment required of large plans might have remained limited to the flat rate portion of the premium only. However, the proposal's substantial reduction in the number of plans required to make the early filing would not then have been possible without significant revenue loss to the PBGC. Another possibility would have been to base the early payment required of large plans on the amount of the previous year's premium only, without the option of paying an estimate. However, the lack of an estimation option might have created problems for plans that underwent very substantial contraction (as through spinoff of most of their participants) or substantially improved their funding during the year preceding the premium payment year.

Another approach (the "maximum simplicity" approach) would have returned to the pre-Grace Commission practice of having all plans pay their premiums on the same schedule, with the due date for all plans deferred to the Form 5500 due date. This approach would have solved all the due date problems discussed above. However, it would have entailed an unacceptable loss of revenue to the PBGC, due to the deferral of premium receipts from large plans.

A third approach (the "legislative change" approach) would have sought a statutory amendment moving the premium determination date back one year, from the last day of the plan year *preceding* the premium payment year to the last day of the plan year *before* the plan year preceding the premium payment year. The premium due date would then have been accelerated to the beginning of the premium payment year for all plans.

Since the extended due date of the applicable Form 5500 would have fallen in the tenth month of the preceding plan year, this approach would have avoided the need to pay premiums before the relevant data had to be filed on Form 5500. It would also have eliminated estimated premium payments and reconciliation by making the early payment the only payment. However, it would have involved a substantial additional cost for small plans, which currently pay relatively late in the premium payment year.

Also, the use of older determination data would have made premiums lag behind changes in participant counts and funding levels. This would have tended to favor plans with increasing participant counts and single-employer plans with deteriorating funding levels by making their premiums lower than under the current system. But plans with declining participant counts and single-employer plans with improving funding levels would have been disadvantaged because their premiums would have been higher than under the current system.

In addition, creating a one-year gap between the premium determination date and the beginning of the premium payment year would have created significant complexities regarding the premium obligations of plans involved in mergers, consolidations and spinoffs during the period between the earlier determination date and the beginning of the premium payment year.

A fourth approach (the "combined filing" approach) would also have called for all plans to pay premiums just once a year, at the beginning of each premium payment year. The payment would have been a combination of two components. One component would have been a reconciliation for the prior year, based on the Form 5500 data filed during the prior year for the year preceding the prior year. The second component would have been a preliminary payment for the current year equal to the prior year's total premium. If the reconciliation involved an additional payment, it would have been added to the preliminary premium for the current year, without any penalties or interest. If the reconciliation generated a credit, it would have been subtracted from the preliminary payment for the current year.

As with the legislative change approach, the applicable Form 5500 due date under the combined filing approach would have been well before the premium due date when the Form 5500 data would be needed. Estimates would also have been avoided, and although there would have been reconciliation filings, they would have been combined with the preliminary premium filings so that plans would not have had to file twice a year. But accelerating most of the premium to the beginning of the year would have meant increased costs for plans, particularly for small plans.

Furthermore, plans with declining participant counts and single-employer plans with improving funding would have been disadvantaged under the combined filing approach in much the same way as under the legislative change approach because, although the preliminary payment would eventually have been reconciled, the reconciliation date would have been a whole year after the preliminary payment. (A plan would have been allowed to reconcile earlier only if it also paid the preliminary premium for the following year at the same time.)

A fifth approach (the "two-system" approach) would have combined the maximum simplicity approach for small plans with the combined filing approach for large plans, giving the advantages of both approaches. However, large plans with declining participant counts and large single-employer plans with improving funding would have had the same kinds of problems as under the combined filing approach. In addition, the difference in payment rules for large and small plans would have been great enough so that different forms and instructions for large and small plans might have been needed.

Compliance with Rulemaking Guidelines

The PBGC has determined that this amendment is not a "major rule" for purposes of Executive Order 12291 (46 FR 13193 (February 17, 1981)) because it will not have an annual effect on the economy of $100 million or more; or create a major increase in costs or prices for consumers, individual industries, or geographic regions; or have significant adverse effects on competition, employment, investment, or innovation, or on the ability of United States-based enterprises to compete with foreign-based enterprises in domestic or export markets. This determination is based on the fact that this amendment would have no significant effect on the overall financial burden of PBGC premiums on plans in general, but rather would only shift those burdens to a limited extent among classes of plans, primarily away from smaller plans and toward larger plans (especially larger underfunded plans); and on the fact that this amendment would tend to decrease the nonfinancial burden of paying PBGC premiums by making the premium payment process simpler.

Under section 605(b) of the Regulatory Flexibility Act, the PBGC certifies that this amendment will not have a significant economic impact on a substantial number of small entities. The amendment will tend to shift the financial burden of PBGC premiums away from smaller plans and toward larger plans (especially larger underfunded plans), and will tend to decrease the non-financial burden of paying PBGC premiums by making the premium payment process simpler. For these reasons, compliance with sections 603 and 604 of the Regulatory Flexibility Act is waived.

List of Subjects in 29 CFR Part 2610

Employee benefit plans, Penalties, Pension insurance, Pensions, and Reporting and recordkeeping requirements.

In consideration of the foregoing, the PBGC proposes to amend part 2610 of subchapter H of chapter XXVI of title 29, Code of Federal Regulations, as follows:

PART 2610—PAYMENT OF PREMIUMS

1. The authority citation for part 2610 continues to read as follows:

Authority: 29 U.S.C. 1302(b)(3), 1306, 1307 (1988 & Supp. I 1989), as amended by sec. 12021, Public Law 101-508, 104 Stat. 1388, 1388-573.

2. In §2610.1, the second sentence and the last three sentences of paragraph (a) are revised to read as follows:

§ *2610.1 Purpose and scope.*

(a) *Purpose.* * * * Subpart A contains rules that apply to both single-employer and multiemployer plans with respect to all premium payment years. * * *

Subpart B contains the premium rates, due dates and computational rules for premium payment years beginning after 1987. Subpart C contains the premium rates and due dates for premium payment years beginning before 1988.

* * *

3. Section 2610.2 is revised to read as follows:

§ *2610.2 Definitions.*

(a) *In general.* For purposes of this part:

Act means the Employee Retirement Income Security Act of 1974, as amended.

Code means the Internal Revenue Code of 1986, as amended.

Form 5500 means the Form 5500 series annual report prescribed by the Internal Revenue Service, the Department of Labor and the PBGC.

Multiemployer plan means a plan described in section 4001(a)(3) of the Act.

New plan means a plan that became effective within the premium payment year and includes a plan resulting from a consolidation or spinoff. A plan that meets this definition is considered to be a new plan for purposes of this part even if the plan constitutes a successor plan within the meaning of section 4021(a) of the Act.

Newly covered plan means a plan that is not a new plan and that was not covered by title IV of the Act pursuant to section 4021 of the Act immediately before the premium payment year.

PBGC means the Pension Benefit Guaranty Corporation.

Plan year means the calendar, policy or fiscal year on which the records of the plan are kept.

Premium payment year means the plan year for which the premium is being paid.

Short plan year means a plan year that is less than twelve full months.

Single-employer plan means a plan described in section 4001(a)(15) of the Act.

(b) *"Participant" for premium payment years beginning after 1992.* For purposes of this part, for a premium payment year beginning after 1992, "participant" means the same as it does for purposes of the Form 5500 for the plan year preceding the premium payment year (or, in the case of a new plan, or a newly covered plan that was not required to file Form 5500 for the plan year preceding the premium payment year, the Form 5500 prescribed for plan years beginning one year before the first day of the plan's first premium payment year).

(c) *"Participant" for premium payment years beginning before 1993.* For purposes of this part, for a premium payment year beginning before 1993, "participant" means any individual who is included in one of the categories described in paragraphs (c)(1)-(c)(3) of this section, subject to the provisions of paragraph (c)(4) of this section.

(1) *Active.* (i) Any individual who is currently in employment covered by the plan and who is earning or retaining credited service under the plan. This category includes any individual who is considered covered under the plan for purposes of meeting the minimum coverage requirements, but who, because of offset or other provisions (including integration with Social Security benefits), does not have any accrued benefits.

(ii) Any non-vested individual who is not currently in employment covered by the plan but who is earning or retaining credited service under the plan. This category does not include a non-vested former employee who has incurred a break in service the greater of one year or the break in service period specified in the plan.

(2) *Inactive*—(i) *Inactive receiving benefits.* Any individual who is retired or separated from employment covered by the plan and who is receiving benefits under the plan. This category does not include an individual to whom an insurer has made an irrevocable commitment to pay all the benefits to which the individual is entitled under the plan.

(ii) *Inactive entitled to future benefits.* Any individual who is retired or separated from employment covered by the plan and who is entitled to begin receiving benefits under the plan in the future. This category does not include an individual to whom an insurer has made an irrevocable commitment to pay all the benefits to which the individual is entitled under the plan.

(3) *Deceased.* Any deceased individual who has one or more beneficiaries who are receiving or entitled to receive benefits under the plan. This category does not include an individual if an insurer has made an irrevocable commitment to pay all the benefits to which the beneficiaries of that individual are entitled under the plan.

(4) For plan years beginning before September 2, 1975, a retiree or former employee for whom a fully paid-up immediate or deferred annuity has been purchased shall be treated as a "participant" for purposes of this part if such individual retains a legal claim against the plan for benefits or if the plan retains a participating interest in the annuity policy.

4. Section 2610.4 is revised to read as follows:

§ 2610.4 Filing address.

Except as may otherwise be provided by instructions in the PBGC Annual Premium Payment Package, any form or payment required to be filed or paid under the provisions of this part shall be mailed to Pension Benefit Guaranty Corporation, P.O. Box 105655, Atlanta, GA 30348-5655, or delivered to Nations Bank Retail Lockbox Processing Center, PBGC Lockbox 105655, 6000 Feldwood Road, 5 Southside East, College Park, GA 30349.

5. Section 2610.5 is revised to read as follows:

§ 2610.5 Date of filing.

(a) *Premium payment years beginning after 1992.* (1) Any form or payment required to be filed or paid under the provisions of this part with respect to a premium payment year beginning after 1992 shall be deemed filed or paid on the earlier of—

(i) The date on which it is mailed, as evidenced by a legible United States Postal Service postmark, registered mail receipt, or other proof of the date of mailing with the United States Postal Service, or

(ii) Five days before the date on which it is received by the PBGC.

(2) For purpses of this section, if the PBGC receives a form or payment on the first business day following a weekend or a federal holiday, then the PBGC shall be deemed to have received the form or payment on the day after the last business day preceding the weekend or holiday. The term *business day* as used in this section means any day that is not a Saturday, a Sunday, or a federal holiday.

(b) *Premium payment years beginning before 1993.* (1) Any form or payment required to be filed or paid under the provisions of this part with respect to a premium payment year beginning before 1993 shall be deemed filed or paid on the date on which it is mailed.

(2) For purposes of this paragraph (b), a form or payment shall be presumed to have been mailed on the date on which it is postmarked

by the United States Postal Service, or three days prior to the date on which it is received by the PBGC if it does not contain a legible United States Postal Service postmark.

6. In § 2610.8, paragraphs (b)(4) and (b)(5) are revised to read as follows:

§ 2610.8 Late payment penalty charges.

* * *

(b) *Waiver of penalty charge.* * * *

(4) With respect to the period of 30 days after the date of any PBGC bill for the premium payment necessary to reconcile the premium paid with the actual premium due, if the bill is paid within that 30-day period; or

(5) With respect to any premium payment (excluding any variable rate portion of the premium under § 2610.22(a)(2)) for a premium payment year beginning before 1993, if a plan that is required to make a reconciliation filing described in § 2610.25(e)(2)(iii) or § 2610.34(b)—

(i) paid at least 90 percent of the flat rate portion of the premium due for the premium payment year by the due date specified in § 2610.25(e)(2)(i) or § 2610.34(a); or

(ii) paid by the due date specified in § 2610.25(e)(2)(i) or § 2610.34(a) an amount equal to the premium that would be due for the premium payment year, computed using the flat per capita premium rate for the premium payment year and the participant count upon which the prior year's premium was based; and

(iii) pays 100 percent of the premium due for the premium payment year under § 2610.22 (excluding any variable rate portion of the premium under § 2610.22(a)(2)), § 2610.32, or § 2610.33, as applicable, on or before the due date for the reconciliation filing under § 2610.25(e)(2)(iii) or § 2610.34(b), as applicable.

7. Section 2610.21 is revised to read as follows:

§ 2610.21 Purpose and scope.

This subpart provides rules for computing and procedures for paying premiums for plan years beginning after 1987.

8. In § 2610.22, paragraph (a) is amended by revising its heading; paragraphs (a)(3) introductory text and (a)(3)(i)-(a)(3)(v) are redesignated as paragraphs (f) introductory text and (f)(1)-(f)(5) respectively; redesignated paragraphs (f) introductory text and (f)(5) are amended by revising the references "(a)(3)", "(a)(3)(i)", "(a)(3)(ii)", "(a)(3)(iii)", "(a)(3)(iv)", and "(a)(3)(v)" (wherever they appear) to read "(f)", "(f)(1)", "(f)(2)", "(f)(3)", "(f)(4)", and "(f)(5)" respectively; paragraph (c) is removed; paragraph (b) is redesignated as paragraph (c); redesignated paragraph (c) is amended by revising the reference "paragraph (a)" to read "paragraphs (a) and (b)"; redesignated paragraph (f) is amended by revising its heading and by removing the first sentence of its introductory text; paragraph (d) is revised; and new paragraphs (a)(3), (b), and (e) are added, to read as follows:

§ 2610.22 Premium rates.

(a) *Single-employer plans.* * * *

(3) *Cap on variable rate amount.* In no event shall the variable rate amount determined under paragraph (a)(2) of this section exceed $34 per participant (for premium payment years beginning in 1988, 1989, or 1990) or $53 per participant (for premium payment years beginning after 1990), or (for premium payment years beginning before 1993) such lesser amount as may be determined under paragraph (f) of this section.

(b) *Multiemployer plans.* For a premium payment year beginning on or after January 1, 1988, the premium paid by a multiemployer plan for basic benefits guaranteed under section 4022A(a) of the Act is equal to the number of participants in the plan on the last day of the plan year preceding the premium payment year multiplied by:

(1) For premium payment years beginning before September 27, 1988, $2.20; and

(2) For premium payment years beginning after September 26, 1988, $2.60.

* * *

(d) *Special refund rule for certain short plan years.* A plan described in this paragraph that pays the full premium due for a short plan year that begins after 1988 is entitled, upon request, to a refund of a portion of the premium. The amount of the refund will be determined by prorating the premium for the short plan year by the number of months (treating a part of a month as a month) in the short plan year. A plan is described in this paragraph if—

(1) the plan is a new or newly covered plan that becomes effective for premium purposes on a date other than the first day of its first plan year;

(2) the plan adopts an amendment changing its plan year, resulting in a short plan year;

(3) the plan's assets are distributed pursuant to the plan's termination, in which case the short plan year for purposes of computing the amount of the refund under this paragraph shall be deemed to end on the asset distribution date or, if later (in the case of a single-employer plan), the date 30 days before the PBGC receives the plan's post-distribution certification; or

(4) the plan is a single-employer plan, and a trustee of the plan is appointed pursuant to section 4042 of the Act, in which case the short plan year for purposes of computing the amount of the refund under this paragraph shall be deemed to end on the date of appointment.

(e) *Special credit rule for certain short plan years.* A plan described in paragraph (d)(1) or (d)(2) of this section is entitled at its option to a credit for a portion of the premium for a short plan year, in lieu of a refund under paragraph (d) of this section, under the circumstances described in this paragraph (e). A plan described in paragraph (d)(1) of this section may claim the credit against the premium due for an initial short plan year that begins after 1992. A plan described in paragraph (d)(2) of this section that pays the full premium due for a short plan year may claim the credit for the short plan year against the premium due for the following full plan year if the full plan year begins after 1992. In either case, the amount of the credit shall be determined in the same manner as the amount of a refund under paragraph (d) of this section, and the credit shall be claimed in accordance with instructions in the PBGC Annual Premium Payment Package.

(f) *Variable rate cap reduction for premium payment years beginning before 1993.*

* * *

9. In § 2610.23, paragraph (a) is amended by adding, after the reference "paragraph (c)" in the first sentence of the introductory text, the reference "or (f)"; paragraph (c) is redesignated as paragraph (f); paragraph (e) is amended by adding, after the reference "paragraphs (a) through (d)", the reference "and (f)"; redesignated paragraph (f) is amended by revising the references "(c)(1)", "(c)(2)", "(c)(3)", "(c)(4)", and "(c)(5)" (wherever they appear) to read "(f)(1)", "(f)(2)", "(f)(3)", "(f)(4)", and "(f)(5)" respectively; paragraph (b)(2) is amended by revising the second, third and fourth sentences; paragraph (d) is amended by revising the heading and introductory text; redesignated paragraph (f) is amended by revising the heading and the first sentence of the introductory text; and paragraph (c) is added, to read as follows:

§ 2610.23 *Determination of unfunded vested benefits.*

* * *

(b) *Unfunded vested benefits.* * * *

(2) *Actuarial value of assets.* * * *

Contributions owed for any plan year preceding the premium payment year shall be included for premium payment years beginning during 1988 and, for premium payment years beginning after 1988, shall be included for plans with 500 or more participants as of the last day of the plan year preceding the premium payment year and may be included for any other plan. However, contributions may be included only to the extent such contributions have been paid into the plan on or before the earlier of the due date specified in § 2610.25(b)(1), (b)(2)(ii), (e)(1), or (e)(2)(ii) (as applicable) or the date that the full amount of the premium (including any variable rate portion) is paid. Contributions included that are paid after the last day of the plan year preceding the premium payment year shall be discounted at the plan asset valuation rate (on a simple or compound basis in accordance with the plan's discounting rules) to the last day of the plan year preceding the premium payment year to reflect the date(s) of payment. * * *

(c) *Simplified filing method for premium payment years after 1992—* (1) *In general.* In lieu of determining the amount of a plan's unfunded vested benefits pursuant to paragraph (a) of this section for a premium payment year beginning after 1992, the plan administrator may, subject to the restrictions in paragraphs (c)(1)(i) and (c)(1)(ii) of this section, calculate the amount of the plan's unfunded vested benefits under this paragraph (c). The computation shall be done, using the plan's Form 5500 Schedule B for the plan year preceding the premium payment year, as follows. The value of the plan's vested benefits shall be adjusted in accordance with paragraphs (c)(2) through (c)(5) of this section to reflect accruals for the plan year preceding the premium payment year and the difference between the interest rate prescribed in paragraph (b)(1) of this section and the plan's current liability interest rate or rates. The value of plan assets shall be adjusted in accordance with paragraph (c)(6) of this section to reflect contributions for the plan year preceding the premium payment year. The resulting unfunded vested benefits amount (the adjusted value of vested benefits minus the adjusted value of assets) shall be further adjusted in accordance with paragraph (c)(7) of this section to reflect the passage of time from the date of the adjusted Schedule B data (the first day of the plan year preceding the premium payment year) to the last day of the plan year preceding the premium payment year. (An alternative calculation method for premium payment years beginning before 1993 is described in paragraph (f) of this section.)

(i) A plan's unfunded vested benefits may be calculated under this paragraph (c) only if neither of the plan's current liability interest rates required to be entered in line 12c(i) of the plan's Form 5500 Schedule B for the plan year preceding the premium payment year exceeds the interest rate prescribed in paragraph (b)(1) of this section by more than six percentage points.

(ii) The unfunded vested benefits of a plan with 500 or more participants as of the last day of the plan year preceding the premium payment year may be calculated under this paragraph (c) only in accordance with the provisions of paragraph (d) of this section, and only if the amount of the plan's unfunded vested benefits determined pursuant to paragraph (a) of this section does not exceed the amount of such unfunded vested benefits calculated under this paragraph (c) and an enrolled actuary so certifies in accordance with the Premium Payment Package.

(2) *Vested benefits adjustment factors.* In the simplified filing method described in this paragraph (c), the vested benefits values required to be entered in item 6d of Schedule B shall be adjusted in accordance with paragraphs (c)(3), (c)(4), and (c)(5) of this section using factors from the tables set forth in this paragraph (c)(2), and the sum of the three vested benefits values as so adjusted shall be used in determining unfunded vested benefits under paragraph (c)(7) of this section. For each adjustment, a Table 1 factor shall be used if the required interest rate prescribed in paragraph (b)(1) of this section (the "Premium Interest Rate") is less than the applicable current liability interest rate specified in paragraph (c)(3), (c)(4), or (c)(5) of this section (the "Funding Interest Rate"), and a Table 2 factor shall be used if the Premium Interest Rate equals or exceeds the applicable Funding Interest Rate. The factor for each adjustment shall be taken from the line in the appropriate table on which appears, in column A, the range of values that includes the amount (expressed as a percentage, rounded to the nearest hundredth of one percent) by which the Premium Interest Rate differs from the applicable Funding Interest Rate, and from the column specified in paragraph (c)(3), (c)(4), or (c)(5) of this section (based, in the case of paragraphs (c)(4) and (c)(5) of this section, on the assumed retirement age required to be entered in line 12d of Schedule B).

TABLE 1
[To be used when the Premium Interest Rate is less than the Funding Interest Rate]

Column A		Column B	Column C			
If the Funding Interest Rate minus the Premium Interest Rate (to the nearest hundredth of a percent) is—		The factor for pay-status benefits is—	The factor for pre-pay-status benefits (based on the plan's assumed retirement age) is—			
at least	but not over		for ages under 60	for ages 60-61	for ages 62-63	for ages over 63
0.01	0.25	1.02	1.04	1.04	1.05	1.05
.26	.50	1.03	1.08	1.09	1.10	1.11
.51	.75	1.05	1.12	1.13	1.15	1.16
.76	1.00	1.06	1.16	1.18	1.20	1.22
1.01	1.25	1.08	1.20	1.23	1.26	1.29

Column A		Column B	Column C			
If the Funding Interest Rate minus the Premium Interest Rate (to the nearest hundredth of a percent) is—		*The factor for pay-status benefits is—*	*The factor for pre-pay-status benefits (based on the plan's assumed retirement age) is—*			
at least	but not over		for ages under 60	for ages 60-61	for ages 62-63	for ages over 63
1.26	1.50	1.10	1.24	1.28	1.31	1.35
1.51	1.75	1.11	1.29	1.33	1.38	1.42
1.76	2.00	1.13	1.34	1.39	1.44	1.49
2.01	2.25	1.15	1.39	1.45	1.51	1.57
2.26	2.50	1.17	1.44	1.50	1.58	1.65
2.51	2.75	1.19	1.49	1.57	1.65	1.73
2.76	3.00	1.20	1.54	1.63	1.72	1.82
3.01	3.25	1.22	1.60	1.70	1.80	1.92
3.26	3.50	1.24	1.66	1.77	1.89	2.01
3.51	3.75	1.26	1.72	1.84	1.97	2.11
3.76	4.00	1.28	1.78	1.92	2.06	2.22
4.01	4.25	1.30	1.85	2.00	2.16	2.33
4.20	4.50	1.32	1.91	2.08	2.26	2.45
4.51	4.75	1.34	1.98	2.16	2.36	2.57
4.76	5.00	1.36	2.06	2.25	2.47	2.70
5.01	5.25	1.38	2.13	2.34	2.58	2.84
5.26	5.50	1.41	2.21	2.44	2.70	2.98
5.51	5.75	1.43	2.29	2.54	2.82	3.13
5.76	6.00	1.45	2.37	2.64	2.95	3.29

TABLE 2
[To be used when the Premium Interest Rate equals or exceeds the Funding Interest Rate]

Column A		Column B	Column C			
If the Premium Interest Rate minus the Funding Interest Rate (to the nearest hundredth of a percent) is—		*The factor for pay-status benefits is—*	*The factor for pre-pay-status benefits (based on the plan's assumed retirement age) is—*			
at least	but not over		for ages under 60	for ages 60-61	for ages 62-63	for ages over 63
0.00	0.25	1.00	1.00	1.00	1.00	1.00
.26	.50	.98	.97	.96	.96	.95
.51	.75	.97	.95	.92	.91	.91
.76	1.00	.95	.92	.89	.88	.86
1.01	1.25	.94	.90	.85	.84	.82
1.26	1.50	.92	.87	.82	.80	.78
1.51	1.75	.91	.85	.79	.77	.75
1.76	2.00	.90	.83	.76	.73	.71
2.01	2.25	.88	.80	.73	.70	.68
2.26	2.50	.87	.78	.70	.67	.64
2.51	2.75	.86	.76	.68	.64	.61
2.76	3.00	.84	.74	.65	.62	.58
3.01	3.25	.83	.72	.62	.59	.56
3.26	3.50	.83	.70	.60	.56	.53
3.51	3.75	.80	.68	.58	.54	.50
3.76	4.00	.79	.66	.55	.52	.48??
4.01	4.25	.78	.64	.53	.49	.46
4.26	4.50	.77	.63	.51	.47	.44
4.51	4.75	.76	.61	.49	.45	.41
4.76	5.00	.74	.59	.47	.43	.39
5.01	5.25	.73	.58	.45	.41	.37
5.26	5.50	.72	.56	.44	.39	.36
5.51	5.75	.71	.55	.42	.38	.34
>5.75	>5.75	.70	.53	.40	.36	.32

(3) *Adjusted value of vested benefits—retirees and beneficiaries.* In the simplified filing method described in this paragraph (c), the adjusted value of vested benefits for retirees and beneficiaries shall be the value of such benefits required to be entered in column (2) on line 6d(i) of Schedule B, multiplied by the appropriate factor determined under paragraph (c)(2) of this section. The factor shall be determined using the Funding Interest Rate required to be entered in the post-retirement column on line 12c(i) of Schedule B and shall be taken from column B of the appropriate table in paragraph (c)(2) of this section.

(4) *Adjusted value of vested benefits—terminated vested participants.* In the simplified filing method described in this paragraph (c), the adjusted value of vested benefits for terminated vested participants shall be the value of such benefits required to be entered in column (2) on line 6d(ii) of Schedule B, multiplied by the appropriate factor determined under paragraph (c)(2) of this section. The factor shall be determined using the greater of the Funding Interest Rates required to

be entered in the pre-retirement and post-retirement columns on line 12c(i) of Schedule B and shall be taken from column C of the appropriate table in paragraph (c)(2) of this section and from the subcolumn of column C that is headed by the age range that includes the plan's assumed retirement age.

(5) *Adjusted value of vested benefits—active participants.* In the simplified filing method described in this paragraph (c), the adjusted value of vested benefits for active participants shall be the sum of the value of such benefits required to be entered in column (2) on line 6d(iii) of Schedule B and the expected accruals for the plan year preceding the premium payment year required to be entered on line 6e of Schedule B, multiplied by the appropriate factor determined under paragraph (c)(2) of this section. The factor shall be determined using the same Funding Interest Rate, and shall be taken from the same column and subcolumn, as specified for terminated vested participants' benefits under paragraph (c)(4) of this section.

(6) *Adjusted value of plan assets.* In the simplified filing method described in this paragraph (c), the adjusted value of plan assets that shall be used in determining unfunded vested benefits under paragraph (c)(7) of this section shall be the sum of—

(i) the value of such assets required to be entered on line 8b of Schedule B (if the amount on line 8b was determined as of the first day of the plan year preceding the premium payment year) or on line 6c of Schedule B (if the amount on line 8b was determined as of a date other than the first day of the plan year preceding the premium payment year), plus

(ii) an amount equal to 0.95 times the total amount of contributions required to be entered in columns (b) and (c) of item 7 of Schedule B.

(7) *Adjusted value of unfunded vested benefits.* In the simplified filing method described in this paragraph (c), the amount of the plan's unfunded vested benefits shall be the product of—

(i) the sum of the adjusted values of vested benefits determined under paragraphs (c)(3), (c)(4), and (c)(5) of this section minus the adjusted value of plan assets determined under paragraph (c)(6) of this section, multiplied by

(ii) the sum of 1 plus the required interest rate prescribed in paragraph (b)(1) of this section (expressed as a decimal fraction of 1, not as a percentage).

(d) *Significant events.* The significant events described in this paragraph shall be reflected in the assumptions used in determining a plan's unfunded vested benefits under paragraph (a) of this section to the extent required by paragraph (a) of this section. A plan with 500 or more participants as of the last day of the plan year preceding the premium payment year may use the simplified filing method described in paragraph (c) of this section or the alternative calculation method described in paragraph (f) of this section if no significant event, as described in this paragraph, has occurred between the first day and the last day of the plan year preceding the premium payment year and an enrolled actuary so certifies in accordance with the Premium Payment Package. If a significant event has occurred between those dates, such a plan may use the simplified filing method or alternative calculation method only if an enrolled actuary makes an appropriate adjustment to the value of unfunded vested benefits to reflect the occurrence of the signficant event and certifies to that fact in accordance with the Premium Payment Package. The significant events described in this paragraph are—

* * *

(f) *Alternative calculation method for premium payment years before 1993.* In lieu of determining the amount of a plan's unfunded vested benefits pursuant to paragraph (a) of this section for a premium payment year beginning before 1993, the plan administrator may calculate the amount of the plan's unfunded vested benefits under this paragraph (f) using the plan's Form 5500, Schedule B, for the plan year preceding the premium payment year. * * *

* * *

10. In § 2610.24, paragraph (c) is redesignated as paragraph (h); paragraph (d) is amended by revising the reference "§ 2610.22(a)(3)" to read "§ 2610.22(f)"; paragraph (g) is amended by revising the reference "(e)(1) and (e)(2)" to read "(f)(1) and (f)(2)"; redesignated paragraph (h) is amended by adding, after the words *"unfunded vested benefits"* in the heading, the words *"for premium payment years beginning before 1993"* and by revising the words "on or after January 1, 1989" in the first sentence of the introductory text to read "after 1988 and before 1993"; redesignated paragraphs (h) introductory text, (h)(2), (h)(3), and (h)(4) are amended by revising the references "§ 2610.23(c)", "§ 2610.23(c)(1)", and "§ 2610.23(c)(5)" (wherever they appear) to read "§ 2610.23(f)", "§ 2610.23(f)(1)", and "§ 2610.23(f)(5)", respectively; paragraph (a)(3) is revised; and new paragraph (c) is added, to read as follows:

§ *2610.24 Variable rate exemptions and special rules.*

(a) *Exemptions.* * * *

(3) *Section 412(i) plans.* A plan is described in this paragraph if the plan satisfied all criteria listed in section 412(i) of the Code and the regulations thereunder on the last day of the plan year preceding the premium payment year and the plan administrator so certifies, in accordance with the Premium Payment Package.

* * *

(c) *Special rule for determining unfunded vested benefits for premium payment years beginning after 1992 for plans terminating in distress or involuntary terminations.* With respect to premium payment years beginning after 1992, a plan described in this paragraph (c) may deter-

mine its unfunded vested benefits by using the special simplified filing method set forth in this paragraph, but only if neither of the plan's current liability interest rates required to be entered in line 12c(i) of the Schedule B described in paragraph (c)(1) of this section exceeds the interest rate prescribed in § 2610.23(b)(1) by more than six percentage points; and, in the case of a plan with 500 or more participants as of the last day of the plan year preceding the premium payment year, only in accordance with the provisions of § 2610.23(d), and only if the amount of the plan's unfunded vested benefits determined pursuant to § 2610.23(a) does not exceed the amount of such unfunded vested benefits determined under this paragraph (c) and an enrolled actuary so certifies in accordance with the Premium Payment Package. (A similar special rule for premium payment years before 1993 is described in paragraph (h) of this section.) A plan is described in this paragraph if it has issued notices of intent to terminate in a distress termination in accordance with section 4041(a)(2) of the Act with a proposed termination date on or before the last day of the plan year preceding the premium payment year, or if the PBGC has instituted proceedings to terminate the plan in accordance with section 4042 of the Act and has sought a termination date on or before the last day of the plan year preceding the premium payment year. Pursuant to this paragraph, a plan shall determine its unfunded vested benefits in accordance with the simplified filing method in § 2610.23(c), except that—

(1) The calculation shall be based on the plan's Form 5500 Schedule B for the plan year that includes (in the case of a distress termination) the proposed termination date or (in the case of an involuntary termination) the termination date sought by the PBGC, or, if no Schedule B is filed for that plan year, on the Schedule B for the immediately preceding plan year;

(2) All references in § 2610.23(c) and § 2610.23(d) to the first day of the plan year preceding the premium payment year shall be deemed to refer to the first day of the plan year for which the Schedule B was filed;

(3) If the Schedule B described in paragraph (c)(1) of this section is for a plan year beginning after 1988, then § 2610.23(c)(5) shall be applied by using, instead of the amount required to be entered on line 6e of Schedule B, an amount equal to the product of—

(i) The amount required to be entered on line 6e of Schedule B, multiplied by

(ii) the number of years (rounded to the nearest hundredth of a year) between the date of the Schedule B data and (in the case of a distress termination) the proposed termination date or (in the case of an involuntary termination) the termination date sought by the PBGC;

(4) If the Schedule B described in paragraph (c)(1) of this section is for a plan year beginning before 1989, then—

(i) the reference to "column (2)" in § 2610.23(c)(3) shall be ignored;

(ii) Section 2610.23(c)(4) shall not be applied; and

(iii) Section 2610.23(c)(5) shall be applied by using, instead of the amount required to be entered in column (2) on line 6d(iii) of Schedule B, the amount required to be entered on line 6d(ii) of Schedule B, and instead of the amount required to be entered on line 6e of Schedule B, an amount equal to the product of—

(A) Seven percent of the amount required to be entered on line 6d(ii) of Schedule B, multiplied by

(B) The number of years (rounded to the nearest hundredth of a year) between the date of the Schedule B data and (in the case of a distress termination) the proposed termination date or (in the case of an involuntary termination) the termination date sought by the PBGC;

(5) Section 2610.23(c)(6) shall not be applied, and the adjusted value of plan assets shall be the value of such assets required to be entered on line 8b of Schedule B (if the amount on line 8b was determined as of the first day of the plan year preceding the premium payment year) or on line 6c of Schedule B (if the amount on line 8b was determined as of a date other than the first day of the plan year preceding the premium payment year), adjusted in accordance with § 2610.23(b)(2); except that the amount of all contributions that are included in the value of assets and that were made after the first day of the plan year preceding the premium payment year shall be discounted to such first day at the interest rate prescribed in § 2610.23(b)(1) for the premium payment year, compounded annually except that simple interest may be used for any partial years; and

(6) For purposes of applying § 2610.23(c)(7), the quantity described in § 2610.23(c)(7)(ii) shall be modified by raising it to a power, the exponent being the number of years (rounded to the nearest hun-

dredth of a year) between the date of the Schedule B data and the last day of the plan year preceding the premium payment year.

* * *

11. In §2610.25, paragraphs (b), (c), and (d) are removed; paragraphs (e) and (f) are redesignated as paragraphs (c) and (d); paragraph (a) is amended by revising the last sentence; redesignated paragraph (c) is amended by revising the last sentence; and new paragraphs (b) and (e) are added, to read as follows:

§2610.25 Filing requirement.

[NOTE: The PBGC has adopted final regulations relating to Prop. Regs. §2610.25(b)(1), §2610.25(b)(2)(ii), and §2610.25(b)(3)(i). The change in the premium filing due date was originally proposed for the 1993 plan year. However, the finalized change is effective beginning with the 1999 plan year. PBGC Final Reg. §4007.11 was published in the Federal Register on December 14, 1998 (63 FR 68684) and is at ¶ 15,371J.

(a) *General rule.* * * * The premium forms and payments shall be filed no later than the applicable due dates specified in paragraph (b) of this section (for premium payment years beginning after 1992) or paragraph (e) of this section (for premium payment years beginning after 1987 and before 1993).

(b) *Due dates for premium payment years beginning after 1992.* For premium payment years beginning after 1992, the due date generally applicable to small plans is prescribed in paragraph (b)(1) of this section and the due dates generally applicable to large plans are prescribed in paragraph (b)(2) of this section; paragraphs (b)(3) and (b)(4) of this section prescribe special rules for new and newly covered plans and for plans that change plan years; and paragraph (b)(5) of this section defines the terms "large plan" and "small plan" for purposes of this paragraph (b).

(1) *Small plans; in general.* The due date for a small plan (except as provided in paragraphs (b)(3) and (b)(4) of this section) is the last day of the ninth full calendar month following the end of the plan year preceding the premium payment year.

(2) *Large plans; in general.* For a large plan (except as provided in paragraphs (b)(3) and (b)(4) of this section)—

(i) The fifteenth day of the first full calendar month following the end of the plan year preceding the premium payment year is the due date for so much of the premium as does not exceed the amount of the premium required to be paid for the plan year preceding the premium payment year (determined without regard to any refund or credit for a short premium payment year under §2610.22(d) or (e)); and

(ii) the due date for any portion of the premium that exceeds the amount described in paragraph (b)(2)(i) of this section is the last day of the ninth full calendar month following the end of the plan year preceding the premium payment year.

(3) *New and newly covered plans.* The due date for the first premium payment year of coverage of any new plan or newly covered plan (as defined in §2610.2) is the latest of—

(i) The last day of the ninth full calendar month that begins on or after the later of—

(A) The first day of the premium payment year, or

(B) The day on which the plan becomes effective for benefit accruals for future service;

(ii) 90 days after the date of the plan's adoption; or

(iii) 90 days after the date on which the plan becomes covered by title IV of the Act pursuant to section 4021 of the Act.

(4) *Plans that change plan years.* For a plan that changes its plan year, each due date for the short plan year shall be the applicable due date specified in paragraph (b)(1), (b)(2), or (b)(3) of this section, and each due date for the plan year that follows the short plan year shall be the later of—

(i) The applicable due date specified in paragraph (b)(1) or (b)(2) of this section; or

(ii) 90 days after the date on which the amendment changing the plan year was adopted.

(5) *Definition of "large plan" and "small plan."* For purposes of this paragraph (b), a "large plan" is a plan that was required to pay premiums for 5,000 or more participants for the plan year preceding the premium payment year, and a "small plan" is a plan that was required to pay premiums for fewer than 5,000 participants for the plan year preceding the premium payment year.

(c) *Continuing obligation to file.* * * * The entire premium computed under this subpart must be paid for that plan year, whether or not the plan is entitled to a refund for a short plan year pursuant to §2610.22(d)(3) or (4).

* * *

(e) *Due dates for premium payment years beginning after 1987 and before 1993.* For premium payment years beginning after 1987 and before 1993, the due date generally applicable to small plans is prescribed in paragraph (e)(1) of this section and the due dates generally applicable to large plans are prescribed in paragraph (e)(2) of this section; paragraphs (e)(3) and (e)(4) of this section prescribe special rules for new and newly covered plans and for plans that change plan years; and paragraph (e)(5) of this section defines the terms "large plan" and "small plan" for purposes of this paragraph (e).

(1) *Small plans; in general.* The due date for a small plan (except as provided in paragraphs (e)(3) and (e)(4) of this section) is the fifteenth day of the eighth full calendar month following the month in which the premium payment year begins.

(2) *Large plans; in general.* For a large plan (except as provided in paragraphs (e)(3) and (e)(4) of this section)—

(i) The due date for the multiemployer premium required by §2610.22(b) and for the flat rate portion of the single-employer premium required by §2610.22(a)(1) is the last day of the second full calendar month following the close of the plan year preceding the premium payment year; and

(ii) The due date for the variable rate portion of the single-employer premium required by §2610.22(a)(2) is the fifteenth day of the eighth full calendar month following the month in which the premium payment year begins.

(iii) If the number of plan participants on the last day of the plan year preceding the premium payment year is not known by the date specified in paragraph (e)(2)(i) of this section, a reconciliation filing (on the form prescribed by this part) and any required premium payment or request for refund shall be made by the date specified in paragraph (e)(2)(ii) of this section.

(3) *New and newly covered plans.* The due date for the first premium payment year of coverage of any new plan or newly covered plan (as defined in §2610.2) is the latest of—

(i) The fifteenth day of the eighth full calendar month following the month in which the plan year begins or, if later, in which the plan becomes effective for benefit accruals for future service;

(ii) 90 days after the date of the plan's adoption; or

(iii) 90 days after the date on which the plan becomes covered by Title IV of the Act pursuant to section 4021 of the Act.

(4) *Plans that change plan years.* For a plan that changes its plan year, each due date for the short plan year shall be the applicable due date specified in paragraph (e)(1), (e)(2), or (e)(3) of this section, and each due date for the plan year that follows the short plan year shall be the later of—

(i) The applicable due date specified in paragraph (e)(1) or (e)(2) of this section; or

(ii) 30 days after the date on which the amendment changing the plan year was adopted.

(5) *Definition of "large plan" and "small plan."* For purposes of this paragraph (e), a "large plan" is a plan that was required to pay premiums for 500 or more participants for the plan year preceding the premium payment year, and a "small plan" is a plan that was required to pay premiums for fewer than 500 participants for the plan year preceding the premium payment year.

* * *

12. Section 2610.31 is revised to read as follows:

§2610.31 Purpose and scope.

This subpart provides rules for calculating and procedures for paying premiums for plan years beginning before 1988.

13. In §2610.33, paragraph (d) is removed; paragraph (a)(1) is amended by revising the table; and paragraph (b) is revised, to read as follows:

§2610.33 Multiemployer premium rates.

(a) * * *

(1) * * *

For premium payment years	Rate
After Sept. 26, 1980, and before Sept. 27, 1984	$1.40
After Sept. 26, 1984, and before Sept. 27, 1986	1.80
After Sept. 26, 1986, and before 1988	2.20

* * *

(b) *New and newly covered plans.* For any new plan or newly covered plan (as defined in §2610.2), the plan administrator shall pay the applicable premium under paragraph (a) of this section for each individual who is a participant in the plan on the date the plan becomes covered by section 4021(a) of the Act.

* * *

14. In §2610.34, paragraphs (a)(7), (a)(8)(ii), (a)(9)(iv), and (b)(6) are removed; paragraph (a)(8)(i) is amended by removing the introductory text and by redesignating paragraphs (a)(8)(i)(A)-(D) as paragraphs (a)(8)(i)-(iv) respectively; paragraphs (a)(8), (a)(9), and (a)(10) are redesignated respectively as paragraphs (a)(7), (a)(8), and (a)(9); paragraphs (a) introductory text, (a)(5)(i), (a)(5)(ii), (a)(6)(i), and (a)(6)(ii), and redesignated paragraphs (a)(7), (a)(8) introductory text, (a)(8)(ii)(A), (a)(8)(ii)(B), and (a)(8)(iii)(A), and (a)(8)(iii)(B) are amended by revising the references "(a)(7)", "(a)(7)(ii)", "(a)(8)", "(a)(9)", and "(a)(10)" (wherever they appear) to read "(a)(6)", "(a)(6)", "(a)(7)", "(a)(8)", and "(a)(9)" respectively; redesignated paragraph (a)(9) is amended by revising the introductory text; and paragraph (c) is amended by revising the last sentence, to read as follows:

§2610.34 Filing requirement.

(a) * * *

(9) For purposes of paragraphs (a)(5), (a)(6), (a)(8), (b)(4), and (b)(5) of this section, the number of participants in a plan year is determined as of the following dates:

* * *

(c) *Continuing obligation to file.* * * * The entire premium computed under this subpart must be paid for that plan year.

* * *

15. Appendix B to part 2610 is amended by revising the introductory text preceding the table to read as follows:

Appendix B—Interest Rates for Valuing Vested Benefits

The following table lists the required interest rates to be used in valuing a plan's vested benefits under §2610.23(b) and in calculating a plan's adjusted vested benefits under §2610.23(c)(2) and (e)(1):

* * *

Issued in Washington, DC, this 6th day of April, 1992.

James B. Lockhart III,

Executive Director, Pension Benefit Guaranty Corporation.

[FR Doc. 92-8242 Filed 4-9-92; 8:45 am]

¶ 20,533C   Reserved.

Proposed Reg. §§2647.1, 2647.2, and 2647.9, relating to the reduction or waiver of complete withdrawal liability, were formerly reproduced at this paragraph.

The final regulations appear at ¶ 15,671A, ¶ 15,671B, and ¶ 15,671I.]

¶ 20,533D   Reserved.

Proposed regulations designed to conform 29 CFR Parts 2606, 2612, 2615, 2622, and 2623 to current law, including the Single Employer Pension Plan Amendments Act of 1986 and the Pension Protection Act, were formerly reproduced at this paragraph.

The final regulations are at ¶ 15,315, ¶ 15,325, ¶ 15,429G-21—¶ 15,429G-26, ¶ 15,461—¶ 15,465B, and ¶ 15,623—¶ 15,623I.]

¶ 20,533E   Reserved.

Proposed regulations that would update the mortality assumptions used in valuing plan benefits in terminated single-employer pension plans trusteed by the PBGC were formerly reproduced at this paragraph.

The final regulations are at ¶ 15,620C, ¶ 15,620H, ¶ 15,620M—¶ 15,620O, ¶ 15,620Z, ¶ 15,687H and ¶ 15,687W.]

¶ 20,533F   Reserved.

Proposed Reg. §§2609.1—2609.6, governing the PBGC's use of administrative offset in collecting late premiums, late payment penalties, and other debts owed to it by plan sponsors, were formerly reproduced at this paragraph.

The final regulations appear at ¶ 15,328A—¶ 15,328G.]

¶ 20,533G   Reserved.

Proposed Regs. §§2671.1—2671.9 regarding the PBGC's notice requirements for underfunded plans were formally reproduced at this paragraph.

The final regulations appear at ¶ 15,403A—¶ 15,403L.]

¶ 20,533H

Proposed regulation on 29 CFR Part 2510: Multiple Employer Welfare Arrangements: Collective Bargaining Agreements.—Reproduced below is the text of proposed regulations concerning when an employee benefit plan is established or maintained pursuant to a collective bargaining agreement and, therefore, is excluded from the definition of a multiple employer welfare arrangement (MEWA). Such plans are not subject to state insurance law regulation under ERISA Sec. 514(b)(6). The proposed regulations establish specific criteria for determining that an agreement is a collective bargaining agreement and criteria for determining when an employee benefit plan or other arrangement is established or maintained pursuant to such an agreement.

The proposed regulations were published in the *Federal Register* on August 1, 1995 (60 FR 39208). The comment period was extended to November 16, 1995 on September 29, 1995 by 60 FR 50508. The proposed regulations are reproduced with the preamble below.

ERISA Sec. 3.

¶20,533C

DEPARTMENT OF LABOR

Pension and Welfare Benefits Administration

29 CFR Part 2510

RIN 1210-AA48

Proposed Regulation for Plans Established or Maintained Pursuant to Collective Bargaining Agreements Under Section 3(40)(A)

AGENCY: Pension and Welfare Benefits Administration, Department of Labor.

ACTION: Notice of Proposed Rulemaking.

SUMMARY: This document contains a proposed regulation under the Employee Retirement Income Security Act of 1974, as amended, 29 U.S.C. 1001-1461 (ERISA or the Act), setting forth specific criteria that must be met in order for the Secretary of Labor (the Secretary) to find that an agreement is a collective bargaining agreement for purposes of this section. The proposed regulation also sets forth criteria for determining when an employee benefit plan is established or maintained under or pursuant to such an agreement. Employee benefit plans that meet the requirements of the proposed regulation are excluded from the definition of "multiple employer welfare arrangements" under section 3(40) of ERISA and consequently are not subject to state regulation of multiple employer welfare arrangements as provided for by the Act. If adopted, the proposed regulation would affect employee welfare benefit plans, their sponsors, participants, and beneficiaries as well as service providers to plans.

DATES: Written comments concerning this proposed rule must be received by November 16, 1995. [Extended 9/29/95 by 60 FR 50508].

ADDRESSES: Interested persons are invited to submit written comments (preferably three copies) concerning the proposals herein to: Pension and Welfare Benefits Administration, Room N-5669, U.S. Department of Labor, 200 Constitution Ave., N.W., Washington, DC 20210. Attention: Proposed Regulation Under Section 3(40). All submissions will be open to public inspection at the Public Documents Room, Pension and Welfare Benefits Administration, U.S. Department of Labor, Room N-5638, 200 Constitution Ave., N.W., Washington, DC 20210.

FOR FURTHER INFORMATION CONTACT: Mark Connor, Office of Regulations and Interpretations, Pension and Welfare Benefits Administration, U.S. Department of Labor, Rm N-5669, 200 Constitution Ave., N.W., Washington, D.C. 20210 (telephone (202) 219-8671) or Cynthia Caldwell Weglicki, Office of the Solicitor, Plan Benefits Security Division, U.S. Department of Labor, Rm N-4611, 200 Constitution Ave., N.W., Washington, D.C. 20210 (telephone (202) 219-4592). These are not toll-free numbers.

SUPPLEMENTARY INFORMATION:

Background

Notice is hereby given of a proposed regulation under section 3(40) of ERISA, 29 U.S.C. 1002(40). Section 3(40)(A) defines the term multiple employer welfare arrangement (MEWA) in pertinent part as follows:

The term "multiple employer welfare arrangement" means an employee welfare benefit plan, or any other arrangement (other than an employee welfare benefit plan), which is established or maintained for the purpose of offering or providing any benefit described in paragraph (1) [of section 3 of the Act] to the employees of two or more employers (including one or more self-employed individuals), or to their beneficiaries, except that such term does not include any such plan or other arrangement which is established or maintained—

(i) under or pursuant to one or more agreements which the Secretary finds to be collective bargaining agreements . . . .

This provision was added to ERISA by the Multiple Employer Welfare Arrangement Act of 1983, Sec. 302(b), Pub. L. 97-473, 96 Stat. 2611, 2612 (29 U.S.C. 1002(40)), which also amended section 514(b) of ERISA. Section 514(a) of the Act provides that state laws which relate to employee benefit plans are generally preempted by ERISA. Section 514(b) sets forth exceptions to the general rule of section 514(a) and subjects employee benefit plans that are MEWAs to various levels of state regulation depending on whether or not the MEWA is fully insured. Sec. 302(b), Pub. L. 97-473, 96 Stat. 2611, 2613 (29 U.S.C. 1144(b)(6)).[1]

The Multiple Employer Welfare Arrangement Act legislation was introduced to counter what the Congressional drafters termed abuse by the "operators of bogus 'insurance' trusts." 128 Cong. Rec. E2407 (1982) (Statement of Congressman Erlenborn). In his comments, Congressman Erlenborn noted that certain MEWA operators had been successful in thwarting timely investigations and enforcement activities of state agencies by asserting that such entities were ERISA plans exempt from state regulation by the terms of section 514 of ERISA. The goal of the bill, according to Congressman Erlenborn, was to remove "any potential obstacle that might exist under current law which could hinder the ability of the States to regulate multiple employer welfare arrangements to assure the financial soundness and timely payment of benefits under such arrangements." *Id*. This concern was also expressed by the Committee on Education and Labor in the Activity Report of the Pension Task Force (94th Congress, 2d Session, 1977) cited by Congressman Erlenborn:

It has come to our attention, through the good offices of the National Association of State Insurance Commissioners, that certain entrepreneurs have undertaken to market insurance products to employers and employees at large, claiming these products to be ERISA covered plans. For instance, persons whose interest is in the profiting from the provision of administrative services are establishing insurance companies and related enterprises. The entrepreneur will then argue that his enterprise is an ERISA benefit plan which is protected under ERISA's preemption provision from state regulation.

Id. As a result of the addition of section 514(b)(6), certain state laws regulating insurance apply to employee benefit plans that are MEWAs. However, the definition of a MEWA in section 3(40) provides that an employee benefit plan is not a MEWA if it is established or maintained pursuant to an agreement which the Secretary finds to be a collective bargaining agreement. Such a plan is therefore not subject to state insurance law regulation under section 514(b)(6). This exclusion is necessary to avoid disrupting the activities of legitimate Taft-Hartley plans.

While the Multiple Employer Welfare Arrangement Act of 1983 significantly enhanced the states' ability to regulate MEWAs, problems in this area continue to exist as the result of the exception for collectively bargained plans contained in the 1983 amendments. This exception is now being exploited by some MEWA operators who, through the use of sham unions and collective bargaining agreements, market fraudulent insurance schemes under the guise of collectively bargained welfare plans exempt from state insurance regulation.[2] Another problem in this area involves the use of collectively bargained arrangements as vehicles for marketing health care coverage nationwide to employees and employers with no relationship to the bargaining process or the underlying agreement.

The Department believes that regulatory guidance in this area is necessary to ensure that (1) state insurance regulators have ascertainable guidelines to help identify and regulate MEWAs operating in their jurisdiction and (2) sponsors of employee health benefit programs will be able to determine independently whether their plans are established or maintained pursuant to collective bargaining agreements for pur-

---

[1] The Multiple Employer Welfare Arrangement Act of 1983 added section 514(b)(6) which provides a limited exception to ERISA's preemption of state insurance laws that allows states to exercise regulatory authority over employee welfare benefit plans that are MEWAs. Section 514(b) provides, in relevant part, that:

(6)(A) Notwithstanding any other provision of this section—(i) in the case of an employee welfare benefit plan which is a multiple employer welfare arrangement and is fully insured (or which is a multiple employer welfare arrangement subject to an exemption under subparagraph (B)), any law of any State which regulates insurance may apply to such arrangement to the extent that such law provides—

(I) standards, requiring the maintenance of specified levels of reserves and specified levels of contributions, which any such plan, or any trust established under such a plan, must meet in order to be considered under such law able to pay benefits in full when due, and

(II) provisions to enforce such standards, and

(ii) in the case of any other employee welfare benefit plan which is a multiple employer welfare arrangement, in addition to this title, any law of any State which regulates insurance may apply to the extent not inconsistent with the preceding sections of this title.

Thus an employee welfare benefit plan that is a MEWA remains subject to state regulation to the extent provided in section 514(b)(6)(A). MEWAs which are not employee benefit plans are unconditionally subject to state law.

[2] In addition, the Department has received requests to make individual determinations concerning the status of particular plans under section 3(40). *See, e.g., Ocean Breeze Festival Park v. Reich*, 853 F. Supp. 906, 910 (1994) (denying motion for mandamus and granting leave to amend complaint); *summary judgement granted sub nom. Virginia Beach Policemen's Benevolent Association, et al. v. Reich* 881 F. Supp. 1059 (E.D.Va. 1995); *Amalgamated Local Union No. 355 v. Gallagher*, No. 91 CIV 0193(RR) (E.D.N.Y. April 15, 1991).

poses of section 3(40)(A) without imposing the additional burden of having to apply to the Secretary for an individual finding.[3]

The proposed regulation first establishes specific criteria that the Secretary finds must be present in order for an agreement to be a collective bargaining agreement for purposes of section 3(40) and, second, establishes certain criteria applicable to determining when an employee benefit plan or other arrangement is established or maintained under or pursuant to such an agreement for purposes of section 3(40). In this regard, the Department notes that section 3(40) not only requires the existence of a *bona fide* collective bargaining agreement, but also requires that the plan be "established or maintained" pursuant to such an agreement. The Department believes that, in establishing the exception under section 3(40)(A)(i) of the Act, Congress intended to accommodate only those plans established or maintained to provide benefits to bargaining unit employees on whose behalf the plans where collectively bargained. For this reason, the Department believes that the exception under section 3(40)(A)(i) should be limited to plans providing coverage primarily to those individuals covered under collective bargaining agreements. Accordingly, the criteria in the proposed regulation relating to whether a plan or other arrangement qualifies as "established or maintained" is intended to ensure that the statutory exception is only available to plans whose participant base is predominately comprised of the bargaining unit employees on whose behalf such benefits were negotiated.

The proposed regulation would, upon adoption, constitute the Secretary's finding for purposes of determining whether an agreement is a collective bargaining agreement pursuant to section 3(40) of the Act. The Department does not intend to make individual findings or determinations concerning an entity's compliance with the proposed regulation. The criteria contained in the proposed regulation are designed to enable entities and state insurance regulatory agencies to determine whether the requirements of the statute are met. Under the proposed regulation, entities seeking to comply with these criteria must, upon request, provide documentation of their compliance with the criteria to the state or state agency charged with investigating and enforcing state insurance laws.

Description of the Proposal

Proposed § 2510.3-40(a) follows the language of section 3(40)(A) of the Act and states that the term multiple employer welfare arrangement does not include an employee welfare benefit plan which is established or maintained under or pursuant to one or more agreements which the Secretary finds to be collective bargaining agreements. Proposed § 2510.3-40(b) provides criteria which the Secretary finds to be essential for an agreement to be collectively bargained for purposes of section 3(40)(A) of the Act. Proposed § 2510.3-40(c) sets forth requirements concerning individuals covered by the employee welfare benefit plan that must be satisfied in order for an employee welfare benefit plan to be considered established or maintained under or pursuant to a collective bargaining agreement as defined in § 2510.3-40(b). Proposed § 2510.3-40(d) provides definitions of the terms "employee labor organization" and "supervisors and managers" for purposes of this section. Proposed § 2510.3-40(e) explains that a plan does not satisfy the requirements of this section if the plan or any entity associated with the plan (such as the employee labor organization or the employer) fails or refuses to comply with the requests of a state or state agency with respect to any documents or other evidence in its possession or control that are necessary to make a determination concerning the extent to which the plan is subject to state insurance law. Proposed § 2510.3-40(f) provides that, in a proceeding brought by a state or state agency to enforce the insurance laws of the state, nothing in the proposed regulation shall be construed to prohibit allocation of the burden of proving the existence of all the criteria required by this section to the entity seeking to be treated as other than a MEWA.

Under the proposed regulation, a plan that fails to meet the applicable criteria would be a MEWA and thus subject to state insurance laws as provided in section 514(b)(6) of ERISA.

Each subsection of the proposed regulation is described in detail below.

1. General Rule and Scope

Proposed regulation 29 CFR 2510.3-40 establishes criteria which must be met for a plan to be established or maintained under or pursuant to one or more agreements which the Secretary finds to be collective bargaining agreements for purposes of section 3(40) of the Act. The proposed regulation is not intended to apply to or affect any other provision of federal law.[4]

In the Department's view, the exclusion of collectively bargained plans or other arrangements from the definition of a MEWA in section 3(40)(A) is an exception to the general statutory rule. Thus the entity asserting the applicability of the provisions concerning collectively bargained plans in section 3(40) has the burden of providing evidence of compliance with the conditions of the statutory exception and the criteria set forth in the proposed regulation.[5] Accordingly, if an entity's status as established or maintained pursuant to one or more agreements which satisfy the criteria of the proposed regulation is challenged by a state or state agency, the entity seeking to be treated as other than a MEWA must produce sufficient evidence to establish that all of the requirements of the proposed regulation have been met.[6]

2. Definition of a Collective Bargaining Agreement

Proposed § 2510.3-40(b) establishes criteria that an agreement must meet in order to be a collective bargaining agreement for purposes of this section. An agreement constitutes a collective bargaining agreement only if the agreement is in writing and is executed by or on behalf of an employer of employees described in § 2510.3-40(c)(1) and by representatives of an employee labor organization meeting the requirements of § 2510.3-40(d)(1). In addition, the agreement must also be the result of good faith, arms-length bargaining binding signatory employers and the employee labor organization to the terms of the agreement for a specified project or period of time, and the agreement must be one which cannot be unilaterally amended or terminated. The Department notes that agreements in which an employer adopts all provisions of an existing agreement binding an employer and an employee labor organization to the terms and conditions of a collective bargaining agreement, such as a pattern agreement, will not fail to satisfy the requirements of proposed § 2510.3-40(b) if the original agreement as initially adopted satisfied the requirements of this section. The Department has also determined that collective bargaining agreements containing an agreement not to strike and providing that the collective bargaining agreement will terminate upon the initiation of a strike, often called "no strike" provisions, will not fail to satisfy the proposed regulation solely by reason of such provisions.

Proposed § 2510.3-40(b)(6) requires that a collective bargaining agreement may not provide for termination of the agreement solely as a result of the failure to make contributions to the plan. Proposed § 2510.3-40(b)(7) provides that an agreement will not constitute a collective bargaining agreement under this section if, in addition to the provision of health coverage, the agreement encompasses only the minimum requirements mandated by law with respect to the terms and conditions of employment (*e.g.*, minimum wage and workers' compensation). The phrase "terms and conditions of employment" as used in the proposed regulation is intended to have the same meaning and application as in case law decided under the National Labor Relations Act, 29 U.S.C. § 151 *et seq.* (NLRA), and would include wages, hours of work and other matters of employment such as grievance procedures and seniority rights. For purposes of this section, the expiration of a collective bargaining agreement will not in and of itself prevent the agreement from satisfying the requirements under the proposed regulation if the agreement, although expired, continues in force.

3. Plans Established or Maintained

The proposed regulation also establishes certain criteria to determine when a plan is established or maintained under or pursuant to one or more collective bargaining agreements for purposes of section 3(40). Proposed § 2510.3-40(c) provides that in situations where a plan covers both individuals who are members of a group or bargaining unit represented by an employee labor organization as defined in proposed § 2510.3-40(d)(1) as well as other individuals, the plan will not be considered to be established or maintained pursuant to one or more collective bargaining agreements unless no less than 85% of the individuals covered by the plan are present or certain former employees and their beneficiaries, excluding supervisors and managers as defined in paragraph (d)(2), who are currently or who were previously covered by a collective bargaining agreement.[7] In addition, three groups of individuals may participate in the plan but are not counted in determining the total number of individuals covered by the plan for purposes of calculating the 85% limitation: (1) present or former employees of the plan or of a related plan established or maintained pursuant to the same collective bargaining agreement; (2) present or former employees of the employee labor organization as defined in paragraph (d)(1) that is a signatory to the collective bargaining agreement pursuant to which the plan is maintained, and (3) beneficiaries of individuals in groups (1) and (2).

For purposes of the proposed regulation, the term "former employee" is limited to individuals who are receiving workers' compensation or disability benefits, continuation coverage pursuant to the Consolidated Omnibus Budget Reconciliation Act (COBRA) (Part 6 of title I of ERISA, 29 U.S.C. §§ 1161-1168), or who have retired or separated from employment after working for more than 1000 hours a year for at least three years for a signatory employer or employee organization, or the plan or related plan. For purposes of paragraph (c)(4), to be considered an employee of the plan, a related plan, or the signatory employee labor organization, an individual must work at least (A) 15 hours a week or 60 hours a month during the period of coverage under the plan, or (B) have worked at least 1000 hours in the last year and currently be on *bona fide* leave based on sickness or disability of the individual or the individual's family or on earned vacation time.

The proposed regulation requires that the plan satisfy the 85% limitation on the last day of each of the previous five calendar quarters unless the plan has not been in existence for five calendar quarters. If the plan or other arrangement has been in existence for a shorter period of time, it must satisfy the 85% limitation on the last day of each calendar quarter during which it has been in existence.

Through the requirement that no less than 85% of individuals covered by the plan be present or former bargaining unit members, the proposed regulation intends to treat as MEWAs arrangements that permit individuals to participate in an employee welfare benefit plan solely as a result of membership or affiliation with an entity and not as a result of the individuals being legitimately represented in collective bargaining by a *bona fide* employee labor organization.[8] The Department believes that the 85% limitation in the proposed regulation is consistent with the purpose of the statutory exception in section 3(40)(A)(i) of ERISA for employee welfare benefit plans which are established or maintained as the result of collective bargaining on behalf of employees concerning the terms and conditions of their employment. To the extent that the Department's position as indicated in Advisory Opinion 91-06A (January 15, 1991) to Gerald Grimes, Oklahoma Insurance Commissioner (concerning a trust that provided health care and other benefits to "associate members" of a labor organization who were not represented by the organization in collective bargaining), appears to express a different position, it would be superseded by the adoption of a final regulation that incorporates this requirement.

4. Definition of Employee Labor Organization

Proposed § 2510.3-40(d)(1) defines the term "employee labor organization" for purposes of this section. Proposed § 2510.3-40(d)(1)(i) provides that, with respect to a particular collective bargaining agreement, an employee labor organization must represent the employees of each signatory employer in one of two ways. All of a signatory employer's bargaining units covered by the collective bargaining agreement must either be certified by the National Labor Relations Board, or the employee labor organization must be lawfully recognized by the signatory employer as the exclusive representative for the employer's bargaining unit employees covered by the collective bargaining agreement. Such representation must take place without employer interference or domination. For purposes of the proposed regulation, employer interference or domination in the formation, administration, or operation of the employee labor organization includes taking an active part in organizing an employee organization or committee to represent employees; bringing pressure upon employees to join an employee organization; improperly favoring one of two or more employee organizations that are competing to represent employees; or otherwise unlawfully promoting or assisting in the formation or operation of the employee organization.

Under proposed § 2510.3-40(d)(1)(ii), an employee labor organization must operate for a substantial purpose other than that of offering or providing health coverage. Proposed § 2510.3-40(d)(1)(iii) states that an employee labor organization may not pay commissions, fees, or bonuses to individuals other than full-time employees of the employee labor organization in connection with the solicitation of employers or participants with regard to a collectively bargained plan. In addition, under subsection (d)(1)(iv), the term "employee labor organization" does not include an organization that utilizes the services of licensed insurance agents or brokers for soliciting employers or participants in connection with a collectively bargained plan. Proposed § 2510.3-40(d)(1)(v) requires an employee labor organization to be a "labor organization" as defined in section 3(i) of the Labor-Management Reporting and Disclosure Act, 29 U.S.C. § 402(i). Proposed § 2510.3-40(d)(1)(vi) also requires an employee labor organization to qualify as a tax-exempt labor organization under section 501(c)(5) of the Internal Revenue Code of 1986. It is the view of the Department that these criteria are necessary to distinguish organizations that provide benefits through legitimate employee representation from organizations that are primarily in the business of marketing commercial insurance products.

5. Supervisors and Managers

Proposed § 2510.3-40(d)(2) defines the terms "supervisors and managers" for purposes of this section. Proposed § 2510.3-40(d)(2) defines as "supervisors and managers" those employees of a signatory employer to a collective bargaining agreement who, acting on behalf of the employer, have the authority to hire, transfer, suspend, layoff, recall, promote, discharge, assign, reward, or discipline other employees, or who have responsibility to direct other employees or to adjust their grievances, or who have power to make effective recommendations concerning any of the actions described above. In order to be considered a supervisor or manager, an individual must be able to use independent judgement in the exercise of authority, responsibility, and power, and that exercise must be more than a routine or clerical function.

6. Failure to Provide Documents

The proposed regulation provides that even if a plan meets the requirements of subsections 2510.3-40(b) and (c) of this section, it will not be considered to be established or maintained pursuant to an agreement that the Secretary finds to be a collective bargaining agreement if an entity, plan, employee labor organization or employer which is a party to the agreement fails or refuses to provide documents or evidence in its possession or control to a state or state agency which reasonably requests documents or evidence in order to determine the status of any entity either under the proposed regulation or under state insurance laws. While the proposed regulation enumerates criteria designed to enable entities to determine whether the requirements of the statute are met, the Department intends that, when requested to do so, entities will provide documentation of their compliance with the criteria to the state or state agency charged with investigating and enforcing state insurance laws. An entity seeking to be treated as other than a MEWA under the provisions of the proposed regulation has the burden of producing sufficient documents and other evidence to prove that it meets the criteria of the proposed regulation and is therefore entitled to application of the statutory exemption from the definition of a MEWA.

The Department anticipates that states or state agencies, including any commission, board or committee charged with investigating and enforcing state insurance laws, will utilize existing jurisdiction under state laws to require the production of documents and other evidence.

---

[7] Although the proposed regulation itself does not impose any specific restrictions concerning individuals who may be included in the 15%, the entity as a whole must comply with the requirements of section 3(1) of ERISA in order to be an employee welfare benefit plan covered by the Act. Section 3(1) provides that status as an ERISA covered plan is dependent on the composition and attributes of the participant base as well as the characteristics of the employer and employee organization. *See, e.g., Bell v. Employee Security Benefits Association*, 437 F. Supp. 382 (1977); Advisory Opinion 93-32 (letter to Mr.

Kevin Long, December 16, 1993); Advisory Opinion 85-03A (letter to Mr. James Ray, January 15, 1985); Advisory Opinion 77-59 (letter to Mr. William Hager, August 26, 1977).

[8] A number of instances have been brought to the Department's attention where entities have attempted to utilize purported collective bargaining agreements as a basis for marketing insurance coverage, generally under the guise of "associate membership," to non-bargaining unit individuals and unrelated employers. *See, e.g., Empire Blue Cross and Blue Shield v. Consolidated Welfare*, 830 F. Supp. 170 (E.D.N.Y. 1993).

Where the entity's compliance with the criteria of the proposed regulation is disputed by a state or state agency, the Department expects that the state or state agency will use its existing authority under state law to bring the matter before the appropriate state adjudicatory body to determine the facts. The proposed regulation does not restrict the authority of the state or state agency to reinvestigate the entity at any time if it believes the entity is not in compliance with the proposed regulation or with state laws.

7. Allocation of Burden of Proof

The proposed regulation provides that, in a proceeding brought by a state or a state agency to enforce the insurance laws of the state, nothing in the proposed regulation shall be read or construed to prohibit the allocation of the burden of proving the existence of all criteria required by this section to the entity seeking to be treated as other than a MEWA. The proposed regulation enumerates criteria designed to enable entities to determine whether the requirements of the statute are met. However, as discussed in paragraph *1. General Rule and Scope, supra,* the Department believes that when challenged, the entity asserting the applicability of an exception has the burden of providing evidence of compliance with each of the terms of the proposed regulation.

Regulatory Flexibility Act

The Regulatory Flexibility Act of 1980 requires each Federal agency to perform a Regulatory Flexibility Analysis for all rules that are likely to have a significant economic impact on a substantial number of small entities. Small entities include small businesses, organizations, and governmental jurisdictions. The Pension and Welfare Benefits Administration has determined that, if adopted, this proposed rule may have a significant economic impact on a substantial number of small entities. Accordingly, as provided in section 603 of the Regulatory Flexibility Act (5 U.S.C. § 601, *et seq.*), the following initial regulatory flexibility analysis is provided:

(1) PWBA is considering the proposed regulation because it believes that regulatory guidance in this area is necessary to ensure (a) that state insurance regulators have ascertainable guidelines to help identify and regulate MEWAs operating in their jurisdictions, and (b) that sponsors of employee welfare benefit plans will be able to determine independently whether their plans are excepted plans under section 3(40)(A) of ERISA. A more detailed discussion of the agency's reasoning for issuing the proposed regulation is found in the Background section, above.

(2) The objective of the proposed regulation is to provide guidance on the application of an exception to the definition of the term "multiple employer welfare arrangement" (MEWA) which is found in section 3(40) of ERISA and applies to certain employee welfare benefit plans. The legal basis for the proposed regulation is found at ERISA section 3(40) (29 U.S.C. 1002(40)); an extensive list of authority may be found in the Statutory Authority section, below.

(3) No accurate estimate of the number of small entities affected by the proposed regulation is available. No small governmental jurisdictions will be affected. It is estimated that a substantial number of small businesses and organizations will be affected, due to the fact that it is precisely those entities, seeking group health care coverage, that are most harmed by unscrupulous entrepreneurs who purport to provide employee health benefits. In a report entitled "Employee Benefits: States Need Labor's Help Regulating Multiple Employer Welfare Arrangements," the United States General Accounting Office (GAO) calculated that between January 1988 and June 1991, fraudulent MEWAs left at least 398,000 participants and their beneficiaries with $123 million in unpaid medical claims and left many other participants without the health insurance they had paid for.[9] By restricting fraudulent and financially unsound MEWAs, the proposed regulation may limit the sources of health care coverage offered to small businesses. On the other hand, MEWAs that either meet the section 3(40) criteria or meet state regulatory standards are less likely to demonstrate the type of fraudulent or imprudent activity that prompted Congressional action. The GAO Report indicated that, during the January 1988 and June 1991 period, more than 600 MEWAs failed to comply with state insurance laws and some violated criminal statutes.[10] Consequently, small entities will receive a benefit from the reduced incidence of fraud and insolvency among the pool of MEWAs in the marketplace. To the extent that MEWAs themselves are small entities, they too will be affected by the proposed regulation.

(4) No identical reporting or recordkeeping is required under the proposed rule. However, this regulation clarifies the information that must be provided upon request to state authorities by those MEWAs wishing to take advantage of the exception under section 3(40)(A) of ERISA. The information to be provided will vary depending upon the entity involved but will include a written collective bargaining agreement and records on the individuals covered by the plan for at least the last five calendar quarters. Such information is routinely prepared and held in the ordinary course of business under current law by most small entities. It is anticipated that the preparation of some of these documents would require the professional skills of an attorney, accountant, or other health benefit plan professional; however, the majority of the recordkeeping may be handled by clerical staff.

(5) No federal rules have been identified that duplicate, overlap or conflict with the proposed rule.

(6) No significant alternatives which would minimize the impact on small entities have been identified. The proposed regulation is less costly in comparison with the alternative methods of determining compliance with section 3(40), such as case-by-case analysis by PWBA of each employee welfare benefit plan, or litigation. The costs of such alternatives would be unduly burdensome on small entities. No federal reporting is required. Instead, the proposed regulation would create standards by which the MEWAs may be reviewed by the states. It would be inappropriate to create an alternative with lower compliance criteria, or an exemption under the proposed regulation, for small MEWAs because those are the entities which pose a higher degree of risk of non-performance due to their increased likelihood of being under-funded or otherwise having inadequate reserves to meet the benefits claims submitted for payment.

Executive Order 12866 Statement

Under Executive Order 12866 (58 FR 51735, Oct. 4, 1993), the Department must determine whether the regulatory action is "significant" and therefore subject to review by the Office of Management and Budget (OMB) and the requirements of the Executive Order. Under section 3(f), the order defines a "significant regulatory action" as an action that is likely to result in a rule (1) having an annual effect on the economy of $100 million or more, or adversely and materially affecting a sector of the economy, productivity, competition, jobs, the environment, public health or safety, or State, local or tribal governments or communities (also referred to as "economically significant"); (2) creating a serious inconsistency or otherwise interfering with an action taken or planned by another agency; (3) materially altering the budgetary impacts of enti tlement, grants, user fees, or loan programs or the rights and obligations of recipients thereof; or (4) raising novel legal or policy issues arising out of legal mandates, the President's priorities, or the principles set forth in the Executive Order.

Pursuant to the terms of the Executive Order, the Department has determined that this program creates a improved method for statutory compliance that will reduce paperwork and regulatory compliance burdens on state governments, businesses, including small businesses and organizations, and make better use of scarce federal resources, in accord with the mandates of the Paperwork Reduction Act, the Regulatory Flexibility Act, and the President's priorities. The Department believes this notice is "significant" under category (4), *supra,* and subject to OMB review on that basis.

Paperwork Reduction Act

The proposed regulation does not contain any information collection or recordkeeping requirements as those terms are defined under the Paperwork Reduction Act because the information to be provided on request to state authorities will vary in each instance depending on the entity involved. Consequently, there is no requirement that the entities comply with identical reporting or recordkeeping requirements. 5 CFR § 1320.7(c). Thus, the proposed regulation imposes no additional federal paperwork burden and the Paperwork Reduction Act does not apply.

Statutory Authority

This regulation is proposed pursuant to section 3(40) of ERISA (Pub. L. 97-473, 96 Stat. 2611, 2612, 29 U.S.C. 1002(40)) and section 505 (Pub. L. 93-406, 88 Stat. 892, 894, 29 U.S.C. 1135) of ERISA and under Secretary of Labor's Order No. 1-87, 52 FR 13139, April 21, 1987.

List of Subjects in 29 CFR Part 2510

Employee benefit plans, Employee Retirement Income Security Act, Pension and Welfare Benefit Administration.

Proposed Regulation

[9] GAO/HRD-92-40 (March 1992) at 2.

[10] *Id.*

For the reasons set out in the preamble, the Department proposes to amend Part 2510 of Chapter XXV of Title 29 of the Code of Federal Regulations as follows:

PART 2510—[AMENDED]

1. The authority for Part 2510 is revised to read:

Authority: Secs. 3(2), 111(c), 505, Pub. L. 93-406, 88 Stat. 852, 894 (29 U.S.C. 1002(2), 1031, 1135); Secretary of Labor's Order No. 27-74, 1-86 (51 FR 3521, January 28, 1986), 1-87 (52 FR 13139, April 21, 1987), and Labor Management Services Administration Order No. 2-6.

Section 2510.3-40 is also issued under sec. 3(40), Pub. L. 97-473, 96 Stat. 2611, 2612, (29 U.S.C. 1002(40)).

Section 2510.3-101 is also issued under sec. 102 of Reorganization Plan No. 4 of 1978, 43 FR 47713, 3 CFR 1978 Comp., p. 332, effective under E.O. 12108, 44 FR 1065, 3 CFR 1978 Comp. p. 275 and sec. 11018(d) of Pub. L. 99-272, 100 Stat. 82.

Section 2510.3-102 is also issued under sec. 102 of Reorganization Plan No. 4 of 1978, 43 FR 47713, 3 CFR 1978 Comp., p. 332, effective under E.O. 12108, 44 FR 1065, 3 CFR Comp., p. 275.

2. Part 2510 is amended by adding new Section 2510.3-40 to read:

§ *2510.3-40 Plans Established or Maintained Pursuant to One or More Collective Bargaining Agreements.*

(a) *General.* Section 3(40)(A) of the Employee Retirement Income Security Act of 1974 (the Act) provides that the term "multiple employer welfare arrangement" (MEWA) does not include an employee welfare benefit plan or other arrangement which is established or maintained under or pursuant to one or more agreements which the Secretary of Labor (the Secretary) finds to be a collective bargaining agreement(s). The purposes of the proposed regulation are to establish specific criteria that the Secretary finds must be met for an agreement to be a collective bargaining agreement and to establish criteria for determining when an employee benefit plan is established or maintained pursuant to such an agreement.

(b) *Collective Bargaining Agreement.* The Secretary finds, for purposes of section 3(40)(A) of the Act, that an agreement constitutes a collective bargaining agreement only if the agreement—

(1) is in writing;

(2) is executed by, or on behalf of, an employer of employees represented by an employee labor organization;

(3) is executed by an employee labor organization;

(4) is the product of good faith, arms-length bargaining between one or more employers and an employee labor organization or uniformly incorporates and binds one or more employers and an employee labor organization to the terms and conditions of another agreement which as originally negotiated and adopted satisfies the requirements of this section;

(5) binds signatory employers and the employee labor organization to the terms of the agreement for a specified project or period of time, cannot be unilaterally amended or terminated and contains procedures for amending the terms and conditions of the agreement;

(6) does not terminate solely as a result of failure to make contributions to the plan; and

(7) in addition to the provision of health coverage, provides more than the minimum requirements mandated by law with respect to the terms and conditions of employment (*e.g.*, provides for more than minimum wage and workers' compensation).

(c) *Established or Maintained.* An employee benefit plan is not established or maintained under or pursuant to one or more collective bargaining agreements for purposes of section 3(40)(A) of the Act unless not less than 85 percent of the individuals covered by the plan are—

(1) employees, excluding supervisors and managers, currently included in one or more groups or bargaining units of employees covered by one or more collective bargaining agreements as defined in paragraph (b) of this section which expressly refer to the plan and provide for contributions thereto; or

(2) persons who were formerly employees described in paragraph (c)(1) of this section who are receiving workers' compensation or disability benefits, COBRA continuation coverage pursuant to Part 6 of title I of ERISA, 29 U.S.C. 1161-1168, or who have retired or separated from employment after working more than 1,000 hours a year for at least three years; or

(3) beneficiaries of individuals included in paragraphs (c)(1) and (2) of this section.

(4) For purposes of this subsection, the following individuals covered by the plan or other arrangement shall not be counted in determining the total number of individuals covered by the plan—

(i) employees of the plan or another plan established or maintained pursuant to the same collective bargaining agreement(s);

(ii) employees of an employee labor organization that meets the requirements of paragraph (d)(1) of this section and that is a signatory to the collective bargaining agreement(s) pursuant to which the plan is maintained;

(iii) persons who were formerly employees described in paragraphs (c)(4)(i) and (ii) of this section who are receiving workers' compensation or disability benefits, COBRA continuation coverage pursuant to Part 6 of title I of ERISA, 29 U.S.C. §§ 1161-1168, or who have retired or separated from employment after working more than 1,000 hours a year for at least three years; or

(iv) beneficiaries of individuals included in paragraphs (c)(4)(i), (ii) and (iii);

(v) provided that, for purposes of paragraphs (c)(4)(i) and (ii) of this section, in order to be an employee, an individual must work at least:

(A) 15 hours a week or 60 hours a month during the period of coverage under the plan, or

(B) have worked more than 1,000 hours in the last year and currently be on *bona fide* leave based on sickness or disability of the individual or the individual's family or on earned vacation time.

(5) For purposes of calculating whether the 85% limitation has been met, a plan or other arrangement must satisfy the requirements of paragraphs (c)(1) through (4) of this section on the last day of—

(i) each of the previous five calendar quarters; or

(ii) if the plan has been in existence for fewer than five calendar quarters, every calendar quarter during which the plan has been in existence.

(d) *Definitions.*

(1) *Employee Labor Organization.* For purposes of this section, an "employee labor organization" shall mean an organization that—

(i) represents, with respect to a particular collective bargaining agreement, the employees of each signatory employer to the agreement where:

(A) all of the employer's bargaining units covered by the agreement are certified by the National Labor Relations Board, or

(B) the employee labor organization is lawfully recognized by the signatory employer (*e.g.*, without employer interference or domination) as the exclusive bargaining representative for the employer's bargaining unit employees covered by the agreement;

(ii) provides substantial representational services to employees regarding the terms and conditions of their employment in addition to health coverage;

(iii) does not pay commissions, fees, or bonuses to individuals, other than full-time employees of the employee labor organization, in connection with the solicitation of employers or participants;

(iv) does not utilize the services of licensed insurance agents or brokers for soliciting employers or participants;

(v) is a "labor organization" as defined in section 3(i) of the Labor-Management Reporting and Disclosure Act, 29 U.S.C. section 402(i); and

(vi) qualifies as a tax-exempt labor organization under section 501(c)(5) of the Internal Revenue Code of 1986.

(2) *Supervisors and Managers.* For purposes of this section, "supervisors and managers" shall mean any employees of a signatory employer to an agreement described in paragraph (b) of this section who, acting in the interest of the employer, have—

(i) authority to hire, transfer, suspend, layoff, recall, promote, discharge, assign, reward or discipline other employees; or

(ii) responsibility to direct other employees or to adjust their grievances; or

(iii) power to make effective recommendations concerning the actions described in paragraphs (d)(2)(i) and (ii) of this section; as long as the exercise of the authority, responsibility and power in paragraphs

(d) (2) (i), (ii) or (iii) of this section is not of a merely routine or clerical nature, but requires the use of independent judgment.

(e) *Failure to Provide Documents or Other Necessary Evidence.* This section shall not apply to any plan or other arrangement if, in conjunction with an investigation or proceeding by a state or state agency, the plan, arrangement, any employee labor organization or employer which is a party to the agreement(s) at issue fails or refuses to provide the state or state agency with any document or other evidence in its possession or control that is reasonably requested by the state or state agency for the purpose of determining the status of the plan or other arrangement under state insurance laws or under this section.

(f) *Allocation of Burden of Proof*

In a proceeding brought to enforce state insurance laws, nothing in the proposed regulation shall be construed to prohibit a state or state agency from allocating the burden of proving the existence of all the criteria required by this section to the entity seeking to be treated as other than a MEWA.

Signed at Washington, DC, this 26th day of July 1995.

Olena Berg

Assistant Secretary,

Pension and Welfare Benefits Administration

¶ 20,533I   Reserved.

Proposed Reg. §§ 2629.1-2629.12 relating to the PBGC Missing Participant Program were formerly reproduced at this paragraph. The final regulations begin at ¶ 15,530A. Schedule MP and its instructions appear at ¶ 10,818.]

¶ 20,533J

Proposed rule on 29 CFR Parts 2509, 2520 and 2550: Obsolete rulings.—Reproduced below is a proposed rule issued by the Pension and Welfare Benefits Administration to remove certain interpretive bulletins and regulations under ERISA that the DOL believes are obsolete. These generally provided transitional relief for plan sponsors, plan administrators and others subject to Title 1 of ERISA during the first several years after ERISA was enacted. They are considered obsolete because the periods or dates of applicability have expired, they merely provide notice of a rescission or withdrawal of prior guidance or regulations, or were rendered ineffective by a subsequent Supreme Court decision.

The proposed rule was filed with the Federal Register on April 2, 1996 and published in the Federal Register on April 3, 1996. (61 FR 14690).

The regulations were finalized effective July 1, 1996 (61 FR 33847). The changes implemented by the final regulations are reflected at ¶ 14,231F, ¶ 14,231G, ¶ 14,244, ¶ 14,245, ¶ 14,246, ¶ 14,246A, ¶ 14,247H, ¶ 14,247Y, ¶ 14,249A, ¶ 14,249C, ¶ 14,249D, ¶ 14,249K, ¶ 14,521, ¶ 14,522, ¶ 14,771B, ¶ 14,771C, ¶ 14,775, ¶ 14,841, ¶ 14,844A, ¶ 14,844B, and ¶ 14,845, ¶ 14,875, ¶ 14,876, ¶ 14,881.

¶ 20,533K

Pension Benefit Guaranty Corporation: Proposed rule: Reportable events: Retirement Protection Act of 1994.—Reproduced below is the preamble and text of a proposed rule issued by the Pension Benefit Guaranty Corporation that revises reportable event regulations to conform to changes made by the Retirement Protection Act of 1994. The proposed rule also add three new reportable events and discusses waivers and timing of filing requirements.

The proposed regulations were filed with the *Federal Register* on July 23, 1996 and published in the *Federal Register* on July 24, 1996 (61 FR 38409).

The regulations were finalized December 2, 1996 (61 FR 63988). The regulations are reproduced at ¶ 15,315A, ¶ 15,461, ¶ 15,461A, ¶ 15,461B, ¶ 15,461C, ¶ 15,461D, ¶ 15,461E, ¶ 15,461F, ¶ 15,461G, ¶ 15,462, ¶ 15,462A, ¶ 15,462B, ¶ 15,462C, ¶ 15,462D, ¶ 15,462E, ¶ 15,462F, ¶ 15,462G, ¶ 15,462H, ¶ 15,462I, ¶ 15,462J, ¶ 15,462K, ¶ 15,462L, ¶ 15,462M, ¶ 15,462N, ¶ 15,462O, ¶ 15,463, ¶ 15,463A, ¶ 15,463B, ¶ 15,463C, ¶ 15,463D, ¶ 15,463E, ¶ 15,463F, ¶ 15,463G, ¶ 15,464 and ¶ 15,651B. The preamble is reproduced at ¶ 23,929E.

¶ 20,533L

Proposed Regulation: Premium audit program: Penalty assessment policy.—Reproduced below is the preamble and text of a proposed rule issued by the Pension Benefit Guaranty Corporation (PBGC) that will require plan administrators to make available to the agency certain plan records supporting premium filings, such as records relating to the number of plan participants as well as records reflecting any plan underfunding. The PBGC proposes to amend the existing regulation to provide for such submission within 30 days of receipt of the PBGC's request.

The proposed regulation was published in the *Federal Register* on December 17, 1996 (61 FR 66247).

The regulation was finalized August 8, 1997 (62 FR 36663). The regulation is reproduced at ¶ 15,371I. The preamble is reproduced at ¶ 23,935I.

¶ 20,533M

Proposed regulations: Equal Employment Opportunity Commission: Age Discrimination in Employment Act of 1967: Benefits waivers.—The Equal Employment Opportunity Commission has issued a proposed regulation to provide guidance on waivers of rights and claims under the Age Discrimination in Employment Act (ADEA) as amended by the Older Workers Benefit Protection Act of 1990 (OWBPA) (P.L. 101-433). The OWBPA requires that all waivers to ADEA rights and claims be knowing and voluntary.

Under the proposed regulation, exit incentive programs and other employment termination programs need not constitute an employee benefit plan for purposes of ERISA. An employer may or may not have an ERISA severance plan in connection with its OWBPA program.

The proposed regulations were published in the *Federal Register* on March 10, 1997 (62 FR 10787).

The final regulations were finalized June 6, 1998 (63 FR 30624). The regulations are reproduced at ¶ 15,750J. The preamble is reproduced at ¶ 23,943F.

¶ 20,533N

Pension Benefit Guarantee Corporation: Proposed rule: Standard termination process: Single-employer plans.—Reproduced below is a proposed rule issued by the PBGC to extend deadlines and simplify the standard termination process for single-employer plans. Specifically, the filing deadline for a standard termination notice would be extended from 120 days to 180 days after the proposed termination date. Plan administrators would have 120 days, instead of 60 days, to distribute plan assets after receipt of an IRS clearance letter. There would be a new requirement that administrators must inform participants of state guarantees applicable to their benefits. Also, standard termination packages would include a model notice of intent to terminate. Effective March 14, 1997, penalties are waived for late filing of post-distribution certification if it is filed within 90 days after the distribution deadline.

The proposed regulation was filed with the *Federal Register* on March 11, 1997 and published in the *Federal Register* on March 14, 1997 (62 FR 12508).

The regulations were finalized November 7, 1997 (62 FR 60424). The regulations are reproduced at ¶ 15,315A, ¶ 15,361D, ¶ 15,423, ¶ 15,440A, ¶ 15,440A-1, ¶ 15,440A-2, ¶ 15,440A-3, ¶ 15,440A-4, ¶ 15,440A-5, ¶ 15,440A-6, ¶ 15,440A-7, ¶ 15,440F, ¶ 15,440F-1, ¶ 15,440F-2, ¶ 15,440F-3, ¶ 15,440F-4, ¶ 15,440F-5, ¶ 15,440F-6, ¶ 15,440F-7, ¶ 15,440F-8, ¶ 15,440F-9, ¶ 15,440F-10, ¶ 15,440J, ¶ 15,440J-1, ¶ 15,440J-2, ¶ 15,440J-3, ¶ 15,440J-4, ¶ 15,440J-5, ¶ 15,440J-6, ¶ 15,440J-7, ¶ 15,440J-8, ¶ 15,440J-9, ¶ 15,530A, ¶ 15,530B, ¶ 15,530C, ¶ 15,530D, ¶ 15,530E, ¶ 15,530F, ¶ 15,530G, ¶ 15,530H, ¶ 15,530I, ¶ 15,530J, ¶ 15,530K, ¶ 15,530L, ¶ 15,530M, and ¶ 15,530N. The preamble is reproduced at ¶ 23,938Q.

¶ 20,533O

Proposed rules: Pension and Welfare Benefits Administration: Definition of ERISA plan assets: SIMPLE IRAs: Salary reduction elective contributions.—The Pension and Welfare Benefits Administration has issued a proposed amendment to a final regulation which would clarify when salary reduction elective contributions to SIMPLE IRAs must become plan assets. The amendment would harmonize the ERISA Title I definition of plan assets (with respect to participant contributions) with Code rules that govern the timing of deposits for SIMPLE IRAs. The proposed amendment aims to simplify plan establishment and administration for small businesses.

The proposed regulation was published in the *Federal Register* on March 27, 1997 (62 FR 14760).

The regulation was finalized effective November 25, 1997 (62 FR 62934). The regulation is reproduced at ¶ 14,139N.

¶ 20,533P

Proposed rules: Pension and Welfare Benefits Administration: Civil monetary penalties.—The Pension and Welfare Benefits Administration has issued proposed regulations to adjust civil monetary penalties under ERISA pursuant to the requirements of the Federal Civil Penalties Inflation Adjustment Act of 1990, as amended by the Debt Collection Improvement Act of 1996 (the Act). The Act requires that certain penalties, which are listed as dollar amounts under ERISA, be adjusted for inflation. Penalties listed as percentages are not required to be adjusted. The adjusted penalties will apply only to violations taking place after the new penalty is effective.

The proposed regulation was published in the *Federal Register* on April 18, 1997 (62 FR 19078).

The regulations were finalized effective July 29, 1997 (62 FR 40696). The regulation is reproduced at ¶ 14,929A, ¶ 14,929B, ¶ 14,929C, ¶ 14,929D, and ¶ 14,929E. The preamble is reproduced at ¶ 23,935W.

¶ 20,533Q

Proposed rules: Pension Benefit Guaranty Corporation: Mergers and transfers: Multiemployer plans.—The PBGC has issued proposed regulations to clarify the application of current PBGC regulations on mergers and transfers between multiemployer plans to plans terminated by mass withdrawal. Under the proposed regs, transactions involving plans that have been terminated by mass withdrawal under ERISA are subject to the merger and transfer rules, and, unless they are *de minimis* transactions, the transactions are governed by the higher-level valuation standard and "safe harbor" solvency test.

The proposed regulations were published in the *Federal Register* on May 1, 1997 (62 FR 23700).

The regulations were finalized May 4, 1998 (63 FR 24421). The regulations are reproduced at ¶ 15,700A, ¶ 15,700B, ¶ 15,700C, ¶ 15,700D, ¶ 15,700E, ¶ 15,700F, ¶ 15,700G, ¶ 15,700H, ¶ 15,700I and ¶ 15,700J. The preamble is reproduced at ¶ 23,942N.

¶ 20,533R

Pension Benefit Guaranty Corporation: Proposed rule: Recoupment: Overpayment.—The PBGC has proposed amendments to its existing regulation governing recoupment of benefit overpayments that would stop the reduction of monthly benefits once the overpayment has been repaid.

The proposed regulations, were published in the *Federal Register* on December 18, 1997 (62 FR 66319).

The regulations were finalized May 28, 1998 (63 FR 29353). The regulations are reproduced at ¶ 15,424, ¶ 15,424A, ¶ 15,424B, ¶ 15,440J-1 and ¶ 15,530B. The preamble is reproduced at ¶ 23,943.

¶ 20,533S

Proposed rules: Pension and Welfare Benefits Administration: Insurance company general accounts.—The PWBA has issued proposed regulations to clarify which assets held by an insurer are plan assets for purposes of Title I of ERISA in instances where an insurer issues policies to or for the benefit of an employee benefit plan, and such policies are supported by assets of the insurer's general account. The proposed regulations also provide guidance with respect to the application of Title I to the general account assets of insurers. The proposed regulations were introduced as a result of amendments to ERISA Sec. 401 made by the Small Business Job Protection Act of 1996, which mandated the guidance.

The proposed regulations, which were published in the *Federal Register* on December 22, 1997 (62 FR 66908), are reproduced below.

The regulations were finalized January 5, 2000 (65 FR 613). The regulations are reproduced at ¶ 14,714. The preamble is reproduced at ¶ 24,805C.

¶ 20,533T

Pension Benefit Guaranty Corporation: Proposed rule: Terminations: Single-employer plan: Guaranteed benefits: Lump sum payments.—The PBGC has issued proposed regulations to increase the maximum value of benefits payable by the PBGC as a lump sum from $3,500 to $5,000. ERISA Sec. 203(e), which specifies the maximum amount that a plan may pay in a single installment to a participant or a surviving spouse without their consent, was amended to increase the maximum value from $3,500 to $5,000. Accordingly, the PBGC has proposed to amend its regulations to increase various thresholds from $3,500 to $5,000.

The proposed regulations were published in the *Federal Register* on April 30, 1998 (63 FR 23693)

The regulations were finalized July 15, 1998 (63 FR 38305). The regulations are reproduced at ¶ 15,421F, ¶ 15,449U, ¶ 15,475A, ¶ 15,475C, ¶ 15,531A, ¶ 15,531D ¶ 15,715G, ¶ 15,715H, ¶ 15,715I. The preamble is reproduced at ¶ 23,943Y.

¶ 20,533U

PWBA proposed regulations: Pension and welfare benefit plans: Summary plan descriptions (SPDs).—The Pension and Welfare Benefits Administration (PWBA) has proposed regulations that would change ERISA's summary plan description (SPD) requirements for pension and welfare benefit plans. These changes would clarify the information that must be included in a group health plan SPD and would require the SPD to identify whether the plan is intended to comply with ERISA Sec. 404(c), if it is a pension plan, or ERISA Sec. 733(a), if it is a welfare plan. These changes would also require that SPDs include a description of QDRO and QMCSO procedures, respectively; the authority of all ERISA plan sponsors to terminate, amend or eliminate benefits under the plan; and a description of the rights and obligations of participants and beneficiaries on termination, amendment or elimination of benefits.

The proposed regulations and preamble, were published in the *Federal Register* on September 9, 1998 (63 FR 48376), are reproduced below.

The PWBA has extended the deadline for comments to December 9, 1998 (63 FR 58335, October 30, 1998).

The regulations were finalized November 21, 2000 (65 FR 70225). The regulations are reproduced at ¶ 14,223, ¶ 14,225 and ¶ 14,429B. The preamble is reproduced at ¶ 24,805N.

¶ 20,533V

Proposed rules: Pension and Welfare Benefits Administration: Employee Retirement Income Security Act of 1974; Rules and Regulations for Administration and Enforcement; Claims Procedure.—The Pension and Welfare Benefits Administration has issued proposed regulations revising the minimum requirements for benefit claims procedures of employee benefit plans covered by Title I of the Employee Retirement Income Security Act of 1974. The proposed regulations establish new standards for the processing of group health disability, pension, and other employee benefit plan claims filed by participants and beneficiaries.

For group health plans and certain plans providing disability benefits, the new standards are intended to ensure more timely benefit determinations, improved access to information on which a benefit determination is made, and greater assurance that participants and beneficiaries will be afforded a full and fair review of denied claims.

The proposed regulations were published in the *Federal Register* on September 9, 1998 (63 FR 48390).

The regulations were finalized November 21, 2000 (65FR 70246). The regulations are reproduced at ¶ 14,931. The preamble is reproduced at ¶ 24,805O.

¶ 20,533W

PBGC: Proposed Rule: Valuation of Benefits: Use of Single Set of Assumptions for All Benefits.—The PBGC is proposing an amendment to its regulations to provide for the use of a single, modified version of its annuity assumptions for allocating assets to lump-sum and annuity benefits. Use of the modified version will be implemented some time after the year 2000. Existing lump-sum assumptions will be used at least through the year 2000.

The proposed rule was published in the *Federal Register* on October 26, 1998 (63 FR 57229) and is reproduced below.

The regulations were finalized on March 17, 2000 (65 FR 14751, 14753). The regulations are reproduced at ¶ 15,421F, ¶ 15,424C, ¶ 15,475A—15,475C, ¶ 15,475E—15,475G and ¶ 15,530B. The preamble is reproduced at ¶ 24,805H.

¶ 20,533X

PWBA: Annual reporting regulations: Form 5500 series: Proposed revisions.—The PWBA has issued proposed amendments to ERISA's annual reporting and disclosure requirements. The amendments are necessary to ensure that the regulations conform to the revisions to the annual return/report forms in the Form 5500 series that employee pension and welfare benefit plan administrators are required to file.

The proposed amendments were published in the *Federal Register* on December 10, 1998 (63 FR 68370).

The regulations were finalized on April 19, 2000 (65 FR 21067). The regulations are reproduced at ¶ 14,231A, ¶ 14,231B, ¶ 14,231C, ¶ 14,231D, ¶ 14,231E, ¶ 14,231F, ¶ 14,231I, ¶ 14,231J, ¶ 14,231K, ¶ 14,231L, ¶ 14,247A, ¶ 14,247U, ¶ 14,247W, ¶ 14,247X, ¶ 14,247Z and ¶ 14,249H. The preamble is reproduced at ¶ 24,805J.

¶ 20,533Y

PWBA: Proposed rules: Electronic technology: Communication and recordkeeping.—The PWBA has issued proposed rules addressing electronic communications of certain information by employee benefit plans and minimum standards for maintenance and retention of employee benefit records in electronic form.

The proposed rules were published in the *Federal Register* on January 28, 1999 (64 FR 4505). The regulations were finalized on April 9, 2002 (67 FR 17264) and are reproduced at ¶ 14,249 and ¶ 14,270B.

¶ 20,533Z

PBGC: Proposed rules: Premium payments: Late payment penalty: Safe harbors.—The PBGC has issued proposed regulations which would expand current safe-harbor rules regarding the payment of premiums. The goal of the proposed rules is to expand the existing safe harbors (CCH PENSION PLAN GUIDE ¶ 15,371G) and encourage self-correction of incorrect premium payments in three situations, which are outlined in detail in the full text below.

The proposed rules were published in the *Federal Register* on April 27, 1999 (64 FR 22589).

The regulations were finalized on November 26, 1999 (64 FR 66383). The regulations are reproduced at ¶ 15,371G. The preamble is reproduced at ¶ 24,805B.

¶ 20,534

Proposed regulations: Equal Employment Opportunity Commission (EEOC): Age Discrimination in Employment Act (ADEA): Older Workers Benefit Protection Act (OWBPA): Severance pay: Waivers.—The EEOC has issued proposed regulations to address issues related to the United States Supreme Court's decision in *Oubre v. Entergy Operations, Inc.* (CCH PENSION PLAN GUIDE ¶ 23,939T). Under the regulations, an individual alleging that a waiver agreement was not knowing and voluntary under the ADEA is not required to tender back any consideration received as a precondition for challenging that waiver agreement. As was the case in *Oubre v. Entergy Operations, Inc.*, consideration for such a waiver may include severance benefits or other employee benefits.

The proposed regulations were published in the *Federal Register* on April 23, 1999 (64 FR 19952).

The regulations were finalized on December 11, 2000 (65 FR 77438). The regulations are reproduced at ¶ 15,750K. The preamble is reproduced at ¶ 24,805Q.

¶ 20,534A

Proposed regulations: Summary plan descriptions (SPDs): Summaries of material modifications (SMMs): Plan descriptions.—The PWBA has issued proposed regulations to remove certain superseded regulations from the Code of Federal Regulations. The superseded regulations pertain to filing SPDs, SMMs and plan descriptions with the DOL. The Taxpayer Relief Act of 1997 created amendments to ERISA and these documents are no longer required to be filed with the DOL, but are to be made available to the DOL upon request.

The preamble and text of the proposed regulations reproduced below were published in the Federal Register on August 5, 1999 (64 FR 42792).

ERISA Sec. 102 , ERISA Sec. 103 and ERISA Sec. 104 .

DEPARTMENT OF LABOR

Pension and Welfare Benefits Administration

29 CFR Parts 2520 and 2560

RIN 1210-AA66

Removal of Superseded Regulations Relating to Plan Descriptions and Summary Plan Descriptions, and Other Technical Conforming Amendments

AGENCY: Pension and Welfare Benefits Administration, Department of Labor.

ACTION: Notice of Proposed Rulemaking.

SUMMARY: This document sets forth a proposed rule that would remove certain provisions from the Code of Federal Regulations (CFR) that were superseded, in whole or in part, by amendments of the Employee Retirement Income Security Act of 1974 (ERISA) enacted as part of the Taxpayer Relief Act of 1997 (TRA '97). These TRA '97 amendments eliminated the requirements that plan administrators file summary plan descriptions (SPDs) and summaries of material modifications (SMMs) with the Department of Labor (Department). The amendments also eliminated all requirements pertaining to plan descriptions. In addition to removing superseded regulations from the CFR, this proposed rule would make miscellaneous technical amendments to the CFR designed to correct affected cross-references.

DATES: Written comments concerning the proposed regulation must be received by October 4, 1999.

ADDRESSES: Written comments (preferably three copies) should be sent to: Office of Regulations and Interpretations, Room N-5669, Pension and Welfare Benefits Administration, U.S. Department of Labor, 200 Constitution Avenue, NW, Washington, DC 20210; Attention: Proposed SPD/Plan Description Regulations. All submissions will be open to public inspection at the Public Documents Room, Pension and Welfare Benefits Administration, Room N-5638, 200 Constitution Avenue, NW, Washington, DC.

FOR FURTHER INFORMATION CONTACT: Jeffrey J. Turner, Office of Regulations and Interpretations, Pension and Welfare Benefits Administration, U.S. Department of Labor, (202) 219-8671 (not a toll-free number).

SUPPLEMENTARY INFORMATION:

Overview

TRA '97 amended sections 101(b), 102, and 104(a)(1) of ERISA to eliminate the requirements that plan administrators file SPDs, SMMs, and plan descriptions with the Department.[1] TRA '97 also amended section 104(b) of ERISA to eliminate the requirement that plan administrators furnish plan descriptions to participants and beneficiaries. These statutory amendments superseded, in whole or in part, the Department's regulations that implemented the SPD, SMM, and plan description filing requirements. This proposed rule would remove those superseded regulations from the CFR.[2] This proposed rule also would make several technical conforming amendments to reflect the fact that regulatory relief from certain plan description, SPD, and SMM requirements is no longer needed in light of TRA '97 and to correct affected regulatory and statutory cross-references in parts 2520 and 2560 of Chapter XXV of Title 29 of the CFR. A chart identifying each regulation that would be changed by this proposed rule is printed below.

Removal of Superseded Regulations

This proposed rule would remove, in whole or in part, the following superseded regulations from 29 CFR part 2520, which pertain to reporting and disclosure under ERISA. This proposed rule also would reserve certain removed sections of the CFR to preserve the continuity of codification in the CFR.

Regulations Superseded in Whole

This proposed rule would remove and reserve §§ 2520.102-1 and 2520.104a-2. These sections require plan administrators to file a plan description with the Department in accordance with §§ 101(b)(2) and 104(a)(1)(B) of ERISA.[3] They were superseded by paragraphs (a) and (c) of § 1503 of TRA '97, which eliminated §§ 101(b)(2) and 104(a)(1)(B) of ERISA.

This proposed rule would remove and reserve § 2520.104a-3. This section implements sections 101(b)(1) and 104(a)(1)(C) of ERISA, which require plan administrators to file with the Department a copy of any SPD that is required to be furnished to participants covered under the plan and beneficiaries receiving benefits under the plan. Section 2520.104a-3 was superseded by paragraphs (a) and (c) of section 1503 of TRA '97, which eliminated sections 101(b)(1) and 104(a)(1)(C) of ERISA.

This proposed rule would remove and reserve §§ 2520.104a-4 and 2520.104a-7. These sections implement §§ 101(b)(3), 102(a)(2), and 104(a)(1)(D) of ERISA, which require plan administrators to file with the Department a copy of summaries of material modifications in the terms of the plan and summaries of any changes in the information required to be in the SPD. Sections 2520.104a-4 and 2520.104a-7 were

---

[1] Prior to 1979, the administrator of an employee benefit plan subject to the provisions of Part 1 of Title I of ERISA was required to file with the Department a plan description (Form EBS-1) to satisfy the statutory filing requirements of section 104(a) and 29 CFR 2520.104a-2. *See* 41 FR 16957 (April 23, 1976). In 1979, the Department amended 29 CFR 2520.104a-2 (44 FR 31639 (June 1, 1979)), to provide that the administrator of an employee benefit plan would satisfy the plan description filing requirements of section 104(a)(1)(B) by filing with the Department a SPD and an updated SPD in accordance with section 104(a)(1)(C) and the regulations thereunder.

[2] Under a separate notice, the Department will promulgate proposed regulations to implement new sections 502(c)(6) and 104(a)(6) of ERISA. Section 502(c)(6) provides that

if, within 30 days of a request by the Department to a plan administrator for documents under section 104(a)(6), the plan administrator fails to furnish the material requested to the Department, the Department may assess a civil penalty against the plan administrator of up to $100 a day from the date of such failure, but in no event in excess of $1,000 per request. Section 104(a)(6) provides that the administrator of any employee benefit plan must furnish to the Department, upon request, any documents relating to the employee benefit plan, including but not limited to, the latest SPD, and the bargaining agreement, trust agreement, contract, or other instrument under which the plan is established or operated.

[3] *See supra* note 1.

superseded by paragraphs (a) and (c) of § 1503 of TRA '97, which eliminated § § 101(b)(3), 102(a)(2), and 104(a)(1)(D) of ERISA.

Regulations Superseded in Part

This proposed rule would amend § 2520.104-20 to reflect the fact that certain of the reporting relief granted by that regulation is no longer needed in light of TRA '97. Specifically, § 2520.104-20 exempts certain unfunded or insured welfare plans with fewer than 100 participants from, among others, the requirements to file plan descriptions, SPDs, and SMMs with the Department. Inasmuch as plan descriptions, SPDs, and SMMs are no longer required to be filed under ERISA as amended by TRA '97, this proposed rule would amend § 2520.104-20(a) to remove the provisions that grant relief from such filing requirements. The amendments made by this proposed rule would not otherwise change the relief available in § 2520.104-20.

This proposed rule would similarly amend § 2520.104-21 to reflect the fact that the SPD, SMM, and plan description filing relief granted by that regulation is no longer needed in light of the TRA '97 elimination of those filing requirements. Specifically, § 2520.104-21 provides a limited exemption from, among others, the requirements to file SPDs, SMMs, and plan descriptions with the Department for welfare benefit plans that cover fewer than 100 participants at the beginning of the plan year, are part of a group insurance arrangement, and that otherwise satisfy the conditions of § 2520.104-21(b). This proposed rule would amend § 2520.104-21(a) by removing the provisions on SPDs, SMMs, and plan descriptions because these documents are no longer required to be filed under ERISA as amended by TRA '97. The amendments made by this proposed rule would not otherwise change the relief available in § 2520.104-21.[4]

This proposed rule would further amend § § 2520.104-20 and 2520.104-21 to reflect the fact that the need for relief under ERISA from the requirement to disclose plan descriptions was eliminated by TRA '97. These section exempt eligible welfare plans from the requirement to: (1) Furnish upon written request of any participant or beneficiary a copy of the plan description, and (2) make copies of the plan description available in the principle office of the administrator and such other places as may be necessary for examination by any participant or beneficiary. This proposed rule would amend § § 2520.104-20(a)(2) and

(3) and 2520.104-21(a)(1) and (2) by removing the provisions on disclosing plan descriptions because plan descriptions are no longer required to be furnished or made available under ERISA as amended by TRA '97.

This proposed rule would amend § § 2520.104-26 and 2520.104-27 to reflect the fact that the need for relief under ERISA from the requirement to file plan descriptions, SPDs, and SMMs was eliminated by TRA '97. These regulations provide certain unfunded dues financed welfare and pension plans maintained by employee organizations with a limited exemption from, among others, the requirement to file plan descriptions and a simplified option for complying with the filing and disclosure requirements applicable to SPDs. This proposed rule would amend § § 2520.104-26 and 2520.104-27 by removing the provisions on plan descriptions and would further amend § § 2520.104-26 and 2520.104-27 to remove the simplified option provisions for filing SPDs because plan descriptions and SPDs are no longer required to be filed with the Department under ERISA as amended by TRA '97. The proposal is not otherwise intended to change the relief available under these sections.

Technical Conforming Amendments

This proposal also would make technical changes that are needed to conform certain cross references in the CFR to sections of ERISA as amended by TRA '97. For example, § 2520.104a-5 refers to section 104(a)(1)(A) of ERISA as the authority for the requirement to file annual reports with the Department. After TRA '97, the correct citation is to § 104(a)(1) of ERISA. Similar technical changes are also being made to conform internal CFR cross references.

Effective Date

This regulation is proposed to be effective 60 days after publication of a final rule in the **Federal Register.** If adopted, the proposed amendments implementing TRA '97 would be applicable as of the August 5, 1997, effective date of section 1503 of TRA '97.

Quick Reference Chart

The chart below lists each section of 29 CFR parts 2520 and 2560 that would be affected by this proposed rule and includes a brief description of the proposed change.

QUICK REFERENCE CHART

CFR section(s)	Remove	Add	Reason(s)
2520.102-1	The whole section	"Reserved"	All "plan description" requirements eliminated from ERISA.
2520.102-4	The last sentence	Nothing	SPD filing requirement eliminated.
2520.103-1(a)	"section 104(a)(1)(A)"	"section 104(a)(1)"	Cross reference correction.
2520.103-5(a), (c)(1)(i), (c)(1)(iii), (c)(2)(ii), (c)(2)(iii), and (c)(3).	"section 104(a)(1)(A)"	"section 104(a)(1)"	Cross reference correction.
2520.103-12(a)	"section 104(a)(1)(A)"	"section 104(a)(1)"	Cross reference correction.
2520.104-4(a)	Last sentence	Nothing	SPD filing requirement eliminated.
2520.104-20(a) (introductory text)	"any of the following documents: Plan description, copy of summary plan description, description of material modification in the terms of a plan or change in the information required to be included in the plan description,".	Nothing	All "plan description" requirements eliminated from ERISA, SPD filing requirement eliminated, and SMM filing requirement eliminated.
2520.104-20(a)(2)	"plan description,"	Nothing	All "plan description" requirements eliminated from ERISA.
2520.104-20(a)(3)	"plan description and"	Nothing	All "plan description" requirements eliminated from ERISA.
2520.104-20(c)	"(section 104(a)(1))"	"(section 104(a)(6))"	Requirement to furnish documents to the Department upon request—moved to different paragraph of ERISA section 104.
2520.104-21(a) (introductory text)	"with the Secretary any of the following documents: Plan description, copy of summary plan description, description of material modification in the terms of a plan or change in the information required to be included in the plan description, and terminal report. In addition, the administrator of a plan exempted under this section:".	After the word file, add: "with the Secretary a terminal report or furnish upon written request of any participant or beneficiary a copy of any terminal report as required by section 104(b)(4) of the Act.".	All "plan description" requirements eliminated from ERISA, SPD filing requirement eliminated, and SMM filing requirement eliminated.
2520.104-21(a)(1)	All of (a)(1)	Nothing	All "plan description" requirements eliminated from ERISA.
2520.104-21(a)(2)	All of (a)(2)	Nothing	All "plan description" requirements eliminated from ERISA.
2520.104-21(c) (second parenthetical).	"section 104(a)(1)(A)"	"section 104(a)(1)"	Cross reference correction.
2520.104-21(c) (third parenthetical).	"section 104(a)(1)"	"section 104(a)(6)"	Requirement to furnish documents to the Department upon request—moved to different paragraph of ERISA section 104.
2520.104-23(b)(2)	"104(a)(1)"	"104(a)(6)"	Requirement to furnish documents to the Department upon request—moved to different paragraph of ERISA section 104.

---

[4] *See* 63 FR 68370, 68388 (Dec. 10, 1998) (eliminating references to requirements to file plan descriptions, SPDs, and SMMs in § 2520.104-21-(d)(3) as part of proposed amendments to annual reporting regulations).

CFR section(s)	Remove	Add	Reason(s)
2520.104-24(b)	"104(a)(1)"	104(a)(6)"	Requirement to furnish documents to the Department upon request—moved to different paragraph of ERISA section 104.
2520.104-25	"104(a)(1)"	"104(a)(6)"	Requirement to furnish documents to the Department upon request—moved to different paragraph of ERISA section 104.
2520.104-26(a)	All of paragraph (a), (a)(1), (a)(2), and (a)(3).	New paragraph (a), (a)(1), and (a)(2).	Paragraph (a) needed to be restructured to reflect the fact that all "plan description" requirements and the SPD filing requirement were eliminated from ERISA.
2520.104-27(a)	All of paragraph (a), (a)(1), (a)(2), and (a)(3).	New paragraph (a), (a)(1), and (a)(2).	Paragraph (a) needed to be restructured to reflect the fact that all "plan description" requirements and the SPD filing requirement were eliminated from ERISA.
2520.104-41(b)	"section 104(a)(1)(A)"	"section 104(a)(1)"	Cross reference correction.
2520.104-43(a)	"section 104(a)(1)(A)"	"section 104(a)(1)"	Cross reference correction.
2520.104-44(d)	"section 104(a)(1)(A)"	"section 104(a)(1)"	Cross reference correction.
2520.104a-2	Whole section	"Reserved"	All "plan description" requirements eliminated from ERISA.
2520.104a-3	Whole section	"Reserved"	SPD filing requirement eliminated.
2520.104a-4	Whole section	"Reserved"	SMM filing requirement eliminated.
2520.104a-5(a)	"section 104(a)(1)(A)"	"section 104(a)(1)"	Cross reference correction.
2520.104a-5(a)(1)	All text in paragraph (a)(1)	"Reserved"	Provision obsolete.
2520.104a-7	Whole section	"Reserved"	SMM filing requirement eliminated.
2520.104b-1(b)(3)	"plan description"	Nothing	All "plan description" requirements eliminated from ERISA.
2520.104b-3(f)	All of para. (f)	Nothing	Part of paragraph (f) was superseded by TRA '97 and the rest of the paragraph has become obsolete as a result of the removal of § 2520.104a-3 by this rule.
2520.104b-3(g)	All of para. (g)	Nothing	Paragraph (g) was superseded by TRA '97 and as a result of the removal of § 2520.104a-3 by this rule.
2560.502c-2(a)	"section 101(b)(4)"	"section 101(b)(1)"	Cross reference correction.

Executive Order 12866 Statement

Under Executive Order 12866, the Department must determine whether the regulatory action is "significant" and therefore subject to the requirements of the Executive Order and subject to review by the Office of Management and Budget (OMB). Under section 3(f), the order defines a "significant regulatory action" as an action that is likely to result in a rule: (1) Having an annual effect on the economy of $100 million or more, or adversely and materially affecting a sector of the economy, productivity, competition, jobs, the environment, public health or safety, or State, local or tribal governments or communities (also referred to as "economically significant"); (2) creating serious inconsistency or otherwise interfering with an action taken or planned by another agency; (3) materially altering the budgetary impacts of entitlement grants, user fees, or loan programs or the rights and obligations of recipients thereof; or (4) raising novel legal or policy issues arising out of legal mandates, the President's priorities, or the principles set forth in the Executive Order. Pursuant to the terms of the Executive Order, it has been determined that this action is not significant within the meaning of the Executive Order.

Paperwork Reduction Act

The rule being issued here is not subject to the requirements of the Paperwork Reduction Act of 1995 (44 U.S.C. 3501 *et seq.*) because it does not contain an "information collection request" as defined in 44 U.S.C. 3502(3).

Regulatory Flexibility Act

The Regulatory Flexibility Act, 5 U.S.C. 601 *et seq.*, requires each Federal agency to perform an initial regulatory flexibility analysis for all proposed rules unless the head of the agency certifies that the rule will not, if promulgated, have a significant economic impact on a substantial number of small entities. Small entities include small businesses, organizations, and governmental jurisdictions. Because this proposed rule would remove certain provisions of the CFR and make a number of technical amendments to the CFR designed to correct cross-references affected by amendments to ERISA enacted as part of TRA '97, the proposed rule would have no impact, independent of the statutory change eliminating the SPD and SMM filing requirements, on small plans. As a result, the undersigned certifies that this proposed rule, if promulgated, would not have a significant impact on a substantial number of small entities. The factual basis for this certification is the same regardless of whether one uses the definition of small entity found in regulations issued by the Small Business Administration (13 CFR 121.201) or one defines small entity, on the basis of section 104(a)(2) of ERISA, as an employee benefit plan with fewer than 100 participants.

Small Business Regulatory Enforcement Fairness Act

The proposed rule being issued here is subject to the provisions of the Small Business Regulatory Enforcement Fairness Act of 1996 (5 U.S.C. 801 *et seq.*) and, if finalized, will be transmitted to Congress and the Comptroller General for review. The rule is not a "major rule" as that term is defined in 5 U.S.C. 804, because it is not likely to result in: (1) An annual effect on the economy of $100 million or more; (2) a major increase in costs or prices for consumers, individual industries, or federal, State, or local government agencies, or geographic regions; or (3) significant adverse effects on competition, employment, investment, productivity, innovation, or on the ability of United States-based enterprises to compete with foreign-based enterprises in domestic or export markets.

Unfunded Mandates Reform Act

For purposes of the Unfunded Mandates Reform Act of 1995 (Pub. L. 104-4), as well as Executive Order 12875, this proposed rule does not include any Federal mandate that may result in expenditures by State, local, or tribal governments, and will not impose an annual burden of $100 million or more on the private sector.

Statutory Authority

This proposed rule is promulgated pursuant to the authority contained in section 505 of ERISA (Pub. L. 93-406, 88 Stat. 894, 29 U.S.C. 1135) and sections 101(b) and 104(a)(1) of ERISA, as amended, and under the Secretary of Labor's Order No. 1-87, 52 FR 13139, April 21, 1987.

List of Subjects

29 CFR Part 2520

Employee benefit plans, Employee Retirement Income Security Act, Group health plans, Pension plans, Welfare benefit plans.

29 CFR Part 2560

Claims, Employee benefit plans, Employee Retirement Income Security Act, Law enforcement, Pensions.

For the reasons set forth above, parts 2520 and 2560 of Chapter XXV of Title 29 of the Code of Federal Regulations are amended as follows:

PART 2520—RULES AND REGULATIONS FOR REPORTING AND DISCLOSURE

1. The authority citation for Part 2520 continues to read as follows:

Authority: Secs. 101, 102, 103, 104, 105, 109, 110, 111 (b)(2), 111(c), and 505, Pub. L. 93-406, 88 Stat. 840-52 and 894 (29 U.S.C. 1021-1025, 1029-31, and 1135); Secretary of Labor's Order No. 27-74, 13-76, 1-87, and Labor Management Services Administration Order 2-6.

Sections 2520.102-3, 2520.104b-1 and 2520.104b-3 also are issued under sec. 101(a), (c) and (g)(4) of Pub. L. 104-191, 110 Stat. 1936,

1939, 1951 and 1955 and, sec. 603 of Pub. L. 104-204, 110 Stat. 2935 (29 U.S.C. 1185 and 1191(c)).

2. Section 2520.102-1 is removed and reserved.

3. Revise section 2520.102-4 to read as follows:

§ 2520.102-4 Option for different summary plan descriptions.

In some cases an employee benefit plan may provide different benefits for various classes of participants and beneficiaries. For example, a plan amendment altering benefits may apply to only those participants who are employees of an employer when the amendment is adopted and to employees who later become participants, but not to participants who no longer are employees when the amendment is adopted. (See § 2520.104b-4). Similarly, a plan may provide for different benefits for participants employed at different plants of the employer, or for different classes of participants in the same plant. In such cases the plan administrator may fulfill the requirement to furnish a summary plan description to participants covered under the plan and beneficiaries receiving benefits under the plan by furnishing to each member of each class of participants and beneficiaries a copy of a summary plan description appropriate to that class. Each summary plan description so prepared shall follow the style and format prescribed in § 2520.102-2, and shall contain all information which is required to be contained in the summary plan description under § 2520.102-3. It may omit information which is not applicable to the class of participants or beneficiaries to which it is furnished. It should also clearly identify on the first page of the text the class of participants and beneficiaries for which it has been prepared and the plan's coverage of other classes. If the classes which the employee benefit plan covers are too numerous to be listed adequately on the first page of the text of the summary plan description, they may be listed elsewhere in the text so long as the first page of the text contains a reference to the page or pages in the text which contain this information.

4. Section 2520.103-1(a), introductory text, is amended by removing the term "section 104(a)(1)(A)" and adding, in its place, the term "section 104(a)(1)".

5. Section 2520.103-5 is amended by removing the term "section 104(a)(1)(A)" from paragraphs (a), introductory text, (c)(1)(i), (c)(1)(iii), (c)(2)(ii), (c)(2)(iii) and (c)(3) and adding, in their place, the term "section 104(a)(1)".

6. Section 2520.103-12 is amended by removing from paragraph (a) the term "section 104(a)(1)(A)" and adding, in its place, the term "section 104(a)(1)".

7. Revise paragraph (a) of § 2520.104-4 to read as follows:

§ 2520.104-4 Alternative method of compliance for certain successor pension plans.

(a) *General.* Under the authority of section 110 of the Act, this section sets forth an alternative method of compliance for certain successor pension plans in which some participants and beneficiaries not only have their rights set out in the plan, but also retain eligibility for certain benefits under the terms of a former plan which has been merged into the successor. This section is applicable only to plan mergers which occur after the issuance by the successor plan of the initial summary plan description under the Act. Under the alternative method, the plan administrator of the successor plan is not required to describe relevant provisions of merged plans in summary plan descriptions of the successor plan furnished after the merger to that class of participants and beneficiaries still affected by the terms of the merged plans.

* * * * *

8. Revise the introductory text in paragraph (a) and paragraphs (a)(2), (a)(3), and (c) of § 2520.104-20 to read as follows:

§ 2520.104-20 Limited exemption for certain small welfare plans.

(a) *Scope.* Under the authority of section 104(a)(3) of the Act, the administrator of any employee welfare benefit plan which covers fewer than 100 participants at the beginning of the plan year and which meets the requirements of paragraph (b) of this section is exempted from certain reporting and disclosure provisions of the Act. Specifically, the administrator of such plan is not required to file with the Secretary an annual or terminal report. In addition, the administrator of a plan exempted under this section—

* * * * *

(2) Is not required to furnish upon written request of any participant or beneficiary a copy of the annual report and any terminal report, as required by section 104(b)(4) of the Act;

(3) Is not required to make copies of the annual report available for examination by any participant or beneficiary in the principal office of the administrator and such other places as may be necessary, as required by section 104(b)(2) of the Act.

(b) * * *

(c) *Limitations.* This exemption does not exempt the administrator of an employee benefit plan from any other requirement of Title I of the Act, including the provisions which require that plan administrators furnish copies of the summary plan description to participants and beneficiaries (section 104(b)(1)) and furnish certain documents to the Secretary of Labor upon request (section 104(a)(6)), and which authorize the Secretary of Labor to collect information and data from employee benefit plans for research and analysis (section 513).

* * * * *

9. Amend § 2520.104-21 by revising paragraphs (a) and (c) to read as follows:

§ 2520.104-21 Limited exemption for certain group insurance arrangements.

(a) *Scope.* Under the authority of section 104(a)(3) of the Act, the administrator of any employee welfare benefit plan which covers fewer than 100 participants at the beginning of the plan year and which meets the requirements of paragraph (b) of this section is exempted from certain reporting and disclosure provisions of the Act. Specifically, the administrator of such plan is not required to file with the Secretary a terminal report or furnish upon written request of any participant or beneficiary a copy of any terminal report as required by section 104(b)(4) of the Act.

* * * * *

(c) *Limitations.* This exemption does not exempt the administrator of an employee benefit plan from any other requirement of title I of the Act, including the provisions which require that plan administrators furnish copies of the summary plan description to participants and beneficiaries (section 104(b)(1)), file an annual report with the Secretary of Labor (section 104(a)(1)) and furnish certain documents to the Secretary of Labor upon request (section 104(a)(6)), and authorize the Secretary of Labor to collect information and data from employee benefit plans for research and analysis (section 513).

* * * * *

10. Section 2520.104-23 is amended by removing from paragraph (b)(2) the term "104(a)(1)" and adding, in its place, the term "104(a)(6)".

11. Section 2520.104-24 is amended by removing from paragraph (b) the term "104(a)(1)" and adding, in its place, the term "104(a)(6)".

12. Section 2520.104-25 is amended by removing the term "104(a)(1)" and adding, in its place, the term "104(a)(6)".

13. In § 2520.104-26, revise paragraph (a) to read as follows:

§ 2520.104-26 Limited exemption for certain unfunded dues financed welfare plans maintained by employee organizations.

(a) *Scope.* Under the authority of section 104(a)(3) of the Act, a welfare benefit plan that meets the requirements of paragraph (b) of this section is exempted from the provisions of the Act that require filing with the Secretary an annual report and furnishing a summary annual report to participants and beneficiaries. Such plans may use a simplified method of reporting and disclosure to comply with the requirement to furnish a summary plan description to participants and beneficiaries, as follows:

(1) In lieu of filing an annual report with the Secretary or distributing a summary annual report, a filing is made of Report Form LM-2 or LM-3, pursuant to the LMRDA and regulations thereunder, and

(2) In lieu of a summary plan description, the employee organization constitution or by-laws may be furnished in accordance with § 2520.104b-2 to participants and beneficiaries together with any supplement to such document necessary to meet the requirements of § § 2520.102-2 and 2520.102-3.

* * * * *

14. In § 2520.104-27, revise paragraph (a) to read as follows:

§ 2520.104-27 Alternative method of compliance for certain unfunded dues financed pension plans maintained by employee organizations.

(a) *Scope.* Under the authority of section 110 of the Act, a pension benefit plan that meets the requirements of paragraph (b) of this section is exempted from the provisions of the Act that require filing with the Secretary an annual report and furnishing a summary annual report to participants and beneficiaries. Such plans may use a simplified method of reporting and disclosure to comply with the requirement to furnish a summary plan description to participants and beneficiaries, as follows:

(1) In lieu of filing an annual report with the Secretary or distributing a summary annual report, a filing is made of Report Form LM-2 or LM-3, pursuant to the LMRDA and regulations thereunder, and

(2) In lieu of a summary plan description, the employee organization constitution or by-laws may be furnished in accordance with § 2520.104b-2 to participants and beneficiaries together with any supplement to such document necessary to meet the requirements of §§ 2520.102-2 and 2520.102-3.

* * * * *

15. Section 2520.104-41 is amended by removing from paragraph (b) the term "section 104(a)(1)(A)" and adding, in its place, the term "section 104(a)(1)".

16. Section 2520.104-43 is amended by removing from paragraph (a) the term "section 104(a)(1)(A)" and adding, in its place, "section 104(a)(1)".

17. Section 2520.104-44 is amended by removing from paragraph (d) the term "section 104(a)(1)(A)" and adding, in its place, "section 104(a)(1)".

18. Section 2520.104a-2 is removed and reserved.

19. Section 2520.104a-3 is removed and reserved.

20. Section 2520.104a-4 is removed and reserved.

21. Section 2520.104a-5 is amended by removing the term "section 104(a)(1)(A)" and adding, in its place, the term "section 104(a)(1)".

22. Section 2520.104a-5 is amended by removing and reserving paragraph (a)(1).

23. Section 2520.104a-7 is removed and reserved.

24. Section 2520.104b-1 is amended by removing from the second sentence of paragraph (b)(3) the term "plan description,".

25. In § 2520.104b-3 paragraphs (f) and (g) are removed and reserved.

PART 2560—RULES AND REGULATIONS FOR ADMINISTRATION AND ENFORCEMENT

26. The authority citation for part 2560 continues to read as follows:

Authority: Secs. 502, 505 of ERISA, 29 U.S.C. 1132, 1135, and Secretary's Order 1-87, 52 FR 13139 (April 21, 1987).

Section 2560.502-1 also issued under sec. 502(b)(2), 29 U.S.C. 1132(b)(2).

Section 2560.502i-1 also issued under sec. 502(i), 29 U.S.C. 1132(i).

Section 2560.503-1 also issued under sec. 503, 29 U.S.C. 1133.

§ 2560.502c-21 [Amended]

27. Section 2560.502c-2 is amended by removing from paragraph (a)(1) and (a)(2) the term "section 101(b)(4)" each time it appears and adding, in its place, the term "section 101(b)(1)".

Signed at Washington, D.C., this 28th day of July 1999.

Richard M. McGahey,

Assistant Secretary,

Pension and Welfare Benefits Administration,

Department of Labor.

[FR Doc. 99-19860 Filed 8-4-99; 8:45 am]

¶ 20,534B

Proposed regulations: Summary plan descriptions (SPDs): Summaries of material modifications (SMMs): Plan descriptions: Civil penalties: Liability.—The Taxpayer Relief Act of 1997 (TRA '97) created amendments to ERISA relating to filing of SPDs, SMMs and plan descriptions. Under TRA '97, these documents are no longer required to be filed with the DOL, but are to be made available to the DOL upon request. The PWBA has proposed civil penalties against administrators for a failure or refusal to provide plan documents to the DOL upon request. Administrators will be jointly and severally liable for all assessed penalties. The liability will be a personal liability of the administrator, not a liability of the plan.

The proposed regulations were published in the *Federal Register* on August 5, 1999 (64 FR 42797). The final regulations were published in the *Federal Register* on January 7, 2002 (67 FR 777) and are reproduced at ¶ 14,248G, ¶ 14,925E, and ¶ 14,928Q. The preamble to the final regulations is reproduced at ¶ 24,805W.

ERISA Sec. 104 and ERISA Sec. 502.

¶ 20,534C

PWBA: Department of Health and Human Services (HHS): Proposed regulations: National Medical Support Notice: Qualified medical child support order (QMCSO): Group health plans.—The PWBA and HHS have jointly issued a proposed regulation that introduces a National Medical Support Notice (Notice) to be used by state agencies in enforcing health care coverage provisions of child support orders. The DOL and HHS developed this Notice pursuant to the Child Support Performance and Incentive Act of 1998 (CSPIA). This regulation would amend ERISA Sec. 609(a) and require administrators of group health plans to treat the Notice as a qualified medical child support order.

The preamble and text of the proposed regulations were published in the *Federal Register* on November 15, 1999 (64 FR 62054). The regulations were finalized December 27, 2000 (65 FR 82127), effective January 26, 2001. The regulations are reproduced at ¶ 15,047H and ¶ 15,047I. The preamble is reproduced at ¶ 24,805R.

¶ 20,534D

PWBA: Proposed regulations: Small pension plans: Annual report: Form 5500: Independent qualified public accountant (IQPA): Audit: Waiver.—The PWBA has issued proposed regulations increasing the eligibility requirements for plans with 100 or fewer participants to qualify for a waiver of the annual examination and report of IQPA's. Under the proposed regulations, the PWBA is also requiring enhanced disclosure to participants and beneficiaries and increased bonding, under certain circumstances, as further conditions of eligibility for a waiver.

The preamble and text of the proposed regulations were published in the *Federal Register* on December 1, 1999 (64 FR 67436). The regulations were finalized October 19, 2000 (65 FR 62957), effective December 18, 2000. The regulations are reproduced at ¶ 14,247U and ¶ 14,247Z. The preamble is reproduced at ¶ 24,805M.

¶ 20,534E

PWBA/DOL: Proposed regulations: Multiple employer welfare arrangements (MEWAs): Collective bargaining agreements.—The Department of Labor has issued proposed regulations setting forth criteria for the exclusion of certain welfare benefit plans from the definition of MEWAs. The criteria would be used to determine if an employee welfare benefit plan was established or maintained under one or more collective bargaining agreements, thereby triggering ERISA preemption.

The proposed regulations were published in the *Federal Register* on October 27, 2000 (65 FR 64481). The regulations were finalized April 9, 2003 (68 FR 17471). The regulations are reproduced at ¶ 14,139C. The preamble is reproduced at ¶ 24,806J.

ERISA Sec. 3.

¶ 20,534F

PWBA/DOL: Proposed regulations: Administrative hearings: Multiple employer welfare arrangements (MEWAs): Collective bargaining agreements.—The Department of Labor has issued proposed regulations regarding administrative hearings, to accompany proposed regulations setting forth criteria for the exclusion of certain welfare benefit plans from state regulation. The hearings would only be available to plans against whom a state's jurisdiction or law has been asserted, and that are claiming ERISA preemption as collectively bargained plans, as opposed to being MEWAs.

The proposed regulations were published in the *Federal Register* on October 27, 2000 (65 FR 64498). The final regulations were published in the *Federal Register* on April 9, 2003 (68 FR 17484) and are effective June 9, 2003. The preamble to the final regulations is reproduced at ¶ 24,806H; the final regulations are reproduced at ¶ 14,789Z-1 through ¶ 14,789Z-10.

¶ 20,534G

PBGC: Proposed regulations: Benefit payments: Amendment of current payments method.—The PBGC has issued proposed regulations to amend its current benefit method payment. The proposed amendments give participants more choices of annuity benefit forms, add rules regarding distribution of payments the PBGC owes to a participant at the time of death, and clarify what it means to be able to retire under plan provisions within Title IV of ERISA. The proposed regulations amend the PBGC's current regulations on Benefits Payable in Terminated Single-Employer Plans, Aggregate Limits on Guaranteed Benefits, and Allocation of Assets in Single-Employer Plans.

The proposed regulation was published in the *Federal Register* on December 26, 2000 (65 FR 81456).

The preamble to the final regulations, which was published in the *Federal Register* on April 8, 2002 (67 FR 16949), can be found at ¶ 24,805Y. The regulations are reproduced at ¶ 15,421C , ¶ 15,421E , ¶ 15,421F , ¶ 15,421G , ¶ 15,421H , ¶ 15,421I , ¶ 15,422 , ¶ 15,422D , ¶ 15,424 , ¶ 15,425 , ¶ 15,425A , ¶ 15,425B , ¶ 15,425C , ¶ 15,425D , ¶ 15,426 , ¶ 15,426A , ¶ 15,426B , ¶ 15,426C , ¶ 15,429M , ¶ 15,471A , and ¶ 15,472C .

ERISA Sec. 4022, ERISA Sec. 4022B, ERISA Sec. 4044.

¶ 20,534H

Pension and Welfare Benefits Administration (PWBA) proposed regulations: IRS: Bona fide wellness programs: Health Insurance Portability and Accountability Act of 1996 (HIPAA): Nondiscrimination requirements.—The PWBA, in conjunction with the IRS and the Department of Health and Human Services, has issued proposed regulations to establish and elucidate the meaning of "bona fide wellness program" with regard to nondiscrimination provisions of the Code and ERISA, as added by HIPAA.

The proposed regulations, which were published in the *Federal Register* on January 8, 2001 (66 FR 1421), are reproduced below. The IRS's proposed regulations are at ¶ 20,255.

ERISA Sec. 702.

[Billing Codes: 4830-01-P; 4510-29-P; 4120-01-P]

DEPARTMENT OF THE TREASURY

Internal Revenue Service

26 CFR Part 54

[REG-114084-00]

RIN 1545-AY34

DEPARTMENT OF LABOR

Pension and Welfare Benefits Administration

29 CFR Part 2590

RIN 1210-AA77

DEPARTMENT OF HEALTH AND HUMAN SERVICES

Health Care Financing Administration

45 CFR Part 146

RIN 0938-AK19

Notice of Proposed Rulemaking for Bona Fide Wellness Programs

AGENCIES: Internal Revenue Service, Department of the Treasury; Pension and Welfare Benefits Administration, Department of Labor; Health Care Financing Administration, Department of Health and Human Services.

ACTION: Notice of proposed rulemaking and request for comments.

SUMMARY: This proposed rule would implement and clarify the term "bona fide wellness program" as it relates to regulations implementing the nondiscrimination provisions of the Internal Revenue Code, the Employee Retirement Income Security Act, and the Public Health Service Act, as added by the Health Insurance Portability and Accountability Act of 1996.

DATES: Written comments on this notice of proposed rulemaking are invited and must be received by the Departments on or before

[INSERT DATE 90 DAYS AFTER PUBLICATION OF THIS DOCUMENT IN THE FEDERAL REGISTER].

ADDRESSES: Written comments should be submitted with a signed original and three copies (except for electronic submissions to the Internal Revenue Service (IRS) or Department of Labor) to any of the addresses specified below. Any comment that is submitted to any Department will be shared with the other Departments.

Comments to the IRS can be addressed to:

CC:M&SP:RU (REG-114084-00)

Room 5226

Internal Revenue Service

POB 7604, Ben Franklin Station

Washington, DC 20044

In the alternative, comments may be hand-delivered between the hours of 8 a.m. and 5 p.m. to:

CC:M&SP:RU (REG-114084-00)

Courier's Desk

Internal Revenue Service

1111 Constitution Avenue, NW.

Washington DC 20224

Alternatively, comments may be transmitted electronically via the IRS Internet site at:

http://www.irs.gov/tax regs/regslist.html.

Comments to the Department of Labor can be addressed to:

U.S. Department of Labor

Pension and Welfare Benefits Administration

200 Constitution Avenue NW., Room C-5331

¶20,534F

Washington, DC 20210

Attention: Wellness Program Comments

Alternatively, comments may be hand-delivered between the hours of 9 a.m. and 5 p.m. to the same address. Comments may also be transmitted by e-mail to: Wellness@pwba.dol.gov.n

Comments to HHS can be addressed to:

Health Care Financing Administration

Department of Health and Human Services

Attention: HCFA-2078-P

P.O. Box 26688

Baltimore, MD 21207

In the alternative, comments may be hand-delivered between the hours of 8:30 a.m. and 5 p.m. to either:

Room 443-G

Hubert Humphrey Building

200 Independence Avenue, SW.

Washington, DC 20201

or

Room C5-14-03

7500 Security Boulevard

Baltimore, MD 21244-1850

All submissions to the IRS will be open to public inspection and copying in room 1621, 1111 Constitution Avenue, NW., Washington, DC from 9 a.m. to 4 p.m.

All submissions to the Department of Labor will be open to public inspection and copying in the Public Documents Room, Pension and Welfare Benefits Administration, U.S. Department of Labor, Room N-1513, 200 Constitution Avenue, NW., Washington, DC from 8:30 a.m. to 5:30 p.m.

All submissions to HHS will be open to public inspection and copying in room 309-G of the Department of Health and Human Services, 200 Independence Avenue, SW., Washington, DC from 8:30 a.m. to 5 p.m.

FOR FURTHER INFORMATION CONTACT: Russ Weinheimer, Internal Revenue Service, Department of the Treasury, at (202) 622-6080; Amy J. Turner, Pension and Welfare Benefits Administration, Department of Labor, at (202) 219-4377; or Ruth A. Bradford, Health Care Financing Administration, Department of Health and Human Services, at (410) 786-1565.

SUPPLEMENTARY INFORMATION:

Customer Service Information: Individuals interested in obtaining additional information on HIPAA's nondiscrimination rules may request a copy of the Department of Labor's booklet entitled "Questions and Answers: Recent Changes in Health Care Law" by calling the PWBA Toll-Free Publication Hotline at 1-800-998-7542 or may request a copy of the Health Care Financing Administration's new publication entitled "Protecting Your Health Insurance Coverage" by calling (410) 786-1565. Information on HIPAA's nondiscrimination rules and other recent health care laws is also available on the Department of Labor's website (http://www.dol.gov/dol/pwba) and the Department of Health and Human Services' website (http://hipaa.hcfa.gov).

Background

The Health Insurance Portability and Accountability Act of 1996 (HIPAA), Public Law 104-191, was enacted on August 21, 1996. HIPAA amended the Internal Revenue Code of 1986 (Code), the Employee Retirement Income Security Act of 1974 (ERISA), and the Public Health Service Act (PHS Act) to provide for, among other things, improved portability and continuity of health coverage. HIPAA added section 9802 of the Code, section 702 of ERISA, and section 2702 of the PHS Act, which prohibit discrimination in health coverage. However, the HIPAA nondiscrimination provisions do not prevent a plan or issuer from establishing discounts or rebates or modifying otherwise applicable copayments or deductibles in return for adherence to programs of health promotion and disease prevention. Interim final rules implementing the HIPAA provisions were first made available to the public on April 1, 1997 (published in the **Federal Register** on April 8, 1997, 62 FR 16894) (April 1997 interim rules).

In the preamble to the April 1997 interim rules, the Departments invited comments on whether additional guidance was needed concerning, among other things, the permissible standards for determining bona fide wellness programs. The Departments also stated that they

intend to issue further regulations on the nondiscrimination rules and that in no event would the Departments take any enforcement action against a plan or issuer that had sought to comply in good faith with section 9802 of the Code, section 702 of ERISA, and section 2702 of the PHS Act before the additional guidance is provided. The new interim regulations relating to the HIPAA nondiscrimination rules (published elsewhere in this issue of the **Federal Register**) do not include provisions relating to bona fide wellness programs. Accordingly, the period for good faith compliance continues with respect to those provisions until further guidance is issued. Compliance with the provisions of these proposed regulations constitutes good faith compliance with the statutory provisions relating to wellness programs.

Overview of the Proposed Regulations

The HIPAA nondiscrimination provisions generally prohibit a plan or issuer from charging similarly situated individuals different premiums or contributions based on a health factor. In addition, under the interim regulations published elsewhere in this issue of the **Federal Register**, cost-sharing mechanisms such as deductibles, copayments, and coinsurance are considered restrictions on benefits. Thus, they are subject to the same rules as are other restrictions on benefits; that is, they must apply uniformly to all similarly situated individuals and must not be directed at individual participants or beneficiaries based on any health factor of the participants or beneficiaries. However, the HIPAA nondiscrimination provisions do not prevent a plan or issuer from establishing premium discounts or rebates or modifying otherwise applicable copayments or deductibles in return for adherence to programs of health promotion and disease prevention. Thus, there is an exception to the general rule prohibiting discrimination based on a health factor if the reward, such as a premium discount or waiver of a cost-sharing requirement, is based on participation in a program of health promotion or disease prevention. The April 1997 interim rules, the interim regulations published elsewhere in this issue of the **Federal Register**, and these proposed regulations refer to programs of health promotion and disease prevention allowed under this exception as "bona fide wellness programs." In order to prevent the exception to the nondiscrimination requirements for bona fide wellness programs from eviscerating the general rule contained in the HIPAA nondiscrimination provisions, these proposed regulations impose certain requirements on wellness programs providing rewards that would otherwise discriminate based on a health factor.

A wide range of wellness programs exist to promote health and prevent disease. However, many of these programs are not subject to the bona fide wellness program requirements. The requirements for bona fide wellness programs apply only to a wellness program that provides a reward based on the ability of an individual to meet a standard that is related to a health factor, such as a reward conditioned on the outcome of a cholesterol test. Therefore, without having to comply with the requirements for a bona fide wellness program, a wellness program could—

• Provide voluntary testing of enrollees for specific health problems and make recommendations to address health problems identified, if the program did not base any reward on the outcome of the health assessment;

• Encourage preventive care through the waiver of the copayment or deductible requirement for the costs of well-baby visits;

• Reimburse employees for the cost of health club memberships, without regard to any health factors relating to the employees; or

• Reimburse employees for the costs of smoking cessation programs, without regard to whether the employee quits smoking.

A wellness program that provides a reward based on the ability of an individual to meet a standard related to a health factor violates the interim regulations published elsewhere in this issue of the **Federal Register** unless it is a bona fide wellness program. Under these proposed regulations, a wellness program must meet four requirements to be a bona fide wellness program.

First, the total reward that may be given to an individual under the plan for all wellness programs is limited. A reward can be in the form of a discount, a rebate of a premium or contribution, or a waiver of all or part of a cost-sharing mechanism (such as deductibles, copayments, or coinsurance), or the absence of a surcharge. The reward for the wellness program, coupled with the reward for other wellness programs with respect to the plan that require satisfaction of a standard related to a health factor, must not exceed a specified percentage of the cost of employee-only coverage under the plan. The cost of employee-only coverage is determined based on the total amount of employer and employee contributions for the benefit package under which the employee is receiving coverage.

The proposed regulations specify three alternative percentages: 10, 15, and 20. The Departments welcome comments on the appropriate level for the percentage. Comments will be taken into account in determining the standard for the final regulations.

Several commenters on the April 1997 regulations suggested that the amount of a reward should be permitted if it is actuarially determined based on the costs associated with the health factor measured under the wellness program. However, in some cases, the resulting reward (or penalty) might be so large as to have the effect of denying coverage to certain individuals. The percentage limitation in the proposed regulations is designed to avoid this result. The percentage limitation also avoids the additional administrative costs of a reward based on actuarial cost.

The Departments recognize that there may be some programs that currently offer rewards, individually or in the aggregate, that exceed the specified percentage. However, as noted below in the economic analysis, data is scarce regarding practices of wellness programs. Thus, the Departments specifically request comments on the appropriateness of the specified percentage of the cost of employee-only coverage under a plan as the maximum reward for a bona fide wellness program, including whether a larger amount should be allowed for wellness programs that include participation by family members (i.e., the specified percentage of the cost of family coverage). Note also that, as stated above, the period for good faith compliance continues with respect to whether wellness programs satisfy the statutory requirements. While compliance with these proposed regulations constitutes good faith compliance with the statutory provisions, it is possible that, based on all the facts and circumstances, a plan's wellness program that provides a reward in excess of the specified range of percentages of the cost of employee-only coverage may also be found to meet the good faith compliance standard.

Under these proposed regulations, the second requirement to be a bona fide wellness program is that the program must be reasonably designed to promote good health or prevent disease for individuals in the program. This requirement prevents a program from being a subterfuge for merely imposing higher costs on individuals based on a health factor by requiring a reasonable connection between the standard required under the program and the promotion of good health and disease prevention. Among other things, a program is not reasonably designed to promote good health or prevent disease unless the program gives individuals eligible for the program the opportunity to qualify for the reward under the program at least once per year. In contrast, a program that imposes a reward or penalty for the duration of the individual's participation in the plan based solely on health factors present when an individual first enrolls in a plan is not reasonably designed to promote health or prevent disease (because, if the individual cannot qualify for the reward by adopting healthier behavior after initial enrollment, the program does not have any connection to improving health).

The third requirement to be a bona fide wellness program under these proposed regulations is that the reward under the program must be available to all similarly situated individuals. The April 1997 interim rules provided that if, under the design of the wellness program, enrollees might not be able to achieve a program standard due to a health factor, the program would not be a bona fide wellness program. These proposed regulations increase flexibility for plans by allowing plans to make individualized adjustments to their wellness programs to address the health factors of the particular individuals for whom it is unreasonably difficult to qualify for the benefits under the program. Specifically, the program must allow any individual for whom it is unreasonably difficult due to a medical condition (or for whom it is medically inadvisable to attempt) to satisfy the initial program standard an opportunity to satisfy a reasonable alternative standard. The examples clarify that a reasonable alternative standard must take into account the relevant health factor of the individual who needs the alternative. A program does not need to establish the specific reasonable alternative standard before the program commences. To satisfy this third requirement for being a bona fide wellness program, it is sufficient to determine a reasonable alternative standard once a participant informs the plan that it is unreasonably difficult for the participant due to a medical condition to satisfy the general standard (or that it is medically inadvisable for the participant to attempt to achieve the general standard) under the program.

Many commenters asked how the bona fide wellness program requirements apply to programs that provide a reward for not smoking.

An example in the proposed regulations clarifies that if it is unreasonably difficult for an individual to stop smoking due to an addiction to nicotine[1] , the individual must be provided a reasonable alternative standard to obtain the reward.

The fourth requirement to be a bona fide wellness program under the proposed regulations is that all plan materials describing the terms of the program must disclose the availability of a reasonable alternative standard. The proposed regulations include model language that can be used to satisfy this requirement; examples also illustrate substantially similar language that would satisfy the requirement.

The proposed regulations contain two clarifications of this fourth requirement. First, plan materials are not required to describe specific reasonable alternative standards. It is sufficient to disclose that some reasonable alternative standard will be made available. Second, any plan materials that describe the general standard would also have to disclose the availability of a reasonable alternative standard. However, if the program is merely mentioned (and does not describe the general standard), disclosure of the availability of a reasonable alternative standard is not required.

Economic Impact and Paperwork Burden

Summary - Department of Labor and Department of Health and Human Services

Under the proposed regulation, health plans generally may vary employee premium contributions or benefit levels across similarly situated individuals based on health status factors only in connection with bona fide wellness programs. The regulation establishes four requirements for such bona fide wellness programs. It (1) limits the permissible amount of variation in employee premium or benefit levels; (2) requires that programs be reasonably designed to promote health or prevent disease; (3) requires programs to permit plan participants who for medical reasons would incur unreasonable difficulty to satisfy the programs' initial wellness standards to satisfy reasonable alternative standards instead; and (4) requires certain plan materials to disclose the availability of such alternative standards. The Departments carefully considered the costs and benefits attendant to these requirements. The Departments believe that the benefits of these requirements exceed their costs.

The Departments anticipate that the proposed regulation will result in transfers of cost among plan sponsors and participants and in new economic costs and benefits.

Economic benefits will flow from plan sponsors' efforts to maintain wellness programs' effectiveness where discounts or surcharges are reduced and from plans sponsors' provision of reasonable alternative standards that help improve affected plan participants' health habits and health. The result will be fewer instances where wellness programs merely shift costs to high risk individuals and more instances where they succeed at improving such individuals' health habits and health.

Transfers will arise because the size of some discounts and surcharges will be reduced, and because some plan participants who did not satisfy wellness programs' initial standards will satisfy alternative standards. These transfers are estimated to total between $18 million and $46 million annually. (The latter figure is an upper bound, reflecting the case in which all eligible participants pursue and satisfy alternative standards.)

New economic costs may be incurred if reductions in discounts or surcharges reduce wellness programs' effectiveness, but this effect is expected to be very small because reductions will be small and relatively few plans and participants will be affected. Other new economic costs will be incurred by plan sponsors to make available reasonable alternative standards where required. The Departments were unable to estimate these costs but are confident that these costs in combination with the transfers referenced above will not exceed the estimate of the transfers alone. Affected plan sponsors can satisfy the proposed regulation's third requirement by making available any reasonable standard they choose, including low cost alternatives. It is unlikely that plan sponsors would choose alternative standards whose cost, in combination with costs transferred from participants who satisfy them, would exceed the cost of providing discounts or waiving surcharges for all eligible participants.

Executive Order 12866 - Department of Labor and Department of Health and Human Services

Under Executive Order 12866, the Departments must determine whether a regulatory action is "significant" and therefore subject to the

---

[1] Under the *Diagnostic and Statistical Manual of Mental Disorders*, Fourth Edition, American Psychiatric Association, 1994 (DSM IV), nicotine addiction is a medical condition. See also Rev. Rul. 99-28, 1999-25 I.R.B. 6 (June 21, 1999), citing a report of the Surgeon General stating that scientists in the field of drug addiction agree that nicotine, a substance common to all forms of tobacco, is a powerfully addictive drug.

requirements of the Executive Order and subject to review by the Office of Management and Budget (OMB). Under section 3(f), the order defines a "significant regulatory action" as an action that is likely to result in a rule (1) having an annual effect on the economy of $100 million or more, or adversely and materially affecting a sector of the economy, productivity, competition, jobs, the environment, public health or safety, or State, local or tribal governments or communities (also referred to as "economically significant"); (2) creating serious inconsistency or otherwise interfering with an action taken or planned by another agency; (3) materially altering the budgetary impacts of entitlement grants, user fees, or loan programs or the rights and obligations of recipients thereof; or (4) raising novel legal or policy issues arising out of legal mandates, the President's priorities, or the principles set forth in the Executive Order.

Pursuant to the terms of the Executive Order, it has been determined that this action raises novel policy issues arising out of legal mandates. Therefore, this notice is "significant" and subject to OMB review under Section 3(f)(4) of the Executive Order. Consistent with the Executive Order, the Departments have assessed the costs and benefits of this regulatory action. The Departments' assessment, and the analysis underlying that assessment, is detailed below. The Departments performed a comprehensive, unified analysis to estimate the costs and benefits attributable to the interim regulation for purposes of compliance with Executive Order 12866, the Regulatory Flexibility Act, and the Paperwork Reduction Act.

Statement of Need for Proposed Action

These interim regulations are needed to clarify and interpret the HIPAA nondiscrimination provisions (Prohibiting Discrimination Against Individual Participants and Beneficiaries Based on Health Status) under Section 702 of the Employee Retirement Income Security Act of 1974 (ERISA), Section 2702 of the Public Health Service Act, and Section 9802 of the Internal Revenue Code of 1986. The provisions are needed to ensure that group health plans and group health insurers and issuers do not discriminate against individuals, participants, and beneficiaries based on any health factors with respect to health care premiums. Additional guidance was required to define bona fide wellness programs.

Costs and Benefits

The Departments anticipate that the proposed regulation will result in transfers of cost among plans sponsors and participants and in new economic costs and benefits. The economic benefits of the regulation will include a reduction in instances where wellness programs merely shift costs to high risk individuals and an increase in instances where they succeed at improving such individuals' health habits and health. Transfers are estimated to total between $18 million and $46 million annually. The Departments were unable to estimate new economic costs but are confident that these costs in combination with the transfers referenced above will not exceed the estimate of the transfers alone. The Departments believe that the regulation's benefits will exceed its costs. Their unified analysis of the regulation's costs and benefits is detailed later in this preamble.

Regulatory Flexibility Act - Department of Labor and Department of Health and Human Services

The Regulatory Flexibility Act (5 U.S.C. 601 et seq.) (RFA) imposes certain requirements with respect to Federal rules that are subject to the notice and comment requirements of section 553(b) of the Administrative Procedure Act (5 U.S.C. 551 et seq.) and which are likely to have a significant economic impact on a substantial number of small entities. Unless an agency certifies that a proposed rule will not have a significant economic impact on a substantial number of small entities, section 603 of the RFA requires that the agency present an initial regulatory flexibility analysis (IRFA) at the time of the publication of the notice of proposed rulemaking describing the impact of the rule on small entities and seeking public comment on such impact. Small entities include small businesses, organizations and governmental jurisdictions.

For purposes of analysis under the RFA, PWBA proposes to continue to consider a small entity to be an employee benefit plan with fewer than 100 participants. The basis of this definition is found in section 104(a)(2) of the Employee Retirement Income Security Act of 1974 (ERISA), which permits the Secretary of Labor to prescribe simplified annual reports for pension plans which cover fewer than 100 participants. Under section 104(a)(3), the Secretary may also provide for exemptions or simplified annual reporting and disclosure for welfare benefit plans. Pursuant to the authority of section 104(a)(3), the Department of Labor has previously issued at 29 C.F.R. §§ 2520.104-20, 2520.104-21, 2520.104-41, 2520.104-46 and 2520.104b-10 certain simplified reporting provisions and limited exemptions from reporting and disclosure requirements for small plans, including unfunded or insured welfare plans covering fewer than 100 participants and which satisfy certain other requirements.

Further, while some large employers may have small plans, in general most small plans are maintained by small employers. Thus, PWBA believes that assessing the impact of this proposed rule on small plans is an appropriate substitute for evaluating the effect on small entities. For purposes of their unified IFRA, the Departments adhered to PWBA's proposed definition of small entities. The definition of small entity considered appropriate for this purpose differs, however, from a definition of small business which is based on size standards promulgated by the Small Business Administration (SBA) (13 CFR 121.201) pursuant to the Small Business Act (15 U.S.C. 631 et seq.). The Departments therefore request comments on the appropriateness of the size standard used in evaluating the impact of this proposed rule on small entities.

Under this proposed regulation, health plans generally may vary employee premium contributions or benefit levels across similarly situated individuals based on health factors only in connection with bona fide wellness programs. The regulation establishes four requirements for such bona fide wellness programs.

The Departments estimate that 36,000 plans with fewer than 100 participants vary employee premium contributions or benefit levels across similarly situated individuals based on health factors. While this represents just 1 percent of all small plans, the Departments nonetheless believe that it represents a substantial number of small entities. The Departments also note that at least some premium discounts or surcharges may be large. Premium discounts associated with wellness programs are believed to range as high as $560 per affected participant per year. Therefore, the Departments believe that the impact of this regulation on at least some small entities may be significant. Having reached these conclusions, the Departments carried out an IRFA as part of their unified analysis of the costs and benefits of the regulation. The reasoning and assumptions underlying the Departments' unified analysis of the regulation's costs and benefits are detailed later in this preamble.

The regulation's first requirement caps maximum allowable variation in employee premium contribution and benefit levels. The Departments estimate that 9,300 small plans will be affected by the cap. These plans can comply with this requirement by reducing premiums (or increasing benefits) by $1.1 million on aggregate for those participants whose premiums are higher (or whose benefits are lower) due to health factors. This would constitute an ongoing, annual transfer of cost of $1.1 million, or $122 on average per affected plan. The regulation does not limit small plans' flexibility to transfer this cost back evenly to all participants in the form of small premium increases or benefit cuts.

The regulation's second requirement provides that wellness programs must be reasonably designed to promote health or prevent disease. Comments received by the Departments and available literature on employee wellness programs suggest that existing wellness programs generally satisfy this requirement. The requirement therefore is not expected to compel small plans to modify existing wellness programs. It is not expected to entail economic costs nor to prompt transfers.

The third requirement provides that rewards under wellness programs must be available to all similarly situated individuals. In particular, programs must allow individuals for whom it would be unreasonably difficult due to a medical condition to satisfy initial program standards an opportunity to satisfy reasonable alternative standards. The Departments believe that some small plans' wellness programs do not currently satisfy this requirement and will have to be modified.

The Departments estimate that 21,000 small plans' wellness programs include initial standards that may be unreasonably difficult for some participants to meet. These plans are estimated to include 18,000 participants for whom the standard is in fact unreasonably difficult to meet. (Many small plans are very small, having fewer than 10 participants, and many will include no participant for whom the initial standard is unreasonable difficult to meet for a medical reason.) Satisfaction of alternative standards by these participants will result in transfers of cost as they qualify for discounts or escape surcharges. If all of these participants request and then satisfy an alternative standard, the transfer would amount to $5 million annually. If one-half request alternative standards and one-half of those meet them, the transfer would amount to $1 million.

In addition to transfers, small plans will also incur new economic costs to provide alternative standards. However, plans can satisfy this requirement by providing inexpensive alternative standards, and have the flexibility to select whatever reasonable alternative standard is most desirable or cost efficient. Plans not wishing to provide alternative standards also have the option of abolishing health-status based variation in employee premiums. The Departments expect that the economic cost to provide alternatives combined with the associated transfer cost of granting discounts or waiving surcharges will not exceed the transfer cost associated with granting discounts or waiving surcharges for all participants who qualify for an alternative, estimated here at $1 million to $5 million, or about $55 to $221 per affected plan. Plans have the flexibility to transfer some or all of this cost evenly to all participants in the form of small premium increases or benefit cuts.

The fourth requirement provides that plan materials describing wellness plan standards must disclose the availability of reasonable alternative standards. This requirement will affect the 36,000 small plans that apply discounts or surcharges. These plans will incur economic costs to revise affected plan materials. The 5,000 to 18,000 small plan participants who will succeed at satisfying these alternative standards will benefit from these disclosures. The disclosures need not specify what alternatives are available, and the regulation provides model language that can be used to satisfy this requirement. Legal requirements other than this regulation generally require plans and issuers to maintain accurate materials describing plans. Plans and issuers generally update such materials on a regular basis as part of their normal business practices. This requirement is expected to represent a negligible fraction of the ongoing, normal cost of updating plans' materials. This analysis therefore attributes no cost to this requirement.

Special Analyses—Department of the Treasury

It has been determined that this notice of proposed rulemaking is not a significant regulatory action as defined in Executive Order 12866. Therefore, a regulatory assessment is not required. It also has been determined that this notice of proposed rulemaking does not impose a collection of information on small entities and is not subject to section 553(b) of the Administrative Procedure Act (5 U.S.C. chapter 5). For these reasons, the Regulatory Flexibility Act (5 U.S.C. chapter 6) does not apply pursuant to 5 U.S.C. section 603(a), which exempts from the Act's requirements certain rules involving the internal revenue laws. Pursuant to section 7805(f) of the Internal Revenue Code, this notice of proposed rulemaking will be submitted to the Chief Counsel for Advocacy of the Small Business Administration for comment on its impact on small business.

Paperwork Reduction Act

Department of Labor and Department of the Treasury

This Notice of Proposed Rulemaking includes a requirement that if the plan materials describe the standard required to be met in order to qualify for a reward such as a premium discount or waiver of a cost-sharing requirement, they must also disclose the availability of a reasonable alternative standard. However, plan materials are not required to describe specific reasonable alternatives. The proposal also includes examples of disclosures which would satisfy the requirements of the proposed rule.

Plan administrators of group health plans covered under Title I of ERISA are required to make certain disclosures about the terms of a plan and material changes in terms through a Summary Plan Description or Summary of Material Modifications pursuant to sections 101(a) and 102(a) of ERISA. Group health plans and issuers also typically make other informational materials available to participants, either as a result of state and local requirements, or as part of their usual business practices in connection with the offer and promotion of health care coverage to employees.

While this proposal may cause group health plans to modify informational materials pertaining to wellness programs, the Departments conclude that it creates no new information collection requirements, and that the overall impact on existing information collection activities will be negligible. First, as described earlier, it is estimated that the proposed reasonable alternative requirements for bona fide wellness programs will impact a maximum of 22,000 plans and 229,000 participants. These numbers are very small in comparison with the 2.5 million ERISA group health plans that cover 65 million participants, and 175,500 state and local governmental plans that cover 11.5 million participants.

In addition, because model language is provided in the proposal, these modifications are expected to require a minimal amount of effort, such that they fall within the provision of OMB regulations in 5 CFR 1320.3(c)(2). This provision excludes from the definition of collection of information language which is supplied by the Federal government for disclosure purposes.

Finally, the Department of Labor's methodology in accounting for the burden of the Summary Plan Description (SPD) and Summary of Material Modifications (SMM), as currently approved under OMB control number 1210-0039, incorporates an assumption concerning a constant rate of revision in these disclosure materials which is based on plans' actual reporting on the annual report/return (Form 5500) of their rates of modification. This occurrence of SPD revisions is generally more frequent than the minimum time frames described in section 104(b) and related regulations. The annual hour and cost burdens of the SMM/SPD information collection request is currently estimated at 576,000 hours and $97 million. Because the burden of modifying a wellness program's disclosures is expected to be negligible, and readily incorporated in other revisions made to plan materials on an ongoing basis, the methodology used already accounts for this type of change. Therefore, the Department concludes that the modification described in this proposal to the information collection request is neither substantive nor material, and accordingly it attributes no burden to this regulation.

Department of Health and Human Services

Under the Paperwork Reduction Act of 1995, we are required to provide 60-day notice in the **Federal Register** and solicit public comment before a collection of information requirement is submitted to the Office of Management and Budget (OMB) for review and approval. In order to fairly evaluate whether an information collection should be approved by OMB, section 3506(c)(2)(A) of the Paperwork Reduction Act of 1995 requires that we solicit comment on the following issues:

•The need for the information collection and its usefulness in carrying out the proper functions of our agency.

•The accuracy of our estimate of the information collection burden.

•The quality, utility, and clarity of the information to be collected.

•Recommendations to minimize the information collection burden on the affected public, including automated collection techniques.

§ 146.121 Prohibiting discrimination against participants and beneficiaries based on a health factor.

(f) *Bona fide wellness programs* Paragraph (1)(iv) requires the plan or issuer to disclose in all plan materials describing the terms of the program the availability of a reasonable alternative standard required under paragraph (f)(1)(iii) of this section. However, in plan materials that merely mention that a program is available, without describing its terms, the disclosure is not required. This requirement will affect the estimated 1,300 nonfederal governmental plans that apply premium discounts or surcharges. The development of the materials is expected to take 100 hours for nonfederal governmental plans. The corresponding burden performed by service providers is estimated to be $38,000.

We have submitted a copy of this rule to OMB for its review of the information collection requirements. These requirements are not effective until they have been approved by OMB. A notice will be published in the **Federal Register** when approval is obtained.

If you comment on any of these information collection and record keeping requirements, please mail copies directly to the following:

Health Care Financing Administration,

Office of Information Services,

Information Technology Investment Management Group,

Division of HCFA Enterprise Standards,

Room C2-26-17, 7500 Security Boulevard,

Baltimore, MD 21244-1850,

Attn: John Burke HCFA-2078-P,

and

Office of Information and Regulatory Affairs,

Office of Management and Budget,

Room 10235, New Executive Office Building,

Washington, DC 20503,

Attn.: Allison Herron Eydt, HCFA-2078-P.

Small Business Regulatory Enforcement Fairness Act

The proposed rule is subject to the provisions of the Small Business Regulatory Enforcement Fairness Act of 1996 (5 U.S.C. 801 et seq.) and, if finalized, will be transmitted to Congress and the Comptroller General for review. The rule is not a "major rule" as that term is defined in 5 U.S.C. 804, because it is not likely to result in (1) an annual effect on the economy of $100 million or more; (2) a major increase in costs or prices for consumers, individual industries, or federal, State, or local government agencies, or geographic regions; or (3) significant adverse effects on competition, employment, investment, productivity, innovation, or on the ability of United States-based enterprises to compete with foreign-based enterprises in domestic or export markets.

Unfunded Mandates Reform Act

For purposes of the Unfunded Mandates Reform Act of 1995 (Public Law 104-4), as well as Executive Order 12875, this proposed rule does not include any Federal mandate that may result in expenditures by State, local, or tribal governments, nor does it include mandates which may impose an annual burden of $100 million or more on the private sector.

Federalism Statement - Department of Labor and Department of Health and Human Services

Executive Order 13132 (August 4, 1999) outlines fundamental principles of federalism, and requires the adherence to specific criteria by federal agencies in the process of their formulation and implementation of policies that have substantial direct effects on the States, the relationship between the national government and States, or on the distribution of power and responsibilities among the various levels of government. Agencies promulgating regulations that have these federalism implications must consult with State and local officials, and describe the extent of their consultation and the nature of the concerns of State and local officials in the preamble to the regulation.

In the Departments' view, these proposed regulations do not have federalism implications, because they do not have substantial direct effects on the States, the relationship between the national government and States, or on the distribution of power and responsibilities among various levels of government. This is largely because, with respect to health insurance issuers, the vast majority of States have enacted laws which meet or exceed the federal standards in HIPAA prohibiting discrimination based on health factors. Therefore, the regulations are not likely to require substantial additional oversight of States by the Department of Health and Human Services.

In general, through section 514, ERISA supersedes State laws to the extent that they relate to any covered employee benefit plan, and preserves State laws that regulate insurance, banking, or securities. While ERISA prohibits States from regulating a plan as an insurance or investment company or bank, HIPAA added a new preemption provision to ERISA (as well as to the PHS Act) preserving the applicability of State laws establishing requirements for issuers of group health insurance coverage, except to the extent that these requirements prevent the application of the portability, access, and renewability requirements of HIPAA. The nondiscrimination provisions that are the subject of this rulemaking are included among those requirements.

In enacting these new preemption provisions, Congress indicated its intent to establish a preemption of State insurance requirements only to the extent that those requirements prevent the application of the basic protections set forth in HIPAA. HIPAA's Conference Report states that the conferees intended the narrowest preemption of State laws with regard to health insurance issuers. H.R. Conf. Rep. No. 736, 104th Cong. 2d Session 205 (1996). Consequently, under the statute and the Conference Report, State insurance laws that are more stringent than the federal requirements are unlikely to "prevent the application of" the HIPAA nondiscrimination provisions.

Accordingly, States are given significant latitude to impose requirements on health insurance issuers that are more restrictive than the federal law. In many cases, the federal law imposes minimum requirements which States are free to exceed. Guidance conveying this interpretation was published in the **Federal Register** on April 8, 1997 and these regulations do not reduce the discretion given to the States by the statute. It is the Departments' understanding that the vast majority of States have in fact implemented provisions which meet or exceed the minimum requirements of the HIPAA non-discrimination provisions.

HIPAA provides that the States may enforce the provisions of HIPAA as they pertain to issuers, but that the Secretary of Health and Human Services must enforce any provisions that a State fails to substantially enforce. When exercising its responsibility to enforce the provisions of HIPAA, HCFA works cooperatively with the States for the purpose of addressing State concerns and avoiding conflicts with the exercise of State authority.[2] HCFA has developed procedures to implement its enforcement responsibilities, and to afford the States the maximum opportunity to enforce HIPAA's requirements in the first instance.

HCFA's procedures address the handling of reports that States may not be enforcing HIPAA's requirements, and the mechanism for allocating enforcement responsibility between the States and HCFA. To date, HCFA has had occasion to enforce the HIPAA non-discrimination provisions in only two States.

Although the Departments conclude that these proposed regulations do not have federalism implications, in keeping with the spirit of the Executive Order that agencies closely examine any policies that may have federalism implications or limit the policy making discretion of the States, the Department of Labor and HCFA have engaged in numerous efforts to consult with and work cooperatively with affected State and local officials.

For example, the Departments were aware that some States commented on the way the federal provisions should be interpreted. Therefore, the Departments have sought and received input from State insurance regulators and the National Association of Insurance Commissioners (NAIC). The NAIC is a non-profit corporation established by the insurance commissioners of the 50 States, the District of Columbia, and the four U.S. territories, that among other things provides a forum for the development of uniform policy when uniformity is appropriate. Its members meet, discuss, and offer solutions to mutual problems. The NAIC sponsors quarterly meetings to provide a forum for the exchange of ideas, and in-depth consideration of insurance issues by regulators, industry representatives, and consumers. HCFA and Department of Labor staff have attended the quarterly meetings consistently to listen to the concerns of the State Insurance Departments regarding HIPAA issues, including the nondiscrimination provisions. In addition to the general discussions, committee meetings and task groups, the NAIC sponsors the following two standing HIPAA meetings for members during the quarterly conferences:

• HCFA/DOL Meeting on HIPAA Issues (This meeting provides HCFA and Labor the opportunity to provide updates on regulations, bulletins, enforcement actions and outreach efforts regarding HIPAA.)

• The NAIC/HCFA Liaison Meeting (This meeting provides HCFA and the NAIC the opportunity to discuss HIPAA and other health care programs.)

In their comments on the 1997 interim rules, the NAIC suggested that the permissible standards for determining bona fide wellness programs ensure that such programs are not used as a proxy for discrimination based on a health factor. The NAIC also commented that the nondiscrimination provisions of HIPAA "are especially significant in their impact on small groups, and particularly in small groups, where there is a great potential for adverse selection and gaming." One State asked that the Departments' final nondiscrimination provisions be as consumer-protective as possible. Finally, another State described already-existing State regulation of issuers offering wellness programs in that State and asked that standards for bona fide wellness programs be left to the States.

The Departments considered these views very carefully when formulating the wellness program proposal. While allowing plans a great deal of flexibility in determining what kinds of incentives best encourage the plan's own participants and beneficiaries to pursue a healthier lifestyle, the Departments proposal ensures that individuals have an opportunity to qualify for the premium discount or other reward. If an individual is unable to satisfy a wellness program standard due to a health factor, plans are required to make a reasonable alternative standard available to the individual. In addition, the Departments reiterate their position that State insurance laws that are more stringent than the federal requirements are unlikely to "prevent the application of" the federal law and therefore are saved from preemption. Therefore, these more protective State laws continue to apply for individuals receiving health insurance coverage in connection with a group health plan.

The Departments welcome further comment on these issues from the States in response to this proposal.

The Departments also cooperate with the States in several ongoing outreach initiatives, through which information on HIPAA is shared among federal regulators, State regulators, and the regulated community. In particular, the Department of Labor has established a Health Benefits Education Campaign with more than 70 partners, including HCFA, NAIC and many business and consumer groups. HCFA has sponsored four conferences with the States—the Consumer Outreach and Advocacy conferences in March 1999 and June 2000, the Implementation and Enforcement of HIPAA National State-Federal Confer-

---

[2] This authority applies to insurance issued with respect to group health plans generally, including plans covering employees of church organizations. Thus, this discussion of federalism applies to all group health insurance coverage that is subject to the PHS Act, including those church plans that provide coverage through a health insurance issuer (but not to church plans that do not provide coverage through a health insurance issuer). For additional information relating to the application of these nondiscrimination rules to church plans, see the preamble to regulations being proposed elsewhere in this issue of the **Federal Register** regarding section 9802(c) of the Code relating to church plans.

ences in August 1999 and 2000. Furthermore, both the Department of Labor and HCFA websites offer links to important State websites and other resources, facilitating coordination between the State and federal regulators and the regulated community.

In conclusion, throughout the process of developing these regulations, to the extent feasible within the specific preemption provisions of HIPAA, the Departments have attempted to balance the States' interests in regulating health plans and health insurance issuers, and the rights of those individuals that Congress intended to protect through the enactment of HIPAA.

Unified Analysis of Costs and Benefits - Department of Labor and Department of Health and Human Services

Introduction

Under the proposed regulation, health plans generally may vary employee premium contributions or benefit levels across similarly situated individuals based on health factors only in connection with bona fide wellness programs. The regulation establishes four requirements for such bona fide wellness programs.

A large body of literature, together with comments received by the Departments, demonstrate that well-designed wellness programs can deliver benefits well in excess of their costs. For example, the U.S. Centers for Disease Control and Prevention estimate that implementing proven clinical smoking cessation interventions can save one year of life for each $2,587 invested. In addition to reduced mortality, benefits of effective wellness programs can include reduced absenteeism, improved productivity, and reduced medical costs. The requirements contained in the proposed regulation were crafted to accommodate and not impair such beneficial programs, while combating discrimination in eligibility and premiums for similarly situated individuals as intended by Congress.

Detailed Estimates

Estimation of the economic impacts of the four requirements is difficult because data on affected plans' current practices are incomplete, and because plans' approaches to compliance with the requirements and the effects of those approaches will vary and cannot be predicted. Nonetheless, the Departments undertook to consider the impacts fully and to develop estimates based on reasonable assumptions.

Based on a 1993 survey of employers by the Robert Wood Johnson Foundation, the Departments estimate that 1.6 percent of large plans and 1.2 percent of small plans currently vary employee premium contributions across similarly situated individuals and will be subject to the four requirements for bona fide wellness programs. This amounts to 32,000 plans covering 1.2 million participants. According to an industry survey by Hewitt Associates, just more than one-third as many plans vary benefit levels across similarly situated individuals as vary premiums. This amounts to 11,000 plans covering 415,000 participants. The Departments separately considered the effect of each of the four requirements on these plans. For purposes of its estimates, the Departments assumed that one-half of the plans in the latter group are also included in the former, thereby estimating that 37,000 plans covering 1.4 million participants will be subject to the four requirements for bona fide wellness programs.

Limit on Dollar Amount—Under the first requirement, any discount or surcharge, whether applicable to employee premiums or benefit levels, must not exceed a specified percentage of the total premium for employee-only coverage under the plan. The proposed regulations specify three alternative percentages: 10, 15, and 20. For purposes of this discussion, the Departments examine the midpoint of the three alternative percentages, 15 percent.

The Departments lack representative data on the magnitude of the discounts and surcharges applied by affected plans today. One leading consultant practicing in this area believes that wellness incentive premium discounts ranged from about $60 to about $480 annually in 1998, averaging about $240 that year. Expressed as a percentage of average total premium for employee-only coverage that year, this amounts to a range of about 3 percent to 23 percent and an average of about 11 percent. This suggests that most affected plans, including some whose discounts are somewhat larger than average, already comply with the first requirement and will not need to reduce the size of the discounts or surcharges they apply. It appears likely, however, that a sizeable minority of plans—perhaps a few thousand plans covering a few hundred thousand participants—will need to reduce the size of their discounts or surcharges in order to comply with the first requirement. The table below summarizes the Departments' assumptions regarding the size of discounts and surcharges at year 2000 levels, expressed in annual amounts.

The Departments considered the potential economic effects of requiring these plans to reduce the size of their discounts or surcharges. These effects are likely to include transfers of costs among plan sponsors and participants, as well as new economic costs and benefits.

Single employee total premium		$2,448
Discount or Surcharge		
low	3%	$70
average	11%	$280
high	23%	$560
Cap on discount or surcharge	15%	$367

Transfers will arise as plans reduce discounts and surcharges. Plan sponsors can exercise substantial control over the size and direction of these transfers. Limiting the size of discounts and surcharges restricts only the differential treatment of participants who satisfy wellness program standards and those who do not. It does not, for example, restrict plans sponsors' flexibility to determine the respective employer and employee shares of base premiums. Possible outcomes include a transfer of costs to plan sponsors from participants who satisfy wellness program standards, from plan sponsors to participants who do not satisfy the standards, from participants who satisfy the standards to those who do not, or some combination of these.

The Departments developed a very rough estimate of the total amount of transfers that might derive from this requirement. The Departments' estimate assumes that (1) all discounts and surcharges take the form of employee premium discounts; (2) discounts are distributed evenly within both the low-to-average range and the average-to-high range, and are distributed across these ranges such that their mean equals the assumed average; and (3) 70 percent of participants qualify for the discount. This implies that just more than one-fourth of plans with discounts or surcharges will be impacted by the cap, and that these plans' current discounts and surcharges exceed the cap by $86 on average. The 9,600 affected plans could satisfy this requirement by reducing premiums for the 106,000 participants who do not qualify by $86 annually, for an aggregate, ongoing annual transfer of approximately $9 million. The Departments solicit comments on their assumptions and estimate, and would welcome information supportive of better estimates.

New economic costs and benefits may arise if changes in the size of discounts or surcharges result in changes in participant behavior.

Net economic welfare might be lost if some wellness programs' effectiveness is eroded, but the magnitude and incidence of such effects is expected to be negligible. Consider a wellness program that discounts premiums for participants who take part in an exercise program. It is plausible that, at the margin, a few participants who would take part in order to obtain a discount of between $368 and $560 annually will not take part to obtain a discount of $367. This might represent a net loss of economic welfare. This effect is expected to be negligible, however. Based on the assumptions specified above, just 248,000 participants now qualifying for discounts would be affected. Reductions in discounts are likely to average about $86 annually, which amounts to $7 per month or $3 per biweekly pay period. Employee premiums are often deducted from pay pre-tax, so the after tax value of these discounts may be even smaller. Moreover, the proposed regulation caps only discounts and surcharges applied to similarly situated individuals in the context of a group health plans. It does not restrict plan sponsors from employing other motivational tools to encourage participation in wellness programs. According to the Hewitt survey, among 408 employers that offered incentives for participation in wellness programs, 24 percent offered awards or gifts and 62 percent varied life insurance premiums, while just 14 percent varied medical premiums.

On the other hand, net economic welfare likely will be gained in instances where large premium differentials would otherwise have served to discourage enrollment in health plans by employees who did not satisfy wellness program requirements. Consider a plan that provides a very large discount for non-smokers. The very high employee premiums charged to smokers might discourage some from enrolling in the plan at all, and some of these might be uninsured as a result. It seems unlikely that the plan sponsor would respond to the first requirement of the proposed regulation by raising premiums drastically for all non-smokers, driving many out of the plan. Instead, the plan sponsor would reduce premiums for smokers, and more smokers would enroll. This would result in transfers to newly enrolled smokers from the plan sponsor (and possibly from non-smokers if the plan sponsor makes other changes to compensation). But it would also result in net gains in economic welfare from reduced uninsurance.

The Departments believe that the net economic gains from prohibiting discounts and surcharges so large that they could discourage enrollment based on health factors outweigh any net losses that might derive from the negligible reduction of some employees' incentive to participate in wellness programs. Comments are solicited on the magnitude of these and any other effects and on the attendant costs and benefits.

Reasonable Design—Under the second requirement, the program must be reasonably designed to promote health or prevent disease. The Departments believe that a program that is not so designed would not provide economic benefits, but would serve merely to transfer costs from plan sponsors to targeted individuals based on health factors. This requirement therefore is not expected to impose economic costs but might prompt transfers of costs from otherwise targeted individuals to their plans' sponsors (or to other participants in their plans if plan sponsors elect to pass these costs back evenly to all participants). Comments received by the Departments and available literature on employee wellness programs, however, suggest that existing wellness programs generally satisfy this requirement. The requirement therefore is not expected to compel plans to modify existing wellness programs. It is not expected to entail economic costs nor to prompt transfers. The Departments would appreciate comments on this conclusion and information on the types of existing wellness programs (if any) that would not satisfy requirement.

Uniform Availability—The third requirement provides that rewards under the program must be available to all similarly situated individuals. In particular, the program must allow any individual for whom it would be unreasonably difficult due to a medical condition to satisfy the initial program standard an opportunity to satisfy a reasonable alternative standard. Comments received by the Departments and available literature on employee wellness programs suggest that some wellness programs do not currently satisfy this requirement and will have to be modified. Based on the Hewitt survey, the Departments estimate that among employers that provide incentives for employees to participate in wellness programs, 18 percent require employees to achieve a low risk behavior to qualify for the incentive, 79 percent require a pledge of compliance, and 38 percent require participation in a program. (These numbers sum to more than 100 percent because wellness programs may apply more than one criterion.) Depending on the nature of the wellness program, it might be unreasonably difficult due to a medical condition for at least some plan participants to achieve the behavior or to comply with or participate in the program.

The Departments identified three broad types of economic impact that might arise from the third requirement. First, affected plans will incur some economic cost to make available reasonable alternative standards. Second, additional economic costs and benefits may arise depending on the nature of alternatives provided, individuals' use of these alternatives, and any changes in the affected individuals' behavioral and health outcomes. Third, some costs may be transferred from individuals who would fail to satisfy programs' initial standards, but who will satisfy reasonable alternative standards once available (and thereby qualify for associated discounts), to plan sponsors (or to other participants in their plans if plan sponsors elect to pass these costs back evenly to all participants).

The Departments note that some plans that apply different discounts or surcharges to similarly situated individuals and are therefore subject to the requirement may not need to provide alternative standards. The requirement provides that alternative standards need not be specified or provided until a participant for whom it is unreasonably difficult due to a medical condition to satisfy the initial standard seeks such an alternative. Some wellness programs' initial standards may be such that no participant would ever find them unreasonably difficult to satisfy due to a medical condition. The Departments reviewed Hewitt survey data on wellness program standards and criteria. Based on their review they estimate that 20,000 of the 35,000 potentially affected plans have initial wellness program standards that might be unreasonably difficult for some participants to satisfy due to a medical condition. Moreover, because alternatives need not be made available until they are sought by qualified plan participants, it might be possible for some these plans to go for years or even indefinitely without needing to make available an alternative standard. This could be particularly likely for small plans. The most common standards for wellness programs pertain to smoking, blood pressure, and cholesterol levels, according to the Hewitt Survey. Based on U.S. Centers for Disease Control and Management data on the incidence of certain health habits and conditions in the general population, the Departments estimate that among companies with 5 employees, about one-fourth probably employ no smokers, and about one-third probably employ no one with high blood pressure or cholesterol. Approximately 96 percent of all plans with potentially difficult initial wellness program standards have fewer than 100 participants.

How many participants might qualify for, seek, and ultimately satisfy alternative standards? The Departments lack sufficient data to estimate these counts with confidence. Rough estimates were developed as follows. The Departments examined the Hewitt survey of wellness program provisions and U.S. Centers for Disease Control and Prevention statistics on the incidence of certain health habits and conditions in the general population in order to discern how wellness programs' initial standards might interact with plan participants' health habits and health status. Based on these data, it appears that as many as 29 percent of participants in plans with discounts or surcharges, or 394,000 individuals, might fail to satisfy wellness programs' initial standards. Of these, approximately 229,000 are in the 22,000 plans which apply standards that might be unreasonably difficult due to a medical condition for some plan participants to satisfy, the Departments estimate. The standards would in fact be unreasonably difficult to satisfy for some subset of these individuals—148,000 by the Departments' estimate. The Departments lack any basis to estimate how many of these will avail themselves of an alternative standard, or how many that do will succeed in satisfying that standard. To estimate the potential impact of this requirement, the Departments considered two assumptions: an upper bound assumption under which all 148,000 individuals seek and satisfy alternative standards, and an alternative assumption under which one-half (or 74,000) seek an alternative and one-half of those (37,000) satisfy it.

Where plans are required to make available reasonable alternative standards, what direct costs will they incur? The regulation does not prescribe a particular type of alternative standard that must be provided. Instead, it permits plan sponsors flexibility to provide any reasonable alternative. The Departments expect that plans sponsors will select alternatives that entail the minimum net costs (or, stated differently, the maximum net benefits) that are possible. Plan sponsors may select low-cost alternatives, such as requiring an individual for whom it would be unreasonably difficult to quit smoking (and thereby qualify for a non-smoker discount) to attend a smoking cessation program that is available at little or no cost in the community, or to watch educational videos or review educational literature. Plan sponsors presumably will select higher-cost alternatives only if they thereby derive offsetting benefits, such as a higher smoking cessation success rate. The Departments also note that the number of plans with initial wellness program standards that might be unreasonably difficult for some participants to satisfy is probably small (having been estimated at 22,000, or 1 percent of all plans), as is the number of individuals who would take advantage of alternative standards (estimated at between 74,000 and 148,00, or between 0.1 percent and 0.2 percent of all participants).

It seems reasonable to presume that the net cost plan sponsors will incur in the provision of alternatives, including transfers as well as new economic costs and benefits, will not exceed the transfer cost of providing discounts (or waiving surcharges) for all plan participants who qualify for alternatives, which is estimated below at between $9 million and $37 million. It is likely that many plan sponsors will find more cost effective ways to satisfy this requirement, and that the true net cost to them will therefore be much smaller than this. The Departments have no basis for estimating the magnitude of the cost of providing alternative standards or of potential offsetting benefits, however, and therefore solicit comments from the public on this question.

What other economic costs and benefits might arise where alternative standards are made available? A large number of outcomes are possible. Consider a program that provides premium discounts for non-smokers.

It is possible that some individuals who would have quit smoking in order to qualify for a discount will nonetheless find it unreasonably difficult to quit and will obtain the discount while continuing to smoke by satisfying an alternative standard. This would represent a net loss of economic welfare from increased smoking.

On the other hand, consider individuals who, in the context of the initial program, are unable or unwilling to quit smoking. It seems likely that some of these individuals could quit with appropriate assistance, and that some alternative standards provided by plan sponsors will provide such assistance. In such cases, a program which had the effect of shifting premium costs to smokers would be transformed into one that successfully reduced smoking. This would represent a net gain of economic welfare.

Which scenario is more likely? The Departments have no concrete basis for answering this question, and therefore solicit comments on it. However, the Departments note that plan sponsors will have strong motivation to identify and provide alternative standards that have positive net economic effects. They will be disinclined to provide alternatives that undermine their overall wellness program and worsen behavioral and health outcomes, or that make financial rewards available absent meaningful efforts by participants to improve their health habits and health. Instead they will be inclined to provide alternatives that sustain or reinforce plan participants' incentive to improve their health habits and health, and/or that help participants make such improvements. It therefore seems likely that gains in economic welfare from this requirement will equal or outweigh losses. The Departments anticipate that the requirement to provide reasonable alternative standards will reduce instances where wellness programs serve only to shift costs to higher risk individuals and increase instances where programs succeed at helping high risk individuals improve their health habits and health.

What transfers of costs might derive from the availability of (and participants' satisfaction of) alternative standards? The transfers arising from this requirement may take the form of transfers to participants who satisfy new alternative wellness program standards from plan sponsors, to such participants from other participants, or some combination of these. The Departments estimated potential transfers as follows. Assuming average annual total premiums for employee-only coverage of $2,448,[3] the maximum allowable discount of 15 percent amounts to $367 per year. As noted earlier, discounts under existing wellness programs appear to average about 11 percent (or $280 per year for a plan costing $2,448), ranging from 3 percent ($70) to 23 percent ($560). Reducing all discounts greater than $367 per year to that amount will reduce the average, perhaps to about $251. Assuming that the 37,000 to 148,000 participants who satisfy alternative standards would not have satisfied the wellness programs' initial standards, the transfers attributable to their discounts and hence to this requirement would amount to between $9 million and $37 million. The Departments solicit comments on their assumptions and estimates regarding transfers that may derive from this requirement.

Disclosure of Alternatives' Availability— The fourth requirement provides that plan materials describing wellness plan standards must disclose the availability of reasonable alternative standards. This requirement will affect the 37,000 plans that apply discounts or surcharges. These plans will incur economic costs to revise affected plan materials. The 37,000 to 148,000 participants who will succeed at satisfying these alternative standards will benefit from these disclosures. The disclosures need not specify what alternatives are available, and the regulation provides model language that can be used to satisfy this requirement. The Departments generally account elsewhere for plans' cost of updating such materials to reflect changes in plan provisions as required under various disclosure requirements and as is part of usual business practice. This particular requirement is expected to represent a negligible fraction of the ongoing cost of updating plans' materials, and is not separately accounted for here.

List of Subjects

26 CFR Part 54

Excise taxes, Health care, Health insurance, Pensions, Reporting and recordkeeping requirements.

29 CFR Part 2590

Employee benefit plans, Employee Retirement Income Security Act, Health care, Health insurance, Reporting and recordkeeping requirements.

* * *

For the reasons set forth above, 29 CFR Part 2590 is proposed to be amended as follows:

PART 2590 [AMENDED]—RULES AND REGULATIONS FOR HEALTH INSURANCE PORTABILITY AND RENEWABILITY FOR GROUP HEALTH PLANS

1. The authority citation for Part 2590 continues to read as follows:

Authority: Secs. 107, 209, 505, 701-703, 711-713, and 731-734 of ERISA (29 U.S.C. 1027, 1059, 1135, 1171-1173, 1181-1183, and 1191-1194), as amended by HIPAA (Public Law 104-191, 110 Stat. 1936), MHPA and NMHPA (Public Law 104-204, 110 Stat. 2935), and WHCRA (Public Law 105-277, 112 Stat. 2681-436), section 101(g)(4) of HIPAA, and Secretary of Labor's Order No. 1-87, 52 FR 13139, April 21, 1987.

2. Section 2590.702 is proposed to be amended by adding text to paragraph (b) to read as follows:

§ 2590.702 Prohibiting discrimination against participants and beneficiaries based on a health factor.

* * * * *

(f) *Bona fide wellness programs*—(1) *Definition.* A wellness program is a bona fide wellness program if it satisfies the requirements of paragraphs (f)(1)(i) through (f)(1)(iv) of this section. However, a wellness program providing a reward that is not contingent on satisfying a standard related to a health factor does not violate this section even if it does not satisfy the requirements of this paragraph (f) for a bona fide wellness program.

(i) The reward for the wellness program, coupled with the reward for other wellness programs with respect to the plan that require satisfaction of a standard related to a health factor, must not exceed [10/15/20] percent of the cost of employee-only coverage under the plan. For this purpose, the cost of employee-only coverage is determined based on the total amount of employer and employee contributions for the benefit package under which the employee is receiving coverage. A reward can be in the form of a discount, a rebate of a premium or contribution, or a waiver of all or part of a cost-sharing mechanism (such as deductibles, copayments, or coinsurance), or the absence of a surcharge.

(ii) The program must be reasonably designed to promote good health or prevent disease. For this purpose, a program is not reasonably designed to promote good health or prevent disease unless the program gives individuals eligible for the program the opportunity to qualify for the reward under the program at least once per year.

(iii) The reward under the program must be available to all similarly situated individuals. A reward is not available to all similarly situated individuals for a period unless the program allows—

(A) A reasonable alternative standard to obtain the reward to any individual for whom, for that period, it is unreasonably difficult due to a medical condition to satisfy the otherwise applicable standard for the reward; and

(B) A reasonable alternative standard to obtain the reward to any individual for whom, for that period, it is medically inadvisable to attempt to satisfy the otherwise applicable standard for the reward.

(iv) The plan or issuer must disclose in all plan materials describing the terms of the program the availability of a reasonable alternative standard required under paragraph (f)(1)(iii) of this section. (However, in plan materials that merely mention that a program is available, without describing its terms, this disclosure is not required.) The following language, or substantially similar language, can be used to satisfy this requirement: "If it is unreasonably difficult due to a medical condition for you to achieve the standards for the reward under this program, or if it is medically inadvisable for you to attempt to achieve the standards for the reward under this program, call us at [insert telephone number] and we will work with you to develop another way to qualify for the reward." In addition, other examples of language that would satisfy this requirement are set forth in Examples 4, 5, and 6 of paragraph (f)(2) of this section.

(2) *Examples.* The rules of this paragraph (f) are illustrated by the following examples.:

Example 1. (i) *Facts.* A group health plan offers a wellness program to participants and beneficiaries under which the plan provides memberships to a local fitness center at a discount.

(ii) *Conclusion.* In this *Example 1*, the reward under the program is not contingent on satisfying any standard that is related to a health factor. Therefore, there is no discrimination based on a health factor under either paragraph (b) or (c) of this section and the requirements for a bona fide wellness program do not apply.

Example 2. (i) *Facts.* An employer sponsors a group health plan. The annual premium for employee-only coverage is $2,400 (of which the employer pays $1,800 per year and the employee pays $600 per year). The plan implements a wellness program that offers a $240 rebate on premiums to program enrollees.

(ii) *Conclusion.* In this *Example 2*, the program satisfies the requirements of paragraph (f)(1)(i) of this section because the reward for the wellness program, $240, does not exceed [10/15/20] percent of the total annual cost of employee-only coverage, [$240/$360/$480]. ($2,400×[10/15/20]%=[$240/$360/$480].)

Example 3. (i) *Facts.* A group health plan gives an annual premium discount of [10/15/20] percent of the cost of employee-only coverage to participants who adhere to a wellness program. The wellness program consists solely of giving an annual cholesterol test to participants.

---

[3] Average level based on the Kaiser Family Foundation/Health Research and Education Trust *Survey of Employer-Sponsored Health benefits, 1999*, projected by the Departments to 2000 levels.

Those participants who achieve a count under 200 receive the premium discount for the year.

(ii) *Conclusion.* In this *Example 3*, the program is not a bona fide wellness program. The program fails to satisfy the requirement of being available to all similarly situated individuals because some participants may be unable to achieve a cholesterol count of under 200 and the plan does not make available a reasonable alternative standard for obtaining the premium discount. (In addition, plan materials describing the program are required to disclose the availability of the reasonable alternative standard for obtaining the premium discount.) Thus, the premium discount violates paragraph (c) of this section because it may require an individual to pay a higher premium based on a health factor of the individual than is required of a similarly situated individual under the plan.

Example 4. (i) *Facts.* Same facts as *Example 3*, except that if it is unreasonably difficult due to a medical condition for a participant to achieve the targeted cholesterol count (or if it is medically inadvisable for a participant to attempt to achieve the targeted cholesterol count), the plan will make available a reasonable alternative standard that takes the relevant medical condition into account. In addition, all plan materials describing the terms of the program include the following statement: "If it is unreasonably difficult due to a medical condition for you to achieve a cholesterol count under 200, or if it is medically inadvisable for you to attempt to achieve a count under 200, call us at the number below and we will work with you to develop another way to get the discount." Individual *D* is unable to achieve a cholesterol count under 200. The plan accommodates *D* by making the discount available to *D*, but only if *D* complies with a low-cholesterol diet.

(ii) *Conclusion.* In this *Example 4*, the program is a bona fide wellness program because it satisfies the four requirements of this paragraph (f). First, the program complies with the limits on rewards under a program. Second, it is reasonably designed to promote good health or prevent disease. Third, the reward under the program is available to all similarly situated individuals because it accommodates individuals for whom it is unreasonably difficult due to a medical condition to achieve the targeted count (or for whom it is medically inadvisable to attempt to achieve the targeted count) in the prescribed period by providing a reasonable alternative standard. Fourth, the plan discloses in all materials describing the terms of the program the availability of a reasonable alternative standard. Thus, the premium discount does not violate this section.

Example 5. (i) *Facts.* A group health plan will waive the $250 annual deductible (which is less than [10/15/20] percent of the annual cost of employee-only coverage under the plan) for the following year for participants who have a body mass index between 19 and 26, determined shortly before the beginning of the year. However, any participant for whom it is unreasonably difficult due to a medical condition to attain this standard (and any participant for whom it is medically inadvisable to attempt to achieve this standard) during the plan year is given the same discount if the participant walks for 20 minutes three days a week. Any participant for whom it is unreasonably difficult due to a medical condition to attain either standard (and any participant for whom it is medically inadvisable to attempt to achieve either standard during the year) is given the same discount if the individual satisfies a reasonable alternative standard that is tailored to the individual's situation. All plan materials describing the terms of the wellness program include the following statement: "If it is unreasonably difficult due to a medical condition for you to achieve a body mass index between 19 and 26 (or if it is medically inadvisable for you to attempt to achieve this body mass index) this year, your deductible will be waived if you walk for 20 minutes three days a week. If you cannot follow the walking program, call us at the number above and we will work with you to develop another way to have your deductible waived, such as a dietary regimen."

(ii) *Conclusion.* In this *Example 5*, the program is a bona fide wellness program because it satisfies the four requirements of this paragraph (f). First, the program complies with the limits on rewards under a program. Second, it is reasonably designed to promote good health or prevent disease. Third, the reward under the program is available to all similarly situated individuals because it generally accommodates individuals for whom it is unreasonably difficult due to a medical condition to achieve (or for whom it is medically inadvisable to attempt to achieve) the targeted body mass index by providing a reasonable alternative standard (walking) and it accommodates individuals for whom it is unreasonably difficult due to a medical condition (or for whom it is medically inadvisable to attempt) to walk by providing an alternative standard that is reasonable for the individual. Fourth, the plan discloses in all materials describing the terms of the program the availability of a reasonable alternative standard for every individual. Thus, the waiver of the deductible does not violate this section.

Example 6. (i) *Facts.* In conjunction with an annual open enrollment period, a group health plan provides a form for participants to certify that they have not used tobacco products in the preceding twelve months. Participants who do not provide the certification are assessed a surcharge that is [10/15/20] percent of the cost of employee-only coverage. However, all plan materials describing the terms of the wellness program include the following statement: "If it is unreasonably difficult due to a health factor for you to meet the requirements under this program (or if it is medically inadvisable for you to attempt to meet the requirements of this program), we will make available a reasonable alternative standard for you to avoid this surcharge." It is unreasonably difficult for Individual *E* to stop smoking cigarettes due to an addiction to nicotine (a medical condition). The plan accommodates *E* by requiring *E* to participate in a smoking cessation program to avoid the surcharge. *E* can avoid the surcharge for as long as *E* participates in the program, regardless of whether *E* stops smoking (as long as *E* continues to be addicted to nicotine).

(ii) *Conclusion.* In this *Example 6*, the premium surcharge is permissible as a bona fide wellness program because it satisfies the four requirements of this paragraph (f). First, the program complies with the limits on rewards under a program. Second, it is reasonably designed to promote good health or prevent disease. Third, the reward under the program is available to all similarly situated individuals because it accommodates individuals for whom it is unreasonably difficult due to a medical condition (or for whom it is medically inadvisable to attempt) to quit using tobacco products by providing a reasonable alternative standard. Fourth, the plan discloses in all materials describing the terms of the program the availability of a reasonable alternative standard. Thus, the premium surcharge does not violate this section.

* * * * *

Signed at Washington, DC this *28th* day of *December*, 2000.

Leslie B. Kramerich

Assistant Secretary, Pension and Welfare Benefits Administration U.S. Department of Labor

---

¶ 20,534I

PBGC: Proposed regulations: Penalties: Late payments: Information penalty: Reasonable cause: Aggravating and mitigating factors.— The PBGC has issued proposed regulations concerning the assessment of penalties against a plan for late payments or failing to provide certain notices or other material information that is required under ERISA Sec. 4071. The proposed regulations state that penalties for late payments may be waived "for reasonable cause" and that the PBGC may take "aggravating and mitigating factors" into account when assessing an information penalty.

The preamble and proposed regulations reproduced below were published in the *Federal Register* on January 12, 2001 (66 FR 2856).

ERISA Sec. 4003 , ERISA Sec. 4007 and ERISA Sec. 4071 .

PENSION BENEFIT GUARANTY CORPORATION

29 CFR Parts 4003, 4007, and 4071

RIN 1212-AA95

Assessment of and Relief From Penalties

AGENCY: Pension Benefit Guaranty Corporation.

ACTION: Proposed rule.

SUMMARY: The PBGC has issued a number of policy statements about penalties over the last few years. Some of these policy statements have been incorporated into the PBGC's regulations. For the convenience of the public, the PBGC is now proposing to codify in its regulations an expanded version of the remaining penalty policy statements. Among other things, this expanded version of the PBGC's penalty policies would explain in general terms the meaning of "reasonable cause" for penalty waivers and the guidelines for assessing penalties under ERISA section 4071.

DATES: Comments must be received on or before March 13, 2001.

ADDRESSES: Comments may be mailed to the Office of the General Counsel, Pension Benefit Guaranty Corporation, 1200 K Street, NW., Washington, DC 20005-4026, or delivered to Suite 340 at the above address. Comments also may be sent by Internet e-mail to reg.comments@pbgc.gov. Comments will be available for inspection at the PBGC's Communications and Public Affairs Department in Suite 240 at the above address during normal business hours.

FOR FURTHER INFORMATION CONTACT: Harold J. Ashner, Assistant General Counsel, or Deborah C. Murphy, Attorney, Pension Benefit Guaranty Corporation, Office of the General Counsel, Suite 340, 1200 K Street, NW., Washington, DC 20005-4026, 202-326-4024. (For TTY/TTD users, call the Federal relay service toll-free at 1-800-877-8339 and ask to be connected to 202-326-4024.)

SUPPLEMENTARY INFORMATION: The PBGC administers the pension plan termination insurance program under Title IV of the Employee Retirement Income Security Act of 1974 (ERISA). When a single-employer plan terminates without sufficient assets to provide all benefits, the PBGC steps in to ensure that participants and beneficiaries receive their plan benefits, subject to certain legal limits. The PBGC also provides financial assistance to multiemployer plans that become unable to pay benefits.

ERISA and the PBGC's regulations require the payment of premiums to the PBGC and the providing of certain information to the PBGC and to other persons. To promote the effective operation of the insurance program under Title IV, ERISA authorizes the PBGC to assess penalties if premiums are paid late and if certain notices and other material information are not timely provided. (See ERISA sections 4007 and 4071 and the PBGC's regulations on Payment of Premiums (29 CFR Part 4007) and Penalties for Failure to Provide Certain Notices or Other Material Information (29 CFR Part 4071).) The PBGC has published four notices in the Federal Register since mid-1995 describing its penalty policies under sections 4007 and 4071.

This proposed rule would expand and codify the policies described in two of those notices: those published July 18, 1995 (60 FR 36837), and December 17, 1996 (61 FR 66338). (The 1995 notice in turn replaced an earlier penalty policy notice published March 3, 1992 (at 57 FR 7605).) The policy guidance would be placed in appendices to the premium payment regulation and the regulation on Penalties for Failure to Provide Certain Notices or Other Material Information. In addition, the PBGC's regulation on Rules for Administrative Review of Agency Decisions (29 CFR Part 4003) would be amended to cover penalties assessed under section 4071.

The policies described in the other two notices have already been codified in PBGC regulations.

The PBGC's regulations on Termination of Single-Employer Plans (29 CFR Part 4041) and Missing Participants (29 CFR Part 4050) reflect the PBGC's Statement of Policy published March 14, 1997 (at 62 FR 12521), announcing penalty relief for late filing of post-distribution certifications in connection with a plan termination.

Section 4007.8 of the PBGC's premium payment regulation reflects the PBGC's Statement of Policy published December 2, 1996 (at 61 FR 63874), announcing a new policy regarding the rate at which premium penalties accrue (1 percent or 5 percent per month depending on whether the premium underpayment is self-corrected). Thus, once the amendments in this rule became effective, all of the PBGC's penalty policies under sections 4007 and 4071 would be in the Code of Federal Regulations. (This rule does not deal with penalties under ERISA section 4302, which applies only to multiemployer plans.)

This rule would not affect the use of any other remedies available to the PBGC and would not address the settlement of legal disputes involving penalties, either alone or in the context of other legal issues.

Compliance With Rulemaking Guidelines

The PBGC has determined that this action is not a "significant regulatory action" under the criteria set forth in Executive Order 12866.

Although the PBGC is publishing this rule as a proposed rule, the rule is not subject to notice and comment rulemaking requirements under section 553 of the Administrative Procedure Act because it deals only with general statements of PBGC policy and with PBGC procedural rules. Because no general notice of proposed rulemaking is required, the Regulatory Flexibility Act does not apply. See 5 U.S.C. 601(2), 603, 604.

List of Subjects

29 CFR Part 4003

Administrative practice and procedure, Organization and functions (Government agencies), Pension insurance, Pensions.

29 CFR Part 4007

Penalties, Pension insurance, Pensions, Reporting and recordkeeping requirements.

29 CFR Part 4071

Penalties.

For the reasons given above, the PBGC proposes to amend 29 CFR parts 4003, 4007, and 4071 as follows.

PART 4003—RULES FOR ADMINISTRATIVE REVIEW OF AGENCY DECISIONS

1. The authority citation for part 4003 continues to read as follows:

Authority: 29 U.S.C. 1302(b)(3).

2. In § 4003.1, paragraph (a) is amended by removing the words "(b)(1) through (b)(4)" and adding in their place the words "(b)(1) through (b)(5)" and by removing the words "(b)(5) through (b)(10)" and adding in their place the words "(b)(6) through (b)(11)"; paragraphs (b)(5) through (b)(10) are redesignated as paragraphs (b)(6) through (b)(11); and a new paragraph (b)(5) is added to read as follows:

§ 4003.1 Purpose and scope.

* * * * *

(b) Scope * * *

* * * * *

(5) Determinations with respect to penalties under section 4071 of ERISA.

* * * * *

PART 4007—PAYMENT OF PREMIUMS

3. The authority citation for part 4007 continues to read as follows:

Authority: 29 U.S.C. 1302(b)(3), 1303(a), 1306, 1307.

4. In § 4007.8, the introductory text of paragraph (a) is amended by removing the words "The charge will be based on" and adding in their place the words "The amount determined under this paragraph (a) will be based on"; and paragraphs (c) and (d) are revised to read as follows:

§ 4007.8 Late payment penalty charges.

* * * * *

(c) Reasonable cause waivers. The PBGC will waive all or part of a late payment penalty charge if the PBGC determines that there is reasonable cause for the late payment. Policy guidelines for applying the "reasonable cause" standard are in §§ 32 through 35 of the Appendix to this part.

(d) Other waivers. The PBGC may waive all or part of a late payment penalty charge in other circumstances without regard to whether there is reasonable cause. Policy guidelines for waivers without reasonable cause are in § 31(b)(1), (b)(3), and (b)(4) of the Appendix to this part.

* * * * *

5. An appendix is added to part 4007 to read as follows:

Appendix to Part 4007—Policy Guidelines on Penalties

Sec.

General Provisions

1 What is the purpose of this Appendix?

2 What defined terms are used in this Appendix?

3 What is the purpose of a premium penalty?

Procedures

11 What are the basic rules for assessing and reviewing premium penalties?

12 What should I know about preliminary notices of premium penalties?

13 What should I know about premium penalty determinations?

14 What should I know about review of premium penalty determinations?

Premium Penalty Assessment

21 What are the rules for assessing a premium penalty?

22 How do premium penalties apply to small plans?

Waiver Standards

31 What are the standards for waiving a premium penalty?

32 What is "reasonable cause"?

33 What kinds of facts does the PBGC consider in determining whether there is reasonable cause for a failure to pay a premium?

34 What are some situations that might justify a "reasonable cause" waiver?

35 What are some situations that might justify a partial "reasonable cause" waiver?

General Provisions

Section 1 What Is the Purpose of this Appendix?

This appendix sets forth principles and guidelines that we intend to follow in assessing, reviewing, and waiving premium penalties. However, this is only general policy guidance. Our action in each case is guided by the facts and circumstances of the case.

Section 2 What Defined Terms Are Used in This Appendix?

The following terms are defined in part 4001 of this chapter: contributing sponsor, ERISA, PBGC, person, plan, and plan administrator. In addition, in this appendix:

(a) Premium penalty means a penalty under ERISA section 4007 and § 4007.8 of this part for failing to pay all or part of a premium on time.

(b) Waiver means reduction or elimination of a premium penalty that is being or has been assessed.

(c) We means the PBGC.

(d) You means (according to the context)—

(1) A plan administrator, contributing sponsor, or other person, if—

(i) The person's action or inaction may be the basis for a premium penalty assessment,

(ii) The person may be required to pay the premium penalty, or

(iii) The person is requesting review of the premium penalty; or

(2) An employee or agent of, or advisor to, any of these persons.

Section 3 What Is the Purpose of a Premium Penalty?

The basic purpose of a premium penalty is to encourage you to pay premiums on time. Premium penalties should be fair, simple, effective, and easy to administer. Therefore,—

(a) We assess a lower (one percent) premium penalty if you correct a premium underpayment yourself before we issue a written notice that there is or may be a premium delinquency;

(b) We assess a higher (five percent) premium penalty if you do not self-correct before we issue a notice; and

(c) We waive premium penalties, in whole or in part, if there is reasonable cause or in other appropriate circumstances.

Procedures

Section 11 What Are the Basic Steps for Assessing and Reviewing Premium Penalties?

(a) *Overview.* There are typically three steps in the premium penalty assessment and review process:

(1) A preliminary notice (discussed in § 12), which gives you an opportunity to submit information relating to the premium penalty assessment, or to simply pay the amount owed;

(2) A premium penalty determination (discussed in § 13) that assesses the premium penalty; and

(3) A review of the premium penalty determination (discussed in § 14).

(b) *Relationship to premium procedures.* (1) When we assess a premium penalty for a late premium payment, the late payment often has already been made. However, if the premium has not been paid when we assess a premium penalty, we will generally assess and review the premium (and any related interest) at the same time as we assess and review the penalty. Differences in premium penalty procedures depending on whether the premium has or has not been paid are noted in §§ 12 and 13.

(2) A premium penalty stops accruing when the premium is paid.

(c) *Debt collection.* Our regulation on Debt Collection (29 CFR Part 4903) provides that we may collect amounts that you owe to us (such as

premium penalties) by reducing other amounts that the government owes to you (such as tax refunds). Procedures under our debt collection regulation may run separately or together with the premium penalty assessment and review procedures.

(d) *Decision-making standards and guidelines.* At each stage of the premium penalty assessment and review process, we evaluate the circumstances by the same standards and apply the same guidelines in deciding whether to assess or waive a premium penalty and how much the premium penalty should be. However, we may have more information when we review a premium penalty than we had when we originally assessed it, and that may make our decision on review different from our original premium penalty determination.

(e) *Providing information to the PBGC.* (1) It is your responsibility to raise any facts and issues that you want us to consider in making premium penalty assessment or waiver decisions and to support your contentions with documentation such as correspondence and police, fire, or insurance reports. If you want us to consider information that you believe we already have in connection with another case, you should identify the information specifically enough so that we can determine whether we have the information, locate it in our files, and review it.

(2) Since premium penalties are assessed for paying a premium late, it is important that you bring to our attention any information or arguments that tend to show that you were not required to pay a premium or that you paid the premium on time.

(f) *Terminology.* There is a slight difference between the terminology we use in this appendix and the terminology we use in our regulation on Rules for Administrative Review of Agency Decisions (29 CFR Part 4003), which governs our issuance and review of premium penalty determinations:

(1) "Initial determination" in the administrative review regulation means the same as "premium penalty determination" in this appendix, and

(2) "Reconsideration of an initial determination" in the administrative review regulation means the same as "review of a premium penalty determination" in this appendix.

Section 12 What Should I Know About Preliminary Notices of Premium Penalties?

Before we make a premium penalty determination, we want you to have an opportunity to give us any information you think we should consider. In most cases, therefore, we send a preliminary notice to tell you that we intend to assess a premium penalty and the reason for the premium penalty. (In some cases, we may skip this preliminary step— for example, if we contact you by telephone to discuss the matter or if we need to make the assessment quickly in order to preserve our right to collect the premium penalty in court.) You may respond to a preliminary notice by submitting any information you want us to consider before we make a premium penalty determination. The preliminary notice will state the time within which you should respond (typically 30 days).

(a) *If premium already paid.* If, by the time we issue a preliminary notice stating that we intend to assess a premium penalty, you have already paid the late premium, the notice ordinarily tells you the amount of the premium penalty that we intend to assess. (The notice also ordinarily tells you the amount of any interest due on the late premium.) If you pay the amount stated in the preliminary notice without requesting relief, that is the end of the matter.

(b) *If premium not already paid.* If, by the time we issue a preliminary notice stating that we intend to assess a premium penalty, you have not already paid the late premium, the notice ordinarily tells you the amount of premium due and the amount of the premium penalty that has accrued up through the date of the preliminary notice. (The preliminary notice also ordinarily tells you the amount of interest that has accrued on the late premium up through the date of the preliminary notice.) If you pay the amount stated in the preliminary notice within 30 days after the date of the preliminary notice without requesting relief, that is the end of the matter. If you do not pay the amount of unpaid premium within 30 days after the date of the preliminary notice, the premium penalty will continue to accrue (subject to the premium penalty cap).

Section 13 What Should I Know About Premium Penalty Determinations?

As the second step in the premium penalty assessment and review process—after a preliminary notice—we make a premium penalty determination (unless, in response to the preliminary notice, you pay the full premium penalty without requesting relief). (If we skip the preliminary notice step, the premium penalty assessment is the first step in the process.) The premium penalty determination notifies you of the reason for the premium penalty (even if we have already issued a preliminary notice stating the reason) and takes into account any information you may have submitted to us in response to a preliminary notice. We also tell you when and where to send your payment, and we tell you about requesting review of the premium penalty determination. (Complete rules for premium penalty determinations and for requesting review are in part 4003 of this chapter.)

(a) *If premium already paid.* If, by the time we issue a premium penalty determination, you have already paid the late premium, the determination tells you the amount of the premium penalty that we are assessing (taking into account any waiver of all or part of the premium penalty) and how we determined the amount of the premium penalty. (The premium penalty determination also ordinarily tells you the amount of any interest due on the late premium.) If you pay the amount stated in the premium penalty determination without requesting review, that is the end of the matter.

(b) *If premium not already paid.* If, by the time we issue a premium penalty determination, you have not already paid the late premium, the premium penalty determination tells you the amount of premium due and the amount of the premium penalty that has accrued up through the date of the premium penalty determination. (The premium penalty determination also ordinarily tells you the amount of interest that has accrued on the late premium up through the date of the premium penalty determination.) If you pay the amount stated in the premium penalty determination within 30 days after the date of the premium penalty determination without requesting review, that is the end of the matter. If you do not pay the amount of unpaid premium within 30 days after the date of the premium penalty determination, the premium penalty will continue to accrue (subject to the premium penalty cap).

Section 14 What Should I Know About Review of Premium Penalty Determinations?

(a) *Timing.* (1) *General rule.* In general, you must request review of a premium penalty determination within 30 days after the date of the determination; if you do not do so, the determination becomes effective, and we may take steps to collect the premium penalty. In addition, you may not be able to raise in court some legal defenses that you might have against collection of the premium penalty, because you have failed to exhaust administrative remedies. (In some cases, the 30-day limitation for requesting review may be extended or waived. See §§ 4003.4 and 4003.5 of the administrative review regulation. If we notify you that we may attempt to collect a debt resulting from a premium penalty determination by referring it for offset against federal payments that may be due you, you will have at least 60 days to request review. See § 4003.32 of the administrative review regulation.)

(2) *Determinations effective immediately.* We may, in our discretion, make a premium penalty determination effective on the date we issue it—for example, if our ability to bring a collection action in court is about to be cut off by the statute of limitations. If we make a premium penalty determination effective immediately, you are not required to request review by us in order to exhaust your administrative remedies. This means that you have the right to raise legal defenses against collection of the premium penalty in court even if you do not request that we review the determination. (See § 4003.22(b) of the administrative review regulation.) If you do request review by the PBGC, we may review the determination.

(b) *Review of determination.* If you request review of a premium penalty determination within the required time, we review the determination and notify you of the results of the review. This review takes into account any information you may have submitted to us in response to a preliminary notice or a premium penalty determination notice or with your request for review.

(c) *Premium penalty accrual during review.* Requesting review of a premium penalty does not make the premium penalty stop accruing. A premium penalty stops accruing on the date when you pay the premium or, if you pay the premium within 30 days after the date of a PBGC bill for the premium, on the date of the bill. In addition, if you request review of a premium penalty, we may waive the portion of the premium penalty that accrues during review if you make a non-frivolous argument that you were not required to pay the premium, as described in § 31(b)(4) of this Appendix.

Premium Penalty Assessment

Section 21 What Are the Rules for Assessing a Premium Penalty?

The rules for assessing a premium penalty are in § 4007.8 of this part. A premium penalty is assessed for failure to pay a premium on time. In general, the amount of a premium penalty is based on the number of

months from the due date to the date of payment, subject to a floor of $25 and a ceiling of 100 percent of the unpaid premium. The premium penalty rate is generally—

(a) 1 percent per month (for all months) on any amount of unpaid premium that you pay on or before the date we issue a written notice that there is or may be a premium delinquency (e.g., a premium bill, a letter initiating a premium compliance review, or a letter questioning a failure to make a premium filing), or

(b) 5 percent per month (for all months) on any amount of unpaid premium that you pay after that date.

Section 22 How Do Premium Penalties Apply to Small Plans?

Since small plan premiums are generally lower than large plan premiums, premium penalties are also generally lower for small plans than for large plans. This is because premium penalties accrue (each month) as a percentage of your premium underpayment.

Waiver Standards

Section 31 What Are the Standards for Waiving a Premium Penalty?

(a) *Facts and circumstances.* In deciding whether to waive a premium penalty in whole or in part, we consider the facts and circumstances of each case.

(b) *Waivers.* (1) *Provisions of law.* We waive all or part of a premium penalty if a statute or regulation requires that we do so. For example, ERISA section 4007(b) and § 4007.8(b) of this part provide for a waiver in certain circumstances involving business hardship; § 4007.8(f) and (g) of this part provides for waivers if certain "safe harbor" tests are met; and § 4007.8(e) of this part provides for a waiver of any premium penalty that accrues after the date of a premium bill if you pay the premium within 30 days after the date of the bill.

(2) *Reasonable cause.* We waive a premium penalty if you show reasonable cause for a failure to pay a premium on time. See §§ 32 through 35 for guidelines on "reasonable cause" waivers. If there is reasonable cause for only part of a failure to pay a premium, we waive the premium penalty only for that part. In determining whether "reasonable cause" exists, we do not consider either—

(i) The likelihood or cost of collecting the premium penalty, or

(ii) The costs and risks of enforcing the premium penalty by litigation.

(3) *Erroneous legal interpretations.* We may waive all or part of a premium penalty if the failure to pay a premium on time that gives rise to the premium penalty is based on your reliance on an erroneous interpretation of the law.

(i) *If you disclose the interpretation to us.* If a failure to pay a premium on time results from your reliance on an erroneous interpretation of the law, we will waive a premium penalty that arises from the failure if you promptly and adequately call our attention to the interpretation and the relevant facts, and the erroneous interpretation is not frivolous. If the interpretation affects a filing that you make with us, you should call our attention to the interpretation with the filing. If you rely on the interpretation to justify not making a filing with us, you should call our attention to the interpretation in a notice submitted to us by the time and in the manner prescribed for the filing not made.

(ii) *If you do not disclose the interpretation to us.* If a failure to pay a premium on time results from your reliance on an erroneous interpretation of the law, and you do not promptly and adequately call our attention to the interpretation and the relevant facts, we may nevertheless waive a premium penalty if the weight of authority supporting the interpretation is substantial in relation to the weight of opposing authority and it is reasonable for you to rely on the interpretation.

(4) *Pendency of review.* If you request review of a premium penalty (as described in § 14 of this Appendix), and you make a non-frivolous argument in your request for review that you were not required to pay the premium, we waive the portion of the premium penalty that accrues during the review process. (If you make a non-frivolous argument that you were not required to pay a portion of the premium, we apply this rule to that portion.)

(5) *Other circumstances.* We may waive all or part of a premium penalty in other circumstances if we determine that it is appropriate to do so. We intend to exercise this waiver authority only in narrow circumstances, primarily if we determine that assessing a premium penalty, or assessing the full amount of a premium penalty, would be inconsistent with the purposes of Title IV of ERISA. For example—

(i) We may waive all or part of a premium penalty if a premium underpayment reflected on a premium form is insignificant and is caused by an inadvertent mathematical error (such as a transposition of digits) on the form. In determining whether and to what extent to grant a waiver in a case of this kind, we consider such factors as how insignificant the underpayment is, whether you have a history of compliance, and whether the underpayment results from an isolated error rather than from a number of errors.

(ii) We may waive all or part of a premium penalty if the law changes shortly before the date a premium payment is due and the premium payment that you make by the due date would have been correct under the law as in effect before the change. In determining whether and to what extent to grant a waiver in a case of this kind, we consider such factors as the length of time between the change in the law and the premium due date, the nature and timing of any publicity given to the change in the law, the complexity of the legal issues, and your general familiarity with those issues.

(c) *Action or inaction of outside parties.* If an accountant, actuary, lawyer, pension consultant, or other individual or firm that is not part of your organization assists you in complying with PBGC requirements, we apply our waiver authority as if the outside individual or firm were part of your organization, as described in § 32(c) of this Appendix.

Section 32 What Is "Reasonable Cause"?

(a) *General rule.* In general, there is "reasonable cause" for a failure to pay a premium on time to the extent that—

(1) The failure arises from circumstances beyond your control, and

(2) You could not avoid the failure by the exercise of ordinary business care and prudence.

(b) *Overlooking legal requirements.* Overlooking legal requirements does not constitute reasonable cause.

(c) *Action or inaction of outside parties.* In some cases an accountant, actuary, lawyer, pension consultant, or other individual or firm that is not part of your organization may assist you in complying with PBGC requirements. If the outside individual's or firm's action, inaction, or advice causes or contributes to a failure to pay a premium on time, our analysis is generally the same as if the outside individual or firm were part of your organization. (In the case of an outside individual who is part of a firm, we generally consider both the individual and the firm to be part of your organization.) Thus, if a failure to pay a premium on time arises from circumstances within the control of the outside individual or firm, or could be avoided by the exercise of ordinary business care and prudence by the outside individual or firm, there is generally no reasonable cause for the failure. The fact that you exercised care and prudence in selecting and monitoring the outside individual or firm is not a basis for a reasonable cause waiver. (However, you may have recourse against the outside individual or firm.)

(d) *Size of organization.* If an organization or one or more of its employees is responsible for taking action, the size of the organization may affect what ordinary business care and prudence would require. For example, ordinary business care and prudence would typically require a larger organization to establish more comprehensive backup procedures than a smaller organization for dealing with situations such as computer failure, the loss of important records, and the inability of an individual to carry out assigned responsibilities. Thus, there may be reasonable cause for a small organization's failure to pay a premium on time even though, if the organization were larger, the exercise of ordinary business care and prudence would have avoided the failure.

(e) *Amount of premium underpayment.* In general, the larger a premium, the more care and prudence you should use to make sure that you pay it on time. Thus, there may be reasonable cause for a small underpayment even though, under the same circumstances, we would conclude that a larger underpayment could have been avoided by the exercise of ordinary business care and prudence.

Section 33 What Kinds of Facts Does the PBGC Consider in Determining Whether There is Reasonable Cause for a Failure to Pay a Premium?

In determining whether a failure to pay a premium on time arose from circumstances beyond your control and whether you could have avoided the failure by the exercise of ordinary business care and prudence—and thus whether waiver of a premium penalty for reasonable cause is appropriate—we consider facts such as the following:

(a) *What event or circumstance caused the underpayment and when the event happened or the circumstance arose.* The dates you give should clearly correspond with the underpayment upon which the premium penalty is based.

(b) *How that event or circumstance kept you from paying the premium on time.* The explanation you give should relate directly to the failure to pay a premium that is the subject of the premium penalty.

(c) *Whether the event or circumstance was beyond your control.*

(d) *Whether you could have anticipated the event or circumstance.*

(e) *How you responded to the event or circumstance, including what steps you took (and how quickly you took them) to pay the premium and how you conducted other business affairs.* Knowing how you responded to the event or circumstance may help us determine what degree of business care and prudence you were capable of exercising during that period and thus whether the failure to pay the premium could or could not have been avoided by the exercise of ordinary business care and prudence.

Section 34 What Are Some Situations That Might Justify a "Reasonable Cause" Waiver?

The following examples illustrate some of the reasons often given for failures to pay premiums for which we may assess penalties. The situation described in each example may constitute reasonable cause, and each example lists factors we consider in determining whether to grant a premium penalty waiver for reasonable cause in a case of that kind.

(a) An individual with responsibility for taking action was suddenly and unexpectedly absent or unable to act. We consider such factors as the following: the nature of the event that caused the individual's absence or inability to act (for example, the resignation of the individual or the death or serious illness of the individual or a member of the individual's immediate family); the size of the organization and what kind of backup procedures it had to cope with such events; how close the event was to the deadline that was missed; how abrupt and unanticipated the event was; how the individual's absence or inability to act prevented compliance; how expensive it would have been to comply without the absent individual; whether and how other business operations and obligations were affected; how quickly and prudently a replacement for the absent individual was selected or other arrangements for compliance were made; and how quickly a replacement for the absent individual took appropriate action.

(b) A fire or other casualty or natural disaster destroyed relevant records or prevented compliance in some other way. We consider such factors as the following: the nature of the event; how close the event was to the deadline that was missed; how the event caused the failure to pay the premium; whether other efforts were made to get needed information; how expensive it would have been to comply; and how you responded to the event.

(c) You reasonably relied on erroneous oral or written advice given by a PBGC employee. We consider such factors as the following: whether there was a clear relationship between your situation and the advice sought; whether you provided the PBGC employee with adequate and accurate information; and whether the surrounding circumstances should have led you to question the correctness of the advice or information provided.

(d) You were unable to obtain information (including records and calculations) needed to comply. We consider such factors as the following: what information was needed; why the information was unavailable; when and how you discovered that the information was not available; what attempts you made to get the information or reconstruct it through other means; and how much it would have cost to comply.

Section 35 What Are Some Situations That Might Justify a Partial "Reasonable Cause" Waiver?

(a) Assume that a fire destroyed the records needed to compute a premium payment. If in the exercise of ordinary business care and prudence it should take you one month to reconstruct the records and pay the premium, but the payment was made two months late, it might be appropriate to waive that part of the premium penalty attributable to the first month the payment was late, but not the part attributable to the second month.

(b) Assume that a plan administrator underpaid the plan's flat-rate premium because of reasonable reliance on erroneous advice from a PBGC employee, and also underpaid the plan's variable-rate premium because the plan actuary used the wrong interest rate. A PBGC audit revealed both errors. The PBGC billed the plan for a premium penalty of $5,000—$1,000 for underpayment of the flat-rate premium and $4,000 for underpayment of the variable-rate premium. The plan administrator requested a waiver of the premium penalty. While the erroneous PBGC advice constituted reasonable cause for underpaying the flat-rate premium, there was no showing of reasonable cause for the error in the variable-rate premium. Therefore, we would waive only the part of the premium penalty based on underpayment of the flat-rate portion of the premium ($1,000).

PART 4071—PENALTIES FOR FAILURE TO PROVIDE CERTAIN NOTICES OR OTHER MATERIAL INFORMATION

6. The authority citation for part 4071 is revised to read as follows:

Authority: 28 U.S.C. 2461 note; 29 U.S.C. 1302(b)(3), 1371.

7. Section 4071.1 is amended by adding at the end of the section the following sentence:

§ 4071.1 Purpose and scope.

* * * This part also provides policy guidelines for assessing and reviewing penalties under ERISA section 4071.

8. A new § 4071.4 and a new appendix are added to part 4071 to read as follows:

§ 4071.4 Assessment and review of penalties.

Policy guidelines for assessing, reviewing, and waiving penalties under ERISA section 4071 are in the Appendix to this part.

Appendix to Part 4071—Policy Guidelines on Penalties

Sec.

General Provisions

1 What is the purpose of this Appendix?

2 What defined terms are used in this Appendix?

3 What is the purpose of an information penalty?

Procedures

11 What are the basic rules for assessing and reviewing information penalties?

12 What should I know about preliminary notices of information penalties?

13 What should I know about information penalty determinations?

14 What should I know about review of information penalty determinations?

Information Penalty Assessment

21 Where can I find the general principles that the PBGC follows in assessing information penalties and how the PBGC applies those principles to specific cases?

22 What are the general principles that the PBGC follows in deciding whether to assess an information penalty and, if so, the amount or rate of information penalty to assess?

23 What aggravating factors does the PBGC consider?

24 What mitigating factors does the PBGC consider?

25 What if multiple persons must give a notice?

26 What if multiple persons must get a notice?

27 What if a single event or circumstance leads to multiple failures to provide section 4071 information?

28 What special guidance is there for specific types of cases?

Waiver Standards

31 What are the standards for waiving an information penalty?

32 What is "reasonable cause"?

33 What kinds of facts does the PBGC consider in determining whether there is reasonable cause for a failure to provide section 4071 information?

34 What are some situations that might justify a "reasonable cause" waiver?

35 What is a situation that might justify a partial "reasonable cause" waiver?

General Provisions

Section 1 What Is the Purpose of This Appendix?

Section 4071 of ERISA authorizes us to assess a penalty if you do not provide certain notices or other material information within the time limit specified in ERISA or in PBGC regulations. Some of the notices and other material information covered by section 4071 have to be provided to us, and some have to be provided to other parties, such as plan participants. This appendix sets forth principles and guidelines that we intend to follow in assessing, reviewing, and waiving information penalties. However, this is only general policy guidance. Our action in each case is guided by the facts and circumstances of the case.

Section 2 What Defined Terms Are Used in This Appendix?

The following terms are defined in part 4001 of this chapter: contributing sponsor, controlled group, employer, ERISA, PBGC, person, plan, plan administrator, and standard termination. In addition, in this appendix:

(a) *Information penalty* means a penalty under ERISA section 4071 for failing to provide section 4071 information on time.

(b) *Section 4071 information* means any notice or other material information that you are required to provide to us or to another party under subtitles A-D of title IV of ERISA, or under section 302(f)(4) or 307(e) of Title I of ERISA, or under PBGC regulations implementing any of these provisions. Whether a particular item of information is "material" depends on the facts and circumstances.

(c) *Waiver* means reduction or elimination of an information penalty that is being or has been assessed.

(d) *We* means the PBGC.

(e) *You* means (according to the context)—

(1) A plan administrator, contributing sponsor, or other person, if—

(i) The person's action or inaction may be the basis for an information penalty assessment,

(ii) The person may be required to pay the information penalty, or

(iii) The person is requesting review of the information penalty; or

(2) An employee or agent of, or advisor to, any of these persons.

Section 3 What Is the Purpose of an Information Penalty?

The basic purpose of an information penalty is to encourage you to provide section 4071 information on time. Information penalties should be fair, simple, effective, and easy to administer. Therefore—

(a) We assess lower information penalties for plans of small businesses and for failures to provide section 4071 information that are speedily corrected;

(b) We assess higher information penalties if the facts and circumstances warrant it; and

(c) We waive information penalties, in whole or in part, if there is reasonable cause or in other appropriate circumstances.

Procedures

Section 11 What Are the Basic Steps for Assessing and Reviewing Information Penalties?

(a) *Overview.* There are typically three steps in the information penalty assessment and review process:

(1) A preliminary notice (discussed in § 12), which gives you an opportunity to submit information bearing on the information penalty assessment;

(2) An information penalty determination (discussed in § 13) that assesses the information penalty; and

(3) A review of the information penalty determination (discussed in § 14).

(b) *Debt collection.* Our regulation on Debt Collection (29 CFR Part 4903) provides that we may collect amounts that you owe to us (such as information penalties) by reducing other amounts that the government owes to you (such as tax refunds). Procedures under our debt collection regulation may run separately or together with the information penalty assessment and review procedures.

(c) *Decision-making standards and guidelines.* At each stage of the information penalty assessment and review process, we evaluate the circumstances by the same standards and apply the same guidelines in deciding whether to assess or waive an information penalty and how much the information penalty should be. However, we may have more information when we review an information penalty than we had when we originally assessed it, and that may make our decision on review different from our original information penalty determination.

(d) *Providing information to the PBGC.* (1) It is your responsibility to raise any facts and issues that you want us to consider in making information penalty assessment or waiver decisions and to support your contentions with documentation such as correspondence and police, fire, or insurance reports. If you want us to consider information that you believe we already have in connection with another case, you should identify the information specifically enough so that we can determine whether we have the information, locate it in our files, and review it.

(2) Since information penalties are assessed for providing section 4071 information late, it is important that you bring to our attention any

information or arguments that tend to show that you were not required to provide the section 4071 information or that you provided the section 4071 information on time.

(e) *Terminology.* There is a slight difference between the terminology we use in this appendix and the terminology we use in our regulation on Rules for Administrative Review of Agency Decisions (29 CFR Part 4003), which governs our issuance and review of information penalty determinations:

(1) "Initial determination" in the administrative review regulation means the same as "information penalty determination" in this appendix, and

(2) "Reconsideration of an initial determination" in the administrative review regulation means the same as "review of an information penalty determination" in this appendix.

Section 12 What Should I Know About Preliminary Notices of Information Penalties?

Before we make an information penalty determination, we want you to have an opportunity to give us any information you think we should consider. In most cases, therefore, we send a preliminary notice to tell you that we intend to assess an information penalty and the reason for the information penalty. (In some cases, we may skip this preliminary step—for example, if we contact you by telephone to discuss the matter or if we need to make the assessment quickly in order to preserve our right to collect the information penalty in court.) You may respond to a preliminary notice by submitting any information you want us to consider before we make an information penalty determination. The preliminary notice will state the time within which you should respond (typically 30 days).

(a) If section 4071 information already provided. If, by the time we issue a preliminary notice stating that we intend to assess an information penalty, you have already provided the late section 4071 information, the notice ordinarily tells you the amount of the information penalty that we intend to assess. If the preliminary notice states an amount of information penalty and you pay the amount stated in the preliminary notice without requesting relief, that is the end of the matter.

(b) If section 4071 information not already provided. If, by the time we issue a preliminary notice stating that we intend to assess an information penalty, you have not already provided the late section 4071 information, the notice ordinarily tells you the rate of penalty that we intend to assess. Providing the section 4071 information will cut off further accrual of the information penalty.

Section 13 What Should I Know About Information Penalty Determinations?

As the second step in the information penalty assessment and review process—after a preliminary notice—we make an information penalty determination (unless, in response to a preliminary notice that states an amount of information penalty, you pay the full information penalty without requesting relief). (If we skip the preliminary notice step, the information penalty assessment is the first step in the process.) The information penalty determination notifies you of the reason for the information penalty (even if we have already issued a preliminary notice stating the reason) and takes into account any information you may have submitted to us in response to a preliminary notice. We also tell you when and where to send your payment, and we tell you about requesting review of the information penalty determination. (Complete rules for information penalty determinations and for requesting review are in part 4003 of this chapter.)

(a) If section 4071 information already provided. If, by the time we issue an information penalty determination, you have already provided the late section 4071 information, the determination tells you the amount of the information penalty that we are assessing (taking into account any waiver of all or part of the information penalty) and how we determined the amount of the information penalty. If the information penalty determination states an amount of information penalty and you pay the amount stated in the information penalty determination without requesting review, that is the end of the matter.

(b) If section 4071 information not already provided. If, by the time we issue an information penalty determination, you have not already provided the late section 4071 information, the determination ordinarily tells you the rate of penalty that we intend to assess. Providing the section 4071 information will cut off further accrual of the information penalty.

Section 14 What Should I Know About Review of Information Penalty Determinations?

(a) Timing. (1) General rule. In general, you must request review of an information penalty determination within 30 days after the date of

the determination; if you do not do so, the determination becomes effective, and we may take steps to collect the information penalty. In addition, you may not be able to raise in court some legal defenses that you might have against collection of the information penalty, because you have failed to exhaust administrative remedies. (In some cases, the 30-day limitation for requesting review may be extended or waived. See §§ 4003.4 and 4003.5 of the administrative review regulation. If we notify you that we may attempt to collect a debt resulting from an information penalty determination by referring it for offset against federal payments that may be due you, you will have at least 60 days to request review. See § 4003.32 of the administrative review regulation.)

(2) *Determinations effective immediately.* We may, in our discretion, make an information penalty determination effective on the date we issue it—for example, if our ability to bring a collection action in court is about to be cut off by the statute of limitations. If we make an information penalty determination effective immediately, you are not required to request review by us in order to exhaust your administrative remedies. This means that you have the right to raise legal defenses against collection of the information penalty in court even if you do not request that we review the determination. (See § 4003.22(b) of the administrative review regulation.) If you do request review by the PBGC, we may review the determination.

(b) *Review of determination.* If you request review of an information penalty determination within the required time, we review the determination and notify you of the results of the review. This review takes into account any information you may have submitted to us in response to a preliminary notice or an information penalty determination notice or with your request for review.

(c) *Information penalty accrual during review.* Requesting review of an information penalty does not make the information penalty stop accruing. An information penalty stops accruing when you provide the section 4071 information. In addition, if you request review of an information penalty, we may waive the portion of the information penalty that accrues during review if you make a non-frivolous argument that you were not required to provide the section 4071 information or that you were (and still are) unable to provide it, as described in Sec. 31(b)(4) of this Appendix.

Information Penalty Assessment

Section 21 Where Can I Find the General Principles That the PBGC Follows in Assessing Information Penalties and how the PBGC Applies Those Principles to Specific Cases?

The general principles that we follow in deciding whether to assess an information penalty and, if so, the amount or rate of information penalty to assess are explained in the following sections of this Appendix:

(1) Section 22 contains basic guidance.

(2) Sections 23 and 24 describe some aggravating and mitigating factors.

(3) Sections 25 through 27 describe how we generally treat situations involving multiple persons and multiple failures to provide section 4071 information.

(4) Section 28 contains special guidance for specific types of cases.

Section 22 What Are the General Principles That the PBGC Follows in Deciding Whether To Assess an Information Penalty and, if so, the Amount or Rate of Information Penalty to Assess?

(a) *Facts and circumstances.* In deciding whether to assess an information penalty for a failure to provide section 4071 information on time and, if so, what rate or amount of information penalty to assess, we consider the facts and circumstances of the failure.

(b) *Aggravating and mitigating factors.* Among the facts and circumstances we consider are aggravating and mitigating factors such as those described in §§ 23 and 24 of this Appendix. Aggravating factors tend to make it more likely that we will assess an information penalty, and mitigating factors tend to make it less likely. If we do assess an information penalty, aggravating factors tend to increase the rate or amount of the information penalty we assess, and mitigating factors tend to decrease the rate or amount. An aggravating or mitigating factor may apply to all or only some of the section 4071 information that is not provided and to all or only some days of a delinquency.

(c) *Effect of plan size.*

(1) *Likelihood of assessment.* In general, the likelihood that we will assess an information penalty is strongly influenced by the number of participants in your plan (as determined under paragraph (e)(2) of this section). Thus, for example, we are much less likely to assess an information penalty if your plan has fewer than 100 participants (espe-

cially for a first violation) than if your plan has more than 1,000 participants (whether or not it is a first violation). This reflects differences in the ordinary business care and prudence standard for large and small plans (see § 32(c)) and in their access to professional help in monitoring their activities and meeting PBGC requirements.

(2) *Amount or rate of information penalty.* The effect of plan size on the amount or rate of an information penalty is explained in paragraphs (e)(1)(ii) and (e)(1)(iii) of this section.

(d) *Waivers.* We may also reduce or eliminate an information penalty if we have information showing that a partial or complete waiver of the information penalty is appropriate. Waivers are explained in §§ 31 through 35 of this Appendix.

(e) *Basic amount or rate of information penalty.* If we assess an information penalty, the starting point for determining the rate or amount of the information penalty is the rate or amount determined under this section. The amount or rate may be higher or lower based on considerations such as those described in paragraphs (a) through (c) of this section and §§ 23 through 28 of this Appendix.

(1) *Basic guidelines.* Although ERISA section 4071 allows us to assess an information penalty up to $1,100 per day for each failure to provide section 4071 information, the information penalties we assess are generally much lower under the following guidelines.

(i) *Daily amount.* The information penalty is generally $25 a day for the first 90 days that the section 4071 information is late, and $50 for each day thereafter.

(ii) *Limit on total information penalty.* The total information penalty generally does not exceed $100 times the number of participants.

(iii) *Reduction for small plans.* If there are fewer than 100 participants in your plan, we generally reduce the daily information penalty based on the ratio of the number of participants to 100, subject to a floor of $5 a day.

(2) *How we count the number of participants.* For purposes of the per-participant cap and the small plan reduction described in paragraphs (e)(1)(ii) and (e)(1)(iii) of this section, we generally count participants in the following ways:

(i) *In plan terminations.* For a failure to provide section 4071 information under part 4041 of this chapter (dealing with standard and distress plan terminations), we generally use the number of persons entitled to distributions of benefits in the plan termination. For example, if you are a plan administrator, and you are late in certifying to us that all benefits were properly distributed in a plan termination, the information penalty generally should not exceed $100 times the number of persons entitled to distributions of benefits in the plan termination.

(ii) *In other cases.* For any other failure to provide section 4071 information, we generally use the number of participants reported on the PBGC Form 1 premium declaration that you most recently filed before the date of the failure, unless the number of participants has changed significantly since the Form 1 was filed. However, if clearly appropriate in a particular case, we may use a different method of determining the number of participants (e.g., adding up the number of participants in two or more plans).

(3) *Examples.* The following examples illustrate the basic guidelines for assessing information penalties under this section. In these examples, assume that you are the plan administrator of a terminating plan and that you file your post-distribution certification late.

(i) *General rule.* If your plan has 112 participants, and you file 306 days after the last day on which you could have made an information-penalty-free filing, the total information penalty should ordinarily be $11,200, as shown in the following table. (Note that in this example, the cap of $100 times the number of participants applies.)

	Daily rate	Total information penalty
Days 1-90	$25	$2,250 ($25 × 90 days).
Days 91-306	$50	$10,800 ($50 × 216 days).
Total for all days (uncapped)		$13,050 ($2,250 + $10,800).
Total capped information penalty.		$11,200 ($100 × 112 participants).

(ii) *Small plan rule.* If your plan has 15 participants, and you file 100 days after the last day on which you could have made an information-penalty-free filing, the total information penalty should ordinarily be $525, as shown in the following table. (Note that in this example, the total information penalty is less than the cap of $100 times the number of participants, i.e., $1,500 ($100 × 15).)

	Daily rate	Total information penalty
Days 1-90	$5 (minimum daily information penalty, since 15/100 × $25 = $3.75).	$450 ($5 × 90 days).
Days 91-100	$7.50 (15/100 × $50)	$75 ($7.50 × 10 days).
Total for all days		$525 ($450 + $75).

Section 23 What Aggravating Factors Does the PBGC Consider?

The aggravating factors that we consider are the following. (We do not consider the absence of mitigating factors to be an aggravating factor.)

(a) *Harmfulness.* Failure to provide section 4071 information on time where the failure is—or has the potential of being—particularly harmful to participants or the PBGC is an aggravating factor. (This may be true even though, by the time we receive the information, any possible harm has been avoided.) Harmfulness may depend on the importance, time-sensitivity, and quantity of section 4071 information you fail to provide on time and on the size of your plan.

(b) *Pattern or practice.* A pattern or practice of failure to provide section 4071 information is an aggravating factor.

(c) *Willfulness.* Willful failure to comply is an aggravating factor.

Section 24 What Mitigating Factors Does the PBGC Consider?

(a) The mitigating factors that we consider are the following (We do not consider the absence of aggravating factors to be a mitigating factor.):

(1) *First-time requirement.* It is a mitigating factor if your failure to provide section 4071 information is a violation of a requirement that applies to you for the first time.

(2) *Self-correction.* It is a mitigating factor if you—

(i) Correct your failure to provide section 4071 information promptly after you discover the failure, and

(ii) Notify us on your own initiative of your failure to provide the section 4071 information before we notify you that you have or may have failed to provide the section 4071 information.

(3) *Corrective action.* It is a mitigating factor if you cooperate with us by taking appropriate corrective action and establishing procedures designed to ensure future compliance.

(b) *Example.* A mid-size company with a pension plan covering 750 participants mistakenly made a quarterly contribution that was too low. The company did not immediately realize that the contribution was too low and did not make a reportable events report to the PBGC. As soon as the company discovered its error, it made a corrective contribution, telephoned the PBGC to alert us to the problem, and promptly filed the required reportable event notice. The company had never before failed to make all required contributions, and both the plan and the company were financially healthy. At the PBGC's request, the plan administrator put in place new procedures to avoid future reporting failures. Under the circumstances, the PBGC might assess no information penalty or might assess an information penalty of less than the amount that would be called for under § 22.

Section 25 What if Multiple Persons Must Give a Notice?

If each of two or more persons is responsible for providing substantially identical section 4071 information to us or to another person or persons, and the information is not provided as required, we may—

(a) Assess an information penalty against any one or more of the persons without regard to whether we assess an information penalty against any other of the persons; and

(b) Determine the amount of information penalty assessed against any person without regard to the amount assessed against any other person.

Section 26 What if Multiple Persons Must Get a Notice?

In general, if you have to give substantially identical notices to multiple persons, we generally assess only a single information penalty for failure to provide the notices as required, regardless of how many persons did not receive a notice as required. However:

(a) The number of persons you did not provide notice to as required may affect the amount of daily information penalty we assess. For example, if you are a plan administrator and you fail to give a Participant Notice under Part 4011 of this chapter as required, we generally assess only one information penalty. But if your plan is quite large, the information penalty we assess is likely to be greater than if the plan were small.

(b) If there are aggravating factors, we may, in addition to assessing a higher information penalty under § 22(b), assess a separate information penalty for each person to whom you failed to give a notice.

Section 27 What if a Single Event or Circumstance Leads to Multiple Failures to Provide Section 4071 Information?

If there are multiple failures to provide section 4071 information relating to a single event or circumstance, we generally assess a separate information penalty for each failure. For example, suppose you are a contributing sponsor of a plan and you fail to make several required contributions to the plan because of a single failure to determine that contributions are necessary for the year. The failure to notify us of each missed contribution is a separate failure for which we generally assess a separate information penalty.

Section 28 What Special Guidance is There for Specific Types of Cases?

The following is special guidance for applying the general assessment principles in specific types of cases:

(a) *Premium information requirements.* If you file a complete, correct premium form (Form 1, Schedule A, Form 1-ES) late, with the full premium payment, we do not assess an information penalty except in unusual cases. The premium penalty for late payment is usually an adequate penalty.

(b) *Plan termination information requirements.* If you fail to file or issue a notice required for a plan termination under Part 4041 of this chapter on time, and we issue a notice of noncompliance nullifying the termination, we do not also assess an information penalty for your failure to file or issue the required notice on time.

(c) *Reportable event post-event notice requirements.* If we assess an information penalty for a failure by a large plan or employer to file a notice of a reportable event under ERISA section 4043, other than an advance notice under ERISA section 4043(b) (which is discussed in paragraph (d) of this section), the amount or rate may be much higher than the basic amount or rate that would be determined under § 22(e) of this Appendix. Such failures usually are—or have the potential of being—particularly harmful to participants or the PBGC if they involve large plans or employers. For example, if you do not give us a required notice of a controlled group member's bankruptcy filing, the controlled group member's assets may be distributed to other creditors before we can file our claims for plan underfunding, and we may therefore be unable to recover on our claims or otherwise participate in the bankruptcy proceedings.

(d) *Reportable event advance notice requirements.* We virtually always assess an information penalty if you fail to file an advance notice of a reportable event under ERISA section 4043(b), and we generally assess the full $1,100-per-day information penalty. This information is generally so time-sensitive and significant that the maximum information penalty is warranted in virtually every case, without regard to whether there are aggravating circumstances in the particular case, because of the need for strong deterrence of violations of this kind.

(e) *Missed contribution notice requirements.* We virtually always assess an information penalty if you fail to file a missed contribution notice (Form 200) under ERISA section 302(f)(4), and we generally assess the full $1,100-per-day information penalty. This information is very time-sensitive because it is the basis for filing a lien under section 302(f) for the protection of the plan. Thus, the maximum information penalty is warranted in virtually every case, without regard to whether there are aggravating circumstances in the particular case, because of the need for strong deterrence of violations of this kind. The fact that the contribution is ultimately made does not undo the potential for harm that exists while the contribution is outstanding. However, we may reduce the information penalty rate for any period during which

the notice remains unfiled after the missed contribution is made—for example, from $1,100 per day to $100 per day.

(f) *Employer reporting requirements.* We virtually always assess an information penalty if you fail to file a financial and actuarial information report under ERISA section 4010, covering plans with very high underfunding, and we generally assess the full $1,100-per-day information penalty. Failures to file financial and actuarial information reports generally are—or have the potential of being—so harmful to participants or the PBGC that the maximum information penalty is warranted in virtually every case, without regard to whether there are aggravating circumstances in the particular case, because of the need for strong deterrence of violations of this kind.

Waiver Standards

Section 31 What are the Standards for Waiving an Information Penalty?

(a) *Facts and circumstances.* In deciding whether to waive an information penalty in whole or in part, we consider the facts and circumstances of each case.

(b) *Waivers.* (1) *Provisions of law.* We waive all or part of an information penalty if a statute or regulation requires that we do so. For example, § 4041.29(b) of this chapter provides that we do not assess an information penalty for a late post-distribution certification except to the extent that you file it more than 90 days after the distribution deadline under § 4041.28(a) of this chapter; and 4050.6(b)(2) of this chapter contains a similar provision for the late filing of information and certifications regarding missing participants in a terminating plan.

(2) *Reasonable cause.* We waive an information penalty if you show reasonable cause for a failure to provide section 4071 information on time. See §§ 32 through 35 for guidelines on "reasonable cause" waivers. If there is reasonable cause for only part of a failure to provide section 4071 information, we waive the information penalty only for that part. In determining whether "reasonable cause" exists, we do not consider either—

(i) The likelihood or cost of collecting the information penalty, or

(ii) The costs and risks of enforcing the information penalty by litigation.

(3) *Erroneous legal interpretations.* We may waive all or part of an information penalty if the failure to provide section 4071 information on time that gives rise to the information penalty is based on your reliance on an erroneous interpretation of the law.

(i) *If you disclose the interpretation to us.* If a failure to provide section 4071 information on time results from your reliance on an erroneous interpretation of the law, we will waive an information penalty that arises from the failure if you promptly and adequately call our attention to the interpretation and the relevant facts, and the erroneous interpretation is not frivolous. If the interpretation affects a filing that you make with us, you should call our attention to the interpretation with the filing. If you rely on the interpretation to justify not making a filing with us, you should call our attention to the interpretation in a notice submitted to us by the time and in the manner prescribed for the filing not made. If the interpretation affects information that you provide to persons other than us, you should call our attention to the interpretation when you provide the information by sending us a notice addressed to Technical Assistance Branch, Insurance Operations Department, PBGC, 1200 K Street, NW., Washington, DC 20005-4026. If you rely on the interpretation to justify not providing information to persons other than us, you should call our attention to the interpretation by sending a notice to the above address by the time prescribed for providing the information that is not provided.

(ii) *If you do not disclose the interpretation to us.* If a failure to provide section 4071 information on time results from your reliance on an erroneous interpretation of the law, and you do not promptly and adequately call our attention to the interpretation and the relevant facts, we may waive an information penalty that arises from the failure if the weight of authority supporting the interpretation is substantial in relation to the weight of opposing authority and it is reasonable for you to rely on the interpretation.

(4) *Pendency of review.* If you request review of an information penalty (as described in § 14 of this Appendix), and you make a non-frivolous argument that you were not required to provide the section 4071 information or that you were (and still are) unable to provide it, we waive the portion of the information penalty that accrues during the review process. (If you make a non-frivolous argument that you were not required (or were unable) to provide a portion of the section 4071 information, we apply this rule to that portion.) The waiver also applies to the post-review period (the period after we complete our review) if

you pay the information penalty within 30 days after the date of our decision and provide the section 4071 information by the time specified in the notice of our decision, which is normally also 30 days after the date of the decision, but may be less depending on the importance of the information. Otherwise, the waiver does not apply to the period from the date of our decision until you provide the section 4071 information.

(5) *Other circumstances.* We may waive all or part of an information penalty in other circumstances if we determine that it is appropriate to do so. We intend to exercise this waiver authority only in narrow circumstances, primarily if we determine that assessing an information penalty, or assessing the full amount of information penalty that might otherwise be appropriate under the guidelines in this appendix, would be inconsistent with the purposes of Title IV of ERISA. For example, we may waive all or part of an information penalty if the law changes shortly before the date when section 4071 information must be provided and the information you provide by that date would have been correct under the law as in effect before the change. In determining whether and to what extent to grant a waiver in a case of this kind, we consider such factors as the length of time between the change in the law and the date by which the section 4071 information must be provided, the nature and timing of any publicity given to the change in the law, the complexity of the legal issues, and your general familiarity with those issues.

(c) *Action or inaction of outside parties.* If an accountant, actuary, lawyer, pension consultant, or other individual or firm that is not part of your organization assists you in complying with PBGC requirements, we apply our waiver authority as if the outside individual or firm were part of your organization, as described in § 32(c) of this Appendix.

Section 32 What Is "Reasonable Cause"?

(a) *General rule.* In general, there is "reasonable cause" for a failure to provide section 4071 information on time to the extent that—

(1) The failure arises from circumstances beyond your control, and

(2) You could not avoid the failure by the exercise of ordinary business care and prudence.

(b) *Overlooking legal requirements.* Overlooking legal requirements does not constitute reasonable cause.

(c) *Action or inaction of outside parties.* In some cases an accountant, actuary, lawyer, pension consultant, or other individual or firm that is not part of your organization may assist you in complying with PBGC requirements. If the outside individual's or firm's action, inaction, or advice causes or contributes to a failure to provide section 4071 information on time, our analysis is generally the same as if the outside individual or firm were part of your organization. (In the case of an outside individual who is part of a firm, we generally consider both the individual and the firm to be part of your organization.) Thus, if a failure to provide section 4071 information on time arises from circumstances within the control of the outside individual or firm, or could be avoided by the exercise of ordinary business care and prudence by the outside individual or firm, there is generally no reasonable cause for the failure. The fact that you exercised care and prudence in selecting and monitoring the outside individual or firm is not a basis for a reasonable cause waiver. (However, you may have recourse against the outside individual or firm.)

(d) *Size of organization.* If an organization or one or more of its employees is responsible for taking action, the size of the organization may affect what ordinary business care and prudence would require. For example, ordinary business care and prudence would typically require a larger organization to establish more comprehensive backup procedures than a smaller organization for dealing with situations such as computer failure, the loss of important records, and the inability of an individual to carry out assigned responsibilities. Thus, there may be reasonable cause for a small organization's failure to provide section 4071 information on time even though, if the organization were larger, the exercise of ordinary business care and prudence would have avoided the failure.

(e) *Potential seriousness of failure to provide section 4071 information on time.* In general, the more potentially serious or harmful a failure to provide section 4071 information on time would be, the more care and prudence you should use to make sure that you provide it on time. Thus, there may be reasonable cause for a minor failure even though, under the same circumstances, we would conclude that a more serious failure could have been avoided by the exercise of ordinary business care and prudence.

Section 33 What Kinds of Facts Does the PBGC Consider in Determining Whether There is Reasonable Cause for a Failure to Provide Section 4071 Information?

In determining whether a failure to provide section 4071 information on time arose from circumstances beyond your control and whether you could have avoided the failure by the exercise of ordinary business care and prudence—and thus whether waiver of an information penalty for reasonable cause is appropriate—we consider facts such as the following:

(a) What event or circumstance caused the failure and when the event happened or the circumstance arose. The dates you give should clearly correspond with the failure upon which the information penalty is based.

(b) How that event or circumstance kept you from providing the section 4071 information on time. The explanation you give should relate directly to the failure to provide section 4071 information that is the subject of the information penalty.

(c) Whether the event or circumstance was beyond your control.

(d) Whether you could have anticipated the event or circumstance.

(e) How you responded to the event or circumstance, including what steps you took (and how quickly you took them) to provide the section 4071 information and how you conducted other business affairs. Knowing how you responded to the event or circumstance may help us determine what degree of business care and prudence you were capable of exercising during that period and thus whether the failure to provide section 4071 information could or could not have been avoided by the exercise of ordinary business care and prudence.

Section 34 What Are Some Situations That Might Justify a "Reasonable Cause" Waiver?

The following examples illustrate some of the reasons often given for failures to provide section 4071 information for which we may assess penalties. The situation described in each example may constitute reasonable cause, and each example lists factors we consider in determining whether we should grant an information penalty waiver for reasonable cause in a case of that kind.

(a) An individual with responsibility for taking action was suddenly and unexpectedly absent or unable to act. We consider such factors as the following: the nature of the event that caused the individual's absence or inability to act (for example, the resignation of the individual or the death or serious illness of the individual or a member of the individual's immediate family); the size of the organization and what kind of backup procedures it had to cope with such events; how close the event was to the deadline that was missed; how abrupt and unanticipated the event was; how the individual's absence or inability to act prevented compliance; how expensive it would have been to comply without the absent individual; whether and how other business operations and obligations were affected; how quickly and prudently a replacement for the absent individual was selected or other arrangements for compliance were made; and how quickly a replacement for the absent individual took appropriate action.

(b) A fire or other casualty or natural disaster destroyed relevant records or prevented compliance in some other way. We consider such factors as the following: the nature of the event; how close the event was to the deadline that was missed; how the event caused the failure to provide section 4071 information; whether other efforts were made to get needed information; how expensive it would have been to comply; and how you responded to the event.

(c) You reasonably relied on erroneous oral or written advice given by a PBGC employee. We consider such factors as the following: whether there was a clear relationship between your situation and the advice sought; whether you provided the PBGC employee with adequate and accurate information; and whether the surrounding circumstances should have led you to question the correctness of the advice or information provided.

(d) You were unable to obtain information (including records and calculations) needed to comply. We consider such factors as the following: what information was needed; why the information was unavailable; when and how you discovered that the information was not available; what attempts you made to get the information or reconstruct it through other means; and how much it would have cost to comply.

Section 35 What Is a Siuation That Might Justify a Partial "Reasonable Cause" Waiver?

Assume that a fire destroyed the records needed for a required filing of section 4071 information. If in the exercise of ordinary business care and prudence it should take you one month to reconstruct the records and prepare the filing, but the filing was made two months late, it might be appropriate to waive that part of the information penalty attributable to the first month the filing was late, but not the part attributable to the second month.

Issued in Washington, D.C., this 5th day of January, 2001.

David M. Strauss,

Executive Director, Pension Benefit Guaranty Corporation.

[FR Doc. 01-686 Filed 1-11-01; 8:45 am]

¶ 20,534J

PBGC proposed regulations: System of Records: Personnel Security Investigation Records: Contract employees: Privacy Act of 1974.—The PBGC has issued a proposed regulation which would amend its current regulations to protect the identity of sources of confidential background information on individuals who work for, or who are being considered for work for the PBGC as contractors or as employees of contractors.

The proposed regulation was published in the *Federal Register* on April 2, 2001 (66 FR 17518).

The preamble to the final regulations, which was published in the *Federal Register* on June 14, 2001 (66 FR 32221), can be found at ¶ 24,805U. The amended portion of the regulations appears at ¶ 15,721B.

¶ 20,534K

PBGC proposed regulations: Appeals board: Administrative review.—The PBGC has proposed to amend its regulation on Administrative Review of Agency Decisions to expedite the appeals process by authorizing a single member of the PBGC's Appeals Board to decide routine appeals. The PBGC would continue to use three-member panels for cases that involve a significant issue of law or a precedent-setting issue.

The proposed regulation was published in the *Federal Register* on March 27, 2002 (67 FR 14663).

The regulation was finalized on July 22, 2002 (67 FR 47694). The final regulation is at ¶ 15,334J. The preamble is at ¶ 24,221.

¶ 20,534L

PBGC proposed regulations: Electronic filing: Issuance rules: Computation-of-time rules: Electronic record retention rules.—The PBGC is attempting to provide filers with increased flexibility with regard to electronic filing as set forth in Title IV of ERISA by issuing proposed regulations designed to minimize existing electronic filing limitations. Filing addresses currently set forth in existing regulations would be put in PBGC form instructions and on the PBGC website at www.pbgc.gov. Additionally, the existing distribution and derivation tables in ERISA Part 4000 would also be moved to the PBGC website.

The proposed regulations, which were published in the *Federal Register* on February 14, 2003 (68 FR 7454), are reproduced below.

PENSION BENEFIT GUARANTY CORPORATION

29 CFR Parts 4000, 4003, 4007, 4010, 4011, 4022, 4041, 4041A, 4043, 4050, 4062, 4203, 4204, 4207, 4208, 4211, 4219, 4220, 4221, 4231, 4245, 4281, 4901, 4902, 4903 and 4907

RIN 1212-AA89

Rules on Filings, Issuances, Computation of Time, and Electronic Means of Record Retention

AGENCY: Pension Benefit Guaranty Corporation.

ACTION: Proposed rule.

SUMMARY: We propose, consistent with the Government Paperwork Elimination Act, to remove requirements from our regulations that might limit electronic filing with us or electronic issuances to others. The proposed rules will give us flexibility to keep pace with ever-changing technology. In addition, they simplify and consolidate our rules on what methods you may use to send us a filing or provide an issuance to someone other than us, on how to determine the date we treat you as having made your filing or provided your issuance, and on how to compute various periods of time (including those for filings with us and for issuances to third parties). Finally, they provide rules for maintaining records by electronic means.

DATES: Comments must be received by April 15, 2003.

ADDRESSES: Comments may be mailed to the Office of the General Counsel, Pension Benefit Guaranty Corporation, 1200 K Street, NW., Washington, DC 20005-4026, or delivered to Suite 340 at the above address. Comments also may be sent by Internet e-mail to reg.comments@pbgc.gov, or by fax to 202-326-4112. We will make all comments available on our Web site, http://www.pbgc.gov. Copies of comments also may be obtained by writing the PBGC's Communications and Public Affairs Department (CPAD) at Suite 240 at the above address or by visiting or calling CPAD during normal business hours (202-326-4040).

FOR FURTHER INFORMATION CONTACT: Harold J. Ashner, Assistant General Counsel, or Thomas H. Gabriel, Attorney, Office of the General Counsel, PBGC, 1200 K Street, NW., Washington, DC 20005-4026; 202-326-4024. (For TTY/TDD users, call the Federal relay service toll-free at 1-800-877-8339 and ask to be connected to 202-326-4024.)

SUPPLEMENTARY INFORMATION: These proposed rules are part of our ongoing implementation of the Government Paperwork Elimination Act (GPEA) and are consistent with the Office of Management and Budget directive to remove regulatory impediments to electronic trans-

actions. They address electronic means for filings with us, issuances to third parties, and recordkeeping. They build in the flexibility needed to allow us to continue to expand the availability of electronic options as technology advances. Under the proposal, much of the detailed information on permitted electronic means will be on our Web site, http://www.pbgc.gov, which will be updated from time to time.

The proposed rules make it easier for you to make a filing or provide an issuance on time by treating most types of submissions as filed or issued on the date sent (provided you meet certain requirements) rather than on the date received. In addition, under the proposal, the rules are easier to use—they are simpler, more uniform, and appear together in a single part of the regulations. The proposal makes similar simplifying changes to the rules for computing periods of time.

Under this proposal, our filing, issuance, computation-of-time, and electronic record-retention rules are consolidated in new subparts A through E of part 4000.

• New subpart A tells you what methods you may use for sending a filing to us. These new rules will apply to any filing with us under our regulations where the particular regulation calls for their application. For these purposes, we treat any payment to us under our regulations as a filing.

• New subpart B tells you what methods you may use to issue a notice or otherwise provide information to any person other than us. These new rules will apply to any issuance (except a payment) under our regulations where the particular regulation calls for their application.

• New subpart C tells you how we will determine the date you send us a filing and the date you provide an issuance to someone other than us (such as a participant). These new rules will apply to any filing or issuance under our regulations where the particular regulation calls for their application.

• New subpart D tells you how to compute time periods. These new rules will apply to any time period under our regulations (e.g., for filings with us and issuances to third parties) where the particular regulation calls for their application.

• New subpart E tells you how to comply with any recordkeeping requirement under our regulations using electronic means.

Existing Part 4000's distribution and derivation tables, which show the changes that occurred as a result of the PBGC's July 1, 1996, reorganization and renumbering of its regulations (61 FR 32574), will be moved to the PBGC's Web site at http://www.pbgc.gov, and combined with similar tables showing the changes that occurred as a result

¶20,534L

of the PBGC's June 29, 1981, reorganization and renumbering of its regulations (46 FR 32574). A note at the beginning of the PBGC's regulations will refer users to the PBGC's Web site for the tables.

Method of Filing

We are trying to provide as much flexibility as possible in filing methods. The proposed rules allow you to file any submission with us by hand, mail, or commercial delivery service, and refer you to our Web site, http://www.pbgc.gov, for current information on electronic filing, including permitted methods, fax numbers, and e-mail addresses. The instruction booklets and forms used for certain filings with us also will describe electronic and other filing methods, as appropriate, and will be available on our Web site.

Where To File

Under the proposed rule, we are removing the filing addresses from our regulations and putting them on our Web site, http://www.pbgc.gov, and in the instructions to our forms; addresses will also be available through our Customer Service Center, 1-800-400-7242 (for participants), or 1-800-736-2444 (for practitioners). (TTY/TDD users may call the Federal relay service toll-free at 1-800-877-8339 and ask to be connected to the appropriate number.) Because we have different addresses for different types of filings, you should make sure to use the appropriate address for your type of filing. For example, some filings (such as premium payments) must be sent to a bank, while other filings (such as the Standard Termination Notice (Form 500)) must be sent to the appropriate department at our offices in Washington, DC.

Method of Issuance

The proposed rules on methods of issuance permit you to use any method of issuance, provided you use measures reasonably calculated to ensure actual receipt of the material by the intended recipient. Posting is not a permissible method of issuance under the rules of this part. (However, for certain issuances, posting is specifically permitted by the regulation governing the particular issuance.)

The proposed rules include a safe-harbor method for providing an issuance by electronic media. The proposed safe-harbor method generally tracks the Department of Labor's final rules (67 FR 17264 (April 9, 2002)) concerning disclosure of certain employee benefit plan information through electronic media, as set out at 29 CFR 2520.104b-1. Our safe-harbor method would be available to any person using electronic media to satisfy issuance obligations under our regulations.

These proposed rules on methods of issuance do not address compliance with the Electronic Signatures in Global and National Commerce Act, Pub. L. 106-229, 114 Stat. 464 (2000) (codified at 15 U.S.C. 7001-7006) ("E-SIGN").

Date of Filing or Issuance

The proposed rules tell you how we will determine the date you filed your submission with us and the date you provided your issuance to someone other than us (such as a participant). In some cases, other PBGC rules relating to issuances to third parties refer to when an issuance is received. (For instance, when there is a request for abatement (regulation § 4207.3), interest is credited to the employer if the plan sponsor does not issue a revised payment schedule reflecting the credit or make the required refund within 60 days after receipt by the plan sponsor of a complete abatement application action.) These proposed rules would not affect those other receipt rules for issuances to third parties. Similarly, these proposed rules would not affect any receipt rule for filings with the PBGC, except to the extent these rules describe how to determine when a document is received (for instance, filings received by the PBGC after 5 p.m. are treated as received on the next business day).

Date of Filing in General

Under the proposed rule, we will treat most types of submissions as filed on the date you send the submission to us if you comply with certain requirements. The requirements vary depending on the method of filing you use. We may ask you for evidence of when you sent a submission to us.

There are a few types of submissions to us that we always treat as filed when received (not when sent), no matter what method you use: (1) Applications for benefits and related submissions (unless the instructions for the applicable forms provide for an earlier date), (2) advance notices of reportable event (under subpart C of section 4043), (3) notices of missed contributions exceeding $1 million (under subpart D of section 4043), and (4) requests for approval of a multiemployer plan amendment. The "filed-when-received" rule is necessary for these submissions because we may need to act quickly to provide benefit payments, to protect participants or premium payers, or to act within a statutory time frame.

In these cases, as well as cases where you do not meet the requirements for your filing date to be the date you send your submission, your filing date is the date we receive your submission. However, if we receive your submission after 5 p.m. (our time) on a business day, or anytime on a weekend or Federal holiday, we will treat it as received on the next business day.

Date of Issuance in General

Under the proposed rule, we will treat most types of issuances to third parties as provided on the date you send the issuance if you comply with certain requirements. The requirements vary depending on the method of issuance you use. The proposed rules for determining the date of an issuance generally track the proposed rules for determining the date of a filing; however, there are some differences for issuances using electronic means. An electronic issuance meeting the proposed safe harbor will have the benefit of the "send-date" rule. An electronic issuance that meets the general standard for issuances (i.e., using measures reasonably calculated to ensure actual receipt), but not the safe harbor, will be deemed issued on the date received by the intended recipient.

Filing and Issuance by U.S. Postal Service

If you send your submission to us, or provide an issuance to someone else, by First-Class Mail (or another at least equivalent class), and you properly mail it by the last scheduled collection of the day, your filing or issuance date is the date you mail it. If you properly mail it later than the last scheduled collection or on a day when there is no scheduled collection, your filing or issuance date is the date of the next scheduled collection.

If your submission or issuance has a legible U.S. Postal Service postmark, we will presume your filing or issuance date is the date of the postmark. However, you may prove an earlier date. The same rules apply if your submission or issuance has a legible postmark made by a private postage meter (but no legible U.S. Postal Service postmark) and arrives at the proper address by the time reasonably expected.

Filing and Issuance Using the Postal Service of a Foreign Country

If you send your submission to us, or provide an issuance to someone else, using the postal service of a foreign country, your filing or issuance date is the date of receipt at the proper address.

Filing and Issuance by Commercial Delivery Service

If you send your submission to us, or provide an issuance to someone else, by a commercial delivery service that meets certain requirements (described below) and you properly deposit your submission or issuance by the last scheduled collection of the day, your filing or issuance date is the date you deposit your submission or issuance; if you properly deposit it later than the last scheduled collection or on a day when there is no scheduled collection, your filing or issuance date is the date of the next scheduled collection.

To benefit from this "send-date" rule, you must use: (1) A "designated delivery service" under Internal Revenue Code §7502(f) (our Web site, http://www.pbgc.gov, will list the designated delivery services), or (2) a service for which it is reasonable to expect that your submission or issuance will arrive at the proper address by 5 p.m. on the second business day after the date of collection.

Filing and Issuance by Hand Delivery

If you hand deliver your submission or issuance, your filing or issuance date is the date of receipt at the proper address. A hand-delivered issuance need not be delivered while the intended recipient is physically present. For example, unless you have reason to believe that the intended recipient will not receive the notice within a reasonable amount of time, a notice is deemed to be received when you place it in the intended recipient's office mailbox.

Filing and Issuance by Electronic Delivery

You may submit most types of filings to PBGC electronically. If you do, the filing date for your submission is the date you transmit it to us at the proper address, provided (1) you comply with the technical requirements for that type of submission (our Web site, http://www.pbgc.gov, tells you when electronic filing is permitted and, if so, identifies the technical requirements for each type of submission), and (2) when sending an e-mail with an attachment, you include, in the body of the e-mail, the name and telephone number of the person for us to contact if we are unable to read the attachment.

Under certain circumstances, you may provide issuances electronically. An electronic issuance meeting the proposed safe harbor will have the benefit of a "send-date" rule. An electronic issuance that meets the general standard for issuances (i.e., using measures reasonably calculated to ensure actual receipt), but not the safe harbor for electronic filings, will be deemed issued on the date received by the intended recipient. For any issuance in the form of an e-mail, you must include, in the body of the e-mail, the name and telephone number of the person to contact if the recipient is unable to read the attachment.

Filing and Issuance by Submission of Computer Disk

For most types of filings with PBGC, you may send us your submission on a computer disk (e.g., a CD-ROM or floppy diskette). Similarly, you may be able to provide certain issuances on computer disk. For filings, you must comply with the technical requirements for that type of submission. For issuances, you must meet certain safe-harbor requirements. For both filings and issuances, you must include, in a paper cover letter or on the disk's label, the name and telephone number of the person to contact if we or the intended recipient is unable to read the disk. The rules for determining the filing or issuance date of your submission of a computer disk will apply as if you sent us a paper version of your submission.

Requirement To Resend

If you have reason to believe that we or the intended recipient has not received your electronic or paper filing or issuance (or has received it in a form that is not useable), you must promptly resend it. If you do so, we will treat it as filed or issued on the original filing or issuance date. If you are not prompt, your filing or issuance date will be the filing or issuance date of the resubmission or reissuance.

De Minimis Issuance Errors

We will not treat your issuance as untimely based on your failure to provide it to a participant or beneficiary in a timely manner if the failure resulted from administrative error and involved only a de minimis percentage of intended recipients, provided that you resend the issuance to the intended recipient promptly after discovering the error. (Under our existing regulations, this rule applies only to standard and distress termination issuances; the proposed rule applies it to all our issuances under our regulations.)

Computation of Time

The proposed computation-of-time rules tell you how to compute time periods under our regulations (e.g., for filings with us and issuances to third parties) where the particular regulation calls for their application. (Some of our regulations will contain specific exceptions or modifications to these proposed rules.)

When computing a time period (whether counting forwards or backwards) under these rules, exclude the day of the act, event, or default that begins the period; include the last day of the period; and if the last day is a weekend or Federal holiday, extend or shorten the period (whichever benefits you in complying with the time requirement) to the next regular business day. The weekend and holiday rule also applies to deadlines for which counting is not required, such as "the last day" of a plan year.

For example, suppose that you miss a required minimum funding contribution of $2 million that has a November 13, 2003, due date. Under our regulations, you are required to file a notice of a missed contribution (Form 200) no later than 10 days after the due date for the missed contribution. To determine your deadline, count November 14 as day 1, November 15 as day 2, November 16 as day 3, and so on. Therefore, November 23 is day 10. Since November 23, 2003, is a Sunday, you will have until Monday, November 24, 2003, to file the notice.

As another example, suppose you are required to file an advance notice of reportable event for a transaction that is effective December 16, 2003. Under our regulations, the notice is due at least 30 days before the effective date of the event. To determine your deadline, count December 15 as day 1, December 14 as day 2, December 13 as day 3, and so on. Therefore, November 16 is day 30. Since November 16, 2003, is a Sunday, you will have until Monday, November 17, 2003, to file the notice.

If a time period is measured in months, you would first identify the day of the calendar month on which you start counting (i.e., the date of the act, event, or default that triggers the period). Then you would look to the corresponding day of the calendar month in which you stop counting. For example, a one-month period measured from January 15 ends (if counting forward) on February 15 or (if counting backward) on December 15. In this example, as in most cases where you are counting months, the day of the calendar month in which the period starts (the 15th) corresponds to the same numbered day of the calendar month in which the period ends. There are two special rules that apply where you start counting on a day that is at or near the end of a calendar month:

- If you start counting on the last day of a calendar month, the corresponding day of any later (or earlier) calendar month is the last day of that calendar month. For example, for a three-month period measured from November 30, the corresponding day (if counting forward) is the last day of February (the 28th or 29th) or (if counting backward) the last day of August (the 31st).

- If you start counting on the 29th or 30th of a calendar month, the corresponding day of February is the last day of February. For example, for a one-month period measured from January 29, the corresponding day is the last day of February (the 28th or 29th).

Electronic Means of Record Retention

The proposed rule provides guidance on record maintenance and retention using electronic means. The proposed rule generally tracks the Department of Labor's final rules (67 FR 17264 (April 9, 2002)) for retaining records by electronic means, set out at 29 CFR 2520.107-1.

You remain responsible for following our electronic recordkeeping rules, even if you rely on others for help. For example, if a service provider to a plan administrator creates, maintains, retains, prepares, or keeps physical custody of the plan's records, the plan administrator must ensure that the service provider complies with these rules.

The proposed recordkeeping requirements are consistent with the goals of E-SIGN and are designed to facilitate voluntary use of electronic records while ensuring continued accuracy, integrity and accessibility of records required to be kept under our regulations. The requirements are justified by the importance of the records involved, are substantially equivalent to the requirements imposed on records that are not electronic records, will not impose unreasonable costs on the acceptance and use of electronic records, and do not require, or accord greater legal status or effect to, the implementation or application of a specific technology or technical specification for performing the functions of creating, storing, generating, receiving, communicating, or authenticating electronic records.

Paperwork Reduction Act

Under the Paperwork Reduction Act (PRA), 44 U.S.C. 3501-3520, an agency may not conduct or sponsor, and a person is not required to respond to, a collection of information unless it displays a currently valid Office of Management and Budget (OMB) control number. The information collection requirements related to the regulations that would be affected by this proposed action were previously approved by OMB. We are requesting OMB's approval of the proposed changes in our filing, issuance, computation-of-time, and recordkeeping rules.

The proposed rules will promote the use of appropriate automated, electronic, or other technological collection techniques or other forms of information technology in connection with the approved information collections. Although the proposed rules are expected to make the information collections more convenient to the public by allowing use of electronic means, expanding the choice of filing, issuance, and recordkeeping methods, and giving the benefit of a "when-sent" filing or issuance date for most types of submissions, we do not expect the changes to materially affect burden and are therefore not revising the annual burden estimates currently approved by OMB for each of our regulations.

We invite comment from the public on any issues arising under the Paperwork Reduction Act relating to this proposed rule. We specifically seek public comments to:

- Evaluate whether the proposed collection of information is necessary for the proper performance of the functions of the agency, including whether the information will have practical utility;

- Evaluate the accuracy of the estimate of the burden of the proposed collection of information, including the validity of the methodology and assumptions used;

- Enhance the quality, utility, and clarity of the information to be collected; and

- Minimize the burden of the collection of information on those who are to respond, including through the use of appropriate automated, electronic, mechanical, or other technological collection techniques or other forms of information technology, e.g., permitting electronic submission of responses.

Compliance With Rulemaking Guidelines

The PBGC has determined, in consultation with the Office of Management and Budget, that this proposed rule is not a "significant regulatory action" under Executive Order 12866.

We certify under section 605(b) of the Regulatory Flexibility Act that the proposed rule will not have a significant economic impact on a substantial number of small entities. The proposed rule does not affect the underlying requirements (e.g., to file a submission with us, provide an issuance to a third party, or retain records) to which the proposed rules would apply. Nor does the final rule require any plan or other entity to make use of electronic media for either disclosure or record-keeping purposes or to change the method it currently uses. Entities may avoid both any marginal cost and any beneficial impacts by simply retaining their existing paper-based or electronic methods of compliance with disclosure requirements or existing paper-based methods of compliance with recordkeeping requirements. (For those entities that already use electronic media for recordkeeping purposes, any expense associated with conforming their procedures to the minimum standards in this proposal would be marginal.) We do not expect the economic impact (if any) associated with the proposed changes to be significant for entities of any size, and therefore certify that the proposed rule would not have a significant economic impact on a substantial number of small entities. Accordingly, sections 603 and 604 of the Regulatory Flexibility Act do not apply.

List of Subjects

29 CFR Part 4000

Pension insurance, Pensions, Reporting and recordkeeping requirements.

29 CFR Part 4003

Administrative practice and procedure, Pension insurance.

29 CFR Part 4007

Employee benefit plans, Penalties, Pension insurance, Reporting and recordkeeping requirements.

29 CFR Part 4010

Employee benefit plans; Penalties; Pension insurance; Reporting and recordkeeping requirements.

29 CFR Part 4011

Employee benefit plans, Pension insurance, Reporting and record-keeping requirements.

29 CFR Part 4022

Employee benefit plans, Pension insurance, Reporting and record-keeping requirements.

29 CFR Part 4041

Employee benefit plans, Pension insurance, Reporting and record-keeping requirements.

29 CFR Part 4041A

Employee benefit plans, Pension insurance, Reporting and record-keeping requirements.

29 CFR Part 4043

Employee benefit plans, Pension insurance, Reporting and record-keeping requirements.

29 CFR Part 4050

Employee benefit plans, Pension insurance, Reporting and record-keeping requirements.

29 CFR Part 4062

Employee benefit plans, Pension insurance, Reporting and record-keeping requirements.

29 CFR Part 4203

Employee benefit plans, Pension insurance, Reporting and record-keeping requirements.

29 CFR Part 4204

Employee benefit plans, Pension insurance, Reporting and record-keeping requirements.

29 CFR Part 4207

Employee benefit plans, Pension insurance.

29 CFR Part 4208

Employee benefit plans, Pension insurance, Reporting and record-keeping requirements.

29 CFR Part 4211

Employee benefit plans, Pension insurance, Reporting and record-keeping requirements.

29 CFR Part 4219

Employee benefit plans, Pension insurance, Reporting and record-keeping requirements.

29 CFR Part 4220

Employee benefit plans, Pension insurance, Reporting and record-keeping requirements.

29 CFR Part 4221

Employee benefit plans, Pension insurance.

29 CFR Part 4231

Employee benefit plans, Pension insurance, Reporting and record-keeping requirements.

29 CFR Part 4245

Employee benefit plans, Pension insurance, Reporting and record-keeping requirements.

29 CFR Part 4281

Employee benefit plans, Pension insurance, Reporting and record-keeping requirements.

29 CFR Part 4901

Freedom of information.

29 CFR Part 4902

Privacy.

29 CFR Part 4903

Claims, Government employees, Income taxes.

29 CFR Part 4907

Administrative practice and procedure, Civil rights, Equal employment opportunity, Federal buildings and facilities, Individuals with disabilities.

For the reasons set forth above, the PBGC proposes to amend 29 CFR parts 4000, 4003, 4007, 4010, 4011, 4022, 4041, 4041A, 4043, 4050, 4062, 4203, 4204, 4207, 4208, 4211, 4219, 4220, 4221, 4231, 4245, 4281, 4901, 4902, 4903 and 4907 of 29 CFR chapter XL as follows:

1. Add the following note above the heading for Subchapter A of Chapter XL:

Note: PBGC's regulations were substantially reorganized and renumbered effective June 29, 1981 (at 46 FR 32574) and July 1, 1996 (at 61 FR 34002). Distribution and derivation tables showing the changes that occurred as a result of these amendments are available on the PBGC's Web site at http://www.pbgc.gov.

2. Revise part 4000 to read as follows:

PART 4000—FILING, ISSUANCE, COMPUTATION OF TIME, AND RECORD RETENTION

Subpart A—Filing Rules §

4000.1 What are these filing rules about?

4000.2 What definitions do I need to know for these rules?

4000.3 What methods of filing may I use?

4000.4 Where do I file my submission?

4000.5 Does the PBGC have discretion to waive these filing requirements?

Subpart B—Issuance Rules

4000.11 What are these issuance rules about?

4000.12 What definitions do I need to know for these rules?

4000.13 What methods of issuance may I use?

4000.14 What is the safe-harbor method for providing an issuance by electronic media?

4000.15 Does the PBGC have discretion to waive these issuance requirements?

Subpart C—Determining Filing and Issuance Dates

4000.21 What are these rules for determining the date of a filing or issuance about?

4000.22 What definitions do I need to know for these rules?

4000.23 When is my submission or issuance treated as filed or issued?

4000.24 What if I mail my submission or issuance using the U.S. Postal Service?

4000.25 What if I use the postal service of a foreign country?

4000.26 What if I use a commercial delivery service?

4000.27 What if I hand deliver my submission or issuance?

4000.28 What if I send a computer disk?

4000.29 What if I use electronic delivery?

4000.30 What if I need to resend my filing or issuance for technical reasons?

4000.31 Is my issuance untimely if I miss a few participants or beneficiaries?

4000.32 Does the PBGC have discretion to waive any requirements under this part?

Subpart D—Computation of Time

4000.41 What are these computation-of-time rules about?

4000.42 What definitions do I need to know for these rules?

4000.43 How do I compute a time period?

Subpart E—Electronic Means of Record Retention

4000.51 What are these record retention rules about?

4000.52 What definitions do I need to know for these rules?

4000.53 May I use electronic media to satisfy PBGC's record retention requirements?

4000.54 May I dispose of original paper records if I keep electronic copies?

Authority: 29 U.S.C. 1082(f), 1302(b)(3).

Subpart A—Filing Rules

§ 4000.1 What are these filing rules about?

Where a particular regulation calls for their application, the rules in this subpart A of part 4000 tell you what filing methods you may use for any submission (including a payment) to us. They do not cover an issuance from you to anyone other than the PBGC, such as a notice to participants. Also, they do not cover filings with us that are not made under our regulations, such as procurement filings, litigation filings, and applications for employment with us. (Subpart B tells you what methods you may use to issue a notice or otherwise provide information to any person other than us. Subpart C tells you how we determine your filing or issuance date. Subpart D tells you how to compute various periods of time. Subpart E tells you how to maintain required records in electronic form.)

§ 4000.2 What definitions do I need to know for these rules?

You need to know two definitions from § 4001.2 of this chapter: *PBGC* and *person*. You also need to know the following definitions:

Filing means any notice, information, or payment that you submit to us under our regulations.

Issuance means any notice or other information you provide to any person other than us under our regulations.

We means the PBGC.

You means the person filing with us.

§ 4000.3 What methods of filing may I use?

(a) *Paper filings.* You may file any submission with us by hand, mail, or commercial delivery service.

(b) *Electronic filings.* Current information on electronic filings, including permitted methods, fax numbers, and e-mail addresses, is—

(1) On our Web site, http://www.pbgc.gov;

(2) In our various printed forms and instructions packages; and

(3) Available by contacting our Customer Service Center at 1200 K Street, NW, Washington, DC, 20005-4026; telephone 1-800-400-7242 (for participants), or 1-800-736-2444 (for practitioners). (TTY/TDD users may call the Federal relay service toll-free at 1-800-877-8339 and ask to be connected to the appropriate number.)

§ 4000.4 Where do I file my submission?

To find out where to send your submission, visit our Web site at http://www.pbgc.gov, see the instructions to our forms, or call our Customer Service Center (1-800-400-7242 for participants, or 1-800-736-2444 for practitioners; TTY/TDD users may call the Federal relay service toll-free at 1-800-877-8339 and ask to be connected to the appropriate number.) Because we have different addresses for different types of filings, you should make sure to use the appropriate address for your type of filing. For example, some filings (such as premium payments) must be sent to a specified bank, while other filings (such as the Standard Termination Notice (Form 500)) must be sent to the appropriate department at our offices in Washington, DC.

§ 4000.5 Does the PBGC have discretion to waive these filing requirements?

We retain the discretion to waive any requirement under this part, at any time, if warranted by the facts and circumstances.

Subpart B—Issuance Rules

§ 4000.11 What are these issuance rules about?

Where a particular regulation calls for their application, the rules in this subpart B of part 4000 tell you what methods you may use to issue a notice or otherwise provide information to any person other than us (e.g., a participant or beneficiary). They do not cover payments to third parties. In some cases, the PBGC regulations tell you to comply with requirements that are found somewhere other than in the PBGC's own regulations (e.g., requirements under the Internal Revenue Code (Title 26 of the United States Code)). If so, you must comply with any applicable issuance rules under those other requirements. (Subpart A tells you what filing methods you may use for filings with us. Subpart C tells you how we determine your filing or issuance date. Subpart D tells you how to compute various periods of time. Subpart E tells you how to maintain required records in electronic form.)

§ 4000.12 What definitions do I need to know for these rules?

You need to know two definitions from § 4001.2 of this chapter: *PBGC* and *person*. You also need to know the following definitions:

Filing means any notice, information, or payment that you submit to us under our regulations.

Issuance means any notice or other information you provide to any person other than us under our regulations.

We means the PBGC.

You means the person providing the issuance to a third party.

§ 4000.13 What methods of issuance may I use?

(a) *In general.* You may use any method of issuance, provided you use measures reasonably calculated to ensure actual receipt of the material by the intended recipient. Posting is not a permissible method of issuance under the rules of this part.

(b) *Electronic safe-harbor method.* Section 4000.14 provides a safe-harbor method for meeting the requirements of paragraph (a) of this section when providing an issuance using electronic media.

§ 4000.14 What is the safe harbor method for providing an issuance by electronic media?

(a) *In general.* Except as otherwise provided by applicable law, rule or regulation, you satisfy the requirements of § 4000.13 if you follow the methods described at paragraph (b) of this section when providing an issuance by electronic media to any person described in paragraph (c) or (d) of this section.

(b) *Issuance requirements.* (1) You must take appropriate and necessary measures reasonably calculated to ensure that the system for furnishing documents—

(i) Results in actual receipt of transmitted information (e.g., using return-receipt or notice of undelivered electronic mail features, conducting periodic reviews or surveys to confirm receipt of the transmitted information); and

(ii) Protects confidential information relating to the intended recipient (e.g., incorporating into the system measures designed to preclude unauthorized receipt of or access to such information by anyone other than the intended recipient);

(2) You prepare and furnish electronically delivered documents in a manner that is consistent with the style, format and content requirements applicable to the particular document;

(3) You provide each intended recipient with a notice, in electronic or non-electronic form, at the time a document is furnished electronically, that apprises the intended recipient of—

(i) The significance of the document when it is not otherwise reasonably evident as transmitted (e.g., "The attached participant notice contains information on the funding level of your defined benefit pension plan and the benefits guaranteed by the Pension Benefit Guaranty Corporation."); and

(ii) The intended recipient's right to request and obtain a paper version of such document; and

(4) You give the intended recipient, upon request, a paper version of the electronically furnished documents.

(c) *Employees with electronic access.* This section applies to a participant who—

(1) Has the ability to effectively access the document furnished in electronic form at any location where the participant is reasonably expected to perform duties as an employee; and

(2) With respect to whom access to the employer's electronic information system is an integral part of those duties.

(d) *Any person.* This section applies to any person who—

(1) Except as provided in paragraph (d)(2) of this section, has affirmatively consented, in electronic or non-electronic form, to receiving documents through electronic media and has not withdrawn such consent;

(2) In the case of documents to be furnished through the Internet or other electronic communication network, has affirmatively consented or confirmed consent electronically, in a manner that reasonably demonstrates the person's ability to access information in the electronic form that will be used to provide the information that is the subject of the consent, and has provided an address for the receipt of electronically furnished documents;

(3) Prior to consenting, is provided, in electronic or non-electronic form, a clear and conspicuous statement indicating:

(i) The types of documents to which the consent would apply;

(ii) That consent can be withdrawn at any time without charge;

(iii) The procedures for withdrawing consent and for updating the participant's, beneficiary's or other person's address for receipt of electronically furnished documents or other information;

(iv) The right to request and obtain a paper version of an electronically furnished document, including whether the paper version will be provided free of charge;

(v) Any hardware and software requirements for accessing and retaining the documents; and

(4) Following consent, if a change in hardware or software requirements needed to access or retain electronic documents creates a material risk that the person will be unable to access or retain electronically furnished documents,

(i) Is provided with a statement of the revised hardware or software requirements for access to and retention of electronically furnished documents;

(ii) Is given the right to withdraw consent without charge and without the imposition of any condition or consequence that was not disclosed at the time of the initial consent; and

(iii) Again consents, in accordance with the requirements of paragraph (d)(1) or paragraph (d)(2) of this section, as applicable, to the receipt of documents through electronic media.

§ 4000.15 Does the PBGC have discretion to waive these issuance requirements?

We retain the discretion to waive any requirement under this part, at any time, if warranted by the facts and circumstances.

Subpart C—Determining Filing and Issuance Dates

§ 4000.21 What are these rules for determining the filing or issuance date about?

Where the particular regulation calls for their application, the rules in this subpart C of part 4000 tell you how we will determine the date you send us a filing and the date you provide an issuance to someone other than us (such as a participant). These rules do not cover payments to third parties. In addition, they do not cover filings with us that are not made under our regulations, such as procurement filings, litigation filings, and applications for employment with us. In some cases, the PBGC regulations tell you to comply with requirements that are found somewhere other than in the PBGC's own regulations (e.g., requirements under the Internal Revenue Code (Title 26 of the United States Code)). In meeting those requirements, you should follow any applicable rules under those requirements for determining the filing and issuance date. (Subpart A tells you what filing methods you may use for filings with us. Subpart B tells you what methods you may use to issue a notice or otherwise provide information to any person other than us. Subpart D tells you how to compute various periods of time. Subpart E tells you how to maintain required records in electronic form.)

§ 4000.22 What definitions do I need to know for these rules?

You need to know two definitions from § 4001.2 of this chapter: *PBGC* and *person.* You also need to know the following definitions:

Business day means a day other than a Saturday, Sunday, or Federal holiday.

We means the PBGC.

You means the person filing with us or the person providing the issuance to a third party.

§ 4000.23 When is my submission or issuance treated as filed or issued?

(a) *Filed or issued when sent.* Generally, we treat your submission as filed, or your issuance as provided, on the date you send it, if you meet certain requirements. The requirements depend upon the method you use to send your submission or issuance (see §§ 4000.24 through 4000.29). (Certain filings are always treated as filed when received, as explained in paragraph (b)(2) of this section.)

(b) *Filed or issued when received.* (1) *In general.* If you do not meet the requirements for your submission or issuance to be treated as filed or issued when sent (see §§ 4000.24 through 4000.32), we treat it as filed or issued on the date received in a permitted format at the proper address.

(2) *Certain filings always treated as filed when received.* We treat the following submissions as filed on the date we receive your submission, no matter what method you use:

(i) *Applications for benefits.* An application for benefits or related submission (unless the instructions for the applicable forms provide for an earlier date);

(ii) *Advance notices of reportable events.* Information required under subpart C of part 4043 of this chapter, dealing with advance notice of reportable events;

(iii) *Form 200 filings.* Information required under subpart D of part 4043 of this chapter, dealing with notice of certain missed minimum funding contributions; and

(iv) *Requests for approval of multiemployer plan amendments.* A request for approval of an amendment filed with the PBGC pursuant to part 4220 of this chapter.

(3) *Determining our receipt date for your filing.* If we receive your submission at the correct address by 5 p.m. (our time) on a business day, we treat it as received on that date. If we receive your submission at the correct address after 5 p.m. on a business day, or anytime on a weekend or Federal holiday, we treat it as received on the next business day. For example, if you send your fax or e-mail of a Form 200 filing to us in Washington, DC, on Friday, March 15, from California at 3 p.m. (Pacific standard time), and we receive it immediately at 6 p.m. (our time), we treat it as received on Monday, March 18.

§ 4000.24 What if I mail my submission or issuance using the U.S. Postal Service?

(a) *In general.* Your filing or issuance date is the date you mail your submission or issuance using the U.S. Postal Service if you meet the requirements of paragraph (b) of this section, and you mail it by the last scheduled collection of the day. If you mail it later than that, or if there is no scheduled collection that day, your filing or issuance date is the date of the next scheduled collection. If you do not meet the requirements of paragraph (b), your filing or issuance date is the date of receipt at the proper address.

(b) *Requirements for "send date."* Your submission or issuance must meet the applicable postal requirements, be properly addressed, and you must use First-Class Mail (or a U.S. Postal Service mail class that is at least the equivalent of First-Class Mail, such as Priority Mail or Express Mail). However, if you are filing an advance notice of reportable event or a Form 200 (notice of certain missed contributions), see § 4000.23(b); these filings are always treated as filed when received.

(c) *Presumptions.* We make the following presumptions—

(1) *U.S. Postal Service postmark.* If you meet the requirements of paragraph (b) of this section and your submission or issuance has a legible U.S. Postal Service postmark, we presume that the postmark date is the filing or issuance date. However, you may prove an earlier date under paragraph (a) of this section.

(2) *Private meter postmark.* If you meet the requirements of paragraph (b) of this section and your submission or issuance has a legible postmark made by a private postage meter (but no legible U.S. Postal Service postmark) and arrives at the proper address by the time reasonably expected, we presume that the metered postmark date is your filing or issuance date. However, you may prove an earlier date under paragraph (a) of this section.

(d) *Examples.* (1) You mail your issuance using the U.S. Postal Service and meet the requirements of paragraph (b) of this section. You deposit your issuance in a mailbox at 4 p.m. on Friday, March 15 and the next scheduled collection at that mailbox is 5 p.m. that day. Your issuance date is March 15. If on the other hand you deposit it at 6 p.m. and the next collection at that mailbox is not until Monday, March 18, your issuance date is March 18.

(2) You mail your submission using the U.S. Postal Service and meet the requirements of paragraph (b) of this section. You deposit your submission in the mailbox at 4 p.m. on Friday, March 15, and the next scheduled collection at that mailbox is 5 p.m. that day. If your submission does not show a March 15 postmark, then you may prove to us that you mailed your submission by the last scheduled collection on March 15.

§ 4000.25 What if I use the postal service of a foreign country?

If you send your submission or issuance using the postal service of a foreign country, your filing or issuance date is the date of receipt at the proper address.

§ 4000.26 What if I use a commercial delivery service?

(a) *In general.* Your filing or issuance date is the date you deposit your submission or issuance with the commercial delivery service if you meet the requirements of paragraph (b) of this section, and you deposit it by the last scheduled collection of the day for the type of delivery you use (such as two-day delivery or overnight delivery). If you deposit it later than that, or if there is no scheduled collection that day, your filing or issuance date is the date of the next scheduled collection. If you do not meet the requirements of paragraph (b), your filing or issuance date is the date of receipt at the proper address. However, if you are filing an advance notice of reportable event or a Form 200 (notice of certain missed contributions), see § 4000.23(b); these filings are always treated as filed when received.

(b) *Requirements for "send date."* Your submission or issuance must meet the applicable requirements of the commercial delivery service, be properly addressed, and—

(1) *Delivery within two days.* It must be reasonable to expect your submission or issuance will arrive at the proper address by 5 p.m. on the second business day after the next scheduled collection; or

(2) *Designated delivery service.* You must use a "designated delivery service" under section 7502(f) of the Internal Revenue Code (Title 26 of the United States Code). Our Web site, http://www.pbgc.gov, lists those designated delivery services. You should make sure that both the provider and the particular type of delivery (such as two-day delivery) are designated.

(c) *Example.* You send your submission by commercial delivery service using two-day delivery. In addition, you meet the requirements of paragraph (b). Suppose the deadline for two-day delivery at the place you make your deposit is 8 p.m. on Friday, March 15. If you deposit your submission by the deadline, your filing date is March 15. If, instead, you deposit it after the 8 p.m. deadline and the next collection at that site for two-day delivery is on Monday, March 18, your filing date is March 18.

§ 4000.27 What if I hand deliver my submission or issuance?

Your filing or issuance date is the date of receipt of your hand-delivered submission or issuance at the proper address. A hand-delivered issuance need not be delivered while the intended recipient is physically present. For example, unless you have reason to believe that the intended recipient will not receive the notice within a reasonable amount of time, a notice is deemed to be received when you place it in the intended recipient's office mailbox. Our Web site, http://www.pbgc.gov, and the instructions to our forms, identify the proper addresses for filings with us.

§ 4000.28 What if I send a computer disk?

(a) *In general.* We determine your filing or issuance date for a computer disk as if you had sent a paper version of your submission or issuances if you meet the requirements of paragraph (b) of this section.

(1) *Filings.* For computer-disk filings, we may treat your submission as invalid if you fail to meet the requirements of paragraph (b)(1) or (b)(3) of this section.

(2) *Issuances.* For computer-disk issuances, we may treat your issuance as invalid if—

(i) You fail to meet the requirements ("using measures reasonably calculated to ensure actual receipt") of § 4000.13(a), or

(ii) You fail to meet the contact information requirements of paragraph (b)(3) of this section.

(b) *Requirements.* To get the filing date under paragraph (a) of this section, you must meet the requirements of paragraphs (b)(1) and (b)(3) To get the issuance date under paragraph (a), you must meet the requirements of paragraphs (b)(2) and (b)(3).

(1) *Technical requirements for filings.* For filings, your electronic disk must comply with any technical requirements for that type of submission (our Web site, http://www.pbgc.gov, identifies the technical requirements for each type of filing).

(2) *Technical requirements for issuances.* For issuances, you must meet the safe-harbor requirements of § 4000.14.

(3) *Identify contact person.* For filings and issuances, you must include, in a paper cover letter or on the disk's label, the name and telephone number of the person to contact if we or the intended recipient is unable to read the disk.

§ 4000.29 What if I use electronic delivery?

(a) *In general.* Your filing or issuance date is the date you electronically transmit your submission or issuance to the proper address if you meet the requirements of paragraph (b) of this section. Note that we always treat an advance notice of reportable event and a Form 200 (notice of certain missed contributions) as filed when received.

(1) *Filings.* For electronic filings, if you fail to meet the requirements of paragraph (b)(1) or (b)(3) of this section, we may treat your submission as invalid.

(2) *Issuances.* For electronic issuances, we may treat your issuance as invalid if—

(i) You fail to meet the requirements ("using measures reasonably calculated to ensure actual receipt") of § 4000.13(a), or

(ii) You fail to meet the contact information requirements of paragraph (b)(3) of this section.

(b) *Requirements.* To get the filing date under paragraph (a), you must meet the requirements of paragraphs (b)(1) and (b)(3). To get the issuance date under paragraph (a), you must meet the requirement of paragraphs (b)(2) and (b)(3).

(1) *Technical requirements for filings.* For filings, your electronic submission must comply with any technical requirements for that type of submission (our Web site, http://www.pbgc.gov, identifies the technical requirements for each type of filing).

(2) *Technical requirements for issuances.* For issuances, you must meet the safe-harbor requirements of § 4000.14.

(3) *Identify contact person.* For an e-mail submission or issuance with an attachment, you must include, in the body of your e-mail, the name and telephone number of the person to contact if we or the intended recipient needs you to resubmit your filing or issuance.

(c) *Failure to meet address requirement.* If you send your electronic submission or issuance to the wrong address (but you meet the requirements of paragraph (b) of this section), your filing or issuance date is the date of receipt at the proper address.

§ 4000.30 What if I need to resend my filing or issuance for technical reasons?

(a) *Request to resubmit.* (1) *Filing.* We may ask you to resubmit all or a portion of your filing for technical reasons (for example, because we are unable to open an attachment to your e-mail). In that case, your submission (or portion) is invalid. However, if you comply with the request or otherwise resolve the problem (e.g., by providing advice that allows us to open the attachment to your e-mail) by the date we specify, your filing date for the submission (or portion) that we asked you to resubmit is the date you filed your original submission. If you comply with our request late, your submission (or portion) will be treated as filed on the date of your resubmission.

(2) *Issuance.* The intended recipient may, for good reason (of a technical nature), ask you to resend all or a portion of your issuance (for example, because of a technical problem in opening an attachment to your e-mail). In that case, your issuance (or portion) is invalid. However, if you comply with the request or otherwise resolve the problem (e.g., by providing advice that the recipient uses to open the attachment to your e-mail), within a reasonable time, your issuance date for the issuance (or portion) that the intended recipient asked you to resend is the date you provided your original issuance. If you comply with the request late, your issuance (or portion) will be treated as provided on the date of your reissuance.

(b) *Reason to believe submission or issuance not received or defective.* If you have reason to believe that we have not received your submission (or have received it in a form that is not useable), or that the intended recipient has not received your issuance (or has received it in a form that is not useable), you must promptly resend your submission or issuance to get your original filing or issuance date. However, we may require evidence to support your original filing or issuance date. If you are not prompt, or you do not provide us with any evidence we may require to support your original filing or issuance date, your filing or issuance date is the filing or issuance date of your resubmission or reissuance.

§ 4000.31 Is my issuance untimely if I miss a few participants or beneficiaries?

The PBGC will not treat your issuance as untimely based on your failure to provide the issuance to a participant or beneficiary in a timely manner if—

(a) The failure resulted from administrative error;

(b) The failure involved only a de minimis percentage of intended recipients; and

(c) You resend the issuance to the intended recipient promptly after discovering the error.

§ 4000.32 Does the PBGC have discretion to waive any requirements under this part?

We retain the discretion to waive any requirement under this part, at any time, if warranted by the facts and circumstances.

Subpart D—Computation of Time

§ 4000.41 What are these computation-of-time rules about?

The rules in this subpart D of part 4000 tell you how to compute time periods under our regulations (e.g., for filings with us and issuances to third parties) where the particular regulation calls for their application. (There are specific exceptions or modifications to these rules in § 4007.6 of this chapter (premium payments), § 4050.6(d)(3) of this chapter (payment of designated benefits for missing participants), and § 4062.10 of this chapter (employer liability payments). In some cases, the PBGC regulations tell you to comply with requirements that are found somewhere other than in the PBGC's own regulations (e.g., requirements under the Internal Revenue Code (Title 26 of the United States Code)). In meeting those requirements, you should follow any applicable computation-of-time rules under those other requirements. (Subpart A tells you what filing methods you may use for filings with us. Subpart B tells you what methods you may use to issue a notice or otherwise provide information to any person other than us. Subpart C tells you how we determine your filing or issuance date. Subpart E tells you how to maintain required records in electronic form.)

§ 4000.42 What definitions do I need to know for these rules?

You need to know two definitions from § 4001.2 of this chapter: *PBGC* and *person*. You also need to know the following definitions:

Business da y means a day other than a Saturday, Sunday, or Federal holiday.

We means the PBGC.

You means the person responsible, under our regulations, for the filing or issuance to which these rules apply.

§ 4000.43 How do I compute a time period?

(a) *In general.* If you are computing a time period to which this part applies, whether you are counting forwards or backwards, the day after (or before) the act, event, or default that begins the period is day one, the next day is day two, and so on. Count all days, including weekends and Federal holidays. However, if the last day you count is a weekend or Federal holiday, extend or shorten the period (whichever benefits you in complying with the time requirement) to the next regular business day. The examples in paragraph (d) of this section illustrate these rules.

(b) *When date is designated.* In some cases, our regulations designate a specific day as the end of a time period, such as "the last day" of a plan year or "the fifteenth day" of a calendar month. In these cases, you simply use the designated day, together with the weekend and holiday rule of paragraph (a) of this section.

(c) *When counting months.* If a time period is measured in months, first identify the date (day, month, and year) of the act, event, or default that begins the period. The corresponding day of the following (or preceding) month is one month later (or earlier), and so on. For example, two months after July 15 is September 15. If the period ends on a weekend or Federal holiday, follow the weekend and holiday rule of paragraph (a) of this section. There are two special rules for determining what the corresponding day is when you start counting on a day that is at or near the end of a calendar month:

(1) *Special "last-day" rule.* If you start counting on the last day of a calendar month, the corresponding day of any calendar month is the last day of that calendar month. For example, a three-month period measured from November 30 ends (if counting forward) on the last day of February (the 28th or 29th) or (if counting backward) on the last day of August (the 31st).

(2) *Special February rule.* If you start counting on the 29th or 30th of a calendar month, the corresponding day of February is the last day of February. For example, a one-month period measured from January 29 ends on the last day of February (the 28th or 29th).

(d) *Examples.* (1) *Counting backwards.* Suppose you are required to file an advance notice of reportable event for a transaction that is effective December 31. Under our regulations, the notice is due at least 30 days before the effective date of the event. To determine your deadline, count December 30 as day 1, December 29 as day 2, December 28 as day 3, and so on. Therefore, December 1 is day 30. Assuming that day is not a weekend or holiday, your notice is timely if you file it on or before December 1.

(2) *Weekend or holiday rule.* Suppose you are filing a notice of intent to terminate. The notice must be issued at least 60 days and no more than 90 days before the proposed termination date. Suppose the 60th day before the proposed termination date is a Saturday. Your notice is timely if you issue it on the following Monday even though that is only 58 days before the proposed termination date. Similarly, if the 90th day before the proposed termination date is Wednesday, July 4 (a Federal holiday), your notice is timely if you issue it on Tuesday, July 3, even though that is 91 days before the proposed termination date.

(3) *Counting months.* Suppose you are required to issue a Participant Notice two months after December 31. The deadline for the Participant Notice is the last day of February (the 28th or 29th). If the last day of February is a weekend or Federal holiday, your deadline is extended until the next day that is not a weekend or Federal holiday.

Subpart E—Electronic Means of Record Retention

§ 4000.51 What are these record retention rules about?

The rules in this subpart E of part 4000 tell you what methods you may use to meet any record retention requirement under our regulations if you choose to use electronic means. The rules for who must retain the records, how long the records must be maintained, and how records must be made available to us are contained in the specific part where the record retention requirement is found. (Subpart A tells you what filing methods you may use for filings with us and how we determine your filing date. Subpart B tells you what methods you may use to issue a notice or otherwise provide information to any person other than us. Subpart C tells you how we determine your filing or issuance date. Subpart D tells you how to compute various periods of time.)

§ 4000.52 What definitions do I need to know for these rules?

You need to know two definitions from § 4001.2 of this chapter: *PBGC* and *person*. You also need to know the following definitions:

We means the PBGC.

You means the person subject to the record retention requirement.

§ 4000.53 May I use electronic media to satisfy PBGC's record retention requirements?

General requirements. You may use electronic media to satisfy the record maintenance and retention requirements of this chapter if:

(a) The electronic recordkeeping system has reasonable controls to ensure the integrity, accuracy, authenticity and reliability of the records kept in electronic form;

(b) The electronic records are maintained in reasonable order and in a safe and accessible place, and in such manner as they may be readily inspected or examined (for example, the recordkeeping system should be capable of indexing, retaining, preserving, retrieving and reproducing the electronic records);

(c) The electronic records are readily convertible into legible and readable paper copy as may be needed to satisfy reporting and disclosure requirements or any other obligation under section 302(f)(4), section 307(e), or Title IV of ERISA;

(d) The electronic recordkeeping system is not subject, in whole or in part, to any agreement or restriction that would, directly or indirectly, compromise or limit a person's ability to comply with any reporting and disclosure requirement or any other obligation under section 302(f)(4), section 307(e), or Title IV of ERISA;

(e) Adequate records management practices are established and implemented (for example, following procedures for labeling of electronically maintained or retained records, providing a secure storage environment, creating back-up electronic copies and selecting an off-site storage location, observing a quality assurance program evidenced by regular evaluations of the electronic recordkeeping system including periodic checks of electronically maintained or retained records; and retaining paper copies of records that cannot be clearly, accurately or completely transferred to an electronic recordkeeping system); and

(f) All electronic records exhibit a high degree of legibility and readability when displayed on a video display terminal or other method of electronic transmission and when reproduced in paper form. The term "legibility" means the observer must be able to identify all letters and numerals positively and quickly to the exclusion of all other letters or numerals. The term "readability" means that the observer must be able to recognize a group of letters or numerals as words or complete numbers.

§ 4000.54 May I dispose of original paper records if I keep electronic copies?

You may dispose of original paper records any time after they are transferred to an electronic recordkeeping system that complies with the requirements of this subpart, except such original records may not be discarded if the electronic record would not constitute a duplicate or substitute record under the terms of the plan and applicable federal or state law.

PART 4003—RULES FOR ADMINISTRATIVE REVIEW OF AGENCY DECISIONS

3. The authority citation for part 4003 continues to read as follows:

Authority: 29 U.S.C. 1302(b)(3).

4. Revise § 4003.9 to read as follows:

§ 4003.9 Method and date of filing.

(a) *Method of filing.* The PBGC applies the rules in subpart A of part 4000 of this chapter to determine permissible methods of filing with the PBGC under this part.

(b) *Date of filing.* The PBGC applies the rules in subpart C of part 4000 of this chapter to determine the date that a submission under this part was filed with the PBGC.

5. Revise § 4003.10 to read as follows:

§ 4003.10 Computation of time.

The PBGC applies the rules in subpart D of part 4000 of this chapter to compute any time period under this part.

§ 4003.33 [Amended]

6. Amend § 4003.33 to add the sentence "See § 4000.4 of this chapter for information on where to file." to the end of the paragraph.

§ 4003.53 [Amended]

7. Amend § 4003.53 to add the sentence "See § 4000.4 of this chapter for information on where to file." to the end of the paragraph.

PART 4007—PAYMENT OF PREMIUMS

8. The authority citation for part 4007 continues to read as follows:

Authority: 29 U.S.C. 1302(b)(3), 1303(a), 1306, 1307.

9. Revise § 4007.3 to read as follows:

§ 4007.3 Filing requirements; method of filing.

(a) *Filing requirements.* The estimation, declaration, reconciliation and payment of premiums shall be made using the forms prescribed by and in accordance with the instructions in the PBGC annual Premium Payment Package. The plan administrator of each covered plan must file the prescribed form or forms, and any premium payments due, no later than the applicable due date specified in § 4007.11.

(b) *Method of filing.* The PBGC applies the rules in subpart A of part 4000 of this chapter to determine permissible methods of filing with the PBGC under this part.

10. Revise § 4007.5 to read as follows:

§ 4007.5 Date of filing.

The PBGC applies the rules in subpart C of part 4000 of this chapter to determine the date that you filed your submission under this part with the PBGC.

11. Revise § 4007.6 to read as follows:

§ 4007.6 Computation of time.

The PBGC applies the rules in subpart D of part 4000 of this chapter to compute any time period under this part. However, for purposes of

determining the amount of a late payment interest charge under § 4007.7 or of a late payment penalty charge under § 4007.8, the rules in part 4000.43 of this chapter governing weekends and Federal holidays do not apply.

12. Revise paragraphs (a) and (c)(1) of § 4007.10 to read as follows:

§ 4007.10 Recordkeeping; audits; disclosure of information.

(a) *Retention of records to support premium payments.* (1) *In general.* All plan records, including calculations and other data prepared by an enrolled actuary or, for a plan described in section 412(i) of the Internal Revenue Code (Title 26 of the United States Code), by the insurer from which the insurance contracts are purchased, that are necessary to support or to validate premium payments under this part shall be retained by the plan administrator for a period of six years after the premium due date. Records that must be retained pursuant to this paragraph include, but are not limited to, records that establish the number of plan participants and that reconcile the calculation of the plan's unfunded vested benefits with the actuarial valuation upon which the calculation was based.

(2) *Electronic recordkeeping.* The plan administrator may use electronic media for maintenance and retention of records required by this part in accordance with the requirements of subpart E of part 4000 of this chapter.

* * * * *

(c) *Providing record information.* (1) *In general.* The plan administrator shall make the records retained pursuant to paragraph (a) of this section available to the PBGC upon request for inspection and photocopying (or, for electronic records, inspection, electronic copying, and printout) at the location where they are kept (or another, mutually agreeable, location) and shall submit information in such records to the PBGC within 45 days of the date of the PBGC's written request therefor, or by a different time specified therein.

* * * * *

PART 4010—ANNUAL FINANCIAL AND ACTUARIAL INFORMATION REPORTING

13. Revise the authority citation for part 4010 to read as follows:

Authority: 29 U.S.C. 1302(b)(3), 1310.

14. Revise paragraphs (c), (d) and (e) of § 4010.10 to read as follows:

§ 4010.10 Due date and filing with the PBGC.

* * * * *

(c) *How and where to file.* The PBGC applies the rules in subpart A of part 4000 of this chapter to determine permissible methods of filing with the PBGC under this part. See § 4000.4 for information on where to file.

(d) *Date of filing.* The PBGC applies the rules in subpart C of part 4000 of this chapter to determine the date that a submission under this part was filed with the PBGC.

(e) *Computation of time.* The PBGC applies the rules in subpart D of part 4000 of this chapter to compute any time period under this part.

PART 4011—DISCLOSURE TO PARTICIPANTS

15. The authority citation for part 4011 continues to read as follows:

Authority: 29 U.S.C. 1302(b)(3), 1311.

16. Revise § 4011.9 to read as follows:

§ 4011.9 Method and date of issuance of notice; computation of time.

(a) *Method of issuance.* The PBGC applies the rules in subpart B of part 4000 of this chapter to determine permissible methods of delivery of the Participant Notice. The Participant Notice may be issued together with another document, such as the summary annual report required under section 104(b)(3) of ERISA for the prior plan year, but must be in a separate document.

(b) *Issuance date.* The PBGC applies the rules in subpart C of part 4000 of this chapter to determine the date the Participant Notice was issued.

(c) *Computation of time.* The PBGC applies the rules in subpart D of part 4000 of this chapter to compute any time period for issuances under this part.

PART 4022—BENEFITS PAYABLE IN TERMINATED SINGLE-EMPLOYER PLANS

17. The authority citation for part 4022 continues to read as follows:

Authority: 29 U.S.C. 1302, 1322, 1322b, 1341(c)(3)(D), and 1344.

18. Amend § 4022.9 by adding paragraph (d) to read as follows:

§ 4022.9 Time of payment; benefit applications.

* * * * *

(d) *Filing with the PBGC.* (1) *Method and date of filing.* The PBGC applies the rules in subpart A of part 4000 of this chapter to determine permissible methods of filing with the PBGC under this part. Benefit applications and related submissions are treated as filed on the date received by the PBGC unless the instructions for the applicable form provide for an earlier date. Subpart C of part 4000 of this chapter provides rules for determining when the PBGC receives a submission.

(2) *Where to file.* See § 4000.4 of this chapter for information on where to file.

(3) *Computation of time.* The PBGC applies the rules in subpart D of part 4000 of this chapter to compute any time period for filing under this part.

PART 4041—TERMINATION OF SINGLE-EMPLOYER PLANS

19. The authority citation for part 4041 continues to read as follows:

Authority: 29 U.S.C. 1302(b)(3), 1341, 1344, 1350.

20. Amend § 4041.3 as follows:

a. Revise paragraphs (a), (b), and (c)(1) to read as follows:

b. Remove paragraph (c)(2);

c. Add the word "or" to the end of paragraph (c)(3)(i);

d. Remove paragraph (c)(3)(ii) and redesignate paragraph (c)(3)(iii) as paragraph (c)(3)(ii);

e. Redesignate paragraphs (c)(3) through (c)(6) as paragraphs (c)(2) through (c)(5).

§ 4041.3 Computation of time; filing and issuance rules.

(a) *Computation of time.* The PBGC applies the rules in subpart D of part 4000 of this chapter to compute any time period under this part. A proposed termination date may be any day, including a weekend or Federal holiday.

(b) *Filing with the PBGC.* (1) *Method and date of filing.* The PBGC applies the rules in subpart A of part 4000 of this chapter to determine permissible methods of filing with the PBGC under this part. The PBGC applies the rules in subpart C of part 4000 of this chapter to determine the date that a submission under this part was filed with the PBGC.

(2) *Where to file.* See § 4000.4 of this chapter for information on where to file.

(c) *Issuance to third parties.* The following rules apply to affected parties (other than the PBGC). For purposes of this paragraph (c), a person entitled to notice under the spin-off/termination transaction rules of § 4041.23(c) or § 4041.24(f) is treated as an affected party.

(1) *Method and date of issuance.* The PBGC applies the rules in subpart B of part 4000 of this chapter to determine permissible methods of issuance under this part. The PBGC applies the rules in subpart C of part 4000 of this chapter to determine the date that an issuance under this part was provided.

* * * * *

21. Revise § 4041.5 to read as follows:

§ 4041.5 Record retention and availability.

(a) *Retention requirement.* (1) *Persons subject to requirement; records to be retained.* Each contributing sponsor and the plan administrator of a plan terminating in a standard termination, or in a distress termination that closes out in accordance with § 4041.50, must maintain all records necessary to demonstrate compliance with section 4041 of ERISA and this part. If a contributing sponsor or the plan administrator maintains information in accordance with this section, the other(s) need not maintain that information.

(2) *Retention period.* The records described in paragraph (a)(1) of this section must be preserved for six years after the date when the post-distribution certification under this part is filed with the PBGC.

(3) *Electronic recordkeeping.* The contributing sponsor or plan administrator may use electronic media for maintenance and retention of records required by this part in accordance with the requirements of subpart E of part 4000 of this chapter.

(b) *Availability of records.* The contributing sponsor or plan administrator must make all records needed to determine compliance with section 4041 of ERISA and this part available to the PBGC upon request

for inspection and photocopying (or, for electronic records, inspection, electronic copying, and printout) at the location where they are kept (or another, mutually agreeable, location) and must submit such records to the PBGC within 30 days after the date of a written request by the PBGC or by a later date specified therein.

PART 4041A—TERMINATION OF MULTIEMPLOYER PLANS

22. The authority citation for part 4041A continues to read as follows:

Authority: 29 U.S.C. 1302(b)(3), 1341a, 1441.

23. Revise § 4041A.3 to read as follows:

§ 4041A.3 Method and date of filing; where to file; computation of time; issuances to third parties.

(a) *Method and date of filing.* The PBGC applies the rules in subpart A of part 4000 of this chapter to determine permissible methods of filing with the PBGC under this part. The PBGC applies the rules in subpart C of part 4000 of this chapter to determine the date that a submission under this part was filed with the PBGC.

(b) *Where to file.* See § 4000.4 of this chapter for information on where to file.

(c) *Computation of time.* The PBGC applies the rules in subpart D of part 4000 of this chapter to compute any time period for filing or issuance under this part.

(d) *Method and date of issuance.* The PBGC applies the rules in subpart B of part 4000 of this chapter to determine permissible methods of issuance under this part. The PBGC applies the rules in subpart C of part 4000 of this chapter to determine the date that an issuance under this part was provided.

PART 4043—REPORTABLE EVENTS AND CERTAIN OTHER NOTIFICATION REQUIREMENTS

24. The authority citation for part 4043 continues to read as follows:

Authority: 29 U.S.C. 1082(f), 1302(b)(3), 1443.

25. Revise § 4043.5 to read as follows:

§ 4043.5 How and where to file.

The PBGC applies the rules in the instructions to the applicable PBGC reporting form and subpart A of part 4000 of this chapter to determine permissible methods of filing with the PBGC under this part. See § 4000.4 for information on where to file.

26. Amend § 4043.6 by removing paragraph (d) and revising paragraphs (a) and (b) and the paragraph heading of paragraph (c) to read as follows:

§ 4043.6 Date of filing.

(a) *Post-event notice filings.* The PBGC applies the rules in subpart C of part 4000 of this chapter to determine the date that a submission under subpart B of this part was filed with the PBGC.

(b) *Advance notice and Form 200 filings.* Information filed under subpart C or D of this part is treated as filed on the date it is received by the PBGC. Subpart C of part 4000 of this chapter provides rules for determining when the PBGC receives a submission.

(c) *Partial electronic filing; deemed filing date.* * * *

* * * * *

27. Revise § 4043.7 to read as follows:

§ 4043.7 Computation of time.

The PBGC applies the rules in subpart D of part 4000 of this chapter to compute any time period under this part.

PART 4050—MISSING PARTICIPANTS

28. The authority citation for part 4050 continues to read as follows:

Authority: 29 U.S.C. 1302(b)(3), 1350.

29. Amend § 4050.6 by revising paragraph (d) to read as follows:

§ 4050.6 Payment and required documentation.

* * * * *

(d) *Filing with the PBGC.* (1) *Method and date of filing.* The PBGC applies the rules in subpart A of part 4000 of this chapter to determine permissible methods of filing with the PBGC under this part. The PBGC applies the rules in subpart C of part 4000 of this chapter to determine the date that a submission under this part was filed with the PBGC.

(2) *Where to file.* See § 4000.4 of this chapter for information on where to file.

(3) *Computation of time.* The PBGC applies the rules in subpart D of part 4000 of this chapter to compute any time period for filing under this part. However, for purposes of determining the amount of an interest charge under § 4050.6(b) or § 4050.12(c)(2)(iii), the rules in § 4000.43 of this chapter governing weekends and Federal holidays do not apply.

PART 4062—LIABILITY FOR TERMINATION OF SINGLE-EMPLOYER PLANS

30. The authority citation for part 4062 continues to read as follows:

Authority: 29 U.S.C. 1302(b)(3), 1362-1364, 1367, 1368.

31. Revise § 4062.9 to read as follows:

§ 4062.9 Method and date of filing; where to file.

(a) *Method of filing.* The PBGC applies the rules in subpart A of part 4000 of this chapter to determine permissible methods of filing with the PBGC under this part. Payment of liability must be clearly designated as such and include the name of the plan.

(b) *Filing date.* The PBGC applies the rules in subpart C of part 4000 of this chapter to determine the date that a submission under this part was filed with the PBGC.

(c) *Where to file.* See § 4000.4 of this chapter for information on where to file.

32. Revise § 4062.10 to read as follows:

§ 4062.10 Computation of time.

The PBGC applies the rules in subpart D of part 4000 of this chapter to compute any time period under this part. However, for purposes of determining the amount of an interest charge under § 4062.7, the rules in § 4000.43 of this chapter governing weekends and Federal holidays do not apply.

PART 4203—EXTENSION OF SPECIAL WITHDRAWAL LIABILITY RULES

33. The authority citation for part 4203 continues to read as follows:

Authority: 29 U.S.C. 1302(b)(3).

34. Amend § 4203.4 by revising paragraphs (a) and (c) to read as follows:

§ 4203.4 Requests for PBGC approval of plan amendments.

(a) *Filing of request.* (1) *In general.* A plan shall apply to the PBGC for approval of a plan amendment which establishes special complete or partial withdrawal liability rules. The request for approval shall be filed after the amendment is adopted. PBGC approval shall also be required for any subsequent modification of the plan amendment, other than a repeal of the amendment which results in employers being subject to the general statutory rules on withdrawal.

(2) *Method and date of filing.* The PBGC applies the rules in subpart A of part 4000 of this chapter to determine permissible methods of filing with the PBGC under this part. The PBGC applies the rules in subpart C of part 4000 of this chapter to determine the date that a submission under this part was filed with the PBGC.

* * * * *

(c) *Where to file.* See § 4000.4 of this chapter for information on where to file.

* * * * *

PART 4204—VARIANCES FOR SALE OF ASSETS

35. The authority citation for part 4204 continues to read as follows:

Authority: 29 U.S.C. 1302(b)(3), 1384(c).

36. Amend § 4204.11 as follows:

a. In the first sentence of paragraph (b), remove the word "filed" and add in its place the word "submitted".

b. Add new paragraph (e) to read as follows:

§ 4204.11 Variance of the bond/escrow and sale-contract requirements.

* * * * *

(e) *Method and date of issuance.* The PBGC applies the rules in subpart B of part 4000 of this chapter to determine permissible methods of issuance under this subpart. The PBGC applies the rules in subpart C of part 4000 of this chapter to determine the date that an issuance under this subpart was provided.

37. Amend § 4204.21 by revising paragraphs (a) and (c) to read as follows:

§ 4204.21 Requests to PBGC for variances and exemptions.

(a) *Filing of request.* (1) *In general.* If a transaction covered by this part does not satisfy the conditions set forth in subpart B of this part, or if the parties decline to provide to the plan privileged or confidential financial information within the meaning of section 552(b)(4) of the Freedom of Information Act (5 U.S.C. 552), the purchaser or seller may request from the PBGC an exemption or variance from the requirements of section 4204(a)(1)(B) and (C) of ERISA.

(2) *Method of filing.* The PBGC applies the rules in subpart A of part 4000 of this chapter to determine permissible methods of filing with the PBGC under this subpart.

* * * * *

(c) *Where to file.* See § 4000.4 of this chapter for information on where to file.

* * * * *

PART 4207—REDUCTION OR WAIVER OF COMPLETE WITHDRAWAL LIABILITY

38. The authority citation for part 4207 continues to read as follows:

Authority: 29 U.S.C. 1302(b)(3), 1387.

39. Amend § 4207.10 by revising paragraph (c) to read as follows:

§ 4207.10 Plan rules for abatement.

* * * * *

(c) *Where to file.* See § 4000.4 of this chapter for information on where to file.

* * * * *

40. Add § 4207.11 to read as follows:

§ 4207.11 Method and date of filing and issuance; computation of time.

(a) *Method of filing.* The PBGC applies the rules in subpart A of part 4000 of this chapter to determine permissible methods of filing with the PBGC under this part.

(b) *Method of issuance.* The PBGC applies the rules in subpart B of part 4000 of this chapter to determine permissible methods of issuance under this part.

(c) *Date of issuance.* The PBGC applies the rules in subpart C of part 4000 of this chapter to determine the date that an issuance under this part was provided.

PART 4208—REDUCTION OR WAIVER OF PARTIAL WITHDRAWAL LIABILITY

41. Revise the authority citation for part 4208 to read as follows:

Authority: 29 U.S.C. 1302(b)(3), 1388(c) and (e).

42. Amend § 4208.9 by revising paragraph (c) to read as follows:

§ 4208.9 Plan adoption of additional abatement conditions.

* * * * *

(c) *Where to file.* See § 4000.4 of this chapter for information on where to file.

* * * * *

43. Add § 4208.10 to read as follows:

§ 4208.10 Method and date of filing and issuance; computation of time.

(a) *Method of filing.* The PBGC applies the rules in subpart A of part 4000 of this chapter to determine permissible methods of filing with the PBGC under this part.

(b) *Method of issuance.* The PBGC applies the rules in subpart B of part 4000 of this chapter to determine permissible methods of issuance under this part.

(c) *Date of issuance.* The PBGC applies the rules in subpart C of part 4000 of this chapter to determine the date that an issuance under this part was provided.

PART 4211—ALLOCATING UNFUNDED VESTED BENEFITS TO WITHDRAWING EMPLOYERS

44. Revise the authority citation for part 4211 to read as follows:

Authority: 29 U.S.C. 1302(b)(3), 1391(c)(1), (c)(2)(d), (c)(5)(B), (c)(5)(D), and (f).

45. Amend § 4211.22 by revising paragraphs (a) and (c) to read as follows:

§ 4211.22 Requests for PBGC approval.

(a) *Filing of request.* (1) *In general.* A plan shall submit a request for approval of an alternative allocation method or modification to an allocation method to the PBGC in accordance with the requirements of this section as soon as practicable after the adoption of the amendment.

(2) *Method of filing.* The PBGC applies the rules in subpart A of part 4000 of this chapter to determine permissible methods of filing with the PBGC under this subpart.

* * * * *

(c) *Where to submit.* See § 4000.4 of this chapter for information on where to file.

* * * * *

PART 4219—NOTICE, COLLECTION AND REDETERMINATION OF WITHDRAWAL LIABILITY

46. The authority citation for part 4219 continues to read as follows:

Authority: 29 U.S.C. 1302(b)(3), 1388(c) and (e).

47. Amend § 4219.17 by revising paragraphs (a), (d) and (e) to read as follows:

§ 4219.17 Filings with PBGC.

(a) *Filing requirements.* (1) *In general.* The plan sponsor shall file with PBGC a notice that a mass withdrawal has occurred and separate certifications that determinations of redetermination liability and reallocation liability have been made and notices provided to employers in accordance with this subpart.

(2) *Method of filing.* The PBGC applies the rules in subpart A of part 4000 of this chapter to determine permissible methods of filing with the PBGC under this subpart.

(3) *Computation of time.* The PBGC applies the rules in subpart D of part 4000 of this chapter to compute any time period under this subpart for filing with the PBGC.

* * * * *

(d) *Where to file.* See § 4000.4 for information on where to file.

(e) *Date of filing.* The PBGC applies the rules in subpart C of part 4000 of this chapter to determine the date that a submission under this part was filed with the PBGC.

* * * * *

§ 4219.19 [Redesignated as § 4219.20]

48. Redesignate § 4219.19 as § 4219.20.

49. Add a new § 4219.19 to read as follows:

§ 4219.19 Issuances to third parties; methods and dates.

The PBGC applies the rules in subpart B of part 4000 of this chapter to determine permissible methods of issuance under this subpart. The PBGC applies the rules in subpart C of part 4000 of this chapter to determine the date that an issuance under this subpart was provided. The PBGC applies the rules in subpart D of part 4000 of this chapter to compute any time period for issuances to third parties under this subpart.

PART 4220—PROCEDURES FOR PBGC APPROVAL OF PLAN AMENDMENTS

50. The authority citation for part 4220 continues to read as follows:

Authority: 29 U.S.C. 1302(b)(3), 1400.

51. Amend § 4220.3 by revising paragraphs (a) and (c) and adding paragraph (f) to read as follows:

§ 4220.3 Requests for PBGC approval.

(a) *Filing of request.* (1) *In general.* A request for approval of an amendment filed with the PBGC in accordance with this section shall constitute notice to the PBGC for purposes of the 90-day period specified in section 4220 of ERISA. A request is treated as filed on the date on which a request containing all information required by paragraph (d) of this section is received by the PBGC. Subpart C of part 4000 of this chapter provides rules for determining when the PBGC receives a submission.

(2) *Method and date of filing.* The PBGC applies the rules in subpart A of part 4000 of this chapter to determine permissible methods of filing with the PBGC under this part.

* * * * *

(c) *Where to file.* See § 4000.4 of this chapter for information on where to file.

* * * * *

(f) *Computation of time.* The PBGC applies the rules in subpart D of part 4000 of this chapter to compute any time period under this part.

PART 4221—ARBITRATION OF DISPUTES IN MULTIEMPLOYER PLANS

52. The authority citation for part 4221 continues to read as follows:

Authority: 29 U.S.C. 1302(b)(3), 1401.

§ 4221.4 Appointment of the arbitrator. [Amended]

53. Amend paragraph (c) of § 4221.4 by revising the second sentence to read as follows:

* * * * *

(c) *Challenge and withdrawal.* * * * The request for withdrawal shall be served on all other parties and the arbitrator by hand or by certified or registered mail (or by any other method that includes verification or acknowledgment of receipt and meets the requirements of § 4000.14 of this chapter) and shall include a statement of the circumstances that, in the requesting party's view, affect the arbitrator's impartiality and a statement that the requesting party has brought these circumstances to the attention of the arbitrator and the other parties at the earliest practicable point in the proceedings. * * *

* * * * *

54. Amend § 4221.6 by revising paragraph (b) to read as follows:

§ 4221.6 Hearing.

* * * * *

(b) After the time and place for the hearing have been established, the arbitrator shall serve a written notice of the hearing on the parties by hand, by certified or registered mail, or by any other method that includes verification or acknowledgment of receipt and meets the requirements of § 4000.14 of this chapter.

* * * * *

55. Revise § 4221.12 to read as follows:

§ 4221.12 Calculation of periods of time.

The PBGC applies the rules in subpart D of part 4000 of this chapter to compute any time period under this part.

56. Revise § 4221.13 to read as follows:

§ 4221.13 Filing and issuance rules.

(a) *Method and date of filing.* The PBGC applies the rules in subpart A of part 4000 of this chapter to determine permissible methods of filing with the PBGC under this part. The PBGC applies the rules in subpart C of part 4000 of this chapter to determine the date that a submission under this part was filed with the PBGC.

(b) *Where to file.* See § 4000.4 of this chapter for information on where to file.

(c) *Method and date of issuance.* The PBGC applies the rules in subpart B of part 4000 of this chapter to determine permissible methods of issuance under this part. The PBGC applies the rules in subpart C of part 4000 of this chapter to determine the date that an issuance under this part was provided.

§ 4221.14 PBGC-approved arbitration procedures. [Amended]

57. Revise the third sentence of paragraph (c) of § 4221.14 to read: "The application shall include:".

PART 4231—MERGERS AND TRANSFERS BETWEEN MULTIEMPLOYER PLANS

58. The authority citation for part 4231 continues to read as follows:

Authority: 29 U.S.C. 1302(b)(3), 1411.

59. Amend § 4231.8 by revising paragraphs (a), (c), and (d) to read as follows:

§ 4231.8 Notice of merger or transfer.

(a) *Filing of request.* (1) *When to file.* Except as provided in paragraph (f) of this section, a notice of a proposed merger or transfer must be filed not less than 120 days before the effective date of the transaction. For purposes of this part, the effective date of a merger or transfer is the earlier of—

(i) The date on which one plan assumes liability for benefits accrued under another plan involved in the transaction; or

(ii) The date on which one plan transfers assets to another plan involved in the transaction.

(2) *Method of filing.* The PBGC applies the rules in subpart A of part 4000 of this chapter to determine permissible methods of filing with the PBGC under this part.

(3) *Computation of time.* The PBGC applies the rules in subpart D of part 4000 of this chapter to compute any time period for filing under this part.

* * * * *

(c) *Where to file.* See § 4000.4 of this chapter for information on where to file.

(d) *Date of filing.* The PBGC applies the rules in subpart C of part 4000 of this chapter to determine the date that a submission under this part was filed with the PBGC. For purposes of paragraph (a) of this section, the notice is not considered filed until all of the information required by paragraph (e) of this section has been submitted.

* * * * *

PART 4245—NOTICE OF INSOLVENCY

60. The authority citation for part 4245 continues to read as follows:

Authority: 29 U.S.C. 1302(b)(3), 1426(e).

61. Amend § 4245.3 as follows:

a. In the first sentence of paragraph (a) remove the words "interested parties, as defined in paragraph (d) of this section" and add in their place the words "interested parties, as defined in paragraph (e) of this section".

b. Redesignate paragraph (d) as paragraph (e).

c. Revise paragraph (c) and add new paragraph (d) to read as follows:

§ 4245.3 Notice of insolvency.

* * * * *

(c) *Delivery to PBGC; filing date.* (1) *Method of delivery.* The PBGC applies the rules in subpart A of part 4000 of this chapter to determine permissible methods of filing with the PBGC under this part.

(2) *Filing date.* The PBGC applies the rules in subpart C of part 4000 of this chapter to determine the date that a submission under this part was filed with the PBGC.

(d) *Delivery to interested parties; issuance date.* (1) *Method of delivery.* The PBGC applies the rules in subpart B of part 4000 of this chapter to determine permissible methods of delivery for the notice of insolvency. In addition to the methods permitted under subpart B of part 4000, the plan sponsor may notify interested parties, other than participants and beneficiaries who are in pay status when the notice is required to be delivered, by posting the notice at participants' work sites or publishing the notice in a union newsletter or in a newspaper of general circulation in the area or areas where participants reside. Notice to a participant shall be deemed notice to that participant's beneficiary or beneficiaries.

(2) *Issuance date.* The PBGC applies the rules in subpart C of part 4000 of this chapter to determine the date that the notice of insolvency was issued.

* * * * *

§ 4245.4 [Amended]

62. Amend the introductory language of paragraph (b) by removing the words "an interested party, as defined in § 4245.3(d)" and adding in their place the words "interested parties, as defined in § 4245.3(e)".

§ 4245.5 [Amended]

63. Amend § 4245.5 as follows:

a. In the first sentence of paragraph (a) remove the words "interested parties, as defined in § 4245.3(d)" and add in their place the words "interested parties, as defined in § 4245.3(e)".

b. Revise paragraph (d) and add paragraph (e) to read as follows:

§ 4245.5 Notice of insolvency benefit level.

* * * * *

(d) *Method of delivery to PBGC; filing date.* (1) *Method of delivery.* The PBGC applies the rules in subpart A of part 4000 of this chapter to determine permissible methods of filing with the PBGC under this part.

(2) *Filing date.* The PBGC applies the rules in subpart C of part 4000 of this chapter to determine the date that a submission under this part was filed with the PBGC.

(e) *Method of delivery to interested parties; issuance date.* (1) *Method of delivery.* The PBGC applies the rules in subpart B of part 4000 of this

chapter to determine permissible methods of delivery for the notice of insolvency benefit levels. In addition to the methods permitted under subpart B of part 4000, the plan sponsor may notify interested parties, other than participants and beneficiaries who are in pay status or reasonably expected to enter pay status during the insolvency year for which the notice is given, by posting the notice at participants' work sites or publishing the notice in a union newsletter or in a newspaper of general circulation in the area or areas where participants reside. Notice to a participant shall be deemed notice to that participant's beneficiary or beneficiaries.

(2) *Issuance date.* The PBGC applies the rules in subpart C of part 4000 of this chapter to determine the date that the notice of insolvency benefit levels was issued.

§ 4245.6 [Amended]

64. In § 4245.6, amend the introductory language of paragraph (b) by removing the words "interested parties, as defined in § 4245.3(d)" and adding in their place the words "interested parties, as defined in § 4245.3(e)".

65. Revise § 4245.7 to read as follows:

§ 4245.7 PBGC address.

See § 4000.4 of this chapter for information on where to file.

66. Add § 4245.8 to read as follows:

§ 4245.8 Computation of time.

The PBGC applies the rules in subpart D of part 4000 of this chapter to compute any time period for filing or issuance under this part.

PART 4281—DUTIES OF PLAN SPONSOR FOLLOWING MASS WITHDRAWAL

67. Revise the authority citation for part 4281 to read as follows:

Authority: 29 U.S.C. 1302(b)(3), 1341(a), 1399(c)(1)(D), and 1441.

68. Revise § 4281.3 to read as follows:

§ 4281.3 Filing and issuance rules.

(a) *Method of filing.* The PBGC applies the rules in subpart A of part 4000 of this chapter to determine permissible methods of delivery for filings with the PBGC under this part.

(b) *Method of issuance.* See § 4281.32(c) for notices of benefit reductions, § 4281.43(e) for notices of insolvency, and § 4281.45(c) for notices of insolvency benefit level.

(c) *Date of filing.* The PBGC applies the rules in subpart C of part 4000 of this chapter to determine the date that a submission under this part was filed with the PBGC.

(d) *Date of issuance.* The PBGC applies the rules in subpart C of part 4000 of this chapter to determine the date that an issuance under this part was provided.

(e) *Where to file.* See § 4000.4 of this chapter for information on where to file.

(f) *Computation of tim* e. The PBGC applies the rules in subpart D of part 4000 of this chapter to compute any time period for filing or issuance under this part.

69. Revise paragraph (c) of § 4281.32 to read as follows:

§ 4281.32 Notices of benefit reductions.

* * * * *

(c) *Method of issuance to interested parties.* The PBGC applies the rules in subpart B of part 4000 of this chapter to determine permissible methods of delivery for the notice of benefit reduction. In addition to the methods permitted under subpart B of part 4000, the plan sponsor may notify interested parties, other than participants and beneficiaries who are in pay status when the notice is required to be delivered or who are reasonably expected to enter pay status before the end of the plan year after the plan year in which the amendment is adopted, by posting the notice at participants' work sites or publishing the notice in a union newsletter or in a newspaper of general circulation in the area or areas where participants reside. Notice to a participant shall be deemed notice to that participant's beneficiary or beneficiaries.

* * * * *

70. Revise paragraphs (e) and (f) of § 4281.43 to read as follows:

§ 4281.43 Notices of insolvency and annual updates.

* * * * *

(e) *Notices of insolvency—method of issuance to interested parties.* The PBGC applies the rules in subpart B of part 4000 of this chapter to determine permissible methods of delivery for the notice of insolvency. In addition to the methods permitted under subpart B of part 4000, the plan sponsor may notify interested parties, other than participants and beneficiaries who are in pay status when the notice is required to be delivered, by posting the notice at participants' work sites or publishing the notice in a union newsletter or in a newspaper of general circulation in the area or areas where participants reside. Notice to a participant shall be deemed notice to that participant's beneficiary or beneficiaries.

(f) *Annual updates—method of issuance.* The PBGC applies the rules in subpart B of part 4000 of this chapter to determine permissible methods of delivery for the annual update to participants and beneficiaries. In addition to the methods permitted under subpart B of part 4000, the plan sponsor may notify interested parties by posting the notice at participants' work sites or publishing the notice in a union newsletter or in a newspaper of general circulation in the area or areas where participants reside. Notice to a participant shall be deemed notice to that participant's beneficiary or beneficiaries.

71. Revise paragraph (c) of § 4281.45 to read as follows:

§ 4281.45 Notices of insolvency benefit level.

* * * * *

(c) *Method of issuance.* The notices of insolvency benefit level shall be delivered to the PBGC and to plan participants and beneficiaries in pay status or reasonably expected to enter pay status during the insolvency year. The PBGC applies the rules in subpart B of part 4000 of this chapter to determine permissible methods of delivery for the notice of insolvency benefit levels.

PART 4901—EXAMINATION AND COPYING OF PENSION BENEFIT GUARANTY CORPORATION RECORDS

72. Revise the authority citation for part 4901 to read as follows:

Authority: 5 U.S.C. 552, 29 U.S.C. 1302(b)(3), E.O. 12600, 52 FR 23781, 3 CFR, 1987 Comp., p.235.

73. Add § 4901.6 to read as follows:

§ 4901.6 Filing rules; computation of time.

(a) *Filing rules.* (1) *Where to file.* See § 4000.4 of this chapter for information on where to file a submission under this part with the PBGC.

(2) *Method of filing.* The PBGC applies the rules in subpart A of part 4000 of this chapter to determine permissible methods of filing with the PBGC under this part.

(3) *Date of filing.* The PBGC applies the rules in subpart C of part 4000 of this chapter to determine the date that a submission under this part was filed with the PBGC.

(b) *Computation of time.* The PBGC applies the rules in subpart D of part 4000 of this chapter to compute any time period under this part.

74. Revise § 4901.11 to read as follows:

§ 4901.11 Submittal of requests for access to records.

A request to inspect or copy any record subject to this subpart shall be submitted to the Disclosure Officer, Pension Benefit Guaranty Corporation. Such a request may be sent to the Disclosure Officer or made in person between the hours of 9 a.m. and 4 p.m. on any working day in the Communications and Public Affairs Department, PBGC, 1200 K Street, NW., Suite 240, Washington, DC 20005-4026. To expedite processing, the request should be prominently identified as a "FOIA request."

75. Revise paragraph (a) of § 4901.15 to read as follows:

§ 4901.15 Appeals from denial of requests.

(a) *Submittal of appeals.* If a disclosure request is denied in whole or in part by the disclosure officer, the requester may file a written appeal within 30 days from the date of the denial or, if later (in the case of a partial denial), 30 days from the date the requester receives the disclosed material. The appeal shall state the grounds for appeal and any supporting statements or arguments, and shall be addressed to the General Counsel, Pension Benefit Guaranty Corporation. See part 4000.4 of this chapter for information on where to file. To expedite processing, the words "FOIA appeal" should appear prominently on the request.

* * * * *

76. Revise paragraph (c) of § 4901.33 to read as follows:

§ 4901.33 Payment of fees.

* * * * *

(c) *Late payment interest charges.* The PBGC may assess late payment interest charges on any amounts unpaid by the 31st day after the date a bill is sent to a requester. Interest will be assessed at the rate prescribed in 31 U.S.C. 3717 and will accrue from the date the bill is sent.

PART 4902—DISCLOSURE AND AMENDMENT OF RECORDS PERTAINING TO INDIVIDUALS UNDER THE PRIVACY ACT

77. The authority citation for part 4902 continues to read as follows:

Authority: 5 U.S.C. 552a.

78. Revise paragraphs (a) and (b) of § 4902.3 to read as follows:

§ 4902.3 Procedures for determining existence of and requesting access to records.

(a) Any individual may submit a request to the Disclosure Officer, Pension Benefit Guaranty Corporation, for the purpose of learning whether a system of records maintained by the PBGC contains any record pertaining to the requestor or obtaining access to such a record. Such a request may be sent to the Disclosure Officer or made in person between the hours of 9 a.m. and 4 p.m. on any working day in the Communications and Public Affairs Department, PBGC, 1200 K Street, NW., Suite 240, Washington, DC 20005-4026.

(b) Each request submitted pursuant to paragraph (a) of this section shall include the name of the system of records to which the request pertains and the requester's full name, home address and date of birth, and shall prominently state the words, "Privacy Act Request." If this information is insufficient to enable the PBGC to identify the record in question, or to determine the identity of the requester (to ensure the privacy of the subject of the record), the disclosure officer shall request such further identifying data as the disclosure officer deems necessary to locate the record or to determine the identity of the requester.

* * * * *

79. Revise paragraph (c) of § 4902.5 to read as follows:

§ 4902.5 Procedures for requesting amendment of a record.

* * * * *

(c) An individual who desires assistance in the preparation of a request for amendment of a record shall submit such request for assistance in writing to the Deputy General Counsel, Pension Benefit Guaranty Corporation. The Deputy General Counsel shall respond to such request as promptly as possible.

80. Revise paragraph (c) of § 4902.6 to read as follows:

§ 4902.6 Action on request for amendment of a record.

* * * * *

(c) An individual who desires assistance in preparing an appeal of a denial under this section shall submit a request to the Deputy General Counsel, Pension Benefit Guaranty Corporation. The Deputy General Counsel shall respond to the request as promptly as possible, but in no event more than 30 days after receipt.

81. Revise paragraph (a) of § 4902.7 to read as follows:

§ 4902.7 Appeal of a denial of a request for amendment of a record.

(a) An appeal from a denial of a request for amendment of a record under § 4902.6 shall be submitted, within 45 days of receipt of the denial, to the General Counsel, Pension Benefit Guaranty Corporation, unless the record subject to such request is one maintained by the Office of the General Counsel, in which event the appeal shall be submitted to the Deputy Executive Director, Pension Benefit Guaranty Corporation. The appeal shall state in detail the basis on which it is made and shall clearly state "Privacy Act Request" on the first page. In addition, the submission shall clearly state "Privacy Act Request" on the envelope (for mail, hand delivery, or commercial delivery), in the subject line (for e-mail), or on the cover sheet (for fax).

* * * * *

82. Add § 4902.10 to read as follows:

§ 4902.10 Filing rules; computation of time.

(a) *Filing rules.* (1) *Where to file.* See § 4000.4 of this chapter for information on where to file a submission under this part with the PBGC.

(2) *Method of filing.* The PBGC applies the rules in subpart A of part 4000 of this chapter to determine permissible methods of filing with the PBGC under this part.

(3) *Date of filing.* The PBGC applies the rules in subpart C of part 4000 of this chapter to determine the date that a submission under this part was filed with the PBGC.

(b) *Computation of time.* The PBGC applies the rules in subpart D of part 4000 of this chapter to compute any time period for filing under this part.

PART 4903—DEBT COLLECTION

83. The authority citation for part 4903 continues to read as follows:

Authority: 29 U.S.C. 1302(b); 31 U.S.C. 3701, 3711(f), 3720A; 4 CFR part 102; 26 CFR 301.6402-6.

84. Amend § 4903.2 by adding paragraphs (c) and (d) to read as follows:

§ 4903.2 General.

* * * * *

(c) The PBGC applies the rules in subpart A of part 4000 of this chapter to determine permissible methods of filing with the PBGC under this part. The PBGC applies the rules in subpart C of part 4000 of this chapter to determine the date that a submission under this part was filed with the PBGC. See § 4000.4 for information on where to file.

(d) The PBGC applies the rules in subpart D of part 4000 of this chapter to compute any time period for filing under this part.

85. Revise paragraph (b)(2) of § 4903.24 to read as follows:

§ 4903.24 Request for offset from other agencies.

* * * * *

(b)(1) * * *

(2) All such requests should be directed to the Director, Financial Operations Department. See § 4000.4 of this chapter for information on where to file.

* * * * *

PART 4907—ENFORCEMENT OF NONDISCRIMINATION ON THE BASIS OF HANDICAP IN PROGRAMS OR ACTIVITIES CONDUCTED BY THE PENSION BENEFIT GUARANTY CORPORATION

86. The authority citation for part 4907 continues to read as follows:

Authority: 29 U.S.C. 794, 1302(b)(3).

87. Revise paragraph (c) of § 4907.170 to read as follows:

§ 4907.170 Compliance procedures.

* * * * *

(c) The Equal Opportunity Manager shall be responsible for coordinating implementation of this section.

(1) *Where to file.* See § 4000.4 of this chapter for information on where to file complaints under this part.

(2) *Method of filing.* The PBGC applies the rules in subpart A of part 4000 of this chapter to determine permissible methods of filing with the PBGC under this part.

(3) *Date of filing.* The PBGC applies the rules in subpart C of part 4000 of this chapter to determine the date that a submission under this part was filed with the PBGC.

(4) *Computation of time.* The PBGC applies the rules in subpart D of part 4000 of this chapter to compute any time period under this part.

* * * * *

Issued in Washington, DC, this 4th day of February, 2003.

Steven A. Kandarian,

Executive Director,

Pension Benefit Guaranty Corporation.

¶ 20,534M

EBSA proposed regulations: COBRA: Notice requirements: Health care continuation coverage: Model notices.—EBSA has issued proposed rules setting minimum standards for the notices required of group health plans to participants and beneficiaries who would lose coverage, regarding their opportunity to obtain continued coverage at group rates for a limited period of time. The proposed rules include model notices. Final regulations were issued, effective July 26, 2004 and applicable to notice obligations that arise on or after the first day of the first plan year beginning on or after November 26, 2004. See ¶ 15,046B-1, ¶ 15,046B-2, ¶ 15,046B-3, ¶ 15,046B-4, ¶ 15,046B-5, ¶ 15,046B-6, and ¶ 24,806M. According to the final regulation preamble, pending the applicability of the final rules, EBSA will view compliance with either the proposed rules or the final rules to constitute good faith compliance with the COBRA statutory notice requirements.

The proposed regulations, which were published in the *Federal Register* on May 28, 2003 (68 FR 31832), are reproduced below.

Part V

Department of Labor

Employee Benefits Security Administration

29 CFR Part 2590

Health Care Continuation Coverage; Proposed Rule

DEPARTMENT OF LABOR

Employee Benefits Security Administration

29 CFR Part 2590

RIN 1210-AA60

Health Care Continuation Coverage

AGENCY: Employee Benefits Security Administration, Labor.

ACTION: Proposed regulations.

SUMMARY: This document contains proposed regulations implementing the notice requirements of the health care continuation coverage (COBRA) provisions of Part 6 of title I of the Employee Retirement Income Security Act of 1974 (ERISA). The continuation coverage provisions generally require group health plans to provide participants and beneficiaries who under certain circumstances would lose coverage (qualified beneficiaries) the opportunity to elect to continue coverage under the plan at group rates for a limited period of time.

The proposed rules set minimum standards for the timing and content of the notices required under the continuation coverage provisions and establish standards for administering the notice process. This document also contains model forms for use by administrators of single-employer group health plans to satisfy their obligation to provide general notices and election notices. These proposed regulations, if finalized, would affect administrators of group health plans, participants and beneficiaries (including qualified beneficiaries) of group health plans, and the sponsors and fiduciaries of such plans.

DATES: Written comments on these proposed regulations should be received by the Department of Labor on or before July 28, 2003.

ADDRESSES: Comments (preferably at least three copies) should be addressed to the Office of Regulations and Interpretations, Employee Benefits Security Administration, Room N-5669, U.S. Department of Labor, 200 Constitution Avenue NW., Washington, DC 20210. Attn: COBRA Notice Regulations. Comments also may be submitted electronically to e-ORI@EBSA.dol.gov. All comments received will be available for public inspection at the Public Disclosure Room, N-1513, Employee Benefits Security Administration, 200 Constitution Avenue NW., Washington, DC 20210.

FOR FURTHER INFORMATION CONTACT: Lisa M. Fields or Suzanne M. Adelman, Office of Regulations and Interpretations, Employee Benefits Security Administration, (202) 693-8523. This is not a toll-free number.

SUPPLEMENTARY INFORMATION:

Background

The continuation coverage provisions, sections 601 through 608 of title I of ERISA, were enacted as part of the Consolidated Omnibus Budget Reconciliation Act of 1985 (COBRA), which also promulgated parallel provisions that became part of the Internal Revenue Code (the Code) and the Public Health Service Act (the PHSA).[1] See Code

---

[1] The Code and PHSA COBRA provisions, although very similar in other ways, are not identical to the COBRA provisions in title I of ERISA in their scope of application. The PHSA provisions apply only to State and local governmental plans, and the Code provisions

section 4980B; PHSA, 42 U.S.C. 300bb-1 et seq. These provisions are commonly referred to as the COBRA provisions, and the continuation coverage that they mandate is commonly referred to as COBRA coverage. The COBRA provisions of title I of ERISA generally require that "any group health plan"[2] offer "qualified beneficiaries" the opportunity to elect "continuation coverage" following certain events that would otherwise result in the loss of coverage ("qualifying events").[3] Continuation coverage is a temporary extension of the qualified beneficiary's previous group health coverage. The right to elect continuation coverage allows individuals to maintain group health coverage under adverse circumstances and to bridge gaps in health coverage that otherwise could limit their access to health care.

COBRA, as enacted, provides that the Secretary of Labor (the Secretary) has the authority under section 608 to carry out the provisions of part 6 of title I of ERISA. The Conference Report that accompanied COBRA divided interpretive authority over the COBRA provisions between the Secretary and the Secretary of the Treasury (the Treasury) by providing that the Secretary has the authority to issue regulations implementing the notice and disclosure requirements of COBRA, while the Treasury is authorized to issue regulations defining the required continuation coverage.[4] Under its authority to interpret the COBRA provisions, the Treasury has issued final regulations that provide rules for determining which plans are subject to the COBRA provisions, who is or can become a qualified beneficiary, which events constitute qualifying events, what COBRA obligations exist in the case of mergers and acquisitions, and the nature of the continuation coverage that must be offered. See Treas. Reg. §§ 54.4980B-1 through 54.4980B-10. These proposed rules implementing the notice requirements of the COBRA provisions of Part 6 of title I of ERISA would apply for purposes of the COBRA provisions of section 4980B of the Code.[5]

COBRA Notice Requirements

Section 606(a)(1) requires group health plans to provide a written notice containing general information about COBRA rights to each covered employee and his or her spouse when coverage under the plan commences. Sections 606(a)(2) and 606(a)(3) require the plan administrator to be notified when a qualifying event occurs, and the nature of the qualifying event determines whether the employer or the covered employee and qualified beneficiary must give this notice to the plan administrator.[6] Section 606(a)(4) requires a plan administrator who has received a notice of qualifying event to provide each qualified beneficiary with a notice of such beneficiary's rights under the COBRA provisions. The provision of an election notice starts the running of the 60-day period during which qualified beneficiaries may elect continuation coverage. See section 605(1)(C).

The maximum period for which a plan is obliged to provide COBRA coverage is 36 months, but in certain circumstances a plan is required to provide only 18 months of continuation coverage (after a qualifying event that is termination or reduction in hours of a covered employee's employment). The COBRA provisions require an 18-month period of COBRA coverage to be extended to a longer period in only two circumstances: if a qualified beneficiary is or becomes disabled, or if a second qualifying event occurs. Sections 602(2) and 606(a)(3) require notice of a disability to be provided as a prerequisite to the disability extension. The right to an extension of continuation coverage based on the occurrence of a second qualifying event is based on providing notice of such second qualifying event pursuant to section 606(a)(3).

The Trade Act of 2002, Public Law 107-210, enacted on August 6, 2002, amended section 605 of ERISA to add a new subsection (b). This new subsection provides a second 60-day COBRA election period for certain individuals who become eligible for trade adjustment assistance (TAA) pursuant to the Trade Act of 1974.[7] New section 605(b)(1) provides that an individual who is either an eligible TAA recipient under section 35(c)(2) of the Code or an eligible alternative TAA recipient under section 35(c)(3) of the Code (collectively, a TAA-eligible individual), and who did not elect continuation coverage during the 60-day COBRA election period that was a direct consequence of the TAA-related loss of coverage,[8] may elect continuation coverage during a 60-day period that begins on the first day of the month in which he or she is determined to be a TAA-eligible individual, provided such election is made not later than 6 months after the date of the TAA-related loss of coverage. The individual may elect coverage for both himself or herself and his or her family. Any continuation coverage elected during the second election period will begin with the first day of the second election period, and not on the date on which coverage originally lapsed. However, the time between the loss of coverage and the start of the second election period will not be counted for purposes of determining whether the individual has had a 63-day break in coverage under section 701(c)(2) of ERISA (and corresponding provisions of the PHSA and the Code).

The new second COBRA election period is intended to assist individuals who become TAA-eligible in taking advantage of a new tax credit, also created by the Trade Act of 2002. Under the new tax provisions, individuals who become eligible for TAA assistance can take a tax credit of 65% of premiums paid for qualified health insurance. The Trade Act of 2002 provides for advance payment of the tax credit to health insurers, beginning in 2003. COBRA continuation coverage is one of the types of health insurance that qualifies for the tax credit. Because of the importance of the right to elect COBRA continuation coverage as a TAA-eligible individual, it is the view of the Department that information on the possible availability of a new second election period in the event of TAA eligibility should, pursuant to 29 CFR 2520.102-3(o), be included in the summary plan description of a group health plan as part of the discussion of continuation coverage provisions.

It is anticipated that information on the right to a second COBRA election, together with other information on trade adjustment assistance and the health coverage tax credit, will also be made available to potentially eligible individuals through the State Workforce Agencies in connection with the certification process for trade adjustment assistance.

Overview of Proposed Regulations

The provision of timely and adequate notifications regarding COBRA rights, the occurrence of qualifying events, and election rights is critical to the effective exercise of COBRA rights. Failure to meet notice requirements may cause a qualified beneficiary to lose COBRA rights or may conversely cause a plan administrator to be subject to fines or other adverse consequences. In the Department's view, regulatory guidance establishing clearer standards for the administration of the COBRA notice processes would reduce the risks both to plans and to qualified beneficiaries by providing certainty as to how the notice obligations can be met.[9] The attached proposed regulations are intended to provide the necessary guidance.

(Footnote Continued)

grant COBRA rights to individuals who would not be considered participants or beneficiaries under ERISA. See PHSA, 42 U.S.C. 300bb-8; Code section 5000(b)(1).

[2] A group health plan is not subject to the COBRA provisions for any calendar year if all employers maintaining such plan normally employed fewer than 20 employees on a typical business day during the preceding calendar year. See section 601(b).

[3] Each of the quoted terms is specifically defined in the COBRA provisions. In particular, the term group health plan is defined in section 607(1) to mean an employee welfare benefit plan as defined in section 3(1) that provides medical care (as defined in section 213(d) of the Code) to participants or beneficiaries directly or through insurance, reimbursement, or otherwise. The Department notes that employee welfare benefit plans under ERISA include, inter alia, plans sponsored by unions for their members as well as plans sponsored by employers for their employees. Such union-sponsored plans would not involve employers in any sponsorship capacity, nor would they necessarily cover individuals all of whom are employees. Although the proposed regulations use the terms "employer" and "employee," as do the COBRA provisions, in assigning duties, they are intended to apply to all group health plans, as defined in section 607(1), subject to COBRA.

[4] H.R. Conf. Rep. No. 99-453, 99th Cong., 1st Sess., at 562-63 (1985). The Conference Report further indicates that the Secretary of Health and Human Services, who is to issue regulations implementing the continuation coverage requirements for State and local governments, must conform the actual requirements of those regulations to the regulations issued by the Secretary and the Treasury. Id. at 563.

[5] As noted in footnote 1, above, certain COBRA provisions (such as the definitions of group health plan, employee and employer) are not identical in the Code and title I of

ERISA. The Treasury has reviewed these rules and concurs that, in those cases in which the statutory language is not identical, §§ 2590.606-1 through 2590.606-4 would nonetheless apply to the COBRA provisions of sec. 4980B of the Code, except to the extent that such regulations are inconsistent with the statutory language of the Code.

[6] When the qualifying event is the death of the covered employee, the termination or reduction of hours of the covered employee's employment, the covered employee's becoming entitled to Medicare, or a bankruptcy proceeding of the employer, the notice obligation falls on the employer. For the other qualifying events (divorce or legal separation or a dependent child's ceasing to be a dependent under the terms of the plan), the notice obligation falls on the covered employee or qualified beneficiary.

[7] Pursuant to the Trade Act of 1974 (19 U.S.C. 2101 et seq.), workers whose employment is adversely affected by international trade (increased imports or a shift in production to another country) may become entitled to receive TAA, which primarily consists of career counseling, up to two years of training, income support during training, job search assistance, and relocation allowances.

[8] Section 605(a)(1) of ERISA provides that the election period is the period which: (A) begins not later than the date on which coverage terminates under the plan by reason of a qualifying event; (B) is of at least 60 days' duration; and (C) ends not earlier than 60 days after the later of the date coverage terminates or the date of the notice.

[9] On September 23, 1997, the Department issued a Request for Information (RFI) to assess public views on the advisability of developing regulations on the COBRA notice provisions. 62 FR 49894 (Sept. 23, 1997). The Department received 15 comments in

The proposed guidance comprises four separate regulations. Section 2590.606-1 covers the general notice. Section 2590.606-2 creates rules for employer-provided notices of the occurrence of a qualifying event. Section 2590.606-3 addresses the responsibilities of qualified beneficiaries to provide notice of a qualifying event or a disability. Finally, § 2590.606-4 deals with the election notice and other notices that plan administrators must provide subsequent to the election of COBRA coverage. As part of this proposal, the Department is also including, for public comment, model forms for two of the administrator's notices: the general notice and the election notice.[10] The model forms are appended, respectively, to § 2590.606-1 and § 2590.606-4. Each model allows for inclusion of plan-specific information to reflect the circumstances of a particular plan. It should be noted, however, that these models have been designed for use primarily by single-employer plans and do not reflect the special rules or practices that may apply in the case of other types of group health plans, such as multiemployer plans or plans sponsored by unions for their members.[11] The Department specifically requests comment on what, if any, changes should be made to the model forms to adequately reflect current practice and meet the needs of plan administrators, participants, and beneficiaries.

These proposed regulations establish minimum timing and content requirements for the required notices and set forth general rules for administering the COBRA notice process. The goal of this regulatory initiative is to create certainty and uniformity in this process, while also improving the consistency and quality of information provided to participants and beneficiaries about their COBRA rights. The Department believes that the proposed regulations, which would provide clear, uniform rules for the required notices, would make it easier for plans and employers to comply with COBRA notice requirements. The Department proposes to make these regulations, in their final form, effective and applicable as of the first day of the first plan year that occurs on or after January 1, 2004.

The Department notes that the Conference Report that accompanied COBRA states that "pending the promulgation of regulations, employers are required to operate in good faith compliance with a reasonable interpretation of these [COBRA] substantive rules, notice requirements, etc."[12] In the absence of final regulations, this continues to be the standard by which the Department will judge plan operations in this area. The publication of these proposed regulations should not be considered to relieve plan administrators of their obligation to meet this standard. In particular, the Department notes that, effective with publication of these proposed regulations, the Department will no longer consider use of the model general notice in ERISA Technical Release 86-2 (June 26, 1986) (TR 86-2) to be good faith compliance with the requirements of section 606(a)(1).[13]

§ 2590.606-1 General Notice

Section 606(a)(1) requires each group health plan covered under COBRA to provide a written notice "at the time of commencement of coverage" to each covered employee and spouse (if any) of the employee. Proposed § 2590.606-1 establishes rules for both when this general notice must be provided and what information it must contain.

Paragraph (c) of the regulation sets forth the required minimum content of a general notice. These content requirements cover basic information regarding COBRA and the rights and responsibilities of qualified beneficiaries that a participant or beneficiary would need to know before the occurrence of a qualifying event in order to be able to protect his or her COBRA rights. In particular, paragraph (c) requires the general notice to describe the plan's requirements for notices that must be provided by qualified beneficiaries, such as the notice of a qualifying event involving divorce, separation, or a dependent's becoming no longer eligible for coverage as a dependent.

Paragraph (b) of the regulation establishes a 90-day period for the furnishing of the general notice, beginning with the date on which the covered employee or spouse first becomes covered under the plan. If the plan administrator must provide an election notice to the employee or to his or her spouse or dependent during the first 90 days of coverage, however, paragraph (b) requires the general notice to be provided at that earlier time. This provision protects participants and beneficiaries during the first 90 days of coverage by ensuring that they receive all of the information they need to understand their rights when the information is most necessary.

Paragraph (e) further permits plans to satisfy the general notice requirement by including the information described in paragraphs (c)(1), (2), (3), (4), and (5) in the summary plan description (SPD) of the plan and providing the SPD at a time that complies with the timing requirements for the general notice. The Department anticipates that many, and perhaps most, plans would prefer to take advantage of the reduced cost and added efficiency of providing a single disclosure document that satisfies both the general notice requirement and the SPD requirement. If a plan chooses to satisfy both disclosure obligations by furnishing a single document, the plan must ensure that the document satisfies both the general notice content requirements and the SPD content requirements.[14]

Paragraph (f) provides that delivery of the general notice should be made in accordance with the standards of 29 CFR 2520.104b-1, including the standards for use of electronic media. Paragraph (d) permits delivery of a single notice addressed to a covered employee and the covered employee's spouse at their residence, provided the plan's latest information indicates that both reside at that address. A single notice would not be permitted, however, if a spouse's coverage under the plan begins at a different time from the covered employee's coverage, unless the spouse's coverage begins before the date on which the notice must be provided to the covered employee. Further, in-hand furnishing of the general notice at the workplace to a covered employee is deemed to be adequate delivery to the employee, although such delivery to the employee would not constitute delivery to the spouse.

The appendix to this section contains a model general notice that plan administrators may use to satisfy the content requirements of the regulation. The model general notice allows for inclusion of plan-specific information, including designation of the appropriate COBRA administrative contact and description of specific plan procedures, and provides alternatives to reflect the plan's practices regarding premium payment requirements, dates on which continuation coverage will begin, and whether bankruptcy could be a qualifying event under the specific plan. While the Department intends that use of an appropriately completed model notice, when finalized, would be considered compliance with the content requirements of the regulation, the Department does not intend to require its use and anticipates that a variety of other notices could satisfy the requirements of the regulation. The Department requests comment on whether the proposed model general notice adequately reflects current practice and provides plans with sufficient flexibility to describe individual plans' specific COBRA provisions.

§ 2590.606-2 Employer's Notice of Qualifying Event

Section 606(a)(2) requires an employer to provide notice to the plan administrator of a qualifying event that is either the employee's termination of employment or reduction in hours of employment, the employee's death, the employee's becoming enrolled in Medicare, or the commencement of a proceeding in bankruptcy with respect to the employer. Proposed § 2590.606-2 addresses this notice obligation of employers.

Paragraph (b) of the regulation provides that an employer shall notify the plan administrator of a qualifying event no later than 30 days after the date of the qualifying event. However, paragraph (b) further provides that, for any plan under which continuation coverage begins, pursuant to section 607(5), with the date of loss of coverage, the 30-day period for providing the notice of qualifying event must also begin with the date of loss of coverage, rather than the date of the qualifying event. Paragraphs (b) and (d) also recognize that multiemployer plans may have different notice periods, as permitted under sections 606(a)(2) and 606(b).

(Footnote Continued)

response to that RFI. These proposed regulations take into account the views expressed in those comments.

[10] Of the 15 comments received in response to the COBRA notice RFI, 11 commenters advocated that the Department develop model plan administrators' notices.

[11] The model election notice, further, is not designed to be used when bankruptcy is the qualifying event.

[12] H.R. Conf. Rep. No. 99-453, at 563.

[13] On June 26, 1986, the Department issued TR 86-2 to provide guidance to employers on the then newly enacted COBRA provisions. The Department provided, with TR 86-2, a model general notice to assist group health plans with the immediate necessity of providing a general notice by the effective date of COBRA, which came into force as of the beginning of the first plan year on or after July 1, 1986. The Department indicated that use of the model notice would be considered good faith compliance with the requirements of section 606(a)(1). The TR 86-2 model notice was intended to inform participants and beneficiaries, for the first time, of the passage of COBRA and educate them about the new COBRA rights. Because of the variety of subsequent statutory amendments, the TR 86-2 model notice no longer adequately reflects the COBRA provisions.

[14] The SPD content regulation, § 2520.102-3, specifies other information, in addition to description of COBRA rights, that must be included in an SPD for a group health plan. See, e.g., § 2520.102-3(j)(2), (3), (l).

Paragraph (c) of the regulation requires that an employer provide the plan administrator sufficient information to enable the administrator to determine the identity of the plan, the covered employee, the qualifying event, and the date of the qualifying event.

§ 2590.606-3 Qualified Beneficiary's Notices

Under section 606(a)(3), each covered employee or qualified beneficiary is responsible for notifying the plan administrator of a qualifying event that is either the divorce or legal separation of the employee from his or her spouse or a dependent's becoming no longer eligible to be covered as a dependent under the plan. This notice must be provided within 60 days after the occurrence of the qualifying event. Proposed § 2590.606-3 provides guidance with respect to this notice obligation and other notice obligations of qualified beneficiaries, such as the notice of disability or second qualifying event.

Paragraph (b) of the regulation requires plans to establish reasonable procedures for the furnishing of notices by covered employees and qualified beneficiaries and sets general standards for what will be considered reasonable.[15] A plan's procedures generally would be deemed reasonable if they are described in the plan's SPD, specify who is designated to receive notices and specify the means qualified beneficiaries must use for giving notice and the required content of the notice. Paragraph (b) further provides that, if a plan does not have reasonable procedures for qualified beneficiaries' notices, notice will be deemed to have been provided if certain information adequately identifying a specific qualifying event is communicated to any of the parties that would customarily be considered in charge of the plan. Paragraph (b) provides that plans may require notices to be submitted via a specific form, if the form is easily available to qualified beneficiaries without cost, and may require specific information to be provided.

Paragraph (d) provides that a plan may not reject an incomplete notice as untimely if the notice is provided within the plan's time limits and contains enough information to enable the plan administrator to identify the plan, the covered employee and qualified beneficiar(ies), the qualifying event or disability determination, and the date on which it occurred. However, if a timely notice fails to supply all of the information required under the plan's procedures, the plan administrator can require qualified beneficiaries to supply the missing information.

Paragraph (c) provides that the statutory time limits for the qualified beneficiaries' notices are minimum time limits and that plans can provide for longer notice periods. The proposed regulation specifies, however, that a plan's time limit for providing any of the qualified beneficiaries' notices could not begin to run unless and until the plan had satisfied the general notice requirements of section 606(a)(1) with respect to the affected qualified beneficiaries.

Paragraph (c) further requires that a plan structured in accordance with section 607(5) to begin continuation coverage with the date of loss of coverage, rather than the date on which a qualifying event occurs, must provide that the 60-day period for qualified beneficiaries' notices also begins with the date of loss of coverage.[16] Paragraph (e) provides that any of the qualified beneficiary notice obligations can be satisfied with respect to all qualified beneficiaries affected by a single qualifying event through a single notice and that any individual representing the qualified beneficiaries can provide the required notice.

With respect to the notice of disability required to be provided under section 606(a)(3), paragraph (c) specifies that qualified beneficiaries can be required by a plan to provide the disability notice within 60 days of the date of the Social Security Administration's determination of disability and before the end of the initial period of 18 months of continuation coverage. Under the proposed regulation, therefore, failure to provide the disability notice within those time limits, if required by the plan, could be a basis for concluding that notice had not been timely provided under section 606(a)(3). Paragraph (c) makes clear, however, that plans may not decline to provide the disability extension

for failure to provide a timely disability notice unless the affected qualified beneficiaries were adequately notified, in advance, of the notice obligation. The regulation further specifies that plans may adopt more generous notice requirements.

§ 2590.606-4 Plan Administrator's Notice Obligations

Section 606(a)(4) requires a plan administrator to notify each qualified beneficiary who is entitled to elect continuation coverage of his or her COBRA rights. Section 606(c) requires a plan administrator to provide such notice within 14 days after the plan administrator is notified of a qualifying event. Proposed § 2590.606-4 provides guidance on the requirements of sections 606(a)(4) and 606(c). The regulation describes timing and content requirements for election notices, requires administrators to notify individuals if continuation coverage is determined not to be available, and requires plan administrators to provide notice when continuation coverage terminates before the end of the maximum period for such coverage.

Paragraph (b) of the regulation sets forth the information that must be included in an election notice.[17] In addition to identifying significant pertinent facts, such as the names and contact information for plan administrators and (if different) COBRA administrators and the qualified beneficiaries and qualifying event, the election notice must describe the continuation coverage being made available and the manner in which the qualified beneficiaries' COBRA rights must be exercised, making clear that each qualified beneficiary has an independent right to elect continuation coverage.[18] The notice must explain the plan's payment requirements, payment schedule, and payment policies (including grace periods and the consequences of late payment or nonpayment). If the plan makes alternative coverage available or provides any conversion options, the notice must describe those options and alternatives and explain how choosing them would affect continuation coverage rights. The notice must also specifically state that it does not fully describe continuation coverage or other rights under the plan and that more complete information is available in the plan's summary plan description or from the plan administrator.

The notice must inform qualified beneficiaries of the consequences of not electing continuation coverage under the plan.[19] The Department is concerned that many participants and beneficiaries will not take into account the possible effects of not electing COBRA coverage on other rights they may have to secure health care coverage (e.g., limitations on pre-existing condition exclusions, guaranteed right to purchase individual coverage without a pre-existing condition exclusion, special enrollment rights). The regulation (and model election notice, discussed below) are designed to remind participants and beneficiaries of these considerations as part of the continuation coverage election process.

If continuation coverage is offered for only a maximum of 18 months, the notice must also provide information on possible extensions of that period due to disability or second qualifying events, including detailed instructions on any notices required to be given by qualified beneficiaries.

Paragraph (b) of the regulation coordinates the running of the statutory 14-day time limit for providing an election notice with circumstances that could affect that period, such as a plan's adoption of the alternative limits permitted under section 607(5), or the special rules for multiemployer plans. Paragraph (e) further provides rules permitting a single election notice to be provided to multiple qualified beneficiaries who are part of a single family unit.

If a plan administrator receives a notice of a qualifying event pursuant to § 2590.606-3 from a participant or beneficiary not eligible to receive continuation coverage under the plan, paragraph (c) of the regulation requires the administrator to provide notice to the individual(s) explaining why he or she is not entitled to such coverage. When a participant or beneficiary submits a notice of qualifying event, there is an expectation of coverage on the part of the participant or beneficiary.

---

[15] ERISA does not mandate that qualified beneficiaries provide notices of qualifying event. A qualified beneficiary may not wish to elect continuation coverage and may therefore decide to forgo providing the notice of qualifying event without violating the COBRA provisions.

[16] Section 607(5) requires coordination of the running of the employer's period for providing notice of qualifying event with the beginning of the continuation coverage period.

[17] The regulation requires an administrator to provide an election notice only when it has been determined that a qualified beneficiary is entitled to elect continuation coverage. In this regard, the Department notes that it is the administrator's responsibility, as a fiduciary, to determine whether individuals who are named in a notice of qualifying event are entitled to continuation coverage and that disputes may arise over the correctness of the administrator's determinations. These proposed regulations are not intended to provide guidance on the substantive rights provided by the COBRA provisions, as such issues are beyond the scope of the Department's authority. The administrator, in reaching decisions

on COBRA issues, must apply the COBRA provisions as interpreted by the Treasury regulations. For example, Treasury has determined that a qualifying event does not occur when an employee begins a family or medical leave from employment under the Family and Medical Leave Act (FMLA), but may occur if the individual does not return to work at the end of the FMLA leave. 26 CFR 54.4980B-10.

[18] The notice could either provide a full description of the offered coverage (including separate options) or make specific reference to relevant portions of the plan's SPD, along with information on how to obtain the SPD.

[19] In particular, paragraph (b) requires the notice to include an explanation of the effect of electing or not electing continuation coverage on rights guaranteed under the Health Insurance Portability and Accountability Act of 1996 (HIPAA), which became Part 7 of title I of ERISA. See § 2590.606-4(b)(4)(vi). The model election notice contains specific language that would carry out this requirement.

Requiring notice in such circumstances is intended to avoid problems attendant to misunderstandings in this area. The notice is subject to the same timing requirements as those applicable to election notices.

Paragraph (d) of the regulation requires a specific notice to be provided to qualified beneficiaries in the event that the administrator terminates a period of continuation coverage before the end of its maximum duration. The COBRA provisions permit early termination of continuation coverage in a number of circumstances, such as when the employer ceases to offer group health coverage to its employees or when the required premium payment is not timely paid. In the Department's view, providing a notice of early termination serves an important administrative function and permits qualified beneficiaries to take appropriate next steps to protect their access to health coverage, either on a group or individual basis. Accordingly, the proposed regulation requires plan administrators to give specific notice of early termination of continuation coverage. Such notice must be provided as soon as administratively practicable after the termination decision is made, must explain why and when the continuation coverage is being terminated, and must describe any rights to other coverage the qualified beneficiaries will have upon termination. Nothing in these proposed regulations is intended to prevent a plan administrator from combining, for ease of administration, the furnishing of an early termination notice to a qualified beneficiary with the furnishing of the certificate of creditable coverage that must be provided to the qualified beneficiary under Part 7 of ERISA.

The appendix to this section contains a model election notice for plan administrators to use in discharging this notice obligation. The model election notice, like the model general notice, allows for inclusion of plan-specific information and provides alternatives, where appropriate, to tailor specific notices to reflect specific plan design. Among the alternatives, the model election notice includes language about the new 65% tax credit under the Trade Act that may be used if an administrator believes employees might be eligible for trade adjustment assistance. The model is intended for use only by single-employer group health plans and does not reflect the special rules that may apply to other plans, such as multiemployer plans or union-sponsored plans. Because of the complexity of the applicable rules, the model is also not intended for use when bankruptcy is the qualifying event.

Use of an appropriately completed model election notice under final regulations would be considered by the Department compliance with the content requirements of the regulation. However, the Department does not intend to require use of the model election notice and anticipates that plans could satisfy the requirements of the regulation through other types of notices. As with the proposed model general notice, the Department specifically solicits public comment on whether the model election notice adequately reflects current COBRA administrative practice and provides sufficient flexibility to be used by a majority of group health plans, as well as suggestions as to how the model could be improved.

Regulatory Impact Analysis

Summary

The Department expects these proposed regulations to benefit both plan sponsors and participants. They will dispel plan administrators' uncertainty about how to comply with COBRA notice provisions and reduce the risk of inadvertent violations. They will help participants and beneficiaries to understand how to exercise their COBRA rights thereby averting costly disputes and lost opportunities to elect COBRA coverage. This will result in an increase in the number of COBRA elections by qualified beneficiaries. These benefits of the regulation are expected to outweigh its costs.

New administrative costs imposed by these regulations are limited because plan sponsors and administrators already distribute notices pursuant to the COBRA statute, and many of their existing practices are likely to already satisfy the requirements of these proposed regulations. The Department estimates the new administrative costs to be $2.4 million in the first year that the regulations are effective and $0.9 million annually in subsequent years. The $0.9 million ongoing annual cost is attributable to the new requirements to notify qualified beneficiaries when continuation coverage is not available or has been terminated before the maximum period of coverage has ended. The additional $1.5 million first-year cost reflects the cost to plans to review existing notices and procedures, to make any necessary revisions, and to develop the new notices.

The Department also expects the number of COBRA elections to increase slightly, resulting in an increased subsidy from employers to COBRA enrollees, i.e., those qualified beneficiaries who elect continuation coverage. Employers can charge COBRA enrollees the full average cost of coverage plus an administrative charge, but those electing

continuation coverage tend to have higher than average costs and therefore as a group enjoy a subsidy from plan sponsors equal to about one-third of the cost of their coverage. If COBRA elections increase by between 0.5 percent and 1.0 percent, the amount of the subsidy will increase by a similar proportion, or between $12 million and $24 million annually. This cost to plan sponsors represents an even larger benefit to the new enrollees. Absent COBRA continuation coverage, these enrollees might purchase insurance individually, and such individual policies generally provide less coverage per dollar than the group policies continued under COBRA. Alternatively, they might go without any coverage and thereby place their finances and possibly their health at risk.

Executive Order 12866

Under Executive Order 12866, the Department must determine whether the regulatory action is "significant" and therefore subject to the requirements of the Executive Order and subject to review by the Office of Management and Budget (OMB). Under section 3(f), the order defines a "significant regulatory action" as an action that is likely to result in a rule (1) having an annual effect on the economy of $100 million or more, or adversely and materially affecting a sector of the economy, productivity, competition, jobs, the environment, public health or safety, or State, local or tribal governments or communities (also referred to as "economically significant"); (2) creating serious inconsistency or otherwise interfering with an action taken or planned by another agency; (3) materially altering the budgetary impacts of entitlement grants, user fees, or loan programs or the rights and obligations of recipients thereof; or (4) raising novel legal or policy issues arising out of legal mandates, the President's priorities, or the principles set forth in the Executive Order.

Pursuant to the terms of the Executive Order, it has been determined that this action is "significant" within the meaning of section 3(f)(4) of the Executive Order and therefore subject to review by the Office of Management and Budget (OMB). Accordingly, the Department has undertaken an assessment of the costs and benefits of this regulatory action. The analysis is summarized below.

As noted earlier in this preamble, COBRA provides that under specific circumstances participants and beneficiaries may elect to continue group health coverage temporarily following events that would otherwise result in the loss of coverage. Within its authority to issue implementing guidance concerning the notice and disclosure provisions of COBRA, the Department is proposing these regulations to address concerns raised by plan administrators, participants, and beneficiaries about the content, timing, and format of the notices required by the statute.

Costs—The Department considered economic costs and benefits in its consideration of alternatives and formulation of this proposal. The Department estimates that the regulations will increase administrative costs by $2.4 million in the first year and $0.9 million annually in subsequent years. Reflecting instances in which clear guidance will avert a lost opportunity to elect COBRA coverage, the Department also expects the number of COBRA elections to increase slightly. As a result, a portion of the cost of health care coverage will transfer from those new COBRA enrollees to plan sponsors, thereby increasing the subsidy from employers to COBRA enrollees by between 0.5 percent and 1.0 percent, or between $12 million and $24 million annually. This transfer represents a cost to plan sponsors and a benefit to COBRA enrollees. Both the administrative cost and the transfer cost will be borne by the 415,000 group health plans, covering a total of about 111 million participants and their dependents, that are currently required to offer continuation coverage.

The administrative cost of these regulations is expected to be modest, primarily because COBRA's statutory provisions have been in effect since 1986. As a result, most group health plans, plan administrators, and health insurance issuers already have developed forms and procedures for the administration of COBRA notices. The Department's estimates recognize only the cost of changes to existing practices that are likely to be associated with these rules; they exclude the pre-regulation impact of the statute itself.

Economies of scale also tend to moderate COBRA administrative costs because the majority of notice obligations are met through the purchase of COBRA administrative services from a number of providers that is small relative to the number of group health plans they serve. Nonetheless, group health plan sponsors, plan administrators, and professional service providers have stated a need for guidance, the implementation of which is expected to result in their reconsideration of their notices and procedures in light of the specific provisions of these regulations and model notices. The estimate includes the cost of professional time for the entities administering continuation coverage for all group health plans to conduct such a review. The estimate is grounded in an assumption as to the entity expected to perform the needed work (e.g., a health insurer or professional administrator); the assumption should not be interpreted to bear on any party's legal responsibility for COBRA compliance.

The Department assumes that the percentage of qualified beneficiaries who lose the opportunity to elect COBRA coverage because they receive inadequate notice is very small. A portion of the cost of health care for those qualified beneficiaries would be transferred to plan sponsors to the extent that the inadequacies would be corrected as a result of the adoption of clearer and more uniform standards in connection with this guidance. The transfer arises because surveys indicate that although qualified beneficiaries who elect COBRA coverage pay the applicable cost of coverage plus an administrative charge for continuation coverage, the average cost of continuation coverage to the sponsor is somewhat higher than the amount paid by the qualified beneficiary. This normally constitutes a subsidy of the continuation coverage by the plan sponsor. However, where qualified beneficiaries have lost the opportunity to elect the COBRA coverage to which they are entitled, they may bear the entire cost of their health care rather than the cost and administrative charge for group coverage. Averting the lost opportunity would result in a transfer of cost from the qualified beneficiary denied coverage to the plan sponsor that is equivalent to the subsidy, assuming the former participant or dependent is paying the entire cost of his or her health care.

The amount of this transfer is estimated at between $12 million and $24 million per year. In deriving this estimate, the Department observed that the number of inquiries the Department receives annually concerning COBRA, about 59,000, is equivalent to just more than 1 percent of the estimated 5 million annual COBRA qualifying events. It is likely that some but not all of these inquiries reflect notice inadequacies that these regulations would correct. The Department also noted that approximately 19 percent of qualifying events result in elections, and that the average subsidy from plan sponsors to COBRA enrollees amounts to about $2,500. If between 0.5 percent and 1.0 percent of qualifying events involve missed opportunities due to inadequate notice, and 19 percent of those events would have resulted in elections, then the regulations would increase COBRA enrollees by between 4,750 and 9,500, increasing the aggregate subsidy by between $12 million and $24 million. Expressed in unit costs, for every one percent increase in the number of participants that were wrongfully denied continuation health coverage, there is an estimated incremental increase in cost of $24 million to plan sponsors or approximately $58 per plan.

The transfer cost, together with the $2.4 million in administrative costs, is equal to only one-hundredth of 1 percent or less of total group health plan costs to companies subject to COBRA. Because the magnitude of the overall increase in costs to plans is small, the Department believes that it will not have a consequential effect on the availability of health coverage for employees, but welcomes comment on these assumptions.

Benefits—The benefits of these proposed rules will arise from improved administrative efficiency, reduced exposure to risk, and from the potential avoidance of some unnecessary losses of group health plan coverage by otherwise qualified beneficiaries.

Inconsistent procedures, and notices that are not fully compliant as to content, timing, and form are known to generate questions, delays, disputes, and duplications of effort that require the expenditure of additional resources by both plan administrators and participants and beneficiaries to resolve. Although the magnitude of the costs and potential savings associated with administrative inefficiencies is unknown, clearer and more uniform standards should serve to avoid the otherwise unnecessary expense associated with rectifying procedural and substantive notice inadequacies.

Providing greater certainty to plan sponsors and plan administrators as to how their notice obligations can be met should also limit risks to both plans and qualified beneficiaries. Plan sponsors and plan administrators who comply with this guidance should be less likely to be subjected to costly disputes, litigation, or penalties as a result of their compliance with this guidance. Improvements in the consistency and quality of information provided to participants and dependents is expected to help them understand their rights and limit their risk of losing the opportunity to elect COBRA coverage.

The benefits of improved efficiency and reduced risk cannot be specifically quantified. The beneficial impact of preventing lost opportunities to elect continuation coverage can be estimated, however. The benefit to enrollees will exceed the financial value of the transfer insofar as the enrollees will gain access to high-value group coverage,

rather than a choice between buying generally lower-value individual insurance or going without coverage altogether. Qualified beneficiaries who lose group health plan coverage due to inadequate notice may be faced with a choice between purchasing individual coverage at a rate significantly higher than a plan's group rate or going without coverage for a period of time. The uninsured bear the risk of catastrophic losses. They are also known to seek preventive care less frequently and to delay or forgo treatment, which may lead to less favorable health outcomes and higher social costs for acute care at a later time. Interruptions in group health plan coverage can ultimately limit the portability of group coverage, as well. A reduction of the numbers of losses of coverage that result from notification failures will also result in efficiency gains to the extent that the qualified beneficiaries elect group health plan coverage rather than individual coverage. Individual coverage is more costly and less efficient due in large part to significantly higher costs of individual policy administration.

Alternatives—The Department gave thorough consideration to the need for guidance on the COBRA notice provisions and to the alternative forms that guidance might take. Being aware that most plan administrators and service providers make use of established forms and procedures, the Department did not wish to impose the costs likely to arise from reviews and changes to forms and procedures likely to result from the issuance of guidance unless it was actually valuable to plan administrators and qualified beneficiaries. Public comments received in response to the 1997 RFI, and information received from a range of interested parties by the Department in the conduct of its compliance assistance, outreach, and enforcement activities, however, persuaded the Department that guidance would be beneficial.

The Department also considered whether an informational booklet or question and answer publication rather than regulatory guidance would serve to provide the needed general information and address administrative complexities. Ultimately, the Department determined that while such publications might be helpful, they would not provide plan administrators with the certainty to meet their stated needs. Similarly, in its deliberations concerning the inclusion of model notices, the Department concluded that promulgation of models would encourage improved uniformity and information quality while providing greater certainty to plan administrators that their notices and procedures conform to the requirements of the statute. Because use of the models is voluntary, it is considered to provide this greater certainty without unnecessarily restricting plan administrators' continued use of existing notices and procedures that are appropriate as to content and timing.

Because the direct costs of this proposal arise from disclosure provisions, additional details concerning the data and assumptions used in developing these estimates may be found in the Paperwork Reduction Act section of this preamble. As required, the paperwork burden estimates include an analysis of the cost of the statutory provisions underlying these proposed regulations.

Paperwork Reduction Act

As part of its continuing effort to reduce paperwork and respondent burden, the Department of Labor conducts a preclearance consultation program to provide the general public and federal agencies with an opportunity to comment on proposed and continuing collections of information in accordance with the Paperwork Reduction Act of 1995 (PRA 95) (44 U.S.C. 3506(c)(2)(A)). This helps to ensure that requested data can be provided in the desired format, reporting burden (time and financial resources) is minimized, collection instruments are clearly understood, and the impact of collection requirements on respondents can be properly assessed.

Currently, EBSA is soliciting comments concerning the proposed information collection request (ICR) included in this Notice of Proposed Rulemaking with respect to the Health Care Continuation Coverage Provisions of Part 6 of title I of ERISA. A copy of the ICR may be obtained by contacting the PRA addressee shown below.

The Department has submitted a copy of the proposed information collection to OMB in accordance with 44 U.S.C. 3507(d) for review of its information collections. The Department and OMB are particularly interested in comments that:

- Evaluate whether the proposed collection of information is necessary for the proper performance of the functions of the agency, including whether the information will have practical utility;

- Evaluate the accuracy of the agency's estimate of the burden of the collection of information, including the validity of the methodology and assumptions used;

- Enhance the quality, utility, and clarity of the information to be collected; and

- Minimize the burden of the collection of information on those who are to respond, including through the use of appropriate automated, electronic, mechanical, or other technological collection techniques or other forms of information technology, e.g., permitting electronic submission of responses.

Comments should be sent to the Office of Information and Regulatory Affairs, Office of Management and Budget, Room 10235, New Executive Office Building, Washington, DC 20503; Attention: Desk Officer for the Employee Benefits Security Administration. Although comments may be submitted through July 28, 2003, OMB requests that comments be received within 30 days of publication of the Notice of Proposed Rulemaking to ensure their consideration.

PRA Addressee: Address requests for copies of the ICR to Joseph S. Piacentini, Office of Policy and Research, U.S. Department of Labor, Employee Benefits Security Administration, 200 Constitution Avenue, NW., Room N-5718, Washington, DC 20210. Telephone (202) 693-8410; Fax: (202) 219-5333. These are not toll-free numbers.

The Department is issuing these proposed rules to set minimum standards for the timing and content of the notices required under the continuation coverage provisions of Part 6 of title I of ERISA, and to establish uniform standards for administering the notice process. In very general terms, the statute requires that qualified beneficiaries be offered the opportunity to elect to continue group health coverage after losses of coverage due to death of the employee, termination of employment or reduction of hours, divorce or legal separation of the covered employee from the employee's spouse, the covered employee's becoming entitled to Medicare, or bankruptcy of an employer that affects covered retirees. Qualified beneficiaries may include employees, the spouse of a covered employee and dependent children of the covered employee. Coverage can extend for 18 or 36 months, depending on the nature of the qualifying event. The plan administrator must notify COBRA participants when their coverage is terminated earlier than its maximum duration. Additional distributions of notices may be required when a COBRA enrollee experiences a second qualifying event.

Each of the sections of the proposed regulations includes an information collection request. The specific regulatory requirements of each section are described in detail earlier in this preamble. The information collection provisions are identified and very briefly described below. The actual provisions of the proposed regulation rather than this summary should be referred to for COBRA compliance purposes.

§ 2590.6061—*General Notice*. This section describes the plan administrator's obligation to provide a general notice of COBRA rights to participants and their spouses who newly become covered under a group health plan. These general notices may be included in the Summary Plan Description. A model general notice has been drafted to assist plan administrators with compliance and reduce compliance burden.

§ 2590.6062—*Employer's notice of qualifying event*. These notices are required to be provided by employers to plan administrators whenever a qualifying event occurs that is an employee's termination of employment or reduction of hours, death, or enrollment in Medicare.

§ 2590.6063—*Qualified beneficiary's notices*. Qualified beneficiaries are responsible for notifying the plan administrator of a qualifying event that is the divorce or legal separation of the employee and spouse, or a dependent's becoming no longer eligible for coverage as a dependent under the plan.

§ 2590.6064—*Plan administrator's notice obligations*. Plan administrators are required to notify each qualified beneficiary who is entitled to elect continuation coverage of his or her rights under COBRA. Paragraph (d) requires specific notice to be provided to qualified beneficiaries in the event that the administrator terminates continuation coverage prior to the end of its maximum duration. A single notice may be sent to multiple qualifying beneficiaries known to reside at a single address, although they each have separate COBRA election rights. A model election notice has been drafted to assist with compliance and reduce compliance burden.

In order to estimate the burden of compliance with the statute and these proposed rules, the Department used data from several sources and made a number of assumptions. It should be noted that this Paperwork Reduction Act analysis includes the cost of the statute as well as the cost of the discretion exercised in this rulemaking. These costs were developed in the manner described below.

In order to develop estimates of the cost of the review, revision, development, and distribution of COBRA notices, it was first necessary to determine the numbers of participants and dependents in plans that are required to offer COBRA coverage (generally plans with 20 or more participants), the numbers of dependents who reside at addresses that are different from other related participants, and the rates of the occurrence of the qualifying events that give rise to notice obligations. The participants and dependents identified in available data sets represent the group of qualified beneficiaries who will have qualifying events. Estimates of the number of entities such as group health insurance issuers and professional administrators that would review their COBRA notices, the number that would consequently revise their COBRA notices, and the time required to do so for each type of notice was also required.

The Department developed its estimates of 55,778,300 employees and 55,002,439 dependents, 67,000 of whom reside at different addresses, and 2,461,000 COBRA enrollees from the February and March 2001 Current Population Survey (CPS; Census Bureau household surveys), the 2000 Medical Expenditure Panel Survey, Household and Insurance Components (MEPS; joint Census Bureau and Agency for Healthcare Policy and Research surveys of households and private establishments), and the 1996 Panel of the Survey of Income and Program Participation (SIPP; a Census Bureau longitudinal household survey). Frequency rates for qualifying events were also developed from MEPS and SIPP.

An estimate of the number of plans covering these employees and dependents was also needed. About 50,000 group health plans file the Form 5500—Annual Return/Report of Employee Benefit Plan. These are generally plans with 100 or more participants that are defined for purposes of regulatory analyses as large plans. Because the majority of small group health plans are not required to file Form 5500, the number of such plans must be estimated from other data sources. CPS and MEPS data can be used to derive an estimate of the number of establishments that offer group health coverage by size of establishment. The establishments with fewer than 20 employees can be excluded based on establishment size variables. While the count of establishments with 20 to 99 employees that do offer coverage will vary to some degree from a count of plans because some plans include multiple establishments, it is considered to offer a reasonable proxy for the number of small plans and the distribution of participants and dependents between large and small plans. Using this approach, it can be assumed that these proposed rules would affect a total of about 415,000 plans, 50,000 of which are large, and 365,000 of which are small. The number of participants in large plans is estimated at 43.5 million. The number of participants in small plans is estimated to be 12.3 million.

The Department has assumed that all administrators for these plans will review their existing forms and procedures in response to promulgation of this guidance, and that some of those plan administrators will additionally need to revise their notices and procedures. The Department is aware that, for a large majority of plans, administration of COBRA general notices and election notices is performed by service providers rather than the plans themselves. In order to derive an estimate of the number of entities that will review forms and procedures, the Department looked at the number of health insurers offering group products and the number of professional administrators providing services to group health plans. This results in an estimate of about 3,000 entities that perform COBRA administration for the majority of all plans. All of these entities are expected to review all of their notices and procedures in response to regulatory guidance.

These reviews are assumed to require 2 hours each for the general notice and election notice requirements, and 1 hour each for the employer notice requirements, the employee notice requirements, and for development of a new notice of early termination of COBRA coverage. Employer and employee notices may need to be developed. These 3,000 reviews are expected to be conducted by professionals at the level of financial managers at a cost of $68 per hour.[20] No cost has been included for the new notice of unavailability of continuation coverage because there is currently no basis for determining the number of these notices that might be sent. The Department has assumed, however, that due to the clear and consistent information provided in the general notice, plan administrators will distribute a limited number of these notices annually, and that the associated cost would be very small.

---

[20] Wage rates are based on National Occupational Employment and Wage Estimates from the Occupational Employment of the Bureau of Labor Statistics for 2000, adjusted for compensation rate growth, additional compensation costs, and overhead.

In order to estimate the number of service providers that would be required to revise their existing notices, the Department examined its data pertaining to the nature of telephone inquiries it receives. These data show that about 59,000 inquiries pertaining to COBRA are received each year. Although the portion of these inquiries that pertain to notice provisions is unknown, as is the number of COBRA notification issues that do not give rise to contact with the Department, this number provides the only available proxy for a rate of notice-related difficulties. Given the roughly 5 million COBRA election notices provided each year, the rate of notice inadequacies is assumed to be about 1%. The actual rate might range from .5% to 1% because inquiries do pertain to issues other than notices, but 1% has been used for purposes of these estimates.

For the purpose of determining the number of service providers involved in preparing and distributing the 1% of COBRA notices that may require revision, the Department took into consideration the fact that service providers are known to use standardized forms, and that a small number of service providers are known to provide COBRA administration to a very large number of plans. Reasoning that the rate of notice inadequacies would be higher if the providers serving the majority of plans made use of notices and procedures that were not adequate as to content and timing, the Department assumed that more than 1% of the providers to the remaining fewer plans would be required to revise notices and procedures. Although the actual number is not known, the Department has assumed that 3%, or 90, service providers will need to make revisions. Modification is assumed to require an additional two hours at $68 for each notice in use.

The start-up costs that arise from this proposal pertain to the review and revision of existing forms and procedures and the development of the new early termination notices. The cost of distribution of the termination notices will be an ongoing operating cost.

Ongoing operating costs arise from completing the forms upon the occurrence of each event that gives rise to a notice obligation with information specific to the dates, plan, employee, spouse, or dependent children, and from distributing the completed forms. No completion or distribution cost is attributed to the general notice, except where dependents reside at separate addresses, as the required information is expected to be included in the Summary Plan Description. No burden is included for completing the employer's notices because they involve adding information that the employer has at hand in its customary personnel practices. Similarly, no completion burden is calculated for the qualified beneficiaries' notices because this information is limited, readily accessible, and would be provided as a usual practice by only the qualified beneficiary who wished to continue coverage. Otherwise, the cost of completion of notices is expected to be incurred at a rate of $34 per hour for 5 minutes for election notices and 1 minute for termination notices.

Postage and materials for distribution are estimated at $0.38 per notice. No assumption has been made as to the number of these notices that will be distributed electronically. Plan administrators are not precluded from using electronic disclosure methods that comply with regulations at 29 CFR.104b-1(b) and (c). However, the Department believes that due to the nature of the rights and obligations involved in COBRA notice requirements, most plan administrators tend not to choose electronic distribution methods for COBRA notices. The Department requests comments on the use of electronic technology in COBRA notice administration. The application of these assumptions results in estimates of the distribution of 2,809,000 employer notices, 651,000 employee notices, 4,699,000 plan administrator election notices, and 1,000,000 early termination notices each year.

The preparation and distribution of these notices is accounted for as cost rather than hours because most COBRA administration is accomplished through the purchase of services for which fees are paid. The Department welcomes comments on its assumptions and methodology for arriving at these estimates. The number of notices of unavailability of continuation coverage cannot be reasonably estimated.

Type of Review: New collection.

Agency: Employee Benefits Security Administration, Department of Labor.

Title: Notice Requirements of the Health Care Continuation Coverage Provisions.

OMB Number: 1210-0NEW.

Affected Public: Individuals or households; business or other for-profit; not-for-profit institutions.

Respondents: 415,000.

Frequency of Response: On occasion.

Responses: 9,159,000.

Estimated Total Burden Hours: None.

Total Annualized Capital/Startup Costs: $1,452,500.

Total Burden Cost (Operating and Maintenance): $17,386,200.

Total Annualized Cost: $18,838,700.

Regulatory Flexibility Act

The Regulatory Flexibility Act (5 U.S.C. 601 et seq.) (RFA) imposes certain requirements with respect to Federal rules that are subject to the notice and comment requirements of section 553(b) of the Administrative Procedure Act (5 U.S.C. 551 et seq.) and that are likely to have a significant economic impact on a substantial number of small entities. Unless an agency certifies that a proposed rule will not have a significant economic impact on a substantial number of small entities, section 603 of the RFA requires that the agency present an initial regulatory flexibility analysis at the time of the publication of the notice of proposed rulemaking describing the impact of the rule on small entities and seeking public comment on such impact. Small entities include small businesses, organizations and governmental jurisdictions.

For purposes of analysis under the RFA, EBSA proposes to continue to consider a small entity to be an employee benefit plan with fewer than 100 participants. The basis of this definition is found in section 104(a)(2) of the Act which permits the Secretary to prescribe simplified annual reports for pension plans, which cover fewer than 100 participants. Under section 104(a)(3), the Secretary may also provide for exemptions or simplified annual reporting and disclosure requirements for welfare benefit plans. Pursuant to the authority of section 104(a)(3), the Department has previously issued at 29 CFR 2520.104-20, 2520.104-21, 2520.104-41, 2520.104-46 and 2520.104b-10 certain simplified reporting provisions and limited exemptions from reporting and disclosure requirements for small plans, including unfunded or insured welfare plans covering fewer than 100 participants that satisfy certain other requirements.

Further, while some large employers may have small plans, in general most small plans are maintained by small employers. Thus, EBSA believes that assessing the impact of this proposed rule on small plans is an appropriate substitute for evaluating the effect on small entities. The definition of small entity considered appropriate for this purpose differs, however, from a definition of small business which is based on size standards promulgated by the Small Business Administration (SBA) (13 CFR 121.201) pursuant to the Small Business Act (15 U.S.C. 631 et seq.). EBSA therefore requests comments on the appropriateness of the size standard used in evaluating the impact of this proposed rule on small entities. On this basis, EBSA has determined that the proposed regulation will not have a significant impact on a substantial number of small entities. In support of this conclusion, the Department has conducted an initial regulatory flexibility analysis, which is summarized below.

EBSA is proposing the regulation to provide plans and qualified beneficiaries with greater certainty as to how the notice obligations of COBRA can be met. The Department is considering this action because inquiries to the Department as well as public comment in response to the 1997 RFI indicated that service providers and plan administrators would welcome guidance that would provide greater administrative efficiency and reduce exposure to risk resulting from procedural or substantive failures to meet notification requirements. At the same time, improvements in the quality of information provided to participants and beneficiaries is expected to help them understand their rights and limit their risk of losing the opportunity to elect the COBRA coverage that is required to be offered.

The COBRA provisions of title I of ERISA require a group health plan to offer qualified beneficiaries the opportunity to elect continuation coverage when they would otherwise lose group health coverage as a result of certain events described in the statute as "qualifying events." Under section 608, the Secretary has the authority to carry out the provisions of Part 6 of title I of ERISA. Further, the Conference Report that accompanied COBRA provided that the Secretary has the authority to issue regulations implementing the notice and disclosure provisions of section 606 of ERISA. The Department's objective in issuing the proposed regulations is to provide guidelines that will assure plan administrators that they are in compliance with the notification provisions of COBRA and that participants and beneficiaries have sufficient information to exercise their COBRA rights. Small plans will benefit from clarifications about the content and timing of notices and from the likelihood that fewer determinations about COBRA coverage will be delayed, disputed, or appealed. In addition, an increased number of qualified beneficiaries in small health plans will be able to obtain group health plan continuation coverage.

The Department believes that, because of the expertise required, small plans will use service providers to review notices and to modify or adapt Department models for use by the plan administrator. Generally, COBRA service providers offer plans on-going administrative services such as notifying employees about their group health plan continuation coverage, distributing and processing election forms, collecting and applying premium payments, and monitoring COBRA compliance. Small plans, in particular, are less likely to have in-house capabilities to handle these administrative tasks. For a service provider, reviewing and adopting or modifying forms for plans will result in some direct cost. Service providers may choose to absorb some of the cost in order to maintain competitive products; others may charge the cost to their client plans. Where these costs are charged to plans, the cost will most likely be minimized because of the economies of scale inherent in the use of standardized forms and procedures. At the same time, costs to small plans are further reduced because of the large number of small plans that share the cost burden; there are approximately seven times as many small plans as large plans. Finally, to further reduce costs, the Department has provided two model notices that can be adapted by service providers for use by individual plans.

The cost estimates for small plan compliance recognize only the cost of changes to existing practices associated with the proposed regulation; they exclude the impact of the statute itself. Costs result first from the likelihood that service providers will develop or modify two notices currently required to be sent to a plan administrator, and the requirement to develop and implement the new early termination notice described in the proposed regulation. No cost is attributable to the new notice of unavailability of continuation coverage. Finally, small plans will incur transfer costs as a result of an increase in the number of elections of continuation coverage by qualified beneficiaries who would have lost the opportunity to elect COBRA coverage absent improved notices and procedures.

The Department estimates that there are approximately 2.5 million plans with fewer than 100 participants that are considered small group health plans under the Department's definition. Among these, COBRA applies to only those plans with 20 or more employees or 365,000 plans, with approximately 12.3 million participants. While the majority of group health plans subject to COBRA are small plans, participation in those plans represents only about 22% of participation in all plans covered by COBRA. Based on the analysis below, the cost to small group health plans to review and adapt or modify existing notices is estimated at $275,900. The cost to develop the new early notice of termination is estimated at $254,300. The total cost to small plans for a service provider's assistance in reviewing, modifying, or developing notices is estimated to be $530,200, or $1.45 per small plan. The comparable average cost to large plans is $37.38 per plan.

Employers with small plans will also incur transfer costs as a result of increased numbers of qualified beneficiaries who will elect continuation coverage. A portion of the cost of health care coverage previously borne by individuals will be transferred from those new COBRA enrollees to plan sponsors under the proposed regulations. For small plans, the per-plan transfer costs are considerably less than for large plans due to there being fewer participants. The potential transfer cost to small plans is estimated to range between $2.6 million and $5.2 million, depending on the number of qualified beneficiaries who will elect COBRA coverage. The rate of potential losses of opportunity to elect COBRA coverage is estimated to fall between .5% and 1%. This represents an average of $7-$14 per small plan. The comparable cost to large plans ranges from $9.4 million to $18.7 million, an average of $185-$370 per plan. At the upper bound, the cost of the proposed regulation for 365,000 small plans is estimated to be $5.7 million, or $15.45 per plan.

Although the basis for the proposed regulation lies in the notice and disclosure provisions of section 606 of title I of ERISA, the proposed regulation does not duplicate, overlap, or conflict with other relevant federal rules. COBRA notification provisions have been in effect for many years. As such, most plan administrators and service providers have developed procedures to comply with their statutory obligations. The proposed regulation merely seeks to provide additional, detailed guidance that will clarify a plan's administrative obligations while assuring plan administrators and service providers that, in complying with the proposed regulation, they have satisfied their statutory obligations. A discussion of alternatives to the proposed regulation that the Department considered appears above in the discussion under Executive Order 12866.

The Department has attempted to minimize the burden of the review and potential revision of existing notices that will be undertaken in response to this guidance by including model notices that can be adapted to plans' specific circumstances. This should lessen the use of resources for small and large plans alike.

Unfunded Mandates Reform Act

For purposes of the Unfunded Mandates Reform Act of 1995 (Pub. L. 104-4), as well as Executive Order 12875, this proposed rule does not include any federal mandate that may result in expenditures by state, local, or tribal governments in the aggregate of more than $100 million, or increased expenditures by the private sector of more than $100 million.

Small Business Regulatory Enforcement Fairness Act

The rule being issued here is subject to the Congressional Review Act provisions of the Small Business Regulatory Enforcement Fairness Act of 1996 (5 U.S.C. 801 et seq.) and, if finalized, will be transmitted to Congress and the Comptroller General for review. The rule is not a "major rule" as that term is defined in 5 U.S.C. 804, because it is not likely to result in (1) an annual effect on the economy of $100 million or more; (2) a major increase in costs or prices for consumers, individual industries, or federal, state, or local government agencies, or geographic regions; or (3) significant adverse effects on competition, employment, investment, productivity, innovation, or on the ability of United States-based enterprises to compete with foreign-based enterprises in domestic or export markets.

Federalism Statement

Executive Order 13132 (August 4, 1999) outlines fundamental principles of federalism and requires the adherence to specific criteria by federal agencies in the process of their formulation and implementation of policies that have substantial direct effects on the States, the relationship between the national government and the States, or on the distribution of power and responsibilities among the various levels of government. This proposed rule would not have federalism implications because it has no substantial direct effect on the States, on the relationship between the national government and the States, or on the distribution of power and responsibilities among the various levels of government. Section 514 of ERISA provides, with certain exceptions specifically enumerated, that the provisions of Titles I and IV of ERISA supersede any and all laws of the States as they relate to any employee benefit plan covered under ERISA. The requirements implemented in this proposed rule do not alter the fundamental provisions of the statute with respect to employee benefit plans, and as such would have no implications for the States or the relationship or distribution of power between the national government and the States.

List of Subjects in 29 CFR Part 2590

Employee benefit plans, Health care, Health insurance, Pensions, Reporting and recordkeeping requirements.

For the reasons set forth in the preamble, the Department proposes to amend Subchapter L, Part 2590 of Title 29 of the Code of Federal Regulations as follows:

Subchapter L—Group Health Plans

PART 2590—RULES AND REGULATIONS FOR GROUP HEALTH PLANS

1. The heading of subchapter L is revised to read as shown above.

2. The heading of part 2590 is revised to read as shown above.

3. The authority citation for part 2590 is revised to read as follows:

Authority: 29 U.S.C. 1027, 1059, 1135, 1161-1168, 1169, 1181-1183, 1185, 1185a, 1185b, 1191, 1191a, 1191b, and 1191c; sec. 401(b), Pub. L. 105-00, 112 Stat. 645; and Secretary of Labor's Order No. 1-2003, 68 FR 5374 (Feb. 3, 2003).

4. The following new sections are added to subpart A of part 2590:

Subpart A—Continuation Coverage, Qualified Medical Child Support Orders, Coverage for Adopted Children

§

2590.606-1 General notice of continuation coverage.

Appendix to § 2590.606-1.

2590.606-2 Notice requirement for employers.

2590.606-3 Notice requirements for covered employees and qualified beneficiaries.

2590.606-4 Notice requirements for plan administrators. Appendix to § 2590.606-4.

§ 2590.606-1. General notice of continuation coverage.

(a) *General.* Pursuant to section 606(a)(1) of the Employee Retirement Income Security Act of 1974, as amended (the Act), the administrator of a group health plan subject to the continuation coverage requirements of Part 6 of title I of the Act shall provide, in accordance with this section, written notice to each covered employee and spouse of the covered employee (if any) of the right to continuation coverage provided under the plan.

(b) *Timing of notice.* The notice required by paragraph (a) of this section shall be furnished to each employee and each employee's spouse, not later than the earlier of:

(1) The date that is 90 days after the date on which such individual's coverage under the plan commences, or, if later, the date that is 90 days after the date on which the plan first becomes subject to the continuation coverage requirements; or

(2) The first date after commencement of coverage of either the covered employee or the spouse on which the administrator is required, pursuant to § 2590.606-4(b), to furnish the covered employee, spouse, or dependent child of such employee notice of a qualified beneficiary's right to elect continuation coverage.

(c) *Content of notice.* The notice required by paragraph (a) of this section shall be written in a manner calculated to be understood by the average plan participant and shall contain the following information:

(1) The name of the plan under which continuation coverage is available, and the name, address and telephone number of the party responsible under the plan for the administration of continuation coverage benefits;

(2) A general description of the continuation coverage under the plan, including identification of the classes of individuals who may become qualified beneficiaries, the types of qualifying events that may give rise to the right to continuation coverage, the obligation of the employer to notify the plan administrator of the occurrence of certain qualifying events, the maximum period for which continuation coverage may be available, when and under what circumstances continuation coverage may be extended beyond the applicable maximum period, and the plan's requirements applicable to the payment of premiums for continuation coverage;

(3) An explanation of the plan's requirements regarding the responsibility of a qualified beneficiary to notify the administrator of a qualifying event that is a divorce, legal separation, or a child's ceasing to be a dependent under the terms of the plan, and a description of the plan's procedures for providing such notice;

(4) An explanation of the plan's requirements regarding the responsibility of qualified beneficiaries who are receiving continuation coverage to provide notice to the administrator of a second qualifying event (such as divorce or legal separation, death of covered employee, covered employee's becoming enrolled in Medicare, and child's loss of dependent child status) or a determination by the Social Security Administration, under title II or XVI of the Social Security Act (42 U.S.C. 401 et seq. or 1381 et seq.),

that a qualified beneficiary is disabled, and a description of the plan's procedures for providing such notices;

(5) An explanation of the importance of keeping the administrator informed of the current addresses of all participants or beneficiaries under the plan who are or may become qualified beneficiaries; and

(6) A statement that the notice does not fully describe continuation coverage or other rights under the plan and that more complete information regarding such rights is available from the plan administrator and in the plan's summary plan description.

(d) *Single notice rule.* A plan administrator may satisfy the requirement to provide notice in accordance with this section to a covered employee and the covered employee's spouse by furnishing a single notice addressed to both the covered employee and the covered employee's spouse, if, on the basis of the most recent information available to the plan, the covered employee's spouse resides at the same location as the covered employee. The prior sentence shall not apply if a spouse's coverage under the plan commences after the date on which the covered employee's coverage commences, unless the spouse's coverage commences before the date on which the notice required by this section is required to be provided to the covered employee.

(e) *Notice in summary plan description.* A plan administrator may satisfy the requirement to provide notice in accordance with this section by including the information described in paragraphs (c)(1), (2), (3), (4), and (5) of this section in a summary plan description meeting the requirements of § 2520.102-3 of this title furnished in accordance with paragraph (b) of this section.

(f) *Delivery of notice.* The notice required by this section shall be furnished in a manner consistent with the requirements of § 2520.104b-1 of this title, including paragraph (c) of that section relating to the use of electronic media.

(g) *Model notice.* The appendix to this section contains a model notice that is intended to assist administrators in discharging the notice obligations of this section. Use of the model notice is not mandatory. The model reflects the requirements of this section as they would apply to single-employer group health plans and must be modified if used to provide notice with respect to other types of group health plans, such as multiemployer plans or plans established and maintained by employee organizations for their members. In order to use the model notice, administrators must appropriately add relevant information where indicated in the model notice, select among alternative language, and supplement the model notice to reflect applicable plan provisions. Items of information that are not applicable to a particular plan may be deleted. Use of the model notice, appropriately modified and supplemented, will be deemed to satisfy the notice content requirements of paragraph (c) of this section.

APPENDIX TO § 2590.606-1
MODEL GENERAL NOTICE OF COBRA CONTINUATION COVERAGE RIGHTS
(For use by single-employer group health plans)

** CONTINUATION COVERAGE RIGHTS UNDER COBRA**

Introduction

You are receiving this notice because you have recently become covered under [*enter name of group health plan*] (the Plan). This notice contains important information about your right to COBRA continuation coverage, which is a temporary extension of coverage under the Plan. The right to COBRA continuation coverage was created by a federal law, the Consolidated Omnibus Budget Reconciliation Act of 1985 (COBRA). COBRA continuation coverage can become available to you and to other members of your family who are covered under the Plan when you would otherwise lose your group health coverage. **This notice generally explains COBRA continuation coverage, when it may become available to you and your family, and what you need to do to protect the right to receive it.** This notice gives only a summary of your COBRA continuation coverage rights. For more information about your rights and obligations under the Plan and under federal law, you should either review the Plan's Summary Plan Description *or* get a copy of the Plan Document from the Plan Administrator.

The Plan Administrator is [*enter name, address and telephone number of Plan Administrator*]. [*If the Plan Administrator administers COBRA continuation coverage, add the following:* The Plan Administrator is responsible for administering COBRA continuation coverage.] [*If the Plan Administrator does not administer COBRA continuation coverage, add the following:* COBRA continuation coverage for the Plan is administered by [*enter name, address and telephone number of party responsible for administering COBRA continuation coverage*].

COBRA Continuation Coverage

COBRA continuation coverage is a continuation of Plan coverage when coverage would otherwise end because of a life event known as a "qualifying event." Specific qualifying events are listed later in this notice. COBRA continuation coverage must be offered to each person who is a "qualified beneficiary." A qualified beneficiary is someone who will lose coverage under the Plan because of a qualifying event. Depending on the type of qualifying event, employees, spouses of employees, and dependent children of employees may be qualified beneficiaries. Under the Plan, qualified beneficiaries who elect COBRA continuation coverage [*choose and enter appropriate information:* must pay *or* are not required to pay] for COBRA continuation coverage.

If you are an employee, you will become a qualified beneficiary if you will lose your coverage under the Plan because either one of the following qualifying events happens:

(1) Your hours of employment are reduced, or

(2) Your employment ends for any reason other than your gross misconduct.

If you are the spouse of an employee, you will become a qualified beneficiary if you will lose your coverage under the Plan because any of the following qualifying events happens:

    (1) Your spouse dies;

    (2) Your spouse's hours of employment are reduced;

    (3) Your spouse's employment ends for any reason other than his or her gross misconduct;

    (4) Your spouse becomes enrolled in Medicare (Part A, Part B, or both); or

    (5) You become divorced or legally separated from your spouse.

Your dependent children will become qualified beneficiaries if they will lose coverage under the Plan because any of the following qualifying events happens:

    (1) The parent-employee dies;

    (2) The parent-employee's hours of employment are reduced;

    (3) The parent-employee's employment ends for any reason other than his or her gross misconduct;

    (4) The parent-employee becomes enrolled in Medicare (Part A, Part B, or both);

    (5) The parents become divorced or legally separated; or

    (6) The child stops being eligible for coverage under the plan as a "dependent child."

[If the Plan provides retiree health coverage, add the following paragraph:]

Sometimes, filing a proceeding in bankruptcy under title 11 of the United States Code can be a qualifying event. If a proceeding in bankruptcy is filed with respect to [*enter name of employer sponsoring the plan*], and that bankruptcy results in the loss of coverage of any retired employee covered under the Plan, the retired employee is a qualified beneficiary with respect to the bankruptcy. The retired employee's spouse, surviving spouse, and dependent children will also be qualified beneficiaries if bankruptcy results in the loss of their coverage under the Plan.

The Plan will offer COBRA continuation coverage to qualified beneficiaries only after the Plan Administrator has been notified that a qualifying event has occurred. When the qualifying event is the end of employment or reduction of hours of employment, death of the employee, [*add if Plan provides retiree health coverage:* commencement of a proceeding in bankruptcy with respect to the employer,] or enrollment of the employee in Medicare (Part A, Part B, or both), the employer must notify the Plan Administrator of the qualifying event [*choose and enter option applicable to this Plan: (1)* within 30 days of any of these events *or (2)* within 30 days following the date coverage ends.]

For the other qualifying events (divorce or legal separation of the employee and spouse or a dependent child's losing eligibility for coverage as a dependent child), you must notify the Plan Administrator. The Plan requires you to notify the Plan Administrator within 60 days [or enter longer period permitted under the terms of the Plan] after the qualifying event occurs. You must send this notice to: [*Enter name of appropriate party*]. [*Add description of any additional Plan procedures for this notice, including a description of any required information or documentation*.]

Once the Plan Administrator receives notice that a qualifying event has occurred, COBRA continuation coverage will be offered to each of the qualified beneficiaries. For each qualified beneficiary who elects COBRA continuation coverage, COBRA continuation coverage will begin [*Enter the option applicable to this Plan: (1)* on the date of the qualifying event *or (2)* on the date that Plan coverage would otherwise have been lost].

COBRA continuation coverage is a temporary continuation of coverage. When the qualifying event is the death of the employee, enrollment of the employee in Medicare (Part A, Part B, or both), your divorce or legal separation, or a dependent child losing eligibility as a dependent child, COBRA continuation coverage lasts for up to 36 months.

When the qualifying event is the end of employment or reduction of the employee's hours of employment, COBRA continuation coverage lasts for up to18 months. There are two ways in which this 18-month period of COBRA continuation coverage can be extended.

Disability extension of 18-month period of continuation coverage

If you or anyone in your family covered under the Plan is determined by the Social Security Administration to be disabled at any time during the first 60 days of COBRA continuation coverage and you notify the Plan Administrator in a timely fashion, you and your entire family can receive up to an additional 11 months of COBRA continuation coverage, for a total maximum of 29 months. [*insert and modify to reflect actual plan provisions on this notice:* You must make sure that the Plan Administrator is notified of the Social Security Administration's determination within 60 days of the date of the determination and before the end of the 18-month period of COBRA continuation coverage.] This notice should be sent to: [*Enter name of appropriate party*]. [*Add description of any additional Plan procedures for this notice, including a description of any required information or documentation*.]

Second qualifying event extension of 18-month period of continuation coverage

If your family experiences another qualifying event while receiving COBRA continuation coverage, the spouse and dependent children in your family can get additional months of COBRA continuation coverage, up to a maximum of 36 months. This extension is available to the spouse and dependent children if the former employee dies, enrolls in Medicare (Part A, Part B, or both), or gets divorced or legally separated. The extension is also available to a dependent child when that child stops being eligible under the Plan as a dependent child. **In all of these** cases, you must make sure that the Plan Administrator is notified of the second qualifying event within 60 days of the second qualifying event [or *enter longer period if permitted under the terms of the Plan*]. This notice must be sent to: [*Enter name of appropriate party*]. [*Add description of any additional Plan procedures for this notice, including a description of any required information or documentation.*]

If You Have Questions

If you have questions about your COBRA continuation coverage, you should contact [*enter name of appropriate party*] or you may contact the nearest Regional or District Office of the U.S. Department of Labor's Employee Benefits Security Administration (EBSA). Addresses and phone numbers of Regional and District EBSA Offices are available through EBSA's website at **www.dol.gov/ebsa**.

Keep Your Plan Informed of Address Changes

In order to protect your family's rights, you should keep the Plan Administrator informed of any changes in the addresses of family members. You should also keep a copy, for your records, of any notices you send to the Plan Administrator.

§ 2590.606-2. Notice requirement for employers.

(a) *General.* Pursuant to section 606(a)(2) of the Employee Retirement Income Security Act of 1974, as amended (the Act), except as otherwise provided in this section, the employer of a covered employee under a group health plan subject to the continuation coverage requirements of Part 6 of title I of the Act shall provide, in accordance with this section, notice to the administrator of the plan of the occurrence of a qualifying event that is the covered employee's death, termination of employment (other than by reason of gross misconduct), reduction in hours of employment, Medicare entitlement, or a proceeding in a case under title 11, United States Code, with respect to the employer from whose employment the covered employee retired at any time.

(b) *Timing of notice.* The notice required by this section shall be furnished to the administrator of the plan—

(1) In the case of a plan that provides, pursuant to section 607(5) of the Act, that continuation coverage and the applicable period for providing notice under section 606(a)(2) of the Act shall commence with the date of loss of coverage, not later than 30 days after the date on which a qualified beneficiary loses coverage under the plan due to the qualifying event;

(2) In the case of a multiemployer plan that provides, pursuant to section 606(a)(2) of the Act, for a longer period of time within which employers may provide notice of a qualifying event, not later than the end of the period provided pursuant to the plan's terms for such notice; and

(3) In all other cases, not later than 30 days after the date on which the qualifying event occurred.

(c) *Content of notice.* The notice required by this section shall include sufficient information to enable the administrator to determine the plan, the covered employee, the qualifying event, and the date of the qualifying event.

(d) *Multiemployer plan special rules.* This section shall not apply to any employer that maintains a multiemployer plan, with respect to qualifying events affecting coverage under such plan, if the plan provides, pursuant to section 606(b) of the Act, that the administrator shall determine whether such a qualifying event has occurred.

§ 2590.606-3. Notice requirements for covered employees and qualified beneficiaries.

(a) *General.* In accordance with the authority of sections 505 and 606(a)(3) of the Employee Retirement Income Security Act of 1974, as amended (the Act), this section sets forth requirements for group health plans subject to the continuation coverage requirements of Part 6 of title I of the Act with respect to the responsibility of covered employees and qualified beneficiaries to provide the following notices to administrators:

(1) Notice of the occurrence of a qualifying event that is a divorce or legal separation of a covered employee from his or her spouse;

(2) Notice of the occurrence of a qualifying event that is a beneficiary's ceasing to be covered under a plan as a dependent child of a participant;

(3) Notice of the occurrence of a second qualifying event after a qualified beneficiary has become entitled to continuation coverage with a maximum duration of 18 (or 29) months;

(4) Notice that a qualified beneficiary entitled to receive continuation coverage with a maximum duration of 18 months has been determined by the Social Security Administration, under title II or XVI of the Social Security Act (42 U.S.C. 401 et seq. or 1381 et seq.) (SSA), to be disabled at any time during the first 60 days of continuation coverage; and

(5) Notice that a qualified beneficiary, with respect to whom a notice described in paragraph (a)(4) of this section has been provided, has subsequently been determined by the Social Security Administration, under title II or XVI of the SSA to no longer be disabled.

(b) *Reasonable procedures.*

(1) A plan subject to the continuation coverage requirements shall establish reasonable procedures for the furnishing of the notices described in paragraph (a) of this section.

(2) For purposes of this section, a plan's notice procedures shall be deemed reasonable only if such procedures:

(i) Are described in the plan's summary plan description required by § 2520.102-3 of this title;

(ii) Specify the individual or entity designated to receive such notices;

(iii) Specify the means by which notice may be given;

(iv) Describe the information concerning the qualifying event or determination of disability that the plan deems necessary in order to provide continuation coverage rights consistent with the requirements of the Act; and

(v) Comply with the requirements of paragraphs (c), (d), and (e) of this section.

(3) A plan's procedures will not fail to be reasonable, pursuant to this section, solely because the procedures require a covered employee or qualified beneficiary to utilize a specific form to provide notice to the administrator, provided that any such form is easily available, without cost, to covered employees and qualified beneficiaries.

(4) If a plan has not established reasonable procedures for providing a notice required by this section, such notice shall be deemed to have been provided when a written or oral communication identifying a specific qualifying event is made in a manner reasonably calculated to bring the information to the attention of any of the following:

(i) In the case of a single-employer plan, either the organizational unit that has customarily handled employee benefits matters of the employer, or any officer of the employer;

(ii) In the case of a plan to which more than one unaffiliated employer contributes, or which is established or maintained by an employee organization, either the joint board, association, committee, or other similar group (or any member of any such group) administering the plan, or the person or organizational unit to which claims for benefits under the plan customarily have been referred; or

(iii) In the case of a plan the benefits of which are provided or administered by an insurance company, insurance service, or other similar organization subject to regulation under the insurance laws of one or more States, the person or organizational unit that handles claims for benefits under the plan or any officer of the insurance company, insurance service, or other similar organization.

(c) *Periods of time for providing notice.* A plan may establish a reasonable period of time for furnishing any of the notices described in paragraph (a) of this section, provided that any time limit imposed by the plan with respect to a particular notice may not be shorter than the time limit described in this paragraph (c) with respect to that notice.

(1) *Time limits for notices of qualifying events.* The period of time for furnishing a notice described in paragraph (a)(1), (2), or (3) of this section may not end before the date that is 60 days after the later of:

(i) In the case of a plan that provides, pursuant to section 607(5) of the Act, that continuation coverage and the applicable period for providing notice under section 606(a)(2) of the Act shall commence with the date of loss of coverage, the date on which the qualified beneficiary loses (or would lose) coverage under the plan as a result of the qualifying event;

(ii) In the case of any plan other than a plan described in paragraph (c)(1)(i) of this section, the date on which the relevant qualifying event occurs; or

(iii) The date on which the qualified beneficiary is informed, through the furnishing of the plan's summary plan description or the notice described in § 2590.606-1, of both the responsibility to provide the notice and the plan's procedures for providing such notice to the administrator.

(2) *Time limits for notice of disability determination.*

(i) Subject to paragraph (c)(2)(ii) of this section, the period of time for furnishing the notice described in paragraph (a)(4) of this section may not end before the date that is 60 days after the later of:

(A) The date of the disability determination by the Social Security Administration; or

(B) The date on which the qualified beneficiary is informed, through the furnishing of the summary plan description or the notice described in § 2590.606-1, of both the responsibility to provide the notice and the plan's procedures for providing such notice to the administrator.

(ii) Notwithstanding paragraph (c)(2)(i) of this section, a plan may require the notice described in paragraph (a)(4) of this section to be furnished before the end of the first 18 months of continuation coverage.

(3) *Time limits for notice of change in disability status.* The period of time for furnishing the notice described in paragraph (a)(5) of this section may not end before the date that is 30 days after the later of:

(i) The date of the final determination by the Social Security Administration, under title II or XVI of the SSA, that the qualified beneficiary is no longer disabled; or

(ii) The date on which the qualified beneficiary is informed, through the furnishing of the plan's summary plan description or the notice described in § 2590.606-1, of both the responsibility to provide the notice and the plan's procedures for providing such notice to the administrator.

(d) *Required contents of notice.*

(1) A plan may establish reasonable requirements for the content of any notice described in this section, provided that a plan may not deem a notice to have been provided untimely if such notice, although not containing all of the information required by the plan, is provided within the time limit established under the plan in conformity with paragraph (c) of this section and the administrator is able to determine from such notice the plan, the covered employee and qualified beneficiary(ies), the qualifying event or disability, and the date on which the qualifying event (if any) occurred.

(2) An administrator may require a notice that does not contain all of the information required by the plan to be supplemented with the additional information necessary to meet the plan's reasonable content requirements for such notice before the notice is deemed to have been provided in accordance with this section.

(e) *Who may provide notice.* With respect to each of the notice requirements of this section, any individual who is either the covered employee, a qualified beneficiary with respect to the qualifying event, or any representative acting on behalf of the covered employee or qualified beneficiary may provide the notice, and the provision of notice by one individual shall satisfy any responsibility to provide notice on behalf of all related qualified beneficiaries with respect to the qualifying event.

(f) *Plan provisions.* To the extent that a plan provides a covered employee or qualified beneficiary a period of time longer than that specified in this section to provide notice to the administrator, the terms of the plan shall govern the time frame for such notice.

(g) *Additional rights to continuation coverage.* Nothing in this section shall be construed to preclude a plan from providing, in accordance with its terms, continuation coverage to a qualified beneficiary although a notice requirement of this section was not satisfied.

§ 2590.606-4. *Notice requirements for plan administrators.*

(a) *General.* Pursuant to section 606(a)(4) of the Employee Retirement Income Security Act of 1974, as amended (the Act), the administrator of a group health plan subject to the continuation coverage requirements of Part 6 of title I of the Act shall provide, in accordance with this section, notice to each qualified beneficiary of the qualified beneficiary's rights to continuation coverage under the plan.

(b) *Notice of right to elect continuation coverage.* (1) Except as provided in paragraph (b)(2) or (3) of this section, upon receipt of a notice of qualifying event furnished in accordance with § 2590.606-2 or § 2590.606-3, the administrator shall furnish to each qualified beneficiary, not later than 14 days after receipt of the notice of qualifying event, a notice meeting the requirements of paragraph (b)(4) of this section.

(2) In the case of a plan with respect to which an employer of a covered employee is also the administrator of the plan, except as provided in paragraph (b)(3) of this section, a notice meeting the requirements of paragraph (b)(4) of this section shall be furnished not later than 44 days after:

(i) In the case of a plan that provides, pursuant to section 607(5) of the Act, that continuation coverage and the applicable period for providing notice under section 606(a)(2) of the Act shall commence with the date of loss of coverage, the date on which a qualified beneficiary loses coverage under the plan due to the qualifying event; or

(ii) In all other cases, the date on which the qualifying event occurred.

(3) In the case of a plan that is a multiemployer plan, a notice meeting the requirements of paragraph (b)(4) of this section shall be furnished not later than the later of:

(i) The end of the time period provided in paragraph (b)(1) of this section; or

(ii) The end of the time period provided in the terms of the plan for such purpose.

(4) The notice required by this paragraph (b) shall be written in a manner calculated to be understood by the average plan participant and shall contain the following information:

(i) The name of the plan under which continuation coverage is available; and the name, address and telephone number of the party responsible under the plan for the administration of continuation coverage benefits;

(ii) Identification of the qualifying event;

(iii) Identification of each qualified beneficiary who is recognized by the plan as being entitled to elect continuation coverage with respect to the qualifying event, and the date on which coverage under the plan will terminate (or has terminated) unless continuation coverage is elected;

(iv) A statement that each individual who is a qualified beneficiary with respect to the qualifying event has an independent right to elect continuation coverage, that a covered employee or a qualified beneficiary who is the spouse of the covered employee (or was the spouse of the covered employee on the day before the qualifying event occurred) may elect continuation coverage on behalf of all other qualified beneficiaries with respect to the qualifying event, and that a parent or legal guardian may elect continuation coverage on behalf of a minor child;

(v) An explanation of the plan's procedures for electing continuation coverage, including an explanation of the time period during which the election must be made, and the date by which the election must be made;

(vi) An explanation of the consequences of failing to elect or waiving continuation coverage, including an explanation that a qualified beneficiary's decision whether to elect continuation coverage will affect the future rights of qualified beneficiaries to portability of group health coverage, guaranteed access to individual health coverage, and special enrollment under Part 7 of title I of the Act, with a reference to where a qualified beneficiary may obtain additional information about such rights; and a description of the plan's procedures for revoking a waiver of the right to continuation coverage before the date by which the election must be made;

(vii) A description of the continuation coverage that will be made available under the plan, if elected, including the date on which such coverage will commence, either by providing a description of the coverage or by reference to the plan's summary plan description;

(viii) An explanation of the maximum period for which continuation coverage will be available under the plan, if elected; an explanation of the continuation coverage termination date; and an explanation of any events that might cause continuation coverage to be terminated earlier than the end of the maximum period;

(ix) A description of the circumstances (if any) under which the maximum period of continuation coverage may be extended due either to the occurrence of a second qualifying event or a determination by the Social Security Administration, under title II or XVI of the Social Security Act (42 U.S.C. 401 et seq. or 1381 et seq.) (SSA), that the qualified beneficiary is disabled, and the length of any such extension;

(x) In the case of a notice that offers continuation coverage with a maximum duration of less than 36 months, a description of the plan's requirements regarding the responsibility of qualified beneficiaries to provide notice of a second qualifying event and notice of a disability determination under the SSA, along with a description of the plan's procedures for providing such notices, including the times within which such notices must be provided and the consequences of failing to provide such notices. The notice shall also explain the responsibility of qualified beneficiaries to provide notice that a disabled qualified beneficiary has subsequently been determined to no longer be disabled;

(xi) A description of the amount, if any, that each qualified beneficiary will be required to pay for continuation coverage;

(xii) A description of the due dates for payments, the qualified beneficiaries' right to pay on a monthly basis, the grace periods for payment, the address to which payments should be sent, and the consequences of delayed payment and nonpayment;

(xiii) A description of any opportunity provided under the plan for other health coverage for which the covered employee or qualified beneficiary may be eligible, either as an alternative to continuation coverage or in addition to continuation coverage (e.g., alternative coverage on a group basis under the plan, an option to enroll under an individual conversion health plan after exhaustion of continuation coverage, retiree health coverage), an explanation of how election of such other coverage would affect the qualified beneficiaries' continuation coverage rights under the plan and rights to guaranteed access to individual health coverage;

(xiv) An explanation of the importance of keeping the administrator informed of the current addresses of all participants or beneficiaries under the plan who are or may become qualified beneficiaries; and

(xv) A statement that the notice does not fully describe continuation coverage or other rights under the plan, and that more complete information regarding such rights is available in the plan's summary plan description or from the plan administrator.

(c) *Notice of unavailability of continuation coverage.* (1) In the event that an administrator who receives a notice of qualifying event furnished in accordance with § 2590.606-3 determines that an individual is not entitled to continuation coverage under Part 6 of title I of the Act, the administrator shall provide to such individual an explanation as to why the individual is not entitled to elect continuation coverage.

(2) The notice required by this paragraph (c) shall be furnished by the administrator in accordance with the time frame set out in paragraph (b) of this section that would apply if the administrator had determined that the individual was entitled to elect continuation coverage.

(d) *Notice of termination of continuation coverage.* (1) The administrator of a plan that is providing continuation coverage to one or more qualified beneficiaries with respect to a qualifying event shall provide, in accordance with this paragraph (d), notice to each such qualified beneficiary of any termination of continuation coverage that takes effect earlier than the end of the maximum period of continuation coverage applicable to such qualifying event.

(2) The notice required by this paragraph (d) shall be written in a manner calculated to be understood by the average plan participant and shall contain the following information:

(i) The reason that continuation coverage has terminated earlier than the end of the maximum period of continuation coverage applicable to such qualifying event;

(ii) The date of termination of continuation coverage; and

(iii) Any rights the qualified beneficiary may have under the plan or under applicable law to elect an alternative group or individual coverage, such as a conversion right.

(3) The notice required by this paragraph (d) shall be furnished by the administrator as soon as practicable following the administrator's determination that continuation coverage shall terminate.

(e) *Special notice rules.* The notices required by paragraphs (b), (c), and (d) of this section shall be furnished to each qualified beneficiary or individual, except that—

(1) An administrator may provide notice to a covered employee and the covered employee's spouse by furnishing a single notice addressed to both the covered employee and the covered employee's spouse, if, on the basis of the most recent information available to the plan, the covered employee's spouse resides at the same location as the covered employee; and

(2) An administrator may provide notice to each qualified beneficiary who is the dependent child of a covered employee by furnishing a single notice to the covered employee or the covered employee's spouse, if, on the basis of the most recent information available to the plan, the dependent child resides at the same location as the individual to whom such notice is provided.

(f) *Delivery of notice.* The notices required by this section shall be furnished in any manner consistent with the requirements of § 2520.104b-1 of this title, including paragraph (c) of that section relating to the use of electronic media.

(g) *Model notice.* The appendix to this section contains a model notice that is intended to assist administrators in discharging the notice obligations of this section. Use of the model notice is not mandatory. The model reflects the requirements of this section as they would apply to single-employer group health plans and must be modified if used to provide notice with respect to other types of group health plans, such as multiemployer plans or plans established and maintained by employee organizations for their members. In order to use the model notice, administrators must appropriately add relevant information where indicated in the model notice, select among alternative language and supplement the model notice to reflect applicable plan provisions. Items of information that are not applicable to a particular plan may be deleted. Use of the model notice, appropriately modified and supplemented, will be deemed to satisfy the notice content requirements of paragraph (b)(4) of this section.

APPENDIX TO § 2590.606-4
MODEL COBRA CONTINUATION COVERAGE ELECTION NOTICE
(For use by single-employer group health plans)

[Enter date of notice]

Dear: *[Enter Name of Employee,*
     Spouse, Dependent Children, as appropriate]

This notice contains important information about your right to continue your health care coverage in the *[enter name of group health plan]* **(the Plan).**

Please read the information contained in this notice very carefully. This notice provides important information concerning your rights and what you have to do to continue your health care coverage under the Plan. If you have any questions concerning the information in this notice or your rights to coverage, you should contact *[enter name of party responsible for COBRA administration for the Plan, with telephone number and address]*.

If you do not elect to continue your health care coverage by completing the enclosed "Election Form" and returning it to us, your coverage under the Plan will end on *[enter date]* due to:

    ☐ End of employment   ☐ Reduction in hours of employment
    ☐ Death of employee   ☐ Divorce or legal separation
    ☐ Enrollment in Medicare   ☐ Loss of dependent child status

Each of the following persons is entitled to elect to continue health care coverage under the Plan:

    ☐ Employee – *[enter name]*
    ☐ Spouse (or former spouse of employee) *[enter name]*
    ☐ Dependent children *[enter name(s)]*

Because of the event (checked above) that will end your coverage under the Plan, you *[and/or, as appropriate,* your spouse, and dependent children] are entitled to continue your health care coverage for up to _____ months *[enter 18 or 36 months as appropriate]*. If you elect to continue your coverage under the Plan, your continuation coverage will begin on *[enter date]* and can last until *[enter date]*.

Your continuation coverage will cost: *[enter amount each qualified beneficiary would be required to pay for each option per month of coverage and any other permitted coverage periods.]*

IMPORTANT - To elect continuation coverage you MUST complete the enclosed "Election Form" and return it to us. You may mail it to the address shown on the Election Form *[or describe other acceptable means of submission]*. **The completed Election Form must be post-marked by** *[enter date]* *[or received by [enter date] if submitted by other means]*. **If you do not submit a completed Election Form by this date, you will lose your right to elect**

continuation coverage. **Important information about your rights is provided to you on the pages after the Election Form.**

COBRA CONTINUATION COVERAGE ELECTION FORM

[Name of Employee / Spouse / Dependent Children (as appropriate)]

IMPORTANT: This form must be completed and returned by mail *[or describe other means of submission and due date]*. **If mailed, it must be post-marked no later than** *[enter date]*. **Send completed form to:**

[Enter Name and Address]

I (We) elect to continue our coverage in the *[enter name of plan]* (the Plan) as indicated below:

Name	Date of Birth	Relationship to Employee	SSN (or other identifier)
a. _____			
b. _____			
c. _____			
d. _____			

Type of coverage elected (check only one):

☐ *[enter description of option]*

☐ *[enter description of option]*

☐ *[enter description of option]*

_____   _____
Signature   Date

_____   _____
Print Name   Relationship to individual(s) listed above

_____
_____

_____   _____
Print Address   Telephone number

IMPORTANT INFORMATION ABOUT YOUR COBRA CONTINUATION COVERAGE RIGHTS

What is continuation coverage?

Federal law requires that most group health plans (including this Plan) give employees and their families the opportunity to continue their health care coverage when there is a "qualifying event" that would result in a loss of coverage under an employer's plan. Depending on the type of qualifying event, "qualified beneficiaries" can include the employee covered under the group health plan, a covered employee's spouse, and dependent children of the covered employee.

Continuation coverage is the same coverage that the Plan gives to other participants or beneficiaries under the Plan who are not receiving continuation coverage. Each qualified beneficiary who elects continuation coverage will have the same rights under the Plan as other participants or beneficiaries covered under the Plan, including [add if applicable: open enrollment and] special enrollment rights. The persons listed on page one of this notice have been identified by the Plan as qualified beneficiaries entitled to elect continuation coverage. Specific information describing continuation coverage can be found in the Plan's summary plan description (SPD), which can be obtained from [enter name, address and telephone number of appropriate party (Plan Administrator or other party)].

How long will continuation coverage last?

In the case of a loss of coverage due to end of employment or reduction in hours of employment, coverage may be continued for up to 18 months. In the case of losses of coverage due to an employee's death, divorce or legal separation, the employee's enrollment in Medicare or a dependent child ceasing to be a dependent under the terms of the plan, coverage may be continued for up to 36 months. Page one of this notice shows the maximum period of continuation coverage available to the listed qualified beneficiaries.

Continuation coverage will be terminated before the end of the maximum period if any required premium is not paid on time, if a qualified beneficiary becomes covered under another group health plan that does not impose any pre-existing condition exclusion for a pre-existing condition of the qualified beneficiary, if a covered employee enrolls in Medicare, or if the employer ceases to provide any group health plan for its employees. Continuation coverage may also be terminated for any reason the Plan would terminate coverage of a participant or beneficiary not receiving continuation coverage (such as fraud).

[If the maximum period of coverage of this notice is 18 months, add the following three paragraphs:]

How can you extend the length of continuation coverage?

If you elect continuation coverage, an extension of the maximum period of 18 months of coverage may be available if a qualified beneficiary is disabled or a second qualifying event occurs. You must notify [*enter name of COBRA administrator*] of a disability or a second qualifying event in order to extend the period of continuation coverage. Failure to provide notice of a disability or second qualifying event may affect the right to extend the period of continuation coverage.

Disability

An 11-month extension of coverage may be available if any of the qualified beneficiaries is disabled. The Social Security Administration (SSA) must determine that the qualified beneficiary was disabled at some time during the first 60 days of continuation coverage, and you must notify [*enter name of COBRA administrator*] of that fact within 60 days of the SSA's determination and before the end of the first 18 months of continuation coverage. All of the qualified beneficiaries listed on page one of this notice who have elected continuation coverage will be entitled to the 11-month disability extension if one of them qualifies. If the qualified beneficiary is determined by SSA to no longer be disabled, you must notify [*enter name of COBRA administrator*] of that fact within 30 days of SSA's determination.

Second Qualifying Event

An 18-month extension of coverage will be available to spouses and dependent children who elect continuation coverage if a second qualifying event occurs during the first 18 months of continuation coverage. The maximum amount of continuation coverage available when a second qualifying event occurs is 36 months. Such second qualifying events include the death of a covered employee, divorce or separation from the covered employee, the covered employee's enrolling in Medicare, or a dependent child's ceasing to be eligible for coverage as a dependent under the Plan. You must notify [*enter name of COBRA administrator*] within 60 days after a second qualifying event occurs.

How can you elect continuation coverage?

Each qualified beneficiary listed on page one of this notice has an independent right to elect continuation coverage. For example, both the employee and the employee's spouse may elect continuation coverage, or only one of them. Parents may elect to continue coverage on behalf of their dependent children only. A qualified beneficiary must elect coverage by the date specified on the Election Form. Failure to do so will result in loss of the right to elect continuation coverage under the Plan. A qualified beneficiary may change a prior rejection of continuation coverage any time until that date.

In considering whether to elect continuation coverage, you should take into account that a failure to continue your group health coverage will affect your future rights under federal law. First, you can lose the right to avoid having pre-existing condition exclusions applied to you by other group health plans if you have more than a 63-day gap in health coverage, and election of continuation coverage may help you not have such a gap. Second, you will lose the guaranteed right to purchase individual health insurance policies that do not impose such pre-existing condition exclusions if you do not get continuation coverage for the maximum time available to you. Finally, you should take into account that you have special enrollment rights under federal law. You have the right to request special enrollment in another group health plan for which you are otherwise eligible (such as a plan sponsored by your spouse's employer) within 30 days after your group health coverage ends because of the qualifying event listed above. You will also have the same special enrollment right at the end of continuation coverage if you get continuation coverage for the maximum time available to you.

How much does continuation coverage cost?

Generally, each qualified beneficiary may be required to pay the entire cost of continuation coverage. The amount a qualified beneficiary may be required to pay may not exceed 102 percent of the cost to the group health plan (including both employer and employee contributions) for coverage of a similarly situated plan participant or beneficiary who is not receiving continuation coverage (or, in the case of an extension of continuation coverage due to a disability, 150 percent). The required payment for continuation coverage for the qualified beneficiaries listed on page one of this notice is described on page one.

[*If employees might be eligible for trade adjustment assistance, the following information may be added*: The Trade Act of 2002 created a new tax credit for certain individuals who become eligible for trade adjustment assistance (eligible individuals). Under the new tax provisions, eligible individuals can either take a tax credit or get advance payment of 65% of premiums paid for qualified health insurance, including continuation coverage. If you have questions about these new tax provisions, you may call the Health Care Tax Credit Customer Contact Center toll-free at 1-866-628-4282. TTD/TTY callers may call toll-free at 1-866-626-4282. More information about the Trade Act is also available at www.doleta.gov/tradeact/2002act_index.asp.

When and how must payment for continuation coverage be made?

First payment for continuation coverage

If you elect continuation coverage, you do not have to send any payment for continuation coverage with the Election Form. However, you must make your first payment for continuation coverage within 45 days after the date of your election. (This is the date the Election Notice is post-marked, if mailed.) If you do not make your first payment for continuation coverage within that 45 days, you will lose all continuation coverage rights under the Plan.

Your first payment must cover the cost of continuation coverage from the time your coverage under the Plan would have otherwise terminated [*if Plan permits, add:* unless you request that your continuation coverage begin only with the date of your Election Notice] up to the time you make the first payment. You are responsible for making sure that the amount of your first payment is enough to cover this entire period. You may contact [*enter appropriate contact information, e.g., the Plan Administrator or other party responsible for COBRA administration under the Plan*] to confirm the correct amount of your first payment.

Your first payment for continuation coverage should be sent to:

[*enter appropriate payment address*]

Periodic payments for continuation coverage

After you make your first payment for continuation coverage, you will be required to pay for continuation coverage for each subsequent month of coverage. [*Enter additional information on other due dates for payments if Plan permits other periodic payment schedules.*] Under the Plan, these periodic payments for continuation coverage are due on the [*enter due day for each month of coverage*]. [*If Plan offers other payment schedules, enter with appropriate dates:* You may instead make payments for continuation coverage for the following coverage periods, due on the following dates:]. If you make a periodic payment on or before its due date, your coverage under the Plan will continue for that coverage period without any break. The Plan [*select one:* will *or* will not] send periodic notices of payments due for these coverage periods.

Periodic payments for continuation coverage should be sent to:

[*enter appropriate payment address*]

Grace periods for periodic payments

Although periodic payments are due on the dates shown above, you will be given a grace period of 30 days [*or enter longer period permitted by Plan*] to make each periodic payment. Your continuation coverage will be provided for each coverage period as long as payment for that coverage period is made before the end of the grace period for that payment. [*If Plan suspends coverage during grace period for nonpayment, enter and modify as necessary:* However, if you pay a periodic payment later than its due date but during its grace period, your coverage under the Plan will be suspended as of the due date and then retroactively reinstated (going back to the due date) when the periodic payment is made. This means that any claim you submit for benefits while your coverage is suspended may be denied and may have to be resubmitted once your coverage is reinstated.]

If you fail to make a periodic payment before the end of the grace period for that payment, you will lose all rights to continuation coverage under the Plan.

[*If Plan provides any election of other health coverage besides continuation coverage (such as alternative coverage in lieu of continuation coverage, individual conversion rights, etc.), enter description of all such coverages and explain how election of such other coverages would affect continuation coverage rights under the Plan. The following are two separate examples of such a description:*]

Can you elect other health coverage besides continuation coverage?

Under the Plan, you have the right to elect alternative group health coverage for a period of six months at no cost to you instead of the continuation coverage described in this Notice. If you elect this six-month alternative coverage, you will lose all rights to the continuation coverage described in this Notice. You should also note that if you enroll in the alternative group health coverage you lose your right under federal law to purchase individual health insurance that does not impose any pre-existing condition limitations when your alternative group health coverage ends. You must contact [*add appropriate contact information*] if you wish to elect alternative coverage.

-- *OR* --

Under the Plan, you have the right, when your group health coverage ends, to enroll in an individual health insurance policy, without providing proof of insurability. The benefits provided under such an individual conversion policy may not be identical to those provided under the Plan. You may exercise this right in lieu of electing continuation coverage, or you may exercise this right after you have received the maximum continuation coverage available to you. You should note that if you enroll in an individual conversion policy you lose your right under federal law to purchase individual health insurance that does not impose any pre-existing condition limitations when your conversion policy coverage ends.

For more information

This notice does not fully describe continuation coverage or other rights under the Plan. More information about continuation coverage and your rights under the Plan is available in your summary plan description or from the Plan Administrator. You can get a copy of your summary plan description from: [*Enter name, address and telephone number of appropriate party (plan administrator or other party)*].

For more information about your rights under ERISA, including COBRA, the Health Insurance Portability and Accountability Act (HIPAA), and other laws affecting group health plans, contact the U.S. Department of Labor's Employee Benefits Security Administration (EBSA) in your area or visit the EBSA website at www.dol.gov/ebsa.

Keep Your Plan Informed of Address Changes

In order to protect your family's rights, you should keep the Plan Administrator informed of any changes in the addresses of family members. You should also keep a copy, for your records, of any notices you send to the Plan Administrator.

Signed at Washington, DC, this 20th day of May, 2003.

Ann L. Combs,

Assistant Secretary,

Employee Benefits Security Administration,

Department of Labor.

¶ 20,534N

Equal Employment Opportunity Commission (EEOC): Proposed regulations: Age Discrimination in Employment Act: Retiree health benefits: Medicare: State-sponsored retiree health benefits program.—The EEOC has issued proposed regulations that exempt from the prohibitions of the Age Discrimination in Employment Act of 1967 the altering, reducing, or eliminating of employer-provided retiree health benefits when retirees become eligible for Medicare or a state-sponsored retiree health benefits program.

The proposed regulations, which were published in the *Federal Register* on July 14, 2003 (68 FR 41542), are reproduced below.

EQUAL EMPLOYMENT OPPORTUNITY COMMISSION

29. CFR Parts 1625 and 1627

RIN 3046-AA72

Age Discrimination in Employment Act; Retiree Health Benefits

AGENCY: U.S. Equal Employment Opportunity Commission.

ACTION: Notice of proposed rulemaking.

SUMMARY: The U.S. Equal Employment Opportunity Commission (Commission or EEOC) proposes to amend its regulations governing age discrimination in employment to exempt from the prohibitions of the Age Discrimination in Employment Act of 1967 the practice of altering, reducing or eliminating employer-sponsored retiree health benefits when retirees become eligible for Medicare or a State-sponsored retiree health benefits program. This exemption will ensure that the application of the ADEA does not discourage employers from providing health benefits to their retirees.

DATES: Comments must be received by September 12, 2003. The Commission will consider any comments received on or before the closing date and thereafter adopt final regulations. Comments received after the closing date will be considered to the extent practicable.

ADDRESSES: Written comments should be submitted to Frances M. Hart, Executive Officer, Office of the Executive Secretariat, U.S. Equal Employment Opportunity Commission, 1801 L Street, NW., Washington, DC 20507. As a convenience to commentators, the Executive Secretariat will accept comments transmitted by facsimile ("FAX") machine. The telephone number of the FAX receiver is (202) 663-4114 (This is not a toll free number). Only comments of six or fewer pages will be accepted via FAX transmittal. This limitation is necessary to assure access to the equipment. Receipt of fax transmittals will not be acknowledged, except that the sender may request confirmation of receipt by calling the Executive Secretariat staff at (202) 663-4078 (voice) or (202) 663-4077 (TTY). (These are not toll free numbers). Copies of comments submitted by the public will be available for review on weekdays, except federal holidays, at the Commission's library, Room 6502, 1801 L Street, NW., Washington, DC, between the hours of 9:30 a.m. and 5 p.m.

FOR FURTHER INFORMATION CONTACT: Lynn A. Clements, Special Assistant to the Legal Counsel, Office of Legal Counsel, at (202) 663-4624 (voice) or (202) 663-7026 (TTY) (These are not toll free numbers). This notice is also available in the following formats: large print, braille, audio tape, and electronic file on computer disk. Requests for this notice in an alternative format should be made to the Publications Information Center at 1-800-669-3362.

SUPPLEMENTARY INFORMATION: Section 9 of the Age Discrimination in Employment Act of 1967, 29 U.S.C. 621 et seq. (ADEA or Act), provides that EEOC "may establish such reasonable exemptions to and from any or all provisions of [the Act] as it may find necessary and proper in the public interest." Implicit in this authority is the recognition that the application of the ADEA could, in certain circumstances, foster unintended consequences that are not consistent with the purposes of the law and are not in the public interest. Such circumstances are rare. Accordingly, EEOC's exercise of this authority has been limited and tempered with great discretion.

After an in-depth study, the Commission believes that the practice of altering, reducing or eliminating employer-sponsored retiree health benefits when retirees become eligible for Medicare or a State-sponsored retiree health benefits program presents a circumstance that warrants Commission exercise of its ADEA exemption authority. For the reasons that follow, and pursuant to its authority under Section 9 of the Act, the EEOC proposes in this notice of proposed rulemaking

(NPRM) to add a new section 32 to part 1625 of Title 29 of the Code of Federal Regulations exempting such coordination of employer-sponsored retiree health benefits with Medicare or a State-sponsored retiree health benefits program from all prohibitions of the ADEA.

Basis for Exemption

In August 2001, the Commission announced that it would study the relationship between the ADEA and employer-sponsored retiree health benefit plans that alter, reduce or eliminate benefits upon eligibility for Medicare or a comparable State-sponsored retiree health benefits program. To begin the process, EEOC developed an internal Retiree Health Benefits Task Force headed by its Legal Counsel. The Task Force met with a wide range of Commission stakeholders, including employers, employee groups, labor unions, human resource consultants, benefit consultants, actuaries and state and local government representatives. The Task Force also reviewed available survey data regarding employer-sponsored retiree health benefits; analyzed the May 2001 United States General Accounting Office's Report to the Chairman of the United States's Senate Committee on Health, Education, Labor and Pensions entitled "Retiree Health Benefits: Employer-Sponsored Benefits May Be Vulnerable to Further Erosion;" and reviewed numerous professional articles discussing the continued erosion of retiree health benefits.

As a result of its study, the Commission has concluded, as discussed in greater detail below, that the number of employers providing retiree health benefits has declined considerably over the last ten years, even though many retired individuals rely on such employer-sponsored plans for affordable health coverage. Various factors have contributed to this erosion, including the increased cost of health care coverage, an increased demand for such coverage as large numbers of workers near retirement age, and changes in the way accounting rules treat the long-term costs of providing retiree health benefits. The Commission believes that concern about the potential application of the ADEA to employer-sponsored retiree health benefits is adversely affecting the continued provision of this important retirement benefit.

Employers Are Not Obligated To Provide Retiree Health Care

Employers are not legally obligated to provide retiree health benefits and many do not. In fact, in 2001, only about "one-third of large employers and less than 10% of small employers offer[ed] retiree health benefits."[1] Employers who choose to provide retiree health benefits are not required to provide such benefits indefinitely, absent some contractual agreement to the contrary. Employers that do offer retiree health benefits, however, often do so to maintain a competitive advantage in the marketplace—using these and other benefits to attract and retain the best talent available to work for their organizations.

Likewise, employer-sponsored retiree health benefits clearly benefit employees. In many cases, employers offer retiree health benefits as a bridge to Medicare so that younger retirees have access to affordable health care benefits when they leave the workforce before reaching the age of Medicare eligibility. Often those benefits are more generous than Medicare benefits because, for example, the employer simply includes younger retirees in its group plan for existing employees. In other cases, employers wish to offer their retirees age 65 and older health benefit plans that supplement the coverage provided under Medicare so that these retirees have access to comprehensive health care benefits at a time when their health care needs may be greatest. The Commission believes that it is in the best interest of both employers and employees for the Commission to pursue a policy that permits employers to offer these benefits to the greatest extent possible.

The Rising Cost of Health Care

The cost of employee health care has increased consistently for several years, making it difficult for employers to continue to provide

---

[1] Hearing Before the House Comm. on Education and the Workforce, 107th Cong. (2001) (statement of William J. Scanlon, Director of Health Care Services, GAO).

retiree health benefits. One report estimates that employers will experience a double-digit increase in their health care costs in 2003 for the third consecutive year.[2] Two widely-cited surveys of employer-sponsored health plans—(1) the Health Research and Educational Trust survey sponsored by The Henry J. Kaiser Family Foundation (Kaiser/ HRET) and (2) the William M. Mercer, Incorporated survey (formerly produced by Foster Higgins) (Mercer/Foster Higgins)—estimate that premiums for employer-sponsored health insurance increased an average of about 11% in 2001.[3] The 2002 Kaiser/HRET study found monthly premium costs for employer-sponsored health insurance rose 12.7% between the Spring of 2001 and 2002, while early results from the 2002 Mercer/Foster Higgins study estimate that health care costs increased almost 15% in 2002.[4] The 2001 Kaiser/HRET survey found that these large changes in premiums would affect small employers, defined as those employing between 3-199 workers, at a greater rate than larger employers.[5] Indeed, the 2002 Kaiser/HRET survey suggests that there may be evidence of erosion in the number of small employers offering health benefits; the study reports that the number of small employers offering such benefits dropped 6% between 2000 and 2002.[6] Many employers and benefit experts believe that the rising cost of prescription drug coverage, in particular, has heavily contributed to the rising cost of health care, with 64% of employers responding to the 2001 Kaiser/HRET study citing "higher spending for drugs" as a significant factor in health insurance premium increases.[7]

In addition to the rising cost of health care generally, increased longevity and, thus, increased numbers of retirees, will continue to mean larger and more frequent payments for health care services on behalf of retired workers. The United States General Accounting Office (GAO) projects that, by 2030, the number of people age 65 or older will be double what it is today, while the number of individuals between the ages of 55 and 64 will increase 75 percent by 2020.[8] It is well-established that utilization of health care services generally rises with age.[9] Thus, the demand for and cost of retiree health coverage is likely to grow significantly in the next few years, while there will be comparatively fewer active workers to subsidize such benefits.[10] The 2000 Mercer/Foster Higgins National Survey of Employer-Sponsored Health Plans showed substantial cost increases for retiree health care coverage between 1999 and 2000, with a 10.6 percent increase for retirees under age 65 and a 17 percent increase for those over 65.[11] A 2002 study by The Henry J. Kaiser Family Foundation and Hewitt Associates (Kaiser/Hewitt) found that retiree health care costs increased an average of 16% between 2001 and 2002 for employers with at least 1000 employees.[12]

Changes in accounting rules also have dramatically impacted the way employers account for the long-term costs of providing retiree health benefits.[13] In 1990, the Financial Accounting Standards Board, which is charged with establishing U.S. standards of financial accounting and reporting, promulgated new rules for retiree health accounting, referred to as Financial Accounting Standards Number 106 or FAS 106. FAS 106 requires employers to apportion the costs of retiree health over the working lifetime of employees and to report unfunded retiree health benefit liabilities in accordance with generally accepted accounting principles beginning with fiscal years after December 15, 1992. Because "the recognition of these liabilities in financial statements dramatically impacts a company's calculation of its profits and losses,"[14] some companies have said that FAS 106 led to reductions in reported income, thus creating an incentive to reduce expenditures for employee benefits such as retiree health.

The Incentive for Employers To Reduce Health Care Costs

As a result of these increased costs and accounting changes, employers have actively examined ways to reduce health care costs, including by reducing, altering or eliminating retiree health coverage.[15] During hearings before the U.S. House of Representative's Committee on Education and the Workforce in November 2001, the GAO's Director of Health Care Services testified that only "one-third of large employers and less than 10% of small employers offer retiree health benefits."[16] The 2001 Mercer/Foster Higgins study shows that the number of employers with 500 or more workers who offer retiree health coverage decreased by 17 percent between 1993 and 2001 for both pre- and post-Medicare eligible retirees.[17] The 2002 Kaiser/HRET survey similarly found that a declining percentage of large companies (those with at least 200 employees) offer retiree health benefits; only 34 percent of such employers offered retiree health coverage in 2002, compared to 66 percent of similar companies in 1988.[18] Another survey completed by Hewitt Associates LLC estimates a 15 percent decline in the number of large employers providing pre-age 65 retiree health coverage between 1991 and 2000 and an 18 percent decrease in the number of large employers providing health benefits to retirees age 65 or older during the same period.[19] The 2002 Kaiser/Hewitt retiree health study concluded that this trend will continue, with one in five large employers likely to eliminate retiree health coverage for future retirees within the next three years.[20]

Of those employers offering retiree health benefits, most are more likely to offer such benefits to early retirees and not to Medicare-eligible retirees. A report issued by Kaiser, HRET and The Commonwealth Fund (Kaiser/HRET/Commonwealth) estimates that only 23%

[2] Hewitt Associates LLC, "Health Care Cost Increases Expected to Continue Double-Digit Pace in 2003," (Lincolnshire, IL: Hewitt Associates LLC Oct. 14, 2002).

[3] The Henry J. Kaiser Family Foundation & Health Research and Educational Trust, "Employer Health Benefits, 2001 Annual Survey" (Menlo Park, CA: The Henry J. Kaiser Family Foundation and Health Research and Educational Trust 2001); William M. Mercer, "Mercer/Foster Higgins National Survey of Employer-Sponsored Health Plans 2001" (New York, N.Y.: William M. Mercer Inc. 2002). The 2001 Kaiser/HRET study, conducted between January and May 2001, surveyed more than 2,500 randomly selected public and private companies in the United States. The 2001 Mercer/Foster Higgins study used a national probability sampling of public and private employers and the results represent about 600,000 employers.

[4] The Henry J. Kaiser Family Foundation & Health Research and Educational Trust, "Employer Health Benefits, 2002 Annual Survey" (Menlo Park, CA: The Henry J. Kaiser Family Foundation and Health Research and Educational Trust 2002); Mercer Human Resource Consulting LLC, "Rate Hikes pushed employers to drop health plans, cut benefits in 2002—but average cost still rose," (New York, N.Y.: Mercer Human Resource Consulting LLC December 9, 2002). The 2002 Kaiser/HRET study surveyed 3,262 randomly selected public and private employers.

[5] The Henry J. Kaiser Family Foundation & Health Research and Educational Trust, "Employer Health Benefits, 2001 Annual Survey" (Menlo Park, CA: The Henry J. Kaiser Family Foundation and Health Research and Educational Trust 2001).

[6] The Henry J. Kaiser Family Foundation & Health Research and Educational Trust, "Employer Health Benefits, 2002 Annual Survey" (Menlo Park, CA: The Henry J. Kaiser Family Foundation and Health Research and Educational Trust 2002).

[7] The Henry J. Kaiser Family Foundation & Health Research and Educational Trust, "Employer Health Benefits, 2001 Annual Survey" (Menlo Park, CA: The Henry J. Kaiser Family Foundation and Health Research and Educational Trust 2001).

[8] U.S. General Accounting Office, "Retiree Health Benefits: Employer-Sponsored Benefits May Be Vulnerable to Further Erosion," GAO Doc. No. GAO-01-374, at 17 (May 2001).

[9] Anna M. Rappaport, "Planning for Health Care Needs in Retirement," in Forecasting Retirement Needs and Retirement Wealth, 288, 288-294 (Olivia S. Mitchell et al. eds., University of Pennsylvania Press 2000).

[10] U.S. General Accounting Office, "Retiree Health Benefits: Employer-Sponsored Benefits May Be Vulnerable to Further Erosion," GAO Doc. No. GAO-01-374, at 17-18 (May 2001).

[11] Anna M. Rappaport, "Postemployment Benefits: Retiree Health Challenges and Trends—2001 and Beyond," in Compensation and Benefits Management, 52, 56 (Autumn

2001) (citing William M. Mercer, "Mercer/Foster Higgins National Survey of Employer-Sponsored Health Plans 2000" (New York, N.Y.: William M. Mercer Inc. 2001).

[12] The Henry J. Kaiser Family Foundation & Hewitt Associates LLC, "Kaiser/Hewitt 2002 Retiree Health Survey" (Menlo Park, CA: The Henry J. Kaiser Family Foundation and Hewitt Associates LLC 2002). This online survey, conducted between July and September 2002, represents information from 435 private employers (with at least 1000 employees) that currently offer retiree health benefits.

[13] Anna M. Rappaport, "FAS 106 and Strategies for Managing Retiree Health Benefits," in Compensation and Benefits Management, 37 (Spring 2001); Paul Fronstin, "Retiree Health Benefits: Trends and Outlook," EBRI Issue Brief No. 236 (Employee Benefit Research Institute Aug. 2001).

[14] Paul Fronstin, "Retiree Health Benefits: Trends and Outlook," EBRI Issue Brief No. 236, at 3 (Employee Benefit Research Institute Aug. 2001).

[15] A survey by THAP!, Andersen and CalPERS found that both public and private employers considered controlling health care costs as a top business issue for the next two to three years. THAP! et al., "Productive Workforce Survey: Report of Findings, Private Employer/Public Agency" (THAP!, Andersen and CalPERS Aug. 2001); see also Anna M. Rappaport, "Postemployment Benefits: Retiree Health Challenges and Trends—2001 and Beyond," in Compensation and Benefits Management, 52, 56 (Autumn 2001) ("Companies seeking to reduce costs are closely examining retiree medical benefits.").

[16] Hearing Before the House Comm. on Education and the Workforce, 107th Cong. (2001) (statement of William J. Scanlon, Director of Health Care Services, GAO).

[17] William M. Mercer, "Mercer/Foster Higgins National Survey of Employer-Sponsored Health Plans 2001" (New York, NY: William M. Mercer, Inc. 2002).

[18] The Henry J. Kaiser Family Foundation & Health Research and Educational Trust, "Employer Health Benefits, 2002 Annual Survey" (Menlo Park, CA: The Henry J. Kaiser Family Foundation and Health Research and Educational Trust 2002).

[19] Hewitt Associates LLC, "Trends in Retiree Health Plans" (Lincolnshire, IL: Hewitt Associates LLC 2001). This conclusion is based on information from Hewitt Associates database of 1,020 large employers, including 85% of Fortune 100 companies and 57% of Fortune 500 companies.

[20] The Henry J. Kaiser Family Foundation & Hewitt Associates LLC, "Kaiser/Hewitt 2002 Retiree Health Survey" (Menlo Park, CA: The Henry J. Kaiser Family Foundation and Hewitt Associates LLC 2002); see also The Henry J. Kaiser Family Foundation & Health Research and Educational Trust, "Employer Health Benefits, 2002 Annual Survey" (Menlo Park, CA: The Henry J. Kaiser Family Foundation and Health Research and Educational Trust 2002) (11% of large employers predict they will eliminate retiree health benefits for future retirees).

of employers with at least 200 workers offered retiree health benefits to Medicare-age retirees in 2001. This is a decline of more than 10 percentage points in a three-year period.[21]

As the number of employers offering retiree health coverage declines, so has the incentive to provide future retirees with such coverage. Unions report that meaningful negotiations about the future provision of employer-sponsored retiree health benefits are becoming increasingly futile. Union representatives have informed EEOC that increasing numbers of employers have refused to include retiree health among the benefits to be provided to employees. A significant number of employers have agreed to provide retiree health only if the benefit terminates when the retiree becomes eligible for Medicare.

Alternatives to employer-sponsored retiree health coverage are costly, offer fewer benefits, and may be limited in availability, particularly for retirees not yet eligible for Medicare.[22] Under provisions of the Consolidated Omnibus Budget Reconciliation Act of 1985, 29 U.S.C. 1161 et seq. (COBRA), retirees under the age of 65 may be eligible for temporary health coverage from either their spouse's employer or their former employer, although the retiree may be required to pay the entire premium. Other retirees under age 65 must obtain coverage in the private individual insurance market, which often is prohibitively expensive or provides limited benefits.[23] Those unable to afford coverage in the private insurance market rely on public insurance, pay for health care out of pocket, or are uninsured. Retirees age 65 or older often rely on Medicare as their primary source of health coverage. Nonetheless, many retirees in this age group rely on employer-sponsored benefits to cover Medicare's cost-sharing requirements or gaps in Medicare coverage. Retirees who do not have access to employer-sponsored supplemental coverage must obtain private individual "Medicare supplement" insurance, which can be prohibitively expensive, particularly if prescription drug coverage is desired.[24] For these reasons, employer-sponsored retiree health coverage is a valuable benefit for older persons that should be protected and preserved to the greatest extent possible.

Interplay Between the ADEA and Employer-Sponsored Retiree Health Benefits

Section 4 of the ADEA makes it unlawful for an employer to discriminate against any individual with respect to "compensation, terms, conditions, or privileges or employment, because of such individual's age." 29 U.S.C. 623(a)(1). In 1989, the Supreme Court held in Public Employees Retirement Sys. of Ohio v. Betts, 492 U.S. 158, 109 S. Ct. 256 (1989), that the ADEA, nevertheless, did not prohibit discrimination in employee benefits, such as health insurance. In response to the Supreme Court's decision in Betts, Congress enacted the Older Workers Benefit Protection Act of 1990, Pub. L. No. 101-433, 104 Stat. 978 (1990) (OWBPA), which amended the ADEA and defined the term "compensation, terms, conditions or privileges of employment" in Section 4 of the Act as including employee benefits. 29 U.S.C. 630(l).

For many years after, however, there was little discussion about the interplay between the ADEA and the provision of retiree health benefits by employers. Many employers relied on legislative history to the OWBPA which states that the practice of eliminating, reducing, or altering employer-sponsored retiree health benefits with Medicare eligibility is lawful under the ADEA. Specifically, employers looked to a joint "Statement of Managers" clarifying several proposed amendments to the OWBPA, which was entered into the congressional records of both the House and Senate and accompanied the final compromise bill. On the subject of "retiree health," the Statement says:

Many employer-sponsored retiree medical plans provide medical coverage for retirees only until the retiree becomes eligible for Medicare. In many of these cases, where coverage is provided to retirees only until they attain Medicare eligibility, the value of the employer-

provided retiree medical benefits exceeds the value of the retiree's Medicare benefits. Other employers provide medical coverage to retirees at a relatively high level until the retirees become eligible for Medicare and at a lower level thereafter. In many of these cases, the value of the medical benefits that the retiree receives before becoming eligible for Medicare exceeds the total value of the retiree's Medicare benefits and the medical benefits that the employer provides after the retirees attains Medicare eligibility. These practices are not prohibited by this substitute. Similarly, nothing in this substitute should be construed as authorizing a claim on behalf of a retiree on the basis that the actuarial value of employer-provided health benefits available to that retiree not yet eligible for Medicare is less than the actuarial value of the same benefits available to a younger retiree.

Final Substitute: Statement of Managers, 136 Cong. Rec. S25353 (Sept. 24, 1990); 136 Cong. Rec. H27062 (Oct. 2, 1990).

In August 2000, the United States Court of Appeals for the Third Circuit became the first federal court of appeals to examine whether an employer's coordination of its retiree health plans with Medicare eligibility violated the ADEA. Erie County Retirees Ass'n v. County of Erie, 220 F.3d 193 (3rd Cir. 2000). Prior to 1992, Erie County offered current employees and retirees separate but similar traditional indemnity health insurance coverage. Id. at 196. In February 1998, however, in an effort to control escalating health benefit costs, the county began to require all eligible retirees over age 65 to accept a coordinated health care plan provided through a health maintenance organization (HMO) and Medicare. Eligible retirees had to have Medicare Part B Medical Insurance in order to participate in the plan. Id. at 197. Retirees not yet eligible for Medicare continued to be covered by a traditional indemnity plan until October 1998 when they were transferred to a hybrid point of service plan where each insured could select between an HMO and the traditional indemnity option on an as-needed basis. Id. In a class action lawsuit, the Medicare-eligible retirees alleged that the county violated the ADEA by offering them health insurance coverage that was inferior to that offered to the county's younger retirees. Id. at 193. In examining whether the county's practice violated the Act, the Third Circuit held that the Statement of Managers language was not controlling and that the ADEA prohibits an employer from treating "retirees differently with respect to health benefits based on Medicare eligibility," unless the employer can meet any of the affirmative defenses provided in section 4 of the ADEA. Id. at 213-14.[25] The one affirmative defense examined in detail by the Third Circuit was the equal benefit/equal cost defense set forth in 29 U.S.C. 623(f)(2)(B)(i). The equal benefit/equal cost defense has been part of the ADEA's regulatory framework since 1967.[26] Consistent with Congress' concern that employers might not hire older workers because many employee benefits become more costly with age, Department of Labor and EEOC regulations interpreted section 4(f)(2) of the ADEA as permitting employers to offer lower levels of certain employee benefits to older workers as long as the benefit cost incurred on behalf of older workers is no less than that incurred for younger workers. 29 CFR 1625.10. In the OWBPA, Congress adopted this test in section 4(f)(2)(B)(i) of the ADEA, thereby codifying the EEOC's equal benefit/equal cost rule.

In Erie County, the Third Circuit found that the costs Medicare incurs on behalf of retirees over age 65 cannot be considered when evaluating whether an employer has satisfied the equal cost prong and remanded the case so the district court could determine whether the county could nonetheless meet the equal benefit/equal cost test. Id. at 216. On remand, the county conceded that it could not meet the equal cost prong using the Third Circuit's formulation of the test. Erie County Retirees Ass'n v. County of Erie, 140 F. Supp.2d 466, 477 (W.D. Pa. 2001). The district court then found that the county did not provide equal benefits to its retirees because (1) age 65 retirees were required to pay a greater portion of the total cost of their health insurance

[21] The Henry J. Kaiser Family Foundation et al., "Erosion of Private Health Insurance Coverage For Retirees: Findings from the 2000 and 2001 Retiree Health and Prescription Drug Coverage Survey" (Menlo Park, CA: The Henry J. Kaiser Family Foundation, Health Research and Educational Trust, and The Commonwealth Fund 2002); see also The Henry J. Kaiser Family Foundation & Health Research and Educational Trust, "Employer Health Benefits, 2002 Annual Survey" (Menlo Park, CA: The Henry J. Kaiser Family Foundation and Health Research and Educational Trust 2002) (96% of employers with at least 200 employees offer health benefits to pre-age 65 retirees, while only 72% of large employers offer health benefits to retirees age 65 and above).

[22] U.S. General Accounting Office, "Retiree Health Benefits: Employer-Sponsored Benefits May Be Vulnerable to Further Erosion," GAO Doc. No. GAO-01-374, at 20-24 (May 2001).

[23] U.S. General Accounting Office, "Retiree Health Benefits: Employer-Sponsored Benefits May Be Vulnerable to Further Erosion," GAO Doc. No. GAO-01-374, at 20-22 (May 2001).

[24] U.S. General Accounting Office, "Retiree Health Benefits: Employer-Sponsored Benefits May Be Vulnerable to Further Erosion," GAO Doc. No. GAO-01-374, at 22-24 (May

2001). GAO estimates that Medigap coverage costs an average of $1,300 per year. Hearing Before the House Comm. on Education and the Workforce, 107th Cong. (2001) (statement of William J. Scanlon, Director of Health Care Services, GAO).

[25] The Commission submitted an amicus curiae brief in Erie County, asserting, based on the plain language of the ADEA, that (1) retirees are covered by the ADEA and (2) employer reliance on Medicare eligibility in making distinctions in employee benefits violated the ADEA, unless the employer satisfied one of the Act's specified defenses or exemptions. In its October 2000 Compliance Manual Chapter on "Employee Benefits," the Commission explicitly adopted the position taken by the Third Circuit in Erie County as its national enforcement policy. When the Commission announced in August 2001 that it wished to further study the relationship between the ADEA and employer-sponsored retiree health plans, the Commission unanimously voted to rescind those portions of its Compliance Manual that discussed the Erie County decision.

[26] In Public Employees Retirement Sys. of Ohio v. Betts, 492 U.S. 158, 109 S. Ct. 256 (1989), the Supreme Court held that the equal benefit/equal cost test did not apply to the ADEA. Congress believed the test should apply, and the regulatory equal benefit/equal cost test was codified in the OWBPA.

premiums than younger retirees; (2) the health plan offered to older retirees did not allow participants to alternate between different forms of coverage, while the plan offered to younger retirees did; and (3) the health plan for younger retirees did not restrict participants to a prescription drug formulary, while the plan for older retirees did contain such a restriction. Id. at 475-77.

Many benefit experts cautioned that the Erie County decision would exacerbate the erosion of employer-sponsored retiree health benefits.[27] The Erie County decision means, among other things, that an employer who voluntarily provides its pre-age 65 retirees with a bridge to Medicare (with the intent to terminate all employer-sponsored retiree coverage at that time) can do so without ADEA implications only if the benefits provided by the bridge coverage are either the same as or less generous than those provided by Medicare. Stated otherwise, in every instance where employer-provided bridge coverage exceeds Medicare coverage, the employer would be prevented by the ADEA from ending its coverage when retirees become eligible for Medicare. The Commission is concerned that many employers will respond to this outcome, given the dramatic cost increases for retiree health benefits, not by incurring additional costs for retiree benefits that supplement Medicare, but rather by reducing or eliminating health coverage for retirees who are not yet eligible for Medicare.

In fact, this is ultimately what happened in Erie County. In an attempt to comply with the court's ruling, the county transferred younger retirees from the hybrid point of service plan—where each retiree had the ability to select between HMO or traditional indemnity plan coverage on an as-needed basis—to an HMO plan similar to that available to retirees over age 65 that did not provide such an option. Erie County Retirees Ass'n v. County of Erie, 192 F. Supp.2d 369, 372 (W.D. Pa. 2002). The county also required employees not yet eligible for Medicare to pay a monthly amount for such coverage equal to the monthly amount of Medicare Part B premiums that retirees over age 65 paid. Id. The result, therefore, is a decrease in health benefits for retirees generally; older retirees receive no better health benefits, while younger retirees must pay more for health benefits that offer fewer choices.

Alternative Proposals

In considering the proper regulatory approach, EEOC closely examined whether it would be possible to apply the equal benefit/equal cost test in its regulations to the practice of coordinating employer-sponsored retiree health benefits with Medicare or a State-sponsored retiree health benefits program. The Commission evaluated various proposals that would have allowed employers to take the cost of Medicare into account when assessing whether they satisfied the equal cost test. The Commission also considered the feasibility of implementing regulations under the ADEA that would require employers to adopt or maintain benefits programs that supplement Medicare in order to satisfy the equal benefits test.

After extensive study, however, it does not appear that retiree health costs or benefits can be reasonably quantified in a regulation. Unlike valuation of costs associated with life insurance or long-term disability benefits, calculating retiree health costs is complex due to the multitude of variables, including types of plans, levels and types of coverage, deductibles, and geographical areas covered. In addition, the subjective nature of some health benefits, such as a greater choice in providers, makes any such valuation more complicated.

Even allowing an employer to take into account the "cost" of Medicare is problematic because the government's cost to provide Medicare services does not reflect what similar benefits would cost an employer in the marketplace. Nor can an employer's Medicare tax obligation, pursuant to the Federal Insurance Contributions Act, 26 U.S.C. 3101 et seq. (FICA), be considered the "cost" of any specific retiree's Medicare benefits inasmuch as most retirees have been employed by multiple employers over the course of their careers and employer FICA contributions are paid into a general Medicare fund that is not employee-specific. Additionally, the fact that employees themselves pay for a portion of the cost of Medicare further complicates cost valuation.

The Commission therefore believes that quantifying the cost to employers of post-Medicare retiree health benefits under any formulation of the equal cost test would not be practicable. This is particularly true for employers who maintain multiple plans for different categories of employees. Even for employers with only one plan, the variability in health claims data from year to year can be great. As a result, calculating retiree health benefit expenses would be cost prohibitive for many employers. Thus, even if it were possible to capture the myriad of complexities involved in a retiree health cost analysis in a regulation, the likelihood is that far too many employers might simply reduce or eliminate existing retiree health benefit plans instead of attempting to comply with such a regulation.

Further complicating compliance with many of the alternative proposals considered by the Commission is the fact that employers do not have the same flexibility in designing retiree health benefit programs as they do when designing other types of retirement benefit programs, such as cash-based retirement incentives. For example, providing supplemental health benefits to retirees who are eligible for Medicare may require that the employer obtain and administer a separate policy just for that coverage. Many employers are unable or unwilling to bear such a burden. Instead, if faced with such a choice, employers are more likely to simply eliminate retiree health coverage altogether—for retirees under and over age 65. Furthermore, future changes in the private health insurance market or in Medicare likely would necessitate further regulatory action were the Commission to adopt many of the alternative proposals considered. The Commission does not believe that it is possible to apply the equal benefit/equal cost test, or a variant of that rule, to the rapidly changing landscape of retiree health care.

The Commission therefore believes that application of the equal cost/equal benefit rule, or a variant of that rule, to the practice of coordinating retiree health benefits with Medicare or a State-sponsored retiree health benefits program would not allow employers to readily and cost-efficiently determine which practices are, and are not, permissible and therefore would not fully alleviate employers' concerns about offering retiree health benefits. It is clear that small and medium-sized employers, and those unable to hire sophisticated employee benefit professionals, would be most affected by a complicated rule. In light of the other factors affecting an employer's decision to provide retiree health benefits, the Commission believes that the current regulatory framework of the ADEA does not provide a sufficient safe harbor to protect and preserve the important employer practice of providing health coverage for retirees.

This lack of regulatory protection may cause a class of people—retirees not yet 65—to be left without any health insurance. It also may contribute to the loss of valuable employer-sponsored coverage that supplements Medicare for retirees age 65 and over. Because almost 60% of retirees between the ages of 55 to 64 rely on employer-sponsored health coverage as their primary source of health coverage,[28] and about one-third of retirees over age 65 rely on employer-provided retiree health plans to supplement Medicare,[29] the Commission believes that such a result is contrary to the public interest and necessitates regulatory action.

The Commission's Proposed Exemption

When enacting the ADEA, Congress recognized that enforcement of the Act required a case-by-case examination of employment practices.[30] In light of this recognition, Congress authorized the Commission to "establish such reasonable exemptions to and from any or all provisions of [the Act] as it may find necessary and proper in the public interest." 29 U.S.C. 628. Pursuant to that authority, the Commission proposes a narrowly drawn exemption that permits the practice of coordinating employer-provided retiree health coverage with eligibility for Medicare or a State-sponsored retiree health benefits program and shows due regard for the remedial purposes of the ADEA. Section 2(b) of the Act firmly establishes the goal of "encouraging employers and workers [to] find ways of meeting problems arising from the impact of age on employment." 29 U.S.C. 621(b). Unrestricted coordination of employer-sponsored retiree health benefits with Medicare or a State-Sponsored health benefits program permits employers to provide a valuable benefit to early retirees who otherwise might not be able to

---

[27] See Anna M. Rappaport, "Postemployment Benefits: Retiree Health Challenges and Trends—2001 and Beyond," in Compensation and Benefits Management, 52, 55 (Autumn 2001) (Erie County will force employers to examine the application of the ADEA to their retiree health plans with "little or no legal precedent"); Paul Fronstin, "Retiree Health Benefits: Trends and Outlook," EBRI Issue Brief No. 236, at 12-14 (Employee Benefit Research Institute Aug. 2001) ("because of the legal and cost concerns raised by the Erie County decision, [employers] are more likely to cut back on benefits for early retirees" or eliminate retiree health benefits).

[28] Hearing Before the House Comm. on Education and the Workforce, 107th Cong. (2001) (statement of William J. Scanlon, Director of Health Care Services, GAO). Of the

56.8% of retirees covered by employer-sponsored health coverage in 1999, 36.3% were covered in their own name and 20.5% received health benefits through a spouse. Paul Fronstin, "Retiree Health Benefits: Trends and Outlook," EBRI Issue Brief No. 236, at 6-7 (Employee Benefit Research Institute Aug. 2001).

[29] The Henry J. Kaiser Family Foundation et al., "Erosion of Private Health Insurance Coverage For Retirees: Findings from the 2000 and 2001 Retiree Health and Prescription Drug Coverage Survey," at iv (Menlo Park, CA: The Henry J. Kaiser Family Foundation, Health and Research Educational Trust and The Commonwealth Fund April 2002).

[30] H.R. Rep. No. 90-805 (1967), reprinted in 1967 U.S.C.C.A.N. 2213; S. Rep. 90-723 (1967).

afford health insurance coverage and allows employers to provide valuable supplemental health benefits to retirees who are eligible for Medicare.

The proposed exemption shows due regard for the Act's prohibition against arbitrary age discrimination in employment—a central concern of Congress when it enacted the ADEA. The exemption also is consistent with the Act's purpose of promoting the employment of older persons and is in accord with the Statement of Managers. See Final Substitute: Statement of Managers, 136 Cong. Rec. 25353 (Sept. 24, 1990); 126 Cong. Rec. H.27062 (Oct. 2, 1990).[31] Therefore, the Commission believes that the remedial purposes of the Act will be better served by allowing employers to coordinate retiree health benefits with Medicare or a State-sponsored retiree health benefits program.

Effect of Exemption

As with any exemption from remedial legislation, the proposal is a narrow exemption from the prohibitions of the ADEA. The exemption permits employee benefit plans to lawfully provide health benefits for retired participants that are altered, reduced or eliminated when the participant is eligible for Medicare health benefits or for health benefits under a State-sponsored retiree health benefits program. No other aspects of ADEA coverage or benefits other than retiree health benefits are affected by this exemption.

The proposed exemption would become effective on the date of publication of a final rule in the Federal Register. It is intended that the exemption shall apply to existing, as well as newly created, employer-provided retiree health benefit plans. As the Appendix to the proposed exemption indicates, it also is intended that the exemption shall apply to dependent and/or spousal health benefits that are included as part of the health benefits provided to retired participants. However, dependent and/or spousal benefits need not be identical to the health benefits provided for retired participants. Consequently, dependent and/or spousal benefits may be altered, reduced or eliminated pursuant to the exemption whether or not the health benefits provided for retired participants are similarly altered, reduced or eliminated.

Additional Amendments

In addition to the proposed exemption discussed above, the Commission proposes to redesignate subpart C of part 1627 as subpart C of part 1625 of Chapter XIV of Title 29 of the Code of Federal of Regulations. Subpart C of part 1627 currently includes two sections. The first, which will be redesignated as section 1625.30, outlines procedures by which the Commission may exercise its exemption authority under Section 9 of the ADEA. The second, redesignated as section 1625.31, explains the parameters of an already existing exemption for special employment programs. Redesignation does not alter either the procedures by which the Commission may exercise its exemption authority under Section 9 of the ADEA or the Special Employment Programs exemption.

Comments

The Commission invites comments on this proposed exemption from all interested parties, including employee rights organizations, labor unions, employers, benefits groups, actuaries, and state and local governments. In particular, the Commission would welcome comments on other types of government-sponsored retiree health benefit programs, including state and local government retiree health plans, that are comparable to Medicare.

In proposing this exemption, the Commission coordinated with other federal agencies in accord with Executive Order 12067, and incorporated, where appropriate, agency comments in the proposal.

Executive Order 12866 and Regulatory Flexibility Act

The proposed rule has been drafted and reviewed in accordance with Executive Order 12866, section 1(b), Principles of Regulation. This rule is considered a "significant regulatory action" under section 3(f)(4) of that Order and was reviewed by the Office of Management and Budget (OMB). The Commission does not believe that the proposed exemption will have a significant impact on small business entities under the Regulatory Flexibility Act because it imposes no economic or reporting burdens on such firms.

The ADEA applies to all employers with at least 20 employees. 29 U.S.C. 630(b). The Act prohibits covered employers from discriminat-

ing in employment against any individual who is at least 40 years of age. 29 U.S.C. 623, 631. The Bureau of Labor Statistics estimates that there are 74,347,000 individuals in the U.S. labor force that are age 40 or above.[32] According to Census Bureau information, approximately 1,976,216 establishments employed 20 or more employees in 2000.[33]

The proposed exemption would apply to all covered employers who provide health benefits to their retirees. In 2001, the GAO concluded that about one-third of large employers and less than 10% of small employers provided such benefits to current retirees.[34] According to the GAO, in 1999, such employer-sponsored health plans were relied on by 10 million retired individuals aged 55 and over as either their primary source of coverage or a supplement to Medicare coverage.[35]

The proposal—which exempts certain practices from regulation—will decrease, not increase, costs to covered employers by reducing the risks of liability for noncompliance with the statute. When the Third Circuit held that the practice of coordinating retiree health benefits with Medicare eligibility was unlawful unless an employer could meet the equal benefit/equal cost test, there was widespread concern that employers who currently provide such retiree health benefits would either have to provide greater benefits to older retirees or reduce benefits for younger retirees to comply. The Commission believes that, if required to make a choice between paying more or less to comply with the ADEA, many employers will choose to pay less by reducing or eliminating health coverage for retirees who are not yet eligible for Medicare. This result is particularly likely given the rising costs of health care in general. The proposed exemption seeks to eliminate this incentive by making clear that the ADEA permits employers to freely coordinate the provision of retiree health benefits with Medicare eligibility. This approach also benefits the significant number of employees who rely on employer-sponsored retiree health coverage and otherwise would have to obtain retiree health coverage in the private individual marketplace at substantial personal expense.

The proposed exemption has no reporting requirements. A major concern regarding the inequitable impact of regulation on small firms is that reporting and accompanying record keeping requirements can be as costly to smaller firms as large ones. The absence of reporting requirements eliminates this concern.

It is not likely that the proposed regulation will disrupt the efficient functioning of the economy and private market forces. Until recently, when structuring retiree health benefits, many employers relied on legislative history to the OWBPA which states that the practice of eliminating, reducing, or altering employer-sponsored retiree health benefits with Medicare eligibility is lawful under the ADEA. The proposed regulation permits the practice of unrestricted coordination of retiree health benefits with Medicare eligibility to continue.

Under other proposals considered by the Commission, many employers would have been forced to discontinue retiree health coverage if they could not afford the required actuarial analysis. It is clear that small and medium-sized employers, and those unable to hire sophisticated employee benefit professionals, would be most affected by a complicated rule. Larger employers who maintain multiple plans for different categories of employees also would face significant expense complying with alternative proposals. Even for employers with only one plan, the variability in health claims data from year to year can be great. As a result, calculating retiree health benefit expenses under alternative proposals considered by the Commission would have been cost prohibitive for many employers.

List of Subjects

29. CFR Part 1625

Advertising, Aged, Employee benefit plans, Equal employment opportunity, Retirement.

29. CFR Part 1627

Aged, Equal employment opportunity, Reporting and recordkeeping requirements.

For the Commission.

Cari M. Dominguez, Chair.

---

[31] While the Third Circuit in Erie County did not find the Statement of Managers controlling, the Commission, in the exercise of its exemption authority, is free to take a broader look at the legislative record in determining whether the proposed exemption is consistent with the Act's purpose of promoting the employment of older persons. The Statement of Managers strongly suggests that it is.

[32] Bureau of Labor Statistics, U.S. Department of Labor, Current Population Survey (April 2003).

[33] Census Bureau, U.S. Department of Commerce, Statistics of U.S. Businesses (2000).

[34] Hearing Before the House Comm. on Education and the Workforce, 107th Cong. (2001) (statement of William J. Scanlon, Director of Health Care Services, GAO).

[35] U.S. General Accounting Office, "Retiree Health Benefits: Employer-Sponsored Benefits May Be Vulnerable to Further Erosion," GAO Doc. No. GAO-01-374, at 1 (May 2001).

For the reasons discussed in the preamble, the Equal Employment Opportunity Commission proposes to amend 29 CFR chapter XIV as follows:

PART 1627—RECORDS TO BE MADE OR KEPT RELATING TO AGE: NOTICES TO BE POSTED

1. Revise the heading of Part 1627 to read as set forth above.

2. The authority citation for 29 CFR Part 1627 shall continue to read as follows:

Authority: § 7, 81 Stat. 604; 29 U.S.C. 626; sec. 11, 52 Stat. 1066, 29 U.S.C. 211; sec. 12, 29 U.S.C. 631, Pub L. 99-592, 100 Stat. 3342; sec. 2, Reorg. Plan No. 1 of 1978, 43 FR 19807.

3. In § 1627.1, remove paragraph (b) and redesignate paragraph (c) as new paragraph (b).

4. In Part 1627, redesignate Subpart C and sections 1627.15 and 1627.16 as Subpart C of Part 1625 and sections 1625.30 and 1625.31, respectively.

PART 1625—AGE DISCRIMINATION IN EMPLOYMENT ACT

5. The authority citation for 29 CFR Part 1625 is revised to read as follows:

Authority: 81 Stat. 602; 29 U.S.C. 621; 5 U.S.C. 301; Secretary's Order No. 10-68; Secretary's Order No. 11-68; § 9, 81 Stat. 605; 29 U.S.C. 628; sec. 12, 29 U.S.C. 631, Pub. L. 99-592, 100 Stat. 3342; sec. 2, Reorg. Plan No. 1 of 1978, 43 FR 19807.

6. In newly redesignated Subpart C of Part 1625, revise the heading of newly redesignated § 1625.31 and the first sentence of paragraph (a) to read as follows:

§ 1625.31 Special employment programs.

(a) Pursuant to the authority contained in section 9 of the Act and in accordance with the procedure provided therein and in § 1625.30(b) of this part, it has been found necessary and proper in the public interest to exempt from all prohibitions of the Act all activities and programs under Federal contracts or grants, or carried out by the public employment services of the several States, designed exclusively to provide employment for, or to encourage the employment of, persons with special employment problems, including employment activities and programs under the Manpower Development and Training Act of 1962, Public Law No. 87-415, 76 Stat. 23 (1962), as amended, and the Economic Opportunity Act of 1964, Public Law No. 88-452, 78 Stat. 508 (1964), as amended, for persons among the long-term unemployed, handicapped, members of minority groups, older workers, or youth. * * *

* * * * *

7. Add section 1625.32 to Subpart C of Part 1625 to read as follows:

§ 1625.32 Coordination of retiree health benefits with Medicare and State health benefits.

(a) *Definitions.* (1) Employee benefit plan means an employee benefit plan as defined in 29 U.S.C. 1002(3).

(2) Medicare means the health insurance program available pursuant to Title XVIII of the Social Security Act, 42 U.S.C. 1395 et seq.

(3) Comparable State health benefit plan means a State-sponsored health benefit plan that, like Medicare, provides retired participants who have attained a minimum age with health benefits, whether or not the type, amount or value of those benefits are equivalent to the type, amount or value of the health benefits provided under Medicare.

(b) *Exemption.* Some employee benefit plans provide health benefits for retired participants that are altered, reduced or eliminated when the participant is eligible for Medicare health benefits or for health benefits under a comparable State health benefit plan. Pursuant to the authority contained in section 9 of the Act, and in accordance with the procedures provided therein and in § 1625.30(b) of this part, it is hereby found necessary and proper in the public interest to exempt from all prohibitions of the Act such coordination of retiree health benefits with Medicare or a comparable State health benefit plan.

(c) *Scope of exemption.* This exemption shall be narrowly construed. It does not apply to the use of eligibility for Medicare or a comparable State health benefit plan in connection with any act, practice or benefit of employment not specified in paragraph (b) of this section. Nor does it apply to the use of the age of eligibility for Medicare or a comparable State health benefit plan in connection with any act, practice or benefit of employment not specified in paragraph (b) of this section.

Appendix to § 1625.32—Questions and Answers Regarding Coordination of Retiree Health Benefits with Medicare and State Health Benefits

Q1. Why is the Commission issuing an exemption from the Act?

A1. The Commission recognizes that while employers are under no legal obligation to offer retiree health benefits, some employers choose to do so in order to maintain a competitive advantage in the marketplace—using these and other benefits to attract and retain the best talent available to work for their organizations. Further, retiree health benefits clearly benefit workers, allowing such individuals to acquire affordable health insurance coverage at a time when private health insurance coverage might otherwise be cost prohibitive. The Commission believes that it is in the best interest of both employers and employees for the Commission to pursue a policy that permits employers to offer these benefits to the greatest extent possible.

Q2. Does the exemption mean that the Act no longer applies to retirees?

A2. No. Only the practice of coordinating retiree health benefits with Medicare (or a comparable State health benefit plan) as specified in paragraph (b) of this section is exempt from the Act. In all other contexts, the Act continues to apply to retirees to the same extent that it did prior to the issuance of this section.

Q3. May employers continue to offer "Medicare carve-out plans" that deduct from the health benefits provided to Medicare-eligible retirees those health benefits that Medicare provides, while continuing to provide to Medicare-eligible retirees those health benefits that Medicare does not provide?

A3. Yes. Employers may continue to offer such "carve-out plans'and make Medicare the primary payer of health benefits for Medicare-eligible retirees. Employers may also continue to offer "carve-out plans" to those retirees eligible for health benefits pursuant to a comparable State health benefit plan and make the comparable State health plan the primary payer of health benefits for these State-eligible retirees.

Q4. Does the exemption also apply to dependent and/or spousal health benefits that are included as part of the health benefits provided for retired participants?

A4. Yes. Because dependent and/or spousal health benefits are benefits provided to the retired participant, the exemption applies to these benefits, just as it does to the health benefits for the retired participant. However, dependent and/or spousal benefits need not be identical to the health benefits provided for retired participants. Consequently, dependent and/or spousal benefits may be altered, reduced or eliminated pursuant to the exemption whether or not the health benefits provided for retired participants are similarly altered, reduced or eliminated.

Q5. Does the exemption permit employers to use Medicare (or comparable State health benefit plan) eligibility, or the age of Medicare eligibility (or the age of eligibility for a comparable State health benefit plan) as a basis for other acts, practices or decisions regarding retirees?

A5. No. Employer use of Medicare (or comparable State health benefit plan) eligibility or the age of Medicare eligibility (or the age of eligibility for a comparable State health benefit plan) in a manner other than as specified in paragraph (b) of this section likely would be considered reliance upon an age-defined factor. Reliance upon an age-defined factor in making distinctions in employee benefits violates the Act, unless the employer satisfies one of the Act's specified defenses or exemptions.

Q6. Does the exemption apply to existing, as well as to newly created, employee benefit plans?

A6. Yes. The exemption applies to all retiree health benefits that coordinate with Medicare (or a comparable State health benefit plan) as specified in paragraph (b) of this section, whether those benefits are provided for in an existing or newly created employee benefit plan.

Q7. Does the exemption apply to health benefits that are provided to current employees who are at or over the age of Medicare eligibility (or the age of eligibility for a comparable State health benefit plan)?

A7. No. The exemption applies only to retiree health benefits, not to health benefits that are provided to current employees. Thus, health benefits for current employees must be provided in a manner that comports with the requirements of the Act. Moreover, under the laws governing the Medicare program, an employer must offer to current employees who are at or over the age of Medicare eligibility the same health benefits, under the same conditions, that it offers to any current employee under the age of Medicare eligibility.

[FR Doc. 03-17738 Filed 7-11-03; 8:45 am]

¶ 20,540

Employee Benefits Security Administration (EBSA)—Investment advisers—State registration—Securities and Exchange Commission (SEC).—.—Reproduced below is the text of a proposed rule which would require state-registered investment advisers that wish to obtain or maintain investment manager status under ERISA to electronically register through a centralized electronic filing system established by the SEC in conjunction with state securities authorities. The electronic system, known as the Investment Adviser Registration Depository (IARD), would become the only way which state-registered investment advisers could satisfy ERISA's filing requirements for investment adviser status.

The proposed regulation was published in the Federal Register on December 9, 2003 (68 FR 68709) and was finalized on August 24, 2004 (69 FR 52119). The final regulations appear at ¶ 14,139A and ¶ 14,879. The preamble is reproduced at ¶ 24,8060.

ERISA § 3(38)(B)(ii).

Part III

Department of Labor

Employee Benefits Security Administration

29 CFR Part 2510

Electronic Registration Requirements for Investment Advisers To Be Investment Managers Under Title I of ERISA; Proposed Rule

DEPARTMENT OF LABOR

Employee Benefits Security Administration

29 CFR Part 2510

RIN 1210-AA94

Electronic Registration Requirements for Investment Advisers To Be Investment Managers Under Title I of ERISA

AGENCY: Employee Benefits Security Administration, Department of Labor.

ACTION: Notice of proposed rulemaking.

SUMMARY: This document contains a proposed regulation relating to the definition of investment manager in section 3(38)(B) of Title I of the Employee Retirement Income Security Act of 1974 (ERISA). Under the proposed regulation, in lieu of filing a copy of their state registration forms with the Secretary of Labor, state-registered investment advisers seeking to obtain or maintain investment manager status under Title I of ERISA would have to electronically register through the Investment Adviser Registration Depository (IARD) as an investment adviser with the state in which they maintain their principal office and place of business. The IARD is a centralized electronic filing system, established by the Securities and Exchange Commission (SEC) in conjunction with state securities authorities. The IARD enables investment advisers to satisfy SEC and state registration obligations through the use of the Internet, and current filing information in the IARD database is readily available to the Department and the general public via the Internet. If adopted, the proposed regulation would make electronic registration through the IARD the exclusive method for state-registered investment advisers to satisfy filing requirements for investment manager status under section 3(38)(B)(ii) of Title I of ERISA. The proposed regulation would affect plan trustees, investment managers, other fiduciaries, and plan participants and beneficiaries.

DATES: Written comments (either in print or electronic format) are invited and must be submitted to the Department of Labor on or before February 9, 2004.

ADDRESSES: Interested persons are invited to submit written comments (preferably with three copies) to the Office of Regulations and Interpretations, Room N-5669, Employee Benefits Security Administration, U.S. Department of Labor, 200 Constitution Ave., NW., Washington, DC 20210, Attention: ERISA Investment Manager Electronic Registration NPRM. Written comments may also be sent by Internet to the following address: E-ORI.EBSA@dol.gov. All submissions received will be available for public inspection and copying from 8:30 a.m. to 4:30 p.m. at the Public Disclosure Room, Employee Benefits Security Administration, U.S. Department of Labor, Room N-1513, 200 Constitution Ave. NW., Washington, DC 20210.

FOR FURTHER INFORMATION CONTACT: Florence M. Novellino, Office of Regulations and Interpretations, Employee Benefits Security Administration, U.S. Department of Labor, Washington, DC 20210, telephone (202) 693-8518 (not a toll free number).

SUPPLEMENTARY INFORMATION:

Background

Under Title I of the Employee Retirement Income Security Act of 1974 (ERISA), named fiduciaries of plans may appoint investment managers to manage assets of the plan. If the investment manager is a registered investment adviser, bank or insurance company, and meets the other requirements for being an "investment manager" as defined in section 3(38) of ERISA, the plan trustees are relieved from certain liabilities relating to the investment manager's performance.[1]

In 1996, the National Securities Market Improvement Act (NSMIA) amended the Investment Advisers Act of 1940 (Advisers Act) to divide certain investment adviser regulatory responsibilities, including the registration requirements, between the Securities and Exchange Commission (SEC) and the states. Prior to 1996, most investment advisers were required to register with the SEC and in each state in which they were doing business. Pursuant to paragraph (1) of section 203A(a) of the Advisers Act, and SEC rule at 17 CFR 275.203A-1, certain investment advisers are prohibited from registering with the SEC but must register with the state in which the adviser maintains it principal office and place of business.[2] The legislative history of NSMIA indicates that this division of regulatory responsibilities was intended, among other things, to encourage the SEC and state regulators to create a uniform system for "one-stop" filing that would benefit investors, reduce regulatory and paperwork burdens for registered investment advisers, and facilitate supervision of investment advisers.[3]

The SEC implemented that legislative intent at the federal level by publishing a final rule in September of 2000 at 17 CFR 275.203-1 which made electronic filing with the Investment Adviser Registration Depository (IARD) mandatory for SEC-registered advisers. Additionally, all states accept forms filed via the IARD to satisfy state registration requirements, and many mandate state registration via the IARD.[4] Accordingly, the IARD has become a "one-stop" Internet-based centralized filing system that enables investment advisers to satisfy filing obligations with both federal and state securities regulators. Pertinent state registration information in the IARD database is available on the Internet to the general public through the Investment Adviser Public Disclosure (IAPD) Web site that may be directly accessed through the SEC's Web site or through links from various state and investor Web sites. The IAPD Web site contains investment adviser registration data, including information about current registration forms, registration status, services provided, fees charged, and disclosures about certain conflicts of interest and disciplinary events, if any. The IAPD Web site includes information on investment advisers that currently are registered with the SEC or a state, and also contains information on invest-

---

[1] Section 402(c)(3) of ERISA states that a plan may provide that with respect to control or management of plan assets a named fiduciary may appoint an investment manager or managers to manage (including the power to acquire and dispose of) plan assets. Section 405(d) of ERISA provides in part that, if an investment manager or managers have been appointed under section 402(c)(3), then no trustee shall be liable for the acts or omissions of such investment manager or managers, or be under an obligation to invest or otherwise manage any asset of the plan which is subject to the management of such investment manager.

[2] Specifically, subject to certain exceptions, investment advisers fall into three categories under the NSMIA amendments. First, investment advisers having assets under management of less than $25 million generally are prohibited from registering with the SEC but must register with the state regulatory authority in the state where the investment adviser maintains its principal office and place of business. Those with at least $25 million but less than $30 million may register with the SEC in lieu of filing with state authorities. Those with $30 million or more must register with the SEC. Section 203A(a) of the Advisers Act is codified at 15 U.S.C. 80b-3a(a). See also 17 CFR 275.203A-2 for exemptions from the prohibition for certain investment advisers registering with the SEC.

[3] S. Rep. No. 104-293, at 5 (1996).

[4] The State of Wyoming has not promulgated a state investment adviser regulation requirement; therefore all Wyoming-based investment advisers are required to register under the Advisers Act with the SEC via the IARD. See 65 FR 57438, 57445 (Sept. 22, 2000).

ment advisers that were registered in the previous two years but are no longer registered.

Section 3(38)(B) of Title I of ERISA was also amended to reflect the above-described changes to the investment adviser registration requirements under the Advisers Act.[5] Specifically, section 3(38)(B) of ERISA requires that, to be an investment manager under Title I, an investment adviser must: (i) be registered with the SEC under the Advisers Act of 1940, or (ii) if not registered under such Act by reason of paragraph (1) of section 203A(a) of such Act, be registered as an investment adviser under the laws of the state in which it maintains its principal office and place of business and, at the time the investment adviser last filed the registration form it most recently filed with such state in order to maintain its registration under the laws of such state, it also filed a copy of such form with the Secretary of Labor.

To implement the filing requirements in section 3(38)(B)(ii) of ERISA, the Department announced on January 14, 1998, that state-registered investment advisers seeking to qualify, or remain qualified, as investment managers must file a copy of their most recent state registration form for the state in which it maintains its principal office and place of business with the Department prior to November 10, 1998, and thereafter file with the Department copies of any subsequent filings with that state. The ongoing obligation to file copies with the Department was, however, to be temporary in nature and remain in effect until a centralized database containing the state registration forms, or substantially similar information, was available to the Department.[6]

The current requirement to file with the Department copies of state registration filings already accessible to the Department and the general public via the IAPD Web site places an unnecessary administrative burden on the regulated community. The requirement also results in the Department allocating resources to receive, sort, and store paper copies of information readily available in electronic form. It is the Department's view that use of the IARD as a centralized electronic database would improve the ability of the Department, plan fiduciaries, and plan participants and beneficiaries to readily access registration information regarding investment advisers eligible to be investment managers of ERISA-covered plans. As noted above, not only does the SEC require electronic filing through the IARD for registration under the Advisers Act, but most states also require IARD filing for compliance with state investment adviser registration requirements. While a few states do not make electronic filing through the IARD mandatory, as noted above, all states permit investment advisers to use the IARD to satisfy registration requirements. As described more fully below, the Department believes the majority of investment managers of ERISA-covered plans already file registration forms electronically through the IARD under the Advisers Act or under applicable state securities laws. In the Department's view, the benefits to plan trustees, plan participants and beneficiaries, and the Department of this proposed regulation outweigh the relatively small incremental cost that some investment managers may incur to file state registration filings through the IARD.

Summary of the Proposed Regulation

The proposed regulation would add § 2510.3-38 to title 29 of the Code of Federal Regulations. Section 2510.3-38(a) would describe the general filing requirement with the Secretary set forth in section 3(38)(B)(ii) applicable to state-registered investment advisers seeking to become or remain investment managers under Title I of ERISA. The regulation would also make clear that its purpose is to establish the exclusive means to satisfy that filing obligation. Section 2510.3-38(b) would provide that, for a state-registered investment adviser to satisfy the filing requirement in section 3(38)(B)(ii) of ERISA, it must electronically file the required registration forms through the IARD. Section 2510.3-38(b) would also provide that submitting a copy of state registration forms to the Secretary does not constitute compliance with section 3(38)(B)(ii) of ERISA. Section 2510.3-38(c) would define the term "Investment Adviser Registration Depository" and "IARD" for purposes of the regulation as the centralized electronic depository described in 17 CFR 275.203-1. Finally, § 2510.3-38(d) would provide a cross-reference to the SEC Internet site at http://www.sec.gov/iard for information on filing investment advisor registration forms with the IARD.

Effective Date and Interim Reliance

This regulation is proposed to be effective 60 days after publication of a final rule in the Federal Register. If adopted, the proposed regulation would be applicable to investment adviser registration filings due after the effective date of the final regulation. Until the effective date of the final regulation, investment advisers seeking to obtain or maintain investment manager status under Title I of ERISA will be treated as having met the filing obligations with the Secretary of Labor described in section 3(38)(B)(ii) of ERISA for any registration filing due on or after the date the proposed regulation is published in the Federal Register if they satisfy the conditions of the proposed regulation.

Regulatory Impact Analysis

Summary

The Department has undertaken this proposed rulemaking for the purpose of establishing a single and readily accessible source of consistent information about the registration of investment advisers that are investment managers by virtue of meeting the requirements of section 3(38)(B)(ii) of ERISA. The Department believes the regulation, if implemented as proposed, would benefit plan fiduciaries, investment advisers, and ultimately the participants and beneficiaries of employee benefit plans. Although the anticipated benefits of the proposal are not quantified here, they are expected to more than justify its relatively modest estimated cost.

The estimated cost of the implementation of electronic registration through the IARD for approximately 500 advisers that submitted copies of their state registrations to the Secretary of Labor, and that currently register in only those states that do not mandate IARD filing, is just under $400,000. Ongoing annual costs are estimated at $50,000. These costs will be offset by efficiency gains for plan fiduciaries and for investment advisers that wish to be appointed by plan fiduciaries. As a result of the electronic registration requirement, plan fiduciaries will be able to access a single source of registration information regardless of the size or location of the adviser, and advisers may more readily demonstrate their eligibility to be investment managers in order to gain appointments by plan fiduciaries. Over time, these investment managers may also reduce the handling of paper and the time required to complete the Form ADV, which is the joint SEC and state registration form that is also currently accepted by all the states for State registration purposes. Electronic availability of registration information will also support better and more transparent decision making with respect to the appointment of investment managers, which ultimately benefits the participants and beneficiaries of the plans involved.

Discussion

The proposal would benefit plan fiduciaries that wish to appoint an investment manager pursuant to section 402(c)(3) of ERISA. Under section 405(d)(1) of ERISA, plan fiduciaries are not liable for the acts or omissions of the investment manager, and have no obligation to invest assets subject to management by the investment manager. The centralized source of readily accessible registration information offered by the IARD will help plan fiduciaries more efficiently locate information needed to determine whether advisers they may consider appointing are eligible to be an investment manager under ERISA. The source and format of information will no longer differ based on the size or principal business location of the adviser.

Uniform use of the IARD for all advisers who wish to be or remain as investment managers under ERISA will benefit these advisers as well. The change to electronic filing will not change the incentives for investment advisers to become investment managers under ERISA, but should promote increased efficiency for doing so. Advisers are not required to be an investment manager to conduct advisory activities for any customer. The Department assumes that an adviser's decision whether to meet the definition of investment manager under ERISA is based on factors unrelated to the form or format of their registration. It is therefore expected that those state-registered advisers who filed paper copies of their state registration forms with the Secretary chose to do so to gain an advantage in securing appointments by plan fiduciaries.

In any case, this proposed regulation will not change the content of the filings for these advisers because all states accept the joint SEC and state filing form (Form ADV) for state registration, and with certain exceptions, all of the copies submitted to the Secretary were made on

---

[5] See sec. 308(b)(1) of Title III of NSMIA and Act of November 10, 1997, § 1, Pub. L. 105-72, 111 Stat. 1457.

[6] Pub. L. 105-72 provided that a fiduciary shall be treated as meeting the requirement for filing a copy of the required state registration form with the Secretary if a copy of the form

(or substantially similar information) is available to the Secretary from a centralized electronic or other record-keeping database. See Act of November 10, 1997, § 1(b), Pub. L. 105-72, 111 Stat. 1457.

Form ADV.[7] Mandatory use of the IARD will, however, change the format and manner in which the information is transmitted. While the Department expects advisers to incur a cost to establish a procedure for electronic filing through the IARD plus an annual fee, the change to an electronic format and transmission method is expected to be more efficient and less costly over time. Use of the IARD will reduce the paper handling, filing, and mailing costs associated with providing copies to the State or States as well as to the Secretary, and reduce handling to obtain and reproduce signatures. The SEC cited similar efficiency gains in its regulatory impact analysis of the final rule implementing mandatory electronic filing for federally regulated advisers. Securities and Exchange Commission, Electronic Filing by Investment Advisers; Final Rule, 65 FR 57438, Sept. 22, 2000.

The proposed regulation will directly affect only those investment advisers who wish to become or remain as investment managers under section 3(38) of ERISA, who generally have $25 million or less under management and consequently do not register with the SEC, and who register only in states that do not mandate use of the IARD to satisfy state registration requirements. Copies of registration forms submitted to the Secretary by State-registered investment advisers indicate that about 500 State-registered advisers have registered in only a non-IARD state.[8] Prior to the implementation of the IARD and many States' decisions to mandate use of the IARD to meet state adviser registration requirements, about 1,500 advisers provided paper copies of their state registration forms to the Secretary. Based on the data contained in those filings, about 1,000 of these already have the capability to file electronically because they are required to register in states that mandate use of the IARD. The Department therefore assumes that this proposed regulation would affect only those advisers that register only in non-IARD states.

Under existing requirements, State-registered advisers incur a State registration filing fee with every State in which they are required to register, plus postage and handling fees for their submissions. Such fees vary by State. Most if not all of the 500 advisers potentially affected by this proposed regulation now register in only one state. When advisers registered only in non-IARD States register through the IARD, the appropriate state registration fee will be forwarded to the state, such that there will be no net change in state filing fees.

The Advisers Act and Form ADV allow for the requirement that states be provided registration statements. To facilitate state registration, the registrant checks the appropriate boxes on the form for each applicable state, and the IARD then distributes the required information electronically to those states. States will be unaffected because they will continue to receive existing fees, although they will be transmitted in a different manner.

These advisers would, however, newly incur the IARD initial filing fee of $150 for advisers of the size under consideration here, and an annual filing fee of $100. It is also expected that the 500 state-registered advisers will incur a cost for the set-up of the electronic filing capability, and an expenditure of time to adjust internal procedures and put existing information into an electronic format. Filing fees for the first year are expected to total $75,000 in the first year and $50,000 in each subsequent year for these advisers.

The cost of the electronic filing set-up is not known. The SEC did not quantify the cost of set-up in the final rule cited above that pertained to mandatory use of the IARD for registration with the SEC. However, for the purpose of this discussion, the cost for establishment of electronic filing capability has been estimated to be $500, or $250,000 for the 500 advisers affected. This is a one-time cost based on available information on annual fees charged to SEC registrants by commercial providers of service in the industry.[9] An examination of a sample of the 500 individual filings showed that many of the advisers in question already use the software of a single provider for completing their Form ADV. Because this provider performs services to IARD filers who are currently SEC registrants as well, we have assumed that their range of services includes a method of facilitating electronic filing. It is also assumed that all advisers make use of electronic technology in the normal course of business and will not be required to make substantial technological changes as a result of this proposal.

A one-time cost is also estimated for the time required for the adviser to adjust its internal procedures to input data electronically, if necessary. A comparison of a sample of the paper filings received with IARD data indicated that these advisers had not also filed electronically with

IARD. It seems likely that many advisers already prepare the forms electronically, regardless of whether they submit them electronically. To account for preparation for electronic transmission, it has been estimated that the advisers will incur the cost of two hours of a financial professional's time at $68 per hour, for a cost of $136 per adviser and a total of $68,000.

The estimated one-time cost of this proposal totals $393,000. The ongoing cost of maintaining registration information and completing and filing Form ADV is not accounted for here because the advisers prepare and file such forms to meet state registration requirements and would continue to do so without regard to this proposed regulation. The ongoing incremental cost of this proposal is therefore $100 per adviser per year, or $50,000.

The Department considered alternatives to this proposal, including issuing no guidance and implementing a standard that would provide the adviser an option to either file a print copy of its state registration or make use of the IARD. The value of greater efficiency through the elimination of dual sources of registration information and promotion of greater accessibility of consistent information through electronic methods was considered to outweigh the relatively modest estimated cost of about $800 per adviser in the first year, and $100 per adviser in each subsequent year. As a result, the Department elected to issue this proposal and seek public comment on its views.

Executive Order 12866

Under Executive Order 12866, the Department must determine whether the regulatory action is "significant" and therefore subject to the requirements of the Executive Order and subject to review by the Office of Management and Budget (OMB). Under section 3(f), the order defines a "significant regulatory action" as an action that is likely to result in a rule (1) having an annual effect on the economy of $100 million or more, or adversely and materially affecting a sector of the economy, productivity, competition, jobs, the environment, public health or safety, or State, local or tribal governments or communities (also referred to as "economically significant"); (2) creating serious inconsistency or otherwise interfering with an action taken or planned by another agency; (3) materially altering the budgetary impacts of entitlement grants, user fees, or loan programs or the rights and obligations of recipients thereof; or (4) raising novel legal or policy issues arising out of legal mandates, the President's priorities, or the principles set forth in the Executive Order.

Pursuant to the terms of the Executive Order, it has been determined that this action is "significant" within the meaning of section 3(f)(4) of the Executive Order and has therefore been reviewed by OMB. The Department has also undertaken the assessment of the costs and benefits of this regulatory action presented above.

Paperwork Reduction Act

As part of its continuing effort to reduce paperwork and respondent burden, the Department of Labor conducts a preclearance consultation program to provide the general public and federal agencies with an opportunity to comment on proposed and continuing collections of information in accordance with the Paperwork Reduction Act of 1995 (PRA 95) (44 U.S.C. 3506(c)(2)(A)). This helps to ensure that requested data can be provided in the desired format, reporting burden (time and financial resources) is minimized, collection instruments are clearly understood, and the impact of collection requirements on respondents can be properly assessed.

Currently, EBSA is soliciting comments concerning the proposed information collection request (ICR) included in this Notice of Proposed Rulemaking concerning Electronic Registration Requirements for Investment Advisers to be Investment Managers Under Title I of ERISA (ERISA Investment Manager Electronic Registration). A copy of the ICR may be obtained by contacting the individual identified in the PRA Addresses section below.

The Department has submitted a copy of the proposed information collection to OMB in accordance with 44 U.S.C. 3507(d) for review of its information collections. The Department and OMB are particularly interested in comments that:

• Evaluate whether the proposed collection of information is necessary for the proper performance of the functions of the agency, including whether the information will have practical utility;

---

[7] Several exceptions were observed; in those cases, the adviser submitted a copy of the State's action on their registration, such as a license or approval form, rather than the registration form itself. In each case, other advisers' filings for the same State were examined to confirm that the state did accept Form ADV filings.

[8] California, Florida, Kentucky, South Carolina, and West Virginia at the time of this writing.

[9] Such fees are used here as a proxy only; the fees do not pertain specifically to electronic set-up or transmission.

• Evaluate the accuracy of the agency's estimate of the burden of the collection of information, including the validity of the methodology and assumptions used;

• Enhance the quality, utility, and clarity of the information to be collected; and

• Minimize the burden of the collection of information on those who are to respond, including through the use of appropriate automated, electronic, mechanical, or other technological collection techniques or other forms of information technology, e.g., permitting electronic submission of responses.

Comments should be sent to the Office of Information and Regulatory Affairs, Office of Management and Budget, Room 10235, New Executive Office Building, Washington, DC 20503; Attention: Desk Officer for the Employee Benefits Security Administration. Although comments may be submitted through February 9, 2004, OMB requests that comments be received within 30 days of publication of the Notice of Proposed Rulemaking to ensure their consideration.

PRA Addresses: Address requests for copies of the ICR to Joseph S. Piacentini, Office of Policy and Research, U.S. Department of Labor, Employee Benefits Security Administration, 200 Constitution Avenue, NW., Room N-5718, Washington, DC 20210. Telephone (202) 693-8410; Fax: (202) 219-5333. These are not toll-free numbers.

The Department is issuing these proposed rules to establish the uniform availability of investment adviser registration information in a centralized electronic database. The proposed rule would affect investment advisers that register with the states rather than SEC by virtue of the requirements of NSMIA, who do not currently register electronically through the IARD, and who wish to fall within the definition of investment manager for purposes of ERISA section 3(38)(B). Such advisers currently file a paper copy of the applicable state registration form with the Secretary of Labor pursuant to section 3(38)(B)(ii) of the statute. The information collection is found in the proposed regulation at section 2520.3-38(b). The basis for the burden estimates is found in the discussion above.

Type of Review: New collection.

Agency: Employee Benefits Security Administration, Department of Labor.

Title: ERISA Investment Manager Electronic Registration.

OMB Number: 1210-0NEW.

Affected Public: Individuals or households; Business or other for-profit.

Respondents: 500.

Frequency of Response: Annually.

Responses: 500.

Estimated Total Burden Hours: 1,000.

Total Annualized Capital/Startup Costs: $275,000.

Total Burden Cost (Operating and Maintenance): $50,000.

Total Annualized Cost: $325,000.

After the year of implementation, the startup cost will be fully defrayed. The ongoing annual operating and maintenance cost will be $50,000.

Unfunded Mandates Reform Act

For purposes of the Unfunded Mandates Reform Act of 1995 (Pub. L. 104-4), as well as Executive Order 12875, this proposed rule does not include any federal mandate that may result in expenditures by State, local, or tribal governments in the aggregate of more than $100 million, or increased expenditures by the private sector of more than $100 million.

Small Business Regulatory Enforcement Fairness Act

The rule being issued here is subject to the Congressional Review Act provisions of the Small Business Regulatory Enforcement Fairness Act of 1996 (5 U.S.C. 801 et seq.) and, if finalized, will be transmitted to Congress and the Comptroller General for review. The rule is not a "major rule" as that term is defined in 5 U.S.C. 804, because it is not likely to result in (1) an annual effect on the economy of $100 million or more; (2) a major increase in costs or prices for consumers, individual industries, or Federal, State, or local government agencies, or geographic regions; or (3) significant adverse effects on competition, employment, investment, productivity, innovation, or on the ability of United States-based enterprises to compete with foreign-based enterprises in domestic or export markets.

Regulatory Flexibility Act

The Regulatory Flexibility Act (5 U.S.C. 601 et seq.) (RFA) imposes certain requirements with respect to federal rules that are subject to the notice and comment requirements of section 553(b) of the Administrative Procedure Act (5 U.S.C. 551 et seq.) and that are likely to have a significant economic impact on a substantial number of small entities. Unless an agency certifies that a proposed rule will not have a significant economic impact on a substantial number of small entities, section 603 of the RFA requires that the agency present an initial regulatory flexibility analysis at the time of the publication of the notice of proposed rulemaking describing the impact of the rule on small entities and seeking public comment on such impact. Small entities include small businesses, organizations and governmental jurisdictions.

For purposes of analysis under the RFA, EBSA normally considers a small entity to be an employee benefit plan with fewer than 100 participants, on the basis of the definition found in section 104(a)(2) of ERISA. However, this proposed regulation pertains to investment advisers that are prohibited from registering with the SEC pursuant to section 203(A) of the Advisers Act and SEC rules. This generally includes those advisers that have assets of less than $25 million under management. In its final rule relating to Electronic Filing by Investment Advisers (65 FR 57445, note 86), the SEC states that for purposes of the Advisers Act and the RFA, an investment adviser generally is a small entity if (a) it manages assets of less than $25 million reported on its most recent Schedule I to Form ADV, (b) it does not have total assets of $5 million or more on the last day of the most recent fiscal year, and (c) it is not in a control relationship with another investment adviser that is not a small entity (Rule 0-7 under the Advisers Act).

Because the entities potentially affected by this rule are similar if not identical to those that fall within the SEC definition of small entity for RFA purposes, and because the regulation is expected to have a direct impact on an existing cost of doing business that investment advisers would assume without regard to this proposal, but no economic impact that would be passed on to employee benefit plans, the Department considers it appropriate in this limited circumstance to use the SEC definition for evaluating potential impacts on small entities. The Department invites comments on its election to use this definition. Using this definition, the Department certifies that this proposed regulation would not have a significant economic impact on a substantial number of small entities. The factual basis for this conclusion is described below.

The SEC States that of about 20,000 investment advisers in the United States, some 12,000 do not file with them. As discussed above, approximately 500 investment advisers are expected to incur costs under this regulation. This represents 2.5 percent of the approximately 20,000 advisers doing business in the U.S., or 4 percent of the 12,000 small advisers that do not currently file with the SEC. Thus the number of advisers that will incur costs under this regulation is substantial neither in absolute terms nor as a fraction of the universe of all or of small advisers.

In addition, the economic impact of the proposal is not expected to be significant for any small entity. Seeking investment manager status for purposes of ERISA is not mandatory; small advisers presumably make efforts to meet the terms of the ERISA investment manager definition only when they compute a net benefit for doing so. The proposed regulation will mandate electronic submission of small adviser's registration information, but will not change the content or other requirements for those registrations. The average cost for affected advisers is estimated to be small: about $800 in the initial year, and $100 in each following year. It is possible that some portion of this cost will be passed on to plans.

On this basis, the Department certifies that this proposed regulation would not have a significant economic impact on a substantial number of small entities. The Department invites comments on the potential impact of this proposed regulation on small entities, and on ways in which costs may be limited within the stated objectives of this proposal.

Federalism Statement

Executive Order 13132 (August 4, 1999) outlines fundamental principles of federalism and requires the adherence to specific criteria by federal agencies in the process of their formulation and implementation of policies that have substantial direct effects on the States, on the relationship between the national government and the States, or on the distribution of power and responsibilities among the various levels of government. This proposed rule does not have federalism implications because it has no substantial direct effect on the States, on the relationship between the national government and the States, or on the distribution of power and responsibilities among the various levels of government. Section 514 of ERISA provides, with certain exceptions specifically enumerated, that the provisions of Titles I and IV of ERISA supersede any and all laws of the States as they relate to any employee benefit plan covered under ERISA. Although the requirements in this proposed rule do alter the fundamental reporting and disclosure requirements of section 3(38)(B) of ERISA with respect to state-registered investment managers, because the duty of these state-registered advisers to report to the states exists independently of ERISA, and the proposed rule merely prescribes that investment advisers seeking ERISA investment manager status use a specific filing method that is accepted by all states and available as a choice in all states for registration purposes, there is neither a direct implication for the States, nor is there a direct effect on the relationship or distribution of power between the national government and the States. This proposal only affects those State-registered investment advisers who choose to seek investment manager status under section 3(38) of ERISA, advisers not seeking such status are unaffected by this proposed regulation.

Statutory Authority

The proposed regulation would be adopted pursuant to the authority contained in section 505 of ERISA (Pub. L. 93-406, 88 Stat. 894; 29 U.S.C. 1135), and the Act of November 10, 1997, § 1, Pub. L. 105-72, 111 Stat. 1457, and under Secretary of Labor's Order 1-2003, 68 FR 5374 (Feb. 3, 2003).

List of Subjects in 29 CFR Part 2510

Employee benefit plans, Employee Retirement Income Security Act, Pensions, Plan assets.

PART 2510—[AMENDED]

1. The authority citation for part 2510 is revised to read as follows:

Authority: 29 U.S.C. 1002(2), 1002(21), 1002(37), 1002(38), 1002(40), 1031, and 1135; Secretary of Labor's Order 1-2003, 68 FR 5374; § 2510.3-101 also issued under sec. 102 of Reorganization Plan No. 4 of 1978, 43 FR 47713, 3 CFR, 1978 Comp., p. 332 and E.O. 12108, 44 FR 1065, 3 CFR, 1978 Comp., p. 275, and 29 U.S.C. 1135 note. § 2510.3-102 also issued under sec. 102 of Reorganization Plan No. 4 of 1978, 43 FR 47713, 3 CFR, 1978 Comp., p. 332 and E.O. 12108, 44 FR 1065, 3 CFR, 1978 Comp., p. 275. Section 2510.3-38 is also issued under § 1, Pub. L. 105-72, 111 Stat. 1457.

2. Add § 2510.3-38 to read as follows:

§ 2510.3-38 *Filing requirements for State registered investment advisers to be investment managers.*

(a) *General.* Section 3(38) of the Act sets forth the criteria for a fiduciary to be an investment manager for purposes of section 405 of the Act. Subparagraph (B)(ii) of section 3(38) of the Act provides that, in the case of a fiduciary who is not registered under the Investment Advisers Act of 1940 by reason of paragraph (1) of section 203A(a) of such Act, the fiduciary must be registered as an investment adviser under the laws of the State in which it maintains its principal office and place of business, and, at the time the fiduciary files registration forms with such State to maintain the fiduciary's registration under the laws of such State, also files a copy of such forms with the Secretary of Labor. The purpose of this section is to set forth the exclusive means for investment advisers to satisfy the filing obligation with the Secretary described in subparagraph (B)(ii) of section 3(38) of the Act.

(b) *Filing requirement.* To satisfy the filing requirement with the Secretary in section 3(38)(B)(ii) of the Act, a fiduciary must be registered as an investment adviser with the State in which it maintains its principal office and place of business and file through the Investment Adviser Registration Depository (IARD), in accordance with applicable IARD requirements, the information required to be registered and maintain the fiduciary's registration as an investment adviser in such State. Submitting to the Secretary investment adviser registration forms filed with a State does not constitute compliance with the filing requirement in section 3(38)(B)(ii) of the Act.

(c) *Definitions.* For purposes of this section, the term "Investment Adviser Registration Depository" or "IARD" means the centralized electronic depository described in 17 CFR 275.203-1.

(d) *Cross reference.* Information for investment advisers on how to file through the IARD is available on the Securities and Exchange Commission Web site at http://www.sec.gov/iard.

Signed at Washington, DC this 3rd day of December, 2003.

Ann L. Combs,

Assistant Secretary, Employee Benefits Security Administration, U.S. Department of Labor.

[FR Doc. 03-30435 Filed 12-8-03; 8:45 am]

¶ 20,534P

Employee Benefits Security Administration (EBSA)—Mandatory distributions—Automatic rollovers— Safe harbors—Individual retirement accounts (IRAs).—Reproduced below is the text of a proposed rule which provides guidance from EBSA that facilitates the satisfaction of fiduciary responsibilities with regard to automatic rollovers of certain mandatory distributions to IRAs. The safe harbor set forth in the proposed rule requires the proper selection of an individual retirement plan provider and provides conditions for the proper investment of funds in connection with the automatic rollover.

The proposed regulation was published in the Federal Register on March 2, 2004 (69 FR 9899).

The regulations were finalized and published in the Federal Register on September 28, 2004 (69 FR 58017). The final rules are effective March 28, 2005. The regulations appear at ¶ 14,742A and the preamble is reproduced at ¶ 24,806P.

Part II

Department of Labor

Employee Benefits Security Administration

29 CFR Part 2550

Fiduciary Responsibility Under the Employee Retirement Income Security Act of 1974 Automatic Rollover Safe Harbor; Proposed Rule

DEPARTMENT OF LABOR

Employee Benefits Security Administration

29 CFR Part 2550

RIN 1210-AA92

Fiduciary Responsibility Under the Employee Retirement Income Security Act of 1974 Automatic Rollover Safe Harbor

AGENCY: Employee Benefits Security Administration, Labor.

ACTION: Proposed regulation.

SUMMARY: This document contains a proposed regulation that, upon adoption, would establish a safe harbor pursuant to which a fiduciary of a pension plan subject to Title I of the Employee Retirement Income Security Act of 1974, as amended (ERISA), will be deemed to have satisfied his or her fiduciary responsibilities in connection with automatic rollovers of certain mandatory distributions to individual retirement plans. This proposed regulation, if finalized, would affect

employee pension benefit plans, plan sponsors, administrators and fiduciaries, and plan participants and beneficiaries.

DATES: Written comments on the proposed regulation should be received by the Department of Labor on or before April 1, 2004.

ADDRESSES: Comments (preferably at least three copies) should be addressed to the Office of Regulations and Interpretations, Employee Benefits Security Administration, Room N-5669, U.S. Department of Labor, 200 Constitution Avenue NW., Washington, DC 20210. Attn: Automatic Rollover Regulation. Comments also may be submitted electronically to e-ori@dol.gov. All comments received will be available for public inspection at the Public Disclosure Room, N-1513, Employee Benefits Security Administration, 200 Constitution Avenue NW., Washington, DC 20210.

FOR FURTHER INFORMATION CONTACT: Lisa M. Alexander or Kristen L. Zarenko, Office of Regulations and Interpretations, Employee Benefits Security Administration, (202) 693-8510. This is not a toll-free number.

SUPPLEMENTARY INFORMATION:

Background

Under the Internal Revenue Code of 1986, as amended (Code), tax-qualified retirement plans are permitted to incorporate provisions requiring an immediate distribution to a separating participant without the participant's consent if the present value of the participant's vested accrued benefit does not exceed $5,000.[1] A distribution by a plan in compliance with such a provision is termed a mandatory distribution, commonly referred to as a "cash-out". Separating participants may choose to roll the cash-out, which is an eligible rollover distribution,[2] into an eligible retirement plan,[3] or they may retain the cash-out as a taxable distribution. Within a reasonable period of time prior to making a mandatory distribution, plan administrators are required to provide a separating participant with a written notice explaining, among other things, the following: the Code provisions under which the participant may elect to have the cash-out transferred directly to an eligible retirement plan and that if an election is not made, such cash-out is subject to the automatic rollover provisions of Code section 401(a)(31)(B); the provision requiring income tax withholding if the cash-out is not directly transferred to an eligible retirement plan; and the provisions under which the distribution will not be taxed if the participant transfers the account balance to an eligible retirement plan within 60 days of receipt.[4]

As part of the Economic Growth and Tax Relief Reconciliation Act of 2001 (EGTRRA),[5] section 401(a)(31) of the Code was amended to require that, absent an affirmative election by the participant, certain mandatory distributions from a tax-qualified retirement plan be directly transferred to an individual retirement plan[6] of a designated trustee or issuer. Specifically, section 657(a) of EGTRRA added a new section 401(a)(31)(B)(i) to the Code to provide that, in the case of a trust that is part of an eligible plan,[7] the trust will not constitute a qualified trust unless the plan of which the trust is a part provides that if a mandatory distribution of more than $1,000 is to be made and the participant does not elect to have such distribution paid directly to an eligible retirement plan or to receive the distribution directly, the plan administrator must transfer such distribution to an individual retirement plan. Section 657(a) of EGTRRA also added a notice requirement in section 401(a)(31)(B)(i) of the Code requiring the plan administrator to notify the participant in writing, either separately or as part of the notice required under section 402(f) of the Code, that the participant may transfer the distribution to another individual retirement plan.[8]

Section 657(c)(2)(A) of EGTRRA directed the Department of Labor (Department) to issue regulations providing safe harbors under which 1) a plan administrator's designation of an institution to receive the automatic rollover and 2) the initial investment choice for the rolled-over funds would be deemed to satisfy the fiduciary responsibility provisions of section 404(a) of ERISA. Section 657(c)(2)(B) of EGTRRA states that the Secretaries of Labor and Treasury may provide, and shall give consideration to providing, special relief with respect to the use of low-cost individual retirement plans for purposes of Code section 401(a)(31)(B) automatic rollovers and for other uses that promote the preservation of assets for retirement income.

Section 657(c)(2)(A) of EGTRRA further provides that the Code provisions requiring automatic rollovers of certain mandatory distributions to individual retirement plans will not become effective until the Department of Labor issues safe harbor regulations.

On January 7, 2003, the Department published a notice in the Federal Register requesting information on a variety of issues relating to the development of a safe harbor pursuant to section 657(c)(2)(A) and (B) of EGTRRA.[9] In response to this request for information (RFI), the Department received 17 comment letters. Copies of these http://www.dol.gov/ebsa/regs/cmt-rolloverRFI.html.

Set forth below is an overview of the proposed safe harbor regulation and a review of the comments received in response to the RFI.

Overview of Proposal

Scope

Consistent with the directive in section 657(c)(2)(A) of EGTRRA, paragraph (a)(1) of § 2550.404a-2 provides that the proposed safe harbor applies only to the automatic rollover of a mandatory distribution described in section 401(a)(31)(B) of the Code. At present, such distributions are limited to nonforfeitable accrued benefits (generally

referred to as vested benefits), the present value of which is in excess of $1,000, but less than or equal to $5,000. For purposes of determining the present value of such benefits, section 401(a)(31)(B) references Code section 411(a)(11). Section 411(a)(11)(A) of the Code provides that, in general, if the present value of any nonforfeitable accrued benefit exceeds $5,000, such benefit may not be immediately distributed without the consent of the participant. Section 411(a)(11)(D) of the Code also provides a special rule that permits plans to disregard that portion of a nonforfeitable accrued benefit that is attributable to amounts rolled over from other plans (and earnings thereon) in determining the $5,000 limit. Inasmuch as section 401(a)(31)(B) of the Code requires the automatic rollover of mandatory distributions, as determined under section 411(a)(11), which would include prior rollover contributions, the proposal provides safe harbor coverage for the automatic rollover of mandatory distributions containing such prior rollover contributions. One commenter on the RFI suggested that the safe harbor should extend to amounts of $1,000 or less. While the Department agrees with the commenter that similar considerations may be relevant to such rollovers, the Department did not adopt this suggestion in light of Congress's direction to provide a safe harbor for automatic rollovers of mandatory distributions described in section 401(a)(31)(B) of the Code.

Paragraph (b) of the proposed regulation provides that, if the conditions of the safe harbor are satisfied, fiduciaries will be deemed to have satisfied their fiduciary duties under section 404(a) of ERISA with respect to both the selection of an individual retirement plan provider and the investment of funds in connection with an automatic rollover of a mandatory distribution described in section 401(a)(31)(B) of the Code to an individual retirement plan, within the meaning of section 7701(a)(37) of the Code.

The proposal makes clear that the standards set forth in the proposed regulation apply solely for purposes of determining compliance with the safe harbor and that such standards are not intended to represent the exclusive means by which a fiduciary might satisfy his or her duties under ERISA with respect to automatic rollovers of mandatory distributions described in section 401(a)(31)(B) of the Code.

As noted above, section 657(c)(2)(B) of EGTRRA provides that the Secretary of the Treasury and the Secretary of Labor shall consider and may provide special relief with respect to the use of low-cost individual retirement plans. The Department considered the provision of such special relief and believes that the framework of the safe harbor encourages the use of low-cost individual retirement plans for purposes of rollovers under section 401(a)(31)(B) of the Code. The Department specifically invites public comment on whether, given the conditions of the proposal, further relief is necessary in this regard. If so, commenters are encouraged to specifically address what relief is necessary and why, as well as identify approaches to providing such relief.

Conditions

Safe harbor relief under the proposed regulation is dependent on a fiduciary satisfying six conditions. In general, the conditions address: (1) The amount of mandatory distributions; (2) qualifications for an individual retirement plan; (3) permissible investment products; (4) permissible fees and expenses; (5) required disclosures to participants and beneficiaries; and 6) prohibited transactions. Each of the conditions is discussed below.

The first condition, described in paragraph (c)(1) of the proposed regulation, provides that, for the automatic rollover of mandatory distributions, the present value of the nonforfeitable accrued benefit, as determined under section 411(a)(11) of the Code, does not exceed the maximum amount permitted under section 401(a)(31)(B) of the Code. This condition was discussed in "Scope", above.

The second condition, described in paragraph (c)(2) of the proposed regulation, provides that the mandatory distribution be directed to an individual retirement plan within the meaning of section 7701(a)(37) of the Code. Section 7701(a)(37) defines the term individual retirement

---

[1] Code sections 411(a)(11) and 417(e). See Code section 411(a)(11)(D) for circumstances where the amount of a cash-out may be greater than $5,000, based on a participant's prior rollover contribution into the plan.

[2] See Code section 402(f)(2)(A).

[3] See Code section 402(f)(2)(B).

[4] Code section 402(f)(1).

[5] Pub. L. 107-16, June 7, 2001, 115 Stat. 38.

[6] Section 401(a)(31)(B)(i) of the Code requires the transfer to be made to an "individual retirement plan", which section 7701(a)(37) of the Code defines to mean an individual retirement account described in section 408(a) and an individual retirement annuity described in section 408(b).

[7] Section 657(a)(1)(B)(ii) of EGTRRA defines an "eligible plan" as a plan which provides for an immediate distribution to a participant of any "nonforfeitable accrued benefit for which the present value (as determined under section 411(a)(11) of the Code) does not exceed $5,000." The Treasury and the IRS have advised the Department that the requirements of Code section 401(a)(31)(B) apply to a broad range of retirement plans including plans established under Code sections 401(a), 401(k), 403(a), 403(b) and 457. The Department notes that the safe harbor proposed herein applies only to employee benefit pension plans covered under title I of ERISA. See infra fn. 15.

[8] Conforming amendments to Code sections 401(a)(31) and 402(f)(1) were also made by section 657 of EGTRRA.

[9] 68 FR 991.http://www.dol.gov/ebsa/regs/fedreg/proposed/2003000281.htm.

plan to mean an individual retirement account described in section 408(a) of the Code and an individual retirement annuity described in section 408(b) of the Code. Accordingly, a bank, insurance company, financial institution or other provider of an individual retirement plan under the safe harbor is required to satisfy the requirements of the Code and regulations issued thereunder.[10] This approach is consistent with the majority of comments received in response to the RFI. These commenters argued that additional criteria are unnecessary and, if imposed, may only serve to limit the number of providers available or willing to establish and maintain the small rollover accounts covered by the safe harbor. Other commenters suggested that the fiduciaries should be required to consider an individual retirement plan provider's financial stability, taking into account such matters as credit ratings or insurance coverage. The Department is unaware of any problems attributable to weaknesses in the existing Code and regulatory standards for individual retirement plan providers. The Department, therefore, believes that, given the limited scope of the proposed safe harbor, existing Code and regulatory standards are sufficiently protective of separating participants and their beneficiaries who would become individual retirement plan account holders, without imposing unnecessary burdens on either plans or individual retirement plan providers.

The third condition, described in paragraph (c)(3) of the proposed regulation, defines the type of investment products in which a mandatory distribution can be invested under the safe harbor. Specifically, the proposal provides for the investment of mandatory distributions in investment products designed to preserve principal and provide a reasonable rate of return, whether or not such return is guaranteed, consistent with liquidity, and taking into account the extent to which charges can be assessed against an individual retirement plan. For this purpose, the product must be offered by a state or federally regulated financial institution, and must seek to maintain a stable dollar value equal to the amount invested in the product by the individual retirement plan.

For purposes of this condition, a "regulated financial institution" is defined in the proposal as a bank or savings association, the deposits of which are insured by the Federal Deposit Insurance Corporation; a credit union, the member accounts of which are insured within the meaning of section 101(7) of the Federal Credit Union Act; an insurance company, the products of which are protected by state guarantee associations; or an investment company registered under the Investment Company Act of 1940.

This condition reflects the Department's view that, given the nature and amount of the automatic rollovers, investments under the safe harbor should be designed to minimize risk, preserve assets for retirement and maintain liquidity. Such safe harbor investment products would typically include money market funds maintained by registered investment companies,[11] and interest-bearing savings accounts and certificates of deposit of a bank or a similar financial institution. In addition, safe harbor investment products would include "stable value products" issued by a regulated financial institution that are fully benefit-responsive to the individual retirement plan account holder. Such products must provide a liquidity guarantee by a financially responsible third party of principal and previously accrued interest for liquidations or transfers initiated by the individual retirement plan account holder exercising his or her right to withdraw or transfer funds under the terms of an arrangement that does not include substantial restrictions to the account holder's access to the assets of the individual retirement plan.

The majority of the commenters on the RFI supported inclusion in the safe harbor of an investment product that favored retention of principal and income over growth. A number of commenters suggested that, in addition to such products, the safe harbor should include investment products identical or similar to those in which the participant had directed his or her investments prior to the mandatory distribution. Some argued that retaining such investments outside the plan might, in fact, result in some cost savings (e.g., lower administrative expenses, avoiding termination charges, etc.). Some commenters also argued for inclusion of participant investments in qualifying employer securities as a safe harbor investment option. The Department does not believe that an investment strategy adopted by a participant while in a defined contribution plan or chosen by a plan fiduciary at a particular point in time would necessarily continue to be appropriate for

the participant in the context of an automatic rollover, particularly given the relatively small account balances covered by the safe harbor. For this reason, the Department did not adopt these suggestions.

The fourth condition addresses the extent to which fees and expenses can be assessed against an individual retirement plan, including the investments of such plan. Most of the commenters on the RFI argued that the safe harbor should permit fees and expenses attendant to the establishment and maintenance of an individual retirement plan to be charged against the assets in the individual retirement plan and the safe harbor should not impose limits on such fees and expenses, noting that competition in the marketplace will serve to control costs. These commenters also noted that the costs attendant to maintaining individual retirement plans to handle mandatory distributions will be higher than for other types of accounts, because the amounts contributed are small, future contributions are unlikely, and the account holders generally will be passive or not in contact with the individual retirement plan providers.

There is nothing in the safe harbor that would preclude establishment, maintenance and other fees and expenses from being charged against the individual retirement plan of an account holder. On the other hand, the safe harbor does establish limits on the amount of such fees and expenses that can be charged against an individual retirement plan. While the Department agrees that competition in the marketplace may serve to keep administrative and investment management costs down, the Department nonetheless believes that, given the importance of cost considerations in connection with the selection of service providers by plan fiduciaries generally and the importance of protecting principal in connection with automatic rollover distributions, the safe harbor should contain some limits on the fees and expenses that may be assessed against an individual retirement plan established for mandatory distributions. In this regard, the Department attempted to strike a balance in the proposal between the application of a marketplace principle and the investment goal of preserving principal.

Under paragraph (c)(4) of the proposed regulation, fees and expenses attendant to an individual retirement plan, including investments of such plan, (e.g., establishment charges, maintenance fees, investment expenses, termination costs and surrender charges) may not exceed certain limits. The first limit, provided in paragraph (c)(4)(i), is intended to ensure that fees and expenses charged to individual retirement plans established in connection with a mandatory distribution are not inconsistent with the marketplace. This limit provides that the fees and expenses charged to such plans may not exceed the fees and expenses charged by the provider for comparable individual retirement plans established for rollover distributions that are not subject to the automatic rollover provisions of section 401(a)(31)(B) of the Code.

The second limit, provided in paragraph (c)(4)(ii), is intended to protect the investment principal by providing that fees and expenses attendant to the individual retirement plan may be charged only against the income earned by the plan, with the exception of charges assessed for the establishment of the plan. The Department understands that in some instances providers will charge a one-time, typically small, fee to set up an individual retirement plan. While providers are not required to limit establishment charges to the income earned by individual retirement plans, these charges, nonetheless, may not exceed establishment charges assessed against comparable individual retirement plans established for rollover distributions that are not subject to the automatic rollover provisions of section 401(a)(31)(B) of the Code. If a provider, therefore, imposes no establishment or set-up charge on its comparable individual retirement plan customers, it may not impose a charge on plans established for rollover distributions under section 401(a)(31)(B) of the Code.

The fifth condition is intended to ensure that participants and beneficiaries are informed of the plan's procedures governing automatic rollovers, including an explanation about the nature of the investment product in which the mandatory distribution will be invested, and how fees and expenses attendant to the individual retirement plan will be allocated (i.e., the extent to which expenses will be borne by the account holder alone or shared with the distributing plan or plan sponsor). In addition, the disclosure must identify a plan contact for further information concerning the plan's procedures, individual retirement plan providers, and the fees and expenses attendant to the

---

[10] For example, with respect to individual retirement accounts, 26 CFR 1.408-2(b)(2)(i) provides that the trustee of an individual retirement account must be a bank (as defined in section 408(n) of the Code and regulations thereunder) or another person who demonstrates, in the manner described in paragraph (e) of the regulation, to the satisfaction of the Internal Revenue Service, that the manner in which the trust will be administered will be consistent with section 408 of the Code and regulations thereunder. With respect to individual retirement annuities, 26 CFR 1.408-3 describes, among other things, require-

ments that must be met in order to maintain the tax-qualified status of such annuity arrangements.

[11] Regarding money market mutual funds, prospectuses for such funds generally state that "an investment in the [money market mutual] Fund is not insured or guaranteed by the Federal Deposit Insurance Corporation or any other government agency. Although the Fund seeks to preserve the value of your [the investor's] investment at $1.00 per share, it is possible to lose money by investing in the Fund."

individual retirement plan. In this regard, paragraph (c)(5) of the proposed regulation conditions safe harbor relief on the furnishing of this information to the plan's participants and beneficiaries in a summary plan description (SPD) or a summary of material modifications (SMM) in advance of an automatic rollover. For purposes of this condition, a plan contact can be identified by reference to a person, position or office, along with an address and phone number of the contact. It is anticipated that the contact, in response to requests from separated participants on whose behalf distributions have been made to an individual retirement plan, would be able to identify the individual retirement plan provider to whom a distribution was made for the particular participant.

One commenter on the RFI argued against the establishment of any new disclosure requirements under the safe harbor, given the requirements that already exist under the Code. Another commenter argued that the safe harbor should require individual notices to each separated participant on whose behalf an individual retirement plan is established informing him or her of the provider's name, address and phone number, and any other information needed by the account holder to take action with regard to the distributed funds.

This condition is consistent with the Department's statement in a footnote to Revenue Ruling 2000-36 requiring that plan provisions governing the default direct rollover of distributions, including the participant's ability to affirmatively opt out of the arrangement, must be described in the plan's SPD furnished to participants.[12] We believe this approach to disclosure similarly serves to ensure that participants and beneficiaries are provided, and have access to, sufficient information about automatic rollovers, while avoiding the imposition of unnecessary costs and burdens on pension plans and individual retirement plan providers.

Paragraph (c)(6) of the proposed regulation conditions safe harbor relief on the plan fiduciary not engaging in prohibited transactions in connection with the selection of an individual retirement plan provider or investment product, unless such actions are covered by a statutory or administrative exemption issued under section 408(a) of ERISA. In this regard, the Department is publishing a proposed class exemption in today's Federal Register that is intended to deal with prohibited transactions resulting from an individual retirement plan provider's selection of itself as the provider of an individual retirement plan and/or issuer of an investment held by such plan in connection with mandatory distributions from the provider's own pension plan. Specifically, the proposed exemption is intended to permit a bank or other regulated financial institution as defined therein to (1) select itself or an affiliate as the individual retirement plan trustee, custodian or issuer to receive automatic rollovers from its own plan and (2) select its own funds or investment products for automatic rollovers from its own plan. In the absence of this exemption, a bank or other financial institution would be required to direct automatic rollovers from its own plan for its own employees to a competitor as the individual retirement plan provider.

Miscellaneous Issues

In response to the Department's RFI, a number of commenters identified possible legal impediments that fiduciaries, banks and other financial institutions might encounter in connection with automatic rollovers. These impediments included perceived conflicts with state laws on signature requirements and escheat, Code requirements, and requirements under the USA PATRIOT Act.[13]

With regard to Code requirements that may possibly conflict with or impede the establishment of individual retirement plans for purposes of automatic rollovers of mandatory distributions under section 401(a)(31)(B) of the Code, the Department has been informed that staff of the Department of the Treasury and the Internal Revenue Service are reviewing the current rules and regulations affecting such distributions and that guidance addressing the application of these rules to the automatic rollover of mandatory distributions is anticipated in advance of or simultaneously with the Department's issuance of a final safe harbor regulation.

With regard to the provisions of the USA PATRIOT Act (Act), a number of commenters pointed out that the customer identification and verification provisions of the Act may preclude banks and other financial institutions from establishing individual retirement plans without the participation of the participant or beneficiary on whose behalf the fiduciary is required to make an automatic rollover. In most of the situations where a fiduciary is required to make an automatic rollover to an individual retirement plan, the participant or beneficiary is unable to be located or is otherwise not communicating with the plan concerning the distribution of plan benefits. Accordingly, if the customer identification and verification provisions of the Act were construed to require participant or beneficiary participation when an individual retirement plan is established on his or her behalf, fiduciaries will be unable to comply with the automatic rollover requirements of the Code and utilize this safe harbor. Commenters also noted that such an interpretation of the Act would limit the ability of fiduciaries to make distributions from terminating defined contribution plans on behalf of missing plan participants and beneficiaries.

In response to these issues, Treasury staff, along with staff of the other Federal functional regulators,[14] have advised the Department that they interpret the customer identification and verification (CIP) requirements of section 326 of the Act and implementing regulations to require that banks and other financial institutions implement their CIP compliance program with respect to an account, including an individual retirement plan, established by an employee benefit plan in the name of a former participant (or beneficiary) of such plan, only at the time the former participant or beneficiary first contacts such institution to assert ownership or exercise control over the account. CIP compliance will not be required at the time an employee benefit plan establishes an account and transfers the funds to a bank or other financial institution for purposes of a distribution of benefits from the plan to a separated employee.[15] In January 2004, Treasury staff, along with staff of the other Federal functional regulators, issued guidance on this matter in the form of a question and answer, published in a set of "FAQs: Final CIP Rule," on the regulators" Web sites.[16]

Issues raised by commenters concerning the possible application of state laws are beyond the scope of this regulation.

Effective Date

As discussed above, section 657(c)(2)(A) of EGTRRA provides that the requirements of section 401(a)(31)(B) of the Code requiring automatic rollovers of mandatory distributions to individual retirement plans do not become effective until the Department issues final safe harbor regulations. Inasmuch as it appears clear that Congress did not intend fiduciaries to be subject to the automatic rollover requirements under the Code in the absence of a safe harbor, the Department believes the effective date of the rollover requirement must be determined by reference to the effective date of the final safe harbor regulation, that is the date on which plan fiduciaries may avail themselves of the relief provided by the safe harbor. In this regard, the Department is proposing to make the final safe harbor regulation effective 6 months after the date of publication in the Federal Register in order to afford plan fiduciaries adequate time to amend their plans, distribute required disclosures and identify institutions and products that would afford relief under the final safe harbor regulation.

Request for Comments

The Department invites comments from interested persons on all aspects of the proposed safe harbor provided herein, including the proposed effective date. Comments (preferably at least three copies) should be addressed to the Office of Regulations and Interpretations, Employee Benefits Security Administration, Room N-5669, U.S. Department of Labor, 200 Constitution Avenue NW., Washington, DC 20210. Attn: Automatic Rollover Regulation. Comments also may be submitted electronically to e-ori@dol.gov. All comments received will be available for public inspection at the Public Disclosure Room, N-1513, Employee Benefits Security Administration, 200 Constitution Avenue NW., Washington, DC 20210.

The Department has limited the comment period to 30 days in order to issue a final regulation on the earliest possible date, taking into account Congress's expectation that regulations would be issued in June 2004. The Department believes that, in light of the earlier published request for information and the limited number of issues presented for consideration by the proposal, the provided 30-day comment period affords interested persons an adequate amount of time to analyze the proposal and submit comments thereon.

---

[12] Revenue Ruling 2000-36, 2000-2 C.B. 140.

[13] Pub. L. No. 107-56, October 26, 2001, 115 Stat. 272.

[14] The term "other Federal functional regulators" refers to the other agencies responsible for administration and regulations under the Act.

[15] It is the Department's understanding that this interpretation applies to a broad spectrum of employee benefit plans including those covered by title I of ERISA and those established under Code provisions.

[16] See FAQs: Final CIP Rule at: http://www.occ.treas.gov/10.pdf http://www.fincen.gov/finalciprule.pdf http:// www.ots.treas.gov/docs/25188.pdf http:// www.fdic.gov/news/news/financial/2004/FIL0404a.html

Regulatory Impact Analysis

Summary

The purpose of this proposed regulation is to establish conditions under which a fiduciary will be deemed to satisfy the fiduciary obligations under section 404(a) of ERISA in connection with the automatic rollover of a mandatory distribution as described in amended Code section 401(a)(31)(B). The EGTRRA amendment is estimated to have significant costs and benefits in that it annually will provide 241,000 former participants with preserved retirement savings of about $249 million and immediate tax savings of about $71 million. Included in those 241,000 participants are 98,000 who are assumed to be passive or non-responsive. Establishing individual retirement plans for these participants for automatic rollovers of mandatory distributions will reduce ordinary plan administrative expenses attributable to those participants by an estimated $9.5 million in the first year.

The amendment will generate one-time administrative compliance costs of an estimated $139 million, and individual retirement plan establishment and maintenance fees totaling $14.4 million in the first year. Automatic rollovers of mandatory distributions may give rise to other costs as well, such as investment expenses, termination charges, and surrender charges, but the magnitude of some of those expenses will relate to the actual investment products selected. The range of possible costs that relate to investment products is considered too broad to support meaningful estimates.

The savings that will arise from this safe harbor are expected to substantially outweigh its costs and transfers. The guidance provided by this proposed regulation is expected to result in an aggregate savings of administrative compliance costs for plans of about $92 million by lessening the time required to select an individual retirement plan provider, investment product, and fee structure that are consistent with the provisions of Code section 401(a)(31)(B) and ERISA section 404(a) with respect to automatic rollovers of mandatory distributions. Other benefits not quantified here are expected to accrue to fiduciaries through greater certainty and reduced exposure to risk, and to former plan participants through the proposed regulatory standards concerning individual retirement plan providers, investment products, preservation of principal, rates of return, liquidity, and fees and expenses.

One-time costs associated with modifying a summary plan description or summary of material modifications to satisfy the safe harbor conditions are expected to amount to about $13 million.

The proposed safe harbor will preserve the principal amounts of automatic rollovers of mandatory distributions by ensuring that the various fees and expenses that apply to the individual retirement plans established for mandatory distributions are not more costly than those charged by the provider to individual retirement plans for comparable rollover distributions that are not subject to the automatic rollover provisions of Code section 401(a)(31)(B). If adopted as proposed, this guidance may also result in a transfer of individual retirement plan costs to other individual retirement plans or to plan sponsors to the extent that earnings and available profit are less than the fees that the individual retirement plan provider would ordinarily charge for comparable individual retirement plans.

Further discussion of costs and benefits and the data and assumptions underlying these estimates will be found below.

Executive Order 12866 Statement

Under Executive Order 12866, the Department must determine whether a regulatory action is "significant" and therefore subject to the requirements of the Executive Order and subject to review by the Office of Management and Budget (OMB). Under section 3(f) of the Executive Order, a "significant regulatory action" is an action that is likely to result in a rule (1) having an annual effect of the economy of $100 million or more, or adversely and materially affecting a sector of the economy, productivity, competition, jobs, the environment, public health or safety, or State, local or tribal governments or communities (also referred to as "economically significant"); (2) creating serious inconsistency or otherwise interfering with an action taken or planned by another agency; (3) materially altering the budgetary impacts of entitlement grants, user fees, or loan programs or the rights and obligations of recipients thereof; or (4) raising novel legal or policy issues arising out of legal mandates, the President's priorities, or the principles set forth in the Executive Order. OMB has determined that this action is significant under section 3(f)(4) because it raises novel legal or policy issues arising from the President's priorities. Accordingly, the Department has undertaken an analysis of the costs and benefits of the proposed regulation. OMB has reviewed this regulatory action.

Costs and Benefits of the EGTRRA Amendment

The impact of the amendment to Code section 401(a)(31) is distinguishable from the impact of the proposed regulation, and is expected to affect, in the aggregate, fiduciaries, plan participants, and certain regulated financial institutions. Fiduciaries will incur initial administrative expenses to select providers and investment products. Plan participants who may otherwise receive a cash distribution and pay ordinary income tax and penalties on the amount distributed will not pay those taxes because the amounts would have been retained in the pension system to earn additional tax-deferred income for retirement. As a result of the amendment, certain costs and fees will also be incurred by pension plans in connection with automatic rollovers and the investments for individual retirement plans. Finally, certain regulated financial institutions will receive additional deposits and earnings potential, and incur costs and charge fees for account maintenance.

After the effective date of the amendment, plans that currently mandate immediate distributions for amounts of greater than $1,000 but not exceeding $5,000 will, absent an affirmative election of a different alternative, make direct transfers of these distributions to an individual retirement plan. To implement this change, fiduciaries and their professional service providers will need to review the new requirements and select individual retirement plan providers and investment products. The amount of time required for this activity will vary, but based on 680,000 retirement plans and an assumed hourly rate of $68, the aggregate cost of each hour is over $46 million. An effort involving an average of 3 hours would result in an aggregate one-time cost of about $139 million. For this estimate we have conservatively assumed that all plans provide for such mandatory distributions and will need to take action to implement procedures for automatic rollovers to individual retirement plans. The proportion of pension plans that provide for such mandatory distributions is not known, but is believed based on anecdotal evidence to be very high. This total cost may be lessened to the extent that fewer plans will need to address the automatic rollover requirement, or that the assistance of service providers to multiple plans results in greater efficiency.

The Census Bureau's 1996 Survey of Program Participation (SIPP), Wave 7 Pension Benefits Module collected information as to the number, uses, and values of lump sum distributions from private pension plans in 1997. The survey responses show whether a distribution was mandatory or voluntary, and whether the amount involved was "Rolled over into another plan, an IRA, or an individual retirement annuity" ("rolled over"). The number of lump sum distributions between $1,001 and $5,000 that were characterized as mandatory and put to other specific uses enumerated in the survey instrument ("lump sums") has been used for the purpose of this analysis to approximate the number of participants in plans with mandatory distribution provisions that might fail to make an affirmative election. The number of automatic rollovers of mandatory distributions that will occur because of the Code amendment may be smaller than the number of lump sums because some of these participants may have made an affirmative election. It seems reasonable to assume that distributions rolled over would have involved an affirmative election, and that the number of participants making affirmative elections will be largely unchanged. The number of lump sums is assumed to represent an upper bound of the number of participants potentially affected by the automatic rollover provisions of Code section 401(a)(31)(B).

SIPP data show that in 1997 about 143,000 mandatory lump sum distributions of $1,001 to $5,000 were made. Using the midpoint of the reported groupings of distribution amounts (e.g., $1,500 for $1,001 to $1,999) the total amount of retirement savings distributed was about $415 million, or an average of $2,900 per former participant. The account balances and present values of accrued benefits ("accounts") of an additional 98,000 participants were left in plans during the same year for reasons that are not known. Although there is some uncertainty with respect to this assumption, this number has been used here as a proxy for a number of participants that did not receive mandatory distributions because they were passive or non-responsive. Assuming that the accounts of these participants were comparable in size and would also be automatically rolled over after the amendment is effective, the aggregate amount of automatic rollovers of mandatory distributions to individual retirement plans for 241,000 participants would be about $699 million per year ($415 million plus $284 million). Only $415 million of this total represents retirement savings that would not otherwise have been preserved, given that the $284 million was already maintained in retirement plans.

The amount of some mandatory distributions subject to the automatic rollover requirements of section 401(a)(31)(B) of the Code may be more than $5,000. This can occur where the present value of the nonforfeitable accrued benefits immediately distributable includes additional funds attributable to prior rollover contributions (and the earnings thereon).

The Department did not attempt to estimate the number or dollar amount of mandatory distributions eligible for relief under the proposed safe harbor regulation that may exceed $5,000. Adequate data to support such estimates are not currently available.

The Department believes it is probable that the number of mandatory distributions containing prior rollover contributions that will be subject to the automatic rollover requirement of section 401(a)(31)(B) of the Code will be small but the number of plans affected and the dollar amount of some of these mandatory distributions might be large.

A large majority of 401(k) plan participants are in plans that accept rollover contributions, according to the Bureau of Labor Statistics. There is some evidence, however, that rollovers into qualified plans are infrequent, which suggests that the number of participants whose accounts include amounts attributable to prior rollover contributions may be small. The number of such participants that will eventually become the owners of an automatic rollover individual retirement plan will be further limited by a number of factors, on which no data are available. Some plans will not mandate distribution of accounts that include prior rollover contributions and therefore exceed $5,000. Some accounts of participants with prior rollover contributions will accumulate more than $5,000 of additional contributions, thereby becoming ineligible for mandatory distributions. Some participants whose accounts do not accumulate more than $5,000 will affirmatively direct, upon leaving employment, the disposition of their accounts. Compared with other participants, those with prior rollover contributions, especially those with large rollover contributions, may be more likely to accumulate more than $5,000 from new contributions and more likely to affirmatively direct the disposition of their accounts.

The Department invites comments on the potential economic impact of the safe harbor established by this proposed regulation in connection with the mandatory distributions of accounts valued at more than $5,000.

The Joint Committee on Taxation's May 26, 2001 estimates of budget effects for this provision of EGTRRA indicated revenue losses on the order of about $30 million per year, which suggests a substantially lower estimate of the aggregate preservation of retirement savings, amounting to about $83 million for private plan participants. The reason for this difference is unknown. Interpreting these differing estimates as ends of a range, ordinary income tax and penalty savings are expected to amount to between $30 million and $112 million per year, while aggregate retirement savings are expected to increase by between $83 million and $415 million per year. For purposes of discussion, midpoint values of $71 million and $249 million are used here. These savings for former participants and distributions of amounts previously retained in plans also represent increased deposits to regulated financial institutions.

The establishment and maintenance of individual retirement plans for automatic rollovers of mandatory distributions will generate costs to individual retirement plans that may be defrayed by administrative fees to the extent that the individual retirement plan providers charge them. Certain investments may also generate fees. Some individual retirement plan providers may have termination fees, and some investments may have surrender charges associated with them that would be incurred at a later time when a former participant chose to exercise control over the account. With interpretive guidance, fiduciaries and the regulated financial institutions will have increased certainty regarding the limitations on costs, fees, and charges for individual retirement plans. In the absence of the proposed safe harbor and the fiduciary's desire to make use of the safe harbor, such costs and fees could be paid by plan sponsors or charged to individual retirement plans. However, it has been assumed here that in the absence of guidance, most fees would be charged against individual retirement plans. Aggregate annual establishment fees for rollovers arising from the amendment each year are estimated to range from a negligible amount to $2.4 million at the upper end of a range based on typical establishment fees for comparable individual retirement plan rollovers that range from no charge to $10 per account. Annual maintenance fees, which typically range from $7 to $50, with a mid-point of $29, are estimated to range from $1.7 million to $12 million, implying a mid-point estimate of $6.9 million, for individual retirement plans established in the first year. Assuming that individual retirement plans continue to be established at a constant rate of 241,000 plans per year and that, at an upper bound, no account holders assume control of their plans, maintenance fees would continue to grow at an average rate of $6.9 million annually.

As noted earlier, although establishment and maintenance fees are relatively predictable based on comparable individual retirement plans

for rollover distributions available in the marketplace, the types of investment products available and the actual choices that may be made by fiduciaries are considered to be too variable to support a meaningful estimate of investment fees, termination charges, and surrender fees.

Plans will benefit from administrative cost savings under the Code amendment for those 98,000 accounts that previously remained in pension plans but are assumed to be subject to mandatory rollover provisions under EGTRRA. Ordinary administrative costs that typically range from $45 to $150 per participant will be saved when accounts are rolled over, reducing plan expenses by about $4.4 million to $14.7 million, or an average of $9.5 million in the first year. Assuming an annual rollover of 98,000 accounts that would remain in pensions plans, cost savings to plans would continue to increase at an average of $9.5 million per year. The cost savings realized in each year will continue to accumulate through the future years that the accounts would otherwise have remained in the pension plan.

For the estimated 8 percent of these accounts that were in defined benefit plans, a small savings of approximately $144,000 would be realized from reduced funding risk and corresponding premium payments to the Pension Benefit Guaranty Corporation (PBGC).

Benefits and Costs of the Proposed Regulation

The proposed regulation will benefit fiduciaries by affording them greater assurance of compliance and reduced exposure to risk. Specificity as to the types of entities that may receive the rollovers, the investment choices, and the limitations on fees will lessen the time required to comply with the EGTRRA amendment. The substantive conditions of the safe harbor will benefit former participants by directing their retirement savings to individual retirement plans, providers, regulated financial institutions, and investment products that minimize risk and offer preservation of principal and liquidity. The limitation of fees and expenses will also benefit individual retirement plan account holders. Fees and expenses for the individual retirement plans will be limited under the safe harbor to those that would be charged by the provider to comparable individual retirement plans established for rollover distributions that are not subject to automatic rollover provisions of the Code, thereby preserving principal. The limitation of maintenance fees to the extent of income earned will also serve to maintain principal.

The benefits of greater certainty for fiduciaries and protection of participants cannot be specifically quantified. The proposed regulation is, however, expected to reduce one-time startup administrative compliance costs by as much as $92 million by narrowing the range of individual retirement plan providers and investment products fiduciaries might otherwise consider, assuming a savings of 2 of the 3 hours that compliance would otherwise require.

No estimate is made for the impact of the limitation on fees charged to the subject individual retirement plans compared to those charged by individual retirement plan providers for comparable individual account plans established for rollover distributions that are not subject to section 401(a)(31)(B) of the Code because the Department is not aware of a basis for judging whether and in what magnitude providers would charge different fees absent the safe harbor.

The proposal may affect the manner in which fees and expenses would otherwise have been allocated among plan sponsors and individual retirement plans. Under section 2550.404a-2(c)(4)(ii) of the proposed regulation, fees and expenses may be charged only against the income earned by the individual retirement plan. In some instances, particularly in the case of smaller individual retirement plans and when interest rates are low, the credited interest, together with any profit the individual retirement plan provider might otherwise derive from holding the plan, may not cover the cost incurred by the provider to maintain the plan. The Department believes that in these circumstances individual retirement plan providers will offset or subsidize any such uncovered costs either through increased maintenance fees on larger automatic rollovers, through increased administrative charges to plan sponsors, or possibly both. Because such uncovered costs (if any) derive from a provision of this proposed regulation, any associated offsets or subsidies would be attributable to it as well. The Department would welcome comments on the probable incidence and magnitude of any such uncovered costs and associated offsets or subsidies.

Plans will incur costs in connection with the proposed safe harbor to modify summary plan descriptions or provide a summary of material modifications. This cost is estimated to be about $13 million.

Alternatives

In preparation for drafting the proposed regulation, the Department published an RFI (68 FR 991) requesting comment on issues relating to the development of safe harbors for automatic rollovers and assistance in drafting regulations. The Department received 17 comments from the general public, service providers, and professional associations involved with pension planning, investing, and retirement accounts. Commenters opined on potential costs, issues of fiduciary liability and prohibited transaction relief, technical considerations involving state and federal laws, disclosures to participants, and draft language for the proposed regulation. Responses to the RFI informed the drafting process by permitting the Department to consider alternatives for achieving the regulatory objective at the initial stages. A more detailed discussion of the comments and the considerations given the alternatives by the Department is provided earlier in the preamble.

Paperwork Reduction Act

This Notice of Proposed Rulemaking is not subject to the requirements of the Paperwork Reduction Act of 1995 (44 U.S.C. 3501 et seq.) because it does not contain a "collection of information" as defined in 44 U.S.C. 3502(3). It is expected that this proposed rule will result in a modification of retirement plan Summary Plan Descriptions, an information collection request approved separately under OMB control number 1210-0039. However, this modification is not considered to be substantive or material in the context of that information collection request as a whole. In addition, the methodology for calculating burden under the Paperwork Reduction Act for the Summary Plan Description takes into account a steady rate of change in Summary Plan Descriptions that is estimated to accommodate the change that would be made by this proposed rulemaking. As a result, the Department has not made a submission for OMB approval in connection with this rulemaking.

Regulatory Flexibility Act

The Regulatory Flexibility Act (5 U.S.C. 601 et seq.) (RFA) imposes certain requirements with respect to Federal rules that are subject to the notice and comment requirements of section 553(b) of the Administrative Procedure Act (5 U.S.C. 551 et seq.) and which are likely to have a significant economic impact on a substantial number of small entities. Unless an agency determines that a proposed rule is not likely to have a significant economic impact on a substantial number of small entities, section 603 of the RFA requires that the agency present an initial regulatory flexibility analysis at the time of the publication of the notice of proposed rulemaking describing the impact of the rule on small entities and seeking public comment on such impact. Small entities include small businesses, organizations and governmental jurisdictions.

For purposes of analysis under the RFA, the Employee Benefits Security Administration (EBSA) proposes to continue to consider a small entity to be an employee benefit plan with fewer than 100 participants. The basis of this definition is found in section 104(a)(2) of ERISA, which permits the Secretary of Labor to prescribe simplified annual reports for pension plans which cover fewer than 100 participants. Under section 104(a)(3), the Secretary may also provide for exemptions or simplified annual reporting and disclosure for welfare benefit plans. Pursuant to the authority of section 104(a)(3), the Department has previously issued at 29 CFR 2520.104-20, 2520.104-21, 2520.104-41, 2520.104-46 and 2520.104b-10 certain simplified reporting provisions and limited exemptions from reporting and disclosure requirements for small plans, including unfunded or insured welfare plans covering fewer than 100 participants and which satisfy certain other requirements.

Further, while some large employers may have small plans, in general small employers maintain most small plans. Thus, EBSA believes that assessing the impact of this proposed rule on small plans is an appropriate substitute for evaluating the effect on small entities. The definition of small entity considered appropriate for this purpose differs, however, from a definition of small business which is based on size standards promulgated by the Small Business Administration (SBA) (13 CFR 121.201) pursuant to the Small Business Act (15 U.S.C. 631 et seq.). EBSA therefore requests comments on the appropriateness of the size standard used in evaluating the impact of this proposed rule on small entities. The Department does not expect that the financial institutions potentially impacted by this proposal will be small entities.

EBSA has preliminarily determined that this rule will not have a significant economic impact on a substantial number of small entities. In support of this determination, and in an effort to provide a sound basis for this conclusion, EBSA has prepared the following initial regulatory flexibility analysis.

Section 657(c)(2)(A) of EGTRRA directed the Department to issue regulations providing safe harbors under which a plan administrator's designation of an institution to receive automatic rollovers of mandatory distributions pursuant to section 401(a)(31)(B) of the Code and the initial investment choice for the rolled-over funds would be

deemed to satisfy the fiduciary responsibility provisions of section 404(a) of ERISA. This EGTRRA provision further provided that the Code provisions requiring automatic rollovers of certain mandatory distributions to individual retirement plans would not become effective until the Department issued safe harbor regulations. Before issuing this proposal, the Department requested comments on the potential design of the safe harbor.

The conditions set forth in this proposed regulation are intended to satisfy the EGTRRA requirement that the Department prescribe regulations providing for safe harbors, while meeting the objectives of offering greater certainty to fiduciaries concerning their compliance with the requirements of ERISA section 404(a), and of preserving assets of former plan participants for retirement income purposes. In describing the financial institutions, investment products, and fee arrangements that fall within the safe harbor, the Department has attempted to strike a balance between the interests of fiduciaries, individual retirement plan providers, and the investment goal of preserving principal.

The proposed rule would impact small plans that include provisions for the mandatory distribution of accounts with a value exceeding $1,000 and not greater than $5,000. It has been assumed for the purposes of this analysis that all plans include such provisions, although the number may actually be somewhat lower. On this basis, it is expected that the proposal will affect 611,800 small plans. The proportion of the total of 241,000 participants estimated to be affected annually by the amendment to Code section 401(a)(31)(B) that were in small plans is not known. Similarly, there are no available data on the number of participants that will separate from employment with account balances of more than $5,000 (because of prior rollover contributions) that may be, depending on the provisions of the distributing plans, automatically rolled over under EGTRRA. It is assumed that all 611,800 small plans will need to address compliance with the Code amendment and section 404(a) of ERISA.

As described above, the costs and benefits of the Code amendment and safe harbor proposal are distinguishable, and estimated separately. As also noted, the proposed regulation is expected to substantially reduce the cost of compliance with the Code amendment. The initial cost of the Code amendment for small plans is expected to be about $124 million. The one-time savings from the proposed regulation is estimated at about $83 million for small plans compared with $9 million for large plans, due to the significantly larger number of small plans. The condition of the safe harbor requiring disclosure of specific information in a summary plan description or summary of material modification is expected to result in costs of about $11 million. Preparation of this information is in most cases accomplished by professionals that provide services to employee benefit plans. Where fiduciaries prepare these materials themselves, it is assumed that persons at the professional level of budget analysts or financial managers will complete the necessary work.

The benefits of greater certainty afforded fiduciaries by the safe harbor are substantial but cannot be specifically quantified.

Prior to publication of this proposed regulation, the Department published an RFI requesting comments and suggestions from the general public on developing guidelines to assist fiduciaries in selecting institutions and investment products for individual retirement plans. The Department specifically requested in the RFI that commenters, "address the anticipated annual impact of any proposals on small businesses and small plans (plans with fewer than 100 participants)." The Department received three comments that pertained specifically to small plans, the first of which cautioned that plan sponsors would be deterred from sponsoring plans with a mandatory distribution provision by placement of any additional burdens on them. Another comment indicated that, because of technological improvements, the burden on small plans would be manageable. Finally, a third commenter noted that annual costs would not be any higher for small plans.

To the Department's knowledge, there are no federal regulations that might duplicate, overlap, or conflict with the proposed regulation for safe harbors under section 404(a) of ERISA.

Congressional Review Act

The notice of proposed rulemaking being issued here is subject to the provisions of the Congressional Review Act provisions of the Small Business Regulatory Enforcement Fairness Act of 1996 (5 U.S.C. 801 et seq.) and, if finalized, will be transmitted to the Congress and the Comptroller General for review.

Unfunded Mandates Reform Act

Pursuant to provisions of the Unfunded Mandates Reform Act of 1995 (Pub. L. 104-4), this rule does not include any Federal mandate that may result in expenditures by State, local, or tribal governments, or the private sector, which may impose an annual burden of $100 or more.

Federalism Statement

Executive Order 13132 (August 4, 1999) outlines fundamental principles of federalism and requires the adherence to specific criteria by federal agencies in the process of their formulation and implementation of policies that have substantial direct effects on the States, the relationship between the national government and the States, or on the distribution of power and responsibilities among the various levels of government. This proposed rule would not have federalism implications because it has no substantial direct effect on the States, on the relationship between the national government and the States, or on the distribution of power and responsibilities among the various levels of government. Section 514 of ERISA provides, with certain exceptions specifically enumerated, that the provisions of Titles I and IV of ERISA supersede any and all laws of the States as they relate to any employee benefit plan covered under ERISA. The requirements implemented in this proposed rule do not alter the fundamental provisions of the statute with respect to employee benefit plans, and as such would have no implications for the States or the relationship or distribution of power between the national government and the States.

List of Subjects in 29 CFR Part 2550

Employee benefit plans, Exemptions, Fiduciaries, Investments, Pensions, Prohibited transactions, Real estate, Securities, Surety bonds, Trusts and trustees.

For the reasons set forth in the preamble, the Department proposes to amend Subchapter F, Part 2550 of Title 29 of the Code of Federal Regulations as follows:

SUBCHAPTER F—FIDUCIARY RESPONSIBILITY UNDER THE EMPLOYEE RETIREMENT INCOME SECURITY ACT OF 1974

PART 2550—RULES AND REGULATIONS FOR FIDUCIARY RESPONSIBILITY

1. The authority citation for part 2550 is revised to read as follows:

Authority: 29 U.S.C. 1135; sec. 657, Pub. L. 107-16, 115 Stat. 38; and Secretary of Labor's Order No. 1-2003, 68 FR 5374 (Feb. 3, 2003). § 2550.401b-1 also issued under sec. 102, Reorganization Plan No. 4 of 1978, 43 FR 47713 (Oct. 17, 1978), 3 CFR, 1978 Comp. 332, effective Dec. 31, 1978, 44 FR 1065 (Jan. 3, 1978), 3 CFR, 1978 Comp. 332. § 2550.401c-1 also issued under 29 U.S.C. 1101. § 2550.404c-1 also issued under 29 U.S.C. 1104. § 2550.407c-3 also issued under 29 U.S.C. 1107. § 2550.408b-1 also issued under 29 U.S.C. 1108(b)(1) and sec. 102, Reorganization Plan No. 4 of 1978, 3 CFR, 1978 Comp. p. 332, effective Dec. 31, 1978, 44 FR 1065 (Jan. 3, 1978), and 3 CFR, 1978 Comp. 332. § 2550.412-1 also issued under 29 U.S.C. 1112.

2. Add § 2550.404a-2 to read as follows:

§ 2550.404a-2 Safe harbor for automatic rollovers to individual retirement plans.

(a) *In general.* (1) Pursuant to section 657(c) of the Economic Growth and Tax Relief Reconciliation Act of 2001, Public Law 107-16, June 7, 2001, 115 Stat. 38, this section provides a safe harbor under which a fiduciary of an employee pension benefit plan subject to Title I of the Employee Retirement Income Security Act of 1974, as amended (the Act), 29 U.S.C. 1001 et seq., will be deemed to have satisfied his or her fiduciary duties under section 404(a) of the Act in connection with an automatic rollover of a mandatory distribution described in section 401(a)(31)(B) of the Internal Revenue Code of 1986, as amended (the Code).

(2) The standards set forth in this section apply solely for purposes of determining whether a fiduciary meets the requirements of this safe harbor. Such standards are not intended to be the exclusive means by which a fiduciary might satisfy his or her responsibilities under the Act with respect to automatic rollovers of mandatory distributions described in section 401(a)(31)(B) of the Code.

(b) *Safe harbor.* A fiduciary that meets the conditions of paragraph (c) of this section is deemed to have satisfied his or her duties under section 404(a) of the Act with respect to both the selection of an individual retirement plan provider and the investment of funds in connection with an automatic rollover of a mandatory distribution described in section 401(a)(31)(B) of the Code to an individual retirement plan, within the meaning of section 7701(a)(37) of the Code.

(c) *Conditions.* With respect to an automatic rollover of a mandatory distribution described in section 401(a)(31)(B) of the Code, a fiduciary shall qualify for the safe harbor described in paragraph (b) of this section if:

(1) The present value of the nonforfeitable accrued benefit, as determined under section 411(a)(11) of the Code, does not exceed the maximum amount under section 401(a)(31)(B) of the Code;

(2) The mandatory distribution is to an individual retirement plan within the meaning of section 7701(a)(37) of the Code;

(3)(i) The mandatory distribution is invested in an investment product designed to preserve principal and provide a reasonable rate of return, whether or not such return is guaranteed, consistent with liquidity, and taking into account paragraph (c)(4) of this section. For this purpose, the product must be offered by a state or federally regulated financial institution, as defined in paragraph (c)(3)(ii) of this section, and must seek to maintain a stable dollar value equal to the amount invested in the product by the individual retirement plan, and

(ii) For purposes of this section, a regulated financial institution shall be: a bank or savings association, the deposits of which are insured by the Federal Deposit Insurance Corporation; a credit union, the member accounts of which are insured within the meaning of section 101(7) of the Federal Credit Union Act; an insurance company, the products of which are protected by state guarantee associations; or an investment company registered under the Investment Company Act of 1940;

(4)(i) Fees and expenses attendant to the individual retirement plan, including investments of such plan, (e.g., establishment charges, maintenance fees, investment expenses, termination costs and surrender charges) shall not exceed the fees and expenses charged by the individual retirement plan provider for comparable individual retirement plans established for rollover distributions that are not subject to the automatic rollover provisions of section 401(a)(31)(B) of the Code, and

(ii) Fees and expenses attendant to the individual retirement plan may be charged only against the income earned by the individual retirement plan, with the exception of charges assessed for the establishment of the individual retirement plan;

(5) Participants have been furnished a summary plan description, or a summary of material modifications, that describes the plan's automatic rollover provisions effectuating the requirements of section 401(a)(31)(B) of the Code, including an explanation that the mandatory distribution will be invested in an investment product designed to preserve principal and provide a reasonable rate of return and liquidity, a statement indicating how fees and expenses attendant to the individual retirement plan will be allocated, and the name, address and phone number of a plan contact (to the extent not otherwise provided in the summary plan description or summary of material modifications) for further information concerning the plan's automatic rollover provisions, the individual retirement plan provider and the fees and expenses attendant to the individual retirement plan; and

(6) Both the fiduciary's selection of an individual retirement plan and the investment of funds would not result in a prohibited transaction under section 406 of the Act, unless such actions are exempted from the prohibited transaction provisions by a prohibited transaction exemption issued pursuant to section 408(a) of the Act.

Signed at Washington, DC, this 24th day of February, 2004.

Ann L. Combs, Assistant Secretary, Employee Benefits Security Administration, Department of Labor.

[FR Doc. 04-4551 Filed 3-1-04; 8:45 am]

¶ 20,534Q

Veterans' Employment and Training Service: Uniformed Services Employment and Reemployment Rights Act of 1994: Protected pension benefits: Protections against discrimination and retaliation: Employer statutory defenses.—The Department of Labor has issued proposed regulations that are designed to clarify the rights of employees and the attendant responsibilities of employers under the Uniformed Services Employment and Reemployment Rights Act of 1994 (USERRA). In addition to reemployment rights and protections from retaliation and discrimination, USERRA entitles veterans returning to employment from uniformed military service to the restoration of pension and profit-sharing benefits that would have accrued but for the employee's military service. Specifically, the reemployed veterans military service is considered served with the employer for purposes of benefit accrual. A reemployed veteran is also entitled to accrued benefits that are contingent on the making of, or derived from, employee contributions or elective deferrals, to the extent that the employee makes payments to the plan with respect to contributions or deferrals.

The proposed regulations were published in the *Federal Register* on September 20, 2004 (69 FR 56265). The final regulations were published in the *Federal Register* on December 19, 2005 (70 FR 75246). The preamble to the final regulations is reproduced at ¶ 24,806U.

¶ 20,534R

Pension Benefit Guaranty Corporation (PBGC): Electronic filing requirements: Financial statements: Actuarial information.—The PBGC has issued a proposed rule which would: require that certain identifying, financial and actuarial information be filed electronically in a standardized format; require the filing of additional items of supporting information that are readily available to the filer; and require a filer for the previous year, who does not believe a filing is required for the current year, to demonstrate why there is no current filing requirement.

The proposed regulation, which was reproduced here, was published in the Federal Register on December 28, 2004 (69 FR 77679), and corrected on January 12, 2005 (70 FR 2080). The final regulations were published in the *Federal Register* on March 9, 2005 (70 FR 11540). The preamble to the final regulations is reproduced at ¶ 24,806R.

¶ 20,534S

Employee Benefits Security Administration: Health plans: HIPAA: Family and Medical Leave Act: Tolling of time periods: Creditable coverage.—The Employee Benefits Security Administration has issued proposed regulations relating to the interaction between the Health Insurance Portability and Accountability Act (HIPAA) and the Family and Medical Leave Act (FMLA). Under the proposed regulations, the beginning of the period that is used for determining whether a significant break in coverage has occurred (generally 63 days) is tolled in cases in which a certificate of creditable coverage is not provided on or before the day coverage ceases. In those cases, the significant break-in-coverage period is tolled until a certificate is provided but not beyond 44 days after the coverage ceases. These rules are being jointly issued with the Internal Revenue Service. Comments must be received by March 30, 2005.

The proposed regulations, which were published in the Federal Register on December 30, 2004 (69 FR 78799), are reproduced below.

DEPARTMENT OF LABOR

Employee Benefits Security Administration

29 CFR Part 2590

RIN 1210-AA54

Notice of Proposed Rulemaking for Health Coverage Portability: Tolling Certain Time Periods and Interaction With the Family and Medical Leave Act Under HIPAA Titles I and IV

AGENCIES: Internal Revenue Service, Department of the Treasury; Employee Benefits Security Administration, Department of Labor; Centers for Medicare & Medicaid Services, Department of Health and Human Services.

ACTION: Notice of proposed rulemaking and request for comments.

SUMMARY: These proposed rules would clarify certain portability requirements for group health plans and issuers of health insurance coverage offered in connection with a group health plan. These rules propose to implement changes made to the Internal Revenue Code, the Employee Retirement Income Security Act, and the Public Health Service Act enacted as part of the Health Insurance Portability and Accountability Act of 1996.

DATES: Written comments on this notice of proposed rulemaking are invited and must be received by the Departments on or before March 30, 2005.

ADDRESSES: Written comments should be submitted with a signed original and three copies (except for electronic submissions) to any of the addresses specified below. Any comment that is submitted to any Department will be shared with the other Departments.

Comments to the IRS can be addressed to: CC:PA:LPD:PR (REG-130370-04), Room 5203, Internal Revenue Service, POB 7604, Ben Franklin Station, Washington, DC 20044.

In the alternative, comments may be hand-delivered between the hours of 8 a.m. and 4 p.m. to: CC:PA:LPD:PR (REG-130370-04), Courier's Desk, Internal Revenue Service, 1111 Constitution Avenue, NW., Washington, DC 20224.

Alternatively, comments may be transmitted electronically via the IRS or via the Federal eRulemaking Portal at *www.regulations.gov* (IRS-REG-130370-04).

Comments to the Department of Labor can be addressed to: U.S. Department of Labor, Employee Benefits Security Administration, 200 Constitution Avenue NW., Room C-5331, Washington, DC 20210, *Attention:* Proposed Portability Requirements.

Alternatively, comments may be hand-delivered between the hours of 9 a.m. and 5 p.m. to the same address. Comments may also be transmitted by e-mail to: *e-ohpsca.ebsa@dol.gov*.

Comments to HHS can be submitted as described below: In commenting, please refer to file code CMS-2158-P. Because of staff and resource limitations, we cannot accept comments by facsimile (FAX) transmission.

You may submit comments in one of three ways (no duplicates, please):

1. *Electronically.* You may submit electronic comments on specific issues in this regulation to *http://www.cms.hhs.gov/regulations/ecomments*. (Attachments should be in Microsoft Word, WordPerfect, or Excel; however, we prefer Microsoft Word.)

2. *By mail.* You may mail written comments (one original and two copies) to the following address ONLY:

Centers for Medicare & Medicaid Services, Department of Health and Human Services, Attention: CMS-2158-P, P.O. Box 8017, Baltimore, MD 21244-8010.

Please allow sufficient time for mailed comments to be received before the close of the comment period.

3. *By hand or courier.* If you prefer, you may deliver (by hand or courier) your written comments (one original and two copies) before the close of the comment period to one of the following addresses. If you intend to deliver your comments to the Baltimore address, please call telephone number (410) 786-7195 in advance to schedule your arrival with one of our staff members. Room 445-G, Hubert H. Humphrey Building, 200 Independence Avenue, SW., Washington, DC 20201; or 7500 Security Boulevard, Baltimore, MD 21244-1850.

(Because access to the interior of the HHH Building is not readily available to persons without Federal Government identification, commenters are encouraged to leave their comments in the CMS drop slots located in the main lobby of the building. A stamp-in clock is available for persons wishing to retain a proof of filing by stamping in and retaining an extra copy of the comments being filed.)

Comments mailed to the addresses indicated as appropriate for hand or courier delivery may be delayed and received after the comment period.

Submission of comments on paperwork requirements. You may submit comments on this document's paperwork requirements by mailing your comments to the addresses provided at the end of the "Collection of Information Requirements" section in this document.

All submissions to the IRS will be open to public inspection and copying in room 1621, 1111 Constitution Avenue, NW., Washington, DC from 9 a.m. to 4 p.m.

All submissions to the Department of Labor will be open to public inspection and copying in the Public Disclosure Room, Employee Benefits Security Administration, U.S. Department of Labor, Room

N-1513, 200 Constitution Avenue, NW., Washington, DC from 8:30 a.m. to 4:30 p.m.

All submissions timely submitted to HHS will be available for public inspection as they are received, generally beginning approximately three weeks after publication of a document, at the headquarters for the Centers for Medicare & Medicaid Services, 7500 Security Boulevard, Baltimore, MD 21244, Monday through Friday of each week from 8:30 a.m. to 4:00 p.m. To schedule an appointment to view public comments, phone 410-786-7195.

FOR FURTHER INFORMATION CONTACT:

Dave Mlawsky, Centers for Medicare & Medicaid Services (CMS), Department of Health and Human Services, at 1-877-267-2323 ext. 61565; Amy Turner, Employee Benefits Security Administration, Department of Labor, at (202) 693-8335; or Russ Weinheimer, Internal Revenue Service, Department of the Treasury, at (202) 622-6080.

SUPPLEMENTARY INFORMATION:

Customer Service Information

To assist consumers and the regulated community, the Departments have issued questions and answers concerning HIPAA. Individuals interested in obtaining copies of Department of Labor publications concerning changes in health care law may call a toll free number, 1-866-444-EBSA (3272), or access the publications on-line at *www.dol.gov/ebsa,* the Department of Labor's Web site. These regulations as well as other information on the new health care laws are also available on the Department of Labor's interactive web pages, Health *E* laws. In addition, CMS's publication entitled "Protecting Your Health Insurance Coverage" is available by calling 1-800-633-4227 or on the Department of Health and Human Services' Web site (www.cms.hhs.gov/hipaa1), which includes the interactive webpages, HIPAA Online. Copies of the HIPAA regulations, as well as notices and press releases related to HIPAA and other health care laws, are also available at the above-referenced Web sites.

Background

The Health Insurance Portability and Accountability Act of 1996 (HIPAA), Public Law 104-191, was enacted on August 21, 1996. HIPAA amended the Internal Revenue Code of 1986 (Code), the Employee Retirement Income Security Act of 1974 (ERISA), and the Public Health Service Act (PHS Act) to provide for, among other things, improved portability and continuity of health coverage. Interim final regulations implementing the HIPAA provisions were first made available to the public on April 1, 1997 (published in the **Federal Register** on April 8, 1997, 62 FR 16894) (April 1997 interim rules). On December 29, 1997, the Departments published a clarification of the April 1997 interim rules as they relate to excepted benefits. On October 25, 1999, the Departments published a notice in the **Federal Register** (64 FR 57520) soliciting additional comments on the portability requirements based on the experience of plans and issuers operating under the April 1997 interim rules.

After consideration of all the comments received on the portability provisions, the Departments are publishing final regulations elsewhere in this issue of the **Federal Register**. These proposed rules address additional and discrete issues for which the Departments are soliciting further comment before promulgating final regulations.

Overview of the Proposed Regulations

1. Rules Relating to Creditable Coverage—26 CFR 54.9801-4, 29 CFR 2590.701-4, 45 CFR 146.113

Tolling of the 63-Day Break-in-Coverage Rule

These proposed rules would modify the 63-day break-in-coverage rules with one significant substantive change. Under the proposed

rules, the beginning of the period that is used for determining whether a significant break in coverage has occurred (generally 63 days) is tolled in cases in which a certificate of creditable coverage is not provided on or before the day coverage ceases. In those cases, the significant-break-in-coverage period is tolled until a certificate is provided but not beyond 44 days after the coverage ceases.

The Departments have fashioned this tolling rule (and a similar tolling rule for the 30-day period for requesting special enrollment) in an effort to address the inequity of individuals' losing coverage without being aware that the coverage has ended while minimizing the burdens on subsequent plans and issuers that are not responsible for providing the missing or untimely certificates. Numerous situations have come to the attention of the Departments in which an individual's health coverage is terminated but in which the individual does not learn of the termination of coverage until well after it occurs. The statute generally requires that a certificate of creditable coverage be provided at the time an individual ceases to be covered under a plan. The statute, the April 1997 interim rules, and the final regulations (published elsewhere in this issue of the **Federal Register**) all permit a plan or issuer to provide the certificate at a later date if it is provided at a time consistent with notices required under a COBRA continuation provision. The statute also directs the Secretaries to establish rules to prevent a plan or issuer's failure to provide a certificate timely from adversely affecting the individual's subsequent coverage. If a plan or issuer chooses to provide a certificate later than the date an individual loses coverage, as the regulations permit in certain circumstances, these proposed rules provide that an individual should not suffer from this rule of convenience for the plan or issuer. However, to prevent the abuse that might result from an open-ended tolling rule, an outside limit of 44 days is placed on this relief. This reflects the fact that, in most cases, plans and issuers are required to provide certificates within 44 days (although some plans and issuers may be required to provide certificates sooner than 44 days after coverage ceases and some entities are not required to provide certificates at all). The Departments have adopted this uniform limit on the tolling rule for purposes of consistency. New examples have been added to illustrate the tolling rule.

2. Evidence of Creditable Coverage—26 CFR 54.9801-5, 29 CFR 2590.701-5, 45 CFR 146.115

Information in Certificate and Model Certificate

These proposed rules would modify the required elements for the educational statement in certificates of creditable coverage to require a disclosure about the Family and Medical Leave Act. Use of the first model certificate below by group health plans and group health insurance issuers, or use of the appropriate model certificate that appears in the preamble to the related final regulations published elsewhere in this issue of the **Federal Register**, will satisfy the requirements of paragraph (a)(3)(ii) in this section of the final regulations. Similarly, for purposes of complying with those final regulations, State Medicaid programs may use the second version below, or may use the appropriate model certificate that appears in the preamble to those final regulations. Thus, until this proposed regulation is published as a final regulation, entities may use either the model certificate published below, or those published elsewhere in this issue of the **Federal Register**. For entities that choose not to use the model certificates below until this proposed regulation is published as a final regulation, we welcome comments as to the applicability date for using them.

BILLING CODE 4830-01-P

CERTIFICATE OF GROUP HEALTH PLAN COVERAGE

1. Date of this certificate: _____

2. Name of group health plan: _____
_____

3. Name of participant: _____

4. Identification number of participant: _____

5. Name of individuals to whom this certificate applies: _____
_____

6. Name, address, and telephone number of plan administrator or issuer responsible for providing this certificate:_____
_____
_____

7. For further information, call: _____

8. If the individual(s) identified in line 5 has (have) at least 18 months of creditable coverage (disregarding periods of coverage before a 63-day break), check here and skip lines 9 and 10: ___

9. Date waiting period or affiliation period (if any) began: _____

10. Date coverage began: _____

11. Date coverage ended (or if coverage has not ended, enter "continuing"): _____

[Note: separate certificates will be furnished if information is not identical for the participant and each beneficiary.]

Statement of HIPAA Portability Rights

IMPORTANT — KEEP THIS CERTIFICATE. This certificate is evidence of your coverage under this plan. Under a federal law known as HIPAA, you may need evidence of your coverage to reduce a preexisting condition exclusion period under another plan, to help you get special enrollment in another plan, or to get certain types of individual health coverage even if you have health problems.

Preexisting condition exclusions. Some group health plans restrict coverage for medical conditions present before an individual's enrollment. These restrictions are known as "preexisting condition exclusions." A preexisting condition exclusion can apply only to conditions for which medical advice, diagnosis, care, or treatment was recommended or received within the 6 months before your "enrollment date." Your enrollment date is your first day of coverage under the plan, or, if there is a waiting period, the first day of your waiting period (typically, your first day of work). In addition, a preexisting condition exclusion cannot last for more than 12 months after your enrollment date (18 months if you are a late enrollee). Finally, a preexisting condition exclusion cannot apply to pregnancy and cannot apply to a child who is enrolled in health coverage within 30 days after birth, adoption, or placement for adoption.

If a plan imposes a preexisting condition exclusion, the length of the exclusion must be reduced by the amount of your prior creditable coverage. Most health coverage is creditable coverage, including group health plan coverage, COBRA continuation coverage, coverage under an individual health policy, Medicare, Medicaid, State Children's Health Insurance Program (SCHIP), and coverage through high-risk pools and the Peace Corps. Not all forms of creditable coverage are required to provide certificates like this one. If you do not receive a certificate for past coverage, talk to your new plan administrator.

You can add up any creditable coverage you have, including the coverage shown on this certificate. However, if at any time you went for 63 days or more without any coverage (called a break in coverage) a plan may not have to count the coverage you had before the break.

→ Therefore, once your coverage ends, you should try to obtain alternative coverage as soon as possible to avoid a 63-day break. You may use this certificate as evidence of your creditable coverage to reduce the length of any preexisting condition exclusion if you enroll in another plan.

<u>**Right to get special enrollment in another plan.**</u> Under HIPAA, if you lose your group health plan coverage, you may be able to get into another group health plan for which you are eligible (such as a spouse's plan), even if the plan generally does not accept late enrollees, if you request enrollment within 30 days. (Additional special enrollment rights are triggered by marriage, birth, adoption, and placement for adoption.)

➔ Therefore, once your coverage ends, if you are eligible for coverage in another plan (such as a spouse's plan), you should request special enrollment as soon as possible.

<u>**Prohibition against discrimination based on a health factor**</u>. Under HIPAA, a group health plan may not keep you (or your dependents) out of the plan based on anything related to your health. Also, a group health plan may no charge you (or your dependents) more for coverage, based on health, than the amount charged a similarly situated individual.

<u>**Right to individual health coverage.**</u> Under HIPAA, if you are an "eligible individual," you have a right to buy certain individual health policies (or in some states, to buy coverage through a high-risk pool) without a preexisting condition exclusion. To be an eligible individual, you must meet the following requirements:

- You have had coverage for at least 18 months without a break in coverage of 63 days or more;
- Your most recent coverage was under a group health plan (which can be shown by this certificate);
- Your group coverage was not terminated because of fraud or nonpayment of premiums;
- You are not eligible for COBRA continuation coverage or you have exhausted your COBRA benefits (or continuation coverage under a similar state provision); and
- You are not eligible for another group health plan, Medicare, or Medicaid, and do not have any other health insurance coverage.

The right to buy individual coverage is the same whether you are laid off, fired, or quit your job.

➔ Therefore, if you are interested in obtaining individual coverage and you meet the other criteria to be an eligible individual, you should apply for this coverage as soon as possible to avoid losing your eligible individual status due to a 63-day break.

<u>**Special information for people on FMLA leave.**</u> If you are taking leave under the Family and Medical Leave Act (FMLA) and you drop health coverage during your leave, any days without health coverage while on FMLA leave will not count towards a 63-day break in coverage. In addition, if you do not return from leave, the 30-day period to request special enrollment in another plan will not start before your FMLA leave ends.

➔ Therefore, when you apply for other health coverage, you should tell your plan administrator or health insurer about any prior FMLA leave.

<u>**State flexibility**</u>. This certificate describes minimum HIPAA protections under federal law. States may require insurers and HMOs to provide additional protections to individuals in that state.

<u>**For more information.**</u> If you have questions about your HIPAA rights, you may contact your state insurance department or the U.S. Department of Labor, Employee Benefits Security Administration (EBSA) toll-free at 1-866-444-3272 (for free HIPAA publications ask for publications concerning changes in health care laws). You may also contact the CMS publication hotline at 1-800-633-4227 (ask for "Protecting Your Health Insurance Coverage"). These publications and other useful information are also available on the Internet at: http://www.dol.gov/ebsa, the DOL's interactive web pages - Health *E*laws, or http://www.cms.hhs.gov/hipaa1.

CERTIFICATE OF MEDICAID COVERAGE

1. Date of this certificate: _____

2. Name of state Medicaid program:
    _____

3. Name of recipient: _____

4. Identification number of recipient:
    _____

5. Name of individuals to whom this certificate
    applies: _____
    _____

6. Name, address, and telephone number of state
    Medicaid agency responsible for providing this
    certificate: _____
    _____
    _____

7. For further information call: _____

8. If the individual(s) identified in line 5 has (have)
    at least 18 months of creditable coverage
    (disregarding periods of coverage before a 63-
    day break), check here and skip line 9. _____

9. Date coverage began: _____

10. Date coverage ended (or if coverage has not
    ended, enter "continuing"): _____

    *[Note: separate certificates will be furnished if
    information is not identical for the recipient and each
    dependent.]*

Statement of HIPAA Portability Rights

IMPORTANT — KEEP THIS CERTIFICATE. This certificate is evidence of your coverage under this state Medicaid program. Under a federal law known as HIPAA, you may need evidence of your coverage to reduce a preexisting condition exclusion period under a group health plan, to help you get special enrollment in a group health plan, or to get certain types of individual health coverage even if you have health problems.

Preexisting condition exclusions. Some group health plans restrict coverage for medical conditions present before an individual's enrollment. These restrictions are known as "preexisting condition exclusions." A preexisting condition exclusion can apply only to conditions for which medical advice, diagnosis, care, or treatment was recommended or received within the 6 months before your "enrollment date." Your enrollment date is your first day of coverage under the plan, or, if there is a waiting period, the first day of your waiting period (typically, your first day of work). In addition, a preexisting condition exclusion cannot last for more than 12 months after your enrollment date (18 months if you are a late enrollee). Finally, a preexisting condition exclusion cannot apply to pregnancy and cannot apply to a child who is enrolled in health coverage within 30 days after birth, adoption, or placement for adoption.

If a plan imposes a preexisting condition exclusion, the length of the exclusion must be reduced by the amount of your prior creditable coverage. Most health coverage is creditable coverage, including group health plan coverage, COBRA continuation coverage, coverage under an individual health policy, Medicare, Medicaid, State Children's Health Insurance Program (SCHIP), and coverage through high-risk pools and the Peace Corps. Not all forms of creditable coverage are required to provide certificates like this one. If you do not receive a certificate for past coverage, talk to your new plan administrator.

You can add up any creditable coverage you have, including the coverage shown on this certificate. However, if at any time you went for 63 days or more without any coverage (called a break in coverage) a plan may not have to count the coverage you had before the break.

➜ Therefore, once your coverage ends, you should try to obtain alternative coverage as soon as possible to avoid a 63-day break. You may use this certificate as evidence of your creditable coverage to reduce the length of any preexisting condition exclusion if you enroll in a group health plan.

Right to get special enrollment in another plan. Under HIPAA, if you lose your group health plan coverage, you may be able to get into another group health plan for which you are eligible (such as a spouse's plan), even if the plan generally does not accept late enrollees, if you request enrollment within 30 days. (Additional special enrollment rights are triggered by marriage, birth, adoption, and placement for adoption.)

➜ Therefore, once your coverage in a group health plan ends, if you are eligible for coverage in another plan (such as a spouse's plan), you should request special enrollment as soon as possible.

Prohibition against discrimination based on a health factor. Under HIPAA, a group health plan may not keep you (or your dependents) out of the plan based on anything related to your health. Also, a group health plan may not charge you (or your dependents) more for coverage, based on health, than the amount charged a similarly situated individual.

Right to individual health coverage. Under HIPAA, if you are an "eligible individual," you have a right to buy certain individual health policies (or in some states, to buy coverage through a high-risk pool) without a preexisting condition exclusion. To be an eligible individual, you must meet the following requirements:

- You have had coverage for at least 18 months without a break in coverage of 63 days or more;
- Your most recent coverage was under a group health plan;
- Your group coverage was not terminated because of fraud or nonpayment of premiums;
- You are not eligible for COBRA continuation coverage or you have exhausted your COBRA benefits (or continuation coverage under a similar state provision); and
- You are not eligible for another group health plan, Medicare, or Medicaid, and do not have any other health insurance coverage.

The right to buy individual coverage is the same whether you are laid off, fired, or quit your job.

➜ Therefore, if you are interested in obtaining individual coverage and you meet the other criteria to be an eligible individual, you should apply for this coverage as soon as possible to avoid losing your eligible individual status due to a 63-day break.

Special information for people on FMLA leave. If you are taking leave under the Family and Medical Leave Act (FMLA) and you drop health coverage during your leave, any days without health coverage while on FMLA leave will not count towards a 63-day break in coverage. In addition, if you do not return from leave, the 30-day period to request special enrollment in another plan will not start before your FMLA leave ends.

➜ Therefore, when you apply for other health coverage, you should tell your plan administrator or health insurer about any prior FMLA leave.

State flexibility. This certificate describes minimum HIPAA protections under federal law. States may require insurers and HMOs to provide additional protections to individuals in that state.

For more information. If you have questions about your HIPAA rights, you may contact your state insurance department or the U.S. Department of Labor, Employee Benefits Security Administration (EBSA) toll-free at 1-866-444-3272 (for free HIPAA publications ask for publications concerning changes in health care laws). You may also contact the CMS publication hotline at 1-800-633-4227 (ask for "Protecting Your Health Insurance Coverage"). These publications and other useful information are also available on the Internet at: http://www.dol.gov/ebsa or http://www.cms.hhs.gov/hipaa1.

BILLING CODE 4830-01-C

3. Special Enrollment Periods—26 CFR 54.9801-6, 29 CFR 2590.701-6, 45 CFR 146.117

Tolling of the Special Enrollment Period

Under HIPAA, the April 1997 interim rules, and the final regulations, an individual wishing to special enroll following a loss of coverage is generally required to request enrollment not later than 30 days after the loss of eligibility, termination of employer contributions, or exhaustion of COBRA continuation coverage. For individuals whose coverage ceases and a certificate of creditable coverage is not provided on or before the date coverage ceases, this regulation provides for proposed tolling rules similar to those described above for determining a significant break. That is, the special enrollment period terminates at the end of the 30-day period that begins on the first day after the earlier of the date that a certificate of creditable coverage is provided or the date 44 days after coverage ceases.

Modification of Special Enrollment Procedures and When Coverage Begins Under Special Enrollment

The April 1997 interim rules did not establish procedures for processing requests for special enrollment beyond affirming the statutory requirement that requests be made not later than 30 days after the event giving rise to the special enrollment right and providing that the same requirements could be imposed on special enrollees that were imposed on other enrollees (*e.g.,* that the request be made in writing). Some examples in the April 1997 interim rules could be read to suggest that plans and issuers could require individuals requesting special enrollment to file completed applications for health coverage by the end of the special enrollment period.

It has been brought to the Departments' attention that some plans and issuers were imposing application requirements that could not reasonably be completed within the special enrollment period (for example, requiring the social security number of a newborn within 30 days of the birth), effectively denying individuals their right to special enroll their dependents. In this regard, the statute merely requires an employee to request special enrollment, or an individual to seek to enroll, during the special enrollment period. These proposed regulations preserve individuals' access to special enrollment by clarifying that during the special enrollment period individuals are only required to make an oral or written request for special enrollment.

The proposed regulations provide further that after a timely request, the plan or issuer may require the individual to complete all enrollment materials within a reasonable time after the end of the special enrollment period. However, the enrollment procedure may only require information required from individuals who enroll when first eligible and information about the event giving rise to the special enrollment right. While a plan can impose a deadline for submitting the completed enrollment materials, the deadline must be extended for information that an individual making reasonable efforts cannot obtain within that deadline.

Thus, even where a plan requires social security numbers from individuals who enroll when first eligible, the plan must provide an extended deadline for receiving the social security number in the case of a newborn. In no event could a plan deny special enrollment for newborns because an employee could not provide a social security number for the newborn within the special enrollment period.

As regards the effective date of coverage for special enrollments, the proposed rules generally follow the statute, the April 1997 interim final rules, and the final regulations being published elsewhere in this issue of the **Federal Register.** However clarifications of the effective date of coverage are added to conform to the clarification of the special enrollment procedures. Where the special enrollment right results from a loss of eligibility for coverage or marriage, coverage generally must begin no later than the first day of the first calendar month after the date the plan or issuer receives the request for special enrollment. However, if the plan or issuer requires completion of additional enrollment materials, coverage must begin no later than the first day of the first calendar month after the plan or issuer receives enrollment materials that are substantially complete.

Where the special enrollment right results from a birth, coverage must begin on the date of birth. In the case of adoption or placement for adoption, coverage must begin no later than the date of such adoption or placement for adoption. If a plan or issuer requires completion of additional enrollment materials, the plan or issuer must provide benefits once the plan or issuer receives substantially complete enrollment materials. However, the benefits provided at that time must be retroactive to the date of birth, adoption, or placement for adoption.

The Departments welcome comments on these aspects of the proposed rule.

4. Interaction With the Family and Medical Leave Act—26 CFR 54.9801-7, 29 CFR 701-8, 45 CFR 146.120

The proposed rules address how the HIPAA portability requirements apply in situations where a person is on leave under the Family and Medical Leave Act of 1993 (FMLA). A general principle of FMLA is that an employee returning from leave under FMLA should generally be in the same position the employee was in before taking leave. At issue is how to reconcile that principle of FMLA with the HIPAA rights and requirements that are triggered by an individual ending coverage under a group health plan. These proposed regulations provide specific rules that clarify how HIPAA and FMLA interact when the coverage of an employee or an employee's dependent ends in connection with an employee taking leave under FMLA.

With respect to the rules concerning a significant break in coverage, if an employee takes FMLA leave and does not continue group health coverage for any part of the leave, the period of FMLA leave without coverage is not taken into account in determining whether a significant break in coverage has occurred for the employee or any dependents. To the extent an individual needs to demonstrate that coverage ceased in connection with FMLA leave (which would toll any significant break with respect to another plan or issuer), these regulations provide that a plan or issuer must take into account all information that it obtains about an employee's FMLA leave. Further, if an individual attests to the period of FMLA leave and the individual cooperates with a plan's or issuer's efforts to verify the individual's FMLA leave, the plan or issuer must treat the individual as having been on FMLA leave for the period attested to for purposes of determining if the individual had a significant break in coverage. Nonetheless, a plan or issuer is not prevented from modifying its initial determination of FMLA leave if it determines that the individual did not have the claimed FMLA leave, provided that the plan or issuer follows procedures for reconsideration similar to those set forth in the final rules governing determinations of creditable coverage.

The question has arisen whether it would be appropriate to waive the general requirement to provide automatic certificates of creditable coverage in the case of an individual who declines coverage when electing FMLA leave if the individual will be reinstated at the end of FMLA leave. At the time an employee elects FMLA leave, the employer (as well as the employee) may not know if the employee will later return from FMLA leave and elect to be reinstated. Requiring plans and issuers to provide certificates when individuals cease health coverage in connection with FMLA leave may result in some certificates being issued when individuals ceasing coverage will not need the certificates as evidence of coverage (because of later reinstatement). However, automatic issuance likely imposes less burden because the plan or issuer does not need to determine whether a certificate is required. Moreover, automatic issuance eliminates the need for remedial measures if an individual expected to be reinstated in fact is not later reinstated. Thus, these proposed regulations clarify there is no exception to the general rule requiring automatic certificates when coverage ends and provide that if an individual covered under a group health plan takes FMLA leave and ceases coverage under the plan, an automatic certificate must be provided.

With respect to the special enrollment rules, an individual (or a dependent of the individual) who is covered under a group health plan and who takes FMLA leave has a loss of eligibility that results in a special enrollment period if the individual's group health coverage is terminated at any time during FMLA leave and the individual does not return to work for the employer at the end of FMLA leave. This special enrollment period begins when the period of FMLA leave ends. Moreover, the rules that delay the start of the special enrollment period until the receipt of a certificate of creditable coverage continue to operate.

5. Special Rules—Excepted Plans and Excepted Benefits—26 CFR 54.9831-1, 29 CFR 2590.732, 45 CFR 146.145

Determination of Number of Plans

Various provisions in Chapter 100 of the Code, Part 7 of Subtitle B of Title I of ERISA, and Title XXVII of the PHS Act apply when an individual commences coverage or terminates coverage under a group health plan. For example, a certificate of creditable coverage must be provided when an individual ceases to be covered under a group health plan. Under the April 1997 interim rules, it was not always clear whether an individual changing benefit elections among those offered by an employer or employee organization was merely switching between benefit packages under a single plan or was switching from one plan to another. These proposed regulations add rules to remove this uncertainty.

Under these proposed regulations, all medical care benefits made available by an employer or employee organization (including a board of trustees of a multiemployer trust) are generally considered to constitute one group health plan (the default rule). However, the employer or employee organization can establish more than one group health plan if it is clear from the instruments governing the arrangements to provide medical care benefits that the benefits are being provided under separate plans and if the arrangements are operated pursuant to the instruments as separate plans. A multiemployer plan and a nonmultiemployer plan are always separate plans. Under an anti-abuse rule, separate plans are aggregated to the extent necessary to prevent the evasion of any legal requirement.

These rules provide plan sponsors great flexibility while minimizing the burden of making decisions about how many plans to maintain. For example, many employers may wish to minimize the number of certificates of creditable coverage required to be furnished to continuing employees. Under the default rule, because all health benefits provided by an employer are considered a single group health plan, there is no need to furnish a certificate of creditable coverage when an employee merely switches coverage among the options made available by the employer. This need would arise only if the employer designated separate benefit packages as separate plans in the plan documents and only if the benefit packages were also operated pursuant to the plan documents as separate plans.

The anti-abuse rule limits the flexibility of these rules to prevent evasions. For example, a plan sponsor might design an arrangement under which the participation of each of many employees in the arrangement would be considered a separate plan. On the face of it, such an arrangement might appear to satisfy the requirement for a plan being exempt from the requirements of Chapter 100 of the Code, Part 7 of ERISA, and Title XXVII of the PHS Act because on the first day of the plan year each plan would have fewer than two participants who are current employees. This would give the impression that the plans would not have to comply with the prohibitions against discriminating based on one or more health factors, with the restrictions on preexisting condition exclusions, nor with any of the other requirements of Chapter 100 of the Code, Part 7 of ERISA, and Title XXVII of the PHS Act. The anti-abuse rule would require the aggregation of plans under such an arrangement to the extent necessary to make the plans subject to the requirements of Chapter 100 of the Code, Part 7 of ERISA, and Title XXVII of the PHS Act. The anti-abuse rule would apply in similar fashion to prevent the evasion of any other law that applies to group health plans or to the parties administering them or providing benefits under them.

Counting the Average Number of Employees

These proposed regulations add rules for counting the average number of employees employed by an employer during a year.[1] Various rules in Chapter 100 of the Code, Part 7 of ERISA, and Title XXVII of the PHS Act require the determination of such an average number, including the Mental Health Parity Act provisions, the guaranteed access provisions under the PHS Act for small employers, and the exemption from the excise tax under the Code for certain small employers.

Under these proposed regulations, the average number of employees employed by an employer is determined by using a full-time equivalents method. Each full-time employee employed for the entire previous calendar year counts as one employee. Full-time employees employed less than the entire previous calendar year and part-time employees are counted by totaling their employment hours in the previous calendar year (but not to exceed 40 hours for any week) and dividing that number by the annual full-time hours under the employer's general employment practices (but not exceeding 40 hours per week). Any resulting fraction is disregarded. For example, if these calculations produce a result of 50.9, the average number of employees is considered to be 50. If an employer existed for less than the entire previous calendar year (including not being in existence at all), then the determination of the average number of employees is made by estimating the average number of employees that it is reasonably expected that the employer will employ on business days in the current calendar year. For a multiemployer plan, the number of employees employed by the employer with the most employees is attributed to each employer with at least one employee participating in the plan.

Economic Impact and Paperwork Burden

Summary—Department of Labor and Department of Health and Human Services

HIPAA's group market portability provisions, which limit the scope and application of preexisting condition exclusions and establish special enrollment rights, provide a minimum standard of protection designed to increase access to health coverage. The Departments crafted these proposed regulations to secure these protections under certain special circumstances, consistent with the intent of Congress, and to do so in a manner that is economically efficient. The Departments are unable to quantify the regulations' economic benefits and costs, but believe that their benefits will justify their costs.

HIPAA's primary economic effects ensue directly from its statutory provisions. HIPAA's statutory group market portability provisions extend coverage to certain individuals and preexisting conditions not otherwise covered. This extension of coverage entails both benefits and costs. Individuals enjoying expanded coverage will realize benefits, sometimes including improvements in health and relief from so-called "job lock." The costs of HIPAA's portability provisions generally include the cost of extending coverage, as well as certain attendant administrative costs. The Departments believe that the benefits of HIPAA are concentrated in a relatively small population, while the costs are distributed broadly across group plan enrollees. The economic effects of HIPAA's statutory portability provisions are discussed in detail in the preamble to the final regulation under the "Effects of the Statute" of the "Basis for Assessment of Economic Impact" section, published elsewhere in this issue of the **Federal Register**.

By clarifying and securing HIPAA's statutory portability protections, these proposed regulations will help ensure that HIPAA rights are fully realized. The result is likely to be a small increase at the margin in the economic effects of HIPAA's statutory portability provisions.

These proposed regulations are intended to secure and implement HIPAA's group market portability and special enrollment provisions under certain special circumstances. The regulations will secure HIPAA's portability rights for individuals who are not timely notified that their coverage has ended and for individuals whose coverage ends in connection with the taking of leave that is guaranteed under FMLA. The regulations also will clarify and thereby secure individuals' special enrollment rights under HIPAA, and clarify the methodologies to be used by employers to determine the number of plans offered and the average number of individuals employed during a given year.

Additional economic benefits derive from the regulations' clarifications of HIPAA requirements. The regulations will reduce uncertainty and costly disputes between employees, employers and issuers, and promote confidence among employees in health benefits' value, thereby promoting labor market efficiency and fostering the establishment and continuation by employers of group health plans.

Benefits under these regulations will be concentrated among a small number of affected individuals while costs will be spread thinly across group plan enrollees.

Affected individuals will generally include those who would have lost access to coverage for needed medical care after being denied HIPAA portability and/or special enrollment rights due to time spent without coverage prior to receiving a certificate or while on FMLA-guaranteed leave. The benefits of these regulations for any particular affected individual may be significant. As noted above and under "Effects of the Statute" in the "Basis for Assessment of Economic Impact" section of the preamble to the final regulation, published elsewhere in this issue of the **Federal Register**, access to coverage for needed medical care is important to individuals' health and productivity. However, the number of affected individuals, and therefore the aggregate cost of extended access to coverage under these regulations, is expected to be small, for several reasons. First, these regulations extend HIPAA rights only in instances where individuals are not timely notified that their coverage has ended or their coverage ends in connection with the taking of FMLA-guaranteed leave. Second, the period over which this regulation extends rights will often be short, insofar as certificates are often provided promptly after coverage ends and many family leave periods are far shorter than the guaranteed 12 weeks. Third, it is generally in individuals' interest to minimize periods of uninsurance. Individuals are likely to exercise their portability and special enrollment rights as soon as possible after coverage ends, which will often be before any extension of such rights under these regulations becomes effective. Fourth, only a portion of individuals who enroll in health plans in circum-

---

[1] The rules for determining the average number of employees employed by an employer during a year are not used for counting the number employed by the employer on a given day, such as the first day of a plan year.

stances where these regulations alone guarantee their special enrollment or portability rights would otherwise have been denied such rights. Fifth, only a small minority of individuals who avoid a significant break in coverage as a direct result of these regulations would otherwise have lost coverage for needed medical care. (The affected minority would be those who suffer from preexisting conditions, join health plans that exclude coverage for such conditions, and require treatment of such conditions during the exclusion periods.)

Affected individuals may also include some who would have been denied special enrollment rights if plans or issuers failed to recognize their requests for special enrollment or imposed unreasonable deadlines or requirements for completion of enrollment materials.

As noted above, the Departments expect that these regulations will increase at the margin the economic effects of HIPAA's statutory portability provisions. For the reasons stated immediately above, the Departments believe that these increases will be small on aggregate, adding only a small increment to the costs attributable to HIPAA's statutory portability provisions, which themselves amount to a small fraction of one percent of health plan expenditures. Additionally, as with the cost of HIPAA's statutory portability provisions, the majority of these costs will be borne by group plan enrollees. The Departments expect these regulations to have little or no perceptible negative impact on employers' propensity to offer health benefit plans or on the generosity of those plans. In sum, the Departments expect that the benefits of these regulations, which can be very large for a particular affected individual, will justify their costs. The basis for the Departments' conclusions is detailed below.

The Departments solicit comments on their conclusions and their basis for them, and empirical data or other information that would support a fuller or more accurate analysis.

Executive Order 12866—Department of Labor and Department of Health and Human Services

Under Executive Order 12866 (58 FR 551735, Oct. 4, 1993), the Departments must determine whether a regulatory action is "significant" and therefore subject to the requirements of the Executive Order and subject to review by the Office of Management and Budget (OMB). Under section 3(f), the order defines a "significant regulatory action" as an action that is likely to result in a rule: (1) Having an annual effect on the economy of $100 million or more, or adversely and materially affecting a sector of the economy, productivity, competition, jobs, the environment, public health or safety, or state, local or tribal governments or communities (also referred to as "economically significant"); (2) creating serious inconsistency or otherwise interfering with an action taken or planned by another agency; (3) materially altering the budgetary impacts of entitlement grants, user fees, or loan programs or the rights and obligations of recipients thereof; or (4) raising novel legal or policy issues arising out of legal mandates, the President's priorities, or the principles set forth in the Executive Order.

Pursuant to the terms of the Executive Order, the Departments have determined that this action raises novel policy issues arising out of legal mandates. Therefore, this notice is "significant" and subject to OMB review under Section 3(f)(4) of the Executive Order. Consistent with the Executive Order, the Departments have assessed the costs and benefits of this regulatory action. The Departments' assessment, and the analysis underlying that assessment, is detailed below. The Departments performed a comprehensive, unified analysis to estimate the costs and benefits attributable to the regulations for purposes of compliance with Executive Order 12866, the Regulatory Flexibility Act, and the Paperwork Reduction Act.

Statement of Need for Proposed Action

These proposed regulations clarify and interpret the HIPAA portability provisions under Section 701 of the Employee Retirement Income Security Act of 1974 (ERISA), Section 2701 of the Public Health Service Act, and Section 9801 of the Internal Revenue Code of 1986. The regulations are needed to secure and implement HIPAA's portability rights for individuals who are not timely notified that their coverage has ended and for individuals whose coverage ends in connection with the taking of leave that is guaranteed under FMLA, and to clarify and secure individuals' special enrollment rights under HIPAA.

Economic Effects

As noted above, HIPAA's primary economic effects ensue directly from its statutory provisions. HIPAA's statutory group market portability provisions extend coverage to certain individuals and preexisting conditions not otherwise covered. This extension of coverage entails both benefits and costs. The economic effects of HIPAA's statutory portability provisions is summarized above and discussed in detail under the "Basis for Assessment of Economic Impact" section of the preamble to the final regulation, published elsewhere in this issue of the **Federal Register**.

Also as noted above, by clarifying and securing HIPAA's statutory portability protections, these regulations will help ensure that HIPAA rights are fully realized. The result is likely to be a small increase at the margin in the economic effects of HIPAA's statutory portability provisions. The benefits of these regulations will be concentrated among a small number of affected individuals, while their costs will be spread thinly across plans and issuers. The regulations also will reduce uncertainty about health benefits' scope and value, thereby promoting employee health benefit coverage and labor market efficiency. The Departments believe that the regulations' benefits will justify their cost. The Departments assessment of the expected economic effects of the regulation are summarized above and discussed in detail below.

Regulatory Flexibility Act—The Department of Labor and Department of Health and Human Services

The Regulatory Flexibility Act (5 U.S.C. 601 *et seq.*) (RFA), imposes certain requirements with respect to Federal rules that are subject to the notice and comment requirements of section 553(b) of the Administrative Procedure Act (5 U.S.C. 551 *et seq.*) and which are likely to have a significant economic impact on a substantial number of small entities. Section 603 of the RFA stipulates that an agency, unless it certifies that a proposed rule will not have a significant economic impact on a substantial number of small entities, must present an initial regulatory flexibility analysis at the time of publication of the notice of proposed rulemaking that describes the impact of the rule on small entities and seeks public comment on such impact. Small entities include small businesses, organizations, and governmental jurisdictions.

For purposes of analysis under the RFA, the Departments consider a small entity to be an employee benefit plan with fewer than 100 participants. The basis for this definition is found in section 104(a)(2) of ERISA, which permits the Secretary of Labor to prescribe simplified annual reports for pension plans which cover fewer than 100 participants. Under section 104(a)(3), the Secretary may also provide for simplified annual reporting and disclosure if the statutory requirements of part 1 of Title I of ERISA would otherwise be inappropriate for welfare benefit plans. Pursuant to the authority of section 104(a)(3), the Department of Labor has previously issued at 29 CFR 2520.104-20, 2520.104-21, 2520.104-41, 2520.104-46 and 2520.104b-10 certain simplified reporting provisions and limited exemptions from reporting and disclosure requirements for small plans, including unfunded or insured welfare plans covering fewer than 100 participants and which satisfy certain other requirements.

Further, while some small plans are maintained by large employers, most are maintained by small employers. Both small and large plans may enlist small third party service providers to perform administrative functions, but it is generally understood that third party service providers transfer their costs to their plan clients in the form of fees. Thus, the Departments believe that assessing the impact of this rule on small plans is an appropriate substitute for evaluating the effect on small entities. The definition of small entity considered appropriate for this purpose differs, however, from a definition of small business based on size standards promulgated by the Small Business Administration (SBA) (13 CFR 121.201) pursuant to the Small Business Act (5 U.S.C. 631 *et seq.*). The Department of Labor solicited comments on the use of this standard for evaluating the effects of the proposal on small entities. No comments were received with respect to the standard. Therefore, a summary of the initial regulatory flexibility analysis based on the 100 participant size standard is presented below.

The economic effects of HIPAA's statutory provisions on small plans are discussed extensively under the "Regulatory Flexibility Act—Department of Labor and Department of Health and Human Services" section of the preamble to the final regulation, published elsewhere in this issue of the **Federal Register**.

By clarifying and securing HIPAA's statutory portability protections, these regulations will help ensure that these benefits are fully realized. The result is likely to be a small increase in the economic effects of HIPAA's statutory provisions. The Departments were unable to estimate the amount of this increase. However, the direct financial value of coverage extensions pursuant to HIPAA's statutory portability provisions are estimated to be approximately $180 million for small plans, or a small fraction of one percent of total small plan expenditures.[2]

The regulations also will reduce uncertainty about health benefits' scope and value, thereby promoting employee health benefit coverage, including coverage under small plans, and labor market efficiency.

The benefits of these regulations will be concentrated among a small number of affected small group plan enrollees, while their costs will be spread thinly across small group plans enrollees. The benefits of these regulations for any particular affected individual, which may include improved health and productivity, may be significant. However, as previously noted, the number of affected individuals, and therefore the aggregate cost of these regulations, is expected to be small. The Departments believe that the benefits to affected individuals of the application of these regulations to small plans justify the cost to small plans of such application. The basis for the Departments' conclusions is detailed below.

The Departments generally expect the impact of the regulations on any particular small plan to be small. A very large majority of small plans are fully insured, so the cost will fall nominally on issuers rather than from plans. Issuers are expected to pass this cost back to plans and enrollees, but will spread much of it across a large number of plans, thereby minimizing the impact on any particular plan. However, it is possible that small plans that self-insure, or fully insured small plans whose premiums are tied closely to their particular claims experience, might bear all or most of the cost associated with extensions of coverage attributable directly to these regulations. The Departments have no way to quantify the incidence or magnitude of such costs, and solicit comments on such incidence and magnitude, and on whether these regulations would have a significant impact on a substantial number of small plans.

Special Analyses—Department of the Treasury

Notwithstanding the determinations of the Departments of Labor and of Health and Human Services, for purposes of the Department of the Treasury this notice of proposed rulemaking is not a significant regulatory action. Because this notice of proposed rulemaking does not impose a collection of information on small entities and is not subject to section 553(b) of the Administrative Procedure Act (5 U.S.C. chapter 5), the Regulatory Flexibility Act (5 U.S.C. chapter 6) does not apply pursuant to 5 U.S.C. 603(a), which exempts from the Regulatory Flexibility Act's requirements certain rules involving the internal revenue laws. Pursuant to section 7805(f) of the Internal Revenue Code, this notice of proposed rulemaking will be submitted to the Chief Counsel for Advocacy of the Small Business Administration for comment on its impact on small business.

Paperwork Reduction Act

Department of Labor

These proposed regulations include three separate collections of information as that term is defined in the Paperwork Reduction Act of 1995 (PRA 95), 44 U.S.C. 3502(3): the Notice of Enrollment Rights, Notice of Preexisting Condition Exclusion, and Certificate of Creditable Coverage. Each of these disclosures is currently approved by the Office of Management and Budget (OMB) through October 31, 2006 in accordance with PRA 95 under control numbers 1210-0101, 1210-0102, and 1210-0103.

Department of the Treasury

These proposed regulations include a collection of information as that term is defined in PRA 95: the Notice of Enrollment Rights, Notice of Preexisting Condition Exclusion, and Certificate of Creditable Coverage. Each of these disclosures is currently approved by OMB under control number 1545-1537.

Department of Health and Human Services

These proposed regulations include three separate collections of information as that term is defined in PRA 95: the Notice of Enrollment Rights, Notice of Preexisting Condition Exclusion, and Certificate of Creditable Coverage. Each of these disclosures is currently approved

by OMB through June 30, 2006 in accordance with PRA 95 under control number 0938-0702.

Small Business Regulatory Enforcement Fairness Act

The rule being issued here is subject to the provisions of the Small Business Regulatory Enforcement Fairness Act of 1996 (5 U.S.C. 801 *et seq.*) and, if finalized, will be transmitted to Congress and the Comptroller General for review. The rule is not a "major rule" as that term is defined in 5 U.S.C. 804, because it is not likely to result in (1) an annual effect on the economy of $100 million or more; (2) a major increase in costs or prices for consumers, individual industries, or federal, state, or local government agencies, or geographic regions; or (3) significant adverse effects on competition, employment, investment, productivity, innovation, or on the ability of United States-based enterprises to compete with foreign-based enterprises in domestic or export markets.

Unfunded Mandates Reform Act

Section 202 of the Unfunded Mandates Reform Act of 1995 requires that agencies assess anticipated costs and benefits before issuing any rule that may result in an expenditure in any 1 year by state, local, or tribal governments, in the aggregate, or by the private sector, of $100 million. These proposed regulations have no such mandated consequential effect on state, local, or tribal governments, or on the private sector.

Federalism Statement Under Executive Order 13132— Department of Labor and Department of Health and Human Services

Executive Order 13132 outlines fundamental principles of federalism. It requires adherence to specific criteria by federal agencies in formulating and implementing policies that have "substantial direct effects" on the States, the relationship between the national government and States, or on the distribution of power and responsibilities among the various levels of government. Federal agencies promulgating regulations that have these federalism implications must consult with State and local officials, and describe the extent of their consultation and the nature of the concerns of State and local officials in the preamble to the regulation.

In the Departments' view, these proposed regulations have federalism implications because they may have substantial direct effects on the States, the relationship between the national government and States, or on the distribution of power and responsibilities among the various levels of government. However, in the Departments' view, the federalism implications of these proposed regulations are substantially mitigated because, with respect to health insurance issuers, the vast majority of States have enacted laws which meet or exceed the federal HIPAA portability standards.

In general, through section 514, ERISA supersedes State laws to the extent that they relate to any covered employee benefit plan, and preserves State laws that regulate insurance, banking or securities. While ERISA prohibits States from regulating a plan as an insurance or investment company or bank, HIPAA added a new section to ERISA (as well as to the PHS Act) narrowly preempting State requirements for issuers of group health insurance coverage. Specifically, with respect to seven provisions of the HIPAA portability rules, states may impose stricter obligations on health insurance issuers.[3] Moreover, with respect to other requirements for health insurance issuers, states may continue to apply state law requirements except to the extent that such requirements prevent the application of HIPAA's portability, access, and renewability provisions.

In enacting these new preemption provisions, Congress intended to preempt State insurance requirements only to the extent that they prevent the application of the basic protections set forth in HIPAA. HIPAA's conference report states that the conferees intended the narrowest preemption of State laws with regard to health insurance issuers. H.R. Conf. Rep. No. 736, 104th Cong. 2d Session 205 (1996). State insurance laws that are more stringent than the federal requirements are unlikely to "prevent the application of" the HIPAA portability provisions, and be preempted. Accordingly, States have significant latitude to impose requirements on health insurance insurers that are more restrictive than the federal law.

---

[2] Computer runs using Medical Expenditure Survey Household Component (MEPS-HC) and the Robert Wood Johnson Employer Health Benefits Survey determined that the share of covered private-sector job leavers at small firms average 35 percent of all covered private sector job leavers. From this, we inferred that the financial burden borne by small plans is approximately 35 percent of the total expenditures by private-sector group health plans which was estimated to be $515 million.

[3] States may shorten the six-month look-back period prior to the enrollment date; shorten the 12-month and 18-month maximum preexisting condition exclusion periods;

increase the 63-day significant break in coverage period; increase the 30-day period for newborns, adopted children, and children placed for adoption to enroll in the plan with no preexisting condition exclusion; further limit the circumstances in which a preexisting condition exclusion may be applied (beyond the federal exceptions for certain newborns, adopted children, children placed for adoption, pregnancy, and genetic information in the absence of a diagnosis; require additional special enrollment periods; and reduce the HMO affiliation period to less than 2 months (3 months for late enrollees).

Guidance conveying this interpretation of HIPAA's preemption provisions was published in the **Federal Register** on April 8, 1997, 62 FR 16904. These proposed regulations clarify and implement the statute's minimum standards and do not significantly reduce the discretion given the States by the statute. Moreover, the Departments understand that the vast majority of States have requirements that meet or exceed the minimum requirements of the HIPAA portability provisions.

HIPAA provides that the States may enforce the provisions of HIPAA as they pertain to issuers, but that the Secretary of Health and Human Services must enforce any provisions that a State fails to substantially enforce. To date, CMS enforces the HIPAA portability provisions in only one State in accordance with that State's specific request to do so. When exercising its responsibility to enforce the provisions of HIPAA, CMS works cooperatively with the State for the purpose of addressing the State's concerns and avoiding conflicts with the exercise of State authority. CMS has developed procedures to implement its enforcement responsibilities, and to afford the States the maximum opportunity to enforce HIPAA's requirements in the first instance. CMS's procedures address the handling of reports that States may not be enforcing HIPAA's requirements, and the mechanism for allocating responsibility between the States and CMS. In compliance with Executive Order 13132's requirement that agencies examine closely any policies that may have federalism implications or limit the policymaking discretion of the States, the Department of Labor and CMS have engaged in numerous efforts to consult and work cooperatively with affected State and local officials.

For example, the Departments sought and received input from State insurance regulators and the National Association of Insurance Commissioners (NAIC). The NAIC is a non-profit corporation established by the insurance commissioners of the 50 States, the District of Columbia, and the four U.S. territories. In most States the Insurance Commissioner is appointed by the Governor, in approximately 14 States, the insurance commissioner is an elected official. Among other activities, it provides a forum for the development of uniform policy when uniformity is appropriate. Its members meet, discuss and offer solutions to mutual problems. The NAIC sponsors quarterly meetings to provide a forum for the exchange of ideas and in-depth consideration of insurance issues by regulators, industry representatives and consumers. CMS and the Department of Labor staff have consistently attended these quarterly meetings to listen to the concerns of the State Insurance Departments regarding HIPAA portability issues. In addition to the general discussions, committee meetings, and task groups, the NAIC sponsors the standing CMS/DOL meeting on HIPAA issues for members during the quarterly conferences. This meeting provides CMS and the Department of Labor with the opportunity to provide updates on regulations, bulletins, enforcement actions, and outreach efforts regarding HIPAA.

The Departments received written comments on the interim regulation from the NAIC and from ten States. In general, these comments raised technical issues that the Departments considered in conjunction with similar issues raised by other commenters. In a letter sent before issuance of the interim regulation, the NAIC expressed concerns that the Departments interpret the new preemption provisions of HIPAA narrowly so as to give the States flexibility to impose more stringent requirements. As discussed above, the Departments address this concern in the preamble to the interim regulation.

In addition, the Departments specifically consulted with the NAIC in developing these proposed regulations. Through the NAIC, the Departments sought and received the input of State insurance departments regarding certain insurance industry definitions, enrollment procedures and standard coverage terms. This input is generally reflected in the discussion of comments received and changes made in Section B— Overview of the Regulations of the preamble to the final regulations published elsewhere in this issue of the **Federal Register**.

The Departments have also cooperated with the States in several ongoing outreach initiatives, through which information on HIPAA is shared among federal regulators, State regulators and the regulated community. In particular, the Department of Labor has established a Health Benefits Education Campaign with more than 70 partners, including CMS, NAIC and many business and consumer groups. CMS has sponsored conferences with the States—the Consumer Outreach and Advocacy conferences in March 1999 and June 2000, and the Implementation and Enforcement of HIPAA National State-Federal Conferences in August 1999, 2000, 2001, 2002, and 2003. Furthermore, both the Department of Labor and CMS Web sites offer links to important State web sites and other resources, facilitating coordination between the State and federal regulators and the regulated community.

Throughout the process of developing these regulations, to the extent feasible within the specific preemption provisions of HIPAA, the Departments have attempted to balance the States' interests in regulating health insurance issuers, and the Congress' intent to provide uniform minimum protections to consumers in every State. By doing so, it is the Departments' view that they have complied with the requirements of Executive Order 13132.

Pursuant to the requirements set forth in Section 8(a) of Executive Order 13132, and by the signatures affixed to proposed final regulations, the Departments certify that the Employee Benefits Security Administration and the Centers for Medicare & Medicaid Services have complied with the requirements of Executive Order 13132 for the attached proposed regulation, Notice of Proposed Rulemaking for Health Coverage Portability: Tolling and Certain Time Periods and Interaction with the Family and Medical Leave Act under HIPAA Titles I & IV (RIN 1210-AA54 and RIN 0938-AL88), in a meaningful and timely manner.

Basis for Assessment of Economic Impact—Department of Labor and Department of Health and Human Services

As noted above, the primary economic effects of HIPAA's portability provisions ensue directly from the statute. The Department's assessment of the economic effects of HIPAA's statutory portability provisions and the basis for the assessment is presented in detail under the "Basis for Assessment of Economic Impact" section of the preamble to the final regulation, published elsewhere in this issue of the **Federal Register**. By clarifying and securing HIPAA's statutory portability protections, these regulations will help ensure that HIPAA rights are fully realized. The result is likely to be a small increase in the economic effects of HIPAA's statutory portability provisions.

Additional economic benefits derive from the regulations' clarifications of HIPAA's portability requirements. The regulations provide clarity through both their provisions and their examples of how those provisions apply in various circumstances. By clarifying employees' rights and plan sponsors' obligations under HIPAA's portability provisions, the regulations will reduce uncertainty and costly disputes over these rights and obligations. They will promote employers' and employees' common understanding of the value of group health plan benefits and confidence in the security and predictability of those benefits, thereby improving labor market efficiency and fostering the establishment and continuation of group health plans by employers.[4]

These proposed regulations are intended to secure and implement HIPAA's group market portability provisions under certain special circumstances. The regulations will secure HIPAA's portability rights for individuals who are not timely notified that their coverage has ended and for individuals whose coverage ends in connection with the taking of leave that is guaranteed under FMLA. The regulations also will clarify and thereby secure individuals' special enrollment rights under HIPAA, and clarify the methodologies to be used by employers to determine the number of plans offered and the average number of individuals employed during a given year.

The benefits of these regulations will be concentrated among a small number of affected individuals.

Affected individuals will generally include those who would have lost access to coverage for needed medical care after forfeiting HIPAA portability and/or special enrollment rights due to time spent without

---

[4] The voluntary nature of the employment-based health benefit system in conjunction with the open and dynamic character of labor markets make explicit as well as implicit negotiations on compensation a key determinant of the prevalence of employee benefits coverage. It is likely that 80% to 100% of the cost of employee benefits is borne by workers through reduced wages (see for example Jonathan Gruber and Alan B. Krueger, "The Incidence of Mandated Employer-Provided Insurance: Lessons from Workers Compensation Insurance," in, David Bradford, ed., *Tax Policy and Economy,* pp:111-143 (Cambridge, MA: MIT Press, 1991); Jonathan Gruber, "The Incidence of Mandated Maternity Benefits," *American Economic Review,* Vol. 84 no. 3 (June 1994), pp. 622-641; Lawrence H. Summers, "Some Simple Economics of Mandated Benefits," *American Economic Review,* Vol. 79, No. 2 (May 1989), pp:177-183; Louise Sheiner, "Health Care Costs, Wages, and Aging," Federal Reserve Board of Governors working paper, April 1999; Mark Pauly and Brad Herring, *Pooling Health Insurance Risks* (Washington, DC: AEI Press, 1999), Gail A. Jensen and Michael A. Morrisey, "Endogenous Fringe Benefits, Compensating Wage Differentials and Older Workers," *International Journal of Health Care Finance and Economics* Vol 1, No. 3-4 (forthcoming), and Edward Montgomery, Kathryn Shaw, and Mary Ellen Benedict, "Pensions and Wages: An Hedonic Price Theory Approach," *International Economic Review,* Vol. 33 No. 1 (Feb. 1992.), pp:111-128.) The prevalence of benefits is therefore largely dependent on the efficacy of this exchange. If workers perceive that there is the potential for inappropriate denial of benefits they will discount their value to adjust for this risk. This discount drives a wedge in the compensation negotiation, limiting its efficiency. With workers unwilling to bear the full cost of the benefit, fewer benefits will be provided. The extent to which workers perceive a federal regulation supported by enforcement authority to improve the security and quality of benefits, the differential between the employers costs and workers willingness to accept wage offsets is minimized.

coverage prior to receiving a certificate or while on FMLA-guaranteed leave. Affected individuals may also include some who would have been denied special enrollment rights if plans or issuers failed to recognize their requests for special enrollment or imposed unreasonable deadlines or requirements for completion of enrollment materials. The benefits of these regulations for any particular affected individual may be large. As noted above, access to coverage for needed medical care is important to individuals' health and productivity. However, the number of affected individuals, and therefore the aggregate cost of extended access to coverage under these regulations, is expected to be small, for several reasons.

First, these regulations extend HIPAA rights only in instances where individuals do not receive certificates immediately when coverage ends or their coverage ends in connection with the taking of FMLA-guaranteed leave. The Departments know of no source of data on the timeliness with which certificates are typically provided. The final regulations that accompany these proposed regulations permit plans to provide certificates with COBRA notices, up to 44 days after coverage ends. Plans, however, often do have the option of providing certificates immediately when coverage ends or even in advance, for example as part of exit packages given to terminating employees or in mailings to covered dependents in advance of birthdays that will end their eligibility for coverage. With respect to FMLA-protected leave, data provided in a 1996 report to Congress suggests that the number of employees who lose coverage in connection with FMLA-protected leave is likely to be small. The report notes that over an 18-month period just 1.2 percent of surveyed employees took what they reported to be FMLA leave. A similar survey of employers found that 3.6 percent of employees took such leave. Nearly all of those taking leave continued their health coverage. (This is not surprising, given that FMLA requires covered employers to extend eligibility for health insurance to employees on FMLA-protected leave on the same terms that applied when the employees were not on leave.) Just 9 percent of leave-takers reported that they lost some kind of employee benefit, with one-third of these reporting that they lost health insurance.[5] Putting these numbers together and converting to an annual basis, in a given year between 0.02 percent and 0.07 percent of employees, or well under one in one thousand, might lose health coverage in connection with FMLA-protected leave. Many of these will ultimately exercise their right to be reinstated in the job from which they took leave and to exercise their FMLA-guaranteed right to resume their previous health coverage. Therefore, the number of employees who will lose coverage and then, later and at the conclusion of FMLA-protected leave, enjoy extended portability rights under HIPAA as a result of these regulations, is likely to be very small.

Second, the period over which this regulation extends rights will often be short, insofar as certificates are often provided promptly after coverage ends and many family leave periods are far shorter than the guaranteed 12 weeks. As noted above, plans generally are required to provide certificates no later than 44 days after coverage ends and may provide them sooner. According to the aforementioned report to Congress on FMLA-protected leave, 41 percent of employees taking FMLA-protected leave did so for less than 8 days. Fifty-eight percent were on leave for less than 15 days, and two-thirds were on leave for less than 29 days. (FMLA protects leaves of up to 12 weeks, or 84 days.)

Third, it is generally in individuals' interest to minimize periods of uninsurance. Individuals are likely to exercise their portability and special enrollment rights as soon as possible after coverage ends, which will often be before any extension of such rights under these regulations becomes effective. Over one 36-month period prior to HIPAA, 71 percent of Americans had continuous coverage—that is, incurred not even a single, one-month break in coverage. Just 4 percent were uninsured for the entire period. About one-half of observed spells without insurance lasted less than 5 months. As noted above, few employees taking FMLA-protected leave had a lapse in health coverage.

Fourth, only a portion of individuals who enroll in health plans in circumstances where these regulations alone guarantee their special enrollment or portability rights would otherwise have been denied such rights. HIPAA special enrollment and portability requirements, both as specified under the final regulations and as modified under these proposed regulations, are minimum standards. Plans are free to provide additional enrollment opportunities.

Fifth, only a small minority of individuals who avoid a significant break in coverage solely as a direct result of these regulations would otherwise have lost coverage for needed medical care. The affected minority would be those who suffer from preexisting conditions, join health plans that exclude coverage for such conditions, and require treatment of such conditions during the exclusion periods. GAO estimated that HIPAA could ensure continued coverage for up to 25 million Americans.[6] More recent estimates suggest that the number of individual policy holders and their dependents which could be helped by HIPAA's portability provisions are more in the 14 million range.[7] As noted above, however, the number of workers and dependents actually gaining coverage for a preexisting condition due to credit for prior coverage following a job change under HIPAA will be smaller than this. Both GAO's and our estimates of people who could benefit include all job changers with prior coverage and their dependents, irrespective of whether their new employer offers a plan, whether their new plan imposed a preexisting condition exclusion period, and whether they actually suffer from a preexisting condition. Accounting for these narrower criteria, CBO estimated that, at any point in time, about 100,000 individuals would have a preexisting condition exclusion reduced for prior creditable coverage. An additional 45,000 would gain added coverage in the individual market. The CBO estimate demonstrates that the number of individuals actually gaining coverage for needed medical services will be a small fraction of all those whose right to such coverage HIPAA's portability provisions guarantee. Accordingly, the Departments expect that the number gaining coverage for needed services as a direct result of these regulations will be a small fraction of the already small number whose right to such coverage these regulations would establish.

The Departments attempted to estimate the number of individuals who might avoid a break in coverage because of the provision of these proposed regulations that tolls the break until the individual receives a certification but not more than 44 days. The Departments examined coverage patterns evident in the Survey of Income and Program Participation (SIPP), a longitudinal household survey that tracks transitions in coverage. SIPP interviews households once every four months. The Departments estimate that, in a given year, about 7 million individuals have breaks in coverage lasting 4 months or less. The survey data suffer from so-called "seam bias"—respondents tend to report that status as unchanged over 4-month increments. Of the 7 million reporting breaks of 4 months or less, 6.5 million report breaks of exactly 4 months. This finding is consistent with the more general finding that breaks of 4 months or less are far more common than longer breaks. It seems likely that the 7 million breaks of 4 months or less actually included proportionate or disproportionately large shares of breaks of 1 or 2 months. Assuming the breaks are actually distributed evenly by length between 1 day and 4 months, then about one-half of the breaks, or 3.5 million breaks, would have lasted less than 63 days and therefore would not have constituted breaks for purposes of HIPAA's portability protections even without reference to the provision of this proposed regulation that tolls the break until the individual receives a certification but not more than 44 days. Approximately three-fourths of the remaining breaks or about 2.6 million breaks, would have lasted between 1 and 44 additional days and thereby potentially have been tolled until the individuals received their certifications but not more than 44 days. Thus 2.6 million provides a reasonable upper bound on the number of individuals who might avoid a break in coverage in a given year because of this tolling provision. It is not known what fraction of these would subsequently join group health plans that include preexisting condition exclusions while suffering from and requiring additional care for preexisting conditions. Comparing GAO's (20 million or more) and our (14 million) estimates of the number of individuals who could potentially benefit from HIPAA's portability protections (individuals with prior creditable coverage who join new health plans in a given year) with the CBO estimate of the number who might actually have added group coverage for needed care (100,000) produces a ratio of about 1 percent. If this proportion holds for group health plan enrollees who avoid breaks because of this tolling provision, then an upper bound of about 26,000 individuals annually might gain coverage for needed care under the proposed regulation's provision treating coverage under such programs as creditable coverage.

---

[5] Commission on Family and Medical Leave and U.S. Department of Labor, *A Workable Balance: Report to Congress on Family and Medical Leave Policies,* transmitted April 30, 1996.

[6] U.S. General Accounting Office, Report HEHS-95-257, "Health Insurance Portability: Reform Could Ensure Continued Coverage for up to 25 Million Americans," September 1995.

[7] We calculated these estimates using internal runs off the MEPS-HC. These runs gave the number of total job changers, total job changers that had employer-sponsored insurance (ESI), and whether this coverage had been for less than 12 months or not. Estimates for dependents were based off the ratio of policy-holders to total dependents from the March 2003 Current Population Survey (March CPS). It should be noted, however, that the EBSA estimate of 14 million does not include estimate of individuals no longer eligible for COBRA continuation coverage or individuals facing job lock, while the GAO numbers do.

The Departments considered whether certain individuals whose HIPAA portability rights these proposed regulations would extend may be disproportionately likely to be in (or have dependents who are in) poor health. Specifically, individuals taking FMLA-protected leave, especially those who elect not to be reinstated in their prior jobs following FMLA-protected leave, may be so likely. On the other hand, individuals in such circumstances are also particularly unlikely to allow their health insurance from their prior job to lapse while they are on leave. Accordingly, most such individuals' special enrollment periods and countable breaks in coverage (if any) would probably have begun at the conclusion of the FMLA-protected leave even in absence of these proposed regulations. The Departments are therefore uncertain whether individuals who would exercise HIPAA portability rights extended solely by these regulations would be more costly to insure than others exercising HIPAA portability rights, and solicit comments on this question.

Affected individuals may also include some who would have been denied special enrollment rights if plans or issuers failed to recognize their requests for special enrollment or imposed unreasonable deadlines or requirements for completion of enrollment materials.

As noted above, the Departments expect that these regulations will result in a small increase in the economic effects of HIPAA's statutory provisions. For the reasons stated immediately above, the Departments believe that this increase will be small on aggregate, adding only a small increment to the cost attributable to HIPAA's statutory portability provisions, which themselves amount to a small fraction of one percent of health plan expenditures. Thus the increase will be negligible relative to typical year-to-year increases in premiums charged by issuers, which can amount to several percentage points or more. Therefore, the Departments expect these regulations to have little or no perceptible negative impact on employers' propensity to offer health benefit plans or on the generosity of those plans. In sum, the Departments expect that the benefits of these regulations, which can be very large for a particular affected individual, will justify their costs.

List of Subjects

26 CFR Part 54

Excise taxes, Health care, Health insurance, Pensions, Reporting and recordkeeping requirements.

29 CFR Part 2590

Continuation coverage, Disclosure, Employee benefit plans, Group health plans, Health care, Health insurance, Medical child support, Reporting and recordkeeping requirements.

45 CFR Part 146

Health care, Health insurance, Reporting and recordkeeping requirements, and State regulation of health insurance.

Proposed Amendments to the Regulations

Employee Benefits Security Administration

29 CFR Chapter XXV

For the reasons set forth above, 29 CFR Part 2590 is proposed to be amended as follows:

PART 2590—RULES AND REGULATIONS FOR GROUP HEALTH PLANS

1. The authority citation for Part 2590 continues to read as follows:

Authority: 29 U.S.C. 1027, 1059, 1135, 1161-1168, 1169, 1181-1183, 1181 note, 1185, 1185a, 1185b, 1191, 1191a, 1191b, and 1191c, sec. 101(g), Pub. L. 104-191, 101 Stat. 1936; sec. 401(b), Pub. L. 105-200, 112 Stat. 645 (42 U.S.C. 651 note); Secretary of Labor's Order 1-2003, 68 FR 5374 (Feb. 3, 2003).

2. Section 2590.701-4 is amended by revising paragraphs (b)(2)(iii) and (b)(2)(iv) and adding *Examples 4* and *6* in paragraph (b)(2)(v) as follows:

§ *2590.701-4 Rules relating to creditable coverage.*

* * * * *

(b) *Standard method.* * * *

(2) *Counting creditable coverage.* * * *

(iii) *Significant break in coverage defined.* A *significant break in coverage* means a period of 63 consecutive days during each of which an individual does not have any creditable coverage, except that periods described in paragraph (b)(2)(iv) of this section are not taken into account in determining a significant break in coverage. (See also § 2590.731(c)(2)(iii) regarding the applicability to issuers of state insur-

ance laws that require a break of more than 63 days before an individual has a significant break in coverage for purposes of state insurance law.)

(iv) *Periods that toll a significant break.* Days in a waiting period and days in an affiliation period are not taken into account in determining whether a significant break in coverage has occurred. In addition, for an individual who elects COBRA continuation coverage during the second election period provided under the Trade Act of 2002, the days between the date the individual lost group health plan coverage and the first day of the second COBRA election period are not taken into account in determining whether a significant break in coverage has occurred. Moreover, in the case of an individual whose coverage ceases, if a certificate of creditable coverage with respect to that cessation is not provided on or before the date coverage ceases, then the period that begins on the first date that an individual has no creditable coverage and that continues through the earlier of the following two dates is not taken into account in determining whether a significant break in coverage has occurred:

(A) The date that a certificate of creditable coverage with respect to that cessation is provided; or

(B) The date 44 days after coverage ceases.

(v) *Examples.* The rules of this paragraph (b)(2) are illustrated by the following examples:

* * * * *

Example 4. (i) *Facts.* Individual *B* terminates coverage under a group health plan, and a certificate of creditable coverage is provided 10 days later. *B* begins employment with Employer *R* and begins enrollment in *R*'s plan 60 days after the certificate is provided.

(ii) *Conclusion.* In this *Example 4*, even though *B* had no coverage for 69 days, the 10 days before the certificate of creditable coverage is provided are not taken into account in determining a significant break in coverage. Therefore, *B*'s break in coverage is only 59 days and is not a significant break in coverage. Accordingly, *B*'s prior coverage must be counted by *R*'s plan.

* * * * *

Example 6. (i) *Facts.* Employer *V* sponsors a group health plan. Under the terms of the plan, the only benefits provided are those provided under an insurance policy. Individual *D* works for *V* and has creditable coverage under *V*'s plan. *V* fails to pay the issuer the premiums for the coverage period beginning March 1. Consistent with applicable state law, the issuer terminates the policy so that the last day of coverage is April 30. *V* goes out of business on July 31. On August 15 *D* begins employment with Employer *W* and enrolls in *W*'s group health plan. *W*'s plan imposes a 12-month preexisting condition exclusion on all enrollees. *D* never receives a certificate of creditable coverage for coverage under *V*'s plan.

(ii) *Conclusion.* In this *Example 6*, the period from May 1 (the first day without coverage) through June 13 (the date 44 days after coverage under *V*'s plan ceases) is not taken into account in determining a 63-day break in coverage. This is because, in cases in which a certificate of creditable coverage is not provided by the date coverage is lost, the break begins on the date the certificate is provided, or the date 44 days after coverage ceases, if earlier. Therefore, even though *D*'s actual period without coverage was 106 days (May 1 through August 14), because the period from May 1 through June 13 is not taken into account, *D*'s break in coverage is only 62 days (June 14 through August 14). Thus, *D* has not experienced a significant break in coverage, and *D*'s prior coverage must be counted by *W*'s plan.

* * * * *

3. Section 2590.701-5 is amended by redesignating paragraphs (a)(3)(ii)(H)(*5*) and (*6*) as paragraphs (a)(3)(ii)(H)(*6*) and (*7*), respectively, and by adding a new paragraph (a)(3)(ii)(H)(*5*) as follows:

§ *2590.701-5 Evidence of creditable coverage.*

(a) *Certificate of creditable coverage.* * * *

(3) *Form and content of certificate.* * * *

(ii) *Required information.* * * *

(H) * * *

(*5*) The interaction with the Family and Medical Leave Act;

* * * * *

4. Section 2590.701-6 is amended by revising paragraphs (a)(1), (a)(4), (b)(1), (b)(3), and *Example 2* in paragraph (b)(4), and adding *Examples 3, 4,* and *5* in paragraph (b)(4) as follows:

§ *2590.701-6 Special enrollment periods.*

(a) *Special enrollment for certain individuals who lose coverage*—(1) *In general.* A group health plan, and a health insurance issuer offering health insurance coverage in connection with a group health plan, is required to permit current employees and dependents (as defined in § 2590.701-2) who are described in paragraph (a)(2) of this section to enroll for coverage under the terms of the plan if the conditions in paragraph (a)(3) of this section are satisfied. Paragraph (a)(4) of this section describes procedures that a plan or issuer may require an employee to follow and describes the date by which coverage must begin. The special enrollment rights under this paragraph (a) apply without regard to the dates on which an individual would otherwise be able to enroll under the plan.

* * * * *

(4) *Applying for special enrollment and effective date of coverage*—(i) *Request.* A plan or issuer must allow an employee a period of at least 30 days after an event described in paragraph (a)(3) of this section (loss of eligibility for coverage, termination of employer contributions, or exhaustion of COBRA continuation coverage) to request enrollment (for the employee or the employee's dependent). For this purpose, any written or oral request made to any of the following constitutes a request for enrollment—

(A) The plan administrator;

(B) The issuer;

(C) A person who customarily handles claims for the plan (such as a third party administrator); or

(D) Any other designated representative.

(ii) *Tolling of period for requesting special enrollment.* (A) In the case of an individual whose coverage ceases, if a certificate of creditable coverage with respect to that cessation is not provided on or before the date coverage ceases, then the period for requesting special enrollment described in paragraph (a)(4)(i) of this section does not end until 30 days after the earlier of —

(*1*) The date that a certificate of creditable coverage with respect to that cessation is provided; or

(*2*) The date 44 days after coverage ceases.

(B) For purposes of this paragraph (a)(4), if an individual's coverage ceases due to the operation of a lifetime limit on all benefits, coverage is considered to cease on the earliest date that a claim is denied due to the operation of the lifetime limit. (Nonetheless, the date of a loss of eligibility for coverage is determined under the rules of paragraph (a)(3) of this section, which provides that a loss of eligibility occurs when a claim that would meet or exceed a lifetime limit on all benefits is incurred, not when it is denied.)

(C) The rules of this paragraph (a)(4)(ii) are illustrated by the following examples:

Example 1. (i) *Facts.* Employer *V* provides group health coverage through a policy provided by Issuer *M.* Individual *D* works for *V* and is covered under *V*'s plan. *V* fails to pay *M* the premiums for the coverage period beginning March 1. Consistent with applicable state law, *M* terminates the policy so that the last day of coverage is April 30. On May 15, *M* provides *D* with a certificate of creditable coverage with respect to *D*'s cessation of coverage under *V*'s plan.

(ii) *Conclusion.* In this *Example 1,* the period to request special enrollment ends no earlier than June 14 (which is 30 days after May 15, the day a certificate of creditable coverage is provided with respect to *D*).

Example 2. (i) *Facts.* Same facts as *Example 1,* except *D* is never provided with a certificate of creditable coverage.

(ii) *Conclusion.* In this *Example 2,* the period to request special enrollment ends no earlier than July 13. (July 13 is 74 days after April 30, the date coverage ceases. That is, July 13 is 30 days after the end of the 44-day maximum tolling period.)

Example 3. (i) *Facts.* Individual *E* works for Employer *W* and has coverage under *W*'s plan. *W*'s plan has a lifetime limit of $1 million on all benefits under the plan. On September 13, *E* incurs a claim that would exceed the plan's lifetime limit. On September 28, *W* denies the claim due to the operation of the lifetime limit and a certificate of creditable coverage is provided on October 3. *E* is otherwise eligible to enroll in the group health plan of the employer of *E*'s spouse.

(ii) *Conclusion.* In this *Example 3,* the period to request special enrollment in the plan of the employer of *E*'s spouse ends no earlier than November 2 (30 days after the date the certificate is provided) and

begins not later than September 13, the date *E* lost eligibility for coverage.

(iii) *Reasonable procedures for special enrollment.* After an individual has requested enrollment under paragraph (a)(4)(i) of this section, a plan or issuer may require the individual to complete enrollment materials within a reasonable time after the end of the 30-day period described in paragraph (a)(4)(i) of this section. In these enrollment materials, the plan or issuer may require the individual only to provide information required of individuals who enroll when first eligible and information about the event giving rise to the special enrollment right. A plan or issuer may establish a deadline for receiving completed enrollment materials, but such a deadline must be extended for information that an individual making reasonable efforts does not obtain by that deadline.

(iv) *Date coverage must begin.* If the plan or issuer requires completion of additional enrollment materials in accordance with paragraph (a)(4)(iii) of this section, coverage must begin no later than the first day of the first calendar month beginning after the date the plan or issuer receives enrollment materials that are substantially complete. If the plan or issuer does not require completion of additional enrollment materials, coverage must begin no later than the first day of the first calendar month beginning after the date the plan or issuer receives the request for special enrollment under paragraph (a)(4)(i) of this section.

(b) *Special enrollment with respect to certain dependent beneficiaries*— (1) *In general.* A group health plan, and a health insurance issuer offering health insurance coverage in connection with a group health plan, that makes coverage available with respect to dependents is required to permit individuals described in paragraph (b)(2) of this section to be enrolled for coverage in a benefit package under the terms of the plan. Paragraph (b)(3) of this section describes procedures that a plan or issuer may require an individual to follow and describes the date by which coverage must begin. The special enrollment rights under this paragraph (b) apply without regard to the dates on which an individual would otherwise be able to enroll under the plan.

* * * * *

(3) *Applying for special enrollment and effective date of coverage*—(i) *Request.* A plan or issuer must allow an individual a period of at least 30 days after the date of the marriage, birth, adoption, or placement for adoption (or, if dependent coverage is not generally made available at the time of the marriage, birth, adoption, or placement for adoption, a period of at least 30 days after the date the plan makes dependent coverage generally available) to request enrollment (for the individual or the individual's dependent). For this purpose, any written or oral request made to any of the following constitutes a request for enrollment—

(A) The plan administrator;

(B) The issuer;

(C) A person who customarily handles claims for the plan (such as a third party administrator); or

(D) Any other designated representative.

(ii) *Reasonable procedures for special enrollment.* After an individual has requested enrollment under paragraph (b)(3)(i) of this section, a plan or issuer may require the individual to complete enrollment materials within a reasonable time after the end of the 30-day period described in paragraph (b)(3)(i) of this section. In these enrollment materials, the plan or issuer may require the individual only to provide information required of individuals who enroll when first eligible and information about the event giving rise to the special enrollment right. A plan or issuer may establish a deadline for receiving completed enrollment materials, but such a deadline must be extended for information that an individual making reasonable efforts does not obtain by that deadline.

(iii) *Date coverage must begin*—(A) *Marriage.* In the case of marriage, if the plan or issuer requires completion of additional enrollment materials in accordance with paragraph (b)(3)(ii) of this section, coverage must begin no later than the first day of the first calendar month beginning after the date the plan or issuer receives enrollment materials that are substantially complete. If the plan or issuer does not require such additional enrollment materials, coverage must begin no later than the first day of the first calendar month beginning after the date the plan or issuer receives the request for special enrollment under paragraph (b)(3)(i) of this section.

(B) *Birth, adoption, or placement for adoption.* Coverage must begin in the case of a dependent's birth on the date of birth and in the case of a dependent's adoption or placement for adoption no later than the date of such adoption or placement for adoption (or, if dependent coverage is not made generally available at the time of the birth, adoption, or placement for adoption, the date the plan makes dependent coverage available). If the plan or issuer requires completion of additional enrollment materials in accordance with paragraph (b)(3)(ii) of this section, the plan or issuer must provide benefits (including benefits retroactively to the date of birth, adoption, or placement for adoption) once the plan or issuer receives enrollment materials that are substantially complete.

(4) Examples. * * *

Example 2. (i) *Facts.* Individual *D* works for Employer *X. X* maintains a group health plan with two benefit packages—an HMO option and an indemnity option. Self-only and family coverage are available under both options. *D* enrolls for self-only coverage in the HMO option. Then, a child, *E,* is placed for adoption with *D.* Within 30 days of the placement of *E* for adoption, *D* requests enrollment for *D* and *E* under the plan's indemnity option and submits completed enrollment materials timely.

(ii) *Conclusion.* In this *Example 2, D* and *E* satisfy the conditions for special enrollment under paragraphs (b)(2)(v) and (b)(3) of this section. Therefore, the plan must allow *D* and *E* to enroll in the indemnity coverage, effective as of the date of the placement for adoption.

Example 3. (i) *Facts.* Same facts as *Example 1.* On March 17 (two days after the birth of *C*), *A* telephones the plan administrator and requests special enrollment of *A, B,* and *C.* The plan administrator sends *A* an enrollment form. Under the terms of the plan, enrollment is denied unless a completed form is submitted within 30 days of the event giving rise to the special enrollment right (in this case, *C*'s birth).

(ii) *Conclusion.* In this *Example 3,* the plan does not satisfy paragraph (b)(3) of this section. The plan may require only that *A* request enrollment during the 30-day period after *C*'s birth. *A* did so by telephoning the plan administrator. The plan may not condition special enrollment on filing additional enrollment materials during the 30-day period. To comply with paragraph (b)(3) of this section, the plan must allow *A* a reasonable time after the end of the 30-day period to submit any additional enrollment materials. Once these enrollment materials are received, the plan must allow whatever coverage is chosen to begin on March 15, the date of *C*'s birth.

Example 4. (i) *Facts.* Same facts as *Example 3,* except that *A* telephones the plan administrator to request enrollment on April 13 (29 days after *C*'s birth). Also, under the terms of the plan, the deadline for submitting the enrollment form is 14 days after the end of the 30-day period for requesting special enrollment (thus, in this case, April 28, which is 44 days after *C*'s birth). The form requests the same information for *A, B,* and *C* (name, date of birth, and place of birth) as well as a copy of *C*'s birth certificate. *A* fills out the enrollment form and delivers it to the plan administrator on April 28. At that time *A* does not have a birth certificate for *C* but applies on that day for one from the appropriate government office. *A* receives the birth certificate on June 1 and furnishes a copy of the birth certificate to the plan administrator shortly thereafter.

(ii) *Conclusion.* In this *Example 4, A, B,* and *C* are entitled to special enrollment under the plan even though *A* did not satisfy the plan's requirement of providing a copy of *C*'s birth certificate by the plan's 14-day deadline. While a plan may establish such a deadline, the plan must extend the deadline for information that an individual making reasonable efforts does not obtain by that deadline. *A* delivered the enrollment form to the plan administrator by the deadline and made reasonable efforts to furnish the birth certificate that the plan requires.

Example 5. (i) *Facts.* Same facts as *Example 4.* On May 3 (after *A* has delivered the enrollment form to the plan administrator but before *A* provides the birth certificate), *A* submits claims for all medical expenses incurred for *B* and *C* from the date of *C*'s birth.

(ii) *Conclusion.* In this *Example 5,* the plan must pay all of the claims submitted by *A.* Because the plan requires that individuals seeking special enrollment complete additional enrollment materials, it is required to provide benefits once it receives enrollment materials that are substantially complete. The form that *A* submitted on April 28 was substantially complete. Because *C*'s birth is the event giving rise to the special enrollment right, on April 28 *A, B,* and *C* become entitled to benefits under the plan retroactive to the date of *C*'s birth.

* * * * *

5. Section 2590.701-8 is added to read as follows:

§ 2590.701-8 Interaction with the Family and Medical Leave Act.

(a) *In general.* The rules of §§ 2590.701-1 through 2590.701-7 apply with respect to an individual on leave under the Family and Medical

Leave Act of 1993 (29 U.S.C. 2601) (FMLA), and apply with respect to a dependent of such an individual, except to the extent otherwise provided in this section.

(b) *Tolling of significant break in coverage during FMLA leave.* In the case of an individual (or a dependent of the individual) who is covered under a group health plan, if the individual takes FMLA leave and does not continue group health coverage for any period of FMLA leave, that period is not taken into account in determining whether a significant break in coverage has occurred under § 2590.701-4(b)(2)(iii).

(c) *Application of certification provisions*—(1) *Timing of issuance of certificate*—(i) In the case of an individual (or a dependent of the individual) who is covered under a group health plan, if the individual takes FMLA leave and the individual's group health coverage is terminated during FMLA leave, an automatic certificate must be provided in accordance with the timing rules set forth in § 2590.701-5(a)(2)(ii)(B) (which generally require plans and issuers to provide certificates within a reasonable time after coverage ceases).

(ii) In the case of an individual (or a dependent of the individual) who is covered under a group health plan, if the individual takes FMLA leave and continues group health coverage for the period of FMLA leave, but then ceases coverage under the plan at the end of FMLA leave, an automatic certificate must be provided in accordance with the timing rules set forth in § 2590.701-5(a)(2)(ii)(A) (which generally require plans and issuers to provide a certificate no later than the time a notice is required to be furnished for a qualifying event under a COBRA continuation provision).

(2) *Demonstrating FMLA leave.* (i) A plan or issuer is required to take into account all information about FMLA leave that it obtains or that is presented on behalf of an individual. A plan or issuer must treat the individual as having been on FMLA leave for a period if—

(A) The individual attests to the period of FMLA leave; and

(B) The individual cooperates with the plan's or issuer's efforts to verify the individual's FMLA leave.

(ii) Nothing in this section prevents a plan or issuer from modifying its initial determination of FMLA leave if it determines that the individual did not have the claimed FMLA leave, provided that the plan or issuer follows procedures for reconsideration similar to those set forth in § 2590.701-3(f).

(d) *Relationship to loss of eligibility special enrollment rules.* In the case of an individual (or a dependent of the individual) who is covered under a group health plan and who takes FMLA leave, a loss of eligibility for coverage under § 2590.701-6(a) occurs when the period of FMLA leave ends if —

(1) The individual's group health coverage is terminated at any time during FMLA leave; and

(2) The individual does not return to work for the employer at the end of FMLA leave.

6. Section 2590.732 is amended by adding paragraphs (a)(2) and (e) to read as follows:

§ 2590.732 Special rules relating to group health plans.

(a) *Group health plan.* * * *

(2) *Determination of number of plans.* The number of group health plans that an employer or employee organization (including for this purpose a joint board of trustees of a multiemployer trust affiliated with one or more multiemployer plans) maintains is determined under the rules of this paragraph (a)(2).

(i) Except as provided in paragraph (a)(2)(ii) or (iii) of this section, medical care benefits provided by a corporation, partnership, or other entity or trade or business, or by an employee organization, constitute one group health plan, unless—

(A) It is clear from the instruments governing the arrangement or arrangements to provide medical care benefits that the benefits are being provided under separate plans; and

(B) The arrangement or arrangements are operated pursuant to such instruments as separate plans.

(ii) A multiemployer plan and a nonmultiemployer plan are always separate plans.

(iii) If a principal purpose of establishing separate plans is to evade any requirement of law, then the separate plans will be considered a single plan to the extent necessary to prevent the evasion.

* * * * *

(e) *Determining the average number of employees*—(1) *Scope.* Whenever the application of a rule in this part depends upon the average number of employees employed by an employer, the determination of that number is made in accordance with the rules of this paragraph (e).

(2) *Full-time equivalents.* The average number of employees is determined by calculating the average number of full-time equivalents on business days during the preceding calendar year.

(3) *Methodology.* For the preceding calendar year, the average number of full-time equivalents is determined by—

(i) Determining the number of employees who were employed full-time by the employer throughout the entire calendar year;

(ii) Totaling all employment hours (not to exceed 40 hours per week) for each part-time employee, and for each full-time employee who was not employed full-time with the employer throughout the entire calendar year;

(iii) Dividing the total determined under paragraph (e)(3)(ii) of this section by a figure that represents the annual full-time hours under the employer's general employment practices, such as 2,080 hours (although for this purpose not more than 40 hours per week may be used); and

(iv) Adding the quotient determined under paragraph (e)(3)(iii) of this section to the number determined under paragraph (e)(3)(i).

(4) *Rounding.* For purposes of paragraph (e)(3)(iv) of this section, all fractions are disregarded. For instance, a figure of 50.9 is deemed to be 50.

(5) *Employers not in existence in the preceding year.* In the case of an employer that was in existence for less than the entire preceding calendar year (including an employer that was not in existence at all), a determination of the average number of employees that the employer employs is based on the average number of employees that it is reasonably expected the employer will employ on business days in the current calendar year.

(6) *Scope of the term "employer".* For purposes of this paragraph (e), employer includes any predecessor of the employer. In addition, all persons treated as a single employer under section 414(b), (c), (m), or (o) of the Internal Revenue Code are treated as one employer.

(7) *Special rule for multiemployer plans.* (i) With respect to the application of a rule in this part to a multiemployer plan (as defined in section 3(37) of the Act), each employer with at least one employee participating in the plan is considered to employ the same average number of employees. That number is the highest number that results by applying the rules of paragraphs (e)(1) through (6) of this section separately to each of the employers.

(ii) The rules of this paragraph (e)(7) are illustrated by the following example:

Example. (i) *Facts.* Twenty five employers have at least one employee who participates in Multiemployer Plan *M.* Among these 25 employers, Employer *K* has 51 employees, determined under the rules of paragraphs (e)(1) through (6) of this section. Each of the other 24 employers has fewer than 50 employees.

(ii) *Conclusion.* With respect to the application of a rule in this part to *M,* each of the 25 employers is considered to employ 51 employees.

Signed at Washington, DC, this 1st day of December, 2004.

Ann L. Combs,

Assistant Secretary, Employee Benefits Security Administration, U.S. Department of Labor.

¶ 20,534T

Employee Benefits Security Administration (EBSA): Defined benefit plans: Multiemployer plans: Annual Funding Notice.— The Employee Benefits Security Administration (EBSA) has released a proposed regulation that would provide increased financial disclosure to participants and beneficiaries of multiemployer defined benefit plans. The annual funding notice, which would also be sent to relevant labor organizations, employers, and the PBGC, would include a statement noting whether the plan's funded current liability percentage was at least 100 percent.

The proposed regulations, which were published in the Federal Register on February 4, 2005 (70 FR 6305), are reproduced below.

Part VII

Department of Labor

Employee Benefits Security Administration

29 CFR Part 2520

Annual Funding Notice for Multiemployer Defined Benefit Pension Plans; Proposed Rule

DEPARTMENT OF LABOR

Employee Benefits Security Administration

29 CFR Part 2520

RIN 1210-AB00

Annual Funding Notice for Multiemployer Defined Benefit Pension Plans

AGENCY: Employee Benefits Security Administration, DOL.

ACTION: Proposed rule.

SUMMARY: This document contains a proposed regulation that, upon adoption, would implement the notice requirement in section 101(f) of the Employee Retirement Income Security Act of 1974. Section 103 of the Pension Funding Equity Act of 2004 (PFEA '04) amended section 101 of ERISA by adding a new subsection (f), which requires the administrator of a multiemployer defined benefit plan to provide participants, beneficiaries, and certain other parties, including the Pension Benefit Guaranty Corporation, with an annual funding notice indicating, among other things, whether the plan's funded current liability percentage is at least 100 percent. This document also contains a model notice that may be used by plan administrators in discharging their duties under section 101(f). This proposed regulation, upon adoption, will affect plan administrators, participants, and beneficiaries of multiemployer defined benefit pension plans, as well as labor organizations representing such participants or beneficiaries and employers that have an obligation to contribute under such plans.

DATES: Written comments on the proposed regulation should be received by the Department of Labor on or before March 7, 2005. See "C. Request for Comments," in the SUPPLEMENTARY INFORMATION section.

ADDRESSES: Comments should be addressed to the Office of Regulations and Interpretations, Employee Benefits Security Administration, Room N-5669, U.S. Department of Labor, 200 Constitution Avenue NW., Washington, DC 20210, Attn: PFEA '04 Project. Comments also may be submitted electronically to e-ORI@dol.gov. All comments received will be available for public inspection at the Public Disclosure Room, N-1513, Employee Benefits Security Administration, 200 Constitution Avenue NW., Washington, DC 20210.

FOR FURTHER INFORMATION CONTACT: Stephanie L. Ward, Office of Regulations and Interpretations, Employee Benefits Security Administration, (202) 693-8500. This is not a toll-free number.

SUPPLEMENTARY INFORMATION:

Background

Section 103(a) of the Pension Funding Equity Act of 2004, Pub. L. 108-218 (PFEA '04), which was enacted on April 10, 2004, added section 101(f) to the Employee Retirement Income Security Act of 1974, as amended (ERISA or the Act). Section 101(f) provides that the administrator of a defined benefit plan which is a multiemployer plan shall for each plan year furnish a plan funding notice to each plan participant and beneficiary, to each labor organization representing such participants or beneficiaries, to each employer that has an obligation to contribute under the plan, and to the Pension Benefit Guaranty Corporation. Section 103(b) of PFEA '04 amended section 502(c)(1) of ERISA to provide that any administrator who fails to meet the requirements of section 101(f) with respect to a participant or beneficiary may, in a court's discretion, be personally liable to such participant or beneficiary in the amount of up to $100 a day from the date of such failure or refusal and the court may in its discretion order such other relief as it deems proper. Section 103(c) of PFEA '04 provides that the Secretary of Labor shall, not later than 1 year after the date of the enactment of PFEA '04, issue regulations (including a model notice) necessary to implement the amendments made by section 103. Section 103(d) of PFEA '04 provides that the amendments made by section 103 of PFEA '04 shall apply to plan years beginning after December 31, 2004.

Overview of Proposed Regulation

Paragraph (a) of the proposed regulation implements the requirements set forth in section 101(f)(1) of the Act. This section in general requires the administrator of a multiemployer defined benefit pension plan to furnish annually a notice of the plan's funded status to the plan's participants and beneficiaries and other specified interested parties (each labor organization representing such participants or beneficiaries, each employer that has an obligation to contribute under the plan, and the Pension Benefit Guaranty Corporation (PBGC)). Those persons entitled to the notice are further clarified in paragraph (f) of the proposed regulation.

Paragraph (a)(2) provides a limited exception to the requirement to furnish the annual funding notice. Under the exception, the plan administrator of a plan receiving financial assistance from the PBGC is not required to furnish the annual funding notice to the parties otherwise entitled to such notice. The Department, after consulting with the PBGC, is of the view that such notice would be of little, if any, value to such parties in light of the PBGC's authority and responsibility under title IV of ERISA with respect to insolvent multiemployer plans.[1]

Paragraph (b) of the proposed regulation sets forth the content requirements of the notice required under section 101(f). Paragraph (b) requires that the identification and financial information included in the notice is consistent with the information included in the plan's Annual Return/Report filed for the plan year to which the notice relates.

Specifically, paragraph (b)(1)-(4) provides that the notice shall include: The name of the plan; the address and phone number of the plan administrator and the plan's principal administrative officer (if different from the plan administrator); the plan sponsor's employer identification number (currently line 2(b) of the Annual Return/Report Form 5500); and the plan number (currently line 1(b) of the Annual Return/Report Form 5500).

Paragraph (b)(5)-(8) further provides that the notice shall include information relevant to the plan's funding, including: a statement as to whether the plan's funded current liability percentage (calculated by dividing the actuarial value of the plan's assets (currently line 1b(2) of the Schedule B of the Annual Return/Report Form 5500) by the current liability (currently line 2b(4), column (3), of the Schedule B of the Annual Return/Report Form 5500) for the plan year to which the notice relates is at least 100 percent (and, if not, the actual percentage); a statement of the market value of the plan's assets (currently line 1b(1) of the Schedule B of the Annual Return/Report Form 5500) and the valuation date, the amount of benefit payments for the plan year to which the notice relates (currently line 2e(4) of the Schedule H of the Annual Return/ Report Form 5500), and the ratio of the assets to the benefit payments for the plan year to which the notice relates; a summary of the rules governing insolvent multiemployer plans, including the limitations on benefit payments and any potential benefit reductions and suspensions (and the potential effects of such limitations, reductions, and suspensions on the plan); and a general description of the benefits under the plan that are eligible to be guaranteed by the PBGC, along with an explanation of the limitations on the guarantee and the circumstances under which such limitations apply.

Paragraph (b)(9) of the proposed regulation permits inclusion in the notice of any additional information that the administrator determines would be helpful to understanding the information required to be contained in the notice.

Paragraphs (c) and (e) of the proposed regulation, respectively, set forth the form and manner requirements relating to the notice. Paragraph (c) of the proposed regulation provides that notices shall be written in a manner calculated to be understood by the average plan participant. See 29 CFR 2520.102-2. Paragraph (e) of the proposed regulation provides that notices (except for notices to the PBGC) shall be furnished in a manner consistent with the requirements of 29 CFR 2520.104b-1. Collectively, these requirements are intended to ensure that notices are written so that the average plan participant can understand them, and that they are provided in a form reasonably accessible to those individuals eligible to receive the notice. In addition, the Department believes that plan administrators already are familiar with the rules in § § 2520.102-2 and 2520.104b-1, thereby easing the burden of compliance with this regulation.

The Department worked with the PBGC to develop model language for use in connection with funding notices. Such language is set forth in a model notice in the appendix to the regulation. Use of the model notice is not mandatory. However, paragraph (g) of the proposed regulation provides that, by using the model notice, the plan administrator will be deemed to satisfy its duties with respect to the requirements of paragraphs (b) and (c) of the proposed regulation, except with respect to information referenced in paragraph (b)(9) of the regulation.

Paragraph (d) provides that notices shall be furnished within 9 months after the close of the plan year, unless the Internal Revenue Service has granted an extension of time to file the annual report, in which case the notice shall be furnished within 2 months after the close of the extension period. This paragraph implements the requirements of section 101(f)(3) of the Act, which provides that annual funding notices shall be provided to recipients no later than two months after the deadline (including extensions) for filing the annual report for the plan year to which the notice relates.

Paragraph (f) of the proposed regulation delineates the persons to whom funding notices required by this section must be furnished. In an effort to limit administrative burdens and costs attendant to compliance with this notice requirement, paragraph (f) of the proposal limits an administrator's disclosure obligation to only individuals who are participants on the last day of the plan year to which the notice relates, beneficiaries receiving benefits under the plan on the last day of the plan year to which the notice relates, labor organizations representing participants under the plan on the last day of the plan year to which the notice relates, and each employer that, as of the last day of the plan year to which the notice relates, is a party to the collective bargaining agreement(s) pursuant to which the plan is maintained or who otherwise may be subject to withdrawal liability. By focusing on a person's status on the last day of the previous plan year, the plan administrator is thereby relieved of additional costs of tracking and providing notice to individuals, labor organizations and employers who may no longer have an interest in the plan's funding condition.

Paragraph (f)(4) provides a more detailed clarification of which employers are entitled to an annual funding notice. Specifically, the language "is a party to the collective bargaining agreement(s) pursuant to which the plan is maintained" therein is intended to cover not only employers that have a present obligation to contribute under the plan, but also those whose obligation may be temporarily suspended due to a funding holiday granted by the plan's board of trustees. In addition, the Department, through its use of the phrase "or who otherwise may be subject to withdrawal liability," intends to make it clear that, in the case of plans that cover employees in the building and construction industry, entertainment industry, or trucking, household goods moving and public warehousing industries, notice is required for any employer that, as of the last day of the plan year to which the notice relates, has ceased to have an obligation to contribute under the plan, but has continued exposure to withdrawal liability pursuant to section 4203(b), (c), or (d) of ERISA. The clarification in paragraph (f)(4) is intended to ensure that all employers that have a direct financial interest in the plan's funding status will receive a notice.

Request for Comments

The Department invites comments from interested persons on all aspects of the proposed regulation. Comments should be addressed to the Office of Regulations and Interpretations, Employee Benefits Security Administration, Room N-5669, U.S. Department of Labor, 200 Constitution Avenue NW., Washington, DC 20210, Attn: PFEA '04 Project. Comments also may be submitted electronically to e-ORI@dol.gov. All comments received will be available for public inspection at the Public Disclosure Room, N-1513, Employee Benefits Security Administration, 200 Constitution Avenue NW., Washington, DC 20210.

The Department has limited the comment period to 30 days in order to issue a final regulation on the earliest possible date, taking into account Congress' expectation that regulations would be issued not later than one year from enactment of the PFEA '04, which was April 10, 2004. The Department believes that, in light of the limited number of issues presented for consideration by the proposal, the provided 30-day comment period affords interested persons an adequate amount of time to analyze the proposal and submit comments.

---

[1] The provisions of title IV of ERISA that apply in the context of a plan's receipt of financial assistance from the PBGC (sections 4245(e) and 4281(d)) ensure that participants and beneficiaries of insolvent plans are adequately informed of, among other things, their plan's funding status (including for participants in pay status, their individual benefit levels), and PBGC's benefit guarantees. In addition, PBGC receives plan financial information before providing financial assistance. Inasmuch as the foregoing title IV provisions are largely duplicative of the requirements in section 101(f) of ERISA, an exception from the requirements of section 101(f) for plans receiving financial assistance necessarily would reduce administrative costs to these plans, thereby increasing the plan's available resources for benefit payments.

Regulatory Impact Analysis

Summary

This proposed regulation contains a model notice and other guidance necessary to implement the amendments made by new section 101(f) of ERISA, as enacted by section 103(a) of PFEA '04. The regulation, if adopted as proposed, will offer a model notice to administrators of multiemployer defined benefit plans, which is expected to mitigate burden and contribute to the efficiency of compliance.

The multiemployer defined benefit plan funding notice provision of PFEA '04 was enacted amid concerns about persisting low interest rates and declines in equity values, each of which has an increasing effect on contribution requirements and a decreasing effect on the funding levels of defined benefit plans. More complete and timelier disclosures were considered an important element of measures enacted in PFEA '04 to strengthen the long-term health of the defined benefit pension system. Increasing the transparency of information about the funding status of multiemployer plans for participants and beneficiaries, the labor organizations representing them, contributing employers, and PBGC will afford all parties interested in the financial viability of these plans greater opportunity to monitor their funding status.

According to a March 2004 Report by the General Accounting Office[2] the regulatory framework within which multiemployer plans operate shifts certain financial risks away from the government and by implication the taxpayer. Contributing employers to multiemployer plans share the risk of funding benefits for all participants, not just those in their employment, and face specific liabilities if they withdraw from the plans. Participants in multiemployer plans face lower benefit guaranties than those in single-employer plans. According to the GAO report, these factors create incentives for participants and employers to work together constructively to find solutions to plans' financial difficulties. These notices will provide timely disclosure of information concerning the funding status of these plans to support the effort of all interested parties to monitor their financial condition and take action where necessary.

The regulation would further afford plan administrators greater certainty that they have discharged their notice obligation under section 101(f). The proposed regulation is also intended to clarify certain terms used in section 101(f) for the general purpose of delineating those persons entitled to receive the notice. The benefits of greater efficiency, certainty, and clarity are expected to be substantial, but cannot be specifically quantified.

The cost of the multiemployer defined benefit plan notices is expected to amount to $777,000 in the year of implementation, and $644,000 in each subsequent year. The total estimated cost includes the one-time development of a notice by each plan, and the annual preparation and mailing by the administrators of all multiemployer defined benefit plans of the required notices to plan participants and beneficiaries, specified labor organizations, employers that have an obligation to contribute to these plans, and to the Pension Benefit Guaranty Corporation. The first year estimate is higher to account for the time required for plan administrators to adapt and review the model notice.

In this proposed regulation, the Department has attempted to provide guidance to assist administrators to meet this objective the most economically efficient way possible. Because the costs of this proposal arise from notice provisions in PFEA '04, the data and methodology used in developing these estimates are more fully described in the Paperwork Reduction Act section of this analysis of regulatory impact.

Executive Order 12866

Under Executive Order 12866 (58 FR 51735), the Department must determine whether a regulatory action is "significant" and therefore subject to review by the Office of Management and Budget (OMB). Section 3(f) of the Executive Order defines a "significant regulatory action" as an action that is likely to result in a rule (1) having an annual effect on the economy of $100 million or more, or adversely and materially affecting a sector of the economy, productivity, competition, jobs, the environment, public health or safety, or State, local or tribal governments or communities (also referred to as "economically significant"); (2) creating serious inconsistency or otherwise interfering with an action taken or planned by another agency; (3) materially altering the budgetary impacts of entitlement grants, user fees, or loan programs or the rights and obligations of recipients thereof; or (4) raising novel legal or policy issues arising out of legal mandates, the Presi-

dent's priorities, or the principles set forth in the Executive Order. It has been determined that this proposed regulation is significant within the meaning of section 3(f)(4) of the Executive Order. OMB has, therefore, reviewed this proposed regulation pursuant to the Executive Order.

Paperwork Reduction Act

As part of its continuing effort to reduce paperwork and respondent burden, the Department of Labor conducts a preclearance consultation program to provide the general public and federal agencies with an opportunity to comment on proposed and continuing collections of information in accordance with the Paperwork Reduction Act of 1995 (PRA 95) (44 U.S.C. 3506(c)(2)(A)). This helps to ensure that requested data can be provided in the desired format, reporting burden (time and financial resources) is minimized, collection instruments are clearly understood, and the impact of collection requirements on respondents can be properly assessed.

Currently, EBSA is soliciting comments concerning the proposed information collection request (ICR) included in the proposed regulation regarding the Annual Funding Notice for Defined Benefit Multiemployer Pension Plans. A copy of the ICR may be obtained by contacting the PRA addressee shown below.

The Department has submitted a copy of the proposed information collection to OMB in accordance with 44 U.S.C. 3507(d) for review of its information collections. The Department and OMB are particularly interested in comments that:

Evaluate whether the proposed collection of information is necessary for the proper performance of the functions of the agency, including whether the information will have practical utility;

Evaluate the accuracy of the agency's estimate of the burden of the collection of information, including the validity of the methodology and assumptions used;

Enhance the quality, utility, and clarity of the information to be collected; and

Minimize the burden of the collection of information on those who are to respond, including through the use of appropriate automated, electronic, mechanical, or other technological collection techniques or other forms of information technology, e.g., permitting electronic submission of responses.

Comments should be sent to the Office of Information and Regulatory Affairs, Office of Management and Budget, Room 10235, New Executive Office Building, Washington, DC 20503; Attention: Desk Officer for the Employee Benefits Security Administration. Although comments may be submitted through April 5, 2005, OMB requests that comments be received within 30 days of publication of the Notice of Proposed Rulemaking to ensure their consideration.

PRA Addressee: Address requests for copies of the ICR to Gerald B. Lindrew, Office of Policy and Research, U.S. Department of Labor, Employee Benefits Security Administration, 200 Constitution Avenue, NW., Room N-5647, Washington, DC 20210. Telephone (202) 693-8410; Fax: (202) 219-5333. These are not toll-free numbers.

The information collection provisions of this proposed regulation are found in § 2520.101-4. A model notice is provided in the Appendix to § 2520.101-4 to facilitate compliance and moderate the burden attendant to supplying notices to participants and beneficiaries, labor organizations, contributing employers, and PBGC as required by PFEA '04 and the proposed regulation. Use of the model notice is not mandatory; however, use of the model will be deemed to satisfy the requirements for content, style, and format of the notice, except with respect to any other information the plan administrator elects to include. This proposed regulation is also intended to clarify certain of the PFEA '04 requirements as to content, style and format, manner of furnishing, and persons entitled to receive notice.

In order to estimate the potential costs of the notice provisions of section 101(f) of ERISA and this proposed regulation, the Department estimated the number of multiemployer defined benefit plans, and the numbers of participants, beneficiaries receiving benefits, labor organizations representing participants, and employers that have an obligation to contribute to these plans. The PBGC Pension Insurance Data Book 2003 indicates that as of September 30, 2003, there were 1,623 multiemployer defined benefit plans with 9.7 million participants and beneficiaries receiving benefits. These estimates are based on premium filings with PBGC for 2002, projected by PBGC to 2003, gener-

---

[2] See GAO-04-423 Private Pensions. Multiemployer Plans Face Short and Long-Term Challenges. U.S. General Accounting Office, March 2004. General Accounting Office name changed to Government Accountability Office effective July 7, 2004.

ally the most recent information currently available. This total has been adjusted to 1,595 to reflect the exception from the requirement to furnish a funding notice for years in which a plan is receiving financial assistance from PBGC.

The Department is not aware of a direct source of information as to the number of labor organizations that represent participants of multiemployer defined benefit plans and that would be entitled to receive notice under section 101(f). As a proxy for this number, the Department has relied on information supplied by the Department's Employment Standards Administration, Office of Labor Management Standards, as to the number of labor organizations that filed required annual reports for their most recent fiscal year, generally 2002, at this time. The Department adjusted the number provided by excluding labor organizations that appeared to represent only state, local, and federal governmental employees to account for the fact that such employees are generally unlikely to be participants in plans covered under Title I of ERISA. The resulting estimate of labor organizations entitled to receive notice is 21,000. Although this number has been used for purposes of this analysis, it is believed that this number is an upper bound for the actual number of labor organizations that will receive notice because it is likely that some labor organizations do not represent participants in defined benefit plans, or that some labor organizations represent only participants in single employer plans not subject to section 101(f).

The Department is also unaware of a source of information for the current number of employers obligated to contribute to multiemployer defined benefit plans. PBGC assisted with development of an estimate of this number by providing the Department with a tabulation on their 1987 premium filings of the number of employers contributing to multiemployer defined benefit plans at that time. This was the last year this data element was required to be reported. The Department has attempted to validate that 1987 figure by dividing the number of participants in multiemployer defined benefit plans in the industries in which these plans are most concentrated, such as construction, trucking, and retail food sales,[3] by the average number of employees per firm in those industries based on data published by the Office of Advocacy, U.S. Small Business Administration for 2001. This computation resulted in a figure that was similar in magnitude, but somewhat higher than the 277,600 employers reported in the PBGC premium filing data. As a result, the Department has used 300,000 for its estimate of the number of contributing employers to whom the required notice will be sent.

For purposes of its estimates of regulatory impact, then, the Department has assumed that each plan will develop a notice, and that each year the multiemployer defined benefit plan notices will be prepared and sent by the administrators of 1,595 plans to 9.7 million participants and beneficiaries, 21,000 labor organizations, and 300,000 contributing employers, and to PBGC, for a total of about 10 million notices.

It is assumed that the availability of a model notice as provided in paragraph (f) will lessen the time otherwise required by a plan administrator to draft a required notice. In developing burden estimates, the Department has included one hour for reviewing and adapting the model notice, and 30 minutes for completing the notice for each plan. Reviewing and adapting the notice is expected to be performed by service providers, specifically by legal counsel at an hourly rate of $83. This accounts for the estimated burden of developing the notice, which amounts to about $133,000 for the 1,595 plans. Completing the notice by adding information relevant to each year is expected to take 30 minutes in the first year of implementation, as well as in subsequent years, and it is expected to be performed by the same professionals who are accounted for as preparing the Summary Annual Report (SAR) for plans, namely financial professionals at the rate of $68 per hour. The assumed preparation cost to plans to complete the notice is therefore about $55,000 per year. The total cost to plans to develop and complete the notice in the year of implementation is about $187,000.

The estimated distribution costs for the notices are based on separate assumptions for participant and beneficiary notices versus the labor organization, contributing employer, and PBGC notices. The distribution cost for the notices to participants and beneficiaries is relatively modest compared to the number of notices because it is assumed that these notices will be provided at the same time and as part of the same mailing as the Summary Annual Report. The mailing costs for the SAR are already accounted for in the ICR for the SAR, currently approved under OMB Control Number 1210-0040. Therefore, only an additional materials cost is accounted for in the estimate of

distribution costs for participant and beneficiary notices, which totals $292,000.

Distribution cost estimates for the notices to labor organizations, employers, and PBGC include $0.40 for materials and postage, and two minutes at a clerical wage rate of about $17 for each notice. Total distribution costs to labor organizations, contributing employers, and PBGC, therefore, are expected to total about $316,000. Distribution costs for all notices are estimated at $608,000.

In order to estimate the hour burden of preparation and distribution of the notices, the Department has generally relied on the same assumptions used for estimates of the burden of SAR preparation and distribution. Specifically, it is assumed that 100% of notices are developed by service providers, and that 90% of notices are prepared and distributed by service providers. Those activities are appropriately accounted for as cost burden, for which plans pay service providers. The remaining 10% of notices prepared and distributed in house by plan administrators are appropriately accounted for as hour burden. Materials and mailing costs are considered direct cost burden, as well. The Department has not accounted here for reductions in mailing and material costs that might arise from the electronic distribution of some notices. Although such distribution may be deemed to satisfy the requirements of section 2520.104b-1(b)(1) with respect to fulfilling the disclosure obligation if conditions of section 2520.104b-1(c) are satisfied, it is assumed for purposes of these estimates that these funding notices are less likely to be provided electronically due to the nature of the industries involved and the relationships of the parties affected by this requirement since the active workers affected often do not have access to e-mail at their workplaces. The resulting hour and cost burden estimates are shown below. The Department requests comments on the data, assumptions, and methodology used in arriving at these estimates of economic impact and PRA 95 burden.

Type of Review: New.

Agency: Department of Labor, Employee Benefits Security Association.

Title: Multiemployer Defined Benefit Plan Funding Notice.

OMB Number: 1210-NEW.

Affected Public: Individuals or households; Business or other for-profit; Not-for-profit institutions.

Respondents: 1,595.

Frequency of Response: Annual.

Responses: 10,048,000.

Estimated Total Burden Hours: 1,155.

Total Annualized Capital/Startup Costs: $133,000.

Total Annual Cost (Operating and Maintenance): $644,000.

Total Annualized Cost: $777,000.

OMB will consider comments submitted in response to this request in its review of the request for approval of the ICR; these comments will also become a matter of public record.

Regulatory Flexibility Act

The Regulatory Flexibility Act (5 U.S.C. 601 et seq.) (RFA) imposes certain requirements with respect to Federal rules that are subject to the notice and comment requirements of section 553(b) of the Administrative Procedure Act (5 U.S.C. 551 et seq.) and which are likely to have a significant economic impact on a substantial number of small entities. Unless an agency certifies that a proposed rule is not likely to have a significant economic impact on a substantial number of small entities, section 603 of the RFA requires that the agency present an initial regulatory flexibility analysis at the time of the publication of the notice of proposed rulemaking describing the impact of the rule on small entities and seeking public comment on such impact. Small entities include small businesses, organizations and governmental jurisdictions.

For purposes of analysis under the RFA, the Employee Benefits Security Administration (EBSA) proposes to continue to consider a small entity to be an employee benefit plan with fewer than 100 participants. The basis of this definition is found in section 104(a)(2) of ERISA, which permits the Secretary of Labor to prescribe simplified annual reports for pension plans that cover fewer than 100 participants. Under section 104(a)(3), the Secretary may also provide for exemp-

---

[3] Multiemployer Plans Face Short and Long-Term Challenges. U.S. General Accounting Office, March 2004. General Accounting Office name changed to Government Accountability Office effective July 7, 2004. See GAO-04-423 Private Pensions.

tions or simplified annual reporting and disclosure for welfare benefit plans. Pursuant to the authority of section 104(a)(3), the Department has previously issued at 29 CFR 2520.104-20, 2520.104-21, 2520.104-41, 2520.104-46 and 2520.104b-10 certain simplified reporting provisions and limited exemptions from reporting and disclosure requirements for small plans, including unfunded or insured welfare plans covering fewer than 100 participants and which satisfy certain other requirements.

Further, while some large employers may have small plans, in general small employers maintain most small plans. Thus, EBSA believes that assessing the impact of this proposed rule on small plans is an appropriate substitute for evaluating the effect on small entities. The definition of small entity considered appropriate for this purpose differs, however, from a definition of small business that is based on size standards promulgated by the Small Business Administration (SBA) (13 CFR 121.201) pursuant to the Small Business Act (15 U.S.C. 631 et seq.). EBSA therefore requests comments on the appropriateness of the size standard used in evaluating the impact of this proposed rule on small entities. The Department does not expect that the plans potentially impacted by this proposal will be small entities. However, the Department requests comments on the potential impact of proposal on small entities, and on ways in which any burdens on small entities might be minimized.

EBSA has preliminarily determined that this rule will not have a significant economic impact on a substantial number of small entities. In support of this determination, EBSA has prepared the following initial regulatory flexibility analysis.

Section 103(c) of PFEA '04 provides that the Secretary of Labor shall issue regulations (including a model notice) necessary to implement the amendments made by new section 101(f) of ERISA, as enacted by section 103(a) of PFEA '04. Section 101(f) of ERISA requires the administrator of a multiemployer defined benefit pension plan to furnish annually a notice of the plan's funded status to the plan's participants and beneficiaries and other specified interested parties (each labor organization representing such participants and beneficiaries, each employer that has an obligation to contribute under the plan, and the PBGC).

The conditions set forth in this proposed regulation are intended to satisfy the PFEA '04 requirement that the Secretary prescribe regulations (including a model notice) necessary to implement the amendments made by section 103.

The proposed rule would impact small plans that are multiemployer defined benefit pension plans. It is expected that the proposal will affect approximately 10 small plans, and 800 participants in small plans.

The initial cost of the funding notice for small plans is expected to be about $82 per plan. Preparation of this information is in most cases accomplished by professionals that provide services to employee benefit plans.

The benefits of greater certainty afforded fiduciaries by the model notice are substantial but cannot be specifically quantified.

To the Department's knowledge, there are no federal regulations that might duplicate, overlap, or conflict with the proposed regulation for multiemployer defined benefit pension plan funding notices under section 101(f) of ERISA.

Congressional Review Act

The rules being issued here are subject to the Congressional Review Act provisions of the Small Business Regulatory Enforcement Fairness Act of 1996 (5 U.S.C. 801 et seq.) and if finalized will be sent to Congress and the Comptroller General for review. The rule is not a "major rule" as that term is defined in 5 U.S.C. 804, because it is not likely to result in (1) an annual effect on the economy of $100 million or more; (2) a major increase in costs or prices for consumers, individual industries, or Federal, State, or local government agencies, or geographic regions; or (3) significant adverse effects on competition, employment, investment, productivity, innovation, or on the ability of United States-based enterprises to compete with foreign-based enterprises in domestic and export markets.

Unfunded Mandates Reform Act

For purposes of the Unfunded Mandates Reform Act of 1995 (Pub. L. 104-4), as well as Executive Order 12875, this proposed regulation does not include any Federal mandate that may result in expenditures by State, local, or tribal governments, and does not impose an annual burden exceeding $100 million on the private sector.

Federalism Statement

Executive Order 13132 (August 4, 1999) outlines fundamental principles of federalism and requires the adherence to specific criteria by Federal agencies in the process of their formulation and implementation of policies that have substantial direct effects on the States, on the relationship between the national government and the States, or on the distribution of power and responsibilities among the various levels of government. This final rule does not have federalism implications because it has no substantial direct effect on the States, on the relationship between the national government and the States, or on the distribution of power and responsibilities among the various levels of government. Section 514 of ERISA provides, with certain exceptions specifically enumerated that are not pertinent here, that the provisions of Titles I and IV of ERISA supersede any and all laws of the States as they relate to any employee benefit plan covered under ERISA. The requirements implemented in this final rule do not alter the fundamental reporting and disclosure requirements of the statute with respect to employee benefit plans, and as such have no implications for the States or the relationship or distribution of power between the national government and the States.

List of Subjects in 29 CFR Part 2520

Accounting, Employee benefit plans, Pensions, Reporting and recordkeeping requirements.

For the reasons set forth in the preamble, the Department of Labor proposes to amend 29 CFR part 2520 as follows:

PART 2520—RULES AND REGULATIONS FOR REPORTING AND DISCLOSURE

1. The authority citation for part 2520 is revised to read as follows:

Authority: 29 U.S.C. 1021-1025, 1027, 1029-31, 1059, 1134 and 1135; and Secretary of Labor's Order 1-2003, 68 FR 5374 (Feb. 3, 2003). § 2520.101-2 also issued under 29 U.S.C. 1132, 1181-1183, 1181 note, 1185, 1185a-b, 1191, and 1191a-c. §§ 2520.102-3, 2520.104b-1 and 2520.104b-3 also issued under 29 U.S.C. 1003,1181-1183, 1181 note, 1185, 1185a-b, 1191, and 1191a-c. §§ 2520.104b-1 and 2520.107 also issued under 26 U.S.C. 401 note, 111 Stat. 788. Section 2520.101-4 also issued under sec. 103 of Pub. L. 108-218.

2. Add the following new section and related appendix to subpart A:

§ *2520.101-4 Annual funding notice for multiemployer defined benefit pension plans.*

(a) *In general.* (1) Except as provided in paragraph (a)(2) of this section, pursuant to section 101(f) of the Act, the administrator of a defined benefit, multiemployer pension plan shall furnish annually to each person specified in paragraph (f) of this section a funding notice that conforms to the requirements of this section.

(2) A plan administrator shall not be required to furnish a funding notice for any plan year for which the plan is receiving financial assistance from the Pension Benefit Guaranty Corporation pursuant to section 4261 of ERISA.

(b) *Content of notice.* A funding notice shall, consistent with the information included in the plan's Annual Return/Report Form 5500 filed for the plan year to which the funding notice relates, include the following information:

(1) The name of the plan;

(2) The address and phone number of the plan administrator and the plan's principal administrative officer (if different from the plan administrator);

(3) The plan sponsor's employer identification number;

(4) The plan number;

(5) A statement as to whether the plan's funded current liability percentage (as defined in section 302(d)(8)(B)) for the plan year to which the notice relates is at least 100 percent (and, if not, the actual percentage);

(6) A statement of the market value of the plan's assets (and valuation date), the amount of benefit payments, and the ratio of the assets to the payments for the plan year to which the notice relates;

(7) A summary of the rules governing insolvent multiemployer plans, including the limitations on benefit payments and any potential benefit reductions and suspensions (and the potential effects of such limitations, reductions, and suspensions on the plan);

(8) A general description of the benefits under the plan which are eligible to be guaranteed by the Pension Benefit Guaranty Corporation, along with an explanation of the limitations on the guarantee and the circumstances under which such limitations apply; and

(9) Any additional information that the plan administrator elects to include, provided that such information is necessary or helpful to understanding the mandatory information in the notice.

(c) *Style and format of notice.* Funding notices shall be written in a manner calculated to be understood by the average plan participant.

(d) *When to furnish notice.* A funding notice shall be furnished within 9 months after the close of the plan year, unless the Internal Revenue Service has granted an extension of time to file the annual report, in which case such furnishing shall take place within 2 months after the close of the extension period.

(e) *Manner of furnishing notice.* (1) Except as provided in paragraph (e)(2) of this section, funding notices shall be furnished in any manner consistent with the requirements of § 2520.104b-1 of this chapter, including paragraph (c) of that section relating to the use of electronic media.

(2) Notice shall be furnished to the Pension Benefit Guaranty Corporation in a manner consistent with the requirements of part 4000 of this title.

(f) *Persons entitled to notice.* Persons entitled to notice under this section include:

(1) Each participant covered under the plan on the last day of the plan year to which the notice relates;

(2) Each beneficiary receiving benefits under the plan on the last day of the plan year to which the notice relates;

(3) Each labor organization representing participants under the plan on the last day of the plan year to which the notice relates;

(4) Each employer that, as of the last day of the plan year to which the notice relates, is a party to the collective bargaining agreement(s) pursuant to which the plan is maintained or who otherwise may be subject to withdrawal liability pursuant to section 4203 of the Act; and

(5) *The Pension Benefit Guaranty Corporation.*

(g) *Model notice.* The appendix to this section contains a model notice that is intended to assist plan administrators in discharging their notice obligations under this section. Use of the model notice is not mandatory. However, use of the model notice will be deemed to satisfy the requirements of paragraphs (b) and (c) of this section, except with respect to information referenced in paragraph (b)(9) of this section.

Appendix to § 2520.101-4—Annual Funding Notice for [Insert name of pension plan]

Introduction

This notice, which federal law requires all multiemployer plans to send annually, includes important information about the funding level of [insert name, number, and EIN of plan] (Plan). This notice also includes information about rules governing insolvent plans and benefit payments guaranteed by the Pension Benefit Guaranty Corporation (PBGC), a federal agency. This notice is for the plan year beginning [insert beginning date] and ending [insert ending date] (Plan Year).

Plan's Funding Level

The Plan's "funded current liability percentage" for the Plan Year was [insert percentage—see instructions below]. In general, the higher the percentage, the better funded the plan. The funded current liability percentage, however, is not indicative of how well a plan will be funded in the future or if it terminates.

(Instructions: For purposes of computing the "funded current liability percentage," insert ratio of actuarial value of assets to current liability, expressed as a percentage. If the percentage is equal to or greater than 100 percent, you may insert "at least 100 percent.")

Plan's Financial Information

The market value of the Plan's assets as of [insert valuation date] was [insert amount]. The total amount of benefit payments for the Plan Year was [enter amount]. The ratio of assets to benefit payments is [enter amount calculated by dividing the value of plan assets by the total benefit payments]. This ratio suggests that the Plan's assets could provide for approximately [enter amount calculated above] years of benefit payments in annual amounts equal to what was paid out in the Plan Year. However, the ratio does not take into account future changes in total benefit payments or plan assets.

Rules Governing Insolvent Plans

The law has special rules governing insolvent multiemployer pension plans. A plan is insolvent for a plan year if its available financial resources are not sufficient to pay benefits when due for the plan year.

An insolvent plan must reduce benefit payments to the highest level that can be paid from the plan's available financial resources. If such resources are not enough to pay benefits at a level specified by law (see Benefit Payments Guaranteed by the PBGC, below), the plan must apply to the PBGC for financial assistance. The PBGC, by law, will loan the plan the amount necessary to pay benefits at the guaranteed level. Reduced benefits may be restored if the plan's financial condition improves.

A plan that becomes insolvent must provide prompt notification of the insolvency to participants and beneficiaries, contributing employers, labor unions representing participants, and PBGC. In addition, participants and beneficiaries also must receive information regarding whether, and how, their benefits will be reduced or affected as a result of the insolvency, including loss of a lump sum option. This information will be provided for each year the plan is insolvent.

Benefit Payments Guaranteed by the PBGC

The PBGC guarantees only vested benefits. Specifically, it guarantees a monthly benefit payment equal to 100 percent of the first $11 of the Plan's monthly benefit accrual rate, plus 75 percent of the next $33 of the accrual rate, times each year of credited service. The maximum guaranteed payment for a vested retiree, therefore, is $35.75 per month times each year of credited service.

Example 1: If a participant with 10 years of credited service has an accrued monthly benefit of $500, the accrual rate for purposes of determining the PBGC guarantee would be determined by dividing the monthly benefit by the participant's years of service ($500/10), which equals $50. The guaranteed amount for a $50 monthly accrual rate is equal to the sum of $11 plus $24.75 (.75 x $33), or $35.75. Thus, the participant's guaranteed monthly benefit is $357.50 ($35.75 x 10).

Example 2: If the participant in Example 1 has an accrued monthly benefit of $200, the accrual rate for purposes of determining the guarantee would be $20 (or $200/10). The guaranteed amount for a $20 monthly accrual rate is equal to the sum of $11 plus $6.75 (.75 x $9), or $17.75. Thus, the participant's guaranteed monthly benefit would be $177.50 ($17.75 x 10).

In calculating a person's monthly payment, the PBGC will disregard any benefit increases that were made under the plan within 60 months before insolvency. Similarly, the PBGC does not guarantee pre-retirement death benefits to a spouse or beneficiary (e.g., a qualified pre-retirement survivor annuity), benefits above the normal retirement benefit, disability benefits not in pay status, or non-pension benefits, such as health insurance, life insurance, death benefits, vacation pay, or severance pay.

Where To Get More Information

For more information about this notice, you may contact [enter name of plan administrator and, if applicable, principal administrative officer], at [enter phone number and address]. For more information about the PBGC and multiemployer benefit guarantees, go to PBGC's Web site, http://www.pbgc.gov, or call PBGC toll-free at 1-800-400-7242 (TTY/TDD users may call the Federal relay service toll free at 1-800-877-8339 and ask to be connected to 1-800-400-7242).

Signed at Washington, DC, this 31st day of January, 2005.

Ann L. Combs, Assistant Secretary, Employee Benefits Security Administration, Department of Labor.

[FR Doc. 05-2151 Filed 2-3-05; 8:45 am]

¶ 20,534U

Pension Benefit Guaranty Corporation (PBGC): Cessation of operations: Single employer: Withdrawal liability.—The PBGC has proposed a rule for computing liability under ERISA § 4063(b) when there is a plant shutdown or substantial cessation of operations by an employer in an " ERISA § 4062(e) event." Such an event occurs when more than 20% of employee-participants in an employer-sponsored plan are separated from employment when the employer ceases operations at a facility in any of its locations without terminating the plan for remaining employees. When such an event occurs, the employer is treated as if it were a substantial employer withdrawing from a multiemployer plan.

The proposed regulation was published in the Federal Register on February 25, 2005 (70 FR 9258).

PENSION BENEFIT GUARANTY CORPORATION

29 CFR Parts 4062 and 4063

RIN 1212-AB03

Liability Pursuant to Section 4062(e) of ERISA

AGENCY: Pension Benefit Guaranty Corporation.

ACTION: Proposed rule.

SUMMARY: The PBGC proposes to amend its regulations to provide a rule for computing liability under section 4063(b) of the Employee Retirement Income Security Act of 1974 ("ERISA") when there is a substantial cessation of operations by an employer as described by section 4062(e) of ERISA.

DATES: Comments must be received on or before April 26, 2005.

ADDRESSES: Comments may be mailed or delivered to the Legislative and Regulatory Department, Pension Benefit Guaranty Corporation, 1200 K Street, NW., Washington, DC 20005-4026. Comments also may be submitted electronically through the PBGC's Web site at http://www.pbgc.gov/regs, or by fax to (202) 326-4112. The PBGC will make all comments available on its Web site, http://www.pbgc.gov.

Copies of the comments may also be obtained by writing to the PBGC's Communications and Public Affairs Department at Suite 240 at the above address or by visiting that office or calling (202) 326-4040 during normal business hours. (TTY and TDD users may call the Federal relay service toll-free at 1-800-877-8339 and ask to be connected to 202-326-4040.)

FOR FURTHER INFORMATION CONTACT: James J. Armbruster, Acting Director, or James L. Beller, Attorney, Legislative and Regulatory Department, Pension Benefit Guaranty Corporation, 1200 K Street, NW., Washington, DC 20005-4026, (202) 326-4024. (TTY and TDD users may call the Federal relay service toll-free at 1-800-877-8339 and ask to be connected to (202) 326-4024.)

SUPPLEMENTARY INFORMATION: This proposed rule is part of the Pension Benefit Guaranty Corporation's (PBGC's) ongoing effort to streamline regulation and improve administration of the pension insurance program.

Section 4062(e) of ERISA provides special rules that apply when "an employer ceases operations at a facility in any location and, as a result of such cessation of operations, more than 20 percent of the total number of his employees who are participants under a plan established and maintained by him are separated from employment" (a "section 4062(e) event"). In the case of a section 4062(e) event, the employer "shall be treated with respect to that plan as if he were a substantial employer under a plan under which more than one employer makes contributions and the provisions of §§ 4063, 4064, and 4065 shall apply."

Section 4063(b) imposes liability upon a substantial employer that withdraws from a multiple employer plan. This section 4063(b) liability represents the withdrawing employer's share of the total liability to the PBGC that would arise if the plan were to terminate without enough assets to pay all benefit liabilities. (In general, the total liability to the PBGC upon termination of a plan is the amount of the plan's unfunded benefit liabilities, together with interest). The section 4063(b) liability payment made by the employer is held in escrow by the PBGC. If the plan terminates within five years, the section 4063(b) liability payment is treated as part of the plan's assets. If the plan does not terminate within five years, the liability payment is returned to the employer. The statute also provides that, in lieu of the liability payment, the contributing sponsor may be required to furnish a bond to the PBGC in an amount not exceeding 150% of the section 4063(b) liability.

The statute also specifies a method of computing the amount of the section 4063(b) liability. Section 4063(b) provides that "[t]he amount of liability shall be computed on the basis of an amount determined by the [PBGC] to be the amount described in section 4062 for the entire plan, as if the plan had been terminated by the [PBGC] on the date of the withdrawal, multiplied by a fraction (1) the numerator of which is the total amount required to be contributed to the plan by such contributing sponsor for the last 5 years ending prior to the withdrawal, and (2) the denominator of which is the total amount required to be contributed to the plan by all contributing sponsors for such last 5 years."

In sum, section 4063(b) imposes liability and provides a method for determining the amount of that liability—i.e., for determining the withdrawing employer's portion of the total liability to the PBGC that would arise if the plan terminated.

Section 4062(e) provides that, when a section 4062(e) event occurs, the employer is treated as a substantial employer under a multiple employer plan. Thus, section 4062(e) creates liability that is analogous to the section 4063(b) liability arising when a substantial employer withdraws from a multiple employer plan. Section 4062(e) does not, however, provide any details as to how this analogy is to be implemented—i.e., how the total liability is to be apportioned with respect to the cessation of operations.

As explained above, when a substantial employer withdraws from a multiple employer plan, section 4063(b) allocates liability to that withdrawing employer based upon the ratio of the employer's required contributions to all required contributions for the five years preceding the withdrawal. The PBGC has found that application of this statutory allocation formula is relatively straightforward when determining withdrawal liability under a multiple employer plan because it is easy to verify what contributions were required to be made by the withdrawing employer and what contributions were required to be made by all of the contributing employers.

In contrast, when there is a section 4062(e) event, there is by definition only one employer that contributes to the plan. When there is only one employer, the numerator and denominator used to determine the liability under section 4063(b) would always be equal. Thus, it is impracticable to use the allocation method described in section 4063(b) to determine the liability arising upon a section 4062(e) event. Instead, the PBGC has been using the method proposed in this rule to determine that liability on a case-by-case basis.

Section 4063(b) of ERISA provides that "in addition to and in lieu of" the manner of computing the liability prescribed in that provision, the PBGC "may also determine the liability on any other equitable basis prescribed by the [PBGC] in regulations." Pursuant to that authority, the PBGC is proposing in this rule a simple, practicable, and equitable method for determining the liability for a section 4062(e) event. Specifically, the PBGC proposes to compute that liability by multiplying the total liability under section 4062 by a fraction (1) the numerator of which is the number of the employer's employees who are participants under the plan and are separated from employment as a result of the cessation of operations, and (2) the denominator of which is the total number of the employer's employees who were participants under the plan before taking into account the cessation of operations. The PBGC would determine the total liability under section 4062 as if the plan had been terminated by the PBGC immediately after the cessation of operations rather than on "the date of the withdrawal" (as specified in section 4063(b)), which does not literally apply in the case of a section 4062(e) event.

By providing a simple and transparent method for determining the amount of this liability, this rule will allow plan sponsors who experience a section 4062(e) event (or believe they may experience a section 4062(e) event) to readily determine their liability (or expected liability). Although the proposed rule would specify a method for determining the amount of the liability imposed by statute, it would not affect the imposition of liability. Moreover, because the PBGC has generally followed this method on a case-by-case basis, the proposed rule would have little or no effect on the amount of liability.

Nothing in this proposed rule would affect the computation of liability incurred when there is a withdrawal of a substantial employer from a multiple employer plan under ERISA section 4063.

Compliance With Rulemaking Guidelines

The PBGC has determined, in consultation with the Office of Management and Budget, that this proposed rule is a "significant regulatory action" under Executive Order 12866. The Office of Management and Budget, therefore, has reviewed this notice under Executive Order 12866.

The PBGC certifies under section 605(b) of the Regulatory Flexibility Act that this proposed rule would not have a significant economic impact on a substantial number of small entities. A section 4062(e) event is generally not relevant for small employers. Most small employers sponsoring defined benefit plans tend not to have multiple operations. For these small employers, the shutdown of operations would be accompanied by plan termination. Section 4062(e) protection is only relevant when the plan is ongoing after the cessation of operations. Thus, the change would not have a significant economic impact on a substantial number of small entities. Accordingly, sections 603 and 604 of the Regulatory Flexibility Act do not apply.

List of Subjects

29 CFR Part 4062

Employee Benefit Plans, Pension insurance, Reporting and record-keeping requirements.

29 CFR Part 4063

Employee Benefit Plans, Pension insurance, Reporting and record-keeping requirements.

For the reasons set forth above, the PBGC proposes to amend parts 4062 and 4063 of 29 CFR chapter LX as follows:

PART 4062—LIABILITY FOR TERMINATION OF SINGLE-EMPLOYER PLANS

1. The authority citation for part 4062 continues to read as follows:

Authority: 29 U.S.C. 1302(b)(3), 1362-1364, 1367, 1368.

2. Amend § 4062.1 by adding the following sentence after the first sentence to read as follows:

§ 4062.1 Purpose and scope.

* * * * *

This part also sets forth rules for determining the amount of liability incurred under section 4063 of ERISA pursuant to the occurrence of a cessation of operations as described by section 4062(e) of ERISA.

* * * * *

§ § 4062.8, 4062.9, and 4062.10 [Redesignated]

3. Redesignate § § 4062.8, 4062.9, and 4062.10 as § § 4062.9, 4062.10, and 4062.11, respectively.

4. Add new § 4062.8 to read as follows:

§ 4062.8 Liability pursuant to section 4062(e).

If, pursuant to section 4062(e) of ERISA, an employer ceases operations at a facility in any location and, as a result of such cessation of operations, more than 20% of the total number of the employer's employees who are participants under a plan established and maintained by the employer are separated from employment, the PBGC will determine the amount of liability under section 4063(b) of ERISA to be the amount described in section 4062 of ERISA for the entire plan, as if

the plan had been terminated by the PBGC immediately after the date of the cessation of operations, multiplied by a fraction—

(a) The numerator of which is the number of the employer's employees who are participants under the plan and are separated from employment as a result of the cessation of operations; and

(b) The denominator of which is the total number of the employer's employees who were participants under the plan before taking the cessation of operations into account.

§ 4062.3 [Amended]

5. In paragraph (b) of § 4062.3, remove the references to "§ 4062.8(c)" and "4062.8(b)" and add the references to "§ 4062.9(c)" and "§ 4062.9(b)" in their places, respectively.

§ 4062.7 [Amended]

6. In paragraph (a) of § 4062.7, remove the reference to "§ 4062.8" and add in its place the reference "§ 4062.9".

PART 4063—LIABILITY OF SUBSTANTIAL EMPLOYER FOR WITHDRAWAL FROM SINGLE-EMPLOYER PLANS UNDER MULTIPLE CONTROLLED GROUPS AND OF EMPLOYER EXPERIENCING A CESSATION OF OPERATION

7. The authority citation for part 4063 continues to read as follows:

Authority: 29 U.S.C. 1302(b)(3).

8. Revise paragraph (a) of § 4063.1 to read as follows:

§ 4063.1 Cross-references.

(a) Part 4062 of this chapter sets forth rules for determination and payment of the liability incurred, under section 4062(b) of ERISA, upon termination of any single-employer plan and, to the extent appropriate, determination of the liability incurred with respect to multiple employer plans under sections 4063 and 4064 of ERISA. Part 4062 also sets forth rules for determining the amount of liability incurred under section 4063 of ERISA pursuant to the occurrence of a cessation of operations as described by section 4062(e) of ERISA.

* * * * *

Issued in Washington, DC, this 22nd day of February, 2005.

Bradley D. Belt, Executive Director, Pension Benefit Guaranty Corporation.

[FR Doc. 05-3702 Filed 2-24-05; 8:45 am]

¶ 20,534V

Pension Benefit Guaranty Corporation (PBGC): Electronic filing requirements: Financial statements: Actuarial information.—The PBGC has issued a proposed rule which would require that certain identifying, financial and actuarial information be filed electronically in a standardized format and would also require the filing of additional items of supporting information that are readily available to the filer.

The proposed regulation was published in the Federal Register on March 9, 2005 (70 FR 11592).

PENSION BENEFIT GUARANTY CORPORATION

29 CFR Parts 4000 and 4007

RIN 1212-AB02

Electronic Premium Filing

AGENCY: Pension Benefit Guaranty Corporation.

ACTION: Proposed rule.

SUMMARY: The PBGC proposes to require electronic filing of premium declarations. The requirement would become effective for plans with 500 or more participants starting with the 2006 plan year and for smaller plans starting with the 2007 plan year. Plans could apply to the PBGC for exemptions on a case-by-case basis. The PBGC has instituted an on-line e-filing facility ("My Plan Administration Account," or "My PAA"), and during 2005 will upgrade My PAA to accept electronic filings made with the use of vendor or proprietary software.

DATES: Comments must be received on or before May 9, 2005.

ADDRESSES: Comments may be mailed or delivered to the Legislative & Regulatory Department, Pension Benefit Guaranty Corporation, 1200 K Street, NW., Washington, DC 20005-4026. Comments also may be submitted electronically through the PBGC's Web site at http://www.pbgc.gov/regs,

or by fax to 202-326-4112. The PBGC will make all comments available on its Web site, http://www.pbgc.gov. Copies of the comments may also be

obtained by writing to the PBGC's Communications and Public Affairs Department at Suite 240 at the above address or by visiting that office

or calling 202-326-4040 during normal business hours. (TTY and TDD users may call the Federal relay service toll-free at 1-800-877-8339 and ask to be connected to 202-326-4040.)

FOR FURTHER INFORMATION CONTACT: James J. Armbruster, Acting Director, or Deborah C. Murphy, Attorney, Legislative & Regulatory Department, Pension Benefit Guaranty Corporation, 1200 K Street, NW., Washington, DC 20005-4026, 202-326-4024. (For TTY/TTD users, call the Federal relay service toll-free at 1-800-877-8339 and ask to be connected to 202-326-4024.)

SUPPLEMENTARY INFORMATION: This proposed rule is part of an ongoing implementation of the Government Paperwork Elimination Act by the Pension Benefit Guaranty Corporation ("PBGC") and is consistent with the Office of Management and Budget's directive to remove regulatory impediments to electronic transactions. The rule addresses electronic submission of premium filings required under the PBGC's regulation on Payment of Premiums (29 CFR Part 4007) and builds in the flexibility needed to allow the PBGC to update the electronic filing process as technology advances.

The PBGC administers the pension insurance programs under Title IV of the Employee Retirement Income Security Act of 1974 ("ERISA"). Pension plans covered by Title IV must pay annual premiums to the PBGC. Premium filings must include information to identify the plans for which premiums are paid and to demonstrate that the amounts paid are correct.

The PBGC has been processing premium filings for 30 years. The volume of filings processed annually is in the tens of thousands. Processing methods have become progressively more automated, and the PBGC now uses specially designed premium forms that can be read by optical character recognition ("OCR") devices. Even with OCR, however, the PBGC has found that the capture of data from paper premium forms and its translation into electronic data files is an imperfect process that inevitably gives rise to errors that can be difficult and burdensome to detect and correct. These errors cause problems for both the PBGC and premium filers, because they can lead to the issuance of improper bills for premiums that have in fact been paid, to delays in the processing of refund requests, to erroneous filing histories, etc.

Consistent with the Government Paperwork Elimination Act, and with a view to reducing problems of this kind, the PBGC introduced optional electronic premium filing for plan years beginning in 2004 using a facility on its Web site (http://www.pbgc.gov) called "My Plan Administration Account" ("My PAA"). To make a premium filing using My PAA, a plan administrator or other pension practitioner logs onto a secure account on the PBGC's Web site and enters necessary information in on-line forms screens. My PAA enables practitioners to route premium filings among themselves electronically for the addition of information and for electronic certification and to submit completed filings to the PBGC with the click of a mouse. The information submitted can be loaded directly into the PBGC's data processing systems, thus eliminating the errors inherent in the OCR data capture process. Premium payments are also made on line as part of the filing process.

My PAA streamlines the premium filing process for users, and it makes the PBGC's processing of premium filings faster and more accurate. Thus it has the potential to reduce the number of erroneous bills, to speed up refund processing, and in general to improve significantly the PBGC's ability to perform its premium collection functions while enhancing service to premium payers.

The PBGC is now engaged in a project to create another premium e-filing method, to be operational in mid-2005, to accommodate pension practitioners who may prefer to continue using private sector software—either purchased annually from a commercial developer or developed "in-house"—for preparing premium filings. The PBGC will issue standards for structuring a computer file containing premium filing information; by incorporating those standards into their software, developers will give software users the ability to create premium data files that they will be able to upload to the PBGC through the PBGC's web site (probably through the existing My PAA portal). Using this new method, practitioners will be able to prepare premium filing information using their own software and then put the information into files that meet PBGC formatting standards and electronically transmit them to the PBGC. The PBGC expects to continue accepting premium payments from such filers in the same way it does now, by paper check, wire transfer, or Automated Clearing House.

Against this background, the PBGC is proposing to eliminate paper premium forms and to require electronic filing of annual premium information submissions for large plans (those with 500 or more participants) for plan years beginning after 2005 and for all plans for plan years beginning after 2006. The PBGC would grant case-by-case exemptions to the electronic filing requirement in appropriate circumstances for filers that demonstrated good cause for exemption. (The submission of information specially requested by the PBGC in connection with a premium compliance review would not be affected by this change, nor would there be a requirement for payment to be made electronically.)

The PBGC invites public comment on this proposal, including the 500-participant cutoff that is used to determine whether a plan is required to begin e-filing in 2006 or 2007 (and is also used to determine whether a plan must pay the flat-rate premium early under 29 CFR 4007.11(a)(2), whether contributions may or must be included in assets under 29 CFR 4006.4(b)(2)(iv) in determining the variable-rate premium, whether significant events must be taken into account under 29 CFR 4006.4(d) when using the alternative calculation method for the variable-rate premium, whether a fully funded plan qualifies for a variable-rate premium exemption under 29 CFR 4006.5(a)(1), and whether a plan may base its variable-rate premium on accrued rather than vested benefits under 29 CFR 4006.5(b)).

Compliance With Rulemaking Guidelines

The PBGC has determined, in consultation with the Office of Management and Budget ("OMB"), that this proposed rule is a "significant regulatory action" under Executive Order 12866. OMB has therefore reviewed this proposed rule under Executive Order 12866.

The PBGC certifies under section 605(b) of the Regulatory Flexibility Act that the amendments in this rule would not have a significant economic impact on a substantial number of small entities. The PBGC expects electronic premium filing to be no more burdensome than

paper filing for filers generally and will grant exemptions from the electronic filing requirement for good cause in appropriate circumstances. Accordingly, as provided in section 605 of the Regulatory Flexibility Act (5 U.S.C. 601 et seq.), sections 603 and 604 do not apply.

The PBGC is submitting the information requirements contained in this proposed rule to OMB for review and approval under the Paperwork Reduction Act. Copies of the PBGC's request may be obtained free of charge by contacting the PBGC Communications and Public Affairs Department, suite 240, 1200 K Street, NW., Washington, DC 20005, 202-326-4040. This proposed rule would modify paperwork collections under both part 4000 (OMB control number 1212-0059) and part 4007 (OMB control number 1212-0009).

The PBGC needs the information required to be submitted under part 4007 to identify the plans for which premiums are paid and to determine whether the amounts paid are correct.

The PBGC estimates that it will receive premium filings annually from about 28,900 plan administrators and that the total annual burden of the collection of information will be about 3,478 hours and $18,172,550. (These estimates include paper and electronic filings.)

Comments on the paperwork provisions under this proposed rule should be mailed to the Office of Information and Regulatory Affairs, Office of Management and Budget, Attention: Desk Officer for the Pension Benefit Guaranty Corporation, Washington, DC 20503. Although comments may be submitted through May 9, 2005, the Office of Management and Budget requests that comments be received on or before April 8, 2005 to ensure their consideration. Comments may address (among other things)—

Whether the proposed collection of information is needed for the proper performance of the PBGC's functions and will have practical utility;

The accuracy of the PBGC's estimate of the burden of the proposed collection of information, including the validity of the methodology and assumptions used;

Enhancement of the quality, utility, and clarity of the information to be collected; and

Minimizing the burden of the collection of information on those who are to respond, including through the use of appropriate automated, electronic, mechanical, or other technological collection techniques or other forms of information technology, e.g., permitting electronic submission of responses.

List of Subjects

29 CFR Part 4000

Pension insurance, Pensions, Reporting and recordkeeping requirements.

29 CFR Part 4007

Penalties, Pension insurance, Pensions, Reporting and recordkeeping requirements.

For the reasons given above, the PBGC proposes to amend 29 CFR parts 4000 and 4007 as follows.

PART 4000—FILING, ISSUANCE, COMPUTATION OF TIME, AND RECORD RETENTION

1. The authority citation for part 4000 continues to read as follows:

Authority: 29 U.S.C. 1082(f), 1302(b)(3).

2. In § 4000.3, paragraph (a) is amended by removing "You may file" and adding in its place "Except for premium declarations, you may file; by redesignating paragraph (b) as paragraph (c) and revising its heading to read "Information on electronic filings."; and by adding a new paragraph (b) to read as follows:

§ 4000.3 What methods of filing may I use?

* * * * *

(b) *Required electronic filings.* You must file premium declarations electronically except to the extent that the PBGC grants an exemption for good cause in appropriate circumstances.

(1) This electronic filing requirement applies to filings for—

(i) Plan years beginning after 2005 for plans that were required to pay premiums for 500 or more participants for the plan year preceding the premium payment year and

(ii) Plan years beginning after 2006 for all other plans.

(2) This electronic filing requirement does not apply to information you file to comply with a request we make under § 4007.10(c) of this

chapter (dealing with providing record information in connection with a premium compliance review).

3. In § 4000.4, remove the last sentence and add two new sentences in its place to read as follows:

§ 4000.4 Where do I file my submission?

* * * You do not have to provide an address for electronic premium submissions made through our web site. We are responsible for ensuring that such submissions go to the proper place.

4. In § 4000.23, add a new sentence at the end of paragraph (a) and at the end of paragraph (b)(3) to read as follows:

§ 4000.23 When is my submission or issuance treated as filed or issued?

(a) * * * A submission made through our web site is considered to have been sent when you perform the last act necessary to indicate that your submission is filed and cannot be further edited or withdrawn.

(b) * * *

(3) * * * A submission made through our web site is considered to have been received when we receive an electronic signal that you have performed the last act necessary to indicate that your submission is filed and cannot be further edited or withdrawn.

5. In § 4000.29, add three new sentences at the end of paragraph (a) introductory text to read as follows:

§ 4000.29 What if I use electronic delivery?

(a) * * * A submission made through our web site is considered to have been transmitted when you perform the last act necessary to indicate that your submission is filed and cannot be further edited or withdrawn. You do not have to provide an address for electronic premium submissions made through our web site. We are responsible for ensuring that such submissions go to the proper place.

* * * * *

PART 4007—PAYMENT OF PREMIUMS

6. The authority citation for part 4007 continues to read as follows:

Authority: 29 U.S.C. 1302(b)(3), 1303(a), 1306, 1307.

7. Section 4007.3 is revised to read as follows:

§ 4007.3 Filing requirement; method of filing.

The estimation, declaration, reconciliation, and payment of premiums shall be made in accordance with the instructions posted on the PBGC's Web site (http://www.pbgc.gov). No later than the applicable due date specified in § 4007.11, the plan administrator of each covered plan shall file in the prescribed format the prescribed information and any premium payments due. Information must be filed electronically except to the extent that the PBGC grants an exemption for good cause in appropriate circumstances. The requirement to file electronically applies to filings for plan years beginning after 2005 for plans that were required to pay premiums for 500 or more participants for the plan year preceding the premium payment year and to filings for plan years beginning after 2006 for all other plans. (The requirement to file electronically does not apply to information filed to comply with a PBGC request under § 4007.10(c) (dealing with providing record information in connection with a premium compliance review).)

8. Section 4007.4 is revised to read as follows:

§ 4007.4 Where to file.

See § 4000.4 of this chapter for information on where to file.

Issued in Washington, DC, this 3rd day of March, 2005.

Bradley D. Belt, Executive Director, Pension Benefit Guaranty Corporation.

[FR Doc. 05-4536 Filed 3-8-05; 8:45 am]

¶ 20,534W

Employee Benefits Security Administration (EBSA): Prohibited transactions: Qualified termination administrators (QTAs): Plan termination: Individual retirement plans.—Reproduced below is the text of an EBSA proposed rule that establishes standards for determining when an individual account plan has been abandoned, guidelines for winding up the plan's affairs and distributing benefits, and guidance with regard to who may initiate and carry out the termination process. The proposed rule was issued in conjunction with a proposed prohibited transaction class exemption (see ¶ 16,707).

The proposed regulation was published in the Federal Register on March 10, 2005 (70 FR 12045).

Department of Labor

Employee Benefits Security Administration

29 CFR Parts 2520, 2550, et al.

Termination of Abandoned Individual Account Plans and Proposed Class Exemption for Services Provided in Connection With the Termination of Abandoned Individual Account Plans; Proposed Rule and Notice

DEPARTMENT OF LABOR

Employee Benefits Security Administration

29 CFR Parts 2520, 2550, and 2578

RIN 1210-AA97

Termination of Abandoned Individual Account Plans

AGENCY: Employee Benefits Security Administration, Labor.

ACTION: Proposed Regulations.

SUMMARY: This document contains three proposed regulations under the Employee Retirement Income Security Act of 1974 (ERISA or the Act) that, upon adoption, would facilitate the termination of, and distribution of benefits from, individual account pension plans that have been abandoned by their sponsoring employers. The first proposed rule would establish a regulatory framework pursuant to which financial institutions and other entities holding the assets of an abandoned individual account plan can terminate the plan and distribute benefits to the plan's participants and beneficiaries, with limited liability. The second proposed rule provides a fiduciary safe harbor for use in connection with making rollover distributions from terminated plans on behalf of participants and beneficiaries who fail to make an election regarding a form of benefit distribution.

Appendices to these rules contain model notices for use in connection therewith. The third proposed rule would establish a simplified method for filing a terminal report for abandoned individual account plans. These proposed regulations, if adopted, would affect fiduciaries,

plan service providers, and participants and beneficiaries of individual account pension plans.

DATES: Written comments on the proposed regulations should be received by the Department of Labor on or before May 9, 2005.

ADDRESSES: Comments should be addressed to the Office of Regulations and Interpretations, Employee Benefits Security Administration, Room N-5669, U.S. Department of Labor, 200 Constitution Avenue NW., Washington, DC 20210, Attn: Abandoned Plan Regulation. Comments also may be submitted electronically to e-ORI@dol.gov. All comments received will be available for public inspection at the Public Disclosure Room, N-1513, Employee Benefits Security Administration, 200 Constitution Avenue NW., Washington, DC 20210.

FOR FURTHER INFORMATION CONTACT: Jeffrey J. Turner or Stephanie L. Ward, Office of Regulations and Interpretations, Employee Benefits Security Administration, (202) 693-8500. This is not a toll-free number.

SUPPLEMENTARY INFORMATION:

Background

Thousands of individual account plans have, for a variety of reasons, been abandoned by their sponsors. Financial institutions holding the assets of these abandoned plans often do not have the authority or incentive to perform the responsibilities otherwise required of the plan administrator with respect to such plans. At the same time, participants and beneficiaries are frequently unable to access their plan benefits. As a result, the assets of many of these plans are diminished by ongoing administrative costs, rather than being paid to the plan's participants and beneficiaries.

Over the past few years, the Department of Labor's Employee Benefits Security Administration (EBSA) has seen an increase in the number of requests for assistance from participants who are unable to obtain access to the money in their individual account plans. According to these participants, even though a bank or other service provider of the plan may be holding their money, neither the bank nor the participants are able to locate anyone with authority under the plan to authorize benefit distributions.

In some cases, plan abandonment occurs when the sponsoring employer ceases to exist by virtue of a formal bankruptcy proceeding. In other cases, abandonment occurs because the plan sponsor has been incarcerated, died, or simply fled the country. Whatever the causes of abandonment, participants in these so-called "orphan plan" or "abandoned plan" situations are effectively denied access to their benefits and are otherwise unable to exercise their rights guaranteed under ERISA. At the same time, benefits in such plans are at risk of being significantly diminished by ongoing administrative expenses, rather than being distributed to participants and beneficiaries.

EBSA responded to those participants' requests for assistance with a series of enforcement initiatives, including the National Enforcement Project on Orphan Plans (NEPOP), which began in 1999. NEPOP focuses primarily on identifying abandoned plans, locating their fiduciaries, if possible, and requiring those fiduciaries to manage and terminate (including making benefit distributions to participants and beneficiaries) the plans in accordance with ERISA. When no fiduciary can be found, the Department often requests a federal court to appoint an independent fiduciary to manage, terminate, and distribute the assets of the plan. EBSA had opened 1,354 civil cases involving orphan plans as of September 30, 2004. In the over 800 orphan plan cases closed with results through September 30, 2004, there were approximately 50,000 participants affected and $250 million in assets involved. As of September 30, 2004, there were 372 active cases involving orphan plans.

During 2002, the ERISA Advisory Council created the Working Group on Orphan Plans to study the causes and extent of the orphan plan problem. On November 8, 2002, after public hearings and testimony, the Advisory Council issued a report, entitled Report of the Working Group on Orphan Plans,[1] concluding that the problems posed by abandoned plans are very serious and substantial for plan participants, administrators, and the government. In particular, the Report states that "[p]lan participants may suffer economic hardship as a result of their inability to obtain a distribution from an orphan plan; plan service providers may be besieged with requests for distributions, although unauthorized to act; and the government may be forced to handle the termination of hundreds or thousands of plans that have been abandoned." Although the Advisory Council's Report estimated that abandoned plans currently represent only about two percent of all defined contribution plans and less than one percent of total plan assets for such plans, the Report also indicated that the orphan plan problem may grow in difficult economic times.

Taking into account the problem of abandoned plans and the Department's efforts to date, the Advisory Council generally recommended measures (whether regulatory, legislative, or both) to encourage service providers to voluntarily terminate abandoned plans and distribute assets to participants and beneficiaries. Specific recommendations of the Advisory Council included new regulations setting forth criteria for determining when a plan is abandoned, procedures for terminating abandoned plans and distributing assets, and rules defining who may terminate and wind up such plans.

The Department carefully considered the recommendations of the Advisory Council, as well as the comments of the various parties testifying at the public hearing, in developing the proposed regulations contained in this document, which are being promulgated by the Department pursuant to its authority in sections 403(d)(1), 404(a), and 505 of ERISA.

Overview of Proposed Abandoned Plan Regulation—29 CFR 2578.1

Generally, this proposed regulation, upon adoption, would establish standards and procedures under title I of ERISA that will facilitate the voluntary, safe and efficient termination of abandoned plans, increasing the likelihood that participants and beneficiaries receive the greatest retirement benefit under the circumstances. Specifically, the proposed

regulation establishes standards for determining when a plan may be considered abandoned and deemed terminated, procedures for winding up the affairs of the plan and distributing benefits to participants and beneficiaries, and guidance on who may initiate and carry out the winding-up process.

Qualified Termination Administrator

All determinations of plan abandonment, as well as related activities necessary to the termination and winding up of an abandoned individual account plan, under this regulation, may be performed only by a "qualified termination administrator" or "QTA." In this regard, paragraph (g) of the proposal provides that a person or entity can qualify as a termination administrator only if it, first, is eligible to serve as a trustee or issuer of an individual retirement plan that is within the meaning of section 7701(a)(37) of the Internal Revenue Code (Code)[2] and, second, if it holds assets of the plan on whose behalf it will serve as the QTA. While the Department believes that a person undertaking to terminate and wind up an abandoned individual account plan should, for purposes of the relief provided by the regulation, be subject to Federal standards and oversight, the Department invites public comment on whether, and how, the definition of a "qualified termination administrator" might be expanded to include other parties.[3] Comments on this subject should address financial, operational, regulatory, and other safeguards on which "QTA" status might be conditioned to protect the interest of the plan's participants and beneficiaries.

Finding of Plan Abandonment

Paragraph (b) of proposed § 2578.1 defines when a plan is abandoned for purposes of the regulation. In this regard, paragraph (b) provides that a QTA may find an individual account plan to be abandoned when there have been no contributions to (or distributions from) a plan for a continuous 12-month period, or where facts and circumstances known to the QTA (such as a plan sponsor's liquidation under title 11 of the United States Code, or communications from plan participants and beneficiaries regarding the plan sponsor, benefit distributions, or other plan information) suggest that the plan is or may become abandoned. See § 2578.1(b)(1)(i). The latter standard is intended to permit immediate findings of abandonment where known facts and circumstances clearly obviate the need for 12 consecutive months of plan inactivity. The testimony of various service providers (such as banks, insurance companies, and mutual funds) makes it clear that they frequently acquire knowledge of abandonment, even though contributions or distributions may have occurred within the past 12 months. For example, in some cases, employees of defunct businesses appear personally or call the bank requesting distributions. Under these circumstances, requiring a 12-month wait before taking some action appears to be of little or no benefit to the plan participants, and possibly even harmful to their interests.

A second condition to a finding of abandonment is that the QTA must, following reasonable efforts to locate or communicate with the known plan sponsor, determine that the plan sponsor no longer exists, cannot be located, or is unable to maintain the plan. See § 2578.1(b)(1)(ii). For this purpose, the proposal describes specific steps that would constitute "reasonable efforts" by a QTA to locate or communicate with the plan sponsor. See § 2578.1(b)(3) and (4).[4] Among other things, a reasonable effort would include furnishing notice to the plan sponsor of the QTA's intent to terminate the sponsor's individual account plan and distribute benefits to the plan's participants and beneficiaries. The proposal describes other information that must be contained in the notice to the plan sponsor. To facilitate compliance with this notification requirement, the Department has developed a model notice to plan sponsors for use by QTAs. This model notice, the use of which would be voluntary on the part of the QTA, is contained in Appendix A to the proposed rule.

With respect to the phrase "unable to maintain the plan" in paragraph (b)(1)(ii), the testimony given to the Advisory Council's Working Group suggests that imprisonment is perhaps the most common reason why a plan sponsor might be considered unable to maintain its plan. This phrase, however, should not be understood to be so limited

---

[1] A copy of the Report can be found at http://www.dol.gov/ebsa/publications/AC110802_report.html.

[2] Section 7701(a)(37) defines the term individual retirement plan to mean an individual retirement account described in section 408(a) of the Code and an individual retirement annuity described in section 408(b) of the Code.

[3] The subject regulation is not intended to limit, in any way, the ability of other parties who may be acting pursuant to court appointment, court order, or otherwise acting on behalf of the sponsor of the plan, to terminate and wind up the affairs of a pension plan, without regard to whether the plan is considered abandoned under this regulation. The proposed definition of "qualified termination administrator" does not include such parties

because they are empowered to take steps to terminate and wind up the affairs of a plan without regard to any authority that might be conferred by the regulation.

[4] The steps described in paragraphs (b)(3) and (4) of the proposed regulation are not intended to be the exclusive method by which a QTA can satisfy the standard of reasonableness in paragraph (b)(1) of the regulation. These steps represent merely what the Department considers to be an appropriate level of effort to locate or communicate with the plan sponsor, given the unique circumstances surrounding abandoned plans, the other requirements and safeguards in the regulation relating to findings of abandonment, and the cost associated with other generally available methods of locating missing plan sponsors. The Department, nevertheless, invites public comment on whether, and how, these steps might be augmented to further reduce the possibility that a QTA might err in concluding that a plan has been abandoned, when in fact the plan sponsor can be located.

in nature. Rather, the Department intends for this phrase to encompass physical, mental, legal, financial, or other impediments that, in the judgment of the QTA, prevent the sponsor from making contributions to and administrating the plan in accordance with the documents and instruments governing the plan.

Deemed Terminations

Following a QTA's finding that a plan has been abandoned, the plan will be deemed to be terminated under the proposal on the ninetieth (90th) day following the date on which the QTA provides notice of its determination of plan abandonment and its election to serve as a QTA to the U.S. Department of Labor. See § 2578.1(c). The furnishing of notice to the Department, in conjunction with the 90-day delay in the deemed termination of the plan, is intended to afford the Department an opportunity to review the circumstances of the proposed plan termination and, if appropriate, object to the termination. If the Department objects to a termination, the plan will not be deemed terminated until such time as the Department informs the QTA that the Department's concerns have been addressed. See § 2578.1(c)(2)(i).

The proposal would also permit (but does not require) the Department, in its sole discretion, to waive some or all of the 90-day waiting period described above. This might happen, for example, in the case of plans with few participants and few assets or if the facts relating to the abandonment are not very complicated, and if it is reasonably apparent to the Department that the proposed termination would be unlikely to put the participants' interests at risk. If the Department were to waive some or all of the 90-day period in a particular case, the plan involved would be deemed terminated when the Department furnished notification of the waiver to the QTA. See § 25781(c)(2)(ii).

Paragraph (c)(3) of § 2578.1 provides that the above referenced notice to the Department must be signed and dated by the QTA and include certain information about the QTA and the abandoned plan. Information about the QTA includes the name, EIN, address and phone number of the QTA, a description of the steps it took to locate or communicate with the known plan sponsor, a statement that it elects to terminate and wind up the plan, and an itemized estimate of any expenses the QTA expects to pay (including to itself) as part of the process contemplated by the proposed regulation. The notice must also identify whether the QTA or its affiliate is, or within the past 24 months has been, the subject of an investigation, examination, or enforcement action by specified federal authorities. Information about the plan includes the name of the plan, an estimate of the number of participants in the plan, an estimate of total assets of the plan held by the QTA, identification of known service providers of the plan, and the last known address of the plan sponsor. The Department believes that the required information will be sufficient to allow the Department to assess whether it should object to a proposed termination.

To facilitate compliance with this notification requirement, the Department has developed a model notice for use by QTAs in notifying the Department of plan abandonment. This model notice, the use of which would be voluntary on the part of QTAs, is contained in Appendix B to the proposed rule.

The Department is considering whether this notification, as well as the notification required by § 2578.1(d)(2)(viii) of the proposed regulation, should be required to be submitted to the Department electronically. The Department, therefore, specifically invites comment on whether, and to what extent, the Department should either mandate or provide for the electronic submission of these notices and what, if any, cost or cost savings might result to plans because of either such a requirement or such an opportunity to submit electronically.

Winding Up the Affairs of the Plan

A number of witnesses appearing before the Advisory Council's Working Group on Orphan Plans indicated that they would be more likely to participate in a formal process for terminating abandoned plans if the Department established specific guidelines on how to wind up such plans. Paragraph (d) of § 2578.1 is intended to provide that guidance. Paragraph (d)(1) of the proposed regulation prescribes the general authority of the QTA to take steps that are necessary or appropriate to wind up the affairs of the plan and distribute benefits to the plan's participants and beneficiaries.

Paragraph (d)(2) of § 2578.1 sets forth specific steps that a QTA must take and, with respect to most such steps, specifies the standards applicable to carrying out the particular activity (e.g., gathering plan records, engaging service providers, paying reasonable expenses, etc.). The prescribed standards are intended to both clarify and limit the responsibilities and liability of QTAs in connection with the termination and winding up of an abandoned plan.

Paragraph (d)(2)(i) of the proposal deals with locating and updating plan records. Several witnesses appearing before the Advisory Council's Working Group identified incomplete or inaccurate plan records as a possible impediment to winding up the affairs of abandoned plans. In responding to this testimony, the Advisory Council's Report recommended that the Department provide guidance on the extent to which the records of abandoned plans must be updated before benefits may be distributed. Paragraph (d)(2)(i)(A) of the proposal provides that the QTA shall undertake reasonable and diligent efforts to locate and update plan records necessary to determine benefits payable under the plan. In recognition of the fact that there will be circumstances where locating, recreating or updating plan records, may, even when possible, be so costly that the plan's participants and beneficiaries will be better off with benefits being determined on less than complete or accurate records, the proposal, at paragraph (d)(2)(i)(B), provides that the QTA shall not have failed to act reasonably and diligently merely because it determines in good faith that updating the records is either impossible or involves significant cost to the plan in relation to the total assets of the plan.

Paragraph (d)(2)(ii) of the proposal provides that the QTA must use reasonable care in calculating the benefits payable based on the plan records assembled. This provision, in conjunction with paragraph (d)(2)(i), is intended to ensure accuracy for the greatest number of distributions, while making it clear that the Department does not expect a QTA to assemble perfect records in every case.

Testimony before the Advisory Council's Working Group indicated a need to address whether and under what circumstances plan assets could be utilized to compensate service providers as part of the termination and winding up process. Paragraphs (d)(2)(iii) and (iv) of the proposal are intended to address the issues relating to the engagement of service providers and the payment of expenses in connection with the termination and winding up of an abandoned plan.

Paragraph (d)(2)(iii) of the proposal provides the QTA with the authority to engage, on behalf of the plan, such service providers as are necessary for the QTA to wind up the affairs of the plan and distribute benefits to the plan's participants and beneficiaries. Paragraph (d)(2)(iv)(A) makes clear that reasonable expenses incurred in connection with the termination and winding up of the plan may be paid from plan assets.

Paragraph (d)(2)(iv)(B) provides guidance concerning when expenses incurred in connection with the termination and winding up of an abandoned plan will be considered "reasonable." In this regard, the Department notes that the guidance provided by that paragraph applies solely for purposes of determining the reasonableness of expenses incurred in connection with the exercise of a QTA's authority under this regulation to terminate and wind up an abandoned plan. Specifically, paragraph (d)(2)(iv)(B) provides that an expense shall be considered reasonable if: the expense is for services necessary to wind up the affairs of the plan and distribute benefits to the plan's participants and beneficiaries; such expense is consistent with industry rates for the provided services, based on the experience of the QTA; such expense is not in excess of rates charged by the QTA (or affiliate) to other customers for comparable services, if the QTA (or affiliate) provides comparable services to other customers; and the payment of the expense would not constitute a prohibited transaction or is otherwise exempt by virtue of an individual or class exemption from ERISA's prohibited transaction rules.

The reference to "industry rates" and "based on the experience of the QTA" in paragraph (d)(2)(iv)(B)(2)(i) is intended to enable QTAs, who possess knowledge about the services needed for a plan termination and industry rates for such or similar services, but who do not perform these services for plans, to engage or retain service providers without going through a potentially time-consuming and costly bidding process. By permitting QTA's to rely on their own industry expertise, we believe QTAs can minimize plan termination costs and, thereby, maximize the benefits payable to a plan's participants and beneficiaries.

The rule in paragraph (d)(2)(iv)(B)(2)(ii) is intended to augment the protections provided under the industry rates standard discussed above. Under this rule, if a QTA performs termination and winding up services for customers other than abandoned plans under this regulation, the fees it charges the other customers for such services shall serve as limits for fees for comparable services needed by the abandoned plans.

The Department anticipates that QTAs may wish to be compensated for services they or an affiliate render in connection with the termination and winding up of an abandoned plan. In the absence of an exemption, however, a QTA's decision to compensate itself from plan assets for such services would constitute a prohibited transaction under section 406 of ERISA, thereby making such payment unreasonable under this regulation. See § 2578.1(d)(2)(iv)(B)(3). To address this problem, the Department is publishing in the Notice section of today's Federal Register a proposed class exemption pursuant to which QTAs or their affiliates can be reimbursed or compensated for services performed pursuant to this regulation, following its adoption.

In addition to locating and updating plan records, calculating benefits and engaging service providers, the QTA shall, as one of its duties in winding up the affairs of a plan, notify each of the plan's participants and beneficiaries concerning the termination of their plan. In general, paragraph (d)(2)(v)(A) provides that the notice furnished to participants and beneficiaries include: a statement that the plan has been terminated; a statement of the participant's or beneficiary's account balance and a description of the distribution options available under the plan; a request for the participant or beneficiary to make an election with respect to the form of distribution; a statement explaining that in the event the participant or beneficiary fails to make an election his or her account balance will be rolled over into an individual retirement plan (i.e., individual retirement account or annuity) or other account (in the case of a non-spousal beneficiary) and invested in an investment product that is designed to preserve principal and provide a reasonable rate of return and liquidity; and the name, address, and telephone number of a person to contact with questions or for additional information.[5] Nothing in the regulation would preclude a QTA from also including its e-mail address in this notice.

Appendix C to this section contains a model notice to participants and beneficiaries. The model allows for inclusion of plan-specific information, including a description of the process for electing a form of distribution. While the Department intends that use of an appropriately completed model notice would be considered compliance with the content requirements of paragraph (d)(2)(v)(A) of the proposed regulation, the Department does not intend to require its use and anticipates a variety of other notices could satisfy the requirements of the regulation.

This notice shall be furnished to the last known address of participants and beneficiaries in accordance with the requirements of 29 CFR 2520.104b-1(b)(1). See § 2578.1(d)(2)(v)(B)(1). If the notice is returned undelivered to the QTA, however, the QTA, consistent with the duties of a fiduciary under section 404(a)(1) of ERISA, shall take steps to locate and notify the missing participant or beneficiary before distributing benefits. See § 2578.1(d)(2)(v)(B)(2). A QTA may ensure compliance with this standard by following previous fiduciary guidance issued by the Department in the context of missing participants. See EBSA Field Assistance Bulletin No. 2004-02 (Sept. 30, 2004).

Paragraph (d)(2)(vi) of the proposal addresses distributions of benefits to participants and beneficiaries. The general rule under that paragraph is that a QTA is required to distribute benefits in accordance with elections of participants or beneficiaries. See § 2578.1(d)(2)(vi)(A). In the absence of a timely election by a participant or beneficiary, however, the individual's benefits must be directly rolled over into an individual retirement plan (or other account in the case of a non-spousal beneficiary) in accordance with proposed 29 CFR 2550.404a-3. See § 2578.1(d)(2)(vi)(B).

The last step in the winding-up process is for the QTA to notify the Department that all benefits have been distributed in accordance with the regulation. Paragraph (d)(2)(viii) of the proposal sets forth the content requirements of this notification, which is referred to in the regulation as the final notice. Among other things, the final notice is required to include: A statement that the plan has been terminated and all assets held by the QTA have been distributed to the plan's participants and beneficiaries on the basis of the best available information; a statement that the special terminal report meeting the requirements of proposed 29 CFR 2520.103-13 is attached to the final notice; a statement that plan expenses were paid out of plan assets by the QTA in accordance with applicable federal law; and, in cases where the QTA paid itself 20 percent or more than it had estimated it would be paying itself, a statement acknowledging and explaining the overrun.

Appendix D to this section contains a model final notice. The model allows for inclusion of plan-specific information. While the Department intends that use of an appropriately completed model notice would be

considered compliance with the content requirements of paragraph (d)(2)(viii) of the proposed regulation, the Department does not intend to require its use and anticipates a variety of other notices could satisfy the requirements of the proposed regulation.

Plan Amendments

Paragraph (d)(3) of section 2578.1 provides that the terms of the plan shall, for purposes of title I of ERISA, be deemed amended to the extent necessary to allow the QTA to wind up the plan in accordance with this regulation. The purpose of this provision is to enable QTAs to avoid the potentially significant costs attendant to amending the plan to permit what is otherwise permissible under this regulation. For example, a QTA may, without regard to plan terms, engage or replace service providers and pay expenses attendant to winding up and terminating the plan from plan assets.

Limited Liability of Qualified Termination Administrator

In a further effort to limit the liability of a QTA, paragraph (e) of the proposed regulation provides that, if a QTA carries out its responsibilities with regard to winding up the affairs of the plan in accordance with paragraph (d)(2) of the regulation, the QTA is deemed to satisfy any responsibilities it may have under section 404(a) of ERISA with respect to such activity, except for selecting and monitoring service providers. In addition, with respect to its selection and monitoring duties, if the QTA selects and monitors service providers consistent with the prudence requirements in part 4 of ERISA, the QTA will not be held liable for the acts or omissions of the service providers with respect to which the QTA does not have knowledge.

Internal Revenue Service

The Advisory Council's Working Group on Orphan Plans recommended that the Department coordinate with the Internal Revenue Service (IRS) in the development of this proposed regulation in order to prevent participants and beneficiaries of abandoned plans, insofar as possible under the Code, from losing the favorable tax treatment otherwise accorded distributions from qualified plans. The Department, therefore, has conferred with representatives of the IRS regarding the qualification requirements under the Code as applied to plans that would be terminated pursuant to this proposed regulation. The IRS has advised the Department that it will not challenge the qualified status of any plan terminated under this regulation or take any adverse action against, or seek to assess or impose any penalty on, the QTA, the plan, or any participant or beneficiary of the plan as a result of such termination, including the distribution of the plan's assets, provided that the QTA satisfies three conditions. First, the QTA, based on plan records located and updated in accordance with paragraph (d)(2)(i) of the proposed regulation, reasonably determines whether, and to what extent, the survivor annuity requirements of sections 401(a)(11) and 417 of the Code apply to any benefit payable under the plan.[6] Second, each participant and beneficiary has a nonforfeitable right to his or her accrued benefits as of the date of deemed termination under paragraph (c)(1) of the proposed regulation, subject to income, expenses, gains, and losses between that date and the date of distribution. Third, participants and beneficiaries must receive notification of their rights under section 402(f) of the Code. This notification should be included in, or attached to, the notice described in paragraph (d)(2)(v) of the proposed regulation. Notwithstanding the foregoing, the IRS reserves the right to pursue appropriate remedies under the Code against any party who is responsible for the plan, such as the plan sponsor, plan administrator, or owner of the business, even in its capacity as a participant or beneficiary under the plan.

Overview of Proposed Safe Harbor for Rollovers From Terminated Individual Account Plans—29 CFR 2550.404a-3

Under proposed § 2578.1, as discussed above, if a participant or beneficiary fails to elect a form of benefit distribution, the QTA is required to distribute that person's benefits in the form of a direct rollover into an individual retirement plan (or other account in the case of a rollover on behalf of a non-spousal beneficiary). See § 2578.1(d)(2)(vi)(B). In a different context, the Department previously took the position that the selection of IRA providers and investments for purposes of a default rollover pursuant to a plan provision is a

---

[5] A QTA is not required under this regulation to select an individual retirement plan provider (or other account provider in cases of non-spousal beneficiaries) as of the date it furnishes to participants and beneficiaries the notice described in paragraph (d)(2)(v) of the proposal. The Department, however, believes that efficient QTAs routinely will know who, even at that early juncture, eventually will be the individual retirement plan (or other account) provider, particularly in those cases where the QTA has selected, or intends to select, itself (or an affiliate) to be the individual retirement plan (or other account) provider. Accordingly, in situations in which a QTA, at the time the notice in paragraph (d)(2)(v) is furnished, has selected or knows who it will select to provide individual

retirement plan services (or other account services in the case of non-spousal beneficiaries), such notice also must include an identification of the individual retirement plan (or other account) provider and, if known, a statement of the fees, if any, that will be paid from the participant or beneficiary's individual retirement plan (or other account in the case of non-spousal beneficiaries), such as establishment or maintenance fees. See § 2578.1(d)(2)(v)(A)(5)(ii)&(iii); § 2550.404a-3(e)(v)&(vi).

[6] These Code sections, and regulations thereunder, set forth qualified joint and survivor and qualified preretirement survivor annuity requirements and related notice, election and consent rules.

fiduciary act.[7] The Department, therefore, is concerned that this position, in the absence of guidance regarding ERISA's fiduciary standards in the context of directly rolling over benefits under proposed § 2578.1, could make potential QTAs apprehensive about assuming the status of a QTA, solely for fear of fiduciary liability in connection with such rollovers.

Accordingly, the Department is proposing a fiduciary safe harbor, at 29 CFR 2550.404a-3, for QTAs that roll over distributions pursuant to proposed § 2578.1(d)(2)(vi)(B). This fiduciary safe harbor was modeled on the fiduciary safe harbor recently adopted by the Department for the automatic rollover of mandatory distributions described in section 401(a)(31)(B) of the Code.[8] If the conditions of the safe harbor are met, a QTA would be deemed to have satisfied the requirements of section 404(a) of the Act with respect to both the selection of an individual retirement plan provider (or other account provider in the context of a rollover on behalf of a non-spousal beneficiary) and the investment of the distributed funds.

The safe harbor has three conditions, set forth in paragraph (d) of the proposed regulation. First, each distribution must be rolled over into an individual retirement plan, as defined in section 7701(a)(37) of the Code or, in the case of a distribution on behalf of a non-spousal distributee,[9] to an account (other than an individual retirement plan) maintained by an entity that is eligible to serve as a trustee or issuer of an individual retirement plan. Second, in connection with each such distribution, the QTA and the individual retirement plan provider (or other account provider in the context of a rollover on behalf of a non-spousal beneficiary) must enter into a written agreement that provides that: Rolled-over funds must be invested in an investment product designed to preserve principal and provide a reasonable rate of return, whether or not such return is guaranteed, consistent with liquidity; the investment product selected for the rolled-over funds shall seek to maintain a stable dollar value equal to the amount invested in the product by the individual retirement plan (or other account in the context of a rollover on behalf of a non-spousal beneficiary); fees and expenses attendant to the individual retirement plan (or other account in the context of a rollover on behalf of a non-spousal beneficiary), including investments of such plan, do not exceed certain limits; and, the participant or beneficiary on whose behalf the QTA makes a direct rollover shall have the right to enforce the terms of the contractual agreement establishing the individual retirement plan (or other account in the context of a rollover on behalf of a non-spousal beneficiary), with regard to his or her rolled-over funds, against the individual retirement plan or other account provider. Third, if the QTA designates itself as the transferee of rollover proceeds, such designation must be exempt from the restrictions imposed by section 406 of ERISA pursuant to section 408(a) of ERISA.[10]

The Department, in developing this safe harbor for QTAs of abandoned plans, observed strong similarities between QTAs of abandoned plans and fiduciaries of terminated defined contribution plans generally. In particular, in either situation, the QTA or fiduciary will find that the winding-up process may be severely complicated or even postponed indefinitely if participants or beneficiaries fail to affirmatively elect a form of distribution. In such cases, the responsible decision maker is faced with a choice of either halting the winding-up process or finishing it in the absence of an affirmative direction from a participant or beneficiary regarding the distribution of his or her benefits.

The Department, therefore, has concluded that the sound administration of ERISA is furthered by not limiting the applicability of § 2550.404a-3 to QTAs. Rather, the Department is proposing to make available safe harbor relief to fiduciaries in connection with rollover distributions from any terminated defined contribution plan, without regard to whether the particular plan is considered abandoned pursuant to proposed section 2578.1, whenever the participant or beneficiary on whose behalf the rollover is being made fails to affirmatively elect a form of distribution.

Of course, as with abandoned plans, the safe harbor is not available unless plan fiduciaries satisfy certain notification requirements before making a rollover distribution. See § 2550.404a-3(e).[11] To facilitate

compliance with this notice requirement, the Department has developed a model notice for use by fiduciaries to notify participants and beneficiaries of their distribution options and to request that each such participant or beneficiary elect a form of distribution. This model notice, the use of which would be voluntary, is contained in the appendix to this proposed regulation.

Finally, the Department, after consulting with the IRS, has decided to limit the applicability of the fiduciary safe harbor to rollovers from tax qualified plans. Specifically, with respect to rollover distributions from plans that are not abandoned plans under section 2578.1, such plans must be in compliance with the requirements of section 401(a) of the Code at the time of each rollover distribution. See § 2550.404a-3(a)(2)(ii). In the context of a rollover distribution from an abandoned plan, the safe harbor is available if such plan is intended to be maintained as a tax-qualified plan in accordance with the requirements of section 401(a) of the Code, even if such plan is not operationally qualified at the time of a rollover distribution pursuant to section 2578.1. See § 2550.404a-3(a)(2)(i). The Department invites comments on whether the safe harbor should be made available to fiduciaries for rollovers from arrangements described in section 403 of the Code, where such arrangements are covered by title I of ERISA.

Overview of Proposed Reporting Regulation—29 CFR 2520.103-13

Several witnesses before the Advisory Council's Working Group on Orphan Plans testified that, in order to be successful, a program for terminating and winding up abandoned plans must include relief from the annual reporting requirements in section 103 of ERISA. In this regard the Advisory Council recommended the creation of special reporting rules for abandoned plans, placing emphasis on relief from the requirement to engage an independent qualified public accountant. The Council also recommended that the Department make clear the extent to which the QTA, rather than the plan administrator (within the meaning of section 3(16) of ERISA), would be responsible for missing or deficient annual reports for plan years preceding the year in which the plan is deemed terminated.

The Department is proposing to add to part 2520 of the Code of Federal Regulations a new section 2520.103-13 to provide annual reporting relief relating to abandoned plan filings by QTAs. This proposed regulation addresses the content, timing, and method of filing rules for the reporting requirement imposed on qualified termination administrators pursuant to proposed 29 CFR 2578.1(d)(2)(vii). In addition to basic identifying information of the plan and QTA, the report would, as proposed, be required to specify the plan's total assets as of a particular date, termination expenses paid by the plan, and the total amount of distributions, along with other relevant information. This report would be required to be filed within 2 months after the month in which all of the plan's affairs have been completed (except for the requirements in 29 CFR 2578.1(d)(2)(vii) and (viii)). This report would be required to be filed on the Form 5500 in accordance with the special instructions for abandoned plans terminated pursuant to 29 CFR 2578.1. The filing of this report with the Department would be accomplished when a report meeting the requirements of proposed section 2520.103-13 is furnished to the Department as an attachment to the notice described in section 2578.1(d)(2)(viii).

Paragraph (e) of proposed 2520.103-13 is intended to address concerns regarding the responsibilities of QTAs under part 1 of title I of ERISA. This paragraph clarifies that a QTA is not subject to the generally applicable reporting requirements in part 1 of title I of ERISA, and that the filing of a report in accordance with this section does not relieve the plan's administrator (within the meaning of section 3(16) of ERISA) of any obligation it has under ERISA. Similarly, any failure by the QTA to meet the requirements of 29 CFR 2520.103-13 does not for that reason make the QTA subject to the requirements of part 1 of title I of ERISA, although it would prevent compliance with section 2578.1.

Effective Date

The Department is considering making these three proposed regulations, i.e., sections 2578.1, 2550.404a-3, and 2520.103-13, effective 60

---

[7] See Rev. Rul. 2000-36, n. 1, where the Department stated that the selection of an IRA trustee, custodian or issuer and IRA investment for purposes of a default rollover pursuant to a plan provision would constitute a fiduciary act under ERISA; see also EBSA Field Assistance Bulletin 2004-02 (Sept. 30, 2004).

[8] See 69 FR 58018 (Sept. 28, 2004).

[9] See 26 CFR 1.402(c)-2, Q&A—12.

[10] Section 406 of the Act prohibits certain transactions involving plans and parties in interest with respect to those plans. Pursuant to section 408(a) of ERISA, the Department may grant an exemption from the restrictions imposed by section 406 of ERISA upon finding that such exemption is administratively feasible, in the interests of the plan and its

participants and beneficiaries and protective of the rights of participants and beneficiaries. The Department is publishing a proposed class exemption in today's Federal Register that is intended to deal with prohibited transactions resulting from a QTA's selection of itself as the provider of an individual retirement plan (or other account provider in the context of a rollover on behalf of a non-spousal beneficiary) and/or issuer of an investment held by such plan.

[11] The Department notes that the notice requirement in paragraph (e) of the proposed safe harbor does not relieve a plan administrator of its obligation to notify participants or beneficiaries of their rights under section 402(f) of the Code. Section 402(f) notification should be included in, or attached to, the notice described in paragraph (e) of this proposed safe harbor.

days after the date of publication of final rules in the Federal Register. The Department invites comments on whether the final regulations should be made effective on an earlier or later date.

Regulatory Impact Analysis

Summary

This regulatory initiative consists of three proposed regulations. One proposal, entitled Rules and Regulations for Abandoned Plans, establishes procedures and standards for the termination of, and distribution of benefits from, an abandoned pension plan. The second proposal, entitled Safe Harbor for Rollovers From Terminated Individual Account Plans, provides relief from ERISA's fiduciary responsibility rules in connection with a rollover distribution on behalf of a missing or unresponsive plan participant. The last proposal, entitled Special Terminal Report for Abandoned Plans, provides annual reporting relief for terminated abandoned plans.

Rules and Regulations for Abandoned Plans (29 CFR 2578.1)

The standards and procedures set forth in this proposed regulation are intended to facilitate the voluntary, safe, and efficient termination of individual account plans that have been abandoned and to increase the likelihood that participants and beneficiaries will receive the greatest retirement benefit practicable under the circumstances. Participants and beneficiaries that had previously been denied access to their benefits because there was no authority willing or able to assume responsibility for the abandoned plan will be able to direct the QTA concerning the distribution of their account balances as permitted under the terms of the plan and federal regulations.

Without this regulation, plans that have been abandoned by a plan sponsor might eventually be terminated through government enforcement or other legal action. However, information gathered by the Advisory Council's Working Group suggests that more often the assets of abandoned plans continue to be diminished by ongoing administrative expenses at the same time that participants and beneficiaries are denied access to their benefits. The Department assumes for purposes of its analysis of the impact of these proposed rules that most plans that would currently meet the criteria for a finding of abandonment would remain abandoned without the establishment of a regulatory framework and specific standards and procedures such as those described in this proposed regulation. It is also assumed that an accumulated number of plans meeting the criteria for abandonment would be terminated and wound up pursuant to these rules, and that a smaller number of plans would become abandoned and terminated in future years.

Although certain costs will be incurred and paid from plan assets in the course of the termination and winding up of abandoned plans pursuant to this regulation, the qualitative and quantitative benefits of the regulation are expected to be both numerous and substantial. The most significant qualitative benefit of the regulation will arise from the facilitation of the voluntary termination of abandoned plans. It is assumed, for purposes of cost estimates presented here, that all fees and expenses for terminating an abandoned plan, to the extent that they are reasonable, will be charged to the plan.

Absent the proposed regulation, the persons or other entities holding assets of abandoned plans would not in most cases have the authority or incentive to see that such plans are terminated and that benefits are distributed to participants and beneficiaries. The specificity of the proposed standards and procedures, along with provisions that limit the liability of the QTA in certain circumstances, will support the rights of participants and beneficiaries by establishing the authority and incentive for a QTA to wind up the affairs of an abandoned plan. The requirements pertaining to the timing and content of notices to the Department and to the participants and beneficiaries, as well as guidance that addresses the obligations of the QTA with respect to the condition of plan records, selection and monitoring of service providers, payment of fees and expenses, and requirements for plan amendments and continued tax qualification, will serve to protect the benefits of affected participants and beneficiaries in the course of the termination and winding up of abandoned plans.

The termination of plans that would otherwise remain abandoned also has quantitative economic implications. The termination of these plans in accordance with the regulation would serve to maximize the benefits ultimately payable to participants and beneficiaries in two important ways. First, termination would preclude the ongoing payment of administrative expenses that diminish assets but only minimally contribute to the management of the plan. In addition, the

specific standards and procedures of the proposed regulation would limit the costs that would otherwise be associated with plan termination. Each of these in turn would moderate the extent to which individual account balances of the abandoned plan would be drawn upon for plan administration.

Costs will be incurred and paid from plan assets to wind up the affairs of abandoned plans. However, these costs are meaningful only in the context of the savings of administrative expenses that would otherwise have continued to be paid indefinitely absent the termination. An assessment of the net effect of the termination cost and administrative savings is complicated by the fact that the cost is incurred once, while the savings would occur repeatedly in future years of what would otherwise be continuing abandonment.

In analyzing the costs and potential savings, and relying on available data and certain assumptions described in detail later in this discussion, the Department compared the aggregate projected termination costs of an estimated number of potentially abandoned plans with the present value of future ongoing administrative costs for those plans. This comparison shows that while the termination costs exceed administrative savings in the year of termination, by the end of the next year and thereafter, the termination has prevented the payment of a significantly greater aggregate expense, resulting in a substantial preservation of retirement benefits.

In the absence of direct measures for the number of abandoned plans, the Department, based on Form 5500 data and certain assumptions, estimates that there are approximately 4,000 abandoned plans at present.[12] Assuming 4,000 abandoned plans, and based on Form 5500 data and certain assumptions concerning ordinary plan termination expenses and typical annual administrative expenses, the Department estimates that the aggregate termination cost for those abandoned plans amounts to $8.4 million, while one year of ongoing administrative costs would amount to $7.7 million. However, by the end of the next following year, termination will have had the effect of saving $6.6 million. In other words, the net benefit in administrative cost savings for facilitating termination of abandoned plans would be $6.6 million for plans that would have remained abandoned for two years. If these plans remained abandoned for five years, it is estimated that the net benefit of facilitating termination would exceed $27 million.

These net benefits represent plan assets preserved for retirement benefits.

These estimates are, however, based on what is known about average ordinary administrative expenses and the way those expenses compare with plan termination costs. The Department has crafted the proposed regulation with the intention of increasing efficiency and significantly reducing the administrative cost of terminating abandoned plans through specificity as to procedures, timing, obligations pertaining to records, selection and monitoring of service providers, payment of fees and expenses, plan amendments, tax qualification issues, and reporting. The Department has also proposed models for required notices in an effort to increase efficiency and reduce the cost of termination. The cost for completing and mailing notices for currently abandoned plans is estimated at $652,300; additional annual costs for plans that become abandoned in the future are $87,340. These costs are explained more fully in the section of the preamble related to the Paperwork Reduction Act.

Because the circumstances of abandoned plans are thought to vary considerably, the estimates of savings in termination costs that might arise from efficiency gains are subject to some uncertainty. However, each 10% reduction in the cost of termination is estimated to produce savings in excess of $800,000. Assuming that the specific provisions of the proposed regulation would increase efficiency and reduce costs by at least 20%, about $1.7 million in termination costs would be saved, further preserving retirement benefits for participants and beneficiaries of currently abandoned plans. In this circumstance, the benefits of these terminations exceed their administrative costs by about $900,000 in the year of termination. Similar effects will be seen for the somewhat smaller number of plans that become abandoned from year to year.

It is estimated that the net benefit of the proposed regulation might vary considerably relative to actual efficiency gains and the duration of plan abandonment. For plans potentially abandoned at this time, this net benefit is expected to range from at least $900,000, to $6.6 million if abandonment continued for a year beyond the year of termination, to $27 million if abandonment continued for four years beyond the year of termination. In future years, termination of an additional 1,650 plans

---

[12] Testimony before the Advisory Council suggests that the number of abandoned plans might be nearer to 2%. If this witness's experience is representative, approximately 11,700 plans could be considered abandoned plans.

annually is expected to result in a net benefit ranging from about $400,000, to $2.7 million at the year beyond the year of termination, to $14.5 million at the fourth year beyond the year of termination. A more detailed discussion of the data, assumptions, and methodology underlying this analysis will be found below.

Safe Harbor for Rollovers From Terminated Individual Account Plans (29 CFR 2550.404a-3)

In addition to plans that are terminated by a QTA because of abandonment, other individual account plans may terminate as a result of a plan sponsor's voluntary decision to discontinue the plan. Similar to a QTA's experience with abandoned plans, a plan administrator or service provider responsible for distributing assets from individual accounts may find that certain participants and beneficiaries fail to elect a form of distribution because they are either missing or unresponsive. In order to select an institution and an investment for rolling over account balances of missing or unresponsive participants or beneficiaries, fiduciaries would benefit from a safe harbor that will limit their liability under section 404(a) of ERISA. Accordingly, fiduciaries that comply with the requirements of this proposed regulation will be deemed to have complied with section 404(a) of ERISA in connection with a rollover from a terminated plan, including an abandoned plan, into an individual retirement plan or other account.

Costs related to establishing individual retirement plans and other accounts and selecting institutions and investments for rolled over accounts, have been accounted for in the Department's regulation on Fiduciary Responsibility Under the Employee Retirement Income Security Act of 1974 Automatic Rollover Safe Harbor (69 FR 58018). The cost for the proposed regulation is attributable only to the Notice to Participants that must be provided to affected participants and beneficiaries informing them about the termination and the need to make an election concerning the distribution of their benefits. The cost for the Notice to Participants in currently abandoned plans is estimated at $207,800. Annual costs for notifying the 56,500 participants in terminating plans, including abandoned plans, estimated to be missing or unresponsive on an ongoing basis are $149,500.

Qualitative benefits will accrue to fiduciaries that rollover accounts under this proposed regulation through greater certainty and reduced exposure to risk, and to former participants through regulatory standards concerning: individual retirement plan or other account providers; investment products, including preservation of principal, rates of return, and liquidity; fees and expenses; and, disclosure.

Special Terminal Report for Abandoned Plans (29 CFR 2520.103-13)

The proposed regulation simplifies the content, timing, and method for final reporting by a QTA to the Department. No cost has been attributed to this proposed regulation, nor has the benefit been estimated.

Executive Order 12866 Statement

Under Executive Order 12866, the Department must determine whether a regulatory action is "significant" and therefore subject to the requirements of the Executive Order and subject to review by the Office of Management and Budget (OMB). Under section 3(f) of the Executive Order, a "significant regulatory action" is an action that is likely to result in a rule (1) having an annual effect on the economy of $100 million or more, or adversely and materially affecting a sector of the economy, productivity, competition, jobs, the environment, public health or safety, or State, local or tribal governments or communities (also referred to as "economically significant"); (2) creating serious inconsistency or otherwise interfering with an action taken or planned by another agency; (3) materially altering the budgetary impacts of entitlement grants, user fees, or loan programs or the rights and obligations of recipients thereof; or (4) raising novel or policy issues arising out of legal mandates, the President's priorities, or the principles set forth in the Executive Order. OMB has determined that this action is significant under section 3(f)(4) because it raises novel legal or policy issues arising from the President's priorities. Accordingly, the Department has undertaken an analysis of the costs and benefits of the proposed regulations. OMB has reviewed this regulatory action. Costs

Rules and Regulations for Abandoned Plans (29 CFR 2578.1)

Under the proposed regulation, individual account plans that are found to be abandoned will incur certain costs and fees in connection with the termination and winding up of the plan. These expenses include, among others, the costs associated with determining whether the plan is, in fact, abandoned, as well as notifying participants and the government of the abandonment. There may also be expenses associated with updating records, distributing benefits, and reporting.

The total expense will arise from the number of plans abandoned. However, the actual number of abandoned plans is not known. To estimate for purposes of this analysis the number of plans that might be abandoned, the Department examined the contribution and distribution activity of individual account pension plans as reported on Form 5500 filings. This information would not by itself indicate whether any plan was abandoned; nor do Form 5500 filings indicate that a plan is abandoned. It is assumed, however, that a QTA would normally have access to more information about a specific plan than can be extracted from Form 5500 data. Nonetheless, Form 5500 data was considered the only source of information for approximating a number of plans that could be considered abandoned based on contribution and distribution activity.

To arrive at its estimate, the Department reviewed the number of plans that filed a Form 5500 in 1999 indicating that no contributions had been received by the plan and no distributions had been made to participants or beneficiaries. Reports by these same filers were compared for each year from 2000 to 2002 in order to determine whether there had been contributions to or distributions from those plans. The Department considered plans to be potentially abandoned for the purpose of this analysis if neither form of activity was present throughout this period. The Department has used this methodology for its estimate of the number of potentially abandoned plans because preliminary analyses of Form 5500 data for plans without contributions and distributions in only a 12-consecutive-month period showed that a portion of those plans resumed activity or terminated in subsequent years. This methodology is merely thought to produce a reasonable estimate that allows for observed variations in plan financial activity from year to year; it does not bear on the actual requirements of a QTA with respect to a finding of abandonment set out in the proposed rules.

This approach yielded an estimate of about 4,000 plans that may be currently abandoned. Because witnesses before the Working Group indicated that most plans were small plans with 20 or fewer participants, it is estimated that the 4,000 plans include 78,500 participants. Other analysis of Form 5500 data suggests that, going forward, an estimated 1,650 plans, with 33,000 participants, and an estimated $868 million in assets, may be abandoned annually. These estimates do not include any abandoned plans that did not file in 1999 or later.

Using the Form 5500 to estimate the number of plans that may have been abandoned results in a fair degree of uncertainty. The fact that a plan has filed an annual report indicates that certain obligations are being met with regard to administration of the plan and that there may be other circumstances that would explain a lack of financial activity. For example, a lack of contributions or distributions from a profit sharing plan may not necessarily indicate that the plan has been abandoned. Testimony by service providers before the Working Group and information gathered under NEPOP indicate, however, that continued administrative activity does not mean that a plan is not abandoned. It is also possible that additional efforts by a QTA in connection with a potential finding of abandonment would reveal that any given plan did not meet the standard for a finding of abandonment. The number of plans actually abandoned, and therefore the number of participants in those plans, may be lower. While each of these factors introduces uncertainty into the estimates, without the advantage of additional information available to a QTA that makes a timely inquiry into the activities of a potentially abandoned plan, the Department believes it is reasonable to rely on the 4,000 plans that showed no activity with regard to contributions or distributions over a four-year period, and the 1,650 plans expected to be abandoned on an annual basis going forward, for reasonable approximations of the number of abandoned plans that might be terminated pursuant to these rules.

The Department has estimated the net impact of the proposed regulation by comparing the ongoing administrative costs for maintaining an abandoned plan with the cost for terminating such a plan. The Department has assumed that termination costs will be significantly affected by the degree to which plan administration was maintained following abandonment. There is expected to be an inverse relationship between ongoing administrative costs and termination costs of abandoned plans, such that a well-maintained plan would be less costly to terminate, and a less-well-maintained plan would be relatively more costly to terminate. Where service providers to the plan have continued to fulfill their contractual obligations, and participants in these more well-maintained plans can be located, the costs for terminating such plans are assumed to be at the lower end of a range. At the higher end of the range are abandoned plans that have not been administered consistent with ERISA's standards, such as where reporting and recordkeeping activities have been discontinued.

Based on available information regarding plans in general, the ongoing administrative costs for abandoned plans are estimated to range from approximately $900 to $3,000 per plan annually, or $3.5 million to

$11.8 million annually for 4,000 currently abandoned plans. Testimony before the Working Group indicated that terminating an abandoned plan can add ten percent to the ordinary expenses related to plan administration. As such, termination costs are expected to range from $1,000 to $3,300 per plan, or $3.9 million to $13 million for all potentially abandoned plans. Weighting the number of abandoned plans equally between those that have been more and less actively administered produces an aggregate annual administrative cost for 4,000 abandoned plans of approximately $7.7 million; the one-time cost to terminate these same plans would be $8.4 million based on these assumptions. Similarly, the annual administrative costs for the 1,650 plans estimated to be abandoned annually is estimated at $3.2 million; while the one-time termination cost would be $3.5 million. The actual proportions of more and less actively administered plans may be different from those assumed.

Although this aspect of the analysis suggests that termination is more costly than ongoing administration, the future savings of ongoing expenses that result from termination will continue through the entire period that the plan would otherwise have remained abandoned. Because costs and savings occur in different years, a single-year comparison of expenses does not adequately account for the net impact of termination under these proposed regulations, as is addressed in the discussion of benefits that follows.

The Department expects that one-time termination costs may in fact be less than one year's ongoing administrative expense as a result of its efforts in these proposed regulations to increase efficiency through establishment of specific standards and procedures, and through clarifying and limiting the responsibilities and liabilities of the QTA. The aggregate termination cost savings that would arise from this greater efficiency is subject to uncertainty. However, each 10% reduction in the cost of termination is assumed to produce savings in excess of $800,000. Assuming that the provisions of these proposed regulations would increase efficiency and reduce costs by at least 20%, $1.7 million in termination costs would be saved, and total one-time termination costs would amount to $6.7 million. Savings of about $700,000 would arise from greater efficiency in terminating plans abandoned in future years, reducing ongoing estimated termination costs from $3.5 million to $2.8 million.

Finally, the Department has estimated the cost for a QTA to complete the notices required to be furnished to the Department, plan sponsor, and participants at $652,300 for currently abandoned plans. Future costs for notices for the 1,650 plans estimated to be abandoned on an annual basis are $87,340. These costs are explained in more detail in the Paperwork Reduction Act section of the preamble.

Safe Harbor for Rollovers From Terminated Individual Account Plans (29 CFR 2550.404a-3)

The safe harbor in section 2550.404a-3 requires the furnishing of a notification to participants and beneficiaries informing them of the termination and the options available for the distribution of assets in an account. The number of notices to be sent and the cost for these notices is based on the number of missing or non-responsive individuals whose account balances are likely to be rolled over by a fiduciary.

Based on data about terminating plans that are not abandoned plans from the year 2000 Form 5500 Annual Report, the Department estimates that, annually, there are 2.3 million participants and beneficiaries in terminating plans. Although the number that will fail to make an election concerning distribution of the assets in their account balances is not known, other information about participants and beneficiaries in defined benefit plans has led the Department to assume that the number is approximately 1%, or 23,500 annually. As such, in order to take advantage of the safe harbor under section 404(a), plan administrators will be required to furnish 23,500 Notices to Participants. The cost for these notices, at 2 minutes per notice and $.38 each for mailing, is $62,170.

Special Terminal Report for Abandoned Plans (29 CFR 2520.103-13)

There are no costs attributable to the changes in annual reporting for abandoned plans in the proposed regulation. Simplified reporting represents a benefit to abandoned plans, as explained below. Benefits

Rules and Regulations for Abandoned Plans (29 CFR 2578.1)

The proposed regulation would have qualitative and quantitative benefits. The standards and procedures set forth here are intended to facilitate the voluntary, safe, and efficient termination of individual account pension plans that have been abandoned, and to increase the likelihood that participants and beneficiaries will receive the greatest retirement benefit practicable under the circumstances.

The most significant qualitative benefit of the regulation will arise from the facilitation of the voluntary termination of abandoned plans.

Absent the proposed standards and procedures, along with provisions that limit the liability of the QTA in certain circumstances, the persons or other entities holding assets of abandoned plans would not in most cases have the authority or incentive to see that such plans are terminated in accordance with applicable requirements, and that benefits are distributed to participants and beneficiaries.

The termination of abandoned plans upon adoption of the regulation would allow participants and beneficiaries that have been unable to access their benefits to elect, according to procedures established by the QTA, a form of distribution for the balance in their individual accounts. The requirements addressing the obligations of the QTA with regard to winding up the affairs of an abandoned plan will serve to protect the benefits of affected participants and beneficiaries in the course of the termination and winding up process. Benefits ultimately payable to participants and beneficiaries are maximized in two important ways. First, termination would preclude the ongoing payment of administrative expenses that diminish assets but only minimally contribute to the management of the plan. In addition, the specific standards and procedures of the proposed regulation would limit the costs that would otherwise be associated with plan termination. Each of these in turn would moderate the extent to which benefits were drawn upon for plan administration.

Costs to be paid from plan assets to wind up the affairs of abandoned plans are meaningful only in the context of the savings of administrative expenses that would otherwise have continued to be paid absent the termination. A comparison of the termination cost with administrative savings is complicated by the fact that the cost is incurred once, while the savings would be incurred repeatedly throughout the years the plan would have been abandoned. To address this timing difference, the Department has estimated the present value of future ongoing administrative expenses using a 3% discount rate over a period from one year after the year of termination to five years after termination. The actual duration of abandonment cannot be determined with certainty; however, a period from one to five years is thought to offer a reasonable illustration of potential administrative cost savings that could arise in future years from the termination of abandoned plans.

The comparison of estimated termination costs of $8.4 million with the present value of future administrative costs discounted over the range of durations noted above shows that while the termination costs exceed the $7.7 million savings in the year of termination, the present value of administrative expenses to be paid in the year following termination exceeds the estimated termination cost by $6.6 million, resulting in a substantial preservation of retirement benefits. The present value of administrative expenses estimated to be paid over the five years following termination exceeds the termination cost by $27 million. Similarly, the cost of termination of the 1,650 plans assumed to be abandoned each year would be slightly greater than ongoing costs in the year of termination, but termination would have had the effect of saving over $2.8 million by the end of the next year, and $11.6 million if the plans remained abandoned for five years. These net benefits would also represent plan assets preserved for retirement benefits.

As noted earlier, the estimates of savings in termination costs that might arise from efficiency gains are subject to some uncertainty. However, each 10% reduction in the cost of termination of existing plans that are potentially abandoned is assumed to produce savings in excess of $800,000. Assuming that the specific provisions of the proposed regulation would increase efficiency and reduce costs by at least 20%, an additional $1.7 million in termination costs would be saved, further preserving retirement benefits for participants and beneficiaries of currently abandoned plans. In this circumstance, the benefits of these terminations exceed their costs by about $900,000 in the year of termination. Efficiency gains for the 1,650 plans that become abandoned from year to year are expected to amount to $710,000, such that the benefits of termination of these abandoned plans exceed their termination costs by about $400,000.

Safe Harbor for Rollovers From Terminated Individual Account Plans (29 CFR 2550.404a-3)

By providing a safe harbor for plan fiduciaries that roll over individual account balances, the Department has increased certainty concerning compliance with ERISA section 404(a) for fiduciaries that designate institutions and investment products for rolled over accounts and has expanded the opportunity for retirement savings for plan participants. The benefits of greater certainty to fiduciaries under the safe harbor, and of savings protection for participants, cannot be specifically quantified. The proposed regulation will provide qualitative benefits to fiduciaries by affording them greater assurance of compliance and reduced exposure to risk; the substantive conditions of the safe harbor will likewise benefit former participants by directing their retirement savings to individual retirement plan and other account providers, regulated financial institutions, and investment products that minimize risk and offer preservation of principal and liquidity. The Department welcomes comments on the data, assumptions, and estimates presented in this analysis.

Special Terminal Report for Abandoned Plans (29 CFR 2520.103-13)

The proposed regulation provides simplified annual reporting to the Department for QTAs that wind up the affairs of an abandoned plan. The time-savings resulting from abbreviated reporting requirements will reduce administrative costs to abandoned plans and increase benefits to participants and beneficiaries.

Paperwork Reduction Act

As part of its continuing effort to reduce paperwork and respondent burden, the Department of Labor conducts a preclearance consultation program to provide the general public and Federal agencies with an opportunity to comment on proposed and continuing collections of information in accordance with the Paperwork Reduction Act of 1995 (PRA 95) (44 U.S.C. 3506(c)(2)(A)). This helps to ensure that requested data will be provided in the desired format, reporting burden (time and financial resources) is minimized, collection instruments are clearly understood, and the impact of collection requirements on respondents can be properly assessed.

Currently, the Department is soliciting comments concerning the information collection request (ICR) included in the Proposed Regulations on Termination of Abandoned Individual Account Plans (29 CFR 2578.1), the Safe Harbor for Rollovers From Terminated Individual Account Plans (29 CFR 2550.404a-3), and the Proposed Class Exemption for Services Provided in Connection with the Termination of Abandoned Individual Account Plans. A copy of the ICR may be obtained by contacting the person listed in the PRA Addressee section below.

The Department has submitted a copy of the proposed information collection to OMB in accordance with 44 U.S.C. 3507(d) for review of its information collections. The Department and OMB are particularly interested in comments that:

Evaluate whether the proposed collection of information is necessary for the proper performance of the functions of the agency, including whether the information will have practical utility;

Evaluate the accuracy of the agency's estimate of the burden of the collection of information, including the validity of the methodology and assumptions used;

Enhance the quality, utility, and clarity of the information to be collected; and

Minimize the burden of the collection of information on those who are to respond, including through the use of appropriate automated, electronic, mechanical, or other technological collection techniques or other forms of information technology, e.g., permitting electronic submission of responses.

Comments should be sent to the Office of Information and Regulatory Affairs, Office of Management and Budget, Room 10235, New Executive Office Building, Washington, DC 20503; Attention: Desk Officer for the Employee Benefits Security Administration. Although comments may be submitted through May 9, 2005 OMB requests that comments be received within 30 days of publication of the Notice of Proposed Rulemaking to ensure their consideration.

PRA Addressee: Address requests for copies of the ICR to Gerald B. Lindrew, Office of Policy and Research, U.S. Department of Labor, Employee Benefits Security Administration, 200 Constitution Avenue, NW., Room N-5647, Washington, DC 20210. Telephone: (202) 693-8410; Fax: (202) 219-5333. These are not toll-free numbers.

The burden estimates for this ICR are derived from notice requirements in two proposed regulations and a recordkeeping requirement in a proposed class exemption as follows: the Regulations for Abandoned Plans (29 CFR 2578.1); the Safe Harbor for Rollovers From Terminated Individual Account Plans (29 CFR 2550.404a-3) (together, "terminating plans"); and, the Proposed Class Exemption for Services Provided in Connection with the Termination of Abandoned Individual Account Plans. A Notice to Participants is required under two of the proposed regulations. The burden for all other notices is attributable only to the Regulations for Abandoned Plans. No burden has been estimated for the third proposed regulation, Special Terminal Report for Abandoned Plans (29 CFR 2520.103-13), because the proposal simplifies ERISA annual reporting requirements for abandoned plans. All burdens under the two proposed regulations are considered cost burdens because a terminating plan will most likely use a service provider or a QTA to inform participants, plan sponsors, and the Department about the

termination. The burden under the proposed exemption is an hour burden.

Terminating Plans

Terminating plans that roll over the account balances of participants and beneficiaries that are either missing or unresponsive, must, in order to take advantage of the safe harbor under 29 CFR 2550.404a-3 of ERISA, send to participants and beneficiaries a notice that includes information about their right to elect a form of distribution for their benefits.

Notice to Participants (29 CFR 2578.1(d)(2)(v) and (29 CFR 2550.404a-3(e))

Fiduciaries that terminate plans are required to notify participants and beneficiaries about such terminations and the need to elect a form of distribution for the assets in their accounts. The Department has provided two models for this notice, only one of which will require completion, depending on whether the plan is an abandoned plan. At 2 minutes per notice, the cost to complete 78,500 notices for currently abandoned plans is $177,933. Mailing costs, at $.38 per notice, are $29,830.

Ongoing costs for completing and mailing 33,000 notices to participants and beneficiaries in 1,650 plans estimated to be abandoned annually in the future, as well as to 23,500 missing or unresponsive participants and beneficiaries in terminated plans that are not abandoned plans, are estimated at $149,500 for a total of 56,500 Notices to Participants.

Rules and Regulations for Abandoned Plans (29 CFR 2578.1)

The information collection provisions of these rules are intended: To ensure that, in the case of an abandoned plan, a plan sponsor has been determined to be unavailable to fulfill its responsibilities to the plan before further action is taken by a QTA; to facilitate federal oversight of the actions taken by a QTA in winding up the affairs of an abandoned plan; to ensure that participants and beneficiaries are apprised of actions that might affect their rights and benefits under the plan; and to provide for a final notice and reporting regarding the resolution of the affairs of the plan. The Department has included model notices that may be used to satisfy these notice requirements, and has provided for reporting in the format of the Form 5500, for purposes of minimizing compliance burden.

As described in detail earlier, the Department assumes that there are currently 4,000 abandoned plans with 78,500 participants, and that in each future year, 1,650 plans with a total of 33,000 participants will become abandoned.

Most tasks involved in normal plan administration, such as calculating or distributing benefits, recordkeeping, and reporting are not accounted for as burden in this proposed regulation because they are either part of the usual business practices of plans, or have already been accounted for in ICRs for other statutory and regulatory provisions under Title I of ERISA.

The proposed regulation requires that a QTA notify, at different times and under different circumstances: the plan sponsor, or, if unable to do so, service providers that might know the whereabouts of the plan sponsor; the Department; and, participants and beneficiaries of the plan. Because the termination and winding up of an abandoned plan will be performed by a QTA or other service providers that will develop and distribute the required notices and report, the burden for this collection of information is considered a cost burden. Hourly costs are estimated at $68 per hour for a QTA. Supplies and postage costs include: regular mail, $.38; certified mail, $2.68; certified mail, return receipt requested, $4.43. The costs for the notices that make up the ICR in the proposed regulations, for both the 4,000 currently abandoned plans and the 1,650 plans estimated to be abandoned annually in the future, are analyzed below.

Notice of Intent to Terminate (paragraph (b)(5)). The Department has provided a model notice of intent to terminate, which is sent by a QTA to the sponsor of a plan that the QTA suspects is abandoned. The QTA will add to the model, identifying information about the plan sponsor and the QTA. The notice is estimated to require 2 minutes of a QTA's time per letter for a cost of $9,067 for the 4,000 currently abandoned plans. Mailing costs for the 4,000 currently abandoned plans amount to $4.43 for each notice or a total of $17,720. Prospective annual costs for QTA time and mailings for 1,650 plans are estimated to be $11,050.

Notice to Plan Sponsor Sent to Current Address (paragraph (b)(4)). If the Notice of Intent to Terminate was not acknowledged as received by the plan sponsor (or its agent) at the address known to the QTA, the QTA must contact known service providers to the plan in an attempt to obtain a current address for the plan sponsor. If any service provider responds to the QTA with a current address for the plan sponsor, the QTA must re-send the Notice of Intent to Terminate to the new address provided by the service provider(s). Because there is no relevant data for estimating the number of notices that may be required to be sent to additional addresses, the Department has assumed that all plans will be required to send one such notice. Mailing costs for the 4,000 currently abandoned plans are $4.43 for each notice, or $17,720. Prospective annual mailing costs for 1,650 plans are $7,310.

Notice to the Department (paragraph (c)(3)). Once a QTA has found that a plan has been abandoned, it notifies the Department of the abandonment and its intention to serve as a QTA. A model notice has been provided that is to be completed by the QTA. A QTA will require an estimated 75 minutes to complete the model form at a cost of $350,720. Mailing is expected to be by certified mail, at $2.68 each, or $10,720 for 4,000 plans. Ongoing annual costs for preparation and mailing for 1,650 plans are estimated at $144,672.

Final Notice (paragraph (d)(2)(viii)). Upon payment of all plan expenses and distribution of assets, the QTA is required to notify the Office of Enforcement, EBSA, that all benefits have been distributed in accordance with the regulation. If fees and expenses paid by the QTA (or its affiliate) exceed by 20 percent the QTA's initial estimate of costs, the amount of increased fees and expenses, along with an explanation for the increase, are to be included in the Final Notice. QTAs will require an estimated ten minutes to complete the notice at a cost of $45,300 for 4,000 plans. Mailing, including the cost of the Terminal Report that will be filed with the Final Notice, is estimated at $1.00 for a cost of $4,000. Estimated annual costs for future abandoned plans are $20,350 for 1,650 plans.

Safe Harbor for Rollovers From Terminated Individual Account Plans (29 CFR 2550.404a-3)

Written Agreement (paragraph (d)(2)). A fiduciary that rolls over assets from an individual account plan into an individual retirement plan or other account must enter into a written agreement with the individual retirement plan or other account provider. The agreement must include provisions related to investment products, rates of return, and fees and expenses among other requirements. The Department understands that it is customary business practice for agreements related to the establishment of individual retirement plans or other accounts to be set forth in writing and that no new burden is created by this requirement.

Special Terminal Report for Abandoned Plans (29 CFR 2520.103-13)

The rules and regulations described in section 2520.103-13 of the proposed regulation would establish a simplified method for filing a Terminal Report for abandoned individual account plans. The Terminal Report is required to be sent to EBSA along with the Final Notice. No cost is estimated for completing the special Terminal Report because it is assumed that this report will be less burdensome than the annual report that would otherwise be required to be filed by a plan.

Proposed Exemption

Under the proposed regulation on Termination of Abandoned Individual Account Plans, a QTA that terminates an abandoned plan would be permitted to distribute participant or beneficiary account balances by rolling them over into an individual retirement plan or other account. The proposed exemption, also published in today's Federal Register, among other provisions, provides relief from the restrictions of section 406(a)(1)(A) through (D), 406(b)(1) and (b)(2) of ERISA and from the taxes imposed by section 4975(a) and (b) of the Code, by reason of section 4975(c)(1)(A) through (E) of the Code, for QTAs of plans that have been abandoned to select and pay themselves or an affiliate for services to the plans. In addition, for participants or beneficiaries that are missing or nonresponsive, a QTA would be permitted to: Designate itself or an affiliate as provider of an individual retirement plan or other account for the rolled over balance; select a proprietary investment product as the initial investment; and, pay itself or the affiliate fees in connection with the rollover. In order to ensure that the records necessary to determine whether the conditions of the proposed exemption have been met and are available for examination by participants, the IRS, and the Department, the Department has included a condition in the proposed exemption requiring a QTA to maintain such records for a period of six years.

Banks, insurance companies, and other financial institutions that provide services to abandoned plans and their participants and beneficiaries will act in accordance with customary business practices, which would include maintaining the records required under the terms of the proposed class exemption. Accordingly, the recordkeeping burden attributable to the proposed exemption will be handled by the QTA and is expected to be small. Assuming that all QTAs will take advantage of

the proposed exemption, and that each abandoned plan will have a separate QTA, the start up hour burden attributable to recordkeeping for QTAs of currently abandoned plans, at one hour for each QTA, is 4,000 hours; the on-going hour burden for QTAs of plans that may be abandoned in the future is 1,650 hours annually.

Type of Review: New collection.

Agency: Employee Benefits Security Administration, Department of Labor.

Title: Notices for Terminated Individual Account Plans.

OMB Number: 1210-0NEW.

Affected public: Individuals or households; business or other for-profit; not-for-profit institutions.

Respondents: 10,123.

Responses: 157,590.

Frequency of Response: On occasion.

Estimated Total Burden Hours: 5,650.

Total Annualized Capital/Startup Costs: $652,300.

Total Burden Cost (Operating and Maintenance): $333,000.

Total Annualized Costs: $985,300.

Regulatory Flexibility Act

The Regulatory Flexibility Act (5 U.S.C. 601 et seq.) (RFA) imposes certain requirements with respect to Federal rules that are subject to the notice and comment requirements of section 553(b) of the Administrative Procedure Act (5 U.S.C. 551 et seq.) and which are likely to have a significant economic impact on a substantial number of small entities. Unless an agency determines that a proposed rule is not likely to have a significant economic impact on a substantial number of small entities, section 603 of the RFA requires that the agency present an initial regulatory flexibility analysis at the time of the publication of the notice of proposed rulemaking describing the impact of the rule on small entities and seeking public comment on such impact. Small entities include small businesses, organizations and governmental jurisdictions.

For purposes of analysis under the RFA, EBSA proposes to continue to consider a small entity to be an employee benefit plan with fewer than 100 participants. The basis of this definition is found in section 104(a)(2) of ERISA that permits the Secretary of Labor to prescribe simplified annual reports for pension plans that cover fewer than 100 participants. Under section 104(a)(3), the Secretary may also provide for exemptions or simplified annual reporting and disclosure for welfare benefit plans. Pursuant to the authority of section 104(a)(3), the Department has previously issued at 29 CFR 2520.104-20, 2520.104-21, 2520.104-41, 2520.104-46 and 2520.104b-10 certain simplified reporting provisions and limited exemptions from reporting and disclosure requirements for small plans, including unfunded or insured welfare plans, covering fewer than 100 participants and which satisfy certain other requirements.

Further, while some large employers may have small plans, in general small employers maintain most small plans. Thus, EBSA believes that assessing the impact of these proposed rules on small plans is an appropriate substitute for evaluating the effect on small entities. The definition of small entity considered appropriate for this purpose differs, however, from a definition of small business which is based on size standards promulgated by the Small Business Administration (SBA) (13 CFR 121.201) pursuant to the Small Business Act (15 U.S.C. 631 et seq.). EBSA therefore requests comments on the appropriateness of the size standard used in evaluating the impact of these proposed rules on small entities.

EBSA has preliminarily determined that these proposed rules may have a significant beneficial economic impact on a substantial number of small entities. In an effort to provide a sound basis for this conclusion, EBSA has prepared the following initial regulatory flexibility analysis. Efficiency gains are assumed to arise from the Department's efforts to provide specific standards and procedures, and to address questions concerning what are reasonable efforts to satisfy these standards. The model notices provided as part of the proposed regulations are also intended to minimize compliance burdens.

To the Department's knowledge, there are no federal regulations that might duplicate, overlap, or conflict with the provisions of the proposed regulations.

Rules and Regulations for Abandoned Plans (29 CFR 2578.1)

As explained earlier in the preamble, in drafting the proposed regulation, the Department relied on recommendations in a 2002 report to the

ERISA Advisory Council by the Working Group on Orphan Plans. Witnesses before the Working Group testified that regulatory action should be undertaken that would allow for the termination of abandoned plans and the distribution of assets to participants and beneficiaries. The conditions set forth in this proposed regulation are intended to facilitate voluntary, safe, and efficient terminations of abandoned plans, and to increase the likelihood of participants and beneficiaries receiving the greatest retirement benefit practicable under the circumstances. The proposed rules would meet the objectives of providing the authority and incentive for termination by offering greater certainty to QTAs concerning their compliance with the requirements of ERISA section 404(a), to the extent applicable, and of preserving future retirement assets for plan participants. Streamlined procedures for terminating and winding up an abandoned plan will reduce some of the cost that would otherwise have been incurred to terminate abandoned plans.

The proposed rules would impact participants and beneficiaries, abandoned individual account plans, entities that provide a variety of services to plans, and financial institutions and entities acting as QTAs that undertake the termination of individual account plans that have been abandoned.

As described earlier in the preamble, the Department determined that there are 4,000 currently abandoned plans, with 78,500 participants. Another 1,650 plans, with 33,000 participants, are expected to be abandoned annually in subsequent years. All plans are assumed to be small plans with approximately 20 participants. Currently small abandoned plans represent less than 1% of all small plans; the 1,650 small plans expected to be abandoned annually hereafter represent less than ½ of 1% of all small plans. The 5,650 small plans potentially affected may still be considered a substantial number, however.

Because essentially all abandoned plans are assumed to be small plans, the more detailed discussion earlier in the preamble on the costs and benefits of the proposed regulation is applicable to this analysis of costs and benefits under the RFA. In summary, the net benefits of terminating the 4,000 plans currently assumed to be abandoned range from $900,000 for efficiency gains, to $6.6 million in administrative cost savings if the plans had remained abandoned for one year following the year of termination, or $27 million if the plans had remained abandoned for five years following termination. The estimated beneficial impact on small plans therefore ranges from $225 per plan to $1,650 per plan, or $6,750 per plan over five years. The per-plan net benefits are very similar for the 1,650 plans assumed to be abandoned in future years.

Safe Harbor for Rollovers From Terminated Individual Account Plans (29 CFR 2550.404a-3)

The proposed regulation provides safe harbor protection under section 404(a) of ERISA for fiduciaries that terminate small plans and roll over balances into individual retirement plans or other accounts for participants and beneficiaries that failed to elect a form of distribution for their benefits. Fiduciaries will benefit from increased confidence that they have fulfilled their fiduciary obligations under ERISA, and plan participants will benefit from increased retirement savings. In particular, the two model Notices to Participants provided by the Department will contribute to lower administrative costs for small plans that terminate. Based on an estimated 78,500 participants in currently abandoned plans, the initial cost to small plans is estimated at $207,800. The annual cost to ongoing terminating plans is considerably less in future years when current small abandoned plans will have been terminated, an estimated 95,820.

Special Terminal Report for Abandoned Plans (29 CFR 2520.103-13)

The proposed regulation provides simplified annual reporting to the Department for QTAs that wind up the affairs of small abandoned plans. The resulting time-savings will reduce administrative costs thereby increasing benefits to participants and beneficiaries. No cost has been attributed to this proposed regulation.

Congressional Review Act

The notice of proposed rulemaking being issued here is subject to the provisions of the Congressional Review Act provisions of the Small Business Regulatory Enforcement Fairness Act of 1996 (5 U.S.C. 801 et seq.) and, if finalized, will be transmitted to the Congress and the Comptroller General for review.

Unfunded Mandates Reform Act

For purposes of the Unfunded Mandates Reform Act of 1995 (Pub. L. 104-4), as well as Executive Order 12875, the proposed rules do not include any federal mandate that may result in expenditures by state, local, or tribal governments in the aggregate of more than $100 million, or increased expenditures by the private sector of more than $100 million.

Federalism Statement

Executive Order 13132 (August 4, 1999) outlines fundamental principles of federalism and requires the adherence to specific criteria by federal agencies in the process of their formulation and implementation of policies that have substantial direct effects on the States, the relationship between the national government and the States, or on the distribution of power and responsibilities among the various levels of government. The proposed rules would not have federalism implications because it has no substantial direct effect on the States, on the relationship between the national government and the States, or on the distribution of power and responsibilities among the various levels of government. Section 514 of ERISA provides, with certain exceptions specifically enumerated, that the provisions of Titles I and IV of ERISA supersede any and all laws of the States as they relate to any employee benefit plan covered under ERISA. The requirements implemented in the proposed rules do not alter the fundamental provisions of the statute with respect to employee benefit plans, and as such would have no implications for the States or the relationship or distribution of power between the national government and the States.

List of Subjects

29 CFR Part 2578

Employee benefit plans, Pensions, Retirement.

29 CFR Part 2520

Accounting, Employee benefit plans, Pensions, Reporting and recordkeeping requirements.

29 CFR Part 2550

Employee benefit plans, Employee Retirement Income Security Act, Employee stock ownership plans, Exemptions, Fiduciaries, Investments, Investments foreign, Party in interest, Pensions, Pension and Welfare Benefit Programs Office, Prohibited transactions, Real estate, Securities, Surety bonds, Trusts and Trustees.

For the reasons set forth in the preamble, the Department of Labor proposes to amend 29 CFR chapter XXV as follows:

Subchapter G—Administration And Enforcement Under The Employee Retirement Income Security Act Of 1974

1. Add part 2578 to subchapter G to read as follows:

PART 2578—RULES AND REGULATIONS FOR ABANDONED PLANS

§

§ *2578.1 Termination of abandoned individual account plans.*

Appendix A to § 2578.1 Notice of Intent to Terminate Plan

Appendix B to § 2578.1 Notification of Plan Abandonment and Intent to Serve as Qualified Termination Administrator

Appendix C to § 2578.1 Notice of Plan Termination

Appendix D to § 2578.1 Final Notice

Authority: 29 U.S.C. 1135; 1104(a); 1103(d)(1).

§ *2578.1 Termination of abandoned individual account plans.*

(a) *General.* The purpose of this part is to establish standards for the termination and winding up of an individual account plan (as defined in section 3(34) of the Employee Retirement Income Security Act of 1974 (ERISA or the Act)) with respect to which a qualified termination administrator (as defined in paragraph (g) of this section) has determined there is no responsible plan sponsor or plan administrator within the meaning of section 3(16)(B) and (A) of the Act, respectively, to perform such acts.

(b) *Finding of abandonment.* (1) A qualified termination administrator may find an individual account plan to be abandoned when:

(i) Either:

(A) No contributions to, or distributions from, the plan have been made for a period of at least 12 consecutive months immediately preceding the date on which the determination is being made; or

(B) Other facts and circumstances (such as a filing by or against the plan sponsor for liquidation under title 11 of the United States Code, or communications from participants and beneficiaries regarding distributions) known to the qualified termination administrator suggest that the plan is or may become abandoned by the plan sponsor; and

(ii) Following reasonable efforts to locate or communicate with the plan sponsor, the qualified termination administrator determines that the plan sponsor:

(A) No longer exists;

(B) Cannot be located; or

(C) Is unable to maintain the plan.

(2) Notwithstanding paragraph (b)(1) of this section, a qualified termination administrator may not find a plan to be abandoned if, at anytime before the plan is deemed terminated pursuant to paragraph (c) of this section, the qualified termination administrator receives an objection from the plan sponsor regarding the finding of abandonment and proposed termination.

(3) A qualified termination administrator shall, for purposes of paragraph (b)(1)(ii) of this section, be deemed to have made a reasonable effort to locate or communicate with the plan sponsor if the qualified termination administrator sends to the last known address of the plan sponsor, and in the case of a plan sponsor that is a corporation, to the address of the person designated as the corporation's agent for service of legal process, by a method of delivery requiring acknowledgement of receipt, the notice described in paragraph (b)(5) of this section.

(4) If receipt of the notice described in paragraph (b)(5) of this section is not acknowledged pursuant to paragraph (b)(3) of this section, the qualified termination administrator shall be deemed to have made a reasonable effort to locate or communicate with the plan sponsor if the qualified termination administrator contacts known service providers (other than itself) of the plan and requests the current address of the plan sponsor from such service providers and, if such information is provided, the qualified termination administrator sends to each such address, by a method of delivery requiring acknowledgement of receipt, the notice described in paragraph (b)(5) of this section.

(5) The notice referred to in paragraph (b)(3) of this section shall contain the following information:

(i) The name and address of the qualified termination administrator;

(ii) The name of the plan;

(iii) The account number or other identifying information relating to the plan;

(iv) A statement that the plan may be terminated and benefits distributed pursuant to 29 CFR 2578.1 if the plan sponsor fails to contact the qualified termination administrator within 30 days;

(v) The name, address, and telephone number of the person, office, or department that the plan sponsor must contact regarding the plan;

(vi) A statement that if the plan is terminated pursuant to 29 CFR 2578.1, notice of such termination will be furnished to the U.S. Department of Labor's Employee Benefits Security Administration; and

(vii) The following statement: "The U.S. Department of Labor requires that you be informed that, as a fiduciary or plan administrator or both, you may be personally liable for costs, civil penalties, excise taxes, etc. as a result of your acts or omissions with respect to this plan. The termination of this plan will not relieve you of your liability for any such costs, penalties, taxes, etc."

(c) *Deemed termination.* (1) Except as provided in paragraph (c)(2) of this section, if a qualified termination administrator finds, pursuant to paragraph (b)(1) of this section, that an individual account plan has been abandoned, the plan shall be deemed to be terminated on the ninetieth (90th) day following the date on which a notice of plan abandonment, as described in paragraph (c)(3) of this section, is furnished to the U.S. Department of Labor.

(2) If, prior to the ninetieth (90th) day following the date on which notice, in accordance with paragraph (c)(3) of this section, is furnished to the U.S. Department of Labor, the Department notifies the qualified termination administrator that it—

(i) Objects to the termination of the plan, the plan shall not be deemed terminated under paragraph (c)(1) of this section until the qualified termination administrator is notified that the Department has withdrawn its objection;

(ii) Waives the 90-day period described in paragraph (c)(1), the plan shall be deemed terminated upon the qualified termination administrator's receipt of such notification.

(3) Following a qualified termination administrator's finding, pursuant to paragraph (b)(1) of this section, that an individual account plan has been abandoned, the qualified termination administrator shall furnish to the U.S. Department of Labor a notice of plan abandonment that is signed and dated by the qualified termination administrator and that includes the following information:

(i) Qualified termination administrator information. (A) The name, EIN, address, and telephone number of the person electing to be the qualified termination administrator, including the address, e-mail address, and telephone number of the person signing the notice (or other contact person, if different from the person signing the notice);

(B) A statement that the person (identified in paragraph (c)(3)(i)(A) of this section) is a qualified termination administrator within the meaning of paragraph (g) of this section and elects to terminate and wind up the plan (identified in paragraph (c)(3)(ii)(A) of this section) in accordance with the provisions of this section; and

(C) An identification whether the person electing to be the qualified termination administrator or its affiliate is, or within the past 24 months has been, the subject of an investigation, examination, or enforcement action by the Department, Internal Revenue Service, or Securities and Exchange Commission concerning such entity's conduct as a fiduciary or party in interest with respect to any plan covered by the Act;

(ii) *Plan information.* (A) The name, address, telephone number, account number, EIN, and plan number of the plan with respect to which the person is electing to serve as the qualified termination administrator;

(B) The name and last known address and telephone number of the plan sponsor;

(C) The estimated number of participants in the plan;

(iii) *Findings.* A statement that the person electing to be the qualified termination administrator finds that the plan (identified in paragraph (c)(3)(ii)(A) of this section) is abandoned pursuant to paragraph (b) of this section. This statement shall include an explanation of the basis for such a finding, specifically referring to the provisions in paragraph (b)(1) of this section, and a description of the specific steps (set forth in paragraphs (b)(3) and (b)(4) of this section) taken to locate or communicate with the known plan sponsor;

(iv) *Plan asset information.* (A) The estimated value of the plan's assets held by the person electing to be the qualified termination administrator;

(B) The length of time plan assets have been held by the person electing to be the qualified termination administrator, if such period of time is less than 12 months; and

(C) An identification of any assets with respect to which there is no readily ascertainable fair market value, as well as information, if any, concerning the value of such assets;

(v) *Service provider information.* (A) The name, address, and telephone number of known service providers (e.g., record keeper, accountant, lawyer, other asset custodian(s)) to the plan; and

(B) An identification of any services considered necessary to wind up the plan in accordance with this section, the name of the service provider(s) that is expected to provide such services, and an itemized estimate of expenses attendant thereto expected to be paid out of plan assets by the qualified termination administrator; and

(vi) A statement that the information being provided in the notice is true and complete based on the knowledge of the person electing to be the qualified termination administrator, and that the information is being provided by the qualified termination administrator under penalty of perjury.

(4) For purposes of calculating the 90-day period referred to in paragraph (c)(1) of this section, the notice described in paragraph (c)(3) of this section shall be considered furnished to the Department:

(i) Upon mailing, if accomplished by United States Postal Service certified mail or Express mail;

(ii) Upon receipt by the delivery service, if accomplished using a "designated private delivery service" within the meaning of 26 U.S.C. 75029 (f); or

(iii) In the case of any other method of furnishing, upon receipt by the Department.

(d) *Winding up the affairs of the plan.* (1) In any case where an individual account plan is deemed to be terminated pursuant to paragraph (c) of this section, the qualified termination administrator shall take steps as may be necessary or appropriate to wind up the affairs of the plan and distribute benefits to the plan's participants and beneficiaries.

(2) For purposes of paragraph (d)(1) of this section, the qualified termination administrator shall:

(i) *Plan records.* (A) Undertake reasonable and diligent efforts to locate and update plan records necessary to determine the benefits payable under the terms of the plan to each participant and beneficiary.

(B) For purposes of paragraph (d)(2)(i)(A) of this section, a qualified termination administrator shall not have failed to make reasonable and diligent efforts to update plan records merely because the administrator determines in good faith that updating the records is either impossible or involves significant cost to the plan in relation to the total assets of the plan.

(ii) *Calculate benefits.* Use reasonable care in calculating the benefits payable to each participant or beneficiary based on plan records described in paragraph (d)(2)(i) of this section.

(iii) *Engage service providers.* Engage, on behalf of the plan, such service providers as are necessary for the qualified termination administrator to wind up the affairs of the plan and distribute benefits to the plan's participants and beneficiaries in accordance with paragraph (d)(1) of this section.

(iv) *Pay reasonable expenses.* (A) Pay, from plan assets, the reasonable expenses of carrying out the qualified termination administrator's authority and responsibility under this section.

(B) Expenses of plan administration shall be considered reasonable solely for purposes of paragraph (d)(2)(iv)(A) of this section if:

(1) Such expenses are for services necessary to wind up the affairs of the plan and distribute benefits to the plan's participants and beneficiaries,

(2) Such expenses: (i) Are consistent with industry rates for such or similar services, based on the experience of the qualified termination administrator, and

(ii) are not in excess of rates charged by the qualified termination administrator (or affiliate) for same or similar services provided to customers that are not plans terminated pursuant to this section, if the qualified termination administrator (or affiliate) provides same or similar services to such other customers, and

(3) The payment of such expenses would not constitute a prohibited transaction under the Act or is exempted from such prohibited transaction provisions pursuant to section 408(a) of the Act.

(v) *Notify participants.* (A) Furnish to each participant or beneficiary of the plan a notice containing the following:

(1) The name of the plan;

(2) A statement that the plan has been determined to be abandoned by the plan sponsor and, therefore, has been terminated pursuant to regulations issued by the U.S. Department of Labor;

(3)(i) A statement of the account balance and the date on which it was calculated by the qualified termination administrator, and

(ii) The following statement: "The actual amount of your distribution may be more or less than the amount stated in this letter depending on investment gains or losses and the administrative cost of terminating your plan and distributing your benefits.";

(4) A description of the distribution options available under the plan and a request that the participant or beneficiary elect a form of distribution and inform the qualified termination administrator (or designee) of that election;

(5)(i) A statement explaining that, if a participant or beneficiary fails to make an election within 30 days from receipt of the notice, the qualified termination administrator (or designee) will roll over the account balance of the participant or beneficiary directly to an individual retirement plan (i.e., individual retirement account or annuity) or other account (in the case of distributions described in § 2550.404a-3(d)(1)(ii) of this chapter) and the account balance will be invested in an investment product designed to preserve principal and provide a reasonable rate of return and liquidity;

(ii) A statement of the fees, if any, that will be paid from the participant or beneficiary's individual retirement plan, if such information is known at the time of the furnishing of this notice; and

(iii) The name, address and phone number of the individual retirement plan provider, if such information is known at the time of the furnishing of this notice; and

(6) The name, address, and telephone number of the qualified termination administrator and, if different, the name, address and phone number of a contact person (or entity) for additional information concerning the termination and distribution of benefits under this section.

(B)(1) For purposes of paragraph (d)(2)(v)(A) of this section, a notice shall be furnished to each participant or beneficiary in accordance with the requirements of § 2520.104b-1(b)(1) of this chapter to the last known address of the participant or beneficiary; and

(2) In the case of a notice that is returned to the plan as undeliverable, the qualified termination administrator shall, consistent with the duties of a fiduciary under section 404(a)(1) of ERISA, take steps to locate and provide notice to the participant or beneficiary prior to making a distribution pursuant to paragraph (d)(2)(vi) of this section. If, after such steps, the qualified termination administrator is unsuccessful in locating and furnishing notice to a participant or beneficiary, the participant or beneficiary shall be deemed to have been furnished the notice and to have failed to make an election within the 30-day period described in paragraph (d)(2)(vi) of this section.

(vi) *Distribute benefits.* (A) Distribute benefits in accordance with the form of distribution elected by each participant or beneficiary.

(B) If the participant or beneficiary fails to make an election within 30 days from receipt of the notice described in paragraph (d)(2)(v) of this section, distribute benefits in the form of a direct rollover in accordance with § 2550.404a-3 of this chapter.

(C) For purposes of distributions pursuant to paragraph (d)(2)(vi)(B) of this section, the qualified termination administrator may designate itself (or an affiliate) as the transferee of such proceeds, and invest such proceeds in a product in which it (or an affiliate) has an interest, only if such designation and investment is exempted from the prohibited transaction provisions under the Act pursuant to section 408(a) of Act.

(vii) *Special Terminal Report for Abandoned Plans.* File the Special Terminal Report for Abandoned Plans in accordance with § 2520.103-13 of this chapter.

(viii) *Final Notice.* No later than two months after the end of the month in which the qualified termination administrator satisfies the requirements in paragraph (d)(2)(i) through (d)(2)(vi) of this section, furnish to the Office of Enforcement, Employee Benefits Security Administration, U.S. Department of Labor, 200 Constitution Ave., NW., Washington, DC 20210, a notice, signed and dated by the qualified termination administrator, containing the following information:

(A) The name, EIN, address, e-mail address, and telephone number of the qualified termination administrator, including the address and telephone number of the person signing the notice (or other contact person, if different from the person signing the notice);

(B) The name, account number, EIN, and plan number of the plan with respect to which the person served as the qualified termination administrator;

(C) A statement that the plan has been terminated and all assets held by the qualified termination administrator have been distributed to the plan's participants and beneficiaries on the basis of the best available information;

(D) A statement that the Special Terminal Report for Abandoned Plans meeting the requirements of § 2520.103-13 of this chapter is attached to this notice;

(E) A statement that plan expenses were paid out of plan assets by the qualified termination administrator in accordance with the requirements of paragraph (d)(2)(iv) of this section;

(F) If fees and expenses paid to the qualified termination administrator (or its affiliate) exceed by 20 percent or more the estimate required by paragraph (c)(3)(v)(B) of this section, a statement that actual fees and expenses exceeded estimated fees and expenses and the reasons for such additional costs; and

(G) A statement that the information being provided in the notice is true and complete based on the knowledge of the qualified termination administrator, and that the information is being provided by the qualified termination administrator under penalty of perjury.

(3) The terms of the plan shall, for purposes of title I of ERISA, be deemed amended to the extent necessary to allow the qualified termination administrator to wind up the plan in accordance with this section.

(e) *Limited liability of qualified termination administrator.* (1) Except as otherwise provided in paragraph (e)(2) of this section, to the extent that the responsibilities enumerated in paragraph (d)(2) of this section involve the exercise of discretionary authority or control that would make the qualified termination administrator a fiduciary within the meaning of section 3(21) of the Act, the qualified termination administrator shall be deemed to satisfy its responsibilities under section

404(a) of the Act to the extent the qualified termination administrator complies with the requirements of paragraph (d)(2) of this section.

(2) A qualified termination administrator shall be responsible for the selection and monitoring of any service provider (other than monitoring an individual retirement plan provider selected pursuant to paragraph (d)(2)(vi)(B) of this section) determined by the qualified termination administrator to be necessary to the winding up of the affairs of the plan, as well as ensuring the reasonableness of the compensation paid for such services. To the extent that a qualified termination administrator, in accordance with the requirements of section 404(a)(1) of the Act, selects and monitors a service provider, and does not otherwise enable the service provider to commit fiduciary breaches, the qualified termination administrator shall not be liable for the acts or omissions of the service provider with respect to which the qualified termination administrator does not have knowledge.

(f) *Continued liability of plan sponsor.* Nothing in this section shall serve to relieve or limit the liability of any person other than the qualified termination administrator due to a violation of ERISA.

(g) *Qualified termination administrator.* A termination administrator is qualified under this section only if:

(1) It is eligible to serve as a trustee or issuer of an individual retirement plan, within the meaning of section 7701(a)(37) of the Internal Revenue Code, and

(2) It holds assets of the plan that is considered abandoned pursuant to paragraph (b) of this section.

APPENDIX A TO § 2578.1

NOTICE OF INTENT TO TERMINATE PLAN

[*Date of notice*]

[*Name of plan sponsor*]
[*Last known address of plan sponsor*]

Re: [*Name of plan and account number or other identifying information*]

Dear [*Name of plan sponsor*]:

We are writing to advise you of our concern about the status of the subject plan. Our intention is to begin the process of terminating the plan in accordance with federal law if you do not contact us within 30 days of your receipt of this notice.

Our basis for taking this action is that {*insert the following language in the brackets*: [our records reflect that there have been no contributions to, or distributions from, the plan within the past 12 months] *or* [*if the basis is under § 29 CFR 2578.1(b)(1)(i)(B), provide a description of the facts and circumstances indicating plan abandonment*]}.

We are sending this notice to you because our records show that you are the sponsor of the subject plan. The U.S. Department of Labor requires that you be informed that, as a fiduciary or plan administrator or both, you may be personally liable for all costs, civil penalties, excise taxes, etc. as a result of your acts or omissions with respect to this plan. The termination of this plan will not relieve you of your liability for any such costs, penalties, taxes, etc. Federal law also requires us to notify the U.S. Department of Labor, Employee Benefits Security Administration, of the termination of any abandoned plan.

Please contact [*name, address, and telephone number of the person, office, or department that the sponsor must contact regarding the plan*] within 30 days in order to prevent this action.

Sincerely,

[*Name and address of qualified termination administrator or appropriate designee*]

APPENDIX B TO § 2578.1

NOTIFICATION OF PLAN ABANDONMENT AND INTENT TO SERVE AS QUALIFIED TERMINATION ADMINISTRATOR

[*Date of notice*]

Abandoned Plan Coordinator, Office of Enforcement
Employee Benefits Security Administration
U.S. Department of Labor
200 Constitution Ave., NW
Suite 600
Washington, DC, 20210

Re: Plan Identification   Qualified Termination Administrator
      [*Plan name and plan number*]   [*Name*]
      [*EIN*]   [*Address*]
      [*Plan account number*]   [*E-mail address*]
      [*Address*]   [*Telephone number*]
      [*Telephone number*]   [*EIN*]

Abandoned Plan Coordinator:

Pursuant to 29 CFR 2578.1(b), we have determined that the subject plan has been abandoned by its sponsor. We are eligible to serve as a Qualified Termination Administrator for purposes of terminating and winding up the plan in accordance with 29 CFR 2578.1, and hereby elect to do so.

We find that the plan is abandoned within the meaning of 29 CFR 2578.1(b) because [*check the appropriate box below and provide additional information as necessary*]:

☐   There have been no contributions to, or distributions from, the plan for a period of at least 12 consecutive months immediately preceding the date of this letter. Our records indicate that the date of the last contribution or distribution was [*enter appropriate date*].

☐   The following facts and circumstances suggest that the plan is or may become abandoned by the plan sponsor [*add description below*]:

_____
_____
_____

We have also determined that the plan sponsor [*check appropriate box below*]:

☐ No longer exists

☐ Cannot be located

☐ Is unable to maintain the plan

We have taken the following steps to locate or communicate with the known plan sponsor [*provide an explanation below*]:

_____

_____

_____

Part I – <u>Plan Information</u>

---

1. Estimated number of individuals (participants and beneficiaries) with accounts under the plan: [*number*]

2. Plan assets held by Qualified Termination Administrator:
    A.   Estimated value of assets of the plan: [*value*]
    B.   Months we have held plan assets, if less than 12:   [*number*]

    C.   Hard to value assets [*select "yes" or "no" to identify any assets with no readily ascertainable fair market value, and include for those identified assets the best known estimate of their value*]:

		Yes	No	
(a)	Partnership/joint venture interests	☐	☐	[*value*]
(b)	Employer real property	☐	☐	[*value*]
(c)	Real estate (other than (b))	☐	☐	[*value*]
(d)	Employer securities	☐	☐	[*value*]
(e)	Participant loans	☐	☐	[*value*]
(f)	Loans (other than (e))	☐	☐	[*value*]
(g)	Tangible personal property	☐	☐	[*value*]

3. Name and last known address and telephone number of plan sponsor:

    _____

    _____

    _____

Part II – <u>Known Service Providers of the Plan</u>

	Name	Address	Telephone
1.			
2.			
3.			

Part III – <u>Services and Related Expenses to be Paid</u>

	Services	Service Provider	Estimated Cost
1.			
2.			
3.			

Part IV – <u>Investigation</u>

In the past 24 months [*check one box*]:

☐ Neither we nor our affiliates are or have been the subject of an investigation, examination, or enforcement action by the Department, Internal Revenue Service, or Securities and Exchange Commission concerning such entity's conduct as a fiduciary or party in interest with respect to any plan covered by the Act.

☐ We or our affiliates are or have been the subject of an investigation, examination, or enforcement action by the Department, Internal Revenue Service, or Securities and Exchange Commission concerning such entity's conduct as a fiduciary or party in interest with respect to any plan covered by the Act.

Part V – <u>Contact Person</u> [*enter information only if different from signatory*]:

[*Name*]
[*Address*]
[*E-mail address*]
[*Telephone number*]

Under penalties of perjury, I declare that I have examined this notice and to the best of my knowledge and belief, it is true, correct and complete.

[*Signature*]
[*Title of person signing on behalf the Qualified Termination Administrator*]
[*Address, e-mail address, and telephone number*]

APPENDIX C TO § 2578.1

NOTICE OF PLAN TERMINATION

[*Date of notice*]

[*Name and last known address of plan participant or beneficiary*]

Re: [*Name of plan*]

Dear [*Name of plan participant or beneficiary*]:

We are writing to inform you that your retirement plan, identified above, has been terminated pursuant to regulations issued by the U.S. Department of Labor. The plan was terminated because it was abandoned by [*enter the name of the plan sponsor*].

Your account balance on [*date*] is/was [*account balance*]. We will be distributing this money as permitted under the terms of the Plan and federal regulations. The actual amount of your distribution may be more or less than the amount stated in this letter depending on investment gains or losses and the administrative cost of terminating your plan and distributing your benefits.

Your distribution options under the Plan are [*add a description of the Plan's distribution options*]. It is very important that you elect one of these forms of distribution and inform us of your election. The process for informing us of this election is [*enter a description of the election process established by the qualified termination administrator*].

[*If this notice is for a participant or participant's spouse, complete and include the following paragraph.*]

If you do not make an election within 30 days from your receipt of this notice, your account balance will be transferred directly to an individual retirement plan. {*If the name of the provider of the individual retirement plan is known, include the following sentence:* The name of the provider of the individual retirement plan is [*name, address and phone number of the individual retirement plan provider*].} Pursuant to federal law, your money in the individual retirement plan would then be invested in an investment product designed to preserve principal and provide a reasonable rate of return and liquidity. {*If fee information is known, include the following sentence:* Should your money be transferred into an individual retirement plan, [*enter the name of the financial institution*] charges the following fees for its services: [*add statement of fees, if any, that will be paid from the participant or beneficiary's individual retirement plan*].}

[*If this notice is for a beneficiary other than the participant's spouse, complete and include the paragraph below rather than the paragraph above.*]

If you do not make an election within 30 days from your receipt of this notice, your account balance will be transferred directly to an account maintained by [*name, address and phone number of the financial institution if known, otherwise insert the following language*: a bank or insurance company or other similar financial institution.].   Pursuant to federal law, your money would then be invested in an investment product designed to preserve principal and provide a reasonable rate of return and liquidity. {*If fee information is known, include the following sentence*: Should your money be transferred into such an account, [*enter the name of the financial institution*] charges the following fees for its services: [*add statement of fees, if any, that will be paid from the participant or beneficiary's individual retirement plan*].}

For more information about the termination, your account balance, or distribution options, please contact [*name, address, and telephone number of the qualified termination administrator and, if different, the appropriate contact person*].

Sincerely,

[*Name of qualified termination administrator or appropriate designee*]

APPENDIX D TO § 2578.1

FINAL NOTICE

[*Date of notice*]

Abandoned Plan Coordinator, Office of Enforcement
Employee Benefits Security Administration
U.S. Department of Labor
200 Constitution Ave., NW
Suite 600
Washington, DC, 20210

Re: <u>Plan Identification</u>   <u>Qualified Termination Administrator</u>
        [*Plan name and plan number*]   [*Name*]
        [*Plan account number*]   [*Address and e-mail address*]
        [*EIN*]   [*Telephone number*]
                                         [*EIN*]

Abandoned Plan Coordinator:

Part I – <u>General Information</u>

The termination and winding-up process of the subject plan has been completed pursuant to 29 CFR 2578.1. Benefits were distributed to participants and beneficiaries on the basis of the best available information pursuant to 29 CFR 2578.1(d)(2)(i). Plan expenses were paid out of plan assets pursuant to 29 CFR 2578.1(d)(2)(iv). A Special Terminal Report for Abandoned Plans meeting the requirements of 29 CFR 2520.103-13 is attached to this notice.

Part II – <u>Contact Person</u> [*complete only if different from signatory*]

[*Name*]
[*Address and e-mail address*]
[*Telephone number*]

[*Include Part III only if fees and expenses paid to the QTA (or its affiliate) exceeded by 20 percent or more the estimate required by 29 CFR 2578.1(c)(3)(v)(B).*]

Part III – <u>Expenses Paid to Qualified Termination Administrator</u>

The actual fees and/or expenses we received in connection with winding up the Plan exceeded by {*insert either*: [20 percent or more] *or* [*the actual percentage*]} the estimate required by 29 CFR 2578.1(c)(3)(v)(B). The reason or reasons for such additional costs are [*provide an explanation of the additional costs*].

Under penalties of perjury, I declare that I have examined this notice and to the best of my knowledge and belief, it is true, correct and complete.

[*Signature*]

[*Title of person signing on behalf the Qualified Termination Administrator*]

[*Address, e-mail address, and telephone number*]

Attachment

Subchapter C—Reporting And Disclosure Under The Employee Retirement Income Security Act Of 1974

PART 2520—RULES AND REGULATIONS FOR REPORTING AND DISCLOSURE

2. The authority citation for part 2520 continues to read as follows:

Authority: 29 U.S.C. 1021-1025, 1027, 1029-31, 1059, 1134 and 1135; and Secretary of Labor's Order 1-2003, 68 FR 5374 (Feb. 3, 2003). §2520.101-2 also issued under 29 U.S.C. 1132, 1181-1183, 1181 note, 1185, 1185a-b, 1191, and 1191a-c. §§2520.102-3, 2520.104b-1 and 2520.104b-3 also issued under 29 U.S.C. 1003,1181-1183, 1181 note, 1185, 1185a-b, 1191, and 1191a-c. §§2520.104b-1 and 2520.107 also issued under 26 U.S.C. 401 note, 111 Stat. 788. Section 2520.101-4 also issued under sec. 103 of Pub. L. 108-218.

3. Add § 2520.103-13 to read as follows:

§ *2520.103-13 Special terminal report for abandoned plans.*

(a) *General.* The terminal report required to be filed by the qualified termination administrator pursuant to § 2578.1(d)(2)(vii) of this chapter shall consist of the items set forth in paragraph (b) of this section. Such report shall be filed in accordance with the method of filing set forth in paragraph (c) of this section and at the time set forth in paragraph (d) of this section.

(b) *Contents.* The terminal report described in paragraph (a) of this section shall contain:

(1) Identification information concerning the qualified termination administrator and the plan being terminated.

(2) The total assets of the plan as of the date the plan was deemed terminated under § 2578.1(c) of this chapter, prior to any reduction for termination expenses and distributions to participants and beneficiaries.

(3) The total termination expenses paid by the plan and a separate schedule identifying each service provider and amount received, itemized by expense.

(4) The total distributions made pursuant to § 2578.1(d)(2)(vi) of this chapter and a statement regarding whether any such distributions were transfers under § 2578.1(d)(2)(vi)(B) of this chapter.

(c) *Method of filing.* The terminal report described in paragraph (a) shall be filed:

(1) On the most recent Form 5500 available as of the date the qualified termination administrator satisfies the requirements in § 2578.1(d)(2)(i) through § 2578.1(d)(2)(vi) of this chapter;

(2) In accordance with the Form's instructions pertaining to terminal reports of qualified termination administrators; and

(3) As an attachment to the notice described in § 2578.1(d)(2)(viii) of this chapter.

(d) *When to file.* The qualified termination administrator shall file the terminal report described in paragraph (a) within two months after the end of the month in which the qualified termination administrator satisfies the requirements in § 2578.1(d)(2)(i) through § 2578.1(d)(2)(vi) of this chapter.

(e) *Limitation.* (1) Except as provided in this section, no report shall be required to be filed by the qualified termination administrator under part 1 of title I of ERISA for a plan being terminated pursuant to § 2578.1 of this chapter.

(2) Filing of a report under this section by the qualified termination administrator shall not relieve any other person from any obligation under part 1 of title I of ERISA.

Subchapter F—Fiduciary Responsibility Under The Employee Retirement Income Security Act Of 1974

PART 2550—RULES AND REGULATIONS FOR FIDUCIARY RESPONSIBILITY

4. The authority citation for part 2550 is revised to read as follows:

Authority: 29 U.S.C. 1135; and Secretary of Labor's Order No. 1-2003, 68 FR 5374 (Feb. 3, 2003). §2550.401b-1 also issued under sec. 102, Reorganization Plan No. 4 of 1978, 43 FR 47713 (Oct. 17, 1978), 3 CFR, 1978 Comp. 332, effective Dec. 31, 1978, 44 FR 1065 (Jan. 3, 1978), 3 CFR, 1978 Comp. 332. §2550.401c-1 also issued under 29 U.S.C. 1101. §2550.404c-1 also issued under 29 U.S.C. 1104. §2550.407c-3 also issued under 29 U.S.C. 1107. § 2550.404a-2 also issued under 26 U.S.C. 401 note (sec. 657, Pub. L. 107-16, 115 Stat. 38). §2550.408b-1 also issued under 29 U.S.C. 1108(b)(1) and sec. 102, Reorganization Plan No. 4 of 1978, 3 CFR, 1978 Comp. p. 332, effective Dec. 31, 1978, 44 FR 1065 (Jan. 3, 1978), and 3 CFR, 1978 Comp. 332. §2550.412-1 also issued under 29 U.S.C. 1112.

5. Add § 2550.404a-3 and its appendix to read as follows:

§ *2550.404a-3 Safe Harbor for Rollovers From Terminated Individual Account Plans.*

(a) *General.* (1) This section provides a safe harbor under which a fiduciary (including a qualified termination administrator, within the meaning of § 2578.1(g) of this chapter) of a terminated individual account plan, as described in paragraph (a)(2) of this section, will be deemed to have satisfied its duties under section 404(a) of the Employee Retirement Income Security Act of 1974, as amended (the Act)), 29 U.S.C. 1001 et seq., in connection with a rollover of a distribution, described in paragraph (b) of this section, to an individual retirement plan or other account.

(2) This section shall apply to an individual account plan only if—

(i) In the case of an individual account plan that is an abandoned plan within the meaning of § 2578.1 of this chapter, such plan was intended to be maintained as a tax-qualified plan in accordance with the requirements of section 401(a) of the Internal Revenue Code of 1986 (Code); or

(ii) In the case of any other individual account plan, such plan is maintained in accordance with the requirements of section 401(a) of the Code at the time of the distribution.

(3) The standards set forth in this section apply solely for purposes of determining whether a fiduciary meets the requirements of this safe harbor. Such standards are not intended to be the exclusive means by which a fiduciary might satisfy his or her responsibilities under the Act with respect to making rollovers described in this section.

(b) *Distributions.* This section shall apply to the rollover of a distribution from a terminated individual account plan to an individual retirement plan or other account if, in connection with such distribution:

(1) The participant or beneficiary, on whose behalf the rollover will be made, was furnished notice in accordance with paragraph (e) of this section or, in the case of an abandoned plan, § 2578.1(d)(2)(v) of this chapter, and

(2) The participant or beneficiary failed to elect a form of distribution within 30 days of the furnishing of the notice described paragraph (b)(1) of this section.

(c) *Safe harbor.* A fiduciary that meets the conditions of paragraph (d) of this section shall, with respect to a distribution described in paragraph (b) of this section, be deemed to have satisfied its duties under section 404(a) of the Act with respect to both the selection of an individual retirement plan provider or other account provider and the

¶20,534W

investment of funds in connection with a rollover distribution described in this section.

(d) *Conditions.* A fiduciary shall qualify for the safe harbor described in paragraph (c) of this section if:

(1)(i) Except as provided in paragraph (d)(1)(ii) of this section, the distribution is to an individual retirement plan within the meaning of section 7701(a)(37) of the Code;

(ii) In the case of a distribution on behalf of a distributee other than a participant or spouse, within the meaning of section 402(c) of the Code, such distribution is to an account (other than an individual retirement plan) with an institution eligible to establish and maintain individual retirement plans within the meaning of section 7701(a)(37) of the Code.

(2) The fiduciary enters into a written agreement with the individual retirement plan or other account provider that provides:

(i) The rolled-over funds shall be invested in an investment product designed to preserve principal and provide a reasonable rate of return, whether or not such return is guaranteed, consistent with liquidity;

(ii) For purposes of paragraph (d)(2)(i) of this section, the investment product selected for the rolled-over funds shall seek to maintain, over the term of the investment, the dollar value that is equal to the amount invested in the product by the individual retirement plan or other account;

(iii) The investment product selected for the rolled-over funds shall be offered by a state or federally regulated financial institution, which shall be: A bank or savings association, the deposits of which are insured by the Federal Deposit Insurance Corporation; a credit union, the member accounts of which are insured within the meaning of section 101(7) of the Federal Credit Union Act; an insurance company, the products of which are protected by state guaranty associations; or an investment company registered under the Investment Company Act of 1940;

(iv) All fees and expenses attendant to an individual retirement plan or other account, including investments of such plan, (e.g., establishment charges, maintenance fees, investment expenses, termination costs and surrender charges) shall not exceed the fees and expenses charged by the individual retirement plan or other account provider for comparable individual retirement plans or other accounts established for reasons other than the receipt of a rollover distribution under this section; and

(v) The participant or beneficiary on whose behalf the fiduciary makes a direct rollover shall have the right to enforce the terms of the contractual agreement establishing the individual retirement plan or other account, with regard to his or her rolled-over account balance, against the individual retirement plan or other account provider.

(3) Both the fiduciary's selection of an individual retirement plan or other account and the investment of funds would not result in a prohibited transaction under section 406 of the Act, unless such actions are exempted from the prohibited transaction provisions by a prohibited transaction exemption issued pursuant to section 408(a) of the Act.

(e) *Notice to participants and beneficiaries.* (1) *Content.* Each participant or beneficiary of the plan shall be furnished a notice containing the following:

(i) The name of the plan;

(ii) A statement of the account balance, the date on which the amount was calculated, and, if relevant, an indication that the amount to be distributed may be more or less than the amount stated in the notice, depending on investment gains or losses and the administrative cost of terminating the plan and distributing benefits;

(iii) A description of the distribution options available under the plan and a request that the participant or beneficiary elect a form of distribution and inform the plan administrator (or other fiduciary) identified in paragraph (e)(1)(vii) of this section of that election;

(iv) A statement explaining that, if a participant or beneficiary fails to make an election within 30 days from receipt of the notice, the plan will directly roll over the account balance of the participant or beneficiary to an individual retirement plan (i.e., individual retirement account or annuity) or other account (in the case of distributions described in paragraph (d)(1)(ii)) and the account balance will be invested in an investment product designed to preserve principal and provide a reasonable rate of return and liquidity;

(v) A statement explaining what fees, if any, will be paid from the participant or beneficiary's individual retirement plan or other account, if such information is known at the time of the furnishing of this notice;

(vi) The name, address and phone number of the individual retirement plan or other account provider, if such information is known at the time of the furnishing of this notice; and

(vii) The name, address, and telephone number of the plan administrator (or other fiduciary) from whom a participant or beneficiary may obtain additional information concerning the termination.

(2) *Manner of furnishing notice.* (i) For purposes of paragraph (e)(1) of this section, a notice shall be furnished to each participant or beneficiary in accordance with the requirements of § 2520.104b-1(b)(1) of this chapter to the last known address of the participant or beneficiary; and

(ii) In the case of a notice that is returned to the plan as undeliverable, the plan fiduciary shall, consistent with its duties under section 404(a)(1) of ERISA, take steps to locate the participant or beneficiary and provide notice prior to making the rollover distribution. If, after such steps, the fiduciary is unsuccessful in locating and furnishing notice to a participant or beneficiary, the participant or beneficiary shall be deemed to have been furnished the notice and to have failed to make an election within 30 days for purposes of paragraph (b)(2) of this section.

APPENDIX TO § 2550.404a-3

NOTICE OF PLAN TERMINATION

[*Date of notice*]

[*Name and last known address of plan participant or beneficiary*]

Re: [*Name of plan*]

Dear [*Name of plan participant or beneficiary*]:

This notice is to inform you that [*name of the plan*] (the Plan) has been terminated and we are in the process of winding it up.

Your account balance in the Plan on [*date*] is/was [*account balance*]. We will be distributing this money as permitted under the terms of the Plan and federal regulations. [*If applicable, insert the following sentence:* The actual amount of your distribution may be more or less than the amount stated in this notice depending on investment gains or losses and the administrative cost of terminating your plan and distributing your benefits.]

Your distribution options under the Plan are [*add a description of the Plan's distribution options*]. It is very important that you elect one of these forms of distribution and inform us of your election. The process for informing us of this election is [*enter a description of the Plan's election process*].

[*If this notice is for a participant or participant's spouse, complete and include the following paragraph.*]

If you do not make an election within 30 days from your receipt of this notice, your account balance will be transferred directly to an individual retirement plan. {*If the name of the provider of the individual retirement plan is known, include the following sentence:* The name of the provider of the individual retirement plan is [*name, address and phone number of the individual retirement plan provider*].} Pursuant to federal law, your money in the individual retirement plan would then be invested in an investment product designed to preserve principal and provide a reasonable rate of return and liquidity. {*If fee information is known, include the following sentence:* Should your money be transferred into an individual retirement plan, [*enter the name of the financial institution*] charges the following fees for its services: [*add statement of fees, if any, that will be paid from the participant or beneficiary's individual retirement plan*].}

[*If this notice is for a beneficiary other than the participant's spouse, complete and include the paragraph below rather than the paragraph above.*]

If you do not make an election within 30 days from your receipt of this notice, your account balance will be transferred directly to an account maintained by [*name, address and phone number of the financial institution if known, otherwise insert the following language*: a bank or insurance company or other similar financial institution.]. Pursuant to federal law, your money would then be invested in an investment product designed to preserve principal and provide a reasonable rate of return and liquidity. {*If fee information is known, include the following sentence:* Should your money be transferred into such an account, [*enter the name of the financial institution*] charges the following fees for its services: [*add statement of fees, if any, that will be paid from the participant or beneficiary's individual retirement plan*].}

For more information about the termination, your account balance, or distribution options, please contact [*name, address, and telephone number of the plan administrator or other appropriate contact person*].

Sincerely,

[*Name of plan administrator or appropriate designee*]

Signed at Washington, DC, this 2nd day of March, 2005.   [FR Doc. 05-4464 Filed 3-9-05; 8:45 am]

Ann L. Combs, Assistant Secretary, Employee Benefits Security Administration, Department of Labor.

¶ 20,534X

Pension Benefit Guaranty Corporation: Benefit valuation: Terminating plans: Mortality assumptions.—The Pension Benefit Guaranty Corporation has issued proposed regulations relating to the mortality assumptions used in its benefit valuation regulations, which provide rules for valuing benefits in a single-employer plan that terminates in a distress or voluntary termination. According to the PBGC, the updated mortality assumptions would better conform to those used by private-sector insurers in pricing group annuities. Under the proposed regulations, the PBGC's mortality tables contained in Appendix A to Part 4044 would be updated from a version of the 1983 Group Annuity Mortality (GAM-83) Tables to a version of 1994 Group Annuity Mortality Basic (GAM-94 Basic) Tables, in order to reflect longer life expectancies and to conform to updated tables used by insurance companies. Comments must be received on or before May 13, 2005.

The proposed regulations, published in the Federal Register on March 14, 2005 (70 FR 12429), were previously reproduced below. The final regulations were published in the Federal Register on December 2, 2005 (70 FR 72205); the preamble to the final regulations is reproduced at ¶ 24,806T.

¶ 20,534Y

Employee Benefits Security Administration (EBSA): Form 5500: Defined benefit plans: Welfare plans: Multiemployer plans: Electronic filing.— The DOL and the Employee Benefits Security Administration (EBSA) have released proposed regulations which would require Form 5500 filers to transmit 100% of annual returns/reports electronically, for plan years beginning on or after January 1, 2007. Therefore, the 100% electronic filing requirement would affect Form 5500 filings due in 2008. Upon adoption, the regulations would impact employee pension and welfare benefit plans, plan sponsors, administrators, and service providers to plans subject to Title I of ERISA.

The proposed regulations, which were published in the Federal Register on August 30, 2005 (70 FR 51542), are reproduced below.

DEPARTMENT OF LABOR

Employee Benefits Security Administration

29 CFR Part 2520

RIN 1210-AB04

Electronic Filing of Annual Reports

AGENCY: Employee Benefits Security Administration, Department of Labor.

ACTION: Proposed regulation.

SUMMARY: This document contains a proposed regulation that, upon adoption, would establish an electronic filing requirement for certain annual reports required to be filed with the Department of Labor by plan administrators and other entities. The Employee Retirement Income Security Act of 1974 (ERISA) and the Internal Revenue Code (the Code), and the regulations issued thereunder, impose certain annual reporting obligations on pension and welfare benefit plans, as well as

on certain other entities. These annual reporting obligations generally are satisfied by filing the Form 5500 Series. Currently, the Department of Labor, the Pension Benefit Guaranty Corporation, and the Internal Revenue Service (the Agencies) use an automated document processing system — the ERISA Filing Acceptance System — to process the Form 5500 Series filings. As part of the Department's efforts to update and streamline the current processing system, the Department has determined that improvements and cost savings in the filing processes can best be achieved by adopting a wholly electronic filing processing system and eliminating the currently accepted paper filings. The Department believes that a wholly electronic system will result in, among other things, reduced filer errors and, therefore, reduced correspondence and potential for filer penalties; more timely data for public disclosure and enforcement, thereby enhancing the protections for participants and beneficiaries; and lower annual report processing costs, benefiting taxpayers generally. As part of the move to a wholly electronic filing system, the regulation contained in this document would, upon adoption, require Form 5500 filings made to satisfy the annual reporting obligations under Title I of ERISA to be made electronically. In order to ensure an orderly and cost-effective migration to an electronic filing system by both the Department and Form 5500 filers, under the proposal the requirement to file electronically would not apply until plan years beginning on or after January 1, 2007, with the first electronically filed forms due in 2008. Upon adoption, this regulation would affect employee pension and welfare benefit plans, plan sponsors, administrators, and service providers to plans subject to Title I of ERISA.

DATES: Written comments must be received by the Department of Labor on or before October 31, 2005.

ADDRESSES: Comments should be addressed to the Office of Regulations and Interpretations, Employee Benefits Security Administration (EBSA), Room N-5669, U.S. Department of Labor, 200 Constitution Avenue, NW, Washington, D.C. 20210. Attn: Form 5500 E-filing regulation (RIN 1210-AB04). Comments also may be submitted electronically to *e-ori@dol.gov* or by using the Federal eRulingmaking Portal: *www.regulations.gov* (follow instructions provided for submission of comments). EBSA will make all comments available to the public on its website at *www.dol.gov/ebsa*. The comments also will be available for public inspection at the Public Disclosure Room, N-1513, EBSA, U.S. Department of Labor, 200 Constitution Avenue, NW, Washington, D.C. 20210.

FOR FURTHER INFORMATION CONTACT: Yolanda R. Wartenberg, Office of Regulations and Interpretations, Employee Benefits Security Administration, (202) 693-8510. This is not a toll-free number.

SUPPLEMENTARY INFORMATION:

Background

Sections 104(a) and 4065 of the Employee Retirement Income Security Act of 1974, as amended (ERISA), and sections 6057(b) and 6058(a) of the Internal Revenue Code of 1986, as amended (the Code), and the regulations issued under those sections, impose certain annual reporting and filing obligations on pension and welfare benefit plans, as well as on certain other entities.[1] Plan administrators, employers, and others generally satisfy these annual reporting obligations by filing the Form 5500 Annual Return/Report of Employee Benefit Plan, together with any required attachments and schedules for the particular plan (Form 5500).[2]

Currently, the Department of Labor, the Pension Benefit Guaranty Corporation, and the Internal Revenue Service (the Agencies) use an automated document processing system — the ERISA Filing Acceptance System (EFAST) -maintained by the Department of Labor (the Department) to process annual reports. Using the EFAST system, the Department annually receives and processes approximately 1.4 million filings. For the 2002 plan year, these filings translated into approximately 25 million paper pages.

Developed in 1998 and 1999, the EFAST system relies on a mixture of filing and processing methods to accept, compile, and monitor the Form 5500 filings. The EFAST system currently accepts filings generated using any of three different formats: (1) government printed "hand-print" forms, which must be filed on paper; (2) computer-generated paper forms identical in format to government-printed hand-print forms, which also must be filed on paper and are treated in processing the same as hand-print forms; and (3) computer-generated forms in which 2D bar code technology is used to encode filer data (known as the "machine-print" version of the forms), which may be filed either on paper or electronically. As indicated, only the computer-generated machine-print forms may be filed electronically, and the Agencies currently accept machine-print filings through any of the following electronic methods of transmission: (1) via modem using file transfer protocol (FTP), or (2) on magnetic or optical media, such as CD-ROM,

computer diskette, or magnetic tape. To process the different filing formats, the system uses a variety of computer technologies, such as optical character recognition technology to read data from the hand-print forms; 2D bar-coding technology to read coded filer information printed on the "machine-print" forms submitted on paper; scanning technology to retain images of paper filings; etc.

A private contractor performs the EFAST processing under a time-limited contract with EBSA. The end of the time-limited contracting cycle and the beginning of another contracting cycle present a significant opportunity for EBSA to evaluate the system and to make changes to take advantage of technological advances. In connection with that process, in March, 2004, the Department posted a request for public comments (Request for Comment) on its website relating to updating the current EFAST processing system.[3]

The Request for Comment set out the Department's preference for enhanced electronic filing and described in detail its understanding of the deficiencies in the EFAST design that impede use of the current electronic filing option. The Request for Comment stated that the Department's goal in developing a new processing system is to make it "more accessible to its user base through Internet and Web-based technology, devoid of paper to the greatest extent possible, faster, less expensive, and more accurate" and to ensure that "electronic filing becomes more convenient and beneficial for all users and stakeholders." The Department noted that "[t]he full benefits of electronic processing have not . . . been realized . . . because [EFAST's] electronic filing option has been underutilized."[4] The Request for Comment noted the benefits to be gained from electronic filing, explaining that, compared with electronic filings, using paper-based forms is less accurate in terms of data capture and less efficient in terms of processing — paper filings take three times as long as electronic filings to process and have nearly twice as many errors, which often trigger follow-up letters from the Agencies seeking corrections or clarifications concerning the filed information. Such filings may also result in the imposition of penalties under ERISA and the Code.

Signaling the Department's interest in moving to an electronic filing system for the Form 5500 Series, the Request for Comment specifically requested comment on whether a reduction in the available filing methods, up to and including adoption of an electronic filing mandate, would be an appropriate solution to the problems caused by underutilization of electronic filing.

In response to the Request for Comment, the Department received many constructive and useful comments from a diverse group of interested parties, including small business owners, sponsors and administrators of small and large plans, actuaries, accountants, entrepreneurs involved in the development and sale of EFAST-approved software, and firms that prepare Form 5500 filings for a wide variety of employee benefit plans.[5] Public comment was largely in accord with the Department's analysis of EFAST's technical deficiencies as laid out in the Request for Comment.

Based on what appears to be a consensus as to the current technical deficiencies of EFAST, the Department has begun the technical process necessary for the development of a new processing system. At the same time, the Agencies separately are undertaking a comprehensive review of the Form 5500 Series in an effort to determine what, if any, design or data changes should be made, in anticipation of the new processing system. Neither the technical project for development of a new processing system, nor the Form 5500 Series project, however, is the subject of this proposal.[6] Any Form or related regulation changes will be proposed for public comment as part of a separate rulemaking.

The subject of this proposal is the Department's determination that any new processing system designed to replace EFAST must have as its core component a requirement that all Form 5500s be submitted

---

[1] Other filing requirements may apply to employee benefit plans under ERISA or to other benefit arrangements under the Code, and such other filing requirements are not within the scope of this proposal. For example, Code sec. 6033(a) imposes an additional reporting and filing obligation on organizations exempt from tax under Code sec. 501(a), which may be related to retirement trusts that are qualified under sec. 401(a) of the Code. Code sec. 6047(e) also imposes an additional reporting and filing obligation on pension benefit plans that are employee stock ownership plans (ESOPs).

[2] For purposes of the annual reporting requirements under the Code, certain pension benefit arrangements that cover only business owners or partners (and their spouses), which are not employee benefit plans under Title I of ERISA, are permitted to file the Form 5500-EZ to satisfy filing requirements under the Code. *See* instructions to the Form 5500-EZ to determine who may currently file the Form 5500-EZ.

[3] The Request for Comment may be reviewed at: http://www.efast.dol.gov/efastrfc.html.

[4] The Department specifically identified technical deficiencies involving the process for obtaining and using electronic signatures, the use of outdated transmission methods, and the continued use of paper for post-filing communications. The Request for Comment suggested various technical design changes to address these and other deficiencies,

including creating an Internet-based method of filing; requiring that approved software be designed only for Internet transmission of computer-generated filings; adopting improved data exchange technology based on widely-accepted standards, such as XML; improving the technical handling of third-party attachments and attestations; and eliminating differences in treatment between paper and electronic filings with respect to acceptance and rejection.

[5] Comments received in response to the Request for Comment may be reviewed at: http://www.dol.gov/ebsa/regs/cmt_efastrfc.html.

[6] In connection with this proposal, the Department is providing in this document further information respecting the technical design and Form 5500 content projects underway within the Department concerning the Form 5500 Series. The Department believes the information about those two other projects will assist the public in evaluating this proposal; however, the Department notes that it is not asking for public comment at this time on those two separate projects. The proposal contained in this notice concerns only the mandate of electronic filing. The public will have adequate separate opportunity for public comment on the Form 5500 regulatory initiative prior to its finalization and ample time to make necessary practical changes prior to implementation of the new processing system.

through electronic means. The Department's determination that electronic filing must be the sole method available under the new processing system is not dependent on the extent or type of data that will be required of filers or the form or forms in which it must be provided; nor is it dependent on the exact software or hardware that will ultimately be devised to accommodate electronic filing, either by the Federal government or by the private sector. Rather, this determination arises from the Department's conclusion that electronic filing will benefit plan sponsors, participants and beneficiaries, and the taxpayer, based on the Department's investigation and analysis, described more fully below, of the practical alternatives. The proposal for an electronic filing requirement contained in this notice is therefore being published in advance of the other projects related to the Form 5500 Series and processing because the Department has concluded, based on considerations explained more fully below, that it is essential to the success of any redesign of EFAST that it provide filers and other affected parties adequate time to make the transition to a fully electronic method of filing the Form 5500 Series. Given the importance of the contemplated transition, the Department is publishing this proposal separately to describe the reasoning behind its conclusion and to solicit public comment on how best to proceed with the transition to electronic filing.

Public Comment and Alternatives

Virtually all of the public comments submitted in response to the Request for Comment recognized the value of electronic filing over paper filing and expressed support for increasing the use of electronic filing. The majority of comments also endorsed the concept of a gradual transition to 100 percent electronic filing. A clear consensus among commenters further favored the development of a secure Internet website on which a filer could file the Form 5500 through direct input of data, provided it was cost-free to the filer. Nonetheless, the commenters opposed an immediate mandate of electronic filing as the next step in EFAST development. The commenters argued that an immediate mandate would impose economic burdens on small businesses and small plans, which may not have easy access to the Internet. The commenters urged the Department to make only incremental changes, building on the current system and taking into account the substantial investments that the filing public has already made to accommodate EFAST. One representative commenter, speaking on behalf of a large number of large employers and service providers to employers of all sizes, suggested that, although electronic filing provides many advantages to both the public and the government, the Department should phase in any mandate over time by market segment, starting first with the largest employers who are already familiar with electronic filing, such as is required by the Securities and Exchange Commission. Other commenters asked the Department to allow sufficient time for experimentation and testing before inaugurating a mandate.

In developing this proposed regulation, the Department sought to advance two main goals. One was to maximize the speed, efficiency, and accuracy with which annual reports are transmitted, accepted, and processed, thereby enhancing the protection of participants' rights. The other was to minimize the burden placed on filers. In pursuit of these goals, the Department considered and analyzed several alternatives, taking into account the costs and benefits attendant to each. These included the following: (1) creating a new processing system that could continue to process both electronic and paper submissions without limitation; (2) continuing the present, primarily paperbased processing system on an interim basis alongside a new, solely electronic processing system; (3) developing a new, primarily electronic processing system with a temporary capacity to process a limited number of paper filings, which would be made available under criteria targeting those filers most likely to desire a longer transition period; and (4) transitioning to a new, solely electronic processing system under a uniformly applicable requirement to file electronically.

The Department considered the costs and benefits of each of these alternatives, and its economic analysis is described below under the heading "Regulatory Impact Analysis." Based on its analysis of the alternatives, the Department has concluded that the maintenance of any paper filing system, even on a reduced scale and/or for limited periods of time, which would be required under any of the first three

alternatives, would be inherently inefficient and unnecessarily costly. It is also the Department's view that any economic benefit that might accrue to some class of filers under those alternatives would be outweighed by the benefits to participants and beneficiaries at large, and to the Department and taxpayers generally, of implementing a single, wholly electronic system. Accordingly, the Department has decided to propose adoption of a uniform requirement to file electronically, as detailed further below.[7]

In so doing, the Department believes that transitioning to a new wholly electronic processing system will not present the problems suggested by the public responses to the Request for Comment. First, as explained more fully below, the Department intends to ensure that the new processing system will remedy the existing technical difficulties that underlie the perceived limitations of EFAST's current electronic filing design and will provide an electronic filing process that will be simpler, easier, and more attractive to filers.

Second, the Department does not believe that transitioning to the new processing system will impose undue burdens on small plans or small employers. Rather, the Department's analysis indicates that filers' costs of transitioning from paper filing to electronic transmission will be relatively modest and surpassed by benefits that will accrue in subsequent years.

Finally, the Department intends to delay implementation of any electronic mandate until the due date for the filing of Form 5500 Series for the plan year beginning in 2007, generally July 2008 or later. The Department believes that this substantial time delay of the proposed full electronic mandate will provide the public with adequate time to make adjustments in advance of the implementation of the new filing system.

The Department's conclusions concerning the public comments and alternatives are grounded in the Regulatory Impact Analysis presented below.

The Department invites comment on the need for an exception to accommodate any potentially significant impediments to some filers' transition to electronic filing. Commenters are encouraged to provide specific examples of such impediments, as well as to address the specific conditions for, and necessary scope of, relief under a hardship exception.

Electronic Filing

After careful consideration of the comments on the Request for Comment, as well as the need to develop a more efficient, cost-effective processing system for annual return/reports, the Department has determined, consistent with the goals of E-government, as recognized by the Government Paperwork Elimination Act[8] and the E-Government Act of 2002,[9] to require electronic filing of the Form 5500 to satisfy the reporting requirements of section 104(a) of Title I of ERISA. A mandate of electronic filing of benefit plan information, among other program strategies, will facilitate EBSA's achievement of its Strategic Goal of "enhancing pension and health benefits of American workers." EBSA's strategic goal directly supports the Secretary of Labor's Strategic Goals of "protecting workers benefits" and of "a competitive workforce," as well as promoting job flexibility and minimizing regulatory burden.[10] A cornerstone of our enforcement program is the collection, analysis, and disclosure of benefit plan information. Requiring electronic filing of benefit plan information, with the resulting improvement in the timeliness and accuracy of the information, would, in part, assist EBSA in its enforcement, oversight, and disclosure roles, which ultimately enhance the security of plan benefits. As the Government Accountability Office noted in its June, 2005, report on the Form 5500 Series,[11] the current necessity for handling paper filings under EFAST creates a substantial delay between receipt of a filing and the availability of its information for any enforcement and oversight purposes. Stating that "the abundance of paper filings results in long processing times," the GAO estimated, for purposes of illustration, that the processing time for a paper filing under EFAST averages 90 days from date of receipt where no filing errors are detected.[12] Electronic filing would eliminate virtually all of this processing time, improving outcomes for all of the users of the Form 5500 information. In this regard, the PBGC has advised the Department that electronic filing will enable PBGC to receive important

---

[7] This approach is congruent with recommendations of the Government Accountability Office, which, in a June, 2005, Report to Congressional Committees, stated that "[g]iven the improved timeliness and reduced errors associated with electronic filing, Labor, IRS and PBGC should require the electronic filing of the Form 5500." *See Private Pension - Government Actions Could Improve the Timeliness and Content of Form 5500 Pension Information* (GAO-05-491) at 44. The Report went on to state "[i]n doing so, Labor should also make improvements to the current electronic filing process to make it less burdensome, such as revising the procedure for signing and authenticating an electronic filing."

[8] Title XVII, Pub. L. 105-277, 112 Stat. 2681 (Oct. 21, 1998).

[9] Pub. L. 107-347, 116 Stat. 2899 (Dec. 17, 2002).

[10] For further information on the Department of Labor's Strategic Plan and EBSA's relationship to it, *see* http://www.dol.gov/_sec/stratplan/main.htm.

[11] *See* fn. 7, above.

[12] *See Private Pensions - Government Actions Could Improve the Timeliness and Content of Form 5500 Pension Information* (GAO-05-491) at 28, fig. 9 at 32. GAO also noted that, where errors in a filing are detected, additional processing delays of up to 120 more days occur.

information about defined benefit plans more quickly and efficiently, improving the PBGC's ability to monitor plan funding; calculate bankruptcy claims; estimate the impact of non-bankruptcy reportable events; evaluate exposure and expected claims; study plan formation and termination trends; and assess compliance with PBGC premium requirements.

In order to ensure an orderly and cost-effective migration to an electronic filing requirement and a new processing system, the requirement to file the Form 5500 electronically would apply only to annual return/reports required to be filed under ERISA section 104(a) for plan years beginning on or after January 1, 2007.

For purposes of the annual reporting requirements under section 4065 of Title IV of ERISA, the Pension Benefit Guaranty Corporation (PBGC) has advised the Department that a plan administrator's electronic filing of a Form 5500 for purposes of ERISA section 104(a), together with the required attachments and schedules and otherwise in accordance with the instructions to the Form, will be treated as satisfying the administrator's annual reporting obligation under section 4065 of Title IV of ERISA.[13] Similarly, for purposes of the annual filing and reporting requirements of the Code, the Internal Revenue Service (IRS) has advised the Department that, although there are no mandatory electronic filing requirements for a Form 5500 under the Code or the regulations issued thereunder, the electronic filing of a Form 5500 by plan administrators, employers, and certain other entities for purposes of ERISA section 104(a), together with the required attachments and schedules and otherwise in accordance with the instructions to the Form, will be treated as satisfying the annual filing and reporting requirements under Code sections 6058(a) and 6059(a). The IRS intends that plan administrators, employers, and certain other entities that are subject to various other filing and reporting requirements under Code sections 6033(a), 6047(e), and 6057(b) must continue to satisfy these requirements in accordance with IRS revenue procedures, publications, forms, and instructions.

With respect to annual reporting and filing obligations imposed by the Code but not required under section 104(a) of ERISA, such as are currently satisfied by the filing of the Form 5500-EZ, the IRS has advised the Department that it is currently working with taxpayers to explore how best to make a transition from paper filing to electronic filing in a manner that minimizes the burdens on taxpayers and practitioners. In this regard, the IRS has promulgated regulations mandating or permitting electronic filing of certain returns filed by pension and welfare benefit plans.[14]

With regard to the development of a new annual return/report electronic processing system, the Department is committed to resolving the electronic filing impediments identified by commenters on the Request for Comment, in particular those impediments relating to electronic signatures, attachments, and attestations furnished by third parties (e.g., accountants, actuaries, etc.).

It is anticipated that the new electronic filing system will incorporate the Internet as the sole medium for transmission of all filings and that the system will incorporate immediate validity and accuracy checks that will reduce both the error and rejection rate of filings and eliminate much of the costly post-filing paper correspondence and related potential penalties. The Department does not anticipate charging any filing fees in connection with the new system.

It is intended that the new electronic filing system will provide more than one vehicle for the electronic submission of annual return/reports. First, it is intended that the new filing system will offer users of approved, privately developed Form 5500 computer software (service providers to plans as well as plan administrators) a secure Internet-based method for transmission of Form 5500s created through the use of the software. This Internet-based transmission process will supercede all of the other currently available methods of transmitting machine-print versions of the Form 5500, including use of computer diskette, CD-ROM, magnetic tape, and modem. As the Department made clear in the Request for Comment, in making a transition to 100 percent electronic filing, the Department does not intend to supplant private software developers, vendors, or service providers to plans. Rather, it is contemplated that the new system will continue to provide support to these private industries, and the Department believes that filers will continue to rely on a variety of privately developed software products and services to facilitate plan administration, including the preparation and filing of the annual return/report. Indeed, it is ex-

pected that third-party software will remain the primary means of producing Form 5500s, with the simple difference that the reports will be filed electronically rather than through the use of paper. It is intended that service providers and software developers that provide value-added services for plan sponsors will be able to incorporate the new system's method of transmission into their services effectively and efficiently. Software file specifications will be non-proprietary so that users of different software may freely share information across different platforms. In this regard, the Department specifically invites public comment on how best to configure the new electronic filing architecture to provide the necessary flexibility to accommodate the needs of the diverse community of employee benefit plans.

Second, the Department also intends to include in the new system, as a separate filing method, a dedicated, secure Internet website through which plan administrators (or other return/report preparers) will be able to input data and to complete and submit Form 5500 filings on an individual plan-by-plan basis. It is anticipated that the Internet website will provide the filer with the capability of entering and saving data for an individual filing through multiple sessions, authorizing input for that filing from multiple parties (service providers, accountants, actuaries, etc.), uploading attachments, saving return/reports to a repository, and retrieving, updating, and editing stored filings, as well as creating and submitting amended filing data to EBSA.

As mentioned above, in connection with implementation of the redesign of EFAST, the Department, in coordination with the IRS and the PBGC, is conducting a thorough content review of the Form 5500. This review will be conducted as a three-agency regulatory initiative and will provide notice and comment opportunities for the public. The Department intends to consider, in conducting the content review of the Form 5500, changes that would facilitate electronic filing, as well as recommendations made by the ERISA Advisory Council on electronic reporting and on reporting by health and welfare plans.[15] That regulatory project will undertake to produce revised forms to be used for annual return/reports for the 2007 plan year, which will be due to be filed in 2008, when the new processing system will be implemented and the electronic filing requirement will begin to apply. Within the next few months, the Department intends to publish a separate notice inviting public comment on proposed changes to the Form 5500 and related rules.

Proposed Rule

The proposed rule contained in this notice is necessary to establish a requirement for the electronic filing of the Form 5500 for purposes of the annual reporting provisions of Title I of ERISA. Although at this time it is not possible to provide full technical details regarding the new electronic filing system, as many of the technological aspects of the redesign are still in development, filing requirements and compliance instructions will be provided to filers in advance of any due date for filing the Form 5500 under a final regulation requiring electronic submissions.

The proposal, upon adoption, would add a new section 2520.104a-2, Electronic Filing of Annual Reports, to Subpart E of Part 2520 of Title 29 of the Code of Federal Regulations. The proposal provides that any Form 5500 Annual Return/Report to be filed with the Secretary of Labor (Secretary) for any plan year beginning on or after January 1, 2007, shall be filed electronically in accordance with instructions and such other guidance as the Secretary may provide, applicable to such annual report. Because the Form 5500 is also filed by certain non-plan entities, such as common or collective trusts, pooled separate accounts, and entities described in 29 CFR 2520.103-12, which file for the fiscal year ending with or within the plan year for which a plan's annual report is filed, the proposal makes further reference to the first "reporting year" beginning on or after January 1, 2007, for such entities.

The proposal is intended to ensure that all Form 5500s filed with the Department, as well as any statements or schedules required to be attached to the report, including those filed by administrators (29 CFR 2520.103-1(a)(2) and (e)), group insurance arrangements (29 CFR 2520.103-2), common or collective trusts and pooled separate accounts (29 CFR 2520.103-3, 2520.103-4, and 2520.103-9), and entities described in 29 CFR 2520.103-12, are required (to the extent of the Department's authority) to be filed electronically. Following the development of a new electronic filing system, the Department intends to provide specific instructions and guidance concerning methods of filing in the instructions for the annual report form(s) and via its website.

---

[13] It should be noted that all administrators of plans required to file reports under ERISA sec. 4065 also are required to file reports for purposes of sec. 104(a) of ERISA.

[14] *See*, e.g., 26 CFR 301.6033-4T (mandating electronic filing of certain corporate income tax returns and returns of organizations required to be filed under Code sec. 6033); 26 CFR

1.6033-4T (returns required to be filed on magnetic media under 26 CFR 301.6033-4T must be filed in accordance with IRS revenue procedures, publications, forms, or instructions).

[15] *See*, e.g., *Report of the ERISA Advisory Council Working Group on Electronic Reporting* (Nov. 8, 2002), at http://www.dol.gov/ebsa/publications/AC_1108a02_report.html.

As indicated above in the discussion under "Electronic Filing," the proposal would not apply to any reporting requirements imposed solely under the Code (i.e., not required under section 104(a) of ERISA). As discussed above, issues relating to transition from paper filing to electronic filing for such reporting requirements are under consideration at the IRS. Accordingly, the regulation would not apply to any attachment, schedule, or report required to be completed by a tax-qualified pension benefit plan solely in order to provide the IRS with information concerning compliance with Code section 410(b) for a plan year, even if such attachment, schedule, or report is required to accompany the Form 5500 Annual Report/Return for that year. The proposal also would not apply to attachments, schedules, or reports that the IRS requires (1) under Code section 6033(a) to be filed by a trustee of a trust created as part of an employee benefit plan described in Code section 401(a) or by a custodian of a custodial account described in Code section 401(f), or (2) under Code section 6047(e) to be filed with respect to an employee stock ownership plan (ESOP).

The proposal, at 29 CFR 2520.104a-2(b), makes clear that the requirement to file annual reports electronically does not affect a person's record retention or disclosure obligations. In other words, the obligations of persons to retain records for purposes of sections 107 and 209 of ERISA would not be altered by the fact that the annual report would be required to be filed in electronic form. Similarly, a plan administrator's obligation to make the latest annual report available for examination and to furnish copies upon request, in accordance with sections 104(b)(2) and 104(b)(4) of ERISA, will not be affected by an electronic filing requirement.

Conforming changes are being proposed to 29 CFR 2520.103-1(f) [contents of the annual report], 2520.103-2(c) [contents of the annual report for a group insurance arrangement], 2520.103-9(d) [direct filing for bank or insurance carrier trusts and accounts], and 2520.103-12(f) [limited exception and alternative method of compliance for annual reporting of investments in certain entities].

Regulatory Impact Analysis

Summary

The Department has considered the potential costs and benefits of this proposed regulation. Costs to plans would consist mainly of a one-time, transition or start-up cost to make the change to electronic filing, generally to be incurred in 2008, which is estimated to be $23 million. Benefits to plans would include ongoing savings on material and postage and efficiency gains from the early detection and correction of more potential filing errors in the course of electronic filing, estimated to total $10 million annually, and realized each succeeding year beginning in 2008. Over time the ongoing savings attributable to this proposed regulation are expected to outweigh its one-time transition costs. Aggregate savings are estimated to exceed aggregate costs by $23 million over the first five years (discounting future savings at a rate of 7 percent).

Additional benefits are expected to accrue to the government and the public in the forms of substantially reduced processing costs and more timely availability of accurate filing data for use in enforcement and for other purposes of benefit to plans and participants.

Executive Order 12866 Statement

Under Executive Order 12866, the Department must determine whether a regulatory action is "significant" and therefore subject to the requirements of the Executive Order and subject to review by the Office of Management and Budget (OMB). Under section 3(f) of the Executive Order, a "significant regulatory action" is an action that is likely to result in a rule (1) having an annual effect on the economy of $100 million or more, or adversely and materially affecting a sector of the economy, productivity, competition, jobs, the environment, public health or safety, or State, local or tribal governments or communities (also referred to as "economically significant"); (2) creating serious inconsistency or otherwise interfering with an action taken or planned by another agency; (3) materially altering the budgetary impacts of entitlement grants, user fees, or loan programs or the rights and obligations of recipients thereof; or (4) raising novel legal or policy issues arising out of legal mandates, the President's priorities, or the principles set forth in the Executive Order. OMB has determined that this action is significant under section 3(f)(4) because it raises novel legal or policy issues arising from the President's priorities. Accord-

ingly, the Department has undertaken below an analysis of the costs and benefits of the proposed regulation.

Regulatory Flexibility Act

The Regulatory Flexibility Act (5 U.S.C. 601 et seq.) (RFA) imposes certain requirements with respect to Federal rules that are subject to the notice and comment requirements of section 553(b) of the Administrative Procedure Act (5 U.S.C. 551 et seq.) and which are likely to have a significant economic impact on a substantial number of small entities. Unless an agency determines that a proposed rule is not likely to have a significant economic impact on a substantial number of small entities, section 603 of the RFA requires that the agency present an initial regulatory flexibility analysis at the time of the publication of the notice of proposed rulemaking describing the impact of the rule on small entities and seeking public comment on such impact. Small entities include small businesses, organizations, and governmental jurisdictions.

For purposes of analysis under the RFA, EBSA proposes to continue to consider a small entity to be an employee benefit plan with fewer than 100 participants. The basis of this definition is found in section 104(a)(2) of ERISA, which permits the Secretary to prescribe simplified annual reports for pension plans that cover fewer than 100 participants. Under section 104(a)(3) of ERISA, the Secretary may also provide for exemptions or simplified annual reporting and disclosure for welfare benefit plans. Pursuant to the authority of section 104(a)(3), the Department has previously issued at 29 CFR 2520.104-20, 2520.104-21, 2520.104-41, 2520.104-46, and 2520.104b-10 certain simplified reporting provisions and limited exemptions from reporting and disclosure requirements for small plans, including unfunded or insured welfare plans that cover fewer than 100 participants and satisfy certain other requirements.

Further, while some large employers may have small plans, in general small employers maintain most small plans. Thus, EBSA believes that assessing the impact of these proposed rules on small plans is an appropriate substitute for evaluating the effect on small entities. The definition of small entity considered appropriate for this purpose differs, however, from a definition of small business that is based on size standards promulgated by the Small Business Administration (SBA) (13 CFR 121.201) pursuant to the Small Business Act (15 U.S.C. 631 et seq.). EBSA therefore requests comments on the appropriateness of the size standard used in evaluating the impact of these proposed rules on small entities.

These proposed rules may have a significant impact on a substantial number of small entities. The Department has therefore prepared an initial regulatory flexibility analysis, presented below under the heading "Small Plans." Additional relevant material also appears below under the heading "Alternatives Considered."

Costs and Benefits

The Department has considered the potential costs and benefits of this proposed regulation. Costs to plans would include a one-time transition or start-up cost to make the change to electronic filing, estimated to be $23 million. Benefits would include ongoing savings on material and postage and efficiency gains from the early detection and correction of more potential filing errors in the course of electronic filing, estimated to total $10 million annually. Over time the ongoing savings attributable to this proposed regulation are expected to outweigh its one-time transition costs. Aggregate savings are estimated to exceed aggregate costs by $23 million over the first five year (discounting future savings at a rate of 7 percent). Additional benefits are expected to accrue to the government and the public in the forms of reduced processing costs and more timely availability of accurate filing data. Beyond that, it is not immediately clear how the costs and benefits of mandatory electronic filing will compare with that of current filing modes, and the Department invites comments on this point.

The costs and benefits of this proposed regulation would accrue primarily to 832,000 plans that file Form 5500.[16] Non-plan entities that file Form 5500 generally do so in their capacity as service providers to plans and therefore are expected to pass their own costs and benefits from the regulation on to the plans they serve.[17]

Transition Costs

The proposed regulation would entail some one-time transition costs, incurred in making the transition to electronic filing. The magnitude of

---

[16] The economic analysis of the proposed regulation pertains only to those plans that file a Form 5500 to satisfy filing requirements under Title I of ERISA. Because the Form 5500-EZ is filed to satisfy filing requirements under the Code, data related to Form 5500-EZ filers is not included in this analysis.

[17] Economic theory predicts that producers in competitive markets pass costs and savings on to buyers.

the transition costs is likely to vary with filers' previous filing methods, reflecting the extent to which their existing filing infrastructure supports electronic filing. It is also expected that different filers will make the transition to electronic filing in different ways, depending on their circumstances and preferences. It is intended that all filers will have a number of methods of electronic filing from which to choose. For example, filers may enter information directly into a government-provided website (using their own Internet service or one available for a fee at a local business center or free of charge at a public library or other facility). They may use commercial software equipped for electronic filing. They may hire a service provider (or rely on an existing relationship with a service provider) to provide electronic filing services.

In 2002, the bulk of all filings, 87 percent, were submitted on machine-print forms; 12 percent were submitted on hand-print forms; and 1 percent were submitted electronically.

Hand-print Filers -Hand-print filers as a group are likely to face larger transition costs than others. These filers by and large currently file government printed forms, filled out by hand or by using a typewriter.[18] Like all other filers, they will have the option of preparing and submitting their filings via a government provided website. It is likely that many (but not all) already have the electronic infrastructure (mainly a personal computer and Internet service) to support electronic filing. It is also likely that others will have access to the Internet at no charge at a local library or other location.[19] Nonetheless, hand-print filers are likely to incur some expense to learn about the new requirement, and some will incur additional costs, such as in locating and becoming familiar with Internet access, as well as in establishing a secured filing account.

For the 104,000 current hand-print filers, the Department estimates a onetime, aggregate transition cost to electronic filing of $12 million. This assumes that a professional-level employee, who costs the plans on average $58.80 per hour in wages, benefits, and overhead,[20] would require on average two hours to make the transition to electronic filing. The cost might be devoted to one or more one-time, transition activities such as learning about the electronic filing system, registering for a secure filing account, selecting and acquiring software, selecting and hiring a service provider, or locating an Internet access site and becoming familiar with a web-based interface. Different types of transition activities will have different costs. Selecting and hiring a service provider might be an example of a potential activity that would cost more than average, while registering for a secure account might be an example of one that would cost less. The activities and the cost will vary from filer to filer. For example, transition activities might be limited and costs low for a filer that is a highly experienced Internet user already carrying out other aspects of business management (such as buying supplies and selling products, reporting wages to SSA, etc.) on line. Activities might be more extensive and costs higher for a filer lacking Internet and computing expertise who needs to acquire a computer and Internet connection or select and hire a service provider. The Department invites comments on transitional activities and costs.

Machine-print Filers - Machine-print filers as a group are likely to incur smaller transition costs than hand-print filers. It is likely that a large proportion of machine-print filings are prepared by service providers, while the remainder are prepared by filers using commercial software. Filers that currently rely on service providers to prepare and submit their filings may opt to continue in this manner, relying on the service provider to file electronically. Service providers' transition costs will be passed back to and spread across the filers they serve. Other machine-print filers may rely on the vendors of their software to incorporate electronic filing features into the 2007 plan-year software (probably as part of an otherwise normal annual software update typically carried out to incorporate any form and instruction changes). It is likely that a majority already have the Internet service required for such software features to function, and some that currently do not have such service would have acquired it by the time the plan-year 2007 filings are due (for reasons unrelated to this regulation). For many machine-print filers the transition to electronic filing will be largely transparent, but will nonetheless entail at least some activities, such as registration for a secure filing account.

For the 726,000 current machine-print filers, the Department estimates a one-time, aggregate transition cost to electronic filing of $11 million. This assumes that one-half of machine-print filers will rely entirely on their existing service providers to make the transition and that the service providers will spread their own transition costs across the filers they serve. The Department, lacking data on the number of affected service providers, did not attempt to estimate their transition cost, and such costs are not included here. Because these costs would be spread across filers, the amount passed on to any single filer is expected to be minimal. The remaining one-half of machine-print filers are assumed to shoulder the transition costs themselves. The Department's estimate assumes that these filers will require on average thirty minutes of a professionallevel employee's time to make the transition to electronic filing. The Department invites comments on these transition costs.

Ongoing Costs and Benefits

Preparation Costs - This proposed regulation pertains to the filing, and not to the preparation, of the Form 5500. However, it is possible that, for some filers, mandatory electronic filing would prompt changes in preparation methods. For example, hand-print filers may currently prepare their filings using a government printed form and a typewriter. Such filers might prepare future filings by entering information into a government website. The Department considered the cost of making such transitions in preparation methods to be part of the overall transition cost of the proposed regulation, included in the estimates presented above.

With respect to ongoing preparation costs, it is likely that some filers will incur higher costs in connection with new preparation methods prompted by this regulation and enabled by the new electronic filing system than with their current methods, but that others will incur lower costs. For example, it is not immediately determinable whether entering information into a website will take more or less time than typing it onto a paper form. The Department expects that commercial preparation software will incorporate features that ease preparation, such as integrated access to form instructions and automatic filling of data fields based on entries in other fields or in prior filings. The Department also intends that the new government filing website interface will be designed with attention to ease of preparation. Lacking an immediate basis to quantify the magnitude or costs and savings from possible changes in preparation methods, the Department did not attribute any such costs or savings to this proposed regulation, but invites comments on the potential magnitude of any such costs and benefits.

Filing Cost Savings -Filing costs generally are expected to be reduced by the implementation of this proposed regulation. Savings are foreseen from the elimination of materials and mailing costs and from a reduction in filing errors and subsequent corrections.

Electronic transmission will eliminate certain costs otherwise attendant to paper filing, including materials and postage. The Department estimates that, by changing to electronic filing, 829,000 plans will benefit from approximately $900,000 in cost-savings annually, assuming savings of $0.0167 per sheet of paper and $0.57 for postage per filing.

In addition, automated checks for errors and omissions upon electronic transmission, together with automated error checks and integrated instructions common to filing preparation software, will ease compliance with reporting requirements. Importantly, these features will reduce the need for subsequent amendments to submitted filings, as well as helping to avoid reporting penalties that might otherwise be assessed for deficient filings.

Historically, filers that use a software-based system generally have fewer filing errors. In 2002, 7 percent and 16 percent of electronic and machine-print filings, respectively, had filing errors compared to 40 percent of hand-print filings. The filing errors include items such as missing signatures, attestations, schedules, or back-up documents that resulted in an incomplete filing. As a result of filer errors and the need for additional information or clarifications about Form 5500 filings for the 2002 plan year, the Department mailed 160,000 letters to filers requesting corrections or additions. This process ultimately delays the final submission and requires plans to incur additional costs to address

---

[18] A very small fraction of all hand-print filers, typically a few percent, files computer-generated forms that are similar to and processed in the same way as government printed forms. These filers might tend to incur smaller transition costs than other hand-print filers. Because of their small numbers and the difficulties in separately identifying them in the data used for this analysis, the Department did not attempt to adjust its estimates to reflect this possible difference. This omission may slightly bias upwards the estimated aggregate transition cost for hand-print filers.

[19] This assumption is consistent with observations made by the ERISA Advisory Council Working Group on Electronic Reporting in its Nov. 8 Report. *See* fn. 15, above.

[20] The total labor cost is derived from wage and compensation data from the Bureau of Labor Statistics' (BLS) 2004 National Occupational Employment and Wage Estimates from the Occupational Employment Survey and BLS 2004 Employment Cost for Compensation. This data can be found at: http://www.bls.gov/news.release/ocwage.t01.htm and http://www.bls.gov/news.release/archives/ecec_09152004.pdf. The estimate assumes a 3 percent annual rate of compensation growth and includes an overhead component, which is a multiple of compensation based on the Government Cost Estimate.

deficiencies. The electronic filing system's intended error detection capability may largely eliminate the Department's need to forward correspondence to plans with deficient filings. This enhancement is likely to save time for filers. If the need for correspondence can be eliminated, the aggregate annual cost savings to affected filers could be as high as $10 million, assuming elimination of correspondence with the Department saves an average of one hour of a professional's time, at an average of $58.80 per hour, plus the value of associated postage and materials. A disproportionate share of this savings, estimated at $2.4 million, would accrue to current hand-print filers (reflecting their historically higher filing error rates), while $7.1 million would accrue to machine-print filers. The Department (and by extension taxpayers) would realize additional savings from this reduced need to correct filing errors.

Societal Benefits

Additional benefits are expected to accrue to the government and the public in the forms of reduced processing costs and more timely availability of accurate filing data.

Participants will benefit from the transition to a fully electronic method of filing. The new filing procedures will provide participants and beneficiaries with access to more accurate plan information since software-based forms are generally less prone to error, the new system will process filings more quickly, and reports disclosing information about plans' administrative and financial status will be available to the public sooner than would otherwise be possible. This improved access can enhance the quality of interaction between plans, participants, and beneficiaries.

The Federal government and the public at large will also benefit from the change to electronic filing. The decrease in correspondence will constitute immediate savings to the Federal government that will, in turn, yield savings to the taxpayers. Finally, improvements in the accuracy of the data contained in submitted filings and the expected acceleration in processing may make possible more timely production of reliable national statistics on private employee benefit plans. Such statistics historically have been produced at a substantial lag of up to four years after the end of the filing year.

Additional Considerations

Proliferation of Technology - In proposing this regulation, and in assessing its economic impacts, the Department took into consideration the high and increasing rates of use of electronic information technologies by businesses, including by small businesses in particular. Such technologies include office computing hardware and software that process, organize, store, and transmit information electronically. The proliferation of such technologies, and of expertise and familiarity with using them, is expected to moderate the cost of compliance with this proposed regulation.

The Department believes that most filers already have access to a computer and the Internet. The use of computers and the Internet has become the norm among U.S. businesses. Most or all industries in the economy are beginning to use the Internet as a means of conducting at least some of their daily operations and to remain competitive. Moreover, it is possible that plan sponsors as a group are more likely than other companies to be using information technologies. The Department believes that few, if any, plan sponsors will purchase a computer or subscribe to Internet service for the sole purpose of electronically filing their Form 5500. (If some do, they may realize collateral benefits as they put their newly acquired technologies to additional uses.) Furthermore, the Department believes that the number of firms offering pension and welfare plans that do not have a computer and/or Internet access is a relatively small number, especially given the substantial growth of computer and Internet usage over the past decade. The Department also believes that the number of plans that will not have a computer or Internet access by the year 2008 will be small.

The Department's views on the proliferation of technologies are grounded in its review of various studies of the topic.

According to a 2002 study for the SBA,[21] the Internet offers unparalleled new opportunities for small businesses. Fifty-seven percent of small businesses already used the Internet; of those most had their own websites; and more than one-third were selling their products on line.[22] Of those not using the Internet, two-thirds did use computers.[23]

The most popular uses of the Internet among small firm users were communicating with customers and suppliers (83 percent), gathering business information (80 percent), and purchasing goods and services (61 percent).[24] Some also used the Internet to conduct banking or other financial transactions (27 percent) or bid on contracts (21 percent). Most firms with websites either broke even financially or made money through use of the sites.

Also according to this study, use of Internet technology is growing. Among small firms with websites, two-thirds had been operating the site for less than one year.[25] Business use of on-line technologies is being driven up by increasing use of such technologies by consumers. Increasing availability and use of affordable, fast broad-band Internet services is helping to drive both trends. Market forecasters predicted rapid growth in world e-commerce, reaching as much as several trillion dollars by 2004.[26]

A 2003 report by SBA[27] found that self-employed computer users numbered 10.5 million in 2000, up from 9.2 million two years earlier. Over the same two years, self-employed individuals' access to the Internet increased by 50 percent, reaching 83 percent of all such individuals.

A 2004 study for SBA[28] of small firms with fewer than 500 employees found that only 27 percent did not currently subscribe to Internet service.

Benefits of E-government - The proposed regulation will advance the goals of administration articulated in the Government Paperwork Elimination Act and the E-Government Act of 2002.

The Department expects this proposed regulation to advance the general trend toward the efficiencies of E-government. Federal, State, and local government agencies have already implemented numerous E-government initiatives.[29] These initiatives reduce the government's burden on businesses by eliminating redundant collection of data. Citizens receive faster, more convenient services from a more responsive and informed government.[30] According to one study, citizens see the most important benefits of E-government as increased government accountability to citizens (36 percent), greater public access to information (23 percent), and more efficient/cost-effective government (21 percent).[31] The GAO has indicated that government agencies that reported using the Internet as a medium for core business operations delivered information and services more quickly, less expensively, and to wider groups of users.[32]

Another study suggests that one of the most powerful ways to reduce compliance costs is through E-government. Web-enabling can save businesses and citizens a considerable amount of time and money, as the following examples demonstrate: (1) The State of Oregon's on-line permitting and reporting process for building construction approvals saved Oregon's construction industry $100 million annually. Deloitte's estimate suggests that if governments at all levels were to follow Oregon's lead, the United States' construction industry, as a whole, could save in the range of $15 billion to $20 billion annually. (2) The SBA's Business Compliance One Stop website saves businesses about $526 million a year, by helping them find, understand, and comply with regulations. (3) In Canada, the province of British Columbia's OneStopBC website cuts down on government paperwork costs for businesses by allowing on-line business license registrations. The cost

---

[21] Joanne H. Pratt, "E-Biz: Strategies for Small Business Success" 32 (2002) (prepared for the SBA Office of Advocacy), available at http://www.sba.gov/advo/research/rs220tot.pdf.

[22] Id. at 6.

[23] Id.

[24] Id. at 6-8.

[25] Id. at 11.

[26] Id. at 23-24.

[27] SBA Office of Advocacy, "Self Employment and Computer Usage," 3 (2003), available at http://www.sba.gov/ADVO/stats/sepc.pdf.

[28] Stephen B. Pociask, TeleNomic Research, LLC, "A Survey of Small Businesses' Telecommunications Use and Spending" 71 (2004) (prepared for SBA Office of Advocacy), available at http://www.sba.gov/advo/research/rs236tot.pdf.

[29] See, e.g., "Electronic Government: Challenges Must Be Addressed with Effective Leadership and Management," Hearing on S.803 Before the Senate Comm. in Governmental Affairs, 106th Cong. 1 (July 11, 2001) (statement of David McClure, Director, Information Technology Management Issues, GAO), available at http://www.gao.gov/new.items/d01959t.pdf.

[30] Susie Trinkle, Capella Univ., "Moving Citizens from in line to Online: How the Internet is Changing How Government Serves its Citizens" (Sept. 10, 2001, available at http://oma.od.nih.gov/ma/bps/bpkm/Resource/Y_MovingCitizensFromLineOn.doc.

[31] Hart-Teeter, "E-Government: the Next American Revolution" (Sept. 28, 2000) available at http://www.excelgov.org/displaycontent.asp?keyword=mReleases&NewsItemID=2559.

[32] Testimony of David A. McClure, GAO, before the Subcommittee on Government Management, Information and Technology, Committee on Government Reform, House of Representatives (2000), as reported in Karen Laynea and Jungwoo Leeb, *Government Information Quarterly* 18 (2001), 122-136.

savings to businesses are estimated to be in the range of $14 million to $27 million annually.[33]

Time Rebates -Time considerations affect all interactions and activities in business. When citizens and businesses can go on line, instead of waiting in line, they can obtain faster, more convenient access to government services.[34] E-government can provide what has come to be described as a "time rebate" — cutting down on the time it takes to comply with government regulations and to complete transactions.

For example, the Commonwealth of Pennsylvania's "PA Open for Business" website allows a business to enter all the information needed to register with the State in one place, instead of having to go to five different agencies. A process that once took days or weeks has been reduced to one hour.[35]

The Department intends that the new electronic filing system will be equipped to streamline submissions and reduce time and burden on filers. The proposed regulation should benefit all parties because the information contained in the Form 5500 would be directly entered into the Department's records. This would improve transaction accuracy, reduce cycle times, improve cost efficiencies, enhance information accessibility, and provide more timely availability of the information contained in the Form 5500 return/reports.

Alternatives Considered

As noted earlier in this preamble, before electing to pursue the approach taken in this proposed regulation, the Department considered alternative options for reconfiguring the filing methods for the Form 5500 Series, focusing in particular on the gradual approach advocated generally in the public comments. The following discusses three such alternatives that the Department considered but rejected, along with the reasons why each was rejected in favor of a uniform requirement to file electronically beginning with filings for the 2007 plan year. Fuller discussion of the third alternative, which would provide a time-limited exception from mandatory electronic filing for certain small plans, follows under the heading "Small Plans."

First, the Department considered developing a new processing system that could continue to process both electronic and paper submissions without limitation. Such a system might be popular with the filing public and might result over time in virtually complete conversion to electronic filing, provided that the new system successfully incorporated the contemplated technological advances. Such a "dual method" processing system would permit filers to choose between electronic and paper filing. It therefore would likely appear to some filers to be more cost-efficient than the uniform requirement to file electronically that the Department is proposing. However, while a "dual method" processing system might be popular with some filers, such a system would perpetuate the inefficiencies inherent in paper filings -larger number of filing errors, required correspondence with filers, increased likelihood of civil penalties, delays in reviews of filings, and increased risks to participants and beneficiaries resulting from erroneous data or delayed enforcement. It therefore does not appear to be in the interest of plans or participants to maintain such a system. In addition, the maintenance of such a system would entail additional costs for the Federal government (and by extension taxpayers) because it would be necessary to incorporate into the system the ability to receive and process a potentially large number of paper filings. In the Department's view, the additional costs for such a complex processing system would be virtually prohibitive for the Federal government in light of current budgetary constraints on the Federal government generally and on the Department in particular. Under such constraints, maintaining a paper filing system would consume resources that would be better devoted to enhancing the system's electronic filing capabilities or carrying out other Department functions.

Second, the Department considered the alternative of continuing the present paper processing system on a short-term interim basis during the initial years of operating a new, solely electronic processing system. This alternative would enable filers to gain familiarity with the new paperless system as part of the transition process. As with the prior approach, this approach would continue, albeit for a limited period, the current inefficiencies of a paper system and the substantial costs of maintaining tandem operations, particularly since continuing the old processing system would require "sole source" non-competitive yearly contractual negotiations with the current contractor, with ever increasing additional costs. For example, in fiscal year 2006 the Department requested an additional $2.1 million to maintain current operations in the first year of a sole source contract.

Third, the Department considered developing a new processing system that would have the temporary capacity to process paper filings from a targeted group of filers under an exception from the electronic filing requirement. For reasons described below under "Small Plans," the Department considered it appropriate to limit the exception to small plans that had previously filed government printed "hand-print" forms and that are not subject to the audit requirement. The Department believes that making such an exception available, at least for the first few years of operating the new processing system, might provide a small net benefit to at least some proportion of this class of filers. However, the Department believes this potential benefit, which could amount (as explained further below) to as little as $14 per plan on average for 74,000 plans or as much as $249 per plan on average for 7,400 plans, is outweighed by the benefits to participants and beneficiaries at large, and to the Department and taxpayers generally, of implementing a single, wholly electronic filing system beginning with reports for the 2007 plan year. The maintenance of any paper system, even on a reduced scale, is inherently inefficient and unnecessarily costly and could undermine full realization of the potential benefits of electronic filing for ERISA compliance and enforcement, thereby exposing some plans and participants to unnecessary risk. Accordingly, the Department rejected this alternative, along with the other two considered alternatives, in favor of a uniform requirement to file electronically.

The Department's consideration of this third alternative, and its basis for rejecting it in favor of a uniform requirement to file electronically, is detailed below under the heading "Small Plans."

Small Plans

The Department believes this regulation may have a significant impact on a substantial number of small plans. As for all other plans, costs and benefits for small plans are expected to vary with the plans' circumstances. Most will likely incur moderate transition costs and subsequently realize moderate ongoing savings. Some, however, may experience larger impacts, including both larger transition costs and/or ongoing net cost increases rather than ongoing net savings. For example, some small plans may lack experience with or easy access to the Internet. Such plans may incur larger than typical transition costs to gain access to the Internet (or to enlist a service provider with access) and may find it more time consuming, and therefore more costly, to prepare their filing on a government website (or to interact with a service provider) than to prepare their filing using a government printed form that is completed "by hand" and filed on paper through the mails. The Department expects that only a minority of plans might be so affected, but that minority might nonetheless represent a substantial number.

The Department therefore conducted an initial regulatory flexibility analysis, repeating the above analysis while limiting the scope to include only small plans - that is, those with fewer than 100 participants. On that basis, it is estimated that 667,000 small plans will incur one-time transition costs of $18 million, including $9 million for 78,000 current hand-print filers and $9 million for 589,000 current machine-print filers. It is further estimated that small plans would realize ongoing materials and postage savings of approximately $700,000 annually and could realize up to $7 million in savings annually from the elimination of the need to correct deficient filings (including $2 million accruing to hand-print filers and $5 million to machine-print), for a total of approximately $8 million in annual savings. As with all other plans, over time the aggregate ongoing savings realized by small plans are expected to outweigh their aggregate one-time transition costs. Over five years, savings are estimated to exceed costs by $17 million (discounting future savings at a rate of 7 percent). The Department believes that impacts may vary among small plans, depending for example on their (or their service providers') access to and familiarity with associated technologies, and possibly on their size. The Department, however, lacks a basis on which to estimate such variations. The Department invites comments on this assessment of the impact of the proposed regulation on small plans.

The Department also assessed the costs and benefits of alternative approaches. As noted above, the Department considered proposing a temporary exception from the requirement to file electronically for certain small plans. The Department undertook to develop as an alternative to a uniform electronic filing requirement an exception provision that would maximize benefits and minimize costs to affected parties including plans, participants, and taxpayers.

---

[33] William D. Eggers, Global Director, Deloitte Research-Public Sector, "Citizen Advantage: Enhancing Economic Competitiveness Through e-Government" 1 (2004).

[34] Gassan Al-Kibsi; Kito de Boer; Mona Mourshed; Nigel P. Rea; "Putting citizens on-line, not in line," McKinsey Quarterly 2001 no. 2.

[35] *See* Eggers, *supra* note 25 at 7, 14.

The Department first considered the criteria that should be adopted to designate filers eligible to continue to file on paper under the exception. The Department selected as the first criterion plan size. Small plans (and the small businesses that sponsor them) may be less likely than large ones to use computers and the Internet or to have current expertise in such usage. They may be harder pressed to devote resources to making a transition to electronic filing. Moreover, transition costs may be largely fixed costs (invariant to plan size) and therefore more burdensome to small than to large plans. The Department considered alternative plan size thresholds, including plans with fewer than 100, fewer than 25, or fewer than 10 participants. The threshold of fewer than 100 participants seemed most desirable. It is consistent with the threshold used for other distinctions in annual reporting requirements and therefore would not add additional complexity to reporting requirements. In addition, the overall systems requirements associated with an exception for plans with fewer than 100 participants would be expected to differ little from those associated with an exception limited to smaller plans. The cost of building, maintaining and periodically updating a system capable of accepting and processing paper filings is largely invariant to the number of paper filings to be accepted. Moreover, the number of plans eligible for the exception would not vary much across the thresholds considered. Among plans not subject to the audit requirement and filing by the hand-print method, the Department estimates that 74,000 have fewer than 100 participants, 59,000 fewer than 25, and 46,000 fewer than 10.

The second criterion identified by the Department was past filing method. As noted above, it is likely that hand-print filers will confront higher average transition costs than machine-print filers. Machine-print filers currently prepare their filings electronically, even if they do not file them electronically. In contrast, some fraction of hand-print filers may be entirely without computing infrastructure.

A third criterion identified by the Department was potential risk to participants. As noted above, hand-print filings are more prone to error than machine-print or electronic filings. In addition, processing of paper filings is inherently slower than processing of electronic filings. Therefore, continued acceptance of paper filings has the potential to slow both detection of ERISA violations and enforcement actions to address such violations.[36] The Department therefore considered approaches that would limit the exception to situations where risks of violations (and associated threats to participants) were less, such as in connection with plans that, because of the presence of other safeguards and/or absence of certain risks, were not required to provide financial audits with their annual reports.

Finally, the Department considered the appropriate duration of such an exception. To accommodate such an exception, the Department's new processing system would need to incorporate an ability to receive and process some number of paper filings. The incorporation of this ability into the system would entail a relatively large, up-front development cost, followed by smaller but substantial ongoing costs to process paper filings. It therefore seemed reasonable to consider as the duration of such an exception the expected minimum "lifetime" of the new system (which corresponds to the expected duration of the contract that will develop and maintain it), which is five years. The Department next considered whether a five-year exception would be sufficient to accomplish the exception's goal of easing small plans' transition to electronic filing. Assuming continued rapid proliferation of computer and Internet usage, it seems likely that five years would be sufficient to accomplish this goal.

Based on this reasoning, the Department considered, as an alternative to a uniform 100 percent electronic filing requirement, a five-year exception for plans that: (1) have fewer than 100 participants, (2) previously filed their annual reports using government printed "hand-print" forms, and (3) are not subject to the audit requirement for annual reporting under Title I of ERISA. The Department estimates that use of these criteria would create a class of 74,000 filers eligible for the temporary exception from electronic filing.

As noted above, small plans are estimated to face an aggregate transition cost of $18 million, followed by ongoing annual savings of $8 million. Over time the aggregate savings will outweigh the cost. But, also as noted above, a disproportionate share of the transition cost, $9 million, is estimated to accrue to the small minority of small plans that file via the hand-print method. The savings accruing to these filers, being attributable to reduced materials and postage and, more important, reduced filing errors, if proportionate to their numbers, will amount to $2 million.

The Department undertook to carefully consider the potential costs and benefits to small plans of the exception defined above. Approximately 74,000 plans could be eligible for the exception. The Department considered two potential scenarios.

In the first scenario, the Department assumed that all eligible plans would file on paper, for an average of three of the five years for which paper filings would be permitted. The Department assumed further that these plans' average transition costs and ongoing savings would be the same as the average assumed earlier for all small plan hand-print filers.[37] The Department also assumed that, by taking advantage of the exception, these filers would reduce their transition cost to the level assumed earlier to be incurred by machine-print filers, but would delay commencement of the ongoing savings available through electronic filing until they began filing electronically (on average after three years). In this scenario, the 74,000 filers taking advantage of the exception would reduce their transition costs by $6.5 million on aggregate, while sacrificing $5.5 million in potential ongoing savings, thereby realizing a net benefit of approximately $1 million, or $14 per filer.

In the second scenario, the Department considered the possibility that the transition cost might vary widely across filers. The Department assumed that just 10 percent of eligible filers would take advantage of the exception (again for an average of three years), but that these filers would face a transition cost (absent the exception) of three times the average assumed for all hand-print filers. Other assumptions were the same as in the first scenario. In this scenario, 7,400 filers taking advantage of the exception would reduce their transition costs by $2.4 million on aggregate, while sacrificing $550,000 in potential ongoing savings, thereby realizing a net benefit of approximately $1.8 million, or $249 per filer.

On the basis of these scenarios, the Department believes that some filers would likely benefit from the exception. However, as noted above, the potential net benefit to a given filer from the exception would be modest. In the first scenario, the average net benefit would amount to just $12 per plan using the exception; in the second, $249 per plan. Further, the availability of the exception would create significant risks to participants and costs to the government (and taxpayers). As discussed above, the maintenance of any paper system, even on a relatively small scale, is inherently inefficient and costly. Also, as discussed above, paper filings take longer to process and therefore pose unnecessary compliance risks. Therefore, the Department concluded that the potential benefit of a limited exception would be outweighed by the associated cost to the government (and to taxpayers) and the potential risks to participants and that adoption of a limited exception could not be justified. For these reasons, the Department rejected the alternative of providing an exception in favor of a uniform requirement to file electronically.

Paperwork Reduction Act

This proposed regulation does not introduce, or materially modify, any information collection requirement, but furthers the Department's goal of automating the submission of the Form 5500 return/report. As such, this notice of proposed rulemaking is not subject to the requirements of the Paperwork Reduction Act of 1995 (44 U.S.C. 3501 et seq.) because it does not contain a "collection of information" as defined in 44 U.S.C. 3502(3).

Congressional Review Act

The notice of proposed rulemaking being issued here is subject to the provisions of the Congressional Review Act provisions of the Small Business Regulatory Enforcement Fairness Act of 1996 (5 U.S.C. 801 et seq.) and, if finalized, will be transmitted to the Congress and the Comptroller General for review.

Unfunded Mandates Reform Act

Pursuant to provisions of the Unfunded Mandates Reform Act of 1995 (Pub. L. 104-4), this rule does not include any Federal mandate that may result in expenditures by State, local, or tribal governments, or the private sector, which may impose an annual burden of $100 million or more.

List of Subjects in 29 CFR Part 2520

Employee benefit plans, pensions, reporting and recordkeeping requirements

For the reasons set forth in the preamble, the Department proposes to amend 29 CFR part 2520 as follows:

---

[36] This concerns not merely reporting violations, but all potential ERISA violations, including those which might directly jeopardize plan assets or participants' benefits.

[37] This assumption seems reasonable insofar as an estimated 94 percent of all small hand-print filers were not subject to the audit requirement and therefore would be eligible for the exception.

1. The authority section of Part 2520 continues to read as follows:

Authority: 29 U.S.C. 1021-1025, 1027, 1029-31, 1059, 1134, and 1135; Secretary of Labor's Order 1-2003, 68 FR 5374 (Feb. 3, 2003). Sec. 2520.101-2 also issued under 29 U.S.C. 1132, 1181-1183, 1181 note, 1185, 1185a-b, 1191, and 1191a-c. Secs. 2520.102-3, 2520.104b-1, and 2520.104b-3 also issued under 29 U.S.C. 1003, 1181-1183, 1181 note, 1185, 1185a-b, 1191, and 1191a-c. Secs. 2520.104b-1 and 2520.107 also issued under 26 U.S.C. 401 note, 111 Stat. 788.

2. Add § 2520.104a-2 after § 2520.104a-1 to read as follows:

§ 2520.104a-2 Electronic Filing of Annual Reports.

(a) Any Form 5500 Annual Return/Report (including accompanying statements or schedules) to be filed with the Secretary for any plan year (or reporting year, in the case of common or collective trusts, pooled separate accounts, and similar non-plan entities) beginning on or after January 1, 2007, shall be filed electronically in accordance with the instructions, and such other guidance as the Secretary may provide, applicable to such report.

(b) Nothing in paragraph (a) of this section is intended to alter or affect the duties of any person to retain records or to disclose information to participants, beneficiaries, or the Secretary.

3. Amend § 2520.103-1 by revising paragraph (f) as follows:

§ 2520.103-1 Contents of the annual report.

* * * * *

(f) *Electronic filing.* Except as provided in § 2520.104a-2 of this chapter, the Form 5500 "Annual Return/Report of Employee Benefit Plan" may be filed electronically or through other media in accordance with the instructions accompanying the form, provided the plan administrator maintains an original copy, with all required signatures, as part of the plan's records.

4. Amend § 2520.103-2 by revising paragraph (c) as follows:

§ 2520.103-2 Contents of the annual report for a group insurance arrangement.

* * * * *

(c) *Electronic filing.* Except as provided in § 2520.104a-2 of this chapter, the Form 5500 "Annual Return/Report of Employee Benefit Plan" may be filed electronically or through other media in accordance with the instructions accompanying the form, provided the trust or other entity described in § 2520.104-43(b) maintains an original copy, with all required signatures, as part of the trust's or entity's records.

5. Amend § 2520.103-9 by revising paragraph (d) as follows:

§ 2520.103-9 Direct filing for bank or insurance carrier trusts and accounts.

* * * * *

(d) *Method of filing.* Except as provided in § 2520.104a-2 of this chapter, the Form 5500 "Annual Return/Report of Employee Benefit Plan" may be filed electronically or through other media in accordance with the instructions accompanying the form, provided the bank or insurance company which maintains the common or collective trust or pooled separate account maintains an original copy, with all required signatures, as part of its records.

6. Amend § 2520.103-12 by revising paragraph (f) as follows:

§ 2520.103-12 Limited exemption and alternative method of compliance for annual reporting of investments in certain entities.

* * * * *

(f) *Method of filing.* Except as provided in § 2520.104a-2 of this chapter, the Form 5500 "Annual Return/Report of Employee Benefit Plan" may be filed electronically or through other media in accordance with the instructions accompanying the form provided the entity described in paragraph (c) of this section maintains an original copy, with all required signatures, as part of its records.

Signed at Washington, D.C., this *23d* day of *August*, 2005.

Ann L. Combs

Assistant Secretary

Employee Benefits Security Administration

[The next page is 1657.]

Topical Index

References are to paragraph (¶) numbers.

Topical Index
References are to paragraph (¶) numbers.